The World Book Dictionary

Volume one A-K

Edited by:
Clarence L. Barnhart
Robert K. Barnhart

Prepared in Cooperation with
World Book, Inc.
Publishers of
The World Book Encyclopedia

William H. Nault, Publisher
Robert O. Zeleny, Editor in Chief

A Thorndike-Barnhart Dictionary

World Book, Inc.
a Scott Fetzer company
Chicago London Sydney Toronto

The World Book Dictionary

World Book, Inc.
525 West Monroe
Chicago, IL 60661

Printed in the United States of America
ISBN 0-7166-0292-X
Library of Congress Catalog Card Number 91-75273

Trademarks or other proprietary names are
entered in this dictionary and so marked;
if the proper designation is missing,
no legal status should be assumed.

A/IB

Contents

Volume one: A-K

Volume two: L-Z

About this book

THE WORLD BOOK DICTIONARY provides information about the meaning, spelling, and pronunciation of the most important and most frequently used words and phrases in the English language. It records facts about the use of these words in both the spoken and written language. And it includes the origin, history, and development of thousands of words.

THE WORLD BOOK DICTIONARY is published under the supervision of the noted American lexicographer, Clarence L. Barnhart. Although this dictionary is more comprehensive than any of the Thorndike-Barnhart school dictionaries, it is based on the same principles that have been thoroughly tested and widely accepted by experts and the public. Revisions are made on a yearly basis.

A complete reference library

Just as THE WORLD BOOK ENCYCLOPEDIA records the events and developments of our time through regular revisions, so THE WORLD BOOK DICTIONARY keeps a running record of the words that tell of these events and developments. These two reference books are the only encyclopedia and dictionary that are edited to supplement each other. Together, they form a reference library for the family as well as the classroom. As a service to owners of the dictionary, the publishers include a special dictionary supplement in each annual edition of THE WORLD BOOK YEAR BOOK. This section contains the most important new words and meanings of the year.

Many authorities consulted

THE WORLD BOOK DICTIONARY is the creation of a lexicographical staff with more than forty years experience in making dictionaries. The staff carried out the editorial policies established by an international committee of distinguished scholars, including renowned linguists, phoneticians, and scholars of English language and literature. The policies of THE WORLD BOOK DICTIONARY and their execution are critically reviewed by this advisory committee and by the editors of THE WORLD BOOK ENCYCLOPEDIA. Special consultants in more than seventy fields of knowledge supply comments and suggestions. Distinguished etymologists have served as consulting editors.

Policies and objectives

From its inception, THE WORLD BOOK DICTIONARY has aimed to be useful to all members of the family and to students of various ages. Their needs were studied by the editors and the members of the advisory committee and a series of editorial policies were formulated.

The editors of THE WORLD BOOK DICTIONARY agreed on the importance of: (1) writing definitions so that they are clear, informative, and easy to understand; (2) defining in a simple manner those words likely to be used by younger readers so that they can readily understand the meanings; (3) listing definitions with the most commonly used meaning first instead of listing them in historical order as do many dictionaries; (4) presenting informative illustrative sentences that help to clarify meanings; (5) ensuring the accuracy of THE WORLD BOOK DICTIONARY by consulting with experts in special fields; (6) placing information so that it can be obtained easily and quickly by the reader; (7) correlating information in the dictionary with information in THE WORLD BOOK ENCYCLOPEDIA.

THE WORLD BOOK DICTIONARY is based on an extensive quotation file containing more than three million quotations collected by experienced readers over a period of more than thirty-five years. These are culled from a wide sampling of contemporary magazines, newspapers, scholarly and technical journals, and books. Through an extensive reading program, the dictionary staff of editors and researchers constantly accumulate information on words, meanings, and usages. Correspondents from Australia, Canada, Great Britain, South Africa, and other parts of the English-speaking world regularly furnish evidence of new regional usages. In addition, the staff carefully reviews THE WORLD BOOK ENCYCLOPEDIA to uncover new words, meanings, and usages incorporated in that publication as part of its ongoing revision program.

The quotation file ensures that this dictionary presents a complete and up-to-date record of the working vocabulary of the English language. It is a principal source of editorial decisions. Without it, the editors would have to turn to secondary sources. Thus, this dictionary is a complete, up-to-date dictionary of modern word usage.

Content

THE WORLD BOOK DICTIONARY contains 225,000 terms in the working vocabulary of English—the vocabulary used by educated people to communicate with each other and needed by them to understand the world they live in and the world of the past. By concentrating on vocabulary in actual use, this dictionary is able to provide fuller definitions and more illustrative sentences than it could if it were to include all possible obsolete, archaic, or excessively technical terms. By limiting entries to the really useful ones, entries are easier to find and space is gained in which to explain them adequately.

Because this dictionary was designed especially for use with THE WORLD BOOK ENCYCLOPEDIA, biographical and geographical information, which more properly belongs in an encyclopedia, is not included. But the names of plants and animals are included, even though the encyclopedia gives more extensive information for many of these, including the scientific names used in classifying plants and animals according to genus and species. Excluding such encyclopedic information from the dictionary means that more space can be given to word meanings, illustrative sentences, usage notes, word origins and histories, synonyms, and illustrations.

Ease of use

Several features make this dictionary especially easy to use. For example, thumb tabs marked with a letter or letters of the alphabet are located along the edges of each volume, and guide words at the tops of pages make finding words quick and easy. All entries (words, phrases, abbreviations, foreign words) are arranged in a single alphabetical listing rather than appearing in separate categories.

The typography of this dictionary has much to do with its ease of use. After testing various type faces, the editors and designers chose the sans-serif Spectra for the body of the dictionary and sans-serif Roma for the supplemental material. These two type faces were selected not only for their modern appearance, but also because they are easy to read. Again, in the interests of readability, the type was set ragged right. This not only achieves even word spacing so that the eye travels smoothly across the column, it also reduces the need for hyphenation, which improves readability.

The arrangement of entries also contributes to ease of use. Entries and cross-references are printed in boldface (heavy) type. This makes them easy to find. Different kinds of Spectra type are used to highlight the various kinds of information provided in each entry. For example: boldface roman is used for entries; lightface roman is used for definitions; and italic is used for illustrative sentences and phrases. Boldface type is also used to identify idioms, which are now provided in one alphabetical list at the end of the appropriate entry. A lightface bar between syllables of entry words replaces the standard convention of periods or centered dots which confused many children. All separate parts of speech relating to an entry are now placed in separate paragraphs, so that the reader can distinguish their meanings easily and quickly. Variant spellings and names are not defined, but the reader is referred by an equal sign to the preferred form where the definition is given. Thus: baryon number = mass number. Etymologies are in brackets following a definition or the several definitions of an entry. To make etymologies easier to understand, words are spelled out, thus excluding abbreviations, such as OF for Old French.

Simplified pronunciation key

The pronunciation key, an adaptation of the International Phonetic Alphabet, employs a minimum number of special symbols, thus enabling the user of this dictionary to find current English pronunciations easily. Pronunciations given are those which the editors consider to be in current use among educated speakers of English in the United States, and in representative areas of Canada. Where variations of pronunciation are common, two or more pronunciations are indicated.

Illustrations

More than 3,000 illustrations were specially created to help extend and clarify definitions. All illustrations were carefully researched by the staff of THE WORLD BOOK ENCYCLOPEDIA so that they are factually correct in every detail. The illustrations were drawn by artists especially commissioned to work on THE WORLD BOOK DICTIONARY. The decision to use line drawings instead of other illustration styles was made to ensure clarity of detail and compatibility with the type face used, and to give the dictionary a look of uniformity and cohesiveness.

Entries were singled out for illustration when it was thought the reader might have difficulty visualizing a concept, or in those instances where illustrations provided additional information as in charts, biological and geological drawings, tables, and chemical formulas. Each illustrated entry is indicated by an asterisk. Many illustrations include parts that are labeled. All labels, except those that are self-evident combinations of words, appear as entries in other parts of the dictionary. Such entries are cross-referred to the illustration containing them.

Special articles

Supplementing the dictionary proper are 124 pages of other interesting, educational material. The supplement includes a "Guide to the dictionary," which explains the various kinds of signs, symbols, abbreviations, and other types of "shorthand" used by the makers of this dictionary to conserve space. The guide also explains and gives directions for using this dictionary as efficiently as possible. Vocabulary inventories—researched, compiled, and tested for the needs of students from grade three through college—help students test their knowledge of words. Special articles on vocabulary development point up how important and valuable a good vocabulary is for effective communication.

"How to write effectively," one of the sections included in the supplement, illustrates the various steps to be followed in preparing school assignments, such as book reports, term papers, and other kinds of writing, such as letters of various kinds. In addition, the supplement includes easy to read articles on subjects such as slang and jargon, codes and ciphers, and a short history of the English language. It gives lists of the words most commonly misspelled and tells how to avoid spelling and writing traps.

The supplement gives important information on how to change measures into and out of metric units. It includes a list of weights and measures and their metric equivalents, and signs and symbols including those pertaining to astronomy, biology, business, commerce, engineering, electrical plans and equipment, plumbing, computer programming, mapping, and meteorology. Various types of important alphabets such as the International Phonetic Alphabet, the Initial Teaching Alphabet, Braille, Esperanto, and the hand alphabet are explained and illustrated.

Editorial resources of two organizations

THE WORLD BOOK DICTIONARY is the result of the combined efforts of two publishing organizations. In producing this edition, policies of past revisions were reconsidered and new points of view were introduced to make a dictionary that meets the needs of today's users.

The editorial responsibility for the dictionary proper is that of Clarence L. Barnhart, Robert K. Barnhart, and the staff of Barnhart Books, one of three permanent staffs in the United States engaged in commercial English lexicography.

The writing and editing of special articles was carried out by the staff of THE WORLD BOOK ENCYCLOPEDIA, which was also responsible for reviewing the dictionary proper for its consistency with the encyclopedia and its appropriateness for users of THE WORLD BOOK ENCYCLOPEDIA. All illustrations in the dictionary were researched, labeled, and captioned by the staff of the encyclopedia, and provided by artists especially commissioned by the encyclopedia.

By sharing the responsibilities of authorship and the correlation of the dictionary and THE WORLD BOOK ENCYCLOPEDIA, we have produced a modern dictionary for use in the home and the classroom.

The Editors

International editorial advisory committee

author of *Introduction to Survey of Scottish Dialects;* coauthor of *Patterns of Language.*

James B. McMillan, Professor of English, University of Alabama; author of *Writing and Thinking* and *Annotated Bibliography of Southern American English.*

Bertil Malmberg, Professor of Linguistics, University of Lund, Sweden; editor of *Studia Linguistica* and *IRAL;* author of *La Phonétique,* and *Phonetics, New Trends in Linguistics, Structural Linguistics and Human Communication, Estudios de fonética hispanica, Phonétique générale et romane, Linguistique générale et romane,* and *Manuel de phonétique générale.*

Albert H. Marckwardt, Professor Emeritus of English and Linguistics, Princeton University; author of *Introduction to the English Language, American English, Linguistics and the Teaching of English.*

David D. Murison, Senior Lecturer in Scottish Language, Universities of Aberdeen and St. Andrews, Scotland; editor of *The Scottish National Dictionary.*

Ralph G. Nichols, Professor Emeritus of Rhetoric, University of Minnesota; author of *Complete Course in Listening;* coauthor of *Are You Listening?, Listening and Speaking, Learn to Listen, Speak and Write, Introduction to the Field of Speech, Practical Speech Making.*

Noel E. Osselton, Professor of English Language University of Newcastle-Upon-Tyne, Newcastle, England; Chairman of the European Association for Lexicography; author of *Branded Words in English Dictionaries before Johnson* and *The Dumb Linguists;* coeditor of Ten Bruggencate's *English-Dutch, Dutch-English Dictionary.*

Ladislas Országh, General editor of *Angol-Magyar Szótár: Magyar-Angol Szótár* [English-Hungarian and Hungarian-English Dictionary]; formerly, Professor of English at the University of Debrecen, Hungary.

Robert C. Pooley, Emeritus Professor of English, University of Wisconsin; author of *Grammar and Usage in Textbooks in English, Teaching English Usage, Teaching English Grammar.*

Thomas Pyles, Emeritus Professor of English and Linguistics, Northwestern University; author of *Words and Ways of American English, The Origins and Development of the English Language,* and *The English Language: A Brief History;* coauthor of *English: An Introduction to Language.*

Randolph Quirk, Quain Professor of English, University College, University of London; director of the Survey of English Usage; author of *The Use of English, The English Language and Images of Matter, The Linguist and The English Language;* coauthor of *An Old English Grammar, Investigating Linguistic Acceptability, Elicitation Experiments in English, A Grammar of Contemporary English, A University Grammar of English,* and *Old English Literature—A Practical Introduction.*

Abgar Renault, Professor of English Literature, University of Minas Gerais, Brazil; author of *Structure and Psychology of the English Language,* and *The Termination -ing (An essay on the English gerund).*

M. H. Scargill, Professor of Linguistics and Department Head, University of Victoria, Canada; director of Lexicographical Center for Canadian English; coeditor of *Dictionary of Canadian English* series and *Dictionary of Canadianisms;* author of *An English Handbook* and *Modern Canadian English Usage.*

John Spencer, Director, The Institute of Modern English Language Studies, University of Leeds, Leeds, England; editor of *Language in Africa, Language in West Africa, Journal of West African Languages,* and *The West African Language Monograph Series;* coauthor of *Linguistics and Style,* and *Modern Poems of the Commonwealth.*

Robert P. Stockwell, Professor of Linguistics and former Chairman, Department of Linguistics, UCLA; coauthor of *Patterns of Spanish Pronunciation, Sounds of English and Spanish, Grammatical Structures of English and Spanish, The Major Syntactic Structure of English, Foundations of Syntactic Theory;* coeditor of *Linguistic Change and Generative Theory.*

J. L. M. Trim, Fellow of Selwyn College, Cambridge; University Lecturer and Head of Department of Linguistics, University of Cambridge; author of *English Pronunciation Illustrated.*

R. W. Zandvoort, Professor of English (Emeritus), University of Groningen, The Netherlands; founder and past editor of *English Studies, a Journal of English Letters and Philology;* author of *A Handbook of English Grammar.*

Special consultants

Alexander, A. E., B.Sc., Ph.D. Fellow, A.A.A.S. Pres., A. E. Alexander Research Company; Editor: *National Jeweler, The Swiss Watch and Jewelry Journal;* American editor: *International Diamond Annual.* (Gem; Jewelry)

Allon, John E., B.Sc. F.R.Ae.S., A.M.I.Mech.E., A.F.A.I.A.A., F.B.I.S. Head of the Aerodynamics, Projects and Assessment Dept., Weapons Division, A. V. Roe and Co., Ltd. (England); Author: *Aerodynamics: A Space Age Survey;* Coeditor: *Spaceflight Technology.* (Aviation and Aerodynamics)

Banton, Michael Parker, Ph.D., D.Sc. Prof., Sociology, U. of Bristol; Author: *White and Coloured; West African City; The Policeman in the Community; Roles; Race Relations; Racial Minorities.* (Sociology)

Barnes, Clive, B.A. Dance Critic, *The Spectator.* Assoc. Ed., *Dance and Dancers;* Author: *Ballet in Britain since the War: Frederick Ashton and his Ballets.* (Dancing)

Baur, John I. H., B.A., M.A. Director Emeritus, Whitney Museum of American Art; Author: *Revolution and Tradition in Modern American Art;* Coauthor: *American Art of Our Century.* (Fine Arts)

Black, Michael H., M.A. Chief Ed. and Education Secretary, Cambridge U. Press (England); Contributor: *New English Larousse, Cambridge History of the Bible.* (Literature; Poetry)

Blythe, David, Director, Nottingham Photo Centre, Nottingham (England). (Photography)

Bonavia, Michael Robert, M.A., Ph.D., F.C.I.T. Formerly Special Project Advisor, British Railways Board; Author: *The Economics of Transport* (Railroad)

Borth, Christy, Former Asst. Managing Director, AMA. Author: *Masters of Mass Production; True Steel; Pioneers of Plenty; Mankind on the Move: A History of Roads.* (Automobile)

Bray, Charles W., Ph.D. Fellow, A.A.A.S.; Special Research Director, Research Group in Psychology and the Social Sciences, Smithsonian Institution; Author: *Psychology and Military Proficiency.* (Psychology)

Bretz, J Harlen, B.A., Ph.D. Fellow, A.A.A.S.; Emeritus Prof., Geology, U. of Chicago. (Geology)

Brewington, C. B., J.P., B.Sc. (Hons)., C. Eng., F.I.C.E., F.R.S.A., Deputy Director (Planning), Trent Polytechnic, Nottingham, England. (Building Trade; Civil Engineering)

Brobeck, Florence, B.Sc. Former Women's Editor, *New York Herald Tribune* and *American Weekly;* Former Assoc. Editor, *McCall's;* Author: *The Family Book of Home Entertaining; The New Cook It in a Casserole; Chafing Dish Cookery; Cooking With Curry.* (Cooking)

Buckingham, A. D., M.Sc., M.A., Ph.D., F.R.A.C.I., F.R.I.C., F.Inst.P., F.R.S., Prof., Chemistry, Cambridge U., Fellow, Pembroke College, Cambridge. (Chemistry)

Cain, A. J., M.A., D.Phil. F.L.S. Prof., Zoology, Dept. of Zoology, Liverpool U.; Author: *Animal Species and Their Evolution;* Editor: *Function and Taxonomic Importance.* (Zoology; Entomology; Animal Classification)

Cameron, Jessie C., Dom.Sc.Cert. (London), Cordon Bleu (Paris). Formerly Principal, Totley Hall Training College of Housecraft (England); Author: *Skill in Cookery.* (Homemaking)

Campbell, Victor E., A.B., B.S. Director, Clergy-Industry Relations, NAM; Editor: *Dateline;* Author: *Youth to Work!—In Your Community.* (Religion)

Carter, Will, Free lance designer, calligrapher and letter carver; Author: *Italic Handwriting.* (Handwriting)

Cleeton, Glen U., B.S., A.M. Fellow and Diplomate, American Psychological Assn.; Dean Emeritus, School of Printing Management, and Dean Emeritus, Div. of Humanities and Social Sciences, Carnegie-Mellon U.; Consulting editor, Graphic Arts, *McGraw-Hill Encyclopedia of Science and Technology.* Author: *Making Work Human;* Coauthor: *General Printing; Executive Ability.* (Printing)

Clegg, Hugh A., M.A., M.D. F.R.C.P. Former editor: *British Medical Journal;* Editor: Proceedings of First and Second World Conferences on Medical Education. (Medicine)

Copeland, Joseph J., A.B., Ph.D. Prof., Botany, The City College of New York; Pres., Asa Wright Nature Centre, Arima Valley, Trinidad. Author: *Yellowstone Thermal Myxophyceae.* (Plant Classification)

Cortelyou, Warren P., Ph.D. Prof., Chemistry, Towson (Md.) State College; Chmn., Chemistry staff. (Chemistry)

Dent, Harold Collett, B.A. F.R.S.A., Hon.F.E.I.S., Hon.F.C.P. Formerly Prof. of Education and Director, Inst. of Education, U. of Sheffield; Author: *Education in Transition; The Education Act 1944; The Educational System of England and Wales.* (Education)

Drew, David, B.A. Former Music Critic, *The New Statesman* (England); Author: *Kurt Weill: A Critical Biography; Modern French Music.* (Music)

Drewry, John Eldridge, A.B., B.J., A.M. Dean Emeritus and Prof. Emeritus, Journalism, Henry W. Grady School of Journalism, U. of Ga. Author: *Book Reviewing; Concerning the Fourth Estate;* Editor: *Post Biographies of Famous Journalists.* (Journalism)

Duncan, James Playford, M.E., D.Sc., M.I.Mech.E., M.I. Prod.E., Ch.E., P.Eng. British Columbia, Prof. and Head of Dept. of Mechanical Engineering, U. of British Columbia. (Automobile; Mechanical Engineering)

Eckstein, Beatrice Saward, B.Sc. Head of Dept. of Geography, Westhill College of Education; Former Lecturer in Geography, U. of Birmingham (England); Author: climatic maps in *Oxford Atlas.* (Meteorology)

Edmondson, Thomas Holden, Ph.C. Medical Information Officer, Nottingham (England). (Pharmacy)

Eyles, Dennis S., Asst. Chief Chemist, Crystal Product Co., Ltd. (England). (Cosmetics)

Eysenck, H. J., Ph.D., D.Sc. Prof., Psychology, Inst. of Psychiatry, U. of London; Fellow, A.P.A., B.P.S. Editor: *Behavior Research and Therapy;* Author: *Dynamics of Anxieties and Hysteria;* Editor: *Handbook of Abnormal Psychology.* (Psychiatry; Psychology)

Fishbein, Morris, M.D., D.Phar. (Hon.), LL.D. (Hon.) F.R.S.M. Prof., Medicine Emeritus, U. of Chicago and U. of Ill.; Medical editor: *Family Health;* Former editor: *Journal of the American Medical Association;* Author: *Modern Home Medical Adviser; Popular Medical Encyclopedia.* (Anatomy and Physiology; Medicine)

Ford-Robertson, Francis C., O.B.E., B.Sc., M.A. Indian Forest Service (Retired). Director and Editor: *Terminology of Forest Science, Technology, Practice and Products.* (Forest and Forest Products)

Gaster, Theodor H., M.A., Ph.D., D.D., D.Lit. Prof. Emeritus, Religion, Barnard College, Columbia College; Former Chief, Hebraic Section, Library of Congress; Author: *Thespis: Ritual, Myth and Drama in the Ancient Near East; The Oldest Stories in the World;* Editor: *The New Golden Bough; The Dead Sea Scriptures in English Translation; Myth, Legend and Custom in the Old Testament.* (Mythology)

Glass, Irving R., B.S., Ph.D. Exec. Vice-President, The Tanners' Council of America; Author: *American Leathers; Inventory Valuation for Tanners.* (Leather)

Grannis, Chandler B., A.B. Editor-at-Large, formerly Editor-in-Chief, *Publishers' Weekly;* Editor: *What Happens in Book Publishing;* Author: *Heritage of the Graphic Arts.* (Publishing)

Green, Neville, F.L.A. Physical Sciences Librarian, The University, Nottingham (England); Editor: *Directory of British Photo-Reproduction Services,* second ed. (Library)

Greig, Peter, B.A. Commandeur, Commanderie de Bordeaux; Chevalier de la Confrérie des Chevaliers du Tastevin; L'Ordre du Mérite Agricole; Author: *Wine and Food Newsletter* (1936-1960). (Wines and Liquors)

Guillebaud, Claude William, M.A. C.B.E. Emeritus Reader in Economics, Cambridge U.; Fellow, St. John's College, Cambridge; Member, Council, Royal Economic Soc.; Editor: *Variorum Edition of Alfred Marshall's Principles of Economics.* (Economics)

Guppy, Nicholas, M.A. F.R.G.S., F.Z.S. Former Asst. Conservator of Forests, British Guiana; Research Associate, New York Botanical Garden; Author: *Wai-Wai: Through the Forests North of the Amazon, A Young Man's Journey.* (Biology)

Harper, Norman, F.G.A., F.R.G.S., F.N.J.A., F.Inst.D. Sr. Lecturer (Retired), School of Silversmithing and Jewellery, Birmingham College of Arts and Crafts, England. Author: *An Introduction to Gemstones, The Hallmarking of Gold and Silver, Textbook on Gem Diamonds.* (Gem; Jewelry)

Hartsook, Jane, B.F.A., M.F.A. Director, Greenwich House Pottery, A School of Ceramics. (Ceramics)

Heflin, Woodford A., A.B., M.A., Ph.D. Prof. Emeritus, International Studies, Air University; Editor: *USAF Dictionary* and *Aerospace Glossary;* Co-editor: *Astronautical Multilingual Dictionary.* (Aviation and Astronautics)

Hibben, Frank Cummings, Ph.D. Prof., Anthropology and Director of Museum, U. of New Mexico; Author: *Prehistoric Man in Europe; Treasure in the Dust; The Lost Americans.* (Archaeology)

Hoijer, Harry, Ph.D. Prof., Dept. of Anthropology, U. of Calif. (Anthropology)

Horn, Stanley F., D.Lit. Editor: *The Southern Lumberman;* A Director of the Forest History Society; Author: *Army of Tennessee; This Fascinating Lumber Business.* (Forest and Forest Products)

Ivins, George H., A.B., M.A. Prof., Education and Chmn. of the Dept., Roosevelt U.; Maud E. Scott Distinguished Prof., Fundamental Education. (Education)

Jaklitsch, J. J., Jr., B.M.E. Editor: American Soc. of Mechanical Engineers: *Mechanical Engineering; Transactions of the A.S.M.E.* (Mechanical Engineering)

Jensen, Rue, B.S., M.S., D.V.M., Ph.D., D.V.Sc. Prof., Pathology, Dean, College Veterinary Medicine, Director Agricultural Experiment Station, Vice-President for Research, Director Diagnostic Laboratory, Colo. State U.; Coauthor: *Diseases of Feedlot Cattle; Diseases of Sheep.* (Veterinary Medicine)

Jessup, Walter E., A.B., C.E. Fellow, American Soc. of Civil Engineers; Consulting Engineer; Former Editor: *Civil Engineering;* Coauthor: *Law and Specifications for Engineers and Scientists.* (Civil Engineering)

Jewell, Andrew, B.Sc. Associate Director, Institute of Agricultural History and Keeper of the Museum of English Rural Life, U. of Reading (England). (Agriculture)

Jirak, Karel B., Dr. Jur., Diploma in Musicology; Member, Czech Academy of Arts and Sciences; Retired Prof. and Chmn., Dept. of Theory and Composition, Chicago Musical College, Roosevelt U.; Former Teacher of Theory and Composition, State Conservatory, Prague; Author: *Musical Forms;* biographies of Mozart, Fibich, Jan Herman, Dvorak. (Music)

Jones, John Moss, B.Sc. (Hons.), M.S., Dip.Met.Min. Assoc. Member, Institutes of Mining Engineers; Associate Member, British Inst. of Management; Former Member of Faculty, Colo. School of Mines. (Mining)

Jungerman, Martha E., B.Sc., M.Sc. Member, AHEA, The Fashion Group, National Home Fashions League, Inter-Society Color Council, Color Marketing Group, Color Coordinator, W. T. Grant Company; Lecturer: Columbia U., NYU, Temple U., The Fashion Inst. of Technology, and Philadelphia College of Textiles and Science. (Clothing)

Kehr, Ernest A., M.A., K.G.C.H.S., R.D.P., F.R.P.S.L. Director, Stamp News Bureau; Exec. Chmn., Philatelic Press Club; Stamp News Editor: *Long Island Newsday;* Author: *The Romance of Stamp Collecting.* (Stamps)

King, R. A., M.A., C.Eng., F.I.E.E. Senior lecturer in Electrical Engineering, Imperial College of Science and Technology, U. of London. (Electricity and Electronics)

Kingsford, R. J. L., M.A. Formerly Secretary to the Syndics, Cambridge U. Press (England); member of the London Board of Directors, Yale University Press. (Publishing)

Kirk, Albert, M.B.E., F.M.I.O.P. Consultant to the Graphic Arts; First Head of the Technical Department of the British Federation of Master Printers (now British Industries Printing Federation). (Printing)

Klots, Alexander B., Ph.D. F.R.E.S. Prof., Biology, The City College of N.Y.; Research Assoc., American Museum of Natural History; Author: *A Field Guide to the Butterflies; Living Insects of the World.* (Zoology; Animal Classification)

Kunitz, Stanley, A.B., A.M., Litt.D. (Hon.) Adjunct Prof. of Writing, School of the Arts, Columbia Univ.; Consultant in Poetry, Library of Congress; Author: *The Testing Tree; A Kind of Order; A Kind of Folly;* Editor: *Yale Series of Younger Poets.* (Literature; Poetry)

Lampe, Geoffrey W. H., (Rev. Prof.) M.C., D.D. Ely Prof. of Divinity, Cambridge U.; Author: *The Seal of the Spirit; A Patristic Greek Lexicon.* (Religion)

Landis, Benson Y., Ph.D., L.H.D., LL.D. Ed. of Research Publications, National Council of the Churches of Christ in the U.S.A.; Editor: *Yearbook of American Churches.* (Deceased) (Religion)

Leach, Sir Edmund R., M.A., Ph.D., F.B.A. Prof. of Social Anthropology and Provost of King's College, Cambridge U.; Author: *Political Systems of Highland Burma; Pul Eliya: a Village of Ceylon; Rethinking Anthropology; A Runaway World?; Claude Lévi-Strauss.* (Anthropology)

Leaman, Gladys Lucille, A.B., B.S. in L.S. Periodicals Librarian, Roosevelt U. (Library)

Lejeune, C. A., B.A., D.Litt. (Hon.) Former Film Critic, *Sunday Observer* (England); Author: *Cinema; Chestnuts in Her Lap.* (Motion Picture)

Linsley, E. Gorton, B.S., M.S., Ph.D. Fellow, A.A.A.S. Dean of the College of Agricultural Sciences, Emeritus, Prof. Emeritus, Entomology, Assoc. Director, Emeritus, Agricultural Experiment Station, U. of Calif.; Coauthor: *Methods and Principles of Systematic Zoology.* (Entomology)

Little, George T., Ph.D. Prof., Political Science, U. of Vt.; Editor: *Handbook for International Relief Administrators.* (Political Science)

MacDougall, A. J., M.Met. F.I.M. Sr. Lecturer, Dept. of Metallurgy, U. of Sheffield (England). (Metallurgy)

Maddison, Francis Romeril, M.A. Curator, Museum of the History of Science, Oxford U.; Author: *A Supplement to a Catalogue of Scientific Instruments in the Collection of J. A. Billmeir, Esq., C.B.E.;* "Scientific Instruments" in *The Concise Encyclopedia of Antiques; Mechanical Uni-*

verse; The Astrarium of Giovanni de' Dondi; Hugo Holt and the Rojas Astrolabe Projection. (Horology)

Marshall, Geoffrey, M.A., Ph.D. F.B.A. Fellow of Queen's College, Oxford U.; Author: *Parliamentary Sovereignty and the Commonwealth; Some Problems of the Constitution; Police and Government; Constitutional Theory.* (Political Science)

Mason, J. F. A., M.A., D.Phil., F.S.A. Student of Christ Church, Oxford U.; University Lecturer, Tutor in History, and Librarian, Christ Church, Oxford; Coauthor: *Christ Church and Reform 1850-1867.* (History)

Mason, John, F.R.S.A. Proprietor of the "Twelve by Eight," private press and paper mill; Author: *Papermaking as an Artistic Craft.* (Bookbinding)

Mayham, Stephen L., Ph.B. Honorary Member, Soc. of Cosmetic Chemists; Assoc. Member, Food and Drug Officials of the U.S.A.; Hon. Pres., The Toilet Goods Assn., Inc.; Author: *Marketing Cosmetics.* (Cosmetics)

McKenna, J. Fenton, B.A., M.A., Ph.B., LL.B., J.D., LL.D. Dean, School of Creative Arts, San Francisco State U. (Theater)

McLintock, Gordon (Rear Admiral), LL.D. Supt., U.S. Merchant Marine Academy; Author: *Learn —And Live; Cargo Handling Analysis; Kings Point—Education for Seafarers.* (Ship and Shipping)

McVittie, George C., M.A., Ph.D. F.R.A.S. Prof. and Head of Dept. of Astronomy, U. of Ill.; Secretary, AAS; Author: *General Relativity and Cosmology; Fact and Theory in Cosmology;* Editor: *Problems of Extra-Galactic Research.* (Astronomy)

Mulhern, George M., B.S., M.S. Director of Public Relations, Lockheed Electronics Co., A Div. of Lockheed Aircraft Corp.; Former Head, General Information Dept., Public Relations and Publications Div., Bell Telephone Laboratories. (Electricity and Electronics)

Nayler, J. L., M.A., C.Eng., F.R.Ae.S., F.A.I.A.A., F.B.I.S. Former Secretary, British Aeronautical Research Council and Commonwealth Advisory Aeronautical Research Council; Author: *Dictionary of Aeronautical Engineering; Dictionary of Astronautics; Dictionary of Mechanical Engineering.* (Aviation and Aerodynamics)

Orens, Irving Peary, B.S., M.A., Ph.D. Fellow, A.A.A.S.; Prof., Physics and Dean Emeritus of the Grad. Div., New Jersey Institute of Technology (Formerly Newark College of Engineering); Author: "Nuclear Radiation Shielding" in *Engineering Materials Handbook; Industrial Uses of Radio-Isotopes.* (Physics)

Osol, Arthur, B.Sc., M.Sc., Ph.D., LL.D., Sc.D. Fellow A.A.A.S., American Inst. of Chemists; Pres. and Prof. of Chemistry, Philadelphia College of Pharmacy and Science; Editor-in-chief, *Dispensatory of the United States of America;* Chmn. Editorial Board, *Blakiston's New Gould Medical Dictionary* and *Remington's Pharmaceutical Sciences.* (Pharmacy)

Pickup, Clifford, B.A., B.Sc., A.M.C.T., A.R.I.B.A. Sr. Lecturer in Architecture, Manchester Polytechnic, Manchester (England). (Architecture)

Pine, Leslie Gilbert, B.A., F.A.M.S., F.S.A.Scot, F.J.I., F.R.S.A. Barrister-at-Law, Tuner Temple; Assoc., Zoological Soc. of London; Member, Institute Internacional de Genealogia y Heráldica; Former Managing Editor: *Shooting Times and Country Magazine;* Former Editor: *Burke's Peerage, Burke's Landed Gentry;* Author: *American Origins; Trace Your Ancestors; Teach Yourself Heraldry and Genealogy; The Story of Surnames.* (Heraldry)

Plant, Sir Arnold, Kt. Bach. B.Com., B.Sc. (Econ.). Hon. LLD. Vice-President, R.Econ.S. Emeritus Prof., Commerce (with special reference to Business Administration), U. of London; Former Prof. and Dean of the Faculty of Commerce, U. of Cape Town (South Africa); Editor: *Some Modern Business Problems;* Author: *1974 Selected Economic Essays and Addresses.* (Trade)

Radford, Charles, B.Sc., F.R.I.C., F.I.Ceram, Senior Lecturer, College of Ceramics, North Staffordshire College of Technology (England). Author: *Calculations in Ceramics.* (Ceramics)

Ragland, Edward F., Vice-President, The Tobacco Institute, Inc. (Tobacco)

Reynolds, Thomas Herbert, B.Sc. A.Inst.P. District Insp. of Schools, Manchester Education Authority (England). (Physics)

Roalfe, William R., LL.B., LL.D. Prof. of Law Emeritus, School of Law, Northwestern U.; Author: *The Libraries of the Legal Profession.* (Law)

Roberts, J. Reginald, M.B.E., D.P.A., F.I.W.M.A. Formerly Chief Insp. of Weights and Measures, City of Manchester (England); Author: *The Training of the Weights and Measures Official in Great Britain.* (Weights and Measures)

Roehrich, Jean Louis, Graduate Technician Watchmaker (Geneva Horological Inst., Switzerland); Formerly Horological Ed., *National Jeweler Magazine.* (Horology)

Sanders, Irwin T., Ph.D. Fellow, American Sociological Soc., American Anthropological Assn., Rural Sociological Soc., Eastern Sociological Soc., Codirector, Community Sociology Training Program, Boston University; Author: *The Community: An Introduction to a Social System; Rainbow in the Rock.* (Sociology)

Schary, Dore, D.H.L., D.F.A. Pres., Dore Schary Productions; Author: *Sunrise at Campobello; For Special Occasions; Case History of a Movie; Devil's Advocate; The Highest Tree;* Coauthor: *Storm in the West; Herzl.* (Motion Picture)

Scott, Robert F., Tech. Editor, *Radio Electronics Magazine;* Electronics R & D consultant. (Electricity and Electronics)

Simon, André Louis, President-Founder of The International Wine and Food Soc.; Author: *The Concise Encyclopedia of Gastronomy; The Cheeses of the World; The History of the Wine Trade in England; The Noble Grapes and Great Wines of France.* (Cooking; Wines and Liquors)

Smith, Weston, B.C.S. Pres., Weston Smith Associates; Lecturer, Grad. School of Bus. Admin. NYU; Editor: *Survey of Shareholder Relations; Survey of Financial Relations Activities of Corporate Management; National Directory of Financial Publicists.* (Economics; Trade)

Smythe, Arthur R., D.V.S.M. F.R.C.V.S. Former Prof., Materia Medica and Toxicology, Royal Veterinary College, and Examiner of Materia Medica and Toxicology, Royal College of Veterinary Surgeons (England). (Veterinary Medicine)

Strange, John G., A.C., D.Sc. (Hon.) LL.D. (Hon.) Pres. and Treas., The Inst. of Paper Chemistry. (Paper)

Sunderman, James F. (Maj.), USAF, B.A., M.S. Chief, Magazine and Book Branch, and Chief, U.S.A.F. Book Program, Office of the Secretary of the Air Force: Former Instructor in History, U. of Miami; Editor: *Early Air Pioneers; World War II in the Air: The Pacific; World War II in the Air: Europe; Journey Into Wilderness.* (Military Science)

Sutherland, Carol Humphrey Vivian, M.A., D.Litt. Keeper of the Heberden Coin Room, Ashmolean Museum, Oxford U.; Student of Christ Church, Oxford; Vice-President, Royal Numismatic Soc.; Pres., International Numismatic Commission; Author: *Coinage in Roman Imperial Policy; Art in Coinage; Gold;* Coeditor: *Roman Imperial Coinage.* (Coins)

Thomas, Jack, Public Relations Consultant; Former Chief Feature-Writer, *Empire News* (England); Author: *No Banners; Given in Evidence; British Coaster;* Coauthor: *Tiger Squadron.* (Journalism; Sports)

Townsend, J. F., Editor: *Paper Packs* and *The Paper Market* (England). (Paper)

Treitel, G. H., B.C.L., M.A. Fellow, Magdalen College and All Souls Reader in English Law, Oxford U.; Visiting Prof., U. of Chicago Law School; Author: *Law of Contract; An Outline of the Law of Contract.* (Law)

Tyrwhitt-Drake, Sir Garrard, Kt., D.L., J.P. Chmn. Maidstone Corp. Museum; Chmn., The Tyrwhitt-Drake Carriage Museum Committee; Author: *My Life with Animals; The English Circus and Fairground.* (Carriage)

Urmson, James O., M.A. Fellow of Corpus Christi College, Oxford U.; Author: *Philosophical Analysis; The Emotive Theory of Ethics;* Editor: *The Encyclopedia of Western Philosophy.* (Philosophy)

Villiers, Alan, F.R.G.S. Vice-Pres., Soc. for Nautical Research; Trustee, National Maritime Museum (England); Member, HMS Victory Technical Advisory Committee, British Maritime Trust; Sailing-ship Master; Author: *The Way of a Ship; The Sons of Sinbad; By Way of Cape Horn; Captain Cook; The War with Cape Horn; Posted Missing; Falmouth for Orders.* (Ship and Shipping)

Wadsworth, James R., V.M.D., M.S. Animal Pathologist, U. of Vermont; Author: *Neoplasia in Captive Zoo Species; Some Clinicopathologic Considerations in Veterinary Oncology.* (Veterinary Medicine)

Walton, Ernest Charles, M.B.E., B.Eng., Ph.D., C.Eng., F.I.E.E. Formerly Head of Electrical Engineering and Physics Dept., Leeds College of Technology (England); Author: "The Electrical Properties of Galvanised Steel Conductors for Overhead Transmission Lines," *I.E.E. Journal,* Vol. 66; Coauthor: *Electrotechnology,* Vol. 1. (Electricity and Electronics)

Wheatland, Cynthia McAdoo, Former Interior Decoration Editor: *The Ladies' Home Journal.* (Homemaking)

Wichmann, Arthur P., B.S., M.S. Fellow, A.A.A.S. Emeritus Prof., Dept. of Metallurgical Engineering, Colorado School of Mines; Author: Chapter IX in *Mineral Resources of Colorado,* First Sequel. (Metallurgy)

Wiggin, Maurice, B.A. M.I.J. Television Critic, Out of Doors Editor, and Book Reviewer, *The Sunday Times* (England); Author: *In Spite of the Price of Hay; Troubled Waters; The Passionate Angler.* (Radio and Television)

Wilcockson, William Howson, M.A. F.G.S. Former Reader in Geology, U. of Sheffield (England); Editor: *Sections of Strata of the Yorkshire Coalfield.* (Geology)

Woodcock, Les, Assoc. Editor: *Sports Illustrated Magazine;* Sports consultant and author of *Collier's Encyclopedia Yearbook.* (Sports)

Editorial staff

Using your language

Speaking and writing are your most important forms of communication. Yet, you may not always express your thoughts and ideas as clearly as you would like to. You may be unsure of which words to choose to convey exactly what you mean. Or you may have problems with spelling, grammar, or punctuation. *Using your language* provides information that will help you with these mechanical aspects of English.

If you know something about the history of English, you will have a better understanding of your language. "Where English comes from," pages *14-16,* is an overview of how and why words become part of English; why the meaning or spelling of some words changes; why and how new words are invented; and why some words that were once popular are now old-fashioned or obsolete.

"Making words," pages *17-20,* will help you understand the structure of words. This section explains roots, prefixes, suffixes, and combining forms. It explains how an understanding of these word parts can help you increase your vocabulary and avoid spelling errors. It lists some of the most commonly used prefixes, suffixes, and combining forms, gives their meanings, and illustrates how each is used.

"Learning to spell correctly," pages *21-22,* will help you with spelling problems that may arise when a word is changed to show number, person, tense, or comparison. It lists spelling rules and exceptions to the rules.

"Common misspellings," page *23,* lists words commonly misspelled because of confusing pronunciations or because they contain silent letters.

"Parts of speech," pages *24-25,* explains the traditional approach to grammar. Here, the eight parts of speech are defined and the use of each is explained and illustrated.

"Capitalization" and "Punctuation," pages *26-31,* show how to use these aspects of language to make reading easier and meaning clearer.

If you want to avoid being a dull writer or conversationalist, read "Choosing the right word," page *32.*

"Writing and spelling traps," pages *33-38,* is a representative list of words that have different meanings, but may be misused because they sound alike or are similar in form.

The final section, "Vocabulary inventories," pages *39-63,* explains why a good vocabulary is an asset, and gives you an opportunity to test your word power through graded vocabulary inventories and answers.

Where English comes from

The English language has existed for hundreds of years. Many words came into English from various European languages. For example, St. Augustine and other Latin-speaking missionaries to England used such words as *bishop* and *priest.* Latin was the language of scholarship and religion. Wherever Latin scholars, missionaries, and government officials exerted important influence, Latin words became known. When the Scandinavians invaded and settled in Britain, some words beginning with *sk-* were adopted into English. For example, *skill, skirt,* and *sky.* The Scandinavians also contributed important pronouns such as *their, them,* and *they.* Words of French origin include *army, blue, chair, dinner, government, jolly, mayor, paper,* and *towel. Balcony, piano,* and *pizza* come from Italy; *fiesta* and *siesta,* from Spain; *orchestra,* from Greece; *boomerang,* from Australia; *vodka,* from Russia; and *igloo,* from the Eskimos.

English is always growing and changing. Words constantly are being added and falling into disuse. Many words that you hear, speak, and read today were not part of the language your grandparents used. Look in a dictionary published at that time and you will not find such words as *astronaut, culture shock, miniskirt, rolamite,* and *microfiche.* Every time new inventions, scientific discoveries, art forms, or fashions appear that do not have names to identify them, new words must be invented or old words given new applications, or taken from other languages.

When words are not used, they become obsolete. Obsolete words are included in the dictionary because they are part of our history and our culture. You will want to know what they mean when you read them in old books or hear them used in plays written a long time ago. Before the automobile was a common form of transportation, people traveled in *buggies* drawn by horses. Now when you hear or see the word *buggy* you are inclined to think of something old-fashioned or insect-ridden.

Many words have changed their meanings. For example, *sly* and *crafty* people were once described as "pretty." At one time, when people wanted to picture someone as *stupid* and *ignorant* they referred to that person as "nice." Today, if someone tells us we are "nice" and "pretty," we feel flattered, not insulted.

These are only a few of the ways in which language changes and grows. By knowing how words become part of a language, you discover important clues to social, political, and cultural changes that take place in the history of a country using that language.

The story of how English originated is a fascinating one.

How English began

English comes from a common ancestral language believed to have existed a very long time ago. It has been called *Indo-European.* About 4,500 years ago, the people who spoke varying forms of this language split into groups that drifted into Europe and parts of Asia. Different speech communities developed within these widespread groups eventually giving rise to several languages including Latin, from which many of the languages spoken in Europe today developed. One group of Indo-European languages is known as Germanic, and this is the primary parent language of English and German.

Warrior-adventurers, who spoke Germanic, invaded what is now Great Britain about A.D. 450. The invaders—called Angles, Saxons, and Jutes—all spoke similar dialects. The people they conquered, known as Britons, spoke Celtic. The Celtic language included Latin words because conquering Roman troops occupied Britain from A.D. 43 until the 400's. The troops had to return home to defend Rome against invading armies. The Germanic tribes conquered Britain after the Romans left.

As the invading tribes took over and settled in Britain, the Celtic languages gradually retreated. Since the Celtic people were forced to communicate with their rulers, the history of the English language begins with the take-over of Britain by the Germanic tribes. As a result, Celtic made only a small contribution to the English vocabulary with words such as *crag* and *bin.* However, many place names were adopted from the Celtic. Among them are *Avon, Kent, London, Ouse,* and *Thames.* Small groups of people living in Ireland, Wales, and the Scottish Highlands still speak varieties of Celtic such as Scottish Gaelic, Welsh, Breton, and recently revived Irish.

Old English

The Angles and Saxons occupied a large part of Britain. The name of one of the former tribes eventually became the name of the land they occupied, *England.* The Anglo-Saxon language, now usually called Old English, became firmly established in Britain in the period from the A.D. 500's to 1066.

Even as this happened, changes were taking place. Latin-speaking Roman and Celtic missionaries under St. Augustine, began spreading Christianity in Britain. The introduction of Christianity exerted a great impact on the English language. Religion brought with it many new ideas and customs. And Christianity used Latin. In their attempt to identify and deal with all these new ideas and customs, the Anglo-Saxons did not hesitate to borrow from Latin the special vocabulary needed for the new religious life. Among the words taken from Church Latin which still survive are:

Latin	Old English	Modern English
abbātis	abbod	abbot
candēla	candel	candle
altāre	altar	altar
āmēn	amen	amen
apostolus	apostol	apostle

However, users of Old English did not borrow as heavily from Latin and other languages in this period as they did later when there was greater communication with the Continent. Sometimes they changed the meanings of native words. The word for Easter (*eastron*) originally was the name for the spring festival honoring the goddess of dawn. *Geōl* (Yule), the name of the festival held to celebrate the passing of the shortest day of the year, came to denote Christmas.

Native ingenuity was shown in creating new words by combining two native words in much the same way as we now combine words such as *space* and *worthy* to form *spaceworthy.* Old English words such as *lœcecraft* (leechcraft), meaning medicine, and *handbōc* (handbook), meaning manual, illustrate this practice.

The growth of the Old English vocabulary during this period of language history reflects the growth of English culture. Because of the Church's influence, scholarship was encouraged and Britain began its rise as one of the intellectual leaders of Europe.

Toward the end of the 700's, hardy Vikings from Denmark, Norway, and Sweden began invading and settling in many parts of Britain. By the 1000's, a Danish king ruled Britain. As a result of the invasions from the Danish peninsula, many Scandinavian words became part of English. These did not identify new ideas and objects. They were everyday words for which the English already had terms and expressions.

Why did the Scandinavian words exist side by side with English words instead of replacing them? The Scandinavian invaders were Germanic people like the Anglo-Saxons. Their cultures were similar and their languages enough alike so that they understood one another. Many words were exactly alike, such as *father, husband, house, life, man, mother, summer, wife,* and *winter.* Other words were so much alike they were used interchangeably.

Although the Scandinavians and the English fought each other, many Scandinavians settled peacefully in Britain, married English women, and raised families. Often both languages were spoken in the same household. Where different words existed for the same thing, the Old English word usually won out, but there were some exceptions. The results of this absorption of language through close contact is seen in the histories of such words from Scandinavia as *skirt, skill, window, leg, gasp, birth, glitter, they, their, them, egg.*

Scholars believe that at least 900 words of Scandinavian origin have survived in modern Standard English. Many more are still in use in Great Britain. They are found in dialects spoken in regions heavily settled by the Swedes, Danes, and Norse in those early days.

Middle English

Old English began to undergo a great change when the Normans invaded England from France in 1066. Until then, in spite of the Latin brought in by the introduction of Christianity, the influence on English was overwhelmingly Germanic. The Normans began a process that brought many French words into the English language. They replaced the English as rulers, chief landholders, and church officials and Norman-French became the language of the ruling class. However, the common people continued to speak English.

Norman-French and Old English existed side by side until political and social changes began to favor the use of English by all classes. The Normans lost control of their territory in France in the early 1200's. Confined to Britain, the Normans began to learn English. Eventually, it replaced French as the language of the ruling class, the schools, and the courts. By the end of what is known as the Middle English period (1100-1500), English again had established itself as the major language in Britain.

During this period, English continued to borrow words from French and from Latin. In the English we now speak, more than half of the words in common use come from these two sources. Many words from Old English and Anglo-French that are roughly synonymous exist side by side today. For example, *dress* and *clothes, aid* and *help, royal* and *kingly.* In addition, trade between Britain and the Low Countries, especially Holland, accounts for the inclusion of perhaps as many as 2,500 words of Dutch origin in the English language. Some examples are: *boom* (at the bottom of a sail), *deck, easel, etch, freight, furlough,* and *stoop* (porch or entrance).

Before the Norman invasion, a great change in English was beginning to shift grammatical and pronunciation patterns. However, the coming of the Normans accelerated these changes. Everyday use, growth of dialects, and contact with foreign languages caused inflections (word endings) to lose their distinctive meanings and their usefulness. Instead of depending on word endings to give exact meaning to a sentence, as had been the case in Old English, word order became the important indicator.

In Old English, for example, *To his þeowum se fæder cwæð,* meaning "The father said to his servants" or "To his servants the father said," would have the same meaning no matter how the words were placed in the sentence. The *-um* ending on þeow(um) would always indicate who was being spoken to. In modern English, if we shift word order to make the sentence read "His servants said to the father," the meaning would be quite different.

English still retains some inflections, including plurals and the verb endings. But Middle English had far fewer inflections than Old English.

Modern English

The Modern English period, starting about 1500, has been concerned for the most part with regulating and standardizing the language. But attempts to fix English into a permanent form failed. The way a language is used gives it life, and usage produces change.

However, fixing a language and freezing its usages into a form that tolerates no change is different from trying to standardize its spelling so that communication between inhabitants of various regions of the country is easy and effective.

Several factors contributed to establishing Standard English spelling and some forms of usage and many of the traits that exist in modern English. These factors included the introduction of the printing press into England in 1477 by William Caxton, the revival of interest in literature, and the growth of popular education.

The need for standardization was recognized as early as the mid-1300's. From that time, the London dialect (East Midland) was gradually adopted from the four main dialects in existence (Northern, East and West Midland, and Southern) as the basis for Standard English. The choice was made because the London dialect was the language of contracts and commerce and the speech of the ruling court. All official documents originating there were written in the London dialect. Furthermore, the translation of the Book of Common Prayer and the King James version of the Bible became tremendous forces for elevated English.

Before Caxton, literary works were written for the most part in the dialect of the author. Spoken dialects continued for a long time and, indeed, still exist. But, by the end of the 1400's, the London dialect was becoming accepted literary usage.

By the early part of the 1600's, more than 20,000 different works were printed in England alone. Books were available to all who could read and afford them. The printed word helped to make spelling more uniform. Up until that time spelling usually varied from region to region.

From the 1500's through the 1700's, many writers experimented with words. Over 10,000 new words entered the English language. Many of these were taken from Latin and Greek by scholars who wanted to replace the forms earlier adopted from French. Translators and writers believed the language was rough, unpolished, and incapable of doing what Latin and Greek had done, and what Italian could do.

They set about enlarging the vocabulary, chiefly by translating words from Greek and Latin. More than twenty-five per cent of modern English words come almost directly from classical languages. Very often we have two words that go back to the same Latin original—one brought in by the Normans, and one taken in directly. For example, words such as *paint* and *picture, certainty* and *certitude.* The adoption of Greek and Latin forms became so abundant and so outrageous that many of these borrowings were dubbed "inkhorn terms" because of their bookishness. However, some of these terms were useful and necessary and they have survived to this day. Among them are *conduct, dexterity, extinguish, scientific,* and *spurious.*

American and British English

After the British colonized America, the English language used by Americans began to change from that in the old country. The biggest factor in this change involved the need to create or adopt words to identify unfamiliar objects. Animals, trees, food, and the physical features of the land were different. The Americans took words from the Indians to identify a raccoon, a tomahawk, a papoose, and a wigwam. When there were no appropriate words, they did what their ancestors had done. They combined words and gave them new meanings. The combination of *garter* and *snake* produced a word to describe a crawling creature they had never seen before. They named the sweet, edible root of a vine belonging to the morning-glory family, *sweet potato.* They adapted from the Narraganset Indians the name for the fruit of a plant of the gourd family, the *squash.*

The growth of American nationalism led to a desire for cultural as well as political independence from the mother country. This, too, influenced American English, as in conscious attempts to reform spelling so that in time, *musick* became *music,* and *labour* became *labor.* New ideas in the arts and sciences and the coming to America of people from many different countries had a powerful effect on American English.

Changes have not been so extensive that we speak a new language. Many Americans may not know that when an Englishman says *fitment* he means an *alteration,* and that the British *goods wagon* is the American *freight car.* But, for the most part, Americans and Britons communicate easily because grammatical and phonetic patterns have not changed, though many words or lexical content are different.

The gap between American and British English has become smaller in recent times, especially with the great increases in the ease of transportation and communication. Neither the Americans nor the British have any qualms about appropriating words from other languages when they express concepts better than native words can. The British have taken American words such as *telephone, jazz,* and *typewriter.* Americans take words from many languages.

English has also changed in other countries where it is used. Canadians, Australians, New Zealanders, and others have adapted English to fit their own needs. Although all English-speaking people can generally understand each other, each English-speaking country has developed distinctive ways of using the language. For example, New Zealanders refer to a *section* (a building lot in a city), Australians to a *mob* (a group of animals), and Canadians to a *chesterfield* (an overstuffed sofa).

As long as travel and trade exist between nations, as long as large groups of people continue to settle in countries other than their native lands, and as long as the sciences and the arts progress, new ideas, new words, and new usages of words will continue to keep language changing and growing.

Making words

You can often learn the spelling and meaning of words more easily when you know how they are put together. Three parts or elements go into the making of many words: *roots, affixes,* and *combining forms.*

A root gives a word its basic or etymological meaning. It may be a word in itself or a word part. *View,* meaning "sight" or "to look at," is a root word. *Port,* which is a Latin form, means "to carry." It is a root that is also a word part in Latin. It is found in Anglicized Latin borrowings as in the words *portable, porter,* and *import.*

Affixes are added before or after words or word parts to modify the meaning of a root. *Re-* is added before *view* to make the word *review,* meaning "to look at again." The affix *-er* can be added to *view,* to make a word meaning "a person who looks at," or to *review,* to make a word meaning "a person who looks at again." An affix placed at the beginning of a word or word part is called a prefix. An affix at the end is a suffix. Prefixes and suffixes may be a syllable, syllables, or a word.

The root word *fold* means "to bend or double over." Add the prefix *un-,* meaning "the opposite," and you have *unfold,* which means "to open up what has been doubled over." Add the suffix *-er,* meaning "performer of an act," and you have *folder,* "something or someone that folds."

A list of prefixes and suffixes commonly used in word building follows on pages *18-19. Attachable, attaching, reattach,* and *unattached* have the same root. Can you identify the root, prefixes, and suffixes? Look up the prefixes and suffixes in the lists that follow and see how they modify the meaning of the root.

Suffixes often change a word's part of speech. (For a full discussion of parts of speech, see pages *24* through *25.*) The adjective *sad* is made into a noun by adding *-ness,* which means "the state of being." The noun *courage* is changed into an adjective by adding the suffix *-ous,* meaning "full of." Writers commonly use the suffix *-ly* to make adverbs: *glad, gladly; correct, correctly.*

Suffixes also are used with adjectives and adverbs to indicate increasing degree. The suffix *-er* forms the comparative, and *-est* forms the superlative for many words: *greater, greatest; faster, fastest; prettier, prettiest.*

Another element used in building words is called a combining form. This is a special form of a word joined with another word or word part to make a combined word. *Tele-,* meaning "having to do with or operating over a long distance" (from the Greek *têle,* meaning "far off") and *-phone,* meaning "sound" (from the Greek *phōnḗ,* meaning "sound") combine to make *telephone. Bio-,* meaning "life or living things" (from the Greek *bíos,* meaning "life") and *-logy,* meaning "science of" (from the Greek *lógos,* meaning "deal with or discuss") combine to form *biology. Cosmology, geology,* and *hydrology* are made the same way. Another example is the combining form *auto,* which can be used with other combining forms and words such as *biography, graph,* and *mobile.* Many combining forms are well-established in English, but are borrowed from Latin or Greek words, or may originate from other languages, such as French and German.

A list of combining forms that can be used with other word elements to create thousands of words follows on page *20.*

Word parts and spelling

Understanding the building of words helps you to spell. Those who realize that *tele-* is a combining form meaning "operating over long distances" are unlikely to make the errors of spelling *telephone* or *telemeter* as *telaphone* or *telameter.* Often, the addition of a suffix does not change the spelling of a root word: *heiress, greenish, brighten, joyful.* In some cases, however, the suffix requires a variation in the spelling of the root word: *desirable, victorious, truly.* At times, the prefix calls for insertion of a hyphen before the rest of the word: *co-conspirator, anti-imperialist.* Guidelines for spelling words made by adding affixes appear in the spelling section on pages 21-22, and the rules for using a hyphen on page 28.

Understanding unfamiliar words

Understanding something about the function of roots, affixes, and combining forms will often help you recognize many new or unfamiliar words. If you know the meanings of such combining forms as *photo-* (meaning "light" and "photographic"); *-meter* (meaning "device for measuring"); *chrono-* (meaning "time"); and *-graph* (meaning "something written, drawn or pictured" and "an instrument that writes, draws or pictures, or records"), you can construct and determine the meaning of many words, such as the following:

photochemistry
photocopy
photometer
photograph
photochronograph
chronometer
chronophotograph
chronograph

Once you know that words are made up of elements in predictable positions, you can break down a word into its parts. You may know the meanings of these parts, or you can easily look them up. The lists of prefixes, suffixes, and combining forms help you do this.

Many English words are made up of roots and affixes that are derived from Latin and Greek. For example, consider the word *interplanetary.* It is composed of the prefix, inter- (from the Latin *inter,* meaning "among; between"); the root word, planet (from the Greek *planḗtēs* [*astḗrēs*], meaning "wandering stars"); and the suffix, -ary (from the Latin *-ārius,* meaning "place for; belonging to"). Thus, the definition of the word *interplanetary* is "situated between the planets; in the region of the planets." Sometimes, two combining forms are joined to make a word. For example, Anglo- (from the Latin *Anglī,* meaning "English") and -phile (from the Greek *phílos,* meaning "lover of") are two combining forms joined to make the word *Anglophile* which is defined as "a friend or admirer of England and the English."

You see how knowing word organization can enrich your vocabulary. Once you understand unfamiliar words, you are able to use them in speaking and writing. The more words that you can use, the better you can make your ideas and opinions understood by others. Thus, you have learned to communicate more effectively.

Following are lists of selected prefixes, suffixes, and combining forms. Any element listed may change its form when being used to make a word. For example, the combining form *auto* sometimes drops the final *o* when added to word parts beginning with vowels: *autism, autarchy.*

Prefixes

Prefix	Meaning	Example
a-	on, in, into	afire, abed
	in the act of	aflutter
	not	apolitical
ab-; a-	from, away, off	abdicate; aperture
ad-; a-; ac-	to, toward	adverb; ascribe; accede
	at, near	adjacent
an-	not	anastigmatic
	without	anarchy
ana-; an-	back, again	anachronism
	up, upward	anode
ante-	before	antedate
anti-	against, opposed to	antiaircraft
	not, opposite of	antisocial
apo-	from, away, off	apocryphal
arch-; archi-	chief, principal	archbishop; architect
	extreme, ultra	archconservative
bi-	two	bisect
	twice, once every two	biannual
cata-	down, downward	cataract
	against	catapult
circum-	around, on all sides	circumlocution
cis-	on this side of	cislunar
co-	with, together	cooperate
	joint, fellow	coauthor
com-; col-; con-	with, together, altogether	combine; collaborate; congress
contra-	against	contradict
de-	to do the opposite of	decentralize
	down, lower	depress
	away, off	derail
	to remove, take away	defrost
demi-	half, partial	demigod
	smaller than ordinary	demitasse
di-; dis-	twice, double, two	diphthong; dissyllable
dia-; di-	through, across	diameter; diocese
dis-	opposite, lack of	dishonest
	apart, away	dismiss
dys-	bad, defective	dysfunction
en-; em-	to cause to be, make	enable; employ
	to put in, put on	enthrone; emblem
epi-; ep-	on, upon, above, in addition, toward	epidemic; epitaph; ephemeral
eu-	good, well, true	euphoria
ex-; e-	former, formerly	ex-president
	out of, from, out	exhale; emerge
	thoroughly, utterly	exterminate; evaporate
extra-	outside, beyond	extraordinary
fore-	front, in front	forepaw
	before, beforehand	foregoing
hemi-	half	hemisphere
hyper-	over, excessive, above, exceedingly	hypercritical, hypersensitive
hypo-	under, beneath	hypodermic
	to a lesser degree	hypothyroid
in-; il-; im-; ir-	not, lack of, opposite of	incorrect; illegal; impatient; irregular
	in, into, on, upon	inscribe; illuminate; imbibe; irrigate
infra-	below, beneath	infrastructure

Prefix	Meaning	Example
inter-	one with the other	intercommunicate
	between, among	interpose
intra-	within, inside	intramural
intro-	inward, within, into	introduce
meta-	between, among	metacarpus
	change of state	metabolism
	behind, after	metathorax
mis-	bad, badly	misgovern
	wrong, wrongly	mispronounce
non-	not, opposite of lack of, failure	nonbreakable, nonliving
ob-; op-; of-; o-	against, in the way, hindering	obstruct; oppose; omit
	inversely, contrary	oblate
	toward, to	obvert; offer
	on, over	obtuse
para-	beside, near	parathyroid
	beyond	parapsychology
	related to, subordinate to	paramedical, paralegal
	disordered condition	paranoia
per-	throughout	perpetual
peri-	around, surrounding	perimeter
post-	after in time	postwar
	after in space	postnasal
	after and caused by	postoperative
pre-	before	prewar
pro-	forward	proceed
	forth, out	proclaim
	on the side of	pro-British
	in place of, acting as	proconsul
	before, preceding	prologue
	in front of	proscenium
quasi-	partly	quasi-judicial
re-	again, anew	reappear
	back	repay
semi-	exactly half	semicircle
	about half, partly	semicivilized
sub-	under, below	subnormal
	down, further, again	subdivide
	near, nearly	subtropical
	lower, subordinate	subhead
super-	over, above	superimpose
	besides, further	superadd
	in high proportion	superabundant
	surpassing	supernatural
syn-; sy-; syl-; sym-	with, together, jointly	synagogue; system; syllogism; symbol
trans-	across, over, through	transcontinental
	beyond, on the other side of	transcend, transoceanic
	to or into a different condition	transform, transmigration
ultra-	beyond	ultraviolet
	extremely	ultramodern
un-	not	unequal
	the opposite of	ungodly
uni-	one, a single	unicellular
up-	up	update
vice-	one who acts in place of another	vice-president, viceroy

Suffixes

Suffix	Meaning	Example
-able	that can be	obtainable
	suitable for; giving	comfortable
	inclined to	peaceable
	fit to; deserving of	wearable, lovable
-age	action; process	breakage
	group; collection of	baggage
	state or rank of	peerage
	cost of; fee for	postage
	house or place of	orphanage, anchorage
-al, -ial	having the nature of	ornamental; facial
	act of	arrival
-an; -ean; -ian	native of	American; European
	having to do with	Shakespearian
-ana; -iana	collection of; about	Americana; Burnsiana
-ance; -ancy	act of	resistance
	thing that	conveyance
	quality or state of	buoyancy
-ant	state or condition of	defiant
	one who	assistant
-ary	place for	infirmary
	collection of	statuary
	having to do with	legendary
-ate	having to do with	collegiate
	make or cause to be	alienate
	produce	ulcerate
	supply or treat with	aerate
	combine with	oxygenate
-ation	act or process of	computation
-cle, -cule	little, small	particle; molecule
-cy	state of being	bankruptcy
	position or rank	captaincy
-dom	rank or realm of	kingdom
	condition of	freedom
-ed	having, or having characteristics of	long-legged, bigoted, honeyed
-en	cause to be; make	blacken
	cause to have	strengthen
	to become	sicken
	made of; have look of	silken
	plural	oxen
-ence	state of being	indifference
-ent	one who	president
-er, -ier, -yer	one who does or is concerned with	reporter; cashier; lawyer
	person living in	New Yorker
	more (comparative)	smarter
	action or process of	waiver
-ery	the art of	cookery
	the condition of	slavery
	quality or action of	knavery
	a place where	bindery
-ese	having to do with	Chinese
-esque	in the style of	Romanesque
	like a	statuesque
-ess	female	heiress
-est	most (superlative)	smartest
-et	little, small	owlet
-ette	little, small	dinette
-ful	full of	cupful, playful
-fy	make or cause to be	electrify, simplify

Suffix	Meaning	Example
-hood	state of being	childhood
-ible	can be, able to be	divisible
-ic	having to do with	atmospheric
	having the nature of	heroic
	containing	alcoholic
	made or caused by	volcanic
	like; similar to	meteoric
-ical	of the nature of	critical, political
-ing	act of person or thing	acting, running
-ion	act or process of	admission
	state or condition	subjection
-ish	somewhat	sweetish
	like a	childish
	having to do with	English
	tending to	bookish
-ism	act or practice of	baptism
	quality or condition	heroism
	doctrine or theory	Darwinism
	expert in	botanist
	one who believes in	socialist
-ite	native of	Denverite
	descendant of	Israelite
	follower of	Jacobite
-itis	inflammation of	tonsillitis
-ity	state of	acidity
-ive	having to do with	sportive
-ize	become or resemble	Americanize
	treat or combine with	oxidize
-less	without	meatless
	that does not	tireless
	that cannot be	countless
-let	little, small	booklet
-like	like; similar to	homelike
-ling	little, small	duckling
-ly	in a manner	cheerfully
	like a	ghostly
-ment	act or state of	enjoyment
	condition of being	amazement
	product or result of	pavement
-most	most (superlative)	uppermost
-ness	state or quality of	greatness
-oid	like, similar to	adenoid, spheroid
-or	person or thing that does something	auditor, actor, elevator
	act, state, quality, or condition	error, horror, labor, terror
-ory	place for	conservatory
	tending or inclined to	conciliatory
-osis	abnormal condition	psychosis
-ous	full of	poisonous
-ry	occupation or work of	dentistry
	collection of	citizenry
-ship	condition of being	partnership
	office or occupation	authorship
	act, power, or skill	horsemanship
-some	tending to	meddlesome
-ster	person who	trickster
-tion	act or state of	locomotion
-ule	little, small	capsule, globule
-ure	act or process of	closure
-ward	toward; leading to	homeward

Combining forms

Form	Meaning	Example
aero-	atmosphere	aerospace
agro-	field, soil	agrology
ambi-	both	ambidextrous
amphi-	around; on both sides	amphitheater
archaeo-	primitive, ancient	archaeology
astro-	star; heavenly body	astrophysics
atmo-	vapor, steam	atmosphere
auto-	self	autobiography
baro-	atmospheric pressure	barometer
biblio-	books	bibliography
bio-	life; of living things	biochemistry
calci-	lime, calcium	calciferous
cardio-	heart	cardiology
centi-	one hundred	centipede
	one hundredth	centimeter
centro-	center, central	centrobaric
chromato-, chromo-	color, pigment	chromatology, chromoplast
chrono-	time	chronometer
-cide	killer	insecticide
cosmo-	world, universe	cosmological
counter-	against	counteract
cranio-	skull	craniology
crypto-	hidden, secret	cryptography
cyclo-	circle	cyclotron
cyto-	cell	cytogenesis
deca-	ten	decade
deci-	one tenth	decibel
dextro-	toward the right	dextrorotatory
ecto-	to or on the outside	ectoderm
electro-	electric	electromagnet
endo-	inner	endoderm
equi-	equal	equivalence
ethno-	race, nation	ethnology
ferro-	contains iron	ferronickel
fibro-	fiber, fibrous	fibrovascular
-gamous	marrying, joining	bigamous
-gamy	marriage	polygamy
geo-	earth	geology
-gram	something written	telegram
-graph	instrument that writes	seismograph
-graphy	to write	biography
-gynous	woman, female	misogynous
gyro-	circle	gyroscope
hecto-	a hundred	hectogram
helio-	the sun	helioscope
hema-, hemo-	blood	hemachrome, hemolymph
hepta-	seven	heptagon
hexa-	six	hexagon
holo-	whole	holocaust
homo-	the same; equal	homogenous
hydro-	water	hydroplane
hypno-	sleep, hypnosis	hypnology
hypo-	under, below	hypodermic
ideo-	idea	ideograph
iso-	equal, alike	isobar
kilo-	one thousand	kilometer
lacto-	milk	lactoprotein
leuco-	without color	leucocyte
levo-	toward the left	levorotatory
litho-	stone, stony	lithography

Form	Meaning	Example
-logy	science of	biology
macro-	large	macrocosm
mal-	bad, poor	maladjusted
mega-	large	megaphone
-meter	a device for measuring	chronometer
micro-	small	microcosm
	one millionth	microfarad
mid-	middle	midnight
milli-	one thousandth	millimeter
-monger	dealer, seller	fishmonger
mono-	one, single	monorail
multi-	many, much	multiform
nano-	one billionth	nanosecond
neo-	new, recent	neoplasm
neuro-	nerve	neurosurgery
nitro-	nitric acid	nitrocellulose
oct-, octa-, octo-	eight	octet, octachord, octopus
omni-	all, completely	omnipotent
ortho-	straight, correct	orthopedics
paleo-	old, ancient	paleography
pan-	all	Pan-American
-pathy	feeling	antipathy
	disease	psychopathy
pedo-	child, children	pedodontics
penta-	five	pentameter
phil-, philo-	loving; fond of	philanthropy, philobiblic
-phobia	fear, hatred	acrophobia
phon-, phono-	sound	phonics, phonometer
photo-	light	photograph
phyto-	plant	phytochemistry
pico-	one trillionth	picofarad
poly-	many	polynomial
pyro-	having to do with fire	pyromania
quadr-, quadri-	four	quadrangle, quadrilateral
schizo-	split, divided	schizophrenic
sept-	seven	septangular
sex-	six	sexangular
spectro-	spectrum	spectroscope
spermato-	seed, sperm	spermatocyte
sporo-	spore	sporogenesis
-stat	stabilizing instrument	thermostat
stereo-	solid	stereobate
	three dimensional	stereoscopic
tel-, tele-	operating over long distances	telelectric, telescope
tera-	one trillion	teravolt
tetra-	four	tetrahedron
theo-	a god or gods	theology
thermo-	heat	thermodynamics
topo-	place	topography
tri-	three	triangle
tricho-	hair, hairlike	trichosis
vaso-	blood vessel	vasoconstrictor
xeno-	stranger	xenophobia
xero-	dry	xeroderma
xylo-	wood, woody	xylophone
zoo-	animal	zoology
zygo-	yoke, paired	zygomorphic

Learning to spell correctly

You can learn to spell any word in this dictionary, or all of them if you want. You begin by looking up the word. "Spelling and looking up words," on pages *122-123* explains how to look up a word that you cannot spell.

Once you have looked it up, make the word yours by following these steps:

1. Write the word neatly and clearly.
2. Close your eyes and visualize the word in your mind.
3. Spell the word out loud.
4. Study the syllables if it has more than one.
5. Pronounce the word out loud.
6. Study its meaning; it may have more than one.
7. Make up a sentence with the word.
8. Use the word at every opportunity in writing and talking.

Once you learn how to spell a word, most spelling problems arise when the word is changed to show number, person, tense, or comparison.

To help you with these problems, a list of spelling rules is given below. Don't try to memorize the rules. Remember that they can be found on these pages. When you have a spelling problem look it up here, and learn the rules and exceptions by using them.

Which is correct?	Correct spelling	This rule explains why	Some exceptions
beleive or believe relieve or releive sliegh or sleigh	**believe** **relieve** **sleigh**	Use *i* before *e* except after *c* or when sounded as *a* as in neighbor and weigh.	*counterfeit, either, foreign, forfeit, height, leisure, seize, weird*
handkerchieves, handkerchiefs, or handkerchiefes	**handkerchiefs**	Most singular words are made plural by adding *s.*	Some nouns ending in *f* or *fe* form the plural by changing the *f* or *fe* to *ve* and adding *s: knives, elves, halves, calves, leaves, loaves, sheaves, shelves, wives.*
armys or armies	**armies**	Nouns ending in *y* preceded by a consonant, form the plural by changing *y* to *i* and adding *es.*	Proper names ending in *y* form the plural by adding *s:* "There are four *Marys* in this class."
monkeys or monkies	**monkeys**	Nouns ending in *y* preceded by a vowel, form the plural by adding *s.*	*soliloquies*
churchs or churches topazs or topazes	**churches** **topazes**	Words ending in *ch, j, s, ss, sh, x,* or *z* are made plural by adding *es.*	
cameos or cameoes radioes or radios	**cameos** **radios**	Nouns ending in *o* preceded by a vowel, form the plural by adding *s.*	
tomatos or tomatoes volcanoes or volcanos	**tomatoes** (both)	Nouns ending in *o* preceded by a consonant, form the plural by adding *es.*	Some words add *s* only: *silos, dittos, dynamos.* In other cases, either *s* or *es* is correct: *buffalos* or *buffaloes.* Check the dictionary if you are not sure.
brother-in-laws or brothers-in-law cupsful or cupfuls	**brothers-in-law** **cupfuls**	Compound nouns add *s* to the main word to form a plural. Add *s* to words ending in *ful.*	

Which is correct?	Correct spelling	This rule explains why	Some exceptions
1920s or 1920's four 7's or four 7s	**1920's** **7's**	Form the plural of numbers, dates, letters, and signs by adding *'s*.	
desireable or desirable caring or careing	**desirable** **caring**	Words ending in *e*, drop the final *e* before adding a suffix beginning with a *vowel*.	*mileage, saleable*
humaneness or humanness arrangement or arrangment	**humaneness** **arrangement**	Words ending in *e*, keep the final *e* before adding a suffix beginning with a *consonant*.	*argument, duly, ninth, wholly*
changeable or changable advantagous or advanta-geous	**changeable** **advantageous**	Words ending in soft-sounding *ce* or *ge*, retain the final *e* when adding suffixes.	
canoing or canoeing lovly or lovely	**canoeing** **lovely**	Words ending in *e* preceded by a vowel, keep the *e* before adding a suffix, except a suffix beginning with *e*.	*truly*
dying or dieing	**dying**	Words ending in *ie*, change the *ie* to *y* before adding a suffix.	
prefered or preferred begining or beginning	**preferred** **beginning**	Words ending in a consonant preceded by a single vowel, double the consonant before adding a vowel suffix.	*crocheting, ricocheted, filleted*
benefiting or benefitting revealling or revealing boilling or boiling	**benefiting** **revealing** **boiling**	Words ending in a consonant preceded by more than one vowel, or not accented on the last syllable, do not double the final consonant.	
accidentaly or accidentally	**accidentally**	Words ending in one *l*, keep the final *l* before a suffix beginning with *l*.	Words ending in *ll* drop one *l* before an *ly* suffix: *hilly, fully.*
allready or already mouthfull or mouthful	**already** **mouthful**	Omit one *l* in adding prefixes or suffixes ending in *ll*.	
supplyed or supplied occupys or occupies	**supplied** **occupies**	Words ending in *y* preceded by a consonant, change *y* to *i* before a suffix, unless suffix begins with *i*.	Words of one syllable ending in *y*, keep the *y* before a suffix: *shy, shyly; dry, dryly.*
stayed or staied	**stayed**	Words ending in *y* preceded by a vowel, retain the *y* before a suffix.	*daily, laid, paid, said, slain*
dissatisfy or disatisfy imortal or immortal	**dissatisfy** **immortal**	Prefixes *dis-, il-, im-, mis-, over-, re-*, and *un-* do not change the spelling of the root word.	

Common misspellings

How many times have you heard people say, "if you do not know how to spell a word, look it up in the dictionary"? But how do you find a word that you cannot spell? You can begin by pronouncing the word, then referring to **Common Spellings of English Sounds** on pages *122-123.* If you think you know the spelling, but cannot find the word, check the spelling rules and exceptions on the two previous pages. You might have switched an *e* and *i,* or added a prefix or suffix without making the correct change in the root. Lastly, you can try different ways of pronouncing and spelling a word, then look for these varieties in the dictionary.

One of the most common reasons for misspelling is mispronunciation. For example, you may develop the habit of saying *goverment,* and spelling it that way instead of *government.* Some words have confusing sounds or silent letters. You might spell *maritime* as *maratime,* or *fasten* as *fasen.* Words that sound alike but have different meanings can be tricky. You might use *principal* when you mean *principle,* or *affect* instead of *effect.* Becoming familiar with Common Mistakes on pages *33* through *38* can help you avoid this.

Following is a list of commonly misspelled words. These words can be used in spelling bees.

abscess
acceptance
accommodate
according
accustomed
achievement
acquaintance
acquire
adequate
adjourned
affidavit
analysis
anesthetic
antarctic
anticipation
anxiety
appetite
approximately
arctic
artificial
assassin
assess
athletics
attorneys
auxiliary

bankruptcy
benefit
bough
brief
bureau

cafeteria
campaign
cancellation
candidate
capacity
casserole
census
cessation
challenge
characteristic
circuit
civilized
collateral
colloquial
colonel
commitment
committee
comparatively
complaint
condemn
condescend
confidential
conscience

conscious
consensus
consequently
continuous
controversy
convenience
corporation
correlate
correspondence
counsel
counterfeit
courteous
crisis
criticism
curiosity
cylinder

debtor
definitely
descend
despair
diaphragm
dilemma
dining
disappear
disappoint
discipline
dissipate
distinguish
dormitory

effervescent
efficacy
efficiency
eligible
eliminate
ellipse
encouraging
enthusiasm
equipped
esteemed
exaggerating
except
exceptionally
excessive
executive
exhibition
exhilarating
existence

facilities
fallacy
fascinating
feasible
fictitious

financial
foliage
forego
fortunately

gauge
guarantee

handkerchief
haphazard
harass
height
hemorrhage
hydraulic
hygiene
hypocrisy

icicle
immediately
immense
inalienable
incidentally
inconvenience
indelible
indictment
indispensable
inevitable
inferred
initial
installation
intellectual
intermittent
intimate
irrelevant
irresistible

jeopardize
journal

laboratory
leisure
license
lieutenant
livelihood

maintenance
management
manufacturer
mathematics
miniature
molecule
monotonous
mortgage
murmur
mutual

necessarily
ninety
noticeable

occasionally
occurred
offense
official
omitted
opportunities
ordinarily

pamphlet
paradise
parallel
parenthesis
partial
participate
peaceable
peculiar
perceive
peril
perpendicular
perseverance
petition
philosophy
physician
plateau
plausible
pneumonia
politician
possess
practically
precisely
predecessor
prior
probability
privilege
psychology
pursuit

receipt
receiving
recommend
referred
reign
relevant
remembrance
reminisce
remiss
remittance
rendezvous
representative
requisition
restaurant

reticence
ridiculous

satisfactorily
schedule
scissors
seize
separate
shepherd
sheriff
simultaneous
skiing
solemn
sorority
specific
spontaneous
statistics
statutes
strength
substantial
succeeded
succession
sufficient
supplement
surveillance
suspicion
sustenance
sympathy
synchronous

temporarily
tentative
terrestrial
thoroughly
tournament
tourniquet
tragedy
transferred

unanimous
undoubtedly
unique
unison
unmanageable
unnecessary
utilize

vacancy
vague
veil

warrant
weird
wretched
wrought

Parts of speech

Every word in this dictionary belongs to one of eight parts of speech: nouns, pronouns, adjectives, verbs, adverbs, prepositions, conjunctions, and interjections.

In fact, many words belong to more than one part of speech, depending on how they are used. A noun is a word used as the name of a person, place, thing, event, or quality. *Cream* is a noun when you speak of cream for coffee. An adjective describes or modifies a noun, so that *cream* becomes an adjective when you speak of banana cream pie. A verb is a word that expresses action. *Cream* becomes a verb when you cream butter and sugar together to make a cake.

You have to know how a word is used in a sentence to label it properly. But that's not as hard as it sounds. Once you get the hang of it, you can sort words into their categories with little trouble.

Nouns

Nouns are the easiest to recognize. You are a noun. So is every person, every place, and every thing: *Susan, man, Mrs. Smith, England, Michigan, ocean, truck, car, Golden Gate Bridge.*

There are two kinds of nouns: common and proper. Proper nouns name particular persons, places, or things: *Susan, England,* and *Golden Gate Bridge* are proper nouns. Common nouns do not tell us the particular person, place, or thing, and they are not capitalized. *Man, ocean,* and *truck* are common nouns.

Common nouns are divided into three groups: abstract, concrete, and collective.

Abstract nouns name qualities, actions, and ideas: *courage, helpfulness, loyalty.* Most of the time, you use *the* before abstract nouns, but not *a.* Ordinarily, you would not say *a* helpfulness.

Concrete nouns name things that you can see or touch: *door, pencil, car.* Most of the time, you use either *a* or *the* before a concrete noun, depending on the meaning you want to convey. Also, concrete nouns can be plural—*doors, pencils, cars*—whereas you would not ordinarily say *courages* or *helpfulnesses.*

Collective nouns are singular, but they refer to a group of persons or things: *team, class, herd, set.* Collective nouns are usually followed by singular verbs: "Our *team was* defeated." But they can be followed by a plural verb, especially where they emphasize the individuals more than the group: "The *people were* discontented."

Pronouns

Pronouns take the place of nouns. Our language would be cumbersome without them. You could say, "Mrs. Smith asked John to be careful with Mrs. Smith's car when John borrowed the car to take John's date home." But it is easier to say, "Mrs. Smith asked John to be careful with her car when he borrowed it to take his date home."

The noun that is replaced or referred to by the pronoun is called the antecedent. Every pronoun must have an antecedent, either stated or understood. In our example, *Mrs. Smith, John,* and *car* are antecedents, and the pronouns *her, he, his,* and *it* relieve you of the necessity of repeating the nouns.

There are five kinds of pronouns: personal, relative, interrogative, demonstrative (definite), and indefinite.

Personal pronouns stand for the name of a person, a place, or a thing. English has seven personal pronouns: *I, you, he, she, it, we,* and *they.* All seven are subject form. They "do" the action. Any one will take the place of a noun in the sentence: ". . . saw Mary."

Each of the seven personal pronouns has an object form. The object forms are: *me, you, him, her, it, us,* and *them.* They receive some kind of action. Some action happens "to" them. Any one will take the place of a noun in the sentence: "Mary saw. . . ."

In speaking and writing, people often misuse personal pronouns in sentences with verbs such as *is, are, am, was, were,* and *to be.* After such verbs, the subject form of the personal pronoun is always used: "It is *I.*"

Choosing the right pronoun to follow a preposition—such as *to, for, at, between*—can be troublesome, too. Prepositions call for the object form of the pronoun. "She talked to Mary and *me.*" (Not Mary and *I.*)

If we add *self* or *selves* to a personal pronoun, it becomes a compound form: *myself, yourself, herself, itself, ourselves, themselves.* This form may be intensive (giving emphasis) or reflexive (expressing action turned back on the subject). Do not use the compound form when you should use a simple personal pronoun. It is wrong to say "My brother and *myself* are going." You may say "I *myself* am going" (intensive), and you may also say "He shaves *himself*" (reflexive).

Relative pronouns serve a double purpose. First, they connect two clauses (groups of words containing a subject and a verb): "She did not buy the same book *that* he did." Second, they relate back to a noun or a pronoun in a preceding clause. "She went with the boy *who* lives on Oak Street." Words frequently used as relative pronouns are *that, what, which, who, whom, whose.* Compound relative pronouns in common use are *whatever, whichever,* and *whoever.*

Interrogative pronouns—*what, which,* and *who*—are used to ask questions. They ask the identity, the nature, or the possessor of whatever is in question. "*Who* was there?" "*Which* of the books is yours?"

Demonstrative pronouns. *That, these, this,* and *those* answer the question "Which?" by pointing out a particular person or thing. They are sometimes called definite pronouns. "*That* is all wrong." "*This* is the one I want." "*Those* are too expensive." "*These* are just perfect."

Indefinite pronouns also answer the question "Which?" But in so doing, they do not refer to definite persons or things. "*Somebody* took my pencil." "*Neither* will do the job." Other indefinite pronouns include *both, each, many, one, other.* Like demonstrative pronouns, many indefinite pronouns are adjectives. "*Both* boys were absent." "*Neither* book is mine."

Adjectives

An *old* man; a *black* cat; a *long* bill. *Old, black,* and *long* are adjectives. Each is used to modify, or to give a more exact meaning to, a noun. It is not just any man, it is an *old* man; it is not just any cat, it is a *black* cat; it is not just any bill, it is a *long* bill.

Descriptive adjectives describe a quality or condition of a noun: a *short* stick, a *sad* girl, a *grassy* slope. Limiting adjectives single out the object talked about or indicate quantity:

this book, *that* ring, *two* words. Notice that some limiting adjectives are regularly used as pronouns (*that, these, this, those*). *A, an,* and *the,* also limiting adjectives, are sometimes called articles.

Phrases and clauses may also serve as adjectives. "The man *with the green hat* saw me." In addition to modifying nouns, adjectives modify a word or group of words that is acting as a noun: "*Going to school* (noun) is *necessary* (adjective)."

Verbs

The most important word in a sentence is the verb. A verb expresses action or a state of being. In "John the ball," we have a subject, *John,* and we have an object, *ball.* But only after adding a verb, such as *threw,* do we have action, and a sentence. "John threw the ball." Sometimes the action is mental rather than physical. "She *believed* the story."

Not all verbs express action. Those that do not may be either linking verbs or auxiliary verbs. Linking verbs join the subject of the sentence to another word, in order to make a statement. "Sara *felt* ill." The verb *felt* links the subject *Sara,* with the word *ill,* to make a statement about Sara's health. Some linking verbs regularly used are *appear, be, grow, look, remain, seem, smell, stay, taste.*

Auxiliary verbs are used with other verbs to form a verb tense, voice, or mood. "I studied" becomes "I *have* studied," with the addition of the helping, or auxiliary verb, *have.* Other common auxiliary verbs are *be, do, may, will.*

Verbs may be either transitive or intransitive. A transitive verb takes an object. "He *lifted* the hammer." An intransitive verb does not take an object. "They *ran* fast." Many verbs are transitive in some sentences and intransitive in others. "She *sang* the song." (Transitive) "She could not *sing.*" (Intransitive)

Adverbs

Adverbs, like adjectives, give a more exact meaning to other words. But adjectives modify only nouns, and words acting as nouns. Adverbs modify verbs, adjectives, other adverbs, entire sentences, or clauses. "The boat was *absolutely* waterproof." (Adverb modifying adjective) "The radio worked *unusually* well." (Adverb modifying adverb) "I went to school *yesterday.*" (Adverb modifying sentence)

An adverb *usually* answers the questions: *How? When? Where?* or *To what extent?* "He ran *quickly* down the road." (How) "She went to school *today.*" (When) "She dropped the ball there." (Where) "John sang *loudly.*" (To what extent).

Interrogative adverbs ask questions. "*Where* did she go?" "*Why* did she go?" Other common interrogative adverbs are *when* and *how.*

Conjunctive adverbs appear between clauses and serve the double function of connecting the two clauses and modifying one. "You signed a contract; *therefore,* we demand payment." Other conjunctive adverbs are *however, moreover, nevertheless, otherwise, still.*

Words commonly used as adverbs are *almost, fast, very,* and most words ending in *-ly: badly, sorely.*

Prepositions

Prepositions may be short words (*in, for, on, to*), long words (*alongside, concerning*), or groups of words (*in spite of, as far as*). But they all do the same thing. They show the relation of one word (usually a noun or a pronoun) to some other word in the sentence. Some of the relations are:

Position—"The book is *on* the table."
Direction—"He walked *toward* the door."
Time—"She left *before* him."

Words frequently used as prepositions are *at, between, by, down, for, in, of, on, over, toward, up, with.*

Conjunctions

Conjunctions join together words or word groups. There are coordinating, correlative, and subordinating conjunctions.

Coordinating conjunctions are the simplest, linking two words or word groups that are grammatically the same. "She bought meat *and* potatoes." Other coordinating conjunctions are *but* and *yet.*

When two coordinating conjunctions are used together, they are called correlative conjunctions. "*Both* Henry *and* Bill are gone." Other correlative conjunctions are *either . . . or, though . . . yet.*

Subordinating conjunctions connect a subordinate clause to the main clause of a sentence. In the following instance, the subordinating conjunction *because* introduces the subordinate clause. "Mary was happy *because* she found her mother at home." Other subordinating conjunctions include *as, before, if, since, unless.*

Interjections

Ah! Alas! Oh! Ouch! These are interjections. A unique characteristic of interjections is that they bear no grammatical relation to other words in a sentence. They neither affect other words—as do adjectives—nor are they affected by other words—as are nouns. A second property held in common by interjections is that they all express emotion. *Ouch!* It hurts. *Alas!* It is a shame. *Ah!* Here comes Mary.

This traditional system of classifying the parts of speech and showing how they function in sentences is one of several approaches in teaching English. Two other approaches are discussed on the following page.

Capitalization

Capital (large) letters are used in writing to make reading easier. They distinguish specific or proper names from general or common names. They signal the beginning of new sentences, quotes, and thoughts. English has many rules for using capitals. The main ones follow:

What to capitalize	Examples
Proper nouns	John Jones Chicago Bill of Rights
Proper adjectives	Paris fashions Kennedy administration Persian rugs
Personified nouns	All Nature sang. Let not Evil triumph.
The first word of a sentence, a phrase, or a word that has the force of a sentence	What are you doing? Nothing. Stop!
The first word of a direct quotation	Bob called, "Hurry up."
The first word of a complete statement following a colon (:)	This is our conclusion: The trial was fair.
The first words and all important words in titles of books, magazines, newspapers, songs, and other writings. (Capitalize *a; an; and; the;* prepositions, and conjunctions only when they come at the beginning or end of a title or when they consist of five or more letters.)	Ivanhoe *Business Week* *Evening News* "Roll Out the Barrel"
The pronoun *I* and the interjection *O*	I was right. Rejoice, O ye people
The days of the week, months, and holidays	Tuesday February Easter Christmas
Words used instead of, or as part, of a family member's name	I asked Father for a dollar. He called Uncle Bob.
Nicknames, titles, and their abbreviations	Old Hickory Senator Brown Dr. Ph.D.
Specific political and geographical subdivisions	Chicago Queens County Italian Sioux Indians
Specific rivers, mountains, and other geographical features	Amazon River Rocky Mountains Atlantic Ocean
Specific streets, highways, buildings, and other locations	Michigan Avenue Empire State Bldg. Fifth Ave.
Political parties, religious denominations, and their members	Democratic Party Baptist Church Republicans
Organizations, business firms, and institutions	Camp Fire General Motors Columbia University
Sacred writings and words that refer to a Supreme Being	Bible Holy Writ God Trust in Him Vishnu
Specific historical events, wars, treaties, documents, etc.	Louisiana Purchase World War II Treaty of Ghent
Branches, departments, and other divisions of government	Congress Parliament Department of State
Specific trains, planes, ships, satellites, submarines, and other vehicles	*Golden State Limited* *Concorde* *Titanic* *Sputnik* *Nautilus*
Stars, planets, constellations, and other heavenly bodies	Sirius Mars Big Dipper Milky Way
Creeds and confessions of faith	Nicene Creed Augsburg Confession
Specific historical periods	Age of Reason Renaissance
Military decorations	Purple Heart Navy Cross Victoria Cross
Preface, contents, chapter, index, and other parts of a book when referred to specifically	This point is explained in Chapter 10 and is listed both in the Index and Contents

Punctuation

Punctuation is used to make written language clearer. The following rules will show you the main uses for each punctuation mark. The punctuation marks follow in alphabetical order.

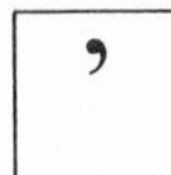

Use the Apostrophe:

1. To show omission of one or more letters, one or more words, or figures in a number.

can't (cannot) 'cause (because)
'45 (1745) five o'clock (five of the clock)

2. To show possession by means of the possessive case of nouns.

Singular	**Plural**
a cat's paws	the girls' lunches
Jack's coat	the Browns' home

But:
Do not use the apostrophe with possessives of personal pronouns.

The dog broke *its* leg. Here is *your* book.

3. To show plurals of numbers, letters, and words discussed as words.

4's all A's no *but's*

Use Brackets:

1. For parentheses within parentheses.

(That was the color [red] he preferred.)

2. To correct a mistake in a direct quote.

"The artist Le[o]nardo painted it."

3. To indicate explanations or your own comments within quotations.

He replied, "That's [Cleveland] where I was born."

4. To indicate stage and acting directions.
CHARLES [waving his arms] Away with you!

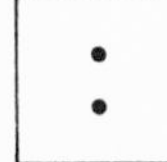

Use the Colon:

1. After a statement followed by a list.

Campers must take these items: bedding, linen, and cooking utensils.

2. After a statement followed by a clause that extends, explains, or amplifies the statement.

Judges have a double duty: They must protect the innocent and punish the guilty.

3. After the salutation of a business letter.

Dear Sir: Gentlemen: Dear Ms. Harris:

4. To separate hours from minutes in indicating time.

2:40 P.M.

5. To separate parts of a citation.

Elementary English XLIV:114-123 Exodus 4:1

Use the Comma:

1. To separate the day of the month, or a special day, from the year.

July 20, 1969 Independence Day, 1776

2. To separate the parts of an address.

He lives at 230 Lake Street, Oak Park, Illinois 60302.
ABC Company, 200 Park Ave., New York, New York 10017

3. After the greeting of an informal letter.

Dear Alice, Dear Uncle John,

4. After the closing of a letter.

Affectionately, Sincerely yours,

5. Before any title or its abbreviation that follows a person's name.

H. W. McDowell, M.D. Byron Phelps, Dean of Men
Sarah Caldwell, Secretary Melvin Brown, Ph.D.

6. Between words or phrases in a series.

Go up the road, across the river, and into the park.
The paper can be white, yellow, or blue.

7. To set off the name of a person spoken to.

Bill, here is your cap. Here, Bill, is your cap.

8. To set off words or phrases that suggest a break in thought, such as *however, of course,* and *moreover.*

You find, however, that small ones are rare.
The winner, of course, received the blue ribbon.

9. To set off *first, second, no, yes, oh,* and similar words when they introduce a sentence.

Yes, the letter came. First, who is not coming?

10. To set off groups of digits in large numbers.

4,342 65,001 210,563,270

11. To separate unrelated numbers in a sentence.

By 1960, 30,000 people lived in the city.

12. To set off words that explain or define other words (apposition).

Janet Jones, my cousin, won a speech award.
The ball ricocheted, or bounced, off a brick wall.

13. To set off phrases and dependent clauses preceding the main clause of a sentence.

By the end of the week, most of the work was done.
To be a good jumper, a person needs strong legs.
Although the children were poorly dressed, they looked healthy.

14. To set off phrases or clauses that add to the main thought of a sentence but are not essential to it.

Climbing, Joe skinned his leg.
The girls, busy as they were, found time to help.
The final reports, which were completed today, give all totals.

15. To separate long coordinate clauses of a compound sentence.

The building collapsed, but no one was hurt.
Snow fell during the night, and the ground froze.
But:
He sang and he danced.
The thunder rumbled and the lightning flashed.

16. To set off coordinate phrases modifying the same noun.

This lake is as deep as, but smaller than, Lake Erie.

17. Between parts of a sentence that suggest contrast or comparison.

The more people he met, the lonelier he felt.
The sooner we get started, the sooner we'll finish.
The more he saw of her, the more he liked her.

18. To indicate the omission of one or more words.

The first game was exciting; the second, dull.
For:
The first game was exciting; the second game was dull.

19. To separate identical or similar words in a sentence.

Who he was, is a mystery. Let them go in, in pairs.

20. To separate adjacent words that might be mistakenly joined in reading a sentence.

To an Asian, Americans are foreigners.
Just as we walked in, the window broke.

Use the Dash:

1. In place of *to* between numbers or dates.

You will find helpful information on pages 27–36.
The years 1930–1936 were hard ones for the family.

2. Between proper names showing terminals of airplanes, buses, ships, and trains.

The New York–Chicago flight was late.

3. Before a summarizing statement introduced by *all, this,* or similar words.

Bob, Bill, Harry—all found summer jobs.
To defeat every opponent—this was his ambition.

4. Before a repeated word or expression.

He was a gentleman—a gentleman of the old school.

5. To emphasize or define a part of a sentence.

The Declaration of Independence—that historic document —was written in 1776.

6. To indicate an "aside" or a point of view of the speaker.

You may—though I doubt it—enjoy this book.

7. To suggest halting or hesitant speech.

"Well—I—ah—I didn't know," he stammered.

8. To indicate a sudden break or interruption in a sentence.

"I'm sorry, sir, but—." He was already through the gate.

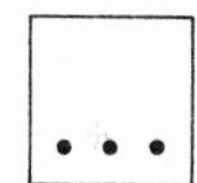

Use Ellipses:

1. Within a quotation to indicate places where a word or words have been omitted.

"The house . . . was built in 1935."
For:
"The house on Elm Street was built in 1935."

2. At the end of a quotation to indicate words omitted before the period. Be sure to include the period.

"He was a giant of a man. . . ."
For:
"He was a giant of a man and was highly respected."

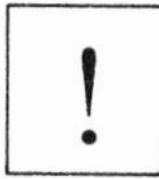

Use the Exclamation Mark:

1. After a word, phrase, or sentence that expresses strong or sudden feeling.

Ouch! That hurts! Good for you!

2. To emphasize a command or strong point of view.

Come here at once! We won't discuss this again!

3. To show sarcasm, irony, or amusement.

You are a fine one to talk about lazy people!
That should be an easy job for you!

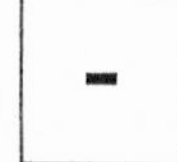

Use the Hyphen:

1. To mark the division of a word at the end of a line. Here are some general rules for using the hyphen in this way.

You may divide a word only between syllables. Divide it in such a way that each part of the hyphenated word contains at least two letters. If you are uncertain where to break a word into syllables, consult the dictionary. Avoid dividing a word in a way that might lead to incorrect pronunciation. For example, *omnipotent* is pronounced om nip′ə tent. Do not hyphenate omnipo-tent; the correct way is omnip-otent. Remember that pronunciation is not an accurate guide to syllabication. For instance, the word *babble,* pronounced bab′əl, is broken into syllables as *bab-ble.*

Avoid dividing a word in a place where either part of the hyphenated word forms a word by itself; for example, tar-tan.

Do not divide a word that is a number or a figure, a contraction, an abbreviation, a word of one syllable, or a word of five letters or less. For example, eighty-five, wouldn't, UNESCO, joint, flora.

Here are specific rules for hyphenating words at the end of a line. You may divide:

a. Between double consonants unless the root ends in the double consonant.

run-ning   remit-tance   col-lection
But:
Divide after a double consonant if the root ends in the double consonant.
roll-ing   bless-edly   miss-ing

b. Before a suffix only if it has three or more letters.

port-able   transi-tion   argu-ment
But not:
writ-er   person-al   horri-fy

c. After a prefix only if it has three or more letters.

trans-mission   anti-climax   pro-logue
But not:
a-symmetry   bi-cycle   en-circle

d. A compound word only where a hyphen already occurs in the word.

first-class   vice-president   self-reliant
Not:
vice-pres-ident   self-re-liant   ep-och-making

2. To join word parts and to separate word parts, use a hyphen:

a. In compound numbers between 21 and 99.

thirty-six   thirty-sixth   ninety-one

b. Between the two parts of fractions when used as modifiers, unless one part of the fraction contains a hyphen.

two-thirds vote   one twenty-second piece
one-fourth capacity   twenty-one thirtieths
But:
Do not use the hyphen between the numerator and denominator when the fraction is a noun.
He bought one half.   He took three tenths.

c. After the prefix *re-* to prevent confusion with other words beginning with these letters.

re-lay a carpet   re-cover a chair
But:
a relay race   recover from an illness

d. After a prefix: when the prefix ends with the same letter with which the root word begins; when the root word begins with *w* or *y;* or when the root word begins with a capital letter.

de-emphasize   co-worker   pre-Columbian

Exceptions occur when the dictionary shows that the preferred spelling is without the hyphen, as in *cooperate.*

e. Between the parts of a compound adjective when it appears before the word it modifies.

drive-in movie   would-be actor   foreign-born person
But:
The client was foreign born.

f. In compounds containing a prepositional phrase, unless the dictionary shows that the preferred spelling is without the hyphen, as in *coat of arms.*

mother-in-law   man-about-town

g. After any prefix that precedes a proper noun or adjective.

un-American   pre-Revolutionary   pro-Communists

h. After each item in a series when the last item requires a hyphen.

first-, second-, and third-grade pupils

i. After *great* in describing generations or descent.

great-great-grandfather   great-grandmother

j. To spell out a word or a name.

s-e-p-a-r-a-t-e   D-i-s-r-a-e-l-i

Do not hyphenate a compound adjective that includes an adverb ending in *ly* even when the adjective is used before the word or phrase it modifies.

It was a slowly moving train.
Not:
It was a slowly-moving train
But:
It was a slow-moving train.

Check your dictionary for words beginning with the prefixes *ante, after, non, pro, pre, super, ultra,* and *well.* Some of these words are hyphenated; some are not. Also check compound words beginning or ending with the words *book, boy, child, dealer, girl, like, maker, man, mill, payer, shop, store,* and *work.* Examples:

man-hours of work   man in white   manslaughter

Use Parentheses:

1. Around explanatory material in a sentence when this material has no essential connection with the rest of the sentence.

To make holes, use an awl (a sharp, pointed tool).

2. To enclose sources of information within a sentence.

The population of Boise is 74,990 (1970 census).

3. Around numbers or letters that indicate subdivisions of a sentence.

This committee has three duties: (a) to solicit members, (b) to collect dues, and (c) to send receipts.

4. Around figures which repeat a number written out.

Enclosed is five dollars ($5.00).

Put marks of punctuation inside the parentheses when they belong with the parenthetical matter.

Carol's question ("Whom did you take to the dance?") produced a chill in the air.
But:
John walked to the store in all that snow (even though I asked him not to).

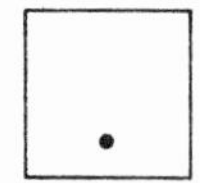

Use the Period:

1. After a sentence.

It is cold outside.

2. After a command given without emphasis.

Please hurry.

3. After initials.

J. P. Jones

4. After an abbreviation or each part of many abbreviations. (Exceptions are listed in the dictionary entry for the word or abbreviation.)

A.M. C.O.D. lbs. Mr. Mrs. Ph.D. Prof. yds.
But:
AFL-CIO AWOL ICBM NAACP NBC

5. After each number or letter that begins a heading in an outline.

Why I Like to Read
I. Satisfies my curiosity
A. About people
B. About things

Use the Question Mark:

1. After a direct question.

How old is Bill?

2. After a statement followed by a short question.

It's cold outside, isn't it?

3. After a word that indicates a question.

What? How? Why?

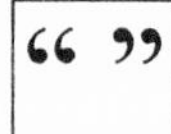

Use Quotation Marks:

1. To enclose the exact words of a speaker.

Mary exclaimed, "I refuse to go!"

2. Around each part of a direct quotation when explanatory words come between the parts.

"This material," said the clerk, "washes easily."
"It will not fade," he added. "The colors are fast."

3. To enclose quoted words or phrases within a sentence.

The leader told us we must "put our shoulders to the wheel."

Enclose a quotation within a quotation in single quotation marks.

"I do not understand your statement: 'He obtained the stock illegally.' "

British usage is opposite, with single quotation marks for most uses and double ones for quotations within quotations.

4. Around the titles of songs or poems.

We all sang "America."
The child recited "Little Miss Muffet."

5. Around the titles of lectures, sermons, pamphlets, handbooks, chapters of a book, magazine articles, and other titled material that is less than a whole book.

"Rescued" was the longest chapter in the book.

6. Around a word or phrase explained or defined by the rest of the sentence.

The "crib" in cribbage is made up of discards from players' hands.

7. Around a word to which attention is called in general writing. (In formal writing, underscore the word.)

You have spelled "parallel" incorrectly.

8. Around a technical or trade name.

Many people use "Jell-Right."

9. Before the beginning of each stanza of a quoted poem and after the last stanza.

The teacher recited these lines from Lord Tennyson's "The Eagle":

"He clasps the crag with crooked hands;
Close to the sun in lonely lands,
Ring'd with the azure world, he stands.

"The wrinkled sea beneath him crawls;
He watches from his mountain walls,
And like a thunderbolt he falls."

10. Before each paragraph of continuous quoted material and after the last paragraph. They are not used at the end of intermediate paragraphs.

"Green told us that the venture turned out to be a complete failure.
"Upon hearing this, Smith knew he was a ruined man. He quickly left the room.

"We have not heard from him since that night. Not even his wife knows where he is. I don't know if he is dead or alive."

Commas and periods are placed inside closing quotation marks (in United States usage).

We all sang "America."

Semicolons and colons are placed outside closing quotation marks.

John said, "I'll call you tomorrow"; but I haven't heard from him.
Here's what he did when he said, "I'll go":
He closed the window and walked out the door.

Question marks and exclamation points are placed inside the closing quotation marks if they belong to the quotation.

"Get out!" she shouted.
But:
How surprised I was to hear her say, "You have written the best essay in the class"!
"Are you going to the movies tonight?" he asked.
But:
What did he mean when he said, "I didn't know you were here"?

Use the Semicolon:

1. Between parts of a compound sentence when they are not joined by the conjunctions *and, but, for, nor,* or *or.*

I must leave you now; you can visit me later.

2. Before a conjunction connecting independent clauses when either clause contains commas.

During the summer, he accomplished nothing; but during the winter, he finished writing his book.

3. After each clause in a series of three or more clauses.

Bells rang; whistles shrieked; horns blared; and people screamed.

4. Before words like *therefore, however,* and *nevertheless* when they connect two independent clauses.

Mr. Black is a busy man; nevertheless, he has agreed to help us with our fund-raising project.

5. After listings when commas occur within the list.

You will need to call Mr. H. H. Hall, of the First Ward; Mr. Henry Griffin, of the Third Ward; and Mr. R. J. Troy of the Council.

6. Before explanatory expressions such as *for example, for instance, that is,* and *namely.*

There are several reasons why this is a good factory site; namely, proximity to fuel, availability of raw materials, good shipping facilities, and an abundance of skilled labor.

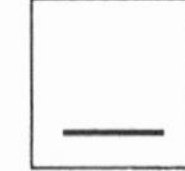

Use Underlining

In manuscript, for words that should appear in italics when set in type, underline:

1. The name of any book or complete volume.

Tom Sawyer describes boyhood near the Mississippi River.

2. The name of a magazine or periodical.

There are amusing cartoons in The New Yorker.

3. Any foreign word that is not commonly used in English. These words have such labels as *Latin, French,* or *Italian* in the dictionary.

The treasurer made an ad interim report.

4. The names of ships, paintings, and works of art.

Titanic
The Last Supper
Rodin's sculpture The Thinker

5. Any words considered not for their grammatical meaning but as words.

But, for, and or are all conjunctions.

Use the Virgule:

1. Between two words to indicate that the meaning of either word pertains.

The man and/or his wife may cash the check.

2. As a dividing line in dates, fractions, and abbreviations.

4/4/76   3/4   1/2   c/o   B/L

3. When recording bibliographical information to indicate the ends of lines in a title or subtitle.

The/ World Book/ Encyclopedia/ A/ Volume 1

4. With a run-in passage of poetry to indicate where one line ends and another begins.

"This above all: to thine own self be true,/ And it must follow, as the night the day,/ Thou canst not then be false to any man."

Choosing the right word

English contains more words than most languages. Because it is a rich blend of words from Latin, French, Greek, and other languages, English has many words with similar meanings. These words are called *synonyms.*

Using words with different shades of meaning adds richness, color, variety, and excitement to your language. The careful use of synonyms helps you communicate accurately and effectively. But wrong choices among words of similar meaning may leave a listener, or reader, with unclear or mistaken impressions.

Repetition of the same words makes reading and conversation dull and monotonous. Instead of always saying a person, thing, or event is *nice,* you can substitute more precise words such as *pleasant, enjoyable, delightful, attractive, lovely, charming, engaging, fascinating, thrilling, enchanting.* Rather than repeatedly describing a food that you like as *delicious,* you can call the food *savory, tasty, palatable, piquant, delectable, elegant, scrumptious, flavorful, appetizing, mouth-watering, luscious.*

The word *said* is often overworked in writing that includes conversation. Take this paragraph, for example:

> "What kind of entertainment shall we have for our class party?" Joan *said.* Tim and David thought for a while. "How about a Punch-and-Judy show?" Tim *said.* "That's a good idea!" David *said.* "Oh, no, that's too silly!" Joan *said.* "Why don't we act out a mystery instead?" Tim thought hard. Then he *said,* "Let's write our own play."

The paragraph would be clearer and more interesting written this way:

> "What kind of entertainment shall we have for our class party?" Joan *asked.* Tim and David thought for a while. "How about a Punch-and-Judy show?" Tim *suggested.* "That's a good idea!" David *shouted.* "Oh, no, that's too silly!" Joan *objected.* "Why don't we act out a mystery instead?" Tim thought hard. Then he *replied,* "Let's write our own play."

Some synonyms are interchangeable; either word can be used in a sentence without changing the meaning of the sentence. There is no difference in meaning between "The *small* boy with the *little* dog lives in the red house," and "The *little* boy with the *small* dog lives in the red house." Other synonyms are the same in one meaning of the words, but they differ in other meanings. You might say that a classmate is *dull* or *stupid.* You would not say that a knife is *stupid,* or that a jackass is *dull.* You could *mislay* or *misplace* your wallet, but you only *misplace* your trust.

How to find synonyms

Synonyms appear after the definition of many words. When a word has more than one definition, synonyms are often given after each definition. The synonyms are preceded by the boldface label **SYN**. Examples are:

boun|te|ous (boun′tē əs), *adj.* **1** given freely; generous: *The rich man gave bounteous gifts to the poor.* **SYN**: liberal, beneficent, munificent. **2** plentiful; abundant: *Because of the spring rains, the farmers had a bounteous crop.* **SYN**: copious. [alteration of Middle English *bountyvous* < Old French *bontif, -ive* full of goodness < *bonté* goodness, bounty] — **boun′te|ous|ly**, *adv.* — **boun′te|ous|ness**, *n.*

can|died (kan′dēd), *adj.* **1** cooked in sugar; glazed with sugar: *candied sweet potatoes.* **2** *Figurative.* made sweet or agreeable: *candied words of praise.* **SYN**: honeyed. **3** preserved or encrusted with sugar: *candied ginger. I roamed about in a daze, smelling the popcorn and candied apples* (Atlantic). **4** turned into sugar: *candied honey.* **SYN**: crystallized.

The dictionary includes synonym studies for many words. Synonym studies can help you write better. They explain the shades of meaning in a synonym that affect its use. They include illustrative sentences that will help you to decide when one word can be appropriately substituted for another word.

re|cov|er (ri kuv′ər), *v., n.* — ***v.t.*** **1** to get back (something lost, taken away, or stolen); regain: *to recover a lost ring, to recover one's temper or health.* **2** to make up for (something lost or damaged): *to recover lost time.* **3** to bring back to life, health, one's senses, or normal condition: *Our men ... took up three men; one of which was just drowning, and it was a good while before we could recover him* (Daniel Defoe). **4** to get back to the proper position or condition: *He started to fall but recovered himself.* **5** to obtain by judgment in a law court: *to recover damages.* **6** to regain in usable form; reclaim. Many useful substances are now recovered from materials that used to be thrown away. **7** to rescue; deliver. **8** to return (a bayonet, sword, or the like) to a certain position, as after use. **9** *Archaic.* to get to; reach.
— ***v.i.*** **1** to get well; get back to a normal condition: *She is recovering from a cold. The man recovered of the bite—The dog it was that died* (Oliver Goldsmith). **2** to obtain judgment in one's favor in a law court. **3** *Sports.* to make a recovery.
— ***n.*** *Sports.* a recovery, especially a getting back to the proper position in fencing or boxing.
[< Anglo-French *recoverer,* Old French *recovrer* < Latin *recuperāre.* See etym. of doublet **recuperate.**]
— ***Syn.*** *v.t.* **1 Recover, reclaim, retrieve** mean to get something back. **Recover** means to get something back again after losing it: *He recovered the stolen furs.* **Reclaim** means to get something back after temporarily giving it up: *At the end of the trip we reclaimed our luggage.* **Retrieve** means to get something back after letting it lapse or deteriorate: *It took him a long time to retrieve his reputation.*

You may be referred to another entry to find a synonym study. Under synonyms for *aware,* you will find this note: "See syn. under **conscious.**"

a|ware (ə wãr′), *adj.* having knowledge; realizing; conscious: *I was too sleepy to be aware how cold it was. She was not aware of her danger.* **SYN**: See syn. under **conscious.** [Old English *gewær*] — **a|ware′ness**, *n.*

Turning to *conscious,* you find that the synonym study deals with both *aware* and *conscious.*

con|scious (kon′shəs), *adj., n.* — ***adj.*** **1** knowing; having experience; aware: *He was conscious of a sharp pain.* **2** able to feel; awake: *About five minutes after fainting I became conscious again.* **3** known to oneself; felt: *conscious guilt. Talking is more often conscious than breathing is.* **4** meant; intended; intentional: *a conscious lie, conscious humor.* **SYN**: deliberate. **5** self-conscious; shy; embarrassed: *She was a little conscious in her manner because of her old-fashioned dress.* **6** *Figurative.* knowing or sharing in human actions or secrets. **7** *Obsolete.* knowing something together with another. **8** *Obsolete.* guilty.
— ***n.*** **the conscious,** *Psychology.* the group of mental processes of which the individual is aware, in contrast to unconscious mental activity ...
— ***Syn.*** **1 Conscious, aware** mean knowing that something exists. **Conscious** emphasizes the idea of realizing or knowing in one's mind that one sees, feels, hears, or otherwise senses something, either physically or emotionally: *He was conscious of a great uneasiness among the spectators.* **Aware** emphasizes the idea of merely noticing something one sees, smells, hears, tastes, feels, or is told: *I was aware that someone was talking, but not conscious of what was said.*

Writing and spelling traps

In English, there are many words that sound alike or look alike, but have different meanings. There are also a number of words and phrases that are sometimes used incorrectly. Such words and phrases are often confusing and lead to errors in usage or spelling. The following list has been compiled from many sources. It is representative, but not exhaustive. The italicized usage notes included under entries in this dictionary offer additional examples and more details on many of the words and phrases below.

ability, capability. *Ability* is the skill to perform; *capability* is the ability of a person to learn or to do something or of a thing to do something. The captain has the *ability* to steer the ship. The ship has a *capability* of thirty knots.

accept, except. The first, always a verb, means to take or receive; the second, sometimes a verb, means to exclude; as preposition, it means excluding. She will *accept* the conditions *except* those that deal with her personal life.

adapt, adept, adopt. *Adapt* means to make suitable; *adept* to be skilled or expert; *adopt* to take for one's own.

adjoin, adjourn. The first means to be next to; the second, to put off until later.

advice, advise. The first means an opinion. The second means to give counsel. He *advised* me about buying that house, but I didn't take his *advice.*

affect, effect. Usually *affect* is a verb meaning to influence. *Effect* used as a noun means result; as a verb it means to bring to pass. The new law *affected* the crime rate, and this *effect* was largest in the cities.

agree to, agree with. You *agree to* a plan, but *agree with* another person.

aid, aide. *Aid* means to give help; an *aide* is an assistant.

air, heir. *Air* is the gas we breathe; *heir* is someone who inherits property.

allay, ally. *Allay* means to put at rest, *ally* to unite. The countries *allied* (became *allies*) to *allay* the possibility of attack.

all right, alright. *All right* is always all right, but *alright* is not all right.

all together, altogether. *All together* means everyone in a group. *Altogether* means completely or entirely. *Altogether* there are 14 persons when the group is *all together.*

allude, elude. You *allude* to (refer indirectly to) a book, but you *elude* (slip away from) a bore.

allusion, illusion. You make an *allusion* by referring indirectly to a person or thing, while an *illusion* is an unreal or misleading appearance.

although, though. *Although* usually introduces a clause that precedes the main clause, *though* usually introduces one that follows. *Although* many have succeeded, he failed completely, *though* he tried hard.

amiable, amicable. *Amiable* describes a friendly, good-natured person; *amicable* describes a peaceful, friendly relationship.

among, between. *Among* usually refers to more than two and *between* refers to two. The main pieces were divided *among* the group. The remainder was split *between* Tom and Bill.

ante, anti. *Ante* means before, *anti* means against.

anyplace, anywhere. Use *anywhere.* This same holds true for *everywhere, nowhere,* and *somewhere.*

appraise, apprise. The former means to estimate value; the latter, to inform. He *appraised* the vase, then *apprised* the owner of its value.

arms, alms. The first refers to part of the body or weapons; the second, to gifts to the poor.

as large as, larger than. The first is used when you want to say that something is two or more times bigger than something else; the latter, compares two things. Colorado is three times *as large as* Maine, but Texas is *larger than* Colorado.

as, like. Use *as* to introduce a clause, *like* to introduce a phrase. Do *as* I do, and you'll find the work will be *like* play.

ascent, assent. The first refers to going up; the second, to agreement or consent.

assay, essay. He wrote an *essay* (composition) on how to *assay* (analyze) gold ore.

averse, adverse. You are probably *averse* (opposed) to *adverse* (bad) weather conditions.

average refers to the quantity involved, not to the person. Americans eat an *average* of 8 pounds of cheese per person annually; but not: The average American eats 8 pounds of cheese annually.

bases, basis. The *bases* (underlying supports, or series of stations) were built on the *basis* (groundwork) of a survey.

beau, bough, bow. He *bowed* and extended his hand to his sister's *beau* (suitor) when they met under the *bough* (main branch) of the tree.

bell, belle. As the *bells* rang, the *belles* (beautiful women) came into the hall.

beside, besides. *Beside* means by the side of; *besides* means also or in addition to. *Besides* his hat and coat, he left his shoes *beside* the river.

biannual, biennial. *Biannual* means twice a year; *biennial* means every two years.

block, bloc. *Block* means many things, but a *bloc* means only a group of persons combined for a purpose.

born, borne. *Born* means bring into life; *borne* to carry or support.

bouillon, bullion. The first is soup, the second refers to gold and silver.

breach, breech. *Breach* refers to an opening; *breech* refers to the lower or back part of something.

bring, take. *Bring* indicates motion toward a speaker; *take* indicates motion away. *Bring* the soup to him and *take* the plates from the table.

calendar, calender. The first is a table showing the divisions of a year; the second, a machine that presses cloth or paper.

callous, callus. *Callous* is an adjective meaning hard or unfeeling; *callus* is a noun referring to a hard, thickened place on the skin. Only a *callous* person would not feel pity when they saw the *calluses* on his skin.

can, may. *Can* implies ability; *may* implies permission. Mary *may* drive the car, if she *can.*

cannon, canon. The first is an artillery weapon; the second, a church rule or law.

canvas, canvass. *Canvas* is a type of cloth; *canvass* means to examine, discuss, or solicit.

capital, capitol. *Capital* refers to the city or town in which the government of a country, state, or province is located. Congress meets in a building called a *capitol.*

casual, causal. The former means uncertain or informal in manner; the latter refers to the cause of.

censor, censure. As a verb, the former means to act as a censor; the latter means to blame or criticize. He *censured* him for *censoring* the letter.

cents, scents, sense. *Cents* refers to money, *scents* to smells, and *sense* to the mind.

cession, session. *Cession* means handing over to another; *session* is a meeting or time period.

charted, charter. *Charted* involves maps. *Charter* concerns a written grant or order.

choral, coral, corral. *Choral* refers to a chorus; *coral* to tiny sea animals and the reefs they build; *corral* to an animal pen.

cite, sight, site. *Cite* means to quote or refer to; *sight* deals with seeing; *site* is a position or place.

clench, clinch. *Clench* means to close tightly; *clinch* is to fasten or settle decisively. She *clenched* her teeth as she *clinched* the deal.

click, clique. *Click* is a sound; *clique* is a group of people.

climactic, climatic. *Climactic* refers to a climax; *climatic* to the climate.

coarse, course. *Coarse* means rough or vulgar; *course* can be onward movement, a track, or a series of studies.

compare, contrast. *Compare* is commonly used in two senses: (1) to point out likenesses (compare to) and (2) to examine two or more objects to find both likenesses and differences (compare with). *Contrast* means to point out differences.

compare to, compare with. *Compare to* means to point out general or metaphorical resemblances. *Compare with* means to note specific similarities or differences between persons or things of the same kind. He *compared* the sea *to* a woman, and his paintings of waves were tranquil *compared with* those of Jones.

complement, compliment. The first is something that completes; the second refers to praise.

compose, comprise. The parts *compose* the whole; the whole is *comprised* of the parts.

confidant, confident. The first is a trusted person; the second refers to firm belief.

core, corps. *Core* refers to the central part; *corps* is a group of people.

corespondent, correspondent. The first involves a divorce; the second involves letters or journalism. The *correspondent* wrote about the divorce case in which Smith was named *corespondent.*

council, counsel. *Council* is an assemblage of people; *counsel* means advise.

continual, continuous. *Continual* implies a recurrence at frequent intervals; *continuous* means extending uninterruptedly. The *continual* hammering gave him a *continuous* headache.

coward, cowered. The first is someone who lacks courage; the second refers to crouching from danger, or in fear.

credible, creditable. The first means believable; the second bringing honor or praise.

cue, queue. You receive a *cue* as a hint, but you wait in a *queue* (line of people) or wear your hair in one (a braid).

currant, current. *Currants* are seedless raisins or tart berries. *Current* refers to flow or to present time.

decree, degree. *Decree* is something ordered by authority, while *degree* is a stage in a process or an academic award.

defer, differ. The first means to put off or yield; the second, to be unlike or disagree.

descent, dissent. *Descent* refers to coming or going down; *dissent* means to disagree.

desert, dessert. Do not confuse *desert* (a place of little rainfall) with *dessert* (sweets or the like served at the end of a meal).

desolate, dissolute. A desert is *desolate* (barren); people who have no morals are *dissolute.*

disburse, disperse. You *disburse* (pay out) money, but you *disperse* (distribute) handbills.

discomfit, discomfort. *Discomfit* means to overthrow, defeat, or embarrass; *discomfort* refers to uneasiness.

discreet, discrete. The former means careful and sensible, the latter means distinct or separate from others. It was a *discreet* action consisting of two *discrete* maneuvers.

distract, detract. *Distract* means to draw away or confuse; *detract,* to take away from. The defect *distracts* your attention and *detracts* from the value.

ecology, environment. *Ecology* is the study of the relationship of living things to each other and their *environment* (surrounding conditions). Pollution affects the *environment; ecology* attempts to determine how.

either means one or the other, not both. Do not say, There are lions behind *either* door when there are lions behind *both* doors. Either is followed by *or,* not *nor.*

elicit, illicit. *Elicit* is a verb meaning to draw out something that is hidden or held back; *illicit* is an adjective meaning unlawful or improper. The police *elicited* from him the hiding place of the *illicit* drug.

emigrate, immigrate. A person *emigrates,* or moves out of, one country and *immigrates,* or moves into, a new place or another country. The *emigrant* from Poland was finally given permission to *immigrate* to the U.S.

eminent, imminent. Do not say someone is *eminent* (distinguished) when you mean his arrival is *imminent* (about to occur).

ensure, insure. Both words mean *to make certain,* but *insure* usually is confined to the meaning *guarantee against loss.* His house was *insured* against fire to *ensure* that he would have money to buy another if it burned down.

envelop, envelope. The first is a verb meaning to wrap or cover; the second, a noun referring to stationery or an enclosing covering.

equable, equitable. *Equable* means uniform; *equitable* means fair. *Equable* distribution is the only *equitable* way.

errand, errant. Do not refer to a short trip, or the purpose of the trip, as an *errant,* which means wandering or incorrect.

exalt, exult. *Exalt* means to raise in rank or to fill with pride; *exult* means to rejoice.

extant, extent. *Extant* means still existing; *extent* means the amount to which something extends. The animal is *extant* and roams the whole *extent* of the range.

fair, fare. *Fare* refers to a price for travel or to food; *fair* means just, not bad, or not dark.

farther, further. *Farther* refers to physical distance; *further,* to abstract relationships of degree or quantity. Smithville was *farther* from the capital than Johnstown and it was *further* behind Johnstown in cultural development.

feint, faint. *Feint* refers to a false appearance or movement; *faint* means not clear or weak, or to lose consciousness.

fewer, less. *Fewer* refers to number, *less* to degree or quantity. There were *fewer* fans and *less* enthusiasm.

fish, fishes. *Fish* is the plural for many of one kind, but *fishes* is used when writing of different species. Halibut, mackerel, and salmon are the most abundant *fishes* in those waters.

flair, flare. The first refers to perception or talent; the second, to flaming up or spreading out.

flew, flu, flue. The insect *flew* down the *flue* (chimney passage) and bit the man with the *flu* (influenza).

flounder, founder. As a verb the first means to struggle; the second, to stumble or sink. They *floundered* for life jackets, as the boat began to *founder.*

flout, flaunt. He *flouts* (treats with contempt) his work, but *flaunts* (displays boldly) his clothes.

fondling, foundling. The first refers to treating lovingly; the second is a noun meaning a deserted child.

foreword, forward. A *foreword* is an introduction or preface; *forward* means ahead or onward.

formally, formerly. *Formally* means in a formal manner. *Formerly* means in the past.

frees, freeze, frieze. Jonathan *frees* the captives tied below the *frieze* (ornamental band around a building or room), so they do not *freeze* to death.

fulsome means disgusting or offensive, not ample or abundant.

gait, gate. He had a swinging *gait* (way of walking) as he came through the *gate.*

gamble, gambol. You may *gambol* (frolic) if you win a risky *gamble* (game of chance).

gamut, gantlet, gauntlet. *Gamut* refers to the whole range of something. *Gantlet* is a method of punishment. *Gauntlet* is a glove.

gild, guild. *Gild* means to cover with gold; *guild* is a society or union.

grate, great. It is not so *great* to have to clean the *grate* (fireplace). It *grates* on your nerves.

grisly, gristly, grizzly. The *grisly* (frightening) *grizzly* (grayish) bear gnawed on the *gristly* (tough) gazelle.

hail, hale. Besides small pieces of ice, *hail* means to shout in welcome. *Hale* means strong and well.

hallow, hollow. *Hallow* refers to holy or sacred; *hollow* means empty inside.

hangar, hanger. A *hangar* is a shelter for airplanes; a *hanger* is someone who hangs things or a device for hanging clothes.

hoard, horde. *Hoard* means to save or store away; *horde* is a crowd or swarm.

hoarse, horse. Do not confuse *hoarse* (a rough, deep voice) with *horse* (an animal).

hospitable, hospital. *Hospitable* refers to friendly treatment, *hospital* is a place for sick or injured persons.

idle, idol. *Idle* means doing nothing; *idol* is an object that is worshipped.

imply, infer. A speaker *implies.* A hearer *infers.* He *implied* that he would be late; I *inferred* that he meant very late.

incite, insight. Do not confuse *incite* (the act of stirring up) with *insight* (understanding or wisdom).

incredible, incredulous. The former means unbelievable; the latter means unbelieving. They felt *incredulous* about his *incredible* story.

inequity, iniquity. *Inequity* refers to unfairness; *iniquity,* to wickedness.

ingenious, ingenuous. *Ingenious* means clever, skillful; *ingenuous* means frank, simple, sincere.

insolate, insulate. The former means to expose to the sun; the latter means to keep from losing heat or cold, or to set apart.

intense, intents. *Intense* means very strong; *intents* means purposes. She felt *intense* about her career *intents.*

interment, internment. Do not confuse *interment* (burial) and *internment* (confinement).

interstate, intrastate, intestate. *Interstate* means between states; *intrastate* means within a state; *intestate* means without a will.

its, it's. *It's* is a contraction of it is. *Its* name is Fido; *it's* a special breed.

jam, jamb. He was *jammed* (squeezed) against the door *jamb* (side of the door) by the fat man eating *jam* (food).

key, quay, cay. *Key* refers to a locking device. *Key* and *cay* both refer to a low island or reef. *Quay* is a landing place for ships.

knead, need. *Knead* is to mix by pressing; need refers to a lack of something.

knight, night. *Knight* is an honorable rank. *Night* is the dark time of a day.

later, latter. *Later* means more late, *latter* means the second of two. John and Joe were *late,* but the *latter* was *later.*

lay, lie. *Lay* is the action word. *Lie* is the state of laying. However, the past tense of *lie* is *lay. Lay* the medicine on the table. It is for the boy who *lay* (not laid) in the wet grass so long that he will have to *lie* in bed for a few days.

lean, lien. *Lean* means to incline, rest against, or without fat. *Lien* means a legal right on another's property.

leave, let. *Leave alone* means to depart from, or allow (cause) to be in solitude. *Let alone* means to be undisturbed. He talked the robber into *letting her alone;* later he had to go home and *leave her alone.*

lend, loan. *Lend* is used as a verb; *loan* is usually used as a noun. Please *lend* me a book.

less, fewer. *Less* refers to degree or quantity; *fewer,* to number. The Bears have *fewer* good linemen than the Vikings and these linemen have *less* experience.

lesser, lessor. *Lesser* means the less important of two. *Lessor* is a person who grants a lease.

liable, libel. *Liable* means likely or bound by law; *libel* refers to a false or damaging statement.

load, lode. You *load* a truck, but you mine a *lode* (vein) of metal ore.

loath, loathe. *Loath* means unwilling; *loathe* is to feel a strong dislike.

lose, loose. *Lose* means to stop having. *Loose* (verb) means to set free, or (adjective) not fastened.

main, mane. *Main* refers to the most important; *mane* refers to long neck hair on a horse and lion.

manner, manor. *Manner* refers to a way of behaving or happening; *manor* is part of an estate where the owner lives.

mantel, mantle. You put things on the *mantel* of a fireplace, but you wear a *mantle.*

maybe, may be. *Maybe* is an adverb or noun; *may be* is a verb form. *Maybe* you will have better luck next spring when you *may be* stronger.

mean, mien. *Mean* refers to the significance of something or to quality or grade. *Mien* refers to a way of acting or looking. He had a stern *mien,* but this did not *mean* he lacked compassion.

median, mean, average. *Median* refers to the middle. *Mean* and *average* refer to the total of all components divided by number of components. The *median* income of Moeburg is $12,500; its *mean* summer temperature is 72°F.

medal, meddle. *Medal* refers to an award or commemorative coin; *meddle* refers to interfering in another's affairs.

metal, mettle. *Metals* are elements and alloys such as iron and steel. *Mettle* is the quality of a disposition; a person's spirit.

moat, mote. *Moat* is a protective ditch; *mote* is a speck of dust.

moral, morale. Do not write *moral* (concerning right conduct) when you mean *morale* (mental condition as regards courage and confidence).

morning, mourning. Do not write *morning* (the early part of the day) when you mean *mourning* (sorrow or wearing black).

naval, navel. *Naval* refers to warships and the navy; *navel* is the depression in the middle surface of the abdomen below the waist.

neither should be followed by *nor,* not *or.*

ordinance, ordnance. Do not confuse *ordinance* (a rule or law) with *ordnance* (military weapons).

over, more than. *Over* refers to relationships in space; *more than* is used with numbers. The airplane flew *over* a city with a population of *more than* 500,000.

pail, pale. Do not write *pail* (a bucket) when you want to refer to *pale* (something without much color or light, a narrow pointed board, or an enclosure).

pain, pane. You suffer *pain* as a hurt, but *pane* usually refers to a single division of a window or door.

pair, pairs. *Pair* is singular, but can be used as a plural after a numeral or an adjective of number such as several. She bought a *pair* of gloves and six *pairs* (or *pair*) of socks.

palate, palette, pallet. *Palate* is the roof of the mouth or the sense of taste. *Palette* is a set of colors or the thin board on which colors are mixed. *Pallet* may mean *palette,* or a poor bed, or a potter's blade, or a low platform on which loads are stacked.

passed, past. The past tense and past participle of *pass* are *passed. Past* is the adjective, adverb, and preposition. As he *passed* the house, he thought of *past* troubles and good times.

peak, peek, pique. He was *piqued* (angry) because he could not reach the *peak* (top); in fact he did not even get close enough to *peek* (look) at the summit (peak).

peddle, pedal. When you sell something, you *peddle* it. When you ride a bicycle, you *pedal* it.

peer, pier. *Peer* refers to a person equal in ability, age, and so on, or to look closely. *Pier* is a structure extending out into the water.

personal, personnel. *Personal* has to do with a person's private affairs; *personnel* refers to people employed in an organization.

plane, plain. *Plane* is a level, a flat surface, or a carpenter's tool. *Plain* means uncomplicated, or a flat stretch of land.

pole, poll. You can raise a flag on a *pole,* but you count the opinions or votes in a *poll.*

pore, pour. *Pour* (cause to flow) the chemicals through the *pores* (very small openings).

practical, practicable. The former means having to do with action rather than theory; the latter means capable of being done. My *practical* scheme was to make the job *practicable* by removing several obstacles.

pray, prey. Man *prays* (communicates) to God, but *preys* on (hunts) animals.

preceding, previous. *Preceding* means to come before; *previous* means to come before at other times. In 1925, we made more money than in the *preceding* year, but not as much as in *previous* years.

prescribe, proscribe. You *prescribe* when you order or direct something; you *proscribe* when you prohibit or condemn something.

pretense, pretext. A *pretext* is put forward to conceal a truth. A *pretense* is intended to conceal personal feelings.

principle, principal. The former is a basic truth or guiding rule; the latter, a dominant or leading person or thing.

rain, reign, rein. Be sure to distinguish between *rain* (water falling from the clouds), *reign* (a period of power or rule), and *rein* (a strap to control an animal).

raise, raze. Do not write *raise* (lift up) when you mean *raze* (tear down).

reluctant, reticent. If you do not want to act you are *reluctant.* If you do not want to speak, you are *reticent.*

respectfully, respectively. The former means in a courteous manner, the latter in the order given. The soldiers took their *respective* positions and *respectfully* saluted the old captain.

role, roll. We play a *role* in life, but we *roll* objects along or into a ball.

root, route. *Root* refers to part of a plant; *route* means a road or way to go. (*Route* is sometimes pronounced like *rout,* which means a defeat and disorderly retreat.)

sac, sack. *Sac* refers to a baglike part in an animal or plant; *sack* usually means a bag of cloth or paper.

sail, sale. A *sail* goes on a boat; a *sale* involves exchanging money and goods.

serge, surge. *Serge* is a type of cloth; *surge* refers to a rising of waves or feelings.

set, sit. *Set* means to cause to sit; *sit* means to be seated. I *set* the projector on the table, then chose to *sit* in the big chair.

species, specie. *Species* refers to a kind or class; *specie,* to money in the form of coin.

shear, sheer. *Shear* means to cut or break; while *sheer* can refer to being very thin, a steep grade, or to turn from a course.

sloe, slough, slow. If you *slow* down and think, you will not confuse *sloe* (a fruit) with *slough* (a muddy, swampy place or skin that is cast off).

soar, sore. When you *soar* you rise to great heights, but when you are *sore* you feel hurt or angry.

speciality, specialty. Use *speciality* when you mean the special character of something; use *specialty* when referring to a special line of work or business. American history is the *speciality* of that college and his *specialty* is the Civil War period.

stationary, stationery. *Stationary* means fixed, *stationery* means writing materials.

straight, strait. *Straight* means direct or without a curve; *strait* is a narrow passage between two bodies of water.

such as, like. Use *such as* for examples; *like* for resemblances. Some ships, *such as* ocean liners, are *like* small cities.

tail, tale. Do not confuse *tail* (the hindmost part of an animal, or object), with *tale* (the story of an event).

team, teem. Do not write *team* (a group of people) when you mean *teem* (to be full).

tear, tier. You cry *tears* or *tear* a piece of paper, but *tiers* are a series of rows arranged one above the other.

temperatures get higher or lower, not warmer or cooler.

tenant, tenet. A *tenant* is an occupant or renter; a *tenet* is a doctrine or belief.

that, which. *That* is preferred in clauses that restrict a thought. *Which* is nonrestrictive, adding subsidiary information. The river *that* forms the boundary between Texas and Mexico is the Rio Grande, *which* has its source in Colorado.

then, than. Use *than* in comparisons; *then* when time is involved, or you mean also. This train is faster *than* that one, but *then* it has a more powerful locomotive.

their, there, they're. *Their* is the possessive form of *they* and means belong to. *There* means in or at that place. *They're* means they are. *They're* going to buy *their* equipment *there.*

tic, tick. Do not confuse *tic* (an involuntary twitch) with *tick* (the sound of a timepiece, or a blood-sucking insect).

timber, timbre. Use *timber* when writing about wood; *timbre* when referring to sound or resonance.

tortuous, torturous. The first means full of twists and turns; the second refers to inflicting pain. The sun was *torturous* as he rode through the *tortuous* ravines.

track, tract. *Track* refers to a path, or a sport; *tract* to a stretch of land or water.

unique means the only one of its kind. Something cannot be very unique, quite unique, somewhat unique, or rather unique; but it can be rare, odd, or unusual.

vain, vane. *Vain* refers to having too much pride, or to not succeeding; *vane* is a blade or flag that moves with wind or water.

vial, vile. *Vial* refers to a small container or to an outpouring of wrath; *vile* means bad or foul.

waive, wave. *Waive* refers to giving something up; *wave* refers to movements like the surge or swell of water.

weather, whether. You should not confuse *weather* (the condition of the atmosphere) with an expression of choice or alternative.

were, was. *Were* is used when a statement is contrary to fact, expresses a wish, or states a doubtful situation. *Was* is used for statements of fact in the past. If he *were* here, he would be as wise as he *was* during the war.

wet, whet. *Wet* is the opposite of dry; *whet* is to sharpen by rubbing or to make keen.

whither, wither. Use *whither* to mean to what place; *wither* to mean a loss of freshness or vigor.

who, whom. *Whom* refers to someone who has been the object of an action. *Who* is used for the person who is the actor. We cannot determine *who* is cheating *whom.*

who's, whose. *Who's* means who is; *whose* is the possessive. I do not know *who's* putting *whose* things in the closet.

wrack, rack. Use *wrack* when you mean ruin or destruction; *rack* when you refer to strain, or torture, or to a frame.

wrest, rest. *Wrest* means to pull away, or take by force; *rest* refers to ease, or lack of activity.

wry, rye. *Rye* is a cereal grain, while *wry* refers to twisted or distorted. He made a *wry* face when he tasted the drink made from fermented *rye.*

Increasing your word power

A good vocabulary goes hand in hand with your ability to think logically and to learn easily and quickly. Language helps you to understand yourself and the world around you. A good vocabulary and your ability to use words correctly and effectively can be your passport to worlds of interesting and exciting information. You can travel in the past, in the present, and in the future through the words you read or hear. You can learn to use words to help transport others to the worlds you have discovered.

Words can help you achieve the poise and popularity that come with self-confidence. A good vocabulary makes school work easier and more rewarding. When you are ready to go to work, your skill in expressing your opinions and ideas will help you get a good job. Your associates and superiors will admire your ability. Words are important socially, too. Everyone enjoys the company of an interesting and articulate person. As you grow and mature, your vocabulary should grow and mature, too. Have you ever wondered *how* your vocabulary grows?

In your preschool years, all the things around you, plus the effort your parents made to introduce new experiences to you and to identify objects for you, were the most important elements in laying the foundation for a good vocabulary. Even before you could talk, you learned words by hearing them and remembering what they meant. This listening vocabulary was your first vocabulary. Long before you were able to utter a single understandable word, you had begun to recognize some of the words you heard. You repeated words that your parents and other members of your family used and you realized that words are very useful. You did not have to point to objects or scream at the top of your voice to get what you wanted. Words were a more efficient way to make yourself understood, and they did not require as much physical energy as pointing and screaming. You had taken the first steps in acquiring a speaking vocabulary.

The first words you spoke were the names of things. You learned words relating to food and people. You used words to show action and to describe how you felt. Your earliest vocabulary probably contained words like *mama, dada, baby, dog, bad, good, hot, cold, give, go,* and *cry.*

These words seem short and simple, and you might think that you used all short words when you were just learning to use words at all. In fact, you used short words of only three kinds—*nouns,* the names of things; *adjectives,* to describe the nouns; and *verbs,* to express action. If you were like most children, you did not properly use a group of words that are short and seem simple, such as *I* and *me, we* and *us, him* and *her, you* and *they.* These words, called *pronouns,* stand for the names of people or things. They are among the trickiest words in our language. When you first used them, you may have said such things as "Me want it." Gradually you learned to pick the right word, such as *she, her,* or *hers,* until you could use the main pronouns in their proper contexts. As you grew older, your thoughts and your needs were becoming more and more complex. You constantly needed more and more words to express your ideas. You listened and learned.

As your vocabulary grew, you began to understand that things could be separated into *general* and *specific* categories. This awareness of differences added many more words to your vocabulary. For example, you learned that although all dogs are called *dogs,* there are many varieties (*poodle, collie, greyhound*) just as there are many kinds of flowers, buildings, trees, birds, and people. At about the same time, you learned that your *apples, bananas,* and *cherries* are all kinds of *fruit,* that *corn* and *spinach* are both *vegetables,* and that *meat, fruit,* and *vegetables,* as well as *bread, cake,* and *milk,* are all forms of *food.*

By the time you were ready to enter school, you already had a stock of more than 2,000 words in your vocabulary.

When you entered the first grade, you could probably recognize such words as *cat, dog,* and *ball* in print. In school, you were taught to read by associating the words you already knew with the printed or written symbols (letters) that make up words. In time, you began to read words that may not have related at all to any of your first-hand experiences. You may never have ridden in an *airplane,* or seen a *barn,* or been on a *train,* but when you learned to read, these new words became part of your vocabulary.

As you read, your vocabulary was made even larger by all the words you saw around you—in advertisements, on labels, road signs, television, and anything else in print that caught your eye and interested you.

While you were learning to read, you were also learning to write. You began to understand how words are put together and how to recognize the names of things (nouns), action words (verbs), descriptive words (adjectives and adverbs), and words that have no meaning themselves but help to make sentences by relating words to each other (conjunctions and function words such as prepositions). You began to understand the importance of putting words in a particular order in a sentence if you wanted to communicate exactly what you meant. You discovered that the English language has interesting peculiarities. For example, some words look and sound exactly alike, but do not have the same meaning. The word *chest* may be a box for storing things, a piece of furniture, or part of the body. Other words sound alike, but have neither the same spelling or the same meaning; words like *mail* and *male.*

As you listened and read, you found also that words die out when they are not used and that some words even change meanings. You learned that new words constantly join the thousands that already exist in English because each time a new thing is discovered or invented, a new word has to be created to help you identify it.

When you entered the intermediate grades and began to write compositions, you were suddenly made aware of how important it was to be able to express what you wanted to say with precision. You learned that some words are different in sound and spelling but have the same or nearly the same meanings. These words, called synonyms, are invaluable additions to your vocabulary. They not only help you to express yourself with exactness, they make your writing and conversation more interesting by adding variety. You knew now that the simple, easy-to-spell words were not always the ones you wanted to use. Perhaps your teacher suggested rules, such as the following, to help you increase your vocabulary.

1 Be alert for new words in everything you hear.

2 Keep a vocabulary notebook. In it, list new words and their meanings. Be sure you know how to pronounce them.

3 Read widely. Newspapers, books, encyclopedias, and magazines will give you new words.

4 Use your dictionary to make sure you can pronounce, spell, and use correctly any of the new words you have discovered.

5 Try out new words when you speak and write.

6 Set yourself a vocabulary goal. Try to learn and use at least one new word a day.

In junior high school, your social and school activities continue to expand. They open up many opportunities for an increased vocabulary. You are certain to make new friends who have talents and interests that differ from your own. They will introduce new words to your vocabulary.

Your hobbies, the school trips you take, your participation in after-school activities will also expose you to new words. For example, if you play in the school band, you will learn the names of band instruments and musical terms such as *coda* and *diminuendo.* In your art class, you may learn such words as *chiaroscuro, easel,* and *patina.*

In high school, you read and write more than ever before. And when you read, you ask questions about the author's words. Does the author use the proper words to express his idea? Do his words make what he says more interesting and colorful? Is there a rhythm and tone when certain words are used that disappears if they are changed or are put in a different order?

You go through the same process when you hear speeches. Is the speaker using "empty words," words that sound fine, but mean little or nothing? Are his words organized properly? Do his words persuade you to his way of thinking? What words would you have used to make his ideas clearer and more meaningful to your audience?

All of these questions you then apply to your own writing.

Vocabulary tests and your ability to use words with discrimination make up a large part of almost any test you are likely to take either in school or in industry. By improving your vocabulary, by making your vocabulary grow as you grow, you improve your chances for success in high school, in college entrance tests, and in tests for any job that interests you.

This section contains a group of vocabulary inventories. They are arranged by grade level, with a separate inventory for each grade from the 3rd through the 12th and one for college level. (Thus these inventories meet the needs of a wide age range, starting with children of 8 or 9 in the third grade.)

Vocabulary inventories

Vocabulary inventories are designed to provide you with a quick check on your word-power. Each inventory consists of a list of words that you are likely to know and use at the grade level indicated. There are 60 words for 3rd grade, 90 words apiece for 4th and 5th grade, and 120 words each for the following grades. Of course, children know many more than 60 words by the time they reach the 3rd grade. But the words included are designed to test the range of each person's vocabulary at the grade-level indicated.

After each word, the inventory offers you a set of three possible definitions. In many cases, the word listed is one you already know in another meaning. For example, you know that *green* is a color. But, at the third grade level, you are likely also to know that you may say a banana is green when it is *not ripe.* The meaning being tested is somewhat more difficult than just a plain color.

If you are using the inventory as a self-testing device, list your choices for all the words in the inventory at the grade level you choose. Then check your answers against the full list of answers beginning on page *59.*

Example:

30. boast
a. complain
b. ask
c. brag

You would list *c. brag,* then check your answer on page *59* and find that you are right.

In some cases, you may feel that the answer given does not define the word in the way your choice does. If you question whether the definition is correct, check the word in the dictionary itself. Suppose your question is about *escape:*

40. escape
a. get free
b. go up
c. come in

You may have chosen *c. come in,* because you imagine a situation in which you *come in* to *escape* a fierce storm outside. Or you might possibly have picked *b. go up,* because you have in mind a situation in which you *go up* to *escape* from a deep dungeon. But, in both these cases, the definition you chose has the basic idea of getting free in it.

3rd grade

For each of the words listed below, choose the best definition. Answers are on page *59*.

1. note
a. good grade
b. short letter
c. funny joke

2. hike
a. small rocket
b. nickname
c. long walk

3. mash
a. cut
b. crush
c. peel

4. cab
a. bus
b. ship
c. taxi

5. pitch
a. throw
b. trip
c. run

6. club
a. deep cut
b. heavy stick
c. good deed

7. land
a. go ashore
b. rent
c. use

8. bill
a. great sea wave
b. large rock
c. bird's beak

9. pack
a. barrel
b. route
c. bundle

10. snack
a. hiding place
b. small meal
c. low stool

11. melon
a. fruit
b. tree
c. road

12. merry
a. very red
b. good to eat
c. full of fun

13. often
a. never
b. many times
c. later

14. silent
a. strong
b. quiet
c. noisy

15. trip
a. stumble
b. catch
c. laugh

16. plain
a. wooden
b. funny
c. simple

17. green
a. not ripe
b. very sweet
c. melted

18. weak
a. not happy
b. not sleepy
c. not strong

19. lower
a. make noise
b. let down
c. make strong

20. whip
a. beat
b. smell
c. hop

21. clearing
a. small forest
b. open space
c. large flock

22. gift
a. tooth
b. seed
c. present

23. tablet
a. writing pad
b. picnic table
c. small bag

24. choose
a. talk about
b. give up
c. pick out

25. explain
a. make clear
b. discover
c. mix up

26. act
a. part of a play
b. part of a song
c. part of a war

27. wink
a. hand signal
b. horn signal
c. eye signal

28. simple
a. hard
b. wrong
c. easy

29. fluffy
a. long and wide
b. bright and shiny
c. soft and light

30. boast
a. complain
b. ask
c. brag

31. chilly
a. quite warm
b. very hot
c. rather cold

32. glad
a. happy
b. sad
c. angry

33. lumber
a. rolls of cloth
b. pieces of wood
c. piles of dirt

34. crippled
a. huge
b. small
c. lame

35. tornado
a. brave soldier
b. strong windstorm
c. calm weather

36. measure
a. find money
b. find size
c. find fun

37. cartoon
a. funny picture
b. funny song
c. heavy box

38. arrive
a. stay
b. begin
c. come

39. squaw
a. Irish dance
b. Indian woman
c. fruit grower

40. escape
a. get free
b. go up
c. come in

41. cozy
a. dark
b. comfortable
c. dirty

42. wrench
a. tool
b. dish
c. key

43. missing
a. hungry
b. tired
c. absent

44. false
a. quite small
b. growing wild
c. not real

45. nurse
a. depend on
b. take care of
c. give away

46. magnet
a. catches birds
b. attracts iron
c. fixes glass

47. leap
a. walk
b. see
c. jump

48. nightmare
a. bad dream
b. white horse
c. warm room

49. mermaid
a. farm girl
b. older lady
c. fishlike woman

50. moccasin
a. Indian shoe
b. pirate flag
c. Eskimo dog

51. branch
a. mark on cattle
b. part of tree
c. water on grass

52. bitter
a. sharp-tasting
b. bright-looking
c. rough-feeling

53. swallow
a. building
b. tree
c. bird

54. hockey
a. flower
b. game
c. fish

55. lullaby
a. cage for bird
b. dish for food
c. song for baby

56. repay
a. give back
b. take from
c. wish for

57. calfskin
a. wood
b. leather
c. metal

58. invent
a. make something new
b. fill a hole
c. hunt all around

59. verse
a. pail of water
b. part of poem
c. long story

60. gem
a. horn
b. glove
c. jewel

4th grade

For each of the words listed below, choose the best definition. Answers are on page *59*.

1. ability
a. learning
b. skill
c. hope

2. bashful
a. shy
b. bold
c. harmful

3. incorrect
a. uncertain
b. wrong
c. probably right

4. fake
a. not loyal
b. false
c. unhealthy

5. forgetful
a. failing to do
b. unable to remember
c. meaning to do

6. frown
a. appear busy
b. look angry
c. be ready

7. suffer
a. get excited
b. complain
c. have pain

8. clue
a. reason
b. riddle
c. helpful fact

9. fret
a. worry
b. rejoice
c. celebrate

10. marvelous
a. wonderful
b. dull
c. sparkling

11. visible
a. torn
b. can be seen
c. brave

12. confess
a. admit
b. describe
c. brag

13. ordinary
a. different
b. common
c. strange

14. halt
a. stop
b. avoid
c. rise

15. locate
a. cut off
b. bring about
c. find

16. imagine
a. try to explain
b. put in order
c. picture in one's mind

17. lengthen
a. make longer
b. take away
c. shrink

18. pretend
a. tend toward
b. make believe
c. hide something

19. solve
a. find the answer
b. make a riddle
c. look for facts

20. wept
a. cleaned
b. brushed off
c. cried

21. decision
a. good deed
b. mistake
c. judgment reached

22. miss
a. grab something
b. capture
c. fail to hit

23. obedience
a. lack of discipline
b. following orders
c. power to enforce

24. pride
a. being careless
b. being understanding
c. being proud

25. smear
a. paint
b. throw out
c. mark or stain

26. surround
a. follow
b. shut in on all sides
c. be near

27. active
a. motionless
b. hasty
c. lively

28. brave
a. foolish
b. calm
c. fearless

29. convince
a. make a person believe
b. speak softly
c. trick a person into

30. retire
a. exchange for something
b. go back again
c. stop working

31. disapprove
a. be sorry for
b. refuse to reply
c. show dislike of

32. signature
a. your name in writing
b. stamp of approval
c. heavy truck

33. talent
a. attitude
b. natural ability
c. understanding

34. earnings
a. leftovers
b. food supplies
c. pay for work

35. glamorous
a. ragged
b. overdressed
c. fascinating

36. wickedness
a. being playful
b. being bad
c. being sorry

37. nonsense
a. lack of skill
b. need to be clear
c. foolishness

38. replace
a. put back
b. renew
c. treat badly

39. splendid
a. round
b. very good
c. narrow

40. unkind
a. cruel
b. not known
c. jealous

41. awkward
a. awful
b. playful
c. clumsy

42. downhearted
a. discouraged
b. ill
c. excited

43. fantastic
a. simple
b. harmful
c. strange

44. liberty
a. patriotism
b. goodness
c. freedom

45. mystery
a. secret
b. cause
c. untrue event

46. self-confidence
a. being shy
b. belief in yourself
c. selfishness

47. tender
a. soft
b. clear
c. thin

48. income
a. money earned
b. money spent
c. invitation

49. uncomfortable
a. unkind
b. unwilling
c. uneasy

50. voyage
a. warehouse
b. ocean trip
c. pirate

51. aid
a. help
b. try
c. repair

52. habit
a. lack of method
b. usual way of doing
c. reason for doing

53. press
a. teachers
b. broadcasters
c. newspapers

54. recount
a. reorder
b. repay
c. count again

55. section
a. smallest slice
b. more than one-half
c. part

56. perfect
a. without fault
b. almost right
c. very difficult

57. uncertain
a. proven
b. not sure
c. very certain

58. unexpected
a. not interested
b. amazing
c. without warning

59. unimportant
a. of special value
b. not important
c. unable to be carried

60. drowsy
a. filthy
b. sleepy
c. bored

61. statement
a. something said
b. proof
c. harsh word

62. disgraceful
a. harmful
b. sorrowful
c. shameful

63. dungeon
a. office
b. storeroom
c. cell

64. roam
a. run slowly
b. wander
c. walk with a purpose

65. shortage
a. too small an amount
b. part that shrinks
c. early death

66. password
a. correct answer
b. secret word
c. warning

67. stupid
a. smart but slow
b. lazy
c. without good sense

68. useless
a. of no value
b. of some value
c. of great value

69. elastic
a. will not bend
b. breaks easily
c. springs back

70. display
a. show
b. hide
c. stop

71. misplace
a. lose
b. enjoy
c. ruin

72. comedian
a. hard worker
b. funny person
c. popular singer

73. slender
a. quick
b. long and thin
c. weak

74. theft
a. mystery
b. robbery
c. what remains

75. echo
a. repeated sound
b. loud explosion
c. steady beat

76. festival
a. trip
b. serious event
c. entertainment

77. result
a. what happens
b. purpose
c. cause of something

78. uninvited
a. not difficult
b. not reasonable
c. not asked

79. permission
a. amount to be paid
b. approval to do
c. give in

80. disaster
a. great misfortune
b. wrong guess
c. drama

81. license
a. liquid
b. permission
c. belief

82. appearance
a. attitude
b. outward look
c. method

83. graze
a. lift
b. eat grass
c. sleep lightly

84. distrust
a. investment
b. doubt
c. failure

85. fare
a. money for a ride
b. right by law
c. proper share

86. rumble
a. low noise
b. crumbled material
c. evil remark

87. importance
a. imported goods
b. useful purpose
c. value

88. sameness
a. slight difference
b. something without purpose
c. being alike

89. transport
a. look closely at an object
b. say with force
c. carry from one place to another

90. transplant
a. plant in another place
b. plant in a row
c. dig ground before planting

5th grade

For each of the words listed below, choose the best definition. Answers are on page *59.*

1. outstanding
a. important
b. difficult
c. certain

2. forbidden
a. not allowed
b. not clear
c. not thoughtful

3. bleach
a. rip apart
b. rub together
c. make whiter

4. nasty
a. not pleasant
b. rainy
c. healthy

5. sorrowful
a. sad
b. alone
c. mean

6. suggestion
a. weak excuse
b. strict order
c. possible idea

7. transfer
a. change over
b. rub out
c. buy

8. vanish
a. miss
b. disappear
c. paint

9. enjoyable
a. pleasant
b. hurtful
c. hopeful

10. penalty
a. gain
b. rule
c. punishment

11. truthful
a. honest
b. frightened
c. guilty

12. unsafe
a. unlocked
b. dangerous
c. free of charge

13. zone
a. shiny metal
b. definite place
c. cold air

14. advice
a. helpful opinion
b. unwanted information
c. bad decision

15. combine
a. discuss in detail
b. join together
c. cut apart

16. difficult
a. unusual
b. simple
c. hard

17. effort
a. sharp tool
b. hard try
c. small insult

18. consult
a. behave well
b. eat up
c. seek advice

19. normal
a. insane
b. funny
c. usual

20. notice
a. skip
b. tell
c. see

21. press
a. repair
b. squeeze
c. turn

22. recall
a. misplace
b. remember
c. forget

23. equip
a. sell
b. give
c. furnish

24. greedy
a. needing to be cleaned
b. wanting too much
c. going too fast

25. similar
a. alike
b. distant
c. well-dressed

26. adulthood
a. average size
b. full growth
c. admission price

27. modern
a. up-to-date
b. official
c. regular

28. rude
a. not polite
b. not sincere
c. too proud

29. cruelty
a. dishonesty
b. deep regret
c. unkind treatment

30. defend
a. refuse to attend
b. search for weapons
c. guard from harm

31. forgiveness
a. shame
b. pardon
c. approval

32. furious
a. careless
b. angry
c. sad

33. identify
a. try
b. guess
c. recognize

34. luxury
a. bad bargain
b. extra comfort
c. necessary purchase

35. objectionable
a. disagreeable
b. additional
c. lovable

36. anxious
a. inactive
b. sure
c. eager

37. excellence
a. below average
b. one of many
c. rare goodness

38. dramatize
a. talk about
b. act out
c. change over

39. flexible
a. very strong
b. easily bent
c. higher than others

40. expand
a. make larger
b. release pressure
c. tighten up

41. gossip
a. unfriendly talk
b. happy event
c. complete explanation

42. paralyze
a. act slowly
b. make powerless
c. speed up

43. pledge
a. promise
b. request
c. faith

44. replacement
a. ruined material
b. substitute
c. worn part

45. unfamiliar
a. not well-known
b. much the same
c. connected to another

46. unsatisfactory
a. not good enough
b. man-made
c. more than needed

47. clatter
a. evil talk
b. slow movement
c. confused noise

48. carefree
a. without authority
b. honest
c. without worry

49. delay
a. tie together
b. shake slowly
c. put off until later

50. powerless
a. unsure
b. tired
c. weak

51. postpone
a. delay
b. send
c. quit

52. threat
a. reasonable request
b. helpful offer
c. possible harm

53. amuse
a. make smile
b. make angry
c. make mistakes

54. boldness
a. seriousness
b. good sense
c. courage

55. compress
a. squeeze together
b. take prisoner
c. stretch out

56. grief
a. sorrow
b. fear
c. excitement

57. simplify
a. smooth out
b. make easier
c. figure out

58. account
a. something extra
b. short term
c. business record

59. deadline
a. end of a race
b. time limit
c. fishing equipment

60. quiver
a. hold tight
b. shake
c. scream

61. billboard
a. large sign
b. horse-drawn cart
c. steam engine

62. attractive
a. different
b. pleasing
c. unusual

63. opinion
a. purpose
b. belief
c. test

64. complexion
a. emblem
b. skin color
c. childhood disease

65. discourage
a. spend foolishly
b. talk at length
c. lessen hope

66. generally
a. in part
b. usually
c. entirely

67. ambition
a. desire for success
b. fear of others
c. lack of confidence

68. advisable
a. honest
b. useless
c. wise

69. bagpipe
a. large insect
b. musical instrument
c. colorful robe

70. motto
a. nickname
b. story
c. saying

71. accomplish
a. seek
b. finish
c. hope for

72. distress
a. trouble
b. debate
c. sadness

73. victorious
a. has won
b. has fought
c. has watched

74. pace
a. price
b. silence
c. rate

75. reasonableness
a. foolish for no reason
b. making good sense
c. ability to work

76. escort
a. shout
b. cover head
c. go along with

77. intelligence
a. ability to learn
b. deserving blame
c. great happiness

78. advertisement
a. polite act
b. paid announcement
c. rare condition

79. blunder
a. stupid mistake
b. loud noise
c. low hedge

80. reexamine
a. solve without doubt
b. prove by reason
c. test again

81. brutal
a. cruel
b. large
c. clever

82. visual
a. can be divided
b. can be heard
c. can be seen

83. captivity
a. officer's rank
b. being held against one's will
c. goods taken illegally

84. fragile
a. heavy
b. easily broken
c. disagreeable

85. eternal
a. ending quickly
b. rushing wildly
c. lasting forever

86. column
a. vertical part of a page
b. frying pan
c. long coat

87. confederation
a. act of conquering
b. states joined together
c. disagreement among partners

88. navigate
a. go to the movies
b. run a ship
c. peel an apple

89. mold
a. growth on bread
b. glass pot
c. secret meeting

90. confused
a. set apart
b. mixed up
c. acting natural

6th grade

For each of the words listed below, choose the best definition. Answers are on page *60.*

1. allowable
a. more than usual
b. strange
c. permitted

2. bonus
a. center part
b. important paper
c. something extra

3. just
a. fair
b. harsh
c. selfish

4. admirer
a. wild animal
b. one who approves
c. one who dislikes

5. anniversary
a. bitter enemy
b. musical composition
c. yearly event

6. brilliance
a. brightness
b. confidence
c. rudeness

7. capable
a. not needed
b. having great value
c. able to do

8. frequent
a. careless
b. impolite
c. happening often

9. gratitude
a. debt owed
b. being thankful
c. amount given

10. leadership
a. necessary action
b. willingness to give
c. ability to guide

11. portable
a. easily carried
b. forbidden
c. told in secret

12. abolish
a. eat rapidly
b. do away with
c. take prisoner

13. estimate
a. wander off course
b. follow close behind
c. judge approximately

14. generosity
a. self-confidence
b. lack of understanding
c. willingness to share

15. impatience
a. loss of silence
b. boldness of manner
c. unwillingness to wait

16. lawful
a. not governed by rules
b. allowed by law
c. stolen by force

17. loyalty
a. being uncertain
b. being faithful
c. being hopeful

18. magical
a. mysterious
b. successful
c. silent

19. majority
a. smallest group
b. greater part
c. amount less than half

20. supreme
a. clear
b. weak
c. highest

21. symbol
a. cloak
b. emblem
c. waterway

22. vow
a. deep wound
b. tool for drawing
c. solemn promise

23. absentee
a. something ordinary
b. escaped prisoner
c. person not present

24. combat
a. game
b. riddle
c. fight

25. counterfeit
a. false
b. below average
c. incomplete

26. disciple
a. follower
b. leader
c. director

27. disregard
a. treat with care
b. wear down
c. pay no attention to

28. document
a. furnish written proof
b. find a mistake
c. act a story

29. insert
a. put in
b. erase
c. force apart

30. wisdom
a. distant land
b. great learning
c. religion

31. columnist
a. architect
b. disloyal person
c. newspaper writer

32. deserve
a. receive punishment
b. be worthy of
c. take care of

33. fiction
a. great discovery
b. made-up story
c. historical event

34. minor
a. less important
b. very certain
c. fully grown

35. panic
a. uncontrolled fear
b. childhood disease
c. laughable event

36. reassemble
a. separate into parts
b. guard from harm
c. put together again

37. reconsider
a. think over again
b. continue to fight
c. tighten up

38. ridiculous
a. stiff
b. laughable
c. artistic

39. slogan
a. motto
b. apartment
c. jacket

40. strict
a. lightweight
b. stern
c. fast

41. vacate
a. leave empty
b. store up supplies
c. discover by accident

42. voluntary
a. done by choice
b. done by force
c. done by accident

43. accustomed
a. far away
b. usual
c. exact

44. advantageous
a. helpful
b. errorless
c. confused

45. annual
a. with flowers
b. yearly
c. part time

46. grant
a. hold back
b. give
c. tell a secret

47. hesitate
a. remain firm
b. offer an excuse
c. be undecided

48. imperfect
a. having faults
b. most excellent
c. repaired

49. radar
a. large telescope
b. sun's energy
c. radio wave locator

50. ruling
a. joke
b. mistake
c. decision

51. abbreviation
a. short form of word
b. folk song
c. dramatic play

52. eliminate
a. number
b. get rid of
c. light up

53. thigh
a. part of arm
b. part of leg
c. part of neck

54. czar
a. pirate
b. emperor
c. peasant

55. yearn
a. long for
b. be jealous over
c. be afraid of

56. shatter
a. break into pieces
b. nail down tightly
c. handle quietly

57. blueprint
a. blue flower
b. famous painting
c. building plan

58. item
a. one dozen
b. separate thing
c. pile of goods

59. site
a. location
b. tent
c. battleground

60. kindling
a. entrance hall
b. firewood
c. small boat

61. mishap
a. planned event
b. unlucky accident
c. repaired object

62. playwright
a. writes plays
b. plans contests
c. teaches school

63. heighten
a. frighten away
b. make tighter
c. make taller

64. henceforth
a. never again
b. from now on
c. once in a while

65. raid
a. quick death
b. long war
c. sudden attack

66. gong
a. wind instrument
b. saucer-shaped bell
c. small drum

67. thump
a. sharp scream
b. dull sound
c. low whistle

68. halo
a. ring of light
b. leafy crown
c. silken robe

69. tamper
a. suggest calmly
b. meddle improperly
c. speak honestly

70. meddlesome
a. shy
b. scanty
c. interfering

71. severe
a. raw
b. thin
c. harsh

72. stupidity
a. lack of intelligence
b. sudden hunger
c. weakened condition

73. concern
a. worry
b. courage
c. regret

74. deceive
a. split
b. lie
c. promise

75. illegal
a. not lawful
b. not desirable
c. secret

76. vicinity
a. amusement park
b. region nearby
c. sticky liquid

77. associate
a. connect
b. figure out
c. avoid

78. collision
a. expensive mistake
b. hitting together
c. working hard

79. foresight
a. looking ahead
b. failing to remember
c. offering to help

80. reliable
a. dependable
b. dangerous
c. repeating

81. solution
a. answer
b. clue
c. mystery

82. eclipse
a. cut off light
b. carry messages
c. wash with chemicals

83. jagged
a. square
b. rattling
c. uneven

84. opponent
a. teammate
b. house guest
c. person on other side

85. absorbing
a. very interesting
b. very difficult
c. tired out

86. conduct
a. simplicity
b. explanation
c. behavior

87. inability
a. lack of skill
b. false reasoning
c. overfed

88. piracy
a. bad storm
b. robbery at sea
c. type of banking

89. transform
a. make larger
b. change
c. heal

90. rampage
a. decayed leaves
b. wild outbreak
c. act of heroism

91. secrecy
a. sharing knowledge
b. concealing from others
c. finding out

92. temptation
a. attraction
b. sin
c. protection

93. approximately
a. accurately
b. nearly
c. usually

94. core
a. unit of measurement
b. innermost part
c. ruined piece

95. dignity
a. lack of importance
b. poor judgment
c. degree of worth

96. migrate
a. sleep a long time
b. suffer a headache
c. move to another place

97. honorable
a. shy
b. honest
c. well-known

98. plywood
a. large tree
b. type of oven
c. board made of thin layers

99. benefit
a. game
b. help
c. duty

100. confide
a. mark off with lines
b. set afire
c. tell as a secret

101. contentment
a. serious thought
b. satisfaction
c. enclosed area

102. debtor
a. finished sketch
b. person who owes money
c. small, gray cat

103. part
a. join
b. seek
c. separate

104. pose
a. agree
b. protect
c. pretend

105. adviser
a. tennis player
b. heating lamp
c. person who gives opinion

106. persuade
a. win over
b. cover up
c. pass by

107. pursuit
a. chase
b. warm clothing
c. cause of trouble

108. laxative
a. tall grass
b. stomach medicine
c. saltshaker

109. endorse
a. approve
b. waste
c. avoid

110. landscape
a. cave-in
b. area fenced in
c. scenery

111. nuisance
a. long story
b. something that annoys
c. famous person

112. humid
a. damp
b. cool
c. breezy

113. nominate
a. forget completely
b. put up for election
c. repeat aloud

114. meditation
a. overeating
b. silly conduct
c. quiet thinking

115. amateur
a. not a professional
b. not working
c. house guest

116. incinerator
a. gentle breeze
b. waste burner
c. long trip

117. hoarse
a. sounding rough and deep
b. sticky
c. old and weary

118. finance
a. provide money for
b. dance around a tree
c. open a store

119. urgent
a. unable to last
b. demanding immediate attention
c. helpless in defeat

120. occasional
a. happening very seldom
b. happening now and then
c. very unusual

7th grade

For each of the words listed below, choose the best definition. Answers are on page *60.*

1. charitable
a. not trustworthy
b. helpful to others
c. shamefully bold

2. conduct
a. guide
b. build
c. separate

3. impure
a. not clean
b. free from harm
c. not serious

4. demolish
a. reshape
b. destroy
c. argue

5. purposely
a. exactly
b. intentionally
c. quickly

6. vouch
a. guarantee
b. capture
c. argue

7. establish
a. be responsible for
b. check over
c. set up

8. portion
a. divide into shares
b. plan ahead
c. remain in place

9. ungrateful
a. unthankful
b. clever
c. shy

10. version
a. unusually good idea
b. deep-seated hatred
c. one side of a story

11. discard
a. throw aside
b. mix up
c. take apart

12. omit
a. leave out
b. change slightly
c. hide from view

13. handicap
a. prize awarded
b. final score
c. added hindrance

14. infrequent
a. occurring seldom
b. full of changes
c. slow moving

15. parade
a. make noise
b. march
c. have fun

16. unconcerned
a. without order
b. not busy
c. not interested

17. violate
a. break a law
b. approve orders
c. paint various colors

18. inseparable
a. unable to meet
b. unable to be parted
c. unable to answer

19. abnormal
a. average
b. disgusting
c. irregular

20. calculate
a. figure out
b. look over
c. cut through

21. decrease
a. become less
b. pull together
c. smooth out

22. insistent
a. noisy
b. demanding
c. humble

23. vivid
a. very bright
b. noisy
c. angry

24. hazardous
a. incorrect
b. dangerous
c. difficult

25. decent
a. harmless
b. proper
c. rude

26. necessitate
a. take back
b. cause to be needed
c. make risky

27. congregate
a. assemble
b. discover
c. sort out

28. improbable
a. hard to enter
b. not likely
c. quick to act

29. journalist
a. tour guide
b. traveler
c. newswriter

30. magnificence
a. hugeness
b. generosity
c. splendor

31. dismissal
a. sending away
b. rest period
c. long speech

32. lawsuit
a. list of rules
b. court case
c. black robe

33. mute
a. damaged
b. silent
c. unseen

34. observable
a. noticeable
b. usable
c. important

35. cluster
a. miser
b. bunch
c. small car

36. mutiny
a. revolt
b. false statement
c. court action

37. obvious
a. filled up
b. easily seen
c. unusually difficult

38. recent
a. brief
b. important
c. new

39. salvage
a. save from loss
b. paint like new
c. investigate thoroughly

40. voluntarily
a. at the present time
b. willingly
c. helpfully

41. reserve
a. earn
b. devote
c. keep back

42. examination
a. investigation
b. long report
c. political meeting

43. forfeit
a. nag at constantly
b. lose as a penalty
c. bring to a sudden halt

44. autopsy
a. perfumed pad
b. difficult problem
c. examination after death

45. technician
a. small detail
b. skilled person
c. assistant

46. suspense
a. uncertainty
b. difficulty
c. support

47. transformation
a. long time
b. source of power
c. complete change

48. percentage
a. part of a whole
b. delicious food
c. brilliant sunlight

49. devilment
a. amusement
b. mischief
c. danger

50. oddity
a. something left over
b. type of poem
c. strange thing

51. unruly
a. easily managed
b. hard to control
c. sought after

52. intrigue
a. rescue operation
b. secret plotting
c. careful selection

53. quake
a. whirl
b. roll
c. shake

54. versus
a. against
b. with
c. under

55. balk
a. gladly help
b. willingly leave
c. stubbornly refuse

56. amputate
a. cut off limbs
b. drive swiftly
c. pay debts

57. depose
a. elect a leader
b. put out of office
c. organize a group

58. bicker
a. quarrel
b. destroy
c. feel ashamed

59. bribe
a. make comfortable
b. influence with a reward
c. put in danger

60. humiliate
a. approve
b. oppose
c. shame

61. antiseptic
a. fights rumors
b. kills disease germs
c. helps plant growth

62. leukemia
a. uneducated person
b. loud noise
c. blood cancer

63. fillet
a. thin slice of meat
b. portion of fruit
c. cool drink

64. cleaver
a. blunt club
b. pointed stick
c. cutting tool

65. haven
a. camper's packsack
b. place of shelter
c. mythical place

66. endear
a. make tired
b. win affection
c. cause suspicion

67. javelin
a. hand spear
b. heavy weight
c. flat disc

68. lock
a. part of a canal
b. front of a chair
c. back of a ship

69. lyre
a. metal box
b. screwdriver
c. small harp

70. coddle
a. treat tenderly
b. handle roughly
c. speak honestly

71. tempo
a. musical instrument
b. usual rhythm
c. painting process

72. uphold
a. display
b. put aside
c. support

73. charitable
a. angry
b. kind and forgiving
c. tearful

74. repulsive
a. gathering friends
b. causing strong dislike
c. working alone

75. ignite
a. set on fire
b. extinguish
c. freeze

76. transmit
a. let in
b. send over
c. cut off

77. contradict
a. explain carefully
b. lie to
c. disagree with

78. safeguard
a. issue a warning
b. keep safe
c. give orders

79. toxic
a. poisonous
b. spreading
c. healthful

80. efficient
a. poor
b. capable
c. sickly

81. linger
a. stay on
b. walk away
c. clamp together

82. rations
a. sneakers
b. gold coins
c. food issued

83. vary
a. agree with
b. make different
c. explain fully

84. weld
a. exercise power
b. cheat out of
c. join together

85. elasticity
a. stiffness
b. ability to stretch
c. hopelessness

86. venturesome
a. daring
b. outrageous
c. timid

87. detection
a. failure
b. mystery
c. discovery

88. royally
a. grandly
b. forcefully
c. faithfully

89. testimony
a. close questioning
b sign of friendship
c. statement of evidence

90. ineffective
a. incapable
b. incomplete
c. eternal

91. quest
a. decision
b. travel
c. search

92. omelet
a. fat chicken
b. small hole
c. beaten egg, fried or baked

93. acknowledge
a. decide
b. admit
c. wonder

94. unaware
a. not conscious
b. not certain
c. not complete

95. besiege
a. surround to capture
b. attempt to escape
c. plan ahead

96. humbleness
a. courage
b. modesty
c. mystery

97. unintelligible
a. not sociable
b. not understandable
c. not comfortable

98. avalanche
a. sliding snow
b. general store
c. part of a church

99. redeem
a. buy back
b. save up
c. call off

100. botanist
a. student of plants
b. sewing machine
c. wire basket

101. hysteria
a. climbing plant
b. unconscious state
c. senseless excitement

102. discipline
a. question
b. punish
c. succeed

103. minute
a. very small
b. quite simple
c. slyly quick

104. bewitch
a. annoy greatly
b. follow closely behind
c. put under a spell

105. excess
a. houseboat
b. narrow scarf
c. too big a supply

106. inviting
a. entertaining
b. well-mannered
c. tempting

107. volume
a. list
b. money
c. amount

108. adaptable
a. spiteful
b. too cold
c. fits new condition

109. exasperate
a. make an exception
b. make angry
c. spend foolishly

110. induce
a. persuade
b. make less
c. flatter

111. respiration
a. leaking
b. breathing
c. running

112. mongrel
a. cruel person
b. homeless wanderer
c. mixed breed

113. predicate
a. part of sentence
b. spot on leaf
c. hard material

114. untimely
a. not graceful
b. not sensible
c. at the wrong time

115. priceless
a. extremely valuable
b. highly exaggerated
c. quite useless

116. react
a. advertise
b. wrap up
c. respond to

117. drift
a. wind-piled snow
b. patchwork
c. wagon

118. patience
a. keep hidden
b. ability to endure
c. unreasonable action

119. metropolitan
a. belonging to the world
b. belonging to large cities
c. belonging to the country

120. unaccountable
a. not necessary
b. unable to be explained
c. having a large number

8th grade

For each of the words listed below, choose the best definition. Answers are on page *61*.

1. purify
a. set in order
b. make clean
c. look ahead

2. fierce
a. wild
b. quick
c. hungry

3. infinity
a. part of speech
b. small particle
c. being without end

4. medicated
a. containing medicine
b. stretched out
c. badly hurt

5. offend
a. hurt the feelings of
b. bring together sharply
c. interfere with

6. disadvantage
a. accident
b. loss
c. luck

7. operative
a. at the right time
b. overly simple
c. in working order

8. outlook
a. problem solved
b. way of thinking
c. destructive force

9. rage
a. act violently
b. be sick
c. have fun

10. universal
a. most important
b. not understood
c. existing everywhere

11. zoology
a. study of mathematics
b. study of animals
c. study of rocks

12. disable
a. make useless
b. argue against
c. make unhappy

13. mindful
a. thoughtless
b. stubborn
c. careful

14. option
a. example
b. choice
c. law

15. pessimistic
a. unwilling
b. gloomy
c. curious

16. plane
a. medical instrument
b. average score
c. flat surface

17. progress
a. work hard
b. change the subject
c. go ahead

18. regular
a. gentle
b. usual
c. not common

19. superlative
a. mysterious
b. above all others
c. not exact

20. tributary
a. unexpected gift
b. mild suffering
c. emptying stream

21. hoodoo
a. avoid using
b. make fun of
c. bring bad luck

22. papier-mâché
a. French rifle
b. fine writing paper
c. wet modeling paper

23. retrial
a. opposite direction
b. discovery
c. second test

24. tariff
a. tax on imports
b. freight of ship
c. colorful garment

25. veto
a. legislate
b. reject
c. argue

26. adaptation
a. taking charge
b. developing ability
c. changing to fit

27. hocus-pocus
a. trickery
b. talent
c. mixture

28. ineligible
a. not qualified
b. lasting temporarily
c. difficult to understand

29. sane
a. amusing
b. sensible
c. friendly

30. sympathize
a. cry unreasonably
b. share another's feeling
c. make comfortable

31. tradition
a. rules of etiquette
b. beliefs from the past
c. written history

32. hearing
a. severe scolding
b. court session
c. rehearsal period

33. interval
a. wrong application
b. great explosion
c. time between

34. pickle
a. preserve
b. cut up
c. fry slowly

35. solar
a. single
b. of the sun
c. central

36. administer
a. manage
b. change
c. seek

37. decagon
a. pony cart
b. ten-sided figure
c. desert

38. falter
a. reach
b. hesitate
c. catch

39. ferocious
a. quick-tempered
b. cone-bearing
c. savagely cruel

40. engulf
a. put to shame
b. spoil
c. swallow up

41. mournful
a. joyful
b. sorrowful
c. hateful

42. originate
a. cancel out
b. defend against
c. cause to be

43. quintet
a. sugary dessert
b. selfish person
c. set of five

44. warrant
a. justify
b. resist
c. capture

45. variable
a. changeable
b. possible
c. exact

46. hostile
a. entertaining
b. unfriendly
c. rugged

47. imperil
a. put in danger
b. cure with medicine
c. force to do

48. isolate
a. reduce pressure
b. blow up
c. place apart

49. racist
a. idiot
b. believes own race is best
c. impatient person

50. ruinous
a. rough-edged
b. not competent
c. destructive

51. memento
a. souvenir
b. mother
c. fruit

52. vagabond
a. witch
b. tramp
c. feline

53. endorse
a. sift out
b. hunt
c. sign back of a check

54. passion
a. strong feeling
b. tall rock
c. place of rest

55. galaxy
a. western lands
b. political group
c. star system

56. indictment
a. court conviction
b. legal accusation
c. serious gossip

57. bounteous
a. plentiful
b. little
c. none

58. supplement
a. add to
b. take from
c. stay the same

59. flounder
a. perform faultlessly
b. struggle awkwardly
c. think carefully

60. charade
a. hairstyle
b. guessing game
c. high chair

61. convulsion
a. changing formation
b. meek gesture
c. violent disturbance

62. ruthless
a. without hate
b. without mercy
c. without help

63. hacienda
a. large estate
b. Japanese fan
c. lamb stew

64. hypocrite
a. ally
b. pretender
c. patient

65. fiancée
a. engaged woman
b. money problem
c. captive soldier

66. misshapen
a. deformed
b. masculine
c. fortunate

67. listless
a. too tired to care
b. energetic
c. without love

68. ingratitude
a. not being thankful
b. not being mean
c. not being wise

69. morale
a. land form
b. physical condition
c. mental condition

70. legible
a. hard to catch
b. impossible to believe
c. easy to read

71. venture
a. admire
b. prepare
c. dare

72. aptitude
a. judgment
b. ability
c. emotion

73. execute
a. outlaw
b. carry out
c. begin

74. heritage
a. education
b. collection
c. inheritance

75. illusion
a. unknown reason
b. soft spot
c. false idea

76. undaunted
a. not afraid
b. safe
c. lonely

77. gale
a. waterfall
b. cabin
c. strong wind

78. injurious
a. harmful
b. unable to judge
c. very noisy

79. mulish
a. stubborn
b. noisy
c. thoughtful

80. pen name
a. assumed name
b. book title
c. trademark

81. radiate
a. make flexible
b. admire greatly
c. shine brightly

82. random
a. define
b. not correct
c. by chance

83. gabardine
a. dancing teacher
b. kind of cloth
c. flat frying pan

84. monopolize
a. talk too much
b. control exclusively
c. get together

85. petrify
a. defend from evil
b. turn into stone
c. make angry

86. sophisticated
a. active
b. lovely
c. worldly-wise

87. surplus
a. extra quantity
b. needed amount
c. raised price

88. eminent
a. talkative
b. well-educated
c. distinguished

89. lair
a. public telephone
b. long porch
c. wild animal's den

90. rustle
a. jump up and down
b. make a drawing
c. make a whispering sound

91. sober
a. serious
b. crabby
c. unoriginal

92. utility
a. cleanliness
b. disappointment
c. usefulness

93. belated
a. delayed
b. unimportant
c. lonely

94. inedible
a. sure to happen
b. unfit to eat
c. not exact

95. jubilant
a. wise
b. rejoicing
c. brilliant

96. contraption
a. band of thieves
b. charity ball
c. gadget

97. impish
a. crabby
b. sickly
c. mischievous

98. intensify
a. make clear
b. make stronger
c. make smaller

99. narrate
a. admire greatly
b. tell a story
c. pull out

100. persistent
a. very earnest
b. continuing steadily
c. easily seen

101. realm
a. large amount
b. kingdom
c. circle

102. wretch
a. short poem
b. bad person
c. valuable jewel

103. technique
a. idea
b. skill
c. attitude

104. mutilate
a. punish severely
b. disfigure
c. take by force

105. blissful
a. sincere
b. disturbed
c. joyful

106. testify
a. make a guess
b. give evidence
c. lie about

107. ramble
a. melt away
b. destroy
c. wander

108. gallery
a. kitchen
b. balcony
c. boat

109. obituary
a. puffy cloud
b. death notice
c. heavy cloth

110. shameful
a. filled with humility
b. dishonorable
c. very shy

111. rash
a. careless
b. tasteless
c. unsure

112. smolder
a. crush out
b. make dirty
c. burn slowly

113. defect
a. mental or physical weakness
b. long wait
c. bad joke

114. clansman
a. traveling salesman
b. one of a related group
c. grocer

115. ratio
a. light coloring
b. iron bar
c. relationship of numbers

116. legion
a. group of soldiers
b. religious ceremony
c. distinguished person

117. nausea
a. small insect
b. sickness in stomach
c. book of poems

118. novelty
a. something new
b. anything that explodes
c. kind of lock

119. prominent
a. easily led
b. very precise
c. well-known

120. unanimous
a. in complete agreement
b. not helpful to others
c. foolishly happy

9th grade

For each of the words listed below, choose the best definition. Answers are on page *67*.

1. relic
a. keepsake
b. strategy
c. victory

2. dedicated
a. serious
b. devoted
c. reliable

3. fantasy
a. historical event
b. imaginary happening
c. spiritual guidance

4. wood pulp
a. material for papermaking
b. unnatural growth
c. clump of trees

5. coma
a. unconsciousness
b. serious injury
c. muscular twitch

6. misinterpret
a. disbelieve
b. treat badly
c. misunderstand

7. circulate
a. pass around
b. push
c. connect

8. ordain
a. set up shop
b. officially appoint
c. take a train

9. undefined
a. unexpected
b. not explained
c. completely free

10. phase
a. administrative problem
b. nervous ailment
c. stage of development

11. preferable
a. partly necessary
b. more honorable
c. more desirable

12. inhospitable
a. uninviting
b. uncomfortable
c. ill

13. amnesia
a. blood disease
b. insanity
c. loss of memory

14. client
a. opponent
b. customer
c. partner

15. nucleus
a. unknown quality
b. central part
c. fertile area

16. transfigure
a. cause mutilation
b. change the appearance of
c. bring action against

17. dissociate
a. introduce
b. join
c. separate

18. acuteness
a. necessity
b. sharpness
c. slyness

19. decelerate
a. gain speed
b. fix boundaries
c. slow down

20. encounter
a. meet with
b. examine carefully
c. surround completely

21. segment
a. section
b. surplus
c. boundary

22. timidity
a. shyness
b. childishness
c. gentleness

23. stabilize
a. make firm
b. require evidence
c. make unavailable

24. dawdle
a. bargain
b. waste time
c. sketch

25. predicament
a. bad situation
b. healing lotion
c. expected result

26. revise
a. change
b. recollect
c. criticize

27. snag
a. irritate
b. catch
c. steal

28. absorption
a. soaking up
b. concentration
c. giving off

29. incision
a. division
b. opinion
c. cut

30. deceit
a. mystery
b. dishonesty
c. vanity

31. wretched
a. miserable
b. humble
c. bent over

32. befuddle
a. despise
b. confuse
c. disregard

33. misfit
a. error
b. bad choice
c. something insuitable

34. commissioner
a. salesman
b. assistant
c. official in charge

35. consumer
a. owner
b. arranger
c. user

36. bantam
a. colorful drape
b. type of nut
c. small-sized fowl

37. misadventure
a. lesson
b. bad luck
c. crime

38. premier
a. prize awarded
b. first in rank
c. acknowledged fact

39. archdeacon
a. tropical fish
b. encyclopedia
c. high church official

40. commentator
a. chief officer
b. news critic
c. strong ruler

41. incriminate
a. interfere with
b. accuse of a crime
c. cause unhappiness

42. pigment
a. weary traveler
b. coloring matter
c. minor ailment

43. strategy
a. reasonable conclusion
b. skillful planning
c. eventual goal

44. data
a. appointment
b. amount
c. information

45. elaborate
a. sift ashes
b. give more details
c. escape

46. post
a. regulate
b. thrust
c. make public

47. defiance
a. open resistance
b. agreement
c. unfriendliness

48. quorum
a. trial by jury
b. public meeting
c. legal majority

49. domestic
a. ordinary
b. tame
c. grown-up

50. irrational
a. unbelievable
b. responsible
c. unreasonable

51. aloof
a. withdrawn
b. futile
c. generous

52. impel
a. force
b. situate
c. slay

53. cumbersome
a. late
b. considerate
c. clumsy

54. beau
a. parent
b. recluse
c. sweetheart

55. superfluous
a. talkative
b. more than needed
c. supplementary

56. whim
a. ponderous movement
b. sudden notion
c. firm decision

57. floriculture
a. fencing
b. zookeeping
c. flower growing

58. molten
a. worn
b. melted
c. disguised

59. canny
a. indifferent
b. shrewd
c. wild

60. tranquil
a. peaceful
b. erratic
c. sullen

61. entice
a. drag
b. employ
c. tempt

62. nonchalant
a. excited
b. indifferent
c. radical

63. renegade
a. traitor
b. hobo
c. judge

64. pugnacious
a. thrifty
b. fond of fighting
c. feeling inadequate

65. maladjustment
a. embarrassment
b. criticism
c. poor fit

66. jovial
a. emphatic
b. without fear
c. full of fun

67. disengage
a. release
b. wish
c. hold

68. confront
a. hide carefully
b. speak softly
c. face boldly

69. gaunt
a. healthy
b. talented
c. thin

70. titanic
a. old
b. huge
c. ridiculous

71. luscious
a. delicious
b. secretive
c. expensive

72. unforeseen
a. mistaken
b. private
c. unexpected

73. alloy
a. business partner
b. alcoholic beverage
c. metallic mixture

74. dehydrate
a. make small
b. rinse with chemicals
c. remove moisture

75. scoff
a. refuse to recognize
b. cause to detest
c. make fun of

76. vengeance
a. revenge
b. neglect
c. patience

77. fickle
a. sickly
b. unwanted
c. changing

78. anatomy
a. function of history
b. structure of animals
c. relation to stars

79. panorama
a. false statement
b. wide view
c. large bed

80. municipal
a. of a state
b. of a country
c. of a city

81. incline
a. glorify
b. slant
c. insult

82. ban
a. throw out
b. fence in
c. prohibit

83. conspire
a. plot
b. die
c. command

84. disrupt
a. break up
b. confuse
c. burst out

85. short-sighted
a. too eager to please
b. not trustworthy
c. lacking in foresight

86. typical
a. characteristic
b. precise
c. brief

87. zany
a. spicy
b. noisy
c. crazy

88. antibiotic
a. pirate
b. false statement
c. disease-killing drug

89. apportion
a. distribute
b. give a decision
c. carry off

90. leeway
a. margin of safety
b. water route
c. modern highway

91. hemisphere
a. small icebox
b. high mountain
c. half a globe

92. graphic
a. in chart or diagram form
b. circular
c. wrong

93. commend
a. order
b. advise
c. praise

94. rearmament
a. moving in one direction
b. supplying weapons again
c. secret code

95. by-product
a. imported product
b. new product
c. extra product

96. distribute
a. seize from others
b. mix several kinds
c. give out in shares

97. lurk
a. cut off
b. dye green
c. wait out of sight

98. embargo
a. leaving a port
b. order closing ports
c. freight of a ship

99. mechanize
a. put in order
b. rebuild completely
c. replace by machinery

100. temperament
a. disposition
b. self-control
c. violence

101. hypochondria
a. confusion
b. wild excitement
c. imaginary sickness

102. vain
a. difficult
b. useless
c. criminal

103. benzine
a. quick-burning oil
b. camp table
c. heavy bombing

104. asphyxiation
a. poisoning
b. suffocation
c. weariness

105. revert
a. win acclaim
b. go back to
c. turn upside down

106. inclination
a. cause
b. belief
c. preference

107. condemnation
a. strong disapproval
b. illegal seizure
c. high praise

108. deficient
a. incomplete
b. careless
c. hard-working

109. citation
a. replacement
b. defender
c. special honor

110. cholera
a. a disease
b. bright light
c. failure

111. papyrus
a. smiling face
b. ancient paper
c. witty saying

112. hoax
a. wishful thought
b. contrary opinion
c. practical joke

113. rebuttal
a. the argument against
b. supporter
c. distribution

114. mangy
a. grand
b. shabby
c. neutral

115. gratify
a. greet
b. please
c. give

116. feudalism
a. social system in the Middle Ages
b. order of knights
c. family disagreement

117. revolutionize
a. use original ideas
b. accept present condition
c. make a great change

118. ravenous
a. very hungry
b. powerful
c. showy

119. granular
a. brightly lighted
b. resentful
c. composed of grains

120. mariner
a. sailor
b. wanderer
c. beggar

10th grade

For each of the words listed below, choose the best definition. Answers are on page *62*.

1. manual
a. not expressive
b. machine-made
c. done by hand

2. capsize
a. overturn
b. seize
c. measure

3. overcome
a. conquer
b. aspire
c. disinfect

4. coincide
a. attempt something alone
b. go bankrupt
c. occur at same time

5. questionable
a. positive
b. doubtful
c. untruthful

6. recognition
a. thought
b. desire
c. acknowledgment

7. narrative
a. story
b. ocean voyage
c. coastline

8. devise
a. imitate
b. confuse
c. invent

9. sanctuary
a. roadside inn
b. place of safety
c. type of sculpture

10. appreciate
a. rise in value
b. decrease in importance
c. eliminate completely

11. distinction
a. proper dress
b. special quality
c. loss of property

12. mystify
a. endanger
b. burglarize
c. bewilder

13. concentrate
a. scatter widely
b. bring together
c. mix up

14. delusion
a. overconfidence
b. original idea
c. false belief

15. negligent
a. cautious
b. careless
c. improper

16. slander
a. hand tool
b. false report
c. court order

17. flawless
a. without fear
b. irresponsible
c. perfect

18. monotone
a. type of organ
b. means of transportation
c. sameness of tone

19. skim
a. spill
b. read fast
c. drain

20. sonic
a. clothlike
b. of sound
c. forbidden

21. perpetual
a. continuous
b. uneasy
c. serious

22. sequence
a. connected series
b. incomplete plan
c. expensive material

23. descendant
a. fallen ruler
b. minus quantity
c. offspring

24. jeopardy
a. danger
b. hindsight
c. probability

25. project
a. regulation
b. plan
c. obstacle

26. unavoidable
a. inevitable
b. untrue
c. decided by majority

27. receptacle
a. container
b. wire
c. wrapper

28. misconstrue
a. suspect others
b. draw to scale
c. interpret incorrectly

29. mural
a. wallpainting
b. stonelike mineral
c. sea shell

30. yield
a. surrender
b. fight vigorously
c. cast aside

31. exquisite
a. very lovely
b. necessary
c. mannerly

32. clique
a. select group
b. delicate tap
c. French model

33. arid
a. quite spoiled
b. unusually smelly
c. very dry

34. brocade
a. woven with raised designs
b. stamped with ink
c. edged with lace

35. laboriously
a. with deep feeling
b. with hard work
c. without interest

36. peril
a. geometric figure
b. sudden loss
c. danger

37. await
a. start suddenly
b. delay momentarily
c. look forward to

38. impel
a. force
b. suggest
c. ignore

39. remorse
a. walled enclosure
b. deep regret
c. refinement

40. scraggly
a. lost
b. ragged
c. unwanted

41. abusive
a. foolish
b. insulting
c. stubborn

42. avert
a. dislike thoroughly
b. turn aside
c. state forcefully

43. reimburse
a. owe to
b. pay back
c. remember

44. intangible
a. insecure
b. not touchable
c. indirect

45. premonition
a. acknowledgment
b. forewarning
c. battle equipment

46. oblivious
a. deceiving
b. odd
c. unaware

47. remnant
a. part left
b. animal characteristic
c. bargain sale

48. boycott
a. bazaar
b. sleeping bag
c. refusal to buy

49. skeptical
a. inclined to doubt
b. lacking in reality
c. disobedient

50. tyranny
a. hilly countryside
b. unjust use of power
c. illegal seizure

51. abhor
a. be angry at
b. detest
c. shock

52. contradict
a. deny
b. blame
c. accept

53. galvanize
a. trick
b. mix up
c. prevent rust

54. blazer
a. sport jacket
b. fur hat
c. silk stocking

55. tousled
a. tired
b. mussed
c. dirty

56. diligent
a. truthful
b. hard-working
c. slow-witted

57. courtly
a. polite
b. loyal
c. wrong

58. acclimated
a. feel dismayed
b. become accustomed
c. grow tired

59. pliable
a. unable to persuade
b. grossly incompetent
c. easily bent

60. dubious
a. doubtful
b. quarrelsome
c. retired

61. crescendo
a. increase in loudness
b. stay the same
c. decrease in loudness

62. foundling
a. lost cause
b. baby deer
c. deserted child

63. glucose
a. kind of plant
b. kind of meat
c. kind of sugar

64. cower
a. crouch fearfully
b. stand erectly
c. speak purposefully

65. dissuade
a. persuade not to do
b. create an invention
c. force to fight

66. infuriate
a. cross-examine
b. make angry
c. breathe inward

67. cochlea
a. center of eye
b. part of inner ear
c. part of brain

68. artisan
a. skilled workman
b. common laborer
c. airplane pilot

69. certitude
a. confusion
b. felony
c. certainty

70. magistrate
a. camera
b. advertisement
c. judge

71. ruffle
a. annoy
b. spread evenly
c. deceive

72. celestial
a. nautical
b. heavenly
c. musical

73. unsung
a. questionable
b. not celebrated
c. effortless

74. confiscate
a. set afire
b. destroy
c. take and keep

75. fervent
a. gracious
b. very earnest
c. weak

76. contraband
a. wide belt
b. smuggled goods
c. subtle tone

77. diversity
a. variety
b. dwelling place
c. lecture

78. disproportionate
a. undeserving of trust
b. less important
c. lacking in balance

79. harass
a. burden
b. torment
c. amuse

80. somber
a. tinted
b. glamorous
c. dark

81. relinquish
a. repair
b. plant
c. give up

82. habitat
a. usual behavior
b. riding costume
c. dwelling place

83. imperative
a. preferred above others
b. workable
c. vitally necessary

84. unscrupulous
a. soiled
b. inefficient
c. lacking principle

85. time-honored
a. old and respected
b. conservative
c. outdated

86. shrewdness
a. distaste
b. insult
c. keenness

87. séance
a. fast, irregular dance
b. formal lecture
c. talk with spirits

88. replenish
a. improve
b. resupply
c. make new again

89. eloquence
a. logical arrangement
b. fine speaking
c. false appeal

90. endowment
a. gift to provide income
b. building contract
c. large down payment

91. chasm
a. optical device
b. deep gap
c. mineral

92. accommodating
a. foolish
b. helpful
c. fearless

93. dormant
a. inactive
b. stale
c. separate

94. beauteous
a. beautiful
b. spiritual
c. undeveloped

95. enliven
a. make difficult
b. make expensive
c. make cheerful

96. trek
a. faucet
b. mathematical unit
c. journey

97. vault
a. show force
b. leap over
c. apply pressure

98. brine
a. very salty water
b. large cat
c. poisonous snake

99. curdle
a. thicken
b. dull
c. blend

100. acquit
a. put next to
b. change quickly
c. free from a charge

101. stagnate
a. pierce suddenly
b. become sluggish
c. reach upward

102. distort
a. label
b. twist out of shape
c. scream

103. mock
a. sincere
b. not real
c. destructive

104. discretion
a. evil scheme
b. good judgment
c. bold action

105. rigamarole
a. trouble
b. nonsense
c. carelessness

106. documentary
a. live wire
b. factual presentation
c. long, full cape

107. notorious
a. widely known
b. talented
c. badly constructed

108. sack
a. rob by force
b. remove temporarily
c. investigate thoroughly

109. rivalry
a. companionship
b. duet
c. contest

110. obsolete
a. extremely tall
b. always free
c. out of date

111. blare
a. fancy cake
b. low-heeled shoe
c. loud noise

112. bliss
a. great happiness
b. sharp blow
c. patch of cloth

113. priority
a. side by side
b. come first
c. have depth

114. bigoted
a. intolerant
b. esteemed
c. talkative

115. facsimile
a. hairless dog
b. loud thunder
c. exact copy

116. vanity
a. fear
b. jealousy
c. pride

117. exploit
a. wise choice
b. daring deed
c. clear statement

118. foundry
a. metal-molding factory
b. mark of disgrace
c. money earned

119. nutritious
a. orderly arrangement
b. good for nothing
c. valuable as food

120. scandalize
a. offend by wrongdoing
b. argue insistently
c. persuade effectively

11th grade

For each of the words listed below, choose the best definition. Answers are on page *62*.

1. idolize
a. make bright
b. admire much
c. decorate elaborately

2. nomad
a. dwarf
b. warrior
c. wanderer

3. reliability
a. attention
b. endurance
c. trustworthiness

4. clarify
a. explain
b. disprove
c. solve

5. petite
a. shy
b. unique
c. little

6. resolute
a. determined
b. fearful
c. complacent

7. coax
a. bury
b. punish
c. persuade

8. precede
a. go before
b. come after
c. fall between

9. chaos
a. roaring fire
b. great confusion
c. destruction

10. conglomerate
a. broken apart
b. water-soaked
c. clustered together

11. evacuation
a. terror
b. withdrawal
c. accumulation

12. merge
a. bet
b. combine
c. separate

13. simile
a. image
b. sure thing
c. comparison

14. differentiate
a. make useless
b. make distinction
c. make similar

15. detract
a. take away
b. make shorter
c. change abruptly

16. flabbergasted
a. embarrassed
b. misled
c. astonished

17. progression
a. forward movement
b. helpful suggestion
c. successful action

18. temperance
a. moderation
b. honesty
c. wisdom

19. turbulent
a. nervous
b. violent
c. dramatic

20. frequency
a. large amount
b. rate of occurrence
c. stage of development

21. hybrid
a. farm machine
b. nobleman's servant
c. mixed offspring

22. luxurious
a. modern and streamlined
b. scarce and old
c. rich and comfortable

23. zealous
a. enthusiastic
b. envious
c. proud

24. witticism
a. good decision
b. clever remark
c. harsh criticism

25. brief
a. test
b. negotiate
c. summarize

26. contaminate
a. prohibit illegally
b. make impure
c. make enemies

27. recipient
a. helper
b. receiver
c. owner

28. enthrall
a. charm
b. weep
c. wonder

29. omnipotent
a. just
b. all-powerful
c. merciful

30. remote
a. very silent
b. not interested
c. far away

31. anticipate
a. recall
b. move into action
c. look forward to

32. carnivorous
a. flesh-eating
b. greedy
c. wild

33. valiant
a. cautious
b. warlike
c. brave

34. alien
a. gangster
b. stranger
c. official

35. eccentric
a. odd
b. holy
c. intellectual

36. prelude
a. explanation
b. symptom
c. introduction

37. reinforce
a. carry out
b. press inward
c. make stronger

38. unsound
a. secret
b. not tested
c. not dependable

39. moderate
a. excessive
b. easy
c. medium

40. philosophical
a. highly studious
b. thoughtfully wise
c. not religious

41. affiliate
a. distinguish
b. associate
c. separate

42. discord
a. lack of obedience
b. lack of harmony
c. unreasonable sadness

43. gall
a. outlet
b. overboldness
c. wild herb

44. heretic
a. cruel savage
b. opponent of accepted belief
c. advocate of court action

45. antagonist
a. opponent
b. disbeliever
c. hero

46. cardinal
a. serious
b. main
c. definite

47. federated
a. having smooth edges
b. joined together
c. insincere

48. reminiscent
a. thoughtful of others
b. recalling past events
c. sensible under stress

49. slovenly
a. untidy
b. bad-tempered
c. disobedient

50. chaste
a. hurried
b. pure
c. wily

51. apex
a. flat field
b. choppy sea
c. highest point

52. ostracize
a. blend
b. burn
c. banish

53. encompass
a. include
b. follow
c. defeat

54. decrepit
a. old and feeble
b. new and shiny
c. last and most

55. coronet
a. ring
b. crown
c. staff

56. moralize
a. explain right and wrong
b. refuse to cooperate
c. think out slowly

57. inadvertent
a. miserable
b. unintentional
c. recognizable

58. harrowing
a. weakening
b. disturbing
c. sickening

59. cistern
a. automobile
b. water tank
c. soft cloth

60. adamant
a. extremely hard
b. spongy
c. especially smooth

61. foyer
a. bedroom
b. entrance hall
c. basement

62. maltreat
a. pet
b. rejoice
c. abuse

63. chassis
a. framework
b. tall building
c. social club

64. unsavory
a. unpleasant in taste
b. sharp to touch
c. good to smell

65. betrothal
a. divorce
b. engagement
c. contest

66. gyrate
a. jump
b. whirl
c. slide

67. chivalrous
a. unreasonable
b. courteous
c. meddlesome

68. naïve
a. like a child
b. experienced
c. helpful

69. primeval
a. ancient
b. modern
c. futuristic

70. sinister
a. quiet
b. evil
c. afraid

71. category
a. class
b. list
c. summary

72. frenzy
a. great excitement
b. sadness
c. great intelligence

73. embark
a. treat badly
b. quarrel noisily
c. begin a voyage

74. fraudulent
a. troublesome
b. clever
c. dishonest

75. resumption
a. immediate result
b. beginning again
c. brief pause

76. abhorrent
a. hateful
b. jealous
c. sticky

77. ornate
a. too expensive
b. highly decorated
c. very rare

78. converge
a. come together
b. discuss reasonably
c. split up

79. futile
a. useless
b. difficult
c. small

80. pacifist
a. believer in peace
b. sleeping pill
c. friendly person

81. traverse
a. cut in half
b. overtake
c. go across

82. assent
a. agree
b. assume
c. state

83. fishmonger
a. fish bait
b. fish recipe
c. dealer in fish

84. ovation
a. operatic performance
b. important conference
c. enthusiastic approval

85. solidify
a. isolate
b. harden
c. prove

86. obsolete
a. out-of-date
b. hidden
c. unimportant

87. obstructive
a. complicated
b. hindering
c. causing ruin

88. subterranean
a. of the sea
b. underground
c. rocky

89. application
a. desire
b. rejection
c. use

90. mandate
a. juicy fruit
b. an order
c. sloping position

91. squatter
a. ranch hand
b. idle worker
c. illegal settler

92. abrasive
a. doubtful story
b. scratchy material
c. cowardly person

93. exotic
a. romantic
b. fragrant
c. strange

94. practicable
a. of great value
b. can be done
c. almost completed

95. option
a. a right to buy
b. fancy table mat
c. support of a cause

96. repercussion
a. aftereffect
b. muffled sound
c. argument

97. terminate
a. lengthen
b. decide
c. finish

98. chromosome
a. gene-carrier
b. two-wheeled bike
c. lace

99. balm
a. tropical fish
b. fragrant ointment
c. glass lid

100. eradicate
a. get rid of
b. fail to justify
c. set free

101. exultation
a. rising up
b. great rejoicing
c. outward explosion

102. begrudge
a. dig from beneath
b. insult without reason
c. be reluctant to give

103. decamp
a. dig a hole
b. leave secretly
c. sleep soundly

104. perception
a. greed
b. power
c. awareness

105. diverse
a. varied
b. numerous
c. crossed

106. opinionated
a. stubborn in belief
b. well-informed
c. masterful

107. abyss
a. deep empty space
b. graceful animal
c. bird call

108. comprehensive
a. including much
b. standing out
c. valued highly

109. irreconcilable
a. very sad
b. off the subject
c. unable to agree

110. attune
a. bring into harmony
b. match wits
c. make up for

111. tentative
a. experimental
b. confused
c. closely related

112. appalled
a. confused
b. dismayed
c. saddened

113. ruse
a. trick
b. sneer
c. mistake

114. unwarranted
a. not biased
b. not justified
c. useless

115. registrar
a. official recorder
b. slogan
c. kind of beetle

116. deplorable
a. comfortable
b. shameful
c. vigorous

117. secession
a. majority vote
b. formal withdrawal
c. slowing down

118. obelisk
a. worn spot
b. disagreement
c. tall stone shaft

119. zygote
a. fertilized egg
b. painting
c. gold leaf

120. yoke
a. frame for carrying loads
b. front of a building
c. story with a lesson

12th grade

For each of the words listed below, choose the best definition. Answers are on page *63*.

1. martyr
a. sufferer for a belief
b. brave warrior
c. religious fanatic

2. controversial
a. debatable
b. exciting
c. significant

3. explicable
a. able to be shared
b. able to be explained
c. exposed to air

4. genial
a. pleasant
b. humorous
c. magical

5. loathsome
a. disgusting
b. sneaky
c. forward

6. prevalent
a. widespread
b. prejudiced
c. illegal

7. trivial
a. unimportant
b. inexpensive
c. exhausting

8. fracas
a. fried veal
b. intricate puzzle
c. noisy quarrel

9. diffuse
a. very small
b. spread out
c. glowing softly

10. extemporaneous
a. not measurable
b. at the same time
c. without preparation

11. vogue
a. alternative
b. legend
c. fashion

12. incontinence
a. large amount
b. lack of restraint
c. special coloring

13. abandon
a. feeling of embarrassment
b. extreme violence
c. freedom from restraint

14. portly
a. weary
b. stout
c. cheerful

15. deficit
a. shortage
b. credit
c. payment

16. statute
a. crime
b. law
c. branch of government

17. skeptic
a. weakling
b. pretender
c. doubter

18. perceive
a. be aware of
b. solve methodically
c. agree upon

19. opportune
a. valuable
b. timely
c. urgent

20. groundless
a. intentionally false
b. without end
c. without cause

21. anthology
a. collection of writings
b. detailed outline
c. musical score

22. deliberate
a. confine secretly
b. argue bitterly
c. consider carefully

23. emancipation
a. poor health
b. setting free
c. formal discourse

24. lament
a. mourn
b. criticize
c. reminisce

25. mania
a. habit
b. joke
c. craze

26. pessimism
a. impatience of others
b. pursuit of material gain
c. belief in the worst

27. persevere
a. continue trying
b. think about
c. toil without effort

28. linear
a. small star
b. magician
c. length measure

29. obsession
a. spicy sauce
b. mail chute
c. inescapable feeling

30. serenity
a. calmness
b. shrewdness
c. good fortune

31. perjure
a. steal away
b. swear falsely
c. injure slightly

32. begrimed
a. dirty
b. having whiskers
c. wealthy

33. eczema
a. skin disease
b. triangle
c. notebook

34. grotesque
a. sharp-pointed
b. evilly mean
c. unnatural in appearance

35. interpose
a. ask unnecessarily
b. place between
c. distribute evenly

36. grimace
a. carpenter's tool
b. ugly smile
c. tight grip

37. melancholy
a. disease
b. boredom
c. sadness

38. annotation
a. false name
b. added comments
c. journey in space

39. diabolic
a. gloomy
b. devilish
c. medicinal

40. zither
a. stringed instrument
b. fast horse
c. animal cry

41. potency
a. good nature
b. power
c. cruelty

42. laud
a. announce
b. praise
c. disturb

43. oligarchy
a. rule by a few
b. religious group
c. body of delegates

44. oppress
a. keep down
b. relieve tension
c. improve the quality of

45. askew
a. stupid
b. twisted
c. amusing

46. materialist
a. muffin tin
b. puff of smoke
c. lover of possessions

47. submissive
a. merciful
b. obedient
c. patient

48. destitution
a. extreme poverty
b. payment for injury
c. written law

49. extortion
a. nasty reply
b. getting by force
c. taking out

50. quagmire
a. puzzle
b. marsh
c. deep hole

51. defunct
a. lively
b. dead
c. dangerous

52. bequeath
a. take by force
b. leave by will
c. buy with money

53. wan
a. blotchy
b. soft
c. pale

54. amass
a. pile up
b. tear down
c. share among many

55. thwart
a. hinder
b. help
c. hope

56. divulge
a. make double
b. make known
c. make tall

57. breadth
a. depth
b. width
c. height

58. edify
a. eat
b. close
c. instruct

59. avid
a. clumsy
b. eager
c. stupid

60. furl
a. roll up
b. hand out
c. close in

61. verbose
a. simple
b. tame
c. wordy

62. disavow
a. disclaim
b. prevent
c. imitate

63. impregnable
a. unwilling
b. unconquerable
c. unpunished

64. martial
a. musical
b. warlike
c. silent

65. paltry
a. shared
b. cultured
c. worthless

66. halitosis
a. bad breath
b. stomach ulcer
c. skin disease

67. buttress
a. support
b. cover
c. tunnel

68. grotto
a. cave
b. game
c. jewel

69. commingle
a. decompose
b. separate
c. blend

70. discommode
a. accommodate
b. suggest
c. disturb

71. hypothetical
a. assumed as true
b. belonging to the people
c. in small quantities

72. lacerate
a. stitch closely
b. decorate completely
c. tear roughly

73. obliterate
a. insult
b. blot out
c. ignore

74. regal
a. royal
b. joyous
c. lawful

75. nurture
a. distribute fairly
b. care for
c. allow to spoil

76. renounce
a. forecast danger
b. give up
c. emphasize strongly

77. quench
a. exert pressure on
b. apply a rough finish to
c. extinguish

78. garble
a. dress in rags
b. scramble a message
c. fire a furnace

79. indignation
a. deep hatred
b. scornful anger
c. lack of manners

80. plausible
a. distorted
b. simplified
c. believable

81. habitable
a. friendly
b. ordinary
c. livable

82. influx
a. huge quantity
b. inward flow
c. vicious attack

83. ingrained
a. flowering
b. deeply rooted
c. sinful

84. itinerary
a. idle wanderer
b. plan of travel
c. limit of the law

85. precedent
a. example set
b. unexpected result
c. furious overflowing

86. mean
a. average
b. result
c. majority

87. query
a. question
b. riddle
c. suggestion

88. ode
a. poem
b. type of egg
c. musical instrument

89. exonerate
a. free from blame
b. make clear
c. accuse of evil

90. rebuff
a. brutal irony
b. sudden check
c. false logic

91. improvise
a. prepare offhand
b. plan carefully
c. retreat from

92. maverick
a. juicy fruit
b. loose dress
c. unbranded steer

93. compassion
a. pity
b. anger
c. sensitivity

94. orient
a. acquaint with a situation
b. whirl around
c. whistle shrilly

95. fortitude
a. stinginess
b. courage to endure
c. honesty

96. frigate
a. sailing ship
b. country store
c. chest of drawers

97. pillage
a. bombard
b. plunder
c. reinforce

98. automaton
a. pilot
b. robot
c. monarch

99. decapitate
a. behead
b. avoid
c. divide

100. hassock
a. child's toothbrush
b. gardening tool
c. footstool

101. patriarch
a. youthful leader
b. military formation
c. religious founder

102. indifferent
a. neither good nor bad
b. ugly
c. difficult

103. recoil
a. move slowly
b. draw back
c. wave around

104. lackadaisical
a. wishy-washy
b. very imaginative
c. unhealthy

105. lambaste
a. sneeze
b. beat or scold
c. carry a load

106. inborn
a. bent inward
b. hidden from sight
c. present from birth

107. laxity
a. neatness
b. carelessness
c. stupidity

108. amphibious
a. for land and sea
b. countrified
c. double-jointed

109. impassioned
a. very reasonable
b. full of feeling
c. coldly indifferent

110. dilemma
a. difficult choice
b. humorous situation
c. unsolved mystery

111. callous
a. having a deep voice
b. nervous
c. not sensitive

112. carbine
a. short, light rifle
b. baby carriage
c. shoelace

113. transcend
a. decline
b. surpass
c. travel

114. caption
a. peaked hat
b. title
c. rowboat

115. abashed
a. shattered
b. ashamed
c. disappointed

116. consecrate
a. make holy
b. bring together
c. hide well

117. refract
a. make smaller
b. bend light rays
c. take back again

118. inveterate
a. aged
b. dishonest
c. habitual

119. erroneous
a. mutilated
b. weird
c. mistaken

120. focus
a. central point
b. ring-tailed monkey
c. coffee bean

College level

For each of the words listed below, choose the best definition. Answers are on page *63*.

1. nebulous
a. not happy
b. not distinct
c. not creative

2. pellagra
a. spotted horse
b. large fruit
c. dietary disease

3. omniscient
a. peaceful
b. all knowing
c. lazy

4. rancid
a. not necessary
b. very important
c. spoiled

5. oblivion
a. authoritative
b. forgetfulness
c. hairiness

6. reamer
a. reasoned principle
b. silly conclusion
c. a finishing tool

7. optimum
a. best amount
b. indigestion
c. sorrow

8. manifest
a. easy to see
b. selfish
c. noble

9. contingent
a. depending upon
b. circular
c. very poor

10. icon
a. thin pipe
b. type of bacteria
c. religious picture

11. papacy
a. small dog
b. inheritance
c. pope's term of office

12. decadent
a. strict
b. morally decaying
c. lengthy

13. larder
a. young insect
b. Asian mammal
c. food-storage place

14. parenthetical
a. explanatory
b. involved
c. spread throughout

15. ambrosia
a. wide-brimmed hat
b. heavenly food
c. trap

16. proviso
a. result
b. condition
c. cause

17. abet
a. fight hard
b. assist
c. swear to be true

18. libretto
a. beautiful writing
b. art style
c. words of an opera

19. chastise
a. punish
b. praise
c. decorate

20. admonish
a. pull hard
b. scold gently
c. sink slowly

21. civility
a. sharpness
b. insanity
c. courtesy

22. adherence
a. bluntness
b. attachment
c. eroding

23. degenerate
a. delivery wagon
b. person of evil character
c. short comment

24. prowess
a. result
b. gap
c. skill

25. furlong
a. horse's hoof
b. one-eighth mile
c. long curl

26. attest
a. mix together
b. give proof
c. make easy

27. abstention
a. rushing forward
b. ironing out
c. holding off

28. catholic
a. flattering
b. calming
c. all-embracing

29. deluge
a. evil leader
b. mansion
c. great flood

30. batiste
a. small flute
b. large box
c. cotton cloth

31. facile
a. easily done
b. impertinent
c. thrifty

32. gamete
a. elf
b. matured germ cell
c. small fish

33. indeterminate
a. premature
b. not fixed
c. pale

34. manna
a. flavor
b. illness
c. food from heaven

35. lethargy
a. lack of interest
b. unable to breathe
c. united front

36. maim
a. beautify
b. cripple
c. protest

37. intuitive
a. stubborn
b. instinctive
c. attractive

38. lamentation
a. loud grief
b. reasonable argument
c. without purpose

39. malfeasance
a. official wrongdoing
b. senseless act
c. dirty word

40. foible
a. weakness
b. nerve
c. poison

41. incongruous
a. united
b. out of harmony
c. concealed

42. magisterial
a. very dull
b. judge-like
c. hard-working

43. pensive
a. in deep thought
b. unsuitable
c. very particular

44. recant
a. carry on
b. spread out
c. withdraw statement

45. pangs
a. cereal
b. cure-all
c. sharp pains

46. sagacity
a. keen judgment
b. good looks
c. poor health

47. elixir
a. happy feeling
b. cure-all
c. poor connection

48. implicitly
a. without appetite
b. overflowing
c. without question

49. luminosity
a. radiance
b. sadness
c. anger

50. indolence
a. hopelessness
b. laziness
c. fatigue

51. caulk
a. make strong
b. make dirty
c. make watertight

52. bovine
a. cowlike
b. curved
c. relaxed

53. defile
a. monopolize
b. pollute
c. spin

54. brandish
a. set on fire
b. keep repeating
c. shake threateningly

55. cajole
a. cook with spices
b. make fun of
c. persuade by flattery

56. evasion
a. artful escape
b. drawing board
c. Spanish shawl

57. incarnation
a. taking human form
b. glowing object
c. unpleasant experience

58. forthright
a. troublesome
b. straightforward
c. courageous

59. caldron
a. volcanic ash
b. dance marathon
c. large kettle

60. introspection
a. devouring food
b. sensing trouble
c. examining oneself

61. servitude
a. slavery
b. density
c. wastefulness

62. palpitate
a. squeeze hard
b. beat rapidly
c. drip constantly

63. ravage
a. lay waste
b. overtax
c. outshine

64. quiescent
a. teasing
b. wrinkled
c. calm

65. paradox
a. example
b. contradiction
c. musical box

66. ire
a. stupidity
b. happiness
c. anger

67. dole
a. large table
b. small portion
c. country house

68. cassock
a. priest's gown
b. kind of thermometer
c. songbird

69. demitasse
a. short skirt
b. small cup
c. ice-cream cone

70. reprehensible
a. remedial
b. primitive
c. blameworthy

71. aneroid
a. nervous disorder
b. kind of barometer
c. mechanical breakdown

72. discursive
a. not keeping to point
b. hopeless
c. bitter

73. fissure
a. flashy dress
b. deep crack
c. cattle disease

74. emulsion
a. physical ailment
b. long-range plan
c. suspension in fluid

75. irrevocable
a. without blame
b. disrespectful
c. cannot be undone

76. permeable
a. can soak through
b. awakens pity
c. out of fashion

77. pathos
a. is dishonest
b. awakens pity
c. shows cruelty

78. eulogize
a. crowd together
b. praise highly
c. make happy

79. floe
a. sailboat
b. mass of moving ice
c. bucket

80. intersperse
a. put here and there
b. control tightly
c. lead easily

81. phototropism
a. peacock feather
b. outer edge
c. turning toward light

82. indubitable
a. certain
b. ridiculous
c. dizzy

83. interaction
a. strengthening
b. controlling
c. acting and reacting

84. papaw
a. clown
b. fleshy fruit
c. prizefighter

85. rector
a. brimless hat
b. minister
c. athletic contest

86. placenta
a. afterbirth
b. large butterfly
c. unknown address

87. schizophrenia
a. plan of action
b. personality disorder
c. fishing boat

88. repression
a. stating
b. keeping down
c. fast walk

89. scuttle
a. sleep soundly
b. talk with spirits
c. sink on purpose

90. postulate
a. summarize
b. take for granted
c. salute

91. proverbial
a. well known
b. rural
c. graceful

92. emit
a. irritate
b. send forth
c. make feeble

93. incorrigible
a. cannot read
b. cannot see
c. cannot be reformed

94. zealot
a. four-wheeled carriage
b. enthusiast
c. critic

95. abrogate
a. descry
b. abolish
c. refinance

96. perpetuity
a. forever
b. optional
c. excellent

97. gesticulate
a. entertain friends
b. dance wildly
c. make motions to express ideas

98. dispenser
a. takes food
b. hands out
c. prays for

99. cantata
a. tall grass
b. clap of thunder
c. musical composition

100. scull
a. light racing boat
b. garter snake
c. alligator pear

101. zircon
a. part of speech
b. big book
c. mineral

102. yokel
a. yellow bird
b. sea captain
c. country fellow

103. toxemia
a. card game
b. bracelet
c. form of blood poisoning

104. disconcert
a. throw into confusion
b. take out
c. compliment

105. implore
a. beg
b. free
c. give in

106. rampant
a. stubborn
b. curious
c. unchecked

107. chronic
a. constant
b. disturbing
c. simple

108. grueling
a. singular
b. very tiring
c. dangerous

109. cadenza
a. rope chair
b. brilliant musical flourish
c. fancy bakery

110. masticate
a. exercise
b. drink
c. chew

111. refraction
a. obligation
b. deflection of light
c. punishment

112. reprimand
a. keep down
b. scold strongly
c. make conform

113. coagulate
a. assist
b. thicken
c. appeal to

114. euphuism
a. lie detector
b. immoral act
c. flowery expression

115. elocution
a. uncomfortable situation
b. art of public speaking
c. broken promise

116. inconclusive
a. dishonest
b. unhealthy
c. proving nothing

117. indomitable
a. without money
b. cannot be subdued
c. lacks ability

118. flounce
a. wide ruffle
b. horse's mane
c. flat roof

119. cohorts
a. partners
b. models
c. narrow shelves

120. peerless
a. without sound
b. without equal
c. without love

Now that you have tested your word power, you will want to know how strong it is. The answers to vocabulary inventories are on pages *59* through *63*. Turn to the page that lists the answers to the vocabulary inventory for your grade level to find out whether your word power is above average, average, or below average. Scoring for grade levels is as follows:

3rd grade (answers are on page *59*)
54 to 60, above average
42 to 53, average
41 or under, below average

4th and 5th grades (answers are on page *59*)
81 to 90, above average
72 to 80, average
71 or under, below average

6th and 7th grades (answers are on page *60*)
108 to 120, above average
84 to 107, average
83 or under, below average

8th and 9th grades (answers are on page *61*)
108 to 120, above average
84 to 107, average
83 or under, below average

10th and 11th grades (answers are on page *62*)
108 to 120, above average
84 to 107, average
83 or under, below average

12th grade and college level (answers are on page *63*)
108 to 120, above average
84 to 107, average
83 or under, below average

3rd grade

1. **note** (b) short letter
2. **hike** (c) long walk
3. **mash** (b) crush
4. **cab** (c) taxi
5. **pitch** (a) throw
6. **club** (b) heavy stick
7. **land** (a) go ashore
8. **bill** (c) bird's beak
9. **pack** (c) bundle
10. **snack** (b) small meal
11. **melon** (a) fruit
12. **merry** (c) full of fun
13. **often** (b) many times
14. **silent** (b) quiet
15. **trip** (a) stumble
16. **plain** (c) simple
17. **green** (a) not ripe
18. **weak** (c) not strong
19. **lower** (b) let down
20. **whip** (a) beat
21. **clearing** (b) open space
22. **gift** (c) present
23. **tablet** (a) writing pad
24. **choose** (c) pick out
25. **explain** (a) make clear
26. **act** (a) part of a play
27. **wink** (c) eye signal
28. **simple** (c) easy
29. **fluffy** (c) soft and light
30. **boast** (c) brag
31. **chilly** (c) rather cold
32. **glad** (a) happy
33. **lumber** (b) pieces of wood
34. **crippled** (c) lame
35. **tornado** (b) strong windstorm
36. **measure** (b) find size
37. **cartoon** (a) funny picture
38. **arrive** (c) come
39. **squaw** (b) Indian woman
40. **escape** (a) get free
41. **cozy** (b) comfortable
42. **wrench** (a) tool
43. **missing** (c) absent
44. **false** (c) not real
45. **nurse** (b) take care of
46. **magnet** (b) attracts iron
47. **leap** (c) jump
48. **nightmare** (a) bad dream
49. **mermaid** (c) fishlike woman
50. **moccasin** (a) Indian shoe
51. **branch** (b) part of tree
52. **bitter** (a) sharp-tasting
53. **swallow** (c) bird
54. **hockey** (b) game
55. **lullaby** (c) song for baby
56. **repay** (a) give back
57. **calfskin** (b) leather
58. **invent** (a) make something new
59. **verse** (b) part of poem
60. **gem** (c) jewel

4th grade

1. **ability** (b) skill
2. **bashful** (a) shy
3. **incorrect** (b) wrong
4. **fake** (b) false
5. **forgetful** (b) unable to remember
6. **frown** (b) look angry
7. **suffer** (c) have pain
8. **clue** (c) helpful fact
9. **fret** (a) worry
10. **marvelous** (a) wonderful
11. **visible** (b) can be seen
12. **confess** (a) admit
13. **ordinary** (b) common
14. **halt** (a) stop
15. **locate** (c) find
16. **imagine** (c) picture in one's mind
17. **lengthen** (a) make longer
18. **pretend** (b) make believe
19. **solve** (a) find the answer
20. **wept** (c) cried
21. **decision** (c) judgment reached
22. **miss** (c) fail to hit
23. **obedience** (b) following orders
24. **pride** (c) being proud
25. **smear** (c) mark or stain
26. **surround** (b) shut in on all sides
27. **active** (c) lively
28. **brave** (c) fearless
29. **convince** (a) make a person believe
30. **retire** (c) stop working
31. **disapprove** (c) show dislike of
32. **signature** (a) your name in writing
33. **talent** (b) natural ability
34. **earnings** (c) pay for work
35. **glamorous** (c) fascinating
36. **wickedness** (b) being bad
37. **nonsense** (c) foolishness
38. **replace** (a) put back
39. **splendid** (b) very good
40. **unkind** (a) cruel
41. **awkward** (c) clumsy
42. **downhearted** (a) discouraged
43. **fantastic** (c) strange
44. **liberty** (c) freedom
45. **mystery** (a) secret
46. **self-confidence** (b) belief in yourself
47. **tender** (a) soft
48. **income** (a) money earned
49. **uncomfortable** (c) uneasy
50. **voyage** (b) ocean trip
51. **aid** (a) help
52. **habit** (b) usual way of doing
53. **press** (c) newspapers
54. **recount** (c) count again
55. **section** (c) part
56. **perfect** (a) without fault
57. **uncertain** (b) not sure
58. **unexpected** (c) without warning
59. **unimportant** (b) not important
60. **drowsy** (b) sleepy
61. **statement** (a) something said
62. **disgraceful** (c) shameful
63. **dungeon** (c) cell
64. **roam** (b) wander
65. **shortage** (a) too small an amount
66. **password** (b) secret word
67. **stupid** (c) without good sense
68. **useless** (a) of no value
69. **elastic** (c) springs back
70. **display** (a) show
71. **misplace** (a) lose
72. **comedian** (b) funny person
73. **slender** (b) long and thin
74. **theft** (b) robbery
75. **echo** (a) repeated sound
76. **festival** (c) entertainment
77. **result** (a) what happens
78. **uninvited** (c) not asked
79. **permission** (b) approval to do
80. **disaster** (a) great misfortune
81. **license** (b) permission
82. **appearance** (b) outward look
83. **graze** (b) eat grass
84. **distrust** (b) doubt
85. **fare** (a) money for a ride
86. **rumble** (a) low noise
87. **importance** (c) value
88. **sameness** (c) being alike
89. **transport** (c) carry from one place to another
90. **transplant** (a) plant in another place

5th grade

1. **outstanding** (a) important
2. **forbidden** (a) not allowed
3. **bleach** (c) make whiter
4. **nasty** (a) not pleasant
5. **sorrowful** (a) sad
6. **suggestion** (c) possible idea
7. **transfer** (a) change over
8. **vanish** (b) disappear
9. **enjoyable** (a) pleasant
10. **penalty** (c) punishment
11. **truthful** (a) honest
12. **unsafe** (b) dangerous
13. **zone** (b) definite place
14. **advice** (a) helpful opinion
15. **combine** (b) join together
16. **difficult** (c) hard
17. **effort** (b) hard try
18. **consult** (c) seek advice
19. **normal** (c) usual
20. **notice** (c) see
21. **press** (b) squeeze
22. **recall** (b) remember
23. **equip** (c) furnish
24. **greedy** (b) wanting too much
25. **similar** (a) alike
26. **adulthood** (b) full growth
27. **modern** (a) up-to-date
28. **rude** (a) not polite
29. **cruelty** (c) unkind treatment
30. **defend** (c) guard from harm
31. **forgiveness** (b) pardon
32. **furious** (b) angry
33. **identify** (c) recognize
34. **luxury** (b) extra comfort
35. **objectionable** (a) disagreeable
36. **anxious** (c) eager
37. **excellence** (c) rare goodness
38. **dramatize** (b) act out
39. **flexible** (b) easily bent
40. **expand** (a) make larger
41. **gossip** (a) unfriendly talk
42. **paralyze** (b) make powerless
43. **pledge** (a) promise
44. **replacement** (b) substitute
45. **unfamiliar** (a) not well-known
46. **unsatisfactory** (a) not good enough
47. **clatter** (c) confused noise
48. **carefree** (c) without worry
49. **delay** (c) put off until later
50. **powerless** (c) weak
51. **postpone** (a) delay
52. **threat** (c) possible harm
53. **amuse** (a) make smile
54. **boldness** (c) courage
55. **compress** (a) squeeze together
56. **grief** (a) sorrow
57. **simplify** (b) make easier
58. **account** (c) business record
59. **deadline** (b) time limit
60. **quiver** (b) shake
61. **billboard** (a) large sign
62. **attractive** (b) pleasing
63. **opinion** (b) belief
64. **complexion** (b) skin color
65. **discourage** (c) lessen hope
66. **generally** (b) usually
67. **ambition** (a) desire for success
68. **advisable** (c) wise
69. **bagpipe** (b) musical instrument
70. **motto** (c) saying
71. **accomplish** (b) finish
72. **distress** (a) trouble
73. **victorious** (a) has won
74. **pace** (c) rate
75. **reasonableness** (b) making good sense
76. **escort** (c) go along with
77. **intelligence** (a) ability to learn
78. **advertisement** (b) paid announcement
79. **blunder** (a) stupid mistake
80. **reëxamine** (c) test again
81. **brutal** (a) cruel
82. **visual** (c) can be seen
83. **captivity** (b) being held against one's will
84. **fragile** (b) easily broken
85. **eternal** (c) lasting forever
86. **column** (a) vertical part of a page
87. **confederation** (b) states joined together
88. **navigate** (b) run a ship
89. **mold** (a) growth on bread
90. **confused** (b) mixed up

6th grade

1. **allowable** (c) permitted
2. **bonus** (c) something extra
3. **just** (a) fair
4. **admirer** (b) one who approves
5. **anniversary** (c) yearly event
6. **brilliance** (a) brightness
7. **capable** (c) able to do
8. **frequent** (c) happening often
9. **gratitude** (b) being thankful
10. **leadership** (c) ability to guide
11. **portable** (a) easily carried
12. **abolish** (b) do away with
13. **estimate** (c) judge approximately
14. **generosity** (c) willingness to share
15. **impatience** (c) unwillingness to wait
16. **lawful** (b) allowed by law
17. **loyalty** (b) being faithful
18. **magical** (a) mysterious
19. **majority** (b) greater part
20. **supreme** (c) highest
21. **symbol** (b) emblem
22. **vow** (c) solemn promise
23. **absentee** (c) person not present
24. **combat** (c) fight
25. **counterfeit** (a) false
26. **disciple** (a) follower
27. **disregard** (c) pay no attention to
28. **document** (a) furnish written proof
29. **insert** (a) put in
30. **wisdom** (b) great learning
31. **columnist** (c) newspaper writer
32. **deserve** (b) be worthy of
33. **fiction** (b) made-up story
34. **minor** (a) less important
35. **panic** (a) uncontrolled fear
36. **reassemble** (c) put together again
37. **reconsider** (a) think over again
38. **ridiculous** (b) laughable
39. **slogan** (a) motto
40. **strict** (b) stern
41. **vacate** (a) leave empty
42. **voluntary** (a) done by choice
43. **accustomed** (b) usual
44. **advantageous** (a) helpful
45. **annual** (b) yearly
46. **grant** (b) give
47. **hesitate** (c) be undecided
48. **imperfect** (a) having faults
49. **radar** (c) radio wave locator
50. **ruling** (c) decision
51. **abbreviation** (a) short form of word
52. **eliminate** (b) get rid of
53. **thigh** (b) part of leg
54. **czar** (b) emperor
55. **yearn** (a) long for
56. **shatter** (a) break into pieces
57. **blueprint** (c) building plan
58. **item** (b) separate thing
59. **site** (a) location
60. **kindling** (b) firewood
61. **mishap** (b) unlucky accident
62. **playwright** (a) writes plays
63. **heighten** (c) make taller
64. **henceforth** (b) from now on
65. **raid** (c) sudden attack
66. **gong** (b) saucer-shaped bell
67. **thump** (b) dull sound
68. **halo** (a) ring of light
69. **tamper** (b) meddle improperly
70. **meddlesome** (c) interfering
71. **severe** (c) harsh
72. **stupidity** (a) lack of intelligence
73. **concern** (a) worry
74. **deceive** (b) lie
75. **illegal** (a) not lawful
76. **vicinity** (b) region nearby
77. **associate** (a) connect
78. **collision** (b) hitting together
79. **foresight** (a) looking ahead
80. **reliable** (a) dependable
81. **solution** (a) answer
82. **eclipse** (a) cut off light
83. **jagged** (c) uneven
84. **opponent** (c) person on other side
85. **absorbing** (a) very interesting
86. **conduct** (c) behavior
87. **inability** (a) lack of skill
88. **piracy** (b) robbery at sea
89. **transform** (b) change
90. **rampage** (b) wild outbreak
91. **secrecy** (b) concealing from others
92. **temptation** (a) attraction
93. **approximately** (b) nearly
94. **core** (b) innermost part
95. **dignity** (c) degree of worth
96. **migrate** (c) move to another place
97. **honorable** (b) honest
98. **plywood** (c) board made of thin layers
99. **benefit** (b) help
100. **confide** (c) tell as a secret
101. **contentment** (b) satisfaction
102. **debtor** (b) person who owes money
103. **part** (c) separate
104. **pose** (c) pretend
105. **adviser** (c) person who gives opinion
106. **persuade** (a) win over
107. **pursuit** (a) chase
108. **laxative** (b) stomach medicine
109. **endorse** (a) approve
110. **landscape** (c) scenery
111. **nuisance** (b) something that annoys
112. **humid** (a) damp
113. **nominate** (b) put up for election
114. **meditation** (c) quiet thinking
115. **amateur** (a) not a professional
116. **incinerator** (b) waste burner
117. **hoarse** (a) sounding rough and deep
118. **finance** (a) provide money for
119. **urgent** (b) demanding immediate attention
120. **occasional** (b) happening now and then

7th grade

1. **charitable** (b) helpful to others
2. **conduct** (a) guide
3. **impure** (a) not clean
4. **demolish** (b) destroy
5. **purposely** (b) intentionally
6. **vouch** (a) guarantee
7. **establish** (c) set up
8. **portion** (a) divide into shares
9. **ungrateful** (a) unthankful
10. **version** (c) one side of a story
11. **discard** (a) throw aside
12. **omit** (a) leave out
13. **handicap** (c) added hindrance
14. **infrequent** (a) occurring seldom
15. **parade** (b) march
16. **unconcerned** (c) not interested
17. **violate** (a) break a law
18. **inseparable** (b) unable to be parted
19. **abnormal** (c) irregular
20. **calculate** (a) figure out
21. **decrease** (a) become less
22. **insistent** (b) demanding
23. **vivid** (a) very bright
24. **hazardous** (b) dangerous
25. **decent** (b) proper
26. **necessitate** (b) cause to be needed
27. **congregate** (a) assemble
28. **improbable** (b) not likely
29. **journalist** (c) newswriter
30. **magnificence** (c) splendor
31. **dismissal** (a) sending away
32. **lawsuit** (b) court case
33. **mute** (b) silent
34. **observable** (a) noticeable
35. **cluster** (b) bunch
36. **mutiny** (a) revolt
37. **obvious** (b) easily seen
38. **recent** (c) new
39. **salvage** (a) save from loss
40. **voluntarily** (b) willingly
41. **reserve** (c) keep back
42. **examination** (a) investigation
43. **forfeit** (b) lose as a penalty
44. **autopsy** (c) examination after death
45. **technician** (b) skilled person
46. **suspense** (a) uncertainty
47. **transformation** (c) complete change
48. **percentage** (a) part of a whole
49. **devilment** (b) mischief
50. **oddity** (c) strange thing
51. **unruly** (b) hard to control
52. **intrigue** (b) secret plotting
53. **quake** (c) shake
54. **versus** (a) against
55. **balk** (c) stubbornly refuse
56. **amputate** (a) cut off limbs
57. **depose** (b) put out of office
58. **bicker** (a) quarrel
59. **bribe** (b) influence with a reward
60. **humiliate** (c) shame
61. **antiseptic** (b) kills disease germs
62. **leukemia** (c) blood cancer
63. **fillet** (a) thin slice of meat
64. **cleaver** (c) cutting tool
65. **haven** (b) place of shelter
66. **endear** (b) win affection
67. **javelin** (a) hand spear
68. **lock** (a) part of a canal
69. **lyre** (c) small harp
70. **coddle** (a) treat tenderly
71. **tempo** (b) usual rhythm
72. **uphold** (c) support
73. **charitable** (b) kind and forgiving
74. **repulsive** (b) causing strong dislike
75. **ignite** (a) set on fire
76. **transmit** (b) send over
77. **contradict** (c) disagree with
78. **safeguard** (b) keep safe
79. **toxic** (a) poisonous
80. **efficient** (b) capable
81. **linger** (a) stay on
82. **rations** (c) food issued
83. **vary** (b) make different
84. **weld** (c) join together
85. **elasticity** (b) ability to stretch
86. **venturesome** (a) daring
87. **detection** (c) discovery
88. **royally** (a) grandly
89. **testimony** (c) statement of evidence
90. **ineffective** (a) incapable
91. **quest** (c) search
92. **omelet** (c) beaten egg, fried or baked
93. **acknowledge** (b) admit
94. **unaware** (a) not conscious
95. **besiege** (a) surround to capture
96. **humbleness** (b) modesty
97. **unintelligible** (b) not understandable
98. **avalanche** (a) sliding snow
99. **redeem** (a) buy back
100. **botanist** (a) student of plants
101. **hysteria** (c) senseless excitement
102. **discipline** (b) punish
103. **minute** (a) very small
104. **bewitch** (c) put under a spell
105. **excess** (c) too big a supply
106. **inviting** (c) tempting
107. **volume** (c) amount
108. **adaptable** (c) fits new condition
109. **exasperate** (b) make angry
110. **induce** (a) persuade
111. **respiration** (b) breathing
112. **mongrel** (c) mixed breed
113. **predicate** (a) part of sentence
114. **untimely** (c) at the wrong time
115. **priceless** (a) extremely valuable
116. **react** (c) respond to
117. **drift** (a) wind-piled snow
118. **patience** (b) ability to endure
119. **metropolitan** (b) belonging to large cities
120. **unaccountable** (b) unable to be explained

8th grade

1. **purify** (b) make clean
2. **fierce** (a) wild
3. **infinity** (c) being without end
4. **medicated** (a) containing medicine
5. **offend** (a) hurt the feelings of
6. **disadvantage** (b) loss
7. **operative** (c) in working order
8. **outlook** (b) way of thinking
9. **rage** (a) act violently
10. **universal** (c) existing everywhere
11. **zoology** (b) study of animals
12. **disable** (a) make useless
13. **mindful** (c) careful
14. **option** (b) choice
15. **pessimistic** (b) gloomy
16. **plane** (c) flat surface
17. **progress** (c) go ahead
18. **regular** (b) usual
19. **superlative** (b) above all others
20. **tributary** (c) emptying stream
21. **hoodoo** (c) bring bad luck
22. **papier-mâché** (c) wet modeling paper
23. **retrial** (c) second test
24. **tariff** (a) tax on imports
25. **veto** (b) reject
26. **adaptation** (c) changing to fit
27. **hocus-pocus** (a) trickery
28. **ineligible** (a) not qualified
29. **sane** (b) sensible
30. **sympathize** (b) share another's feeling
31. **tradition** (b) beliefs from the past
32. **hearing** (b) court session
33. **interval** (c) time between
34. **pickle** (a) preserve
35. **solar** (b) of the sun
36. **administer** (a) manage
37. **decagon** (b) ten-sided figure
38. **falter** (b) hesitate
39. **ferocious** (c) savagely cruel
40. **engulf** (c) swallow up
41. **mournful** (b) sorrowful
42. **originate** (c) cause to be
43. **quintet** (c) set of five
44. **warrant** (a) justify
45. **variable** (a) changeable
46. **hostile** (b) unfriendly
47. **imperil** (a) put in danger
48. **isolate** (c) place apart
49. **racist** (b) believes own race is best
50. **ruinous** (c) destructive
51. **memento** (a) souvenir
52. **vagabond** (b) tramp
53. **endorse** (c) sign back of a check
54. **passion** (a) strong feeling
55. **galaxy** (c) star system
56. **indictment** (b) legal accusation
57. **bounteous** (a) plentiful
58. **supplement** (a) add to
59. **flounder** (b) struggle awkwardly
60. **charade** (b) guessing game
61. **convulsion** (c) violent disturbance
62. **ruthless** (b) without mercy
63. **hacienda** (a) large estate
64. **hypocrite** (b) pretender
65. **fiancée** (a) engaged woman
66. **misshapen** (a) deformed
67. **listless** (a) too tired to care
68. **ingratitude** (a) not being thankful
69. **morale** (c) mental condition
70. **legible** (c) easy to read
71. **venture** (c) dare
72. **aptitude** (b) ability
73. **execute** (b) carry out
74. **heritage** (c) inheritance
75. **illusion** (c) false idea
76. **undaunted** (a) not afraid
77. **gale** (c) strong wind
78. **injurious** (a) harmful
79. **mulish** (a) stubborn
80. **pen name** (a) assumed name
81. **radiate** (c) shine brightly
82. **random** (c) by chance
83. **gabardine** (b) kind of cloth
84. **monopolize** (b) control exclusively
85. **petrify** (b) turn into stone
86. **sophisticated** (c) worldly-wise
87. **surplus** (a) extra quantity
88. **eminent** (c) distinguished
89. **lair** (c) wild animal's den
90. **rustle** (c) make a whispering sound
91. **sober** (a) serious
92. **utility** (c) usefulness
93. **belated** (a) delayed
94. **inedible** (b) unfit to eat
95. **jubilant** (b) rejoicing
96. **contraption** (c) gadget
97. **impish** (c) mischievous
98. **intensify** (b) make stronger
99. **narrate** (b) tell a story
100. **persistent** (b) continuing steadily
101. **realm** (b) kingdom
102. **wretch** (b) bad person
103. **technique** (b) skill
104. **mutilate** (b) disfigure
105. **blissful** (c) joyful
106. **testify** (b) give evidence
107. **ramble** (c) wander
108. **gallery** (b) balcony
109. **obituary** (b) death notice
110. **shameful** (b) dishonorable
111. **rash** (a) careless
112. **smolder** (c) burn slowly
113. **defect** (a) mental or physical weakness
114. **clansman** (b) one of a related group
115. **ratio** (c) relationship of numbers
116. **legion** (a) group of soldiers
117. **nausea** (b) sickness in stomach
118. **novelty** (a) something new
119. **prominent** (c) well-known
120. **unanimous** (a) in complete agreement

9th grade

1. **relic** (a) keepsake
2. **dedicated** (b) devoted
3. **fantasy** (b) imaginary happening
4. **wood pulp** (a) material for papermaking
5. **coma** (a) unconsciousness
6. **misinterpret** (c) misunderstand
7. **circulate** (a) pass around
8. **ordain** (b) officially appoint
9. **undefined** (b) not explained
10. **phase** (c) stage of development
11. **preferable** (c) more desirable
12. **inhospitable** (a) uninviting
13. **amnesia** (c) loss of memory
14. **client** (b) customer
15. **nucleus** (b) central part
16. **transfigure** (b) change the appearance of
17. **dissociate** (c) separate
18. **acuteness** (b) sharpness
19. **decelerate** (c) slow down
20. **encounter** (a) meet with
21. **segment** (a) section
22. **timidity** (a) shyness
23. **stabilize** (a) make firm
24. **dawdle** (b) waste time
25. **predicament** (a) bad situation
26. **revise** (a) change
27. **snag** (b) catch
28. **absorption** (a) soaking up
29. **incision** (c) cut
30. **deceit** (b) dishonesty
31. **wretched** (a) miserable
32. **befuddle** (b) confuse
33. **misfit** (c) something unsuitable
34. **commissioner** (c) official in charge
35. **consumer** (c) user
36. **bantam** (c) small-sized fowl
37. **misadventure** (b) bad luck
38. **premier** (b) first in rank
39. **archdeacon** (c) high church official
40. **commentator** (b) news critic
41. **incriminate** (b) accuse of a crime
42. **pigment** (b) coloring matter
43. **strategy** (b) skillful planning
44. **data** (c) information
45. **elaborate** (b) give more details
46. **post** (c) make public
47. **defiance** (a) open resistance
48. **quorum** (c) legal majority
49. **domestic** (b) tame
50. **irrational** (c) unreasonable
51. **aloof** (a) withdrawn
52. **impel** (a) force
53. **cumbersome** (c) clumsy
54. **beau** (c) sweetheart
55. **superfluous** (b) more than needed
56. **whim** (b) sudden notion
57. **floriculture** (c) flower growing
58. **molten** (b) melted
59. **canny** (b) shrewd
60. **tranquil** (a) peaceful
61. **entice** (c) tempt
62. **nonchalant** (b) indifferent
63. **renegade** (a) traitor
64. **pugnacious** (b) fond of fighting
65. **maladjustment** (c) poor fit
66. **jovial** (c) full of fun
67. **disengage** (a) release
68. **confront** (c) face boldly
69. **gaunt** (c) thin
70. **titanic** (b) huge
71. **luscious** (a) delicious
72. **unforeseen** (c) unexpected
73. **alloy** (c) metallic mixture
74. **dehydrate** (c) remove moisture
75. **scoff** (c) make fun of
76. **vengeance** (a) revenge
77. **fickle** (c) changing
78. **anatomy** (b) structure of animals
79. **panorama** (b) wide view
80. **municipal** (c) of a city
81. **incline** (b) slant
82. **ban** (c) prohibit
83. **conspire** (a) plot
84. **disrupt** (a) break up
85. **shortsighted** (c) lacking in foresight
86. **typical** (a) characteristic
87. **zany** (c) crazy
88. **antibiotic** (c) disease-killing drug
89. **apportion** (a) distribute
90. **leeway** (a) margin of safety
91. **hemisphere** (c) half a globe
92. **graphic** (a) in chart or diagram form
93. **commend** (c) praise
94. **rearmament** (b) supplying weapons again
95. **by-product** (c) extra product
96. **distribute** (c) give out in shares
97. **lurk** (c) wait out of sight
98. **embargo** (b) order closing ports
99. **mechanize** (c) replace by machinery
100. **temperament** (a) disposition
101. **hypochondria** (c) imaginary sickness
102. **vain** (b) useless
103. **benzine** (a) quick-burning oil
104. **asphyxiation** (b) suffocation
105. **revert** (b) go back to
106. **inclination** (c) preference
107. **condemnation** (a) strong disapproval
108. **deficient** (a) incomplete
109. **citation** (c) special honor
110. **cholera** (a) a disease
111. **papyrus** (b) ancient paper
112. **hoax** (c) practical joke
113. **rebuttal** (a) the argument against
114. **mangy** (b) shabby
115. **gratify** (b) please
116. **feudalism** (a) social system in the Middle Ages
117. **revolutionize** (c) make a great change
118. **ravenous** (a) very hungry
119. **granular** (c) composed of grains
120. **mariner** (a) sailor

10th grade

1. **manual** (c) done by hand
2. **capsize** (a) overturn
3. **overcome** (a) conquer
4. **coincide** (c) occur at same time
5. **questionable** (b) doubtful
6. **recognition** (c) acknowledgment
7. **narrative** (a) story
8. **devise** (c) invent
9. **sanctuary** (b) place of safety
10. **appreciate** (a) rise in value
11. **distinction** (b) special quality
12. **mystify** (c) bewilder
13. **concentrate** (b) bring together
14. **delusion** (c) false belief
15. **negligent** (b) careless
16. **slander** (b) false report
17. **flawless** (c) perfect
18. **monotone** (c) sameness of tone
19. **skim** (b) read fast
20. **sonic** (b) of sound
21. **perpetual** (a) continuous
22. **sequence** (a) connected series
23. **descendant** (c) offspring
24. **jeopardy** (a) danger
25. **project** (b) plan
26. **unavoidable** (a) inevitable
27. **receptacle** (a) container
28. **misconstrue** (c) interpret incorrectly
29. **mural** (a) wallpainting
30. **yield** (a) surrender
31. **exquisite** (a) very lovely
32. **clique** (a) select group
33. **arid** (c) very dry
34. **brocade** (a) woven with raised designs
35. **laboriously** (b) with hard work
36. **peril** (c) danger
37. **await** (c) look forward to
38. **impel** (a) force
39. **remorse** (b) deep regret
40. **scraggly** (b) ragged
41. **abusive** (b) insulting
42. **avert** (b) turn aside
43. **reimburse** (b) pay back
44. **intangible** (b) not touchable
45. **premonition** (b) forewarning
46. **oblivious** (c) unaware
47. **remnant** (a) part left
48. **boycott** (c) refusal to buy
49. **skeptical** (a) inclined to doubt
50. **tyranny** (b) unjust use of power
51. **abhor** (b) detest
52. **contradict** (a) deny
53. **galvanize** (c) prevent rust
54. **blazer** (a) sport jacket
55. **tousled** (b) mussed
56. **diligent** (b) hard-working
57. **courtly** (a) polite
58. **acclimated** (b) become accustomed
59. **pliable** (c) easily bent
60. **dubious** (a) doubtful
61. **crescendo** (a) increase in loudness
62. **foundling** (c) deserted child
63. **glucose** (c) kind of sugar
64. **cower** (a) crouch fearfully
65. **dissuade** (a) persuade not to do
66. **infuriate** (b) make angry
67. **cochlea** (b) part of inner ear
68. **artisan** (a) skilled workman
69. **certitude** (c) certainty
70. **magistrate** (c) judge
71. **ruffle** (a) annoy
72. **celestial** (b) heavenly
73. **unsung** (b) not celebrated
74. **confiscate** (c) take and keep
75. **fervent** (b) very earnest
76. **contraband** (b) smuggled goods
77. **diversity** (a) variety
78. **disproportionate** (c) lacking in balance
79. **harass** (b) torment
80. **somber** (c) dark
81. **relinquish** (c) give up
82. **habitat** (c) dwelling place
83. **imperative** (c) vitally necessary
84. **unscrupulous** (c) lacking principle
85. **time-honored** (a) old and respected
86. **shrewdness** (c) keenness
87. **séance** (c) talk with spirits
88. **replenish** (b) resupply
89. **eloquence** (b) fine speaking
90. **endowment** (a) gift to provide income
91. **chasm** (b) deep gap
92. **accommodating** (b) helpful
93. **dormant** (a) inactive
94. **beauteous** (a) beautiful
95. **enliven** (c) make cheerful
96. **trek** (c) journey
97. **vault** (b) leap over
98. **brine** (a) very salty water
99. **curdle** (a) thicken
100. **acquit** (c) free from a charge
101. **stagnate** (b) become sluggish
102. **distort** (b) twist out of shape
103. **mock** (b) not real
104. **discretion** (b) good judgment
105. **rigamarole** (b) nonsense
106. **documentary** (b) factual presentation
107. **notorious** (a) widely known
108. **sack** (a) rob by force
109. **rivalry** (c) contest
110. **obsolete** (c) out of date
111. **blare** (c) loud noise
112. **bliss** (a) great happiness
113. **priority** (b) come first
114. **bigoted** (a) intolerant
115. **facsimile** (c) exact copy
116. **vanity** (c) pride
117. **exploit** (b) daring deed
118. **foundry** (a) metal-molding factory
119. **nutritious** (c) valuable as food
120. **scandalize** (a) offend by wrongdoing

11th grade

1. **idolize** (b) admire much
2. **nomad** (c) wanderer
3. **reliability** (c) trustworthiness
4. **clarify** (a) explain
5. **petite** (c) little
6. **resolute** (a) determined
7. **coax** (c) persuade
8. **precede** (a) go before
9. **chaos** (b) great confusion
10. **conglomerate** (c) clustered together
11. **evacuation** (b) withdrawal
12. **merge** (b) combine
13. **simile** (c) comparison
14. **differentiate** (b) make distinction
15. **detract** (a) take away
16. **flabbergasted** (c) astonished
17. **progression** (a) forward movement
18. **temperance** (a) moderation
19. **turbulent** (b) violent
20. **frequency** (b) rate of occurrence
21. **hybrid** (c) mixed offspring
22. **luxurious** (c) rich and comfortable
23. **zealous** (a) enthusiastic
24. **witticism** (b) clever remark
25. **brief** (c) summarize
26. **contaminate** (b) make impure
27. **recipient** (b) receiver
28. **enthrall** (a) charm
29. **omnipotent** (b) all-powerful
30. **remote** (c) far away
31. **anticipate** (c) look forward to
32. **carnivorous** (a) flesh-eating
33. **valiant** (c) brave
34. **alien** (b) stranger
35. **eccentric** (a) odd
36. **prelude** (c) introduction
37. **reinforce** (c) make stronger
38. **unsound** (c) not dependable
39. **moderate** (c) medium
40. **philosophical** (b) thoughtfully wise
41. **affiliate** (b) associate
42. **discord** (b) lack of harmony
43. **gall** (b) overboldness
44. **heretic** (b) opponent of accepted belief
45. **antagonist** (a) opponent
46. **cardinal** (b) main
47. **federated** (b) joined together
48. **reminiscent** (b) recalling past events
49. **slovenly** (a) untidy
50. **chaste** (b) pure
51. **apex** (c) highest point
52. **ostracize** (c) banish
53. **encompass** (a) include
54. **decrepit** (a) old and feeble
55. **coronet** (b) crown
56. **moralize** (a) explain right and wrong
57. **inadvertent** (b) unintentional
58. **harrowing** (b) disturbing
59. **cistern** (b) water tank
60. **adamant** (a) extremely hard
61. **foyer** (b) entrance hall
62. **maltreat** (c) abuse
63. **chassis** (a) framework
64. **unsavory** (a) unpleasant in taste
65. **betrothal** (b) engagement
66. **gyrate** (b) whirl
67. **chivalrous** (b) courteous
68. **naive** (a) like a child
69. **primeval** (a) ancient
70. **sinister** (b) evil
71. **category** (a) class
72. **frenzy** (a) great excitement
73. **embark** (c) begin a voyage
74. **fraudulent** (c) dishonest
75. **resumption** (b) beginning again
76. **abhorrent** (a) hateful
77. **ornate** (b) highly decorated
78. **converge** (a) come together
79. **futile** (a) useless
80. **pacifist** (a) believer in peace
81. **traverse** (c) go across
82. **assent** (a) agree
83. **fishmonger** (c) dealer in fish
84. **ovation** (c) enthusiastic approval
85. **solidify** (b) harden
86. **obsolete** (a) out-of-date
87. **obstructive** (b) hindering
88. **subterranean** (b) underground
89. **application** (c) use
90. **mandate** (b) an order
91. **squatter** (c) illegal settler
92. **abrasive** (b) scratchy material
93. **exotic** (c) strange
94. **practicable** (b) can be done
95. **option** (a) a right to buy
96. **repercussion** (a) aftereffect
97. **terminate** (c) finish
98. **chromosome** (a) gene-carrier
99. **balm** (b) fragrant ointment
100. **eradicate** (a) get rid of
101. **exultation** (b) great rejoicing
102. **begrudge** (c) be reluctant to give
103. **decamp** (b) leave secretly
104. **perception** (c) awareness
105. **diverse** (a) varied
106. **opinionated** (a) stubborn in belief
107. **abyss** (a) deep empty space
108. **comprehensive** (a) including much
109. **irreconcilable** (c) unable to agree
110. **attune** (a) bring into harmony
111. **tentative** (a) experimental
112. **appalled** (b) dismayed
113. **ruse** (a) trick
114. **unwarranted** (b) not justified
115. **registrar** (a) official recorder
116. **deplorable** (b) shameful
117. **secession** (b) formal withdrawal
118. **obelisk** (c) tall, stone shaft
119. **zygote** (a) fertilized egg
120. **yoke** (a) frame for carrying loads

12th grade

1. **martyr** (a) sufferer for a belief
2. **controversial** (a) debatable
3. **explicable** (b) able to be explained
4. **genial** (a) pleasant
5. **loathsome** (a) disgusting
6. **prevalent** (a) widespread
7. **trivial** (a) unimportant
8. **fracas** (c) noisy quarrel
9. **diffuse** (b) spread out
10. **extemporaneous** (c) without preparation
11. **vogue** (c) fashion
12. **incontinence** (b) lack of restraint
13. **abandon** (c) freedom from restraint
14. **portly** (b) stout
15. **deficit** (a) shortage
16. **statute** (b) law
17. **skeptic** (c) doubter
18. **perceive** (a) be aware of
19. **opportune** (b) timely
20. **groundless** (c) without cause
21. **anthology** (a) collection of writings
22. **deliberate** (c) consider carefully
23. **emancipation** (b) setting free
24. **lament** (a) mourn
25. **mania** (c) craze
26. **pessimism** (c) belief in the worst
27. **persevere** (a) continue trying
28. **linear** (c) length measure
29. **obsession** (c) inescapable feeling
30. **serenity** (a) calmness
31. **perjure** (b) swear falsely
32. **begrimed** (a) dirty
33. **eczema** (a) skin disease
34. **grotesque** (c) unnatural in appearance
35. **interpose** (b) place between
36. **grimace** (b) ugly smile
37. **melancholy** (c) sadness
38. **annotation** (b) added comments
39. **diabolic** (b) devilish
40. **zither** (a) stringed instrument
41. **potency** (b) power
42. **laud** (b) praise
43. **oligarchy** (a) rule by a few
44. **oppress** (a) keep down
45. **askew** (b) twisted
46. **materialist** (c) lover of possessions
47. **submissive** (b) obedient
48. **destitution** (a) extreme poverty
49. **extortion** (b) getting by force
50. **quagmire** (b) marsh
51. **defunct** (b) dead
52. **bequeath** (b) leave by will
53. **wan** (c) pale
54. **amass** (a) pile up
55. **thwart** (a) hinder
56. **divulge** (b) make known
57. **breadth** (b) width
58. **edify** (c) instruct
59. **avid** (b) eager
60. **furl** (a) roll up
61. **verbose** (c) wordy
62. **disavow** (a) disclaim
63. **impregnable** (b) unconquerable
64. **martial** (b) warlike
65. **paltry** (c) worthless
66. **halitosis** (a) bad breath
67. **buttress** (a) support
68. **grotto** (a) cave
69. **commingle** (c) blend
70. **discommode** (c) disturb
71. **hypothetical** (a) assumed to be true
72. **lacerate** (c) tear roughly
73. **obliterate** (b) blot out
74. **regal** (a) royal
75. **nurture** (b) care for
76. **renounce** (b) give up
77. **quench** (c) extinguish
78. **garble** (b) scramble a message
79. **indignation** (b) scornful anger
80. **plausible** (c) believable
81. **habitable** (c) livable
82. **influx** (b) inward flow
83. **ingrained** (b) deeply rooted
84. **itinerary** (b) plan of travel
85. **precedent** (a) example set
86. **mean** (a) average
87. **query** (a) question
88. **ode** (a) poem
89. **exonerate** (a) free from blame
90. **rebuff** (b) sudden check
91. **improvise** (a) prepare offhand
92. **maverick** (c) unbranded steer
93. **compassion** (a) pity
94. **orient** (a) acquaint with a situation
95. **fortitude** (b) courage to endure
96. **frigate** (a) sailing ship
97. **pillage** (b) plunder
98. **automaton** (b) robot
99. **decapitate** (a) behead
100. **hassock** (c) footstool
101. **patriarch** (c) religious founder
102. **indifferent** (a) neither good nor bad
103. **recoil** (b) draw back
104. **lackadaisical** (a) wishy-washy
105. **lambaste** (b) beat or scold
106. **inborn** (c) present from birth
107. **laxity** (b) carelessness
108. **amphibious** (a) for land and sea
109. **impassioned** (b) full of feeling
110. **dilemma** (a) difficult choice
111. **callous** (c) not sensitive
112. **carbine** (a) short, light rifle
113. **transcend** (b) surpass
114. **caption** (b) title
115. **abashed** (b) ashamed
116. **consecrate** (a) make holy
117. **refract** (b) bend light rays
118. **inveterate** (c) habitual
119. **erroneous** (c) mistaken
120. **focus** (a) central point

College level

1. **nebulous** (b) not distinct
2. **pellagra** (c) dietary disease
3. **omniscient** (b) all knowing
4. **rancid** (c) spoiled
5. **oblivion** (b) forgetfulness
6. **reamer** (c) a finishing tool
7. **optimum** (a) best amount
8. **manifest** (a) easy to see
9. **contingent** (a) depending upon
10. **icon** (c) religious picture
11. **papacy** (c) pope's term of office
12. **decadent** (b) morally decaying
13. **larder** (c) food-storage place
14. **parenthetical** (a) explanatory
15. **ambrosia** (b) heavenly food
16. **proviso** (b) condition
17. **abet** (b) assist
18. **libretto** (c) words of an opera
19. **chastise** (a) punish
20. **admonish** (b) scold gently
21. **civility** (c) courtesy
22. **adherence** (b) attachment
23. **degenerate** (b) person of evil character
24. **prowess** (c) skill
25. **furlong** (b) one-eighth mile
26. **attest** (b) give proof
27. **abstention** (c) holding off
28. **catholic** (c) all-embracing
29. **deluge** (c) great flood
30. **batiste** (c) cotton cloth
31. **facile** (a) easily done
32. **gamete** (b) matured germ cell
33. **indeterminate** (b) not fixed
34. **manna** (c) food from heaven
35. **lethargy** (a) lack of interest
36. **maim** (b) cripple
37. **intuitive** (b) instinctive
38. **lamentation** (a) loud grief
39. **malfeasance** (a) official wrongdoing
40. **foible** (a) weakness
41. **incongruous** (b) out of harmony
42. **magisterial** (b) judge-like
43. **pensive** (a) in deep thought
44. **recant** (c) withdraw statement
45. **pangs** (c) sharp pains
46. **sagacity** (a) keen judgment
47. **elixir** (b) cure-all
48. **implicitly** (c) without question
49. **luminosity** (a) radiance
50. **indolence** (b) laziness
51. **caulk** (c) make watertight
52. **bovine** (a) cowlike
53. **defile** (b) pollute
54. **brandish** (c) shake threateningly
55. **cajole** (c) persuade by flattery
56. **evasion** (a) artful escape
57. **incarnation** (a) taking human form
58. **forthright** (b) straightforward
59. **caldron** (c) large kettle
60. **introspection** (c) examining oneself
61. **servitude** (a) slavery
62. **palpitate** (b) beat rapidly
63. **ravage** (a) lay waste
64. **quiescent** (c) calm
65. **paradox** (b) contradiction
66. **ire** (c) anger
67. **dole** (b) small portion
68. **cassock** (a) priest's gown
69. **demitasse** (b) small cup
70. **reprehensible** (c) blameworthy
71. **aneroid** (b) kind of barometer
72. **discursive** (a) not keeping to point
73. **fissure** (b) deep crack
74. **emulsion** (c) suspension in fluid
75. **irrevocable** (c) cannot be undone
76. **permeable** (a) can soak through
77. **pathos** (b) awakens pity
78. **eulogize** (b) praise highly
79. **floe** (b) mass of moving ice
80. **intersperse** (a) put here and there
81. **phototropism** (c) turning toward light
82. **indubitable** (a) certain
83. **interaction** (c) acting and reacting
84. **papaw** (b) fleshy fruit
85. **rector** (b) minister
86. **placenta** (a) afterbirth
87. **schizophrenia** (b) personality disorder
88. **repression** (b) keeping down
89. **scuttle** (c) sink on purpose
90. **postulate** (b) take for granted
91. **proverbial** (a) well known
92. **emit** (b) send forth
93. **incorrigible** (c) cannot be reformed
94. **zealot** (b) enthusiast
95. **abrogate** (b) abolish
96. **perpetuity** (a) forever
97. **gesticulate** (c) make motions to express ideas
98. **dispenser** (b) hands out
99. **cantata** (c) musical composition
100. **scull** (a) light racing boat
101. **zircon** (c) mineral
102. **yokel** (c) country fellow
103. **toxemia** (c) form of blood poisoning
104. **disconcert** (a) throw into confusion
105. **implore** (a) beg
106. **rampant** (c) unchecked
107. **chronic** (a) constant
108. **grueling** (b) very tiring
109. **cadenza** (b) brilliant musical flourish
110. **masticate** (c) chew
111. **refraction** (b) deflection of light
112. **reprimand** (b) scold strongly
113. **coagulate** (b) thicken
114. **euphuism** (c) flowery expression
115. **elocution** (b) art of public speaking
116. **inconclusive** (c) proving nothing
117. **indomitable** (b) cannot be subdued
118. **flounce** (a) wide ruffle
119. **cohorts** (a) partners
120. **peerless** (b) without equal

How to write effectively

Good writing is more than correct writing. You may use correct spelling, punctuation, and grammar and still produce an unsatisfactory piece of writing. To be good, writing must be interesting. *How to write effectively* deals with the creative aspect of writing. It provides information on how to use words and organize your ideas and thoughts so that you can capture and hold the attention of the reader.

"Improving your writing," pages *66-67,* tells how to take advantage of the various connotations of words to add color and interest to your writing. It explains how to construct paragraphs; how to use language clearly and concisely; and how to avoid monotony by using various sentence patterns.

"Writing term papers," page *68,* tells how to choose a subject; how to plan and research it; how to write the first draft of your paper; and how to prepare the final copy.

To write an effective paper, you should organize your material into an outline before you begin the actual writing. "Preparing an outline," page *69,* shows how an outline can help you develop your subject in a clear and interesting way. It explains and illustrates two types of outlines—the topic outline and the sentence outline.

"Writing book reports," page *70,* describes the four basic parts all book reports must include, and lists the standard forms to be used for bibliography entries.

Footnotes are an important part of a research paper. Various types of footnotes may be used, but all have a definite order and form. "Preparing footnotes," page *71,* describes these forms and gives the various types of footnotes that are used in citing sources of information, such as books, pamphlets, magazines, and encyclopedias.

"Preparing manuscripts," pages *72-73,* tells how an author's manuscript should be prepared before submitting it to a publisher, and how the manuscript is handled by the publisher before publication. The article discusses copy editing. It provides a chart of proofreader's marks, explains what each means, and how each is used in correcting manuscripts.

"Letter writing," pages *74-75,* discusses business letters, letters of application, order letters, complaint letters, letters to the editor, and informal notes.

"Using the right forms of address," pages *76-79,* provides important information on some of the ways to address titled persons, such as United States officials, Commonwealth officials, foreign officials to the United States, and clergymen.

Improving your writing

In your articles, letters, and reports, are you able to say exactly what you want to say in the most effective way? If not, and you want to improve your writing, take a close look at your choice of words, your sentences, and your paragraphs. These are the basic units of written communication.

Writing better sentences

You may be writing grammatically correct—even precise—sentences, but correct writing alone will not ensure success as a writer. Good writing is also interesting writing. To catch and hold a reader's attention, you must create effective, readable sentences.

Choosing your words

When you write a sentence, choose words that are specific. Use exact descriptive words instead of vague or general ones. Compare the sentence, "David likes his hobby," with "David takes pride in his stamp collection."

Take advantage of a word's various connotations, or shades of meaning. For example, *slow* has two synonyms which also mean "taking a long time to do something or to happen": *leisurely* and *deliberate*. Even though all three words suggest taking longer than usual or necessary, *leisurely* implies slowness because there is plenty of time, and *deliberate* suggests slowness because of care, thought, or self-control.

Use figures of speech (words used in an imaginative sense rather than a literal sense) in order to make a point more effectively and in a fresh or vigorous way. Look at these examples: "The fog crept in on little cat feet." "The troops came down like a wolf on the fold . . ." But avoid using overworked figures of speech, such as "getting down to brass tacks." To be effective, figures of speech should be natural.

Unnecessary words obscure ideas. Get rid of so-called "deadwood," words or phrases that add nothing to the meaning of a sentence. "We were not aware of the fact that Mary had gone" is more simply stated "We didn't know Mary had gone."

Avoid circumlocutions, or roundabout ways of saying things. Do not say indirectly what you can say directly. For this reason, try to use active verbs because they are more direct, natural, and emphatic than passive verbs. Compare: "In the course of John's stay in Canada, he was introduced to the girl who was later to become his wife" and "While John was in Canada, he met his future wife."

Use repetition to emphasize a point. Repeat an important word, phrase, or idea to stress it, as in the sentence, "For Brutus is an honourable man; so are they all, all honourable men."

Sentence patterns

Choose the kind of sentence that best conveys what you want to say. A *simple sentence* (subject and predicate) can help emphasize a point, as in "The sky looked ominous." A *compound sentence* (two main clauses joined by a conjunction such as *and* or *but*) can express two related ideas of equal importance: "Yesterday the temperature was 50, but today it reached only 45." A *complex sentence* (a main clause and one or more subordinate clauses) will help you to relate two ideas that are not of equal importance: "The school prom will be held here, even though this hall is not centrally located." This type of sentence is a good device for emphasis. Putting the less important ideas in subordinate clauses gives emphasis to the ideas in the main clause.

Vary the pattern and length of your sentences to avoid monotony. Most sentences tend to be declarative statements: "John went to the circus." An occasional question, exclamation, or command lends variety. A mixture of long and short sentences also helps. Look at this paragraph:

> Originally an Indian village, "Old Montreal" represents 300 years of Canadian history and folklore. What can you see there? A few of the dramatic sights are the oldest church in Montreal and the fur depot of the North West Company. Take a walking tour down the narrow cobblestone streets. You'll take a trip into the past!

Constructing better paragraphs

Once you have stated your ideas in sentences, arrange the sentences in paragraphs. A paragraph contains sentences that work together to develop one phase of a subject, to make one idea clear to the reader. Each new indentation signals the reader that another idea is going to be discussed. To be effective and pleasing, a paragraph should have unity, adequate development, and coherence.

Unity. All the sentences in a paragraph should develop one topic or phase of a subject. A topic sentence states in general terms the main thought or point of the paragraph. The other sentences help develop that thought or point. Usually a topic sentence comes at the beginning of the paragraph; but it may come at the end to summarize the ideas developed in the paragraph. The following paragraph begins with a topic sentence.

> *The International Flag Code is the sign language of the sea.* It contains 40 flags and pennants, which may be combined in various ways to spell out messages. There are 26 flags to represent the letters of the alphabet and 10 numeral pennants to stand for zero through nine. The code also contains an "answering pennant" as well as three "substitute pennants" for repeating letters and figures.

The topic sentence helps you clarify your ideas in your own mind, suggests the details you need to support it, and enables a reader to identify the main point of each paragraph.

Adequate development. A paragraph is adequately developed when it contains enough specific details to support the topic sentence. The following examples illustrate the kinds of details you can use:

1. Reasons. You may need reasons to support an opinion. In this paragraph, the topic sentence is supported by reasons:

> The successful farmer manages his farm on the basis of sound information, not guesswork. He keeps records of all his expenses, year after year. He watches government reports on farm production and on market prices of farm products. He experiments with newly developed seeds, fertilizers, and chemicals that prevent crop and livestock diseases. He visits displays of farm machinery to learn about new labor-saving equipment. The information he gathers helps him to make profitable decisions.

2. **Examples.** A specific example can clarify your point.

> There is no longer any reason for certain rules of etiquette. For example, many gentlemen still walk on the outside when accompanying a lady on the street. This practice originated when streets were muddy. Gentlemen walked on the outside to protect ladies from the mud splashed by passing carriages. Now most streets are paved.

3. **Similarities and differences.** Some topics are best explained by comparing or contrasting them to other examples.

> Soccer was the forerunner of American football. As in football, there are 11 men on each of two opposing teams. But in football, there are seven men in the line and four in the backfield. In soccer, there are five men in the first line, three in the second line, and two in front of the goalkeeper.

4. **Statistics and facts.** You may find that you need statistics or facts to prove certain points.

> Many persons consider Babe Ruth baseball's greatest hitter. In 22 seasons of regular play, he hit 714 home runs. He hit 60 of them in one year, 1927.

5. **Incidents.** Relating an incident is often the best way of making a point.

> Weather forecasting is better left to meteorologists. We discovered that last winter. According to an old superstition, the ground hog comes out of its burrow on February 2. If it sees its shadow, it returns underground for six more weeks. Thus a sunny February 2 means six more weeks of winter. The sun was shining last February 2, so the boys in my neighborhood decided to postpone the camping trip we had planned for the first weekend in March. The first Saturday in March turned out to be a beautiful spring day. . . .

Coherence. If a paragraph is adequately developed and unified but still lacks effectiveness, it probably lacks coherence; that is, the thoughts are not easy to follow. To correct the problem, make sure that (1) the details in each paragraph are arranged in logical order and (2) the sentences are well linked so that the reader is able to follow your thoughts easily from one sentence to the next. Here are some logical ways to order the details in a paragraph. The method you choose will depend on your purpose and what you are writing about.

Chronological order. If you are writing a story or telling someone how to do something, you may want to arrange your details according to a time sequence. This is a very common and simple arrangement.

Space order. If you are writing a description, you may want to describe things from left to right or begin with the nearest feature and move to the most distant one. You might also begin with a noticeable feature of something and then describe a less apparent characteristic.

If your description does not fit into chronological or space order, you may want to arrange details in order of importance, interest, or difficulty. Still other methods are to go from the general to the particular, from the particular to the general, or from the familiar to the unfamiliar.

No matter what type of order you decide on, a paragraph will not be coherent unless the sentences are tied together. Each sentence must follow the preceding one logically and smoothly.

To connect sentences, you will probably use both direct and indirect links. Direct links are such words as *next, meanwhile, for example, in addition, however.* These words help to show the relationship between the thoughts in your sentences.

Indirect links are less obvious, but often more effective. They add variety to your writing by avoiding repetition of direct links. Indirect links include (1) use of pronouns to refer to a noun in a preceding sentence, (2) repetition of key words or phrases, and (3) substitution of a synonym to recall important words in previous sentences. Here is an example: "The Island of The Blue Dolphins was my home. I had no other. It would be my home until the men returned in their ship. But even if they came soon, I could not live without a roof or a place to store food. I would have to build a house."

The same types of links can be used to provide transitions between paragraphs.

Writing term papers

When assigned a term paper, you are asked to read, to take notes, to organize your thoughts, and to write at length on a subject that interests you. Each of the following steps is important.

Step 1: Choosing a subject. Choose a subject of interest to you, one you know something about, or one that has special meaning for you. Do not try to cover too much. Limit your subject to a specific topic. Instead of "The History of the United States Space Program," try "The Apollo Moon Landing Project." And make sure that your topic is treated in the reference sources available to you.

Step 2: Plan your work. Take time to do some background reading in a good general encyclopedia, and to make a preliminary outline. Certain questions about your subject have probably already occurred to you. If your topic is "The Apollo Moon Landing Project," you will want to know when it started; how; where; who were the main people involved in it; why the United States decided to go to the moon; and whether or not the project was a success. Using these questions as a start, set up possible divisions of your subject to guide you in your research.

Step 3: Locating information. To find information on your subject at your school or community library, consult such reference guides as:

The card catalog (to locate books)

Reader's Guide to Periodical Literature (to locate magazine articles)

The New York Times Index and *Facts on File* (for information on current or recent events reported in newspapers)

Use file cards to make a working bibliography—a list of the books, magazine articles, and newspaper stories you think may be helpful. Be sure to record all the information about each source. You will need this for your final bibliography.

You may also want to interview people who have experience in the field you are exploring. If so, prepare your questions in advance of the interview.

Step 4: Reading and taking notes. You will find ordinary file cards helpful for recording information and ideas you may want to use in your paper. You can easily sort these cards to organize information. Your note cards should contain:

1. *Slug.* A "slug" is a short heading that shows the mainhead or subhead in your preliminary outline. It is a guide to where the information should go and will simplify the organization of your paper later.

2. *Source Number.* This number, keyed to your working bibliography, shows the source for the information.

3. *Page Number.* Enter the number of the page used for each note. Then you can recheck quickly and easily, if necessary. You may also need page numbers for a footnote if you quote or paraphrase an author.

4. *Body of Note.* There is no set form for notes. You may write a few words as a reminder, a summary, or a direct quotation. Write clearly and legibly so that when you use the note you will be able to read it.

Step 5: Sorting notes and outlining. Now you are ready to organize your material and prepare your final outline. Scan your note cards and sort them according to slugs to make your outline (see page *69*). By now the paper you intend to write should have taken definite form in your mind. Read through your notes and tentatively assign your material to the logical divisions of your subject. Now you are ready to build the final outline and write your first draft.

Step 6: Writing and revising. In your first draft, do not concern yourself with grammar, syntax, punctuation, or spelling. Just try to record your ideas clearly and logically. Write on one side of the paper, leaving wide margins and space between lines for insertions and corrections. When your first draft is completed, you can tackle the polishing and revision.

Your revision should be done in three steps:

1. *Check the content.* Read your paper carefully, looking for gaps in the flow of thought. Check to see that each idea is adequately developed. Add concrete examples where they improve clarity. Check to see that your ideas are in logical sequence and that your vocabulary is adequate to express them.

2. *Check for style and interest.* Vary your sentences in length and pattern. Pay special attention to the opening—will it catch your reader's attention?—and to the conclusion—does it give a polished ending or summary to the paper?

3. *Check the mechanics.* Look for careless or uncertain spelling and check these words in the dictionary. Correct any grammatical errors. Be sure you have used the proper punctuation. Indent paragraphs and make certain that each paragraph contains only those sentences that pertain to the particular facet of the subject you are writing about. If you quote or paraphrase authors, give them credit in footnotes.

Step 7: Preparing the final copy. A typed paper is neat and easy to read. If you cannot type, write your paper neatly in ink. In addition to the text, your term paper may include:

1. *Title page.* This page contains the title, your name, and the date. It also may contain the name of your school, the course, and the instructor.

2. *Preface.* Add this page if you want to explain your reason for choosing a subject, describe problems you encountered, or express gratitude to someone.

3. *Table of contents* (outline).

4. *Bibliography.* See page *70.*

5. *Appendix.* Any diagrams, charts, lists, graphs, or other information which you referred to in your paper should be supplied in this section.

Step 8: Submitting the paper. Assemble the parts of your paper in this order:

1. Title page
2. Preface
3. Table of contents
4. Text
5. Bibliography
6. Appendix

Fasten your paper in the upper left-hand corner or insert it in a manuscript-sized folder.

Preparing an outline

How many times have you had to write a paper, speech or report and, even with lots of ideas or material, not known how to begin? How often have you read an article that contained interesting material but became dull or confusing because it was not organized properly or never came to a conclusion? Both you and the authors of dull articles could be helped by a good outline.

If you are working from note cards, arrange the cards in what seems to be the most logical way. Then use the cards to build your outline. Look first for obvious divisions. These will become the main heads in your outline. Then see how the main heads can be subdivided. Each subhead must relate to the main head—and you cannot have fewer than two subheads under any main head. When you are finished, your outline should show the order of events, their importance, and their relationship to one another.

You may use either a *topic* outline or a *sentence* outline, depending on how you like to work. Or, if you are doing a short, simple paper, an informal plan or work outline may be all you need. The longer and more complicated the material, the more you need a carefully constructed outline.

One of the first things that becomes apparent when you look at an outline is the definite form and the style for capitalization and punctuation.

The outline starts off with the title centered at the top. All main headings are identified by Roman numerals (I, II, etc.). Subheadings, identified by capital letters (A, B, etc.) are indented under the main heads. The sub-subheadings are again indented and follow Arabic numerals (1, 2, etc.). Any items under the sub-subheadings would be indented again and would follow lower-case letters (a, b, etc.). All letters and numerals are followed by periods.

You will also notice that in either a topic outline or a sentence outline, parallel items are phrased in the same way. That is, all main heads are similar, all subheadings under one heading are phrased alike, and so on.

A topic outline consists of brief phrases or short clauses for all heads. Notice that the first word of each heading and subheading, as well as any proper noun, is capitalized. There are no periods after the phrases. Here is an example of a topic outline:

Why I like to read

I. A method of satisfying my curiosity
  A. About people
    1. In ages past
    2. In the present
    3. In the future
  B. About things
    1. Historical events
    2. Scientific discoveries
    3. Language development
    4. Current happenings
    5. Art happenings

II. A major form of entertainment
  A. Allows me to experience adventure
  B. Shows me the beauty of life
  C. Cheers me with humor
  D. Thrills me with mystery

III. A help to me as a person
  A. Keeps me up to date
  B. Increases my vocabulary
  C. Broadens my understanding
  D. Interests me in more things

A sentence outline is divided and organized in much the same way as a topic outline, but each heading is a complete sentence. Such an outline takes more time because you must put your information into specific statements. But it has several advantages: (1) It helps you to state your points more clearly and completely; (2) It saves time later when you transfer the sentences in your outline to your final presentation; and (3) The main heads can serve as your topic sentences. Here is a sentence outline:

Why be a coin collector?

I. Coin collecting is a hobby people of all ages and both sexes can enjoy.
  A. It satisfies the collecting urge of young people.
  B. It provides entertaining pastime for older people.
  C. It is an interesting hobby for those who are ill or disabled.

II. Today the number of coin collectors in this country reaches into the millions.
  A. Many people have been collecting for years.
  B. Each day, probably as many as a thousand new people begin to collect coins.
  C. Numismatic clubs are forming rapidly.

III. Coin collecting is a rewarding hobby.
  A. The value of a coin rarely decreases.
    1. Often you can sell the coin to another hobbyist at a profit.
    2. Frequently coins are in such demand that the collectors' price goes up several dollars each year.
  B. You can learn much about history, art, and business from this hobby.
  C. The association with other collectors—people of all ages with different experiences and backgrounds—helps your personal and social development.
  D. Your investment of time and money may pay large dividends.

As soon as you begin to write your outline, you sort out all the haphazard ideas and thoughts you have concerning your topic, and put them into a logical order. Then, when you read your outline, you can see at a glance whether or not you have organized the main divisions of your subject according to their importance and interest. Also, your outline should show you, clearly and concisely, how the subdivisions relate to one another and to the main division under which they fall, and how each of the main divisions relates to your overall subject. You may want to refine the first draft of your outline before you begin to write your paper, speech, or report.

A good outline helps you to develop your subject in an interesting and readable manner. You may use a topic outline or a sentence outline. No matter which kind of outline you choose to use, it will prove as valuable to you as the blueprint to the builder or a map to a hiker.

Documenting research reports

A research report or term paper is not like a book report. A research report has a broader topic and is much longer. Another major difference is that a research report makes extensive use of documentation in the form of footnotes and a bibliography. To document a source is to give credit to the person you have quoted or whose ideas you have used. Every time you use words, ideas, facts, or statistics from a book, magazine, newspaper, or other source you must credit the source in a footnote. All such sources must also be listed in the bibliography at the end of your report.

Preparing footnotes

Footnotes are an important part of any research paper. You should give credit in a footnote whenever you quote a source directly, use another's opinions or ideas, or rely on someone else's facts, figures, or statements that might be questioned.

Every footnote in a research paper has a number. Footnotes are usually numbered consecutively throughout the paper, beginning with 1. The number of the footnote appears after the sentence, fact, or quotation you are crediting, and is raised slightly above the line. At the bottom of the page, place the same numeral before the footnote, again slightly raised above the line. Type a line about 1½ inches long between the text and the footnotes.

There are a number of different ways to write footnotes. Use the form your teacher prefers. Just be certain that, whatever form you use, you are consistent. Notice that in the style followed here, the footnote contains only enough information to identify the source. It is not as complete as will be the entry in the bibliography (see the bibliographic entries on the following page).

This is one way you might footnote a quotation from a book:

> Of all the shots in a hockey game, the one goaltenders dread most is the slap shot. Slap shots have been measured at 119 miles per hour.[1]

---

[1] Bobby Hull, Hockey Is My Game, p. 127.

All footnotes follow a certain order and style. When the source is a book, the most common form for a footnote gives the parts in this order: author (first name first), title of the book (underlined), and page. Put commas between the parts of the footnote and a period at the end. The first line of each footnote is indented. Additional lines are single spaced and begin flush with the left margin of the paper. Leave a line of space between footnotes.

When the source is a magazine, give the author's name (first name first), the title of the article (in quotation marks), the name of the magazine (underlined), the date of the issue, and the page. If no author's name is given, then start with the title of the article.

For newspaper articles, use the title of the article (in quotation marks), the name of the newspaper (underlined), the date, the section number (if there is one), and the page.

If the source is an encyclopedia article, give the author's name if it is known (first name first), the title of the article (in quotation marks), the name of the encyclopedia (underlined), the edition or year of publication, and the volume and page. If only the author's initials appear at the end of the article, the list of authors in the front matter will usually provide the full name. If there is no author, start the footnote with the title of the article.

Here are some examples of basic footnote forms:

1. A book with one author:

[1] Jim Hunt, The Men in the Nets: Hockey's Tortured Heroes, p. 7.

2. A book with two authors:

[2] Frank R. Donovan and Bruce Catton, Ironclads of the Civil War, p. 19.

3. A book with an editor:

[3] Frank B. Freidel, ed., Union Pamphlets of the Civil War, 1861-1865, p. 13.

4. A work by an institution:

[4] South African Information Service, Art in South Africa, p. 22.

5. A magazine article:

[5] Rudolf F. Graf, "Build an Electronic Guard to Foil Car Thieves," Popular Science Monthly, October 1968, p. 140.

6. A newspaper article:

[6] "Mayors Seek Greater U.S. Effort Against Drugs," The New York Times, May 6, 1971, p. 19.

7. An encyclopedia article:

[7] Abraham H. Lass, "How to Do Research," The World Book Encyclopedia, 1982, Vol. 22, p. 27.

For later references to the same source, you can use a shortened form of footnote. The exact form of the footnote will depend upon what it refers to and where it falls.

If the source is the same work and page number as in the preceding footnote, use *ibid.* If only the page is different, place a comma after *ibid.* and give the new page. When you use *ibid.,* underline it and put a period after it because it is the abbreviation for the Latin *ibidem,* meaning "in the same place."

[30] Oscar Lewis, The Children of Sanchez, p. 68.

[31] Ibid.

[32] Ibid., p. 130.

To refer to a source quoted earlier, but not in the immediately preceding footnote, give the last name of the author (if you have not quoted another author with the same last name) and the page number. If the full title of the source is not listed on the same page, you can include a shortened form of the title.

[1] Bobby Hull, Hockey Is My Game, p. 127.

[2] Jim Hunt, The Men in the Nets: Hockey's Tortured Heroes, p. 7.

[3] Hull, p. 130.

If you use more than one book or article by the same author, subsequent references to that author need include only the last name, the title, and the page:

[16] Oscar Lewis, The Children of Sanchez, p. 200.

[17] Lewis, La Vida, p. 30.

Footnotes are more than just common courtesy or honesty. They also make it possible for an interested reader to go to the source for further information.

Preparing the bibliography

Your bibliography, which goes at the end of your paper, is a list of all the sources you used, whether you quoted from them or not. The bibliography has two functions. First, it shows how far you went in researching your topic by indicating the range of your sources. Second, it shows the reader where to look for additional information if the topic is of interest.

Arrange the entries in your bibliography in alphabetical order according to the last names of the authors or the first main words in the titles when there is no author. When a source has more than one author, list the authors in the same order that the source does. If there are more than two authors, you may use *et. al.*, meaning "and others," after the first author's name.

Do not number the entries. Start each entry at the left margin. When an entry runs more than one line, the additional lines should be indented. All entries should be single spaced, with a full line of space between entries.

If the bibliography includes more than one work by the same author, use a long dash in place of the name in all entries after the first. The titles should be listed in alphabetical order.

There are various ways to present the information in bibliographic entries. You should use the form your teacher prefers. And whatever form you use, you should be consistent.

For a book: Author (last name first), title (underlined), place of publication, publisher, and year of publication.

For a magazine article: Author (last name first), title of the article (in quotation marks), name of the magazine (underlined), date of publication, and the page or pages on which the article appears.

For a newspaper article: Author (last name first) if known, title of the article (in quotation marks), name of the newspaper (underlined), date of issue, section (if any), and page.

For an encyclopedia article: author (last name first) if known, title of the article (in quotation marks), name of the encyclopedia, date of publication, volume, and page.

Here is a sample bibliography showing various types of entries:

Bradbury, Ray, *et al.* Mars and the Mind of Man. New York: Harper and Row, 1973.

Donovan, Frank R., and Catton, Bruce. Ironclads of the Civil War. New York: American Heritage, 1964.

Freidel, Frank B., ed. Union Pamphlets of the Civil War. Cambridge: Harvard University Press, 1967.

Graf, Rudolf F. "Build an Electronic Guard to Foil Car Thieves." Popular Science Monthly, October 1968, p. 140.

Hull, Bobby. Hockey Is My Game. New York: McKay, 1967.

Lass, Abraham H. "How to Do Research." The World Book Encyclopedia, 1982, Vol. 22, p. 27.

Lewis, Oscar. La Vida. New York: Random House, 1966.

———. A Study in Slum Culture. New York: Random House, 1968.

"Mayors Seek Greater U.S. Effort Against Drugs." The New York Times, May 6, 1971, p. 19.

Writing book reports

The purpose of a book report is threefold: First, you want to acquaint your readers with the book. Second, you want to give them your carefully thought-out opinion of it. Third, you want to help readers decide whether they would like to read the book.

There is no standard form for a book report. However, every book report should contain the following four parts:

1. Identification. Give the title and author's name. If the book is one with which your readers may not be familiar, identify it further. Give the name of the publisher, the place and year of publication, the price, and the number of pages. If the book is part of a series, state that fact and tell where it comes in the series. You may list the information at the beginning of your report, or incorporate it within the report. If you identify the book at the beginning of your report, your list should follow this order: author's name (last name first); title (underlined); place of publication; name of the publisher; year of publication.

2. Classification. A word or phrase early in your report helps the reader keep in mind the type of book on which you are reporting; mystery, biography, humor, adventure, and so on. Your reader can then mentally compare it with similar books he has read.

3. Description. A skillful book report gives an overall view of a book without giving away its outcome. Your description of a book may include quotations or brief sketches of scenes or action that you think are representative of the book. Take notes while reading. It will save you the time and trouble of thumbing through the book later to relocate quotations or other information.

4. Evaluation. Your opinion is the most important part of the report. It may be either your immediate reaction to the book or a judgment based on further study. In either case, your opinion should be definite and clear. It should be supported with facts. You will want to comment on characterizations, plot, and recurring themes. Compare or contrast it to other books you've read. Write a word of criticism or praise while reading. It will help you recall your impression of the material after you have finished the book.

In addition to these four parts you may want to include other material. You may want to trace the imagery to show how the author uses it to bring out a theme. Or you may want to point out effective symbols that an author uses.

Writing book reports can be a valuable exercise in clear thinking and precise writing. It also gives you the opportunity to improve your writing and to develop a style of your own.

Preparing manuscripts

If you contribute or submit an article to a newspaper, magazine, or other publication, it should be prepared in a professional way. Once you have done this, and mailed or delivered the manuscript, your responsibility ends. But you might want to know what happens to the manuscript, sometimes called copy, after it reaches an editor and the printer.

The author's manuscript

Your manuscript should be neatly typed, double-spaced, using only one side of the paper. If possible, begin each page with a paragraph. Avoid hyphenating words at the end of lines, and never divide a word from one page to another.

Pages. Number the pages consecutively at the top. Type the word *more* at the bottom of each page except the last. On the last page, type an end mark, such as # # #, below the last line of your manuscript.

Corrections. Write or type the correction above the line. Be neat and be sure that your writing is clear.

Spelling. Consult your dictionary for preferred spelling, and stick to that spelling throughout your manuscript.

Capitalization and punctuation. Be consistent with an accepted style, such as the one suggested in this dictionary, pages *26-31*. But keep in mind that every publication has its own style and that your copy may be changed to conform to "house" rules.

Copy editing

When your manuscript reaches the publisher, an editor is assigned to copy edit your manuscript. It is the editor's responsibility to see that what the author has said is clear, accurate, and orderly; to see that capitalization and punctuation are correct; and to mark the manuscript in such a way that the typesetter will have no difficulty setting it in type.

Both editor and typesetter need to know and use the same set of marks. These marks, called proofreaders' marks, are used in marking the manuscript for the typesetter and in correcting proofs. In the manuscript, the proof marks are indicated either on a line or between lines; on a galley or page proof, the proofreaders' marks are put in the margin left or right, next to the line in which the correction is to be made. Marks in the line indicate where the correction should be made. All corrections should be neatly and clearly indicated.

Proofreading

After your manuscript has been set in type, the typesetter prints a proof, which is compared with the original copy by a proofreader, the editor, and sometimes the author. There is more than one way to indicate errors in proofs, but the style shown is one commonly used by many editors and proofreaders. All directions to the printer that are not to be set in type should be circled.

Proofreaders' marks

Punctuation marks

Mark in copy	Mark in margin	Meaning
said the queen^Now	⊙	Insert period
Are you asking me^	?	Insert question mark
"No^" he shouted	!	Insert exclamation mark
Now, here^you see	^,	Insert comma
Everything^s going well	'	Insert apostrophe
other day^today isn't	;	Insert semicolon
in the following^	:	Insert colon
Looking^Glass	=	Insert hyphen
for 1940^1941	1/N	Insert en dash
It was^or was it?	1/M	Insert em dash
He was going^to the	. . .	Insert ellipsis
^That is it.^	"/"	Insert quotation marks
It^the book^was	(/)	Open and close parentheses
We new^sic^she would	[/]	Open and close brackets
CO2	2	Use subscript
X3	3	Use superscript

Operational marks

Mark in copy	Mark in margin	Meaning
The rule is, nver	e/	Insert missing letter
The story will long	be/	Insert missing word
yesterday,	ℊ	Delete
tomorroow, and	ℊ	Delete and close up
inthemarket	#/#	Insert space
the base ball team	⁀	Close up space
Now is the best of	eq #	Space evenly
This will be time to	⁀/	Less space
yesterday—never but	tr	Transpose words
down the valley. This	¶	Paragraph
was not what he wanted. It would make trouble	no ¶	No paragraph; copy should be run in
Chapter 6	Sp	Spell out
By all day in the	out; see copy	Copy out
every other bight	night/?	Is this correct?
By all means, you should tell them	‖	Align type
She saw it was right	stet	Let it stand
You will understand	]	Move to the right
This is the way	[	Move to the left
All the time	□	Indent one em
All the time	□□	Indent two ems
We use words to	=	Straighten line
Vice objected to	9	Inverted letter
If you would tell	w.f.	Wrong font
Heading	][	Center
he left for home	⊗	Broken letter

Type style

Mark in copy	Mark in margin	Meaning
Now, not later	ital	Set in italic
If you *please*,	rom	Set in roman
Introduction	bf	Set in boldface
The Book	bf ital	Set in boldface italic
THE team was ready	lc	Set in lower case
the king	caps	Set in upper case
the book	c+lc	Set in upper and lower case
in 450 B.C.	sc	Set in small caps
the book	c+sc	Set in caps and small caps

Letter writing

Every letter you write, whether business or personal, should meet the requirements of any good piece of writing. It should be clear, informative, and well organized. It is customary to follow the standard forms used by most persons.

A letter can be divided into a specific number of parts.

A business letter always has six parts. They are (1) the heading, (2) the inside address, (3) the salutation, (4) the body, (5) the complimentary close, and (6) the signature.

A personal letter is less formal and has fewer parts. The inside address is never used, and if you write to a friend very often, you may omit all but the date from the heading.

1. Heading is written in the upper left-hand or right-hand corner of the letter sheet. It consists of three lines: your street address; the city, state, and ZIP Code; and the date. You may use either the block form or the indented form. The block form is most often used in business letters.

Block form	**Indented form**
1632 Romer Road	132 Fifth Avenue
Chicago, Illinois 60610	Albany, New York 12220
November 6, 1975	November 12, 1975

Do not use punctuation at the end of a line unless the last word is abbreviated. Never abbreviate the name of the month. If the letter sheet has a letterhead, add the date two or three spaces below. You may put it flush with the right-hand margin or in the center of the page. The heading and the inside address are single-spaced.

2. Inside address is always used in a business letter. Place it four spaces below the heading, flush with the left-hand margin. The inside address includes the recipient's name and title, the name of the company, the company's address, the city, state, and ZIP Code.

When you write to an individual in a company, use the person's personal and business titles (Ms. Alice Keating, Director) or his or her professional and business titles (Dr. George Bussey, President). When the person's business title is long, place it on the second line.

Avoid abbreviations in the address unless it is customary. For instance, use *St. Louis* not *Saint Louis.* Use *N.E.* not *North East.* Write out in full the number names of streets and avenues ten and below. For instance, write *Sixth Avenue* or *Tenth Street,* but *57th Street.*

3. Salutation or greeting in a personal letter is usually followed by a comma. In a business letter, place the salutation at least two lines below the inside address. If the letter is short you may leave more space. When you write to an individual in a company, use the person's name followed by a colon (Dear Mrs. Brown:). When you write directly to a company, use *Gentlemen:* or *Dear Sir:,* or *Ms.*

4. Body begins two lines below the salutation. If you type the body single space, double-space between paragraphs. The body is the most important part of a letter. It should contain all the information you want the recipient to have. In a business letter, you should state all you have to say as briefly as possible. Always use prepositions, articles, and pronouns where they are necessary to good grammar. Avoid beginning a letter with expressions such as *Answering yours of, Am writing in reply to, etc.*

5. Complimentary close is placed two lines below the body of the letter. Align it either with the left-hand margin or with the heading (see example on page *75*). Only the first word in the complimentary close is capitalized. A comma follows the complimentary close. Some correct complimentary closes are: *Sincerely yours, Yours truly, Yours sincerely, Respectfully yours, Very truly yours, Cordially yours,* and *Yours very truly.*

6. Signature is written under the complimentary close. Be sure the signature is legible. In a business letter, the name is typed two lines below the written signature. Never put *Mr.* in front of a man's signature. *Miss* or *Mrs.* enclosed in parentheses can be put in front of a woman's signature.

The envelope

Use the same style (block or indented) on the envelope that you use in the heading of your letter. Center the address a little below the middle of the envelope. The city and state usually appear on one line, but they may be written on separate lines. Be sure to include the Zip Code.

Special business letters

1. Letters of application. These should include all the information you want your prospective employer to have. Give your age and list all previous school and job experience. Explain clearly and concisely why you are qualified for the job. Describe similar tasks performed for other employers. Be sure your letter is neat and well organized, and that your grammar, spelling, and punctuation are correct.

2. Order letters. Give an exact description of the goods you order. Supply details such as size, color, and style. Give the catalog number if you have it. State the quantity you want, the price, and how you want your order shipped (freight, parcel post, or express). Tell whether you intend to pay for it by credit card, check, money order, or C.O.D.

3. Complaint letters. The purpose of a complaint letter is to get a mistake corrected as soon as possible. Do not antagonize the recipient by being sarcastic or rude. A clear explanation of what is wrong and a courteous request for correction of the error will bring more effective results.

4. Letters to the editor. Be sure you know the subject you intend to write about before you compose such a letter. You can make your point more convincing when you know the facts about an issue. Say something constructive, and say it clearly and briefly. Avoid threats and insults no matter how much you may disagree with the editorial policy of the paper.

Informal notes

Informal notes take the same form as personal letters except that they are shorter and concern one specific item rather than several.

1. Invitations and replies. All necessary details should be included in the invitation. Be specific about time, date, and place. Informal invitations should be hand written. Reply promptly to written invitations.

2. Thank-you notes. Thank friends for their hospitality or the gift you received, or for an act of kindness.

Business letter and envelope

A 23 Fremont Street
Chillicothe, Ohio 45601
January 4, 1975

B Marsden Manufacturing Company
342 West 41st Street
New York, N.Y. 10036

C Gentlemen:

D Recently I read in Syndicate Store Merchandising that your company is now manufacturing a new line of adjustable storage racks and bins.

I am planning to open a new variety store in a recently opened shopping center. Because of the large number of items that I will carry, many of them seasonal, I will need a highly flexible arrangement in the stock room.

Will you please send me any information or descriptive literature on this line that is available. Also kindly let me know the name and address of your local representative.

E Very truly yours,

F James Gregory

James Gregory

James Gregory
23 Fremont Street
Chillicothe, Ohio 45601

Marsden Manufacturing Company
342 West 41st Street
New York, N.Y. 10036

A Heading
B Inside address
C Salutation
D Body
E Complimentary close
F Signature

Personal letter and envelope

A 316 Azalea Drive
Athens, Georgia 30601
December 26, 1975

B Dear Bob,

C How nice to hear from you and what good news that you are coming here next week on business. It must be three years since we last saw each other and a lot has happened since then. We have a new home now with a guest room and expect you to stay with us.

Let me know when you are arriving and I will meet you at the airport.

D Sincerely yours,
E Sue

S. L. Arendt
316 Azalea Drive
Athens, Georgia 30601

Mr. Robert Breen
6 North Adams Avenue
Madawaska, Maine 04756

A Heading
B Salutation
C Body
D Complimentary close
E Signature

Using the right forms of address

The following pages include a listing of some titled persons and the forms you use to address them in writing and speaking. Not every dignitary you might have occasion to address is included. Nor are the forms necessarily the only correct ones.

Address forms for women are the same as for men, except where indicated. A safe form for closing business, or formal, letters is "Very truly yours." Personal, or informal, letters can be closed with "Sincerely yours."

United States Officials

President of the United States

In speaking: Mr. *or* Madam President *or* Sir *or* Madam

In writing:
The President
The White House
Washington, D.C. 20500
Mr. *or* Madam President: (*business*)
My dear Mr. *or* Madam President: (*personal*)
The President and Mrs. [Mr.] Green (*address*)

Closing: Respectfully, (*business*)
Very respectfully, (*personal*)

Vice-President of the United States

In speaking: Mr. *or* Madam Vice-President *or* Sir *or* Madam

In writing:
The Vice-President
Executive Office Building
Washington, D.C. 20501
Mr. *or* Madam Vice-President: (*business*)
My dear Mr. *or* Madam Vice-President: (*personal*)
The Vice-President and Mrs. [Mr.] Green (*address*)

Cabinet Members (except Attorney General)

In speaking: Mr. Secretary *or* Mr. Green
Madam Secretary *or* Miss, Mrs., *or* Ms. Smith

In writing:
The Honorable John Green
The Honorable Mary Smith
Secretary of State
Sir: *or* Madam: (*business*)
My dear Mr. *or* Madam Secretary: (*personal*)
The Secretary of State and Mrs. [Mr.] Green (*address*)

Attorney General; Postmaster General

In writing:
The Attorney General
The Postmaster General
Sir: *or* Madam: (*business*)
My dear Mr. *or* Madam Attorney General:
My dear Mr. *or* Madam Postmaster General: (*personal*)
(*The other forms are the same as for Cabinet members.*)

Chief Justice of the Supreme Court

In speaking: Mr. *or* Madam Chief Justice

In writing:
The Chief Justice
The Supreme Court Bldg.
Washington, D.C. 20543
Sir: *or* Madam: (*business*)
My dear Mr. *or* Madam Chief Justice: (*personal*)
The Chief Justice and Mrs. [Mr.] Green (*address*)

Associate Justices of the Supreme Court

In speaking: Mr. *or* Madam Justice *or*
Mr. *or* Madam Justice Green

In writing:
Mr. (Miss, Mrs., *or* Ms.) Justice Green
Sir: *or* Madam: (*business*)
My dear Mr. *or* Madam Justice: (*personal*)
Mr. [Madam] Justice and Mrs. [Mr.] Green (*address*)

Speaker of the House of Representatives

In speaking: Mr. *or* Madam Speaker *or*
Mr. *or* Madam Green

In writing:
The Honorable John Green
The Honorable Mary Smith
Speaker of the House of Representatives
Sir: *or* Madam: (*business*)
My dear Mr. *or* Madam Green: (*personal*)
The Speaker of the House of Representatives and Mrs. [Mr.] Green (*address*)

United States Senators

In speaking: Senator Green

In writing:
The Honorable John Green
The Honorable Mary Smith
United States Senate
Washington, D.C. 20510
Sir: *or* Madam: (*business*)
My dear Senator Green: (*personal*)
The Honorable and Mrs. John Green (*address*)
The Honorable Mary Smith and Mr. Smith (*address*)

Closing: Respectfully, *or* Sincerely yours,

United States Representatives

In speaking: Mr. Green *or* Miss, Mrs., *or* Ms. Smith

In writing:
The Honorable John Green
The Honorable Mary Smith
House of Representatives
Washington, D.C. 20515
Sir: *or* Madam: (*business*)
My dear Mr. *or* Miss, Mrs., *or* Ms. Green: (*personal*)
The Honorable and Mrs. John Green (*address*)
The Honorable Mary Smith and Mr. Smith (*address*)

Closing: Respectfully, *or* Sincerely yours,

United States Ambassadors

In speaking: Mr. *or* Madam Ambassador

In writing:
The Honorable John Green
The Honorable Mary Smith
Sir: *or* Madam: (*business*)
My dear Mr. *or* Madam Ambassador: (*personal*)
The Honorable and Mrs. John Green (*address*)
The Honorable Mary Smith and Mr. Smith (*address*)

Closing: Respectfully yours,

(*Although it is permissible to refer to United States ambassadors as "American" ambassadors, it is wise not to do so, because other Western Hemisphere ambassadors are also very conscious of being Americans.*)

Governors

In speaking: Governor Green

In writing:
The Honorable John Green
The Honorable Mary Smith
Governor of New York

Sir: *or* Madam: (*business*)
My dear Governor: (*personal*)
The Honorable John Green and Mrs. Green (*address*)
The Honorable Mary Smith and Mr. Smith (*address*)

Closing: Respectfully, *or* Sincerely yours,

State Senators and Representatives

(*State legislators are addressed in the same manner as United States Senators and Representatives. Official letters are sent to them at their seats of government.*)

Mayors

In speaking: Mayor Green *or* Mr. *or* Madam Mayor

In writing:
The Honorable John Green
The Honorable Mary Smith

Sir: *or* Madam: (*business*)
My dear Mayor Green: (*personal*)
The Honorable and Mrs. [Mr.] Green (*address*)

Judges

In speaking: Mr. *or* Madam Justice

In writing:
The Honorable John Green
The Honorable Mary Smith

Sir: *or* Madam: (*business*)
My dear Mr. *or* Madam Justice (*personal*)
The Honorable and Mrs. [Mr.] Green (*address*)

President or Chancellor of a University

In speaking: President Green *or* Chancellor Green

In writing:
President John Green
Dear Sir: *or* Madam: (*business*)
Dear President Green: *or* Chancellor Green: (*personal*)

Commonwealth Officials

Reigning King or Queen

In speaking: Your Majesty *or* Sir *or* Ma'am

In writing:
His Majesty the King
Her Majesty the Queen
Buckingham Palace
London,
England (*on cables and envelopes only*)

May it please Your Majesty:

Closing: Yours very respectfully, *or*
Yours respectfully,

Nonreigning Members of the Royal Family

In speaking: Your Royal Highness

In writing:
H.R.H. the Prince of Wales
Sir:

H.R.H. the Duchess of Trent
Madam:

Closing: Yours very respectfully, *or* Respectfully yours,

Governor General

In speaking: Your Excellency

In writing:
His *or* Her Excellency
The Right Honourable John Green
The Right Honourable Mary Smith
Governor General of Canada

Sir: *or* Madam:

(*The wife* [*husband*] *of the Governor General is called Her* [*His*] *Excellency.*)

(Their Excellencies Governor General and Mrs. [Mr. or other title] Smith)

Closing: I have the honour to be, Sir,
Your Excellency's obedient servant

Prime Minister

In speaking: Your Excellency *or* Mr. *or* Madam Prime Minister *or in Britain,* Mr. *or* Madam Green

In writing:
The Right Honourable John Green,
Prime Minister

Sir: *or* Madam: *or in some countries*
Excellency: (*business*)
Dear Mr. *or* Madam Green: *or*
My Dear Mr. *or* Madam Green (*personal*)

Closing: Yours respectfully, (*business*)
Yours sincerely, (*personal*)

Members of the House of Lords

In speaking: My Lord

In writing:
The Right Honourable
the Viscount (Duke, Earl) Green
The House of Lords

My Lord: (*business*)
Dear Lord Green: (*personal*)
(*Do not use the abbreviation "M.P." for members of the House of Lords.*)

Members of Parliament

In speaking: Sir *or* Mr. *or* Madam Green

In writing:
Sir John Green, Bt., M.P. (with title)
John Green, Esq., M.P. (without title)
Mary Smith, M.P.
House of Commons

Dear Sir *or* Madam: (*business*)
Dear Mr. *or* Madam Green: (*personal*)

Closing: Yours very truly, (*business*)
Yours sincerely, (*personal*)

Members of the Senate

In speaking: Sir *or* Madam *or* Senator Green

In writing:
The Honourable John Green

Dear Sir *or* Madam:

Closing: Yours sincerely,

Members of the House of Commons

In speaking: Sir *or* Madam *or* Mr. Green

In writing:
John H. Green, Esq., M.P.

Dear Sir *or* Madam:

Closing: Yours sincerely,

Foreign Officials in the United States

Foreign Ambassadors to the United States

In speaking: Mr. *or* Madam Ambassador

In writing:
His (Her) Excellency
The Ambassador of Australia

Sir: *or* Madam: (*business*)
My dear Mr. *or* Madam Ambassador: (*personal*)
His [Her] Excellency, the Ambassador of Australia, and Mrs. [Mr.] Green (*address*)

Closing: Yours very truly, (*business*)
Yours sincerely, (*personal*)

Secretary-General of the United Nations

In speaking: Mr. *or* Madam Secretary-General

In writing:
His (Her) Excellency
John Green
Secretary-General of the United Nations

My dear Mr. *or* Madam Secretary-General:

Representatives to the United Nations

(*Each member nation awards its own titles to its individual representatives to the United Nations, and they should be so addressed. You may use the forms for Ambassador as a general guide for addressing United Nations representatives.*)

Clergymen

The correct form for closing all business letters to clergymen is "Respectfully yours" *and for closing personal letters,* "Sincerely yours." *These terms are preceded by another sentence, where indicated. When writing to a clergyman, use a precise street address.*

Protestant Clergymen

Most Protestant clergymen are addressed as ministers with or without doctorate; see below. Exceptions for the Protestant Episcopal and Methodist churches, the Anglican Church of Canada, and the Church of England are listed.

Protestant Episcopal Bishops

In speaking: Bishop Green

In writing:
The Right Reverend John Green

Right Reverend Sir: (*business*)
My dear Bishop: (*personal*)

Protestant Episcopal Archdeacon

In speaking: Sir *or* Archdeacon

In writing:
The Venerable John Green, D.D.

Venerable Sir: (*business*)
My dear Archdeacon: (*personal*)

Protestant Episcopal Dean

In speaking: Sir, Dean, *or* Dean Green

In writing:
The Very Reverend
John Green, D.D., S.T.D.

Very Reverend Sir: (*business*)
My dear Dean Green: (*personal*)

Protestant Episcopal Canon

In speaking: Sir *or* Canon Green

In writing:
The Reverend John Green

Reverend Sir: (*business*)
My dear Canon Green: (*personal*)

Methodist Bishops

In speaking: Bishop Green

In writing:
The Reverend John Green

Reverend Sir: (*business*)
My dear Bishop: (*personal*)

Anglican Church of Canada

The forms of address are similar to the addresses for equivalent clergy of the Protestant Episcopal Church. The primate and archbishops of the Canadian church are addressed as "The Most Reverend" *rather than* "The Right Reverend." *In informal situations,* "Mr." *is often placed before the title, such as,* "Mr. Dean." *Canons are referred to as* "The Reverend Canon."

Church of England Archbishops

In speaking: Your Grace

In writing:
The Most Reverend
The Lord Archbishop of Canterbury

Your Grace: (*business*)
My dear Archbishop: (*personal*)

Closing: I have the honour to be,
Most Reverend Sir,
Your obedient servant, *etc.*

Church of England Bishops

In speaking: My Lord

In writing:
The Right Reverend
The Lord Bishop of Bristol

My Lord: *or* My Lord Bishop:

Closing: I am, Right Reverend Sir, *etc.*

Church of England Deans and Canons

These clergymen are addressed the same as their counterparts in the Anglican Church of Canada.

Protestant Clergymen

In speaking: Sir, *or* Doctor Green

In writing:
The Reverend John Green, (D.D.)

Reverend Sir: (*business*)
My dear Mr. *or* Dr. Green: (*personal*)

Roman Catholic Clergymen

Pope

In speaking: Your Holiness *or* Most Holy Father

In writing:
His Holiness, the Pope, *or*
His Holiness
Pope John XXIV

Your Holiness:

Closing: Your Holiness, Most Humble Servant, *etc.*

Cardinals

In speaking: Your Eminence

In writing:
His Eminence
John Cardinal Green
Your Eminence: *or less formally,*
My dear Cardinal Green:

Closing: I have the honor to be,
Your Eminence, *etc.*

Roman Catholic Archbishops

In speaking: Your Excellency *or* Archbishop Green

In writing:
The Most Reverend John Green
Your Excellency: *or*
Most Reverend Sir: (*business*)
My dear Archbishop: *or*
Dear Archbishop Green: (*personal*)

Closing: I have the honor to be,
Your Excellency, *etc.*

Roman Catholic Bishops

In speaking: Your Excellency
or Bishop Green

In writing:
The Most Reverend (*in America*)
The Right Reverend (*in Canada and Britain*)
Your Excellency: *or*
Most Reverend Sir: (*business*)
My dear Bishop: *or*
Dear Bishop Green: (*personal*)

Closing: I have the honor to be,
Your Excellency, *etc.*

Roman Catholic Priests

In speaking: Father Green

In writing:
The Reverend Father John Green,
Reverend Father: (*business*)
Dear Father Green: (*personal*)

Closing: I am, Reverend Father, *etc.*

Jewish Clergymen

Rabbis with Doctorate

In speaking: Doctor Green or Rabbi Green

In writing:
Rabbi John H. Green, D.D.
Sir: (*business*)
My dear Rabbi Green: (*personal*)

Rabbis without Doctorate

In speaking: Rabbi Green

In writing:
Rabbi John Green,
Sir: (*business*)
My dear Rabbi Green: (*personal*)

Cantors

In speaking: Cantor Green

In writing:
Cantor John Green
Sir: (*business*)
My dear Cantor Green: (*personal*)

Greek Orthodox Clergymen

Patriarch

In speaking: Your Holiness

In writing:
His Holiness
The Ecumenical Patriarch of Constantinople
Your Holiness:

Greek Orthodox Archbishops

In speaking: Your Eminence

In writing:
The Most Reverend John
Archbishop of North America
Your Eminence:

Greek Orthodox Bishops

In speaking: Your Grace

In writing:
The Right Reverend John
Bishop of Olympus
Right Reverend Sir: (*business*)
My dear Bishop: (*personal*)

Greek Orthodox Priests

In speaking: Father *or* Father Green

In writing:
The Very Reverend John Green
My dear Father Green:

Using different languages

To most of us, language consists of the spoken or written word. But language may take other forms. For example, it may be a system of special gestures made with the hands or with flags; or a system of signs and symbols other than numbers or letters; or a special vocabulary used by persons who belong to a particular profession, trade, or social group. *Using different languages* deals with the sounds and alphabets of several widely used languages. It explains and illustrates some of the different forms language takes. It will help you understand how they function, and how to recognize them should you encounter them.

Languages are based on alphabets. Alphabets usually are composed of letters or characters that are arranged in a specific order to represent various sounds. "Alphabets," pages *82-83,* compares various alphabets, including the Roman alphabet, Braille, Esperanto, the Initial Teaching Alphabet, the international Morse code, and the hand alphabet.

"Language sounds," pages *84-90,* explains the International Phonetic Alphabet and includes charts and pronunciation guides to illustrate how you can learn to say foreign words without an accent. The charts include the sounds of English, French, German, Italian, Russian, and Spanish.

"Codes and ciphers," page *91,* describes some of the methods used to write and decipher the secret messages in codes and ciphers.

"Signs and symbols," pages *92-97,* lists and defines many important signs and symbols, among which are those that pertain to astronomy, biology, business, commerce, engineering, electrical plans and equipment, plumbing, computer programming, mapping, and meteorology.

"Slang and jargon," page *98,* tells why slang and jargon are used, and by whom; why slang and jargon words and phrases change constantly; and why most of them are short-lived.

"Measures and weights," pages *99-105,* gives information to help you change measures into and out of metric units. It lists customary measures and metric measures, including length, distance, surface or area, and volume and capacity.

Because most names have a definite meaning, names are a kind of language too. "First names," pages *106-111,* lists hundreds of first names for men and women; tells what each means; and gives the language of origin.

Alphabets

Roman alphabet	Braille	Hand alphabet (finger spelling)	Esperanto	
Aa	⠁	A	Aa	
Bb	⠃	B	Bb	
Cc	⠉	C	Cc	Ĉĉ
Dd	⠙	D	Dd	
Ee	⠑	E	Ee	
Ff	⠋	F	Ff	
Gg	⠛	G	Gg	Ĝĝ
Hh	⠓	H	Hh	Ĥĥ
Ii	⠊	I	Ii	
Jj	⠚	J	Jj	Ĵĵ
Kk	⠅	K	Kk	
Ll	⠇	L	Ll	
Mm	⠍	M	Mm	
Nn	⠝	N	Nn	
Oo	⠕	O	Oo	
Pp	⠏	P	Pp	
Qq	⠟	Q		
Rr	⠗	R	Rr	
Ss	⠎	S	Ss	Ŝŝ
Tt	⠞	T	Tt	
Uu	⠥	U	Uu	Ŭŭ
Vv	⠧	V	Vv	
Ww	⠺	W		
Xx	⠭	X		
Yy	⠽	Y		
Zz	⠵	Z	Zz	

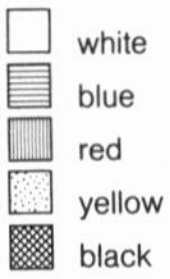

white
blue
red
yellow
black

Initial Teaching Alphabet		International Flag Code	International Morse code	Semaphore
a as in father **æ** as in rate	**au** as in taut **a** as in apple		•—	A
b as in *b*ig			—•••	B
c as in cat	**ch** as in *ch*ick		—•—•	C
d as in *d*og			—••	D
e as in egg	**ee** as in meet		•	E
f as in *f*ill			••—•	F
g as in gate			——•	G
h as in *h*at			••••	H
i as in *i*t	**ie** as in t*ie*		••	I
j as in *j*ig			•———	J
k as in *k*ilt			—•—	K
l as in *l*amp			•—••	L
m as in *m*an			——	M
n as in *n*et	**ng** as in si*ng*		—•	N
o as in hot **œ** as in toe **ω** as in book	**oo** as in moon **ou** as in vow **oi** as in *oi*l		———	O
p as in *p*ig			•——•	P
			——•—	Q
r as in *r*un	**r** as in father (used only after e, i, o, u, y)		•—•	R
s as in sad **sh** as in *sh*ip	**3** as in vision **z** as in rose		•••	S
t as in *t*ap **th** as in *th*in	**th** as in *th*en		—	T
ue as in due	**u** as in *u*gly		••—	U
v as in *v*an			•••—	V
w as in *w*ill	**wh** as in *wh*en		•——	W
			—••—	X
y as in *y*ell			—•——	Y
z as in zoo			——••	Z

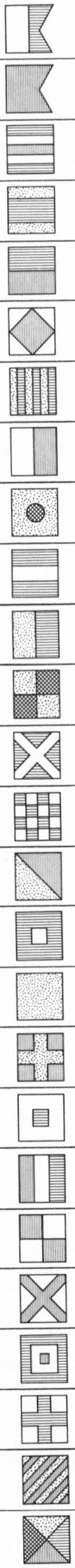

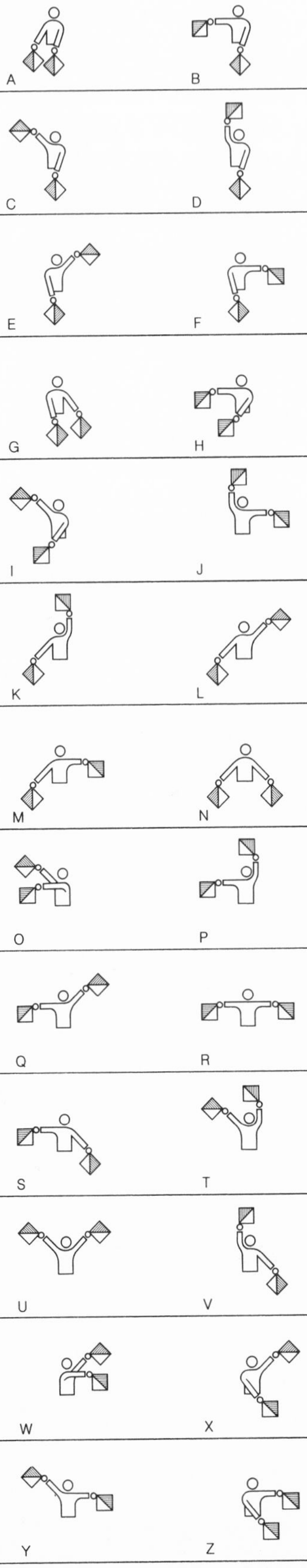

International Phonetic Alphabet

If you went to a concert in Germany, you might hear music by Tschaikowskij. If you went to a concert in Italy, you might hear the same work, but the composer's name would be spelled Ciajkovskij. In English, we spell his name much as the French do, Tchaikovsky. All of us are trying to spell a Russian name in a way that will show how it is pronounced in our language. Scholars use the International Phonetic Alphabet for this. Other systems exist for writing sounds, but the IPA is the most widely used. When you read tʃaikʰɔfski in IPA, you can say the word, regardless of spelling.

The consonant and vowel charts on these pages do not contain all the sounds made in all the languages of the world. They have been simplified to concentrate on the sounds used in English, French, German, Italian, Russian, and Spanish. With these charts and the pronunciation guides on the pages that follow, you can learn to say foreign words without an accent. Just follow these steps:

1. Read the word in one of the languages.

2. Look up the letters in the pronunciation guide, then the sounds of the letters in IPA symbols.

3. Check the symbols with these charts.

You make language sounds with air exhaled from your lungs. You vary the sounds by changing the shape and size of the passages through which the air moves, including your mouth, nose, and *glottis* (the opening between your vocal chords). You vary the shape of your mouth by moving your jaw and lips and by changing the way you hold your tongue in relation to your alveolar ridge or gum ridge, your *palate* (the roof of your mouth), and your *uvula* (the fleshy part of your soft palate). The loudest sounds are *voiced* (produced by vibrations of your vocal chords). Other sounds are called *voiceless* if you do not use your vocal chords in making them.

These charts show individual sounds in fairly pure form, but each sound can be affected by other sounds in the same word. No chart could show all these variations. In the chart of vowels, the indications of tongue, lip, and jaw positions are more descriptions of the vowel sounds than instructions on how to make the sounds. In both charts, phonetic transcriptions appear in brackets [ ], spellings in parentheses ( ), and translations in quotation marks " ".

Consonants

Manner of formation		**Shaping the sound** **Bilabial** (both lips)	**Labiodental** (lower lip and upper front teeth)	**Dental** (tongue tip against upper front teeth)	**Alveolar** (tongue tip behind upper front teeth)
Stop (complete stoppage of exhaled air)	**Aspirated** (voiceless, puff of air follows release of stoppage)	pʰ [pʰap] (pop)			tʰ [tʰap] (top)
	Unaspirated (voiceless, no puff or air)	p often in [pɛt] (bet) Sp. [paɾa] (para) "for"		t Sp. [toɾo] (toro) "bull"	t often in [tɛt] (debt)
	Voiced	b [əbʌv] (above)		d Sp. [dos] (dos) "two"	d [tʰədei] (today)
Affricate (begins as a stop, ends as a fricative, as ch in "chin"	**Voiceless**	pf Ger. [pfotə] (Pfote) "paw"			ts Ger. [tsu] (zu) "to"
	Voiced				dz It. [dzɛɾɔ] (zero) "zero"
Fricative (air forced through a narrow opening)	**Voiceless**		f [fʊt] (foot)	θ [θɪk] (thick)	s [sɪk] (sick)
	Voiced	β Sp. [laβaɾ] (lavar) "to wash" —like a very relaxed [b]	v [vest] (vest)	ð [ðɪs] (this)	z [zoun] (zone)
Nasal (air flows through nose)		m [kʰa:m] (calm)		n Sp. [naða] (nada) "nothing"	n [snæk] (snack)
Lateral (air flows around sides of tongue while front of tongue touches roof of mouth or teeth)				l Ger. [bal] (Ball) "ball" —pronounce [l] while tongue is in position for [ɛ] as in "wet"	
				ɫ [baɫ] (ball) —body of tongue pushed back to make throat opening narrow	
Trill (or roll) (exhaled air causes tongue tip to vibrate)				r Sp. [pero] (perro) "dog"	
Tap (single rapid contact of tongue)				ɾ often in [baɾəm](bottom) Sp. [peɾo] (pero) "but"	

Vowels

Tongue position		Front: Lips neutral or spread	Front: Lips rounded	Central: Lips rounded	Central: Lips neutral or spread	Back: Lips neutral	Back: Lips rounded	Jaw opening
High **(tense vowels are often held longer than lax vowels)**	**Tense**	i [fit] (feet)	y Ger. [fy:lən] (fühlen) "to feel" —[i] with rounded lips	ʉ [bʉtʰ] (boot) often a diphthong, as in [sɪʉt] (suit) —the American "oo" sound has a tongue position more forward than the [u] of the other five languages	ɨ Rus. [dɨm] (ДЫМ) "smoke"		u Ger. [ʁu:m] (Ruhm) "praise" —similar to English [bʉtʰ] (boot)	Close
(lax vowels are not as closely rounded as tense vowels)	**Lax**	ɪ [fɪt] (fit)	ʏ Ger. [fʏlən] (füllen) "to fill" —[ɪ] with rounded lips		ɪ usually in [dzɪst] (*just* a minute)		ʊ [bʊk] (book) Ger. [ʁʊm] (Rum) "rum"	
Mid	**Tense**	e Ger. [de:nən] (dehnen) "to extend" —similar to English [beitʰ] (bait)	ø Ger. [gø:tə] (Goethe) —[e] with rounded lips	ɜ British [bɜ:d] (bird) ə [ðəmæn] (the man)—neutral lips Fr. [ləvæ̃] (le vin) "the wine" —rounded Ger [bonə] (bohne) "bean" —neutral lips ɚ [bɚd] (bird) —often rounded			o Ger. [zo:n] (Sohn) "son" —similar to English [bout] (boat)	Half Close
	Lax	ɛ [lɛs] (less)	œ Ger. [gœt əʁ] (Goetter) "gods" —[ɛ] with rounded lips			ʌ [ɹʌ:b] (rub)	ɔ Ger. [zɔnə] (Sonne) "sun" —often in English [fɔə] (for)	Half Open
Low		æ [læs] (lass)			a [daun] (down) Fr. [ale] (aller) "to go"	ɑ [ɹɑ:b] (rob)	ɒ [sɒ:] (saw)	Open

Semivowels

Also called glides. When a glide follows a vowel, the vowel symbol is often used with a tie ‿ joining it to the next.	j [jɛt] (yet) [saj] or [sai] (sigh)	ɥ Fr. [ɥitʰ] (huit) "eight" Fr. [œɥ] or [œy] (oeil) "eye"	ɹ [ɹɛd] (red)—usually rounded before a vowel [faɹ] or [faə] (far) —usually neutral lips after a vowel		w [wɛt] (wet) [naw] or [nau] (now)

If air escapes through the nose during a vowel, the vowel is nasalized.
Examples: [mæ̃n] (man), Fr. [bõ] (bon) "good"

Palato-Alveolar **(tongue tip farther back, tongue slightly grooved)**	**Palatal*** **(front of tongue against hard palate and gum ridge)**	**Velar** **(back of tongue against soft palate)**	**Uvular** **(back of tongue against uvula)**	**Glottal** **(windpipe opening closed or partially closed)**
		kʰ [kʰɑp] (cop)		
		k often in [kɛt] (get) Sp. [kaɾa] (cara) "dear"		ʔ [ʔoʔou] (oh-oh!)
		ɡ [əɡou] (ago)		
tʃ [tʃik] (cheek) Sp. [tʃiko] (chico) "little" —English [tʃ] usually aspirated				
dʒ [ɛdʒ] (edge) It. [dʒa] (gia) "once"				
ʃ [ʃɪpʰ] (ship)	ç often in [çuu] (hue) Ger. [iç] (ich) "I" —tongue is shaped for [i] but friction noise is made	x Rus. [ɛxə] (Эхо) "echo" —like a very relaxed [kʰ]	χ Ger. [daχ] (Dach) "roof" —reminiscent of gargling	h [hɛd] (head)
ʒ [mɛʒə] (measure) Fr. [ʒon] (jaune) "yellow"	j Sp. [jeɡaɾ] (llegar) "arrive" —like an energetic [j] in [jɛs] (Yes!)	ɣ Sp. [djeɣo] (Diego) —like a very relaxed [ɡ]	ʁ Ger. [fa:ʁən] (fahren) "to drive"	
	ɲ Sp. [aɲo] (año) "year" —somewhat like [nj] in [kʰænjən] (canyon)	ŋ [sɪŋ] (sing)		
	ʎ It. [fɔʎa] (foglia) "leaf" —somewhat like [lj] in [mɪljən] (million)			
			ʀ Ger. [fa:ʀən] (fahren) "to drive"	

* A palatalized or "soft" consonant is one made with the tongue in position for [j] during and immediately after the consonant.
Examples: [kʲut] (cute), Rus. [nʲet] (Нет) "no"

French

French words are stressed on the final syllable: dor*mir* "to sleep," bene*vole* "benevolent," benedic*tion* "blessing."

Final e is not counted as a symbol.

Letters	Sounds	Spelling and pronunciation
ch	ʃ	chaud [ʃo] hot
or	k	chaos [kaos] chaos for words of Latin or Greek origin
gn	ɲ	ligne [liɲ] wood
ph	f	sphère [sfɛʁ] sphere
A nasal vowel occurs when a syllable ends with a single nasal (m *or* n). The nasal is deleted. The four nasal vowels are:		
ai, ei, i	æ̃	faim [fæ̃] hunger
a, e	ɒ̃	entre [ɒ̃tʁ] between
o	õ	bon [bõ] good
u	ʌ̃	brun [bʁʌ̃] brown
eau, au	o	beauté [bote] beauty *not* [əu] as in [bəut] boat
oeu, eu	ø	yeux [jø] eyes
ou	ɥ	bouche [buʃ] mouth *not* [əu] as in [bəuθ] both *not* [ʊu] as in [mʊud] mood
a	a	laver [lave] to wash
b	b	baton [batõ] stick
c	k	cacher [kaʃe] to hide *not* [kʰ] as in [kʰæʃ] cash
ç	s	reçu [ʁəsy] received
d	d	dette [dɛt] debt
ai, ei, é,	e	penser [pɒ̃se] to think
-ed, -er, -ez		pied [pje] foot But before [l], ai and ei are [aj] and [ɛj]. -er and -ez are pronounced [e] only if they are verb endings
è, ê	ɛ	bête [bɛt] beast
e	ɛ	elle [ɛl] she when e is stressed
or	ə	demain [dəmæ̃] tomorrow when e is not stressed

Letters	Sounds	Spelling and pronunciation
f	f	fini [fini] finished
g	g	glace [glas] ice
h	h	never pronounced. See rule 18 haut [o] high
i	i	midi [midi] noon
j	ʒ	joli [ʒɔli] pretty
k	k	kiosque [kjɔsk] kiosk
l	l	loup [lu] wolf *not* "dark" [l] as in [mɪɫ] mill.
m	m	âme [am] soul
n	n	jaune [ʒon] yellow
o	ɔ	globe [glɔb] globe
p	p	perle [pɛʁl] pearl *not* [pʰ] as in [pʰɛn] pen
qu	k	quand [kɒ̃] when *not* [kʰ] as in [kʰɒf] cough
r	ʁ	mer [mɛʁ] sea [r] is not common, but acceptable *not* [ɹ] as in [mɛɹ] mare
s	s	seul [sœl] only
t	t	tasse [tas] coffee cup *not* [tʰ] as in [tʰɛn] ten
u	y	user [yze] to use *not* [ʊu] as in [mʊud] mood *not* [jʊu] as in [jʊuz] use
v	v	vache [vaʃ] cow
w	v	wagon [vagõ] railroad car many foreign words have [w]
x	ks	taxi [taksi] taxi
y	i	y [i] there
z	z	zéro [zeʁo] zero

Adjustment rules

1. [k, g] before the letters e, i become [s, ʒ] respectively: centre [sɒ̃tʁ] center, gens [ʒɒ̃] people, chaise [ʃɛːz] chair. For two [k]'s together, only the first one is changed: accepter [aksɛpte] accept.

2. If [gu] is followed by e, i, the [u] is deleted: guerre [gɛːʁ] war, guider [gide] to guide.

3. [ks] becomes [gz] or [z] in many words: exact [ɛgzakt] exact, dixième [dizjɛm] tenth.

4. Single [s] between vowels becomes [z]: chose [ʃoːz] thing, lisez [lize] you read.

5. [t] becomes [s] in most suffixes before the letters [ie, ia, io]: patient [pasjɒ̃] patient, initial [inisjal] initial. *Not* [ʃ] as in [ləuʃən] lotion.

6. If word-final [il] follows a vowel, it becomes [j]: travail [tʁavaj] work, oeil [œj] eye. If [ill] is not at the beginning of a word, it becomes [j]: feuille [fœj] leaf, oreille [ɔʁɛj] ear. If there is no vowel before [ill], the [i] remains: fille [fij] girl. But mille [mil] thousand, distiller [distile] to distill.

7. [o] becomes [wa] before [i]: loyal [lwajal] loyal, voyage [vwajaʒ] voyage.

8. [i, u, y] before a vowel become the glides [j, w, ɥ] respectively: pied [pje] foot, oui [wi] yes, huit [ɥit] eight.

9. Double consonants are pronounced as single.

10. Final [ə] is deleted: monde [mõd] world, arrivée [aʁive] arrived, bouche [buʃ] mouth.

11. The verb ending [ɒ̃t] is deleted: ils parlent [ilpaʁl] they speak, but comment [kɔmɒ̃] how.

12. [ʁ, l] at end of words become voiceless [χ, l̥] respectively if they follow a voiceless consonant: autre [otχ] other, siècle [sjɛkl̥] century.

13. [e, ø] in closed syllables (a syllable ending in one or more consonants) become [ɛ, œ] respectively: aime [ɛm] likes, neuf [nœf] nine.

14. Stressed vowels before [v, ʁ, z, ʒ], the voiced fricatives, are usually lengthened: pauvre [poːvʁ] poor, neige [nɛːʒ] snow, dur [dyːʁ] hard, beurre [bœːʁ] butter.

15. Final consonants are usually deleted: clef [kle] key, grand [gʁɒ̃] large, part [paʁ] part. But there are many exceptions: lis [lis] lily, arc [aʁk] bow, il [il] he. This rule does not apply if [ə] or [ɒ̃t] have already been deleted.

16. [ɔ] becomes [o] at end of word and before [z]: mot [mo] word, oser [oze] to dare.

17. If a word is followed by a vowel, rule 15 may not apply vous avez [vuzave] you have, but vous prenez [vupʁəne] you take. [ks] when linked in this way becomes [z]. les Beaux Arts [lebozaːʁ] the fine arts.

18. [h] is always deleted. But some examples of [h] are the so-called "aspirated" h, which serves only to prevent liaison: les herbes [lezɛʁb] the herbs, les/hanches [leɒ̃ʃ] the hips.

German

German words are usually stressed on the first syllable: *Mutter* "mother," *gross*zügig "generous." There are, however, a few prefixes that do not take stress, such as ge-, ver-, ent-, emp-, er-, zer-. Examples are *sa*gen "say," ge*sagt* "said," *ste*hen "stand," ver*ste*hen "understand." Also, the words wo "where" and da "there" are not stressed when they form question words or adverbs, such as wor*über* "what about," da*von* "from there." There are a few isolated exceptions as well, such as Fa*mi*lie "family." (All German nouns are capitalized.)

Letters	Sounds	Spelling and pronunciation
ä, æ	ɛ	Männer [mɛnəʁ] men
		not [ei] as in [mein] mane
		not [ɑ] as in [mɑ] ma
ai, ei	ai	mein [main] my
au	au	Auge [augə] eye
		not [ɒ] as in [ɒf] off
äu, eu, aeu	ɔi	Heu [hɔi] hay
		not [jʉ] as in [jʉnət] unit
ie	ii	Lied [li:tʰ] song
ö, œ	ø	König [kʰø:niç] king
		not [ɚ] as in [kʰɚl] curl
		not [ei] as in [kʰein] cane
ü, ue	y	kühn [kʰy:n] bold
		not [jʉ] as in [kʰjʉt] cute
		not [ʊu] as in [kʰʊup] coop
ck	kk	Ecke [ɛkə] corner
chs	ks	Ochs [ɔks] ox
ch	çç	mich [miç] me
		not [ʃ] as in [wɪʃ] wish
dt	tt	Stadt [ʃtatʰ] city
ng	ŋŋ	Ring [ʁɪŋ] ring
		not [ŋg] as in [fɪŋgɚ] finger
ph	f	Phrase [fʁa:zə] phrase
sch	ʃʃ	Schiff [ʃɪf] ship
qu	kv	Quelle [kʰvɛlə] source
		not [kw] as in [kʰwɪt] quit
ß	ss	naß [nas] wet
a	a	Mann [man] man
b	b	Buch [bux] book
c	k, ts	foreign words only. [ts] before front vowels, [k] before back vowels.
d	d	oder [odəʁ] or
e	e	See [ze:] lake
f	f	auf [auf] on
g	g	Geld [gɛltʰ] money
h	h	Haus [haus] house
i	i	Mutti [mʊti] mom
j	j	ja [ja] yes
		not [dʒ] as in [dʒɛt] jet
k	k	Kuh [kʰu:] cow
l	l	Liebe [li:bə] love
		not "dark" [ɫ] as in [ɒɫ] all
m	m	Macht [maxtʰ] power
n	n	Nacht [naxtʰ] night
o	o	Ofen [o:fən] oven
		not [ɔu] as in [hɔuɫ] hole
p	p	Opa [opa] grandpa
r	ʁ	rot [ʁo:tʰ] red
		trilled [r] is also acceptable
		not [ɹ] as in [ɹɛd] red
s	s	Wurst [vʊʁstʰ] sausage
t	t	Mutter [mʊtəʁ] mother
u	u	Schuh [ʃu:] shoe
		not [ʊu] as in [dʊu] do
v	f	Vater [fatəʁ] father
w	v	Welle [vɛlə] wave
x	ks	Hexe [hɛksə] witch
y	y	foreign words only
z	ts	zehn [tse:n] ten
		not [z] as in [zɪp] zip

Adjustment rules

1. The suffix -ig in the last syllable becomes [içç] : heilig [hailiç] holy; erniedrigt [ɛʁnidʁiçtʰ] humbled.

2. [h] after a vowel is deleted, but makes the vowel long: Ehre [e:ʁə] honor.

3. Double vowels are long: Aal [a:l] eel; Lied [li:tʰ] song.

4. A stressed vowel before one consonant is usually lengthened; a vowel before two or more consonants remains short: Miete [mi:tə] rent; Mitte [mɪtə] middle; sechs [zɛks] six.

5. Short [i, y, e, ø, u, o] become [ɪ, ʏ, ɛ, œ, ʊ, ɔ] respectively: füllen [fʏlən] fill; elf [ɛlf] eleven; Butter [bʊtəʁ] butter.

6. Single [s] not next to any consonant becomes [z]: Sohn [zo:n] son; Hase [ha:zə] hare.

7. [sp, st] at beginning of word becomes [ʃp, ʃt]: Stern [ʃtɛʁn] star; spielen [ʃpi:lən] to play.

8. Double consonants (having been used as cues for vowel length) become single: Ofen [o:fən] oven; offen [ɔfən] open; echt [ɛçtʰ] real.

9. [ç] after back vowels [u, ʊ, o, ɔ, a] becomes [x]: acht [axtʰ] eight; Loch [lɔx] hole; not [k] as in [sɑkt] socked or [lʊk] look.

10. [b, d, g, v, z] at end of word become [p, t, k, f, s] respectively (that is, voiced stops and fricatives become voiceless): und [ʊntʰ] and; Sarg [zaʁkʰ] coffin; ab [apʰ] away; Haus [haus] house; sagt [zaktʰ] says.

11. [p, t, k] at beginning of stressed syllable or end of word are aspirated or "exploded" (that is, they sound like English [p, t, k]): geputzt [gɛpʰʊtstʰ] cleaned; kalt [kʰaltʰ] cold.

12. Unstressed [ɛ] in final syllables becomes [ə]: bitte [bɪtə] please; helfen [hɛlfən] to help; Messer [mɛsəʁ] knife.

13. Stressed syllables beginning with vowels are typically preceded by a glottal stop [ʔ]: aber [ʔabəʁ] but; einatmen [ʔainʔatmən] inhale.

Many German words are compounds, such as Speise "food" + Karte "card" = Speisekarte "menu." The adjustment rules apply to each word in a compound separately. Some words will be pronounced incorrectly if the compound's parts are not identified correctly. Liebestreue "faithfulness in love" is pronounced [li:bəstʰʁɔiə], not [li:bəʃtʁɔiə], because the parts are Liebes + Treue, not Liebe + Streue.

Italian

The best guess as to where Italian words are stressed is the next-to-last (penultimate) syllable: par*la*re "to speak," *ba*cio "kiss," genuina*men*te "truly." But many words are stressed on the last syllable, or two syllables before it. Some of these stress shifts are part of the grammatical pattern. For example, first and second person singular future verbs are stressed on the last syllable: cante*ro* "I will sing," cante*ra* "he will sing." Adjectives formed from -ibile, -istico, and some other suffixes have the stress shifted to the left: umo*ris*tico "humorous," vi*si*bile "visible." An incorrect stress may change the meaning of the word: *net*tare "nectar," net*ta*re "to clean"; *noc*ciolo "kernel," noc*cio*lo "nut-tree." (Stress is not marked on this page if it falls on the next-to-last syllable).

The letters e, o, and z each have two basic sounds. Choosing the right one requires looking the word up in a dictionary. Most dictionaries use a standard set of diacritical marks for this purpose (see the list of basic sounds). Unstressed e and o are always [ɛ] and [ɔ], with a tendency to be more like [e] and [o] if [e] or [o] appears in the word.

Letters	Sounds	Spelling and pronunciation
gn	ɲ	sdegno [zdeɲɔ] scorn
		like [nj] as in [mɛnjʊu] menu, but
		the tongue is shaped for [j]
		during the [n].
a	a	mano [manɔ] hand
b	b	basta [basta] enough
		not [p] as in [pæθ] bath
c	k	capo [kapɔ] head
		not [kʰ] as in [kʰɑɹ] car
d	d	Dio [diɔ] God
		not [t] as in [tid] deed
		also, must be dental
e	e	venti [venti] twenty
		usual diacritical mark is é
		not [ɛi] as in [vɛin] vane
or	ɛ	venti [vɛnti] winds
		usual diacritical mark is è
f	f	forza [fɔrtsa] force
g	ɡ	gamba [ɡamba] leg
		not [k] as in [kʌn] gun
h	h	never pronounced. See rule 7
		vecchio [vɛk:jɔ] old
i	i	libro [librɔ] book
j, k		foreign words only
l	l	miele [mjɛlɛ] honey
		not "dark" [ɫ] as in [mɛɫən] melon
m	m	amare [amarɛ] to love

Letters	Sounds	Spelling and pronunciation
n	n	nero [nerɔ] black
		must be dental
o	o	rotto [rot:ɔ] broken
		usual diacritical mark is ó
		not [ou] as in [ɹout] wrote
or	ɔ	dotto [dɔt:ɔ] learned
		usual diacritical mark is ò
p	p	pane [panɛ] bread
		not [pʰ] as in [pʰʌn] pun
q	k	questo [kwestɔ] this
		not [kʰ] as in [kʰwɪɫt] quilt
r	r	ragazza [raɡat:sa] girl
		not [ɹ] as in [ɹʌɡ] rug
s	s	sole [solɛ] sun
t	t	tutto [tut:ɔ] all
		not [tʰ] as in [tʰʊut] toot
		also, must be dental
u	u	chiuso [kjuzɔ] closed
		not [ʊu] as in [kʰjʊut] cute
		not [ʊ] as in [kʰʊd] could
v	v	vino [vinɔ] wine
w, x, y		foreign words only
z	dz	mezzo [mɛd:zɔ] half
		usual diacritical mark is ẓ
or	ts	mezzo [met:sɔ] overripe
		no diacritical mark means [ts]
		not [z] as in [izi] easy

Adjustment rules

1. If [gl] appears between a vowel (on the left) and unstressed [i] (on the right), it becomes [ʎʎ]: figlio [fiʎ:ɔ] son, tògliere [tɔʎ:ɛrɛ] to seize. Pronounce "light" [l] with tongue shaped for [i].

2. [k, ɡ] become [tʃ, dʒ] if there is a following [e, ɛ] or [i]: giro [dʒirɔ] circle, geloso [dʒɛlozɔ] jealous, cielo [tʃɛlɔ] heaven.

3. Unstressed [i] is deleted if there is a palatal consonant [tʃ, dʒ, ʎ, ɲ] on the left and a vowel on the right: figlio [fiʎ:ɔ] son, veggia [ved:ʒa] cask, but Lucia [lutʃia] Lucia, oggi [ɔd:ʒi] today.

4. [stʃ] becomes [ʃ] whenever the spellings "sci" or "sce" appear: uscio [uʃɔ] entrance, scelta [ʃelta] choice.

5. [n] followed by [ɡ] or [k] becomes [ŋ].: banca [baŋka] bench, inglese [iŋɡlezɛ] English. Similarly, [n] before [b, p] or [m] becomes [m]: un poco [umpɔkɔ] a little bit. In general, nasals take the place of articulation of a following consonant.

6. Single [s] between vowels or before a voiced consonant becomes [z]: mìsero [mizɛrɔ] misery, sbandire [zbandirɛ] banish, but salve [salvɛ] hail, scala [skala] scale, esso [ɛs:ɔ] this. There are many speakers who have both [s] and [z] between vowels. For those dialects, many exceptions must be learned.

7. [h] is deleted. It serves only to prevent [i] from affecting [k] and [ɡ]: ghiaia [ɡjaja] gravel, chiave [kjavɛ] key.

8. Unstressed [i, u] before vowels become [j, w] respectively: uomo [wɔmɔ] man, chiesa [kjɛza] church.

9. Double consonants are lengthened. Vowels are somewhat lengthened before single consonants (vowel length has not been transcribed): machia [makja] treachery, macchia [mak:ja] speck; sono [sonɔ] I am, sonno [son:ɔ] sleep. For [ts, dz, tʃ, dʒ], the [t, d] portions are lengthened: regia [rɛdʒa] royal, reggia [rɛd:ʒa] palace. [dz] or [ts] between vowels always counts as doubled. Single [r] is usually a single tap of the tongue.

Russian

Each Russian word (not counting compounds) has one stressed syllable, marked in dictionaries with an acute accent: **ми́рный** [mʲirnɨi] peace; **билéт** [bʲilʲɛt] ticket. It is not marked in ordinary writing. A few clues for stress location come directly from the spelling. For example, **ё** is always stressed and the suffix-**ист** is always stressed (**марксист** [mɑrksʲist] marxist). But stress location usually changes depending upon the grammatical form of a word: **вдова́** [vdɑvɑ] widow, **вдо́вы** [vdɔvɨ] widows; **я учу́** [ja utʃu] I teach, **он у́чит** [ɔnutʃit] he teaches.

Letters	Sounds	Spelling and pronunciation
а	ɑ	**мать** [mɑtʲ] mother
б	b	**брак** [brɑk] marriage *not* like English voiceless unaspirated [p] as in [pi] be
в	v	**водка** [vɔtkə] vodka
г	g	**глава** [glɑvɑ] leader *not* [k] as in [kʊd] good
д	d	**да** [dɑ] yes *not* [t] as in [tɪp] dip; also, must be dental, *not* like English alveolar [d]
е	jɛ	**есть** [jɛstʲ] to eat
ё	jɔ	**ёлка** [jɔlkə] Christmas tree
ж	ʒ	**одежда** [ɑdʲɛʒdə] clothes tongue touches roof of mouth farther back than for English [ʒ] as in [mɛʒə] measure
з	z	**глаза** [glɑzɑ] eyes
и	ji	**книга** [knʲigə] book
й	i	**чай** [tʃɑi] tea
к	k	**конь** [kɔnʲ] horse
л	ɫ	**слово** [slɔvə] word [ɫ] is more precise. **л** is at least as "dark" as English [ɫ] as in [mɪɫ] mill
м	m	**храм** [xrɑm] temple
н	n	**нос** [nɔs] nose must be dental
о	ɔ	**кто** [ktɔ] who

Letters	Sounds	Spelling and pronunciation
п	p	**правда** [prɑvdə] truth
р	r	**роман** [rɑmɑn] novel *not* [ɹ] as in [ɹɛd]
с	s	**стул** [stul] chair
т	t	**там** [tɑm] there must be dental
у	u	**друг** [druk] friend *not* [ʊu] as in [dɹʊup] droop
ф	f	**факт** [fɑkt] fact
х	x	**плохо** [plɔxə] bad *not* [k] as in [pʰɑkət] pocket
ц	ts	**отец** [ɑtʲɛts] father
ч	tʃ	**часы** [tʃisɪ] clock
ш	ʃ	**школа** [ʃkɔlə] school like **ж**, tongue contacts roof of mouth farther back than English [ʃ] as in [ʃi] she
щ	ʃtʃ	**борщ** [bɔrʃtʃ] borscht
ъ		**объект** [ɑbjɛkt] object not pronounced. Prevents rule 6 from operating
ы	ɨ	**сын** [sɨn] son *not* [ɪ] as in [sɪn] sin
ь	j	**бальшое** [balʲʃɔjə] big
э	ɛ	**эта** [ɛtə] that
ю	ju	**юбка** [jupkə] skirt
я	ja	**я** [ja] I

Adjustment rules

1. Unstressed [jɛ] and [ji] after [ʒ, ʃ, or ts] become [ɪ]: **тоже** [tɔʒɪ] also; **жир** [ʒɪr] fat.

2. Unstressed [ɑ] or [ɛ] after [j] becomes [i] if it is not the last segment in the word: **театр** [tʲiɑtr] theater; **пятно** [pʲitnɔ] spot. Word-final [jɛ] becomes [jə].

3. Unstressed [ɔ] becomes [ɑ]: **окно** [ɑknɔ] window.

4. [ɑ] following a stressed syllable becomes [ə]: **мясо** [mʲɑsə] meat; **зона** [zɔnə] zone.

5. Stressed [ɔ, ɛ] tend to become [ɔə, ɛə]: **это** [ɛətə] this; **хорошо** [xɑrɑʃɔə] good.

6. A consonant followed directly by [j] with no **ъ** in between absorbs the [j]. The body of the tongue is shaped for [j] during the consonant, resulting in a palatalized or *soft* consonant: **весь** [vʲɛsʲ] all; **сталь** [stɑlʲ] steel. This rule does not apply to [ʒ, ʃ, ts], which always remain hard. It applies redundantly to [tʃ] and [ʃtʃ] which are always soft anyway.

7. [j] drops out after [ʒ, ʃ, ts]: **жена** [ʒɛnɑ] wife; **шея** [ʃɛjə] neck. Rules 6 and 7 can only apply once to each consonant: **мужья** [muʒjɑ] husbands.

8. A vowel between two soft consonants is fronted: [ɑ, ɔ, u] become [æ, œ, y] respectively: **пять** [pʲætʲ] five; **тётя** [tʲœtʲə] aunt.

9. Voiced obstruents (stops or fricatives) at the ends of words become voiceless: [b, d, g, v, z, ʒ] become [p, t, k, f, s, ʃ] respectively: **год** [gɔt] year; **молодёжь** [mɑlɑdʲɔʃ] youth; **поезд** [pɔjist] train.

10. When two obstruents appear together, the first one takes the voicing of the second: **отдать** [ɑd:ɑtʲ] give back; **сдавать** [zdɑvɑtʲ] deliver. This rule operates across words as well: **к дому** [gdɔmu] to the house.

11. [s, z] take on the tongue position of a following [ʃ, ʒ, or ʃtʃ]: **сжатие** [ʒ:ɑtʲijə] pressure.

12. [p, t, k] are aspirated slightly at end of words, and nowhere else, unlike English, which requires aspiration at beginning of words: **там** [tɑm] there, not [tʰ] as in English [tʰɑm] Tom.

Spanish

Spanish words ending in a vowel, n, or s, are usually stressed on the next-to-last syllable: c*a*sa "house," *ha*blan "they speak." Words ending in other consonants are usually stressed on the last syllable: co*mer* "to eat," lati*tud* "latitude." Words that do not follow this rule have the stressed vowel marked with an acute accent: también "also," habló "he spoke."

Letters		Sounds	Spelling and pronunciation
a		a	nada [naða] nothing
*b		b	bueno [bwɛnɔ] good
			not [p] as in [pɔi] boy
*c		k	casa [kasa] house
ch		tʃ	chico [tʃikɔ] small
*d		d	donde [dɔndɛ] where
			not [t] as in [tɔɹ] door
			also, must be dental
e		ɛ	comer [kɔmɛr] to eat
f		f	familia [familja] family
*g		ɡ	gordo [ɡɔrdɔ] fat
			not [k] as in [kɑt] got
h		silent	haber [aβɛr] to have
*i		i	niña [niɲa] girl
j		h	jugar [huɣar] to play
			in most of the Western Hemisphere
	or	x	[xuɣar]
			mainly in northern Spain
k			foreign words only
l		l	ley [lɛi] law
			not "dark" [ɫ] as in [pʰʊɫ] pull
ll		j	caballo [kaβajɔ] horse
			in most of the Western Hemisphere
	or	ʎ	[kaβaʎɔ]
			mainly in northern Spain. Pronounce "light" [l] with the tongue shaped for [i]
*m		m	mucho [mutʃɔ] much
*n		n	no [nɔ] no
			must be dental
ñ		ɲ	año [aɲɔ] year
			Pronounce [n] with the tongue shaped for [i]
o		ɔ	coro [kɔrɔ] choir
p		p	puerta [pwɛrta] door
			not [pʰ] as in [pʰɔɹ] pour
qu		k	quizás [kisas] perhaps
			not [kʰ] as in [kʰiz] keys
			not [kʰw] as in [kʰwɪz] quiz
r		r	pero [pɛɾɔ] but
*rr		r	perro [pɛr:ɔ] dog
			not [ɹ] as in [pʰɛɹ] pair
*s		s	ser [sɛr] to be
t		t	tía [tia] aunt
			not [tʰ] as in [tʰi] tea
			also, must be dental
*u		u	mujer [muhɛr] woman
			not [jʊu] as in [mjʊut] mute
			not [ʊu] as in [mʊud] mood
v		b	verdad [bɛrðað] truth
w			foreign words only
x		ks	extraño [ɛkstraɲɔ] strange
y		i	hoy [ɔi] today
z		s	luz [lus] light
			in most of the Western Hemisphere
	or	θ	[luθ]
			mainly in northern Spain

*Adjustment rules

1. [b,d,k,g] remain unchanged after nasals, [l], or silence: mandar [mandar] to command, buenas noches [bwɛnaznɔtʃɛs] good evening. In all other cases, these sounds are produced with little energy; a complete stop is not made, resulting in an approximate [β, ð, ɣ]: nada [naða] nothing, esta bueno [ɛstaβwɛnɔ] it's good, vagar [baɣar] to wander, una vaca [unaβaka] a cow.

2. [g] before [e, i] becomes [h] ([x] in northern Spain): gente [hɛntɛ] people, girar [hirar] to revolve.

3. [gu] before [e, i] becomes [g]: guerra [gɛr:a] war, guitarra [gitar:a] guitar. Two dots above the u means this rule does not apply: agüero [agwerɔ] omen.

4. [i] before vowels becomes [j]: diablo [djaβlɔ] devil, ciudad [sjuðað] city. If there is no consonant before [j], it is pronounced with the tongue in position for [i] as usual, but with a narrow opening for the airstream, resulting in friction noise. This is more precisely transcribed [ĵ]: ayuda [aĵuða] aid.

5. [k] before [e, i] becomes [s] ([θ] in northern Spain): centro [sɛntrɔ] center, cielo [sjɛlɔ] heaven.

6. [m, n] take on the place of articulation of a following consonant: tengo [tɛŋgɔ] I have, un peso [umpɛsɔ] a peso, en vez de [ɛmbɛzdɛ] in place of.

7. Single [r] is reduced to a single tap, double [r] is strongly trilled: pero [pɛɾɔ] but, perro [pɛr:ɔ] dog.

8. [s] before a voiced consonant becomes [z]: mismo [mizmɔ] same, los huevos [lɔzwɛvɔs] the eggs, es verdad [ɛzβɛrðað] it's true. This rule operates freely across word boundaries, as do rules 7 and 8.

9. [u] before vowels becomes [w]: guardar [gwardar] to guard, bueno [bwɛnɔ] good.

10. For convenience, precise vowel qualities have not been transcribed. e is between [e] and [ɛ], and o is between [o] and [ɔ]. They are not diphthongs like English [ei] and [ou].

Codes and ciphers

Codes and ciphers are systems of writing messages containing secret information. Code systems differ from cipher systems. A code system may use a single word or a number to stand for a complete message. A cipher system uses a separate letter, number, or other symbol for each letter of the *plaintext* (ordinary language) message. Both codes and ciphers are based on formulas called *keys.* The receiver of a *cryptogram* (a message in code or cipher) must have the key to unlock the secret information. In cipher systems, the key may be a letter, number, or other symbol arranged in a special pattern throughout the cryptogram. In code systems, the key is a code group or number.

Changing plaintext into codes and ciphers is called *encoding* or *enciphering.* Finding the secret information in the cryptogram is called *decoding* or *deciphering.* The art of using and solving codes and ciphers is called *cryptography* from the Greek *kryptós,* meaning hidden, and *graphíā,* meaning writing. Breaking a code or a cipher is called *cryptanalysis.*

Since code systems use a secret vocabulary in which a code number or a code group may stand for a complete message, code systems require the use of *code books.* Words, phrases, and sentences that are used in special operations, such as naval intelligence, are compiled in a kind of dictionary. Each of the plaintext terms is given a code number or a code group. For example, the code group BANAT might mean the word "attack" and the code group BANEV might mean the phrase "attack progressing satisfactorily." Sometimes the code equivalents are listed next to the plaintext terms. But for greater secrecy, often two separate code books are compiled—one listing the plaintext terms, and the other containing the code equivalents.

Code books include *syllabary groups.* These are used to encode or decode proper names and words that may not have been included in the code book. For example, the word AUSTRALIA would be encoded with the syllable codes for AUS TRAL IA.

Cipher systems are variations of the basic methods of *substitution* and *transposition.* In the substitution method, letters, numbers, and other symbols in the plaintext keep their original positions, but are replaced by other letters, numbers, or symbols. For example, the message WILL ARRIVE AT SEVEN might be enciphered XJMM BSSJWF BU TFWFO. Here, each letter was replaced by the one immediately following it in the alphabet. To make this simple substitution a bit more complex, the letters are grouped in units of five. Now the cryptogram reads: XJMMB SSJWF BUTFW FOGCB. Because there were fewer than five letters in the last group, meaningless letters called nulls were added. In this example, the nulls are GCB. The same message might have been enciphered: ZLOOD UULYH DWVHY HQKFG. Here, each letter in the plaintext was replaced by the third letter to its right in the alphabet.

Another substitution method uses a key word in which no letter is repeated, a plaintext alphabet, and a cipher alphabet. The key word is put at the beginning of the cipher alphabet. The plaintext alphabet is written either above or below the cipher alphabet. In this example, the key word is CUSTOMER, and the words to be enciphered are HELP IS COMING.

Cipher: C U S T O M E R A B D F G H I J K L N P Q V W X Y Z
Plain: A B C D E F G H I J K L M N O P Q R S T U V W X Y Z

By substituting letters in the cipher alphabet for the letters in the plaintext and grouping them in five-letter units with nulls, HELP IS COMING is enciphered ROFJA NSIGA HERCP.

In transposition ciphers, the plaintext letters are kept, but they may be jumbled or rearranged in a special pattern. For example, the secret message is WILL ARRIVE AT SEVEN. The message received by the correspondent reads: WLARV ASVNI LRIET EEROC. This cryptogram was enciphered by first writing the plaintext in two lines, in this manner:

W L A R V A S V N
I L R I E T E E

These two lines were then combined into a single line

W L A R V A S V N I L R I E T E E

and regrouped into units of five letters. Nulls were added to the last group to make five letters.

Columnar transposition is another kind of transposition cipher. The letters of the plaintext message are arranged in columns under a key word whose letters are numbered according to the sequence of the letters in the alphabet. In this example, the key word is WATER. The letter A is number 1, E is 2, R is 3, T is 4, and W is 5. The plaintext message WATCH FOR WOMAN IN WHITE is arranged in five-letter rows under the key-word numbers.

W	A	T	E	R
5	1	4	2	3
W	A	T	C	H
F	O	R	W	O
M	A	N	I	N
W	H	I	T	E

To get the final cipher, the columns are taken in numerical order, and arranged in groups of five letters each. In this example, the final cipher reads: AOAHC WITHO NETRN IWFMW. To decipher the cryptogram, the cryptographer reverses the process.

Yet another method is to replace each plaintext letter with a two-cipher letter. This is called *biliteral substitution.* The cipher is arranged in a matrix with five key letters at the head and five different key letters at the side. The plaintext alphabet is arranged in five rows, with five letters in each row. I and J are grouped as one letter. Then, each plaintext letter is replaced by one key letter from the head and one from the side. In this example, the plaintext FRIEND is enciphered AR FU OR PB GT OB.

	A	F	G	O	P
B	A	B	C	D	E
R	F	G	H	IJ	K
T	L	M	N	O	P
U	Q	R	S	T	U
V	V	W	X	Y	Z

The cryptographer could have used key numbers instead of key letters. If the key numbers at the head were 1 2 5 7 9, and those at the side were 3 4 6 8 10, the cryptogram for FRIEND would be 14 28 74 93 56 73.

A form of hidden writing that is neither code nor cipher is also used to transmit secret information. Significant letters may be concealed in a seemingly ordinary sentence to make up a message. For example, the first letter of each word in HAVE ENDORSED LONG-RANGE PLANS is extracted to spell out HELP. The sender of a message might use plaintext words for which there are prearranged secret equivalents so that the sentence SALLY ARRIVES ON EVENING TRAIN might mean STRIKE IS ON.

Signs and symbols

Astronomy

Astronomical bodies

☉ the sun; Sunday
⊖ center of sun
☾, ☽ or ◐ the moon; Monday
☽, ◐, ☽ or ☽ the moon, first quarter
● new moon
○ full moon
☾, ◑, ☾ or ☾ the moon, last quarter
♂ Mars; Tuesday
☿ Mercury; Wednesday
♃ Jupiter; Thursday
♀ Venus; Friday
♄ Saturn; Saturday
♁, ⊕ or ⊖ Earth
♅ or ♅ Uranus
♆ Neptune
♇ Pluto
⚳ or ① Ceres, first asteroid discovered
⚴ or ② Pallas
⚵ or ③ Juno
⚶ or ④ Vesta
✳ or ✱ fixed star
☄ comet
◎ planetary nebula
⬭ galaxy

Signs of position

☌ conjunction
✱ sextile; indicating two heavenly bodies 60 degrees apart
□ quadrature; indicating a heavenly body that is 90 degrees from another
△ trine; indicating two heavenly bodies 120 degrees distant from each other
☍ opposition, or 180 degrees apart
☊ ascending node
☋ descending node
♈ vernal equinox
♎ autumnal equinox
α, RA or AR right ascension
β celestial latitude
δ, Decl. declination
θ sidereal time
λ celestial or geographical longitude; wave length
′ minute (of arc)
″ second (of arc)

Signs of Zodiac

Spring

♈ Aries, the Ram
♉ Taurus, the Bull
♊ or ♊ Gemini, the Twins

Summer

♋ or ♋ Cancer, the Crab
♌ Leo, the Lion
♍ Virgo, the Virgin

Autumn

♎ Libra, the Balance
♏ Scorpio, the Scorpion
♐ or ♐ Sagittarius, the Archer

Winter

♑ or ♑ Capricorn, the Goat
♒ Aquarius, the Water Bearer
♓ or ♓ Pisces, the Fishes

Basic

╲, ⃠, X or ⊗ (red) prohibition
○ (red) restriction
△ (red) warning
→ direction
⇢ motion
↰ left
↱ right
⇧ up
⇩ down
⇥ in
⇤ out
⏽ on
⭘ off
+ increase
− decrease
○ empty
● full
⌢ continuously variable
& ampersand; and. See **ampersand.**
&c et cetera; and so forth. See usage note under **etc.**
© copyright, copyrighted
® registered trademark
′ foot, feet
″ inch, inches
X by, combined with in multiplication or relative dimensions: *a room that is 10′ X 20′*
¶ paragraph
″ ditto; indicating the same as the above
* born. Also see **asterisk** (def. 1)
† died. Also see **dagger** (def. 2)
‡ double dagger. See **double dagger.**
§ section
♠ (in cards) spade
♡ heart
♢ diamond
♣ club
☞ index

Biology

♂, ♁ or □ male
♀ or ○ female
⚲ neuter
☿ or ⚥ hermaphrodite
◇ sex unknown or unspecified
X (of a hybrid) crossed with
P parent or parental generation
F filial generation
F_1, F_2, etc. the first, second, etc. filial generation
+ possessing a specified characteristic, or longer than
− lacking a specified characteristic, or shorter than
= identical with
♃ a perennial plant or herb
△ an evergreen
✱ Northern Hemisphere
✱ Southern Hemisphere
I✱ Old World
✱I New World
∞ indefinitely numerous
! specimen seen by the author; certainty, verified
? doubt or uncertainty
§ section or division of a genus

△ head
□ thorax
▷ abdomen
⊖ egg
⊕ larva
☽ pupa

Business

Money

$ dollar
¢ cent(s)
₡ colón(es) (Costa Rica, El Salvador)
£ pounds sterling
/, s. shilling, shillings
d old penny or pence: *The stamp cost 2½d.*
Cr.$ cruzeiro (Brazil)
D. Kr. krone (Denmark)
DM Deutsche Mark (Germany)
Drs. drachmae (Greece)
Esc. escudo (Portugal)
F franc (France)
I. £ pounds sterling (Israel)
N. Kr. krone (Norway)
P. peso (Mexico)
₱ peso (Philippines)
p new pence
Ptas. pesetas (Spain)
Rs. rupees (India)
RUB. ruble (U.S.S.R.)
S. Frs. francs (Switzerland)
S. Kr. krona (Sweden)
¥ yen (Japan)

Commerce

a/c account; account current
@ at
B/E, B E bill of exchange
B/L bill of lading
c/d, C/D (in bookkeeping) carried down
c/f, C/F (in bookkeeping) carried forward
c. & f. cost and freight
c.l., C/L carload, carload lots
℅ care of; (in bookkeeping) carried over
c/s, C/S cases
l/c, L/C letter of credit
P & L profit and loss; (in bookkeeping) a record to show net profit or loss
s. d., S/D sight draft
(before a figure) number: *# 10 envelopes;* (after a figure or figures) pounds
% per cent; order of
℔ per

Chemistry

+ plus; positive charge
− single bond; negative charge
⬡ benzene
→ yields
⇄ reversible reaction
↓ precipitate
↑ gas expelled
‰ salinity; parts per hundred
′ valence
⌐ or ⌙ joined
= give or form
≡ or ⇔ is equivalent

Elements

Symbol	Name	Atomic number
Ac	Actinium	89
Ag	Silver	47
Al	Aluminum	13
Am	Americium	95
Ar	Argon	18
As	Arsenic	33
At	Astatine	85
Au	Gold	79
B	Boron	5
Ba	Barium	56
Be	Beryllium	4
Bi	Bismuth	83
Bk	Berkelium	97
Br	Bromine	35
C	Carbon	6
Ca	Calcium	20
Cd	Cadmium	48
Ce	Cerium	58
Cf	Californium	98
Cl	Chlorine	17
Cm	Curium	96
Co	Cobalt	27
Cr	Chromium	24
Cs	Cesium	55
Cu	Copper	29
Dy	Dysprosium	66
Er	Erbium	68
Es	Einsteinium	99
Eu	Europium	63
F	Fluorine	9
Fe	Iron	26
Fm	Fermium	100
Fr	Francium	87
Ga	Gallium	31
Gd	Gadolinium	64
Ge	Germanium	32
H	Hydrogen	1
He	Helium	2
Hf	Hafnium	72
Hg	Mercury	80
Ho	Holmium	67
I	Iodine	53
In	Indium	49
Ir	Iridium	77
K	Potassium	19
Kr	Krypton	36
La	Lanthanum	57
Li	Lithium	3
Lu	Lutetium	71
Lw	Lawrencium	103
Md	Mendelevium	101
Mg	Magnesium	12
Mn	Manganese	25
Mo	Molybdenum	42
N	Nitrogen	7
Na	Sodium	11
Nb	Niobium	41
Nd	Neodymium	60
Ne	Neon	10
Ni	Nickel	28
No	Nobelium	102
Np	Neptunium	93
O	Oxygen	8
Os	Osmium	76
P	Phosphorus	15
Pa	Protactinium	91
Pb	Lead	82
Pd	Palladium	46
Pm	Promethium	61
Po	Polonium	84
Pr	Praseodymium	59
Pt	Platinum	78
Pu	Plutonium	94
Ra	Radium	88
Rb	Rubidium	37
Re	Rhenium	75
Rh	Rhodium	45
Rn	Radon	86
Ru	Ruthenium	44
S	Sulfur	16
Sb	Antimony	51
Sc	Scandium	21
Se	Selenium	34
Si	Silicon	14
Sm	Samarium	62
Sn	Tin	50
Sr	Strontium	38
Ta	Tantalum	73
Tb	Terbium	65
Tc	Technetium	43
Te	Tellurium	52
Th	Thorium	90
Ti	Titanium	22
Tl	Thallium	81
Tm	Thulium	69
U	Uranium	92
V	Vanadium	23
W	Tungsten	74
Xe	Xenon	54
Y	Yttrium	39
Yb	Ytterbium	70
Zn	Zinc	30
Zr	Zirconium	40

Diacritical marks

(to distinguish sounds or values of letters)

´ acute (as in the French word *née*)
` grave (as in the French word *père*)
~ tilde (as in the Spanish word *piñata*)
^ circumflex (as in the word *rôle*)
– macron (as used in pronunciation: *āge, īce, ūse*)
˘ breve (as used in pronunciation: *tăp, rĭp, fŏb*)
¨ dieresis (as in the word *Noël*)
¸ cedilla (as in the word *façade*)

Engineering and construction

Architectural plans

—·— or ℄ centerline

←→ dimension line

〰 short breakline

---- phantom line

—— extension line

------ hidden line

cutting plane

sectioning

Electrical plans Circuits

—— direct current

∼ alternating current

≈ audio frequency

crossed wires

joined wires

single phase

2 phase, 3-wire

2 phase, 4-wire

3 phase, 3-wire

3 phase Delta

2- and 3-phase tee connected

3 phase, 3-wire vee connected

start of winding

preset control

preset tapping

adjustable tapping

ground

Equipment

lighting panel

power panel

—— branch circuit; concealed in ceiling or wall

-·-·- branch circuit; concealed in floor

---- branch circuit; exposed

(G) generator

(M) motor

push button

buzzer

bell

battery

electricity meter

multicell battery, the long line is always positive

battery with polarity indicated

one-cell battery

ground

double headset receiver

antenna

dipole antenna

loop antenna

alternating current source

variable

fixed capacitor

variable capacitor

electrolytic capacitor

variable capacitor with a moving plate

resistor

variable resistor

vacuum tube

gas-filled tube

vacuum tube with grid

vacuum tube with filament

vacuum tube with plate

vacuum tube with cathode

inductor with air core

inductor with magnetic core

variable inductor

transformer with air core

transformer with iron core

p-n-p type transistor

n-p-n type transistor

inductor

diode

controlled rectifier

lamp bulb

piezoelectric crystal unit

amplifier

loudspeaker

microphone

cathode-ray tube (TV)

fuse

circuit breaker

recording head

playback head

erase head

photosensitivity

male female connectors

Outlets

outlet, single

outlet, wall

outlet, ceiling

(E) (E) electric outlet; used when circle alone might be confused with other symbols

(B) (B) blanked outlet

(D) drop cord

(F) (F) fan outlet

(J) (J) junction box

(L) (L) lamp holder

(L)PS (L)PS lamp holder with pull switch

(S) (S) pull switch

(V) (V) outlet for vapor discharge lamp

(X) (X) exit light outlet

(C) (C) clock outlet

duplex outlet

duplex outlet, split wired

duplex outlet, special purpose

1,3 convenience outlet other than duplex (1 = single, 3 = triplex, etc.)

WP weatherproof convenience outlet

R range outlet

S switch and convenience outlet

R radio and convenience outlet

special purpose outlet

floor outlet

(T) thermostat

S single pole switch

S2 double pole switch

S3 three-way switch

S4 four-way switch

SD automatic door switch

Mechanical

compressor

pneumatic compressor. △ indicates hydraulic compressor

hydraulic motor. ▼ indicates pneumatic motor

hydraulic pump

oscillating motor

(C) (G) pump, rotary and centrifugal. G indicates gas engine drive; D, diesel; M, motor; T, turbine; E, steam; C, circulating water; D, concentrate; F, boiler feed; O, oil; S, service

(G) blower, gas. Other letters as above.

engine, gas

turbine

heat exchanger

air-cooled condenser

water-cooled condenser

pipeline junction

crossed pipelines

low pressure steam supply

low pressure steam return

medium pressure steam supply

high pressure steam supply

- pneumatic flow direction
- hydraulic flow direction
- waste water
- cold water
- hot water supply
- hot water return
- vent pipe
- -CH- chilled water line
- -F- fuel line
- -G- gas line
- -V- vacuum line
- threaded pipe joint
- flanged pipe joint
- welded pipe joint
- bell and spigot pipe joint
- soldered pipe joint
- union, threaded. Other types of unions are indicated by the same type of symbols used with pipe joints
- tee joint, threaded. flanged, welded, etc. indicated in the same manner as above
- cross joint, threaded
- 90° elbow, threaded
- concentric reducer
- threaded bushing
- expansion joint flange
- check valve
- gate valve
- globe valve
- cock valve
- diaphragm valve
- safety valve
- stopcock
- pressure gauge
- thermometer

Plumbing

- bath
- shower head
- urinal
- water closet
- bidet
- WH water heater. DU means dental unit; HWT, hot water tank
- meter
- R range. B, bath; L, lavatory; S, sink; W, water storage; DW, dishwasher; LT, laundry tray
- DF drinking fountain. FD means fountain drain
- water cistern

Programming for computers

- process
- decision
- preparation
- merge
- extract
- collate
- sort
- manual input
- input/output
- online storage
- document
- punched card
- deck of cards
- punched tape
- magnetic tape
- magnetic disk
- display
- communication link
- terminal interruption

Mapping

- (red) superhighway, divided highway. Other colors indicate toll or interstate
- interchange
- no interchange
- paved main highway (various colors)
- secondary road (various colors)
- unpaved road
- broken line indicates under construction
- bridge
- tunnel
- railroad tracks
- international boundary
- state or provincial
- county
- township
- reservation
- capital city
- cities, towns
- 64 U.S. Interstate Highways
- 66 6 6 U.S. Highways (Alternate, By-pass)
- 23 state and provincial highways
- 284 secondary state, county, and provincial highways
- K county trunk highways
- Trans-Canada Highway
- 11 Mexican and Central American Highways
- U.S. and Canadian Nat'l Parks
- U.S. National Cemeteries, Historic Sites
- U.S. National Monuments
- points of interest
- 17 interchange numbers and names
- airports (commercial, military, municipal)
- state and provincial parks (with camping facilities)
- state and provincial parks (no camping facilities)
- state memorials, monuments, historic sites
- recreational areas and campsites
- colleges
- ports of entry
- springs and wells
- ranger stations

Mathematics

+ plus; positive; denoting approximate accuracy: *pi is equal to 3.14159+*
— minus; negative; denoting approximate accuracy
× times; multiplied by
· multiplied by
÷ divided by
= equals, is equal to
≠ not equal to
≈ nearly equal to
± plus or minus; positive or negative
∓ minus or plus; negative or positive
< less than
> greater than
≦ equal to or less than
≧ equal to or greater than
≮ not less than
≯ not greater than
≡ identical with
≢ not identical with
~ or ∝ proportional to
≐ approaches
→ approaches limits of
⇔ equivalent
: is to; divided by
! or ⌞ factorial product
Σ sum
∝ varies as; is directly proportional to
√ radical sign, indicating square root of
¹, ², ³ (at the right of a symbol or numeral) indicating that it is raised to the first, second, third, etc., power
∜ (²√, ³√, ⁴√, ⁵√, ⁶√), the radical sign used with indices, indicating the second, third, fourth, fifth, sixth root of
0 infinitesimal; zero
∞ infinity
() parentheses
[ ] brackets
{ } braces
— vinculum (above letters)
(these four: indicate that the enclosed quantities should be treated as a single unit)
f or *F* function
∫ integral
g the acceleration of gravity
∠; ∠s angle; angles
△; △s triangle; triangles
▱ parallelogram
▭ rectangle
□ square
○; ⓢ circle; circles
⊥ perpendicular to
∥ parallel to
π the Greek letter pi, representing the ratio of the circumference of any circle to its diameter; equal to 3.14159+
∂ or δ differential; variation
⌒ arc of circle
° degree, degrees
′ minute, minutes
″ second, seconds
≅ or ≡ congruent to
∴ therefore; hence
∵ since; because
≜ equilateral
≚ equiangular
/ single bond of affinity (between letters)
∺ geometrical proportion
∸ difference between
{ } or ∅ empty set
ε is a member of a set; j ε B
∉ is not a member of a set; k ∉ B
| such that
↔ is equivalent to; A ⟷ Z
U universal set
⊂ is included in; A ⊂ N
∪ union; A ∪ B
∩ intersection; J ∩ K

Meteorology

⊙ sunshine
rain
✱ snow
⊠ snow on ground
floating ice crystals
▲ hail
△ sleet
V frostwork
⊔ hoarfrost
≡ fog
∞ haze
T thunder
sheet lightning
thunderstorm
↖ direction
dust or sand storm
)(tornado
tropical storm
hurricane
∀ squall
visibility reduced by smoke
◎ wind calm
— wind 1-2 knots, about 1-2 (statute) mph (1.8-3.6 km/hr.)
wind 8-12 knots, 9-14 (statute) mph (14-23 km/hr.)
wind 13-17 knots, 15-20 (statute) mph (24-32 km/hr.)
wind 48-52 knots, 55-60 (statute) mph (89-97 km/hr.)
warm front, aloft
warm front, surface
cold front, aloft
cold front, surface
occluded front
stationary front
○ clear sky
scattered clouds, covering 10 per cent or less of sky
cloud cover, 20-30 per cent
cloud cover, 40 per cent
cloud cover, 50 per cent
broken clouds, covering 60-90 per cent of sky
broken clouds, 60 per cent
broken clouds, 70-80 per cent
broken clouds, 90 per cent
⊕ overcast

Nautical

Buoys

BC 7 black can #7
BS 1 black spar #1
RN 2 red nun #2
HBS horizontally banded spar
VS vertically striped spar

Lights

⊙ stationary light
floating light
stationary light #3, flashing green, visible for 9 statute miles
stationary white light, flashing in groups of two or more flashes
red buoy #28, with quick flashing red light
range lights, with true course heading

Landmarks

SPIRE ⊙ spire
STACK ⊙ stack
MAST ⊙ TR ⊙ mast or tower
FP ⊙ flagpole
tanks
buildings

Other chart symbols

submerged electrical cable (do not anchor)
limits of dredging
✱ + rock
area uncovers at low water
swamp area
triangulation station (fixed point for surveying, usually not visible from a boat).
NWS SIG STA National Weather Service Signal Station

Weather warnings

small craft advisory (red)
gale warning (red over red)
storm warning (black inside red)
night small craft advisory (red over white)
night gale warning (white over red)
night storm warning (red over red)

Traffic

International signs

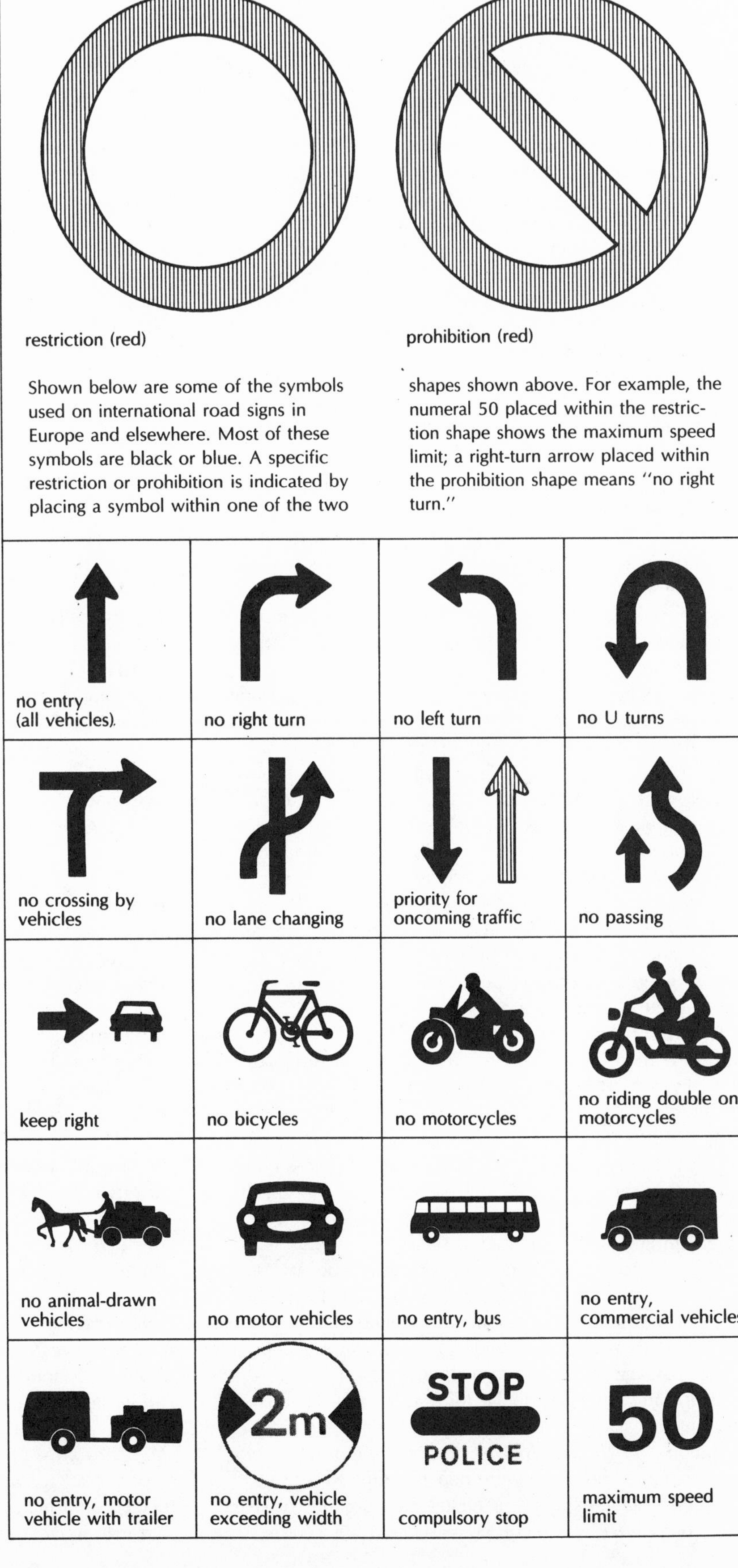
restriction (red)
prohibition (red)
Shown below are some of the symbols used on international road signs in Europe and elsewhere. Most of these symbols are black or blue. A specific restriction or prohibition is indicated by placing a symbol within one of the two shapes shown above. For example, the numeral 50 placed within the restriction shape shows the maximum speed limit; a right-turn arrow placed within the prohibition shape means "no right turn."
no entry (all vehicles)
no right turn
no left turn
no U turns
no crossing by vehicles
no lane changing
priority for oncoming traffic
no passing
keep right
no bicycles
no motorcycles
no riding double on motorcycles
no animal-drawn vehicles
no motor vehicles
no entry, bus
no entry, commercial vehicles
2m
STOP
POLICE
50
no entry, motor vehicle with trailer
no entry, vehicle exceeding width
compulsory stop
maximum speed limit

Slang and jargon

Slang is a special language used to describe ideas and things in new and novel ways. It may give standard words new meanings. Some examples are *square, drag, creep,* and *soul.* Or, it may create new words to fill particular needs. Some examples are *disk jockey, hippie,* and *funky.*

Slang may be vivid and forceful or crude and offensive. It is used because it gives people a sense of freedom and boldness, and allows them to poke fun at established institutions and violate language taboos. It is a nonviolent way to rebel against *finks, fuddy-duddies,* and *squares.*

Humor is often an ingredient of slang. When a teen-ager says, "If I'm not back at the pad in an hour, my old man will lose his cool!" his or her friends know exactly what that means. And the slang is funnier and has more visual impact than the standard "If I'm not home in an hour, my father will be angry." The same is true when a criminal says "The bims went bam and took me to the slammer," which means, "The police arrested me and took me to jail." In both cases, the speaker was facing an unpleasant situation and the use of slang helped to present an image of courage that the speaker may not have felt.

Slang helps to "break the ice" more easily than standard language. It creates an immediate sense of belonging among members of a particular group and excludes outsiders who are unfamiliar with the special language. Persons who share the same interests invent words and phrases to describe their special experiences and beliefs. Teen-agers, musicians, entertainers, and certain ethnic groups have large slang vocabularies. Often, slang vocabularies pass into general use. This may happen when the general public prefers a slang word or phrase to one in standard use, or when there is no standard word or phrase to fill a particular need. *Hoax,* meaning an act that is performed with the intention of deceiving, was slang in George Washington's day. It is probably an alteration of the word *hocus* which comes from *hocus-pocus,* a term used by swindlers in the Middle Ages.

When slang passes into general use, a group may invent new slang in order to maintain its exclusiveness. This helps explain why slang changes and grows and why there are so many slang words for the same things. For example, *bread, bacon, geetus, gelt, gravy,* and *moola* are a few of the slang words used to describe money.

The use of slang has almost always been rejected by some and welcomed by others. Ambrose Bierce, an American journalist, described slang as "the speech of him who robs the literary garbage cans on their way to the dump." But H. L. Mencken, the American editor and critic, described slang as "the most powerful of all stimulants that keep language alive and growing." He believed that "some of the most pungent and valuable words in English, especially American English," originated as slang.

No one knows exactly how or when slang began. No one even knows the origin of the word *slang.* But slang has existed for thousands of years, and it is found in almost every country. Although slang is widely used, it is not accepted as polite language or used in formal writing.

Most slang remains popular for only a short time. Then it dies out for lack of use. Expressions such as *blue fizzle* (bad recitation), *off the cob* (naive), and *cooking on the front burner* (doing very well) were popular some twenty years ago. Other slang expressions endure for hundreds of years. The word *booze* was recorded as slang in the 1200's. The expressions *beat it* and *It's Greek to me* were used by Shakespeare.

Some slang words enter the ranks of Standard English in a comparatively short time. Others wait hundreds of years to achieve this status. The word *hairdo* (slang for coiffure) became part of Standard English in less than twenty years. But *strenuous,* slang in the 1500's, was not accepted into Standard English until the 1900's.

A slang dictionary published in 1785 contained the words *duds, grub, hush money, leery,* and *pigheaded.* Of these, only *pigheaded* passed into standard use. The word *grub* remains slang. *Duds, hush money,* and *leery* are now considered as informal usage. The words *jaywalk* (slang in 1919), *racket* (1920), and *kibitz* (1935) also achieved informal status.

Slang survives or becomes part of informal language when it fills the need to characterize things in fresh ways, imparts new meanings to standard words, or offers the advantage of economy of speech by allowing a speaker to make a point forcefully and vividly with a minimum number of words. Despite the multitude of slang words and phrases that have been created through the years, comparatively few survive. Slang that fulfills the requirements of Standard English, namely the ability to communicate precise meaning or a shade of meaning, eventually ceases to be slang and becomes part of Standard English.

Jargon

Jargon has several meanings. It may mean gibberish; or a language that is not understood; or, as it is used here, the words and expressions invented by members of a special occupation or profession. It is sometimes picked up by the general public and becomes part of common slang. Here are some examples:

astronautics: *A-OK* (all systems go), *auntie* (antimissile missile), *bird* (booster rocket or missile), *buy the farm* (have a fatal crash), *glitch* (trouble), *kluge* (temporary repair)

logging: *bear fighting* (separating wood strips from boards), *boar's nest* (lumber camp), *camp strawberries* (beans), *carry the balloon* (look for work), *gut hammer* (dinner gong), *saw-log* (toothpick)

medicine: *admiral* (male nurse), *bang* (injection), *coconut grove* (skull fracture), *corn husker* (chiropodist), *finger joint* (chiropractor's office), *lollypop* (thermometer), *ward mama* (hospital nurse)

restaurant service: *a burn* (malted), *Adam and Eve on a raft* (two poached eggs on toast), *bubble dancer* (dishwasher), *cremated* (well done), *mahogany* (whole wheat), *through the garden* (with lettuce and tomato), *81* (water), *86* (no more left)

truck driving: *aviator* (speeding driver), *big hat* (state trooper), *cackle crate* (truck hauling live poultry), *deadheading* (running empty), *hood lifter* (garage mechanic), *lay on air* (apply brakes), *sheep herder* (driver with questionable ability), *rags* (bad tires), *smoke ham* (pass another vehicle), *tailboard artist* (one who thinks he is a perfect driver), *woodchuck* (driver with a low job seniority), *pots* (flares placed on a highway to warn traffic of an obstruction or hazard), *pajama wagon* (a sleeper tractor).

Words for size

If people in different countries used different words to describe the same sizes and weights, trade and other forms of communication involving measurement would be difficult and confusing. Two major systems of measurement standards are used worldwide to avoid these problems. One is the *metric system.* Dating back to the 1790's, it is the most widely used. The *customary,* or *English, system of measurement,* developed in England beginning about the 1200's, was used throughout the English-speaking world until the early 1970's. Today, the United States is the only major country in the world that has not adopted the metric system.

Converting measurements

The table opposite provides a quick and handy way to convert customary units to approximate metric units and metric units to approximate customary units. If a more exact conversion is needed, the tables on the following pages can be used. Simply look up the unit you are dealing with and multiply that unit by either its metric or customary equivalent. For example, suppose you wanted to change 10 furlongs to meters. You will find furlong in the "Length and distance table" on page 100. The metric equivalent of 1 furlong is 201.168 meters. To make the conversion, multiply the number of furlongs, 10, by the number of meters, 201.168, in one furlong: 10 × 201.168 = 2,011.68 meters. So, 10 furlongs equal 2,011.68 meters.

If you are dealing with imperial measures, the customary and metric equivalents are in the tables at the bottom of page 101 and the top of page 102.

Metric conversion table

This table will help you change measurements into and out of metric units. To use it, look up the unit you know in the left-hand column and multiply it by the number in the center column. Your answer will be approximately the number of metric units shown in the right-hand column.

When you know:	Multiply by:	To find:
Length and distance		
inches	25	millimeters
inches	2.5	centimeters
feet	30	centimeters
feet	0.3	meters
yards	0.9	meters
miles	1.6	kilometers
millimeters	0.04	inches
centimeters	0.4	inches
meters	3.3	feet
meters	1.1	yards
kilometers	0.6	miles
Surface or area		
square inches	6.5	square centimeters
square feet	0.09	square meters
square yards	0.83	square meters
square miles	2.6	square kilometers
acres	0.4	hectares
square centimeters	0.16	square inches
square meters	1.2	square yards
square kilometers	0.4	square miles
hectares	2.4	acres
Volume and capacity		
ounces (fluid)	30	milliliters
pints	0.47	liters
quarts	0.95	liters
gallons	3.8	liters
milliliters	0.034	ounces (fluid)
liters	2.1	pints
liters	1.06	quarts
liters	0.26	gallons
Weight and mass		
ounces	28	grams
pounds	0.45	kilograms
tons	0.9	metric tons
grams	0.035	ounces
kilograms	2.2	pounds
metric tons	1.1	tons
Temperature		
degrees Fahrenheit	0.55 (after subtracting 32)	degrees Celsius
degrees Celsius	1.8 (then add 32)	degrees Fahrenheit

Length and distance

Customary		Metric
1 inch (in.)		2.54 cm
1 foot (ft.)	12 in.	30.48 cm
1 yard (yd.)	3 ft.	0.9144 m
1 rod (rd.)	5½ yd.	5.0292 m
1 furlong (fur.)	40 rd., or ⅛ mi.	201.168 m
1 statute mile (mi.)	5,280 ft.	1.6093 km
1 league (statute)	3 mi.	4.8280 km

Metric		Customary
1 nanometer (nm)		0.00000003937 in.
1 micron (μ)	1,000 nm	0.00003937 in.
1 millimeter (mm)	1,000 μ	0.03937 in.
1 centimeter (cm)	10 mm	0.3937 in.
1 decimeter (dm)	10 cm	3.937 in.
1 meter (m)	10 dm	39.37 in.
1 dekameter (dam)	10 m	393.7 in.
1 hectometer (hm)	10 dkm	328.0833 ft.
1 kilometer (km)	10 hm	0.62137 mi.

Nautical

		Customary	Metric
1 span		9 in.	22.8 cm
1 fathom (fm.)	8 spans	6 ft.	1.83 m
1 cable's length	120 fathoms	720 ft.	219.46 m
1 nautical mile, or 1 international nautical mile		6,076.11549 ft., or 1.150779 statute mi.	1.852 km
1 league (nautical)	3 nautical miles	3.452338 statute mi.	5.556 km
1 degree	60 nautical miles (nominal)	69.046740 statute mi.	111.119266 km

Surveyor's, or Gunter's, chain

		Customary	Metric
1 link (li.)		7.92 in.	20.12 cm
1 chain (ch.)	100 li.	66 ft.	20.12 m
1 furlong (fur.)	10 ch.	660 ft.	201.168 m
1 statute mile (mi.)	8 fur.	5,280 ft.	1.6093 km

Engineer's chain

		Customary	Metric
1 link (li.)		1 ft.	30.48 cm
1 chain (ch.)	100 li.	100 ft.	30.48 m
1 mile (mi.)	52.8 ch.	5,280 ft.	1.6093 km

Surface or area

Customary		Metric
1 square inch (sq. in.)		6.4516 cm²
1 square foot (sq. ft.)	144 sq. in.	0.0929 m²
1 square yard (sq. yd.)	9 sq. ft.	0.8361 m²
1 square rod (sq. rd.)	30¼ sq. yd.	25.293 m²
1 acre (A.)	160 sq. rd.	0.4047 ha
1 square mile (sq. mi.)	640 A.	258.9988 ha, or 2.590 km²

Metric		Customary
1 square millimeter (mm²)		0.002 sq. in.
1 square centimeter (cm²)	100 mm²	0.155 sq. in.
1 square decimeter (dm²)	100 cm²	15.5 sq. in.
1 square meter (m²)	100 dm²	1,550 sq. in.
1 square dekameter (dam²)	100 m²	119.6 sq. yd.
1 square hectometer (hm²)	100 dam²	2.4711 acres
1 square kilometer (km²)	100 hm²	247.105 acres or 0.3861 sq. mi.

Metric land measurement

Metric		Customary
1 centiare (ca)		1,550 sq. in.
1 are (a)	100 ca	119.6 sq. yd.
1 hectare (ha)	100 a	2.4711 acres
1 square kilometer (km²)	100 ha	247.105 acres, or 0.3861 sq. mi.

Surveyor's land measurement

		Customary	Metric
1 square link (sq. li.)		62.73 sq. in.	404.686 cm^2
1 square pole (sq. p.)	625 sq. li.	30.25 sq. yd.	25.293 m^2
1 square chain (sq. ch.)	16 sq. p.	484 sq. yd.	404.686 m^2
1 acre (A.)	10 sq. ch.	4,840 sq. yd.	4,046.856 m^2
1 section (sec.)	640 A.	1 sq. mi.	2.589 km^2
1 township (tp.)	36 sec.	36 sq. mi.	93.240 km^2

Volume and capacity

Volume measurement

Customary		Metric
1 cubic inch (cu. in.)		16.387 cm^3
1 cubic foot (cu. ft.)	1,728 cu. in.	0.0283 m^3
1 cubic yard (cu. yd.)	27 cu. ft.	0.7646 m^3

Metric		Customary
1 cubic millimeter (mm^3)		0.00006 cu. in.
1 cubic centimeter (cm^3)	1,000 mm^3	0.0610 cu. in.
1 cubic decimeter (dm^3)	1,000 cm^3	0.0353 cu. ft.
1 cubic meter (m^3)	1,000 dm^3	1.308 cu. yd.
1 cubic dekameter (dam^3)	1,000 m^3	1,308 cu. yd.
1 cubic hectometer (hm^3)	1,000 dam^3	1,308,000 cu. yd.

Metric capacity measure

Metric		Customary
1 milliliter (ml)		0.0610 cu. in.
1 centiliter (cl)	10 ml	0.6103 cu. in.
1 deciliter (dl)	10 cl	6.1025 cu. in.
1 liter (l)	10 dl	61.025 cu. in., or 1.057 liquid qt., or 0.908 dry qt.
1 dekaliter (dal)	10 l	610.25 cu. in.
1 hectoliter (hl)	10 dal	6,102.55 cu. in.
1 kiloliter (kl)	10 hl	35.316 cu. ft., or 264.179 gal., or 28.38 bu.

Household capacity measurement

Customary			Metric
1 teaspoon		1/6 fl. oz.	4.9 ml
1 tablespoon	3 teaspoons	½ fl. oz.	14.8 ml
1 cup	16 tablespoons	8 fl. oz.	236.6 ml
1 pint	2 cups	16 fl. oz.	473.2 ml
1 quart	2 pints	32 fl. oz.	946.3 ml
1 gallon	4 quarts	128 fl. oz.	3.785 l

Customary liquid capacity measurement

Customary			Metric
1 gill (gi.)		7.219 cu. in.	0.1183 l
1 pint (pt.)	4 gi.	28.875 cu. in.	0.4732 l
1 quart (qt.)	2 pt.	57.75 cu. in.	0.9463 l
1 gallon (gal.)	4 qt.	231 cu. in.	3.7854 l
1 barrel (liquids) (bbl.)	31.5 gal.	4.21 cu. ft.	119.24 l
1 barrel (petroleum) (bbl.)	42 gal.	5.61 cu. ft.	158.98 l

Imperial	Customary		Metric
1 imperial quart	1.201 U.S. qt.	69.354 cu. in.	1.13652 l
1 imperial gallon	1.201 U.S. gal.	277.42 cu. in.	4.54609 l

Customary dry capacity measurement

Customary			Metric
1 pint (pt.)		33.600 cu. in.	550.61 cm^3
1 quart (qt.)	2 pt.	67.20 cu. in.	1,101.22 cm^3
1 peck (pk.)	8 qt.	537.61 cu. in.	8,809.77 cm^3
1 bushel (bu.)	4 pk.	2,150.42 cu. in.	0.035239 m^3
1 barrel (bbl.)		4.08 cu. ft.	0.115627 m^3

Imperial	Customary		Metric
1 imperial quart	1.032 U.S. qt.	69.354 cu. in.	1,136.52 cm^3
1 imperial bushel	1.032 U.S. bu.	2,219.36 cu. in.	0.03637 m^3

Apothecaries' fluid measurement

		Customary	Metric
1 minim or drop (min. or m)		0.002083 fl. oz.	0.0616 ml
1 fluid dram (fl. dr. or *f*ʒ)	60 min.	0.125 fl. oz.	3.6966 ml
1 fluid ounce (fl. oz. or *f*℥)	8 fl. dr.	1 fl. oz.	0.0296 l
1 pint (O.)	16 fl. oz.	16 fl. oz.	0.4732 l
1 gallon (C.)	8 O.	128 fl. oz.	3.7853 l

Shipping capacity measurement

		Customary	Metric
1 barrel bulk		5 cu. ft.	0.1416 m^3
1 shipping ton, or 1 measurement ton, or 1 freight ton,	**8 barrels bulk**	40 cu. ft.	1.1327 m^3
1 displacement ton		35 cu. ft.	0.9911 m^3
1 register ton		100 cu. ft.	2.8317 m^3

Weight and mass

Avoirdupois weight

		Metric
1 grain (gr.)		0.0648 g
1 dram (dr.)	27.34375 gr.	1.7718 g
1 ounce (oz.)	16 dr.	28.3495 g
1 pound (lb.)	16 oz.	453.5924 g, or 0.4536 kg
1 hundredweight (cwt.)	100 lb.	45.3592 kg
1 short ton	2,000 lb.	907.18 kg, or 0.9072 t

Special British units	Customary	Metric
1 stone (st.)	14 lb.	6.35 kg
1 hundredweight (cwt.)	112 lb.	50.80 kg
1 long ton	2,240 lb.	1,016.05 kg, or 1.0160 t

Metric weight

		Avoirdupois
1 milligram (mg)		0.0154 gr.
1 centigram (cg)	10 mg	0.1543 gr.
1 decigram (dg)	10 cg	1.5432 gr.
1 gram (g)	10 dg	15.4324 gr.
1 dekagram (dag)	10 g	0.3527 oz.
1 hectogram (hg)	10 dag	3.5274 oz.
1 kilogram (kg)	10 hg	2.2046 lb.
1 quintal (q)	100 kg	220.46 lb.
1 metric ton (t)	1,000 kg	2,204.62 lb.

Apothecaries' weight

		Avoirdupois	Metric
1 grain (gr.)		0.002286 oz.	0.0648 g
1 scruple (s. ap. or ℈)	20 gr.	0.04571 oz.	1.296 g
1 dram (dr. ap. or ʒ)	3 s. ap.	0.1371 oz.	3.888 g
1 ounce (oz. ap. or ℥)	8 dr. ap.	1.0971 oz.	31.1035 g
1 pound (lb. ap. or ℔)	12 oz. ap.	13.1657 oz.	373.24 g, or 0.3732 kg

Troy weight

		Avoirdupois	Metric
1 grain (gr.)		0.002286 oz.	0.0648 g
1 pennyweight (dwt.)	24 gr.	0.054857 oz.	1.56 g
1 ounce (oz. t.)	20 dwt.	1.0971 oz.	31.1035 g
1 pound (lb. t.)	12 oz. t.	13.1657 oz.	373.24 g, or 0.3732 kg

Temperature

Fahrenheit (°F.) temperatures

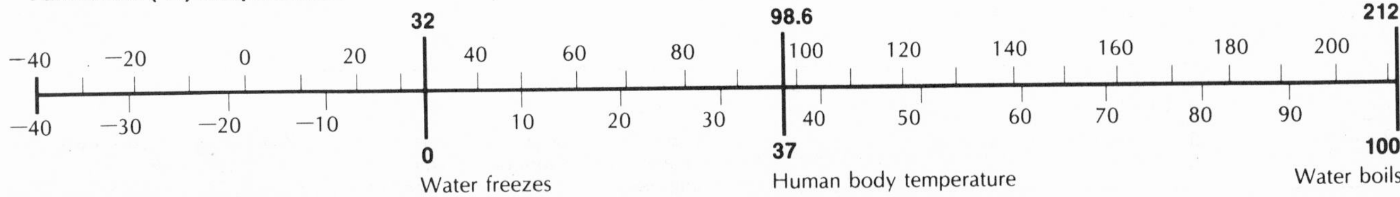

Celsius (°C) temperatures

Time

1 picosecond (ps)		0.000000000001 s
1 nanosecond (ns)		0.000000001 s
1 microsecond (μs)	1,000 ns	0.000001 s
1 millisecond (ms)	1,000 μs	0.001 s
1 second (s)	1,000 ms	1/3,600 hr.
1 minute (min.)	60 s	1/60 hr.
1 hour (hr.)	60 min.	
1 day (da.)	24 hr.	
1 week (wk.)	7 da.	
1 lunar year (yr.)	354 da.	
1 solar year	365 1/4 da.	
1 calendar year	365 da.	
1 leap year	366 da.	
1 decade	10 yr.	
1 century	100 yr.	
1 millennium	1,000 yr.	

Other measures

Circular and angular measurement

Degrees

1 second (″)		1/1,296,000 circle
1 minute (′)	60 seconds	1/21,600 circle
1 degree (°)	60 minutes	1/360 circle
1 quadrant, or 1 right angle	90 degrees	¼ circle
1 circumference	4 quadrants	1 circle

Radians

0.017454 radians (rad.)	1°
1 radian	57.2958°
2π radians	360°

Mils

1 mil	0.056250°
17.778 mils	1°
6,400 mils	360°

Counting measure

1 dozen (doz.)		12 units
1 gross (gr.)	12 doz.	144 units
1 great gross	12 gr.	1,728 units

Paper measure

1 quire (qr.)	24 or 25 sheets
1 ream (rm.)	20 quires
1 perfect ream	516 sheets
1 bundle (bdl.)	2 reams

Printing measure

		Customary	Metric
1 point		approx. 1/72 or 0.013837 in.	0.3514598 mm
1 pica	12 points	approx. 1/6 or 0.166044 in.	4.2175176 mm

Wood measurement

Customary		Metric
1 board foot (bd. ft.)	144 cu. in. (1 ft. X 1 ft. X 1 in.)	.00236 m³
1 cord foot (cd. ft.)	16 cu. ft. (4 ft. X 4 ft. X 1 ft.)	0.4531 m³
1 cord (cd.)	8 cd. ft. (4 ft. X 4 ft. X 8 ft.)	3.625 m³

Metric		Customary
1 stere	1 m³	1.3079 cu. yd., or 0.2759 cord

Lumber

Lumber is bought and sold by nominal sizes, but these differ from the actual sizes of the finished or surfaced wood. The following actual sizes apply to minimum-dressed dry softwood.

Nominal size, inches	Actual size, inches	Board feet per foot of length
1 x 2	¾ x 1½	1/6
1 x 4	¾ x 3½	1/3
1 x 6	¾ x 5½	½
1 x 8	¾ x 7¼	2/3
1 x 10	¾ x 9¼	5/6
1 x 12	¾ x 11¼	1
2 x 2	1½ x 1½	1/3
2 x 4	1½ x 3½	2/3
2 x 6	1½ x 5½	1
2 x 8	1½ x 7¼	1 1/3
2 x 10	1½ x 9¼	1 2/3
2 x 12	1½ x 11¼	2
3 x 6	2½ x 5½	1½
4 x 4	3½ x 3½	1 1/3
4 x 6	3½ x 5½	2
4 x 8	3½ x 7¼	2 2/3
4 x 10	3½ x 9¼	3 1/3

Nails

Penny size (d)	Length, inches	Length, centimeters	Common nails per pound	Casing nails per pound	Finishing nails per pound
2	1	2.5	875	1,000	1,350
3	1¼	3.2	550	625	850
4	1½	3.8	300	450	600
6	2	5.1	175	225	300
8	2½	6.4	100	150	200
10	3	7.6	65	95	125
16	3½	8.8	45	70	
20	4	10.0	30		
50	5½	13.8			

Screws

Wood screw number	Body diameter, inches	Body diameter, centimeters	Shank hole, wood drill number	Thread hole, wood drill number
0	1/16	.156	2	
2	3/32	.234	3	2
5	1/8	.313	4	3
7	5/32	.390	5	4
9	3/16	.470	6	5
12	7/32	.547	7	6
14	1/4	.625	8	7
16	9/32	.703	9	8
18	5/16	.781	10	9

Miscellaneous measures and weights

Angstrom is a unit once used with the metric system to measure small distances. It equals 0.0000001 of a millimeter (0.0000000039 inch).
Assay Ton, used for testing ore, equals 29.167 grams (1.029 ounces).
Bolt, used in measuring cloth, equals 120 feet (36.6 meters).
Butt, formerly used for liquids, commonly equals 126 gallons of wine (477 liters).
Catty, used to measure tea and other materials, weighs about 1 1/3 pounds (0.6 kilogram).
Chaldron, a capacity measure, equals 36 imperial bushels (1.31 cubic meters).
Cubit, in the customary system, is 18 inches (46 centimeters). It is based on the length of the forearm.
Ell, used in measuring cloth, equals 45 inches (114 centimeters).
Firkin, used to measure lard or butter, equals either about 9 imperial gallons (40.9 liters) or about 56 pounds (25 kilograms).
Fortnight is a period of 14 days.
Hand, used to measure the height of horses, from the ground to the withers, equals 4 inches (10 centimeters).
Hogshead, used to measure liquids, equals 63 gallons (238 liters).
Kilderkin, used to measure liquids, equals 18 imperial gallons (82 liters).
Knot is a speed of 1 nautical mile (1.1508 statute miles or 1.852 kilometers) per hour.
Light-Year, the distance light travels in a year. It is about 5.88 trillion miles (9.46 trillion kilometers).
Line, used to measure buttons, is 1/40 inch (0.6 millimeter).
Load, of earth or gravel, equals 1 cubic yard (0.76 cubic meter).
Mole is a metric base unit for the amount of a substance. It equals 602,257,000,000,000,000,000,000 atoms, molecules, or whatever other elemental particles are being measured.
Nail, used in measuring cloth, equals 2.25 inches (5.72 centimeters).
Palm equals 3 or 4 inches (8 or 10 centimeters).
Perch, used for masonry, equals 24.75 cubic feet (0.7 cubic meter).
Perch, a measure of length in the customary system, equals 1 rod (5.03 meters).
Pin, used to measure liquids, equals 4½ gallons (17 liters).
Pipe, used to measure liquids, equals 126 gallons (477 liters).
Pole, a measure of length in the customary system, equals 1 rod (5.03 meters).
Puncheon, used to measure liquids, equals 84 gallons (318 liters).
Quarter, used to measure grain, equals 25 pounds (11 kilograms).
Rood, used to measure land, equals ¼ acre (0.1 hectare).
Score is a group of 20.
Skein, used to measure yarn, equals 360 feet (110 meters).
Tierce, used to measure liquids, equals 42 gallons (159 liters).
Tun, used to measure liquids, equals 252 gallons (954 liters).
Vara, used to measure land, equals 33 1/3 inches (84.6 centimeters) in Texas; 33 inches (84 centimeters) in California; and from 32 to 43 inches (81 to 109 centimeters) in Spain, Portugal, and Latin-American countries.

Wire

Wire size is indicated by gauge, or diameter. *American,* or *Brown and Sharpe,* is the standard gauge used in the United States for copper and other electric wire. Sometimes the *imperial* gauge of England is used. The *steel wire gauge* is the standard for steel wire in the United States.

Diameter in inches

Gauge No.	American or Brown & Sharpe	Steel wire	Imperial or British
00000000			
0000000		0.4900	0.500
000000		0.4615	0.464
00000		0.4305	0.432
0000	0.4600	0.3938	0.400
000	0.4096	0.3625	0.372
00	0.3648	0.3310	0.348
0	0.3249	0.3065	0.324
1	0.2893	0.2830	0.300
2	0.2576	0.2625	0.276
3	0.2294	0.2437	0.252
4	0.2043	0.2253	0.232
5	0.1819	0.2070	0.212
6	0.1620	0.1920	0.192
7	0.1443	0.1770	0.176
8	0.1285	0.1620	0.160
9	0.1144	0.1483	0.144
10	0.1019	0.1350	0.128
11	0.09074	0.1205	0.116
12	0.08081	0.1055	0.104
13	0.07196	0.0915	0.092
14	0.06408	0.0800	0.080
15	0.05707	0.0720	0.072
16	0.05082	0.0625	0.064
17	0.04526	0.0540	0.056
18	0.04030	0.0475	0.048
19	0.03589	0.0410	0.040
20	0.03196	0.0348	0.036
21	0.02846	0.0317	0.032
22	0.02535	0.0286	0.028
23	0.02257	0.0258	0.024
24	0.02010	0.0230	0.022
25	0.01790	0.0204	0.020
26	0.01594	0.0181	0.018
27	0.01419	0.0173	0.0164
28	0.01264	0.0162	0.0149
29	0.01126	0.0150	0.0136
30	0.01003	0.0140	0.0124
31	0.008928	0.0132	0.0116
32	0.007950	0.0128	0.0108
33	0.007080	0.0118	0.0100
34	0.006304	0.0104	0.0092
35	0.005614	0.0095	0.0084
36	0.005000	0.0090	0.0076
37	0.004453	0.0085	0.0068
38	0.003965	0.0080	0.0060
39	0.003531	0.0075	0.0052
40	0.003145	0.0070	0.0048
41		0.0066	0.0044
42		0.0062	0.0040
43		0.0060	0.0036
44		0.0058	0.0032
45		0.0055	0.0028
46		0.0052	0.0024
47		0.0050	0.0020
48		0.0048	0.0016
49		0.0046	0.0012
50		0.0044	0.0010

Diameter in centimeters

Gauge No.	American or Brown & Sharpe	Steel wire	Imperial or British
00000000			
0000000		1.2446	1.27
000000		1.1723	1.18
00000		1.0935	1.10
0000	1.168	1.0003	1.02
000	1.040	0.9208	0.945
00	0.9266	0.8408	0.884
0	0.8252	0.7786	0.823
1	0.7348	0.7189	0.762
2	0.6543	0.6668	0.701
3	0.5827	0.6190	0.640
4	0.5189	0.5723	0.589
5	0.4620	0.5258	0.538
6	0.4115	0.4877	0.488
7	0.3665	0.4496	0.447
8	0.3264	0.4115	0.406
9	0.2906	0.3767	0.366
10	0.2588	0.3429	0.325
11	0.2305	0.3061	0.295
12	0.2053	0.2680	0.264
13	0.1828	0.2325	0.234
14	0.1628	0.2032	0.203
15	0.1450	0.1829	0.183
16	0.1291	0.1588	0.163
17	0.1150	0.1372	0.142
18	0.1024	0.1207	0.122
19	0.09116	0.1042	0.102
20	0.08118	0.0884	0.0914
21	0.07229	0.0806	0.0813
22	0.06439	0.0727	0.0711
23	0.05733	0.0656	0.0610
24	0.05105	0.0585	0.0559
25	0.04547	0.0519	0.0508
26	0.04049	0.0460	0.0457
27	0.03604	0.0440	0.0417
28	0.03211	0.0412	0.0378
29	0.02860	0.0381	0.0345
30	0.02548	0.0356	0.0315
31	0.02268	0.0336	0.0295
32	0.02019	0.0326	0.0274
33	0.01798	0.0300	0.0254
34	0.01601	0.0265	0.0234
35	0.01426	0.0242	0.0213
36	0.01270	0.0229	0.0193
37	0.01131	0.0216	0.0173
38	0.01007	0.0204	0.0152
39	0.008969	0.0191	0.0132
40	0.007988	0.0178	0.0122
41		0.0168	0.0112
42		0.0158	0.0102
43		0.0153	0.0091
44		0.0148	0.0081
45		0.0140	0.0071
46		0.0132	0.0061
47		0.0127	0.0051
48		0.0122	0.0041
49		0.0117	0.0030
50		0.0112	0.0025

First names— where they come from and what they mean

Almost everyone wants to know what her or his first name, or given name, means. The following list provides this information for many common names. Women's names which are the same or similar to given men's names are omitted. Also excluded are minor variations in spelling of these names. Meanings separated by commas denote the fact that the name is composed of two words or name-elements with different meanings. Semicolons indicate disagreement between authorities over the meanings, or that the names arose in different languages. Those names noted as Hebrew or Aramaic come from the Bible.

Women's names

A

Abigail (*Hebrew*) My father rejoices.
Ada, Adah (*Hebrew*) Ornament.
Adelaide, Adeline (*Germanic*) Noble, kind.
Adriana (*Latin*) Of the Greek city of Adria.
Agatha (*Greek*) Good.
Agnes (*Latin*) Lamb; sacred and pure.
Aileen (*Greek*) Light.
Alberta (*Germanic*) Noble, bright.
Alethea (*Greek*) Truth.
Alexa, Alexandria (*Greek*) Helper of men.
Alice, Alison (*Germanic*) Noble, kind.
Allegra (*Old French-Latin*) Sprightly; cheerful.
Alma (*Latin*) Kind; from the river Alma.
Alva (*Latin*) White.
Amanda (*Latin*) Lovable.
Amity (*Latin*) Friendly.
Anastasia (*Greek*) Arise again.
Andrea (*Greek*) Brave.
Angela (*Greek*) Angelic.
Ann, Anna, Anne (*Hebrew*) Grace; God has been gracious.
Annabel (*Scottish*) Lovable or amiable.
Antoinette (*Latin*) Inestimable.
April (*Latin*) Open; from the month.
Arabella (*Germanic, Scottish*) Eagle, heroine; lovable.
Ariadne (*Greek*) Most holy.
Arlene (*Celtic*) Pledge.
Athena (*Greek*) From Athena, the goddess of wisdom.
Audrey (*Germanic*) Noble, strength.
Augusta (*Latin*) Exalted or venerable.
Aurora (*Latin*) Dawn.
Ava (*Latin*) Bird.

B

Barbara (*Greek*) Stranger.
Beatrice (*Latin*) She who blesses.
Bella (*Latin*) Beautiful; oath of God.
Benita (*Latin*) Blessed.
Bernadette, Bernadine (*Germanic*) Bear, firm.
Bernice (*Greek*) Bringer of victory.
Bertha (*Germanic*) Bright.
Beryl (*Greek*) From the jewel beryl.
Betty (*Hebrew*) Oath of God.
Beulah (*Hebrew*) Married.
Beverly (*Old English*) From Beverley, England.
Blanche (*Latin-French*) White or fair.
Blossom (*Old English*) Flower or bloom.
Bonita (*Latin-French*) Good.
Brenda (*Norse*) Sword.
Bridget (*Celtic*) Strength.
Buena (*Spanish*) Good.

C

Camilla (*Etruscan*) Attendant at a sacrifice.
Candace (*Latin*) Glowing.
Candita (*Latin*) White.
Cara (*Celtic*) Friend.
Carla, Carlotta (*Germanic*) Man.
Carmen (Hebrew, Latin) Garden of God; song.
Carol, Caroline (*Germanic-Old French*) Man; song of joy.
Cassandra (*Greek*) Helper of men.
Catherine (*Greek*) Pure.
Cecelia, Celia (*Latin*) Blind; the heavens.
Celeste (*Latin*) Heavenly.
Charis (*Greek*) Loving; grace.
Charity (*Latin*) Charitable.
Charlotte (*Germanic*) Man.
Charmian (*Greek*) A little joy.
Chenoa (*American Indian*) White dove.
Cherry (*Latin*) Charitable.
Cheryl (*Germanic*) Man.
Chloe (*Greek*) Bloom.
Christabel (*Greek*) Christ's beauty.
Christiana (*Latin*) Christian.
Christine (*Old English*) Christened one.
Cindy (*Greek*) From Mt. Cynthus; Diana, moon goddess.
Clara, Clare, Clarissa (*Latin*) Bright.
Claribel (*Latin*) Bright and fair.
Claudette (*Latin*) Little lame one.
Claudia (*Latin*) Lame.
Clematis (*Greek*) Clinging vine.
Clemence, Clementine (*Latin*) Mild, merciful.
Cleopatra (*Greek*) Fame of her father.
Clotilda (*Germanic*) Loud, battle.
Colette (*Latin-French*) People's victory.
Colleen (*Celtic*) Girl.
Columbia, Columbine (*Latin*) Dove.
Concordia (*Latin*) Harmony.
Constance (*Latin*) Firm of purpose.
Consuela (*Spanish*) Consolation.
Cora, Corinne (*Greek*) Maiden.
Coral, Coralie (*Greek*) Bright colored stone.
Cordelia (*Celtic, Germanic*) Sea daughter; heart.
Cornelia (*Latin*) Hornlike.
Crystal (*Greek*) Clear ice; frost.
Cymbaline (*Celtic*) Lord of the sun.
Cynthia (*Greek*) From Mt. Cynthus; Diana, moon goddess.

D

Dagmar (*Danish*) Glory of the Danes.
Dahlia (*Swedish*) Valley; flower dahlia.
Daisy (*Old English*) Day's eye; flower daisy; pearl.
Dama (*Latin*) Lady.

Damaris (*Greek*) Gentle.
Daphne (*Greek*) The laurel tree.
Darlene, Daryl (*Old English*) Tenderly beloved.
Dawn (*Old English*) Break of day.
Deanna (*Latin*) Bright as day.
Deborah, Debra (*Hebrew*) The bee.
Deidre, Deirdre (*Celtic*) Sorrow.
Delia, Della (*Greek*) From the island of Delos.
Delicia (*Latin*) Delightful.
Delight (*Germanic*) Pleasurable.
Denise (*Latin*) Belonging to Dionysus, Greek god of wine.
Desirée (*Latin-French*) Desired.
Diane (*Latin*) From Diana, Greek moon goddess.
Dinah (*Hebrew*) Judgment.
Dolores (*Spanish*) Of the sorrows (Mary).
Donna (*Latin*) Lady.
Dora (*Greek*) Gift.
Dorcas (*Greek*) Gazelle.
Doris (*Greek*) Of the sea; of the Dorian people.
Dorothy (*Greek*) Gift of God.
Dulcia (*Latin*) Sweet.

E

Easter (*Old English*) From Eostre, the Old English goddess of spring.
Eda, Edith (*Old English*) Rich, war.
Eden (*Hebrew*) Delight.
Edna (*Hebrew*) Delight.
Effie (*Greek*) Of fair fame; worship of the gods.
Eileen, Elaine, Eleanor (*Greek*) Light; bright one.
Electra (*Greek*) Bright or shining.
Elissa, Eliza, Elizabeth (*Hebrew*) Oath of God.
Ella (*Old English, Norman-French*) Elfin; all.
Ellen (*Greek*) Light; the bright one.
Elma (*Greek*) Amiable.
Eloise (*Germanic-French*) Hale, wide; hear, fight.
Elsa, Elsie (*Hebrew*) Oath of God.
Emerald (*Latin*) Transparent green beryl, the emerald.
Emily (*Latin-Germanic*) Affable; worker.
Emma (*Germanic*) Universal.
Enid (*Welsh*) Soul or life; woodlark.
Enrica (*Germanic*) Home, rule.
Erica (*Germanic-Latin*) Rule, heather.
Ermentrude (*Germanic*) Universal, strength.
Ernestine (*Germanic*) Grave or serious; earnest.
Esmé (*Greek*) The emerald.
Esmeralda (*Greek-Spanish*) The emerald.
Estelle (*Latin*) A star.
Esther (*Hebrew-Persian*) Myrtle; a star.
Ethel (*Old English*) Noble.
Etta (*Germanic*) Small or little.
Eunice (*Greek*) Happy victory.
Euphemia (*Greek*) Of fair fame; worship of the gods.
Eva, Eve (*Hebrew*) Life; lively.
Evangeline (*Greek*) Bearer of good tidings.
Evelyn (*Celtic-Latin*) Pleasant; life; hazel.

F

Faith (*Latin*) Faithful.
Fanny (*Germanic*) Free.
Fay (*Latin-Old French*) Faithful; fairy or elf.
Felicia (*Latin*) Happiness.
Felipa (*Greek*) Lover of horses.
Fifi (*Hebrew-French*) He shall add.
Flavia (*Latin*) Yellow.
Flora (*Latin*) A flower.
Florence, Florenda (*Latin*) Flourishing; of Florence.
Frances, Francesca (*Germanic*) Free.
Freda, Frederica, Frieda (*Germanic*) Peace, rule.

G

Gabrielle (*Hebrew*) God is my strength.
Gail, Gale (*Old English*) Gay.
Gay (*French-Germanic*) Merry.
Genevieve (*Celtic*) White or fair lady.
Georgia (*Greek*) An earth worker or farmer.
Geraldine, Germaine (*Germanic*) Spear, rule.
Gertrude (*Germanic*) Spear, strength.
Gladys (*Latin-Welsh*) Lame; ruler.
Gloria (*Latin*) Glorious; song of praise to God.
Godiva (*Old English*) God, gift.
Grace (*Latin*) Thanksgiving.
Greta, Gretchen (*Greek*) A pearl.
Guenevere, Gwynne (*Celtic*) White, fair lady.
Gwendolyn (*Celtic*) White-browed.

H

Hannah (*Hebrew*) Grace; God has been gracious.
Harriet (*Germanic*) Home, rule.
Hazel (*Old English*) Of the hazel tree.
Heather (*Scottish*) Of the shrub heather.
Hedda (*Old English*) Robe.
Helen (*Greek*) Light.
Helga (*Norse*) Holy.
Hephzibah (*Hebrew*) On whom is my delight.
Hermione (*Greek*) Of the earth; of Hermes, messenger god.
Hester (*Persian*) A star.
Hilda (*Germanic*) War or battle.
Hildegarde (*Germanic*) War, knowledge.
Holly (*Old English*) Of the shrub holly.
Hope (*Old English*) Expectation of something desired.
Hyacinth (*Greek-Irish*) Of the plant hyacinth.

I

Ida (*Germanic*) Work; industrious.
Ileana (*Greek*) From ancient Ilium, or Troy.
Imogene (*Latin, Celtic*) Image; girl or daughter.
Inez (*Greek-Spanish*) Lamb; sacred and pure.
Ingrid (*Old Norse*) Daughter.
Iona (*Greek*) Violet-colored stone.
Irene (*Greek*) Peace; messenger of peace.
Iris (*Greek*) Rainbow.
Irma (*Germanic*) Universal.
Irvette (*Old English*) Sea friend.
Isabel (*Hebrew-French*) Oath of God, oath of Baal.
Ivy (*Germanic*) Clinging; from the plant ivy.

J-K

Jackie (*Hebrew*) Gracious gift of God.
Jacqueline (*Hebrew*) May God protect; the supplanter.
Jane, Janet, Jean (*Hebrew*) Gracious gift of God.
Jemima (*Hebrew*) Dove.
Jennifer (*Celtic*) White wave.
Jenny, Jessica (*Hebrew*) Gracious gift of God.
Jewel (*Latin*) Precious stone.
Jill (*Latin-Greek*) Downy-face, youthful.
Joan, Johanna (*Hebrew*) Gracious gift of God.
Jocelyn (*Latin, Germanic*) Merry; a Goth.
Josephine (*Hebrew*) May God add.
Joyce (*Old French*) Joyful; merry.
Judith, Judy (*Hebrew*) Praised; a Jewess.
Julia, Juliet (*Latin-Greek*) Downy-face, youthful.
June (*Latin*) Youthful; from the month.
Justine (*Latin*) Just.
Karen (*Greek-Danish*) Pure.
Karla (*Germanic*) Man.
Katharine, Kathleen (*Greek*) Pure.
Kay (*Greek, Latin*) Pure; rejoicing.
Kirsten (*Latin*) Christian.

L

Lana (*Greek*) Light.
Laura, Laurel, Loretta (*Latin*) Laurel, victory.
Lee (*Old English*) Dweller at the meadow.
Leila (*Arabic*) Darkness.
Leilani (*Hawaiian*) Heavenly wreath.
Lenora (*Greek*) Light; the bright one.
Leslie (*Scottish*) From Leslie, garden of hollies.
Letitia (*Latin*) Joy or gladness.
Lillian (*Greek-Hebrew*) From the lily; oath of God.

Lily (*Latin*) From the flower lily.
Linda (*Germanic*) Serpent; lithe.
Lisa (*Hebrew*) Oath of God.
Lois (*Germanic, Greek*) Hear, fight; more desirable.
Lola (*Spanish, Germanic*) Of the sorrows (Mary); man.
Lori (*Latin*) The laurel, symbol of victory.
Lotus (*Latin*) From the flower lotus.
Louisa, Louise (*Germanic-French*) Hear, fight.
Lucia, Lucille, Lucy (*Latin*) Light.
Lulu (*Persian*) Pearl.
Lydia (*Greek*) A woman of Lydia.
Lynn (*Old English*) Dweller at or near a pool.

M

Mabel (*Latin*) Lovable; amiable.
Madeline (*Aramaic*) Woman from Magdala; tower.
Mae, May (*Hebrew, Latin*) *See* MARY; from goddess Maia.
Mamie (*Hebrew*) Pet form, *see* MARY.
Margaret (*Greek*) A pearl.
Maria, Marian, Marilyn (*Hebrew*) *See* MARY.
Marie (*Hebrew-French*) *See* MARY.
Marjorie (*Greek-French*) A pearl.
Marlene (*Hebrew*) *See* MARY; elevated.
Martha (*Aramaic*) Lady, mistress.
Mary (*Hebrew*) Bitterness; wished-for child; rebellion.
Matilda, Maud (*Germanic*) Might, war.
Maxine (*Latin-French*) The greatest.
Melanie (*Greek*) Black.
Melissa (*Greek*) Honeybee.
Melody (*Latin*) Musical quality.
Mercedes (*Spanish*) Of mercies (Mary).
Merle (*Latin*) A blackbird.
Mildred (*Old English*) Mild, power.
Millicent, Millie (*Germanic*) Work, strength.
Minnette (*Hebrew, Germanic*) *See* MARY; small.
Miranda (*Latin*) Worthy of admiration.
Muriel (*Celtic*) Sea-white.
Myrtle (*Greek*) From the shrub myrtle.

N-O-P-Q

Nancy, Nanette (*Hebrew*) Grace; God has been gracious.
Naomi (*Hebrew*) Pleasantness.
Natalie (*Latin*) Birthday (of Christ).
Nellie (*Greek*) Light.
Nita (*Hebrew-Spanish*) Gracious gift of God.
Nola (*Celtic*) Noble or famous.
Nora, Norah (*Latin-Irish*) Honor.
Norma (*Latin*) Model or pattern.
Octavia (*Latin*) The eighth born.
Olga (*Old Norse*) Holy.
Olive, Olivia (*Latin*) From the olive.
Ophelia (*Greek*) Serpent; assistance.
Pamela (*Greek*) All honey.
Pansy (*Greek*) From the flower pansy.
Patricia (*Latin*) Noble or patrician.
Paula, Pauline (*Latin*) Small.
Pearl (*Old French*) A pearl.
Peggy (*Greek*) Pearl.
Penelope (*Greek*) Weaver.
Phoebe (*Greek*) Bright.
Phyllis (*Greek*) A green leaf or bough.
Priscilla (*Latin*) The ancient.
Prudence (*Latin*) The discreet or prudent person.
Queenie (*Old English*) Wife of a king.
Quintina (*Latin*) The fifth born.

R

Rachel (*Hebrew*) Ewe.
Rebecca (*Hebrew*) Cow; snare.
Regina (*Latin*) Queen.
Rhea (*Greek*) From Rhea, the goddess of fertility.
Rhoda (*Greek*) Rose.
Rita (*Greek*) Pearl.
Roberta (*Germanic*) Fame, bright.
Rosa, Rose, Rosalie (*Latin*) A rose.
Rosamond (*Germanic*) Horse, protection.
Rosemary (*Latin*) From the shrub rosemary; dew of the sea.
Ruby (*Latin*) From the gem ruby; red.
Ruth (*Hebrew-Germanic*) Friend, beauty; fame.

S

Sabina (*Latin*) Sabine; of an ancient Italian tribe.
Sally (*Hebrew*) Princess.
Sandra, Zandra (*Greek*) Helper of men.
Sapphira (*Greek*) From the gem sapphire.
Sara, Sarah (*Hebrew*) Princess.
Selma (*Germanic*) Divine, helmet.
Sharon (*Hebrew*) Plain or level country.
Sheila (*Latin-Irish*) Blind.
Shirley (*Old English*) From Shireley, England.
Sibyl (*Greek*) A prophetess.
Silvia, Sylvia (*Latin*) Wood or forest.
Sonja, Sonya (*Greek-Russian*) Wisdom.
Stella (*Latin*) Star.
Susan, Suzanne (*Hebrew*) Lily.

T-U-V

Teresa, Theresa (*Greek*) The harvester.
Thelma (*Greek*) Nursling.
Una (*Latin, Celtic*) The one; famine.
Ursula (*Latin*) Little she-bear.
Valerie (*Latin*) Valorous.
Vanessa (*Latin*) Butterfly; grace of God.
Vera (*Latin, Slavonic*) True; faith.
Veronica (*Latin*) True image.
Viola (*Latin*) From the violet.
Virginia (*Latin*) Pertaining to spring.
Vivian (*Latin*) Animated; alive.

W-X

Wanda (*Germanic*) Stem; a wanderer.
Wendy (*Welsh*) White-browed.
Wilhelmina, Wilma (*Germanic*) Resolution, helmet.
Winifred (*Germanic-Celtic*) Friend, peace; reconciliation.
Xenia (*Greek*) Hospitable.

Y-Z

Yolande (*Latin-French*) Violet.
Yvette, Yvonne (*Hebrew-French*) Gracious gift of God.
Zena (*Persian*) Woman.
Zoe (*Greek*) Life.

Men's names

A

Aaron (*Hebrew*) Lofty mountain.
Abel (*Hebrew*) Vanity; son.
Abner (*Hebrew*) Father of light.
Abraham (*Hebrew*) Exalted father; father of multitudes.
Adam (*Hebrew*) Man of red earth.
Adolf, Adolph (*Germanic*) Noble, wolf.
Adrian (*Latin*) Of the Greek city Adria.
Alan, Allan (*Celtic*) Comely or fair; harmony.
Alastair (*Greek-Scottish*) Helper of men.
Albert (*Germanic*) Noble, bright.
Alden (*Old English*) Old, friend.
Aldric (*Germanic*) Old, rule.
Alexander, Allister (*Greek*) Helper of men.
Alfonso, Alonzo, Alphonso (*Germanic*) Noble, ready.
Algernon (*Norman-French*) Bewhiskered.
Aloysius (*Germanic*) Hear, fight.
Ambrose (*Greek*) Immortal.
Amos (*Hebrew*) A burden-bearer; carried.
Andrew (*Greek*) Manly.
Angus (*Celtic*) One choice; unique choice.
Anthony (*Latin*) Inestimable; strength.
Archibald (*Germanic*) Simple, bold.
Argus (*Greek*) Vigilant.
Arno, Arnold (*Germanic*) Eagle.
Arthur (*Celtic, Norse*) Noble bear-man; Thor's eagle.
Asa (*Hebrew*) God has given.
Asher (*Hebrew*) Bearer of salvation.
Ashley (*Old English*) Ash tree meadow.
Aubrey (*Germanic*) Elf, rule.
August, Austin (*Latin*) Exalted, majestic.
Avery (*Old English*) Boar, battle.

B

Baldwin (*Germanic*) Bold, friend.
Barnabas (*Hebrew*) Son of prophecy; son of encouragement.
Barrett (*Germanic*) Bear, rule.
Barry (*Celtic*) Looking straight at the mark; spear.
Bartholomew (*Hebrew*) Son of Talmai (furrow).
Basil (*Greek*) Kingly.
Benedict (*Latin*) Blessed.
Benjamin (*Hebrew*) Son of my right hand; son of the south.
Bentley (*Old English*) Bent grass clearing.
Berman (*Old English*) Bearkeeper.
Bernard (*Germanic*) Bear, stern.
Bert, Bertram (*Germanic*) Bright.
Blaine (*Celtic*) Thin or lean.
Blair (*Celtic*) A plain or level land.
Blake (*Old English*) Black.
Boris (*Slavonic*) Stranger.
Bradley (*Old English*) Broad meadow.
Brant (*Norse*) Sword.
Brent (*Old English*) Steep hill.
Brian (*Celtic*) Strong.
Bruce (*Old French*) From Brieuse in Normandy.
Bruno (*Germanic*) Dark-complexioned; brown.
Bryan (*Celtic*) Strong.
Byrne (*Germanic*) Bear.
Byron (*Germanic*) From the cottage.

C

Caesar (*Latin*) Hairy.
Caleb (*Hebrew*) Dog.
Calvert (*Old English*) Herdsman; calf herd.
Calvin (*Latin*) Bald.
Carl (*Germanic*) Man.
Carlton (*Old English*) Peasant's farm.
Carlyle (*Germanic*) Fortified city.
Carol (*Celtic*) Battle-mighty; warrior.
Casey (*Celtic*) Valorous.
Caspar (*Persian*) Treasure.
Cecil (*Latin*) Blind.
Cedric (*Celtic*) Chieftain.
Charles (*Germanic*) Man.
Chauncy (*Old French*) From Chancey in France.
Chester (*Old English*) Fortified town.
Christian (*Latin*) Follower of Christ.
Christopher (*Greek*) Christ-bearer.
Clarence (*Latin*) Illustrious.
Clark (*Old English*) Learned man; clergyman.
Claude (*Latin*) Lame.
Clayton (*Old English*) Town on clay bed.
Clement (*Latin*) Merciful.
Clifford (*Old English*) Fort at a cliff.
Clinton (*Old English*) Hill enclosure.
Clyde (*Welsh*) Fame.
Colin (*Greek-Irish*) People's victory.
Conrad (*Germanic*) Bold, counsel.
Constantine (*Latin*) Constant or firm of purpose.
Cornelius (*Latin*) The cornel tree; hornlike.
Craig (*Gaelic*) Mountain crag.
Curtis (*Old French*) Courteous.
Cuthbert (*Old English*) Famous, bright.
Cyril (*Greek*) Lordly.
Cyrus (*Persian*) The sun; throne.

D

Dale (*Old English*) Valley.
Damon (*Greek*) Taming.
Dan (*Hebrew*) Judged.
Dana (*Scandinavian*) From Denmark.
Daniel (*Hebrew*) Judged of God.
Daryl (*Old English*) Beloved; darling.
David (*Hebrew*) Beloved; friend; commander.
Dean (*Old English*) Valley.
Denis, Dennis (*Greek*) Of Dionysus, god of wine.
Derek, Derrick (*Germanic*) Folk, rule.
Dexter (*Latin*) Right hand.
Dirk (*Germanic*) Folk, rule.
Doane (*Old English*) Hill slope.
Dominic (*Latin*) Of the Lord; Sunday.
Donald (*Celtic*) World mighty; proved chieftain.
Dougal (*Celtic*) Dark stranger.
Douglas (*Celtic*) Dark gray; dark blue.
Dudley (*Old English*) Dudda's meadow.
Duff (*Celtic*) Dark; black.
Duke (*Latin*) Leader.
Duncan (*Celtic*) Brown warrior.
Dunstan (*Old English*) Brown, stone; hill, stone.
Durward (*Scottish*) Doorkeeper.
Dwight (*Germanic*) White.

E

Earl, Earle (*Old English*) Nobleman.
Ebenezer (*Hebrew*) Stone of help.
Eden (*Hebrew*) Delight.
Edgar (*Old English*) Rich, spear.
Edmund (*Old English*) Rich, protection.
Edsel (*Old English*) Rich, self.
Edward (*Old English*) Rich, guardian.
Edwin (*Old English*) Rich, friend.
Egbert (*Old English*) Sword, bright.
Egmont (*Old English*) Sword, protection.
Elbert (*Old English*) Noble, bright.
Eli, Ely (*Hebrew*) My God; Yahveh is God; the highest.
Elias, Elijah, Eliot, Ellis (*Hebrew*) Yahveh is God.
Elmer (*Old English*) Noble, fame.
Elmo (*Greek*) Amiable.
Elsdon (*Hebrew-English*) Ellis' valley.
Elson (*Hebrew*) Son of Elias.
Elwin (*Germanic*) Elf, friend.
Emanuel (*Hebrew*) God is with us.
Emery, Emory (*Germanic*) Work, rule.
Emil (*Germanic*) Industrious; work.
Emile (*Latin-French*) Affable.
Emmet (*Germanic*) Industrious.
Enoch (*Hebrew*) Follower; initiated.

Enos (*Hebrew*) Mortal man.
Erasmus (*Greek*) Beloved; amiable.
Eric (*Old Norse*) Ever king.
Ernest (*Old English*) Grave, serious.
Errol (*Latin*) Wandering.
Erwin (*Old English*) Sea, friend.
Esmond (*Old English*) Grace, protector.
Ethelbert (*Old English*) Noble, bright.
Eugene (*Greek*) Well-born; noble.
Eustace (*Greek*) Steadfast; rich in harvest.
Evan (*Hebrew-Celtic*) Gracious gift of God.
Evelyn (*Celtic-Latin*) Pleasant; life; hazel.
Everett (*Germanic*) Boar, hard.
Ewan, Ewen (*Celtic*) Well-born; a youth.
Ezra (*Hebrew*) Helper.

F

Fabian (*Latin*) Bean-grower.
Farley (*Old English*) Fern-covered clearing.
Felix (*Latin*) Happy or fortunate.
Ferdinand (*Germanic*) Journey, venture.
Fergus (*Celtic*) Manly strength; man's choice.
Flavian (*Latin*) Yellow.
Flobert (*Germanic*) Wise, bright.
Floyd (*Celtic*) Gray.
Francis, Frank (*Germanic*) Free.
Franklin (*Germanic*) Freeman or freeholder.
Frederick (*Germanic*) Peace, rule.

G

Gabriel (*Hebrew*) Man of God; God is my strength.
Garland (*Old French*) Crowned for victory.
Garrett, Garrick, Garth (*Germanic*) Spear, firm.
Gary (*Celtic*) Hunting dog.
Gascon, Gaston (*Old French*) Native of Gascony.
Geoffrey (*Germanic*) God, peace; district of land, peace.
Geordie, George (*Greek*) Earthworker or farmer.
Gerald (*Germanic*) Spear, rule.
Gerard (*Germanic*) Spear, hard.
Gilbert (*Germanic*) Pledge, bright.
Giles (*Greek*) Shield bearer; young goat.
Gilroy (*Latin-Celtic*) Servant of the king.
Glen (*Welsh*) Valley.
Godfrey (*Germanic*) God, peace.
Godwin (*Germanic*) God, friend.
Gordon (*Old English*) Spacious hill; three-cornered hill.
Graham (*Old English*) Gray homestead.
Grant (*Latin*) Great or large.
Granville (*Old French*) Large town.
Gregory (*Greek*) Watchman.
Griffith (*Welsh*) Strong fighter; ruddy.
Grover (*Old English*) Dweller in or near a small wood.
Gustav (*Germanic*) Goth, staff.
Guy (*Germanic*) Sensible; leader; wood.

H-I

Hamilton (*Old English*) Treeless hill.
Harley (*Old English*) Hare, woods.
Harold (*Old Norse*) Army, power.
Harrison (*English*) Son of Harry.
Harry (*Germanic*) Home, rule.
Harvey (*Celtic, Old French*) Bitter; warrior; carnage worthy.
Hector (*Greek, Gaelic*) Defender; horseman.
Henry (*Germanic*) Home, rule.
Herbert (*Germanic*) Army, bright.
Herman (*Germanic*) Army, man.
Hilary (*Latin*) Cheerful.
Hiram (*Hebrew*) Brother is exalted; noble.
Hobart, Hubert (*Germanic*) Mind, bright.
Homer (*Greek*) A security or pledge.
Horace (*Latin*) Timekeeper.
Hosea (*Hebrew*) Salvation.
Howard (*Old English*) Sword, guardian; hedge warden.
Hugh, Hugo (*Germanic*) Mind or spirit.
Humphrey (*Germanic*) Giant, peace.
Hyman (*Hebrew*) Life.
Ian (*Hebrew-Celtic*) Gracious gift of God.
Ichabod (*Hebrew*) Without glory.
Ira (*Aramaic*) Watchful; stallion.
Irving (*Old English*) Green river; sea, friend.
Isaac (*Hebrew*) He laughs, or the laughter.
Isidore (*Greek*) Gift of Isis, the Egyptian moon goddess.
Ivan (*Hebrew*) Gracious gift of God.

J-K

Jack (*Hebrew*) Gracious gift of God.
Jacob, James (*Hebrew*) May God protect; supplanter.
Jarvis (*Germanic*) Spear, servant.
Jasper (*Persian*) Master of the treasure.
Jefferson (*Old English*) Son of Geoffrey.
Jeffrey (*Germanic*) *See* GEOFFREY.
Jerome (*Greek*) Holy name.
Jerrold (*Germanic*) Spear, rule.
Jesse (*Hebrew*) God exists.
Jethro (*Hebrew*) Excellent.
Joel (*Hebrew*) Yahveh is God.
John, Jonathan (*Hebrew*) Gracious gift of God.
Jonas (*Hebrew*) Dove.
Joseph (*Hebrew*) May God add.
Joshua (*Hebrew*) God is salvation; Yahveh helps.
Joslyn (*Latin*) The just; merry.
Julius (*Latin*) Downy-bearded; youthful.
Junior (*Latin*) The younger.
Justin (*Latin*) Just or upright.
Karl (*Germanic*) Manly.
Keith (*Gaelic*) The wind; woods.
Kelvin (*Celtic*) Warrior friend.
Kenneth (*Celtic*) Handsome or comely.
Kent (*Old English*) Open country.
Kermit (*Celtic*) God of arms.
Kerwin (*Germanic*) Love, friend.
Kevin (*Celtic*) Handsome birth.
Kirby (*Germanic*) Village with a church.

L

Laird (*Scottish*) Landed proprietor.
Lambert (*Germanic*) Land, bright.
Lars, Laurence, Lawrence (*Latin*) Laurel, victory.
Leander (*Greek*) Lion man.
Lee (*Old English*) Dweller at the meadow.
Leland (*Old English*) From the meadow land.
Leo, Leon (*Latin*) Lion.
Leonard (*Germanic*) Lion, stern.
Leopold (*Germanic*) People, bold.
Leroy (*Old French-Latin*) The king.
Leslie (*Celtic*) Garden of hollies; gray fort.
Lester (*Latin-English*) Dwellers on Legra River.
Lewis (*Latin*) Hear, fight.
Lincoln (*Latin-Old English*) Lake colony.
Llewellyn (*Celtic*) Leader or ruler; lionlike.
Lloyd (*Celtic*) Brown; gray.
Loren (*Latin*) The laurel, symbol of victory.
Louis, Luis (*Latin-French*) Hear, fight.
Lowell (*Old English*) Beloved; little wolf.
Lucius, Luke (*Latin*) Light.
Luther (*Germanic*) Fame, warrior.
Lyle (*French-Latin*) From the small island.
Lyman (*Old English, Celtic*) Homestead by a wood; snow birth.
Lynn (*Old English*) Pool or lake.

M

Malcolm (*Celtic*) Servant of Columba.
Manuel (*Hebrew*) God is with us.
Marcus, Mark (*Latin*) Of Mars, god of war.
Mario (*Hebrew, Latin*) Bitterness; of Mars, god of war.
Marlin (*Old English, Celtic*) The merlin, sparrow hawk; sea-hill.
Marmaduke (*Celtic*) Sea leader.
Marshall (*Old French*) Official in charge of horses.
Martin (*Latin*) Of Mars, god of war.
Marvin (*Germanic*) Fame, friend.

Matthew (*Hebrew*) Gift of God.
Maurice (*Latin*) Moorish or dark-skinned.
Max, Maximillian (*Latin*) The greatest.
Melvin (*Celtic*) Chieftain.
Merle (*Latin-Old French*) Blackbird.
Merton (*Old English*) Sea, farm.
Meyer (*Germanic*) Head servant; farmer.
Michael (*Hebrew*) Who is like God.
Miles, Milo (*Latin*) Soldier.
Milton (*Old English*) Middle homestead; mill homestead.
Monroe (*Celtic*) From the red marsh.
Morgan (*Welsh*) Great, bright.
Morris (*Latin*) Moorish or dark-skinned.
Morton (*Old English*) Homestead by a marsh.
Moses (*Coptic*) Son; boy.
Murray (*Middle English*) Merry.
Myron (*Greek*) Fragrant.

N-O

Nathan (*Hebrew*) Gift of God.
Nathaniel (*Hebrew*) Gift of God.
Neil (*Celtic*) A champion.
Nelson (*Celtic-Germanic*) Son of Neil.
Neville (*Latin*) New town.
Newton (*Old English*) New town.
Nicholas (*Greek*) People's victory.
Noel (*Latin*) Christmas.
Norman (*Old English*) A northman; Norwegian.
Norval (*Germanic*) Man from the north.
Olaf (*Old Norse*) Ancestor's relics.
Oliver (*Latin*) From the olive.
Oran, Orin (*Celtic*) White of skin.
Orval, Orville (*Old French*) Gold town.
Osbert (*Germanic*) Divine, bright.
Oscar (*Old English*) Divine, spear.
Otto (*Germanic*) Wealthy.
Owen (*Latin-Celtic*) Well-born; young warrior.

P-Q

Patrick (*Latin*) Noble or patrician.
Paul (*Latin*) Small.
Percy (*Old French*) Persius' estate.
Peregrine (*Latin*) Wanderer; stranger.
Peter (*Greek*) A rock.
Philbert (*Germanic*) Very, bright.
Philip (*Greek*) Lover of horses.
Pierre (*Greek-French*) A rock.
Prescott (*Old English*) Priest's cottage.
Quentin (*Latin*) The fifth.
Quincy (*Old French-Latin*) Quintus' estate.

R

Radford (*Old English*) Red ford.
Ralph (*Germanic*) Counsel, wolf.
Ramsey (*Old English*) Ram's isle.
Randal, Randolph (*Germanic*) Shield, wolf.
Raphael (*Hebrew*) Healed by God.
Raymond (*Germanic*) Counsel, protection.
Reginald (*Germanic*) Might, power.
Reuben (*Hebrew*) Behold a son; substitute.
Rex (*Latin*) King.
Richard (*Germanic*) Rule, hard.
Robert, Robin (*Germanic*) Fame, bright.
Roderick (*Germanic*) Fame, rule.
Rodney (*Old English*) Road, servant.
Roger (*Germanic*) Fame, spear.
Roland (*Germanic*) Fame, land.
Rolf, Rollo (*Germanic*) Fame, wolf.
Ronald (*Germanic-Scottish*) Might, power.
Roosevelt (*Dutch*) Rose field.
Roscoe (*Old English*) Roe, wood.
Roy (*Celtic-Old French*) Red; king.
Rudolph (*Germanic*) Fame, wolf.
Rufus (*Latin*) Red-haired.
Russell (*Old French*) Little red; red head.

S

Samson (*Hebrew*) Sun's man; resplendent.
Samuel (*Hebrew*) His name is God; name of God; God hath heard.
Sanders (*Greek*) Helper of men.
Sanford (*Old English*) Sandy river crossing.
Saul (*Hebrew*) Requested; desire.
Scott (*Celtic*) One from Scotland or Ireland.
Sebastian (*Greek*) Venerable.
Selwyn (*Old English*) House, friend.
Septimus (*Latin*) The seventh.
Seth (*Hebrew*) The appointed.
Sewell (*Germanic*) Victory, power.
Sextus (*Latin*) The sixth.
Shelby (*Old English*) Village where willows grow.
Sheldon (*Old English*) Steep-sided valley, flat-topped hill.
Sherman (*Old English*) The shearman or cutter.
Sidney (*Celtic*) A telescoping of St. Denis.
Sigfried (*Germanic*) Victory, peace.
Sigmund (*Germanic*) Victory, protection.
Silas (*Latin*) Of the forest.
Simeon, Simon (*Hebrew*) God has heard; hearkening; snub-nosed.
Soloman (*Hebrew*) Peaceful.
Stanislas (*Slavonic*) War camp; camp glory.
Stanley (*Old English*) Stony meadow.
Stephen, Steven (*Greek*) Crown or garland.
Stewart, Stuart (*Old English*) One in charge of the household.

T-U-V

Terrence (*Latin*) Soft or tender.
Theodore (*Greek*) Gift of God.
Theodoric (*Germanic*) People, rule.
Thomas (*Aramaic*) A twin.
Timothy (*Greek*) Honoring God.
Titus (*Latin*) Safe.
Ulric (*Germanic*) Wolf, rule.
Ulysses (*Latin*) The hater.
Valentine (*Latin*) Valorous, healthy.
Vaughn (*Celtic*) Little.
Vernon (*Old French*) Alder grove.
Victor (*Latin*) Conqueror.
Vincent (*Latin*) Conquering.

W-X-Y-Z

Wallace (*Old English-Scottish*) A Welshman.
Walter (*Germanic*) Rule, army.
Ward (*Germanic*) Guardian.
Washington (*Old English*) Homestead of Wassa's people; manor of the Wessyngs.
Wayne (*Old English*) Wagon.
Wendell (*Germanic*) Wanderer.
Wesley (Old English) West meadow.
Whitney (*Old English*) White island.
Wilbur (*Germanic*) Resolution, bright.
Willard (*Germanic*) Resolution, hard.
William, Willis (*Germanic*) Resolution, helmet.
Winston (*Old English*) Winec's homestead; friend, stone.
Woodrow (*Old English*) Row of trees.
Xavier (*Spanish-Arabic*) New house; brilliant.
Xerxes (*Greek-Persian*) King.
Yates (*Old English*) Gate.
Zaccheus (*Hebrew*) The righteous one; pure.
Zebulun (*Hebrew*) Habitation.
Zenas (*Greek*) Gift of Zeus, the chief Greek god.

Using this dictionary

All dictionaries are not alike. Words, definitions, and etymologies may be arranged in different ways in different dictionaries. The use of terms and symbols may vary. To get the most out of this dictionary, you should be familiar with the methods and principles it uses. *Using this dictionary* provides information that will help you find the words you look up quickly and efficiently. It will make it easier for you to understand definitions, word origins, syllabication, punctuation, and other components of a dictionary entry.

"Guide to the dictionary," pages *114-119,* explains the special terms, symbols, and abbreviations used in this dictionary. It explains how to look up words; how to recognize preferred spelling when two or more acceptable spellings appear for an entry; how to divide a word into syllables; how pronunciations are indicated; and how definitions are arranged. It explains and illustrates the kinds of labels that are used in this dictionary to indicate entries that are not part of standard speech or writing. It explains and illustrates the various forms of cross references, figurative usages, synonyms and synonym studies, and the function of usage notes in this dictionary.

"Origin of words," pages *120-121,* describes the symbols found in etymologies and illustrates how each is used. It gives a step-by-step explanation of how to trace a word from its origin to its present usage; explains why some etymologies appear within the entry while others are placed at the end of an entry. It provides information on cross references to etymologies, and, through a sampling of the etymologies, gives you a fascinating glimpse into the lives of people long ago.

"Spelling and looking up words," pages *122-123,* includes a table of common spellings of English sounds to help you find words in this dictionary when you are unsure of spellings. It explains why one spelling may be preferred to another, and which spelling to choose when there are two or more acceptable spellings.

There are more sounds in English than there are letters in the alphabet. To make up for the lack of letters, this dictionary uses certain symbols and marks. "Pronunciation," page *124,* explains the symbols and the diacritical marks that appear above some symbols. It includes a complete pronunciation key.

Guide word **Main entry** **Subentry** **Guide word**

218 **blow**

• **blowgun** definition 1

• **blucher** definition 1

• **blowtorch** definition 1

blue pencil 219

Guide to the dictionary

You use your dictionary to expand your knowledge of words so that you can communicate effectively in both written and spoken language. A good vocabulary broadens your understanding of what you read or hear and increases your ability to speak and write well. This dictionary contains thousands of words you can use to express your thoughts in a clear, interesting way. It tells how to spell and pronounce words. It gives their meanings and origins and tells how to use words in sentences. If you want to know where to put a hyphen when you need to divide a word at the end of a line, or if you want to know whether a word is considered slang, this dictionary has the answers.

In order to give you such information and much more in a limited space, lexicographers use special terms, signs, symbols, and abbreviations. If you want to get the most out of your dictionary, you should know what each of these means and how it is used. This section interprets, explains, and illustrates the special terms used in this dictionary.

Alphabetical order

To find the word you are looking up without wasting time and effort, you should know how this dictionary is arranged The words or phrases you look up are called *entries.* They are listed in alphabetical order, letter by letter. For example, the entry *newcomer* appears before the entry *New Covenanters,* which comes before *new-create.*

Thumb tabs and guide words

How do you find the word you want without having to search through a lot of pages? Thumb tabs marked with letter or letters of the alphabet are located along the edge of each volume. Suppose you are looking up the word *boss.* First, you find the thumb tab marked B and open the dictionary there. Then, since the second letter of *boss* is *o,* and *o* falls near the middle of the alphabet, you turn to the middle of the B section. You will see a *guide word* in the top outside corner of each page. Guide words lead you to the word you are looking for. The guide word at the top of a left-hand page repeats the first main entry on that page. The guide word at the top of a right-hand page repeats the last main entry on that page. For example, the guide word on page 232 is *born-again,* and the guide word on page 233 is *bottom.* A glance at the guide words *born-again* and *bottom* tells you at once that *boss,* the word you are looking up, must be on one of these two pages.

If you know how a word sounds but are unsure of the spelling, read the section "Spelling and looking up words," on pages *122* and *123* before you begin to look up the word.

Main entries

Main entries are the words or phrases in boldface (heavy) type that extend into the margin. A main entry may be a single word; a compound word (two words combined into one); a phrase; an abbreviation; a letter of the alphabet; or part of a word such as a prefix, suffix, or combining form. Here are examples of the kinds of main entries you will find in this dictionary:

Single-word entry:

cake (kāk), *n., v.,* **caked, cak|ing.** —*n.* **1** a baked mixture of flour, sugar, eggs, flavoring, and other things, usually including shortening and baking

Compound-word entry:

boat|load (bōtʹlōdʹ), *n.* **1** as much or as many as a boat can hold or carry. **2** the load that a boat is carrying

Phrase entry:

cakes and ale, good things; pleasures of life:

Abbreviation entry:

adv., an abbreviation for the following:
1 ad valorem.
2 adverb.
3 advertisement.
4 against (Latin, *adversus*).

Letter-of-the-alphabet entry:

B[1] or **b** (bē), *n., pl.* **B's** or **Bs, b's** or **bs. 1** the

Part-of-a-word entry:

auto-[2], *combining form.* automobile; vehicle:

Subentries

A subentry is an expression that uses the main-entry word but has a special meaning of its own. Subentries appear under the overall heading of the main entry because the most important word in the subentry is the main-entry word. For example, you will find several subentries, including *miss the boat,* listed under the main entry *boat.* Like the main entry, a subentry is printed in boldface type, but it does not extend into the margin. Each subentry has its own definition and most have illustrative sentences.

boat (bōt), *n., v.* —*n.* **1** a small, open vessel for . . .
miss the boat, *Informal.* to miss an opportunity; lose one's chances: *The buyer missed the boat and never got the house when he offered too low a bid.*

Spelling

A word may have more than one acceptable spelling. When two or more spellings of the same word are used almost equally in speech and writing, they appear as a single entry joined by "or."

a|dapt|er or **a|dap|tor** (ə dapʹtər), *n.* **1** a person or thing that adapts. **2** a device for fitting parts to each other or a machine to a different use.

When a particular spelling is the preferred one, and the alternate spelling belongs in a different alphabetical place, the preferred spelling is the main-entry word. The alternate spelling appears at the end of the entry. Such alternate spellings also appear as separate entries and are cross-referred to the preferred spelling.

ba|bies'-breath (bāʹbēz brethʹ), *n.* **1** a tall plant bearing numerous clusters of small, fragrant, white or pink flowers on branching stalks; gypsophila. Babies'-breath is a member of the pink family and is often grown in rock gardens. **2** any of various other plants bearing somewhat similar flowers often pink or rose. Also, **baby's-breath.**

ba|by's-breath (bāʹbēz brethʹ), *n.* = babies'-breath.

For more on spelling, see "Spelling and looking up words," on pages *122* and *123.*

Syllables

How can you be sure of putting a hyphen in the right place when you come to the end of a line and find you have room for only part of a word? All you need do is look up the word and see how it is divided into syllables in your dictionary.

A syllable is the part of a word usually pronounced as a unit. It may be a vowel sound or a vowel sound with one or more consonants. Vertical lines appear between syllables to show how the word is divided. For example, *ad|sorb|a|bil|i|ty* has six syllables. You can divide *adsorbability* wherever there is a vertical line. Words of only one syllable are never divided. For more on how to divide words when you come to the end of a line, see "Use the Hyphen," page *28.*

Syllables are not indicated in phrase entries when each word in the phrase appears in its own alphabetical place in the dictionary. For example, *laboratory* is divided into syllables, but *laboratory animal* is not.

Pronunciation and stress

You will find the pronunciation of a word in the parentheses following the main-entry word. When there are several pronunciations, the preferred pronunciation is given first. The syllables that differ from the preferred pronunciation follow the preferred pronunciation.

de|nun|ci|a|to|ry (di nunʹsē ə tôrʹē, -tōrʹ-; -shē-),

A special system of symbols is used to show the pronunciation of words. This system is explained in a pronunciation key at the foot of almost every right-hand page.

Stress is the relative force with which a syllable is to be pronounced. It is indicated by an accent mark following the stressed syllable. In most words of more than one syllable, some syllables are pronounced with more force than others. In this dictionary, a bold accent [**ʹ**] shows the greater or primary stress. A lighter accent [ʹ] shows syllables of lesser or secondary stress.

ba|by-sit (bāʹbē sitʹ), *v.i.,* **-sat, sit|ting. 1** to take care of a child or children while the parents are away for a while. **2** *Figurative.* to take care of

For more on pronunciation, see "Pronunciation," on page *124.*

Parts of speech

Parts of speech are abbreviated and italicized following the pronunciation of main-entry words. You have only to look at these abbreviations to see the various ways a word can be used in a sentence. For example, *n., adj., v.* following the entry *bobtail,* tells you that bobtail is used as a noun, as an adjective, and as a verb. Each part of speech is defined in a separate paragraph labeled with the part of speech in boldface italics.

bob|tail (bobʹtālʹ), *n., adj., v.* —*n.* **1** a short tail, or a tail cut short. **2** an animal having such a tail.
—***adj.*** **1** having such a tail. **2** *Figurative.* cut short or incomplete: *Chances favor a "bobtail" bill wrapping up pet schemes* (Wall Street Journal).
—***v.t.*** **1** to cut short the tail of. **2** *Figurative.* to cut short sometimes, so as to make incomplete.

The parts of speech and their abbreviations are:

noun **n.**
transitive verb **v.t.**
intransitive verb **v.i.**
pronoun **pron.**

adjective **adj.**
adverb **adv.**
preposition **prep.**
conjunction **conj.**
interjection **interj.**

For more on parts of speech, see pages *23* and *24.*

Inflections

Inflections are the forms of a word that show grammatical differences such as the plurals of nouns, the past tense and present participle of verbs, and the comparative forms of adjectives and adverbs. Regular inflections, such as adding *s* or *es* to form the plural of a noun, adding *ed* to form the past tense of a verb, adding *ing* to form the present participle, or adding *er* or *est* to show comparison in adjectives and adverbs are not shown in the dictionary when they do not present spelling problems. When there are irregularities, the dictionary shows them in boldface type following the part-of-speech label.

can|dy (kan′dē), *n., pl.* **-dies**, *v.,* **-died**, **-dy|ing**,

a|wake (ə wāk′), *v.,* **a|woke** or **a|waked**, **a|waked** or (*especially British*) **a|wo|ken**, **a|wak-ing**, *adj.* — ***v.i.*** **1** to come out of sleep; wake up;

crust|y (krus′tē), *adj.,* **crust|i|er**, **crust|i|est**. **1** of

For more on inflections, see "Spelling and looking up words," pages *122* and *123.*

Singular and plural

Most noun entries in the dictionary are singular and become plural by adding *s* or *es.* But some nouns generally used in the plural do not end in *s* or *es.* When these are main entries, they are designated plural after the part-of-speech label and referred to the singular form.

men (men), *n.* **1** plural of **man**.

Some nouns are used only in the plural form. When these are main entries, they are designated by the abbreviation pl. following the part of speech. For example,

mo|res (môr′āz, ēz; mōr′-), *n.pl.*

When a singular noun main-entry word has an irregular plural form, the abbreviation pl. and the plural form follow the part-of-speech label. For example,

foot (füt), *n., pl.* **feet**

When a plural form is given as the main entry, but is used in both plural and singular forms depending on usage, definitions are preceded by the labels *sing. in use* or *pl. in use.*

dy|nam|ics (dī nam′iks), *n.* **1** *sing. in use.* the branch of physics dealing with the motion of bodies and the action of forces on bodies either in motion or at rest. Dynamics includes kinematics, kinetics, and statics. **2** *sing. in use.* the science of force acting in any field. **3** *pl. in use.* the forces, physical or moral, at work in any field: *the dynamics of education.* **4** *pl. in use.* the variation and contrast of force or loudness in the production of musical sounds.

Definitions

Definitions give the meanings of entries. They follow the part-of-speech label. In this dictionary, the definitions are normally listed with the most commonly used meaning first. (In some other dictionaries, the definitions are listed in historical order, with the oldest meanings first.) Words that have more than one meaning have numbered definitions.

When a definition has both a number and the letter *a* in boldface type, it means that such definitions are followed by one or more definitions that are closely related to it. Each of these related definitions has a boldface letter. In this example, definition **1a** is followed by definition **b,** and definition **4a** is followed by definitions **b** and **c.**

ba|by (bā′bē), *n., pl.* **-bies**, *adj., v.,* **-bied**, **-by|ing** — ***n.*** **1a** a very young child, especially one too young to walk or speak; infant: *A hungry baby will usually cry.* **SYN**: nursling. **b** the young of an animal: *a mother cat and her babies.* **2** the youngest of a family or group: *She may be the baby of the group, but she's as smart as any of us.* **3** *Figurative.* a person who acts like a baby; childish person: *Don't be a baby and cry over that little scratch.* **4** *Especially U.S. Slang.* **a** a girl or young woman, especially a sweetheart; babe. **b** any person or thing: *That boxer is a tough baby. Instead of a hundred miles an hour, you bring this baby in at almost twice that* (Harper's). **c** *Figurative.* a plan, idea, or project, which is the chief interest or responsibility of a person or group: *The Air Force, claiming that all pilot instruction is their baby, took over training of Army helicopter pilots from the Army* (Newsweek).

Some definitions are followed by semicolons and words that extend or clarify the definition. Such words are closely related to, or may be synonyms for, the main-entry word.

blam|a|ble (blā′mə bəl), *adj.* deserving blame; faulty; blameworthy. **SYN**: guilty, censurable, culpable. Also, **blameable**. — **blam′a|ble|ness**, *n.* — **blam′a|bly**, *adv.*

Illustrative sentences and phrases

This dictionary provides sentences and phrases to help you to understand and remember the meanings of words by showing them in actual use. The phrases or sentences are set off from the definition by a colon.

awe (ô), *n., v.,* **awed**, **aw|ing**. — ***n.*** **1** great wonder; a feeling of wonder and reverence inspired by anything of great beauty, sublimity, majesty, or power: *We feel awe when we stand near vast mountains, or when we think of God's power and glory.*

Restrictive or usage labels

Restrictive or usage labels tell you that a particular word is not part of standard speech and writing or that it has a special meaning in certain circumstances. Such words may be out-of-date; words you might use if you belonged to a particular group, or profession; or words that you would find only in special kinds of writing, such as poetry. When a word has such a restricted use, an italicized label appears with the definition and applies only to that particular definition.

Here are the restrictive labels used in this dictionary, with examples:

Archaic means that the word is no longer in general use. It may be found in special contexts, such as law, or in special styles of writing, such as the Scriptures. Sometimes modern writers use archaic words to give their writings an old-fashioned flavor.

cai|tiff (kā′tif), *n., adj.* — ***n.*** *Archaic.* a mean, cowardly person. **SYN**: coward.
— ***adj.*** cowardly and mean: *A territory Wherein were bandit earls and caitiff Knights* (Tennyson).

Combining form means a special form of a word that can be combined with another word or part of a word to convey a particular meaning. Often combining forms come from other languages, especially Greek and Latin. When combining forms are added together, the new word has the same meaning as the combined meanings of its parts.

denti-, *combining form.* of a tooth or teeth; dental: *Dentiform = of the form of a tooth.* Also, **dento-**. [< Latin *dēns, dentis* tooth]

For more on combining forms, see "Making words," on pages *17-19.*

Dialect means that the word is spoken in a certain district of a country or by a certain group of people. A word used mainly in regional speech is indicated by a regional label.

clink[3] (klingk), *v.t., v.i. Dialect.* to clinch.

ca|jon (kä hōn′), *n., pl.* **-jo|nes** (-hō′nās). *Southwestern U.S.* a narrow canyon or gorge with vertical sides. [< Spanish *cajón* large box < *caja* box]

English-speaking variations. Labels such as *Australian, British, Canadian, Scottish,* and *U.S.* are used to indicate words, meanings, and spellings used in specific English-speaking countries.

chook (chu̇k), *n. Australian Informal.* a chicken. [probably imitative]

can|di|da|ture (kan′də də chər, -dā′-), *n. British.* candidacy: *At one time his candidature seemed likely to lead to further divisions in the party* (London Times).

ba|biche (bä bēsh′), *n. Canadian.* thongs or lacings of rawhide, sinew, or gut, used especially to make snowshoes, snares, and other items of wood and leather exposed to the weather. [< Canadian French *babiche* < an Algonkian word]

airt (ärt), *n., v. Scottish.* **—*n.*** a point of the compass; a direction.
—*v.t.* to direct; guide.
[< Scottish Gaelic *àird* direction; high place]

bounty jumper, *U.S.* a person who enlisted as a soldier during the Civil War for the sake of the bounty offered and then deserted.

Foreign language labels, such as *French, German,* and *Latin,* indicate that an entry is a foreign word or phrase widely used in English. The entry also gives each term's literal meaning.

ad un|guem (ad ung′gwem), *Latin.* **1** to a nicety. **2** (literally) to a fingernail (as work brought to the final touch or test with the fingernail).

Informal means that the word or phrase may often be used in everyday conversation or writing, but that it is not used in formal speech or writing.

cage|y (kā′jē), *adj.,* **cag|i|er, cag|i|est**. *Informal.* shrewd and cautious; sharp and wary:

Obsolete means that the word is found only in writings of an earlier time or in modern writings that imitate the style of earlier writings.

couth[2] (küth), *v., adj.* ***—v.*** *Obsolete.* a past tense and past participle of **can**.

Poetic means that the word is found in poetry or in poetic prose. Such words are not used in ordinary speech or writing.

a|wea|ry (ə wir′ē), *adj. Poetic.* weary; tired (of):

Prefix indicates a syllable, or word put in front of a word or word part to alter its meaning or to form a new word.

en-[1], *prefix.* **1** to cause to be; make, as in *enable, enfeeble.*
2 to put in; put on, as in *encircle, enthrone.*
3 other meanings, as in *enact, encourage, entwine. En-* changes the meaning of a verb little or not at all except to make it more emphatic. Also, **em-** before *b, p,* and sometimes *m.*

Some common prefix entries are followed by a list of words containing the prefix but not separately defined in the dictionary. Such lists of words occur after the entries non-, pre-, and re-.

pre-, *prefix.* **1** before: *Prewar = before the war. Pre-Cambrian = before the Cambrian.*
2 beforehand: *Preview = view beforehand.*
3 before, as in position or space; in front of: *Premolar = in front of the molars.*
[< Latin *prae-* < *prae* before]
▶When **pre-** is joined to a root with initial *e*, the latter has usually been spelled with *ë* or preceded by the hyphen: *preëmpt, pre-empt;* most writers and editors now omit these marks: *preempt, preexistence.* The hyphen is also used before roots with an initial capital letter: *pre-Christian.* Otherwise prefix and root are joined directly without any mark: *preoccupy, prescription.*

Words not separately defined in this dictionary appear in the following listing:

pre|ab′do|men
pre′ac|cept′
pre′ac|cept′ance
pre|ac′cess
pre′ac|ces′si|ble
pre′ac|cord′
pre′ac|count′
pre′ac|cu′mu|late
pre′ac|cu|mu|la′tion
pre′ac|cu|sa′tion
pre′ac|cuse′
pre′ac|knowl′edge
pre′ac|knowl′edg|ment
pre′ac|quaint′
pre′ac|quaint′ance
pre′ac|quire′
pre′ac|quired′
pre′ac|quit′
pre′ac|quit′tal
pre|act′
pre|ac′tion
pre′a|dapt′
pre′a|dapt′a|ble
pre′ad|ap|ta′tion
pre′ad|just′
pre′ad|just′a|ble
pre′ad|just′ment
pre′ad|min′is|tra′tion
pre′ad|min′is|tra′tive
pre′ad|min′is|tra′tor
pre′ad|mis′sion
pre′ad|mit′
pre′ad|mon′ish
pre′ad|mo|ni′tion
pre′ad|o|les′cent
pre′a|dopt′
pre′a|dop′tion
pre′a|dult′
pre′a|dult′hood
pre′ad|vert′en|cy
pre′ad|vert′ent
pre|ad′ver|tise
pre′ad|ver|tise′ment
pre|ad′ver|tis′er
pre′ad|vice′
pre′ad|vis′a|ble
pre′ad|vise′
pre′ad|vis′er

For more on prefixes, see "Making words," pages *17-19.*

Professional terms, such as *Dentistry* or *Photography,* indicate terms pertaining to the arts, sciences, or technology.

chorale prelude, *Music.* an organ composition based on a chorale.

a|vow|ry (ə vou′rē), *n., pl.* **-ries**. *Law.* an avowal of an act.

Slang means that the word is not considered Standard English. It may be a new word or phrase created by a particular group to express an idea more vividly than words now in standard speech. Or it may be a standard word whose meaning has been changed to convey a concept quite different from the original. Slang is often used to achieve a special effect in speaking or writing.

cag|er (kā′jər), *n. U.S. Slang.* a basketball player:

square . . . 18. *Slang.* not up to date; too conventional or old-fashioned. . .

For more on slang, see "Slang and jargon," page *98.*

Substandard indicates that the word does not conform to accepted standards of speech and writing.

ain't (ānt), *Substandard or Dialect.* **1** am not; is not. **2** are not. **3** have not; has not.
▶ Ain't is not acceptable in formal English. Careful speakers and writers do not use *ain't* because its use even in informal English is subject to sharp criticism, though *ain't* is used habitually. . .

Suffix indicates a syllable or word put at the end of a word to form another word with a different meaning, or to form an inflectional ending.

-en², *suffix added to nouns to form adjectives.* made of; having the look of, as in woolen, silken, wooden, ashen. [Old English *-en*]

For more on suffixes, see "Making words," pages *17-20.*

Trademark means that the word's use is protected or restricted by law. A trademark is used by a manufacturer to distinguish his product from the product of others.

Da·cron (dā′kron, dak′ron), *n. Trademark.* an artificial fiber or fabric that does not wrinkle or fade easily. It is used for shirts, dresses, suits, and . . .

Unfriendly use indicates that the word is normally used to insult or belittle.

Boche or **boche** (bosh, bôsh), *n. Unfriendly Use.* **1** a German soldier. **2** any German. [< French army slang *boche* < *tête de boche* blockhead, earlier *tête de caboche* < *caboche* skull]

Cross references

Cross references show you where to find additional information about a word in another place in the dictionary. In this dictionary, cross references are given for preferred spellings; related etymologies; illustrations; equivalent terms; usage notes; synonyms; and subentries that are related to main entries other than those under which they appear.

Preferred spellings:

disc brake = disk brake.

Related etymologies:

a·waked . . . [fusion of Olde English *āwacian* and *awōc, onwōc,* past tense forms of *awæcnian,* earlier *onwæcnian* awaken. See related etym. at **wake**.]

Illustrations:

bob·cat (bob′kat′), *n.* **1** the wildcat or lynx of North America; bay lynx. See picture under **lynx**.

Equivalent terms:

can·dle·ber·ry (kan′del ber′ē), *n., pl.* **-ries**. **1a** = wax myrtle. **b** = bayberry. **2** = candlenut. **3** the fruit of any of these plants.

Usage notes:

a·wait (ə wāt′), *v.t.* **1** to wait for; look forward to: ► See **wait** for usage note.

Synonyms:

a·ware (ə wãr′), *adj.* having knowledge; realizing; conscious: *I was too sleepy to be aware how cold it was. She was not aware of her danger.* SYN: See syn. under **conscious**.

Subentry cross references:

do away with. See under **do¹**.
where away? See under **where**.

Homographs

Words that have the same spelling but different meanings and origins are called homographs. In this dictionary, each one of a group of homographs appears as a separate main entry with its own superscript (raised) number.

boil¹ (boil), *v., n.* — ***v.i.*** **1** to bubble up and give off steam or vapor: *Water boils when heated to 212 degrees Fahrenheit.* **2a** to have its contents . . . [<Old French *boillir* < Latin *bullīre* seethe < *bulla* a bubble] — **boil′a·ble**, *adj.*

boil² (boil), *n.* a painful, red swelling on the skin, formed by pus around a hard core; furuncle. Boils are often caused by infection. [Old English *bȳle*]

Run-on words

Run-on words are formed by adding suffixes to the main-entry word. They appear in boldface type after the main-entry words from which they are formed. They are divided into syllables and the stressed syllables are marked. Run-on words are not defined because the meaning is clear from the main-entry definitions.

bound·less (bound′lis), *adj.* **1** not limited; infinite: *Outer space is boundless.* **2** vast: *the boundless ocean. He has boundless energy.* — **bound′less·ly**, *adv.* — **bound′less·ness**, *n.*

Etymology

The etymology of a word traces its origin and development to its present use. In this dictionary, etymologies appear in square brackets following entry definitions. The etymologies use two important symbols: <, meaning "derived from" or "taken from," and +, meaning "and." For example, the etymology of *cousin* is

[<Old French *cousin, cosin* < Latin *cōnsōbrīnus* mother's sister's child < *com-* together + *soror* sister]

The English word is derived from Latin words through Old French. Etymologies are not given for words whose origins are obvious. For example, the etymology for choralist is not given because it is derived from choral, which has its own etymology. In cases where the most important use of the word represents a modern part of speech derived from an older one, a brief note ("[<verb]") indicates the fact, as in *affray* or *affront.*

For more on etymology, see "Origin of words," pages *120* and *121.*

Illustrations

Illustrations make difficult concepts easier to understand and supply information that expands the definition. All entries that have illustrations in their own right are marked by an asterisk. Entries that are illustrated within the illustration of another entry are cross-referred to that entry.

air·frame (ãr′frām′), *n.* the framework of an airplane, not including the engine or engines, of a ballistic missile, or of a dirigible. See picture under **airship**.

air·ship** (ãr′ship′), *n., v.,* **-shipped, -ship·ping**. — ***n. **1** a balloon that can be steered; a dirigible. An airship is filled with a gas that is lighter than air, and is driven by propeller. **2** *Obsolete.* an airplane.
— ***v.t.*** *U.S.* to ship by aircraft: *to airship supplies to Greenland.*

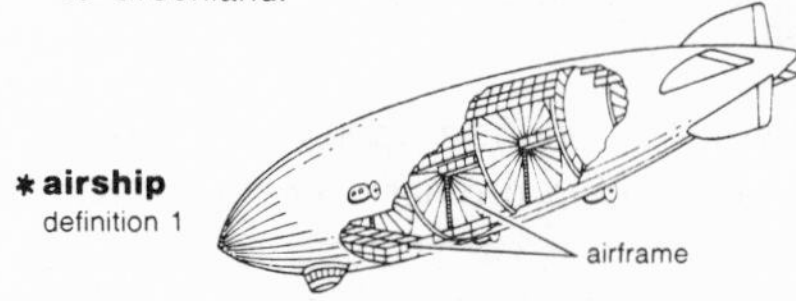

***airship**
definition 1

Synonyms

Synonyms are words that have the same or nearly the same meaning. In this dictionary, a synonym you can use in place of the word defined appears immediately after the definition, as in definitions 2 and 3 in the example below. But sometimes you need help in picking the one word that best expresses your meaning. In such cases, a *synonym study* explains the shades of meaning. The synonym study in this example applies to definition 1. Synonyms have one kind of label (SYN:) and synonym studies, which are always separate paragraphs, another (—*Syn.*).

ar|gu|ment (är′gyə mənt), *n.* **1** a discussion by persons who disagree; dispute: *He won the argument by producing figures to prove his point.* **2** giving reasons for or against something; debate: *Let us not waste time in argument.* SYN: discussion. **3** a reason or reasons given for or against something: *His arguments in favor of a new school are very persuasive.* SYN: rationale. **4** a short statement or summary of what is in a book, poem, or the like. SYN: abstract, theme. **5** *Mathematics.* an independent variable on whose value the value of a function depends. [<Latin *argūmentum* < *arguere* make clear]
—*Syn.* **1 Argument, controversy, dispute** mean presentation of varying opinions by persons who disagree on some question. **Argument** suggests an intellectual encounter in which each side uses facts and reasons to try to convince the other: *His strong arguments persuaded me to accept his conclusions.* **Controversy** tends to suggest a more or less formal argument between groups, often carried on in writing or speeches: *The controversy over American schools still continues.* **Dispute** suggests contradicting rather than reasoning, and applies to an argument marked by feeling: *The dispute over the property was settled in court.*

For more on synonyms, see "Choosing the right word," on page *32.*

Usage notes

Some words are often misused because they sound alike (as in *affect* and *effect*) or are similar in form (as in *disinterested* and *uninterested*). This dictionary provides notes to help clarify the use of such words so that you can avoid making mistakes. Usage notes are indicated by a boldface arrow [▶]. They explain when and how such words are used and show them in context in illustrative sentences.

dis|in|ter|est|ed (dis in′tər əs tid, -tris-; -tə res′-), *adj.* **1** free from selfish motives; impartial; fair: *An umpire makes disinterested decisions. Never have statesmen needed so much the disinterested wisdom which a philosophic temper alone can give* (Manchester Guardian). SYN: unbiased, unprejudiced. **2** not interested; unconcerned; uninterested: *A disinterested pupil can spoil a class. He was tired, preoccupied, disinterested* (Dayton Rommel). —**dis|in′ter|est′ed|ly,** *adv.* —**dis|in′ter|est′ed|ness,** *n.*
▶ **Disinterested** and **uninterested** can be used to make a useful distinction of meaning. *Uninterested* means having no concern about the matter and paying no attention: *I find it difficult to entertain anyone so uninterested in everything I suggest doing.* In careful usage, *disinterested* means having no reason or desire to be anything but strictly impartial and fair: *A judge should be disinterested.* Increasingly, however, *disinterested* is being used with the meaning of *uninterested.* Because of this, it is wise to make sure that context makes the intended meaning of *disinterested* unmistakable.

In cases of comparison, the usage note is given under the main-entry word that is alphabetically first. For example, in the comparison between *disinterested* and *uninterested,* the usage note is under *disinterested.* A cross reference appears under the entry *uninterested.*

Usage notes are also given for other types of entries that may present usage problems. Some examples include the use of certain titles in speaking and writing (see *Reverend*), the proper way to list academic degrees (see *degree*), and the use of certain prefixes, suffixes, prepositions, and the like.

Figurative usage

Definitions and illustrative sentences or phrases are labeled *Figurative* when the word defined is used out of its usual, matter-of-fact sense. Words used figuratively are usually exaggerated or used imaginatively to make speech and writing more forceful, colorful, or beautiful.

In this dictionary, the label *Figurative* precedes a definition when the meaning is figurative only and not used in a literal sense, as in *dislocate,* definition 2. When the meaning of the main-entry word is literal, but the illustrative sentence or phrase gives only the figurative meaning, it is preceded by (*Figurative.*) in parentheses as in *dislocation,* definition 1. When the figurative meaning of an illustrative sentence or phrase is self-evident, it is preceded by the label *Figurative:* and no definition is given, as in *deploy,* definition 3.

dis|lo|cate (dis′lō kāt), *v.t.,* **-cat|ed, -cat|ing. 1** to put out of joint: *The football player dislocated his shoulder when he fell.* **2** *Figurative.* to put out of order; disturb; upset: *Our plans for the picnic were dislocated by the rain.* SYN: disarrange, disconcert. **3** to put out of place; displace.

dis|lo|ca|tion (dis′lō kā′shən), *n.* **1** the act of dislocating: (*Figurative.*). *His dislocation of the family's plans did not upset the children.* **2** the state of being dislocated. **3** *Physics.* an imperfection in the crystal structure of a metal or other solid resulting from the absence of an atom or atoms in one or more layers of a crystal.

de|ploy (di ploi′), *v., n.*—*v.t.* **1** to spread out (troops, military units, or other forces) from a column into a long battle line. **2** to distribute (forces) in convenient positions for future use: *A fleet of ships were deployed over the line area in which the astronauts were expected to land.* **3** *Figurative: . . . an English poet deploying all the forces of his genius* (Matthew Arnold).

Origin of words

By studying the etymology of a word, you can trace its evolution from when and how it was first used to its present form and usage. You can see how it relates to earlier English forms, and to words in languages other than English. Look carefully at etymologies and you will find words that have changed their meanings and spellings with usage.

Etymology

The etymology for a word always appears in square brackets near the end of the entry. It may include one or both of these symbols: < which means "derived from" or "taken from," and + which means "and."

com|punc|tion (kəm pungk′shən), *n.* **1** uneasiness of the mind because of wrongdoing; pricking of the conscience; regret; remorse: *He had no compunction about having eaten up a whole box of cookies. . . . a remorse and compunction for former sins* (John Donne). **SYN**: contrition. **2** a slight or passing regret; being temporarily sorry: *He threw out the rowdy without compunction.* [< Late Latin *compunctiō, -ōnis* pricking, remorse < Latin *compungere* < *com-* (intensive) + *pungere* to prick] —**com|punc′tion|less,** *adj.*

You can see from this etymology that the word *compunction* is derived from the Latin *compungere,* which comes from *com-* and *pungere,* meaning *to prick.* The meaning of the English *compunction* is much the same as the meaning of its earlier form. But see how the meaning of *comrade* has changed from an earlier word meaning *roommate.*

com|rade (kom′rad; *especially British* kom′rid, kum′-), *n.* **1** a companion and friend: *The two boys were close comrades and did everything together.* **2** a person who shares in what another is doing; fellow worker; partner. **3** a fellow member of a union, political party, or other group: *Members of the Communist Party are often called comrades.* **4** = comrade in arms. [< Middle French *camarade* < Spanish *camarada* roommate < Latin *camera* vault < Greek *kamárā*]

A short etymology within an entry indicates that the meaning of one part of speech is actually derived from the meaning of another, as in *affray.*

af|fray (ə frā′), *n., v.—n.* a noisy quarrel; fight in public; brawl. In law, an affray is fighting in a public place so as to frighten others. [< Old French *effrei* < *effreer;* see the verb]
—*v.t. Archaic.* to frighten.
[< Anglo-French *afrayer,* variant of Old French *effreer,* ultimately < Latin *ex-* out of + unrecorded Frankish *frithu* peace]

Word origin indicators

When the etymology of an entry is undetermined, this dictionary indicates "origin uncertain" or "origin unknown." When a word origin is uncertain but possibly related to another word, this dictionary indicates "origin uncertain. Compare . . ." When the origin of a word is almost certain but still unproved, this dictionary indicates "apparently" or "perhaps."

dab[3] . . . [origin uncertain]

clour . . . [origin unknown]

clem . . . [origin uncertain. Compare Dutch and German *klemmen* pinch.]

dad . . . [apparently < children's speech]

Back formations

When a longer word such as a noun is shortened to form a new verb, the new shorter word is a back formation, because the process usually works the other way. The noun *admonition* was shortened to form the verb *admonish,* and the noun *burglar* was shortened to form the verb *burgle.*

Doublets

Doublets are two or more words that come from a common source, but came into English by different routes. For example, *cadence, cadenza,* and *chance* are doublets.

cadence . . .
[< French *cadence* < Italian *cadenza* < Vulgar Latin *cadentia* < Latin *cadere* fall. See etym. of doublets **cadenza, chance.**]

cadenza . . .
[<Italian *cadenza.* See etym. of doublets **cadence, chance.**]

chance . . .
[< Old French *cheance* < Vulgar Latin *cadentia* a falling < Latin *cadero* fall. See etym. of doublets **cadence, cadenza.**]

By looking at the etymologies of these three words, you can see that *cadence* is taken from the French; that *cadenza* is from the Italian; and that *chance* is from the Old French. But all three go back to the Latin *cadere.*

Related etymologies

Words that are derived from different forms of the same original word are indicated in etymologies by "See related etym. at . . ." For example, *adult* and *adolescent* have related etymologies because both are derived from different forms of the Latin *adolēscere,* meaning *to grow up.*

adult . . .
[< Latin *adultus,* past participle of *adolēscere* < *ad-* to + *alēscere* grow up. See related etym. at **adolescent.**] —**a|dult′ness,** *n.*

adolescent . . .
[< Latin *adolēscēns, -entis,* present participle of *adolēscere* grow up < *ad-* to + *alēscere* grow up. See related etym. under **adult.**] —**ad′o|les′cent|ly,** *adv.*

Cross references

Cross references to etymologies save space and avoid unnecessary repetition. Even more important, they help you to see at a glance those words that have a common ancestor. When two or more words are derived from the same origin, this dictionary gives only one etymology in detail. Other related etymologies are cross-referred to the detailed etymology with the words "See etym. under . . ." For example, *abstention* and *abstinence* are derived from the Latin *abstinere,* meaning *withhold.* The more detailed etymology is given under *abstinence.*

abstention . . .
[< Late Latin *abstentiō, -ōnis* < Latin *abstinēre* withhold; see etym. under **abstinence**]

abstinence . . .
[< Latin *abstinentia* < *abstinēns, -entis,* present participle of *abstinēre* withhold < *abs-* from + *tenēre* hold]

Interesting facts

The etymology that appears after entries in this dictionary tells, in capsule form, the origin and history of the word defined. By studying etymologies, you can trace a word back to its origin; you can see how some words change their meanings with time; and you can learn many interesting facts about how people lived in the past, and in various parts of the world. Here are some examples:

Words that have changed their meanings:

ex|plore (ek splôr′, -splōr′), *v.,* **-plored, -plor|ing.**
—*v.t.* **1** to travel in (little-known lands or seas)

for the purpose of discovery: *Admiral Byrd explored much of Antarctica.* **2** to go over carefully; look into closely; examine: *to explore a possibility. The children explored the new house from attic to cellar.* **SYN**: investigate, scrutinize. See syn. under **search**. **3** *Medicine.* to examine by touch, for example with a probe: *The surgeon explored the wound.* **4** *Obsolete.* to search for; search out: *Let some prophet . . . Explore the cause of great Apollo's rage* (Alexander Pope).
—***v.i.*** to carry out a methodical searching operation; engage in exploration: *Some geologists explore for oil.*
[< Latin *explōrāre* investigate, spy out, (originally) cry out (at the sight of game or an enemy) < *ex-* out + *plōrāre* weep, cry]

scan|dal (skan′dəl), *n., v.*, **-daled, -dal|ing** or (*especially British*) **-dalled, -dal|ling.** —***n.*** **1** a shameful action, condition, or event that brings disgrace or shocks public opinion: *It was a scandal for the city treasurer to take tax money for his own use. The state-government scandals of 1939-1940 retired him to private life when he first was governor* (Newsweek). **2** damage to reputation; disgrace: *to avoid scandal at all costs. O the disgrace of it! The scandal, the incredible come-down* (Max Beerbohm). **SYN**: discredit, disrepute, dishonor. **3** public talk about a person that will hurt his reputation; evil gossip; slander; defamation: *You'll have no scandal while you dine, but honest talk and wholesome wine* (Tennyson). **SYN**: calumny. **4** discredit to religion caused by irreligious conduct or moral lapse.
—***v.t.*** **1** *Archaic.* to spread scandal about (a person); defame. **2** *Obsolete.* to disgrace.
be the scandal of, to scandalize: *The visiting dignitaries who got into a public brawl were the scandal of the town.*
[< Latin *scandalum* (cause for) offense, temptation < Greek *skándalon* scandal, offense; (originally) trap with a springing device. See etym. of doublet **slander**.]

sham|poo (sham pü′), *v.*, **-pooed, -poo|ing,** *n.*
—***v.t.*** **1** to wash (the hair, the scalp, or a rug) with a soapy or other cleansing preparation. **2** to wash the hair or scalp of (a person). **3** *Archaic.* to massage.
—***n.*** **1** the act of washing the hair, the scalp, or a rug, with a soapy or other cleansing preparation. **2** a preparation used for shampooing: *a liquid shampoo.* **3** *Archaic.* a massage.
[Anglo-Indian < Hindustani *chāmpō,* imperative (literally) press, knead < Sanskrit *cap* knead]

How some foods got their names;

co|co (kō′kō), *n., pl.* **-cos,** *adj.* —***n.*** **1** = coconut palm. **2** = coconut.
—***adj.*** made of the rind or husk of the coconut: *a coco mat.* Also, **cocoa.**
[< Portuguese *coco* grinning face (because of the resemblance of the shell's base to a monkey face)]

ketch|up (kech′əp), *n.* **1** a sauce to use with meat, fish, etc. Tomato ketchup is made of tomatoes, onions, salt, sugar, and spices. **2** a sauce made from mushrooms, walnuts, etc. Also **catchup, catsup, katchup, katsup.** [< Chinese *ké-tsiap* brine of pickled fish, or < Malay *kĕchap* smack the lips]

punch[3] (punch), *n.* a drink made of different liquids, often fruit juices, mixed together. [probably < Hindustani *pānch* five < Sanskrit *pañca* (because of the number of ingredients in the drink)]

sau|sage (sô′sij), *n.* chopped pork, beef, or other meats, seasoned and usually stuffed into a thin tube: *The frankfurter . . . is the most popular sausage in the world* (John C. Ayres). [< Old North French *saussiche,* Old French *saucisse* < Vulgar Latin *salcīcia* < Latin *salere* to salt < *sāl, salis* salt. Compare etym. under **sauce.**]

sau|terne or **Sau|terne** (sō tėrn′, sô-), *n.* **1** Also, **sauternes** or **Sauternes.** a sweet white wine made in the region south of Bordeaux, France: *In bad years the Sauternes are less sweet, but there's no such thing as "dry Sauternes"* (Atlantic). **2** a similar wine made elsewhere. [< *Sauternes,* a town in France near where the grapes are grown]

How some methods of cooking foods got their names;

braise (brāz), *v.t.,* **braised, brais|ing.** to brown (meat) quickly in fat and then cook long and slowly in a covered pan with a very little liquid. [< French *braiser* < Old French *braise* hot charcoal < a Germanic word] —**brais′er,** *n.*

poach[2] (pōch), *v.t.* **1** to cook (an egg) by breaking it into boiling water. **2** to cook (any of various foods, especially fish) by simmering for a short time in a liquid. [< Old French *pochier* (literally) to put in a bag (because the yolk is thought of as enclosed in the white of the egg) < *poche* cooking spoon < Late Latin *popia,* perhaps < a Gaulish word]

sau|té (sō tā′, sô-), *adj., n., v.,* **-téed, -té|ing.**
—***adj.*** cooked or browned in a little fat, usually quickly and over a hot fire.
—***n.*** a dish of food cooked or browned in a little fat.
—***v.t.*** to fry quickly in a little fat: *crabmeat sautéed with butter.*
[< French *sauté,* past participle of *sauter* to jump < Latin *saltāre* hop, dance (frequentative) < *salīre* to leap]

How some house furnishings got their names;

can|o|py (kan′ə pē), *n., pl.* **-pies,** *v.,* **-pied, -py|ing.** —***n.*** **1** a covering fixed over a bed, throne, or entrance, or carried on poles over a person: *There is a striped canopy over the entrance to . . .*
[< Old French *canape,* learned borrowing from Medieval Latin *canapēum* < Latin *cōnōpēum* a couch with mosquito curtains < Greek *kōnṓpion* (originally) of Canopus]

car|pet (kär′pit), *n., v., adj.* —***n.*** **1a** a heavy, woven fabric for covering floors and stairs. **b** a covering made of this fabric. Carpets are usually tacked or nailed to the floor; rugs are not. **2** anything like a carpet: (*Figurative.*) *He walked on a carpet of grass. . . .*
[< Medieval Latin *carpeta, carpita* thick cloth < Vulgar Latin *carpīre* to pick, card (wool) < Latin *carpere*] —**car′pet|less,** *adj.*

cup (kup), *n., v.,* **cupped, cup|ping.** —***n.*** **1** a hollow, rounded dish to drink from. Most cups have handles. **2** as much as a cup holds; cupful. . . .
[Old English *cuppe* < Late Latin *cuppa* < Latin *cūpa* tub] —**cup′like′,** *adj.*

dish (dish), *n., v.* —***n.*** **1** anything to serve food in, such as a plate, bowl, cup, or saucer. Dishes can be made of glass, pottery, or plastic, but paper plates are usually not called dishes. *She brought forth butter in a lordly dish* (Judges 5:25). . . .
[Old English *disc* < Latin *discus* < Greek *diskos* discus, platter. See etym. of doublets **dais, desk, discus,** and **disk.**]

rug[1] (rug), *n.* **1** a heavy floor covering usually covering only part of a room's floor: *a rag rug, a grass rug.* **2** a thick, warm cloth used as covering: *The Indian wrapped his woolen rug around . . .*
[< Scandinavian (compare Norwegian dialectal *rugga* coarse coverlet)]

ta|ble (tā′bəl), *n., adj., v.,* **-bled, -bling.** —***n.*** **1** a piece of furniture having a smooth, flat top on legs: *a dining table, a surgeon's operating table.* **2** a table upon which food is served: to set the silverware on a table. **3** food put on a table to be eaten; fare: *Your mother sets a good table.* **4** the entertainment of a family or guests at a table; eating; feasting. **5** the persons seated at a table especially at a dinner or for discussion: *The . . .*
[Old English *tabule, tabele,* ultimately < Latin *tabula* slab for writing or painting]

How the first barricades were built;

bar|ri|cade (bar′ə kād′, bar′ə kād), *n., v.,* **-cad|ed, -cad|ing.** —***n.*** **1** a rough, hastily made barrier for defense: *The soldiers cut down trees to make a barricade across the road.* **SYN**: fortification, rampart. **2** *Figurative.* any barrier or obstruction. **SYN**: block, obstacle, impediment.
—***v.t.*** **1** to block or obstruct with a barricade: *The soldiers barricaded the road with fallen trees.* **2** to shut in or out with, or as if with, a barricade.
[< French *barricade* < Provençal *barricada* < *barrica* barrel < *barril* (barrels of earth were the first barricades)] —**bar′ri|cad′er,** *n.*

Words become full of life and carry greater meaning if you study and use their etymologies.

Spelling and looking up words

Almost everyone is unsure of how to spell some words, especially words that are pronounced one way and spelled another. The dictionary gives you the correct spelling. But how do you look up a word you cannot spell?

Before you give up in despair, try to decide exactly what you need to know. If you want to spell the word *separate,* but cannot remember whether an *a* or an *e* follows the *p,* all you need do is check *sepa-*. If you want to spell the word *wagon,* but cannot remember whether to use one *g* or two, look up *wagg-* and see what you find. Your greatest problems will be in words that have a combination of letters that do not look like the sounds they represent—the *a* sounds of *plaid, half,* and *laugh* for example, or the silent letters that begin *gnaw, knife,* and *pneumonia.* Before you look up these words in the dictionary, check the table of Common spellings of English sounds on these pages. It will help you find the words you cannot spell.

Spelling

Some words have more than one acceptable spelling. When one spelling is used almost as often as another, the two spellings appear together in a single entry joined by "or."

cal|o|rie or **cal|o|ry**

Alternate spellings may be combined in a single entry when: an entry can be written with or without a hyphen, such as *orangutan* or *orang-utan;* an entry can be written with a capital or a lower case letter, such as *burley* or *Burley;* an entry can be written with or without a possessive ending, as in *bachelor's* or *bachelor hall;* an entry can be written in the singular or the plural, such as *Canterbury bell* or *bells;* an abbreviation can be written with or without periods, as in *GI* (no periods) or *G.I.*

In cases where the two forms of the word are not equally used or belong in different alphabetical places, the alternate spelling appears at the end of the entry for the preferred spellings, introduced by the word *also,* as in *catabolism* . . . Also, *katabolism.* Such alternate spellings appear in their own alphabetical places in the dictionary, but only as cross references to the preferred spelling, such as *katabolism* = *catabolism.*

When the pronunciation of an alternate form differs from the pronunciation of the preferred spelling, the alternate form has a separate cross-reference entry.

i|o|dide (ī′ə dīd, -did), *n.* a compound of iodine with another element or radical; a salt of hydriodic acid. [< *iod-* + *-ide*]
i|o|did (ī′ə did), *n.* = iodide.

When more than one spelling is given for an entry, which should you choose? Where several forms are combined in a single entry joined by "or," the first spelling is considered the more commonly used.

co|deine or **co|dein** (kō′dēn), *n.* a white, crystalline drug obtained from opium and used to relieve pain and coughs, and to cause sleep:

quan|dong or **quan|dang** (kwon′dong′), *n.* **1** an Australian tree related to the sandalwood, that has an edible fruit and a nutlike seed with an edible kernel. **2** the fruit of this tree. **3** the seed or kernel. [< the native Australian name]

You will be among the majority if you choose *codeine* and *quandong.*

When different spellings of the same word are listed as separate entries, the spelling of the defined entry is preferred to the entry that is cross referred.

co|coa|nut (kō′kə nut′, -nət), *n., adj.* = coconut.

co|co|nut (kō′kə nut′, -nət), *n., adj.* —***n.*** **1** the large, round, brown, hard-shelled nut of the coconut palm. Coconuts have a white lining that is good to eat and a whitish or clear liquid called coconut milk, used as a drink. The white lining is cut up into shreds and used for cakes, puddings, and pies. **2** the fruit of the coconut palm, containing the nut within a thick, ovoid, fibrous husk: *The coconut yields six commercial products: copra, coconut oil, coconuts, shredded coconut, oil cake, and coir fiber* (Colby and Foster). **3** = coconut palm.
—***adj.*** of or made from the fruit of the coconut.
Also, **cocoanut**.

You should choose *coconut.*

Inflections

Inflections or inflected forms are the forms of a word that show grammatical differences such as the plurals of nouns, the past tense and present participle of verbs, and the comparative forms of adjectives and adverbs. Most inflections are regular. That is, they follow simple rules, such as the rule to add *s* to the end of a singular noun to form the plural. For more on spelling rules, see "Learning to spell correctly" on page *20.* This dictionary does not list regular inflections. When the spelling of an inflected form is *irregular,* it is shown in boldface type after the part of speech designation:

bab|ble (bab′əl), *v.,* **-bled, -bling,** *n.* —***v.i.*** **1** to make sounds like a baby: *My baby brother babbles and coos in his crib.* **2** to talk foolishly; prattle: *She babbled on and on about her new dress.*

e|mul|si|fy (i mul′sə fī), *v.t.,* **-fied, -fy|ing.** to make or turn (an oil, fat, resin, or other substance) into an emulsion: *Juice from the pancreas emulsifies fat in the digestion of food.*

Only the syllable or syllables that differ from the spelling of the main entry are given:

ad|vance (ad vans′, -väns′), *v.,* **-vanced, -vancing,** *n., adj.* —***v.t.*** **1** to put or move forward; push forward: *The general advanced the troops.* **2** to help forward; further: *The President's speech ad-*

ka|tab|a|sis (kə tab′ə sis), *n., pl.* **-ses** (-sēz). **1** a military retreat, especially that of Cyrus the Younger and the Greeks who fought against Artaxerxes. **2** the act or process of going down. [< Greek *katábasis* descent < *katabainein* to go down]

Common irregular inflections have main entries themselves:

da|ta (dā′tə, dat′ə, dä′tə), *n.pl. of* **da|tum**. things known or granted; information; facts: *Names,*

me|di|a[1] (mē′dē ə), *n.* **1** a plural of **medium**: *Newspapers, magazines, and billboards are important media for advertising.* **2** = medium (def. 2). **3** = mass media.
▶See **medium** for usage note.

When two or more spellings are listed for inflected forms, the one listed first is the most acceptable.

a|quar|i|um (ə kwãr′ē əm), *n., pl.* **i|ums, -i|a** (-ē ə). **1** a pond, tank, or glass bowl in which living fish and other water animals and water plants are kept. **2** a building used for showing collec-

ge|nus (jē′nəs), *n., pl.* **gen|e|ra** or **ge|nus|es.** **1** any group of similar things; kind; sort; class: *Assuming, however, that there still exists the genus serious reader* (Hayden Carruth). **2** a

Some inflected forms are spelled one way in American English and another way in British English. These spellings are labeled:

bev|el (bev′əl), *n., v.,* **-eled, -el|ing** or (*especially British*) **-elled, -el|ling.** *adj.*—***n.*** **1** a sloping edge or surface. There is often a bevel on the frame

Common spellings of English sounds

This table shows the various sounds of English and the most common spellings for those sounds. It will help you find words in this dictionary when you are unsure of how to spell them. Many words are pronounced differently from the way they are written. For example, *laugh* is pronounced (*laf*) and *phrase* is pronounced (*frāz.*) If you are unsure of how a word begins or ends or of some of the letters in between, this table will give you the clues you need to look it up in the dictionary. See page *124* for a key to the symbols.

Symbol	Spelling
a	h***a***t, pl***ai***d, h***a***lf, l***au***gh
ā	***a***ge, ***ai***d, g***ao***l, g***au***ge, s***ay***, br***ea***k, v***ei***n, w***eigh***, th***ey***
â	c***a***re, ***ai***r, pr***ay***er, wh***e***re, p***ea***r, th***ei***r
ä	f***a***ther, h***a***lf, l***au***gh, s***e***rgeant, h***ea***rt
b	***b***ad, ra***bb***it
ch	***ch***ild, wa***tch***, righ***te***ous, ques***ti***on, fu***tu***re
d	***d***id, a***dd***, fill***ed***
e	m***a***ny, ***ae***sthetic, s***ai***d, s***ay***s, l***e***t, br***ea***d, h***ei***fer, l***eo***pard, fr***ie***nd, b***u***ry
ē	C***ae***sar, qu***ay***, ***e***qual, t***ea***m, b***ee***, rec***ei***ve, p***eo***ple, k***ey***, mach***i***ne, bel***ie***ve, ph***oe***nix
ėr	p***ear***l, st***er***n, f***ir***st, w***or***d, j***our***ney, t***ur***n, m***yr***tle
ər	li***ar***, moth***er***, elix***ir***, hon***or***, hon***our***, aug***ur***, zeph***yr***
f	***f***at, e***ff***ort, lau***gh***, ***ph***rase
g	***g***o, e***gg***, ***gh***ost, ***gu***est, catalo***gue***
h	***h***e, ***wh***o
hw	***wh***eat
i	***E***nglish, b***ee***n, b***i***t, s***ie***ve, w***o***men, b***u***sy, b***ui***ld, h***y***mn
ī	***ai***sle, ***ay***e, h***eigh***t, ***ey***e, ***i***ce, l***ie***, h***igh***, b***uy***, sk***y***, r***ye***
j	bri***dg***e, ver***du***re, sol***di***er, tra***g***ic, exa***gg***erate, ***j***am
k	***c***oat, a***cc***ount, ***ch***emistry, ba***ck***, a***cq***uire, sa***cque***, ***k***ind, fo***lk***, li***qu***or
l	***l***and, te***ll***
m	dra***chm***, paradi***gm***, ca***lm***, ***m***e, cli***mb***, co***mm***on, sole***mn***
n	***gn***aw, ***kn***ife, ***mn***emonic, ***n***o, ma***nn***er, ***pn***eumonia
ng	i***n***k, lo***ng***, to***ngue***
o	w***a***tch, h***o***t
ō	b***eau***, y***eo***man, s***ew***, ***o***pen, b***oa***t, t***oe***, ***oh***, br***oo***ch, s***ou***l, th***ough***, l***ow***
ô	***a***ll, Ut***ah***, w***al***k, t***au***ght, l***aw***, ***o***rder, br***oa***d, b***ough***t
oi	b***oi***l, b***oy***
ou	h***ou***se, b***ough***, n***ow***
p	cu***p***, ha***pp***y
r	***r***un, ***rh***ythm, ca***rr***y, ***wr***ong
s	***c***ent, ni***ce***, ***ps***ychology, ***s***ay, ***sc***ent, ***sch***ism, mi***ss***
sh	o***ce***an, ma***ch***ine, spe***ci***al, ***psh***aw, ***s***ure, ***sch***ist, con***sci***ence, nau***se***ous, ***sh***e, ten***si***on, ***iss***ue, mi***ssi***on, na***ti***on
t	stopp***ed***, bou***ght***, ***pt***omaine, ***t***ell, ***Th***omas, bu***tt***on
th	***th***in
ŦH	***th***en, brea***the***
u	c***o***me, d***oe***s, fl***oo***d, tr***ou***ble, c***u***p
u̇	w***o***lf, g***oo***d, sh***ou***ld, f***u***ll
ü	man***eu***ver, thr***ew***, ad***ieu***, m***o***ve, sh***oe***, f***oo***d, cr***ou***p, thr***ough***, r***u***le, bl***ue***, fr***ui***t
v	o***f***, Ste***ph***en, ***v***ery, fli***vv***er
w	ch***o***ir, q***u***ick, ***w***ill
y	opin***i***on, hallelu***j***ah, ***y***es
yü	b***eau***ty, f***eu***d, qu***eue***, f***ew***, ad***ieu***, v***iew***, ***u***se, c***ue***, ***you***, ***yu***le
z	ha***s***, di***sc***ern, sci***ss***ors, ***x***ylophone, ***z***ero, bu***zz***
zh	gara***ge***, mea***s***ure, divi***si***on, a***z***ure, bra***zi***er
ə	***a***lone, fount***ai***n, mom***e***nt, penc***i***l, c***o***mplete, cauti***ou***s, circ***u***s

Pronunciation

Say aloud the words *far, fat,* and *face,* and you can hear immediately that there are more sounds in English than letters in the alphabet. To make up the difference, this dictionary uses a special set of symbols that tell you how to pronounce the words you look up. The pronunciation follows the word in this way: **dic|tion|ar|y** (dik′shə ner′ē). Each symbol represents a specific sound, as indicated in the short pronunciation key on almost every right-hand page in this dictionary.

Diacritical marks appear above some symbols. These marks indicate specific sounds for the symbols with which they appear. The diacritical marks are:

circumflex (sėr′kəm fleks)—the mark over the ô, as in *order.*

dieresis (dī er′ ə sis)—two dots over the ä, as in *father,* or the ü, as in *rule.*

macron (mā′kron)—the long mark over the ā, as in *age;* the ē, as in *equal;* the ī, as in *ice;* and the ō, as in *open.*

single dot—over the ė in the ėr, as in *term,* and over the u̇, as in *full.*

tilde (til′ də)—the curved mark over the ã, as in *care.*

Stress marks show which syllables to emphasize. A heavy stress mark [′] follows the syllable with primary or strong accent. A light stress mark [′] follows the syllable with secondary or lighter accent.

Some words taken from foreign languages are spoken with sounds that otherwise do not occur in English. Symbols for these sounds are given in the complete pronunciation key on this page.

Complete pronunciation key

a	hat, cap	oi	oil, voice
ā	age, face	ou	house, out
ã	care, air	p	paper, cup
ä	father, far	r	run, try
b	bad, rob	s	say, yes
ch	child, much	sh	she, rush
d	did, red	t	tell, it
e	let, best	th	thin, both
ē	equal, see	ᴛʜ	then, smooth
ėr	term, learn	u	cup, butter
f	fat, if	u̇	full, put
g	go, bag	ü	rule, move
h	he, how	v	very, save
i	it, pin	w	will, woman
ī	ice, five	y	young, yet
j	jam, enjoy	z	zero, breeze
k	kind, seek	zh	measure, seizure
l	land, coal		
m	me, am	ə	represents:
n	no, in	a	in about
ng	long, bring	e	in taken
o	hot, rock	i	in pencil
ō	open, go	o	in lemon
ô	order, all	u	in circus

Non-English sounds

Y	as in French *du.* Pronounce ē with the lips rounded as for English ü in *rule.*
œ	as in French *peu.* Pronounce ā with the lips rounded as for ō.
N	as in French *bon.* The N is not pronounced, but shows that the vowel before it is nasal.
H	as in German *ach.* Pronounce k without closing the breath passage.
à	as in French *ami.* The quality of this vowel is midway between the a of *hat* and the ä of *far,* but closer to the former.

A a

* **A**[1] or **a**[1] (ā), *n., pl.* **A's** or **As, a's** or **as. 1** the first letter of the alphabet. There are two *a*'s in *afraid.* **2** any sound represented by this letter. **3** used as a symbol for: **a** the first (of an actual or possible series): *stateroom A on a ship, company A in an infantry battalion.* **b** the best (of its kind or class): *Grade A milk.* **c** a known quantity (used especially in algebraic equations, along with *b, c,* etc.; *x, y,* and *z* most commonly represent unknown quantities). **4** the highest grade (in schools and colleges): *to get an A in English.* **5** *Music.* **a** the sixth tone in the scale of C major. **b** a symbol representing this tone. **c** a key, string, valve, or finger hole, that produces this tone. **d** the scale or key that has A as its keynote: *a symphony in A.*
from A to Z, from beginning to end: *The African countries need everything from A to Z in medicine* (London Times).

a in the treble clef

* **A**[1]
definition 5b
a in the bass clef

A[2] (ā), *n., pl.* **A's.** anything shaped like the letter A.

a[2] (*unstressed* ə; *stressed* ā), *adj. or indefinite article.* **1a** any: *Is there a pencil in the box? A tree has leaves. Call a doctor.* **b** one like; another (before proper names or nouns used as the type of a class): *a Daniel come to judgment . . .* (Shakespeare). *She is a saint among women.*
2 one: *My mother wants a pound of butter.*
3a the same: *two at a time.* **b** a particular: *too high a price.* **c** one kind of: *Chemistry is a science.* **d** a certain; some: *a matter of doubt, a great many friends.* **4** a single: *not a chance, not a one.* [variant of *an*[1]]
▶See **an**[1] for usage note.
▶Though **a** regularly precedes other modifiers, it follows *many, such, what,* and any adjective preceded by *as, how, so,* or *too,* as in *many a man, what a bore, as great a bore.*

a[3] (*unstressed* ə; *stressed* ā), *adj. or indefinite article* (*originally a prep.*). to or for each; every: *Thanksgiving comes once a year. He earns ten dollars a day.* [Old English *on* on]

a[4] (ə), *pron. British Dialect.* **1** he. **2** she. **3** it. **4** they. [Middle English *a*]

a[5] (ə), *v.t. Dialect.* have: *I should a thought of it.* [Middle English *a,* contraction of *have*]
▶Now often written solid (*I shoulda thought of it*) and, in representations of English speech, *of* (əv). See **of** for another usage note.

a[6] (ə), *prep. Obsolete or Dialect.* of: *John a Gaunt, cup a tea.* [Middle English *a,* for *of*]

a' (ä, ô), *adj. Scottish.* all: *A man's a man for a' that . . .* (Robert Burns).

a-[1], *prefix.* **1** on____; in____; into____: *Abed = in bed.*
2 in the act of____: *Aflutter = in the act of fluttering.*
3 in a____condition: *Aweary = in a weary condition.*
4 to ____; toward____: *Aside = to one side.* [Middle English *a,* Old English *an, on*]
▶**a-**[1]. There is a strong tendency to avoid placing adjectives originally formed with *a-* + noun (such as *asleep, alive*) before a noun which they qualify. We say *a man who is asleep* and *a man asleep,* but usually not *an asleep man.*

a-[2], *prefix.* the form of **ab-**[1] before *m, p,* and *v,* as in *amentia, aperture, avert.*

a-[3], *prefix.* the form of **ad-** before *sc, sp,* and *st,* as in *ascribe, aspire, astringent.*

a-[4], *prefix.* **1** not____: *Apolitical = not political.*
2 without____: *Atonal = without tone.*
▶The prefix **a-** is the form of **an-**[1] before consonants except *h.*
▶**A-,** meaning "not," "without," or "lacking," is of Greek origin and is found in words taken directly, or through Latin, from Greek, as in *apathetic,* meaning "without feeling." As a naturalized English prefix, it is also used in new formations, as in *asocial, areligious.* It is called "alpha privative" from *alpha,* the name of the Greek letter corresponding to our letter *a,* and *privative,* meaning "taking away, depriving." *A-* corresponds to English *un-* and Latin *in-.*

a (no period), an abbreviation or symbol for the following:
1 ampere or amperes.
2 are (100 square meters).
3 (in scoring baseball, basketball, hockey, and other team games) assist or assists.
4 atto-.
5 before (Latin, *ante*): *a 1600 = before 1600.*
6 *Astronomy.* a semimajor axis, defining a planet's mean distance from the sun (one of the five orbital elements describing any planet).

a., an abbreviation or symbol for the following:
1 about.
2 *Commerce.* **a** accepted. **b** approved.
3 acre or acres.
4 adjective.
5 alto.
6 *Heraldry.* argent.
7 before (Latin, *ante*): *a. 1600 = before 1600.*

A (no period), an abbreviation or symbol for the following:
1 absolute (temperature).
2 adenine.
3a America. **b** American.
4 ampere or amperes.
5 angstrom unit or units.
6 anode.
7 April.
8 (formerly) argon (chemical element). Now, **Ar** (no period).
9 (in scoring baseball, basketball, hockey, and other team games) assist or assists.
10a atomic fission. **b** atomic weight. Odd and even A are denoted by o and + respectively.
11 Australian (used with the symbol for *dollar* or (formerly) *pound*): *$A250.*
12 one of the four major blood factors or groups widely used to determine blood compatibility in transfusions. A person with A type blood can receive blood of either the A or O group.
13 (in financial rating) the third highest rank.
14 the first in a series of narrow shoe widths (followed in degree of narrowness by AA, etc.).

Å or **A°**, angstrom unit or units.

A., 1 acre or acres. **2** adult. **3** answer.

A-1 (ā'wun'), *adj. Informal.* A one; first-rate.

A 1, 1 (of a ship) in the best condition (from a double symbol used originally by Lloyd's Register, "A" applying to the hull and "1" to the engines, rigging, and other operating equipment). **2** *Informal.* A one; first-rate.

a|a (ä'ä), *n.* lava hardened into a rough, slaggy, brittle mass. [< Hawaiian *'a'a*]

AA (no periods), an abbreviation or symbol for the following:
1 achievement age.
2 air-to-air.
3 antiaircraft.
4 author's alteration.
5 (in financial rating) the second highest rank.
6 the second in a series of narrow shoe widths (followed in degree of narrowness by AAA).

A.A., an abbreviation for the following:
1 Alcoholics Anonymous.
2 antiaircraft.
3 Associate in Arts.
4 Automobile Association (of Great Britain).

AAA (no periods) an abbreviation for the following:
1 Agricultural Adjustment Administration (of the United States).
2 American Automobile Association.
3 (in financial rating) the highest rank.
4 the third in a series of narrow shoe widths (preceded in degree of width by AA).

A.A.A., 1 Amateur Athletic Association (of Great Britain). **2** American Arbitration Association.

A.A.A.A. or **AAAA** (no periods), American Association of Advertising Agencies.

A.A.A.L., American Academy of Arts and Letters.

A.A.A.S. or **AAAS** (no periods), **1** American Academy of Arts and Sciences. **2** American Association for the Advancement of Science.

AAF (no periods) or **A.A.F.,** Army Air Forces (of the United States).

AAM (no periods), air-to-air missile.

A and M (no periods) or **A. & M.,** *Informal.* Agricultural and Mechanical (in U.S. college names): *Texas A and M.*

A. & R. or **a. and r.,** artists and repertory (department of a phonograph record company).

A.A.R., Association of American Railroads.

aard|vark (ärd'värk'), *n.* a burrowing mammal of southern and eastern Africa with a piglike snout, very strong claws, and a long tail. The aardvark feeds at night with its long, sticky tongue on ants and termites. [< Afrikaans *aardvark* < Dutch *aarde* earth + *varken* pig]

aard|wolf (ärd'wu̇lf'), *n., pl.* **-wolves.** a mammal of southern and eastern Africa, resembling the hyena somewhat, to which it is related, but with small, weak teeth. It feeds chiefly on termites and other insects and on carrion. [< Afrikaans *aardwolf* < Dutch *aarde* earth + *wolf* wolf]

Aar|on (ãr'ən), *n.* (in the Bible) the older brother of Moses and the first high priest of the Israelites. The Jewish priesthood is traditionally said to descend from his tribe (Levi) and, in particular, from Aaron's sons.

Aa|ron|ic (ãr on'ik), *adj.* **1a** of or descended from Aaron. **b** Levitical. **2** of or having to do with the lesser order of the Mormon priesthood for young men 12 to 20 years old, comprising the offices of priest, teacher, and deacon. **3** priestly.

Aar|on|ite (ãr'ə nīt), *n.* **1** a descendant of Aaron. **2** a Levite.

Aaron's beard, = rose of Sharon (def. 2).

Aaron's rod, 1 any of several tall plants with long, flower-bearing main stems, especially a kind of goldenrod. **2** (in the Bible) the rod with which Aaron performed miracles. It turned into a serpent. Exodus 7:10. Later it blossomed and bore almonds. Numbers 17:8. **3** an architectural ornament consisting of a rod with leaves sprouting on either side, or of a rod with a snake twined around it.

AARP (no periods), American Association of Retired Persons.

A.A.S., 1 American Academy of Sciences. **2** Fellow of the American Academy (Latin, *Academiae Americanae Socius*).

aas|vo|gel (äs'fō'gəl), *n. Afrikaans.* a vulture.

A.A.U. or **AAU** (no periods), Amateur Athletic Union (of the United States).

A.A.U.P. or **AAUP** (no periods), American Association of University Professors.

A.A.U.W. or **AAUW** (no periods), American Association of University Women.

Ab (ab, äb), *n.* the eleventh (or, in leap year, the twelfth) month of the Jewish civil year, and the fifth month of the ecclesiastical year, beginning in July or in the first part of August. [< Hebrew *ābh*]

ab-[1], *prefix.* from; away; away from; off: *Abnormal = away from normal.* Also: **a-** before *m, p, v;* **abs-** before *c, t.* [< Latin *ab-* < *ab* off, away from]

ab-[2], *prefix.* the form of **ad-** before *b,* as in *abbreviate.*

ab-[3], a prefix in the names of theoretical electromagnetic units of measurement, such as *abampere* or *abhenry,* in the centimeter-gram-second system of measurement. [< *ab*(solute)]

ab., about.

a.b., 1 able-bodied (seaman). **2** *Baseball.* (times) at bat.

Ab (no period), *Chemistry.* alabamine (the name originally used for *astatine*).

AB (no periods), one of the four major blood factors or groups widely used to determine blood compatibility in transfusions. A person with AB type blood can receive blood of either the AB, A, B, or O group.

A.B., 1 able-bodied (seaman). **2** *Baseball.* (times) at bat. **3** Also, **B.A.** Bachelor of Arts, a college degree usually given in the United States for four years' study (or the equivalent) beyond high school and generally with the emphasis on liberal arts (Latin, *Artium Baccalaureus*).
▶Some American colleges and universities use the abbreviation **A.B.,** others **B.A.** British universities use *B.A.*

* **A**[1]
definition 1

Script letters look like examples of fine penmanship. They appear in many formal uses, such as invitations to social functions.

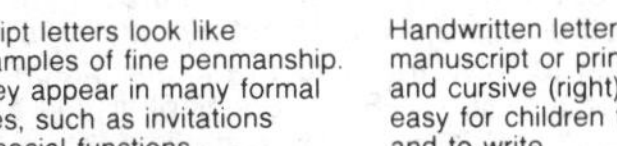
Handwritten letters, both manuscript or printed (left) and cursive (right), are easy for children to read and to write.

Aa *Aa*
Roman letters have *serifs* (finishing strokes) adapted from the way Roman stonecutters carved their letters. This is *Times Roman* type.

Aa ***Aa***
Sans-serif letters are often called *gothic.* They have lines of even width and no serifs. This type face is called *Helvetica.*

Aa Aa
Between roman and gothic, some letters have thick and thin lines with slight flares that suggest serifs. This type face is *Optima.*

Computer letters can be sensed by machines either from their shapes or from the magnetic ink with which they are printed.

a|ba (ä′bə, ə bä′), *n.* **1** a gownlike, sleeveless outer garment worn by Arabs. **2** a woolen fabric, usually striped, made in Arabia, Syria, and neighboring countries. **3** a coarse, thick, heavily felted woolen cloth, originally made and worn by Hungarian peasants. Also, **abba, abaya.** [< Arabic *'abā'a*]

***aba**
definition 1

ABA (no periods), abscisic acid.

a|ba|ca or **a|ba|cá** (ä′bə kä′), *n.* **1** a strong fiber made from the leaves of a Philippine plant, used for making rope, fabrics, and matting; Manila hemp: *Many of the natives wear abacá slippers* (Colby and Foster). **2** the plant itself, related to the banana and now also grown in Central America. [< Spanish *abacá* < Tagalog *abaká*]

ab|a|cist (ab′ə sist), *n.* a person skilled in using an abacus: *A Japanese abacist trounced an American operating a modern calculating machine* (New York Times).

a|back (ə bak′), *adv. Archaic.* backward.
taken aback, a suddenly surprised; upset or confused by something unexpected: *John was taken aback by his friend's angry answer.* SYN: disconcerted, abashed, startled. **b** (of a ship) caught by a head wind that presses the sails back against the mast, instantly stopping the ship: *The "Captain" [a ship] was taken as flat aback as could be by a squall striking her from starboard* (London Daily News). **c** (of sails) caught on the forward surface by the wind: *The ship nearly lost its mast when its sails were suddenly taken aback by the shifting gale.*
[Old English *on bæc* toward the back]

ab|ac|ti|nal (ab ak′tə nəl), *adj. Zoology.* **1** located at a distance from the mouth or oral area: aboral. **2** lacking tentacles or rays: *the abactinal end of a sea anemone.* —**ab|ac′ti|nal|ly,** *adv.*

a|bac|u|lus (ə bak′yə ləs), *n., pl.* **-li** (-lī). **1** one of the little cubes or slabs of colored glass, enamel, or stone used in mosaic work or marquetry; tessera. **2** a small abacus. [< Latin *abaculus* (diminutive) < *abacus* abacus; ornamental marble sideboard]

***ab|a|cus** (ab′ə kəs), *n., pl.* **-cus|es, -ci** (-sī). **1** a frame with rows of counters or beads used for adding and other tasks in arithmetic by the ancient Greeks and Romans and in China and other Asian countries. It is also used in schools to teach place value in the number system and to teach blind children arithmetic. **2** a slab forming the top of a capital of a column. See picture under **Doric.** [< Latin *abacus* < Greek *ábax, -akos*]

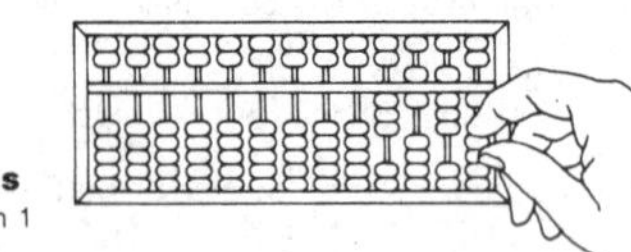
***abacus**
definition 1

A|bad|don (ə bad′ən), *n.* **1** Apollyon, the destroying angel; angel of hell (in the Bible, Revelation 9:11). **2** the place of the lost; bottomless pit; hell.

a|baft (ə baft′, -bäft′), *adv., prep.* —*adv.* at or toward the back of a ship; aft; astern.
—*prep.* back of; behind; astern of.
abaft the mast. See under **mast[1]**.
[< *a-*[1] on + Middle English *baft,* Old English *beæftan* < *be* by + *æftan* behind]

ab|a|lo|ne (ab′ə lō′nē), *n.* a mollusk that can be eaten, especially one native to salt water along the Pacific coast of North America. Its large, rather flat shell is lined with mother-of-pearl. [American English < Mexican Spanish *aulone* < Costanoan (Monterey) *aūlun* red abalone]

ab|am|pere (ab am′pir), *n.* the basic theoretical electromagnetic unit of current in the centimeter-gram-second system, equal to 10 amperes. [< *ab-*[3] absolute + *ampere*]

a|ban|don[1] (ə ban′dən), *v.t.* **1** to give up entirely: *She abandoned her hope of being a nurse.* SYN: relinquish, renounce, drop, discard. **2** to desert, forsake, or leave without intending to return: *A good mother would not abandon her baby. Abandon ship!* SYN: quit. See syn. under **desert[2]**. **3** to give (oneself) up completely (to a feeling or impulse); surrender: *The lost child abandoned himself to despair.* **4** *Obsolete.* to banish. [< Old French *abandoner* put in (one's) jurisdiction < *a bandon* in the power of] —**a|ban′don|er,** *n.* —**a|ban′don|ment,** *n.*

a|ban|don[2] (ə ban′dən), *n.* a yielding to natural impulses; freedom from self-control or restraint: *to dance with youthful abandon. The students on the winning side cheered with abandon.* [< French *abandon*]

a|ban|doned (ə ban′dənd), *adj.* **1** deserted; forsaken: *The boys often play in the abandoned house.* **2** wicked; immoral: *Gangsters live an abandoned life.* SYN: dissolute, profligate, depraved. **3** unrestrained: *abandoned laughter.* —**a|ban′doned|ly,** *adv.*

a|ban|don|ee (ə ban′də nē′), *n. Law.* a person to whom something is abandoned, especially the underwriter to whom the salvage of a wrecked vessel is abandoned.

à bas (à bä′), *French.* down with (the person or thing named): *"A bas le roi!" means "Down with the king!"*

a|base (ə bās′), *v.t.,* **a|based, a|bas|ing. 1** to bring down; make lower in rank, condition, or character: **a** to degrade: *A man who betrays his country abases himself.* SYN: debase, demean, dishonor. **b** to humble; humiliate: *to abase oneself before God.* **2** *Archaic.* to cast down. [< Old French *abaissier* bring low < *a-* to + *baissier* to lower < Vulgar Latin *bassiāre* < Late Latin *bassus* low] —**a|base′ment,** *n.* —**a|bas′er,** *n.*

a|bash (ə bash′), *v.t.* to make uneasy, shy, and somewhat ashamed; embarrass and confuse; disconcert: *The boy was not abashed by the laughter of his classmates. . . . a man whom no denial, no scorn could abash* (Henry Fielding). SYN: chagrin, confound. [< Old French *esbaiss-,* stem of *esbair* be astonished < Vulgar Latin *batāre* gape] —**a|bash′ment,** *n.*

a|bashed (ə basht′), *adj.* embarrassed and confused: *The shy, abashed girl rushed from the room as it filled with strangers.*

a|ba|sia (ə bā′zhə), *n.* total or partial loss of the ability to coordinate the muscles used in walking. [< *a-*[4] not + Greek *básis* a step]

a|bask (ə bask′, -bäsk′), *adv.* in pleasant warmth.

a|bat|a|ble (ə bā′tə bəl), *adj.* that can be abated.

a|bate (ə bāt′), *v.,* **a|bat|ed, a|bat|ing.** —*v.t.* **1** to make less in force or intensity; decrease; diminish: *The medicine abated his pain. Soft words did not abate her fury.* SYN: lessen. **2a** to put an end to (a nuisance or an action): *We can abate the smoke nuisance by heating with gas.* SYN: stop. **b** to render (a writ) null and void. **3** to deduct something from; reduce: *to abate a tax.* **4** *Archaic.* to omit. **5** *Archaic.* to bring down. —*v.i.* **1** to become less in force or intensity; diminish: *Although the rain has abated somewhat, the wind is still blowing very hard.* SYN: lessen. **2a** (of an action or a nuisance) to be at an end. **b** (of a writ) to become null and void. [< Old French *abatre* beat down < *a-* to + *batre* beat < Latin *battuere*] —**a|bat′er, a|bat′or,** *n.*

a|bate|ment (ə bāt′mənt), *n.* **1** a decrease; lessening: *I had much abatement of my hopes; though not a total frustration* (Oliver Cromwell). SYN: diminution, mitigation. **2** an amount abated; reduction. SYN: deduction. **3** the act or process of putting an end to something. **4** *Heraldry.* a mark of dishonor.

ab|a|tis (ab′ə tis), *n., pl.* **-tis. 1** a barricade of trees cut down and placed with their sharpened branches directed toward the enemy. **2** a barricade of barbed wire. [< French *abatis* mass of things thrown down < Old French *abateïs* < *abatre* beat down, fell]

A battery, a low-voltage battery connected to both ends of the filament in an electron tube, for heating the filament.

ab|at|toir (ab′ə twär, -twôr; ab′ə twär′, -twôr′), *n.* **1** a slaughterhouse. **2** a place of physical punishment, such as a boxing or wrestling ring or a bullfighting arena. [< French *abattoir* < *abattre* beat down]

ab|ax|i|al (ab ak′sē əl), *adj.* not in the axis. [< *ab-*[1] from + *axis*[1] + *-al*[1]]

ab|ax|ile (ab ak′səl, -sīl), *adj.* = abaxial.

a|ba|ya (ə bä′yä), *n.* = aba.

ab|ba[1] or **Ab|ba** (ab′ə), *n.* **1** Father (used of the Deity in the Bible, Mark 14:36). **2** an ecclesiastical title in the Syriac and Coptic churches. [< Aramaic *'abbā* father]

ab|ba[2] (ab′ə), *n.* = aba.

ab|ba|cy (ab′ə sē), *n., pl.* **-cies. 1** the position or power of an abbot. **2** the term of office of an abbot. **3** the district or community ruled by an abbot. Also, **abbotcy, abbotship.** [< Late Latin *abbātia* < *abbās, -ātis* abbot. See etym. of doublet **abbey.**]

Ab|bas|id or **Ab|bas|sid** (ə bas′id, ab′ə sid), *n.* any caliph of the dynasty at Baghdad that ruled most of the Moslem world during its height of civilization and splendor from 750 to 1258. This dynasty was descended from Abbas, uncle of Mohammed.

Ab|bas|side (ə bas′īd, ab′ə sīd), *n.* = Abbasid.

ab|ba|te (äb bä′tā), *n., pl.* **-ti** (-tē). (in Italy) an abbot or ecclesiastic. [< Italian *abate*]

ab|ba|tial (ə bā′shəl), *adj.* of or having to do with an abbot, abbess, abbey, or abbacy: *abbatial vestments.* [< Middle French *abbatial,* learned borrowing from Medieval Latin *abbatialis* < Late Latin *abbātia* abbacy < *abbās, -ātis* abbot]

ab|bé (ab′ā, a bā′; *French* à bā′), *n., pl.* **ab|bés** (ab′āz, a bāz′; *French* à bā′). **1** a title of respect used for anyone who is entitled to wear clerical dress, including (during and after the 1600's) tutors, lecturers, and secretaries nominated by the French king to receive the revenues of abbacies during vacancies. **2** a title used in Quebec for an abbot or a priest. [< French *abbé* < Late Latin *abbās, -ātis* abbot]

Ab|be condenser (ä′bə), *Optics.* a lens placed below the object in a compound microscope to deflect light upward through it. [< Ernst *Abbe,* 1840-1905, a German physicist]

Abbe fo|com|e|ter (fō kom′ə tər), *Optics.* an instrument for the precise measurement of the focal length of lenses and mirrors.

ab|bess (ab′is), *n.* a woman who is the head of an abbey of nuns, especially in a religious order that has monasteries under the direction of abbots. [< Old French *abeësse* < Late Latin *abbātissa* < *abbās, -ātis* abbot]

Ab|be|vil|li|an or **Ab|be|vil|le|an** (ab′ə vil′ē ən), *adj.* of or having to do with a paleolithic culture of the glacial period in Europe, in which early recognizable stone tools, crude hand axes, were made. Formerly called **Chellean.** [< *Abbeville,* a city in France, a site of archaeological discoveries + *-an*]

ab|bey (ab′ē), *n., pl.* **-beys. 1a** the building or buildings where monks or nuns live a religious life, ruled by an abbot or abbess; a monastery or convent, the members of which live in seclusion and under vows of celibacy. SYN: cloister. **b** the monks or nuns living there. **2** (in Great Britain) a church or other building that was once an abbey or a part of an abbey: *Westminster Abbey, Newstead Abbey.* [< Old French *abaïe* < Late Latin *abbātia* < *abbās, -ātis* abbot. See etym. of doublet **abbacy.**]

ab|bot (ab′ət), *n.* a man who is the head of an abbey or monastery of monks. [Old English *abbad* < Late Latin *abbās, -ātis* < Late Greek *abbâs* < Aramaic *'abbā* father]

ab|bot|cy (ab′ət sē), *n., pl.* **-cies.** = abbacy.

Abbot of Misrule or **Unreason,** the leader of the festivities in medieval Christmas revels.

ab|bot|ship (ab′ət ship), *n.* = abbacy.

abbr. or **abbrev., 1** abbreviated. **2** abbreviation.

ab|bre|vi|ate (ə brē′vē āt), *v.,* **-at|ed, -at|ing.** —*v.t.* **1** to make shorter; shorten (a word or phrase) so that a part stands for the whole: *We can abbreviate "inch" to "in." "Acre" is abbreviated to "a." by omission, "hour" to "hr." by contraction, and "pound"* (Latin, *"libra"*) *to "lb." by substitution.* SYN: See syn. under **shorten. 2** to make briefer: *to abbreviate a long speech.* SYN: condense, compress, reduce. —*v.i.* to use abbreviation or abbreviations: *She abbreviated so much that it was hard to understand her letters.* [< Late Latin *abbreviāre* (with English *-ate*[1]) < Latin *ad-* to + *brevis* short. See etym. of doublet **abridge.**] —**ab|bre′vi|a′tor,** *n.*

ab|bre|vi|a|tion (ə brē′vē ā′shən), *n.* **1** a shortened form: **a** a part of a word or phrase standing for the whole: *"Dr." is an abbreviation for "Doctor."* An abbreviation may be the initial letter of a word (*a.* for *acre*), the initial letters of the words of a phrase (*A.A.U.P.* for *American Association of University Professors*), the first and last letters of a word (*ft.* for *foot* or *feet*), or the first part of a word (*Esq.* for *Esquire*). **b** a shortened form based on substitution (*d.* for *penny,* Latin, *denarius*). *Abbr:* abbr. **2** a making briefer. SYN: condensation, abridgment. **3** any method of musical notation indicating the repetition of certain notes or passages without writing them out in full.

ab|bre|vi|a|tion|ist (ə brē′vē ā′shə nist), *n.* a person who habitually forms, uses, or advocates using abbreviations: *. . . the continual confusing contribution of the abbreviationists* (James Thurber).

ab|bre|vi|a|to|ry (ə brē′vē ə tôr′ē, -tōr′-), *adj.* shortening or tending to shorten.

A|B|C (ā′bē′sē′), *n.* **1a** facts or skills to be learned first; elementary principles: *Fred learned the ABC of swimming this summer at camp.* **b** a book or other source of elementary principles; basic work: *to write the ABC of modern stagecraft.* **2** the alphabet; ABC's. **3** a book listing alphabetically all British railway stations and showing their passenger service.

ABC (no periods), **1** Advanced Booking Charter (an air travel reservation made at low group-charter rates and far enough in advance for the airline to create a group of travelers). **2** American Bowling Congress. **3** American Broadcasting Companies. **4** Australian Broadcasting Corporation. **5** Audit Bureau of Circulations.

A-B-C book, a primer.

A.B.C.D. or **ABCD** (no periods), Accelerated Business Collection and Delivery (a system employed by the United States Postal Service).

ab|cou|lomb (ab′kü lom′), *n.* a theoretical electromagnetic unit of charge in the centimeter-gram-second system, equal to the quantity of electricity conveyed in one second by a current of one abampere. [< *ab-*[3] absolute + *coulomb*]

ABC powers, Argentina, Brazil, and Chile.

A|B|C's (ā′bē′sēz′), *n.pl.* **1** the alphabet. **2** basic facts or skills; elementary principles; fundamentals; rudiments: *to master the ABC's of golf.*

ABC soil, a cross section of soil having a well-defined A horizon, B horizon, and C horizon.

abc weapons or **ABC weapons**, atomic, biological, and chemical devices and substances, as instruments of war.

Ab|der|ite (ab′də rīt), *n.* a stupid person (because the inhabitants of Abdera, an ancient town in Thrace, were known for their stupidity).

Ab|di|as (ab dī′əs), *n.* = Obadiah, in the Douay Bible.

ab|di|ca|ble (ab′də kə bəl), *adj.* that can be abdicated.

ab|di|cate (ab′də kāt), *v.*, **-cat|ed, -cat|ing.** —*v.t.* to give up (office, power, or authority); renounce formally (a right, claim, or duties); resign: *When the king abdicated his throne, his brother became king.* SYN: relinquish, surrender.
—*v.i.* **1** to renounce office, power, or authority; resign: *Why did the king abdicate?* **2** to withdraw oneself (from): ... *those who abdicate life socially will soon abdicate from life itself* (Time).
[< Latin *abdicāre* (with English *-ate*[1]) renounce < *ab-* away + *dicāre* proclaim] —**ab′di|ca′tor**, *n.*

ab|di|ca|tion (ab′də kā′shən), *n.* an abdicating; giving up an office, power, or authority; resigning, especially under force: *The present Queen [Elizabeth II] owes her early accession as much to the abdication of her uncle as to the rather premature death of her father* (Manchester Guardian Weekly). SYN: renunciation, resignation.

ab|di|ca|tive (ab′də kā′tiv), *adj.* involving abdication.

***ab|do|men** (ab′də mən, ab dō′-), *n.* **1a** the part of the body containing the stomach and the intestines; belly. In man and other mammals the abdomen is a large cavity between the chest (thorax) and the pelvis, and also contains the liver, pancreas, kidneys, and spleen. **b** a corresponding region in vertebrates below mammals. **2** the last of the three parts of the body of insects and many other arthropods, including spiders and crustaceans. [< Latin *abdōmen*]

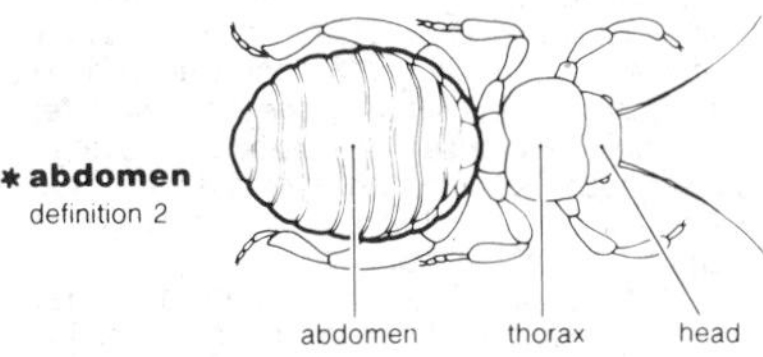

***abdomen** definition 2

ab|dom|i|nal (ab dom′ə nəl), *adj.* of the abdomen; in the abdomen; for the abdomen: *Bending the body exercises the abdominal muscles.* SYN: ventral, visceral. —**ab|dom′i|nal|ly**, *adv.*

abdominal brain, = solar plexus.

ab|dom|i|nous (ab dom′ə nəs), *adj.* = potbellied.

ab|duce (ab düs′, -dyüs′), *v.t.*, **-duced, -duc|ing.** to draw away or aside. [< Latin *abdūcere* lead away < *ab-* away + *dūcere* to lead]

ab|du|cent (ab dü′sənt, -dyü′-), *adj.* pulling or drawing away a part of the body from a given point or center, as a muscle does; abducting.

ab|duct (ab dukt′), *v.t.* **1** to carry off (a person) unlawfully, by force or by trickery; kidnap: *The police caught the man who tried to abduct the boy for ransom.* **2** to pull (a part of the body) away from its normal position, as to raise an arm upward and outward. [< Latin *abductus*, past participle of *abdūcere* lead away < *ab-* away + *dūcere* to lead]

ab|duc|tion (ab duk′shən), *n.* **1** the unlawful carrying off of anyone by force or by trickery; kidnaping. **2** the pulling away of a part of the body from its normal position. **3** *Logic.* a syllogism where the minor premise has no proof.

ab|duc|tor (ab duk′tər), *n.* **1** a person who abducts someone; kidnaper. **2** a muscle that pulls a part of the body away from its normal position by the trunk or main axis. The deltoid muscle of the shoulder is an abductor that raises the arm outward and upward.

a|beam (ə bēm′), *adv., adj.* **1** directly opposite the middle of a ship's side: *Fire a broadside when their ship comes abeam of ours.* **2** straight across a ship; at right angles to the keel of a ship.

a|be|ce|dar|i|an (ā′bi si dãr′ē ən), *n., adj.* —*n.* **1** a person who is learning the alphabet. **2** a beginner; tyro. **3** a teacher of beginners.
—*adj.* **1** of the alphabet. **2** arranged in alphabetical order. **3** primary; rudimentary.
[< Late Latin *ābēcēdārius* having to do with the alphabet < Latin *ā bē cē dē* ABCD]

a|be|ce|dar|i|um (ā′bi si dãr′ē əm), *n., pl.* **-dar|i|a** (-dãr′ē ə). a first book in reading; primer. [< Medieval Latin *abecedarium* alphabet; primer]

a|be|ce|da|ry (ā′bi sē′dər ē), *n., pl.* **-ries**, *adj.* = abecedarian.

a|bed (ə bed′), *adj., adv.* **1** in bed: *The lights were out, and all were thought to be abed* (Samuel Smiles). **2** confined to bed: *Louis being abed with gout* ... (W. H. Dixon).

A|bed|ne|go (ə bed′ni gō), *n.* one of the three Hebrews cast into the fiery furnace by Nebuchadnezzar. Meshach and Shadrach were the other two (in the Bible, Daniel 3:12-30).

a|beg|ging (ə beg′ing), *adj., adv.* in an unwanted or overlooked condition: *In those days, the newer trends in art were going abegging* ... (Show).

A|bel (ā′bəl), *n.* the second son of Adam and Eve. Abel was killed in jealousy by his older brother, Cain (in the Bible, Genesis 4:1-15).

a|bele (ə bēl′, ā′bəl), *n.* the white poplar tree. [< Dutch *abeel* < Old French *albel* < Medieval Latin *albellus* (diminutive) < Latin *albus* white]

a|be|li|a (ə bē′lē ə, -bēl′yə), *n.* a shrub with small, glossy leaves and pink to white, bell-like flowers. [< Clarke *Abel*, 1780-1826, an English naturalist]

A|bel|ian group (ə bēl′yən), *Mathematics.* a group of numbers combined according to commutative law. [< Niels H. *Abel*, 1802-1829, a Norwegian mathematician + *-ian*]

a|bel|mosk (ā′bəl mosk), *n.* a bushy plant of the mallow family, bearing large, showy, yellow blossoms, grown in tropical and semitropical countries for its musky seeds, which are used in perfumes; muskmallow. [< New Latin *Abelmoschus* < Arabic *'abū-l-miskī* father (source) of musk]

A|ben|len (ə ben′lən), *n., pl.* **-len** or **-lens.** a member of a Negrito people living in the northern part of the Philippines.

Ab|er|deen An|gus (ab′ər dēn ang′gəs), any of a breed of small, entirely black, hornless cattle, raised for beef and originally bred in Scotland.

Aberdeen terrier, the Scottish terrier (an unofficial name once common).

Ab|er|do|ni|an (ab′ər dō′nē ən), *adj., n.* —*adj.* of or having to do with Aberdeen (a city in Scotland), its people, or their customs.
—*n.* a native or inhabitant of Aberdeen.

A|ber|glau|be (ä′bər glou′bə), *n. German.* superstition.

ab|er|nath|y|ite (ab′ər nath′ē īt), *n.* a minor ore of uranium in the torbernite group. *Formula:* $K(UO_2)(AsO_4)\cdot 4H_2O$

Ab|er|ne|thy (ab′ər ne′thē), *n., pl.* **-thies.** a hard biscuit sometimes flavored with caraway seeds. [< John *Abernethy*, 1764-1831, English surgeon]

ab|er|rance (ab er′əns), *n.* a wandering or deviating from what is regular, normal, or right.

ab|er|ran|cy (ab er′ən sē), *n.* = aberrance.

ab|er|rant (ab er′ənt), *adj., n.* —*adj.* deviating from what is regular, normal, or right: *a rocket on an aberrant course, aberrant behavior. He likes man to be playful, variedly worshipful, comic, aberrant and unpredictable* (Wall Street Journal). SYN: abnormal, deviant, eccentric.
—*n.* a person who deviates from normal human behavior.
[< Latin *aberrāns, -antis*, present participle of *aberrāre* wander away < *ab-* away + *errāre* wander] —**ab|er′rant|ly**, *adv.*

***ab|er|ra|tion** (ab′ə rā′shən), *n.* **1** a wandering from the right path or usual course of action; straying: *A lie is an aberration from the truth.* **2** an abnormal structure or development; deviation from a standard or ordinary type: ... *changes in chromosome structure are called chromosomal mutations or aberrations* (The Effects of Atomic Weapons). ... *even so-called communism itself might turn out to be a passing aberration in history's long march* (Wall Street Journal). SYN: irregularity, abnormality, mutation. **3** a wandering of the mind; temporary mental disorder: *His peculiarities are no more than harmless aberrations.* SYN: eccentricity. **4** the failure of a lens, mirror, or the like, to bring to a single focus the rays of light coming from one point. Aberration causes a distorted image (spherical aberration) or an image with a colored fringe (chromatic aberration). **5** an apparent displacement of a heavenly body from its actual position, as seen by an observer on the earth, caused by the combined effect of the earth's motion and the noninstantaneous transmission of the light from the heavenly body.

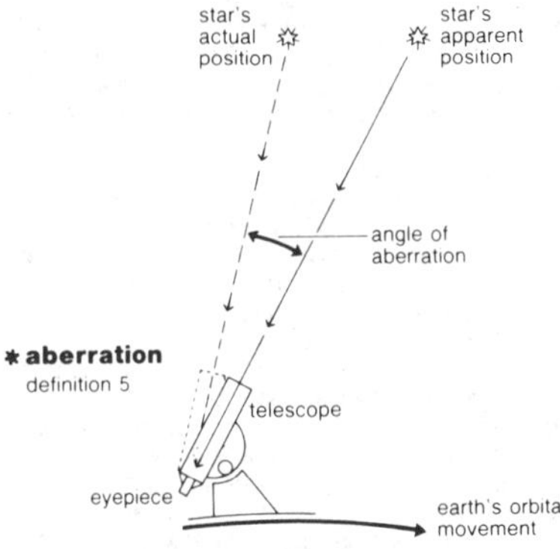

***aberration** definition 5

ab|er|ra|tion|al (ab′ə rā′shə nəl), *adj.* of or characterized by aberration; eccentric; irrational.

ab|er|ra|tion|ist (ab′ə rā′shə nist), *n.* a person who shows aberrant behavior.

a|bet (ə bet′), *v.t.*, **a|bet|ted, a|bet|ting.** **1** to encourage or help, especially in doing something wrong: *One man did the actual stealing, but two others abetted him by attracting the attention of the storekeeper.* SYN: support. **2** to urge on or assist in any way: *Lawson and Haggart are here abetted by Billy Butterfield* ... *and Bill Stegmeyer in thriving performances of eight deep-South standards* (*"Moon Over Miami," "Alabama Bound," etc.*) (Saturday Review). SYN: support. [< Old French *abeter* arouse < *a-* to + *beter* to bait < a Germanic word]

a|bet|ment (ə bet′mənt), *n.* instigation; encouragement: *My wife,* ... *with my approval and abetment, is a working mother* (Harper's).

a|bet|tal (ə bet′əl), *n.* = abetment.

a|bet|ter (ə bet′ər), *n.* a person who abets.

a|bet|tor (ə bet′ər), *n. Especially Law.* a person who abets; abetter.

ab ex|tra (ab ek′strə), *Latin.* from without: ... *a spectator ab extra who can see the whole of a society simultaneously* (New Yorker).

a|bey|ance (ə bā′əns), *n.* a temporary stopping of activity: *The custom was revived after an abeyance of several centuries.*
in abeyance, **a** in a state of suspended action: *Let's hold that question in abeyance until we know more about it. The purchasing agent held his order in abeyance pending completion of the inventory.* **b** *Law.* in a state of waiting for legal ownership or possession: *An inheritance is in abeyance when the rightful owner has not been determined.*
[< Anglo-French *abeiance* (legal) expectation < Old French *abeër* covet < *a-* at, after + *beër* gape < Vulgar Latin *batāre*]

a|bey|ant (ə bā′ənt), *adj.* dormant; latent.

ab|far|ad (ab far′ad, -əd), *n.* a theoretical electromagnetic unit of capacitance in the centimeter-gram-second system, equal to 10^9 farads. [< *ab-*[3] absolute + *farad*]

ab|hen|ry (ab hen′rē), *n., pl.* **-ries** or **-rys.** a theoretical electromagnetic unit of inductance in the centimeter-gram-second system, equal to 10^{-9} henry. [< *ab-*[3] absolute + *henry*]

ab|he|sive (ab hē′siv, -ziv), *adj., n.* —*adj.* not sticking to other material; slippery: *an abhesive plastic.* —*n.* an abhesive substance. [< *ab-*[1] off, away from + (ad)*hesive*]

ab|hor (ab hôr′), *v.t.*, **-horred, -hor|ring. 1** to shrink away from with horror; feel disgust for; hate very, very much: *Most people abhor the thought of war. Many people abhor snakes.* SYN: loathe, detest, abominate. **2** *Obsolete.* to horrify. [< Latin *abhorrēre* shrink back < *ab-* from + *horrēre* shrink] —**ab|hor′rer**, *n.*

ab|hor|rence (ab hôr′əns, -hor′-), *n.* **1** a feeling of horror or disgust; very great hatred: *Mother has an abhorrence of snakes. We, at twenty, had no abhorrence of raw ideas or explicit statement* (New Yorker). SYN: detestation, aversion, antipathy. **2** something hated or detested.

ab|hor|rent (ab hôr′ənt, -hor′-), *adj.* **1** causing horror; disgusting; detestable: *the rioters' abhor-*

rent conduct. 2 contrary or repugnant (to): *abhorrent to nature. Lying and stealing are abhorrent to an honest man.* SYN: loathsome, offensive. 3 having or showing dislike (of): *The Greek of the heroic age was . . . abhorrent of excess* (William E. Gladstone). —**ab|hor'rent|ly**, *adv.*

A|bib (ā'bib), *n.* the first month of the Jewish ecclesiastical year and the seventh of the civil year. Abib was called *Nisan* after the Babylonian Captivity. [< Hebrew *ābhībh* (literally) spring; ear of corn]

a|bid|ance (ə bī'dəns), *n.* the act of abiding.
abidance by, conformity to: *The coach demanded abidance by the rules of the game.*

a|bide[1] (ə bīd'), *v.*, **a|bode** or **a|bid|ed, a|bid|ing.** —*v.t.* 1 to put up with; endure; tolerate: *A good housekeeper can't abide dust. She can't abide him.* SYN: bear, stand. 2 to await submissively; submit to; sustain: *He must abide his fatal doom* (Joanna Baillie). 3 to await defiantly; withstand: *He soon learned to abide . . . terrors which most of my bolder companions shrank from encountering* (Hugh Miller). 4 *Archaic.* to wait for; await: *I will abide the coming of my lord* (Tennyson).
—*v.i.* 1 to stay; remain; wait: *Abide with me for a time. I'll call upon you straight: abide within* (Shakespeare). *He within his ships abode the while* (William Cowper). 2 to continue to live (in a place); reside; dwell: *No martin there in winter shall abide* (John Dryden). 3 to continue (in some state or action): *. . . ye shall abide in my love* (John 15:10). 4 to continue in existence; endure: *Thou hast established the earth, and it abideth* (Psalms 119:90). SYN: last. 5 *Archaic.* to be left. 6 *Obsolete.* to stay behind.
abide by, **a** to accept and follow out; be bound by: *Both teams will abide by the umpire's decision.* **b** to remain faithful to; stand firm by; be true to; fulfill: *Abide by your promise.*
[Old English *ābīdan* stay on, and *onbīdan* wait for] —**a|bid'er**, *n.*
►**Abide**, except in **abide by** and **can't abide**, tends to be used in formal, literary, or poetic contexts. In ordinary speech or informal writing, such synonyms as *stay, remain, wait, live,* or *continue* are more common, and generally more suitable.

a|bide[2] (ə bīd'), *v.t. Archaic.* to pay for; atone for; suffer for.
[< *abide*[1]]
►**abide, aby.** Through confusion of form with *aby,* when that verb was becoming archaic, and through association of sense between *aby* (pay for) *a deed,* and *abide the consequences of a deed, abide* came to be used for *aby,* to pay for, atone for.

a|bid|ing (ə bī'ding), *adj.* continuing; lasting: *an abiding faith, the abiding classics of literature. The old sailor had an abiding love of the sea.* SYN: permanent, steadfast. —**a|bid'ing|ly**, *adv.* —**a|bid'ing|ness**, *n.*

à bien|tôt (à byaɴ tō'), *French.* see you soon; good-by.

ab|i|et|ic acid (ab'ē et'ik), an acid prepared from the resin of some species of pine, larch, and fir and used in soaps, varnishes, and plastics. *Formula:* $C_{20}H_{30}O_2$ [< Latin *abies, -etis* fir tree + English *-ic*]

ab|i|gail (ab'ə gāl), *n.* a lady's maid. [< *Abigail,* a character in Beaumont and Fletcher's play *The Scornful Lady*]

Ab|i|gail (ab'ə gāl), *n.* the wife of Nabal and, after Nabal's death, of David (in the Bible, I Samuel 25:3-42).

a|bil|i|ty (ə bil'ə tē), *n., pl.* **-ties.** 1 the power to do or act: *the ability to think clearly. The old horse still has the ability to work.* SYN: capability, capacity. 2 skill: *Washington had great ability as a general.* 3 power to do some special thing; natural gift; talent: *Musical ability often shows itself early in life.*
[< Middle French *habilité,* learned borrowing from Latin *habilitās* aptness < *habilis* able]
—*Syn.* 2, 3 **Ability, talent** mean special power to do or for doing something. **Ability** applies to a demonstrated physical or mental power to do a certain thing well: *She has developed unusual ability as a dancer.* **Talent** applies to an inborn capacity for doing a special thing: *a child with a remarkable talent for painting.*
►After **ability** the infinitive of a verb preceded by *to* is used, rather than the gerund preceded by *of: A lawyer needs the ability to think clearly,* not *of thinking clearly.* The preposition used after *ability* and before a noun is *in: ability in music.*

A|bim|e|lech (ə bim'ə lek), *n.* a son of Gideon who was set up as king of Israel by the people of Shechem (in the Bible, Judges 9).

ab init., ab initio.

ab in|i|ti|o (ab' i nish'ē ō), *Latin.* from the beginning: *The decree was not a nullity in the sense of being void ab initio* (London Times).

ab in|tra (ab in'trə), *Latin.* from within.

a|bi|o|gen|e|sis (ā'bī ō jen'ə sis, ab'ē ō-), *n.* the supposed transformation of inanimate matter into living matter; spontaneous generation. [(coined by Thomas Huxley in 1870) < *a-*[4] without + *bio-* life + *genesis*]

a|bi|o|ge|net|ic (ā'bī ō jə net'ik, ab'ē ō-), *adj.* of or relating to spontaneous generation. —**a'bi|o|ge|net'i|cal|ly**, *adv.*

a|bi|o|ge|net|i|cal (ā'bī ō jə net'ə kəl, ab'ē ō-), *adj.* = abiogenetic.

a|bi|o|gen|ic (ā'bī ō jen'ik, ab'ē ō-), *adj.* not produced by living organisms; not biogenic: *abiogenic proteins.* —**a'bi|o|gen'i|cal|ly**, *adv.*

a|bi|o|ge|nic|i|ty (ā'bī ō jə nis'ə tē, ab'ē ō-), *n.* the condition of being abiogenic.

a|bi|og|e|nist (ā'bī oj'ə nist, ab'ē oj'-), *n.* a believer in the theory of spontaneous generation.

a|bi|o|log|i|cal (ā'bī ə loj'ə kəl), *adj.* not connected with biology; not biological: *rocks formed by abiological processes.* —**a'bi|o|log'i|cal|ly**, *adv.*

a|bi|ot|ic (ā'bī ot'ik), *adj.* 1 having no life; lifeless. Our abiotic environment includes soil, water, atmosphere, radiation, and the weather. 2 independent of the vital processes of a living organism: *an abiotic effect.*

a|bi|ot|ro|phy (ā'bī ot'rə fē), *n.* a degeneration of cells, tissues, or the like, due to congenital weakness. [< *a-*[4] without + Greek *bíos* life + *trophḗ* nourishment]

ab|ir|ri|tant (ab ir'ə tənt), *n., adj. Medicine.* —*n.* a drug or medicine that relieves irritation.
—*adj.* relieving irritation; soothing.

ab|ir|ri|tate (ab ir'ə tāt), *v.t.,* **-tat|ed, -tat|ing.** *Medicine.* to deaden or lessen irritation in. [< *ab-*[1] away + *irritate*] —**ab|ir'ri|ta'tion**, *n.*

Ab|i|tur (äb'i tůr'), *n. German.* a final examination given to secondary school students, passage of which authorizes matriculation in a university.

ab|ject (ab'jekt, ab jekt'), *adj., n.* —*adj.* 1 so low or degraded as to be hopeless; wretched; miserable: *Many people still live in abject poverty.* 2 deserving contempt; despicable: *abject flattery. Shame on you for your abject fear!* SYN: contemptible, degraded. 3 slavish: *abject submission.* SYN: servile, groveling. 4 *Obsolete.* cast off; rejected.
—*n. Archaic.* an outcast.
[< Latin *abjectus,* past participle of *abjicere* throw down or away < *ab-* down, away + *jacere* to throw] —**ab|ject'ness**, *n.* —**ab|ject'ly**, *adv.*

ab|jec|tion (ab jek'shən), *n.* = abasement.

ab|jec|tive (ab jek'tiv), *adj.* tending to abase; demoralizing: *an abjective influence.*

ab|judge (ab juj'), *v.t.,* **-judged, -judg|ing.** to take away by judicial decision; rule out. [< *ab-*[1] + *judge;* patterned after *adjudge*]

ab|junc|tion (ab jungk'shən), *n. Botany.* abstriction of spores.

ab|jur|a|to|ry (ab jůr'ə tôr'ē, -tōr'-), *adj.* expressing abjuration.

ab|jure (ab jůr'), *v.t.,* **-jured, -jur|ing.** 1 to swear to give up; reject solemnly, formally, or on oath; renounce: *to abjure power, allegiance, or a claim or claimant. An alien must abjure his foreign citizenship before he can become an American citizen.* SYN: forswear. 2 to retract formally or solemnly; repudiate: *to abjure a belief, doctrine, or opinion formerly held.* SYN: recant. 3 to refrain from; avoid: *to abjure humor.*
abjure the realm. See under **realm.**
[< Latin *abjūrāre* deny upon oath < *ab-* away + *jūrāre* swear] —**ab'ju|ra'tion**, *n.* —**ab|jur'er, ab|jur'or**, *n.*

ab|ka|ri (äb kä'rē), *n.* in India: 1 the manufacture and sale of alcoholic liquors. 2 the government tax upon liquors. 3 the licensing of dealers in alcoholic liquors. [< Hindustani *ābkārī* < Persian, (originally) distillation and sale of water < *āb* water + *kār* work]

abl., ablative.

ABL (no periods), Automated Biological Laboratory.

ab|lac|ta|tion (ab'lak tā'shən), *n.* the weaning of a child from the breast. [< Late Latin *ablactātiō, -ōnis* < *ablactāre* wean < *ab-* away, off + *lactāre* suckle]

a|blare (ə blãr'), *adj., adv.* blaring.

ab|las|tin (ab las'tin), *n.* a substance in the blood that impairs the ability of germs to reproduce.
[< *a-*[4] not + Greek *blastós* sprout + English *-in*]

ab|late (ab lāt'), *v.,* **-lat|ed, -lat|ing.** —*v.t.* 1 *Aerospace.* to remove by ablation. 2 to remove by burning away, wearing down, or cutting away.
—*v.i. Aerospace.* to undergo ablation.
[< Latin *ablātus,* past participle of *auferre* carry away; see etym. under **ablative**]

ab|la|tion (ab lā'shən), *n.* 1 *Aerospace.* **a** the disintegration of part of the nose cone on a missile or spacecraft when it reenters the atmosphere. Ablation usually occurs as melting or vaporizing of an outer surface to protect the rest of the structure from excessive heat. **b** the removal or carrying away of heat by melting or vaporization. 2 removal. 3 the removal by surgery of a tumor or a part of the body. 4 the wearing away of a glacier, snow, or other formation by melting or evaporation: *Yet, because there is so little ablation—return of moisture to the atmosphere—this light precipitation has become a glacier of up to a mile or more in depth* (Time).

ablation shield, a type of heat shield that uses up heat by melting and vaporizing. The air stream carries the molten particles and the hot gas vapor away from the spacecraft.

ab|la|ti|val (ab'lə tī'vəl), *adj.* in or having to do with the ablative case.

ab|la|tive (*n., adj. 1* ab'lə tiv; *adj. 2* ab lā'tiv), *n., adj.* —*n. Grammar.* 1 the case in Latin that expresses place from or in which, source, agent, cause, association, or instrument. 2 a case with similar uses in some other inflected languages. 3 a word or construction in this case. *Example: statū* and *quō* in the phrase *in statū quō nunc,* "in the state in which [something] now [is]." *Abbr:* abl.
—*adj.* 1 of or showing the ablative: *ablative case.* 2 *Aerospace.* made to be removed by ablation: *An ablative nosecone is made of light materials, such as fiberglass, which burn and fall away as the missile reenters the atmosphere* (New York Times).
[< Latin *ablātīvus* (literally) of removal (coined by Julius Caesar) < *ablātus,* past participle of *auferre* carry away < *ab-* away + *ferre* carry]
►**ablative case.** In Latin the case conveyed its meaning with or without a preposition. As prepositions were given more weight, the case endings gradually atrophied, as in French. In English, prepositional phrases do the work of Latin ablatives.

ablative absolute, a Latin construction consisting of a noun or pronoun with an adjective, noun, or participle, both in the ablative case, expressing time, occasion, cause, or other circumstance. *Example: Sōle oriente, tenebrae aufugiunt,* "The sun rising (that is, when or because the sun is rising), the shadows flee away." See also **absolute,** *adj.* def. 5a.

ab|la|tor (ab lā'tər), *n. Aerospace.* an ablating substance.

ab|laut (ab'lout, äb'-; *German* äp'lout), *n.* (in Indo-European languages) the systematic substitution of one root vowel sound for another in different inflectional forms or derivatives of a word, as in *ring, rang, rung;* gradation. [< German *Ablaut* (coined by Jakob Grimm) < *ab-* off + *Laut* sound]

a|blaze (ə blāz'), *adj., adv.* 1 on fire; in a blaze; blazing: *The forest was set ablaze by lightning.* 2 shining brightly; flashing or brilliant: *The hotel was ablaze with lights.* 3 in great excitement: *I was ablaze with anger when he kicked my dog.*

a|ble (ā'bəl), *adj.,* **a|bler, a|blest.** 1 having enough power, skill, means, or talent to do something; capable: *Most little children are able to walk before they are able to talk. A cat is able to see in the dark.* 2 having more power or skill than most others have; skillful: *She is an able teacher.* SYN: expert, clever, accomplished. 3 done with skill: *The audience applauded his able speech.* SYN: effective. 4 legally authorized or qualified. 5 having the necessary qualifications: *an able seaman.* [< Old French *hable, able* < Latin *habilis* fit, easily held or handled < *habēre* hold]
—*Syn.* 1 **Able, capable, competent** mean having the skill or means to do or for doing something. **Able** emphasizes power to act or perform: *She is able to earn a living.* **Capable** emphasizes fitness for doing, capacity or ability to do something adequately, or, sometimes, general efficiency: *Washington proved himself capable both as soldier and as administrator.* **Competent** emphasizes possession of sufficient skill or other requirements to do a certain kind of work satisfactorily: *A competent typist is not necessarily a competent secretary.*
►When they do not precede nouns, **able** and **competent** are followed by *to* plus an infinitive, **capable** by *of* plus a gerund: *able to work, competent to perform a task, capable of judging music.*

-able, *suffix.* 1 (*added to verbs*) that can be ____ed; able to be ____ed: *Enjoyable = that can be enjoyed.*
2 (*added to nouns*) suitable for ____; giving ____: *Comfortable = giving comfort.*
3 (*added to nouns*) inclined to ____; such as to ____: *Peaceable = inclined to peace.*
4 (*added to verbs and nouns*) fit to be ____ed; deserving of ____: *Wearable = fit to be worn. Lovable = deserving of love.*
5 (*added to verbs*) liable to be ____: *Breakable = liable to be broken.* [< Old French *-able* < Latin *-ābilis,* a suffix forming adjectives from verbs with infinitives in *-āre,* being one form of the suffix *-bilis*]
►Instead of **-able** a number of words have the

spelling **-ible**, which originally belonged largely to words from Latin infinitives in *-ēre, -ere,* or *-īre* (as in *terrible*). The living suffix is *-able,* used in coining occasional words like *jumpable; -able* is attached to verbs (*actable*), nouns (*actionable*), and even verbal phrases (*get-at-able*) to form adjectives.

a|ble-bod|ied (ā′bəl bod′ēd), *adj.* strong and healthy; physically fit: *All able-bodied barbarians were soldiers* (Bulletin of Atomic Scientists).

able-bodied seaman or **able seaman**, an experienced seaman who can perform all the duties required of a seaman, especially a trained deckhand on a merchant vessel. *Abbr:* A.B.

Able Day, the day of the first atomic-bomb test at Bikini; July 1, 1946 (June 30 in the United States). Also, **A-day**. [American English < *able,* code word for A]

ab|le|gate (ab′lə gāt), *n.* a papal envoy who brings to newly appointed cardinals the insignia of office or presents of honor. [< Latin *ablēgātus,* past participle of *ablēgāre* send away < *ab-* away + *lēgāre* to dispatch]

ab|let (ab′lit), *n. British.* the bleak, a freshwater fish. [< French *ablette*]

a|blins (ā′blinz), *adv. Scottish.* perhaps. Also, **aiblins.**

a|bloom (ə blüm′), *adv., adj.* in bloom; blossoming.

ab|lu|ent (ab′lü ənt), *adj., n.* —*adj.* cleansing; purifying.
—*n.* any cleansing agent; detergent.
[< Latin *abluēns, -entis,* present participle of *abluere;* see etym. under **ablution**]

ab|lu|tion (ab lü′shən), *n.* **1** Often, **ablutions**. a washing or cleansing as a religious ceremony of purification. **2** Often, **ablutions**. a washing or cleansing of one's body: *to perform one's morning ablutions.* **3** the water or other liquid used. **ablutions**, *British.* a public washroom: *The Holemen's dwelling* [*had*] *accommodation for about one hundred souls, with communal ablutions at either end* (Punch).
[< Latin *ablūtiō, -ōnis* < *abluere* wash off < *ab-* away + *lavere* to wash]

ab|lu|tion|ar|y (ab lü′shə ner′ē), *adj.* of or having to do with ablution.

a|bly (ā′blē), *adv.* in an able manner; with skill; capably: *The meeting was ably run by the chairman.* **SYN**: well, competently, cleverly.

ABM (no periods), antiballistic missile.

Ab|na|ki (ab nä′kē), *n., pl.* **-ki** or **-kis**. **1** a member of a confederacy of North American Indians who lived in Maine and eastern Canada in colonial days. **2** the Algonkian language of these tribes.

ab|ne|gate (ab′nə gāt), *v.t.,* **-gat|ed, -gat|ing.** to deny (anything) to oneself; renounce or give up (a privilege or luxury). [< Latin *abnegāre* (with English *-ate*[1]) refuse < *ab-* off, away + *negāre* deny] —**ab′ne|ga′tion**, *n.* —**ab′ne|ga′tor**, *n.*

ab|nor|mal (ab nôr′məl), *adj.* **1** not as it should be; very different from the ordinary conditions, the standard, or a type; unusual: *an abnormal amount of rain. It is abnormal for a man to be eight feet tall.* **SYN**: exceptional, aberrant. See syn. under **irregular**. **2** (of a person) badly adjusted. [< *ab-*[1] off + *normal;* influenced by French *anormal* and Latin *abnormis;* see etym. under **abnormity**] —**ab|nor′mal|ness**, *n.*

ab|nor|mal|i|ty (ab′nôr mal′ə tē), *n., pl.* **-ties**. **1** an abnormal form, feature, or happening: *He described abnormalities of cattle and hens which, he said, had been brought about by excessive development of the milk and egg producing organs* (London Times). **2** an abnormal condition.

ab|nor|mal|ly (ab nôr′mə lē), *adv.* **1** in a manner not normal; irregularly: *to behave abnormally.* **2** to an exceptional degree: *an abnormally hot day.*

abnormal psychology, the study of all forms of abnormal behavior of people, including the identification and classification of mental disorders, their causes, and their treatment; psychopathology. Students in this field are concerned with functional disorders, such as psychoses and neuroses, and organic disorders, such as loss of memory and mental retardation due to brain damage, circulation deficiencies, and similar causes.

ab|nor|mi|ty (ab nôr′mə tē), *n., pl.* **-ties**. **1** abnormality; irregularity. **2** a monstrosity. [< Late Latin *abnormitās* < Latin *abnormis* < *ab-* off + *norma* a rule]

a|bo (a′bō), *n., pl.* **a|bos**. *Australian Slang.* an aborigine.

A|B|O (ā′bē′ō′), *adj., n.* —*adj.* of or having to do with a system of classifying blood factors to determine blood compatibility in transfusions. The main factors or groups are A, B, AB, and O.
—*n.* this system of classification.

a|board (ə bôrd′, -bōrd′), *adv., prep., adj.* —*adv.* **1** on board; in or on a ship, train, bus, or airplane: *Until the children have climbed aboard no car may pass a school bus picking up pupils.* **2** alongside (a ship or shore): *close aboard.*
—*prep.* on board of; on, in, or into (a ship, train, bus, or airplane): *Everybody was soon aboard the train.*
—*adj. Baseball.* on base: *to hit a double with three runners aboard.*

all aboard! *U.S.* everybody on! (a call directing passengers to enter a train, bus, etc., or indicating that all have boarded): *"All aboard!" shouted the conductor, and everyone rushed for the train.*

come (or **get**) **aboard**, *U.S. Informal.* to join: *"When I came aboard the space program," the commander has said, "I felt like the greenest rookie in spring training"* (New York Times).

a|bode (ə bōd′), *n., v.* —*n.* **1** a place to live in; house or home; dwelling: *A simple hut was their abode. But I know thy abode, and thy going out, and thy coming in* (II Kings 19:27). *... one of those shows in which television cameras are conducted through the abodes of famous men* (New York Times). **SYN**: residence, habitation, domicile. **2** a stay or a sojourn in a place.
—*v.* a past tense and a past participle of **abide**[1]: *He abode there one year.* [Old English *ābād*]

ab|ohm (ab ōm′), *n.* a theoretical electromagnetic unit of resistance in the centimeter-gram-second system, equal to 10^{-9} ohm. [< *ab-*[3] absolute + *ohm*]

a|boi|deau (ab′ə dō; *French* à bwȧ dō′), *n., pl.* **-deaus** (-dōz); *French* **-deaux** (-dō′). *Canadian.* aboiteau.

a|boil (ə boil′), *adv., adj.* in a boiling state: *The immediate vicinity was aboil ... a brisk beehive of military efficiency* (Alastair Reed).

a|boi|teau (ab′ə tō; *French* à bwȧ tō′), *n., pl.* **-teaus** (-tōz); *French* **-teaux** (-tō′). *Canadian.* **1** a sluice gate in the dikes along the Bay of Fundy: *The English apparently learned from the Acadians the special arts of building dikes and aboiteaux* (Canadian Geographic Journal). **2** the dike itself. Also, **aboideau**. [< Canadian French *aboiteau*]

a|bol|ish (ə bol′ish), *v.t.* **1** to put an end to; do away with (a law, institution, or custom) completely: *Many people wish that nations would abolish war. Slavery was abolished in the United States in 1865.* **SYN**: annul, stop, suppress. **2** *Obsolete.* to destroy: *Thus ... shall the Bastille be abolished* (Thomas Carlyle). [< French *aboliss-,* stem of *abolir;* fusion of Latin *abolēre* destroy, and *abolēscere* die out] —**a|bol′ish|a|ble**, *adj.* —**a|bol′ish|er**, *n.* —**a|bol′ish|ment**, *n.*
—*Syn.* **1 Abolish, annihilate, extinguish** mean to put an end to something. **Abolish** now usually applies to man-made things other than concrete objects, such as laws or customs, usually long in existence: *The college students voted to abolish all secret societies.* **Annihilate**, more general in application, suggests the use of force and retains its literal meaning of reducing to nothing or of destroying completely: *Three survivors told how the enemy annihilated the regiment.* **Extinguish**, a rather formal word in this sense, applies to things or ideas which die or are blotted out by overpowering force or circumstances: *You may extinguish liberty, but not the love of liberty.*

ab|o|li|tion (ab′ə lish′ən), *n.* **1a** a putting an end to; abolishing: *Abolition of war is one purpose of the United Nations.* **b** (in the 1700's and 1800's) the suppression of Negro slavery. **2** a being abolished; abrogation. [< Latin *abolitiō, -ōnis* < *abolēre* destroy]

ab|o|li|tion|ar|y (ab′ə lish′ə ner′ē), *adj.* destructive.

ab|o|li|tion|ism (ab′ə lish′ə niz əm), *n.* the principle or policy of abolition, especially of Negro slavery.

ab|o|li|tion|ist (ab′ə lish′ə nist), *n., adj.* —*n.* **1** a person who wishes to abolish something, such as an institution or custom. **2** Also, **Abolitionist**. (in the 1700's and 1800's in the United States and Great Britain) a person who favored the compulsory abolition of Negro slavery.
—*adj.* of or having to do with abolitionism or abolitionists: *... abolitionist and retentionist theories of capital punishment* (Observer).

ab|o|ma|sal (ab′ə mā′səl), *adj.* of or having to do with the abomasum: *abomasal feeding.*

ab|o|ma|sum (ab′ə mā′səm), *n., pl.* **-sa** (-sə). the fourth and true stomach of cows, sheep, deer, and other ruminants, in which the food is digested. [< New Latin *abomasum* < Latin *ab-* away + *omāsum* bullock's tripe]

ab|o|ma|sus (ab′ ə mā′səs), *n., pl.* **-si** (-sī). = abomasum.

A-bomb (ā′bom′), *n., v.* —*n.* an atomic bomb.
—*v.t.* to bomb with an atomic bomb or bombs.
—**A′-bomb′er**, *n.*

a|bom|i|na|ble (ə bom′ ə nə bəl, -bom′nə-), *adj.* **1** disgusting; hateful; detestable: *Kidnaping is an abominable act. Shall we pass by this monstrous heap of absurd notions, and abominable practices?* (Edmund Burke). **SYN**: horrible, loathsome, revolting, odious, execrable. **2** very unpleasant; disagreeable: *abominable manners. The weather for the picnic was abominable—rainy, windy, and cold.* **SYN**: distasteful, offensive. [< Old French *abominable,* learned borrowing from Latin *abōminābilis* < *abōminārī* deplore as an ill omen, abominate] —**a|bom′i|na|ble|ness**, *n.* —**a|bom′i|na|bly**, *adv.*

Abominable Snowman, (according to local legends) a manlike or apelike hairy beast supposed to live in the higher parts of the Himalayas. Also called **Yeti**.

a|bom|i|nate (ə bom′ə nāt), *v.t.,* **-nat|ed, -nat|ing.** **1** to feel disgust for; hate very much; loathe: *Players abominate unfairness in an umpire.* **SYN**: detest, abhor, despise, execrate. **2** to dislike: *She abominates hot weather.* [< Latin *abōminārī* (with English *-ate*[1]) deplore as an ill omen < *ab-* off + *ōminārī* prophesy < *ōmen, ōminis* omen]
—**a|bom′i|na′tor**, *n.*

a|bom|i|na|tion (ə bom′ə nā′shən), *n.* **1** anything that arouses strong disgust or loathing; a revolting thing: *Lying lips are abomination to the Lord* (Proverbs 12:22). **2** a feeling of disgust; loathing: *Many people consider smoking with abomination.* **SYN**: hate, detestation. **3** a shamefully wicked action: *If we are going to revive the abomination of expurgatory oaths, why stop at one profession and one kind of objectionable behavior?* (Atlantic). **4** anything strongly disliked.

à bon mar|ché (à bôɴ mär shā′), *French.* at a good price; cheap.

a|bonne|ment (à bôn mäɴ′), *n. French.* subscription.

ab|o|ral (ab ôr′əl, -ōr′-), *adj. Zoology.* having to do with or located away from the mouth or at the opposite end from the mouth. [< *ab-*[1] away from + *oral*] —**ab|o′ral|ly**, *adv.*

ab|o|rig|i|nal (ab′ə rij′ə nəl), *adj., n.* —*adj.* **1** first or earliest so far as science or history gives record; existing from the beginning: *The Indians are the aboriginal inhabitants of America.* **SYN**: indigenous, original, native. **2** of the earliest known inhabitants; primitive: *The use of horses was not an aboriginal custom in America, but was introduced by Europeans.* **SYN**: indigenous.
—*n.* one of the aborigines. —**ab′o|rig′i|nal|ly**, *adv.*
► See **aborigine** for usage note.

ab|o|rig|i|nal|i|ty (ab′ə rij′ə nal′ə tē), *n.* the state or quality of being aboriginal.

ab o|rig|i|ne (ab ə rij′ə nē), *Latin.* from the beginning.

ab|o|rig|i|ne (ab′ə rij′ə nē), *n.* one of the original or earliest known inhabitants of a country or area; a member of the native race, as distinguished from an invader or colonist: *The Eskimos are among the aborigines of North America. Among the Australian Aborigines ... females are excluded from religious spheres (rituals, secret societies, and the like)* (Felix M. Keesing).
aborigines, the plants and animals native to a particular region or area: *I doubt whether any case is on record of an invasion on so grand a scale of one plant over the aborigines* (Charles Darwin).
[singular, back formation from plural; plural < Latin *Aborīginēs* (originally) ancestors of the Romans < *ab orīgine* from the beginning]
► Although recently formed, the singular **aborigine** is in regular use by anthropologists and others in preference to **aboriginal**; and **aborigines** is more common than **aboriginals** in the plural.

a|born|ing (ə bôr′ning), *adv., adj.* while being born or produced: *The plan, which died aborning, would have made two important changes in United States troop dispositions* (New York Times).

a|bort (ə bôrt′), *v., n.* —*v.i.* **1** to fail to develop or come to completion; end a mission, test, or experiment prematurely: *The rocket flight aborted.* **2** to give birth before the embryo can live outside the mother's body because it is still dependent upon her body system to support its own; miscarry. **3** to end prematurely and fruitlessly. **4** *Biology.* to be arrested in growth, as an organ; fail to develop.
—*v.t.* **1** to end or abandon (a mission, test, or experiment) before completion. **2** to cause to give birth prematurely.
—*n.* **1** an aborting or being aborted: *Any malfunction of the power plant, which must be completely automatic, ... will cause an abort and loss of the missile* (Ben I. Funk). **2** *U.S.* a test, opera-

Pronunciation Key: hat, āge, cãre, fär; let, ēqual, tėrm; it, īce; hot, ōpen, ôrder; oil, out; cup, pu̇t, rüle; child; long; thin; ᴛʜen; zh, measure; ə represents a in about, e in taken, i in pencil, o in lemon, u in circus.

tion, or mission, as of a missile launching, broken off or abandoned prior to completion. **3** *U.S.* a mechanism that fails to begin, or to complete, a scheduled operation or test. **4** an aircraft mission, sortie, or flight given up for reasons other than enemy action.
[< Latin *abortus,* past participle of *aborīrī* miscarry < *ab-* amiss + *orīrī* be born] —**a|bort′er**, *n.*

a|bor|ti|cide (ə bôr′tə sīd), *n.* **1** the destroying of a human embryo within the womb, especially by drugs or surgery. **2** an abortifacient. [< Latin *abortus, -ūs* fetus + English *-cide*[2] a killing]

a|bor|ti|fa|cient (ə bôr′tə fā′shənt), *n., adj.* —*n.* a drug or agent used to cause abortion.
—*adj.* causing abortion.
[< Latin *abortus, -ūs* abortion, fetus + *faciēns, -entis,* present participle of *facere* do]

a|bor|tion (ə bôr′shən), *n.* **1a** (in mammals) birth that occurs before the embryo has developed enough to live, usually during the first twelve weeks of pregnancy; miscarriage. **b** the inducing of premature delivery in order to destroy offspring. **2a** the failure of anything to develop properly or to be completed; imperfect development. **b** anything that fails to develop properly, such as an animal, a plan or project, or a building. **3** *Biology.* **a** the failure of an organ to develop beyond an early stage. **b** an imperfectly developed organ. [< Latin *abortiō, -ōnis* < *aborīrī;* see etym. under **abort**]

a|bor|tion|al (ə bôr′shə nəl), *adj.* characterized by failure.

a|bor|tion|ist (ə bôr′shə nist), *n.* a person who induces or seeks to induce an abortion, especially an illegal abortion.

abortion pill, a tablet of synthetic steroid taken to abort a pregnancy by blocking progesterone so that the fertilized egg does not become implanted in the uterus: *The revolutionary new abortion pill, RU 486, is . . . considered by the medical profession to be a far better means of abortion than surgical procedures* (New York Times).

a|bor|tive (ə bôr′tiv), *adj., n.* —*adj.* **1** coming to nothing; unsuccessful; fruitless: *Early attempts to make airplanes fly proved abortive. The League of Nations was part of an abortive effort to secure world peace.* SYN: ineffective, futile. **2** *Biology.* imperfectly formed or developed; rudimentary.
3 born or happening before the right time; premature. **4** causing abortion; abortifacient. **5** ending or shortening the course of a disease.
—*n.* **1** a drug causing abortion; abortifacient. **2** an abortive birth. —**a|bor′tive|ly**, *adv.* —**a|bor′tive|ness**, *n.*

a|bor|tus (ə bôr′təs), *n., pl.* **-tus|es**. *Medicine.* an aborted fetus. [< Latin *abortus;* see etym. under **abort**]

a|bought (ə bôt′), *v. Archaic.* past tense and past participle of **aby** and of **abide**[2].

a|bou|li|a (ə bü′lē ə), *n.* = abulia.

a|bou|lic (ə bü′lik), *adj.* = abulic.

a|bound (ə bound′), *v.i.* **1** to be plentiful or numerous: *Fish abound in the ocean. Rock abounds under the soil.* **2** to be rich (in): *America abounds in oil. Shakespeare's poetry abounds in imagery.* **3** to be well supplied; be filled (with): *The ocean abounds with fish.* SYN: teem, swarm. [< Old French *abonder,* learned borrowing from Latin *abundāre* overflow < *ab-* off + *undāre* rise in waves < *unda* a wave] —**a|bound′ing|ly**, *adv.*

a|bout (ə bout′), *prep., adv.* —*prep.* **1a** having something to do with; of: Black Beauty *is a story about a horse.* SYN: concerning, regarding, respecting. **b** in connection with: *There is something strange about him.* **2** somewhere near; in or close to (a place): *The dog was about the house.* **3** not far from; close to (in time): *Come about three o'clock. About 1850 the westward movement was in full swing.* **4** approximating; near: *He is about my size.* **5** on every side of; around: *A collar goes about the neck. He rubbed his eyes and looked about him.* **6** on or near (one's person); at hand; with: *She has no money about her.* **7** here and there in or on; in many parts of; everywhere in: *papers scattered about the room. The dog ran about the yard.* **8** doing; working at: *An expert worker knows what he is about.*
—*adv.* **1** nearly; almost: *He has about finished his work. The bottle is about empty. This is about the nicest day we've had.* **2** somewhere near: *A stray dog has been lurking about.* **3** toward or on every side; all around: *Look about and tell me what you see.* **4a** in many places; here and there; to and fro: *to shuffle papers about on a desk. The rumor went about that you were ill.* **b** moving around; active; stirring: *He is able to be up and about.* **5** in the opposite direction: *Face about! After swimming across the lake the boys turned about and swam back to shore.* **6** one after another; by turns; in succession: *Turn about is no more than fair play.* **7** *Nautical.* on or to the opposite tack: *to come, put, or go about.*

about to, on the point of; ready to; going to: *The plane is about to take off.*
[Old English *onbūtan* on the outside of]
▶**about**, *prep.* **3**, *adv.* **1** In expressions of time or number there has never been a strong distinction between the preposition (meaning approximately at, roughly in) and the adverb (meaning roughly, approximately) except the presence or absence of an object: *Buddha was born about 560 B.C.* (prep.). *Norsemen reached America in about the year 1000* (adv.). *Come about noon* (prep.). *Games start at about one* (adv.).

a|bout-face (*n.* ə bout′fās′; *v.* ə bout′fās′), *n., v.,* **-faced, -fac|ing**. *Especially U.S.* —*n.* **1** a turning or going in the opposite direction. **2** a shift to the opposite attitude or opinion. **3** the execution of an about face.
—*v.i.* **1** to turn or go in the opposite direction: *After swimming the length of the pool, she about-faced and swam all the way back.* **2** to execute an about face. Also, *British and Canadian,* **about-turn**.

about face, *Especially U.S.* a military command to turn in the opposite direction by placing the right foot behind the left foot and pivoting to the right.

about ship, a command to bring a sailing vessel about.

a|bout-ship (ə bout′ship′), *v.i.* to put a sailing ship on the opposite tack (usually as an infinitive or as a command).

a|bout-town|er (ə bout′tou′nər), *n.* a man or woman who frequents the fashionable night clubs, the theaters, etc., of the city.

a|bout-turn (ə bout′tėrn′), *n., v.i. British and Canadian.* = about-face.

a|bove (ə buv′), *adv., prep., adj., n.* —*adv.* **1** in or at a higher place; overhead or farther up: *There were snowy peaks above. The stairs lead above.* **2** on the upper side or on top: *leaves dark above and light below.* **3** higher in rank or power: *The lawyer who lost his case made an appeal to the court above.* **4** in or from a direction thought of as higher; upstream: *There's good fishing above.* **5** earlier in a book or article: *See what is written above.* **6** above zero: *The temperature is five above.* **7** in heaven.
—*prep.* **1** to or in a higher place than: *a sword above his head. This elevator does not go above the third floor.* **2** higher than; over: *Look above the tall building to see the sun. He kept his head above water. A captain is above a sergeant.* **3** too great in importance for; superior to: *A great person should be above mean actions. The spoiled girl felt above washing dishes.* **4** more than: *The weight is above a ton.* **5** beyond: *Turn at the first corner above the church.*
—*adj.* made or mentioned earlier in a book or article; foregoing: *the above statement.*
—*n.* something that is written above: *Just as I was concluding the above, I received yours* (William Russell).

above all. See under **all**.

above oneself, overly complacent; smug: *"You're a bit above yourself, my dear," she said. "You're only a little girl."* (The Storyteller).

from above, from a higher place, person, authority, etc.: *an order from above.*
[Old English *abufan*]

a|bove-av|er|age (ə buv′av′rij, -ər ij), *adj.* exceeding what is usual; exceptional: *above-average precipitation, to have an above-average intelligence.*

a|bove|board (ə buv′bôrd′, -bōrd′), *adj., adv.* in open sight; without tricks or concealment: *Everything that the mayor did was open and aboveboard (adj.). His campaign was run aboveboard (adv.).* [< *above* + *board* (table); because card-players were required to keep their hands above the table]

a|bove|ground (ə buv′ground′), *adj., adv.* **1** above the surface of the ground: *aboveground testing of nuclear weapons* (adj.), *to build aboveground* (adv.). **2** *U.S.* in the open; not secret or underground. **3** not buried; alive.

a|bove|men|tioned (ə buv′men′shənd), *adj.* mentioned before.

a|bove|stairs (ə buv′stãrz′), *n., adv., adj. British.* —*n.pl.* the living quarters of a house apart from (usually above) the servants' quarters.
—*adv., adj.* upstairs.

a|bove-the-line (ə buv′ᴛʜə līn′), *adj.* (in a financial statement) indicating a current or ordinary revenue or expense: *The Exchequer outturn for 1962-63 was an above-the-line surplus of £353 million* (The Annual Register).

ab o|vo (ab ō′vō), *Latin.* **1** from the origin or very beginning. **2** (literally) from the egg.

a|boz|zo (ə bot′sō), *n., pl.* **-zi** (-sē). *Italian.* **1** a rough drawing or sketch. **2** a written outline or draft.

Abp., archbishop.

abr., **1** abridged. **2** abridgment.

ab|ra|ca|dab|ra (ab′rə kə dab′rə), *n.* **1** a word or formula formerly supposed to have magic power, used in incantations or as a charm to ward off disease. **2** meaningless talk; gibberish. [< Latin *abracadabra*]

a|bra|ço (ə brä′sü), *n., pl.* **-ços** (-süs). *Portuguese.* an embrace. Also, *Spanish,* **abrazo**.

a|brad|ant (ə brā′dənt), *adj., n.* —*adj.* wearing down; abrading. —*n.* an abrasive.

a|brade (ə brād′), *v.t., v.i.,* **a|brad|ed, a|brad|ing**. **1** to wear down or away by rubbing; scrape off: *The skin on Tom's knees was abraded by his fall. Glaciers abrade rocks.* **2** to wear down by friction: (*Figurative.*) *His policies* [*have*] *steadily abraded Ottawa's relations with Washington* (Manchester Guardian Weekly). [< Latin *abrādere* < *ab-* off + *rādere* to scrape] —**a|brad′a|ble**, *adj.* —**a|brad′er**, *n.*

A|bra|ham (ā′brə ham, -həm), *n.* the first patriarch (his son Isaac and his grandson Jacob were the other two). By tradition he was the ancestor of the Jews, through Isaac, and also the ancestor of the Arabs, through his son Ishmael (in the Bible, Genesis 12-25).

A|bra|ham|ic (ā′brə ham′ik), *adj.* of or relating to the patriarch Abraham.

A|bra|ham-man (ā′brə ham′man′), *n., pl.* **-men**. a beggar who wandered about England in the 1500's and 1600's, pretending to be a lunatic.

A|bram (ā′brəm), *n.* the original name of Abraham.

a|bran|chi|al (ā brang′kē əl), *adj.* = abranchiate.

a|bran|chi|an (ā brang′kē ən), *adj., n.* = abranchiate.

a|bran|chi|ate (ā brang′kē it, -āt), *adj., n.* —*adj.* having no gills. —*n.* an animal having no gills. [< *a-*[4] without + Greek *bránchia* gills + English *-ate*[1]]

a|bra|sa|ble (ə brā′sə bəl), *adj.* capable of being abraded or worn down.

a|bra|sion (ə brā′zhən), *n.* **1** a place scraped or worn by rubbing; an abraded spot or surface: *He had an abrasion on his heel where his shoe rubbed.* **2** a wearing away by rubbing; scraping off: *the abrasion of rocks by currents of water laden with sand. Coins become thinner by constant abrasion.* [< Latin *abrāsiō, -ōnis* < *abrādere;* see etym. under **abrade**]

a|bra|sive (ə brā′siv, -ziv), *n., adj.* —*n.* a substance used for smoothing, polishing, grinding, or sharpening: *Sandpaper, pumice, and emery are abrasives.*
—*adj.* **1** wearing away by rubbing; causing abrasion. **2** harsh; rough: *an abrasive voice.* —**a|bra′sive|ly**, *adv.* —**a|bra′sive|ness**, *n.*

à bras ou|verts (á brä zü ver′), *French.* with open arms; eagerly; receptively.

a|brax|as (ə brak′səs), *n.* **1** a mystical Gnostic word, said to represent the Greek numeral letters α, β, ρ, α, ξ, α, ς, amounting to the mystical number 365. **2** an amulet inscribed with it.

a|bra|zo (ä brä′sō, -thō), *n., pl.* **-zos** (-sōs, -thōs). *Spanish.* an embrace. Also, *Portuguese,* **abraço**.

ab|re|act (ab′rē akt′), *v.t. Psychoanalysis.* to express or release (repressed emotions) by reliving the experiences associated with them, as by talking about them.

ab|re|ac|tion (ab′rē ak′shən), *n. Psychoanalysis.* the releasing of repressed emotions by reliving the experiences associated with them, for example by talking about them; catharsis. [translation of German *Abreagierung*]

ab|re|ac|tive (ab′rē ak′tiv), *adj.* of or causing abreaction.

a|breast (ə brest′), *adv., adj.* side by side: *The soldiers marched four abreast* (adv.). *The airplane had four seats, two abreast on each side of the aisle* (adj.).

abreast of (or **with**), up with; alongside of; even with: *Keep abreast of what is going on by reading the newspaper. Keep abreast with the flow of events.*

a|bri (á brē′), *n., pl.* **a|bris** (á brē′). *French.* a shelter, such as a dugout or cave.

a|bridge (ə brij′), *v.t.,* **a|bridged, a|bridg|ing**. **1** to make shorter, especially by using fewer words: *A long story can be abridged by leaving out unimportant parts.* SYN: condense, epitomize. **2** to make less: *The rights of citizens must not be abridged without proper cause.* SYN: curtail, lessen, diminish. **3** to deprive (of): *to abridge citizens of their rights. The legislature therefore cannot abridge the executive power of any rights . . .* (Sir William Blackstone). SYN: divest. **4** to shorten in length of time. [< Old French *abregier* < Late Latin *abbreviāre* < Latin *ad-* to + *brevis* short. See etym. of doublet **abbreviate**.] —**a|bridg′a|ble**, **a|bridge′a|ble**, *adj.* —**a|bridg′er**, *n.*

a|bridged (ə brijd′), *adj.* shortened; condensed: *This book appears in the Reader's Digest in an abridged form. Abbr:* abr.

a|bridg|ment or **a|bridge|ment** (ə brij′mənt), *n.* **1** a shortened form; condensed version, especially of a book or long article: *That one book is an abridgment of a three-volume history. Abbr:*

abr. SYN: abstract, epitome, précis, synopsis, condensation. **2** a making shorter; an abridging. **3** curtailment: *an abridgment of liberties.* SYN: reduction.

a|brim (ə brim′), *adv., adj.* brimming: *eyes abrim with tears.*

a|brin (ā′brin), *n.* a highly poisonous protein found in the Indian licorice or jequirity bean. [< New Latin *Abrus,* genus name of the jequirity + English *-in*]

a|bris|tle (ə bris′əl), *adv., adj.* bristling: ... *a century abristle with dissent* (Time).

a|broach (ə brōch′), *adv., adj.*
set abroach, a to cause to flow or let out liquid: *Hogsheads of ale and claret were set abroach in the streets* (Macaulay). **b** to give rise to; spread far and wide; put in circulation: *What mischiefs he might set abroach* (Shakespeare).

a|broad (ə brôd′), *adv., adj., n.* —*adv., adj.* **1a** outside one's own country; in or to foreign lands (used in the United States especially with reference to Europe): *He is going abroad next year to study in Italy.* **b** out in the open air; out of one's house or abode; outdoors: *My grandfather walks abroad only on warm days.* **2** far and wide; widely: *The news that the astronaut was coming quickly spread abroad.* **3** in circulation; going around; current: *A rumor is abroad that school will close.*
—*n.* foreign lands: *At the close of the reign of Charles the Second, a great part of the iron which was used in the country was imported from abroad* (Macaulay).
be all abroad, a to be far wrong in one's guess or estimate: *The forecasters of a defeat for President Truman in 1948 were all abroad in their reckonings.* **b** to be puzzled: *The latter champion was all abroad ... and had lost all presence of mind* (Thackeray).
[< *a-*[1] on + *broad*]

ab|ro|ga|ble (ab′rə gə bəl), *adj.* that can be abrogated.

ab|ro|gate (ab′rə gāt), *v.t.,* **-gat|ed, -gat|ing.** **1** to abolish (a law, treaty, or custom) by an authoritative act; repeal; cancel: *When war broke out, our country abrogated its trade agreements with the enemy country. The 21st amendment to the Constitution, permitting the manufacture of intoxicating liquor, abrogated the 18th amendment, which prohibited it.* SYN: annul, nullify, invalidate, void. **2** to do away with. [< Latin *abrogāre* (with English *-ate*[1]) repeal < *ab-* away + *rogāre* propose a law] —**ab′ro|ga′tion,** *n.*

ab|ro|ga|tive (ab′rə gā′tiv), *adj.* abrogating; annulling: *an abrogative law.*

ab|ro|ga|tor (ab′rə gā′tər), *n.* a person who abrogates.

a|brupt (ə brupt′), *adj.* **1** showing sudden change; unexpected: *He made an abrupt turn to avoid hitting another car.* SYN: hasty. **2** very steep: *The road made an abrupt rise up the hill.* SYN: precipitous. See syn. under **steep**[1]. **3** short or sudden in speech or manner; blunt: *He was very gruff and had an abrupt way of speaking.* SYN: brusque, curt. **4** passing suddenly from one subject or thought to another; disconnected: *an abrupt style of writing.* **5** *Botany.* suddenly tapering off; truncate. **6** *Geology.* (of adjacent rock formations) having a sharp boundary at the point of contact. [< Latin *abruptus,* past participle of *abrumpere* break off < *ab-* off + *rumpere* break] —**a|brupt′ly,** *adv.* —**a|brupt′ness,** *n.*

a|brup|tion (ə brup′shən), *n.* a sudden breaking off.

abs-, *prefix.* the form of **ab-**[1] before *c* and *t,* as in *abscond, abstain.*

abs., 1 absent. **2a** absolute. **b** absolutely. **3** abstract.

ABS (no periods), **1** acrylonitrile-butadiene-styrene (a heavy-duty plastic). **2** alkyl benzene sulfonate (the basis of most hard detergents). The molecules of ABS cannot be broken down completely in sewage treatment systems.

Ab|sa|lom (ab′sə ləm), *n.* **1** David's favorite son. He rebelled against his father, was defeated in battle, and was later killed (in the Bible, II Samuel 18). **2** a favorite son. **3** a rebellious son.

ab|scess (ab′ses), *n., v.* —*n.* a collection of pus in the tissues of some part of the body. An abscess results from an infection and usually makes a painful sore, often accompanied by inflammation or swelling.
—*v.i.* to form an abscess.
[< Latin *abscessus, -ūs* withdrawal < *abscēdere* withdraw < *abs-* away + *cēdere* go]

ab|scessed (ab′sest), *adj.* having an abscess; diseased with an abscess: *The dentist treated my abscessed tooth.*

ab|scind (ab sind′), *v.t.* to cut off; exscind. [< Latin *abscindere* < *ab-* from + *scindere* to cut]

ab|scise (ab sīz′), *v.i., v.t.,* **-scised, -scis|ing.** to separate or cut off by abscission. [< Latin *abscīsus,* past participle of *abscīdere* < *abs-* away + *caedere* to cut]

ab|scis|ic acid (ab sis′ik), a plant hormone that promotes abscission and dormancy; abscisin. *Abbr:* ABA (no periods). [< *absciss*(sion) + *-ic*]

ab|scis|in (ab sis′ən), *n.* = abscisic acid.

ab|scis|sa (ab sis′ə), *n., pl.* **-scis|sas, -scis|sae** (-sis′ē). the distance of a point in a plane of two axes from the vertical axis (y-axis), measured on a line parallel to the horizontal axis (x-axis). The abscissa and the ordinate together are coordinates of the point. [< Latin (*līnea*) *abscissa* (line) cut off < *abscindere* to tear off < *ab-* off + *scindere* to tear]

ab|scis|sion (ab sizh′ən, -sish′-), *n.* **1** the normal separation of a mature fruit, leaf, or stem from a twig by the formation of a corky layer of young cells at the base. **2** a cutting off, as by surgery. [< Latin *abscissiō, -ōnis* a tearing off, a breaking off < *abscindere;* see etym. under **abscissa**]

abscission layer, = absciss layer.

ab|sciss layer (ab′sis), a corky layer of young cells formed at the base of a fruit, leaf, or stem just before the part falls. It protects the stem from decay.

ab|scond (ab skond′), *v.i.* to go away hurriedly and secretly, especially to avoid punishment; go off and hide: *The dishonest cashier absconded with the bank's money.* SYN: flee, escape, decamp. [< Latin *abscondere* < *abs-* away + *condere* store] —**ab|scond′er,** *n.*

ab|scond|ee (ab skon′dē), *n.* a person who absconds; absconder.

ab|scond|ence (ab skon′dəns), *n.* an absconding; concealment; seclusion.

ab|seil (äb′zīl, äp′-), *n., v.* —*n.* the method of descending a very steep cliff by means of a rope secured at the summit.
—*v.i.* to descend by this means.
[< German *Abseil* < *abseilen,* verb < *ab-* down + *Seil* rope] —**ab′seil|er,** *n.*

ab|sence (ab′səns), *n.* **1** a being away: *absence from work. His absence from school was caused by illness.* **2** a time of being away: *The sailor returned after an absence of two years.* **3** a being without; lack: *Darkness is the absence of light.* SYN: want, deficiency. **4** the condition of being absent-minded. SYN: inattentiveness. [< Old French *absence,* learned borrowing from Latin *absentia* < *absēns, -entis* absent]

absence of mind, the condition of being absent-minded.

ab|sent (*adj., prep.* ab′sənt; *v.* ab sent′), *adj., v., prep.* —*adj.* **1** not present (at a place); away: *Three members of the class are absent today. I will be absent from work tomorrow.* **2** not existing; lacking: *Snow is absent in some countries. In certain fishes the ribs are entirely absent.* **3** absent-minded: *The old man passed us with an absent look. I lost all my gaiety, became absent and thoughtful* (Tobias Smollett).
—*v.t.* to take or keep (oneself) away; withdraw: *Do not absent yourself from school without good reason.*
—*prep.* lacking; without: *Absent more and better research, it seemed sensible to initiate study* (Bulletin of Atomic Scientists).
[< Latin *absēns, -entis,* present participle of *abesse* be away < *ab-* away + *esse* to be] —**ab|sent′er,** *n.* —**ab′sent|ly,** *adv.* —**ab′sent|ness,** *n.*

ab|sen|ta|tion (ab′sən tā′shən), *n.* the act of absenting oneself.

ab|sen|tee (ab′sən tē′), *n., adj.* —*n.* a person who is away or stays away.
—*adj.* of or having to do with an absentee or absentees: *absentee ownership of land, absentee capital, an absentee voter.*

absentee ballot, a ballot of or for a voter who is permitted to vote by mail.

ab|sen|tee|ism (ab′sən tē′iz əm), *n.* **1** the practice or habit of being an absentee, especially from work. **2** an economic system under which a landowner controls the use of land in a country or place where he does not live.

absentee landlord, an owner, especially a landowner, who derives his income from one region, but lives in another.

ab|sen|te re|o (ab sen′tē rē′ō), *Latin, Law.* in the defendant's absence.

ab|sent-mind|ed (ab′sənt mīn′did), *adj.* not aware of or not paying attention to what is going on around one; forgetful or inattentive; preoccupied: *The absent-minded man put salt in his coffee and sugar on his egg.* SYN: abstracted, oblivious, distrait. —**ab′sent-mind′ed|ly,** *adv.* —**ab′sent-mind′ed|ness,** *n.*

absent without leave, (of a soldier, sailor, or other military personnel) away from one's post without permission, but without intending to desert. *Abbr:* A.W.O.L.

ab|sinthe or **ab|sinth** (ab′sinth), *n.* **1** a somewhat bitter, yellowish-green alcoholic drink made from brandy flavored with wormwood, anise, or other herbs. Its manufacture and sale are now forbidden in the United States and a number of other countries. **2** the plant wormwood. **3** a yellowish-green color. [< French *absinthe,* learned borrowing from Latin *absinthium* wormwood < Greek *apsinthion*]

ab|sinth|ism (ab′sin thiz əm), *n.* a diseased condition caused by too much drinking of absinthe.

ab|sit o|men (ab′sit ō′mən), *Latin.* may no harm come (of a thing just said or done).

ab|so|lute (ab′sə lüt), *adj., n.* —*adj.* **1** free from any imperfection or lack; complete; whole: *Try to tell the absolute truth. She did her work with absolute precision.* SYN: entire, pure. **2** not limited in any way; with no limits or restrictions: *Long ago some rulers had absolute power. The patient had absolute confidence in his doctor's ability to perform the operation.* SYN: unrestricted, unlimited, unconditional. **3** established beyond correction; certain; positive: *I had absolute proof that I was not present when the accident occurred.* SYN: infallible. **4** *Physics.* not compared with anything else: **a** independent of arbitrary or variable standards: *absolute zero of temperature.* 273° absolute is the same as 0° centigrade (Celsius). **b** based on some primary units (especially those of length, mass, and time) of invariable value which are taken as fundamental (as contrasted with any system of units based partly on some arbitrary unit, as of gravitation, whose value varies with latitude, altitude, or the like): *the centimeter-gram-second system of absolute units.* **c** based on a system of measurement independent of arbitrary or variable standards: *absolute temperature, absolute velocity, absolute pressure.* **5a** (of certain phrases) having the function of clauses; forming part of a sentence but not connected with it grammatically. In "The train being late, we missed the boat," *the train being late* is an absolute phrase or construction. See also **ablative absolute. b** (of transitive verbs) used without an expressed object. In "Please give freely," *give* is a verb in absolute use. **c** (of adjectives and possessive pronouns) used without a noun. In "There is rest for the weary," *weary* is an adjective in absolute use. In "Your house is larger than his," *his* is a pronoun in absolute use. *Abbr:* abs.
—*n.* anything that is absolute.
absolutes, a fixed and immutable qualities, concepts, or standards: *Exact measurement of any kind must be based upon absolutes.* **b** rigid standards of morality or firmly held beliefs about propriety: *A dogmatic person likes to speak in terms of absolutes.*
the absolute, *Philosophy.* **a** fundamental reality thought of as apart from all special relations or conditions; that which is capable of being thought or conceived by itself alone: *Whatever can be known* (*or conceived*) *out of relation ... is the known Absolute* (James F. Ferrier). **b** that which exists without relation to any other being; the ultimate ground of all things: [*They*] *tell us that the Absolute is unknowable, and that we can therefore know nothing of God* (Henry E. Manning). **c** that which is considered independently of its being subjective or objective: *Schelling pronounced the subject and object identical in the absolute* (Robert A. Vaughn).
[< Latin *absolūtus,* past participle of *absolvere* absolve < *ab-* from + *solvere* loosen] —**ab′so|lute′ly,** *adv.* —**ab′so|lute′ness,** *n.*

absolute address, the specific location where information is stored in a digital computer.

absolute alcohol, ethyl alcohol that is theoretically pure and in practice contains not more than 1 per cent of water by weight.

absolute altimeter, an altimeter measuring altitude by the time required for a radio wave to echo from the surface immediately below. It is absolute in contrast to the measurement by barometric pressure, which is subject to atmospheric conditions.

absolute altitude, the height of a flying object, such as an aircraft or missile, above the earth's surface directly below (rather than above sea level).

absolute ceiling, the maximum altitude above sea level at which a given aircraft or other airborne object can maintain horizontal flight.

absolute comparison, *Grammar.* the use of comparative or superlative forms of adjectives and adverbs in a sense that does not involve comparison. Thus in "I am in the best of health," *best* is an absolute superlative, but in "He was the best student in the class," *best* is a relative superlative.

absolute discharge, *Law.* (in Great Britain) the

Pronunciation Key: hat, āge, cãre, fär; let, ēqual, tėrm; it, īce; hot, ōpen, ôrder; oil, out; cup, pu̇t, rüle; child; long; thin; ᴛʜen; zh, measure; ə represents **a** in about, **e** in taken, **i** in pencil, **o** in lemon, **u** in circus.

discharge of an offender upon payment of a fine or court costs, which is not considered to be a conviction, nor entered in police records as a criminal case.

absolute humidity, the mass of water vapor present in a given volume of air, usually expressed in grams per cubic meter.

absolute idealism, *Philosophy.* a form of idealism which holds that there is only one universal spirit, of which all things are manifestations.

absolute magnitude, the magnitude a given star would have if placed at the distance of 10 parsecs (32.6 light-years) from the earth, used as a basis for expressing the intrinsic brightness of stars.

absolute majority, more than half the total number voting or qualified to vote.

absolute monarchy, a monarchy in which the ruler's power is not limited.

absolute music, music which does not imitate, describe, or represent objective sounds, scenes, or events; abstract music.

absolute ohm, a measure of the resistance of a conductor based on electromagnetic units of the centimeter-gram-second system, equal to 10^9 abohms.

absolute pitch, *Music.* **1** the pitch of a tone determined solely by the frequency of its vibrations per second. **2** a sense of correct pitch, by which some people are able exactly to identify tones by ear; perfect pitch.

absolute pressure, fluid pressure measured above a vacuum (or above zero pressure) in units of force per unit of area.

absolute reality, *Philosophy.* the presence in the universe of a spiritual power greater than man's moral or religious perceptions.

ab|so|lutes (ab′sə lüts), *n.pl.* See under **absolute.**

***absolute scale**, a scale in which temperatures are measured from absolute zero, such as the Kelvin scale or the Rankine scale.

absolute system, a system of absolute units.

absolute temperature, a temperature measured from or expressed in degrees above absolute zero.

absolute unit, a unit defined directly in terms of the fundamental units of mass, length, and time, as opposed to relative measurements.

absolute value, the value of a real number regardless of any accompanying sign: *The absolute value of +3, or of −3, is 3.*

absolute zero, the temperature at which substances would have no heat whatever, and all molecules would stop moving. Theoretically, it is the lowest temperature, −273.15 degrees centigrade (Celsius) or −459.67 degrees Fahrenheit.

ab|so|lu|tion (ab′sə lü′shən), *n.* **1** a freeing from guilt or punishment for sin; forgiveness of sins declared by ecclesiastical authority: *After confession, after absolution, When my whole soul was white I prayed for them* (Longfellow). **2** a freeing or freedom from guilt or blame. SYN: pardon, exoneration, exculpation, acquittal. **3** the declaration that frees a person from guilt or punishment for sin: *The Absolution or Remission of Sins, To be pronounced by the Priest alone, standing* (Book of Common Prayer). **4** release from a duty or promise. SYN: discharge, acquittance, exemption. **5** remission of penance or other ecclesiastical sentence.

ab|so|lut|ism (ab′sə lü tiz′əm), *n.* **1** a system or form of government in which the ruler has unrestricted power; despotism. SYN: tyranny, autocracy, totalitarianism. **2** positiveness. **3** *Philosophy.* the doctrine of an absolute idealism.

ab|so|lut|ist (ab′sə lü′tist), *n., adj.* —*n.* a person who favors or supports absolutism.
—*adj.* despotic: *... the return under Soviet rule to some of the darkest practices of absolutist tsarism* (Wall Street Journal).

ab|so|lut|is|tic (ab′sə lü tis′tik), *adj.* of absolutists or absolutism.

ab|so|lu|tize (ab′sə lü tīz), *v.t.*, **-tized, -tiz|ing.** to make absolute; declare perfect, unconditional, or complete: *The forms that characterize man's religious thought ... are culturally contingent; yet the early Christian philosophers absolutized them* (Saturday Review).

ab|sol|u|to|ry (ab sol′yə tôr′ē, -tōr′), *adj.* absolving.

ab|solv|a|ble (ab sol′və bəl, -zol′-), *adj.* that can be absolved; deserving absolution. —**ab|solv′a|ble|ness**, *n.* —**ab|solv′a|bly**, *adv.*

ab|solve (ab solv′, -zolv′), *v.t.*, **-solved, -solv|ing. 1** to declare free from sin, guilt, or blame or their penalties or consequences: *My brother was absolved of blame for the accident. The priest absolved the man after he confessed his sin and did penance.* SYN: exonerate, acquit. **2** to set free (from a duty or obligation); release: *I absolve you from your promise to go.* SYN: exempt. [< Latin *absolvere* < *ab-* from + *solvere* loosen. See etym. of doublet **assoil.**] —**ab|solv′er**, *n.*

ab|sol|vent (ab sol′vənt, -zol′-), *adj., n.* —*adj.* absolving.
—*n.* a person who absolves.

ab|so|nant (ab′sə nənt), *adj.* = discordant. [< Latin *ab-* off + *sonāns, -antis,* present participle of *sonāre* to sound]

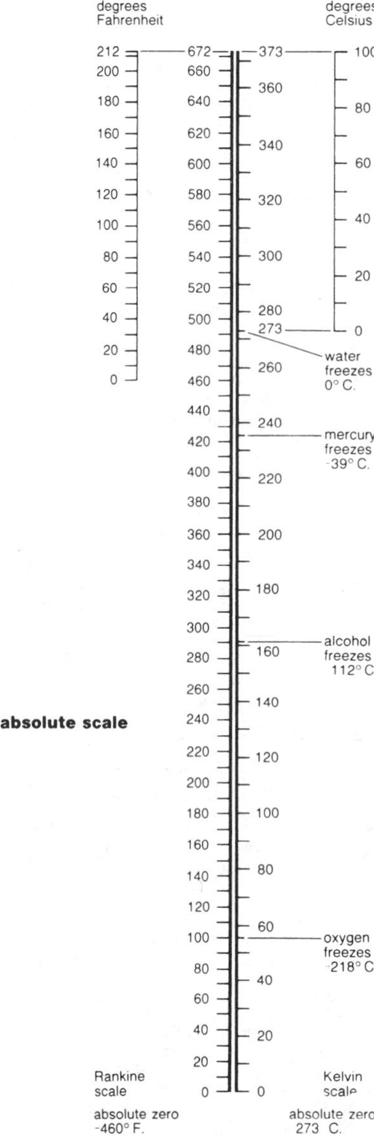

***absolute scale**

absolute scale (degrees absolute)

ab|sorb (ab sôrb′, -zôrb′), *v.t.* **1** to take in or suck up (a liquid or gas); soak or blot up: *The sponge absorbed the spilled milk. Water can absorb ammonia.* See picture under **adsorb. 2** to take in and make a part of itself; assimilate: *The United States has absorbed millions of immigrants.* **3** to take in and hold rather than reflect: *Rugs absorb sounds and make a house quieter. Anything black absorbs most of the light rays that fall on it.* **4** *Figurative.* to take up all the attention of; interest very much: *Building a dam in the brook absorbed the boy so completely that he did not hear us call him to lunch.* SYN: engross. **5** *Figurative.* to grasp with the mind; understand: *to absorb the full meaning of a remark.* **6** to take in and endure; sustain: *The boxer absorbed the punches without buckling under the assault. North Vietnam could absorb considerable punishment ... without any decisive economic effect* (New York Times). **7** to accept and pay (an increased cost, tax, or the like) without adding it to the price of a product or services: *The manufacturer absorbed the increase in overhead and did not raise his prices.* **8** *Biology.* to take (digested food, oxygen, or the like) into the bloodstream by osmosis: *Digested food is absorbed into the bloodstream in the intestines.* [< Latin *absorbēre* swallow up < *ab-* from + *sorbēre* suck in] —**ab|sorb′er**, *n.*
—*Syn.* **2 Absorb, assimilate** mean to take something in, both literally and as used figuratively with reference to ideas. **Absorb** means to swallow up a thing so that it loses its individual character or disappears: *Large companies sometimes absorb smaller ones.* **Assimilate** adds to *absorb* the idea of converting what is absorbed into an essential part of what has taken it in: *A person who reads intelligently assimilates what he reads by making it a part of his own thoughts and thinking.*

ab|sorb|a|bil|i|ty (ab sôr′bə bil′ə tē, -zôr′-), *n.* an absorbable condition or quality.

ab|sorb|a|ble (ab sôr′bə bəl, -zôr′-), *adj.* that can be absorbed.

ab|sorb|ance (ab sôr′bəns, -zôr′-), *n. Physics.* the common logarithm of the absorptivity of a substance.

ab|sorb|an|cy (ab sôr′bən sē, -zôr′-), *n.* **1** = absorbency. **2** = absorptivity (def. 2). **3** = absorbance.

ab|sorbed (ab sôrbd′, -zôrbd′), *adj.* very much interested; completely occupied; engrossed: *I was so absorbed that I did not hear the bell ring. He eyed the coming tide with an absorbed attention* (Dickens). —**ab|sorb′ed|ly**, *adv.* —**ab|sorb′ed|ness**, *n.*

ab|sor|be|fa|cient (ab sôr′bə fā′shənt, -zôr′-), *adj., n.* —*adj.* causing or aiding absorption.
—*n.* any substance causing or aiding absorption. [< Latin *absorbēre* absorb + *faciēns, -entis,* present participle of *facere* do]

ab|sorb|en|cy (ab sôr′bən sē, -zôr′-), *n.* **1** an absorbent quality or condition. **2** the degree to which a substance is absorbent.

ab|sorb|ent (ab sôr′bənt, -zôr′-), *adj., n.* —*adj.* taking in, or able to take in, moisture, light, or heat: *Absorbent paper towels are used to dry the hands.*
—*n.* any substance that absorbs moisture, light, or heat.

absorbent cotton, fluffy raw cotton from which the wax has been removed, used to dress small wounds, or as a swab for putting on or wiping away salves, lotions, or other liquid.

ab|sorb|ing (ab sôr′bing, -zôr′-), *adj.* extremely interesting; engrossing: *The explorer told us the absorbing story of his adventures.* —**ab|sorb′ing|ly**, *adv.*

ab|sorp|tance (ab sôrp′təns, -zôrp′-), *n.* = absorptivity (def. 2).

ab|sorp|ti|om|e|ter (ab sôrp′shē om′ə tər, -zôrp′-), *n.* an instrument for measuring the absorption of a gas by a liquid.

ab|sorp|ti|o|met|ric (ab sôrp′shē ō met′rik, -zôrp′-), *adj.* of or involving the measurement of the absorption of gas by a liquid.

ab|sorp|tion (ab sôrp′shən, -zôrp′-), *n.* **1** the act or process of absorbing; a taking up and holding: *A paper towel dries up spilled milk by absorption. In the absorption of light rays by black objects, light energy is changed to heat energy.* **2** *Figurative.* the condition of being absorbed, especially showing great interest (in something): *The children's absorption in their game was so complete that they did not notice the first few drops of rain.* **3a** *Physiology.* the process of taking (digested food, oxygen, or the like) into the bloodstream by osmosis. **b** *Botany.* the process of taking inorganic salts in solution into root hairs from soil water by osmosis. [< Late Latin *absorptiō, -ōnis* < Latin *absorbēre;* see etym. under **absorb**]

absorption band, a dark bank or bands in a continuous spectrum of white light caused by the natural or artificial absorption of the wavelengths of light radiating from the luminous molecules of a chemical element in a gaseous state.

absorption coefficient, **1** a constant for a material indicating the degree to which it absorbs radiation, atomic particles, rays of light, etc., that pass through it. **2** the rate at which the human body absorbs a particular substance, usually expressed in milligrams per kilogram of body weight per hour.

absorption line, a dark line in a continuous spectrum of white light caused by the natural or artificial absorption of the wavelengths of light radiating from the atoms of a chemical element in a gaseous or liquid state: *Some 66 [chemical elements] have been found in the atmosphere of the sun by their telltale absorption lines in the solar spectrum* (Armin Deutsch).

absorption spectrum, a continuous spectrum broken by dark lines or bands, formed by passing white light or other electromagnetic radiation through a gas or liquid. The lines or bands indicate the presence of a particular chemical element or compound by the absorption of certain frequencies. The dark lines or bands are caused by the transfer of energy when the element is excited to incandescence and its wavelengths of light are absorbed by passing through the cooler vapors of the same element.

ab|sorp|tive (ab sôrp′tiv, -zôrp′-), *adj.* able to absorb; absorbent. —**ab·sorp′tive·ly,** *adv.* —**ab·sorp′tive·ness,** *n.*

ab·sorp·tiv·i·ty (ab′sôrp tiv′ə tē, -zôrp-), *n.* **1** = absorbency. **2** *Physics.* the ratio of the radiant energy absorbed by a surface to the total of the energy striking the surface.

ab·squat·u·late (ab skwoch′ə lāt), *v.i.,* **-lat·ed, -lat·ing.** *U.S. Slang.* to run away; flee; abscond: *Anybody who has read a thriller by Ian Fleming is bloody well aware why the Russians have absquatulated with so many of Britain's state secrets. It's that blinking British Agent 007* (Time). [American English < *ab-*[1] + *squat;* influenced by *abscond* and *capitulate*] —**ab·squat′u·la′tion,** *n.*

abs. re., absente reo.

ab·stain (ab stān′), *v.i.* **1** to do without something; hold oneself back; refrain (from): *If you abstain from eating candy and rich foods, you will not be so fat. When the cigars were passed, he abstained. He abstained from smoking.* SYN: forbear, desist. See syn. under **refrain**[1]. **2** to refrain from voting: *Six members voted in favor of the motion, five members voted against it, and four members abstained. So the motion was adopted.* [< Old French *abstenir,* learned borrowing from Latin *abstinēre* withhold < *abs-* from + *tenēre* hold]

ab·stain·er (ab stā′nər), *n.* a person who abstains, especially from the use of alcoholic liquor.

ab·ste·mi·ous (ab stē′mē əs), *adj.* **1** sparing in eating and drinking; moderate; temperate: *My sister is abstemious in her eating habits; she never eats too much. Abstemious, refusing luxuries, not sourly and reproachfully, but simply as unfit for his habit* (Emerson). **2** very plain; restricted: *an abstemious diet.* SYN: sparing. [< Latin *abstēmius* (with English *-ous*) < *abs-* off + unrecorded *tēmum* strong drink] —**ab·ste′mi·ous·ly,** *adv.* —**ab·ste′mi·ous·ness,** *n.*

ab·sten·tion (ab sten′shən), *n.* **1** the act of abstaining; abstinence: *He gave several reasons for his abstention from signing the contract.* **2** the fact of not voting: *There were six votes in favor, five against, and four abstentions.* **3** a person who abstains, especially a voter who does not vote. [< Late Latin *abstentiō, -ōnis* < Latin *abstinēre* withhold; see etym. under **abstinence**]

ab·sten·tion·ist (ab sten′shə nist), *n., adj.* —*n.* a person who practices abstention, especially in political affairs.

—*adj.* abstaining; not interfering: *an abstentionist policy or group.*

ab·sten·tious (ab sten′shəs), *adj.* = abstemious.

ab·sterge (ab stėrj′), *v.t.,* **-sterged, -sterg·ing. 1** to wipe off; clean by wiping. **2** *Medicine.* to purge. [< Latin *abstergēre* < *abs-* away + *tergēre* wipe, cleanse]

ab·ster·gent (ab stėr′jənt), *adj., n.* —*adj.* cleansing.

—*n.* a cleansing agent; detergent.

ab·ster·sion (ab stėr′shən, -zhən), *n.* the act or process of cleansing, scouring, or purging. [< Late Latin *abstersiō, -ōnis* < Latin *abstergēre* wipe off; see etym. under **absterge**]

ab·ster·sive (ab stėr′siv), *adj., n.* = abstergent. —**ab·ster′sive·ness,** *n.*

ab·sti·nence (ab′stə nəns), *n.* an abstaining; partly or entirely giving up certain pleasures, food, or drink: *abstinence from meat during Lent. His doctor recommended abstinence from coffee and tobacco. Buddhists favor "the Middle Way" between abstinence and self-indulgence.* SYN: self-denial, continence. See also **total abstinence.** [< Latin *abstinentia* < *abstinēns, -entis,* present participle of *abstinēre* withhold < *abs-* from + *tenēre* hold]

ab·sti·nen·cy (ab′stə nən sē), *n.* = abstinence.

ab·sti·nent (ab′stə nənt), *adj.* abstaining, especially from self-indulgence; abstemious. —**ab′sti·nent·ly,** *adv.*

ab·stract (*adj.* ab′strakt, ab strakt′; *v. 1, 3, 4* abstrakt′; *v. 2, n.* ab′strakt), *adj., v., n.* —*adj.* **1** thought of apart from any particular object, real thing, or actual instance; not concrete: *Sweetness is abstract; a lump of sugar is concrete. Truth is an abstract concept.* **2** expressing or naming a quality, idea, or other concept, rather than a particular object or concrete thing: *Honesty is an abstract noun.* See also **abstract noun, abstract number. 3** hard to understand; difficult; abstruse: *The atomic theory of matter is so abstract that it can be fully understood only by advanced students.* SYN: profound. **4** concerned with ideas or concepts rather than actual particulars or instances; not practical or applied; ideal or theoretical: *abstract reasoning, abstract mathematics.* SYN: visionary. **5** not representing any actual object or concrete thing; having little or no resemblance to real or material things, especially in art that avoids the use of ordinary conventional designs and the representation of material things, animals, or persons: *We saw many abstract paintings in the Museum of Modern Art. The interest of an abstract picture is exclusively decorative* (London Times). SYN: nonrepresentational, nonobjective.

—*v.t.* **1** to think of (a quality, such as color, weight, or truth) apart from any object or real thing having that quality or any actual instance: *We can abstract the idea of redness from the color of all red objects.* **2** to make an abstract of; summarize: *Try to abstract this story for a book report.* SYN: abridge. **3a** to take away; remove: *Iron is abstracted from ore.* SYN: extract. **b** to take away secretly, slyly, or dishonestly. SYN: steal, purloin. **4** to withdraw (the attention); divert. SYN: detach, disengage.

—*n.* **1** a brief statement of the main ideas or important points of an article, book, case in court, or other printed material; summary: *The students will write brief summaries of scientific treatises, earning $2.50 for each such abstract* (Wall Street Journal). SYN: abridgment, digest, compendium. **2** an abstract of title. *Abbr:* abs. **3** a work of abstract art; abstraction: *a geometric abstract in red and yellow.* **4** an abstract idea or term; abstraction: *the abstract called capitalism.*

in the abstract, in theory rather than in practice: *10 percent of society understands in the abstract the meaning of "freedom"* (Maclean's).

[< Latin *abstractus,* past participle of *abstrahere* draw away < *abs-* away + *trahere* draw] —**ab·stract′er, ab·strac′tor,** *n.* —**ab′stract·ly,** *adv.* —**ab′stract·ness,** *n.*

ab·stract·ed (ab strak′tid), *adj.* lost in thought; absent-minded. SYN: preoccupied. —**ab·stract′ed·ly,** *adv.* —**ab·stract′ed·ness,** *n.*

abstract expressionism, a style of abstract painting intended primarily to express the artist's emotions or state of mind during a creative experience, as by freely splattering or staining the canvas with paint: *Abstract expressionism, if it is to survive, must have a purpose and a form to fit that purpose* (New Yorker).

abstract expressionist, 1 a painter who produces works of abstract expressionism. **2** of or having to do with abstract expressionism: *De Kooning's canvas reaffirms the abstract expressionist credo that the very effort of painting is what paintings should be about* (Time).

ab·strac·tion (ab strak′shən), *n.* **1** the idea of a quality thought of apart from any particular object or real thing having that quality; abstract idea, concept, or term: *Whiteness, courage, hope, sorrow, and length are abstractions. A line that has no width is only an abstraction.* **2** the formation of an abstract idea or concept: *. . . abstraction is nothing more than leaving out of a number of resembling ideas what is peculiar to each* (Joseph Priestley). **3a** a taking away; removal: *the abstraction of iron from ore. After the abstraction of the juice from an orange, only the pulp and peel are left.* **b** secret, sly, or dishonest removal; purloining. **4** the state of being lost in thought; absent-mindedness: *In a fit of abstraction he forgot to eat lunch.* **5** a work of abstract art: *a group of abstractions in oil and water color.* **6** abstractionism: *The recent emphasis on extreme abstraction . . . raises questions which go to the very basis of artistic expression* (New York Times).

ab·strac·tion·al (ab strak′shə nəl), *adj.* having to do with abstraction: *. . . music so astringent . . . that it amounts to abstractional design* (New York Times).

ab·strac·tion·ism (ab strak′shə niz əm), *n.* **1** the theory or principles of abstract art. **2** the art or practice of making abstractions, especially in art: *Making mobiles is a type of abstractionism.*

ab·strac·tion·ist (ab strak′shə nist), *n.* **1** an artist who produces works of abstract art: *The abstractionist, though, works in symbols, not depicting the object but suggesting it* (New Yorker). **2** an idealist; a dreamer.

ab·strac·tive (ab strak′tiv), *adj.* **1** having the power of abstraction. **2** of or having the nature of an abstract or summary. —**ab·strac′tive·ly,** *adv.* —**ab·strac′tive·ness,** *n.*

abstract music, = absolute music.

abstract noun, a common noun that refers to a quality, idea, action, or state, rather than to a physical object, tangible thing, or specific being. *Youth* is an abstract noun in "the vigor of youth," a collective noun in "the youth of our country," and a concrete noun in "a youth."

abstract number, a number which does not relate to a particular object or thing, as 4 or 6 distinguished from 4 apples or 6 cats.

abstract of title, a summarized account of past ownership of a piece of real estate, going back as far as legally necessary, to establish current ownership.

ab·strict (ab strikt′), *v.t., v.i.* to separate by abstriction.

ab·stric·tion (ab strik′shən), *n.* branched spore formation in certain fungi in which portions of the spore-bearing filament (hypha) are separated by the formation of walls (septa); abjunction. [< *ab-*[1] away + Late Latin *strictiō, -ōnis* a drawing together < Latin *stringere* to bind tight]

ab·struse (ab strüs′), *adj.* hard to understand; difficult: *If you do not master arithmetic, you will find algebra complicated and abstruse. The fields of inquiry run from simple mechanics to abstruse atomic energy* (Wall Street Journal). SYN: esoteric, recondite, obscure, arcane. [< Latin *abstrūsus,* past participle of *abstrūdere* conceal < *abs-* away + *trūdere* thrust] —**ab·struse′ly,** *adv.* —**ab·struse′ness,** *n.*

ab·stru·si·ty (ab strü′sə tē), *n.* **1** *no pl.* abstruse character; obscurity: *The abstrusity of some legal documents baffles most laymen.* **2** *pl.* **-ties.** an abstruse point or matter: *. . . there were criminal lawyers deeply versed in the abstrusities and tricks of the criminal law* (Theodore Dreiser).

ab·surd (ab sėrd′, -zėrd′), *adj., n.* —*adj.* plainly not true, logical, or sensible; so contrary to reason that it is laughable; foolish; ridiculous: *The idea that the number 13 brings bad luck is absurd.* SYN: preposterous. See syn. at **ridiculous.**

—*n.* situations and ideas that represent the absurdity of the human condition: *students of the absurd, the literature of the absurd.*

[< Latin *absurdus* out of tune, senseless] —**ab·surd′ly,** *adv.* —**ab·surd′ness,** *n.*

ab·surd·ism (ab sėr′diz əm), *n.* the principles and practices of the absurdists: *. . . the austere absurdism of great dramatists like Beckett and Pinter* (Renata Adler).

ab·surd·ist (ab sėr′dist), *n., adj.* —*n.* a playwright who uses the techniques of the Theater of the Absurd: *The absurdist presents fantasy as reality, or reality as fantasy* (Saturday Review).

—*adj.* of or having to do with the Theater of the Absurd: *absurdist comedy, absurdist dialogue.*

ab·surd·i·ty (ab sėr′də tē, -zėr′-), *n.* **1** *no pl.* absurd quality or condition; lack of sense; foolishness: *the absurdity of superstition. You can see the absurdity of wearing shoes on your head and hats on your feet.* **2** *pl.* **-ties.** something absurd; a ridiculous or unreasonable action, statement, or custom: *To say that every father has a daughter is an absurdity.*

ABT (no periods), American Ballet Theatre.

ab·u·def·duf (ab′yə def′duf), *n.* any one of a genus of small, agile, tropical marine fish that hide in crevices in rocks or coral reefs; damselfish. [< New Latin *Abudefduf* the genus name]

a·build·ing (ə bil′ding), *adj. Especially U.S.* in the process of being built: *What many call the New Europe is abuilding around the European Economic Community, better known as the Common Market* (Wall Street Journal).

a·bu·li·a (ə byü′lē ə), *n.* loss of the ability to make decisions, characteristic of schizophrenia. Also, **aboulia.** [< Greek *aboulíā* indecision < *a-* without + *boulḗ* will]

a·bu·lic (ə byü′lik), *adj.* **1** of or having to do with abulia. **2** characterized by abulia. Also, **aboulic.**

a·bun·dance (ə bun′dəns), *n.* **1** a quantity that is more than enough; great plenty; full supply: *There is such an abundance of apples this year that many are not being picked. Oil, the greatest source of Venezuela's wealth, continues to flow in abundance* (Atlantic). SYN: profusion, superfluity. **2** a plentiful supply of money and possessions; wealth: *In the near future technology was going to create abundance and everyone would have enough of everything* (Saul Bellow). SYN: affluence.

a·bun·dant (ə bun′dənt), *adj.* **1** more than enough; very plentiful: *The trapper had an abundant supply of food for the winter.* SYN: ample, bountiful, profuse. **2** having more than enough; abounding (in); rich: *The fishermen found a river abundant in salmon. The Lord . . . abundant in goodness and truth* (Exodus 34:6). [< Old North French *abundant,* learned borrowing from Latin *abundāns, -antis,* present participle of *abundāre* abound < *ab-* off + *undāre* rise in waves < *unda* a wave] —**a·bun′dant·ly,** *adv.* —**a·bun′dant·ness,** *n.*

abundant number, a whole number whose divisors have a sum greater than twice this number. The number 18 is an abundant number because the sum of its divisors (18, 9, 6, 3, 2, 1) is greater than 2 × 18.

abundant year, the longest of the three common years of the Jewish calendar, having 355 days; perfect year.

ab u·no dis·ce om·nes (ab yü′nō dis′ē om′nēz), *Latin.* from one learn all.

ab ur·be con·di·ta (ab ėr′bē kon′di tə), *Latin.*

Pronunciation Key: hat, āge, cãre, fär; let, ēqual, tėrm; it, īce; hot, ōpen, ôrder; oil, out; cup, pu̇t, rüle; child; long; thin; ᴛʜen; zh, measure; ə represents a in about, e in taken, i in pencil, o in lemon, u in circus.

since the founding of the city (of Rome, about 753 B.C.). *Abbr:* A.U.C.

a·bus·age (ə byü′sij), *n.* = abuse.

a·buse (*v.* ə byüz′; *n.* ə byüs′), *v.*, **a·bused, a·bus·ing,** *n.* **—*v.t.*** **1** to use wrongly; make bad use of; misuse: *Do not abuse the privilege of using the library by loud talking.* **2** to treat badly; mistreat: *The angry boy abused his dog by beating it. Don't abuse your eyes by reading in a bad light.* **SYN:** injure. **3** to use harsh and insulting language about or to: *Instead of debating the issues the candidates abused each other.* **SYN:** revile, malign. **4** *Archaic.* to impose on; mislead; deceive. [< Old French *abuser* < *abus;* see noun]
—*n.* **1** a wrong or bad use: *Talking too loud is an abuse of your library privileges. The people hated the wicked king for his abuse of power.* **SYN:** misapplication, misuse. **2** harsh or severe treatment: *The abuse of the helpless prisoner made him bitter.* **SYN:** injury. **3** a bad practice or custom: *Slavery is an abuse. Abuses multiply when citizens are indifferent.* **4** harsh and insulting language. **SYN:** vituperation. **5** *Archaic.* deception. [< Old French *abus,* learned borrowing from Latin *abūsus, -ūs* a wasting < *abūtī* misuse < *ab-* away + *ūtī* use] **—a·bus′a·ble,** *adj.* **—a·bus′er,** *n.*

a·bu·sive (ə byü′siv, -ziv), *adj.* **1** using harsh and insulting language; reviling: *You're an . . . abusive . . . bad old creature* (Dickens). **SYN:** scurrilous, opprobrious, reproachful. **2** containing abuse; harsh and insulting: *an abusive letter.* **3** treating roughly or cruelly. **4** wrongly used; misapplied. **5** *Archaic.* corrupt. **—a·bu′sive·ly,** *adv.* **—a·bu′sive·ness,** *n.*

a·bus·tle (ə bus′əl), *adj.* bustling; stirring: *a house abustle with preparations for the holidays.*

a·but (ə but′), *v.,* **a·but·ted, a·but·ting.** **—*v.t.*** to border on; adjoin; meet: *A shed abuts the barn.*
—*v.i.* to touch at one end or edge; end at; border (on): *The sidewalk abuts on the street.*
[< Old French *abouter* join end to end (< *a-* to + *bout* a striking), and *abuter* touch with an end (< *a-* to + *but* end)] **—a·but′ter,** *n.*

a·bu·ti·lon (ə byü′tə lon), *n.* **1** any one of several plants of the mallow family having bell-shaped, yellow or white flowers often veined with red; flowering maple. **2** the flower of any of these plants. [< New Latin *Abutilon* < Arabic *'abūtīlūn*]

***a·but·ment** (ə but′mənt), *n.* **1a** a support for an arch or bridge. **b** the point or place where the support joins the thing supported. **2** the fact, state, or place of abutting.

*** abutment**
definition 1a

a·but·tal (ə but′əl), *n.* the fact or state of abutting.
abuttals, the parts of a piece of land which abut on other land: *The land is set forth by bounds and abuttals* (Nathaniel Bacon).

a·but·ting (ə but′ing), *adj.* = adjacent.

a·buzz (ə buz′), *adj., adv.* **1** buzzing; filled with buzzing sounds. **2** filled with noises of activity: *The retail shoe industry is abuzz with talk of a big boom just ahead* (Wall Street Journal).

ab·volt (ab vōlt′), *n.* an electromagnetic unit of electromotive force in the centimeter-gram-second system, equal to 10^{-8} volt. [< *ab-*[3] absolute + *volt*]

Ab·wehr (äp′vār′), *n. German.* the German counterintelligence system in World War II.

a·by or **a·bye** (ə bī′), *v.t.,* **a·bought, a·by·ing.** *Archaic.* **1** to pay the penalty for; atone for. **2** to suffer; endure. [< Old English *ābyg-,* stem of *ābycgan* pay for] ►See **abide**[2] for usage note.

a·bysm (ə biz′əm), *n.* = abyss. [< Old French *abisme* < Medieval Latin *abysmus,* alteration of Late Latin *abyssus* abyss]

a·bys·mal (ə biz′məl), *adj.* **1** too deep or great to be measured; bottomless: *abysmal ignorance.* **SYN:** immeasurable, unfathomable. **2** *Informal.* extremely bad; of very low quality; miserable: *The system of teaching was abysmal* (Punch). **3** of or having to do with the greatest depths of the ocean. **—a·bys′mal·ly,** *adv.*

a·byss (ə bis′), *n.* **1** a bottomless or very great depth; a very deep crack in the earth: *The mountain climber stood at the edge of a cliff overlooking an abyss four thousand feet deep.* **SYN:** chasm. **2** *Figurative.* anything too deep or great to be measured; lowest depth: *Failure after failure plunged him into an abyss of despair.* **3** the chaos before the Creation. [< Late Latin *abyssus* < Greek *ábyssos* < *a-* without + *byssós* bottom]

a·byss·al (ə bis′əl), *adj.* **1** of or inhabiting the depths of the ocean to which light does not penetrate: *an abyssal mollusk.* **2** = unfathomable. **3** = plutonic: *abyssal rock.*

abyssal plain, a deep, extremely level undersea plain, such as the plain lying about 750 miles to 1,000 miles off the eastern coast of North America, with deposits of clay, silt, and sand apparently laid down by the action of a dense current of sediments, or turbidity current, moving along the sea floor.

Ab·ys·sin·i·an (ab′ə sin′ē ən), *n., adj.* **—*n.*** a person born or living in Abyssinia (Ethiopia).
—*adj.* of or having to do with Abyssinia.

Abyssinian cat, any one of a breed of medium-sized cats with long, tapering tails, small paws, and short, silky hair with dark-colored tips.

ab·zyme (ab′zīm), *n.* an antibody that is chemically modified to function as an enzyme: *Enzymatic antibodies, or abzymes, . . . perform a range of chemical jobs such as making or breaking specific bonds between the amino acids that make up proteins* (Science News). [< *ab-*[1] + (en)*zyme*]

ac-, *prefix.* the form of **ad-** before *c, k,* and *q,* as in *accede, acknowledgment, acquaint.*

ac., acre or acres.

a.c. or **a-c,** alternating current (of electricity).
►These abbreviations are now widely used as modifiers: *an a.c. motor.*

Ac (no period), **1** actinium (chemical element). **2** alto-cumulus (clouds).

AC (no periods), **1** *U.S.* Air Corps (before World War II). **2** alternating current.

A/C or **a/c** (no periods), *Commerce.* **1** account. **2** account current.

A.C., **1** *British.* aircraftsman. **2** alternating current. **3** before Christ (Latin, *ante Christum*).

a·ca·cia (ə kā′shə), *n.* **1** a tree or shrub of the pea family, with (usually) finely divided leaves, that grows mostly in tropical or warm regions throughout the world. In the United States, acacias are common from Texas to California. Certain species in Australia produce tannin; others in Africa produce gum arabic; still others in India and Southeast Asia yield catechu. **2** a locust tree of North America, with thorny branches and clusters of white flowers. **3** gum arabic. [< Latin *acacia* < Greek *akakiā* a thorny Egyptian tree]

acad., **1** academic. **2** academy.

ac·a·deme (ak′ə dēm′), *n.* **1** an academy; school; university. **2** the world of scholars; academic life.

Ac·a·deme (ak′ə dēm′), *n.* the Academy (the park or grove near Athens where Plato taught).

a·cad·e·mese (ə kad′ə mēz′), *n.* academic jargon: *The dominant rhetoric is academese relieved by flashes of cliché* (Dwight Macdonald).

ac·a·de·mi·a (ak′ə dē′mē ə), *n.* academic life; academe: *Writers too turn their talents to other kinds of communities—to the world of academia or the Army, bohemia or business* (Harper's). [< Latin *acadēmīa* academy]

ac·a·dem·ic (ak′ə dem′ik), *adj., n.* **—*adj.*** **1** of or having to do with schools, colleges, universities, and their studies; scholarly: *the academic world, academic research. The academic year begins when school opens in September.* **SYN:** scholastic. **2** concerned with general education rather than commercial, technical, or professional education: *History and French are academic subjects; typewriting and bookkeeping are commercial subjects.* **SYN:** humanistic. **3** not arising in practice; not practical; hypothetical; theoretical: *"Which came first, the chicken or the egg?" is an academic question. Wilson, one of the least academic of our critics, is also one of the most thorough* (Saturday Review). **SYN:** speculative. **4** following fixed rules and traditions; formal: *academic verse, academic painting.* **SYN:** conventional.
—*n.* **1** a college student or teacher. **2** an academician. **—ac′a·dem′i·cal·ly,** *adv.*

Ac·a·dem·ic (ak′ə dem′ik), *adj.* belonging to Plato's school of philosophy; skeptical.

ac·a·dem·i·cal (ak′ə dem′ə kəl), *adj.* = academic: *academical discourses.*

ac·a·dem·i·cals (ak′ə dem′ə kəlz), *n.pl.* = academic dress.

academic dress, the cap and gown worn by a teacher or student, now in the United States usually only at graduation exercises or on other special occasions.

academic freedom, **1** the freedom of a teacher or student to investigate or discuss controversial political, economic, and social issues and problems without fear of interference or loss of standing. **2** the freedom of an academic institution to decide what subjects it shall teach and how it will teach them.

academic gown, a long, loose, flowing outer garment worn by a member or graduate of a college or university.

a·cad·e·mi·cian (ə kad′ə mish′ən, ak′ə də-), *n.* **1** a member of an academy or society for encouraging literature, science, or art: *The academicians of France rejected terms of science in their first essay* (Samuel Johnson). **2** an artist, writer, or composer more notable for mastery of conventional forms than for originality: *a dry academician.* **3** a college student or teacher; an academic.

ac·a·dem·i·cism (ak′ə dem′ə siz əm), *n.* **1** conformity to convention or tradition in art, literature, or music. **2** formalism; pedantry.

academic rank, *U.S. and Canada.* the rank of a member of the faculty of a college or university. The four commonest ranks are instructor, assistant professor, associate professor, professor.

academic year, the official annual period of sessions of a college or university.

a·cad·e·mism (ə kad′ə miz əm), *n.* = academicism.

a·cad·e·mist (ə kad′ə mist), *n.* = academician.

a·cad·e·mize (ə kad′ə mīz), *v.t.,* **-mized, -miz·ing.** **1** to organize into an academy. **2** to make academic. **3** to regulate as if by academic rules.

a·cad·e·my (ə kad′ə mē), *n., pl.* **-mies.** **1** a place for instruction: **a** a private high school. **b** a school where some special skill or subject can be studied: *a riding academy. West Point is a military academy.* **c** (formerly) a college, university, or other institution of higher learning. **2** a group of authors, scholars, artists, musicians, or scientists organized to encourage literature, research, art, music, or science. The Royal Academy of London promotes the arts.
the Academy, the park or grove near ancient Athens where Plato taught: *[The] Academy . . . was a large enclosure of ground which was once the property of a citizen at Athens named Academus* (John Robinson).
[< Latin *acadēmīa* < Greek *Akadēmeia,* the grove where Plato taught]

Academy Award, *U.S.* one of the awards made annually by the Academy of Motion Picture Arts and Sciences; Oscar.

A·ca·di·an (ə kā′dē ən), *n., adj.* **—*n.*** **1** a native or inhabitant of Acadia (region in southeastern Canada), especially a French settler there or one of his descendants: *With 230,000 Acadians, New Brunswick is now almost French Canadian . . .* (Maclean's). **2** a descendant of French Acadians who moved to Louisiana; Cajun.
—*adj.* **1** of Acadia or Acadians. **2** *Geology.* of or having to do with a time when mountains were formed, in or near the Devonian.

ac·a·jou (ak′ə zhü), *n.* **1a** the cashew tree. **b** its fruit. **2** a gum or resin from its bark. [< French *acajou*]

a·cal·cu·li·a (ə kal′kyü′lē ə), *n.* a form of aphasia involving loss of ability to solve even simple arithmetic problems. [< New Latin *acalculia* < *a-*[4] + Latin *calculāre* calculate]

ac·a·leph (ak′ə lef), *n.* (in early zoological classification) a member of a group of animals including both the coelenterates and the ctenophores. [< New Latin *Acalepha* < Late Latin *acalēphē* < Greek *akalḗphē* stinging nettle]

ac·a·lephe (ak′ə lēf), *n.* = acaleph.

ac·a·na·ceous (ak′ə nā′shəs), *adj. Botany.* prickly. [< Latin *acanos* thistle + English *-aceous*]

a·can·tha (ə kan′thə), *n., pl.* **-thae** (-thē). **1** *Botany.* a prickle. **2** *Zoology.* a spine or prickly fin. **3** *Anatomy.* **a** a spinous process of a vertebra. **b** the vertebral column. [< Greek *ákantha*]

ac·an·tha·ceous (ak′ən thā′shəs), *adj.* **1** belonging to the acanthus family of plants. **2** having prickles; being prickly. [< Greek *ákantha* thorn + English *-aceous*]

ac·an·thas·ter (ak′ən thas′tər), *n.* the crown-of-thorns starfish, a large predator of coral islands and reefs throughout the Pacific: *They can stay alive for six months without eating, but when they eat they eat heartily: a big acanthaster can kill fifty years of coral growth in a night* (New Yorker). [< New Latin *Acanthaster* (*planci*), the species name < Greek *ákantha* thorn + *astḗr* star]

a·can·thine (ə kan′thin, -thēn), *adj.* **1** of an acanthus. **2** resembling an acanthus.

a·can·tho·ceph·a·lan (ə kan′thə sef′ə lən), *n.* any one of a large group of parasitic worms that have backward-curving hooks at their front ends for attaching themselves to the intestines of vertebrates. They lack a digestive tract, food being taken in through the body wall. [< Greek *ákantha* thorn + *kephalḗ* head + English *-an*]

ac·an·tho·di·an (ak′ən thō′dē ən), *n.* any one of several extinct sharklike fishes, living from the late Silurian into the Permian period, representing the earliest known vertebrates with jaws.

a·can·thoid (ə kan′thoid), *adj.* **1** shaped like a spine. **2** having spines. [< Greek *ákantha* thorn + English *-oid*]

a·can·tho·log·i·cal (ə kan′thə loj′ə kəl), *adj.* of or having to do with acanthology.

ac·an·thol·o·gy (ak′ən thol′ə jē), *n.* the study of spines. [< Greek *ákantha* thorn + English *-logy*]

ac·an·thop·ter·yg·i·an (ak′ən thop′tə rij′ē ən), *n., adj.* — ***n.*** any one of a group of fishes with hard, spiny rays in the dorsal and anal fins, including the sunfish, perch, bass, porgy, mackerel, and swordfish. — ***adj.*** of or belonging to this group. [< Greek *ákantha* thorn + *pterygia,* plural, fins + English *-an*]

a·can·thous (ə kan′thəs), *adj.* = acanthoid.

***a·can·thus** (ə kan′thəs), *n., pl.* **-thus·es, -thi** (-thī). **1** any one of several plants somewhat like the thistle, found especially around the Mediterranean. The leaves of the acanthus have many narrow, pointed lobes, and are sometimes spiny. **2** an architectural ornament patterned on the leaves of these plants, popular in ancient Greek and Roman times. [< Latin *acanthus* < Greek *ákanthos* < *akē* thorn]

***acanthus**
definitions 1, 2
leaf flower ornament

acanthus family, a large family of plants found mainly in tropical areas. The leaves of the plants are usually simple, but the petals are irregular and coiled. Many kinds are grown for decoration. The bear's-breech and clockvine are members of the acanthus family.

a cap·pel·la or **a ca·pel·la** (ä′ kə pel′ə; *Italian* ä′käp pel′lä), of choral music or singers: **1** without instrumental accompaniment. **2** with an accompaniment in unison with the vocal part, as in early church music. [< Italian *a cappella* in the manner of chapel music]

a ca·pric·cio (ä′ kə prē′chō; *Italian* ä′ kä prēt′chō), *Music.* with the expression and time to be rendered as the performer pleases. [< Italian *a capriccio* at will]

a·car·i·an (ə kãr′ē ən), *n., adj.* = acaridan.

ac·a·ri·a·sis (ak′ə rī′ə sis), *n.* an infestation of plant, animal, or man with mites or ticks. [< New Latin *acariasis* < Greek *akarí* mite + New Latin *-asis,* suffix forming names of diseases]

a·car·i·cide (ə kar′ə sīd), *n.* a substance for killing acarids. [< *acari*(d) + *-cide*[1]]

ac·a·rid (ak′ər id), *n.* any one of an order of small arachnids that includes the mites and ticks. [< New Latin *Acaridae* < Greek *akarí* mite]

a·car·i·dan (ə kar′ə dən), *n., adj.* — ***n.*** = acarid. — ***adj.*** of or belonging to the acarids.

ac·a·rine (ak′ə rīn, -rēn), *n., adj.* = acaridan.

ac·a·roid (ak′ə roid), *adj.* of or like an acarid.

acaroid gum or **resin,** a red resin obtained especially from the trunk of the Australian grass tree, used in varnishes.

ac·a·rol·o·gist (ak′ə rol′ə jist), *n.* a person who studies ticks and mites.

ac·a·rol·o·gy (ak′ə rol′ə jē), *n.* the study of ticks and mites. [< Greek *akarí* + English *-logy*]

a·car·pel·ous or **a·car·pel·lous** (ā kär′pə ləs), *adj.* (of a flower) having no carpels.

a·car·pous (ā kär′pəs), *adj.* (of a plant) not producing fruit; sterile. [< Greek *ákarpos* (with English *-ous*) < *a-* without + *karpós* fruit]

ac·a·rus (ak′ər əs), *n., pl.* **-a·ri** (-ə rī). a mite or tick. [< New Latin *Acarus* < Greek *akarí*]

a·cat·a·lec·tic (ā kat′ə lek′tik), *adj., n.* — ***adj.*** (of a line of verse) having the complete number of syllables in the last foot; complete.
— ***n.*** such a line of verse.
[< Late Latin *acatalēcticus,* alteration of *acatalēctus* < Greek *akatálēktos*]

a·cat·a·lep·sy (ə kat′ə lep′sē), *n. Philosophy.* incomprehensibility. [< Greek *akatalēpsíā* < *a-* not + *katálēpsis* a grasping]

a·cat·a·lep·tic (ə kat′ə lep′tik), *adj., n. Philosophy.* — ***adj.*** incomprehensible; not to be known with certainty.
— ***n.*** a person who believes that we can know nothing with certainty.

a·cau·dal (ā kô′dəl), *adj.* without a tail. [< *a-*[4] not + Latin *cauda* tail + English *-al*[1]]

a·cau·date (ā kô′dāt), *adj.* = acaudal.

ac·au·les·cence (ak′ô les′əns), *n.* the condition of being or appearing to be without a stem.

ac·au·les·cent (ak′ô les′ənt), *adj.* of plants: **1** stemless. **2** apparently stemless. [< *a-*[4] not + *caulescent*]

a·cau·line (ā kô′lin, -līn), *adj.* = acaulescent.

a·cau·lose (ā kô′lōs), *adj.* = acaulescent.

a·cau·lous (ā kô′ləs), *adj.* = acaulescent.

a·caus·al (ā kô′zəl, a-), *adj.* not causal; not having to do with cause and effect. [< *a-*[4] not + *causal*]

a·cau·sal·i·ty (ā kô zal′ə tē, a-), *n.* acausal quality or agency.

acc., an abbreviation for the following:
1 accompaniment.
2 according.
3 account.
4 *Grammar.* accusative.

Ac·ca·di·an (ə kā′dē ən), *adj., n.* = Akkadian.

ac·cede (ak sēd′), *v.i.,* **-ced·ed, -ced·ing. 1** to give in; agree; assent (to): *Please accede to my request.* SYN: yield, acquiesce. **2** to become a party (to): *Our government acceded to the treaty.* **3** to come, attain, or succeed (to an office or dignity): *When the king died, his oldest son acceded to the throne.* [< Latin *accēdere* approach, enter upon < *ad-* to + *cēdere* move, go] — **ac·ced′er,** *n.*

ac·ced·ence (ak sē′dəns), *n.* the act of acceding; entering upon or agreeing to.

accel., *Music.* accelerando.

ac·cel·er·a·ble (ak sel′ər ə bəl), *adj.* that can be accelerated.

ac·cel·er·an·do (ak sel′ə rän′dō; *Italian* ät chā′lä-rän′dō), *adj., adv., n., pl.* **-dos, -di** (-dē). *Music.*
— ***adj., adv.*** gradually increasing in speed (used as a direction).
— ***n.*** a gradual increase of speed.
[< Italian *accelerando* accelerating]

ac·cel·er·ant (ak sel′ər ənt), *n., adj.* — ***n.* 1** something that causes acceleration. **2** *Chemistry.* a positive catalyst; accelerator.
— ***adj.*** accelerating.

ac·cel·er·ate (ak sel′ə rāt), *v.,* **-at·ed, -at·ing.**
— ***v.t.* 1a** to cause (anything in motion or process) to go or move faster; speed up: *The engineer accelerates a train by turning on more power.* SYN: hurry, quicken. **b** to hasten the operation of (a process). **2** to cause to happen sooner; hasten: *Sunshine, fresh air, and rest often accelerate a person's recovery from sickness.* SYN: expedite. **3** *Physics.* to change the velocity of (a moving object). **4** *Education.* **a** to complete (a course of study) in less than the usual time: *to take accelerated math.* **b** to advance (a student) at a rate faster than average: *skipping grades to accelerate bright pupils.*
— ***v.i.* 1** to increase in speed; go faster: *The more power the engineer turns on, the more the train accelerates. Stock prices surged yesterday as volume accelerated sharply* (New York Times). **2** to change in velocity. **3** *Education.* to complete a course of study in less than the usual time: *... undergraduates who go to summer sessions to accelerate* (New York Times).
[< Latin *accelerāre* (with English *-ate*[1]) quicken < *ad-* to + *celer* swift]

ac·cel·er·at·ed depreciation (ak sel′ə rā′tid), *Accounting.* the charging of depreciation of assets such as machinery and buildings at a rate faster than the normal rate.

ac·cel·er·at·ed·ly (ak sel′ə rā′tid lē), *adv.* at a faster rate; with increasing speed.

ac·cel·er·a·tion (ak sel′ə rā′shən), *n.* **1** an accelerating; speeding up or hastening: *Turning on more power causes the acceleration of a train. Acceleration of tooth decay is caused by lack of care.* **2** increased speed: *No, sir; you cannot conceive with what acceleration I advance towards death* (Samuel Johnson). **3** *Physics.* **a** a change in velocity. An increase in velocity is expressed as positive acceleration; a decrease in velocity is expressed as negative acceleration. **b** the rate of this change. **4** *U.S. and Canada.* the advancement of superior students to grades matching their abilities, regardless of a normal schedule of promotion.

acceleration clause, a clause in a contract stating that the seller may demand immediate payment in full of the outstanding balance if the buyer fails to meet one of the installment payments due.

acceleration of gravity, the rate of change in velocity of a freely falling body, caused by the force of gravity. The rate varies slightly with changes in latitude and altitude. At sea level, in the approximate latitude of New York City, it is 32.16 feet per second in each second of the fall of the body.

ac·cel·er·a·tive (ak sel′ə rā′tiv), *adj.* tending to accelerate; quickening.

ac·cel·er·a·tor (ak sel′ə rā′tər), *n.* the thing that causes an increase in the speed of anything: **a** the pedal or lever that controls the speed of a motor vehicle by regulating the flow of fuel to the engine. **b** *Nuclear Physics.* a particle accelerator. **c** *Chemistry.* any substance that hastens a reaction, usually as a catalyst. **d** *Photography.* any substance or device that shortens the time of exposure or development. **e** *Physiology.* any muscle, nerve, or secretion that increases the speed of a bodily function.

ac·cel·er·a·to·ry (ak sel′ər ə tôr′ē, -tōr′-), *adj.* accelerative; quickening.

ac·cel·er·o·graph (ak sel′ər ə graf, -gräf), *n.* a device for measuring the pressures developed by the combustion of an explosive in a closed, or nearly closed space, for example as in a cannon or underground. [< *acceler*(ate) + *-graph*]

ac·cel·er·om·e·ter (ak sel′ə rom′ə tər), *n.* **1** an instrument for measuring acceleration, such as that of a moving vehicle, aircraft, or rocket. **2** a device for measuring the pressure of gases at any point within a gun. [< *acceler*(ate) + *-meter*]

ac·cent (*n.* ak′sent; *v.* ak′sent, ak sent′), *n., v.*
— ***n.* 1** the greater force or stronger tone of voice given to certain syllables or words. Accent is controlled by a change of pitch or by stress: *In "letter" the accent is on the first syllable.* **2** a mark sometimes written or printed to show the spoken force of a syllable, such as those in yes′ter day, to day′, and to mor′row. Some words have two accents, a stronger or primary accent (′) and a weaker or secondary accent ('), such as those in ac'a dem′ic. In this dictionary, (′) is used to show primary accent and (') to show secondary accent, for example in **ac·cel·er·a·tor** (ak sel′ə rā'tər). Weakest accent is often left unmarked. **3** a different way of pronouncing heard in different parts of the same country, or in the speech of a person speaking a language that is not his own: *a Southern accent. My father was born in Germany and still speaks English with a German accent.* **4** a distinguishing mark, character, or tone: *The accent of humor characterizes his writings. Shakespeare's writing has the accent of greatness.* **5** *Informal.* marked interest, favor, or approval; emphasis; stress: *Mother puts a considerable accent on good manners.* **6** one of three marks, called acute (´), grave (`), and circumflex (ˆ), used in French (*blasé, à la carte, tête-à-tête*), Greek, and some other languages to indicate the quality of the vowel or as a conventional feature of the spelling. **7a** emphasis on certain words or syllables in a line of poetry to give them rhythm. **b** a mark placed above or next to a stressed syllable. In "The stag′/at eve′/had drunk′/his fill′," the accents are on *stag, eve, drunk,* and *fill.* **8a** a mark at the right of a number indicating minutes of a degree, two such marks indicating seconds, as in 20°10′30″ (read *20 degrees, 10 minutes, 30 seconds*). **b** one, two, or three marks at the right of a number used to denote feet, inches, and lines (twelfths of an inch), as in 3′6″7‴ (read *3 feet, 6 inches, 7 lines*). **c** a mark placed at the right of a letter so that it may be used to represent different mathematical quantities, as in a′, a″, a‴ (read *a prime, a double prime* or *a second, a triple prime* or *a third;* in British usage this is read *a dash, a double dash, a triple dash*). **9** *Music.* **a** emphasis on certain notes or chords. **b** a symbol for this. **10** a touch of color or light which serves to bring the features of a structure into relief or furnish a contrast in a scheme of color.
— ***v.t.* 1** to pronounce or mark with an accent: *Is "acceptable" accented on the first or second syllable?* **2** *Figurative.* to emphasize; accentuate.
accents, a a tone of voice: *The little girl spoke to her doll in tender accents.* **b** speech; language: *Winds! on your wings to heaven her accents bear* (John Dryden).
[< Latin *accentus, -ūs* (literally) song added to (speech) < *ad-* to + *cantus, -ūs* a singing < *canere* sing] — **ac′cent·less,** *adj.*
— ***Syn.*** *v.t.* **2 Accent, accentuate,** both meaning to emphasize, are sometimes confused. In general use, **accent** means to mark or say something with emphasis: *Throughout his speech the President accented the gravity of the situation.* **Accentuate** means to give emphasis to something by intensifying it or making it conspicuous: *Her white dress accentuated the redness of her sunburned arms.*

accent mark, accent (*n.* defs. 2, 6, and 9b).

ac·cen·tor or **ac·cent·er** (ak sen′tər), *n.* **1** any one of several birds noted for their melodious song, especially the hedge sparrow. **2** a person who sings a leading part.

ac·cents (ak′sents), *n.pl.* See under **accent.**

ac·cen·tu·al (ak sen′chü əl), *adj.* **1** of accent; formed by accent. **2** characterized by a pattern of stressed and unstressed syllables. Most English poetry is accentual; ancient Greek and Latin poetry is quantitative. SYN: rhythmical. — **ac·cen′tu·al·ly,** *adv.*

ac·cen·tu·al·i·ty (ak sen′chü al′ə tē), *n.* the quality of being accentual.
accentualities, accentual characteristics: *With an insight into the accentualities ... of modern*

Pronunciation Key: hat, āge, cãre, fär; let, ēqual, tėrm; it, īce; hot, ōpen, ôrder; oil, out; cup, pu̇t, rüle; child; long; thin; ᴛʜen; zh, measure; ə represents **a** in about, **e** in taken, **i** in pencil, **o** in lemon, **u** in circus.

Saxon (Charles Lamb).

ac·cen·tu·ate (ak sen′chü āt), *v.t.,* **-at·ed, -at·ing.** **1** to call special attention to; emphasize; intensify: *The twinkle in her eyes accentuated her smile.* SYN: See syn. under **accent. 2** to pronounce with an accent; stress. **3** to mark with an accent; place an accent or accents on. **4** to increase the severity of; aggravate: *The problem is accentuated by a shortage of teachers and classrooms* (Atlantic).
[< Medieval Latin *accentuare* (with English *-ate*[1]) < Latin *accentus* accent] **—ac·cen′tu·a′tor,** *n.*

ac·cen·tu·a·tion (ak sen′chü ā′shən), *n.* **1** an accentuating; emphasis. **2** manner of pronunciation. **3** the marking of accent or stress in speech.

ac·cept (ak sept′), *v.t.* **1** to take or receive (what is offered or given); consent to take: *I accept your gift gratefully.* SYN: See syn. under **receive. 2** to consent to; say yes to: *She asked me to go to the party and I accepted her invitation.* **3** to take as true or satisfactory; believe: *The teacher won't accept your excuse.* SYN: acknowledge. **4** to receive with liking and approval: *I soon accepted the new student as a friend. The design of the new car was not accepted by the public. Scholars now generally accept Einstein's theory of relativity.* SYN: approve. **5** to undertake as a responsibility: *My sister accepted a position as cashier.* SYN: assume. **6** *Commerce.* to sign and agree to pay: *to accept a promissory note.* **7** to receive (a committee report) as satisfactory. **8** to understand; construe: *Can we accept this interpretation of the manuscript as correct?* **9** *Medicine.* to take into the body without rejecting: *A mouse whose thymus has been removed . . . will accept a skin graft from an unrelated animal, whereas normal mice invariably reject such foreign grafts* (Scientific American). **—*v.i.*** to say yes to an invitation; accept a suggestion or offer: *I was invited and I accepted.*
[< Latin *acceptāre* (frequentative) < *accipere* receive < *ad-* to + *capere* take]
▶**Accept, except** are often confused because they are similar in sound. *Accept,* always a verb, has as its basic meaning "to take *to* (oneself)" and is a synonym of *receive: He accepted the gift. Except,* sometimes a verb, sometimes a preposition, has a basic sense of taking *out:* the verb is a synonym of *omit, exclude;* the preposition is a synonym of *but: We can call his career brilliant if we except that one blunder he made in his last speech. Everyone except John went home.*

ac·cept·a·bil·i·ty (ak sep′tə bil′ə tē), *n.* the quality of being satisfactory or acceptable.

ac·cept·a·ble (ak sep′tə bəl), *adj.* **1** likely to be gladly received or accepted; agreeable: *Flowers are an acceptable gift to a sick person.* SYN: pleasing, welcome. **2a** good enough; satisfactory: *The singer gave an acceptable performance but it was not outstanding. He received an acceptable mark on the test but his sister won honors.* SYN: passable. **b** capable of being tolerated; bearable: *. . . a defence system would work to the extent of reducing damage but not to the extent of making nuclear war acceptable* (London Times). **—ac·cept′a·ble·ness,** *n.* **—ac·cept′a·bly,** *adv.*

ac·cept·ance (ak sep′təns), *n.* **1** the act of taking what is offered or given to one: *The teacher's acceptance of the flowers they brought delighted the children.* **2** favorable reception; approval: *The violinist played with marked acceptance.* **3** the act of taking as true and satisfactory; belief: *The acceptance of the atomic theory by physicists has led to many scientific discoveries.* **4** *Commerce.* **a** a promise or signed agreement to pay a draft or bill of exchange when it is due. **b** the draft or bill of exchange itself. **c** the sum specified by it: *an acceptance of $10,000.* **5** the state or condition of being accepted: *She was thrilled by her acceptance into the club.*

acceptance house or **accepting house,** = merchant bank.

acceptance rate, *Commerce.* the rate of interest demanded or paid on an acceptance.

ac·cept·an·cy (ak sep′tən sē), *n.* willingness to receive; receptiveness.

ac·cept·ant (ak sep′tənt), *adj., n.* **—*adj.*** receptive. **—*n.*** a person who accepts.

ac·cep·ta·tion (ak′sep tā′shən), *n.* **1** the usual meaning; the generally accepted meaning: *It is more important to know the acceptation of a word than its derivation.* **2** favorable reception; approval: *That hypothesis will have a better claim to acceptation* (J. A. Brown). **3** a taking as true and satisfactory; belief.

ac·cept·ed (ak sep′tid), *adj.* conventional; approved. **—ac·cept′ed·ly,** *adv.* **—ac·cept′ed·ness,** *n.*

ac·cept·er (ak sep′tər), *n.* a person who accepts something offered or given.

ac·cep·tive (ak sep′tiv), *adj.* **1** suitable for acceptance; acceptable. **2** ready to accept: *. . . reverently acceptive of every Victorian formula* (Edmund Gosse).

ac·cep·tor (ak sep′tər, -tôr), *n.* **1** a person who accepts; accepter. **2** a person who signs a draft or bill of exchange and agrees to pay it. **3** *Chemistry.* an atom sharing two electrons in a bond with another atom but contributing neither electron. **4** *Radio.* a circuit that allows ready reception of a particular frequency and no other.

ac·cess (*n.* ak′ses; *v.* ak′səs, ak ses′), *n., v.* **—*n.*** **1** the right or privilege to approach, enter, or use; admittance: *All children have access to the library during the afternoon.* SYN: admission. **2** approach to places, persons, or things: *Access to mountain towns is often difficult because of poor roads. Have you access to people who can help you get work?* SYN: accessibility. **3** a way or means of approach; entrance: *A ladder provided the only access to the attic.* (*Figurative.*) *A minister must try every access to the conscience.* **4** an attack (of disease): *the access of her asthma in the spring.* **5** *Figurative.* an outburst, as of anger. **6** increase; accession. **7** the act of coming toward; approach: *the access of winter.* SYN: onset. **8** = access time. **—*v.t.*** **1** to obtain access to; reach: *The pallets run . . . in open, parallel passageways, which can only be accessed from each end* (New Scientist). **2** to retrieve (data) from a computer: *. . . the ability of a program to access a remote data set as if it were local with no special planning* (David J. Farber).
[< Old French *acces* attack, learned borrowing from Latin *accessus, -ūs* a coming to < *accēdere* approach < *ad-* to + *cēdere* move, go]

ac·ces·sa·ry (ak ses′ər ē), *n., pl.* **-ries,** *adj. Law.* = accessory.

ac·ces·si·bil·i·ty (ak ses′ə bil′ə tē), *n.* **1** the condition of being easy to reach or get at. **2** openness to influence.

ac·ces·si·ble (ak ses′ə bəl), *adj.* **1** easy to get at; easy to reach or enter: *tools readily accessible on an open rack. A telephone should be put where it will be accessible.* SYN: convenient. **2** that can be entered or reached: *This rocky island is accessible only by helicopter.* SYN: approachable. **3** that can be obtained: *Not many facts about the kidnapping were accessible.* SYN: available.
accessible to, capable of being influenced by; susceptible to: *An open-minded person is accessible to reason.*
—ac·ces′si·ble·ness, *n.* **—ac·ces′si·bly,** *adv.*

ac·ces·sion (ak sesh′ən), *n., v.* **—*n.*** **1** the act of attaining to a right, office, or station; attainment: *The king's death was followed by the prince's accession to the throne.* **2a** an increase; addition: *The accession of 40 new pupils overcrowded the school.* **b** that which is added: *There are many new novels in the accessions to the library.* **3** agreement; assent; adherence (to a plan or view): *We got her accession to the plan.* **4** the action of coming near; approach; access. **5** *Law.* an addition to property by natural growth or artificial improvement.
—*v.t.* *Especially U.S.* to record (additions to a library) by entering the titles and authors in a file, list, or register.

ac·ces·sion·al (ak sesh′ə nəl), *adj.* of or due to accession; giving increase or enlargement; additional.

accession book, a blank book in which the titles of books, periodicals, or pamphlets received by a library are entered, with all necessary details.

accession number, the number given to a book, periodical, or pamphlet when it is entered in an accession book.

ac·ces·sit (ak ses′it), *n.* a certificate or prize awarded to a student of second (or lower) merit in British and French schools. [< Latin *accessit* he has come near < *accedere* to approach; see etym. under **access**]

ac·ces·so·ri·al (ak′sə sôr′ē əl, -sōr′-), *adj.* auxiliary; accessory.

ac·ces·so·rize (ak ses′ə rīz), *v.t.,* **-rized, -riz·ing.** *U.S.* to supplement with accessories: *We accessorized the outfit with a matching turban* (McCall's).

ac·ces·so·ry (ak ses′ər ē), *n., pl.* **-ries,** *adj.* **—*n.*** **1** an extra thing added to help something of more importance; subordinate or nonessential part or detail: *A heater is a useful accessory to a car. All the accessories to her costume—hat, gloves, shoes, and purse—were perfectly matched.* SYN: auxiliary, adjunct. **2** *Law.* a person who has helped in a crime or has helped to hide it; one who knowingly helps an offender in the commission of a felony and thus shares in guilt, although not present at the time and place of the violation: *By not reporting the theft he became an accessory.* SYN: See syn. under **accomplice.**
—*adj.* **1** helping in producing some effect; added; extra: *His tie supplied an accessory bit of color, which was very pleasing.* SYN: additional, supplementary. **2** helping to commit or hide a crime; helping in a felony. **3** nonessential.
accessory after the fact, a person who hides an offender against the law, helps him to escape, or fails to report the offense: *Near relatives who aid a criminal are not regarded as accessories after the fact in many states* (Fred E. Inbau).
accessory before the fact, a person who supports or encourages an offender against the law in committing a felony: *By helping the thieves plan the bank robbery, he was an accessory before the fact.*
[< Medieval Latin *accessorius* < Latin *accēdere* be added] **—ac·ces′so·ri·ly,** *adv.* **—ac·ces′so·ri·ness,** *n.*

accessory bud, an additional bud forming in or near the leaf axil, such as a bud on a young stem of the red maple. See picture under **bud**[1].

accessory fruit, a fruit having conspicuous fleshy parts that accompany or surround an ovary or ovaries, such as an apple or strawberry.

access road, a secondary road leading from or to a main road.

access speed, = access time (def. 1).

access time, 1 the time required to retrieve information from the memory of a computer; access speed: *Access time . . . can range from a fraction of a microsecond to several seconds or minutes* (Scientific American). **2** *Television.* a period of time set aside by a network to show programs of affiliates, educational programs, and the like.

ac·ciac·ca·tu·ra (ät chäk′kä tü′rä), *n. Music.* **1** an appoggiatura that is sounded as briefly as possible. **2** a grace note played on an organ with its principal note and immediately released, while the principal note is held. [< Italian *acciaccatura* < *acciaccare* crush]

ac·ci·dence (ak′sə dəns), *n.* the part of grammar dealing with those changes in the forms of words that show case, number, person, tense, voice, mood, degree, or other relationships.

ac·ci·dent (ak′sə dənt), *n.* **1** something that happens by chance and results in loss, damage, or death; undesirable or unfortunate occurrence: *She was hurt in an automobile accident.* SYN: misfortune, mishap, disaster, calamity. **2** something that happens without being planned, intended, wanted, or known in advance: *A series of lucky accidents led the explorer to his discovery. Their meeting was an accident. The story of my life, And the particular accidents gone by, Since I came to this isle* (Shakespeare). **3** chance: *Prizes of accident as oft as merit* (Shakespeare). SYN: fortune, luck. **4** any nonessential quality: *Some men classify objects by color and size and other accidents of appearance* (Emerson). **5** an irregularity in surface or structure.
by accident, by chance; not on purpose: *I met an old friend by accident.*
[< Latin *accidēns, -entis,* present participle of *accidere* happen < *ad-* to + *cadere* fall]

***accidental**
definition 1

ac·ci·den·tal** (ak′sə den′təl), *adj., n.* **—*adj. **1** happening by chance; not planned; unexpected: *an accidental death by drowning. Breaking the dish was accidental; he did not mean to do it. Our accidental meeting led to our becoming friends. The freedom of science is so important to its progress just because it allows the accidental to occur* (Bulletin of Atomic Scientists). SYN: unintentional, fortuitous, casual. **2** nonessential; not necessary; incidental: *Songs are essential to musical comedy, but accidental to Shakespeare's plays.* SYN: subsidiary. **3** *Music.* of or having to do with an accidental.
—*n.* **1** *Music.* a sign used to show a change of pitch from the key signature; a flat, a sharp, or a natural just before the note to be changed. **2** *Music.* the tone indicated by any of these. **3** a nonessential property.
accidentals = accidental lights.
—ac′ci·den′tal·ness, *n.*
—*Syn.* *adj.* **2 Accidental, incidental** mean not essential or of primary importance. **Accidental** emphasizes that what it describes is not an essential or necessary part or result of some larger thing or scheme of things: *The lost earrings were accidental to the costume and the audience never noticed they were missing.* **Incidental** emphasizes that what it describes, although perhaps necessary, is subordinate to something else in importance: *The grant covers tuition, board, and room at the university, but not incidental expenses like laundry and haircuts.*

accidental color, a complementary color seen after fixing the eye for a time on a particular color and then turning the eye away. A person staring at a blue object and then turning his glance away will see the color yellow, as blue and yellow are complementary or accidental colors.

accidental lights, combinations of light and shade painted into a picture, especially to make certain subjects stand out from the rest of the picture, such as light streaming through foliage; accidentals.

ac|ci|den|tal|ly (ak′sə den′tə lē, -dent′lē), *adv.* without being planned; by chance; not on purpose; unintentionally.

accidental president, a Vice-President of the United States who becomes President because of the death or resignation of the President. Harry S Truman was an accidental president.

ac|ci|dent|ed (ak′sə den′tid), *adj.* having irregularities of surface.

accident insurance, insurance against accidental personal injury suffered by the insured.

ac|ci|dent|ly (ak′sə dent′lē), *adv.* = accidentally.

ac|ci|dent-prone (ak′sə dənt prōn′), *adj.* tending to have or cause accidents: *Youthfulness alone does not make drivers accident-prone* (Maclean's). — **ac′ci|dent-prone′ness**, *n.*

ac|cid|i|a (ak sid′ē ə), *n.* = accidie.

ac|ci|die (ak′sə dē), *n.* sloth; torpor; loss of interest in life: *Advisory committees, if they are confined to pure advice and never get near the point of action, fade away into a kind of accidie* (C. P. Snow). [< Medieval Latin *accidia,* alteration of Late Latin *acēdia.* See etym. of doublet **acedia.**]

ac|cip|i|ter (ak sip′ə tər), *n.* **1** any one of several short-winged hawks having a long tail and able to fly at great speed, such as a goshawk or Cooper's hawk. They live mostly by preying on other birds. **2** any bird of prey. [< Latin *accipiter* < *accipere* take to oneself < *ad-* to + *capere* take]

ac|cip|i|tral (ak sip′ə trəl), *adj.* = accipitrine.

ac|cip|i|trine (ak sip′ə trin, -trīn), *adj.* **1** of or having to do with hawks, especially accipiters. **2** hawklike; raptorial.

ac|claim (ə klām′), *v., n.* — *v.t.* **1** to welcome with loud approval; praise highly; applaud: *The crowd acclaimed the fireman for rescuing two people from the burning house.* SYN: extol. **2** to proclaim or announce with signs of approval; hail: *The newspapers acclaimed the fireman a hero.* **3** *Canadian.* to elect to an office without opposition.
— *v.i.* to shout applause.
— *n.* a shout or show of approval; applause; welcome: *The astronaut was welcomed with great acclaim.* SYN: acclamation, plaudits.
[< Latin *acclāmāre* shout approval (or disapproval) of < *ad-* toward + *clāmāre* cry out] — **ac|claim′er**, *n.*

ac|cla|ma|tion (ak′lə mā′shən), *n.* **1** a shout of welcome or show of approval by a crowd; applause: *When the President stood up to speak, he was greeted by the acclamation of the crowd.* **2** *Canadian.* an electing without opposition.
by acclamation, with an oral vote in which the votes are not counted, particularly an overwhelming vote of approval: *All the members said "Aye," and so the chairman was elected by acclamation.*

ac|clam|a|to|ry (ə klam′ə tôr′ē, -tōr′-), *adj.* expressing acclamation: *He was sent out again by the acclamatory voice of the nation* (Robert Chambers).

ac|cli|ma|ta|tion (ak′lə mə tā′shən), *n.* = acclimation.

ac|cli|mate (ə klī′mit, ak′lə māt), *v.t., v.i.,* **-mat|ed, -mat|ing.** *Especially U.S.* to accustom or become accustomed to a new climate, surroundings, or conditions; acclimatize: *to acclimate settlers. The penguin has acclimated itself to antarctic conditions.* (*Figurative.*) *I have not been long enough at this table to get well acclimated* (Oliver Wendell Holmes). [< French *acclimater* < *a-* to + *climat* climate] — **ac|cli′mat|a|ble**, *adj.*

ac|cli|ma|tion (ak′lə mā′shən), *n.* an adjusting by an animal or plant to a new climate or other environmental conditions. Acclimation generally takes place within the lifetime of an individual.

ac|cli|ma|ti|za|tion (ə klī′mə tə zā′shən), *n.* = acclimation: *There is an increase in the total volume of blood in the process of acclimatization to a warmer climate* (Thomas A. Blair).

ac|cli|ma|tize (ə klī′mə tīz), *v.t., v.i.,* **-tized, -tiz|ing.** to adjust to new conditions; acclimate: *You can't expect a refugee to escape one day and to start building ... the next. Refugees must first get acclimatized over here* (Atlantic). — **ac|cli′ma|tiz′a|ble**, *adj.* — **ac|cli′ma|tiz′er**, *n.*

ac|cliv|i|tous (ə kliv′ə təs), *adj.* sloping upward; acclivous.

ac|cliv|i|ty (ə kliv′ə tē), *n., pl.* **-ties.** an upward slope of ground. SYN: ascent. [< Latin *acclīvitās* < *acclīvis* ascending < *ad-* toward + *clīvus* rising ground]

ac|cli|vous (ə klī′vəs), *adj.* rising with a slope. [< Latin *acclīvus* (with English *-ous*)]

ac|co|lade (ak′ə lād′, -läd′; ak′ə lād, -läd), *n.* **1** something awarded as an honor; praise in recognition of merit or an accomplishment: *It [a book] carries accolades of approval from several American critics and poets* (London Times). **2** a tap on the shoulder with the flat side of a sword given in making a man a knight. Formerly an embrace or kiss was given instead. **3** *Music.* a vertical line or brace connecting two or more staves. **4** *Architecture.* a curved molding above an arched opening. [< French *accolade,* alteration of Old French *acolee* an embrace about the neck < *acoler* to embrace < Vulgar Latin *accollāre* < Latin *ad-* to + *collum* neck]

ac|com|mo|da|ble (ə kom′ə də bəl), *adj.* = adaptable. — **ac|com′mo|da|ble|ness**, *n.*

ac|com|mo|date (ə kom′ə dāt), *v.,* **-dat|ed, -dat|ing.** — *v.t.* **1** to have room for; hold comfortably: *This airplane is large enough to accommodate over 400 passengers.* SYN: See syn. under **contain.** **2** to help out; oblige: *He wanted change for a dollar, but I could not accommodate him.* SYN: serve. **3** to supply; furnish: **a** to supply with a place to sleep or live for a time, and sometimes with food as well: *Can the inn accommodate a party of five for two weeks?* **b** to provide (a person) with a loan of money. **4** to make fit; make suitable; adjust: *We must accommodate ourselves to our changed circumstances. My eyes soon accommodated themselves to seeing objects in the darkness.* SYN: fit, adapt. See syn. under **adjust.** **5** to bring to harmony or agreement; reconcile: *He tried to accommodate the dispute between the friends.* SYN: harmonize, compose.
— *v.i.* **1** to become adjusted; be adapted. **2** to settle differences; agree.
[< Latin *accommodāre* (with English *-ate*[1]) < *ad-* to + *commodāre* make fit < *com-* with + *modus* measure] — **ac|com′mo|da′tor**, *n.*

ac|com|mo|dat|ing (ə kom′ə dā′ting), *adj.* willing to do favors; obliging: *My teacher was accommodating enough to lend me a dollar.* — **ac|com′mo|dat′ing|ly**, *adv.*

ac|com|mo|da|tion (ə kom′ə dā′shən), *n.* **1** anything that supplies a want or gives aid; a help, favor, or convenience: *It will be an accommodation to me if you will meet me tomorrow instead of today.* **2** Often, **accommodations. a** a room or lodgings and sometimes food as well: *Can we find accommodations at the hotel for the night? ... restaurants, hotels, and other places of public accommodation* (New York Times). **b** Usually, **accommodations.** a reserved seat, berth, or room on a train, airplane, bus, or ship: *Can I secure accommodations on the Chicago train today?* **3** willingness to help out. **4** *U.S.* a loan. **5** the process of fitting or being fitted to a purpose or situation; adjustment; adaptation: *The accommodation of our desires to a smaller income took some time.* **6** the automatic adjustment of the lens of the eye to see objects at different distances. The eye muscles adjust the thickness and curvature of the lens and the diameter of the pupil so as to produce an accurate focus. **7** a settlement of differences; reconciliation; compromise: *The bankrupt and the men to whom he owed money arranged an accommodation.* **8** a process by which individuals or social groups adjust to one another so as to overcome conflicts. **9** a professional favor, especially a discount in a fee. **10** an accommodation bill, draft, or note.

accommodation bill, draft, or **note**, a bill, draft, or note drawn, accepted, or endorsed by one person to enable another person to obtain credit by or to raise money on it.

ac|com|mo|da|tion|ist (ə kom′ə dā′shə nist), *n., adj. U.S.* — *n.* a Negro who favors accommodation with the white establishment.
— *adj.* of or relating to accommodationists.

accommodation ladder, a stairway or ladder hung over a ship's side on which people may climb up from or down to small boats.

ac|com|mo|da|tions (ə kom′ə dā′shənz), *n.pl.* See under **accommodation** (*n.* def. 2).

accommodation sale, the sale of a commodity by one dealer to another for resale.

accommodation train, *U.S.* a train that stops at all, or nearly all, stations.

ac|com|mo|da|tive (ə kom′ə dā′tiv), *adj.* = accommodating. — **ac|com′mo|da′tive|ness**, *n.*

ac|com|pa|ni|ment (ə kum′pə ni mənt), *n.* **1** anything that goes along with something else; something added: *Cranberry sauce is a usual accompaniment to turkey. The rain was an unpleasant accompaniment to our ride.* SYN: concomitant, appendage. **2** *Music.* a vocal or instrumental part that helps or enriches the main part; a subsidiary instrumental or vocal part to sustain a voice or voices or a solo instrument: *She sang to a violin and piano accompaniment.*

ac|com|pa|nist (ə kum′pə nist), *n.* a person who plays a musical accompaniment.

ac|com|pa|ny (ə kum′pə nē), *v.,* **-nied, -ny|ing.** — *v.t.* **1** to go along with: *May we accompany you on your walk? (Figurative.) I had a doughnut accompanied by a glass of milk.* **2** to be or happen along with: *Fire is accompanied by heat. The rain was accompanied by a high wind.* **3** to cause to be attended by; supplement (with): *He accompanied his speech with gestures.* **4** to play or sing a musical accompaniment for or to: *She accompanied the singer on the piano.*
— *v.i.* to play or sing a musical accompaniment.
[< Middle French *accompagner* < Old French *acompaignier* take as a companion < *a-* to + *compaignier* < *compain* companion] — **ac|com′pa|ni|er**, *n.*
— *Syn. v.t.* **1 Accompany, attend, escort** mean to go with someone or something. **Accompany** means to go along as a companion: *He accompanied his friend to the airport.* One who **attends** goes along as a subordinate: *Many courtiers attended the queen on her journey.* To **escort** is to go with as a sign of especial attention or courtesy, or as a protection: *He escorted a girl to the dance. Secret Service men escort the President and his family everywhere.*

ac|com|pa|ny|ist (ə kum′pə nē ist), *n.* = accompanist.

ac|com|plice (ə kom′plis), *n.* **1** a person who knowingly aids another in committing a crime or other wrong act: *The thief had an accomplice who let him into the building. He was an accomplice in the murder of the German foreign minister* (Harper's). **2** an associate. [earlier *a complice* a confederate < Middle French *complice,* learned borrowing from Late Latin *complex, -icis* < Latin *complicāre* fold together < *com-* together + *plicāre* fold]
— *Syn.* **1 Accomplice, confederate, accessory** in technical (legal) use mean partner in crime. **Accomplice** applies to a person who deliberately gives help of any kind in connection with an unlawful act or crime, whether before, during, or after the act itself: *Without an accomplice to open the door the thief could not have gotten into the building so easily.* **Confederate** applies to a person who joins with others, or another, for the purpose of committing an unlawful act: *The head of the smuggling ring has not been found, but his confederates are in jail.* **Accessory** applies to a person not present during a criminal act who aids in planning or executing it or who hides the criminal or helps him escape.

ac|com|plish (ə kom′plish), *v.t.* **1** to succeed in completing; fulfill, perform, or carry out (an undertaking, plan, or promise): *Did you accomplish your purpose?* SYN: achieve, effect, attain. **2** to actually do; finish: *to accomplish nothing. Fred can accomplish more in a day than any other boy in his class.* SYN: complete, execute. See syn. under **do**[1]. **3** to complete (a distance): *to accomplish a journey.* **4** to perfect; polish. [< Old French *acompliss-,* stem of *acomplir* < Vulgar Latin *accomplēre* < Latin *ad-* to + *complēre* fill up] — **ac|com′plish|a|ble**, *adj.* — **ac|com′plish|er**, *n.*

ac|com|plished (ə kom′plisht), *adj.* **1** carried out or completed; done: *With their work accomplished the boys went out to play. The division of Germany is an accomplished fact.* **2** expert; skilled: *an accomplished surgeon. Only an accomplished dancer can perform with this ballet company.* **3** skilled in social arts and graces: *an accomplished host.*

ac|com|plish|ment (ə kom′plish mənt), *n.* **1** something that has been done with knowledge, skill, or ability; completed undertaking; achievement: *The teacher was proud of her pupils' accomplishments.* SYN: attainment. **2** special skill: *She was a girl of many accomplishments: she could draw and sing, sew and cook.* SYN: acquirement. **3** a doing; carrying out; completion: *The accomplishment of his purpose took three months.* SYN: consummation, fulfillment.

ac|compt (ə kount′), *n., v. Archaic.* account.

ac|cord (ə kôrd′), *v., n.* — *v.i.* to be in harmony; be consistent; agree (with): *His account of the accident accords with yours.* SYN: correspond, harmonize, concur.
— *v.t.* **1** to grant freely; award: *Accord him praise for his good work.* **2** *Archaic.* to reconcile; harmonize.
— *n.* **1** agreement; harmony: *Most people are in accord in their desire for peace.* **2** an agreement, often an informal one, between nations: *an accord with France.* **3** harmony of colors or of pitch and tone. **4** *Law.* a private, friendly arrangement between parties settling a controversy without re-

Pronunciation Key: hat, āge, cãre, fär; let, ēqual, tėrm; it, īce; hot, ōpen, ôrder; oil, out; cup, pu̇t, rüle; child; long; thin; ᴛʜen; zh, measure; ə represents **a** in about, **e** in taken, **i** in pencil, **o** in lemon, **u** in circus.

sort to a lawsuit.
of one's own accord, without being asked or without suggestion from another: *A boy who washes behind his ears of his own accord is indeed unusual. Whether . . . lots were actually cast to select the person to do the deed, or whether the discussions simply inspired Bresci to act of his own accord, is not certain* (Barbara Tuchman).
with one accord, in complete agreement; unanimously: *The club members voted with one accord to raise the dues. These all continued with one accord in prayer and supplication* (Acts 1:14).
[< Old French *acorder* < Vulgar Latin *accordāre* < Latin *ad-* to + *cor, cordis* heart] **—ac|cord'a|ble**, *adj.* **—ac|cord'er**, *n.*

ac|cord|ance (ə kôr'dəns), *n.* **1** agreement or harmony; conformity: *What he did was in accordance with what he said.* **2** the act of according or granting: *accordance of privilege.*

ac|cord|ant (ə kôr'dənt), *adj.* **1** in harmony; agreeing: *True religion is a relation, accordant with reason and knowledge, which man establishes with the infinite life surrounding him* (Leo Tolstoy, quoted by J. W. R. Scott). **2** *Geology.* that meet or join one another without break or noticeable irregularity: *accordant mountain tops, accordant valleys.* **—ac|cord'ant|ly**, *adv.*

ac|cor|da|tu|ra (ä kôr'dä tü'rä), *n.* the series of tones to which a stringed instrument is usually tuned.
[< Italian *accordatura*]

ac|cord|ing (ə kôr'ding), *adv., adj.* **—*adv.*** accordingly.
—*adj.* agreeing; in harmony.
according as, to the extent that; in proportion as: *According as you have informed yourself, you will be able to answer the questions. . . . according as we have the courage to face the implications of . . . new knowledge* (Saturday Review).
according to, a in agreement with: *He came according to his promise.* **b** in proportion to; on the basis of: *You will be ranked according to the work you do. Spend according to your income.* **c** on the authority of; as said by: *According to this book, cats and tigers are related.*

ac|cord|ing|ly (ə kôr'ding lē), *adv.* **1** in a way that agrees with something that has been expected or stated; correspondingly: *These are the rules; you can act accordingly or leave the club.* **2** for this reason; therefore; consequently: *He was too sick to stay; accordingly, we sent him home. Skates were something of a rarity, and, accordingly, it was normal to see a pair divided, with the older brother lunging and coasting on one runner and the kid brother hopping along on the other* (Edward Weeks).

ac|cor|di|on** (ə kôr'dē ən), *n., adj.* **—*n. a musical wind instrument with a bellows, metal reeds, and keys. An accordion is shaped like a rectangle and is played by forcing air through the reeds by compressing the bellows.
—*adj.* having folds like the bellows of an accordion: *a skirt with accordion pleats.*
[< German *Akkordion* < *Akkord* concord of sounds < French *accord*]

***accordion**

accordion

concertina

ac|cor|di|on|ist (ə kôr'dē ə nist), *n.* a person who plays an accordion.

ac|cost (ə kôst', -kost'), *v., n.* **—*v.t.*** to come up and speak to; speak to first; address: *A stranger accosted him, asking for directions.* SYN: greet, hail.
—*n.* *Rare.* an accosting.
[< French *accoster* move up to < Vulgar Latin *accostāre* < Latin *ad-* to + *costa* side]

ac|couche (ə küsh'), *v.,* **-couched, -couch|ing.**
—*v.i.* to assist in childbirth.
—*v.t.* *U.S. Informal.* to produce; create: . . . *his blissful intimation that he had helped to accouche the Ninth Symphony* (S. J. Perelman).
[< French *accoucher*]

ac|couche|ment (ə küsh'mənt; *French* á küsh-mäN'), *n.* confinement for childbirth; delivery of a baby. [< French *accouchement*]

ac|cou|cheur (ak'ü shėr'; *French* á kü shœr'), *n.* **1** a man who helps women in childbirth; male midwife. **2** an obstetrician.
[< French *accoucheur*]

ac|cou|cheuse (ak'ü shüz'; *French* á kü shœz'), *n.* a midwife.

ac|count (ə kount'), *n., v.* **—*n.*** **1** a statement telling in detail about an event or thing; report; description: *The boy gave his father an account of the ball game. Please give me an account of everything as it happened.* SYN: story, narrative. **2** a statement explaining one's conduct, especially to a superior. **3** a statement of reasons, causes, or the like, explaining some event: *No satisfactory account has yet been given of these phenomena.* **4** importance or value; worth: *This torn notebook is of little account.* **5a** a record of money received and spent: *Jack keeps a written account of the way he spends his allowance. All stores, banks, and factories keep accounts.* **b** a record of business dealings, as between a bank and a depositor. **c** a detailed statement of money due; a periodic record of purchases for which a customer at a store is billed: *My father settles his accounts on the tenth of each month.* **6** a charge account. **7** a bank account. **8a** the services that an advertising agency does for a client. **b** the client. *Abbr:* acct.
—*v.i.* **1** to give a statement of money received or spent: *You will have to account to the auditor next week.* **2** to pay the penalty (for).
—*v.t.* **1** to hold to be; consider: *Solomon was accounted wise. A trout is accounted delicious eating. In law, an accused person is accounted innocent until he is proved guilty.* **2** to assign; impute.
account for, a to tell what has been done with; answer for: *The treasurer of the club had to account for the money paid to him and spent by him.* **b** to give a satisfactory reason for; explain: *Late frosts accounted for the poor fruit crop.* **c** to cause the death or capture of: *The soldiers accounted for two enemy snipers. The persecuted animals bolted above ground: the terrier accounted for one, the keeper for another* (Thackeray).
bring to account, to make (someone) answer for his conduct: *After breaking the law repeatedly, the hoodlum was finally caught and brought to account.*
call to account, a to demand an explanation of: *The treasurer was called to account for the shortage of funds.* **b** to scold; rebuke; reprimand: *The principal called the boys to account for their bad behavior in class. He waits in fear and trembling the visit of a very ill-natured relative who . . . is coming to call him to a stern account* (London Times).
for account of, on behalf of: *A very considerable portion are shipped for account of the manufacturers* (Thomas Tooke).
give a good (or **bad**) **account of oneself**, to conduct oneself well (or badly); do something in a way that reflects much (or little) credit on oneself: *He is their most reliable ballplayer—he always gives a good account of himself.*
gone to one's account, died: *He has gone to his account. God forgive him!* (Frederick Marryat).
on account, as part payment: *I bought my new camera by paying a dollar a week on account.*
on account of, a because of: *The game was put off on account of rain.* **b** for the sake of: *[Bacon] valued geometry chiefly, if not solely, on account of those uses, which to Plato appeared so base* (Macaulay).
on any account, for any reason; under any conditions: *He was brought up not to lie on any account.*
on no account, for no reason; under no conditions; certainly not: *On no account should you lie. He recommends the king on no account to remove Granvelle from the administration* (William H. Prescott).
on one's account, for one's sake: *Don't wait on my account.*
on one's own account, for one's own purpose and at one's own risk: *The repairman left his regular job and has gone into business on his own account.*
take account of, a to make allowance for; consider: *Before making your summer plans you should take account of the wishes of your family.* **b** to make a note of; notice: *The auctioneer tried to take account of all the signals made by the bidders on the floor.*
take into account, to make allowance for; reckon with; consider: *You must take into account the wishes of all the class in planning a picnic. Let us, then, before we go behind "Das Kapital," take into account the tremendous effect which it produces on us the first time we read it* (Edmund Wilson).
turn to account, to get advantage or profit from: *The new pitcher turned the coach's advice to good account in the next inning.*
[< Old French *acont* < *aconter* < *a-* to (< Latin *ad-*) + *conter* < Latin *computāre* count < *com-* together + *putāre* reckon. Compare etym. under **compute**.]

ac|count|a|bil|i|ty (ə koun'tə bil'ə tē), *n.* the state of being held responsible for carrying out one's obligations; responsibility: . . . *most accountability programs reflect no effort to discover successful methods and materials. Rather they are exercises in blame-placing in which teachers are made the scapegoats for all educational and societal shortcomings* (Albert Shanker).

ac|count|a|ble (ə koun'tə bəl), *adj.* **1** liable to be called to account; responsible; answerable: *Each person is accountable for his own work.* **2** explainable: *His bad temper is easily accountable; he has had a toothache all day.* SYN: explicable. **—ac|count'a|ble|ness**, *n.* **—ac|count'a|bly**, *adv.*

ac|count|an|cy (ə koun'tən sē), *n.* the work of an accountant; the examining or keeping of business accounts; accounting: *He joined the British Linen Bank . . . but he then decided to study chartered accountancy* (New Scientist).

ac|count|ant (ə koun'tənt), *n.* a person who examines or manages business accounts; one whose profession is examining or interpreting business accounts and financial records. *Accountants analyze, interpret, and draw conclusions from the accounts that the bookkeeper records.* **—ac|count'ant|ship**, *n.*

account book, a book in which accounts of receipts and expenditures are kept.

account current, = account (*n.* def. 5c).

account executive, an executive in an advertising agency or other business firm who negotiates with a client and directs the work done for a client or clients.

ac|count|ing (ə koun'ting), *n.* **1** the art, practice, or system of keeping, analyzing, and interpreting business accounts. Accounting enables companies and governmental agencies to summarize and report in an understandable fashion a large number of transactions. **2** a statement of accounts. **3** a reckoning up or balancing of accounts.

accounting machine, a mechanical or electronic device for solving accounting problems.

ac|counts payable (ə kounts'), **1** the sums currently due to creditors by a company or person. **2** a record of them.

accounts receivable, **1** the sums currently due to a company or person. **2** a record of them.

ac|cou|ple (ə kup'əl), *v.t.,* **-pled, -pling.** *Obsolete.* to join; couple.
[< Old French *accoupler* < Vulgar Latin *accōpulāre* < Latin *ad-* to + *cōpula* bond] **—ac|cou'ple|ment**, *n.*

ac|cou|ter (ə kü'tər), *v.t.,* **-tered, -ter|ing.** to furnish with clothing or equipment; equip; outfit; array, especially in military attire: *Knights were accoutered in armor.* [< French *accoutrer* < Middle French *accoustrer* < *a-* to + *coustre* a vestry keeper]

ac|cou|ter|ment (ə kü'tər mənt), *n.* the process of accoutering or being accoutered.
accouterments, a a soldier's equipment with the exception of his weapons and clothing. A belt, blanket, and knapsack are parts of a soldier's accouterments. **b** personal equipment; clothes; outfit: *This man from Paris was now so disguised by his leather accouterments . . . that his closest friend might have passed by without recognizing him* (Thomas Hardy).

ac|cou|tre (ə kü'tər), *v.t.,* **-tred, -tring.** *Especially British.* to accouter.

ac|cou|tre|ment (ə kü'tər mənt), *n.* *Especially British.* accouterment.

ac|cred|it (ə kred'it), *v.t.* **1** to give credit or authority to: *The president will accredit you as his representative.* SYN: authorize. **2** to send or provide with credentials: *An ambassador is accredited to a foreign country to represent his government there.* **3** to recognize as coming up to an official standard. **4** to accept as true; believe; trust: *My sister is always truthful and anything she says will be accredited.* SYN: See syn. under **credit.** **5** to consider as belonging or due (to a person); ascribe; attribute: *We accredit the invention of the telephone to Alexander Graham Bell.* SYN: See syn. under **credit.**
accredit with, to give (a person) credit for (something); regard (a person) as having: *I accredited him with more sense than his silly behavior suggests.*
[< French *accréditer* < *à-* to + *crédit* credit]

ac|cred|i|ta|tion (ə kred'ə tā'shən), *n.* **1** *U.S.* recognition of a school, college, hospital, agency for social work, or the like, as coming up to an official standard: *There is a need for more uniform accreditation and certification standards* (Daniel Tanner). **2** credentials: *His staff announced routine receipt of accreditations for the new Ambassadors* (Time).

ac|cred|it|ed (ə kred'ə tid), *adj.* **1** recognized as coming up to an official standard: *Some colleges will accept without examination the graduates of accredited high schools.* **2** worthy of acceptance, belief, or trust: *Einstein was an accredited authority in mathematics.* **3** provided with credentials: *an accredited diplomat.*

ac|cres|cence (ə kres′əns), *n.* **1** growth. **2** = accretion.

ac|cres|cent (ə kres′ənt), *adj.* **1** growing; increasing. **2** *Botany.* growing larger after flowering. [< Latin *accrēscēns, -entis,* present participle of *accrēscere* grow, be added to; see etym. under **accrete**]

ac|crete (ə krēt′), *v.,* **-cret|ed, -cret|ing,** *adj.* —*v.i.* to grow together; adhere (to).
—*v.t.* to add as by growth.
—*adj. Botany.* grown together.
[< Latin *accrētus,* past participle of *accrēscere* grow, be added to < *ad-* to + *crēscere* grow]

ac|cre|tion (ə krē′shən), *n.* **1** a growing together of separate things: *A glacier is formed by the accretion of many particles of frozen packed snow.* **2** an increase in size by natural growth or gradual external addition. **3** a whole that results from such growths or additions. **4** a thing added; addition. **5** growth in size. **6** *Law.* the increase in area of a piece of land, beach, etc., by the washing up of soil.

ac|cre|tion|ar|y (ə krē′shə ner′ē), *adj.* characterized or formed by accretion: *the debate [as to] whether the moon's rocks are volcanic or accretionary in origin* (New Scientist).

accretion disk or **disc,** *Astronomy.* a disk-shaped formation of gases or other interstellar matter around a black hole, neutron star, or other celestial body: *This formation, called an accretion disk, may be very important in some stellar birth sequences. In our own solar system ... the planets and asteroids formed from the accretion disk as the sun grew in the embryo core* (Stephen P. Maran).

ac|cre|tive (ə krē′tiv), *adj.* of or by accretion: *accretive growth.*

ac|croach (ə krōch′), *v.t. Archaic.* to usurp. [< Old French *accrocher* to draw with a hook < *a-* to + *croc* a hook] —**ac|croach′ment,** *n.*

ac|cro|chage (ä krô shäzh′), *n. French.* **1** *Art.* a method or style of hanging up paintings. **2** *Military.* a skirmish. **3** (literally) a hooking.

ac|cru|al (ə krü′əl), *n.* **1** an accruing: *Money left in a savings bank increases by the accrual of interest.* **2** the amount accrued or accruing.

accrual basis, a method of accounts in which the expenses incurred and income earned for a particular period are shown, whether or not actual cash payments and receipts have been made or received during that period.

ac|crue (ə krü′), *v.,* **-crued, -cru|ing.** —*v.i.* **1** to come as a natural product or result: *Ability to think clearly will accrue to you from good habits of study.* SYN: amass, accrete. **2** to grow or arise as the product of money invested: *Interest begins to accrue when the loan is granted.* SYN: accumulate. —*v.t.* to obtain or derive (from): *... and denied that South Korea would accrue any benefits from Japan's growing industrial power* (New York Times). SYN: collect, gather.
[< obsolete *accrue* an increase < Old French *acreüe* < *acreistre* to increase < Latin *accrēscere* < *ad-* to + *crēscere* grow]

ac|crued expense (ə krüd′), expense incurred but not yet paid.

accrued income, income earned but not yet received.

accrued interest, interest that has accumulated at a given time but has not yet been paid.

ac|crue|ment (ə krü′mənt), *n.* = accrual.

acct., *Commerce.* **1** account. **2** accountant.

ac|cul|tur|al (ə kul′chər əl), *adj.* involving or produced by acculturation.

ac|cul|tur|ate (ə kul′chə rāt), *v.,* **-at|ed, -at|ing.** —*v.t.* to cause (an individual or a group) to adopt the culture or cultural elements of another group: *The Navajo would ... become "acculturated," that is learn the white man's ways* (New York Times). —*v.i.* to become acculturated.

ac|cul|tur|a|tion (ə kul′chə rā′shən), *n.* **1** the adoption by an individual or a group of the culture patterns of another group; a process of social change caused by the interaction of significantly diverse cultures; cultural leveling or homogeneity: *About a third of this class is Italian, and a great many of the families are still in process of acculturation to American life* (Robert W. White). **2** a child's conditioning to the patterns of a particular society.

ac|cul|tur|a|tion|al (ə kul′chə rā′shə nəl), *adj.* of or having to do with acculturation.

ac|cul|tur|a|tive (ə kul′chə rə tiv), *adj.* associated with or leading to acculturation: *Not infrequently acculturative processes result in considerable social disturbances* (Beals and Hoijer).

ac|cul|tur|ize (ə kul′chə rīz), *v.t., v.i.,* **-ized, -iz|ing.** = acculturate.

ac|cum|ben|cy (ə kum′bən sē), *n.* the state of being accumbent.

ac|cum|bent (ə kum′bənt), *adj.* **1** *Botany.* lying against something. **2** reclining, as at a table. [< Latin *accumbēns, -entis,* present participle of *accumbere* lie down < *ad-* to, + *-cumbere* lie down]

ac|cu|mu|la|ble (ə kyü′myə lə bəl), *adj.* that can be accumulated.

ac|cu|mu|late (ə kyü′myə lāt), *v.,* **-lat|ed, -lat|ing.** —*v.t.* to collect little by little; amass; heap up by degrees: *He accumulated a fortune by hard work.*
—*v.i.* to grow into a heap by degrees; pile up; gather: *Dust and cobwebs had accumulated in the house while she was gone.*
[< Latin *accumulāre* (with English *-ate*[1]) < *ad-* in addition + *cumulāre* heap up < *cumulus* heap]
—*Syn. v.t.* **Accumulate, amass** mean to collect large amounts. **Accumulate** emphasizes the idea of heaping up, little by little over a period of time: *Through the years he accumulated sufficient money to buy a farm when he retired.* **Amass** emphasizes the idea of gathering a large amount to oneself within a relatively short time: *Before he was forty he amassed a fortune.*

ac|cu|mu|la|tion (ə kyü′myə lā′shən), *n.* **1** material collected; mass: *His accumulation of old papers filled three boxes.* SYN: aggregation. **2** *Figurative.* a collecting together; amassing: *The accumulation of useful knowledge is one result of reading.* SYN: amassment. **3** growth by continuous additions, as the addition of interest to principal. SYN: accrual, accretion.

ac|cu|mu|la|tive (ə kyü′myə lā′tiv), *adj.* **1** arising from accumulation; cumulative. **2** tending to accumulate wealth; hoarding; acquisitive. —**ac|cu′mu|la′tive|ly,** *adv.* —**ac|cu′mu|la′tive|ness,** *n.*

ac|cu|mu|la|tor (ə kyü′myə lā′tər), *n.* **1** a person or thing that accumulates. **2** any of various devices that collect, store, or absorb energy: **a** *British.* a storage battery. **b** a cylinder or apparatus that serves to equalize pressure in a hydraulic system or to accumulate energy for intermittent use. **c** an elastic section in a chain or rope to prevent breaking under a sudden strain. **3** a unit in a computer, totalizator, or the like, in which the totals or results of arithmetical operations are registered.

ac|cu|ra|cy (ak′yər ə sē), *n.* the state of being without errors or mistakes; exactness; correctness; precision: *Arithmetic problems must be solved with accuracy.*

ac|cu|rate (ak′yər it), *adj.* **1** without errors or mistakes; precisely correct; exactly right: *You must take care to be accurate in arithmetic. An airplane pilot must have an accurate watch. Military power is no longer an accurate measure of national security* (James Reston). SYN: See syn. under **correct. 2** making few or no errors; precise: *an accurate observer.* SYN: careful. [< Latin *accūrātus* done with care, past participle of *accūrāre* take care of < *ad-* to + *cūrāre* take care < *cūra* care] —**ac′cu|rate|ly,** *adv.* —**ac′cu|rate|ness,** *n.*

ac|curs|ed (ə kėr′sid, -kėrst′), *adj.* **1** that deserves to be cursed; annoying and troublesome; hateful; detestable: *Colonel Sibthorpe ... prayed that hail and lightning might descend from heaven on the accursed thing* (Lytton Strachey). SYN: execrable, damnable. **2** under a curse; doomed: *And the city shall be accursed* (Joshua 6:17). SYN: ill-fated. —**ac|curs′ed|ly,** *adv.* —**ac|curs′ed|ness,** *n.*

ac|curst (ə kėrst′), *adj.* = accursed.

accus., accusative (case).

ac|cus|a|ble (ə kyü′zə bəl), *adj.* liable to be accused.

ac|cus|al (ə kyü′zəl), *n.* = accusation.

ac|cu|sa|tion (ak′yu̇ zā′shən), *n.* **1** the offense charged: *The accusation against him was that he had stolen ten dollars from the store.* **2** a charge of being something bad, of doing something wrong, or of having broken the law: *The taint of accusation often ruins a reputation.* **3** an accusing or being accused.

ac|cu|sa|ti|val (ə kyü′zə tī′vəl), *adj.* having to do with the accusative case.

ac|cu|sa|tive (ə kyü′zə tiv), *adj., n.* —*adj.* showing the direct object. *Me, us, him,* and *them* are in the accusative case, or, as usually said for English words, the objective case.
—*n.* **1a** the objective case. **b** a corresponding case in Latin, Greek, and many other inflectional languages used as the direct object of a verb, sometimes as the subject of an infinitive, or as the object of a preposition, to indicate the goal of action or motion toward. *Galliam* in *Caesar Galliam vīcit,* meaning "Caesar conquered Gaul," is in the accusative. **2** a word used as the object of a verb or preposition. **3** the form of pronouns used for the object of a verb or preposition in English, such as *me, us, him, them.* The term *objective* is more commonly used in modern English grammar. *Abbr:* acc.
[< Latin *accūsātīvus,* translation of Greek (*ptôsis*) *aitiātikḗ* (case) of what is caused] —**ac|cu′sa|tive|ly,** *adv.*

ac|cu|sa|to|ri|al (ə kyü′zə tôr′ē əl, -tōr′-), *adj.* having to do with an accuser. —**ac|cu′sa|to′ri|al|ly,** *adv.*

ac|cu|sa|to|ry (ə kyü′zə tôr′ē, -tōr′-), *adj.* containing an accusation; accusing: *an accusatory glance.*

ac|cuse (ə kyüz′), *v.,* **-cused, -cus|ing.** —*v.t.* **1** to charge with having done something wrong, with being something bad, or with having broken the law: *The driver was accused of speeding. He was accused as accessory to the crime.* SYN: denounce, arraign, indict. See syn. under **charge. 2** to place the blame on; find fault with; blame; censure: *The President accused Congress for the delay in passing his program. She sent for Blanche to accuse her face to face* (Tennyson). *Accusing the times is but excusing ourselves.*
—*v.i.* to bring an accusation: *He accused no more, But dumbly shrank before accusing throngs Of thought* (George Eliot).
[< Old French *acuser* < Latin *accūsāre* < *ad-* against + *causa* cause, reason]

ac|cused (ə kyüzd′), *adj., n.* —*adj.* charged with a crime or other offense.
—*n.* **the accused,** *Law.* the person or persons formally charged with a crime or an offense in a court of law: *The trial took place before a military tribunal, the accused having been arrested following the boycott* (Observer).
▶**accused, defendant.** In strict legal usage, the defendant is the party sued in a civil suit. *Defendant* is not formally correct for *the accused* in a criminal court but is popularly so used.

ac|cus|er (ə kyü′zər), *n.* a person who accuses another.

ac|cus|ing|ly (ə kyü′zing lē), *adv.* in an accusing manner.

ac|cu|sive (ə kyü′siv), *adj.* disposed to accuse; accusing; accusatory.

ac|cus|tom (ə kus′təm), *v.t.* to make familiar by use or habit; get used; train: *to accustom a hunting dog to the noise of a gun. A good traveler can accustom himself to almost any kind of food.* SYN: familiarize, habituate. [< Old French *acostumer* < *a-* to + *costume* custom, ultimately < Latin *cōnsuētūdo* < *cōnsuēscere* accustom < *com-* with + *suēscere* accustom]

ac|cus|tomed (ə kus′təmd), *adj.* usual; customary: *Soon the sick boy was well and in his accustomed place at school.* SYN: habitual, wonted, familiar.
accustomed to, used to; in the habit of: *The farmer was accustomed to hard work. She is accustomed to jogging daily.*
—**ac|cus′tomed|ness,** *n.*

ACD (no periods), a solution of acid, citrate, and dextrose, used as a preservative in storing blood for transfusions.

ACDA (no periods), Arms Control and Disarmament Agency (of the United States).

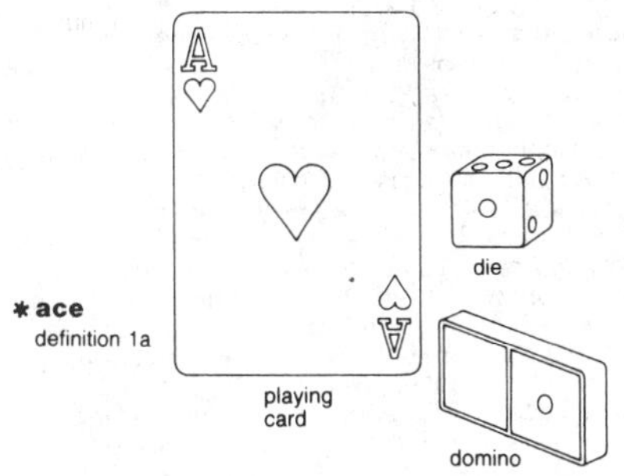

***ace** definition 1a

***ace** (ās), *n., adj., v.,* **aced, ac|ing.** —*n.* **1a** a playing card, domino, or side of a die having one spot. In most card games the ace is the highest and winning card of its suit. **b** the single spot or point by which such a playing card, side of a die, or domino is marked. **2a** (in tennis, handball, and certain other games) a point won by a single stroke, especially a serve that the opponent fails to return. **b** *Golf.* a hole in one. **3a** a person expert at something: *He is an ace at basketball.* **b** a combat pilot who has shot down five or more enemy aircraft. **4** *Figurative.* a very small quantity; a trifle: *I may peradventure be an ace before thee* (Robert Burton). **5** *U.S. Slang.* **a** a dollar bill. **b** a one-year prison term.
—*adj. U.S. Informal.* having very great skill; expert: *Beside him sat young Lord Birt, ace flier* (Harper's).
—*v.t.* **1** to score an ace against (an opponent in tennis and other net games) by delivering a service which the opponent misses: *He gave the club*

Pronunciation Key: hat, āge, cãre, fär; let, ēqual, tėrm; it, īce; hot, ōpen, ôrder; oil, out; cup, pu̇t, rüle; child; long; thin; ᴛʜen; zh, measure; ə represents **a** in about, **e** in taken, **i** in pencil, **o** in lemon, **u** in circus.

pro a good game, aced him three times (Time). **2** *U.S. Slang.* to achieve a high mark in.

ace in the hole, 1 *Informal.* anything decisive or conclusive held in reserve to use at a critical time. **2** an ace dealt face down in the gambling game of stud poker.

ace out, *U.S. Informal.* to get the better of; come out on top of; defeat; outdo: *Boeing Co. aces out General Dynamics for the first big defense deal of the 1980s, the $4 billion cruise missile contract* (Time).

within an ace of, on the very point of: *I came within an ace of making my fortune* (Washington Irving).

[< Old French *as* < Latin *as, assis* the smallest unit (of coinage or measure)]

a|ce|di|a (ə sē′dē ə), *n.* sloth; torpor; loss of interest in life: *Pursewarden's suicide is attributed to acedia, or boredom with life* (Time). [< Late Latin *acēdia* < Greek *akēdíā* < *a-* not + *kêdos* care. See etym. of doublet **accidie.**]

ace-high (ās′hī′), *adj. U.S. Informal.* greatly respected; highly esteemed.

A|cel|da|ma (ə sel′də mə), *n.* **1** a field near Jerusalem in which Judas committed suicide after his betrayal of Jesus (in the Bible, Acts 1:18-19). **2** any scene of violent death or slaughter.

a|cel|lu|lar (ā′sel′yə lər), *adj.* lacking cells; not cellular: *Alan Boyden ... attacked the concept of protozoans being identified as acellular rather than unicellular* (Malcolm T. Jollie).

AcEm (no periods), actinium emanation.

ac|e|naph|thene (as′ə naf′thēn, -nap′-) *n.* a hydrocarbon obtained from coal tar, used in making dyes, insecticides, plastics, etc. *Formula:* $C_{12}H_{10}$ [< *ace*(tic) + *naphthene*]

a|cen|tric (ā sen′trik), *adj.* **1** having no center. **2** not on center.

-aceous, *adjective suffix.* having the appearance of; of or like; containing, as in *arenaceous, cretaceous, herbaceous, sebaceous. -aceous* is used in botany as a termination of adjectives accompanying New Latin names ending in *-aceae* for various families of plants, as in *liliaceous* (New Latin *Liliaceae*, the lily family). [< Latin *-āceus*]

a|ceph|a|lan (ā sef′ə lən), *adj., n.* —***adj.*** belonging to the class of mollusks, including the bivalves, not having a distinct head.
—***n.*** any one of these headless mollusks.
[< Late Latin *acephalus* headless (< Greek *aképhalos* < *a-* without + *kephalē̂* head)]

a|ce|phal|ic (ā′sə fal′ik), *adj.* = acephalous.

a|ceph|a|lous (ā sef′ə ləs), *adj.* **1** headless. **2** *Zoology.* lacking a distinct head; having no part of the body specially organized as the seat of the senses. **3** having no leader. [< Late Latin *acephalus* (with English *-ous*)]

a|ce|qui|a (ə sā′kyə), *n. Southwestern U.S.* an irrigation canal or ditch. [American English < Spanish *acequia* < Arabic *assāqiya*]

ac|e|ra|ceous (as′ə rā′shəs), *adj.* belonging to the maple family of trees and shrubs. [< Latin *acer* maple + English *-aceous*]

ac|er|ate (as′ər it, -ə rāt), *adj.* = acerose.

a|cerb (ə sėrb′), *adj.* **1** sharp in taste; sour or bitter: *an acerb substance.* **SYN:** acid, acrid. **2** *Figurative.* sharp and harsh in manner; severe: *acerb wit. ... the dark, acerb, and caustic little professor* (Charlotte Brontë). **SYN:** acrimonious. [< Latin *acerbus* bitter] —**a|cerb′ly,** *adv.*

ac|er|bate¹ (as′ər bāt), *v.t.,* **-bat|ed, -bat|ing. 1** to make sour, bitter, or harsh to the taste. **2** *Figurative.* to exasperate; embitter. [< Latin *acerbāre* (with English *-ate*¹) < *acerbus* bitter]

a|cer|bate² (ə sėr′bit, -bāt; as′ər bāt), *adj.* exasperated; embittered; acerb.

a|cer|bic (ə sėr′bik), *adj.* = acerb: ... *one of the lengthiest and most acerbic feuds ever waged* (Time). —**a|cer′bi|cal|ly,** *adv.*

a|cer|bi|ty (ə sėr′bə tē), *n., pl.* **-ties. 1** sharpness of taste; sourness or bitterness. **2** *Figurative.* harshness of manner, tone, or language; severity. **SYN:** acrimony. [< French *acerbité,* learned borrowing from Latin *acerbitās* < *acerbus* bitter]

ac|e|ren|to|mon (as′ə ren′tə mon), *n.* a primitive wingless insect with no antennae, no eyes, and front legs used as organs of touch. [< New Latin *acerentomon* < Greek *ákeros* without antennae, acerous + *éntomon* insect]

ac|er|o|la (as′ə rō′lə), *n.* **1** a deep-red fruit about the size of a large cherry, with a tart flavor; Puerto Rican cherry; Barbados cherry; West Indian cherry. It is the richest known natural source of vitamin C. **2** the small, bushy tree on which this fruit grows, native to the West Indies, parts of Mexico, Central America, and northern South America. [< American Spanish *acerola* < Spanish *acerola* azarole]

ac|er|ose (as′ə rōs), *adj.* needle-shaped and stiff, as the leaves or needles of the pine. [< Latin *acerōsus* full of chaff < *acus, -eris* chaff, but taken as < *acus, -ūs* needle]

ac|er|ous (as′ər əs), *adj.* without horns, antennae, or tentacles. [< Greek *ákeros* (with English *-ous*) < *a-* without + *kéras* horn]

a|cer|vate (ə sėr′vit, -vāt), *adj. Botany.* growing in closely compacted clusters; heaped. [< Latin *acervātus,* past participle of *acervāre* heap up < *acervus* heap] —**a|cer′vate|ly,** *adv.*

ac|es (ā′siz), *adj. U.S. Slang.* of the highest quality or excellence; tops.

a|ces|cence (ə ses′əns), *n.* process of souring.

a|ces|cen|cy (ə ses′ən sē), *n.* = acescence.

a|ces|cent (ə ses′ənt), *adj.* **1** likely to turn sour or acid. **2** slightly sour; acidulous. [< Latin *acēscēns, -entis,* present participle of *acēscere* to sour]

acet-, *combining form.* the form of **aceto-** before vowels, as in *acetal, acetaldehyde, acetanilide.*

ac|e|tab|u|lar (as′ə tab′yə lər), *adj.* like an acetabulum; cup-shaped.

ac|e|tab|u|lum (as′ə tab′yə ləm), *n., pl.* **-lums, -la** (-lə). **1** the cup-shaped socket at the base of the hipbone into which the ball-shaped top of the thighbone (femur) fits. **2** *Zoology.* any cup-shaped structure, such as a sucker on the ventral side of a parasitic flatworm. [< Latin *acētābulum* (originally) a cup-shaped vinegar holder < *acētum* vinegar]

ac|e|tal (as′ə tal), *n.* **1** a colorless, volatile liquid with an etherlike odor, found in old wines, brandy, etc., used especially as a hypnotic or soporific and as a solvent. *Formula:* $C_6H_{14}O_2$ **2** any one of a class of organic compounds obtained by the reaction of aldehydes or ketones with alcohols. **3** = acetal resin.

ac|et|al|de|hyde (as′ə tal′də hīd), *n.* a colorless, highly volatile, fragrant substance, used as a source of acetic acid, as a solvent, as a solid fuel (canned heat), and in the synthesis of many other compounds; aldehyde. *Formula:* CH_3CHO

acetal resin, a thermoplastic material obtained by polymerization of formaldehyde. Acetal resins are tough, stiff, springy, and have a high melting point. They are used as a substitute for metals, in automobile and appliance parts, and in hardware.

ac|et|am|id (as′ə tam′id, ə set′ə mid), *n.* = acetamide.

ac|et|am|ide (as′ə tam′īd, -id; ə set′ə mīd, -mid), *n.* a white, readily soluble, crystalline solid used in organic synthesis. It is the amide of acetic acid. *Formula:* C_2H_5NO [< *acet-* + *amide*]

ac|e|ta|min|o|phen (as′ə tə min′ə fən), *n.* a crystalline drug derived from acetanilide and used instead of aspirin, especially in cases of hemorrhagic and allergic disorders. *Formula:* $C_8H_9NO_2$

ac|et|an|i|lid (as′ə tan′ə lid), *n.* = acetanilide.

ac|et|an|i|lide (as′ə tan′ə līd, -lid), *n.* a drug used in medicines to lessen pain and fever; antifebrin. It is a white, soluble, crystalline compound. Acetanilide may destroy blood cells, weaken heart muscles, and even cause death after long use. *Formula:* C_8H_9NO [< *acet-* + *anilide*]

ac|e|tar|sone (as′ə tär′sōn), *n.* an arsenical compound used in the treatment of amebic dysentery. *Formula:* $C_8H_{10}NO_5$ As [< *acet-* + *ars*(enic)]

ac|e|tate (as′ə tāt), *n.* **1** a salt or ester of acetic acid. **2** any one of a group of synthetic resins or fibers made from cellulose acetate: *Color-fast acetate is also being made up into myriad items from wedding gowns to raincoats, umbrellas, curtains, ribbons* (Wall Street Journal). [< *acet-*]

ac|e|tat|ed (as′ə tā′tid), *adj.* treated with acetic acid; formed into an acetate.

a|ce|ta|zol|a|mide (ə sē′tə zol′ə mīd), *n.* = acetazoleamide.

a|ce|ta|zol|e|a|mide (ə sē′tə zol′ē ə mīd, -zol′ə-) *n.* a diuretic used in treating epilepsy, peptic ulcers, and certain forms of hepatitis. *Formula:* $C_4H_6N_4O_3S_1$ [< *acet-* + (di)*azole* + *amide*]

a|ce|tic (ə sē′tik, -set′ik), *adj.* of, producing, or derived from vinegar or acetic acid. [< Latin *acētum* vinegar + English *-ic*]

acetic acid, a sour, colorless acid present in vinegar, that is responsible for the tart taste and pungent odor. It is a compound of hydrogen, carbon, and oxygen, and is used in the manufacture of acetates and pharmaceuticals, in organic synthesis, and as a solvent for various gums and resins. *Formula:* $C_2H_4O_2$

acetic anhydride, an acrid, colorless liquid used in the manufacture of cellulose acetate. It is the anhydride of acetic acid. *Formula:* $C_4H_6O_3$

a|cet|i|fi|ca|tion (ə set′ə fə kā′shən), *n.* the action of converting into vinegar or acetic acid.

a|cet|i|fy (ə set′ə fī), *v.t., v.i.,* **-fied, -fy|ing.** to turn into vinegar or acetic acid. [< Latin *acētum* vinegar + English *-fy*] —**a|cet′i|fi′er,** *n.*

ac|e|tim|e|ter (as′ə tim′ə tər), *n.* an apparatus for measuring the quantity of acetic acid in a solution, especially in vinegar. [< French *acétimètre* < Latin *acētum* vinegar + French *-mètre* -meter]

ac|e|tim|e|try (as′ə tim′ə trē), *n.* **1** the determination of the strength of vinegar. **2** the measurement of the proportion of acetic acid in any substance.

ac|e|tize (as′ə tīz), *v.i.,* **-tized, -tiz|ing.** to become sour; acetify.

aceto-, *combining form.* acetic acid or acetyl: *Acetoglyceride = a chemical substance formed by treating glyceride with acetic acid.* Also, **acet-** before vowels. [< Latin *acētum* vinegar]

ac|e|to|a|ce|tic acid (as′ə tō ə sē′tik, ə sē′tō-; -set′ik), = diacetic acid.

a|ce|to|glyc|er|ide (ə sē′tō glis′ə rīd), *n.* a substance formed by treating animal or vegetable fats or oils, such as lard, or soybean or peanut oil, with acetic acid. It is used especially to retard spoilage in certain foods and cosmetic ointments.

ac|e|tom|e|ter (as′ə tom′ə tər), *n.* = acetimeter.

ac|e|tom|e|try (as′ə tom′ə trē), *n.* = acetimetry.

ac|e|tone (as′ə tōn), *n.* a colorless, sweet-smelling, highly inflammable liquid, the simplest ketone, used as a solvent for oils and other organic compounds and in making varnishes and pharmaceuticals. *Formula:* C_3H_6O [< *acet-*]

acetone bodies, *Medicine.* a group of ketones resulting from incomplete oxidation of fats, the presence of which in urine is a characteristic symptom of diabetes; ketone bodies.

ac|e|to|ne|mi|a (as′ə tō nē′mē ə), *n.* **1** an excess of acetone bodies in the blood, as in diabetes; ketosis. **2** ketosis of cattle. [< *acetone* + *-emia*]

ac|e|ton|ic (as′ə ton′ik), *adj.* of or derived from acetone.

ac|e|to|ni|trile (as′ə tō nī′trəl), *n.* a colorless liquid prepared from acetamide, used in organic synthesis, especially as a purification agent and solvent. *Formula:* C_2H_3N [< *aceto-* + *nitrile*]

ac|e|to|nu|ri|a (as′ə tō nůr′ē ə, -nyůr′-), *n.* an excess of acetone bodies in the urine, as in diabetes; ketonuria. [< *acetone* + *-uria*]

ac|e|to|phe|net|i|din (as′ə tō fə net′ə din, ə sē′tō-), *n.* = phenacetin.

ac|e|to|phe|none (as′ə tō fē nōn′, ə sē′tō-), *n.* a colorless liquid used in making perfumes. *Formula:* C_8H_8O [< *aceto-* + *phen*(yl) + *-one*]

ac|e|tose (as′ə tōs), *adj.* sour; acetous.

ac|e|tous (as′ə təs, ə sē′-), *adj.* **1** producing or containing vinegar or acetic acid. **2** tasting like vinegar; sour. [< Late Latin *acētōsus* < Latin *acētum* vinegar]

a|ce|tum (ə sē′təm), *n.* **1** *Pharmacy.* a solution of certain drugs in dilute acetic acid. **2** vinegar. [< Latin *acētum* vinegar]

ac|e|tyl (as′ə təl, ə sē′-), *n. Chemistry.* the univalent radical of acetic acid and its derivatives. *Formula:* CH_3CO- [< *acet-* + *-yl*]

a|cet|y|late (ə set′ə lāt), *v.t.,* **-lat|ed, -lat|ing.** *Chemistry.* to add one or more acetyl radicals to (an organic compound): *Fully acetylated cotton is another treated cotton that combines the textile's good natural qualities with some desirable synthetic qualities* (Scientific American). —**a|cet′y|la′tion,** *n.*

a|ce|tyl|cho|line (ə sē′təl kō′lēn, -lin; -kol′ēn, -in), *n.* a substance produced in nerve tissue and closely associated with the transmission of nerve impulses in the body. It is a derivative of choline. Produced synthetically, it is used in treating high blood pressure, amblyopia, etc. *Formula:* $C_7H_{17}O_2N$ *Abbr:* ACH (no periods).

ac|e|tyl|cho|lin|es|ter|ase (as′ə təl kō′lə nes′tə-rās, -kol′ə-), *n.* = cholinesterase.

acetyl coenzyme A, *Biochemistry.* a compound important as an intermediate in metabolism, as an acetylating agent, and in other biochemical functions. *Formula:* $C_{25}H_{38}N_7O_{17}P_3S$

a|cet|y|lene (ə set′ə lēn, -lin), *n.* a colorless gas that burns with a bright light, and very hot flame. It is used for preparing other compounds to make synthetic fibers and plastics. It is also used in lighting and, combined with oxygen, for welding and cutting metals. *Formula:* C_2H_2 [< *acetyl*]

acetylene series, a series of unsaturated hydrocarbons having the general formula C_nH_{2n-2}

acetylene torch, = oxyacetylene torch.

a|cet|y|len|ic (ə set′ə lē′nik, -lin′ik), *adj.* prepared from or resembling acetylene.

ac|e|tyl|ic (as′ə til′ik), *adj.* of or having to do with acetyl.

a|cet|y|lide (ə set′ə līd), *n.* a compound formed by the replacement of one or both of the hydrogen atoms of acetylene by a metal. [< *acetyl*]

ac|e|tyl|meth|a|dol (as′ə təl meth′ə dol), *n.* a drug used as a substitute for morphine for the relief of pain.

ac|e|tyl|sal|i|cyl|ic acid (as′ə təl sal′ə sil′ik, ə sē′-), = aspirin.

ace|y-deuc|y or **ace|y-deuce|y** (ā′sē dü′sē, -dyü′-), *n. U.S.* a variety of backgammon.

ac.-ft., acre-foot or acre-feet.

ach (äʜ), *interj. German.* oh! ah!

ACH (no periods), acetylcholine.

A|chae|an (ə kē′ən), *adj., n.* —***adj.* 1** of Achaia (a region and country in ancient Greece, in the Peloponnesus) or the Achaeans. **2** having to do with a league of cities formed in southern Greece

in 280 B.C. **3** Greek.
—*n.* **1** a native or inhabitant of Achaia. **2** (in Homer) any Greek. Also, **Achaian, Achean.**

Ach|ae|me|ni|an (ak′ə mē′nē ən), *adj., n.* —*adj.* of or having to do with the Achaemenids or their language.
—*n.* **1** an Achaemenid. **2** the Persian language of the Achaemenids.
[< Latin *Achaemenius* (< *Achaemenes* < Greek *Achaiménēs* < Old Persian *Hakhāmanis* legendary ancestor of the Achaemenids) + English *-an*]

Ach|ae|me|nid (ak′ə mē′nid, ə kē′mə-), *n., pl.* **-me|nids, -me|ni|des** (-men′ə dēz), *adj.* —*n.* a member of an ancient royal family of Persia, beginning with Cyrus the Great, about 558 B.C., and ending with Darius III, who was overthrown by Alexander the Great in 330 B.C.
—*adj.* of the Achaemenids; Achaemenian.
[< Greek *Achaimenídēs* < *Achaiménēs*]

A|cha|ian (ə kā′ən, -kī′-), *adj., n.* = Achaean.

ach|a|la|sia (ak′ə lā′zhə), *n. Medicine.* inability of a muscular organ to relax: *achalasia of the esophagus, sphincteral achalasia.* [< New Latin *achalasia* < *a-*[4] without + Greek *chálasis* a slackening]

a|char|ne|ment (à shàr nə mäɴ′), *n. French.* bloodthirsty fury; ferocity.

a|char|ya (ä chär′yə), *n.* a Hindu teacher, scholar, or spiritual leader. [< Hindi *āchārya*]

A|cha|tes (ə kā′tēz), *n.* **1** the faithful companion (*"fidus Achates"*) of Aeneas in Virgil's *Aeneid.* **2** a faithful comrade.

ache (āk), *n., v.,* **ached, ach|ing.** —*n.* a continuous pain, especially a dull or heavy pain: *The boy lay still trying to forget the ache in his back. Muscular aches follow hard exercise.* **SYN:** See syn. under **pain.** [Old English *æce*]
—*v.i.* **1** to be in continuous pain; suffer pain; hurt: *My arm aches.* **2** to have pity or sympathy; feel: *She ached for the hurt little dog.* **3** *Informal.* to be eager; wish very much: *During the hot days of August we all ached to go swimming. The lonely girl aches for home.* **SYN:** long, yearn.
[Old English *acan*] —**ach′ing|ly,** *adv.*

A|che|an (ə kē′ən), *adj., n.* = Achaean.

Ach|e|lo|us (ak′ə lō′əs), *n. Greek Mythology.* the river god, represented as a bull with a human head.

a|chene (ā kēn′), *n. Botany.* any small, dry, hard fruit consisting of one seed with a thin outer covering that does not burst open when ripe, such as the sunflower seed. Also, **achenium, akene.** [< New Latin *achaenium* < Greek *a-* not + *chainein* gape (because it ripens without bursting)]

a|che|ni|al (ā kē′nē əl), *adj.* **1** having to do with an achene. **2** like an achene.

a|che|ni|um (ā kē′nē əm), *n., pl.* **-ni|a** (-nē ə). = achene.

A|cher|nar (ā′kər när), *n.* the brightest star in the constellation Eridanus.

Ach|er|on (ak′ə ron), *n. Greek and Roman Mythology.* **1** one of the five rivers of Hades. See also **Styx.** **2** the lower world; Hades.

A|cheu|li|an or **A|cheu|le|an** (ə shü′lē ən), *adj.* of or having to do with a culture of the middle and lower paleolithic age in Europe and North Africa. It followed the Abbevillian and was characterized by more symmetrical biface tools with greater cutting surface. [< French *acheuléen* < Saint-*Acheul,* a region in France]

à che|val (à shə vàl′), *French.* **1** on horseback. **2** astride.

a|chieve (ə chēv′), *v.,* **a|chieved, a|chiev|ing.**
—*v.t.* **1** to carry out to a successful end; accomplish; do: *Did you achieve all that you expected to today? He soon learned that you cannot achieve much without work. ... they would concentrate their resources to achieve an efficient means of delivery* (New York Herald Tribune). **SYN:** complete, effect, execute, perform. **2** to reach by one's own efforts; get by effort: *He achieved fame as a swimmer. Newton and Einstein achieved distinction in mathematics.* **SYN:** gain, attain, win.
—*v.i.* to bring about a result intended: *Still achieving, still pursuing, Learn to labor and to wait* (Longfellow).
[< Old French *achever* < Vulgar Latin *accapāre* < Latin *ad-* to + *caput* a head] —**a|chiev′a|ble,** *adj.* —**a|chiev′er,** *n.*

a|chieve|ment (ə chēv′mənt), *n.* **1** something achieved or won by exertion; some plan or action carried out with courage or unusual ability: *Sailing a submarine under the North Pole was a great achievement. Martin Luther King, Jr., won the Nobel prize for his achievements in behalf of civil rights.* **SYN:** accomplishment, feat. See syn. under **exploit.** **2** an achieving; completion: *The achievement of one's aim comes only out of hard work.*

achievement age, the measure of how much a student has learned, determined by an achievement test and expressed as the (tabulated) average age of other students making the same score. Also, *especially British,* **attainment age.**

achievement quotient, the ratio of a student's achievement age to his actual age, usually multiplied by 100. *Abbr:* AQ (no periods). Also, *especially British,* **attainment quotient.**

achievement test, a test intended to measure quantitatively the results of learning or teaching. Also, *especially British,* **attainment test.**

Ach|il|le|an (ak′ə lē′ən), *adj.* **1** of Achilles. **2** like Achilles, who was noted for his bravery, his invulnerability (except in the heel), and his unrelenting wrath.

A|chil|les (ə kil′ēz), *n.* **1** *Greek Legend.* the greatest Greek warrior at the siege of Troy; the hero of Homer's *Iliad.* Thetis, his mother, held him by the heel when she dipped him into the river Styx to make him invulnerable. After he killed Hector, Paris killed him by shooting an arrow into his heel. **2** *Astronomy.* an asteroid which revolves around the sun and oscillates about points equally distant from Jupiter and the sun.

Achilles' heel, a weak point; vulnerable place: *Despite chronic shortages of some foods, farm production cannot be considered the Achilles' heel of Russia's economy* (Wall Street Journal).

Achilles' spear, *Greek Legend.* the spear of Achilles, the rust of which was made into a cure for wounds inflicted by it.

Achilles' tendon, the strong tendon at the back of the leg that connects the muscles in the calf with the bone of the heel.

a|chim|e|nes (ə kim′ə nēz), *n.* any one of a genus of tropical American herbs, cultivated for their flowers, which resemble gloxinias. [< Latin *achaemenis* an Indian plant < Greek *achaimenis*]

Ach|i|nese (ach′ə nēz′, -nēs′), *adj., n., pl.* **-nese.**
—*adj.* of or having to do with Achin (or Atjeh), a province of Sumatra, its people, or their language.
—*n.* **1** a native or inhabitant of Achin. **2** the Indonesian language of the Achinese.

A|chit|o|phel (ə kit′ə fel), *n.* Ahithophel, in the Douay and Vulgate Bibles. This spelling is well known through John Dryden's use in *Absalom and Achitophel.*

***ach|kan** (uch′kən), *n.* a close-fitting jacket of three-quarter length, worn by men in India, for formal or semiformal dress. [< Hindustani *ackan*]

***achkan**

a|chlam|y|date (ə klam′ə dāt), *adj.* having no mantle: *an achlamydate mollusk.*

ach|la|myd|e|ous (ak′lə mid′ē əs), *adj. Botany.* lacking a calyx and a corolla. [< *a-*[4] not + Greek *chlamýs, -ydos* mantle + English *-ous*]

a|chlor|hy|dri|a (ā′klôr hī′drē ə), *n. Medicine.* the absence of hydrochloric acid in the gastric juice. [< *a-*[4] without + *chlorhydric,* variant of *hydrochloric* (acid)]

a|chlor|hy|dric (ā′klôr hī′drik), *adj.* of or having to do with achlorhydria.

a|cho|lic (ā kō′lik, ā kol′ik), *adj.* free from or deficient in bile.

ach|o|lur|i|a (ak′ə lůr′ē ə), *n. Medicine.* a kind of jaundice marked by the absence of bile pigment in the urine. [< Greek *ácholos* lacking bile + English *-uria*]

ach|o|lur|ic (ak′ə lůr′ik), *adj.* of or having to do with acholuria.

a|chon|drite (ā kon′drīt), *n.* a stony meteorite that does not contain small embedded grains of minerals (chondrules).

a|chon|drit|ic (ā kon′drit′ik), *adj.* of or resembling achondrites.

a|chon|dro|pla|sia (ā kon′drə plā′zhə), *n.* dwarfism characterized by extreme shortness of the limbs and a disproportionately large head, due to a disorder of skeletal growth in fetal life. [< *a-*[4] without + Greek *chóndros* cartilage + *plásis* a molding]

a|chon|dro|pla|si|ac (ā kon′drə plā′zhē ak, -zē-), *adj., n.* = achondroplastic.

a|chon|dro|plas|tic (ā kon′drə plas′tik), *adj., n.*
—*adj.* **1** of or having to do with achondroplasia. **2** suffering from achondroplasia.
—*n.* a person who has achondroplasia.

a|chor|dal (ā kôr′dəl), *adj.* **1** lacking a chord. **2** = achordate.

a|chor|date (ā kôr′dāt), *adj., n.* —*adj.* lacking a notochord.
—*n.* an achordate animal. [< New Latin *Achordata* the collective name of such animals < Latin *a-* without + *chorda* chord[2]]

ach|ro|ite (ak′rō īt), *n.* a colorless variety of tourmaline. [< Greek *áchroia* absence of color + English *-ite*[1]]

ach|ro|mat (ak′rə mat), *n.* **1** = achromatic lens. **2** a color-blind person.

ach|ro|mat|ic (ak′rə mat′ik), *adj.* **1** refracting white light without breaking it up into the colors of the spectrum: *an achromatic telescope.* **2** without color; colorless. **3** *Biology.* consisting of material stained with difficulty by the usual stains or dyes: *achromatic cells.* **4** *Music.* without accidentals; not modulated. [< Greek *achrṓmatos* colorless] —**ach′ro|mat′i|cal|ly,** *adv.*

a|chro|ma|tic|i|ty (ā krō′mə tis′ə tē), *n.* = achromatism.

achromatic lens, a compound lens corrected for chromatic aberration; achromat.

a|chro|ma|tin (ā krō′mə tin), *n. Biology.* that portion of the mitotic cell nucleus or of individual chromosomes which, under the action of staining agents, remains less highly colored than the rest.

a|chro|ma|tism (ā krō′mə tiz əm), *n.* **1** freedom from chromatic aberration. **2** lack of color.

a|chro|ma|tize (ā krō′mə tīz), *v.t.,* **-tized, -tiz|ing.** to make achromatic; remove color from. —**a|chro′ma|ti|za′tion,** *n.*

a|chro|ma|top|si|a (ā kro′mə top′sē ə), *n.* total color blindness.

a|chro|ma|tous (ā krō′mə təs), *adj.* **1** lacking color. **2** having less color than normal.

a|chro|mic (ā krō′mik), *adj.* lacking color.

a|chro|mo|trich|i|a (ā krō′mə trik′ē ə), *n.* a graying of the hair in humans, or of the fur in animals, caused by a deficiency in the diet. [< Greek *áchrōmos* colorless + *thríx, trichós* a hair]

a|chro|mous (ā krō′məs), *adj.* = achromic.

Ach|ro|my|cin (ak′rə mī′sin), *n. Trademark.* tetracycline (an antibiotic drug).

Ach|tung (äʜ′tůng), *interj. German.* attention! (used as a command or warning).

ach|y (ā′kē), *adj. Informal.* full of aches: [*Crying*] *would only make her eyes achy and puffy and swollen in the morning* (Shirley Ann Grau).

ac|i|cle (as′ə kəl), *n.* = acicula.

a|cic|u|la (ə sik′yə lə), *n., pl.* **-lae** (-lē). a needlelike part: *The spines or bristles of some plants and the crystals of certain minerals are aciculae.* [< Late Latin *acicula,* variant of *acucula* pin (diminutive) < Latin *acus* needle]

a|cic|u|lar (ə sik′yə lər), *adj.* needle-shaped.
—**a|cic′u|lar|ly,** *adv.*

a|cic|u|late (ə sik′yə lit), *adj.* **1** having aciculae. **2** acicular; needle-shaped.

a|cic|u|lat|ed (ə sik′yə lā′tid), *adj.* = aciculate.

a|cic|u|lum (ə sik′yə ləm), *n., pl.* **-lums, -la** (-lə). a slender needlelike part or bristly structure: **a** *Botany.* an acicula. **b** *Zoology.* a seta. [< *acicula* (as if that were from a Latin plural)]

ac|id (as′id), *n., adj.* —*n.* **1a** a chemical compound with a sour or bitter taste that usually unites with a base to form a salt. Acids have a *pH* value of less than 7. They change blue litmus paper to red and yield hydrogen ions in a water solution. Hydrochloric acid and sulfuric acid are two common kinds. *Certain bacteria cause some foods to form acids that eat their way slowly through the enamel of the teeth.* **b** any ionic or molecular substance which can give up a proton. **c** any molecule or ion that can attach itself to a pair of electrons from a base, forming a covalent bond. **2** a substance with a sour taste like that of vinegar. **3** *Slang.* LSD (lysergic acid diethylamide), a hallucinogen: *The hippies say there is not much acid* (*LSD*) *around now, but that grass* (*marijuana*) *is plentiful* (New York Times).
—*adj.* **1** of acids; having the properties of an acid: *Blue litmus paper turns red in an acid solution.* **2** sharp or biting to the taste; sour: *Lemons are an acid fruit.* **SYN:** tart. See syn. under **sour.** **3** *Figurative.* sharp in manner or temper; caustic: *an acid tongue. Mother made an acid comment about my disorderly room.* **4** containing a large proportion of silica; acidic: *Granite is an acid rock.* **5** containing more acid than is normal. **6** having a *pH* factor of less than 7; having a relatively high concentration of hydrogen ions (contrasted with *alkaline* especially as a characteristic of soil).
[< Latin *acidus* sour < *acēre* be sour] —**ac′id|ly,** *adv.* —**ac′id|ness,** *n.*

acid drop, *British.* a candy made of sugar

Pronunciation Key: hat, āge, cãre, fär; let, ēqual, tėrm; it, īce; hot, ōpen, ôrder; oil, out; cup, pu̇t, rüle; child; long; thin; ᴛʜen; zh, measure; ə represents a in about, e in taken, i in pencil, o in lemon, u in circus.

strongly flavored with tartaric acid.

ac|id-fast (as′id fast′, -fäst′), *adj.* **1** retaining dye when treated with acid to remove the dye: *Tubercle bacilli are acid-fast.* **2** differentiated by such a stain from closely related forms. **—ac′id-fast′ness**, *n.*

ac|id-form|ing (as′id fôr′ming), *adj.* **1** producing a high proportion of acid residue during metabolism. **2** acidiferous.

ac|id|head (as′id hed′), *n. Slang.* a person addicted to LSD: *He aroused the ire of acidheads when he argued that the pleasures of drug taking are not worth the perils* (Time).

a|cid|ic (ə sid′ik), *adj.* **1a** forming acid. **b** of an acid or acids: *acidic ions.* **c** having the properties of an acid: *acidic resins.* **2** *Figurative.* sharp and biting in manner or temper; caustic. **3** containing a relatively large proportion of silica: *Granite is an acidic rock.*

ac|i|dif|er|ous (as′ə dif′ər əs), *adj.* yielding an acid.

ac|i|dif|ic (as′ə dif′ik), *adj.* producing acidity or an acid; acidifying.

a|cid|i|fi|ca|tion (ə sid′ə fə kā′shən), *n.* the process of acidifying.

a|cid|i|fy (ə sid′ə fī) , *v.t., v.i.,* **-fied, -fy|ing. 1a** to make or become sour. **b** *Figurative.* to make caustic or turn sour: *His thin existence [was] all acidified into rage* (Thomas Carlyle). **2** to change into an acid. **3** to make or become acid. **—a|cid′i|fi′a|ble**, *adj.* **—a|cid′i|fi′er**, *n.*

ac|i|dim|e|ter (as′ə dim′ə tər), *n.* an instrument for determining the strength of acids or acid solutions.

ac|i|di|met|ric (as′ə də met′rik), *adj.* of or involving acidimetry.

ac|i|di|met|ri|cal (as′ə də met′rə kəl), *adj.* = acidimetric.

ac|i|dim|e|try (as′ə dim′ə trē), *n.* **1** measurement of the strength of acids. **2** determination of the amount of free acid in a solution, usually by titration.

a|cid|i|ty (ə sid′ə tē), *n., pl.* **-ties. 1a** acid quality or condition; sourness: *the acidity of vinegar.* **b** *Figurative: The acidity of his remarks showed the disappointment in his defeat.* **2** the degree of acid quality: *the acidity of a soil.* **3** an excess of acid, especially hyperacidity. **4** *Chemistry.* the number of replaceable —OH groups in the molecule of a base.

ac|i|di|za|tion (as′ə də zā′shən), *n.* = acidification.

ac|i|dize (as′ə dīz), *v.t., v.i.,* **-dized, -diz|ing.** = acidify.

ac|id|less trip (as′id lis), *U.S. Slang.* = sensitivity training.

acid number, a number expressing the degree of acidity of a substance, equal to the number of milligrams of potassium hydroxide required to neutralize the free fatty acids in one gram of the substance; acid value.

a|cid|o|phil (a sid′ə fil), *n.* a cell that stains readily with acid dyes.

ac|i|doph|i|lic (as′ə dof′ə lik), *adj.* of or designating cells that stain with acid dyes. [< *acid* + Greek *phílos* loving, fond + English *-ic*]

ac|i|doph|i|lous (as′ə dof′ə ləs), *adj.* = acidophilic.

ac|i|doph|i|lus milk (as′ə dof′ə ləs), skim milk fermented by a bacterial culture, taken as part of a diet intended to change the bacterial content of the intestine.

ac|i|do|sis (as′ə dō′sis), *n.* a harmful condition in which the blood and tissues are less alkaline than is normal. [< *acid* + *-osis*]

ac|i|dot|ic (as′ə dot′ik), *adj.* **1** of or having to do with acidosis. **2** suffering from acidosis.

acid process, any steel-making process in which the furnace is lined with a siliceous substance and in which pig iron containing little phosphorus is used.

acid radical, a radical formed from an organic acid by the removal from the acid of the univalent radical —OH (an atom of oxygen in combination with an atom of hydrogen); acyl.

acid rain, rain that has a high concentration of sulfuric and nitric acids due to air pollution: *Scandinavian and American researchers suspect that acid rains have killed fish in many lakes in both regions* (Boyce Rensberger).

acid rock, rock'n'roll music with sound and lyrics suggestive of hallucinatory or psychedelic experiences. [< *acid* (LSD)]

acid salt, a salt formed from an acid of which only part of the hydrogen has been replaced by a metal or radical.

acid test, a thorough test to find out the real quality of some person or thing; decisive test: *... political assumptions which, I think, could not long withstand the acid test of logic* (Wall Street Journal).

ac|id-tongued (as′id tungd′), *adj.* sharp-tongued; caustic: *This acid-tongued diplomat has managed to play a controversial role in almost every East-West dispute* (Newsweek).

acid trip, *Slang.* a hallucinatory experience that results from using LSD.

a|cid|u|late (ə sij′ə lāt), *v.t.,* **-lat|ed, -lat|ing. 1** to make slightly acid or sour. **2** *Figurative.* to make caustic or harsh: *a compliment acidulated with some scorn.* **—a|cid′u|la′tion**, *n.*

a|cid|u|lat|ed (ə sij′ə lā′tid), *adj.* **1** slightly acid or sour. **2** *Figurative.* embittered.

a|cid|u|lent (ə sij′ə lənt), *adj.* = acidulous.

a|cid|u|lous (ə sij′ə ləs), *adj.* **1** slightly acid or sour. **2** *Figurative.* caustic; harsh: *It is beautiful, therefore ... to find a woman, George Eliot, departing utterly out of that mood of hate or even of acidulous satire in which Thackeray so often worked* (Sidney Lanier). **—a|cid′u|lous|ly**, *adv.* **—a|cid′u|lous|ness**, *n.*

acid value, = acid number.

ac|id|y (as′ə dē), *adj.* having an acid quality.

ac|i|er|age (as′ē ər ij), *n.* the process of depositing a layer of iron on another metal by electric action. [< French *aciérage* < *acier* steel]

ac|i|er|ate (as′ē ə rāt), *v.t.,* **-at|ed, -at|ing.** *Especially U.S.* to convert (iron) into steel. [< French *acier* steel + English *-ate*[1]]

ac|i|er|a|tion (as′ē ə rā′shən), *n.* conversion into steel.

ac|i|form (as′ə fôrm), *adj.* needle-shaped; acicular. [< Latin *acus* needle + English *-form*]

***ac|i|nac|i|form** (as′ə nas′ə fôrm), *adj.* scimitar-shaped: *acinaciform leaves.* [< Latin *acīnacēs* scimitar (< Greek *akīnákēs*) + English *-form*]

***acinaciform**

ac|i|nar (as′ə nər), *adj. Anatomy.* having to do with an acinus or acini.

a|cin|i|form (ə sin′ə fôrm), *adj.* clustered like grapes; acinous. [< Latin *acinus* grape, berry + English *-form*]

ac|i|nose (as′ə nōs), *adj.* = acinous.

ac|i|nous (as′ə nəs), *adj.* composed of or resembling a cluster of small berries; consisting of acini. [< Latin *acinōsus* grapelike < *acinus* grape, berry]

ac|i|nus (as′ə nəs), *n., pl.* **-ni** (-nī). **1** *Botany.* **a** one of the small, fleshy berries (drupelets) that make up such compound fruits as the blackberry. **b** the compound fruit that they compose. **c** the stone or seed of a grape or berry. **d** a berry which grows in clusters, such as grapes or currants. **2** *Anatomy.* a minute lobule; one of the small terminal sacs with constricted lumen in a lung or exocrine gland. [< Latin *acinus*]

ac|i|pen|ser|id (as′ə pen′sər id), *adj., n.* **—*adj.*** = acipenseroid.
—*n.* an acipenseroid fish, such as the sturgeon.

ac|i|pen|ser|oid (as′ə pen′sə roid), *adj.* of or having to do with a group of fishes that includes the sturgeons and related forms. [< Latin *acipenser* a fish, believed to be the sturgeon + English *-oid*]

A|cis (ā′sis), *n. Greek Myth.* a youth who fell in love with Galatea and was slain by Polyphemus in a jealous rage. His blood became the river Acis, in Sicily.

ack-ack or **Ack-Ack** (ak′ak′), *n. Slang.* **1** antiaircraft fire. **2** antiaircraft artillery. [British radio operator's code word for *AA* (*antiaircraft*)]

ac|kee (ak′ē, a kē′), *n.* **1** a tropical tree of the soapberry family, native to West Africa, whose fruit contains oily seeds embedded in a white, spongy aril. **2** the aril, which is cooked and eaten as a vegetable. Also, **akee.** [< a native word in western Africa]

ack em|ma (ak em′ə), *British Slang.* the radio operator's word for *a.m.*

ac|knowl|edge (ak nol′ij), *v.t.,* **-edged, -edg|ing. 1** to admit to be true or to exist: *He acknowledges his own faults.* **SYN:** grant, concede, confess, avow, own. See syn. under **admit. 2** to recognize the authority or claims of: *The boys acknowledged the pitcher to be the best player on the baseball team.* **3** to express appreciation of or make known that one has received (a favor, service, gift, or message): *She acknowledged the gift with a pleasant letter. I acknowledged her letter at once.* **4** *Law.* **a** to recognize as genuine; certify: *to acknowledge a deed before a notary public.* **b** to admit (a debt or other liability). **5** to respond to: *He acknowledged the greeting with a nod.* [blend of obsolete *acknow* admit, and *knowledge*, verb, admit] **—ac|knowl′edge|a|ble**, *adj.* **—ac|knowl′edged|ly**, *adv.* **—ac|knowl′edg|er**, *n.*

ac|knowl|edg|ment or **ac|knowl|edge|ment** (ak nol′ij mənt), *n.* **1** something given or done to show that one has received a favor, service, gift, or message: *The supermarket's receipt was acknowledgment that the groceries had been paid for. The winner waved in acknowledgment of the crowd's cheers. What is the grateful acknowledgment of a friend's kindness?* **2** admitting that something is true or exists: *acknowledgment of a mistake. The accused man made acknowledgment of his guilt.* **SYN:** admission, concession, confession, avowal. **3** answering; response: *acknowledgment of an introduction.* **4** the recognition of authority, claims, or merit. **SYN:** acceptance. **5** *Law.* **a** an official certificate in legal form. **b** admission of a debt or other liability.

a|clas|tic (ā klas′tik), *adj. Physics.* not refracting. [< Greek *áklastos* unbroken + English *-ic*]

a|clin|ic (ā klin′ik), *adj.* having no magnetic dip or inclination. [< Greek *aklinḗs* not bending + English *-ic*]

***aclinic line**, the magnetic equator, at which a magnetic needle balances horizontally without dipping.

***aclinic line**

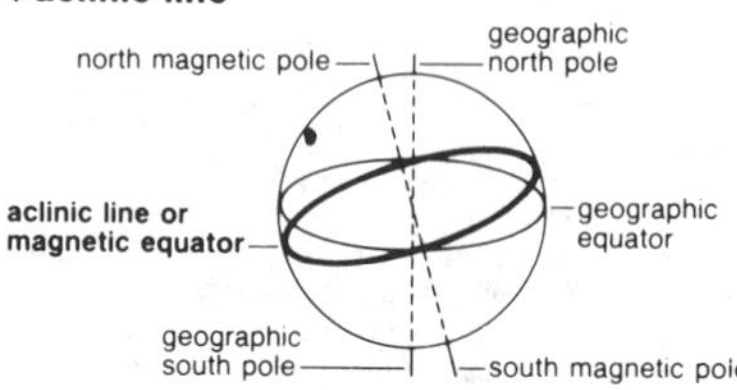

ACLS (no periods), **1** American Council of Learned Societies. **2** Automatic Carrier Landing System.

ACLU (no periods) or **A.C.L.U.**, American Civil Liberties Union.

ac|me (ak′mē), *n.* the highest point: *A baseball player usually reaches the acme of his skill before he is thirty.* **SYN:** apex, culmination, climax. [< Greek *akmḗ* (highest) point]

Ac|me|ist (ak′mē ist), *n.* one of a group of Russian poets of the early 1900's who opposed symbolism and advocated precision and concreteness in poetry.

ac|ne (ak′nē), *n.* a skin disease, especially of adolescence, in which the oil glands in the skin become clogged and inflamed, often causing pimples, particularly on the face. [< Late Greek *aknḗ*, misspelling of Greek *akmḗ* point]

ac|ne|form (ak′nə fôrm), *adj.* **1** of or having to do with acne. **2** resembling acne.

ac|ne|i|form (ak nē′ə fôrm), *adj.* = acneform.

ac|ne ro|sa|ce|a (ak′nē rō zā′shē ə), a disorder, especially of middle age, characterized by pimples and chronic congestion of the blood vessels of the nose and central part of the face.

a|cock (ə kok′), *adv., adj.* in a cocked position.

a|cock|bill (ə kok′bil), *adv. Nautical.* turned upward, as yards tilted at an angle with the deck.

a|coe|lo|mate (ā sē′lə māt, -mit), *adj., n.* **—*adj.*** without either a true or false body cavity (coelom), as the flatworms.
—*n.* an acoelomate worm; flatworm.

a|coe|lous (ā sē′ləs), *adj.* having no digestive tract or body cavity. [< Greek *ákoilos* (with English *-ous*) not hollow < *a-* not + *koîlos* hollow]

a|cold (ə kōld′), *adj. Archaic.* cold; chilled: *Poor Tom's acold* (Shakespeare). *The owl, for all his feathers, was acold* (Keats).

ac|o|lyte (ak′ə līt), *n.* **1a** a person who helps a priest, deacon, or other person in charge of a church service by performing certain subordinate duties; altar boy: *The acolyte lit the candles on the altar.* **b** a person ordained to the fourth and highest minor order in the Roman Catholic Church. **2** a youth who assists with certain parts of the service, but is not a member of the clergy, in some Protestant churches. **3** an assistant; attendant; follower. **4** *Astronomy.* an attendant star; satellite. [< Medieval Latin *acolytus*, alteration of Late Latin *acolūthos* < Greek *akólouthos* follower]

à compte (à kôɴt′), *French.* as part payment; on account.

a|con|i|tase (ə kon′ə tās), *n.* an enzyme that promotes the conversion of citric acid in the process of turning it into aconitic acid for further conversion from a food chemical into physical energy. [< *aconit*(ic) + *-ase*]

ac|o|nite (ak′ə nīt), *n.* **1** a plant with irregular, blue, purple, yellow, or yellow-and-white flowers shaped like hoods. Only a few grow wild in North America, such as monkshood and wolfsbane. Aconite belongs to the crowfoot family and has poisonous roots, leaves, and seeds. **2** a very poisonous drug prepared from the roots of monkshood, and used to relieve inflammation and pain. It contains aconitine, and was formerly used to reduce fever and slow the action of the heart but now is used occasionally in liniments. [< Latin *aconītum* < Greek *akóniton*]

ac|o|nit|ic (ak′ə nit′ik), *adj.* of or having to do with aconite.

aconitic acid, a whitish or yellowish crystalline acid obtained from aconite and bagasse or by dehydration of citric acid. *Formula:* $C_6H_6O_6$

a|con|i|tin (ə kon′ə tin), *n.* = aconitine.

a|con|i|tine (ə kon′ə tēn), *n.* a very poisonous alkaloid derived from the roots of the common European aconite. *Formula:* $C_{34}H_{47}O_{11}N$

ac|o|ni|tum (ak′ə nī′təm), *n.* = aconite.

a|con|ti|um (ə kon′shē əm), *n., pl.* **-ti|a** (-shē ə). any one of several long, delicate threads equipped with stinging cells, arising from the septa of some sea anemones and protruding when the animal contracts. [< New Latin *acontium* < Greek *akóntion* (diminutive) < *ákōn* javelin < *akḗ* point]

★a|corn (ā′kôrn, -kərn), *n.* the nut of an oak tree. [Old English *æcern*]

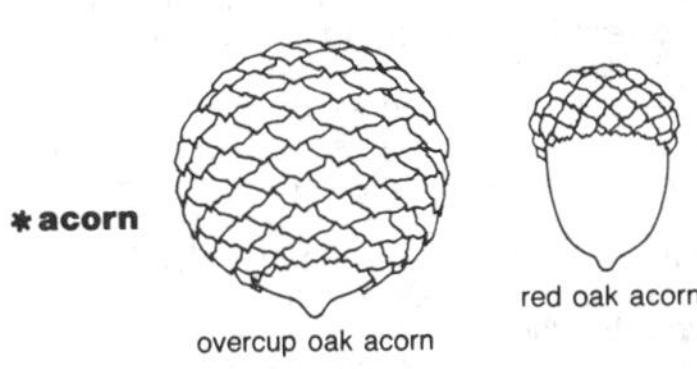

resembling an acorn:

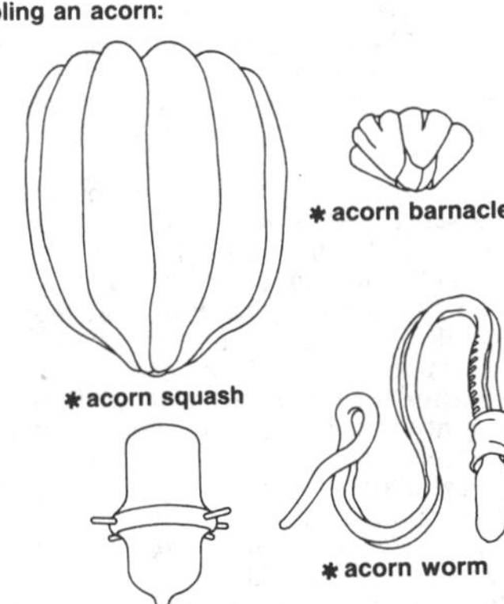

★acorn barnacle, a barnacle that lives on rocks in the sea.

acorn shell, *British.* a rock barnacle.

★acorn squash, a small, dark-green, edible winter squash resembling an acorn in shape, having yellow or orange flesh.

★acorn tube, a small vacuum tube, shaped like an acorn, used at high frequencies, especially in radios.

★acorn worm, a small, wormlike marine animal whose front end looks somewhat like an acorn.

à corps per|du (á kôr per dY′), *French.* impetuously; furiously.

a|cos|mic (ā koz′mik), *adj.* **1** having to do with acosmism. **2** disordered; confused; disharmonious.

a|cos|mism (ā koz′miz əm), *n.* the denial of the existence of a universe, or of a universe as distinct from God. —**a|cos′mist**, *n.*

a|cot|y|le|don (ā′kot ə lē′dən, ə kot′-), *n.* a plant without cotyledons, such as a moss or lichen; cryptogam.

a|cot|y|le|don|ous (ā′kot ə lē′də nəs, ə kot′-), *adj.* having no distinct cotyledons; cryptogamic.

a|cou|chi (ə kü′shē), *n., pl.* **-chis**. a small rodent related to the guinea pig and agouti, native to Guinea. [< French *acouchi* < a native word]

a|cou|chy (ə kü′shē), *n., pl.* **-chies**. = acouchi.

a|cou|me|ter (ə kü′mə tər, -kou′-), *n.* an instrument for measuring keenness of hearing. [< Greek *akoúein* hear + English *-meter*]

a|cous|ma (ə kus′mə), *n., pl.* **-mas, -ma|ta** (-mə tə). *Psychology.* the hearing of imaginary sounds; auditory hallucination. [< Greek *akousma* thing heard < *akoúein* hear]

a|cous|tic (ə küs′tik, -kous′-), *adj.* **1** having to do with the sense or the organs of hearing. **2** having to do with the science of sound (acoustics). **3a** of or having to do with sound waves or sound. **b** actuated, directed, or controlled by sound waves: *an acoustic mine.* **4** designed to absorb or reduce noise: *a ceiling of acoustic tile.* [< Greek *akoustikós* related to hearing < *akoúein* hear] —**a|cous′ti|cal|ly**, *adv.*

a|cous|ti|cal (ə küs′tə kəl, -kous′-), *adj.* = acoustic: *No one can say for sure what the acoustical qualities of an auditorium will be until it is finished* (New Yorker).

acoustical hologram, a picture produced by acoustical holography.

acoustical holography, holography that uses sound waves instead of laser light to produce a three-dimensional picture: *Hence, a hologram can be recorded with sound waves and then reconstructed with light. This technique is called acoustical holography* (Science Journal).

acoustic coupler, a device for transmitting data over telephone circuits without making an electrical connection.

acoustic feedback, *Electronics.* the feedback of sound from the output of a sound system back to the input, such as noise from a loudspeaker reaching the microphone.

ac|ous|ti|cian (ak′ü stish′ən, -ou-), *n.* **1** an expert in acoustics. **2** a person trained in fitting the hard-of-hearing with hearing aids.

ac|ous|tic|i|ty (ak′ü stis′ə tē, -ou-), *n.* acoustic quality or condition.

acoustic mine, a mine that has a small microphone connected to its trigger, exploded by the sound of the propellers of a vessel passing over or near it; sonic mine.

acoustic nerve, an auditory nerve.

acoustic perfume, an overlay of nondescript sound to cover up distracting or annoying noises; white noise: *The most popular form of acoustic perfume, of course, is music—piped, canned, or live* (Eugene Raskin).

acoustic phonetics, study of speech sounds by means of acoustic tools and techniques.

a|cous|tics (ə küs′tiks, -kous′-), *n.pl.* **1** the structural features of an auditorium, hall, or room, that determine how well sounds can be heard or transmitted in it; acoustic qualities: *The acoustics will be particularly poor, as they invariably are in new auditoriums* (Norman Mailer). **2** the science of sound.

►**Acoustics**, meaning acoustic qualities (def. 1), is plural in form and in use: *The acoustics were so good that people in the last row could hear the speaker well. Acoustics,* meaning the science of sound (def. 2), is plural in form and singular in use: *Acoustics is taught in some colleges.*

acoustic torpedo, a torpedo that is guided by sound waves from the target.

acoustic velocity, the rate at which a sound wave travels through a specified medium.

acoustic wave, = sound wave.

acousto-, *combining form.* **1** of sound or acoustic waves: *Acoustoelectronics = the study of the conversion of electronic signals into sound waves.* **2** acoustic and ___: *Acousto-optic modulator = acoustic and optic modulator.*

a|cous|to|e|lec|tron|ics (ə küs′tō i lek′tron′iks, -kous′-; -ē′lek-), *n.* a branch of electronics dealing with the conversion of electrical signals into a flow of acoustic waves traveling along a solid surface.

à cou|vert (á kü ver′), *French.* sheltered from the weather; covered.

ACP (no periods), African, Caribbean, and Pacific countries (group of over 40 nonaligned nations that have a treaty of cooperation with the European Economic Community).

ac|qua al|ta (äk′wä äl′tä), *Italian.* high water: *Venetians are quite accustomed to minor attacks of such acqua alta, which, in the spring and fall, frequently invade the lower floors of houses and submerge the famous square under a foot or so* (New Yorker).

ac|quaint (ə kwānt′), *v.t.* **1** to furnish (a person) with information; make aware; let know; inform: *Acquaint him with your plans for next summer.* **SYN:** tell, apprise. See syn. under **inform**. **2** to make more or less familiar (with): *Let me acquaint you with your new duties.* **SYN:** familiarize.

be acquainted with, to be familiar with or know: *I am acquainted with his plans.*

become acquainted with, to get to know: *We became acquainted with our new neighbors.*

[< Old French *acointer* < Vulgar Latin *accognitāre* make known (frequentative) < Latin *accognōscere* < *ad-* + *cognōscere* come to know well]

ac|quaint|ance (ə kwān′təns), *n.* **1** *pl.* **-anc|es**. a person known to one, but not a close friend: *We have many acquaintances in our neighborhood.* **2** *no pl.* **a** knowledge of persons or things gained from experience with them. Acquaintance is more than mere recognition, and less than familiarity or intimacy. *I have some acquaintance with French, but I do not know it well.* **b** the state of being acquainted, or of knowing people and being known by them: *a man of wide acquaintance.*

cultivate the acquaintance of, to try to get to know (someone) well: *The ambitious young candidate tried to cultivate the acquaintance of the most influential politicians of his state.*

make the acquaintance of, to get to know: *My mother soon made the acquaintance of my new teacher. We spent a day or two in making the general acquaintance of the glacier* (John Tyndall).

scrape acquaintance, to take the trouble to get acquainted: *Her two dearest friends had contrived to scrape acquaintance without introduction* (F. Whishaw).

acquaintance rape, forced sexual intercourse with a person one knows in a casual way: *The use of new terms, like acquaintance rape and date rape, while controversial, has given both men and women the vocabulary they need to express their experiences with both force and precision* (Time).

ac|quaint|ance|ship (ə kwān′təns ship), *n.* **1** the relation between acquaintances: *Their acquaintanceship lasted many years.* **2** personal knowledge; acquaintance: *While Interlingua can be read with little difficulty by almost anyone, books are available which will give a formal acquaintanceship with this international language* (Science News Letter).

ac|quest (ə kwest′), *n.* **1** a thing acquired; acquisition. **2** *Law.* property acquired otherwise than by succession. [< Middle French *acquest,* ultimately < Latin *ad-* to + *quaerere* seek]

ac|qui|esce (ak′wē es′), *v.i.,* **-esced, -esc|ing.** to give consent; accept by keeping silent or by not making objections; agree or submit quietly: *We acquiesced in their plan because we could not suggest a better one.* **SYN:** accede, assent, concur. [< French *acquiescer,* learned borrowing from Latin *acquiēscere* < *ad-* to + *quiēs* rest, quiet] —**ac′qui|esc′ing|ly**, *adv.*

ac|qui|es|cence (ak′wē es′əns), *n.* consent given without making objections; agreeing or submitting quietly; assent.

►**Acquiescence** is distinguished from openly declared consent on the one hand and from opposition or open discontent on the other.

ac|qui|es|cent (ak′wē es′ənt), *adj.* quietly consenting or agreeing; acquiescing. —**ac′qui|es′cent|ly**, *adv.*

ac|quire (ə kwīr′), *v.t.,* **-quired, -quir|ing.** **1** to get by one's own efforts or actions: *He acquired the money for a college education by working summers.* **SYN:** gain, win, attain. **2** to come to have; get as one's own: *to acquire land. He acquired a strong liking for sports at camp.* **SYN:** obtain. **3** to find, take up, and hold: *This . . . robot uses vision to acquire the letters that spell out its name, and arranges them in order* (G. I. Robertson). See syn. under **get**. [< Latin *acquīrere* get (in addition) < *ad-* to + *quaerere* seek] —**ac|quir′a|ble**, *adj.* —**ac|quir′er**, *n.*

ac|quired character or **characteristic** (ə kwīrd′), a change of structure or of function in a plant or animal as a result of use or disuse or in response to the environment. An acquired character cannot be inherited.

ac|quire|ment (ə kwīr′mənt), *n.* **1** the act of acquiring; gaining or getting as one's own: *The acquirement of wealth is one aim of being in business.* **2** something acquired; an accomplishment; attainment: *Her musical acquirements are unusual for a girl of her age.*

ac|qui|si|tion (ak′wə zish′ən), *n., v.* —*n.* **1** the act of acquiring or getting as one's own: *He spent hundreds of hours in the acquisition of skill at the piano. With the acquisition of 19 rare specimens, the collection is unmatched.* **2** a thing acquired or gained; an addition: *The museum's latest acquisition is a painting by Rubens.* **SYN:** gain. —*v.t.* to acquire: *. . . a pencil stub that I'd recently acquisitioned from a desk drawer* (J. D. Salinger). [< Latin *acquīsītiō, -ōnis* < *acquīrere* acquire]

ac|quis|i|tive (ə kwiz′ə tiv), *adj.* **1** fond of acquiring; eager to get (money, goods, ideas, etc.); greedy: *Misers are acquisitive. As a man steeped in the civilized traditions of the West, he knew that there must be rational limits put upon the acquisitive and possessive instincts* (Atlantic). **SYN:** avid, covetous. **2** likely to get and keep: *A great scholar is acquisitive of ideas.* —**ac|quis′i|tive|ly**, *adv.* —**ac|quis′i|tive|ness**, *n.*

ac|quit (ə kwit′), *v.t.,* **-quit|ted, -quit|ting.** **1** to declare (a person) not guilty (of an offense); set free after considering evidence: *The man accused of stealing the money was acquitted.* **SYN:** clear, exonerate, exculpate. **2** to pay off or settle (a debt or claim). **3** *Archaic.* to set free or release (from a duty or obligation).

acquit oneself, to do one's part; behave oneself; conduct oneself: *The soldiers acquitted themselves bravely in battle.*

[< Old French *aquiter* < *a-* to + *quite* free, learned borrowing from Medieval Latin *quitus,* alteration of Latin *quiētus* quiet] —**ac|quit′ter**, *n.*

Pronunciation Key: **h**a**t**, **ā**ge, **c**ã**re**, **f**ä**r**; **l**e**t**, **ē**qual, **t**ė**rm**; **i**t, **ī**ce; **h**o**t**, **ō**pen, **ô**rder; **oi**l, **ou**t; **c**u**p**, **p**u̇**t**, **r**ü**le**; **ch**ild; lo**ng**; **th**in; **ᴛʜ**en; **zh**, measure; **ə** represents **a** in about, **e** in taken, **i** in pencil, **o** in lemon, **u** in circus.

ac|quit|ment (ə kwit′mənt), *n. Obsolete.* acquittal.

ac|quit|tal (ə kwit′əl), *n.* **1** the act of setting free by declaring not guilty; discharge; release: *The jury brought in a verdict of acquittal.* **2** performance (of a duty or obligation).

ac|quit|tance (ə kwit′əns), *n.* **1** a written release from a debt or obligation. **2** the payment of a debt; settlement of a claim. **3** a written statement showing that a debt has been paid; receipt for the full amount.

a|cral|de|hyde (ə kral′də hīd), *n.* = acrolein. [< Latin *ācer, ācris* sharp + English *aldehyde*]

a|cra|ni|al (ā krā′nē əl), *adj.* having no skull.

a|cra|sin (ə krā′sin), *n.* a substance produced by certain amebas as an attractant, causing a group of amebas to aggregate. [< Greek *akrasia* lack of strength or control + English *-in*]

a|crawl (ə krôl′), *adv., adj.* crawling; swarming: *. . . acrawl with Siamese cats and intellectual gentility* (Time).

***a|cre** (ā′kər), *n.* **1** a measure of land, 160 square rods, 4,840 square yards, or 43,560 square feet, or 4,047 square meters. **2** a field (obsolete except in *God's acre*).

acres, a lands; property: *broad acres.* **b** *Informal.* large quantities: *acres of money.*

[Old English *æcer* tilled field]

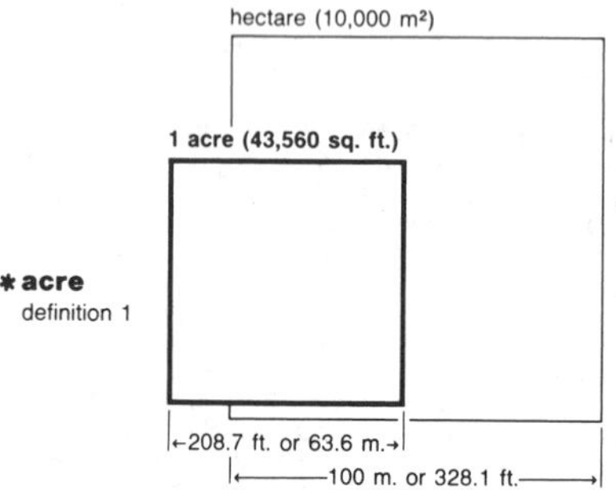

***acre** definition 1

a|cre|age (ā′kər ij), *n.* **1** number of acres; extent in acres: *The acreage of this park is over 800.* **2** *U.S.* a piece of land sold by the acre.

a|cred (ā′kərd), *adj.* having acres; landed (used chiefly in compounds).

a|cre-foot (ā′kər fu̇t′), *n., pl.* **-feet.** a unit of measure of the volume of water in irrigation, equal to an acre of water one foot deep; 43,560 cubic feet or 1,233.5 cubic meters.

a|cre-inch (ā′kər inch′), *n.* 3,630 cubic feet or 102.79 cubic meters; 1/12 of an acre-foot.

a|cres (ā′kərz), *n.pl.* See under **acre**.

ac|rid (ak′rid), *adj.* **1** sharp, bitter, or stinging to the taste, or to the nose, eyes, or skin: *Smoke feels acrid in your nose.* SYN: irritating, corrosive, pungent. **2** *Figurative.* irritating in manner; sharp in temper: *The quarrelsome old man had an acrid disposition.* SYN: caustic, acrimonious. [< Latin *ācer, ācris* sharp] **—ac′rid|ly,** *adv.* **—ac′rid-ness,** *n.*

ac|ri|dine (ak′rə dēn, -din), *n.* a colorless, crystalline compound, obtained from coal tar, used in the synthesis of certain dyes and drugs and as a reagent. *Formula:* $C_{13}H_9N$ [< *acrid* + *-ine*[2]]

a|crid|i|ty (ə krid′ə tē), *n., pl.* **-ties. 1** acrid quality; pungent bitterness; sharpness. **2** a caustic comment.

ac|ri|dol|o|gy (ak′rə dol′ə jē), *n.* the study of locusts. [< Greek *akrís, akrid-* locust + *-logy*]

ac|ri|fla|vine (ak′rə flā′vin, -vēn), *n.* a reddish-yellow powder obtained from acridine, used in solution as an antiseptic and disinfectant. *Formula:* $C_{14}H_{14}N_3Cl$ [< *acri*(dine) + Latin *flāvus* yellow + English *-ine*[2]]

Ac|ri|lan (ak′rə lan), *n. Trademark.* a synthetic fiber produced from acrylonitrile. It somewhat resembles wool in texture and resists wrinkling.

ac|ri|mo|ni|ous (ak′rə mō′nē əs), *adj.* sharp or bitter in temper, language, or manner; caustic: *An acrimonious dispute broke out between the drivers who had the accident. Our interlocutors were never arrogant or acrimonious, but earnestly inquiring, seeking patiently to understand another point of view* (Harper's). SYN: acrid, biting. **—ac′ri|mo′ni|ous|ly,** *adv.* **—ac′ri|mo′ni|ous|ness,** *n.*

ac|ri|mo|ny (ak′rə mō′nē), *n., pl.* **-nies.** sharpness or bitterness in temper, language, or manner; acrid quality. SYN: acerbity, asperity. [< Latin *ācrimōnia* pungency < *ācer, ācris* sharp]

a|crit|i|cal (ā krit′ə kəl), *adj.* not critical: *acritical symptoms, an acritical disease.* **—a|crit′i|cal|ly,** *adv.*

ac|ro|a|mat|ic (ak′rō ə mat′ik), *adj.* abstruse; esoteric. [< Greek *akroāmatikós* designed for hearing < *akroâsthai* hear]

ac|ro|bat (ak′rə bat), *n.* **1** a person who can swing on a trapeze, turn handsprings, walk a tightrope, or do other feats of bodily skill and strength; one highly skilled in gymnastic feats, such as tumbling. **2** *Figurative.* a daring performer. [< French *acrobate* < Greek *akróbatos* going on tiptoe, climbing up high < *ákros* tip (of the toes) + *-batos* going]

ac|ro|bat|ic (ak′rə bat′ik), *adj.* **1** of an acrobat: *Walking a tightrope is an acrobatic feat.* **2** *Figurative.* like an acrobat's: *With an acrobatic leap, he picked the apple off the tree.* **3** of acrobatics. **—ac′ro|bat′i|cal|ly,** *adv.*

ac|ro|bat|ics (ak′rə bat′iks), *n.pl.* **1** the tricks or performances of an acrobat; gymnastic feats: *the acrobatics of a tumbler.* **2** *Figurative.* feats like those of an acrobat: *The children were delighted by the monkey's acrobatics.* **3** stunt flying. **4** the art or skill of an acrobat.

ac|ro|bat|ism (ak′rə bat iz′əm), *n.* = acrobatics.

ac|ro|blast (ak′rə blast), *n.* the structure that forms the acrosome in spermatogenesis. [< Greek *ákros* tip + *blastós* sprout]

ac|ro|car|pous (ak′rə kär′pəs), *adj.* producing fruit at the end or top of the main stem, as certain mosses do. [< Greek *akrókarpos* (with English *-ous*) bearing fruit at the top < *ákros* tip + *karpós* fruit]

ac|ro|cen|tric (ak′rō sen′trik), *adj.* having a centromere near one end: *an acrocentric chromosome.* [< Greek *ákros* extremity + English *centric*]

ac|ro|ce|phal|ic (ak′rō sə fal′ik), *adj., n.* **—adj.** of or characterized by acrocephaly.
—n. an acrocephalic person.

ac|ro|ceph|a|lous (ak′rō sef′ə ləs), *adj.* = acrocephalic.

ac|ro|ceph|a|ly (ak′rō sef′ə lē), *n.* a deformity of the head characterized by a skull that tapers upward to a point. [< Greek *ákros* tip, point + *kephalḗ* head, skull]

ac|ro|dont (ak′rə dont), *adj., n.* **—adj. 1** attached by the base to the edge of the jawbone, without sockets: *acrodont teeth.* **2** having teeth so attached. **—n.** an acrodont animal. Some lizards are acrodonts. [< Greek *ákros* tip + *odoús, odóntos* tooth]

ac|ro|drome (ak′rə drōm), *adj.* having the main veins coming together and uniting at the tip of the leaf: *an acrodrome plant.* [< Greek *ákros* tip + *dromos* a running]

a|crod|ro|mous (ə krod′rə məs), *adj.* = acrodrome.

ac|ro|dyn|i|a (ak′rō din′ē ə), *n.* a disease, especially of very young children, characterized by abnormal redness of the skin and lesions on the hands and feet: *Too much mercury, for example, results in a condition called acrodynia, which killed many babies before its secret was discovered* (New Scientist). [< Greek *ákros* tip, extremity + *odýnē* pain]

ac|ro|gen (ak′rə jən), *n.* a plant growing only at the apex, such as the ferns and mosses. [< Greek *ákros* tip + English *-gen*]

ac|ro|gen|ic (ak′rə jen′ik), *adj.* = acrogenous.

a|crog|e|nous (ə kroj′ə nəs), *adj.* **1** growing from the top or by terminal buds only, as the ferns and mosses do. **2** of or having to do with the acrogens. **—a|crog′e|nous|ly,** *adv.*

a|cro|le|in (ə krō′lē in), *n.* a colorless liquid with an irritating odor, used in chemical warfare as a tear gas; acraldehyde: *Research programs have been undertaken to try to find the substance in smog that causes eye irritation. Such suspects as acrolein . . . have been squirted at volunteer martyrs to science* (Science News Letter). *Formula:* C_3H_4O [< Latin *ācer, ācris* sharp + *olēre* to smell + English *-in*]

ac|ro|lith (ak′rə lith), *n.* an ancient Greek statue with a stone or marble head, legs, and arms, but a wooden body. [< Late Latin *acrolithus* < Greek *akrólithos,* adjective < *ákros* end + *líthos* stone]

ac|ro|lith|ic (ak′rə lith′ik), *adj.* of the nature of an acrolith; formed like an acrolith.

ac|ro|me|gal|ic (ak′rō mə gal′ik), *adj., n.* **—adj. 1** having to do with acromegaly. **2** affected with acromegaly.
—n. a person affected with acromegaly.

ac|ro|meg|a|ly (ak′rō meg′ə lē), *n.* a chronic condition in which the bones of the face, hands, and feet become progressively and permanently enlarged, caused by abnormal activity of the pituitary gland. [< French *acromégalie* < Greek *ákros* end + *mégas, -álou* big]

a|cro|mi|al (ə krō′mē əl), *adj.* of or having to do with the acromion.

a|cro|mi|on (ə krō′mē ən), *n.* the outer, triangular end of the scapula, to which the collarbone is connected and which forms the point of the shoulder. [< Greek *akrṓmion* < *ákros* end, tip + *ômos* shoulder]

ac|ro|nym (ak′rə nim), *n., v.* **—n.** a word formed from the first letters or syllables of other words, such as UNESCO (from *U*nited *N*ations *E*ducational, *S*cientific, and *C*ultural *O*rganization).
—v.t. to make an acronym of; designate by an acronym: *Missiles are frequently acronymed; the TOW stands for "tube-launched, optically traced, wire-guided"* (New York Times Magazine). [< Greek *ákros* tip, end + (dialectal) *ónyma* name]
►See **initialism** for usage note.

ac|ro|nym|ic (ak′rə nim′ik), *adj.* **1** of an acronym or acronyms. **2** formed as an acronym. **—ac′ro-nym′i|cal|ly,** *adv.*

a|cron|y|mous (ə kron′ə məs), *adj.* = acronymic.

a|crop|e|tal (ə krop′ə təl), *adj.* developing from below toward the top or apex (used of the order in which the parts of a plant develop). [< Greek *ákros* tip + Latin *petere* seek + English *-al*[1]] **—a|crop′e|tal|ly,** *adv.*

ac|ro|phobe (ak′rə fōb), *n.* a person affected with acrophobia.

ac|ro|pho|bi|a (ak′rə fō′bē ə), *n.* an abnormal fear of being in high places. [< Greek *ákros* tip, summit + English *-phobia*]

a|croph|o|ny (ə krof′ə nē), *n.* the use of a picture of some object to represent the initial sound, letter, or syllable in the name of that object. Using the picture of an ox, called *aleph* in Phoenician, to represent the sound *a,* is an example of acrophony. [< Greek *ákros* tip, extremity + *phōnḗ* sound]

a|crop|o|lis (ə krop′ə lis), *n.* the high, fortified part or citadel of an ancient Greek city.
the Acropolis, the citadel of Athens on which the Parthenon was built. [< Greek *akrópolis* < *ákros* highest part (of) + *pólis* city]

ac|ro|pol|i|tan (ak′rə pol′ə tən), *adj.* of or having to do with an acropolis.

ac|ro|sin (ak′rə sən), *n.* a spermatic enzyme that digests the protein protective layer around the ovum.

ac|ro|som|al (ak′rə sō′məl), *adj.* of an acrosome.

ac|ro|some (ak′rə sōm), *n.* a minute organ or structure at the front end of a sperm cell. [< Greek *ákros* tip, end + *sôma* body]

ac|ro|spire (ak′rə spīr), *n. Botany.* the first sprout appearing in the germination of grain. [< Greek *ákros* tip, end + *speîra* a coil]

ac|ro|spore (ak′rə spôr, -spōr), *n. Botany.* a spore at the end of a sporophore, as in fungi. [< Greek *ákros* tip, end + *sporá* seed]

a|cross (ə krôs′, -kros′), *prep., adv.* **—prep. 1** from one side to the other of; to the other side of; over: *The cat walked across the street. A bridge was laid across the river.* **2** on the other side of; beyond: *lands across the sea. The woods are across the river.*
—adv. 1 from one side to the other: *What is the distance across? The pool is twenty feet across.* **2** to, on, or at the other side: *At this speed we shall soon be across.* **3** from side to side; crossed; crosswise: *with arms across.*
across the country. See under **country**.
come (or **run**) **across,** to meet or fall in with; find: *We come across hard words in some books. I ran across an old friend yesterday.*
get across (to). See under **get**.
get (or **put**) **across.** See under **get** and **put**.
[< *a-*[1] in, on + *cross*]

a|cross-the-board (ə krôs′ᴛʜə bôrd′, -kros′-; -bōrd′), *adj., adv. U.S.* applying to all members of an industry, union, or other group; general: *Look for an across-the-board cut in civilian payrolls* (Wall Street Journal).

a|cros|tic (ə krôs′tik, -kros′-), *n., adj.* **—n. 1** a composition in verse or an arrangement of words in which the first, last, or certain other letters in each line, taken in order, spell a word or phrase. **2** an acronym. **3** a puzzle to be solved by discovering acrostics from clues. **—adj.** of or like an acrostic. [< Late Latin *achrostichis* < Greek *akrostichis* < *ákros* end (of) + *stíchos* row, line] **—a|cros′ti|cal|ly,** *adv.*

a|cros|ti|cal (ə krôs′tə kəl, -kros′-), *adj.* = acrostic.

ac|ro|te|ri|on (ak′rə tir′ē ən), *n., pl.* **-te|ri|a** (-tir′ē ə). = acroterium.

ac|ro|te|ri|um (ak′rə tir′ē əm), *n., pl.* **-te|ri|a** (-tir′ē ə). **1a** one of the angles of a pediment. **b** an ornament erected on it. **2** a statue or ornament erected on a gable of a building. **3** the ornamented tip of the prow on a galley. [< Latin *acrōtērium* < Greek *akrōtḗrion* summit < *ákros* tip, end]

ac|ro|tism (ak′rə tiz əm), *n.* absence or weakness of the pulse. [< *a-*[4] without + Greek *krótos* a sound of striking + English *-ism*]

ac|ryl|am|ide (ak′rə lam′īd, -id; ə kril′ə mīd, -mid), *n.* the amide of acrylic acid, a colorless, crystalline substance used in making synthetics, plastics, and adhesives. *Formula:* C_3H_5NO

ac|ry|late (ak′rə lāt), *n.* a salt or ester of acrylic acid.

acrylate resin, = acrylic resin.

a|cryl|ic (ə kril′ik), *adj., n.* **—adj. 1** having to do with or containing acrylic acid. **2** derived from

acrylonitrile. **3** of or having to do with acrylics: *acrylic colors, acrylic paintings.*
—*n.* **1** an acrylic resin. **2a** a paint or varnish using an acrylic resin as the medium. **b** a painting done with acrylics: ... *a $2,500 Gordon Smith acrylic* (Maclean's). **3** an acrylic fiber. [< *acr*(olein) + *-yl* + *-ic*]

acrylic acid, a colorless, pungent liquid, soluble in water and alcohol, used in the manufacture of various plastics. *Formula:* $C_3H_4O_2$

acrylic fiber, any of various synthetic textile fibers produced from acrylonitrile. Acrilan, Dynel, and Orlon are acrylic fibers.

acrylic resin, any one of a group of tough, crystal-clear plastics, highly resistant to sunlight and weather, now widely used in automobile accessories, instrument panels, dental plates, and, in emulsion form, as a varnish, paint, or adhesive. They are produced synthetically by polymerizing the esters of acrylic acid or one of its derivatives.

ac|ry|lo|ni|trile (ak′rə lō nī′trəl, -trīl, -trēl; ə kril′-ō nī′-), *n.* a colorless, inflammable, poisonous liquid used in making Buna N synthetic rubber and plastics, and as the basic ingredient of acrylic fiber. *Formula:* CH_2:CH•CN [< *acryl*(ic) + *nitrile*]

A.C.S., antireticular cytotoxic serum, obtained from rabbits' blood injected with spleen and rib marrow of guinea pigs, a substance which may increase the activity and growth of the liver, spleen, and certain other tissues.

A.C.S.R. or **ACSR** (no periods), aluminum cable, steel reinforced (used of transmission lines).

act (akt), *n., v.* —*n.* **1** something done; a doing or performance; a deed: *an act of kindness. Slapping his face was a childish act.* **2** process of doing; action: *The farmer caught the boys in the act of stealing his apples.* **3a** one of the main divisions of a play or opera: *Most modern plays have three acts.* **b** one of several short performances on a program, such as a variety or television show: *We stayed to see the trained dog's act.* **4** the decision of a legislature; law; statute. An act of Congress is a bill that has been passed by Congress. SYN: decree. **5** *Informal, Figurative.* a display of affected or pretended behavior: *She's not angry; she's just putting on an act.* [< Latin *āctus, -ūs* a doing, and *āctum* (thing) done, both < *agere* do]
—*v.i.* **1** to do something: *At the alarm, the firemen acted promptly and saved the burning house. Act, act in the living present* (Longfellow). **2** to have effect: *The medicine acted like magic.* **3** to behave: *The boy acted badly in school. She acts as if she were tired.* **4a** to perform on the stage, in motion pictures, on television, or over the radio; play a part: *He acts very well.* **b** (of a play or role) to be capable of being performed. **5** *Figurative.* to pretend: *Her anger is not genuine; she is acting.* SYN: feign. —*v.t.* **1** to behave like: *Most people act the fool now and then.* **2** *Figurative.* to perform or play the part of (a character) on the stage, in motion pictures, on television, or over the radio; play (a role): *to act Macbeth. The handsome man acts the part of the hero.* SYN: enact. **3** *Obsolete.* to animate.
act as, to carry out the functions of: *to act as chaplain.*
act for, to take the place of; do the work of; act in behalf of: *While the principal was gone, the assistant principal acted for him.*
act on, a to follow; obey: *to act on the principle of the golden rule. I will act on your suggestion.* **b** to have an effect or influence on: *Yeast acts on dough and makes it rise.*
act out, a to portray as an actor: *to act out the heroine's part in detail.* **b** to express (unconscious or repressed feelings, fantasies, or frustrations) by one's actions or behavior: *To observe that children act out the secret wishes of their parents is true enough parlor psychology* (New York Times).
act up, *Informal.* **a** to behave badly: *The spoiled girl acted up whenever company came.* **b** to play tricks; make mischief: *Children often act up on Halloween.* [*The*] *five-year-old had been acting up ... and driving her father up the wall* (Maclean's).
act upon, a to be influenced by and follow: *By acting upon his teacher's advice on how to study, he improved his grades considerably.* **b** to have an effect or influence on: *One sphere will act upon another with a force directly proportional to their quantities of matter* (David Brewster).
get into (or **in on**) **the act**, *Informal.* to join in or take part in an activity, especially in something expedient or fashionable: *As soon as Ping-Pong became fashionable everybody stopped snickering and tried to get in on the act.*
get one's act together, *U.S. Informal.* to get organized; eliminate differences, inconsistencies, and the like: *There I was, ... weeping, feeling like a miserable, self-indulgent, neurotic, middle-aged woman who couldn't get her act together* (Eleanor Coppola).
[< Latin *āctus,* past participle of *agere* do; the development of the English verb *act* has been influenced by the noun *act*]
— *Syn. n.* **1 Act, action** mean a thing done. **Act** applies especially to a single thing done by a single effort in an instant: *It was the act of a moment to plunge into the river and seize the drowning child.* **Action** may apply to more than one act and therefore often suggests continued or repeated effort over a period of time: *The action of the locomotive's pistons was smooth and powerful.*
► In most of its senses **act** in both the United States and Great Britain is modified by adverbs: *He acted badly.* In the sense of "behave," however, *act* is often a linking verb and is followed by a predicate adjective: *He acts wise. Her little boy acts older than he really is.* The former of these examples is perfectly acceptable in American and Canadian use, but nonstandard in British use.

ac|ta (ak′tə), *n.pl.* acts; deeds; proceedings; records. [< Latin *ācta,* plural of *āctum* act]

act|a|bil|i|ty (ak′tə bil′ə tē), *n.* actable quality or condition.

act|a|ble (ak′tə bəl), *adj.* **1** that can be acted (on the stage). **2** that can be done.

Ac|tae|on (ak tē′ən), *n. Greek Mythology.* the hunter who saw Artemis (Diana) bathing. In anger she changed him into a stag, and his own dogs tore him to pieces.

ACT battery, a group of tests similar to the College Boards given to a student applying for admission to a college, covering different fields of knowledge, and also a profile covering the achievements, goals, and special interests of the student.

act-drop (akt′drop′), *n.* (in a theater) a curtain which is lowered between acts.

acte gra|tuit (ákt grä twē′), *French.* an act performed without reason or cause; a gratuitous act: *The hero ... behaves like a personification of Gide's acte gratuit* (*"an action motivated by nothing ... born of itself"*) (Time).

A|C|T|H (ā′sē′tē′āch′), *n.* **1** adrenocorticotropic hormone (a hormone of the pituitary gland which stimulates the cortex of the adrenal gland to produce other hormones). **2** this hormone obtained from animals, used in treating arthritis, rheumatic fever, and certain other disorders; corticotropin. [< *a*(dreno)*c*(ortico)*t*(ropic) *h*(ormone)]

Ac|ti|an (ak′tē ən, -shē-), *adj.* of or having to do with Actium, an ancient town and promontory in western Greece.

Actian games, 1 games held from remote antiquity at Actium in honor of Apollo. **2** a later series of games founded by the Roman emperor Augustus in commemoration of his naval victory near Actium over Antony and Cleopatra (September 2, 31 B.C.).

Ac|ti|di|one (ak′tə dī′ōn), *n. Trademark.* cycloheximide.

ac|tin (ak′tin), *n.* a protein component of muscle fibers that acts with another protein, myosin, in muscle contraction. Actin exists in a globular and a fibrous form. [ultimately < Latin *āctus, -ūs* motion + English *-in*]

ac|ti|nal (ak′tə nəl, ak tī′-), *adj.* **1** having to do with the side of a radiate animal which contains the mouth; oral. **2** having tentacles or rays. [< Greek *aktís, -înos* ray + English *-al*[1]] —**ac′ti|nal|ly**, *adv.*

act|ing (ak′ting), *adj., n.* —*adj.* **1** temporarily taking another's place and doing his duties; substitute: *While the governor was sick, the lieutenant governor was acting governor.* **2** specially prepared for actors' use (provided with full stage directions, etc.): *the acting copy of a play.*
—*n.* the occupation of an actor or actress; the art or fact of playing a part on the stage, in motion pictures, on television, or over the radio.

ac|tin|i|a (ak tin′ē ə), *n., pl.* **-i|ae** (-ē ē), **-i|as.** = sea anemone. [< New Latin *Actinia* < Greek *aktís, -înos* ray]

ac|tin|i|an (ak tin′ē ən), *adj., n.* —*adj.* **1** of a sea anemone. **2** like a sea anemone.
—*n.* = sea anemone.

ac|tin|ic (ak tin′ik), *adj.* **1** producing chemical changes by radiation. **2** of actinism. —**ac|tin′i|cal|ly**, *adv.*

actinic rays, rays of radiant energy, especially from the sun, that produce chemical change. Actinic rays are important in photography. They include green, blue, violet, and ultraviolet rays, X rays, gamma rays, and infrared radiation.

ac|ti|nide (ak′tə nīd), *n.* one of the actinides (series of heavy, radioactive metallic elements with atomic numbers 89 or 90 through 103).

ac|ti|nides (ak′tə nīdz), *n.pl.* the series of chemical elements extending from actinium (atomic number 89) or thorium (atomic number 90) to lawrencium (atomic number 103); actinium, thorium, protactinium, uranium, neptunium, plutonium, americium, curium, berkelium, californium, einsteinium, fermium, mendelevium, nobelium, and lawrencium. The properties of these elements differ only slightly with increasing atomic number.

actinide series, the actinides.

ac|tin|i|form (ak tin′ə fôrm), *adj. Zoology.* having a radiated form, as the sea anemone does.

ac|tin|ism (ak′tə niz əm), *n. Especially U.S.* that action or property in radiant energy which produces chemical changes, for example in photography.

***ac|tin|i|um** (ak tin′ē əm), *n.* a radioactive, metallic chemical element somewhat like radium, found in pitchblende after uranium has been extracted or obtained from radium by bombardment with neutrons. [< New Latin *actinium* < Greek *aktís, -înos* ray of light + New Latin *-ium*]

***actinium**

symbol	atomic number	mass number	oxidation state
Ac	89	227	3

actinium emanation, = actinon.

actinium K, the name originally given to element number 87 by its discoverer, who changed it to *francium* in 1947.

actinium series, the series of isotopes produced by radioactive decay of actinium.

ac|ti|no|bac|il|lo|sis (ak′tə nō bas′ə lō′sis), *n.* a disease of domestic animals, especially cattle, similar to actinomycosis. [< New Latin *Actinobacillus* the bacterium causing it]

ac|tin|o|gram (ak tin′ə gram), *n.* a record made by an actinograph.

ac|tin|o|graph (ak tin′ə graf, -gräf), *n.* a recording actinometer. [< Greek *aktís, -înos* ray of light + English *-graph*]

ac|ti|no|graph|ic (ak′tə nə graf′ik), *adj.* of or measured by an actinograph.

ac|ti|nog|ra|phy (ak tə nog′rə fē), *n.* the recording of intensities of radiant energy by means of an actinograph.

ac|ti|noid (ak′tə noid), *adj.* having the form of rays; radiated. A starfish is actinoid. [< Greek *aktís, -înos* ray + English *-oid*]

ac|tin|o|lite (ak tin′ə līt), *n.* a green variety of amphibole containing iron, usually occurring in needle-shaped crystals. [< Greek *aktís, -înos* ray + English *-lite*]

ac|ti|nol|o|gy (ak′tə nol′ə jē), *n.* the branch of physics dealing with the chemical action of light. [< Greek *aktís, -înos* ray of light + English *-logy*]

ac|ti|nom|e|ter (ak′tə nom′ə tər), *n.* **1** an instrument for measuring the degree of actinic action in radiant energy. **2** *Photography.* an exposure meter; a light meter. [< Greek *aktís, -înos* ray of light + English *-meter*]

ac|ti|no|met|ric (ak′tə nə met′rik), *adj.* of or having to do with actinometry.

ac|ti|no|met|ri|cal (ak′tə nə met′rə kəl), *adj.* = actinometric.

ac|ti|nom|e|try (ak′tə nom′ə trē), *n.* the measurement of intensities of radiant energy.

ac|ti|no|mor|phic (ak′tə nə môr′fik), *adj.* having radial symmetry; radiosymmetrical. [< Greek *aktís, -înos* ray + *morphḗ* form + English *-ic*]

ac|ti|no|mor|phous (ak′tə nə môr′fəs), *adj.* = actinomorphic.

ac|ti|no|my|ces (ak′tə nə mī′sēz), *n.* = actinomycete.

ac|ti|no|my|cete (ak′tə nə mī′sēt), *n.* any one of a group of bacteria found in soil that are structurally similar to certain fungi. Antibiotics such as streptomycin and chloramphenicol are derived from some actinomycetes. [< Greek *aktís, -înos* ray + *mýkēs, -ētos* fungus]

ac|ti|no|my|cin (ak′tə nə mī′sin), *n.* an antibiotic related to streptomycin, developed from actinomycetes.

ac|ti|no|my|co|sis (ak′tə nə mī kō′sis), *n.* a chronic infectious disease of cattle, sheep, hogs, and sometimes man, caused by a parasitic actinomycete; lumpy jaw. It is characterized by the formation of lumpy abscesses about the jaw and tongue.

ac|ti|no|my|cot|ic (ak′tə nə mī kot′ik), *adj.* **1** of an actinomycete. **2** caused by actinomycosis.

ac|ti|non (ak′tə non), *n.* an isotope of radon, formed by the decay of actinium; actinium emanation. [< *actinium*]

ac|tin|o|phage (ak tin′ə fāj), *n.* a bacteriophage that attacks actinomycetes. [< Greek *aktís, -înos* ray + *phageîn* eat]

Pronunciation Key: hat, āge, cãre, fär; let, ēqual, tėrm; it, īce; hot, ōpen, ôrder; oil, out; cup, pu̇t, rüle; child; long; thin; ᴛʜen; zh, measure; ə represents a in about, e in taken, i in pencil, o in lemon, u in circus.

ac|ti|nost (ak′tə nost), *n.* one of the bones in a fish immediately supporting the rays of the pectoral and ventral fins. [< Greek *aktís, -înos* ray + *ostéon* bone]

ac|ti|no|ther|a|py (ak′tə nə ther′ə pē), *n.* the treatment of disease with actinic rays, such as ultraviolet rays, X rays, and radium.

ac|ti|no|zo|an (ak′tə nə zō′ən), *n., adj.* = anthozoan. [< New Latin *Actinozoa* the class name < Greek *aktís, -înos* ray + *zôia,* plural of *zôion* animal]

ac|ti|no|zo|on (ak′tə nə zō′ən, -on), *n., pl.* **-zo|a** (-zō′ə). = anthozoan.

ac|tion (ak′shən), *n.* **1** doing something; the process of acting: *The quick action of the firemen saved the building from being burned down.* **2** physical activity: *A soldier is a man of action.* **3** something done; act: *Giving the dog food was a kind action.* SYN: See syn. under **act**. **4** the effect or influence of one thing on another: *The action of wind on the ship's sails moved the ship over the water.* **5** way of moving or working; mode of acting: *A child can push our lawn mower, because it has such an easy action.* **6** the working parts of a gun, machine, motor, or instrument; mechanism by which something is operated: *The keys of a piano are part of its action.* **7a** combat between military forces; battle; fighting: *My uncle was wounded in action in Vietnam.* SYN: See syn. under **battle**[1]. **b** a part of a battle; a minor battle; a fight: *We fought a brief holding action until the main army escaped.* SYN: See syn. under **battle**[1]. **8** a series of events in a story, play, narrative poem, or the like: *The action of "Hamlet" ends with a funeral procession.* **9** a legal proceeding by one party against another to enforce a right or punish a wrong; lawsuit: *Of 79 underworld personalities . . . seven have left the country; actions against 36 others were tied up in the courts* (Newsweek). **10** appearance of movement: *a photograph filled with action.* **11** lively events: *"Tom Sawyer" is a story packed with action.* **12** *U.S. Slang.* **a** wagers or the money wagered; betting: *His [the bookmaker's] action . . . may not reflect the action of the track* (Atlantic). **b** profits from any business or enterprise: *What most of the militants are asking for is not separation but to be included in, to have a share of the wealth and a piece of the action* (Richard M. Nixon). **c** a place or condition of lively activity, excitement, etc.: *to go where the action is.*

actions, conduct or behavior: *My mother punished me for my rude actions. Actions speak louder than words.*

bring action, to begin a lawsuit: *Action was brought against the newspaper for libel.*

in action, a taking part; active: *All the players stayed in action through the entire game.* **b** working: *The machine is now in action.*

out of action, not operating or working, especially because of damage; inactive: *One hand grenade put the machine gun out of action.*

see action, to take part in a battle: *The Major was on the front lines in World War II and saw action again in Korea.*

take action, a to start working: *The firemen took quick action to put out the fire.* **b** to begin a lawsuit; sue: *The man hurt in the accident has taken action to recover damages for his injury.* **c** to begin to do something: *The medicine will not take action for several hours.*

[< Old French *action,* learned borrowing from Latin *āctiō, -ōnis* < *agere* do] —**ac′tion|less,** *adj.*

ac|tion|a|bil|i|ty (ak′shə nə bil′ə tē), *n.* the state or condition of being actionable; liability to legal action.

ac|tion|a|ble (ak′shə nə bəl), *adj.* giving cause for a lawsuit; justifying a lawsuit: *Wrongful interference was actionable* (London Times). —**ac′tion|a|bly,** *adv.*

ac|tion|al (ak′shə nəl), *adj.* of or having to do with an action or actions.

action current, a change of electric potential in the movement of nerve impulses along the fibers of a sensory or motor nerve.

ac|tion|ist (ak′shə nist), *n.* a person who favors taking immediate action, as in politics: *He is a pragmatic man and not a theorist; an actionist and not a philosophic thinker* (Harper's).

action level, the level of concentration at which a toxic or other unwanted substance in a food or other product is considered hazardous enough to public health to warrant government action: *In Washington, a spokesman for the Food and Drug Administration said that last May the agency established an "action level" of 0.1 part per million for Mirex in fish. Fish containing that level or more will be seized if shipped in interstate commerce* (New York Times).

action painter, an artist who uses or favors action painting; tachiste.

action painting, a style of painting associated with abstract expressionism, in which colors are splashed or daubed on the canvas, allowing impulse rather than conscious effort to control the form and content of the picture; tachisme.

action potential, a difference of electric potential on the surface of a cell, nerve fiber, or muscle fiber resulting from stimulation and associated with the transmission of a nerve impulse.

action spectrum, a chart of the varying intensity of a photochemical or other reaction to light of different wave lengths.

ac|ti|vate (ak′tə vāt), *v.t.,* **-vat|ed, -vat|ing. 1** to make active; cause to act: *The storm of recent protests . . . has also activated many persons in positions of government* (Listener). SYN: impel, motivate, prompt. **2** *Physics.* to make radioactive. **3** *Chemistry.* to make capable of reacting or of speeding up a reaction. **4** to purify (sewage) by treating it with air and bacteria. **5** to make (charcoal, carbon, etc.) capable of absorbing impurities, especially in the form of gases. **6** *U.S.* to make (a military unit) active by assigning personnel and equipment to it and issuing orders for duty to it: *The division has been activated and is approaching combat condition.* —**ac′ti|va′tion,** *n.* —**ac′ti|va′tor,** *n.*

ac|ti|vat|ed alumina (ak′tə vā′tid), a partially calcined form of aluminum oxide, used as a dehydrating and adsorbing agent.

activation analysis, a method of identifying minute amounts of an element by analyzing the radiation given off when a substance containing the element has been bombarded with nuclear particles, especially neutrons.

activation energy, the additional energy needed in an atomic system for a particular process to occur, as for a molecule to enter into a chemical reaction.

ac|tive (ak′tiv), *adj., n.* —*adj.* **1** showing much action; moving or capable of moving rather quickly much of the time; lively: *as active as a kitten. Most children are more active than grown people.* SYN: quick, agile. **2** showing much or constant action; brisk: *an active market.* SYN: vigorous, energetic, bustling. **3** acting; working: *An active volcano may erupt at any time.* SYN: operative. **4** working hard or with energy; busy and energetic; effective: *still active in public affairs at 70. He took an active part in organizing the stamp club.* SYN: diligent. **5** in action, operation, or use: *an active account.* **6** causing action or change. **7** radioactive. **8** *Grammar.* showing the subject of the verb as acting. In "He broke the window," *broke* is in the active voice.

—*n.* **1a** the active voice. **b** a verb form in the active voice. **2** a person or thing that is active: *. . . a determined bloc of Communist "actives" and leaders* (Newsweek).

[< Latin *āctīvus* < *agere* do] —**ac′tive|ly,** *adv.* —**ac′tive|ness,** *n.*

active duty, 1 *U.S.* military service with full pay and regular duties. **2** active service.

active immunity, immunity from a disease due to the production of antibodies by the organism.

active list, a list of officers who are performing, or are immediately available for, military or naval service, at full pay.

active mass, the molecular concentration of the substances involved in a chemical reaction, expressed in terms of mols (gram molecules) per liter.

active repeater, = active satellite.

active satellite, a communications satellite designed to receive, amplify, and retransmit microwave signals of television, radio, or telephone, sent to a distant part of the world: *The Telstar was the first of the active satellites.*

active service, 1 military service in face of the enemy in time of war. **2** active duty.

active site, the part of an enzyme where reactions are catalyzed.

active transport, the moving of fluid through a cell membrane from a less to a more concentrated solution; osmosis.

active voice, *Grammar.* the form of the verb that shows that its subject is performing the action which the verb expresses. In "I wrote a letter," *wrote* is in the active voice. In "A letter was written by me," *was written* is in the passive voice.

ac|tiv|ism (ak′tə viz əm), *n.* **1** the policy or practice of furthering one's political or national interests by every available means, including violence or warfare. **2** the policy or practice of doing things with decision and energy and emphasizing activity. **3** a philosophical theory that assumes the objective reality and active existence of everything.

ac|tiv|ist (ak′tə vist), *n., adj.* —*n.* a person who practices or supports activism: *political activists.* —*adj.* **1** of activism. **2** of or having to do with activists: *activist groups.*

ac|tiv|is|tic (ak′tə vis′tik), *adj.* = activist: *. . . the positive and activistic mysticism of the West* (Evelyn Underhill).

ac|tiv|i|ty (ak tiv′ə tē), *n., pl.* **-ties. 1** the condition of being active; use of power; movement: *mental activity. Children engage in more physical activity than old people.* SYN: exercise. **2** an action; doing: *The activities of enemy spies may be dangerous to our country.* SYN: act, deed. **3** vigorous action; liveliness: *no activity in the market. The activity of the children disturbed the sleeping man.* SYN: bustle, commotion. **4** Often, **activities.** a thing to do; pursuit: *My favorite outdoor activity is playing football. A student who has too many outside activities may find it hard to keep up with his studies.* SYN: occupation. **5** anything active; an active force: *The study of the activities of the living being is called its physiology* (Thomas Huxley). **6** radioactivity.

activity series, = electromotive series.

ac|ti|vize (ak′tə vīz), *v.t.,* **-vized, -viz|ing.** to make active; activate.

act of faith, an act showing or requiring faith.

act of God, a sudden, usually unforeseeable and uncontrollable, natural event. Floods, storms, and earthquakes are called acts of God.

act of war, an act of armed aggression by a nation without a formal declaration of war.

ac|to|my|o|sin (ak′tə mī′ə sin), *n.* a substance consisting of the proteins actin and myosin, found in muscle cells and thought to be the means by which muscles contract and relax.

ac|ton (ak′tən), *n.* **1** a quilted jacket worn in ancient times under mail. **2** a jacket plated with metal. [< Old French *auqueton* < Spanish *alcoton* < Arabic *al-quṭn* the cotton]

ac|tor (ak′tər), *n.* **1** a person who acts on the stage, in motion pictures, on television, or over the radio. **2** a person who does something; doer. [< Latin *āctor* < *agere* do]

ac|tor|ish (ak′tər ish), *adj.* **1** of an actor. **2** like an actor. **3** mannered or unconvincing: *The characters are so actorish . . . that they come to seem phony* (Time).

ac|tor|y (ak′tər ē), *adj.* characterized by theatrical ability, style, or manner: *He's [Rex Harrison] an actory actor, the least frivolous actor I've ever worked with* (Moss Hart).

ac|tress (ak′tris), *n.* a woman or girl actor.

ac|tress|y (ak′trə sē), *adj.* **1** of an actress. **2** like an actress: *Although actressy in many ways, she lacked the old trouper's temperament* (New Yorker). **3** mannered; unconvincing.

Acts (akts), *n.pl.* (*singular in use*). In full, **The Acts of the Apostles.** the fifth book of the New Testament. Acts tells about the beginnings of the Christian Church.

ACTU (no periods), Australian Council of Trade Unions.

ac|tu|al (ak′chü əl), *adj., n.* —*adj.* **1** existing as a fact; real: *What he told us was not a dream but an actual happening.* SYN: true, genuine. See syn. under **real**[1]. **2** now existing; present: *the actual (not the past or future) state of affairs today.* SYN: current. **3** *Obsolete.* active; practical.

—*n. Informal.* a documentary film or broadcast.

[< Old French *actuel,* learned borrowing from Late Latin *āctuālis* practical < Latin *āctus, -ūs* a doing < *agere* do] —**ac′tu|al|ness,** *n.*

actual grace, *Theology.* divine grace establishing in man the ability to perform good acts and avoid evil.

ac|tu|al|ist (ak′chü ə list), *n.* a realist.

ac|tu|a|li|té (àk tʏ à lē tā′), *n. French.* topical or current interest.

actualités, current events; news: *Everything is grist to fashion's mill: art exhibitions, films, plays, and what the French call actualités—things that are happening* (Sunday Times).

ac|tu|al|i|ty (ak′chü al′ə tē), *n., pl.* **-ties. 1** an actual thing; fact: *A trip to the moon is now an actuality. To look at the actualities of the present and take measure of what is best to be done for the future* (George Grote). **2** actual existence; reality: *To sacrifice a truth of actuality to a truth of feeling* (John Ruskin). **3a** a documentary film or broadcast: *Questions about the fairness of interpretation are most likely to arise in connection with what we call "actualities," and most people call "documentaries"* (Harper's). **b** a film, broadcast, or other record that is made while something is happening: *Wartime actuality shots are . . . convincingly integrated* (Punch).

ac|tu|al|ize (ak′chü ə līz, -chə līz), *v.t.,* **-ized, -iz|ing.** to make (a plan or idea) actual; convert into action or a fact. —**ac′tu|al|i|za′tion,** *n.*

ac|tu|al|ly (ak′chü ə lē, -chə lē), *adv.* in fact; really; truly: *Are you actually going to camp this summer or just wishing to go? Gray is actually a mixture of black and white.*

actual sin, *Theology.* a sin committed by an individual of his own will, in contrast with original sin.

ac|tu|ar|i|al (ak′chü ãr′ē əl), *adj.* **1** of actuaries or their work. **2** determined by actuaries: *I produced . . . actuarial tables showing that women are su-*

perior physically (Lorraine Hopkins). —**ac′tu|ar′i|al|ly**, *adv.*

ac|tu|ar|y (ak′chů er′ē), *n., pl.* **-ar|ies.** a person whose work is estimating risks, rates, premiums, and other factors, for insurance companies. The probabilities in their calculations are generally based on recorded statistics of previous occurrences. [< Latin *āctuārius* copyist, account keeper < *āctus, -ūs* public business < *agere* do]

ac|tu|ate (ak′chů āt), *v.t.,* **-at|ed, -at|ing. 1** to put into motion; cause to move; move: *The pump is actuated by a belt driven by an electric motor.* **SYN:** activate. **2** to influence to act; impel: *Kindness actuated him to help the old woman with the heavy bundle.* **SYN:** motivate, prompt. [< Medieval Latin *actuare* (with English *-ate*[1]) < Latin *āctus, -ūs* an act < *agere* do] —**ac′tu|a′|tion**, *n.* —**ac′tu|a′tor, ac′tu|at′er**, *n.*

ac|u|ate (ak′yů it, -āt), *adj.* needle-shaped; sharp-pointed. [< New Latin *acuatus* < Latin *acus, -ūs* needle]

a|cu|i|ty (ə kyü′ə tē), *n.* sharpness; acuteness: *acuity of vision, acuity of wit.* **SYN:** keenness, intensity. [< Medieval Latin *acuitas* < Old French *agüete* < *agu* sharp < Latin *acūtus*]

a|cu|le|a (ə kyü′lē ə), *n., pl.* **-le|ae** (-lē ē). a minute spine on the wing membrane of certain moths. [< New Latin *aculea* < Latin *acūleus* thorn, sting]

a|cu|le|ate (ə kyü′lē it, -āt), *adj.* **1a** having sharp prickles (aculei) growing from the bark; prickly. **b** having minute spines (aculeae) on the wing membranes, as some moths do. **2** equipped with a sting, as a wasp or bee. **3** *Figurative.* pointed; incisive. [< Latin *acūleātus* having prickles or stings, sharp-pointed < *acūleus* thorn, sting]

a|cu|le|at|ed (ə kyü′lē ā′tid), *adj.* = aculeate.

a|cu|le|o|late (ə kyü′lē ə lit), *adj. Botany.* having small prickles. [< Latin *acūleolus* (diminutive) < *acūleus* thorn + English *-ate*[1]]

a|cu|le|us (ə kyü′lē əs), *n., pl.* **-le|i** (-lē ī). **1** a prickle growing from the bark (epidermis), as in the rose or blackberry. **2** the sting of wasps, bees, or other insects. [< Latin *acūleus* thorn]

a|cu|men (ə kyü′mən), *n.* sharpness and quickness in seeing and understanding; keen insight; mental acuteness: *astute political acumen.* **SYN:** discernment, perception. [< Latin *acūmen* point, shrewdness < *acuere* sharpen]

***a|cu|mi|nate** (*adj.* ə kyü′mə nit, -nāt; *v.* ə kyü′mə nāt), *adj., v.,* **-nat|ed, -nat|ing.** —*adj.* tapering to a point; pointed: *acuminate leaves.*
—*v.t.* to make sharp or pointed.
[< Latin *acūminātus,* past participle of *acūmināre* sharpen < *acūmen, -inis* point] —**a|cu′mi|na′tion**, *n.*

***acuminate**

acuminate leaf

a|cu|mi|nous (ə kyü′mə nəs), *adj.* acute; keen: *an acuminous display of talent.*

ac|u|pres|sure (ak′yə presh′ər), *n.* a method of relieving pain, diagnosing illness, etc., by applying pressure where major nerves are close to the skin. [< Latin *acus* needle + English *pressure*]

ac|u|punc|tur|al (ak′yə pungk′chər əl), *adj.* of or having to do with acupuncture: *acupunctural anaesthesia.*

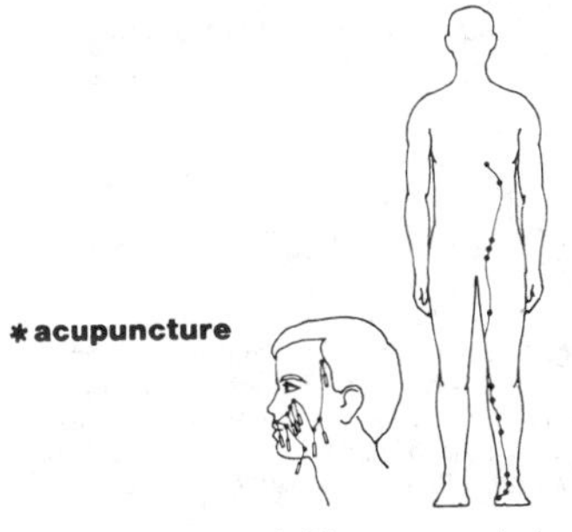

***acupuncture**

some facial puncture points

some body puncture points

***ac|u|punc|ture** (ak′yə pungk′chər), *n.* the puncture of the skin or body tissue with needles, practiced in ancient Chinese medicine and recently introduced into modern Western medicine, especially as a method of producing local anesthesia. [< Latin *acus* needle + English *puncture*]

ac|u|punc|tur|ist (ak′yə pungk′chər ist), *n.* a person who practices acupuncture.

a|cush|la (ə kůsh′lə), *n. Anglo-Irish.* darling. [< Irish *a* oh + *cuisle* pulse (of the heart)]

a|cu|tance (ə kyü′təns), *n. Photography.* the relative sharpness of an image, especially as determined by physical measurements. [< *acute*]

a|cute (ə kyüt′), *adj., n.* —*adj.* **1** acting keenly on the senses; sharp and severe: *A toothache can cause acute pain.* **SYN:** intense. **2** coming quickly to a turning point; brief and severe: *An acute disease like pneumonia reaches a crisis within a short time.* **3** threatening; critical: *The long drought caused an acute shortage of water in the city.* **SYN:** crucial. **4** *Figurative.* quick in perceiving and responding to impressions; keen; sharp: *an acute observer. Dogs have an acute sense of smell.* **5** *Figurative.* quick in discernment; having power to perceive small differences or effects; sharp-witted; shrewd: *an acute thinker.* **SYN:** clever. See syn. under **sharp. 6** high in pitch; shrill: *Some sounds are so acute that we cannot hear them.* **7** having or ending in a sharp point. **SYN:** pointed. **8** having the mark (´) over it: *É is called "e acute" or "acute e."* **9a** less than a right angle. **b** having one or more acute angles.
—*n.* an acute accent.
[< Latin *acūtus,* past participle of *acuere* sharpen] —**a|cute′ly**, *adv.* —**a|cute′ness**, *n.*

***acute accent, 1** a mark placed over a vowel letter of some languages to show the quality of its sound, as in French *abbé,* to show stress, as in Spanish *adiós,* to show vowel length, as in Hungarian *huszár,* or to show raised pitch, as in Greek *Christós.* **2** a mark used to indicate emphasis in pronunciation, as in *ac′tor* (ak′tər).

***acute accent**

definition 1
décembre, sábado

definition 2
ad min′ is tra′ tion

acute angle, an angle less than a right angle; any angle less than 90 degrees. See picture under **angle.**

a|cute-care (ə kyüt′ kãr′), *adj.* designed for the care of patients with serious diseases of relatively short duration; equipped to treat nonchronic diseases: *Citing a "drastically eroded" financial situation, the head of the city's Health and Hospitals Corporation has recommended reducing from 15 to 11 the number of acute-care municipal hospitals* (New York Times).

ACV (no periods), air cushion vehicle.

a|cy|clic (ā sī′klik, -sik′lik), *adj.* **1** not cyclic; arranged spirally rather than in circles or whorls: *acyclic flower parts.* **2** *Chemistry.* having an open-chain structure: *an acyclic compound.*

ac|yl (as′əl), *n.* = acid radical. [< *ac*(id) + *-yl*]

ac|yl|ate (as′ə lāt), *v.t.,* **-at|ed, -at|ing.** to introduce an acid radical (acyl) into (a substance). —**ac′yl|a′tion**, *n.*

ad[1] (ad), *n. Informal.* an advertisement: *. . . the breathless, exotic coquetry of the cosmetic ads* (Saturday Review).
▶**Ad** is the clipped form of *advertisement* in the United States and Canada, and is also spreading in use in Great Britain; **advert** is a form used less often in Great Britain.

ad[2] (ad), *n.* advantage (the first point won in a game of tennis after deuce).

ad-, *prefix.* **1** to; toward, as in *admit, administer, adverb, advert.* **2** at; near, as in *adjacent, adrenal.* Also: **a-** before *sc, sp, st;* **ab-** before *b;* **ac-** before *c, k, q;* **af-** before *f;* **ag-** before *g;* **al-** before *l;* **an-** before *n;* **ap-** before *p;* **ar-** before *r;* **as-** before *s;* **at-** before *t.* [< Latin *ad-* < *ad* to, toward, at]

ad., advertisement.

a.d., *Commerce.* after date.

AD (no periods), **1** adenoid-degenerating (of a type of respiratory disease). **2** Alzheimer's disease.

A/D, analogue to digital (conversion in computers).

A.D. or **AD** (no periods), since Christ was born; after the birth of Christ: *Charlemagne was crowned by the Pope in 800 A.D. From A.D. 100 to A.D. 500 is 400 years.* [for Late Latin *annō Dominī* in the year of our Lord]
▶**A.D.** might be expected to occur only with a particular year: *1376 A.D.* It has long been used, however, in the sense "after Christ," corresponding to B.C., "before Christ": *the 5th century A.D.* With a particular year, it often occurs before the figure: *A.D. 1376.*

A|da or **ADA** (ā′də), *n.* a computer language combining the codes of a variety of other computer languages. [< Augusta *Ada* Byron, 1815-1852, daughter of Lord Byron, who worked with Babbage on an early computer]

ad ab|sur|dum (ad ab sėr′dəm), *Latin.* to an absurdity: *There is a danger that the definition of privileged information may be reduced eventually ad absurdum* (London Times).

a|dac|tyl|ous (ā dak′tə ləs), *adj.* without fingers or toes, or both, usually congenitally so. [< *a-*[4] without + Greek *dáktylos* finger + English *-ous*]

ad|age (ad′ij), *n.* a wise saying that has been much used; a well-known proverb. *Examples:* A new broom sweeps clean. Haste makes waste. **SYN:** saw, maxim, aphorism, epigram. [< French *adage,* learned borrowing from Latin *adagium*]

a|da|gi|et|to (ə dä′jē et′ō, -zhē-), *n., pl.* **-tos.** *Music.* a short adagio. [< Italian *adagietto* (diminutive) < *adagio*]

a|da|gio (ə dä′jō, -zhē ō, -zhō), *adv., adj., n., pl.* **-gios.** —*adv., adj. Music.* somewhat slowly; more slowly than andante (used as a direction).
—*n.* **1** *Music.* a slow part. **2** in ballet: **a** a slow dance in which the female partner performs difficult feats of balancing. **b** the movements practiced in a ballet lesson for development of balance, line, and grace.
[< Italian *adagio* < *ad agio* at ease]

Ad|am[1] (ad′əm), *n.* the first man; father of the human race (in the Bible, Genesis 1:26-5:5).
not known (someone) **from Adam,** *Informal.* to have no acquaintance with (someone): *He called to see my Governor this morning . . . and beyond that I don't know him from Adam* (Dickens).
the old Adam, the human tendency to sin: *An impatience to shake off the old social and political Adam* (George Grote).

***Ad|am**[2] (ad′əm), *adj.* of or exemplifying a delicate, graceful style of furniture and architecture introduced by the brothers Robert and James Adam in the 1700's, that makes use of wreaths, fan ornaments, and like decoration.

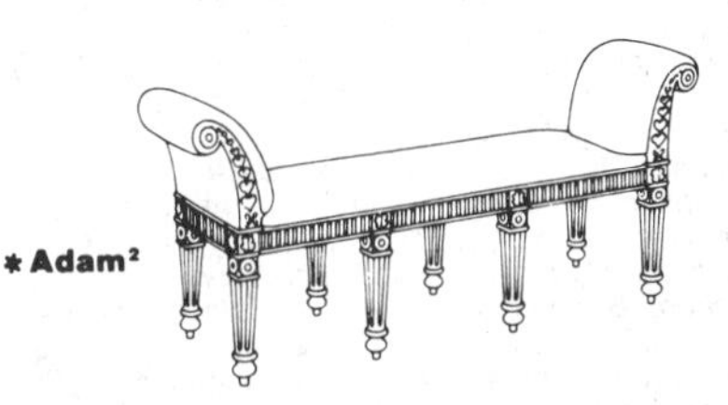

***Adam**[2]

ad|a|man|cy (ad′ə mən sē), *n.* adamant quality.

Ad|am-and-Eve (ad′əm ən ēv′), *n.* = puttyroot.

ad|a|mant (ad′ə mant, -mənt), *adj., n.* —*adj.* **1** not giving in readily; firm and unyielding; immovable: *Columbus was adamant in refusing the requests of his sailors to turn back. She was adamant; but he, too . . . showed no sign of yielding* (Lytton Strachey). **SYN:** inflexible, stubborn, obstinate. **2** too hard to be cut or broken.
—*n.* **1** any extremely hard substance; that which is impregnable to any force. **2** *Obsolete.* any of various extremely hard rocks or minerals.
[< Old French *adamaunt* the hardest stone (= diamond) < Latin *adamās, adamantis* < Greek *adámās, -antos* the hardest metal (= steel) < *a-* not + *damnánai* conquer. See etym. of doublet **diamond.**] —**ad′a|mant|ly**, *adv.*

ad|a|man|tane (ad′ə man′tān), *n.* an organic compound whose structure of carbon atoms is in the shape of a diamond. [< *adamant* + *-ane*]

ad|a|man|tine (ad′ə man′tin, -tēn, -tīn), *adj.* **1** unyielding; firm; immovable: *a risk which severely tried even the adamantine fortitude of Cromwell* (Macaulay) **2** too hard to be cut or broken. **SYN:** unbreakable, impenetrable.

Ad|am|esque (ad′ə mesk′), *adj.* of the style of Robert and James Adam. See **Adam**[2].

A|dam|ic (ə dam′ik), *adj.* **1** of or having to do with Adam. **2** like Adam. —**A|dam′i|cal|ly**, *adv.*

A|dam|i|cal (ə dam′ə kəl), *adj.* = Adamic.

ad|am|ite (ad′ə mīt), *n.* a yellow, hydrous zinc arsenate. [< a proper name + *-ite*[1]]

Ad|am|ite (ad′ə mīt), *n.* **1** a person. **2** a nudist.

Ad|am|it|ic (ad′ə mit′ik), *adj.* **1** of an Adamite. **2** like an Adamite.

Adam's ale, water.

Adam's apple, the slight lump at the front of a person's throat, formed by the thyroid cartilage of the larynx. It is normally more evident in men than in women. Its name derives from the notion that a piece of the forbidden fruit stuck in Adam's throat.

ad|ams|ite (ad′əm zīt), *n.* a yellow, irritant smoke containing a poisonous form of arsenic, that causes sneezing, headache, vomiting, and temporary disablement, used as a harassing agent in chemical warfare; DM (no period). *Formula:* $C_{12}H_9AsClN$ [< Major Roger *Adams,* born 1889, U.S. Army, the inventor + *-ite*[1]]

Ad|am's-nee|dle (ad′əmz nē′dəl), *n.* any one of

Pronunciation Key: h**a**t, **ā**ge, c**ã**re, f**ä**r; l**e**t, **ē**qual, t**ė**rm; **i**t, **ī**ce; h**o**t, **ō**pen, **ô**rder; **oi**l, **ou**t; c**u**p, p**ů**t, r**ü**le; **ch**ild; lo**ng**; **th**in; **ᴛʜ**en; **zh**, measure; **ə** represents **a** in about, **e** in taken, **i** in pencil, **o** in lemon, **u** in circus.

several yuccas, especially a northern species much grown as a garden plant.

a|dan|gle (ə dang′gəl), *adv., adj.* hanging loosely; dangling.

a|dapt (ə dapt′), *v.t.* **1** to make fit or suitable; adjust: *Cats can adapt themselves very well to indoor life. Can you adapt your way of working to the new job? But one of the striking facts of nature is the ability of living things to adapt themselves to practically any environment on earth* (Scientific American). SYN: accommodate, temper. See syn. under **adjust**. **2** to change to fit a different use: *The boys adapted the old barn for use by the club. You can adapt this vacuum cleaner for spraying insecticide. This motion picture has been adapted from a short story.* **—v.i.** to become adjusted: *The Australopithecines . . . were still in the process of adapting to erect progression* (Science).
[< Latin *adaptāre* < *ad-* to + *aptāre* join < *aptus* fitted, joined]
►**Adapt** meaning "make suitable" is followed by the preposition *to: His style is not adapted to adults. Adapt* meaning "revise" is followed by *for* or *from: The story was adapted for the movies. It was adapted from a novel by Sinclair Lewis.*

a|dapt|a|bil|i|ty (ə dap′tə bil′ə tē), *n.* the power to change easily to fit different conditions; adaptable quality: *Japanese architecture has above all the qualities of elasticity and adaptability* (Atlantic).

a|dapt|a|ble (ə dap′tə bəl), *adj.* **1** easily changed to fit different conditions: *Mother has an adaptable schedule.* SYN: flexible, pliant, malleable. **2** changing easily to fit different conditions: *She is an adaptable person.* SYN: flexible, pliant, malleable. **—a|dapt′a|ble|ness**, *n.*

ad|ap|ta|tion (ad′ap tā′shən), *n.* **1a** the act of adapting; changing to fit; adjustment (to different circumstances or conditions, usually over a period of time): *He made a good adaptation to his new school.* **b** the condition of being adapted or made to fit: *His adaptation to school away from home was painful and lonely.* **2** something made by changing to fit different conditions: *A motion picture is often an adaptation of a novel.* **3** a change in structure, form, or habits to fit different conditions: *Wings are adaptations of the front limbs for flight.* **4** adjustment of a sense organ, as the eye, to varying conditions.
►**Adaption**, possibly influenced by the unrelated *adoption,* sometimes occurs; but **adaptation** is the strongly preferred form in all senses.

ad|ap|ta|tion|al (ad′ap tā′shə nəl), *adj.* of or involving adaptation: *The modifications which insect larvae undergo may be divided into two kinds—developmental, and adaptational or adaptive; those which tend to suit them to their own mode of life* (Sir John Lubbock). **—ad′ap|ta′tion|al|ly**, *adv.*

a|dap|ta|tive (ə dap′tə tiv), *adj.* = adaptive.

a|dapt|ed (ə dap′tid), *adj.* fitted; suitable: *Florida has a climate adapted to the growing of oranges.*

a|dapt|ed|ness (ə dap′tid nis), *n.* the state of being adapted or suited; adaptation: . . . *the adaptedness of living matter to its environment* (Beals and Hoijer).

a|dapt|er or **a|dap|tor** (ə dap′tər), *n.* **1** a person or thing that adapts. **2** a device for fitting parts to each other or a machine to a different use.

a|dap|tion (ə dap′shən), *n.* = adaptation.
►See **adaptation** for usage note.

a|dap|tion|al (ə dap′shə nəl), *adj.* = adaptational.

a|dap|tive (ə dap′tiv), *adj.* **1a** of or characterized by adaptation. **b** showing adaptation. **2** serving to adapt. **3** *Biology.* enabling the organism to fit into a certain environment or situation. **—a|dap′|tive|ly**, *adv.* **—a|dap′tive|ness**, *n.*

adaptive convergence, the tendency in distantly related animals or plants to assume similar characteristics, as of form, structure, or habits, under similar conditions. The similar shape of fish and whales is the result of adaptive convergence.

adaptive radiation, the evolution of closely related organisms into strikingly different forms because of different environmental requirements. The diverse forms of bats and mice result from adaptive radiation.

a|dap|to|me|ter (ə dap′tə mē′tər, ad′ap tom′-ə-), *n.* a device for measuring the capacity of the eye to adapt to different conditions of light or distance.

A|dar (ə där′), *n.* the sixth month of the Jewish civil year, and the twelfth month of the ecclesiastical year, beginning in February or early March.
[< Hebrew *adhār*]

Adar She|ni (shā′nē), = Veadar. [< Hebrew *adhār shēnī* (literally) second Adar]

ad a|stra per a|spe|ra (ad as′trə pər as′pər ə), *Latin.* to the stars through difficulties (the motto of Kansas).

a|dat (ä′dät), *n.* (in Indonesia) a system of local customs stressing cooperation; law; custom.
[< Malayan *adat* < Arabic *adālat* equity]

ad|ax|i|al (ad ak′sē əl), *adj.* on the side nearest to the axis. [< *ad-* to + *axis*[1] + *-al*[1]]

A-day (ā′dā′), *n.* **1** = Able Day. **2** the date scheduled for the commencing or completing of anything. [American English < *A*(ble) *Day*]

a|daz|zle (ə daz′əl), *adv., adj.* dazzling; brilliant: *The sky was once again adazzle with stars* (Saturday Review).

ADC[1] (no periods), **1** Aid to Dependent Children (a program of the federal and state governments in the United States to provide financial and medical assistance to needy children and the adults taking care of them). **2** advanced developing country: *Foreign aid has contributed to the rise of a series of economically free and prosperous "ADCs," . . . including South Korea, Singapore, Taiwan, Malaysia, and Thailand* (Time).

ADC[2] (no periods) or **A.D.C.**, **1** aide-de-camp. **2** Air (or Aerospace) Defense Command (of the U.S. Air Force).

ad cap|tan|dum vul|gus (ad kap tan′dəm vul′-gəs), *Latin.* for the purpose of catching the crowd; intended to captivate the public.

add (ad), *v.t.* **1** to find the sum of (numbers or quantities): *Add 8 and 2 and you have 10.* SYN: total. **2** to say further; go on to say or write: *She said good-by and added that she had had a pleasant visit.* **3** to join (one thing to another or others); put together; put with: *Add more wood to the fire. She tasted her lemonade, then added sugar. The author added an index to his book.* SYN: append, attach.
—v.i. 1 to find the sum of numbers or quantities: *The little boy is learning to add and subtract.* **2** to make or form an addition: *The fine day added to the pleasure of the picnic.*
add in, to include: *The figures are complete—the cost of transportation must be added in.*
add up, a *Informal.* to make the correct, desired, or expected total: *The figures made her cry. They wouldn't add up, she said* (Dickens). **b** *Informal.* to make sense; fit together: *The facts just don't add up.* **c** to find the sum of (a column or series of numbers): *This computer can add up a long list of numbers in less than a minute.*
add up to, *Informal.* to amount to: *The President's commission . . . proposes a program . . . which adds up almost to a condition of permanent mobilization* (Baltimore Sun).
[< Latin *addere* < *ad-* to + *dare* put, set]

add., **1a** addenda. **b** addendum. **2** additional. **3** address.

ADD (no periods), attention deficit disorder: *ADD children reported significantly more symptoms of depression and anxiety than the comparison group* (Science News).

add|a|bil|i|ty (ad′ə bil′ə tē), *n.* = addibility.

add|a|ble (ad′ə bəl), *adj.* that can be added. Also, **addible**.

ad|dax (ad′aks), *n.* a large antelope with a heavy body, short legs, and long, loosely spiraled horns. It lives in the deserts of Arabia and North Africa.
[< Latin *addax* < an African word]

add|ed line (ad′id), *Music.* a ledger line.

add|ed-val|ue tax (ad′id val′yü), a sales tax based on the value added to goods at each sales transaction during production and on down to the retailer; value-added tax.

ad|dend (ad′end, ə dend′), *n.* a number or quantity to be added to another number or quantity. In the problem "712 + 365 = ?" 365 is the addend.
[< *addendum*]

ad|den|da (ə den′də), *n., pl. of* **addendum**. a series of appendixes to a book or additions to a document.

ad|den|dum (ə den′dəm), *n., pl.* **-da**. **1** an appendix to a book or document. **2** a thing added or to be added; addition. **3** *Machinery.* that part of a tooth which projects beyond the pitch circle or pitch line of a toothed wheel or rack. [< Latin *addendum,* neuter gerundive of *addere* add]

addendum circle, the circle described by the outer ends of the teeth of a turning gearwheel.

ad|der[1] (ad′ər), *n.* **1a** a small, poisonous snake common in Europe and the only poisonous snake in Great Britain. It belongs to the viper family. **b** any one of several other poisonous snakes of the viper family, such as the puff adder of Africa. **c** any one of several poisonous snakes in the Bible and in the Greek and Roman classics. **d** the death adder of Australia, related to the cobra. **2** any one of several small, harmless snakes of North America, such as the puff adder (hognose snake) and the milk adder (milk snake). [Old English *nǣdre*; in Middle English *a nadder* was taken as *an adder*]

add|er[2] (ad′ər), *n.* **1** a person who adds. **2** a machine for adding. **3** a device that forms the black-and-white signals transmitted on television.
[< *add* + *-er*[1]]

ad|der's-mouth (ad′ərz mouth′), *n.* **1** any one of several small North American orchids with tiny, greenish flowers. **2** any one of several other orchids, especially the snakemouth.

***ad|der's-tongue** (ad′ərz tung′), *n.* **1** a small fern with a spike springing from the base of a frond so as to suggest the mouth and tongue of a snake. **2** *U.S.* the dogtooth violet. **3** the rattlesnake plantain.

***adder's-tongue**
definitions 1, 2, 3
adder's-tongue fern | dogtooth violet | rattlesnake plantain

add|i|bil|i|ty (ad′ə bil′ə tē), *n.* capability of, or fitness for, being added.

add|i|ble (ad′ə bəl), *adj.* = addable.

ad|dict (*n.* ad′ikt; *v.* ə dikt′), *n., v.* **—n. 1** a person who is a slave to a habit: *A drug addict finds it almost impossible to stop using drugs. Doctors, penologists, and policemen disagree on how to control drug distribution and handle addicts* (Newsweek). **2** *Figurative.* a person who is deeply devoted to or a very enthusiastic follower or advocate of something: *a TV addict.*
—v.t. 1 to give (oneself) up to a habit. **2** *Figurative.* to devote (oneself) slavishly to a practice.
[< Latin *addictus,* past participle of *addīcere* give over to < *ad-* to + *dīcere* say, declare]

ad|dict|ed (ə dik′tid), *adj.* slavishly following or unable to give up a habit; strongly inclined: *Most addicted drug users need medical help.* SYN: habituated, accustomed. **—ad|dict′ed|ness**, *n.*

ad|dic|tion (ə dik′shən), *n.* the condition of being a slave to a habit; strong inclination: *Many people are helpless victims of drug addiction. . . . his monotonous addiction to a vein of rather flat-footed Marxist invective* (Edmund Wilson).

ad|dic|tive (ə dik′tiv), *adj.* causing or tending to cause addiction. **—ad|dic′tive|ness**, *n.*

add|ing machine (ad′ing), any one of several machines for calculating or computing by mechanical or electrical means. Adding machines are used to speed up bookkeeping operations.

ad|di|o (äd dē′ō), *interj. Italian.* farewell!

Ad|di|so|ni|an (ad′ə sō′nē ən), *adj.* of or like Joseph Addison or his writing.

Ad|di|son's disease (ad′ə sənz), a chronic, wasting disease of the cortex of the adrenal glands. It is characterized by low blood pressure, weakened muscles, intestinal disturbances, and a brownish discoloration of the skin. [< Thomas *Addison,* 1793-1860, a doctor who described it]

ad|dit|a|ment (ə dit′ə mənt), *n.* anything added; an addition. [< Latin *additāmentum* < *addere* add]

***ad|di|tion** (ə dish′ən), *n.* **1** the adding of one thing to another: *The addition of flour will thicken gravy.* **2** the adding of one number or quantity to another: *2 + 3 = 5 is a simple addition.* **3** anything added: *Cream is a tasty addition to many desserts.* SYN: adjunct, appendage. **4a** *U.S.* a part added to a building. **b** adjoining land added to the land one owns. **c** an area laid out as an extension of existing urban development. **5** *Law.* a title or designation added to a name to show rank, occupation, or other status, such as *Esq.* in "John Doe, Esq."
in addition (to), besides; as well as: *In addition to her work in the school, our teacher gives music lessons after school hours.*
[< Old French *addition,* learned borrowing from Latin *additiō, -ōnis* < *addere* add]

***addition**
definition 2

2 augend
+4 addend
6 sum

2 + 4 = 6 sum (augend, addend)

ad|di|tion|al (ə dish′ə nəl), *adj.* more or added; extra; supplementary: *Mother needs additional help in the kitchen when we have company for dinner. Vital additional acres are being freed for food production* (Observer). **—ad|di′tion|al|ly**, *adv.*

addition fact, a basic statement in addition, such as 2 + 3 = 5.

addition product, = additive compound.

ad|di|tive (ad′ə tiv), *n., adj.* **—n. 1** something added, such as an ingredient to keep food fresh or to improve its flavor, color, texture, or beneficial effect: *Vitamins and preservatives are some of the additives in this bread.* **2** a substance added to gasoline, fuel oil, or other combustible substance, to improve its efficiency.
—*adj.* involving addition; to be added: *an additive process.* **—ad′di|tive|ly**, *adv.*

additive compound, *Chemistry.* a compound

formed by addition, involving conversion of a double bond into a single bond.

additive inverse, either of two numbers whose sum is zero. The additive inverse of +5 is −5; the additive inverse of −5 is +5.

ad|di|tiv|i|ty (ad′ə tiv′ə tē), *n.* the condition of being additive.

ad|di|to|ry (ad′ə tôr′ē, -tōr′-), *adj.* tending to add or enlarge.

ad|dle (ad′əl), *v.*, **-dled, -dling**, *adj.* **—*v.t., v.i.*** **1** to make or become muddled or confused: *I have addled my head with writing all day* (Dickens). **2** to make or become rotten or putrid: *Eggs addle quickly in hot weather.*
—*adj.* **1** muddled or confused (now usually in compounds such as *addlebrained, addleheaded*). **2** rotten: *addle eggs.* SYN: putrid.
[Old English *adela* mud, liquid filth]

ad|dled (ad′əld), *adj.* **1** muddled; confused: *an addled brain.* **2** rotten: *addled eggs.*

ad|dle|pat|ed (ad′əl pā′tid), *adj.* muddled, confused, or stupid: ... *the incredible woolliness of thought ... in which a couple of generations of addlepated theosophist enthusiasts have enveloped the subject* (New Yorker).

add-on (ad′on′, -ôn′), *n., adj.* **—*n.*** an added sum, quantity, or item. **—*adj.*** accessory: *add-on units for heating or air conditioning.*

ad|dress (ə dres′; *also* ad′res, *especially for n. 2*), *n., v.*, **-dressed** or **-drest, -dress|ing.** **—*n.*** **1** a speech, either spoken or written, especially a formal one: *The President made an address to the nation on television.* SYN: discourse, lecture. See syn. under **speech. 2a** the place to which one's mail is directed; place of residence or of business: *Write your name and address on this envelope.* **b** the writing on an envelope, package, or the like, that shows where and to whom it is to be sent. **3** a symbol identifying the area in which certain information is stored in the core of an electronic computer. **4** manner of speaking to another: *A salesman should be a man of pleasant address. His address, I perceived, was abrupt, unceremonious* (Thomas Carlyle). SYN: bearing. **5** skillful management; adroitness: *A good manager solves problems with speed and address. His ready address to extricate himself both in action and discourse; for no man ever resolved quicker, or spoke clearer* (Sir Francis Bacon). SYN: cleverness, tact, dexterity, facility. **6** a formal expression of views to those in authority, especially a request to do a particular thing: *an address from the colonists to the king, listing grievances.* **7** a resolution of both houses of the legislature of Canada or Australia impeaching a judge. [< French *adresse* (< Old French *adresser,* verb), and < English *address,* verb]
—*v.t.* **1** to deliver a speech to: *The President addressed the nation on the subject of war and peace.* **2** to speak or write to; direct (spoken or written words to anyone): *He addressed me as though we were old friends.* **3** to use titles or other set forms in speaking or writing to: *The king was addressed as "Your Majesty."* **4** to write on (an envelope or package) to whom and where it is to be sent: *Please address this letter to Alaska.* **5** to direct to the attention: *to address a warning to a friend. Let us address a petition to the Governor.* **6** to apply (oneself) in speech (to a person): *He addressed himself to the chairman.* **7** to speak directly to: *Address the chair!* **8** to apply or devote (oneself); direct one's energies: *He addressed himself to the task of learning French.* **9** to prepare for a stroke in golf by placing the head of a club behind (the ball). **10** *Commerce.* to consign or entrust to the care of another, as agent or factor. **11** to provide or gain access to (the location of stored information) in a computer: *The hardware is amazingly cheap—and the size of control task is limited only by the amount of memory which can be addressed* (*a 10 bit address handles 1024 program steps*) (New Scientist). **12** *Archaic.* to woo; court. **13** *Obsolete.* **a** to prepare. **b** to arrange.
—*v.i.* *Obsolete.* **1** to prepare. **2** to appeal.
addresses, attentions paid in courtship: *The ... footman persecuted her with his addresses* (Thackeray).
[< Old French *adresser,* earlier *adrecier* < Vulgar Latin *addīrēctiāre* make straight < *ad-* up + *dīrēctiāre* straighten < Latin *dīrēctus* straight] **—ad|dress′er, ad|dres′sor,** *n.*

ad|dress|a|ble (ə dres′ə bəl), *adj.* accessible in the memory of a computer.

address book, a small book of pages, for listing names and addresses.

ad|dress|ee (ə dre sē′, ad′re-), *n.* the person to whom a letter, package, or the like, is addressed.

Ad|dres|so|graph (ə dres′ə graf, -gräf), *n. Trademark.* a machine for printing addresses automatically.

ad|duce (ə düs′, -dyüs′), *v.t.*, **-duced, -duc|ing.** to offer as a reason in support of an argument; give as proof or evidence; bring up as an example; cite: *The principal adduced a record of good marks and leadership to show the boy deserved a scholarship. Reasons good I shall adduce in due time to my peers* (Robert Browning). SYN: present, advance, allege, instance. [< Latin *addūcere* < *ad-* to + *dūcere* lead] **—ad|duc′er,** *n.*

ad|duce|a|ble (ə dü′sə bəl, -dyü′-), *adj.* = adducible.

ad|du|cent (ə dü′sənt, -dyü′-), *adj.* adducting: *adducent muscles.*

ad|duc|i|ble (ə dü′sə bəl, -dyü′-), *adj.* that can be adduced.

ad|duct (ə dukt′), *v.t.* to pull (a part of the body) inward toward the main axis. [< Latin *adductus,* past participle of *addūcere* bring to < *ad-* to + *dūcere* bring]

ad|duc|tion (ə duk′shən), *n.* **1** an adducing; bringing forward arguments. **2** an adducting; a pulling a part of the body inward.

ad|duc|tive (ə duk′tiv), *adj.* tending to lead toward; bringing to something else.

ad|duc|tor (ə duk′tər), *n.* a muscle that adducts, such as the muscle that moves the thumb inward against the fingers.

add-up (ad′up′), *n. U.S. Informal.* the sum total (of a discussion); gist.

a|deem (ə dēm′), *v.t. Law.* to revoke the bequest of (a legacy), especially by operation of law. [< Latin *adimere* take away < *ad-* to + *emere* buy, take]

A|dé|lie penguin (ad′ə lē, ä dā lē′), the smallest and most common of the penguins. [< the *Adélie* Coast, Antarctica]

a|del|o|mor|phic (ə del′ə môr′fik), *adj. Physiology.* having unclear or indeterminate form: *adelomorphic cells.* [< Greek *ádēlos* unseen + *morphḗ* form + English *-ic*]

a|del|phic (ə del′fik), *adj.* **1** of or having to do with brothers or sisters: *Two types of polyandry are practised in Tibet: adelphic, or fraternal, and nonfraternal* (New Scientist). **2** involving related elements. [< Greek *adelphikós* brotherly, sisterly < *adelphós* brother]

a|demp|tion (ə demp′shən), *n. Law.* the revoking of a legacy, especially because the testator, before his death, has disposed of the thing bequeathed. [< Latin *adēmptiō, -ōnis* < *adimere* take away; see etym. under **adeem**]

ad|e|nal|gi|a (ad′ə nal′jē ə), *n.* pain in a gland. [< New Latin *adenalgia* < Greek *adḗn* gland + *álgos* pain]

ad|e|nec|to|my (ad′ə nek′tə mē), *n., pl.* **-mies.** the removal of a gland by surgery.

A|den|ese (ä′dən ēz′, -ēs′; ā′-), *adj., n.* **—*adj.*** of or having to do with Aden (Southern Yemen) or its people. **—*n.*** a native or inhabitant of Aden.

Ad|e|ni (ä′dən ē), *adj., n.* = Adenese.

a|den|i|form (ə den′ə fôrm), *adj.* having a glandlike shape.

ad|e|nine (ad′ə nin, -nēn, -nīn), *n.* a substance present in nucleic acid in cells. It is one of the purine bases in both DNA and RNA. *Formula:* $C_5H_5N_5$ *Abbr:* A (no period). [< Greek *adḗn* gland + English *-ine*[2] (found originally in glands)]

ad|e|ni|tis (ad′ə nī′tis), *n.* inflammation of a gland or glands. [< Greek *adḗn* gland + English *-itis*]

ad|e|no|car|ci|no|ma (ad′ə nō kär′sə nō′mə), *n., pl.* **-mas, -ma|ta** (-mə tə). a cancer that originates in the epithelium of a gland or duct. [< Greek *adḗn, -énos* gland + English *carcinoma*]

ad|e|no|car|ci|nom|a|tous (ad′ə nō kär′sə nom′ə təs), *adj.* **1** of or like an adenocarcinoma. **2** having an adenocarcinoma.

ad|e|no|hy|poph|y|sis (ad′ə nō hī pof′ə sis, -hi-), *n., pl.* **-ses** (-sēz). the part of the pituitary gland comprising the anterior and intermediate lobes. Prolactin is one of the hormones produced by the adenohypophysis. [< Greek *adḗn, -énos* gland + *hypóphysis* outgrowth]

ad|e|noid (ad′ə noid), *adj.* **1** of or having to do with the lymphatic glands or lymphoid tissue. **2** like a gland; glandular. [< Greek *adenoeidḗs* < *adḗn, -énos* acorn, gland + *eîdos* form]

ad|e|noi|dal (ad′ə noi′dəl), *adj.* **1** of lymphoid tissue; adenoid. **2** having adenoids. **3** characteristic of a person having large or swollen adenoids. **—ad′e|noi′dal|ly,** *adv.*

ad|e|noid|ec|to|my (ad′ə noi dek′tə mē), *n., pl.* **-mies.** the removal of the adenoids by surgery.

ad|e|noi|di|tis (ad′ə noi dī′tis), *n.* inflammation of the adenoids.

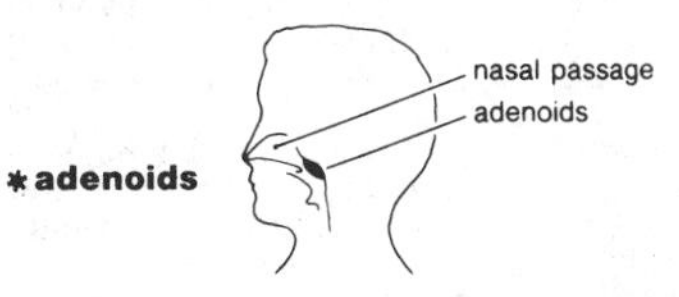

***adenoids**

***ad|e|noids** (ad′ə noidz), *n.pl.* growths in the upper part of the throat, just back of the nose, consisting of glandular tissue. Adenoids can swell up and hinder natural breathing and speaking.

ad|e|nol|o|gy (ad′ə nol′ə jē), *n.* the scientific study of glands, their nature, and their functions.

ad|e|no|ma (ad′ə nō′mə), *n., pl.* **-mas, -ma|ta** (-mə tə). **1** a tumor originating in a gland. **2** a tumor resembling a gland in structure. [< Greek *adḗn* gland + English *-oma*]

ad|e|nom|a|tous (ad′ə nom′ə təs), *adj.* **1** of or like an adenoma; glandular. **2** having an adenoma.

ad|e|no|path|ic (ad′ə nō path′ik), *adj.* **1** of or having to do with adenopathy. **2** having adenopathy.

ad|e|nop|a|thy (ad′ə nop′ə thē), *n.* disease of a gland. [< Greek *adḗn, -énos* gland + English *-pathy*]

a-de|nop|ter|in (ā′də nop′tər in), *n.* a drug derived from folic acid (a vitamin in the B complex), used to treat leukemia.

a|den|o|sine (ə den′ə sēn, -sin), *n.* a substance, composed of adenine and a pentose, found in tissue, especially muscle tissue, and in ribonucleic acid. It is important in muscle contraction and the metabolism of sugars. *Formula:* $C_{10}H_{13}N_5O_4$ [< German *Adenosin* < *Adenin* adenine]

adenosine de|am|i|nase (dē am′ə nās), an enzyme which aids in the breakdown of adenosine into other substances.

adenosine di|phos|phate (dī fos′fāt), a compound of adenosine and two phosphate groups, formed from adenosine triphosphate in the muscles. *Formula:* $C_{10}H_{15}N_5O_{10}P_2$ *Abbr:* ADP (no periods).

adenosine mon|o|phos|phate (mon′ə fos′fāt), **1** = adenylic acid. **2** a cyclic isomer of adenylic acid, functioning as a regulatory agent in many cellular and enzymatic processes; cyclic AMP. *Abbr:* AMP (no periods).

adenosine triphosphate, a compound of adenosine and three phosphate groups. The removal of phosphate releases large amounts of energy which are used for biological reactions, for example in muscle contraction and the metabolism of sugars. *Formula:* $C_{10}H_{16}N_5O_{13}P_3$ *Abbr:* ATP (no periods).

ad|e|not|o|my (ad′ə not′ə mē), *n., pl.* **-mies.** a dissection or incision of a gland.

ad|e|no|vi|ral (ad′ə nō vī′rəl), *adj.* of or like an adenovirus.

ad|e|no|vi|rus (ad′ə nō vī′rəs), *n.* any one of a group of viruses that attack mucous tissues, especially of the respiratory tract.

ad|e|nyl cyc|lase (ad′ə nil sī′klās), an enzyme that converts adenosine triphosphate into adenosine monophosphate or cyclic AMP.

ad|e|nyl|ic acid (ad′ə nil′ik), an acid composed of adenine, ribose, and phosphoric acid, formed in the body from red blood corpuscles and muscle tissue but derived from adenosine. *Formula:* $C_{10}H_{14}N_5O_7P$

a|deph|a|gous (ə def′ə gəs), *adj.* **1** of or having to do with a suborder of beetles that prey on other insects, such as the tiger beetles. **2** voracious; predatory. [< Greek *adēphágos* (with English *-ous*) eating to excess < *ádēn* enough + *phageîn* eat]

a|dept (*adj.* ə dept′; *n.* ad′ept, ə dept′), *adj., n.* **—*adj.*** very skillful; expert: *an adept tennis player. She is adept in music.* SYN: proficient.
—*n.* **1** a thoroughly skilled person; an expert: *He is an adept in working out crossword puzzles.* **2** *Obsolete.* an alchemist.
[< Medieval Latin *adeptus* skilled in alchemy; (originally) past participle of Latin *adipīscī* attain < *ad-* to + *apīscī* reach] **—a|dept′ly,** *adv.* **—a|dept′ness,** *n.*
▶**Adept** is generally followed by *in,* but there is a growing tendency not to fault use of *at: She is adept in getting her own way.*

ad|e|qua|cy (ad′ə kwə sē), *n.* state or condition of being adequate; as much as is needed for a particular purpose; sufficiency: *The adequacy of treatment with antibiotics is being tested.*

ad|e|quate (ad′ə kwit), *adj.* **1** as much as is needed for a particular purpose; sufficient; enough: *His wages are adequate to support his family.* SYN: requisite. See syn. under **enough. 2** suitable or competent: *He is quite adequate for the job.* SYN: satisfactory. [< Latin *adaequātus,* past participle of *adaequāre* equalize < *ad-* + *aequāre* make level < *aequus* equal] **—ad′e|quate|ly,** *adv.* **—ad′e|quate|ness,** *n.*

a|der|min (ə dėr′min), *n.* = pyridoxine.

Pronunciation Key: hat, āge, cãre, fär; let, ēqual, tėrm; it, īce; hot, ōpen, ôrder; oil, out; cup, pu̇t, rüle; child; long; thin; ᴛʜen; zh, measure; ə represents **a** in about, **e** in taken, **i** in pencil, **o** in lemon, **u** in circus.

Ad·es·te Fi·de·les (ä des′tā fi dā′lās; ad es′tē- fi dē′lēz), "O Come, All Ye Faithful" (a hymn often sung as a Christmas carol).

ad e·un·dem (gra·dum) (ad ē un′dəm grā′dəm), *Latin.* to the same (standing), applied to the admission without examination of a student transferring from one college or university to another.

à deux (ä dœ′), *French.* of, for, or between two (people) only: *a dinner à deux.*

ad ex·tra (ad ek′strə), *Latin.* in an outward direction.

ad ex·tre·mum (ad ek strē′məm), *Latin.* at last; finally.

ADF (no periods), **1** aircraft direction finder. **2** automatic direction finder.

ad·fect·ed (ad fek′tid), *adj. Mathematics.* containing different powers of an unknown quantity; compounded. [variant of *affected*]

ad fin., ad finem.

ad fi·nem (ad fī′nəm), *Latin.* to or at the end.

ad glo·ri·am (ad glôr′ē əm, glōr′-), *Latin.* for glory.

ad gus·tum (ad gus′təm), *Latin.* to the taste; to one's liking.

ADH, antidiuretic hormone.

a·dhar·ma (ə där′mə, -dėr′-), *n. Hinduism.* wrong behavior; injustice; unrighteousness. [< Sanskrit *adharma* < *a-* lacking + *dharma* dharma]

ad·here (ad hir′), *v.i.,* **-hered, -her·ing. 1** to stick fast; remain attached (to): *Mud adheres to your shoes. Paint adheres best to a clean, dry surface.* **SYN**: cling. See syn. under **stick**². **2** to hold closely or firmly (to): *He adheres to his ideas even when they are proved wrong. We adhered to our plan in spite of the storm.* **SYN**: cleave, persevere. **3** to be devoted or attached (to); be a follower or upholder; give allegiance (to a party, leader, or belief): *Many people adhere to the church of their parents.* **4** *Obsolete.* to agree. [< Latin *adhaerēre* stick to < *ad-* to + *haerēre* cling] —**ad·her′er**, *n.*

ad·her·ence (ad hir′əns), *n.* **1** a holding to and following closely; steady observance or maintenance: *The coach insisted on rigid adherence to the rules.* **2** attachment or devotion (to a party, leader, or belief); faithfulness. **3** a sticking fast; adhesion.

ad·her·ent (ad hir′ənt), *n., adj.* —*n.* a faithful supporter; follower: *Surrealism still has its numerous adherents* (New Yorker). **SYN**: See syn. under **follower**.
—*adj.* **1** sticking fast; clinging; attached. **2** *Botany.* adnate. —**ad·her′ent·ly**, *adv.*
►**Adherent**. The noun is usually followed by the preposition *of: He is an adherent of the conservative party.*

ad·he·sion (ad hē′zhən), *n.* **1** a sticking fast (to anything); an adhering; attachment. **2a** a following and supporting; faithfulness; adherence. **b** *Figurative.* agreement; assent; *To that treaty Spain and England gave . . . adhesion* (Macaulay). **SYN**: concurrence. **3** *Physics.* the molecular attraction exerted between the surfaces of unlike bodies in contact, such as a solid and a liquid. **4a** the growing together of body tissues that are normally separate, as a result of inflammation or after certain kinds of surgery. **b** Often, **adhesions.** one of the bands or fibers of new tissue by which this is accomplished. **5** *Botany.* adnation. **6** *Anthropology.* the association of two apparently unrelated aspects of culture in a functional relationship, for example when the making of pottery by hand is considered to be woman's work. [< Latin *adhaesiō, -ōnis* < *adhaerēre* adhere]

ad·he·sion·al (ad hē′zhə nəl), *adj.* of or having to do with adhesion.

ad·he·sive (ad hē′siv, -ziv), *n., adj.* —*n.* **1** *U.S.* sticky tape used especially to hold bandages in place; adhesive tape. **2** glue, paste, or other substance for sticking things together. **3** a gummed postage stamp: *The design, by the French artist Pierre Gandon, shows the Arc de Triomphe, with a mass of flowers in the foreground, but this busy 15 fr. adhesive has been criticised by the experts as being "too busy"* (Sunday Times).
—*adj.* **1** sticking and holding fast; adhering easily. **SYN**: sticky. **2** coated with glue, paste, or other sticky substance: *an adhesive label.* **SYN**: gummed. —**ad·he′sive·ly**, *adv.* —**ad·he′sive·ness**, *n.*

adhesive tape, a strip of cloth coated on one surface with a sticky substance, used especially for holding bandages in place.

ad·hib·it (ad hib′it), *v.t.* **1** to attach; affix. **2** to apply as a remedy. **3** to take in; let in; admit. [< Latin *adhibitus,* past participle of *adhibēre* apply, employ in < *ad-* toward + *habēre* hold]

ad·hi·bi·tion (ad′hə bish′ən), *n.* the act of adhibiting; applying, especially as a remedy.

ad hoc (ad hok′, äd hōk′), *Latin.* for a specific purpose; special: *an ad hoc committee. Only individual benefactors and ad hoc grants have made possible the ecological surveys already undertaken* (New Scientist).

ad ho·mi·nem (ad hom′ə nem), *Latin.* **1** appealing to a person's prejudices or emotions rather than to his power to reason: *an argument ad hominem.* **2** (literally) to the man.

ADI (no periods), acceptable daily intake (of a drug, radioactivity, etc.).

ad·i·a·bat (ad′ē ə bat), *n.* a line or curve showing graphically the relationship of pressure and volume or of temperature and entropy of a fluid during an adiabatic process. [< *adiabatic*]

ad·i·a·bat·ic (ad′ē ə bat′ik), *adj. Physics.* **1** occurring without loss or gain of heat. **2** of or having to do with a change of volume of a gas during which no heat enters or leaves it. [< Greek *adiábatos* impassable] —**ad′i·a·bat′i·cal·ly**, *adv.*

adiabatic gradient or **rate**, the rate at which a parcel of air becomes cooler or warmer as it gains or loses altitude, respectively, estimated to be approximately 5.5 degrees Fahrenheit per 1,000 feet, or 1 degree centigrade (Celsius) per 100 meters.

ad·i·an·tum (ad′ē an′təm), *n.* any one of several ferns having delicate wedge-shaped leaflets on slender, black stems, and marginal clusters of spore cases, such as the maidenhair fern. [< Latin *adiantum* < Greek *adianton* unwettable < *a-* not + *diantós* wettable < *diaínein* make wet (because its fronds shed water)]

ad·i·aph·o·ra (ad′ē af′ər ə), *n.pl.* things neither good nor bad; nonessentials in faith or conduct. [< Greek *adiáphora* indifferent things, neuter plural of *adiáphoros* indifferent < *a-* not + *diáphoros* different < *diaphérein* differ < *dia-* apart + *phérein* to bear]

ad·i·aph·o·re·sis (ad′ē af′ə rē′sis), *n.* reduction or absence of perspiration. [< *a-*⁴ without + Greek *diaphórēsis* perspiration < *diaphoreîn* carry through < *dia-* through + *phoreîn* carry]

ad·i·aph·o·ret·ic (ad′ē af′ə ret′ik), *adj., n.* —*adj.* capable of reducing or preventing perspiration. —*n.* any agent or drug that reduces or prevents perspiration.

ad·i·aph·o·rism (ad′ē af′ə riz əm), *n.* religious indifference or moderation.

ad·i·aph·o·rist (ad′ē af′ər ist), *n.* a person characterized by indifference or moderation, especially in religious matters.

ad·i·aph·o·rous (ad′ē af′ər əs), *adj.* neither good nor bad; indifferent.

ad·i·a·ther·man·cy (ad′ē ə thėr′mən sē), *n.* imperviousness to radiant heat.

ad·i·a·ther·ma·nous (ad′ē ə thėr′mə nəs), *adj. Physics.* impervious to radiant heat; not diathermanous.

ad·i·a·ther·mic (ad′ē ə thėr′mik), *adj.* = adiathermanous.

A·di·das or **a·di·das** (ə dē′dəz), *n. Trademark.* a type of athletic equipment, especially footwear and garments. [< *Adi Das*(sler), German manufacturer]

ad i·dem (ad ī′dəm), *Latin.* to the same thing or effect; in agreement: *The essence of a binding agreement is that the parties are ad idem—that their minds are at one* (Sunday Times).

a·dieu (ə dü′, ə dyü′; *French* ä dyœ′), *interj., n., pl.* **a·dieus, a·dieux** (ə düz′, ə dyüz′; *French* ä dyœ′). good-by; farewell: *to make one's adieus.* [< Middle French *adieu* < *à Dieu* to God]

ad inf., ad infinitum.

ad in·fi·ni·tum (ad in′fə nī′təm), *Latin.* without limit; endlessly: *The adversaries appeared equally immovable and equally prolific, . . . ready to beget new successors in interest, and so on, ad infinitum* (New Yorker).

ad int., ad interim.

ad in·te·rim (ad in′tər im), *Latin.* **1** in the meantime: *to serve ad interim.* **2** temporary: *an ad interim report.*

a·di·os (ä′dē ōs′, ad′ē-), *interj., n. Southwestern U.S.* good-by; farewell. [American English < Spanish *adiós* < *a Dios* to God]

ad·i·pate (ad′ə pāt), *n. Chemistry.* a salt or ester of adipic acid. [< *adip*(ic) + *-ate*²]

a·dip·ic (ə dip′ik), *adj.* of or derived from fatty or oily substances. [< Latin *adeps, -ipis* fat]

adipic acid, a fatty acid found in beet juice or prepared synthetically, used in the manufacture of certain plastics, baking powder, etc. *Formula:* $C_6H_{10}O_4$

ad·i·po·cere (ad′ə pə sir), *n.* a soft, waxy substance produced by the decomposition of dead animal bodies buried in moist places or submerged in water. [< French *adipocire* < Latin *adeps, -ipis* fat + French *cire* wax < Latin *cēra*]

ad·i·poc·er·ous (ad′ə pos′ər əs), *adj.* of the nature of or like adipocere.

ad·i·po·ki·net·ic (ad′ə pō ki net′ik), a hormone that controls the release of fatty substances from the adipose cells of insects for use by the flight muscle cells.

ad·i·po·ni·trile (ad′ə pō nī′trəl, -trēl, -trīl), *n.* a chemical used as an intermediate in the manufacture of nylon. *Formula:* $NC(CH_2)_4CN$ [< *adip*(ic acid) + *nitrile*]

ad·i·pose (ad′ə pōs), *adj., n.* —*adj.* consisting of or resembling fat; fatty. [< Medieval Latin *adiposus* < Latin *adeps, -ipis* fat] —**ad′i·pose·ness**, *n.* —*n.* the animal fat stored in fatty tissues.

adipose fin, a small, fatty, fin-shaped projection behind the dorsal fin of certain fishes, such as trout and catfish, that lacks supporting rays.

adipose tissue, animal fat; connective tissue, such as that under the skin and around the kidneys, containing masses of fat-laden cells.

ad·i·po·sis (ad′ə pō′sis), *n. Medicine.* a fatty condition, especially of an organ: *adiposis of the liver.* [< Latin *adeps, -ipis* fat + English *-osis*]

ad·i·pos·i·ty (ad′ə pos′ə tē), *n.* **1** adipose condition; fatness. **2** a tendency to become fat.

a·dip·sin (ə dip′sin), *n.* a chemical substance found primarily in adipose tissue and associated with various types of obesity, such as those due to defects in genes or metabolism: *Some forms of obesity . . . may be tied to a lack of adipsin* (Gina Kolata). [< Latin *adip(i)s* fat + English *-in*²]

ad·i·pyl (ad′ə pəl), *n.* the bivalent radical of adipic acid. *Formula:* $C_6H_8O_2$—

ad·it (ad′it), *n.* **1** an approach; entrance. **2** a horizontal or slightly inclined entrance to a mine. **3** admission; access. [< Latin *aditus, -ūs* < *adīre* approach < *ad-* to + *īre* go]

a·dith·er (ə diᴛʜ′ər), *adv., adj.* in a dither; excited; bustling: *adither with vacationing tourists.*

ad·i·tus (ad′ə təs), *n., pl.* **-tus** or **-tus·es. 1** = adit. **2** *Zoology.* a canal leading inwards, as in sponges. [< Latin *aditus, -ūs;* see etym. under **adit**]

adj., **1** adjective. **2** adjourned. **3** adjudged. **4** adjunct. **5** adjustment.

Adj., adjutant.

ad·ja·cence (ə jā′səns), *n.* = adjacency.

ad·ja·cen·cy (ə jā′sən sē), *n., pl.* **-cies.** the state of being adjacent, or of lying near or adjoining. **adjacencies**, adjoining places or vicinity.

ad·ja·cent (ə jā′sənt), *adj.* lying near or close, or contiguous (to); neighboring or adjoining; bordering; next: *The house adjacent to ours has been sold.* **SYN**: abutting. [< Latin *adjacēns, -entis,* present participle of *adjacēre* lie near < *ad-* near + *jacēre* lie²] —**ad·ja′cent·ly**, *adv.*
►**Adjacent** means lying near or neighboring, but not necessarily touching.

adjacent angles, two angles that have the same vertex and one side in common. See picture under **angle**.

ad·jec·ti·val (aj′ik tī′vəl, aj′ik tə vəl), *adj., n.* —*adj.* **1** of or having to do with an adjective: *-Able is an adjectival suffix.* **2** used as an adjective. —*n.* a word or group of words used as an adjective. —**ad′jec·ti′val·ly**, *adv.*

ad·jec·tive (aj′ik tiv), *n., adj.* —*n.* **1** a word that describes more fully the name of a person, animal, or thing. An adjective is said to modify a noun by qualifying or limiting a word or phrase used as a noun. In "a tiny brook," "The day is warm," "great happiness," and "this pencil," *tiny, warm, great,* and *this* are adjectives; in "a blue shirt," *blue* is a descriptive adjective; in "his book," *his* is a limiting adjective. **2** the form class, or part of speech, in many languages, comprising such words. *Abbr:* adj.
—*adj.* **1** of an adjective. **2** used as an adjective. **3** not standing by itself; dependent. **4** *Law.* relating to procedure; not substantive. **5** requiring the use of a mordant to make permanent: *an adjective dye.* [< Latin (*nōmen*) *adjectīvum,* neuter of *adjectīvus* added < *adjicere* add to < *ad-* to + *jacere* throw] —**ad′jec·tive·ly**, *adv.*
►**Adjectives** can be identified by features of form or of position. Most adjectives can come between an article and a noun, and can stand singly after linking verbs, such as *be* and *seem;* most adjectives can express degrees of comparison by being preceded by *more* and *most* or (in the case of certain short or common adjectives) by taking the endings *-er* and *-est.*

Adj. Gen., Adjutant General.

ad·join (ə join′), *v.t.* **1** to be next to; be in contact with: *His yard adjoins ours. Canada adjoins the United States.* **2** to be very near to: *Our garden adjoins the house.* —*v.i.* to be side by side; be next or close to each other or in contact: *Canada and the United States adjoin.* [< Old French *ajoin-,* stem of *ajoindre* < Latin *adjungere* add < *ad-* to + *jungere* join]

ad·join·ing (ə joi′ning), *adj.* being next or in contact; bordering; adjacent; contiguous: *We have adjoining desks. The twins have adjoining rooms.*

ad·journ (ə jėrn′), *v.t.* **1a** to put off until a later time: *The members of the club voted to adjourn the morning meeting until after lunch.* **b** to put off until a future meeting of the same body: *The committee adjourned consideration of the question.* **2** to suspend the meeting of to a future time or another place, or indefinitely: *The judge decided to adjourn the court for two hours.* **3** to put

off; defer; postpone: *I adjourn what I have to say on this topic* (Emerson). —*v.i.* **1a** to stop business or activity for a time, or indefinitely; recess: *The court adjourned from Friday until Monday.* **b** to transfer the place of meeting: *The committee adjourned to a larger hall.* **2** *Informal.* to go (to another place): *After dinner we adjourned to the living room to talk.*
[< Old French *ajorner* < *a jorn* to a (stated) day < Latin *ad* to + *diurnum* day, neuter of *diurnus* daily < *diēs* day]

ad|journ|ment (ə jėrn′mənt), *n.* **1** an adjourning. **2** a being adjourned. **3** the time during which a court, lawmaking body, or the like, is adjourned. **SYN**: recess.

Adjt., adjutant.

ad|judge (ə juj′), *v.t.*, **-judged, -judg|ing.** **1** to decree or decide by law; judge: *The accused man was adjudged guilty. The boy's case was adjudged in the juvenile court.* **SYN**: rule, pronounce, adjudicate. **2** to award or assign by law; grant: *The property was adjudged to the rightful owner.* **3** to condemn or sentence by law: *The thief was adjudged to prison for two years.* **4** *Archaic.* to deem; consider. [< Old French *ajugier* < Latin *adjūdicāre.* See etym. of doublet **adjudicate.**]

ad|judge|a|ble (ə juj′ə bəl), *adj.* that can be judged.

ad|judg|ment (ə juj′mənt), *n.* = adjudication.

ad|ju|di|cate (ə jü′də kāt), *v.*, **-cat|ed, -cat|ing.** —*v.t.* to decide or settle by law or as an authority; adjudge: *How long will it be before we have a civilized system of adjudicating management-labor disputes?* (New York Times).
—*v.i.* to act as judge or arbitrator; pass judgment: *The court adjudicated on the case.*
[< Latin *adjūdicāre* (with English *-ate*[1]) < *ad-* to + *jūdex, -icis* a judge. See etym. of doublet **adjudge.**] —**ad|ju′di|ca′tor**, *n.*

ad|ju|di|ca|tion (ə jü′də kā′shən), *n.* **1** a passing of judgment. **2** a judgment of a court of law or decision of a judge. **3** the act of a court declaring an ascertained fact: *an adjudication of bankruptcy.*

ad|ju|di|ca|tive (ə jü′də kā′tiv), *adj.* having or deriving from the power to judge; adjudicating.

ad|ju|di|ca|to|ry (ə jü′də kə tôr′ē, -tōr′-), *adj.* judicial: *The President had no power from Congress to remove a member from such an adjudicatory body merely because he wanted his own appointees (Manchester Guardian).*

ad|junct (aj′ungkt), *n., adj.* —*n.* **1** something added that is less important or not necessary, but helpful: *A spare tire is a more important adjunct to a car than a radio.* **SYN**: accessory, auxiliary. **2** an assistant to, or associate of, a more important person. **3** a word or phrase that qualifies or modifies one of the essential elements of a sentence. Adjectives, adjectival phrases, adverbs, adverbial phrases, and some nouns used in a modifying or qualitative position are adjuncts. In "The tired man walked down the village street," *tired* is an adjunct to the subject *man, down the street* is an adjunct to the verb *walked,* and *village* is an adjunct to *street.* **4** *Logic.* a nonessential property or attribute.
—*adj.* **1** subordinate: *adjunct arteries.* **2** accompanying: *adjunct military forces.*
[< Latin *adjūnctus,* past participle of *adjungere* join to < *ad-* to + *jungere* join] —**ad′junct|ly**, *adv.*

ad|junc|tion (ə jungk′shən), *n.* = addition.

ad|junc|tive (ə jungk′tiv), *adj.* forming an adjunct. —**ad|junc′tive|ly**, *adv.*

adjunct professor, = associate professor.

ad|ju|ra|tion (aj′ů rā′shən), *n.* **1** an earnest or solemn appeal: *The prosecutor addressed a strong adjuration to the witness to tell the whole truth.* **2** a solemn charging on oath or under penalty of a curse.

ad|jur|a|to|ry (ə jůr′ə tôr′ē, -tōr′-), *adj.* containing a solemn appeal or command.

ad|jure (ə jůr′), *v.t.*, **-jured, -jur|ing.** **1** to ask earnestly or solemnly: *I adjure you on your honor to speak the truth. She adjured the Duchess to tell her whether the beauty of Albert's character had ever been surpassed* (Lytton Strachey). **SYN**: beg, entreat. **2** to command (a person) on oath or under some penalty (to do something). **SYN**: charge. [< Latin *adjūrāre* put to an oath < *ad-* to + *jūrāre* swear < *jūs, jūris* oath] —**ad|jur′er, ad|ju′ror**, *n.*

ad|just (ə just′), *v.t.* **1** to change (something) to make fit; adapt (one thing to another): *These desks and seats can be adjusted to the height of any child.* **2** to set just right; put in proper order, position, or relation; arrange: *to adjust one's clothes, adjust the aim of a gun to allow for distance and wind. Please adjust the TV so that it is not so loud.* **SYN**: regulate, fix. **3** to settle; arrange satisfactorily: *The boys adjusted their difference of opinion and were friends again.* **SYN**: reconcile. **4** to decide the amount of money to be paid in settlement of (an insurance claim, a bill, or other monies owing).
—*v.i.* **1** to adapt oneself; get used: *Some wild animals never adjust to life in a zoo. Freshmen soon adjust to school life.* **2** to be changed so as to fit different users, for example by changing the angle, focus, or height: *These field glasses adjust with a screw. The new camera has a lens that adjusts automatically.*
[< earlier French *adjuster* < Old French *ajuster* < *a-* for + *juste* straight, right, learned borrowing from Latin *jūstus*]
—*Syn.* *v.t.* **1 Adjust, adapt, accommodate** have in common the idea of fitting one thing or person to another. **Adjust** emphasizes the idea of matching one thing to another: *I have to adjust my expenditures to my income.* **Adapt** emphasizes the idea of making minor changes in a thing (or person) to make it fit, suit, or fit into something: *I adapted the pattern to the material.* **Accommodate** emphasizes that the things to be fitted together are so different that one must be subordinated to the other: *I have to accommodate my desires to my income.*

ad|just|a|bil|i|ty (ə jus′tə bil′ə tē), *n.* the ability to adjust or be adjusted: *My quick adjustability to any circumstance made the second descent of the wall less terrifying ...* (New Yorker).

ad|just|a|ble (ə jus′tə bəl), *adj.* that can be adjusted: *The adjustable lamp on my desk can be placed in various positions.* —**ad|just′a|bly**, *adv.*

ad|just|a|ble-pitch propeller (ə jus′tə bəl-pich′), a propeller with blades that can be set manually at any of several pitches when at rest.

ad|just|ed (ə jus′tid), *adj.* **1** arranged or regulated: *a delicately adjusted spring or balance.* **2** adapted to environmental requirements (usually the second element of a compound): *Well-adjusted people can cope with most situations.* **3** corrected after accounting for variables, contingencies, and other hitherto unrelated factors: *adjusted gross income.* —**ad|just′ed|ness**, *n.*

ad|just|er or **ad|jus|tor** (ə jus′tər), *n.* **1** a thing that adjusts something else. **2** a person who adjusts insurance or other claims. **3** Usually, **adjustor.** a nerve or system of neurons which adjusts the effects of receptor and effector nerves.

ad|just|ive (ə jus′tiv), *adj.* tending or serving to adjust.

ad|just|ment (ə just′mənt), *n.* **1** a changing to make fit; setting right to fit some standard or purpose: *The adjustment of the seats to the right height for the children was necessary for their comfort.* **2** a means of adjusting; a regulating device: *A television set has an adjustment so that we can make the sound loud or soft.* **3** a settlement: *Try to make some adjustment of your differences so that you can work together without quarreling.* **4** an orderly arrangement of parts or elements: *the adjustment of the works of a watch.* **5** *Psychology.* **a** the process by which a person or animal adapts himself to the natural or social conditions around him. **b** the condition or relationship thus obtained: *The city dwellers quickly made an adjustment to village life.* **6** a reduction in the selling price of an article because of slight damage. **7** *Bookkeeping.* the correction of an account, especially an entry made at the end of a period to bring it up to date.

ad|just|ment|al (ə just men′təl), *adj.* of or having to do with adjustment.

ad|ju|tage (aj′ə tij), *n.* a short tube adjusted to an orifice, such as a nozzle or spout. Also, **ajutage.** [< French *ajutage* < Old French *ajuster* adjust]

ad|ju|tan|cy (aj′ə tən sē), *n., pl.* **-cies.** the rank or position of an adjutant in the army.

ad|ju|tant (aj′ə tənt), *n., adj.* —*n.* **1** an army officer who assists the commanding officer of a battalion or larger unit by sending out orders, keeping records, writing letters, and doing other administrative work. *Abbr:* Adj., Adjt. **2** a helper; assistant. **3** = adjutant bird.
—*adj.* helping.
[< Latin *adjūtāns, -antis,* present participle of *adjūtāre* to help (frequentative) < *adjuvāre* assist < *ad-* to + *juvāre* to help]

adjutant bird or **stork**, a very large species of stork of India, Southeast Asia, and Africa, so called because of its stiff gait when walking; marabou.

adjutant general, *pl.* **adjutants general.** an adjutant of a division or larger military unit.

Adjutant General, The, the head of the administrative division of the U.S. Army, in charge of records, decorations, publications, etc. *Abbr:* Adj. Gen.

ad|ju|tant|ship (aj′ə tənt ship), *n.* = adjutancy.

ad|ju|van|cy (aj′ə vən sē), *n.* assistance; help.

ad|ju|vant (aj′ə vənt), *adj., n.* —*adj.* assisting or aiding; auxiliary.
—*n.* **1** a person or thing that helps or assists; helper. **2** a substance added to a medicine to assist its action. **3** a substance that facilitates or enhances the effectiveness of any process or treatment, such as a chemical mixture that increases the body's production of antibodies.
[< Latin *adjuvāns, -antis,* present participle of *adjuvāre* assist < *ad-* to + *juvāre* to help]

Ad|ler|i|an (ad lir′ē ən), *adj.* of or having to do with the Austrian psychiatrist Alfred Adler (1870-1937) or his teachings, especially his theory that life's difficulties can be compensated for by the individual's efforts to overcome them.

ad|less (ad′lis), *adj. U.S. Informal.* without presenting any advertising.

ad|lib (ad lib′), *v.*, **-libbed, -lib|bing,** *adj., adv., n. Informal.* —*v.i., v.t.* to make up as one goes along; improvise (words, music, or gestures not in a script or score); extemporize: *The actor forgot some of his lines and had to adlib his part. The speaker adlibbed a pun.*
—*adj.* made up on the spot; extemporized; improvised: *He wasn't much of a juggler, but his adlib comments to the audience made him popular* (Newsweek).
—*adv.* on the spur of the moment; by making up (words, music, etc.) as one goes along; freely: *The orchestra played adlib. Arnold Toynbee writes his history, instead of dictating adlib on the tape* (New Statesman).
—*n.* music, words, or gestures made up as one goes along: *John Ford, who was directing, let him flounder through a nervous adlib—no prompting* (Saturday Evening Post).
[< *ad lib*(itum)] —**ad|lib′ber**, *n.*

ad lib, **1** without stint: *The same range of curiosity takes in addiction to drugs, suicide ... alcoholism and neuroses ad lib* (London Times). **2** without restraint: *The Greeks and Trojans dashed ad lib about the Plain of Troy, blown only by tailwinds of emotion* (A. J. Liebling). [< *ad lib*(itum)]

ad lib. or **ad libit.**, *Music.* ad libitum.

ad lib|i|tum (ad lib′ə təm), **1** *Music.* to any extent; without restriction. *Ad libitum* is used as a direction to change, omit, or expand a passage of music as much as the player wishes. *Abbr:* ad lib. **2** ad lib: *He implies, indeed, that the world will multiply its future Einsteins virtually ad libitum* (New Yorker). [< Latin *ad libitum* at pleasure]

ad lim|i|na a|pos|to|lo|rum (ad lim′i nə ə pos′tə-lôr′əm), or **ad limina**, *Latin.* **1** to the Holy See at Rome (as in official visits of bishops to the Vatican): *His ... object is to carry out the visit ad limina which bishops are supposed to make every five years* (London Times). **2** to the tombs of the Apostles Peter and Paul (as in a pilgrimage).

ad li|tem (ad lī′təm), *Latin.* for a (particular) lawsuit or legal action.

ad lit|te|ram (ad lit′ər əm), *Latin.* to the letter; exactly; verbatim.

ad loc., ad locum.

ad lo|cum (ad lō′kəm), *Latin.* to or at the place.

Adm., **1** Administrator. **2a** Admiral. **b** admiralty.

ad ma|jo|rem De|i glo|ri|am (äd mä yôr′em de′ē glôr′ē äm), *Latin.* to the greater glory of God (motto of the Society of Jesus, commonly called the Jesuits).

ad|man (ad′man′), *n., pl.* **-men.** *Informal.* a man who prepares advertisements and places them in suitable media; advertising man: *Am I alone in wearying of the complaint ... that the admen are always creating new desires where none existed?* (Punch).

ad|mass (ad′mas), *n., adj. British.* —*n.* **1** advertising designed to reach and appeal to a mass audience. **2** the mass audience sought by such advertising.
—*adj.* of, having to do with, or influenced by admass: *the admass audience, an admass society.*

ad|meas|ure (ad mezh′ər, -mā′zhər), *v.t.*, **-ured, -ur|ing.** to assign to (each person) his rightful share; measure out to; apportion. [< Old French *amesurer* < Medieval Latin *admensurare* < Latin *ad-* to + *mēnsūrāre* to measure] —**ad|meas′ur|er**, *n.*

ad|meas|ure|ment (ad mezh′ər mənt, -mā′-zhər-), *n.* **1** just apportionment of shares in anything. **2** the process of measuring. **3** size; dimensions; proportions.

Ad|me|tus (ad mē′təs), *n. Greek Legend.* the king of Pherae, a city in Thessaly, and husband of Alcestis.

admin., *Especially British.* **1** administration. **2** administrative. **3** administrator.

ad|min|i|cle (ad min′ə kəl), *n.* **1** *Law.* supporting or corroborative evidence. **2** any aid; support; auxiliary. [< Latin *adminiculum* a prop]

ad|mi|nic|u|lar (ad′mə nik′yə lər), *adj.* **1** auxiliary. **2** supporting or corroborative, as of evidence.

ad|min|is|ter (ad min′ə stər), *v.t.* **1** to manage

Pronunciation Key: hat, āge, cãre, fär; let, ēqual, tėrm; it, īce; hot, ōpen, ôrder; oil, out; cup, půt, rüle; child; long; thin; ᴛʜen; zh, measure; ə represents **a** in about, **e** in taken, **i** in pencil, **o** in lemon, **u** in circus.

the affairs of; control (a country, city, business, household, office, or club) on behalf of others; direct: *The Secretary of Defense administers a department of the government. A housewife administers her household.* **SYN**: conduct, manage. **2** to give out; apply; dispense: *The coach administered first aid to the injured player. The priest administered the last rites to the dying man. Judges administer justice and punishment.* **3** to deliver or bestow (a blow, rebuke, or advice to a person or animal). **4** to offer formally: *to administer the oath of allegiance. The witness could not testify until the judge had administered an oath to him to tell the truth.* **SYN**: tender. **5** to settle or take charge of (an estate, trust, or other property) as administrator, executor, or trustee. **6** to control (prices or wages) without regard to the normal pressures of supply and demand; stabilize.

—*v.i.* **1** to be helpful; add something; contribute; minister (to): *to administer to a person's comfort or pleasure. The government administered to the needs of the flood victims.* **2** *Law.* to act officially as administrator, executor, or trustee.

[< Old French *aministrer,* learned borrowing from Latin *administrāre,* ultimately < *ad-* to + *minister* servant]

administered price, a price fixed by a company's administrative action instead of being subject to frequent changes through the interplay of supply and demand on the open market.

ad|min|is|te|ri|al (ad min′ə stir′ē əl), *adj.* = administrative.

ad|min|is|tra|ble (ad min′ə strə bəl), *adj.* that can be administered.

ad|min|is|trant (ad min′ə strənt), *adj., n.* —*adj.* administering.

—*n.* = administrator.

ad|min|is|trate (ad min′ə strāt), *v.t., v.i.,* **-trat|ed, -trat|ing.** = administer.

ad|min|is|tra|tion (ad min′ə strā′shən), *n.* **1** the managing of a business, household, club, or office; management: *a school of business administration, skillful administration of a home. The administration of a big business requires skill in dealing with people.* **SYN**: direction. **2** the group of persons in charge of the management of affairs: *The principal and superintendent of a school are part of the administration of the school.* **3a** the management of public affairs by government officials: *He is experienced in city administration.* **b** the officials as a group; the government. **4a** Usually, **the Administration.** (in the United States) the President, his Cabinet, and the departments of the government run by the members of the Cabinet or by other persons appointed by the President: *The narrow escape of the Administration from total defeat ...* (James G. Blaine). **b** (in Great Britain) the Prime Minister and the Cabinet. **5** the time during which a government holds office; period of office of officials, especially that of a U.S. President: *The Liberal administration in Canada lasted many years. On reviewing the incidents of my administration, I am unconscious of intentional error* (George Washington). **6** a giving out, applying, or dispensing; act or process of administering something: *The Red Cross handled the administration of aid to the refugees.* **SYN**: dispensation, provision. **7** the management or settlement of the estate of a deceased or incompetent person or a minor by administrators or executors, or of a trust by trustees.

[< Latin *administrātiō, -ōnis* < *administrāre;* see etym. under **administer**]

ad|min|is|tra|tion|al (ad min′ə strā′shə nəl), *adj.* = administrative.

ad|min|is|tra|tive (ad min′ə strā′tiv), *adj.* **1** having to do with administration; concerning the management or conduct of affairs; executive: *administrative ability. The Interstate Commerce Commission is an administrative agency of the U.S. government that regulates the rates charged by the railroads.* **2** of the administration: *administrative policies.* —**ad|min′is|tra′tive|ly**, *adv.*

ad|min|is|tra|tor (ad min′ə strā′tər), *n.* **1** a person who administers; manager: *the administrator of a government program.* **2** a person with ability as a manager or executive: *a born administrator.* **3** *Law.* a person appointed by law to settle or take charge of the estate of a person who has died or who is legally incompetent. —**ad|min′is|tra′tor|ship**, *n.*

ad|min|is|tra|trix (ad min′ə strā′triks), *n., pl.* **-trix|es, -tri|ces** (-trə sēz). *Law.* a woman administrator.

ad|mi|ra|bil|i|ty (ad′mər ə bil′ə tē), *n.* the quality of being admirable; admirableness.

ad|mi|ra|ble (ad′mər ə bəl), *adj.* **1** worth admiring; arousing wonder united with approval, esteem, or reverence; wonderful: *Lincoln had an admirable character. What a piece of work is man! ... how express and admirable!* (Shakespeare). **SYN**: praiseworthy. **2** very good; excellent: *Under the doctor's admirable care the sick man soon recovered.* [< Latin *admīrābilis* < *admīrārī* admire] —**ad′mi|ra|ble|ness**, *n.*

ad|mi|ra|bly (ad′mər ə blē), *adv.* in an admirable manner; excellently.

ad|mi|ral (ad′mər əl), *n.* **1a** any naval officer of any one of the four highest ranks. **b** an officer in the U.S. Navy ranking next below a fleet admiral and next above a vice-admiral. **c** an officer in the British navy ranking next below an Admiral of the Fleet. **2a** *Especially British.* the commander of a fleet of fishing or merchant ships. **b** the commander in chief of the navy of a country. **3** either of two species of large, colorful butterflies originally found only in Europe, but now also found in America. It has greatly reduced forelegs. **4** a flagship. *Abbr.:* Adm. [earlier *amiral* < Old French < Arabic *'amīr-al-* chief of. See related etym. at **amir.**] —**ad′mi|ral|ship**, *n.*

Admiral of the Fleet, **1** an officer of the highest rank in the British Navy. **2** *U.S.* a fleet admiral (not an official title).

ad|mi|ral|ty (ad′mər əl tē), *n., pl.* **-ties.** **1a** the branch of law dealing with affairs of the sea and of ships. **b** a court of law dealing with affairs of the sea and of ships. **2** the rank or position of an admiral.

the Admiralty, in Great Britain (until 1963): **a** the government department in charge of naval affairs: *The Admiralty is the only department of state conducted by a board* (A. Lawrence Lowell). **b** the building in London where this department has its headquarters: *The board members are meeting in the Admiralty.*

admiralty law, = maritime law.

admiralty metal, a type of brass containing a small amount of tin, used especially for marine fittings.

ad|mi|ra|tion (ad′mə rā′shən), *n.* **1** a feeling of wonder, pleasure, and approval; delight or satisfaction at something fine or beautiful or well done: *Everyone has admiration for bravery. The beauty of the sunset and the view excited our admiration.* **2** the act of regarding with delight (something fine, great, or beautiful): *The tourists paused in admiration of the beautiful view.* **3** a person or thing that is admired or esteemed (now used only in the phrase *the admiration of*): *My new bike was the admiration of all my friends.* **4** *Archaic.* wonder: *Season your admiration for a while with an attent ear* (Shakespeare).

ad|mire (ad mīr′), *v.,* **-mired, -mir|ing.** —*v.t.* **1** to regard with wonder, pleasure, and approval; feel delight or satisfaction in: *We all admire a brave boy, a beautiful picture, or a fine piece of work.* **SYN**: esteem. **2** to feel or express admiration for: *We all admired my father's new car.* **3** to wonder at; marvel at (now often used ironically or sarcastically): *I admire your nerve.* **4** *U.S. Dialect.* to like (to do something): *We'd sure admire to do that, ma'am* (John Steinbeck).

—*v.i.* **1** to feel or express admiration. **2** *Archaic.* to wonder.

[< Latin *admīrārī* < *ad-* at + *mīrārī* wonder < *mīrus* wonderful] —**ad|mir′er**, *n.* —**ad|mir′ing|ly**, *adv.*

ad|mis|si|bil|i|ty (ad mis′ə bil′ə tē), *n.* the quality or state of being admissible.

ad|mis|si|ble (ad mis′ə bəl), *adj.* **1** capable or worthy of being admitted: *Only adults are admissible to this club.* **2a** permitted by a person in authority or by the rules; allowable: *Is it admissible to swim here?* **SYN**: permissible. **b** that can be considered; reasonable: *an admissible suggestion.* **SYN**: conceivable. **c** *Law.* that can be considered as evidence or proof. —**ad|mis′si|ble|ness**, *n.* —**ad|mis′si|bly**, *adv.*

▶ See **admittable** for usage note.

ad|mis|sion (ad mish′ən), *n.* **1a** the act of allowing (a person, animal, or group) to enter; entrance: *the admission of aliens into a country, the admission of Kentucky as a state into the Union. His admission into the hospital was delayed for lack of beds.* **b** the condition or fact of being admitted: *These books never found admission to the library.* **SYN**: access. **2a** the right, power, or privilege of entering or using a particular place, position, or occupation; permission to enter: *Every elementary school graduate has admission to high school. She applied for admission to the library stacks.* **b** the price paid for the right to enter: *Admission to the show is one dollar.* **3** acceptance into an office or position. **4a** the act of admitting to be true; acknowledging; confession: *His admission that he was to blame kept the others from being punished.* **SYN**: acknowledgment. **b** acceptance as true or valid; confirmation. **c** a fact or point acknowledged; something accepted as true or valid; concession. **SYN**: validation. **5** in a steam or internal-combustion engine: **a** the letting in of the working fluid, as steam, into a cylinder. **b** the point in the cycle of the engine at which this occurs. [< Latin *admissiō, -ōnis* < *admittere;* see etym. under **admit**]

▶ **Admission**, the more frequent term, emphasizes the privileges, rights, etc., of being admitted, while **admittance**, the rarer term, stresses the literal action of letting into a place: *He gained admittance to the park, but without a ticket could not gain admission to the exhibition.*

Admission Day, a legal holiday in Arizona (February 14), California (September 9), and Nevada (October 31), commemorating the respective admission of each of these states into the United States.

ad|mis|sive (ad mis′iv), *adj.* admitting or tending to admit.

ad|mit (ad mit′), *v.,* **-mit|ted, -mit|ting.** —*v.t.* **1** to say (something) is real or true; acknowledge; own; confess: *to admit one's guilt. He admits now that he made a mistake. The soldier refused to admit defeat.* **2a** to accept as true or as a fact: *... admitting the virtues of the late king* (Macaulay). **b** to allow or receive as lawful or valid: *to admit evidence, admit a claim.* **3** to allow (a person or thing) to enter; let in: *He was admitted to school this year. Windows admit light and air to the room.* **4** to allow to use, exercise, or enjoy privileges, of a particular place, position, or occupation: *I was admitted to that club last year.* **5** to give the right to enter to: *This ticket admits one person to the game. Canada has admitted millions of immigrants since World War II.* **6** to allow; concede; grant: *It is necessary to admit the possibility of error. Where the conflict becomes so acute, it is difficult for either side to admit common concepts of morality* (Edmund Wilson). **7** to have room for; be large enough for: *This garage door will admit two cars abreast. The harbor admits many ships.*

—*v.i.* to be a means of entrance; give access (to): *This door admits to the dining room.*

admit of, to give allowance or opportunity for; leave room for: *His answer admits of no reply. They admit of insights, not answers* (New Yorker).

admit to the bar. See under **bar**[1].

[< Latin *admittere* < *ad-* to + *mittere* let go] —**ad|mit′ter**, *n.*

—*Syn. v.t.* **1 Admit, acknowledge, confess** mean to grant or disclose that something is true. **Admit** means to grant or own the existence or truth of something, usually after hesitating and then giving in to outside forces, one's own conscience, or one's judgment: *I admit that you are right.* **Acknowledge** means to declare openly one's knowledge of the existence or truth of something, sometimes reluctantly: *They now have acknowledged defeat.* **Confess** means to admit something about oneself that is unfavorable or criminal: *I confess that I am a coward.*

▶ **Admit** is followed by *to* or *into* when it means "give the right to enter to" or "allow to enter": *Fifty cents will admit you to the game. The butler would not admit him into the house. Admit* is followed by *of* when it means "afford possibility, allow": *His conduct admits of no complaint.*

ad|mit|ta|ble (ad mit′ə bəl), *adj.* that can be admitted to a place or as a fact. Also, **admittible.**

▶ **Admittable**, formerly the equivalent of **admissible**, is usually limited to the more literal sense of *admit* (def. 1).

ad|mit|tance (ad mit′əns), *n.* **1** the right to enter; permission to enter: *There is no admittance to the park after dark. She had admittance to all the theaters free of charge. No admittance except on business!* **2** the act of admitting: *our admittance by the caretaker.* **3** actual entrance. **4** a measure of the ability of an electric circuit to conduct an alternating current; the reciprocal of impedance. **5** (in English law) a formal transfer of title to a copyhold.

▶ See **admission** for usage note.

ad|mit|ta|tur (ad′mə tā′tər), *n. U.S. Obsolete.* a student's certificate of admission to a college. [< Latin *admittātur* let him be admitted]

ad|mit|ted|ly (ad mit′id lē), *adv.* without denial; by general consent: *Admittedly the rules are strict. It is admittedly not easy for a proud nation to admit a serious mistake in judgment* (James P. Warburg).

ad|mit|ti|ble (ad mit′ə bəl), *adj.* = admittable.

ad|mix (ad miks′), *v.t., v.i.,* **-mixed** or **-mixt, -mix|ing.** to add to something else as an ingredient; mix in; mingle. [< Middle English *admixt* admixed < Latin *admixtus,* past participle of *admiscēre* < *ad-* in addition + *miscēre* mix]

ad|mix|ture (ad miks′chər), *n.* **1** the act of mixing. **2** a mixture: *An admixture of flour and water may be used as a paste.* **3** anything added in mixing; ingredient.

Adml., Admiral.

ad|mon|ish (ad mon′ish), *v.t.* **1** to advise (a person) about his faults or warn against something in order that he may be guided to improve: *The*

policeman admonished him not to drive so fast. **SYN**: forewarn. **2** to scold gently; reprove: *The teacher admonished the student for his careless work.* **3** to urge earnestly; advise strongly: *Their guide admonished the mountain climbers to follow him carefully.* **SYN**: exhort. **4** to recall to a duty overlooked or forgotten; remind: *She admonished him of his obligation.* **SYN**: notify. [back formation < *admonition*] —**ad|mon'ish|er**, *n.*
▶ **admonish.** *Of,* not *against,* is used after this rather formal word for "warn": *John admonished them of the impending peril.*

ad|mon|ish|ment (ad mon'ish mənt), *n.* = admonition: *But most Israelis feel that it was worth getting an admonishment in order to put an end to the Egyptian sniping* (Harper's).

ad|mo|ni|tion (ad'mə nish'ən), *n.* **1** an admonishing; gentle reproof or warning: *He received an admonition from his teacher for not doing his homework. Now all these things ... are written for our admonition* (I Corinthians 10:11). **2** counsel; recommendation: *The doctor's admonition was to work out a stiff knee.* [< Old French *amonition,* learned borrowing from Latin *admonitiō, -ōnis* < *admonēre* advise < *ad-* to + *monēre* advise, warn]

ad|mon|i|tor (ad mon'ə tər), *n.* a person who admonishes; admonisher; monitor.

ad|mon|i|to|ri|al (ad mon'ə tôr'ē əl, -tōr'-), *adj.* = admonitory.

ad|mon|i|to|ry (ad mon'ə tôr'ē, -tōr'-), *adj.* containing admonition; admonishing; warning: *The librarian raised an admonitory finger for silence.*

***ad|nate** (ad'nāt), *adj. Botany, Zoology.* (of unlike parts of plants or animals) growing together or adhering throughout their length; congenitally attached. [< Latin *adnātus* grown onto, past participle of *adnāscī* grow upon < *ad-* to + *nāscī* be born. Compare etym. under **agnate.**] —**ad|na'tion**, *n.*

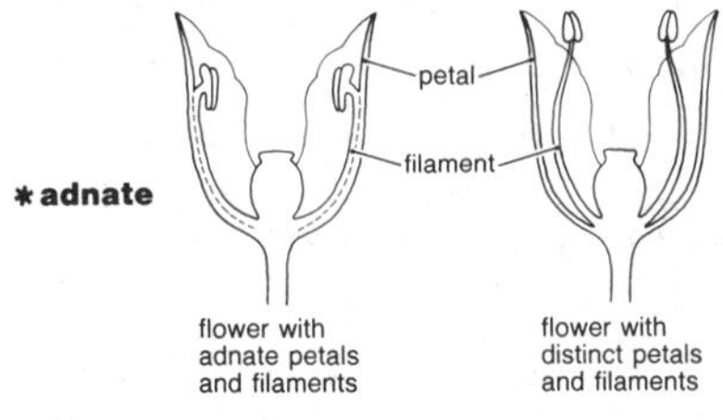

flower with adnate petals and filaments
flower with distinct petals and filaments

ad nau|se|am (ad nô'shē am, -sē-; -əm), *Latin.* to a disgusting extent: *He talks ad nauseam about his family's importance.*

ad|nex|a (ad nek'sə), *n.pl. Anatomy.* parts appended or adjunct to another or others, such as the eyelids and tear glands in relation to the eyeball. [< Latin *adnexa,* neuter plural of *adnexus,* past participle of *adnectere* connect < *ad-* to + *nectere* bind. Compare etym. under **annex.**]

ad|nex|al (ad nek'səl), *adj. Anatomy.* appended or adjunct to another or to other parts.

ad|nom|i|nal (ad nom'ə nəl), *adj.* of or having to do with adnouns; adjectival.

ad|noun (ad'noun), *n.* **1** an adjective used as a noun. *Example: weary* in "no rest for the weary" is an adnoun. **2** an adjective.

a|do (ə dü'), *n.* **1** noisy activity; bustle; fuss: *There was much ado about the party by all the family.* **SYN**: See syn. under **stir**[1]. **2** trouble; difficulty: *with much ado.* [Middle English *at do* to do]

a|do|be (ə dō'bē), *n., adj.* —*n.* **1** brick made of clay baked in the sun, used in building. **2** a building made of such bricks or of sun-dried clay. **3** clay for making such bricks.
—*adj.* built or made of adobe: *Many people in the southwestern United States and in Mexico live in adobe houses.*
[American English < Spanish *adobe* < Arabic *aṭ-ṭūb* the brick]

adobe flat, *Southwestern U.S.* a smooth plain covered with clay deposited by streams which flow only during heavy rains and periods of thawing.

a|do|bo (ə dō'bō), *n.* marinated chicken, or chicken and pork, eaten especially in Latin America and the Philippines. [< Spanish *adobo* (literally) pickle sauce]

ad|o|lesce (ad'ə les'), *v.i.,* **-lesced, -lesc|ing.** *Especially U.S.* **1** to be or become an adolescent. **2** to behave like an adolescent. [back formation < *adolescent*]

ad|o|les|cence (ad'ə les'əns), *n.* **1** growth from childhood to adulthood: *the dreamy, stormy years of adolescence.* **2** the period of growth from childhood to adulthood; youth: *John grew tall during his adolescence.*

ad|o|les|cen|cy (ad'ə les'ən sē), *n.* = adolescence.

ad|o|les|cent (ad'ə les'ənt), *n., adj.* —*n.* a person growing up from childhood to manhood or womanhood, especially, in ordinary use, from about 12 to about 20 years of age: *Nine adolescents, six juveniles and four adults were taken into court yesterday ... Those between 16 and 18 are adolescents and those under 16 are juveniles* (New York Times). **SYN**: teen-ager, youth.
—*adj.* **1** growing up from childhood to adulthood; youthful: *He is still in the adolescent stage of development.* **SYN**: pubescent. **2** of adolescents; during adolescence; characteristic of adolescents: *adolescent self-consciousness. Adolescent friendships often do not last.* **SYN**: juvenile. **3** *Figurative.* immature: *adolescent behavior.* **SYN**: puerile.
[< Latin *adolēscēns, -entis,* present participle of *adolēscere* grow up < *ad-* to + *alēscere* grow up. See related etym. under **adult.**] —**ad'o|les'cent|ly**, *adv.*

Ad|o|nai (ä'dō nī', ad'ə nā'ī), *n.* a Hebrew name for God.

A|don|ic verse or **line** (ə don'ik), a verse or line consisting of a dactyl (–◡◡) and a spondee (– –) or a trochee (–◡).

A|don|is (ə don'is, -dō'nis), *n.* **1** *Greek and Roman Mythology.* a handsome young man who was loved by Aphrodite (Venus). **2a** any extremely handsome young man. **b** a vain young man; a dandy. **3** an asteroid discovered in 1936 whose orbit comes within that of Venus. Adonis is about a mile in diameter. **4** a group of plants that grows wild in Europe and Asia. Some of these plants are cultivated in gardens in North America for their yellow or red flowers.

a|dopt (ə dopt'), *v.t.* **1** to take for your own or as your own choice: *I liked your idea and adopted it. Few Americans would find it easy to adopt Japanese customs. Her [Greece's] whole culture has never ceased to adopt and to adapt alien elements* (Atlantic). **SYN**: embrace, espouse. **2** to accept formally or officially; approve: *The committee adopted the new rule by a vote of five to three.* **SYN**: endorse. **3a** to take (a child of other parents), as approved by law, and bring up as one's own child: *The judge permitted the Browns to adopt the homeless orphan.* **b** to take (anyone) voluntarily into any relationship (as heir, father, friend, or citizen): *His nephew was his adopted heir.* **4** to take (a word) from a foreign language into regular use without (intentionally) changing its form: *In English we have adopted the German words "Gneiss," "Hamburger," "Hornblende," and "Quartz."* **5** (in Great Britain) to accept as the candidate of a political party for election. [< Latin *adoptāre* < *ad-* to + *optāre* choose] —**a|dopt'a|ble**, *adj.* —**a|dopt'er**, *n.*

a|dopt|a|bil|i|ty (ə dop'tə bil'ə tē), *n.* fitness for adoption.

a|dopt|ee (ə dop'tē', ad'op-), *n.* a person who is adopted.

a|dop|tion (ə dop'shən), *n.* **1** the act of adopting: *the adoption of a new name. Our club voted the adoption of some new rules.* **2** the fact or condition of being adopted: *to offer a child for adoption. Joe's adoption by his aunt changed his whole life. New ideas should be carefully tested before their adoption.*

a|dop|tion|ism (ə dop'shə niz əm), *n. Theology.* the doctrine that Christ as man is the Son of God by adoption only. —**a|dop'tion|ist**, *n.*

a|dop|tive (ə dop'tiv), *adj.* **1** related by adoption; adopted: *an adoptive son, one's adoptive country.* **2** tending to adopt: *English is a receptive and adoptive language.* —**a|dop'tive|ly**, *adv.*

a|dor|a|bil|i|ty (ə dôr'ə bil'ə tē, -dōr'-), *n., pl.* **-ties.** the quality of being adorable.

a|dor|a|ble (ə dôr'ə bəl, -dōr'-), *adj.* **1** worthy of being adored. **SYN**: revered, worshipful. **2** *Informal.* attractive or delightful; lovely: *What an adorable dress!* **SYN**: alluring. —**a|dor'a|ble|ness**, *n.* —**a|dor'a|bly**, *adv.*
▶ See **adore** for usage note.

ad|o|ral (ad ôr'əl, -ōr'-), *adj., n. Zoology.* —*adj.* **1** near the mouth: *adoral cilia.* **2** of or having a mouth.
—*n.* an adoral part or function. [< *ad-* to + *oral*]

ad|o|ra|tion (ad'ə rā'shən), *n.* **1** the highest love and admiration. **2** worship; reverence: *the adoration of the Magi.* [< Latin *adōrātiō, -ōnis* < *adōrāre;* see etym. under **adore**]

a|dore (ə dôr', -dōr'), *v.,* **a|dored, a|dor|ing.**
—*v.t.* **1** to love and admire very greatly: *She adores her mother.* **SYN**: revere, idolize. **2** *Informal.* to like very much: *I just adore that dress!* **3** to worship: *"O come let us adore Him," sang the choir at Christmas.* **SYN**: venerate.
—*v.i.* to be an adorer; offer worship.
[< Latin *adōrāre* < *ad-* to + *ōrāre* speak, pray] —**a|dor'er**, *n.* —**a|dor'ing|ly**, *adv.*
▶ **Adore** and **adorable** are often used in informal speech to express general and undiscriminating approval: *I adore hamburgers. What an adorable hat she is wearing!*

a|dorn (ə dôrn'), *v.t.* **1** to add beauty to: *Wild flowers adorned the river bank.* **SYN**: beautify. **2** to put ornaments on; decorate: *She adorned her hair with flowers.* **SYN**: deck. See syn. under **decorate. 3** to make greater the splendor or honor of; add distinction to; grace: *And a new Cibber shall the stage adorn* (Alexander Pope). [< Latin *adōrnāre* < *ad-* + *ōrnāre* fit out] —**a|dorn'er**, *n.* —**a|dorn'ing|ly**, *adv.*

a|dorn|ment (ə dôrn'mənt), *n.* **1** *pl.* **-ments.** something or someone that adds beauty; an ornament; decoration: *Christmas trees decorated with all the traditional adornments. A distinguished judge is an adornment to the bench.* **2** *no pl.* the act of adorning; ornamentation: *She was busy with the adornment of the room for the party. In many societies, particularly in tropical or mild climates, adornment may be wholly divorced from clothing and far more important* (Beals and Hoijer).

a|down (ə doun'), *prep., adv. Poetic.* down: *He did but float a little way Adown the stream of time* (James Russell Lowell). [Old English *of dūne* downward]

ADP (no periods), **1** adenosine diphosphate. **2** automatic data processing.

ad pa|tres (ad pā'trēz), *Latin.* to one's fathers; dead.

ad|press (ad pres'), *v.t.* to press closely to a surface; lay flat. [< Latin *adpressus,* past participle of *adprimere* press to < *ad-* to + *premere* press]

ad quem (ad kwem'), *Latin.* to or at which; (goal) toward which.

ad|ra|di|al (ad rā'dē əl), *adj. Zoology.* situated near or beside a radial part, such as the arm of a starfish. [< *ad-* to + *radial*]

A|dras|tus (ə dras'təs), *n. Greek Legend.* a king of Argos, the only survivor of the Seven against Thebes, whom he led.

ad ref|er|en|dum (ad ref'ə ren'dəm), *Latin.* for further reference or consideration; subject to approval: *The president was given the authority to issue decree laws ad referendum of the Congress* (Raul d'Eca).

ad rem (ad rem'), *Latin.* to the point.

ad|re|nal (ə drē'nəl), *adj., n.* —*adj.* **1** on or near the kidney; suprarenal. **2** of or derived from the adrenal glands.
—*n.* an adrenal gland.
[< *ad-* near + Latin *rēnēs* kidneys + English *-al*[1]] —**ad|re'nal|ly**, *adv.*

ad|re|nal|ec|to|mize (ə drē'nə lek'tə mīz), *v.t.,* **-mized, -miz|ing.** to remove one or both of the adrenal glands from by surgery.

ad|re|nal|ec|to|my (ə drē'nə lek'tə mē), *n., pl.* **-mies.** the surgical removal of one or both of the adrenal glands.

***adrenal gland** or **body**, either of two very small ductless glands, one on the upper part of each kidney, that secrete adrenalin; suprarenal gland. The outer layer or cortex secretes corticosterone and other important steroid hormones and the inner part or medulla secretes adrenalin.

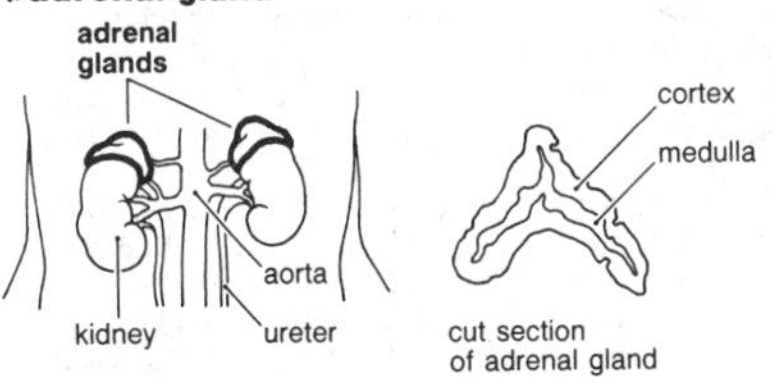

cut section of adrenal gland

ad|ren|al|in (ə dren'ə lin), *n.* a hormone secreted by the inner part or medulla of the adrenal glands; epinephrine. Adrenalin speeds up the heartbeat and thereby increases bodily energy and resistance to fatigue. *Formula:* $C_9H_{13}O_3N$ [< *adrenal* + *-in*]

Ad|ren|al|in (ə dren'ə lin), *n. Trademark.* adrenalin which is artificially produced; epinephrine.

ad|ren|al|ine (ə dren'ə lin, -lēn), *n.* = adrenalin.

ad|ren|er|gic (ad're nėr'jik), *adj.* that is activated by or produces adrenalin: *adrenergic nerve fiber. The intense adrenergic stimulation preceding stress-induced shock is well recognized* (Science). [< *adren*(aline) + Greek *érgon* work + English *-ic*]

ad|ren|in (ə dren'in), *n.* = adrenalin.

ad|ren|ine (ə dren'ēn), *n.* = adrenin (adrenalin).

ad|ren|o|chrome (ə dren'ə krōm), *n.* a compound formed by the oxidation of adrenalin, and capable of converting hemoglobin into methemoglobin. *Formula:* $C_9H_9O_3N$

Pronunciation Key: hat, āge, cãre, fär; let, ēqual, tėrm; it, īce; hot, ōpen, ôrder; oil, out; cup, pu̇t, rüle; child; long; thin; ᴛʜen; zh, measure; ə represents **a** in about, **e** in taken, **i** in pencil, **o** in lemon, **u** in circus.

ad|re|no|cor|ti|cal (ə drē′nō kôr′tə kəl), *adj.* having to do with or derived from the outer layer or cortex of an adrenal gland: *adrenocortical steroids.*

ad|re|no|cor|ti|co|troph|ic (ə drē′nō kôr′tə kō-trof′ik), *adj.* = adrenocorticotropic.

ad|re|no|cor|ti|co|troph|in (ə drē′nō kôr′tə kō-trof′in), *n.* = adrenocorticotropin (ACTH).

ad|re|no|cor|ti|co|trop|ic (ə drē′nō kôr′tə kō-trop′ik), *adj.* stimulating the activity of the adrenal cortex.

ad|re|no|cor|ti|co|trop|in (ə drə′nō kôr′tə kō-trop′in), *n.* = ACTH.

ad|re|no|gen|i|tal (ə drē′nō jen′ə təl), *adj.* of, having to do with, or caused by the effects of the adrenal hormones upon the genital organs.

ad|re|no|lyt|ic (ə drē′nə lit′ik), *adj., n.* **—*adj.*** having to do with or inhibiting the effect of adrenalin or the adrenergic nerves.
—*n.* an adrenolytic drug.

ad|re|no|tro|phic (ə drē′nə trō′fik), *adj.* = adrenotropic.

ad|re|no|trop|ic (ə drē′nə trop′ik), *adj.* stimulating the activity of the adrenal glands.

a|dri|a|my|cin (ā′drē ə mī′sən), *n.* a drug used as an antibiotic and experimentally in the treatment of cancer. It is derived from a kind of streptomyces. [< Italian *adriamicina* < *Adriàtico* Adriatic (Sea) + *-micina* -mycin, as in *streptomycin*]

a|drift (ə drift′), *adv., adj.* **1** floating without being guided; drifting: *During the storm our boat was adrift on the lake.* **2** without guidance or direction; aimless: *The basketball team was adrift while the coach was sick. With no clear-cut ambitions or special aptitudes, he found himself adrift after the war* (New York Times). **3** *Especially British Informal, Figurative.* unattached; unfastened; loose: *The top of your pen is coming adrift and will soon fall.*

a|drip (ə drip′), *adj., adv.* dripping: *... oars adrip with silver foam* (Atlantic Monthly).

a|droit (ə droit′), *adj.* **1** having or showing skill in using the mind; resourceful in reaching one's objective; ingenious; clever: *A good teacher is adroit in asking questions. But this adroit defence failed to make any impression upon Victoria* (Lytton Strachey). **2** having or showing skill in the use of the hands or the body; skillful: *Monkeys are adroit climbers.* **SYN:** deft. See syn. under **dexterous.** [< French *adroit ro* < *à droit* rightly < Old French *a dreit* < Latin *ad* to, *dīrēctus* straight] **—a|droit′ly,** *adv.* **—a|droit′ness,** *n.*

à droite (à drwàt′), *French.* to or on the right.

a|droop (ə drüp′), *adj., adv.* drooping: *Her neck adroop, she last let go her spear* (J. D. Long).

a|dry (ə drī′), *adj., adv. Archaic.* dry; thirsty.

ads., advertisements.

ad|sci|ti|tious (ad′sə tish′əs), *adj.* added or derived from outside; supplemental; additional: *adscititious customs alien to the tribe.* **SYN:** adventitious, extrinsic. [< Latin *adscītus* accepted (ultimately < *ad-* to + *scīre* know) + English *-itious*] **—ad′sci|ti′tious|ly,** *adv.*

ad|script (ad′skript), *adj.* written after (distinguished from *subscript* and *superscript*): *an adscript letter or character.* [< Latin *adscrīptus,* past participle of *adscrībere* write after < *ad-* to + *scrībere* write]

ad|scrip|tion (ad skrip′shən), *n.* = ascription.

***ad|sorb** (ad sôrb′, -zôrb′), *v.t.* to take up and hold (a gas, liquid, or dissolved substance) spread out on the surface in a thin layer of molecules: *Dyes are adsorbed on the fibers of cloth. Consider what happens when a clean surface, e.g., of metal, is exposed to a gas. It has been shown that even a liquid mercury surface rapidly collects a film one molecule thick, a so-called adsorbed layer* (P. R. Rowland). [< *ad-* to + Latin *sorbēre* suck in]

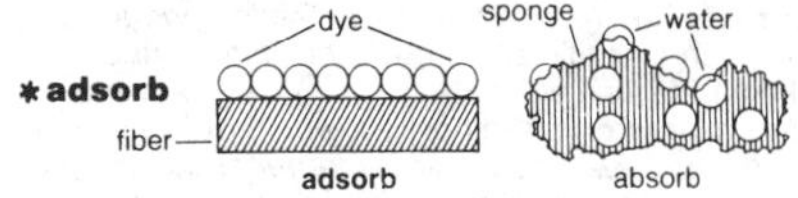

ad|sorb|a|bil|i|ty (ad sôr′bə bil′ə tē, -zôr′-), *n.* the condition or quality of being adsorbable.

ad|sorb|a|ble (ad sôr′bə bəl, -zôr′-), *adj.* that can be adsorbed.

ad|sorb|ate (ad sôr′bāt, -zôr′-), *n.* anything that is adsorbed.

ad|sorb|ent (ad sôr′bənt, -zôr′-), *adj., n.* **—*adj.*** adsorbing readily.
—*n.* a substance that adsorbs readily.

ad|sorp|tion (ad sôrp′shən, -zôrp′-), *n.* **1** the process of adsorbing; condensation of gases, liquids, or dissolved substances on the surface of solids. **2** the condition of being adsorbed.

ad|sorp|tive (ad sôrp′tiv, -zôrp′-), *adj.* **1** of or having to do with adsorption. **2** able to adsorb.

ad|su|ki bean (ad sü′kē, -zü′-), = adzuki bean.

ad|sum (ad′sum), *Latin.* I am here (formerly a student's answer to a roll call).

ad sum|mum (ad sum′əm), *Latin.* to the highest point or degree.

ad|u|lar|i|a (aj′ə lãr′ē ə), *n.* a transparent or translucent variety of feldspar. Moonstone is opalescent adularia. [< New Latin *adularia* < *Adula,* a mountain group in the Swiss Alps]

ad|u|late (aj′ə lāt), *v.t.,* **-lat|ed, -lat|ing.** to praise too much; flatter slavishly: *What is there to adulate in me! Am I particularly intelligent?* (W. S. Gilbert). [< Latin *adūlārī* (with English *-ate* [1]) fawn upon] **—ad′u|la′tor,** *n.*

ad|u|la|tion (aj′ə lā′shən), *n.* too much praise; slavish flattery: *Adulation ever follows the ambitious* (Oliver Goldsmith).

ad|u|la|to|ry (aj′ə lə tôr′ē, -tōr′-), *adj.* characterized by adulation; praising too much; flattering slavishly: *Poujade's own public meetings, held before packed houses of adulatory listeners, were well-disciplined affairs* (Harper's).

a|dult (ə dult′, ad′ult; *see note below*), *adj., n.*
—*adj.* **1** having full size and strength; full-grown; fully developed; grown-up: *an adult person, an adult animal or plant.* **SYN:** mature. **2** of, for, or by grown-up persons: *adult books, adult behavior.*
—*n.* **1a** a person who has reached full growth and development; grown-up person: *Try to behave like an adult. Children want and need adults to set the reasonable limits of their innovating, exploring, and rebelling* (Saturday Review). **b** a person who has reached an age of maturity as defined by law, usually the age of 18, sometimes the age of 21: *Adults must accept full responsibility for their actions.* **2** a plant or animal grown to full size and strength.
[< Latin *adultus,* past participle of *adolēscere* < *ad-* to + *alēscere* grow up. See etym. at **adolescent.**] **—a|dult′ly,** *adv.* **—a|dult′ness,** *n.*
▶**Adult** is pronounced ə dult′ or ad′ult, the choice depending often on the placement of the stress in the following word: *a dult′i de′ as,* but *ad′ult no′tions.*

adult education, education for adults in academic, vocational, or recreational subjects, offered (usually at night) in schools and colleges, or by correspondence: *Adult education has come a long way from the time when its primary concerns were to teach immigrants to speak English* (Time).

a|dul|ter|ant (ə dul′tər ənt), *n., adj.* **—*n.*** a substance used to adulterate something, especially something that destroys purity or quality without greatly altering appearance.
—*adj.* adulterating.

a|dul|ter|ate (*v.* ə dul′tə rāt; *adj.* ə dul′tər it, -tə-rāt), *v., -at|ed, -at|ing, adj.* **—*v.t.*** to add an inferior, impure, or improper substance to; lower the purity or quality of (food, drugs, or other substances) without greatly altering the appearance to increase in bulk or quantity: *It is against the law to adulterate milk with water.* **SYN:** corrupt, debase.
—*adj.* **1** debased by adulteration; adulterated. **SYN:** spurious, counterfeit. **2** = adulterous.
[< Latin *adulterāre* (with English *-ate* [1]), ultimately < *ad-* to + *alter* other] **—a|dul′ter|a′tor,** *n.*

a|dul|ter|a|tion (ə dul′tə rā′shən), *n.* **1** the act or process of adulterating: *We have laws against the adulteration of coffee and tea.* **SYN:** debasement. **2** an adulterated substance; product that has been adulterated.

a|dul|ter|er (ə dul′tər ər), *n.* a person, especially a man, who commits adultery.

a|dul|ter|ess (ə dul′tər is, -tris), *n.* a woman who commits adultery.

a|dul|ter|ine (ə dul′tər in, -tə rīn), *adj.* **1** born of adultery. **2** of or involving adultery. **3** adulterated or spurious. **4** *Historical.* illegal; unlicensed.

a|dul|ter|ous (ə dul′tər əs, -trəs), *adj.* **1** committing adultery. **2** having to do with adultery. **3** *Archaic.* spurious. **—a|dul′ter|ous|ly,** *adv.*

a|dul|ter|y (ə dul′tər ē), *n., pl.* **-ter|ies.** unfaithfulness of a married man to his wife or of his wife to him; voluntary sexual intercourse by a married man with a woman not his wife, or by a married woman with a man not her husband. [< Latin *adulterium* < *adulterāre* defile, ultimately < *ad-* to + *alter* other, different]

a|dult|hood (ə dult′hu̇d), *n.* the condition or time of being an adult: *The adolescent peer group ... occupies the stage between childhood dependence on parents and the social responsibilities of adulthood* (Listener).

adult Western, a story, motion picture, or television play having a Western theme, and designed to appeal to an adult audience.

ad|um|bral (ad um′brəl), *adj.* giving shade; shady.

ad|um|brant (ad um′brənt), *adj.* showing in outline; shadowing forth; adumbrating.

ad|um|brate (ad um′brāt, ad′əm brāt), *v.t.,* **-brat|ed, -brat|ing.** **1** to indicate faintly; outline; sketch: *One may adumbrate a few generic traits, though each has many exceptions* (Harper's). **SYN:** suggest. **2** to foreshadow. **SYN:** typify, symbolize. **3** to overshadow; obscure. **SYN:** darken. [< Latin *adumbrāre* (with English *-ate* [1]) < *ad-* upon + *umbra* shade] **—ad′um|bra′tion,** *n.*

ad|um|bra|tive (ad um′brə tiv), *adj.* faintly indicating or typifying. **—ad|um′bra|tive|ly,** *adv.*

a|dunc (ə dungk′), *adj.* bent or curved inward; hooked: *an adunc bill, beak, or nose.* [< Latin *aduncus* < *ad-* toward + *uncus* a hook]

a|dun|cous (ə dung′kəs), *adj.* = adunc.

ad un|guem (ad ung′gwem), *Latin.* **1** to a nicety. **2** (literally) to a fingernail (as work brought to the final touch or test with the fingernail).

ad|u|rol (ad′ə rol, -rōl), *n.* a crystalline substance produced from hydroquinone, used as a photographic developer. [< German *Adurol*]

a|dust (ə dust′), *adj.* **1** burned: *adust by the sun; (Figurative.) adust with rage.* **2** parched; dried by heat: *adust air.* **3** sunburned: *an adust complexion.* **4** *Figurative.* gloomy; melancholy: *an adus temperament.* [< Latin *adustus,* ultimately < *ad-* + *ūrere* to burn]

ad u|trum|que pa|ra|tus (ad yü trum′kwē pə-rā′təs), *Latin.* prepared for either alternative.

adv., an abbreviation for the following:
1 ad valorem.
2 adverb.
3 advertisement.
4 against (Latin, *adversus*).

Adv., **1** Advent. **2** advocate (lawyer).

ad val., ad valorem.

ad va|lo|rem (ad və lôr′em, -lōr′-), (of taxes, import duties, or other fees) levied in proportion to the certified value of the merchandise or goods: *Ad valorem imports are those goods and materials on which the duty permitting them to enter this country is calculated on their value abroad* (New York Times). *Abbr:* ad val. [< Medieval Latin *ad valorem*]

ad|vance (ad vans′, -väns′), *v.,* **-vanced, -vanc|ing,** *n., adj.* **—*v.t.*** **1** to put or move forward; push forward: *The general advanced the troops.* **2** to help forward; further: *The President's speech advanced the cause of peace.* **SYN:** promote. **3** to put or bring forward; suggest; offer: *to advance an opinion. What plan to win the game can you advance?* **SYN:** propose, present, adduce, propound. **4** to raise to a higher rank or position; promote: *The colonel advanced him from lieutenant to captain.* **5** to put up; raise (prices); make higher; increase: *The grocer advanced the price of milk by two cents.* **6a** to make earlier in time: *to advance the date of the wedding.* **SYN:** quicken, hasten. **b** to make (a watch or clock) read later: *All clocks should be advanced one hour at the beginning of daylight-saving time.* **c** to cause (the sparking action in an internal-combustion engine) to take place earlier in the cycle. **7** to supply beforehand: *The company advanced the salesman funds for expenses.* **8** to lend (money), especially on security: *to advance a loan.* **9** *Archaic.* to raise or lift up, as one's head.
—*v.i.* **1** to go forward; move forward: *The angry crowd advanced toward the building. The troops advanced.* **2** to make progress; improve: *to advance in skill.* **3** to rise in rank or position; be promoted: *He advanced from vice-president to president of the company.* **4** to go up; increase in amount, price, or value; rise: *Milk advanced two cents a quart. The stock advanced three points.* **5** *U.S.* to make the arrangements for a political campaign; be or act as an advance man: *... Jerry Bruno was "advancing" for John Kennedy, Robert Kennedy, Lyndon Johnson, and others* (New Yorker).
—*n.* **1a** forward movement; progress: *The army's advance was very slow.* **b** the distance covered: *An advance of nine miles brought the army to the village.* **c** the order or signal to move forward. **2a** onward movement in any process or course of action; progress: *the advance of knowledge.* **b** a step forward; a degree of progress: *We have made great advances in airplane design. Modern science has brought a great advance in our understanding of the laws of physics.* **3** a rise in amount, price, or value; increase: *There was an advance of two cents a quart in the price of milk.* **4a** the furnishing of money or goods before they are due or as a loan; payment beforehand. **b** money paid or goods furnished before they are due or as a loan: *He asked for an advance on next week's salary.* **5** that which is forward or ahead, as a body of troops: *I got back on the 5th with the advance ...* (U. S. Grant). **6** *U.S.* the arrangements made for a political campaign by an advance man. **7** *U.S.* a copy of a speech, statement, or briefing, released to the press before it is given: *The press office gave out advances of the senator's speech.*
—*adj.* **1** going before: *the advance guard, advance section of a train.* **2** ahead of time: *The teacher gave advance notice of the change of*

the date of our test. Here's an advance look at what some congressmen are cooking up for the next session (Newsweek). **3** made available before the date of general publication or release: *an advance copy of a book.*
advances, approach made to gain something; attempts or offers toward another or others to settle a difference, to make an acquaintance, or the like; attempt at conciliation; overtures: *Bob made the first advances toward making up his quarrel with Dick.*
in advance, a in front; ahead: *The leader of the band marched in advance.* **b** ahead of time: *I paid for my ticket in advance. Children with bad hearts must also be studied carefully so that the surgeon will know in advance what type of operation he will have to perform* (New York Herald Tribune).
in advance of, ahead of: *Leonardo da Vinci was in advance of his time in designing a flying machine.*
[< Old French *avancier* < Vulgar Latin *abantiare* < Latin *abante* from before < *ab* from + *ante* before] —**ad|vanc′er**, *n.* —**ad|vanc′ing|ly**, *adv.*
—***Syn.*** *v.i.* **1 Advance, proceed, move on** mean to move forward. **Advance** emphasizes to move toward a definite end or destination: *In two plays the team advanced to the one-yard line. The infantry advanced three miles to the ridge.* **Proceed** emphasizes continuing to move forward from a definite point, often a temporary stop or intermediate goal: *Leaving New York, the President and his party proceeded to Philadelphia.* **Move on**, a more informal expression, means to move from a stopping place, but does not suggest a destination: *When the ambulance left, the crowd moved on.*

advance agent, = advance man.

ad|vanced (ad vanst′, -vänst′), *adj.* **1** in front of others; forward: *Our army is in an advanced position.* **2** ahead of most others; having greater knowledge or superior skill: *The advanced class has studied history three years.* **3** ahead of others in progress or ideas; based on the most recently developed principles or theories: *The United States has an aircraft of an advanced design.* **4a** very old; far along in life: *His grandfather lived to the advanced age of 90 years.* **b** far along in development: *the advanced stage of a disease.* **5** increased: *greatly advanced prices.* **6** carried far or too far toward an extreme: *advanced political ideas.*

advanced standing, *U.S.* **1** credit granted by a college to a student for work already done elsewhere. **2** the standing of such a student.

advance guard, 1a a body of troops sent or stationed ahead of others, as for protection or reconnaissance. **b** *Figurative: Today's 20 nuclear electric plants are only the advance guard of a much larger host to come* (New York Times). **2** = avant-garde: *It looks like the first really promising development in youthful, advance guard, or experimental writing in a long time* (Newsweek).
—**ad|vance′-guard′**, *adj.*

advance man, *U.S.* **1** a person, similar to a press agent, whose job is to stimulate interest in a play, motion picture, circus, or other entertainment, before its scheduled showing in a particular place. **2** a person who prepares the travel arrangements and publicity for the political campaign of a candidate.

ad|vance|ment (ad vans′mənt, -väns′-), *n.* **1** a moving forward; improvement: *Hard work brought him an advancement in pay. Anatole France, by himself rather timid and lazy, had at that time a Jewish friend, Mme. Caillavet, who made him work, gave him a salon in her house and generally promoted his advancement* (Edmund Wilson). SYN: furtherance, progress. **2** promotion: *Good work won her advancement to a higher position. His hopes of advancement failing in England, Swift returned to Ireland.* (Thackeray).

ad|van|tage (ad van′tij, -vän′-), *n., v.,* **-taged, -tag|ing.** —***n.*** **1** anything that is a benefit or a help in getting something wanted; favorable condition, circumstance, or opportunity: *Good health is always an advantage. One advantage of having a car ... is the opportunity to keep a flexible schedule* (Atlantic). **2** any gain resulting from a better or superior position: *The boy who can think for himself has an advantage when he begins work.* **3** a better or superior position; superiority: *to maintain a scientific advantage by pioneering in research.* (FORMAL) *She has the advantage of Mrs. Allen, who has no money at all.* (INFORMAL) *Now Dick Tracy has the advantage over the racketeer.* SYN: ascendancy. **4** *Tennis.* **a** the first point scored after deuce. **b** the score thus made. In the United States this term is often shortened to *ad,* in Great Britain to *vantage.* **5** *Obsolete.* an opportunity: *Make use of time, let not advantage slip* (Shakespeare).
—***v.t.*** to give an advantage to; help; benefit: *Boston was also advantaged with the neighborhood of the country's oldest college* (James Russell Lowell).
—***v.i.*** to gain an advantage; be benefited: *Many animals advantage by nature's coloration.*
take advantage of, a to use to help or benefit oneself: *Take advantage of your illness to catch up on your reading.* **b** to use unfairly; impose upon: *Don't take advantage of me by asking me to run errands on such a hot day.* **c** to seduce (a woman).
take at advantage, to surprise: *Once it happened that the enemy took him at advantage* (Robert Southey).
to (or **with**) **advantage**, to a good effect; with a useful effect; favorably: *That frame sets off the painting to advantage. Head tilted winningly, she was ... seeking to display herself to advantage* (John Updike).
to one's advantage, to one's benefit or help: *It will be to your advantage to study Spanish before you visit Mexico.*
[< Old French *avantage* < *avant* before < Latin *abante* from before < *ab* from + *ante* before]
—***Syn.*** *n.* **2 Advantage, benefit, profit** mean gains of different kinds. **Advantage** applies to a gain resulting from a position of superiority, of any kind, over others: *In the long run, independent thinking will give us many advantages in every field of science.* **Benefit** usually applies to gain in personal or social improvement: *The general relaxation of the body is one of the chief benefits of swimming.* **Profit** applies especially to material gain, but also to gain in anything valuable or valued, such as knowledge: *There is a profit even in mistakes.*

ad|van|taged (ad van′tijd, -vän′-), *adj.* born or living in good circumstances; provided with advantages; privileged: *Isolated in suburbia the advantaged child goes through school feeling no impact from the social and political issues of the day* (Science News).

ad|van|ta|geous (ad′vən tā′jəs), *adj.* giving advantage; favorable; helpful: *From this advantageous position the scouts can observe three roads.* SYN: beneficial, profitable. —**ad′van|ta′geous|ly**, *adv.* —**ad′van|ta′geous|ness**, *n.*

ad|vec|tion (ad vek′shən), *n.* the transfer of heat, cold, or other properties of air by the horizontal motion of a mass of air. [< Latin *advectiō, -ōnis* a conveying < *advehere* carry to < *ad-* to + *vehere* carry]

ad|vec|tion|al (ad vek′shə nəl), *adj.* = advective.

advection fog, a fog that occurs when a body of relatively warm, moist air moves over a cold surface: *Advection fogs often form in the Newfoundland Banks area, where warm air blows over the cold water of the Labrador Current* (George F. Taylor).

ad|vec|tive (ad vek′tiv), *adj.* of or having to do with the horizontal moving of masses of air, involving the transfer of heat or other properties of air.

ad|vene (ad vēn′), *v.i.,* **-vened, -ven|ing.** to come about as something extraneous or adventitious; supervene: *Unexpected benefits often advene from an invention or a discovery.* [< Latin *advenīre* arrive; see etym. under **advent**]

ad|vent (ad′vent), *n.* a coming or arrival, especially of something infrequent or unusually important: *the advent of a new era, the advent of space exploration. The advent of spring was a time for festivals in ancient days.* [< Latin *adventus, -ūs* < *advenīre* arrive < *ad-* to + *venīre* come]

Ad|vent (ad′vent), *n.* **1** the season of devotion including the four Sundays before Christmas. **2** the coming of Christ into the world; birth of Christ. **3** the second coming of Christ at the millennium; Second Advent.

Ad|vent|ism (ad′ven tiz əm, ad ven′-), *n.* the belief or doctrine that the expected second coming of Christ is near at hand. —**Ad′vent|ist**, *n., adj.*

ad|ven|ti|ti|a (ad′ven tish′ē ə), *n.* a membranous structure covering but not properly belonging to an organ, especially a blood vessel. [< Latin *adventīcia,* neuter plural of *adventīcius;* see etym. under **adventitious**]

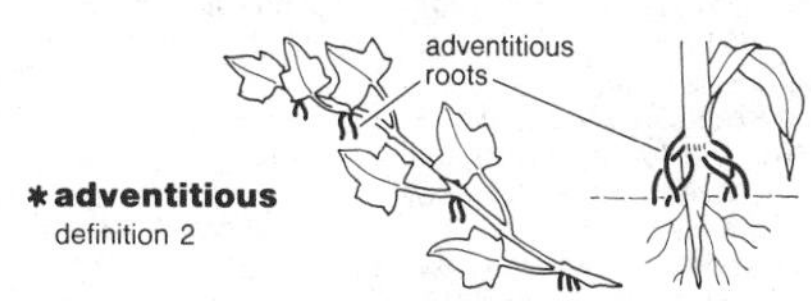

***adventitious**
definition 2

***ad|ven|ti|tious** (ad′ven tish′əs), *adj.* **1** coming from outside; additional; accidental: *The romantic life of the artist gives his painting an adventitious interest.* SYN: casual, extrinsic. **2** *Botany, Zoology.* appearing out of the normal or usual place, such as roots on stems or buds on leaves, or hair where it does not ordinarily grow. [< Latin *adventīcius,* ultimately < *ad-* to + *venīre* come]
—**ad′ven|ti′tious|ly**, *adv.* —**ad′ven|ti′tious|ness**, *n.*

ad|ven|tive (ad ven′tiv), *adj., n. Botany, Zoology.* —***adj.*** introduced into a new environment; not native or established, though growing with cultivation.
—***n.*** a plant or animal not native to the environment: *Many foreign weeds are adventives, until they become naturalized* (Norman Taylor).

Advent Sunday, the first of the four Sundays in Advent; the Sunday nearest to Saint Andrew's Day (November 30).

ad|ven|ture (ad ven′chər), *n., v.,* **-tured, -tur|ing.**
—***n.*** **1** an exciting or unusual experience: *The trip to Alaska was quite an adventure for her.* **2** a bold undertaking, usually exciting and somewhat dangerous: *the daring adventure of rocketing into outer space. Sailing across the Pacific on a raft was a daring adventure.* **3** readiness to take part in exciting or dangerous undertakings; the seeking of excitement or danger: *An explorer must have a spirit of adventure.* **4** a business undertaking; commercial speculation; venture: *an ill-advised adventure in oil stocks.* **5** *Obsolete.* risk; jeopardy; peril. **6** *Obsolete.* fortune; luck.
—***v.t.*** **1** to dare to do; venture on: *So bold Leander would adventure it* (Shakespeare). **2** to expose to danger or loss; risk; hazard: *to adventure one's life.* **3** to venture to say; volunteer.
—***v.i.*** **1** to risk oneself: *Now he adventured on a shore unknown* (Byron). **2** to venture; dare: *She feared she could not safely adventure to do so* (Scott).
[< Old French *aventure* < Latin *adventūra* (*rēs*) (thing) about to happen < *advenīre* arrive < *ad-* to + *venīre* come]

ad|ven|tur|er (ad ven′chər ər), *n.* **1** a person who has or seeks adventures. SYN: daredevil, venturer, adventurist. **2** a soldier ready to serve in any army that will hire him. SYN: soldier of fortune. **3** a person who lives by his wits in ways that are not entirely honest or respectable; one who schemes for money or social position. SYN: intriguer, opportunist. **4** a person who undertakes commercial risks; a speculator. **5** a person who financed early trading ventures.

ad|ven|ture|some (ad ven′chər səm), *adj.* bold and daring; adventurous. —**ad|ven′ture|someness**, *n.*

ad|ven|tur|ess (ad ven′chər is), *n.* **1** a woman who schemes to get money or social position: *The odious little adventuress* [*Becky Sharp*] *making her curtsey* (Thackeray). **2** a woman adventurer.

ad|ven|tur|ism (ad ven′chə riz əm), *n.* the urging or undertaking of a program, policy, or the like, without careful planning. —**ad|ven′tur|ist**, *n.* —**ad|ven′tur|is′tic**, *adj.*

ad|ven|tur|ous (ad ven′chər əs), *adj.* **1** fond of adventures; ready to take risks; rashly daring: *Magellan was a bold, adventurous explorer.* SYN: venturous, venturesome. **2** enterprising; daring: *an adventurous people.* **3** full of danger; involving risk; dangerous; hazardous: *An expedition to the North Pole is an adventurous undertaking.* —**ad|ven′tur|ous|ly**, *adv.* —**ad|ven′tur|ous|ness**, *n.*

ad|verb (ad′vėrb), *n.* **1** a word that tells how, when, or where something happens. In "He walked slowly," "He came late," "I saw her there," and "She sings well," *slowly, late, there,* and *well* are adverbs. Adverbs also tell how much or how little is meant. In "This soup is very good" and "She is rather slow," *very* and *rather* are adverbs. An adverb is used to extend or limit the meaning of a verb (he ran *fast*), an adjective (*exceedingly* bright), another adverb (*very* quickly), or a phrase, clause, or even a whole sentence (*almost* through the wall; *just* what I wanted; *finally,* I went home). Most adverbs are made up of adjectives or participles plus the ending *-ly,* like *badly* in "He rowed badly" and *deservedly* in "She was deservedly popular." **2** a form class or part of speech comprising these or similar words. *Abbr:* adv. [< Latin *adverbium* < *ad-* to + *verbum* verb, word]
▶ Many of the very frequently used adverbs have no formal feature identifying them as adverbs (*soon, there, twice,* etc.). In some recent analyses of English syntax, some of the words which have traditionally been classified as adverbs but are greatly restricted in the part they play in organization of English sentences are separated from the adverb class and assigned to their own classes. For instance, *very, more,*

Pronunciation Key: hat, āge, cãre, fär; let, ēqual, tėrm; it, īce; hot, ōpen, ôrder; oil, out; cup, pu̇t, rüle; child; long; thin; ᴛʜen; zh, measure; ə represents a in about, e in taken, i in pencil, o in lemon, u in circus.

somewhat are sometimes assigned to a class of *intensifiers; therefore* to a class of *sentence connectors.*

ad|ver|bi|al (ad vėr′bē əl), *adj., n.* —*adj.* **1** used as an adverb. In the sentence "He worked as quickly as possible," *as quickly as possible* is an adverbial phrase modifying the verb *worked.* **2** of an adverb; forming adverbs: *-ly is an adverbial suffix.* **3** given to the use of or containing adverbs: *an adverbial style.*
—*n.* an adverbial word or group of words. —**ad-ver′bi|al|ly,** *adv.*

ad|ver|bi|al|i|ty (ad vėr′bē al′ə tē), *n.* the state or quality of being adverbial.

ad|ver|bi|al|ize (ad vėr′bē ə līz), *v.t.,* **-ized, -iz-ing.** to make an adverb of (a word or phrase).

ad ver|bum (ad vėr′bəm), *Latin.* word for word; verbatim.

ad|ver|sar|y (ad′vər ser′ē), *n., pl.* **-sar|ies,** *adj.* —*n.* **1** a person or group opposing or hostile to another person or group; enemy; antagonist: *The United States and Japan were adversaries in World War II.* SYN: foe. **2** a person or group on the other side in a contest; opponent: *Which school is our adversary in this week's football game?* SYN: rival, contestant.
—*adj.* antagonistic; adverse: *"The hearings," Senator Watkins said on the opening day, "are not to be adversary in character"* (New Yorker).
the Adversary, Satan, as the enemy of mankind; the Devil: *Or shall the Adversary thus obtain his end?* (Milton).
[< Latin *adversārius* < *adversus;* see etym. under **adverse**]

ad|ver|sa|tive (ad vėr′sə tiv), *adj., n.* —*adj.* expressing contrast, opposition, or antithesis: *"But" and "yet" are adversative conjunctions.*
—*n.* an adversative word, expression, or proposition. [< Late Latin *adversātīvus,* ultimately < *ad-* against + *vertere* turn] —**ad|ver′sa|tive|ly,** *adv.*

ad|verse (ad vėrs′, ad′vėrs; *see note below*), *adj.* **1** unfriendly in purpose or effect; hostile: *His adverse criticisms discouraged me.* SYN: antagonistic. **2** acting against one's interests; unfavorable; harmful: *adverse circumstances. Dirt and disease are adverse to the best growth of children. An unbalanced diet has an adverse effect upon health.* SYN: injurious, inimical. **3** acting in or coming from a contrary direction; opposing: *Adverse winds hinder planes.* **4** opposite in position. **5** *Botany.* turned toward the stem. [< Latin *adversus* turned against, past participle of *advertere* turn to < *ad-* to + *vertere* turn] —**ad|verse′ly,** *adv.* —**ad|verse′ness,** *n.*
▶ **adverse.** The accent may be placed on either syllable: ad vėrs′ or ad′vėrs. When *adverse* stands alone the stress is usually on the second syllable: *The winds were ad|verse′.* When *adverse* precedes a noun, the stress is usually on the first syllable: *Ad′verse criticism upsets him.*

ad|ver|si|ty (ad vėr′sə tē), *n., pl.* **-ties. 1** a condition of unhappiness, misfortune, or distress; being in unfavorable circumstances, especially unfavorable financial circumstances: *He that never was acquainted with adversity has seen the world but on one side* (Samuel Johnson). SYN: See syn. under **misfortune. 2** a particular misfortune; calamity; hardship: *In trouble, sorrow, need, sickness, or any other adversity* (Book of Common Prayer).

ad|vert[1] (ad vėrt′), *v.i.* **1** to refer (to) in speaking or writing; direct attention: *The speaker adverted to the need for caution on the roads. There is one other obvious contingency in this connection, and to it I shall now advert* (Atlantic). SYN: allude. **2** to turn the attention; take notice or heed; attend (to). [< Latin *advertere* turn to < *ad-* to + *vertere* turn]

ad|vert[2] (ad′vėrt), *n. British Informal.* an advertisement.
▶ See **ad**[1] for usage note.

ad|vert|ence (ad vėr′təns), *n.* a directing or turning of the mind; attention or heed.

ad|vert|en|cy (ad vėr′tən sē), *n.* the quality or habit of attentiveness; heedfulness.

ad|vert|ent (ad vėr′tənt), *adj.* attentive; heedful; noticing. [< Latin *advertēns, -entis,* present participle of *advertere* turn to < *ad-* to + *vertere* turn] —**ad|vert′ent|ly,** *adv.*

ad|ver|tise (ad′vər tīz, ad′vər tīz′), *v.,* **-tised, -tis-ing.** —*v.t.* **1** to give public notice of in newspapers and magazines, over the radio, by television or billboard; announce: *When people lose something valuable, they advertise it in the newspaper.* SYN: publicize. **2** to praise publicly the good qualities of (a product, service or idea) in order to create a demand or promote sales: *Manufacturers advertise products that they wish to sell.* SYN: promote, boost, recommend. **3** to call attention to; make conspicuous; emphasize: *His bad spelling advertises his ignorance.* SYN: proclaim, announce. **4** to notify; inform: *We have advertised our correspondents abroad of our new process.* SYN: advise, apprise. —*v.i.* **1** to ask by public notice (for): *He advertised for a job.* **2** to seek to sell goods or services by advertising; issue advertising: *It pays to advertise.* Also, **advertize.**
[< Middle French *advertiss-,* stem of *advertir* < Latin *advertere* turn to < *ad-* to + *vertere* turn]
—**ad′ver|tis′er,** *n.*

ad|ver|tise|ment or **ad|ver|tize|ment** (ad′vər-tīz′mənt; ad vėr′tis-, -tiz-; ad′vər tīz′-), *n.* **1** a public announcement or printed notice, recommending some product or service, or informing of some need. Advertisements are usually published in a newspaper or magazine, displayed by posters, distributed by circulars, or broadcast over radio or television. *The furniture store has an advertisement in the newspaper of a special sale. A good advertisement attracts by its news value, convinces by its simplicity, and sells by creating desire through common-sense appeal* (Walter J. Carlson). *Abbr:* advt. **2** *Archaic.* information.
▶ **Announcements** often contain news of direct or even vital benefit to the hearer or reader, while **advertisement** suggests the primary motive is to benefit the advertiser, usually by persuading the hearer or reader to part with money.

ad|ver|tis|ing (ad′vər tī′zing, ad′vər tī′-), *n.* **1** the business of preparing, publishing, or circulating advertisements: *In 1931 F.D.R. surprisingly confessed: "If I were starting life over again I would probably give first thought to making advertising my career ... because it combines real imagination with a deep study of psychology"* (Time). **2** advertisements collectively: *Billboards carry advertising. Fashions in advertising change frequently.* **3** a bringing to public notice by radio or television announcements, published notices, posters, or other means: *The store attracted many customers by advertising.*

ad|ver|tize (ad′vər tīz, ad′vər tīz′), *v.t., v.i.,* **-tized, -tiz|ing.** = advertise.

ad|vice (ad vīs′), *n.* **1** an opinion about what should be done; suggestion; recommendation: *To keep well, follow the doctor's advice.* **2** Often, **advices.** news, especially from a distance; information: *Advices of the score from the returning spectators were incomplete. Washington advices indicated the votes will be very close either way* (Wall Street Journal). SYN: report, word. [< Old French *avis* < (*ce*) *m'est a vis* my view is < Vulgar Latin *mihi est vīsum,* for Latin *mihi vidētur* seems (best) to me]
—*Syn.* **1 Advice, counsel** mean an opinion given by a person for the guidance of another. **Advice** is the general word: *I asked her advice about which paint to buy.* **Counsel** is the more formal word, suggesting the giving of a professional or more carefully considered opinion: *The senior asked the bank president for counsel about a career in banking.*

ad|vis|a|bil|i|ty (ad vī′zə bil′ə tē), *n.* the quality of being advisable; fitness; propriety; expediency: *He asked about the advisability of buying a used car. In any case, it was obvious that it would have been impossible for the leadership to have done more than hint at the advisability of moderation* (London Times).

ad|vis|a|ble (ad vī′zə bəl), *adj.* **1** to be advised or recommended; wise; sensible; suitable: *It is not advisable for him to go to school while he is still sick. A hot-air furnace is not advisable for a large building.* SYN: prudent, expedient. **2** open to advice. —**ad|vis′a|ble|ness,** *n.* —**ad|vis′a|bly,** *adv.*

ad|vise (ad vīz′), *v.,* **-vised, -vis|ing.** —*v.t.* **1** to give advice to; offer an opinion to; counsel: *He advised me to put my money in the bank. Advise him to be cautious.* SYN: caution, warn, admonish. **2** to recommend as a remedy, policy, or plan of action: *His doctor advised complete rest.* SYN: suggest. **3** to give notice to; inform; tell: *We were advised of the dangers before we began our trip. Please advise me of the date of delivery.* SYN: notify, acquaint. —*v.i.* **1** to give advice; recommend: *I shall do as you advise.* **2** *Especially U.S.* to talk over plans; consult (with); confer: *Before buying a house he advised with friends who owned houses.* **3** *Obsolete.* to consider; reflect. [< Old French *aviser* < *avis;* see etym. under **advice**]

ad|vised (ad vīzd′), *adj.* **1** considered: *an ill-advised remark.* SYN: planned, thought-out. **2** informed: *Keep me advised.*

ad|vis|ed|ly (ad vī′zid lē), *adv.* after careful consideration; deliberately: *We speak advisedly and from experience when we say that this was the general feeling* (Harriet Martineau).

ad|vis|ee (ad vī′zē, ad′vī zē′), *n.* **1** a person who is advised. **2** *Education, especially U.S.* a student assigned to an adviser.

ad|vise|ment (ad vīz′mənt), *n.* careful consideration; consultation: *The lawyer took our case under advisement and said he would give us an answer in two weeks.*

ad|vis|er or **ad|vi|sor** (ad vī′zər), *n.* **1** a person who gives advice: *a political adviser on foreign affairs.* SYN: counselor, mentor. **2** *U.S.* a teacher or other person appointed to advise a student or students.

ad|vi|so|ry (ad vī′zər ē), *adj., n., pl.* **-ries.** —*adj.* **1** having power to advise, but not to determine or direct policy: *an advisory committee.* SYN: consultative. **2** containing advice: *to offer an advisory opinion.*
—*n.* **1** a bulletin or report to advise of developments: *An advisory by the Weather Service warned of a hurricane.* **2** a recommendation; report: *An executive ... was quite disturbed over an advisory presented to him by his firm's legal counsel* (Drug Trade News). —**ad|vi′so|ri|ly,** *adv.*

ad vi|vum (ad vī′vəm), *Latin.* (of portraits) life-like.

ad|vo|caat (ad′vō kät′), *n.* a Dutch eggnog. [< Dutch *advocatenborrel* (literally) lawyer's drink < *advocaat* lawyer + *borrel* drink]

ad|vo|ca|cy (ad′və kə sē), *n.* **1** the act of speaking or writing in favor of something; public recommendation; support: *The President's advocacy of the plan won support for it.* **2a** the profession or art of pleading a case before a court. **b** the pleading of a case: *A lawyer's professional advocacy of a case does not always imply his private belief in it.* [< Middle French *advocacie,* learned borrowing from Medieval Latin *advocatia* < Latin *advocātus* an advocate]

advocacy journalism, journalism that promotes a particular point of view, especially in news articles.

advocacy planning, a form of city planning in which advice and cooperation is sought from nonprofessional people, such as businessmen, homeowners, and civic groups, who would be affected by a particular plan.

ad|vo|cate (*v.* ad′və kāt; *n.* ad′və kit, -kāt), *v.,* **-cat|ed, -cat|ing,** *n.* —*v.t.* to speak or write in favor of; recommend publicly (a measure, policy, belief, or theory); support: *He advocates building more good roads.* SYN: urge. [< noun]
—*n.* **1** a person who speaks in favor; one who pleads or argues publicly for something, such as a proposal, belief, or theory; supporter: *He is an advocate of better school buildings.* SYN: champion. **2** a person who pleads or speaks for another; intercessor; defender: *The advocates of Charles have very dexterously contrived to conceal ... the real nature of this transaction* (Macaulay). **3** a lawyer who pleads the cause of anyone in certain courts of law: *Lord Birkett ... was one of the great advocates of his age ... he was an unsurpassed pleader* (Manchester Guardian Weekly). **4 Advocate,** Christ (in the Bible, I John 2:1). *Come, thou Advocate and Saviour, Manifest thy wondrous grace* (John Wesley).
[< Old French *avocat,* learned borrowing from Latin *advocātus,* (originally) past participle of *advocāre* summon < *ad-* to + *vocāre* call]
▶ **Advocate** (def. 3) survives as the technical title in courts of certain countries and regions which retain substantial elements of the Roman law, such as Scotland. It is also the title used in the British admiralty courts, and certain special British tribunals, but not in ordinary English law courts, where **barrister** is used.

ad|vo|ca|tion (ad′və kā′shən), *n.* **1** the process by which a Scottish or papal superior court brings an action before itself from an inferior court. **2** = advocacy.

ad|vo|ca|tor (ad′və kā′tər), *n.* = advocate (defs. 1 and 2).

ad|voc|a|to|ry (ad vok′ə tôr′ē, -tōr′-), *adj.* of or having to do with an advocate.

ad|vo|ca|tus di|a|bo|li (ad′və kā′təs dī ab′ə lī), *Latin.* **1** a devil's advocate, appointed to argue against a proposed beatification or canonization in the Roman Catholic Church. **2** an adverse critic, especially one whose criticism is solicited in order to test the supporter's judgment.

ad|vow|ee (ad′vou ē′), *n.* a person who has a right of advowson in English law. [< Old French *avoue* < Latin *advocātus* an advocate]

ad|vow|son (ad vou′zən), *n.* the right, in English law, to select and name the person to be appointed to a vacant church benefice or living. It is considered a right of property and as such can be sold. [< Old North French *advowson,* Old French *avoëson* < Latin *advocātiō, -ōnis,* ultimately < *ad-* to + *vocāre* call]

advt., advertisement.

ad|wom|an (ad′wům′ən), *n., pl.* **-wom|en.** *U.S. Informal.* a woman whose business is advertising; advertising woman.

ad|y|na|mi|a (ad′ə nā′mē ə), *n.* physical weakness or debility; asthenia. [< Greek *adynamiā* < *a-* without + *dýnamis* power]

ad|y|nam|ic (ad′ə nam′ik, ā′dī-), *adj.* physically weak; asthenic.

ad|y|tum (ad′ə təm), *n., pl.* **-ta** (-tə). **1** the innermost part of an ancient Greek or Roman temple, open only to the priests. **2** *Figurative.* an inner room; a sanctum. [< Latin *adytum* < Greek *ády-ton,* neuter of *ádytos* not to be entered < *a-* not + *dýein* enter]

***adz** or **adze** (adz), *n., v.,* **adzed, adz|ing.** —*n.* a tool somewhat like an ax, used for shaping heavy timbers. The blade is set across the end of the handle and curves inward. —*v.t.* to shape with an adz. [Old English *adesa*]

***adz**

ad|zu|ki bean (ad zü′kē), a variety of kidney bean widely grown for food in China and Japan. Also, **adsuki bean.** [< Japanese *azuki*]

ae (ā), *adj. Scottish.* one.

ae., at the age of. See **aet.**

Ae|a|cus (ē′ə kəs), *n. Greek Mythology.* a son of Zeus, grandfather of Achilles, and one of the three judges of Hades.

AEC (no periods) or **A.E.C.,** Atomic Energy Commission (of the United States, abolished in 1974). See **ERDA, NRC.**

ae|ci|al stage (ē′shē əl), the phase in the life cycle of certain rust fungi in which aecia (spores) are produced.

ae|cid|i|al stage (i sid′ē əl), *British.* aecial stage.

ae|cid|i|o|spore (i sid′ē ə spôr, -spōr), *n. British.* an aeciospore.

ae|cid|i|um (i sid′ē əm), *n., pl.* **-i|a** (-ē ə). *British.* an aecium.

ae|ci|o|spore (ē′sē ə spôr, -spōr), *n.* a spore produced in an aecium, having two nuclei.

ae|ci|o|stage (ē′sē ə stāj), *n.* = aecial stage.

ae|ci|um (ē′shē əm, -sē-), *n., pl.* **-ci|a** (-shē ə, -sē-). a cup-shaped structure which produces chains of spores (aeciospores), formed by the fusion of spores of opposite mating types of certain rust fungi. They usually appear on the lower surface of the leaf of the host plant. Also, *British,* **aecidium.** [< New Latin *aecium* < Greek *aikīā* injury < *aikḗs* unseemly]

AECL (no periods), Atomic Energy of Canada Limited.

a|ë|des (ā ē′dēz), *n.* **1** any mosquito of the species that transmits yellow fever and dengue; tiger mosquito. **2** any other mosquito of the same genus. [< New Latin *Aedes* < Greek *aēdḗs* unpleasant < *a-* without + *ēdos* pleasure]

ae|dile (ē′dīl), *n.* an elected official in ancient Rome in charge of promoting public games and circuses, maintaining public order, supervising traffic, and superintending public buildings and lands, the marketplace, and food and water supplies. Also, **edile.** [< Latin *aedīlis,* probably (originally) a temple official < *aedēs* temple] —**ae′dile-ship,** *n.*

Ae|ë|tes (ē ē′tēz), *n. Greek Legend.* a king of Colchis, from whom the Golden Fleece was stolen by Jason and Medea, Aeëtes' daughter.

A.E.F. or **AEF** (no periods), **1** Allied Expeditionary Force (during World War II). **2** American Expeditionary Forces or Force (soldiers sent to Europe by the United States during World War I).

Ae|ge|an (ē jē′ən), *adj.* **1** of or in the Aegean Sea, between Greece and Asia Minor, or the islands in it. **2** of or having to do with the first great European civilization (from about 3000 to about 1100 B.C.) that flourished on Crete and nearby islands, during the Bronze Age and spread to Greece before 1400 B.C.

ae|ger (ē′jər), *n.* = aegrotat. [< Latin *aeger* sick]

ae|ge|ri|id (i jir′ē id), *n. Zoology.* a moth of a family having mainly transparent, scaleless wings; a clearwing. [< New Latin *Aegeriidae* the family name < Latin *Aegeria,* a nymph]

Ae|ge|us (ē′jē əs, -jüs), *n. Greek Legend.* the father of Theseus who, thinking his son was dead, threw himself into the Aegean Sea.

ae|gi|lops (ē′jə lops, ej′ə-), *n.* = egilops.

Ae|gi|ne|tan sculptures or **marbles** (ē′jə nē′-tən), a collection of sculptures dating from the 400's B.C., discovered in 1811 on the island of Aegina, off the southeastern coast of Greece.

Ae|gir (ā′gir, ē′jir), *n.* the Old Norse god of the sea, husband of Ran.

ae|gis (ē′jis), *n.* **1** Also, **Aegis.** *Greek Mythology.* the shield or breastplate used by Zeus or by his daughter Athena. According to one legend the shield was made by Hephaestus (Vulcan) for Zeus. Whenever Athena went on a mission for Zeus, she carried the Aegis with her as a sign of authority. **2** *Figurative.* protecting influence or care; protection: *the aegis of the law.* SYN: shield, shelter. **3** *Figurative.* sponsorship; auspices: *The conference on world health was held under the aegis of the United Nations.* Also, **egis.** [< Latin *aegis* < Greek *aigís*]

Ae|gis|thus (i jis′thəs), *n. Greek Legend.* the lover of Clytemnestra, and her accomplice in murdering her husband, Agamemnon. He was, in turn, killed by Agamemnon's son, Orestes.

ae|gro|tat (i grō′tat), *n.* **1** a medical certificate given at certain British and Canadian universities to a student too ill to attend an examination. **2** the unclassified degree awarded to a student on the basis of this certificate. Also, **aeger.** [< Latin *aegrōtat* he is sick]

Ae|gyp|to|pith|e|cus (i jip′tō pith′ə kəs), *n.* an extinct anthropoid ape of the early Miocene whose remains were discovered in 1966 in the Fayum desert region of Egypt. [< New Latin *Aegyptopithecus* < Greek *Aígyptos* Egypt + *píthē-kos* ape]

ae|lu|ro|phile (i lůr′ə fīl, -lyůr′-), *n.* = ailurophile. [< Greek *aílouros* cat + English *-phile*]

ae|lu|ro|phil|i|a (i lůr′ə fil′ē ə, -lyůr′-), *n.* = ailurophilia. [< Greek *aílouros* cat + English *-philia*]

ae|lu|ro|phobe (i lůr′ə fōb, -lyůr′-), *n.* = ailurophobe. [< Greek *aílouros* cat + English *-phobe*]

ae|lu|ro|pho|bi|a (i lůr′ə fō′bē ə, -lyůr′-), *n.* = ailurophobia. [< Greek *aílouros* cat + English *-phobia*]

Ae|ne|as (i nē′əs), *n. Greek and Roman Legend.* a Trojan hero, son of Anchises and Aphrodite (Venus). After the fall of Troy, he escaped from the burning city carrying his father and leading his little son. After years of wandering he reached Italy, where his descendants supposedly founded Rome.

Ae|ne|id (i nē′id), *n.* a long poem by Virgil telling the story of the wanderings and adventures of Aeneas. It is a Latin epic poem in twelve books, completed about 19 B.C.

ae|ne|o|lith|ic (ā′nē ə lith′ik), *adj.* chalcolithic. [< Latin *aēneus* of bronze + Greek *líthos* stone + English *-ic*]

a|e|ne|ous (ā ē′nē əs), *adj.* bronze-colored (used especially of insects). [< Latin *aēneus* (with English *-ous*) brazen]

ae|o|li|an (ē ō′lē ən), *adj.* **1** of or produced by the winds: *aeolian sandstone.* **2** carried by the winds: *aeolian soil.* [< Latin *Aeolius* of *Aeolus,* god of the winds (< Greek *Aíolos* < *aiólos* changeful) + English *-an*]

Ae|o|li|an[1] (ē ō′lē ən), *adj.* of Aeolus. Also, **Eolian.**

Ae|o|li|an[2] (ē ō′lē ən), *adj., n.* —*adj.* belonging to a certain branch of the Greek people that lived in Boeotia, Thessaly, and Asia Minor.
—*n.* a member of this branch. Also, **Eolian.**

***aeolian harp** or **lyre,** a box that gives out musical sounds when currents of air blow across the six or more tuned strings fitted over openings in its top, causing the strings to vibrate; wind harp.

***aeolian harp**
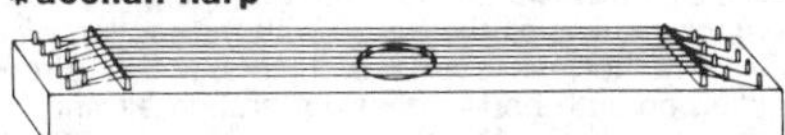

Aeolian mode, 1 one of the modes in ancient Greek music, characterized as grand and stately. **2** a mode of medieval church music, beginning and ending on the note A.

Ae|ol|ic (ē ol′ik), *n., adj.* —*n.* one of the great groups of dialects of ancient Greece, spoken in Aeolis, Lesbos, Thessaly, and Boeotia.
—*adj.* of Aeolis. Also, **Eolic.**

ae|o|li|na (ē′ə lī′nə), *n.* = aeoline.

ae|o|line (ē′ə līn), *n. Music.* **1** a soft organ stop. **2** = harmonica. [< *Aeolus* + *-ine*[1]]

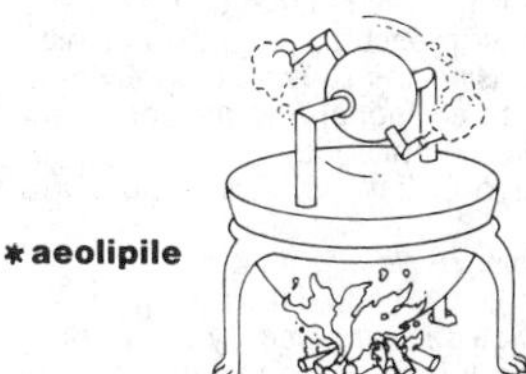
***aeolipile**

***ae|o|li|pile** or **ae|o|li|pyle** (ē′ə lə pīl, ē ol′ə-), *n.* an apparatus demonstrating the principle of the jet engine, said to have been invented by Hero of Alexandria, consisting of a boiler connected to a pivoted spherical vessel having two tubes bent at right angles to the pivot. Reaction to jets of steam escaping through the tubes causes the vessel to rotate. Also, **eolipile, eolipyle.** [< Latin *aeolipila* < *Aeolus* god of the winds + *pila* ball]

ae|o|lo|trop|ic (ē′ə lə trop′ik), *adj. Physics.* varying in properties and behavior along different axes or directions; anisotropic. [< Greek *aiólos* changeful + *tropḗ* a turning + English *-ic*]

ae|o|lot|ro|pism (ē′ə lot′rə piz əm), *n. Physics.* = anisotropy.

ae|o|lot|ro|py (ē′ə lot′rə pē), *n. Physics.* = anisotropy.

Ae|o|lus (ē′ə ləs), *n.* **1** *Greek Mythology.* the god of the winds. **2** a legendary king of Thessaly.

ae|on (ē′ən, -on), *n.* = eon.

ae|o|ni|an (ē ō′nē ən), *adj.* eternal. Also, **eonian.** [< Greek *aiṓnios* eternal (< *aiṓn* age) + English *-an*]

ae|py|or|nis (ē′pē ôr′nis), *n.* a gigantic, extinct, flightless bird of Madagascar; elephant bird. [< Greek *aipýs* high + *órnis* bird]

ae|quo a|ni|mo (ē′kwō an′ə mō), *Latin.* with an even mind; calmly; tranquilly.

ae|quor|in (i kwôr′ən), *n.* a protein in certain jellyfish which causes them to glow in the presence of calcium, extracted for use as a natural source of luminescence. [< New Latin *Aequorea* the genus name of the jellyfish (< Latin *aequor* the level sea < *aequus* level, even) + English *-in*]

aer-, *combining form.* the form of **aero-** used sometimes before vowels, as in *aerate.* [< Latin *āēr* air < Greek *āḗr*]

ae|rar|i|an (ē rãr′ē ən), *n., adj.* in ancient Rome: —*n.* one of the lowest class of Roman citizens, who paid only a poll tax but had no right to vote.
—*adj.* connected with the public treasury; fiscal. [< Latin *aerārius* fiscal (< *aes, aeris* copper, money) + English *-an*]

aer|ate (ãr′āt), *v.t.,* **-at|ed, -at|ing. 1** to expose to and mix with air: *Water in some reservoirs is aerated and purified by spraying it high into the air.* **2** to fill with a gas; charge or mix with gas, often under pressure: *Soda water is water that has been aerated with carbon dioxide.* **3** to expose to chemical action with oxygen: *Blood is aerated in the lungs.* **4** to expose to air. [< *aer-* + *-ate*[1]] —**aer|a′tion,** *n.* —**aer′a|tor,** *n.*

aer|at|ed water (ãr′ā tid), = mineral water.

aer|en|chy|ma (ãr eng′kə mə), *n.* a type of tissue containing large air spaces, found especially in the stems of certain aquatic plants. [< Greek *āḗr* air + *énchyma* infusion < *encheîn* pour in < *en-* in + *cheîn* pour]

ae|re per|en|ni|us (ir′ē pə ren′ē əs), *Latin.* more lasting than bronze (from Horace's line *exegi monumentum ære perennius,* "I have completed a monument more lasting than bronze").

aer|i|al (*n.* ãr′ē əl; *adj.* ãr′ē əl, ā ir′-), *n., adj.* —*n.* **1** a long wire or set of wires or rods used in radio, television, and radar for sending out or receiving electromagnetic waves; antenna.
2 *American Football.* a forward pass: *Jerry Harper hit Johnny Bell with an aerial good for 50 yards and a score* (New York Times). [< adjective]
—*adj.* **1a** of or for aircraft; having to do with aviation in any way: *an aerial ferry.* **b** carried out by or seen from aircraft: *aerial farming, aerial spraying, an aerial view of the city.* **2** living in the air: **a** growing in the air instead of in soil: *The banyan tree has aerial roots.* **b** floating or flying in the air: *Petrels are the most aerial and oceanic of birds* (Charles Darwin). **3** of or having to do with the air; atmospheric: *aerial currents.* **4** extending high into the air; lofty: *aerial mountains.* SYN: airy. **5a** as light as air; ethereal: *sweet, faint, aerial music.* SYN: delicate. **b** as thin as air; unsubstantial; imaginary: *aerial beings, fine and aerial distinctions.* SYN: immaterial. **6** *Archaic.* consisting of air; gaseous.
[< Latin *aerius* (< Greek *āérios*) + English *-al*[1]]
—**aer′i|al|ly,** *adv.* —**aer′i|al|ness,** *n.*
▶**aerial.** The pronunciation in four syllables, ā ir′-ē əl, is often made necessary by the meter in reading poetry and is still the preferred pronunciation in the more literary uses of the word: *moving with aerial grace.* In the more common senses (*aerial warfare*) pronunciation with three syllables is established and natural.
▶See **air** for another usage note.

aerial bar, a high trapeze, as in a circus.

aer|i|al|ist (ãr′ē ə list), *n.* an acrobat who performs feats on a trapeze, tightrope, or the like.

aer|i|al|i|ty (ãr′ē al′ə tē, ā ir′-), *n.* airiness; unsubstantiality.

aerial ladder, a very long ladder that can be extended, such as is used by firemen.

aerial mine, 1 a mine designed to be dropped

Pronunciation Key: hat, āge, cãre, fär; let, ēqual, tėrm; it, īce; hot, ōpen, ôrder; oil, out; cup, pu̇t, rüle; child; long; thin; ᴛʜen; zh, measure; ə represents **a** in about, **e** in taken, **i** in pencil, **o** in lemon, **u** in circus.

from an aircraft into water. **2** a very heavy bomb, especially one slowed in its descent by a parachute.

aerial perspective, the branch of perspective that has to do with the variations of light, shade, and color in objects that are drawn or painted according to their distances from the observer, the quantity of light falling on them, and the medium through which they are seen.

aerial photograph, a vertical or oblique photograph taken from an aircraft, for military, meteorological, or mapping purposes.

aerial photography, the process or technique of taking photographs from aircraft.

aerial railway or **aerial tramway**, overhead cables or rails from which a car is suspended to move persons and things across a river, canyon, or other difficult place to cross.

aerial rocket, a rocket launched from an aircraft.

aerial survey, a survey of land made by means of aerial photographs.

aerial tanker, an airplane used to refuel other airplanes while in the air.

aerial torpedo, a torpedo designed to be released from a low-flying aircraft into water (no longer used).

***aer|ie** or **aër|ie** (ãr′ē, ir′-), *n.* **1** the nest of an eagle, hawk, or other bird of prey, usually built in a lofty place. **2** the young eagles, hawks, or other birds in such a nest. **3** *Figurative.* a house, castle, or the like, placed high on a rock or mountainside. Also, **aery, aëry, eyrie, eyry.** [< Medieval Latin *aeria* < Old French *aire* < Latin *ārea* open space, or *ager, agrī* field]

***aerie** definition 1

aer|ied or **aër|ied** (ãr′ēd, ir′-), *adj.* having an aerie or aeries: *an aeried crag.*

aer|if|er|ous (ãr if′ər əs, ā′ə rif′-), *adj.* conveying air. [< Latin *āēr, āeris* air + English *-ferous*]

aer|i|fi|ca|tion (ãr′ə fə kā′shən, ā ir′-), *n.* an aerifying or being aerified, as by bubbling air through.

aer|i|form (ãr′ə fôrm, ā ir′-), *adj.* **1** having the form of air; gaseous: *substances existing in an aeriform state.* **2** *Figurative.* unsubstantial; unreal: *aeriform figures, aeriform attainments.* [< Latin *āēr, āeris* air + English *-form*]

aer|i|fy (ãr′ə fī, ā ir′-), *v.t.,* **-fied, -fy|ing.** **1** to force air into; fill with air; aerate. **2** to convert into vapor or gas. [< Latin *āēr, āeris* air + English *-fy*]

aer|o or **a|ër|o** (ãr′ō), *adj.* **1** of or having to do with aviation or flying; aeronautical. **2** of or for aircraft: ... *the success of the industry in selling airliners and aero engines abroad* (Observer).

aero- or **aëro-**, *combining form.* **1** air; the air; of the air: *Aeroplane = airplane. Aerometer = air meter.*
2 atmosphere; atmospheric: *Aerospace = space in the atmosphere. Aerology = science of the atmosphere.*
3 gas; of gas or gases: *Aerodynamics = dynamics of gases.*
4 of or for aircraft: *Aerobatics = aircraft acrobatics. Aerodrome = landing field for aircraft.*
[< Greek *āēr, āéros* air]

▶**aero-**. When the combining form **aero-** was new in English, it was usually pronounced in three syllables as ā′ə rō- or ā′ər ə-, and the form *aëro-* was preferred in many words because it clearly indicated these pronunciations. With the frequent use of the many words containing it, however, it has come to be pronounced ãr′ō- or ãr′ə- rather generally in both North America and Great Britain, and the spelling *aëro-* has become rare.

aer|o|al|ler|gen (ãr′ō al′ər jən), *n.* any allergen carried by the air, such as pollen or germs.

aer|o|bac|ter (ãr′ō bak′tər), *n.* any one of a genus of aerobic bacteria that ferment sugars with the production of various acids. [< New Latin *Aerobacter* the genus name < *aero-* + *bacterium*]

aer|o|bal|lis|tic (ãr′ō bə lis′tik), *adj.* of or having to do with aeroballistics.

aer|o|bal|lis|tics (ãr′ō bə lis′tiks), *n.* the study of the behavior of projectiles fired from aircraft.

aer|o|bat|ic (ãr′ə bat′ik), *adj.* having to do with or characterized by aerobatics.

aer|o|bat|ics (ãr′ə bat′iks), *n.* **1** the performance of tricks or stunts with an aircraft in flight, such as loops; stunt flying. **2** the art of performing such maneuvers: *The merit of aerobatics is that everything depends on the skill of the pilot; an old and slow aircraft is not a handicap and may even be an advantage* (London Times). [< *aero-* (plane) + (acro)*batics*]

aer|obe (ãr′ōb), *n.* a microorganism, especially any of various bacteria, which can live only in the presence of oxygen. [ultimately < Greek *āēr, āéros* air + *bíos* life]

aer|o|bic (ãr ō′bik), *adj.* **1** living and growing only where there is atmospheric oxygen: *aerobic bacteria.* **2** having to do with or caused by aerobic bacteria. **3** of or having to do with aerobics: *The cardinal requirement of aerobic exercise is that it must tax the person's capacity* (Time). [ultimately < Greek *āēr, āéros* air + *bíos* life] —**aer|o′bi|cal|ly**, *adv.*

aer|o|bics (ãr ō′biks), *n.* **1** a system of exercises based on a correlation of oxygen consumption and physical fitness, and designed to promote the supply and use of oxygen by the body. **2 Aerobics,** a trademark for this system.

aer|o|bi|o|log|i|cal (ãr′ō bī′ə loj′ə kəl), *adj.* of or having to do with aerobiology.

aer|o|bi|ol|o|gist (ãr′ō bī ol′ə jist), *n.* a person who studies aerobiology.

aer|o|bi|ol|o|gy (ãr′ō bī ol′ə jē), *n.* the branch of biology that deals with the way bacteria, viruses, pollen, and the like, are carried through the air.

aer|o|bi|o|sis (ãr′ō bī ō′sis), *n.* life sustained by an organism in the presence of oxygen (contrasted with *anaerobiosis*).

aer|o|bi|ot|ic (ãr′ō bī ot′ik), *adj.* of or characterized by aerobiosis; aerobic.

aer|o|bi|um (ãr ō′bi əm), *n., pl.* **-bi|a** (-bē ə). = aerobe.

aer|o|dist (ãr′ō dist), *n.* a tellurometer adapted to aircraft use for geographical survey. [< *aero-* + *dist*(ance)]

aer|o|do|net|ics (ãr′ō də net′iks), *n.* the art or study of gliding and soaring flight. [< Greek *āerodónētos* soaring (< *āēr, āéros* air + *doneîn* shake) + English *-ics*]

aer|o|drome (ãr′ə drōm), *n. Especially British.* = airdrome; airport.

aer|o|drom|ics (ãr′ə drom′iks), *n. Obsolete.* the science of flying.

aer|o|dy|nam|ic (ãr′ō dī nam′ik, -di-), *adj.* of or having to do with aerodynamics. —**aer′o|dy|nam′i|cal|ly**, *adv.*

aer|o|dy|nam|i|cal (ãr′ō dī nam′ə kəl, -di-), *adj.* = aerodynamic.

aerodynamic heating, the heating of the leading edge or surface of an object moving through the atmosphere at high speed, caused by friction with the air.

aer|o|dy|nam|i|cist (ãr′ō dī nam′ə sist, -di-), *n.* a person who studies aerodynamics: *But as soon as man began to probe into the high atmosphere with jet airplanes and rockets, aerodynamicists became aware that they must begin to pay attention not only to the gross behavior of air but also to the behavior of its individual molecules* (Scientific American).

aer|o|dy|nam|ics (ãr′ō dī nam′iks, -di-), *n.* the branch of physics that deals with the motion of air and other gases around objects, and of forces acting on both bodies passing through air and other gases: *Rockets are powerful research tools ... in aerodynamics* (Science News).

aer|o|dyne (ãr′ə dīn), *n.* any heavier-than-air aircraft. [< *aero-* + Greek *dýnamis* power]

aer|o|e|las|tic (ãr′ō i las′tik), *adj.* of or having to do with aeroelasticity.

aer|o|e|las|tic|i|ty (ãr′ō i las′tis′ə tē, -ē′las-), *n.* **1** the movement or deformation of an aircraft component or other elastic structure under the stress of aerodynamic forces. **2** the branch of mechanics that deals with such movement or deformation.

aer|o|em|bo|lism (ãr′ō em′bə liz əm), *n.* a harmful blocking of blood vessels by nitrogen bubbles in the blood and body tissues, caused by a sudden reduction of air pressure, as in skin divers and other divers rising too rapidly, tunnel workers leaving pressurized caissons, and aviators ascending rapidly to high altitudes.

aer|o-en|gine (ãr′ō en′jən), *n. British.* an aircraft engine.

aer|o|foil (ãr′ə foil), *n. British.* an airfoil.

aer|o|gel (ãr′ə jel), *n.* a colloidal solution of a solid in which a liquid is replaced by a gas or by air, thus producing a high degree of porosity. [< *aero-* + *gel*]

aer|o|gen (ãr′ə jən), *n.* any one of various species of gas-producing bacteria. [< *aero-* + *-gen*]

aer|o|gen|er|a|tor (ãr′ō jen′ə rā tər), *n.* a generator driven by the wind.

aer|o|gen|ic (ãr′ō jen′ik), *adj.* **1** gas-producing: *aerogenic bacteria.* **2** having the form of air or gas; aeriform: *The inhalable, or aerogenic, form of the vaccine gives greater immunity than does the injected form* (Science News Letter). [< *aero-* + *-gen* + *-ic*]

aer|o|gram (ãr′ə gram), *n.* **1** a radiogram. **2** the record made by an aerograph. **3** = air letter.

aer|o|gramme (ãr′ə gram), *n.* = air letter.

aer|o|graph (ãr′ə graf, -gräf), *n.* an instrument carried high into the upper atmosphere by an airplane, balloon, or kite to record pressure, temperature, humidity, and other atmospheric conditions.

aer|og|ra|pher (ãr og′rə fər), *n.* a person who studies aerographics or describes atmospheric conditions.

aer|o|graph|ic (ãr′ə graf′ik), *adj.* **1** of aerography. **2** of aerographics.

aer|o|graph|i|cal (ãr′ə graf′ə kəl), *adj.* = aerographic.

aer|o|graph|ics (ãr′ə graf′iks), *n.* the study of the air or atmospheric conditions.

aer|og|ra|phy (ãr og′rə fē), *n.* description of the air or atmospheric conditions.

aer|o|lite (ãr′ə līt), *n.* a meteorite made up entirely or almost entirely of stone. [< *aero-* + *-lite*]

aer|o|lit|ic (ãr′ə lit′ik), *adj. U.S.* made up entirely or almost entirely of stone, as a meteorite.

aer|o|log|ic (ãr′ə loj′ik), *adj.* of or having to do with aerology. —**aer′o|log′i|cal|ly**, *adv.*

aer|o|log|i|cal (ãr′ə loj′ə kəl), *adj.* = aerologic: *Through aerological investigations scientists have learned much about the atmosphere and the weather* (J. V. Finch).

aer|ol|o|gist (ãr ol′ə jist), *n.* a person who studies aerology.

aer|ol|o|gy (ãr ol′ə jē), *n.* **1** the branch of meteorology that deals with the properties and phenomena of the upper atmosphere. **2** = meteorology.

aer|o|mag|net|ic (ãr′ō mag net′ik), *adj.* having to do with magnetism in, or the action of magnetic force on, elements of the atmosphere, especially in the upper layers: *an aeromagnetic survey.*

aer|o|man|cy (ãr′ə man′sē), *n.* **1** divination by the air or atmospheric phenomena. **2** *Obsolete.* the forecasting of the weather. [< Greek *āēr, āéros* air + *manteíā* divination]

aer|o|me|chan|ic (ãr′ō mə kan′ik), *n., adj.* —*n.* **1** a mechanic who works on aircraft. **2** an expert in aeromechanics.
—*adj.* = aeromechanical.

aer|o|me|chan|i|cal (ãr′ō mə kan′ə kəl), *adj.* of or having to do with aeromechanics.

aer|o|me|chan|ics (ãr′ō mə kan′iks), *n.* the branch of physics that deals with the motion (aerodynamics) and equilibrium (aerostatics) of air and other gases.

aer|o|med|i|cal (ãr′ō med′ə kəl), *adj.* of or having to do with aeromedicine.

aer|o|med|i|cine (ãr′ō med′ə sən), *n.* aviation medicine.

aer|o|me|te|or|o|graph (ãr′ō mē′tē ər ə graf, -gräf), *n.* a meteorograph used in aircraft and other flying objects.

aer|om|e|ter (ãr om′ə tər), *n.* an instrument for determining the weight or density of air and other gases.

aer|o|met|ric (ãr′ə met′rik), *adj.* having to do with aerometry or an aerometer.

aer|om|e|try (ãr om′ə trē), *n.* the science of pneumatics.

aer|o|naut (ãr′ə nôt), *n.* **1** the pilot of an airship or balloon; balloonist. **2** a person who travels in an airship or balloon. **3** the pilot of an airplane. [< *aero-* + Greek *naútēs* sailor]

aer|o|nau|tic (ãr′ə nô′tik), *adj.* = aeronautical.

aer|o|nau|ti|cal (ãr′ə nô′tə kəl), *adj. U.S.* of or having to do with aeronautics or aeronauts: *aeronautical engineering, aeronautical meteorology.* —**aer′o|nau′ti|cal|ly**, *adv.*

aer|o|nau|tics (ãr′ə nô′tiks), *n.* the science or art having to do with the design, manufacture, and operation of aircraft.

aer|o|neu|ro|sis (ãr′ō nu̇ rō′sis, -nyu̇-), *n.* a nervous disorder affecting aviators, usually caused by excessive flying and characterized by such symptoms as gastric distress, irritability, and insomnia.

aer|o|nom|i|cal (ãr′ə nom′ə kəl), *adj.* of or having to do with aeronomy.

aer|on|o|mist (ãr on′ə mist), *n.* a person who studies aeronomy.

aer|on|o|my (ãr on′ə mē), *n.* the science that deals with the physical and chemical conditions of the upper atmosphere, especially the changes occurring as the result of radiation from outer space. [< *aero-* + Greek *némein* manage]

aer|o-o|ti|tis me|di|a (ãr′ō ō tī′tis mē′dē ə), inflammation of the middle ear caused by differences between the air pressure in the cavity of the middle ear and that of the atmosphere that occur from sudden changes of altitude in flying.

aer|o|pause (ãr′ə pôz), *n.* **1** the limit of man's penetration in the atmosphere at any particular time. **2** the upper limit of manned airborne flight. [< *aero-* + Greek *paûsis* a ceasing]

aer|o|pha|gi|a (ãr′ə fā′jē ə), *n.* an abnormal swallowing of air, sometimes associated with hysteria. [< *aero-* + Greek *phageîn* eat]

aer|oph|a|gy (ār of′ə jē), *n.* = aerophagia.

aer|o|phi|lat|e|list (ār′ō fə lat′ə list), *n.* a collector of airmail stamps.

aer|o|phi|lat|e|ly (ār′ō fə lat′ə lē), *n.* the business or hobby of collecting and trading airmail stamps.

aer|o|pho|bi|a (ār′ə fō′bē ə), *n.* a morbid fear of air or gases, especially of drafts.

aer|o|phore (ār′ə fôr, -fōr), *n.* a portable respirator for the use of firemen, miners, and others, containing chemicals designed to revive exhaled air passing through it or to make smoke-filled air breathable.

aer|o|pho|tog|ra|phy (ār′ō fə tog′rə fē), *n.* = aerial photography.

aer|o|phys|ics (ār′ō fiz′iks), *n.* the branch of physics that deals with the atmosphere; aerodynamics and aerostatics.

aer|o|phyte (ār′ə fīt), *n.* a plant nourished by the air instead of the soil; air plant; epiphyte.

aer|o|plane (ār′ə plān), *n. Especially British.* = airplane. ▶ See **airplane** for usage note.

aer|o|pulse (ār′ō puls), *n.* = pulsejet.

aer|o|res|o|na|tor (ār′ō rez′ə nā tər), *n.* = pulsejet.

aer|o|scep|sis (ār′ō skep′sis), *n. Zoology.* the ability to perceive the state of the atmosphere. [< *aero-* + Greek *sképsis* perception]

aer|o|scep|sy (ār′ō skep′sē), *n. Zoology.* aeroscepsis.

aer|o|scope (ār′ə skōp), *n.* an instrument for collecting dust, bacteria, spores, or other contaminants from the air for microscopic investigation.

aer|o|scop|ic (ār′ə skop′ik), *adj.* having to do with exercising aeroscopy.

aer|os|co|py (ār os′kə pē), *n. Zoology.* perception or observation of atmospheric conditions, as by insects and snails.

aer|o|shell (ār′ō shel′), *n.* a parachutelike device used to decelerate a spacecraft making a soft landing.

aer|o|sid|er|ite (ār′ō sid′ə rīt), *n.* a meteorite consisting mainly of metallic iron.

aer|o|sid|er|o|lite (ār′ō sid′ər ə līt), *n.* a meteorite containing both iron and stone.

aer|o|sol (ār′ə sol, -sōl), *n.* **1** very fine colloidal particles of a solid or liquid substance suspended in the air or in some other gas. Smoke and fog are common aerosols. **2** an aerosol bomb or container.

***aerosol bomb**, **can**, or **container**, a can containing an insecticide, cosmetic, or other product under pressure, that may be released as a spray or mist; spray can.

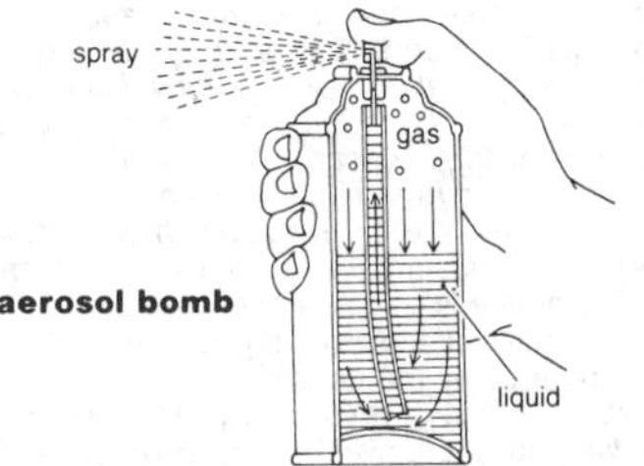

***aerosol bomb**

aerosol cloud, a man-made spray or mist in which disease-producing or chemical agents are suspended.

aer|o|sol|ize (ār′ə sol īz), *v.t.*, **-ized**, **-iz|ing**. **1** to discharge in a fine colloidal suspension of spray or mist. **2** to produce or package in aerosol form: *aerosolized drugs.* —**aer′o|sol′i|za′tion**, *n.*

aer|o|sol|o|scope (ār′ə sol′ə skōp), *n.* an instrument capable of detecting and counting microscopic particles, such as dust or germs, carried in the air. [< *aerosol* + *-scope*]

aer|o|space (ār′ə spās), *n.* **1** the field of science, technology, and industry dealing with the flight of rockets and other spacecraft through the atmosphere or the space beyond it: *Aerospace ... has provided more jobs for last June's engineering graduates than any other field of business or industry* (Science News Letter). **2** the earth's atmosphere and the space beyond it, especially the space in which rockets, satellites, and other spacecraft operate.

aerospace engineering, engineering that deals with the design and development of aircraft and space vehicles. Aerospace engineers also design testing equipment such as wind tunnels.

aerospace medicine, = space medicine.

aerospace plane, a craft that is part airplane and part spaceship which has no wings and looks like an enormous bathtub; lifting body. It is designed to ride into space on top of a rocket and return to earth after completing its mission.

aer|o|stat (ār′ə stat), *n.* any lighter-than-air aircraft, such as a balloon or dirigible. [< French *aérostat* < Greek *āēr, āéros* air + *statós* standing]

aer|o|stat|ic (ār′ə stat′ik), *adj.* **1** of or having to do with aerostatics. **2** of or having to do with an aerostat.

aer|o|stat|i|cal (ār′ə stat′ə kəl), *adj.* = aerostatic.

aer|o|stat|ics (ār′ə stat′iks), *n.* the branch of physics that deals with the static equilibrium of air and other gases, and of solid objects suspended or moving in them.

aer|o|sta|tion (ār′ə stā′shən), *n. U.S.* **1** the art or science of operating lighter-than-air aircraft. **2** *Obsolete.* aerostatics.

aer|o|tac|tic (ār′ə tak′tik), *adj. Biology.* moving toward or away from oxygen or air: *The bacteria under the coverslip ... are "positively aerotactic," aggregating around the edges where the oxygen concentration is higher than in the centre* (New Scientist).

aer|o|tax|is (ār′ə tak′sis), *n. Biology.* movement of an organism or part of an organism toward or away from oxygen or air. [< *aero-* + Greek *táxis* arrangement]

aer|o|tech|ni|cal (ār′ō tek′nə kəl), *adj.* of or having to do with aeronautical production and research.

aer|o|tech|no|log|i|cal (ār′ō tek′nə loj′ə kəl), *adj.* = aerotechnical: *... that any aerotechnological gap which once existed between the U.S.S.R. and the Western powers is all but closed* (Science News Letter).

aer|o|ther|a|peu|tics (ār′ō ther′ə pyü′tiks), *n.* a method of treating disease by varying the pressure or composition of the air breathed.

aer|o|ther|a|py (ār′ō ther′ə pē), *n.* = aerotherapeutics.

aer|o|ther|mo|dy|nam|ic (ār′ō thėr′mō dī nam′ik, -di-), *adj.* of or having to do with aerothermodynamics.

aer|o|ther|mo|dy|nam|i|cist (ār′ō thėr′mō dī nam′ə sist), *n.* a person skilled in aerothermodynamics.

aer|o|ther|mo|dy|nam|ics (ār′ō thėr′mō dī nam′iks, -di-), *n.* the branch of thermodynamics that deals with the relations between heat and mechanical energy in air and other gases, especially in their applications to changes induced by the motions of bodies in the medium.

aer|o|train (ār′ə trān′), *n.* a high-speed train that combines the air-cushion element of the hovercraft and the single-rail feature of the monorail: *The aerotrain [will] provide rapid transportation between cities that are too close for economic air travel* (Time).

ae|ru|gi|nous (i rü′jə nəs), *adj.* having the nature or color of verdigris; bluish-green. [< Latin *aerūginōsus* < *aerūgō, -inis* aerugo]

ae|ru|go (i rü′gō), *n.* **1** the rust of copper or brass; verdigris. **2** *Rare.* the rust of metals in general. [< Latin *aerūgō* < *aes, aeris* brass]

aer|y[1] or **aër|y**[1] (ār′ē), *adj. Poetic.* **1** aerial; lofty. **2** ethereal. [< Latin *āerius* < Greek *āérios* < *āēr, āéros* air]

aer|y[2] or **aër|y**[2] (ār′ē, ir′-), *n., pl.* **aer|ies**, **aër|ies**. an aerie (eagle's nest).

Aes|chy|le|an (es′kə lē′ən; *especially British* ēs′kə lē′ən), *adj.* of or in the rather outspoken style of the ancient Greek dramatist Aeschylus: *an Aeschylean tragedy.*

aes|cu|la|ceous (es′kyə lā′shəs), *adj.* belonging to the same family as the horse chestnut. [< Latin *aesculus* kind of oak + English *-aceous*]

Aes|cu|la|pi|an (es′kyə lā′pē ən; *especially British* ēs′kyə lā′pē ən), *adj., n.* —*adj.* **1** of or having to do with Aesculapius. **2** of or having to do with the healing art; medical. —*n.* a physician.

Aes|cu|la|pi|us (es′kyə lā′pē əs; *especially British* ēs′kyə lā′pē əs), *n.* **1** the Roman god of medicine and healing (identified with the Greek god Asclepius). **2** a physician.

aes|cu|lin (es′kyə lin), *n.* = esculin.

Ae|sir (ā′sir, ē′-), *n. pl.* the chief Scandinavian gods and goddesses (Odin, Thor, Balder, Loki, Tyr, Freya, etc.), who lived in Asgard. [< Old Icelandic *æsir* gods]

Ae|so|pi|an (i sō′pē ən), *adj.* **1** of Aesop. **2** composed by Aesop or in his manner: *a fable in the Aesopian style.* Also, **Esopian**.

aes|the|o|met|ric (es′thē ō met′rik), *adj.* of or having to do with aestheometry: *aestheometric designs.*

aes|the|om|e|try (es′thē om′ə trē), *n.* a method of making geometric designs on a board, cloth, or the like, by means of needle and thread, used especially in teaching geometry and art. [< *aesthe(tics)* + *(ge)ometry*]

aes|the|sia (es thē′zhə), *n.* the perception of the external world by the senses; feeling; sensibility. Also, **esthesia**. [< Greek *aísthēsis* a perceiving]

aes|the|si|om|e|ter (es thē′zē om′ə tər, -sē-), *n.* = esthesiometer.

aes|the|sis (es thē′sis), *n.* = aesthesia.

aes|thete (es′thēt; *especially British* ēs′thēt), *n.* **1** a person who pretends to appreciate or be specially sensitive to the beautiful in nature or art; one who gives too much attention to beauty. **2** a person who appreciates or is sensitive to beauty in nature or art. Also, **esthete**. [< Greek *aisthētḗs* one who perceives]

aes|thet|ic (es thet′ik; *especially British* ēs thet′ik), *adj., n.* —*adj.* **1** having to do with the beautiful, as distinguished from the useful, scientific, or moral; based on or determined by beauty rather than by practical or moral considerations: *The committee laid stress on aesthetic elements, such as architecture and design* (Claude M. Berkeley). **2** (of persons) having or showing an appreciation of beauty in nature and art. **3** (of things) showing good taste; artistic; pleasing: *an aesthetic wallpaper. The ruins have a romantic or an impersonal, aesthetic appeal to all people, but to the Greeks they are a living force* (Atlantic).
—*n.* **1** an aesthetic philosophy or point of view: *Once again, Balanchine tamed an alien movement to his own distinctive personal aesthetic* (Doris Hering). **2** an aesthete. Also, **esthetic**. [< Greek *aisthētikós* sensitive; see etym. under **aesthetics**] —**aes|thet′i|cal|ly**, *adv.*

aes|thet|i|cal (es thet′ə kəl; *especially British* ēs thet′ə kəl), *adj.* of or having to do with aesthetics. Also, **esthetical**.

aes|the|ti|cian (es′thə tish′ən; *especially British* ēs′thə tish′ən), *n.* an expert in or student of aesthetics: *The aesthetician studies art in a theoretical way* (Thomas Munro). Also, **esthetician.**

aes|thet|i|cism (es thet′ə siz əm; *especially British* ēs thet′ə siz əm), *n.* **1** the belief in beauty as the basic standard of value in human life, underlying all moral or materialistic considerations. **2** a great love for and sensitivity to beauty and the arts. Also, **estheticism**.

aes|thet|i|cist (es thet′ə sist; *especially British* ēs thet′ə sist), *n.* = aesthetician.

aes|thet|i|cize (es thet′ə sīz; *especially British* ēs thet′ə sīz), *v.t.*, **-cized**, **-ciz|ing**. to make aesthetic or agreeable to refined taste.

aes|thet|ics (es thet′iks; *especially British* ēs thet′iks), *n.* the study of beauty in art and nature; philosophy of beauty or taste; theory of the fine arts. Also, **esthetics**. [< German *Aesthetik* < New Latin *aesthetica* < Greek *aisthētikós* sensitive < *aisthánesthai* perceive]

aes|ti|val (es′tə vəl, es tī′-; *especially British* ēs′tə vəl, ēs tī′-), *adj.* = estival.

aes|ti|vate (es′tə vāt; *especially British* ēs′tə vāt), *v.i.*, **-vat|ed**, **-vat|ing**. = estivate.

aes|ti|va|tion (es′tə vā′shən; *especially British* ēs′tə vā′shən), *n.* = estivation.

aes|ti|va|tor (es′tə vā′tər; *especially British* ēs′tə-vā′tər), *n.* = estivator.

aet. or **aetat.**, at the age of (usually at death); aged (a designated figure); *Here lies John Richards, aet. 71.* Also, **ae.** [abbreviation of Latin *aetātis*, genitive of *aetās* age]

AET (no periods) or **A.E.T.**, a crystalline chemical compound used in the prevention and treatment of radiation sickness. *Formula:* $C_3H_{11}Br_3N_3S$ [< *A*(mino) *E*(thyl) (iso)*T*(hiouronium)]

ae|ta|tis su|ae (ē tā′tis sü′ē; ī tä′tis sü′ī), *Latin.* in his—th year; aged—(a shortened form of **anno aetatis suae**).

aeth|el|ing (ath′ə ling), *n.* = atheling.

ae|ther (ē′thər), *n.* = ether.

ae|the|re|al (i thir′ē əl), *adj.* = ethereal.

ae|thri|o|scope (ē′thrē ə skōp, eth′rē-), *n.* an instrument for measuring minute variations of temperature due to different conditions of the sky. [< Greek *aithría* open sky + English *-scope*]

ae|ti|o|log|ic (ē′tē ə loj′ik), *adj.* = etiologic.

ae|ti|o|log|i|cal (ē′tē ə loj′ə kəl), *adj.* = etiological.

ae|ti|ol|o|gist (ē′tē ol′ə jist), *n.* = etiologist.

ae|ti|ol|o|gy (ē′tē ol′ə jē), *n.* = etiology.

Ae|to|li|an (i tō′lē ən), *adj., n.* —*adj.* of or having to do with the ancient Greek region of Aetolia or its people.
—*n.* an inhabitant of ancient Aetolia.

AEW (no periods), airborne early warning (radar for enemy ships and aircraft).

af-, *prefix.* the form of **ad-** before *f*, as in *affix.*

a.f., audio frequency.

Af., **1** Africa. **2** African.

AF (no periods), **1** Air Force, especially the United States Air Force. **2** Anglo-French. **3** audio frequency. **4** autofocus in a camera.

AFA (no periods), American Federation of Arts.

a|far (ə fär′), *adv.* far away; at a great distance: *Abraham ... saw the place afar off* (Genesis 22:4).

from afar, from far off; from a distance: *I saw*

Pronunciation Key: hat, āge, cãre, fär; let, ēqual, tėrm; it, īce; hot, ōpen, ôrder; oil, out; cup, pu̇t, rüle; child; long; thin; ᴛʜen; zh, measure; ə represents a in about, e in taken, i in pencil, o in lemon, u in circus.

him coming down the road from afar.

A·far (ə fär′, ä fär′), *n.* **1** a member of a nomadic tribe of Hamitic origin in Somalia, Ethiopia, and Djibouti; Danakil. **2** this tribe.

a·fa·ra (ä fä′rä), *n.* any one of a species of trees native to Nigeria, the wood of which is light-colored and resembles teak in its grain; limba. [< a native word]

AFB (no periods) or **A.F.B.**, Air Force Base.

AFC (no periods), automatic frequency control.

a·feard or **a·feared** (ə fird′), *adj. Archaic or Dialect.* afraid; frightened.

a·fe·brile (ā fē′brəl, -feb′rəl), *adj.* without fever.

aff (af, äf), *prep., adv. Scottish.* off.

af·fa·bil·i·ty (af′ə bil′ə tē), *n.* the quality that makes a person easy to talk to; courteous and pleasant ways. SYN: amiability, geniality.

af·fa·ble (af′ə bəl), *adj.* **1** easy to talk to; courteous and pleasant in receiving and responding to the conversation or approaches of others: *Our principal is a very friendly and affable man.* SYN: approachable, amiable. **2** gracious: *an affable smile.* [< French *affable,* learned borrowing from Latin *affābilis* easy to speak to < *affārī* speak to < *ad-* to + *fārī* speak] —**af′fa·ble·ness,** *n.*

af·fa·bly (af′ə blē), *adv.* in an affable manner; courteously.

af·fair (ə fãr′), *n.* **1** thing to do; matter of business; job; task: *The President has many affairs to look after. The project was an important but time-consuming affair.* SYN: activity. **2** a particular action or happening: *The party on Saturday was a jolly affair.* **3** a private concern: *That's my own affair.* **4** a thing; matter: *The mechanism of a clock is a complicated affair.* **5** an amorous or romantic experience, especially a temporary one; love affair; romance. **6** an important or notorious case: *the Dreyfus affair.* **7** *U.S. Informal.* a festive or ceremonious occasion, such as a banquet, wedding, or dinner: *a catered affair.*

affairs, matters of interest, especially public or business matters: *men of affairs. The reasonableness of something is rarely a motive in human affairs* (Barbara W. Tuchman).

[< Old French *afaire* < *a faire* to do < Latin *ad* to, *facere* do]

af·faire (å fãr′), *n. French.* **1** a love affair (short for *affaire d'amour* or *affaire de coeur*). **2** any affair, especially some sensational event or legal case, often involving political scandal or intrigue: *Since the days of the Dreyfus case, one of the perennial features of French government has been l'affaire—that unique combination of intrigue, scandal, and politics that seems to . . . suggest the existence of deep, deadly and corrupt forces . . .* (Time).

af·faire d'a·mour (å fãr′då mür′), *French.* **1** a love affair. **2** (literally) an affair of love.

af·faire de coeur (å fãr′də kœr′), *French.* **1** a love affair. **2** (literally) an affair of the heart.

af·faire d'hon·neur (å fãr′dô nœr′), *French.* **1** a duel. **2** (literally) an affair of honor.

affair of honor, = duel.

af·fairs (ə fãrz′), *n.pl.* See under **affair.**

af·fect[1] (*v.* ə fekt′; *n.* af′ekt), *v., n.* —*v.t.* **1** to produce a result on; have an effect on; act on; influence or change: *The small amount of rain last year affected the growth of crops. The disease affected his mind so that he lost his memory. Nothing you say will affect my decision.* **2** to touch the heart of; stir the feelings of: *The stories of starving children so affected him that he gave all his spare money to their aid.* SYN: move.

—*n. Psychology.* the felt or affective component of a stimulus or motive to action.

[< Latin *affectus,* past participle of *afficere* act on < *ad-* to + *facere* do]

►See **affect**[2] for usage note.

af·fect[2] (ə fekt′), *v.t.* **1** to pretend to have or feel: *He affected ignorance of the fight, but we knew that he had seen it.* SYN: feign, simulate, profess. See syn. under **pretend.** **2** to use because one prefers to; choose to use, wear, own, etc.; fancy: *He affects carelessness in dress.* **3** to make a show of liking; adopt falsely or ostentatiously: *to affect a taste for abstract art.* [< Middle French *affecter,* learned borrowing from Latin *affectāre* strive for < *afficere* act on < *ad-* to + *facere* do] —**af·fect′er,** *n.*

►**Affect** and **effect** are often confused in writing, partly because they are pronounced very similarly or identically, and partly because *to affect* is synonymous with *to have an effect on.* But in the general vocabulary *affect* is used only as a verb, whereas *effect* is most commonly used as a noun: *Overwork has had a serious effect on his health. Overwork has seriously affected his health.* In formal English *effect* is also a verb meaning most commonly "to cause or bring about": *The new coach effected a marked change in the students' attitude toward sports.* Notice that the object of the verb *affect* is the person or thing influenced, while the object of *effect* is the change or result of the influence: *to effect an improvement by affecting the people concerned.*

af·fec·ta·tion (af′ek tā′shən, -ik-), *n.* **1** an artificial way of talking or acting put on to impress others; pretense: *Her roughness is an affectation; she is really a quiet, gentle girl.* SYN: show, pose. **2** a mannerism, choice of language, or the like, that indicates a tendency toward this: *Her little affectations seem silly.* SYN: peculiarity.

af·fect·ed[1] (ə fek′tid), *adj.* **1** acted on; influenced: *Everyone felt affected by the war.* **2** influenced injuriously: *She froze her feet and the affected toes were numb.* **3** moved in feeling; stirred up. **4** inclined. [< *affect*[1] + *-ed*[2]]

af·fect·ed[2] (ə fek′tid), *adj.* **1** put on for effect; not natural; pretended; artificial: *an affected welcome, an affected tone of voice.* SYN: unnatural, pretentious. **2** behaving, speaking, or writing unnaturally for effect: *He is too picked, too spruce, too affected, too odd* (Shakespeare). [< *affect*[2] + *-ed*[2]] —**af·fect′ed·ly,** *adv.* —**af·fect′ed·ness,** *n.*

af·fect·ing (ə fek′ting), *adj.* touching the heart; moving the feelings: *The refugee told an affecting story of hunger and suffering.*

af·fec·tion (ə fek′shən), *n.* **1** a feeling of warm liking and tender attachment; fondness; tenderness: *Mothers have affection for their children. His gentleness and kind ways increased his dog's affection for him.* SYN: See syn. under **love.** **2** an unhealthy condition; disease: *He is suffering from an affection of the ear.* SYN: ailment. **3** feeling; inclination: *The world of ideas is first arranged in six broad categories of abstract relations, space, matter, intellect, volition and affections* (Simeon Potter). **4** *Archaic.* disposition; tendency.

af·fec·tion·al (ə fek′shə nəl), *adj.* implying affection; relating to the affections: *The affectional bond is often very strong at the inception of marriage, but it does not always endure* (Ogburn and Nimkoff). —**af·fec′tion·al·ly,** *adv.*

af·fec·tion·ate (ə fek′shə nit), *adj.* **1** having or showing affection; fond; tender: *an affectionate child, an affectionate farewell. The soldier received an affectionate letter from his sister.* SYN: warm; devoted. **2** *Obsolete.* headstrong. —**af·fec′tion·ate·ly,** *adv.* —**af·fec′tion·ate·ness,** *n.*

af·fec·tioned (ə fek′shənd), *adj. Archaic.* disposed.

af·fec·tion·less (ə fek′shən lis), *adj.* deprived of affection: *an affectionless youngster. Children from affectionless and disrupted homes are disproportionately involved in crime and delinquency* (Morris and Hawkins).

af·fec·tive (ə fek′tiv), *adj.* **1** of or having to do with the feelings; emotional. **2** arousing emotion; concerning emotion: *It may be noted that the difference between "Green was my valley" and "My valley was green" is that the first sentence has greater affective suggestiveness* (Simeon Potter). —**af·fec′tive·ly,** *adv.*

af·fec·tiv·i·ty (af′ek tiv′ə tē), *n. Psychology.* the relative intensity of response to a feeling or emotion.

af·fect·less (ə fekt′lis), *adj.* unfeeling; unemotional: *How do people become so "affectless"—so unaffected by the suffering of other people?* (Katherine Gauss Jackson). —**af·fect′less·ly,** *adv.* —**af·fect′less·ness,** *n.*

af·fen·pin·scher (ä′fən pin′shər), *n.* any one of a breed of small dogs having stiff, black fur, pointed ears, a prominent chin, and mustachelike tufts of hair.

[< German *Affenpinscher* < *Affe* monkey, ape + *Pinscher* pinscher]

af·fer·ence (af′ər əns), *n.* the action or excitation of afferent nerves.

***afferent**

in blood vessels: **in nerves:**

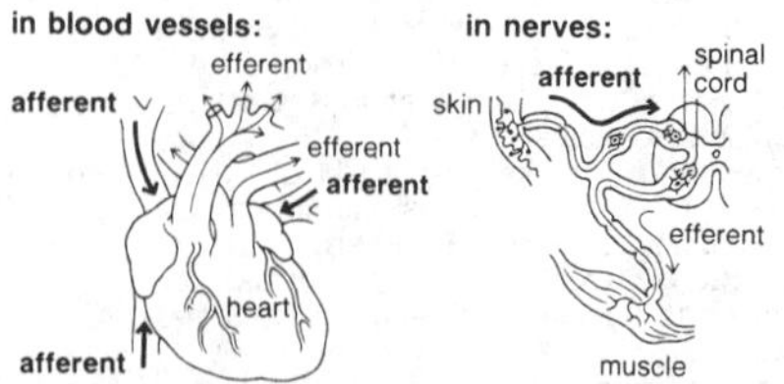

***af·fer·ent** (af′ər ənt), *adj.* carrying inward to a central organ or point (contrasted with *efferent*). Afferent nerves carry stimuli from nerve endings to the spinal cord. [< Latin *afferēns, -entis,* present participle of *afferre* bring to < *ad-* to + *ferre* bring]

af·fet·tu·o·so (ä fet′tü ō′sō), *adj., adv. Music.* with feeling; tender. [< Italian *affettuoso*]

af·fi·ance (ə fī′əns), *v.,* **-anced, -anc·ing,** *n.* —*v.t.* to promise (oneself or another) in marriage; engage; betroth: *James and Beth are affianced to each other.*

—*n.* **1** the pledging of faith; betrothal: *Affiance made, my happiness begun* (Edmund Spenser). SYN: engagement, troth. **2** *Archaic.* trust; confidence.

[< Old French *afiance* < *afier* to trust < Medieval Latin *affidare* < Latin *ad-* to + Vulgar Latin *fīdāre* to trust < Latin *fīdus* faithful] —**af·fi′anc·er,** *n.*

af·fi·anced (ə fī′ənst), *adj.* promised in marriage; engaged; betrothed.

af·fi·ant (ə fī′ənt), *n. Law, U.S.* a person who makes an affidavit. [< Old French *affiant,* present participle of *afier;* see etym. under **affiance**]

af·fiche (ä fēsh′), *n.* = poster: *Colin turned out the best affiches since Toulouse-Lautrec . . . seizing a subject's single feature and turning it into an artistic shop sign* (Time). [< French *affiche* < *afficher* to affix]

af·fi·da·vit (af′ə dā′vit), *n.* a statement written down and sworn to be true. An affidavit is usually made before a judge or notary public or, in Great Britain, a commissioner of oaths. [< Medieval Latin *affidavit* he has stated on oath]

af·fil·i·a·ble (ə fil′ē ə bəl), *adj.* that can be affiliated.

af·fil·i·ate (*v.* ə fil′ē āt; *n.* ə fil′ē it, -āt), *v.,* **-at·ed, -at·ing,** *n.* —*v.t.* **1** to join in close association; connect: *Though the two clubs did not have the same members, they were affiliated with each other.* SYN: associate. **2** to attach to or associate with a larger company or organization, often as a branch. **3** to bring into relationship; adopt. **4** *Law.* to fix the paternity of. **5** to trace the origin or connection of; ascribe.

—*v.i.* to associate oneself; connect; be joined (with): *to affiliate with a political party.*

—*n.* **1** an organization or group associated with other similar organizations or groups. **2** *U.S.* a person or organization that is associated with a larger organization; branch organization; subsidiary: *Our local automobile club is an affiliate of the national automobile club.*

[< Medieval Latin *affiliare* (with English *-ate*[1]) adopt < Latin *ad-* to + *fīlius* son]

►Individuals or groups of individuals **affiliate** "*with* an organization" in the United States, "*to* an organization" in Great Britain.

af·fil·i·at·ed (ə fil′ē ā′tid), *adj.* associated; connected: *The American Automobile Association [has] 753 affiliated clubs and branches* (Newsweek).

af·fil·i·a·tion (ə fil′ē ā′shən), *n.* association; connection; relation: *Our hospital has an affiliation with the medical school of the university. The population is sparse, with few affiliations with the Afghans* (Science). SYN: relationship, kinship.

af·fi·nal (ə fī′nəl), *adj., n.* —*adj.* **1** having a common origin or source. **2** related by marriage: *This establishes affinal (in-law) relationships between clans and binds them into a still larger unit: the tribe* (Scientific American).

—*n.* a relative by marriage; kinsman.

af·fine (ə fīn′), *adj., n.* —*adj. Mathematics.* having to do with or designating a transformation that carries parallel lines to parallel lines and finite points to finite points: *affine geometry.*

—*n.* a relative by marriage.

[< French *affiné* < *affin* kin by marriage, learned borrowing from Latin *affīnis* < *ad fīnem* at the border] —**af·fine′ly,** *adv.*

af·fined (ə fīnd′), *adj.* **1** related; connected. **2** *Obsolete.* bound; obligated.

af·fin·i·ta·tive (ə fin′ə tā′tiv), *adj.* of the nature of affinity. —**af·fin′i·ta′tive·ly,** *adv.*

af·fin·i·tive (ə fin′ə tiv), *adj.* closely connected: *the affinitive bond between identical twins.*

af·fin·i·ty (ə fin′ə tē), *n., pl.* **-ties.** **1** a natural attraction to a person or liking for a thing: *She has an affinity for dancing. If you have an affinity for mathematics, you will probably enjoy physics.* **2** relationship; connection: *There is an affinity between Swedes and Norwegians.* **3** relationship by marriage (distinguished from *consanguinity*). **4** *Biology.* a resemblance between species, genera, breeds, or other natural groupings that makes a common ancestry probable. **5** the force that attracts certain chemical elements to others and keeps them combined. **6** a person to whom one is especially attracted. **7** *Figurative.* resemblance; likeness.

[< Old French *affinite,* learned borrowing from Latin *affīnitās* < *affīnis* kin by marriage < *ad fīnem* at the border]

affinity card, a credit card issued at special rates to members of an affinity group: *The affinity card . . . is a Visa or MasterCard that a university, union, club, or some other group issues to its members* (Washington Post).

affinity group, any formally organized group, club, or other organization.

af·firm (ə fėrm′), *v.t.* **1** to declare to be true; say firmly; assert: *The prisoner affirmed his innocence. The Bible affirms that God is love.* SYN: aver, maintain, avouch. **2** to confirm; ratify: *The higher court affirmed the lower court's decision.*

SYN: validate, corroborate. —*v.i.* 1 to declare solemnly, but without taking an oath. SYN: vouch. 2 to make a solemn assertion.
[< Old French *afermer* < Latin *affirmāre* < *ad-* to + *firmāre* strengthen < *firmus* strong, true]
—**af|firm′er**, *n.*
▶ **Affirm** is used when a speaker or writer puts forward his own statement as true. **Confirm** is used when he corroborates, ratifies, or establishes a statement already made.

af|firm|a|ble (ə fėr′mə bəl), *adj.* that can be affirmed or asserted. —**af|firm′a|bly**, *adv.*

af|firm|ance (ə fėr′məns), *n.* 1 the act of affirming; assertion. 2 confirmation.

af|firm|ant (ə fėr′mənt), *n., adj.* —*n.* a person who affirms. —*adj.* affirming.

af|fir|ma|tion (af′ər mā′shən), *n.* 1 a positive statement; an assertion. 2 a solemn declaration having the legal force of an oath, made by Quakers and others whose religion or conscience forbids the taking of an oath. 3 the act of confirming anything established, especially laws; ratification; confirmation.

af|firm|a|tive (ə fėr′mə tiv), *adj., n.* —*adj.* 1 saying that some statement is a fact; answering "yes"; affirming: *Her answer to my question was affirmative.* 2 arguing in favor of a question being formally debated: *the affirmative side.* 3 positive in manner. 4 *Logic.* containing no negative or implicitly negative (private) terms in a proposition. *Example:* "All men are equal."
—*n.* a word or statement that says "yes" or agrees: *"I will" is an affirmative.*
in the affirmative, expressing agreement by saying "yes"; agreeing: *The principal replied in the affirmative when we requested that we have an afternoon off for a class picnic.*
the affirmative, the side arguing in favor of a question being formally debated: *The affirmative presented a strong argument, but the negative won the debate.*
—**af|firm′a|tive|ly**, *adv.* —**af|firm′a|tive|ness**, *n.*

affirmative action, *U.S.* any plan or program that promotes the employment of women and of members of minority groups. —**af|firm′a|tive-ac′tion**, *adj.*

af|firm|a|to|ry (ə fėr′mə tôr′ē, -tōr′-), *adj.* = affirmative.

af|fix (*v.* ə fiks′; *n.* af′iks), *v., n.* —*v.t.* 1 to stick on; fasten (to): *She affixed an airmail stamp to her letter.* SYN: fix. See syn. under **attach**. 2 to add, especially at the end: *The President affixed his signature to the bill.* 3 to make an impression of (a seal). 4 *Figurative.* to connect with; attach: *to affix blame.*
—*n.* 1 something joined or attached; an addition. SYN: attachment, adjunct, addendum. 2 a syllable or syllables added to a word or the base of a word to change its meaning or use; a prefix, suffix, or infix. In our language affixes are either prefixes like *un-* and *re-* or suffixes like *-ly* and *-ness.* The sign *-bi-* in Latin *legebit* "He will read" is an infix.
[< Medieval Latin *affixare,* ultimately < Latin *ad-* to + *fīgere* fasten] —**af|fix′er**, *n.*

af|fix|al (ə fik′səl), *adj.* of, having to do with, or of the nature of an affix.

af|fix|a|tion (ə fik sā′shən), *n.* 1 the forming of an affix or affixes: *Of all morphological processes affixation is by far the most common* (Simeon Potter). 2 the act of affixing; affixture.

af|fix|ture (ə fiks′chər), *n.* 1 the act or process of affixing. 2 something affixed.

af|fla|tion (ə flā′shən), *n.* = inspiration.

af|fla|tus (ə flā′təs), *n.* an overmastering impulse or compelling force; inspiration, especially divine inspiration: *There is a strong evangelical excitement ..., an afflatus of that mood of direct revelation in reformed Christianity—the same mood that produced the Quakers and Shakers* (New Yorker). [< Latin *afflātus, -ūs* a blast, breath < *afflāre* blow upon < *ad-* on + *flāre* blow]

af|flict (ə flikt′), *v.t.* 1 to cause pain to; trouble very much; distress: *My grandfather is afflicted with arthritis. The pangs of conscience afflicted him.* SYN: torment, harass. 2 *Archaic.* to cast down. [< Latin *afflīctus,* past participle of *afflīgere* dash against < *ad-* upon + *flīgere* dash]
—**af|flict′er**, *n.* —**af|flict′ing|ly**, *adv.*

af|flic|tion (ə flik′shən), *n.* 1 a state of pain, trouble, or distress; misery: *The country suffered from the affliction of war. The Queen your Mother, in most great affliction of spirit, hath sent me to you* (Shakespeare). SYN: wretchedness, tribulation. 2 a cause of pain, trouble, or distress; misfortune: *His blindness is an affliction.*

af|flic|tive (ə flik′tiv), *adj.* causing misery or pain; distressing. —**af|flic′tive|ly**, *adv.*

af|flu|ence (af′lü əns), *n.* 1 wealth; riches: *The United States is a country of great affluence.* SYN: opulence. 2 *Figurative.* an abundant supply; great abundance: *We have had an affluence of rain this month. Winter ... with its affluence of snows* (Longfellow). SYN: profusion. 3 *Archaic.* a flowing toward a particular point. [< Middle French *affluence,* learned borrowing from Latin *affluentia* < *affluēns, -entis;* see etym. under **affluent**]

af|flu|ent (af′lü ənt), *adj., n.* —*adj.* 1 having wealth; rich; wealthy: *an affluent person.* 2 *Figurative.* abundant; plentiful. SYN: copious, plenteous. 3 flowing freely.
—*n.* 1 a stream flowing into a larger stream or body of water; a tributary. 2 an affluent person: *To young affluents the holidays signify a generous portion of normally adult fare* (London Times).
[< Latin *affluēns, -entis,* present participle of *affluere* flow toward < *ad-* to + *fluere* flow] —**af′flu|ent|ly**, *adv.*

affluent society, a society with an abundant supply and consumption of luxury products and services: *Motor cars, now regarded as a symbol of the affluent society, are not seen* [*in Russia*] *in anything like the numbers evident in Western countries* (J. V. Davidson-Houston). [< *The Affluent Society* (1958), by John Kenneth Galbraith, born 1908, an American economist]

af|flux (af′luks), *n.* a flow toward or to a place or part. [< Medieval Latin *affluxus* < Latin *affluere* flow toward < *ad-* to + *fluere* flow]

af|force (ə fôrs′, -fōrs′), *v.t.,* **-forced, -forc|ing.** to reinforce or strengthen (a jury, court, or other legal body) by adding new members. [< Old French *aforcer,* ultimately < Latin *ad-* to + *fortis* strong] —**af|force′ment**, *n.*

af|ford (ə fôrd′, -fōrd′), *v.t.* 1 to have or spare the money for: *Can we afford a new car?* 2 to manage to give, spare, or have: *A busy man can't afford a delay. Can you afford the time?* SYN: bear. 3 to be able without difficulty or harm; have the means: *He cannot afford to waste so much time. I can't afford to take the chance.* SYN: manage. 4 to give as an effect or a result; provide: *Reading this story will afford real pleasure.* SYN: confer, bestow. 5 to furnish from natural resources; yield: *Our garden affords a good supply of fresh vegetables. Some trees afford resin.* SYN: supply. 6 to grant: *Kind heav'n afford him everlasting rest* (Alexander Pope). SYN: give. [Old English *geforthian* to further, accomplish] —**af|ford′a|ble**, *adj.*
▶ **Afford** in the sense of def. 1 is usually preceded by *can, can't, be able* (or *unable*) *to,* or the like, and often followed by an infinitive: *We can afford to sell cheap.*

af|for|est (ə fôr′ist, -for′-), *v.t.* to change (open land) into forest. [< Medieval Latin *afforestare* < *ad-* to + *foresta* forest]

af|for|est|a|tion (ə fôr′ə stā′shən, -for′-), *n.* 1 the changing of open land into forest. 2 the territory afforested.

af|for|est|ment (ə fôr′ist mənt, -for′-), *n.* = afforestation (def. 1).

af|fran|chise (ə fran′chīz), *v.t.,* **-chised, -chis|ing.** = enfranchise. [< Old French *afranchiss-,* stem of *afranchir* < *a* + *franchir* to free < *franc* free; (originally) a Frank]

af|fray (ə frā′), *n., v.* —*n.* a noisy quarrel; fight in public; brawl. In law, an affray is fighting in a public place so as to frighten others. [< Old French *effrei* < *effreer;* see the verb]
—*v.t. Archaic.* to frighten.
[< Anglo-French *afrayer,* variant of Old French *effreer,* ultimately < Latin *ex-* out of + unrecorded Frankish *frithu* peace]

af|freight (ə frāt′), *v.t.* to lease (a vessel) while its owners remain in charge of its operation.
—**af|freight′er**, *n.* —**af|freight′ment**, *n.*

af|fri|cate (af′rə kit), *n. Phonetics.* a sound which begins as a stop and ends as a fricative. The *ch* in *chin* is an affricate because it starts like *t* and ends almost as *sh.* [< Latin *affricātus,* past participle of *affricāre* rub against < *ad-* against + *fricāre* rub]

af|fri|ca|tion (af′rə kā′shən), *n. Phonetics.* the act of sounding an affricate; turning a sound into an affricate.

af|fric|a|tive (ə frik′ə tiv), *n., adj. Phonetics.* —*n.* = affricate. —*adj.* consisting of or having to do with an affricate.

af|fright (ə frīt′), *v., n. Archaic.* —*v.t.* to excite with sudden fear; frighten.
—*n.* 1 sudden fear; fright; terror. 2 a cause of terror.
[Old English *āfyrhtan* < *ā-* (intensive) + *fyrhtan* frighten]

af|front (ə frunt′), *n., v.* —*n.* 1 a word or act intended to show disrespect or contempt; open insult: *To be called a coward is an affront.* SYN: See syn. under **insult**. 2 a slight or injury to one's dignity. SYN: indignity. [< verb]
—*v.t.* 1 to insult openly; offend purposely: *The boy affronted his teacher by making a face at her. The people of the village were affronted by the superior airs of the wealthy newcomer.* 2 to face courageously and defiantly; confront. 3 *Archaic.* to face toward; front on; face.
[< Old French *afronter* (originally) strike on the forehead, defy, face < Vulgar Latin *affrontāre* to face, defy < Latin *ad-* to + *frōns, frontis* forehead] —**af|front′er**, *n.*

af|fron|tive (ə frun′tiv), *adj. Archaic.* affronting; insulting.

af|fuse (ə fyüz′), *v.t.,* **-fused, -fus|ing.** *Archaic.* to pour (water or other liquid) on a person or thing. [< Latin *affūsus,* past participle of *adfundere* pour upon < *ad-* on + *fundere* pour]

af|fu|sion (ə fyü′zhən), *n.* a pouring of water on a person, as in a form of baptism, or by a doctor treating fever.

Af|ghan (af′gən, -gan), *n., adj.* —*n.* 1 a person born or living in Afghanistan. 2 the principal language of Afghanistan; Pashto or Pushtu. 3 an Afghan hound. —*adj.* of Afghanistan, its people, or their language.

af|ghan (af′gən, -gan), *n.* a blanket or shawl made of knitted or crocheted wool or synthetic fiber, often in a special pattern. [< *Afghan*]

Afghan hound, any one of a breed of large, swift hunting dogs, originally bred in Afghanistan. It has a narrow head, large and drooping ears, a heavy coat of silky hair, and a long lock of hair at the top of the head. The Afghan hound is used for hunting gazelles, hares, and leopards in Africa.

af|ghan|i (af gan′ē), *n.* the unit of money of Afghanistan, equal to 100 puls.

Af|ghan|i (af gan′ē), *adj.* = Afghan.

a|fi|brin|o|gen|e|mi|a (ā′fī brin′ə jə nē′mē ə), *n.* bleeding caused by the lack of fibrinogen in the blood. [< *a-*[1] + *fibrinogen* + *-emia* < Greek *haîma* blood]

a|fi|cio|na|da (ə fē′syə nä′də; *Spanish* ä fē′thyō nä′ᴛʜä), *n., pl.* **-das.** a woman aficionado. [< Spanish *aficionada,* feminine of *aficionado*]

a|fi|cio|na|do (ə fē′syə nä′dō; *Spanish* ä fē′thyō nä′ᴛʜō), *n., pl.* **-dos.** 1 a person who is very enthusiastic about some sport or hobby or a special field; devotee; enthusiast: *To crime-story aficionados the bulky bachelor doctor looks like a perfect Agatha Christie character* (Newsweek). 2 a person who takes a very great interest in bullfighting although not a bullfighter. [< Spanish *aficionado* (literally) fond of]

a|field (ə fēld′), *adv.* 1 away from home; away: *He wandered far afield in foreign lands.* 2 out of the right way; off the beaten track; astray: *We seem to have gone far afield; we are lost.* (*Figurative.*) *The discussion has gotten far afield of the main topic.* 3 in or on the field; to the field: *The general decided to put another army afield.*

a|fi|ko|men (ä′fi kō′mən), *n. Judaism.* a piece of ceremonial matzoth set aside to be eaten at the end of the Passover feast or Seder. It is hidden by the head of the family, and at the end of the Seder the children search for it, the finder receiving a reward. [< Hebrew *āphīqōmān,* ultimately probably < Greek *epíkōmon,* neuter of *epíkōmos* of or for a festival < *epí* for + *kômos* festival]

a|fire (ə fīr′), *adj., adv.* 1 on fire; burning. SYN: ablaze. 2 *Figurative.* enthusiastic.

AFL (no periods), **A.F.L.**, or **A.F. of L.**, American Federation of Labor (organization of craft unions, founded in 1886 and merged with the CIO in 1955).

A.F.L. or **AFL** (no periods), American Football League.

a|flame (ə flām′), *adj., adv.* 1 in flames; on fire. 2 in a glow; glowing. 3 *Figurative.* in a glow of excitement or eagerness; enthusiastic.

a|flare (ə flãr′), *adj., adv.* flaring: *Bushy white hair aflare, drooping mustache aquiver ... he is a little deaf but alert as a lion* (Time).

af|la|tox|in (af′lə tok′sən), *n.* a poisonous substance produced in certain plants, especially peanuts, by a common mold: *The tumors in trout were shown to be caused by aflatoxin, a naturally occurring carcinogen ... The trout feed was contaminated by the aflatoxin* (Atlantic). [< *A*(*spergillus*) *fla*(*vus*), the mold + *toxin*]

AFL-CIO (no periods) or **A.F.L.-C.I.O.**, a labor organization formed by the merger in 1955 of the craft unions of the American Federation of Labor (AFL) and the industrial unions of the Congress of Industrial Organizations (CIO).

a|float (ə flōt′), *adv., adj.* 1 floating on the water or in the air: *He had ten balloons afloat at one time.* 2 on shipboard; at sea. 3 *Figurative.* adrift: *penniless and afloat in a strange city.* 4 flooded: *After the rain the whole cellar was afloat.* 5 *Figurative.* being spread; in circulation; going around: *Rumors of a revolt were afloat.* 6 existing or operating without financial difficulties: *to* *keep an enterprise afloat.* **7** fully started or launched: *to set afloat a new venture.*

a|flut|ter (ə flut′ər), *adj., adv.* **1** fluttering or waving: *The flags were aflutter in the breeze.* **2** *Figurative.* in a flutter; excited: *The whole village was aflutter with the news.*

A.F. of L. See **AFL**.

a|foot (ə fu̇t′), *adv., adj.* **1** on foot; by walking: *Did you come all the way afoot?* **2** *Figurative.* going on; in progress: *Great preparations for the dinner were afoot in the kitchen. There is mischief afoot.* **3** on the move; moving; astir: *Not a person in the house was yet afoot.*

a|fore (ə fôr′, -fōr′), *adv., prep., conj. Archaic and Dialect.* before. [Old English *onforan* (< *on foran* in front), and *ætforan* < *æt* at + *foran* in front]

a|fore|hand (ə fôr′hand′, -fōr′-), *adv., adj. Archaic or Dialect.* beforehand.

a|fore|men|tioned (ə fôr′men′shənd, -fōr′-), *adj.* spoken of before; mentioned earlier; aforesaid. SYN: abovementioned.

a|fore|said (ə fôr′sed′, -fōr′-), *adj.* spoken of before; mentioned earlier.

a|fore|thought (ə fôr′thôt′, -fōr′-), *adj., n.* **—adj.** thought out beforehand; deliberately planned: *The evil deed was planned with malice aforethought.*
—n. = premeditation.

a|fore|time (ə fôr′tīm′, -fōr′-), *adv., adj. Archaic.*
—adv. formerly.
—adj. former; previous.

A-for|ma|tion (ā′fôr mā′shən), *n.* (in football) an offensive formation with most of the line to one side of the quarterback and the backfield to the other side.

a for|ti|o|ri (ā fôr′shē ôr′ī, -ōr′-; -ē), for a still stronger reason. Thus if *B* exceeds *C*, and *C* is proved greater than *X*, then *B* is *a fortiori* greater than *X*. *If an agreement for nuclear or conventional disarmament is impossible, then World Government is, a fortiori, also impossible* (Bulletin of Atomic Scientists). [< Latin *ā* from, *fortiōrī* (*argūmentō*) stronger (reason)]

a|foul (ə foul′), *adv., adj.* in a tangle; in a collision; entangled: *Raising the sail was impossible with the lines afoul.*
run (or **fall**) **afoul of,** to get into trouble with: *He will run afoul of the law if he steals. There is also, of course, that inevitable day when their man . . . runs afoul of the authorities for the last time and is sent home* (Time).

AFP (no periods), alphafetoprotein.

Afr., **1** Africa. **2** African.

a|fraid (ə frād′), *adj.* **1** feeling fear; frightened; alarmed: *She is afraid of the dark.* **2** unwilling because of fear: *Shy people are often afraid to speak up.* **3** sorry to have to say: *I'm afraid I must ask you to leave now. I'm afraid you are wrong about that.* [(originally) past participle of archaic *affray* to frighten]
—*Syn.* **1 Afraid, frightened, terrified** mean feeling fear. **Afraid,** which is never used before the noun, means being in a mental state of fear which may have either a real or an imagined cause and may be brief or last long: *He is sometimes afraid of snakes.* **Frightened,** commonly used instead of *afraid* before the noun, particularly means suddenly made afraid, often only momentarily, by a real and present cause: *The frightened child ran home.* **Terrified** means suddenly filled with a very great and paralyzing fear: *Terrified by heights, I couldn't bring myself to look at the bottom of the canyon.*

A-frame (ā′frām′), *n., adj.* **—n.** **1** a frame shaped like the letter *A*, used as a support for a pulley, as a skeleton support for a building, etc. **2** a house built on an A-frame.
—adj. built on an A-frame: *an A-frame cottage.*

af|reet (af′rēt, ə frēt′), *n. Arabian Mythology.* a powerful evil demon, giant, or jinni. Also, **afrit, afrite.** [< Arabic *'ifrīt*]

a|fresh (ə fresh′), *adv.* once more; again: *If you spoil your drawing, start afresh.*

Af|ric (af′rik), *adj. Poetic.* African.

Af|ri|can (af′rə kən), *adj., n.* **—adj.** **1** of Africa; from Africa; having to do with Africa, its peoples, their languages, or their ways of life. **2** of or having to do with a black person or black people.
—n. **1** a person born or living in Africa, especially a person belonging to one of the native tribes of Africa. **2** a black person.

Af|ri|ca|na (af′rə kä′nə, -kan′ə, -kā′nə), *n.pl.* **1** a collection of books, documents, facts, or other literary material about Africa. **2** a collection of things, such as textiles, tools, or handcrafted products made in Africa, especially before the introduction of mechanized technology. **3** anecdotes, folklore, songs, or other things about Africa or typical of one or more of the African cultures.

Af|ri|can-A|mer|i|can (af′rə kən ə mer′ə kən), *adj., n.* = Afro-American: *. . . the movement the Rev. Jesse Jackson is spearheading to officially declare us African-Americans* (Washington Post).

African daisy, a plant related to the aster, having flowers that resemble daisies.

Af|ri|can|der (af′rə kan′dər), *n.* = Afrikaner.

Af|ri|can|der|ism (af′rə kan′də riz əm), *n.* = Afrikanderism.

African elephant, an elephant of the genus native to Africa, usually larger and fiercer than the elephant found in Asia. See picture under **elephant.**

Af|ri|ca|ner (af′rə kä′nər), *n.* = Afrikaner.

African gray, a West African parrot of a gray color with a bright-red tail, one of the commonest of cage birds.

African horse sickness, a disease of horses most prevalent in Africa, caused by a virus transmitted by a species of gnat. It is characterized by fever, swelling on the skin, and is usually fatal.

Af|ri|can|ism (af′rə kə niz′əm), *n.* **1** a word, phrase, or meaning originating or more widely used among Africans speaking English than among other speakers of English. **2** devotion or loyalty to Africa or to black culture and to its customs and traditions. **3** a custom or trait peculiar to Africa or to black culture.

Af|ri|can|ist (af′rə kə nist), *n.* **1** a person who studies African history, culture, art, etc. **2** a supporter of African nationalism or interests.

Af|ri|can|i|za|tion (af′rə kə nə zā′shən), *n.* **1** the act of making African, as in converting into an African language. **2** the turning over to Africans or placing in their custody: *Africanization of the civil service.*

Af|ri|can|ize (af′rə kə nīz), *v.t.,* **-ized, -iz|ing.** **1** to make African, as in customs, language, or ownership. **2** to turn over to Africans or place in their custody: *Technical services are even less Africanized* (Atlantic).

Africanized bee or **honeybee,** = killer bee (def. 2).

African lily, a variety of agapanthus, grown for its blue or white flowers.

African lion hound, = Rhodesian ridgeback.

African mahogany, a timber tree grown in Africa that has softer, lighter, and more brittle wood than the true or American mahogany.

African marigold, a common variety of marigold, larger than the French marigold.

African oak, **1** a hard, heavy, dark-brown wood, valued especially in shipbuilding. **2** the African tree it comes from, of the spurge family.

African rosewood, a West African tree or its light, elastic wood.

African sleeping sickness, = sleeping sickness (def. 1).

African snail, a large snail of the western coast of Africa, the East Indies, and the Pacific Islands, that destroys flowers, vegetables, and young rubber plants.

African teak, = African oak.

African violet, a tropical plant, with (usually) violet, white, or pink flowers and heart-shaped, fuzzy leaves, often grown as a house plant. It belongs to the gesneria family and is a perennial, native to Africa.

A|fri|di (ä frē′dē), *n., pl.* **-di** (-dē), **-dis** (-dēz). any of a Pathan people now living in both India and Pakistan and native to the Khyber Pass region. Traditionally they are known for their warlike habits and feuding.

Af|ri|kaans (af′rə käns′, -känz′), *n., adj.* **—n.** a dialect of Dutch spoken in South Africa which developed from the Dutch of the colonists who came in the 1600's; South African Dutch; Taal.
—adj. of Afrikaans; using or speaking Afrikaans: *an Afrikaans writer, the Afrikaans press.*
[< Afrikaans variant of Dutch *afrikansch* African]

Af|ri|kan|der (af′rə kan′dər), *n.* **1** = Afrikaner. **2** a breed of red cattle from South Africa having a hump and other similarities to heat-resistant Brahman cattle. It has been used mostly for breeding experiments.

Af|ri|kan|der|dom (af′rə kan′dər dəm), *n.* = Afrikanerdom.

Af|ri|kan|der|ism (af′rə kan′də riz əm), *n.* any Afrikaans word, expression, usage, etc., carried over into the English spoken in South Africa.

Af|ri|ka|ner or **Af|ri|kaa|ner** (af′rə kä′nər), *n., adj.* **—n.** a white person born in South Africa of European, especially Dutch or Huguenot, ancestry; Boer: *You know he spoke Afrikaans like an Afrikaner* (Alan Paton).
—adj. of or having to do with an Afrikaner or Afrikaners.

Af|ri|ka|ner|dom (af′rə kä′nər dəm), *n.* the realm or domain of Afrikaners, especially as the dominant group in South Africa: *Apartheid will be pursued with . . . vigour until African nationalism submerges Afrikanerdom* (Manchester Guardian).

af|rit or **af|rite** (af′rēt, ə frēt′), *n.* = afreet.

***Af|ro** (af′rō), *n., pl.* **-ros,** *adj.* **—n.** a style of bushy, curly hair, resembling that of some African black tribes.
—adj. **1** of or in the style of an Afro: *Afro haircuts, an Afro wig.* **2** African-American: *an Afro club, Afro clothes.* [< *Afro-*]

Afro-, *combining form.* **1** African: *Afro-Socialism* = *African Socialism.*
2 African and: *Afro-European trade* = *African-and-European trade.*
[< Latin *Āfer, -frī* African]

Af|ro-A|mer|i|can (af′rō ə mer′ə kən), *adj., n.*
—adj. of or having to do with black Americans or their characteristics or culture: *In Africa, however, they [drum solos] are an appreciable element in the tribal musical repertory, and hold such a place in the musical tradition that in the New World they are everywhere a part of Afro-American music and its derivatives, such as jazz* (Melville J. Herskovits). **—n.** an American black.

Af|ro-A|sian (af′rō ā′zhən, -ā′shən), *adj., n.*
—adj. of or having to do with Africans and Asians as a group, or with their common aspirations.
—n. a native or inhabitant of one of the Afro-Asian countries: *Some Afro-Asians here are talking of a censure motion* (Manchester Guardian Weekly).

Af|ro-A|si|at|ic (af′rō ā′zhē at′ik, -shē-), *adj.* of or having to do with a family of languages spoken throughout northern Africa and southwestern Asia that includes the Semitic and Hamitic languages.

Af|ro|cen|tric (af′rō sen′trik), *adj.* regarding Africa as the source and center of African-American culture: *Bethel is proudly Afrocentric—a bright mural of African faces is painted over the altar* (Time).

Af|ro-Cu|ban (af′rō kyü′bən), *adj.* of or having to do with black Cubans or their culture.

Af|ro-Eur|o|pe|an (af′rō yu̇r′ə pē′ən), *adj.* of or having to do with both Africa and Europe: *The aims of the new party are: the formation at once of an Afro-European government . . .* (Manchester Guardian Weekly).

à froid (á frwä′), *French.* without prejudice or passion; calmly and coldly; objectively: *However, examined à froid, the thing appears to make a lot of sense* (New Yorker).

af|ror|mo|si|a (af′rōr mō′zē ə), *n.* a strong West African hardwood resembling teak. [< New Latin *afrormosia* the species name]

AFSCME (no periods), American Federation of State, County and Municipal Employees.

aft (aft, äft), *adv., adj. Nautical.* **—adv.** at, near, or toward the stern; abaft. SYN: astern, behind.
—adj. in or near the stern.
[Old English *æftan* from behind]

AFT (no periods) or **A.F.T.,** American Federation of Teachers.

af|ter (af′tər, äf′-), *prep., adv., adj., conj., n.*
—prep. **1** going or coming in the rear of; behind: *You come after me in line. Wave after wave washed over the ship.* SYN: See syn. under **behind.** **2** next to; following: *Day after day I waited for a letter from my friend.* **3a** in search of; in pursuit of: *The dog ran after the rabbit.* **b** *Figurative: He was after me to get my homework done.*
4 about; concerning: *Your aunt asked after you.*
5 later than: *After supper we can go.* **6** because of; as a result of: *After the big dinner, I couldn't finish my dessert. After the selfish way she has acted, how can you like her?* SYN: considering.
7 in spite of; notwithstanding: *After all her suffering, she still manages to be cheerful.* **8** in imitation of; in agreement with: *He wrote a fable after the manner of Aesop.* **9** lower in rank or importance than: *A major comes after a colonel.* **10** according to: *to act after one's own ideas.* **11** in honor of; for: *He was named after his father.* **12** in proportion to; in accordance with: *O Lord, deal not with us after our sins* (Book of Common Prayer).
—adv. **1** behind; in the rear: *Jill came tumbling after* (nursery rhyme). **2** later; afterward: *I ran so hard I panted for five minutes after.*
—adj. **1** later; following; subsequent: *In after years the sailor did not get home often.* **2** nearer or toward the stern of the ship: *the after sails.*
—conj. later than the time that: *After he goes, we shall eat.*
—n. *Informal.* afternoon: *The only thing on the tab this after is an open-heart [operation] at two* (New Yorker).
after all. See under **all.**
after you, please go ahead: *He held open the door for the lady and said politely, "after you."*
[Old English *æfter* more to the rear, later, (originally) comparative of *af* off, away]

***Afro**

af|ter|beat (af′tər bēt′, äf′-), *n. Music.* a note or notes, especially of the accompaniment, that follow the beat.

af|ter|birth (af′tər bėrth′, äf′-), *n.* the placenta and membranes expelled from the uterus shortly after birth.

af|ter|bod|y (af′tər bod′ē, äf′-), *n., pl.* **-bod|ies.** the stern or rear part of a ship, aircraft, or rocket.

af|ter|brain (af′tər brān′, äf′-), *n.* the portion of a hindbrain from which the medulla oblongata develops; myelencephalon.

af|ter|burn|er (af′tər bėr′nər, äf′-), *n.* a device in the engine of a jet plane which supplies additional fuel to the exhaust and reignites it, thus increasing the thrust of the plane so that bursts of very high speed can be obtained. See picture under **airplane.**

af|ter|burn|ing (af′tər bėr′ning, äf′-), *n.* **1** the irregular burning of fuel following the principal combustion in an engine, as in a rocket engine after fuel is cut off. **2** a second burning in a jet engine, by an injection of fuel in an afterburner.

af|ter|care (af′tər kãr′, äf′-), *n.* **1** the care or nursing of convalescent patients after treatment, especially following childbirth or surgery. **2** care and assistance given to inmates of certain institutions, such as former mental patients or convicts, after their discharge.

af|ter|clap (af′tər klap′, äf′-), *n.* a subsequent and unexpected stroke, as of misfortune.

af|ter|cool|er (af′tər kü′lər, äf′-), *n.* a device for cooling the air compressed by a compressor, supercharger, etc.; air-cooler.

af|ter|crop (af′tər krop′, äf′-), *n.* a second crop from land in the same year.

af|ter|damp (af′tər damp′, äf′-), *n.* a suffocating mixture of gases, chiefly carbon dioxide, nitrogen, and carbon monoxide, found in coal mines after an explosion of firedamp.

af|ter-dark (af′tər därk′, äf′-), *adj.* of or for the evening or night: *after-dark costumes, after-dark bus runs.*

af|ter|deck (af′tər dek′, äf′-), *n.* the part of a deck toward or near the stern of a ship.

af|ter-din|ner (af′tər din′ər, äf′-), *adj.* following a dinner or banquet: *an after-dinner speech, after-dinner coffee.* **SYN:** postprandial.

af|ter|ef|fect (af′tər i fekt′, äf′-), *n.* **1** a result that follows later, or that begins rather long after the cause has disappeared; a delayed effect: *The aftereffect of the explosion was a great fire.* **2** a secondary effect of a drug, disease or the like; side effect.

af|ter|feed (af′tər fēd′, äf′-), *n.* grass that grows after a first crop has been cut, and that is used for pasture instead of being cut again.

af|ter|glow (af′tər glō′, äf′-), *n.* **1** the glow remaining after something bright has gone: **a** the glow in the sky after sunset. **b** luminous trail, such as of a meteor or meteorite. **c** a lingering impression of brightness, as an afterimage. **2** *Figurative.* a pleasurable feeling following something greatly enjoyed: *There is a lilt to her song that always leaves an afterglow* (Wall Street Journal).

af|ter|grass (af′tər gras′, äf′tər gräs′), *n.* a second growth of grass in a mowed field, or grass growing among the stubble after harvest.

af|ter|growth (af′tər grōth′, äf′-), *n.* a second stage of growth or development, usually one that is not expected or desired.

af|ter|guard (af′tər gärd′, äf′-), *n.* **1** the amateur crew and owner of a yacht, distinguished from hired sailors. **2** the seamen assigned to duty on the poop of a ship.

af|ter|heat (af′tər hēt′, äf′-), *n.* the heat released by radioactive decay in an atomic reactor: *Recovered gas would then be used to drive a gas turbine for power generation ... The afterheat could be used for air-conditioning houses* (Science News).

af|ter|hours (af′tər ourz′, äf′-), *adj.* of or in time following the normal work shift, business day, or usual duties: *The informal afterhours exchanges ... make these otherwise tiring congresses rewarding* (Newsweek).

af|ter|im|age (af′tər im′ij, äf′-), *n. Psychology.* a visual or other sensation that persists or recurs after the stimulus causing it has ceased to act.

af|ter|life (af′tər līf′, äf′-), *n.* **1** life after death. **2** *Figurative.* the later period of one's life: *What happened to the graduates of Oxford and Cambridge in afterlife?* (Atlantic).

af|ter|light (af′tər līt′, äf′-), *n.* **1** the glow in the sky after sunset; twilight. **2** *Figurative.* the period following some event: *In the afterlight of last November's unpleasantness, some important changes appear to have been made in Senator G.* (Harper's).

af|ter|math (af′tər math, äf′-), *n.* **1a** a result or consequence, especially of something destructive: *The aftermath of war is hunger and disease.* **b** the period following some event: *In the aftermath of any election, the immediate duty of the professional politician is to review and reshuffle the portfolio of his loyalties* (Alistair Cooke). **2** a second mowing or crop of grass from land in the same season. [< *after* + *math*² a mowing]

af|ter|most (af′tər mōst, äf′-), *adj.* **1** nearest the stern of a ship: *the aftermost hatch.* **2** last in order or time; hindmost.

af|ter|noon (*n.* af′tər nün′, äf′-; *adj.* af′tər nün′, äf′-), *n., adj.* **—*n.*** **1a** the time from noon to evening. *Abbr:* p.m., P.M. **b** *Especially British.* the time between lunch and either dark or six o'clock, whichever comes sooner. (English lunch is usually 1:00-2:00.) **2** *Figurative.* the latter part: *a man in the afternoon of life.*
—*adj.* in or suitable for the afternoon: *an afternoon dress.*

af|ter|noon|er (af′tər nü′nər, äf′-), *n. U.S.* a newspaper appearing in the afternoon: *In 1954, The [Los Angeles] Mirror switched to standard size and absorbed the opposition afternooner, The Daily News* (Newsweek).

af|ter|noons (af′tər nünz′, äf′-), *adv.* during the afternoon; in the afternoon: *He is too busy afternoons to take a nap.*

afternoon tea, 1 light refreshments, including tea, served in the afternoon. **2** a social gathering including such a meal.

af|ter|pains (af′tər pānz′, äf′-), *n.pl.* the pains that follow childbirth: *Afterpains are caused by contractions of the womb.* (*Figurative.*) *afterpains of conscience following a dishonorable act.*

af|ter|part (af′tər pärt′, äf′-), *n.* the aft part of a ship or boat; stern.

af|ter|piece (af′tər pēs′, äf′-), *n.* **1** a short play performed after a longer one. **2** an afterword: *Evelyn Waugh encouraged her to write this work [a biography], and Waugh himself contributed an afterpiece* (New Yorker).

af|ter|rip|en|ing (af′tər rī′pə ning, äf′-), *n.* the further development of seeds or fruits by enzymatic action after harvesting or picking: *Other seeds will only begin to germinate after a certain period from harvesting has elapsed, this being generally termed afterripening* (Science News).

af|ters (af′tərz, äf′-), *n.pl. British Informal.* the course which follows the main course of a meal; dessert: *... apple Charlotte and macaroons for afters* (Colin Watson).

af|ter-sales (af′tər sālz′, äf′-), *adj. British.* after being sold: *after-sales service of motor cars.*

af|ter|sen|sa|tion (af′tər sen sā′shən, äf′-) *n. Psychology.* a sensation which persists after its stimulus has ceased, such as an afterimage.

af|ter|shaft (af′tər shaft′, äf′tər shäft′), *n.* **1** a supplementary feather growing out from the underside of a feather. **2** the shaft of such a feather.

af|ter-shave (af′tər shāv′, äf′-), *n.,* or **after-shave lotion,** shaving lotion applied after shaving to soothe the skin.

af|ter|shock (af′tər shok′, äf′-), *n.* **1** a lesser shock coming after the main shock of an earthquake. **2** *Figurative.* any delayed effect; aftereffect: *the aftershock of dismissal.*

af|ter-ski (af′tər skē′, äf′-), *adv., adj., n.* = après-ski.

af|ter|taste (af′tər tāst′, äf′-), *n.* **1** a taste that is noticed in the mouth after eating or drinking. **2** *Figurative.* a feeling such as of pleasure or, usually, regret after something done or experienced; retrospective feeling.

af|ter-tax (af′tər taks′, äf′-), *adj.* that remains after taxes, especially income taxes, are paid; net: *after-tax earnings.*

af|ter-the|a|ter (af′tər thē′ə tər, äf′-), *adj.* following attendance or a performance at the theater: *an after-theater party.*

af|ter|thought (af′tər thôt′, äf′-), *n.* **1** a thought that comes too late to be used. **2** a second or later thought or explanation: *The fact that I agree with Bohr's fundamental ideas ... is the result of my own thinking, although ... mine was only an afterthought, stimulated by Bohr's forethought* (Max Born).

af|ter|time (af′tər tīm′, äf′-), *n.* the future.

af|ter|treat|ment (af′tər trēt′mənt, äf′-), *n.* a follow-up treatment given to a manufactured article to improve or finish it: *The new product, which is still at the development stage, does not require this wet-hot aftertreatment* (New Scientist).

af|ter|ward (af′tər wərd, äf′-), *adv.* at a later time; afterwards; subsequently. [Old English *æfterweard*]

af|ter|wards (af′tər wərdz, äf′-), *adv.* afterward; later: *The bud was small at first, but afterwards it became a large flower.* [< *afterward* + adverbial genitive *-s*]

af|ter|word (af′tər wėrd′, äf′-), *n.* something written at the conclusion of a book, play, or other work, as an epilogue or the like: *In the narrative and the afterword, there is also an unfolding of one of the most remarkable states in history* (Saturday Review).

af|ter|world (af′tər wėrld′, äf′-), *n.* a world after death.

aft|most (aft′mōst, äft′-), *adj. Nautical.* aftermost.

Af|to|ni|an (af tō′nē ən), *adj. Geology.* of or having to do with the first interglacial stage in the topographical development of North America. [< *Afton,* a town in Wyoming]

af|to|sa (af tō′sə), *n.* = foot-and-mouth disease. [< Spanish *aftoso* aphthous < *afta* thrush, a disease]

af|wil|lite (af wil′īt), *n.* a rare, colorless, monoclinic crystalline form of hydrous calcium silicate, found in Ireland, Africa, and the United States. *Formula:* $3CaO \cdot 2SiO_2 \cdot 3H_2O$ [< *A*lpheus *F. Will*iams, who discovered it + *-ite*¹]

ag-, *prefix.* the form of **ad-** before *g,* as in *agglutinate, aggrandize.*

Ag (no period), **1a** agricultural. **b** agriculture. **2** *Chemistry.* silver (Latin, *argentum*).

Ag., 1a agricultural. **b** agriculture. **2** August.

A.G., 1 adjutant general. **2** attorney general.

a|ga (ä′gə), *n.* a Moslem title of respect. Also, **agha.** [< Turkish *aga*]

a|gain (ə gen′; *especially British* ə gān′; *see note below*), *adv.* **1** another time; once more: *Come again to play. Say that again. Try again.* **SYN:** anew, afresh. **2** in return; in reply; back: *to answer again. He laughed till the glasses in the sideboard rang again* (Dickens). **3** to the same place or person; back: *I walked to town and back again.* **4** on the other hand; yet: *It may rain, and again it may not.* **SYN:** further, furthermore. **5** moreover; besides: *And then again, what do his fine words amount to?*

again and again, many times over; repeatedly; often; frequently: *Again and again the firemen were driven back as the flames flared up. Our leaders tell us, again and again, that we are the richest and most powerful nation on earth* (Martha Gellhorn).

as much again, a twice as much or as many: *I have $10, but I need as much again to buy a $20 camera.* **b** as much as has already been spent, accounted for, etc.: *It will cost you not only all you have spent but also as much again to do the job right.*

[Old English *ongēan, ongegn* toward; opposite, against; back; again < *on* on + *gegn* direct]

▶**Again** and **against** are pronounced both with (ā) and (e) in Great Britain, but the former is much less common than it once was. In the United States, ə gān′and ə gānst′are rather infrequent and are often thought of as affectations when used by Americans.

a|gainst (ə genst′; *especially British* ə gānst′), *prep., conj.* **—*prep.*** **1** in opposition to; contrary to: *It is against the law to cross the street when the light is red. This is against the rules of the game. The dogs fought against the lion.* **2** actively opposed; hostile to: *Why are you against me?* **3a** so as to strike; upon: *Rain beats against the window.* **b** in the opposite direction to; so as to meet: *We will sail against the wind.* **4** directly opposite to; in front of; facing toward: *over against the wall.* **5** in contact with: *The ladder is leaning against the wall.* **6** in contrast to or with: *The ship appeared against the sky.* **7** in preparation for: *Squirrels store up nuts against the winter. [I am] saving up money against the next time I might have to go to New York* (A. J. Liebling). **8** so as to defend or protect from: *An umbrella is a protection against rain.* **9** in return for: *to trade one thing against another.*
—*conj.* *Archaic.* by the time that; before.
[Middle English *agenes* < *agen,* Old English *ongegn* again + adverbial genitive *-s* (the *-t* is a later addition)] **—a|gainst′ness,** *n.*
▶For a note on pronunciation, see **again.**

***a|gal** (ä′gäl, ä gäl′), *n.* a cord wound around a head covering at the temples, worn by any of various Arab peoples. [< Arabic *'iqāl*]

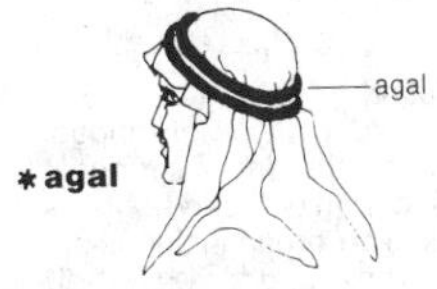

***agal**

ag|a|lac|ti|a (ag′ə lak′tē ə), *n.* a lack or deficiency of milk in a mother after childbirth. [< New Latin *agalactia* < Greek *agalaktíā* < *a-* without + *gála, gálaktos* milk]

a|gal|loch (ə gal′ək), *n.* the fragrant wood of a kind of East Indian tree; aloes. [< New Latin *agallochum* < Greek *agállochon*]

a|gal|lo|chum (ə gal′ə kəm), *n.* = agalloch.

Pronunciation Key: hat, āge, cãre, fär; let, ēqual, tėrm; it, īce; hot, ōpen, ôrder; oil, out; cup, pu̇t, rüle; child; long; thin; ᴛʜen; zh, measure; ə represents **a** in about, **e** in taken, **i** in pencil, **o** in lemon, **u** in circus.

ag|al|mat|o|lite (ag′əl mat′ə līt), *n.* any one of various grayish or greenish minerals; figure stone; pagodite. It is soft enough to be carved into ornaments and figurines, especially in China, and is also used for glazing pottery. [< Greek *ágalma, -atos* statue + English *-lite*]
ag|al|wood (ag′əl wu̇d′), *n.* the fragrant wood of a kind of East Indian tree; aloes. [< *agal*(loch)]
ag|a|ma (ag′ə mə), *n.* any one of a genus of small lizards related to the iguanas, but having acrodont dental development, found in the Mediterranean region, in southern Asia, and in Africa. [< New Latin *Agama* < Spanish; origin uncertain]
Ag|a|mem|non (ag′ə mem′non, -nən), *n. Greek Legend.* the leader of the Greeks in the Trojan War, a king of Mycenae. He was the brother of Menelaus and the father of Orestes, Electra, and Iphigenia. On his return from the war, he was killed by Clytemnestra, his unfaithful wife, and her lover, Aegisthus.
a|gam|ete (ā gam′ēt, ā gə mēt′), *n.* an asexual reproductive cell.
ag|a|mi (ag′ə mē), *n., pl.* **-mis.** a trumpeter, a bird of South America related to the cranes. [< French *agamy* < native name in Guiana]
a|gam|ic (ā gam′ik, ə gam′-), *adj. Biology.* **1** = asexual. **2** (of ova) not requiring fertilization by the male. [< Late Latin *agamus* (< Greek *ágamos* unmarried < *a-* without + *gámos* marriage) + English *-ic*]
a|gam|i|cal|ly (ā gam′ə klē, ə gam′-), *adv.* in an agamic or asexual manner; asexually.
ag|a|mid (ag′ə mid), *n.* = agama.
a|gam|ma|glob|u|li|ne|mi|a (ā gam′ə glob′yə lə-nē′mē ə), *n. Medicine.* the absence of gamma globulin in the blood: *Occasionally, human beings are born without the capacity to form the anti-body-containing gamma globulins. Those suffering from such agammaglobulinemia die soon of infection unless massive antibiotic therapy is used* (Isaac Asimov). [< *a-*[4] without + *gamma globulin* + *-emia*]
a|gam|o|gen|e|sis (ā gam′ə jen′ə sis, ag′ə mō-), *n. Biology.* asexual reproduction. [< Greek *ágamos* unmarried + English *genesis*]
a|gam|o|ge|net|ic (ā gam′ə jə net′ik, ag′ə mō-), *adj. Biology.* propagating without sex; reproducing or being reproduced without sexual union.
ag|a|mous (ag′ə məs), *adj.* **1** = agamic (asexual). **2** = cryptogamous.
a|gan|gli|on|ic (ā gang′glē on′ik), *adj.* having no ganglia.
ag|a|pan|thus (ag′ə pan′thəs), *n.* any one of the varieties of a South African perennial plant of the amaryllis family, including the African lily, with clusters of blue or white flowers with yellow anthers: *Agapanthus is in full bloom on the mountain in January* (A. H. Hamer). [< New Latin *Agapanthus* the genus name < Greek *agápē* love + *ánthos* flower]
a|gape[1] (ə gāp′, -gap′), *adv., adj.* **1** with the mouth wide open in wonder or surprise: *Their rich retinue . . . Dazzles the crowd, and sets them all agape* (Milton). **2** wide open; gaping: *with mouth agape.* [< *a-*[1] + *gape*]
a|ga|pe[2] (ag′ə pē), *n., pl.* **-pae** (-pē). **1** a communal meal among the early Christians, as an expression of brotherly love, originally combined with the celebration of the Lord's Supper; love feast. **2** unselfish brotherly love: *Thus, it is from repression of agape, love of one's fellow man, . . . that anxiety springs* (Time). [< Greek *agápē* love]
a|gar (ā′gər, ag′ər, ā′gər), *n.* **1** a jellylike extract obtained from certain seaweeds, used in making cultures for bacteria and fungi, in food processing, as a glue, as a mild laxative, and in certain Oriental soups and jellies. Agar is a complex carbohydrate. **2** a culture medium containing agar. [< *agar-agar*]
a|gar-a|gar (ā′gər ā′gər, ag′ər ag′ər, ā′gər ā′gər), *n.* = agar. [< Malay]
ag|a|ric (ag′ər ik, ə gar′-), *n.* **1** a type of fungus having blade-shaped gills on the under surface of an umbrellalike structure on which naked spores are produced; gill fungus. The group includes toadstools, edible mushrooms, and several shelf-like fungi. **2** a corklike fungus that grows on trees. [< Latin *agaricum* < Greek *agarikón* < *Agariā* a place in Sarmatia]
a|gar|i|ca|ceous (ə gar′ə kā′shəs), *adj.* belonging to a large family of fungi that includes the common mushrooms.
agaric acid, = agaricic acid.
ag|a|ric|ic acid (ag′ə ris′ik), a white, crystalline powder, odorless and almost tasteless, contained in agaric. *Formula:* $C_{22}H_{40}O_7\ 1\frac{1}{2}H_2O$
agaric mineral, = rock milk.
ag|ate[1] (ag′it), *n.* **1** a kind of quartz with colored stripes, cloudy colors, or mosslike formations. **2** a marble used in games that looks like agate. **3** a piece of this quartz. **4** a burnisher, die plate, or other tool made of it. **5** *U.S.* a size of printing type (5½ point), called *ruby* in England. The term survives largely in the phrase *agate line.* [< Old French *agathe,* alteration of *acate,* learned borrowing from Latin *achātēs* < Greek *achátēs*] —**ag′ate|like′,** *adj.*
a|gate[2] (ə gāt′), *adv. Scottish and Northern English.* on the way; going. [< *a-*[1] on + obsolete *gate* way, path]
agate line, *U.S.* a measure of print, about 1/14 inch deep and one column wide, used as a unit of space in advertising.
ag|ate|ware (ag′it wār′), *n.* **1** cooking dishes, cups, or other household utensils made of iron or steel coated with variegated enamel. **2** pottery colored to look like agate.
ag|a|tho|de|mon or **ag|a|tho|dae|mon** (ag′ə thə dē′mən), *n.* a good spirit; good genius (contrasted with *cacodemon*). [< Greek *agathodaimōn* < *agathós* good + *daimōn* a spirit]
ag|a|tif|er|ous (ag′ə tif′ər əs), *adj.* containing or yielding agate.
ag|at|ize (ag′ə tīz), *v.t.,* **-ized, -iz|ing.** to change into agate; make like agate.
à gauche (à gōsh′), *French.* to the left; on the left.
a|ga|ve (ə gä′vē, -gā′-), *n.* any one of a group of chiefly Mexican-American desert plants having a dense cluster of rigid, fleshy leaves with spines along the edges and at the tips. Soap, alcoholic drinks, and rope are made from some kinds of agave. The century plant and sisal are agaves. [< New Latin *Agave* < Greek *Agaúē,* a proper name < *agauós* noble]
agave family, a group of herbs and shrublike plants, especially adapted to desert life, closely related to the lily and amaryllis families, and including the century plant, yucca, bowstring hemp, and tuberose.
a|ga|vose (ə gä′vōs), *n.* a sugar found in the sap of the century plant. *Formula:* $C_{12}H_{22}O_{11}$ [< *agave* + *-ose*[2]]
a|gaze (ə gāz′), *adv.; adj.* gazing.
agcy., agency.
age (āj), *n., adj., v.,* **aged, ag|ing** or **age|ing.** —*n.* **1** time of life; length of life from birth on: *His age is ten.* **2** the length of time anything has existed: *Turtles live to a great age. The bristlecone pines and the redwoods of California have the greatest age of any living thing.* **3** a particular period or stage of life: *middle age. Grandfather has reached old age.* **4** the latter part of life; old age: *the wisdom of age.* **5** the full or average term of life: *The age of a horse is 25 to 30 years.* **6** a period in history: *the golden age, the atomic age, the Bronze Age. We are living in the age of jet planes and space travel.* SYN: epoch, era. **7** a generation: *ages yet unborn.* **8** *Psychology.* the level of a person's development mentally, educationally, emotionally, or otherwise. **9** the effects of growing old: *He has begun to show his age.* **10** the period in which a person's lifetime falls; his generation: *Galileo was in advance of his age.* **11** a period in the earth's history; eon: *the ice age.*
—*adj.* aged: *The star of the piece is John Jennings, age twenty-eight* (Edith Oliver).
—*v.i.* **1** to grow old: *He is aging fast.* **2** to become mature: *Wine is put in casks to age.*
—*v.t.* **1** to make old; produce the effects of age in: *Worry ages a person.* **2** to bring to full growth; mature, especially by keeping in storage: *to age wine. This cheese must be aged for a year before it is ripe enough to eat.*
ages, a *Informal.* a long time or seemingly long time: *I haven't seen you for ages!* **b** a long, indefinite stretch of time; hundreds of years: *the work of ages.*
come of age, to reach full development or maturity: *Army men feel the aircraft won't really come of age until maintenance costs are brought down sharply* (Wall Street Journal).
of age, at the time of life when a person is considered ready for adult rights and responsibilities, fixed by law, formerly at 21, and now often at 18: *You cannot vote unless you are of age.*
[< Old French *aage* < Gallo-Romance *aetāticum* < Latin *aetās, -ātis* age]
-age, *suffix forming nouns from other nouns or from verbs.* **1** the act of _____ing: *Breakage = act of breaking.*
2 a group or collection of _____s: *Baggage = group of bags.*
3 the condition or rank of _____s: *Peerage = rank of peers.*
4 the cost of or fee for _____ing: *Postage = cost of posting (mailing).*
5 a home for _____s: *Orphanage = home for orphans.*
[< Old French *-age* < Latin *-āticum* < nouns in *-ā* + *-ticum,* neuter of *-ticus* < Greek *-tikós*]
age area, *Anthropology.* the age of a culture trait as determined by the relative size of the area over which it has spread.
age class, = age group.
a|ged (ā′jid *for adj. 1, 3, n.;* ājd *for adj. 2, 4*), *adj., n.* —*adj.* **1** having lived a long time; old: *The aged woman was wrinkled and bent.* SYN: elderly. **2** of the age of: *A child aged six must go to school.* **3** characteristic of old age: *aged wrinkles.* **4** improved by aging: *aged cheese.*
—*n.* elderly people: *a home for the aged, care of the aged.* —**a′ged|ly,** *adv.* —**a′ged|ness,** *n.*
a|gee (ə jē′), *adv., adj. Dialect.* to one side; awry; ajar. Also, **ajee.**
age group, a group of people of about the same age: *The youth culture is the special set of mores, customs, roles and values of youth considered as a distinctive, separate age group* (American Scholar).
age|ing (ā′jing), *n.* = aging.
age|ism (ā′jiz əm), *n.* discrimination against old or elderly people, especially in employment and housing.
age|ist (ā′jist), *adj.* discriminating against old or elderly people; practicing ageism: *Our ageist society usually lumps all old people into one great, gray mass* (Maggie Kuhn).
age|less (āj′lis), *adj.* never growing old or out of date; never coming to an end: *the ageless wisdom of the Bible.* —**age′less|ly,** *adv.*
age|long (āj′lông′, -long′), *adj.* lasting a long time; everlasting: *agelong legends.*
age mate, a member of the same age group.
a|gen|cy (ā′jən sē), *n., pl.* **-cies.** **1** a business of a person or company that acts for another: *An agency rented our house for us. Employment agencies help workers to get jobs, and find workers for people who need them.* **2** the office of such a person or company. **3** a special department of the government concerned with the administration of affairs within a specific field: *The agency in charge of intelligence activities for the United States is the Central Intelligence Agency.* **4** any organization or bureau providing a public service: *The international agencies chiefly concerned with marine pollution are the Food and Agricultural Organization, the World Health Organization, and the United Nations Development Program* (Walter Sullivan). **5** *U.S.* an Indian agency. **6** means of producing effects; action or operation: *Snow is drifted by the agency of the wind.* SYN: instrumentality. [< Medieval Latin *agentia* < Latin *agēns, -entis,* present participle of *agere* do]
agency shop, a factory or business firm in which employees pay union dues or equivalent fees whether they belong to the union or not.
a|gen|da (ə jen′də), *n., pl. of* **a|gen|dum** (ə jen′-dəm). **1** a list of things to be dealt with or done; business to be brought before a meeting of a committee, council, board, or other group: *The agenda for today's club meeting includes reading of committee reports, admission of new members, and planning of the month's activities.* **2** *Figurative: . . . an expanding agenda of political and human problems* (Adlai E. Stevenson). *The TC is . . . an auto with a hidden agenda: the prestige it brings to Chrysler will spill over onto the company's more utilitarian offerings* (Vanity Fair). **3** *Theology.* matters of practice as contrasted with matters of belief or credenda. [< Latin *agenda* things to be done, neuter plural gerundive of *agere* do]
►**Agenda** is now established in general use as a singular (*The agenda has already been settled*), and the plural *agendas* is now also relatively common.
A|gene (ā′jēn), *n. Trademark.* a bleaching agent formerly used to bleach flour. *Formula:* NCl_3
ag|e|ne|si|a (aj′ə nē′sē ə), *n.* = agenesis.
a|gen|e|sis (ā jen′ə sis), *n. Medicine.* **1** sexual impotence or sterility. **2** absence or incomplete development of a part or organ. [< *a-*[4] without + Greek *génnēsis* producing]
a|ge|nize (ā′jə nīz), *v.t.,* **-nized, -niz|ing.** to bleach with Agene.
a|gent (ā′jənt), *n.* **1** a person or company that acts for another: *I made my brother my agent while I was out of the city. An insurance agent will insure your property against losses from accidents. Abbr:* agt. SYN: representative, deputy, intermediary. **2** a law-enforcement officer: *a federal agent.* **3** a member of the government secret service; secret agent. **4a** any power or cause that produces an effect by its action: *Yeast is the agent that causes bread to rise. Electricity is an important agent of convenience in the modern home. Many insects are agents of fertilization. Conscience is a moral agent.* **b** a person who produces an effect: *I was still to be the willful agent of all my own miseries* (Daniel Defoe). **c** any substance or force capable of causing a chemical reaction: *a catalytic agent.* **5** means; instrument: *Graphite is used as a lubricating agent.* **6** *Informal.* a traveling salesman. **7** *British.* a candidate's campaign manager. **8** *U.S., Historical.* a road agent; highwayman. [< Latin *agēns, -entis,* present participle of *agere* do]

a|gent-gen|er|al (ā′jənt jen′ər əl, -jen′rəl), *n., pl.* **a|gents-gen|er|al.** a representative in England of certain of the Canadian provinces, Australian states, etc., under the leadership of a high commissioner.

a|gen|tial (ā jen′shəl), *adj.* **1** of or in the capacity of an agent or an agency. **2** = agentive.

a|gen|ti|val (ā′jən tī′vəl), *adj.* = agentive.

a|gen|tive (ā′jən tiv), *adj., n.* **—*adj.*** having the grammatical function of indicating a person or thing that performs an action. The *-er* of *builder* is an agentive suffix.
—*n.* a grammatical form or element that expresses or denotes an agent.

agent noun, a noun that indicates an agent (a person or thing acting), especially a noun that indicates the person or thing doing the act expressed by a verb, such as *binder, creator, runner,* and *sleeper,* in relation to *bind, create, run,* and *sleep.*

Agent Orange, a highly toxic herbicide used for defoliation and crop destruction: *... Agent Orange ... had been rained down by the tens of thousands of tons, and over some five million acres, in herbicidal warfare operations in South Vietnam* (New Yorker). [so called from the color of the code stripe on its container]

a|gent pro|vo|ca|teur (á zhäɴ′prô vô kà tœr′), *pl.* **a|gents pro|vo|ca|teurs** (á zhäɴ′prô vô kà-tœr′). *French.* a person secretly hired to join a group of persons in order to induce or incite the members of the group to do something unlawful that will make them liable to punishment: *... that the charges against Mr. Bouman were unfounded and that an agent provocateur had tried to trap him into bribery* (London Times).

a|gent|ry (ā′jən trē), *n., pl.* **-ries.** the business of an agent.

Age of Aquarius, (in astrology) an age of unprecedented freedom and fellowship now newly dawning upon earth.

age of consent, the minimum age, as fixed by law, at which a person is considered competent to act in his or her own behalf, as in marriage.

age of discretion, *Law.* fourteen years.

Age of Fishes, the Devonian age.

Age of Mammals, the Cenozoic age.

Age of Reason, the period in Europe from the 1600's to the late 1700's in which philosophers emphasized the use of reason as the best method of learning truth. John Locke, Descartes, Diderot, Rousseau, and Voltaire were leaders.

Age of Reptiles, the Mesozoic age.

age-old (āj′ōld′), *adj.* having existed for a very long time; very old; ancient: *age-old customs.*

ag|er|a|tum (aj′ə rā′təm, ə jer′ə-), *n.* **1** any one of a genus of chiefly tropical American garden plants of the composite family. Certain species have small, dense flower heads, usually blue, sometimes white or pinkish. **2** any one of several other composite plants, usually having blue flowers. [< New Latin *Ageratum* < Greek *agḗraton* < *agḗratos* ageless < *a-* not + *gēráskein* grow old]

a|ges (ā′jəz), *n.pl.* See under **age.**

a|geu|si|a (ə gyü′sē ə), *n.* partial or total loss of the sense of taste. [< New Latin *ageusia* < Greek *a-* without + *geûsis* sense of taste]

ag|ger (aj′ər), *n.* **1** a mound of earth, especially an earthen rampart around an ancient Roman camp. **2** a Roman road. [< Latin *agger*]

Ag|ge|us (ə gē′əs), *n.* = Haggai (in the Douay Bible).

Ag|gie (ag′ē), *n. U.S. Slang.* **1** Usually, **Aggies,** *pl.* a group representing an agricultural college, such as an athletic team. **2** a student at an agricultural college.

ag|gie (ag′ē), *n.* a playing marble made of agate.

ag|gior|na|men|to (ä jôr′nä men′tō), *n.* **1** *Italian.* (in the Roman Catholic Church) the modernization of old customs and practices. **2** (literally) an updating.

***agglomerate**
definition 2

ag|glom|er|ate** (*v.* ə glom′ə rāt; *n., adj.* ə glom′-ər it, -ə rāt), *v.,* **-at|ed, -at|ing,** *n., adj.* **—*v.t., v.i. to gather together in a mass; cluster or heap together; gather; amass. **SYN:** accumulate, collect.
—*n.* **1** a loose or rough mass or collection; a cluster: *The United States ... has always been an agglomerate of peoples who came—or whose ancestors came—from different lands to find their future* (C. L. Sulzberger). **2** a rock of angular volcanic fragments fused by heat.
—*adj.* **1** packed together in a mass. **2** gathered into a cluster or mass, but not cohering, as some types of flowers.
[< Latin *agglomerāre* (with English *-ate*[1]) wind onto a ball < *ad-* to + *glomus, -eris* ball]

ag|glom|er|at|ic (ə glom′ə rat′ik), *adj. Geology.* having the nature of an agglomerate.

ag|glom|er|a|tion (ə glom′ə rā′shən), *n.* **1** a mass of things gathered or clustered together: *an agglomeration of stars. The buildings are huge agglomerations of aluminum and glass* (David Boroff). **2** the act of agglomerating. **3** an agglomerated condition.

ag|glom|er|a|tive (ə glom′ə rā′tiv), *adj.* tending to agglomerate.

ag|glu|ti|na|ble (ə glü′tə nə bəl), *adj.* that can be agglutinated.

ag|glu|ti|nant (ə glü′tə nənt), *adj., n.* **—*adj.*** uniting closely, as glue; adhesive.
—*n.* any sticky or viscous substance that causes objects to stick together. [< Latin *agglūtināns, -antis,* present participle of *agglūtināre;* see etym. under **agglutinate**]

ag|glu|ti|nate (*v.* ə glü′tə nāt; *adj.* ə glü′tə nit, -nāt), *v.,* **-nat|ed, -nat|ing,** *adj.* **—*v.t.*** **1** to unite or fasten as with glue; stick or join together. **SYN:** cement. **2** to form (words) by joining words, or words and affixes, together with little or no change in form. **SYN:** compound. **3** (in immunology) to cause (cells) to clump together.
—*v.i.* **1** to become agglutinated; join or clump together; undergo agglutination.**2** to turn into glue.
—*adj.* **1** stuck or joined together: *"Never-to-be-forgotten" is an agglutinate word.* **2** agglutinative (def. 2).
[< Latin *agglūtināre* (with English *-ate*[1]) < *ad-* to + *glūtināre* to glue < *glūten, -inis* glue]

agglutinating language, a language characterized by combining into a single word fixed combining forms that never blend with one another. The Finno-Ugric languages are agglutinating languages.

ag|glu|ti|na|tion (ə glü′tə nā′shən), *n.* **1** the process of agglutinating, especially the clumping together of bacteria or red blood cells, caused usually by the introduction of antibodies to such cells. **2** an agglutinated condition. **3** a mass or group formed by the sticking together of separate things. **4** the forming of words by joining together words that retain their individual form and meaning.

ag|glu|ti|na|tive (ə glü′tə nā′tiv), *adj.* **1** tending to stick together; adhesive: *Glue is an agglutinative substance.* **2** forming words by agglutination: *Turkish is probably the most highly agglutinative tongue now spoken by men* (Simeon Potter).

ag|glu|ti|nin (ə glü′tə nin), *n.* an antibody that causes bacteria or blood cells to stick together in clumps. [< *agglutin*(ate) + *-in*]

ag|glu|tin|o|gen (ag′lü tin′ə jən), *n.* any one of a group of antigens which stimulate the production of agglutinins.

ag|gra|da|tion (ag′rə dā′shən), *n. Geology.* the filling up of a bay, valley, or the like with silt or other debris from a stream, river, or sea, thus raising its level.

ag|gra|da|tion|al (ag′rə dā′shə nəl), *adj. Geology.* of or having to do with the process of aggradation.

ag|grade (ə grād′), *v.,* **-grad|ed, -grad|ing.** *Geology.* **—*v.t.*** to raise the level of (a bay, valley, or other enclosed area) by filling it up with silt or other debris.
—*v.i.* to raise the level of a bay, valley, or other enclosed area. [< *ad-* up to + *grade,* as in *degrade*]

ag|gran|diz|a|ble (ag′rən dī′zə bəl), *adj.* that can be aggrandized.

ag|gran|dize (ag′rən dīz, ə gran′-), *v.t.,* **-dized, -diz|ing.** **1** to make greater or larger in power; increase the rank or wealth of: *The dictator sought to aggrandize himself by new conquests.* **SYN:** exalt. **2** to increase in size or intensity; magnify; enlarge. **SYN:** augment, enhance. [< French *agrandiss-,* stem of *agrandir,* ultimately from Latin *ad-* to + *grandis* great] **—ag′gran|diz′er,** *n.*

ag|gran|dize|ment (ə gran′diz mənt), *n.* **1** a making greater, larger, or more powerful: *Production in a free country can always suffer because under monolithic government all production can go to the aggrandizement of the state* (William Faulkner). **2** an increase in power, wealth, rank, or the like.

ag|gra|vate (ag′rə vāt), *v.t.,* **-vat|ed, -vat|ing.** **1a** to make worse or more severe: *His bad temper was aggravated by a headache.* **SYN:** increase, augment, intensify, exacerbate. **b** to make more burdensome or more offensive: *A lie will only aggravate your guilt.* **SYN:** increase, augment, intensify, exacerbate. **2** *Informal.* to annoy; irritate; exasperate: *He aggravated his sister by pulling her hair. The whispering in class aggravates our teacher.* **SYN:** provoke. **3** *Obsolete.* to add weight to. [< Latin *aggravāre* (with English *-ate*[1]) to make heavier < *ad-* on + *gravis* heavy. See etym. of doublet **aggrieve.**] **—ag′gra|vat′ing|ly,** *adv.* **—ag′gra|va′tor,** *n.*
►**Aggravate** as a synonym of *annoy, exasperate, irritate, provoke,* is sometimes condemned by prescriptive grammarians, but is established in informal use and found in the works of standard writers: *Threats only served to aggravate people in such cases* (Thackeray).

aggravated assault, *Law.* assault committed with the intention of committing an additional offense: *Aggravated assault includes assault with intent to kill or to inflict serious bodily injury, whether or not a dangerous weapon is used* (Morris and Hawkins).

ag|gra|va|tion (ag′rə vā′shən), *n.* **1** the act of making worse or more severe. **2** the condition of being made worse or more severe. **3** something that aggravates, such as a circumstance that adds to the unpleasantness of anything or intensifies an evil. **4** *Informal.* an annoyance; irritation, or other exasperation.

ag|gra|va|tive (ag′rə vā′tiv), *adj.* that tends to aggravate.

ag|gre|ga|ble (ag′rə gə bəl), *adj.* that may be aggregated or lumped together (with other property): *Parliamentary estates were aggregable with the marriage settlement funds* (Westminster Gazette).

ag|gre|gate (*n., adj.* ag′rə git, -gāt; *v.* ag′rə gāt), *n., adj., v.,* **-gat|ed, -gat|ing.** **—*n.*** **1** total amount; sum: *The aggregate of all the gifts was over $100.* **2** a mass of separate things joined together; combined mass; collection: *A lump of sugar is an aggregate of sugar crystals.* **3** any material, such as sand or gravel, that is mixed with water and cement to make concrete. **4** *Geology.* rock composed of several different mineral constituents capable of being separated by mechanical means: *Granite is a type of aggregate.*
—*adj.* **1a** total. **b** gathered together in one mass or group. **SYN:** combined, collective. **2** *Botany.* consisting of many florets arranged in a dense mass: *an aggregate flower.* **3** *Geology.* composed of different mineral fragments united into one rock by heat, as granite.
—*v.t.* **1** to amount to; come to; total: *The money collected will aggregate $1,000.* **2** to gather together in a mass or whole; collect; unite: *Granite is made of small particles aggregated together.* **SYN:** mass.
—*v.i.* to come together in a mass; accumulate.
in the aggregate, taken together; considered as a whole; collectively: *The payments on our house amount in the aggregate to a big sum of money. Our judgment of a man's character is derived from observing a number of successive acts, forming in the aggregate his general course of conduct* (George C. Lewis).
[< Latin *aggregātus,* past participle of *aggregāre* add to, ultimately < *ad-* to + *grex, gregis* flock] **—ag′gre|gate′ly,** *adv.* **—ag′gre|gate′ness,** *n.* **—ag′gre|ga′tor,** *n.*

aggregate fruit, a fruit composed of a cluster of ripened ovaries that were separate in the flower, such as the blackberry and raspberry (distinguished from *simple fruit* and *multiple fruit*).

ag|gre|ga|tion (ag′rə gā′shən), *n.* **1** the collecting of separate things into one mass or whole: *the aggregation of white corpuscles.* **2** the group or mass collected. **SYN:** gathering, collection, assemblage.

aggregation signs, the parentheses, braces, or brackets used in algebra to enclose a symbol or group of symbols.

ag|gre|ga|tive (ag′rə gā′tiv), *adj.* **1** tending to aggregate; collective. **2** social; gregarious.

ag|gre|ga|to|ry (ag′rə gə tôr′ē, -tōr′-), *adj.* like an aggregate; collected into a whole.

ag|gress (ə gres′), *v.i.* to make the first attack; commit the act of hostility that begins a quarrel, war, etc.: *You can't carve a new nation out of an old country without aggressing against a people who have lived there for centuries* (Wall Street Journal). **—*v.t.*** to commit aggression against; attack: *He is making the most of his ... position as the aggressed and injured* (New Yorker). [< Latin *aggressus,* past participle of *aggredī* approach, attack < *ad-* to + *gradī* to step]

ag|gres|sion (ə gresh′ən), *n.* **1** the first step in an attack or a quarrel; an unprovoked attack: *A country that sends its army to occupy another country is guilty of aggression.* **2** the practice of making assaults or attacks on the rights or territory of others as a method or policy. **3** any attack, infringement, or encroachment: *... aggression upon their ancient liberties* (Scott).

Pronunciation Key: hat, āge, cãre, fär; let, ēqual, tėrm; it, īce; hot, ōpen, ôrder; oil, out; cup, pu̇t, rüle; child; long; thin; ᴛʜen; zh, measure; ə represents **a** in about, **e** in taken, **i** in pencil, **o** in lemon, **u** in circus.

4 *Psychology.* an act or attitude of hostility, usually arising from feelings of inferiority or frustration.

ag|gres|sive (ə gres′iv), *adj.* **1** taking the first step in an attack or a quarrel; ready to attack others; attacking: *Which was the aggressive one, Joan or James? An aggressive country is always ready to start a war.* **SYN**: quarrelsome. **2** characterized by aggression; offensive: *an aggressive war.* **3** *Informal, Figurative.* very active; energetic: *The police are making an aggressive campaign against driving too fast.* **4** *Figurative.* too confident and certain; assertive; self-assertive; pushing: *an aggressive person. Her aggressive manner irritated her classmates.* —**ag|gres′sive|ly**, *adv.* —**ag|gres′sive|ness**, *n.*

ag|gres|siv|i|ty (ə gre siv′ə tē), *n.* the quality or condition of being aggressive: *A third factor has been the rapid multiplication of drugs which offer effective control of depression and violent aggressivity* (Israel Zwerling).

ag|gres|sor (ə gres′ər), *n.* one that begins an attack or a quarrel, especially a nation that starts a war by committing aggression: *As illegal aggressors* [*they*] *acquired no belligerent rights under international law* (London Times). *There is nothing more easy than to break a treaty ratified in all the usual forms, and yet neither party be the aggressor* (Oliver Goldsmith). **SYN**: assailant, invader.

ag|grieve (ə grēv′), *v.t.*, **-grieved, -griev|ing.** to injure unjustly; cause grief or trouble to: *His friend's insult aggrieved him.* [< Old French *agrever* < Latin *aggravāre.* See etym. of doublet **aggravate.**]

► **Aggrieve** is now rare except in the passive: *Both were alike aggrieved by the tyranny of a bad king* (Macaulay).

ag|grieved (ə grēvd′), *adj.* **1** injured or wronged in one's rights, relations, or position, especially one's legal rights: *to make amends to an aggrieved person.* **2** feeling injured or wronged; troubled; distressed: *He was aggrieved at the insult from his friend.*

ag|griev|ed|ly (ə grē′vid lē), *adv.* in an aggrieved manner.

ag|grieve|ment (ə grēv′mənt), *n.* a being or feeling aggrieved; resentment; grievance: *He bent his head but that did not hide the aggrievement, indignation, that was in his voice* (Eudora Welty).

ag|gro (ag′rō), *n. British Slang.* rowdy and violent activities, such as those of skinheads. Also, **agro.** [< *aggravation*]

a|gha (ä′gə), *n.* = aga.

a|ghast (ə gast′, -gäst′), *adj.* struck with surprise or horror; filled with shocked amazement: *My friend's suggestion that we should run away from home left my sister aghast.* [past participle of obsolete *agast* terrify < Old English *on-* on + *gæstan* frighten. See related etym. at **ghost.**] —**a|ghast′ness**, *n.*

ag|ile (aj′əl; *especially British* aj′īl), *adj.* **1** moving quickly and easily; active; lively; nimble: *as agile as a cat. An acrobat has to be agile.* **SYN**: sprightly, spry, brisk. **2** *Figurative.* quick in thinking; alert: *You need an agile mind to solve puzzles.* **SYN**: quick-witted. [< Latin *agilis* < *agere* move] —**ag′ile|ly**, *adv.* —**ag′ile|ness**, *n.*

a|gil|i|ty (ə jil′ə tē), *n.* **1** the ability to move quickly and easily; liveliness; nimbleness: *He has the agility of a monkey.* **2** *Figurative.* alertness: *a man of great mental agility. He solved the complex problem with astounding agility.*

a|gin[1] (ə gin′), *prep. Informal or Dialect.* against; opposed to: *Progress, I'm agin it!* [variant of *against*]

a|gin[2] (ə gin′), *adv. Informal or Dialect.* again; once more: *Well, fellers, here I am agin.* [variant of *again*]

ag|ing (ā′jing), *n.* **1** a becoming old or older. **2** the process of maturing: *the aging of meat.* Also, **ageing.**

ag|i|o (aj′ē ō, aj′ō), *n., pl.* **-i|os. 1** a premium paid in the exchange of money to allow for the difference in value of two different kinds of currencies. **2** this difference expressed as a percentage. **3** a premium or discount on bills of exchange from other countries. **4** = agiotage. [< Italian *aggio,* variant of *agio* ease]

ag|i|o|tage (aj′ē ə tij, aj′ə-), *n.* **1** the business of exchange; moneychanging. **2** speculation in stocks. [< French *agiotage* < *agioter* speculate < Italian *aggio* agio]

a|gist (ə jist′), *v.t.* to take in (cattle or other stock) for feeding or pasturing, at a certain rate. [< Anglo-French, Old French *agister* < *a-* to + *gister* to lodge, ultimately < Latin *jacēre* to lie] —**a|gis′ter, a|gis′tor**, *n.*

a|gist|ment (ə jist′mənt), *n.* **1** the taking in of livestock to feed or pasture at a certain rate. **2** the rate charged for this or profit made by doing it. **3** any charge levied upon the owner or occupier of pasture lands.

ag|i|ta|ble (aj′ə tə bəl), *adj.* **1** capable of being agitated or shaken. **2** that may be debated or discussed. [< French *agitable* < Latin *agitābilis* < *agitāre;* see etym. under **agitate**]

ag|i|tate (aj′ə tāt), *v.,* **-tat|ed, -tat|ing.** —*v.t.* **1** to move or shake vigorously: *The slightest wind will agitate the leaves of some trees.* **2a** to disturb or excite (a person): *She was much agitated by the unexpected news of her brother's illness.* **b** to disturb or excite (the thoughts or feelings of): *This had agitated my thoughts for two hours* (Daniel Defoe). **SYN**: perturb, discompose, disquiet. **3** to argue about; discuss vigorously and publicly: *The antislavery leaders agitated the question of slavery for many years.* **4** *Archaic.* to contemplate.

—*v.i.* to keep arguing about and discussing a matter vigorously to arouse public interest and feeling: *to agitate for a shorter working day.*

[< Latin *agitāre* (with English *-ate*[1]) move to and fro < *agere* drive, move]

ag|i|tat|ed (aj′ə tā′tid), *adj.* disturbed; excited; expressing agitation: *... an agitated countenance* (Thackeray). —**ag′i|tat′ed|ly**, *adv.*

ag|i|ta|tion (aj′ə tā′shən), *n.* **1** a vigorous moving or shaking: *Agitation of the leaves in the breeze made a rustling sound.* **2** a disturbed, upset, or troubled state; disturbance; excitement: *Because of her agitation over the unexpected illness of her brother, she could not sleep.* **SYN**: turmoil, unrest. **3** vigorous argument or discussion to arouse public interest and feeling: *There was much agitation for and against slavery before the Civil War.* **SYN**: debate.

ag|i|ta|tion|al (aj′ə tā′shə nəl), *adj.* of or having to do with agitation: *He said that the difference between the Congress Party and the other political parties in the country was that the former avoided slogans and concentrated on work whereas the other parties had adopted an agitational approach* (Times of India). —**ag′i|ta′tion|al|ly**, *adv.*

a|gi|ta|to (ä′jē tä′tō), *adj., adv. Music.* in an agitated manner; hurried and restless in style (generally in combination with *allegro* or *presto*). [< Italian *agitato*]

ag|i|ta|tor (aj′ə tā′tər), *n.* **1** a person who stirs up public feeling for or against something; one who tries to make people discontented with things as they are. **2** a device or machine for shaking, stirring, or mixing, as in some washing machines.

ag|it|prop (aj′ət prop′), *adj., n.* —*adj.* serving the combined purposes of agitation and propaganda. —*n.* a person who is both agitator and propagandist.

[< Russian *agitprop* < *agitatsiya* agitation + *propaganda* propaganda]

A|gla|ia (ə glā′ə), *n. Greek Mythology.* one of the three Graces.

a|glare (ə glãr′), *adj., adv.* glaring: *Drivers were blinded by the wet pavement aglare with headlights.*

a|gleam (ə glēm′), *adj., adv.* gleaming: *a Christmas tree agleam with lights.*

a|glee (ə glē′), *adv. Scottish.* = agley.

ag|let (ag′lit), *n.* **1** the metal tag at the end of a shoelace or other lace or cord. **2** = aiguillette. Also, **aiglet.** [< unrecorded Middle French *aguillette* (diminutive) < Old French *aguille* needle, ultimately < Latin *acus.* See etym. of doublet **aiguillette.**]

a|gley or **a|gly** (ə glē′, -glī′), *adv. Scottish.* out of the right way; wrong; awry. Also, **aglee.** [< *a-*[1] on, at + Scottish *gley* a squint]

a|glim|mer (ə glim′ər), *adj., adv.* glimmering.

a|glint (ə glint′), *adj., adv.* glinting; gleaming: *glasses aglint in the sun.*

Ag|li|pay|an (ag′lə pī′ən), *adj., n.* —*adj.* of or having to do with the Philippine Independent Church, a native Roman Catholic church founded by Bishop Gregorio Aglipay in 1902. —*n.* a member of this church.

a|glit|ter (ə glit′ər), *adv., adj.* glittering: *aglitter with brass buttons.*

a|glos|sal (ā glos′əl), *adj.* having no tongue.

a|glos|sate (ā glos′āt), *adj.* = aglossal.

a|glow (ə glō′), *adv., adj.* glowing: *Pensacola at sundown finds streets busy and shops aglow* (Time). (*Figurative.*) *The baby's cheeks were aglow with health.*

a|gly|cone (ā glī′kōn), *n.* the nonsugar part of a glycoside molecule. [< *a-*[4] + Greek *glykýs* sweet + English *-one*]

ag|ma (ag′mə), *n. Phonetics.* a nasal consonant, such as *m, n,* or *ng* (as in *thing*). [< Late Greek *agma* the nasalized *g*]

ag|mi|nate (ag′mə nit, -nāt), *adj.* arranged in a group or cluster. [< Latin *agmen, -inis* a troop + English *-ate*[1]]

ag|mi|nat|ed (ag′mə nā′tid), *adj.* = agminate.

ag|nail (ag′nāl′), *n.* **1** a hangnail. **2** a whitlow. [Old English *angnægl* corn (on the toe) < *ang-* tight, painful + *nægl* nail]

ag|nate (ag′nāt), *n., adj.* —*n.* **1** *Anthropology.* a kinsman descended from a common male ancestor through male links only. **2** a kinsman on the father's side.

—*adj.* **1** related on the father's side, or through male descent only. **2** *Figurative.* allied; akin. [< Latin *agnātus,* past participle of *agnāscī* be born in addition < *ad-* to + *gnāscī* be born. Compare etym. at **adnate.**]

ag|na|than (ag′nə thən), *adj. Zoology.* having no lower jaw; jawless: *an agnathan fish.* [< *a-*[4] + Greek *gnáthos* jaw + English *-an*]

ag|nat|ic (ag nat′ik), *adj. Anthropology.* related by common descent through male links only.

ag|na|tion (ag nā′shən), *n.* **1** *Anthropology.* the relationship of agnates. **2** descent from a common male ancestor, even though female links have intervened. **3** kinship by descent.

Ag|ni (ag′nē-, ug′-), *n. Hinduism.* a principal Vedic god, god of fire, the sun, and lightning, and mediator between mankind and the gods. [< Sanskrit *agni* fire, Agni]

ag|nize (ag nīz′), *v.t.,* **-nized, -niz|ing.** *Archaic.* **1** to recognize. **2** to acknowledge. [< Latin *agnōscere* < *ad-* to + *gnōscere* get to know; on analogy of English *recognize*]

ag|no|men (ag nō′mən), *n., pl.* **-nom|i|na** (-nom′ə nə). **1** an additional name given to an ancient Roman to commemorate some characteristic or achievement, as in Publius Cornelius Scipio *Africanus* (so called because of his victories in Africa against the Carthaginians). See also **cognomen. 2** any additional name, as in Eric *the Red.* [< Latin *agnōmen* < *ad-* to + *nōmen* name; *-g-* by influence of *agnōscere* (see etym. under **agnize**)]

ag|nom|i|nal (ag nom′ə nəl), *adj.* of or having to do with an agnomen.

ag|no|si|a (ag nō′sē ə), *n. Medicine.* the inability to recognize familiar objects, caused by an impairment of the brain. [< New Latin *agnosia* < Greek *a-* without + *gnōsis* a knowing]

ag|nos|tic (ag nos′tik), *n., adj.* —*n.* a person who believes that nothing is known or can be known about the existence of God or about things outside of human experience. **SYN**: skeptic, unbeliever, freethinker.

—*adj.* of agnostics or their beliefs. [(coined by Thomas Huxley) < Greek *ágnōstos* not to be known, not knowing (< *a-* not + *gnōstós* (to be) known) + English *-ic*] —**ag|nos′ti|cal|ly**, *adv.*

ag|nos|ti|cism (ag nos′tə siz əm), *n.* the belief or intellectual attitude of agnostics: *One meets few atheists, though many agnostics. But the agnosticism is humble and open rather than self-satisfied* (Atlantic).

ag|nos|tid (ag nos′tid), *n. Geology.* a small, blind trilobite of the Cambrian period. [< New Latin *Agnostidae* the family name < Greek *ágnōstos* unknown]

ag|nus cas|tus (ag′nəs kas′təs), a shrub or small tree, related to verbena, with spikes of purplish-blue or white flowers; chaste tree. [< Latin *agnus* the shrub (< Greek *ágnos*), and *castus* pure, chaste]

Ag|nus De|i (ag′nəs dē′ī; än′yůs de′ē), **1a** an image of a lamb as a symbol of Christ. **b** (in the Roman Catholic Church) a wax medallion stamped with this figure and blessed by the Pope. **2a** a part of the Mass that begins "Agnus Dei." **b** a musical adaptation of this, sung as part of the Mass or as an anthem. [< Latin *Agnus Deī* Lamb of God]

a|go (ə gō′), *adj., adv.* —*adj.* gone by; past (always placed after the noun): *I met her two years ago.*

—*adv.* in the past: *He lived here long ago.* [Old English *āgān* gone by]

a|gog (ə gog′), *adj., adv.* —*adj.* full of expectation or excitement; eager; curious; excited: *The children were all agog to see their presents.*

—*adv.* with eagerness, curiosity, or excitement. [< Middle French *en gogues* in good humor]

a|gog|ic (ə goj′ik, ə gō′gik), *adj. Music.* effected by or involving a lengthening of the time value of a note: *agogic accents, agogic nuances. Indian music, unlike African, is not dynamic. Its rhythms are agogic* (Listener). [< German *agogisch* < Greek *agōgē* a leading away < *ágein* to lead]

a|gog|i|cal (ə goj′ə kəl, ə gō′gə kəl), *adj. Music.* agogic.

a|gog|ics (ə goj′iks, ə gō′giks), *n. Music.* the use of agogic accents: *His interpretations are by no means devoid of color or agogics* (*stresses, rubatos, etc., not indicated in the score*) (Harold C. Schonberg).

à go-go (ə gō′gō), *Slang.* go-go: *... hostess à go-go of Arthur, Manhattan discothèque* (Time). [< French *à go-go*]

a|go|ing (ə gō′ing), *adj. Dialect.* in motion or operation; going.

set agoing, to cause to start: *Watches must be wound up to set them agoing* (Richard Bentley).

ag|on (ag′ōn, -on), *n., pl.* **a|go|nes** (ə gō′nēz). **1** a contest for a prize in athletics or artistic competitions at the ancient Greek games. 2 a debate or conflict between the main characters in ancient Greek plays. [< Greek *agōn* < *ágein* to conduct, celebrate]

ag|o|nal (ag′ə nəl), *adj.* of or having to do with agony: *He showed slow, agonal respiratory efforts* (San Francisco Chronicle).

a|gone (ə gôn′, -gon′), *adj. Archaic.* past; ago. [< past participle of obsolete *ago* to go away]

a|gon|ic (ə gon′ik, ā-), *adj.* not forming an angle. [< *a-*[4] + Greek *gōníā* angle]

agonic line, the irregular north-south line of places where a compass does not vary from true north.

ag|o|nise (ag′ə nīz), *v.i., v.t.* **-nised, -nis|ing.** *British.* agonize.

ag|o|nist (ag′ə nist), *n.* 1 a contender for a prize, as in athletics; contestant. 2 *Physiology.* a muscle which on contracting is counteracted or opposed by the movement of another muscle (the antagonist). 3 *Medicine.* a drug whose action is counteracted or opposed by another drug (the antagonist).

ag|o|nis|tic (ag′ə nis′tik), *adj.* 1 of or having to do with the athletic or other contests of the ancient Greeks. 2 athletic. 3 strained; forced. 4 combative. [< Greek *agōnistikós* < *agōnízesthai* contend < *agōn* contest < *ágein* to conduct, celebrate] **—ag′o|nis′ti|cal|ly,** *adv.*

ag|o|nis|ti|cal (ag′ə nis′tə kəl), *adj.* = agonistic.

ag|o|nize (ag′ə nīz), *v.,* **-nized, -niz|ing.** **—*v.i.*** 1 to feel great anguish; suffer agony. 2 *Figurative.* to strive painfully; struggle: *to agonize over a problem.* **—*v.t.*** to cause to suffer extreme pain; torture. [< Late Latin *agōnizāre* < Greek *agōnízesthai* contend, struggle < *agōn* a contest < *ágein* to conduct, celebrate] **—ag′o|niz′er,** *n.*

ag|o|niz|ed|ly (ag′ə nī′zid lē), *adv.* in an agonized manner.

ag|o|niz|ing (ag′ə nī′zing), *adj.* causing very great pain, suffering, anguish, or anxiety; tormenting: *agonizing suspense.* **—ag′o|niz′ing|ly,** *adv.*

agonizing reappraisal, any complete reassessment of a situation, especially one involving painful or unpleasant changes: *Many agonizing reappraisals have been directed to British Industry in the postwar period* (New Scientist).

ag|o|ny (ag′ə nē), *n., pl.* **-nies.** 1a very great suffering of body or mind: *Nobody can stand for long the agony of a severe toothache.* SYN: torment. **b** *Figurative.* very great suffering of mind; extreme mental pain or suffering: *The loss of her husband filled her with agony.* SYN: torment, woe. 2 a sudden, powerful emotion: *With cries and agonies of wild delight ...* (Alexander Pope). 3 Often, **agonies.** the struggle often preceding death: *the agonies of death, mortal agony.* 4 a struggle, especially one involving a crisis: *the agony of war.* [< Late Latin *agōnia* < Greek *agōníā* a struggle < *agōn* contest, assembly < *ágein* to conduct, celebrate]

▶**Agony** is often used in informal English in a light vein in such expressions as: *My shoes hurt; I'm in agony. I have to do my Latin sometime; I might as well get the agony over now.*

agony column, *Slang, especially British.* 1 a newspaper column of classified advertisements for personal messages, appeals for charity, missing persons, or the like. 2 a newspaper column devoted to personal advice in response to readers' questions.

ag|o|ra[1] (ag′ər ə), *n., pl.* **-rae** (-rē), **-ras.** the market place in an ancient Greek city. [< Greek *agorā* < *ageirein* to assemble]

the Agora, the assembly place of ancient Athens, where citizens debated matters of public interest.

a|go|ra[2] (ä gə rä′), *n., pl.* **-rot** (-rot′). a unit of money of Israel, a coin equal to 1/100 of an Israeli pound. [< Hebrew *agōrāh*]

ag|o|ra|phobe (ag′ər ə fōb), *n.* a person with an abnormal fear of being in open places.

ag|o|ra|pho|bi|a (ag′ər ə fō′bē ə), *n.* an abnormal fear of being in open places: *While still in his prime he developed agoraphobia and went to live underground* (New Yorker). [< *agora*[1] + *-phobia*]

ag|o|ra|pho|bic (ag′ər ə fō′bik), *adj., n.* **—*adj.*** of or having to do with agoraphobia: *... a windowless interior, haunting in its agoraphobic stillness* (London Times). **—*n.*** = agoraphobe.

a|gou|a|ra (a gü ä′rə), *n.* a South American species of raccoon, about the size of a fox, that feeds on crustaceans and mollusks. [< Spanish *aguará*]

a|gou|ti (ə gü′tē), *n., pl.* **-tis** or **-ties.** 1 a rodent of tropical America, about the size of a rabbit. It is usually brownish or grizzled in color and is related to the guinea pig. 2 an alternation of light and dark bands in the hair of various rodents. [< French *agouti* < Spanish *agutí* < Tupi (perhaps West Indies) name]

a|gou|ty (ə gü′tē), *n., pl.* **-ties.** = agouti.

agr., 1 agricultural. 2 agriculture. 3 agriculturist.

AGR (no periods) or **A.G.R.,** advanced gas-cooled reactor (an atomic reactor using carbon dioxide or other gas as a coolant).

a|gra (ə grô′), *n. Anglo-Irish.* = darling. [< Irish *a grādh* O love!]

a|graffe or **a|grafe** (ə graf′), *n.* 1 a clasp or hook for fastening clothing or armor. 2 a small cramp iron used in building. [< Middle French *agrafe* < *agrafer* to hook]

àgrands frais (á gräN fre′), *French.* at great expense.

a|gran|u|lo|cyte (ā gran′yə lə sīt), *n. Medicine.* a nongranular leucocyte.

a|gran|u|lo|cyt|ic (ā gran′yə lə sit′ik), *adj. Medicine.* of or like an agranulocyte.

agranulocytic angina, = agranulocytosis.

a|gran|u|lo|cy|to|sis (ā gran′yə lō sī tō′sis), *n. Medicine.* an acute disease with high fever, ulcers in mouth and throat, and a sharp decrease of granulocytes, following a massive infection or treatment with certain coal-tar drugs.

Ag|ra|pha (ag′rə fə), *n.pl.* sayings ascribed to Jesus, not in the Bible but in other early Christian literature. [< Greek *ágrapha* (*rhêmata*) unwritten (sayings)]

a|graph|i|a (ā graf′ē ə), *n.* a form of aphasia involving partial or complete inability to write (contrasted with *alexia*). [< New Latin *agraphia* < Greek *a-* without + *-graphíā* act of writing]

a|graph|ic (ā graf′ik), *adj.* characterized by the inability to write.

a|grar|i|an (ə grãr′ē ən), *adj., n.* **—*adj.*** 1a having to do with farming land, its use, or its ownership. **b** for the support and advancement of farmers and farming: *an agrarian movement.* 2 agricultural. 3 growing wild in the fields, as certain plants. **—*n.*** a person who favors a new or more equitable division of rural land. [< Latin *agrārius* (< *ager, agrī* field)]

a|grar|i|an|ism (ə grãr′ē ə niz′əm), *n.* 1 political agitation or civil dissension arising from dissatisfaction with the existing tenure of the land. 2 the principle of a more equitable division of rural land. 3 promotion of the farmer's interests, especially by political means.

a|grav|ic (ā grav′ik), *adj.* having no gravity; weightless: [< *a-*[4] not + *grav* (ity) + *-ic*]

a|gree (ə grē′), *v.,* **a|greed, a|gree|ing.** **—*v.i.*** 1 to have the same feeling or opinion: *We all agree in liking the teacher. I agree with your argument.* SYN: concur. 2 to be in harmony; be consistent; correspond: *All accounts of the accident seem to agree. Your story agrees with mine.* 3 to get along well together: *Brothers and sisters don't always agree as well as they should.* 4 to say that one is willing (to); consent; assent: *He agreed to go with us.* 5 to come to an understanding, especially in settling a dispute: *The workers and employers agreed on the terms for settling the strike.* 6 *Grammar.* (in inflected languages) to have the same gender, number, case, or person, as another word. In the sentences "The man is going," "The men are going," the subjects and the verbs agree in person and number. *A Latin adjective must agree with its noun in gender, number, and case.*

—*v.t.* to say (something) is real or true; admit; grant; concede: *John agreed that he had been thoughtless.*

agree with, to have a good effect on; suit: *The food did not agree with me; it made me sick.*

[< Old French *agreer* < *a gre* to (one's) liking < Latin *ad* to, *grātum,* neuter, pleasing]

—*Syn.* **—*v.i.*** 2 **Agree, correspond, coincide** mean to be consistent. **Agree** means to be consistent or harmonious in all essentials and without differences or contradictions: *All the reports agree about the magnitude of the disaster.* **Correspond** means to agree or to equal in essentials or as a whole, in spite of superficial differences: *The Canadian Dominion Day corresponds to the American Independence Day.* **Coincide** means to agree so closely as to be identical: *His tastes coincide with mine.*

a|gree|a|bil|i|ty (ə grē′ə bil′ə tē), *n.* the quality of being agreeable.

a|gree|a|ble (ə grē′ə bəl), *adj.* 1 giving pleasure; pleasant; pleasing: *The boy had a charming and agreeable manner.* SYN: See syn. under **pleasant.** 2 ready to agree; willing: *agreeable to a suggestion. If Mother is agreeable, we can go to the show this afternoon.* SYN: conformable. 3 in agreement; suitable (to): *music agreeable to the occasion.* **—a|gree′a|ble|ness,** *n.* **—a|gree′a|bly,** *adv.*

a|greed (ə grēd′), *adj.* 1 fixed by common consent: *to pay the agreed price.* 2 in agreement: *Are you all agreed, Lords?* (Shakespeare).

a|gree|ment (ə grē′mənt), *n.* 1 an understanding reached by two or more persons, groups of persons, or nations among themselves. Nations make treaties; certain persons make contracts; both are agreements. SYN: pact, covenant, compact. 2 the act of coming to an understanding, especially in settling a dispute: *Every obstacle to agreement has been removed.* SYN: settlement. 3 sameness of feeling or opinion: *There was perfect agreement between the two friends. They tried to shape their thought and deed in noble agreement* (George Eliot). SYN: concurrence, accord. 4 harmony; correspondence: *And what agreement hath the temple of God with idols?* (II Corinthians 6:16). SYN: concord, consonance. 5 *Grammar.* (in inflected languages) correspondence between words in number, case, gender, or person; concord. There is agreement in "that man" but lack of agreement in "those man."

a|gré|ga|tion (á grā gá syôN′), *n. French.* admission by examination to the rank of agrégé.

a|gré|gé (á grā zhā′), *n. French.* an academic rank obtained by competitive examination entitling the holder to teach in a lycée or university.

a|gré|ment (á grā mäN′), *n., pl.* **-ments** (-mäN′). *French.* 1 the acceptance of a foreign diplomat by the country to which he is going to go. 2 (literally) agreement; approval.

agréments, agreeable features or accessories; ornaments; charms: *He delights in the agréments of wealth and rank.*

a|gres|tal (ə gres′təl), *adj.* = agrestial.

a|gres|tial (ə gres′chəl), *adj.* 1 having to do with or inhabiting the fields; wild. 2 *Botany.* growing wild in cultivated land, as weeds. [< Latin *agrestis* (< *ager, agrī* field) + English *-al*[1]]

a|gres|tic (ə gres′tik), *adj.* 1 rural; rustic. 2 unpolished; uncouth.

a|gres|ti|cal (ə gres′tə kəl), *adj.* = agrestic.

ag|ri|busi|ness (ag′rə biz′nis), *n.* the business of producing, processing, and distributing agricultural products.

agric., 1 agricultural. 2 agriculture. 3 agriculturist.

ag|ri|cul|tur|al (ag′rə kul′chər əl), *adj.* 1 of farming; having to do with farming; connected with agriculture: *A hoe is an agricultural tool. Bananas rank among the chief agricultural products of South America* (Preston E. James). 2 promoting the interests or the study of agriculture: *an agricultural college.* **—ag′ri|cul′tur|al|ly,** *adv.*

agricultural engineering, the branch of engineering that deals with the development of farmland, the improvement of farming, erosion control, and irrigation.

ag|ri|cul|tur|al|ist (ag′rə kul′chər ə list), *n. U.S.* = agriculturist.

agricultural paper, negotiable instruments, such as notes and acceptances, used in agricultural transactions.

ag|ri|cul|ture (ag′rə kul′chər), *n.* the science, art, or occupation of cultivating the soil to make crops grow; the raising of crops and farm animals; farming. SYN: husbandry, tillage. [< Late Latin *agricultūra* < Latin *ager, agrī* land + *cultūra* cultivation]

ag|ri|cul|tur|ist (ag′rə kul′chər ist), *n.* 1 a farmer. 2 an expert in farming.

ag|ri|mo|ny (ag′rə mō′nē), *n., pl.* **-nies.** 1 a plant of the rose family with slender stalks of feathery leaves and small, yellow flowers, whose roots are used as an astringent. 2 any of various similar plants, especially the hemp agrimony. [< Latin *agrimōnia,* variant of *argemōnia* < Greek *argemōnē*]

a|grin (ə grin′), *adj., adv.* grinning: *His hard features were revealed all agrin ... with glee* (Charlotte Brontë).

ag|ri|o|log|i|cal (ag′rē ə loj′ə kəl), *adj.* of or having to do with agriology.

ag|ri|ol|o|gist (ag′rē ol′ə jist), *n.* a person who studies agriology.

ag|ri|ol|o|gy (ag′rē ol′ə jē), *n.* the comparative study of the customs of uncivilized peoples. [< Greek *ágrios* wild, savage (< *agrós* open country) + English *-logy*]

ag|ro (ag′rō), *n.* = aggro.

agro-, *combining form.* 1 field; soil: *Agrology = soil science.* 2 agriculture: *Agrochemical = a chemical used in agriculture.* 3 agricultural and ____: *Agro-industrial = agricultural and industrial.* [< Greek *agrós*]

ag|ro|bac|te|ri|a (ag′rō bak tir′ē ə), *n.pl.* bacteria present in the soil: *The usual procedure for introducing a new gene into plant cells is to insert the gene into agrobacteria and then let the bacteria infect protoplasts* (Daniel L. Hartl).

ag|ro|bac|te|ri|al (ag′rō bak tir′ē əl), *adj.* of or having to do with agrobacteria: *The agrobacterial plasmid seems an ideal vehicle for moving selected genes into plants* (Science News).

ag|ro|bi|o|log|ic (ag′rō bī′ə loj′ik), *adj.* = agrobiological.

ag|ro|bi|o|log|i|cal (ag′rō bī′ə loj′ə kəl), *adj.* of or having to do with agrobiology. **—ag′ro|bi′o|log′i|cal|ly**, *adv.*

ag|ro|bi|ol|o|gist (ag′rō bī ol′ə jist), *n.* a person who studies agrobiology.

ag|ro|bi|ol|o|gy (ag′rō bī ol′ə jē), *n.* the study of plant nutrition and growth in relation to the condition and constituents of the soil, especially to increase crops.

ag|ro|chem|i|cal (ag′rō kem′ə kəl), *n., adj.* **—*n.*** any chemical product, such as an insecticide, used in agriculture. **—*adj.*** of agro chemicals: *agrochemical manufacturers, the agrochemical industry.*

ag|ro|cit|y (ag′rō sit′ē), *n., pl.* **-cit|ies.** = agrogorod. [partial translation of Russian *agrogorod*]

ag|ro|cli|mat|ic (ag′rō klī mat′ik), *adj.* of or having to do with agroclimatology.

ag|ro|cli|ma|tol|o|gy (ag′rō klī′mə tol′ə jē), *n.* the branch of climatology that deals with the effects of weather upon crops: *Agroclimatology can advise as to whether such crops are likely to succeed in a given locality* (Scientific American).

ag|ro|go|rod (ag′rō gôr′əd; *Russian* ä grä gô′rət), *n., pl.* **-go|rods, -go|ro|da** (-gôr′ə dä′). an amalgamation of farm communities in Russia into a single unit, resembling a city in its administrative structure. [< Russian *agrogorod*]

ag|ro-in|dus|tri|al (ag′rō in dus′trē əl), *adj.* involving or combining agriculture and industry; agricultural and industrial.

ag|ro-in|dus|try (ag′rō in′də strē), *n., pl.* **-tries.** 1 an agricultural industry. 2 an agro-industrial complex.

ag|ro|log|ic (ag′rə loj′ik), *adj.* = agrological.

ag|ro|log|i|cal (ag′rə loj′ə kəl), *adj.* of or having to do with agrology. **—ag′ro|log′i|cal|ly**, *adv.*

a|grol|o|gist (ə grol′ə jist), *n.* a person who studies agrology.

a|grol|o|gy (ə grol′ə jē), *n.* the branch of agriculture that deals with soils; science of soils.

ag|ro|ma|ni|a (ag′rə mā′nē ə), *n.* an abnormal desire to live in open fields, apart from all other persons, sometimes as a manifestation of schizophrenia. [< *agro-* + *mania*]

ag|ro|nom|ic (ag′rə nom′ik), *adj.* of or having to do with agronomy.

ag|ro|nom|i|cal (ag′rə nom′ə kəl), *adj.* = agronomic.

ag|ro|nom|ics (ag′rə nom′iks), *n.* = agronomy.

a|gron|o|mist (ə gron′ə mist), *n.* a person who studies agronomy.

a|gron|o|my (ə gron′ə mē), *n.* the study of soil and the improvement of crop production; science of managing farmland; husbandry. [< Greek *agronómos* an overseer of land (< *agrós* land + *-nómos*, related to *némein* manage) + English *-y*[3]]

a|gros|to|log|ic (ə gros′tə loj′ik), *adj.* of or having to do with agrostology.

a|gros|to|log|i|cal (ə gros′tə loj′ə kəl), *adj.* = agrostologic.

ag|ros|tol|o|gist (ag′rə stol′ə jist), *n.* a person who studies agrostology.

ag|ros|tol|o|gy (ag′rə stol′ə jē), *n.* the branch of botany that deals with grasses. [< Greek *ágrōstis* a kind of grass + English *-logy*]

ag|ro|tech|ny (ag′rə tek′nē), *n.* the science of preserving raw farm products and converting them into manufactured commodities, as in dairying or canning. [< *agro-* + Greek *téchnē* art, skill]

ag|ro|town (ag′rō toun′), *n.* = agrogorod. [partial translation of Russian *agrogorod*]

a|ground (ə ground′), *adv., adj.* 1 stranded on the shore or on the bottom in shallow water: *The ship ran aground and stuck in the sand* (adv.). *It is still aground* (adj.). 2 *Figurative.* in or into difficulties: *Their plans ran aground for lack of money.*

AGS (no periods) or **A.G.S.**, alternating gradient synchrotron.

agt., agent.

a|gua (ä′gwä), *n. Spanish.* water.

a|gua|miel (ä′gwä myel′), *n.* the juice of certain species of the agave, from which pulque and tequila are made. [< Spanish *aguamiel* < *agua* water + *miel* honey]

a|guar|dien|te (ä′gwär dyen′tā), *n.* 1 a coarse brandy of Spain and Portugal. 2 any crudely distilled liquor, usually made from sugar cane, drunk in Latin America and the southwestern United States. [American English < Spanish *aguardiente* < *agua* water + *ardiente* burning]

a|gue (ā′gyü), *n.* 1 a malarial fever with alternating chills and sweating at regular intervals. 2 *Figurative.* any fit of shaking or shivering; a chill. [< Middle French *aguë*, learned borrowing from Latin (*febris*) *acūta* severe (fever)]

a|gue-cake (ā′gyü kāk′), *n.* an enlarged and hardened spleen, from chronic malaria.

a|gue|weed (ā′gyü wēd′), *n.* 1 the common boneset or thoroughwort of North America. 2 a species of gentian bearing clusters of five blue flowers.

a|gui|nal|do (ä′gē näl′dō), *n., pl.* **-dos.** *Spanish.* 1 an annual bonus, especially one given at Christmas in Argentina and certain other Spanish-speaking countries. 2 (in Puerto Rico) an ornamental plant related to the morning-glory.

a|gu|ish (ā′gyü ish), *adj.* 1 of or like ague. 2 liable to have ague. 3 causing ague. **—a′gu|ish|ly**, *adv.*

a|gush (ə gush′), *adj., adv.* gushing: *The cider mill . . . all agush with sweet juice* (Hawthorne).

ah (ä), *interj., n., pl.* **ah's** or **ahs.** **—*interj.*** an exclamation of pain, sorrow, regret, pity, admiration, surprise, joy, dislike, or contempt. The meaning of *ah* varies according to the way it is spoken. **—*n.*** the interjection or exclamation *ah.* [perhaps < Old French *ah*]

a.h., ampere-hour or ampere-hours.

A.H., in the year of the Hegira, which was, in the Christian reckoning, A.D. 622 (Latin, *anno Hegirae*).

a|ha (ä hä′), *interj.* an exclamation of triumph, satisfaction, surprise, or joy. [< *ah* + *ha*]

A|hab (ā′hab), *n.* a king of Israel who was led to the worship of idols by his wife Jezebel (in the Bible, I Kings 16:29-33).

A|has|u|e|rus (ə haz′yü ir′əs, -hazh′ü-), *n.* a Persian king, the husband of Esther, mentioned in the Bible in the books of Ezra and Esther.

à haute voix (à ōt vwä′), *French.* 1 aloud. 2 (literally) in a loud voice.

AHD (no periods), arteriosclerotic heart disease.

a|head (ə hed′), *adv.* 1 in front; before: *Walk ahead of me. Breakers ahead!* 2 forward; onward: *Go ahead with this work for another week.* 3 in advance; earlier: *Columbus was ahead of his times in his belief that the world was round.*

be ahead, a to be winning: *Our team is ahead by 6 points.* **b** to have more than is needed: *We're ahead $10 on the budget.*

get ahead, to succeed: *It takes hard work to get ahead in business.*

get ahead of, to do or be better than; surpass; outdistance; excel: *If she works hard she will get ahead of her sister in arithmetic.*

a|hem (ə hem′), *interj., n.* **—*interj.*** a sound made by coughing or clearing the throat, sometimes used to attract attention, express doubt, or gain time. **—*n.*** the interjection or exclamation *ahem: His answer amounted to a courteous ahem.* [extended form of *hem*]

AHF (no periods), antihemophilic factor.

AHG (no periods), antihemophilic globulin.

a|hi (ä′hē), *n. Hawaiian.* the bluefin, a tuna.

a|him|sa (ə him′sä), *n.* the doctrine of nonviolence: *The thinkers of Brahmanism, of Samkhya, of Jainism, as well as of Buddhism, exalt nonviolence, which they call ahimsa; indeed, they consider it as the sublime principle* (Albert Schweitzer). [< Sanskrit *ahimsā* < *a-* not + *himsā* injury]

a|his|tor|i|cal (ā′his tôr′ə kəl, -tor′-), *adj.* not historical; without regard for history: *Theories of social change are, . . . often ahistorical and devoid of cultural concreteness* (Hinkle and Hinkle).

A|hith|o|phel (ə hit′ə fel), *n.* a counselor who joined Absalom in his revolt against David (in the Bible, II Samuel 15-17).

Ah|ma|diy|ya (ä′mə dē′yə), *n.* an Islamic sect, especially in Pakistan, whose members work as missionaries throughout the world.

a|hold[1] (ə hōld′), *n. U.S. Dialect or Informal.* a hold: *He also passes notes to me during school . . . and if the teacher got ahold of one I would just die in my seat* (Chicago Sun-Times).

a|hold[2] (ə hōld′), *adv. Nautical.* near or close to the wind: *lay a ship ahold.*

-aholic, *combining form.* a person who is obsessed with or addicted to something; a ____ addict: *Foodaholic = a person who is obsessed with food or eating. I had considered myself just another enthusiastic fan of pro football, not an abuser, a footballaholic* (Washington Post). [abstracted from *workaholic*]

A horizon, the top layer of soil through which moisture seeps downward, dissolving the chemical elements, such as sodium, calcium, and magnesium, and carrying them away to the rivers and the sea.

a|horse (ə hôrs′), *adv., adj.* on horseback.

a|hoy (ə hoi′), *interj.* a call used chiefly by sailors to attract the attention of someone at a distance: *The sailors in the lifeboat shouted "Ship ahoy!" to the passing freighter.* [< *a(h)* + *hoy*, probably a variant of *hey*]

Ah|ri|man (är′i mən), *n.* the spirit of ignorance and evil in the Zoroastrian religion.

a|hu (ä′hü), *n.* a raised platform at a Polynesian temple site. [< Hawaiian and Tahitian *ahu*]

a|hull (ə hul′), *adv. Nautical.* with sails furled and helm lashed to the lee side: *We finally lay ahull, stops on and heavy spars secure* (Atlantic).

a|hum (ə hum′), *adj., adv.* humming: *Ahum with ideas, Leopold . . . was soon seeking out more adventurous governments* (Time).

a|hun|gered (ə hung′gərd), *adj. Archaic.* hungry.

A|hu|ra Maz|da (ä′hůr ə maz′də), Ormazd (the Zoroastrian spirit of good).

ai[1] (ī, ä′ē), *n., pl.* **ais** (īz, ä′ēz). the three-toed sloth of South and Central America. [< Portuguese *ai* < Tupi (Brazil)]

ai[2] (ī), *interj.* oh! alas!

AI (no periods), 1 airborne intercept (radar that detects enemy aircraft). 2 Amnesty International. 3 artificial insemination. 4 artificial intelligence.

ai|blins (ā′blinz), *adv. Scottish.* possibly; perhaps. [< *able* + dialectal suffix *-lings* condition]

aid (ād), *v., n.* **—*v.t.*** 1 to give support to; help; assist: *The Red Cross aids flood victims.* SYN: See syn. under **help.** 2 to help in bringing about: *This new medicine may aid your recovery.* SYN: facilitate, further, promote, forward. **—*v.i.*** to give assistance; help. [< Middle French *aider* < Old French *aidier* < Latin *adjūtāre* (frequentative) < *adjuvāre* < *ad-* to + *juvāre* help]

—*n.* 1 help; assistance: *When my arm was broken, I could not dress without aid.* SYN: support, succor. 2 a person or a thing, such as a tool or instrument, that helps; helper; assistant: *She was a nurse's aid for a time. A dishwasher is an aid to housewives.* 3 *U.S.* an aide-de-camp; aide. 4a a customary payment from a feudal vassal to his lord. **b** the right of a feudal lord to require his vassals to contribute money when the lord's eldest son was knighted, when his eldest daughter married, and when ransom was needed to release the lord from captivity. 5 a grant of money to the British Crown, made by Parliament, for an extraordinary purpose; subsidy.

what (something) is in aid of, *British Informal.* what the purpose of (something) is: *It was difficult for his mother to make out what all of his bellowing was in aid of until he stopped shouting.*

[< Old French *aide* < Late Latin *adjūta* < *adjuvāre;* see the verb] **—aid′er**, *n.*

AID (no periods), Artificial Insemination by Donor.

A|ï|da (ä ē′də), *n.* 1 an opera by Giuseppe Verdi, first produced in 1871. 2 its heroine, an Ethiopian princess.

aid|ance (ā′dəns), *n.* aid; help; assistance.

aid|ant (ā′dənt), *adj., n.* **—*adj.*** aiding; helpful. **—*n.*** an assistant or auxiliary: *The court is now called upon to be an aidant to the enforcement of a judgment given by a Portuguese court* (Sir Robert Phillimore).

aid-de-camp (ād′də kamp′), *n., pl.* **aids-de-camp.** *Especially U.S.* = aide-de-camp.

aide (ād), *n.* 1 a helper; an assistant, often to a person of high rank: *a presidential aide, a diplomatic aide.* 2 = aide-de-camp.

aide-de-camp (ād′də kamp′; *French* ed′də käN′), *n., pl.* **aides-de-camp** (ādz′də kamp′; *French* ed′-də käN′). 1 a military officer who acts as an assistant to a superior officer by taking and sending messages and acting as a secretary: *Edmund Randolph . . . served as General George Washington's aide-de-camp during the Revolutionary War* (Frank E. Vandir). 2 any assistant; aide: *the indefatigable aide-de-camp of the Commissioner.* [< French *aide-de-camp* (literally) camp assistant]

aide-mé|moire (ed′mā mwär′), *n. French.* 1 something to stimulate the memory, such as a calendar note. 2 a memorandum summarizing the discussion and the agreements arrived at in a meeting: *The Soviet aide-mémoire of 1958 stated that the Soviet Union was prepared to sign a peace treaty with the whole of Germany* (Terence Prittie).

aid|ful (ād′fəl), *adj. U.S.* helpful.

aid|less (ād′lis), *adj.* without help; unassisted; helpless.

aid|man (ād′man′, -mən), *n., pl.* **-men.** *Military.* a member of the medical service.

aid post, *British.* an aid station.

AIDS (ādz), *n.* acquired immune deficiency syndrome, a viral disease that attacks and breaks down the body's immune system, leading to serious and usually fatal infections and to a form of sarcoma: *Like hepatitis, AIDS could be transmitted by intimate sexual contact or blood* (Newsweek).

aid station, *U.S.* the first-aid post of a regiment or battalion, just behind the line of battle, for the first medical treatment of the wounded.

AIDS virus, the retrovirus that causes AIDS; HIV: *Because its genes are made up of RNA instead of the usual DNA, the AIDS virus is classified as a retrovirus* (Donald P. Francis).

a|i|ga (ä ē′gə), *n.* the Samoan family unit, consisting of a group of close relatives along the female or male line. [< Samoan *'aiga*]

ai|glet (ā′glit), *n.* = aglet.

ai|gret (ā′gret, ā gret′), *n.* = aigrette.

ai|grette (ā′gret, ā gret′), *n.* 1a a tuft of feathers worn as an ornament on the head, on a helmet, or the like. **b** anything shaped or used like this. 2 = egret. [< French *aigrette* egret]

ai|guille (ā gwēl′, ā′gwēl), *n.* a slender, sharply

pointed peak of rock, especially in the Alps. [< French *aiguille*, ultimately < a diminutive form of Latin *acus* needle]

ai|guil|lette (ā′gwi let′), *n.* an ornamental cord, braid, or loop on a dress uniform; aglet. [< earlier French *aiguillette* (diminutive, altered) < Old French *aguille* needle < Late Latin *acūcula* (diminutive) < Latin *acus.* See etym. of doublet **aglet**.]

AIH (no periods), Artificial Insemination by Husband.

ai|ki|do (ī kē′dō), *n.* a Japanese method of fighting without weapons, using holds, throws, and movements designed to make an opponent lose his balance: *The disciple of aikido ... does not flee or resist the attacker but, instead, blends with him* (New York Times). [< Japanese *aikidō*]

ail (āl), *v., n.* —*v.t.* to be the matter with; trouble: *Find out what ails that crying child.* **SYN:** afflict, distress.
—*v.i.* to be ill; feel sick; be indisposed: *She has been ailing for a week.*
—*n.* pain or disease; trouble; illness: *It was necessary for them to have remedies for their ails* (Casper Lederer). [Old English *eglan*]

ai|lan|thic (ā lan′thik), *adj.* of or having to do with the ailanthus.

ai|lan|thus (ā lan′thəs), *n.* a tree native to Asia with many leaves and clusters of small, greenish flowers, often used as a shade tree; tree of heaven. The flowers of some ailanthus trees have a somewhat disagreeable odor. [alteration of New Latin *ailantus* < Amboinese *ai lanto* < *ai lanit* tree of heaven; form influenced by Greek *ánthos* flower]

ailanthus moth, a moth, once of some commercial importance as a source of silk, native to China, introduced into the eastern United States. Its larvae feed on ailanthus leaves.

***ai|ler|on** (ā′lə ron), *n.* a hinged, movable part on the rear edge of an airplane wing used for banking, rolling, or balancing the airplane. [< French *aileron*, alteration of Old French *aleron* (diminutive) < *ele* wing < Latin *āla*]

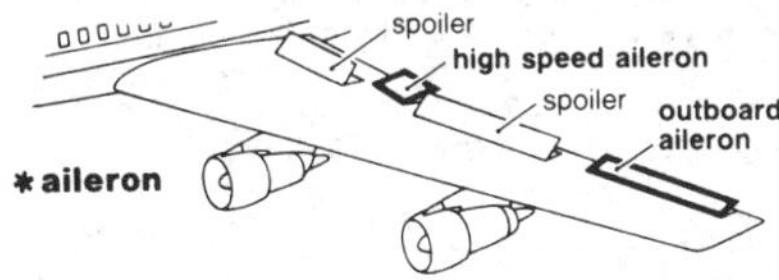

***aileron**

ai|le|va|tor (ā′lə vā′tər), *n.* = elevon.

ail|ing (ā′ling), *adj.* **1** sick; unwell: *... an obviously ailing and incapacitated man* (Observer). **2** *Figurative.* not in a sound condition; doing poorly: *The bankrupt company was a financially ailing concern for years.*

ail|ment (āl′mənt), *n.* an illness; sickness, especially a minor disorder of the body or mind, as distinguished from an acute or specific disease; sickness: *His ailment was only an upset stomach.* **SYN:** malady, complaint.

ai|lu|ro|phile (ā lu̇r′ə fīl, -lyu̇r′-), *n.* a person who has great affection for cats. Also, **aelurophile**.

ai|lu|ro|phil|i|a (ā lu̇r′ə fil′ē ə, -lyu̇r′-), *n.* a great affection for cats. Also, **aelurophilia**.

ai|lu|ro|phobe (ā lu̇r′ə fōb, -lyu̇r′-), *n.* a person who has a morbid fear or hatred of cats. Also, **aelurophobe**.

ai|lu|ro|pho|bi|a (ā lu̇r′ə fō′bē ə, -lyu̇r′-), *n.* a morbid fear or hatred of cats. Also, **aelurophobia**.

aim (ām), *v., n.* —*v.t.* **1** to point or direct (a weapon or blow) in order to hit a target: *to aim a gun.* **SYN:** level. **2** to direct (words or acts) so as to influence a certain person or action: *The coach aimed his talk at the boys who had not played fair.* **3** *Obsolete.* to guess. **4** *Obsolete.* to devise.
—*v.i.* **1** to point or direct something, such as a gun or blow, in order to hit: *He aimed at the lion but missed.* **2** to direct one's efforts; try: *She aims for perfection. We aim to please our customers.* **SYN:** aspire. **3** *U.S. Informal, Figurative.* to have in mind as a purpose; intend: *I aim to go.* **4** *Obsolete.* to guess.
—*n.* **1** the act of pointing or directing at something. **2** the ability to point or direct a weapon or blow: *His aim was so poor that he missed the door and hit the window with a snowball.* **3** the direction aimed in; line of sighting: *Your aim must allow for the wind.* **4** *Figurative.* the object of efforts; purpose; intention; goal: *Her aim was to do two years' work in one. O Happiness! our being's end and aim!* (Alexander Pope). **SYN:** intent, design, object. **5** *Obsolete.* a guess; conjecture. [< Old French *esmer* < Latin *aestimāre* appraise, and Old French *aesmer* < Vulgar Latin *adaestimāre.* See etym. of doublet **esteem**.] —**aim′a|ble**, *adj.* —**aim′er**, *n.* —**aim′less**, *adj.* —**aim′less|ly**, *adv.* —**aim′less|ness**, *n.*

AIM (no periods), American Indian Movement.

ai|mak (ī′mak, ā′mak), *n.* **1** one of the provinces of Mongolia. **2** a Mongolian clan. [< Mongolian *aimak*]

ain (ān), *adj. Scottish.* **1** one. **2** own.

aî|né, *fem.* **aî|née** (e nā′), *adj. French.* elder or eldest (used after a proper name).

ain|hum (ān′hum), *n. Medicine.* a painful constriction of the toe by a fibrous ring, afflicting people especially in tropical climates. In extreme cases, the toe falls off. [< an African word]

Ai|no (ī′nō), *n., pl.* **-nos.** = Ainu.

ain't (ānt), *Substandard or Dialect.* **1** am not; is not. **2** are not. **3** have not; has not.
▶**Ain't** is not now acceptable in formal English. Careful speakers and writers do not use *ain't*, because its use even in informal English is subject to sharp criticism, though *ain't* is used habitually by many Americans. It is almost never employed by cultivated speakers except as a deliberate illiteracy, usually for humorous effect as in "It ain't necessarily so." A case for *ain't* as a contraction for *am not*, etc., has been advanced by a number of language specialists, including H. W. Fowler; but the prevailing practice of writers and speakers of standard English is to avoid it. Compare also with **an't**.

Ai|nu (ī′nu), *n., pl.* **-nu** or **-nus**. **1** a member of an aboriginal, light-skinned people in northern Japan, now becoming extinct: *The Ainu survive in northern Japan in much the same relation to the Japanese as the Indians occupy to the whites in the United States, except that the contact has been longer and the Ainu are fewer* (A. L. Kroeber). **2** their language. It is as yet unclassified but unrelated to Japanese. Also, **Aino**.

air¹ (ãr), *n., v., adj.* —*n.* **1** the mixture of gases that surrounds the earth; atmosphere. Air consists chiefly of nitrogen and oxygen, along with carbon dioxide, argon, hydrogen, and small quantities of neon, helium, and other inert gases. It is odorless, tasteless, and invisible. We breathe air, and it directly or indirectly supports every form of life on earth. **2** the space overhead; sky: *Birds fly in the air.* **3** air in motion; a light wind; breeze: *a hot, summer day without a breath of air.* **4** fresh air: *He opened the window to let some air into the overheated room.* **5a** a simple melody or tune: *an old Scottish air, a traditional air.* **b** a piece of music designed to be played or sung as a solo: *D'Indy's Symphony on a French Mountain Air, a traditional air.* **c** the leading part of a piece of music that predominates and gives character to it. In part music it is usually the soprano. **6** *Figurative.* public mention: *He gave air to his opinions.* **SYN:** publicity. **7** the general character or appearance of anything: *An air of mystery surrounds the deserted house.* **SYN:** aura. **8** way; look; manner; bearing: *The famous man had an air of importance.* **SYN:** mien. **9** the medium through which radio waves travel; airways: *to fill the air with advertising.* **10** *Informal.* the personnel and equipment comprised by an air force: *French tactical air flies 1,000 sorties in six days* (Newsweek). **11** *Philately.* an airmail stamp. **12** *Obsolete.* breath.
—*v.t.* **1a** to put out in the air: *to air a blanket. It is good to air your clothes often.* **b** to let fresh air through: *Open the windows and air the room.* **SYN:** ventilate. **c** *British.* to warm and remove all dampness from: *Air the sheets before you put them on the bed.* **2** *Figurative.* to make known; express publicly: *Do not air your troubles too often.* **SYN:** expose, display. **3** to take on a stroll: *to air the dog.* **4** *Informal.* to broadcast by radio or television, or both: *The game was aired to all parts of the country.*
—*v.i.* to take the air; take a walk or ride.
—*adj.* **1** having to do with aviation; done by means of aircraft: *air photography.* **2** of or having to do with aircraft: *air safety, an air armada.* **SYN:** aerial.

airs, unnatural or affected manners: *Your friends will laugh if you put on airs.*

clear the air, to remove emotional tensions, misunderstanding, mistrust, or the like: *His explicit declaration in reply to Mr. Parnell's speech ... has cleared the air* (Manchester Examiner).

get the air, *U.S. Slang.* **a** to be discharged from a job: *She took off from work so often that she finally got the air.* **b** to be rejected as a suitor: *After he got the air, he moped in a lovesick trance for weeks.*

give the air, *U.S. Slang.* to dismiss, especially contemptuously: *Jim gives the air too freely to opinions he doesn't happen to agree with.*

in the air, **a** going around; being spread: *Wild rumors were in the air.* **b** *Figurative.* uncertain; unsettled: *Plans for the picnic are still in the air since we can't decide where to go.*

off the air, **a** not engaged in broadcasting: *This station is off the air from midnight to six in the morning.* **b** not being broadcast: *We used to watch that show, but it's off the air now.*

on the air, **a** broadcasting: *The station has been on the air since 1960.* **b** being broadcast: *Is that radio show still on the air?*

out of thin air, **a** out of nothing visible or concrete: *The problem ... involved the task of establishing out of thin air a program* (Bulletin of Atomic Scientists). **b** out of nowhere: *The little man appeared out of thin air* (London Times).

take air, *British.* to spread about among people; become known: *The story has taken air among all the neighbors.*

take the air, **a** to go outdoors; take a walk or ride: *On such a nice day, one should get out and take the air.* **b** *U.S.* to start broadcasting: *The new radio station will take the air next week.*

up in the air, **a** uncertain; unsettled: *The date of the wedding is still up in the air.* **b** *Informal.* very angry or excited: *The driver was up in the air about his parking ticket.*

walk (or **tread**) **on air**, to be very gay or pleased: *The boys are walking on air because their team won the game. ... treading on air at the way he'd handled the deal* (S. J. Perelman).
[< Old French *air* < Latin *āēr, āeris* < Greek *āēr, āéros*]
▶**Air, aerial** are often interchangeable before nouns. When their meanings differ, *air* frequently has to do with aviation: *air power, air dominance,* or (as an attributive noun) with atmospheric air: *air density, air temperature. Aerial* frequently modifies something other than air that is at home in, soars in, is used in, or reaches into the air: *aerial towers, aerial spirits, an aerial root.*

air² (ãr), *adv., adj. Scottish.* early; soon. [Middle English *ar*, Old English *ǣr.* See etym. of doublet **ere**.]

Air Academy, *U.S.* the Air Force Academy.

air age, the era of human history marked by the use of aircraft in war and as a means of public transport. The preliminaries began well before 1910 but effective and general use came only about 1939.

air alert, **1** a state of readiness for defense against enemy aircraft, when aircraft get into the air ready for immediate response to orders. **2** the signal to get aircraft into the air for such defense.

air arm, = air force.

air-a|tom|ic (ãr′ətom′ik), *adj.* based on or involving the use of atomic bombs carried by aircraft or of missiles armed with atomic warheads: *air-atomic defense.*

air attack, an attack by aircraft.

air|bag (ãr′bag′), *n.*, or **air bag**, a safety device consisting of a plastic bag that inflates in front of a passenger in an automobile collision to keep him from being thrown forward.

air base, a headquarters and airfield for military aircraft.

air battery, a battery that uses zinc or another metal as the fuel and pressurized air as the oxidizing agent.

air bearing, a bearing using the pressure of thin jets of air to support weights, eliminate friction, etc.

air bed, *British.* an air mattress.

***air bladder**, a sac in most fishes and various animals and plants that is filled with air. The air bladder of a fish is also called the *swim bladder* and adjusts the specific gravity of the fish to the water pressure at varying depths.

***air bladder**

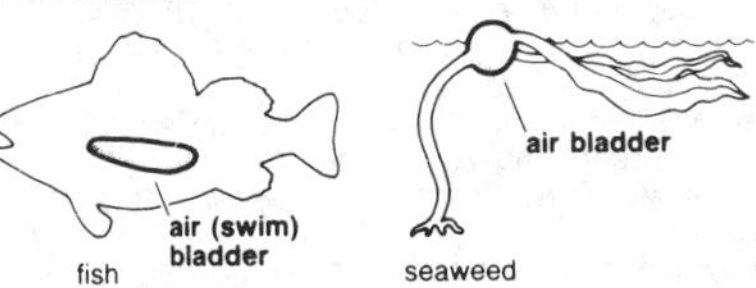

air blast, **1** a stream of air, especially one produced by mechanical means. **2** the shock caused by a very fast movement of air or of an object through the air, such as that of a missile reentering the earth's atmosphere. **3** the downward or outward pressure wave set up by an atomic explosion in the air.

air|boat (ãr′bōt′), *n.* a small flat-bottomed boat driven by an airplane propeller mounted on the boat and revolving in the air, used for travel in large swamps and flooded areas: *Skim through the Everglades in an airboat* (New Yorker).

air|borne (ãr′bôrn′, -bōrn′), *adj.* **1a** supported by the air; off the ground: *Within 15 minutes the*

Pronunciation Key: hat, āge, cãre, fär; let, ēqual, tėrm; it, īce; hot, ōpen, ôrder; **oi**l, **ou**t; cup, pu̇t, rüle; **ch**ild; lo**ng**; **th**in; **ᵺ**en; **zh**, measure; ə represents **a** in about, **e** in taken, **i** in pencil, **o** in lemon, **u** in circus.

bombers can be airborne. The kite was finally airborne. **b** carried in aircraft: *airborne troops.* **c** having its aircraft in the air: *an airborne patrol.* **2** carried by air: *airborne seeds, airborne contamination from industrial pollution.*

air|bound (ãr′bound′), *adj.* stopped up by an accumulation of air, as a pipe.

***air brake**, **1** a brake or system of brakes operated by forcing compressed air against a piston or pistons. **2** = speed brake.

***air brake**
definition 1

brake applied:
air pressure lowered by engineer
to engine
valve closed
brake cylinder
from rest of train
brake shoe
wheel
air from reservoir

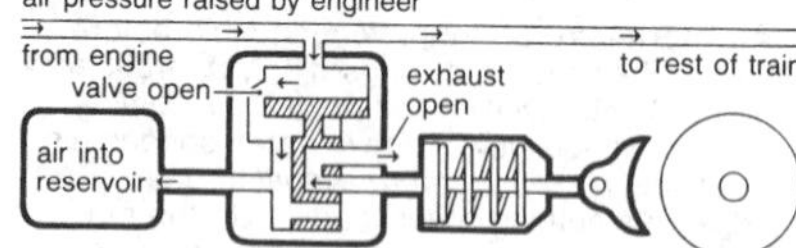

air|bra|sive (ãr′brā′siv), *adj.* that cleans, smooths, or cuts by the action of abrasive particles propelled at high speeds by compressed air from a nozzle: *an airbrasive drill.* [< *air* + (a)*brasive*]

air-break switch (ãr′brāk′), a switch in which an electric circuit is interrupted in the air.

air-breath|er (ãr′brē′ᴛʜər), *n.* a missile whose engine uses oxygen from the atmosphere to oxidize its fuel.

air-breath|ing (ãr′brē′ᴛʜing), *adj.* **1** that takes in oxygen from the atmosphere to oxidize its fuel: *air-breathing missiles.* **2** that respirates or breathes air as a natural process: *air-breathing insects.*

air brick, a brick perforated for ventilation.

air bridge, a link between two or more places by aircraft: *Three companies have formed an air bridge between Rio and São Paulo, which provides nonreservation flights every half hour* (London Times).

***air|brush** (ãr′brush′), *n., v.* —*n.* a device somewhat like an atomizer, operated by compressed air, that is used to spray paint on a surface.
—*v.t.* to paint or touch up with an airbrush: *The Times airbrushed out the player and printed his shadow* (Time).

***airbrush**

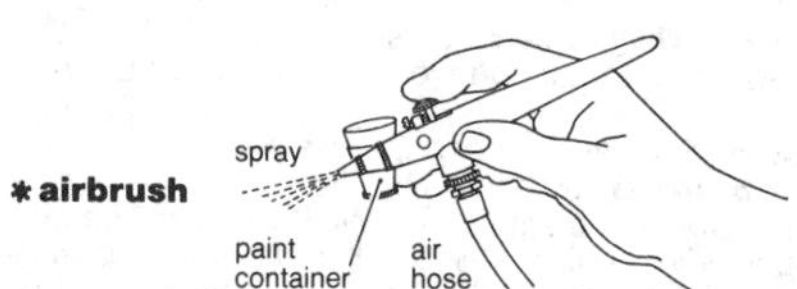

air|burst (ãr′bėrst′), *n.* an explosion of a bomb in the air, above the surface of the earth: *In a high airburst, the fireball will not touch the ground, and there will be no local fallout* (Bulletin of Atomic Scientists).

air|bus (ãr′bus′), *n.* a very large jet aircraft for carrying passengers on short flights.

air cargo, cargo transported by aircraft; air freight.

air carrier, an aircraft that carries freight.

air castle, a daydream; castle in the air.

Air Cav, Air Cavalry.

Air Cavalry, a unit of the United States Army transported to combat areas by aircraft, especially helicopters.

air cell, a tiny cavity for air in an organism. The air sacs of a bird are air cells.

air chamber, any compartment filled with air, especially a trap in a pump or other hydraulic system to prevent excessive pressures when the pump is suddenly stopped or started.

air cleaner, a device that removes impurities from a stream of gas or air.

air coach, *U.S.* **1** a class of air travel with lower fares than first class. **2** a commercial aircraft with comparatively low fares. **3** such aircraft collectively.

air|cock (ãr′kok′), *n.* a small valve for letting air in or out.

air compressor, a device that pushes together, or compresses, air, and holds it under pressure, especially as a source of power for a pneumatic drill, pump, or other device.

air-con|di|tion (ãr′kən dish′ən), *v.t.* **1** to supply (a building, room, car, or other enclosed area) with the equipment for air conditioning. **2** to treat (the air within a building, car, or other enclosed area) by means of air conditioning.

air-con|di|tioned (ãr′kən dish′ənd), *adj.* having air conditioning: *In air-conditioned buildings the air is kept at the most comfortable temperature.*

air conditioner, equipment used to air-condition a building, room, car, or other enclosed area.

air conditioning, a means of treating air in a building, room, car, or other enclosed area, to free it from dust and to regulate its temperature and amount of moisture: *Air conditioning is the use of a refrigerant which is cooled by pressure changes in a condenser and cycled through a coil. Air then is blown over the cold coil* (Wall Street Journal).

air control, **1** military control of an airspace. **2** control of a hostile force or nation by means of a superior air or space power. **3** = air traffic control.

air-cool (ãr′kül′), *v.t.* **1** to remove heat from (an internal-combustion engine) by forcing air on or around the cylinders. **2** to remove heat from (a room or other enclosed area) by blowing cool air in. —**air′-cool′er**, *n.*

air-cooled (ãr′küld′), *adj.* cooled by having air blown on it.

air-cool|ing (ãr′kü′ling), *n.* the reduction of heat by passing a current of air through or over heated areas.

air-core (ãr′kôr′, -kōr′), *adj. Electricity.* having a nonmetallic core: *an air-core transformer.*

air-cored (ãr′kôrd′, -kōrd′), *adj.* = air-core.

Air Corps, the air arm of the U.S. Army from 1926 to 1941, a predecessor of the U.S. Air Force.

air corridor, a passage or corridor over foreign-controlled territory open to aircraft as specified by government ruling or international agreement: *Along Western air corridors to Berlin, Soviet MIG-17s began making closeup inspections of U.S. passenger liners* (Time).

air cover, **1** a force of aircraft protecting a land or sea operation, a convoy, or other group. **2** the protection given by such a force: *The training of the Royal Air Force is ... to provide in daylight air cover for the craft carrying the troops and for the naval forces protecting them, and close support during the attack* (Louis Mountbatten).

air|craft (ãr′kraft′, -kräft′), *n., pl.* **-craft.** **1** an airplane, airship, helicopter, or balloon; any machine for flying in the air that is supported in flight by buoyancy (such as a balloon), or by the action of air (such as an airplane), or by reaction to one or more jet streams (such as a rocket). **2** such machines collectively or as a class; airplanes, airships, helicopters, or balloons: *The rapid development of aircraft that could take off and land vertically soon might make obsolete many large airports and long runways* (New York Times).

***aircraft carrier**, a warship designed as a base for aircraft, with a large, flat deck on which to land or take off.

***aircraft carrier**

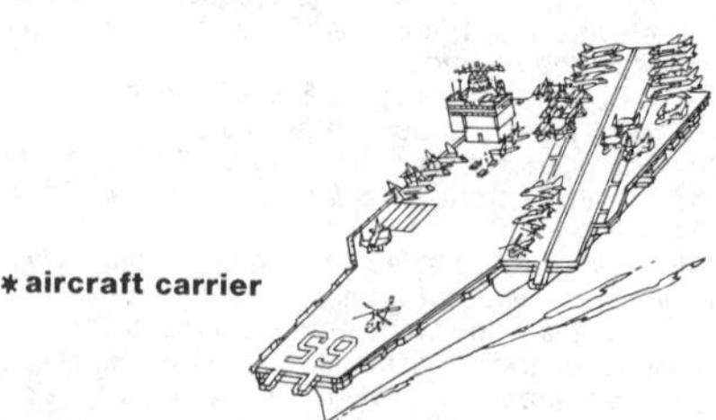

air|craft|man (ãr′kraft′mən, -kräft′-), *n., pl.* **-men.** = aircraftsman.

air|crafts|man (ãr′krafts′mən, -kräfts′-), *n., pl.* **-men.** **1** an enlisted man of the lowest rating in the Royal Air Force. **2** his equivalent in most other countries of the Commonwealth of Nations.

air|crafts|wom|an (ãr′krafts′wu̇m′ən, -kräfts′-), *n., pl.* **-wom|en.** an enlisted woman in the Royal Air Force who is equivalent in rank to an aircraftsman.

air|craft|wom|an (ãr′kraft′wu̇m′ən, -kräft′-), *n., pl.* **-wom|en.** = aircraftswoman.

air|crew (ãr′krü′), *n.* the crew that flies an aircraft but does not service it (distinguished from *ground crew*).

air|crew|man (ãr′krü′mən), *n., pl.* **-men.** a member of a crew that flies in an aircraft.

air-cure (ãr′kyu̇r′), *v.t.,* **-cured, -cur|ing.** to cure (tobacco or lumber) by the action of the air alone, without heating it. Air-cured tobacco is dried by leaving the leaf out in the sun, and then in constant circulation of air in well-ventilated barns.

air current, atmospheric flow; wind.

air curtain, a mass of air heated or cooled and circulated around the entrance of a store, building, or the like, to hold in or keep out warm air, according to the season, serving in place of a conventional door.

air cushion, **1** a cushion inflated with air instead of being stuffed. **2** a device by which pressure or shock is absorbed by air.

air cushion vehicle, a vehicle that travels a few feet above the surface of land or water on a cushion of air produced by a system of fans; ground effect machine; hovercraft. *Abbr:* ACV.

air cylinder, a cylinder filled with air and having a piston, for checking the recoil of a gun.

air defense, a system of defense against air attack, using aircraft, missiles, and other weapons, and electronic detection of attacking aircraft.

air door, = air curtain.

air drag, = air resistance.

air-driv|en (ãr′driv′ən), *adj.* deriving its power from compressed air: *an air-driven dental drill.*

air|drome (ãr′drōm′), *n. U.S.* an airport. Also, *especially British,* **aerodrome.**

air|drop (ãr′drop′), *n., v.,* **-dropped, -drop|ping.** —*n.* the act or system of delivering food, supplies, cargo, or persons by parachute from aircraft in flight: *But Army rescue teams radioed that in many cases where food was urgently needed it was impossible to attempt airdrops* (New York Times).
—*v.t.* to deliver (food, supplies, cargo, or persons) by parachute from aircraft in flight.

air-dry (ãr′drī′), *v.,* **-dried, -dry|ing,** *adj.* —*v.t.* to dry by airing.
—*adj.* so dry that no evaporation takes place.

air duct, a pipe or duct for conveying outside air into a building.

Aire|dale (ãr′dāl), *n.,* or **Airedale terrier**, a large terrier having a wiry brown or tan coat with dark markings. Airedales were originally bred to hunt small game. [< *Airedale,* a valley in Yorkshire, England]

air edition, an edition of a newspaper or magazine, printed on very thin paper or with fewer pages than usual, for shipping to distribution points by air.

air embolism, an often fatal condition in which rupture of a lung introduces air into the pulmonary veins causing clotting and a loss of circulation in arteries of the brain.

air engine, a motor driven by the force of heated or compressed air.

air-en|trained concrete (ãr′en trānd′), concrete containing billions of tiny air cells in each cubic foot that are formed by adding soaplike resinous or fatty materials to the cement or concrete when it is mixed. The cells give the water in concrete enough room to expand as it freezes.

air-ex|press (ãr′ik spres′), *v.t.* to transport by air express.

air express, the shipment of merchandise by aircraft.

air|fare (ãr′fãr′), *n.* the price of a trip by airplane.

air ferry, an aircraft or system of aircraft for the transport of persons and cargo between fixed points. The later term is *air bridge.*

air|field (ãr′fēld′), *n.* the landing area of an airport or air base.

air filter, a mechanical or electronic component in an air cleaner that filters dust, pollen, or other contaminants from the air.

***airfoil**

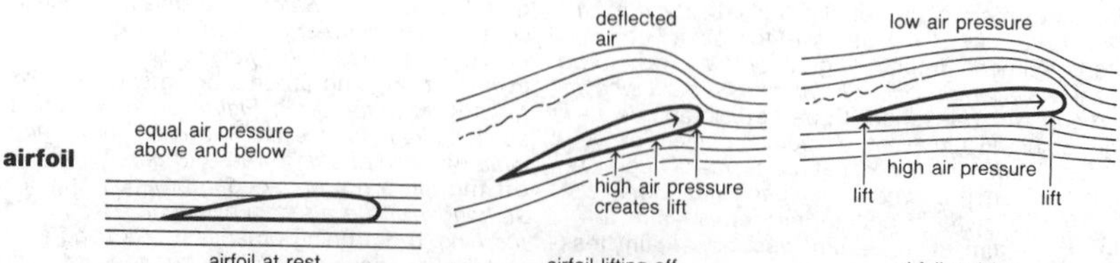

Pronunciation Key: hat, āge, cãre, fär; let, ēqual, tėrm; it, īce; hot, ōpen, ôrder; oil, out; cup, pu̇t, rüle; child; long; thin; ᴛʜen; zh, measure; ə represents **a** in about, **e** in taken, **i** in pencil, **o** in lemon, **u** in circus.

air fleet, **1** military aircraft, under a single commanding officer, used for a particular kind of mission or within a particular theater of operations. **2** an air force.

air|flow (ãr′flō′), *n., adj.* —*n.* **1** a natural movement of air. **2** the flow of air around and relative to an object moving in air.
—*adj.* **1** streamlined: *airflow design.* **2** that is produced by air currents: *airflow patterns around cumulus clouds.*

* **air|foil** (ãr′foil′), *n.* **1** a wing, aileron, rudder, or other surface designed to help lift or control an aircraft. See picture below on preceding page. **2** a spoiler or similar device designed to help keep a car firmly on the road at high speeds.

air force, **1** the branch of the military forces that uses aircraft. **2** the largest tactical unit of this branch.

Air Force, **1** *U.S.* a separate branch of the armed forces of the United States, created in 1947, that includes aviation personnel, equipment, etc. *Abbr:* AF (no periods), A.F. **2** *British.* the Royal Air Force.

Air Force Academy, the officer-training service school of the U.S. Air Force, near Colorado Springs, Colorado.

Air Force blue, **1** *U.S.* the shade of medium blue officially adopted by the U.S. Air Force for its standard uniforms. **2** *British.* the shade of medium blue-gray similarly used in the R.A.F.

air|frame (ãr′frām′), *n.* the framework of an airplane, not including the engine or engines, of a ballistic missile, or of a dirigible. See picture under **airship**.

air-freight (ãr′frāt′), *v.t.* to ship (something) by air freight.

air freight, **1** freight transported by aircraft. **2** the class of cargo by which this is comprised: *to ship by air freight.*

air|freight|er (ãr′frā′tər), *n.* **1** an aircraft that carries freight. **2** a person or company engaged in the business of operating such aircraft.

air gap, the space in an electric motor or dynamo between the armature and the core.

air gas, = producer gas.

air|glow (ãr′glō′), *n. Astronomy.* a faint glow in the sky, not visible to the naked eye, believed due to chemical reactions in the upper atmosphere.

air gun, **1** an air rifle or air pistol. **2** a device utilizing compressed air to force grease, putty, or some similar substance into or onto something.

air hammer, **1** a pneumatic drill, especially one used for breaking up pavement. **2** a pneumatic hammer used in riveting.

air|head (ãr′hed′), *n.* **1** a position established in enemy territory which can be reached and supplied by air: *Each airhead is an internal island to which every fighting man must be carried by air, plus every pound of equipment and food for its maintenance* (Newsweek). **2** *Slang.* a stupid person; blockhead: *One of the many airheads who move torpidly through...[the film] Raise the Titanic says in a throat-clutching voice: "A ship that big down that deep!?!?* (Maclean's).

air hole, **1** a hole that air can pass through. **2** an open space in the ice on a body of water. **3** *U.S.* an air pocket.

air|hop (ãr′hop′), *v.,* **-hopped**, **-hop|ping**, *n. U.S. Slang.* —*v.i.* to make frequent short trips by plane. —*n.* a short trip by plane.

air hostess, *British.* an airline hostess.

air|house (ãr′hous′), *n.* a temporary building made of woven nylon, inflated and kept erect by air pressure, and coated with polyvinyl chloride.

air hunger, *Medicine.* shortness of breath from lack of oxygen, symptomatic of acidosis.

air|i|ly (ãr′ə lē), *adv.* in an airy manner.

air|i|ness (ãr′i nis), *n.* airy quality.

air|ing (ãr′ing), *n.* **1** exposure to air, as for drying or warming: *She gave the rug a thorough airing.* **2** a walk, ride, drive, or the like, outdoors. **3** *Figurative.* exposure to public notice or discussion: *The proposed rule is due for an airing at the next school assembly.*

air jacket, **1** a space in which air is circulated to absorb excess heat, such as in a machine. **2** *British.* an inflatable life jacket.

air|land (ãr′land′), *v.t.* to land and unload (troops or supplies) from aircraft.

air lane, a regular route used by aircraft; airway.

air-launch (ãr′lônch′, -länch′), *v.t.* to launch from a flying aircraft.

air layering, a method of causing a branch or stem to form roots for planting, by making a cut halfway through the branch and wrapping it in moist earth or moss. New roots form in the area of the cut.

air|less (ãr′lis), *adj.* **1** without fresh air; stuffy. **2** without a breeze; still. —**air′less|ness**, *n.*

air letter, **1** a lightweight sheet of paper, often designed to fold and seal as an envelope, with a message on its inner surfaces. **2** any letter sent by air mail; airmail letter.

air|lift (ãr′lift′), *n., v.* —*n.* **1** a system of using aircraft to transport passengers and freight to a place when existing land routes are closed or inadequate: *Medical supplies were brought by airlift to the flooded villages.* **2** the aircraft used. **3** the passengers or freight transported by such a system.
—*v.t.* to transport by airlift: *Enough planes were provided to airlift two army divisions.*

air|lift|ing (ãr′lif′ting), *n.* = airlift (def. 1).

airlift pump, a pump used in oil wells and in mines consisting of a pipe for conducting air to the bottom of a long drop pipe that is submerged below the liquid. The mixture of air and liquid that is formed is lighter than the liquid outside the drop pipe, forcing the liquid to rise.

air|line (ãr′līn′), *n.* **1** a system of transporting people and things by aircraft. **2** the company owning or operating such a system. **3** a route for aircraft; airway; air lane. **4** *Especially U.S.* a straight line through the air.

air-line (ãr′līn′), *adj. Especially U.S.* **1** shortest possible: *the air-line distance to Chicago.* **2** straight: *an air-line highway.*

airline hostess or **stewardess**, *U.S.* a stewardess on an airliner. Also, *British,* **air hostess**.

air|lin|er (ãr′lī′nər), *n.* a large passenger airplane.

air|load (ãr′lōd′), *n.* **1** the total weight carried by an aircraft in flight exclusive of the aircraft itself, computed as the weight of the passengers, crew, cargo, and fuel. **2** the aerodynamic force imposed upon a moving airfoil or other object.

air lock, **1** an airtight compartment between places where there is a difference in air pressure. The pressure in an air lock can be raised or lowered. **2** a decompression chamber. **3** the blocking of a liquid's flow, as through a tube, caused by the presence of air.

air|log (ãr′lôg′, -log′), *n.* **1** the log kept by the pilot or commanding officer of an aircraft. **2** a device for recording the distance traveled by a missile in the air.

air mail, = airmail, *n.*

air|mail (ãr′māl′), *n., v., adj.* —*n.* **1** mail sent by aircraft. **2** a system of sending mail by aircraft.
—*v.t.* to send (anything) by airmail: *Please airmail this letter.*
—*adj.* **1** sent or to be sent by aircraft: *an airmail letter.* **2** of or having to do with the carrying of mail by air.

air|man (ãr′mən), *n., pl.* **-men**. **1** the pilot of an aircraft; aviator. **2** one of the crew of an aircraft. **3** an enlisted man ranking above an airman basic in the U.S. Air Force.

airman basic, an enlisted man of the lowest rank in the U.S. Air Force, comparable in grade to a private.

airman first class, an airman of the highest rank in the U.S. Air Force, ranking next below a sergeant.

air|man|ship (ãr′mən ship), *n.* skill in aviation.

air map, a map consisting of or based on aerial photographs.

air|mark (ãr′märk′), *v.t.* to mark as a guide for pilots of aircraft: *to airmark a landing strip.* —**air′mark′er**, *n.*

air marshal, a rank in the Royal Air Force corresponding to vice-admiral or lieutenant general.

air mass, a large body of air within the atmosphere that has nearly uniform temperature and humidity at any given level and moves horizontally over great distances without changing.

air mattress, a pad that can be inflated to serve as a life raft, mattress, etc.

Air Medal, a decoration awarded to any person in the U.S. Air Force or air force of another branch of military service, for meritorious achievement while flying.

air mile, a nautical mile, 6076.11549 feet, used as a measure of distance in the flight of aircraft.

air-mind|ed (ãr′mīn′did), *adj.* **1** interested in aviation. **2** fond of air travel. —**air′-mind′ed|ness**, *n.*

Air Ministry, the department of the British government in charge of military aviation, and formerly also of civil aviation.

air miss, a very narrow escape from collision between aircraft.

air|mo|bile (ãr′mō bēl′), *adj. U.S.* moved to the front by air: *airmobile combat troops.*

air mosaic, a map consisting of strips of film taken by successive photographs from airplanes with special cameras. An air mosaic gives a bird's-eye view of the landscape.

air|om|e|ter (ãr om′ə tər), *n.* **1** a container for holding and measuring air. **2** an apparatus for measuring the quantity or rate of flow of air.

air|park (ãr′pärk′), *n.* a small airport.

air passage, **1** accommodations for a trip by aircraft: *to book air passage from London to Rome.* **2** any conduit for air, such as the nose or windpipe.

air piracy, the hijacking of aircraft; skyjacking.

air pirate, a person who commits air piracy; skyjacker.

air pistol, a pistol that shoots a single pellet or dart, worked by compressed air.

* **air|plane** (ãr′plān′; ãr′ə plān′; *see note below*), *n., v.,* **-planed**, **-plan|ing**. —*n. U.S.* a flying machine that has one or more planes or wings and is driven by one or more propellers or jet engines or a rocket engine. An airplane is an aircraft heavier than air, supported in flight by the action of the air flowing past or thrusting upward on its fixed wings. See picture below. Also, *especially British,* **aeroplane**. —*v.i.* to fly in an airplane.
[< French *aéroplane* < *aéro-* air + stem of *planer* soar, learned borrowing from Latin *plānus* level]
▶**Airplane, aeroplane**. In written use, *airplane* is the usual form in the United States (and official in the government), whereas *aeroplane* is more often used in Great Britain in addition to *aircraft.* In speech, however, the pronunciation ãr′ə plān′is frequent in the United States, even in reading the form *airplane.*

airplane carrier, *U.S.* an aircraft carrier.

airplane cloth, *U.S.* **1** a plain, tightly woven, sturdy cotton fabric used as a luggage covering and in some garments. **2** a similar linen fabric used to cover the frames of older airplanes.

airplane luggage, *U.S.* very lightweight luggage, made especially for air travel.

airplane spin, *Wrestling.* a throw used especially by professional wrestlers. One wrestler lifts his opponent on his shoulders, whirls him about, and throws him down.

air plant, a plant not connected with the ground and seeming to live on air; epiphyte: *Many orchids are air plants.*

air|play (ãr′plā′), *n.* the amount of broadcast time for a phonograph record: *The "underground" promotion man for the record company knew that reviews influenced FM airplay and availability in stores* (Harper's).

air pocket, a downward current of air that causes an airplane to lose altitude suddenly. An air pocket is caused by the sudden sinking of cooled air.

air pollution, the contamination of the air especially by industrial waste gases, fuel exhaust, or smoke: *The correlation of the number of deaths from bronchitis with both airborne dust and smoke is so pronounced that air pollution plays a major role* (New Scientist).

air|port (ãr′pôrt′, -pōrt′), *n.* a station with a field for airplanes to land and take off from, and buildings for keeping, repairing, and servicing airplanes and usually also for passengers; an area, especially on land, used regularly by aircraft.

air|post (ãr′pōst′), *adj. British.* airmail: *an airpost stamp.*

air post, *British.* air mail.

air|pow|er (ãr′pou′ər), *n.* the capacity of a nation to wage war in and from the air by means of military aircraft or missiles.

air pressure, **1** pressure caused by the weight of the air; atmospheric pressure. Winds are caused by the flow of air from an area of high air pressure to an area of low air pressure. **2** the pressure of compressed air. **3** pressure on a

***airplane**

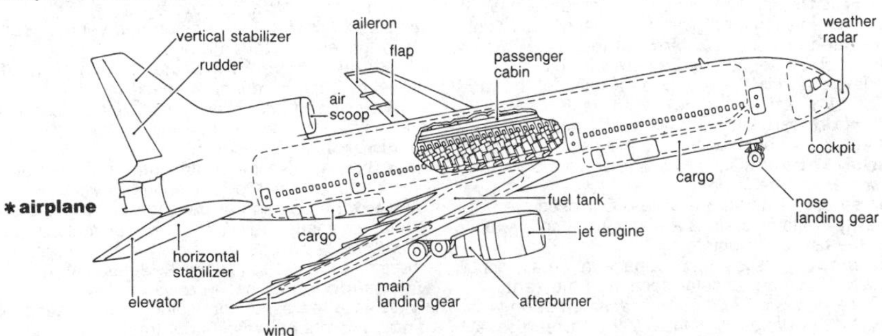

moving object by the air it strikes.
air|proof (ãr′prüf′), *adj., v.* **—*adj.*** impervious to air.
—*v.t.* to make (something) airproof.
air pump, an apparatus for forcing air into or through something, or for drawing it out, or for compressing it.
air raid, an attack by enemy aircraft, especially by bombers.
air raider, an aircraft, especially a bomber, that engages in an air raid.
air-raid shelter (ãr′rād′), a place for protection during an air raid.
air resistance, opposition by the air to any body moving through it, such as an aircraft or projectile.
air rifle, a gun that uses compressed air to shoot a single pellet or dart; air gun.
air rights, the rights, by lease or purchase, to possession and use of space above an existing installation: *Air rights are valuable chiefly in the nation's largest cities, such as New York and Chicago, where buildings already jam most useable ground space* (Wall Street Journal).
air route, **1** a path or course followed by aircraft: *the shortest air route from Chicago to Tokyo.* **2** markings on a chart giving point of departure, course, and destination for an aircraft flight.
airs (ãrz), *n.pl.* See under **air**.
air sac, **1** an alveolus: *The air from the bronchial tubes flows into millions of air sacs, called alveoli, which make up the spongelike mass of each lung* (Arthur C. Guyton). **2** an air-filled space in different parts of the body of a bird, connected with the lungs. It aids in breathing and in regulating body temperature. **3** a thin-walled enlargement in the trachea of an insect, resembling a sac.
air-sac disease (ãr′sak′), chronic respiratory disease in domestic fowl.
air sampling, the taking of samples of air for analysis, especially to count the pollen in it, or to analyze the amount of contamination from industrial wastes, fuel exhaust, or smoke, or to detect radioactive fallout.
air|scape (ãr′skāp), *n. U.S.* a view from very high up, as from an aircraft.
air scoop, a shovellike opening that conveys a flow of air to an aircraft engine during flight. See picture under **airplane**.
air|screw (ãr′skrü′), *n. British.* an aircraft propeller.
air service, transportation of people or things by aircraft.
Air Service, the aviation branch of the U.S. Army between 1907 (officially 1920) and 1926, a predecessor of the U.S. Air Force.
air shaft, a passage for letting fresh air in, as to a mine, tunnel, or building; air well.
air|ship** (ãr′ship′), *n., v.,* **-shipped, -ship|ping.** **—*n. **1** a balloon that can be steered; a dirigible. An airship is filled with a gas that is lighter than air, and is driven by propeller. **2** *Obsolete.* an airplane.
—*v.t.* *U.S.* to ship by aircraft: *to airship supplies to Greenland.*

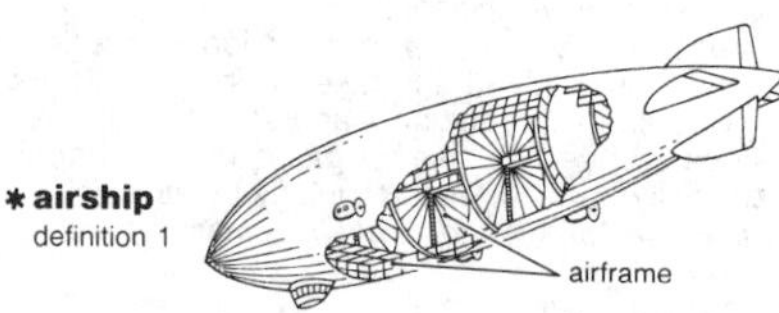

***airship**
definition 1

air shower, a large number of secondary rays, consisting of electrons, positrons, mesons, and photons, created when a primary cosmic ray enters the atmosphere.
air|shut|tle (ãr′shut′əl), *v.i., v.t.,* **-tled, -tling.** to travel by air shuttle: *We airshuttled to Washington the other morning* (New Yorker).
air shuttle, **1** air service, usually without passenger reservations, running on a frequent schedule between two cities. **2 Air-Shuttle**, a service mark for such air service by Eastern Airlines.
air|sick (ãr′sik′), *adj.* sick as a result of the motion of aircraft. **—air′sick′ness**, *n.*
air-slake (ãr′slāk′), *v.t.,* **-slaked, -slak|ing.** to slake (lime) by exposure to moist air.
air-slaked (ãr′slākt′), *adj.* slaked by moist air: *air-slaked lime.*
air space, **1** any more or less enclosed area or cavity containing air. **2** any gas-filled space found in the tissues of plants.
air|space (ãr′spās′), *n.* **1** space in the air, especially above a particular section of the earth: *China protested that its airspace had been violated by foreign airplanes.* **2** the limited space in the air occupied by a formation of aircraft. **3** the space used in an aerial maneuver.
air speed, the speed of an aircraft in relation to the speed of the air, as distinguished from ground speed.
air-speed indicator (ãr′spēd′), a flight instrument that shows air speed.
air-spray (ãr′sprā′), *v.t.* to apply (a liquid) in a spray controlled by air pressure.
air spring, any device that utilizes the elasticity of compressed air to absorb or resist shock.
air staff, a group of officers in the U.S. Air Force that advises a commanding officer in planning and carrying out military operations.
air|stream (ãr′strēm′), *n.* the relative flow of air around or against an object in flight, usually in a direction opposite to that of the object's flight.
air strike, an attack by aircraft upon a target: *130 guerrillas had been killed, 100 of them by immediate air strikes* (New York Times).
air|strip (ãr′strip′), *n.* **1** a paved or cleared runway for aircraft, often made hastily for temporary use; landing strip. **2** a small airport.
air survey, a topographical survey consisting of or based on aerial photographs.
air suspension, a method of suspending a vehicle, such as an automobile, on its axles, that utilizes a piston supported by a chamber of compressed air instead of a metal spring at each suspension point.
airt (ãrt), *n., v. Scottish.* **—*n.*** a point of the compass; a direction.
—*v.t.* to direct; guide.
[< Scottish Gaelic *àird* direction; high place]
air taxi, a passenger airplane for short-distance flights: *Air taxis link the 600 cities served by scheduled airlines with more than 6,000 communities that are not ... and perform hundreds of functions from serving as ambulances to charting forest fires* (Time).
air terminal, **1** a building at an airport for boarding and discharging passengers from aircraft. **2** a terminal for passengers going to or coming from an airport.
airth (ãrth), *n., v.t. Scottish.* airt.
air|tight (ãr′tīt′), *adj.* **1** so tight that no air or gas can get in or out. **2** *Especially U.S. Informal, Figurative.* having no weak points or loopholes open to attack: *an airtight alibi. The team had an airtight defense.* **SYN**: unassailable.
air time, **1** the moment when a particular radio or television program begins to be broadcast: *three minutes to air time.* **2** an amount of broadcasting time; minutes or hours of broadcasting, especially as sold by radio or television stations or networks for commercials: *to spend $100,000 for air time.*
air-to-air (ãr′tů ãr′), *adj., adv.* passing between two flying aircraft, as a rocket launched by one to destroy another: *air-to-air missiles, air-to-air defense, air-to-air refueling.*
air-to-ground (ãr′tů ground′), *adj., adv.* passing from a flying aircraft to the ground: *air-to-ground missiles.*
air-to-sur|face (ãr′tů sėr′fis), *adj., adv.* passing from a flying aircraft to something on the ground or the surface of the sea: *an air-to-surface signal.*
air-to-un|der|wa|ter (ãr′tů un′dər wôt′ər, -wot′-), *adj., adv.* passing from a flying aircraft to a vessel under the water: *air-to-underwater communication.*
air tourist, = air coach.
air tractor, an aircraft specially designed for crop dusting and spraying.
air traffic, the aircraft landing or taking off or in flight in a given area: *heavy air traffic at the airport.*
air traffic control, **1** the control of the movements of aircraft to promote safe, orderly, and rapid traffic. **2** a licensed or governmental agency providing this service.
air transport, **1** the business of transporting people or cargo by airplane. **2** an airplane that carries chiefly cargo. **3** a military aircraft that carries personnel, supplies, and equipment.
air-trans|port|a|ble (ãr′trans pôr′tə bəl, -pōr′-), *adj.* that can be transported by air.
air trap, a pocket for catching and venting foul air or gases, as from a drain.
air travel, **1** travel by airplane. **2** the amount of travel by airplane during a specified period.
air|trav|el|er (ãr′trav′lər, -ə lər), *n.* a person who travels by air.
air umbrella, = air cover.
air valve, a valve for controlling the flow of air into or out of pipes or enclosures.
air vent, an opening or passage to allow the entrance or escape of air: *Steam radiators usually must have air vents to let the air out so that the steam can come in* (Wilbur L. Beauchamp).
air vesicle, an air sac in a water plant.
air vessel, a vessel containing or conducting air; an air chamber; a respiratory tract.
air|ward (ãr′wərd), *adv.* upward.
air|wards (ãr′wərdz), *adv.* = airward.
air washer, a row of nozzles that spray water inside an air conditioner to keep the air moist and free of dust.
air|wave (ãr′wāv′), *n.* = airway (def. 3).
airwaves, radio or television broadcasting: *Pure conversation ... has been shockingly absent from the airwaves* (New York Times).
air|way (ãr′wā′), *n.* **1** a route for aircraft; air lane; airline. **2** a passage for air: *A thin tube, known as an endotracheal catheter, has been put down her windpipe to assure her a clear and controllable airway throughout the operation* (Harper's). **3** *U.S.* a specified radio frequency.
airways, *U.S. Informal.* channels for radio or television broadcasting: *There was a big surge in radio spot advertising and the airways were filled with lots of new jingles* (C. J. Shuttleworth).
air well, = air shaft.
air wing, the air arm of an army or navy.
air|wom|an (ãr′wům′ən), *n., pl.* **-wom|en. 1** a civilian woman pilot; an aviatrix. **2** an enlisted woman in an air force (not now in official use).
air|wor|thi|ness (ãr′wėr′ᴛʜē nis), *n.* the condition of an aircraft fit and safe for flight.
air|wor|thy (ãr′wėr′ᴛʜē), *adj.* (of aircraft) fit and safe for flight.
air|y (ãr′ē), *adj.,* **air|i|er, air|i|est. 1** with air moving through it; well supplied with fresh air: *a large, airy room.* **2** light as air; graceful; delicate: *She sang an airy tune.* **3** light-hearted; gay: *the children's airy laughter.* **4** breezy: *a high, airy hill.* **5** of air; in the air; aerial: *The sky was filled with birds and other airy creatures.* **6** reaching high in the air; lofty: *airy pinnacles.* **7** like air; not solid or substantial: *airy plans, airy phantoms of the mind.* **SYN**: flimsy, unreal. **8** *Figurative.* unnatural; affected: *an airy tone of voice.* **9** *Figurative.* flippant: *airy criticism.*
air|y-fair|y (ãr′ē fãr′ē), *adj. Informal.* **1** delicate; light; airy: *airy-fairy creatures.* **2** fanciful; dreamy; impractical: *Not airy-fairy schemes ... but in detail and in writing, so that we know what we are considering* (London Times).
aisle (īl), *n.* **1** a passage between rows of seats in a hall, theater, or school. **2a** a similar passage in a church. In some large, elaborate churches the aisles are parallel to the main passage (the nave), and usually set off by pillars. **b** any similar part, as of choir or transept. **c** the nave itself. **3** *U.S., Figurative.* any long, narrow passage, as between rows of trees in a forest. **SYN**: corridor.
down the aisle, *Informal.* to the altar for a marriage ceremony: *The parents hoped that the oldest of their daughters would be the first down the aisle.*
roll in the aisles, *Slang.* to respond enthusiastically to something funny: *He has kept Italian audiences rolling in the aisles for 40 years or more* (London Times).
[< Middle French *ele* < Latin *āla* wing; influenced in form by French *aile* and English *isle*, and in meaning by English *alley*]
aisled (īld), *adj.* having an aisle or aisles.
aisle-sit|ter (īl′sit′ər), *n. U.S. Informal.* a person who sits next to the aisle, especially a drama critic.
ait[1] (āt), *n. British Dialect.* a small island in a river or lake; islet. [Middle English *eyt* < Old English *īgeoth* islet < *īeg* island]
ait[2] (āt), *n. Scottish.* oat.
aitch (āch), *n., pl.* **aitch|es**, *adj.* **—*n.*** the letter *H, h.*
—*adj.* in the form of a capital *H.*
[respelling of earlier *ache* < French, the name of the letter *H, h*]
aitch|bone (āch′bōn′), *n.* **1** the rumpbone, especially of a steer. **2** a cut of beef taken from or including this bone. Also, **edgebone.** [Middle English *an ache-bone*, misdivision of earlier *a nache(-bone)* < Old French *nache* < Late Latin *natica* < Latin *natis* buttock]
aitch|less (āch′lis), *adj. British.* that does not aspirate his *h*'s: *The aitchless millionaire ... goes to an elocutionist and learns a B.B.C. accent* (George Orwell).
Ait|ken Bible (āt′kən), the first Bible printed in English in America (by Robert Aitken, Philadelphia, 1782).
AJA (no periods) or **A.J.A.**, Americans of Japanese ancestry.
a|jan|gle (ə jang′gəl), *adv., adj.* jangling: *You arrive at the track, already exhausted and with nerves ajangle* (Life).
a|jar[1] (ə jär′), *adv., adj.* slightly open: *Please leave the door ajar.* [Middle English *on char* on the turn; *char*, Old English *cerr* turn]
a|jar[2] (ə jär′), *adv., adj.* not in harmony; discordant. [< *a-*[1] in + *jar*[2] discord]
A|jax (ā′jaks), *n. Greek Legend.* **1** a Greek hero at the siege of Troy, second only to Achilles in strength and courage. Ajax killed himself when the armor of Achilles was awarded to Odysseus (Ulysses). **2 Ajax the Lesser**, another Greek

hero at Troy, second to Achilles in swiftness.

a|jee (ə jē′), *adv., adj. Scottish.* agee.

a|jin|gle (ə jing′gəl), *adv., adj.* jingling: *Peasant pockets were ajingle with the proceeds of the nation's fourth bumper crop* (Time).

a|jog (ə jog′), *adv., adj.* at a jog; jogging.

aj|o|wan (aj′ə wən), *n.* the fruit or seed of an Oriental plant of the parsley family, used for flavoring and to produce an aromatic oil similar to that obtained from thyme. [< a Javanese word]

aj|u|ga (aj′ə gə), *n.* = bugleweed (def. 1). [< New Latin *Ajuga* the genus name]

a|jut (ə jut′), *adj.* that juts out; projecting: *There he is, jaw ajut, teeth softly agleam, ... the whole man fairly overflowing with aplomb* (Newsweek).

aj|u|tage (aj′ə tij), *n.* = adjutage.

a|jut|ment (ə jut′mənt), *n.* = projection.

AK (no period), Alaska (with postal Zip Code).

a.k.a. or **AKA** (no periods), also known as.

a|ka|mai (ä kä mī′), *adj. Hawaiian.* clever; smart.

A|kan (ä′kän), *n., pl.* **A|kan** or **A|kans.** **1** a group of peoples inhabiting Ghana and other parts of western Africa. **2** the Kwa language of these peoples.

a|ke|bi (ä′kā bē), *n.* **1** a hardy Asiatic vine with dark-green leaves. **2** a fiber derived from it, used in making baskets. **3** its seeds, which yield an oil sometimes used in cooking. [< a Japanese word]

ak|ee (ak′ē, ə kē′), *n.* = ackee.

A|ke|la (ə kē′lə), *n.* a title given by cub scouts to a cubmaster or den mother. [< *Akela,* the leader of the wolves in *The Jungle Book,* by Rudyard Kipling]

a|kene (ā kēn′), *n.* = achene.

* **a|kim|bo** (ə kim′bō), *adj., adv.* with the hands on the hips and the elbows bent outward: *to stand with arms akimbo.* [Middle English *in kenebowe,* perhaps, in keen bow, at a sharp angle]

***akimbo**

a|kin (ə kin′), *adj., adv.* **—*adj.*** **1** of the same kind; alike; similar: *Most boys are akin in their love of sports.* **2** belonging to the same family; related by blood: *Your cousins are akin to you.* **3** cognate. SYN: analogous. **—*adv.*** of kin.
[for *of kin*]
▶As an adjective, **akin** is used only as a complement. **Kin**, not **akin**, is used in technical anthropology.

ak|i|ne|sia (ak′ə nē′zhə), *n. Medicine.* the complete or partial loss of the power to move. [< Greek *akīnēsíā* quiescence < *a-* without + *kī́nēsis* motion]

ak|i|net|ic (ak′ə net′ik), *adj.* of or characterized by akinesia.

A|ki|ta (ä kē′tä), *n.* any of a breed of medium-sized dogs of Japan, with a sharp nose and pointed ears. [< *Akita,* a city in northern Japan]

Ak|ka|di|an (ə kā′dē ən, -kä′-), *n., adj.* **—*n.*** **1** the eastern division of the Semitic languages, spoken during ancient times in Mesopotamia. **2** any language of this division, such as Assyrian. **3** the ancient non-Semitic language of Babylonia; Sumerian. **4** one of the ancient inhabitants of Akkad (northern Babylonia).
—*adj.* **1** of Akkad. **2** of or in the Semitic language of the Akkadians. **3** Sumerian. Also, **Accadian.**

ak|ro|te|ri|on (ak′rə tir′ē ən), *n., pl.* **-te|ri|a** (-tir′ē ə). = acroterium. [< Greek *akrōtḗrion;* see etym. under **acroterium**]

Ak|ti|vist (äk ti vist′), *n., pl.* **-vis|ten** (-vis′tən). (in East Germany) a worker who exceeds his quota; Stakhanovite. [< German *Aktivist* (literally) activist]

ak|to|graph (ak′tə graf, -gräf), *n.* an apparatus for recording the period or frequency of an animal's activity. [< German *Aktograph* < *Akt* act + *-graph* graph]

ak|u (äk′ü), *n. Hawaiian.* the bonito or skipjack, related to tuna.

a|kva|vit (ä′kvä vēt′, äk′vä vēt), *n.* = aquavit.

al-, *prefix.* the form of **ad-** before *l,* as in *allure, ally.*

-al[1], *suffix added to nouns to form adjectives.* of; like; having the nature of: *Natural = of nature; like nature. Ornamental = having the nature of ornament.* [< Latin *-ālis* having to do with]

-al[2], *suffix added to verbs to form nouns.* the act of ___ing: *Arrival = the act of arriving. Refusal = the act of refusing.* [< Latin *-ālia,* neuter plural of *-ālis*]

Al (no period), aluminum (chemical element).

AL (no periods), **1** Alabama (with postal Zip Code). **2** or **AL.**, Anglo-Latin. **3** *Baseball.* American League.

A.L., Anglo-Latin.

a|la (ā′lə), *n., pl.* **a|lae** (ā′lē). **1** a wing. **2** any winglike structure: **a** one of the lateral cartilages of the nose. **b** one of the two side petals of any flower shaped like a sweet pea. **3** an armpit. [< Latin *āla*]

a la or **à la** (ä′ lə; *French* à là), in the manner of; in the style of: *If we are talking about a massed conventional aggression à la World War II, aerial inspection can provide adequate warning* (Bulletin of Atomic Scientists). [< French *à la*]
▶**a la, à la.** Although originally French, *a la* is now regarded as an English preposition: *a la Hollywood.* In formal writing and some advertising (for cosmetics and fashionable clothes), the French spelling is usually used: *à la.*

Ala., Alabama.

ALA (no periods), American Library Association.

A.L.A. Australian Library Association.

al|a|ba|do (al′ə bä′dō; *Spanish* ä lä bä′dō), *n., pl.* **-dos.** (in Mexico) a religious ballad or folk song. [< Spanish *alabado* praised < *alabar* to praise]

Al|a|bam|a (al′ə bam′ə), *n., pl.* **-bam|a** or **-bam|as.** **1** a member of a Muskhogean tribe of Indians, now living mostly in Texas. **2** this tribe. **3** the language of this tribe. [American English < Choctaw *alba ayamule* I clear the thicket]

Al|a|bam|an (al′ə bam′ən), *adj., n.* **—*adj.*** of or having to do with Alabama or its people.
—*n.* a native or inhabitant of Alabama.

Al|a|bam|i|an (al′ə bam′ē ən), *adj., n.* = Alabaman.

al|a|bam|ine (al′ə bam′ēn, -in), *n.* a rare, unisolated chemical element, now called astatine. [< *Alabama* + *-ine*[2]]

al|a|bas|ter (al′ə bas′tər, -bäs′-), *n., adj.* **—*n.*** **1** a smooth, white or delicately shaded, translucent stone, a variety of gypsum. Alabaster is considered a soft stone, often carved into ornaments and vases. **2** a variety of calcite that is somewhat translucent and often streaked like marble.
—*adj.* **1** made of alabaster: *an alabaster vase.* **2** *Figurative.* smooth and white like alabaster: *her alabaster throat.*
[< Latin *alabaster* < Greek *alábastros* (alabaster) vase]

al|a|bas|trine (al′ə bas′trin, -bäs′-), *adj.* of or resembling alabaster.

à la belle é|toile (à là bel′ ā twàl′), *French.* **1** in the open air at night. **2** (literally) at the beautiful star.

à la bonne heure (à là bô nœr′), *French.* **1** all right; splendid. **2** (literally) at the good hour.

à la carte (ä′ lə kärt′; *French* à là kàrt′), with a stated price for each dish (instead of one price for the whole meal, *table d'hôte* or *prix fixe*): *There is only one menu at Chez Paugé, and all the dishes are à la carte* (Craig Claiborne). [< French *à la carte* according to the bill of fare]

à la chi|noise (à là shē nwàz′), *French.* in the Chinese style.

a|lack (ə lak′), *interj. Archaic.* an exclamation of sorrow or regret; alas: *Alack! our friend is gone* (Tennyson). [Middle English *alacke*]

a|lack|a|day (ə lak′ə dā′), *interj. Archaic.* alack; alas.

a|lac|ri|tous (ə lak′rə təs), *adj.* full of alacrity; brisk. SYN: quick, prompt, lively, willing.

a|lac|ri|ty (ə lak′rə tē), *n.* **1** brisk and eager action; liveliness: *Although the man was very old, he still moved with alacrity.* SYN: celerity, briskness, sprightliness. **2** prompt and cheerful willingness: *He accepted with grateful alacrity* (Scott). SYN: eagerness. [< Latin *alacritās* < *alacer, -cris* brisk]

A|lad|din (ə lad′ən), *n.* a youth in *The Arabian Nights,* who found a magic lamp and a magic ring. By rubbing either one of them he could call either of two powerful spirits (jinn) to do whatever he asked.

a|lae (ā′lē), *n.* plural of **ala.**

à la fran|çaise (à là fräɴ sez′), *French.* in the French style.

à la grecque (à là grek′), *French.* in the Greek style.

à la ja|po|naise (à là zhà po nez′), *French.* in the Japanese style.

à la king (ä′ lə king′), creamed with pimento, green pepper, and mushrooms: *chicken à la king.*

a|la|li|a (ə lā′lē ə), *n.* a partial or total loss of the power of speech, due to a functional disorder. [< *a-*[4] without + Greek *laliā́* (act of) talking]

Al|a|man|ni (al′ə män′nē), *n.* = Alemanni.

al|a|me|da (al′ə mā′də, -mē′-), *n. Southwestern U.S.* a public walk shaded with poplars or other trees. [< Spanish *alameda* < *álamo* poplar tree, alamo]

à l'a|mé|ri|caine (à là mā′rē ken′), *French.* in the American style: *The moon ... is where French businessmen think guaranteed wages à l'américaine belong* (New Yorker).

al|a|mo (al′ə mō, ä′lə-), *n., pl.* **-mos.** *Southwestern U.S.* a poplar tree, especially a cottonwood. [American English < Spanish *álamo;* origin uncertain]

a|la|mode (*n.* al′ə mōd; *adv., adj.* ä′lə mōd′, al′ə-), *n., adv., adj.* **—*n.*** a lightweight, glossy silk, used especially for scarfs.
—*adv., adj.* = à la mode.

à la mode or **a la mode** (ä′ lə mōd′, al′ ə), **1** according to the prevailing fashion; in style; fashionable. **2** served with ice cream: *pie à la mode.* **3** cooked with vegetables: *beef à la mode.* [< French *à la mode* in the fashion]

al|a|mort (al ə môrt′), *adj.* **1** in a half-dead condition. **2** melancholy; spiritless. [< French *à la mort*]

à la New|burg (ä′ lə nü′bėrg, nyü′-), served in a rich white sauce made with cream, yolks of eggs, butter, and wine or flavoring.

à l'an|glaise (à läɴ glez′) *French.* in the English style: *... red plush carpets and a winter garden and five-o'clock tea à l'anglaise* (New Yorker).

A|la|ni (ə lā′nī), *n.pl.* a people of Scythian origin who lived in the Caucasus and fought on the side of the Huns and the Vandals.

al|a|nine (al′ə nēn, -nin), *n.* a crystalline amino acid, occurring in several proteins. *Formula:* $C_3H_7NO_2$ [< *al*(dehyde) + inserted *-an-* + *-ine*[2]]

Al|a|ouite (al ə wit′), *n.* = Alawite.

a|lap (ä läp′), *n.* the rhythmless introductory section of a raga: *This was the percussionless alap in Desh Malhar, a raga tuned to the rains* (London Times). [< Sanskrit *alāp*]

à la page (à là pàzh′), *French.* up-to-date; modern.

à la pa|ri|sienne (à là pà rē zyen′), *French.* in the Parisian style.

a|lar (ā′lər), *adj.* **1** of or like a wing or wings; alary. **2** winged; alate. **3** = axillary. [< Latin *ālāris* < *āla* a wing]

à la ri|gueur (à là rē gœr′), *French.* strictly speaking; if absolutely necessary.

a|larm (ə lärm′), *n., v.* **—*n.*** **1** sudden fear; excitement caused by fear of danger; fright: *The deer darted off in alarm.* SYN: apprehension; consternation. See syn. under **fear.** **2** a warning of approaching danger: *This is no false alarm.* **3a** a signal giving such warning: *a fire alarm.* **b** a bell or other device that makes a noise to warn or waken people: *a burglar alarm.* **4** a call to arms or action: *Paul Revere gave the alarm to the towns near Boston.* **5** *Fencing.* appel.
—*v.t.* **1** to make uneasy; fill with sudden fear; frighten: *The breaking of a branch under my foot alarmed the deer. He was alarmed because his friends were so long in returning.* SYN: See syn. under **frighten.** **2** to warn (anyone) of approaching danger: *Alarm everyone quickly; the house is full of smoke.* **3** *Obsolete.* to call to arms.
[< Old French *alarme* < Italian *allarme* < *all'arme!* to arms!]

alarm clock, a clock that can be set to ring or sound at any desired time.

a|larm|ing (ə lär′ming), *adj.* causing alarm; frightening: *He failed to show any sense of urgency in dealing with a situation that has become so acute and alarming* (London Times). **—a|larm′ing|ly,** *adv.*

a|larm|ism (ə lär′miz əm), *n.* the attitude and habits of alarmists.

a|larm|ist (ə lär′mist), *n., adj.* **—*n.*** a person who is easily alarmed or alarms others needlessly or on very slight grounds: *The alarmists cry out that there is a danger of World War Three* (Wall Street Journal).
—*adj.* of or having to do with an alarmist or alarmism.

a|lar|um (ə lar′əm, -lär′-), *n. British or Archaic.* alarm.

a|lar|ums and excursions (ə lar′əmz, -lär′-), an archaic stage direction for a conventionalized skirmish.

à la russe (à là rʏs′), *French.* in the Russian style.

a|la|ry (ā′lər ē, al′ər-), *adj.* **1** of or having to do with wings; alar. **2** wing-shaped. [< Latin *ālārius* < *āla* wing]

a|las (ə las′, -läs′), *interj.* an exclamation of sorrow, grief, regret, pity, dread, or concern: *Alas! poor Yorick* (Shakespeare). [< Old French *a* ah + *las* miserable < Latin *lassus* weary]

Alas., Alaska.

a|las|ka (ə las′kə), *n.* **1** a type of wool and cotton yarn. **2** *British.* a dress or coating fabric made of

---

Pronunciation Key: hat, āge, cãre, fär; let, ēqual, tėrm; it, īce; hot, ōpen, ôrder; oil, out; cup, pu̇t, rüle; child; long; thin; ᴛʜen; zh, measure; ə represents **a** in about, **e** in taken, **i** in pencil, **o** in lemon, **u** in circus.

this yarn. [< *Alaska,* the state]

Alaska cod, a species of cod found in the northern Pacific ocean.

A|las|kan (ə las′kən), *adj., n.* **—*adj.*** of or having to do with Alaska or its people.
—*n.* a native or inhabitant of Alaska.

Alaskan king crab = king crab (def. 2).

Alaskan malamute, any one of an Alaskan breed of large, strong dogs having a gray, or black and white, coat and commonly used for pulling sleds. Also **malamute, malemute, malemiut.** [< an Eskimo word]

Alaska Standard Time, the standard time in central Alaska, and all of Hawaii, two hours behind Pacific Standard Time.
▶*Hawaii Standard Time* and *Alaska Standard Time* are names used in different areas of the same time zone.

A|las|tor (ə las′tər), *n.* **1** *Greek Mythology.* an epithet of Zeus in the capacity of avenger. **2** (in medieval demonology) the executor of the sentence to kill.

a|las|trim (ə las′trim), *n.* a contagious eruptive fever, regarded as a mild form of smallpox. [< Portuguese *alastrar* to spread]

a|late (ā′lāt), *adj.* having wings or winglike parts; winged; alar. [< Latin *ālātus* < *āla* wing]

a|lat|ed (ā′lā tid), *adj.* = alate.

a|la|tion (ā lā′shən), *n.* **1** winged condition or form. **2** the manner in which wings are formed or placed, as in insects.

Al|a|wi (al′ə wē), *n.* = Alawite.

Al|a|wite (al ə wit′), *n.* one of a Moslem sect in Syria that regards Ali, the son-in-law of Mohammed, as the true successor of Mohammed. Also, **Alaouite.**

alb (alb), *n.* a white linen robe with narrow sleeves, worn by Roman Catholic and some Anglican priests at the Communion service. [< Late Latin *alba* < Latin *vestis alba* white robe]

Alb., **1** Albanian. **2** Albany. **3** Albert. **4** Alberta (Canada; not in official use).

al|ba[1] (äl′bə, al′-), *n.* a traditional Provençal song, usually describing the parting of lovers at dawn. [< Old Provençal *alba* dawn < Vulgar Latin *alba lūx* white light]

al|ba[2] (al′bə), *n.* the white tissue of the brain. [< New Latin *alba,* feminine of Latin *albus* white]

Alba., Alberta (Canada; not in official use).

al|ba|core (al′bə kôr, -kōr), *n., pl.* **-cores** or (*collectively*) **-core. 1** a large fish related to the tuna, with long pectoral fins; germon. It has light-colored flesh valued for canning and is found in all tropical seas. **2** any of various related marine food or game fishes. Also, **albicore.** [< Portuguese *albacora* < Arabic *al-bakura*]

Al|ba|ni|an (al bā′nē ən, -bān′yən), *adj., n.* **—*adj.*** of or having to do with Albania, a European country between Yugoslavia and Greece, its people, their language, or their way of life.
—*n.* 1 a native or inhabitant of Albania, the European country. **2** the language of Albania, a member of the Indo-European family.

al|ba|ta (al bā′tə), *n.* = German silver. [< Latin *albāta* clothed in white < *albus* white]

***al|ba|tross** (al′bə trôs, -tros), *n., pl.* **-tros|ses** or (*collectively*) **-tross. 1** a very large, web-footed sea bird related to the petrels. The albatross is the largest ocean bird and can fly long distances. **2** *Figurative.* a great or intolerable burden: *The Turks carefully hung the albatross of responsibility around Washington's neck* (Atlantic). [variant of obsolete *alcatras* frigate bird < Portuguese *alcatraz* pelican < Arabic *al-ghaṭṭās* a sea eagle]

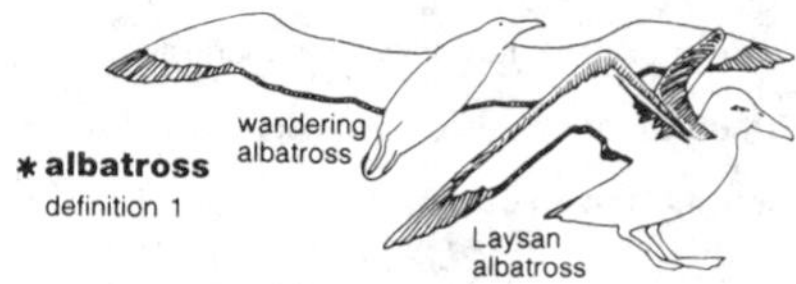

***albatross** definition 1

al|be|do (al bē′dō), *n., pl.* **-dos. 1** the ratio of light reflected to light received by a planet or other heavenly body: *Neptune's albedo, or reflecting power, is a little less than that of Venus* (E. C. Slipher). **2** *Nuclear Physics.* the ratio of the number of neutrons coming out of a medium (not itself a source) to the number of neutrons entering it. **3** the white and spongy inner part of the rind of a citrus fruit that contains the jelling substance pectin. [< Latin *albēdō* whiteness < *albus* white]

al|be|it (ôl bē′it), *conj.* although; even though; even if: *Albeit he has failed twice, he is not discouraged.* **SYN:** though, notwithstanding. [Middle English *al be it* although it be]

Al|be|marle pippin (al′bə märl), a yellowish apple with a rare winelike flavor; Yellow Newtown.

al|ber|go (äl ber′gō), *n. Italian.* an inn: *He asked one of the piazza-loungers if there were a decent hotel nearby, and got directed to a small albergo* (Harper's).

al|ber|gue (äl ber′gā), *n. Spanish.* an inn: *Albergues resemble American motels, and stand along the main highways* (Walter C. Langsam).

Al|ber|ich (äl′bər ɪʜ), *n. German Legend.* the powerful king of the dwarfs and head of the Nibelungs.

Al|ber|tan (al bėr′tən), *n., adj.* **—*n.*** a native or inhabitant of Alberta, Canada.
—*adj.* of or having to do with Alberta.

al|bert|ite (al′bər tīt), *n.* a jet-black, lustrous, bituminous mineral resembling asphalt. [< *Albert* county, New Brunswick + *-ite*[1]]

al|bes|cence (al bes′əns), *n.* a becoming white.

al|bes|cent (al bes′ənt), *adj.* becoming white; whitish; blanched. [< Latin *albēscēns, -entis,* present participle of *albēscere* become white < *albus* white]

al|bi|core (al′bə kôr, -kōr), *n., pl.* **-cores** or (*collectively*) **-core.** = albacore.

Al|bi|gen|ses (al′bə jen′sēz), *n.pl.* the members of a religious sect that originated in southern France in the 1000's. They were stigmatized as heretics and their movement was suppressed during the 1200's. [< New Latin *Albigenses* < *Albiga* Albi, a city in southern France]

Al|bi|gen|si|an (al′bə jen′sē ən, -shən), *adj., n.* **—*adj.*** of or having to do with the Albigenses.
—*n.* one of the Albigenses.

al|bin|ic (al bin′ik), *adj.* = albinistic.

al|bi|nism (al′bə niz əm), *n.* the absence of color; condition of being an albino: ... *albinism (a condition in which all pigmentation is lacking) is a recessive characteristic in man as it is in other animals* (Beals and Hoijer).

al|bi|nis|tic (al′bə nis′tik), *adj.* **1** of albinism. **2** having albinism.

al|bi|no (al bī′nō; *especially British* al bē′nō), *n., pl.* **-nos. 1** a person who from birth has a pale, milky skin, very light hair, and pink eyes with deep-red pupils, because of the absence of coloring pigment in the skin, hair, and eyes. **2** a plant or an animal with pale, defective coloring. [< Portuguese *albino* < *albo* < Latin *albus* white]

al|bi|no|ism (al bī′nō iz əm; *especially British* albē′nō iz əm), *n.* = albinism.

Al|bi|on (al′bē ən), *n. Poetic.* England: *the white cliffs of Albion.*

Al|bi|re|o (al bī′rē ō), *n.* the star representing the head of the swan in the constellation Cygnus.

al|bite (al′bīt), *n.* a feldspar, usually white, occurring in granite and other igneous rocks. *Formula:* $NaAlSi_3O_8$ [< Latin *albus* white + English *-ite*[1]]

al|bit|ic (al bit′ik), *adj.* of the nature of or containing albite.

al|bit|i|cal (al bit′ə kəl), *adj.* = albitic.

al|biz|zi|a (al bit′sē ə, -biz′ē ə), *n.* any one of a group of trees of tropical Asia and Africa, related to the acacia, and valued for its hard, strong, and durable wood. Certain species of albizzia are cultivated for ornament in Europe and America. [< New Latin *Albizzia* the genus name < *Albizzi,* name of a family of nobles in Tuscany that introduced the tree in Italy]

ALBM (no periods), air-launched ballistic missile.

al|bum (al′bəm), *n.* **1a** a book with blank pages for holding things like photographs, autographs, and postage stamps. **b** a case for a phonograph record. **c** a single, long-playing phonograph record. **2** a set of phonograph records or tape recordings. **3** a scrapbook. **4** *U.S.* a register for visitors at a public place (called a *visitors' book* in England). [< Latin *album* tablet, neuter of *albus* white]

al|bu|men (al byü′mən), *n.* **1** the white of an egg, consisting mostly of albumin dissolved in water. See diagram under **egg**[1]. **2** *Botany.* the food for a young plant stored in a seed; endosperm. **3** *Chemistry.* albumin. [< Late Latin *albūmen* < Latin *albus* white]

al|bu|men|ize (al byü′mə nīz), *v.t.,* **-ized, -iz|ing.** to treat with albumen or an albuminous solution.

al|bu|min (al byü′mən), *n. Chemistry.* a protein found in the white of an egg, milk, blood serum, lymph, and many other animal and plant tissues and juices. Albumin is composed of nitrogen, carbon, hydrogen, oxygen, and a little sulfur, especially $C_{72}H_{112}N_{18}O_{22}S$. It is soluble in water and can be coagulated by heat. [< French *albumine* < Late Latin *albūmen, -inis* white of egg < Latin *albus* white]

al|bu|mi|nate (al byü′mə nāt), *n.* **1** a nearly insoluble protein resulting from the action of an alkali or an acid upon albumin. **2** a compound formed by the union of an albumin, as with a metal.

al|bu|min|i|za|tion (al byü′mə nə zā′shən), *n.* the act or process of albuminizing.

al|bu|min|ize (al byü′mə nīz), *v.t.,* **-ized, -iz|ing. 1** to change into albumin. **2** to treat with albumin; albumenize. **—al|bu′min|i|za′tion,** *n.* **—al|bu′min|iz′er,** *n.*

al|bu|mi|noid (al byü′mə noid), *n., adj.* **—*n.*** a substance like albumin; a protein. Albuminoids are obtained chiefly from animal connective tissues and bones, and are characterized by insolubility.
—*adj.* like albumin.

al|bu|mi|noi|dal (al byü′mə noi′dəl), *adj.* of the nature of an albuminoid.

al|bu|mi|nose (al byü′mə nōs), *adj.* = albuminous.

al|bu|mi|nous (al byü′mə nəs), *adj.* **1** of or like albumin. **2** containing albumin.

al|bu|mi|nu|ri|a (al byü′mə nůr′ē ə, -nyůr′-), *n.* the presence of albumin in the urine. [< Late Latin *albūmen, -inis* albumen + English *-uria*]

al|bu|mi|nu|ric (al byü′mə nůr′ik, -nyůr′-), *adj.* causing or characterized by albuminuria.

al|bu|mose (al′byə mōs), *n.* a compound derived from albumins by the action of proteolytic enzymes; proteose. [< *album(in)* + *-ose*[2]]

al|bur|nous (al bėr′nəs), *adj.* of or like alburnum.

al|bur|num (al bėr′nəm), *n.* the lighter, softer, and more recently formed wood between the inner bark and the harder center, or heartwood, of a tree; sapwood. [< Latin *alburnum* < *albus* white]

al|ca|hest (al′kə hest), *n.* = alkahest.

Al|ca|ics (al kā′iks), *n.pl.* Alcaic lines or stanzas.

Al|ca|ic stanza (al kā′ik), a four-line stanza of 11-11-9-10 syllables invented by the Greek poet Alcaeus and later modified by the Roman poet Horace. Example:

O mighty-mouth'd inventor of harmonies,
O skill'd to sing of Time or Eternity,
God-gifted organ-voice of England,
Milton, a name to resound for ages.
(Tennyson)

al|caide or **al|cayde** (al kād′; *Spanish* äl kī′ᴛʜā), *n.* **1** a commander of a Spanish fortress. **2** a warden of a Spanish prison. [< Spanish *alcaide* < Arabic *al-qā'id* the commander]
▶**Alcaide** is sometimes confused with **alcalde**, with respect to both spelling and meaning, but, unlike *alcalde, alcaide* is seldom, if ever, used of a person in a country where Spanish (or, less often, Portuguese) is not the dominant language.

al|cal|de (al kal′dē; *Spanish* äl käl′dā), *n.* **1** *U.S.* a mayor or justice of the peace (in regions of former Spanish influence). **2** the mayor of a Spanish or Portuguese town who also has the powers of a judge. [< Spanish *alcalde* < Arabic *al-qāḍī* the judge]

al|can|na (al kan′ə), *n.* henna, especially the shrub from which the coloring matter is obtained. [< Spanish *alcana* < Arabic *al-ḥinnā'*]

al|cap|ton (al kap′tən), *n.* = alkapton.

al|cap|to|nu|ri|a (al kap′tə nůr′ē ə, -nyůr′-), *n.* = alkaptonuria.

al|ca|zar (al′kə zär, al kaz′ər; *Spanish* äl kä′thär), *n.* a palace, castle, or fortress in Spain, originally of the Spanish Moors. [< Spanish *alcázar* < Arabic *al-qasr* the castle < Latin *castrum* fort]

Al|ca|zar (al′kə zär, al kaz′ər; *Spanish* äl kä′thär), *n.* a palace of the Moorish kings at Seville, Spain. It was later occupied by the Spanish royal family.

Al|ces|tis (al ses′tis), *n. Greek Legend.* the wife of King Admetus, whose life she saved by sacrificing her own with such rare wifely devotion that Hercules rescued her from Hades, and thus restored her to life.

al|chem|ic (al kem′ik), *adj.* = alchemistic.

al|chem|i|cal (al kem′ə kəl), *adj.* of alchemy or alchemists; alchemistic. **—al|chem′i|cal|ly,** *adv.*

al|che|mist (al′kə mist), *n.* **1** a person who studied a combination of chemistry and magic in the Middle Ages. **2** *Figurative.* a person with great and often seemingly mysterious power to affect the course of events or to change one thing into another.

al|che|mis|tic (al′kə mis′tik), *adj.* of or having to do with alchemy or alchemists.

al|che|mis|ti|cal (al′kə mis′tə kəl), *adj.* = alchemistic.

al|che|mize (al′kə mīz), *v.t.,* **-mized, -miz|ing.** to transmute by alchemy; transform.

al|che|my (al′kə mē), *n.* **1** a combination of chemistry, magic, and philosophy, studied in the Middle Ages. Alchemy tried to find or prepare a substance which would turn cheaper metals into gold and silver and which would also cure any ailment and prolong human life. *In its fullest sense alchemy was a philosophical system containing a complex and mobile core of rudimentary science and elaborated with astrology, religion, mysticism, magic, theosophy and many other constituents. Alchemy dealt not only with the mysteries of matter but also with those of creation and life; it sought to harmonize the human individual with the universe surrounding him* (Scientific American). **2** *Figurative.* a magical or mysterious power or process of transforming one thing into another: *the lovely alchemy of spring.* [< Old French *alkemie,* learned borrowing from Medieval Latin *alchimia* < Arabic *alkīmiyā'* <

Late Greek *chymeíā* art of alloying metals < Greek *chýma* ingot < *cheîn* pour]

Al|ci|des (al sī'dēz), *n. Greek Legend.* Hercules.

al|ci|dine (al'sə dīn, -din), *adj.* of or like the family of birds that includes the auks and puffins. [< New Latin *Alcidae* the auk family < Scandinavian (compare Old Icelandic *ālka* auk) + English *-ine*[1]]

ALCM (no periods), air-launched cruise missile.

Alc|me|ne (alk mē'nē), *n. Greek Legend.* the mother of Hercules, by Zeus, and wife of Amphitryon.

al|co|hol (al'kə hôl, -hol), *n.* **1** the colorless liquid in wine, beer, whiskey, gin, and other fermented and distilled liquors that makes them intoxicating; grain alcohol; ethyl alcohol; ethanol. Alcohol is used in medicines, in manufacturing, and as a fuel. It is commercially prepared from grain, potatoes, and molasses. *Formula:* C_2H_5OH **2** whiskey, gin, or any other intoxicating liquor containing this liquid. **3** *Chemistry.* any of a group of similar organic compounds. Alcohols contain a hydroxyl group and react with certain acids to form esters. Wood alcohol or methyl alcohol, CH_3OH, is very poisonous. [< Medieval Latin *alcohol* (originally) fine powder, (later) essence < Arabic *al-kuhl* powdered antimony]

al|co|hol|ate (al'kə hôl āt, -hol-), *n.* **1** an alcohol in which the hydrogen of the hydroxyl is replaced by a metal. **2** a compound or solution containing alcohol.

alcohol dehydrogenase, an enzyme found in yeast and liver, essential to the metabolism and production of alcohols.

al|co|hol|ic (al'kə hôl'ik, -hol'-), *adj., n.* —*adj.* **1** of alcohol: *alcoholic fumes. This wine has a high alcoholic content.* **2** containing alcohol: *Whiskey and gin are alcoholic liquors.* **3** caused by alcohol: *alcoholic dehydration.* **4** suffering from the excessive use of intoxicating liquors; having alcoholism: *More than 75 per cent of . . . alcoholic patients have benefited from the drug [meprobamate] during the withdrawal period* (Newsweek).

—*n.* a person who has the habit of drinking too much intoxicating liquor: *An alcoholic is one whose drinking harmfully and definitely interferes with his job standing and ability, his reputation or his home life* (Marguerite Clark).

al|co|hol|i|cal|ly (al'kə hôl'ə klē, -hol'-), *adv.* in an alcoholic manner; after the manner of alcohol.

al|co|hol|ic|i|ty (al'kə hô lis'ə tē, -ho-), *n.* alcoholic quality.

al|co|hol|ism (al'kə hô liz'əm, -ho-), *n.* **1** a disease which has as its chief symptom the inability to stop drinking alcoholic liquors to excess: *The only effective cure for alcoholism comes through personal and social psychotherapy* (Floyd L. Ruch). **2** a diseased condition of the body caused by drinking too much alcoholic liquor. **3** alcohol poisoning.

al|co|hol|ize (al'kə hôl īz, -hol-), *v.t.,* **-ized, -iz|ing.** **1** to change into alcohol. **2** to add alcohol to. **3** to make drunk; intoxicate. —**al'co|hol'i|za'tion,** *n.*

al|co|hol|om|e|ter (al'kə hô lom'ə tər, -ho-), *n.* an instrument for finding the percentage of alcohol in a liquid. It is a type of hydrometer.

al|co|hol|y|sis (al'kə hôl'ə sis, -hol'-), *n.* decomposition by the action of alcohol. [< *alcohol* + *lysis*]

al|com|e|ter (al kom'ə tər), *n. U.S.* a drunkometer. [< *alco*(hol) + *meter*]

Al|cor (al kôr'), *n.* a star, visible to the naked eye, in Ursa Major. Alcor is the smaller partner star of Mizar.

Al|co|ran (al'kō rän', -ran'), *n.* the Koran. [< Old French *alcoran* < Arabic *al-qur'ān* the Koran]

Al|co|ran|ic (al'kō ran'ik), *adj.* **1** of or having to do with the Koran. **2** of or having to do with Islamic theology.

al|co|sol (al'kə sol, -sōl), *n. Chemistry.* a colloidal solution in alcohol.

al|cove (al'kōv), *n.* **1** a small room or recess opening out of a larger room. SYN: nook. **2** a recess or large, hollow space in a wall. SYN: niche. **3** *Archaic.* a bower; summerhouse. [< French *alcôve* < Spanish *alcoba* < Arabic *al-qubba* the vaulted chamber]

al|cy|on (al'sē ən), *adj., n.* = halcyon.

Al|cy|o|ne (al sī'ə nē), *n.* **1** *Greek Mythology.* **a** the daughter of Aeolus. She was changed into a kingfisher. **b** one of the Pleiades. **2** the brightest star in the Pleiades. [< Latin *Alcyonē* < Greek *Alkyónē* < *alkyṓn, -ónos* sea kingfisher]

Ald., alderman.

Al|deb|a|ran (al deb'ər ən), *n.* a red star, the brightest star in the constellation Taurus. [< Arabic *al-dabarān* the follower (that is, of the Pleiades)]

al|de|hyde (al'də hīd), *n.* **1** any one of a group of organic chemical compounds having the radical CHO, derived from the primary alcohols by oxidation, and yielding acids on further oxidation. Formaldehyde is an aldehyde produced by the oxidation of methyl alcohol. **2** a transparent, colorless liquid with a characteristic smell, produced by the partial oxidation of ordinary alcohol; acetaldehyde. *Formula:* CH_3CHO [< New Latin *al*(cohol) *dehyd*(rogenatum) dehydrogenized alcohol]

al|de|hy|dic (al'də hī'dik), *adj.* **1** of the nature of aldehydes. **2** resembling the aldehydes.

al den|te (äl den'tā), *Italian.* firm to the tooth; cooked so as not to be too soft: *The ravioli were well made, but they were far too al dente and served lukewarm* (Craig Claiborne).

***al|der** (ôl'dər), *n.* a tree or shrub somewhat like a birch. Alders usually grow in wet land and have clusters of catkins that develop into small, woody cones. The light, soft wood is used in cabinetwork; the bark is used for tanning and dyeing. [< Old English *alor*]

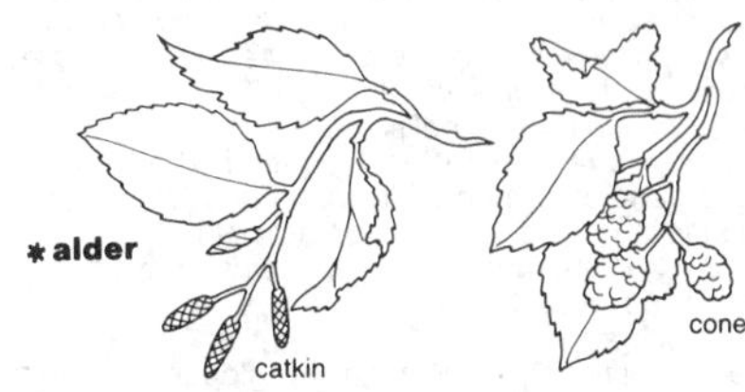

***alder**

al|der|man (ôl'dər mən), *n., pl.* **-men.** **1** (in certain cities of the United States) a member of a council that governs a city. An alderman is usually elected by the voters of a certain ward or district and represents them on the council. **2** (in English and Irish cities and boroughs) a senior elected councilor who ranks next to the mayor in importance: *The aldermen and councilors followed the Lord Mayor in the procession to the Cathedral.* **3** (in Anglo-Saxon times) a chief or lord. [Old English *ealdormann* < *ealdor* elder, chief + *mann* man]

al|der|man|cy (ôl'dər mən sē), *n.* the office of alderman; aldermanship.

al|der|man|ic (ôl'dər man'ik), *adj.* **1** of or like an alderman. **2** suitable for an alderman.

al|der|man|ry (ôl'dər mən rē), *n., pl.* **-ries.** *U.S.* a ward or district represented by an alderman.

al|der|man|ship (ôl'dər mən ship), *n.* the office of alderman.

Al|der|ney (ôl'dər nē), *n., pl.* **-neys.** any one of a breed of dairy cattle that originated in Alderney (one of the Channel Islands).

Al|dine (ôl'dīn, -dēn), *adj., n.* —*adj.* **1** printed or published by Aldus Manutius of Venice or his family (mainly between 1494 and 1597). **2a** printed or designed in imitation of the books printed or the type faces used by this family. **b** bound in the manner of Aldus.

—*n.* an edition, book, or style of type in the Aldine manner.

Aldm., alderman.

al|dol|ase (al'də lās), *n.* an enzyme occurring in muscle tissue. [< *ald*(ehyde) + *-ol*[1] + *-ase*]

al|dose (al'dōs), *n.* a sugar containing any one of a group of organic chemical compounds having the radical CHO and the OH radical on the C atom adjacent to the CHO group. [< *ald*(ehyde) + *-ose*[2]]

al|dos|te|rone (al dos'tə rōn), *n.* a hormone of the adrenal cortex which controls the salt and water balance in the body; electrocortin. [< *ald*(ehyde) + *ster*(ol) + *-one*]

al|dos|te|ron|ism (al dos'tər ə niz'əm), *n. Medicine.* a hormonal imbalance, with the symptoms of hypertension and muscular weakness, and characterized by excessive retention of sodium and excessive loss of potassium.

al|drin (al'drin), *n.* a very powerful insecticide derived from naphthalene, effective against insects that infest the soil, such as locusts and grasshoppers. *Formula:* $C_{12}H_8Cl_6$ [< Diels-*Ald*(e)*r* reaction (an important organic reaction) + *-in*]

ale (āl), *n.* a strong beer made by fermentation from malt and flavored with hops. Ale is heavier and more bitter and contains more alcohol than other beer. *I would give all my fame for a pot of ale and safety* (Shakespeare). [Old English *alu*]

a|leak (ə lēk'), *adv., adj.* leaking.

a|le|a|tor|ic (ā'lē ə tôr'ik, -tor'-), *adj. Music.* consisting of random or chance elements: *Aleatoric music is that in which the instrumentalists have complete leeway . . . to finish the thoughts of the composer* (New York Times). [< Latin *āleātōrius* aleatory + English *-ic*]

a|le|a|to|ry (ā'lē ə tôr'ē, -tōr'-), *adj., n.* —*adj.* **1** dependent on an uncertain event; contingent. **2** having to do with good or bad luck. **3** = aleatoric.

—*n.* aleatoric music: *Improvisation is one form of aleatory* (New York Times).

[< Latin *āleātōrius* < *āleātor* dice player < *ālea* a gambling game with dice]

a|lec|i|thal (ə les'ə thəl), *adj.* having little or no yolk: *alecithal eggs.* [< *a-* [4] without + Greek *lékithos* yolk + English *-al*[1]]

ale|con|ner (āl'kon'ər), *n.* **1** an inspector of measures in English public houses (pubs). **2** *Historical.* an official who tasted ale and beer to determine their quality or purity. [Middle English *ale* ale + *conner,* Old English *cunnere* examiner]

A|lec|to (ə lek'tō), *n. Greek and Roman Mythology.* one of the three Furies. (Megaera and Tisiphone were the other two.)

a|lec|try|o|man|cy (ə lek'trē ə man'sē), *n.* divination by means of a rooster picking up grains of corn. [< Greek *alektryṓn* rooster + *manteíā* divination]

a|lee (ə lē'), *adv., adj.* on or toward the side of a ship that is away from the wind. SYN: leeward, lee. [< Scandinavian (compare Old Icelandic *ā hlē* < *ā* on + *hlē* shelter, lee)]

a|lef (ä'ləf, ā'-), *n.* = aleph.

ale|house (āl'hous'), *n.* a place where ale or beer is sold to be drunk on the premises; bar; public house; pub.

Al|e|man|ni (al'ə män'nē), *n.* a group of Germanic tribes that occupied the region from the Main to the Danube in the first part of the 200's A.D. Also, **Alamanni.**

Al|e|man|nic (al'ə man'ik), *n.* a High German dialect spoken in southwestern Germany, Alsace, and Switzerland.

a|lem|bic (ə lem'bik), *n.* **1** a glass or metal container, formerly used in chemistry for distilling. **2** *Figurative.* something that transforms or refines: *Imagination is the alembic of the mind.* [< Medieval Latin *alambicus* < Arabic *al-'anbīq* the still < Late Greek *ámbīx, -īkos* alembic < Greek, vessel narrowing toward the brim]

a|lem|bi|cate (ə lem'bə kāt), *v.t.,* **-cat|ed, -cat|ing.** to distill in an alembic.

A|len|çon (ə len'sən, -son), *n.,* or **Alençon lace,** **1** a fine needle-point lace made by hand in France. **2** a reproduction of it made by machine. [< *Alençon,* a city in France]

a|leph (ä'ləf, ā'-), *n.* the first letter of the Hebrew alphabet, representing a glottal stop. Also, **alef.** [< Hebrew *'āleph* (literally) ox]

a|leph-null (ä'ləf nul', ā'-), *n.* the cardinal number of an infinite set of whole numbers.

A|lep|po boil (ə lep'ō), = Oriental sore.

Aleppo pine, a pine native to southern Europe and the Near East, whose wood has been used for shipbuilding since very ancient times. [< *Aleppo,* a city in Syria]

a|lerce (ə lėrs'), *n.* **1** a large pine that resembles the California redwood. **2** the wood used by the Moors in their buildings, obtained from the sandarac tree of Morocco. [< Spanish *alerce* < Arabic *al-'arz* the cedar]

a|lert (ə lėrt'), *adj., n., v.* —*adj.* **1** watchful and keen; wide-awake: *A good hunting dog is alert to every sound and movement in the field.* SYN: attentive, vigilant. See syn. under **watchful.** **2** quick in action; lively; nimble: *A sparrow is very alert in its movements.* SYN: brisk, active. **3** ready to speak, think, or act.

—*n.* **1** a signal warning of approaching enemy aircraft, a hurricane, or other threatening danger. **2** the period of time after this warning until the danger has passed: *The hurricane alert is over.* **3** a signal, especially to troops, to be ready for action.

—*v.t.* **1** to warn against and prepare for an air attack, a hurricane, or other threatening danger. **2** to call to arms; notify (troops, police, or other forces) to get ready for action. **3** to make alert; warn: *Despite alerted antiaircraft and fighter defenses, the Liberators pressed home low-level attack through oil fires and intense smoke, wrecking the refineries* (Time).

on the alert, ready at any instant for what is coming; on the lookout; wide-awake; watchful: *A sentry must be on the alert. The Government is on the alert and will take the necessary steps to maintain security and stability* (London Times).

[< French *alerte* < Italian *all'erta* on the watch] —**a|lert'ly,** *adv.* —**a|lert'ness,** *n.*

à l'es|pa|gnole (à les pà nyōl'), *French.* in the Spanish style.

a|leu|ki|a (ə lü'kē ə), *n.* diminution or absence of leucocytes from the blood. [< New Latin *aleukia* < *a-* without + *leuk-* white (cell) + *-ia* -y[3]]

a|leu|ro|man|cy (ə lůr'ə man'sē), *n.* divination by meal or flour, practiced by the ancients. [< French *aleuromancie* < Greek *áleuron* flour +

Pronunciation Key: hat, āge, cãre, fär; let, ēqual, tėrm; it, īce; hot, ōpen, ôrder; oil, out; cup, pu̇t, rüle; child; long; thin; ᴛʜen; zh, measure; ə represents **a** in about, **e** in taken, **i** in pencil, **o** in lemon, **u** in circus.

manteiā divination]

a|leu|ro|nat (ə lůr′ə nat), *n.* flour made of aleurone, used especially in making bread for diabetic persons. [< *aleurone*]

a|leu|rone (ə lůr′ōn, al′yə rōn), *n.* a mixture of minute protein granules found in seeds and grains. [< Greek *áleuron* flour < *aleîn* grind]

aleurone grains, granules of protein that form a single layer of cells comprising the outer cellular layer of the endosperm.

a|leu|ron|ic (al′yə ron′ik), *adj.* of or having to do with aleurone.

Al|e|ut (al′ē üt), *n.* **1** one of an Eskimo people living on the Aleutian Islands and the Alaska Peninsula. **2** the language of this people, distantly related to Eskimo. [< Russian *aleút*]

A|leu|tian (ə lü′shən), *adj., n.* **—*adj.*** of the Aleuts or the Aleutian Islands.
—*n.* an Aleut.

A level, *British.* the advanced level; highest level of examination given to secondary school students who wish to obtain a General Certificate of Education.

al|e|vin (al′ə vin), *n.* a very young fish, especially a very young salmon. [< French *alevin,* ultimately < Latin *allevāre* lift up, rear < *ad-* to + *levāre* raise]

ale|wife[1] (āl′wīf′), *n., pl.* **-wives.** a woman who keeps an alehouse or pub. [< *ale* + *wife*]

ale|wife[2] (āl′wīf′), *n., pl.* **-wives.** a sea fish found in great numbers along the U.S. Atlantic Coast, related to the herring and the shad, but inferior as food. It swims up rivers to spawn in spring and is also common in the Mississippi Valley and landlocked in some of the Great Lakes region. [American English; earlier *aloofe;* origin uncertain]

al|ex|an|der or **Al|ex|an|der** (al′ig zan′dər), *n.* a cocktail made with gin or brandy, mixed with crème de cacao and cream. [probably < *Alexander* the Great]

Al|ex|an|dri|an (al′ig zan′drē ən, -zän′-), *adj., n.* **—*adj.*** **1** of Alexandria (city in Egypt). **2** of Alexander the Great. **3** of alexandrine verse. **4a** of or belonging to the school of Greek literature which flourished in Alexandria under the Ptolemies (323 B.C. to 30 B.C.). **b** of or belonging to the schools of philosophy in Alexandria in the 100's and 200's A.D. that gave rise to Neoplatonism.
—*n.* a member or follower of any of the Alexandrian schools of literature and philosophy.

Al|ex|an|dri|an|ism (al′ig zan′drē ə niz′əm), *n.* **1** the style and characteristics of the Alexandrian literary school. **2** the methods and doctrines of the Alexandrian philosophical schools.

al|ex|an|drine or **Al|ex|an|drine** (al′ig zan′drin, -zän′-; *also British* al′ig zän′drīn), *n., adj.* **—*n.*** a line of verse having six iambic feet, with a caesura (pause) after the third foot. *Example:*
"He seeks′/out might′/y charms′,/
to trou′/ble sleep′/y minds′."/
—*adj.* of such a line or such poetry.
[< French *alexandrin* (because this meter was used in Old French poems on *Alexander* the Great)]
▶**Alexandrine** is the usual French heroic verse and is used in English to vary the usual heroic verse of five feet.

al|ex|an|drite (al′ig zan′drīt, -zän′-), *n.* a dark-green variety of chrysoberyl which looks red under artificial light, used as a gem. [< Russian *aleksandrit* < *Aleksandr,* later Alexander II of Russia + *-ite*[1]]

a|lex|i|a (ə lek′sē ə), *n.* a cerebral disorder characterized by loss of the ability to read, or to read aloud; word blindness (contrasted with *agraphia*). [< New Latin *alexia* < Greek *a-* without + *léxis* speech < *légein* speak; patterned on *agraphia*]

a|lex|in (ə lek′sin), *n.* a substance present in normal blood serum which is capable of destroying bacteria or other foreign substances; complement. [< German *Alexin* < Greek *aléxein* ward off]

al|ex|in|ic (al′ek sin′ik), *adj.* of or like the alexins.

a|lex|i|phar|mic (ə lek′sə fär′mik), *adj., n.* **—*adj.*** warding off or counteracting the effects of poison; antidotal.
—*n.* an antidote. [< Greek *alexiphármakos* < *aléxein* ward off + *phármakon* poison]

al|fa (al′fə), *n.,* or **alfa grass,** (in North Africa) esparto. [< Arabic *ḥalfā′*]

Al|fa (al′fə), *n. U.S.* a code name for the letter *a,* used in transmitting radio messages.

al|fal|fa (al fal′fə), *n. Especially U.S.* a plant with leaves like clover, deep roots, and bluish-purple flowers; lucerne. Alfalfa is grown as food for horses and cattle and can be cut several times a season and dried as hay. It belongs to the pea family. [< Spanish *alfalfa* < Arabic *al-'faṣfaṣ*]

alfalfa weevil, a tawny red insect native to Europe and Asia that has spread widely in the alfalfa-growing regions of the United States.

al|fa|qui (al′fə kē′), *n.* an Islamic theologian. [< Spanish *alfaquí* < Arabic *al-faqīh*]

al|fil|a|ri|a or **al|fil|e|ri|a** (al fil′ə rē′ə), *n.* a European plant of the geranium family, now widely naturalized as a forage plant in dry areas of the western and southwestern United States; red-stem filaree. [American English < American Spanish *alfilerilla* < Spanish *alfiler* pin < Arabic *al-khilāl* wooden pin, peg, toothpick]

al|fi|le|ril|la (al fil′ə ril′ə), *n.* = alfilaria.

al fi|ne (äl fē′nā), *Music.* to the end. Used as a direction, with *da capo* (from the beginning) or *dal segno* (from the sign), to indicate the repetition of a passage. [< Italian *al fine*]

al|for|ja (al fôr′jə), *n.* **1** *Southwestern U.S.* a saddlebag. **2** a cheek pouch, especially of a baboon. [< Spanish *alforja* knapsack < Arabic *al-khurj* the saddlebag]

al|fres|co (al fres′kō), *adv., adj.,* or **al fresco,** in the open air; outdoors: *We dined alfresco (adv.). We dined at an alfresco café (adj). He in his al fresco progress is nearer to nature than they are, nearer to the simple life* (London Times). [< Italian *al fresco* in the cool]

Al|fvén wave (äl vān′), a magnetohydrodynamic wave generated by motion within an electrically conducting plasma in a magnetic field. [< Hannes *Alfvén,* born 1908, a Swedish physicist, who discovered it]

alg., algebra.

ALG (no periods), antilymphocyte globulin.

al|ga (al′gə), *n., pl.* **al|gae.** one of the algae.

al|gae (al′jē), *n.pl.* a group of simple organisms that can make their own food. Algae contain chlorophyll but lack true stems, roots, or leaves. Some algae float free in water and form scum on rocks; these are single-celled. Others, such as the seaweeds and some freshwater plants like them, may be very large; those are multicellular. The two main groups of algae are the blue-green algae that are sometimes classified with bacteria as protists, and all other algae—the green algae, the brown algae, and the red algae—which are classified as plants. [< Latin *algae,* plural of *alga* seaweed]

al|gae|cide (al′jə sīd), *n.* potassium permanganate or other poison used to kill algae.

al|gal (al′gəl), *adj., n.* **—*adj.*** of or like algae.
—*n.* one of the algae.

al|gar|ro|ba or **al|ga|ro|ba** (al′gə rō′bə), *n.* **1** the mesquite bush or pod. **2** the carob tree or fruit. [< Spanish *algarroba* < Arabic *al-kharrūba*]

al|gate (ôl′gāt), *adv. Dialect.* **1** always. **2** however. [< *all* + *gate*[3]]

al|gates (ôl′gāts), *adv. Dialect.* algate.

al|ge|bra (al′jə brə), *n.* **1** the branch of mathematics that uses both letters and numbers to show relations between quantities. In algebra quantities are denoted by letters, negative numbers as well as ordinary numbers are used, and problems are solved in the form of equations. The equation $x + y = x^2$ is a way of stating, by algebra, that the sum of two quantities equals the square of one of them. *Algebra is a shorthand used to arrive at answers to general problems instead of solving each separately by the boring and inefficient process of plain arithmetic* (Harper's). **2** a textbook or treatise on this science. [< Medieval Latin *algebra* < Arabic *al-jabr* the bone setting; reduction (that is, of parts to a whole)]

al|ge|bra|ic (al′jə brā′ik), *adj.* of or having to do with algebra; used in algebra: *$(a + b)$ $(a - b) = a^2 - b^2$ is an algebraic statement.*

al|ge|bra|i|cal (al′jə brā′ə kəl), *adj.* = algebraic.

al|ge|bra|i|cal|ly (al′jə brā′ə klē), *adv.* by means of algebra or of algebraic processes.

al|ge|bra|ist (al′jə brā′ist), *n.* a person who studies algebra.

al|ge|bra|ize (al′jə brə īz), *v.t.,* **-ized, -iz|ing. 1** to solve by algebra. **2** to reduce to algebraic form: *When a child throws out his five fingers ... he has algebraized before he can speak* (Blackwood's Magazine).

Al|gen|ib (al gen′ib), *n.* a star in the wing of the constellation Pegasus.

Al|ge|ri|an (al jir′ē ən), *adj., n.* **—*adj.*** of or having to do with Algiers, Algeria, their people, or their way of life.
—*n.* a person born or living in Algiers or Algeria.

Al|ge|rine (al′jə rēn), *adj., n.* = Algerian.

al|get|ic (al jet′ik), *adj.* having to do with or producing pain. [< Greek *algeîn* to feel pain + English *-ic*]

al|gi|cide (al′jə sīd), *n.* = algaecide.

al|gid (al′jid), *adj.* cold; chilly (used especially of the cold stage of a fever). [< Latin *algidus* < *algēre* be cold]

al|gid|i|ty (al jid′ə tē), *n.* coldness, especially the cold stage of a fever; chilliness.

al|gin (al′jin), *n.* a gelatinous compound found in certain (especially brown) algae, used in plastics, and as a food emulsifier and thickener. [< *alg*(a) + *in*]

al|gin|ate (al′jə nāt), *n.* **1** = algin. **2** a type of yarn made from algin.

al|gin|ic acid (al jin′ik), = algin. *Formula:* $(C_6H_8O_6)_n$

al|goid (al′goid), *adj.* resembling algae.

Al|gol (al′gol), *n.* a binary star in the constellation Perseus that varies in apparent brightness periodically because its brighter component is eclipsed by the fainter. [< Arabic *al-ghūl* the ghoul, demon]

ALGOL or **Al|gol** (al′gol), *n.* a computer language for scientific work: *Scientific problems have to be expressed in an algebraic system known as ALGOL* (New Scientist). [< *Algo*(rithmic) *l*(anguage)]

al|go|lag|ni|a (al′gə lag′nē ə), *n.* pleasure or gratification obtained by inflicting or experiencing pain; masochism or sadism. [< Greek *álgos* pain + *lagneiā* lust]

al|go|log|i|cal (al′gə loj′ə kəl), *adj.* of or having to do with algology.

al|gol|o|gist (al gol′ə jist), *n.* a person who studies algology.

al|gol|o|gy (al gol′ə jē), *n.* the branch of botany that deals with algae; phycology. [< *alg*(a) + *-logy*]

al|gom|e|ter (al gom′ə tər), *n.* an instrument for measuring the sensitiveness of the skin to pain caused by pressure. [< Greek *álgos* pain + English *-meter*]

al|go|met|ric (al′gə met′rik), *adj.* of or having to do with measurement by means of an algometer.

Al|gon|ki|an (al gong′kē ən), *n., adj.* **—*n.*** **1** the most widespread family of North American Indian languages, including the languages of the Arapaho, Blackfoot, Cheyenne, Ojibwa, Delaware, Sauk and Fox, and Shawnee tribes. **2** an Indian belonging to an Algonkian tribe. **3** the late Proterozoic geological period or system of rocks.
—*adj.* **1** of or having to do with this family of languages. **2** late Proterozoic.
[American English < *Algonqu*(in) + English *-ian*]

Al|gon|kin (al gong′kin), *n.* = Algonquin.

Al|gon|qui|an (al gong′kē ən, -kwē-), *n., adj.* = Algonkian.

Al|gon|quin (al gong′kin, -kwin), *n.* **1** a group of tribes of North American Indians that lived in eastern Canada, in the valleys of the Ottawa River and the northern tributaries of the St. Lawrence. They were early allies of the French against the Iroquois. **2** an Indian belonging to any of these tribes. **3** the Algonkian language of any of these tribes.
[American English < French *Algonquin* < an American Indian word]

al|go|phil|i|a (al′gə fil′ē ə), *n.* love of pain; abnormal pleasure derived from suffering. [< Greek *álgos* pain + English *-philia*]

al|go|pho|bi|a (al′gə fō′bē ə), *n.* excessive fear of pain. [< Greek *álgos* pain + English *-phobia*]

al|gor (al′gôr), *n.* a chill, especially the start of a fever. [< Latin *algor,* related to *algēre* be cold]

al|go|rism (al′gə riz əm), *n.* **1** the Arabic or decimal system of arithmetical notation, with the figures from 1 to 9 and zero. **2** = algorithm. [< Old French *algorisme,* learned borrowing from Medieval Latin *algorismus* < Arabic *al-khuwārizmī* al-Khowarizmi, author of a famous work on algebra]

al|go|rithm (al′gə riᴛʜ əm), *n.* a formal procedure for any mathematical operation: *the division algorithm.*

al|go|rith|mic (al′gə rith′mik), *adj.* of an algorithm; having to do with or according to algorithms: *Human methods of solving problems fall into two categories; in one, an exhaustive examination of all possible solutions is undertaken; the other relies on shortcuts or inspired guesses. The first method is called algorithmic and the second heuristic* (F. H. George).

al|gous (al′gəs), *adj.* **1** of or like algae. **2** abounding in algae.

al|gua|cil (al′gwə sēl′), *n., pl.* **-cils, -ci|les** (-sē′lās). = alguazil.

al|gua|zil (al′gwə zēl′), *n., pl.* **-zils.** a constable or policeman, in Spain.

al|gum (al′gum), *n.* an unidentified tree mentioned in the Bible, probably a kind of sandalwood. II Chronicles 2:8. See also **almug.** [< Hebrew *'algūm*]

Al|ham|bra (al ham′brə), *n.* the palace of the Moorish kings at Granada, Spain. The Alhambra was the last stronghold of the Moors in Europe and was captured in 1492.

Al|ham|bra|ic (al′ham brā′ik), *adj.* = Alhambresque.

Al|ham|bresque or **al|ham|bresque** (al′ham-bresk′), *adj.* in the ornate and elaborate style of the Alhambra.

a|li|as (ā′lē əs), *n., pl.* **-as|es,** *conj.* **—*n.*** a name used by a person instead of his real name, to hide who he is; assumed name; other name: *The spy's real name was Harrison, but he sometimes went by the alias of Johnson.* **SYN:** pseudonym.

—conj. otherwise called; with the assumed name of: *The thief's name was Jones, alias Williams.*
[< Latin *aliās* otherwise]
▶In law, this word is still often written in italics (Harrison *alias* Harvey). In this use "alias" stands for the Latin *alias dictus,* meaning "otherwise called."

A|li Ba|ba (ä′lē bä′bə; al′ē bab′ə), a poor woodcutter in *The Arabian Nights* who discovers a treasure hidden in a cave by forty thieves.

al|i|bi (al′ə bī), *n., pl.* **-bis**, *v.,* **-bied**, **-bi|ing**. *—n.* **1** *Law.* the plea or fact that an accused person was somewhere else when an offense was committed: *Immediately after the robbery the gang scattered to establish alibis.* **2** *U.S. Informal.* an excuse: *What is your alibi for failing to do your homework?*
—v.i. U.S. Informal. to make an excuse: *He alibied for her that she was very busy when they asked him why she didn't visit them.*
—v.t. U.S. Informal. to make an excuse for.
[< Latin *alibī* elsewhere]

al|i|bil|i|ty (al′ə bil′ə tē), *n.* nutritiousness.

al|i|ble (al′ə bəl), *adj.* nutritive; nourishing. [< Latin *alibilis* < *alere* nourish]

Al|ice band (al′is), *Especially British.* a wide, colored headband: *The bridesmaids had white silk and wool dresses ... and green velvet Alice bands on their heads* (London Times).

Alice blue, a pale-blue color.

Al|ice-in-Won|der|land (al′is in wun′dər land′), *adj. Informal.* dreamlike; fantastic; unreal: *... the Alice-in-Wonderland flavor of government proceedings* (Wall Street Journal). [< *Alice's Adventures in Wonderland,* a fantasy (1865) by Lewis Carroll, 1832-98, an English writer and mathematician]

al|i|cy|clic (al′ə sī′klik, -sik′lik), *adj., n. —adj.* (of certain organic compounds) reacting like fatty (aliphatic) compounds, but differing structurally in containing a carbon ring.
—n. a group of organic compounds that have the principal carbon atoms arranged in closed ring structures. Most alicyclics are derived from petroleum or coal tar.

Al|id (al′id), *n.* = Shiite. [< *Ali,* the son-in-law of Mohammed]

al|i|dad (al′ə dad), *n.* = alidade.

∗**al|i|dade** (al′ə dād), *n.* **1** a measuring instrument consisting of a sighting device, such as a telescope, attached to a straightedge, used especially in surveying, to make a map or a scale drawing of a given area. **2** a similar device used in lookout towers to locate forest fires. [< Medieval Latin *alhidada* < Arabic *al-'iḍāda* pointer (of an astrolabe)]

∗**alidade**
definition 1

al|ien (āl′yən, ā′lē ən), *n., adj., v. —n.* **1** a resident foreigner. Aliens are not citizens of the country in which they live, and therefore owe their loyalty to another country. **2** a person belonging to a different ethnic or social group; stranger; foreigner. **3** a person excluded.
—adj. **1** of or by another country; foreign: *alien conquerors, alien domination. French is an alien language to Americans.* **2** having the legal status of an alien: *an alien resident.* **3** entirely different from one's own; strange: *alien customs.* **4** not in agreement; opposed, adverse, or repugnant: *Unkindness is alien to her nature.*
—v.t. to alienate; transfer: *The executive ... could not alien any part of our territory* (Thomas Jefferson).
[< Old French *alien,* learned borrowing from Latin *aliēnus* < *alius* another]

al|ien|a|bil|i|ty (āl′yə nə bil′ə tē, ā′lē ə-), *n.* the quality or state of being transferable.

al|ien|a|ble (āl′yə nə bəl, ā′lē ə-), *adj.* that can be transferred to another owner: *alienable property.*

al|ien|age (āl′yə nij, ā′lē ə-), *n.* the state of being an alien; the legal standing of an alien: *Exemption from military service ... on the ground of alienage* (Abraham Lincoln).

al|ien|ate (āl′yə nāt, ā′lē ə-), *v.t.,* **-at|ed**, **-at|ing**. **1** to turn away in feeling; turn from affection to indifference, dislike, or hatred; make unfriendly: *The American colonies were alienated from England by disputes over trade and taxation. He was alienated from his sister by her foolish acts. The cruelties of the terrorists, from which the Chinese were themselves the main sufferers, alienated public opinion* (Atlantic). **SYN:** estrange. **2** to transfer the ownership of (property, a property right, etc.) to another: *Enemy property was alienated during the war.* **3** *Figurative.* to turn away; transfer.

al|ien|a|tion (āl′yə nā′shən ā′lē ə-), *n.* **1** a turning away in feeling or affection: **a** the act of alienating; making unfriendly. **SYN:** estrangement. **b** the state of being alienated; not feeling interested in or involved with one's family, associates, or society: *The condition that sociologists call "alienation," the mass society in which the old securities vanish and the individual feels adrift in an alien world, are secular facts about which party programs do nothing* (Harper's). **2** the transfer of the ownership of property to another. **3** mental disease; insanity.

alienation of affections, *Law.* the turning or taking away by another of affectionate feeling, or love, especially that of husband and wife for each other.

al|ien|a|tor (āl′yə nā′tər, ā′lē ə-), *n.* a person who transfers property.

al|ien|ee (āl′yə nē′, ā′lē ə-), *n.* a person to whom property is transferred.

alien enemy, *Law.* an alien in a country at war with the country to which he owes allegiance.

al|ien|er (āl′yə nər, ā′lē ə-), *n.* = alienator.

a|li|e|ni ju|ris (ā′lē ē′nī jür′is), *Latin.* under the authority of another.

al|ien|ism (āl′yə niz əm, ā′lē ə-), *n.* **1** the quality or condition of being alien. **2** the study or treatment of mental diseases.

al|ien|ist (āl′yə nist, ā′lē ə-), *n.* a psychiatrist, especially one who testifies in a law court. [< French *aliéniste* < Latin *aliēnus* insane; earlier, strange]
▶**Alienist** was formerly a general term for a psychiatrist, and in law it still designates an expert qualified to testify about the sanity of a person.

al|ien|or (āl′yə nər, ā′lē ə-), *n.* = alienator.

al|i|es|ter|ase (al′ə es′tə rās), *n.* an enzyme that decomposes fatty-acid esters. [< *ali*(phatic) + *esterase*]

a|lif (ä′lif), *n.* the first letter of the Arabic alphabet. [< Arabic *'alif*]

al|i|form (al′ə fôrm, ā′lə-), *adj.* having the shape of a wing; winglike. [< Latin *āla* wing + English *-form*]

a|light[1] (ə līt′), *v.i.,* **a|light|ed** or (*Poetic*) **a|lit**, **a|light|ing**. **1** to get down; get off; dismount: *to alight from a bus. He alighted from the horse.* **SYN:** descend. **2** to come down from the air and lightly settle; come down from flight: *The bird alighted on our window sill.* **SYN:** land, light. **3** to come by chance; happen: *I alighted on just the book I needed in the library. ... we alighted upon a sign which manifestly referred to billiards* (Mark Twain). [Old English *ālīhtan* < *ā-* away, out + *līhtan* lighten < *līht* light (in weight)]

a|light[2] (ə līt′), *adv., adj.* **1** on fire; lighted: *Is the kindling alight?* **2** lighted up; aglow: (*Figurative.*) *Her face was alight with happiness.* [Old English *ālīht* illuminated, past participle of *ālīhtan* to light up]

a|lign (ə līn′), *v.t.* **1** to bring into line; arrange or adjust in a straight line: *The marksman aligned the sights of his gun with the distant target. The garageman aligned the front wheels of our car.* **2** to join with others for or against a cause: *Germany was aligned with Japan in World War II.*
—v.i. to form a line; fall into line: *The troops aligned.* Also, **aline**.
[< French *aligner* < Old French *alignier* < *a-* to + *lignier* < Latin *līnea* line] **—a|lign′er**, *n.*

a|lign|ment (ə līn′mənt), *n.* **1** arrangement in a straight line; formation in a line or pattern of lines: *The troops were in perfect alignment.* **2** a bringing into line. **3** the line or lines so formed. **4** a joining of persons or groups having similar interests, ideals, etc., for a common purpose: *The establishment of the Common Market resulted in a new European alignment.* **5** *Electronics.* the adjustment or synchronization of circuits or components so that they perform properly. **6** *Civil Engineering.* a ground plan. **7** parallel rows of large stones erected in the New Stone and Bronze ages in western Europe. Also, **alinement**.

a|like (ə līk′), *adv., adj. —adv.* **1** in the same way; similarly: *Robert and his father walk alike.* **2** in or to the same degree; equally: *Both were implicated alike.*
—adj. like one another; similar: *These twins are very much alike.* **SYN:** akin, analogous, resembling.
[Old English *onlīc*] **—a|like′ness**, *n.*

al|i|ment (al′ə mənt), *n., v. —n.* **1** food; nourishment. **SYN:** nutriment, provender. **2** *Figurative.* means of support; sustenance. **SYN:** maintenance, prop. **3** *Scottish.* alimony.
—v.t. **1** to give aliment to: (*Figurative.*) *They will furnish him money literally to aliment a civil war* (Thomas Jefferson). **SYN:** feed. **2** to maintain by an allowance. **SYN:** support.
[< Latin *alimentum* < *alere* nourish]

al|i|men|tal (al′ə men′təl), *adj.* of food; nourishing. **—al′i|men′tal|ly**, *adv.*

al|i|men|ta|ry (al′ə men′tər ē, -trē), *adj.* **1** having to do with food and nutrition. **2** nourishing; nutritious. **3** providing support or sustenance.

∗**alimentary canal**, the parts of the body through which food passes while it is being digested and from which wastes are eliminated. In mammals, the mouth, esophagus, stomach, intestines, and anus are parts of the alimentary canal.

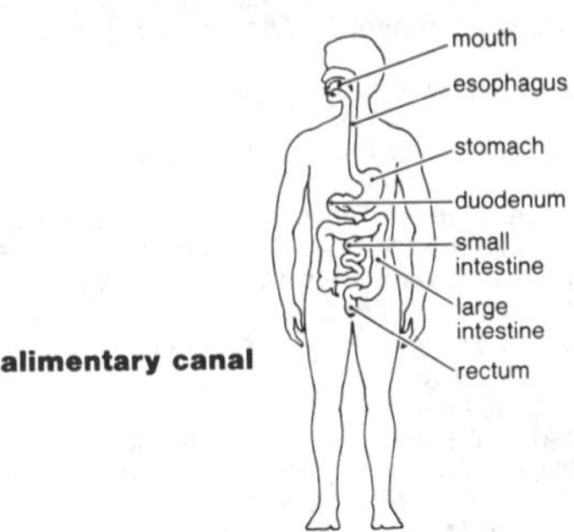

∗**alimentary canal**

al|i|men|ta|tion (al′ə men tā′shən), *n.* **1** nourishment; nutrition. **2** maintenance; support: *The alimentation of poor children ... was extended or increased by fresh endowments* (Charles Merivale).

al|i|men|ta|tive (al′ə men′tə tiv), *adj.* nutritive; alimentary. **—al′i|men′ta|tive|ly**, *adv.* **—al′i|men′ta|tive|ness**, *n.*

al|i|mo|ny (al′ə mō′nē), *n.* **1a** a fixed sum of money paid regularly under orders from a court to a woman or man for support of the spouse, or former spouse. **2** supply of the means of living; maintenance. [< Latin *alimōnia* sustenance < *alere* nourish]
▶In the United States, **alimony** is paid after a divorce, or after a legal separation, or until a decision is reached by the court. In English law, *alimony* is ordered during the course of a suit for separation or divorce or following a judicial separation; following divorce the term is **maintenance**, though in popular British use *alimony* covers it also.

à l'im|pro|viste (à laɴ prô vēst′), *French.* unexpectedly; suddenly: *There were a lot of jeeps on the road whose occupants had taken off, like us, à l'improviste, and as these vehicles passed the truck, the soldier up top would throw cases of K rations down into their rear seats* (New Yorker).

a|line (ə līn′), *v.t., v.i.,* **a|lined**, **a|lin|ing**. = align. **—a|lin′er**, *n.*

A-line (ā′līn′), *adj., n. —adj.* resembling the outline of the letter A in shape: *An A-line dress, skirt, etc.*
—n. a woman's garment with a triangular or A-shaped line formed especially by a flaring tunic and skirt.

a|line|ment (ə līn′mənt), *n.* = alignment.

Al|i|oth (al′ē oth), *n.* a bright star, of the second magnitude, in the handle of the Big Dipper (Ursa Major). [< Arabic *'alyat* fat sheep's tail]

al|i|ped (al′ə ped), *adj., n. —adj.* having the toes connected by a winglike membrane, as a bat.
—n. an aliped animal.
[< Latin *ālipēs, -pedis* < *āla* wing + *pēs* foot]

al|i|phat|ic (al′ə fat′ik), *adj., n. Chemistry. —adj.* of or designating a class of organic compounds in which the carbon atoms form chains with open ends rather than rings; fatty. Carbohydrates, ethers, and alcohols are aliphatic compounds.
—n. an aliphatic compound: *Today the oil industry—once a source of aliphatics—also produces cheap aromatics* (New Scientist).
[< Greek *áleiphar, -atos* fat, oil + English *-ic*]

al|i|quant (al′ə kwənt), *adj., n. Rare. —adj.* not dividing a number or quantity without a remainder. *Example:* 6 is an aliquant part of 20, for 3 times 6 are 18, leaving a remainder of 2.
—n. an aliquant part.
[< Latin *aliquantus* some, considerable]

al|i|quot (al′ə kwət), *adj., n. —adj.* dividing a number or quantity without leaving any remainder. *Example:* 6 is an aliquot part of 18.
—n. an aliquot part.
[< Latin *aliquot* a few]

al·i·sphe·noid (al′ə sfē′noid), *adj., n.* —***adj.*** of or having to do with either of two bones at the base of the skull that form the greater wings of the sphenoid.
—***n.*** an alisphenoid bone.
[< Latin *āla* wing + English *sphenoid*]

al·i·sphe·noi·dal (al′ə sfi noi′dəl), *adj.* = alisphenoid.

a·list (ə list′), *adv., adj.* having a list; tilted: *The foundering ship lay alist, its decks awash on the port side.*

a·lit (ə lit′), *v. Poetic.* alighted; a past tense and a past participle of **alight**[1]: *The bird alit upon a branch.*

à l'i·ta·lienne (á lē tá lyen′), *French.* in the Italian style.

a·lit·er·a·cy (ā lit′ər ə sē), *n.* lack of interest in reading or literature.

a·lit·er·ate (ā lit′ər it), *n., adj.* —***n.*** a person who shows no interest in reading or literature: *These are the "aliterates," people who know how to read but just don't bother* (Newsday).
—***adj.*** showing no interest in reading or literature: *an aliterate society.*
[< *a-*[4] + (il)*literate*]

a·li·tur·gic (al′ə tėr′jik), *adj.* not liturgical (applied especially to certain days on which the Eucharistic service is not to be celebrated).

a·li·tur·gi·cal (al′ə tėr′jə kəl), *adj.* = aliturgic.

a·li·un·de (ā′lē un′dē), *adv., adj. Law.* from another source. [< Latin *aliunde* < *alius* other + *unde* whence]

a·live (ə līv′), *adj.* **1** having life; living: *The snake was still alive and wriggled into the bushes after the car hit it.* **2** in continued activity or operation; in full force; active: *We celebrate Memorial Day to keep alive the memory of soldiers and sailors who have died for their country. Keep the principles of liberty alive.* **SYN:** unextinguished, unabated. **3** of all living: *He was the happiest man alive.* **4** *Figurative.* full of energy; lively; active: *Though father is retired he is very much alive.* **SYN:** brisk, vivacious. **5** connected to a source of electricity; live. **6** connected for broadcasting or recording.
alive to, noticing; awake to; sensitive to: *Are you alive to what is going on? In Tam [a Cambodian officer] impressed me as a sensitive man, alive to the suffering and fear of the people among whom he lived* (Donald Kirk).
alive with, full of; swarming with: *The street was alive with people, women rushing through their last-minute marketing, people coming home from work* (James T. Farrell).
look alive! See under **look.**
man alive! See under **man.**
[Old English on *līfe* in life] —**a·live′ness,** *n.*
►**Alive** is usually placed after its noun (*every man alive*) or in the predicate: *His father is alive.* In recent usage, however, *alive* is sometimes placed in attributive position: *If you want an alive theater, you will get it* (Harper's). *Ann Frank . . . achieved immortality as a Jewish heroine through her poignantly alive diary* (Saturday Night).

a·li·yah (ä lē yä′), *n. Hebrew.* **1** immigration to Israel by Jews. **2** (literally) ascent.

al·i·za·ri (al′ē zä′rē), *n.* a commercial name of madder in the Near East. [< French, Spanish *alizari* < Arabic *al-'aṣāra* the extract]

a·liz·a·rin (ə liz′ər in), *n.* a red, crystalline dye prepared from coal tar, formerly obtained from madder. *Formula:* $C_{14}H_8O_4$ [< French *alizarine* < *alizari* madder, alizari]

a·liz·a·rine (ə liz′ər in, -ə rēn), *n.* = alizarin.

al·ka·hest (al′kə hest), *n.* the universal solvent sought by the alchemists. Also, **alcahest.** [< Medieval Latin *alkahest* (supposedly coined by Paracelsus)]

al·ka·hes·tic (al′kə hes′tik), *adj.* all-dissolving.

al·ka·le·mi·a (al′kə lē′mē ə), *n.* an abnormal increase in the alkalinity of the blood. [< *alkal*(i) + *-emia*]

al·ka·les·cence (al′kə les′əns), *n.* **1** the process of becoming alkaline. **2** = alkalescency.

al·ka·les·cen·cy (al′kə les′ən sē), *n.* the tendency to become alkaline; slight alkaline character.

al·ka·les·cent (al′kə les′ənt), *adj., n.* —***adj.*** tending to become alkaline; slightly alkaline.
—***n.*** an alkalescent substance.

al·ka·li (al′kə lī), *n., pl.* **-lis** or **-lies,** *adj.* —***n.*** **1** any one of a group of bitter-tasting substances that neutralize acids and form salts with them, and turn red litmus paper blue. Alkalis are soluble in water and often produce caustic solutions. Lye and ammonia are two common alkalis. In its most restricted, but most usual sense, *alkali* is applied only to the hydrates of lithium, sodium, potassium, rubidium, cesium, francium, and ammonium. In a more general sense it is applied to the hydrates of the alkaline-earth metals, and also to the alkaloids. **2** the soluble part of the ashes of marine plants, chiefly the carbonates of sodium or potassium; soda ash. **3** any salt or mixture of salts that neutralizes acids. Some desert soils contain much alkali, which is usually harmful to crops. **4** *Western U.S.* a region abounding in alkali: *Sunrise found the white stage lurching eternally on across the alkali* (Owen Wister).
—***adj.*** alkaline: *an alkali base.*
[< Middle French *alcali* < Arabic *al-qalī* the ashes of saltwort]

alkali bee, a bee of the northwestern United States that pollinates alfalfa.

al·ka·lic (al′kə lik, al kal′ik), *adj.* **1** characterized by high alkali content: *alkalic igneous rock.* **2** alkaline.

alkali disease, *U.S.* a disease of livestock, especially in western parts of the United States, caused by eating grass containing selenium absorbed from the soil.

alkali feldspar, feldspar containing sodium and potassium in varying amounts. Microcline and orthoclase are alkali feldspars.

al·ka·li·fi·a·ble (al′kə lə fī′ə bəl, al kal′ə-), *adj.* that can be alkalified (alkalized).

alkali flat, *Western U.S.* an arid plain at the bottom of an undrained basin, containing an excess of alkali in its soil: *In a slick alkali flat which was surfaced like steel* (Mark Twain).

al·ka·li·fy (al′kə lə fī, al kal′ə-), *v.t., v.i.,* **-fied, -fy·ing.** to make or become alkaline; alkalize.

alkali land, = alkali soil.

alkali metal, any one of the group of univalent metals that includes lithium, sodium, potassium, rubidium, cesium, and francium.

al·ka·lim·e·ter (al′kə lim′ə tər), *n.* an instrument or standard solution for determining the quantity of an alkali in a solution or compound.

al·ka·lim·e·try (al′kə lim′ə trē), *n.* determination of the amount of alkali in a solution or compound.

al·ka·line (al′kə līn, -lin), *adj.* **1** of or like an alkali: *an alkaline reaction.* **2** containing an alkali. **3** containing more alkali than is normal. **4** having a *p*H factor of more than 7; having a relatively low concentration of hydrogen ions (contrasted with *acid,* especially as a characteristic of soil).

al·ka·line-earth metals (al′kə līn ėrth′, -lin-), a group of chemical elements, calcium, strontium, barium, radium, beryllium, and magnesium. Older tables omit the last three.

alkaline earths, the oxides of the alkaline-earth metals. Some authorities exclude one or more.

al·ka·lin·i·ty (al′kə lin′ə tē), *n.* alkaline quality or condition: *She built instruments to measure the degree of acidity or alkalinity shown by the color of the juices she extracted from the plants* (Science News Letter).

alkali soil, soil containing soluble mineral salts, in quantities sufficient to restrict or prevent the growth of plants, found usually in arid regions.

al·ka·lize (al′kə līz), *v.t., v.i.,* **-lized, -liz·ing.** to make or become alkaline or an alkali. —**al′ka·li·za′tion,** *n.* —**al′ka·liz′er,** *n.*

al·ka·loid (al′kə loid), *n., adj.* —***n.*** any one of a large group of alkaline substances containing nitrogen and found in or obtained from many plants. Atropine, quinine, nicotine, morphine, caffeine, strychnine, and cocaine are alkaloids. Most alkaloids are colorless, crystalline, have a bitter taste, are used as drugs, and may be highly poisonous.
—***adj.*** = alkaloidal.
[< *alkal*(i) + *-oid*]

al·ka·loi·dal (al′kə loi′dəl), *adj.* of or having to do with an alkaloid or alkaloids.

al·ka·lo·sis (al′kə lō′sis), *n.* an excess of alkali in the blood and body tissue. [< *alkal*(i) + *-osis*]

al·kane (al′kān), *n.* any of the methane series of saturated aliphatic hydrocarbons. [< *alk*(yl) + *-ane*]

al·ka·net (al′kə net), *n.* **1a** a European variety of borage whose roots yield alkannin, a red coloring matter; redroot. **b** the root. **c** the red coloring matter; alkannin. **2** any one of various similar plants, especially the European bugloss.
[< Spanish *alcana* < Arabic *al-hinnā'* the henna (shrub)]

al·kan·nin (al kan′ən), *n.* a deep-red coloring matter obtained from alkanet; anchusin. [< New Latin *Alkanna* the alkanet genus + English *-in*]

al·kap·ton (al kap′tən), *n.* a substance that causes urine to turn dark through oxidation; homogentisic acid. It is present in alkaptonuria. Also, **alcapton.** [< *alk*(ali) + Greek *háptein* fasten, combine]

al·kap·to·nu·ri·a (al kap′tə nůr′ē ə, -nyůr′-), *n.* a disorder of metabolism, marked by the presence of a brownish-yellow, acidic substance in the urine which turns it dark or black. Also, **alcaptonuria.**
[< *alkapton* + *-uria*]

al·kap·to·nu·ric (al kap′tə nůr′ik, -nyůr′-), *adj.* causing or characterized by alkaptonuria.

al·ke·ken·gi (al′kə ken′jē), *n.* **1** a plant of the nightshade family, bearing an edible, slightly acid, scarlet fruit, loosely enclosed in a large, red calyx. **2** its fruit.
[< Medieval Latin *alkekengi* < Arabic *al-kākanj* the nightshade]

al·kene (al′kēn), *n.* any of the ethylene series of unsaturated aliphatic hydrocarbons; olefin. [< *alk*(yl) + *-ene*]

al·ki (al′kē), *n.* by-and-by (the American Indian motto of the state of Washington).

Al·ko·ran (al′kō rän′, -ran′), *n.* = Alcoran (the Koran).

al·ky (al′kē), *n., pl.* **-kies.** *U.S. Slang.* **1** alcohol: *Seems there'd been a card game and a lot of alky drinking* (Baltimore Sun). **2** an alcoholic.
[< *alcohol*]

al·kyd (al′kid), *n., adj.* —***n.*** an alkyd resin.
—***adj.*** of or containing an alkyd resin: *an alkyd paint.*
[< *alc*(ohol) + (ac)*id*]

alkyd resin, any one of a group of sticky resins that become plastic when heated and are used especially in paints and lacquer. Alkyd resins are derived from phthalic acid and glycerol, or similar substances.

al·kyl (al′kəl), *n., adj.* —***n.*** a univalent radical occurring in aliphatic hydrocarbon derivatives from which a hydrogen atom has been removed. *Formula:* C_nH_{2n+1} —See also **aryl.**
—***adj.*** of or having to do with an alkyl: *alkyl sulfate.*
[< *alk*(ali) + *-yl*]

al·kyl·a·mine (al′kə lə mēn′, -lam′in), *n.* an amine formed by the replacement of hydrogen in ammonia by an alkyl.

al·kyl·ate (al′kə lāt), *n., v.,* **-at·ed, -at·ing.** —***n.*** a high-octane substance produced in petroleum refining, important as a component of aviation gasoline.
—***v.t.*** to introduce an alkyl into (an organic compound). —**al′kyl·a′tion,** *n.*

al·kyl·at·ing agent (al′kə lā ting), *Biochemistry.* any one of a class of cytotoxic chemicals that produce their poisonous effects by alkylation: *One of the four major groups of new anti-cancer drugs [is the group of] alkylating agents which act as cell poisons* (Harper's).

al·kyl·ene (al′kə lēn), *n.* any divalent hydrocarbon radical with the two free valences attached to different carbon atoms, as in the ethylene series.

al·kyne (al′kīn), *n.* any one of the acetylene series of unsaturated, open-chain hydrocarbons.
[< *alky*(l) + *-ine*[2]]

all (ôl), *adj., pron., n., adv.* —***adj.*** **1** every one of: *all men, all those present. All the children came. You all know the teacher.* **2** the whole of: *The mice ate all the cheese. All America rejoiced at the end of the war.* **SYN:** entire, complete. **3** the greatest possible: *He made all haste to reach home in time.* **4** every (kind, sort, or manner of something): *all sorts of arguments.* **5** any whatever; any: *The prisoner denied all connection with the crime.* **6** nothing but; only: *This plane carries all cargo and no passengers.* **7** *U.S. Dialect* (*Pennsylvania Dutch*). completely used up (always in the predicate): *The butter is all.*
—***pron.*** **1** the whole number; everyone: *All of us are going.* **2** everything: *All is well. All that glitters is not gold.* **3** the whole amount or extent: *All of the bread has been eaten.*
—***n.*** **1** everything one has: *He lost his all in the fire.* **2** a whole; entirety.
—***adv.*** **1** wholly; entirely: *all tired out. The cake is all gone. He is all deaf in one ear and half deaf in the other.* **SYN:** completely. **2** only; exclusively: *money spent all on pleasure.* **3** each; apiece: *The score was even at forty all.*
above all, before everything else: *Above all, he loves his work.*
after all, when everything has been considered; nevertheless: *I see that you came after all. Yet after all he was a mere mortal* (Washington Irving).
all and sundry, all, both collectively and individually: *give notice to all and sundry.*
all but, nearly; almost: *She is all but nine years old.*
all in, *Informal.* worn out; weary; exhausted: *After the race, the horse was all in.*
all in all, a everything: *They are all in all to each other.* **b** when everything has been taken into account: *All in all, I think he did a good job.* **c** completely: *And trust me not at all or all in all* (Tennyson).
all of, as much as; no less than; fully: *all of fifteen minutes, all of half a page.*
all over, a everywhere: *I looked all over for your glasses.* **b** done with; finished: *The game is all over.*
all square. See under **square.**
all that, so very; so extremely: *I never knew Jessie Matthews was all that good at knitting* (Punch).
all the, as much . . . as: *A touch of the iron is all the care this dress needs* (New York Times).
all there, *Informal.* **a** wide-awake; alert: *It was his excusable boast . . . that when anything was wanted he was "all there"* (James Payn). **b** not crazy; sane: *Hans Jansen was what is commonly*

called "not all there" (Margaret S. Gatty).
all told. See under **told.**
and all, and all the rest of it; and so on: *George, you don't remember me, it's such a long time and all* (John O'Hara). *With smithy, bellows, tongs, anvil, and all* (Scott).
(as) all get-out. See under **get-out.**
at all, a under any conditions: *I was surprised that he came at all considering the hard storm.* **b** in any way: *The teacher was not at all disturbed by the interruption.*
for all (that), in spite of; notwithstanding: *The price was high, but for all that he bought the gift.*
in all, counting every person or thing; altogether: *There were 100 men in all.*
once (and) for all, finally or decisively: *to settle a matter once and for all.*
[Old English *eall*]
▶**All** was formerly used to form a true compound in writing, as in *almighty, already,* and *always,* but today it usually stands in loose combination with or without a hyphen, and retains a clear syntactic relation to the word following, as (1) an adjective (*all fours, all-American*), (2) a noun, as a possessive (*All-father,* meaning "father of all") or as a direct object (*allheal,* meaning "heals all"), or (3) an adverb (*all-around, all-powerful*).

***al|la bre|ve** (ä′lə brā′vā) , **1** a musical measure having two or four beats, in which a half note represents one beat, to be played or sung twice as fast as the notation would suggest. **2** using or having this measure **3** the character or symbol indicating this measure. [< Italian *alla breve* in brief style]

***alla breve**
definition 3

Al|lah (al′ə, ä′lə), *n.* the Moslem name for the one Supreme Being, or God. [< Arabic *Allāh*]

al|la|man|da (al′ə man′də), *n.* a tropical American plant of the dogbane family, cultivated in hothouses for its large, funnel-shaped, yellow flowers. [< New Latin *Allamanda,* the genus name < J.N.S. *Allamand,* Swiss scientist of the 1700's]

all-A|mer|i|can (ôl′ə mer′ə kən), *adj., n.* **—*adj.*** **1** *Sports.* selected as the best of its class in the United States: *He was chosen as the quarterback on this year's all-American football team.* **2** made up entirely of Americans or American elements: *The ship had an all-American crew.* **3** representing the whole United States. **4** typically or thoroughly of the United States; characteristically American: *... the all-American passion for breaking records* (Atlantic).
—*n.* **1** *Sports.* a player selected as one of the best in the United States at his position. **2** a hypothetical team made up of college players, each selected as best in the United States at his position.

al|lan|ite (al′ə nīt), *n.* a brownish-black, monoclinic mineral related to epidote, sometimes occurring in granite and other igneous rocks. [< Thomas *Allan,* 1777-1833, English mineralogist]

al|lan|to|ic (al′ən tō′ik), *adj.* of or relating to the allantois.

al|lan|toid (ə lan′toid), *adj., n.* **—*adj.*** **1** of the allantois. **2** like the allantois in shape. **—*n.*** = allantois.

al|lan|toi|dal (al′ən toi′dəl), *adj.* = allantoid.

al|lan|to|in (ə lan′tō in), *n.* an oxidation product of uric acid, used to stimulate growth of healthy tissue in wounds, ulcers, or the like. *Formula:* $C_4H_6N_4O_3$ [< *allanto*(is) + *-in*]

al|lan|to|is (ə lan′tō is), *n.* an appendage on the embryos of reptiles, birds, and mammals, developing as a membranous sac from the posterior portion of the yolk sac. It is important in the formation of the umbilical cord and the placenta in mammals. [< New Latin *allantois,* new singular for earlier *allantoides* < Greek *allāntoeidēs* sausage-shaped < *allâs, -ântos* sausage + *eîdos* shape]

al|la pri|ma (ä′lə prē′mə), of or in a style of painting in which the pigments are laid on the canvas in thick, heavy masses, instead of washes, glazes, or repeated coats. [< Italian *alla prima* at first]

al|lar|gan|do (äl′lär gän′dō), *adv., adj., n., pl.* **-dos, -di** (-dē). *Music.* **—*adv.*, *adj.*** gradually becoming slower and louder.
—*n.* a musical passage that becomes gradually slower and louder: *The conductor laid a heavy hand on texture and rhythm and applied monstrous allargandi at the close of quick movements* (London Times).
[< Italian *allargando*]

all-a|round (ôl′ə round′), *adj. U.S.* **1** able to do many things; useful in many ways; not limited or specialized: *He is an all-around football player—he runs, passes, and punts. "While we're always looking for good students, you men can help us by keeping a sharp eye out for real all-around boys who, incidentally, have some athletic ability"* (Saturday Review). **2** including all; all-inclusive: *the best all-around American city school exhibit.* Also, *Especially British,* **all-round.** [American English < *all* + *around*] **—all′-a|round′ness,** *n.*

all-a|round|er (ôl′ə roun′dər), *n. U.S.* an all-around person.

al|la vos|tra sa|lu|te (äl′lä vôs′trä sä lü′tā), *Italian.* to your health!

al|lay (ə lā′), *v.t.,* **-layed, -lay|ing. 1** to put at rest; quiet: *His fears were allayed by the news that his family was safe.* SYN: pacify, calm, quell. **2** to make less; relieve (pain, thirst, trouble, or other suffering); check: *Her fever was allayed by the medicine.* SYN: alleviate, mitigate. **3** to make less; weaken. [Old English *ālecgan* < *ā-* away, off + *lecgan* to lay] **—al|lay′er,** *n.* **—al|lay′ment,** *n.*

all clear, a signal indicating the end of an air raid or other danger.

all|com|ers (ôl′kum′ərz), *n.pl. British.* anyone who comes, especially to participate in a contest.

all-day (ôl′dā′), *adj.* for or through the whole day; lasting all day: *an all-day conference.*

al|lée (à lā′), *n. French.* **1** a walk or path, especially one between shrubs or trees in a garden: *There is a green courtyard whose hedges Auguste, the old gardener, keeps in fine shape, and an allée of chestnuts* (Harper's). **2** a mall; avenue.

al|le|ga|tion (al′ə gā′shən), *n.* **1** a positive statement, usually made without proof: *He makes so many wild allegations that no one will believe him. It is composed of fantastic allegations presented as facts* (Harper's). SYN: statement, declaration. **2** a positive statement that one is prepared to prove; assertion: *The lawyer's allegation was proved.* SYN: affirmation. **3a** the act of making a charge before a legal tribunal. **b** the charge undertaken to be proved. **4** the act of alleging or declaring. [< Latin *allēgātiō, -ōnis* < *allēgāre* send a message, cite < *ad-* to + *lēgāre* to commission < *lēx, lēgis* law]

al|lege (ə lej′), *v.t.,* **-leged, -leg|ing. 1** to state positively; assert; declare: *This man alleges that his watch has been stolen.* **2** to assert without proof; claim: *The alleged theft never really happened. Where much is alleged something must be true* (Edward Gibbon). *Union headquarters are investigating the latest case of alleged interference with voting in a recent election* (London Times). SYN: affirm. **3** to give as a reason, excuse, or argument; bring forward: *He was tardy this morning and alleges that his bus was late.* **4** *Archaic.* to quote (an author, work, etc.); cite. [< Anglo-French *alegier,* alteration of Old French *esligier* buy free and clear (< Latin *ex-* out + *lītigāre* bring suit), but with meaning of Latin *allēgāre* cite, charge] **—al|lege′a|ble,** *adj.* **—al|leg′er,** *n.*

al|leg|ed|ly (ə lej′id lē), *adv.* according to what is or has been alleged: *He allegedly failed to support his family.*

Al|le|ghe|ny spurge (al′ə gā′nē, al′ə gā′-), a low, creeping, evergreen plant of the box family, found in the southern United States. It is a kind of pachysandra.

al|le|giance (ə lē′jəns), *n.* **1** the loyalty owed by a citizen to his country or government; obligation of a subject to his ruler: *I pledge allegiance to the flag. His allegiance has never been questioned.* SYN: duty, obligation. **2** *Figurative.* faithfulness to a person, cause, or the like; loyalty to any person or thing; devotion: *We owe allegiance to our friends. His allegiance to his brother lasted all his life.* SYN: fidelity. [Middle English *alegeaunce* < Medieval Latin *ligeantia* < Late Latin *ligius* liege]

al|le|giant (ə lē′jənt), *adj., n.* **—*adj.*** giving allegiance; loyal.
—*n.* a person who owes allegiance.

al|le|gor|ic (al′ə gôr′ik, -gor′-), *adj.* = allegorical.

al|le|gor|i|cal (al′ə gôr′ə kəl, -gor′-), *adj.* **1** explaining or teaching something by a story; using allegory: *The parables in the Bible are allegorical.* **2** consisting of or occurring in allegory: *an allegorical character. The oldest of these show the twelve months as allegorical ladies holding flowers, fruits, and other symbols of the season* (Harper's). **—al′le|gor′i|cal|ly,** *adv.* **—al′le|gor′i|cal|ness,** *n.*

al|le|go|rism (al′ə gôr′iz əm, -gōr′-, -gər-), *n.* **1** the use of allegory. **2** the allegorical method of interpreting Scripture.

al|le|go|rist (al′ə gôr′ist, -gōr′-, -gər-), *n.* a person who uses allegory or writes allegorically.

al|le|go|ris|tic (al′ə gə ris′tik), *adj.* = allegorical.

al|le|go|rize (al′ə gə rīz), *v.,* **-rized, -riz|ing.**
—*v.t.* **1** to make into an allegory. **2** to treat or explain as an allegory.
—*v.i.* to use allegory. **—al′le|gor′i|za′tion,** *n.* **—al′le|go|riz′er,** *n.*

al|le|go|ry (al′ə gôr′ē, -gōr′-), *n., pl.* **-ries. 1** a story that is told to explain or teach something, especially a long and complicated story with an underlying meaning different from the surface meaning of the story itself. The parables in the Bible are allegories. *Bunyan's "Pilgrim's Progress" and Spenser's "The Faerie Queene" are well-known allegories in English.* **2** a method of speaking or writing characterized by this kind of figurative description. [< Latin *allēgoria* < Greek *allēgoriā* < *allēgoreîn* speak figuratively < *állos* other + *agoreúein* speak, speak publicly < *agorâ* assembly]
▶An **allegory,** a **fable,** or a **parable** is a story made up to present ideas in a concrete, vivid way. The incidents of an *allegory* may stand for political, spiritual, or romantic situations; its characters may be types (*Mr. Worldly Wiseman*) or personifications (*Courtesy, Jealousy*). The characters of a *fable* are animals or inanimate objects that by acting and talking like human beings call attention to human weaknesses or desired virtues and teach a common-sense lesson that is usually stated at the end: *Aesop's fables.* A *parable* is a short story of everyday life used to teach a moral by comparison: *Jesus used the parable of the mustard seed to show how a small beginning can produce great results.*

al|le|gret|to (al′ə gret′ō), *adj., adv., n., pl.* **-tos.** *Music.* **—*adj.*** quick, but not so quick as *allegro.*
—*adv.* in allegretto tempo; somewhat briskly, but less so than *allegro.*
—*n.* an allegretto part in a piece of music.
[< Italian *allegretto* (diminutive) < *allegro* allegro]

al|le|gro (ə lā′grō, -leg′rō), *adj., adv., n., pl.* **-gros.** *Music.* **—*adj.*** quick and lively, but not so quick as *presto.*
—*adv.* in quick time; briskly.
—*n.* a quick, lively part in a piece of music.
[< Italian *allegro* < Latin *alicer, alecris,* unrecorded variant of *alacer, -cris* brisk]

al|lel (ə lel′), *n.* = allele.

al|lele (ə lēl′), *n.* **1** either of a pair of alternative characteristics, such as tallness and dwarfness, potentially present in the germ cell. **2** a gene, especially one gene of a pair that bear these characteristics. [short for *allelomorph*]

al|le|lic (ə lē′lik, -lel′ik), *adj.* of or having to do with an allele or alleles: *Two genes are said to be allelic if they normally occupy the same place on a chromosome* (Bulletin of Atomic Scientists).

al|le|lism (ə lē′liz əm, -lel′iz-), *n.* the state or condition of being allelic or an allele.

al|le|lo|mi|met|ic (ə lē′lə mi met′ik, -lel′ə-; -mī-), *adj.* of or characterized by imitativeness within a group; imitative of one another: *All the sheep in a flock, or all the fish in a school, or all the dogs in a pack, tend to do the same thing at the same time. Scientifically, this is termed allelomimetic behavior* (Science News Letter). [< Greek *allēlōn* of each other + English *mimetic*]

al|le|lo|morph (ə lē′lə môrf, -lel′ə-), *n.* **1** *Genetics.* = allele. **2** *Chemistry.* one of two or more substances having the same atoms but differing in their bonds or molecular arrangement. [< Greek *allēlōn* of each other + *morphē* form]

al|le|lo|mor|phic (ə lē′lə môr′fik, -lel′ə-), *adj.* = allelic.

al|le|lo|mor|phism (ə lē′lə môr′fiz əm, -lel′ə-), *n.* = allelism.

al|le|lu|ia or **al|le|lu|iah** (al′ə lü′yə), *interj., n.* **—*interj.*** "Praise ye the Lord!"; the Latin and liturgical form of **hallelujah.**
—*n.* a hymn of praise to the Lord: *We hear the Easter peals and sing our Alleluias today* (Sunday Times).
alleluias, *Informal.* unrestrained praise for anything: *His latest novel was received with a chorus of alleluias from the critics.*
[< Latin *allēlūja* < Greek *allēloúia* < Hebrew *hăllәlū-yāh* praise ye Jehovah]

al|le|mande (al′ə mand′; *French* àl mäɴd′), *n.* **1** any one of various German dances popular in France in the 1700's, in which the participants hold hands. **2** the music for any of these dances. **3** *Music.* a piece of music, in duple time, forming one of the movements of the classical suite, such as in those of Bach and Handel. **4** = quadrille. [< French (*danse*) *allemande* German (dance)]

all-em|brac|ing (ôl′em brā′sing), *adj.* including all, especially in an indiscriminate or sweeping manner: *... the Buddhist goal of universal and all-embracing love* (Atlantic).

all-en|com|pass|ing (ôl′en kum′pə sing), *adj.* = all-embracing.

Pronunciation Key: hat, āge, cãre, fär; let, ēqual, tėrm; it, īce; hot, ōpen, ôrder; oil, out; cup, pu̇t, rüle; child; long; thin; ᴛʜen; zh, measure; ə represents a in about, e in taken, i in pencil, o in lemon, u in circus.

* **Al|len screw** (al′ən), a screw having a hexagonal socket sunk in its head, and threaded to the top, used as a set screw or plug.

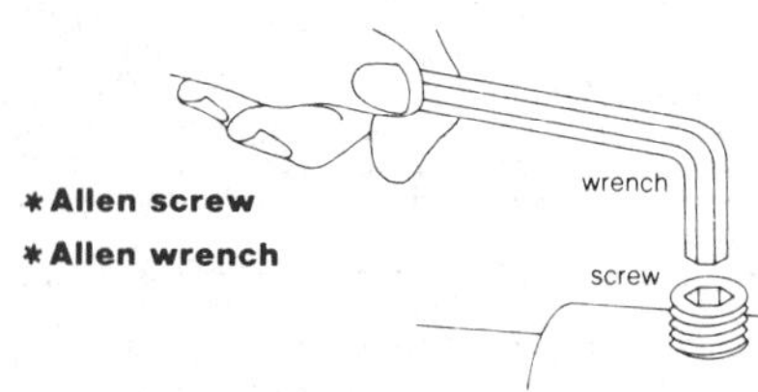

* **Allen screw**
* **Allen wrench**

* **Allen wrench**, a tool to adjust Allen screws, having a hexagonal tip to fit the socket in the screw and a handle bent at a right angle.

al|ler|gen (al′ər jən), *n.* any substance that causes or reveals an allergy in a particular individual or individuals: *One of the major allergens causing asthma is house dust* (Alexander Paton). [< *aller*(gy) + *-gen*]

al|ler|gen|ic (al′ər jen′ik), *adj.* of or caused by an allergen: *Asthma is an allergenic condition that affects the bronchi of the lung* (Edwin Diamond). **—al′ler|gen′i|cal|ly**, *adv.*

al|ler|gic (ə lėr′jik), *adj.* **1** having an allergy (to): *to be allergic to pollens. Some people who are allergic to eggs cannot eat them without breaking into a rash.* **2** of or caused by allergy: *Hay fever is an allergic reaction.* **3** *Slang.* having a strong dislike; opposed (to): *allergic to work. She is allergic to camping.* **—al|ler′gi|cal|ly**, *adv.*

al|ler|gist (al′ər jist), *n.* a doctor who specializes in treating allergies.

al|ler|go|log|i|cal (al′ər jə loj′ə kəl), *adj.* of or having to do with allergology.

al|ler|gol|o|gist (al′ər jol′ə jist), *n.* an expert in or student of allergology; allergist.

al|ler|gol|o|gy (al′ər jol′ə jē), *n.* the study of allergies. [< *allerg*(y) + *-logy*]

al|ler|gy (al′ər jē), *n., pl.* **-gies.** **1** unusual sensitiveness to certain substances such as particular kinds of pollen, food, hair, or cloth. Hay fever and asthma are common allergies. Headaches or hives are common signs of allergy. Allergies differ in symptoms according to the substance. **2** = anaphylaxis. **3** *Slang, Figurative.* a strong dislike: *an allergy to picnics, an allergy for work.* [< New Latin *allergia* < Greek *állos* different, other + *érgon* action]

al|leth|rin (ə leth′rin), *n.* an insecticide resembling natural pyrethrum in its properties, but produced synthetically. *Formula:* $C_{19}H_{26}O_3$ [< Greek *állos* different + English (pyr)*ethr*(um) + *-in*]

al|le|vi|ate (ə lē′vē āt), *v.t.,* **-at|ed, -at|ing.** **1** to make easier to endure (suffering of the body or mind); relieve: *Heat often alleviates pain.* **SYN:** allay, mitigate. **2** to lessen or lighten; diminish: *Business should not flee from the problems facing the city, but should stay and help alleviate them* (New York Times). [< Late Latin *alleviāre* (with English *-ate*[1]) to lighten < Latin *ad-* to + *levis* light (in weight)] **—al|le′vi|a′tor**, *n.*

al|le|vi|a|tion (ə lē′vē ā′shən), *n.* **1** the act of alleviating: *the alleviation of taxes.* **2** the condition of being alleviated; relief. **3** something that alleviates: *His friend's sympathy was an alleviation of his grief.*

al|le|vi|a|tive (ə lē′vē ā′tiv), *adj., n.* **—*adj.*** alleviating. **—*n.*** anything that alleviates.

al|le|vi|a|to|ry (ə lē′vē ə tôr′ē, -tōr′-), *adj.* alleviating.

all-ex|pense (ôl′ek spens′), *adj.* covering payment of all ordinary or incidental expenses, such as transportation and accommodations: *. . . an eight-day escorted all-expense trip to Colorado Springs* (New York Times).

all-ex|pens|es-paid (ôl′ek spen′səz pād′), *adj.* all-expense: *I should not like to see every student coming here guaranteed a four-year all-expenses-paid scholarship* (Atlantic).

al|ley[1] (al′ē), *n., pl.* **-leys.** **1** *Especially U.S.* a narrow back street in a city or town, especially one running between rows of houses or buildings. **2** *British Dialect.* a narrow street in a city or town. **3** a path in a park or garden, bordered by trees, shrubbery, or bushes: *. . . with alleys of trees along the embankment* (Robert Louis Stevenson). **4a** a long, narrow lane along which the ball is rolled in bowling; bowling alley. **b** Often, **alleys.** a building containing a number of alleys for bowling.

down (or **up**) **one's alley**, *Informal.* easy or pleasing for one; suited to one's abilities or tastes: *Anything relating to the making, designing, or repairing of handbags is right up Artkraft's alley* (Vogue).

[< Old French *alee* a going < *aler* go]

al|ley[2] (al′ē), *n., pl.* **-leys.** a large, white or colored marble used to shoot at the other marbles in the game of marbles. [short for *alabaster*]

alley cat, *U.S.* **1** a cat of unknown parentage, such as often roams the back streets of cities. **2** *Slang.* a person, especially a girl or woman, considered as similar to such a cat, especially in her way of life, fierceness of temper, and lack of moral character.

al|ley|way (al′ē wā′), *n.* **1** *Especially U.S.* an alley in a city or town. **2** a narrow passageway: *Newer ships have protected alleyways below deck that the men can use in foul weather* (Wall Street Journal).

al|lez-vous-en (á lā vü zäɴ′), *interj. French.* be off with you! go away! get out!

all-faith (ôl′fāth′), *adj. U.S.* of or for all the religious faiths, especially Catholic, Protestant, and Jewish: *an all-faith chapel.*

All-fa|ther (ôl′fä′ᴛʜər), *n.* **1** the Father of all; God. **2** the chief god in a religion having a number of gods, as Zeus, Jupiter, or Odin.

all-fired (ôl′fīrd′), *adj., adv. U.S. Informal.* **—*adj.*** unusual; excessive: *You could've hired a rig from the livery stable if you was in such an all-fired hurry* (New Yorker).
—*adv.* excessively; inordinately. **—all′-fired′ly**, *adv.*

All Fools' Day, April 1, April Fools' Day.

all fours, **1** all four legs of an animal. **2** the arms and legs of a person; hands and knees: *The baby crawled on all fours.* **3** seven-up (card game).

be (or **stand**) **on all fours**, *Especially British.* to be on a level or exactly comparable (with): *The decision I have quoted is on all fours with this case* (London Daily News).

run on all fours, *Especially British.* to move smoothly: *. . . though the comparison should not exactly run on all fours when examined* (London Daily Telegram).

all-hail (ôl′hāl′), *n., v.* **—*n.*** a salutation of "all hail!"
—*v.t.* *Archaic.* to salute with "all hail!"

all hail, an exclamation of greeting or welcome.

All|hal|low|mas or **All|hal|low|mass** (ôl′hal′ō-məs), *n.* the feast of All Saints' Day.

All|hal|lows (ôl′hal′ōz), *n.* **1** November 1, All Saints' Day. **2** = Allhallowmas. [< *all* + *hallow*[1], Old English *hālga* holy man < *hālig* holy]

All Hallow summer, = St. Martin's summer; Indian summer.

All|hal|low|tide (ôl′hal′ō tīd′), *n.* the time of year of All Saints' Day.

all|heal (ôl′hēl′), *n.* **1** = valerian (the plant). **2** = selfheal.

al|li|a|ble (ə lī′ə bəl), *adj.* that can be allied.

al|li|a|ceous (al′ē ā′shəs), *adj.* **1** of or belonging to the genus of plants that includes the onion, garlic, chive, and leek. **2** having a smell or taste resembling any of these; garliclike. [< Latin *allium* garlic + English *-aceous*]

al|li|ance (ə lī′əns), *n.* **1** a union formed by agreement; joining of interests. A joining of national interests by treaty is an alliance. A marriage may be a family alliance. **SYN:** coalition. **2** the nations or persons that belong to such a union. **SYN:** league. **3** any joining of efforts or interests by persons, families, states, or organizations: *an alliance between church and state.* **SYN:** association, connection, fusion. **4** similarity in structure or descent; relationship. **SYN:** kinship, affinity. [< Old French *aliance* < *alier* unite < Latin *alligāre* bind to < *ad-* to + *ligāre* bind]

al|li|cin (al′ə sin), *n.* a substance having antibacterial properties, found in the juice of garlic. *Formula:* $C_6H_{10}OS_2$ [< Latin *allium* garlic + *-cin*, as in *streptomycin*]

al|lied (ə līd′, al′īd), *adj.* **1** united by agreement or treaty; combined for some special purpose: *allied armies. France, Great Britain, Russia, and the United States were allied nations during World War II.* **2** associated; connected: *allied banks.* **SYN:** affiliated. **3** similar in structure or descent; related: *Allied animals, such as the dog and the wolf, look somewhat alike.* **SYN:** kindred.
▶The terms **allied** and **Allied** are frequently stressed on the first syllable when used before a noun, as in *the allied armies.*

Al|lied (ə līd′, al′īd), *adj.* of or by the Allies.

al|lies (al′īz, ə līz′), *n.* plural of **ally.**

Al|lies (al′īz, ə līz′), *n.pl.* **1** the countries that fought against Germany, Austria-Hungary, Turkey, and Bulgaria in World War I. **2** the countries that fought against Germany, Italy, and Japan in World War II. **3** (during the latter part of World War II) the United Nations.

al|li|ga|tion (al′ə gā′shən), *n. Arithmetic.* a method of finding the relations between the proportions and prices of ingredients of a mixture and the cost of the mixture itself. [< Latin *alligātiō, -ōnis* < *alligāre* bind to < *ad-* to + *ligāre* bind]

* **al|li|ga|tor** (al′ə gā′tər), *n., adj., v.* **—*n.*** **1** a large reptile with a rather thick skin, similar to the crocodile but having a shorter and flatter head. There are two species of alligators. One lives in the rivers and marshes of the southeastern United States and the other in and near the lower Yangtze River in China. **2** leather prepared from the skin of an alligator. **3** an amphibian vehicle for carrying troops and supplies ashore. **4** *Slang.* a jazz enthusiast who is not a musician. **5** a machine that has a strong jaw or jaws, such as one for bringing the balls of iron from a puddling furnace into compact form for handling, or a kind of rock breaker.
—*adj.* of or having the appearance of alligator (leather): *alligator shoes.*
—*v.i.* *U.S.* to develop cracks, ridges, or small blisters: *The paint alligators . . . under the first hot sun* (New York Times).
[< Spanish *el lagarto* the lizard < Latin *lacertus* lizard]

* **alligator**
definition 1

* **alligator clip**, a terminal at the end of a wire with narrow jaws, used to make temporary electrical connections: *One end of the spring is attached to a battery terminal, and the alligator clip is made fast to one lead of the motor* (Scientific American). See picture below.

* **alligator gar**, any one of various freshwater gars of the lower Mississippi Valley, Mexico, Cuba, and Central America, which attain to lengths of over seven feet. See picture below.

* **alligator pear**, = avocado. See picture below.

* **alligator shears**, large shears used for cutting heavy metal. See picture below.

* **alligator snapping turtle** or **snapper**, a large, freshwater snapping turtle of the southeastern United States. It is the largest freshwater turtle of North America, sometimes growing to about 3 feet in length and weighing up to 140 pounds. See picture below.

alligator weed, an aquatic plant with long, narrow leaves, commonly found in inland waters of the southeastern United States, where it is a troublesome weed, impeding navigation.

* **alligator wrench**, a tool with strong, V-shaped jaws, one or both of which are toothed, used for twisting pipes. See picture below.

all-im|por|tant (ôl′im pôr′tənt), *adj.* extremely important; essential; vital: *There are many who consider that the "conquest of space" for prestige is all-important.*

all-in (ôl′in′), *adj.* **1** *British.* inclusive of all: *an all-in rate.* **2** with no restrictions: *all-in wrestling.*

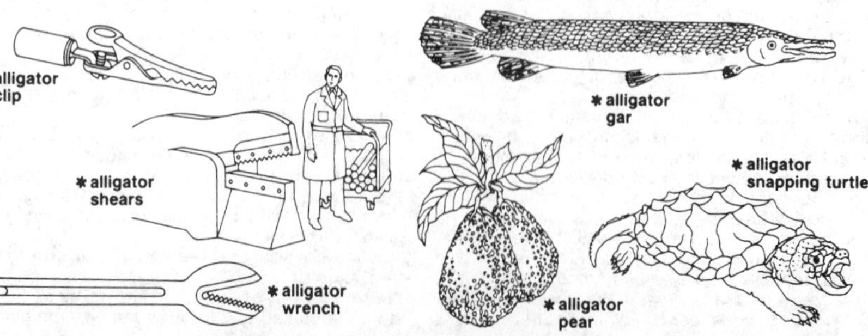

all-in|clu|sive (ôl′in klü′siv), *adj.* including all; all-embracing: *an all-inclusive price.*
all-in-one (ôl′in wun′), *n.* a foundation garment consisting of a corset and attached brassiere.
al|lit|er|ate (ə lit′ə rāt), *v.,* **-at|ed, -at|ing.** *—v.i.* **1** to have the same first sound or the same first letter. **2** to use alliteration.
—v.t. to speak or write (anything) with alliteration. [< Latin *ad-* to + *lītera* letter + English *-ate*[1]]
al|lit|er|a|tion (ə lit′ə rā′shən), *n.* the repetition of the same first sound or the same first letter in a group of words or line of poetry. *Example:* "The *s*un *s*ank *s*lowly" contains alliteration of *s.*
al|lit|er|a|tive (ə lit′ə rā′tiv), *adj.* having words beginning with the same sound or letter. **—al|lit′er-a′tive|ly,** *adv.* **—al|lit′er|a′tive|ness,** *n.*
al|lit|er|a|tor (ə lit′ə rā′tər), *n.* a person who uses alliteration.
al|li|um (al′ē əm), *n.* any plant of the genus that includes the onion, garlic, and chive. [< Latin *allium* garlic]
all|ness (ôl′nis), *n.* totality; universality.
all-night (ôl′nīt′), *adj.* **1** for or through the whole night; lasting all night: *an all-night sitting of Parliament. Jordan's all-night curfew was lifted last week* (Time). **2** operating or serving throughout the night: *After arriving late at night, we drank coffee in an all-night cafe* (Bill Sertl).
allo-, *combining form.* **1** other; others: *Allocentric = viewing others as the center.*
2 variant or different: *Allograph = variant form of a grapheme. Allophone = different sound.*
[< Greek *állos* other]
al|lo|ca|ble (al′ə kə bəl), *adj.* that can be allocated or assigned: *Some $5.5 billion of the long-term debt, the agency said, is not readily allocable* (Wall Street Journal).
al|lo|cate (al′ə kāt), *v.t.,* **-cat|ed, -cat|ing. 1** to set or lay aside for a special purpose; assign or allot; apportion: *The Ford Foundation allocated millions of dollars for cancer research.* **SYN:** distribute. **2** to fix the place of; locate. [< Medieval Latin *allocare* (with English *-ate*[1]) < Latin *ad-* to, at + *locāre* to place < *locus* a place]
al|lo|ca|tion (al′ə kā′shən), *n.* **1** an allocating; allotment; distribution; assignment. **SYN:** apportionment. **2** the share, portion, or thing allocated. **3** *Accounting.* a system of distributing income and expenses among the departments of a business.
al|lo|cen|tric (al′ə sen′trik), *adj.* having or viewing others as the center of things; accepting or recognizing the importance, superiority, or other attribute of another person or group: *Which alternative one chooses for himself is likely to be determined by the degree to which one is ethnocentric or allocentric* (Alfred L. Kroeber). [< *allo-* + *centric*]
al|lo|chro|mat|ic (al′ə krə mat′ik), *adj.* exhibiting variety of color, as a gem. [< *allo-* + *chromatic*]
al|loch|ro|ous (ə lok′rō əs), *adj.* having various colors, as a mineral. [< Greek *allóchroos* (with English *-ous*) changed in color < *állos* other + *chroiā́* color]
al|loch|tho|nous (ə lok′thə nəs), *adj.* formed or coming from somewhere else; not native. [< Greek *állos* other + *chthṓn* earth + English *-ous*]
al|lo|cor|tex (al′ə kôr′teks), *n.* the oldest part of the cerebral cortex; archipallium. [< *allo-* + *cortex*]
al|lo|cu|tion (al′ə kyü′shən), *n.* a formal or official address, especially by the Pope. [< Latin *allocūtiō, -ōnis* < *alloquī* to address < *ad-* to + *loquī* speak]
al|lod (al′od), *n.* an allodium; freehold.
al|lo|di|al (ə lō′dē əl), *adj.* **1** held in absolute ownership. **2** of or having to do with the holding of land in absolute ownership. Also, **alodial.**
al|lo|di|um (ə lō′dē əm), *n., pl.* **-di|a** (-dē ə). land held in absolute ownership without rent, service, or other restriction; freehold (contrasted with *feud*). Also, **allod, alod, alodium.** [< Medieval Latin *allodium* < Frankish (compare Old High German *alōd*)]
al|log|a|mous (ə log′ə məs), *adj.* of or caused by allogamy.
al|log|a|my (ə log′ə mē), *n.* cross-fertilization (contrasted with *autogamy*). [< *allo-* + *-gamy*]
al|lo|ge|ne|ic (al′ə jə nē′ik), *adj.* = allogenic.
al|lo|gen|ic (al′ə jen′ik), *adj.* genetically unlike: *grafts of allogenic bone marrow.* [< *allo-* + *-gen* + *-ic*]
al|lo|graft (al′ə graft, -gräft), *n.* = homograft.
al|lo|graph (al′ə graf, -gräf), *n. Linguistics.* one of the variant forms of a grapheme. The letters *f* in *fun, ff* in *ruff,* and *gh* in *tough* are allographs. [< *allo-* + *-graph*]
al|lom|er|ism (ə lom′ə riz əm), *n.* variability in chemical constitution with similarity in crystalline form. [< Greek *állos* other + *méros* part + English *-ism*]
al|lom|er|ous (ə lom′ər əs), *adj.* alike in crystalline form, but different in chemical constitution.
al|lo|met|ric (al′ə met′rik), *adj.* of or characterized by allometry.
al|lom|e|try (ə lom′ə trē), *n.* the relative growth rate of one part of an organism with reference to the rest, as a result of which its relative size changes with age. [< *allo-* + *-metry*]
al|lo|morph (al′ə môrf), *n.* **1** one of the variant forms of a morpheme. *Ad-* in *adjust, ac-* in *acquire,* and *al-* in *allocate* are some allomorphs of the morpheme *ad-.* **2** = allotrope. [< *allo-* + *morph*]
al|lo|mor|phic (al′ə môr′fik), *adj.* = allotropic.
al|lo|mor|phism (al′ə môr′fiz əm), *n.* = allotropy.
al|lons (á lôɴ′), *v.i. French.* let's go! hurry up!
al|lo|nym (al′ə nim), *n.* **1** the name of another person, especially of a better-known person, used by an author as his in the publishing of a work. **2** a work published under another's name. [< Greek *állos* other + dialectal *ónyma* name]
al|lon|y|mous (ə lon′ə məs), *adj.* published under the name of someone, especially of a better-known person, other than the real author.
al|lo|path (al′ə path), *n.* **1** a doctor who uses allopathy. **2** a person who favors allopathy.
al|lo|path|ic (al′ə path′ik), *adj.* of allopathy; using allopathy.
al|lo|path|i|cal|ly (al′ə path′ə klē), *adv.* by, in, or as related to allopathy.
al|lop|a|thist (ə lop′ə thist), *n.* = allopath.
al|lop|a|thy (ə lop′ə thē), *n.* the method of treating a disease by using remedies to produce effects different from those caused by the disease treated (contrasted with *homeopathy*). [< German *Allopathie* < Greek *állos* different + *-pátheia* effect < *páthos* suffering]
al|lo|pat|ric (al′ə pat′rik), *adj.* designating two species or populations whose natural ranges are usually adjacent but do not overlap. [< Greek *állos* other + *patriā́* clan + English *-ic*]
al|lo|phane (al′ə fān), *n.* a translucent, uncrystallized mineral, hydrous aluminum silicate, with a sky-blue, green, brown, or yellow color. [< Late Greek *allophanḗs* < *állos* different + *phaínesthai* appear]
al|lo|phone (al′ə fōn), *n.* any one of several slightly different speech sounds that are heard as the same sound by speakers of a given language or dialect; one of the individual sounds belonging to a single phoneme. *Example:* The *t* in *take* and the *t* in *atom* are allophones of the phoneme *t.* [< *allo-* + *phone*[2]]
al|lo|phon|ic (al′ə fon′ik), *adj.* of or having to do with allophones: *Spontaneous changes must have their origin in allophonic variation* (Harold Allen).
al|lo|phyl|i|an (al′ə fil′ē ən), *adj. Archaic.* not Indo-European or Semitic: *Basque and Finnish are allophylian languages.* [< Latin *allophȳlus* (< Greek *allóphȳlos* < *állos* other + *phȳlḗ* tribe) + English *-ian*]
al|lo|plasm (al′ə plaz′əm), *n.* a differentiated form of protoplasm, such as the protoplasm which develops into cilia and flagella. [< *allo-* + (proto)*plasm*]
al|lo|plas|tic (al′ə plas′tik), *adj.* **1** shaping or altering the environment: *alloplastic adaptation.* **2** of or having to do with alloplasty.
al|lo|plas|ty (al′ə plas′tē), *n.* the replacement of the body's tissues and organs with synthetic substances, especially plastics. [< *allo-* + Greek *plastós* molded]
al|lo|pol|y|ploid (al′ə pol′i ploid), *n. Genetics.* a polyploid organism in which the different sets of chromosomes originate from different species. See also **amphidiploid.** [< *allo-* + *polyploid*]
al|lo|pu|ri|nol (al′ə pyůr′ə nol), *n.* a drug that inhibits the enzyme causing the formation of uric acid in the body, used especially in the treatment of gout. [< *allo-* + *purine* + *-ol*[1]]
all-or-none (ôl′ôr nun′), *adj.* = all-or-nothing: *This transfer is an "all-or-none" process, the electron getting all of the photon's energy or none at all* (Sears and Zemansky).
all-or-noth|ing (ôl′ôr nuth′ing), *adj.* either completely effective or ineffective; admitting no fine distinctions: *G-6-PD is an all-or-nothing substance: the enzyme is either produced in the normal amount, or is not produced at all* (Time).

***allosaur**

***al|lo|saur** (al′ə sôr), *n.* = allosaurus.
al|lo|sau|rus or **Al|lo|sau|rus** (al′ə sôr′əs), *n.* a carnivorous dinosaur of the Jurassic period, fossil remains of which have been found in North America, often attaining to a length of over 30 feet and a height of 15 feet. [< New Latin *Allosaurus,* the genus name < Greek *állos* + *saûrus* lizard]
al|lo|some (al′ə sōm), *n. Genetics.* **1** a chromosome that is not typical; an irregular or abnormal chromosome. **2** a sex chromosome. [< *allo-* + *-some*[3]]
al|lo|ster|ic (al′ə ster′ik), *adj.* of or having to do with interactions produced by enzymes indirectly or not at the active or catalytic site: *allosteric effects or activity.* **—al′lo|ster′i|cal|ly,** *adv.*
al|lo|ster|y (ə los′tər ē), *n.* allosteric property or effect.
al|lot (ə lot′), *v.t.,* **-lot|ted, -lot|ting. 1** to divide and distribute in parts or shares: *The profits from the candy sale have been allotted equally to the Boy Scouts and the Girl Scouts.* **2** to give as a share, task, duty, or the like; assign: *The teacher allotted each boy a part in the Christmas play.* **SYN:** See syn. under **assign. 3** to appropriate (anything) to a special purpose; allocate: *Ten years I will allot to the attainment of knowledge* (Samuel Johnson). [< Middle French *allotir* < Old French *aloter* < *a-* to + *lot* lot < a Germanic word] **—al|lot′ta|ble,** *adj.* **—al|lot′ter,** *n.*
—Syn. **1 Allot, apportion** mean to give out in shares. **Allot** emphasizes giving set amounts for a definite purpose or to particular persons, and does not suggest the way in which the shares are set or distributed: *The Government is ready to allot homesteads in that area.* **Apportion** emphasizes division and distribution according to a fair plan, usually in proportions settled by some rule: *The reward money was apportioned among those who had helped in the rescue.*
al|lo|the|ism (al′ə thē′iz əm), *n.* the worship of other gods. [< Greek *állos* other + English *theism*]
al|lot|ment (ə lot′mənt), *n.* **1** division and distribution in parts or shares: *The allotment of profits was made Monday.* **2a** the share, part, or portion allotted: *Your allotment was four dollars.* **b** that part of a serviceman's pay which he designates to be sent to his family or dependents. **3** *British.* a small plot of land rented or assigned to someone for gardening.
al|lot|ri|oph|a|gy (ə lot′rē of′ə jē), *n.* an appetite for substances unsuitable for food. [< Greek *allótrios* foreign (< *állos* other) + *phageîn* eat]
al|lo|trope (al′ə trōp), *n.* an allotropic form.
al|lo|trop|ic (al′ə trop′ik), *adj.* occurring in two or more forms that differ in physical and chemical properties but not in the kind of atoms of which they are composed. Oxygen gas and ozone are allotropic forms of the element oxygen; they are gases composed of the same kind of atoms, but ozone is more active than oxygen, is heavier, and has an irritating odor. [< Swedish *allotropi* (< Greek *állos* another + *trópos* way) + English *-ic*] **—al′lo|trop′i|cal|ly,** *adv.*
al|lo|trop|i|cal (al′ə trop′ə kəl), *adj.* = allotropic.
al|lo|tro|pic|i|ty (al′ə trə pis′ə tē), *n.* the quality of being allotropic.
al|lot|ro|pism (ə lot′rə piz əm), *n.* = allotropy.
al|lot|ro|py (ə lot′rə pē), *n.* the property or fact of being allotropic.
all' ot|ta|va (äl′ lōt tä′vä), *Music.* a musical direction (8va) to play notes an octave higher or lower than written, higher if *8va* is above the staff, lower if *8va* is below the staff. [< Italian *all'ottava* at the octave]
al|lot|tee (ə lot′ē′), *n.* a person to whom something is allotted.
al|lo|type (al′ə tīp′), *n.* **1** *Biology.* a single specimen of the opposite sex of the specimen (holotype) on which a description of a species, variety, etc., is based. **2** *Genetics.* any of several different characteristics shown by inheritable amino-acid sequences at various positions on polypeptide chains, indicating genetic variations. [< *allo-* + *type*]
al|lo|typ|ic (al′ə tip′ik), *adj. Genetics.* of or having to do with an allotype: *an allotypic character, an allotypic determinant.*
all-out (ôl′out′), *adj., adv. Informal.* *—adj.* greatest possible; complete: *He made an all-out effort to get on the team.*
—adv. to the utmost extent or degree: *to go all-out to win. We found we had to row all-out to keep up with the . . . flyers* (Atlantic).
all-out|er (ôl′ou′tər), *n. Informal.* an all-out devotee, supporter, follower, or the like.
all|o|ver (*adj.* ôl′ō′vər; *n.* ôl′ō′vər), *adj., n.* *—adj.* **1** covering the whole surface: *an allover pattern.*

Pronunciation Key: hat, āge, cãre, fär; let, ēqual, tėrm; it, īce; hot, ōpen, ôrder; oil, out; cup, pu̇t, rüle; child; long; thin; ᴛʜen; zh, measure;
ə represents a in about, e in taken, i in pencil, o in lemon, u in circus.

2 having a pattern that is repeated over the whole surface of a fabric, especially an embroidered or lace fabric: *One dress of white surah [has] an allover diamond print in charcoal* (New Yorker).
—*n.* a fabric with such a pattern.

al|low (ə lou′), *v.t.* **1** to let (someone) do something; permit (something) to be done: *The class was not allowed to leave until the bell rang. They do not allow swimming at this beach.* **SYN:** See syn. under **permit**. **2** to let have; give as an allowance or share: *His father allows him $2 a week as spending money.* **SYN:** grant, yield, assign. **3** to accept as true; admit; acknowledge; recognize: *The judge allowed the claim of the man whose property was damaged.* **4** to add or subtract to make up for something: *to allow an extra hour for traveling time. The trip will cost you only $20, but you ought to allow $5 more for extra expenses.* **5** to permit to happen, especially through carelessness or neglect: *to allow a cake to burn.* **6** *U.S. Dialect.* to say; think: *... Brer Rabbit he 'low he was on his way to Miss Meadows* (Joel Chandler Harris). **7** *Archaic.* to approve; sanction.
allow as how, *U.S. Dialect.* to admit or concede that: *Grant allows as how maybe Sherman is right* (New Yorker).
allow for, to take into consideration; provide for: *She purposely made the dress larger to allow for shrinking when it was washed. Don't forget to allow for changes in the weather.*
allow of, to permit; admit: *But the window, too, allowed of a double vision* (Encounter).
[< Old French *alouer* approve < Latin *allaudāre* (< *ad-* to + *laudāre* praise), confused with Old French *alouer* assign < Medieval Latin *allocare* allocate] —**al|low′er**, *n.*

al|low|a|bil|i|ty (ə lou′ə bil′ə tē), *n.* the quality of being allowable; allowableness.

al|low|a|ble (ə lou′ə bəl), *adj., n.* —*adj.* allowed by law or by a person in authority; permitted by the rules or by custom or usage; not forbidden: *In some parks it is allowable to walk on the grass.* **SYN:** permissible, legitimate.
—*n.* **1** that which is or may be allowed. **2** *U.S.* the amount of oil a producer is permitted to take from an oil well in a given period, as specified by state or federal authority: *Cutbacks in oil production allowables during the second half by state regulatory bodies may lower crude oil production for the year* (Wall Street Journal). —**al|low′a|ble|ness**, *n.* —**al|low′a|bly**, *adv.*

al|low|ance (ə lou′əns), *n., v.,* **-anced, -anc|ing.** —*n.* **1** a limited share set apart; definite portion or amount given out to meet expenses or requirements: *My weekly allowance is $2.* **SYN:** allotment. **2** an amount added or subtracted to make up for something; discount: *The salesman offered us an allowance of $500 on our old car; so we got a $3500 car for $3000.* **3** an allowing; conceding: *allowance of a claim.* **SYN:** admission, acceptance. **4** tolerance: *allowance of slavery.* **5** *Machinery.* the permissible variation in the dimensions of parts that fit together, as a shaft and a bearing. **6** a handicap in the form of an advantage, in certain sports. **7** (in coinage) the permissible variation from the standard in minting.
—*v.t.* **1** to put (anyone) upon an allowance. **2** to limit to a fixed, regular amount.
make allowance (for) or **make allowances (for)**, to take into consideration; allow for: *You should make allowance for the wishes of others.*

al|low|ed|ly (ə lou′id lē), *adv.* by general allowance; admittedly: *It may allowedly be used in all cases* (Thomas De Quincey).

al|lox|an (ə lok′sən), *n.* a compound produced by oxidation of uric acid, that causes diabetes when injected into test animals. *Formula:* $C_4H_2N_2O_4$ [< *all*(antoin) + *ox*(alic acid) + *-an*]

al|loy (*n.* al′oi, ə loi′; *v.* ə loi′), *n., v.* —*n.* **1** a metal made by mixing and fusing together two or more metals, or a metal and some other substance. Brass is an alloy of copper and zinc. Alloys are often harder, lighter, and stronger than the pure metals of which they are composed. **2** an inferior metal mixed with a more valuable one: *This ring is not pure gold; there is some alloy in it.* **3** *Figurative.* any injurious addition; impurity: *The only alloy in our enjoyment of the vacation was the rainy weather.* **4** relative purity, fineness, or quality of metals. [< French *aloi* < Old French *alei* < *aleier;* see the verb]
—*v.t.* **1** to make into an alloy. **2** to strengthen, lighten, harden, or make less valuable by mixing with an inferior metal. **3** *Figurative.* to make lower or less valuable by mixing with something bad; debase: *Her happiness was alloyed by the thought that other people were suffering.*
[< French *aloyer* < Old French *aleier* combine < Latin *alligāre* < *ad-* to + *ligāre* bind. See etym. of doublet **ally**, verb.]

alloy metallurgy, = physical metallurgy.

alloy steel, carbon steel to which additional alloying elements such as chromium, nickel, and manganese have been added to make it harder or more resistant to corrosion or to give it some other special property.

all-per|vad|ing (ôl′pər vā′ding), *adj.* thoroughly or extremely pervasive; permeating all: *an all-pervading principle.*

all-pow|er|ful (ôl′pou′ər fəl), *adj.* omnipotent; almighty: *He is still not the all-powerful dictator that Stalin was* (Newsweek).

all-pur|pose (ôl′pėr′pəs), *adj.* that can be used for any purpose: *an all-purpose thread. All-purpose flour is as suitable for pastry and cakes as it is for bread.*

all ready, quite ready; completely ready.
▶ See note under **already**.

all-right (ôl′rīt′), *adj. U.S. Slang.* very good or excellent of its kind; very dependable: *Don't worry about him; he's an all-right fellow.*

all right, **1** without error; correct: *The answers were all right.* **2** satisfactory; acceptable: *The work was not done very well; but it was all right. The substitute material should be all right.* **3** in a satisfactory way: *The engine seemed to be working all right.* **4** in good health: *I was ill for a week, but I'm all right now.* **5** yes: *"Will you come with me?" "All right."* **6** without doubt; certainly: *He is smart, all right!*
▶ See **alright** for usage note.

all|right|nik (ôl′rīt′nik), *n. Slang.* a person who is smug and self-satisfied with his money or status: *Most of us are allrightniks—doing okay* (Herbert Gold). [< *all right* + *-nik*, a Slavic personal suffix; originally Yiddish slang]

all-risk (ôl′risk′), *adj.* covering against all kinds of losses except those specifically excluded by the terms of the policy: *all-risk insurance.*

all-risks (ôl′risks′), *adj.* = all-risk.

all-round (ôl′round′), *adj. Especially British.* all-around.

all-round|er (ôl′roun′dər), *n. Especially British.* all-arounder.

All Saints' Day, November 1, a church festival honoring all the saints; Allhallows.

all|seed (ôl′sēd′), *n.* any one of various plants producing a large quantity of seed, especially: **a** a kind of goosefoot. **b** the knotgrass.

all-sky camera (ôl′skī′), an astronomical instrument for photographing the sky from horizon to horizon, consisting of a convex mirror facing the sky and a camera pointed down at its center.

all|sorts (ôl′sôrts′), *n.pl. Especially British.* assorted candies: *... hoards of liquorice allsorts* (Punch).

All Souls' Day, November 2 (or the next day if November 2 is a Sunday), a day when services are held in the Roman Catholic Church and prayers said for all the souls in purgatory.

all|spice (ôl′spīs′), *n.* **1** a spice having a flavor suggesting a mixture of cinnamon, nutmeg, and cloves. **2** the berry of the West Indian and Central American pimento tree from which this spice is made. **3** the tree itself; pimento.

all-star (ôl′stär′), *adj., n.* —*adj.* made up of the best players or performers: *an all-star show. He has been named to an all-star team.*
—*n.* a member of an all-star team, cast, or other group.

all-ter|rain vehicle (ôl′te rān′, -ter′ān), a strong, lightweight automobile designed for use on rough, sandy, or marshy terrain. *Abbr:* ATV (no periods).

all|thorn (ôl′thôrn′), *n.* a desert shrub of the southwestern United States and Mexico, having tiny, scalelike leaves and branches terminating in hard, sharply pointed tips.

all-time (ôl′tīm′), *adj. U.S. Informal.* **1** of or for time within memory: *an all-time box office favorite.* **2** of or for all time up to the present: *an all-time track record.* **3** outstripping all others of all time: *an all-time high in farm production.*

all together, everyone in a group: *We found the boys all together in a group.*
▶ **All together** (two words) is an adjective phrase; **altogether** is an adverb.

al|lude (ə lüd′), *v.i.,* **-lud|ed, -lud|ing.** to refer indirectly (to); mention slightly in passing: *Do not ask him about his failure; do not even allude to it.* **SYN:** hint, intimate, insinuate, advert. See syn. under **refer**. [< Latin *allūdere* play with < *ad-* to + *lūdere* play]

al|lu|mette (à ly met′), *n. French.* a match for lighting a fire.

all-up weight (ôl′up′), *Especially British.* the gross weight of an aircraft.

al|lure (ə lůr′), *v.,* **-lured, -lur|ing,** *n.* —*v.t.* to tempt or attract very strongly; fascinate; charm: *Circus life allured him with its action and excitement.* **SYN:** See syns. under **charm** and **lure**.
—*v.i.* to be attractive or fascinating.
—*n.* great charm; attractiveness; fascination: *the allure of the sea.*
[< Middle French *alurer* < Old French < *a-* to + *leurre* a lure < a Germanic word. See related etym. at **lure**.] —**al|lure′ment**, *n.* —**al|lur′er**, *n.*

al|lur|ing (ə lůr′ing), *adj.* strongly attracting; tempting: *an alluring advertisement, an alluring prospect, alluring terms.* —**al|lur′ing|ly**, *adv.* —**al|lur′ing|ness**, *n.*

al|lu|sion (ə lü′zhən), *n.* **1** slight or incidental mention made in passing; indirect reference: *John was hurt by any allusion to his failure.* **SYN:** hint, intimation, insinuation, suggestion. **2** a reference by something quoted or mentioned in passing, especially to something presumed to be well known: *His writings are filled with classical allusions.* [< Latin *allūsiō, -ōnis* < *allūdere* play with < *ad-* to + *lūdere* play]
▶ See **illusion** for usage note.

al|lu|sive (ə lü′siv), *adj.* containing an allusion; full of allusions: *"How do you mean, Nature?" asked Larry, who did not understand the allusive conversation of intellectual men but appreciated it nonetheless* (New Yorker). —**al|lu′sive|ly**, *adv.* —**al|lu′sive|ness**, *n.*

al|lu|vi|al (ə lü′vē əl), *adj., n.* —*adj.* **1** consisting of, or formed by sand, silt, or mud left by flowing water: *an alluvial plain.* A delta is an alluvial deposit at the mouth of a river. **2** found in silt or sand (alluvium) left by flowing water.
—*n.* alluvial soil.

alluvial fan or **cone**, *Geology.* a fan-shaped deposit of sand, silt, or mud formed at the point where a stream emerges from a ravine into a plain or other relatively flat area. See picture under **valley**.

al|lu|vi|on (ə lü′vē ən), *n.* **1** = alluvium. **2** the wash or flow of water against a shore. **3** a flood. **4** *Law.* the formation of new land by the slow deposits made by flowing water or waves. [< Latin *alluviō, -ōnis* < *alluere* wash against < *ad-* against + *lavere* wash]

al|lu|vi|um (ə lü′vē əm), *n., pl.* **-vi|ums, -vi|a** (-vē ə). the deposit of sand, silt, or mud left by flowing water. [< Late Latin *alluvium*, neuter of *alluvius* alluvial < Latin *alluere* wash against < *ad-* against + *lavere* wash]

all-weath|er (ôl′weᴛʜ′ər), *adj. Especially U.S.* that can be used in all kinds of weather: *an all-weather highway. Bus schedules, moreover, are often highly irregular and the street corner is hardly an all-weather waiting room* (Harper's).

al|ly (*n.* al′ī, ə lī′; *see note below; v.* ə lī′), *n., pl.* **-lies**, *v.,* **-lied, -ly|ing.** —*n.* **1** a person, group, or nation united with another for some special purpose: *England and France have been allies in some wars, though they have fought against each other in others.* See also **Allies**. **SYN:** associate, confederate. **2** a helper; supporter: (*Figurative.*) *Science instead of being the enemy of religion, becomes its ally* (Henry Thomas Buckle). **3** a related animal, plant, form, or thing.
—*v.t.* **1** to combine for some special purpose; unite by formal agreement: *The premier of Belgium signed a treaty that allied his country to France.* **2** to associate; connect: *This newspaper is allied with three others.* **SYN:** affiliate. **3** to relate by similarity, as of structure or descent; connect by a common origin: *Dogs are allied to wolves.*
—*v.i.* to join or unite; enter into alliance: *to ally against the common enemy.*
[< Old French *allier*, alteration of *aleier* < Latin *alligāre* < *ad-* to + *ligāre* bind. See etym. of doublet **alloy**, verb.]
▶ **ally.** The two pronunciations of the noun may often be used by the same speaker, the choice between them being determined by position of the word in a sentence and the cadence preferred.
▶ See **allied** for another usage note.

-ally, *suffix forming adverbs.* in a ___ic manner: *Basically = in a basic manner. Tragically = in a tragic manner.* [< *-al*[1] + *-ly*[1]]

all-year (ôl′yir′), *adj.* for the whole year; lasting throughout the year; in operation year-round: *an all-year harbor, all-year air conditioning.*

al|lyl (al′əl), *n.* a univalent, unsaturated, open-chain radical found in the liquids yielded especially by pressing garlic, onion, and mustard seeds. *Formula:* $CH_2{:}CHCH_2$— [< Latin *allium* garlic + English *-yl*]

allyl alcohol, a colorless, poisonous liquid used in the synthesis of organic chemicals. The vapor given off by it is so irritating to the eyes and mucous membranes that it has sometimes been used in chemical warfare. *Formula:* $CH_2{:}CHCH_2OH$

allyl chloride, a colorless, poisonous liquid used in making allyl alcohol and allyl resin. *Formula:* $CH_2{:}CHCH_2Cl$

al|lyl|ic (ə lil′ik), *adj.* of or having to do with allyl; characterized by the presence of allyl.

allyl resin, any one of a group of durable, virtu-

ally colorless resins prepared from allyl alcohol.
allyl sulfide, the colorless or yellowish oil which gives onions and garlic their taste and smell. *Formula:* $(C_3H_5)_2S$
al|lyl|thi|o|u|re|a (al′əl thī′ō yü rē′ə, -yůr′ē-), *n.* = thiosinamine.
al|ma or **al|mah** (al′mə), *n.* (in Egypt) a girl who has been trained as a professional singer and dancer. Also, **alme, almeh.** [< Arabic *'ālimah* an instructed female]
Al|ma|gest (al′mə jest), *n.* **1** the great astronomical treatise written by Ptolemy (Greek astronomer of Alexandria) about 140 A.D. **2** Also, **almagest.** any of various medieval books on astrology and alchemy. [< Old French *almageste* < Arabic *al-majistī* < *al* the + Greek *megístē* (*sýntaxis*) the greatest (composition)]
Al|ma Ma|ter (al′mə mä′tər; äl′mə; mā′tər), **1** a title given by the ancient Romans to several goddesses, especially to Ceres. **2** = alma mater. [< Latin *alma māter* bounteous mother]
al|ma ma|ter (al′mə mä′tər; äl′mə; mā′tər), **1** a person's school, college, or university, at which he is or has been a student: [*He*] *turned over the stock* (*valued at $1,900*) *to his alma mater, Gonzaga University* (Newsweek). **2** a school's official or particular song. [< *Alma Mater*]
al|ma|nac (ôl′mə nak), *n.* **1** a reference book published every year, often containing summaries of information on particular subjects. **2** a calendar that also gives information about the weather, sun, moon, stars, tides, church holidays, and other facts. [< Medieval Latin *almanachus* < Spanish *almanaque* < Arabic *almanākh*, apparently < Late Greek *almenichiakón* calendar]
al|ma|nack (ôl′mə nak), *n. Archaic.* = almanac.
al|man|dine (al′mən dēn, -din), *n.* **1** a variety of garnet with a deep red color. **2** *U.S.* a violet variety of spinel. [earlier *alabandine* < Late Latin *alabandīna* (*gemma*) (gem) of Alabanda, a city of Caria]
al|man|dite (al′mən dīt), *n.* = almandine (def. 1).
al|me or **al|meh** (al′mə), *n.* = alma.
al|me|mar (al mē′mär), *n.* the platform in a synagogue on which stands the lectern used by the reader of the Law and the Prophets; bimah. [alteration of Arabic *al-minbar* the pulpit (of the mosque)]
al|might|y (ôl mī′tē), *adj., adv., n.* — ***adj.*** **1** possessing all power; all-powerful: *O God Almighty, Blessed Saviour* (Tennyson). **SYN:** omnipotent. **2** having great power: ... *Truth's almighty charms* (William Cowper). **3** *U.S. Informal.* great: *almighty nonsense.*
— ***adv.*** *U.S. Informal.* exceedingly; very: ... *an almighty fine girl* (Mark Twain).
— ***n.*** **Almighty** or **the Almighty**, God; the Deity: *thou Almighty! in whose hand is fate* (Alexander Pope).
[Old English *ealmihtig* < *eall* all + *mihtig* mighty] — **al|might′i|ly**, *adv.* — **al|might′i|ness**, *n.*
almighty dollar, *U.S. Informal.* money thought of as all-powerful.
al|mi|qui (äl mē′kē), *n.* the solenodon of Cuba. [< Spanish *almiquí*]
al|mi|rah (al mī′rə), *n.* a cupboard or wardrobe, in India. [< Hindustani *almārī* < Portuguese *almario* < Latin *armārium.* See etym. of doublet **ambry, armoire.**]
***al|mond** (ä′mənd, am′ənd; äl′mənd, al′-), *n.* **1a** the edible, flattish, oval-shaped nut in the peachlike fruit of a tree growing in warm regions. **b** the tree that the fruit grows on. It belongs to the rose family. **2** any of various similar fruits or the trees on which they grow. **3** something shaped like an almond. **4** a pale-tan color; biscuit. **5** a kind of pigeon. [< Old French *almande* < Medieval Latin *amandula* < Latin *amygdala* < Greek *amygdálē*] — **al′mond|like′**, *adj.*

***almond** definition 1a

al|mond-eyed (ä′mənd īd′, am′ənd-; äl′mənd-, al′-), *adj.* having eyes that appear to be oval-shaped and to have pointed ends.
al|mon|er (al′mə nər, ä′mə-), *n.* **1** *Historical.* a person who distributes alms for a king, a monastery, or a person of rank. **2** *British.* **a** a social worker attached to a hospital. **b** an officer in the royal household. [< Old French *almosnier* < Late Latin *elēmosinārius* almsgiver < Latin *eleēmosyna* alms]
al|mon|ry (al′mən rē, ä′mən-), *n., pl.* **-ries.** a place where alms are distributed. [< Old French *aumosnerie* < *almosnier* almoner]
al|most (ôl′mōst, ôl mōst′), *adv., adj.* — ***adv.*** nearly; all but; very near to: *Nine is almost ten. I almost missed the train. He was almost within sight of the city.*
— ***adj.*** near; virtual: *Huston consulted them about the finer points of cowboy life with almost reverence* (Manchester Guardian Weekly).
almost never, scarcely ever: *The old lady almost never goes outside in the winter.*
almost no, scarcely any: *We have almost no milk left after the boys drank so much for lunch.*
[Old English *eall mǣst* nearly]
▶ See **most** for usage note.
alms (ämz, älmz), *n. sing. or pl.* **1** money or gifts to help the poor; charity: *The beggar asked for alms. To scatter from our abundance occasional alms is not enough* (William Ellery Channing). **SYN:** dole, benefaction. **2** *Archaic, Figurative.* a good deed; a charity. [Old English *ælmysse* < Vulgar Latin *alēmosyna* < Latin *eleēmosyna* < Greek *eleēmosýnē* pity, alms, ultimately < *éleos* pity]
alms box, *British.* a box kept in or just outside a church for alms.
alms-deed (ämz′dēd′, älmz′-), *n. Archaic.* a charitable deed.
alms|giv|er (ämz′giv′ər, älmz′-), *n.* a person who helps the poor with money or other gifts.
alms|giv|ing (ämz′giv′ing, älmz′-), *n.* the giving of help to the poor.
alms|house (ämz′hous′, älmz′-), *n.* a home for persons who do not have enough money to live on and who are supported at public expense or (in Great Britain) by private charity.
alms|man (ämz′mən, älmz′-), *n., pl.* **-men. 1** a person supported by alms. **2** a giver of alms: *King John also was a great almsman* (Edward A. Freeman).
alms|wom|an (ämz′wům′ən, älmz′-), *n., pl.* **-wom|en. 1** a woman supported by alms. **2** a woman who gives alms.
al|mu|can|tar (al′myə kan′tər), *n. Astronomy.* **1** a small circle on the celestial sphere parallel to the horizon or horizontal plane; a parallel or circle of altitude. **2** an astronomical instrument consisting of a telescope crossed by horizontal wires and mounted on a box floating on mercury. By using it to note the rise of a star in the east and the setting of a star in the west an observer can accurately correct a timepiece and determine latitude. [< French *almicantarat* < Medieval Latin *almucantarath* < Arabic *al-muqanṭarāt*, plural, ultimately < *qanṭara* bridge]
al|muce (al′myüs), *n.* = amice[2]. [probably < Medieval Latin *almutia.* Compare etym. under **amice[2].**]
al|mug (al′mug), *n.* an unidentified tree mentioned in the Bible (I Kings 10:11, 12). See also **algum.** [< Hebrew *'almūg*]
al|ni|co (al′nə kō), *n.* an alloy of iron in combination with aluminum, nickel, cobalt and small amounts of other elements. Alnico is permanently magnetic and can lift up to 60 times its own weight. [< *al*(uminum) + *ni*(ckel) + *co*(balt)]
al|o|ca|sia (al′ə kā′zhə), *n.* any one of certain tropical herbs having low leaves and reddish berries. [< New Latin *Alocasia*, variation of *Colocasia* the taro genus < Greek *kolokasiā* root of an Egyptian bean]
al|od (al′od), *n.* = allodium.
a|lo|di|al (ə lō′dē əl), *adj.* = allodial.
a|lo|di|um (ə lō′dē əm), *n., pl.* **-di|a** (-dē ə). = allodium.
al|oe (al′ō), *n.* **1** a plant related to the lily, having a long spike of flowers and thick, narrow, fleshy leaves. It grows chiefly in South Africa and other warm, dry climates. **2** *U.S.* the century plant. [< Latin *aloē* < Greek *alóē*]
al|oes (al′ōz), *n.pl.* (*sing. in use*). **1a** a bitter drug made from the dried juice of the leaves of certain aloes, used chiefly as a laxative. **b** the juice of these leaves. **2** the fragrant wood or resin of a kind of East Indian tree; lignaloes.
▶ **Aloes**, the drug, is plural in form and singular in use: *Aloes is sometimes used as a tonic.*
al|o|et|ic (al′ō et′ik), *adj., n.* — ***adj.*** of the nature of aloes; having aloes as an ingredient, as a medicine.
— ***n.*** an aloetic medicine.
a|loft (ə lôft′, -loft′), *adv., adj.* **1** far above the earth; up in the air; high up: *Some birds fly thousands of feet aloft.* **2** in or into the air; off from the ground. **3** high above the deck of a ship; up among the sails, rigging, or masts of a ship: *The sailor scrambled aloft to get a better view of the distant shore.* [< Scandinavian (compare Old Icelandic *ā lopti* in the air)]
a|log|i|cal (ā loj′ə kəl), *adj.* not involving logic; not based upon reason or formed by an act of judgment: *Language is neither logical nor illogical, but alogical* (Harold Allen). — **a|log′i|cal|ly**, *adv.*
a|lo|ha (ə lō′ə, ä lō′hä), *interj., n.* — ***interj.*** **1** greetings; hello. **2** good-by; farewell.
— ***n.*** (in Hawaii) love.
[< a Hawaiian word]
***aloha shirt**, a brightly colored, variously patterned, lightweight sports shirt, usually worn without a jacket.

***aloha shirt**

Aloha State, a nickname for Hawaii.
al|o|in (al′ō in), *n.* the bitter, purgative principle of aloes, that crystallizes in pale-yellow needles. *Formula:* $C_{20}H_{19}O_9$ [< *aloe* + *-in*]
a|lone (ə lōn′), *adj., adv.* — ***adj.*** **1** apart from other persons or things; quite by oneself; solitary: *She was alone in the empty house.* **SYN:** lone, isolated, unaccompanied, single. **2** without anyone else; only: *One boy alone can do this work. I alone remained.* **3** without anything more: *Meat alone is not adequate food for most people.*
— ***adv.*** **1** apart from other persons or things: *to walk alone, live alone. One tree stood alone on the hill.* **2** and nothing more; only; merely; exclusively: *He did the job for money alone.*
go it alone. See under **go[1].**
leave alone, not bother; not meddle with: *The principal is busy at his desk; you'd better leave him alone.*
let alone, a not bother; not meddle with: *If everyone will let him alone he will get his work done.* **b** not to mention: *It would have been a hot day for summer, let alone early spring.*
let well enough alone, to be satisfied with conditions and not try to change them: *He's the kind of mechanic who can't let well enough alone and is always tampering with the motor to make it work better.*
[Old English *eall* all (completely) + *āna* alone]
— **a|lone′ness**, *n.*
▶ **Alone** is most often used predicatively; when used attributively it always follows, never precedes, its noun: *Iron alone rusts.*
a|long[1] (ə lông′, -long′), *prep., adv.* — ***prep.*** **1** on or by the whole length of; from one end to or toward the other of; lengthwise of: *to walk along a river. Trees are planted along the street.* **2** on or during: *We met along the way.*
— ***adv.*** **1** from one end to the other; lengthwise: *Cars are parked along by the stadium.* **2** onward; forward: *March along quickly.* **3** *U.S.* together with someone or something: *He took his dog along. You should take a tent along if you are going camping.* **4** *U.S. Informal.* somewhere near; around: *along about four o'clock.*
all along, all the time: *He knew the answer all along. I have all along declared this to be a neutral paper* (Joseph Addison).
along of, *Dialect.* in company with; together with: *Father and I went out one day along of Captain Gooden* (Yankee Doodle).
along with, in company with; together with: *I'll go along with you.*
be along, *Informal.* to come to a place: *I will be along about evening.*
get along, *Informal.* **a** to manage with at least some success: *She gets along very well on her salary. Some of these halls turn out to be smaller than represented, but I have no doubt, to use an American expression, that we shall "get along"* (Dickens). **b** to agree: *They got along well as partners.* **c** go away! *Why don't you leave, take off, get along!* **d** to move forward; advance: *Let's get along or we'll be late. I have only just set out upon my travels, and shall learn better manners as I get along* (Laurence Sterne). **e** to succeed; prosper: *He is getting along in his new business. She expressed supreme contempt for men who had no knack of getting along in the world* (Joel Chandler Harris).
right along. See under **right.**
[Old English *andlang* stretching away, the length of < *and-* opposite + *lang* long]
a|long[2] (ə lông′, -long′), *adv.*
along of or, formerly, **along on**, *British Dialect.* because of: *An't my heart been heavy and watchful along of him and you?* (Dickens).
a|long|shore (ə lông′shôr′, -long′-; -shōr′), *adv.* **1** near or along the shore. **2** on the shore.
a|long|side (ə lông′sīd′, -long′-), *adv., prep.*
— ***adv.*** at the side; close to the side; side by side: *Anchor alongside.*
— ***prep.*** by the side of; side by side with; beside:

Pronunciation Key: hat, āge, cãre, fär; let, ēqual, tėrm, it, īce; hot, ōpen, ôrder; oil, out; cup, pu̇t, rüle; child; long; thin; ᴛʜen; zh, measure; ə represents **a** in about, **e** in taken, **i** in pencil, **o** in lemon, **u** in circus.

Park alongside the curb. The boat was tied up alongside the wharf.

alongside of, beside; next to: *If you stay alongside of me, you won't get lost.*

a|loof (ə lüf′), *adv., adj.* —***adv.*** **1** at some distance but within view; away; apart: *One boy stood aloof from all the others.* **2** without community of feeling: *to stand aloof from family joys and sorrows.*
—***adj.*** unsympathetic; not interested; withdrawn; reserved: *an aloof manner. Because of her shyness Jane seemed to be very aloof. Her aloof manner kept her from making many friends.* **SYN**: distant.
[< *a-*[1] on + obsolete *loof* luff, windward, probably < Dutch *loef*] —**a|loof′ly**, *adv.* —**a|loof′ness**, *n.*

al|o|pe|ci|a (al′ə pē′shē ə, -sē-), *n.* partial or complete loss of hair, as from disease; baldness. [< Latin *alōpecia* < Greek *alōpekíā* (originally) fox mange < *alṓpēx, -ekos* fox]

alopecia a|re|a|ta (ãr′ē ā′tə), loss of hair in sharply defined patches. [< New Latin *alopecia areata*]

al|o|pe|coid (al′ə pē′koid, ə lop′ə-), *adj.* of or like a fox; foxlike; vulpine. [< Greek *alṓpēx, -ekos* fox + English *-oid*]

Al|o|rese (al′ə rēz′, -rēs′), *n., pl.* **-rese**, *adj.* —***n.*** a native or inhabitant of the island of Alor in Indonesia.
—***adj.*** of Alor or its people.

a|lors (á lôr′), *interj. French.* then: *He raises his eyebrows and smiles. "Alors, adieu"* (James Baldwin).

a|loud (ə loud′), *adv.* **1** loud enough to be heard; not in a whisper: *He spoke aloud, although he was alone. She read the story aloud to the others.* **SYN**: audibly. **2** in a loud voice; loudly: *The wounded man groaned aloud with pain.* **SYN**: vociferously.

à l'ou|trance (à lü träɴs′), *French.* to the utmost; to the very end: *Gilbert Scott was the Hector, and Palmerston the Achilles of this early Victorian duel à l'outrance* (London Times). See also **à outrance**.

a|low[1] (ə lō′), *adv. Archaic or Nautical.* below; down. [< *a-*[1] on + *low*[1]]

a|low[2] (ə lō′, -lou′), *adj., adv. British Dialect.*
—***adj.*** blazing.
—***adv.*** on fire. [< *a-*[1] on + *low*[3] flame < a Scandinavian word]

alp (alp), *n.* **1** a high mountain. **2** mountain grassland occurring especially above the timber line. [< Latin *Alpēs* the Alps]

Alp (alp), *n.* a single peak of the Alps (mountain system in Europe).

al|pac|a (al pak′ə), *n.* **1a** a sheeplike animal of South America, with long, soft, silky hair or wool. It is a mammal closely related to, but somewhat smaller than, the llama. **b** its long, soft, and silky wool. **c** a warm, lightweight cloth made from this wool. **2a** a glossy, wiry cloth made of wool and cotton, usually black or gray. **b** an imitation of this made from rayon or cotton. [< Spanish *alpaca* < Quechua]

al|par|ga|ta (äl′pär gä′tä), *n. Spanish.* a sandal of cloth, especially canvas, with braided rope sole: *spinning and twisting heavy jute yarns for alpargatas* (Glasgow Herald).

al|peen (al′pēn), *n.* a stout-headed stick; cudgel. [< Irish Gaelic *ailpín*]

al|pen|glow (al′pən glō′), *n.* a rosy glow from the setting or rising sun often seen on or near the peaks of mountains. [partial translation of German *Alpenglühen* < *Alpen* Alps + *Glühen* glow]

***al|pen|horn** (al′pən hôrn′), *n.* a long, powerful wooden horn used especially in the Alps of Switzerland and Austria for calling cattle and for signals; alphorn; alpine horn. [< German *Alpenhorn*]

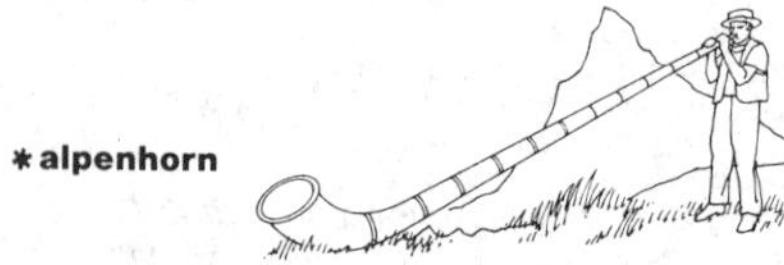

***alpenhorn**

al|pen|stock (al′pən stok′), *n.* a strong staff with an iron point, used as an aid in climbing mountains. [< German *Alpenstock*]

al|pes|trine (al pes′trin), *adj.* **1** growing on mountains below the timber line; subalpine. **2** of or having to do with high mountains, especially the Alps. [< Medieval Latin *alpestris* + English *-ine*[1]]

***al|pha** (al′fə), *n.* **1** the first letter of the Greek alphabet, corresponding to the English *A, a.* **2** the beginning; first in a series. **3** the first, largest, or other most important feature of a series, especially as a symbol. **4** one of several possible positions of atoms or groups which are substituted in a compound: *alpha iron.* [< Latin *alpha* < Greek *álpha* < Semitic (compare Hebrew *'āleph* the first letter of the Hebrew alphabet)]

***alpha** definition 1

A	α
capital letter	lower-case letter

Al|pha (al′fə), *n.* the principal (usually, the brightest) star in a constellation. Thus, the polestar is referred to by astronomers as Alpha Ursae Minoris (α Ursae Minoris), because it is the principal star in the constellation Ursa Minor.

alpha and omega, the first and the last; the beginning and the end: *I am Alpha and Omega, the beginning and the ending, saith the Lord* (Revelation 1:8). [because alpha and omega are the first and last letters of the Greek alphabet]

al|pha|bet (al′fə bet), *n., v.* —***n.*** **1** the letters of a language arranged in their usual order, not as they are in words. The English alphabet is a b c d e f g h i j k l m n o p q r s t u v w x y z. **2** a set of letters or characters representing sounds, used in writing a language. The English alphabet has only 26 letters to represent more than 40 sounds. **3** *Figurative.* parts to be learned first; elementary principles. **SYN**: rudiments, fundamentals.
—***v.t.*** to alphabetize.
[< Latin *alphabētum* < Greek *alphábētos* < *álpha* A + *bêta* B]

al|pha|be|tar|i|an (al′fə bə tãr′ē ən), *n.* a person who is learning the alphabet.

al|pha|bet|ic (al′fə bet′ik), *adj.* alphabetical: *The apparent ancestor of most of the alphabetic writing is that developed for the Phoenician language* (Henry A. Gleason, Jr.).

al|pha|bet|i|cal (al′fə bet′ə kəl), *adj.* **1** arranged by letters in the order of the alphabet: *Dictionary entries are listed in alphabetical order.* **2** of the alphabet. **3** using or expressed by an alphabet: *Mandarin Chinese is a deliberate literary medium created by Hu Shih and his helpers. Mao will now make its orthography alphabetical by edict* (Simeon Potter). —**al′pha|bet′i|cal|ly**, *adv.*

al|pha|bet|ize (al′fə bə tīz), *v.t.,* **-ized, -iz|ing.** **1** to arrange in the usual order of the letters of the alphabet: *Alphabetize the words in your spelling lesson.* **2** to express by an alphabet.
—**al′pha|bet′i|za′tion**, *n.* —**al′pha|bet|iz′er**, *n.*

alphabet soup, **1** soup cooked with pieces of dried flour paste shaped in the letters of the alphabet. **2** *U.S. Slang.* abbreviations, especially of government agencies: *Not even F.D.R.'s New Deal (WPA, PWA, NRA, etc., etc.) managed to cook up such a rich alphabet soup.* (Time).

alpha brass, brass consisting of a solid solution containing up to 38 percent zinc.

alpha cellulose, a highly refined and purified form of cellulose, used as a filler, especially in plastics, in surgery, and in filters.

Alpha Cen|tau|ri (sen tôr′ī), a star system consisting of three stars, but appearing to the naked eye as a single star of a minus magnitude, in the constellation Centaurus. [< Latin *alpha* alpha + *Centaurus, -ī* centaur]

Alpha Cru|cis (krü′sis), the brightest star in the Southern Cross (Crux) and one of the twenty brightest stars in the heavens. [< Latin *alpha* alpha + *crux, crucis* cross]

alpha decay, the disintegration of a radioactive substance through the emission of alpha particles.

al|pha|fe|to|pro|tein (al′fə fē′tə prō′tēn, -tē in), *n.* a protein of undetermined function produced in the liver by the fetus and by persons suffering from some diseases, such as hepatitis. A high level of alphafetoprotein in the blood serum of a pregnant woman indicates possible defects of the brain and central nervous system in the fetus. *Abbr:* AFP (no periods).

alpha globulin, one of the fractions of globulin, containing enzymes and hormones.

al|pha-he|lix (al′fə hē′liks), *n.* the molecular structure of many proteins, made up of a single spiral or coil of amino acid with a line of hydrogen bonds as its backbone.

Alpha Her|cu|lis (hėr′kyə lis), the largest star in the galactic system that contains the sun and earth. [< Latin *alpha* alpha + *Herculēs, -is* Hercules]

alpha iron, a soft, ductile, magnetic form of iron.

Alpha Leonis, = Regulus.

al|pha|mer|ic (al′fə mer′ik), *adj.* = alphanumeric.

al|pha|met|ic (al′fə met′ik), *n.* an arithmetical puzzle or calculation using letters instead of numerals, each letter representing a specific digit. [< *alpha*(bet) + (arith)*metic*]

al|pha|nu|mer|ic (al′fə nü mer′ik, -nyü-), *adj.* using both letters and numbers: *an alphanumeric computer.*

alpha particle, *Physics.* a positively charged particle consisting of two protons and two neutrons, released at a very high speed in the disintegration of radium and other radioactive substances. By the acquisition of two electrons it becomes an atom of helium. See diagram under **disintegration**.

alpha privative, the prefix **a-**[4] when used to mean "not" or "without," as in *asymmetrical.*

alpha rays or **alpha radiation**, *Physics.* a stream of alpha particles: *Alpha radiation consists of ... high-energy particles [that] have low penetrating ability. The skin of a mammal or the exoskeleton of an insect will stop most alpha radiation* (R. G. Wiegert).

alpha rhythm, the normal pattern of electrical oscillations in the adult brain while a person is awake but with eyes closed, recorded by an electroencephalograph in the frequency of 8 to 13 hertz per second. In childhood and old age the rate is slower.

al|pha|scope (al′fə skōp), *n.* a device connected to a computer on which letters, numerals, and symbols are displayed on a cathode-ray tube screen. [< *alpha*numeric (using both letters and numbers) + *-scope*]

alpha test, any one of a series of intelligence tests consisting mainly of questions on verbal and numerical relations, especially one given to recruits by the U.S. Army in World War I. See also **beta test**.

al|pha|to|coph|er|ol (al′fə tə kof′ə rōl, -rol), *n.* the most potent form of vitamin E. *Formula:* $C_{29}H_{50}O_2$ [< *alpha* + *tocopherol*]

Alpha Ursae Minoris, the polestar; North Star.

alpha waves, = alpha rhythm.

Al|phe|ratz (al′fə rats), *n.* the brightest star in the constellation Andromeda.

Al|phe|us (al fē′əs), *n. Greek Mythology.* a river god who fell in love with the nymph Arethusa. To help her escape him, Artemis changed her into a fountain.

Al|phonse and Gas|ton (al′fonz and gas′tən), two persons who treat each other with exaggerated or ridiculous courtesy. [< the names of the characters in a comic strip by Frederick Burr Opper, 1857-1937, an American illustrator]

alp|horn (alp′hôrn′), *n.* = alpenhorn.

al|pho|sis (al fō′sis), *n.* lack of pigment in the skin, as in albinism. [< Latin *alphus* a white spot on the skin (< Greek *alphós* dull-white leprosy)]

al|pine (al′pīn, -pin), *adj., n.* —***adj.*** **1** of or like high mountains: *alpine terrain.* **SYN**: mountainous, montane. **2** very high. **SYN**: mountainous, montane. **3** growing at high elevations, especially on mountains above the timber line: *alpine plants.*
—***n.*** an alpine plant.

Al|pine (al′pīn, -pin), *adj., n.* —***adj.*** **1** of or like the Alps (a mountain system in southern Europe). **2** very high and craggy like the Alps; lofty. **3** of or having to do with ski racing that includes the downhill and slalom (distinguished from *Nordic*).
—***n.*** **1** one of the generally recognized principal subgroups of the Caucasian racial group in Europe. Alpines are characterized by a relatively broader and rounder head than the Nordic or Mediterranean, medium height, and brunette complexion. They include the Slavs as well as many of the peoples of central Europe. **2** a member of this group.

Alpine bearberry, an evergreen shrub related to the common bearberry, but having black berries rather than red ones.

Alpine bistort, a dwarf species of the bistort.

Alpine fescue, a variety of sheep fescue that grows above the timber line from the Rocky Mountains westward.

Alpine fir, a fir native to western North America, growing especially in mountainous regions and having a pale-yellow or white wood of commercial value for lumber.

alpine garden, a kind of rock garden in which plants are grown under conditions resembling those in which alpine plants thrive.

Alpine goat, a breed of goats bred for their milk.

alpine horn, = alpenhorn.

Alpine ibex, the best-known species of ibex, found in the Alps and certain other mountainous regions of Europe.

Al|pin|ism or **al|pin|ism** (al′pə niz əm), *n.* the climbing of high mountains, especially the Alps; art or practice of a mountaineer. —**Al′pin|ist, al′pin|ist**, *n.*

al|read|y (ôl red′ē), *adv.* **1** before this time: *We arrived at noon but you had already left.* **2a** by this time; even now: *You are half an hour late already.* **b** *Especially U.S. Informal.* this very instant; right now (used for emphasis, to express impatience, etc.): *Let's go already! What is it already?* [for *all ready*]

► **All ready**, as distinguished from the adverb **already**, is used as an adjective phrase meaning "quite ready" or "completely ready": *The workmen were all ready to start their next job.*

al|right (ôl rīt′), *adv., adj. Informal.* all right.
▶**All right** is the correct spelling of both the adjective phrase (*He is all right*) and the sentence adverb meaning yes, certainly (*All right, I'll come*). The spelling **alright** is not used in formal and in most informal writing. Occasionally *alright* is found in advertising and in comic strips, but it is not as yet generally acceptable.

ALS (no periods), **1** Also, **a.l.s.** amyotrophic lateral sclerosis. **2** antilymphocyte serum. **3** Automatic-Landing System.

Al|sa|tia (al sā′shə), *n.* a former name of Whitefriars in London. Alsatia was a sanctuary for debtors and lawbreakers from the 1300's until 1697.

Al|sa|tian (al sā′shən), *adj., n.* —*adj.* **1** of or having to do with Alsace (region in northeastern France) or its people. **2** of or belonging to Alsatia.
—*n.* **1** a person born or living in Alsace. **2** (in Great Britain and Commonwealth countries) = German shepherd. **3a** a debtor or criminal in sanctuary. **b** a Bohemian person; adventurer.

Alsatian dog, (in Great Britain and Commonwealth countries) = German shepherd.

al|sike clover, or **al|sike** (al′sīk, -sik; ôl′-), *n.* a kind of tall clover with whitish flowers that become pink, native to Europe but now widely cultivated also in the United States and elsewhere for forage. It is sometimes called *Swedish clover.* [< *Alsike,* Sweden, a habitat of the plant]

al|si|na|ceous (al′sə nā′shəs), *adj.* **1** of or having to do with the pink family; caryophyllaceous. **2** allied to or resembling the chickweed. [< Latin *alsīnē* a luxuriant plant, perhaps chickweed (< Greek *alsínē*) + English *-aceous*]

Al Si|rat (al si rät′), **1** (in Moslem literature) the bridge over hell to paradise, narrow and sharp as the edge of a sword blade. **2** (in the Koran) the "right way"; the difficult path of true religion. [< Arabic *alsirāt* the road < Late Latin *strāta* street]

al|so (ôl′sō), *adv.* **1** in addition; besides; too: *That dress is pretty; it is also inexpensive.* syn: further, likewise, furthermore. **2** *Obsolete.* likewise. [Old English *ealswā* entirely so]
▶**Also** is a weak connective; ordinarily *and* will do its work better: *He came with tents, cooking things, and* [better than *also*] *about fifty pounds of photographic equipment.*

al|soph|i|la (al sof′ə lə), *n.* any one of a genus of Australian tree ferns, one variety of which is often raised indoors. [< New Latin *Alsophila* < Greek *álsos* grove + *philos* loving]

al|so-ran (ôl′sō ran′), *n.* **1** an unsuccessful contestant; a loser. **2** any horse that finishes behind the first three in a race, and thus wins nothing.

al|stroe|me|ri|a (al′strə mir′ē ə), *n.* any one of a genus of South American herbs of the amaryllis family, having leafy stems and colorful flowers. [< New Latin *Alstroemeria* < Baron Claude *Alstroemer,* 1736-1796, a Swedish botanist]

alt (alt), *adj., n. Music.* —*adj.* high in pitch. —*n.* the first octave above the treble staff: *Your ladyship's absolutely in alt ... Yes, in alt ... you have raised your voice a full octave higher* (George Colman). [< Italian *alto* high]

alt., **1** alternate. **2** altitude. **3** alto.

Alta., Alberta (a province in Canada).

al|ta fescue (al′tə), a variety of fescue grown in the humid areas of Tennessee, Missouri, and Kansas for hay and pasture.

Al|tai|an (al tā′ən, -tī′-), *n., adj.* —*n.* **1** a member of a Tartar tribe of the Altai Mountains. **2** a person belonging to any of the Ural-Altaic peoples.
—*adj.* = Altaic.

Al|ta|ic (al tā′ik), *adj., n.* —*adj.* **1** of or having to do with a family of languages that includes Turkish, Mongolian, and Manchu. **2** of or having to do with the Altai Mountains (a mountain system in central Asia) or the region in and around them.
—*n.* the Altaic family of languages. [< *Altai,* an Asian mountain chain + English *-ic*]

Al|ta|ir (al tä′ir), *n.* a star of the first magnitude, in the constellation Aquila. It is about ten times as bright as the sun. [< Arabic *al-ṭā'ir* the bird, (literally) flyer]

al|tar (ôl′tər), *n.* **1** a table or stand in the most sacred part of a church, synagogue, or temple, always thought of as the central point of worship: *The priest knelt in prayer before the altar.* (*Figurative.*) *The stones which construct the sacred altar of peace* (Edmund Burke). **2** a block of stone, mound of turf, or other raised place, on which to make sacrifices or burn offerings to a god. **3** *Figurative.* a place consecrated to devotional observances: *the family altar.*
lead to the altar, to marry: [*He*] *leads her to the village altar* (Tennyson).
[Old English *altar* < Latin *altāre,* related to *adolēre* burn up]

al|tar|age (ôl′tər ij), *n.* money offered at an altar, or received by a priest for services at an altar.

altar boy, a boy or man who helps a priest during certain religious services; acolyte.

altar bread, bread, or unleavened wafers, used in the ceremony of the Holy Eucharist or Holy Communion.

altar cloth, a decorative cloth placed on an altar.

al|tar|piece (ôl′tər pēs′), *n.* a decorated panel or wall behind and above an altar in a church; reredos.

altar rail, a railing in front of an altar, especially one that separates the altar area from the rest of the chancel; communion rail.

al|tar|wise (ôl′tər wīz′), *adv.* in an altar's position.

alt|az|i|muth (al taz′ə məth), *n.* an instrument for determining the apparent position of a heavenly body. It consists of a telescope that can be moved up and down and in a circle, and is mounted so that its angle from north and from the horizontal can be read on scales. A theodolite is a portable altazimuth. [< *alt*(itude) + *azimuth*]

al|ter (ôl′tər), *v.t.* **1** to make different; change the appearance of; vary: *If this coat is too large, a tailor can alter it to fit you.* syn: modify. **2** *U.S. and Australia.* **a** to castrate (a male animal). **b** to spay (a female animal). —*v.i.* to become different: *Since her trip to Europe, her whole outlook has altered.* syn: See syn. under **change**.
[< Middle French *altérer,* learned borrowing from Late Latin *alterāre* < Latin *alter* other]

alter., alteration.

al|ter|a|bil|i|ty (ôl′tər ə bil′ə tē), *n.* the quality of being alterable; alterableness.

al|ter|a|ble (ôl′tər ə bəl), *adj.* that can be altered.

al|ter|a|ble|ness (ôl′tər ə bəl nis), *n.* the quality of being alterable; alterability.

al|ter|a|bly (ôl′tər ə blē), *adv.* in a manner that can be altered.

al|ter|ant (ôl′tər ənt), *adj., n.* —*adj.* causing alteration.
—*n.* **1** something that causes alteration. **2** a reagent used in dyeing, to modify or change a color.

al|ter|a|tion (ôl′tə rā′shən), *n.* **1** a change in the character, appearance, or form of anything; altered or changed condition: *Mother made some alterations in my new dress. Love is not love which alters when it alteration finds* (Shakespeare). *The atom and hydrogen bombs have led to great alterations in military planning.* **2** an altering; the act of making some change in a thing: *The alteration of our house took three months.*

al|ter|a|tive (ôl′tə rā′tiv), *adj., n.* —*adj.* **1** causing change; having the power to cause change. **2** gradually restoring the healthy bodily functions.
—*n.* a remedy that gradually restores health.

al|ter|cate (ôl′tər kāt, al′-), *v.i.,* **-cat|ed, -cat|ing.** to dispute angrily; quarrel. syn: wrangle. [< Latin *altercārī* (with English *-ate*[1]) < *alter* the other]

al|ter|ca|tion (ôl′tər kā′shən, al′-), *n.* an angry dispute; quarrel: *The two teams had an altercation over the umpire's decision.* syn: wrangle.

al|tered (ôl′tərd), *n. Slang.* a hot rod modified or rebuilt for a drag race; an altered dragster.

altered chord, *Music.* a chord affected by an accidental and thus changed in character.

altered state of consciousness, any deviation from the normal activity of the mind or brain: *Drug experience can be understood only if it is viewed as an altered state of consciousness rather than as a pharmacological event* (Andrew Weil). *Telepathy, clairvoyance, mystical transports, and other altered states of consciousness may be latent in most, if not all, of us* (New Yorker). *Abbr:* ASC (no periods).

al|ter e|go (al′tər ē′gō, ôl′-; eg′ō), **1** a very intimate friend or close associate: *Marx's alter ego, Engels, wrote that, when the aims of the Revolution had been accomplished, the state would "wither away"* (New York Times). **2** another aspect of one's nature: *"Well, really," said Letty to her alter ego, "you ought to be ashamed of yourself"* (Michael Strange). [< Latin *alter ego*]

al|ter i|dem (al′tər ī′dem, ôl′-), *Latin.* another self; second self; alter ego.

al|tern (ôl′tərn, al′-), *adj. Archaic.* alternate. [< Latin *alternus* in turn, alternate < *alter* the other]

al|ter|nant (ôl tėr′nənt, al-), *adj.* **1** alternating. **2** composed of alternate layers.

al|ter|na|ri|a (al′tər nãr′ē ə, ôl′-), *n.* any one of a genus of fungi which cause fruit and vegetable blight, mold, or rot. [< New Latin *Alternaria* < Latin *alternāre* alternate (because of their form)]

al|ter|nat (âl ter ná′), *n.* rotation of precedence, a practice in diplomacy by which several states claiming equality with one another take each in turn the first place, as in the signing of treaties. [< French *alternat* (literally) alternation]

***al|ter|nate** (*v.* ôl′tər nāt, al′-; *adj., n.* ôl′tər nit, al′-), *v.,* **-nat|ed, -nat|ing,** *adj., n.* —*v.i.* **1** to occur by turns, first one and then the other; happen or be arranged by turns. Squares and circles alternate in this row: □ ○ □ ○ □ ○ □ ○. *Night and day alternate. The countryside of England alternates between hills and valleys. Good times seem to alternate with bad.* **2** to take turns: *Lucy and her sister will alternate in setting the table.* syn: rotate. **3a** (of an electric current) to reverse direction at regular intervals: *Some electric currents alternate 120 times a second.* **b** to produce or be operated by such a current.
—*v.t.* **1** to arrange by turns; do or perform by turns: *He alternated work and pleasure.* **2** to interchange regularly: *The ailing man alternated two hours of work with one hour of rest.*
—*adj.* **1** placed or occurring by turns; first one and then the other: *The row has alternate squares and circles.* syn: intermittent. **2** every other: *We get milk on alternate days because it is not delivered every day.* **3** to or for each other; reciprocal: *alternate acts of kindness.* **4** *Botany.* **a** placed singly at different heights along a stem; not opposite: *alternate leaves.* **b** placed opposite to the spaces between other organs: *petals which are alternate with sepals.*
—*n.* **1** *U.S.* a person appointed to take the place of another if necessary; a substitute: *We have several alternates on our team. If the delegate is present to vote the alternate is silent; if from any cause the delegate is absent, the alternate steps into his shoes* (James Bryce). **2** a person or thing that alternates.
[< Latin *alternāre* (with English *-ate*[1]) < *alternus* every second one < *alter* the other]
—**al′ter|nate|ness**, *n.* —**al′ter|nat′ing|ly**, *adv.*

***alternate**
adj., definition 4a

alternate angles, two angles, both interior or both exterior but not adjacent, formed when two lines are crossed by a third, on opposite sides of the third. If the two lines are parallel, the alternate angles are equal.

al|ter|nate|ly (ôl′tər nit lē, al′-), *adv.* **1** by turns; first one and then the other: *There is a sort of delight which is alternately mixed with terror and sorrow, in the comtemplation of death* (Richard Steele). **2** on each side in turn.

al|ter|nat|ing current (ôl′tər nā′ting, al′-), an electric current in which the electricity flows regularly in one direction and then the other, usually reversing 120 times per second. *Abbr:* a.c.

alternating gradient synchrotron, a particle accelerator similar to the synchrotron, but having a series of C-shaped magnets facing in opposite directions which create an alternating field, enabling particles to be accelerated to very high energies. *Abbr:* AGS (no periods).

al|ter|na|tion (ôl′tər nā′shən, al′-), *n.* an alternating; occurring by turns, first one and then the other: *There is an alternation of red and white stripes in the flag of the United States.*

***alternation of generations**, *Genetics.* the regular alternation of forms or of mode of reproduction in successive generations of an animal or plant; heterogenesis.

***alternation of generations**

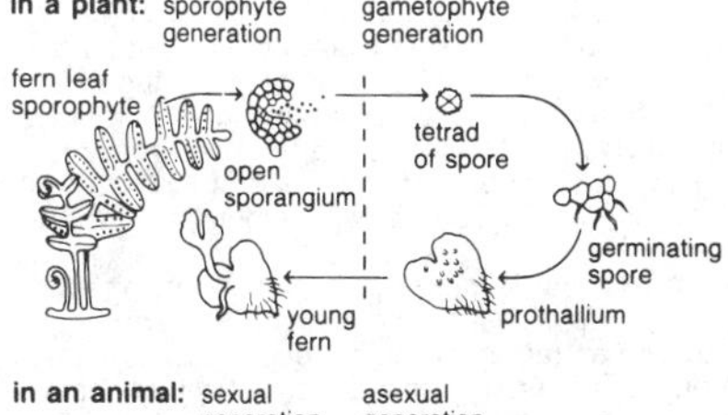

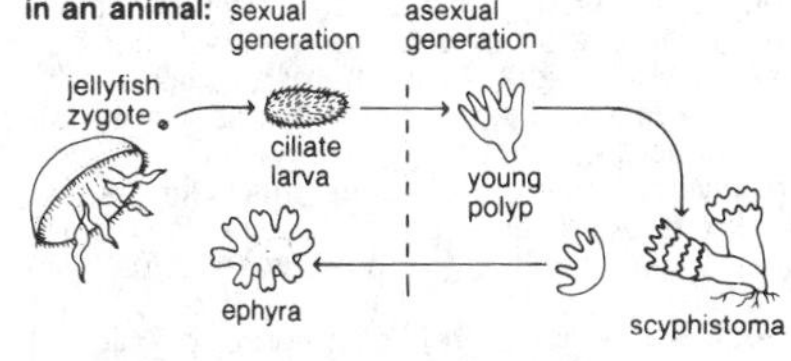

al|ter|na|tive (ôl tėr′nə tiv, al-), *n., adj.* —*n.* **1** a choice between two things: *Her father gave her the alternative of staying in high school or going to work.* syn: See syn. under **choice**. **2** a choice

Pronunciation Key: hat, āge, cãre, fär; let, ēqual, tėrm; it, īce; hot, ōpen, ôrder; oil, out; cup, pu̇t, rüle; child; long; thin; ᴛʜen; zh, measure; ə represents **a** in about, **e** in taken, **i** in pencil, **o** in lemon, **u** in circus.

from among more than two things: *If you don't want steak for dinner, there are several alternatives.* SYN: selection. See syn. under **choice**. 3 one of the things to be chosen: *She chose the first alternative and stayed in school. My decided preference is for the fourth and last of these alternatives* (William E. Gladstone).

—*adj.* 1 giving or requiring a choice between only two things: *We discussed the alternative plans of having a picnic or taking a trip on a boat.* 2 giving a choice from among more than two things: *There are several alternative routes from Chicago to New York.* —**al|ter'na|tive-ness**, *n.*

▶**Alternative** comes from the Latin word *alter,* meaning "other" or "the second of two." Some formal writers, mindful of origin, confine its meaning to one of two possibilities, but it is commonly used to mean one of several possibilities.

alternative conjunction, 1 an adversative conjunction; conjunction connecting two terms but contrasting their meaning. *Examples:* but, yet, however. 2 a disjunctive conjunction, connecting two terms but disconnecting their meaning. *Examples:* either ... or, neither ... nor.

alternative energy, power and heat derived from sources other than fossil fuels (petroleum, coal, natural gas) or nuclear fission: *The institute's work will cover ... a survey of existing energy resources, including an assessment of alternative (renewable) energy sources such as solar energy, geothermal energy, biogas, and wind power* (Don Hinrichsen).

al|ter|na|tive|ly (ôl tėr'nə tiv lē, al-), *adv.* in an alternative manner; in a manner that admits the choice or possibility of one out of two things.

alternative school, *Especially U.S.* a school that provides a different curriculum from the conventional elementary or high school program in an effort to educate students by changing the learning environment.

alternative technology, the application of conservation to industrial and agricultural practices: *It is quite possible to envisage a future society in which widespread use is made of wind energy, methane, organic farming, geodesic domes, and all other alternative technology* (New Scientist).

al|ter|na|tor (ôl'tər nā'tər, al'-), *n.* a dynamo or generator for producing an alternating electric current: *Alternators ... keep the current flowing even while the engine's idling* (Harper's).

al|the|a or **al|thae|a** (al thē'ə), *n.* 1 the rose of Sharon, a flowering garden shrub of the mallow family, having showy flowers. 2 any one of certain other plants of the mallow family, such as the hollyhock and marsh mallow: *Althea grows in great beauty in all parts of the Mississippi Valley* (Western Monthly Review). [< Latin *althaea* < Greek *althaíā* wild mallow]

Al|the|a (al thē'ə), *n. Greek Legend.* the mother of Meleager.

Al|thing (äl'thing, ôl'-), *n.* the parliament of Iceland, composed of an upper and a lower house having equal power. It has been in existence since A.D. 930, and is the oldest parliament in the world. [< Old Icelandic *althing* whole assembly]

al|tho or **al|tho'** (ôl ᴛʜō'), *conj. U.S. Informal.* although.

alt|horn (alt'hôrn'), *n.* a brass musical instrument related to the saxhorn and similar to the French horn, usually pitched in E flat or B flat, used especially in military bands in place of the French horn. See picture under **French horn**. Also, **alto, alto horn**. [< Italian *alto* high + English *horn*]

al|though (ôl ᴛʜō'), *conj.* in spite of the fact that; though. [Old English *eall* all, completely + *thāh* though]

al|ti|graph (al'tə graf, -gräf), *n.* a recording altimeter. [< Latin *alti-* (< *altus* high) + *-graph*]

al|tim|e|ter (al tim'ə tər, al'tə mē'-), *n.* any instrument for measuring altitude, especially an instrument in an aircraft or other flying object that measures its height above the earth's surface, such as an aneroid barometer that shows the atmospheric pressure at any given altitude, or a radio device. Some other instruments, such as quadrants or sextants, permit calculation of altitude by trigonometry. [< Latin *alti-* (< *altus* high) + English *-meter*]

al|tim|e|try (al tim'ə trē), *n.* the art or practice of measuring altitudes, as with an altimeter or by trigonometry.

al|ti|pla|no (äl'ti plä'nō), *n.* high, upland plains, especially those of Bolivia, Peru, and certain other countries in or adjoining the Andes, reaching altitudes of more than 15,000 feet above sea level. [< American Spanish *altiplano* < Latin *altus* high + *plānus* level]

al|tis|o|nant (al tis'ə nənt), *adj.* high-sounding, as words; pompous; lofty. [< Latin *alti-* (< *altus* high) + English *sonant*]

al|tis|si|mo (al tis'ə mō; *Italian* äl tēs'sē mō), *adj., n. Music.* —*adj.* highest. —*n.* the second octave above the treble staff. [< Italian *altissimo* < Latin *altissimus,* superlative of *altus* high]

al|ti|tude (al'tə tüd, -tyüd), *n.* 1 height above sea level or some other level on the earth's surface: *The airplane was flying at an altitude of 30,000 feet.* SYN: elevation. See syn. under **height**. 2 height above sea level: *The altitude of Denver is 5,280 feet.* 3 a high place; region of great height: *At some altitudes snow never melts.* 4 the vertical distance from the base of a geometrical figure to its highest point. 5 *Astronomy.* the height of a star, planet, or other heavenly body expressed as its angular distance above the horizon. 6 *Figurative.* position of high rank or great power. SYN: stature. 7 (in space navigation) the distance of a spacecraft from the surface of a reference body, such as the moon.
altitudes, elevated regions; great heights.
[< Latin *altitūdō* < *altus* high]

altitude chamber, a sealed room in which the conditions of flying at high altitudes are simulated in order to determine the ability of the human body to adjust to them.

altitude sickness, a condition of the body that results from too little oxygen in the blood, which may be characterized by shortness of breath, fatigue, dizziness, headache, faulty judgment, and nausea: *At about 10,000 to 12,000 feet ... people begin to show symptoms of altitude sickness* (Scientific American).

al|ti|tu|di|nal (al'tə tü'də nəl, -tyü'-), *adj.* of or having to do with altitude.

al|ti|tu|di|nous (al'tə tü'də nəs, -tyü'-), *adj.* having much altitude; high; lofty (used affectedly or humorously).

al|to (al'tō), *n., pl.* **-tos**, *adj. Music.* —*n.* 1a the lowest woman's voice; contralto. b the highest man's voice; countertenor. 2 a singer with such a voice. 3 a part in music for such a voice or for an instrument of similar range. 4a an instrument playing such a part, as a viola, recorder, or althorn. b = althorn.
—*adj.* of or for an alto; that can sing or play an alto part: *an alto voice, an alto saxophone.*
[< Italian *alto* < Latin *altus* high]

alto clef, the C clef when the clef symbol is placed on the third line of the staff.

al|to-cu|mu|lus or **al|to|cu|mu|lus** (al'tō kyü'myə ləs), *n., pl.* **-li** (-lī). a fleecy cloud formation consisting of a layer of small, white or grayish-white, rounded clouds, usually with shaded portions, at heights of from 8,000 to 20,000 feet. [< Latin *altus* high + English *cumulus*]

alto flute, a type of large flute that has wider holes than the regular flute.

al|to|geth|er (ôl'tə geᴛʜ'ər), *adv., n.* —*adv.* 1 to the whole extent; completely; entirely: *The house was altogether destroyed by fire.* SYN: wholly, totally, thoroughly. 2 on the whole; considering everything: *Altogether, he was well pleased.* 3 in all; all included: *Altogether there were 14 books.*
—*n.* 1 a whole. 2 a state of being unclothed; the nude: *The model posed in the altogether.*
[Middle English *altogeder*]
▶The adverb **altogether** is distinguished from the adjective phrase **all together** meaning "everyone in a group": *We found the boys all together in the kitchen.*

alto horn, = althorn.

al|to-re|lie|vo (al'tō ri lē'vō), *n., pl.* **-vos**. 1 sculpture in which the figures stand out at least half their thickness from the background; high relief. 2 a carving or piece of sculpture in high relief: *a fine bust of queen Elizabeth on onyx, alto-relievo in profile* (Horace Walpole). [< Italian *altorilievo*]

al|to-stra|tus (al'tō strā'təs), *n., pl.* **-ti** (-tī). a sheetlike formation of gray or bluish clouds with an ill-defined base occurring at heights of from 6,500 to 20,000 feet. [< Latin *altus* high + English *stratus*]

al|tri|cial (al trish'əl), *adj.* of or having to do with birds that are born blind, usually without feathers, and thus helpless for some time after hatching (contrasted with *precocial*). [< New Latin *altrices* those that nourish, plural of Latin *altrīx, -īcis* a nurse + English *-al*[1]]

al|tru|ism (al'trü iz əm), *n.* 1 unselfish devotion to the interests and welfare of others; disinterested regard for others as a principle of action; unselfishness. SYN: philanthropy, humanitarianism. 2 *Zoology.* self-sacrificing behavior by an animal or group that benefits another animal or group: *Wilson concentrates in particular on altruism ... such behavior include ... cooperation among animals in warning against danger* (E. M. Wood). [< French *altruisme* < Italian *altrui* of or for others < Latin *alter* other]

al|tru|ist (al'trü ist), *n.* a person who works for the welfare of others; unselfish person: *He drew an affecting portrait of himself as an altruist whose sole aim was to provide adequate housing* (New Yorker).

al|tru|is|tic (al'trü is'tik), *adj.* 1 thoughtful of the welfare of others; unselfish. 2 *Zoology.* characterized by altruism: *altruistic social animals.*

al|tru|is|ti|cal|ly (al'trü is'tə klē), *adv.* benevolently; unselfishly.

al|u|del (al'yə del), *n.* a glass or earthenware apparatus resembling a pear-shaped pot, but open at both ends so that the neck of one can be fitted into the bottom of another, formerly used as a condenser in sublimation. [< Old French *alutel* < Arabic *al-uthāl*]

***al|u|la** (al'yə lə), *n., pl.* **-lae** (-lē). a set of three or four quill-like feathers growing at a small joint in the middle of a bird's wing; bastard wing. [< New Latin *alula* (diminutive) < Latin *āla* wing]

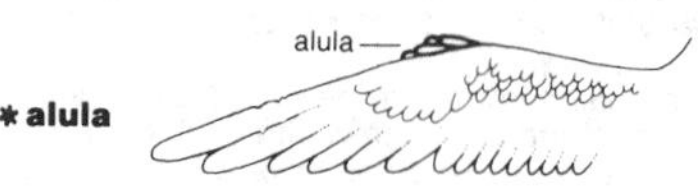

***alula**

al|u|lar (al'yə lər), *adj.* of or designating an alula.

al|um (al'əm), *n.* 1 a whitish mineral salt used in medicine and in dyeing; potash alum. A pencil of alum is sometimes used to stop the bleeding of a small cut. *Formula:* $KAl(SO_4)_2 \cdot 12H_2O$ 2 a colorless, crystalline salt containing ammonia, used in baking powder, foam fire extinguishers, the purification of drinking water, and in medicine; ammonia alum. *Formula:* $NH_4Al(SO_4)_2 \cdot 12H_2O$ 3 any one of a group of double salts analogous to and including potash alum, formed by the union of the sulfate of a trivalent metal, such as aluminum, chromium, or iron, with the sulfate of a monovalent alkali metal or ammonium. 4 *U.S.* = aluminum sulfate. [< Old French *alum* < Latin *alūmen*]

a|lu|mi|na (ə lü'mə nə), *n.* a mineral occurring in nature as corundum, found mainly in bauxite and in clay or loam; aluminum oxide. Emery, rubies, and sapphires are crystalline forms of alumina colored by various impurities. Alumina is used in making aluminum, porcelain, and abrasives. *Formula:* Al_2O_3 [< New Latin *alumina* < Latin *alūmen, -inis* alum]

a|lu|mi|nate (ə lü'mə nāt), *n.* a salt in which alumina acts toward the stronger bases as an acid.

a|lu|mi|nif|er|ous (ə lü'mə nif'ər əs), *adj.* yielding or containing aluminum, alumina, or alum. [< Latin *alūmen, -inis* alum + English *-ferous*]

a|lu|mi|nite (ə lü'mə nīt), *n.* a hydrated sulfate of alumina used in tanning, dyeing, and purifying water. *Formula:* $Al_2O_3SO_3 \cdot 9H_2O$

al|u|min|i|um (al'yə min'ē əm; *especially Canadian* ə lü'mə nəm), *n., adj. British and Canadian.* aluminum. [< *alumin*(um) + New Latin *-ium,* a suffix meaning "metal"]

a|lu|mi|nize (ə lü'mə nīz), *v.t.,* **-nized, -niz|ing.** to treat, coat, or impregnate with aluminum.

a|lu|mi|nog|ra|phy (ə lü'mə nog'rə fē), *n.* the art or process of producing and printing from aluminum plates instead of lithographic stones. [< *aluminum* + *-graphy*]

a|lu|mi|non (ə lü'mə non), *n.* an acid dye used for determining the presence of the aluminum ion. *Formula:* $C_{22}H_{23}N_3O_9$

a|lu|mi|no|sil|i|cate (ə lü'mə nō sil'ə kit, -kāt), *n.* a compound of aluminum and silicon with a metal oxide or other radical (such as albite). Feldspars and zeolites are aluminosilicates.

a|lu|mi|no|ther|mic (ə lü'mə nō thėr'mik), *adj.* of or having to do with aluminothermy.

a|lu|mi|no|ther|mics (ə lü'mə nō thėr'miks), *n.pl.* (*sing. in use*). = aluminothermy.

a|lu|mi|no|ther|my (ə lü'mə nō thėr'mē), *n.* 1 the chemical combination of oxygen and aluminum to produce a high temperature and reduction of compounds of other metals. 2 the science dealing with such processes. [< *alumin*(um) + Greek *thérmē* heat]

a|lu|mi|nous (ə lü'mə nəs), *adj.* 1 of or containing alum. 2 of or containing aluminum. [< Latin *alūminōsus* < *alūmen, -inis* alum]

***a|lu|mi|num** (ə lü'mə nəm), *n., adj.* —*n.* a silver-white metal that is strong, very light, and does not tarnish or rust easily. Aluminum is widely used in alloys, and for making pots and pans, automobile and aircraft parts, and instruments. It is a metallic chemical element, found abundantly in nature but occurring only in combination with other elements (its compounds make up more than 15 per cent of the crust of the earth).
—*adj.* of or containing aluminum. [< *alumina*]

***aluminum**

symbol	atomic number	atomic weight	oxidation state
Al	13	26.9815	3

aluminum acetate, a white, crystalline powder used as a waterproofing and fireproofing agent in textile manufacturing, as a mordant in dyeing, and as a disinfectant. *Formulas:* (normal) $Al(C_2H_3O_2)_3$; (basic) $Al(C_2H_3O_2)_2OH$

aluminum brass, a tough, hard kind of aluminum bronze.

aluminum bromide, a colorless or yellowish-white, crystalline compound used in organic synthesis. *Formula:* $AlBr_3 \cdot 6H_2O$

aluminum bronze, any one of certain alloys of copper and aluminum with small amounts of another metal or metals, as iron, nickel, or manganese, used in making firearms, marine fittings, etc. Some aluminum bronzes are equal to steel in hardness and strength.

aluminum chloride, a colorless or yellowish, crystalline compound used as a deodorant, as a disinfectant, and as a preservative for wood. In its anhydrous form it is used in the catalytic cracking of petroleum. *Formula:* $AlCl_3 \cdot 6H_2O$

aluminum hydroxide, a white, odorless, tasteless powder used in waterproofing, in dyeing, as a glaze in ceramics, and in medicines. *Formula:* $Al(OH)_3$

aluminum oxide, = alumina.

aluminum paint, a paint with insulating qualities produced by mixing flakes of aluminum with varnish and lacquer.

aluminum sulfate, a white, crystalline salt, commercially available as a powder or in crystalline form, used in dyeing, medicine, water purification, as well as in the leather and paper industries. *Formula:* $Al_2(SO_4)_3$

a|lu|mi|num|ware (ə lü′mə nəm wãr′), *n.*, or **aluminum ware**, kitchen utensils and other articles made of aluminum.

a|lum|na (ə lum′nə), *n., pl.* **-nae**. *Especially U.S.* a woman graduate or former student of a certain school, college, or university. [American English < Latin *alumna*]

a|lum|nae (ə lum′nē), *n.* plural of **alumna.**
▶See **alumni** for usage note.

a|lum|ni (ə lum′nī), *n., pl. of* **alumnus**. graduates or former students of a school, college, or university. "Alumni" may mean either men graduates or both men and women.
▶**Alumnae** and **alumni** must not be confused in writing. Difficulty arises in speech because, in the Roman pronunciation of the Latin, "ae" is pronounced (ī) and "i" is pronounced (ē), while in the English pronunciation, the situation is reversed.

a|lum|nus (ə lum′nəs), *n., pl.* **-ni**. **1** a graduate or former student of a certain school, college, or university. **2** *Figurative.* a person who is a former resident, contributor, fellow worker, or who had some capacity in association with others: *Many a famous writer is an alumnus of a local newspaper or literary magazine.* [American English < Latin *alumnus* foster son < *alere* nourish]

al|um|root (al′əm rüt′, -rụ̇t′), *n.* **1a** any one of several plants of the saxifrage family having astringent roots. **b** = crane's-bill. **2** the root of any of these.

alum stone, = alunite.

a|lun-a|lun (ä′lün ä′lün), *n.* a village square, in Malaya. [< Malay *alun-alun*]

A|lun|dum (ə lun′dəm), *n. Trademark.* an abrasive resembling corundum, made by fusing alumina under intense heat.

al|u|nite (al′yə nīt), *n.* a mineral consisting typically of common (potash) alum together with normal hydrate of aluminum. It is used as a fertilizer. *Formula:* $K_2SO_4 \cdot Al_2(SO_4)_3 \cdot HAl(OH)_3$ [< Old French *alun* alum + English *-ite*[1]]

al|ve|o|la (al vē′ə lə), *n., pl.* **-lae**. = alveolus.

al|ve|o|lae (al vē′ə lē), *n., pl. of* **alveola**. = alveoli.

al|ve|o|lar (al vē′ə lər), *adj.* **1** of or having to do with the part of the jaws where the sockets of the teeth are. **2a** of or like an alveolus. **b** containing alveoli. **3** *Phonetics.* formed by bringing the tip of the tongue near or against the alveoli. English *t* and *d* are alveolar consonants.

alveolar ridge, the ridge on each jaw containing the bony sockets of the teeth.

al|ve|o|late (al vē′ə lit, -lāt), *adj.* having many small cavities; pitted like a honeycomb.

al|ve|o|lat|ed (al vē′ə lā′tid), *adj.* = alveolate.

al|ve|o|la|tion (al vē′ə lā′shən), *n.* alveolate condition, formation, or structure.

al|ve|o|li (al vē′ə lī), *n., pl. of* **alveolus**. *Phonetics.* the ridge behind and above the upper front teeth.

al|ve|o|lus (al vē′ə ləs), *n., pl.* **-li**. **1** *Anatomy and Zoology.* a small cavity, pit, or cell, especially: **a** one of the air sacs of the lungs. **b** one of a cluster of acini at the end of a duct of a gland. **2** the bony socket of a tooth. **3** one of the cells of a honeycomb. [< Latin *alveolus* (diminutive) < *alveus* cavity]

al|ve|o|pal|a|tal (al vē′ə pal′ə təl), *adj. Phonetics.* intermediate between alveolar and palatal.

al|vine (al′vin, -vīn), *adj.* having to do with the abdomen; intestinal. [< Medieval Latin *alvinus* < Latin *alvus* the belly]

al|way (ôl′wā), *adv. Archaic.* always.

al|ways (ôl′wiz, -wāz), *adv.* **1** every time; at all times: *Night always follows day. Water always has some air in it.* **2** all the time; continually: *Home is always a cheerful place at holiday time. I am always available for advice. The Lord be with us always.* SYN: forever, unceasingly, perpetually, uninterruptedly, invariably. [Middle English *all* + *wayes,* genitive singular of *way* way]

a|lys|sum (ə lis′əm), *n.* **1** a plant of the mustard family, having small, yellow or white flowers, sometimes rose or pink. **2** = sweet alyssum. [< New Latin *Alyssum* the genus name < Greek *álysson* madwort, neuter of *álysşos* curing madness < *a-* without + *lýssa* madness, fury]

Alz|hei|mer's disease (ôlts′hī′mərz), a form of senile psychosis found at an early age, characterized by progressive deterioration of memory and other mental activity: *Alzheimer's disease ... is believed to be irreversible* (New York Times). [< Alois *Alzheimer*, 1864-1915, a German pathologist, who first described it]

am (am; *unstressed* əm), *v.* the form of the verb **be** used with *I* in the present tense; first person singular, present indicative of **be:** *The little boy said, "I am six years old. I am going to school." I am,* you *are,* and he *is* are present indicative forms of the verb **be**. [Old English *eom*]

am-, *combining form.* the form of **ambi-** before *p*, as in *amplexicaul, amputate.*

a.m., **1** before noon: *School begins at 9 a.m.* **2** the time from midnight to noon. [for Latin *ante merīdiem*]
▶Except in tables and the headlines of newspapers, the abbreviations **a.m.** and **p.m.** are usually written in small letters. In ordinary text they are used only with figures for specific hours: *from 2 to 4 a.m.*

Am (no period), americium (chemical element).

Am., **1** America. **2** American.

AM (no periods), amplitude modulation.

A.M., **1** before noon; the time from midnight to noon. See also **a.m.** **2** in the year of the world (Latin, *anno mundi*). **3** *U.S.* Master of Arts (Latin, *Artium Magister*). Also, **M.A.**

a|ma (ä′mä), *n., pl.* **a|ma**. *Japanese.* a woman pearl diver.

a|mac|rine (ā mak′rīn, am′ə krīn), *adj., n.* —*adj.* not having long fibers: *amacrine nerve cells.* —*n.* an amacrine cell of the retina which conducts signals to the ganglia.
[< Greek *a-* not + *makrós* long + *is, -in-* muscle, fiber]

am|a|da|vat (am′ə də vat′), *n.* a small, finchlike songbird, brown with white spots, native to India, often kept as a cage bird. [< *Ahmadabad*, a city in India from which the birds were exported]

Am|a|dis of Gaul (am′ə dis), the title and hero of a celebrated medieval romance of chivalry.

am|a|dou (am′ə dü), *n.* a soft, spongy substance made by steeping the more solid portion of certain fungi that grow on trees in a solution of saltpeter; punk; German tinder; touchwood; agaric. It was formerly used as tinder and in medicine as a styptic. [< French *amadou*]

a|mah (ä′mə, am′ə), *n.* in India, China, etc.: **a** a baby's nurse. **b** a maid. [Anglo-Indian < Portuguese *ama* wet nurse]

a|main (ə mān′), *adv.* **1** at full speed. **2** with full force; violently. **3** in haste; at once. **4** exceedingly; greatly. [< *a-* in + *main* force]

am|al|dar (am′əl där), *n.* (in India) a manager, agent, or the like, especially a collector of revenue. Also, **amildar**. [< Hindustani *'amaldār*]

A|mal|e|kite (ə mal′ə kīt), *n.* a member of an ancient tribe of robber Bedouins south of the Dead Sea, supposed to be the descendants of Esau (in the Bible, Genesis 36:12; Numbers 13:29).

a|mal|gam (ə mal′gəm), *n.* **1** an alloy of mercury with some other metal or metals. Silver amalgam is used as fillings for teeth. Tin amalgam has been used for silvering mirrors. **2** *Figurative.* a mixture or blend of different things: *an amalgam of good and evil, an amalgam of strength and weakness.* SYN: amalgamation, combination. [< Medieval Latin *amalgama*, perhaps < Arabic *al-malghama* the amalgam < Greek *málagma* emollient < *malássein* soften]

a|mal|gam|a|ble (ə mal′gə mə bəl), *adj.* that can be amalgamated.

a|mal|gam|ate (ə mal′gə māt), *v.,* **-at|ed, -at|ing,** *adj.* —*v.t.* **1** to combine to form a whole; unite (any things that are distinct, such as elements, ideas, or parts); merge: *The company amalgamated its three sales offices. Many different stocks have been amalgamated in the United States.* SYN: mix, blend. **2** to combine mercury with (another metal). —*v.i.* **1** to become united; be combined: *The two stores amalgamated to form one big store.* SYN: mix, blend. **2** to enter into combination with mercury.
—*adj.* combined: *amalgamate languages.*
—**a|mal′gam|a′tor**, *n.*

a|mal|gam|a|tion (ə mal′gə mā′shən), *n.* **1** the act or process of amalgamating. **2** the state or condition of being amalgamated. **3** the result of amalgamating; a uniform whole formed of previously distinct elements, societies, etc.; combination; blend; union: (*Figurative.*) *Our nation is an amalgamation of many different peoples.* **4** a method for collecting gold from other materials by using mercury.

a|mal|gam|a|tive (ə mal′gə mā′tiv), *adj.* that amalgamates or tends to amalgamate.

a|mal|gam|ize (ə mal′gə mīz), *v.t.,* **-ized, -iz|ing.** = amalgamate.

Am|al|thae|a or **Am|al|the|a** (am′əl thē′ə), *n. Greek and Roman Mythology.* the goat that nursed the infant Zeus (Jupiter). One of her horns (horn of Amalthaea) would become full of anything its owner wished.

A|man|a (ə man′ə), *adj.* of or having to do with the Amana Church Society, a religious community in eastern Iowa which originated in 1714 as a German Protestant sect.

a|man|dine (ä′mən dēn′, am′ən-), *adj.* made or served with almonds: *trout amandine.* [< French *amandine* < *amande* almond < Old French *almande;* see etym. under **almond**]

A|man|ist (ə man′ist), *n.* a member of the Amana Church Society.

*** am|a|ni|ta** (am′ə nī′tə), *n.* any fungus of a group composed chiefly of very poisonous mushrooms, such as the death cup. [< New Latin *Amanita* < Greek *amānîtai* a type of fungus]

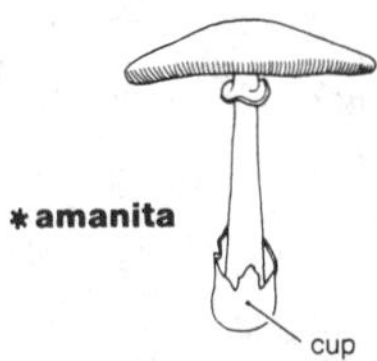

***amanita**

A|man|ite (ə man′īt), *n.* a member of a religious group, the Amana Church Society, that leads a simple life, with the strong helping the weak.

a|man|ta|dine (ə man′tə dēn), *n.* a synthetic drug that prevents influenza infection by inhibiting the penetration of the influenza virus into cells. [alteration of *adamantane*]

a|man|u|en|sis (ə man′yụ̇ en′sis), *n., pl.* **-ses** (-sēz). a person who writes down what another says, or who copies what another has written. [< Latin *āmanuēnsis* < (*servus*) *ā manū* secretary]
▶**Amanuensis** and **secretary** are seldom, if ever, interchangeable in modern use. The former now suggests a definite closeness of relationship, especially through a common interest in some scholarly or literary undertaking: *His wife served as his faithful amanuensis through all seven versions of the manuscript.*

am|a|ranth (am′ə ranth), *n.* **1** an annual plant with showy, purple, greenish, or crimson flowers. One variety is love-lies-bleeding. **2** a purple or purplish-red color. **3** *Poetic.* an imaginary flower that never fades. [< Latin *amarantus* < Greek *amárantos* everlasting < *a-* not + *maráinein* wither; influenced in form by Greek *ánthos* flower]

am|a|ran|tha|ceous (am′ə ran thā′shəs), *adj.* belonging to the amaranth family.

amaranth family, a group of dicotyledonous plants, chiefly weedy herbs of warm regions, including the amaranth, cockscomb, and some of the pigweeds.

am|a|ran|thine (am′ə ran′thin, -thīn), *adj.* **1** never-fading; undying. **2** purple or purplish-red. **3** of or like the amaranth.

am|a|relle (am′ə rel′), *n.* any cultivated variety of sour cherry having light-red fruit and nearly colorless juice. [probably < earlier Flemish *amarelle,* apparently < Italian *amarella* (diminutive) < *amaro* < Latin *amārus* bitter]

am|a|ret|to (am′ə ret′tō), *n., pl.* **-tos**. an Italian liqueur with an almond taste. [< Italian *amaretto* < *amaro* bitter]

am|a|ryl|li|da|ceous (am′ə ril′ə dā′shəs), *adj.* belonging to the amaryllis family.

am|a|ryl|lis (am′ə ril′is), *n.* a lilylike bulbous plant with clusters of large, red, white, purple, or pink flowers; belladonna lily. [< Latin *amaryllis* < Greek *Amaryllís,* typical name of a country girl]

Am|a|ryl|lis (am′ə ril′is), *n.* a name for a country girl in pastoral poetry.

Pronunciation Key: hat, āge, cãre, fär; let, ēqual, tėrm; it, īce; hot, ōpen, ôrder; oil, out; cup, pụ̇t, rüle; child; long; thin; ᴛʜen; zh, measure; ə represents **a** in about, **e** in taken, **i** in pencil, **o** in lemon, **u** in circus.

***amaryllis family**, a group of perennial herbs resembling those of the lily family, including the narcissus, amaryllis, snowdrop, and onion. Their seeds are monocotyledonous and come from an inferior ovary. See picture below.

a|mass (ə mas′), *v.t.* to heap together; pile up, especially for oneself; accumulate; collect: *The miser amassed a fortune for himself.* **SYN**: gather, hoard, aggregate. See syn. under **accumulate**. [< Old French *amasser* < *a-* to + *masse* mass < Latin *massa* kneaded dough] —**a|mass′a|ble**, *adj.* —**a|mass′er**, *n.* —**a|mass′ment**, *n.*

a|mate (ə māt′), *v.t.*, **a|mat|ed, a|mat|ing.** *Archaic.* to dismay; daunt: *A half-blown flow'ret which cold blasts amate* (Keats). [< Old French *amater* < *a-* to + *mater* beat or cast down < *mat* dejected]

A|ma|te|ra|sü (ä′mä te rä′sü), *n.* the goddess of the sun, in the Shinto religion, from whom by Japanese tradition the emperor of Japan is supposed to be descended.

am|a|teur (am′ə chůr, -chər, -tyůr, -tůr, -tər; am′ə-tėr′; *see note below*), *n., adj.* —*n.* **1** a person who does something for pleasure, not for money or as a profession: *For an amateur, our science teacher is a pretty accurate weather forecaster.* **2** an athlete who is not a professional: *Only amateurs are permitted to compete in the Olympic games. An amateur is one who engages in sports merely for the enjoyment he gets from them and who never capitalizes on his athletic skills to any degree whatsoever* (New York Times). **3** a person who does something rather poorly: *You can tell from his painting that he is an amateur, completely without training.* **4** a superficial student or worker; dabbler. **SYN**: dilettante.

—*adj.* **1** of an amateur; made or done by amateurs: *amateur painting, amateur baseball. Our school has an amateur orchestra.* **2** being an amateur: *an amateur golfer, an amateur pianist.* [< French *amateur* < Old French, learned borrowing from Latin *amātor, -ōris* lover < *amāre* to love]

► Of the various pronunciations of **amateur** in current use, (am′ə tėr′) is closest to the French, while (am′ə chər) or (am′ə tər) exhibits the greatest degree of Anglicization.

am|a|teur|ish (am′ə chůr′ish, -tyůr′-, -tůr′-, -tėr′-), *adj.* done as an amateur might do it; not expert; not very skillful: *Mr. Scarpini, whose fluency and muscularity I admired last year when he appeared with the orchestra in a Prokofieff concerto, disclosed a flimsy, not to say amateurish, approach to Mozart's subtle melodies* (New Yorker). —**am′a|teur′ish|ly,** *adv.* —**am′a|teur′ish-ness**, *n.*

am|a|teur|ism (am′ə chů riz′əm, -chə-, -tyů-, -tů-, -tə-; am′ə tėr′iz əm), *n.* **1** an amateurish way of doing things. **2** the position or rank of an amateur: *We must try to understand the Russian's conception of amateurism and professionalism* (Atlantic).

am|a|teur|ship (am′ə chůr ship, -chər-, -tyůr-, -tůr-, -tər-; am′ə tėr′ship), *n.* the quality, character, or status of an amateur.

A|ma|ti (ä mä′tē), *n.* a violin, cello, or other stringed instrument, made at Cremona, Italy, by Nicolò Amati (1596-1684), or a member of his family. These instruments are considered among the first of the modern type.

am|a|tive (am′ə tiv), *adj.* amorous. [< Latin *amātus,* past participle of *amāre* to love + English *-ive*] —**am′a|tive|ly**, *adv.* —**am′a|tive|ness**, *n.*

am|a|tol (am′ə tol, -tōl), *n.* a powerful explosive made of ammonium nitrate and TNT. [< *am*(monium) + (trinitro)*tol*(uene)]

am|a|to|ri|al (am′ə tôr′ē əl, -tōr′-), *adj.* = amatory.

am|a|to|ri|ous (am′ə tôr′ē əs, -tōr′-), *adj.* = amatory. —**am′a|to′ri|ous|ness**, *n.*

am|a|to|ry (am′ə tôr′ē, -tōr′-), *adj.* of love; expressing love; having to do with making love or with lovers: *an amatory look. Valentine cards often have amatory verses on them.* **SYN**: amorous, erotic. [< Latin *amātōrius* < *amāre* to love]

am|au|ro|sis (am′ô rō′sis), *n.* partial or complete loss of vision through loss of power of the optic nerve, without noticeable external change in the eye. [< Greek *amaúrōsis* < *amaurós* dim]

am|au|rot|ic (am′ô rot′ik), *adj.* of or characterized by amaurosis.

amaurotic idiocy, a fatal disease of children caused by degeneration of the cells of the central nervous system, transmitted genetically as a result of two recessive alleles; Tay-Sachs disease.

a max|i|mis ad mi|ni|ma (ā mak′sə məs admin′ə mə), *Latin.* from the greatest to the least: *They are likely to be sold bad insurance, make bad realty investments, and sing away their legal right a maximis ad minima* (New Yorker).

a|maze (ə māz′), *v.*, **a|mazed, a|maz|ing,** *n.* —*v.t.* **1** to surprise greatly; strike and overwhelm with sudden wonder; astound: *She was so amazed by the surprise party that she could not think of a thing to say. And they were all amazed at the mighty power of God* (Luke 9:43). **SYN**: astonish. See syn. under **surprise**. **2** *Archaic.* to bewilder; perplex: *How vainly men themselves amaze* (Andrew Marvell).

—*n. Archaic or Poetic.* amazement.

[Old English *āmasian*]

a|mazed (ə māzd′), *adj.* greatly surprised: *an amazed look.* **SYN**: astonished, astounded. —**a|maz′ed|ly**, *adv.* —**a|maz′ed|ness**, *n.*

a|maze|ment (ə māz′mənt), *n.* **1** great surprise; sudden and overwhelming wonder; astonishment: *The girl was filled with amazement when she first saw the ocean.* **2** *Archaic.* **a** overwhelming fear. **b** bewilderment. **c** stupefaction.

a|maz|ing (ə mā′zing), *adj.* very surprising; causing amazement; wonderful; astonishing; astounding. —**a|maz′ing|ly**, *adv.*

Am|a|zon (am′ə zon, -zən), *n.* **1** *Greek Legend.* one of a race of women warriors supposed to have lived near the Black Sea. **2** the Amazon ant. [< Latin *Amāzōn* < Greek *Amazṓn;* origin uncertain]

am|a|zon (am′ə zon, -zən), *n.* **1** a tall, strong, aggressive woman. **2** any one of certain parrots of Central and South America. **3** a hummingbird.

Amazon ant, any one of certain European and American red ants with long, sharp jaws that are so curved they cannot feed themselves or dig nests. They carry off and enslave young ants of other species to do this work for them.

Am|a|zo|ni|an (am′ə zō′nē ən), *adj.* **1** of the Amazon River (in South America) or the region it drains. **2** of the Amazons. **3** Also, **amazonian**. (of a woman) like an Amazon; aggressive or warlike: *Mrs. Preston, a Russian, was as Amazonian and fair as Mme. Floquet was elfin and swart* (New Yorker).

Am|a|zon|ism (am′ə zon′iz əm, am′ə zən-), *n.* a condition in which women take on the work, attitudes, and other roles attributed to men; Amazonian state or character.

am|a|zon|ite (am′ə zə nīt), *n.* a semiprecious stone, a bright, bluish-green variety of feldspar. [for *Amazon* stone (< the *Amazon* River) + *-ite*[1]]

Amazon stone, = amazonite.

amb-, *combining form.* the form of **ambi-** before vowels, as in *ambages.*

Amb., ambassador.

am|ba|ges (am bā′jēz, am′bə jiz), *n.pl.* **1** indirect ways; delaying tactics. **2** ambiguities; circumlocutions. **3** *Archaic.* circuitous paths. [< Middle French *ambages,* learned borrowing from Latin *ambāgēs* < *ambi-* about + *agere* drive]

am|ba|gious (am bā′jəs), *adj.* **1** roundabout. **2** *Archaic.* winding. —**am|ba′gious|ly**, *adv.* —**am|ba′gious|ness**, *n.*

am|ba|ry or **am|ba|ri** (am bär′ē), *n.* **1** the fiber of an Asian plant of the mallow family, used especially for making ropes and cloth, as a substitute for hemp or jute. **2** the plant itself, a species of hibiscus. [< Hindustani *ambārā,* ultimately < Sanskrit]

am|bas|sade (am′bə sād′, am′bə sād), *n. Archaic.* an embassy.

am|bas|sa|dor (am bas′ə dər, -dôr), *n.* **1** a representative of the highest rank sent by one government or ruler to another: *Our ambassador to France lives in Paris, the capital of France, and speaks and acts in behalf of the government of the United States.* **2** a representative sent by one government or ruler to a meeting of an organization, usually an international organization concerning political affairs: *the Canadian ambassador to the United Nations, the Danish ambassador to NATO.* **3** any official messenger, agent, or representative with some special errand: *Miles Standish chose John Alden to be his ambassador.* **4** *Figurative.* any member of a particular group thought of as representing the qualities, traits, or habits of his group: *A tourist abroad can be an ambassador of good will for his country.* Also, **embassador**. [< Middle French *ambassadeur* < Italian *ambasciatore*] —**am|bas′sa|dor|ship**, *n.*

am|bas|sa|dor-at-large (am bas′ə dər ət lärj′), *n., pl.* **am|bas|sa|dors-at-large.** a minister accredited to no government in particular, but appointed on or for a special occasion.

ambassador extraordinary, an ambassador sent on a special mission.

am|bas|sa|do|ri|al (am bas′ə dôr′ē əl, -dōr′-), *adj.* of an ambassador or ambassadors: *a conference on the ambassadorial level.*

ambassador plenipotentiary, an ambassador having full power to sign treaties.

am|bas|sa|dress (am bas′ə dris), *n.* **1** a woman ambassador. **2** the wife of an ambassador.

am|bas|sage (am′bə sij), *n.* = embassage.

am|bas|sy (am′bə sē), *n., pl.* **-sies.** = embassy.

am|batch (am′bach), *n.* a leguminous tree or shrub of tropical Africa, with very light, spongy wood. [< a native name]

am|ber (am′bər), *n., adj.* —*n.* **1** a hard yellow or yellowish-brown gum, the resin of fossil pine trees. Amber is translucent and easily polished and is used for jewelry and pipestems. It develops a negative charge of static electricity when rubbed. **2** the color of amber; yellow or yellowish brown.

—*adj.* **1** made of amber: *I have a necklace with amber beads.* **2** yellow or yellowish-brown: *She has amber hair.*

[< Old French *ambre* < Arabic *'anbar* ambergris]

am|ber|fish (am′bər fish′), *n., pl.* **-fish|es** or (*collectively*) **-fish.** = amber jack.

am|ber|gris (am′bər grēs, -gris), *n.* a waxlike, fragrant substance of a grayish color, sometimes found floating in tropical seas. Ambergris originates as a secretion in the intestines of some sperm whales and is used to fix odors in making perfumes. [< Middle French *ambre gris* gray amber]

Am|be|ri|na (əm′bə rē′nə), *n.* glassware colored by adding gold to the glass. It ranges in color from pale amber-yellow to rich ruby-red.

am|ber|ite (am′bə rīt), *n.* an explosive, a variety of smokeless powder.

amber jack, **1** a game and food fish of the Atlantic from New Jersey to Brazil. **2** = yellowtail (def. 2).

am|ber|oid (am′bə roid), *n.* synthetic amber. It is made by heating small scraps of amber under pressure. Also, **ambroid**.

am|ber|seed (am′bər sēd′), *n.* = ambrette.

ambi-, *combining form.* both: *Ambidextrous = dextrous with both hands.* Also, **am-** before *p;* **amb-** before vowels. [< Latin *ambi-* around, or < *ambō* both]

am|bi|ance (am′bē əns), *n.* **1** surroundings; atmosphere: *The movement in the streets is of a different quality—the bustling headlong zest that makes the ambiance of Paris street life* (Atlantic). **2** arrangement of accessories to support or intensify the main effect of a piece of art, especially decorative art. [< French *ambiance*]

am|bi|col|or|ate (am′bə kul′ə rit, -rāt), *adj.* **1** colored on both sides. **2** showing ambicoloration.

am|bi|col|or|a|tion (am′bə kul′ə rā′shən), *n.* an abnormal coloration on both sides of a flatfish instead of having the underside white. [< *ambi-* + *coloration*]

am|bi|dex|ter (am′bə dek′stər), *adj., n.* —*adj.* = ambidextrous.

—*n.* an ambidextrous person.

[< Late Latin *ambidexter* < Latin *ambi-* both, doubly + *dexter* right-handed]

am|bi|dex|ter|i|ty (am′bə dek ster′ə tē), *n.* **1** the ability to use both hands equally well. **2** *Figurative.* unusual skillfulness. **3** deceitfulness.

am|bi|dex|trous (am′bə dek′strəs), *adj.* **1** able to use both hands equally well. **2** *Figurative.* more than usually skillful. **3** deceitful. —**am′bi|dex′trous|ly**, *adv.* —**am′bi|dex′trous|ness**, *n.*

am|bi|ence (am′bē əns), *n.* = ambiance.

am|bi|ens (am′bē enz), *n.* a muscle of the leg of certain birds (so called from the way in which it

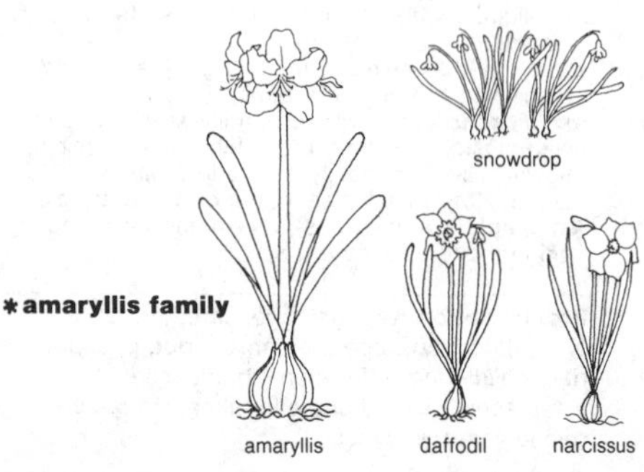

***amaryllis family**

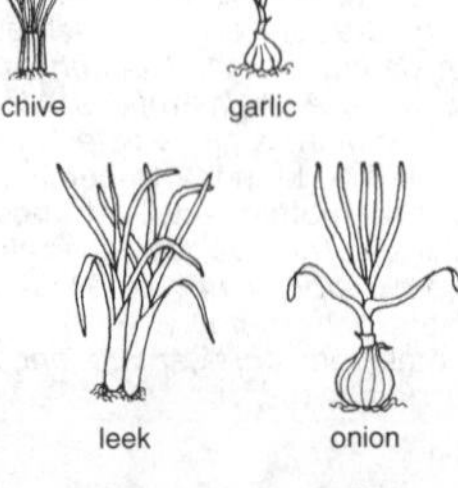

winds about the limb in passing from the hip to the foot). [< Latin *ambiēns* ambient]

am|bi|ent (am′bē ənt), *adj.* all around; surrounding; encompassing: *The flowers made the ambient air fragrant. Opening to the ambient light* (Milton). [< Latin *ambiēns, -entis,* present participle of *ambīre* surround < *ambi-* around + *īre* go]

am|bien|te (am byen′tā), *n. Spanish, Italian.* surroundings; atmosphere.

am|bi|gu|i|ty (am′bə gyü′ə tē), *n., pl.* **-ties.** **1** the possibility of two or more meanings: *The ambiguity of the speaker's statement made it hard to tell which side he was on.* **2** a word or expression that can have more than one meaning: *Answer me without ambiguities.* **3** lack of clarity; vagueness; uncertainty. [< Latin *ambiguitās* < *ambiguus* ambiguous]

am|big|u|ous (am big′yu̇ əs), *adj.* **1** having more than one possible meaning; permitting more than one interpretation or explanation. The sentence "After John hit Dick he ran away" is ambiguous because one cannot tell which boy ran away. SYN: equivocal. See syn. under **obscure.** **2** not clearly defined; not clear; doubtful; uncertain: *He was left in an ambiguous position by his friend's failure to appear and help him.* SYN: vague. **3** of doubtful position or classification: *an ambiguous character.* [< Latin *ambiguus* (with English *-ous*) < *ambigere* be uncertain, wander < *ambi-* in two ways + *agere* drive] —**am|big′u|ous|ly,** *adv.* —**am|big′u|ous|ness,** *n.*

am|bi|lat|er|al (am′bə lat′ər əl), *adj.* on both sides.

am|bi|sex|u|al (am′bə sek′shü əl), *adj.* **1** of or characteristic of both sexes. **2** attracted to both sexes; bisexual.

am|bi|son|ic (am′bi son′ik), *adj.* having to do with recorded sound that simulates the directional qualities of the sound it reproduces. [< Latin *ambi-* surrounding + English *sonic*]

am|bi|son|ics (am′bi son′iks), *n.pl.* ambisonic sound reproduction.

am|bit (am′bit), *n.* **1a** the limits of a district, region, or other area. **b** *Figurative.* the scope of an action, policy, or law. **2** a circuit; circumference. [< Latin *ambitus, -ūs* circuit < *ambīre* go around, surround < *ambi-* around + *īre* go]

am|bi|tend|en|cy (am′bə ten′dən sē), *n. Psychology.* the simultaneous existence in an individual of opposing or contradictory tendencies.

am|bi|tion (am bish′ən), *n., v.* —*n.* **1** a strong desire for fame, success, honor, wealth, or other position; seeking after a high position or great power: *Because he was filled with ambition, he worked after school and on Saturdays.* SYN: aspiration. **2** a thing for which one has a strong desire: *Her ambition was to be a great actress.*
—*v.t. Informal.* to be ambitious of; desire strongly; seek eagerly.
[< Latin *ambitiō, -ōnis* a canvassing for votes < *ambīre* go around < *ambi-* around + *īre* go] —**am|bi′tion|less,** *adj.*

am|bi|tious (am bish′əs), *adj.* **1** having or guided by ambition; full of ambition: *an ambitious young man.* SYN: aspiring. **2** desiring strongly; eager: *The actor was ambitious of success. Gamblers are ambitious for money.* **3** arising from ambition; showing ambition: *He had an ambitious plan for building a rocket.* SYN: bold, audacious. **4** too greatly aspiring; showy; pretentious: *an ambitious style.* —**am|bi′tious|ly,** *adv.* —**am|bi′tious|ness,** *n.*

am|bit|ty (am bit′ē), *adj.* of or designating glass that becomes devitrified while it is being worked. [apparently < French *ambité*]

am|biv|a|lence (am biv′ə ləns), *n.* the state or condition of having conflicting attitudes or feelings, as love and hate, about the same person at the same time. [< *ambi-* double + Latin *valentia* value < *valēns, -entis,* present participle of *valēre* be worth, strong]

am|biv|a|len|cy (am biv′ə lən sē), *n., pl.* **-cies.** = ambivalence.

am|biv|a|lent (am biv′ə lənt), *adj.* acting in opposite ways; having or showing conflicting attitudes or feelings: *Modern science has always been somewhat ambivalent. It has always been both the pure knowledge of the universe and power over nature* (Bulletin of Atomic Scientists). —**am|biv′a|lent|ly,** *adv.*

am|bi|ver|sion (am′bə vėr′zhən, -shən), *n.* the state or condition of being an ambivert.

am|bi|vert (am′bə vėrt), *n.* a person with qualities intermediate between those of an introvert and those of an extrovert. [< *ambi-* both + *-vert,* as in *introvert*]

am|ble (am′bəl), *n., v.,* **-bled, -bling.** —*n.* **1** the way a horse or mule goes when it lifts first the two legs on one side and then the two on the other; pace; rack. **2** an easy, slow pace in walking: *the amble of a fat dog.*
—*v.i.* **1** to go at an amble: *My horse can amble and trot.* **2** to walk at an easy, slow pace. SYN: saunter, stroll.
[< Old French *ambler* < Latin *ambulāre* walk] —**am′bler,** *n.* —**am′bling|ly,** *adv.*

am|blyg|o|nite (am blig′ə nīt), *n.* a whitish, translucent mineral, lithium aluminum fluophosphate. *Formula:* $Li(AlF)PO_4$ [< German *Amblygonit* < Latin *amblygōnius* obtuse-angled (< Greek *amblygōnios* < *amblýs* blunt + *gōniā* angle) + *-ite*[1]]

am|bly|o|pi|a (am′blē ō′pē ə), *n.* dimness of sight, without apparent organic defect; lazy eye. If it continues, it may lead to amaurosis. [< Late Latin *amblyōpia* < Greek *amblyōpíā* < *amblýs* dull, blunt + *ōps* eye]

am|bly|op|ic (am′blē op′ik), *adj.* of or characterized by amblyopia.

am|bly|pod (am′bli pod), *n.* any one of an extinct order of North American hoofed mammals of the Eocene period, having horns and a single tusk, but otherwise resembling the elephant somewhat. [< New Latin *Amblypoda* < Greek *amblýs* blunt + *poús, podós* foot]

am|bo (am′bō), *n., pl.* **-bos.** a raised desk or pulpit used in early Christian churches, for the reading of the Gospel and in making announcements. [< Medieval Latin *ambo* < Greek *ámbōn* crest]

am|bo|cep|tor (am′bə sep′tər), *n. Medicine.* = immune body. [< Latin *ambō* both + English (re)ceptor (because it is assumed to have an affinity for both the antigen and the complement)]

Am|boi|na button or **Am|boy|na button** (am boi′nə), = yaws.

Amboina wood or **Amboyna wood,** the mottled wood of a tree of Malaysia, used for inlays and ornamental cabinetwork. [< *Amboina,* Indonesia]

Am|boi|nese (am′boi nēz′, -nēs′), *adj., n., pl.* **-nese.** —*adj.* of the island of Amboina, Indonesia, its people, or their language.
—*n.* **1** a native or inhabitant of Amboina. **2** the Malay dialect spoken by the Amboinese.

Am|bo|nese (am′bə nēz′, -nēs′), *adj., n., pl.* **-nese.** = Amboinese.

am|brette (am bret′), *n.* the musky seed of the abelmosk, used in perfumery; amberseed. [< French *ambrette* (diminutive) < *ambre* amber]

am|broid (am′broid), *n.* = amberoid.

am|bro|sia (am brō′zhə), *n.* **1** *Greek and Roman Mythology.* the food of the gods. It was the substance that gave immortality. **2** *Figurative.* something especially pleasing to taste or smell. **3** a dessert of grated coconut meat and sliced oranges and, sometimes, sliced bananas. **4** = beebread. **5** any one of various plants of a genus of weeds allied to wormwood; ragweed. **6** a fungus cultivated as a food by certain burrowing beetles. [< Latin *ambrosia* < Greek *ambrosíā* < *ámbrotos* of the gods < *a-* not + *brotós* mortal]

ambrosia beetle, a wood-boring beetle found in tree trunks.

am|bro|si|a|ceous (am brō′zē ā′shəs), *adj.* belonging or related to the genus of plants of the composite family that includes the ragweeds. [< *ambrosia* + *-aceous*]

am|bro|sial (am brō′zhəl), *adj.* **1** like ambrosia; especially delicious or sweet-smelling. **2** *Figurative.* worthy of the gods; divine: *The pièce de résistance is ambrosial piano . . .* (New Yorker). —**am|bro′sial|ly,** *adv.*

am|bro|sian (am brō′zhən), *adj.* = ambrosial.

Am|bro|sian chant (am brō′zhən), a mode of chanting or singing introduced by Saint Ambrose in the cathedral of Milan about 384.

am|bro|type (am′brə tīp), *n.* one of the earliest types of photograph, consisting of a glass negative with a black backing (by means of which the negative was made to appear as a positive). [(coined by James Ambrose Cutting, 1814-1867, the inventor) < Greek *ámbrotos* immortal]

am|bry (am′brē), *n., pl.* **-bries.** *Archaic.* **1** a storehouse. **2** a pantry or cupboard. **3** a locker or recess in a church for storing sacramental vessels, vestments, etc. [alteration of *almarie* < Old French *armarie,* learned borrowing from Latin *armārium* < *arma* tools. See etym. of doublet **armoire, almirah.**]

ambs|ace (āmz′ās′, amz′-), *n.* **1** both aces; double aces, the lowest possible cast at dice. **2** bad luck; misfortune. **3** the smallest point. Also, **amesace.** [< Old French *ambes as* both aces < Latin *ambās* both, *as* smallest unit]

am|bu|la|cral (am′byə lā′krəl), *adj.* of or having to do with an ambulacrum or the ambulacra.

am|bu|la|crum (am′byə lā′krəm), *n., pl.* **-cra** (-krə). any of the radial areas of an echinoderm, containing a series of perforations through which the tubular organs of locomotion are protruded and withdrawn. [< Latin *ambulācrum* a tree-lined walk < *ambulāre* to walk]

am|bu|lance (am′byə ləns), *n.* **1** an automobile, boat, or aircraft equipped to carry sick, injured, or wounded persons. **2** (formerly) a moving hospital accompanying an army; field hospital. [< French *ambulance* < (*hôspital*) *ambulant* mobile (hospital), ultimately < Latin *ambulāre* to walk]

am|bu|lance-chas|ing (am′byə ləns chā′sing), *adj. U.S. Informal.* characteristic of or designating lawyers who encourage accident victims to become their clients and sue for damages. —**ambulance chaser.**

am|bu|lant (am′byə lənt), *adj.* **1** moving about; walking; ambulatory. **2** performed with players in motion: *the ambulant music of a marching band.* **3** *Law.* ambulatory; not fixed. [< Latin *ambulāns, -antis,* present participle of *ambulāre* to walk about]

am|bu|late (am′byə lāt), *v.i.,* **-lat|ed, -lat|ing.** to walk; move about. [< Latin *ambulāre* (with English *-ate*[1])] —**am′bu|la′tion,** *n.* —**am′bu|la′tor,** *n.*

am|bu|la|to|ry (am′byə lə tôr′ē, -tōr′-), *adj., n., pl.* **-ries.** —*adj.* **1** having to do with walking; fitted for walking: *the ambulatory life of a sheepherder.* **2** capable of walking; not bedridden: *an ambulatory patient.* **3** moving from place to place: *The Lapps live in ambulatory villages, moving with their herds of reindeer.* SYN: itinerant. **4** *Figurative.* not fixed; changeable: *A man's will is ambulatory until his death.*
—*n.* a covered place for walking, such as the aisle of a church surrounding the choir and apse or the cloister of a monastery.

am|bu|lette (am′byə let′), *n.* a small bus, van, or similar vehicle designed to carry elderly or handicapped people: *The Holmes Ambulance service . . . operates the so-called ambulette vans to transport as many as four wheelchair or ambulatory patients* (New York Times).

am|bus|cade (am′bə skād′), *n., v.t., v.i.,* **-cad|ed, -cad|ing.** = ambush. [< Middle French *embuscade* < Italian *imboscata* < *imboscare* to lie in wait in the woods] —**am′bus|cad′er,** *n.*

am|bus|ca|do (am′bə skā′dō), *n., pl.* **-dos.** *Archaic.* an ambuscade (ambush).

am|bush (am′bu̇sh), *n., v.* —*n.* **1** the place where soldiers or other persons are hidden so that they can make a surprise attack on an approaching enemy: *The soldiers lay in ambush, waiting for the signal to open fire.* **2** a surprise attack on an approaching enemy from some hiding place; act or condition of lying in wait to attack: *Indians often trapped their enemies by ambush, instead of meeting them in open battle.* **3** soldiers or others hidden to make such a surprise attack.
—*v.t.* **1** to attack unexpectedly and from a hidden position: *Our men ambushed the retreating enemy.* SYN: waylay, ambuscade. **2** *Archaic.* to put (soldiers or others) in hiding for a surprise attack: *The major ambushed his troops in the woods on either side of the road.*
—*v.i.* to wait in hiding to make a surprise attack.
[< Middle French *embusche* < Old French *embuscher* < *en-* in + *busche* wood, bush < Vulgar Latin *būsca*] —**am′bush|er,** *n.*

ambush bug, any of a group of predatory insects which attack other insects from concealment, especially in flowers.

am|bush|ment (am′bu̇sh mənt), *n.* the act or position of ambushing; an ambush.

am|bys|to|ma (am bis′tə mə), *n.* any one of a genus of salamanders native to the United States and Central America. [< New Latin *Ambystoma* < Greek *amblýs* blunt + *stóma* mouth]

am|bys|to|mid (am bis′tə mid), *n.* = ambystoma.

A.M.D.G., ad majorem Dei gloriam ("for the greater glory of God"; motto of the Society of Jesus).

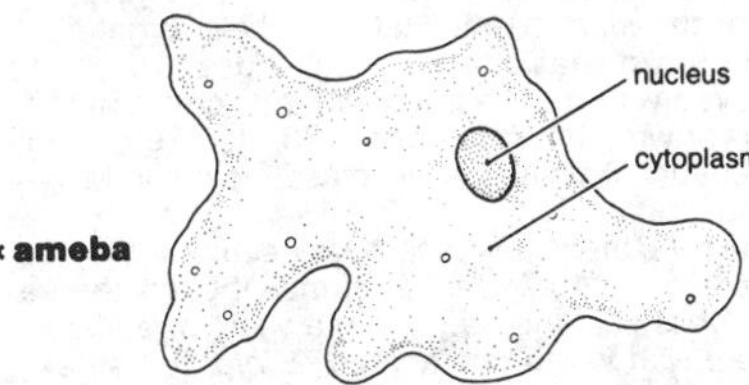

*** ameba**

***a|me|ba** (ə mē′bə), *n., pl.* **-bas, -bae** (-bē). an extremely small and very simple animal made up of only one cell. Amebas are so small that they cannot be seen without a microscope. Many amebas live in fresh and salt water; others live in soil or as parasites in other animals. They move and take in food by forming temporary fingerlike projections (pseudopods) that are constantly changing shape. Amebas are protozoans and are usually classified as rhizopods; they consist of a shapeless mass of protoplasm enclosed by a flexible membrane and contain one or more nuclei. Also, **amoeba.** [< New Latin *amoeba* <

Greek *amoibê* change] —**a|me′ba|like′**, *adj.*

a|me|ban (ə mē′bən), *adj.* **1** of or having to do with an ameba or amebas. **2** like an ameba. Also, **amoeban**.

am|e|be|an (am′ə bē′ən), *adj.* = amoebean.

am|e|bi|a|sis (am′ə bī′ə sis), *n.* an infection or disease caused by amebas, as amebic dysentery. Also, **amoebiasis**. [< *ameb*(a) + *-iasis*]

a|me|bic (ə mē′bik), *adj.* **1** of or like an ameba or amebas. **2** characterized or caused by amebas or similar protozoans: *amebic dysentery.* Also, **amoebic**.

amebic dysentery, a type of dysentery, now widely distributed, caused by a species of ameba and usually accompanied by intestinal ulcers.

a|me|bi|cid|al (ə mē′bə sī′dəl), *adj.* of or designating an amebicide. Also, **amoebicidal**.

a|me|bi|cide (ə mē′bə sīd), *n.* a substance for killing amebas. Also, **amoebicide**. [< *ameba* + *-cide*[1]]

a|me|bid (ə mē′bid), *n.* **1** = ameba. **2** an amebalike animal. Also, **amoebid**.

a|me|bi|form (ə mē′bə fôrm), *adj.* = ameboid. Also, **amoebiform**.

a|me|bo|cyte (ə mē′bə sīt), *n.* an amebalike cell, as a leucocyte. Also, **amoebocyte**. [< *ameba* + *-cyte*]

a|me|boid (ə mē′boid), *adj.* **1** of or like an ameba; like that of an ameba: *ameboid movements.* **2** related to amebas. Also, **amoeboid**.

a|me|bu|la (ə mē′byə lə), *n., pl.* **-las, -lae** (-lē). a microscopically small ameba or amebalike organism. [< New Latin *amoebula* (diminutive) < *amoeba* ameba]

âme dam|née (äm dä nā′), *French.* **1** a lost soul; person who is damned. **2** a person who blindly follows another; tool.

a|meer (ə mir′), *n.* = emir.

am|el|corn (am′əl kôrn′), *n.* a kind of wheat (spelt) cultivated to some extent in Europe, especially for its starch. [< German *Amelkorn* < Latin *amylum* starch + German *Korn* grain]

a|mel|io|ra|ble (ə mēl′yər ə bəl, -mē′lē ər-), *adj.* that can be improved.

a|mel|io|rant (ə mēl′yər ənt, -mē′lē ər-), *n.* something that ameliorates.

a|mel|io|rate (ə mēl′yə rāt, -mē′lē ə-), *v.,* **-rat|ed, -rat|ing.** —*v.t.* to make better, especially more tolerable, satisfactory, prosperous, or the like; improve: *Smoke control has ameliorated living conditions in the city.* SYN: mitigate, relieve.
—*v.i.* to become better: *Living conditions in the city ameliorated with smoke control.*
[< French *améliorer* (with English *-ate*[1]), ultimately from Late Latin *meliōrāre* < Latin *melior* better] —**a|mel′io|ra′tor**, *n.*

a|mel|io|ra|tion (ə mēl′yə rā′shən, -mē′lē ə-), *n.* **1** the process of making better. **2** the condition of being made better; improvement. **3** an improvement.

a|mel|io|ra|tive (ə mēl′yə rā′tiv, -mē′lē ə-), *adj.* tending to ameliorate; improving. —**a|mel′io|ra′tive|ly**, *adv.*

a|mel|io|ra|to|ry (ə mēl′yə rə tôr′ē, -tōr′-; -mē′lē ə-), *adj.* = ameliorative.

a|mel|o|blast (ə mel′ə blast), *n.* a cell which forms dental enamel: *Yet to make perfect enamel each enamel-forming cell must stay healthy until the work is done, for the ameloblasts, unlike most other cells of the body, cannot reproduce* (Scientific American). [< Old French *esmal* enamel + Greek *blastós* germ]

Am|e|lung glass (am′ə lung), glassware engraved with mottoes, monograms, crests, and flower wreaths, made from 1784 to 1795 by John Frederick Amelung at his glass factory in Maryland.

a|men (ā′men′, ä′-; *see note below*), *interj., n., adv., v.* —*interj.* **1** so be it; may it become true. *Amen* is said after a prayer, a wish, or a statement with which one agrees. **2** *Informal.* an expression of approval.
—*n.* the word *amen*, as at the end of a prayer.
—*adv. Archaic.* truly; verily.
—*v.t.* **1** to say "amen" to; sanction or approve. **2** to end or finish.
[< Late Latin *āmēn* < Greek *āmēn* < Hebrew *'āmēn* truly]
▶The pronunciation (ä′men′) is ordinarily employed in singing. In spoken use the choice between this pronunciation and (ā′men′) is in part dependent on the practice in different religious groups.

A|men (ä′mən), *n.* = Amon.

a|me|na|bil|i|ty (ə mē′nə bil′ə tē, -men′ə-), *n.* the state or condition of being amenable.

a|me|na|ble (ə mē′nə bəl, -men′ə-), *adj.* **1** open to influence, suggestion, or advice; submissive; responsive: *Dick is reasonable and amenable to persuasion.* SYN: compliant, tractable. **2** accountable or answerable to some jurisdiction or authority: *People living in a country are amenable to its laws.* SYN: liable, responsible. **3** *Figurative.* that can be tested by a problem: *amenable to mathematical analysis.* [< French *amener* (< *a-* to + *mener* lead < Latin *mināre* drive with shouts < *minae* threats) + *-able* -able] —**a|me′na|ble|ness**, *n.* —**a|me′na|bly**, *adv.*

a|men corner (ā′men′), *U.S. Informal.* **1** the part of a church occupied by the worshipers who assist the preacher with occasional and irregular responses. **2** *Figurative.* any rallying place.

a|mend (ə mend′), *v., n.* —*v.t.* **1** to change the form of (a law, bill, or motion.) by addition, omission, or alteration of language: *The Constitution of the United States was amended so that women could vote.* **2** to change for the better; improve: *It is time you amended your poor table manners. The mayor is making a greater effort to amend conditions in the slums.* **3** to free from faults; make right; correct: *The spelling in my theme was amended by the teacher.* SYN: emend, rectify. **4** *Archaic.* to repair; mend.
—*v.i.* to reform oneself: *After he criticized me, I took pains to amend.*
—*n.* See **amends**.
[< Old French *amender* < Latin *ēmendāre* < *ex-* out + *menda* fault. See etym. of doublet **emend**.] —**a|mend′a|ble**, *adj.* —**a|mend′er**, *n.*

a|mend|a|to|ry (ə men′də tôr′ē, -tōr′-), *adj. U.S.* that amends; corrective.

a|mende (ə mend′; *French* à mäɴd′), *n.* reparation, as for wrong done; amends. [< French *amende*]

a|mende ho|no|ra|ble (á mäɴd′ô nô rá′blə), *French.* **1** public apology and reparation such as to reestablish the honor of a person who has been injured or offended. **2** *Figurative.* any open or formal apology and reparation: *He is under the distinct impression that his book—a chatty, friendly portrait of Napoleon's strange, brief exile on the island of Elba in 1814-15—is a sort of belated amende honorable to a great character who was shabbily used by the British* (New York Times).

a|mend|ment (ə mend′mənt), *n.* **1** a change made or offered in a law, bill, or motion by addition, omission, or alteration of language: *The Constitution of the United States has over twenty amendments.* **2** the act of making such a change or alteration. **3** a change for the better; improvement. **4** a change made to remove an error; correction. **5** *Law.* alteration or correction in any process, pleading, proceeding at law or in equity.

a|mends (ə mendz′), *n.sing. or pl.* **1** something given or paid to make up for a wrong or injury done; payment for loss; satisfaction; compensation: *to make amends to a person who was imprisoned unjustly. If you carelessly took more than your share of the money, you should make amends at once by returning the extra amount.* SYN: reparation, recompense. **2** *Obsolete.* improvement in health; recovery. [< Old French *amendes* penalties, plural of *amend* reparation < *amender* to amend]

a|mene (ə mēn′), *adj. Rare.* pleasant; agreeable. [< Latin *amoenus*]

a|men|i|ty (ə men′ə tē, -mē′nə-), *n., pl.* **-ties.** **1** a pleasant way; polite act: *Saying "Thank you" and holding the door open for another to pass through are amenities that should be taught to young children.* SYN: courtesy, civility, comity. **2** a pleasant feature; a thing which makes life easier and more pleasant: *Television, telephones, and automobiles are among the amenities of modern life.* SYN: convenience. **3** the quality of being pleasant; pleasantness; agreeableness: *We went to Hawaii to enjoy the amenity of a warm climate.* SYN: gentleness, mildness, clemency.
amenities, *Especially British.* modern conveniences such as plumbing and lighting: *The castle is in good repair, but it lacks the amenities.*
[< Latin *amoenitās* < *amoenus* pleasant]

a|men|or|rhe|a or **a|men|or|rhoe|a** (ā men′ə rē′ə), *n.* failure to menstruate. [< New Latin *amenorrhea* < Greek *a-* not + *mēn* month + *rhoiā* flux < *rheîn* to flow]

a|men|or|rhe|ic or **a|men|or|rhoe|ic** (ā men′ə rē′ik), *adj.* of or having to do with amenorrhea.

A|men-Ra (ä′mən rä′), *n.* = Amon-Re.

a men|sa et tho|ro (ā men′sə et thō′rō), *Latin.* from board and bed (designating a legal separation in which the husband continues to support the wife but no longer lives with her).

am|ent[1] (am′ənt, ā′mənt), *n.* a long, slender, scaly flower spike that grows on willows, birches, alders, and poplars; catkin. [< Latin *āmentum* thong of a javelin]

a|ment[2] (am′ənt, ā′mənt), *n. Psychology.* a person suffering from amentia; an idiot.

am|en|ta|ceous (am′ən tā′shəs), *adj.* **1** consisting of or like an ament. **2** bearing catkins; amentiferous. [< *ament*[1] + *-aceous*]

a|men|tia (ā men′shə), *n.* **1** a deficiency in intellectual development, such as imbecility or idiocy. **2** temporary confused condition caused by insanity. [< Latin *āmentia* < *āmēns, -mentis* < *ā-* off + *mēns* the mind]

am|en|tif|er|ous (am′ən tif′ər əs), *adj.* bearing catkins; amentaceous: *The pussy willow is amentiferous.* [< *ament*[1] + *-ferous*]

a|men|ti|form (ə men′tə fôrm), *adj.* having the shape of a catkin. [< *ament*[1] + *-form*]

Amer., **1** America. **2** American.

Am|er|a|sian (am′ər ā′zhən, -shən), *adj., n.* —*adj.* of mixed American and Asian descent: ... *the hundreds of thousands of rejected, mixed-blooded "Amerasian" youths who since 1945 have been fathered by American servicemen from Korea to Viet Nam* (Time).
—*n.* a person of mixed American and Asian descent.

a|merce (ə mėrs′), *v.t.,* **a|merced, a|merc|ing.** **1** to punish by an arbitrary fine; fine (a person) that amount which seems proper to the court. **2** *Archaic.* to punish. [< Anglo-French *amercier* < *a merci* at the mercy (of)] —**a|merc′er**, *n.*

a|merce|a|ble (ə mėr′sə bəl), *adj.* subject to amercement.

a|merce|ment (ə mėrs′mənt), *n.* **1** the act of amercing; imposition of a discretionary fine. **2** the fine imposed.

A|mer|i|ca-First|er (ə mer′ə kə fėrs′tər), *n. U.S.* a member or supporter of the America First Committee, an isolationist group that sought to keep the U.S. neutral before it entered World War II.

A|mer|i|can (ə mer′ə kən), *adj., n.* —*adj.* **1** of or having to do with the United States; in the United States: *Many immigrants become American citizens.* **2** native only to the Western Hemisphere: *the American eagle. Cacao, tomatoes, corn, and tobacco are American plants.* **3** of or in the Western Hemisphere: *the Amazon, the Mississippi, and other American rivers.*
—*n.* **1a** a person born or living in the United States; citizen of the United States, or of the earlier British colonies, not belonging to one of the aboriginal races: *The people of Alaska are Americans.* **b** a person born or living in North or South America; native or inhabitant of the Western Hemisphere: *The citizens of Mexico, Canada, and Argentina are Americans.* **c** = American Indian. **2** = American English: *"In the Clearing," a new collection by Robert Frost ... is written in American, a language that still has a good deal of life and heart in it* (New Yorker). *Abbr:* Am.

A|mer|i|ca|na (ə mer′ə kä′nə, -kan′ə, -kā′nə), *n.pl.* **1** a collection of books, documents, facts, or other literary material about America, especially its history. **2** a collection of early American furniture, textiles, or other, usually handcrafted, products. **3** anecdotes, folklore, or other thing, about America, or typical of America and American culture: *Freak shows are a vanishing item of Americana* (Harper's). [< *America* + *-ana*]

American aloe, *U.S.* a common name for the century plant, though the century plant is botanically unrelated to the aloes.

American arbor vitae, a species of arbor vitae found in eastern United States that grows to a height of 60 feet.

American ash, the white ash tree, the species most common in North America.

American Beauty, a hybrid variety of cultivated rose, with deep-pink to crimson flowers.

American bittersweet, a twining shrub of the staff-tree family with an orange or orange-yellow pod which opens to display crimson or scarlet seeds.

***American bond**, a method of bricklaying in which four to six layers of bricks with the sides exposed are between single layers of bricks laid flat with the ends exposed; common bond.

***American bond**

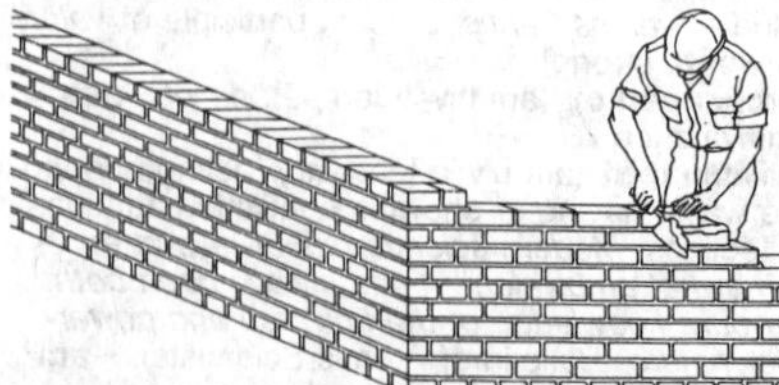

American brant, a wild goose of North America that breeds in the Arctic and winters along the Atlantic coast of North America.

American chameleon, a lizard of the southeastern United States, especially North and South Carolina.

American cheese, the most common variety of Cheddar made in America, usually deep yellow in color, less often white; ordinary yellow cheese.

American class, any one of several breeds of chicken developed in the United States and Canada, including the Plymouth Rock, New Hampshire, Wyandotte, Rhode Island Red, and

Rhode Island White breeds.

American cockroach, a large cockroach native to subtropical America, now established in many parts of the world.

American copper, a small butterfly that attacks other butterflies, and sometimes even birds and dogs.

American cowslip, = shooting star.

American crocodile, a crocodile that lives in the extreme south of Florida, on the larger West Indian Islands, and in Central America and areas near it.

American Dream, the American way of life, especially as expressed in expectation of achievement: *Salesmen like this are very much part of the American Dream. Each one is out on his own . . . He thinks he's free, that it's just up to him how well he does* (Vincent Canby).

American eagle, the bald eagle. The coat of arms of the United States has a design of the American eagle on it.

American egret, a species of tall, handsome egret with fine, white plumage.

American elm, the species of elm native to the United States; white elm.

* **American Empire**, of or designating an American version of the Empire style of furniture, developed after the Revolutionary War by Duncan Phyfe and his followers: *The American Empire furniture is generally large and heavy, and has straight lines.*

* **American Empire**

American English, the form of English spoken and written in the United States: *American English came, not chiefly from British local dialects, but from standard British of the seventeenth century* (John Kenyon).

A|mer|i|can|ese (ə mer′ə kə nēz′, -nēs′), *n.* the slang, colloquialisms, inflections, and the like, of general American speech as distinguished from other forms of English, such as those spoken in Great Britain, Australia, and Canada: *The shoddiness of Mr. Chase's prefabricated Americanese is shown immediately by comparison with such genuine masters as Dashiell Hammett or Raymond Chandler* (Sunday Times).

American football, the game of football as it is played in the United States (especially as distinguished from *Rugby* and *soccer* or *association football*).

American foxhound, a usually white, medium-sized hunting dog with different-sized patches of black or tan, or both. It is trained to hunt foxes by following their foot scent.

American hellebore, a plant of the lily family, having yellow-green flowers, native to North America. Its poisonous roots are sometimes dried and powdered for use as an insecticide.

American holly, a species of holly whose leaves and berries are used as decorations. It is commonest in the southeastern United States. See picture under **deciduous**.

American hornbeam, a species of hornbeam native to North America; ironwood.

American Indian, a member of one of the aboriginal peoples of North and South America, or the West Indies, often excepting the Eskimos; an Indian.

▶**American Indian—red Indian**. The latter is the popular term in the English-speaking world outside of North America.

A|mer|i|can|ise (ə mer′ə kə nīz), *v.t., v.i.,* **-ised, -is|ing.** *British.* Americanize.

A|mer|i|can|ism (ə mer′ə kə niz′əm), *n.* **1** devotion or loyalty to the United States and to its customs and traditions. **2** a word, phrase, or meaning originating or more widely used in American English than in other varieties of English: *The term* exclamation point *is an Americanism* (Mitford M. Mathews). **3** a custom or trait peculiar to the United States.

A|mer|i|can|ist (ə mer′ə kə nist), *n.* a person who studies subjects relating to either of the American continents, such as their history, ethnography, or geography.

American ivy, = Virginia creeper.

A|mer|i|can|i|za|tion (ə mer′ə kə nə zā′shən), *n.* the act or process of Americanizing.

A|mer|i|can|ize (ə mer′ə kə nīz), *v.t., v.i.,* **-ized, -iz|ing.** to make or become American in habits, customs, or character: *The heroine of the play was an Americanized French girl. The process whereby individuals or groups once dissimilar become similar, that is, become identified in their interests and outlook, is termed assimilation. . . . Usually, when this process is mentioned, we think of immigrants being "Americanized"* (Ogburn and Nimkoff).

American leopard, = jaguar.

American linden, = basswood.

American lotus, = water chinquapin.

A|mer|i|can|ly (ə mer′ə kən lē), *adv.* in an American manner: *. . . incredibly, Americanly rich* (Illustrated London News).

American marten, the species of marten native to North America, related to the weasel.

American merganser, a North American variety of fish-eating duck that has a glossy greenish-black head and upper neck.

American merlin, = pigeon hawk.

American mink, **1** the species of mink native to North America, now the commonest species of wild mink. **2** its fur, much valued for use in making women's coats, stoles, and hats.

American mountain ash, the species of mountain ash common in eastern North America.

A|mer|i|can|ness (ə mer′ə kən nis), *n.* American character or quality.

A|mer|i|ca|no (ä mā′rē kä′nō), *n., pl.* **-nos.** a cocktail composed of sweet vermouth and bitters mixed with soda water. [< Spanish *Americano* (literally) American]

A|mer|i|can|oc|ra|cy (ə mer′ə kə nok′rə sē), *n.* (in Communist use) American government; rule by Americans.

A|mer|i|can|oid (ə mer′ə kə noid), *n., adj.* **—*n.*** a member of any of various tribes of northeastern Siberia bearing physical resemblances to the Indians of northwestern North America.

—*adj.* of or having to do with the Americanoids or their languages: *Americanoid dialects.*

A|mer|i|ca|nol|o|gist (ə mer′ə kə nol′ə jist), *n.* a foreign expert on United States policies, leaders, culture, and the like: *a Soviet Americanologist.*

A|mer|i|can|o|phile (ə mer′ə kan′ə fīl, -fil), *n.* a friend or admirer of the United States or its people.

A|mer|i|can|o|phil|i|a (ə mer′ə kan′ə fil′ē ə), *n.* friendship for or devotion to the United States, its culture, or its people.

A|mer|i|can|o|phobe (ə mer′ə kan′ə fōb), *n.* a person who fears or hates the United States or its people.

American organ, *Especially British.* a melodeon.

American Party, **1** a party prominent in the United States between 1853 and 1856, which wanted to permit only native-born citizens to participate in the government. See also **Know-Nothing**. **2** a party founded in 1969 in the United States that believes each state should decide for itself whether to have segregated schools.

American plan, *U.S.* a system used in hotels where one price covers room, board, and service (contrasted with *European plan*).

American plum, any of several cultivated varieties of cold-resistant plums with amber flesh and skin that grow wild east of the Rocky Mountains.

American redstart, a warbler with a striking black color and salmon markings that looks somewhat like a small oriole.

American Revised Version, a revision of the Bible, published in the United States in 1901. It included changes not accepted for the English or Revised Version.

American sable, = American marten.

American saddle horse, any one of a breed of fine saddle horses, bred in America from utility stock and thoroughbreds in colonial times, noted for their appearance, carriage, and intelligence. Usually five-gaited, they are used for both riding and driving.

American Selling Price, the wholesale price of certain domestic American products, used in customs valuation as the standard for assessing the duty to be paid on imported products of the same kind. *Abbr:* ASP (no periods).

American Sign Language, the system of communication by manual gestures used by the deaf in North America.

American snipe, the species of snipe native to North America, found in marshy places and hunted as game; Wilson's snipe.

American Spanish, the dialect of Spanish spoken in South and Central America and the West Indies.

American Standard Version, = American Revised Version.

American system, the policy of fostering American industries, by means of high tariff duties, and of encouraging internal development: *The chief issue of Monroe's first administration was "the American system" proposed and named by Henry Clay.*

American trotting horse, a standardbred horse, considered the best for harness racing.

American trypanosomiasis, = Chagas' disease.

American water spaniel, any one of a breed of hunting dogs having a thick, closely curled coat that is usually solid liver or dark chocolate brown.

American white hellebore, = American hellebore.

American widgeon, the species of widgeon native to North America; baldpate.

American woodbine, the Virginia creeper or American ivy.

American woodcock, the common woodcock of the eastern United States and southern Canada: *The American woodcock . . . has short legs and a tail, and a long bill with a sensitive tip* (Alfred M. Bailey).

American yew, = ground hemlock.

America's Cup, a cup first won in a race by the schooner *America* in 1851, and since then awarded to the winner of a sailboat race held approximately once every six years.

* **am|er|i|ci|um** (am′ə rish′ē əm), *n.* an artificial, radioactive, metallic chemical element produced from plutonium by bombardment with high-energy alpha particles. [< New Latin *americium* < English *America* + *-ium*, a suffix meaning "metallic element"]

* **americium**

symbol	atomic number	mass number	oxidation state
Am	95	243	6, 5, 4, 3

Am|er|ind (am′ər ind), *n., adj.* = Amerindian. [< *Amer*(ican) *Ind*(ian)]

Am|er|in|di|an (am′ər in′dē ən), *n., adj.* **—*n.*** **1** = American Indian. **2** (sometimes) = Eskimo. **—*adj.*** of or having to do with American Indians.

Am|er|in|dic (am′ər in′dik), *adj.* of or having to do with Amerindians.

am|er|is|tic (am′ə ris′tik, ā′mə-), *adj. Biology.* not meristic; unsegmented.

Am|er|toy (am′ər toi), *n.* any one of an American breed of toy dogs similar to the toy Manchester terrier but smaller. [< *Amer*(ican) + *toy*]

ames|ace (āmz′ās′, amz′-), *n.* = ambsace.

Am|es|lan (am′əs lan), *n.* = American Sign Language: *Among the sign languages, the deaf in the United States use two principal means of communication, Ameslan and finger-spelling* (Eugene Linden).

Ames test (āmz), a test for detecting cancer-producing substances by measuring their relative ability to cause a mutation: *The Ames test . . . uses a highly specialized strain of bacteria that is very susceptible to mutations to measure mutagenic effect* (Harper's). [< Bruce *Ames*, an American biochemist]

a|meth|o|caine (ə meth′ə kān), *n.* = tetracaine hydrochloride.

am|e|thop|te|rin (am′ə thop′tər in), *n.* one of the group of so-called antagonists of folic acid, used in the treatment of leukemia, especially in children; methotrexate. *Formula:* $C_{20}H_{22}N_8O_5$

am|e|thop|te|rine (am′ə thop′tə rēn, -tər in), *n.* = amethopterin.

am|e|thyst (am′ə thist), *n., adj.* **—*n.*** **1** a purple or violet variety of quartz, used for jewelry. **2** a rare violet-colored variety of corundum or sapphire, used for jewelry; oriental amethyst. **3** a purplish or violet color.

—*adj.* purple or violet.

[< Old French *ametiste*, learned borrowing from Latin *amethystus* < Greek *améthystos* the amethyst, (thought to be) a preventive of intoxication < *a-* not + *méthy* wine] **—am′e|thyst|like′**, *adj.*

am|e|thys|tine (am′ə this′tin, -tīn), *adj.* **1** violet. **2** of amethyst.

amethystine python, a variety of python living in Australia and the East Indies.

am|e|tro|pi|a (am′ə trō′pē ə), *n.* astigmatism, myopia, or other abnormal conditions of the eye with respect to refraction. [< New Latin *ametropia* < Greek *ámetros* irregular (< *a-* without + *métron* measure) + *-ōpia* < *ōps* eye]

am|e|trop|ic (am′ə trop′ik), *adj.* of or denoting ametropia.

Am|ex (am′əks), *n. U.S.* American Stock Exchange.

Am|har|ic (am har′ik, äm här′-), *n., adj.* **—*n.*** the official and literary language of Ethiopia since the 1300's, a Semitic language of the Ethiopic group. **—*adj.*** of or denoting this language.

a|mi (á mē′), *n. French.* **1** a friend. **2** a lover.

a|mi|a|bil|i|ty (ā′mē ə bil′ə tē), *n.* the quality of being amiable; good nature; friendliness; pleasantness.

Pronunciation Key: hat, āge, cãre, fär; let, ēqual, tėrm; it, īce; hot, ōpen, ôrder; oil, out; cup, pu̇t, rüle; child; long; thin; ᴛʜen; zh, measure; ə represents a in about, e in taken, i in pencil, o in lemon, u in circus.

a|mi|a|ble (ā′mē ə bəl), *adj.* **1** good-natured and friendly; pleasant and agreeable: *She is an amiable girl and gets along with everyone.* **SYN**: engaging, sweet-tempered, amicable. **2** *Archaic.* lovable or lovely. [< Old French *amiable* < Late Latin *amīcābilis* < Latin *amīcus* friend. See etym. of doublet **amicable**.] —**a′mi|a|ble|ness**, *n.* —**a′mi|a|bly**, *adv.*

am|i|an|thus (am′ē an′thəs), *n.* a variety of asbestos with long, flexible, pearly white fibers. [< Latin *amiantus* < Greek *amiantos* (*líthos*) (literally) undefiled stone < *a-* not + *miainein* to defile]

am|ic (am′ik), *adj.* **1** of or resembling an amide or amine. **2** having to do with ammonia.

am|i|ca|bil|i|ty (am′ə kə bil′ə tē), *n.* the quality of being amicable; friendliness.

am|i|ca|ble (am′ə kə bəl), *adj.* having or showing a friendly attitude; peaceable: *Instead of fighting, the two nations settled their quarrel by amicable negotiation.* **SYN**: harmonious. [< Late Latin *amīcābilis* < Latin *amīcus* friend. See etym. of doublet **amiable**.] —**am′i|ca|ble|ness**, *n.* —**am′i|ca|bly**, *adv.*

am|ice[1] (am′is), *n.* an oblong piece of white linen, usually with an embroidered cross, worn under the alb by priests at Mass. It is placed around the neck and over the shoulders. [< Old French *amit,* learned borrowing from Latin *amictus* cloak < *amicīre* wrap < *ambi-* about + *jacere* throw]

am|ice[2] (am′is), *n.* a furred hood, or a hood with cape attached, with long ends hanging down, formerly worn by the clergy. Also, **almuce**. [< Old French *aumusse* < Medieval Latin *almutia;* origin uncertain]

a|mi|cus cu|ri|ae (ə mī′kəs kyůr′ē ē; ə mē′kəs kyůr′ē ī), *Law.* a person with no interest in a case who is called in to advise the judge. [< New Latin *amicus curiae* friend of the court]

a|mi|cus hu|ma|ni ge|ne|ris (ə mī′kəs hyü mā′nī jen′ər is), *Latin.* a friend to mankind; philanthropist.

a|mi|cus us|que ad a|ras (ə mī′kəs us′kwē ad ā′ras), *Latin.* **1** a friend except when religion forbids. **2** a friend to the last extremity. **3** (literally) a friend all the way to the altars.

a|mid[1] (ə mid′), *prep.* in the middle of; surrounded by; among: *The little church stood unharmed amid the ruins of the burned village.* [Middle English *amidde* < Old English *on middan*]

am|id[2] (am′id), *n. Rare.* amide.

A|mi|dah (a mē′dä), *n.* the most solemn prayer in the Jewish liturgy. It is composed of nineteen short benedictions recited while standing. [< Hebrew *′ămīdhāh*]

am|i|date (am′ə dāt), *v.t.*, **-dat|ed, -dat|ing.** to make into an amide. —**am′i|da′tion**, *n.*

am|ide (am′īd, -id), *n.* **1** any one of a group of organic compounds having the univalent radical $-CONH_2$, or a similar radical, obtained by substituting the $-NH_2$ radical for the $-OH$ group of a corresponding acid. **2** a compound in which a metal is substituted for one of the hydrogen atoms of ammonia. [< *am*(monia) + *-ide*]

a|mid|ic (ə mid′ik), *adj.* of or derived from an amide.

am|i|din (am′ə din), *n.* starch dissolved in water. [< French *amidon* (< Latin *amylum* starch) + English *-in*]

Am|i|dism (am′ə diz əm), *n.* a form of Mahayana Buddhism which places faith above works: *... easygoing Amidism, in which a paradise called "Pure Land" awaits the intense faithful who repeats a simple prayer* (Time). [< *Amida,* name of the Buddha who taught Amidism + English *-ism*]

a|mi|do (ə mē′dō, am′ə-), *adj.* **1** of or containing an amide or amides. **2** (occasionally) amino. [< *amide*]

a|mi|do|gen (ə mē′də jən, -mid′ə-), *n.* a univalent radical, $-NH_2$, occurring in the amides and amines. [< *amide* + *-gen*]

am|i|dol (am′ə dol, -dōl), *n.* a crystalline powder produced from phenol, used in photographic developing. *Formula:* $C_6H_8N_2O{\cdot}2HCl$ [< *amid*(e) + *-ol*[1]]

am|i|done (am′ə dōn), *n.* = methadone.

a|mi|do|py|rine (ə mē′dō pī′rēn), *n. Especially British.* aminopyrine.

a|mid|ship (ə mid′ship), *adv.* = amidships.

a|mid|ships (ə mid′ships), *adv.* **1** in or toward the middle of a ship; halfway between the bow and stern. **2** *Informal, Figurative.* in the middle: *The boxer doubled over from a blow received amidships. The parked vehicle was struck amidships by the skidding bus.*

a|midst (ə midst′), *prep.* = amid[1]. [Middle English *amidde* + adverbial genitive *-s* (the *-t* is a later addition)]

a|mie (á mē′), *n. French.* **1** a feminine friend. **2** a mistress; sweetheart.

Am|i|gen (am′ə jən), *n. Trademark.* a predigested form of protein produced by the hydrolysis of milk, meat, and certain other protein foods. It is used in the treatment of protein deficiency.

a|mi|go (ə mē′gō), *n., pl.* **-gos.** friend. [American English < Spanish *amigo* < Latin *amīcus*]

am|il|dar (am′əl där), *n.* = amaldar.

a|mil|len|ni|al|ism (ā′mə len′ē əl iz′əm), *n.* the doctrine that the millennium is the long period of time between Christ's first coming and His second coming (not necessarily the 1000 years before).

am|in (am′in), *n.* = amine.

am|i|na|tion (am′ə nā′shən), *n.* conversion into an amino compound: *New reaction mechanisms are postulated in which amination of phosphorylated acids gives rise directly to the corresponding amino acid* (New Scientist).

a|mine (ə mēn′, am′in), *n.* any one of a group of organic compounds obtained from ammonia by replacement of one or more of the three hydrogen atoms by univalent hydrocarbon radicals. [< *am*(monia) + *-ine*[2]]

a|mi|no (ə mē′nō, am′ə-), *adj.* of or containing the $-NH_2$ group combined with a nonacid radical. [< *amine*]

amino acid, any one of a group of complex organic compounds of nitrogen, hydrogen, carbon, and oxygen that combine in various ways to form the proteins that make up living matter. They contain the radicals $-NH_2$ and $-COOH$. *There are eight or 10 amino acids regarded as essential to nutrition because they are the building blocks of the proteins which make up the bulk of the cells of the human body* (Wall Street Journal).

amino acid dating, a method of dating dead organic matter by measuring the amount of change in the structure of the amino acids present after death: *When properly used, this dating method has important advantages over the radiocarbon technique ... fossils can be dated over a period of 15,000 to 100,000 years ... amino acid dating can be completed in two days using only 10g of a sample* (New Scientist).

a|mi|no|ben|zo|ic acid (ə mē′nō ben zō′ik, am′ə-), a substance found in yeast, especially brewers' yeast, which is part of the vitamin B complex, and apparently essential to the growth of some animal species and bacteria. It is a constituent of folic acid. *Formula:* $C_7H_7NO_2$

amino group or **radical**, the monovalent radical $-NH_2$

a|mi|no|phyl|line (ə mē′nō fil′ēn, am′ə-; -in), *n.* a poisonous, white or yellowish compound consisting of theophylline and ethylenediamine, used to treat bronchial asthma and heart conditions. *Formula:* $C_{16}H_{28}N_{10}O_6$ [< *amino* + Greek *phýllon* leaf + English *-ine*[2]]

a|mi|no|plast (ə mē′nə plast, am′ə-), *n.* any one of various resins prepared from amino or amido compounds. [< *amino* + Greek *plastós* molded]

a|mi|no|plas|tic (ə mē′nə plas′tik, am′ə-), *adj.* of or having to do with an aminoplast or aminoplasts.

a|mi|nop|ter|in (am′ə nop′tər in), *n.* a yellow crystalline compound used in treating leukemia and as a poison to kill rodents. *Formula:* $C_{19}H_{20}N_8O_5{\cdot}2H_2O$ [< *amino-* + Greek *pterón* wing, feather + English *-in*]

a|mi|no|py|rine (ə mē′nō pī′rēn, -rin; am′ə-), *n.* a crystalline drug used as an antipyretic and as an analgesic in treating colds and pain. *Formula:* $C_{13}H_{17}N_3O$ [< *amino* + Greek *pŷr* fire + English *-ine*[2]]

a|mir (ə mir′), *n.* = emir. Also, **ameer**. [< Arabic *′amīr* commander. See related etym. at **admiral**.]

a|mir|ate (ə mir′āt), *n.* = emirate. [*amir* + *-ate*[3]]

Am|ish (am′ish, ä′mish), *n., pl.* **Am|ish**, *adj.* —*n.* a very strict Mennonite sect, founded in the late 1600's. Its members are found today chiefly in eastern Pennsylvania, and in parts of Ohio, Indiana, Illinois, Iowa, and Canada.
—*adj.* of or having to do with this sect or its members.
[American English < Jacob *Amman,* a Swiss Mennonite preacher in the 1600's + *-ish*]

Am|ish|man (am′ish mən, ä′mish-), *n., pl.* **-men.** a member of the Amish sect; one of the Amish: *The Amishman ... produces his milk without the help of machinery* (New York Times).

a|miss (ə mis′), *adv., adj.* —*adv.* not the way it should be; out of order; at fault; in a wrong way; wrongly: *You must be tired; your work is going amiss today.*
—*adj.* improper; wrong: *Something is amiss when a boy will not eat for days.*
take amiss, to be offended at (something not intended to offend): *Don't take it amiss if the teacher checks your answers.*
[Middle English *a mis* in error, at fault]

am|i|to|sis (am′ə tō′sis), *n.* a method of cell division in which the cell separates into new cells without an exact division of the chromosomes: *It is probably safe to say that the cells which are thought to divide by amitosis are those for which we have not developed a sufficiently refined technique to see mitosis* (A. M. Winchester). [< *a-*[4] not + *mitosis*]

am|i|tot|ic (am′ə tot′ik), *adj.* reproducing without mitosis: *In both plants and animals, amitotic division of cells usually indicates a diseased or degenerative condition* (Harbaugh and Goodrich). —**am′i|tot′i|cal|ly**, *adv.*

am|i|ty (am′ə tē), *n., pl.* **-ties.** peace and friendship; friendly relations; friendliness: *a treaty of amity and commerce. If there were true amity between nations, there would be no wars.* **SYN**: good will, friendship, harmony. [< Middle French *amitié* < Old French *amistie* < Vulgar Latin *amīcitās* < Latin *amīcus* friend]

AMM (no periods), anti-missile missile.

am|me|ter (am′mē′tər, am′ē′-), *n.* an instrument for measuring in amperes the strength of an electric current. [< *am*(pere) + *-meter*]

am|mi|a|ceous (am′ē ā′shəs), *adj. Botany.* of or belonging to the parsley family; apiaceous. [< Latin *ammi* parsley plant (< Greek *ámmi*) + English *-aceous*]

am|min (am′in), *n.* = ammine.

am|mine (am′ēn, ə mēn′), *n.* **1** any one of a group of inorganic compounds containing ammonia molecules and a metallic salt. **2** (infrequently) an ammonia molecule as found in such a compound.

am|mo (am′ō), *n. Informal.* ammunition.

am|mo|cete or **am|mo|coete** (am′ə sēt), *n.* the larva of a lamprey. The anatomy of ammocetes is typical of chordates, and they are therefore often used in zoology courses as representative. They are blind and toothless, and look like worms. They live in the sand and mud of the stream bottom for several years. [< Greek *ámmos* sand + *koítē* bed]

Am|mon (am′ən), *n.* **1** the Greek and Roman name for Amon, whom the Greeks identified with Zeus, the Romans with Jupiter. He was represented with horns like a ram's. **2** an epithet of Zeus or Jupiter as worshiped in Egypt.

am|mo|nal (am′ə nal), *n.* a high explosive consisting of a mixture of ammonium nitrate and aluminum. [< *ammon*(ium) + *al*(uminum)]

am|mo|nia (ə mōn′yə, -mō′nē ə), *n.* **1** a colorless, soluble gas, consisting of one part nitrogen and three parts hydrogen, that has a very strong, pungent, and suffocating smell and a strong alkaline reaction. Ammonia can be condensed to a colorless liquid under pressure and cold. *Formula:* NH_3 **2** this gas dissolved in water; spirits of hartshorn. Ammonia is used for cleaning and for making fertilizers and many other products, such as explosives and plastics. *Formula:* NH_4OH [< New Latin *ammonia* (so named because obtained from *sal ammoniac*)]

ammonia alum, = alum (def. 2).

am|mo|ni|ac (ə mō′nē ak), *n., adj.* —*n.* **1** a gum resin used for medicines and as a cement for porcelain; gum ammoniac. **2** ammonium chloride; sal ammoniac. —*adj.* = ammoniacal.
[< Latin *Ammōniacum* < Greek *ammōniakós* of Ammon (the gum was said to come from near the shrine of *Ammon* in Libya)]

am|mo|ni|a|cal (am′ə nī′ə kəl), *adj.* of or containing ammonia: *Ammonia may be sold as concentrated ammoniacal liquor from which chemical manufacturers can produce anhydrous ammonia* (London Times).

am|mo|ni|ate (ə mō′nē āt), *v.t.*, **-at|ed, -at|ing.** to combine or treat with ammonia. —**am|mo′ni|a′tion**, *n.* —**am|mo′ni|a′tor**, *n.*

ammonia water, ammonia gas dissolved in water; ammonia (def. 2).

am|mon|ic (ə mon′ik, -mō′nik), *adj.* of or derived from ammonia.

am|mon|i|cal (ə mon′ə kəl), *adj.* = ammonic.

am|mon|i|fi|ca|tion (ə mon′ə fə kā′shən), *n.* **1** the process of ammonifying. **2** the condition of being ammonified. **3** the production of ammonia in the decomposition of organic matter, especially through the action of bacteria.

am|mon|i|fy (ə mon′ə fī), *v.*, **-fied, -fy|ing.** —*v.t.* to combine with ammonia or ammonium compounds. —*v.i.* to be ammonified.

am|mo|nite (am′ə nīt), *n.* the fossil shell of a mollusk extinct in the Cretaceous period, coiled in a flat spiral and up to 6 feet in diameter. [< New Latin *ammonites* < Latin *cornū Ammōnis* horn of Ammon (represented as a ram)]

Am|mon|ite (am′ə nīt), *n.* a member of a Semitic tribe that inhabited the region of Palestine east of the Jordan River. The Ammonites were descended from the son of Lot (in the Bible, Deuteronomy 2:19, 20).

am|mo|ni|um (ə mō′nē əm), *n.* a univalent basic radical whose compounds or salts are similar to those of the alkali metals. It never appears in a free state by itself, but acts as a unit in chemical reactions. *Formula:* NH_4 [< New Latin *ammonium* < *ammonia* ammonia]

ammonium alum, = alum (def. 2).

ammonium bicarbonate, white, soluble crystals used in making dyes, in compounds for fire extinguishers, and (in baking) as a substitute for yeast. *Formula:* NH_4HCO_3

ammonium carbonate, colorless, soluble crystals used in smelling salts, baking powder, glues, and adhesives. *Formula:* $(NH_4)_2CO_3$

ammonium chloride, a white, crystalline compound used in dry cells, in medicine, in printing on cloth, and in fertilizers; sal ammoniac. *Formula:* NH_4Cl

ammonium hydroxide, an alkali formed when ammonia gas dissolves in water; ammonia (def. 2). *Formula:* NH_4OH

ammonium nitrate, colorless crystals, or a white, soluble powder, used as a source of nitrogen in soil fertilization and in the manufacture of explosives. *Formula:* NH_4NO_3

ammonium sulfate, colorless crystals, or a white, soluble powder, used especially in fertilizers. *Formula:* $(NH_4)_2SO_4$

am|mo|noid (am′ə noid), *n.* any cephalopod of an extinct order comprising the ammonites and their allies. [< New Latin *Ammonoidea* the name of the order < *ammonites* ammonite]

am|mo|nol|y|sis (am′ə nol′ə sis), *n.* decomposition by the action of ammonia. [< *ammonia* + Greek *lýsis* a loosening]

am|mo|no|lyt|ic (ə mō′nə lit′ik), *adj.* of or produced by ammonolysis.

am|moph|i|lous (ə mof′ə ləs), *adj.* that lives or grows in sand. [< Greek *ámmos* sand + *phílos* loving (with English *-ous*)]

am|mu|ni|tion (am′yə nish′ən), *n., v.* **—*n.*** **1** bullets, shells, gunpowder, shot, and bombs that can be exploded or fired from guns or other weapons; military explosives and missiles to be used against an enemy. **2** a thing or things that can be shot, hurled, or thrown. **3** *Figurative.* any means of attack or defense; an error, mistake, or the like, that can be used against someone: *The candidate's foolish remarks gave fresh ammunition to his opponents.* **4** (formerly) any military supplies; munitions.
—*v.t.* to supply with ammunition.
[< obsolete French *amunition,* used for *munition* munitions]

am|ne|sia (am nē′zhə), *n.* complete or partial loss of memory caused by injury to the brain, or by disease or shock. [< New Latin *amnesia* < Greek *amnēsiā́* forgetfulness < *a-* not + *mimnḗskesthai* recall]

am|ne|si|ac (am nē′zhē ak, -zē-), *adj., n.* = amnesic.

am|ne|sic (am nē′sik, -zik), *adj., n.* **—*adj.*** of, causing, or characterized by loss of memory.
—*n.* a person who has amnesia.

am|nes|tic (am nes′tik), *adj.* = amnesic.

am|nes|ty (am′nə stē), *n., pl.* **-ties**, *v.,* **-tied, -ty|ing.** **—*n.*** **1** a general pardon or conditional offer of pardon for past offenses against a government: *After order was restored, the king granted amnesty to those who had rebelled against him.* **2** the granting of such a pardon. **3** a forgetting or intentional overlooking: *By mutual amnesty men avoid seeing the drift of each other's statements* (Contemporary Review).
—*v.t.* to give amnesty to; pardon.
[< Latin *amnēstia* < Greek *amnēstiā́* oblivion < *a-* not + *mimnḗskesthai* recall]

am|ni|o|cen|te|sis (am′nē ō sen tē′sis), *n.* the insertion of a special hypodermic needle into the amnion to remove a sampling of fetal cells from the amniotic fluid for diagnostic purposes: *Amniocentesis can tell expectant parents that their child will be genetically defective* (Science News). [< New Latin *amniocentesis* < Greek *amníon* amnion + *kéntēsis* act of puncturing]

am|ni|og|ra|phy (am′nē og′rə fē), *n.* X-ray examination of the amnion. [< *amnio*(n) + *-graphy*]

am|ni|on (am′nē ən), *n., pl.* **-ni|ons, -ni|a** (-nē ə). a membrane forming the inner sac which encloses the embryo or fetus of the higher vertebrates, such as mammals, birds, and reptiles. The amnion is filled with a serous fluid that protects the embryo or fetus and keeps it moist. See also **chorion**. See picture under **embryo**. [< Late Latin *amnion* < Greek *amníon* (diminutive) < *amnós* lamb]

am|ni|on|ic (am′nē on′ik), *adj.* of or having to do with the amnion; amniotic: *The embryo is surrounded by another membrane, the amnion, which contains the amnionic fluid, in which the embryo floats* (A. M. Winchester).

am|ni|o|scope (am′nē ə skōp), *n.* an illuminated endoscope for examining the amnion and its contents. [< *amnio*(n) + *-scope*]

am|ni|os|co|py (am′nē os′kə pē), *n.* examination by means of an amnioscope.

am|ni|ote (am′nē ōt), *n. Zoology.* any one of the group of vertebrates that develop amnions in their embryonic stages. [< New Latin *Amniota*]

am|ni|ot|ic (am′nē ot′ik), *adj.* **1** of or inside the amnion. **2** having an amnion: *an amniotic cavity.* [< *amnios,* older variant of *amnion*]

amniotic fluid, the serous fluid, enclosed by the amnion, in which the embryo or fetus develops: *The amnion forms a closed sac about the embryo and is filled with a watery amniotic fluid that keeps the embryo moist and protects it against shock or adhesions* (Tracy I. Storer).

am|o|bar|bi|tal (am′ō bär′bə tôl, -tal), *n.* a crystalline barbiturate used as a sedative and hypnotic; Amytal. *Formula:* $C_{11}H_{18}N_2O_3$

am|o|di|a|quin (am′ō dī′ə kwin), *n.* a yellowish synthetic drug used in the treatment of malaria. *Formula:* $C_{20}H_{22}ClN_3O$ [< *am*(in)*o* + *di*(chloro)-*quin*(oline)]

a|moe|ba (ə mē′bə), *n., pl.* **-bas, -bae** (-bē). = ameba.

a|moe|ban (ə mē′bən), *adj.* = ameban.

am|oe|be|an or **am|oe|bae|an** (am′ə bē′ən), *adj.* alternately responsive, as verses in dialogue form. Also, **amebean**.

am|oe|bi|a|sis (am′ə bī′ə sis), *n.* = amebiasis.

a|moe|bic (ə mē′bik), *adj.* = amebic.

a|moe|bi|cid|al (ə mē′bə sī′dəl), *adj.* = amebicidal.

a|moe|bi|cide (ə mē′bə sīd), *n.* = amebicide.

a|moe|bid (ə mē′bid), *n.* = amebid.

a|moe|bi|form (ə mē′bə fôrm), *adj.* = amebiform.

a|moe|bo|cyte (ə mē′bə sīt), *n.* = amebocyte.

a|moe|boid (ə mē′boid), *adj.* = ameboid.

a|mok (ə muk′, -mok′), *adv., adj., n.* **—*adv., adj.*** = amuck.
—*n.* a violent nervous disorder among the Malays, characterized by rushing about in a murderous frenzy and attempting to kill anyone in the way.
[< Malay *amok*]

a|mo|le (ə mō′lē; *Spanish* ä mō′lā), *n.* **1** any one of several plants of Mexico and the southwestern United States whose roots and juice can be used like soap. **2** the root or juice used as soap. [American English < Mexican Spanish *amole* < Nahuatl *amolli* soap]

A|mon (ä′mən), *n.* the chief god of the ancient Egyptians. His main center of worship was in Thebes in Upper Egypt. Also, **Amen**.

à mon a|vis (á môɴ ná vē′), *French.* in my opinion.

a|mong (ə mung′), *prep.* **1** a part of; one of; in the number or class of: *The United States and Russia are among the largest countries of the world. That book is the best among modern novels.* **2** in with; in the company of: *His brothers were among the crowd. He fell among thieves.* **3** surrounded by; in the center of: *There is a house among the trees.* **4** in comparison with; as distinguished from: *one among many.* **5** to each of; with a portion for each of: *Divide the fruit among the boys.* **6** by the combined action of: *You have, among you, spoiled the child.* **7** by, with, or through the whole of; throughout: *In hard times there is often political unrest among the people.*
among ourselves, yourselves, or **themselves,** each with all the others; as a group; mutually: *The children quarreled among themselves, never with outsiders.*
[Old English *on gemang* in a crowd]
► **among, between.** *Among* implies more than two objects: *They distributed the provisions among the survivors. Between* is always used when only two are concerned: *They divided the prize between the two boys.* When *between* is used of several, it tends to suggest the individuals involved more than the situation: *The family of seven hadn't a pair of shoes between them.*

a|mongst (ə mungst′), *prep. Especially British.* among. [< *among* + adverbial genitive *-s* (the *-t* is a later addition)]

A|mon-Re (ä′mən rā′), *n.* Amon, worshiped as the sun god. Also, **Amen-Ra**.

a|mon|til|la|do (ə mon′tə lä′dō; *Spanish* ä mōn′tē-lyä′ᴛʜō), *n., pl.* **-dos** (-dōz; *Spanish* -ᴛʜōs). a moderately dry, light-colored sherry. [< Spanish *amontillado,* ultimately < *Montilla,* Spain]

a|mo|ra (ä mō′rä), *n., pl.* **a|mo|ra|im** (ä mō rä′im). the head of a school for the study of Jewish law and tradition that grew up in Babylonia. About 500 A.D. these schools finished compiling the Gemara. [< Hebrew *amōrā′* expounder]

a|mor|al (ā môr′əl, -mor′-; a-), *adj.* **1** not classifiable as good or bad because not involving any question of morality; nonmoral. **2** unable to distinguish between right and wrong. [< *a-*[4] not + *moral*] **—a|mor′al|ly,** *adv.*

a|mor|al|ism (ā môr′ə liz əm, -mor′-), *n.* indifference to morality; amoral attitude; amorality: *He emphasizes the dogmatic imperialism and complete amoralism of Communism* (Wall Street Journal). **—a|mor′al|ist,** *n.*

a|mo|ral|i|ty (ā′mə ral′ə tē, am′ə-), *n.* the quality of being amoral.

am|o|ret|to (am′ə ret′ō; *Italian* ä′mō rāt′tō), *n., pl.* **-ret|ti** (-ret′ē; *Italian* -rāt′tē). a cupid. [< Italian *amoretto* (diminutive) < *amore* love]

am|o|ri|no (am′ə rē′nō, ä′mə-), *n., pl.* **-ni** (-nē). = amoretto. [< Italian *amorino* (diminutive) < *amore* love]

am|o|rist (am′ər ist), *n.* a person devoted to love or love-making; a gallant. [< Latin *amor* love + English *-ist*]

am|o|ris|tic (am′ə ris′tik), *adj.* **1** of an amorist. **2** like an amorist.

Am|o|rite (am′ə rīt), *n.* **1** a member of an ancient Semitic people that inhabited the highlands of Palestine and Syria (Canaan) before their conquest by the Israelites. In the 1900's B.C. the Amorites built a state in Babylonia, with its capital at Babylon. **2** the Semitic language of these people.

am|o|ro|so (am′ə rō′sō, ä′mə-), *adv., adj. Music.* with love or tenderness. [< Italian *amoroso* loving < Late Latin *amōrōsus* < Latin *amor* love]

am|o|rous (am′ər əs), *adj.* **1** showing love or fondness; loving: *an amorous letter to one's sweetheart.* **SYN:** ardent, tender, passionate, fond, devoted. **2** having to do with love or courtship: *amorous flirtation.* **3** inclined to love; fond of making love: *an amorous disposition, an amorous knight.* **SYN:** amatory. **4** in love: *So amorous is Nature of whatever she produces* (John Dryden). **SYN:** enamored. [< Old French *amorous* < *amour* love < Latin *amor*] **—am′o|rous|ly,** *adv.* **—am′o|rous|ness,** *n.*

a|mor pa|tri|ae (ā′môr pā′trē ē, pat′rē ē), *Latin.* love of one's country; patriotism.

a|mor|phic (ə môr′fik), *adj.* = amorphous.

a|mor|phism (ə môr′fiz əm), *n.* amorphous condition or quality.

a|mor|phous (ə môr′fəs), *adj.* **1a** having no definite form; shapeless; formless: *The ghost was an amorphous being that drifted with mist.* **b** *Biology.* without the definite shape or organization found in most higher animals or plants: *An ameba is amorphous.* **c** *Geology.* occurring in a continuous mass, without stratification or cleavage. **2** of no particular type or pattern; anomalous; unclassifiable. **3** not consisting of crystals; uncrystallized; noncrystalline: *Glass is amorphous; sugar is crystalline.* [< Greek *ámorphos* (with English *-ous*) < *a-* without + *morphḗ* shape] **—a|mor′phous|ly,** *adv.* **—a|mor′phous|ness,** *n.*

a|mort (ə môrt′), *adj. Archaic.* **1** lifeless; inanimate. **2** *Figurative.* spiritless; dejected. [< French *à mort* at death]

am|or|tise (am′ər tīz, ə môr′-), *v.t.,* **-tised, -tis|ing.** *Especially British.* amortize. **—am′or|ti|sa′tion,** *n.*

am|or|tize (am′ər tīz, ə môr′-), *v.t.,* **-tized, -tiz|ing.** **1** to set money aside regularly in a special fund to accumulate at interest, for future paying or settling of (a debt or other liability). **2** *Law.* to convey (property) to a body, especially an ecclesiastical body, which does not have the right to sell or give it away, as in mortmain. [< Old French *amortiss-,* stem of *amortir* deaden < *a-* to + *mort* death < Latin *mors, mortis*] **—am′or|tiz′a|ble,** *adj.* **—am′or|ti|za′tion,** *n.* **—a|mor′tize|ment,** *n.*

A|mos (ā′məs), *n.* **1** a Hebrew prophet and social reformer who lived in the 700's B.C. **2** a book of the Old Testament containing his prophecies.

am|o|site (am′ə sīt), *n.* a form of asbestos containing a small amount of magnesium, found in South Africa. As it is highly resistant to heat and acid, it is used in insulation and filters. [< *A*(sbestos) *M*(ines) *o*(f) *S*(outh Africa) + *-ite*[1]]

a|mo|tion (ə mō′shən), *n. Archaic.* removal or ejection, as from a position or office. [< Latin *āmōtiō, -ōnis* < *āmovēre* remove < *ā-* off + *movēre* move]

a|mount (ə mount′), *n., v.* **—*n.*** **1** the total sum; quantity to which anything mounts up or reaches: *What is the amount of the bill for the groceries?* **2** the full value, effect, extent, or force: *The amount of evidence against him is great.* **SYN:** significance, import. **3** the quantity or number (of something); a quantity viewed as a whole: *a great amount of intelligence. No amount of coaxing would make the dog leave his master.* **4** the sum of the principal and interest due on a loan. *Abbr:* amt. [< verb]
—*v.i.* **1** to reach or come (to); add up: *The loss from the flood amounts to ten million dollars.* **2** to be equal (to); be equivalent in quantity, value, force, or effect: *Keeping what belongs to another amounts to stealing. Her unfriendly comment amounted to an insult. The Historical Society had been in existence twenty years, but ... it hadn't amounted to a hill of beans* (New Yorker).
[< Old French *amonter* < *amont* < Latin *ad* to, *mōns, montis* mountain]

Pronunciation Key: hat, āge, cãre, fär; let, ēqual, tėrm, it, īce; hot, ōpen, ôrder; oil, out; cup, pu̇t, rüle; child; long; thin; ᴛʜen; zh, measure;
ə represents **a** in about, **e** in taken, **i** in pencil, **o** in lemon, **u** in circus.

▶**amount, number**. *Amount* is used of things viewed in the bulk, weight, or sum; *number* is used of persons or things that can be counted: *an amount of milk, a number of cans of milk.*

a|mour (ə mür′), *n.* **1** a love affair. **2** a secret love affair. [< Old French *amour* < Old Provençal < Latin *amor, amōris* love]

am|ou|rette (am′ə ret′), *n.* a passing love affair. [< French *amourette*]

a|mour-pro|pre (à mür′prô′prə), *n.*, or **amour propre**, *French.* conceit; self-esteem: *I am a plastic surgeon—I am not God. All you can do now is cover your imperfections with amour-propre* (New Yorker).

a|move (ə müv′), *v.t.*, **a|moved, a|mov|ing**. *Law.* to remove.

amp (amp), *n. U.S. Slang.* the amplifier of a high-fidelity set. [< *amp*(lifier)]

amp., **1** amperage. **2** ampere or amperes.

AMP (no periods), **1** adenosine monophosphate. **2** ampere or amperes.

am|pe|lop|sis (am′pə lop′sis), *n.* any one of a group of climbing vines or shrubs of the grape family, to which the pepper vine belongs. [< New Latin *Ampelopsis* < Greek *ámpelos* vine + *ópsis* appearance]

am|per|age (am′pər ij, am pir′-), *n.* the strength of an electric current expressed in amperes.

am|pere (am′pir, am pir′), *n.* the unit for measuring the strength of an electric current. It is the amount of current one volt can send through a resistance of one ohm. Ordinary light bulbs take from ¼ to ½ ampere. *Abbr:* amp. [< André M. *Ampère,* 1775-1836, a French physicist]

am|pere-hour (am′pir our′), *n.* the quantity of electricity (3,600 coulombs) transferred by a current of one ampere in one hour. *Abbr:* a.h.

am|pere-me|ter (am′pir mē′tər), *n.* = ammeter.

ampere turn, **1** a unit of magnetomotive force, the force produced by a current of one ampere passing through one complete loop of a coil. **2** the loop itself.

am|per|o|met|ric (am′pər ə met′rik), *adj.* of or having to do with the measurement of amperage: *amperometric titration.*

***am|per|sand** (am′pər sand), *n.* the sign meaning "and." It is often used in the titles of business firms. [alteration of *and per se and* (literally) "& by itself = and"]

***ampersand**

&

Jones, Smith & Co.

wages & hours

am|phet|a|mine (am fet′ə mēn, -min), *n.* **1** a drug used as an inhalant or (in solution) as a spray to relieve nasal congestion in colds or hay fever, asthma, and the like. *Formula:* $C_9H_{13}N$ **2** a phosphate or sulfate of amphetamine used in tablet form as a stimulant to combat fatigue, or to reduce the appetite; Benzedrine. **3a** = dextroamphetamine. **b** = methamphetamine. [< *a*(lpha)-*m*(ethyl-beta)-*ph*(enyl)-*et*(hyl)-*amine*]

amphi-, *combining form.* **1** around; on both sides: *Amphitheater = a theater* (*with seats*) *all around.* **2** in two ways; of two kinds: *Amphibious = living in two ways* (*two kinds of environment*). [< Greek *amphi-* both, around < *amphí*]

am|phi|ar|thro|sis (am′fē är thrō′sis), *n., pl.* **-ses** (-sēz). *Anatomy.* a form of articulation which permits slight motion, such as that between the bodies of the vertebrae. [< *amphi-* + Greek *arthrō̂sis* a joining]

am|phi|as|ter (am′fē as′tər), *n. Biology.* the spindle, together with the two asters, that forms during the prophase of mitosis and can be separated from the rest of the cell intact.

Am|phib|i|a (am fib′ē ə), *n.pl.* a class of vertebrates comprising the amphibians. [< New Latin *Amphibia,* neuter plural of *amphibius* < Greek *amphíbios* amphibious]

am|phib|i|an** (am fib′ē ən), *n., pl.* **-i|ans, -i|a** (-ē ə), *adj.* **—*n. **1** one of a class of cold-blooded vertebrates having a usually moist skin without scales. Frogs, toads, newts, and salamanders are amphibians. Their eggs are laid in water, where the young hatch and usually develop as tadpoles (larval stage) that have gills for breathing. Later they develop legs and most develop lungs, though some salamanders never do. **2** an animal that lives both on land and in water but is unable to breathe under water. Crocodiles, seals, and beavers are amphibians. **3** a plant that grows on land or in water. **4** an aircraft that can take off from and land on either land or water. **5** a tank, truck, or other vehicle able to travel across land or water. **6** *Figurative.* a person who has a two-fold character or leads a double life. **—*adj.*** **1** able to live both on land and in water. **2** that can start from and land on either land or water; amphibious.

***amphibian**

definitions 1, 3, 4, 5

definition 1

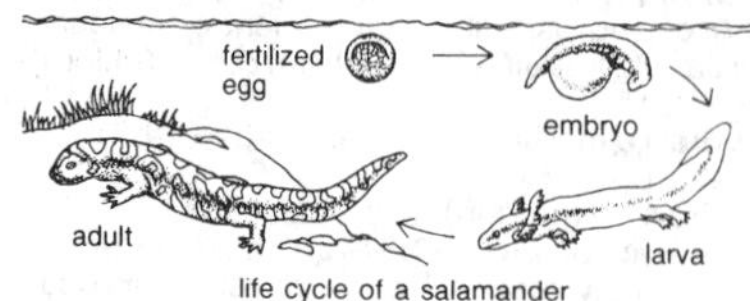

life cycle of a salamander

definition 3

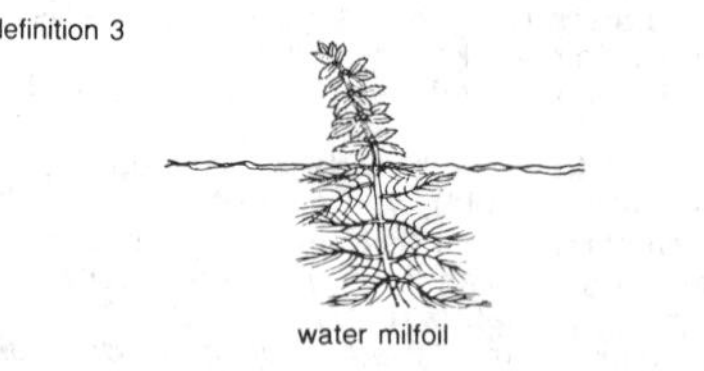

water milfoil

definition 4

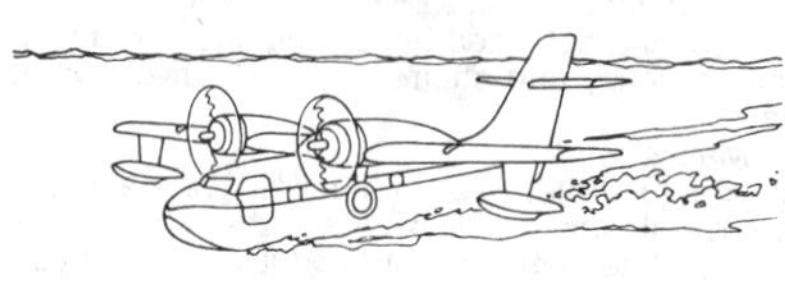

definition 5

am|phib|i|ol|o|gy (am fib′ē ol′ə jē), *n.* the branch of zoology that deals with amphibians.

am|phi|bi|ot|ic (am′fə bī ot′ik), *adj.* living in water at one period of life and on land at another: *A toad is amphibiotic.*

am|phib|i|ous (am fib′ē əs), *adj.* **1** able to live both on land and in water: *Frogs are amphibious.* **2a** able to travel across land or water: *Some tanks are amphibious.* **b** trained for amphibious attack or assault: *amphibious troops.* **3** by the combined action of land, sea, and air forces: *The enemy launched an amphibious attack.* **4** *Figurative.* having two qualities, kinds, natures, or parts. [< Greek *amphíbios* (with English *-ous*) living a double life, amphibious < *amphi-* both + *bíos* life] **—am|phib′i|ous|ly**, *adv.* **—am|phib′i|ous|ness**, *n.*

am|phi|blas|tu|la (am′fə blas′chu̇ lə), *n. Biology.* a blastula in which the cells of one hemisphere differ from those of the other, as in certain sponges.

am|phi|bole (am′fə bōl), *n.* any one of a group of silicate minerals, including asbestos and hornblende. Amphiboles usually consist of a silicate of calcium, magnesium, and one or more other metals, such as iron. [< French *amphibole* < Latin *amphibolus* < Greek *amphíbolos* ambiguous < *amphi-* on both sides + *-bolos* struck]

amphibole group, a group of minerals consisting of amphibole and allied minerals.

am|phi|bol|ic¹ (am′fə bol′ik), *adj.* of or of the nature of an amphibole.

am|phi|bol|ic² (am′fə bol′ik), *adj.* **1** having to do with or characterized by amphibology; ambiguous; equivocal. **2** *Medicine, Rare.* doubtful; uncertain.

am|phib|o|lite (am fib′ə līt), *n.* a rock of metamorphic origin consisting chiefly of amphibole and often containing quartz, garnet, or epidote. [< *amphibo*(le) + *-lite*]

am|phib|o|log|i|cal (am fib′ə loj′ə kəl), *adj.* of or characterized by amphibology; amphibolic; ambiguous; equivocal.

am|phi|bol|o|gy (am′fə bol′ə jē), *n., pl.* **-gies**. **1** an ambiguity in language, usually from uncertainty of the grammatical construction rather than from the meaning of the words forming it. *Example:* Pyrrhus the Romans shall, I say, subdue. **2** a phrase or sentence containing such an ambiguity. [< Late Latin *amphibologia,* alteration of Latin *amphibolia;* see etym. under **amphiboly**]

am|phib|o|lous (am fib′ə ləs), *adj.* = ambiguous: *amphibolous language.*

am|phib|o|ly (am fib′ə lē), *n., pl.* **-lies**. = amphibology. [< Latin *amphibolia* < Greek *amphibolíā* < *amphíbolos* ambiguous < *amphi-* on both sides + *-bolos* struck]

am|phi|brach (am′fə brak), *n.* a foot of three syllables: **a** (in quantitative meter, as Greek or Latin) a short, long, and short, such as in *ămātă.* **b** (in modern or accentual meter) an unaccented, accented, and unaccented, such as in *amus′ing.* [< Latin *amphibrachus* < Greek *amphíbrachys* short at both ends < *amphi-* both + *brachýs* short]

am|phi|brach|ic (am′fə brak′ik), *adj.* of or containing an amphibrach or amphibrachs.

am|phi|car|pic (am′fə kär′pik), *adj.* bearing fruit at two different times, or of two different kinds: *an amphicarpic plant.*

am|phi|car|pous (am′fə kär′pəs), *adj.* = amphicarpic.

am|phi|chro|ic (am′fə krō′ik), *adj.* reacting to an acid or an alkali by change of color, as litmus paper. Amphichroic substances are valuable for chemical tests. [< *amphi-* + Greek *chroiá* color + English *-ic*]

am|phi|chro|mat|ic (am′fə krō mat′ik), *adj.* = amphichroic.

am|phi|coe|lous (am′fə sē′ləs), *adj.* hollowed at both ends; concave on both sides, as the vertebrae of fishes. [< *amphi-* + Greek *koîlos* hollow (with English *-ous*)]

am|phic|ty|on (am fik′tē ən), *n.* a deputy to the council of the Amphictyonic League or to some other amphictyony. [< Greek *amphiktýones,* earlier *amphiktíones* those dwelling around]

am|phic|ty|on|ic (am fik′tē on′ik), *adj.* of or having to do with an amphictyony or amphictyons.

Amphictyonic League, the most famous amphictyony, charged with maintenance and supervision of the temple of Apollo at Delphi and of the Pythian games.

am|phic|ty|o|ny (am fik′tē ə nē), *n., pl.* **-nies**. a federation of ancient Greek city-states, sharing a common religious cult. [< Greek *amphiktyoníā* < *amphiktýones* amphictyons]

am|phi|cyr|tic (am′fə sėr′tik), *adj.* convex on both ends; convex on both sides. [< Greek *amphíkyrtos* gibbous (< *amphi-* on two sides + *kyrtós* curved) + English *-ic*]

am|phi|dip|loid (am′fə dip′loid), *n. Genetics.* a plant that is the result of a cross between two taxonomically different parents and survives because either the chance production of unreduced gametes or the subsequent doubling of the chromosome number provides each chromosome with a homologue for pairing. See also **allopolyploid**.

am|phi|drom|ic (am′fə drom′ik), *adj.* of or having to do with cotidal lines radiating from an amphidromic point. [< Greek *amphidromos* running around (< *amphi-* around + *drómos* running) + English *-ic*]

amphidromic point, a point of no tide, especially the point around which tidal action occurs and from which cotidal lines radiate.

am|phi|gas|tri|um (am′fə gas′trē əm), *n., pl.* **-tri|a** (-trē ə). a small, rudimentary leaf on the underside of the stem of certain liverworts. [< New Latin *amphigastrium* < *amphi-* + Greek *gastḗr, gastrós* belly]

am|phi|ge|an (am′fə jē′ən), *adj. Botany.* extending around the earth, as species of plants found throughout the same latitude. [< *amphi-* + Greek *gê* earth + English *-an*]

am|phi|gor|ic (am′fə gôr′ik, -gor′-), *adj.* having to do with or of the nature of an amphigory.

am|phi|go|ry (am′fə gôr′ē, -gōr′-), *n., pl.* **-ries**. a piece of nonsense writing, especially one which parodies a serious piece of writing: *Lewis Carroll's "You are old, Father William" is an amphigory of a poem by Robert Southey.* [< French *amphigouri*]

am|phi|gou|ri (am′fə gu̇r′ē), *n., pl.* **-ries**. = amphigory.

am|phim|a|cer (am fim′ə sər), *n.* a foot of three syllables: **a** (in quantitative meter, as Greek or Latin) a long, short, and long, such as in *cāritās.* **b** (in modern or accentual meter) an accented, unaccented, and accented, such as in *hu′man-kind′.* [< Latin *amphimacrus* < Greek *amphímakros* (literally) long at both ends < *amphi-* both + *makrós* long]

am|phi|mix|is (am′fə mik′sis), *n. Biology.* the union of the gametes of two organisms; fertilization. [< *amphi-* + Greek *míxis* a mingling]

am|phi|neu|ran (am′fə nu̇r′ən, -nyu̇r′-), *n.* any one of a class of marine mollusks, the chitons, that adhere to rocks. They have bilateral symmetry and calcareous spicules or shells of eight overlapping plates embedded in the cuticle. [< *amphi-* + Greek *neûron* nerve + English *-an*]

Am|phi|on (am fī′ən), *n. Greek Mythology.* a son of Zeus and Antiope, and the husband of Niobe. His skill on the lyre was such that by his music he caused stones to move into place and form the walls of Thebes.

am|phi|ox|us (am′fē ok′səs), *n.* = lancelet. [< New Latin *amphioxus* < Greek *amphi-* both + *oxýs* sharp]

am|phi|phlo|ic (am′fə flō′ik), *adj.* having to do with plant stems that have the phloem on the inner and outer surfaces of the xylem. [< *amphi-* + Greek *phloiós* bark + English *-ic*]

am|phi|pod (am′fə pod), *n., adj.* — ***n.*** any one of a large order of small aquatic crustaceans with four front sets of legs directed forward and three rear sets directed backward, such as the beach fleas.
— ***adj.*** of or having to do with an amphipod or amphipods.
[< New Latin *Amphipoda* < Greek *amphi-* both + *poús, podós* foot]

am|phip|ro|sty|lar (am fip′rə stī′lər), *adj.* = amphiprostyle.

am|phip|ro|style (am fip′rə stīl, am′fə prō′-), *adj., n.* — ***adj.*** having a portico, or a porchlike structure on a building, with columns at each end, but no columns at the sides.
— ***n.*** an amphiprostyle building, such as a Greek temple.
[< Latin *amphiprostȳlōs* < Greek *amphipróstȳlos* < *amphi-* both + *pró* before + *stȳlos* pillar]

am|phis|bae|na (am′fis bē′nə), *n.* **1** a wormlike lizard, found especially in caves or other underground places in the tropics, whose head and tail appear superficially to be indistinguishable and which can move with equal ease either backward or forward. **2** a venomous serpent in early fables, having a head at each end and able to move in either direction. [< Latin *amphisbaena* < Greek *amphísbaina* < *amphís, amphi-* both ways + *baínein* go]

am|phis|bae|nic (am′fis bē′nik), *adj.* of or like an amphisbaena.

am|phis|ci|ans (am fish′ē ənz, -fish′ənz), *n.pl. Archaic.* the people of the Torrid Zone. [< Medieval Latin *amphiscii* (< Greek *amphískioi* < *amphi-* on both sides + *skiā́* shadow) + English *-an* + *-s*[1]]

am|phis|ci|i (am fish′ē ī), *n.pl.* = amphiscians.

am|phi|sty|lar (am′fə stī′lər), *adj.* having columns on two sides or at both ends of a building. [< *amphi-* + Greek *stȳlos* pillar + English *-ar*]

am|phi|the|a|ter (am′fə thē′ə tər), *n.* **1** a circular or oval building with rows of seats around a central open space (the arena). Each row is higher than the one in front of it. **2** *Figurative.* a place of public contest; an arena. **3** something like an amphitheater in shape: *The town was set in an amphitheater of hills.* **4** a semicircular, rising gallery in a theater. [< Latin *amphitheātrum* < Greek *amphithéātron,* ultimately < *amphi-* on all sides + *théātron* theater < *théā* view]

am|phi|the|a|tre (am′fə thē′ə tər), *n. Especially British.* amphitheater.

am|phi|the|at|ric (am′fə thē at′rik), *adj.* = amphitheatrical.

am|phi|the|at|ri|cal (am′fə thē at′rə kəl), *adj.* of or like an amphitheater. — **am′phi|the|at′ri|cal|ly,** *adv.*

am|phi|the|ci|um (am′fə thē′shē əm, -sē-), *n., pl.* **-ci|a** (-shē ə, -sē-). the outer layer of cells in the spore case of mosses, surrounding the endothecium. [< New Latin *amphithecium* < Greek *amphi-* both + *thēkíon* (diminutive) < *thēkē* a chest, box]

am|phit|ri|chous (am fit′rə kəs), *adj.* having one single flagellum at each end of the cell: *amphitrichous bacteria.* [< *amphi-* + Greek *thríx, trichós* hair + English *-ous*]

Am|phi|tri|te (am′fə trī′tē), *n.* the ancient Greek goddess of the sea. She was the wife of Poseidon.

am|phit|ro|pous (am fit′rə pəs), *adj. Botany.* having a partly inverted ovule attached near the middle of one side and parallel with the placenta. [< *amphi-* + Greek *tropḗ* a turning + English *-ous*]

Am|phit|ry|on (am fit′rē ən), *n.* **1** *Greek Legend.* a prince of Thebes, who became the husband of Alcmene. His outward appearance was assumed by Zeus, who gave a feast in Alcmene's honor and became by her the father of Hercules. **2** *Figurative.* **a** a host, especially a lavish host: *The true Amphitryon is the Amphitryon who asks us to dinner* (Molière). **b** anyone acting as a host whose real identity is uncertain.

am|pho|lyte (am′fə līt), *n.* an electrolyte having amphoteric properties. [< Greek *ámphō* both + English (electro)*lyte*]

∗amphora

∗am|pho|ra (am′fər ə), *n., pl.* **-pho|rae** (-fə rē). a tall, two-handled, earthenware jar, used by the ancient Greeks and Romans for storage, such as of grain or oil. Some were pointed at the bottom so they could be thrust into the earth or stored upright in rocks. *Amphorae—the Greek two-handled, oval-bodied vases with pointed base ... have been found wherever Greek commerce extended* (Jennie J. Young). See also **ampulla.** [< Latin *amphora* < Greek *amphoreús,* earlier *amphiphoreús* < *amphi-* on both sides + *phoreús* bearer (referring to the handles)]

am|pho|ral (am′fər əl), *adj.* of or resembling an amphora.

am|phor|ic (am fôr′ik, -for′-), *adj. Medicine.* resembling the sound made by blowing across the mouth of a flask.

am|pho|ter|ic (am′fə ter′ik), *adj.* **1** reacting as a weak acid or as a weak base. **2** reacting as electropositive or as electronegative. [< Greek *amphóteros* (adjective to *ámphō* both) + English *-ic*]

am|pho|ter|i|cin (am′fə ter′ə sin), *n.* an antibiotic used to treat certain fungous infections.

am|pho|ter|ism (am fō′tə riz əm), *n.* the quality of being amphoteric.

amp.-hr., ampere-hour.

am|phur (äm fůr′), *n.* an administrative subdivision of a province (changwat) of Thailand. [< Thai *amphur*]

am|pi|cil|lin (am′pə sil′in), *n.* a semisynthetic penicillin used against Gram-negative bacteria, especially those that have developed a resistance to natural penicillin. [< *am*(ino-benzyl) *p*(en)*icillin*]

am|ple (am′pəl), *adj.,* **-pler, -plest. 1** more than enough; large in kind or degree; abundant; copious; unrestricted: *He has received ample praise for the work he did.* **SYN:** plentiful, unrestrained. **2** as much as is needed; enough; sufficient: *to take an ample supply of food. My allowance is ample for carfare and lunches.* **SYN:** full, complete, adequate. **3** having plenty of room; large; roomy: *A well-designed house has ample closets.* **SYN:** broad, wide, spacious, big, extensive. [< Middle French *ample* < Latin *amplus*] — **am′ple|ness,** *n.*

am|plec|tant (am plek′tənt), *adj. Botany.* twining: *an amplectant tendril.* [< Latin *amplectī* to embrace (< *ambi-* about + *plectere* to wind, weave) + English *-ant*]

∗am|plex|i|caul (am plek′sə kôl), *adj.* nearly surrounding or clasping the stem, as some leaves do at their base. [< New Latin *amplexicaulis,* ultimately < Latin *ambi-* about + *plectere* wind, weave + *caulis* stem]

∗amplexicaul

amplexicaul leaves

am|pli|a|tion (am′plē ā′shən), *n. Archaic.* an enlarging or extending; amplification. [< Latin *ampliātiō, -ōnis* < *ampliāre* widen < *amplius,* neuter comparative of *amplus* ample]

am|pli|a|tive (am′plē ā′tiv), *adj. Logic.* having the function of enlarging or extending a simple concept, or adding to what is already known.

am|pli|dyne (am′plə dīn), *n.* a rotating direct-current machine equipped with brushes and windings which make it capable of absorbing a weak, variable signal and reproducing it at a higher power level with the same variation. It is used for amplification. [< Latin *amplus* ample + English *dyne*]

am|pli|fi|a|ble (am′plə fī′ə bəl), *adj.* that can be amplified: *amplifiable signals.*

am|pli|fi|ca|tion (am′plə fə kā′shən), *n.* **1** a making greater, stronger, or more extensive; expansion: *the amplification of knowledge.* **SYN:** enlargement. **2** a detail or example that amplifies a statement, narrative, or the like: *Your argument needs amplification before I can understand and accept it.* **3** an expanded statement, narrative, or the like. **4** an increase in the strength of an electric current.

am|pli|fi|ca|tive (am′plə fə kā′tiv), *adj.* = amplificatory.

am|plif|i|ca|to|ry (am plif′ə kə tôr′ē, -tōr′-), *adj.* of the nature of enlargement or extension.

am|pli|fi|er (am′plə fī′ər), *n.* **1** a person or thing that amplifies or enlarges. **2a** a vacuum tube, transistor, or other device in a radio, phonograph, etc., for strengthening electrical impulses. **b** an apparatus for making audible the sounds recorded on a phonograph record or tape or for increasing the sound of a public-address system. **3** a loudspeaker.

am|pli|fy (am′plə fī), *v.,* **-fied, -fy|ing.** — ***v.t.*** **1** to make greater; make stronger or larger: *When sound is amplified, it can be heard a greater distance. By advertising widely, a manufacturer can amplify the demand for a product.* **2** to make fuller and more extensive; expand; enlarge: *Please amplify your description of the accident by giving us more details.* **SYN:** develop. **3** to make too much of; exaggerate: *Don't amplify the difficulties of the task.* **SYN:** magnify. **4** to increase the strength of (an electrical impulse): *By turning this knob to the right you can amplify the sound from this radio.*
— ***v.i.*** to write or talk more at length; make additional remarks: *The speaker amplified on so many topics that the audience could not follow him.* **SYN:** expatiate.
[< Middle French *amplifier,* learned borrowing from Latin *amplificāre, amplus* ample + *facere* make]

∗am|pli|tude (am′plə tüd, -tyüd), *n.* **1** the quality of being ample in size; largeness; width; breadth. **2** the quality of being ample in amount; a quantity that is more than enough; abundance; fullness: *A very rich man has an amplitude of money.* **3** *Figurative.* the extent of mental capacity; intellectual scope; breadth of thought. **4** one half the range of a regular vibration. The distance between the position of rest and the highest position in the arc of a pendulum is its amplitude. *A pendulum swinging through an angle of 90 degrees has an amplitude of 45 degrees.* **5** the peak strength of an alternating electric current in a given cycle. **6** the arc along the horizon measured between either true east or west and a point where a line drawn from the zenith through a star or other heavenly body would intersect the horizon. [< Latin *amplitūdō* < *amplus* ample]

∗amplitude
definitions 4, 5, 6

definition 4
45° amplitude: 45° 45°
0°

definition 5

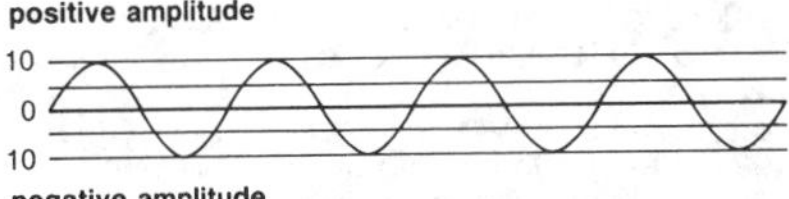

definition 6

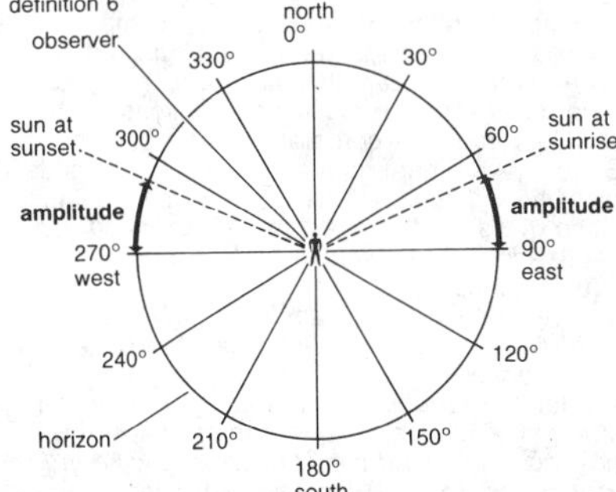

amplitude modulation, deliberate change of the amplitude of radio waves in order to transmit sound or visual waves. Amplitude modulation is used for ordinary radio broadcasting and for the transmission of the picture portion of television. *Abbr:* AM (no periods).

am|pli|tu|din|ous (am′plə tü′də nəs, -tyü′-), *adj.* more than ample, especially in size, abundance, or scope: ... *his amplitudinous performance* (New York Times).

am|ply (am′plē), *adv.* in an ample manner; to an ample degree; sufficiently; liberally; abundantly: *We are amply supplied with food.*

am|poule (am′pül, am pül′), *n.* a small, sealed glass container, usually holding one dose or other specific quantity of a drug or medicine, such as for hypodermic injection. [< French *am-*

Pronunciation Key: hat, āge, cãre, fär; let, ēqual, tėrm, it, īce; hot, ōpen, ôrder; oil, out; cup, pu̇t, rüle; child; long; thin; ᴛʜen; zh, measure; ə represents a in about, e in taken, i in pencil, o in lemon, u in circus.

poule < Latin *ampulla* small bottle]
am|pul (am′pul), *n.* = ampoule.
am|pule (am′pyül), *n.* = ampoule.
am|pul|la (am pul′ə, -půl′-), *n., pl.* **-pul|lae** (-pul′ē, -půl′-). **1** a two-handled bottle or jar used in ancient Rome, especially for holding oil, perfume, or wine. It was patterned after, but smaller than, an amphora. See also **amphora**. **2** a vessel for holding the consecrated oil used in churches for certain religious rites or ceremonies, such as those of unction and coronation. **3** a vessel for the wine and water at Mass. **4** *Anatomy and Zoology.* the dilated portion of a canal or duct in an animal, as of the semicircular canals of the ear. **5** *Botany.* a flask-shaped organ or bladder on an aquatic plant. [< Latin *ampulla* (diminutive) < *amphora* amphora]
am|pul|la|ceous (am′pə lā′shəs), *adj.* having the form of an ampulla; bottle-shaped.
am|pul|lar (am pul′ər), *adj.* = ampullaceous.
am|pul|la|ry (am pul′ər ē), *adj.* = ampullaceous.
am|pu|tate (am′pyə tāt), *v.t.,* **-tat|ed, -tat|ing.** **1** to cut off (all or a portion of a leg, arm, hand, or other part that grows out), usually by surgery: *The doctor amputated the wounded soldier's leg.* **2** *Figurative.* to cut down or lop off (anything); prune: *Despite the defeat of* [*the*] *attempt to amputate our NATO force, pressure continues for reducing this too rapidly* (New York Times). [< Latin *amputāre* (with English *-ate*[1]) < *ambi-* about + *putāre* prune] **—am′pu|ta′tor,** *n.*
am|pu|ta|tion (am′pyə tā′shən), *n.* **1** the act of cutting off, especially all or a portion of a leg, arm, hand, or other part that grows out, usually by surgery: *In this way a surgeon may be able to save a man's leg when it is being threatened with gangrene and amputation* (New York Herald-Tribune). **2** *Figurative.* a cutting down or lopping off of anything; pruning: *During the three days rain cut more than nine hours from the match, and the amputation was fatal* (London Times).
am|pu|tee (am′pyə tē′), *n.* a person who has had all or part of a leg or arm amputated: *In tests on 50 patients, the pneumatic arm enabled amputees to make up to a dozen different movements* (Time).
am|ri|ta or **am|ree|ta** (am rē′tə, um-), *n. Hinduism.* **1** the elixir of immortality. **2** immortality (as that which is conferred by it). [< Sanskrit *ámṛta*, ultimately < *a-* not + *mṛ-* die]
amt (ämt), *n., pl.* **am|ter** (äm′tər), **amts.** the largest local administrative unit of Denmark. [< Danish *amt* < German]
amt., amount.
Am|torg (am′tôrg), *n.* a company organized in 1924 in the United States by the Soviet Union to serve as the buying and selling organization of the Soviet Union in trade between the two countries. [< Russian *Am*(*erikanskaja*) American + *torg*(*ovlja*) trade]
am|trac or **am|track** (am′trak), *n.* a small amphibious vehicle used in military landings during World War II. [< *am*(phibious) + *trac*(tor)]
Am|trak (am′trak′), *n.* National Railroad Passenger Corporation, a corporation of the United States government created to manage essential passenger service of railroads between major cities in the United States. [an irregular shortening of *American Travel and Track*]
amu (no periods), atomic mass unit.
a|muck (ə muk′), *adv., adj., n.* **—*adv.*, *adj.*** in a murderous frenzy; mad with a desire to attack.
—*n.* = amok.
run (or **go**) **amuck, a** to run about in a murderous frenzy; have a crazy desire to attack: *The bull ran amuck and tried to gore everyone in his way.* **b** to behave wildly; disregard rules, instructions, or consequences: *The boy ran amuck, throwing his books all over the floor. I might have run amuck against society, but I preferred that society should run amuck against me* (Thoreau).
[< Malay *amok* engaging furiously in battle, attacking with desperate resolution]
am|u|let (am′yə lit), *n.* some small object, such as a locket or carved image, worn as a magic charm against evil, disease, or harm. **SYN:** talisman, charm. [< Latin *amulētum*]
a|muse (ə myüz′), *v.t.,* **a|mused, a|mus|ing.** **1** to cause to laugh or smile: *The playful puppy running around the room amused the baby.* **2** to keep pleasantly interested; cause to feel cheerful or happy; entertain: *The new toys amused the children.* **3** to cause (time) to pass pleasantly; while away. **4** *Archaic.* to divert so as to deceive; beguile. **5** *Obsolete.* **a** to bewilder. **b** to engage the attention of; attract. [< Old French *amuser* divert < *a-* to + *muser* gape] **—a|mus′a|ble,** *adj.* **—a|mus′er,** *n.*
—*Syn.* **2 Amuse, entertain** mean to keep pleasantly interested. **Amuse** emphasizes the idea of passing time by keeping one's attention occupied with something interesting and pleasing and at the same time light and trivial: *While waiting, she amused herself by counting the cars that passed.* **Entertain** emphasizes greater effort or more elaborate means to hold attention: *Some people entertain themselves by reading; others are entertained by the radio or television.*
a|mused (ə myüzd′), *adj.* pleasantly entertained. **—a|mus′ed|ly,** *adv.*
a|muse|ment (ə myüz′mənt), *n.* **1** the condition of being amused: *The boy's amusement was so great that we all had to laugh with him. I could not conceal my amusement at her surprise.* **2** a thing that amuses, such as an entertainment or sport; anything which pleasantly whiles away the time; means of recreation: *Most outdoor sports are healthy amusements. When we go to the park we always enjoy the swings, slides, and other such amusements. I am a great friend to public amusements; for they keep people from vice* (Samuel Johnson). **SYN:** pastime. [< French *amusement* < *amuser* amuse]
amusement park, an outdoor place of entertainment with such amusements as a Ferris wheel, roller coaster, and booths for various games or for refreshments: *They screamed with each pitch of the boat, as on a roller coaster in an amusement park* (Frederic Morton).
a|mu|si|a (ā myü′zē ə), *n.* loss of the ability to distinguish or express musical sounds. [< New Latin *amusia* < Greek *amousía* lack of music < *a-* not + *mousía* music]
a|mus|ing (ə myü′zing), *adj.* **1** entertaining; diverting: *an amusing book.* **SYN:** pleasing. **2** causing laughter or smiles: *amusing jokes, amusing antics.* **SYN:** funny. **—a|mus′ing|ly,** *adv.* **—a|mus′ing|ness,** *n.*
a|mu|sive (ə myü′ziv, -siv), *adj.* amusing; entertaining.
Am|vets or **AMVETS** (am′vets′), *n.pl.* American Veterans of World War II, Korea, and Vietnam, an organization founded in 1944. [American English < *Am*(erican) *Vet*(eran)*s*]
a|myg|da|la (ə mig′də lə), *n., pl.* **-lae** (-lē). **1** = almond. **2** = tonsil. **3** an almond-shaped body in the lateral ventricle of the brain. [< Medieval Latin *amygdala* tonsil < Latin, almond < Greek *amygdálē*]
a|myg|da|la|ceous (ə mig′də lā′shəs), *adj.* akin to the almond (applied to those plants of the rose family which produce stone fruits, such as the peach). [< *amygdal*(a) + *-aceous*]
a|myg|da|late (ə mig′də lit, -lāt), *adj.* of or like almonds.
a|myg|dale (ə mig′dāl), *n.* a vapor cavity in a volcanic rock, filled with such other minerals as agate or calcite. [< Greek *amygdálē* almond]
a|myg|dal|ic (am′ig dal′ik), *adj.* of or having to do with almonds.
a|myg|da|lin (ə mig′də lin), *n.* a glucoside found in bitter almonds and cherry and peach kernels. *Formula:* $C_{20}H_{27}NO_{11}$
a|myg|da|line (ə mig′də lin, -līn), *adj. Rare.* **1** of or like an almond or almonds. **2** of or like a tonsil or tonsils.
a|myg|da|loid (ə mig′də loid), *n., adj.* **—*n.*** a rock that contains amygdales.
—*adj.* **1** having to do with or of the nature of such a rock. **2** almond-shaped.
[< Greek *amygdálē* almond + English *-oid*]
a|myg|da|loi|dal (ə mig′də loi′dəl), *adj.* = amygdaloid.
a|myg|dule (ə mig′dyül, -dül), *n.* = amygdale.
am|yl (am′əl), *n.* a group of carbon and hydrogen atoms that acts as a unit in forming compounds; any one of various forms of a univalent radical derived from pentane. *Formula:* $—C_5H_{11}$ [< Latin *amylum* (< Greek *ámylon* starch) + English *-yl*]
am|y|la|ceous (am′ə lā′shəs), *adj.* of or like starch; starchy. [< Latin *amylum* starch + English *-aceous*]
amyl acetate, = banana oil.
amyl alcohol, an acrid, oily liquid, the chief constituent of fusel oil: *Amyl alcohol is used mainly in lacquers* (World Book Encyclopedia). *Formula:* $C_5H_{11}OH$
amyl amine, a colorless liquid formed by the decomposition of nitrogenous matter, used as an absorbent for gases, in making oil-soluble soap, and in corrosion inhibitors. *Formula:* $C_5H_{11}NH_2$
am|yl|ase (am′ə lās), *n.* any of various enzymes in saliva and pancreatic juice, or in parts of plants (as germinating seeds), that help to change starch into sugar.
am|yl|ene (am′ə lēn), *n.* any one of a group of unsaturated hydrocarbons of the ethylene series, found in several isomeric forms. *Formula:* C_5H_{10}
a|myl|ic (ə mil′ik), *adj.* having to do with amyl.
amyl nitrite, a yellowish, oily, volatile liquid used as a heart stimulant and as an antidote against certain poisons. *Formula:* $C_5H_{11}NO_2$
am|y|lo|dex|trin (am′ə lō dek′strən), *n.* a white, tasteless, odorless powder formed by the hydrolysis of starch, which turns reddish-brown or red-dish-violet in iodine solutions. [< *amylum* + *dextrin*]
a|myl|o|gen (ə mil′ə jən), *n.* soluble starch. [< *amylum* + *-gen*]
a|myl|o|gen|ic (ə mil′ə jen′ik), *adj.* **1** of or having to do with amylogen. **2** forming starch: *amylogenic leucoplasts.*
am|y|loid (am′ə loid), *n., adj.* **—*n.*** an insoluble, waxy protein developed in diseased degeneration of various organs. **—*adj.*** of or like starch.
[< *amylum* + *-oid*]
am|y|loi|dal (am′ə loi′dəl), *adj.* = amyloid.
am|y|loi|do|sis (am′ə loi dō′sis), *n.* degeneration of the tissues of an organ, characterized by deposits of amyloids. [< *amyloid* + *-osis*]
am|y|lol|y|sis (am′ə lol′ə sis), *n.* the conversion of starch into substances that can be absorbed and utilized by the body, such as certain sugars, by the action of enzymes or acids. [< *amylum* + Greek *lýsis* a loosening]
am|y|lo|lyt|ic (am′ə lə lit′ik), *adj.* of or having to do with amylolysis: *Germination is allowed to proceed from four to six days, during which time amylolytic, i.e. starch-digesting, enzymes are developed in the barley embryos, and the conversion of the starch reserves of the grain to sugar begins* (H. J. Bunker).
am|y|lo|pec|tin (am′ə lə pek′tin), *n.* any starch of a major group of starches having molecules of branched structure and containing some phosphate, distinguished from the other major group, which has molecules of unbranched and probably spiral structure: *Glycogen is an amylopectin.* [< *amylum* + *pectin*]
am|y|lo|plast (am′ə lə plast), *n.* a body in plant cells which forms starch grains. [< *amylum* + Greek *plastós* molded]
am|y|lo|plas|tid (am′ə lə plas′tid), *n.* = amyloplast.
am|y|lop|sin (am′ə lop′sin), *n.* the enzyme (an amylase) in the pancreatic juice that changes starch into simpler compounds such as maltose.
[< *amylum* + (pe)*psin*]
am|yl|ose (am′ə lōs), *n.* **1** any starch of a major group of starches having molecules of unbranched and probably spiral structure, distinguished from the other major group, which has molecules of branched structure. **2** any polysaccharide. [< *amylum* + *-ose*[2]]
am|y|lum (am′ə ləm), *n. Chemistry.* starch, especially cornstarch. [< Latin *amylum* < Greek *ámylon*]
a|myn|o|dont (ə min′ə dont), *n., adj.* **—*n.*** any one of an extinct genus of aquatic animals of the Eocene period, related to the rhinoceros, having large bodies and short, heavy legs.
—*adj.* of or having to do with an amynodont or amynodonts.
[< New Latin *Amynodonta* < Greek *ámȳna* defense + *odoús, odóntos* tooth]
a|my|o|to|ni|a (ā mī′ə tō′nē ə), *n. Medicine.* an atonic condition of the muscles; lack of muscular tone. [< *a-*[4] not + Greek *mys, myós* muscle + *-toniā* tone]
a|my|o|tro|phi|a (ə mī′ə trō′fē ə), *n.* = amyotrophy.
a|my|o|troph|ic (ə mī′ə trof′ik), *adj.* of or having to do with amyotrophy.
amyotrophic lateral sclerosis, a degenerative disease of the nervous system, characterized by atrophy of the muscles; Lou Gehrig's disease. *Abbr:* ALS (no periods).
am|y|ot|ro|phy (am′ē ot′rə fē), *n.* atrophy of the muscles or a muscle. [< *a-*[4] not + Greek *mys, myós* muscle + *trophḗ* nourishment]
Am|y|tal (am′ə tôl, -tal), *n. Trademark.* = amobarbital.
an[1] (an; *unstressed* ən), *adj. or indefinite article.* **1a** any: *Is there an apple for me? An oak has acorns. Please give me an answer.* **b** one like; another (before proper names or nouns used as the type of a class): *an Elijah in modern dress. She is an angel among women.* **2** one: *My mother needs an ounce of butter.* **3** each; every: *John earns fifty cents an hour.* **4a** the same: *two desks to an office.* **b** a particular: *It was too awful an accident to describe.* **c** one kind of: *Painting is an art.* **d** a certain; some: *an occasion for concern, an enormous number of pigeons.* **5** a single: *not an ounce of hope.* [Middle English *an* (unstressed form before vowels) < Old English *ān* one]
▶In modern Standard English the form of the indefinite article is **a** before a word beginning with a consonant sound and **an** before a word beginning with a vowel sound: *a* horse, *a* man, *a* union, but *an* answer, *an* hour. Note that one's choice is determined by the initial sound, not by the spelling. Usage varies before words beginning with *h* in an unstressed syllable, like *historical* or *hotel,* where, because the *h* is commonly silent or weakly articulated, many use *an.* In Great Britain *an* is occasionally used before words like *united* and *euphonious,* which begin with the sound of (y).
▶See **a**[2] for another usage note.

an², **an'** (an; *unstressed* ən), *conj.* **1** *Dialect or Informal.* and. **2** *Archaic.* if. [reduction of *and*]

an-¹, *prefix.* **1** not: *Anastigmatic = not astigmatic.* **2** without: *Anhydrous = without water.* Also, **a-** (before consonant sounds except *h*). [< Greek *an-* not, without]

an-², *prefix.* the form of **ad-** before *n*, as in *annex.*

an-³, *prefix.* the form of **ana-** before vowels, as in *anode.*

-an, *suffix used to form adjectives and nouns, especially from proper nouns.* **1** of or having to do with ___: *Mohammedan = of or having to do with Mohammed.* **2** of or having to do with ___or its people: *Asian = of or having to do with Asia or its people.* **3** a native or inhabitant of ___: *American = a native or inhabitant of America.* **4** a person who knows much about or is skilled in ___: *Historian = a person who knows much about history. Magician = a person skilled in magic.* Also, **-ian**, **-ean.** [< Latin *-ānus*]

an., in the year (Latin, *anno*).

An (no period), actinon (isotope of radon).

AN (no periods), **AN.**, or **A.N.**, Anglo-Norman.

a|na¹ (ā'nə, ä'-), *n.pl. or sing.* **1** a collection of the memorable sayings or table talk of anyone. **2** notes and scraps of information relating to a person or place; literary gossip. See also **-ana.** [< *-ana* anecdotes]
▶**Ana** is construed as a collective singular in the sense of def. 1, and the plural form *anas* exists for it in this sense only.

an|a² (an'ə), *adv.* in equal quantities; so much of each (used of ingredients in prescriptions). [< Medieval Latin *ana* < Greek *aná* at the rate of]

ana-, *prefix.* back; again; thoroughly; up, as in *anachronism, anaplastic, analysis, anabatic, anatomy.* Also, **an-** before vowels. [< Greek *ana-* < *ana* back, up, again]

-ana, *suffix.* a collection of objects, documents, books, facts, or sayings of or about: *Americana = a collection of objects, documents, books, facts, or sayings of or about America.* Also, **-iana.** See also **ana¹**. [< Latin *-āna*, neuter plural of *-ānus* -an]

an|a|bae|na (an'ə bē'nə), *n., pl.* **-nas. 1** any one of a genus of freshwater, blue-green algae found in ponds, reservoirs, and other enclosed, or partly enclosed, bodies of water, which sometimes occur in such large numbers as to give a fishy taste and smell to the water in which they grow. **2** a colony or mass of such algae. [< New Latin *Anabaena* < Greek *anabaínein* ascend (from their habit of rising to the surface)]

an|a|bap|tism (an'ə bap'tiz əm), *n.* a second baptism.

An|a|bap|tism (an'ə bap'tiz əm), *n.* the doctrines or practices of the Anabaptists.

An|a|bap|tist (an'ə bap'tist), *n., adj.* —*n.* a member of a former Protestant sect opposing infant baptism and holding that only baptism of adults who had professed faith was valid. The Anabaptists originated in Switzerland in the 1520's.
—*adj.* of or having to do with the Anabaptists or Anabaptism.
[< New Latin *anabaptista* < Latin *anabaptismus* < Greek *anabaptismós* < *ana-* again + *baptismós* baptism]

***an|a|bas** (an'ə bas), *n.* any one of a genus of freshwater, spiny-finned fishes resembling the perch, found in southern Asia and Africa, such as the climbing fish, which can travel for short distances on land and is said to climb trees. [< New Latin *Anabas* < Greek *anabâs*, aorist participle of *anabaínein* ascend < *ana-* up + *baínein* go]

***anabas**

a|nab|a|sin (ə nab'ə sin), *n.* = anabasine.

a|nab|a|sine (ə nab'ə sēn, -sin), *n.* a liquid alkaloid, similar in molecular structure to nicotine, used as an insecticide. *Formula:* $C_{10}H_{14}N_2$ [< New Latin *Anabasis* a shrub containing anabasine + English *-ine²*]

a|nab|a|sis (ə nab'ə sis), *n., pl.* **-ses** (-sēz). any passage of a large military force through a large area. [< Greek *anábasis* ascent < *ana-* up + *baínein* go]

an|a|bat|ic (an'ə bat'ik), *adj.* moving upward: *an anabatic air current.* [< Greek *anabatikós* pertaining to an ascent < *anábasis* ascent < *ana-* up + *baínein* go]

an|a|bi|o|sis (an'ə bī ō'sis), *n.* **1** a state of apparently suspended animation in which certain aquatic invertebrates survive long periods of drought. **2** revival after apparent death; resuscitation. [< Greek *anabíōsis* < *ana-* again + *bioûn* live]

an|a|bi|ot|ic (an'ə bī ot'ik), *adj.* of or having to do with anabiosis.

an|a|bleps (an'ə bleps), *n.* a small fish of tropical America that swims at the surface of the water and has eyes divided into two parts (the upper parts project above the water, and enable the fish to see through the air; the lower parts function independently under the water); four-eyed fish. [< New Latin *Anableps* < Greek *anablépein* look up < *ana-* up + *blépein* look]

an|a|bol|ic (an'ə bol'ik), *adj.* of or occurring in anabolism: *Anabolic changes require energy, which is derived principally from the oxidation by plants and animals of organic compounds high in energy value* (Harbaugh and Goodrich).

anabolic steroid, any of a group of synthetic hormones that increase the size and strength of muscles, often used by athletes during training: *The IOC* [*International Olympic Committee*] *added anabolic steroids, the socalled body-building drugs, to the list of prohibited substances at the Olympic Games* (D.K.R. Phillips).

a|nab|o|lism (ə nab'ə liz əm), *n.* the process by which food substances are changed into the tissues of a living animal or plant; constructive metabolism (contrasted with *catabolism*). [coined from *metabolism* by substituting Greek *ana-* up]

an|a|branch (an'ə branch, -brănch), *n.* **1** a stream that branches off from a larger stream and loses itself in sand, gravel, and the like. **2** a stream that branches off from a river and reenters it lower down, forming an island. [< *ana-* (stomosing) *branch*]

an|a|canth (an'ə kanth), *n.* any one of an order of North American fishes having soft rays on the fins, ventral fins in thoracic or jugular position, and air bladders (when present) without ducts, such as the cod, pollack, and hake. [< *an-¹* not + Greek *ákantha* thorn]

an|a|can|thin (an'ə kan'thin), *adj.* of or having to do with an anacanth or anacanths.

an|a|can|thine (an'ə kan'thīn, -thin), *adj.* = anacanthin.

an|a|car|di|a|ceous (an'ə kär'dē ā'shəs), *adj.* belonging to a family of trees and shrubs typified by the cashew, and including the sumac, mango, pistachio, and poison ivy. [< New Latin *anacardium* (< Greek *aná* according to + *kardía* heart) + English *-aceous* (from the shape of its fruit)]

an|a|chron|ic (an'ə kron'ik), *adj.* = anachronistic. —**an'a|chron'i|cal|ly**, *adv.*

an|a|chron|i|cal (an'ə kron'ə kəl), *adj.* = anachronistic.

***a|nach|ro|nism** (ə nak'rə niz əm), *n.* **1** the act of placing a person, thing, or event in some time where he or it does not belong; error in fixing a date or dates; erroneous reference of an event, circumstance, or custom to a wrong, especially an earlier, date. It is an anachronism to speak of George Washington riding in an automobile. **2** something placed or occurring out of its proper time; anything out of keeping with a specified time, especially something proper to a former age but not to the present: *The nickel ferry ride to Staten Island is a beautiful anachronism which deserves preservation* (New York Times). [< Greek *anachronismós* < *ana-* back + *chrónos* time]

THE BRITISH
ARE COMING-
THE BRITISH
ARE COMING!

***anachronism**
definition 2

a|nach|ro|nis|tic (ə nak'rə nis'tik), *adj.* having or involving an anachronism. —**a|nach'ro|nis'ti|cal|ly**, *adv.*

a|nach|ro|nis|ti|cal (ə nak'rə nis'tə kəl), *adj.* = anachronistic.

a|nach|ro|nous (ə nak'rə nəs), *adj.* placed or occurring out of the proper time. —**a|nach'ro|nous|ly**, *adv.*

an|a|cid|i|ty (an'ə sid'ə tē), *n.* a deficiency or lack of acid, especially in the stomach. [< *an-¹* not + *acidity*]

a|nac|la|sis (ə nak'lə sis), *n. Prosody.* a change of place between a short syllable and a preceding long one. [< Greek *anáklasis* < *ana-* back + *klân* break]

an|a|clas|tic (an'ə klas'tik), *adj.* **1** *Prosody.* having to do with or characterized by anaclasis. **2** having to do with or produced by refraction of light.

an|a|cli|nal (an'ə klī'nəl), *adj. Geology.* descending in a direction opposite to that of the dip of the rock formation below, as a valley or stream. [< *ana-* + Greek *klínein* to lean + English *-al¹*]

a|nac|li|sis (ə nak'lə sis), *n. Psychoanalysis.* a libidinal attachment to an object, dependent on the previous satisfaction of another desire, such as hunger, by the same object. [< Greek *anáklisis* < *ana-* back + *klínein* lean]

an|a|clit|ic (an'ə klit'ik), *adj.* **1** leaning for support; dependent. **2** *Psychoanalysis.* of or having to do with anaclisis.

an|a|co|lu|thi|a (an'ə kə lü'thē ə), *n.* passing from one construction in a sentence to another before the former is completed, especially a deliberate shift used as a figure of speech to suggest strong emotion. [< Latin *anacoluthia* < Greek *anakolouthía* lack of sequence]

an|a|co|lu|thic (an'ə kə lü'thik), *adj.* of or involving anacoluthia or an anacoluthon; lacking grammatical sequence.

an|a|co|lu|thon (an'ə kə lü'thon), *n., pl.* **-tha** (-thə). **1** a change from one grammatical construction to another in the same sentence, especially one made deliberately for greater force. *Example:* "And he charged him to tell no man: but go, and shew thyself to the priest, and offer for thy cleansing ..." (Luke 5:14). **2** a sentence in which this occurs. [< Late Latin *anacoluthon* < Greek *anakólouthon* < *an-* not + *akólouthos* following]

an|a|con|da (an'ə kon'də), *n.* **1** a very large South American snake that crushes its prey in its coils; water boa. Anacondas live in tropical forests and rivers and are the longest snakes in America, sometimes over 30 feet. They belong to the same family as the boa. **2** any large snake which crushes its prey in its coils, such as the python or boa. **3** (originally) a very large snake of Ceylon (Sri Lanka), a kind of python. [probably < Singhalese *henakandayā* whip snake]

A|nac|re|on|tic or **a|nac|re|on|tic** (ə nak'rē on'tik), *adj., n.* —*adj.* **1** of Anacreon (ancient Greek lyric poet). **2** having the structure or meter of Anacreon's verses (in English, a stanza usually consisting of four lines, rhyming *abab*, each consisting of three trochaic feet plus one accented syllable at the end of the line). **3** having the mood or manner of Anacreon's verses; convivial and amatory.
—*n.* a poem in the manner of Anacreon.

an|a|cru|sis (an'ə krü'sis), *n.* **1** one or more unaccented syllables at the beginning of a line of poetry in which the first foot normally begins with an accented syllable, regarded as separate from and introductory to the remainder of the line. *Example: "From rain'bow/clouds' there/flow' not"* (Shelley). **2** a note or notes that begin a piece or passage of music on a nonaccented beat. [< Greek *anákrousis* < *ana-* up + *kroúein* strike]

an|a|crus|tic (an'ə krus'tik), *adj.* characterized by anacrusis.

an|a|da|ma bread (an'ə dā'mə), a kind of yeast bread made in New England with corn meal and molasses. [origin unknown]

an|a|dem (an'ə dem), *n. Poetic.* a wreath for the head, usually of flowers; garland. [< Latin *anadēma* < Greek *anádēma* < *anadeîn* bind up < *ana-* up + *deîn* bind]

an|a|di|plo|sis (an'ə də plō'sis), *n. Rhetoric.* repetition in the first part of one clause of a prominent word in the latter part of the preceding clause. *Example:* In anticipation he feared death, death that found him unafraid, however. [< Late Latin *anadiplōsis* < Greek *anadíplōsis* < *ana-* back + *diplōsis* a doubling]

a|nad|ro|mous (ə nad'rə məs), *adj.* going up rivers from the sea to spawn, as salmon and shad (contrasted with *catadromous*). [< Late Greek *anádromos* running up(stream) (with English *-ous*) < *ana-* upward + *drameîn* run]

a|nae|mi|a (ə nē'mē ə), *n. Especially British.* anemia.

a|nae|mic (ə nē'mik), *adj. Especially British.* anemic.

an|aer|obe (an ãr'ōb), *n.* **1** an organism that can live without free oxygen. **2** an organism that cannot live in the presence of free oxygen.

an|aer|o|bi|an (an'ãr ō'bē ən), *adj.* = anaerobic. [< New Latin *anaerobium* (< Greek *an-* without + *āér, āéros* air + *bíos* life) + English *-ian*]

an|aer|o|bic (an'ãr ō'bik), *adj.* **1** living, growing, or taking place, where there is no free oxygen. Some anaerobic bacteria get their oxygen from the matter released during fermentation which takes place in the absence of free oxygen. *One important reason for the common practice of keeping*

Pronunciation Key: hat, āge, cãre, fär; let, ēqual, tėrm; it, īce; hot, ōpen, ôrder; oil, out; cup, pu̇t, rüle; child; long; thin; ᴛʜen; zh, measure; ə represents **a** in about, **e** in taken, **i** in pencil, **o** in lemon, **u** in circus.

wounds open and of using cotton or other loose materials for dressings is that air is admitted, thus suppressing the growth of anaerobic bacteria such as those that cause tetanus (Fred W. Emerson). **2** having to do with or caused by anaerobes or by the absence of free oxygen. Also, **anerobic**. — **an'aer|o'bi|cal|ly**, *adv.*

an|aer|o|bi|o|sis (an'ãr ō'bī ō'sis), *n.* the ability of an organism to live and reproduce in the absence of free oxygen.

an|aer|o|bi|ot|ic (an'ãr ō bī ot'ik), *adj.* = anaerobic.

an|aer|o|bi|um (an'ãr ō'bē əm), *n., pl.* **-bi|a** (-bē ə). = anaerobe.

an|aes|the|sia (an'əs thē'zhə), *n. Especially British.* anesthesia.

an|aes|the|si|ol|o|gist (an'əs thē'zē ol'ə jist), *n. Especially British.* anesthesiologist.

an|aes|the|si|ol|o|gy (an'əs thē'zē ol'ə jē), *n. Especially British.* anesthesiology.

an|aes|the|sis (an'əs thē'sis), *n. Especially British.* anesthesis (anesthesia).

an|aes|thet|ic (an'əs thet'ik), *n., adj. Especially British.* anesthetic. — **an'aes|thet'i|cal|ly**, *adv.*

an|aes|the|tise (ə nes'thə tīz), *v.t.,* **-tised, -tis|ing**. *Especially British.* anesthetize. — **an|aes'the|ti|sa'tion**, *n.* — **an|aes'the|tis'er**, *n.*

an|aes|the|tist (ə nes'thə tist), *n. Especially British.* anesthetist.

an|aes|the|tize (ə nes'thə tīz), *v.t.,* **-tized, -tiz|ing**. *Especially British.* anesthetize. — **an|aes'the|ti|za'tion**, *n.* — **an|aes'the|tiz'er**, *n.*

an|a|gen|e|sis (an'ə jen'ə sis), *n.* **1** *Biology.* progressive evolutionary change within a species. **2** *Medicine.* reproduction or regeneration of tissue. [< New Latin *anagenesis* < Greek *ana-* upward + *génesis* creation, genesis]

an|a|glyph (an'ə glif), *n.* **1** an embossed or engraved ornament worked in low relief, such as on a cameo or coin. **2** a picture consisting of two images superimposed, one printed in red, the other in green, viewed with a red light filter over one eye and a green over the other, giving a stereoscopic effect. It is used as a still picture or part of a motion picture. [< Greek *anaglyphḗ* < *ana-* up + *glýphein* carve]

an|a|glyph|ic (an'ə glif'ik), *adj.* of or having to do with an anaglyph or anaglyptics.

an|a|glyph|o|scope (an'ə glif'ə skōp), *n.* a device through which anaglyphs (def. 2) are viewed, consisting of a pair of red and green light filters. [< *anaglyph* + *-scope*]

an|a|glyp|tic (an'ə glip'tik), *adj.* = anaglyphic.

an|a|glyp|tics (an'ə glip'tiks), *n.* the art of carving or decorating in low relief.

an|a|go|ge (an'ə gō'jē), *n.* **1** the spiritual meaning or interpretation, as of Scripture. **2** an Old Testament typification of something in the New Testament. [< Late Latin *anagōgē* < Greek *anagōgḗ* elevation < *ana-* up + *ágein* lead]

an|a|gog|ic (an'ə goj'ik), *adj.* **1** having to do with anagoge; spiritual; mystical. **2** *Psychoanalysis.* of or having to do with unconscious striving toward morally uplifting ideals. — **an'a|gog'i|cal|ly**, *adv.*

an|a|gog|i|cal (an'ə goj'ə kəl), *adj.* = anagogic.

an|a|go|gy (an'ə gō'jē), *n. Obsolete.* anagoge. [< Greek *anagōgḗ*]

***an|a|gram** (an'ə gram), *n.* a word or phrase formed from another by transposing or rearranging the letters. *Examples:* lived—devil; north—thorn.

anagrams, a game in which the players make words by changing and adding letters.

[< New Latin *anagramma* < Greek *anagrammatízein* transpose letters < *ana-* up or back + *grámma, -atos* letter]

***anagram** William Shakespeare = I ask me, has Will a peer?

an|a|gram|mat|ic (an'ə grə mat'ik), *adj.* of or containing an anagram or anagrams. — **an'a|gram|mat'i|cal|ly**, *adv.*

an|a|gram|mat|i|cal (an'ə grə mat'ə kəl), *adj.* = anagrammatic.

an|a|gram|ma|tism (an'ə gram'ə tiz əm), *n.* the making of anagrams.

an|a|gram|ma|tist (an'ə gram'ə tist), *n.* a person who makes anagrams.

an|a|gram|ma|tize (an'ə gram'ə tīz), *v.t.,* **-tized, -tiz|ing**. to make into or use as an anagram or anagrams.

an|a|grams (an'ə gramz), *n.pl.* (*sing. in use*). See under **anagram**.

a|nal (ā'nəl), *adj.* **1** of or having to do with the anus. **2** at or near the anus. **3** *Psychoanalysis.* of or having to do with a pattern of personality traits supposed to have developed from the stage when the child's interest was focused on excretory habits and control of defecation. An anal character is supposed to be manifested by extreme neatness, miserliness, stubbornness, and self-control. — **a'nal|ly**, *adv.*

anal., **1a** analogous. **b** analogy. **2a** analysis. **b** analytic.

an|al|cime (an al'sim, -sīm), *n.* = analcite.

an|al|cite (an al'sīt, an'əl-), *n.* a whitish or slightly tinted variety of zeolite (hydrous aluminum sodium silicate) occurring in trap rocks. *Formula:* $NaAlSi_2O_6 \cdot H_2O$ [< French *analcime* (< Greek *an-* not + *álkimos* strong) + English *-ite*[1]]

an|a|lec|ta (an'ə lek'tə), *n.pl.* analects (especially in referring to Greek or Latin authors). [< Greek *análekta*]

an|a|lects (an'ə lekts), *n.pl.* literary gleanings; collections of fragments or extracts (usually as part of a title): *the Confucian Analects.* [< Greek *análekta* (things) gathered up < *ana-* up + *légein* gather]

an|a|lem|ma (an'ə lem'ə), *n.* a graduated scale representing the sun's declination at any date of the year, drawn on the Torrid Zone of a terrestrial globe, often in the shape of a long figure 8 centered on the equator. [< Latin *analemma* sundial pedestal < Greek *analēmma* a support, ultimately < Greek *ana-* up + *lambánein* take]

an|a|lep|tic (an'ə lep'tik), *adj., n.* — ***adj.*** **1** restorative; strengthening: *an analeptic medicine.* **2** restoring to consciousness.

— ***n.*** a restorative.

[< Late Latin *analēpticus* < Greek *analēptikós*, ultimately < *ana-* up + *lambánein* take]

anal fin, a fin located near the anus on the underside of fishes (contrasted with *dorsal fin*). See picture under **fin**.

an|al|ge|si|a (an'əl jē'zē ə, -sē ə, -zhə, -shə), *n.* deadening, or absence of the sense, of pain without loss of consciousness. See also **anesthesia**. [< New Latin *analgesia* < Greek *analgēsiā* < *an-* without + *algeîn* feel pain]

an|al|ge|sic (an'əl jē'zik, -sik), *adj., n.* — ***adj.*** of or causing analgesia.

— ***n.*** a drug that relieves or lessens pain.

an|al|get|ic (an'əl jet'ik), *adj., n.* = analgesic.

an|a|log (an'ə lôg, -log), *n., adj. U.S.* analogue.

analog computer, an electronic calculating machine or automatic control which deals directly with physical quantities, such as weights, voltages, or lengths, rather than with a numerical code.

an|a|log|ic (an'ə loj'ik), *adj.* of analogy: *Each language has its own fashions in word-composition which may be either extended indefinitely by analogic creation or suffered to fall into desuetude quite unpredictably* (Simeon Potter).

an|a|log|i|cal (an'ə loj'ə kəl), *adj.* **1** based on analogy; using analogy. **2** expressing an analogy, as the *heart* of an apple, the *mouth* of a cave. — **an'a|log'i|cal|ly**, *adv.*

analogical change, *Linguistics.* **1** the alteration of one linguistic form, such as an inflected word, in conformity with another form regarded as similar. The alteration, in children's usage, of *men* to *mans* in conformity with the predominant pattern of forming English plurals is done by analogical change. **2** the replacement of such a form by another regarded as equivalent and perhaps preferable, such as the substitution of *frozen* for the earlier *froren* because of the pattern suggested by other parts of the verb, *freeze* and *froze.*

► **Analogical change** in English has led to a regularization of inflectional endings. As a result, many former inflectional patterns have completely disappeared or persist now in a very few words. The surviving active inflections (such as *-ed* for the past and past participle of verbs) are used with new words entering the language and with words formerly inflected in other ways, as well as with words to which they originally applied. Some words now exist in two forms, the newer based on analogy, such as *crew* and *crowed.* The older form of such a pair is in most instances gradually falling into disuse.

a|nal|o|gise (ə nal'ə jīz), *v.i., v.t.,* **-gised, -gis|ing**. *Especially British.* analogize.

a|nal|o|gist (ə nal'ə jist), *n.* a person who searches for, points out, or argues from analogies.

a|nal|o|gize (ə nal'ə jīz), *v.,* **-gized, -giz|ing**. — ***v.i.*** **1** to use analogy or analogies; speak in or reason from analogy. **2** to show itself analogous; be in general harmony.

— ***v.t.*** to make, or show to be, analogous.

a|nal|o|gon (ə nal'ə gon), *n.* = analogue.

a|nal|o|gous (ə nal'ə gəs), *adj.* **1** alike in some way; similar in the quality or feature that is being thought of, or in circumstances or uses; comparable (to): *The human heart is analogous to a pump. Who can say that the anatomy of modern despotism is significantly analogous to the anatomy of despotism in the declining Roman Empire?* (Bulletin of Atomic Scientists). **SYN:** corresponding, like. **2** *Biology.* corresponding in function, but not in structure and origin: *The wing of a fly is analogous to the wing of a bird.* [< Latin *analogus* (with English *-ous*) < Greek *análogos* proportionate < *aná lógon* according to due ratio] — **a|nal'o|gous|ly**, *adv.* — **a|nal'o|gous|ness**, *n.*

an|a|logue (an'ə lôg, -log), *n., adj.* — ***n.*** **1** an analogous word, thing, circumstance, or situation. **SYN:** parallel. **2** an organ or part analogous to another organ or part (distinguished from *homologue*). **3** a substance which interferes in a biochemical reaction because of its structural similarity to one of the normal reactants.

— ***adj.*** of or having to do with analog computers: *The analogue machine is just what its name implies: a physical analogy to the ... problem* (Scientific American).

[< French *analogue* < Greek *análogos* proportionate, analogous]

analogue computer, = analog computer.

***a|nal|o|gy** (ə nal'ə jē), *n., pl.* **-gies**. **1** a likeness in some ways between things that are otherwise unlike; similarity: *There is an analogy between the human heart and a pump.* **SYN:** resemblance, correspondence, equivalence. **2** comparison of such things: *Historical analogies, as between Napoleon and Hitler, ought not to be carried too far.* **3** *Biology.* correspondence of organs or other parts in function but not in structure and origin (distinguished from *homology*). **4** *Logic.* the inference that things alike in certain respects will be alike in others: *a prediction based on the analogy of history. Deductions based on analogy are frequently open to doubt. Analogy ... proceeds on the basis of similarity between two situations. If the similarity is close enough, one may conjecture that a conclusion which holds in one situation should hold in the other* (Scientific American). **5** *Mathematics.* proportion; agreement of ratios. **6** *Linguistics.* **a** = analogical change: *The similarity between words like "man" and "pan" sometimes causes children to make the analogy "mans" for "men."* **b** the creation of a new word based on the pattern of an old one, as *astronaut* on the model of *Argonaut.* [< Latin *analogia* < Greek *analogiā* proportion, relation < *análogos* analogous]

► One says **analogy** *between* things, and that one thing has *analogy to* or *with* another.

***analogy**
definition 3

analogous:

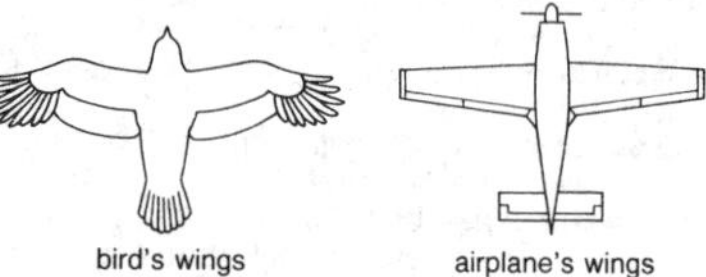

homologous:

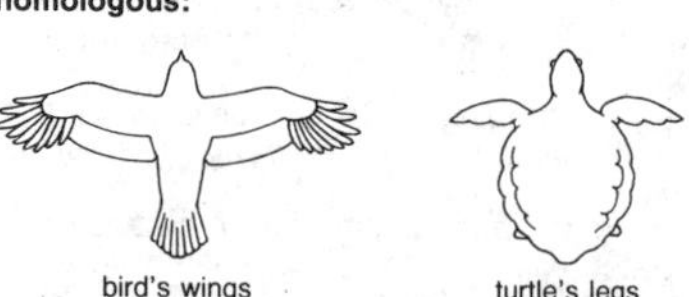

an|al|pha|bet (an al'fə bet), *n.* an illiterate person.

an|al|pha|bete (an al'fə bēt), *n.* = analphabet.

an|al|pha|bet|ic (an'al fə bet'ik, an al'-), *adj., n.* — ***adj.*** **1** illiterate; unlettered. **2** not utilizing a conventional alphabet: *In Jespersen's analphabetic notation each sound is represented by a set of symbols consisting of Greek and Latin letters and Arabic numerals.*

— ***n.*** an illiterate person; analphabet.

a|nal|y|sand (ə nal'ə zand), *n.* a person being psychoanalyzed.

an|a|lyse (an'ə līz), *v.t.,* **-lysed, -lys|ing**. *Especially British.* analyze. — **an'a|lys'er**, *n.*

a|nal|y|sis (ə nal'ə sis), *n., pl.* **-ses** (-sēz). **1a** separation of anything into its parts or elements to find out what it is made of. An analysis of the sentence "Babies like soft food" shows that it is made up of the plural noun *babies,* the verb *like,* the adjective *soft,* and the singular noun *food.* **b** *Figurative.* an examining carefully and in detail. An analysis can be made of a book or a person's character. **c** a statement or table giving the results of an analysis; outline or summary. **2** *Chemistry.* **a** the determination of the kind or amount of the constituents of a substance. **b** the intentional separation of a substance into its ingredients or elements to determine their amount or nature. A chemical analysis of ordinary table salt shows that it is made up of two elements, sodium and chlorine. **3** the diagnosis and treatment of mental disorder;

psychoanalysis. **4** *Physics.* the resolution of light into its prismatic constituents. **5** *Mathematics.* **a** algebraic reasoning as applied to geometry. **b** treatment by the calculus. **6** *Philosophy.* the breaking up of a concept or event into its constituent elements or into its causes to reveal concealed content or form.

in the last (or **final**) **analysis**, in essence; fundamentally; ultimately; basically: *Is not peace, in the last analysis, a matter of human rights?* (John F. Kennedy).

[< Medieval Latin *analysis* < Greek *análysis* a breaking up < *ana-* up + *lýein* loosen]

an|a|lyst (an′ə list), *n.* **1** a person who analyzes or is skilled in analysis. **2** a person who practices psychoanalysis; psychoanalyst.

an|a|lyt|ic (an′ə lit′ik), *adj.* **1** = analytical. **2** *Linguistics.* characterized by the use of separate words, such as auxiliary verbs and prepositions, rather than by the use of inflectional endings. English is an analytic language, whereas Latin is synthetic.

an|a|lyt|i|cal (an′ə lit′ə kəl), *adj.* **1** separating a whole into its parts; of analysis; using analysis as a method or process: *The methods of science are analytical. The detective had an analytical mind.* **2** concerned with or based on analysis. [< Late Latin *analyticus* < Greek *analytikós* < *análysis* a breaking up, analysis]

analytical balance, a precision balance, used especially in analytical chemistry for weighing quantities as small as 1/10,000 of a gram.

analytical chemistry, the branch of chemistry that deals with the determination by analysis of the components making up samples of matter.

analytical cubism, an early form of cubism characterized by simple geometric forms.

analytical geometry, = analytic geometry.

an|a|lyt|i|cal|ly (an′ə lit′ə klē), *adv.* **1** by means of analysis. **2** to or toward analytical methods.

analytical psychology, **1** a system of psychology that uses introspection in the attempt to reduce sensations or emotions to their elements. **2** the school of psychology founded by Carl Jung, differing from Freudian psychology mainly in method of dream interpretation, the concept of a collective unconscious as well as a personal one, and the use of the term *libido* as a will to live, not primarily or necessarily sexual.

analytical table, an arrangement of the prominent characteristics of a group of plants or animals to make identification of specimens easy.

analytic geometry, the use of coordinates and algebra or the calculus to solve problems in geometry.

an|a|ly|tic|i|ty (an′ə lə tis′ə tē), *n.* analytic quality, condition, or character.

an|a|lyt|ics (an′ə lit′iks), *n.* mathematical or algebraic analysis.

an|a|lyze (an′ə līz), *v.t.,* **-lyzed, -lyz|ing.** **1** to separate (anything complex) into its parts or elements to find out what it is made of: *After you analyze a sentence grammatically, you should be able to understand its meaning better.* SYN: resolve. **2a** *Figurative.* to examine carefully and in detail, especially to determine why something has happened or may be expected to happen: *Analyze the situation before you act.* SYN: dissect. **b** *Figurative.* to examine critically the parts or elements of; find out the essential features of: *Many men have tried to analyze the causes of success.* **3** *Chemistry.* to subject to analysis: **a** to determine the nature or amount of the components of (a substance). **b** to separate intentionally (a compound or mixture) into its elements: *A chemist can analyze water into two colorless gases, hydrogen and oxygen.* **4** *Mathematics.* to submit (a problem) to treatment by algebra, and especially by calculus. **5** = psychoanalyze. [< French *analyser* < *analyse* analysis] **—an′a|lyz′a|ble,** *adj.* **—an′a|ly|za′tion,** *n.* **—an′a|lyz′er,** *n.*

an|am|ne|sis (an′am nē′sis), *n.* the recalling of things past; recollection; reminiscence. [< Greek *anámnēsis* < *ana-* back + *mimnēskesthai* call to mind]

an|am|nes|tic (an′am nes′tik), *adj.* recalling to mind. **—an′am|nes′ti|cal|ly,** *adv.*

an|a|mor|phic (an′ə môr′fik), *adj.* of or characterized by anamorphosis.

an|a|mor|phize (an′ə môr′fīz), *v.t.,* **-phized, -phiz|ing.** **1** to represent by anamorphosis. **2** to project with an anamorphoscope.

an|a|mor|pho|scope (an′ə môr′fə skōp), *n.* a special mirror or other device for correcting the distortion of anamorphosis.

an|a|mor|phose (an′ə môr′fōz), *v.t.,* **-phosed, -phos|ing.** to represent by anamorphosis.

an|a|mor|pho|sis (an′ə môr′fə sis, -môr fō′-), *n., pl.* **-ses** (-sēz). **1a** a distorted image or projection that appears in natural form when reflected from a curved mirror, or the like. **b** a method of producing such images or projections; distortion. **2** *Botany.* **a** an anomalous change of form in a plant. **b** a gradual change of form within a group of plants or animals over a long period of time. [< Greek *anamórphōsis* < *anamorphoûn* transform < *ana-* again + *morphḗ* form]

a|na|nas (ə nä′nəs, -nā′-), *n.* = pineapple.

an|an|drous (an an′drəs), *adj. Botany.* lacking stamens: *Anandrous flowers are female.* [< Greek *ánandros* husbandless (with English *-ous*) < *an-* without + *anḗr, andrós* man]

An|a|ni|as (an′ə nī′əs), *n.* **1** a famous liar who, with his wife Sapphira, was struck dead for lying (in the Bible, Acts 5:1-10). **2** *Informal.* any liar, especially one who lies habitually.

an|an|thous (an an′thəs), *adj.* lacking flowers: *an ananthous plant.* [< Greek *ananthḗs* (< *an-* without + *ánthos* flower) + English *-ous*]

an|a|nym (an′ə nim), *n.* a name written or spelled backward. [< Greek *aná* back + dialectal *ónyma* name]

an|a|pest or **an|a|paest** (an′ə pest), *n.* **1** a foot of verse having three syllables: **a** (in modern or accentual meter) two unaccented followed by one accented, as *by the way′.* **b** (in quantitative meter, such as Greek or Latin) two short followed by one long, as *pĭĕtās.* **2** a line of verse composed of or containing such feet. *Example:* "From the cen′/tre all round′/to the sea′/I am lord′/of the fowl′/and the brute′" (Cowper). [< Latin *anapaestus* < Greek *anápaistos* (*dáktylos*) (dactyl) reversed < *ana-* back + *paíein* strike]

an|a|pes|tic or **an|a|paes|tic** (an′ə pes′tik), *adj., n.* **—adj.** of or consisting of anapests. **—n.** an anapestic verse.

an|a|phase (an′ə fāz), *n. Biology.* the third stage in mitosis, characterized by the movement of the two sets of daughter chromosomes to opposite ends of the spindle. It occurs after the metaphase and before the telophase. [< *ana-* up + *phase*]

a|naph|o|ra (ə naf′ər ə), *n. Rhetoric.* the repetition of the same word or words at the beginning of two or more successive verses, clauses, or sentences. *Example:* "Where is the wise? where is the scribe? where is the disputer of this world?" (I Corinthians 1:20). [< Latin *anaphora* < Greek *anaphorā́* < *ana-* back + *phérein* carry]

an|aph|ro|dis|i|a (an af′rə diz′ē ə), *n.* absence or lack of sexual power or desire.

an|aph|ro|dis|i|ac (an af′rə diz′ē ak), *adj., n.* **—adj.** capable of decreasing sexual desire. **—n.** an anaphrodisiac drug or other agent. [< *an-*[1] not + Greek *aphrodīsiakós* aphrodisiac]

an|a|phy|lac|tic (an′ə fə lak′tik), *adj.* **1** of anaphylaxis. **2** producing anaphylaxis: *anaphylactic shock.*

an|a|phy|lac|to|gen (an′ə fə lak′tə jən), *n.* an anaphylactic substance.

an|a|phy|lac|to|gen|ic (an′ə fə lak′tə jen′ik), *adj.* producing anaphylaxis.

an|a|phy|lac|toid (an′ə fə lak′toid), *adj.* having or resembling the symptoms of anaphylaxis.

an|a|phy|lax|is (an′ə fə lak′sis), *n.* increased sensitivity to the action of a normally nontoxic protein upon exposure to it, especially for the second time, sometimes causing severe or even fatal shock. Serum sickness in humans is an instance of relatively mild anaphylaxis. [< *ana-* back + *-phylaxis* protection, as in *prophylaxis*]

an|a|plas|mo|sis (an′ə plaz mō′sis), *n.* a disease of livestock, expecially cattle, caused by a protozoan parasite which infests the blood. [< *ana-* through + *plasma* + *-osis*]

an|a|plas|tic (an′ə plas′tik), *adj.* **1** having to do with or involving plastic surgery. **2** having reverted to a more embryonic form, with increased capacity for multiplication, as in malignant tissue. [< Greek *anaplássein* restore < *ana-* back + *plássein* to shape; patterned on *plastic*]

an|a|plas|ty (an′ə plas′tē), *n.* = plastic surgery. [< *anaplastic*]

an|ap|tot|ic (an′ap tot′ik), *adj.* tending to lose, or having already lost, by phonetic decay, the use of inflections: *English is an anaptotic language.* [< *ana-* back + Greek *áptōtos* indeclinable + English *-ic*]

an|ap|tyc|tic (an′ap tik′tik), *adj.* of or having to do with anaptyxis.

an|ap|tyx|is (an′ap tik′sis), *n. Phonetics.* the insertion of an additional vowel in a word, thus forming an extra syllable, as in (ath′ə lēt) for *athlete* and (el′əm) for *elm.* [< Greek *anáptyxis* an unfolding < *ana-* back + *ptýssein* to fold]

an|arch (an′ärk), *n.* a promoter of anarchy: *Imperial anarchs doubling human woes* (Lord Byron). [< *anarchy*]

an|ar|chic (an är′kik), *adj.* **1** producing anarchy; favoring anarchy; lawless: *an anarchic age.* **2** of or having to do with anarchism as a political theory. **—an|ar′chi|cal|ly,** *adv.*

an|ar|chi|cal (an är′kə kəl), *adj.* = anarchic.

an|ar|chism (an′ər kiz əm), *n.* **1a** the political theory that all systems of government and law are harmful. Believers in anarchism think that all such systems prevent individuals from reaching their greatest development. **b** the practice or support of this belief. **2** disorder and confusion; lawlessness; terrorism.

an|ar|chist (an′ər kist), *n., adj.* **—n.** **1** a person who wants to overthrow established governments and have a world without rulers and laws; advocate of anarchism. **2** a person who promotes disorder and stirs up revolt. **—adj.** anarchistic.

an|ar|chis|tic (an′ər kis′tik), *adj.* of anarchism; like that of anarchists. **—an′ar|chis′ti|cal|ly,** *adv.*

anarcho-, *combining form.* anarchist and ___: *Anarcho-pacifist = anarchist and pacifist.* [< *anarchist*]

an|ar|cho-pac|i|fism (an är′kō pas′ə fiz əm), *n.* the beliefs and practices of persons believing in or following both anarchism and pacifism: *Growing numbers of drop-outs and hippies are gravitating towards ... anarcho-pacifism* (Manchester Guardian Weekly). **—an|ar′cho-pac′i|fist,** *adj., n.*

an|ar|cho-syn|di|cal|ism (an är′kō sin′də kə liz′əm), *n. Especially British.* syndicalism. **—an|ar′-cho-syn′di|cal|ist,** *n.*

an|ar|cho-syn|di|cal|is|tic (an är′kō sin′də kə lis′tik), *adj. Especially British.* syndicalistic.

an|ar|chy (an′ər kē), *n.* **1** an absence of a system of government and law: *After its defeat in war the country was in a state of anarchy. Eternal anarchy amidst the noise of endless wars* (John Milton). **2** disorder and confusion; lawlessness: (*Figurative.*) *... the wild anarchy of drink* (Ben Jonson). SYN: chaos. **3** = anarchism (def. 1). [< Greek *anarchiā́* < *an-* without + *archós* ruler]

an|ar|thri|a (an är′thrē ə), *n.* inability to articulate distinctly in speaking, especially as a result of damage to the brain. [< *an-*[1] not + Greek *árthron* joint, article]

an|ar|throus (an är′thrəs), *adj.* **1** (of animals) without joints. **2** (of Greek nouns) used without the article. [< Greek *ánarthros* (with English *-ous*) < *an-* without + *árthron* joint, article]

an|a|sar|ca (an′ə sär′kə), *n.* a dropsy of considerable extent in the subcutaneous connective tissue; generalized edema. [< *ana-* throughout + Greek *sárx, sarkós* flesh]

an|a|sar|cous (an′ə sär′kəs), *adj.* of or characterized by anasarca.

A|na|sa|zi (ä′nə sä′zē), *n., pl.* **-zi** or **-zis.** **1** a member of a North American Indian group that included the Basket Makers and the Pueblo Indians. **2** the culture typified by this group. [< a Navaho word meaning "ancient"]

a|nas|pid (ə nas′pid), *n.* any one of a group of fossil fishes of the Silurian and Devonian periods, having a heterocercal tail and lacking paired fins. [< Greek *ana-* against + *aspís, -ídos* shield]

an|a|stat|ic (an′ə stat′ik), *adj.* (of print) raised in relief.

an|as|tig|mat (an as′tig mat), *n.* an anastigmatic lens.

an|as|tig|mat|ic (an′ə stig mat′ik, an as′tig-), *adj.* free from astigmatism (applied especially to a compound photographic lens in which each part is designed to compensate for the astigmatic defects of the other); stigmatic. **—an′as|tig|mat′i-cal|ly,** *adv.*

a|nas|to|mose (ə nas′tə mōz), *v.i., v.t.,* **-mosed, -mos|ing.** to communicate or connect by anastomosis.

a|nas|to|mo|sis (ə nas′tə mō′sis), *n., pl.* **-ses** (-sēz). **1** a cross connection between separate parts of any branching system, such as the veins of leaves, veins in the wings of insects, or rivers and their branches. **2** communication between blood vessels in an animal body. [< Late Latin *anastomōsis* < Greek *anastómōsis* provision of an outlet < *ana-* back + *stóma* mouth]

a|nas|to|mot|ic (ə nas′tə mot′ik), *adj.* of or characterized by anastomosis.

a|nas|tro|phe (ə nas′trə fē), *n. Rhetoric.* inversion of the usual order of words or the arrangement of clauses in a sentence. *Example:* "Sweet are the uses of adversity." [< Greek *anastrophḗ* < *ana-* back + *stréphein* turn]

anat., **1** anatomical. **2** anatomy.

an|a|tase (an′ə tās), *n.* a variety of native titanium dioxide; octahedrite. [< French *anatase* < Greek *anátasis* extension < *ana-* up + *teínein* stretch (from its elongated crystals)]

an|a|tex|is (an′ə tek′sis), *n. Geology.* the process by which plutonic rock is melted and regenerated as a magma. [< Greek *anátēxis* a melting < *anatḗkein* to melt < *ana-* up + *tḗkein* to thaw]

a|nath|e|ma (ə nath′ə mə), *n., pl.* **-mas.** **1** a person or thing that is utterly detested or con-

Pronunciation Key: hat, āge, cãre, fär; let, ēqual, tėrm; it, īce; hot, ōpen, ôrder; oil, out; cup, pu̇t, rüle; child; long; thin; ᴛʜen; zh, measure; ə represents **a** in about, **e** in taken, **i** in pencil, **o** in lemon, **u** in circus.

demned: *Because of its uncertainties, steeple-chasing long has been anathema to the betting fraternity* (Wall Street Journal). **SYN:** taboo. **2** any person or thing that has been cursed or consigned to damnation. **3** a solemn curse by church authorities excommunicating some person from the church. **4** the act of denouncing and condemning some person or thing as evil. **5** a curse or imprecation. **SYN:** malediction. [< Latin *anathema* < Greek *anáthema* thing devoted, especially to evil < *ana-* up + *tithénai* set]

anathema maranatha, the term *anathema* supplemented by a phrase meaning "the Lord hath come," apparently added for solemnity, and hence used as an intensified form of *anathema* (in the Bible, I Corinthians 16:22). [< Greek *anáthema* thing devoted to evil + Aramaic *Marán athá* The Lord hath come]

a|nath|e|mat|ic (ə nath′ə mat′ik), *adj.* of or having the nature of an anathema. **—a|nath′e|mat′i|cal|ly,** *adv.*

a|nath|e|mat|i|cal (ə nath′ə mat′ə kəl), *adj.* = anathematic.

a|nath|e|ma|ti|sa|tion (ə nath′ə mə tə zā′shən), *n. British.* anathematization.

a|nath|e|ma|tise (ə nath′ə mə tīz), *v.t., v.i.,* **-tised, -tis|ing.** *British.* anathematize.

a|nath|e|ma|ti|za|tion (ə nath′ə mə tə zā′shən), *n.* an anathematizing or being anathematized.

a|nath|e|ma|tize (ə nath′ə mə tīz), *v.,* **-tized, -tiz|ing.** **—*v.t.*** to pronounce an anathema against; denounce; curse. **—*v.i.*** to utter anathemas; curse. **—a|nath′e|ma|tiz′er,** *n.*

an|a|tine (an′ə tin, -tīn), *adj., n.* **—*adj.*** **1** of or having to do with the duck family. **2** resembling or characteristic of a duck. **—*n.*** a bird of the duck family. [< Latin *anatīnus* < *anas, anatis* duck]

An|a|to|li|an (an′ə tō′lē ən), *adj., n.* **—*adj.*** of or having to do with Anatolia (a region between the Black and Mediterranean seas), its people, or their language. **—*n.*** **1** a native or inhabitant of Anatolia. **2** the language of Anatolia, a dialect of Turkish. **3** a group of extinct languages spoken in ancient Anatolia.

an|a|tom|ic (an′ə tom′ik), *adj.* = anatomical.

an|a|tom|i|cal (an′ə tom′ə kəl), *adj.* **1** connected with the study or practice of anatomy or dissection: *an anatomical treatise.* **2** of or having to do with anatomy; structural: *an anatomical weakness.*

an|a|tom|i|cal|ly (an′ə tom′ə klē), *adv.* in an anatomical manner; as regards structure; by means of anatomy or dissection.

a|nat|o|mist (ə nat′ə mist), *n.* **1** a person who studies anatomy. **2** a person who dissects or analyzes: (*Figurative.*) *the economic anatomists examining the causes of inflation.*

a|nat|o|mi|za|tion (ə nat′ə mə zā′shən), *n.* dissection; analysis.

a|nat|o|mize (ə nat′ə mīz), *v.t.,* **-mized, -miz|ing.** **1** to divide (an animal or plant) into parts to study the structure and relation of the parts; dissect. **2** *Figurative.* to examine the parts of; analyze: *Miss Jenkins has the shrewdness to realize that by anatomizing Elizabeth's neuroses she is expounding her greatness* (New Yorker).

a|nat|o|my (ə nat′ə mē), *n., pl.* **-mies.** **1** the science of the structure of animals and plants, based upon dissection, microscopic observation, and other analyses. Anatomy is a part of biology. *Doctors study human anatomy.* **2** a book about this. **3** the dissecting of animals or plants to study the position and structure of their parts. **4** the structure of an animal or plant: *The anatomy of an earthworm is much simpler than that of a man.* **5** *Figurative.* the detailed examining of the parts or elements of a thing; analysis: *The Anatomy of Melancholy* (Robert Burton). **6** *Archaic.* a skeleton. [< Late Latin *anatomia* < Greek *anatomē* dissection < *ana-* up + *témnein* cut]

***a|nat|o|saur|us** (ə nat′ə sôr′əs), *n., pl.* **-sau|ri** (-sôr′ī). an ornithopod dinosaur with as many as 2,000 teeth. **SYN:** trachodont. [< New Latin *anatosaurus* < Latin *anas, anat-* duck + Greek *saûros* lizard]

***anatosaurus**

a|nat|ro|pous (ə nat′rə pəs), *adj. Botany.* inverted at an early stage of growth of an ovule, so that the micropyle is close to the hilum, and the chalaza is at the opposite end. [< *ana-* back + Greek *tropē* a turn + English *-ous*]

a|nat|to (ə nat′ō, -nä′tō), *n.* = annatto.

an|bu|ry (an′bər ē), *n., pl.* **-ries.** **1** a soft wart on horses and other animals. **2** a disease attacking the roots of turnips, cabbages, and other plants. [perhaps earlier *ang-berry* < Old English *ang-* pain + *berie* berry]

anc., **1** ancient. **2** anciently.

-ance, *suffix forming nouns chiefly from verbs.*
1 the act or fact of ____ing: *Avoidance = the act or fact of avoiding.*
2 the quality or state of being ____ed: *Annoyance = the quality of being annoyed.*
3 a thing that ____s: *Conveyance = a thing that conveys.*
4 what is ____ed: *Contrivance = what is contrived.*
5 the quality or state of being ____ant: *Importance = the quality or state of being important.*
[< French *-ance* < Latin *-antia, -entia*]
▶Although the spelling of words ending in **-ance** and **-ence,** in **-ancy** and **-ency,** and in **-ant** and **-ent** differs, pronunciation of the members of each suffix pair is the same and the accepted spelling must be committed to memory.

an|ces|tor (an′ses tər), *n., v.* **—*n.*** **1** a person from whom one is directly descended, usually one more remote than a parent; forefather. Your grandfathers, your grandmothers, and so on back, are your ancestors. *His ancestors came to America on the Mayflower.* **SYN:** forebear, progenitor. **2** *Figurative.* that from which anything is descended; forerunner. **SYN:** precursor. **3** *Biology.* the early or lower form from which a species or group is descended, according to the theory of evolution: *Dinosaurs and today's reptiles are descendants of common ancestors.* **4** *Law.* a person from whom an inheritance is derived.
—*v.t.* to be the ancestor of: *Their grandfathers ancestored the oldest family in Houston.*
[< Old French *ancestre* < Latin *antecessor* < *antecēdere* < *ante-* before + *cēdere* go. See etym. of doublet **antecessor.**]

ancestor worship, great veneration for or worship of one's ancestors, as a characteristic of certain religions.

an|ces|tral (an ses′trəl), *adj.* **1** of or having to do with ancestors: *England was the ancestral home of the Pilgrims.* **2** inherited from ancestors: *Black hair is an ancestral trait in that family.* **SYN:** hereditary. **—an|ces′tral|ly,** *adv.*

an|ces|tress (an′ses tris), *n.* a woman from whom one is descended.

an|ces|try (an′ses trē), *n., pl.* **-tries.** **1** grandparents and other ancestors: *Many of the early settlers in America had English ancestry.* **SYN:** stock. **2** line of descent from ancestors; lineage: *The king was of noble ancestry.* **3** honorable descent. **SYN:** birth, family.

An|chi|ses (an kī′sēz), *n. Greek and Roman Legend.* a prince of Troy and the father of Aeneas, on whose shoulders Anchises was carried from the flaming city.

an|chor¹** (ang′kər), *n., v.* **—*n. **1** a shaped piece of metal fastened to a rope, chain, or cable lowered from a ship or boat to the bottom of the water to hold the ship or boat in place: *The anchor caught in the mud of the lake bottom and kept the boat from drifting.* **2** *Figurative.* something that makes a person feel safe and secure: *His mother's letters were an anchor to the boy when he went to camp for the first time.* **3** a thing for holding something else in place: *The anchors of the cables of this suspension bridge are set in concrete.* **4** = anchorman or anchorwoman. **5** *U.S.* a department store, convention center, or other project large enough to make a shopping or business area around it safe for investment: *With the confidence provided by the anchor, the neighborhood often flourishes* (New Yorker).
—*v.t.* **1** to hold in place with an anchor: *Can you anchor the boat in this storm?* **2** to hold in place; fix firmly: *The scouts anchored the tent to the ground.* **3** to be the anchorman or anchorwoman of: *to anchor a relay team or a news program.*
—*v.i.* **1** to drop anchor; stop or stay in a place by using an anchor: *The ship anchored in the bay.* **2** to lay hold or be firmly fixed in any way: (*Figurative.*) *His opinion was firmly anchored in faith.* **3** to be or serve as anchorman or anchorwoman.
at anchor, held by an anchor; anchored: *The ship was riding at anchor in the bay.*
cast an anchor to windward, to adopt measures for security: *Policy is based on a desire to cast an anchor to windward, to secure a friend for the United States.*
cast anchor, to let down or drop the anchor: *The boat cast anchor near shore.*
come to anchor, to drop the anchor: *They drifted along the coast and came to anchor in a bay.*
ride at anchor, to be kept at some place by being anchored: *The boat rode at anchor until the storm subsided.*
weigh anchor, to take up the anchor so as to sail away: *They weighed anchor and drifted toward shore.* (*Figurative.*) *Our author weighs up anchors, and once more ... resolves to prove his fortune* (Philip Massinger).
[Old English *ancor* < Latin *ancora* < Greek *ánkȳra*]

***anchor¹**
definition 1

parts of a yachtsman anchor: **other anchors:**

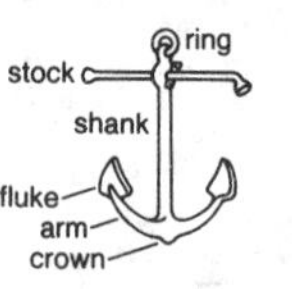

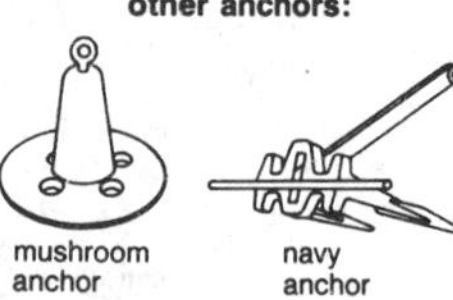

an|chor² (ang′kər), *n. Obsolete.* an anchorite; hermit: *An anchor's cheer in prison be my hope* (Shakespeare). [Old English *ancra*]

an|chor|age (ang′kər ij), *n.* **1** a place to anchor. **2** money paid for the right to anchor. **3** the act or process of anchoring or the state of being anchored: *There is room for the anchorage of 500 ships.* **4** *Figurative.* something to hold onto or depend on.

anchor arm, the part of a cantilever bridge between the shore and the pier.

anchor bend, = fisherman's bend.

an|cho|ress (ang′kər is), *n.* a woman anchorite.

an|cho|ret (ang′kər it, -kə ret), *n.* = anchorite. [< Late Latin *anachōrēta* < Late Greek *anachōrētēs* < Greek *anachōreîn* < *ana-* back + *chōreîn* withdraw]

an|cho|ret|ic (ang′kə ret′ik), *adj.* = anchoritic.

an|cho|rite (ang′kə rīt), *n.* **1** a person who lives alone in a solitary place for religious meditation. **2** a hermit. **SYN:** recluse. [< Medieval Latin *anachorita,* alteration of Late Latin *anachōrēta* anchoret]

an|cho|rit|ic (ang′kə rit′ik), *adj.* **1** of an anchorite. **2** like that of an anchorite.

anchor knot, a knot used especially for attaching a cable to the ring of an anchor.

an|chor|less (ang′kər lis), *adj.* drifting.

an|chor|man (ang′kər man′), *n., pl.* **-men.** **1a** the last man to run or swim on a relay team. **b** the last player to bowl for a team in each frame. **c** the end man of a tug-of-war team. **2** *Radio and Television.* a person who coordinates a broadcast usually by commenting and introducing reports from correspondents in several different cities, countries, or other areas.

anchor plate, a heavy support, often embedded in masonry, to secure the cables of a suspension bridge.

an|chor|wom|an (ang′kər wu̇m′ən), *n., pl.* **-women.** a female anchorman.

an|cho|vet|ta or **an|cho|ve|ta** (an′chə vet′ə), *n.* a small anchovy of the Pacific coast of America, from southern California to Peru, commonly used as bait. [< Spanish *anchoveta* (diminutive) < *anchova* anchovy]

an|cho|vy (an′chō vē, -chə-; an chō′-), *n., pl.* **-vies.** a very small fish that looks somewhat like a herring, especially one abundant in the Mediterranean. Anchovies are preserved by salting or drying and may be packed in oil, made into paste, or used in sauces. [< Spanish, Portuguese *anchova* < Vulgar Latin *apiúva,* alteration of Latin *apua* < Greek *aphýē*]

anchovy pear, **1** a West Indian fruit, somewhat resembling the mango, often pickled. **2** the tree that bears it, related to that which bears the Brazil nut.

an|chu|sa (an chü′zə, ang kyü′sə), *n.* any one of a genus of plants of the borage family, having hairy stems and rough leaves, such as the European bugloss or alkanet. [< Latin *anchūsa* < Greek *ánchousa* alkanet]

an|chu|sin (an chü′zin, ang kyü′sin), *n.* a red dye obtained from a variety of anchusa; alkannin. [< *anchusa* + *-in*]

an|chy|lose (ang′kə lōs), *v.i., v.t.,* **-losed, -los|ing.** = ankylose.

an|chy|lo|sis (ang′kə lō′sis), *n.* = ankylosis.

an|chy|lot|ic (ang′kə lot′ik), *adj.* = ankylotic.

an|cienne no|blesse (äɴ syen′ nô bles′), *French.* **1** the nobles of France before the French Revolution in 1789. **2** the old nobility (of any country, region, or other area).

an|cien ré|gime (äɴ syaɴ′ rā zhēm′), *French.* **1** the social and political structure of France before the French Revolution of 1789. **2** *Figurative.* the old order of things: *Modern jazz ... was not—and is not—a revolution against an ancien régime that would be better off buried* (New Yorker).

an|cient¹ (ān′shənt), *adj., n.* **—*adj.*** **1** of or belonging to times long past: *ancient records. In Egypt, we saw the ruins of an ancient temple*

built six thousand years ago. SYN: early. **2** of the time before the fall of the Western Roman Empire (A.D. 476). **3** of great age; very old: *the ancient hills, an ancient custom. Rome is an ancient city.* SYN: timeworn, hoary. See syn. under **old**. **4** *Figurative.* old-fashioned; antique: *Slang of the past generation is usually an ancient turn of phrase.* SYN: antiquated. **5** *Informal.* no longer news; out of fashion. **6** *Archaic.* having the experience and wisdom of age. SYN: venerable.
—*n.* **1** a very old person; patriarch. **2** a person belonging to an earlier period of the world's history.
the ancients, a people who lived long ago, such as the ancient Greeks, Romans, Egyptians, or Hebrews: *The ancients had no means of distinguishing an alloy from a pure metal* (Science News). **b** the authors, sculptors, painters, and intellectuals of ancient Greece and Rome: *He was deeply read in the ancients* (Henry Fielding).
[< Old French *ancien,* learned borrowing from unrecorded Late Latin *anteānus* < Latin *ante* before] —**an'cient|ness,** *n.*

an|cient² (ān'shənt), *n. Archaic.* **1** a standard; flag. **2** a standardbearer. [< *ensign*]

ancient history, 1 history from the earliest-known times to the fall of the western part of the Roman Empire in A.D. 476. **2** *Informal, Figurative.* a well-known fact or event of the recent past: *You didn't know she'd married? Why, that's ancient history now.*

ancient lights, *British.* windows whose light must not be overshadowed by new building.

an|cient|ly (ān'shənt lē), *adv.* **1** in ancient times. **2** formerly.

Ancient of Days, God, as the Eternal Being (in the Bible, Daniel 7).

ancient regime, = ancien régime.

an|cient|ry (ān'shən trē), *n. Archaic.* **1** the quality of being very old; ancientness. **2** old-fashioned style. **3** antiquity.

an|cil|lar|y (an'sə ler'ē), *adj., n., pl.* **-lar|ies.**
—*adj.* **1** subordinate; dependent; subservient. SYN: subsidiary. **2** assisting; auxiliary: *an ancillary engine in a sailboat.* SYN: accessory.
—*n. British.* **1** a subordinate part; accessory. SYN: subsidiary. **2** an assistant; helper. SYN: accessory.
[< Latin *ancillāris* < *ancilla* handmaid]

an|cip|i|tal (an sip'ə təl), *adj.* having two sharp edges, as the stems of certain plants. [< Latin *anceps, -cipitis* (< *an-,* for *ambi-* double + *caput* head) + English *-al*¹]

an|cip|i|tous (an sip'ə təs), *adj.* = ancipital.

an|cis|troid (an sis'troid), *adj.* hook-shaped. [< Greek *ankistroeidēs* < *ánkistron* a hook + *eîdos* form]

***an|con** (ang'kon), *n., pl.* **an|co|nes** (ang kō'nēz). **1** a projection like a bracket, used to support a cornice, aconsole, or a corbel. **2** *Rare.* the elbow. [< Latin *ancōn* < Greek *ankôn* bend, elbow]

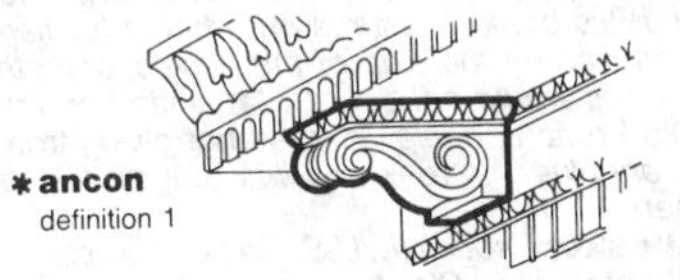

***ancon**
definition 1

An|co|na (ang kō'nə), *n.* a breed of chicken that originated in Italy, resembling the Leghorns.

an|co|nal (ang'kə nəl), *adj.* of or like an ancon.

an|co|ne|al (ang kō'nē əl), *adj.* = anconal.

-ancy, *suffix.* a form of **-ance,** expressing more distinctly the sense of quality or state, as in *ascendancy, buoyancy.*
▶See **-ance** for usage note.

an|cy|los|to|mi|a|sis (an'sə los'tə mī'ə sis), *n.* = hookworm disease. Also, **ankylostomiasis.** [< New Latin *Ancylostoma* the hookworm genus (< Greek *ankýlos* hooked + *stóma* mouth) + English *-iasis*]

and (and; *unstressed* ənd, ən), *conj., n.* —*conj.* **1** as well as: *nice and cold. You can come and go in the car.* **2** added to; with; together with; besides: *4 and 2 make 6. He likes ham and eggs.* **3** as a result: *The sun came out and the grass dried.* **4** *Informal.* to: *Try and do better. Won't you come and see us this weekend?* **5** *Archaic and Dialect.* if; supposing that: *and you please.*
—*n.* the character & used as a symbol for the conjunction *and.* See also **ampersand.**
[Old English *and*]
▶**And** is a coordinating conjunction; that is, it connects words, phrases, or clauses.

AND (and), *n.* a computer logic circuit or operation in which two connected items are true only if each of the items is true. [< *and,* conj.]

and., andante.

An|da|lu|sian (an'də lü'zhən, -shən), *adj., n.*
—*adj.* of Andalusia (region in southern Spain) or its people.
—*n.* **1** a native or inhabitant of Andalusia. **2** any chicken of a breed of medium-sized domestic fowl having black and bluish-black plumage.

an|da|lu|site (an'də lü'sīt), *n.* a very hard silicate of aluminum occurring as a mineral in orthorhombic crystals of various colors.When transparent, it is used as a gem. *Formula:* Al_2SiO_5 [< *Andalusia,* Spain, where first found + *-ite*¹]

An|da|ma|nese (an'də mə nēz', -nēs'), *n., pl.* **-nese,** *adj.* —*n.* **1** one of the Negrito people living in the Andaman Islands in the Bay of Bengal. **2** the language of the Andamanese, of no known relationship to any other language.
—*adj.* of the Andamanese or their language.

an|dan|te (än dän'tā, an dan'tē), *adv., adj., n. Music.* —*adv., adj.* moderately slow: *The movement was played andante* (*adv.*). *an andante movement* (*adj.*).
—*n.* a moderately slow movement; piece of music in this time.
[< Italian *andante* < *andare* walk]

an|dan|ti|no (än'dän tē'nō, an'dan-), *adv., adj., n., pl.* **-nos.** *Music.* —*adv., adj.* slightly faster than *andante.*
—*n.* a musical composition or part of one that is played andantino.
[< Italian *andantino* (diminutive) < *andante*]

An|de|an (an dē'ən, an'dē-), *adj.* of or having to do with the Andes (mountain system in South America).

An|der|mass (an'dər mas'), *n.* = Saint Andrew's Day.

An|der|son shelter (an'dər sən), an air-raid shelter of corrugated iron used in Britain during World War II. [< Sir J. *Anderson,* Home Secretary, 1939-40]

an|des|ine (an'də zin), *n.* a triclinic feldspar. [< *Andes* (mountains) + *-ine*²]

an|des|ite (an'də zīt), *n.* an igneous rock occurring in many varieties, in all of which a high-soda plagioclase is the chief constituent. [< *Andes* (mountains) + *-ite*¹]

***and|i|ron** (and'ī'ərn), *n.* one of a pair of metal supports for wood burned in a fireplace; firedog. Andirons hold the wood above the floor of the fireplace on legs that are short in back and usually have a high ornamental shaft in front to keep the logs from rolling out of the fireplace. [< Old French *andier* (*-iron* by association with *iron*)]

***andiron**

and/or, both or either. "To earn money from stocks and/or bonds" means to earn it from both stocks and bonds or from either stocks or bonds.
▶**And/or** is used chiefly in business and legal writing. It is useful when three choices exist (both items mentioned or either one of the two).

An|dor|ran (an dôr'ən, -dor'-), *adj., n.* —*adj.* of or having to do with Andorra (country between France and Spain), its people, or their language.
—*n.* a native or inhabitant of Andorra.

an|dra|dite (an'drə dīt), *n.* a garnet containing calcium and iron, occurring in a variety of colors, such as red, yellow, green, and brown. *Formula:* $Ca_3Fe_2(SiO_4)_3$ [< José B. d'*Andrad*(a) e Silva, 1763-1838, a Brazilian mineralogist + English *-ite*]

An|dre|a Fer|ra|ra (an'drē ə fə rä'rə), *n.* a sword or sword blade of a kind greatly esteemed in Scotland toward the end of the 1500's and later.

An|drew (an'drü), *n.* one of Christ's twelve apostles, brother of Simon Peter (in the Bible, Mark 3:18). He is the patron saint of Greece, Russia, and Scotland.

an|dro|cen|tric (an'drə sen'trik), *adj.* having man or the male as its center. [< Greek *anêr, andrós* man + English *centric*]

An|dro|cles (an'drə klēz), *n. Roman Legend.* a slave spared in the arena by a lion from whose foot he had pulled a thorn years before.

an|dro|clin|i|um (an'drə klin'ē əm), *n., pl.* **-i|a** (-ē ə). = clinandrium. [< New Latin *androclinium* < Greek *anêr, andrós* man + *klīnê* bed, couch]

An|dro|clus (an'drə kləs), *n.* = Androcles.

an|dro|co|ni|um (an'drə kō'nē əm), *n., pl.* **-ni|a** (-nē ə). a patch of scent scales on the wings of male butterflies. [< New Latin *androconium* < Greek *anêr, andrós* man + *kónis* dust]

an|droc|ra|cy (an drok'rə sē), *n.* the rule of man or the male; male supremacy: *The stage of gynecocracy was succeeded by the stage of androcracy, and the subjection of women was rendered complete* (Lester E. Ward). [< Greek *anêr, andrós* man + *kratós* rule]

an|dro|crat|ic (an'drə krat'ik), *adj.* of or having to do with androcracy.

an|droe|cial (an drē'shəl), *adj.* of or having to do with an androecium.

an|droe|ci|um (an drē'shē əm, -sē-), *n., pl.* **-ci|a** (-shē ə, -sē-). a name given to the whole of the male organs of a flower; the stamens of a flower (correlative to *gynoecium*). [< New Latin *androecium* < Greek *anêr, andrós* man + *oikíon* (diminutive) < *oîkos* house]

an|dro|gen (an'drə jən), *n.* any sex hormone, produced especially by the testes, that induces or strengthens masculine characteristics, such as a beard, large muscles, or a deep voice: *The androgens and estrogens are not sex specific. . . . Both are present in varying amounts in normal men and women* (Science News Letter). [< Greek *anêr, andrós* man + English *-gen*]

an|dro|gen|ic (an'drə jen'ik), *adj.* of or having to do with an androgen. —**an'dro|gen'i|cal|ly,** *adv.*

an|dro|ge|nic|i|ty (an'drə jə nis'ə tē), *n.* the capability of a hormone or other substance to strengthen masculine characteristics.

an|dro|gyne (an'drə jīn, -jin), *n.* **1** *Botany.* an androgynous plant. **2** = hermaphrodite. [< Latin *androgynus* < Greek *andrógynos* < *anêr, andrós* man + *gynê* woman]

an|drog|y|nous (an droj'ə nəs), *adj.* **1** *Botany.* having flowers with stamens and flowers with pistils in the same cluster. **2** = hermaphroditic. **3** of or for both sexes: *Dress will become more androgynous, with class symbols becoming more important than sexual ones* (Time).

an|drog|y|ny (an droj'ə nē), *n.* = hermaphroditism.

an|droid (an'droid), *n., adj.* —*n.* an automaton in the form of a human being. —*adj.* of or having to do with a male: *android glands.* [< New Latin *androides* < Greek *anêr, andrós* man + *eîdos* form]

an|droi|des (an droi'dēz), *n.* = android.

an|drol|o|gy (an drol'ə jē), *n.* the study of male fertility, especially of disorders of the male reproductive system. [< Greek *anêr, andrós* man + English *-logy*] —**an|drol'o|gist,** *n.*

An|drom|a|che (an drom'ə kē), *n. Greek Legend.* the brave and loyal wife of Hector, prince of Troy.

An|drom|e|da (an drom'ə də), *n., genitive* (def. 2) **An|drom|e|dae. 1** *Greek Legend.* a princess of Ethiopia who was chained to the side of a rock as a sacrifice to a sea monster in order to save her country. Perseus killed the monster and married Andromeda. **2** a northern constellation, between Perseus and Pegasus, containing the only spiral nebula in the Northern Hemisphere visible to the unaided eye. **3** Also, **andromeda.** the horticultural name for any one of several evergreen shrubs of the heath family.

An|drom|e|dae (an drom'ə dē), *n.* genitive of **Andromeda** (the constellation).

An|drom|e|did (an drom'ə did), *n.* a shower of meteors occurring in late November and appearing to radiate from a point in the constellation Andromeda: *The Leonids are remarkably swift; the Andromedids surprisingly slow* (Pall Mall Gazette).

an|dro|sphinx (an'drə sfingks), *n.* a sphinx having the head of a man, as distinguished from one with the head of a ram (criosphinx) or of a hawk (hieracosphinx), one of the three types of the ancient Egyptian sphinx. [< Greek *anêr, andrós* man + English *sphinx*]

an|dro|spore (an'drə spôr, -spōr), *n.* = microspore. [< New Latin *androsporus* < Greek *anêr, andrós* man + *spóros* spore, seed]

an|dros|ter|one (an dros'tə rōn), *n.* a sex hormone conducive to certain male characteristics. *Formula:* $C_{19}H_{30}O_2$ [< Greek *anêr, andrós* man + English *ster*(ol) + *-one*]

An|dva|ri (än'dwä rē), *n. Norse Mythology.* a dwarf who was robbed by Loki of his treasure and a magic ring.

ane (ān), *adj., pron. Scottish.* one.

-ane, *suffix forming nouns. Chemistry.* a saturated carbon of the methane series, such as in *butane* or *propane.* [imitative formation patterned on *-ene, -ine,* etc.]

a|near (ə nir'), *adv., prep. Archaic.* near.

an|ec|do|ta (an'ik dō'tə), *n.pl.* historical detail which is unpublished. [see etym. under **anecdote**]

an|ec|dot|age (an'ik dō'tij), *n.* **1** anecdotes collectively. **2** *Humorous.* talkative old age.

an|ec|do|tal (an'ik dō'təl, an'ik dō'-), *adj.* of anecdotes; containing anecdotes: *This book is informal, anecdotal and easy to read.* —**an'ec|do'tal|ly,** *adv.*

an|ec|do|tal|ist (an'ik dō'tə list), *n.* = anecdotist.

an|ec|dote (an'ik dōt), *n.* a short account of some interesting incident or event, especially one in the life of a person: *Many anecdotes are told*

Pronunciation Key: hat, āge, cãre, fär; let, ēqual, tėrm; it, īce; hot, ōpen, ôrder; oil, out; cup, pu̇t, rüle; child; long; thin; ᴛʜen; zh, measure;
ə represents **a** in about, **e** in taken, **i** in pencil, **o** in lemon, **u** in circus.

about Abe Lincoln. SYN: See syn. under **story**[1].
anecdotes, secret, private, or previously unpublished narratives or details of history or biography: *Professing . . . to avoid anecdotes, I say nothing of those famous reconciliations and quarrels* (Edmund Burke). [< Medieval Latin *anecdota* < Late Greek *anékdota* (things) unpublished, ultimately < Greek *an-* not + *ek-* out + *didónai* give]

an|ec|dot|ic (an′ik dot′ik), *adj.* **1** = anecdotal. **2** always ready to tell anecdotes. —**an′ec|dot′i|cal|ly**, *adv.*

an|ec|dot|i|cal (an′ik dot′ə kəl), *adj.* = anecdotic.

an|ec|dot|ist (an′ik dō′tist), *n.* a person who relates anecdotes.

an|e|cho|ic (an′e kō′ik), *adj.* having or admitting no echoes: *an anechoic chamber.*

a|nele (ə nēl′), *v.t.,* **a|neled, a|nel|ing.** *Archaic.* **1** to administer extreme unction to (a person who is dying). **2** to anoint. [Middle English *anelien* < *an-* on + *elien* anoint < Old English *ele* < Latin *oleum* oil]

an|e|lec|tric (an′i lek′trik), *adj., n.* —*adj.* that cannot be electrified by friction.
—*n.* an anelectric substance.

a|ne|mi|a (ə nē′mē ə), *n.* **1** a weak condition caused by not enough red cells in the blood or by a loss of blood. It is characterized by pallor, palpitation of the heart, and a tendency to fatigue. **2** *Figurative.* lack of vigor or strength; weakness. Also, *especially British,* **anaemia.** [< New Latin *anaemia* < Greek *anaimíā* lack of blood < *an-* without + *haîma* blood]

a|ne|mic (ə nē′mik), *adj.* **1** of anemia; having anemia: *anemic symptoms, an anemic child.* **2** *Figurative.* lacking in vigor, strength, or spirit; weak: *an anemic economy, anemic defense.* —**a|ne′mi|cal|ly**, *adv.*

anemic anoxia, decrease in oxygen from the blood caused by deficiency in hemoglobin or alteration of the hemoglobin in the blood by chemicals.

a|nem|o|gram (ə nem′ə gram), *n.* a record of an anemograph. [< Greek *ánemos* wind + *-gram*[1]]

a|nem|o|graph (ə nem′ə graf, -gräf), *n.* = anemometer.

a|nem|o|graph|ic (ə nem′ə graf′ik), *adj.* of or having to do with an anemograph or anemography (anemometry).

an|e|mog|ra|phy (an′ə mog′rə fē), *n. Obsolete.* **1** = anemometry. **2** a treatise on the winds.

an|e|mo|log|i|cal (an′ə mə loj′ə kəl), *adj.* of or having to do with anemology.

an|e|mol|o|gy (an′ə mol′ə jē), *n.* the science of the winds. [< Greek *ánemos* wind + *-logy*]

***an|e|mom|e|ter** (an′ə mom′ə tər), *n.* an instrument for measuring the speed, or pressure, of the wind; wind gauge. [< Greek *ánemos* wind + English *-meter*]

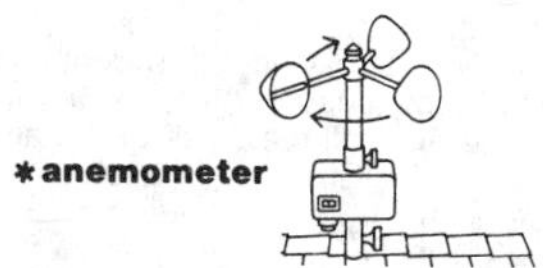
***anemometer**

an|e|mo|met|ric (an′ə mə met′rik), *adj.* of or having to do with an anemometer or anemometry.

an|e|mo|met|ri|cal (an′ə mə met′rə kəl), *adj.* = anemometric.

an|e|mo|met|ro|graph (an′ə mə met′rə graf, -gräf), *n.* = anemograph.

an|e|mom|e|try (an′ə mom′ə trē), *n.* the use of the anemometer; science or process of measuring wind speeds.

a|nem|o|ne (ə nem′ə nē), *n.* **1** a perennial plant of the crowfoot family, with a slender stem and small, white or colored flowers shaped like cups; windflower. It often blossoms early in the spring. The wood anemone is one common kind. **2** = sea anemone (a flowerlike polyp). [< Latin *anemōnē* < Greek *anemṓnē* windflower < *ánemos* wind]

an|e|moph|i|lous (an′ə mof′ə ləs), *adj.* fertilized by pollen carried by the wind, as the flowers of grasses, sedges, and pines; wind-pollinated. [< Greek *ánemos* wind + *phílos* loving (with English *-ous*)]

an|e|moph|i|ly (an′ə mof′ə lē), *n.* fertilization by pollen carried on the wind; wind-pollination.

a|nem|o|scope (ə nem′ə skōp), *n.* any instrument for showing or recording the direction of the wind, such as a weather vane. [< Greek *ánemos* wind + English *-scope*]

an|e|mo|sis (an′ə mō′sis), *n.* a condition of various trees in which the annual layers are separated from one another. It is supposed by some to be due to the action of strong winds upon the trunk, and by others to the action of frost or of lightning. [< Greek *ánemos* wind + English *-osis*]

an|en|ce|pha|li|a (an en′sə fā′lē ə), *n.* = anencephaly.

an|en|ce|phal|ic (an en′sə fal′ik), *adj.* = anencephalous.

an|en|ceph|a|lous (an′en sef′ə ləs), *adj.* lacking a brain.

an|en|ceph|a|lus (an′en sef′ə ləs), *n., pl.* **-li** (-lī). a creature without a brain. [< New Latin *anencephalus* < Greek *anenképhalos* < *an-* without + *enképhalos* brain]

an|en|ceph|a|ly (an′en sef′ə lē), *n.* the absence of a brain: *fetal anencephaly.*

an-end (an end′), *adv. Nautical.* in the direction of the length; directly ahead. [< *an,* obsolete variant of *on,* prep., + *end*]

a|nenst (ə nenst′), *prep.* = anent.

a|nent (ə nent′), *prep.* **1** concerning; about: *I note John DeLury's letter of Feb. 2, anent the rise of productivity of his workers* (Robert Hoskins). **2** *Dialect.* side by side with; beside. [Old English *on emn, on efn* on even (ground with); the *-t* is a later addition]

an|er|gy (an′ər jē), *n.* **1** lack of energy. **2** loss or weakening of an acquired immunity. [< Greek *anergíā* sluggishness, idleness < *an-* without + *érgon* work]

an|er|o|bic (an′ār ō′bik), *adj.* = anaerobic.

an|er|oid (an′ə roid), *adj., n.* —*adj.* using no liquid.
—*n.* = aneroid barometer.
[< French *anéroïde* < Greek *a-* without + Late Greek *nērón* water]

aneroid altimeter, an altimeter that uses air pressure to measure altitude.

***aneroid barometer**, a barometer that is worked by the pressure of air on the elastic lid of an air tight metal box from which the air has been pumped out. A change of pressure causes a pointer attached to the lid to move along a scale.

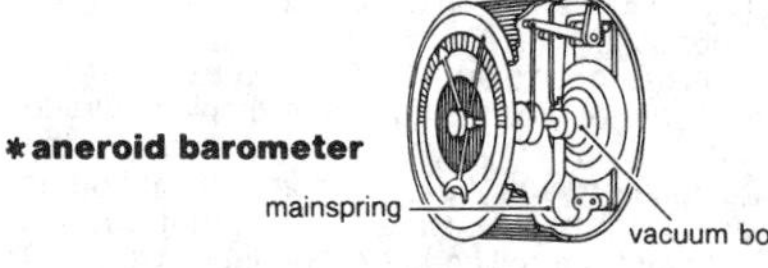

***aneroid barometer**

anes (āns), *adv. Scottish.* once.

an|es|the|sia (an′əs thē′zhə), *n.* loss of the feeling of pain, touch, cold, or other sensation. Anesthesia can be produced by ether, chloroform, novocaine, morphine, or other chemical agent, or by hypnotism, or as the result of hysteria, paralysis, or disease. The entire body (**general anesthesia**) or only a certain area or areas of the body (**local anesthesia**) may be affected. Also, *especially British,* **anaesthesia.** [< New Latin *anaesthesia* < Greek *anaisthēsíā* insensibility < *an-* without + *aísthēsis* sensation]

an|es|the|si|ol|o|gist (an′əs thē′zē ol′ə jist), *n.* a person, usually a doctor, who studies anesthesiology or is an expert in administering anesthesia, especially during an operation.

an|es|the|si|ol|o|gy (an′əs thē′zē ol′ə jē), *n.* the science of administering general and local anesthetics, especially in surgery.

an|es|the|sis (an′əs thē′sis), *n.* = anesthesia.

an|es|thet|ic (an′əs thet′ik), *n., adj.* —*n.* a substance that causes entire or partial loss of the feeling of pain, touch, cold, or other sensation. Ether, chloroform, and procaine are anesthetics used by doctors so that patients will feel no pain.
—*adj.* **1** causing anesthesia: *an anesthetic gas.* **2** of or with anesthesia. **3** *Figurative.* unfeeling.
—**an′es|thet′i|cal|ly**, *adv.*

an|es|the|tist (ə nes′thə tist), *n.* a person who administers anesthesia, especially during an operation. Also, *especially British,* **anaesthetist.**

an|es|the|tize (ə nes′thə tīz), *v.t.,* **-tized, -tiz|ing.** **1** to make (a person, animal, or area of the body) unable to feel pain, touch, cold, or other sensation; make insensible. **2** *Figurative.* to lessen or deaden (the emotional or critical response of a person). Also, *especially British,* **anaesthetise.**
—**an|es′the|ti|za′tion**, *n.* —**an|es′the|tiz′er**, *n.*

an|es|trum (an es′trəm, -ēs′-), *n. Zoology.* the inactive period of the estrous cycle. [< *an-*[1] not + *estrum*]

an|e|thole (an′ə thōl), *n.* the chief constituent of the essential oils of anise and fennel, used as a perfuming agent, especially in soaps and toothpastes. *Formula:* $C_{10}H_{12}O$ [< Latin *anēthum* anise + English *-ole*]

a|neuch (ə nüH′), *n., adj., adv. Scottish.* enough.

an|eu|ploid (an yü′ploid), *adj. Biology.* having a number of chromosomes not a multiple of the haploid number for the species. [< *an-* + Greek *eû* well + *-plous* -fold + *eîdos* form]

an|eu|rin (an′yər in; ə nyůr′-, -nůr′-), *n.* = vitamin B_1 (thiamin).

an|eu|rysm or **an|eu|rism** (an′yə riz əm), *n.* a permanent swelling of an artery or vein, caused by pressure of the blood on a weakened part. Aneurysms are caused congenitally or by disease or injury. [< Greek *aneúrysma* < *ana-* up + *eurýs* wide]

an|eu|rys|mal or **an|eu|ris|mal** (an′yə riz′məl), *adj.* **1** of or caused by aneurysm. **2** affected with aneurysm.

a|new (ə nü′, -nyü′), *adv.* **1** once more; again: *He made so many mistakes he had to begin his work anew.* **2** in a new form or different way: *The architect planned the building anew.* [Old English *of niowe*]

an|frac|tu|os|i|ty (an frak′chů os′ə tē), *n., pl.* **-ties.** **1** the quality or state of being full of windings and turnings. **2** a passage, channel, or crevice full of turnings and windings.

an|frac|tu|ous (an frak′chů əs), *adj.* full of windings and turnings; sinuous; roundabout; circuitous: *On the coast, the anfractuous cliffs are dotted with a series of promontory forts made long before the dawn of history* (Atlantic). [< Late Latin *ānfrāctuōsus* < Latin *ānfrāctus, -ūs* a winding < *an-,* for *ambi-* about, + *frangere* break]

ANG (no periods), American Newspaper Guild.

an|ga|ry (ang′gər ē), *n.* the right of a belligerent nation to seize, use, or destroy property belonging to neutrals. [< Late Latin *angārīa* forced service < Greek *angāreíā* office of the ángaros a messenger]

an|ge|kok or **an|ga|kok** (ang′gə kok), *n.* an Eskimo sorcerer, medicine man, or shaman.

an|gel (ān′jəl), *n., v.* —*n.* **1** a messenger from God; (in some religious beliefs) one of an order of spiritual beings that are attendants of God: *The angels told the shepherds about the birth of Christ.* SYN: seraph, cherub. **2** a conventional representation of such a being, usually as a winged human figure clothed in white: *Angels are painted fair* (Thomas Otway). **3** *Figurative.* a person as pure, innocent, good, or lovely as an angel: *She is an angel among women.* **4** any supernatural (but not divine) spirit, either good or bad: *Every man hath a good and a bad angel attending on him in particular, all his life long* (Robert Burton). **5** *Figurative.* a guardian or attendant spirit: *I to her became Her guardian and her angel* (Tennyson). **6** *Figurative.* a messenger; herald: *Soft breezes, the angels of Spring.* SYN: harbinger. **7** *U.S. Slang.* a person who pays for producing a play; financial backer; sponsor: *But in any show, the initial cost is not nearly so important as operating expenses. They determine how soon—if ever—an angel gets his money back* (Newsweek). **8** an English gold coin in use between 1465 and 1634. **9** an unexplained, invisible phenomenon that causes a radar echo.
—*v.t. U.S. Slang.* to provide financial backing or support for (a play, or other theatrical production). SYN: sponsor, subsidize, finance.

on the side of the angels, on the virtuous or right side; acting worthily or honorably: *O'Brien has been reviled as have few international men . . . but his book reassures one that in his fierce way he was on the side of the angels, something his friends would not doubt* (Canadian Forum).
[< Old French *angele,* learned borrowing from Latin *angelus* < Greek *ángelos* (originally) messenger]

angel cake, *Especially U.S.* angel food cake.

angel dust, *U.S. Slang.* a powerful drug, phencyclidine or PCP, that acts as a depressant. It is used as a narcotic, especially by smoking it when sprinkled on marijuana, mint leaves, or parsley. *Angel dust . . . can create paranoia, restlessness, manic agitation—and it can masquerade as other drugs because its effects sometimes resemble hallucinogens like LSD, or stimulants or depressants* (New York Daily News).

An|ge|le|no (ān′jə lē′nō), *n., pl.* **-nos** or **-noes.** *U.S. Informal.* a native or inhabitant of Los Angeles, California.

an|gel|et (an′jə let), *n.* **1** a little angel. **2** *Obsolete.* a gold coin of half the value of an angel (def. 8). [< Old French *angelet,* diminutive of *angele* angel]

***angelfish**

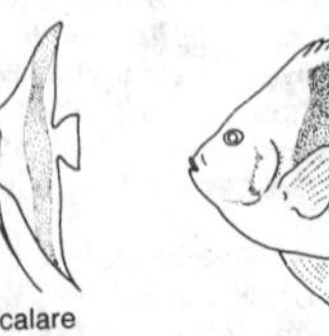
scalare

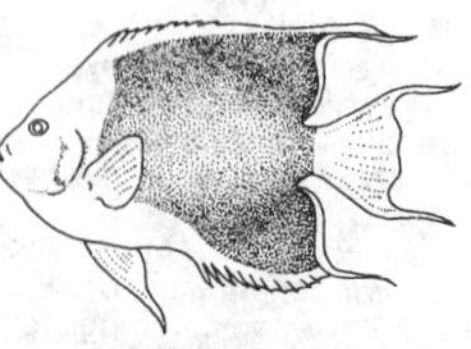
rock beauty

***an|gel|fish** (ān′jəl fish′), *n., pl.* **-fish|es** or (*collectively*) **-fish.** **1** any one of several colorful, tropical marine fish with spiny fins. **2** = scalare.

angel food cake, *Especially U.S.* a very light,

white cake made of the whites of eggs beaten very stiff, with sugar and flour.

an|gel|ic (an jel′ik), *adj.* **1** of angels; heavenly: *angelic messengers. The saint had an angelic vision.* **2** like an angel; pure, innocent, good, or lovely: *an angelic woman. The little baby had an angelic face.* **—an|gel′i|cal|ly,** *adv.*

an|gel|i|ca (an jel′ə kə), *n.* a tall perennial plant of the parsley family used in cooking, in medicine, for flavoring, and in making perfume. Candied angelica is cut into shapes to decorate cakes, etc. [< Medieval Latin *angelica* (from its use as an antidote)]

an|gel|i|cal (an jel′ə kəl), *adj.* = angelic.

angelica oil, a colorless or pale-yellow, aromatic oil obtained from the root or seeds of angelica, used for flavoring.

angelica tree, *U.S.* a small, prickly tree, the Hercules'-club.

angel light, a small, triangular light in the upper and outer part of an arched window, next to the point where the arch springs in Gothic architecture.

an|gel|ol|o|gy (ān′jə lol′ə jē), *n.* the branch of theology that deals with angels.

***an|gel|shark** (ān′jəl shärk′), *n.* a shark having large fins which spread out like wings.

***angelshark**

an|gel|skin (ān′jəl skin′), *n.* = peau d'ange.

an|gels-on-horse|back (ān′jəlz on hôrs′bak′, -ôn-), *n.pl.* oysters wrapped in bacon.

angel's trumpet, any plant of a genus of South American herbs of the nightshade family having large, trumpet-shaped flowers.

An|ge|lus or **an|ge|lus** (an′jə ləs), *n.* **1** a prayer said by Roman Catholics in memory of Christ's assuming human form. **2** the bell **(Angelus bell)** rung at morning, noon, and evening to signal the times this prayer is said. [< Latin *angelus* (the first word in the service)]

an|ger (ang′gər), *n., v.* **—*n.*** **1** the feeling one has toward something or someone that hurts, opposes, offends, or annoys; strong displeasure: *In a moment of anger I hit my brother.* **2** *Dialect.* a painful inflammation. **3** *Obsolete.* grief; trouble. **—*v.t.*** **1** to make angry; arouse anger in: *The boy's disobedience angered his father.* **2** *Dialect.* to irritate or inflame (a sore or wound). **—*v.i.*** to become angry: *He angers easily.* [< Scandinavian (compare Old Icelandic *angr* grief)]
—*Syn.* *n.* **1 Anger, indignation, wrath** mean the feeling of strong displeasure turned against anyone or anything that has hurt or wronged us or others. **Anger** is the general word for the emotion: *He never speaks in anger.* **Indignation,** more formal, means intense anger mixed with scorn, caused by something mean or base and therefore often justified: *The atrocity caused widespread indignation.* **Wrath,** a formal word, means great anger or indignation accompanied by a desire to punish: *the wrath of Achilles. to provoke the wrath of God.*

an|ger|ly (ang′gər lē), *adv. Archaic.* with anger or resentment.

An|ge|vin (an′jə vin), *adj., n.* **—*adj.*** **1** of or from Anjou (old province of France). The Plantagenet family of the kings of England was Angevin. **2** of or belonging to the Plantagenet family.
—*n.* **1** a member of the Plantagenet family. **2** a native or inhabitant of Anjou.
[< French *Angevin* < Medieval Latin *Andegavinus* < *Andegarum* Angers, city in western France]

An|ge|vine (an′jə vin, -vīn), *adj., n.* = Angevin.

an|gi|na (an jī′nə; *in medicine often* an′jə nə), *n.* **1** = angina pectoris. **2** any sudden, acute pain. **3** any inflammation of the throat, such as quinsy, croup, or mumps. [< Latin *angīna* quinsy < *angere* to choke]

an|gi|nal (an jī′nəl), *adj.* of or characterized by angina or angina pectoris.

angina pec|to|ris (pek′tər is), a condition of the heart marked by sharp chest pains and a feeling of suffocation. It is usually associated with a diminished supply of blood to the heart's muscle. [< New Latin *angina pectoris* angina of the chest]

an|gi|nose (an′jə nōs), *adj.* = anginal.

an|gi|nous (an′jə nəs), *adj.* = anginal.

an|gi|o|car|di|o|gram (an′jē ō kär′dē ə gram), *n.* an X-ray photograph of the heart and the thoracic blood vessels. [< Greek *angeîon* receptacle + *kardíā* heart + English *-gram*]

an|gi|o|car|di|o|graph|ic (an′jē ō kär′dē ə graf′ik), *adj.* of or having to do with an angiocardiogram or angiocardiography.

an|gi|o|car|di|og|ra|phy (an′jē ō kär′dē og′rə fē), *n., pl.* **-phies.** examination of the heart and of the thoracic blood vessels by X-ray photography or a fluoroscope. [< Greek *angeîon* receptacle + *kardíā* heart + English *-graphy*]

an|gi|o|car|pous (an′jē ō kär′pəs), *adj.* having a fruit enclosed in a distinct covering. [< New Latin *angiocarpus* (with English *-ous*) < Greek *angeîon* receptacle + *karpós* fruit]

an|gi|o|e|de|ma (an′jē ō i dē′mə), *n.* an allergic condition marked by urticarial swellings on the skin and mucous membranes. [< Greek *angeîon* receptacle + English *edema*]

an|gi|o|gen|in (an′jē ō jen′in), *n.* a protein that promotes the growth of new blood vessels, discovered in human cancer tissue: *Artificially administered angiogenin could be of great benefit to the victims of heart disease by causing new blood vessels to grow in the heart* (Thomas H. Maugh II).

an|gi|o|gram (an′jē ō gram′), *n.* an X-ray photograph of blood vessels, especially of the heart, by the injection of a radiopaque substance into the blood vessels.

an|gi|o|graph|ic (an′jē ō graf′ik), *adj.* of or having to do with angiography.

an|gi|og|ra|phy (an′jē og′rə fē), *n., pl.* **-phies.** X-ray examination of blood vessels by injection of a radiopaque substance into blood vessels.

an|gi|ol|o|gist (an′jē ol′ə jist), *n.* a person who studies angiology or is an expert in angiographic examination.

an|gi|ol|o|gy (an′jē ol′ə jē), *n.* the branch of anatomy that deals with the blood and lymphatic vessels. [< Greek *angeîon* receptacle + *-logy*]

an|gi|o|ma (an′jē ō′mə), *n., pl.* **-mas, -ma|ta** (-mə tə). a tumor produced chiefly by the enlargement of blood or lymphatic vessels. [< New Latin *angioma* < Greek *angeîon* receptacle + *-ōma* -oma]

an|gi|om|a|tous (an′jē om′ə təs, -ō′mə-), *adj.* of or having to do with an angioma or angiomas.

an|gi|o|neu|rot|ic edema (an′jē ō nů rot′ik, -nyů-), = angioedema.

an|gi|o|plas|ty (an′jē ō plas′tē), *n.* a surgical procedure for clearing a passage in an artery, especially by threading a small balloon through the artery and inflating it to clear blood clots and fatty deposits. [< Greek *angeîon* receptacle + *-plastia* a molding]
—an′gi|o|plas′tic, *adj.*

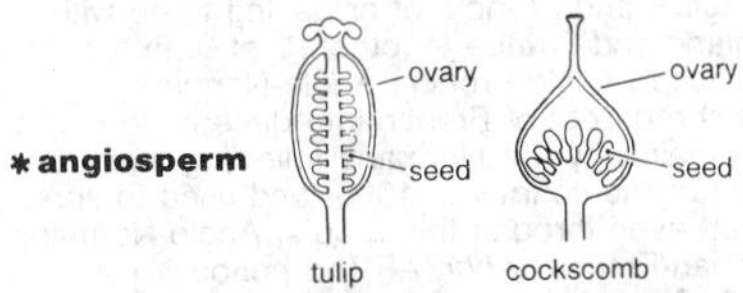

***angiosperm**

***an|gi|o|sperm** (an′jē ə spėrm), *n.* any plant having its seeds enclosed in an ovary or fruit; a flowering plant. Grasses, beans, strawberries, and oaks are angiosperms. The angiosperms are one of the two large subdivisions into which the seed-bearing plants are divided. *Geologic history supports the statement that the angiosperms have been slowly but certainly replacing the gymnosperms during the last 100 million years* (Fred W. Emerson). [< New Latin *angiospermus* < Greek *angeîon* receptacle + *spérma* seed]

an|gi|o|sper|mal (an′jē ə spėr′məl), *adj.* = angiospermous.

an|gi|o|sper|mic (an′jē ə spėr′mik), *adj.* = angiospermous.

an|gi|o|sper|mous (an′jē ə spėr′məs), *adj.* having the seeds enclosed in an ovary.

an|gi|o|ten|sin (an′jē ō ten′sin), *n.* a peptide occurring in the blood that affects the caliber of blood vessels and otherwise alters blood pressure. [< Greek *angeîon* receptacle + English *tens*(ion) + *-in*]

an|gi|ot|o|my (an′jē ot′ə mē), *n., pl.* **-mies.** surgical incision or dissection of a blood or lymphatic vessel. [< Greek *angeîon* receptacle + *-tomíā* a cutting]

an|gi|o|to|nin (an′jē ō tō′nin), *n.* = angiotensin.

ang|klung (ang′klong), *n.* a musical instrument of Malaya and Indonesia, consisting of bamboo pipes of different lengths that are tuned to octaves. [< Malay *angklung*]

Angl., **1** Anglican. **2** Anglicized.

an|gle¹** (ang′gəl), *n., v.,* **-gled, -gling.** **—*n. **1** the space between two lines or surfaces that meet: *Angles are measured in degrees.* **2** the figure formed by two such lines or surfaces. See picture below. **3** the difference in direction between two such lines or surfaces, measured especially in degrees or parts of degrees: *The two roads lie at an angle of about 45 degrees.* **4** a corner of a building, room, or other structure: *We took a picture of the northeast angle of the church.* **5** *Informal, Figurative.* **a** a point of view; an approach to a task or problem often selected to achieve a particular result: *I would like to hear your angle in this dispute. We are dealing with the problem from a new angle.* **b** one aspect or phase of a problem or situation: *There are many angles to this question.* **6** *Slang.* a special, underhanded scheme to make profit; racket.
—*v.i.* **1** to move at an angle: *The chicken angled across the road.* **2** to turn or bend at an angle: *The road here angles to the right.*
—*v.t.* **1** to move or bend in angles. **2** to place at an angle or angles. **3** *Informal, especially U.S. Figurative.* to present (a report, narrative, item of news, or the like) with bias or prejudice; slant: *A good reporter does not angle his story.*
[< Old French *angle* < Latin *angulus*]

an|gle² (ang′gəl), *v.,* **-gled, -gling,** *n.* **—*v.i.*** **1** to fish with a hook and line. **2** *Figurative.* to try to get something by using tricks or schemes: *She angled for an invitation to his party by flattering him. For some years now the Soviet Union has been angling to detach Japan from the western powers* (London Times). **—*n.*** *Archaic.* a fishhook. [Old English *angel* fishhook]

angle bar, **1** a piece of iron or steel used to bolt together the ends of two rails on a railroad track; rail joint. **2** = angle iron.

angle brace, **1** a special brace to drill in corners otherwise difficult to reach. **2** = angle iron.

an|gled (ang′gəld), *adj.* **1** having an angle or angles. **2** placed at angles with each other.

an|gle|doz|er (ang′gəl dō′zər), *n.* a bulldozer with its blade set at a slant to push earth, snow, or other objects to one side.

angle iron, a strip of iron or steel in the shape of an angle, used for joining or bracing two or more pieces at an angle.

an|gle|me|ter (ang′gəl mē′tər), *n.* any one of various instruments used for measuring angles, especially a clinometer.

angle of aberration, the angle between the actual and the apparent position of a star or other heavenly body to an observer. See **aberration** (def. 5).

angle of attack, *U.S.* the acute angle between the chord of an airplane wing or other airfoil and the direction of the relative wind in flight.

angle of deviation, the angle between a ray of light that enters an optical device, prism, etc., and the ray, or any one of the rays, that emerges.

angle of dip, **1** the angle of downward inclination from the horizontal of the needle of a magnetic compass, ranging from 0 degrees at the magnetic equator to 90 degrees at either of the magnetic poles. **2** *Geology.* the angle of downward inclination from the horizontal in a plane of stratification.

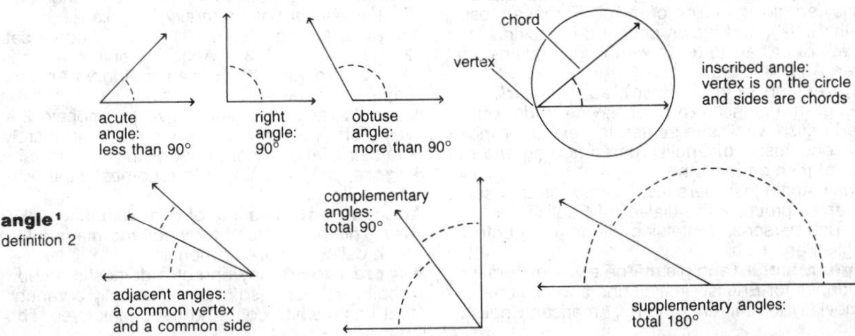

***angle¹** definition 2

Pronunciation Key: hat, āge, cãre, fär; let, ēqual, tėrm; it, īce; hot, ōpen, ôrder; oil, out; cup, půt, rüle; child; long; thin; ᴛʜen; zh, measure; ə represents **a** in about, **e** in taken, **i** in pencil, **o** in lemon, **u** in circus.

***angle of incidence**, 1 the angle that a line or ray of light, or the like, falling upon a surface makes with a line perpendicular to that surface. The angle of incidence is always equal to and adjacent to the angle of reflection. **2a** the angle between the longitudinal axis of an aircraft and the chord of a wing or other horizontal airfoil. **b** *British.* the angle of attack.

***angle of incidence**
definition 1
***angle of reflection**

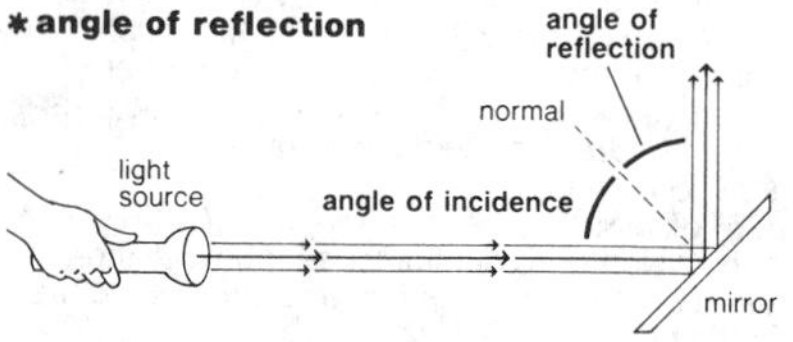

angle of reflection
normal
light source
angle of incidence
mirror

***angle of reflection**, the angle that a line or ray of light, or the like, reflected from a surface, makes with a line perpendicular to that surface.

angle of refraction, the angle that a ray of light or the like refracted at a surface separating two media makes with a line perpendicular to the surface.

angle of repose, the greatest angle of slope from the horizontal at which a heap of loose material will stand without slipping, sliding, or rolling. The angle varies according to the nature of the material.

angle of slip or **slide**, the minimum angle of slope from the horizontal at which loose material, such as earth, will flow or slide downward.

angle of stall, the angle of attack of an airfoil at which the flow of air about the airfoil changes abruptly so that lift is sharply reduced and drag is sharply increased.

angle plate, = angle iron.

an|gle|pod (ang′gəl pod′), *n.* any one of various plants of the milkweed family, especially a species of the southern and central United States.

an|gler (ang′glər), *n.* **1** a person who fishes with a hook and line, especially one who does so for sport. **2** *Figurative.* a person who tries to get something by using tricks and schemes. **3** Also, **angler fish.** a kind of saltwater fish of the Atlantic coasts of Europe and North America, that preys upon small fish which it attracts by the movement of wormlike tendrils or filaments attached to its head and mouth.

An|gles (ang′gəlz), *n.pl.* a West Germanic tribe that, with the Jutes and Saxons, invaded and settled in England in the 400's and 500's A.D. The Angles founded there the kingdoms of East Anglia, Mercia, and Northumbria, and from the Angles the name *England* is derived. [< Late Latin *Anglī* (compare Old English *engle* < *Angul* a district in Schleswig)]

angle shot, *U.S. Informal.* **1** any photograph, or motion-picture or television scene, taken by the camera at an angle, as from the side or upward from below. **2** *Sports.* the directing of a ball, puck, or the like, obliquely across a court, field, or rink.

an|gle|site (ang′glə sīt), *n.* native lead sulfate, occurring in crystalline or granular form. *Formula:* $PbSO_4$ [< *Angles*(ey), Wales, where first found + *-ite*[1]]

an|gle|smith (ang′gəl smith′), *n.* a blacksmith skilled in forging angle irons, beams, and other fittings, into the various forms used in shipbuilding.

an|gle|worm (ang′gəl wėrm′), *n.* = earthworm.

An|gli|a (ang′glē ə), *n.* the Latin name for England.

An|gli|an (ang′glē ən), *adj., n.* **—*adj.*** of or having to do with the Angles, their dialect, or their customs.
—*n.* **1** one of the Angles; an Angle. **2** the dialect of the Angles.

An|glic (ang′glik), *n., adj.* **—*n.*** a simplified form of English worked out by the Swedish scholar R. E. Zachrisson (1880-1937) for use as an auxiliary international language.
—*adj.* = Anglian.

An|gli|can (ang′glə kən), *adj., n.* **—*adj.*** **1** of or having to do with the Church of England or other churches of the same faith or in communion with it elsewhere. **2** *Especially U.S.* English.
—*n.* a member of an Anglican Church.
[< Medieval Latin *Anglicanus* < *Anglicus* English]

Anglican Church, = Church of England.

Anglican Communion, the Church of England and the churches elsewhere conforming with its doctrine and organization, such as the Church of Ireland, the Episcopal Church of Scotland, and the Protestant Episcopal Church of the United States.

An|gli|can|ism (ang′glə kə niz′əm), *n.* the principles and beliefs of the Church of England and other churches of the same faith elsewhere (the Anglican Communion).

An|gli|ce (ang′glə sē), *adv. Medieval Latin.* in English; as it would be said in English: *to visit München, Anglice Munich.*

an|gli|cise (ang′glə sīz), *v.t., v.i.,* **-cised, -cis|ing.** *British.* Anglicize.

An|gli|cism (ang′glə siz əm), *n.* **1** a custom or trait peculiar to the English. **2** *U.S.* a word, phrase, or meaning used in England, but not in widespread use in other English-speaking countries; a Briticism. **3** the state or quality of being characteristically English. [< Medieval Latin *Anglicus* English + English *-ism*]

An|gli|cist (ang′glə sist), *n. Especially U.S.* **1** a person who studies English linguistics. **2** = Anglist.

An|gli|ci|za|tion or **an|gli|ci|za|tion** (ang′glə sə zā′shən), *n.* the act or process of making or becoming English.

An|gli|cize or **an|gli|cize** (ang′glə sīz), *v.t., v.i.,* **-cized, -ciz|ing.** to make or become English in form, pronunciation, habits, customs, or character. "Cajole," "lace," and "cousin" are French words that have been Anglicized.

An|gli|fi|ca|tion (ang′glə fə kā′shən), *n.* = Anglicization.

An|gli|fy (ang′glə fī), *v.t.,* **-fied, -fy|ing.** = Anglicize.

an|gling (ang′gling), *n.* the act, art, or sport of fishing, especially with a hook and line.

An|glist (ang′glist), *n. U.S.* a person who studies England or its history, literature, and the like.

An|glis|tics (ang glis′tiks), *n.* English linguistics. [< *Angl*(o-) + (lingu)*istics*]

An|glo (ang′glō), *n., pl.* **-glos.** *U.S., Southwestern Slang.* a white American of other than Spanish or Mexican descent: *In New Mexico, the line drawn between "Anglo" and "Hispano" is a linguistic, not a racial one. ... The term Anglo designates the non-Hispano, non-Indian portion of the population, whose names may run from Gallagher to Goldstein* (Harper's). [< *Anglo-*]

Anglo-, *combining form.* **1** English: *Anglo-Catholic = English-Catholic.*
2 English and ____: *The Anglo-American alliance = the English-and-American alliance.*
[< Late Latin *Anglī* the English]

An|glo-A|mer|i|can (ang′glō ə mer′ə kən), *adj., n.* **—*adj.*** **1** English and American. **2** of or shared by Anglo-Americans.
—*n.* an American, especially a United States citizen, of English descent.

An|glo-Ca|na|di|an (ang′glō kə nā′dē ən), *adj., n.* **—*adj.*** **1** English and Canadian. **2** of or shared by Anglo-Canadians.
—*n.* a Canadian citizen of English descent.

An|glo-Cath|o|lic (ang′glō kath′ə lik, -kath′lik), *n., adj.* **—*n.*** a member of the Church of England who believes that the Reformation neither cut off nor altered its Catholicism and insists on its Catholic character.
—*adj.* **1** of or having to do with the Church of England as a Catholic church (contrasted with the Roman Catholic and Greek churches); emphasizing the Catholic character of the Church of England. **2** of or having to do with Anglo-Catholics, their practices, or their beliefs.

An|glo-Ca|thol|i|cism (ang′glō kə thol′ə siz əm), *n.* Anglo-Catholic beliefs and practices.

An|glo-French (ang′glō french′), *adj., n.* **—*adj.*** **1** English and French; of or having to do with England and France together. **2** of or in the dialect called Anglo-French; Anglo-Norman.
—*n.* the dialect of French introduced into England mainly by the Normans following their conquest of the country in 1066, and used to some extent even through the 1300's; Anglo-Norman; Norman-French. *Abbr:* AF (no periods).

An|glo-In|di|an (ang′glō in′dē ən), *n., adj.* **—*n.*** **1a** a person of British birth long resident in India, especially one who was, or belonged to the immediate family of, a British Indian civil servant, soldier, or the like. **b** the dialect of English spoken by such persons, containing many words taken directly from the native languages of India, especially Hindi. **2** (officially, in the Republic of India) an Indian citizen of mixed European, especially British, and Indian descent; Eurasian.
—*adj.* of or having to do with Anglo-Indians; that is an Anglo-Indian.

An|glo-I|rish (ang′glō ī′rish), *adj., n.* **—*adj.*** **1** English and Irish. **2a** of or having to do with the English who have settled in Ireland, or their descendants. **b** of English parentage on one side and of Irish on the other.
—*n.* **1** Anglo-Irish persons, thought of as a social or ethnic group. **2** the dialect of English spoken by such persons, containing elements of both English and Irish.

An|glo|ma|ni|a (ang′glə mā′nē ə), *n.* extreme fondness for English institutions and customs, especially for imitating them. [American English < *Anglo-* + Greek *maniā* madness]

An|glo|ma|ni|ac (ang′glə mā′nē ak), *n.* a person who is fond of and imitates the English, especially to an extreme degree in speech and manner; an extreme Anglophile.

An|glo-Nor|man (ang′glō nôr′mən), *n., adj.* **—*n.*** **1** one of the Normans who settled in England between 1066 and 1154. **2** a descendant of an English Norman. **3** = Anglo-French.
—*adj.* English and Norman. *Abbr:* AN (no periods).

An|glo-Nu|bi|an goat (ang′glō nü′bē ən), a breed of milk goat resulting from a cross between Nubian goats and goats from England.

An|glo|phil (ang′glə fil), *n.* = Anglophile.

An|glo|phile (ang′glə fīl, -fil), *n.* a person who greatly admires England, its people, and its culture.

An|glo|phil|i|a (ang′glə fil′ē ə), *n.* a devotion to England, its culture, or its people: *Unlike many Americans who work in England, Wallace has held to a calm course between Anglophilia and Anglophobia* (Newsweek).

An|glo|phil|i|ac (ang′glə fil′ē ak), *adj.* = Anglophilic.

An|glo|phil|ic (ang′glə fil′ik), *adj.* characterized by Anglophilia.

An|glo|phobe (ang′glə fōb), *n.* a person who has a great hatred, distrust, or fear of England or the English.

An|glo|pho|bi|a (ang′glə fō′bē ə), *n.* great hatred, distrust, or fear of England or the English.

An|glo|pho|bic (ang′glə fō′bik), *adj.* of or having to do with Anglophobia.

An|glo|phone or **an|glo|phone** (ang′glə fōn), *n., adj.* **—*n.*** an English-speaking inhabitant of a bilingual or multilingual country.
—*adj.* of Anglophones; English-speaking: *The Anglophone and Francophone clubs reflect the philosophy of Britain and France themselves* (C. L. Sulzberger).
[< French *anglophone* < *anglo-* Anglo- + *-phone* -phone]

An|glo-Sax|on (ang′glō sak′sən), *n., adj.* **—*n.*** **1** a member of the Germanic tribes that invaded England in the 400's and 500's A.D. and ruled most of England until the Norman Conquest in 1066. **2** his speech; the language of these tribes; Old English: *Old English is the best designation for the Germanic dialects of Britain before the Norman Conquest, though the less suitable Anglo-Saxon is often used* (H. A. Gleason, Jr.). **3** a member of the English-speaking world; person who in any period of history has spoken English. **4** a person of English descent. **5** the English language as spoken or written in any part of the world at any date; English. **6** *Figurative.* **a** plain English without long Latin or other foreign words. **b** English words considered too coarse for polite use.
—*adj.* **1** of the Anglo-Saxons. **2** of Anglo-Saxon. **3** having to do with any English-speaking people. *Abbr:* AS (no periods).
[< Medieval Latin *Anglo-Saxones* English Saxons]
▶ **Anglo-Saxon, Old English.** Since the development of the English language has been continuous and uninterrupted, most scholars now prefer to use the term *Old English* when referring to the language of the period before A.D. 1100. This usage is by no means universal, however, and the terms have been employed as exact synonyms in this sense.

An|glo-Sax|on|ism (ang′glō sak′sə niz əm), *n.* **1** the Anglo-Saxon character, spirit, tendencies, etc. **2** an Anglo-Saxon trait or usage.

an|goisse (äɴ gwäs′), *n. French.* **1** (in existentialist philosophy) the sense of fear and anxiety that leads man to question the meaning of life. **2** (literally) anguish.

an|go|la (ang gō′lə), *n.* = angora.

An|go|lan (ang gō′lən, an-), *adj., n.* **—*adj.*** of or having to do with Angola (a former Portuguese colony in southwestern Africa), its people, or their language.
—*n.* a native or inhabitant of Angola.

an|go|lar (ang′gō lär′), *n., pl.* **-la|res** (-lär′ēz). **1** a unit of Angolan money, worth about 3½ cents. **2** a piece of paper money worth one angolar. [< Portuguese *angolar* (literally) Angolan]

An|go|ra (ang gôr′ə, -gōr′-), *n.* **1** = Angora cat. **2** = Angora goat. **3** = Angora rabbit. **4** = mohair. **5** = angora (def. 2). [< earlier *Angora* Ankara, capital of Turkey]

an|go|ra (ang gôr′ə, -gōr′-), *n.* **1** = mohair. **2** a very fluffy yarn or fabric made partly or entirely of the hair of the Angora goat or the Angora rabbit.

Angora cat, a variety of the domestic cat with long, silky hair.

Angora goat, a variety of goat with long, silky hair. This hair is used for wool and made into a cloth called angora or mohair.

Angora rabbit, any one of a domestic breed of rabbits with long, soft hair, especially a variety that has a white coat and deep-pink eyes. The hair is used in making a very fluffy yarn or fabric.

Angora wool, the long, silky hair of the Angora goat, used for wool and made into a cloth called angora or mohair.

an|gos|tu|ra (ang′gə stůr′ə, -styůr′-), *n.* **1** Also, **angostura bark**. the bitter bark of a South American tree of the rue family. **2** Also, **Angostura**. = Angostura Bitters. [< Spanish *angostura* < *Angostura*, a town in Venezuela, from which it was imported]

Angostura Bitters, *Trademark.* a bitter tonic prepared from various barks and roots. It is used as flavoring in certain alcoholic drinks and sometimes in food.

An|gou|lême (äɴ′gyü lem′), *n.* a member of a branch of the royal house of Valois founded by Francis I. The Angoulêmes ruled France from 1515 to 1589.

An|gou|mois grain moth (äng′güm wä′), a moth whose larva infests stored grain. [< *Angoumois*, a former province of France from which it is supposed to have been introduced to the United States]

An|gra Main|yu (ang′grə mī′nyü), (in the Zoroastrian religion) an earlier name of **Ahriman**.

An|gries or **an|gries** (ang′grēz), *n.pl. Informal.* Angry Young Men: *"We're not Beatniks and we're not Angries," said another student* (Maclean's).

an|gri|ly (ang′grə lē), *adv.* in an angry manner; with anger or resentment.

an|gri|ness (ang′grē nis), *n.* **1** the quality of being angry; wrathfulness. **2** an inflamed condition of a wound.

an|gry (ang′grē), *adj.*, **-gri|er, -gri|est.** **1** feeling or showing anger; roused by anger: *I was very angry when he kicked my dog.* **SYN:** irate, enraged, furious, infuriated. **2** raging or stormy; characterized by or suggestive of anger: *The dark clouds made the sky look angry.* **3** expressing anger; moved or caused by anger: *My friend's angry words hurt my feelings.* **4** *Figurative.* inflamed and sore: *An infected cut looks angry.* **5** *Archaic.* irritable.
[< *anger*]

►**angry**. In reference to a thing, *angry at* and *angry about* are used: *I was angry at his slipshod work. Do you ever get angry about the cheating you see?* In reference to a person, *angry with* is general: *He was angry with his son.* Formal English uses *angry at* or *angry with,* making the following distinctions: when the angry feeling is being stressed, *at* is used; when the stress is on the directing of that anger upon a person, *with* is used: *We were angry at the boys for their tardiness. I was so angry with John that he drew back in fear.*

►See **mad** for another usage note.

Angry Young Man or **angry young man**, **1** one of a group of British writers of the 1950's and 1960's characterized by works that bitterly attack or satirize the social and political establishment of Great Britain. **2** any young intellectual rebel: *Burns' career as B.C.* (*British Columbia*) *radio's most popular angry young man was secure* (Maclean's).

Angst (ängst), *n. German.* inordinate fear, fright, or anxiety: *Her ill health and feelings of inferiority obsessed her with a sense of Angst* (Harold Nicolson).

ang|strom or **Ang|strom** (ang′strəm), *n.* = angstrom unit: *One angstrom is 10^{-8} centimeter* (Robert H. Baker).

angstrom or **Angstrom unit**, one ten-millionth of a millimeter, a unit of measurement of the wave length of light. *Symbol:* λ *Abbr:* A., A (no period), Å., A.U. [< Anders J. *Ångström,* 1814-1874, a Swedish physicist]

An|guil|lan (ang gwil′ən), *adj., n.* —*adj.* of or having to do with Anguilla (one of the Leeward Islands, in the West Indies) or its people.
—*n.* a native or inhabitant of Anguilla.

an|guil|li|form (ang gwil′ə fôrm), *adj.* shaped like an eel. [< Latin *anguilla* eel + English *-form*]

an|guine (ang′gwin), *adj.* of or resembling a snake; snakelike: *an anguine lizard.* [< Latin *anguīnus* < *anguis* snake]

an|guish (ang′gwish), *n., v.* —*n.* **1** very great physical pain; great suffering or distress: *He was in anguish until the doctor set his broken leg.* **SYN:** agony, torment. **2** *Figurative.* extreme mental pain or suffering: *the anguish of despair.* **SYN:** agony, torment, woe.
—*v.t.* to cause anguish to: (*Figurative.*) The loss of her son anguished her deeply.
—*v.i.* to suffer anguish: *He had waked and anguished* (John Keats).
[< Old North French *anguisse* < Latin *angustia* tightness < *angustus* narrow]

an|guished (ang′gwisht), *adj.* **1** suffering anguish; distressed with severe pain. **2** *Figurative.* full of grief or anguish; showing anguish; tormented: *an anguished cry. He saw the anguished face of the mother whose child was lost.*

an|gu|lar (ang′gyə lər), *adj.* **1** having an angle or angles; having sharp corners; pointed: *I cut my hand on an angular piece of rock.* **2** consisting of an angle: *an angular point.* **3** measured by an angle. **4** somewhat thin and bony; not plump: *Many basketball players have tall, angular bodies.* **SYN:** gaunt, lank. **5** *Figurative.* stiff and awkward: *angular movements.* **SYN:** clumsy, gawky. [< Latin *angulāris* < *angulus* angle] —**an′gu|lar|ly**, *adv.* —**an′gu|lar|ness**, *n.*

angular acceleration, the rate of change of angular velocity.

angular aperture, the angular breadth of the light which an optical instrument transmits from the point viewed.

angular diameter, = apparent diameter.

angular displacement, the amount of rotation of a rigid body about a fixed axis.

angular gyrus, a part of the left hemisphere of the brain, in which visual images of words are converted into their associated sounds.

an|gu|lar|i|ty (ang′gyə lar′ə tē), *n., pl.* **-ties**. the condition of having many angles or sharp or prominent corners; angular quality or form. **angularities**, sharp corners.

angular measure, = circular measure.

angular momentum, the product of the moment of inertia of a body and its angular velocity: *Angular momentum is . . . extremely important in connection with nuclear physics. Each elementary particle of physics, such as the proton and the neutron, has an angular momentum called spin* (John R. Peirce).

angular velocity, the rate of angular motion about an axis, usually expressed in radians per second.

an|gu|late (*adj.* ang′gyə lit, -lāt; *v.* ang′gyə lāt), *adj., v.*, **-lat|ed, -lat|ing.** —*adj.* **1** formed with corners; cornered. **2** angled; angular.
—*v.t.* to form with angles.
[< Latin *angulātus* < *angulus* angle] —**an′gu|late|ly**, *adv.*

an|gu|lat|ed (ang′gyə lā′tid), *adj.* = angulate.

an|gu|la|tion (ang′gyə lā′shən), *n.* angular formation.

An|gus (ang′gəs), *n.* **1** *Celtic Mythology.* the god of love. **2** = Aberdeen Angus (cattle).

an|gus|ti|fo|li|ate (ang gus′tə fō′lē it, -āt), *adj.* narrow-leaved. [< Latin *angustus* narrow + *folium* leaf + English *-ate*[1]]

an|har|mon|ic (an′här mon′ik), *adj. Physics.* not harmonic.

an|he|dral[1] (an hē′drəl), *adj. Crystallography.* having the molecular structure of a crystal but lacking its external form. [< *an-*[1] lacking + Greek *hédrā* seat, base, surface + English *-al*[1]]

an|he|dral[2] (an hē′drəl), *adj. Aeronautics.* of a wing or tail plane: **1** that slopes upward from the horizontal; positively dihedral. **2** (sometimes) that slopes downward from the horizontal; negatively dihedral. [< *an-*[3] up + Greek *hédrā* seat, base, surface + English *-al*[1]]

an|he|la|tion (an′hə lā′shən), *n.* shortness of breath; panting. [< Latin *anhēlātiō, -ōnis* < *anhēlāre* to pant]

an|hi|dro|sis (an′hə drō′sis), *n.* the inability to secrete perspiration. [< *an-* without + Greek *hidrōs* sweat + English *-osis* condition]

an|hi|drot|ic (an′hə drot′ik), *adj., n.* —*adj.* tending to stop perspiration.
—*n.* a substance or agent that tends to stop perspiration.

an|hin|ga (an hing′gə), *n.* = water turkey. [< Tupi (Brazil) *anhinga*]

an|his|tous (an his′təs), *adj. Biology.* having no recognizable structure. [< *an-* without + Greek *histós* web, tissue + English *-ous*]

an|hun|gered (ən hung′gərd), *adj.* **1** *Archaic.* hungry. **2** *Figurative.* craving; longing: *Anhungered for some joy untried* (James Russell Lowell).

an|hy|drate (an hī′drāt), *v.t.*, **-drat|ed, -drat|ing.** to remove water from; dehydrate. [< *an-* without + Greek *hýdōr* water + English *-ate*[1]]

an|hy|dra|tion (an′hī drā′shən), *n.* = dehydration.

an|hy|drid (an hī′drid), *n.* = anhydride.

an|hy|dride (an hī′drīd, -drid), *n.* **1** any oxide that unites with water to form an acid or base. Sulfur trioxide, SO_3, is the anhydride of sulfuric acid. An anhydride of a nonmetal or of an organic radical is an acid anhydride; an anhydride of a metal is a basic anhydride. **2** any compound which is formed by the removal of water. [< *anhydr*(ous) acid + *-ide*]

an|hy|drite (an hī′drīt), *n.* a white or grayish mineral consisting of anhydrous calcium sulfate, usually granular but sometimes crystalline. *Formula:* $CaSO_4$

an|hy|dro|glu|cose (an hī′drō glü′kōs), *n.* glucose in crystalline form, from which all water has been removed.

an|hy|drous (an hī′drəs), *adj.* **1** without water. **2** *Chemistry.* containing no water of crystallization; not hydrated: *anhydrous ammonia. Many crystals, like diamond, sulfur, quartz, sodium chloride, potassium chlorate, and others, are anhydrous* (Monroe M. Offner). [< Greek *ánydros* (with English *-ous*) < *an-* without + *hýdōr* water]

a|ni (ä′nē), *n., pl.* **a|nis**. a kind of cuckoo with black feathers, inhabiting the warmer parts of America; tickbird. [perhaps < a Tupi (Brazil) word]

an|i|con|ic (an′ī kon′ik), *adj.* not shaped into human form, especially of images of worship: *Certain aniconic sacred things . . . we may call fetishes—the hewn stock or pillar, the meteorite, the axe* (L. R. Farnell). [< *an-*[1] + *iconic*]

an|i|con|ism (an ī′kə niz əm), *n.* the use or worship of aniconic images.

a|nigh (ə nī′), *adv., prep. Dialect or Archaic.* nigh; near.

a|night (ə nīt′), *adv. Archaic.* at night; by night. [Old English *on niht*]

a|nights (ə nīts′), *adv. Archaic.* anight.

an|il (an′əl), *n.* **1** a West Indian shrub of the pea family, from the leaves and stalks of which indigo is made. **2** *Rare.* indigo. [< French *anil* < Portuguese < Arabic *an-nīl* the indigo < Sanskrit *nīlī* < *nīla* dark blue]

an|ile (an′īl, ā′nīl), *adj.* old-womanish; suitable for a weak or doting old woman. [< Latin anīlis < *anus* old woman]

an|i|lide (an′ə lid, -līd), *n.* any compound derived from aniline, containing the univalent radical C_6H_5NH-. [< *anil* + *-ide*]

an|i|lin (an′ə lin), *n.* = aniline.

an|i|line (an′ə lin, -līn), *n.* a poisonous, oily liquid, colorless when pure, obtained from coal tar and especially from nitrobenzene. It is a compound of carbon, nitrogen, and hydrogen and is used in making dyes, perfumes, certain medicines, plastics, and resins. *Formula:* $C_6H_5NH_2$ [< German *Anilin* < *Anil* indigo < French *anil;* see etym. under **anil**]

aniline dye, **1** any dye made from aniline. **2** any one of several chemically related dyes. **3** any artificial dye.

a|nil|i|ty (ə nil′ə tē), *n., pl.* **-ties**. **1** anile condition; dotage. **2** an anile act or notion. [< Latin *anīlitās* < *anīlis* anile]

►**Anility** is a much stronger word than **senility**, tending always to convey a definite feeling of contempt.

anim., *Music.* animato.

an|i|ma (an′ə mə), *n., pl.* **-mae** (-mē). *Latin.* life; soul.

an|i|mad|ver|sion (an′ə mad vėr′zhən, -shən), *n.* unfavorable comment; criticism: *As the years passed, and the royal mourning remained as unrelieved as ever, the animadversions grew more general and more severe* (Lytton Strachey). **SYN:** censure, blame. [< Latin *animadversiō, -ōnis* < *animadvertere;* see etym. under **animadvert**]

an|i|mad|vert (an′ə mad vėrt′), *v.i.* **1** to make criticisms; comment unfavorably; censure. **2** *Archaic.* to observe; remark; note. —*v.t. Obsolete.* to observe.
[< Latin *animadvertere* < *animus* mind + *ad-* to + *vertere* to turn] —**an′i|mad|vert′er**, *n.*

an|i|mal (an′ə məl), *n., adj.* —*n.* **1** any living thing that is not a plant. Most animals can move about, while most plants cannot. Animals feed upon other animals or plants. Many animals have a cavity for digestion and a nervous system, and can inhale oxygen and exhale carbon dioxide. A dog, a bird, a fish, a snake, a fly, and a worm are all animals. Animals are distinguished typically from plants by more advanced types of sensation and response to stimuli. **2** an animal other than man; brute; beast: *a farm stocked with pigs, cows, geese, and various other animals. Man has always considered himself closer to God than the animals are.* **3a** an animal with four feet; quadruped: *Man uses animals as beasts of burden: the elephant in the jungle, the water buffalo in or near the river and marsh, the donkey in the mountains, the horse on the plains, and the camel in the desert.* **b** any mammal, as distinguished from a bird, reptile, and other lower forms. **4** a person who is like a beast in the way that he acts or thinks; brutish or degenerate person: *His intellect is not replenished, he is only an animal, only sensible in the duller parts* (Shakespeare). **5** *Figurative.* any person or thing regarded as strange, different, or unusual: *Monique . . . hasn't yet grasped the English mentality—if there is such an animal* (Maclean's).
—*adj.* **1** of animals; relating to or connected with animals: *the animal world, animal fats.* **2** like that of animals; purely physical: *animal courage, animal cunning. What is important and inspiring . . . is the idea that the human spirit will be able to*

Pronunciation Key: hat, āge, cãre, fär; let, ēqual, tėrm; it, īce; hot, ōpen, ôrder; oil, out; cup, půt, rüle; child; long; thin; ᴛʜen; zh, measure; ə represents a in about, e in taken, i in pencil, o in lemon, u in circus.

master its animal nature through reason (Edmund Wilson). **3** sensual: *animal appetites.*
[< Latin *animal* living being < *anima* life, breath] —**an′i|mal|like′**, *adj.*

—*Syn. n.* **2 Animal, beast, brute** mean a living creature of a lower order than man. **Animal**, the general word, usually suggests nothing more: *He likes animals. Be kind to animals.* **Beast** usually applies to four-legged animals, as distinct from birds, insects, etc.: *We went to the zoo to see the gorillas, elephants, and various other beasts. The horse is a noble beast.* **Brute** emphasizes the lack of ability to reason, the ability popularly thought of as that which sets man apart from animals: *The poor brutes, maddened by fear, dashed back into the center of the fire.*

a|ni|mal bi|pes im|plu|me (an′ə məl bī′pēz im-plü′mē; ä′ni mäl bē′pās im plü′mä), *Latin.* an unfeathered, two-footed animal (a definition of man in the Latin version of Plato's *Politicus*).

animal charcoal, = boneblack.

animal crackers, *U.S.* slightly sweet cookies pressed and baked in the shapes of animals.

an|i|mal|cu|la (an′ə mal′kyə lə), *n.* plural of **animalculum.**

an|i|mal|cu|lae (an′ə mal′kyə lē), *n.pl.* animalcules. [< falsely assumed Latin singular *animalcula*, actually a plural form]

an|i|mal|cu|lar (an′ə mal′kyə lər), *adj.* of animalcules.

an|i|mal|cule (an′ə mal′kyül), *n.* **1** a very tiny animal, usually too small to be seen without the aid of a microscope: *Rotifers and protozoans are animalcules.* **2** *Archaic.* any very small animal, such as a mouse or insect. [< New Latin *animalculum* (diminutive) < Latin *animal* living being]

an|i|mal|cu|line (an′ə mal′kyə lin), *adj.* = animalcular.

an|i|mal|cu|lum (an′ə mal′kyə ləm), *n., pl.* **-la.** = animalcule.

animal flower, a flowerlike animal, such as the sea anemone; a zoophyte.

animal heat, the temperature maintained during life in the body of a warm-blooded vertebrate animal, and necessary for its physiological functions.

animal husbandman, a person skilled in animal husbandry.

animal husbandry, the breeding, raising, and care of farm animals.

an|i|mal|ier (an′ə mə lir′), *n.* an artist who specializes in animal subjects; animalist. [< French *animalier* < *animal* animal]

an|i|mal|ism (an′ə mə liz′əm), *n.* **1** the doctrine that human beings are mere animals without souls. **2** animal existence, nature, activity, or enjoyment: *the healthy animalism of young boys.*

an|i|mal|ist (an′ə mə list), *n.* **1** a believer in animalism. **2** a sensualist. **3** an artist whose chief subject is animal life.

an|i|mal|is|tic (an′ə mə lis′tik), *adj.* **1** of animalism or animalists. **2** = sensual.

an|i|mal|i|ty (an′ə mal′ə tē), *n.* **1** animal nature or character in man. **2** animal life. **3** = animal kingdom.

an|i|mal|ize (an′ə mə līz), *v.t.,* **-ized, -iz|ing. 1** to convert into animal matter, as food by assimilation. **2** to brutalize; sensualize: *It does not bring about ... [an] animalizing of the human, but rather it celebrates man at his human best* (London Times). —**an′i|mal|i|za′tion**, *n.*

animal kingdom, all animals, as distinguished from plants or minerals.

an|i|mal|ly (an′ə mə lē), *adv.* = physically.

animal magnetism, **1** the power to attract physically; physical charm: *... the power of animal magnetism and money in the competition for the top girl* (Atlantic). **2** hypnotism; mesmerism.

animal park, a zoo where animals live in open surroundings similar to their natural habitats instead of being displayed in cages: *In the new animal parks now opening all over the United States ..., animals have the space in which to interact with their own and other species in a natural way* (Barbara Ford).

animal pole, that part of the surface of an egg or ovum having the least yolk, in which is found the most vital protoplasm in the embryo.

animal protein factor, vitamin B_{12} added to animal feed to stimulate growth.

animal spirits, natural liveliness; healthy cheerfulness.

animal starch, = glycogen.

an|i|mate (*v.* an′ə māt; *adj.* an′ə mit), *v.,* **-mat|ed, -mat|ing,** *adj.* —*v.t.* **1** to make lively, gay, or vigorous: *His arrival animated the whole party. Our teacher is able to animate a lecture on a dull subject with witty remarks.* **SYN**: enliven. **2** to arouse to action of any kind: **a** to inspire; encourage: *The soldiers were animated by their captain's brave speech.* **SYN**: inspirit, embolden. **b** to move mentally; stir up; incite: *the motives which animate that great man.* **SYN**: prompt. **3a** to put in motion by causing to act or work: *Windmills are animated by the wind. Among the things the Americans showed were the Lionel train, a model of Norris Dam, some sewing machines, and some mechanical saws—all animated* (New Yorker). **SYN**: actuate, automate. **b** to prepare in the form of an animated cartoon: *to animate a film sequence.* **4a** to be a motive or reason for; give life to; make alive: *Love for her mother animated Alice's work. Poetry, that force which ... animates matter* (Samuel Johnson). **SYN**: quicken, vivify. **b** *Figurative.* to cause to move as if alive: *a field of corn animated by the wind.*

—*adj.* **1** having life; living. Animate nature means all living plants and animals. *Scientists now believe there are many worlds in outer space having animate beings.* **SYN**: alive. **2** lively; vigorous; animated.

[< Latin *animāre* (with English *-ate*[1]) < *anima* life, breath] —**an′i|mate|ly**, *adv.* —**an′i|mat′er**, *n.*

an|i|mat|ed (an′ə mā′tid), *adj.* **1** lively; vigorous: *The boys had an animated discussion about yesterday's baseball game.* **SYN**: spirited. **2** gay; joyful: *an animated smile.* **SYN**: vivacious, buoyant. **3** *Figurative.* seeming to be alive; simulating life: *animated dolls working on batteries.* **4** living; alive; animate. —**an′i|mat′ed|ly**, *adv.*

animated cartoon or **animated drawing**, a series of drawings arranged to be photographed and shown as a motion picture. Each drawing shows a slight change from the one before it, so that when projected in rapid sequence the figures appear to move.

an|i|mat|ing (an′ə mā′ting), *adj.* **1** giving life. **2** rendering lifelike. **3** inspiring; enlivening: *The talk was incessant and animating* (John Tyndall). —**an′i|mat′ing|ly**, *adv.*

an|i|ma|tion (an′ə mā′shən), *n.* **1** liveliness of manner; vigor; spirit: *The boy acted his part as a pirate with great animation.* **SYN**: vivacity. **2** an animating or being animated: *a case of suspended animation.* **SYN** enlivening. **3** the preparation of an animated cartoon. **4** life. **SYN**: aliveness.

an|i|ma|tism (an′ə mə tiz′əm), *n.* the belief that inanimate objects have a form of life and are conscious beings: *Animatism apparently never gives rise to religious sentiments, nor does it inspire the worship of the object said to be animated* (Beals and Hoijer).

a|ni|ma|to (ä′ni mä′tō), *adj. Music.* lively; gay; vigorous; with spirit. [< Italian *animato*]

an|i|ma|tor (an′ə mā′tər), *n.* **1** a person or thing that animates. **2** an artist who makes the drawings forming an animated cartoon.

an|i|mé (an′ə mā, -mē), *n.* any one of several resins or copals, especially: **a** a resin obtained from a tropical American tree, used especially in making varnish. **b** = elemi. [< French *animé* < a native word]

an|i|mism (an′ə miz əm), *n.* **1** the belief that there are living souls in trees, stones, stars, and other objects traditionally thought of as being without souls: *It should be noted that animism, especially where it involves the belief in spirits who dwell in pools, trees, or other similar things, must be distinguished from animatism* (Beals and Hoijer). **2** the belief in the existence of soul distinct from matter; belief in spiritual beings, such as souls, angels, and devils. [< Latin *anima* life, breath, soul + English *-ism*]

a|ni|mis o|pi|bus|que pa|ra|ti (an′ə mis ō′pə-bus′kwē pə rā′tī; ä′ni mēs ō′pi bùs′kwe pä rä′tē), *Latin.* prepared in mind and resources (one of two mottoes of South Carolina, the other being *dum spiro spero*).

an|i|mist (an′ə mist), *n.* a person who believes in some form of animism.

an|i|mis|tic (an′ə mis′tik), *adj.* of or having to do with animism.

an|i|mos|i|ty (an′ə mos′ə tē), *n., pl.* **-ties.** active dislike or enmity; keen hostile feelings; ill will; violent hatred: *Gossips soon earn the animosity of their neighbors.* **SYN**: hostility, hate. [< Latin *animōsitās* < *animōsus* spirited < *animus* spirit]

an|i|mus (an′ə məs), *n.* **1** violent hatred; ill will; active dislike or enmity; animosity. **2** moving spirit; intention. [< Latin *animus* spirit, feeling]

an|i|on (an′ī′ən), *n.* **1** a negatively charged ion. During electrolysis, anions move toward the positive pole (contrasted with *cation*). **2** an atom or group of atoms having a negative charge. [< Greek *aniṓn* (thing) going up, present participle neuter of *aniénai* go up < *ana-* up + *iénai* go]

anion exchange, ion exchange in which the negative ions are exchanged.

an|i|on|ic (an′ī on′ik), *adj.* of or having to do with an anion or anions.

an|i|rid|i|a (an′ī rid′ē ə), *n.* a congenital absence of or defect in the iris of the eye. [< New Latin *aniridia* < Greek *an-* without + *îris, íridos* iris]

a|nis (ä nēs′), *n.* a type of anisette made in Spain. [< Spanish *anís*]

anis-, *combining form.* the form of **aniso-** before vowels, as in *aniseikonia.*

an|is|al|de|hyde (an′ə sal′də hīd), *n.* a pale-yellow liquid, used in perfumes. *Formula:* $C_8H_8O_2$ [< *anis-* + *aldehyde*]

an|ise (an′is), *n.* **1** a plant of the same family as the carrot and parsley, grown especially for its fragrant seeds. **2** the seed, used as a flavoring or in medicine; aniseed. [< Old French *anis*, learned borrowing from Latin *anīsum* < Greek *ánīson*]

an|i|seed (an′ə sēd, an′is sēd′), *n.* the fragrant seed of the anise, used as a flavoring in certain foods and drinks, or in medicine. Its flavor is somewhat like that of licorice. [< *ani*(se) + *seed*]

an|is|ei|ko|ni|a (an′ī sī kō′nē ə), *n.* a condition characterized by the formation of an image in one eye which differs in size or shape from that formed in the other. [< New Latin *aniseikonia* < *ánisos* unequal + Greek *eikṓn* image]

an|is|ei|kon|ic (an′ī sī kon′ik), *adj.* **1** of or having to do with aniseikonia. **2** resembling or characterized by aniseikonia.

anise oil, the essential oil obtained from aniseed, the source of many important chemical derivatives, also used in absinthe and in medicines.

anise seed, = aniseed.

an|i|sette (an′ə zet′, -set′), *n.* a liqueur flavored with aniseed. [< French *anisette* (diminutive) < *anise* anise]

aniso-, *combining form.* **1** unequal: *Anisopterous = having unequal wings.* **2** unlike: *Anisodactylous = having the toes unlike.* Also, **anis-** before vowels. [< Greek *ánisos* < *an-* not + *ísos* like, equal]

an|i|so|car|pic (an ī′sə kär′pik, an′ī-), *adj.* having fewer carpels than other floral parts. [< *aniso-* + Greek *karpós* fruit + English *-ic*]

an|i|so|cy|to|sis (an ī′sə sī tō′sis, an′ī-), *n.* inequality in the size of the red blood corpuscles. [< *aniso-* + *-cyte* + *-osis*]

an|i|so|dac|ty|lous (an ī′sə dak′tə ləs, an′ī-), *adj.* having the toes unlike. [< *aniso-* + *dactyl* + *-ous*]

an|i|so|ga|mete (an ī′sə gə mēt′, -gam′ēt; an′ī-), *n.* either of a pair of conjugating gametes that differ from each other in form or size. [< *aniso-* + *gamete*]

an|i|sog|a|mous (an′ī sog′ə məs), *adj.* of or characterized by anisogamy.

an|i|sog|a|my (an′ī sog′ə mē), *n.* the conjugation of dissimilar gametes, among protozoans and thallophytes. [< *aniso-* + *-gamy*]

an|i|sole (an′ə sōl), *n.* a compound used in perfumery and as a solvent. *Formula:* C_7H_8O [< *anis*(e) + *-ole*]

an|i|som|er|ous (an′ī som′ər əs), *adj.* **a** having irregular or asymmetrical floral parts. **b** having unequal numbers of parts in each whorl. [< *aniso-* + Greek *méros* part + English *-ous*]

an|i|so|met|ric (an ī′sə met′rik, an′ī-), *adj.* of unequal measurement; having nonsymmetrical parts; not isometric: *anisometric crystals.*

an|i|so|me|tro|pi|a (an ī′sə mə trō′pē ə, an′ī-), *n.* inequality in the refractive power of the two eyes. [< *aniso-* + Greek *métron* measure + *ṓps* eye]

an|i|sop|ter|ous (an′ī sop′tər əs), *adj.* having unequal wings. [< *aniso-* + Greek *pterón* wing + English *-ous*]

an|i|so|trop|ic (an ī′sə trop′ik, an′ī-), *adj.* **1** *Physics.* having different properties in different directions; aeolotropic (contrasted with *isotropic*). **2** *Botany.* responding differently or unequally to external stimuli. [< *aniso-* + Greek *tropḗ* a turning + English *-ic*] —**an|i′so|trop′i|cal|ly**, *adv.*

an|i|sot|ro|py (an′ī sot′rə pē), *n.* the state or quality of being anisotropic.

An|jou (an′jü), *n.* a variety of large, late-maturing, russet pears that originated in France but are widely grown in the United States.

an|ker (ang′kər), *n.* a unit of liquid measure for wine and spirits used in the Netherlands, Denmark, Sweden, and certain other north European countries. In the Netherlands (and formerly in England) it is equal to 8½ imperial gallons. [< Dutch *anker* < Medieval Latin *ancheria*]

an|ker|ite (ang′kə rīt), *n.* a mineral closely allied to dolomite, with the magnesia largely replaced by iron, valued as an iron ore. [< German *Ankerit* < Professor M. J. *Anker* of Styria + German *-it* -ite[1]]

ankh (angk), *n.* a T-shaped cross with a loop at the top, in Egyptian art and mythology symbolizing generation or life; crux ansata; ansate cross. See the diagram under **cross.** [< Egyptian *'n-kh* life, the soul]

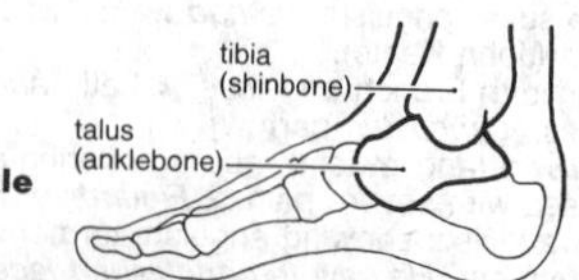

***ankle**

***an|kle** (ang′kəl), *n., v.,* **-kled, -kling.** —*n.* **1** the joint that connects the foot and the leg. Human

beings and all other animals that have feet and bones have ankles. **2** the slender part of the leg between this joint and the calf. The ankle of a human being has seven bones.
—*v.i. U.S. Slang.* to walk, especially in a swaggering fashion: . . . *long-stemmed models ankled through the lobby* . . . (Time).
[< Scandinavian (compare Danish *ankel*)]

an|kle|bone (ang′kəl bōn′), *n.* the principal bone of the ankle; the astragalus or talus.

an|kle-deep (ang′kəl dēp′), *adj., adv.* **1** of a depth sufficient to cover a person's ankles. **2** *Figurative.* deeply immersed: *to be ankle-deep in problems.*

an|klet (ang′klit), *n.* **1** a short sock reaching just above the ankle. **2** a band or chain worn around the ankle. An anklet may be an ornament, a brace, or a fetter.

an|kus (ang′kəs), *n.* an elephant goad combining a sharp hook and a straight point or spike, used in India. [< Hindustani *ankus*]

an|kush (ang′kəsh), *n.* = ankus.

***an|ky|lo|saur** (ang′kə lə sôr), *n.* a dinosaur of the Upper Cretaceous period, having an armor of bony plates: *Despite the weight of their armor and their consequent lack of mobility, ankylosaurs in fossil form have been found in all parts of the world* (William E. Swinton). [< New Latin *Ankylosauria* the suborder name < Greek *ankýlos* crooked + *saûros* lizard]

***ankylosaur**

an|ky|lose (ang′kə lōs), *v.*, **-losed, -los|ing.** —*v.i.* **1** (of joints) to become stiff; undergo ankylosis. **2** (of bones) to grow together; unite by ankylosis.
—*v.t.* to cause to grow together or become stiff, by or as if by ankylosis. Also, **anchylose.**
[< *ankylosis*]

an|ky|lo|sis (ang′kə lō′sis), *n.* **1** a joining together of bones as a result of disease, injury, or corrective surgery. **2** stiffness of a joint caused by this. Also, **anchylosis.** [< Greek *ankýlōsis* < *ankyloûn* to crook < *ankýlos* crooked]

an|ky|los|to|mi|a|sis (ang′kə los′tə mī′ə sis), *n.* = ancylostomiasis.

an|ky|lot|ic (ang′kə lot′ik), *adj.* of or having to do with ankylosis. Also, **anchylotic.**

an|lace (an′lis), *n.* a kind of medieval dagger resembling a heavy knife, broad at the hilt and tapering to a point. [< Old French *alesnaz* < *alesne* awl]

an|la|ge (än′lä gə), *n., pl.* **-gen** (-gən), **-ges** (-gəs). = Anlage.

An|la|ge (än′lä gə), *n., pl.* **-gen** (-gən). *German.* **1a** the first clustering of cells constituting the beginning of an organ or part in the development of an embryo. **b** = blastema. **2** foundation; rudiment. **3** predisposition; inclination.

ann., an abbreviation for the following:
1 annals.
2 annual.
3 annuity.
4 years (Latin, *anni*).

an|na (an′ə), *n.* in India and Pakistan: **1** a former unit of money equal to one-sixteenth of a rupee. **2** a coin having this value. [< Hindustani *ānā* < Sanskrit *ānaka* insignificant]

an|na|berg|ite (an′ə bėr′gīt), *n.* a mineral, hydrous arsenate of nickel, of a fine apple-green color, occurring in capillary crystals or as an earthy mass. *Formula:* $Ni_3As_2O_8 \cdot 8H_2O$ [< *Annaberg,* a region in Germany where it is found + English *-ite*[1]]

an|nal (an′əl), *n.* a record of the events of a single year, or entry of a single item, in a chronicle. [< *annals*]

an|nal|ist (an′ə list), *n.* **1** a writer of annals. **2** = historian. **3** any keeper of records.

an|nal|is|tic (an′ə lis′tik), *adj.* of an annalist or characteristic of annals. —**an′nal|is′ti|cal|ly,** *adv.*

an|nals (an′əlz), *n.pl.* **1** historical records; history: *George Washington holds an important place in the annals of the United States of America.* SYN: chronicles. **2** a written account of events year by year. **3a** a record of any proceedings. **b** any record; story: . . . *the short and simple annals of the poor* (Thomas Gray). SYN: account. [< Latin *annālēs* (*librī*) annual (books); annual record < *annus* year]

An|na|mese (an′ə mēz′, -mēs′), *adj., n., pl.* **-mese.** —*adj.* of or having to do with Annam (a former kingdom, now part of Vietnam), its people, their language, or their way of life. —*n.* **1** a native or inhabitant of Annam. **2** the language spoken by the Annamese; the Vietnamese language.

An|na|mite (an′ə mīt), *adj., n.* = Annamese.

an|nates (an′āts, -its), *n.pl.* the first year's revenue of a see or benefice, paid to the Papal Curia, or (in England, after 1534) to the Crown. [< Middle French *annate* (singular), learned borrowing from Medieval Latin *annata* a year's work < Latin *annus* year]

an|nats (an′ats, -its), *n.pl.* = annates.

an|nat|to (ə nat′ō, -nä′tō), *n.* **1** an orange-red dye obtained from the waxy pulp surrounding the seeds of a small tree native to tropical America, used for coloring textiles, butter, cheese, varnishes, and lacquers. **2** the tree itself. Also, **anatto, anotta, anotto, arnotta, arnotto.** [< Carib (perhaps West Indies) *annoto*]

an|neal (ə nēl′), *v.t.* **1** to make (glass or metals) less brittle by heating and then cooling; temper: *For example, an alloy when cast is usually inhomogeneous and must be annealed at a high temperature, so that the atoms can diffuse to give it a uniform composition throughout* (Science News). **2** *Figurative.* to toughen or harden (the human will, mental attributes, or the like): . . . *the mind to strengthen and anneal* (Sir Walter Scott). **3** *Molecular Biology.* to link up or reconnect complementary sequences of (DNA or RNA molecules): *The DNA . . . was also separated into single strands by heating, and the resulting single strands were then "annealed" with the cellular DNA at a lower temperature* (Scientific American). **4** *Archaic.* to heat (glass or metals) in order to fix colors.
[Old English *anǣlan* < *an-* on + *ǣlan* burn]
—**an|neal′er,** *n.*

an|nec|tent (ə nek′tənt), *adj.* joining one thing to another; providing a connecting link, as between groups of animals. [< Latin *annectēns, -entis,* present participle of *annectere* annex]

an|ne|lid (an′ə lid), *n., adj.* —*n.* any one of a large group of worms with long, soft bodies composed of a series of similar ringlike segments. Earthworms, leeches, and various sea worms are annelids. —*adj.* of or belonging to this group of worms. [< French *annélide* < Old French *annel* ring < Latin *ānellus* (diminutive) < *ānulus* (diminutive) < *ānus* ring]

an|nel|i|dan (ə nel′ə dən), *n., adj.* = annelid.

an|nex (*v.* ə neks′; *n.* an′eks), *v., n.* —*v.t.* **1** to join or add to a larger or more important thing: *The United States annexed Texas in 1845.* **2** to attach as a qualification or limitation: *to annex a clause to a contract.* SYN: subjoin, affix. See syn. under **attach. 3** to add to a book or other writing; append: *a translation with a glossary annexed.* **4** *Informal.* to take as one's own; appropriate, especially without permission.
—*n.* something added or attached: **a** an addition to an existing building; extension; wing: *We are building an annex to the school.* **b** an appendage to a document, book, or other written material. SYN: addition. Also, *especially British,* **annexe.**
[< Medieval Latin *annexare* < Latin *annexus,* past participle of *annectere* < *ad-* to + *nectere* bind] —**an|nex′a|ble,** *adj.*

an|nex|a|tion (an′ək sā′shən), *n.* **1** the act or process of annexing. **2** the state or condition of being annexed: *The annexation of Texas enlarged the United States.* **3** something annexed.
▶**Annexation** often takes the prepositions *to* or *by: the annexation of Texas to the United States, the annexation of Austria by Germany.* Particularly in the United States, the choice of a preposition affects the meaning, the use of *by* tending always to suggest an appropriation by force or the threat of force.

an|nex|a|tion|al (an′ək sā′shə nəl), *adj.* of or having to do with annexation.

an|nex|a|tion|ism (an′ek sā′shə niz əm), *n.* an advocacy or policy of annexation.

an|nex|a|tion|ist (an′ek sā′shə nist), *n., adj.* —*n.* a person who works toward or advocates annexation, especially territorial annexation to or by a country. —*adj.* seeking or advocating territorial annexation: *annexationist policies.*

an|nexe (ə neks′), *n. Especially British.* annex.

an|nex|ment (ə neks′mənt), *n.* = annexation.

an|nex|ure (ə nek′shər), *n. Especially British.* something added or attached, such as an appendix or codicil.

An|nie Oak|ley (an′ē ōk′lē), *U.S. Slang.* **1** a free ticket or pass: *Chilly weather . . . and a substantial rush for "Annie Oakleys" at fistic headquarters today were the only noteworthy developments leading up to the 10-round heavyweight match* (Baltimore Sun). **2** *Baseball.* a base on balls: *Newcombe's Annie Oakley average last season . . . was 3.85* (Richmond News Leader). Also, **Oakley.** [American English < *Annie Oakley,* 1860-1926, a famous rifle woman (referring to the resemblance between punched tickets and her small perforated targets)]

an|ni|hi|la|bil|i|ty (ə nī′ə lə bil′ə tē), *n. Rare.* the quality or state of being annihilable.

an|ni|hi|la|ble (ə nī′ə lə bəl), *adj.* that can be annihilated.

an|ni|hi|late (ə nī′ə lāt), *v.*, **-lat|ed, -lat|ing.** —*v.t.* **1** to destroy completely; wipe out of existence: *An avalanche annihilated the village.* SYN: obliterate, exterminate. See syn. under **abolish. 2** to bring to ruin or confusion: *to annihilate an army.* SYN: destroy. **3** *Nuclear Physics.* to cause the annihilation of: *Electrically neutral particles also have corresponding antiparticles which are annihilated when they encounter each other* (Bulletin of Atomic Scientists).
—*v.i. Nuclear Physics.* to undergo annihilation: *They [the particles] annihilate to yield two new photons with the same total energy as the original photons* (Scientific American).
[< Late Latin *annihilāre* (with English *-ate*[1]) < Latin *ad-* to + *nihil* nothing]

an|ni|hi|la|tion (ə nī′ə lā′shən), *n.* **1** complete destruction. **2** *Nuclear Physics.* the destruction of a particle and antiparticle (such as an electron and positron) by uniting or colliding, the energy being converted into one or more photons of radiation. **3** *Theology.* destruction of both soul and body.

an|ni|hi|la|tion|ism (ə nī′ə lā′shə niz əm), *n. Theology.* the doctrine that the wicked are totally destroyed in both body and soul after death. —**an|ni′hi|la′tion|ist,** *n.*

annihilation radiation, the radiation produced by annihilation (def. 2).

an|ni|hi|la|tive (ə nī′ə lā′tiv), *adj.* such as to annihilate: *annihilative force.*

an|ni|hi|la|tor (ə nī′ə lā′tər), *n.* a person or thing that annihilates.

an|ni|ver|sa|ry (an′ə vėr′sər ē, -vėrs′rē), *n., pl.* **-ries,** *adj.* —*n.* **1** the yearly return of a special date: *a 25th wedding anniversary. Your birthday is an anniversary you like to have remembered.* **2** the celebration of the yearly return of a special date: *My parents invited their friends to their wedding anniversary.*
—*adj.* **1** celebrated each year at the same date: *an anniversary occasion.* **2** having to do with an anniversary: *an anniversary dinner.*
[< Latin *anniversārius* returning annually < *annus* year + *versus,* past participle of *vertere* to turn]

an|no ae|ta|tis su|ae (an′ō ē tā′tis sü′ē; ä′nō ī tä′tis sü′ī), *Latin.* in one's (specified) year of age.

an|no Dom|i|ni (an′ō dom′ə nī), *Latin.* in the year of our Lord; in the year since the birth of Christ. *Abbr:* A.D.

an|no mun|di (an′ō mun′dī), *Latin.* in the year of the world; in the year since the traditional estimated date (4004 B.C.) of the Creation. *Abbr:* A.M.

an|no|na|ceous (an′ə nā′shəs), *adj.* of or belonging to the custard-apple family of trees and shrubs, that includes the custard apple, soursop, sweetsop, and papaw. Also, **anonaceous.** [< New Latin *Annona* the typical genus (< Spanish *anona*) + English *-aceous*]

an|no|tate (an′ə tāt), *v.*, **-tat|ed, -tat|ing.** —*v.t.* to provide with explanatory or critical notes or comments: *Shakespeare's plays are often annotated to make them easier to understand.* SYN: gloss. —*v.i.* to write or insert explanatory or critical notes or comments: *Some people annotate as they read.* SYN: gloss.
[< Latin *annotāre* (with English *-ate*[1]) < *ad-* to + *notāre* to mark < *nota* note] —**an′no|ta′tor,** *n.*

an|no|ta|tion (an′ə tā′shən), *n.* **1a** the act of providing with explanatory or critical notes or comments: *The annotation of Shakespeare's plays required the explanation of many words no longer used.* **b** the condition of being provided with notes: *That book's annotation required hundreds of hours.* **2** a note added to a text, document, or other written material, to explain or criticize: *The editor's annotations were printed in small type at the bottom of the page.*

an|no|ta|tive (an′ə tā′tiv), *adj.* of or using annotations.

an|nounce (ə nouns′), *v.*, **-nounced, -nounc|ing.** —*v.t.* **1** to give formal or public notice of: *to announce a wedding in the papers. Please announce to the children that there will be no school this afternoon.* **2a** to make known the presence or arrival of: *The loudspeaker announced each airplane as it landed at the airport.* **b** to make known the readiness of: *Dinner will soon be announced.* **3** to be or provide evidence of: *A faint glow in the east announced the coming of another day.* **4** to be an announcer for.
—*v.i.* to introduce programs or read news on the radio or television.
announce for, *U.S. Informal.* to make known one's candidacy for (a political office): *Astronaut John Glenn announced for the U.S. Senate* (Time).

Pronunciation Key: hat, āge, cãre, fär; let, ēqual, tėrm; it, īce; hot, ōpen, ôrder; oil, out; cup, pu̇t, rüle; child; long; thin; ᴛʜen; zh, measure; ə represents **a** in about, **e** in taken, **i** in pencil, **o** in lemon, **u** in circus.

[< Old French *anoncier* < Latin *annūntiāre* < *ad-* to + *nūntius* messenger. See etym. of doublet **annunciate.**]

—Syn. v.t. **1 Announce, proclaim, declare** mean to make known formally or publicly. **Announce** means to give formal notice of something of interest to the public or a particular group: *to announce the names of the members of the new cabinet. The proud parents announced the birth of their first baby.* **Proclaim** means to announce publicly and with authority something of importance to the general public: *The President proclaimed an emergency.* **Declare,** often interchangeable with *proclaim* in this sense, means to make known clearly and plainly, usually formally or officially: *An armistice was declared.*

an·nounce·ment (ə nouns′mənt), *n.* **1** the act of announcing; making known: *His announcement of the school holiday was met with shouts and cheers.* **2** what is announced or made known; a public or formal notice: *The chairman made two announcements. Announcements of marriages appear in the newspapers.* **3** a card, note, or the like, by which such notice is conveyed: *to receive an engraved announcement of a marriage in the mail.*

▶ See **advertisement** for usage note.

an·nounc·er (ə noun′sər), *n.* **1** a person or thing that announces. **2** a person who introduces programs, and reads news and advertisements over the radio or on a television broadcast.

an·no ur·bis con·di·tae (an′ō ėr′bis kon′də tē), *Latin.* in the year since the traditional estimated date (753 B.C.) of the founding of the city (Rome), used as the date of reference for the ancient Latin calendar. *Abbr:* A.U.C.

an·noy (ə noi′), *v., n.* *—v.t.* **1** to make somewhat angry; cause uneasiness to, especially by repeated acts; disturb; trouble; vex: *The baby is always annoying his sister by pulling her hair.* SYN: irritate, bother, tease. See syn. under **worry. 2** to hurt or molest: *The bees annoyed the picnickers.* SYN: harry. *—v.i.* to be a cause of trouble; be an upsetting influence.

—n. Archaic. annoyance.

[< Anglo-French *anoier,* Old French *enoier* to weary, vex < Late Latin *inodiāre* make loathsome < Latin *in odiō* in hatred] **—an·noy′er,** *n.*

▶ **annoy.** With reference to a thing, *annoyed at* is used: *I was annoyed at the interruption.* With reference to a person, *annoyed with* is used: *I was annoyed with my sister again.* When it means "molested," *annoyed by* is used: *I was annoyed by hecklers during my speech.*

an·noy·ance (ə noi′əns), *n.* **1a** the state or condition of being annoyed; feeling of dislike or trouble; vexation: *Her face showed her annoyance at the delay.* SYN: discomfort, trouble. **b** the act of annoying: *The principal stopped the annoyance of others by the noisy boys.* **2** something that annoys; nuisance: *The noisy traffic on our street is an annoyance.* SYN: bother, pest.

an·noy·ing (ə noi′ing), *adj.* troublesome; disturbing; vexatious: *an annoying manner. The boy was always annoying his sister by pulling her hair. The campers fought constantly against the annoying presence of mosquitoes.* **—an·noy′ing·ly,** *adv.* **—an·noy′ing·ness,** *n.*

an·nu·al (an′yu̇ əl), *adj., n.* *—adj.* **1** coming once a year: *Your birthday is an annual event.* **2** in a year; for a year: *What is his annual salary?* **3** lasting for a whole year; accomplished during a year: *The earth makes an annual course around the sun.* **4** living but one year or season: *Corn and beans are annual plants.*

—n. **1** a plant that lives but one year or growing season: *Many garden plants are annuals.* **2** a book, journal, or other written matter, published once a year; yearbook.

[< Old French *annuel,* learned borrowing from Late Latin *annuālis* < Latin *annus* year] **—an′nu·al·ly,** *adv.*

an·nu·al·ize (an′yu̇ ə līz), *v.,* **-ized, -iz·ing.** *—v.i.* to write for an annual. *—v.t. U.S.* to compute (income or expenditures) for or as if for a year.

annual parallax, the apparent change or amount of change in the position of a heavenly body as a result of the earth's motion around the sun; heliocentric parallax. It is the angle subtended at the heavenly body by the radius of the earth's orbit.

annual ring, any of the concentric rings of wood (xylem) seen when the stem of a tree or shrub is cut across; growth ring. In most trees a dark ring shows the growth during one summer and early fall, and a somewhat lighter ring shows a spring's growth. By counting these it is possible to tell the age of a tree.

an·nu·i·tant (ə nü′ə tənt, -nyü′-), *n.* a person who receives an annuity. [< *annuit(y)* + *-ant*]

an·nu·it coep·tis (an′yu̇ it sep′tis), *Latin.* He (God) has favored our undertakings (one of the two mottoes on the reverse of the great seal of the United States, adapted from Virgil's *Aeneid*).

an·nu·i·ty (ə nü′ə tē, -nyü′-), *n., pl.* **-ties. 1** a sum of money paid every year or in installments at certain regular times: *Mr. Smith gives his old employees annuities after they retire.* **2** the right to receive or duty to pay such a sum of money. **3** an investment that provides a fixed yearly income during one's lifetime or for a specified time. [< Middle French *annuité* < Medieval Latin *annuitas* < Latin *annus* year]

an·nul (ə nul′), *v.t.,* **-nulled, -nul·ling. 1** to do away with; destroy the force of; make void; cancel: *to annul a plan. The judge annulled the contract because one of the signers was too young.* SYN: abolish, nullify, abrogate. **2** to reduce to nothing; annihilate. [< Late Latin *annūllāre* < Latin *ad-* + *nūllus* of no value] **—an·nul′la·ble,** *adj.* **—an·nul′ler,** *n.*

an·nu·lar (an′yə lər), *adj.* of or having the form of a ring; ringlike; ring-shaped; ringed. [< Latin *ānulāris* (*annulāris* in late and poor manuscripts) < *ānulus* (*annulus*) (diminutive) < *ānus* ring] **—an′nu·lar·ly,** *adv.*

annular eclipse, an eclipse of the sun in which the moon covers the sun incompletely, leaving a narrow uneclipsed ring (annulus) which surrounds the dark moon.

an·nu·lar·i·ty (an′yə lar′ə tē), *n.* annular quality, condition, or form.

annular ligament, a ligament encircling the wrist or ankle.

an·nu·late (an′yə lit, -lāt), *adj.* **1** furnished with rings or ringlike parts. **2** composed of rings or a series of ringlike segments. [< Latin *annulātus* < *annulus* annulus]

an·nu·lat·ed (an′yə lā′tid), *adj.* = annulate.

an·nu·la·tion (an′yə lā′shən), *n.* **1** formation of rings or ringlike divisions. **2** a ringlike structure; a ring.

an·nu·lene (an′yə lēn), *n. Chemistry.* an aromatic cyclic compound with a large ring structure. [< *annul(ar)* + *-ene*]

an·nu·let (an′yə lit), *n.* **1** a little ring. **2** *Architecture.* a narrow, ringlike molding or circlet of wood or stone, particularly one just below a Doric capital. **3** *Heraldry.* a small ring or circle on a shield, used as a mark for the fifth son. [< Latin *ānulus* ring; see etym. under **annulus**]

an·nul·ment (ə nul′mənt), *n.* **1** the act or process of annulling or declaring void. **2** the state or condition of being annulled; cancellation; invalidation: *An annulment of the marriage was granted by the court because the marriage was illegal.*

▶**Annulment** and **divorce** are never synonymous with reference to marriage. An *annulment* is the declaration that a marriage never really existed, or was void from the beginning, that the parties were therefore never mutually married. A *divorce* is the legal dissolution of a previously valid marriage.

an·nu·lose (an′yə lōs), *adj.* = annulate.

an·nu·lus (an′yə ləs), *n., pl.* **-li** (-lī), **-lus·es. 1** a ringlike part, band, or space, such as that on the stem of certain mushrooms. **2** *Geometry.* the region between two concentric circles. [< Latin *ānulus* (*annulus* in late and poor manuscripts) (diminutive) < *ānus* ring]

an·num (an′əm), *n. Latin.* year (especially in the phrase *per annum*).

an·nun·ci·ate (ə nun′sē āt, -shē-), *v.t.,* **-at·ed, -at·ing.** to make known; announce. [< Latin *annūntiāre* (with English *-ate*[1]) < *ad-* + *nūntiāre* announce < *nūntius* message.]

an·nun·ci·a·tion (ə nun′sē ā′shən, -shē-), *n.* = announcement.

the Annunciation, a the announcement by the angel Gabriel to the Virgin Mary that she was to be the mother of Jesus Christ (in the Bible, Luke 1:26-38): *No subject has been more frequently treated by the religious painters than that of the Annunciation* (John Ruskin). **b** a church festival held on March 25 in memory of this event; Annunciation Day: *to celebrate the Annunciation.*

Annunciation Day, Lady Day, March 25, a church holiday in commemoration of the Annunciation.

Annunciation lily, = Madonna lily.

an·nun·ci·a·tor (ə nun′sē ā′tər, -shē-), *n.* **1** *U.S.* an indicator for showing where a signal comes from. **2** a person or thing that announces.

an·nun·ci·a·to·ry (ə nun′sē ə tôr′ē, -tōr′-), *adj.* characterized by annunciation; annunciative.

an·nus mi·ra·bi·lis (an′əs mə rab′ə lis), *pl.* **an·ni mi·ra·bi·les** (an′ī mə rab′ə lēz). *Latin.* year of marvels; wonderful year (applied to various memorable years, especially, in English history, to the year 1666, which is noted for such important events as the great fire of London, and which was commemorated in Dryden's poem *Annus Mirabilis*): *It was in the annus mirabilis of 1922 that Joyce gave us "Ulysses" and Eliot "The Waste Land"* (Saturday Review).

A No. 1, *Informal.* = A one; first-class.

a·no·a (ə nō′ə), *n., pl.* **a·no·as.** a wild ox related to the water buffalo, but much smaller and having nearly straight horns, native to Celebes. [< a native word]

a·no·ci·as·so·ci·a·tion (ə nō′sē ə sō′sē ā′shən, -shē-), *n.* the preventing or minimizing of shock as a result of surgery by the temporary cutting off of the nervous system, either surgically or through local anesthesia, from the area of operation. [< *a-*[4] not + Latin *nocēre* injure]

a·no·ci·a·tion (ə nō′sē ā′shən), *n.* = anociassociation.

an·od·al (an ō′dəl), *adj.* = anodic.

an·ode (an′ōd), *n.* **1** a positively charged electrode. In an electrolytic cell or electron tube, electrons flow from the cathode to the anode. The plate in a vacuum tube is an anode. **2** the negative terminal of a battery or cell that sends out current. The zinc electrode in a dry cell is the anode. [< Greek *ánodos* a way up < *ana-* up + *hodós* way]

an·od·ic (an od′ik), *adj.* of or having to do with an anode. **—an·od′i·cal·ly,** *adv.*

an·od·ise (an′ō dīz), *v.t.,* **-ised, -is·ing.** *British.* anodize.

an·od·ize (an′ə dīz), *v.t.,* **-ized, -iz·ing.** to coat the surface of (a metal) with a protective film by making it the anode of a cell and subjecting it to the action of an electrolyte. **—an′o·di·za′tion,** *n.*

an·o·dyne (an′ə dīn), *n., adj.* *—n.* **1** a medicine or drug that lessens pain. Bromides, chloroform, and ether are anodynes. Aspirin is an anodyne that does not cause unconsciousness. **2** *Figurative.* anything that soothes.

—adj. **1** lessening pain. **2** *Figurative.* soothing.

[< Latin *anōdynus* < Greek *anṓdynos* painless < *an-* without + *odýnē* pain]

an·o·dyn·in (an′ə dī nin), *n.* a substance found in human blood and resembling a hormone. It has long-lasting pain-relieving properties.

an·o·e·sis (an′ō ē′sis), *n.* a state of consciousness in which there is sensation but no thought. [< *a-*[1] + *noesis*]

an·o·et·ic (an′ō et′ik), *adj.* of or having to do with anoesis.

a·noint (ə noint′), *v.t.* **1** to put oil on; cover or rub with ointment; smear: *Anoint sunburned skin with cold cream.* **2** to put oil on (a person) in a ceremony as a sign of consecration to office: *The bishop anointed the new king.* **3** to rub or smear with any other substance or liquid. **4** (in humorous use) to beat soundly; cudgel. [< Old French *enoint,* past participle of *enoindre* < Latin *inunguere* < *in-* on + *unguere* smear] **—a·noint′er,** *n.* **—a·noint′ment,** *n.*

a·noint·ing of the sick (ə noin′ting), = extreme unction.

a·no·le (ə nō′lē), *n.* any one of a genus of American lizards that can change the color of their skin, including the American chameleon. [< New Latin *Anolis;* see etym. under **anolian lizard**]

a·no·li·an lizard (ə nō′lē ən), = American chameleon. [< New Latin *Anolis* the genus name (< a native name in the Antilles) + English *-ian*]

an·o·lyte (an′ə līt), *n.* the part of an electrolyte close to the anode during electrolysis. [< *ano-(de)* + (electro)*lyte*]

a·nom·a·lism (ə nom′ə liz əm), *n.* **1** an anomaly; irregularity. **2** anomalous character.

a·nom·a·lis·tic (ə nom′ə lis′tik), *adj.* **1** of or containing an anomaly; characterized by anomaly. **2** having to do with the anomaly of a planet. **—a·nom′a·lis′ti·cal·ly,** *adv.*

anomalistic month, the time required for the moon to pass from perigee to perigee.

anomalistic year, the time between two successive passages of the perihelion by the earth in its orbit around the sun; 365 days, 6 hours, 13 minutes, and 53.1 seconds.

a·nom·a·lon (ə nom′ə lon), *n. Nuclear Physics.* a hypothetical fragment of a nucleus traveling an unusually short distance after colliding with a target nucleus: *These relatively small anomalons surprised scientists who . . . believed that anamalons, if they exist, would be much larger particles* (Marc Kusinitz). [< *anoma-l(ous)* + *-on*]

a·nom·a·lo·scope (ə nom′ə lə skōp), *n.* an instrument for determining, by his ability to match a given shade of yellow by blending shades of green and red, if or to what extent a person is color-blind. [< Greek *anṓmalos* uneven + *-scope*]

a·nom·a·lous (ə nom′ə ləs), *adj.* **1** departing from the common rule; not conforming to what is usual; irregular: *A position as head of a department, but with no real authority, is anomalous.* SYN: unnatural, exceptional, peculiar. **2** *Biology.* differing from the type; abnormal: *an anomalous structure.* **3** *Grammar.* irregular: *an anomalous inflection.* [< Late Latin *anōmalus* (with English *-ous*) < Greek *anṓmalos* < *an-* not + *homalós* even] **—a·nom′a·lous·ly,** *adv.* **—a·nom′a·lous·ness,** *n.*

anomalous water, = polywater.

a|nom|a|ly (ə nom′ə lē), *n., pl.* **-lies.** **1** something abnormal, especially an animal or plant, that shows deviation from the type: *A dog with six legs would be an anomaly.* **2** departure from a general rule; irregularity: *"A lamb in school is an anomaly," said the teacher to Mary.* **3** *Grammar.* irregularity in inflections. **4** *Astronomy.* the angle between a line from the sun to the earth, or other planet, at a given moment and a line from the sun to the planet's perihelion passage. The angle is counted in the sense of the planet's motion. [< Latin *anōmalia* < Greek *anōmaliā* < *anōmalos;* see etym. under **anomalous**]

a|nom|ic[1] (ə nom′ik, -nō′mik), *adj.* characterized by anomie; lacking direction or purpose; aimless: *Riesman believes . . . some men will adjust, some will fail to adjust, and some will rise above adjustment. Those who fail he calls anomic* (Time).

a|nom|ic[2] (ə nom′ik, -nō′mik), *adj.* of or denoting a form of aphasia in which objects cannot be remembered by name. [< Greek *a-* without + *ónoma* name + English *-ic*]

an|o|mie or **an|o|my** (an′ə mē), *n.* a lack of direction or purpose; condition of aimlessness or rootlessness: *The process of change tends to develop situations in which the old norms no longer restrain individual behavior and new norms are either absent or unacceptable. Such anomie . . . frequently occurs in the development of urban society* (Hinkle and Hinkle). [< French *anomie* < Greek *anomía* lawlessness < *a-* without + *nómos* law]

a|non (ə non′), *adv., interj. Archaic.* **—*adv.*** **1** in a little while; soon; presently. **2** at another time; again. **—*interj.*** coming at once!

ever and anon. See under **ever.**

[Old English *on ān* into one, and *on āne* in one, at once]

anon., anonymous.

an|o|na|ceous (an′ə nā′shəs), *adj.* = annonaceous.

an|o|nym (an′ə nim), *n.* **1** fictitious name; pseudonym. **2** a person whose name is not known or not disclosed. [< Late Latin *anōnymus* anonymous]

an|o|nym|i|ty (an′ə nim′ə tē), *n.* **1** *no pl.* the condition of being anonymous: *This, was part of Lorentz' character, Einstein explained, a kind of nobility which made him work for the well-being of others, preferably in anonymity* (Scientific American). **2** *pl.* **-ties.** a person who is anonymous: *. . . one of those amiable anonymities at a cocktail party* (New Yorker).

a|non|y|mous (ə non′ə məs), *adj.* **1** by or from a person whose name is not known or given: *threats in an anonymous letter. An anonymous book is one published without the name of the author.* **2** having no name; of unknown name; nameless: *This book was written by an anonymous author.* **3** *Figurative.* lacking distinctive character; having no individual features: *The visitor who is admitted passes into a vast, anonymous lobby* (Atlantic). *Abbr:* anon. [< Late Latin *anōnymus* (with English *-ous*) < Greek *anōnymos* < *an-* without + (dialectal) *ónyma* name]

—a|non′y|mous|ly, *adv.* **—a|non′y|mous|ness,** *n.*

a|noph|e|les (ə nof′ə lēz), *n., pl.* **-les,** *adj.* **—*n.*** any one of a genus of mosquitoes that can transmit the protozoans causing malaria to human beings. **—*adj.*** that is or derives from the anopheles: *an anopheles carrier or infection.*

[< New Latin *anopheles* < Greek *anōphelēs* useless, harmful < *an-* without + *óphelos* use, profit]

a|noph|e|line (ə nof′ə lin, -līn), *n., adj.* = anopheles. [< *anophel*(es) + *-ine*[1]]

a|no|rak (ä′nə räk), *n.* a heavy, cloth or leather jacket with a furred hood, worn in arctic regions. [< Eskimo (Greenland) *ánorâq* clothing, dress]

an|o|rec|tic (an′ə rek′tik), *adj.* of or characterized by anorexia; without appetite.

an|o|rec|tous (an′ə rek′təs), *adj.* = anorectic.

an|o|ret|ic (an′ə ret′ik), *adj., n.* **—*adj.*** causing a loss of appetite. **—*n.*** an anoretic drug.

an|o|rex|i|a (an′ə rek′sē ə), *n.* **1** lack of appetite for food. **2** = anorexia nervosa. [< Greek *anorexiā* < *an-* without + *orégein* reach after]

anorexia ner|vo|sa (nėr vō′sə), an unnatural and prolonged aversion to food that causes severe loss of weight: *Anorexia nervosa . . . occurs predominantly among children and adolescents* (Science News).

an|o|rex|ic (an′ə rek′sik), *adj., n.* **—*adj.*** suffering from anorexia: *In a recent case study an anorexic girl saw herself as emaciated, introverted, unsociable and unhappy—the very opposite of being sexually attractive* (London Times). **—*n.*** an anorexic person: *Anorexics tend to sleep fitfully, and when they awake, they experience naturally occurring trancelike periods* (Scientific American). [< *anorex*(ia) + *-ic*]

an|or|gan|ic bone (an′ôr gan′ik), animal bone treated with an organic solvent, for use in bone repair. [< *an-*[1] not + *organic*]

an|or|thic (an ôr′thik), *adj. Mineralogy.* triclinic. [< *an-* not + Greek *orthós* straight + English *-ic*]

an|or|thite (an ôr′thīt), *n.* a lime feldspar in crystals or as a constituent of igneous rocks. [< *an-* not + Greek *orthós* straight + *-ite*[1]]

an|or|thit|ic (an′ôr thit′ik), *adj.* of or containing anorthite.

an|or|tho|clase (an ôr′thə klās, -klāz), *n.* a triclinic feldspar related to microcline, found in certain igneous rocks. [< *an-*[1] not + *orthoclase*]

an|or|tho|site (an ôr′thə sīt), *n.* a granular igneous rock composed chiefly of a soda-lime feldspar, especially labradorite. [< French *anorthose* feldspar + English *-ite*[1]]

an|or|tho|sit|ic (an ôr′thə sit′ik), *adj.* of or containing anorthosite.

an|os|mi|a (an oz′mē ə, -os′-), *n.* loss or lack of the sense of smell. [< New Latin *anosmia* < Greek *an-* without + *osmē* smell < *ózein* to smell]

an|os|mic (an oz′mik, -os′-), *adj.* of or having anosmia.

an|os|tra|can (an os′trə kən), *n.* any one of an order of small, aquatic crustaceans having a relatively large number of uniform, flattened appendages and no carapace. [< New Latin *Anostraca* (< Greek *an-* without + *óstrakon* shell) + *-an*]

an|oth|er (ə nuᴛʜ′ər), *adj., pron.* **—*adj.*** **1** one more: *May I have another glass of milk, please?* **2** not the same; a different: *Show me another kind of hat. That is quite another matter.* **3** similar in one or more respects but not actually the same: *That singer is another Caruso.*

—*pron.* **1a** one more: *He ate a bar of candy and then asked for another.* **b** one of the same kind: *His father was a scholar, and he is another.* **2** a different one: *This pen won't write; please give me another.* **3** the other (used in phrases with *one* so as to refer to the whole of a group or series): *They walked out, one after another.*

[for *an other*]

an|oth|er|guess (ə nuᴛʜ′ər ges′), *adj. Archaic.* of another sort or kind. [alteration of earlier *anothergates* < *another* + *gates,* adverbial genitive of *gate* way]

a|not|ta (ə not′ə), *n.* = annatto.

a|not|to (ə not′ō), *n.* = annatto.

an|o|vu|lar (an ō′vyə lər, -ov′yə-), *adj.* = anovulatory.

an|o|vu|la|to|ry (an ō′vyə lə tôr′ē, -tōr′-; -ov′yə-), *adj.* not connected with ovulation: *anovulatory menstruation.*

an|ox|e|mi|a or **an|ox|ae|mi|a** (an′ok sē′mē ə), *n.* deficiency of oxygen in the blood. [< *an-* without + *ox*(ygen) + *-emia*]

an|ox|e|mic or **an|ox|ae|mic** (an′ok sē′mik), *adj.* of or characterized by anoxemia; having a deficiency of oxygen in the blood.

an|ox|i|a (an ok′sē ə), *n.* lack of sufficient oxygen in the body tissues. Anoxia occurs when the blood flowing through the lungs does not absorb enough oxygen, when the blood cannot carry its full load of oxygen, or when the blood flow slows.

an|ox|ic (an ok′sik), *adj.* of or characterized by anoxia; lacking sufficient oxygen.

ans., **1** answer. **2** answered.

an|sa (an′sə), *n., pl.* **-sae** (-sē). **1** a handle or handlelike part. **2** *Astronomy.* either one of the parts of Saturn's rings, which, when seen obliquely, seemed, in the earlier telescopes, to project like handles on each side of the planet. [< Latin *ānsa*]

An|sar (än′sär), *n., pl.* **An|sar, An|sars, An|sa|ri** (än sä′rē). a member of the largest Islamic sect of Sudan.

an|sate (an′sāt), *adj.* having a handle or something resembling a handle. [< Latin *ānsātus* < *ānsa* handle]

ansate cross, = ankh.

an|sat|ed (an′sā tid), *adj.* = ansate.

An|schau|ung (än′shou′ůng), *n.* **1** view of life; world-view: *. . . the world that gets its Anschauung from the media of romance—whodunits, television, and the flicks* (A. J. Liebling). **2** *Philosophy.* the perception one gets through one's senses; direct sense perception. [< German *Anschauung* view, perception]

An|schluss or **an|schluss** (än′shlůs), *n.* union, especially the political union of Germany and Austria in 1938 under Hitler. [< German *Anschluss*]

an|ser|ine (an′sə rīn, -sər in), *adj.* **1** of, like, or having to do with a goose or geese. **2** stupid; foolish. [< Latin *ānserīnus* < *ānser* goose]

an|ser|ous (an′sər əs), *adj.* stupid; foolish.

an|swer (an′sər, än′-), *v., n.* **—*v.t.*** **1** to reply to; speak or write in response to: *Please answer my question. I will try to answer your letter before the end of the week.* **2** to act or move in response to: *She answered the doorbell.* **3** *Figurative.* to satisfy the needs, requirements, or wishes, of; serve; suit: *This will answer your purpose.* **4** to reply to (a charge): *to answer a summons to appear in court.* **5** to find the solution to: *to answer a problem.* **6** to correspond to: *That stamp is the one answering the description in the catalog.*

—*v.i.* **1** to speak or write in return to a question; make answer; reply: *I asked him a question, but he would not answer.* **2** to reply or respond by act or motion; act in return to a call or signal; respond: *He knocked on the door, but no one answered.* **3** *Figurative.* to meet one's needs, requirements, or wishes; serve: *On the picnic, a newspaper answered for a tablecloth.* **4** to be responsible (for): *The bus driver must answer for the safety of the children in his bus.* **5** to agree with; be similar (to); correspond: *This dog answers to the description of the one we lost.*

—*n.* **1** the words spoken or written in reply, as to a question, letter, remark, or appeal: *The boy gave a quick answer.* **SYN:** rejoinder, retort, return. **2** a gesture or act done in return: *A nod was her only answer.* **3** the solution to a problem: *What is the correct answer to this arithmetic problem?* **4** *Figurative.* a person or thing that corresponds to another: *Agnar Mykle has a somewhat . . . unenviable reputation as the Norwegian answer to Thomas Wolfe* (Manchester Guardian Weekly). **5** *Law.* a defendant's pleading in reply to a charge or accusation; a defense. **6** *Music.* the second entry of the subject of a fugue, in a different voice and usually at the interval of a fourth below or a fifth above. *Abbr:* ans.

answer back, *Informal.* to reply in a rude, impertinent way: *Instead of apologizing the impolite young man kept answering back.*

know all the answers, *Informal.* to have pretensions to complete or infallible knowledge: *[The President] is beset constantly by . . . people who know all the answers and want to give them* (Baltimore Sun).

[Old English *andswaru* < *and-* against + *swerian* swear] **—an′swer|er,** *n.*

—*Syn.* *v.i.* **1 Answer, reply, respond** mean to say something in return to something said, asked, or demanded. **Answer** is the general word meaning to speak or write in return: *I called, but no one answered.* **Reply** is used in more formal style or to suggest more formal answering, as with thought and care: *I sent in my application, and the university replied immediately.* **Respond,** formal in this sense, suggests giving the answer hoped for or counted on: *When we requested information and instructions, the chairman responded.*

an|swer|a|bil|i|ty (an′sər ə bil′ə tē, än′-), *n.* **1** responsibility. **2** the state or quality of being answerable: *He had his era's . . . belief in the answerability of all questions* (Time).

an|swer|a|ble (an′sər ə bəl, än′-), *adj.* **1** responsible or accountable (to someone for something): *The club treasurer is held answerable to the club for the money given to him.* **SYN:** liable, amenable. **2** that can be answered: *That question is easily answerable.* **3** *Archaic.* corresponding. **—an′swer|a|ble|ness,** *n.* **—an′swer|a|bly,** *adv.*

answering machine, a tape-recording device that responds to a telephone call with a recorded message and records a message from the caller.

an|swer|ing service (an′sər ing, än′-), *U.S.* a business which receives telephone calls for a subscriber in his absence, and on his return reports on the calls received.

an|swer|less (an′sər lis, än′-), *adj.* **1** without an answer. **2** = unanswerable.

***ant** (ant), *n.* a small insect that lives in tunnels burrowed in the ground or in wood. Ants live together in large, highly organized groups called colonies of from dozens of individuals to half a million or more. Ants are black, brown, reddish, or yellowish. Ants, bees, and wasps belong to the same group of insects. [Old English *ǣmete*]

***ant**

queen male worker

ant-, *prefix.* the form of **anti-** before vowels and *h,* as in *antacid, anthelmintic.*

-ant, *suffix added to verbs.* **1** (*to form adjectives*) that ___s; ___ing: *Buoyant = that buoys* or *buoying. Compliant = that complies* or *complying. Triumphant = that triumphs* or *triumphing.* **2** (*to form nouns*) one that ___s: *Assistant = one that assists.* See also **-ent.** [< Old French *-ant* < Latin *-āns, -antis* and *-ēns, -entis*]

Pronunciation Key: hat, āge, cãre, fär; let, ēqual, tėrm; it, īce; hot, ōpen, ôrder; oil, out; cup, půt, rüle; child; long; thin; ᴛʜen; zh, measure; ə represents a in about, e in taken, i in pencil, o in lemon, u in circus.

▶ See **-ance** for usage note.

ant., **1a** antiquarian. **b** antiquary. **2** antonym.

an't (änt, ānt), *Informal or Dialect.* **1** am not; is not. **2** are not. **3** have not; has not.

▶ See **ain't** for usage note.

an|ta (an′tə), *n., pl.* **-tae** (-tē). **1** a pilaster or pier, usually having a capital and base, especially one of a pair framing a doorway or portico and formed by prolonging and thickening the walls, such a portico being *in antis.* **2** a pilaster placed opposite a column.
[< Latin *antae* (plural only)]

Ant|a|buse (ant′ə byüs′), *n. Trademark.* disulfiram.

ant|ac|id (ant as′id), *n., adj.* **—*n.*** a substance that neutralizes acids, especially one that is or can be used as a remedy for excess acidity in the stomach. Baking soda and magnesia are antacids.
—*adj.* tending to neutralize acids; counteracting acidity. Also, **anti-acid**.
[< *ant-* + *acid*]

An|tae|an (an tē′ən), *adj.* of or like Antaeus.

An|tae|us (an tē′əs), *n. Greek Mythology.* a giant wrestler who was invincible while touching the earth. Hercules strangled him while holding him in the air.

an|tag|o|nise (an tag′ə nīz), *v.t., v.i.,* **-nised, -nis|ing**. *British.* antagonize.

an|tag|o|nism (an tag′ə niz əm), *n.* **1** active opposition; activity or relation of contending parties or conflicting forces; conflict; hostility: *the antagonism between good and evil. During the argument, the boy's antagonism showed plainly in his face.* **2** an opposing force or principle. **3** *Biology.* the total of the reciprocal interference of one organism with the growth of an unlike organism, under such conditions as lack of food supply: *Antagonism includes the three processes of competition, antibiosis and exploitation* (New Scientist).

an|tag|o|nist (an tag′ə nist), *n.* **1** a person who fights, struggles, or contends against another in a combat or contest of any kind; adversary; opponent: *The knight defeated each antagonist who came against him.* **SYN**: foe, rival. See syn. under **opponent**. **2** a muscle which resists or counteracts another muscle, relaxing while the opposite one contracts, and conversely. **3** a drug which counteracts the effects of another drug (the *agonist*). [< Greek *antagōnistēs* < *antagōnízesthai* struggle against; see etym. under **antagonize**]

an|tag|o|nis|tic (an tag′ə nis′tik), *adj.* acting against or hostile toward each other; mutually opposed; conflicting: *Cats and dogs are often antagonistic.* **SYN**: opposing, hostile. **—an|tag′o|nis′ti|cal|ly**, *adv.*

an|tag|o|nis|ti|cal (an tag′ə nis′tə kəl), *adj.* = antagonistic.

an|tag|o|nize (an tag′ə nīz), *v.,* **-nized, -niz|ing**. **—*v.t.*** **1** to make an enemy of; arouse dislike in: *Her unkind remarks antagonized people who had been her friends.* **2** to oppose actively. **3** to counteract or neutralize.
—*v.i.* to act in opposition or antagonism.
[< Greek *antagōnízesthai* < *anti-* against + *agôn* contest] **—an|tag′o|ni|za′tion**, *n.* **—an|tag′o|niz′er**, *n.*

ant|al|ka|li (ant al′kə lī), *n., pl.* **-lis** or **-lies**. anything that counteracts the action of an alkali, especially within the body.

ant|al|ka|line (ant al′kə līn, -lin), *adj., n.* **—*adj.*** counteracting the action of alkalis.
—*n.* = antalkali.

ant|a|pex (ant ā′peks), *n.* that point on the celestial sphere away from which the sun and solar system are moving.

ant|arc|tic (ant ärk′tik, -är′tik), *adj.* at, around, or near the South Pole; of the south polar region: *The typical antarctic plants are the lichens* (Science News).
the Antarctic, the south polar region: *Rain and disease are practically strangers to the Antarctic* (New Yorker).
[< Latin *antarcticus* < Greek *antarktikós* opposite the north < *anti-* opposite + *arktikós* of the north; see etym. under **arctic**]

***Antarctic Circle** or **antarctic circle**, **1** the imaginary boundary of the south polar region. It runs parallel to the equator at 23 degrees 30 minutes (23°30′) north of the South Pole. **2** = Antarctic Zone.

Antarctic Convergence, the point in the Antarctic Ocean where warmer tropical waters meet the cold polar waters. Air temperatures, cloud formations, and ocean life change abruptly at the convergence.

Antarctic Divergence, the line in the Antarctic Ocean along which a current, formed from westerly winds, meets easterly winds.

Antarctic Zone, the region between the Antarctic Circle and the South Pole, including the Antarctic Ocean and Antarctica.

An|tar|es (an tãr′ēz), *n.* a red star of the first magnitude, the largest and brightest star in the constellation Scorpio. [< Latin *Antarēs* < Greek *Antárēs* < *anti-* like + *Árēs* Mars (from its color)]

ant|ar|thrit|ic (ant′är thrit′ik), *adj., n.* **—*adj.*** preventing or relieving arthritis; used against arthritis.
—*n.* an antarthritic agent.

ant|asth|mat|ic (ant′az mat′ik, -as-), *adj., n.*
—*adj.* preventing or relieving asthma; used against asthma.
—*n.* an antasthmatic agent.

ant bear, **1** a large South American anteater having long front claws, a very slender head, a shaggy, gray coat marked with a black band on the chest, and a large, bushy tail; great anteater. **2** = aardvark.

ant bird, any one of several varieties of birds which feed mainly on ants, especially one of a family of small birds of South America.

ant cattle, aphids which are kept and tended by ants for the sake of their honeydew.

ant cow, an aphid from which ants obtain honeydew.

an|te (an′tē), *n., v.,* **-ted** or **-teed, -te|ing**. **—*n.*** **1** a stake in the game of poker that each player must put up before receiving a hand or drawing new cards. **2** *U.S. Slang.* a sum of money needed, set aside or paid: *Congress decided to increase the ante for pollution control.*
—*v.t.* *Informal.* **1** to put (one's stake) into the pool in poker. **2** to pay (one's share).
ante up, *Informal.* **a** to put in one's ante in poker: *Ante up! ante up, boys—friends I mean—don't back out!* (J. J. Hooper). **b** to pay one's share: *Death ..; and I have been pardners many a time, an' when he passes the word, I'll ante up with a smile* (Horace Vachell).
[< *ante-*]

ante-, *prefix.* **1** before: *Antedate = to date before. Antenatal = before birth.*
2 in front of: *Anteroom = the room in front* (*of another*).
[< Latin *ante-* before]

***ant|eat|er** (ant′ē′tər), *n.* **1** an animal with a long, sticky tongue, that eats ants and termites, such as the ant bear (great anteater) and the tamandua. Anteaters have no teeth but use their very long claws to dig into ant hills. They have long, slender heads and snouts. Their threadlike tongues are thrust into the nests of ants and then pulled back into the mouth covered with ants. **2** any of the pangolins (scaly anteaters). **3** = echidna. **4** = aardvark.

***anteater**
definition 1

an|te-bel|lum (an′tē bel′əm), *adj.* **1** before the war. **2** *Especially U.S.* before the American Civil War: *The setting is the ante-bellum plantation in springtime* (Saturday Review). [American English < Latin *ante bellum* before the war]

an|te|cede (an′tə sēd′), *v.,* **-ced|ed, -ced|ing**.
—*v.t.* **1** to go before or in front of; precede in time or place. **2** *Rare.* to surpass in rank, wealth, or the like.
—*v.i.* to go or come before; come first.
[< Latin *antecēdere* < *ante-* before + *cēdere* go]

an|te|ced|ence (an′tə sē′dəns), *n.* **1** a going before; precedence; priority. **2** apparent motion of a planet from east to west. [< Latin *antecēdentia* < *antecēdēns, -entis* antecedent]

an|te|ced|en|cy (an′tə sē′dən sē), *n.* = antecedence; priority.

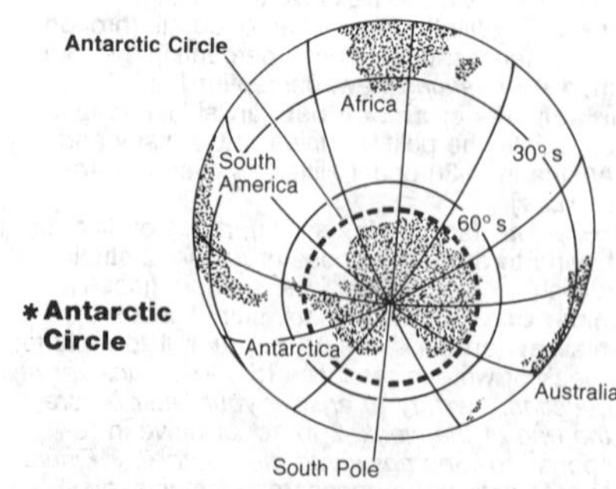

***Antarctic Circle**

an|te|ced|ent (an′tə sē′dənt), *n., adj.* **—*n.*** **1** any word, phrase, or clause to which a word, especially a pronoun, occurring later in a sentence, refers. In "This is the house that Jack built," *house* is the antecedent of *that.* In "I remember the house where I was born," *house* is the antecedent of *where.* In "I was determined to act, and he knew it," the antecedent of *it* is the entire first clause. **2** a previous thing or event; something happening before and leading up to another. **3** *Mathematics.* **a** the first term of a ratio (distinguished from *consequent*). See picture under **consequent**. **b** the first or third term in a proportion. **4** *Logic.* the part of a conditional proposition which states the condition and upon which the other part (the consequent) logically depends. In the proposition "If it rains, we will get wet," *if it rains* is the antecedent.
—*adj.* **1** coming or happening before; preceding; previous: *The cave men lived in a period of history antecedent to written records.* **SYN**: prior, earlier. **2** functioning as an antecedent: *an antecedent clause.*
antecedents, **a** ancestors; ancestry: *He has Scottish antecedents.* **b** the past life or history: *No one knew the antecedents of the mysterious stranger.*
[< Latin *antecēdēns, -entis,* present participle of *antecēdere* < *ante-* before + *cēdere* go]

an|te|ced|ent|ly (an′tə sē′dənt lē), *adv.* = previously.

an|te|ces|sor (an′tə ses′ər, an′tə ses′-), *n.* = predecessor. [< Latin *antecessor* < *antecēdere* < *ante-* before + *cēdere* go]

an|te|cham|ber (an′tē chām′bər), *n.* = anteroom.

an|te|chap|el (an′tē chap′əl), *n.* **1** an anterior (usually smaller) chapel. **2** an anteroom of a chapel.

an|te|choir (an′tē kwīr′), *n.* a space, usually more or less enclosed, in front of the choir of a church.

an|te|church (an′tē chėrch′), *n.* a porch or vestibule of a church.

an|te|com|mun|ion (an′tē kə myün′yən), *n.* that part of the Communion office in the Church of England, which precedes the Communion service proper, and is used on those holy days when there is no Communion.

an|te|court (an′tē kôrt′, -kōrt′), *n.* a front or outer court; forecourt.

an|te|cu|bi|tal (an′tē kyü′bə təl), *adj.* situated at the front of the elbow: *an antecubital vein.*

an|te|date (an′tē dāt, an′tē dāt′), *v.,* **-dat|ed, -dat|ing**, *n.* **—*v.t.*** **1** to be or happen before; precede: *Radio antedated television. Just as the first example of photographic realism, which was produced by the Dutch painters, antedated the camera by at least a century, so the first example of highly organized machines antedated power driven mechanical units by four or five millenniums* (New Yorker). **2** to give an earlier date to (a document or event): *Some states require a person to antedate legal papers to Saturday if they are signed on Sunday.* **3** to anticipate.
—*n.* a date affixed to a document, or assigned to an event, earlier than its actual date.

an|te|di|lu|vi|an (an′tē də lü′vē ən), *adj., n.* **—*adj.*** **1** very old or old-fashioned; antiquated (in a disparaging sense): *antediluvian notions of etiquette.* **2** before the Flood.
—*n.* **1** a very old or old-fashioned person. **2** a person who lived before the Flood.
[< *ante-* + Latin *dīluvium* deluge (< *dīluere* wash away < *dis-* away + *luere* wash) + English *-ian*]

an|te|di|lu|vi|an|ism (an′tē də lü′vē ə niz′əm), *n.* = antiquatedness: *France ... is the home at one and the same time ... of modernism and antediluvianism* (Newsweek).

an|te|fix (an′tē fiks), *n., pl.* **an|ti|fix|es, an|te|fix|a** (an′tē fik′sə). **1** an upright ornament at the lower edge of a tiled roof, placed to conceal the end of a row of convex tiles which cover the joints of the flat tiles. **2** an ornament projecting upward from the top of a cornice. [< Latin *antefīxa,* neuter plural past participle of *antefīgere* < *ante-* in front + *fīgere* make fast]

an|te|fix|al (an′tē fik′səl), *adj.* of or like an antefix.

an|te|flex|ion (an′tē flek′shən), *n.* the process of bending forward or the condition of being bent forward, especially of the uterus; anteversion. [< *ante-* + Latin *flexiō, -ōnis* a bending < *flectere* to bend]

an|te|hall (an′tē hôl′), *n.* a smaller hall opening into a larger one.

***an|te|lope** (an′tə lōp), *n., pl.* **-lope** or **-lopes**. **1** any one of certain mammals of Africa and Asia that are related to goats and cows but resemble the deer in appearance, grace, and speed. Antelope belong to a group of cud-chewing, hoofed animals usually having a single pair of hollow horns that curve backward and do not fork or branch. The hartebeest, black buck, duiker, steenbok, gazelle, and gnu are all antelopes. See the picture opposite on the next page. **2** *U.S.* the pronghorn of the western plains of North America. It is not related to the true antelopes. **3** leather made from the hide of any of these animals. [< Old French *antelop* a mythical savage beast < Medieval Latin *antalopus* < Late Greek *anthólops*]

antelope brush, a grayish shrub of the rose family, found in the arid regions of western North America; bitter brush.

antelope jack rabbit, a large jack rabbit with extremely large ears, an iron-gray body, and whitish sides, common in Arizona and the southwestern United States.

an|te|me|rid|i|an (an′tē mə rid′ē ən), *adj.* before noon; in or having to do with the morning. [< Latin *antemerīdiānus* < *ante merīdiem* before noon]

an|te me|rid|i|em (an′tē mə rid′ē əm), *Latin.* before noon; in the morning; in the period of time between midnight and the following noon. *Abbr:* a.m., A.M.

an|te-mor|tem (an′tē môr′təm), *adj.* before death, especially just before death: *an ante-mortem confession.* [< Latin *ante mortem* before death]

an|te|mun|dane (an′tē mun′dān), *adj.* before the creation of the world. [< *ante-* + *mundane*]

an|te|na|tal (an′tē nā′təl), *adj.* happening or existing before birth; prenatal: *antenatal care.* [< *ante-* + *natal*] —**an′te|na′tal|ly**, *adv.*

an|ten|na (an ten′ə), *n., pl.* **-ten|nae** (-ten′ē) *for 1 and 3,* **-ten|nas** *for 2.* **1** one of the long, slender feelers on the head of an insect, centipede, scorpion, or lobster. Insects and centipedes have one pair of them; lobsters and crabs have two pairs. Some other arthropods, such as spiders, have none. Most antennae are useful primarily as organs of touch, but some are sensitive to odors, sounds, and light. **2** a long wire or set of wires or rods, used in television, radio, or radar for sending out or receiving electromagnetic waves; aerial. **3** *Figurative.* sense of perception: *A resourceful administrator with keen political antennae ...* (Harper's). *American wits at the moment have the antennae for details of cliché that the English have for details of vernacular* (Penelope Gilliatt). [< Latin *antenna* sail yard; of uncertain origin]

an|ten|nae (an ten′ē), *n.* a plural of **antenna** (defs. 1 and 3).

an|ten|nal (an ten′əl), *adj. Zoology.* of or having to do with antennae; bearing antennae: *Entomologists attach contacts to the antennal nerve fibres, which run from the olfactory sense organs to the brain* (New Scientist).

an|ten|na|ry (an ten′ər ē), *adj.* = antennal.

an|ten|nule (an ten′yül), *n. Zoology.* **1** a small antenna or similar organ. **2** one of a pair of small antennae in front of a pair of larger antennae on the head of a crustacean. [< *antenna* + *-ule*, a diminutive suffix]

An|te|nor (an tē′nər), *n. Greek Legend.* a wise old man of Troy who urged, without success, that Helen be returned to Menelaus.

an|te|num|ber (an′tē num′bər), *n.* the preceding number.

an|te|nup|tial (an′tē nup′shəl), *adj.* before marriage. [< *ante-* + *nuptial*]

an|te|or|bi|tal (an′tē ôr′bə təl), *adj.* situated in front of the eye. [< *ante-* + *orbital*]

an|te|par|tum (an′tē pär′təm), *adj.* before childbirth; preceding delivery of a child. [< Latin *ante partum*]

an|te|past (an′tē past, -päst), *n. Archaic.* a foretaste. [< *ante-* + Latin *pāstus* food < *pāscere* to feed]

an|te|pen|di|um (an′tē pen′dē əm), *n., pl.* **-di|a** (-dē ə), **-di|ums.** **1** a hanging, screen, or cloth to cover the front of an altar; frontal. **2** an ornamental cover for the reading desk of a pulpit. [< Medieval Latin *antependium* < Latin *ante-* before + *pendere* hang]

an|te|pe|nult (an′tē pē′nult, -pi nult′), *n.* the third syllable from the end of a word. In *an te ri or, te* is the antepenult. [< Latin (*syllaba*) *antepaenultima* < *ante-* before + *paene* almost + *ultimus* last]

an|te|pe|nul|ti|ma (an′tē pi nul′tə mə), *n.* = antepenult.

an|te|pe|nul|ti|mate (an′tē pi nul′tə mit), *adj., n.* —*adj.* **1** third from the end; last but two. **2** of or having to do with the antepenult: *English and Russian have much in common since they are both strongly stressed tongues showing both penultimate and antepenultimate rhythms* (Simeon Potter).
—*n.* = antepenult.

an|te|porch (an′tē pôrch′, -pōrch′), *n.* an outer, often smaller porch opening into a larger one.

an|te|port (an′tē pôrt′, -pōrt′), *n. Obsolete.* an outer gate or door. [< *ante-* + *port²*]

an|te-post (an′tē pōst′), *adj. British.* made before the event on the race track; occurring prior to post time.

an|te|pran|di|al (an′tē pran′dē əl), *adj.* before dinner. [< *ante-* + Latin *prandium* dinner + English *-al¹*]

ant|er|gic (an tėr′jik), *adj.* acting in opposition to the action of another part, such as a muscle: *antergic contraction.* [< *ant-* + *-ergic*, as in *synergic*]

an|te|ri|or (an tir′ē ər), *adj.* **1** more to the front; fore: *The anterior part of a fish contains the head and gills.* **2** going before; earlier; previous: *Events anterior to the last war forecast its coming.* SYN: prior. [< Latin *anterior*, comparative of *ante* before] —**an|te′ri|or|ly**, *adv.* —**an|te′ri|or|ness**, *n.*

an|te|ri|or|i|ty (an tir′ē ôr′ə tē, -or′-), *n.* the state or quality of being anterior.

an|ter|o|in|fe|ri|or (an′tər ō in fir′ē ər), *adj.* lower front.

an|ter|o|lat|er|al (an′tər ō lat′ər əl), *adj.* front and to one side.

an|te|room (an′tē rüm′, -rům′), *n.* a small room leading to a larger one; a waiting room. SYN: antechamber, vestibule, foyer.

an|ter|o|pa|ri|e|tal (an′tər ō pə rī′ə təl), *adj.* of or having to do with the lateral plates of the skull.

an|ter|o|pos|te|ri|or (an′tər ō pos tir′ē ər), *adj.* front and back; forward and backward.

an|ter|o|ven|tral (an′tər ō ven′trəl), *adj.* front and toward the belly surface.

an|te|type (an′tē tīp′), *n.* a preceding type; an earlier example.

an|te|ver|sion (an′tē vėr′zhən, -shən), *n.* the process of anteverting or the condition of being anteverted; anteflexion, especially of the uterus, so that the broad upper portion is turned toward the pubis. [< Latin *anteversiō, -ōnis* < *antevertere* turn forwards]

an|te|vert (an′tē vėrt′), *v.t.* to bend or tip forward, especially the uterus.

ant|heap (ant′hēp′), *n.* = anthill.

ant|he|li|on (ant hē′lē ən, an thē′-), *n., pl.* **-li|a** (-lē ə). **1** a luminous ring seen, chiefly on high mountains or in polar regions, surrounding the shadow of an object, such as the observer's head, projected on a cloud, fog bank, or the like, opposite to the sun. **2** a bright spot sometimes seen directly opposite and at the same altitude as the sun, caused by reflections from ice and snow. [< Greek *anthēlion* < *anti-* opposite + *hēlios* sun]

ant|he|lix (ant hē′liks), *n., pl.* **-hel|i|ces** (-hel′ə sēz), **-he|lix|es.** = antihelix.

an|thel|min|tic (an′thel min′tik), *adj., n.* —*adj.* destroying or expelling intestinal worms.
—*n.* an anthelmintic agent or remedy.
[< *ant-* against + Greek *hélmins, -inthos* worm + English *-ic*]

an|them (an′thəm), *n., v.* —*n.* **1** a song of praise, devotion, or patriotism: *"The Star-Spangled Banner" is the national anthem of the United States.* **2** a piece of sacred vocal music, usually with words from some passage in the Bible. SYN: hymn, chant. **3** a hymn sung in alternate parts; antiphon.
—*v.t.* to celebrate or praise in an anthem; sing to sacred music.
[< Late Latin *antefana* < *antiphōna* psalm < Greek *anti-* opposed to + *phōnḗ* sound. See etym. of doublet **antiphon.**]

an|the|mi|on (an thē′mē ən), *n., pl.* **-mi|a** (-mē ə). a flat ornament of floral or leaflike forms in a radiating cluster, such as in architectural decoration, embroidery, or vase painting. [< Greek *anthémion* (diminutive) < *ánthemon* flower < *ánthos* flower]

an|the|mis (an′thə mis), *n.* any one of a genus of thistles, the flowers of which resemble those of the daisy. [< Greek *anthemís* camomile]

an|ther (an′thər), *n.* the part of the stamen of a flower that bears the pollen. It is usually a double-celled sac situated at the end of a slender, threadlike stem (filament). See picture under **flower.** [< New Latin *anthera* < Greek *antherá*, feminine of *antherós* flowery < *ánthē* full bloom]

an|ther|al (an′thər əl), *adj.* of or having to do with an anther or anthers.

an|ther|id|i|al (an′thə rid′ē əl), *adj.* of an antheridium.

an|ther|id|i|o|phore (an′thə rid′ē ə fôr, -fōr), *n.* a gametophore that bears only antheridia. [< *antheridium* + *-phore*]

an|ther|id|i|um (an′thə rid′ē əm), *n., pl.* **-i|a** (-ē ə). the part of ferns, mosses, and related plants that produces the male reproductive cells. [< New Latin *antheridium* < *anthera* anther + Greek *-idion*, a diminutive suffix]

an|ther|less (an′thər lis), *adj.* without anthers.

an|ther|o|zo|id (an′thər ə zō′id, an′thər ə zoid), *n.* = spermatozoid: *When the sex cells become mature, the male cell, or antherozoid, swims through the moisture on the plant to the female cell, and fertilizes the egg* (Rolla M. Tryon). [< *anther* + *zooid*]

an|the|sis (an thē′sis), *n.* full bloom: *flowers in the anthesis.* [< Greek *ánthēsis* < *antheîn* to blossom < *ánthos* flower]

ant|hill (ant′hil′), *n.* **1** a heap of dirt piled up by ants around the entrance to their tunnels; antheap. **2** *Figurative.* a congested mass, especially of people: ... *the appalling human anthill of Bengal* (Manchester Guardian Weekly).

an|tho|carp (an′thə kärp), *n.* a fruit having some of its parts consist of tissue other than the ripened ovary, such as the blackberry, strawberry, or fig; accessory fruit; pseudocarp. [< Greek *ánthos* flower + *karpós* fruit]

an|tho|car|pous (an′thə kär′pəs), *adj.* of or having to do with an anthocarp or anthocarps.

an|tho|cy|an (an′thə sī′ən), *n.* = anthocyanin.

an|tho|cy|a|nin (an′thə sī′ə nin), *n.* any one of a group of pigments formed in the cell sap of plants, which produce the deep red, blue, lavender, and purple colors of petals, leaves, roots, or fruits: *Most of the reds, blues, and purples seen in autumn foliage are due to ... anthocyanins* (Fred W. Emerson). [< Greek *ánthos* flower + *kýanos* blue + English *-in*]

an|tho|di|um (an thō′dē əm), *n., pl.* **-di|a** (-dē ə). **1** the flower head, or capitulum, of composite plants; compound flower. **2** the involucre surrounding the flower head of composite plants. [< New Latin *anthodium* < Greek *anthṓdēs* flowerlike + *-ion*, a diminutive suffix]

an|thog|ra|phy (an thog′rə fē), *n.* the botanical description of flowers. [< Greek *ánthos* flower + English *-graphy*]

an|tho|log|i|cal (an′thə loj′ə kəl), *adj.* **1** of or like a literary anthology. **2** *Obsolete.* treating of flowers.

an|thol|o|gist (an thol′ə jist), *n.* a person who makes an anthology; one who selects, arranges, and edits the material for an anthology or for anthologies.

an|thol|o|gize (an thol′ə jīz), *v.,* **-gized, -giz|ing.**
—*v.t.* to make an anthology of or from; use in an anthology.
—*v.i.* to select and put material together in an anthology.

an|thol|o|gy (an thol′ə jē), *n., pl.* **-gies.** **1** a collection of poems or prose selections, usually from various authors, and especially of a particular type, period, or country: *an anthology of 20th-century American poetry.* **2** a collection of paintings, records, or motion pictures: *Wildenstein's Gallery ... exhibits an anthology of watercolours by 14 contemporary French artists* (Manchester Guardian). [< Greek *anthología*, ultimately < *ánthos* flower + *légein* gather]

an|tho|my|i|id (an′thə mī′ī′id), *n.* any one of a family of flies related to the housefly, whose larvae damage crops. [< New Latin *Anthomyiidae* the family name < Greek *ánthos* flower + *myîa* the fly]

an|thoph|a|gous (an thof′ə gəs), *adj.* that eats flowers, as various beetles. [< Greek *ánthos* flower + *phageîn* eat + English *-ous*]

an|thoph|i|lous (an thof′ə ləs), *adj.* that loves flowers, as bees. [< Greek *ánthos* flower + *phílos*

***antelope** definition 1

Grant's gazelle

hartebeest

steenbok

Pronunciation Key: hat, āge, cãre, fär; let, ēqual, tėrm, it, īce; hot, ōpen, ôrder; oil, out; cup, pu̇t, rüle; child; long; thin; ᴛʜen; zh, measure; ə represents **a** in about, **e** in taken, **i** in pencil, **o** in lemon, **u** in circus.

(with English *-ous*) loving]

an|tho|phore (an′thə fôr, -fōr), *n.* an elongation of the receptacle of a flower, between the calyx and the corolla, forming a stalk bearing the corolla, stamens, and pistil. [< French *anthophore,* learned borrowing from Greek *anthophóros* flower-bearing < *ánthos* flower + *phérein* to bear]

an|thoph|o|rous (an thof′ər əs), *adj.* that bears flowers or a flower.

an|tho|phyl|lite (an′thə fil′īt), *n.* a variety of asbestos with short, brittle fibers, used in cement, plasters, paint, and as insulating material. [< New Latin *anthophyllum* clove (because of its color) (< Greek *ánthos* flower + *phýllon* leaf) + English *-ite*[1]]

an|tho|tax|y (an′thə tak′sē), *n.* classification of flowers according to manner of grouping on the stem (inflorescence). [< Greek *ánthos* flower + *táxis* arrangement]

an|tho|zo|an (an′thə zō′ən), *n., adj.* **—*n.*** a sea anemone, coral, or other polyp with radial segments; any one of a class of marine coelenterates with biradial symmetry; an actinozoan.
—*adj.* of or belonging to the anthozoans.
[< New Latin *Anthozoa* (< Greek *ánthos* flower + *zôion* animal) + English *-an*]

an|tho|zo|on (an′thə zō′ən, -on), *n., pl.* **-zo|a** (-zō′ə). = anthozoan.

an|thra|cene (an′thrə sēn), *n.* a colorless, crystalline compound used in making alizarin dyes. It is a complex compound of hydrogen and carbon, obtained in distilling coal tar. *Formula:* $C_{14}H_{10}$ [< Greek *ánthrax, -akos* charcoal + English *-ene*]

an|thrac|ic (an thras′ik), *adj.* of or having to do with the disease anthrax.

an|thra|cite (an′thrə sīt), *n.* a coal that burns with very little smoke or flame; hard coal. It consists almost entirely of carbon. [< Latin *anthracītis* < Greek *anthrakîtis,* name of a fiery gem < *ánthrax* live coal, charcoal]

an|thra|cit|ic (an′thrə sit′ik), *adj.* of or like anthracite.

an|thrac|nose (an thrak′nōs), *n.* any one of various diseases of plants caused by fungi whose mycelia penetrate the tissue of the plant, where they form spores which break through the surface of the tissue and appear as blackish spots; bitter rot. Anthracnose can destroy certain food crops, such as some grains, melons, and beans. [< Greek *ánthrax, -akos* carbuncle, charcoal + *nósos* disease]

an|thra|coid (an′thrə koid), *adj.* resembling anthrax. [< *anthrax* + *-oid*]

an|thra|co|sis (an′thrə kō′sis), *n.* lung disease produced by the inhalation of coal dust. [< New Latin *anthracosis* < Greek *ánthrax, -akos* live coal + New Latin *-osis* -osis]

an|thra|co|there (an′thrə kə thir), *n.* any one of a genus of extinct mammals of the Tertiary period, related to the pig and occasionally growing as large as a rhinoceros. [< New Latin *Anthracotherium* < Greek *ánthrax, -akos* coal + *thēríon* beast]

an|thra|cot|ic (an′thrə kot′ik), *adj.* having to do with or affected by anthracosis.

an|thra|qui|none (an′thrə kwə nōn′, -kwin′ōn), *n.* a hydrocarbon, crystallizing in yellow needles, obtained from anthracene by oxidation, used in making alizarin dyes. *Formula:* $C_{14}H_8O_2$ [< *anthra*(cene) + *quinone*]

an|thrax (an′thraks), *n., pl.* **-thra|ces** (-thrə sēz). **1** an infectious, often fatal, disease of cattle, sheep, and other quadrupeds, that human beings may get from them. **2** a malignant carbuncle that is the usual lesion of this disease. **3** a carbuncle of any sort. [< Late Latin *anthrax* < Greek *ánthrax* carbuncle, live coal]

anthrop-, *combining form.* the form of **anthropo-** before vowels, as in *anthropoid.*

anthrop., 1 anthropological. 2 anthropology.

an|throp|ic (an throp′ik), *adj.* having to do with man; human.

an|throp|i|cal (an throp′ə kəl), *adj.* = anthropic.

anthropo-, *combining form.* man; human being; human: *Anthropology = the science of man.* Also, **anthrop-** before vowels. [< Greek *ánthrōpos* man]

an|thro|po|cen|tric (an′thrə pə sen′trik), *adj.* **1** regarding man as the central fact, and his existence and welfare as the ultimate aim, of the universe. **2** interpreting all things in the universe in terms of man and his values. **—an′thro|po|cen′tri|cal|ly,** *adv.*

an|thro|po|cen|trism (an′thrə pə sen′triz əm), *n.* a belief, doctrine, or attitude in which the universe is regarded as centered about man, or in terms of man.

an|thro|po|gen|e|sis (an′thrə pə jen′ə sis), *n.* the study of the origin and evolution of the human race. [< *anthropo-* + *genesis*]

an|thro|po|ge|net|ic (an′thrə pō jə net′ik), *adj.* of or having to do with anthropogenesis.

an|thro|pog|e|ny (an′thrə poj′ə nē), *n.* = anthropogenesis.

an|thro|po|ge|o|graph|ic (an′thrə pə jē′ə graf′ik), *adj.* = anthropogeographical.

an|thro|po|ge|o|graph|i|cal (an′thrə pə jē′ə graf′ə kəl), *adj.* of or having to do with anthropogeography. **—an′thro|po|ge′o|graph′i|cal|ly,** *adv.*

an|thro|po|ge|og|ra|phy (an′thrə pō jē og′rə fē), *n.* the branch of geography that deals especially with the distribution and environment of man. It is also called *human geography.*

an|thro|pog|o|ny (an′thrə pog′ə nē), *n.* = anthropogenesis.

an|thro|po|graph|ic (an′thrə pə graf′ik), *adj.* of or having to do with anthropography.

an|thro|pog|ra|phy (an′thrə pog′rə fē), *n.* the branch of anthropology that deals especially with the geographical distribution of man. [< *anthropo-* + *-graphy*]

an|thro|poid (an′thrə poid), *adj., n.* **—*adj.*** **1** (of certain apes) manlike; resembling man: *The anthropoid structure of certain apes includes lack of a tail and cheek pouches.* **2** (of human beings) apelike.
—*n.* a manlike ape. Gorillas, chimpanzees, orangutans, and gibbons are anthropoids; lemurs and monkeys are not.
[< Greek *anthrōpoeidēs* < *ánthrōpos* man + *eîdos* shape]

an|thro|poi|dal (an′thrə poi′dəl), *adj.* of anthropoid nature or structure.

anthropoid ape, any ape of the family that includes the gorilla, chimpanzee, gibbon, and orangutan, characterized by their general structural resemblance to man, such as lack of a tail and shape and proportion of various bones, and absence of cheek pouches.

An|thro|poi|de|a (an′thrə poi′dē ə), *n.* a suborder of primates, including monkeys, apes, and man. [< New Latin *Anthropoidea*]

an|thro|po|lat|ric (an′thrə pə lat′rik), *adj.* of or having to do with anthropolatry.

an|thro|pol|a|try (an′thrə pol′ə trē), *n.* the worship of a human being as divine. [< *anthropo-* + Greek *latreiā* worship]

an|thro|po|log|ic (an′thrə pə loj′ik), *adj. Rare.* anthropological.

an|thro|po|log|i|cal (an′thrə pə loj′ə kəl), *adj.* of or having to do with anthropology: *From an anthropological approach, Margaret Mead points out how individuals who grow up in preliterate groups which stress competition become competitive-minded* (Emory S. Bogardus). **—an′thro|po|log′i|cal|ly,** *adv.*

an|thro|pol|o|gist (an′thrə pol′ə jist), *n.* a person who studies anthropology: *Essentially the function of the anthropologist is to integrate the various disciplines dealing with man* (Beals and Hoijer).

an|thro|pol|o|gy (an′thrə pol′ə jē), *n.* the science of man, that deals with his physical characteristics, with the origin and development of races, and with the cultures, customs, and beliefs of mankind: *Most of the sciences dealing with man tend to concentrate on a limited number of aspects. Anthropology has tended to concentrate on the over-all problems, particularly through the concept of culture* (Beals and Hoijer). [< *anthropo-* + *-logy*]

an|thro|pom|e|ter (an′thrə pom′ə tər), *n.* a device for measuring the human body and its proportions. [< *anthropo-* + *-meter*]

an|thro|po|met|ric (an′thrə pə met′rik), *adj.* of or having to do with anthropometry. **—an′thro|po|met′ri|cal|ly,** *adv.*

an|thro|po|met|ri|cal (an′thrə pə met′rə kəl), *adj.* = anthropometric.

an|thro|pom|e|trist (an′thrə pom′ə trist), *n.* a person who studies anthropometry.

an|thro|pom|e|try (an′thrə pom′ə trē), *n.* the branch of anthropology that deals with measurement of the human body and especially its proportions. [< *anthropo-* + *-metry*]

an|thro|po|morph (an′thrə pə môrf′), *n.* a representation of the human form in art: *cartooned anthropomorphs.* [< *anthropo-* + Greek *morphḗ* form]

an|thro|po|mor|phic (an′thrə pə môr′fik), *adj.* attributing human form or qualities to gods, animals, or things: *The religion of ancient Greece was anthropomorphic. Today we speak of the eye of a needle, the finger of a sundial, the hands of a clock, the teeth of a comb or saw, and so on. All these expressions, which seem to be so simple and obvious, imply the use of anthropomorphic similes* (Simeon Potter). [< *anthropo-* + Greek *morphḗ* form + English *-ic*] **—an′thro|po|mor′phi|cal|ly,** *adv.*

an|thro|po|mor|phism (an′thrə pə môr′fiz əm), *n.* the act or practice of attributing human form or qualities to gods, animals, or things. **—an′thro|po|mor′phist,** *n.*

an|thro|po|mor|phize (an′thrə pə môr′fīz), *v.t., v.i.,* **-phized, -phiz|ing.** to attribute human form or qualities to gods, animals, or things. **—an′thro|po|mor′phi|za′tion,** *n.*

an|thro|po|mor|pho|sis (an′thrə pə môr′fə sis), *n.* transformation into human shape. [< *anthropo-* + (meta)*morphosis*]

an|thro|po|mor|phous (an′thrə pə môr′fəs), *adj.* **1** of human form; having the form of a man. **2** = anthropomorphic. **—an′thro|po|mor′phous|ly,** *adv.*

an|thro|po|path|ic (an′thrə pə path′ik), *adj.* of or having to do with anthropopathy. **—an′thro|po|path′i|cal|ly,** *adv.*

an|thro|pop|a|thism (an′thrə pop′ə thiz əm), *n.* = anthropopathy.

an|thro|pop|a|thy (an′thrə pop′ə thē), *n.* the act or practice of attributing human feelings and passions to a god, animal, or thing.

an|thro|poph|a|gi (an′thrə pof′ə jī), *n.pl., sing.* **-gus.** man-eaters; cannibals. [< Latin *anthrōpophagī* (plural) < Greek *anthrōpophágos* maneating < *ánthrōpos* man + *phageîn* eat]

an|thro|po|phag|ic (an′thrə pə faj′ik), *adj.* = cannibalistic.

an|thro|po|phag|i|cal (an′thrə pə faj′ə kəl), *adj.* = cannibalistic.

an|thro|poph|a|gism (an′thrə pof′ə jiz əm), *n.* = cannibalism.

an|thro|poph|a|gist (an′thrə pof′ə jist), *n.* = cannibal.

an|thro|poph|a|gite (an′thrə pof′ə jīt), *n.* = cannibal.

an|thro|poph|a|gous (an′thrə pof′ə gəs), *adj.* = cannibalistic.

an|thro|poph|a|gus (an′thrə pof′ə gəs), *n.* singular of **anthropophagi.**

an|thro|poph|a|gy (an′thrə pof′ə jē), *n.* = cannibalism.

an|thro|poph|u|ism (an′thrə pof′yu̇ iz əm), *n.* the ascription of human nature, functions, or desires, to a god or gods. [< *anthropo-* + Greek *phyḗ* nature + English *-ism*]

an|thro|poph|u|is|tic (an′thrə pof′yu̇ is′tik), *adj.* of or having to do with anthropophuism.

an|thro|po|psy|chic (an′thrə pə sī′kik), *adj.* of or having to do with anthropopsychism.

an|thro|po|psy|chism (an′thrə pə sī′kiz əm), *n.* the attributing of a soul to nature or natural phenomena. [< *anthropo-* + Greek *psȳchḗ* soul + English *-ism*]

an|thro|po|soph|i|cal (an′thrə pə sof′ə kəl), *adj.* of or having to do with the spiritualist doctrine of anthroposophy.

an|thro|pos|o|phy (an′thrə pos′ə fē), *n.* a spiritualist doctrine based upon the assumed perfectibility of man's understanding of himself and mankind. It was developed from Theosophy chiefly by Rudolf Steiner, 1861-1925, an Austrian philosopher. [< *anthropo-* + Greek *sophiā* wisdom]

an|thro|po|tom|i|cal (an′thrə pə tom′ə kəl), *adj.* of or having to do with anthropotomy.

an|thro|pot|o|mist (an′thrə pot′ə mist), *n.* a person who studies anthropotomy.

an|thro|pot|o|my (an′thrə pot′ə mē), *n.* the anatomy of the human body. [< *anthropo-* + Greek *-tomiā* a cutting]

an|thu|ri|um (an thu̇r′ē əm), *n.* any one of a genus of tropical American plants of the arum family having brightly colored leaves. [< New Latin *Anthurium* < Greek *ánthos* flower + *ourā* tail]

an|ti (an′tī, -tē), *n., pl.* **-tis,** *adj., prep. Informal.*
—*n.* a person opposed to something, such as a plan, idea, or political party.
—*adj.* of or belonging to the opposition; opposed; against: *He is inclined to be anti by profession—anti the new* (Manchester Guardian).
—*prep.* opposed to; against: *anti everything new.*
[< *anti-*]

anti-, *prefix.* **1** against; opposed to ___: *Antiaircraft = against aircraft. Antislavery = opposed to slavery.*
2 not; the opposite of ___: *Antisocial = the opposite of social. Antiwarlike = not warlike.*
3 rival ___: *Antipope = rival pope.*
4 preventing or counteracting ___: *Antirust = preventing or counteracting rust. Antiseptic = preventing or counteracting infection.*
5 preventing, curing, or alleviating ___: *Antiscorbutic = preventing, curing, or alleviating scurvy.*
6 (thing) placed opposite ___; (thing) moving or acting in opposition to ___: *Anticathode = the plate opposite the cathode. Antimonsoon = air current moving in the opposite direction from that of a monsoon.*
7 analogue; counterpart: *Antineutron = analogue of a neutron. Anticodon = counterpart of a codon.* Also, **ant-** before vowels and *h.*
[< Greek *anti-* opposite < *antí*]
▶**Anti-** is usually hyphened before root words beginning with a vowel and before proper nouns and adjectives: *anti-imperialistic, anti-intellectual, anti-British, anti-Semitic. Anti-* is pronounced an′tē, or often, more emphatically, an′tī.

an|ti|a|bor|tion (an′tē ə bôr′shən), *adj.* opposed to or prohibiting induced abortions: *antiabortion laws. The antiabortion movement . . . is arguing for the obligations of the family at a time when the family is a declining American institution* (Russell Baker). **—an′ti|a|bor′tion|ism,** *n.* **—an′ti|a|bor′tion|ist,** *n.*

an|ti-ac|id (an′tē as′id), *n., adj.* = antacid.

an|ti-ad|min|is|tra|tion (an′tē ad min′ə strā′shən), *adj.* opposed to the administrative branch of a government or its policies.

an|ti|air (an′tē ãr′), *adj.* = antiaircraft.

an|ti|air|craft (an′tē ãr′kraft′, -kräft′), *adj., n.* **—*adj.*** used in defense against enemy aircraft: *antiaircraft missiles.*
—*n.* **1** an antiaircraft gun. **2** gunfire from antiaircraft guns. *Abbr:* AA (no periods).

an|ti-al|co|hol|ic (an′tē al′kə hôl′ik, -hol′-), *adj.* opposed to the manufacture, sale, or drinking of alcoholic beverages.

an|ti-al|co|hol|ism (an′tē al′kə hô liz′əm, -ho-), *n.* opposition to the manufacture, sale, or drinking of alcoholic beverages; prohibitionism.

an|ti|al|ler|gic (an′tē ə lėr′jik), *adj., n.* **—*adj.*** preventing or inhibiting the action of an allergen.
—*n.* an antiallergic substance, such as an antihistamine.

an|ti-A|mer|i|can (an′tē ə mer′ə kən), *adj.* opposed to the interests or the people of the United States.
▶**anti-American, un-American.** Users of these words should bear in mind that either may tend to convey a strong sense of opprobrium, with the latter now perhaps stronger than the former in its suggestion of activities considered by the user to border upon if not actually to constitute treason.

an|ti-A|mer|i|can|ism (an′tē ə mer′ə kə niz′əm), *n.* anti-American policies, beliefs, or actions: *In Tunisia, . . . anger and frustration erupted in a wave of anti-Americanism and in destruction of U.S. property* (Newsweek).

an|ti-an|a|phy|lac|tic (an′tē an′ə fə lak′tik), *adj.* **1** desensitized to an antigen or antigens. **2** of or having to do with anergy.

an|ti|an|dro|gen (an′tē an′drə jən), *n.* a substance that neutralizes the action of androgens in the body.

an|ti-a|ne|mic (an′tē ə nē′mik), *adj., n.* **—*adj.*** preventing or curing anemia; used against anemia.
—*n.* an anti-anemic agent or remedy, especially vitamin B_{12}.

an|ti|ar (an′tē är), *n.* **1** the upas tree of Java, of the mulberry family. **2** its sap, which is sometimes poisonous. **3** a poison for arrows made from its sap. [< Javanese *antjar*]

an|ti-art (an′tē ärt′), *n., adj.* **—*n.*** **1** any form of art that rejects standard artistic or aesthetic concepts or values: *The combination of formal qualities with crude fact in Cubist collage contained the seeds of anti-art* (New Yorker). **2** = neo-Dada. **—*adj.*** of or having to do with anti-art: *It was not surprising that Miró . . . joined the anti-art iconoclasm of the Dadaists* (Observer).

an|ti-a|tom (an′tē at′əm), *n.* atom of antimatter.

an|ti|bac|te|ri|al (an′tē bak tir′ē əl), *adj., n.* **—*adj.*** that destroys or inhibits the growth or action of bacteria.
—*n.* an antibacterial substance or agent.

an|ti|bal|lis|tic missile (an′tē bə lis′tik), a missile which is designed to intercept and destroy a ballistic missile.

an|ti|bar|y|on (an′tē bar′ē on) *n.* an antiparticle of a baryon, such as an antiproton or antineutron.

an|ti|bil|ious (an′tē bil′yəs), *adj., n.* **—*adj.*** preventing or relieving biliousness; used against biliousness.
—*n.* an antibilious agent or remedy.

an|ti|bi|o|sis (an′tē bī ō′sis), *n.* **1** an association between organisms which is detrimental to one of them. **2** the antagonistic association between a microorganism and an antibiotic. [< *anti-* + Greek *bíōsis* way of life < *bíos* life]

an|ti|bi|ot|ic (an′tē bī ot′ik), *n., adj.* **—*n.*** a substance produced by a living organism, especially a bacterium or a fungus, that destroys or weakens germs. Penicillin is an antibiotic useful in treating scarlet fever and common types of blood poisoning. Tetracycline and streptomycin are antibiotics.
—*adj.* of or having to do with antibiosis or antibiotics; destroying or inhibiting the growth or action of microorganisms through antibiosis: *Antibiotic drugs are well on the way to abolishing diseases caused by bacteria and larger organisms, and even some viruses* (Science News Letter).

an|ti|bish|op (an′tē bish′əp), *n.* a rival, opposing, or spurious bishop. See also **antipope.**

an|ti|bod|y (an′tē bod′ē), *n., pl.* **-bod|ies.** **1** a protein substance produced in the blood or tissues of animals or man that destroys or weakens bacteria or neutralizes the poisons they produce. An antibody is formed in response to some specific antigen, and reacts with or neutralizes that antigen. Antibodies are named according to the type of their activity and include antitoxins, hemolysins, agglutinins, and precipitins. **2** a substance whose action opposes that of some other substance. [translation of German *Antikörper* < Greek *anti-* opposing + German *Körper* body, substance]

an|tic (an′tik), *n., adj., v.,* **-ticked, -tick|ing.** **—*n.*** **1** Often, **antics.** a funny or grotesque gesture or action; a silly trick; caper: *The clown amused the children by his antics.* **2** *Archaic.* a clown: *. . . dancing and hallooing like an antic* (Daniel Defoe).
—*adj.* grotesque, bizarre, or ludicrous, especially in appearance or behavior: *The clown came on with many antic gestures.*
—*v.i.* to perform antics; play the clown.
[< Italian *antico* ancient (with sense of *grottesco* grotesque) < Latin *antīquus* < *ante* before. See etym. of doublet **antique.**]

an|ti|can|cer (an′tē kan′sər), *adj.* used in the treatment or prevention of cancer: *anticancer drugs, an anticancer vaccine.*

an|ti|cap|i|tal|ism (an′tē kap′ə tə liz′əm), *n.* opposition to the principles of capitalism and to the institutions or practices based on them. **—an′ti-cap′i|tal|ist,** *n., adj.*

an|ti|cap|i|tal|is|tic (an′tē kap′ə tə lis′tik), *adj.* = anticapitalist.

an|ti|cat|a|lyst (an′tē kat′ə list), *n. Rare.* a substance which hinders a chemical reaction. [< *anti-* + *catalyst*]

an|ti|cath|ode (an′tē kath′ōd), *n.* **1** the plate, often of platinum, opposite the cathode in an X-ray tube, upon which the cathode rays impinge and produce X rays; target. **2** the anode in a vacuum tube.

an|ti|chlor (an′tē klôr, -klōr), *n.* any substance used to remove excess chlorine from paper pulp or cloth fiber after bleaching.

an|ti|chlo|ris|tic (an′tē klô ris′tik, -klō-), *adj.* of or having to do with an antichlor.

an|ti|cho|lin|er|gic (an′tē kō′lə nėr′jik, -kol′ə-), *adj.* inhibiting cholinergic action; preventing the liberation of acetylcholine at the nerve endings, as by the use of a drug.

an|ti|cho|lin|es|ter|ase (an′tē kō′lə nes′tə rās, -kol′ə-), *n.* a drug or poison that prevents the action of cholinesterase; an anticholinergic substance, such as physostigmine.

An|ti|christ (an′tē krīst′), *n.* the great enemy or opponent of Christ and Christianity, expected to spread destruction through the world only to be defeated and crushed for eternity at the second coming of Christ (I John 2:18).

an|ti|christ (an′tē krīst′), *n.* **1** a person who denies or opposes Christ; an anti-Christian. **2** a false Christ.

an|ti-Chris|tian (an′tē kris′chən), *adj., n.* **—*adj.*** opposed to Christians or to Christianity.
—*n.* an anti-Christian person.

an|ti-Chris|tian|ism (an′tē kris′chə niz əm), *n.* opposition to Christians or to Christianity.

an|ti|church (an′tē chėrch′), *adj.* anticlerical: *growing antichurch pressure of the East German regime* (Time).

an|tic|i|pant (an tis′ə pənt), *adj., n.* **—*adj.*** **1** expectant; anticipative (of). **2** realized or enjoyed in advance; anticipatory (of): *a happiness anticipant of heaven.*
—*n.* a person who anticipates; anticipator.

an|tic|i|pate (an tis′ə pāt), *v.,* **-pat|ed, -pat|ing.** **—*v.t.*** **1** to look forward to; expect: *We anticipated a good time at the party.* **SYN:** foresee, await. See syn. under **expect.** **2** to do before others do; be ahead of in doing: *The Chinese anticipated the European discovery of gunpowder.* **SYN:** antedate, precede. **3** to take care of ahead of time; consider in advance: *Mother anticipated my hunger by baking cookies before I came home from school.* **4** to be before (another) in thinking or acting; forestall: *In the discovery of the South Pole, Scott was anticipated by Amundsen.* **5** to consider or mention before the proper time: *to anticipate a point in the argument.* **6** to cause to happen sooner; hasten; accelerate: *The lazy boy anticipated his dismissal by stealing stamps.* **7** to spend or pay out (money) before it is explicitly placed at one's disposal. **8** to pay (a debt or obligation) before the date it is due.
—*v.i.* to speak of or deal with matters before they arise naturally: *We must not anticipate.*
[< Latin *anticipāre* (with English *-ate*[1]) < *ante* before + *capere* take] **—an|tic′i|pa′tor,** *n.*

an|tic|i|pa|tion (an tis′ə pā′shən), *n.* **1** the act of anticipating; looking forward to; expectation: *The farmer cut more firewood than usual, in anticipation of a cold winter. A pleasure is sometimes greatest in anticipation.* **2** realization, enjoyment, or celebration of an event or experience in advance: *the pleasures of anticipation.* **3** *Law.* **a** the taking into possession or assigning of money from a trust estate before it is properly at one's disposal. **b** a sum thus taken or assigned. **4** *Music.* the introduction of a tone in advance of its chord as a means of varying the melody.

an|tic|i|pa|tive (an tis′ə pā′tiv), *adj.* involving anticipation; having a tendency to anticipate. **—an-tic′i|pa′tive|ly,** *adv.*

an|tic|i|pa|to|ry (an tis′ə pə tôr′ē, -tōr′-), *adj.* anticipating; anticipative: *He feels that without anticipatory investment a free enterprise economy soon gets sick, and that when it does it soon gets very sick* (Atlantic). **—an|tic′i|pa|to′ri|ly,** *adv.*

an|ti|clas|tic (an′tē klas′tik), *adj.* having two opposite curvatures transverse to each other; convex in length and concave in breadth, or vice versa, as a saddle. [< *anti-* + Greek *klastós* broken (< *klân* to break) + English *-ic*]

an|ti|cler|i|cal (an′tē kler′ə kəl), *adj., n.* **—*adj.*** opposed to the influence of the church and clergy, especially in public affairs.
—*n.* an anticlerical person: *In next-door Quebec anticlericals who are themselves Catholics in good standing are trying to put laymen in control [of the schools]* (Harper's).

an|ti|cler|i|cal|ism (an′tē kler′ə kə liz′əm), *n.* opposition to the influence of the church and clergy, especially in public affairs: *. . . a country of lively anticlericalism, Marxist polemics, and half-empty churches* (Time). **—an′ti|cler′i|cal|ist,** *n.*

an|ti|cli|mac|tic (an′tē klī mak′tik), *adj.* of or like an anticlimax. **—an′ti|cli|mac′ti|cal|ly,** *adv.*

an|ti|cli|max (an′tē klī′maks), *n.* **1** an abrupt descent from the important to the trivial or unimportant. *Example:* "Alas! Alas! what shall I do? I've lost my wife and best hat, too!" **2** descent (in importance or interest) contrasting sharply with a previous rise or high point.
[< *anti-* + *climax*]

an|ti|cli|nal (an′tē klī′nəl), *adj., n.* **—*adj.*** of or like an anticline; inclining in opposite directions from a central axis.
—*n.* an anticline.
[< Greek *antiklīnein* (< *anti-* against + *klīnein* to slope, lean) + English *-al*[1]]

an|ti|cline (an′tē klīn), *n. Geology.* a fold of rock strata that bends downward on both sides from its center (contrasted with *syncline*). See picture under **fold**[1].
[< *anticlinal;* patterned on *incline*]

an|ti|cli|no|ri|um (an′tē klī nôr′ē əm, -nōr′-), *n., pl.* **-no|ri|a** (-nôr′ē ə, -nōr′-), **-no|ri|ums.** a mountain range or system in which the folds of strata constitute one huge composite of anticlines and synclines. [< New Latin *anticlinorium* < *anti-* against + Greek *klīnein* to slope + *óros* mountain]

an|ti|clock|wise (an′tē klok′wīz′), *adj., adv.* = counterclockwise.

an|ti|clot|ting (an′tē klot′ing), *adj.* = anticoagulant.

an|tic|ly (an′tə klē), *adv.* = grotesquely.

an|ti|co|ag|u|lant (an′tē kō ag′yə lənt), *n., adj.* **—*n.*** a substance or agent that prevents or slows up coagulation of blood: *Usually, when transfusions are given, . . . an anticoagulant is used to prevent clotting* (World Book Encyclopedia).
—*adj.* that acts as an anticoagulant.

an|ti|co|don (an′tē kō′don), *n. Genetics.* a group of three bases in transfer RNA, corresponding to each codon in messenger RNA: *Transfer RNA loaded with amino acid is thought to "recognize" the codon for that amino acid, perhaps through the binding to the codon of an anticodon of three complementary bases on transfer RNA* (Scientific American).

an|ti|co|in|ci|dence (an′tē kō in′sə dəns), *n.* the prevention of coincidence, especially the arranging of atomic particles in such a way as to avoid unwanted combinations.

an|ti|co|lo|ni|al (an′tē kə lō′nē əl), *adj.* opposed to colonialism: *an anticolonial power.*

an|ti|co|lo|ni|al|ism (an′tē kə lō′nē ə liz′əm), *n.* opposition to colonialism: *The Chinese stress that . . . they too were a colored nation which had to achieve independence through anticolonialism* (Maclean's).

an|ti|co|lo|ni|al|ist (an′tē kə lō′nē ə list), *n., adj.* **—*n.*** an opponent of colonialism.
—*adj.* anticolonial: *The torrent of anticolonialist oratory at the All African People's Conference in Accra . . . seemed to have no end* (Time).

an|ti|com|mu|nism or **an|ti-Com|mu|nism** (an′tē kom′yə niz əm), *n.* opposition to the principles of communism and to the institutions and practices based on them. **—an′ti|com′mu|nist, an′ti-Com′mu|nist,** *n., adj.*

an|ti|con|vul|sant (an′tē kən vul′sənt), *n., adj.* **—*n.*** a drug or agent that prevents or alleviates the effects of convulsions: *When . . . anticonvulsants are effective, they prevent the periodic at-*

Pronunciation Key: hat, āge, cãre, fär; let, ēqual, tėrm; it, īce; hot, ōpen, ôrder; oil, out; cup, pu̇t, rüle; child; long; thin; ᴛʜen; zh, measure; ə represents **a** in about, **e** in taken, **i** in pencil, **o** in lemon, **u** in circus.

tacks which are the manifestation of epilepsy (Harper's).
—***adj.*** that acts as an anticonvulsant.
[< *anti-* + *convuls*(ion) + *-ant*]

an|ti|cor|ro|sive (an′tē kə rō′siv), *n., adj.* —***n.*** a substance or agent that prevents or counteracts corrosion.
—***adj.*** that acts as an anticorrosive.

an|ti|creep (an′tē krēp′), *adj.* preventing creeping (applied to various mechanical devices, such as one for keeping rails from moving lengthwise).

an|ti|creep|ing (an′tē krē′ping), *adj.* = anticreep.

an|ti|cryp|tic (an′tē krip′tik), *adj. Zoology.* that serves to make an animal less conspicuous to its prey, such as natural colorings or markings. [< *anti-* + *cryptic*]

an|tics (an′tiks), *n.pl.* See under **antic** (*n.* def. 1).

an|ti|cy|clone (an′tē sī′klōn), *n.* **1** winds moving ground and away from a center of high pressure, which also moves. The motion of an anticyclone is clockwise in the Northern Hemisphere and counterclockwise in the Southern. **2** an atmospheric disturbance at the edge of such an area. [< *anti-* + *cyclone*]

an|ti|cy|clon|ic (an′tē sī klon′ik), *adj.* of, like, or having to do with an anticyclone. —**an′ti|cy|clon′i|cal|ly,** *adv.*

an|ti|de|pres|sant (an′tē di pres′ənt), *n., adj.* —***n.*** a drug or agent that prevents or alleviates the effects of depression: *The antidepressants ... elevate mood and restore drive and zest for living* (New York Times).
—***adj.*** that acts as an antidepressant.

an|ti|de|riv|a|tive (an′tē də riv′ə tiv), *n.* (in calculus) any function the derivative of which is a given function: *The derivative of X^2 is 2X; an antiderivative of 2X is X^2.*

an|ti|deu|te|ri|um (an′tē dü tir′ē əm, -dyü-), *n.* the analogue in antimatter of deuterium.

an|ti|deu|ter|on (an′tē dü′tə ron, -dyü′-), *n.* the analogue in antimatter of deuteron, consisting of an antiproton and an antineutron.

an|ti|diph|the|rit|ic (an′tē dip′thə rit′ik, -dif′-), *n., adj.* —***n.*** an agent or drug that prevents or cures diphtheria.
—***adj.*** that acts as an antidiphtheritic.

an|ti|dis|crim|i|na|tion (an′tē dis krim′ə nā′shən), *adj.* opposed to discrimination, especially on the basis of race or religion, in education, housing, employment, or recreation: *antidiscrimination legislation.*

an|ti|dis|es|tab|lish|men|tar|i|an (an′tē dis′əstab′lish mən târ′ē ən), *n., adj.* —***n.*** a person who believes in the doctrine of antidisestablishmentarianism.
—***adj.*** of or having to do with the doctrine of antidisestablishmentarianism.

an|ti|dis|es|tab|lish|men|tar|i|an|ism (an′tē-dis′əstab′lish mən târ′ē ə niz′əm), *n.* the doctrine that an established national church, especially the Church of England, should be maintained and should retain its status of formal preeminence with regard to other churches in the same country.

an|ti|di|u|ret|ic (an′tē dī′yů ret′ik), *n., adj.* —***n.*** a drug or agent that reduces or inhibits the elimination of urine.
—***adj.*** that acts as an antidiuretic.

an|ti|do|tal (an′tē dō′təl), *adj.* like an antidote; serving as an antidote. —**an′ti|do′tal|ly,** *adv.*

an|ti|dote (an′tē dōt), *n.* **1** a medicine that counteracts the harmful effect of a poison; remedy: *Milk is an antidote for some poisons.* **2** *Figurative.* a remedy for any evil; counteracting agent: *Education is an antidote for ignorance. Prosperity is a good antidote for political unrest.* [< Latin *antidotum* < Greek *antídoton* given as a remedy, ultimately < *anti-* against + *didónai* give]

an|ti|drom|ic (an′tē drom′ik), *adj. Physiology.* able to conduct impulses in a direction opposite to the usual, as a nerve fiber. [< *anti-* + Greek *drómos* a course + English *-ic*] —**an′ti|drom′i|cal|ly,** *adv.*

an|ti|dump|ing (an′tē dum′ping), *adj.* providing protection against dumping of foreign goods on the domestic market: *antidumping duty, antidumping laws.*

an|ti-e|lec|tron (an′tē i lek′tron), *n.* a positron.

an|ti-en|er|gis|tic (an′tē en′ər jis′tik), *adj.* opposing applied energy.

an|ti-en|zyme (an′tē en′zīm, -zim), *n.* a substance having enzymatic properties that acts to inhibit or reduce the effects of another enzyme: *Discovery that the fungus responsible for Dutch elm disease depends for nutrition on two enzymes formed by it, gave hope that an anti-enzyme may be an effective weapon against this fungus* (Science News Letter).

an|ti|es|tab|lish|ment (an′tē es tab′lish mənt), *adj.* opposed to a country's political, social, and economic establishment: *the antiestablishment movement, antiestablishment slogans.*

an|ti-ev|o|lu|tion|ist (an′tē ev′ə lü′shə nist), *n.* a person opposed to accepting the principles of evolutionary theory.

an|ti|fas|cism or **an|ti-Fas|cism** (an′tē fash′iz əm), *n.* opposition to the principles of fascism and to institutions and practices based on them.

an|ti|fas|cist or **an|ti-Fas|cist** (an′tē fash′ist), *adj., n.* —***adj.*** opposed to the principles of fascism and to the institutions and practices based on them: *The radical young scientists ... were bitterly antifascist* (C. P. Snow).
—***n.*** an antifascist person.

an|ti|fe|brile (an′tē fē′brəl, -feb′rəl), *adj., n.* —***adj.*** tending to reduce fever; antipyretic.
—***n.*** a drug or agent that reduces fever.

an|ti|fe|brin or **an|ti|fe|brine** (an′tē fē′brin, -feb′rin), *n.* = acetanilide. [< *anti-* + Latin *fēbris* fever + English *-in*]

an|ti|fed|er|al (an′tē fed′ər əl, -fed′rəl), *adj.* opposed to federalism. Also, **Antifederal.**

an|ti|fed|er|al|ism (an′tē fed′ər ə liz′əm, -fed′rə-liz-), *n.* opposition to centralization of power at the expense of power held by component states.

an|ti|fed|er|al|ist (an′tē fed′ər ə list, -fed′rə-), *n.* any opponent of federalism.

An|ti|fed|er|al|ist or **An|ti-Fed|er|al|ist** (an′tē-fed′ər ə list, -fed′rə-), *n. U.S.* a member of the Antifederal Party.

Antifederal Party, a political party that opposed the adoption of the Constitution of the United States before 1789.

an|ti|feed|ant (an′tē fē′dənt), *n.* a chemical substance, such as an alkaloid, coumarin, or terpene, that repels plant-eating insects: *New approaches to pest control ... exploit the use of juvenile hormone analogues, "antifeedants," and chemosterilants* (Nature). *If crops were sprayed with efficient, synthetic antifeedants, the pests might turn from crops to weeds* (G. B. Kauffman).

an|ti|fem|i|nism (an′tē fem′ə niz əm), *n.* opposition to feminist principles or doctrine: *Freud's own childish rage and despair find expression in antifeminism, the subjection of love to sex, the acclamation of hate ...* (Maclean's). —**an′ti|fem′i|nist,** *adj., n.*

an|ti|fer|ro|mag|net|ic (an′tē fer′ō mag net′ik), *adj., n.* —***adj.*** that resists being magnetized or is nonmagnetic: *Antiferromagnetic materials behave in some important respects like ferromagnetic materials such as iron, but are much weaker magnetically* (New Scientist).
—***n.*** a substance that exhibits such properties.

an|ti|fer|ro|mag|ne|tism (an′tē fer′ō mag′nə-tiz əm), *n.* the property of resisting magnetization or of being nonmagnetic.

an|ti|fer|til|i|ty (an′tē fėr til′ə tē), *adj.* preventing or reducing fertility; contraceptive: *an antifertility drug.*

an|ti|fluor|i|da|tion (an′tē flůr′ə dā′shən, -flü′-ər ə-), *n.* opposition to the addition of fluorides to drinking water.

an|ti|fluor|i|da|tion|ist (an′tē flůr′ə dā′shə nist, -flü′ər ə-), *n.* a person who opposes the addition of fluorides to drinking water.

an|ti|foam (an′tē fōm′), *n.* a substance that inhibits the formation of foam.

an|ti|foam|ing (an′tē fō′ming), *adj.* inhibiting the formation of foam.

an|ti|fo|lic (an′tē fō′lik, -fol′ik), *n., adj.* —***n.*** any one of a group of compounds that counteract the effects of folic acid.
—***adj.*** having the ability to counteract folic acid.

an|ti|for|eign|ism (an′tē fôr′ə niz əm, -for′-), *n.* opposition to foreign persons, things, or ideas; xenophobia: *Moroccan antiforeignism was largely to blame for the country's economic plight* (Melvin Kranzberg).

an|ti|form (an′tē fôrm′), *adj.* avoiding or opposing traditional forms and materials in art: *"Antiform" art ... calls upon the expressive powers inherent in sheets of rubber, felt, chicken wire, and lead pellets* (Harold Rosenberg).

an|ti|foul|ing (an′tē fou′ling), *adj.* that prevents or reduces encrustation of foreign matter on a surface, as of carbon in a cylinder or on a valve of an internal-combustion engine, of scale or rust in a boiler, or of barnacles below the water line of a ship.

an|ti|freeze (an′tē frēz′), *n.* a substance with a low freezing point added to a liquid to lower its freezing point. Alcohol was used as an antifreeze in automobile radiators because it prevented the water from freezing during cold weather. Now glycol, which does not evaporate at normal engine temperatures, is widely used.

an|ti|fric|tion (an′tē frik′shən), *adj.* preventing or reducing friction.

antifriction alloy, any of various alloys of copper, tin, lead, antimony, or zinc, used especially in bearings.

an|ti|fun|gal (an′tē fung′gəl), *adj.* that destroys or inhibits the growth or action of fungi.

an|ti|fun|gus (an′tē fung′gəs), *n., adj.* —***n.*** an antifungal substance or agent. —***adj.*** = antifungal.

an|ti|gen (an′tə jən), *n.* any protein substance that causes the body to produce antibodies to counteract it. Bacteria are antigens. Antigens also include toxins and foreign blood cells. [< *anti-* + *-gen*]

an|ti|gen|ic (an′tə jen′ik), *adj.* of or like an antigen; functioning as an antigen. —**an′ti|gen′i|cal|ly,** *adv.*

antigenic determinant, the part of an antigen which causes a reaction in the immune system, especially an epitope: *It should be possible to make vaccines consisting of synthetic antigenic determinants rather than natural whole antigens* (Ben Patrusky).

an|ti|ge|nic|i|ty (an′tə jə nis′ə tē), *n.* the state of being an antigen or functioning as an antigen: *The polio vaccines have differed greatly in antigenicity from batch to batch* (Science News).

An|tig|o|ne (an tig′ə nē), *n. Greek Legend.* the daughter of Oedipus and Jocasta who gave her dead brother Polynices a proper burial, though doing so meant her own death, as her uncle, King Creon of Thebes, had forbidden it on pain of death.

an|tig|o|rite (an tig′ə rīt), *n.* a variety of serpentine, occurring in flaky layers in rocks of massive formation. [< *Antigorio,* a valley in Italy, where it is found + *ite*[1]]

an|ti|gov|ern|ment (an′tē guv′ərn mənt, -ər-mənt), *adj.* **1** opposed to the institution or apparatus of government. **2a** opposed to a particular government or its policies: *[The] National Revolutionary Movement, aided by disqualification of some antigovernment candidates, captured 78 seats in the 123-man Assembly* (Time). **b** = anti-administration.

an|ti|grav|i|ty (an′tē grav′ə tē), *n.* a physical force by which the force of gravity is opposed or neutralized: *Antimatter, Einstein said, could possess antigravity* (New Yorker).

an|ti-G suit (an′tē jē′), = G-suit. [< *anti-* + *G,* abbreviation of *gravity*]

an|ti|ha|la|tion (an′tē hā lā′shən, -ha-), *adj., n. Photography.* —***adj.*** preventing or counteracting the effects of halation. —***n.*** the treating of film with an antihalation substance.

an|ti|he|li|um (an′tē hē′lē əm), *n.* the analogue in antimatter of helium.

an|ti|he|lix (an′tē hē′liks), *n., pl.* **-hel|i|ces** (-hel′ə-sēz), **-he|lix|es.** the curved ridge of cartilage within the outer rim (helix) of the human ear. Also, **anthelix.** [< *anti-* + *helix*]

an|ti|he|mo|phil|ic factor (an′tē hē′mə fil′ik, -hem′ə-), a protein in blood plasma that causes clotting. *Abbr:* AHF (no periods).

antihemophilic globulin, = antihemophilic factor. *Abbr:* AHG (no periods).

an|ti|he|ro (an′tē hir′ō), *n., pl.* **-roes.** a main character in a novel, play, story, or poem, who has none of the qualities normally expected of a hero; literary or dramatic protagonist who is typically unheroic, unconventional, and often resentful or contemptuous of accepted social standards and values: *It is ... the tone of the antiheroes of our time: ironic, indignant, footloose, scarred, political* (Observer).

an|ti|he|ro|ic (an′tē hi rō′ik), *adj.* **1** of or having to do with an antihero.

an|ti|his|ta|mine (an′tē his′tə mēn, -min), *n.* a medicine that inhibits or relieves the effects of histamine in the body, used especially in the treatment of colds and of hay fever and certain other allergies.

an|ti|his|ta|min|ic (an′tē his′tə min′ik), *adj., n.* —***adj.*** of or like an antihistamine; functioning as an antihistamine. —***n.*** an antihistamine.

an|ti|hu|man|ism (an′tē hyü′mə niz əm), *n.* any belief or philosophy such as fascism or communism, held in opposition to the philosophy of humanism.

an|ti|hy|dro|gen (an′tē hī′drə jən), *n.* the analogue in antimatter of hydrogen: *The combination of an antiproton with a positron would form an antihydrogen atom* (Hannes Alfvén).

an|ti|hy|per|ten|sive (an′tē hī′pər ten′siv), *n., adj.* —***n.*** a drug or agent that reduces high blood pressure. —***adj.*** that acts as an antihypertensive. [< *anti-* + *hypertensive*]

an|ti|hyp|not|ic (an′tē hip not′ik), *n., adj.* —***n.*** a drug or agent that prevents sleep. —***adj.*** that acts as an antihypnotic. [< *anti-* + *hypnotic*]

an|ti-ic|er (an′tē ī′sər), *n.* any device or substance that prevents or counteracts the formation or accumulation of ice, especially on the wings of an aircraft or the windshield of an automobile.

an|ti-ic|ing (an′tē ī′sing), *n.* the action or function of an anti-icer.

an|ti-im|pe|ri|al|ism (an′tē im pir′ē ə liz′əm), *n.* opposition to imperialism, especially to the acquisition and government of dependent territories: *Anti-imperialism is just as powerful a force in some of the countries absorbed by the Soviet Union as in the Asiatic and African lands which have been or are still under foreign rule* (Wall

Street Journal).

an|ti-im|pe|ri|al|ist (an′tē im pir′ē ə list), *adj., n.* —*adj.* opposed to imperialism.
—*n.* a person opposed to imperialism. —**an′ti-im|pe′ri|al|is′tic,** *adj.*

an|ti-in|te|gra|tion (an′tē in′tə grā′shən), *adj.* opposed to racial integration, especially in schools or housing: *. . . thus bringing in a mixed-race state and . . . weakening Dixie's anti-integration bloc* (Wall Street Journal). —**an′ti-in′te|gra′tion|ist,** *n.*

an|ti-in|tel|lec|tu|al (an′tē in′tə lek′chu̇ əl), *adj., n.* —*adj.* opposed to the practices or pursuits of intellectuals or to intellectual points of view: *What worries me about the real beatniks . . . is that they are profoundly anti-intellectual* (New Yorker). —*n.* an anti-intellectual person.

an|ti-in|tel|lec|tu|al|ism (an′tē in′tə lek′chu̇ ə liz′əm), *n.* opposition to the practices or pursuits of intellectuals or to intellectual points of view: *The cries of anti-intellectualism from one side and anti-Americanism from the other seem to be dominant themes in the postwar era* (Time).

an|ti|ke|to|gen|e|sis (an′tē kē′tə jen′ə sis), *n.* the action of certain substances, such as glucose, that reduces or prevents the excessive formation of ketones in the body, especially in diabetes. [< *anti-* + *keto*(sis) + *genesis*]

an|ti|ke|to|gen|ic (an′tē kē′tə jen′ik), *adj.* of or having to do with antiketogenesis.

an|ti|knock (an′tē nok′), *n.* a substance added to the fuel of an internal-combustion engine to reduce noise caused by too rapid combustion.

an|ti|la|bor (an′tē lā′bər), *adj.* opposed to or thought of as being in opposition to labor, especially organized labor: *an antilabor law.*

an|ti|lamb|da (an′tē lam′də), *n.* a neutral antiparticle, the analogue in antimatter of the lambda particle.

an|ti|le|gom|e|na (an′tē lə gom′ə nə), *n.pl.* certain books of the New Testament whose inspiration was not universally acknowledged in the early church. They include Hebrews, James, Jude, II Peter, II and III John, and Revelation. [< Greek *antilegómena,* ultimately < *anti-* against + *légein* to speak]

an|ti|lep|ton (an′tē lep′ton), *n.* the analogue in antimatter of the lepton: *The antileptons are the positron, the positive muon and the antineutrino* (Scientific American).

an|ti|lib|er|al (an′tē lib′ər əl, -lib′rəl), *adj., n.* —*adj.* opposed to liberalism or to liberals.
—*n.* an antiliberal person.

An|til|o|chus (an til′ə kəs), *n. Greek Legend.* a son of Nestor and friend of Achilles.

antilog., antilogarithm.

an|ti|log|a|rithm (an′tē lôg′ə riᴛʜ əm, -log′-), *n.* the number corresponding to a given logarithm: *Since the logarithm of 100 is 2, the antilogarithm of 2 is 100.*

an|til|o|gism (an til′ə jiz əm), *n.* = antilogy.

an|til|o|gy (an til′ə jē), *n., pl.* **-gies.** a contradiction in terms or ideas, especially one arrived at by contradicting the conclusion of a valid syllogism. [< Greek *antilogía* < *antílogos* contradictory < *anti-* against + *légein* speak]

an|ti|lym|pho|cyte globulin (an′tē lim′fə sīt), an immunosuppressive substance obtained from animals injected with lymphocytes, used to prevent rejection of transplanted organs. *Abbr:* ALG

antilymphocyte serum, = antilymphocyte globulin. *Abbr:* ALS (no periods).

an|ti|ma|cas|sar (an′tē mə kas′ər), *n.* a small covering to protect the back or arms of a chair or sofa against soiling. [< *anti-* against + *Macassar* (oil) a hair oil from Macassar]

an|ti|mag|net|ic (an′tē mag net′ik), *adj.* made with materials that resist magnetization so as to prevent a magnetic field from affecting the speed of the moving parts, especially of a watch.

an|ti|ma|lar|i|a (an′tē mə lãr′ē ə), *adj., n.* = antimalarial.

an|ti|ma|lar|i|al (an′tē mə lãr′ē əl), *adj., n.* —*adj.* preventing or curing malaria; used against malaria. —*n.* an antimalarial agent or drug.

an|ti-Ma|son|ic (an′tē mə son′ik), *adj. U.S.* opposed to Freemasonry.

an|ti|masque or **an|ti|mask** (an′tē mask′, -mäsk′), *n.* a grotesque interlude performed between the acts of a masque for purposes of comedy, contrast, or burlesque.

an|ti|mat|ter or **an|ti-mat|ter** (an′tē mat′ər), *n., adj.* —*n.* physical matter identical in appearance, structure, and other properties, with matter as we know it but with the electric charges of its particles reversed; matter composed of antiparticles: *When normal matter collides with anti-matter, both are annihilated and tremendous amounts of energy are released* (Science News Letter).
—*adj.* of or having to do with antimatter: *an antimatter star or universe.*

an|ti|mere (an′tə mir), *n.* one of the symmetrically corresponding parts of the body of a bilaterally or radially symmetrical animal. [< *anti-* + Greek *méros* part]

an|ti|merg|er (an′tē mėr′jər), *adj.* that opposes, restricts, or prohibits a merger or mergers, especially of business or industrial enterprises: *antimerger legislation.*

an|ti|mer|ic (an′tə mer′ik), *adj.* of or characterized by antimeres.

an|tim|er|ism (an tim′ə riz əm), *n.* the condition of being antimeric.

an|ti|me|tab|o|lite (an′tē mə tab′ə līt), *n.* **1** a substance that interferes in a biochemical reaction by combining with one of the agents in the reaction because of a structural similarity to the normal substance. **2** a compound, especially a drug, used to attack the protein constituents of cancerous or leukemic cells, and thus temporarily retard their growth. [< *anti-* + *metabol*(ism)]

an|ti|mi|cro|bi|al (an′tē mī krō′bē əl), *adj., n.* —*adj.* that destroys or inhibits the growth or action of microbes.
—*n.* an antimicrobial drug or agent: *Nitrofuran products [are] a special class of antimicrobials distinct from antibiotics and sulfonamides* (Wall Street Journal).

an|ti|mi|cro|bic (an′tē mī krō′bik), *adj., n.* = antimicrobial.

an|ti|mil|i|ta|rism (an′tē mil′ə tə riz′əm), *n.* opposition to the military, or to a predominant military interest in government or administration.
—**an′ti|mil′i|ta|rist,** *adj., n.*

an|ti|mil|i|ta|ris|tic (an′tē mil′ə tə ris′tik), *adj.* = antimilitarist.

an|ti|mis|sile or **an|ti-mis|sile** (an′tē mis′əl), *adj., n.* —*adj.* **1** used in defense against ballistic missiles and rockets; designed to intercept and destroy enemy missiles: *an antimissile missile, an antimissile system.* **2** of or having to do with antimissile weapons or systems: *antimissile research.* —*n.* an antimissile weapon, especially an antimissile missile.

an|ti|mi|tot|ic (an′tē mi tot′ik, -mī-), *adj.* capable of retarding mitosis or cell division in malignant tissues.

an|ti|mol|e|cule or **an|ti-mol|e|cule** (an′tē mol′ə kyül), *n.* a molecule of antimatter.

an|ti|mo|nar|chic (an′tē mə när′kik), *adj.* = antimonarchist (def. 1).

an|ti|mo|nar|chi|cal (an′tē mə när′kə kəl), *adj.* = antimonarchist (def. 1).

an|ti|mon|ar|chist (an′tē mon′ər kist), *adj.* **1** opposed to monarchy as an institution. **2** opposed to a particular monarch or claimant to monarchy.

an|ti|mo|ni|al (an′tə mō′nē əl), *adj., n.* —*adj.* containing antimony in combination.
—*n.* an antimonial compound.

an|ti|mo|nic (an′tə mō′nik, -mon′ik), *adj.* **1** of antimony. **2** containing antimony, especially with a valence of 5.

an|ti|mo|nide (an′tə mə nīd), *n.* a compound of antimony and another element. [< *antimon*(y)]

an|ti|mo|ni|ous (an′tə mō′nē əs), *adj.* = antimonous.

an|ti|mon|ite (an′tə mə nīt), *n.* = stibnite. [< Medieval Latin *antimonium* antimony + English *-ite*[1]]

an|ti|mo|nop|o|ly (an′tē mə nop′ə lē), *adj.* **1** opposed to monopoly: *widespread antimonopoly sentiment.* **2** that seeks to prevent or eliminate monopolies: *antimonopoly legislation.*

an|ti|mo|nous (an′tə mō′nəs), *adj.* **1** of antimony. **2** containing antimony, especially with a valence of 3.

an|ti|mon|soon (an′tē mon sün′), *n.* a current of air above a monsoon and moving in the opposite direction.

***an|ti|mo|ny** (an′tə mō′nē), *n.* a brittle, hard, metallic chemical element with a bright, silvery, crystalline texture. Antimony is used chiefly in alloys to make them harder, and its compounds are used to make medicines, pigments, and glass. It is found chiefly in combination, especially in stibnite. [< Medieval Latin *antimonium*]

***antimony**

symbol	atomic number	atomic weight	oxidation state
Sb	51	121.75	±3, +5

antimony glance, = stibnite.

an|ti|mo|nyl (an′tə mə nil, an tim′ə-), *n.* a univalent radical, containing antimony and oxygen, which combines with acid radicals to form salts. *Formula:* SbO- [< *antimon*(y) + *-yl*]

antimony sulfide, **1** the trisulfide of antimony, occurring naturally as stibnite, used especially as a pigment in paints and in making matches and explosives. *Formula:* Sb_2S_3 **2** a sulfide of antimony in the form of an orange-yellow powder, used chiefly as a pigment. *Formula:* Sb_2S_5

an|ti|mu|ta|gen (an′tē myü′tə jən), *n.* any one of various substances that tend to prevent or inhibit mutation. [< *anti-* + *muta*(tion) + *-gen*]

an|ti|my|cin (an′tē mī′sin), *n.* an antibiotic compound, a derivative of streptomycin, used especially against mites. [< *anti-* + (strepto)*mycin*]

an|ti|na|tion|al (an′tē nash′ə nəl, -nash′nəl), *adj.* opposed to one's own nation or to a national party.

an|ti|na|tion|al|ism (an′tē nash′ə nə liz′əm, -nash′nə liz-), *n.* an antinational principle, policy, or belief. —**an′ti|na′tion|al|ist,** *n.*

an|ti|na|tion|al|is|tic (an′tē nash′ə nə lis′tik, -nash′nə-), *adj.* opposed to nationalism.

an|ti|ne|o|plas|tic (an′tē nē′ə plas′tik), *adj.* that retards growth, especially cellular growth.

an|ti|neu|ral|gic (an′tē nu̇ ral′jik, -nyu̇-), *adj., n.* —*adj.* preventing or curing neuralgia; used against neuralgia.
—*n.* an antineuralgic agent or remedy.

an|ti|neu|rit|ic (an′tē nu̇ rit′ik, -nyu̇-), *n., adj.* —*n.* an agent or drug that prevents or cures neuritis.
—*adj.* that acts as an antineuritic.

an|ti|neu|tri|no (an′tē nü trē′nō, -nyü-), *n., pl.* **-nos.** the analogue in antimatter of the neutrino: *In the normal process of emission of a negative electron from a nucleus during beta decay, a neutron changes into a proton plus the electron plus an antineutrino* (New Scientist).

an|ti|neu|tron (an′tē nü′tron, -nyü′-), *n.* the analogue in antimatter of the neutron.

ant|ing (ant′ing), *n.* the practice among certain species of birds of picking up ants and dropping them among their feathers or of rubbing their feathers with them.

ant|in|i|al (an tin′ē əl), *adj.* of or belonging to the antinion.

ant|in|i|on (an tin′ē ən), *n. Anatomy.* the medial frontal part of the skull, farthest from the inion; anterior portion of the cranium. [< *ant-* + *inion*]

an|ti|nod|al (an′tə nō′dəl), *adj. Physics.* of or having to do with an antinode or antinodes.

an|ti|node (an′tə nōd), *n. Physics.* the point or line of maximum displacement of a vibrating body; loop. [< *anti-* + *node*]

an|ti|noise (an′tē noiz′), *adj., n.* —*adj.* **1** opposed to, or directed against, noise: *London, Chicago and Los Angeles are among the large cities now considering antinoise bans* (Wall Street Journal). **2** preventing or lessening noise: *antinoise filters.*
—*n.* a sound used to eliminate noise by having its wavelength neutralize the wavelength of the noise: *Digisonix. . .can send antinoise into a fan duct, canceling sounds that would otherwise spread throughout a factory or building* (New York Times).

an|ti|no|mi|an (an′tə nō′mē ən), *n., adj.* —*n.* a member of any one of several Christian sects denying the necessity of moral law in view of the fact that salvation is freely bestowed by grace.
—*adj.* **1** of or having to do with an antinomian or antinomians. **2** denying the obligatory nature of moral law.
[< Medieval Latin *Antinomi* name of the sect (< Greek *anti-* against + *nómos* law) + English *-an*]

an|ti|no|mi|an|ism (an′tə nō′mē ə niz′əm), *n.* the doctrine or practice of antinomians; denial of the moral law.

an|tin|o|my (an tin′ə mē), *n., pl.* **-mies. 1a** the opposition of one law, rule, or principle to another. **b** *Philosophy.* a contradiction between two principles, conclusions, or inferences which seem equally logical, reasonable, or necessary. **2** *Obsolete.* any law, rule, or principle opposed to another. [< Latin *antinomia* < Greek *antinomía* < *anti-* against + *nómos* law]

an|ti|nov|el (an′tē nov′əl), *n.* a novel that avoids conventional techniques, especially by subordinating action to precise descriptions of physical and mental states: *Like other antinovels, "The Connecting Door" makes a brave attempt to ignore emotion and drama as far as possible* (Listener).

an|ti|nu|cle|ar (an′tē nü′klē ər, -nyü′-), *adj.* **1** opposed to the use of nuclear energy, especially its military use. **2** of or having to do with the nucleus of an anti-atom: *antinuclear particles.*

an|ti|nu|cle|on (an′tē nü′klē on, -nyü′-), *n.* an antineutron or antiproton. [< *anti-* + *nucleon*]

an|ti|nuke (an′tē nük′), *adj.* opposed to the use of nuclear energy for military purposes or for the generation of electricity.

An|ti|o|pe (an tī′ə pē), *n. Greek Mythology.* **1** a princess of Thebes who bore Amphion and Zethus to Zeus and then abandoned them for fear of her father. **2** = Hippolyte.

an|ti-ox|i|dant (an′tē ok′sə dənt), *n.* a substance which checks oxidation.

***an|ti|par|al|lel** (an′tē par′ə lel), *adj.* **1** moving in parallel lines but in opposite directions. **2** of or having to do with the intersection of two straight lines of equal length with a third straight line and

Pronunciation Key: hat, āge, cãre, fär; let, ēqual, tėrm; it, īce; hot, ōpen, ôrder; oil, out; cup, pu̇t, rüle; child; long; thin; ᴛʜen; zh, measure; ə represents a in about, e in taken, i in pencil, o in lemon, u in circus.

forming equal but opposite angles, as in an isosceles trapezoid.

*** antiparallel** definition 2

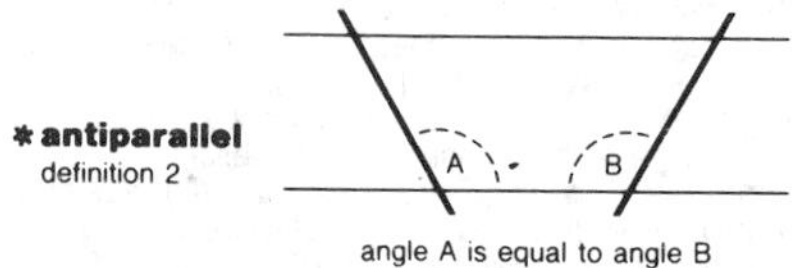

angle A is equal to angle B

an|ti|par|a|sit|ic (an′tē par′ə sit′ik), *n., adj.* —*n.* a drug or agent that destroys or inhibits the growth or action of parasites.
—*adj.* that acts as an antiparasitic.

an|ti|par|ti|cle (an′tē pär′tə kəl), *n.* a particle of antimatter; a unit of matter, such as a positron, antiproton, or antineutron, corresponding in mass and properties to an elementary particle but with an opposite electrical charge or opposite magnetic properties. When an antiparticle collides with a corresponding particle, they destroy each other, thereby releasing great energy. *There is an antiparticle for every known elementary particle* (Science News Letter).

an|ti|par|ty (an′tē pär′tē), *adj.* opposed to the policies or leadership of a party, especially a Communist Party: *Professor D. Tomor-Ochir, secretary of the Central Committee, was expelled for "antiparty, anti-Marxist activities"* (Richard L. Walker).

an|ti|pas|to (än′tē päs′tō), *n., pl.* **-tos.** an appetizer or assortment of appetizers consisting of fish, meats, deviled eggs, peppers, lettuce, olives, and other vegetables. [< Italian *antipasto* < Latin *ante* before + *pāstus* food]
▶**antipasto, hors d'oeuvres.** *Antipasto* is normally restricted to the traditionally Italian appetizer described above: *hors d'oeuvres* is applied somewhat more generally.

an|tip|a|thet|ic (an tip′ə thet′ik, an′ti pə-), *adj.* **1** having antipathy; contrary or opposed in nature or disposition: *Dogs and cats are often antipathetic. Traditional American talkativeness by its nature has been inherently antipathetic to privacy* (Bulletin of Atomic Scientists). **2** arousing antipathy; uncongenial (to): *The very idea had become antipathetic to her.* —**an|tip′a|thet′i|cal|ly,** *adv.*

an|tip|a|thet|i|cal (an tip′ə thet′ə kəl, an′ti pə-), *adj.* = antipathetic.

an|ti|path|ic (an′ti path′ik), *adj.* **1** = antipathetic. **2** *Medicine.* producing contrary symptoms; allopathic.

an|tip|a|thy (an tip′ə thē), *n., pl.* **-thies. 1** a strong or fixed dislike; a feeling against; aversion: *She felt an antipathy to snakes.* SYN: repugnance, abhorrence, disgust. **2** something or someone that arouses such a feeling; an object of aversion or dislike: *The Scots and nonconformists were antipathies of Dr. Johnson.* **3** *Obsolete.* contrariety of feeling, disposition, or nature. [< Latin *antipathīa* < Greek *antipátheia* < *anti-* against + *páthos* feeling]

an|ti|pe|ri|od|ic (an′tē pir′ē od′ik), *n., adj.* —*n.* a drug or agent that cures diseases, especially intermittent fever, that exhibit periodicity.
—*adj.* that acts as an antiperiodic.

an|ti|per|i|stal|sis (an′tē per′ə stal′sis), *n.* reversed peristaltic action of the intestines, by which their contents are carried upward. [< *anti-* + *peristalsis*]

an|ti|per|i|stal|tic (an′tē per′ə stal′tik), *adj.* of or having to do with antiperistalsis; reversing peristaltic action.

an|ti|per|ni|cious anemia factor (an′tē pər-nish′əs), = vitamin BÜù.

an|ti|per|son|nel (an′tē pėr′sə nel′), *adj. Military.* directed against enemy troops rather than against mechanized equipment or supplies: *an antipersonnel mine.*

an|ti|per|spi|rant (an′tē pėr′spər ənt), *n., adj.* —*n.* any one of a number of preparations for inhibiting perspiration, especially in order to prevent body odor.
—*adj.* that is an antiperspirant.

an|ti|pes|ti|len|tial (an′tē pes′tə len′shəl), *adj.* preventing, or used against, a plague or epidemic.

an|ti|pet|al|ous (an′tē pet′ə ləs), *adj.* growing opposite the petals: *antipetalous stamens.*

an|ti|phlo|gis|tic (an′tē flō jis′tik), *n., adj.* —*n.* an agent or drug that counteracts or reduces inflammation.
—*adj.* that acts as an antiphlogistic.

an|ti|phon (an′tə fon), *n.* **1a** a song, hymn, or prayer sung or chanted in alternate parts; a composition consisting of verses or passages sung alternately by two choirs. **b** a short introduction or conclusion (often in the form of plain song) to a psalm or other part of a church service. **2** a verse or verses sung or chanted in response in a church service. [< Late Latin *antiphōna* < Greek *antíphōna* musical accords < *anti-* opposed to + *phōnē* sound. See etym. of doublet **anthem.**]

an|tiph|o|nal (an tif′ə nəl), *adj., n.* —*adj.* like an antiphon; sung or chanted alternately.
—*n.* a book of antiphons; antiphonary. —**an|tiph′o|nal|ly,** *adv.*

an|tiph|o|nar|y (an tif′ə ner′ē), *n., pl.* **-nar|ies,** *adj.* —*n.* a book containing a set or collection of antiphons. —*adj.* = antiphonal. [< Medieval Latin *antiphonarium* < Late Latin *antiphōna* antiphon]

an|tiph|o|ner (an tif′ə nər), *n.* = antiphonary.

an|ti|phon|ic (an′tə fon′ik), *adj.* = antiphonal.

an|tiph|o|ny (an tif′ə nē), *n., pl.* **-nies. 1a** antiphonal singing. **b** an antiphonal response. **2** = antiphon (def. 1a).

an|tiph|ra|sis (an tif′rə sis), *n.* the conscious use of words in a sense opposite to their meaning. [< Latin *antiphrasis* < Greek *antíphrasis* < *anti-* against + *phrázein* speak]

an|ti|phras|tic (an′tē fras′tik), *adj.* of or having to do with antiphrasis; opposed to the ordinary meaning.

an|ti|plas|tic (an′tē plas′tik), *adj., n.* —*adj.* **1** preventing or inhibiting plasticity. **2** *Medicine.* tending to prevent or check the process of healing.
—*n.* an antiplastic substance or agent.

an|tip|o|dal (an tip′ə dəl), *adj.* **1** on the opposite side of the earth. **2** *Figurative.* directly opposite; exactly contrary: *antipodal beliefs.* —**an|tip′o|dal|ly,** *adv.*

an|ti|pode (an′tə pōd), *n.* anything exactly opposite; direct opposite. SYN: antithesis. [singular of *antipodes*]

an|tip|o|de|an (an tip′ə dē′ən), *adj., n.* —*adj.* = antipodal.
—*n.* an inhabitant of an antipodal place.

an|tip|o|des (an tip′ə dēz), *n.pl.* **1** two places on directly opposite sides of the earth: *The North Pole and the South Pole are antipodes.* **2** a place on the opposite side of the earth. **3** *Figurative.* two opposites or contraries: *Hate and love are antipodes.* **4** *Figurative.* the direct opposite. **5** Australia and New Zealand, so known because of their position in relation to that of England. **6** *Obsolete.* those who dwell directly opposite to each other, or directly opposite to us, on the earth. [< Latin *antipodes* < Greek *antípodes,* plural of *antípous* with feet opposite < *anti-* opposite + *poús* foot]
▶**Antipodes** is plural in form and plural or singular in use for defs. 2, 4, and 5.

an|ti|pole (an′tē pōl′), *n.* the opposite pole.

an|ti|pol|lu|tion (an′tē pə lü′shən), *adj.* designed to reduce or prevent pollution: *antipollution devices, an antipollution program.*

an|ti|pope (an′tē pōp′), *n.* a person claiming the papacy in opposition to a canonically chosen pope.

an|ti|pov|er|ty (an′tē pov′ər tē), *adj.* designed to combat poverty on a large scale; organized to help the poor, especially in depressed areas: *The new Act authorises the expenditure of $947 million . . . to be spent on antipoverty projects* (Observer).

an|ti|pro|ton (an′tē prō′ton), *n.* a tiny particle of the same mass as a proton, but negatively charged, created when a proton hits a neutron; the analogue in antimatter of the proton: *Their 1955 discovery of the antiproton . . . came through research with the big atom-smashing bevatron at Berkeley* (Wall Street Journal).

an|ti|pru|rit|ic (an′tē prù rit′ik), *n., adj.* —*n.* a drug or agent that relieves or prevents itching.
—*adj.* that acts as an antipruritic.

an|ti|psy|chot|ic (an′tē sī kot′ik), *n., adj.* —*n.* a drug or agent used or effective in relieving psychotic symptoms.
—*adj.* that acts as an antipsychotic.

an|ti|py|ret|ic (an′tē pī ret′ik), *n., adj.* —*n.* a drug or agent that checks or prevents fever; antifebrile. —*adj.* that acts as an antipyretic.

an|ti|py|rine or **an|ti|py|rin** (an′tē pī′rin), *n.* a white, crystalline drug used as a sedative, analgesic, and antipyretic; phenazone. *Formula:* $C_{11}H_{12}N_2O$ [< *anti-* + *pyr*(etic) + *-ine*]

an|ti|py|rot|ic (an′tē pī rot′ik), *n., adj.* —*n.* a drug or agent that heals or relieves burns. —*adj.* that acts as an antipyrotic. [< *anti-* + Greek *pyrōtikós* burning < *pyroûn* to burn < *pyr* fire]

antiq., 1 antiquarian. **2** antiquity or antiquities.

an|ti|quar|i|an (an′tə kwãr′ē ən), *n., adj.* —*n.* a person who studies or collects relics from ancient times.
—*adj.* of or having to do with antiquities or antiquarians: *The antiquarian section of the museum was full of old furniture.*
[< Latin *antīquārius* (with English *-ian*) < *antīquus* ancient]

an|ti|quar|i|an|ism (an′tə kwãr′ē ə niz′əm), *n.* **1** the profession or pursuits of the antiquarian. **2** an interest in antiquities.

an|ti|quark (an′tē kwôrk′), *n. Nuclear Physics.* one of a hypothetical set of three elementary particles, that are analogues in antimatter to the quark; the antiparticle of quark.

an|ti|quar|y (an′tə kwer′ē), *n., pl.* **-quar|ies.** = antiquarian.

an|ti|quate (an′tə kwāt), *v.t.,* **-quat|ed, -quat|ing. 1** to make old-fashioned, out of date, or obsolete. **2** to cause to appear antique; antique. [< Late Latin *antīquāre* (with English *-ate*[1]) < Latin *antīquus* ancient] —**an′ti|qua′tion,** *n.*

an|ti|quat|ed (an′tə kwā′tid), *adj.* **1** that has grown old but is no longer valued; old-fashioned; out-of-date: *antiquated fashions, antiquated laws. Most science books written 20 years ago are now antiquated.* SYN: obsolete, archaic, outmoded. **2** too old for work or for service: *This antiquated truck is ready for the junk heap.* —**an′ti|quat′ed|ness,** *n.*

an|tique (an tēk′), *adj., n., v.,* **-tiqued, -ti|quing.** —*adj.* **1** old-fashioned; out-of-date: *She wore an antique gown to the costume party.* SYN: antiquated. **2** of or belonging to ancient Greece or Rome. SYN: classic. **3a** of times long ago; from times long ago; ancient: *antique heroes.* SYN: early. **b** of or belonging to a distinctly earlier age than the present; old: *This antique chair was made in 1750.* SYN: early. **4** in the style of times long ago: *An antique gold finish is dull and slightly greenish.* **5** by or in which antiques are bought and sold: *an antique shop, an antique dealer.*
—*n.* **1** something belonging to an earlier age; a piece of china, silver, furniture, or other article, made long ago: *This carved chest is a genuine antique.* **2** antique style, usually of Greek or Roman art: *a statue imitating the antique.* **3** a style of type.
—*v.t.* to make, bind, or finish in an antique style.
—*v.i.* to collect antiques; shop for antiques: *Everybody antiques. Everybody loves the 18th century* (Atlanta Constitution).
[< Latin *antīquus* former, old < *ante* before. See etym. of doublet **antic.**] —**an|tique′ly,** *adv.* —**an|tique′ness,** *n.* —**an|ti′quer,** *n.*

an|tiq|ui|ty (an tik′wə tē), *n., pl.* **-ties. 1** great age; oldness: *the antiquity of man. That vase is of such great antiquity that nobody knows how old it is.* **2** times long ago; early ages of history. Antiquity usually refers to the period between 5000 B.C. and A.D. 476. *Moses and Caesar were two great men of antiquity.* **3** the people of ancient times.
antiquities, a things from times long ago; artifacts, monuments, or records of ancient times: *We visited museums and libraries filled with antiquities.* **b** the customs and life of olden times: *a specialist in the Roman and Greek antiquities.*

an|ti|ra|bic (an′tē rā′bik, -rab′ik), *adj.* = antirabies.

an|ti|ra|bies (an′tē rā′bēz), *adj.* that prevents or immunizes against rabies: *an antirabies vaccine.*

an|ti|ra|chit|ic (an′tē rə kit′ik), *n., adj.* —*n.* a vitamin or other agent that prevents or cures rickets.
—*adj.* that acts as an antirachitic.
[< *anti-* + *rachitic*]

an|ti|rac|ist (an′tē rā′sist), *n., adj.* —*n.* an opponent of racists or racism.
—*adj.* opposed to racists or racism.

an|ti|re|jec|tion (an′tē ri jek′shən), *adj.* designed to combat immunological rejection, especially in transplant surgery: *Doctors abandoned the operation because of high rejection rates. But the new antirejection techniques have revived their interest* (Newsweek).

an|ti|re|li|gious (an′tē ri lij′əs), *adj.* **1** = anticlerical. **2** = irreligious: *He played upon the antireligious sentiment of the younger generation by hammering away disdainfully at . . . personal devotion to the Moslem cult* (Time).

An|ti|re|mon|strant (an′tē ri mon′strənt), *n.* one of the Dutch Calvinists of the 1600's who opposed the Arminian stand adopted by the Remonstrants.

an|ti|rent (an′tē rent′), *adj.* **1** opposed to the payment of rent on land. **2** designating a political party or group in New York between 1839 and 1847 that was opposed to payment of rent on land to the patroons.

an|ti|rent|er (an′tē ren′tər), *n.* a person opposed to the payment of rent, especially a person opposed to paying rent to a patroon in early New York. The New York antirenters were active between 1839 and 1847.

an|ti|rent|ism (an′tē ren′tiz əm), *n.* opposition to the payment of rent on land.

an|ti|rheu|mat|ic (an′tē rü mat′ik), *n., adj.* —*n.* a drug or agent that prevents or relieves rheumatism. —*adj.* that acts as an antirheumatic. [< *anti-* + *rheumatic*]

an|tir|rhi|num (an′tə rī′nəm), *n.* any one of a genus of herbaceous plants of the figwort family; a snapdragon. [< New Latin *Antirrhinum* < Greek *antírrhīnon* < *antírhīnós* like a nose (from its shape)]

an|ti|rust (an′tē rust′), *adj., n.* **—*adj.*** preventing or removing rust.
—*n.* a substance that prevents or removes rust.

an|ti|sa|loon or **an|ti-sa|loon** (an′tē sə lün′), *adj. U.S.* opposed to the existence of saloons, bars, or other places for the sale of alcoholic beverages.

an|ti|sat|el|lite (an′tē sat′ə līt), *adj.* able or intended to be able to seek out and destroy an artificial satellite: *The Air Force successfully carried off another space feat ... that presaged the day of antisatellite weapons* (Wall Street Journal).

an|ti|sci|ence (an′tē sī′əns), *adj., n.* **—*adj.*** = antiscientific. **—*n.*** opposition to science, scientific research, or the scientific method.

an|ti|sci|en|tif|ic (an′tē sī′ən tif′ik), *adj.* opposed to science, scientific research, or the scientific method.

an|ti|scor|bu|tic (an′tē skôr byü′tik), *n., adj.* **—*n.*** a drug or agent that prevents or cures scurvy.
—*adj.* that acts as an antiscorbutic.

antiscorbutic acid, = vitamin C.

an|ti|seg|re|ga|tion (an′tē seg′rə gā′shən), *adj.* opposed to racial segregation, especially in schools or housing.

an|ti|seg|re|ga|tion|ist (an′tē seg′rə gā′shə nist), *n., adj.* **—*n.*** a person who is opposed to racial segregation, especially in schools or housing.
—*adj.* = antisegregation.

an|ti-Sem|ite (an′tē sem′īt, -sē′mīt), *n.* a person whose actions or feelings are characterized by anti-Semitism.
▶**anti-Semite.** This and the following two words are based on a misunderstanding, since Jews form only one group of Semites. Others are Arabs, Druses, and Samaritans.

an|ti-Se|mit|ic (an′tē sə mit′ik), *adj.* prejudiced against Jews.

an|ti-Sem|i|tism (an′tē sem′ə tiz əm), *n.* **1** dislike or hatred for Jews; prejudice against Jews. **2** action or policy reflecting this, ranging from social discrimination to physical persecution.

an|ti|sense (an′tē sens′), *adj. Genetics.* that does not code for a genetic product but serves only to preserve the coding sequence: *Antisense transcription has been described in bacteria [and] in higher forms of life* (Scientific American).

an|ti|sep|al|ous (an′tē sep′ə ləs), *adj.* growing opposite the sepals: *antisepalous stamens.*

an|ti|sep|sis (an′tə sep′sis), *n.* **1** prevention of infection. **2** the process by which microorganisms are prevented from gaining access to, or multiplying in, body tissues injured by accident or surgery; method or medicine that prevents infection.

an|ti|sep|tic (an′tə sep′tik), *adj., n.* **—*adj.*** **1** preventing infection; unfavorable to the growth and activity of the microorganisms of disease, putrefaction, or fermentation. **2** of or using antisepsis. **3** *Figurative.* having a sterilized or sterile quality; coldly or severely immaculate: *an antiseptic nursery, an antiseptic tutor.*
—*n.* a substance that kills or prevents the growth of germs and thus prevents infection. Iodine, hydrogen peroxide, Mercurochrome, alcohol, and boric acid are widely used antiseptics. **—an′ti·sep′ti|cal|ly,** *adv.*

an|ti|sep|ti|cize (an′tə sep′tə sīz), *v.t.*, **-cized, -ciz|ing.** to treat with an antiseptic or antiseptics.

an|ti|se|rum (an′tē sir′əm), *n., pl.* **-se|rums, -se|ra** (-sir′ə). a serum containing antibodies that are specific for certain antigens, such as may be obtained from a person or animal that has been immunized against these antigens.

an|ti|sex|u|al (an′tē sek′shü əl), *adj.* opposed to sexual expression or activity, especially that which is blatantly or publicly displayed.

an|ti|slav|er|y or **an|ti-slav|er|y** (an′tē slā′vər ē, -slāv′rē), *adj., n.* **—*adj.*** opposed to slavery; against slavery. **—*n.*** opposition to slavery.

an|ti|smog (an′tē smog′), *adj.* designed to reduce or eliminate smog.

an|ti|so|cial (an′tē sō′shəl), *adj.* **1** opposed to the principles upon which society is based: *Murder and stealing are antisocial acts.* **2** against the general welfare: *Spitting and littering in public places are examples of antisocial behavior.* SYN: asocial. **3** opposed to friendly relationship and normal companionship with others; not sociable: *Hermits are antisocial. It is ... an antisocial individualism born of an era when spatial distances were extensive* (Emory S. Bogardus). SYN: unsociable.

an|ti|so|cial|ism or **an|ti-So|cial|ism** (an′tē sō′shə liz əm), *n.* opposition to the principles of socialism and to the institutions and practices based on them. **—an′ti|so′cial|ist, an′ti-So′cial|ist,** *adj., n.*

an|ti|so|cial|is|tic or **an|ti-So|cial|is|tic** (an′tē-sō′shə lis′tik), *adj.* = antisocialist.

an|ti|so|lar (an′tē sō′lər), *adj.* opposite the sun.

an|ti|spas|mod|ic (an′tē spaz mod′ik), *n., adj.* **—*n.*** a drug or agent that prevents or relieves spasms.
—*adj.* that acts as an antispasmodic.

an|ti|state (an′tē stāt′), *adj.* antigovernment: ... *his fear of being denounced by an informer for antistate activities* (J. V. Davidson-Houston). [< *anti-* + *state*]

an|ti|stat|ic (an′tē stat′ik), *adj.* designed to prevent or reduce static electricity, especially in synthetic and plastic products: *antistatic sprays.*

an|ti-Stokes line (an′tē stōks′), a line in a spectrum of the same, or higher, frequency as that of the exciting light. It is due to a vibrating molecule's absorption of a light quantum. [see etym. under **Stokes' law**]

an|tis|tro|phe (an tis′trə fē), *n.* **1** the part of an ancient Greek ode sung by the chorus when moving from left to right. **2** a stanza following a strophe and usually in the same meter. [< Late Latin *antistrophē* < Greek *antistrophē* a turning about < *anti-* against + *stréphein* turn]

an|ti|stroph|ic (an′tē strof′ik), *adj.* of or having to do with an antistrophe.

an|ti|sub|ma|rine (an′tē sub′mə rēn), *adj.* for use against submarines.

an|ti|sym|met|ric (an′tē si met′rik), *adj.* **1** *Mathematics.* denoting a function which is transformed into its negative when its variables are interchanged in pairs. **2** *Physics.* denoting a system in which each point has properties opposite to those of a point symmetrically related to it. **—an′ti|sym|met′ri|cal|ly,** *adv.*

an|ti|sym|me|try (an′tē sim′ə trē), *n.* an antisymmetric state or condition.

an|ti|syph|i|lit|ic (an′tē sif′ə lit′ik), *n., adj.* **—*n.*** a drug or agent that prevents or cures syphilis.
—*adj.* that acts as an antisyphilitic.

an|ti|tank (an′tē tangk′), *adj. Military.* designed for use against armored vehicles, especially tanks: *an antitank gun, antitank mines.*

an|tith|e|sis (an tith′ə sis), *n., pl.* **-ses** (-sēz). **1** the direct opposite: *Hate is the antithesis of love.* **2** opposition; contrast (of, between, or to): *the antithesis of theory and fact.* **3** anything opposed, or forming a contrast. **4** contrast of ideas; the expression in balanced constructions of opposed ideas. *Example:* "To err is human; to forgive, divine." **5** either of the two ideas contrasted.
[< Late Latin *antithesis* < Greek *antíthesis* < *anti-* against + *tithénai* to set]

an|ti|thet|ic (an′tə thet′ik), *adj.* **1** of or using antithesis. **2** contrasted; opposite. **—an′ti|thet′i|cal|ly,** *adv.*

an|ti|thet|i|cal (an′tə thet′ə kəl), *adj.* = antithetic: *The poetic image in which the tension of antithetical meanings is most effectively embodied is the metaphor* (Observer).

an|ti|throm|bin (an′tē throm′bin), *n.* an antienzyme that inhibits the action of thrombin in blood serum, preventing the formation of fibrin.

an|ti|thy|roid (an′tē thī′roid), *n., adj.* **—*n.*** a drug or agent that prevents or relieves hyperthyroidism.
—*adj.* that acts as an antithyroid.

an|ti|torque rotor (an′tē tôrk′), a subsidiary rotor, mounted on the tail of a helicopter, that rotates in a vertical plane so as to generate a thrust opposite to the torque of the main rotor.

an|ti|to|tal|i|tar|i|an (an′tē tō tal′ə tãr′ē ən), *adj., n.* **—*adj.*** opposed to totalitarian government: *The antitotalitarian group opposed the ... Law of State Security because it made lack of patriotism a crime and authorized the president to suspend constitutional guarantees* (Amos E. Taylor).
—*n.* an antitotalitarian person.

an|ti|tox|ic (an′tē tok′sik), *adj.* **1** counteracting diseases or poisonings caused by toxins. **2** having to do with or like an antitoxin.

an|ti|tox|in (an′tē tok′sin), *n.* **1** a substance formed in the body that can make a person safe from an infection or disease; an antibody formed in the body in response to the presence of a toxin in the body, which combines with the toxin and thus neutralizes it. **2** a serum containing antitoxin. Diphtheria antitoxin, obtained from the blood of horses infected with diphtheria, is injected into a person to make him immune to diphtheria, or to treat him if already infected.

an|ti|tox|ine (an′tē tok′sin, -sēn), *n.* = antitoxin.

an|ti|trades (an′tē trādz′), *n.pl.* **1** (at tropical latitudes) winds that blow in a direction opposite to the trade winds on a level above them. **2** (at temperate latitudes) the prevailing westerlies.

an|tit|ra|gus (an tit′rə gəs), *n., pl.* **-gi** (-jī). a protuberance toward the rear of the external ear, inside the helix, opposite to the tragus. [< Greek *antítragos* < *anti-* opposite + *trágos* tragus]

an|ti|trust (an′tē trust′), *adj.* opposed to trusts or other business monopolies, especially those contrived by large corporations having enough control of the market to govern trade practices and prices and act to stifle competition: *antitrust legislation.*

an|ti|tu|mor (an′tē tü′mər, -tyü′-), *adj.* used in the treatment or prevention of cancerous tumors.

an|ti|tus|sive (an′tē tus′iv), *adj., n.* **—*adj.*** preventing or relieving cough.
—*n.* an antitussive substance or drug.

an|ti|ty|pal (an′tē tī′pəl), *adj.* = antitypic.

an|ti|type (an′tē tīp′), *n.* **1** a person, thing, or idea adumbrated or represented by an earlier type or symbol, such as a New Testament event prefigured in the Old Testament. **2** an opposite type. [< Late Latin *antitypus* < Greek *antítypos* < *anti-* corresponding to + *týpos* stamp, stroke]

an|ti|typ|ic (an′tē tip′ik), *adj.* of or of the nature of an antitype; fulfilling what has been prefigured by a type or symbol.

an|ti|typ|i|cal (an′tē tip′ə kəl), *adj.* = antitypic.

an|ti-un|ion (an′tē yün′yən), *adj. U.S.* opposed to a labor union or labor unions.

an|ti-un|ion|ism (an′tē yün′yə niz əm), *n.* opposition to labor unions, characterized by refusal to recognize, deal with, or join a union. **—an′ti-un′ion|ist,** *n., adj.*

an|ti|ven|ene (an′tē ven′ēn), *n.* = antivenin.

an|ti|ven|in (an′tē ven′in), *n.* **1** an antitoxin to a venin (a protein toxin in snake and other venom). **2** a serum having such an antitoxin, produced from the blood of animals that have been immunized against snake and other venom and used to modify reaction to the bite of a poisonous animal.

an|ti|vi|ral (an′tē vī′rəl), *adj.* counteracting or destroying a virus or viruses.

an|ti|vi|rot|ic (an′tē vī rot′ik), *adj., n.* **—*adj.*** = antiviral.
—*n.* an antiviral substance or agent.

an|ti|vi|rus (an′tē vī′rəs), *n., adj.* **—*n.*** a culture from which bacteria are filtered, which is diluted or weakened by heating, used in effecting local immunity.
—*adj.* that acts as an antivirus; antiviral: *Antivirus therapy is confined to vaccination: we are still using Jenner's procedure to avoid smallpox* (New Scientist).

an|ti|vi|ta|min (an′tē vī′tə min), *n.* **1** any substance that inhibits or prevents the absorption of a vitamin. **2** an enzyme that destroys vitamins.

an|ti|viv|i|sec|tion (an′tē viv′ə sek′shən), *adj., n.* **—*adj.*** opposed to the practice of vivisection.
—*n.* = antivivisectionism.

an|ti|viv|i|sec|tion|ism (an′tē viv′ə sek′shə-niz əm), *n.* opposition to the practice of vivisection. **—an′ti|viv′i|sec′tion|ist,** *n.*

an|ti|war (an′tē wôr′), *adj.* opposed to war.

an|ti|white (an′tē hwīt′), *adj.* opposed to white people or to the white establishment.

an|ti|world or **an|ti-world** (an′tē wėrld′), *n.* the world of antimatter; a theoretical world in which the charges of all elementary particles are reversed: *The anti-world of atomic nucleons is now complete [with] the discovery of the antineutron as a companion of the antiproton* (Science News Letter).

an|ti|xe|roph|thal|mic (an′tē zir′of thal′mik), *adj., n.* **—*adj.*** preventing or curing xerophthalmia; used against xerophthalmia.
—*n.* an antixerophthalmic agent or remedy.

an|ti-xi-ze|ro (an′tē zī′zir′ō), *n.* the analogue in antimatter of the xi zero.

✱antler
definition 1

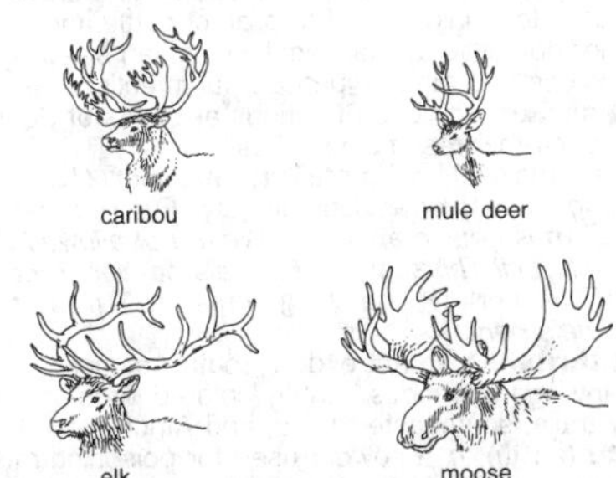

✱ant|ler (ant′lər), *n.* **1** the solid, bony horn of a male deer or of related animals, such as elk, moose, or caribou, usually having one or more branches when fully grown. Antlers are shed once a year and grow back again during the next year. **2** a branch of such a horn. [< Old French *antoillier,* ultimately < Latin *ante* before + *oculus* eye] **—ant′ler|like′,** *adj.*

ant|lered (ant′lərd), *adj.* **1** having antlers. **2** deco-

Pronunciation Key: hat, āge, cãre, fär; let, ēqual, tėrm; it, īce; hot, ōpen, ôrder; oil, out; cup, pu̇t, rüle; child; long; thin; ᴛʜen; zh, measure; ə represents a in about, e in taken, i in pencil, o in lemon, u in circus.

rated with antlers.

ant|ler|less (ant′lər lis), *adj.* without antlers.

antler moth, a nocturnal moth whose larva is destructive of meadowlands.

ant|li|a (ant′lē ə), *n., pl.* **-li|ae** (-lē ē). *Zoology.* the tubelike proboscis of butterflies, moths, and other lepidopterous insects. [< Latin *antlia* a pump < Greek *antlía* buckets]

Ant|li|a (ant′lē ə), *n., genitive* **Ant|li|ae**. a southern constellation between Argo and Hydra.

Ant|li|ae (ant′lē ē), *n.* genitive of **Antlia**.

ant|li|ate (ant′lē it, -āt), *adj.* furnished with an antlia.

ant lion, **1** an insect whose larva digs a pit where it lies in wait to catch ants and other insects as they fall in and are trapped. **2** the larva itself; doodlebug.

ant|o|don|tal|gic (ant ō′don tal′jik), *n., adj.* **—*n.*** a drug or agent that prevents or relieves toothache. **—*adj.*** that acts as an antodontalgic.

An|to|nine (an′tə nīn), *adj.* characteristic of the reign extending from A.D. 138 to 180 of the Roman emperors Marcus Aurelius Antoninus and Antoninus Pius; tranquil.

an|to|no|ma|sia (an′tə nō mā′zhə), *n.* **1** the use of an epithet or title instead of a person's name, as to refer to an ambassador as "His Excellency," or to a judge as "His Honor." **2** the use of a proper name to express a quality, as to call a patient person "a veritable Job." **3** the naming of a fictional character for his chief quality or characteristic, as in *Squire Allworthy.* [< Latin *antonomasia* < Greek *antonomasiā*, ultimately < *anti-* instead + *ónoma* name]

an|to|no|mas|tic (an′tə nō mas′tik), *adj.* characterized by antonomasia.

an|to|nym (an′tə nim), *n.* a word that means the opposite of another word (contrasted with *synonym*). "Hot" is the antonym of "cold." "Sharp," "keen," and "acute" are antonyms of "dull." *Abbr:* ant. [< *ant-* + Greek (dialectal) *ónyma* name; probably suggested by Greek *antōnymiā* pronoun]

an|ton|y|mous (an ton′ə məs), *adj.* of or like an antonym or antonyms.

an|ton|y|my (an ton′ə mē), *n., pl.* **-mies**. **1** the condition of being antonymous; oppositeness in meaning. **2** the study of antonyms. **3** the use or coupling of antonyms for emphasis or amplification. **4** a set, list, or system of antonyms.

An Tos|tal (ən tos′təl), an annual Irish festival of welcome to visitors and tourists.

an|tre (an′tər), *n. Poetic.* a cave; cavern: *... the antre of an ogre* (George Meredith). [< French *antre*, learned borrowing from Latin *antrum* antrum]

an|trorse (an trôrs′), *adj. Botany, Zoology.* bent forward or upward. [< New Latin *antrorsus* < Latin *anter(ior)* in front + *versus* turned] **—an|trorse′ly**, *adv.*

an|trum (an′trəm), *n., pl.* **-tra** (-trə). a cavity, especially one in a bone (often applied to the sinus in the maxilla). [< Latin *antrum* < Greek *ántron* cave]

an|trus|ti|on (an trus′tē ən), *n.* any of a body of men forming the bodyguard or military household of Frankish kings. [< Medieval Latin *antrustio, -onis* < Old High German *trōst* trust, fidelity]

An|try|cide (an′trə sīd), *n. Trademark.* a drug related to quinine, used to protect cattle and other domestic animals against African sleeping sickness and other trypanosomal infections.

ant shrike, any one of various ant birds of South America that resemble shrikes.

ants|y (an′tsē), *adj.*, **ants|i|er, ants|i|est.** *U.S. Slang.* uneasy or anxious; fidgety: *Everyone here in town is getting antsy. ... We're not allowed to march until Thursday, and there's nothing to do* (New Yorker). [< the slang phrase *to have ants in one's pants*]

ant thrush, **1** an ant bird of South America. **2** any one of various brightly colored birds of Australia, southeastern Asia, and Africa; pitta.

an|tu (an′tü), *n.* a powder used for poisoning rats. *Formula:* $C_{11}H_{10}N_2S$ [< *a*(lpha)-*n*(aphthyl)*t*(hio)-*u*(rea), its chemical name]

ANTU (an′tü), *n. Trademark.* antu.

An|tu|rane (an′tə rān), *n. Trademark.* a drug that stimulates the excretion of uric acid, used to treat gout and experimentally to prevent the formation of blood clots. *Formula:* $C_{23}H_{20}N_2O_3S$

A|nu|bis (ə nü′bis, -nyü′-), *n. Egyptian Mythology.* the conductor of the dead, a son of Osiris, identified by the Greeks with Hermes.

a|nu|cle|ar (ā nü′klē ər, -nyü′-), *adj.* lacking a nucleus or nuclei, as a cell: *anuclear erythrocytes.*

a|nu|cle|ate (ā nü′klē it, -nyü′-; -āt), *adj.* lacking a nucleus or nuclei; anuclear.

A number 1, *Informal.* A one; first-class.

an|u|ran (ə nyůr′ən, -nůr′-), *n., adj. Zoology.* **—*n.*** any one of a subclass of amphibians, such as the frog; a salientian. **—*adj.*** = salientian. [< *an-* without + Greek *ourá* tail + English *-an*]

an|u|re|sis (an′yů rē′sis), *n.* = anuria.

an|u|ri|a (ə nyůr′ē ə, -nůr′-), *n.* the absence of urine; inability to urinate. [< New Latin *anuria* < Greek *an-* without + *oûron* urine]

an|u|ric (ə nyůr′ik, -nůr′-), *adj.* of or having to do with anuria; characterized by anuria.

an|u|rous (ə nyůr′əs, -nůr′-), *adj.* tailless; acaudal.

a|nus (ā′nəs), *n.* the opening at the lower end of the alimentary canal, through which solid waste material and undigested food pass from the body. [< Latin *ānus* (earlier) ring]

an|vil** (an′vəl), *n., v.,* **-viled, -vil|ing** or (*especially British*) **-villed, -vil|ling.** **—*n. **1** an iron or steel block on which metals are hammered and shaped. **2** anything resembling a blacksmith's anvil in shape or use, such as the fixed jaw of a measuring instrument or steel bars struck like a blacksmith's anvil: (*Figurative.*) *The hero was hardened on the anvil of war.* **3** the incus, a bone of the middle ear. See picture under **ear**[1].
—*v.t.* to fashion on or as if on an anvil; hammer out (used chiefly in figurative connotations). [Old English *anfilte*]

***anvil**
definition 1

anx|i|e|ty (ang zī′ə tē), *n., pl.* **-ties.** **1** uneasy thoughts or fears about what may happen; troubled, worried, or uneasy feeling: *Mother felt anxiety when my baby brother was so sick. We all felt anxiety when the prairie fire came close to town. Anxiety is one of the major characteristics of our time* (Atlantic). SYN: concern, apprehension, dread, misgiving. **2** eager desire: *Her anxiety to succeed led her to work hard.* **3** *Psychiatry.* a state of fear and mental tension commonly occurring in mental disorders. [< Latin *anxietās* < *anxius* anxious < *angere* choke]

anxiety hysteria, *Psychiatry.* a mental condition between hysteria and anxiety neurosis.

anxiety neurosis, *Psychiatry.* a mental condition characterized by emotional instability, imagined fears, irritability, and a general sense of fatigue.

anx|i|o|lyt|ic (ang zī′ə lit′ik), *n., adj.* **—*n.*** a drug used to relieve anxiety; tranquilizer.
—*adj.* used or tending to relieve anxiety; tranquilizing: *anxiolytic and antidepressant drugs.* [< *anx*(iety) + *lytic*]

anx|ious (angk′shəs, ang′-), *adj.* **1** uneasy because of thoughts or fears of what may happen; troubled; worried: *Mother felt anxious about the children who had been gone an hour too long.* **2** causing uneasy feelings or troubled thoughts; worrying; distressing: *The week of the flood was an anxious time for all of us.* **3** wishing very much; eager: *He was anxious for a bicycle. She was anxious to please her mother.* [< Latin *anxius* (with English *-ous*) troubled < *angere* choke] **—anx′ious|ly**, *adv.* **—anx′ious|ness**, *n.*

▶**anxious.** The idiom is *anxious for* when "eagerly desiring" is meant: *He is anxious for her news.* When "worried" is meant, the idioms are *anxious about*, referring to persons, and *anxious at*, referring to things: *Her mother was anxious about her. They became anxious at her delay.*

anxious seat or **bench**, *U.S.* **1** an uneasy or troubled condition. **2** a seat near the pulpit at a revival meeting for those troubled about their religious life that want to strengthen their faith.

an|y (en′ē), *adj., pron., adv.* **—*adj.*** **1a** one out of many: *Choose any book you like from the books on the shelf.* **b** some out of many or much: *Do any spots show? Is there any fresh fruit left?* **2** every: *Any child knows that.* **3** even a little; even one or two: *He was forbidden to go to any house. There has never been any doubt about that.* **4** in no matter what quantity or number: *Have you any sugar?* **5** enough to be noticed: *He had hardly any money.* **6** no matter how great or how small: *He means to win at any cost.*
—*pron.* **1a** any thing; any part: *Take the cake; I don't want any.* **b** any person: *The Lord is ... not willing that any should perish* (II Peter 3:9). **2** some: *I need more paper; have you any that you can spare?*
—*adv.* **1** even a little: *Do not go any closer.* **2** to some extent or degree; at all: *Has the sick child improved any?* [Old English *ǣnig*]

▶**any.** In comparisons of things of the same class, idiomatic English calls for *any other: This book is better than any other on the same subject.* But: *I think a movie is more entertaining than any book* (not the same class of things).

an|y|bod|y (en′ē bod′ē, -bud′-), *pron., n., pl.* **-bod|ies.** **1** any person; anyone: *Has anybody been here?* **2** *Informal.* an important person: *Is he anybody?*

▶**Anybody, somebody** are both often used to mean "an important person," but the former tends to be interrogatory or negative: *I doubt if he is anybody.* The latter tends to be strongly affirmative, though often sarcastically so: *Look at all those reporters talking to him—they must think he really is somebody.*

an|y|how (en′ē hou), *adv.* **1** in any case; at any rate; anyway; at least: *I can see as well as you, anyhow.* **2** in any way whatever: *The answer is wrong anyhow you look at it.* **3** carelessly; haphazardly: *He dumped the tools into the box just anyhow. [He] was sprawled anyhow on a couch in his hotel room* (New York Times).

an|y|more (en′ē môr′, -mōr′), *adv.* at present; now; currently: *He didn't know anymore, he said, whether he was a Liberal or Conservative* (Harper's). *And of course nobody who is anybody fattens anymore* (Saturday Evening Post).

any more, **1** anything additional; more: *I don't want any more.* **2** further; additional: *Let's not have any more fighting.* **3** currently: *I don't smoke any more. What, after all, can one say that is "original" about William Shakespeare any more?* (American Scholar).

any more than, to a greater extent or more general degree than: *... You cannot ... have democracy in a revolutionary party any more than anywhere else* (Edmund Wilson).

an|y|one (en′ē wun, -wən), *pron.* any person; anybody: *Can anyone go to this movie or is it just for adults? Anyone may come. He is said to have been able ... to detect the place of origin of anyone he met* (Edmund Wilson).

▶**Anyone** is written as one word when the stress is on the *any: Anyone* (en′ē wun) *would know that.* It is two words when the stress is on the *one: I'd like any one* (en′ē wun′) *of them.* When the stress is on *one*, it may refer to a thing or a person.

any one, **1** any single or individual: *in any one city in the United States.* **2** any person or thing.

an|y|place (en′ē plās), *adv. Informal.* anywhere: *[There is in] Kansas more clear weather than anyplace else outside the Rio Grande Valley and southern California* (New Yorker).

an|y|thing (en′ē thing), *n., pron., adv.* **—*n.*** or ***pron.*** **1a** any thing: *Do you have anything to eat? My dog will eat almost anything.* **b** particular thing not mentioned: *Have you anything on your mind you wish to talk about?* **2** a certain amount; part: *Is anything about the plan yet in doubt? Is there anything of the saint in her?* **3** a person of importance: *He isn't anything in the local government though he has lived there for years.*
—*adv.* in any way; at all: *Is your doll anything like mine?*

anything but, not at all: *This room is anything but warm.*

an|y|time (en′ē tīm), *adv.* at any time; no matter when: *You are welcome to visit us anytime.*

an|y|way (en′ē wā), *adv.* **1** in any case; at least: *I am coming anyway, no matter what you say.* **2** in any way whatever. **3** carelessly; anyhow: *He dumped the tools in the box just anyway.*

▶**Anyway** is one word when the *any* is stressed: *I can't do it anyway.* It is two words when the stress is about equal: *Any way I try, it comes out wrong.*

an|y|ways (en′ē wāz), *adv. Informal.* = anyway.

an|y|when (en′ē hwen), *adv. Dialect.* at any time.

an|y|where (en′ē hwãr), *adv.* in any place; at or to any place: *I'll meet you anywhere you say.*

anywhere between, *Informal.* at any point between: *I told them that a reasonable date for the foundation of the monument was anywhere between 1400 and 1700* B.C. (Holiday).

anywhere from, *Informal.* at any point within a stated range: *It will take anywhere from two to three hours to drive there.*

anywhere near, *Informal.* nearly: *The job is not anywhere near done.*

get anywhere, *Informal.* to advance; prosper; succeed: *He was a talented man, but his dislike of hard work prevented him from getting anywhere in the business world.*

an|y|wise (en′ē wīz), *adv.* in any way; to any degree; at all.

ANZAAS (an′zas′), *n.* Australian and New Zealand Association for the Advancement of Science.

An|zac (an′zak), *n.* a soldier from Australia or New Zealand. [< *A*(ustralia) and *N*(ew) *Z*(ealand) *A*(rmy) *C*(orps)]

ANZAM (an′zam), *n.* an alliance of Australia, New Zealand, and Malaysia to protect the approaches

Pronunciation Key: **hat**, **āge**, **cãre**, **fär**; **let**, **ēqual**, **tėrm**; **it**, **īce**; **hot**, **ōpen**, **ôrder**; **oil**, **out**; **cup**, **pu̇t**, **rüle**; **child**; **long**; **thin**; **ᴛʜen**; **zh**, measure; **ə** represents **a** in about, **e** in taken, **i** in pencil, **o** in lemon, **u** in circus.

to southeastern Asia in the Indian Ocean and the Indonesian seas, formed in the 1960's. [< *A*(ustralia) *N*(ew) *Z*(ealand) *M*(alaysia)]

ANZUS (an′zůs), *n.* an alliance of Australia, New Zealand, and the United States for the purpose of mutual defense in the Pacific, formed in 1951. [< *A*(ustralia) *N*(ew) *Z*(ealand) *U*(nited) *S*(tates)]

a.o. or **a/o** (no periods), account of.

***a|o dai** (ä′ō dī′), *pl.* **a|o dais.** a tunic open up each side to the waist and worn with wide pantaloons by Vietnamese women. [< Vietnamese *ao dai*]

***ao dai**

A-OK (no periods) or **A-O.K.** (ā′ō′kā′), *adj., adv., interj. Informal.* OK: *The "A-OK" method of teaching the deaf is to "talk, talk, talk," to them* (Harper's).

A one (ā′ wun′), *Informal.* first-rate; first-class; excellent. Also, **A No. 1, A number 1, A 1.**

A|o|ni|an (ā ō′nē ən), *adj.* of or having to do with Aonia, a region of Boeotia in ancient Greece containing Mount Helicon and associated especially with the Muses.

AOR (no periods), **1** adult-oriented rock; classic rock: *Sales are helped by Zeppelin's status as the backbone of AOR and classic-rock radio* (Rolling Stone). **2** at own risk (a hospital term).

a|o|rist (ā′ər ist), *n., adj.* —*n.* **1** one of the past tenses of Greek verbs. It shows that an action took place at some time in the past without indicating whether the act was completed, repeated, or continued. **2** a tense of similar form or meaning in certain other languages, such as Sanskrit.
—***adj.*** of or in the aorist.
[< Greek *aóristos* indefinite < *a-* not + *hóros* boundary]

a|o|ris|tic (ā′ə ris′tik), *adj.* **1** undefined; indeterminate: *like certain aoristic combinations in music* (George Meredith). **2** of or having to do with an aorist. —**a′o|ris′ti|cal|ly,** *adv.*

a|or|ta (ā ôr′tə), *n., pl.* **-tas, -tae** (-tē). the great artery that carries the blood from the left side (ventricle) of the heart to all parts of the body except the lungs. The aorta is the main trunk of the arterial system and has many branches. See picture under **circulation.** [< New Latin *aorta* < Greek *aortē* the aorta]

a|or|tic (ā ôr′tik), *adj.* of or having to do with the aorta: *an aortic valve, aortic aneurysms.*

a|or|ti|tis (ā′ôr tī′tis), *n.* inflammation of the aorta.

a|or|tog|ra|phy (ā′ôr tog′rə fē), *n., pl.* **-phies.** examination of the aorta by means of arteriographs.

a|ou|dad (ä′ů dad), *n.* a wild sheep native to northern Africa, found also in California, New Mexico, and Texas; barbary sheep. [< French *aoudad* < Berber *audad*]

à ou|trance (á ü träɴs′), *French.* to the utmost; to the very end: *to battle à outrance. . . . Emerson's description of Henry David Thoreau—"a protestant à outrance"* (New Yorker).

ap-[1], *prefix.* the form of **ad-** before *p,* as in *apprehend.*

ap-[2], *prefix.* the form of **apo-** before vowels and *h,* as in *aphelion.*

ap., apothecaries' weight.

Ap., **1** Apostle. **2** April.

AP (no periods), **1** Air Police (the military police of the United States Air Force). **2** American plan. **3** antipersonnel. **4** Associated Press. It often appears in print as a ligature (Ⱥ).

a|pace (ə pās′), *adv.* very soon; swiftly; quickly; fast: *The summer flew by, and the time for school was coming on apace.*

A|pach|e (ə pach′ē), *n., pl.* **A|pach|es** or **A|pach|e.** **1** a member of a tribe of Indians living in the southwestern United States. They were formerly warlike and nomadic. **2** the tribe itself. **3** their language, of the Athapascan stock. [American English, apparently < American Spanish *apache* < Zuñi *ápachu* enemy (their name for the Navajos)]

a|pache (ə päsh′, -pash′; *French* á pásh′), *n., adj.* —*n.* a rough or rowdy person, especially one of a band of toughs or gangsters who operate in Paris and Brussels.
—***adj.*** of or designating a kind of very energetic dance in which the partners are dressed like an apache and his woman.
[< French *apache,* special use of English *Apache*]

a|pa|ge Sa|ta|nas (ap′ə jē sat′ə nəs; ä′pä ge sä′tä näs), *Latin.* begone, Satan!

a|pa|go|ge (ap′ə gō′jē), *n. Logic.* demonstration of a proposition, by showing the impossibility or absurdity of the contrary. [< Greek *apagōgḗ* a leading away]

a|pa|gog|ic (ap′ə goj′ik), *adj. Logic.* of or having to do with apagoge.

a|pa|gog|i|cal (ap′ə goj′ə kəl) *adj. Logic.* of the nature of apagoge.

a|pa|min (ā′pə min), *n.* a substance, derived from bee venom, that is poisonous to nervous tissue, used experimentally in neurology and medicine: *Apamin is the smallest neurotoxic polypeptide known, and it is the only one whose interaction with the spinal cord is well established* (Science). [< Latin *ap*(is) bee + English *amin*(o acid)]

a|pa|nage (ap′ə nij), *n.* = appanage.

a|pa|re|jo (ä′pə rā′hō), *n., pl.* **-jos.** *Southwestern U.S.* a kind of packsaddle, usually of stuffed leather. [American English < Spanish *aparejo* packsaddle, harness]

a|part (ə pärt′), *adv., adj.* —***adv.*** **1** to pieces; in pieces; in separate parts: *He took the watch apart to see how it runs. That old house looks as if it were falling apart.* **2** away from each other: *Keep the dogs apart.* **3** to one side; aside: *He sets some money apart for a vacation each year. All joking apart, do you mean that?* **4** away from others; each by itself; separately; independently: *View each idea apart.* **5** to or in another place; away: *to live apart from one's family.*
—***adj.*** separate: *He became a man apart.*
apart from, besides: *Apart from its cost, the plan was a good one.*
[< Old French *a part* to the side < Latin *ad partem*]

à part (á pár′), *French.* **1** aside: *It seemed to me regrettable that American hotel men don't offer our à part service—serving from a side table rather than plopping everything on one plate in the kitchen* (New Yorker). **2** an aside.

a|part|heid (ä pärt′hāt, -hīt, -hīd), *n.* racial segregation, especially as practiced in the Republic of South Africa. There, segregation of blacks from whites is the law of the South African government. [< Afrikaans *apartheid* < Dutch < *apart* separate]

a|part|ment (ə pärt′mənt), *n.* **1a** a room or group of rooms to live in; flat: *Our apartment is on the second floor of that building.* **b** *U.S.* a single room. **2** an apartment building. [< French *appartement* < Italian *appartamento,* ultimately < *a parte* apart]

apartment building, a building with a number of apartments in it.

apartment hotel, *U.S.* a hotel having furnished apartments for rent to permanent residents.

apartment house, = apartment building.

a|part|ness (ə pärt′nis), *n.* the quality of being or standing apart; aloofness: *Howarth . . . is one of those distant, always lonely figures who search out crowds only to emphasize their own apartness* (Manchester Guardian).

à pas de gé|ant (á pä′də zhā äɴ′), *French.* with a giant's stride or tread: *Up he thunders, à pas de géant, . . . a hint of the mediaeval in his upturning boots* (Punch).

ap|as|tron (ap as′trən), *n. Astronomy.* that point in the orbit of a double star in which one star is farthest away from its primary. [< *ap-*[2] away + Greek *ástron* star]

ap|a|tet|ic (ap′ə tet′ik), *adj.* deceptively resembling the coloration of an animal's environment or the markings of another species. [< Greek *apatētikós* fallacious < *apatân* to deceive]

ap|a|thet|ic (ap′ə thet′ik), *adj.* **1** with little interest or desire for action; indifferent: *The lazy boy's apathetic attitude toward schoolwork annoyed his teacher.* **SYN:** listless. **2** lacking in feeling; unemotional: *His apathetic response to the tragedy showed he did not understand the play.* **SYN:** listless.
[< *apathy,* on analogy of *pathetic*]

ap|a|thet|i|cal (ap′ə thet′ə kəl), *adj.* = apathetic.

ap|a|thet|i|cal|ly (ap′ə thet′ik lē), *adv.* in an apathetic manner.

ap|a|thy (ap′ə thē), *n.* **1** lack of interest in or desire for activity; indifference: *The apathy of the lazy boy was annoying. The citizens' apathy to local affairs resulted in poor government.* **SYN:** unconcern, impassivity. See syn. under **indifference.** **2** lack of feeling: *The miser heard the old beggar's story with apathy.* **SYN:** unfeelingness, insensibility.
[< Latin *apathīa* < Greek *apátheia* < *a-* without + *páthos* feeling]

ap|a|tite (ap′ə tīt), *n.* a native phosphate of lime, varying in color from white to green, blue, violet, and brown, occurring in crystals or masses, and commonly minced for use as a fertilizer. [< Greek *apátē* deceit + English *-ite*[1] (because its diverse forms were often wrongly identified)]

ap|a|to|sau|rus (ap′ə tō sôr′əs), *n.* = brontosaurus.
[< Greek *apatân* to deceive + *saûros* lizard]

APB (no periods), all points bulletin (a police message alerting all patrolmen).

APC (no periods), **1** adenoidal-pharyngeal-conjunctival (virus). **2** aspirin, phenacetin, caffeine.

***ape** (āp), *n., v.,* **aped, ap|ing,** *adj.* —*n.* **1** a large, tailless monkey with long arms, that can stand almost erect and walk on two feet. Chimpanzees, gorillas, orangutans, and gibbons are anthropoid apes. Certain other monkeys, such as the Barbary ape and the macaque, are also called apes: *Many people confuse apes with monkeys, but the two groups of animals differ in many ways* (R.L. Susman). See picture below. **2** any monkey. **3** *Figurative.* a person who imitates or mimics. **4** *Figurative.* **a** a rough, clumsy person. **b** a fool.
—***v.t.*** to imitate; mimic: *The girl aped the way the movie star fixed her hair.*
—***adj.*** *Slang.* wild; excited; enthusiastic: *I advised her to quit acting ape* (S. J. Perelman).
go ape, *Slang.* to become wildly excited: *Seniors . . . chose oval-shaped rings . . . and the kids have really gone ape over them* (Kay Harris).
[Old English *apa*] —**ape′like′,** *adj.*

a|peak (ə pēk′), *adv., adj.* —***adv.*** (of an anchor chain, oars, or a yard) in or into a vertical position or nearly so.
—***adj.*** **1** (of a ship or boat) with the anchor chain running vertically, or nearly so, to the anchor. **2** (of oars or a yard) vertical.

a|pei|ron (ə pī′rən), *n.* the ultimate principle or original source of life (postulated by Anaximander, Greek philosopher of the 500's B.C.). [< Greek *ápeiron,* accusative, the Infinite]

a|pel|la (ə pel′ə), *n.* the general assembly of ancient Sparta.
[< Late Greek *apella*]

ape man, any one of various animals supposed to be evolutionary links between ape and man: *The ape men of Africa who may have been our direct ancestors were probably the prey of wild animals of their day, not the hunters* (Scientific American).

a|per|çu (a′pər sü′; *French* á per sʏ′), *n.* **1** insight gained upon a rapid survey of a subject: *At every point in the argument particular instances lead to a fresh or thought-provoking remark about some artist's work, and the book is as illuminating in such critical apercus as in its general thesis* (London Times). **2** a short outline or sketch.
[< French *aperçu* a quick glance]

a|pe|ri|ent (ə pir′ē ənt), *adj., n.* —***adj.*** mildly purgative; laxative.
—*n.* an aperient medicine or article of diet.
[< Latin *aperiēns, -entis,* present participle of *aperīre* to open]

a|pe|ri|od|ic (ā′pir ē od′ik), *adj.* **1** not periodic; irregular. **2** *Physics.* having irregular vibrations.

a|pe|ri|o|dic|i|ty (ā pir′ē ə dis′ə tē), *n.* aperiodic condition.

a|pé|ri|tif (ə per′ə tēf′; *French* á pā rē tēf′), *n.* an alcoholic drink, especially any of various wines, taken before a meal to stimulate the appetite: *Apéritifs, which Frenchmen like to sip in cafes in the late afternoon, are made by adding alcohol and herbs to wine* (Edward W. Fox). [< French *apéritif*]

a|per|i|tive (ə per′ə tiv), *adj., n.* = aperient.

***ape** definition 1

a|pert (ə pėrt′), *adj.* **1** *Archaic.* open; manifest; unconcealed. **2** *Obsolete.* bold, forward, or pert. [< Old French *apert* < Latin *apertus,* past participle of *aperīre* to open]

ap|er|tom|e|ter (ap′ər tom′ə tər), *n.* a device attached to a microscope for measuring the angular aperture of the objective lens. [< *apert*(ure)]

ap|er|ture (ap′ər chůr, -chər), *n.* **1** an opening; gap; hole: *A window is an aperture for letting in light and air.* **SYN:** orifice, slit. **2** the diameter of the opening through which light passes in a camera, telescope, or other optical instrument. [< Latin *apertūra* < *aperīre* open. See etym. of doublet **overture.**]

aperture card, a key-punch card with one or more openings for holding a microfilm frame or frames, used in data processing, documentation, and the like: *Microfilm copies of patents offered to the public and for examiners' use will be stored in the form of aperture cards, which have space for eight images each* (Science News).

ap|er|tured (ap′ər chůrd, -chərd), *adj.* having an aperture or apertures.

ap|er|y (ā′pər ē), *n., pl.* **-er|ies. 1** pretentious or silly mimicry. **2** a silly or apish action or performance. [< *ape* + *-ry*]

a|pet|al|ous (ā pet′ə ləs), *adj.* having no petals: *apetalous flowers.*

à peu près (ȧ pœ pre′), *French.* almost; nearly.

a|pex (ā′peks), *n., pl.* **a|pex|es, ap|i|ces. 1** the highest point; tip: *The apex of a triangle or of a leaf is the point opposite the base.* **2** *Figurative.* the climax; peak: *a nation at the apex of its power. Camping out on the last night and eating around the campfire was the apex of the boys' vacation.* **3** the point on the celestial sphere toward which the sun and solar system are moving relative to the stars. [< Latin *apex*]

APF (no periods), animal protein factor.

ap|fel|stru|del (ap′fəl strü′dəl; *German* äp′fəl-shtrü′dəl), *n.* a strudel with an apple filling.

a|phaer|e|sis (ə fer′ə sis), *n.* = apheresis.

aph|ae|ret|ic (af′ə ret′ik), *adj.* = apheretic.

a|pha|ki|a (ə fā′kē ə), *n.* lack or loss of the lens of the eye. [< New Latin *aphakia* < *a-* without + Greek *phakós* lentil]

a|pha|kic (ə fā′kik), *n.* a person who has aphakia.

aph|a|nite (af′ə nīt), *n.* a compact rock so uniform in texture that no distinct crystals are visible to the naked eye. [< French *aphanite* < Greek *aphanḗs* not manifest < *a-* not + *phaínein* show forth]

aph|a|nit|ic (af′ə nit′ik), *adj.* of or like aphanite.

a|pha|sia (ə fā′zhə), *n.* total or partial loss of the ability to use or understand words. Aphasia is caused by injury or disease that affects the brain. [< New Latin *aphasia* < Greek *aphasiā* < *a-* without + *phásis* utterance < *phánai* speak]

a|pha|si|ac (ə fā′zē ak), *adj., n. Rare.* aphasic.

a|pha|sic (ə fā′zik, -sik), *adj., n.* **—adj.** of or having to do with aphasia; suffering from aphasia.
—n. a person who has aphasia.

***a|phe|li|on** (ə fē′lē ən, a-), *n., pl.* **-li|ons, -li|a** (-lē ə). **1** the point farthest from the sun in the orbit of a planet or comet. **2** the point in the orbit of any orbiting body farthest from the body about which it revolves. **3** *Figurative.* the furthermost point: *France, which is just now in ... the aphelion or furthest point of political cold* (P. Thompson). [a Grecized form of New Latin *aphelium* < Greek *apo-* away from + *hḗlios* sun]

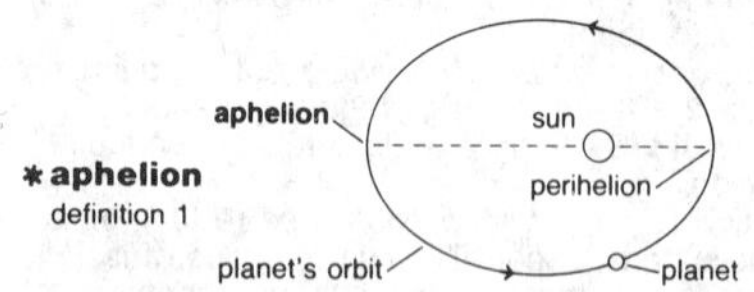

***aphelion**
definition 1

a|phe|li|o|trop|ic (ə fē′lē ə trop′ik), *adj.* bending or turning away from sunlight: *an apheliotropic plant.* **—a|phe′li|o|trop′i|cal|ly,** *adv.*

a|phe|li|ot|ro|pism (ə fē′lē ot′rə piz əm), *n.* the tendency of a plant to bend or turn away from sunlight; negative heliotropism. [< *apheliotrop*(ic)]

a|phe|mi|a (ə fē′mē ə), *n.* a form of aphasia marked by inability to articulate words. [< New Latin *aphemia* < Greek *a-* without + *phḗmē* voice]

a|phem|ic (ə fem′ik), *adj.* of or having to do with aphemia; suffering from aphemia.

a|pher|e|sis (ə fer′ə sis), *n.* omission of a phoneme, particularly an unaccented vowel, from the beginning of a word, or the resulting omission of a letter from the spelling, such as in *state* for *estate.* Also, **aphaeresis.** [< Late Latin *aphaeresis* < Greek *aphaíresis* a taking away < *apo-* away + *haireîn* take]

aph|e|ret|ic (af′ə ret′ik), *adj. Rare.* of the nature of apheresis. Also, **aphaeretic.**

aph|e|sis (af′ə sis), *n.* apheresis in which an unaccented initial vowel is gradually weakened and then lost, such as *possum* for *opossum.* [< Greek *áphesis* a letting go < *aphīénai* < *apo-* off + *hīénai* send]

a|phet|ic (ə fet′ik), *adj.* concerning or produced by aphesis.

aph|e|tize (af′ə tīz), *v.t.,* **-tized, -tiz|ing.** to shorten by aphesis.

a|phi|cide (ā′fə sīd, af′ə-), *n.* an insecticide intended for use especially against aphids.

a|phid (ā′fid, af′id), *n.* a very small insect that lives by sucking juices from plants; plant louse. [< New Latin *aphides,* plural of *aphis* aphis]

a|phid|i|an (ə fid′ē ən), *adj. Rare.* of or having to do with an aphid or aphids.

a|phis (ā′fis, af′is), *n., pl.* **aph|i|des** (af′ə dēz). = aphid. [< New Latin *aphis, -idis* (coined by Linnaeus)]

aphis lion or **wolf,** any one of various insect larvae, such as of the ladybug, that feed on aphids.

a|pho|ni|a (ə fō′nē ə), *n.* loss of voice caused by an abnormal condition of the larynx. [< New Latin *aphonia* < Greek *aphōniā* < *a-* without + *phōnḗ* voice]

a|phon|ic (ə fon′ik), *adj., n.* **—adj. 1** *Phonetics.* **a** without sound; not pronounced. **b** produced without motion of the vocal cords; voiceless. **2** of or characterized by aphonia.
—n. a person who suffers from aphonia.

aph|o|rism (af′ə riz əm), *n.* **1** a short sentence expressing a general truth, piece of practical wisdom, or the like; maxim; proverb. *Example:* "A living dog is better than a dead lion." **SYN:** adage, saw, apothegm. **2** a concise statement of a principle in any science. [< Late Latin *aphorismus* < Greek *aphorismós* definition < *apo-* off + *hóros* boundary] ▶See **epigram** for usage note.

aph|o|ris|mat|ic (af′ə riz mat′ik), *adj.* **1** = aphorismic. **2** = aphoristic.

aph|o|ris|mic (af′ə riz′mik), *adj.* having the form of an aphorism.

aph|o|rist (af′ər ist), *n.* a person who writes or utters aphorisms.

aph|o|ris|tic (af′ə ris′tik), *adj.* of or like aphorisms: *He himself spoke in dark, aphoristic riddles* (Scientific American). **—aph′o|ris′ti|cal|ly,** *adv.*

aph|o|rize (af′ə rīz), *v.i.,* **-rized, -riz|ing.** to write or speak in aphorisms.

a|pho|tic (ā fō′tik), *adj.* without light. [< Greek *áphōs, áphōtos* (< *a-* without + *phôs, phōtós* light) + English *-ic*]

aph|ro|dis|i|ac (af′rə diz′ē ak), *adj., n.* **—adj.** awakening or increasing sexual desire. **—n.** anything that awakens or increases sexual desire, such as a specially concocted drug or food. [< Greek *aphrodīsiakós* < *aphrodīsios* pertaining to *Aphrodītē* Aphrodite]

aph|ro|dis|i|a|cal (af′rə di zī′ə kəl), *adj.* = aphrodisiac.

Aph|ro|di|te (af′rə dī′tē), *n.* **1** the Greek goddess of love and beauty. The Romans called her Venus. **2** a brown butterfly of North America, having black spots. [< Greek *Aphrodītē* (literally) foam-born < *aphrós* foam]

aph|tha (af′thə), *n., pl.* **-thae** (-thē). **1** thrush, a disease especially of infants. **2** one of the round, whitish spots or cankers, especially in the mouth, that characterize this disease. [< Latin *aphtha* < Greek *áphtha,* related to *áptein* to inflame]

aph|thoid (af′thoid), *adj.* resembling an aphtha or aphthae. [< *aphth*(a) + *-oid*]

aph|thous (af′thəs), *adj.* of the nature of or characterized by aphthae.

aphthous fever, foot-and-mouth disease; aftosa.

a|phyl|lous (ə fil′əs), *adj.* destitute of leaves; naturally leafless, as a cactus. [< New Latin *aphyllus* (with English *-ous*) < Greek *áphyllos* < *a-* without + *phýllon* leaf]

a|phyl|ly (ə fil′ē), *n.* the state of being aphyllous.

a|pi|a|ceous (ā′pē ā′shəs), *adj.* = ammiaceous. [< Latin *apium* parsley; (probably originally) liked by bees (< *apis* bee) + English *-aceous*]

a|pi|an (ā′pē ən), *adj.* of or having to do with bees. [< Latin *apiānus* < *apis* bee]

a|pi|ar|i|an (ā′pē ãr′ē ən), *adj.* concerned with bees; having to do with beekeeping.

a|pi|a|rist (ā′pē ər ist), *n.* = beekeeper.

a|pi|ar|y (ā′pē er′ē), *n., pl.* **-ar|ies.** a place where bees are kept; group of beehives. [< Latin *apiārium,* neuter of *apiārius* of bees < *apis* bee]

ap|i|cal (ap′ə kəl, ā′pə-), *adj., n.* **—adj.** of the apex; at the apex; forming the apex. **—n.** *Phonetics.* a sound made by using the tip of the tongue. [< Latin *apex, -icis* + English *-al*[1]] **—ap′i|cal|ly,** *adv.*

apical meristem, *Botany.* the actively growing and dividing tissue at the tip of a root or shoot.

ap|i|ces (ap′ə sēz, ā′pə-), *n.* apexes; a plural of **apex.**

a|pic|u|late (ə pik′yə lit, -lāt), *adj.* ending with a short and abrupt point: *apiculate leaves.* [< New Latin *apiculatus* < *apiculus* tip (diminutive) < Latin *apex, -icis* apex]

a|pic|u|lat|ed (ə pik′yə lā′tid), *adj.* = apiculate.

a|pi|cul|tur|al (ā′pə kul′chər əl), *adj.* of or having to do with apiculture.

a|pi|cul|ture (ā′pə kul′chər), *n.* the raising and care of bees; beekeeping: *Modern apiculture ... has gone far beyond the simple task of providing a pot of honey for the breakfast table* (New York Times). [< Latin *apis* bee + *cultūra* tending]

a|pi|cul|tur|ist (ā′pə kul′chər ist), *n.* a person who practices apiculture; apiarist.

a|pi|dic|tor (ā′pə dik′tər), *n.* an instrument for recording and measuring the sounds in a beehive. [< Latin *apis* bee + Late Latin *dictor* speaker]

a|piece (ə pēs′), *adv.* for each one; each: *These apples are ten cents apiece.* **SYN:** individually, singly, severally. [earlier *a piece* an item]

à pied (ȧ pyā′), *French.* on foot.

ap|i|ko|ros (ap′i kō′rôs), *n., pl.* **-kor|sim** (-kōr′-sim). a Jew who disbelieves in, or is lax in observing, Judaic law: *An apikoros ... was a renegade from the Jewish religion, but the word had the even deeper and more sinister connotation of treachery not merely to the Jewish religion but to God himself* (New Yorker). [< Hebrew *apīqōrōs* < Greek *Epíkouros* Epicurus. Compare etym. under **epicure.**]

ap|i|ol (ap′ē ol, -ōl; ā′pē-), *n.* the active element of parsley seed, obtainable as white crystals and in an oleoresin (liquid or green apiol), sometimes used to reduce fever or as an emmenagogue. *Formula:* $C_{12}H_{14}O_4$ [< Latin *apium* parsley + English *-ol*[1]]

a|pi|ol|o|gist (ā′pē ol′ə jist), *n.* a person who studies apiology.

a|pi|ol|o|gy (ā′pē ol′ə jē), *n.* the scientific study of bees. [< Latin *apis* bee + English *-logy*]

A|pis (ā′pis), *n.* the sacred bull worshiped by the ancient Egyptians.

ap|ish (ā′pish), *adj.* **1** foolish; silly: *That tease always has an apish grin on his face.* **2** like an ape: *The Pithecanthropi ... must have had apish countenances, with a low forehead, immensely heavy brow ridge shadowing the eyes, a broad, flat nose, massive and somewhat projecting jaws—and no chin* (The Observer). **3** senselessly imitative. **—ap′ish|ly,** *adv.* **—ap′ish|ness,** *n.*

a|piv|o|rous (ā piv′ər əs), *adj.* feeding on bees: *Most apivorous birds probably originated in Africa.* [< Latin *apis* bee + *vorāre* devour + English *-ous*]

a|pla|cen|tal (ā′plə sen′təl, ap′lə-), *adj. Zoology.* having no placenta, as monotremes and marsupials. [< *a-*[4] not + *placental*]

ap|la|nat|ic (ap′lə nat′ik), *adj. Optics.* free from aberration, especially from spherical aberration. [< *a-*[4] not + Greek *planētikós* moving, unstable < *planâsthai* wander]

a|plan|a|tism (ə plan′ə tiz əm), *n.* freedom from aberration, especially from spherical aberration. [< *aplanat*(ic) + *-ism*]

a|pla|sia (ə plā′zhə), *n.* incomplete or defective growth and development of a bodily organ or part. [< New Latin *aplasia* < Greek *a-* not + *plássein* to form]

a|plas|tic (ā plas′tik), *adj.* **1** of or having to do with aplasia; characterized by aplasia. **2** characterized by or tending toward irregularity or absence of organic structure.

aplastic anemia, a severe anemia caused by failure of the bone marrow to produce various blood elements, such as red cells, as a result of exposure to certain antibiotic drugs, poisons, large doses of X rays, or for unknown reasons.

a|plen|ty (ə plen′tē), *adv., adj. Informal.* in plenty: *He knew his countryside and its legends faithfully and had stories aplenty about the old characters* (Richard M. Dorson).

ap|lite (ap′līt), *n.* a granite of fine grain, consisting of quartz and feldspar. Also, **haplite.** [< Greek *haplós, haploûs* simple + English *-ite*[1]]

ap|lit|ic (ap lit′ik), *adj.* of or like aplite.

a|plo|ma|do falcon (ä plō mä′dō), a falcon ranging from extreme southwestern United States southward through Mexico. Its habits and food somewhat resemble the sparrow hawk's. [< Spanish *aplomado* leaden, lazy]

a|plomb (ə plom′), *n.* **1** self-possession springing from perfect confidence in oneself; assurance; poise: *He exudes self-confidence and aplomb* (Time). **2** *Rare.* perpendicularity. [< French *aplomb* < earlier *à plomb* according to the plummet]

ap|ne|a or **ap|noe|a** (ap nē′ə), *n.* **1** temporary suspension of breathing. **2** = asphyxia. [< New Latin *apnoea* < Greek *ápnoia* < *a-* without + *pnoḗ* breath]

ap|ne|al or **ap|noe|al** (ap nē′əl), *adj.* of or characterized by apnea.

ap|ne|ic or **ap|noe|ic** (ap nē′ik), *adj.* = apneal.

apo-, *prefix.* **1** from; away; quite; off, as in *apostasy, apocalypse.*
2 (especially in modern scientific terms) standing off or away from each other; detached; separate: *Aposepalous = having separate sepals. Also,* **ap-** before vowels and *h.*

[< Greek *apo-* < *apó* off]

APO (no periods) or **A.P.O.**, Army Post Office.

Apoc., **1** Apocalypse. **2a** Apocrypha. **b** Apocryphal.

a|poc|a|lypse (ə pok′ə lips), *n.* **1** a revelation, especially a revelation or vision of a great world upheaval: *The new writings more and more take the form of apocalypses—that is, of supernatural visions which reveal past, present, and future* (New Yorker). **2** a great upheaval or cataclysm. **3** any of the apocalyptic writings.
the Apocalypse, the last book of the New Testament; book of Revelation: *Pope Clement VII thought that the prophecies of the Apocalypse were about to be fulfilled, and that the end of the world was at hand* (Hugh Trevor-Roper).
[< Latin *apocalypsis* < Greek *apokálypsis* < *apo-* off + *kalýptein* to cover, veil]

a|poc|a|lyp|tic (ə pok′ə lip′tik), *adj., n.* —*adj.* **1** like or giving a revelation especially of violent upheaval: *Among people who see supernatural implications in natural phenomena, tornadoes have long been regarded as the most apocalyptic of storms* (New Yorker). **2** Also, **Apocalyptic.** of or having to do with the Apocalypse. **3** having to do with a class of Jewish and Christian visionary literature written between 200 B.C. and A.D. 200, describing the ultimate triumph of God over evil.
—*n.* **1** = apocalyptist. **2** apocalyptic writing or literature. —**a|poc′a|lyp′ti|cal|ly**, *adv.*

a|poc|a|lyp|ti|cal (ə pok′ə lip′tə kəl), *adj.* = apocalyptic.

a|poc|a|lyp|ti|cism (ə pok′ə lip′tə siz əm), *n.* **1** expectation of the imminent end of the present world, especially as a doctrine derived from the book of Revelation. **2** = Messianism.

a|poc|a|lyp|tist (ə pok′ə lip′tist), *n.* the writer or an interpreter of the Apocalypse.

ap|o|carp (ap′ə kärp), *n.* an ovary or fruit having separate or distinct carpels. [< *apo-* + Greek *karpós* fruit]

ap|o|car|pous (ap′ə kär′pəs), *adj.* having the carpels distinct or separate.

ap|o|cen|ter (ap′ə sen′tər), *n.* the point in the orbit of a heavenly body at which it is farthest from the point around which it revolves. [< *apo-* + *center*]

ap|o|cen|tric (ap′ə sen′trik), *adj.* at or having to do with an apocenter.

ap|o|cen|tric|i|ty (ap′ə sen tris′ə tē), *n.* the property of being apocentric.

ap|o|chro|mat (ap′ə krə mat), *n.* an apochromatic lens.

ap|o|chro|mat|ic (ap′ə krə mat′ik), *adj.* having neither chromatic nor spherical aberration: *an apochromatic lens.* [< *apo-* + *chromatic*]

a|poc|o|pate (ə pok′ə pāt), *v.*, **-pat|ed, -pat|ing,** *adj.* —*v.t.* to shorten by apocope.
—*adj.* apocopated. —**a|poc′o|pa′tion**, *n.*

a|poc|o|pe (ə pok′ə pē), *n.* the dropping out of the last sound, syllable, or letter in a word. *Th′* for *the* and *i′* for *in* are examples of apocope. [< Late Latin *apocopē* < Greek *apokopē* < *apo-* off + *kóptein* to cut]

ap|o|crine (ap′ə krīn), *adj.* of or having to do with a skin gland which feeds a milky-white, odorless fluid to the hair roots and skin surface. Certain occupations, such as mining, cause the secretion to change color and develop an offensive odor. [< *apo-* + Greek *krīnein* separate]

A|poc|ry|pha (ə pok′rə fə), *n.pl.* **1** fourteen books or portions of books of the Old Testament that are included in the Roman Catholic Bible but not generally found in Jewish or Protestant Bibles. The Apocrypha appear in the Septuagint (Greek) and in the Vulgate (Latin) Bibles, but are not accepted as genuine parts of the Biblical canon by the Jews or the Protestants, though sometimes appearing in an appendix in Bibles used by Episcopalians and Lutherans. **2** Also, **apocrypha.** certain early Christian writings rejected from the New Testament. **3** Also, **apocrypha.** (in the Roman Catholic Church) certain religious literature completely rejected as of dubious origin as part of the canon by the weight of authority; pseudepigrapha. *Abbr:* Apoc. [< Late Latin *apocrypha,* neuter plural of *apocryphus* < Greek *apókryphos* hidden < *apo-* away + *krýptein* hide]

a|poc|ry|pha (ə pok′rə fə), *n.pl.* **1** writings or statements of doubtful authorship or authority. **2** = Apocrypha (def. 2). **3** = Apocrypha (def. 3).

A|poc|ry|phal (ə pok′rə fəl), *adj.* **1** of or having to do with the Apocrypha. **2** not canonical.

a|poc|ry|phal (ə pok′rə fəl), *adj.* **1** of doubtful authorship or authority: *apocryphal writings, an apocryphal manuscript of the Middle Ages.* **SYN:** dubious. **2** of doubtful genuineness; false; counterfeit: *There are always many apocryphal stories about a famous person. There are ... many stories of fish and frogs reviving after being found frozen solid in blocks of ice, but these stories must be apocryphal* (Scientific American). **SYN:** sham, spurious, fabricated. —**a|poc′ry|phal|ly,** *adv.* —**a|poc′ry|phal|ness,** *n.*

a|poc|y|na|ceous (ə pos′ə nā′shəs), *adj.* belonging to the dogbane family. [< New Latin *Apocynaceae* the dogbane family < Latin *apocynum* dogbane < Greek *apokynon* < *apo-* away + *kýōn, kynós* dog]

ap|o|cyn|thi|on (ap′ə sin′thē ən), *n.* = apolune. [< *apo-* + Latin *Cynthia* goddess of the moon + Grecized ending *-on*]

ap|od (ap′od), *n., adj.* —*n.* **1** an animal lacking limbs or feet. **2** a fish lacking ventral fins.
—*adj.* = apodal.
[< Greek *ápous, ápodos* footless < *a-* without + *poús, podós* foot]

ap|o|dal (ap′ə dəl), *adj.* **1** (of certain animals) lacking limbs or feet; footless. **2** (of fishes) lacking ventral fins, as the eel. [< *apod* + *-al*[1]]

ap|ode (ap′ōd), *n., adj.* —*n.* = apod.
—*adj.* = apodal.

ap|o|deic|tic (ap′ə dīk′tik), *adj. Especially British.* apodictic. —**ap′o|deic′ti|cal|ly,** *adv.*

ap|o|deic|ti|cal (ap′ə dīk′tə kəl), *adj. Especially British.* apodictic.

a|pod|e|ma (ə pod′ə mə), *n., pl.* **ap|o|dem|a|ta** (ap′ə dem′ə tə). = apodeme.

ap|o|deme (ap′ə dēm), *n.* one of the plates of chitin which extend inward from the exoskeletons of arthropods, supporting their internal organs. [< New Latin *apodema* < Greek *apo-* from, off + *démas* body, frame]

a|po|di|a (ə pō′dē ə), *n.* lack of feet; footless condition. [< New Latin *apodia* < Greek *apodiā* < *a-* without + *poús, podós* foot]

ap|o|dic|tic (ap′ə dik′tik), *adj.* **1** (of a conclusion) following by necessity from its grounds. **2** (of an argument) in which the conclusion follows necessarily from its grounds. [< Latin *apodīcticus* < Greek *apodeiktikós* demonstrative, ultimately < *apo-* off + *deiknýnai* to show] —**ap′o|dic′ti|cal|ly,** *adv.*

ap|o|dic|ti|cal (ap′ə dik′tə kəl), *adj.* = apodictic.

a|pod|o|sis (ə pod′ə sis), *n., pl.* **-ses** (-sēz). the clause stating the result in a conditional sentence (contrasted with *protasis*). In "If I were rich, I would help the poor," *I would help the poor* is the apodosis. [< Greek *apódosis* an answering < *apo-* back + *didónai* give]

ap|o|dous (ap′ə dəs), *adj.* = apodal.

ap|o|dy|te|ri|um (ap′ə də tir′ē əm), *n., pl.* **-te|ri|a** (-tir′ē ə). a room for disrobing in an ancient Greek or Roman bathhouse. [< Latin *apodȳtērium* < Greek *apodytḗrion* < *apodýein* to undress]

ap|o|en|zyme (ap′ō en′zīm, -zim), *n. Biochemistry.* the protein portion of an enzyme system. [< *apo-* + *enzyme*]

ap|o|fer|ri|tin (ap′ō fer′ə tin), *n.* a protein which combines with iron to form ferritin. [< *apo-* + *ferritin*]

ap|o|gam|ic (ap′ə gam′ik), *adj.* of or like apogamy.

a|pog|a|mous (ə pog′ə məs), *adj.* = apogamic. —**a|pog′a|mous|ly,** *adv.*

a|pog|a|my (ə pog′ə mē), *n. Botany.* the production of a sporophyte directly from cells of a gametophyte instead of by the usual sexual process. [< *apo-* + *-gamy*]

ap|o|ge|al (ap′ə jē′əl), *adj. Rare.* of or having to do with an apogee.

ap|o|ge|an (ap′ə jē′ən), *adj.* = apogeal.

***ap|o|gee** (ap′ə jē), *n., v.,* **-geed, -gee|ing.** —*n.* **1a** the point farthest from the earth in the orbit of the moon or other satellite of the earth. **b** the point in the orbit of any satellite body at which it is farthest from the body about which it is in orbit. **2** *Aerospace.* the point farthest from the earth in the trajectory of a ballistic missile. **3** *Figurative.* the furthermost point; highest point; peak; apex: *The Medicis* [*were*] *the lords of Florence during the apogee of the city's power and magnificence* (New York Times).
—*v.i.* to reach or be at an apogee.
[< French *apogée* < Greek *apógeion,* neuter of *apógeios* < *apò gês* from the earth]

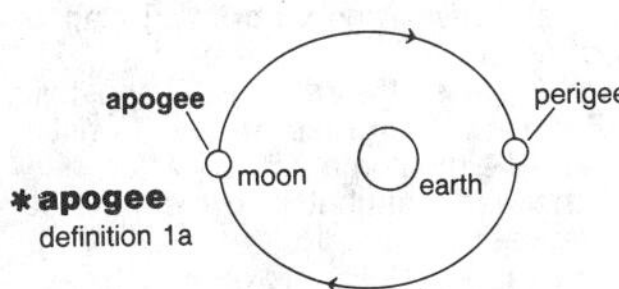

***apogee**
definition 1a

ap|o|ge|o|trop|ic (ap′ə jē′ə trop′ik), *adj.* bending or turning away from the earth: *apogeotropic leaves.* —**ap′o|ge′o|trop′i|cal|ly,** *adv.*

ap|o|ge|ot|ro|pism (ap′ə jē ot′rə piz əm), *n.* a tendency of leaves and other plant parts to bend or turn upward and away from the earth; negative geotropism.

ap|o|graph (ap′ə graf, -gräf), *n.* a copy or transcript, such as of a manuscript. [< Greek *apógraphon*]

à point (à pwaN′), *French.* just enough; just right; to the point (often said of cooking): *No oven could possibly have achieved the crispness of the well-browned fat on that leg of lamb, or that delicate pink meat done à point* (New Yorker).

a|po|lar (ā pō′lər), *adj.* not polar; having no pole.

ap|o|laus|tic (ap′ə lôs′tik), *adj.* having to do with or devoted to enjoyment. [< Greek *apolaustikós* < *apolaúein* to enjoy]

a|po|lit|i|cal (ā′pə lit′ə kəl), *adj.* not concerned with politics or political issues: *The largely rural, nomadic population was generally apolitical and had never known democracy* (Wall Street Journal). —**a′po|lit′i|cal|ly,** *adv.*

Ap|ol|lin|i|an (ap′ə lin′ē ən), *adj.* = Apollonian.

A|pol|lo (ə pol′ō), *n., pl.* **-los.** **1** *Greek and Roman Mythology.* the god of the sun, poetry, music, prophecy, healing, and archery. The Greeks and Romans considered Apollo the highest type of youthful, manly beauty. **2** *Figurative.* an extremely handsome young man. **3** an asteroid, discovered in 1932, having a diameter of about one mile. **4** a butterfly, generally white with dark, eyelike markings on the wings.

Ap|ol|lo|ni|an (ap′ə lō′nē ən), *adj.* **1** of or having to do with Apollo; like Apollo. **2** very handsome: *an Apollonian young man.*

A|pol|lyon (ə pol′yən), *n.* the Devil (in the Bible, Revelation 9:11).

a|pol|o|gete (ə pol′ə jēt), *n.* = apologist.

a|pol|o|get|ic (ə pol′ə jet′ik), *adj., n.* —*adj.* **1** making an apology; expressing regret; acknowledging a fault; excusing failure: *He sent me an apologetic note saying he was sorry for forgetting to come to my party. She spoke in a subdued and apologetic manner.* **2** defending by speech or writing; containing a defense. —*n.* an apologia; an apology; a defense. [< Latin *apologēticus* < Greek *apologētikós* defending, ultimately < *apo-* fully + *légein* tell]

a|pol|o|get|i|cal (ə pol′ə jet′ə kəl), *adj.* = apologetic.

a|pol|o|get|i|cal|ly (ə pol′ə jet′ik lē), *adv.* in an apologetic manner.

a|pol|o|get|ics (ə pol′ə jet′iks), *n.pl.* (*sing. in use*). the branch of theology that deals with the defense of a religious faith on the basis of reason. [see etym. under **apologetic**]

ap|o|lo|gi|a (ap′ə lō′jē ə), *n.* a statement in defense or justification of an idea, belief, religion, or other doctrine; apology in defense of something: *And that, my friend, that was as near as Katy ever got to an explanation or an apologia* (Harper's).

ap|o|lo|gi|a pro vi|ta su|a (ap′ə lō′jē ə prō vī′tə sü′ə), a defense of one's career, beliefs, or policies (from John Henry Cardinal Newman's *Apologia Pro Vita Sua*).

a|pol|o|gise (ə pol′ə jīz), *v.i.,* **-gised, -gis|ing.** *British.* apologize.

a|pol|o|gist (ə pol′ə jist), *n.* a person who defends an idea, belief, religion, or other doctrine, in speech or writing: *Dictators and their apologists like to say that authoritarian government makes for economic efficiency, that loss of liberty is balanced by material gains* (Time).

a|pol|o|gize (ə pol′ə jīz), *v.i.,* **-gized, -giz|ing.** **1** to say one is sorry; make an apology; acknowledge a fault; offer an excuse: *She apologized for hurting my feelings.* **2** to defend an idea, argument, belief, or other doctrine, in speech or writing.
—**a|pol′o|giz′er,** *n.*

ap|o|logue (ap′ə lôg, -log), *n.* a fable with a moral: *Aesop's fables are apologues.* [< Middle French *apologue,* learned borrowing from Latin *apologus* < Greek *apólogos* story < *apo-* fully + *légein* tell]

a|pol|o|gy (ə pol′ə jē), *n., pl.* **-gies.** **1** words saying one is sorry for an offense, fault, or accident; explanation asking pardon: *Will you accept my apology for the trouble I have caused? We made our apologies for being late.* **SYN:** justification. See syn. under **excuse.** **2** explanation of the truth or justice of something; defense in speech or writing; apologia: *an apology for the Christian religion. Thomas Paine's "Common Sense" is a famous apology for American independence and democracy.* **SYN:** justification. See syn. under **excuse.** **3** a poor substitute; makeshift: *One piece of toast is a skimpy apology for a breakfast.* [< Latin *apologia* < Greek *apologiā* a speech in defense, ultimately < *apo-* fully + *légein* tell]

ap|o|lune (ap′ə lün), *n.* that point in the orbit of a body about the moon where it is farthest from the center of the moon; apocynthion; aposelenium. [< *apo-* + French *lune* moon]

Pronunciation Key: hat, āge, cãre, fär; let, ēqual, tėrm, it, īce; hot, ōpen, ôrder; oil, out; cup, pu̇t, rüle; child; long; thin; ᴛʜen; zh, measure; ə represents **a** in about, **e** in taken, **i** in pencil, **o** in lemon, **u** in circus.

ap|o|mic|tic (ap′ə mik′tik), *adj.* of or characterized by apomixis. **—ap′o|mic′ti|cal|ly,** *adv.*

ap|o|mic|ti|cal (ap′ə mik′tə kəl), *adj.* = apomictic.

ap|o|mix|is (ap′ə mik′sis), *n.* reproduction in which union of sexual cells or organs does not occur. Apogamy is an example of apomixis. [< *apo-* + Greek *mixis* a mingling]

ap|o|mor|phi|a (ap′ə môr′fē ə), *n.* = apomorphine.

ap|o|mor|phin (ap′ə môr′fin), *n.* = apomorphine.

ap|o|mor|phine (ap′ə môr′fēn, -fin), *n.* an artificial alkaloid prepared from morphine, used as an emetic. *Formula:* $C_{17}H_{17}NO_2$

ap|o|neu|ro|sis (ap′ə nu̇ rō′sis, -nyu̇-), *n., pl.* **-ses** (-sēz). a whitish, shining, fibrous membrane, an expanded tendon, serving as a fascia for sheathing, or as the end or attachment of, certain muscles. [< Greek *aponeúrōsis* < *aponeuroûsthai* change into a tendon < *apo-* + *neûron* sinew]

ap|o|neu|rot|ic (ap′ə nu̇ rot′ik, -nyu̇-), *adj.* of or having to do with aponeuroses.

ap|o|pemp|tic (ap′ə pemp′tik), *adj., n. Rare.* —*adj.* having to do with farewell; valedictory. —*n.* a farewell hymn.
[< Greek *apopemptikós* < *apópempsis* a sending off]

ap|o|pet|al|ous (ap′ə pet′ə ləs), *adj.* = polypetalous.

a|poph|a|sis (ə pof′ə sis), *n.* a statement that one will not speak of something which one really mentions or hints at. *Example:* "I will not mention his kindness, his charities." [< Late Latin *apophasis* < Greek *apóphasis* < *apophánai* deny < *apo-* off + *phánai* say]

a|poph|o|ny (ə pof′ə nē), *n., pl.* **-nies.** = ablaut. [< *apo-* + Greek *phōnē* sound]

ap|o|phthegm (ap′ə them), *n.* = apothegm.

ap|o|phtheg|mat|ic (ap′ə theg mat′ik), *adj.* = apothegmatic.

ap|o|phtheg|mat|i|cal (ap′ə theg mat′ə kəl), *adj.* = apothegmatical.

a|poph|y|ge (ə pof′ə jē), *n. Rare.* **1** the slight concave spread at the bottom of the shaft of a column, forming a transition to the horizontal lines of the base. **2** a similar but less perceptible spread at the top of the shaft. [< Latin *apophygis* < Greek *apophygḗ* an escape < *apo-* away + *pheúgein* flee]

a|poph|yl|lite (ə pof′ə līt, ap′ə fil′īt), *n.* a mineral consisting of a hydrous silicate of potassium and calcium, sometimes with a trace of fluorine, occurring in crystals or in laminated masses, with a pearly luster. [< French *apophyllite* < Greek *apo-* away + *phýllon* leaf + French *-ite* -ite[1]]

ap|o|phys|e|al (ap′ə fiz′ē əl, -fə zē′-), *adj.* of or having to do with an apophysis.

ap|o|phys|i|al (ap′ə fiz′ē əl), *adj.* = apophyseal.

a|poph|y|sis (ə pof′ə sis), *n., pl.* **-ses** (-sēz). **1** a natural outgrowth or a projection or swelling, especially any process of a vertebra. **2** a swelling at the base of the capsule in certain mosses. [< Greek *apóphysis* < *apo-* off + *phýein* grow]

ap|o|plec|tic (ap′ə plek′tik), *adj., n.* —*adj.* **1** of or causing apoplexy. **2** suffering from apoplexy. **3** showing symptoms of a tendency to apoplexy: (*Figurative.*) *An apoplectic rage turned his speech into jibberish.*
—*n.* a person who has apoplexy; person likely to have apoplexy. **—ap′o|plec′ti|cal|ly,** *adv.*

ap|o|plec|ti|cal (ap′ə plek′tə kəl), *adj.* = apoplectic.

ap|o|plec|ti|form (ap′ə plek′tə fôrm), *adj.* that resembles apoplexy.

apoplectiform septicemia, a fatal disease of poultry, with symptoms like those in apoplexy. It is caused by streptococci that invade the bloodstream.

ap|o|plex|y (ap′ə plek′sē), *n.* a sudden loss or lessening of the power to feel or think or move; stroke. Apoplexy is caused by injury to the brain when a blood vessel breaks or the blood supply becomes obstructed. [< Late Latin *apoplēxia* < Greek *apoplēxíā* < *apo-* off, from + *plēssein* to strike]

ap|o|pyle (ap′ə pīl), *n.* an opening in the radial canal of a sponge for water to pass through. [< *apo-* + Greek *pýlē* gate]

a|port (ə pôrt′, -pōrt′), *adv.* to or toward the port side; to the left of a ship.

ap|o|se|le|ni|um (ap′ə si lē′nē əm), *n.* = apolune. [< *apo-* + New Latin *selenium* < Greek *selḗnē* moon]

ap|o|se|mat|ic (ap′ə sə mat′ik), *adj. Biology.* that serves to warn or alarm enemies: *the aposematic markings of the skunk.*

ap|o|seme (ap′ə sēm), *n.* an aposematic coloring or marking.

ap|o|sep|al|ous (ap′ə sep′ə ləs), *adj.* = polysepalous. [< *apo-* + *sepal* + *-ous*]

ap|o|si|o|pe|sis (ap′ə sī′ə pē′sis), *n.* a sudden halt in the midst of a sentence, as if the speaker were unable or unwilling to proceed. *Example:* "His courage—but surely that speaks for itself." [< Latin *aposiōpēsis* < Greek *aposiṓpēsis* < *apo-* off + *siōpê* silence]

ap|o|si|o|pet|ic (ap′ə sī′ə pet′ik), *adj. Rare.* of or like aposiopesis.

a|pos|ta|size (ə pos′tə sīz), *v.i.,* **-sized, -siz|ing.** = apostatize.

a|pos|ta|sy (ə pos′tə sē), *n., pl.* **-sies.** a complete forsaking of one's religion, faith, political party, or principles: (*Figurative.*) *In 1910 began a series of famed apostasies of disciples who refused to accept Freud's theories unconditionally* (Time). SYN: desertion, defection, lapse. [< Late Latin *apostasia* < Greek *apostasíā* defection < *apo-* away from + *stênai* stand]

a|pos|tate (ə pos′tāt, -tit), *n., adj.* —*n.* a person who completely forsakes his religion, faith, political party, or principles. SYN: renegade, traitor. —*adj.* unfaithful to religion, faith, political party, or principles.

ap|o|stat|ic (ap′ə stat′ik), *adj.* = apostate.

ap|o|stat|i|cal (ap′ə stat′ə kəl), *adj.* = apostate.

a|pos|ta|tize (ə pos′tə tīz), *v.i.,* **-tized, -tiz|ing.** to forsake completely one's religion, faith, political party, or principles.

a pos|te|ri|o|ri (ā pos tir′ē ôr′ī, -ōr′-; -ôr′ē, -ōr′-), **1** from effect to cause; from particular cases to a general rule. **2** based on actual observation or experience. [< Medieval Latin *a posteriori* from the later]

a|pos|til or **a|pos|tille** (ə pos′təl), *n.* a marginal note, comment, or annotation. [< Old French *apostiller* write marginal notes < *a* to + *postille* marginal note]

a|pos|tle or **A|pos|tle** (ə pos′əl), *n.* **1** one of the twelve disciples chosen by Christ to go forth and preach the gospel to all the world. **2** any early Christian leader or missionary: *Saint Paul was frequently called the "Apostle to the Gentiles."* **3** the first Christian missionary to any country or region. **4** *Figurative.* the leader of any reform movement or new belief who shows great vigor in seeking to make it popular or to win converts: *Jean Monnet, ... the principal apostle of a federal Europe, refused to concede defeat* (Newsweek). **5** one of the council of twelve officials of the Mormon Church who help administer the affairs of the church.
the Apostles, Peter (Simon Peter), Andrew, James the Greater (or the Elder), John, Philip, Bartholomew, Thomas (Didymus), Matthew (or Levi), James the Less (or the Younger), Jude (or Judas or Lebbaeus or Thaddaeus), Simon, and Judas Iscariot (later replaced by Matthias): *The glorious company of the Apostles praises Thee* (John Cleveland).
[< Old French *apostle,* learned borrowing from Latin *apostolus* < Greek *apóstolos* messenger < *apo-* off + *stéllein* send]

apostle bird, a short-winged and short-tailed bird, especially numerous in Australia, noted for its chattering noises.

apostle plant, a South American plant of the iris family with showy white and blue flowers.

Apostles' Creed, a statement of belief that contains the fundamental doctrines of Christianity, beginning "I believe in God, the Father Almighty. ..." In its present form (with some variations between the texts of the Roman Catholic and certain Protestant churches) it dates back to the 700's A.D., and is supposed to have been composed by the Apostles.

a|pos|tle|ship (ə pos′əl ship), *n.* = apostolate.

apostle spoon, a silver spoon on the handle of which is the figure of an Apostle, formerly one of a set given to an infant at baptism.

a|pos|to|late (ə pos′tə lit, -lāt), *n.* the rank or office of an apostle.

ap|os|tol|ic or **Ap|os|tol|ic** (ap′ə stol′ik), *adj.* **1** of the Apostles; having to do with an apostle or the Apostles. **2** coming from or originating with the Apostles. **3** of or having to do with the Pope; papal. [< Latin *apostolicus* < Greek *apostolikós* < *apóstolos;* see etym. under **apostle**] **—ap′os|tol′i|cal|ly,** *adv.*

ap|os|tol|i|cal (ap′ə stol′ə kəl), *adj.* = apostolic.

Apostolic Fathers, 1 a group of early Christian writers who lived almost immediately after the Apostles. **2** the works attributed to them, probably written between 95 and 150 A.D.

ap|os|tol|i|cism (ap′ə stol′ə siz əm), *n. Rare.* profession of, or claim to, apostolicity.

a|pos|to|lic|i|ty (ə pos′tə lis′ə tē), *n.* the quality of being apostolic.

apostolic orders, = holy orders (def. 3).

Apostolic See, the bishopric of the Pope at Rome, said to have been established by Peter; the Holy See.

apostolic succession, the unbroken sequence through which religious authority has been handed down from the Apostles to their present-day successors, the regularly ordained bishops and priests. Certain churches (such as the Roman Catholic, Eastern Orthodox, and some churches of the Anglican Communion) maintain that the succession is historical fact and, since it preserves the transmission of divine authority, is the necessary basis for valid performance of certain rites.

***a|pos|tro|phe**[1] (ə pos′trə fē), *n.* a sign of punctuation used:
a to show the omission of one or more letters in the spelling of contractions, as in *can't* for *cannot* and *o'er* for *over.*
b to show the possessive forms of nouns or indefinite pronouns, as in *John's book, the lions' den,* and *everybody's business.*
c to write the plurals of figures, letters of the alphabet, and words discussed as words: *There are two o's in apology and four 9's in 959,990.*
d to show that certain sounds represented in the usual spelling have not been spoken, as in *'lectric* for *electric.*
[< French *apostrophe,* learned borrowing from Late Latin *apostrophus* < Greek *apóstrophos* (*prosōidíā*) omission (mark) < *apo-* away + *stréphein* turn]

***apostrophe**[1]

’

a.
Aren't you going?
b.
Jane's book

a|pos|tro|phe[2] (ə pos′trə fē), *n.* a speech to someone absent or dead as if he were present; words addressed to a lifeless thing or an idea as if it could hear or reply. [< Late Latin *apostrophē* < Greek *apostrophḗ* < *apo-* away from + *stréphein* turn]

ap|os|troph|ic[1] (ap′ə strof′ik), *adj.* of or having to do with the apostrophe (sign of punctuation). [< *apostrophea*[1] + *-ic*]

ap|os|troph|ic[2] (ap′ə strof′ik), *adj.* of or having to do with rhetorical apostrophe; given to the use of rhetorical apostrophe. [< *apostrophe*[2] + *-ic*]

a|pos|tro|phise (ə pos′trə fīz), *v.t., v.i.,* **-phised, -phis|ing.** *British.* apostrophize.

a|pos|tro|phize[1] (ə pos′trə fīz), *v.t., v.i.,* **-phized, -phiz|ing. 1** to mark with an apostrophe or apostrophes. **2** to write or print using an apostrophe or apostrophes. [< *apostrophe*[1] + *-ize*]

a|pos|tro|phize[2] (ə pos′trə fīz), *v.,* **-phized, -phiz|ing.** —*v.i.* to stop, especially in a speech or poem, and address some absent person as if he were present or a thing or idea as if it could appreciate what is said.
—*v.t.* to address an apostrophe to: *Shakespeare apostrophizes judgment in these words: "Oh, judgment! thou art fled to brutish beasts."*
[< *apostrophe*[2] + *-ize*]

apothecaries' measure, a system of fluid measure used in mixing and dispensing liquid drugs. In the United States:

60 minims	= 1 fluid dram	= 3.6966 milliliters
8 fluid drams	= 1 fluid ounce	= 0.0295 liter
16 fluid ounces	= 1 pint	= 0.4732 liter
8 pints	= 1 U.S. gallon or 231 cubic inches or 3.7853 liters	

In Great Britain the pint (being the eighth part of the imperial gallon of 277.420 cubic inches) is divided into 20 fluid ounces, with subdivisions corresponding to use in the United States.

apothecaries' weight, a system of dry weights in which a pound containing 12 ounces is used. Apothecaries' weight is used in mixing drugs and filling prescriptions:

20 grains	= 1 scruple	= 1.296 grams
3 scruples	= 1 dram	= 3.888 grams
8 drams	= 1 ounce	= 31.1035 grams
12 ounces	= 1 pound	= 373.24 grams

a|poth|e|car|y (ə poth′ə ker′ē), *n., pl.* **-car|ies. 1** a person who prepares and sells drugs and medicines; druggist; pharmacist. **2** a person in England and Ireland who formerly prescribed drugs and medicines and sold them as well. [< Late Latin *apothēcārius* shopkeeper < Latin *apotheca* storehouse < Greek *apothḗkē,* related to *apotithénai* to put away < *apo-* away + *tithénai* put]

ap|o|the|cial (ap′ə thē′shəl), *adj.* of or having to do with an apothecium.

ap|o|the|ci|um (ap′ə thē′shē əm, -sē əm), *n., pl.* **-ci|a** (-shē ə, -sē-). the fruiting body of various lichens and fungi, generally an open, more or less cup- or saucer-shaped receptacle. The asci or spore sacs are attached to the inner surface. [< New Latin *apothecium* < Late Greek *apothḗkion* larder (diminutive) < *apothḗkē;* see etym. under **apothecary**]

ap|o|thegm (ap′ə them), *n.* a short, forceful saying; maxim. *Example:* "Beauty is only skin deep." Also, **apophthegm.** [< Greek *apóphthegma* < *apo-* forth + *phthéngesthai* to utter]

ap|o|theg|mat|ic (ap′ə theg mat′ik), *adj.* of or having to do with an apothegm; inclined to use

apothegms. SYN: sententious, pithy. Also, **apo-phthegmatic**. —**ap′o|theg|mat′i|cal|ly**, *adv.*
ap|o|theg|mat|i|cal (ap′ə theg mat′ə kəl), *adj.* = apothegmatic. Also, **apophthegmatical**.
ap|o|theg|ma|tist (ap′ə theg′mə tist), *n.* a maker of apothegms.
ap|o|them (ap′ə them), *n. Rare.* the perpendicular from the center to any one of the sides of a regular polygon; the radius of the circumscribed circle of a regular polygon. [< *apo-* + Greek *théma* thing placed]
a|poth|e|o|sis (ə poth′ē ō′sis, ap′ə thē′ə-), *n., pl.* **-ses** (-sēz). **1a** a glorified ideal: *She is the very apotheosis of a lady.* **b** glorification; exaltation: *the apotheosis of a book.* **2** the raising of a human being to the rank of a god; deification: *The apotheosis of the emperor became a Roman custom.* [< Latin *apotheōsis* < Greek *apothéōsis*, ultimately < *apo-* from + *theós* god]
a|poth|e|o|size (ə poth′ē ə sīz, ap′ə thē′-), *v.t.*, **-sized, -siz|ing.** **1** to glorify; exalt. **2** to raise to the rank of a god; deify.
ap|o|tro|pa|ic (ap′ə trō pā′ik), *adj.* able or believed to be able to ward off evil: *apotropaic charms.* [< Greek *apotrópaios* (< *apotrépein* avert) + English *-ic*]
ap|o|zy|mase (ap′ə zī′mās), *n.* the part of zymase that is composed of protein.
app., an abbreviation for the following:
1 apparent.
2 appendix.
3 appointed.
4 apprentice.
ap|pal (ə pôl′), *v.t., v.i.*, **-palled, -pal|ling.** = appall.
Ap|pa|la|chian (ap′ə lā′chən, -lach′ən), *adj.* **1** of or having to do with the Appalachian Mountains, its regions, or its inhabitants. **2** of or designating geological phenomena associated with the Appalachian Mountains at the end of the Permian period.
Appalachian tea, **1** any one of various shrubs of the eastern United States of the same family as the holly, whose leaves are used locally for brewing a kind of tea. **2** the withe rod, whose leaves are also used for tea. **3** the leaves of either of these.
ap|pall (ə pôl′), *v.*, **-palled, -pall|ing.** —***v.t.*** to fill with horror or fear; dismay; terrify: *The thought of another war appalled us. She was appalled when she saw the river had risen to the doorstep.*
—***v.i.*** *Obsolete.* **1** to become pale. **2a** to fail. **b** to lose flavor; pall. [< Old French *apallir* become, or make, pale < *a-* to + *pale* pale < Latin *pallidus.* See related etym. at **pale**[1].]
ap|pall|ing (ə pô′ling), *adj.* causing horror; dismaying; terrifying; horrifying: *When the Ethiopian comes down into the desert, his mules collapse in the appalling heat* (New Yorker). —**ap|pall′-ing|ly**, *adv.*
Ap|pa|loo|sa (ap′ə lü′sə), *n.* any horse of a small, sturdy breed with dark brown or black spots on a roan background, developed by the Nez Percé Indians of Idaho and Washington. [< *Palouse* River region, where these horses were bred]
ap|pa|nage (ap′ə nij), *n.* **1** land, property, money, benefices, or the like, set aside to support the younger children or vassals of kings, princes, or other royalty. **2** a person's assigned portion; rightful property. **3** something that accompanies; adjunct: *The millionaire had three houses, a yacht, and all the other appanages of wealth.* **4** a territory controlled by another country. Also, **apanage**. [< Old French *apanage* < *apaner* provide with bread, ultimately < Latin *ad-* to + *pānis* bread]
appar., **1** apparent. **2** apparently.
ap|pa|rat (ä′pä rät′), *n.* a political or party organization; administrative machine. [< Russian *apparat* (literally) apparatus < German]
ap|pa|rat|chik (ä′pä rät′chik), *n., pl.* **-chi|ki** (-chi-kē). a political or party official or bureaucrat, especially in a Communist country; a member of an apparat: *a union apparatchik.* [< Russian *apparat* + *-chik* agentive suffix]
ap|pa|ra|tus (ap′ə rā′təs, -rat′əs), *n., pl.* **-tus** or **-tus|es.** **1** anything necessary to carry out a purpose or for a particular use. Tools, special instruments, and machines are apparatus; so are grocer's scales and the equipment in a gymnasium. Test tubes, beakers, and a Bunsen burner are part of the apparatus used in chemistry. SYN: equipment, gear. **2** a mechanism or piece of machinery: *An automobile is a complicated apparatus.* **3** the organs of the body which together perform a particular function. The stomach and intestines are part of our digestive apparatus. **4** a political or party organization; an administrative machine. **5** = apparatus criticus (def. 1). [< Latin *apparātus, -ūs* < *apparāre* prepare < *ad-* + *parāre* make ready]
ap|pa|ra|tus cri|ti|cus (ap′ə rā′təs krit′i kəs), *Latin.* **1** aids in the critical study of a text, such as notes, glosses, bibliographies, and variant readings. **2** a collection of reference books, texts, or other material, to be used in literary work.
ap|par|el (ə par′əl), *n., v.*, **-eled, -el|ing** or (*especially British*) **-elled, -el|ling.** —***n.*** **1** clothing; dress: *Does this store sell women's apparel?* SYN: raiment, garb. See syn. under **dress**. **2** *Figurative.* anything viewed as similar to clothing; that which covers or envelops: *a range of hills in the green apparel of June foliage.* SYN: raiment, garb. See syn. under **dress**.
—***v.t.*** to clothe; dress up; array: *The horseback riders, gaily appareled, formed part of the circus parade.*
[< Old French *apareil* < *apareiller* prepare, fit out, probably ultimately < Latin *apparāre* < *ad-* to + *parāre* make ready]
ap|par|en|cy (ə par′ən sē), *n. Archaic.* **1** the quality of being apparent. **2** the condition or status of being heir apparent.
ap|par|ent (ə par′ənt), *adj.* **1** plain to see; so plain that one cannot help seeing it: *The stain is apparent from across the room.* SYN: plain, perceptible. See syn. under **obvious**. **2** easily understood; evident: *It is apparent that the days become shorter in October and November. It is apparent that you dislike your job.* **3** according to appearances; that appears to be; seeming: *The apparent size of an airplane in the sky is smaller than the airplane really is.* [< Old French *aparant*, present participle of *apareir* < Latin *appārēre;* see etym. under **appear**] —**ap|par′ent|ness**, *n.*
apparent diameter, the diameter of a heavenly body as it appears to the observer; angle subtended by the diameter of a heavenly body at the eye of the viewer; angular diameter.
ap|pa|rente|ment (á pá ränt mäɴ′), *n. French.* a coalition of political parties within a constituency during an election.
ap|par|ent|ly (ə par′ənt lē), *adv.* **1** as far as one can judge by appearances; seemingly: *Apparently he is an honest man.* SYN: ostensibly. **2** clearly; plainly; obviously. SYN: evidently.
apparent magnitude, the brightness of a star as it appears to the unaided eye.
apparent noon, the moment when the sun's center crosses the meridian.
*** apparent position**, the position in which an object appears to be when seen through glass, water, or any other diffracting medium, as distinguished from its true position.

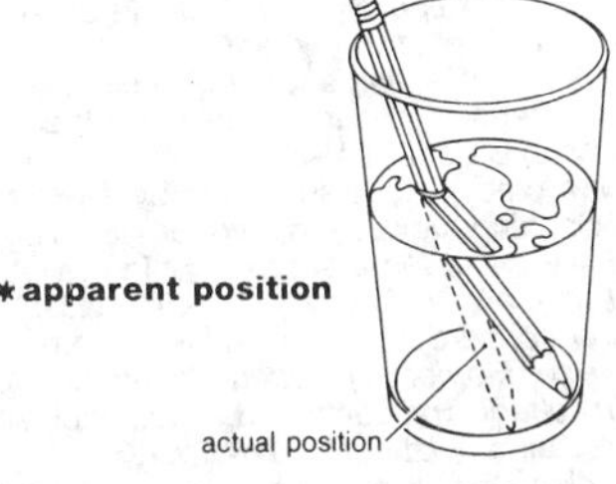

*** apparent position**

apparent solar time, the measure of the day by the apparent positions of the sun, usually determined by the apparent noon.
ap|pa|ri|tion (ap′ə rish′ən), *n.* **1** a supernatural sight or thing; a ghost or phantom: *The apparition, clothed in white, glided through the wall.* SYN: See syn. under **ghost**. **2** the appearing of something strange, remarkable, or unexpected: *The Bible tells us that the shepherds saw the apparition of a bright star where Jesus was born.* [< Late Latin *appāritiō, -ōnis* < Latin, service, servants < *appārēre* appear < *ad-* + *pārēre* come in sight]
ap|pa|ri|tion|al (ap′ə rish′ə nəl), *adj.* of or like a phantom; spectral; immaterial.
ap|par|i|tor (ə par′ə tər), *n.* **1** a messenger or minor officer of an ecclesiastical or, formerly, a civil court. **2** an official in ancient Rome who attended a magistrate to execute his orders. [< Latin *appāritor* < *appārēre;* see etym. under **appear**]
ap|pas|sio|na|ta (äp päs′syō nä′tä), *adj.* the feminine form of **appassionato**.
ap|pas|sio|na|to (äp päs′syō nä′tō), *adj. Music.* impassioned. [< Italian *appassionato*]
ap|peal (ə pēl′), *v., n.* —***v.i.*** **1** to ask earnestly; make an earnest request (to or for); ask for help or sympathy: *The children appealed to their mother to know what to do on a rainy day. I appeal to you to support the Girl Scouts' drive for funds.* **2** to call on some person to decide some matter in one's favor: *When Mother said "No," my little sister would appeal to Father.* **3** *Law.* **a** to ask that a case be taken to a higher court or judge to be heard again. **b** to remove a case formally from an inferior to a higher court for review or retrial. **4** to be attractive, interesting, or enjoyable: *Blue and red appeal to me, but I don't like gray or yellow.*
—***v.t.*** *Law.* **1** to apply for a retrial of (a case) before a higher court. **2** to remove (a case) to a higher court.
—***n.*** **1** an earnest request; call for help or sympathy: *She made one last appeal to her father for permission to go to the party.* SYN: plea, entreaty, petition, solicitation. **2** *Law.* **a** a request to have a case heard again before a higher court or judge: *His execution ... was stayed last week when he filed an appeal* (Newsweek). **b** the right to have a case heard again. **c** the case thus heard. **3** a call on some person to decide a matter in one's favor: *His appeal for another chance was granted.* **4** attraction or interest: *Television has a great appeal for most young people.*
appeal to the country. See under **country**.
[< Old French *apeler* < Latin *appellāre* accost, related to *appellere* < *ad-* up to + *pellere* drive]
—**ap|peal′a|ble**, *adj.* —**ap|peal′er**, *n.*
ap|peal|ing (ə pē′ling), *adj.* **1** that appeals; attractive or interesting. **2** imploring; suppliant. —**ap-peal′ing|ly**, *adv.* —**ap|peal′ing|ness**, *n.*
ap|pear (ə pir′), *v.i.* **1** to be seen; come in sight; become visible: *One by one the stars appear. A ship suddenly appeared on the horizon.* **2** to seem; look: *The apple appeared sound on the outside, but it was rotten inside.* SYN: See syn. under **seem**. **3** to show or present oneself in public; come before the public, especially as a performer: *to appear in a concert, appear as an actor. The singer will appear on the television program today.* **4** to be published: *His latest book appeared a year ago.* **5** to become known to the mind; be plain: *Their error appeared the next day. Our characters appear in our acts.* **6** to present oneself formally: *A person accused of crime must appear before the court.* [< Old French *apareir* < Latin *appārēre* < *ad-* + *pārēre* come in sight] —**ap|pear′er**, *n.*
ap|pear|ance (ə pir′əns), *n.* **1** the act of coming in sight: *John's appearance in the doorway was welcomed with shouts.* **2** the act of coming before the public, especially as a performer: *The singer made her first appearance in a concert in Boston.* **3** outward look; aspect: *The appearance of the old gray house made us think that it was empty.* **4** outward show or seeming; pretense: *The old lady laughs a lot to keep up appearances, so the neighbors won't think she is sick.* SYN: semblance, guise. **5** a thing that appears in sight; object seen. **6** the coming into court of a party to a lawsuit or charge. **7** an apparition. **8** *Philosophy.* that which is perceived subjectively, through the senses, as opposed to that which exists as objective reality.
put in an appearance, to be present and noticed, at least briefly, at a meeting, party, or the like: *A busy congressman may put in an appearance at several different committee meetings in the course of a few hours.*
—***Syn.*** **3 Appearance, aspect** mean the look or looks of a person or thing. **Appearance** is the general word applying to what one sees when he looks at someone or something: *His pleasing appearance wins him many friends.* **Aspect** applies to the appearance at certain times or under certain conditions: *I love the bay in all its aspects, even its stormy, frightening aspect in winter.*
ap|pease (ə pēz′), *v.t.*, **-peased, -peas|ing.** **1** to put an end to by satisfying (an appetite or desire); satisfy: *A good dinner will appease your hunger.* **2** to make calm or quiet; pacify: *He tried to appease the crying child by giving him candy.* **3** to give in to the demands of: *The boy appeased his father and got up from television to finish his homework.* SYN: conciliate, placate, propitiate. [< Old French *apaisier* < *a-* to + *pais* peace < Latin *pāx, pācis*] —**ap|peas′a|ble**, *adj.* —**ap|peas′ing|ly**, *adv.*
—***Syn.*** **2 Appease, pacify** mean to make calm. **Appease** means to calm or quiet a person who is excited, upset, and demanding by making concessions to him: *To appease my angry neighbor, I offered to make good the damage.* **Pacify** means to quiet people or things that are quarreling or fighting among themselves or against some condition, by making peace though not necessarily by eliminating the cause of the disturbance: *She pacified the angry crowd.*
ap|pease|ment (ə pēz′mənt), *n.* the act of appeasing or the condition of being appeased; pacification; satisfaction: *The road of appeasement is not the road to peace, but is surrender on the installment plan* (New York Times).
ap|peas|er (ə pē′zər), *n.* a person who appeases.
ap|pel (á pel′), *n. Fencing.* **1** a stamp of the foot,

Pronunciation Key: hat, āge, cãre, fär; let, ēqual, tėrm; it, īce; hot, ōpen, ôrder; **oi**l, **ou**t; cup, pu̇t, rüle; **ch**ild; lo**ng**; **th**in; **ŧh**en; **zh**, measure; **ə** represents **a** in about, **e** in taken, **i** in pencil, **o** in lemon, **u** in circus.

originally an indication of a coming attack, now often accompanying a feint. **2** a sharp stroke on the opponent's blade, often accompanied by a stamp of the foot, used to secure an opening. [< French *appel (du pied)* a call (with the foot)]

ap·pel·lant (ə pel′ənt), *n., adj.* **—*n.*** a person who appeals, especially one who appeals a decision of a lower court to a higher court.
—*adj.* **1** having to do with appeals. **2** appealing.

ap·pel·late (ə pel′it), *adj.* of or having to do with an appeal or appeals: *An appellate judge hears appeals that question the accuracy of the trial judge's decisions on points of law* (Erwin N. Griswold). [< Latin *appellātus*, past participle of *appellāre;* see etym. under **appeal**]

appellate court, a court having the power to examine again and reverse the decisions of a lower court.

ap·pel·la·tion (ap′ə lā′shən), *n.* **1** a name. **2** a title describing some quality; epithet. In "John the Baptist," the appellation of *John* is *the Baptist.* **3** the act of calling by a name; designation.

ap·pel·la·tive (ə pel′ə tiv), *n., adj.* **—*n.*** **1** a descriptive name. **2** a common noun that can be applied to any member of a class.
—*adj.* that names. **—ap·pel′la·tive·ly**, *adv.*

ap·pel·lee (ap′ə lē′), *n.* the defendant or respondent in a case carried by appeal to a higher court.

ap·pel·lor (ə pel′ôr, ap′ə lôr′), *n.* a person who carries a case by appeal to a higher court.

ap·pend (ə pend′), *v.t.* to add to a larger thing; attach as a supplement: *to append notes to a book. The amendments to the Constitution of the United States are appended to it.* **SYN:** subjoin, affix. [< Latin *appendere* < *ad-* on + *pendere* hang]

ap·pend·age (ə pen′dij), *n.* **1** a thing attached to something larger or more important; addition. **SYN:** adjunct, accessory. **2** *Biology.* any one of various external or subordinate parts. Arms, tails, fins, and legs are appendages.

ap·pend·aged (ə pen′dijd), *adj.* furnished with or having an appendage or appendages.

ap·pend·ance (ə pen′dəns), *n. Law.* the fact of being appendant.

ap·pend·ant or **ap·pend·ent** (ə pen′dənt), *adj., n.* **—*adj.*** **1** added; attached. **SYN:** pertinent, attendant, consequent. **2** *Law.* attached or belonging as an additional but subsidiary right. **—*n.*** **1** an appendage. **2** a subsidiary right or property.

ap·pen·dec·to·my (ap′ən dek′tə mē), *n., pl.* **-mies.** removal of the vermiform appendix by a surgical operation. [American English < *append*(ix) + Greek *ektomē* a cutting out]

ap·pen·di·cec·to·my (ə pen′də sek′tə mē), *n., pl.* **-mies.** = appendectomy.

ap·pen·di·ces (ə pen′də sēz), *n.* a plural of **appendix.**

ap·pen·di·ci·tis (ə pen′də sī′tis), *n.* inflammation of the appendix of the large intestine. [American English < Latin *appendix, -icis* + English *-itis*]

ap·pen·di·cle (ə pen′də kəl), *n.* a small appendage. [< Latin *appendicula* (diminutive) < *appendix, -icis;* see etym. under **appendix**]

ap·pen·dic·u·lar (ap′ən dik′yə lər), *adj.* of or like an appendix.

appendicular skeleton, the skeleton of the limbs (contrasted with *axial skeleton*).

ap·pen·dic·u·late (ap′ən dik′yə lit, -lāt), *adj.* **1** having appendicles or appendages. **2** = appendicular.

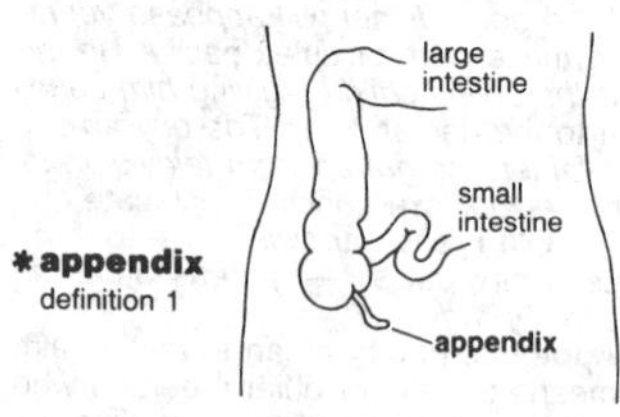

***appendix** definition 1

ap·pen·dix** (ə pen′diks), *n., pl.* **-dix·es** or **-di·ces,** *v.,* **-dixed, -dix·ing.** **—*n. **1** the small, saclike growth attached to the large intestine; vermiform appendix. **2** an addition at the end of a book or document. **SYN:** See syn. under **supplement. 3** a tube located at the bottom of the bag of a dirigible or balloon, by which it is inflated or deflated.
—*v.t.* to provide with an appendix: *The book is illustrated, indexed, and appendixed to a fare-thee-well* (New Yorker).
[< Latin *appendix* < *appendere* < *ad-* on + *pendere* hang]
►The English plural **appendixes** is rapidly overtaking the Latin **appendices.**

appendix ver·mi·for·mis (vėr′mə fôr′mis), = vermiform appendix.

ap·per·ceive (ap′ər sēv′), *v.t.,* **-ceived, -ceiv·ing. 1** to perceive clearly; observe; recognize; notice; remark. **2** *Psychology, Rare.* to comprehend by apperception. [< Old French *aperceivre* < Vulgar Latin *appercipere* < Latin *ad-* to + *percipere* perceive]

ap·per·cep·tion (ap′ər sep′shən), *n.* **1** clear perception; full understanding. **2** *Psychology, Rare.* the assimilation of a new perception by means of a mass of ideas already in the mind. [< French *aperception* < New Latin *apperceptio, -onis* (coined by Leibniz)]

ap·per·cep·tive (ap′ər sep′tiv), *adj.* of or having to do with apperception. **—ap′per·cep′tive·ly,** *adv.*

ap·per·tain (ap′ər tān′), *v.i.* to belong as a part; be connected; pertain; relate: *Forestry appertains to geography, to botany, and to agriculture.* [< Old French *apertenir* < Late Latin *appertinēre* < Latin *ad-* to + *pertinēre* pertain]

Ap·pert process (ä per′), a process of making wire glass, invented by Leon Appert of France. It consists of rolling one sheet of glass and laying meshed wire on it, then rolling another sheet of glass on the top and pressing the wire and the sheets of glass into one solid sheet.

ap·pe·stat (ap′ə stat′), *n.* an area in the hypothalamic region of the brain regarded as the center which controls or regulates the appetite. [(coined by N.H. Jolliffe, born 1901, American nutrition expert) < *appe*(tite) + *-stat*]

ap·pe·tence (ap′ə təns), *n.* **1** the state of longing for, desiring, or craving; appetite; desire. **2** instinctive inclination or tendency. **3** material or chemical attraction or affinity. [< Latin *appetentia* < *appetere* seek after < *ad-* to + *petere* seek]

ap·pe·ten·cy (ap′ə tən sē), *n., pl.* **-cies.** = appetence.

ap·pe·tis·ing (ap′ə tī′zing), *adj. British.* appetizing.

ap·pe·tite (ap′ə tīt), *n.* **1** desire or craving for food: *Michael had no appetite; so they had to coax him to eat.* **SYN:** hunger. **2** *Figurative.* **a** desire or craving: *The lively boys had a great appetite for excitement and amusement.* **SYN:** longing. **b** taste; liking: *The blind man had no appetite for art museums.* [< Old French *appetite*, learned borrowing from Latin *appetītus, -ūs* < *appetere* long for < *ad-* + *petere* seek]

ap·pe·ti·tive (ap′ə tī′tiv), *adj.* of or having to do with appetite.

ap·pe·tiz·er (ap′ə tī′zər), *n.* something that arouses the appetite or gives relish to food. Pickles and olives are appetizers.

ap·pe·tiz·ing (ap′ə tī′zing), *adj.* arousing or exciting the appetite: *Appetizing food always smells delicious.* **—ap′pe·tiz′ing·ly,** *adv.*

Ap·pi·an Way (ap′ē ən), a famous ancient Roman road extending about 366 miles southeast from Rome to Brundisium.

ap·plaud (ə plôd′), *v.i.* to show approval, especially by clapping hands, shouting, or stamping the feet. **—*v.t.*** **1** to show approval of in this way: *The audience applauds anything that pleases it in a play or concert.* **2** to be pleased with; approve; praise: *Mother applauded his decision to remain in school.* **SYN:** commend, laud, extol, acclaim. [< Latin *applaudere* < *ad-* upon + *plaudere* clap] **—ap·plaud′a·ble,** *adj.* **—ap·plaud′er,** *n.* **—ap·plaud′ing·ly,** *adv.*

ap·plause (ə plôz′), *n.* **1** approval shown, especially by clapping the hands, shouting, or stamping the feet: *Applause for the performance rang out from the audience.* **2** approval; praise. **SYN:** acclamation, acclaim, approbation, plaudit, accolade. [< Latin *applausus*, past participle of *applaudere;* see etym. under **applaud**]

ap·plau·sive (ə plô′siv), *adj.* characterized by applause. **—ap·plau′sive·ly,** *adv.*

ap·ple (ap′əl), *n.* **1** the firm, fleshy, somewhat round fruit of a tree widely grown in temperate regions. Apples usually have red, yellow, or green skin, and are eaten either raw or cooked. **2** the tree itself, belonging to the rose family, probably a native of Europe and the temperate regions of western Asia. Its blossom is the state flower of Michigan and Arkansas. **3** the fruit of any of various related trees, such as the crab apple. **4** any such tree. **5** any of various other fruits or fruitlike products, such as the oak apple and love apple or tomato. **6** *U.S. Slang.* a baseball. **7** *U.S. Slang.* an American Indian who thinks and acts like a white man (used in an unfriendly way): *Young Indian activists have been heard . . . to label an Indian bureaucrat, who may have neglected his origins, "an apple"—red on the outside, white on the inside* (New York Times). **8** *U.S. Slang.* a citizens band radio operator who broadcasts illegally, especially by using output of greater power than the law permits. [Old English *æppel*] **—ap′ple·like′,** *adj.*

apple butter, a smooth, dark-brown, somewhat heavy jam made by stewing apples with sugar, spices, and sometimes cider.

ap·ple·cart (ap′əl kärt′), *n.* a cart that carries or is intended to carry apples.
upset the applecart, *Informal.* to disrupt or bring to naught a plan or program of action: *"The recent steel strike did not upset the applecart," he declared* (Wall Street Journal).

ap·ple-cheeked (ap′əl chēkt′), *adj.* having red, blushing, or glowing cheeks.

apple family, a former grouping of plants now classified with the rose family. See also **malaceous.**

apple fly, an adult apple maggot.

apple green, a clear light-green color.

ap·ple-green (ap′əl grēn′), *adj.* of a clear light-green color.

apple gum, a gum tree in Australia, especially one resembling the apple tree and valued for its hard, brown timber.

ap·ple·jack (ap′əl jak′), *n. U.S.* a brandy distilled from hard cider.

ap·ple·knock·er (ap′əl nok′ər), *n. U.S. Slang.* a native of the country, especially a farmer or farm hand (always derogatory in use).

apple leafhopper, a small, slender insect that spreads fire blight in apple orchards and feeds on potatoes and other crops.

apple maggot, the larva of certain insects of the same family as the fruit fly, which feeds on the flesh of apples and carries the organisms of bacterial rot; railroad worm.

apple moss, any moss of a genus with spore capsules shaped like apples.

apple of discord, **1** any cause of jealousy and trouble. **2** *Greek Legend.* a golden apple inscribed "For the fairest" thrown by the goddess of discord into a gathering of the gods. Aphrodite, Athena, and Hera forthwith claimed it, and in return for Aphrodite's promise to him that he might have Helen, the fairest of women, Paris awarded it to Aphrodite. This dispute and the decision of Paris led to the Trojan War.

apple of Peru, coarse annual plant of the nightshade family, bearing solitary, pale-blue flowers.

apple of Sodom, **1** something that appears to be very desirable or attractive but turns out to be wholly disappointing. **2** a fruit described by ancient writers as fair to the eye but turning to smoke and ashes when plucked. **3** a spiny plant found near Jericho that bears small yellow fruits like small apples. It is related to the tomato.

apple of the eye, **1** a person or thing that is valued or cherished. **2** the pupil of the eye.

apple pandowdy, *U.S.* deep-dish apple pie or pudding; pandowdy.

ap·ple-pie (ap′əl pī′), *adj.* having or showing traditional American values and traits: [He] *trades frankly on the appeal of his Horatio Alger career and apple-pie patriotism* (Time). [< the notion that apple pie is a typical old-fashioned American food]

apple-pie order *U.S. Informal.* perfect order or condition.

ap·ple-pol·ish (ap′əl pol′ish), *Informal.* **—*v.t.*** to seek the approval of by ingratiating actions: *To her credit she doesn't apple-polish her ex-boss . . .* (Saturday Review). **—*v.i.*** to curry favor; act like a toady. **—ap′ple-pol′ish·er,** *n.*

ap·ple·sauce (ap′əl sôs′), *n.* **1** apples cut in pieces and cooked with sugar, spices, and water until soft. **2** *Slang.* nonsense.

apple scab, a fungous disease of apple trees characterized by dark blotches on the leaves and lesions on the fruit.

Ap·ple·ton layer (ap′əl tən), = F layer. [< Edward V. *Appleton*, 1892-1965, a British physicist]

ap·ple-tree borer (ap′əl trē′), any one of a large number of beetles that live in the wood or just under the bark of apple trees. The legless grubs hatch from eggs laid on the bark and bore into the wood, often killing the tree.

ap·ple·wood (ap′əl wu̇d′), *n.* the wood of the apple tree, used for firewood and in cabinetmaking.

ap·pli·ance (ə plī′əns), *n.* **1** a thing like a tool or small machine used in doing something, particularly for household use. A can opener is an appliance for opening tin cans. Vacuum cleaners, washing machines, refrigerators, and electric coffeepots are household appliances. **SYN:** tool, instrument, apparatus. **2** a putting into use; applying; application: *The appliance of electricity to household tasks makes housework easier.*

appliance garage, *U.S.* a kitchen cabinet designed to hold appliances such as food processors and toasters.

ap·pli·ca·bil·i·ty (ap′lə kə bil′ə tē), *n.* the quality of being applicable.

ap·pli·ca·ble (ap′lə kə bəl, ə plik′ə-), *adj.* **1** that can be put to practical use; appropriate; suitable: *The rule "Look before you leap" is almost always applicable.* **SYN:** relevant. **2** that can be put on or administered: *This salve is too dry to be easily applicable.* **—ap′pli·ca·ble·ness,** *n.* **—ap′pli·ca·bly,** *adv.*

ap·pli·cant (ap′lə kənt), *n.* a person who applies (for a job, money, position, help, entrance, or office): *Are you an applicant for this job? Many high-school graduates are applicants to college.* **SYN:** petitioner, candidate, aspirant. [< Latin *ap-*

plicāns, -antis, present participle of *applicāre;* see etym. under **apply**]

ap|pli|ca|tion (ap′lə kā′shən), *n.* **1** a spoken or written request for a job, money, position, help, entrance, or office: *I have put in my application to become a boy scout. All applications for tickets must be received within three days. He filled out an application for the position of clerk.* **2a** the act of using; putting to use; use: *the application of atomic energy to manufacturing. The application of what you know will help you solve new problems.* **SYN**: employment, utilization. **b** the act of applying; putting on: *The painter's careless application of paint spattered the floor. Mother suggested the application of a soothing ointment to my chapped skin.* **3** thing applied. Cold cream, ointments, and mustard plasters are applications. **4** continued effort; close attention: *By application to his work he got a better job.* **SYN**: See syn. under **effort.** [< Latin *applicātiō, -ōnis* a joining to < *applicāre;* see etym. under **apply**]

applications satellite, any earth satellite designed for some practical use on earth, such as a weather satellite, a communications satellite, or a navigational satellite: *France had refused to support an expensive European programme for the development of applications satellites to be used for navigation, meteorology, and air traffic control* (John Newell).

ap|pli|ca|tive (ap′lə kā′tiv), *adj. Rare.* **1** applied. **2** applicatory.

ap|pli|ca|tor (ap′lə kā′tər), *n.* an instrument or device for applying medicine, a cosmetic, or paint.

ap|pli|ca|to|ry (ap′lə kə tôr′ē, -tōr′-), *adj.* **1** *Rare.* that can be put into use; practical. **2** *Archaic.* applicable.

ap|plied (ə plīd′), *adj.* put to practical use; used to solve actual problems: *Engineers use applied mathematics to solve the practical problems in building a bridge. Applied research is the conversion of the discoveries of basic research into products, techniques, processes, and services* (Bulletin of Atomic Scientists).

applied science, science that uses facts, laws, and theories to solve practical problems: *Applied science is used in building a bridge, designing a radio, or testing intelligence.*

ap|pli|er (ə plī′ər), *n.* a person or thing that applies.

ap|pli|qué (ap′lə kā′), *n., v.,* **-quéd, qué|ing,** *adj.* —*n.* **1** ornaments made of one material sewed or otherwise fastened on another. **2** work trimmed with such ornaments.
—*v.t.* **1** to trim or ornament with appliqué. **2** to fasten on as appliqué.
—*adj.* **1** trimmed in this way: *an appliqué quilt.* **2** applied in this way to other material: *appliqué trim.*
[< French *appliqué,* past participle of *appliquer,* in Old French *apliquier,* learned borrowing from Latin *applicāre;* see etym. under **apply**]

ap|ply (ə plī′), *v.,* **-plied, -ply|ing.** —*v.t.* **1** to put or lay on or in contact with: *He applied two coats of paint to the table. Mother applied a wet cloth to the bump on my head.* **2** to put to practical use; put into effect; use: *He knows the rule but does not know how to apply it.* **3** to use for a special purpose: *The surplus in our club treasury was applied to paying for the party.* **SYN**: appropriate. **4** to use (a word or words) to refer (to a person or thing): *to apply a nickname. Don't apply that adjective to me.* **5** to set to work and stick to it; turn or keep (oneself or one's attention) on a task or study: *He applied himself to learning French.*
—*v.i.* **1** to be useful or suitable; fit: *When does this rule apply?* **2** to make a request; ask: *He is applying for a job as clerk. They applied to him for help.* **3** to have a bearing on; refer: *This applies to us as much as to them.*
[< Old French *aplier* < Latin *applicāre* < *ad-* on + *plicāre* fold, lay]

***ap|pog|gia|tu|ra** (ə poj′ə tůr′ə, -tyůr′-), *n. Music.* a grace note resolving to an essential note of melody or harmony. An appoggiatura may be either played lightly and very quickly (short appoggiatura) or accented and given its full time value (long appoggiatura). [< Italian *appoggiatura* < *appoggiare* lean, ultimately < Latin *ad-* on + *podium* projecting part]

***appoggiatura**

ap|point (ə point′), *v.t.* **1** to name for an office or position; choose: *George's father was appointed postmaster. Who appointed the new members of the committee?* **SYN**: designate. **2** to decide on; set (a time or place to be somewhere or to meet someone): *We shall appoint eight o'clock as the time to begin. He appointed the schoolhouse as the place for the meeting.* **3** to fix; prescribe: *The law of Moses was appointed by God.* **SYN**: ordain, establish. **4** to furnish; equip: *a fully appointed workshop.* **SYN**: supply.
—*v.i.* to use the legal power of appointment.
[< Old French *apointer* < *a-* to + *point* point < Latin *punctum.* See related etym. at **point.**] —**ap-point′a|ble,** *adj.* —**ap|point′er, ap|poin′tor,** *n.*

ap|point|ee (ə poin tē′, ap′oin-; ə poin′tē), *n.* a person who is appointed to an office or position.

ap|poin|tive (ə poin′tiv), *adj.* subject to or filled by appointment: *Positions in the President's cabinet are appointive.*

ap|point|ment (ə point′mənt), *n.* **1** a meeting with someone at a certain time and place; engagement: *I have an appointment to see the doctor at 4 o'clock.* **2** office or position to which the holder is appointed: *The Secretary of State has a high government appointment.* **SYN**: post. **3** the act of naming for or placing in an office or position; choosing. **4** the disposal of real property, in exercise of an authority conferred for that purpose. **5** direction; decree: *Everything happens by the appointment of Providence.*
appointments, furniture; equipment: *The new hotel has very modern appointments.*

ap|port (ə pôrt′, -pōrt′; *French* à pôr′), *n.* **1** the introduction of a material object or objects at a séance. **2** any material object produced by occult means: ... *a poltergeist bringing unrequested apports* (Punch). [< French *apport* < *apporter* to bring, introduce; see etym. under **rapport**]

ap|por|tion (ə pôr′shən, -pōr′-), *v.t.* to divide and give out in fair shares; distribute according to some rule: *The father's will apportioned his property among his children.* **SYN**: allocate, mete, ration. See syn. under **allot.** [< obsolete French, Old French *apportionner* < *a-* to + *portionner* to divide < Latin *portiō, -ōnis* portion] —**ap|por′-tion|er,** *n.*

ap|por|tion|ment (ə pôr′shən mənt, -pōr′-), *n.* **1** the act of dividing and giving out in fair shares; distribution according to some rule. **2** *U.S.* the determination and assignment of representation (in a legislative body). Apportionment usually involves the establishment of districts from which representatives are elected.

ap|pos|a|ble (ə pō′zə bəl), *adj.* that can be apposed, especially (of the thumb) capable of moving to touch the tip of each of the four fingers.

ap|pose (ə pōz′), *v.t.,* **-posed, -pos|ing. 1** to put next; place side by side. **2** to put (one thing to another); apply: *An official seal was apposed to the document.* [< Old French *apposer* < *a-* to + *poser* put, place, pose[1]]

ap|po|site (ap′ə zit), *adj.* fittingly applied; appropriate; suitable; apt: *That is a very apposite suggestion.* **SYN**: pertinent, relevant, apropos. [< Latin *appositus,* past participle of *appōnere* < *ad-* near + *pōnere* place] —**ap′po|site|ly,** *adv.* —**ap′-po|site|ness,** *n.*

ap|po|si|tion (ap′ə zish′ən), *n.* **1a** a placing together in the same grammatical relation. **b** the relation to a noun or pronoun of another noun or noun equivalent which is added to it as an explanation or identification. In "Mr. Brown, our neighbor, has a new car," *Mr. Brown* and *our neighbor* are in apposition. Words in apposition are equivalent in meaning and have the same grammatical function in the sentence. **2** the act of putting side by side; apposing: *the apposition of thumb and forefinger.* **3** position side by side; juxtaposition. **4** the deposit of successive layers of cell-wall material in plants, thus increasing the thickness of the cell wall.

ap|po|si|tion|al (ap′ə zish′ə nəl), *adj.* of or having to do with apposition; appositive. —**ap′po|si′tion-al|ly,** *adv.*

ap|pos|i|tive (ə poz′ə tiv), *n., adj.* —*n.* a noun or noun equivalent added to another noun or pronoun as an explanation; word, phrase, or clause in apposition. In the sentence, "Mr. Brown, our neighbor, has a new car," *our neighbor* is an appositive.
—*adj.* **1** placed in apposition. **2** of or having to do with apposition. **3** parenthetical; descriptive: *an appositive clause.* —**ap|pos′i|tive|ly,** *adv.*

ap|prais|a|ble (ə prā′zə bəl), *adj.* that can be appraised.

ap|prais|al (ə prā′zəl), *n.* **1** an estimate of the value, amount, or quality: *The tax collector made an appraisal of $15,000 on the farmer's new barn. Their appraisal of the stock was too low.* **2** an appraising; evaluating; valuation: *His appraisal of his crop took him all over his farmland. He did not think the feeling that ... American surplus disposal programmes were interfering with normal trade was "an accurate appraisal"* (London Times).

ap|praise (ə prāz′), *v.t.,* **-praised, -prais|ing. 1** to estimate the value, amount, quality, or merit of; judge: *A teacher should be able to appraise ability and achievement in students.* **SYN**: rate, apprize. See syn. under **estimate. 2** to set a price on; fix the value of: *Property is appraised for taxation.* [apparently < *praise,* verb] —**ap|prais′-ing|ly,** *adv.*

ap|praise|ment (ə prāz′mənt), *n.* = appraisal.

ap|prais|er (ə prā′zər), *n.* **1** a person authorized to fix the value of items such as property, imported goods, or real estate. **2** a person who appraises.

ap|pre|ci|a|ble (ə prē′shē ə bəl, -shə bəl), *adj.* enough to be felt or estimated; noticeable; perceptible: *A slight hill makes an appreciable difference in walking. With more study his grades showed appreciable improvement.* **SYN**: discernible, palpable, marked, significant, considerable.

ap|pre|ci|a|bly (ə prē′shē ə blē, -shə blē), *adv.* to an appreciable degree; by a difference that can be noticed; perceptibly; noticeably: *He is appreciably better.*

ap|pre|ci|ate (ə prē′shē āt), *v.,* **-at|ed, -at|ing.** —*v.t.* **1** to be thankful for: *We appreciate your help.* **2** to think highly of; recognize the worth or quality of; value; enjoy: *Almost everybody appreciates good food.* **SYN**: esteem, prize. See syn. under **value. 3** to be aware of; be sensitive to; recognize; discern: *Do you fully appreciate the risk you are taking? He is a trained musician who can appreciate even very small differences in sounds.* **4** to have an opinion of the value, worth, or quality of; estimate: *Most people can appreciate the importance of exercise for good health. Einstein's knowledge is so specialized I cannot begin to appreciate it.* **SYN**: appraise. **5** to raise in value: *New buildings usually appreciate land.*
—*v.i.* to rise in value: *This land will appreciate greatly as soon as good roads are built. Collections of rare books, paintings and stamps are examples of property that has appreciated in value over the postwar years* (Wall Street Journal).
[< Latin *appretiāre* (with English *-ate*[1]) < *ad-* + *pretium* price. See etym. of doublet **apprise**[2].]
—**ap|pre′ci|at′ing|ly,** *adv.* —**ap|pre′ci|a′tor,** *n.*

ap|pre|ci|a|tion (ə prē′shē ā′shən), *n.* **1** the quality or condition of being thankful for; gratefulness; approval: *He showed his appreciation of her help by sending flowers.* **2** the fact of valuing highly; sympathetic understanding: *She has an appreciation of art and music.* **3** an estimate of the value or quality of something; estimation: *They are mistaken in their appreciation of the country's economic conditions.* **4** favorable criticism: *He has written a fine appreciation of that novel.* **5** a rise in value: *The vogue is to seek appreciation rather than income. The urge is to speculate rather than invest* (Wall Street Journal).

ap|pre|ci|a|tive (ə prē′shē ā′tiv, -shə tiv), *adj.* having appreciation; showing appreciation; recognizing the value: *The lost child was appreciative of the smallest kindness. The audience was noisily appreciative of the singer's performance.*
—**ap|pre′ci|a′tive|ly,** *adv.* —**ap|pre′ci|a′tive-ness,** *n.*

ap|pre|ci|a|to|ry (ə prē′shē ə tôr′ē, -tōr′-; -shə-tôr′-, -tōr′-), *adj.* = appreciative. —**ap|pre′ci|a|to′-ri|ly,** *adv.*

ap|pre|hend (ap′ri hend′), *v.t.* **1** to arrest; seize: *The thief was apprehended and put in jail.* **SYN**: capture. **2** to look forward to with fear; expect anxiously; dread: *A guilty man apprehends danger in every sound. I apprehend no worsening of the situation.* **SYN**: forebode. **3** to become or be conscious of; notice or perceive. **4** to grasp with the mind; understand: *I apprehended his meaning more from his gestures than from the queer sounds he made.* **SYN**: comprehend. **5** to regard; view: *These are the rights and wrongs of the case, as I apprehend them.* **6** *Obsolete.* to lay hold of with the hands; grasp. —*v.i.* **1** to be apprehensive; fear: *I apprehended the consequences with dread.* **2** to grasp ideas; understand. [< Latin *apprehendere* < *ad-* upon + *prehendere* seize] —**ap′pre|hend′er,** *n.*
▶ See **reprehend** for usage note.

ap|pre|hen|si|bil|i|ty (ap′ri hen′sə bil′ə tē), *n.* the quality of being apprehensible.

ap|pre|hen|si|ble (ap′ri hen′sə bəl), *adj.* that can be apprehended; understandable. —**ap′pre|hen′-si|bly,** *adv.*

ap|pre|hen|sion (ap′ri hen′shən), *n.* **1** expectation of misfortune; fear; dread: *The roar of the hurricane filled us with apprehension. Her apprehensions about the dangers of traveling were increased by the accident.* **2** the act of seizing or the state of being seized; arrest: *The appearance*

Pronunciation Key: hat, āge, cãre, fär; let, ēqual, tėrm, it, īce; hot, ōpen, ôrder; oil, out; cup, pu̇t, rüle; child; long; thin; ᴛʜen; zh, measure; ə represents **a** in about, **e** in taken, **i** in pencil, **o** in lemon, **u** in circus.

of the thief's picture in all the papers led to his apprehension. **3** grasp by the mind; understanding: *I do not have a clear apprehension of fractions.* [< Latin *apprehēnsiō, -ōnis* < *apprehendere* < *ad-* upon + *prehendere* seize]

ap|pre|hen|sive (ap'ri hen'siv), *adj.* **1** feeling alarm; afraid, anxious, or worried: *The captain felt apprehensive for the safety of his passengers during the storm at sea.* **2** quick to understand; able to learn. **3** perceptive (of). —**ap'pre|hen'sive|ly,** *adv.* —**ap'pre|hen'sive|ness,** *n.*

ap|pren|tice (ə pren'tis), *n., v.,* **-ticed, -tic|ing.** —*n.* **1** a person learning a trade or art. In return for instruction the apprentice agrees to work for his employer a certain length of time with little or no pay. **2** a beginner; learner.
—*v.t.* to bind or take as an apprentice: *Benjamin Franklin's father apprenticed him to a printer.*
[< Old French *aprentiz* < Latin *apprēndere,* earlier *apprehendere;* see etym. under **apprehend**]

ap|pren|tice|ment (ə pren'tis mənt), *n.* **1** the act of apprenticing. **2** an apprenticeship.

ap|pren|tice|ship (ə pren'tis ship), *n.* **1** the condition of being an apprentice. **2** the time during which one is an apprentice: *During their long apprenticeship the boys also absorbed the community traditions and culture from their elders* (Scientific American).

ap|pressed (ə prest'), *adj.* pressed closely; fitting closely (to).

ap|prise[1] (ə prīz'), *v.t.,* **-prised, -pris|ing.** to give notice to; let know; inform; notify; advise: *We were at once apprised of his change of plans.* Also, **apprize.** [< French *appris,* past participle of *apprendre* learn < Latin *apprēndere,* earlier *apprehendere;* see etym. under **apprehend**] —**ap-pris'er,** *n.* —**ap|prise'ment,** *n.*

ap|prise[2] (ə prīz'), *v.t.,* **-prised, -pris|ing.** = apprize (appraise). [< Old French *apriser, aprisier* < Latin *appretiāre* appreciate. See etym. of doublet **appreciate.**] —**ap|pris'er,** *n.* —**ap|prise'ment,** *n.*

ap|prize[1] (ə prīz'), *v.t.,* **-prized, -priz|ing.** = apprise[1]. —**ap|priz'er,** *n.* —**ap|prize'ment,** *n.*

ap|prize[2] (ə prīz'), *v.t.,* **-prized, -priz|ing.** = appraise. [see etym. under **apprise[2]**] —**ap|priz'er,** *n.* —**ap|prize'ment,** *n.*

ap|proach (ə prōch'), *v., n.* —*v.t.* **1** to come near or nearer to: *Walk softly as you approach the baby's crib.* (*Figurative.*) *The wind was approaching a gale.* **SYN:** near, approximate. **2** to bring or move near (to something): *I ... approached my chair by sly degrees to the fire* (Oliver Goldsmith). **3** to make advances or overtures to: *A group of us approached the principal with the idea of calling a holiday in honor of Martin Luther King.* **4** *Figurative.* to start work on: *to approach a difficult task.* —*v.i.* to come near or nearer: *Winter is approaching.* **SYN:** impend.
—*n.* **1** the act of coming near or nearer; approaching: *Sunset announces the approach of night.* **SYN:** advance, advent. **2** a way by which a place or person can be reached; means of access: *The approach to the house was a narrow path. His best approach to the great man lay through a mutual friend.* **SYN:** accession. **3** *Figurative.* a method of starting work on a task or problem: *He seems to have a good approach to the problem.* **4** nearness in quality, character, time, or condition: *In mathematics there must be more than an approach to accuracy.* **SYN:** approximation. **5** a stroke in golf by which a player tries to hit his ball onto the putting green.
approaches, works thrown up by besiegers for protection in their advances toward a fortress.
[< Old French *aprochier* < Latin *appropiāre* < *ad-* to + *prope* near] —**ap|proach'less,** *adj.*

ap|proach|a|bil|i|ty (ə prō'chə bil'ə tē), *n.* approachable quality or condition.

ap|proach|a|ble (ə prō'chə bəl), *adj.* **1** that can be approached; accessible: *The house on the mountain is approachable only on foot.* **2** easy to approach and talk to; friendly and sociable; affable: *No matter how busy he was, he was always approachable.* —**ap|proach'a|ble|ness,** *n.*

*** approach light,** a light or one of a series of lights placed in front of a runway to indicate a favorable approach for aircraft.

ap|pro|bate (ap'rə bāt), *v.t.,* **-bat|ed, -bat|ing.** *Especially U.S.* to express approbation of. [< Latin *approbāre* (with English *-ate*[1]) < *ad-* + *probāre* prove. See etym. of doublet **approve.**]

ap|pro|ba|tion (ap'rə bā'shən), *n.* **1** favorable opinion; approval: *The teacher gave her approbation to the science committee's class report.* **2** the act of formally and authoritatively approving; sanction.

ap|pro|ba|tive (ap'rə bā'tiv), *adj.* expressing approbation; approving. —**ap'pro|ba'tive|ness,** *n.*

ap|pro|ba|to|ry (ə prō'bə tôr'ē, -tōr'-; ap'rə-; ap'rə bā'tər-), *adj.* = approbative.

ap|proof (ə prüf'), *n. Archaic.* **1** approval: *The self-same tongue, Either of condemnation or approof* (Shakespeare). **2** proof. [< Old French *aprove* < *aprover* approve < Latin *approbāre;* see etym. under **approbate**]

ap|pro|pin|quate (ap'rə ping'kwāt), *v.i.,* **-quat|ed, -quat|ing.** *Archaic.* to come near; approach. [< Latin *appropinquāre* (with English *-ate*[1]) < *ad-* to + *prope* near]

ap|pro|pin|qua|tion (ap'rə ping kwā'shən), *n.* the action of coming near; approach.

ap|pro|pin|qui|ty (ap'rə ping'kwə tē), *n.* nearness, such as of one to another; propinquity.

ap|pro|pri|a|ble (ə prō'prē ə bəl), *adj.* that can be appropriated.

ap|pro|pri|ate[1] (ə prō'prē it), *adj.* right for the occasion; suitable; proper; fitting: *Plain, simple clothes are appropriate for school wear.* **SYN:** meet. See syn. under **fit[1]**. [< Late Latin *appropriātus,* past participle of *appropriāre* < Latin *ad-* + *proprius* one's own] —**ap|pro'pri|ate|ly,** *adv.* —**ap|pro'pri|ate|ness,** *n.*

ap|pro|pri|ate[2] (ə prō'prē āt), *v.t.,* **-at|ed, -at|ing.** **1** to set apart for some special use: *The state legislature has just appropriated additional funds for school aid.* **SYN:** assign, apportion. **2** to take for oneself; take possession of; use as one's own: *You should not appropriate other people's belongings without their permission.* **SYN:** seize, secure. [< Latin *appropriāre* (with *-ate*[1]); see etym. at **appropriate[1]**] —**ap|pro'pri|a'tor,** *n.*

appropriate technology, the use of machinery and methods suited to available conditions, particularly to conditions of underdeveloped areas: *Soap making has become an appropriate technology classic. The oil is locally produced, technology for small scale soap making already exists, the market is local, and soap can be produced for half the price of the nationally advertised brands* (New Scientist).

ap|pro|pri|a|tion (ə prō'prē ā'shən), *n.* **1** a sum of money or other thing appropriated: *The school received an appropriation of five thousand dollars toward the new playground.* **2** the act of appropriating: *The appropriation of the land made it possible to have a park.*

ap|pro|pri|a|tive (ə prō'prē ā'tiv), *adj.* tending to appropriate. —**ap|pro'pri|a'tive|ness,** *n.*

ap|prov|a|ble (ə prü'və bəl), *adj.* worthy or deserving of approval. —**ap|prov'a|ble|ness,** *n.*

ap|prov|al (ə prü'vəl), *n.* **1** favorable opinion; approving; praise: *We all like others to show approval of what we do.* **SYN:** commendation, approbation. **2** permission; consent; sanction: *The principal gave approval for a class picnic.*
approvals, merchandise sent on approval.
on approval, so that the customer can inspect the item and decide whether to buy or return it: *He bought the television set on approval.*

ap|prove (ə prüv'), *v.,* **-proved, -prov|ing.** —*v.t.* **1** to think or speak well of; express one's agreement with or admiration of; be pleased with: *The teacher looked at John's work and approved it.* **SYN:** like. **2** to give consent to; authorize or make legal; confirm; ratify: *Father approved our plans for the summer. Congress approved the President's new appointment for Secretary of State.* **3** to provide proof of; demonstrate; prove; corroborate: *'Tis an old lesson; Time approves it true* (Byron). *What damned error but some sober brow Will bless it, and approve it with a text?* (Shakespeare). **SYN:** laud. See syn. under **praise.**
—*v.i.* to give a favorable opinion (of): *I'm not sure I approve of what you want to do.*
[< Old French *aprover* < Latin *approbāre* < *ad-* + *probāre* prove. See etym. of doublet **approbate.**] —**ap|prov'ing|ly,** *adv.*
—*Syn. v.t.* **2 Approve, sanction, ratify** mean to give consent or support through formal action or through the force of public opinion. **Approve,** the general word, means to consent formally or officially to something one thinks favorably of: *The school board approved the budget.* **Sanction** means to give official authorization or support: *Society does not sanction child labor.* **Ratify** means to give formal approval or confirmation of something of importance, as by a vote: *The club council ratified the by-laws.*

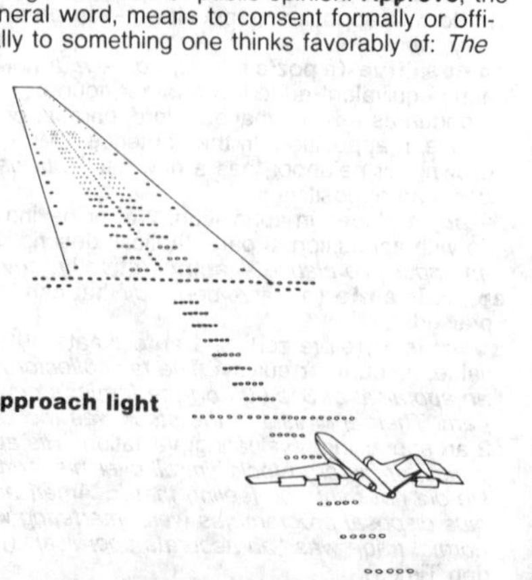

*** approach light**

ap|proved (ə prüvd'), *adj.* **1** regarded with favor. **2** sanctioned; confirmed. —**ap|prov'ed|ly,** *adv.*

approved school, *British.* a reform school for first offenders.

ap|prov|er (ə prü'vər), *n.* **1** a person who approves or commends. **2** a person who proves or offers to prove.

approx., **1** approximate. **2** approximately.

ap|prox|i|mal (ə prok'sə məl), *adj.* close together; contiguous, as surfaces of adjoining teeth.

ap|prox|i|mate (*adj.* ə prok'sə mit; *v.* ə prok'sə-māt), *adj., v.,* **-mat|ed, -mat|ing.** —*adj.* **1** nearly correct: *The approximate length of a meter is 40 inches; the exact length is 39.37 inches.* **2** very near: *approximate leaves.* **3** very like: *a statement approximate to the truth.*
—*v.t.* **1** to come near to; approach: *Your account of what happened approximates the truth, but there are several small errors. The crowd approximated a thousand people.* **2** to bring near.
—*v.i.* to come near or close (to): *All we can expect ... is to approximate to the true solution* (James Stephen).
[< Latin *approximātus,* past participle of *approximāre* < *ad-* + *proximus* nearest, superlative of *prope* near]

ap|prox|i|mate|ly (ə prok'sə mit lē), *adv.* by a close estimate; nearly; about: *We are approximately 200 miles from home. Abbr:* approx.

ap|prox|i|ma|tion (ə prok'sə mā'shən), *n.* **1** a nearly correct amount; close estimate: *25,000 miles is an approximation of the circumference of the earth.* **2** the act of approximating; approach: *Her story was a close approximation to the truth.* **3** the condition of being near.

ap|prox|i|ma|tive (ə prok'sə mā'tiv), *adj.* approximating; approximate: *a first or approximative verification* (John Herschel).

ap|prox|i|ma|tor (ə prok'sə mā'tər), *n.* a person who approximates, or comes near (to).

ap|pui (ä pwē'), *n. French.* support. See also **point d'appui.**

ap|pulse (ə puls'), *n.* a driving upon; approach; impact. [< Latin *appulsus, -ūs* < *appellere* to drive < *ad-* to + *pellere* drive]

ap|pul|sive (ə pul'siv), *adj.* driving upon; impinging.

ap|pur|te|nance (ə pėr'tə nəns), *n.* **1** an addition to something more important; added thing; accessory. A radio in a car is an appurtenance; an engine is a necessity. **2** a minor property, right, or privilege accompanying another that is more important.
appurtenances, a accessories; trappings: *We worry because we have much to lose: homes, cars, television sets, washing machines, freezers, and all the other appurtenances of the wealthy of the world* (Harper's). **b** apparatus; gear: *the appurtenances of war.*
[< Anglo-French *apurtenance,* Old French *appartenance* < *appertenir* appertain]

ap|pur|te|nant (ə pėr'tə nənt), *adj., n.* —*adj.* pertaining; belonging; appertaining (to). —*n.* a thing that appertains: *the mysterious appurtenants ... of Redemption* (Samuel Taylor Coleridge).

Apr., April.

APRA, Australian Performing Rights Association.

a|prax|i|a (ə prak'sē ə), *n.* loss of the ability to perform coordinated or purposeful movements. [< New Latin *apraxia* < Greek *a-* not + *prássein* do]

a|près la guerre or **a|près guerre** (ä pre (lä) ger'), *French.* after the war, especially after World War I or II; postwar: *The shock of defeat led to a weakening of the traditional Japanese social and individual ethics. An après la guerre mentality set in* (London Times).

a|près moi le dé|luge (ä pre mwä' lə dā lyzh'), *French.* when I am (or we are) gone, let happen what will; after me the deluge. The expression is generally attributed to Louis XV of France.

A|pres|o|line (ə pres'ə lēn, -lin), *n. Trademark.* hydralazine: *Apresoline inhibits materials from the kidneys that stimulate high blood pressure* (New York Times).

a|près-ski (ä pre skē'), *adv., adj., n. French.* —*adv., adj.* after skiing: *après-ski wear.* —*n.* after skiing activity.

a|près tout (ä pre tü'), *French.* when all is considered; after all: *Après tout, Bach has said all there is to say in music ...* (Atlantic).

a|près vous (ä pre vü'), *French.* after you.

ap|ri|cate (ap'rə kāt), *v.i., v.t.,* **-cat|ed, -cat|ing.** *Rare.* to bask in or expose to sunlight. [< Latin *aprīcārī* (with English *-ate*[1]) < *aprīcus* exposed to the sun] —**ap'ri|ca'tion,** *n.*

a|pri|cot (ā'prə kot, ap'rə-), *n., adj.* —*n.* **1** a roundish, pale orange-colored fruit about the size of a plum, that has a downy skin something like that of a peach. **2** the tree that it grows on, belonging to the rose family. **3** a pale orange-yellow.

—adj. **1** pale orange-yellow. **2** made of or from apricots: *apricot brandy.*

[earlier *abrecock* < Portuguese *albricoque* < Spanish *albaricoque* < Arabic *al-barqūq* < Late Greek *praikókion*, a borrowing from Latin *prae coquis* early-ripe < *prae* before + *coquere* ripen]

A|pril (ā′prəl), *n.* the fourth month of the year. It has 30 days. *Abbr:* Apr. [< Latin *Aprīlis*]

April fool, a person who gets fooled on April Fools' Day.

April Fools' Day or **April Fool's Day**, April 1, a day observed by fooling people with tricks and jokes; All Fools' Day.

a pri|o|ri (ā prī ôr′ī, -ōr′-; ä prē ôr′ē, -ōr′-), **1** (of reasoning, arguments, or statements) from cause to effect; from a general rule to a particular case. **2** based on opinion or theory rather than on actual observation or experience: *Where we think this book unreasonable and lopsided in its conclusion, is, for instance, in its a priori reasoning that there have been no important or really "modern" composers since Wagner* (New York Times). [< Medieval Latin *a priori* from (something) previous]

a|pri|or|ism (ā′prī ôr′iz əm, -ōr′-), *n.* **1** something assumed as if known a priori: *Unwarrantable apriorisms, . . . pure unproved assumptions* (The American). **2** a priori reasoning or doctrine. **3** *Philosophy.* belief in the doctrine of innate ideas. **—a′pri|or′ist**, *n.*

a|pri|o|ris|tic (ā prī′ə ris′tik), *adj.* **1** having an a priori character: *. . . the emotional and aprioristic idea of a continuous and inherent progress of civilization* (Alfred L. Kroeber). **2** = a priori. **—a|pri′o|ris′ti|cal|ly**, *adv.*

a|pri|or|i|ty (ā′prī ôr′ə tē, -ōr′-), *n.* **1** the quality of being based on or derived from a priori reasoning. **2** practice of a priori reasoning.

a|pron** (ā′prən, -pərn), *n., v.* **—*n. **1** a garment worn over the front part of the body to cover or protect clothes: *a kitchen apron, a carpenter's apron.* **2** an area in front of an airport terminal or hangar on which to park aircraft. **3** the area of a stage in front of the curtain. **4a** a protective structure or layer of material to prevent the washing away of a surface, such as a riverbank, by water. **b** a platform at the bottom of a sluice to intercept the fall of water. **5** a kind of flat conveyor belt. **6** a protective sheet or plate of metal on certain parts of guns, roofs, or machines. **7** a sheet of sand and gravel in front of a glacial moraine. **8** a leather covering for the legs in certain types of open vehicles. **9** a thick mass of skin on the chest of a ram.

—v.t. to provide with or as if with an apron: *Then he aproned me again, stropped his razor, and whipped up a lather* (New Yorker).

[misdivision of Middle English (*a*) *naperon* < Old French *naperon* (diminutive) < *nape* < Latin *mappa* napkin] **—a′pron|like′**, *adj.*

***apron**
definition 3

apron stage, a stage extending into the theater so that the audience faces it on three sides.

apron strings, the cord or cords by which an apron is fastened on the wearer.

tied to the apron strings, dependent on or dominated by (one's mother, wife, or other female associate): *He could not submit to be tied to the apron strings even of the best of wives* (Macaulay).

ap|ro|pos (ap′rə pō′), *adv., adj.* **—*adv.*** **1** fittingly; opportunely. **2** by the way (introducing an incidental observation or question).

—adj. to the point; fitting; suitable: *Your remark is certainly apropos to what we are discussing.*

apropos of, with regard to: *Apropos of the party, what are you going to wear?*

[< French *à propos* to the purpose]

à pro|pos de rien (à prô pō′də ryaɴ′), *French.* apropos of nothing; not pertinent; irrelevant.

a|prowl (ə proul′), *adv., adj.* prowling about; on the prowl: *Along Madison Avenue . . . he bumped into a Dartmouth contemporary . . . aprowl for something to edit* (New Yorker). [< *a-*[1] + *prowl*]

***apse** (aps), *n.* **1** a semicircular or many-sided recess in a church, usually at the east end. The roof of an apse is vaulted or arched. **2** = apsis (def. 1). [< Latin *apsis, -īdis* < Greek *hapsís, -îdos* loop < *háptein* fasten]

ap|si|dal (ap′sə dəl), *adj.* **1** of or having to do with an apse. **2** including or attached to an apse.

ap|sis (ap′sis), *n., pl.* **-si|des** (-sə dēz). **1** either of two points in the elliptical orbit of a heavenly body at one of which, the lower apsis, it is nearest to, and at the other, the higher apsis, farthest from, the body or point about which it is revolving. These two points can be joined by the line of apsides. **2** = apse (def. 1). [< Latin *apsīs, -īdis*]

apt (apt), *adj.* **1** fitted by nature; likely (to): *A careless person is apt to make mistakes.* **SYN:** inclined, liable, prone. **2** right for the occasion; suitable; fitting; appropriate: *His apt reply to the question showed that he had understood it very well.* **SYN:** apposite. **3** quick to learn; intelligent: *Some pupils in our class are more apt than others.* **SYN:** prompt, ready, bright. [< Latin *aptus* joined, fitted] **—apt′ly**, *adv.* **—apt′ness**, *n.*

▶See **likely** for usage note.

apt., apartment.

APT (no periods), **1** advanced passenger train (a train capable of speeds of 150 miles per hour). **2** automatic picture transmission (used to send pictures to earth from artificial satellites). **3** automatically programmed tool (a system of machine-tool automation or numerical control).

ap|ter|al (ap′tər əl), *adj.* **1** without columns along the sides: *the sterile, apteral office buildings of the modern city.* **2** = apterous.

ap|te|ri|um (ap tir′ē əm), *n., pl.* **-ri|a** (-rē ə). one of the featherless spaces on the skin of a bird intervening between the feathered tracts. [< New Latin *apterium* < Greek *ápteros* featherless, wingless; see etym. under **apterous**]

ap|ter|ous (ap′tər əs), *adj.* **1** wingless. Lice are apterous insects. **2** having no winglike expansions, as of stems, seeds, or other plant parts. [< Greek *ápteros* (with English *-ous*) < *a-* without + *pterón* wing]

ap|ter|yg|i|al (ap′tə rij′ē əl), *adj.* lacking wings, fins, or limbs. [< Greek *aptérygos* + English *-ial*]

ap|ter|yx (ap′tər iks), *n., pl.* **-yx|es**. a wingless, or practically wingless, nocturnal bird about the size of a chicken, that has hairlike feathers; kiwi. They live in New Zealand, but are now almost extinct. [< New Latin *apteryx* < Greek *a-* without + *ptéryx* wing]

ap|ti|tude (ap′tə tüd, -tyüd), *n.* **1** natural tendency or talent; ability; capacity: *Edison had a remarkable aptitude for inventing new things.* **SYN:** propensity. **2** readiness in learning; quickness to understand: *He is a pupil of great aptitude.* **SYN:** intelligence. **3** special fitness; appropriateness. [< Late Latin *aptitūdō* < Latin *aptus* joined, fitted. See etym. of doublet **attitude**.]

aptitude test, a test given to a person to find out the sort of work, studies, or skill, for which he is specially suited: *Countless U.S. youths submit themselves to aptitude tests . . . based on Freudian interpretation of personality structure* (Time).

ap|tote (ap′tōt), *n. Grammar.* an indeclinable noun. [< Latin *aptōtum* < Greek *áptōton* < *a-* without + *ptōtós* a falling]

ap|tot|ic (ap tot′ik), *adj.* having no grammatical inflections, as certain languages.

apts., apartments.

A|pu|li|an (ə pyü′lē ən, -pyül′yən), *adj., n.* **—*adj.*** of or having to do with Apulia (district in southeastern Italy).

—n. a native or inhabitant of Apulia.

a|pur|pose (ə pėr′pəs), *adv. Informal.* intentionally; on purpose: *He commenced brushing . . . with a toothbrush he'd bought apurpose* (Walter D. Edmonds).

a|py|ret|ic (ā′pī ret′ik), *adj.* free from fever. [< *a-* not + *pyretic*]

a|py|rex|i|a (ā′pī rek′sē ə), *n.* absence of fever. [< New Latin *apyrexia* < Greek *apyrexíā*]

a|py|rex|i|al (ā′pī rek′sē əl), *adj.* = apyretic.

aq., **1** aqua. **2** aqueous.

Aq., aqua.

AQ (no periods) or **A.Q.**, achievement quotient.

aq|ua (ak′wə, ā′kwə), *n., pl.* **aq|uae** (ak′wē, ā′kwē), **aq|uas**, *adj.* **—*n.*** **1** = water. **2** a liquid solution (used in many descriptive names in pharmacy and chemistry). **3** aquamarine color.

—adj. light bluish-green.

[< Latin *aqua* water]

aqua ammonia, = aqua ammoniae.

aqua am|mo|ni|ae (ə mō′nē ē), ammonia gas dissolved in water. [< New Latin *aqua ammoniae* (literally) water of ammonia]

***apse**
definition 1

aq|ua|cade (ak′wə kād), *n.* a display of swimming, diving, and other aquatic skills before an audience. [< *aqua* + *-cade*]

aq|ua|cul|tur|al (ak′wə kul′chər əl), *adj.* of or having to do with aquaculture. Also, **aquicultural**.

aq|ua|cul|ture (ak′wə kul′chər), *n.* the raising of plants or animals, such as fish or shellfish, in or at the bottom of the sea, a lake, a river, or other body of water. Also, **aquiculture**.

aq|ua|cul|tur|ist (ak′wə kul′chər ist), *n.* a person who engages in aquaculture.

Aq|ua|dag (ak′wə dag), *n. Trademark.* a colloidal suspension of graphite, used in making electrodes or as a lubricant.

aq|ua|farm (ak′wə färm′), *n.* a pond or other body of water used for aquaculture.

aq|ua for|tis, or **aq|ua|for|tis** (ak′wə fôr′tis, ā′kwə-), *n.* = nitric acid. [< New Latin *aqua fortis* (literally) strong water]

***aq|ua|gun** (ak′wə gun′), *n.* a spear or harpoon propelled by a spring or compressed air and released by a trigger, used for underwater hunting.

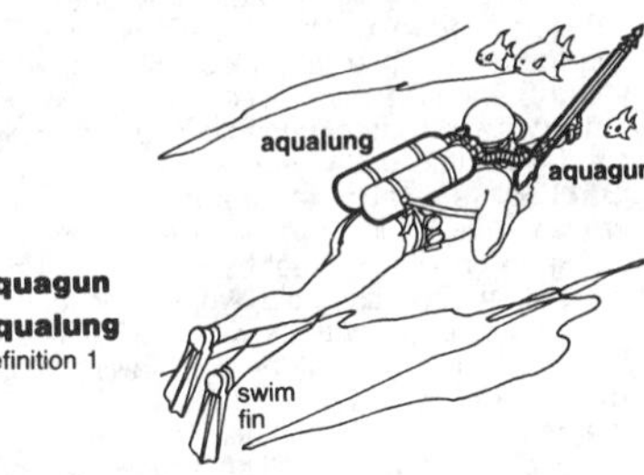

***aquagun**
***aqualung**
definition 1

aq|ua|lung** (ak′wə lung′), *n., v.* **—*n. **1** an underwater breathing device used in skin diving, consisting of one or more cylinders of compressed air strapped to the diver's back, a hose and mouthpiece through which the diver breathes, and sometimes a glass mask placed over the eyes and nose. The supply of air to the diver is regulated automatically by a valve. **2** **Aqua-Lung**, a trademark for this device.

—v.i. to dive using an aqualung. **—aq′ua-lung′er**, *n.*

aq|ua|ma|rine (ak′wə mə rēn′), *n., adj.* **—*n.*** **1** a transparent, bluish-green semiprecious stone that is a variety of beryl. **2** a light bluish-green color.

—adj. light bluish-green.

[< Latin *aqua marīna* seawater (from its color)]

aq|ua|naut (ak′wə nôt), *n.* an underwater explorer: *The experiment proved that aquanauts could live and work for long periods of time hundreds of feet below the surface* (Time). [< *aqua* + *-naut*, as in *astronaut*]

aq|ua|plane (ak′wə plān′), *n., v.,* **-planed, -planing.** **—*n.*** a wide board on which a person rides for sport as he is towed by a speeding motorboat. See also **surfboard**.

—v.i. to ride on an aquaplane for sport.

[< *aqua* + *plane*[1]]

aq|ua|plan|ing (ak′wə plā′ning), *n.* a dangerous skidding effect resulting from a loss of contact between tires and a wet road when a highly compressed film of water builds up between the tires and the road; hydroplaning.

aqua pu|ra (pyůr′ə), pure water. [< New Latin *aqua pura* < Latin *aqua* water, *pūra* clean, pure]

aqua re|gi|a (rē′jē ə), a mixture of nitric acid and hydrochloric acid that will dissolve gold and platinum. [< New Latin *aqua regia* royal water (because it dissolves gold)]

aq|ua|relle (ak′wə rel′), *n.* **1** a painting made with ink and very thin, transparent water colors. **2** the method of painting with ink and transparent water colors. [< French *acquarelle* < Italian *acquerella, acquerello* < Latin *aquārius* of water < *aqua* water]

aq|ua|rel|list (ak′wə rel′ist), *n.* an artist who makes aquarelles.

A|quar|i|an (ə kwãr′ē ən), *adj., n.* **—*adj.*** of or having to do with the Age of Aquarius.

—n. a person belonging to this age, especially when of a younger generation.

A|quar|i|i (ə kwãr′ē ī), *n.* genitive of **Aquarius** (def. 1).

a|quar|ist (ə kwãr′ist), *n.* a person who keeps an aquarium: *These lively instruction books cover just about everything a perplexed aquarist might need to know—from developing a wet thumb for plants to growing and chopping one's own worms* (New York Times). [< *aquar* (ium) + *-ist*]

Pronunciation Key: hat, āge, cãre, fär; let, ēqual, tėrm; it, īce; hot, ōpen, ôrder; oil, out; cup, půt, rüle; child; long; thin; ᴛʜen; zh, measure; ə represents **a** in about, **e** in taken, **i** in pencil, **o** in lemon, **u** in circus.

a|quar|i|um (ə kwãr′ē əm), *n., pl.* **-i|ums, -i|a** (-ē ə). **1** a pond, tank, or glass bowl in which living fish and other water animals and water plants are kept. **2** a building used for showing collections of living fish, water animals, and water plants: *The aquarium had large tanks with glass fronts for different kinds of fish.* [< Latin *aquārium,* neuter of *aquārius* of water < *aqua* water]

A|quar|i|us (ə kwãr′ē əs), *n., genitive* (def. 1) **A|quar|i|i.** **1** a northern constellation supposed to represent a man standing with his left hand extended upward, and with his right hand pouring a stream of water out of a vase; the Water Bearer. **2** the eleventh sign of the zodiac, which the sun enters about January 21. **3** a person born under the sign of Aquarius. [< Latin *Aquārius* < *aqua* water]

a|quat|ic (ə kwat′ik, -kwot′-), *adj., n.* **—*adj.*** **1** growing or living in water: *Water lilies are aquatic plants.* **2** taking place in or on water: *Swimming and sailing are aquatic sports.*
—*n.* a plant or animal that lives in water.
aquatics, sports that take place in or on water. [< Old French *aquatique,* learned borrowing from Latin *aquāticus* watery, inhabiting water < *aqua* water] **—a|quat′i|cal|ly,** *adv.*

a|quat|i|cal (ə kwat′ə kəl, -kwot′-), *adj.* = aquatic.

aq|ua|tint (ak′wə tint′), *n., v.* **—*n.*** a method of etching on copper or steel by the use of a resinous solution and nitric acid, which produces finely granular shaded effects as well as lines resembling those of ink or water-color drawing. **2** an etching made by this process.
—*v.t., v.i.* to etch in aquatint.
[< French *aquatinte* < Italian *acqua tinta* < Latin *aqua* water, and *tīncta* feminine, dyed]

aq|ua|tone (ak′wə tōn), *n.* **1** a photoengraving process in which the design to be reproduced is transferred to a sensitized aluminum plate coated with a mixture of gelatin and celluloid. **2** the print produced by such a process.

a|qua|vit (ä′kvä vēt′, äk′vä vēt), *n.* a strong, colorless alcoholic liquor flavored slightly with caraway, popular especially in the Scandinavian countries, made by redistilling neutral spirits. Also, **akvavit.** [< Danish, Norwegian *akvavit* < Medieval Latin *aqua vitae* water of life]

aqua vi|tae (vī′tē), **1** brandy, whiskey, or any strong alcoholic liquor. **2** = alcohol. [< Medieval Latin *aqua vitae* water of life]

***aq|ue|duct** (ak′wə dukt), *n.* **1** an artificial channel or large pipe for bringing water from a distance. **2** the structure that supports such a channel or pipe. **3** a similar structure by which a canal is carried over a stream, river, or other obstruction. **4** *Anatomy.* a canal or channel in the body, especially a small one in the head. [< Latin *aquaeductus* < *aqua* water *ductus, -ūs* a leading < *dūcere* to lead]

***aqueduct**
definition 1

a|que|ous (ā′kwē əs, ak′wē-), *adj.* **1** of water: *aqueous vapor.* **2** containing water; made with water: *The druggist put the medicine in an aqueous solution.* **3** like water; watery: *Aqueous matter ran from the sore.* **4** produced by the action of water. Aqueous rocks are formed of the sediment carried and deposited by water. **—a′que|ous|ly,** *adv.* **—a′que|ous|ness,** *n.*

aqueous ammonia, ammonia gas dissolved in water.

aqueous humor, the watery liquid which fills the space in the eye between the cornea and the crystalline lens.

aq|ui|cul|tur|al (ak′wə kul′chər əl), *adj.* = aquacultural.

aq|ui|cul|ture (ak′wə kul′chər), *n.* = aquaculture.

aq|ui|cul|tur|ist (ak′wə kul′chər ist), *n.* = aquaculturist.

aq|ui|fer (ak′wə fər), *n.* **1** *Geology.* a stratum of earth or porous rock that contains water: *Like surface streams, water in the aquifers flows underground from the source to discharge points —either wells, swamps, springs, or lakes* (Newsweek). See picture under **artesian well.**
2 anything that carries water. [< Latin *aqui-* (< *aqua* water) *ferre* to carry]

a|quif|er|ous (ə kwif′ər əs), *adj.* conveying or containing water. [< Latin *aqui-* (< *aqua* water)]

aq|ui|fo|li|a|ceous (ak′wə fō′lē ā′shəs), *adj.* belonging to the same family of plants as the holly. [< Latin *aquifolius* having pointed leaves (< *acus* point *folium* leaf) English *-aceous*]

Aq|ui|la (ak′wə lə), *n., genitive* **Aq|ui|lae.** a northern constellation in the Milky Way, between Cygnus and Sagittarius, which contains the star Altair; the Eagle. [< Latin *aquila* eagle]

Aq|ui|lae (ak′wə lē), *n.* genitive of **Aquila.**

aq|ui|le|gi|a (ak′wə lē′jē ə, ā′kwə-), *n.* = columbine. [< Medieval Latin *aquilegia*]

aq|ui|line (ak′wə līn, -lin), *adj.* **1** curved like an eagle's beak; hooked: *an aquiline nose.* **2** of or like an eagle. [< Latin *aquilīnus* < *aquila* eagle]

aq|ui|lin|i|ty (ak′wə lin′ə tē), *n.* aquiline quality, condition, or form.

A|qui|lo (ak′wə lō), *n. Roman Mythology.* the north wind; Boreas.

a|quiv|er (ə kwiv′ər), *adj.* trembling; quivering.

a quo (ā kwō′), *Latin.* from which.

a|quose (ə kwōs′, ā′kwōs), *adj.* abounding in water; watery; aqueous. [< Latin *aquōsus* < *aqua* water]

a|quos|i|ty (ə kwos′ə tē), *n.* = wateriness.

ar (är), *n.* = are[2].

ar-, *prefix.* the form of **ad-** before *r,* as in *arrive.*

-ar, *suffix forming adjectives from nouns.* **1** of or having to do with ___: *Polar = of the pole(s). Nuclear = having to do with a nucleus or nuclei.*
2 like ___: *Stellar = like a star.*
3 of the nature of the ___: *Popular = of the nature of the people.*
[< Latin *-āris*]

ar., **1** argent. **2** aromatic. **3a** arrival. **b** arrive. **c** arrives.

Ar (no period), argon (chemical element).

Ar., 1a Arabian. **b** Arabic. **2** Aramaic. **3** argentum (silver).

AR (no period), Arkansas (in postal Zip Code).

a|ra (ä′rä), *n.* = macaw. [< New Latin *ara*]

ar|a-A (ar′ə ā′), *n.* a drug used to control viral infections. It is made from a sugar derived from gum arabic and a substance present in nucleic acid. Ara-A is effective against encephalitis, hepatitis, and influenza. *Hailed as the most significant advance since the first clinical use of penicillin in 1941, ara-A is derived from a type of sponge found in the Caribbean Sea* (Dianne Rafalik). [< *ara*(binose)-*A*(denine), constituents of the drug]

Ar|ab (ar′əb), *n., adj.* **—*n.*** **1a** a person born or living in Arabia. **b** a member of the native race of Arabia. The Arabs are a Semitic people now widely scattered over southwestern and southern Asia and north, east, and central Africa.
2 = Arabian horse. **3** a homeless little wanderer; child of the streets; street Arab.
—*adj.* of the Arabs; of Arabia: *An Arab maiden brought his food* (Shelley).
[< French *Arabe,* learned borrowing from Latin *Arabs, -abis* < Greek *Áraps, -abos* of Arabia < Arabic *'arabī*]
▶**Arab, Arabian, Arabic** are rarely if ever interchangeable as synonyms in modern use. **Arab** now most commonly applies specifically to the people or to their culture: *the Arab world. Lawrence's Arab forces supported Allenby's English.* **Arabian,** a more historical term, applies to the somewhat vaguely defined territory which is traditionally recognized as the home of these people: *the barren Arabian sands.* **Arabic** applies to the written language of the Arabs, their many spoken dialects, and by extension their literature and other products of their culture: *Arabic poetry.*

Arab., 1 Arabian. **2** Arabic.

ar|a|besque (ar′ə besk′), *n., adj., v.,* **-besqued, -besqu|ing.** **—*n.*** **1** a kind of ornament in which flowers, foliage, fruits, and geometrical figures are represented in a fancifully combined pattern, used especially for the decoration of Arabian Oriental rugs and for walls and ceilings. **2** a ballet pose in which the dancer stands (either erect or bent at the waist) on one leg, extending the other at right angles to it, with the arms held in any of various positions. **3** a fanciful, ornamental musical passage or piece: *... an arabesque of right-hand chords and arpeggios* (Whitney Balliett).
—*adj.* **1** carved or painted in arabesque.
2 *Figurative.* like arabesque; elaborate; fanciful.
—*v.t.* to decorate with or in the style of arabesques. **—*v.i.*** to execute an arabesque in ballet. [< French *arabesque* < Italian *arabesco* < *Arabo* Arab < Latin *Arabs*]

A|ra|bi|an (ə rā′bē ən), *adj., n.* **—*adj.*** of Arabia or the Arabs. **—*n.*** **1** an Arab; person born or living in Arabia. **2** = Arabian horse.
▶See **Arab** for usage note.

Arabian camel, a camel with one hump; dromedary.

Arabian coffee, the common coffee shrub from which arabica coffee is made.

Arabian horse, a swift, graceful horse belonging to a breed of horses originally developed by the Arabs for use in the deserts of Arabia, now used as saddle horses.

Arabian Nights, The, a collection of old tales from Arabia, Persia, and India, dating from the 900's A.D. It contains tales of Ali Baba, Aladdin, and many others and is also known as *The Arabian Nights' Entertainments,* and *A Thousand and One Nights.*

ar|a|bic (ar′ə bik), *adj.* derived from various acacias of Arabia and other Eastern countries, such as gum arabic.

Ar|a|bic (ar′ə bik), *n., adj.* **—*n.*** **1** the language of the Arabs; any one of several Semitic languages related to Hebrew. Arabic is now spoken chiefly in Arabia, Iraq, Syria, Lebanon, Jordan, Egypt, and North Africa. **2** the classical literary language of the Koran.
—*adj.* **1** of the Arabs or their language. **2** belonging to Arabia. **3** coming from the Arabs: *Arabic architecture.*
[< Latin *Arabicus* < *Arabs* Arab]
▶See **Arab** for usage note.

a|rab|i|ca (ə rab′ə kə), *n.* **1** coffee made from the seeds of the common coffee shrub. **2** the seeds from which it is made. [< New Latin (*Coffea*) *arabica,* the coffee shrub]

A|rab|i|cize (ə rab′ə sīz), *v.t.,* **-cized, -ciz|ing.** **1** to make like Arabic; conform to Arabic usage: *Urdu is the Arabicized form of Hindustani.* **2** to render Arabic in culture; Arabize: *Most of the Berbers have been Arabicized, but some 35 percent continue to speak Berber dialects* (Benjamin Rivlin).

Arabic numerals or **figures,** the figures 1, 2, 3, 4, 5, 6, 7, 8, 9, 0. They are called Arabic because they were first made known to Europeans by Arab scholars, but most probably they were derived from India.

ar|a|bil|i|ty (ar′ə bil′ə tē), *n.* the quality or condition of being arable; capability of being used as arable land.

ar|a|bin (ar′ə bin), *n.* an amorphous powder, the principal constituent of gum arabic and certain other plant gums. *Formula:* $C_{10}H_{18}O_9$

a|rab|i|nose (ə rab′ə nōs, ar′ə bə-), *n.* a pentose sugar prepared by the action of sulfuric acid on gum arabic and certain other plant gums. *Formula:* $C_5H_{10}O_5$

ar|a|bis (ar′ə bis), *n.* any plant of a group belonging to the mustard family, including the sicklepod, found chiefly in rocky terrain: *Milk-white arabis haunted by the drowsy booming bees* (Rhoda Broughton). [< New Latin *Arabis* the genus name < Greek *Arabis* Arabian]

Ar|ab|ism (ar′ə biz əm), *n.* **1** the realm of Arab power or influence; Arab nations, collectively. **2** attachment to Arabic culture. **3** advancement of Arab interests and aspirations.

Ar|ab|ist (ar′ə bist), *n.* **1** a person who studies Arabic language, literature, or history. **2** a supporter of Arab interests and aspirations.

Ar|ab|i|za|tion (ar′ə bə zā′shən), *n.* **1** the act or process of bringing under Arab control or rendering Arabic in culture. **2** the condition of being Arabized.

Ar|ab|ize (ar′ə bīz), *v.t.,* **-ized, -iz|ing.** to bring under Arab control or render Arabic in culture. **—Ar′ab|i|za′tion,** *n.*

ar|a|ble (ar′ə bəl), *adj., n.* **—*adj.*** fit for plowing; suitable for producing crops which require plowing and tillage: *There is not much arable land on the side of a rocky mountain.*
—*n.* arable land, now especially such land actually in use.
[< Latin *arābilis* < *arāre* to plow]

Arab League, an organization of Arab nations created in 1945 to promote closer relations among its members.

Ar|a|by (ar′ə bē), *n. Poetic.* Arabia.

ar|a|ca|ri (är′ə sär′ē), *n.* a toucan with a body about 13 inches in length, found in South America from Colombia through Brazil. [< Portuguese *araçari* < Tupi]

a|ra|ceous (ə rā′shəs), *adj.* belonging to the arum family; aroid; aroideous. [< New Latin *Araceae* the arum family (< Latin *arum* arum)]

a|rach|ic acid (ə rak′ik), a fatty acid found in peanut oil, peanut butter, etc. *Formula:* $C_{20}H_{40}O_2$ [< *arach*(is) *-ic*]

ar|a|chi|don|ic acid (ar′ə kə don′ik), an unsaturated acid obtained from lecithin. *Formula:* $C_{20}H_{32}O_2$ [< New Latin *Arachis, -idis* the peanut genus *-onic,* a chemical suffix meaning "acid"]

ar|a|chin (ar′ə kin), *n.* a glyceryl ester of arachic acid. [< *arach*(ic) *-in*]

ar|a|chine (ar′ə kēn), *n.* = arachin.

ar|a|chis (ar′ə kis), *n.* any of various plants, comprising a genus of the pea family, whose pods ripen underground, especially the peanut. [< New Latin *Arachis* < Greek *árakos* a leguminous weed]

arachis oil, = peanut oil.

A|rach|ne (ə rak′nē), *n. Greek Mythology.* a Lydian maiden who dared to challenge Athena to a contest in weaving and was changed by her into a spider. [< Latin *Arachnē* < Greek *Aráchnē* (literally) spider]

a|rach|nid (ə rak′nid), *n., adj.* **—*n.*** a small animal of a large group (arthropods) that includes the

spiders, scorpions, mites, ticks, and daddy-longlegs. An arachnid is closely allied to the insects and crustaceans, but breathes air by means of tracheal tubes or pulmonary sacs and has four pairs of walking legs, no antennae, and no wings. The body is usually divided into only two regions.
—adj. = arachnidan.
[< New Latin *Arachnidae* < Greek *aráchnē* spider, web]

a|rach|ni|dan (ə rak′nə dən), *adj., n.* *—adj.* of or having to do with the arachnids.
—n. = arachnid.

a|rach|nid|i|an (ə rak′nid′ē ən), *adj., n.* = arachnidan.

a|rach|nid|ism (ə rak′nə diz əm), *n.* the diseased condition caused by the bite of a poisonous spider or other arachnid.

a|rach|noid (ə rak′noid), *adj., n.* *—adj.* **1** of or resembling an arachnid. **2** of or designating the delicate serous membrane enveloping the brain and spinal cord, lying between the dura mater and pia mater. **3** like a cobweb. **4** *Botany.* covered with or formed of long, delicate, cobweblike hairs or fibers.
—n. **1** = arachnid. **2** the arachnoid membrane.
[< New Latin *arachnoides* < Greek *arachnoeidēs* cobweblike < *aráchnē* spider, web]

ar|ach|nol|o|gist (ar′ak nol′ə jist), *n.* a person who studies arachnology.

ar|ach|nol|o|gy (ar′ak nol′ə jē), *n.* the branch of zoology that deals with the arachnids. [< Greek *aráchnē* spider + English *-logy*]

Ar|a|go|nese (ar′ə gə nēz′, -nēs′), *adj., n., pl.* **-nese.** *—adj.* of Aragon, a region and former kingdom in northeastern Spain, its people, or their language.
—n. **1** a native or inhabitant of Aragon. **2** the dialect of Spanish spoken in Aragon.

a|rag|o|nite (ə rag′ə nīt, ar′ə gə-), *n.* a mineral, one of the two crystalline forms of calcium carbonate, the other being calcite. Aragonite crystallizes in orthorhombic prisms. [< French *aragonite* < *Aragon,* Spain, where it was found]

ar|a|hat (ur′ə hət), *n.* = arhat.

a|raise (ə rāz′), *v.t.,* **a|raised, a|rais|ing.** *Obsolete.* to raise.

a|rak (ar′ək), *n.* = arrack.

Ar|a|len (är′ə len), *n. Trademark.* chloroquine.

a|ra|li|a (ə rā′lē ə), *n.* = araliad.

a|ra|li|a|ceous (ə rā′lē ā′shəs), *adj.* belonging to the ginseng family, as English ivy. [< New Latin *Aralia* the genus name + English *-aceous*]

a|ra|li|ad (ə rā′lē ad), *n.* an araliaceous plant.

Aram., Aramaic.

Ar|a|mae|an or **Ar|a|me|an** (ar′ə mē′ən), *n., adj.*
—n. **1** a Semite of ancient Syria or Mesopotamia. **2** = Aramaic.
—adj. of Aram (ancient Syria) or its people.
[< Latin *Aramaeus* (< Greek *Aramaîos* of Aram < Hebrew *'ărām* Aram) + English *-an*]

Ar|a|ma|ic (ar′ə mā′ik), *n., adj.* *—n.* a Semitic language or group of dialects in which much Jewish and early Christian literature was written. Aramaic includes Syriac and the language spoken in Palestine at the time of Christ. *One form of Aramaic is of present-day importance as the language of much Rabbinical Jewish literature, while Syriac is a liturgical language in some Eastern churches and the language of much early Christian literature* (H. A. Gleason, Jr.).
—adj. of or in Aramaic.
[< Greek *Aramaîos* Aramaean; patterned on *Hebraic*]

a|ra|ne|id (ə rā′nē id), *n.* a spider. [< New Latin *Araneida* < Latin *arānea* spider]

ar|a|ne|i|dan (ar′ə nē′ə dən), *adj., n.* *—adj.* of or belonging to the order of spiders.
—n. a spider.

ar|a|ne|i|form (ar′ə nē′ə fôrm), *adj.* spiderlike. [< Latin *arānea* spider + English *-form*]

a|ra|ne|ol|o|gy (ə rā′nē ol′ə jē), *n.* the part of zoology that treats of spiders. [< Latin *arānea* spider + English *-logy*]

a|ra|ne|ose (ə rā′nē ōs), *adj.* cobweblike; arachnoid. [< Latin *arānea* spider + English *-ose*[1]]

a|ra|ne|ous (ə rā′nē əs), *adj.* = araneose.

A|rap|a|ho (ə rap′ə hō), *n., pl.* **-ho** or **-hos.** **1** a member of a tribe of North American Indians, originally nomadic, that lived in Colorado and are now settled on reservations in Wyoming and Oklahoma. The Arapaho are Algonkians. **2** the language of this tribe. [American English, perhaps < Pawnee *larapihu* trader]

A|rap|a|hoe (ə rap′ə hō), *n., pl.* **-hoe** or **-hoes.** = Arapaho.

ar|a|pai|ma (ar′ə pī′mə), *n.* a large, edible, freshwater South American fish, sometimes growing to a length of 15 feet. [< Portuguese *arapaima,* perhaps < the Tupi name]

a|ra|ro|ba (ä′rə rō′bə), *n.* **1** a bitter powder used in medicines for skin diseases; Goa powder. **2** the Brazilian tree from which this powder is obtained, having a distinctive pattern of stripes in its wood. [< Portuguese *araroba* < the Tupi name]

a|ras|tra (ə ras′trə), *n.* = arrastra.

A|rau|can (ə rô′kən), *n.* the language of the Araucanians.

Ar|au|ca|na (ar′ô kä′nə), *n.* a type of chicken in South America that produces blue-shelled eggs. [< American Spanish *Araucana* < *Arauco,* a province of Chile + *-ana* (feminine) -an]

Ar|au|ca|ni|an (ar′ô kā′nē ən), *n., adj.* *—n.* **1** a member of a group of South American Indian tribes in Chile and Argentina, whose native dialects make up an independent language family. **2** this language family.
—adj. of or designating the Araucanians or Araucanian.

ar|au|car|i|a (ar′ô kãr′ē ə), *n.* any tree of a genus related to the pine family and native to South America, Australia, and Polynesia, such as the monkey puzzle. One species, the Norfolk Island pine, is grown in dwarf form as a house plant. [< New Latin *Araucaria* < *Arauco,* a province in Chile]

ar|au|car|i|an (ar′ô kãr′ē ən), *adj., n.* *—adj.* of or belonging to an araucaria or to the genus.
—n. a species of this or a closely related genus.

à ra|vir (à rà vēr′), *French.* with charm; ravishingly: . . . *who sing and mime and play the fool à ravir* (Punch).

A|ra|wak (ä′rä wäk), *n.* **1** a member of a South American Indian tribe now living mostly in Brazil. The Arawaks belong to the Arawakan language family. They tend to shortness of stature and lack the fiercely warlike tradition of the Caribs and some other tribes of the same general area, supporting themselves chiefly by agriculture. **2** the language or language family of this tribe.

A|ra|wa|kan (ä′rä wä′kən), *adj., n.* *—adj.* **1** of or denoting the most extensive known family of American Indian languages, now chiefly found in northern South America, but formerly spoken also throughout the West Indies and in a small part of southern Florida. **2** of or having to do with the Arawaks.
—n. **1** an Arawak. **2** the Arawakan language family.

arb (ärb), *n. U.S. Informal.* an arbitrager: *The arbs sometimes play a role in a defensive restructuring when the company wants to get its share price up* (Economist).

ar|ba|lest or **ar|ba|list** (är′bə list), *n.* a powerful medieval crossbow with a steel bow, bent by a special attachment and shooting arrows, balls, or stones. Also, **arblast.** [< Old French *arbaleste* < Late Latin *arcuballista* < Latin *arcus* bow + *ballista* military engine for throwing stones, ultimately < Greek *bállein* to throw]

ar|ba|lest|er (är′bə les′tər), *n.* a soldier armed with an arbalest; crossbowman.

ar|bi|ter (är′bə tər), *n.* **1** a person with full power to judge or decide: *Dress designers are arbiters of ladies' fashion.* **2** a person chosen to decide or settle a dispute; arbitrator. **SYN:** umpire, judge. [< Latin *arbiter* (originally) one who approaches (two disputants) < *ad-* up to + *baetere* go]

ar|bi|ter e|le|gan|ti|a|rum (är′bə tər el′ə gan′shē-ãr′əm), *Latin.* arbiter of elegances; authority on good taste. According to Tacitus, this was the honorary post of the writer Gaius Petronius at the court of Nero. *The Museum's most effective intervention as an arbiter elegantiarum has been in architecture and in home furnishings* (New Yorker).

ar|bi|tra|ble (är′bə trə bəl), *adj.* that can be decided by arbitration; subject to arbitration: *Among arbitrable issues is the question of whether sailors who quit work voluntarily should receive payments* (Wall Street Journal).

ar|bi|trage (är′bə trij; *also, for def.* 1, är′bə-träzh′), *n., v.,* **-traged, -trag|ing.** *—n.* **1a** the calculation of the prices of a given stock, bond, or the like, in different places at the same time with allowance for exchange rates. **b** the buying and selling of stocks, bonds, or the like, at the same time in different markets, taking advantage of differences of price between markets. **2** *Archaic.* arbitration.
—v.i. to engage in arbitrage.
[< Old French *arbitrage* < *arbitrer* arbitrate < Latin *arbitrārī* < *arbiter* arbiter]

ar|bi|trag|er (är′bə trə jər), *n.* a banker or a broker in arbitrage operations.

ar|bi|tra|geur (är′bə trə zhər), *n.* = arbitrager. [< French *arbitrageur* < *arbitrage*]

ar|bi|tral (är′bə trəl), *adj.* of arbiters or arbitration: *an arbitral body, an arbitral decision.* [< Late Latin *arbitrālis* < Latin *arbiter* arbiter]

ar|bit|ra|ment (är bit′rə mənt), *n.* **1** the decision or award made by an arbiter or arbitrator. **2** the power or right to judge and decide; power of absolute and final decision. **3** the act of deciding a dispute as an arbiter or arbitrator. [< Old French *arbitrement,* learned borrowing from Medieval Latin *arbitramentum* < Latin *arbitrārī* arbitrate < *arbiter* arbiter]

ar|bi|trar|y (är′bə trer′ē), *adj., n., pl.* **-trar|ies.** *—adj.* **1** based on one's own wishes, notions, or will; not going by any rule or law: *A good judge tries to be fair and does not make arbitrary decisions or rules.* **2** capricious; uncertain: *an arbitrary character.* **SYN:** unreasonable, changeful. **3** using or abusing unlimited power; tyrannical: *an arbitrary king.* **SYN:** despotic. **4** fixed or determined by chance; not regulated by fixed rule or law; that can be determined as the occasion arises: *an arbitrary name, an arbitrary serial number.* **SYN:** discretionary.
—n. a charge added to a regular rate or wage, for special or extra service: *Firemen were subject . . . to the collective agreement in regard to manning of diesel locomotives* [*and*] *payment of arbitraries* (Economist).
[< Latin *arbitrārius* < *arbiter* arbiter] **—ar′bi|trar′i|ly,** *adv.* **—ar′bi|trar′i|ness,** *n.*

ar|bi|trate (är′bə trāt), *v.,* **-trat|ed, -trat|ing.** *—v.i.* **1** to give a decision in a dispute; act as arbitrator; mediate: *The teacher arbitrated between the two boys in their quarrel. The governor offered to arbitrate between the city and the county in their dispute.* **SYN:** judge. **2** to submit a matter to arbitration.
—v.t. **1** to submit to arbitration; settle by arbitration: *The two nations finally agreed to arbitrate their dispute, and war was avoided.* **2** to give an expert or official decision in regard to; decide or determine. **SYN:** adjudicate. [< Latin *arbitrārī* (with English *-ate*[1]) < *arbiter* arbiter]

ar|bi|tra|tion (är′bə trā′shən), *n.* the settlement of a dispute by the decision of somebody chosen to be the judge, umpire, or arbiter: *to submit the points in a dispute to arbitration. The strike was settled by arbitration. Arbitration differs from mediation in that a definite decision on the issue is handed down by the individuals who serve as arbitrators, and the decision is regarded as binding on the contestants* (Ogburn and Nimkoff).

ar|bi|tra|tion|al (är′bə trā′shə nəl), *adj.* **1** of or involving arbitration. **2** resulting from arbitration.

ar|bi|tra|tive (är′bə trā′tiv), *adj.* having power to arbitrate; done by arbitration.

ar|bi|tra|tor (är′bə trā′tər), *n.* **1** a person chosen to decide or settle a dispute: *A mediator seeks to bring the two sides in a labor dispute together. An arbitrator hears evidence and makes specific recommendations for settlement* (Wall Street Journal). **SYN:** umpire, judge. **2** a person with full power to judge or decide; arbiter. **—ar′bi|tra′tor|ship,** *n.*

ar|bi|tress (är′bə tris), *n.* a woman arbiter or arbitrator.

ar|bo|lo|co (är′bə lō′kō), *n.* a South and Central American composite tree, whose hard wood is used for billiard cues. [< Spanish *árbol* tree]

ar|bor[1] (är′bər), *n.* **1a** a shady place formed by trees or shrubs or often by vines growing on latticework. **b** the latticework itself. **2** *Obsolete.* **a** a plot of ground covered with grass or turf. **b** a flower garden. **c** an orchard. Also, *British,* **arbour.** [< Anglo-French *erber* < Late Latin *herbārium* < Latin *herba* herb, grass; spelling influenced by *arbor*[3]. See etym. of doublet **herbarium.**]

ar|bor[2] (är′bər), *n.* **1** the main shaft or axle of a machine which transmits mechanical force to other moving parts. **2** the axle or spindle on which a wheel revolves, especially in clocks and watches. **3** in the machining of metal and other materials: **a** a shaft that holds the cutting tool or tools. **b** a shaft or bar (mandrel) forced into an object to support it while it is turned. **4** a cork cylinder used to build up a bait-casting reel so that the spool will be half filled with an older line. [< French *arbre,* originally, tree < Latin *arbor, -oris* tree; spelling influenced by Latin *arbor*]

ar|bor[3] (är′bər), *n., pl.* **ar|bo|res.** a tree (used chiefly as part of various names in botany). [< Latin *arbor*]

ar|bo|ra|ceous (är′bə rā′shəs), *adj.* treelike; arboreal. [< *arbor*[3] + *-aceous*]

Arbor Day, a day observed by planting trees in many states of the United States and provinces of Canada, in New Zealand, and in parts of Australia. The date varies in different places.

ar|bo|re|al (är bôr′ē əl, -bōr′-), *adj.* **1** living in or among trees. A squirrel is an arboreal animal. **2** of or like trees. **—ar|bo′re|al|ly,** *adv.*

ar|bored (är′bərd), *adj.* **1** placed in or as if in an arbor; arched over; embowered. **2** furnished with an arbor or arbors. Also, *British,* **arboured.**

ar|bo|re|ous (är bôr′ē əs, -bōr′-), *adj.* **1** abounding in trees; wooded. **2** = arboreal. **3** = arborescent. [< Latin *arboreus* (with English *-ous*) < *arbor* tree]

ar|bo|res (är′bə rēz), *n.* plural of **arbor**[3].

Pronunciation Key: hat, āge, cãre, fär; let, ēqual, tėrm; it, īce; hot, ōpen, ôrder; oil, out; cup, pu̇t, rüle; child; long; thin; ᴛʜen; zh, measure; ə represents **a** in about, **e** in taken, **i** in pencil, **o** in lemon, **u** in circus.

ar|bo|resce (är′bə res′), *v.i.*, **-resced, -res|cing.** to take the form of a tree. [< Latin *arborēscere* < *arbor* tree]

ar|bo|res|cence (är′bə res′əns), *n.* the state of being arborescent.

ar|bo|res|cent (är′bə res′ənt), *adj.* like a tree in structure, growth, or appearance; branching. **—ar′bo|res′cent|ly,** *adv.*

ar|bo|re|tum (är′bə rē′təm), *n., pl.* **-tums, -ta** (-tə). a place where trees and shrubs, especially rare ones, are grown and exhibited for scientific, educational, and other purposes. [< Latin *arborētum* < *arbor* tree]

ar|bor|i|cole (är bôr′ə kōl, -bor′-), *adj.* inhabiting trees. [< French *arboricole* < Latin *arbor* tree + *colere* inhabit]

ar|bo|ric|o|lous (är′bə rik′ə ləs), *adj.* = arboricole.

ar|bo|ri|cul|tur|al (är′bər ə kul′chər əl), *adj.* of or having to do with arboriculture.

ar|bo|ri|cul|ture (är′bər ə kul′chər), *n.* the cultivation of trees and shrubs for use or ornament.

ar|bo|ri|cul|tur|ist (är′bər ə kul′chər ist), *n.* a person who studies arboriculture.

ar|bo|ri|form (är′bər ə fôrm), *adj.* having the form of a tree.

ar|bo|rist (är′bər ist), *n.* **1** a person who studies or cultivates trees. **2** *Rare.* a herbalist.

ar|bor|i|za|tion (är′bər ə zā′shən), *n.* **1** a growth or an appearance resembling the figure of a tree or plant, as in certain minerals or fossils. **2** the process of growing into this shape or of developing such an appearance.

ar|bo|rize (är′bə rīz), *v.i.*, **-rized, -riz|ing.** to have or produce branching formations: *The airways of the lung ... arborize like a tree* (New Scientist).

ar|bo|rous (är′bə rəs), *adj.* = arboreous.

ar|bor|vi|rus (är′bər vī′rəs), *n.* any one of several groups of small viruses transmitted by mosquitoes, ticks, and other arthropods. Yellow fever, dengue, and equine encephalitis are caused by arborviruses. [< *ar* (thropod)-*bor*(ne) *virus*]

ar|bor vi|tae, or **ar|bor|vi|tae** (är′bər vī′tē), *n.* **1** any one of various evergreen trees, especially the white cedar, a common American species with many horticultural varieties, often planted for ornament and for hedges, and the red cedar or giant arbor vitae of the western United States. **2** a treelike appearance, such as that of the cerebellum, produced by the arrangement of the white and gray nerve tissue. [< Latin *arbor vītae* tree of life]

ar|bour (är′bər), *n. British.* arbor[1].

ar|boured (är′bərd), *adj. British.* arbored.

ar|bus|cle (är′bə səl), *n.* a dwarf tree or a shrub of treelike growth. [< Latin *arbuscula* (diminutive) < *arbor* tree]

ar|bute (är′byüt), *n. Poetic.* the European arbutus. [< Latin *arbutus* strawberry tree]

ar|bu|tus (är byü′təs), *n.* **1** a trailing plant of eastern North America, that has clusters of fragrant, pink or white flowers very early in the spring; mayflower; trailing arbutus. The arbutus belongs to the same family as the heath. It is the state flower of Massachusetts and provincial flower of Nova Scotia. **2** any one of several evergreen shrubs or trees of the heath family, having clusters of large, white or pink flowers and red berries, such as the strawberry tree and the madroña. [< Latin *arbutus* strawberry tree]

arc (ärk), *n., v.,* **arced** (ärkt), **arc|ing** (är′king), or **arcked, arck|ing.** **—*n.*** **1** any part of the circumference of a circle. See picture under **circle.** **2** any part of any curved line. **3** a curved stream of brilliant light or sparks formed as a strong electric current jumps from one conductor to another: *a carbon arc.* **4a** the part of a circle which a heavenly body appears to pass through above the horizon; diurnal arc. **b** the part of the same circle below the horizon; nocturnal arc. **5** a band or belt contained between concentric curves or something having this form: *You see a rainbow as an arc when the sun is behind you and the sky in front of you is filled with moisture* (Walter J. Saucier).
—*v.i.* **1** to form an electric arc. **2** to take or follow a curved path: *Ranger 6 arced on a graceful, curving course toward the moon* (Time).
[< Latin *arcus* bow] **—arc′like′,** *adj.*

ARC (ärk), *n.* AIDS-related complex, a milder form of AIDS, characterized by swollen glands, loss of weight, and weakness: *While no patient has been known to recover from AIDS, there is new evidence ... that some ARC patients do get better* (Time).

ar|cade (är kād′), *n., v.,* **-cad|ed, -cad|ing.** **—*n.*** **1** a passageway with an arched roof. **2** a building having such a passageway. **3** any covered passageway: *Some buildings have arcades with small stores along either side.* SYN: gallery, loggia. **4** a row of arches supported by columns or piers. SYN: colonnade.
—*v.t.* to furnish with, or form into, an arcade.
[< French *arcade* < Italian *arcata* < Medieval Latin < *arca* < Latin *arcus* bow, arch]

Ar|ca|di|a (är kā′dē ə), *n.* any region of simple, quiet contentment (from a region of ancient Greece famous in tradition for the simple, contented life of its pastoral people).

Ar|ca|di|an (är kā′dē ən), *adj., n.* **—*adj.*** **1** of Arcadia. **2** like that of Arcadia; ideally rural; rustic. **3** having to do with simple, quiet contentment.
—*n.* **1** an inhabitant of Arcadia. **2** a person with simple, rural tastes.

ar|ca|di|an|ism (är kā′dē ə niz′əm), *n.* rustic or pastoral simplicity, especially in literature: *A spirit of lyrical pathos, and of poetical arcadianism* (David Masson).

Ar|ca|dy (är′kə dē), *n. Poetic.* Arcadia.

ar|ca|na (är kā′nə), *n.pl.* profound secrets: (*Figurative.*) *The arcana of psychoanalysis have formed the basis for a whole generation's small talk* (Reporter). [plural of *arcanum*]

ar|cane (är kān′), *adj.* understood only by a few; secret: *One part of my mind has always been skeptical about dowsers ... At the same time I have had to admit that their arcane rites actually seem to work* (John Fisher). (*Figurative*). *Unfortunately Intourist, upon whose arcane machinations the visitor to Russia depends, had broken down in this instance* (Manchester Guardian Weekly). SYN: mysterious, obscure, esoteric. [< Latin *arcānus* hidden < *arca* chest, box] **—ar|cane′ly,** *adv.*

ar|ca|num (är kā′nəm), *n., pl.* **-nums, -na** (-nə). **1** a secret; mystery (usually in the plural). **2** one of the great secrets that the alchemists sought to discover. **3** a marvelous remedy; an elixir. [< Latin *arcānum,* neuter of *arcānus* hidden, arcane]

ar|ca|to (är kä′tō), *adj.* (of a tone or passage) played by using the bow instead of plucking or pinching the strings. [< Italian *arcato* bowed]

ar|ca|ture (är′kə chər), *n.* **1** a small arcade. **2** an arcade used as a decoration, not as a passage. [< French *arcature* < Italian *arcatura* < Medieval Latin *arcata* < *arca* < Latin *arcus* bow]

arc-back (ärk′bak′), *n.* a flow of current in the wrong direction in a rectifier, caused by a failure to suppress the reverse half of the alternating current cycle.

ar|cel|la (är sel′ə), *n.* an amebalike protozoan enclosed in a hemispherical shell. [< New Latin *arcella* (diminutive) < Latin *arca* chest, box]

arc furnace, an electric furnace in which heat is produced by means of an electric arc between carbon electrodes, or between acarbon electrode and the furnace charge.

arch[1] (ärch), *n., v.* **—*n.*** **1** a curved structure capable of bearing the weight of the material above it. Arches often form the tops of doors, windows, and gateways. **2** a monument in the form of an arch or arches. **3** = archway. **4** = instep: *Fallen arches cause flat feet.* **5** something like an arch: *the great blue arch of the sky.* SYN: vault.
—*v.t.* **1** to bend into an arch; curve: *The wind arched the trees over the road. He arched his eyebrows in mock surprise.* **2** to furnish with an arch: *The rainbow arches the heavens.* **3** to form an arch over; span: *A bridge arched the stream.*
—*v.i.* to form into an arch or arches; curve: *The sky arches overhead.*
[< Old French *arche* bridge arch < Medieval Latin *arca* < Latin *arcus* bow]

arch[2] (ärch), *adj.* **1** playfully mischievous; saucy or pert; waggish: *The little girl gave her mother an arch look and ran away. Miss Price ... manages to create a girlish and innocent character without seeming in the least bit arch or simpering* (Atlantic). SYN: sly, roguish. **2** chief; principal; leading: *The arch rebel of all was Patrick Henry.* **3** *Archaic.* cunning; crafty: ... *a very arch fellow, a downright hypocrite* (John Bunyan). [< *arch-*]

arch-, *prefix.* **1** chief; principal: *Archbishop = principal bishop. Archenemy = chief enemy.*
2 extreme; ultra-: *Archconservative = extreme conservative.*
3 early; primal; primitive: *Archencephalon = primal encephalon (brain).* Also, **archi-.** [< Latin *archi-* < Greek *arche-, archi-* < *archós* ruler]

arch., **1a** archaic. **b** archaism. **2** architecture.

Arch., **1** archbishop. **2** archipelago. **3** architect.

Ar|chae|an (är kē′ən), *adj., n.* = Archean.

ar|chae|bac|te|ri|a (är′kē bak tir′ē), *n.pl.* microorganisms having a different chemical makeup and being genetically distinct from bacteria and higher living organisms; methanogens. Archaebacteria exist in a warm, oxygen-free environment by ingesting carbon dioxide and hydrogen to produce methane.

archaeo-, *combining form.* ancient; primitive: *Archaeopteryx = an ancient bird. Archaeology = study of ancient (things).* [< Greek *archaîos* ancient < *archḗ* beginning]

ar|chae|o|as|tron|o|my (är′kē ə ə stron′ə mē), *n.* the study of the astronomical beliefs and practices of ancient peoples.

ar|chae|o|cyte (är′kē ə sīt), *n. Zoology.* an undifferentiated, itinerant cell, especially an ameboid cell, which gives rise to reproductive cells, such as in the sponge embryo. Also, **archeocyte.** [< *archaeo-* + Greek *kýtos* hollow, cell]

archaeol., **1** archaeological. **2** archaeology.

ar|chae|o|log|ic (är′kē ə loj′ik), *adj.* = archaeological. Also, **archeologic.**

ar|chae|o|log|i|cal (är′kē ə loj′ə kəl), *adj.* of or having to do with archaeology: *An archaeological expedition uncovered the lost city of Troy.* Also, **archeological.** **—ar′chae|o|log′i|cal|ly,** *adv.*

ar|chae|ol|o|gist (är′kē ol′ə jist), *n.* a person who studies archaeology. Also, **archeologist.**

ar|chae|ol|o|gy (är′kē ol′ə jē), *n.* **1** the scientific study of the people, customs, and life of ancient times. Students of archaeology excavate the remains of ancient cities and classify and study tools, artifacts, pottery, monuments, or any other remains in order to reconstruct a picture of life in the past, especially where there were few or no written records available. **2** the materials or data for such a study of a particular culture, such as artifacts, remains, or other records. **3** *Rare.* ancient history. Also, **archeology.** [< Greek *archaiología* < *archaîos* ancient + *-lógos* treating of]

ar|chae|o|mag|net|ism (är′kē ə mag′nə tiz əm), *n.* the measurement of residual magnetism, used as a method to determine the age of an archaeological specimen by relating the permanent magnetism it acquired at its creation to the amount of magnetism retained at the time of measurement.

ar|chae|op|ter|yx (är′kē op′tər iks), *n.* the oldest known fossil bird, having such reptilian characteristics as teeth and a long, bony tail. The archaeopteryx lived in the more recent part of the European Jurassic. Also, **archeopteryx.** [< *archaeo-* + Greek *ptéryx* bird, wing]

ar|chae|or|nis (är′kē ôr′nis), *n.* a fossil bird of the European Upper Jurassic, related to the archaeopteryx. [< *archaeo-* + Greek *órnīs* bird]

Ar|chae|o|zo|ic (är′kē ə zō′ik), *adj., n.* = Archeozoic.

ar|cha|ic (är kā′ik), *adj.* **1** no longer used in ordinary language. The words "in sooth" and "methinks" have become archaic. **2** old-fashioned; out-of-date: *Grandfather's spats and Grandmother's buttoned shoes are archaic forms of dress today. The railroads contend that the present work rules are archaic* (New York Times). SYN: antiquated. **3** ancient: *Archaic statues were dug up from the ruins of old Greek cities.* [< Greek *archāïkós* < *archaîos* ancient < *archḗ* a beginning] **—ar|cha′i|cal|ly,** *adv.*

▶**Archaic** words or meanings survive in certain special contexts, as that of law, or special styles, as that of the Scriptures, or are used by modern writers to give an old-fashioned flavor to writing.

Ar|cha|ic (är kā′ik), *n., adj. Anthropology.* **—*n.*** the oldest culture or series of cultures of a region. **—*adj.*** of or belonging to such a culture or cultures: *Archaic peoples.*

archaic smile, the mouth with upturned corners in Greek sculpture prior to the 400's B.C.

ar|cha|ism (är′kē iz əm, -kā-), *n.* **1** a word or expression no longer in general use. "In sooth" and "methinks" are archaisms meaning "in truth" and "it seems to me." **2** the use of something characteristic of an earlier period in language, music, or art. **3** anything, such as a law or custom, that is archaic or has survived but is thought of as archaic: *Sociologically as well as scenically, Sicily is an archaism* (New Yorker). [< Greek *archāïsmós* < *archāïzein* to archaize < *archaîos* ancient]

ar|cha|ist (är′kē ist, -kā-), *n.* **1** = antiquary. **2** a person who uses archaisms.

ar|cha|is|tic (är′kē is′tik, -kā-), *adj.* **1** of or having to do with an archaist. **2** imitatively archaic; affectedly antique. **—ar′cha|is′ti|cal|ly,** *adv.*

ar|cha|ize (är′kē īz, -kā-), *v.i., v.t.,* **-ized, -iz|ing.** to cause something to be archaic; give an archaic flavor to. **—ar′cha|iz′er,** *n.*

arch|an|gel (ärk′ān′jəl), *n.* **1** (in the Bible) an angel of high rank; leader among the angels. Michael, Gabriel, and Raphael are archangels. **2** (in the Roman Catholic Church) a member of the second lowest of the nine orders of angels. Archangels rank just above angels; seraphim and cherubim are the highest ranks. **3** = angelica. [< Latin *archangelus* < Greek *archángelos* < *arch-* chief + *ángelos* angel]

arch|an|gel|ic (ärk′an jel′ik), *adj.* of or having to do with archangels; like an archangel.

arch|an|gel|i|cal (ärk′an jel′ə kəl), *adj.* = archangelic. **—arch′an|gel′i|cal|ly,** *adv.*

arch|bish|op (ärch′bish′əp), *n.* a bishop of the highest rank. He presides over a church district called an archbishopric or archdiocese. *Abbr:* Abp. [Old English *aercebiscop* < Late Latin *archiepiscopum,* ultimately < Greek *archi-* chief + *epískopos* bishop]

arch|bish|op|ric (ärch′bish′əp rik), *n.* **1** a church district governed by an archbishop; archdiocese. **2** the position, rank, or dignity of an archbishop.

arch|con|serv|a|tive (ärch′kən sėr′və tiv), *adj., n.* **—*adj.*** ultraconservative; reactionary.

—*n.* an extreme conservative; reactionary.

Archd., **1** archdeacon. **2** archduke.

***arch dam**, a dam in the form of an arch which is held up by horizontal thrust from the sides of a valley or gorge.

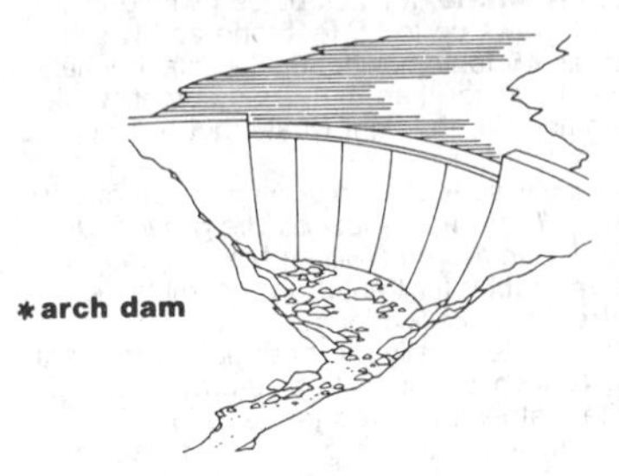

***arch dam**

arch|dea|con (ärch′dē′kən), *n.* **1** an assistant to a bishop in the Church of England. He superintends the work of other members of the clergy. **2** a member of a cathedral chapter in the Roman Catholic Church, formerly possessing great temporal and ecclesiastical powers. [Old English *arcediacon* < Late Latin *archidiāconus*, ultimately < Greek *archi-* chief + *diākonos* deacon]

arch|dea|con|ate (ärch′dē′kə nit), *n.* the office of an archdeacon.

arch|dea|con|ry (ärch′dē′kən rē), *n., pl.* **-ries.** **1** the district under the supervision of an archdeacon. **2** the position or rank of an archdeacon. **3** the residence of an archdeacon.

arch|dea|con|ship (ärch′dē′kən ship), *n.* = archdeaconry (defs. 1 and 2).

arch|di|oc|e|san (ärch′dī os′ə sən), *adj.* of or having to do with an archdiocese.

arch|di|o|cese (ärch′dī′ə sis, -sēs), *n.* the church district governed by an archbishop.

arch|du|cal (ärch′dü′kəl, -dyü′-), *adj.* **1** of an archduke. **2** of an archduchy.

arch|duch|ess (ärch′duch′is), *n.* **1** the wife or widow of an archduke. **2** a princess of the former ruling house of Austria-Hungary.

arch|duch|y (ärch′duch′ē), *n., pl.* **-duch|ies.** the territory under the rule of an archduke or archduchess.

arch|duke (ärch′dük′, -dyük′), *n.* **1** a prince of the former ruling house of Austria-Hungary. **2** the title of the former rulers of various duchies, such as Lorraine and Brabant.

Ar|che|an (är kē′ən), *adj., n.* Pre-Cambrian, especially lower, or older, Pre-Cambrian. Also, **Archaean.** [< *archaeo-* + *-an*]

ar|che|bi|o|sis (är′kə bī ō′səs), *n.* spontaneous generation; abiogenesis: *I should like to live to see archebiosis proved true* (Charles Darwin). [< Greek *arche-* primal + *bíōsis* way of life]

arched (ärcht), *adj.* having an arch or arches.

ar|che|gone (är′kə gōn), *n.* = archegonium.

ar|che|go|ni|al (är′kə gō′nē əl), *adj.* of or having to do with an archegonium.

ar|che|go|ni|ate (är′kə gō′nē it, -āt), *adj.* having archegonia.

ar|che|go|ni|o|phore (är′kə gō′nē ə fôr, -fōr), *n.* an outgrowth of the prothallium which bears archegonia. [< *archegonium* + *-phore*]

ar|che|go|ni|um (är′kə gō′nē əm), *n., pl.* **-ni|a** (-nē ə). the female reproductive organ of plants such as mosses and ferns. The archegonium is a multicellular, flask-shaped organ, containing a single egg and corresponding to the pistil of flowering plants. [< New Latin *archegonium* (diminutive) < Greek *archégonos* founder < *archē* beginning + a root *gen-* to bear]

ar|che|go|sau|rid (är′kə gə sôr′id), *adj., n.* —*adj.* of or belonging to a genus of extinct, lizardlike amphibians of the Permian period. They had well-developed limbs, a fold of enamel and dentine in their teeth, and a length of four or five feet. —*n.* an archegosaurid animal. [< Greek *archēgós* beginning + *saûros* lizard]

Ar|che|lon (är′kə lon), *n.* an extinct marine turtle of the Cretaceous reaching a dozen feet in length. [< New Latin *Archelon* < Greek *arche-* primal + *chelṓnē* tortoise]

arch|en|ceph|a|lon (ärk′en sef′ə lon), *n.* the older or primitive parts of the brain: *The activities of the archencephalon dominate the actions of animals, but the cerebrum in man [now] controls the archencephalon* (Foster Kennedy). [< *arch-* + *encephalon*]

arch|en|e|my (ärch′en′ə mē), *n., pl.* **-mies.** **1** a principal opponent; chief adversary. **2** Often, **Archenemy.** the Devil as the enemy of God and man; Satan.

ar|chen|ter|ic (är′kən ter′ik), *adj.* having to do with the archenteron.

ar|chen|ter|on (är ken′tə ron), *n. Embryology.* the primitive intestinal or alimentary cavity of a gastrula. See picture under **embryo.** [< *arch-* + *enteron*]

ar|che|o|cyte (är′kē ə sīt), *n.* = archaeocyte.

archeol., **1** archeological. **2** archeology.

ar|che|o|log|ic (är′kē ə loj′ik), *adj.* = archaeologic.

ar|che|o|log|i|cal (är′kē ə loj′ə kəl), *adj.* = archaeological. —**ar′che|o|log′i|cal|ly**, *adv.*

ar|che|ol|o|gist (är′kē ol′ə jist), *n.* = archaeologist.

ar|che|ol|o|gy (är′kē ol′ə jē), *n.* = archaeology.

ar|che|op|ter|yx (är′kē op′tər iks), *n.* = archaeopteryx.

Ar|che|o|zo|ic (är′kē ə zō′ik), *n., adj.* —*n.* **1** the geological era before the Proterozoic, when the most primitive life appeared. **2** the rocks formed in this era. —*adj.* of this era or its rocks. [< *archeo-* + Greek *zōē* life]

arch|er (är′chər), *n.* a person who shoots with bow and arrows; bowman. [< Anglo-French *archer*, Old French *archier* < Late Latin *arcārius*, ultimately < Latin *arcus* bow]

Arch|er (är′chər), *n.* a constellation and the ninth sign of the zodiac; Sagittarius.

ar|cher|fish (är′chər fish′), *n., pl.* **-fish|es** or (*collectively*) **-fish.** a small East Indian fish that captures insects as much as three or four feet above the water by shooting water on them, thus causing them to fall.

arch|er|y (är′chər ē), *n.* **1** the practice, sport, or art of shooting with a bow and arrow. **2** archers: *The archery advanced, shooting steadily.* **3** the weapons of an archer; bows and arrows.

ar|che|spore (är′kə spôr, -spōr), *n. Botany.* the cell or group of cells which gives rise to the cells from which spores are developed. [< New Latin *archesporium* < Greek *arche-* primal + *sporá* seed]

ar|che|spo|ri|al (är′kə spôr′ē əl, -spōr′-), *adj.* having to do with or of the nature of an archespore.

ar|che|spo|ri|um (är′kə spôr′ē əm, -spōr′-), *n.* = archespore.

ar|che|typ|al (är′kə tī′pəl), *adj.* of or of the nature of, or constituting an archetype; original: *The book has vitality and charm such as is rarely encountered in so archetypal a specimen of the British countryside mystery* (New York Times). —**ar′che|typ′al|ly**, *adv.*

ar|che|type (är′kə tīp), *n.* the original model or pattern from which copies are made, or out of which later forms develop; prototype: *That little engine is the archetype of huge modern locomotives.* SYN: exemplar. [< Latin *archetypum* < Greek *archétypon*, neuter of *archétypos* original < *arche-* primal + *týpos* stamp]

ar|che|typ|ic (är′kə tip′ik), *adj.* = archetypal.

ar|che|typ|i|cal (är′kə tip′ə kəl), *adj.* = archetypal. —**ar′che|typ′i|cal|ly**, *adv.*

arch|fiend (ärch′fēnd′), *n.* **1** a chief fiend: *There has not yet been devised a way to bring to his knees the archfiend Time* (New Yorker). **2** Also, **Arch Fiend.** the Devil as the chief of the infernal host; Satan.

arch|foe (ärch′fō′), *n.* = archenemy.

arch-grav|i|ty dam (ärch′grav′ə tē), a dam that resists the thrust of the water by using the thrust of the sides of the valley, as in an arch dam, and the thrust of its own weight, as in a gravity dam.

archi-, *prefix.* a form of **arch-,** found mainly in modern loans from Greek or Latin or in words patterned on them, as in *archipallium, archiplasm.*

ar|chi|ben|thal (är′kə ben′thəl), *adj.* belonging to or living in the archibenthos: *The archibenthal species have a greater range than those restricted to . . . the shallow waters of the coast* (Science).

ar|chi|ben|thos (är′kə ben′thos), *n.* the depths of the primitive or Paleozoic ocean. [< Greek *archi-* primal + *bénthos* depth (of the sea)]

ar|chi|blast (är′kə blast), *n.* **1** the formative yolk in an ovum, constituting the germ. **2** = ectoderm. [< *archi-* + Greek *blastós* sprout]

ar|chi|carp (är′kə kärp), *n.* the initial stage of the fruiting body in some ascomycetous fungi. [< *archi-* + Greek *karpós* fruit]

ar|chi|di|ac|o|nal (är′kə dī ak′ə nəl), *adj.* of or having to do with an archdeacon or his office.

ar|chi|di|ac|o|nate (är′kə dī ak′ə nit, -nāt), *n.* = archdeaconate.

ar|chie (är′chē), *n. British Slang.* **1** an ant. **2** *Obsolete.* antiaircraft fire.

Archie Bunker, *Especially U.S.* a bigoted, self-righteous person, especially of the working class: *A self-employed iron worker with a self-described "Archie Bunker" perception of the world . . .* (Ronald Sullivan). [< name of the central character in a television comedy series]

ar|chi|e|pis|co|pa|cy (är′kē ə pis′kə pə sē), *n.* the state or dignity of an archbishop.

ar|chi|e|pis|co|pal (är′kē ə pis′kə pəl), *adj.* of or having to do with an archbishop or an archbishopric: *archiepiscopal authority.* [< Medieval Latin *archiepiscopalis* < Late Latin *archiepiscopus* archbishop] —**ar′chi|e|pis′co|pal|ly**, *adv.*

archiepiscopal cross, the badge or emblem of an archbishop (a Latin cross with the horizontal member doubled and the upper one shorter than the lower one); patriarchal cross.

ar|chi|e|pis|co|pate (är′kē ə pis′kə pit, -pāt), *n.* = archbishopric.

ar|chil (är′kil, -chil), *n.* = orchil. [< Old French *orcheil* < Italian *oricello*; origin uncertain]

ar|chi|mage (är′kə māj), *n.* a chief magician or enchanter; a great wizard. [< Greek *archi-* primal + *mágos* magus]

ar|chi|ma|gus (är′kə mā′gəs), *n., pl.* **-gi** (-jī). *Latin.* archimage.

ar|chi|man|drite (är′kə man′drīt), *n.* in the Greek Church: **1** an abbot of one of the larger monasteries, or sometimes one who supervises several monasteries. **2** a title given to nonmonastic priests of high dignity. [< Late Latin *archimandrīta* < Late Greek *archimandrítēs* < *archi-* chief of + *mándrā* monastery]

Ar|chi|me|de|an (är′kə mē′dē ən, -mə dē′-), *adj.* **1** of or having to do with Archimedes. **2** invented by or attributed to Archimedes: *the Archimedean principle that a body partly or wholly immersed in fluid loses in weight* (New Yorker).

***Archimedean screw**, a device for raising water, attributed to Archimedes. It is made by winding a large screw or a flexible tube in a spiral within an inclined cylinder. Its revolutions cause water to move upward through the spiral chambers.

***Archimedean screw**

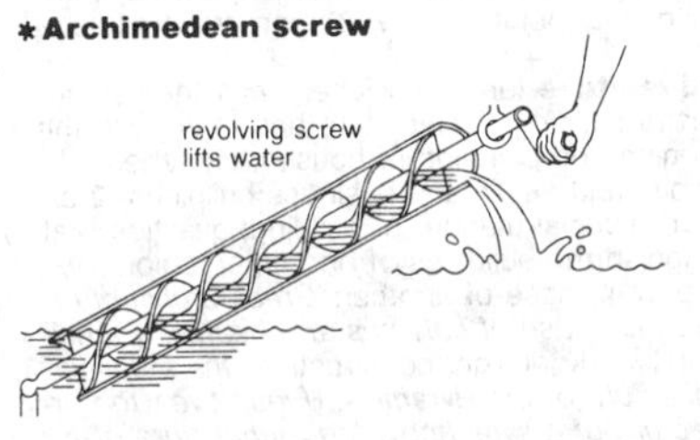

Ar|chi|me|des' principle, (är′kə mē′dēz), the law of physics that an object placed in a fluid loses an amount of weight equal to the weight of the fluid it displaces.

Archimedes' screw, = Archimedean screw.

ar|chine (är shēn′), *n.* = arshin.

arch|ing (är′ching), *n.* **1** a group or line of arches. **2** any arched part.

ar|chi|pal|li|al (är′kə pal′ē əl), *adj.* of or having to do with the archipallium.

ar|chi|pal|li|um (är′kə pal′ē əm), *n.* the part of the pallium responsible for the sense of smell, regarded as the oldest part of the cerebral cortex: *In mammals the archipallium is largest in keen-smelling forms or in primitive ones like the marsupials; it is altogether lost in the dolphins, who roam the seas without smelling* (Alfred L. Kroeber).

ar|chi|pe|lag|ic (är′kə pə laj′ik), *adj.* **1** of or having to do with an archipelago. **2** resembling an archipelago.

ar|chi|pel|a|go (är′kə pel′ə gō), *n., pl.* **-gos** or **-goes.** **1** a group of many islands: *the Japanese archipelago.* The islands between southeast Asia and Australia form the Malay Archipelago. See picture under **peninsula.** **2** a sea having many islands in it. [< Italian *arcipelago* < *arci-* chief, archi- + *pelago* sea, ultimately < Greek *pélagos* (originally) the Aegean]

ar|chi|plasm (är′kə plaz′əm), *n.* **1** the granular protoplasmic substance comprising the asters and spindles of a cell during mitosis. It is a permanent cell constituent. **2** undifferentiated protoplasm. Also, **archoplasm.** [< *archi-* + Greek *plásma* something formed]

ar|chi|plas|mic (är′kə plaz′mik), *adj.* of or of the nature of archiplasm. Also, **archoplasmic.**

archit., architecture.

ar|chi|tect (är′kə tekt), *n., v.* —*n.* **1** a person who designs and lays out plans for buildings, and then sees that these plans are followed by the contractors and workers who actually put up the buildings; a person skilled in architecture. *Abbr:* arch. **2** *Figurative.* a maker; creator: *The student council was the architect of our honor system. Every man is the architect of his own fortune.* SYN: builder, planner, designer.
—*v.t.* to design; construct: *The bathing suit . . . is so cleverly architected within as to be all but surf-proof* (Time).
[< Latin *architectus* < Greek *architéktōn* < *archi-*

Pronunciation Key: hat, āge, cãre, fär; let, ēqual, tėrm; it, īce; hot, ōpen, ôrder; oil, out; cup, pu̇t, rüle; child; long; thin; ᴛʜen; zh, measure; ə represents **a** in about, **e** in taken, **i** in pencil, **o** in lemon, **u** in circus.

chief + *téktōn* builder]

ar|chi|tec|ton|ic (är′kə tek ton′ik), *adj., n.* —*adj.* **1** having to do with architecture, construction, or design, especially as a science. **2** showing skill in construction or design. **3** directive; controlling. **4** having to do with the systematic arrangement of knowledge.
—*n.* = architectonics. [< Latin *architectonicus* < Greek *architektonikós* < *architéktōn* architect] —**ar′chi|tec|ton′i|cal|ly**, *adv.*

ar|chi|tec|ton|i|cal (är′kə tek ton′ə kəl), *adj.* = architectonic.

ar|chi|tec|ton|ics (är′kə tek ton′iks), *n.* **1** the science of architecture. **2** skill in architecture. **3a** any skill considered as resembling this, especially in the design of a work of art. **b** the design or structure of a work of art.

ar|chi|tec|tur|al (är′kə tek′chər əl), *adj.* **1** of architecture; having to do with architecture. **2** according to the principles of architecture.

architectural barrier, any part of a building, sidewalk, or other structure that obstructs access by a handicapped person: *"Architectural barriers" can be curbs which are too high for a person in a wheelchair to negotiate by himself.* (Tuscaloosa News).

architectural engineering, engineering that deals with the planning and construction of all types of buildings.

ar|chi|tec|tur|al|ly (är′kə tek′chər ə lē), *adv.* **1** with regard to architectural principles; from an architectural point of view. **2** in an architectural manner.

ar|chi|tec|ture (är′kə tek′chər), *n.* **1** the science or art of building. Architecture has to do with the designing and planning of houses, churches, schools, and public and business buildings. **2** a style or special manner of building; qualities that distinguish the buildings of one time, region, or group from those of another: *Greek architecture made much use of columns and beams.* **3** architectural work; design; construction: *the massive architecture of the Pyramids.* (*Figurative.*) *the architecture of a symphony, the architecture of a molecule.* **4** a building; structure. [< Latin *architectūra* < *architectus* architect]

ar|chi|trave (är′kə trāv), *n.* **1** the main beam resting on the top of a column or row of columns. See diagram under **entablature**. **2** the molding around a door, window, arch, or panel. [< Italian *architrave* < *archi-* chief (learned borrowing from Latin *archi-*) + *trave* beam < Latin *trabs, trabis*]

ar|chi|val (är kī′vəl; är′kī-, -kə-), *adj.* **1** of or having to do with archives. **2** contained in records.

ar|chive (är′kīv), *n.* a particular collection of documents, especially of an individual: *This historic archive, extending to about 20,000 documents in 107 volumes, contains the official correspondence of the three British commanders in chief in America . . . during the Revolutionary War* (William B. Todd).
▶See **archives** for usage note.

ar|chives (är′kīvz), *n.pl.* **1a** public records or historical documents. **b** *Figurative.* any voluminous record. **2** a place where public records or historical documents are kept. [< Middle French *archives*, learned borrowing from Latin *archīvum*, singular < Greek *archeîa*, plural < *archê* government]

▶**archives—archive**. The use of this word in the singular may be said largely to have disappeared from English in the 1800's, but examples of the singular survive in certain proper names (*Bettmann Archive*) and in literature, especially when reference is made to a particular document: *Some rotten archive, rummaged out of some seldom explored press* (Charles Lamb).

ar|chi|vist (är′kə vist, -kī-), *n.* a keeper of archives: *The foundation will appoint an archivist . . . to fill gaps in available records* (Newsweek).

ar|chi|volt (är′kə vōlt), *n.* **1** a curved molding or other ornamental band around the top of an arch or of an arched opening. **2** the inner curve of an arch; soffit. [< Italian *archivolto* < *arco* arch¹ + *volto* turned, curved]

arch|ly (ärch′lē), *adv.* in an arch or playfully mischievous manner; pertly; saucily.

arch|ness (ärch′nis), *n.* playful mischievousness; pertness; sauciness.

ar|chon (är′kon), *n.* **1** a chief magistrate in ancient Athens. **2** a ruler or president. [< Greek *árchōn*, present participle of *árchein* rule] —**ar′chon|ship**, *n.*

ar|chon|tate (är′kən tāt), *n.* an archon's tenure of office. [< Greek *archont-*, stem of *árchōn* ruler + English *-ate*³]

ar|chon|tic (är kon′tik), *adj.* of or having to do with an archon.

ar|cho|plasm (är′kə plaz′əm), *n.* = archiplasm.

ar|cho|plas|mic (är′kə plaz′mik), *adj.* = archiplasmic.

arch|priest (ärch′prēst′), *n.* **1** a chief priest. **2a** the chief assistant to a bishop, especially one acting as the dean of a cathedral chapter. **b** the highest ranking priest in an archdiocese among the clergy outside the cathedral chapter, especially one acting as a rural dean. **3** the highest ranking priest among the Roman Catholic secular clergy in England between 1598 and 1623.

arch|priest|hood (ärch′prēst′hůd), *n.* the position or office of an archpriest.

arch|ri|val (ärch′rī′vəl), *n.* a principal rival.

archt., architect.

arch|way (ärch′wā′), *n.* **1** an entrance or passageway with an arch over it. **2** an arch covering a passageway.

ar|cif|er|ous (är sif′ər əs), *adj.* of or belonging to a division of amphibians which have a divided sternum, the cartilage tissue of one side of which overlaps the other. [< Latin *arcus* bow]

ar|ci|form (är′sə fôrm), *adj.* bent like a bow; bowshaped; curved. [< Latin *arcus* bow]

arc-jet engine (ärk′jet′), a rocket engine that uses an electric arc to heat the propellant.

arcked (ärkt), *v.* arced; a past tense and a past participle of **arc**.

arck|ing (är′king), *v.* arcing; a present participle of **arc**.

arc lamp, a lamp that produces a brilliant light as a strong electric current jumps from one conductor to another, each usually a carbon electrode.

arc light, **1** the brilliant light given by an arc lamp. **2** = arc lamp.

ar|co (är′kō), *adv. Music.* using the bow, as after a passage of pizzicato. [< Italian *arco* bow < Latin *arcus*]

arc of crisis, a politically unstable area extending in a curve from the Indian subcontinent west to Turkey and south through the Arabian peninsula and northeastern Africa: *In an Administration that was intending to give top priority to the Third World, we have . . . that whole arc of crisis more and more hostile to the U.S.* (Henry Kissinger).

arc|o|graph (är′kə graf, -gräf), *n.* an instrument for drawing an arc of a circle without using a central point.

ar|col|o|gy (är kol′ə jē), *n., pl.* **-gies**. a planned city housed entirely within a single structure of enormous size: *There are arcologies for sea, shore or plain, for populations the size of Sarasota (30,000), Atlanta (400,000) or Dallas (1,000,000)* (Estie Stoll). [(coined by Paolo Soleri, American architect) < *arc*(hitectural) (ec)*ology*]

arc|tic (ärk′tik, är′tik), *adj., n.* —*adj.* **1** at or near the North Pole; of the north polar region: *the arctic fox. They explored the great arctic wilderness of northern Canada.* **2** *Figurative.* extremely cold; frigid. **3** having to do with or situated under Ursa Major or Minor.
—*n.* one of a pair of arctics.
the Arctic, the north polar region. The Arctic has an extremely cold winter but is inhabited by such animals as the reindeer, polar bear, and musk ox. [< Latin *arcticus* < Greek *arktikós* of the Bear (constellation) < *árktos* bear] —**arc′ti|cal|ly**, *adv.*

arctic char or **charr**, a trout of Alaska and northern Canada.

***Arctic Circle** or **arctic circle**, **1** the imaginary boundary of the north polar region. It runs parallel to the equator at 66 degrees 30 minutes (66° 30′) north latitude. **2** the polar region surrounded by this parallel; Arctic Zone.

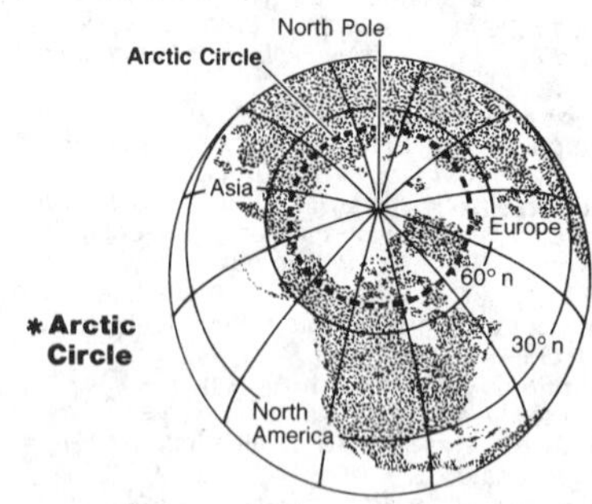

***Arctic Circle**

arctic fox, a fox of arctic regions, bluish- or brownish-gray in summer and white in winter, valued for its fur.

arctic grayling, a grayling of Alaska and northern Canada.

arctic hare, a large hare of both polar regions that is gray in the summer in southern subspecies and white in winter in all subspecies, except for black tips on the ears. In the far North it remains white the year round.

arctic lights, = aurora borealis.

arctic loon, a smaller species of loon that breeds in the northern British Isles and Scandinavia and winters mainly in the Black Sea area.

arctic owl, = snowy owl.

arctic pack, a densely compacted mass of floating ice found in arctic or antarctic waters.

arctic poppy, = Iceland poppy.

arctic right whale, a black baleen whale of the Arctic that grows up to 55 feet long and weighs as much as 45 tons; bowhead; Greenland whale. Its baleen is longer than that of any other whale. It looks much like the right whale, but has no bonnet on its snout.

arc|tics (ärk′tiks, är′tiks), *n.pl.* warm, waterproof overshoes: *There was snow on the ground, but she had her arctics on* (William Maxwell).

arctic seal, rabbit fur treated to resemble seal.

arctic skua, = parasitic jaeger.

arctic tern, a tern native to both polar regions. It is about 17 inches long, with blue-gray, black, and white feathers, and red feet and bill. The arctic tern migrates over a greater distance than any other bird.

arctic trout, = arctic char.

arctic willow, a shrub found in arctic and subarctic North America and Asia. It is one of the chief sources of forage for reindeer and other animals.

arctic wolf, a big, shaggy wolf with a yellowish-white coat that lives in the tundras of arctic North America and Greenland; tundra wolf; white wolf.

Arctic Zone, the region between the Arctic Circle and the North Pole; Frigid Zone.

arc|ti|id (ärk tī′id), *adj., n.* —*adj.* of or belonging to a family of relatively heavy-bodied, broad-winged, spotted or striped moths, such as the tiger moth.
—*n.* an arctiid moth.
[< New Latin *Arctiidae* the family < Greek *árktos* bear (because of their hairy appearance)]

Arc|to|gae|a (ärk′tə jē′ə), *n.* a primary zoogeographical division of the earth's surface, comprising Europe, Asia, Africa, and North America, exclusive of Central America. [< New Latin *Arctogaea* < Greek *árktos* arctic; the north + *gaîa* earth]

Arc|to|gae|al (ärk′tə jē′əl), *adj.* of or having to do with the zoogeographical area known as the Arctogaea.

Arc|to|gae|an (ärk′tə jē′ən), *adj.* = Arctogaeal.

Arc|tu|ri|an (ärk tůr′ē ən, -tyůr′-), *adj.* having to do with or resembling Arcturus (applied to a class of stars having a spectrum like that of Arcturus).

Arc|tu|rus (ärk tůr′əs, -tyůr′-), *n.* a very bright star in the northern sky. It is the brightest star in the constellation Boötes. [< Latin *Arctūrus* < Greek *Arktoûros* < *árktos* the Great Bear (constellation); a bear + *oûros* watcher]

ar|cu|ate (är′kyů it, -āt), *adj.* curved like a bow; arched: *Horns have a tendency to become arcuate in the Goat* (Charles Blake). [< Latin *arcuātus*, past participle of *arcuāre* to bend < *arcus* bow] —**ar′cu|ate|ly**, *adv.*

ar|cu|at|ed (är′kyů ā′tid), *adj.* = arcuate: *Arcuated architecture was perfected by the Medieval builders* (Gilbert Scott).

ar|cu|a|tion (är′kyů ā′shən), *n.* **1** a bowlike curvature. **2** the use of arches in architecture; arched work.

ar|cus se|ni|lis (är′kəs sə nī′lis), *Medicine.* a yellowish band which encircles the cornea with advancing age. [< Latin *arcus senilis* senile arch]

arc-weld (ärk′weld′), *v.t.* to fuse together by arc welding. —**arc′-weld′er**, *n.*

arc welding, a welding process in which the heat used to fuse metals together is produced by an electric arc either between two electrodes or between an electrode and the metal.

ard (ärd), *n.* a primitive type of plow, without a colter, especially widespread in the Mediterranean area. [probably < Arabic *ard* earth, soil]

ARD (no periods), acute respiratory disease.

ar|deb (är′deb), *n.* an Eastern unit of dry measure, in Egypt equal officially to 5.62 U.S. bushels but varying from locality to locality. [< Arabic *'ardabb* < Greek *artábē*]

Ar|den (är′dən), *n.* **1** a district or forest in central England (Warwickshire) and formerly also in eastern England, generally believed to be the scene of Shakespeare's *As You Like It*, though some argue for Ardennes, France. **2** a land of the imagination or of romance.

ar|den|cy (är′dən sē), *n.* the quality of being ardent; ardor.

ar|dent (är′dənt), *adj.* **1** glowing with passion; passionate; impassioned: *ardent love.* SYN: fervent. **2** full of zeal; very enthusiastic; eager: *He is an ardent scout. After reading about the lives of several great Americans, John became an ardent student of American history.* SYN: keen. **3** burning; fiery; hot: *an ardent fever.* **4** glowing: *With flashing flames his ardent eyes were filled* (John Dryden). [< Old French *ardant*, present participle of *ardoir* to burn < Latin *ārdēre* < *āridus* arid] —**ar′dent|ly**, *adv.* —**ar′dent|ness**, *n.*

ardent spirits, strong distilled alcoholic liquors, such as brandy.

Ar|dil (är dil′), *n. Trademark.* a textile fiber made in Great Britain from peanut meal.

Ar|dois signal system (är′dwä), a night signaling system used by ships, made up of pairs of red and white electric lights arranged vertically and operated by a keyboard.

ar|dor (är′dər), *n.* **1** warmth of emotion; passion. SYN: fervor. **2** great enthusiasm; eagerness; zeal: *the ardor of a saint. He spoke with patriotic ardor.* **3** burning heat. **4** *Obsolete.* an effulgent spirit. Also, *British,* **ardour**. [< Anglo-French, Old French *ardour* < Latin *ārdor* < *ārdēre* to burn < *āridus* arid]

ar|dour (är′dər), *n. British.* ardor.

ar|dri (ôr′drē), *n.* the title given to the chief king of ancient Ireland by the rulers of the various small kingdoms. He had almost no power over them. [< Irish Gaelic *ārdrī* high king]

ar|du|ous (är′jü əs), *adj.* **1** hard to do; requiring much effort; difficult: *an arduous lesson.* SYN: laborious. **2** using up much energy; strenuous: *He enjoys an arduous workout in the gymnasium.* **3** hard to climb; steep: *an arduous hill.* [< Latin *arduus* steep (with English *-ous*)] —**ar′du|ous|ly,** *adv.* —**ar′du|ous|ness,** *n.*

are[1] (är; *unstressed* ər), *v.* the form of the verb **be** used with *we, you,* and *they* and any plural noun to indicate the present tense; plural and second person singular, present indicative of **be:** *We are ready. You are next. They are waiting.* We say: I am, you are, he is, she is, it is, we are, you are, they are. [Old English (Northumbrian) *aron*]

are[2] (ãr, är), *n.* a unit of surface measure in the metric system, equal to 100 square meters, or 119.6 square yards. Also, **ar.** [< French *are* < Latin *ārea* area]

ar|e|a (ãr′ē ə), *n.* **1** an amount of surface; extent of surface: *The area of this floor is 600 square feet.* **2** region or district: *The Rocky Mountain area is the most mountainous in the United States.* SYN: tract, stretch, zone. **3** a level, open space: *a playground area.* **4** *Figurative.* range of knowledge or interest; sphere of activity; field: *Our science teacher is familiar with the areas of physics, chemistry, and similar sciences.* SYN: extent, scope, expanse. **5** a yard or court of a building. **6** *British.* a sunken space at the entrance of a cellar or basement; areaway (def. 1). **7a** a portion of the cerebral cortex whose function has been identified: *the sensory area, the speech area.* **b** any other section of the body or a section of one of its organs: *the pulmonary area of the heart.* [< Latin *ārea* piece of level ground]

area bombing, **1** the dropping of bombs from aircraft on a general area instead of on a narrowly defined target. **2** saturation bombing.

area code, a combination of three numerals used to dial directly by telephone from one area of the United States and Canada to another.

area defense, a defense against air or missile attack organized to protect an entire area as distinguished from a point or line.

ar|e|al (ãr′ē əl), *adj.* of or having to do with an area.

area navigation, a system of aircraft navigation by means of airborne computers that permits pilots to take a direct flight path instead of having to receive bearings at prescribed radio-beacon locations.

area rug, a rug for covering a particular area, such as the dining area, of a house or apartment: *Wall-to-wall carpeting gives way to area rugs* (Wall Street Journal).

area scan, a radar scan based on a fixed beam or beams directed to provide continuous surveillance of a particular airspace. See also **sector scan.**

area school, *U.S.* a school serving several districts; consolidated school.

area study, *U.S.* a program of study, usually on the college or university level, which deals with the history, geography, economics, language, literature, and culture of a given geographical area (in Great Britain called *local history*).

ar|e|a|way (ãr′ē ə wā′), *n. U.S.* **1** a sunken area or court at the entrance to a cellar or basement. **2** an area used as a passageway between buildings.

ar|e|a|wide (ãr′ē ə wīd′), *adj.* covering an entire region or district: *an areawide blackout, areawide marketing of a product.*

ar|e|ca (ar′ə kə, ə rē′-), *n.* **1a** any one of a genus of palms that bear the betel nut. **b** = betel nut. **2** any one of a group of related palms. [< Portuguese *areca* < Malayalam *ádekka*]

areca nut, = betel nut.

areca palm, = areca (defs. 1a and 2).

ar|e|co|line (ar′ə kə lēn, ə rē′kə lēn), *n.* a colorless, odorless, and mildly toxic oily alkaloid obtained from the betel nut, used in medicine: *At present, Echinococcus infections are treated with arecoline* (New Scientist). *Formula:* $C_8H_{13}O_2N$ [< *areca* + *-ol*[2] + *-ine*[2]]

A|re|cu|na or **A|re|ku|na** (ä′re kü′nä), *n., pl.* **-na** or **-nas. 1** a member of a tribe of Carib Indians of southeastern Venezuela. **2** the language of this tribe.

a|re|li|gious (ā′ri lij′əs), *adj.* not concerned with religion; indifferent to religion: *T. S. Eliot ... sensed the dilemma of modern, urban and areligious man* (Time). [< *a-*[4] not + *religious*]

a|re|na (ə rē′nə), *n.* **1** the space in an ancient Roman amphitheater in which contests or shows took place: *Gladiators fought with lions in the arena at Rome.* **2** a similar space, surrounded by seats, used today for contests or shows: *a boxing arena.* SYN: ring. **3** a large building in which indoor sports are played. **4** *Figurative.* any place of conflict and trial: *The United Nations is an arena for world debate.* SYN: lists. **5** *Figurative.* a field of endeavor: *the political arena.* SYN: area, sphere. [< later variant of Latin *harēna* sand, sandy place (because the floor of Roman arenas was sand)]

ar|e|na|ceous (ar′ə nā′shəs), *adj.* **1** sandy. **2** = arenicolous. [< Latin *harēnāceus* < *harēna* sand]

arena theater or **stage**, = theater-in-the-round.

ar|e|na|tion (ar′ə nā′shən), *n.* remedial application of hot sand to the body; sand bath. [< Latin *harēnātiō, -ōnis* < *harēna* sand]

a|re|nic (ə rē′nik), *adj.* of or having to do with an arena.

ar|e|nic|o|lous (ar′ə nik′ə ləs), *adj.* living in sand or sandy places. [< Latin *harēna* sand + *colere* inhabit + English *-ous*]

ar|e|nose (ar′ə nōs), *adj.* full of sand; sandy. [< Latin *harēnōsus* < *harēna* sand]

aren't (ärnt, är′ənt), are not.

▶**Aren't** is often used interrogatively in the expression *aren't I,* meaning *am I not,* chiefly to avoid the use of *ain't I* and partly because *am I not* sounds too formal or affected to most speakers: *Why aren't I allowed to stay?* In Great Britain *an't I* (änt ī) is used in this sense.

▶See **ain't** for another usage note.

ar|e|o|cen|tric (ãr′ē ə sen′trik), *adj. Astronomy.* having Mars as center. [< Greek *Áreos* of Mars + English *center* + *-ic*]

a|re|og|ra|pher (ãr′ē og′rə fər), *n.* a person who describes the appearance of Mars.

ar|e|o|graph|ic (ãr′ē ə graf′ik), *adj.* having to do with areography.

ar|e|og|ra|phy (ãr′ē og′rə fē), *n.* **1** the description of the planet Mars. **2** a treatise on the planet Mars. [< Greek *Áreos* of Mars + English *-graphy*]

a|re|o|la (ə rē′ə lə), *n., pl.* **-lae** (-lē), **-las. 1** a ring of color: *the areola about a pustule.* **2** a small area. **3** an interstice: *The spaces between the veins of a leaf or the nervures of an insect's wing are areolae.* [< Latin *āreola* (diminutive) < *ārea* area]

a|re|o|lar (ə rē′ə lər), *adj.* **1** of or like an areola. **2** containing areolae: *Loose, or areolar, tissue ... supports, penetrates, separates, and allows motion between all the different parts and organs within the body* (Irvin Stein).

a|re|o|late (ə rē′ə lit, -lāt), *adj.* marked by or divided into areolae: *The skin of a plant is areolate* (John Lindley). —**ar′e|o|la′tion,** *n.*

a|re|o|lat|ed (ə rē′ə lā′tid), *adj.* = areolate.

ar|e|ole (ãr′ē ōl), *n.* **1** = areola: *A bright star ... surrounded by a blue or violet areole* (Simon Newcomb). **2** one of the small pits or cavities from which the spines, branches, or flowers of the cactus grow. [< French *aréole,* learned borrowing from Latin *āreola*]

a|re|o|let (ə rē′ə let), *n.* **1** a small areola. **2** a small cell or space in an insect's wing.

ar|e|ol|o|gy (ãr′ē ol′ə jē), *n.* the scientific study of the planet Mars. [< Greek *Áreos* of Mars + English *-logy*]

ar|e|om|e|ter (ãr′ē om′ə tər), *n.* = hydrometer. [< Greek *araiós* rare + English *-meter*]

ar|e|om|e|try (ãr′ē om′ə trē), *n.* = hydrometry.

Ar|e|op|a|gite (ar′ē op′ə jīt, -gīt), *n.* a member of the tribunal of the Areopagus.

Ar|e|op|a|git|ic (ar′ē op′ə jit′ik), *adj., n.* —*adj.* of or having to do with the Areopagus.

—*n.* a speech in the style of the orations of Isocrates to the Areopagus.

Ar|e|op|a|gus (ar′ē op′ə gəs), *n.* **1** a hill in Athens, Greece, west of the Acropolis. **2** the oldest and most respected council of ancient Athens, which met there. **3** *Figurative.* any important tribunal. [< Latin *Areopagus* < Greek *Areiópagos* < *Áreios págos* hill of Ares (Mars' hill)]

ar|e|op|a|gy (ar′ē op′ə jē), *n.* an Areopagus or tribunal.

a|re|pa (ä rā′pä), *n., pl.* **-pas.** (in Latin America) a kind of griddlecake made of soaked Indian corn ground into a paste or dough. [< American Spanish *arepa*]

Ar|es (ãr′ēz), *n.* the Greek god of war. The Romans called him Mars.

ar|e|tal|o|gy (ar′ə tal′ə jē), *n., pl.* **-gies.** a narrative of the feats or achievements of a legendary figure: *an aretalogy of Pythagoras.* [< Greek *aretalogiā* < *aretē* manly virtue + *-logiā* -logy]

ar|e|te (ar′ə tā′), *n.* manly virtue; nobility of character; integrity: *The book ends with a plea for ... the cultivation of arete, which "connotes ... decision and self-responsibility," rather than hubris, "a sometimes arrogant pride in our great but limited power"* (Scientific American). *... arete, a unity of mind and body to which the complete man of every age must aspire* (Time). [< Greek *aretē*]

a|rête (ə rāt′), *n.* a sharp ridge on a mountain, especially a rocky edge. See picture under **mountain.** [< French *arête* < Old French *areste* ridge, spine < Vulgar Latin *aresta,* variant of Latin *arista.* See etym. of doublet **arista, arris.**]

Ar|e|thu|sa (ar′ə thü′zə, -sə), *n. Greek Legend.* a nymph who was changed into a stream by Artemis to save her from the pursuing river god Alpheus.

ar|e|thu|sa (ar′ə thü′zə, -sə), *n.* any one of a genus of plants of the orchid family. The common North American species is a small swamp plant with a single, usually pink, fragrant flower. [< *Arethusa*]

arg., **1** *Heraldry.* argent. **2** argentum.

Arg., **1** Argentina. **2** Argentine.

ar|gal[1] (är′gəl), *n.* = argol.

ar|gal[2] (är′gəl), *n.* = argali.

ar|ga|la (är′gə lə), *n.* a large Indian stork; adjutant bird. [< Hindustani *hargīlā*]

ar|ga|li (är′gə lē), *n., pl.* **-li. 1** a large wild sheep of Asia, having long, thick, spirally curved horns. **2** the bighorn, aoudad, or other wild sheep. [< Mongol *argali*]

Ar|gand lamp (är′gənd), an oil or gas lamp with a tubular burner, or wick, admitting air to the flame both from within and without. [< Aimé *Argand,* 1755-1803, a Swiss inventor]

ar|gan tree (är′gən), a Moroccan tree of the sapodilla family that yields a fruit used as a cattle feed and an oil used in cooking. [< Arabic *arjān*]

ar|ga|sid (är′gə sid), *adj., n.* —*adj.* of or belonging to a family of ticks which attack chickens and other fowl, especially in warm climates. —*n.* an argasid tick. [< New Latin *Argasidae* < Greek *ārgós* living without labor]

ar|gent (är′jənt), *n., adj.* —*n.* **1** *Archaic or Poetic.* silver. **2** *Heraldry.* the silver or white tincture in a coat of arms, in engraving represented by a bare surface. —*adj.* = silvery. [< Old French *argent* < Latin *argentum* silver]

ar|gen|tal (är jen′təl), *adj.* **1** of or having to do with silver. **2** resembling silver.

Ar|gen|tan lace (är zhäɴ täɴ′), a variety of needlepoint lace made in France. [< *Argentan,* a commune in France]

ar|gen|tate (är′jən tāt), *adj. Botany.* silvery.

ar|gen|te|ous (är jen′tē əs), *adj.* = silvery. [< Latin *argenteus* < *argentum* silver]

ar|gen|tic (är jen′tik), *adj. Chemistry.* of or containing silver, especially with a valence of 2.

ar|gen|tif|er|ous (är′jən tif′ər əs), *adj.* yielding silver: *an argentiferous ore.* [< Latin *argentum* silver + English *-ferous*]

ar|gen|tine (är′jən tin, -tīn), *adj., n.* —*adj.* **1** of silver. **2** = silvery.

—*n.* **1** = silver. **2** a metal or other material resembling silver in color, such as the scales of certain fish, used in making artificial pearls. [< Latin *argentum* silver + English *-ine*[1]]

Ar|gen|tine (är′jən tēn, -tīn), *adj., n.* —*adj.* of Argentina or its people.

—*n.* a person born or living in Argentina.

the Argentine, Argentina.

Ar|gen|tin|e|an or **Ar|gen|tin|i|an** (är′jən tin′ē ən), *adj., n.* = Argentine.

Argentine ant, a small, brown ant native to South America, a household and orchard pest in the southwestern United States.

Ar|gen|ti|no (är′jən tē′nō), *n., pl.* **-nos.** = Argentine.

ar|gen|tite (är′jən tīt), *n.* a native silver sulfide, an ore of silver found in veins traversing granite and certain other strata of rock. *Formula:* Ag_2S [< Latin *argentum* silver + English *-ite*[1]]

ar|gen|tous (är jen′təs), *adj. Chemistry.* of or containing silver, especially with a valence of 1.

ar|gen|tum (är jen′təm), *n. Chemistry.* silver. *Symbol:* Ag (no period). *Abbr:* Ar. [< New Latin *argentum* < Latin]

Pronunciation Key: hat, āge, cãre, fär; let, ēqual, tėrm; it, īce; hot, ōpen, ôrder; oil, out; cup, pu̇t, rüle; child; long; thin; ᴛʜen; zh, measure; ə represents **a** in about, **e** in taken, **i** in pencil, **o** in lemon, **u** in circus.

ar|gil (är′jil), *n.* clay, especially clay suitable for use in pottery. [< Old French *argille* < Latin *argilla* < Greek *árgīllos* < *argês* shining, white]

ar|gil|la|ceous (är′jə lā′shəs), *adj.* = clayey. [< Latin *argillāceus* (with English *-ous*) < *argilla* argil]

ar|gil|lif|er|ous (är′jə lif′ər əs), *adj.* yielding clay. [< Latin *argilla* argil + English *-ferous*]

ar|gil|lite (är′jə līt), *n.* a schist or slate derived from clay. [< Latin *argilla* argil + English *-ite*[1]]

ar|gil|lous (är jil′əs), *adj.* = clayey. [< Old French *argilus* (with English *-ous*) < Latin *argillōsus* clayey]

ar|gi|nae|mi|a (är′jə nē′mē ə), *n.* an inherited deficiency of the enzyme arginase, resulting in high levels of arginine in the blood and leading to mental retardation and other metabolic abnormalities. [< *argin*(ine) + New Latin *-aemia* condition of the blood (< Greek *haîma* blood)]

ar|gi|nase (är′jə nās), *n.* an enzyme in mammals that breaks down arginine and converts it to urea. [< *argin*(ine) + *-ase*]

ar|gi|nine (är′jə nīn), *n.* one of the amino acids present in plant and animal proteins. It cannot be synthesized by some animals and therefore must be added to their feed. *Formula:* $C_6H_{14}O_2N_4$ [< Latin *argentum* silver + English *-ine*[1] (from the silver color of the first salts discovered)]

Ar|give (är′jīv, -gīv), *adj., n.* — ***adj.*** Greek (of the city of Argos or the region of Argolis, whence came many of those who fought against Troy).
— ***n.*** **1** a native or inhabitant of Argos or Argolis. **2** a Greek.

ar|gle-bar|gle (är′gəl bär′gəl), *n., v.i.,* **-bar|gled, -bar|gling.** *Informal.* = argy-bargy: *Three months of legal argle-bargle ...* (Newsweek). (*n.*) *Me and the minister were just argle-bargling* (D. Moir). (*v.i.*) [originally Scottish reduplication of *argle,* variant of *argue*]

Ar|go (är′gō), *n., genitive* (def. 2) **Ar|gus. 1** *Greek Legend.* the ship in which Jason and his companions sailed in search of the Golden Fleece. **2** a large southern constellation between Canis Major and the Southern Cross.

ar|gol (är′gəl), *n.* crude tartar, gathering in a crust on the sides of containers in which wine is fermented. Also, **argal.** [< Anglo-French *argoil;* origin unknown]

***ar|gon** (är′gon), *n.* a colorless, odorless, inert gas that forms a very small part of the air. It is a chemical element and is used in electric light bulbs and radio tubes. [< New Latin *argon* < Greek *ārgón,* neuter of *ārgós* idle < *a-* without + *érgon* work]

***argon**

symbol	atomic number	atomic weight
Ar	18	39.948

ar|go|naut (är′gə nôt), *n.* = paper nautilus. [see etym. under **Argonaut**]

Ar|go|naut (är′gə nôt), *n.* **1** *Greek Legend.* any one of the men who sailed with Jason in search of the Golden Fleece. **2a** *U.S.* a person who went to California in 1849 in search of gold. **b** *Canadian.* a person who went to British Columbia in 1862 in search of gold. [< Latin *Argonauta* < Greek *Argonaútēs* < *Argô* Argo, the name of Jason's ship + *naútēs* sailor]

Ar|go|nau|tic (är′gə nô′tik), *adj.* of the Argonauts.

ar|go|sy (är′gə sē), *n., pl.* **-sies.** *Historical or Poetic.* **1** a large merchant ship: *Venetian merchants with deep-laden argosies* (Longfellow). **2** a fleet of such ships. [< Italian *Ragusea* (ship) of Ragusa, an Italian port which traded extensively with England in the 1500's]

ar|got (är′gō, -gət), *n.* **1** the jargon or slang of a group of persons; *soldiers' argot.* **SYN:** cant, lingo, patois. **2** the jargon of thieves, intended to conceal meaning from outsiders. [< French *argot;* origin uncertain]

ar|got|ic (är got′ik), *adj.* of the nature of slang; slangy.

ar|gu|a|ble (är′gyü ə bəl), *adj.* capable of being argued; open to argument; debatable: *The point is arguable, but as demands on the school budgets increase, the role of the Federal government will ... grow greater* (Newsweek). — **ar′gu|a|bly,** *adv.*

ar|gue (är′gyü), *v.,* **-gued, -gu|ing.** — ***v.i.*** **1** to give reasons selected to support or refute a point: *He argued for a different policy.* **2** to discuss with someone who disagrees: *John argued with his sister about who should wash the dishes.* **SYN:** debate. See syn. under **discuss. 3** to bring forward reasons against anything; raise objections; dispute: *The senator argued against the passage of the bill. You are always ready to argue.*
— ***v.t.*** **1** to try to prove by reasoning; maintain: *Columbus argued that the world was round.* **SYN:** contend. **2** to persuade by giving reasons: *He argued me into going.* **3** to give reasons for or against (something): *to argue a question.* **SYN:** debate, discuss. **4** to indicate; show; prove: *Her rich clothes argue her to be wealthy.* **SYN:** denote.
argue away (or **off**), to get rid of by argument: *Men ... would argue a dog's tail off* (D'Arcy Thompson).
argue down, to wear down by arguing: *Mrs. Hauser had argued down the landlord on this too* (Harper's).
[< Old French *arguer* < Latin *argūtāre* chatter (frequentative) < *arguere* make clear] — **ar′gu|er,** *n.*

ar|gu|fy (är′gyə fī), *v.,* **-fied, -fy|ing.** *Informal or Dialect.* — ***v.i.*** **1** to argue with childish persistence. **2** to argue; wrangle. **3** to prove or be evidence of something.
— ***v.t.*** to pester or persuade by tiresome argument.
[< *argue* + *-fy*] — **ar′gu|fi′er,** *n.*

ar|gu|ment (är′gyə mənt), *n.* **1** a discussion by persons who disagree; dispute: *He won the argument by producing figures to prove his point.* **2** giving reasons for or against something; debate: *Let us not waste time in argument.* **SYN:** discussion. **3** a reason or reasons given for or against something: *His arguments in favor of a new school are very persuasive.* **SYN:** rationale. **4** a short statement or summary of what is in a book, poem, or the like. **SYN:** abstract, theme. **5** *Mathematics.* an independent variable on whose value the value of a function depends. [< Latin *argūmentum* < *arguere* make clear]
— ***Syn.*** **1 Argument, controversy, dispute** mean presentation of varying opinions by persons who disagree on some question. **Argument** suggests an intellectual encounter in which each side uses facts and reasons to try to convince the other: *His strong arguments persuaded me to accept his conclusions.* **Controversy** tends to suggest a more or less formal argument between groups, often carried on in writing or speeches: *The controversy over American schools still continues.* **Dispute** suggests contradicting rather than reasoning, and applies to an argument marked by feeling: *The dispute over the property was settled in court.*

ar|gu|men|ta|tion (är′gyə men tā′shən), *n.* **1** discussion of reasons for and against anything; debate: *A day was wasted in useless argumentation.* **2** the process of arguing; methodical presentation of arguments; reasoning. **3** a series of arguments.

ar|gu|men|ta|tive (är′gyə men′tə tiv), *adj.* **1** fond of arguing; quarrelsome: *an argumentative disposition.* **SYN:** disputatious. **2** containing argument; controversial: *His style of writing is argumentative and tiresome.* — **ar′gu|men′ta|tive|ly,** *adv.* — **ar′gu|men′ta|tive|ness,** *n.*

ar|gu|men|ta|tor (är′gyə men tā′tər), *n.* one who engages in argumentation.

argument from design, = teleological argument.

ar|gu|men|tum ad ho|mi|nem (är′gyə men′təm ad hom′ə nem), *Latin.* an argument appealing to personal prejudices or interests. See also **ad hominem.**

ar|gu|men|tum ad ig|no|ran|ti|am (är′gyə-men′təm ad ig′nō ran′shē əm), *Latin.* **1** an argument appealing to ignorance. **2** an argument based on an adversary's ignorance.

Ar|gus[1] (är′gəs), *n.* **1** *Greek Mythology.* a giant with a hundred eyes, who was set to watch Io. Hermes killed him, and his eyes were put in the peacock's tail. **2** a watchful guardian.

Ar|gus[2] (är′gəs), *n.* genitive of **Argo** (def. 2).

***ar|gus** (är′gəs), *n.* any one of a group of pheasants native to Asia and noted for the enormous development of the secondary feathers of the wings and middle feathers of the tail, marked with eyelike spots. [< *Argus*[1]]

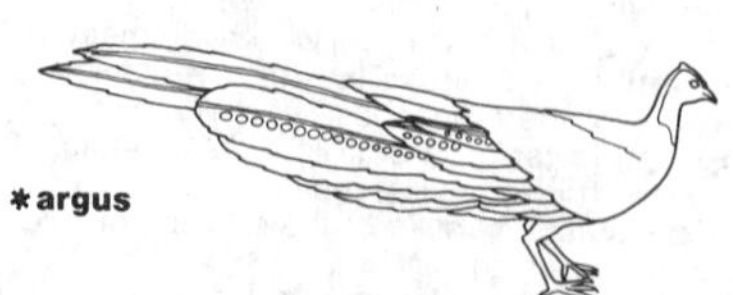

***argus**

Ar|gus-eyed or **ar|gus-eyed** (är′gəs īd′), *adj.* keenly watchful; observant.

ar|gy-bar|gy (är′gē bär′gē), *n., v.,* **-bar|gied, -bar|gy|ing.** *Informal.* — ***n.*** noisy dispute; bickering; wrangling: *... constant interrogation, argy-bargy and palaver* (Punch).
— ***v.i.*** to argue noisily; bicker; wrangle: *... a session where opinionated delegates argy-bargy under a chairman from the National Executive* (New Scientist). Also, **argle-bargle.**
[originally Scottish variant of *argle-bargle*]

ar|gyle or **Ar|gyle** (är′gīl), *adj., n.* — ***adj.*** of or designating a pattern of diamond-shaped areas and lines, in various colors, resembling a plaid, used especially in knitted articles such as socks or neckties.
— ***n.*** an article, especially a sock, having such a pattern.
[special use of variant of *Argyll,* a county in Scotland]

ar|gyr|i|a (är jir′ē ə), *n.* discoloration of the skin due to prolonged use of silver compounds. [< New Latin *argyria* < Greek *árgyros* silver]

ar|gyr|o|dite (är jir′ə dīt), *n.* a rare mineral composed of silver, germanium, and sulfur, occurring in steel-gray crystals having a metallic luster. *Formula:* Ag_8GeS_6 [< Greek *argyrōdês* rich in silver (< *árgyros* silver) + English *-ite*[1]]

Ar|gy|rol (är′jə rōl, -rol), *n. Trademark.* a compound of silver and a protein used in the treatment of inflamed mucous membranes. [< Greek *árgyros* silver]

ar|hat (ur′hət), *n.* a Buddhist who has attained nirvana. [< Sanskrit *arhant* deserving]

a|rhyth|mi|a (ə rith′mē ə), *n.* = arrhythmia.

a|rhyth|mic (ə rith′mik, -rɪᴛʜ′-), *adj.* = arrhythmic. — **a|rhyth′mi|cal|ly,** *adv.*

a|ri|a (ā′rē ə, ār′ē-), *n.* **1** a song for a single voice, often consisting of two or three parts, with instrumental or vocal accompaniment, in an opera, oratorio, or cantata. **2** a song for a voice or instrument; air; melody. [< Italian *aria* < Latin *āera,* accusative, air < Greek *āéra*]

Ar|i|ad|ne (ar′ē ad′nē), *n. Greek Legend.* a daughter of Minos, king of Crete. She fell in love with Theseus and gave him a ball of thread to help him find his way out of the Labyrinth after he killed the Minotaur.

Ar|i|an[1] (ār′ē ən), *adj., n.* — ***adj.*** of or having to do with the doctrine, denounced as heretical, that Christ the Son is subordinate to God the Father, because Christ was begotten of and created by God and so came into being after God.
— ***n.*** a believer in this doctrine.
[< *Arius,* A.D. 250?-336?, a Greek priest + *-an*]

Ar|i|an[2] (ār′ē ən, är′yən), *adj., n.* = Aryan.

Ar|i|an|ism (ār′ē ə niz′əm), *n.* the religious doctrine of Arius (A.D. 250?-336?) that denied the divinity of Christ. Arianism was declared heretical by the Roman Catholic Church in 325 but persisted among the Christian barbarian tribes until the 700's.

Ar|i|an|ize (ār′ē ə nīz), *v.t.,* **-ized, -iz|ing.** to convert to Arianism.

a|ri|bo|fla|vi|no|sis (ā′rī bō flā′və nō′sis), *n.* a condition caused by insufficient riboflavin in the diet.

ar|id (ar′id), *adj.* **1** having very little rainfall; very dry: *an arid climate.* **SYN:** parched. See syn. under **dry. 2** unfruitful because of lack of moisture; barren: *arid soil. Desert lands are arid.* **3** *Figurative.* dull; uninteresting and empty: *an arid, boring speech, an arid, unrewarding field of study.* **SYN:** lifeless. [< Latin *āridus* < *ārēre* be dry] — **ar′id|ly,** *adv.* — **ar′id|ness,** *n.*

a|rid|i|ty (ə rid′ə tē), *n.* **1** *no pl.* arid condition; dryness; barrenness: *Aridity is increased by high evaporation, low humidity, strong winds* (*which remove humid air*) *and by low pressure* (R. N. Elston). **2** *no pl. Figurative.* lack of interest, life, or spirit; dullness: *cultural aridity, technical aridity.* **3** *pl.* **-ties.** *Figurative.* something barren or lifeless: *... such architectural aridities as the cut-rate skyscraper ... and dreary boxlike housing that smothered the human spirit* (Russell Baker).

ar|i|el (ār′ē əl), *n.,* or **ariel gazelle,** a gazelle native to Arabia: *The familiar light-brown gazelle, sometimes called the ... ariel gazelle, is about 2 feet tall* [*and*] *lives in the desert where only a few low shrubs grow* (Victor H. Cahalane). [< Arabic *'ayyil* stag]

Ar|i|el (ār′ē əl), *n.* **1** the airy spirit who served Prospero in Shakespeare's play *The Tempest.* **2** one of the five satellites of the planet Uranus. **3** Jerusalem (in the Bible, Isaiah 29:1,2,7).

Ar|ies (ār′ēz, -ē ēz), *n., genitive* (def. 1) **A|ri|e|tis. 1** a northern constellation between Pisces and Taurus, named from fancied arrangement in the shape of a ram. **2** the first sign of the zodiac; the Ram. The sun enters Aries about March 21. **3** a person born under the sign of Aries. [< Latin *Aries* the Ram]

A|ri|e|tis (ə rī′ə tis), *n.* genitive of **Aries** (def. 1).

ar|i|et|ta (ar′ē et′ə, är′-), *n.* a short air or song. [< Italian *arietta* (diminutive) < *aria* aria]

ar|i|ette (ar′ē et′), *n.* = arietta.

a|right (ə rīt′), *adv.* correctly; rightly: *If I heard you aright, you said you would go.*

A|rik|a|ra (ə rik′ə rə), *n., pl.* **-ra** or **-ras. 1** a member of a tribe of North American Indians of the northern Great Plains. **2** the Caddoan language of this tribe.

ar|il (ar′il), *n.* an outer covering of certain seeds. The aril arises from the stalk (funiculus) of the ovule at or below the hilum. The pulpy inner pod of the bittersweet is an aril. [< New Latin *arillus* < Medieval Latin *arilli* raisins]

ar|il|late (ar′ə lāt), *adj.* having an aril or arils.

ar|il|lat|ed (ar′ə lā′tid), *adj.* = arillate.

ar|il|lode (ar′ə lōd), *n.* an aril not arising from the stalk (funiculus), as in the nutmeg; false aril. [< New Latin *arillus* aril + Greek *eîdos* form]

a|ril|lus (ə ril′əs), *n., pl.* **a|ril|li** (ə ril′ī). = aril.

Ar|i|masp (ar′ə masp), *n., pl.* **-mas|pi** or **-masps.** one of the Arimaspi.

Ar|i|mas|pi (ar′ə mas′pī), *n.pl. Greek Mythology.* a race of one-eyed men of northern Europe who fought with the griffins, trying to wrest from them the gold they guarded.

Ar|i|ma|the|a or **Ar|i|ma|thae|a** (ar′ə mə thē′ə), *n.* a town of ancient Palestine, the home of Joseph of Arimathea. Its location is not now known (in the Bible, Matthew 27:57-60).

a|ri|o|so (ä′rē ō′sō), *adj., adv., n., pl.* **-sos.** *Music.*
—*adj., adv.* like a song.
—*n.* a piece or passage like a song; a vocal part. [< Italian *arioso* songlike < *aria* aria]

a|rise (ə rīz′), *v.i.,* **a|rose, a|ris|en, a|ris|ing. 1** to rise up; get up: *The children arose from their seats to salute the flag. My lady sweet, arise!* (Shakespeare). **SYN:** stand. **2** to move upward; ascend: *Smoke arises from the chimney.* **SYN:** mount. **3a** to come into being or action; come about; appear; begin: *A great wind arose. A cry arose from the stands as the ballplayer was called "out."* **SYN:** originate. **b** to be caused; be started; result (from): *Accidents often arise from carelessness.* **SYN:** proceed. [Old English *ārīsan*]
▶See **rise** for usage note.

a|ris|en (ə riz′ən), *v.* past participle of **arise:** *The prince has not yet arisen from his bed. Trouble had arisen over the ball game.*

a|ris|ta (ə ris′tə), *n., pl.* **-tae** (-tē) **1** the beard of grains and grasses; awn. **2** a bristle at or near the end of the antenna of certain flies. [< Latin *arista* the beard (also, whole ear) of grain. See etym. of doublet **arête, arris.**]

Ar|is|tae|us (ar′ə stē′əs), *n. Greek Mythology.* the son of Apollo and the water nymph Cyrene, famous as a keeper of bees.

ar|is|tarch (ar′ə stärk), *n.* a severe critic. [< *Aristarchus* of Alexandria, died about 145 B.C., a severe critic of the Homeric poems]

Ar|is|tar|chus (ar′ə stär′kəs), *n.* a crater on the moon, the rough floor of which gives off a brighter reflected light than does any other of the moon's craters.

a|ris|tate (ə ris′tāt), *adj.* **1** having aristae. **2** ending in a thin spine. [< Latin *aristātus* < *arista* arista]

a|ris|to (ə ris′tō), *n., pl.* **-tos.** *British Informal.* an aristocrat: ... *the aristos flouncing out their ruffs at the reeking buffoons crowding around the tumbrils* (Punch).

ar|is|toc|ra|cy (ar′ə stok′rə sē), *n., pl.* **-cies. 1** a class of people having a high position in society by birth, rank, or title; nobility. Earls, dukes, and princes belong to the aristocracy. **2** any class of people that is considered superior because of birth, intelligence, culture, or wealth; upper class. **SYN:** élite, gentry, patriciate. **3** government in which the nobles or a privileged upper class rules. **SYN:** oligarchy. **4** a country or state having such a government. **5** a government by the best citizens: ... *the attainment of a truer and truer aristocracy, or government again by the best* (Thomas Carlyle). [< Late Latin *aristocratia* < Greek *aristokratiā* rule of the best born < *áristos* best + *krátos* rule]

a|ris|to|crat (ə ris′tə krat, ar′ə stə-), *n.* **1** a person who belongs to the aristocracy; noble. **2** a person who has the tastes, opinions, manners, or culture of the upper classes. **3** a person who favors government by an aristocracy. [< French *aristocrate* < *aristocratie* < Late Latin *aristocratia* aristocracy]

a|ris|to|crat|ic (ə ris′tə krat′ik, ar′ə stə-), *adj.* **1a** belonging to the upper classes; superior in birth, intelligence, culture, or wealth. **SYN:** noble, patrician, high-born. **b** having to do with an aristocracy. **2** like an aristocrat in appearance, manners, ways, and tastes; stylish or grand: *an aristocratic air.* **3** *Figurative.* snobbish; exclusive. **4** *Figurative.* admirably dignified and restrained; fastidious. **5** favoring aristocrats or government by aristocrats. —**a|ris′to|crat′i|cal|ly,** *adv.*

a|ris|to|crat|i|cal (ə ris′tə krat′ə kəl, ar′ə stə-), *adj.* = aristocratic.

a|ris|toi (ar′ə stoi), *n.pl. Greek.* the aristocracy; upper classes: *His gossipy barrage of light anecdotes and heavy name-dropping should delight hoi polloi and aristoi alike* (Time).

Ar|is|tol (ar′ə stol, -stōl), *n. Trademark.* thymol iodide, a brown powder used in surgery as a substitute for iodoform. *Formula:* $C_{20}H_{24}I_2O_2$ [< Greek *áristos* best + English *-ol*[2]]

a|ris|to|lo|chi|a|ceous (ə ris′tə lō′kē ā′shəs), *adj.* of or belonging to the family of plants that includes the birthwort. [< Latin *aristolochīa* an herb used in childbirth (< Greek *aristolócheia* < *áristos* best + *locheiā* childbirth) + English *-aceous*]

Ar|is|to|phan|ic (ar′is tə fan′ik), *adj.* of, having to do with, or characteristic of the ancient Greek dramatist Aristophanes or his comedies: *Aristophanic drama is farce and celebration in a combination that we have lost touch with* (Atlantic).

Ar|is|to|te|le|an (ar′ə stə tē′lē ən, -tēl′yən), *adj., n. Especially British.* Aristotelian.

Ar|is|to|te|li|an (ar′ə stə tē′lē ən, -tēl′yən), *adj., n.*
—*adj.* of or having to do with Aristotle or his philosophy.
—*n.* **1** a follower or student of Aristotle or his philosophy. Aristotle based much of his thinking upon scientific examination from which he formulated the deductive method of reasoning. **2** a person whose reasoning is characterized by an emphasis on the empirical and the particular as opposed to the hypothetical and the general.

Ar|is|to|te|li|an|ism (ar′ə stə tē′lē ə niz′əm, -tēl′yə-), *n.* the philosophic system or any doctrine of Aristotle.

Aristotelian logic, 1 the logic of Aristotle. **2** = formal logic.

Ar|is|to|tel|ic (ar′ə stə tel′ik), *adj.* = Aristotelian.

a|ris|to|type (ə ris′tə tīp), *n.* **1** a photographic printing process, now obsolete, in which silver salts are used in collodion orgelatin. **2** a print made by such a process. [< Greek *áristos* best + English *type*]

arith., 1 arithmetic. **2** arithmetical.

a|rith|me|tic (*n.* ə rith′mə tik; *adj.* ar′ith met′ik), *n., adj.* —*n.* **1** the art or practice of computing or calculating by means of numbers; the science of positive, real numbers; computation. When you study arithmetic you learn to add, subtract, multiply, and divide. Arithmetic also includes involution and extraction of roots. **2** the study of numbers and their relationship; theory of numbers. **3** a textbook or handbook dealing with arithmetic. **4** calculation; planning: *faulty political arithmetic.*
—*adj.* = arithmetical.
[< Old French *arismetique,* learned borrowing from Latin *arithmētica* < Greek *arithmētikē* (*téchnē*) (art) of counting, ultimately < *arithmós* number]

ar|ith|met|i|cal (ar′ith met′ə kəl), *adj.* **1** of arithmetic; having to do with arithmetic. **2** according to the rules of arithmetic. —**ar′ith|met′i|cal|ly,** *adv.*

arithmetical progression or **series,** a series of numbers in which there is always the same difference, added or subtracted, between a number and the one next after it. *Examples:* 2, 4, 6, 8, 10 is an arithmetical progression in which 2 is added to each number; 8, 5, 2, −1, is an arithmetical progression in which 3 is subtracted from each number.

a|rith|me|ti|cian (ə rith′mə tish′ən, ar′ith-), *n.* a person who studies arithmetic.

arithmetic or **arithmetical mean,** = average (def. 1): *If you add together the numbers of all the eggs and divide by ... the number of hens, you will find the arithmetic average or arithmetic mean* (Albert E. Waugh).

arithmetic unit, the part of a digital computer in which arithmetical operations are performed.

a|rith|me|ti|za|tion (ə rith′mə ti zā′shən), *n.* the process of making any part of mathematics depend on purely arithmetical concepts.

a|rith|me|tize (ə rith′mə tīz), *v.,* **-tized, -tiz|ing.**
—*v.t.* to solve by or state in terms of arithmetic: *to arithmetize a problem.*
—*v.i. Especially British.* to use arithmetic.

ar|ith|mom|e|ter (ar′ith mom′ə tər), *n.* an early form of adding machine. [< Greek *arithmós* number + English *-meter*]

a ri|ve|der|ci (ä rē′vā der′chē), *Italian.* farewell; until we meet again. Also, **arrivederci.**

Ariz., Arizona.

Ar|i|zo|nan (ar′ə zō′nən), *adj., n.* —*adj.* of or having to do with Arizona.
—*n.* a native or inhabitant of Arizona.

Ar|i|zo|na ruby (ar′ə zō′nə), a garnet resembling a ruby in color; Cape ruby; pyrope.

Ar|i|zo|ni|an (ar′ə zō′nē ən), *adj., n.* = Arizonan.

ar|i|zo|nite (ar′ə zō′nīt), *n.* an igneous rock that is an ore of titanium. *Formula:* $Fe_2O_3 \cdot 3TiO_2$ [< *Arizona,* the state where it was discovered + *-ite*[1]]

Ar|ju|na (är′jü nə), *n.* a warrior, son of Indra and one of the heroes of the *Mahabharata* in Hindu epic poetry.

ark (ärk), *n.* **1a** the large boat in which Noah saved himself, his family, and a pair of each kind of animal, from the Flood (in the Bible, Genesis 6-8). **b** *Figurative.* any place of refuge. **2** *U.S.* a large flatboat used to carry freight or as a house in western rivers during the westward movement. **3** *Informal.* **a** any large, clumsy boat: *The barge was a wallowing, leaky old ark.* **b** any large, clumsy vehicle. **c** *U.S.* any large, clumsy dwelling. **4** a cabinet in Jewish synagogues and temples, for housing holy scrolls of the Pentateuch. See also **Ark of the Covenant. 5** *Archaic or Dialect.* a chest, box, or basket.
[Old English *earc* < Latin *arca* chest]

Ark., Arkansas.

Ar|kan|san (är kan′zən), *n.* a native or inhabitant of Arkansas.

Ar|kan|saw|yer (är′kən sô′yər), *n. Informal or Dialect.* = Arkansan.

Ar|kie (är′kē), *n. U.S. Informal.* a migratory farm worker from Arkansas: ... *the "Okies" and "Arkies" in the orchards and vegetable fields of California* (White and Renner). [American English]

Ark of the Covenant, the wooden chest or box in which the Israelites kept the two stone tablets containing the Ten Commandments.

ar|kose (är kōs′), *n.* a sandstone derived from granite, containing small quantities of feldspar and occasionally quartz or mica. [< French *arkose*]

arles (ärlz), *n.pl. or sing. North British Dialect.* money given in confirmation of a bargain or engagement; earnest money. [< diminutive of Old French *eres* (plural) < Latin *arrha,* short for *arrabō* < Greek *arrhabôn*]

bones and joints of the arm:

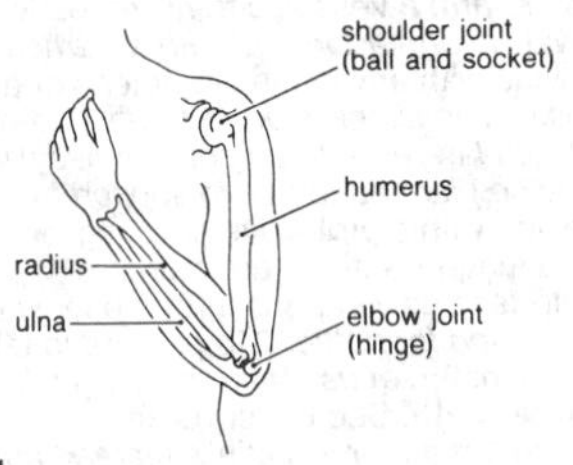

muscles of the arm:

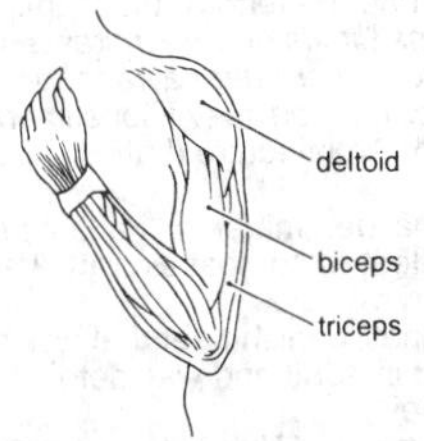

***arm**[1]
definition 1

***arm**[1] (ärm), *n.* **1a** the part of a person's body between the shoulder and the hand, sometimes including the latter. **b** the part between the shoulder and the elbow. **2a** a forelimb or similar organ of any animal. The front legs of a bear or the tentacles of an octopus are sometimes called arms. **b** a cut of meat from this part. **3** something shaped or used like an arm. An armchair has two arms. An inlet is an arm of the sea. **4** a main branch or limb of a tree. **5** an extension or division; branch: *the research arm of a company, the administrative arm of a school, the political arm of an organization.* **6** a part of an instrument or machine projecting from a trunk or axis. **7a** either of the lower cross pieces of an anchor. **b** the part of a yard extending on either side of the mast. **8** the part of a dress, shirt, suit, or other garment covering an arm; sleeve. **9** *Figurative.* power; authority: *The strong arm of the law keeps order in the city.* **10** that upon which a person counts for support or assistance: *Sir Lancelot, my right arm* (Tennyson). **11a** the ability to pitch, throw, or pass with power and speed: *With his arm, he can pitch every day.* **b** a player having this ability: *one of the best arms in the game.* **12** a shoulder-cut of meat.

arm in arm, with arms linked: *She walked arm in arm with her sister.*

at arm's length, away from close contact or familiarity; at a distance: *He learned to hold people at arm's length without seeming unfriendly.*

chance one's arm, *British Informal.* to take a chance; risk a loss or defeat: *From the time that Bolus decided to chance his arm he looked an altogether more dangerous player* (London Times).

in arms, unable yet to walk; very young: *Her little brother was but a babe in arms.*

Pronunciation Key: hat, āge, cãre, fär; let, ēqual, tėrm; it, īce; hot, ōpen, ôrder; oil, out; cup, pu̇t, rüle; child; long; thin; ᴛʜen; zh, measure; ə represents **a** in about, **e** in taken, **i** in pencil, **o** in lemon, **u** in circus.

present arms, a to bring a rifle to a vertical position in front of the body. **b** this position. **c** a command to assume this position.

put the arm on, *Slang.* to get money from; collect funds from; induce to pay: *The use of deception to put the arm on debtors is unlawful* (Wall Street Journal).

twist one's arm, to compel by influence; use pressure on: *. . . a ruthless planner and politically astute enough to twist the Treasury arm for a just cause* (London Times).

with open arms, in a warm, friendly way; cordially: *to welcomed home with open arms.*

[Old English *earm*]—**arm'like',** *adj.*

arm[2] (ärm), *n., v.* **—*n.*** **1** a weapon of any kind. Guns and swords, an ax, or a stick—any of these might be arms for defense or attack. See also **arms. 2a** a combat branch of one of the armed forces, such as the infantry or artillery. **b** one of the armed forces, such as the army, navy, or air force: *During the 1914-18 War he played a very active part in developing the Italian air arm as a member of the staff of the Italian G.H.Q.* (London Times). [singular of *arms*]

—*v.t.* **1a** to supply with weapons: *In colonial days the French armed the Indians to attack the British.* **b** to install guns in or on; equip with armament: *to arm a vessel.* **c** to make ready for use in war: *to arm a torpedo with a warhead.* **2** to provide with any means to defend or attack something: *The skunk is armed with a powerful scent. Each lawyer entered court armed with the evidence he planned to use to support his case.* **3** to provide with a protective covering; armor. **4** to provide a magnet with an armature.

—*v.i.* **1** to take up weapons; prepare for war: *The soldiers armed for battle.* **2** to prepare to take action (against): *Let us arm against injustice.*

arm to the teeth. See under **teeth.**

[< Old French *armer* < Latin *armāre* < *arma* weapons]

Arm., **1** Armenia. **2** Armenian.

ARM (ärm), *n. U.S.* adjustable rate mortgage (a mortgage with an interest rate that changes periodically during the term of the loan): *ARMs with caps [limits on rate increases or decreases] provide greater payment predictability and security for the borrower* (Consumers' Guide).

Ar.M., Master of Architecture (Latin, *Architecturae Magister*).

ar|ma|da (är mä'də, -mā'-), *n.* **1** a large fleet of warships. **2** a fleet of combat aircraft. **3** any large group of military vehicles.

the Armada, the Spanish fleet that was sent to attack England in 1588 and was defeated in the English Channel.

[< Spanish *armada* < Vulgar Latin *armāta* armed force < Latin *armāre* to arm.]

***ar|ma|dil|lo** (är'mə dil'ō), *n., pl.* **-los.** a small, burrowing mammal that has a very hard protective shell of small, bony plates. The armadillo feeds chiefly at night, and some kinds when attacked can roll themselves into a ball inside this armor. Armadillos are found in tropical South America and some parts of southern North America, especially Texas. [< Spanish *armadillo* (diminutive) < *armado* armed (one) < Latin *armātus,* (originally) past participle of *armāre* to arm]

***armadillo**

Ar|ma|ged|don (är'mə ged'ən), *n.* **1** the place of a great and final conflict between the forces of good and evil at the end of the world (in the Bible, Revelation 16:16). **2** *Figurative.* any great and final conflict: *A more effective way to prevent the modern Armageddon from growing beyond the technical possibility of control would be to ban the testing of long-range missiles* (Bulletin of Atomic Scientists).

Ar|ma|gnac (är'mȧ nyȧk'), *n.* a type of dry brandy made in southwestern France.

ar|ma|ment (är'mə mənt), *n.* **1** war equipment and supplies; the weapons, ammunition, and equipment of a military force, vehicle, or installation. Guns, shells, bombs, electronic detection devices, missiles, and all other offensive and defensive equipment of a fort, ship, airplane, or the like, are armament. *Armaments are not so much a cause of war as a consequence of international suspicion and antagonism* (Wall Street Journal). **2** the army, navy, and other military forces of a nation, including both men and equipment. **3** the act or process of arming; preparation for war: *Disarmament is as much a function of national security as is armament* (Saturday Review). **4** equipment or apparatus for resistance or action of any kind: *the defensive armament of plants and animals.* (*Figurative.*) *But when she comes to the cabalettas, she unleashes her full technical armament* (Harper's). [< Latin *armāmenta* implements < *armāre* to arm]

ar|ma|men|tar|i|um (är'mə men tãr'ē əm), *n., pl.* **-i|a** (-ē ə). **1** all the equipment and therapeutic resources of a physician, dentist, hospital, or other health facility: *Morphine in the past has been one of the towering stand-bys of the physician's armamentarium* (New York Times). **2** the equipment or resources of anything: *. . . the armamentarium of up-to-date primary and secondary school techniques* (Scientific American). [< Latin *armāmentārium* arsenal < *armāmenta* implements < *armāre* to arm]

ar|ma|ture (är'mə chər), *n., v.,* **-tured, -tur|ing.** **—*n.*** **1a** a coil of wire wound around an iron core, placed between opposite poles of a magnet in an electric motor or dynamo. In a motor, electric current is sent through coils of wire, which causes the armature to move through the magnetic field between the poles. See picture under **generator. b** a piece of soft iron placed in contact with the poles of a magnet to maintain the magnetic power. **c** the movable part of an electric relay or buzzer, placed in a magnetic field which causes it to move. **2** = armor. **3a** the protective or defensive covering of an animal or plant. A turtle's shell is an armature. **b** any part or organ of an animal or plant serving for offense (teeth, suckers of dodder) or defense (thorns). **4** *Fine Arts.* a framework over which clay or some other substance is applied in modeling. **5** a frame or support for carrying a load or pack. **6** wire wound round and round a cable.

—*v.t.* to provide with an armature.

[< Latin *armātūra* < *armāre* to arm. See etym. of doublet **armor.**]

ar|ma vi|rum|que ca|no (är'mä wi rùm'kwe kä'nō), *Latin.* of arms and the man I sing (the first line of the *Aeneid*).

arm|band (ärm'band'), *n.* **1** a band of cloth worn around the upper arm as a symbol or badge: *a mourning armband of black.* **2** = armlet (def. 1).

arm bar, a wrestling hold in which the opponent's arm is held taut and used as a lever in forcing him to the floor.

arm|chair (ärm'chãr'), *n., adj.* **—*n.*** a chair with pieces at the sides to support a person's arms. **—*adj.*** **1** expressing opinions or theorizing about a subject without being directly involved or having practical experience in it: *an armchair politician. A brilliant performance against the Los Angeles Rams . . . temporarily silenced armchair coaches who argue that he should be benched because of his age* (Time). **2** sharing in another's experiences by reading, hearing, or viewing: *an armchair explorer, armchair travel.*

armed[1] (ärmd), *adj.* **1** having arms: *an armed chair.* **2** having arms of a certain kind: *long-armed.* [*arm*[1] + *-ed*[2]]

armed[2] (ärmd), *adj.* **1** furnished with arms or armor; equipped for war: *an armed boat.* **2** using arms: *an armed attack.* [*arm*[2] + *-ed*[2]]

armed forces, all of the military, naval, and air forces of a country: *They are highly dubious about the wisdom of unbalancing the armed forces [by] placing the emphasis on air and nuclear power at the expense of both the Army and the Navy* (Newsweek).

Armed Forces Day, a day in honor of all the United States armed forces, replacing separate days for each branch, observed the third Saturday in May.

armed neutrality, the status of a nation or nations refraining from war but in readiness for it.

armed robbery, robbery involving the coercive use of a weapon or weapons.

Armen., Armenian.

Ar|me|ni|an (är mē'nē ən, -mēn'yən), *adj., n.* **—*adj.*** **1** of Armenia, its people, or their language. **2** of the Armenian church.

—*n.* **1** a person born or living in Armenia, especially a person whose native language is Armenian. **2** a member of the Armenian Church. **3** the Indo-European language of the Armenians.

Armenian Church, an independent church close to the Orthodox Church in doctrine.

arm|er (är'mər), *n.* a person who arms or equips with arms.

ar|met (är'met), *n.* a defensive head covering introduced in the 1400's. It consisted of a round iron helmet with a projection over the back of the neck and a visor, beaver, and gorget to protect the face and throat. [< Middle French *armet* < Old French *armette* (diminutive) < *arme* arm[2]]

arm|ful (ärm'fùl), *n., pl.* **-fuls.** as much as one arm or both arms can hold: *She carried an armful of groceries to the car.*

arm|guard (ärm'gärd'), *n.* **1** a protective covering for the arm. **2** *Boxing.* defense with the arm.

arm|hole (ärm'hōl'), *n.* a hole for the arm or sleeve in a garment.

ar|mi|ger (är'mə jər), *n.* **1** a person entitled to heraldic arms. **2** a person who attended a knight to bear his armor; squire. [< Medieval Latin *armiger* < Latin, armor bearer < *arma* arms + *gerere* carry]

ar|mig|er|al (är mij'ər əl), *adj.* of the character of an armiger.

ar|mig|er|ous (är mij'ər əs), *adj.* entitled to bear heraldic arms.

ar|mil or **ar|mill** (är'mil), *n. Historical.* a bracelet or armlet, especially one awarded by an official of a government or church in recognition of exemplary action. [< Old French *armille* < Latin *armilla* arm ring, hoop < *armus* shoulder]

ar|mil|la (är mil'ə), *n., pl.* **-mil|lae** (-mil'ē). **1** = armil. **2** = armillary sphere. [< Latin *armilla* < *armus* shoulder]

ar|mil|lar|y (är'mə ler'ē, är mil'ər-), *adj.* **1** like a bracelet. **2** consisting of hoops and rings. [< Latin *armilla* arm ring, hoop (< *armus* shoulder) + English *-ary*]

armillary sphere, an old type of celestial globe or sphere, used for determining celestial positions, consisting of movable metal rings or hoops representing the equator, ecliptic, meridian, and other circles.

arm|ing (är'ming), *n. Nautical.* a piece of tallow at the end of the weight (lead) on a sounding line, used to bring to the surface samples of the sand or other matter covering the bottom.

Ar|min|i|an (är min'ē ən), *adj., n.* **—*adj.*** of Arminius or Arminianism.

—*n.* a believer in Arminian doctrines.

Ar|min|i|an|ism (är min'ē ə niz'əm), *n.* the doctrines of Jacobus Arminius (1560-1609) and his followers, who criticized Calvin's doctrines and believed that there was a chance of salvation for all men through God's grace.

ar|mip|o|tent (är mip'ə tənt), *adj.* mighty in arms or war (originally an epithet of Mars). [< Latin *armipotēns, -entis* < *arma* weapons + *potēns* powerful]

ar|mi|stice (är'mə stis), *n.* a stop in fighting; temporary peace; truce. An armistice is arranged by agreement on all sides, often while a permanent peace is being arranged. [< New Latin *armistitium* < Latin *arma* arms + *sistere* stop, stand]

Armistice Day, *U.S.* November 11, the anniversary of the end of World War I in 1918. It is called *Remembrance Day* in the Commonwealth of Nations. As an official holiday it was renamed *Veterans Day* in the United States in 1954, and between 1971 and 1978 it was celebrated on the fourth Monday in October.

arm|less[1] (ärm'lis), *adj.* **1** without either arm. **2** without any branch.

arm|less[2] (ärm'lis), *adj.* without arms or weapons.

arm|let (ärm'lit), *n.* **1** an ornamental band or bracelet for the upper arm. **2** a small inlet of the sea.

arm|load (ärm'lōd'), *n.* as much as an arm or the arms carry, especially in a cradled position; armful: *an armload of books.*

arm|lock (ärm'lok'), *n.* a wrestling hold in which the opponent's arm is held taut and twisted.

ar|moire (är mwär'), *n.* a large, often ornate cupboard, clothes press, or movable closet, with doors and usually with shelves. [< French *armoire* < Old French *armarie,* learned borrowing from Latin *armārium* cabinet < *arma* weapons. See etym. of doublets **almirah, ambry.**]

ar|mon|i|ca (är mon'ə kə), *n.* = glass harmonica.

ar|mor** (är'mər), *n., v.* **—*n. **1** a covering, usually of metal or leather, worn to protect the body in fighting. See the picture opposite on the next page. **2** any similar kind of protective covering against wear or accident. A diver's suit and the scales of a fish are armor. **3** the steel or iron plates or other protective covering of a warship, aircraft, tank, or fortification; armor plate. **4** the armored forces and equipment, such as the tanks, of a military unit. **5** a protective metal covering wrapped around an electric cable or telephone line. **6** *Figurative.* anything serving as protective or defensive: *the armor of knowledge.*

—*v.t., v.i.* to cover or protect with armor. Also, *British,* **armour.**

[< Old French *armeüre* < Latin *armātūra* < *armāre* to arm. See etym. of doublet **armature.**]

—ar'mor|like', *adj.*

ar|mor|bear|er (är'mər bãr'ər), *n.* an attendant who carried the armor or weapons of a warrior.

ar|mor-clad (är'mər klad'), *n., adj.* **—*n.*** (formerly) an armored war vessel. **—*adj.*** wearing armor; protected by armor; armorplated.

ar|mored (är'mərd), *adj.* **1** covered or protected with armor: *an armored personnel carrier.* **2** using or equipped with armored vehicles: *He served in an armored division.*

armored cable, an electric cable having a protective metal covering of steel wires or of other flexible, rust-resistant material.

armored car, **1** a motor vehicle protected by armor plate against small-arms fire, especially a truck to transport money and other valuables. **2** a military vehicle with similar protection, often carrying a mounted gun, and used especially for reconnaissance.

armored cruiser, one of a class of warships below the battleship class, having less armor and armament and greater speed than a battleship.

armored force, a military assault force of considerable mobility and striking power, made up of tanks supported by infantry and artillery troops.

ar|mor|er (är′mər ər), *n.* **1** a soldier or sailor in charge of firearms and their maintenance, or a member of the armed forces who loads and services weapons aboard a combat airplane. The armorer of a warship takes care of the revolvers, pistols, rifles, and their ammunition on the ship. **2** a manufacturer of firearms. **3** (originally) a person who made or repaired armor: *Now thrive the armorers* (Shakespeare).

ar|mo|ri|al (är môr′ē əl, -mōr′-), *adj., n.* —*adj.* having to do with coats of arms or heraldry.
—*n.* a book showing coats of arms. —**ar|mo′ri|al|ly**, *adv.*

armorial bearings, a coat or coats of arms; heraldic devices.

Ar|mor|ic (är môr′ik, -mor′-), *adj., n.* —*adj.* of or having to do with Brittany, its people, or their language; Breton.
—*n.* **1** a native of Brittany. **2** the Breton language.
[< *Armorica,* an ancient region in France corresponding to Brittany]

Ar|mor|i|can (är môr′ə kən, -mor′-), *adj., n.* = Armoric.

ar|mor|ist (är′mər ist), *n.* an expert in heraldry.

armor plate, steel or iron plating to protect warships, tanks, aircraft, forts, and the like. Armor plate is now usually a specially toughened alloy of steel.

ar|mor|plat|ed (är′mər plā′tid), *adj.* covered or protected by armor plate; ironclad.

ar|mor|y[1] (är′mər ē), *n., pl.* **-mor|ies. 1a** a place where weapons are kept; arsenal. **b** *Figurative: Intense secrecy, sudden surprise, and attack, attack, attack are very much part of the political armory* (Atlantic). **2** *U.S.* a place where weapons are made. **3** *U.S. and Canadian.* a building with a drill hall, offices, and other facilities, for militia: *Night after night we made our way to the Toronto armories, where we right wheeled, shouldered arms, changed arms, left turned and halted with a bang that nearly broke our insteps* (Maclean's). **4** *Archaic.* armor; arms. [< *armor*]

ar|mor|y[2] (är′mər ē), *n.* **1** the art of blazoning arms; heraldry. **2** *Archaic.* heraldic bearings; coats of arms. [< Old French *armoierie* < *armoyer* to blazon with (coats of) arms < *arme* heraldic arms < Latin *arma* weapons]

ar|mour (är′mər), *n., v.t., v.i. British.* armor.

ar|mour|bear|er (är′mər bãr′ər), *n. British.* armorbearer.

ar|mour-clad (är′mər klad′), *n., adj. British.* armor-clad.

ar|moured (är′mərd), *adj. British.* armored.

ar|mour|er (är′mər ər), *n. British.* armorer.

ar|mour|ies (är′mər ēz), *n.pl. Canadian.* armory (def. 3).

ar|mour|y (är′mər ē), *n., pl.* **-mour|ies.** *British.* armory.

arm|pit (ärm′pit′), *n.* the hollow place under the arm at the shoulder; axilla.

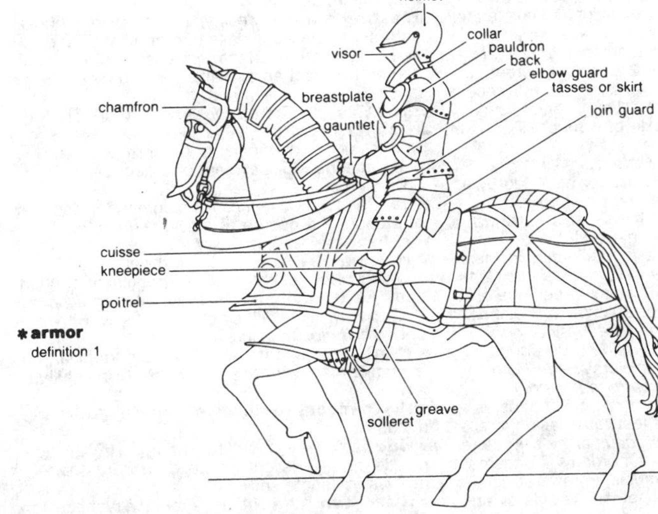

***armor**
definition 1

arm|rest (ärm′rest′), *n.* a support for the arm, especially one on a chair or couch, and on the inside of the door of an automobile.

arms (ärmz), *n.pl.* **1** weapons: *We have the arms we need to fight. The arms race is a symptom of the world's affliction* (Bulletin of Atomic Scientists). *Noncombatant soldiers do not carry arms.* SYN: armament. **2** the use of arms; fighting; war: *A soldier is a man of arms. He had abandoned the business into which his family had put him and had taken up the profession of arms* (Atlantic). SYN: combat, battle. **3a** a design used as a symbol of a family or government; coat of arms. **b** symbols and designs used in heraldry as emblems of official dignity by cities, corporations, clubs, and other organizations. SYN: blazonry.
bear arms, a to serve as a soldier; fight: *The soldier bore arms for his country. . . . the present King . . . has constrained our fellow Citizens . . . to bear Arms against their Country* (Declaration of Independence). **b** to possess and display a coat of arms: *A knight bore his arms on his shield.*
shoulder arms, a to hold a rifle almost upright with the barrel resting in the hollow of the shoulder and the butt in the hand. **b** to bear arms: *Old and young alike shouldered arms to fight against the hated enemy.*
take up arms, to arm for attack or defense: *The settlers took up arms against the Indians.* (*Figurative.*) *You will find it a far easier field to wage war against all the armies . . . than to take up arms against any truth of God* (Nathaniel Ward).
to arms, prepare for battle: *To arms! to arms! the fierce Virago cries* (Alexander Pope).
under arms, a having weapons; equipped for fighting: *The troops were under arms soon after war was declared.* **b** mobilized: *The whole city got under arms* (Dante Gabriel Rossetti).
up in arms, a very angry; in rebellion: *The students were up in arms when their holiday was canceled.* **b** preparing for a battle: *The minutemen were up in arms shortly after the British left Boston.*
[< Old French *armes* < Latin *arma* weapons]

arm|scye (ärm′sī′), *n.* the opening in a garment within which a sleeve is set; armhole. [< *arm*[1] + *scye* opening in a garment]

arms|eye (ärmz′ī′), *n.* = armscye.

arms race, a competition between countries for supremacy in armaments: *The arms race is expanding all the time, the armies, navies, and air forces are being increased continuously* (New York Times).

Arm|strong line (ärm′strông), the altitude level above which low atmospheric pressure would cause body fluids to vaporize if not protected. It is calculated at about 63,000 feet but varies according to circumstances. [< H. G. *Armstrong,* born 1899, a general in the United States Air Force]

arm-twist|er (ärm′twis′tər), *n. U.S. Informal.* a person who uses pressure to influence.

arm-twist|ing (ärm′twis′ting), *n. U.S. Informal.* a compelling by influence; pressure: *After some arm-twisting by fellow union leaders* [*he*] *followed suit* (Time).

ar|mure (är′myər), *n.* a fabric with a pebbled surface resulting from small geometric patterns in weaving, originally of heavy silk, now of many fibers or blends. [< Old French *armeüre* defensive covering < Latin *armātūra* armor < *armāre* to arm < *arma* arms (because the fabric weave resembles armor)]

arm wrestling, a contest of strength between two people, in which the contenders grasp usually right hands, resting their right elbows on a table. Each person tries to force the other's hand down to the table.

ar|my (är′mē), *n., pl.* **-mies. 1** a large, organized group of soldiers trained and armed to fight wars, especially on land: *American armies have fought in many countries.* SYN: troops. **2** Often, **Army.** all the military forces of a nation, except the naval forces and, sometimes, also the air forces. **3** = field army. **4** any group of people organized for a purpose: *The Salvation Army helps the poor.* **5** *Figurative.* a very large number; multitude: *an army of ants.* SYN: throng, host. [< Old French *armee* < Vulgar Latin *armāta* armed force < Latin *armāre* to arm. See etym. of doublet **armada.**]

Army Air Forces, the name from 1941 to 1947 of the aviation branch of the U.S. Army, now part of the Air Force. *Abbr:* **AAF** (no periods), **A.A.F.**

army ant, any one of a group of African and tropical American ants that travel in large numbers. They swarm over and devour even large animals.

army brat, *U.S. Slang.* a child of a soldier in the regular army.

army corps, a large unit of organization in an army, comprising two or more divisions.

Army Day, *U.S.* a day in honor of the United States Army, replaced by Armed Forces Day.

army group, a tactical military unit of organization, comprising two or more armies.

army list, *British.* the official list of all commissioned officers.

army of occupation, an army sent into a defeated or subject country to enforce a treaty, keep order, or maintain a faltering government.

army surplus, obsolete or excess supplies and equipment of the army classified as surplus and often sold or for sale to civilians.

army worm, the larva of a night-flying moth that often travels with large numbers of its kind destroying grain and garden crops.

Ar|nel (är nel′), *n. Trademark.* a synthetic, wrinkle- and shrink-resistant fiber used for shirts, suits, and other articles of clothing.

***ar|ni|ca** (är′nə kə), *n.* **1** a healing liquid applied to bruises and sprains, prepared from the dried flowers, leaves, or roots of the arnica plant. **2** a European plant related to the aster. It is a perennial herb with showy, yellow flowers, native to the north temperate and arctic regions. **3** the dried flowers or roots used in preparing the liquid. [< New Latin *arnica*]

***arnica**
definition 2

ar|ni|cin (är′nə sin), *n.* an acrid, yellowish, crystalline substance in the flowers and roots of arnica, used in preparing arnica, the healing liquid.

Ar|nold|i|an (är nōl′dē ən), *adj., n.* —*adj.* of or characteristic of the English poet and essayist Matthew Arnold (1822-1888), his style, or his writings. —*n.* an admirer of Matthew Arnold.

ar|not|ta (är not′ə), *n.* = annatto.

ar|not|to (är not′ō), *n.* = annatto.

a|roar (ə rôr′), *adj., adv.* roaring: *The papers leap forth from the presses aroar* (Ogden Nash).

ar|oid (ar′oid), *adj., n.* —*adj.* belonging to the arum family; araceous. —*n.* any such plant.
[< *ar*(um) + *-oid*]

a|roi|de|ous (ə roi′dē əs), *adj.* = araceous.

a|roint (ə roint′), *interj., v. Archaic.* —*interj.* Often, **aroint thee!** avaunt! begone!: *Aroint thee, Witch* (Shakespeare).
—*v.t.* to drive away: *Whiskered cats arointed flee* (Elizabeth Barrett Browning). Also, **aroynt.**

a|ro|ma (ə rō′mə), *n.* **1** a pleasant, often spicy, odor; sweet smell; fragrance: *Just smell the aroma of the cake baking in the oven.* SYN: scent, perfume. **2** a distinctive fragrance or flavor: *the aroma of fresh coffee.* SYN: redolence. **3** *Figurative.* a subtle quality: *The room conveyed a delicate aroma of the mysterious East.* SYN: flavor. [< Latin *arōma* < Greek *árōma, -atos* spice]

Pronunciation Key: hat, āge, cãre, fär; let, ēqual, tėrm; it, īce; hot, ōpen, ôrder; oil, out; cup, pu̇t, rüle; child; long; thin; ᴛʜen; zh, measure; ə represents **a** in about, **e** in taken, **i** in pencil, **o** in lemon, **u** in circus.

a|ro|mal (ə rō′məl), *adj.* of or having to do with aroma or aromas.

ar|o|mat|ic (ar′ə mat′ik), *adj., n.* —*adj.* **1** sweet-smelling; spicy; fragrant: *The cinnamon tree has an aromatic inner bark.* **2** of or designating a group of organic chemical compounds containing a closed chain of carbon atoms and mostly having a pleasant odor. They include benzene, its derivatives, naphthalene, anthracene, and others.
—*n.* **1** a plant, drug, or medicine that yields a fragrant smell, such as sage, or certain spices and oils. **2** an aromatic chemical compound: *Benzene, toluene, and xylenes, the three basic aromatics, were once made predominantly from coal* (J. D. Heldman and W. W. Reynolds).
[< Latin *arōmaticus* < Greek *arōmatikós* < *árōma, -atos* spice] —**ar′o|mat′i|cal|ly,** *adv.*

ar|o|mat|i|cal (ar′ə mat′ə kəl), *adj. Obsolete.* aromatic.

a|ro|ma|tic|i|ty (ə rō′mə tis′ə tē), *n.* the chemical property characteristic of aromatic compounds.

aromatic vinegar, a solution of volatile oils in acetic acid, alcohol, and water, used as a stimulant in fainting, fatigue, and similar ailments.

a|ro|ma|ti|za|tion (ə rō′mə tə zā′shən), *n. Chemistry.* the production of aromatic (closed-chain) hydrocarbons from aliphatic (open-chain) hydrocarbons.

a|ro|ma|tize (ə rō′mə tīz), *v.t.,* **-tized, -tiz|ing.** to make aromatic; season with spices: *Aromatized wines include ... French and Italian vermouths. They are famous for their distinctive odor, called bouquet* (J. Bernard Robb).

a|rose (ə rōz′), *v.* past tense of **arise**: *She arose from her chair.*

a|round (ə round′), *prep., adv.* —*prep.* **1** in a circle about: *He has traveled around the world.* **2** closely surrounding: *She had a coat around her shoulders.* **3** on all sides of: *Woods lay around the house.* **4** *Informal.* in many parts of; here and there in; about: *He leaves his books around the house.* **5** *U.S. Informal.* somewhere about; near: *Please stay around the house.* **6** *U.S. Informal.* near in amount, number, time, or other quantity, to; approximately: *That hat cost him around ten dollars. I'll be home around three o'clock.* **7** on the far side of: *just around the corner.*
—*adv.* **1** in a circle: *He spun around like a top.* **2** in circumference: *The tree measures four feet around.* **3** on all sides; in every direction: *A dense fog lay around.* **4** *Especially U.S.* here and there; in many places: *We walked around to see the town.* **5** *U.S. Informal.* somewhere about; near: *Wait around awhile.* **6** in the opposite direction: *Turn around! You are going the wrong way.* **7** going about; out of bed; stirring: *He is now able to be around, but is not yet fully well.* **8** from one to another: *If you pass the book around, everyone can see the pictures.*
have been around, *Informal.* to be experienced in worldly ways; possess wisdom or sophistication: *One could see by his charm and elegant manners that the young prince had been around.*
▶ See **round** for usage note.

a|round-the-clock (ə round′ᴛʜə klok′), *adj.* never stopping; constant: *Steel making is now a continuous-process industry that requires around-the-clock work, seven days a week* (Wall Street Journal).

a|rous|al (ə rou′zəl), *n.* **1** the act of arousing. **2** the fact of being aroused.

a|rouse (ə rouz′), *v.,* **a|roused, a|rous|ing.** —*v.t.* **1** to stir to action; excite: *The attack on Pearl Harbor aroused the whole country. His behavior had aroused suspicion.* **SYN:** stimulate, kindle. **2** to wake up (a person); stir from sleep; awaken: *The noise aroused the sleeping guard.*
—*v.i.* to awaken; bestir oneself. —**a|rous′er,** *n.*

a|row (ə rō′), *adv.* in a row.

a|roynt (ə roint′), *interj., v.t. Archaic.* aroint.

ar|peg|gi|at|ed (är pej′ē ā′tid), *adj.* = arpeggioed.

***ar|peg|gi|o** (är pej′ē ō, -pej′ō), *n., pl.* **-gi|os.** *Music.* **1** the sounding of the notes of a chord in rapid succession instead of together. **2** a chord sounded in this way. [< Italian *arpeggio* < *arpeggiare* play the harp < *arpa* harp < a Germanic word]

***arpeggio**

written played

ar|peg|gi|oed (är pej′ē ōd, -pej′ōd), *adj.* sounded in the manner of an arpeggio, as a chord.

ar|pent (är′pənt; *French* år pän′), *n.* **1** an old French unit of land measure, still sometimes used in parts of North America (especially Quebec and Louisiana) and in certain British colonies, varying from 0.84 to 1.28 acres. **2** an old French unit of linear measure, equal to approximately 11.5 rods. [< French *arpent*]

ar|que|bus (är′kwə bəs), *n.* = harquebus.

ar|que|bus|ier (är′kwə bə sir′), *n.* = harquebusier.

arr., **1a** arranged. **b** arrangement or arrangements. **2a** arrival. **b** arrive.

ar|ra|ca|cha (är′ə kä′chə), *n., pl.* **-chas.** a South American plant of the parsley family, cultivated for its nutritious roots, especially in the Andes. [< Spanish *arracacha* < Quechua]

ar|rack (ar′ək), *n.* any of various strong liquors of Asiatic manufacture, usually made from toddy, molasses, rice, or dates. Also, **arak.** [< Arabic *'araq* (fermented) juice]

ar|rah (ar′ə), *interj. Irish.* an exclamation of surprise, indignation, or the like.

ar|raign (ə rān′), *v., n.* —*v.t.* **1** to bring before a law court to answer a charge: *The cashier was arraigned on a charge of stealing.* **SYN:** charge, indict. **2** to call in question; find fault with; accuse.
—*n.* the act or process of arraigning.
[< Anglo-French *arainer* < Old French *a-* to + *raisnier* speak < Vulgar Latin *ratiōnāre* < Latin *ratiō, -ōnis* argumentation] —**ar|raign′er,** *n.*

ar|raign|ment (ə rān′mənt), *n.* **1** the act of bringing before a court to answer a charge: *the arraignment of the suspects.* **2** unfavorable criticism; a charging with faults; blaming; accusation.

ar|range (ə rānj′), *v.,* **-ranged, -rang|ing.** —*v.t.* **1** to put in the proper, or any desired, order: *to arrange furniture or one's hair. Please arrange the books on the library shelf. He arranged his business so that he could take a vacation in September.* **SYN:** dispose, order, group, organize. **2** to plan; prepare beforehand: *to arrange a dinner, arrange a conference.* **3** to reach an understanding about; settle (a dispute): *The two neighbors have now arranged their differences.* **SYN:** adjust. **4** *Music.* to adapt (a piece of music) to voices or instruments for which it was not written: *This music for the violin is also arranged for the piano. Abbr:* arr.
—*v.i.* **1a** to prepare beforehand; form plans; plan: *Can you arrange to meet me this evening?* **SYN:** contrive. **b** to make preparations; take the necessary steps: *to arrange for a taxi to come and get us.* **2** to come to an understanding; reach agreement: *to arrange with the enemy.*
[< Old French *arangier* < *a-* to + *rangier* assemble < *rang* rank[1] < a Germanic word] —**ar|range′a|ble,** *adj.* —**ar|rang′er,** *n.*

ar|range|ment (ə rānj′mənt), *n.* **1a** the act of putting in order: *The arrangement of the flowers for the wedding took a long time.* **SYN:** disposition, placement. **b** the condition of being put in order: *Careful arrangement of books in the library made them easy to find.* **2** the way or order in which things or persons are put, such as a design or pattern: *You can make six arrangements of the letters A, B, and C.* **SYN:** array. **3** something arranged in a particular way: *Make an arrangement of the chairs to form a circle.* **SYN:** formation. **4** an adjustment, settlement, or agreement: *No arrangement could possibly please everybody.* **5a** the adaptation of a piece of music to voices or instruments for which it was not originally written. **b** a piece so adapted; a transcription: *This piece of music for the piano also has an arrangement for the violin.*
arrangements, plans or preparations for an occasion, function, or act: *All arrangements have been made for our trip to Chicago.*
[< French *arrangement* < *arranger* arrange]

ar|rant (ar′ənt), *adj.* thoroughgoing; downright: *He was such an arrant liar that nobody ever believed him.* **SYN:** absolute, unmitigated, inveterate. [variant of *errant*] —**ar′rant|ly,** *adv.*

ar|ras (ar′əs), *n.* **1** a rich tapestry fabric, with figures and scenes in color. **2** a curtain, screen, or hangings of tapestry. [< *Arras,* a city in France]

ar|ra|sene (ar′ə sēn′), *n.* a kind of embroidery thread with a velvetlike pile of wool or silk. [< *arras*]

ar|ras|tra (ä räs′trə), *n. Historical, Western U.S. and Canada.* a crude mill, usually operated by a mule, for pulverizing gold and silver ores. Also, **arastra.** [American English < Spanish *arrastrar* to harrow < Latin *rastrum* harrow]

ar|ray (ə rā′), *n., v.* —*n.* **1** proper order; regular arrangement: *The troops were formed in battle array.* **SYN:** formation. **2** a display of persons or things; an imposing group: *an array of wedding gifts, an array of problems. The array of good players on the other team made our side look weak.* **3** a military force; soldiers: *Bade his messengers ride forth ... to summon his array* (Macaulay). **SYN:** troops, army. **4** clothes, especially for some special or festive occasion; dress: *bridal array. She wore gorgeous array.* **SYN:** attire. **5** *Mathematics, Statistics.* an orderly arrangement of numbers, terms, or symbols, in rows or columns. **6** *Aerospace.* a group of antennas or similar devices coupled together to increase their effectiveness.
—*v.t.* **1** to put in order for some purpose; arrange: *The general arrayed his troops for the battle.* (*Figurative.*) *His hasty plans were arrayed against a background of hysteria.* **SYN:** marshal, line up. **2** to dress in fine clothes; adorn: *She was arrayed like a queen in her magnificent dress.* (*Figurative.*) *A mountain ... arraying itself in the majesty of darkness* (William Gilpin). **SYN:** attire.
[< Anglo-French *arayer* < Old French *a-* to + *rei* order < a Germanic word] —**ar|ray′er,** *n.* —**ar|ray′ment,** *n.*

ar|ray|al (ə rā′əl), *n.* **1** the act of arraying; muster of a force. **2** array.

ar|rear (ə rir′), *n.* **1** something not done or overdue: *I owe a long arrear of thanks* (Dickens). **2** something held in reserve.
arrears, a money due but not paid; debts: *He collected his arrears of pay.* **b** unfinished work; things not done on time: *I have arrears of correspondence to catch up on.*
in arrears, behind in payments, work, or other commitments: *When this is paid we shall still be in arrears. Spiritual progress is in arrears of material progress.*
[< Old French *ariere, arere* < Vulgar Latin *ad retrō* < Latin *ad* to, *retrō* back]

ar|rear|age (ə rir′ij), *n.* debts; arrears: *Arrearages in scheduled production were eliminated by the end of the quarter* (New York Times). [< Old French *arerage* < *ariere* arrear]

ar|rest (ə rest′), *v., n.* —*v.t.* **1** to seize by authority of the law; take to jail or court: *Policemen arrested the thieves.* **SYN:** apprehend. **2** to stop; check: *Filling a tooth arrests decay. A driver uses brakes to arrest his car's speed.* **SYN:** halt. See syn. under **stop. 3** to catch and hold: *Our attention was arrested by the sound of a shot.* **SYN:** capture.
—*n.* **1** a seizing by authority of the law; taking to jail or court: *We saw the arrest of the burglar.* **SYN:** detention. **2** the act of seizing; seizure. **3** a stopping of anything in motion or progress; checking: *Machines can now take over after an arrest of the heart's function during an operation.* **SYN:** stoppage, pause, check. **4a** a device for stopping the motion of a machine, moving part, or object. **b** a device to stop sparks that rise in smoke.
under arrest, held by the police; in the custody of the police: *The burglar has been placed under arrest.*
[< Old French *arester* < Vulgar Latin *arrestāre* < Latin *ad-* + *restāre* remain < *re-* back + *stāre* stand] —**ar|rest′a|ble,** *adj.* —**ar|rest′er,** *n.* —**ar|rest′ment,** *n.*

ar|rest|ant (ə res′tənt), *n.* a substance that checks the spread of destructive insects and larvae.

ar|rest|a|tion (ə res′tā′shən), *n.* a stopping or checking; arrest: *An interval of puzzled uncertainty naturally follows any sudden arrestation and deflection of the national course* (Allan Nevins).

ar|rest|ee (ə res′tē′), *n.* a person under arrest: *Arrested ... in 1945, he spent a year in American camps and was eventually released as "an erroneous arrestee"* (Atlantic).

arrester gear or **wire,** *British.* arresting gear.

ar|rest|ing (ə res′ting), *adj.* that catches and holds the attention; striking: *The most arresting portrayal of the evening was that given by Irene Hayes, in the role that I somehow think of persistently as Miss Dracula* (New Yorker). —**ar|rest′ing|ly,** *adv.*

arresting gear, *Especially U.S.* the wires, hooks, and other devices installed on an aircraft and across a landing surface, especially on an aircraft carrier, to arrest an aircraft's forward motion after landing.

ar|res|tive (ə res′tiv), *adj.* serving to arrest.

ar|res|tor (ə res′tər), *n.* (in Scots law) a person who legally holds money or property that has been attached for payment of a debt or other obligation.

ar|rêt (å re′), *n. French.* **1** a judgment or decision of a court. **2** a decree of a sovereign authority.

ar|rhi|zal (ə rī′zəl), *adj. Botany.* having no root.

ar|rhi|zous (ə rī′zəs), *adj.* = arrhizal.

ar|rhyth|mi|a (ə rith′mē ə), *n.* irregularity of heartbeat. Also, **arhythmia.** [< New Latin *arrhythmia* < Greek *arrhythmía* lack of rhythm < *a-* without + *rhythmós* measure]

ar|rhyth|mic (ə rith′mik, -riᴛʜ′-), *adj.* irregular; not rhythmic. Also, **arhythmic.** —**ar|rhyth′mi|cal|ly,** *adv.*

ar|rhyth|mi|cal (ə rith′mə kəl, -riᴛʜ′-), *adj.* = arrhythmic.

ar|ride (ə rīd′), *v.t.,* **-rid|ed, -rid|ing.** *Archaic.* to please; gratify; delight. [< Latin *arrīdēre* < *ad-* at + *rīdēre* laugh, smile]

ar|ri|ère-ban (ar′ē ər ban′; *French* å ryer bän′), *n.*

1 the summons of a feudal lord, calling his vassals to military duty. **2** the group of vassals so summoned. [< Old French *ariere-ban,* alteration of *arban, herban* < a Frankish word]

ar|rière-garde (à ryer gärd′), *n. French.* **1** any group, especially in the arts, that is behind or backward, as opposed to the avant-garde. **2** (literally) rear guard.

ar|rière-pen|sée (à ryer päɴ sā′), *n. French.* a thought kept back; mental reservation.

ar|ris (ar′is), *n.* **1** a sharp edge, such as of a squared stone. **2** a sharp ridge: *The fluted shaft of a Doric column has arrises.* [ultimately < Latin *arista* ear of grain. See etym. of doublets **arête, arista.**]

ar|riv|al (ə rī′vəl), *n.* **1** the act of arriving; coming: *She is waiting for the arrival of the train.* **SYN:** advent, appearance. *Abbr:* arr. **2** a person or thing that arrives: *The new arrival is a boy.*

ar|rive (ə rīv′), *v.,* **-rived, -riv|ing.** **—*v.i.*** **1** to reach the end of a journey; come to a place: *When did you arrive in town? Two policemen arrived on the scene of the accident.* **SYN:** See syn. under **come. 2** to come; occur: *The time has arrived for you to study.* **3** to be successful; establish position or reputation: *It took years for Beethoven to arrive as a composer. Abbr:* arr.
—*v.t. Archaic.* to reach; come to.
arrive at, to come to; reach: *You should arrive at school before nine o'clock. We must arrive at a decision soon.*
[< Old French *arriver* come to shore < Vulgar Latin *arrīpāre* < Latin *ad rīpam* to the shore]
—ar|riv′er, *n.*
▶ **Arrive** is followed by *at* when the place reached is a natural stopping point: *We arrived at the bridge, the stadium, the seashore, Chicago* (when city is just a stage in a journey). When a city or town is thought of as the end of a journey *arrive in* is used: *We arrived in Boston a week ago and found rooms in a fine hotel.*

ar|ri|vé (à rē vā′), *n. French.* a person who has recently achieved success, especially by unscrupulous means; an upstart; parvenu.

ar|ri|ve|der|ci (ä rē′vā der′chē), *interj., n. Italian.* a rivederci.

ar|ri|viste (à rē vēst′), *n. French.* an upstart; arrivé; parvenu: *Socially he was ... pretty much an arriviste, and in fine company still something of a duffer* (Atlantic).

ar|ro|ba (är rō′bä), *n.* **1** a unit of weight used in Spain, Portugal, and Latin America (25.36 pounds in Mexico; 32.38 pounds in Brazil). **2** a Spanish liquid measure, varying in different places and according to the liquid. [< Spanish *arroba* < Arabic *ar-rub'* the quarter (of a Spanish quintal)]

ar|ro|gance (ar′ə gəns), *n.* too great pride with contempt of others; haughtiness: *Her arrogance made it hard for us to like her.* **SYN:** overbearingness.

ar|ro|gan|cy (ar′ə gən sē), *n.* = arrogance.

ar|ro|gant (ar′ə gənt), *adj.* too proud and contemptuous of others; haughty. **SYN:** presumptuous, overbearing. See syn. under **haughty.** [< Latin *arrogāns, -antis,* present participle of *arrogāre* to claim < *ad-* + *rogāre* ask] **—ar′ro|gant|ly,** *adv.*

ar|ro|gate (ar′ə gāt), *v.t.,* **-gat|ed, -gat|ing. 1** to claim or take without right: *The despotic king arrogated to himself the power that belonged to the nobles.* **SYN:** appropriate, assume, usurp. **2** to claim for another or assign without good reasons: *He suspiciously arrogated bad motives to other people.* **SYN:** attribute, ascribe. [< Latin *arrogāre* (with English *-ate*[1]) < *ad-* + *rogāre* ask]
—ar′ro|ga′tion, *n.* **—ar′ro|ga′tor,** *n.*

ar|ron|disse|ment (à rôɴ dēs mäɴ′), *n., pl.* **-ments** (-mäɴ′). *French.* **1** the largest administrative subdivision of a department in France. Arrondissements are divided into cantons. **2** an administrative district of Paris.

ar|row (ar′ō), *n., v.* **—*n.*** **1** a slender, pointed shaft or stick for shooting from a bow. **2** anything like an arrow in shape or speed: (*Figurative.*) *Arrows of lightning shot across the sky.* **3** a sign used to show direction or position in maps, on road signs, on traffic lights, and to mark important items in writing.
—*v.t.* **1** to mark with an arrow to show direction or importance: *The most important points are arrowed in the left margin.* **2** to move swiftly toward and penetrate, like an arrow: *... the pickerel would occasionally arrow the surface* (Atlantic).
—*v.i.* to move very swiftly, like an arrow: *... in less than three minutes, the plane arrowed upward to 75,000 feet* (Newsweek).
[Old English *arwe*] **—ar′row|like′,** *adj.*

Ar|row (ar′ō), *n.* = Sagitta.

ar|row|back chair (ar′ō bak′), a chair having a back formed by vertical pieces of wood shaped somewhat like arrows.

***ar|row|head** (ar′ō hed′), *n.* **1** the pointed head or tip of an arrow. An arrowhead is usually shaped like a wedge and made of harder material than the shaft. The Indians made arrowheads of flint. **2** a marsh or water plant, many varieties of which have leaves shaped like arrowheads. **3** *Architecture.* the dart-shaped motif in an egg-and-dart molding. **4** a mark like an arrow or arrowhead used to indicate direction, such as on a map or road marker.

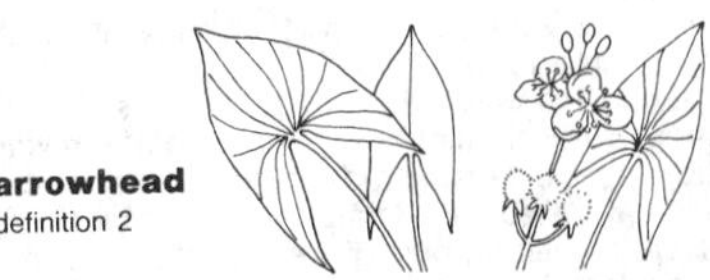
***arrowhead**
definition 2

ar|row-head|ed (ar′ō hed′id), *adj.* shaped like an arrowhead; sagittate; cuneiform.

arrow of time, *Physics.* the direction in which time flows: *In most of the things we experience, the arrow of time, as it is called, is pointed firmly in the future* (Science News). *Accumulated starlight from the cycle subsequent to the one in which we live ... can arise, it seems, if the "arrow of time" is reversed in each cycle of the universe—that is, time flows backwards* (Nature).

ar|row|root (ar′ō rüt′, -růt′), *n.* **1a** an easily digested starch made from the roots of a tropical American plant. **b** the plant from which it is made. **2** a similar starch obtained from other plants, used especially in certain cookies and crackers. [< Arawak *araruta* mealy root]

ar|row|weed (ar′ō wēd′), *n.* a variety of arrowwood, found in the southwestern United States and Mexico.

ar|row|wood (ar′ō wůd′), *n.* viburnum, the flowering dogwood, the wahoo, or other shrub or small tree with tough, straight stems. Arrowwood was formerly used by the Indians for making arrows.

ar|row|worm (ar′ō wėrm′), *n.* any of various small marine worms, characterized by bristles around the mouth.

ar|row|y (ar′ō ē), *adj.* **1** of arrows. **2** like an arrow in shape, speed, or effect: *Arrowy words, each one hitting its mark* (George Eliot).

ar|roy|o (ə roi′ō), *n., pl.* **-roy|os.** *Southwestern U.S.* **1** the dry bed of a stream; gully: *The hard, parched desert ground cannot absorb the torrents of water quickly, and dry gullies, called arroyos, become flooded in a few minutes* (Natt N. Dodge). **2** a small river. [American English < Spanish *arroyo* < Latin *arrugia* mine shaft]

ar|roz con pol|lo (ä rôs′ kôn pō′yō), *Spanish.* rice with chicken (a cooked dish popular in the West Indies).

ars a|mo|ris (ärz′ ä mō′ris), *Latin.* the art of love.

ars ar|ti|um (ärz′ är′tē əm), *Latin.* the art of arts, especially (in scholastic use) logic.

arse (ärs), *n. Slang.* the buttocks. [Old English *ærs, ears*]

ar|se|nal (är′sə nəl), *n.* **1** a building for storing, manufacturing, or repairing weapons and ammunition for an army or navy. **SYN:** armory. **2** a collection or supply of weapons: *... the stockpiling of additional weapons for an already bulging atomic arsenal* (Harper's). **3** *Figurative.* collection; storehouse; supply: *the U.S. space arsenal, a government's arsenal of propaganda. ... the arsenal of perception, sensibility, and diction she can command* (New Yorker). [< Italian *arsenale* < Arabic (*dār*) *aṣ-ṣinā'a* (house) of the manufacturing]

ar|se|nate (är′sə nāt, -nit), *n.* a salt or ester of arsenic acid. [< *arsen*(ic) + *-ate*[2]]

arsenate of lead, = lead arsenate.

ar|se|nic** (*n.* är′sə nik, ärs′nik; *adj.* är sen′ik), *n., adj.* **—*n. **1** a very brittle, grayish-white nonmetallic chemical element which occurs chiefly in combination with other elements. Arsenic has a metallic luster and volatilizes when heated. It forms poisonous compounds with oxygen and is used especially to make insecticides, weedkillers, and certain medicines. **2** a violent, tasteless poison that is a compound of this element; arsenic trioxide.
—*adj.* **1** of arsenic. **2** containing arsenic, especially with a valence of 5.
[< Latin *arsenicum* < Greek *arsenikón* yellow orpiment < Hebrew *zarnīq*]

***arsenic**
definition 1

symbol	atomic number	atomic weight	oxidation state
As	33	74.9216	±3, +5

arsenic acid, a colorless, crystalline compound, used in preparing arsenates. *Formula:* H_3AsO_4

ar|sen|i|cal (är sen′ə kəl), *adj., n.* **—*adj.*** of or containing arsenic: *an arsenical compound.*
—*n.* any one of a group of preparations containing arsenic, used especially as fungicides or drugs.

arsenical pyrite, = arsenopyrite.

ar|sen|i|cate (är sen′ə kāt), *v.t.,* **-cat|ed, -cat|ing.** to combine or treat with arsenic.

arsenic trichloride, a colorless, oily, poisonous liquid, soluble in concentrated hydrochloric acid but decomposed by water, used in luster finishing of ceramics and in the preparation of many arsenic compounds. *Formula:* $AsCl_3$

arsenic trioxide, a violent poison that is a white, tasteless powder, used in industry and in medicine. *Formula:* As_2O_3 or As_4O_6

ar|se|nide (är′sə nīd, -nid), *n.* a compound of arsenic and a metal or other positive element or radical. [< *arsen*(ic) + *-ide*]

ar|se|ni|ous (är sē′nē əs), *adj.* **1** of arsenic. **2** containing arsenic, especially with a valence of 3.

arsenious acid, any of three hypothetical acids of arsenic. *Formulas:* H_3AsO_3 or $HAsO_2$ or $H_4As_2O_5$

ar|se|nite (är′sə nīt), *n.* **1** a salt or ester of arsenious acid. **2** = arsenic trioxide.

ar|se|niu|ret|ed or **ar|se|niu|ret|ted** (är sēn′yə ret′id, -sen′-), *adj.* combined with arsenic to form an arsenide. [< *arsenic* + *-uret,* an old suffix meaning the same as *-ide*]

ar|se|no|py|rite (är′sə nō pī′rīt, är sen′ə-), *n.* a mineral having a metallic luster and silvery gray color that is an important ore of arsenic; mispickel; iron sulfarsenide. *Formula:* FeAsS

ar|se|no|ther|a|py (är′sə nō ther′ə pē), *n.* the treatment of disease by the use of arsenical drugs.

ar|se|nous (är′sə nəs), *adj.* = arsenious.

ars est ce|la|re ar|tem (ärz est sē lā′rē är′tem; ärs est kā lā′re är′tem), *Latin.* it is (true) art to conceal art (that is, to produce a natural effect with no trace of study or effort).

ars gra|ti|a ar|tis (ärz grā′shē ə är′tis; ärs grä′tē ä är′tis), *Latin.* art for art's sake.

ar|shin (är shēn′), *n.* **1** a measure of length in Russia equal to 28 inches or 71.12 centimeters. **2** a Turkish measure of length equal to 100 centimeters or 39.37 inches. Also, **archine.** [< Russian *arshin.* Compare Turkish *arshin* ell, yard.]

ar|sine (är sēn′; är′sēn, -sin), *n.* **1** a colorless, inflammable, highly poisonous gas having a garliclike odor. *Formula:* AsH_3 **2** one of the derivatives of this gas, in which the hydrogen atoms are replaced wholly or in part by organic radicals. [< *ars*(enic) + *-ine*[2]]

ar|sis (är′sis), *n., pl.* **-ses** (-sēz). **1a** the accented syllable of a metrical foot (contrasted with *thesis*). **b** (formerly) the unaccented syllable of a metrical foot. **2** *Music.* the weak or weakest beat in a measure (contrasted with *thesis*); upbeat. [< Latin *arsis* < Greek *ársis* a raising (perhaps of the hand or foot in beating time) < *aírein* to raise]

ars lon|ga, vi|ta bre|vis (ärz lông′gə, vī′tə brē′vis; ärs lông′gä, wē′tä bre′wis), *Latin.* art is long, life is short (a translation from the Greek of Hippocrates).

ar|son (är′sən), *n.* the crime of intentionally and maliciously setting fire to a building or other property. [< Old French *arçon* < Late Latin *ārsiō, -ōnis* a burning < Latin *ārdēre* to burn]

ar|son|ist (är′sə nist), *n.* a person who commits arson.

ars|phen|a|mine (ärs fen′ə mēn, -min; -fenam′in), *n.* a yellowish, hygroscopic, crystalline compound, formerly much used in treating diseases caused by spirochetes, such as syphilis. It was originally called "606" and sold under the trademark of Salvarsan. *Formula:* $C_{12}H_{14}As_2Cl_2N_2O_2{\cdot}2H_2O$

ars po|e|ti|ca (ärz pō et′ə kə), *Latin.* the art of poetry.

art[1] (ärt), *n.* **1** painting, drawing, and sculpture: *She is studying art and music.* **2** paintings, sculptures, and other works of art; artwork: *He went to an exhibit at the museum of art.* **3a.** any form of human activity that is the product of and appeals primarily to the imagination. The fine arts include drawing, painting, and sculpture, and also architecture, poetry, music, and dancing. *The arts are civilization's storehouse of felt values, the rendering of what has seemed important to those of powerful imagination and profound feeling and great mastery of expression* (Harper's). **b** a branch of learning that depends more on special practice than on general principles. Writing compositions is an art; grammar is a science. **c** Usually, **arts,** *pl.* a branch or division of learning, especially in the humanities. History, literature, and philosophy are included among the arts; bi-

Pronunciation Key: **h**a**t**, **ā**ge, **c**ã**re**, **f**ä**r**; **l**e**t**, **ē**qual, **t**ė**rm**, **it**, **ī**ce; **h**o**t**, **ō**pen, **ô**rder; **oil**, **out**; **c**u**p**, **p**ů**t**, **r**ü**le**; **child**; **long**; **thin**; **ᴛʜen**; **zh**, measure; **ə** represents **a** in about, **e** in taken, **i** in pencil, **o** in lemon, **u** in circus.

ology, chemistry, and physics are among the sciences. *She is attending a college of arts and sciences.* **4** these types of activities taken together: *"Classical art is healthy, romantic art sickly," said Goethe* (Listener). *Modern histories of nineteenth-century art are entirely theological in tone* (New Yorker). **5** a set of working principles or methods gained by experience: *the art of war. She understands the art of making friends.* **6a** special skill: *the art of saying things well.* **SYN:** faculty, knack. **b** some kind of skill or practical application of skill. Cooking, sewing, and housekeeping are household arts. **SYN:** craft, vocation. **c** human skill or effort; ingenuity: *This well-kept garden owes more to art than to nature.* **7a** a skillful act. **b** a trick, stratagem, or wile: *The witch deceived the girl by her arts.* **SYN:** craft, guile. **8** *Archaic.* learning in general.
art and part in, concerned both in the planning and the perpetration of (anything); accessory: *You are art and part with us In purging heresy* (Tennyson).
arts, subjects forming a course leading to a preliminary degree: *Literature is one of the liberal arts.*
[< Old French *art* < Latin *ars, artis*]

art² (ärt), *v. Archaic or Poetic.* are (used only with *thou*). "Thou art" means "You are." [Old English *eart*]

art., **1** article. **2** artificial. **3** artist.

ar|tal (är′täl), *n.* plural of **rotl.**

art brut (är bryt′), *French.* **1** a work of art, especially a painting, free of cultural influence and without any particular technique: *He began to collect ... art brut—the art works of children, delinquents, prisoners, schizoids and other mental patients* (Observer). **2** (literally) raw art.

***Art De|co** or **art de|co** (ärt de′kō), a style of ornate, geometrical, and colorful decoration that originated in France in the 1920's. [< French *Art Déco(ratif)* Decorative Art]

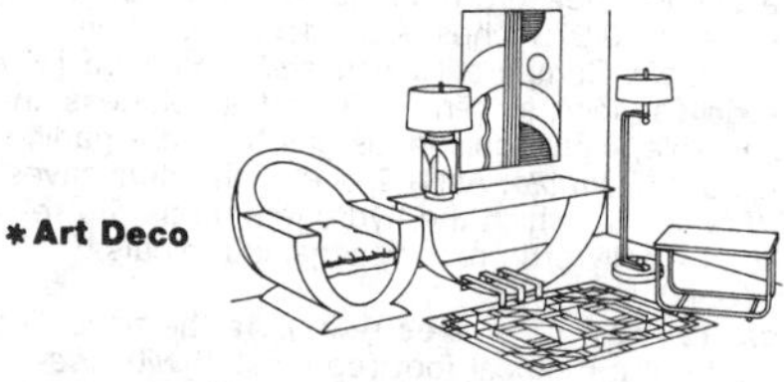

***Art Deco**

ar|te|fact (är′tə fakt), *n. Especially British.* artifact.

ar|te|fac|tu|al (är′tə fak′chü əl), *adj. Especially British.* artifactual.

ar|tel (är tel′), *n.* a cooperative association of workers. [< Russian *artel′* < Italian *artieri* craftsmen]

ar|te|mi|a (är tē′mē ə), *n.* any one of a genus of small crustaceans found in saline waters, used commercially as fish food. [< New Latin *Artemia* < Greek *Ártemis* Artemis]

Ar|te|mis (är′tə mis), *n. Greek Mythology.* the goddess of the hunt, of the forests, of wild animals, and of the moon. She was the twin sister of Apollo and was called Diana by the Romans.

ar|te|mis|i|a (är′tə miz′ē ə, -mish′-), *n.* any one of a genus of plants that includes wormwood. They grow mainly in dry regions of the Northern Hemisphere. An artemisia with silvery gray foliage which keeps all winter is often grown in gardens. [< Latin *artemisia* < Greek *artemisíā* < *Ártemis*]

ar|ter|en|ol (är tir′ə nol), *n.* = norepinephrine. [origin uncertain]

ar|te|ri|al (är tir′ē əl), *adj.* **1** of an artery or the arteries: *hardening of the arterial walls.* **2** contained in the arteries. Arterial blood is bright red because it has been purified and oxygenated by passing through the lungs. **3** serving as a major route of transportation, supply, or access: *Many large arterial highways join the nation's cities.* **4** having a main channel with many branches. —**ar|ter′i|al|ly,** *adv.*

ar|te|ri|al|ize (är tir′ē ə līz), *v.t.,* **-ized, -iz|ing.** to convert (venous blood) into the bright-red blood of the arteries by the action of oxygen in the lungs. —**ar|te′ri|al|i|za′tion,** *n.*

arterio-, *combining form.* artery or arteries: *Arteriotomy = the opening of an artery.* [< Greek *artērio-* artery < *artēríā*]

ar|te|ri|o|gram (är tir′ē ə gram), *n.* **1** an X-ray photograph of an artery. **2** = arteriograph.

ar|te|ri|o|graph (är tir′ē ə graf, -gräf), *n.* **1a** an instrument which makes a graph of the pulsing of an artery. **b** the graph or tracing itself. **2** = arteriogram.

ar|te|ri|o|graph|ic (är tir′ē ə graf′ik), *adj.* of or having to do with an arteriograph.

ar|te|ri|og|ra|phy (är tir′ē og′rə fē), *n.* the art or science of using the arteriograph.

ar|ter|i|o|lar (är tir′ē ō′lər), *adj.* **1** of or having to do with an arteriole. **2** resembling an arteriole.

ar|te|ri|ole (är tir′ē ōl), *n.* a small artery, especially one leading into capillaries. [< New Latin *arteriola* (diminutive) < Latin *artēria* artery < Greek *artēríā*]

ar|te|ri|ol|o|gy (är tir′ē ol′ə jē), *n.* the scientific study of the arteries.

ar|te|ri|o|scle|ro|sis (är tir′ē ō sklə rō′sis), *n.* a progressive thickening and hardening of the walls of the arteries, causing a decrease or loss of circulation and often associated with high blood pressure or with chronic disease of the kidneys. Arteriosclerosis usually occurs in elderly people. [< *arterio-* + *sclerosis*]

ar|te|ri|o|scle|rot|ic (är tir′ē ō sklə rot′ik), *adj., n.* —*adj.* of or having arteriosclerosis.
—*n.* a person who has arteriosclerosis.

ar|te|ri|ot|o|my (är tir′ē ot′ə mē), *n., pl.* **-mies.** the surgical opening of an artery. [< *arterio-* + Greek *-tomíā* a cutting]

ar|te|ri|o|ve|nous (är tir′ē ō vē′nəs), *adj.* of or having to do with both an artery and a vein: *An arteriovenous aneurysm allows a vein and artery to open into one another* (Lois G. Lobb).

ar|te|ri|tis (är′tə rī′tis), *n.* inflammation of an artery or arteries.

ar|ter|y (är′tər ē), *n., pl.* **-ter|ies,** *v.,* **-ter|ied, -ter|y|ing.** —*n.* **1** any of the blood vessels or tubes that carry blood from the heart to all parts of the body. Arteries are membranous, elastic, and muscular and form part of the system of blood vessels. **2** a main road; important channel: *Oceans serve as the main arteries of transportation between continents* (Ernest W. Williams, Jr.). **SYN:** highway, thoroughfare.
—*v.t.* **1** to supply with arteries. **2** to traverse like arteries: *Great rivers arteried every state* (Lucy L. Cameron).
[< Latin *artēria* < Greek *artēríā* artery, windpipe (since the arteries do not contain any blood after death, some of the ancients regarded them as air ducts, branching from the trachea)]

***ar|te|sian well** (är tē′zhən), **1** a deep, drilled well from which water gushes up without pumping, located in a formation where water pressure is sufficient to produce a constant supply of water rising to the surface of the ground. **2** *U.S.* any deep, drilled well. [< French *artésien* of Artois, a province where such wells were first drilled in modern times]

***artesian well**
definition 1

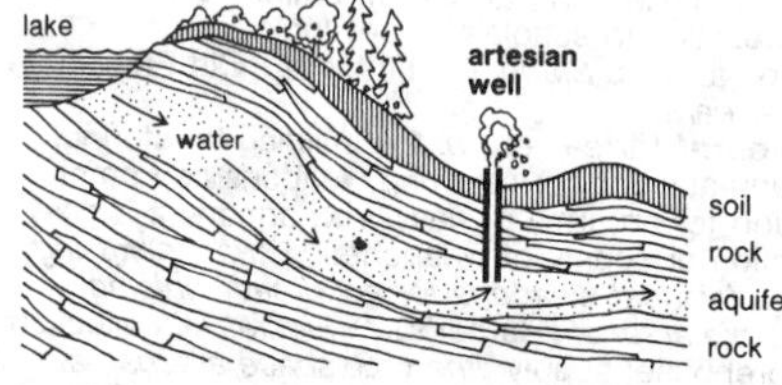

art film, a motion picture that is artistic or avant-garde, especially in theme and technique.

art form, **1** any traditional or recognized medium of expression in the arts, especially in painting, music, or literature: *The sonnet was one of the art forms in Shakespeare's day.* **2** any medium of expression considered to resemble one of these, such as folk singing: *He is hired by The Torch, a progressive weekly full of stories by Africans and given to hailing primitive folkways as major new art forms* (Malcolm Bradbury).

art|ful (ärt′fəl), *adj.* **1** slyly clever; deceitful; crafty: *A swindler uses artful tricks to get people's money away from them.* **SYN:** sly. **2** skillful; clever: *His artful settling of the disagreement won everybody's approval.* **SYN:** adroit. **3** artificial. **4** *Archaic.* having or showing practical or constructive skill. —**art′ful|ly,** *adv.* —**art′ful|ness,** *n.*

art glass, decorative colored glassware, especially of a type developed in the 1800's.

art house, = art theater.

ar|thral|gia (är thral′jə), *n.* pain, especially neuralgic pain, in a joint. [< Greek *árthron* joint + *álgos* pain]

ar|thral|gic (är thral′jik), *adj.* of or affected with arthralgia.

ar|thrit|ic (är thrit′ik), *adj., n.* —*adj.* **1** of arthritis. **2** caused by arthritis. **3** *Figurative.* feeble; decrepit: *... creating a modern railway system out of the present arthritic Victorian organism* (London Times). —*n.* a person who has arthritis. —**ar|thrit′i|cal|ly,** *adv.*

ar|thrit|i|cal (är thrit′ə kəl), *adj. Rare or Obsolete.* arthritic.

ar|thri|tis (är thrī′tis), *n.* an inflammation of a joint or joints of the body. Rheumatism and gout are two kinds of arthritis. [< Latin *arthrītis* < Greek *arthrîtis* < *árthron* joint]

ar|throd|e|sis (är throd′ə sis), *n., pl.* **-ses** (-sēz). immobilization or stabilization of a joint by surgical fusion of the bones. [< Greek *árthron* joint + *désis* a binding]

ar|thro|di|a (är thrō′dē ə), *n., pl.* **-di|ae** (-dē ē). *Anatomy.* a gliding joint; diarthrosis. [< Greek *arthrōdia* < *árthron* joint]

ar|thro|di|al (är thrō′dē əl), *adj.* of or having to do with an arthrodia: *Arthrodial joints are usually provided with ligaments* (Robert Todd).

ar|thro|dire (är′thrə dīr), *n.* any one of a group of placoderms having jointed necks, whose fossils are commonly found in Devonian rocks but persist into the Permian period. [< Greek *árthron* joint + *deirē* neck]

ar|thro|mere (är′thrə mir), *n.* one of the segments or divisions of the body of a jointed or articulate animal. [< Greek *árthron* joint + *méros* portion]

ar|throp|a|thy (är throp′ə thē), *n.* any joint disease. [< Greek *árthron* joint + English *-pathy*]

ar|thro|plas|tic (är′thrə plas′tik), *adj.* of or having to do with arthroplasty.

ar|thro|plas|ty (är′thrə plas′tē), *n.* **1** the making of an artificial joint to replace a natural one. **2** surgery performed on a joint. [< Greek *árthron* joint + *plastós* molded]

ar|thro|pod (är′thrə pod), *n.* any one of a large group of invertebrate animals having segmented (jointed) bodies and hollow, jointed legs. The antennae, wings, and legs of arthropods are articulated in pairs. Insects (such as beetles and bees), arachnids (such as spiders and mites), crustaceans (such as lobsters and crabs), and the extinct trilobites are arthropods. [< New Latin *Arthropoda* < Greek *árthron* joint + *poús, podós* foot]

Ar|throp|o|da (är throp′ə də), *n.pl.* the phylum of invertebrates composed of the arthropods.

ar|throp|o|dal (är throp′ə dəl), *adj.* = arthropodous.

ar|throp|o|dous (är throp′ə dəs), *adj.* of or having to do with the arthropods.

ar|thro|scope (är′thrə skōp), *n.* an instrument for examining the interior of a joint.

ar|thros|co|py (är thros′k ə pē), *n.* examination of the interior of a joint by means of an arthroscope.

ar|thro|sis (är thrō′sis), *n., pl.* **-ses** (-sēz). *Anatomy.* an articulation or suture joining two bones or cartilages. [< Greek *árthrosis* < *árthron* a joint]

ar|thro|spore (är′thrə spôr, -spōr), *n.* any of several spores in certain fungi and algae, that look like a string of beads, produced by the breaking up, or fission, of a hypha. [< Greek *árthron* joint + *sporá* seed]

ar|thro|spor|ic (är′thrə spôr′ik, -spor′-), *adj.* = arthrosporous.

ar|thros|po|rous (är thros′pər əs), *adj.* producing arthrospores.

Ar|thur (är′thər), *n.* a Christian king in medieval and later romances about ancient Britain who gathered about him the famous Knights of the Round Table. The historical person about whom these romances were later spun was probably a British chieftain or the Romano-British general, Aurelius Auriolanus, who, about 500 A.D., successfully halted the Anglo-Saxon conquest for nearly thirty years.

Ar|thu|ri|an (är thür′ē ən), *adj.* **1** of King Arthur, his court, and his knights: *Arthurian legends.* **2** of the romances about them: *an Arthurian scholar.*

ar|ti|ad (är′tē ad), *n., adj.* —*n.* an atom or element whose valence is expressed by an even number. —*adj.* having the valence expressed by an even number. See also **perissad.** [< Greek *ártios* even]

***ar|ti|choke** (är′tə chōk), *n.* **1** a plant somewhat like a thistle, with large prickly leaves; globe artichoke. It is a large, vigorous, composite herb, with divided leaves and a flowering head. **2** its flowering head, which is cooked and eaten as a vegetable before it becomes mature. **3** = Jerusalem artichoke. [< Italian *articiocco* < Old Provençal *arquichaut,* ultimately < Arabic *al-harshūf*]

***artichoke**
definition 1

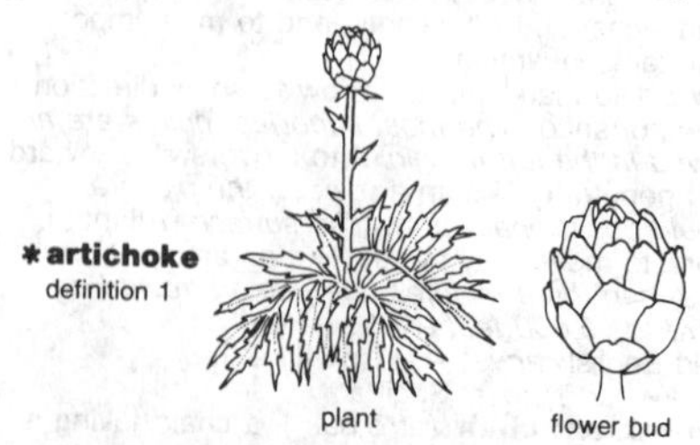

ar|ti|cle (är′tə kəl), *n., v.,* **-cled, -cling.** —*n.* **1** a part of a magazine, newspaper, or book: *There is an article on gardening in the newspaper today.* An article is a written composition on a special

subject, complete in itself. SYN: essay, piece. **2** a clause in a contract, treaty, or statute: *When the Constitution of the United States was adopted it had seven articles.* SYN: provision. **3** a particular thing; item (of the class indicated): *Bread is a main article of food. A desk is an article of furniture.* SYN: object. **4** a piece of goods or property; commodity. **5** *Grammar.* one of the words *a, an,* or *the,* as in *a book, an egg, the boy,* or the corresponding words in certain other languages. *A* and *an* are the **indefinite articles**; *the* is the **definite article**: *One quickly detects a foreigner thru his inaccurate use of the article* (New Yorker). **6** one of the separate charges in an accusation or indictment; a count. **7** *Archaic.* a particular item of business; matter; subject. **8** *Archaic.* a point of time; moment. *Abbr:* art.
—*v.t.* **1** to bind by contract: *The apprentice was articled to serve the master workman for seven years.* **2** to charge; accuse.
—*v.i.* to bring charges; make a specific charge or charges (against).
[< Old French *article,* learned borrowing from Latin *articulus* (diminutive) < *artus* joint]

article of faith, an essential condition of a belief or creed; basic principle: *It is an article of faith with virtually every Gibraltarian that he wants to remain separate from Spain* (Manchester Guardian Weekly).

Articles of Confederation, the constitution adopted by the thirteen original states of the United States in 1781. It was replaced by the present Constitution in 1789.

ar|tic|u|la|ble (är tik′yə lə bəl), *adj.* that can be articulated: *specific and articulable facts.*

ar|tic|u|la|cy (är tik′yə lə sē), *n.* the quality or condition of being articulate; articulateness: . . . *the fast, crisp articulacy of* [*the actor*] *John Gielgud* (London Times).

ar|tic|u|lar (är tik′yə lər), *adj.* of or belonging to the joints: *Arthritis is an articular disease.* [< Latin *articulāris* < *articulus* article]

ar|tic|u|late (*adj., n.* är tik′yə lit; *v.* är tik′yə lāt), *adj., v.,* **-lat|ed, -lat|ing,** *n.* —*adj.* **1** spoken in distinct syllables or words: *A baby cries and gurgles but does not use articulate speech.* SYN: clear, intelligible. **2** able to put one's thoughts into words easily and clearly: *Julia is the most articulate of the sisters.* **3** made up of distinct parts; distinct. **4** having joints; jointed; segmented. The backbone is an articulate structure.
—*v.t.* **1** to speak distinctly; express in clear sounds and words: *The speaker was careful to articulate his words so that everyone in the room could understand him.* SYN: enunciate. **2** to unite by joints: *The two bones are articulated like a hinge.*
—*v.i.* **1** to express oneself in words: *Radio and television announcers are trained to articulate clearly.* SYN: enunciate. **2** to fit together in a joint: *After his knee was injured, he was lame because the bones did not articulate well.*
—*n.* any invertebrate having the body and limbs composed of jointed segments.
[< Latin *articulātus,* past participle of *articulāre* (probably) divide into single joints < *articulus* article] —**ar|tic′u|late|ly,** *adv.* —**ar|tic′u|late|ness,** *n.* —**ar|tic′u|la′tor,** *n.*

ar|tic|u|lat|ed lorry (är tik′yə lā′tid), *British.* truck trailer.

ar|tic|u|la|tion (är tik′yə lā′shən), *n.* **1** the way of speaking; way of pronouncing words and syllables; enunciation: *If you read aloud more slowly, your articulation will be much clearer.* **2** a joint between parts of an animal or plant. **3** the act or manner of connecting by a joint or joints: *The articulation of the bones of the hand is quite complex.* **4** the state of being jointed. **5** *Botany.* **a** a joint or place where separation of two parts takes place naturally, such as at the base of a deciduous leafstalk. **b** a node or the space between such parts. **6** the portion between two joints or nodes in an animal.

ar|tic|u|la|tion|ist (är tik′yə lā′shə nist), *n.* a person who teaches or advocates teaching deaf-mutes to make articulate sounds.

ar|tic|u|la|tive (är tik′yə lā′tiv), *adj.* having to do with or relating to articulation.

ar|tic|u|la|to|ry (är tik′yə lə tôr′ē, -tōr′-), *adj.* of or having to do with vocal articulation: *When we refer to the organs of speech we generally mean those of the articulatory tract from larynx to lips* (Simeon Potter).

ar|ti|fact (är′tə fakt), *n.* **1** anything made by human skill or work, especially a tool or weapon: *Arrowheads and pottery were among the artifacts found at the site of the prehistoric village.* **2** *Biology.* something not naturally present in a tissue or cell. **3** a wave recorded in an electroencephalogram that does not originate in the brain. Also, *especially British,* **artefact.** [< Latin *ars; artis* art + *factus* made, past participle of *facere* make]

ar|ti|fac|ti|tious (är′tə fak tish′əs), *adj.* = artifactual.

ar|ti|fac|tu|al (är′tə fak′chů əl), *adj.* of or having to do with an artifact or artifacts.

ar|ti|fice (är′tə fis), *n.* **1** a clever device; trick; ruse: *She will use any artifice to get her own way.* SYN: maneuver, contrivance. See syn. under **stratagem. 2** trickery; craft: *His conduct is free from artifice.* SYN: cunning, guile, deception. **3** skill or ingenuity. [< Latin *artificium* < *ars, artis* art + *facere* make]

ar|tif|i|cer (är tif′ə sər), *n.* **1** a skilled workman; craftsman. **2** a maker; inventor: *Man . . . is the artificer of his own fortune* (Thomas Carlyle). **3** *British.* an army or navy technician who maintains or repairs equipment: *an engine-room artificer.*

ar|ti|fi|cial (är′tə fish′əl), *adj., n.* —*adj.* **1** made by human skill or labor; not natural: *At night you read by artificial light.* **2** made as a substitute or in imitation; not real: *artificial silk. She made artificial flowers from paper.* SYN: synthetic. **3** put on for effect; affected; pretended; assumed; false: *an artificial tone of voice. When nervous, he had an artificial laugh.* SYN: feigned, hollow. **4** based on prominent points of resemblance or difference rather than natural relationships for biological classification: *Examples of artificial classifications of plants are those that divide them into trees, shrubs, and herbs; into those that grow in wet, moist, and dry locations; and those with regard to color of flowers, without regard to genetic kinship* (Fred W. Emerson). **5** not native to a place; cultivated: *African violets are artificial plants in North America.*
—*n.* an artificial flower.
[< Latin *artificiālis* < *artificium* artifice] —**ar′ti|fi′cial|ly,** *adv.* —**ar′ti|fi′cial|ness,** *n.*
—*Syn. adj.* **1 Artificial, synthetic** mean man-made, not natural. **Artificial** describes that which is produced by human skill and labor, in contrast to that produced in nature, but which often corresponds to natural things or processes: *an artificial leg. Artificial respiration has saved the lives of many people who would have otherwise drowned.* **Synthetic** describes substances put together in a laboratory by chemical combination or treatment of natural materials, often to serve as substitutes for natural products: *When Teflon, a synthetic substance, is used to coat a pan, food can be fried without grease.*

artificial fever, fever produced artificially to kill bacteria.

artificial gene, nucleic acids, sometimes in combination with other substances, that are joined under laboratory conditions to form nucleotides which will perform some genetic function in a living cell: *The researchers worked nine years to complete their artificial gene, and many biologists hailed the feat as proof that DNA molecules are indeed the basis of life* (Earl A. Evans, Jr.).

artificial gravity, a simulation of the force of gravity set up within a space vehicle, typically by centrifugal force, as by rotating a cabin about an axis of a spacecraft.

artificial heart, a plastic device that pumps blood in the body in place of the heart. It consists of two chambers each with a flexible diaphragm inflated by compressed air to pump blood.

artificial horizon, **1** a horizontal reflecting surface, such as a mirror or the surface of mercury or other fluid at rest, used in taking altitudes. **2** an instrument, usually controlled gyroscopically, that indicates the position of the true horizon.

artificial insemination, the introduction of semen into the vagina or cervix of a female by other than natural means.

artificial intelligence, **1** the ability of certain electronic devices to obey spoken commands, show recognition of simple objects, and carry out tasks, such as assembling objects in various ways. **2** the programming of such devices or the means by which they operate.

ar|ti|fi|ci|al|i|ty (är′tə fish′ē al′ə tē), *n.* **1** *no pl.* artificial quality or condition: *the artificiality of a forced smile.* **2** *pl.* **-ties.** something unnatural or unreal: *DeVries . . . takes a long cool look at the artificialities and vanities of contemporary exurbia* (Canadian Saturday Night).

ar|ti|fi|cial|ize (är′tə fish′ə līz), *v.t.,* **-ized, -iz|ing.** to make artificial, or give a semblance of artificiality to: *"The St. Valentine's Day Massacre" . . . artificializes and confuses the tawdry history it is supposed to relate* (Bosley Crowther).

artificial kidney, = hemodialyzer.

artificial life, lifelike organisms created and existing in a computer: *They are creating a field called artificial life, mixing the impulses of biology with the tools of computation* (New York Times).

artificial moon, **1** an earth satellite. **2** any artificial satellite.

artificial person, *Law.* a corporation; person.

artificial radioactivity, radioactivity of a normally stable element, induced by nuclear bombardment.

artificial rain, a fall of rain induced by seeding clouds with pellets of compressed carbon dioxide or any one of certain other substances designed to encourage precipitation.

artificial reality, an environment created by computer graphics that appears three-dimensional and real: *Artificial reality . . . relies on the techniques of interactive computer graphics to create the illusion of navigating* (Time).

artificial respiration, the act, means, or process of restoring normal breathing to a person who has stopped breathing by forcing air alternately into and out of his lungs. It can be accomplished by any of a number of methods.

artificial satellite, a satellite of any celestial body, manufactured and placed in orbit by man.

artificial selection, man's agency in modifying the pressures, and so changing the results, of natural selection, such as in breeding horses for speed, or cattle for beef or milk.

ar|til|ler|ist (är til′ər ist), *n.* **1** a gunner; artilleryman. **2** a person who studies the use of artillery.

ar|til|ler|y (är til′ər ē), *n.* **1** mounted guns or rocket launchers manned by a crew; guns of larger caliber than machine guns; cannon; ordnance. **2** the part of an army that uses and manages such guns. **3** the science and practice of firing and coordinating the firing of guns of larger caliber than machine guns. *Abbr:* art. [< Old French *artillerie* implements of war < *artillier* equip with implements of war < Medieval Latin *articula* (diminutive) < Latin *ars, artis* skill]

ar|til|ler|y|man (är til′ər ē mən), *n., pl.* **-men.** *U.S.* a soldier who belongs to the artillery; gunner.

ar|ti|o|dac|tyl or **ar|ti|o|dac|tyle** (är′tē ō dak′təl), *n., adj.* —*n.* any animal of an order of hoofed quadruped mammals with an even number of toes, usually two or sometimes four, on each foot. Swine, camels, deer, sheep, cattle, and many other animals are artiodactyls. —*adj.* having an even number of toes or digits on each foot. [< Greek *ártios* even-numbered + *dáktylos* finger, toe]

ar|ti|o|dac|tyl|ous (är′tē ō dak′tə ləs), *adj.* = artiodactyl.

ar|ti|san (är′tə zən), *n.* a workman skilled in some industry or trade; craftsman. Carpenters, masons, plumbers, and electricians are artisans. SYN: artificer, mechanic. See syn. under **artist.** [< French *artisan* < Italian *artigiano,* ultimately < Latin *ars, artis* art]

ar|ti|san|al (är′tə zə nəl), *adj.* of or having to do with artisans or artisanry: *What happened to the artisanal life of the area—the jewelry, the exquisite world-renowned rugs?* (Maclean's).

ar|ti|san|ry (är′tə zən rē), *n.* the ability or workmanship of an artisan: *the artisanry of local craftsmen.*

ar|ti|san|ship (är′tə zən ship), *n.* = artisanry.

art|ist (är′tist), *n.* **1** a person who paints pictures. *Abbr:* art. SYN: painter. **2** a person who is skilled in any of the fine arts, such as sculpture, music, or literature. **3** a public performer, especially an actor or singer. SYN: entertainer. **4** a person who does work with skill and good taste. [< Middle French *artiste* < Italian *artista* < Medieval Latin < Latin *ars, artis* art]
—*Syn.* **4 Artist, artisan** mean a person who does work with skill. **Artist** emphasizes use of taste, imagination, and creative ability in addition to skill, and usually applies to a person working in the fine arts: *Her creative interpretation makes that dancer an artist.* **Artisan** emphasizes skill, and applies to a person working in the manual or mechanic arts: *Factories want artisans in all departments.*

ar|tiste (är tēst′), *n.* **1** a professional performer, especially a singer or dancer. **2** a very skillful worker who treats his work as an art, such as a fine cook or dressmaker. [< French *artiste* artist]

ar|tis|tic (är tis′tik), *adj.* **1** done with skill and good taste: *That actress gave an artistic performance.* SYN: tasteful, harmonious. **2** having or showing appreciation of beauty: *She has an artistic way of arranging flowers.* SYN: aesthetic. **3** of art or artists: *Our museum has many artistic works.* **4** having good color and design; pleasing to the senses: *an artistic wallpaper.* SYN: painterly. —**ar|tis′ti|cal|ly,** *adv.*

ar|tis|ti|cal (är tis′tə kəl), *adj.* = artistic.

art|ist|ry (är′tə strē), *n., pl.* **-ries. 1** the workmanship of an artist; artistic quality: *the unmistakable artistry of Rembrandt.* **2** the profession or occupation of an artist.

art|less (ärt′lis), *adj.* **1a** without any trickery, guile, or deceit: *He sets about promoting his plans with an artless good faith which confounds his cynical court* (Saturday Review). **b** made or done without knowledge of social customs; simple: *Small*

Pronunciation Key: hat, āge, cãre, fär; let, ēqual, tėrm; it, īce; hot, ōpen, ôrder; oil, out; cup, pu̇t, rüle; child; long; thin; ᴛʜen; zh, measure; ə represents **a** in about, **e** in taken, **i** in pencil, **o** in lemon, **u** in circus.

children ask many artless questions, such as, "Mother, did you want this lady to come see you?" SYN: candid, naive. **2** not artificial; natural: *artless eloquence. Such artless beauty lies in Shakespeare's wit* (John Dryden). SYN: sincere, ingenuous. **3** without art; unskilled; ignorant. SYN: rude, clumsy, uncultured, unpracticed.
—**art′less|ly**, *adv.* —**art′less|ness**, *n.*

art|mo|bile (ärt′mə bēl), *n. U.S.* a bus or truck that is a traveling branch of an art museum.

art music, professionally composed music of a classical character: *These albums . . . give a fascinating glimpse into the [Spanish] nation's traditions of art music, as opposed to folk music* (New Yorker).

art nou|veau (ärt nü vō′), an ornate style of decoration that originated in Belgium and France about 1895: *In many ways Whistler was the first authentic interior decorator, predicting as he did the style of art nouveau well before it became a popular movement* (Saturday Review). [< French *art nouveau* (literally) new art]

ar|to|type (är′tō tīp), *n.* = collotype.

arts (ärts), *n.pl.* See under **art**[1].

arts and crafts, woodworking, knitting, and similar work involving artistic design.

art song, a song of a classical character, sung at recitals: *In music, there are two types of song: folk songs by unknown artists, and art songs, musical settings of poetic texts* (Scott Goldthwaite).

art-square (ärt′skwãr′), *n.* a square rug of ingrain carpet.

art|sy (är′tsē), *adj.*, **art|si|er, art|si|est.** = arty: *The magazine's bizarre layout and typography look artsy enough to have been dreamed up by a gaggle of interior decorators* (Time).

art|sy-craft|sy (är′tsē kraf′tsē, -kräf′-), *adj.* **1** suggestive of handicraft; not genuinely artistic. **2** not useful or comfortable in design. **3** = arty.

art theater, a theater that specializes in experimental drama, documentary or foreign motion pictures, etc.

art|ware (ärt′wãr′), *n.* articles of artistic or decorative design.

art|work (ärt′wėrk′), *n.* **1** illustration of any sort in a book, magazine, or other printed material. **2** a work or works of art. **3** the production of such work.

art|y (är′tē), *adj.*, **art|i|er, art|i|est.** *Informal.* making a pretense or show of being artistic: *The secret of Huston's direction is that it is sensitive and artistic without being self-consciously arty* (Newsweek). —**art′i|ly**, *adv.* —**art′i|ness**, *n.*

art|y-craft|y (är′tē kraf′tē, -kräf′-), *adj.* = artsy-craftsy.

ar|um (ãr′əm), *n.* **1** a plant having a club-shaped spike of small flowers partly surrounded by a hooded sheath, such as the jack-in-the-pulpit. **2** a plant somewhat like it and belonging to the same family, such as the calla lily. [< Latin *arum* < Greek *áron*]

***arum family**, *Botany.* a group of monocotyledonous perennial herbs, typically having a club-shaped spike of small flowers partly surrounded by a hooded sheath. The family includes the jack-in-the-pulpit, sweet flag, skunk cabbage, calla lily, and cuckoopint. See picture below.

a|run|di|na|ceous (ə run′də nā′shəs), *adj.* **1** of or having to do with a reed. **2** reedlike. [< Latin *harundināceus* (with English *-ous*) < *harundō, -inis* a reed]

A|run|ta (ə run′tə), *n.* **1** a large tribe of Australian aborigines inhabiting central Australia. **2** their language.

a|rus|pex (ə rus′peks, ar′ə speks), *n.* = haruspex.

A.R.V., American Revised Version (of the Bible).

Ar|val Brethren (är′vəl), a group of twelve priests in ancient Rome who offered sacrifices for the renewed fertility of the fields. [< Latin *arvālis* of plowed land]

Ar|vin (är′vən), *n.* a member of the ARVN.

ARVN (no periods), Army of the Republic of (South) Vietnam.

ar|vo (är′vō), *n. Australian Slang.* afternoon.

ar|y (ãr′ē), *adj. U.S. Dialect.* any; some. [< *e'er a* < *ever a*]

-ary, *suffix forming nouns and adjectives.* **1** a place for ______: *Infirmary = place for the infirm.*
2 a collection of ______: *Statuary = collection of statues.*
3 a person or thing that ______s: *Boundary = thing that bounds.*
4 of or having to do with ______: *Legendary = of legend.*
5 being; having the nature of ______: *Secondary = being second.*
6 characterized by ______: *Customary = characterized by custom.* [< Latin *-ārius*, or *-ārium*, neuter]

Ar|y|an (ãr′ē ən, ar′-; är′yən), *adj., n.* —*adj.* **1** of or having to do with a family of languages from which most European languages are descended; Indo-European. **2** *Archaic.* of or having to do with the Indo-Iranian portion of Indo-European. **3** (as used by the Nazis) of a Caucasian who is a gentile, especially of the Nordic type.
—*n.* **1** a person belonging to a prehistoric group of people who spoke the language from which the Indo-European languages are derived. **2** a person supposed to be descended from this prehistoric group of people. **3** the assumed prehistoric language of this people. **4** (as used by the Nazis) a Caucasian who is a gentile, especially of the Nordic type. Also, **Arian**.
[< Sanskrit *ārya* noble]

Ar|y|an|ism (ãr′ē ə niz′əm; ar′-; är′yə-), *n.* **1** the Nazi doctrine of the superiority of the Caucasian gentiles who composed the so-called Aryan race. **2** belief in this doctrine.

Ar|y|an|ize (ãr′ē ə nīz, ar′-; är′yə-), *v.t.*, **-ized, -iz|ing.** **1** to make characteristically Aryan. **2** (as used by the Nazis) to rid of so-called non-Aryan persons or elements. —**Ar′y|an|i|za′tion**, *n.*

ar|y|bal|los (ar′i bal′əs), *n.* **1** a small Greek vase with a ball-shaped body, a single handle, a short neck, and a flared lip. **2** any similar vase, such as one with two handles used by the Incas. [< Greek *arýballos* (originally) a bag or purse made so as to draw close]

ar|yl (ar′əl), *n.* a univalent radical occurring in aromatic hydrocarbon derivatives. See also **alkyl**. [< *ar*(omatic) + *-yl*]

ar|yl|a|mines (ar′ə lə mēnz′, -lam′inz), *n.pl.* a group of amines formed by the substitution of aromatic radicals for one or more of the hydrogen atoms of ammonia.

ar|y|te|noid (ar′ə tē′noid, ə rit′ə-), *adj., n.* —*adj.* having the shape of a ladle or cup (applied to two cartilages of the larynx which regulate the action of the vocal cords, and to several small glands of the larynx).
—*n.* an arytenoid cartilage or other structure.
[< New Latin *arytaenoides* < Greek *arytainoeidēs* < *arýtaina* ladle + *eîdos* shape]

ar|y|te|noi|dal (ar′ə tə noi′dəl, ə rit′ə-), *adj.* **1** shaped like the arytenoids. **2** belonging to the arytenoids.

as[1] (az; *unstressed* əz), *adv., prep., conj., pron.* —*adv.* **1** to the same degree or extent; equally: *as black as coal. The two brothers are as tall as their father.* **2** for example: *Some animals, as dogs and cats, eat meat.*
—*prep.* **1** doing the work of; in the character or role of: *The student acted as teacher. The actor appeared as Macbeth.* **2** in the manner of; like: *They treat him as an equal. Will you fight as men, or die as slaves?*
—*conj.* **1** during the time that; when; while: *She sang as she worked. As they were walking, the rain began.* **2** in the same way that: *Run as I do. Treat others as you wish them to treat you.* **3** to the same degree or extent that: *She worked just so much as she was told to.* **4** because: *We paid him generously, as he had done the work well.* **5** though: *Brave as they were, the danger made them afraid.* **6** that the result was: *The child so marked the picture as to spoil it.*
—*pron.* **1** a condition or fact that: *She is very careful, as her work shows.* **2** that: *Do the same thing as I do.*

as . . . as, to the (specified) degree or extent: *as wise as fair, as strong as ever, as soon as you can.*

as for, about; concerning; referring to: *As for politics, I am indifferent.*

as from, considered formally as dating from: *The contract shall be in effect as from this day.*

as good as. See under **good**.

as if, similar to what it would be if: *You sound as if you were angry.*

as is. See under **is**.

as it were. See under **were**.

as of, beginning on or at (a certain date or time): *The new contract becomes effective as of January 1st.*

as regards. See under **regard**.

as though, similar to the way it would be if: *It looks as though it might rain.*

as to (before a verb), in order to: *He so behaved as to impress the entire company favorably.*

as to, about; concerning; referring to: *I'd like a cat, and I have no preference as to its color.*

as well. See under **well**[1].

as well as. See under **well**[1].

as yet. See under **yet**.

so as (to). See under **so**[1].

such as. See under **such**.

[Old English (unstressed) *ealswā* quite so. See related etym. at **also**.]

►**As to** is often a clumsy substitute for a single preposition, usually *about* or *of*: *Practice usually proves the best teacher as to* (in, for, of) *the use of organ stops.*

►See **because** and **like**[1] for usage notes.

as[2] (as), *n., pl.* **as|ses.** **1** the ancient Roman pound, equal to twelve ounces. **2** an ancient Roman copper coin, worth a few cents. [< Latin *as, assis*]

as-, *prefix.* the form of **ad-** before *s*, as in *assist.*

as (no period), asymmetric.

As (no period), **1** alto-stratus. **2** arsenic (chemical element).

AS (no periods), **1** air-to-surface. **2** Anglo-Saxon.

A.S., **1** Anglo-Saxon. **2** Associate in Science (a college degree).

A|sa (ā′sə), *n.* the third king of Judah (800's B.C.), the champion of Jehovah against worshipers of idols (in the Bible, I Kings 15:8-24).

a|sa|do (ä sä′ᴛʜō), *adj., n., pl.* **-dos** (ᴛʜōs). *Spanish.* —*adj.* roasted.
—*n.* a roast; barbecue.

as|a|fet|i|da or **as|a|foet|i|da** (as′ə fet′ə də), *n.* a gum resin that smells like garlic, formerly used in medicine to prevent spasms. It is obtained from various Asiatic plants of the parsley family. Also, **assafetida, assafoetida.** [< Medieval Latin *asafetida* < *asa* mastic (< Persian *azā*) + Latin *foetidus* stinking]

a|sa|na (ä′sə nə), *n., pl.* **-nas.** any of the prescribed postures or positions in yoga. [< Sanskrit *āsana*]

ASA number or **speed**, a number giving the sensitivity of a type of photographic film to light according to standards set by the American Standards Association.

A|saph|ic (ə saf′ik), *adj.* of or having to do with Asaph, one of the chief singers in the Temple during the time of David and Solomon. He was the head of one guild of singers, the "sons of Asaph."

Asaphic psalms, Psalms 50 and 73-83, which have the name of Asaph superscribed.

A|sa|rah B'Te|bet or **B'Te|beth** (ä sä rä′ bə tā-vāth′, ä sôr′ə bə tā′vəs), a Jewish fast day, the 10th of Tebet, in remembrance of the beginning of the siege of Jerusalem by the Babylonians in 587 B.C. [< Hebrew *'ăsārāh bĕṭebeth* tenth of Tebet]

as|a|rum (as′ər əm), *n.* any one of a genus of low, stemless herbs with dull brownish flowers and aromatic rootstock. The common American species is known as wild ginger or snakeroot. [< New Latin *Asarum* the genus name < Latin *asarum* hazelwort, wild spikenard < Greek *ásaron*]

ASAT (ā′sat), *n.* a hunter-killer satellite able to destroy another satellite: *ASAT . . . has a parabolic "dish" antenna that homes in on the target satellite . . . where it detonates. The ASAT goes off like a super hand grenade* (Time). [< *A*nti-*Sat*ellite interceptor]

as|bes|ti|form (as bes′tə fôrm, az-), *adj.* having the form or appearance of asbestos.

as|bes|tine (as bes′tin, az-), *adj.* **1** of asbestos. **2** having the properties of asbestos.

as|bes|tos (as bes′təs, az-), *n., adj.* —*n.* **1** a substance that does not burn or conduct heat. It usually comes in fibers that can be made into a fabric like cloth or felt. Asbestos is a mineral, a silicate of calcium and magnesium. **2** a fireproof fabric made of these mineral fibers. Asbestos is resistant to both heat and chemical reaction. It is used to make brake linings, cloth, paint, insulating and roofing materials, and fire-resistant clothing.

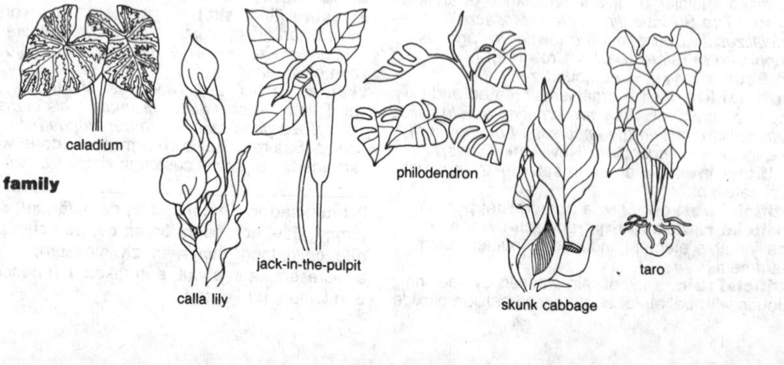

caladium
philodendron
jack-in-the-pulpit
taro
calla lily
skunk cabbage

***arum family**

—*adj.* of or containing asbestos: *asbestos gloves. Some workers wear asbestos suits for protection from fire.*
[< Old French *asbestos* < Latin < Greek *ásbestos* unquenchable (originally applied to quicklime) < *a-* not + *sbennýnai* quench]

asbestos cement, a building material consisting of a mixture of asbestos and cement.

as|bes|to|sis (as′bes tō′sis, az′-), *n.* chronic inflammation and congestion of the lungs caused by excessive inhalation of asbestos dust.

as|bes|tous (as bes′təs, az-), *adj.* = asbestiform.

as|bes|tus (as bes′təs, az-), *n.* = asbestos.

ASC (no periods), altered state of consciousness: *Experiences of ecstasy, mystical union, other "dimensions," rapture, beauty, space-and-time transcendence* [*are*] *all common in ASC's* (Science).

As|ca|ni|us (as kā′nē əs), *n. Roman Legend.* the son of Aeneas, the reputed founder of Alba Longa (from which Rome developed).

ASCAP (no periods) or **A.S.C.A.P.**, American Society of Composers, Authors and Publishers.

as|ca|ri|a|sis (as′kə rī′ə sis), *n.* a disease caused by ascarids in the stomach and intestines, often accompanied by diarrhea and abdominal pain. [< *ascar*(id) + *-iasis*]

as|ca|rid (as′kər id), *n.* a roundworm, pinworm, or similar nematode worm, existing as a parasite in the intestinal tract of vertebrates. [< Greek *askarís, -ídos* an intestinal worm]

as|ca|ris (as′kər is), *n.* **1** a relatively large roundworm common as an intestinal parasite in man, and sometimes in pigs and horses. **2** any other worm of the group of nematode worms.

as|cend (ə send′), *v.i.* **1** to go up; rise; move upward: *He watched the airplane ascend higher and higher. The sun ascended slowly.* (*Figurative.*) *The congressman rapidly ascended to power in Congress and became Speaker of the House.* **2** *Music.* to rise in pitch.
—*v.t.* **1** to climb; go to or toward the top of: *A small party is planning to ascend Mount Everest.* (*Figurative.*) *The prince ascended the throne to become king.* SYN: scale. See syn. under **climb**. **2** to move upward along; go toward the source of: *They ascended the Platte River.*
[< Latin *ascendere* < *ad-* to + *scandere* climb]
—**as|cend′a|ble, as|cend′i|ble,** *adj.*

as|cend|ance or **as|cend|ence** (ə sen′dəns), *n.* = ascendancy.

as|cend|an|cy or **as|cend|en|cy** (ə sen′dən sē), *n.* controlling influence; domination; rule: *Hannibal and the Carthaginians challenged the ascendancy of Rome.* SYN: supremacy, sway, authority.

as|cend|ant or **as|cend|ent** (ə sen′dənt), *adj., n.* —*adj.* **1** moving upward; ascending; rising. **2** *Figurative.* dominant; superior; ruling; controlling: *Under Louis XIV, France had the ascendant position in world politics.* SYN: paramount. **3** near the eastern horizon; rising toward the zenith: *ascendant Venus.* **4** *Botany.* directed or growing upward.
—*n.* **1** a position of power; controlling influence: *Strong minds have undoubtedly an ascendant over weak ones* (Earl of Chesterfield). SYN: superiority, supremacy, domination. **2** *Astrology.* **a** a horoscope. **b** the sign of the zodiac rising above the eastern horizon at a given time. **3** = ancestor.
in the ascendant, **a** in control; supreme; dominant: *Monarchs are no longer in the ascendant in government.* **b** increasing in influence, popularity, or acceptance: *The study of science is in the ascendant in many schools.*

as|cend|er (ə sen′dər), *n.* **1** a person or thing that ascends. **2** *Printing.* **a** the upper part of such lower-case letters as *b, d, h,* and *k.* **b** any such letter.

as|cend|ing (ə sen′ding), *adj.* **1** rising; mounting up; sloping upwards. **2** *Botany.* directed upwards; growing upwards in a gradual curve to an erect position.

ascending axis, the stem of a plant.

ascending colon, the part of the large intestine that ascends on the right side of the abdomen. See diagram under **intestine**.

ascending node, the point at which the orbit of a heavenly body intersects the fundamental plane; node.

as|cen|seur (á säɴ sœr′), *n. French.* an elevator or lift: *We zoomed by practically instant ascenseur to the sixtieth floor* (New Yorker).

as|cen|sion (ə sen′shən), *n.* **1** the act of ascending or going upward; ascent: *a balloon ascension.* **2** *Astronomy.* the rising of a heavenly body above the horizon. [< Latin *ascēnsiō, -ōnis* < *ascendere* ascend]

As|cen|sion (ə sen′shən), *n.* **1** the passing of Christ from earth to heaven, after the Resurrection (in the Bible, Acts 1:9). **2** Ascension Day.

as|cen|sion|al (ə sen′shə nəl), *adj.* **1** of or connected with ascension. **2** of or having to do with ascent.

Ascension Day, a church festival in honor of the Ascension of Christ, observed on the fortieth day after Easter, in the Church of England sometimes called Holy Thursday.

as|cen|sion|ist (ə sen′shə nist), *n.* a person who makes ascensions, such as a balloonist.

As|cen|sion|tide (ə sen′shən tīd′), *n.* the period of ten days from Ascension Day to Whitsun eve.

as|cen|sive (ə sen′siv), *adj.* **1** tending upward; rising. **2** *Grammar.* augmentative; intensifying.

as|cen|sor (ə sen′sər), *n.* = elevator.

as|cent (ə sent′), *n.* **1** the act of going up; upward movement; a rising: *The sudden ascent of the elevator made us dizzy.* **2** *Figurative.* improvement in position or rank; advancement; promotion. **3** a climbing, especially of a ladder or mountain: *The ascent of Mount Everest is difficult.* **4** a place or way that slopes up; way of ascending; upward route: *They climbed up the very steep ascent.* **5** degree of upward slope; gradient: *The gradual ascent of the hill made it easy to climb.* [< *ascend;* patterned on *descent*]

as|cer|tain (as′ər tān′), *v.t.* to find out for certain by trial and research; make sure of; determine: *The detective tried to ascertain the facts about the robbery. The question is how to ascertain what the people really want* (Atlantic). SYN: learn, discover. [< Old French *acertener* < *a-* to + *certain* certain < Latin *certus* sure] —**as′cer|tain′ment,** *n.*

as|cer|tain|a|ble (as′ər tā′nə bəl), *adj.* that can be ascertained. —**as′cer|tain′a|ble|ness,** *n.* —**as′cer|tain′a|bly,** *adv.*

as|ce|sis (ə sē′sis), *n.* the practice of asceticism: *They establish a strict ascesis . . . as a means of a closer communion with the divine* (Edwin Johnson). [< Greek *askēsis* exercise, training < *askeîn* to exercise]

as|cet|ic (ə set′ik), *n., adj.* —*n.* **1** a person who practices unusual self-denial or severe discipline over himself for religious reasons. Fasting is a common practice of ascetics. **2** a person who refrains from pleasures and comforts.
—*adj.* **1** refraining from pleasures and comforts; self-denying. SYN: austere, abstinent. **2** practicing unusual self-denial for religious reasons: *The early ascetic Christians lived in desert places.*
[< Greek *askētikós* < *askētēs* monk < *askeîn* to exercise] —**as|cet′i|cal|ly,** *adv.*

as|cet|i|cal (ə set′ə kəl), *adj.* of or having to do with ascetics or asceticism; ascetic.

as|cet|i|cism (ə set′ə siz əm), *n.* **1** the life or habits of an ascetic; unusual or extreme self-denial. **2** the doctrine that by abstinence and self-denial a person can train himself to be in conformity with God's will.

asc|hel|minth (ask hel′minth), *n.* any microscopic animal of a phylum comprising organisms with a pseudocoel, an unsegmented body surrounded by a cuticle, and a digestive tube with posterior anus, such as the rotifers, gastrotrichans, and nematodes. [< Greek *askós* skin bag + *hélmins, -inthos* worm]

Asch|heim-Zon|dek test (äsh′hīm zon′dek), a test to determine pregnancy by injecting the woman's urine into the ovaries of an immature mouse. [< Paul *Aschheim*, a German pathologist, and Bernhard *Zondek*, a German gynecologist, who discovered the test in 1928]

A|schoff body (ä′shôf), any of certain small nodules found in the heart tissue of a person affected with heart disease caused by rheumatic fever. [< Ludwig *Aschoff*, a German pathologist of the 1900's]

as|ci (as′ī), *n.* plural of **ascus**.

as|cid|i|an (ə sid′ē ən), *n.* **1** any one of several sea animals with a tough, saclike covering, such as the sea squirts. **2** any tunicate. [< Greek *askídion* (diminutive) < *askós* (literally) skin bag]

as|cid|i|um (ə sid′ē əm), *n., pl.* **-i|a** (-ē ə). a baglike or pitcher-shaped part of a plant, such as the leaf of the pitcher plant. [< New Latin *ascidium* < Greek *askídion* ascidian]

a|sci|en|tif|ic (ā′sī ən tif′ik), *adj.* that is not based on or in accord with science or the scientific method: *The philosophy which we are taught is ascientific, not to say antiscientific* (Enzo Boeri).

as|cif|er|ous (ə sif′ər əs), *adj.* = ascigerous.

as|cig|er|ous (ə sij′ər əs), *adj. Botany.* bearing asci. [< New Latin *ascus* sac, bag + Latin *gerere* bear + English *-ous*]

ASCII (as′kē) *n.* American Standard Code for Information Interchange (a computer code representing letters, numbers, and symbols).

as|ci|tes (ə sī′tēz), *n.* dropsy of the abdomen or peritoneum. [< Late Latin *ascītes* < Greek *askītēs* (*hýdrōps*) abdominal (dropsy) < *askós* belly (literally) skin bag]

as|cit|ic (ə sit′ik), *adj.* of or affected with ascites.

as|cle|pi|a|da|ceous (as klē′pē ə dā′shəs), *adj.* belonging to the milkweed family. [< New Latin *Asclepiadaceae* (< *Asclepias;* see etym. under **asclepias**) + English *-ous*]

As|cle|pi|a|de|an (as klē′pē ə dē′ən), *adj., n.* —*adj.* (of a verse in Greek and Latin poetry) consisting of a spondee, two or three choriambs, and an iamb. —*n.* an Asclepiadean verse. [< Late Latin *asclēpiadēus* < Greek *asklēpiádeios* < *Asklēpiádēs*, the poet Asclepiades]

as|cle|pi|as (as klē′pē əs), *n.* any plant of a genus of North American milkweeds. [< New Latin *Asclepias* the genus name < Latin *asclepias* swallowwort < Greek *asklēpiás* < *Asklēpiós* the god Asclepius]

As|cle|pi|us (as klē′pē əs), *n.* **1** the Greek god of medicine and healing, adopted by the Romans under the spelling Aesculapius. **2** *Homeric Legend.* a physician, father of the two physicians of the Greek army.

asco-, *combining form.* ascus; sac: *Ascospore = spore produced in an ascus.* [< New Latin *ascus* < Greek *askós* skin bag, sac]

as|co|carp (as′kə kärp), *n.* a body composed of asci and sterile hyphae in some ascomycetous fungi. It is the mature fruiting body and is exceedingly varied, its structure being a taxonomic character. [< *asco-* + Greek *karpós* fruit]

as|co|car|pous (as′kə kär′pəs), *adj.* of or like ascocarps; having an ascocarp.

as|cog|e|nous (as koj′ə nəs), *adj.* producing asci.

as|co|go|ni|a (as′kə gō′nē ə), *n.* plural of **ascogonium**.

as|co|go|ni|al (as′kə gō′nē əl), *adj.* of or having to do with an ascogonium.

as|co|go|ni|um (as′kə gō′nē əm), *n., pl.* **-ni|a** (-nē ə). the female sex organ in the gametophyte of ascomycetous fungi. [< New Latin *ascogonium* < Greek *askós* skin bag + a root *gen-* to bear]

as|co|li|chen (as′kə lī′kən), *n.* any one of a class of lichens in which the fungus living symbiotically with an alga is an ascomycete.

as|co|my|cete (as′kə mī sēt′), *n.* any one of a large class of fungi characterized by the formation of spores in elongated sacs (asci). Yeasts, truffles, and some molds and mildews are included in this class. [< Greek *askós* skin bag + *mýkēs, -ētos* fungus]

as|co|my|ce|tous (as′kə mī sē′təs), *adj.* of or belonging to the ascomycetes.

A scope, a radarscope that indicates the range of the target but not its bearing.

a|scor|bate (ā skôr′bāt, ə-), *n.* a salt of ascorbic acid. [< *ascorb*(ic) + *-ate*[2]]

a|scor|bic acid (ā skôr′bik, ə-), = vitamin C. [< *a-*[4] not + *scorb*(ut)*ic*]

as|co|spore (as′kə spôr, -spōr), *n.* one of the cluster of spores formed within an ascus.

as|co|spor|ic (as′kə spôr′ik, -spor′-), *adj.* = ascosporous.

as|cos|po|rous (as kos′pər əs; as′kə spôr′-, -spōr′-), *adj.* having ascospores.

***as|cot** (as′kət, -kot), *n.* a necktie with broad ends, resembling a scarf, tied so that the ends may be laid flat, one across the other. [< *Ascot*, in England, where famous horse races are held]

***ascot**

as|cribe (ə skrīb′), *v.t.,* **-cribed, -crib|ing.** **1** to think of as caused by or coming from; assign or attribute (to): *The police ascribed the automobile accident to fast driving. The author of this tale is unknown, but it is ascribed to the brothers Grimm.* SYN: See syn. under **attribute**. **2** to consider as belonging (to): *Men have ascribed their own characteristics to their gods.* [< Old French *ascriv-*, stem of *ascrire* < Latin *ascrībere* < *ad-* to + *scrībere* write] —**as|crib′a|ble,** *adj.*

as|crip|tion (ə skrip′shən), *n.* **1** the act of ascribing: *the ascription of selfishness to a miser.* **2** a statement or words ascribing something. Also, **adscription**. [< Latin *ascrīptiō, -ōnis* addition < *ascrībere* ascribe]

as|cus (as′kəs), *n., pl.* **as|ci.** the elongated sac or cell in which the spores are formed in certain fungi. [< New Latin *ascus* < Greek *askós* skin bag]

as|dic or **As|dic** (az′dik), *n., adj. British.* sonar: *The forward part of the submarine is taken up*

Pronunciation Key: hat, āge, cãre, fär; let, ēqual, tėrm; it, īce; hot, ōpen, ôrder; oil, out; cup, pu̇t, rüle; child; long; thin; ᴛʜen; zh, measure; ə represents **a** in about, **e** in taken, **i** in pencil, **o** in lemon, **u** in circus.

with torpedoes and asdic equipment (Manchester Guardian). [< *A*(llied) *S*(ubmarine) *D*(etection) *I*(nvestigation) *C*(ommittee)]

-ase, a suffix used to form the names of enzymes: *Maltase = an enzyme that decomposes malt.* [< (diast)*ase*]

a|sea (ə sē′), *adv.* **1** on the sea; at sea. **2** to the sea.

ASEAN (as′ē ən, ä′sē-), *n.* Association of South East Asian Nations (group of 6 nations consisting of Brunei, Indonesia, Malaysia, the Philippines, Singapore, and Thailand, organized in 1967 to promote economic progress and political stability in the area).

a|seis|mic (ā sīz′mik), *adj.* free of seismic disturbances: *The aseismic nature of the ridge south and east of southern Africa also suggests that it is at present a dormant ridge* (Nature).

a|se|i|ty (ā sē′ə tē), *n.* underived or independent existence: *The absolute being and aseity of God* (W. R. Smith). [< Latin *a* from (< *ad-*) + *se* oneself + English *-ity*]

a|sen|ta|mi|en|to (ä′sen tä′mē en′tō), *n., pl.* **-tos.** (in Chile) a collective farm established by the government on land expropriated from individual landholders. [< Spanish *asentamiento* (literally) settlement]

a|sep|sis (ə sep′sis, ā-), *n.* **1** aseptic condition. **2** aseptic methods or treatment. [< *a-*[4] without + *sepsis*]

a|sep|tic (ə sep′tik, ā-), *adj., n.* **—*adj.*** **1** free from the living germs causing infection or fermentation: *Surgical instruments are made aseptic by boiling them.* **2** employing all possible measures to exclude germs: *aseptic surgery.*
—*n.* an aseptic substance or preparation.
—a|sep′ti|cal|ly, *adv.*

a|sep|ti|cism (ə sep′tə siz əm, ā-), *n.* the use of aseptic methods.

a|sep|ti|cize (ə sep′tə sīz, ā-), *v.t.,* **-cized, -ciz|ing.** to make aseptic.

a|sex|u|al (ā sek′shů əl), *adj. Biology.* **1** having no sex. **2** independent of sexual processes. The division into two parts by an ameba is a form of asexual reproduction, called fission; budding is another form. *In liverworts, mosses, and some lower animals sexual and asexual reproduction alternate by generations. Reproduction that involves only one "parent" and has no special reproductive structures is termed asexual reproduction* (Tracy I. Storer). **—a|sex′u|al|ly,** *adv.*

a|sex|u|al|i|ty (ā sek′shů al′ə tē), *n.* asexual condition.

a|sex|u|al|ize (ā sek′shů ə līz), *v.t.,* **-ized, -iz|ing.** to make unable to reproduce sexually, by gelding or spaying. **—a|sex′u|al|i|za′tion,** *n.*

As|gard (as′gärd, az′-), *n. Norse Mythology.* the home of the Norse gods and of heroes slain in battle, the location of Valhalla. It could be reached only by the rainbow bridge Bifrost.

ash[1] (ash), *n., v.* **—*n.*** **1** what remains of anything combustible after it has been thoroughly burned; the incombustible residue of organic substances remaining after combustion: *He flicked his cigarette ash into the fireplace.* See also **ashes. 2** fine material thrown out of a volcano in eruption; powdered lava. **3** the light gray color of wood ashes.
—*v.t.* to burn or convert (something) to ashes.
—*v.i.* to form or become ashes.
[Old English *æsce*]

ash[2] (ash), *n.* **1** a timber or shade tree that has a tough wood. The ash has a silver-gray bark, grayish twigs, and straight-grained wood, and belongs to the olive family. **2** its tough, springy wood. [Old English *æsc*]

a|shake (ə shāk′), *adj.* shaking: *Wild swans hid in lilies all ashake* (Elizabeth Barrett Browning).

a|shamed (ə shāmd′), *adj.* **1** feeling shame; disturbed or uncomfortable because one has done something wrong, improper, or silly; feeling embarrassed or disgraced: *I was ashamed when I cried at the movies. The poor girl was ashamed of her ragged dress.* **2** unwilling because of fear of shame; held back by the belief that shame would be felt: *He was ashamed to tell his mother he had failed. A man should never be ashamed to own he has been in the wrong* (Alexander Pope). [Old English *asceamod,* past participle of *asceamian* feel shame < *a-* on + *sceamu* shame] **—a|sham′ed|ly,** *adv.* **—a|sham′ed|ness,** *n.*
—*Syn.* **1 Ashamed, humiliated, mortified, chagrined** mean feeling embarrassed and disgraced. **Ashamed** emphasizes a feeling of having disgraced oneself by doing something wrong, improper, or foolish: *Later he felt ashamed at his lack of self-control.* **Humiliated** emphasizes a painful feeling of being lowered and shamed in the eyes of others: *Parents are humiliated if their children behave badly when guests are present.* **Mortified** means feeling greatly embarrassed and humiliated, sometimes ashamed: *He was mortified when he forgot his speech.* **Chagrined** means embarrassed and annoyed or disappointed: *I was chagrined to find that I had left the tickets at home.*

A|shan|ti (ə shan′tē, -shän′-), *n., pl.* **-ti** or **-tis. 1** a native of the Ashanti region in Ghana. **2** the Kwa language of the Ashanti, closely related to Akan.

ash-bin (ash′bin′), *n. British.* an ashcan; dustbin.

ash blond, a blond with very light or ash-colored hair. **—ash′-blond′,** *adj.*

ash|cake (ash′kāk′), *n. U.S.* a cake baked in or under the ashes of a fire.

ash|can (ash′kan′), *n., v.,* **-canned, -can|ning.**
—*n.* **1** *Especially U.S.* a barrel, drum, or large can for ashes or garbage. **2** *Nautical.* a depth charge.
—*v.t.* *Informal.* to reject; discard; throw out: *The message was ashcanned without ever having been formally delivered* (Wall Street Journal).
throw (cast, or **toss) into the ashcan,** to throw away; discard: *In disregarding the traditional patronage practices of the politicians, ... Mr. Sachs also probably cast into the ashcan his chances of renomination* (New York Times).

Ashcan School, a group of American artists of the early 1900's who painted realistic and typically dark and drab city scenes.

ash-col|ored (ash′kul′ərd), *adj.* having the whitish-gray color of ashes; having a pale grayish tinge.

ash-dry (ash′drī′), *adj.* very dry; parched: *Though [he] is still swaying slightly at bullfight time, his mouth and his spirit are ash-dry* (Time).

ash|en[1] (ash′ən), *adj.* **1a** like ashes; of the color of ashes. **b** *Figurative.* pale; pallid: *an ashen face.* **2** of ashes. [< *ash*[1] + *-en*[2]]

ash|en[2] (ash′ən), *adj.* **1** of the ash tree or its timber. **2** made from the wood of the ash tree. [< *ash*[2] + *-en*[2]]

Ash|er (ash′ər), *n.* **1** the eighth son of Jacob (in the Bible, Genesis 30:12-13). **2** the Israelite tribe that claimed him as ancestor.

a|she|rah (ə shē′rə), *n.* **1** a wooden post, pillar, or trunk of a tree used as a symbol of the goddess Asherah near Canaanite and Phoenician altars devoted to the worship of Baal. **2 Asherah,** the goddess herself, associated with Baal. [< Hebrew *ashērāh*]

ash|er|y (ash′ər ē), *n., pl.* **-er|ies. 1** a place for ashes. **2** a potash or pearlash factory.

ash|es (ash′iz), *n.pl.* **1** what remains of anything combustible after it has been thoroughly burned: *Ashes have to be removed from a fireplace and furnace or there will be no space for a fire.* **2** what remains of a dead human body when burned. **3** a dead body; corpse: *"Peace to their ashes!"* **4** the ruins or remains of a civilization or culture. **5** powdered lava.
the Ashes, the legendary prize for which the cricket matches between England and Australia are played: *If we fail to bring home the Ashes it will certainly not be for want of trying* (Westminster Gazette).

ash|fall (ash′fôl′), *n.* the fall of volcanic or other ash after an eruption or explosion.

ash gray, light gray tinged with green. **—ash′-gray′,** *adj.*

ash|i|ba|ri (ä′shē bä′rē), *n.* a sweep of the foot in judo, designed to drop an opponent on his back. [< Japanese *ashibari*]

a|shim|mer (ə shim′ər), *adv., adj.* in a shimmering state.

a|shine (ə shīn′), *adv., adj.* in a shining state.

a|shiv|er (ə shiv′ər), *adj.* shivering: *She shivered, drew her coat closer and walked out before him, alone, still ashiver* (Saturday Evening Post).

Ash|ke|naz|i (ash′kə naz′ē, äsh′kə nä′zē), *adj.* = Ashkenazic.

Ash|ke|naz|ic (ash′kə naz′ik, äsh′kə nä′zik), *adj.* of or descended from the Ashkenazim.

Ash|ke|naz|im (ash′kə naz′im, äsh′kə nä′zim), *n.pl.* the Jews of Germany, Poland, Russia, etc., and their descendants, as contrasted with the Sephardim or Spanish and Portuguese Jews. [< Hebrew *ashkənāzīm,* plural of *ashkənāzī* a German < *ashkənāz* Germany, originally an ancient kingdom]

ash key, the winged fruit, or samara, of the ash tree.

ash|lar or **ash|ler** (ash′lər), *n.* **1** a square-hewn stone used in building and for pavement. **2** masonry made of ashlars. **3** a similar masonry, usually in thin slabs, used as a facing to a rubble or brick wall. [< Old French *aisselier,* ultimately < a diminutive form of Latin *axis* (earlier *assis*) board]

ash|lared or **ash|lered** (ash′lərd), *adj.* faced with ashlar, as a wall.

ash|lar|ing or **ash|ler|ing** (ash′lər ing), *n.* **1** masonry or a facing of ashlar. **2** a short studding cutting off the angle between the floor and roof in a garret and affording a wall of some height.

ash|man (ash′man′, -mən), *n., pl.* **-men.** a collector of ashes and other refuse.

a|shore (ə shôr′, -shōr′), *adv., adj.* **1** to the shore or to land: *The men rowed the captain ashore.* **2** on the shore; on land: *The sailor had been ashore for months. Samples were drawn for later measurement ashore of salinity ... and level of radioactivity* (Science).

ash|pan (ash′pan′), *n.* a shallow pan, usually set under a grate, for collecting ashes, as in a furnace.

ash|pit (ash′pit′), *n.* a hole for ashes, as under a grate.

ash|plant (ash′plant′), *n.,* or **ashplant cane,** the sapling of the ash tree, cut and used especially as a walking stick or prod.

a|shram (ä′shrəm), *n.* **1** (in India) a small rural retreat for meditation: **2** any similar retreat.

Ash|to|reth (ash′tə reth), *n.* = Astarte.

ash|tray (ash′trā′), *n.* a small dish to put tobacco ashes in.

A|shur (ä′shůr, ash′ər), *n.* the chief god of the Assyrians. Also, **Asshur, Assur, Asur.**

A|shu|ra (ä shü′rä), *n.* a Shiitic fast day commemorating the death of Imam Hussein, grandson of the prophet Mohammed.

Ash|vins (ash′vinz), *n.pl. Hindu Mythology.* the pair of twins responsible for the physical well-being of the world.

Ash Wednesday, the first day of Lent; the seventh Wednesday before Easter. [< the Roman Catholic custom of marking penitents with ashes]

ash|wort (ash′wėrt′), *n.* a composite plant of the southeastern United States, covered with an ash-colored wool.

ash|y (ash′ē), *adj.,* **ash|i|er, ash|i|est. 1** like ashes; pale as ashes; ashen. **2** consisting of ashes. **3** covered with ashes.

A|sia|dol|lar (ā′zhə dol′ər), *n.* a U.S. dollar deposited in Asian banks and used in various money markets of Asia: *U.S. companies flock to buy Asiadollar CDs* (Business Week).

A|sian (ā′zhən, -shən), *n., adj.* **—*n.*** a person born or living in Asia.
—*adj.* of or having to do with Asia; characteristic of its people.

Asian flu, an influenza caused by a strain of virus first identified in Hong Kong in early 1957.

A|si|an|ic (ā′zhē an′ik, -shē-), *adj.* of or having to do with Asia Minor: *... Asianic elements in Greek civilization* (Sir William Ramsay).

A|si|at|ic (ā′zhē at′ik, -shē-), *n., adj.* = Asian. **—A′si|at′i|cal|ly,** *adv.*

Asiatic black bear, = black bear (def. 2).

Asiatic cholera, = cholera (def. 1a).

Asiatic flu, = Asian flu.

A|si|at|i|cize (ā′zhē at′ə sīz, -shē-), *v.t.,* **-cized, -ciz|ing.** to make Asiatic in character or type.

a|side (ə sīd′), *adv., n.* **—*adv.*** **1** on one side; to one side; away: *Move the table aside. He stood aside from the crowd, unnoticed.* **2** away from oneself; off: *I laid my overcoat aside.* **3** out of a person's thoughts or consideration: *Swimming is easier if you can put your fears aside.*
—*n.* **1** words spoken to one side; a remark made in an undertone that others who are present are not supposed to hear: *His low aside, "We've won!" was overheard.* **2** words spoken by an actor which the other actors are supposed not to hear. An actor's asides are usually spoken to the audience. *Those asides—a typical device of this playwright—which the characters deliver to the audience do not really suit the screen* (Manchester Guardian Weekly). **3** a digression: *Some years ago a majority opinion of the Supreme Court, in an aside on the On Lee case, stated: "the use of bifocals, field glasses or telescopes ... is not forbidden even if they focus without [the subject's] knowledge or consent"* (Vance Packard).
aside from, a away from; apart from: *Your remark is aside from the question.* **b** *U.S. Informal.* except for: *Aside from arithmetic, I have finished my homework.*
set aside. See under **set.**

as|i|en|to (as′ē en′tō), *n.* = assiento.

A|sil|ian (ə sil′yən, -zil′-), *adj., n.* = Azilian.

a|si|lid (ə sī′lid), *adj., n.* **—*adj.*** of or belonging to a genus of large, fierce, two-winged flies which prey on other insects. **—*n.*** an asilid fly. [< New Latin *Asilidae* the family name < Latin *asīlus* horsefly]

as|i|nine (as′ə nīn), *adj.* **1** foolish and stupid; obviously silly: *Temper tantrums are asinine.* **2** like that of an ass: *asinine ears.* **3** of asses. [< Latin *asinīnus* < *asinus* ass] **—as′i|nine|ly,** *adv.*

as|i|nin|i|ty (as′ə nin′ə tē), *n., pl.* **-ties. 1** silliness; stupidity. **2** asinine remarks or deeds: *In the train he got an aisle seat and scanned the asininities in the evening paper* (New Yorker).

ask (ask, äsk), *v.t.* **1** to try to find out about by words; inquire: *Ask the way.* **2** to seek the answer to: *Ask any question you wish.* **3** to put a question to; inquire of: *Ask him how old he is.* SYN: query. See syn. under **question. 4** to try to get by words; request: *Ask her to sing. I asked*

permission to leave the table. **5** to claim; demand: *to ask too high a price for a house.* **6** to invite: *She asked ten guests to the party.* **7** to require; call for; need: *This job asks hard work.* **8** *Informal.* to publish the banns of (a person or persons). —*v.i.* **1** to make a request (for); try to get something by words: *Why don't you ask for help?* **2** to try to find out (about); inquire (after): *She asked about our health. Did anyone ask after me while I was ill?*
ask around, *U.S.* to inquire here and there: *I don't know, but ask around—somebody will know.*
ask for it, *Informal.* to invite danger or unpleasant consequences: *By his rude behavior and selfish ways the little bully was just asking for it.*
ask for trouble. See under **trouble**.
ask (someone) **out**, to invite (someone), especially on a date: *He asked her out to dinner.*
for the asking, by merely being asked for; without extra cost or effort: *Free tickets are available for the asking.*
[Old English *āscian*]—**ask'er**, *n.*
—***Syn.*** *v.t.* 1, *v.i.* **2 Ask, inquire** mean to try to find out by a question. **Ask** is the general word meaning to seek information from someone: *I asked about you. Ask someone where that street is.* **Inquire** is more formal, but suggests more strongly going into a subject, asking in an effort to get definite information: *I inquired about you; I wanted to know when you are leaving. You had better inquire how to get there.*
—*v.t.* **4 Ask, request, solicit** mean to try to get by words. **Ask** is the general word: *I asked permission to do it.* **Request**, a more formal word, means to ask in a polite and more formal way: *We request contributions to the library.* **Solicit**, a formal word, means to request respectfully or earnestly: *They are soliciting funds for a new hospital.*

a|skance (ə skans'), *adv.* **1** with suspicion or disapproval: *The students looked askance at the plan to have classes on Saturday.* **2** to one side; sideways. [origin uncertain]

a|skant (ə skant'), *adv.* = askance.

as|ka|ri (as'kər ē), *n., pl.* **-ris** or **-ri**. an African policeman, guard or soldier. [< Arabic *'askarī* soldier]

a|skew (ə skyü'), *adv., adj.* to one side; out of the proper position; turned or twisted the wrong way: *The wind blew her hat askew* (adv.). *Some of his facts and dates are askew* (adj.). SYN: awry, aslant. [perhaps < *a-*[1] on + *skew*]

ask|ing price (as'king, äs'-), *Informal.* the first charge, rate, or price set, especially as a preliminary to bargaining or negotiation: *an asking price of $50,000 for a house.*

ASL (no periods), American Sign Language.

a|slant (ə slant', -slänt'), *adv., prep., adj.* —***adv.*** in a slanting direction.
—***prep.*** slantingly across.
—***adj.*** slanting.

a|sleep (ə slēp'), *adj., adv.* —***adj.*** **1** not awake; sleeping: *The cat is asleep.* **2** *Figurative.* not aware; oblivious: *He is asleep to the danger.* SYN: unmindful; heedless. **3** dull; inactive: *His mind is asleep.* SYN: dormant. **4** having lost the power of feeling; numb: *My foot is asleep.* **5** dead.
—***adv.*** into a condition of sleep: *The tired boy fell asleep.*

a|slope (ə slōp'), *adv., adj.* at a slant; sloping.

ASM (no periods), air-to-surface missile.

As|mo|de|us (az'mə dē'əs, as'-), *n.* **1** an evil spirit of Hebrew demonology, mentioned in the apocryphal Book of Tobit. **2** (later) the king of the demons.

a|so|cial (ā sō'shəl), *adj.* **1** indifferent to social customs or laws; not social: *an asocial act.* **2** reluctant to associate with other people; not sociable: *He was asocial and suspicious of others.* —**a|so'cial|ly**, *adv.*

a|so|ci|al|i|ty (ā sō'shē al'ə tē), *n.* **1** indifference to social customs or laws. **2** reluctance to meet other people; unsociableness.

a|so|ma|tous (ā sō'mə təs), *adj.* without a body; incorporeal. [< Latin *asōmatus* (with English *-ous*) < Greek *asōmatos* < *a-* without + *sôma* body]

asp[1] (asp), *n.* **1** any one of several small, poisonous snakes of Africa, especially the Egyptian cobra. **2** a small, poisonous snake of Europe; adder. **3** any venomous snake. [< Latin *aspis* < Greek *aspis*]

asp[2] (asp), *n. Poetic.* an aspen. [Old English *æspe*]

ASP (no periods), **1** aerospace plane. **2** Also **A.S.P.** American Selling Price.

as|par|a|gin (ə spar'ə jin), *n.* = asparagine.

as|pa|rag|i|nase (as'pə raj'ə nās), *n.* a bacterial enzyme that breaks down asparagine, used especially in the treatment of leukemia; L-asparaginase. [< *asparagine* + *-ase*]

as|par|a|gine (ə spar'ə jēn, -jin), *n.* a crystalline amino acid, the protein constituent of many plants. *Formula:* $C_4H_8N_2O_3$

as|par|a|gus (ə spar'ə gəs), *n.* **1** a plant with scalelike leaves. It is a perennial plant of the lily family, with pulpy red berries and no bulb. The stems have many branches covered with threadlike branchlets, the true leaves being reduced to scales. The green, tender shoots of one kind are used as a vegetable. **2** these shoots. [< Latin *asparagus* < Greek *aspáragos*]

asparagus fern, a variety of asparagus, native to southern Africa, and cultivated as a house plant for its heavy ornamental growth of fine leaves.

a|spar|kle (ə spär'kəl), *adj.* sparkling.

as|par|tame (as par'tām), *n.* an artificial sweetener, several hundred times sweeter than sugar, obtained from aspartic acid and used as a substitute for sugar or saccharin. *Formula:* $C_{14}H_{18}N_2O_5$

as|par|tic acid (as pär'tik), a crystalline amino acid, derived from the juice of asparagus, beets, young sugar cane, or certain seeds. *Formula:* $C_4H_7O_4N$

A.S.P.C.A. or **ASPCA** (no periods), American Society for the Prevention of Cruelty to Animals.

***as|pect** (as'pekt), *n.* **1** one side or part or view (of a subject); one of the ways in which a subject or situation may be looked at or thought about: *We must consider each aspect of this plan before we decide.* **2** the way in which an object appears to the eye; look; appearance: *the aspect of the countryside.* SYN: See syn. under **appearance**. **3** facial expression; countenance: *The judge has a solemn aspect.* SYN: mien, air. **4** the particular direction anything faces or is exposed to: *The house has a sunny southern aspect.* SYN: exposure. **5** the side fronting or facing in a given direction: *The southern aspect of the house is the warmest in winter.* **6 a** *Astronomy.* the relative position of a planet with respect to another planet, the sun, or the moon, as seen from the earth. **b** *Astrology.* the relative positions of the heavenly bodies, especially planets, as determining their supposed influence upon human affairs. **7** *Grammar.* **a** any one of several categories of verb forms in some languages which express action or state as beginning, ending, continuing, or being repeated, rather than indicating time, as does a tense form. For example in such a language, the inceptive aspect of a verb "to strike" might mean "he begins, began, or will begin to strike." **b** the meaning expressed by such a category. **c** (in languages without such forms) a similar meaning otherwise expressed. **d** such categories or their meanings, taken collectively. **8** the position, or presentation, of a plane surface relative to a fluid or gas through which it moves. **9** *Obsolete.* the act of looking at anything; contemplation; gaze.
[< Latin *aspectus* < *aspicere* look at < *ad-* at + *specere* look]

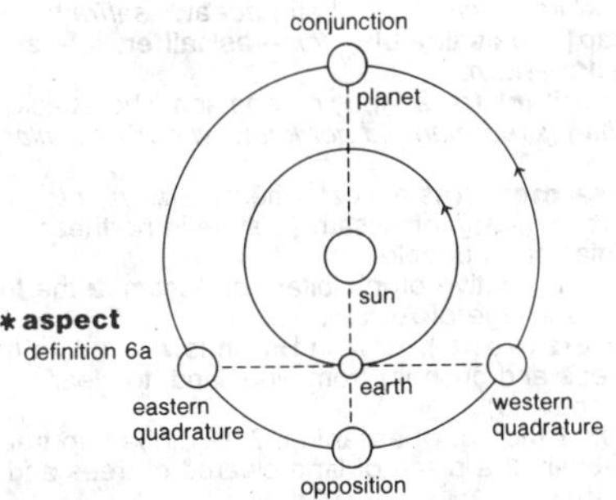

***aspect**
definition 6a

aspect ratio, *Aeronautics.* the ratio of the square of the span of an airfoil to its actual area.

as|pec|tu|al (as pek'chu̇ əl), *adj. Grammar.* of or having to do with aspect.

as|pen (as'pən), *n., adj.* —***n.*** any one of several poplar trees, including the quaking aspen of North America and others of Europe, whose leaves tremble and rustle in the slightest breeze.
—***adj.*** **1** of any of these trees. **2** *Figurative.* quivering; trembling.
[< earlier meaning "of the asp[2]"]

as|per (as'pər), *n.* a Turkish money of account, equal to one 120th of a piaster, formerly a small silver coin. [< French *aspre* < Medieval Greek *áspron, áspros* white, apparently < Latin *asper* (*nummus*) newly minted (coin)]

as|per|ate (as'pə rāt), *v.t.,* **-at|ed, -at|ing.** to make rough. [< Latin *asperāre* (with English *-ate*[1]) < *asper* rough]

as|perge (ə spėrj'), *v.t.,* **-perged, -perg|ing.** to sprinkle: *Their suits, like pieces of planetarium sky, were dead black and thickly asperged with silver* (Punch). [< Latin *aspergere* < *ad-* to + *spargere* sprinkle]—**as'per|ga'tion**, *n.*

as|per|ges or **As|per|ges** (ə spėr'jēz), *n.* **1** the rite of sprinkling altar, clergy, and people with holy water, especially before Sunday High Mass. **2** the anthem intoned during this rite. [< Latin *aspergēs* thou shalt sprinkle]

as|per|gil|lo|sis (as pėr'jə lō'sis), *n., pl.* **-ses** (-sēz). a fatal disease of birds and fowl, caused by any one of several molds, especially aspergilli. It also occurs in domestic animals and (occasionally) in man as an ear or lung infection.

as|per|gil|lum (as'pər jil'əm), *n., pl.* **-gil|la** (-jil'ə), **-gil|lums.** a brush or perforated vessel for sprinkling holy water. [< Latin *aspergere* sprinkle + *-illum*, a diminutive suffix]

as|per|gil|lus (as'pər jil'əs), *n., pl.* **-gil|li** (-jil'ī). any one of a genus of tiny fungi having spore-bearing organs (conidiophores) that resemble the brushes (aspergilla) used for sprinkling holy water. Many common molds, including several commercially useful species, belong to this genus. [< New Latin *Aspergillus* < English *aspergillum*]

as|per|i|fo|li|ate (as'pər ə fō'lē it, -āt), *adj. Botany.* having rough leaves. [< New Latin *asperifolius* (< Latin *asper* rough + *folium* leaf)]

as|per|i|ty (as per'ə tē), *n., pl.* **-ties. 1** harshness or sharpness of temper, especially as shown in tone or manner: *We were dismayed at the asperity in the visitor's voice.* **2** *Figurative.* severity; rigor: *The settlers suffered the asperities of a very cold winter.* **3** roughness or unevenness of a surface. [< Old French *asprete*, learned borrowing from Latin *asperitās* < *asper* rough]

a|sper|mous (ə spėr'məs), *adj. Botany.* without seed. [< Greek *áspermos* (with English *-ous*) < *a-* without + *spérma* seed]

as|perse (ə spėrs'), *v.t.,* **-persed, -pers|ing. 1** to spread damaging or false reports about; slander: *He said law enforcement facts turn the tide . . . upon . . . those who seek to asperse the country's good name* (Baltimore Sun). SYN: calumniate, vilify, traduce. **2** to sprinkle. [< Latin *aspersus*, past participle of *aspergere* sprinkle < *ad-* on + *spargere* sprinkle]—**as|pers'er**, *n.*

as|per|sion (ə spėr'zhən, -shən), *n.* **1** a damaging or false statement; slander: *You should not cast aspersions upon an innocent man.* **2** the act of spreading such reports; defamation; calumniation. **3** *Obsolete.* a sprinkling with water. [< Latin *aspersiō, -ōnis* < *aspergere* sprinkle]

as|per|sive (ə spėr'siv), *adj.* that tends to slander or defame: *aspersive rumors.* —**as|per'sive|ly**, *adv.*

as|per|soir (äs per swär'), *n.* = aspergillum. [< French *aspersoir* < Medieval Latin *aspersorium*]

as|per|so|ri|um (as'pər sôr'ē əm, -sōr'-), *n., pl.* **-so|ri|a** (-sôr'ē ə, -sōr'-), **-so|ri|ums. 1** a container for holy water. **2** = aspergillum. [< Medieval Latin *aspersorium* < Latin *aspersus* sprinkled + *-ōrium* receptacle]

as|phalt (as'fôlt, -falt), *n., adj., v.* —***n.*** **1** a dark-colored substance, much like tar, that is used for waterproofing roofs, building foundations, and other surfaces; mineral pitch. It is found in natural beds in various parts of the world and also obtained by refining crude petroleum. **2** a smooth, hard mixture of this substance with crushed rock or sand. Asphalt is used in surfacing roads.
—***adj.*** of asphalt; made of or covered with asphalt: *an asphalt highway.*
—***v.t.*** to cover, permeate, or seal with asphalt.
[< Late Latin *asphalton* < Greek *ásphaltos* < a Semitic word]

asphalt cement, a refined, semisolid asphalt used for paving.

asphalt cloud, particles of combustible asphalt discharged by an antiballistic missile in the path of an enemy missile or missiles.

as|phal|tene (as fôl'tēn, -fal'-), *n.* a kind of hard, brittle asphalt.

as|phal|tic (as fôl'tik, -fal'-), *adj.* of the nature of or containing asphalt.

as|phal|tite (as fôl'tīt, -fal'-), *n., adj.* —***n.*** a resinous form of asphalt. —***adj.*** = asphaltic.

asphalt jungle, *U.S. Informal.* a slum or other area of a modern city in which violence and crime are common: *Juvenile delinquency last year climbed 9% in the asphalt jungles across the U.S.* (Time).

as|phal|tum (as fal'təm), *n.* = asphalt.

a|spher|ic (ā sfer'ik), *adj. Optics.* not spherical: *an aspheric surface, aspheric mirrors.* —**a'spher'i|cal|ly**, *adv.*

a|spher|i|cal (ā sfer'ə kəl), *adj.* = aspheric.

as|pho|del (as'fə del), *n.* **1** any one of several

Pronunciation Key: hat, āge, câre, fär; let, ēqual, tėrm; it, īce; hot, ōpen, ôrder; oil, out; cup, pu̇t, rüle; child; long; thin; ᴛʜen; zh, measure; ə represents **a** in about, **e** in taken, **i** in pencil, **o** in lemon, **u** in circus.

plants of the lily family with spikes of white, yellow, or pink flowers, especially the yellow asphodel. **2** the immortal flower of the Greek paradise whose pale blossoms covered the Elysian meadows. **3** *Poetic.* the daffodil. [< Latin *asphodelus* < Greek *asphódelos*]

as|phyx|i|a (as fik′sē ə), *n.* suffocation or unconscious condition caused by lack of oxygen and excess of carbon dioxide in the blood, as in choking or drowning. [< New Latin *asphyxia* < Greek *asphyxiā* a stopping of the pulse < *a-* without + *sphýxis* pulse < *sphýzein* to throb]

as|phyx|i|al (as fik′sē əl), *adj.* of or characterized by asphyxia.

as|phyx|i|ant (as fik′sē ənt), *adj., n.* —*adj.* causing asphyxia.
—*n.* a cause of asphyxia.

as|phyx|i|ate (as fik′sē āt), *v.t., v.i.,* **-at|ed, -at|ing.** to suffocate because of lack of oxygen in the blood; produce asphyxia in: *The men trapped in the coal mine were almost asphyxiated by gas before help could reach them.* —**as|phyx′i|a′tion,** *n.* —**as|phyx′i|a′tor,** *n.*

as|pic¹ (as′pik), *n.* a kind of jelly made from meat or fish stock, tomato juice, or the like, and used as a garnish, in salads, and some other dishes. [< French *aspic*]

as|pic² (as′pik), *n. Poetic.* the asp (snake). [< French *aspic,* variant of Old French *aspe* asp < Latin *aspis* < Greek *aspís*]

as|pic³ (as′pik), *n.* a variety of lavender native to southern France and Spain, yielding a volatile, aromatic oil used in perfume. [< Middle French *aspic* < Provençal *aspic* lavender < Latin *spīcum* ear (of a plant)]

as|pi|dis|tra (as′pə dis′trə), *n.* an Asian plant with large, green leaves and very small flowers, much used as a house plant. It is an herb belonging to the lily family. [< New Latin *aspidistra* < Greek *aspís, -idos* shield + *ástron* star]

as|pir|ant (ə spīr′ənt, as′pər-), *n., adj.* —*n.* a person who aspires, especially one who seeks a position of honor: *There are many aspirants to the office of mayor of our town.* **SYN:** See syn. under **candidate.**
—*adj.* aspiring: *Three hundred aspirant pilots started the course with him that summer* (Maclean's).

as|pi|rate (*v.* as′pə rāt; *adj., n.* as′pər it), *v.,* **-rat|ed, -rat|ing,** *adj., n.* —*v.t.* **1** to begin (a word or syllable) with a breathing or *h*-sound. *Hot* is aspirated; *honor* is not. **2** to pronounce with a breathing or *h*-sound. The *h* in *forehead* is often not aspirated. **3** to pronounce (a stop) with a puff of air following or accompanying. *P* is aspirated in *pin* but not in *tip.* **4** to draw by suction. **5** *Medicine.* to remove (fluid) by means of an aspirator.
—*adj.* pronounced with a breathing or *h*-sound; aspirated. The *h* in *here* is aspirate.
—*n.* **1** the sound of *h* in *hot.* **2** an aspirated sound. English *p* is an aspirate in *pat,* but not in *tap.*
[< Latin *aspīrāre* (with English *-ate*¹); see etym. under **aspire**]

as|pi|rat|ed (as′pə rā′tid), *adj.* **1** having a breathing sound or *h*-sound prefixed, added, or blended. **2** pronounced with an emission of breath: *In English these six sounds are all aspirated, p, t, and k more strongly than b, d, and g, because naturally a certain amount of breath energy is used up in vibrating the vocal chords. In stressed syllables t is highly aspirated* (Simeon Potter).

as|pi|ra|tion (as′pə rā′shən), *n.* **1** earnest desire; longing; ambition: *She had aspirations to become an actress.* **2a** an aspirating (of sounds): *the aspiration of "h" in "house." Many people pronounce "where" with no aspiration.* **b** an aspirated sound. **3** the act of drawing air into the lungs; breathing. **4** *Medicine.* the act of removing fluid from a cavity of the body by the use of an aspirator. **5** suction.

as|pi|ra|tor (as′pə rā′tər), *n.* **1** an apparatus or device using suction. **2** an apparatus for creating a partial vacuum by the action of a moving fluid. **3** *Medicine.* an instrument, consisting of a hollow needle or trocar connected with a suction syringe, used in removing fluid from a cavity of the body.

as|pir|a|to|ry (ə spīr′ə tôr′ē, -tōr′-), *adj.* of or suited for aspiration.

as|pire (ə spīr′), *v.i.,* **-pired, -pir|ing. 1** to have an ambition for something; desire earnestly; seek: *Scholars aspire after knowledge. Tom aspired to be captain of the team.* **SYN:** aim, long, crave. **2** to rise high: *On what wings dare he aspire?* (William Blake). **SYN:** tower, soar. [< Latin *aspīrāre* < *ad-* toward + *spīrāre* breathe] —**as|pir′er,** *n.*

as|pi|rin (as′pər in), *n.* a drug used to relieve the pain, especially of headaches and arthritis, and the fever of colds; acetylsalicylic acid. It is a white, crystalline compound, prepared from salicylic acid. *Formula:* $C_9H_8O_4$ [< German *Aspirin* (originally a trademark) < Greek *a-* without + Latin *spīraea* an herb + German *-in* -in² (because aspirin is made without the use of *Spiraea ulmaria,* the natural source of acetylsalicylic acid)]

as|pir|ing (ə spīr′ing), *adj.* **1** = ambitious. **2** rising; soaring. —**as|pir′ing|ly,** *adv.*

a|sprawl (ə sprôl′), *adv., adj.* in a sprawling posture; sprawling.

a|squint (ə skwint′), *adv., adj.* with a squint; squinting. [origin uncertain]

a|squirm (ə skwėrm′), *adv., adj.* squirming; wriggling or writhing: *A swim, even in chlorinated water asquirm with kids, delightfully strips away fatigue* (John Dos Passos).

ASR (no periods) or **A.S.R., 1** airport surveillance radar. **2** air surveillance radar.

ASROC (as′rok), *n.* an antisubmarine rocket launched from a ship. [< *A*(nti) *S*(ubmarine) *Roc*(ket)]

ass¹ (as), *n.* **1** a four-footed, hoofed mammal related to the horse, but smaller, with longer ears and a shorter mane, shorter hair on the tail, and a dark stripe along the back; donkey. It is a patient, stubborn, rather slow, but very sure-footed beast of burden when domesticated. **2** *Figurative.* a stupid, silly, or stubborn person; fool. [Old English *assa,* ultimately < Latin *asinus*]

ass² (as), *n. Slang.* the buttocks. [variant of *arse*]

ass., 1 assistant. **2** association.

as|sa|fet|i|da or **as|sa|foet|i|da** (as′ə fet′ə də), *n.* = asafetida.

as|sa|gai (as′ə gī), *n., pl.* **-gais,** *v.,* **-gaied, -ga|ing.** —*n.* **1** a slender spear or javelin of hard wood, once the chief weapon of the Zulus and some other African tribes. **2** a South African tree of the dogwood family, whose hard wood was formerly used to make these spears.
—*v.t.* to strike or kill with an assagai. Also, **assegai.**
[< Spanish *azagaya* < Arabic *az-zaghāya* < *al-* the + a Berber name]

as|sai¹ (äs sī′), *adv. Music.* very: *"Adagio assai" means very slowly.* [< Italian *assai* very < Vulgar Latin *ad satis* to sufficiency < Latin *ad* to, *satis* enough]

as|sai² (ə sī′), *n.* **1** a tall, slender Brazilian palm. **2** the purple fruit it bears. **3** a beverage made from this fruit. [< Portuguese *assahy,* perhaps < the Tupi (Brazil) name]

as|sail (ə sāl′), *v.t.* **1** to set upon with violence; attack repeatedly with violent blows: *The enemy assailed our fort.* **SYN:** assault. See syn. under **attack. 2** to set upon vigorously with hostile words, arguments, or abuse: *The senators assailed the President on the subject of the treaty.* **3** to come over (a person) strongly, as a feeling does; beset; trouble: *How sharp were the twinges of jealousy that were beginning to assail her* (Theodore Dreiser). [< Old French *assaill-,* stem of *asalir* < Late Latin *assalīre* < Latin *ad-* at + *salīre* to leap] —**as|sail′a|ble,** *adj.* —**as|sail′er,** *n.* —**as|sail′ment,** *n.*

as|sail|ant (ə sā′lənt), *n.* a person who attacks: *The injured man did not know who his assailant was.*

As|sa|mese (as′ə mēz′, -mēs′), *adj., n., pl.* **-mese.** —*adj.* of Assam (a state in northeastern India) or its people.
—*n.* **1** a native or inhabitant of Assam. **2** the Indic language of Assam.

as|sart (ə särt′), *v., n.* in British law: —*v.t.* to grub (trees and bushes) from woodland; to clear (woodland).
—*n.* **1** the act of assarting. **2** a grubbed-up tree or bush. **3** a piece of land cleared of trees and bushes.
[< Anglo-French *assarter,* Old French *essarter* < Medieval Latin *exsartare* < Latin *ex-* out of + *sarrīre* to hoe]

as|sas|sin (ə sas′ən), *n.* **1** a murderer, especially one hired or chosen to murder by a sudden or secret attack. **SYN:** killer. **2** *Figurative.* anyone who harms seriously or destroys, or seeks to do so: *a character assassin.* [< Italian *assassino* < Arabic *ḥashshāshīn* hashish eaters; specifically, the Ismaili fanatics who took hashish when preparing to murder]

as|sas|si|nate (ə sas′ə nāt), *v.t.,* **-nat|ed, -nat|ing. 1** to murder (someone, especially a public personage) by a sudden or secret attack; kill: *President Lincoln was assassinated in April, 1865.* **2** *Figurative.* to harm seriously or destroy (a name, reputation, or the like) by treachery, slander, or sudden attack. [< *assassin* + *-ate*¹]

as|sas|si|na|tion (ə sas′ə nā′shən), *n.* the act of murdering someone, especially a public personage, by a sudden or secret attack; a killing: *The family life of the Lincolns ... had ... painful strains before and after the assassination in Ford's Theater, but after April 14, 1865, the tragic tones multiply* (Newsweek).

as|sas|si|na|tor (ə sas′ə nā′tər), *n.* a person who assassinates; assassin; murderer.

assassin bug, an insect that lives largely on the blood of other insects and sometimes attacks man. It is a heteropterous insect with wings like that of a squash bug and a three-jointed proboscis.

as|sault (ə sôlt′), *n., v.* —*n.* **1** a sudden, vigorous attack made with blows or weapons: *The enemy made an assault on our fort.* **SYN:** onslaught, charge. **2** a sudden and violent attack made on traditions, opinions, or other institutions, with hostile words or actions. **3** *Law.* a threat or attempt to strike or otherwise do physical harm to a person. Any carrying out of the threat or the success of an attempt is immaterial. **4** = rape. **5** the final phase of a military attack; closing with the enemy in hand-to-hand fighting.
—*v.t.* **1** to make an assault on by means of blows, hand-to-hand fighting, or hostile words; attack. **SYN:** See syn. under **attack. 2** *Archaic.* to beset.
—*v.i.* to make an assault. **SYN:** See syn. under **attack.**
[< Old French *asaut* < Vulgar Latin *assaltus,* ultimately < Latin *ad-* at + *salīre* to leap] —**as|sault′a|ble,** *adj.* —**as|sault′er,** *n.*

assault and battery, *Law.* a successful carrying out of threatened or attempted physical attack, as by a blow or beating.

assault boat or **craft,** any small boat used to carry troops and light arms from ship to shore, especially in forcing a landing.

assault carrier, an aircraft carrier that provides a base for an airborne assault or for air support during an assault.

as|sault|ive (ə sôl′tiv), *adj.* **1** *Psychology.* compulsively violent: *... she became assaultive ... and had delusions of persecution* (Science News Letter). **2** *Law.* involving assault: *assaultive offenses such as robbery and homicide.* —**as|sault′ive|ly,** *adv.* —**as|sault′ive|ness,** *n.*

as|say (ə sā′, as′ā), *v., n.* —*v.t.* **1** to analyze (an ore or alloy) to find out the quantity of gold, silver, or other metal in it. **2** to make an assay of; try, test, or examine. **3** *Archaic.* to attempt.
—*v.i.* to contain, as shown by analysis, a certain proportion of metal in ore, or of a particular ingredient in any substance, especially a drug.
—*n.* **1** the analysis of any substance, especially an ore, alloy, or drug, to find out the amount of metal or other ingredient in it by measuring, weighing, or calculating; determination of the proportion of gold or other metal in an ore or alloy or of an ingredient in a drug or other substance: *Hormonal assays showed both astronauts excreted greater amounts of aldosterone in space than on the ground* (Science News). **2** the substance or sample analyzed or tested. **3** a list of the results of assaying any substance, especially an ore, alloy, or drug. **4** a trial, test, or examination: *By no assay of reason ...* (Shakespeare). **5** *Archaic.* an attempt. **6** *Archaic.* the tasting of food or drink intended for another before serving it.
[< Old French *assayer* < Latin *exagium* a weighing < *exigere* weigh, prove < *ex-* out + *agere* to drive] —**as|say′a|ble,** *adj.* —**as|say′er,** *n.*

assay ton, a unit of weight used for testing ore, equivalent to 29.167 grams.

assd., 1 assessed. **2** assigned.

as|se|gai (as′ə gī), *n., pl.* **-gais,** *v.t.,* **-gaied, -ga|ing.** = assagai.

as|sem|blage (ə sem′blij), *n.* **1** a group of persons gathered together; assembly: *an assemblage of all religions and races.* **SYN:** concourse, gathering. **2** a number of things brought together or found together; collection; group: *an assemblage of bare rocks.* **3** the act of bringing or coming together; meeting. **4** the process of putting or fitting together: *That factory foreman supervises assemblage of parts in automobile engines.* **5** an art form made of a random collection of pieces of metal, wood, cloth, and other odds and ends. **6** the state of being assembled.

as|sem|bla|gist (ə sem′blə jist), *n.* an artist who creates assemblages.

as|sem|ble (ə sem′bəl), *v.,* **-bled, -bling.** —*v.t.* **1** to gather together; bring together: *The grandfather had assembled all the members of the family for the annual picnic.* **SYN:** See syn. under **gather. 2** to put together; fit together: *Some boys like to assemble model airplanes.* **SYN:** construct.
—*v.i.* to come together; meet: *Congress assembles in January.* **SYN:** congregate. See syn. under **gather.**
[< Old French *assembler* < Vulgar Latin *assimulāre* bring together < Latin, liken < *ad-* to + *simulāre* imitate]

as|sem|bler (ə sem′blər), *n.* **1** a person or thing that assembles. **2** a computer program or routine for converting instructions in an assembly language into machine language.

assembler language, = assembly language.

as|sem|bly (ə sem′blē), *n., pl.* **-blies. 1** a group of people gathered together for some purpose; meeting: *The principal addressed the school assembly.* A reception or a ball may be called an assembly. **SYN:** gathering, convention, congregation. See syn. under **meeting. 2** a meeting of lawmakers. **SYN:** legislature. **3** the act of coming together; an assembling; meeting: *unlawful assembly.* **4** the act or process of putting together; fitting together: *In Detroit we saw the assembly of the parts which make up an automobile.* **5a** the complete group of parts required to put something together: *the hull assembly of a model boat.* **b** the complete group of parts put together to form a unit: *The rear of an airplane has a tail assembly. The steering assembly of our car was damaged in the accident.* **6** a signal on a bugle or drum for troops to form in ranks. [< Old French *assemblee* < *assembler* assemble]

As|sem|bly (ə sem′blē), *n., pl.* **-blies. 1** the legislature or a legislative body of any one of various countries, states, or other political divisions, as: **a** (in the United States) the lower branch of the state legislature of some states (often called the *General Assembly*). **b** (in Canada) the legislature of a province (often called the *Legislative Assembly*). **2** the legislative assembly of the United Nations (called the *General Assembly*).

assembly language, a coding system of abbreviations, numerals, and additional symbols for programming an electronic computer.

assembly line, a row of workers and machines along which work is passed until the final product is made: *Automobiles are produced on an assembly line where each worker repeats his special task.*

As|sem|bly|man or **as|sem|bly|man** (ə sem′blē mən), *n., pl.* **-men.** a member of an Assembly.

assembly plant, a plant in which the parts of complete units are put together: *an automobile assembly plant.*

assembly room, *British, Archaic.* a ballroom.

As|sem|bly|wom|an or **as|sem|bly|wom|an** (ə sem′blē wu̇m′ən), *n., pl.* **-wom|en.** a woman member of an Assembly.

as|sent (ə sent′), *v., n.* **—*v.i.*** to express agreement; consent; agree: *Everyone assented to the plans for the dance.* **SYN:** concur, acquiesce, comply. See syn. under **consent.**
—*n.* acceptance of a proposal or statement; agreement: *The teacher gave her assent to the plan.*
[< Old French *assentir* < Latin *assentīre* < *ad-* along with + *sentīre* feel, think] **—as|sent′er,** *n.*

as|sen|ta|tion (as′ən tā′shən), *n.* **1** an expression of assent. **2** = flattery.

as|sent|ing|ly (ə sen′ting lē), *adv.* in an assenting manner; so as to express assent.

as|sen|tor (ə sen′tər), *n.* **1** = assenter. **2** a voter who, in addition to the proposer and seconder, endorses the nomination of a candidate in a British election.

as|sert (ə sėrt′), *v.t.* **1** to state positively; declare firmly: *John asserts that he will go whether we do or not.* **SYN:** affirm, maintain, aver. See syn. under **declare. 2** to insist on (a right or a claim); defend; maintain: *Assert your independence.*
assert oneself, to put oneself forward; make demands: *A leader must assert himself sometimes in order to be followed.*
[< Latin *assertus,* past participle of *asserere* to claim < *ad-* to + *serere* join] **—as|sert′a|ble, as|sert′i|ble,** *adj.* **—as|ser′tor, as|sert′er,** *n.*

as|sert|a|tive (ə sėr′tə tiv), *adj.* = assertive.

as|sert|ed|ly (ə sėr′tid lē), *adv.* **1** = assertively. **2** = allegedly.

as|ser|tion (ə sėr′shən), *n.* **1** a positive statement; firm declaration: *His assertion of his innocence was believed by the jury.* **2** the act of insisting on a right or claim: *If you say that you own the book, prove your assertion of ownership.*

as|ser|tive (ə sėr′tiv), *adj.* too confident and certain; positive; forward: *John is an assertive boy, always insisting on his own rights and opinions.* **SYN:** dogmatic. **—as|ser′tive|ly,** *adv.* **—as|ser′tive|ness,** *n.*

assertiveness training, a method of training submissive individuals to behave with confidence, usually by adopting an aggressive attitude: *Cosmetic treatments, charm schools, assertiveness training—nothing helped make her anything except more . . . self-conscious* (TV Guide).

as|ser|to|ry (ə sėr′tər ē), *adj.* affirming; declaratory.

as|es[1] (as′iz), *n.* plural of **ass.**

as|es[2] (as′iz), *n.* plural of **as**[2].

asses' bridge, = pons asinorum. [translation of Late Latin *pōns asinōrum*]

as|sess (ə ses′), *v.t.* **1** to estimate the value of (property or income) for taxation; value (at): *The town clerk has assessed that house at $20,000.* **SYN:** appraise. **2** to fix the amount of (a tax, fine, or damages): *Damages from last week's flood have been assessed at $50,000.* **3** *Especially U.S.* to put a tax on or call for a contribution from (a person, property, or organization): *Each member of the club will be assessed one dollar to pay for the trip.* **4** *Figurative.* to examine critically and estimate the merit, significance, or value of; criticize; evaluate: *The committee met to assess the idea of establishing a new university. It is impossible even for a scientist of genius to assess a lost opportunity of which he was unaware* (Bulletin of Atomic Scientists). **5** to portion out as a tax; apportion. [< Medieval Latin *assessare* fix a tax < Latin *assidēre* < *ad-* by + *sedēre* sit] **—as|sess′a|ble,** *adj.*

assessed valuation, the percentage of the total market value of property used by a government as a basis of taxation.

as|ses|see (as′e sē′), *n.* a person whose property has been assessed.

as|sess|ment (ə ses′mənt), *n.* **1** the act of assessing: (*Figurative.*) *Every assessment of loyalty involves a subjective element* (Bulletin of Atomic Scientists). **2** the amount of tax which is decided to be payable. **3** an official valuation of property for purposes of taxation. **4** valuation in general; appraisal.

as|ses|sor (ə ses′ər), *n.* **1** a person who estimates the value of property or income for taxation. **2** an assistant to a judge chosen because of his special knowledge of a field.

as|ses|so|ri|al (as′ə sôr′ē əl, -sōr′-), *adj.* of or having to do with an assessor or assessors.

as|ses|sor|ship (ə ses′ər ship), *n.* the office, position, or function of an assessor.

as|set (as′et), *n.* **1** something that has value; advantage: *Ability to get along with people is an asset in business.* **2** an item of value. [< *assets*]

as|sets (as′ets), *n.pl.* **1** things of value; all items of value owned by a person or business and constituting the resources of the person or business. Real estate, cash, securities, inventories, patents, and good will are assets. *His assets include a house, a car, stocks, bonds, and jewelry.* (*Figurative.*) *Honesty is one of the judge's most valuable assets.* **2** property that can be used to pay debts. **3** *Accounting.* the entries on a balance sheet that express in terms of money the value of the tangible things or intangible rights which constitute the resources of a person, business, or organization, as of a given date. [< Old French *asez* enough < Latin *ad satis* sufficiently (misunderstood as a plural noun "sufficient things")]

as|set-strip|ping (as′et strip′ing), *n. British.* the use of the assets of a company to finance an unrelated enterprise, such as another holding of a purchasing conglomerate: *Asset-stripping may not be so frequent a motive for takeovers as public opinion tends to assume* (London Times). **—as′set-strip′per,** *n.*

as|sev|er|ate (ə sev′ə rāt), *v.t.,* **-at|ed, -at|ing.** to declare solemnly; state emphatically. **SYN:** affirm, aver. [< Latin *assevērāre* (with English *-ate*[1]) < *ad-* + *sevērus* serious] **—as|sev′er|at′ing|ly,** *adv.* **—as|sev′er|a′tion,** *n.*

as|sev|er|a|tive (ə sev′ə rā′tiv, -sev′ər ə-), *adj.* of or having to do with asseveration; characterized by asseveration.

As|shur (ä′shu̇r, ash′ər), *n.* = Ashur (the chief god of the ancient Assyrians).

as|sib|i|late (ə sib′ə lāt), *v.t.,* **-lat|ed, -lat|ing.** to give a hissing sound to; make sibilant: *"Church" is an assibilated form of "kirk."* [< Latin *assībilāre* (with English *-ate*[1]) hiss at < *ad-* to + *sībilāre* to hiss] **—as|sib′i|la′tion,** *n.*

As|si|de|ans or **As|si|dae|ans** (as′ə dē′ənz), *n.pl.* = Hasidim. [< Greek *Assidaioi* (< Hebrew *hasidim*) + English *-an*]

as|si|du|i|ty (as′ə dü′ə tē, -dyü′-), *n., pl.* **-ties.** careful, steady attention; diligence: *He led her through the artistic splendors of Florence with assiduity* (New Yorker).

as|sid|u|ous (ə sij′u̇ əs), *adj.* working hard and steadily; careful and attentive; diligent: *No error escaped his assiduous attention to detail.* **SYN:** steady, unremitting, untiring. [< Latin *assiduus* (with English *-ous*) < *assidēre* sit at < *ad-* at + *sedēre* sit] **—as|sid′u|ous|ly,** *adv.* **—as|sid′u|ous|ness,** *n.*

as|si|en|to (as′ē en′tō), *n. Historical.* a contract between Spain and a foreign country, or a group of foreign merchants, for supplying African slaves. [< Spanish *assiento,* now *asiento* contract]

as|si|ette (a′sē et′), *n.* **1** *Bookbinding.* a compound of bole, bloodstone, and galena applied to the trimmed edges of pages before gilding. **2** a serving of food; helping. [< French *assiette* (literally) seat, site < *assier* to sit]

as|sign (ə sīn′), *v., n.* **—*v.t.* 1** to give as a task to be done or as a share; allot: *The teacher has assigned ten problems for today.* **2** to appoint (to a post or duty); designate: *The captain assigned two soldiers to guard the gate.* **3** to name definitely; fix; set: *The judge assigned a day for the trial.* **SYN:** settle, determine, specify. **4** to ascribe as belonging to; attribute; refer: *A student should be able to assign events to their places in history.* **5** to transfer or hand over (property or a right) legally: *Mr. Jones assigned his home and farm to his creditors.*
—*n.* a person to whom property or a right is legally transferred.
[< Old French *assigner,* learned borrowing from Latin *assīgnāre* < *ad-* to + *sīgnāre* to mark < *sīgnum* mark] **—as|sign′a|ble,** *adj.* **—as|sign′a|bly,** *adv.*
—*Syn.* *v.t.* 1 Assign, allot mean to give something to a particular person, group, or institution as a share. **Assign** emphasizes giving something that has been established as a share by some plan or principle: *The teacher assigned two acts so that we would finish the play before the holidays.* **Allot** emphasizes giving an amount or part which is set more or less by chance: *Whenever Mother allots our household tasks, I end up with more than my fair share of the work.*

as|sign|a|bil|i|ty (ə sī′nə bil′ə tē), *n.* capability of being assigned.

as|sig|nat (as′ig nat), *n.* a piece of paper money issued between 1789 and 1796 by the French revolutionary government, based on the value of confiscated lands. [< French *assignat* < Latin *assīgnātum* < *assīgnāre* assign]

as|sig|na|tion (as′ig nā′shən), *n.* **1** a secret meeting of lovers. **2** the appointment of a time and place for such a meeting. **3** an allotting; apportionment. **4** the legal transfer, as of property or right. [< Old French *assignacion,* learned borrowing from Latin *assīgnātiō, -ōnis* < *assīgnāre* assign]

as|signed convict (ə sīnd′), a convict in colonial Australia committed to the custody of a settler or a military officer as a servant.

assigned risk, *U.S.* an insurance risk which an insurance company would not normally accept but which, under State law, is assigned on a prorated basis to insurance companies at an extra premium.

as|sign|ee (ə sī′nē′, as′ə-), *n.* **1** a person to whom some right or property is legally transferred. **2** a person who is officially appointed to act for another; deputy.

as|sign|er (ə sī′nər), *n.* a person who assigns, allots, or apportions.

as|sign|ment (ə sīn′mənt), *n.* **1** something assigned, especially a piece of work to be done, or a responsibility allotted to a particular person, group, or organization: *Today's assignment in arithmetic consists of ten problems.* **2** the act of assigning; appointment: *The soldier was informed of his assignment to a new base.* **3a** the legal transfer of some property or right. **b** the document that authorizes this transfer.

as|sign|or (ə sī nôr′, as′ə-), *n.* a person who legally transfers to another some property or right.

as|sim|i|la|bil|i|ty (ə sim′ə lə bil′ə tē), *n.* capability of being assimilated.

as|sim|i|la|ble (ə sim′ə lə bəl), *adj.* that can be assimilated.

as|si|mi|la|do (as′ə mə lä′dō), *n., pl.* **-dos.** a native in Portuguese colonies who is literate or educated and therefore eligible for Portuguese citizenship. [< Portuguese *assimilado* (literally) one who is assimilated]

as|sim|i|late (ə sim′ə lāt), *v.,* **-lat|ed, -lat|ing,** *n.* **—*v.t.* 1a** to change (food) into living tissues; digest: *The human body will not assimilate sawdust.* **b** *Figurative.* to take in and make a part of oneself; absorb: *She reads so much that she does not assimilate it all.* **SYN:** See syn. under **absorb. 2** to make like the people of a nation or other group in customs, viewpoint, character, or other attribute: *We have assimilated immigrants from many lands. By living a long time with the Indians, he was assimilated to them in his thinking and actions.* **SYN:** incorporate. **3** to make (a speech sound, usually a consonant) more like the sound which follows or precedes. **SYN:** adapt. Consonants are frequently assimilated to neighboring consonants; *ads-* becomes *ass-; comr-, corr-; disf-, diff-.* See also **assimilation,** def. 4.
—*v.i.* 1a to be changed into living tissue; be digested: *The woody fibers of plants will not assimilate into the human body.* **b** *Figurative.* to be taken into oneself; absorb: *After he has watched television all day, nothing will assimilate through his senses.* **2** to become like the people of a nation, or other group in customs, viewpoint, character or other attribute: *Many immigrants assimilate readily in this country.* **3** to become like.

Pronunciation Key: hat, āge, cãre, fär; let, ēqual, tėrm; it, īce; hot, ōpen, ôrder; oil, out; cup, pu̇t, rüle; child; long; thin; ᴛʜen; zh, measure; ə represents **a** in about, **e** in taken, **i** in pencil, **o** in lemon, **u** in circus.

—*n.* *Obsolete.* that which is like.
[< Latin *assimilāre* (with English *-ate*[1]), variant of *assimulāre* compare < *ad-* to + *simulāre* imitate] —**as|sim′i|la′tor**, *n.*

as|sim|i|la|tion (ə sim′ə lā′shən), *n.* **1** the act or process of assimilating: *Life depends on the assimilation of food.* **2** the condition of being assimilated. **3** *Sociology.* the process by which immigrants or other newcomers become like the people they are around, adopting the attitudes and cultural patterns of the society into which they have come. **4** the alteration of a speech sound influenced by a neighboring sound, which makes it more like the neighboring sound.

as|sim|i|la|tion|ism (ə sim′ə lā′shə niz əm), *n.* the principles or practices of persons who favor the assimilation of various ethnic groups in a country or region. —**as|sim′i|la|tion|ist**, *n., adj.*

as|sim|i|la|tive (ə sim′ə lā′tiv), *adj.* assimilating; connected with, or promoting assimilation: *the assimilative functions of the body.* —**as|sim′i|la′tive|ness**, *n.*

as|sim|i|la|to|ry (ə sim′ə lə tôr′ē, -tōr′-), *adj.* = assimilative.

As|sin|i|boin or **As|sin|i|boine** (ə sin′ə boin), *n.* **1** a member of a Siouan tribe of northeastern Montana and adjacent parts of Canada. **2** the language of this tribe.

as|sise (ə sēz′), *n.* a geological formation consisting of parallel beds of rock bearing the same types of fossils. [< French *assise* layer (of rock) < *asseoir* to place, seat]

as|sist (ə sist′), *v., n.* —*v.t.* **1** to give aid to; help (a person) either in doing something or when in need: *She assisted her mother with the housework.* SYN: aid, support, succor. See syn. under **help**. **2** to further or promote (an action or process): *These tablets assist digestion.* **3** to be the assistant of (a person).
—*v.i.* **1** to give aid; help: *When all assist, the job can be done quickly.* **2** to be present (at) either as a spectator or as one taking part in a ceremony or observance: *The congregation assists at divine service.* **3** *U.S. Sports.* to help a teammate directly in making a play that scores in basketball, in hockey or soccer, or baseball, or that helps to put a runner out in baseball.
—*n.* **1** *Informal.* an act of assistance; aid; help: *With an assist from my brother we reached the top of the hill. The strongest assist to Canada's claim was the judgment rendered by the World Court* (Canada Month). **2** *U.S. Sports.* a play that assists.
[< Middle French *assister*, learned borrowing from Latin *assistere* < *ad-* by + *sistere* take a stand] —**as|sist′er**, *n.*

as|sist|ance (ə sis′təns), *n.* **1** the act of assisting; help; aid: *I need your assistance.* SYN: support, backing, succor. **2** the help or aid given: *a grant of $2,000 as assistance toward a degree.*

as|sist|ant (ə sis′tənt), *n., adj.* —*n.* **1** a person who assists another, such as a superior in some office or work; helper; aid: *I was her assistant in the library for a time.* **2** a thing or device that helps or aids: *Rhyme and meter are assistants to memory.*
—*adj.* **1** helping; assisting; subordinate: *She is an assistant teacher.* **2** helpful; auxiliary (to): *Beasts of burden are animals assistant to man.*

assistant professor, *Especially U.S. and Canada.* a teacher ranking next below an associate professor and above an instructor.

as|sist|ant|ship (ə sis′tənt ship), *n.* **1** the office or position of assistant. **2** *U.S.* a position below that of an instructor in a college or university, usually held by a graduate student on a part-time basis: *A research assistantship to provide training in science writing will be available for an outstanding graduate student in February* (Science).

as|sis|tor (ə sis′tər), *n. Law.* a person who assists; assister.

as|size (ə sīz′), *n.* **1a** a session of a law court. **b** the time or place of such a session. **2** the action to be decided by a trial. **3** the writ instituting the trial. **4** verdict; judgment. **5** *Scottish.* a trial by jury. **6** *Obsolete.* **a** an ordinance, especially as to measures, weights, or prices. **b** the standard prescribed.
assizes, periodical sessions of a law court formerly held in each county of England: *He will be tried at the local assizes.*
[< Old French *assise* < *asseir* sit at < Vulgar Latin *assedēre* < Latin *assidēre* < *ad-* by + *sedēre* sit. See etym. of doublet **size**[1].]

assn., **ass'n**, or **Assn.**, association.

assoc., **1** associate. **2** association.

as|so|ci|a|bil|i|ty (ə sō′shē ə bil′ə tē, -shə-), *n.* the quality of being associable.

as|so|ci|a|ble (ə sō′shē ə bəl, -shə-), *adj., n.* —*adj.* **1** that can be associated, joined, or connected. **2** belonging to a cooperative economic or trade association of several countries: *Kingston was the venue for the meeting ... between the ACP (Africa, Caribbean, and Pacific) associable states and the EEC* (Sheila Patterson).
—*n.* an associable country or state.
[< French *associable* < Old French *associer*, learned borrowing from Latin *associāre* associate] —**as|so′ci|a|ble|ness**, *n.*

as|so|ci|ate (*v.* ə sō′shē āt; *n., adj.* ə sō′shē it, -āt), *v.*, **-at|ed**, **-at|ing**, *n., adj.* —*v.t.* **1** to connect in thought (with): *We associate turkey with Thanksgiving.* **2** to join as a companion, partner, or friend: *He is associated with his sons in business.* **3** to join; combine in action; unite: *The action of the stream had associated the gold particles with the sand.* —*v.i.* **1** to be friendly or keep company (with): *Do not associate with bad companions.* **2** to combine for a common purpose: *When bad men combine, good men must associate* (Edmund Burke).
—*n.* **1** a thing usually connected with another. **2** companion, partner, or friend: *I am one of his associates at the store.* SYN: ally, colleague. **3** a member of an association or institution without the rights and privileges of full membership.
—*adj.* **1** joined with another or others. SYN: allied. **2** admitted to some, but not all, rights and privileges: *He has been an associate member of the club and will be made a full member this fall.* **3** having a rank next to the highest in its class: *He was an associate editor of the paper.* **4** united in the same group or category. SYN: concomitant. *Abbr:* assoc.
[< Latin *associāre* (with English *-ate*[1]) < *ad-* to + *sociāre* join < *socius* companion]
▶**associate**. Referring to a person, *with* is used after *associate: He is associated with Frisby in a law-firm partnership.* Referring to a thing, *in* is used: *They were associated in several clothing companies.*

associated state, a former colony or protectorate granted complete local autonomy in domestic affairs but under the charge of the colonial power in defense and foreign relations.

Associate in Arts, **1** a degree given by a college or junior college to a person who has completed a two-year course of study. **2** a person who has this degree.

associate professor, *Especially U.S. and Canada.* a college or university teacher ranking next below a professor and above an assistant professor.

as|so|ci|ate|ship (ə sō′shē it ship), *n.* the position or office of an associate.

associate state, = associated state.

as|so|ci|a|tion (ə sō′sē ā′shən, -shē-), *n.* **1** a group of people joined together for some purpose; society: *Will you join the young people's association at our church?* SYN: club. *Abbr:* assn. **2** the act of associating or the condition of being associated: *Association of ideas is an important part of thinking. I look forward to my association with the counselors I will have at camp.* SYN: alliance, union, combination, relation. **3** companionship, partnership, or friendship: *The three old friends had enjoyed a close association over many years.* **4** idea or object connected with another idea in thought; mental connection or union between an object and ideas that have some relation to it: *What association do you make with the color red? Words being arbitrary must owe their powers to association, and have the influence, and that only, which custom has given them* (Samuel Johnson).

as|so|ci|a|tion|al (ə sō′sē ā′shə nəl, -shē-), *adj.* **1** of or having to do with association. **2** of or having to do with an association. —**as|so′ci|a′tion|al|ly**, *adv.*

association area, the part of the brain that brings together the impulses from the sensory areas, sorts them, and sends them to the motor area: *Some sort of relationship, though certainly not a simple one, exists between the size and development of the association areas and what we call mental ability* (Beals and Hoijer).

association football, *Especially British.* soccer.

as|so|ci|a|tion|ism (ə sō′sē ā′shə niz əm, -shē-), *n.* **1** *Psychology.* the theory that the laws of the association of ideas are the fundamental laws of mental action. **2** = Fourierism. —**as|so′ci|a′tion|ist**, *n.*

as|so|ci|a|tion|is|tic (ə sō′sē ā′shə nis′tik), *adj.* of or having to do with associationism or associationists: *associationistic psychology.*

association of ideas, *Psychology.* the tendency of a sensation, perception, feeling, volition, or thought to recall to consciousness others which formerly coexisted in consciousness with it or which are similar to it.

as|so|ci|a|tive (ə sō′shē ā′tiv), *adj.* **1** tending to associate. **2** having to do with association. **3** of or having to do with the associative law: *an associative operation, associative sets.* —**as|so′ci|a′tive|ly**, *adv.*

associative law, *Mathematics.* a law stating that the combinations by which two numbers are added or multiplied will not change their sum or product. *Examples:* $2 + (3 + 5)$ gives the same sum as $(2 + 3) + 5$; $(2 \times 3) \times 5$ gives the same product as $2 \times (3 \times 5)$.

associative memory or **storage**, a computer memory whose data locations are made accessible by its contents; content-addressable memory: *Associative memories can be rated by their storage density* (Michael F. Deering).

as|so|ci|a|tor (ə sō′shē ā′tər), *n.* **1a** a person or thing that joins in association. **b** a confederate; companion. **2** a member of an association.

as|soil (ə soil′), *v.t. Archaic.* **1** to absolve. **2** to atone for. [< Old French *assoill-*, stem of *assoldre* < Latin *absolvere*. See etym. of doublet **absolve**.]

as|so|lu|ta (äs′sō lü′tä), *adj.* **1** designating a rank in an opera or ballet company higher than that of prima donna or prima ballerina; absolute: *prima ballerina assoluta.* **2** = solo. [< Italian *assoluta* < Latin *absolūtus* free, separate, absolute]

as|so|nance (as′ə nəns), *n.* **1** resemblance in sound of words or syllables. *Example:* W*a*ken lords and l*a*dies g*a*y. **2** a substitute for rhyme in which the vowels are alike but the consonants are different. *Examples: brave-vain, lone-show, man-hat, penitent-reticence.* [< French *assonance*, learned borrowing from Latin *assonāns*, present participle of *assonāre* sound in answer < *ad-* to + *sonāre* sound]

as|so|nanced (as′ə nənst), *adj.* characterized by assonance.

as|so|nant (as′ə nənt), *adj., n.* —*adj.* having to do with or characterized by assonance.
—*n.* a word or syllable forming an assonance with another.

as|so|nan|tal (as′ə nan′təl), *adj.* of or having to do with assonance.

as|sort (ə sôrt′), *v.t.* **1** to arrange by kinds; distribute into groups by sorts; sort out; classify: *He assorted the books alphabetically.* SYN: arrange. **2** to furnish with various sorts: *The grocer assorts his stock to meet the varied demands of his customers.* —*v.i.* **1** to agree in sort or kind; fall into a class or group (with): *the two kinds assort well. These buttons do not assort with the samples on the cards.* SYN: match, suit. **2** to associate or keep company (with): *He has always assorted with men of his own age.* [< Middle French *assortir* < *a-* to + *sorte* sort < Latin *sors, sortis* lot] —**as|sort′er**, *n.*

as|sort|a|tive (ə sôr′tə tiv), *adj.* that sorts out; selective: *The result of dating, courting, being engaged may be assortative mating, or the marriage of persons ... that are alike in many important characteristics* (Emory S. Bogardus).

as|sort|ed (ə sôr′tid), *adj.* **1** selected so as to be of different kinds; various: *She served assorted cakes.* **2** arranged by kinds; classified: *There were socks assorted by size on the shelf.* **3** suited to one another; matched: *They are a poorly assorted couple, always quarreling.* **4** including various kinds; miscellaneous: *an assorted collection of books.* SYN: diverse, heterogeneous.

as|sort|ment (ə sôrt′mənt), *n.* **1** the act of sorting out or classifying: *The assortment of so many books would take a long time.* **2** a collection of various kinds: *We have these curtains in an assortment of colors.* **3** a group or class.

A.S.S.R., Autonomous Soviet Socialist Republic.

asst. or **Asst.**, assistant.

as|suage (ə swāj′), *v.t.*, **-suaged**, **-suag|ing**. **1** to calm or soothe (angry or excited feelings); make less intense: *He did all he could to assuage her fears.* SYN: mitigate, soften, allay. **2** to make (physical or mental pain) milder or easier; relieve or lessen: *Aspirin assuages pain.* SYN: alleviate. **3** *Figurative.* to satisfy; appease; quench (appetites or desires): *A drink of water will assuage your thirst.* [< Old French *assouagier*, ultimately < Latin *ad-* + *suāvis* sweet] —**as|suag′er**, *n.* —**as|suage′ment**, *n.*

as|sua|sive (ə swā′siv), *adj., n.* —*adj.* soothing: *Music her soft assuasive voice applies* (Alexander Pope). —*n.* a soothing remedy.
[ultimately < Latin *ad-* + *suāvis* sweet]

as|sume (ə süm′), *v.*, **-sumed**, **-sum|ing**. —*v.t.* **1** to take for granted without actual proof; suppose: *He assumed that the train would be on time.* SYN: presume. **2** to take upon oneself; undertake (an office or responsibility): *to assume leadership. He assumed the responsibility for planning the picnic.* **3** to take on; put on: *The problem has assumed a new form.* **4** to pretend: *Although he saw the accident, he assumed ignorance of it.* SYN: feign, simulate. See syn. under **pretend**. **5** to claim for oneself; appropriate; usurp: *The king's wicked brother tried to assume the throne.* **6** to adopt: *to assume a new partner.* —*v.i.* to be arrogant; claim more than is due; presume. [< Latin *assūmere* < *ad-* to + *sūmere* take] —**as|sum′a|ble**, *adj.* —**as|sum′a|bly**, *adv.* —**as|sum′er**, *n.*

as|sumed (ə sümd′), *adj.* **1** pretended; not real: *The famous stranger was traveling under the assumed name of Smith.* **SYN**: simulated. **2** supposed: *The assumed facts turned out to be untrue.* **3** usurped: *The dictator soon lost his assumed power.* — **as|sum′ed|ly**, *adv.*

as|sum|ing (ə sü′ming), *adj.* **1** taking too much upon oneself; presumptuous: *An assuming manner is irritating to most people.* **2** taking too much for granted: *Gasoline shortages jolted an assuming nature about unlimited natural resources.*

as|sump|sit (ə sump′sit), *n. Law.* **1** an action to recover damages for breach of a promise or contract agreed upon orally or in writing not under seal. **2** an actionable promise or contract. [< Latin *assūmpsit* he has taken (upon himself)]

as|sump|tion (ə sump′shən), *n.* **1** a thing assumed: *His assumption that he would win the prize proved incorrect. Every assertion of fact or system of facts rests on assumptions, avowed or implied* (John E. Owen). **SYN**: supposition, hypothesis, premise, conjecture. **2** unpleasant boldness; arrogance; presumption: *The reporter's assumption in always thrusting himself forward made him disliked.* **3** the act of assuming: *The President's assumption of authority takes place upon his inauguration.* [< Latin *assūmptiō, -ōnis* < *assūmere* assume]

As|sump|tion (ə sump′shən), *n.* **1** a doctrine of the Roman Catholic Church proclaiming the bodily taking up of the Virgin Mary from earth to heaven after her death. **2** a church festival in honor of this on August 15.

as|sump|tive (ə sump′tiv), *adj.* characterized by assumption; assuming; assumed. — **as|sump′tive|ly**, *adv.*

As|sur (ä′sůr, as′ər), *n.* = Ashur (the chief Assyrian god).

as|sur|ance (ə shůr′əns), *n.* **1** a making sure or certain. **2** a statement intended to make a person more sure or certain; positive declaration inspiring confidence: *Her employer gave her his assurance that she would receive a raise in pay.* **SYN**: guarantee, pledge. **3** security, certainty, or confidence: *We have the assurance of final victory.* **SYN**: certitude, trust. **4** confidence in one's own ability; self-confidence: *Joe's hard studying has given him considerable assurance in school.* **SYN**: intrepidity, fearlessness. See syn. under **confidence**. **5** too much boldness; impudence: *He has the assurance to deny all knowledge of the affair.* **SYN**: audacity, presumption. **6** *British.* insurance: *life assurance.*

as|sure (ə shůr′), *v.t.,* **-sured, -sur|ing.** **1** to tell positively or confidently: *They assured us that the plane would be on time. After the fire, the captain of the ship assured the passengers that there was no danger.* **2a** to make (a person) sure or certain; convince: *The man assured himself that the bridge was safe before crossing it.* **b** to give or restore confidence to; encourage: *The father assured his frightened child.* **SYN**: reassure. **3** to make safe; secure: *The calf's life was assured when the leopard fled before the dogs. The company's profits were assured by the popularity of its new product.* **SYN**: ensure. **4** *British.* to make safe against loss; insure: *Have you assured your life?* [< Old French *aseürer* < Vulgar Latin *assēcūrāre* < Latin *ad-* + *sēcūrus* secure] — **as|sur′a|ble**, *adj.*

as|sured (ə shůrd′), *adj., n.* — *adj.* **1** sure; certain: *You may be assured that he is safe.* **SYN**: guaranteed. **2** confident; bold: *The pirate's assured manner outraged the captain.* **3** *British.* insured against loss.

— *n.* **1** a person whose life or property is insured. **2** a person who is the beneficiary of an insurance policy. — **as|sur′ed|ly**, *adv.* — **as|sur′ed|ness**, *n.*

as|sur|er (ə shůr′ər), *n.* **1** a person who assures. **2** *British.* **a** a person who insures; underwriter. **b** a person who insures his life.

as|sur|gen|cy (ə sėr′jən sē), *n.* the state or quality of being assurgent.

as|sur|gent (ə sėr′jənt), *adj.* **1** rising; ascending. **2** *Botany.* curving upward. [< Latin *assurgēns, -entis,* present participle of *assurgere* rise up < *ad-* to + *surgere* rise]

Assyr., Assyrian.

As|syr|i|an (ə sir′ē ən), *adj., n.* — *adj.* of Assyria, its people, or their language.

— *n.* **1** a native or inhabitant of the ancient empire of Assyria. **2** the ancient Semitic language of the Assyrians: *Assyrian or Babylonian ... and Sumerian ... are the chief languages of the vast cuneiform literature from Mesopotamia* (H. A. Gleason, Jr.).

As|syr|i|o|log|i|cal (ə sir′ē ə loj′ə kəl), *adj.* having to do with Assyriology.

As|syr|i|ol|o|gist (ə sir′ē ol′ə jist), *n.* a person who studies Assyriology.

As|syr|i|ol|o|gy (ə sir′ē ol′ə jē), *n.* the study of the language, history, and antiquities of Assyria.

As|syr|o-Bab|y|lo|ni|an (ə sir′ō bab′ə lō′nē ən), *adj.* Assyrian and Babylonian.

AST (no periods) or **A.S.T.**, Atlantic Standard Time.

a|star|board (ə stär′bərd), *adv. Nautical.* to or toward the starboard side of a ship: *Realising what was happening, the tug turned hard aport, the merchantman hard astarboard, and both ran ashore* (Lord Mountbatten).

As|tar|te (as tär′tē), *n.* the goddess of fertility, love, and maturity of the ancient Semites. She was known as Ashtoreth to the Hebrews and as Ishtar to the Babylonians and Assyrians, to whom she was also the goddess of war. She is often identified with the Greek goddess Aphrodite and the Roman goddess Venus.

a|stat|ic (ā stat′ik), *adj.* **1** unstable; unsteady. **2** *Physics.* having no tendency to take a fixed or definite position: *A magnetic needle whose directive power has been neutralized is astatic.* — **a|stat′i|cal|ly**, *adv.*

a|stat|i|cism (ā stat′ə siz əm), *n.* instability; unsteadiness.

***as|ta|tine** (as′tə tēn, -tin), *n.* a radioactive, nonmetallic chemical element produced artificially from bismuth by bombarding it with alpha particles. Astatine is rare, highly unstable, and belongs to the halogen group. Several isotopes of it have been reported. [< Greek *ástatos* unstable + English *-ine*[2]]

***astatine**

symbol	atomic number	mass number	oxidation state
At	85	210	±1, +3, +5, +7

as|tat|ki (as tat′kē), *n.* a petroleum fuel once used in the Soviet Union. [< Russian *ostatki* residue]

as|ter (as′tər), *n.* **1a** a common plant having daisylike flowers with white, pink, blue, or purple petals around a yellow center. **b** its flower. Asters belong to the composite family. Some asters are very small; others are large with many petals. See picture under **composite family**. **2** any plant or flower like this of other genera of the composite family. China asters look much like small chrysanthemums. **3** *Biology.* one of two star-shaped structures found in a cell during mitosis; astrosphere. An aster consists of achromatic fibers radiating from around the centrosphere (containing the centrosome). [< Latin *aster* < Greek *astḗr* star]

as|ter|a|ceous (as′tə rā′shəs), *adj.* of or like an aster or asters.

aster family, a former group of plants, now classified as a subgroup of the composite family, whose blossoms are really compact heads of florets surrounded by small leaves or bracts. The daisy belongs to this group.

as|te|ri|a (as tir′ē ə), *n.* a gem, such as a sapphire, that when cut as a cabochon shows a starlike, luminous figure. [< Latin *asteria* < Greek *astérios* starry < *astḗr* star]

as|te|ri|at|ed (as tir′ē ā′tid), *adj.* having a starlike figure: *Some sapphires are asteriated.*

as|ter|id (as′tər id), *n.* = asteroid (starfish).

***as|ter|isk** (as′tər isk), *n., v.* — *n.* **1** a star-shaped mark used in printing and writing, chiefly to call attention to a footnote or to indicate the omission of words or letters. **2** anything shaped like a star. — *v.t.* to mark with an asterisk; star. [< Late Latin *asteriscus* < Greek *asterískos* (diminutive) < *astḗr* star]

***asterisk**
definition 1

...preliminary figures are given in the report.*

*Report of the Committee...

as|ter|ism (as′tə riz əm), *n.* **1a** a group of stars smaller than a constellation. **b** (formerly) a constellation. **2** the property some crystallized minerals have of showing a starlike luminous figure. **3** three asterisks placed thus (⁂ or ⁎⁎⁎) in printed or written work to direct attention to a passage. [< Greek *asterismós* constellation < *asterízein* to mark with stars < *astḗr* star]

a|stern (ə stėrn′), *adv. Nautical.* **1** at or toward the rear of a ship; aft: *The captain went astern. While we were in motion the only sheltered spot on deck was astern and to port of the cabin and the wheelhouse* (Christopher Rand). **2** backward: *The boat moved slowly astern.* **3** behind: *Some yachts tow small boats astern.*

a|ster|nal (ā stėr′nəl), *adj.* not joined to the sternum: *The floating ribs are asternal.* [< *a-*[4] not + *sternal*]

as|ter|oid (as′tə roid), *n., adj.* — *n.* **1** any one of the thousands of very small objects that revolve about the sun, chiefly between the orbit of Mars and the orbit of Jupiter; planetoid. The mass of the moon is about thirty times the combined mass of all known asteroids. **2** any one of a class of echinoderms, usually having five arms or rays radiating from a central disc, a mouth under this disc, and rows of tubular walking feet; starfish.

— *adj.* **1** starlike. **2** resembling a starfish. [< Greek *asteroeidḗs* starlike < *astḗr* star + *eîdos* form]

as|ter|oi|dal (as′tə roi′dəl), *adj.* of or having to do with asteroids: *A meteorite ... that was launched quite unceremoniously somewhere in the asteroidal belt sometime during the last two billion years ... was recovered recently* (Science News Letter).

as|ter|o|phyl|lite (as′tər ō fil′īt), *n.* a member of a genus of fossil plants, with leaves arranged in whorls, found in the coal formations of Europe and America. [< Greek *astḗr, -eros* star + *phýllon* leaf + *líthos* stone]

aster yellows, a virus disease of aster plants, characterized by yellowing and dwarfing.

as|the|ni|a (as thē′nē ə, as′thə nī′-), *n.* lack or loss of strength; weakness; debility; adynamia. [< New Latin *asthenia* < Greek *asthéneia* < *asthenḗs* weak < *a-* without + *sthénos* strength]

as|then|ic (as then′ik), *adj., n.* — *adj.* **1** of or characterized by asthenia; weak; debilitated; adynamic. **2** characterized by a tall, spare body build: *He thought that schizophrenia was found more frequently among those with the asthenic type of body, characterized by a slender, narrow trunk, long legs, and a narrow, angular face* (Ogburn and Nimkoff).

— *n.* **1** a person who has asthenia. **2** a person of the asthenic type.

as|the|no|pi|a (as′thə nō′pē ə), *n. Medicine.* weakness of the eyes or visual organs. [< New Latin *asthenopia* < Greek *asthenḗs* weak + *ṓps, ōpós* eye]

as|the|nop|ic (as′thə nop′ik), *adj.* having to do with, or suffering from, asthenopia; resembling asthenopia.

as|then|o|sphere (as then′ə sfir), *n.* a region of the earth's mantle directly beneath the lithosphere, having a thickness of a hundred miles or more and consisting of hot, soft, or weak rock material. [< Greek *asthenḗs* weak + English *sphere*]

as|then|o|spher|ic (as then′ə sfer′ik), *adj.* of or having to do with the asthenosphere: *The descending lithosphere displaces asthenospheric material, forcing it upward to form new crust* (Science News).

asth|ma (az′mə, as′-), *n.* a chronic disease that makes breathing difficult and causes coughing. Asthma is an allergy characterized by intermittent or continuous difficulty in breathing and a sense of constriction in the chest. *Asthma attacks the smooth lung muscles instead of the upper respiratory system, and is most commonly caused by mold spores, but it can be caused by anything that can cause hay fever* (New Yorker). [< Greek *âsthma* panting, perhaps < *ázein* breathe hard]

asth|mat|ic (az mat′ik, as-), *adj., n.* — *adj.* **1** of or having to do with asthma. **2** having asthma: *A plump, asthmatic man came panting into the room* (Edgar Maass).

— *n.* a person who has asthma. — **asth|mat′i|cal|ly**, *adv.*

asth|mat|i|cal (az mat′ə kəl, as-), *adj.* = asthmatic.

as|tig|mat|ic (as′tig mat′ik), *adj.* **1** having astigmatism. **2** having to do with or characterized by astigmatism: (*Figurative.*) *the astigmatic views of a bigot.* **3** correcting astigmatism: *astigmatic lenses.* — **as′tig|mat′i|cal|ly**, *adv.*

as|tig|mat|i|cal (as′tig mat′ə kəl), *adj.* = astigmatic.

***astigmatism**
definition 1

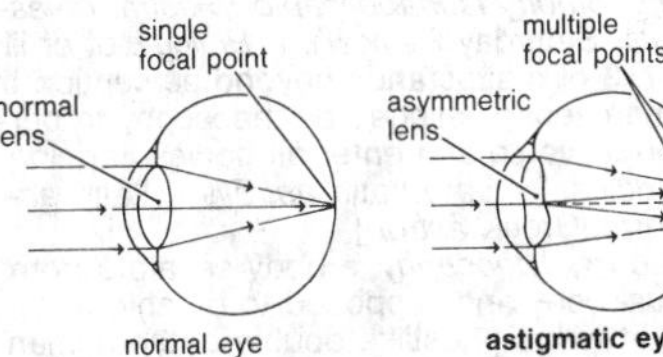

***as|tig|ma|tism** (ə stig′mə tiz əm), *n.* **1** the structural defect of an eye or of a lens that makes ob-

Pronunciation Key: hat, āge, cãre, fär; let, ēqual, tėrm, it, īce; hot, ōpen, ôrder; oil, out; cup, pu̇t, rüle; child; long; thin; ᴛʜen; zh, measure; ə represents **a** in about, **e** in taken, **i** in pencil, **o** in lemon, **u** in circus.

jects look indistinct or gives imperfect images. With perfect focus, all the rays of light, entering through the cornea, converge at one point on the retina; with astigmatism they do not. **2** *Figurative.* inability or refusal to accept what is right or true: *the moral astigmatism of a bigot.* [< *a-*[4] without + Greek *stígma, -atos* point + English *-ism*]

a|stil|be (ə stil′bē), *n.* any plant of a genus of the saxifrage family, having long spikes of small, white flowers. [< New Latin *Astilbe* the genus name < Greek *a-* not + *stilbē̂*, feminine of *stilbós* glittering]

a|stir (ə stėr′), *adv., adj.* **1** in motion; stirring with activity or excitement: (*Figurative.*) *I found Western Europe astir with efforts to rethink current policies, to realign current political groupings* (Harper's). **2** out of bed: *Most farmers are astir early each morning.*

As|to|lat (as′tə lat), *n. Arthurian Legend.* a place thought by some to be in southeastern England (Surrey) near London.

a|stom|a|tous (ā stom′ə təs, -stō′mə-), *adj.* **1** (of animals) having no mouth. **2** (of plants) having no stomata.

as|to|mous (as′tə məs), *adj.* = astomatous. [< Greek *ástomos* (with English *-ous*) < *a-* without + *stóma* mouth]

as|ton|ied (ə ston′ēd), *adj. Archaic.* **1** dazed. **2** filled with consternation; dismayed. **3** astonished. [past participle of Middle English *astonyen* astonish]

as|ton|ish (ə ston′ish), *v.t.* to surprise greatly; amaze: *The gift of ten dollars astonished the little boy.* **SYN:** astound. See syn. under **surprise.** [Middle English *astonyen* < Old French *estoner* < Vulgar Latin *extonāre,* for Latin *attonāre* stupefy < *ad-* at + *tonāre* thunder] —**as|ton′ished|ly,** *adv.* —**as|ton′ish|er,** *n.*

as|ton|ish|ing (ə ston′i shing), *adj.* very surprising; amazing. —**as|ton′ish|ing|ly,** *adv.*

as|ton|ish|ment (ə ston′ish mənt), *n.* **1** great surprise; sudden wonder; amazement. **2** anything that causes great surprise.

as|tound (ə stound′), *v., adj.* —*v.t.* to shock with alarm or surprise; surprise very greatly; amaze: *She was astounded by the news that she had won the contest. I am astounded by the opinion of some of our city high school teachers that the Regents should be made easier because the percentage of failures has increased* (New York Herald Tribune).
—*adj. Archaic.* astonished.
[earlier *astouned,* past participle of *astonyen* < Old French *estoner* astonish] —**as|tound′ment,** *n.*

as|tound|ing (ə stoun′ding), *adj.* shocking with alarm or surprise; amazing. —**as|tound′ing|ly,** *adv.*

astr., **1** astronomer. **2** astronomical. **3** astronomy.

as|tra|chan (as′trə kən), *n.* = astrakhan.

As|tra|chan (as′trə kən), *n.* a tart, usually red, summer variety of apple, of Russian origin.

a|strad|dle (ə strad′əl), *prep., adj., adv.* = astride.

As|trae|a (as trē′ə), *n. Greek Mythology.* the goddess of justice.

as|tra|gal (as′trə gəl), *n.* **1** *Architecture.* **a** a small, convex molding cut into the form of a string of beads. **b** a small, plain, convex molding. **2** the anklebone; astragalus. [< Latin *astragalus* < Greek *astrágalos* (originally) anklebone]

as|trag|a|lar (as trag′ə lər), *adj.* of or having to do with the anklebone.

as|trag|a|lus (as trag′ə ləs), *n., pl.* **-li** (-lī). **1** the uppermost bone of the tarsus; anklebone; talus. **2** = astragal (def. 1). [< Latin *astragalus* < Greek *astrágalos*]

as|tra|khan (as′trə kən), *n.* **1** the curly, furlike wool on the skin of stillborn or very young caracul lambs from Astrakhan. **2** a rough woolen cloth that looks like this. Also, **astrachan.** [< *Astrakhan,* a city and region of Russia]

as|tral (as′trəl), *adj.* **1** of the stars; starry: *Euclidean geometry is inapplicable to astral measurements* (Saturday Review). **2** *Biology.* of or like an aster. **3** of a substance beyond perception by the human senses alleged by theosophy to pervade the universe and enter all bodies, forming astral bodies. [< Late Latin *astrālis* < Latin *astrum* star < Greek *ástron*]

astral body, *Theosophy.* a body separate from the actual body and supposed to be able to leave it at will; a ghostlike double of the human body.

astral lamp, an oil lamp so made that it casts no shadow on the table below.

as|tral|ly (as′trə lē), *adv.* **1** in an astral manner; according to the stars. **2** as an astral body.

a|strand (ə strand′), *adv.* on the strand; stranded: *The tall ship ... Amid the breakers lies astrand* (Scott).

a|stray (ə strā′), *adj., adv.* out of the right way; wandering; off: (*Figurative.*) *Your reasoning is astray on that subject* (adj.). *The gate is open and all the cows have gone astray* (adv.).

as|trict (ə strikt′), *v.t.* **1** to bind up; compress. **2** to bind by moral or legal obligation. **3** to restrict; tie down; limit (to). [< Latin *astrictus,* past participle of *astringere* astringe] —**as|tric′tion,** *n.*

as|tric|tive (ə strik′tiv), *adj., n.* —*adj.* binding; astringent.
—*n.* an astringent. —**as|tric′tive|ly,** *adv.* —**as|tric′tive|ness,** *n.*

a|stride (ə strīd′), *prep., adj., adv.* —*prep.* **1** with one leg on each side of (something): *He sits astride his horse.* **2** on both sides of; extending over or across (something): *Kajang lies astride the tarred road to Singapore* (London Times).
—*adj., adv.* **1** with one leg on each side: *The knight sits astride on his horse.* **2** with legs far apart.

as|tringe (ə strinj′), *v.t.,* **-tringed, -tring|ing.** to bind; constrict; contract. [< Latin *astringere* < *ad-* + *stringere* draw tight]

as|trin|gen|cy (ə strin′jən sē), *n.* the quality of being astringent.

as|trin|gent (ə strin′jənt), *n., adj.* —*n.* a substance that shrinks body tissues and thus checks the flow of blood or other secretions. Alum is an astringent.
—*adj.* **1** having the property of shrinking or contracting tissues. **SYN:** binding, constrictive, styptic. **2** *Figurative.* austere; stern: *The concert* [*was*] *too well upholstered in sound—one wanted something more austere, more astringent, more spiky and less comfortable* (London Times). **3** *Figurative.* caustic; biting: *astringent wit. Several very violent moments, but much good astringent dialogue* (Punch).
[< Latin *astringēns, -entis,* present participle of *astringere* astringe] —**as|trin′gent|ly,** *adv.*

as|tri|on|ics (as′trē on′iks), *n.* the branch of astronautics dealing with electronic instrumentation. [< *astri-* (alteration of *astro-*) + (electr)*onics*]

as|tro (as′trō), *adj.* astronautic: *General Schreiver dealt America her first hand as an astro power* (Kenneth F. Gantz).

astro-, *combining form.* **1** star or other heavenly body or bodies: *Astrochemistry = star or planet chemistry.*
2 space; spacecraft: *Astronaut = space traveler.*
[< Greek *astro-* < *ástron* star]

as|tro|bi|ol|o|gist (as′trō bī ol′ə jist), *n.* a person who studies astrobiology.

as|tro|bi|ol|o|gy (as′trō bī ol′ə jē), *n.* the branch of biology dealing with the discovery or study of life on heavenly bodies; exobiology.

as|tro|bleme (as′trə blēm), *n.* one of the ancient meteoritic scars on the earth's surface. [< *astro-* + Greek *blēma* throw of a missile (< *bállein* to throw)]

as|tro|bot|a|nist (as′trō bot′ə nist), *n.* a person who studies astrobotany.

as|tro|bot|a|ny (as′trō bot′ə nē), *n.* the branch of botany dealing with the discovery or study of plant life on heavenly bodies.

as|tro|chem|ist (as′trō kem′ist), *n.* a person who studies astrochemistry.

as|tro|chem|is|try (as′trō kem′ə strē), *n.* the study of the chemical composition and characteristics of heavenly bodies.

as|tro|com|pass (as′trō kum′pəs), *n.* an optical instrument with which direction, or heading, may be determined by sighting on a celestial body.

as|tro|cyte (as′trə sīt), *n.* a star-shaped neuroglia cell.

as|tro|cy|to|ma (as′trə sī tō′mə), *n., pl.* **-mas, -ma|ta** (-mə tə). a brain tumor consisting of astrocytes. [< *astrocyte* + *-oma*]

as|tro|dome (as′trə dōm), *n.* **1** a very large enclosed area, especially one under a plastic dome: *But maybe in a couple of hundred years' time sailing will take place in gigantic "astrodomes," a hundred times larger than the Houston model* (London Times). **2** a dome of transparent plastic on the top of an aircraft, through which a navigator takes observations of the stars.

as|tro|dy|nam|ics (as′trō dī nam′iks), *n.* the branch of dynamics dealing with the motion of bodies in outer space and the forces acting upon them.

as|tro|gate (as′trə gāt), *v.i.,* **-gat|ed, -gat|ing.** to navigate in a spacecraft. [< *astro-* + (navi)*gate*] —**as′tro|ga′tion,** *n.* —**as′tro|ga′tor,** *n.*

as|tro|ge|ol|o|gist (as′trō jē ol′ə jist), *n.* a person who studies astrogeology.

as|tro|ge|ol|o|gy (as′trō jē ol′ə jē), *n.* the study of the geological characteristics of space and the heavenly bodies.

as|trog|o|ny (ə strog′ə nē), *n.* the genesis or origin of the stars. [< *astro-* + Greek *-goniā* production]

as|tro|graph (as′trə graf, -gräf), *n.* a telescope fitted with a camera, used in astrography.

as|tro|graph|ic (as′trə graf′ik), *adj.* of or having to do with astrography.

as|trog|ra|phy (ə strog′rə fē), *n.* the science of mapping planets and heavenly bodies.

As|tro|jet (as′trō jet′), *n. Trademark.* fan-jet.

astrol., **1** astrologer. **2** astrological. **3** astrology.

as|tro|labe (as′trə lāb), *n.* an astronomical instrument formerly used for measuring the altitude of the sun or stars. It has been largely replaced by the sextant. [< Old French *astrelabe,* learned borrowing from Medieval Latin *astrolabium* < Greek *astrolábos* (originally) taking (the position of) stars < *ástron* star + *lambánein* take]

as|trol|a|try (ə strol′ə trē), *n.* worship of the heavenly bodies. [< *astro-* + Greek *latreiā* worship]

as|trol|o|ger (ə strol′ə jər), *n.* a person who claims to know and interpret the supposed influence of the stars and planets on persons or events: *People believed that if astrologers could foretell happenings in the heavens from the study of stars, they could also foretell events in people's lives* (Beauchamp, Mayfield, and West).

as|tro|lo|gi|an (as′trə lō′jē ən), *n., adj.* —*n.* = astrologer.
—*adj.* = astrological.

as|tro|log|ic (as′trə loj′ik), *adj.* = astrological.

as|tro|log|i|cal (as′trə loj′ə kəl), *adj.* of or having to do with astrology: *Forecasting the end of the world is a favorite pastime of astrological or numerological devotees* (Atlantic). —**as′tro|log′i|cal|ly,** *adv.*

as|trol|o|gist (ə strol′ə jist), *n.* = astrologer.

as|trol|o|gy (ə strol′ə jē), *n.* **1** the study of the stars and planets to reveal their supposed influence on persons or events, and to foretell what will happen; judicial astrology; mundane astrology. **2** *Archaic.* practical astronomy, such as the prediction of tides and eclipses and the fixing of Easter; natural astrology. [< Latin *astrologia* astronomy < Greek *astrologiā* < *astrológos* astronomer < *ástron* star + *-logos* treating of < *légein* speak]

as|tro|med|i|cine (as′trō med′ə sən), *n.* = aerospace medicine.

as|tro|me|te|or|o|log|i|cal (as′trō mē′tē ər ə loj′ə kəl), *adj.* of or having to do with astrometeorology.

as|tro|me|te|or|ol|o|gist (as′trō mē′tē ə rol′ə jist), *n.* a person who studies astrometeorology.

as|tro|me|te|or|ol|o|gy (as′trō mē′tē ə rol′ə jē), *n.* the branch of meteorology dealing with the influence of heavenly bodies on weather.

as|tro|met|ric (as′trə met′rik), *adj.* of or having to do with astrometry.

as|tro|met|ri|cal (as′trə met′rə kəl), *adj.* = astrometric.

as|trom|e|try (ə strom′ə trē), *n.* the branch of astronomy dealing with the measurement of the magnitudes, apparent positions, or motions of the heavenly bodies.

astron., **1** astronomer. **2** astronomical. **3** astronomy.

as|tro|naut (as′trə nôt), *n.* **1** a pilot or member of the crew of a spacecraft: *360,000 pounds of thrust ... boosted astronaut Glenn's 4,100-pound capsule into space* (Science News Letter). **2** a traveler in outer space. [< *astro-* + Greek *naútēs* sailor]
▶ See **cosmonaut** for usage note.

as|tro|nau|tic (as′trə nô′tik), *adj.* of or having to do with astronautics or astronauts: *astronautic research.* —**as′tro|nau′ti|cal|ly,** *adv.*

as|tro|nau|ti|cal (as′trə nô′tə kəl), *adj.* = astronautic: *an astronautical expert.*

as|tro|nau|tics (as′trə nô′tiks), *n.* **1a** the art or science of designing, building, and operating space vehicles. **b** the scientific study of space flight. **2** travel in outer space; space travel.

as|tro|nav|i|ga|tion (as′trō nav′ə gā′shən), *n.* the navigation of an air or space vehicle by means of instruments carried within the vehicle that sight on celestial bodies: *The cardinal principle of astronavigation is to keep far away from gravitational maelstroms* (Time).

as|tron|o|mer (ə stron′ə mər), *n.* a person who studies astronomy; person skilled in astronomy: *Astronomers have seen some clusters of stars that are a million light-years away* (Beauchamp, Mayfield, and West).

Astronomer Royal, **1** the principal astronomer of England. Until 1971, the title was given to the director of the Royal Greenwich Observatory. **2** the principal astronomer of Scotland, who is also director of the Royal Edinburgh Observatory.

as|tro|nom|ic (as′trə nom′ik), *adj.* = astronomical.

as|tro|nom|i|cal (as′trə nom′ə kəl), *adj.* **1** of astronomy; having to do with astronomy: *astronomical calculations. A telescope is an astronomical instrument.* **2** *Figurative.* enormous; like the numbers reported in astronomy; so large as to be beyond comprehension; very great: *Astronomical sums of money are spent on defense by many nations.* —**as′tro|nom′i|cal|ly,** *adv.*

astronomical day, twenty-four hours of mean

solar time reckoned from noon; mean solar day.
astronomical time, mean solar time reckoned from noon through the twenty-four hours.
astronomical unit, the mean distance of the earth from the sun (about 93 million miles), sometimes used as a unit of measurement in expressing distances between planets and stars.
astronomical year, the period of the earth's revolution around the sun; solar year. It lasts 365 days, 5 hours, 48 minutes, 45.51 seconds.
as|tron|o|my (ə stron′ə mē), *n.* **1** the science of the sun, moon, planets, stars, and all other heavenly bodies. It deals with their composition, motions, relative positions, distances, and sizes, as well as with the earth in its relation to them. **2** *pl.* **-mies.** a textbook or treatise on this science. [< Latin *astronomia* < Greek *astronomíā* < *ástron* star + *némein* dictate the laws of]
as|tro|pho|to|graph (as′trō fō′tə graf, -gräf), *n.* a photograph of a heavenly body: . . . *a large astrophotograph of the spiral nebula of Andromeda* (New Yorker).
as|tro|pho|to|graph|ic (as′trō fō′tə graf′ik), *adj.* of or having to do with astrophotography.
as|tro|pho|tog|ra|phy (as′trō fə tog′rə fē), *n.* the photography of heavenly bodies, especially for astronomical purposes.
as|tro|pho|tom|e|ter (as′trō fō tom′ə tər), *n.* a photometer for measuring the intensity of the light of heavenly bodies.
as|tro|pho|to|met|ri|cal (as′trō fō′tə met′rə kəl), *adj.* **1** having to do with the astrophotometer or its use. **2** obtained or made by means of the astrophotometer.
as|tro|pho|tom|e|try (as′trō fō tom′ə trē), *n.* measurement of the intensity of the light of heavenly bodies.
as|tro|phys|i|cal (as′trō fiz′ə kəl), *adj.* **1** of or having to do with astrophysics. **2** of or having to do with the physical and chemical characteristics of heavenly bodies. **—as′tro|phys′i|cal|ly,** *adv.*
as|tro|phys|i|cist (as′trō fiz′ə sist), *n.* a person who studies astrophysics: *The astrophysicists tell us that there is practically no lithium, beryllium, or boron in the universe* (E. P. George).
as|tro|phys|ics (as′trō fiz′iks), *n.* the branch of astronomy that deals with the physical characteristics of heavenly bodies, such as luminosity, temperature, size, mass, and density, and also their chemical composition: *With the advent of the spectrograph and other modern appliances, astrophysics was developed and it is now the most rapidly expanding branch of astronomy* (John C. Duncan).
as|tro|sphere (as′trə sfir), *n.* **1** = aster. **2** = centrosphere.
As|tro|Turf (as′trō tėrf′), *n. Trademark.* a material made with nylon and vinyl that resembles a grassy surface, used for artificial playing fields and lawns.
as|tu|cious or **as|tu|tious** (ə stü′shəs, -styü′-), *adj.* = astute. [< Middle French *astucieux* < Old French *astuce* astuteness, learned borrowing from Latin *astūtia* < *astūtus* astute]
as|tu|ci|ty (ə stü′sə tē, -styü′-), *n.* = *astuteness.*
As|tu|ri|an (as tůr′ē ən), *adj., n.* **—*adj.*** of Asturias (a region of Spain) or its people.
—*n.* **1** a native or inhabitant of Asturias. **2** the dialect of Spanish spoken by Asturians.
as|tute (ə stüt′, -styüt′), *adj.* shrewd, especially with regard to one's own interests; clever; crafty; sagacious: *He was an astute businessman who turned a profit easily.* **SYN:** See syn. under **shrewd.** [< Latin *astūtus* < *astus, -ūs* sagacity] **—as|tute′ly,** *adv.* **—as|tute′ness,** *n.*
As|ty|a|nax (as tī′ə naks), *n. Greek Legend.* the young son of Hector and Andromache, hurled from the walls of Troy by the victorious Greeks because of the prediction that he would restore the Trojan kingdom.
a|sty|lar (ā stī′lər), *adj.* having no columns or pilasters. [< Greek *ástȳlos* (< *a-* without + *stýlos* pillar) + English *-ar*]
A-sub (ā′sub′), *n. Informal.* an atomic submarine.
a|sud|den (ə sud′ən), *adv. Poetic.* suddenly.
a|sun|der (ə sun′dər), *adv., adj.* **—*adv.*** in pieces; into separate parts: *Lightning split the tree asunder.*
—*adj.* apart or separate from each other: *The two armies were miles asunder.*
[Old English *on sundran*]
A|sur (ä′sůr, as′ėr), *n.* = Ashur.
a|swarm (ə swôrm′), *adj.* swarming: . . . *the streets are aswarm with humanity* (New Yorker).
a|sway (ə swā′), *adj.* swaying.
a|swim (ə swim′), *adj.* swimming; overflowing: (*Figurative.*) *The Baltic from Finland to Danzig was aswim with Soviet warships* (Time).
a|swirl (ə swėrl′), *adj.* in a swirl; swirling: *with skirts aswirl.*
a|swoon (ə swün′), *adj.* in a swoon; swooning.
a|syl|lab|ic (ā′sə lab′ik), *adj.* not constituting a syllable; not syllabic.
a|sy|lum (ə sī′ləm), *n.* **1** an institution for the support and care of the mentally ill, the blind, orphans, or other people who are unable to care for themselves. **2** refuge; shelter. In olden times a church might be an asylum for a debtor or a criminal, since no one was allowed to drag a person from the altar. Now asylum is sometimes given by one nation to persons of another nation who are accused of political or other crimes. **SYN:** sanctuary, protection. [< Latin *asȳlum* < Greek *ásȳlon* refuge < *a-* without + *sȳlē* right of seizure]
***a|sym|met|ric** (ā′sə met′rik, as′ə-), *adj.* **1** not symmetrical; lacking symmetry. **2** *Logic.* denoting a relationship between terms which cannot be reversed. In "John is the father of Bill," *is the father of* is asymmetric. **—a′sym|met′ri|cal|ly,** *adv.*

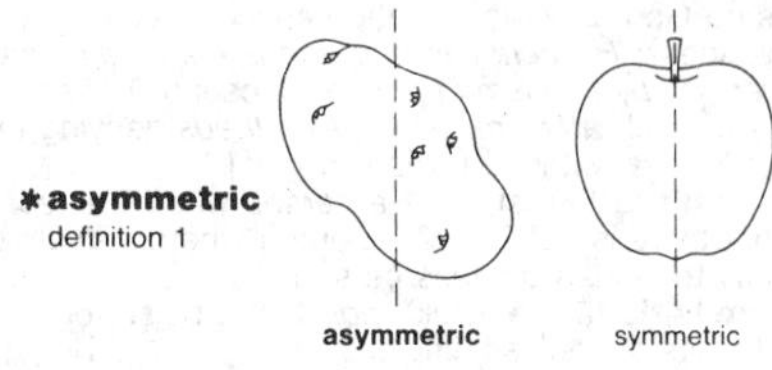

***asymmetric** definition 1

a|sym|met|ri|cal (ā′sə met′rə kəl, as′ə-), *adj.* = asymmetric: *Any object which cannot be divided into corresponding halves by any plane is said to be asymmetrical* (A. Franklin Shull).
asymmetric carbon atom, *Chemistry.* a carbon atom combined directly with four unlike atoms or groups.
a|sym|me|try (ā sim′ə trē, a-), *n.* lack of symmetry. [< Greek *asymmetríā* < *asýmmetros* < *a-* not + *sýmmetros* having symmetry]
a|symp|to|mat|ic (ā′simp tə mat′ik), *adj.* without symptoms: . . . *a patient who is asymptomatic or has only vague or slight symptoms* (Francis Lederer).
as|ymp|to|pi|a (as′im tō′pē ə), *n. Nuclear Physics.* a hypothetical region in which the interactions of high-energy particles approach constant values: *Such fantastic power could finally bring experimenters to . . . "asymptopia": the far-out region on the energy scale where all the complex events inside the atom—and hence the very nature of matter—comes within reach of man's understanding* (Time). [blend of *asymptote* and *utopia*]
***as|ymp|tote** (as′im tōt), *n.* a straight line that continually approaches a curve but does not meet it within a finite distance. [< Greek *asýmptōtos* < *a-* not + *symptōtós* due to coincide < *sympīptein* < *syn-* together + *pīptein* to fall]

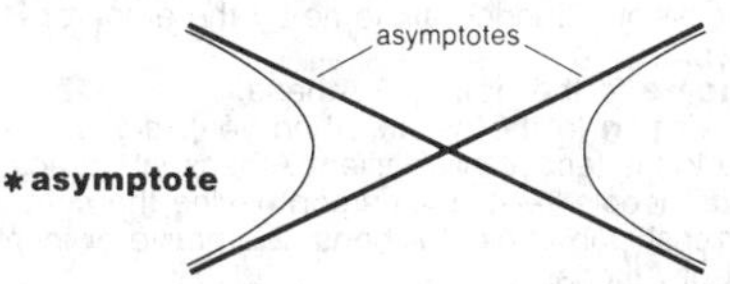

***asymptote**

as|ymp|tot|ic (as′im tot′ik), *adj.* of or having to do with an asymptote. **—as′ymp|tot′i|cal|ly,** *adv.*
as|ymp|tot|i|cal (as′im tot′ə kəl), *adj.* = asymptotic.
a|syn|chro|nism (ā sing′krə niz əm), *n.* asynchronous quality or condition.
a|syn|chro|nous (ā sing′krə nəs), *adj.* not coinciding in time: *Since they all work on a basic system of asynchronous gears . . . their motion is inherently unstable and nonrepetitive* (New Yorker).
a|syn|chro|ny (ā sing′krə nē), *n.* = asynchronism.
as|yn|det|ic (as′ən det′ik), *adj.* **1** not joined by a conjunction. *Examples:* the book I read; the time he was here. **2** without cross references: *an asyndetic catalog.* **—as′yn|det′i|cal|ly,** *adv.*
a|syn|de|ton (ə sin′də ton, -tən), *n.* the omission of conjunctions for emphasis or brevity, as in "Come take it," "Go get him." [< Late Latin *asyndeton* < Greek *asýndeton* < *a-* not + *sýndetos* connected < *syndeîn* connect]
a|syn|er|gy (ā sin′ər jē), *n., pl.* **-gies.** lack of coordination of parts or organs normally acting in harmony. [< *a-* [4] + *synergy*]
a|syn|tac|tic (ā′sin tak′tik), *adj.* loosely put together; irregular; ungrammatical: *If they* [*compounds*] *conform to the grammatical pattern, they are syntactic compounds* (*e.g., radioactive*). *If they fail to conform, they may be termed asyntactic* (*e.g., baby-sitting*) (Simeon Potter).
at (at; *unstressed* ət, it), *prep.* **1** in; on; by; near: *There is someone at the front door. She is at school.* **2** in the direction of; to; toward: *to aim at the mark. Look at me. The dog ran at the cat.* **3** on or near the time of: *at midnight. He goes to bed at nine o'clock.* **4** in a place or condition of: *at right angles. England and France were at war.* **5** through; by way of: *Smoke came out at the chimney.* **6** doing; trying to do; engaged in: *He is at work on a new project.* **7** for: *We bought two books at a dollar each.* **8** because of; by reason of; with: *The shipwrecked sailors were happy at the arrival of the rescuers. She is angry at you.* **9** according to: *She can wiggle her ears at will.* **10** from: *The prisoner got good treatment at the hands of his captors.* [Old English *æt*]
at one. See under **one.**
►**At** is used to show where or, sometimes, when. *At, in* are used to connect a word stating a place or a time to a sentence. *At* is used when the place or time is thought of as a point, such as on a map or a clock. *In* is used when the place or time is thought of as having boundaries and the idea to be expressed is that of being *inside* or *within* the boundaries: *On our trip we stopped at Chicago and stayed two days in New York. We left at noon and drove in the afternoon.*
►See **about** for another usage note.
at-, *prefix.* the form of **ad-** before *t,* as in *attain.*
at., **1** airtight. **2** atmosphere. **3** atomic.
At (no period), astatine (chemical element).
AT (no periods), **1** antitank. **2** appropriate technology. **3** Atlantic Time.
A.T., Atlantic Time.
at|a|bal (at′ə bal), *n.* a kind of kettledrum or tabor used by the Moors. Also, **attabal.** [< Spanish *atabal* < Arabic *aṭ-ṭabl* the drum]
At|a|brine (at′ə brin, -brēn), *n. Trademark.* a yellow, crystalline, synthetic compound, quinacrine hydrochloride, used, especially during World War II, in treating malaria; atebrin; mepacrine. *Formula:* $C_{23}H_{30}ClN_3O \cdot 2HCl \cdot 2H_2O$
a|tac|a|mite (ə tak′ə mīt), *n.* a crystalline or massive form of copper chloride occurring in various shades of green. *Formula:* $Cu_2Cl(OH)_3$ [< *Atacama,* a province in Chile, where it is found]
a|tac|tic (ā tak′tik), *adj.* **1** = irregular. **2** *Medicine.* ataxic. **3** *Grammar.* lacking proper syntax. [< Greek *átaktos* (< *a-* not + *taktós* arranged)]
at|a|ghan (at′ə gan), *n.* = yataghan.
At|a|lan|ta (at′ə lan′tə), *n. Greek Legend.* a maiden famous for her beauty and her speed in running. She promised to marry any suitor who could outrun her, but those who failed were put to death.
at|a|man (at′ə mən), *n., pl.* **-mans.** = hetman. [< Russian *ataman* < Old Russian *vatamanŭ,* perhaps < a Tartar word]
at|a|mas|co lily, or **at|a|mas|co** (at′ə mas′kō), *n.* **1** a plant with a single pink or white, lilylike flower. It belongs to the amaryllis family and is native to the southeastern United States. **2** any plant of the same genus. [American English < Algonkian *ātamāsku* under the grass]
a|ta|rac|tic (at′ə rak′tik), *n., adj.* **—*n.*** any drug that relaxes the muscles and relieves excitement: *Ataractics . . . calm upset people without causing mental depression* (Walter Modell).
—*adj.* that soothes or relaxes the body or mind: *ataractic medicines.*
at|a|rax|i|a (at′ə rak′sē ə), *n. Medicine.* calmness of mind or emotions; tranquillity. [< New Latin *ataraxia* < Greek *ataraxíā* < *a-* not + *taraktós* disturbed]
at|a|rax|ic (at′ə rak′sik), *n., adj.* = ataractic.
at|a|rax|y (at′ə rak′sē), *n.* = ataraxia.
a|taunt (ə tônt′), *adv.* in a fully rigged state; with all sails set. [< French *autant* as much]
a|tav|ic (ə tav′ik), *adj.* **1** of or having to do with a remote ancestor or ancestors. **2** = atavistic.
at|a|vism (at′ə viz əm), *n.* **1** *Biology.* the reappearance in an animal or plant of characteristics of a remote ancestor not found in its immediate ancestors, generally the result of a recombination of genes. **2** reversion to a primitive type. **3** resemblance to a remote ancestor. [< Latin *atavus* ancestor + English *-ism*]
at|a|vist (at′ə vist), *n.* an animal or plant exhibiting atavism.
at|a|vis|tic (at′ə vis′tik), *adj.* **1** having to do with atavism. **2** having a tendency to atavism. **3** characterized by atavism: *It is evident that all animals are ultimately from one primal source. The appearance in the embryo of atavistic survivals and the fact that the process of embryological development is fundamentally the same in all animals further confirm this conclusion* (Beals and Hoijer). **—at′a|vis′ti|cal|ly,** *adv.*
a|tax|i|a (ə tak′sē ə), *n.* **1** loss of normal coordination, especially inability to coordinate voluntary movements of the muscles. **2** = locomotor ataxia. [< New Latin *ataxia* < Greek *ataxíā* < *a-* without + *táxis* order]
a|tax|ic (ə tak′sik), *adj., n.* **—*adj.*** characterized by

Pronunciation Key: hat, āge, cãre, fär; let, ēqual, tėrm; it, īce; hot, ōpen, ôrder; oil, out; cup, pu̇t, rüle; child; long; thin; ᴛʜen; zh, measure; ə represents **a** in about, **e** in taken, **i** in pencil, **o** in lemon, **u** in circus.

or affected with ataxia.
—*n.* a person who has ataxia.

a|tax|ite (ə tak′sīt), *n. U.S.* a composite volcanic rock in which fragments from more than one lava are mixed irregularly. [< Greek *ataxíā* disorder + English *-ite*[1]]

a|tax|y (ə tak′sē), *n.* = ataxia.

ate[1] (āt), *v.* past tense of **eat:** *Father ate his dinner an hour ago.*

a|te[2] (ā′tē), *n.* infatuation or mad impulse, sometimes personified, as in Greek drama.

A|te (ā′tē), *n. Greek Mythology.* the goddess of recklessness and mischief, who incited men to rash deeds, later regarded as the goddess of punishment or revenge.

-ate[1], *suffix forming adjectives, verbs, and nouns.*
1 of or having to do with ____: *Collegiate = having to do with college.*
2 having; containing ____: *Compassionate = having compassion.*
3 having the form of ____; like ____: *Stellate = having the form of a star.*
4 become ____: *Maturate = become mature.*
5 cause to be ____: *Alienate = cause to be alien.*
6 produce ____: *Ulcerate = produce ulcers.*
7 supply or treat with ____: *Aerate = treat with air.*
8 combine with ____: *Oxygenate = combine with oxygen.*
[< Latin *-ātus,* past participle ending of verbs in *-āre*]
▶**-ate**[1] is a living English suffix, chiefly replacing the *-āre* of Latin infinitives, as in *assimilate* from *assimilāre,* and the *-ātus* of Latin participial adjectives, as in *foliate* from *foliātus.*

-ate[2], *suffix forming nouns.* salt made from ____ic acid: *Sulfate = salt made from sulfuric acid.* [special use of *-ate*[1]]

-ate[3], *suffix forming nouns.* office, rule, or condition of ____: *Caliphate = rule of a caliph.* [< Latin *-ātus, -ūs,* an ending of 4th declension nouns]

at|e|brin (at′ə brin), *n.* = Atabrine.

a|tech|nic (ə tek′nik, ā-), *adj., n.* —*adj.* without technical knowledge.
—*n.* a person without technical knowledge.
[< Greek *átechnos* (< *a-* without + *téchnē* skill) + English *-ic*]

at|e|lec|ta|sis (at′ə lek′tə sis), *n. Medicine.* **1** a collapse of the lungs. **2** incomplete expansion of the lungs at birth. [< Greek *atelês* imperfect + *éktasis* expansion]

at|el|ier (at′əl yā), *n.* a workshop, especially of an artist or craftsman; studio: *Cole Porter ... recalls a visit he and Martin paid to the atelier where the costumes for "Can-Can," a period piece, were being made* (New Yorker). [< French *atelier* < Old French *astelier* (originally) pile of chips < *astele* chip, ultimately < Latin *astula*]

a tem|po (ä tem′pō), *Music.* in time; returning to the former speed. [< Italian *a tempo*]

A|ten (ä′tən), *n.* = Aton.

*****A tent**, a tent with sides sloping downwards from a ridgepole: *A ragged A tent sagged away from the prevailing wind* (Elizabeth Robins). [< the letter *A* (because of its shape)]

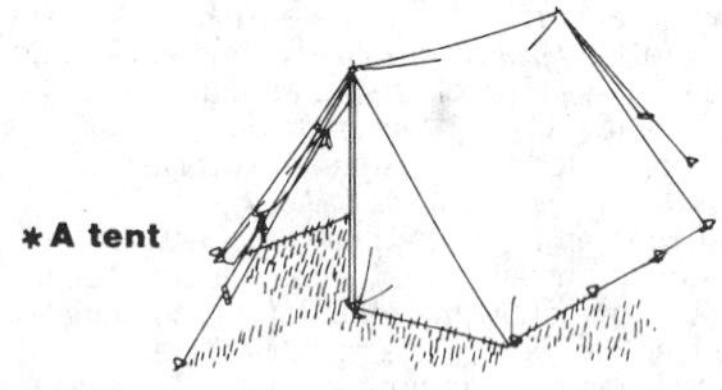

*** A tent**

a ter|go (ā tėr′gō), *Latin.* from behind.

à terre (à ter′), *French.* on the ground: *In the idiom closest to traditional ballet ... the men have no visible problems with turns, either en l'air or à terre* (Saturday Review).

a|te|wa|za (ä′tə wä′zə), *n.* a technique in judo of using tricks of beating or kicking that will paralyze, injure, or kill an opponent. [< Japanese *atewaza* < *ate* a blow + *waza* skilled work]

Ath|a|bas|can or **Ath|a|bas|kan** (ath′ə bas′kən), *n., adj.* —*n.* **1** Athapascan. **2** a member of a tribe of North American Indians living near Lake Athabasca, in western Canada.
—*adj.* of the Athabascan Indians or the Athapascan family of Indian languages.

ath|a|na|sia (ath′ə nā′zhə), *n.* deathlessness; immortality. [< Greek *athanasíā* < *athánatos* immortal < *a-* without + *thánatos* death]

Ath|a|na|sian (ath′ə nā′zhən), *adj., n.* —*adj.* of or having to do with Athanasius, his doctrines, or his defense of the consubstantiality of Jesus with God the Father against the Arians.
—*n.* a person who maintains the doctrines of Athanasius.

Athanasian Creed, a Christian creed or profession of faith of unknown authorship and probably composed around A.D. 430. It is one of the three creeds (with the Apostles' Creed and the Nicene Creed).

a|than|a|sy (ə than′ə sē), *n.* = athanasia.

ath|a|nor (ath′ə nôr), *n.* a towerlike furnace used by alchemists, in which fuel was gravity-fed to provide a continuous source of heat. [< Arabic *at-tannūr* the oven]

Ath|a|pas|can or **Ath|a|pas|kan** (ath′ə pas′kən), *adj., n.* —*adj.* of or denoting a North American language family extending from Alaska and Canada to Mexico, and including the Apache and Navaho. —*n.* an Indian of this stock.

a|the|ism (ā′thē iz əm), *n.* **1** the belief that there is no God. **2** neglect of the service of God; godlessness: *Hypocrisy in one age is generally succeeded by atheism in another* (Joseph Addison). [< French *athéisme* < Greek *átheos* denying the gods < *a-* without + *theós* a god]

a|the|ist (ā′thē ist), *n.* **1** a person who believes that there is no God. **2** a person who ignores his duty to God; a godless person.

a|the|is|tic (ā′thē is′tik), *adj.* **1** of atheism or atheists. **2** godless; impious.

a|the|is|ti|cal (ā′thē is′tə kəl), *adj.* = atheistic. —**a′the|is′ti|cal|ly**, *adv.*

ath|el (ath′əl), *n.* a small, grayish, evergreen tamarisk, native to Asia, widely planted in desert areas, such as the southwestern United States, as a windbreak. [< Arabic *athlah*]

ath|el|ing (ath′ə ling, aŧʜ′-), *n.* an Anglo-Saxon noble or prince, especially a crown prince. [Old English *ætheling* < *æthel* noble family + *-ing* belonging to]

a|the|mat|ic (ā′thi mat′ik), *adj. Music.* having no thematic structure: *There are ... in spite of the "athematic" conception, some well-defined and recognizable melodic and rhythmic shapes* (Manchester Guardian Weekly). [< *a-*[4] not + *thematic*]

A|the|na (ə thē′nə), *n. Greek Mythology.* the goddess of wisdom, arts, industries, and prudent warfare. She was one of the chief divinities of Olympus, and was said to have sprung from the forehead of Zeus. She was often called *Pallas,* or *Pallas Athena.* The Romans called her Minerva.

ath|e|nae|um or **ath|e|ne|um** (ath′ə nē′əm), *n.* **1** a scientific or literary club. **2** a reading room; library. [< Late Latin *Athenaeum* < Greek *Athēnaion* temple of Athena]

Ath|e|nae|um (ath′ə nē′əm), *n.* **1** the temple of Athena at Athens. Poets and learned men gathered there. **2** a school where law, philosophy, grammar, and various other subjects, were taught and where poets and men of letters gathered for discussion, founded at Rome by the emperor Hadrian.

A|the|ne (ə thē′nē), *n.* = Athena.

A|the|ni|an (ə thē′nē ən, -thēn′yən), *adj., n.* —*adj.* of Athens (especially ancient Athens in Greece) or its people. —*n.* **1** a person having the right of citizenship in ancient Athens. **2** a native or inhabitant of Athens.

a|ther|man|cy (ā thėr′mən sē), *n.* athermanous quality or condition.

a|ther|ma|nous (ā thėr′mə nəs), *adj.* not permitting the passage of radiant heat. [< *a-*[4] without + Greek *thermaínein* to heat (< *thérmē* heat) + English *-ous*]

ath|er|o|gen|e|sis (ath′ər ō jen′ə sis), *n.* formation or development of atheroma.

ath|er|o|gen|ic (ath′ər ō jen′ik), *adj.* forming or developing atheroma: *an atherogenic diet of high cholesterol content.*

ath|er|o|ma (ath′ə rō′mə), *n., pl.* **-mas, -ma|ta** (-mə tə). **1** fatty degeneration of the inner walls of the arteries. **2** a fatty deposit clogging an artery. [< Latin *atherōma* < Greek *athérōma* < *athérē* mush + *-ōma*]

ath|er|om|a|tous (ath′ə rom′ə təs), *adj.* of or having to do with atheroma; resembling atheroma: *In two animals kept on the diet for 60 weeks and 57 weeks, atheromatous changes developed* (Science News Letter).

ath|er|o|scle|ro|sis (ath′ər ō sklə rō′sis), *n.* a form of arteriosclerosis in which a deposit of fatty material narrows the interior of the arteries: *In atherosclerosis ... the normally smooth artery lining becomes rougher and narrower* (John W. Ferree). [< Greek *athérē* mush + English *sclerosis*]

ath|er|o|scle|rot|ic (ath′ər ō sklə rot′ik), *adj., n.* —*adj.* of or having to do with atherosclerosis; affected with atherosclerosis.
—*n.* a person who has atherosclerosis.

ath|er|o|sis (ath′ə rō′sis), *n.* = atheroma (def. 1).

ath|e|toid (ath′ə toid), *adj., n.* —*adj.* of or having to do with athetosis; resembling athetosis.
—*n.* an athetoid person. The arms and legs of an athetoid are apt to move away from his body in any direction, even though he does not want them to move at all.
[< Greek *áthetos* not fixed + English *-oid*]

ath|e|to|sis (ath′ə tō′sis), *n.* a condition, usually affecting children, characterized by constant, slow, involuntary movements of the hands and fingers, and of the toes and feet. [< Greek *áthetos* not fixed + English *-osis*]

a|thirst (ə thėrst′), *adj.* **1** keenly desirous (for); eager: *Most young people are athirst for new experiences.* **2** thirsty: *... fatigued and hungry and athirst* (Robert Southey).

ath|lete (ath′lēt, a′thə lēt *see note below*), *n.* a person trained in exercises of physical strength, speed, and skill, especially one who participates or competes in games requiring agility and stamina. Ball players, runners, boxers, and swimmers are athletes. [< Latin *āthlēta* < Greek *āthlētḗs* < *āthleîn* compete < *āthlon* prize]
▶While a′thə lēt has replaced ath′lēt in some quarters, the related words *athletic* and *athletics* do not follow this pattern to such a degree.

athlete's foot, a very contagious, chronic skin disease of the feet, which may be caused by any of several related fungi; ringworm of the feet: *Athlete's foot ... is probably transmitted principally through bath mats, swimming pools, etc.* (Sidonie M. Gruenberg).

athlete's heart, an enlargement of the heart without accompanying disease of the valves, resulting from overexercise.

ath|let|ic (ath let′ik), *adj.* **1** for athletes or athletics: *an athletic field.* **2** of or suited to an athlete; like an athlete: *athletic feats.* **3** having to do with active games and sports: *He joined an athletic association.* **4** active and strong: *He is an athletic boy.* SYN: muscular, vigorous. **5** *Anthropology.* characterized by a robust physique. —**ath|let′i|cal|ly**, *adv.*

athletic foot, = athlete's foot.

ath|let|i|cism (ath let′ə siz əm), *n.* devotion to athletics.

ath|let|ics (ath let′iks), *n.* **1** (*usually pl. in use*) exercises of physical strength, speed, and skill; active games and sports. Atheltics include baseball and basketball. **2** (*usually sing. in use*) the practice and principles of physical training: *Athletics is recommended for every student.*

ath|o|dyd (ath′ə did), *n.* an early name for a ramjet engine. [< *a*(ero) *th*(erm)*o dy*(namic) *d*(uct)]

at-home (ət hōm′), *n., adj.* —*n.* Also, **at home.** an informal reception, usually in the afternoon: *The President of India ... was given an "At Home" by the Governor of Maharashira ... on Wednesday evening* (Times of India).
—*adj.* for use at home; informal: *at-home garb.*

-athon, *combining form.* an activity involving endurance; marathon: *Walkathon = a walking marathon. A weekend telethon ... his competitors derisively rechristened begathon* (TV Guide). [< (*mar*)*athon*]

Ath|o|nite (ath′ə nīt), *adj.* of or having to do with Mount Athos, especially as an important Greek Orthodox monastic center: *Every Athonite community guards ikons and frescoes, manuscripts, and jewels, that would drive the average millionaire collector giddy with desire* (Manchester Guardian Weekly).

Ath|or (ath′ôr), *n.* = Hathor.

a|thrill (ə thril′), *adj.* in a thrill; thrilled; thrilling.

a|throb (ə throb′), *adj.* throbbing.

ath|ro|cyte (ath′rə sīt), *n.* a cell in certain invertebrates which is able to ingest foreign matter, presumably as part of an excretory system. [< Greek *athróos* together + English *-cyte*]

a|thwart (ə thwôrt′), *adv., prep.* —*adv.* across from side to side; crosswise: *Most seats run athwart a rowboat.*
—*prep.* **1** = across. **2** *Nautical.* across the line or course of: *The tug steamed athwart the ship.* **3** *Figurative.* in opposition to; against: *If you come athwart me, 'ware* (Tobias Smollett). [< *a-*[1] on, into + *thwart*]

a|thwart|ships (ə thwôrt′ships), *adv.* from side to side of a ship; crosswise of a ship: *... suitably instrumented in order to show the magnitude and direction of the forces both athwartships and in the fore and aft line* (New Scientist).

a|tilt (ə tilt′), *adj., adv.* **1** at a tilt; tilted: *His cap, atilt, gave him a jaunty air.* **2** *Figurative.* in a tilting encounter: *Break a lance, and run atilt at Death* (Shakespeare).

a|tin|gle (ə ting′gəl), *adj.* tingling; in a tingling or excited condition: *fingers atingle with cold.*

-ation, *suffix added mainly to verbs to form nouns.* **1** act or process of ____ing: *Education = act or process of educating.*
2 condition or state of being ____ed: *Cancellation = condition or state of being canceled.*
3 result of ____ing: *Civilization = result of civilizing.*
[< Latin *-ātiō, -ōnis* < *-āt-* of past participle stems + *-iō, -ōnis,* a noun suffix]

a|tip|toe (ə tip′tō′), *adv., adj.* **1** on tiptoe. **2** *Figurative.* eagerly; with anticipation: *We must go and say straight out to the reader who waits atiptoe to hear what life is* (Virginia Woolf).

a|tishoo (ə chü′, ə tish′ü), *n., pl.* **-oos.** *Informal.* a sneeze. [imitative]

-ative, *suffix added to verbs and nouns to form adjectives.* **1** tending to ____: *Talkative* = *tending to talk.*
2 having to do with ____: *Qualitative* = *having to do with quality.*
[< French *-ative* < Latin *-ātīvus* < *-āt-* of past participle stems + *-īvus*, an adjective suffix]

Atl., Atlantic.

At|lan|tan (at lan′tən), *n.* a native or inhabitant of Atlanta, Georgia.

At|lan|te|an (at′lan tē′ən), *adj.* **1** resembling Atlas; strong: *With Atlantean shoulders fit to bear The weight of mightiest Monarchies* (Milton). **2** of or having to do with the legendary island of Atlantis. [< Latin *Atlantēus* (< Greek *Atlánteios* of Atlas) + English *-an*]

at|lan|tes (at lan′tēz), *n.pl., sing.* **at|las**. *Architecture.* supporting columns or pilasters sculptured as figures, or half figures of men (distinguished from *caryatids,* figures of women). [< Latin *Atlantes* < *Greek Átlantes,* plural of *Átlās* Atlas]

At|lan|thro|pus (at′lan thrō′pəs, at lan′thrə-), *n.* an extinct type of man discovered in Algeria in 1954: *Atlanthropus ... is closely allied to the Java and Peking types of men from the Far East* (L. S. B. Leakey). [< New Latin *Atlanthropus* < Greek *Átlās, -antos* Atlas + *ánthrōpos* man]

At|lan|tic (at lan′tik), *adj.* **1** of the Atlantic Ocean: *The cod is an Atlantic food fish.* **2a** in or over the Atlantic Ocean: *an Atlantic air route.* **b** near or on the Atlantic Ocean: *New Jersey is one of the Atlantic states. The Atlantic sea lanes are full of ship traffic.* **3** of or having to do with NATO (the North Atlantic Treaty Organization) and its member nations: *the Atlantic alliance, the Atlantic community.* **4** = Atlantean (def. 1). [< Latin *Atlanticus* < Greek *Atlantikós* having to do with Atlas]

Atlantic Charter, the joint declaration of President Franklin D. Roosevelt and Prime Minister Winston Churchill on August 14, 1941, about postwar aims of the Allied powers, resulting from a meeting at sea off the coast of Newfoundland.

At|lan|ti|cism (at lan′tə siz əm), *n.* a policy of close cooperation between western European and North American countries, especially within the North Atlantic Treaty Organization (NATO). **—At|lan′ti|cist**, *n.*

Atlantic mackerel, an important food fish of North America, averaging about 18 inches in length and one pound in weight.

Atlantic Pact, = North Atlantic Treaty.

Atlantic puffin, a puffin living on the rocky coasts of the Arctic, having a white breast, underparts, and throat and blackish wings and tail.

Atlantic salmon, the common salmon of the North Atlantic waters, much valued for its taste and as a game fish.

Atlantic Standard Time, the standard time in the zone of the 60th meridian, one hour ahead of Eastern Standard Time. It is used in the easternmost part of Canada. *Abbr:* AST (no periods).

At|lan|tis (at lan′tis), *n.* a legendary island in the Atlantic Ocean said to have sunk beneath the sea. It was first mentioned in the literature of ancient Greece, and located somewhere west of the Pillars of Hercules (Gibraltar).

at-large (at′lärj′), *adj., adv. U.S.* **—*adj.*** representing the whole of a state or region, not merely one political division of it: *No elector may vote for more than two at-large candidates* (Walter A. Gordon). **—*adv.*** by the representative or representatives of the whole of a state or region: *Currently all eight of* [*the State's*] *seats in the House are filled at-large* (Atlanta Constitution).

at|las (at′ləs), *n.* **1** a book of maps. A big atlas has maps of every country. **2** a book of plates or tables illustrating any subject: *an atlas of human anatomy.* **3** the first cervical vertebra, which supports the skull. **4** *Especially British.* a large size of paper, 26 x 34 (or, sometimes, 33) inches. **5** singular of **atlantes**. [< *Atlas,* because a picture of the giant Atlas bearing a globe on his shoulders was common as a first page in early collections of maps]

At|las (at′ləs), *n.* **1** *Greek Mythology.* a giant who supported the heavens on his shoulders. He was said to be a Titan punished for revolt against Zeus. **2** *Figurative.* a person or thing that sustains the burden of anything; mainstay. [< Latin *Atlās* < Greek *Átlās, -antos* < *tlênai* to bear]

Atlas cedar, a North African cedar related to the cedar of Lebanon.

atlas moth, a large silkworm moth with strongly hooked wings, found in Asia and Australia.

at|la|tl (ät′lä təl), *n.* a stick, usually fitted with a thong to hold the butt of a spear, used for throwing spears in pre-Spanish Mexico. [< Nahuatl *atlatl*]

At|li (ät′lē), *n. Norse Legend.* a king whose wife, Gudrun killed him for having killed her brothers.

atm. or **atm** (no period), **1** atmosphere or atmospheres. **2** atmospheric.

ATM (no periods) or **A.T.M.**, automatic teller machine (an electronic machine that makes change, records deposits, etc.): *Most A.T.M. users are also shoppers ... able to "bank" from 8 in the morning until 10 at night* (New York Times).

at|man (ät′mən), *n.* the soul of the individual in Hindu philosophy; the self. [< Sanskrit *ātman* (literally) breath, self]

At|man (ät′mən), *n.* the soul of the universe and source of all individual souls in Hindu philosophy; Brahma. [see etym. under **atman**]

atmo-, *combining form.* vapor or steam: *Atmology* = *science of vapor.* [< Greek *atmós* vapor]

at|mol|y|sis (at mol′ə sis), *n., pl.* **-ses** (-sēz). the separation of mixed gases by partial diffusion through a porous substance. [< *atmo-* + Greek *lýsis* a loosening]

at|mom|e|ter (at mom′ə tər), *n.* an instrument for measuring evaporation.

at|mo|met|ric (at′mə met′rik), *adj.* of or having to do with atmometry.

at|mom|e|try (at mom′ə trē), *n.* the science of measuring evaporation.

***at|mos|phere** (at′mə sfir), *n.* **1** the air that surrounds the earth; the mass of gases that surrounds the earth and is held to it by the force of gravity. **2** the mass of gases that surrounds, or may surround, any heavenly body: *The atmosphere of Venus is cloudy.* **3** the air in any given place: *Most cities no longer have a clear atmosphere. Our cellar has a damp atmosphere.*
4 *Figurative.* mental or moral surroundings; surrounding influence: *Nuns live in a religious atmosphere. Genius can only breathe freely in an atmosphere of freedom* (John Stuart Mill).
5 *Figurative.* the coloring or feeling that pervades a work of art: *music steeped in the atmosphere of old Vienna, the mysterious atmosphere of "Treasure Island."* **6** *Physics.* a unit of pressure equal to 14.7 pounds per square inch or 1033.2 grams per square centimeter. The pressure exerted by the air on the earth's surface at sea level is about one atmosphere. It is defined as the pressure which will support a column of mercury 760 millimeters high at 0 degrees centigrade (Celsius) at sea level. *Abbr:* atm. [< New Latin *atmosphaera* < Greek *atmós* vapor + *sphaîra* sphere] **—at′mos|phere|less**, *adj.*

***atmosphere**
definition 1

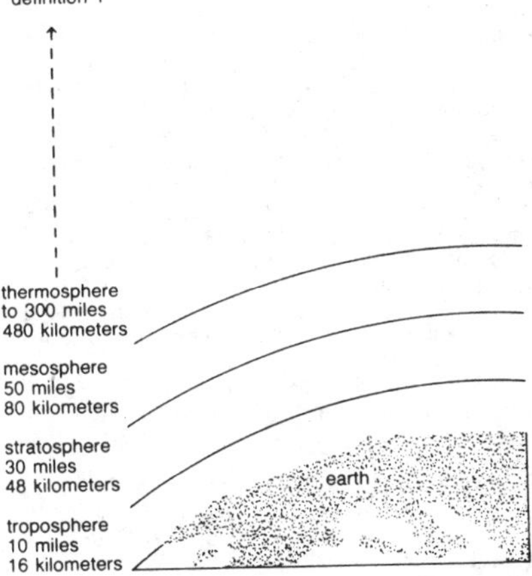

at|mos|pher|ic (at′mə sfer′ik), *adj.* **1** of or having to do with the atmosphere: *Normal atmospheric pressure on the earth's surface at sea level is 14.7 pounds to the square inch.* **2** in the atmosphere: *Atmospheric conditions often prevent observations of the stars.* **3** caused or produced by the action of the atmosphere. **—at′mos|pher′i|cal|ly**, *adv.*

at|mos|pher|i|cal (at′mə sfer′ə kəl), *adj.* = atmospheric.

atmospheric pressure, pressure caused by the weight of the air. The normal atmospheric pressure on the earth's surface at sea level is 14.7 pounds per square inch or 1033.2 grams per square centimeter.

at|mos|pher|ics (at′mə sfer′iks), *n.pl.* interfering sounds in radio communication caused by electric disturbance of the atmosphere; static: *Today it is an accepted fact that "atmospherics" are produced also by a radiation which comes to us direct from the centre of the Galaxy* (Gabriele Rabal).

atmospheric tides, movement of atmospheric masses in a pattern somewhat resembling that of the tides, caused by temperature fluctuations and by gravitation.

at|mos|pher|i|um (at′mə sfer′ē əm), *n.* a room or building with apparatus for simulating atmospheric phenomena: *... the Atmospherium creates thunderstorms from tiny clouds in a matter of minutes* (Saturday Review).

at|mos|phil elements (at′mə sfil), oxygen, nitrogen, and carbon, the elements concentrated in the atmosphere according to the theory that the earth was formed from a cooling mass of hot gases. [< *atmos*(phere) + *-phil*]

at. no., atomic number.

a|to|le (ä tō′lā), *n.* a mush or gruel made of the meal of Indian corn in Spanish-American countries. [< Mexican Spanish *atole* < Nahuatl *atúlli*]

at|oll (at′ol, ə tol′), *n.* a ring-shaped coral island or group of islands enclosing or partly enclosing lagoon. [< Maldivian *atoll,* perhaps < Malayalam *aḍal* uniting]

***at|om** (at′əm), *n.* **1** the smallest particle of a chemical element that can take part in a chemical reaction without being permanently changed. An atom is made up of protons and neutrons in a central nucleus surrounded by electrons. Nearly all of its mass is concentrated in this nucleus. A molecule of water consists of two atoms of hydrogen and one atom of oxygen. *About one hundred million atoms laid side by side are an inch long* (J. L. Crammer and R. E. Peierls). **2** *Figurative.* a very small particle; tiny bit: *There is not an atom of truth in the whole story.* **SYN:** iota, jot, grain, tittle. **3** one of the ultimate particles of matter, according to ancient philosophy, which came together to form the universe. [< Middle French *atome,* learned borrowing from Latin *atomus* < Greek *átomos* indivisible < *a-* without + *tómos* a cutting]

***atom**
definition 1

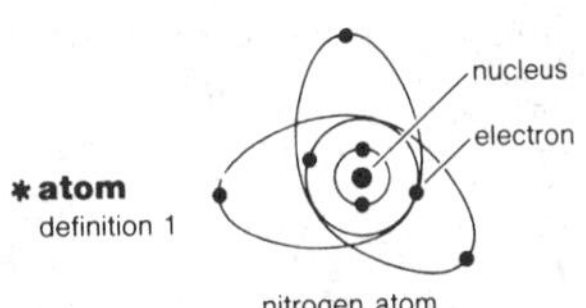

at|om|ar|i|um (at′ə mãr′ē əm), *n.* a room or building for the display of equipment used in atomic research and the presentation of atomic phenomena.

atom bomb, = atomic bomb.

at|om-bomb (at′əm bom′), *v.t.* to destroy or lay waste with atomic bombs.

atom bomber, = atomic bomber.

atom gun, a cyclotron or similar device; atom smasher.

a|tom|ic (ə tom′ik), *adj.* **1** of atoms; having to do with atoms: *atomic research. Scientists have discovered many new atomic particles.* **2** using atomic energy: *an atomic submarine.* **3** of or with atomic bombs: *atomic fallout, atomic warfare.*
4 *Chemistry.* separated into atoms. **5** *Figurative.* extremely small; minute: *particles of atomic size, atomic changes in the atmosphere.* **6** *Informal, Figurative.* very strong; powerful: *an atomic stimulus to business.* **—a|tom′i|cal|ly**, *adv.*

atomic age, the present era, as that marked by the first use of atomic energy: *A resident of the atomic age is constantly and forcibly reminded of change* (Newsweek).

a|tom|i|cal (ə tom′ə kəl), *adj.* = atomic.

atomic bomb, a bomb in which the splitting of atomic nuclei results in an explosion of tremendous force and heat, accompanied by a blinding light. The destructive force of an atomic bomb is due to nearly instantaneous and uncontrolled successive fissions of uranium or plutonium atoms in a chain reaction, each fission releasing tremendous energy and also neutrons which produce the succeeding fission. Also, **A-bomb, atom bomb**. See also **fission bomb**.

atomic bomber, **1** a military aircraft that carries atomic bombs. **2** an aircraft powered by nuclear energy.

atomic breeder, = breeder reactor.

atomic calendar, a device for determining the age of any organic material, based upon a measurement of its radioactive carbon. Thus far it is accurate to a limit of about 40,000 years.

atomic clock, an instrument for measuring time using atomic vibrations as its standard of accuracy rather than the revolution of the earth: *Atomic clocks can be made to measure time with an accuracy approaching one second per 1,000 years* (Scientific American).

atomic cloud, the upward-spiraling mass of radioactive dust and vapor formed by the explosion of a nuclear bomb.

Pronunciation Key: hat, āge, cãre, fär; let, ēqual, tėrm; it, īce; hot, ōpen, ôrder; oil, out; cup, pu̇t, rüle; child; long; thin; ᴛʜen; zh, measure;
ə represents **a** in about, **e** in taken, **i** in pencil, **o** in lemon, **u** in circus.

atomic cocktail, a liquid suspension of radioactive isotopes of iodine, phosphorus, or some other element, given orally in the treatment of some types of cancer.
atomic energy, the energy that exists in atoms; nuclear energy. Some atoms can be made to release some of their energy, either under control (in a reactor) or uncontrolled (in a bomb). Atomic energy is generated through alteration of the nucleus of an atom and is derived chiefly from fission (splitting of heavy nuclei) or sometimes from fusion (combining of light nuclei). *On Aug. 6, 1945, atomic energy literally burst upon the consciousness of the world* (Lewis L. Strauss).
atomic engine, 1 an engine operated by atomic energy. **2** a device for producing atomic energy; reactor.
atomic era, = atomic age.
atomic furnace, a reactor that provides heat for the generation of steam by which turbines or other engines may be run.
a|tom|i|chron (ə tom′ə kron), *n.* = atomic clock. [< *atomi*(c) + Greek *chrónos* time]
atomic hypothesis, = atomic theory.
at|o|mic|i|ty (at′ə mis′ə tē), *n.* **1** *Chemistry.* **a** the number of atoms contained in one molecule of an element. **b** valence. **c** the number of atoms or radicals which can be replaced in the molecule of a compound. **2** atomic state or condition.
atomic mass, the mass of an atom, as expressed on a scale in which the mass of the most abundant isotope of carbon is placed at 12; physical atomic weight.
atomic mass unit, the unit for expressing atomic mass, equal to approximately 1.66×10^{-24} grams. *Abbr:* amu (no periods).
atomic number, the number of protons carried by the nucleus of an atom of a chemical element. The atomic number is used in describing the element and giving its relation to other elements in a series. Atomic numbers range from 1 (hydrogen) to 106 and predicted to at least 110. *The atomic number of uranium is 92. Abbr:* at. no.
atomic physics, the study of atoms and their physical properties, structure, energy, and other physical features.
atomic pile, = reactor.
atomic power, power, especially electric power, produced by atomic energy.
atomic power reactor, = reactor.
atomic reactor, = reactor.
a|tom|ics (ə tom′iks), *n.* atomic physics, especially in technical application.
atomic structure, the physical description of an atom, derived theoretically, but taken as a basic working hypothesis in modern physics.
atomic submarine, a submarine driven by atomic power, capable of remaining underwater for long periods of time.
atomic theory, the theory that all matter is composed of atoms, especially the modern theory that an atom is made up of a nucleus around which electrons revolve.
atomic time, time as measured by an atomic clock: *An atomic time standard . . . would define the second in [terms of] the number of energy waves given off by an atom of cesium* (Wall Street Journal).
atomic warfare, warfare using atomic weapons.
atomic warhead, the warhead of an atomic weapon.
atomic weapon, any weapon utilizing nuclear fission or fusion as its destructive force.
atomic weight, the relative weight of an atom of a chemical element, based on the weight of an atom of carbon, which is taken as 12. Formerly, atomic weights were based on the weight of an atom of oxygen, which was taken as 16. *The atomic weight of hydrogen is 1.00797, of uranium 238.03. Abbr:* at. wt.
at|om|ism (at′ə miz əm), *n.* philosophical doctrine that the universe is composed of minute, separate, and indivisible particles. **—at′om|ist**, *n., adj.*
at|om|is|tic (at′ə mis′tik), *adj.* **1** of atomism. **2** of atomists. **3** of atoms. **—at′om|is′ti|cal|ly**, *adv.*
at|om|is|tics (at′ə mis′tiks), *n. Rare.* nuclear physics.
at|om|ize (at′ə mīz), *v.t.*, **-ized, -iz|ing. 1** to change (a liquid) into a spray of very small drops. **2a** to separate into atoms. **b** *Figurative.* to reduce (anything) to small particles or units; fragmentize: *The antitrust route is one seeking to so atomize the steel industry that harsh competition would keep prices down* (Wall Street Journal). **3** to obliterate (anything) by an atomic explosion: *to atomize a city.* **—at′om|i|za′tion**, *n.*
at|om|iz|er (at′ə mī′zər), *n.* an apparatus used to blow a liquid in a spray of very small drops: *an atomizer for perfume.*
atom smasher, *Informal.* a cyclotron or other particle accelerator: *The atom smasher will fire high energy proton bullets at nuclear targets to explore the fundamental nature of energy and matter* (Wall Street Journal).
atom smashing, *Informal.* the acceleration and bombardment of charged particles in a cyclotron or other particle accelerator.
at|o|my[1] (at′ə mē), *n., pl.* **-mies. 1** *Archaic.* a very small thing; atom. **2** *Archaic or Poetic.* a tiny being; pygmy. [< Latin *atomī,* plural of *atomus* atom]
at|o|my[2] (at′ə mē), *n., pl.* **-mies.** *Archaic.* a skeleton. [< *anatomy,* taken as *an atomy*]
A|ton (ä′ton), *n.* an ancient Egyptian sun god worshiped at Thebes. The Aton is usually represented as a solar disk whose rays end in hands.
a|ton|al (ā tō′nəl), *adj. Music.* having no key; characterized by atonality. [< *a-*[4] not + *tonal*] **—a|ton′al|ly**, *adv.*
a|ton|al|ism (ā tō′nə liz əm), *n. Music.* atonal composition. **—a|ton′al|ist**, *n.*
a|ton|al|is|tic (ā tō′nə lis′tik), *adj. Music.* characterized by atonalism.
a|to|nal|i|ty (ā′tō nal′ə tē), *n. Music.* lack of tonality; absence of relationship between tones or chords and any central keynote.
a|tone (ə tōn′), *v.,* **a|toned, a|ton|ing.** **—*v.i.*** **1** to make up; make amends (for): *He atoned for his unkindness to his sister by taking her to the movies. Nothing can atone for a murder.* **2** to harmonize: *to atone our ideas with our perceptions.*
—*v.t.* **1** to make amends for; expiate: *He atoned his sin by repenting and asking God's forgiveness.* **2** *Archaic.* to conciliate; propitiate: *So heaven, atoned, shall dying Greece restore* (Alexander Pope). **3** *Obsolete.* to bring into unity.
[< *at one,* influenced by *atonement*] **—a|ton′a|ble**, *adj.* **—a|ton′er**, *n.*
a|tone|ment (ə tōn′mənt), *n.* **1** the act or fact of making up for something; giving satisfaction for a wrong, loss, or injury; amends. **SYN:** expiation, reparation. **2** *Archaic.* reconciliation; harmony. **3** Yom Kippur; Day of Atonement.
the Atonement or **atonement**, the reconciliation of God with sinners through the sufferings and death of Christ: *. . . through our Lord Jesus Christ, by whom we have now received the atonement* (Romans 5:11).
[< earlier *at onement* a being in accord; *onement* < Middle English *onen* unite, ultimately < Old English *ān* one]
at|one|ness (at wun′nis), *n.* harmonious relationship.
a|ton|ic (ə ton′ik), *adj., n.* **—*adj.*** **1** *Grammar, Prosody.* unaccented. **2** *Phonetics.* without voice; voiceless; surd. **3** lacking muscular or nervous tone.
—*n.* **1** *Grammar, Prosody.* an unaccented syllable or word. **2** *Phonetics.* a voiceless consonant; surd.
at|o|ny (at′ə nē), *n.* **1** *Medicine.* lack of tone; muscular weakness, especially in a contractile organ; enervation; debility. **2** *Phonetics.* lack of stress. [< Late Latin *atonia* < Greek *atoníā* < *átonos* < *a-* without + *tónos* strain, stress]
a|top (ə top′), *prep., adv.* **—*prep.*** on the top of: *He had a hat atop his head.*
—*adv.* on the top; at the top.
At|o|phan (at′ə fan), *n. Trademark.* cinchopen.
a|top|ic (ə top′ik), *adj.* of or characterized by atopy.
at|o|py (at′ə pē), *n.* a form of allergy that involves hereditary hypersensitivity. [< Greek *atopíā* strangeness < *a-* not + *tópos* place]
à tort (à tôr′), *French.* **1** wrongly. **2** wrong.
à tort et à tra|vers (à tôr′tā à trà ver′), *French.* **1** wrong and crosswise. **2** at random or at cross-purposes.
ATP (no periods), adenosine triphosphate.
A|T|P|ase (ā′tē′pē′ās′), *n. Biochemistry.* the enzyme which aids in the decomposition of adenosine triphosphate. [< *ATP* + *-ase*]
at|ra|bil|i|ar (at′rə bil′ē ər), *adj.* = atrabilious.
at|ra|bil|ious (at′rə bil′yəs), *adj.* **1** melancholy; gloomy; depressed. **2** bad-tempered: *His name . . . soon became a synonym for the atrabilious type of crusader who seems perpetually to be throwing a tantrum* (Time). [< Latin *ātra bīlis* black bile + English *-ous*] **—at′ra|bil′ious|ness**, *n.*
at|ra|ment (at′rə mənt), *n.* **1** blacking. **2** ink. **3** any black fluid. [< Latin *ātrāmentum* < *āter* black]
at|ra|men|tous (at′rə men′təs), *adj.* inky; black as ink.
a|trau|mat|ic (ā′trô mat′ik), *adj.* that prevents or inhibits a traumatic reaction.
a|trem|ble (ə trem′bəl), *adv., adj.* in a trembling manner or state.
a|tre|sia (ə trē′zhə), *n.* **1** the spontaneous degeneration of an egg cell or cells. **2** the absence or closure of a bodily passage: *atresia of the esophagus.* [< New Latin *atresia* < Greek *atrētós* not perforated < *a-* not + *trētós* perforated < *trêsis* opening]
a|tre|sic (ə trē′sik, -zik), *adj.* of or having to do with atresia.
A|treus (ā′trüs, -trē əs), *n. Greek Legend.* a king of Mycenae and the father of Agamemnon and Menelaus.
a|tri|a (ā′trē ə), *n.* plural of **atrium**.
a|tri|al (ā′trē əl), *adj.* of or belonging to an atrium (def. 3): *Normally, the two atria of the heart are separated by a membrane called the atrial septum* (Michael E. De Bakey).
atrial na|tri|u|ret|ic factor or **peptide** (nā′ trē yù ret′ik), = auriculin.
A|tri|dae (ə trī′dē), *n.pl. Greek Legend.* Agamemnon and Menelaus, the sons of Atreus.
a|tri|o|pore (ā′trē ə pôr′), *n. Anatomy.* the outlet of an atrium. [< Latin *ātrium* atrium + Greek *póros* passage]
a|tri|o|ven|tric|u|lar (ā′trē ō ven trik′yə lər), *adj.* having to do with the auricles and ventricles of the heart; auriculoventricular.
atrioventricular bundle, a muscle bundle that conducts heartbeat impulses from the right atrium to the ventricles of the heart; bundle of His.
atrioventricular node, a small mass of tissue in the right auricle of the heart, which receives the heartbeat impulses from the sinoatrial or sinus node and conducts them by way of the atrioventricular bundle; A-V node. It sometimes replaces the sinoatrial node as the heart's pacemaker.
a|trip (ə trip′), *adv.* **1** (of an anchor) just clear of the bottom; barely aweigh: *One ship, with anchor atrip and sails unfurled . . .* (Washington Irving). **2** (of sails or yards) hoisted up.
at|ri|plex (at′ri pleks), *n.* = orach.
[< New Latin *Atriplex* the genus name < Latin *atriplex* orach]
a|tri|um (ā′trē əm), *n., pl.* **a|tri|a. 1** the main room of an ancient Roman house, usually also serving as an entrance hall. **2** a hall or court. **3** *Anatomy.* **a** the auricle of the heart. See the diagram under **heart**. **b** any of various cavities or sacs, especially in certain marine animals.
[< Latin *ātrium*]
at|ro|ce|ru|le|ous (at′rə sə rü′lē əs), *adj.* having a blackish-blue color.
[< Latin *āter* black + *caeruleus* blue (with English *-ous*)]
a|tro|cious (ə trō′shəs), *adj.* **1** very wicked or cruel; very savage or brutal: *Kidnaping is an atrocious crime.* **SYN:** evil, heinous. **2** *Informal.* very bad or unpleasant; abominable: *The boy had the atrocious habit of talking with his mouth full.* **SYN:** execrable. **—a|tro′cious|ly**, *adv.* **—a|tro′cious|ness**, *n.*
a|troc|i|ty (ə tros′ə tē), *n., pl.* **-ties. 1** very great wickedness or cruelty: *Many acts of atrocity are committed in war.* **2** a very cruel or brutal act: *The women and children suffered from the atrocities of war.* **3** *Informal.* a very bad blunder; anything that violates or is thought of as violating good taste, ordinary convention, or the like: *Her dress is an atrocity.* [< Latin *atrōcitās* < *atrōx, -ōcis* gloomy, fierce < *āter* dark, black]
à trois (à trwä′), *French.* for or among three (people) only: *a dinner à trois.*
a|troph|ic (ə trof′ik), *adj.* of or characterized by atrophy.
at|ro|phied (at′rə fēd), *adj.* wasted away; withered.
at|ro|phy (at′rə fē), *n., v.,* **-phied, -phy|ing.** **—*n.*** **1** a wasting away; wasting away of a part or parts of the body, especially through imperfect nourishment or disuse: *Some diseases cause atrophy of the muscles in the legs.* **2** arrested development of an organ of an animal or plant. **3** *Figurative.* a halting in growth or withering of anything: *. . . a chronic atrophy and disease of the whole soul* (Thomas Carlyle).
—*v.i.* to waste away; undergo atrophy: (*Figurative.*) An ability may atrophy if it is not used. (*Figurative.*) The politician's power in a democracy will soon atrophy if he is cut off too long from the people.
—*v.t.* to affect with atrophy: (*Figurative.*) Constant pressure atrophies the mind.
[< Late Latin *atrophia* < Greek *atrophíā* < *a-* without + *trophē* nourishment]
a|tro|pi|a (ə trō′pē ə), *n.* = atropine.
at|ro|pin (at′rə pin), *n.* = atropine.
at|ro|pine (at′rə pēn, -pin), *n.* a poisonous drug obtained from belladonna and similar plants. Atropine relaxes the muscles and dilates the pupil of the eye. *Formula:* $C_{17}H_{23}NO_3$ [< New Latin *Atropa* belladonna plant (< Greek *Átropos* Atropos) + *-ine*[2]]
at|ro|pin|ism (at′rə pə niz′əm), *n.* = atropism.
at|ro|pism (at′rə piz əm), *n.* poisoning by atropine.
At|ro|pos (at′rə pəs), *n. Greek and Roman Mythology.* one of the three Fates (Clotho and Lachesis are the other two). Atropos cuts the thread of life.
a|trous (ā′trəs), *adj.* intensely black. [< Latin *āter* black + English *-ous*]
ATS (no periods), Applications Technology Satel-

lite (a combined weather and communications satellite in synchronous orbit over the equator).

At|si|na (at si′nə), *n., pl.* **-na** or **-nas.** **1** a member of a tribe of Plains Indians now living in Montana: *The Atsina Indians were closely related to the Arapaho in language and customs* (John C. Ewers). **2** the Algonkian language of this tribe.

att., **1** attention. **2** attorney.

at|ta (a′tə), *n.* (in India) wheat flour or meal. [< Punjabi *aṭṭa*]

at|ta|bal (at′ə bal), *n.* = atabal.

at|ta|boy (at′ə boi′), *interj. U.S. Informal.* an exclamation of approval or admiration: *The marines rose from their chairs to encourage the new performer: "Attaboy, soldier! Attaboy!"* (H. L. Foster). [short for *that's the boy*]

at|tac|ca (ät täk′kä), *v.i. Music.* begin at once. [< Italian *attacca* < *attaccare* attack]

at|tach (ə tach′), *v.t.* **1** to fix in place; fasten (to): *The boy attached a rope to his sled.* **2** to join to a person, group, or organization: *The lost dog attached itself to the boy walking home from school.* **3** to add at the end; affix: *The signers attached their names to the Constitution.* **4a** to connect with, especially for duty; assign: *He was attached as mate to the ship "Clio."* **b** to assign, connect, or allocate (a military unit, soldiers, or equipment) temporarily to an organization or commander. **5** to bind by affection; join by sympathy: *She is very much attached to her cousin.* **6** to give to; regard as belonging; attribute: *He attached great importance to rockets.* **7** to take and hold (a person or property) by order of a court of law: *If you owe money to a man, he can attach part of your salary unless you pay him.* SYN: confiscate. **8** *Obsolete.* to fall upon; attack. **—*v.i.*** **1** to fasten itself; belong: *The blame for this accident attaches to the man who destroyed the signal.* **2** to be associated as a circumstance or incident; belong: *the advantages which attach to wealth.* [< Old French *atachier* < *a-* to + Germanic source of Old French *tache* a fastening, nail. See related etym. at **tack.**] **—at|tach′a|ble,** *adj.*

—*Syn.* *v.t.* **1 Attach, affix** mean to add one thing to another. **Attach** is the general word and suggests only joining or fastening one thing to another by some means: *I attached a trailer to the car.* **Affix** is a more formal word and often suggests putting something smaller or less important on another firmly and permanently: *With each new state, a star is affixed to the flag.*

at|ta|ché (at′ə shā′; *especially British* ə tash′ā), *n.* a person on the official staff of an ambassador or minister to a foreign country: *a press attaché.* [< French *attaché,* originally past participle of *attacher,* in Old French *atachier* attach]

attaché case, a flat, rectangular case of leather or plastic for carrying things, such as papers.

at|tached (ə tacht′), *adj.* **1** joined to others; not detached: *Row houses are attached dwellings of the same design.* **2** *Zoology.* fixed to a spot during life; stationary: *Adult barnacles are attached shellfish.*

at|tach|ment (ə tach′mənt), *n.* **1** the act of attaching or the fact or state of being attached; connection: *the attachment of muscles to the bones of the jaw. The attachment of the rope to the sled took less than a minute.* SYN: fastening, joining. **2** anything attached to something else, such as an additional device. Some sewing machines have attachments for making buttonholes. SYN: adjunct, appurtenance. **3** a means of attaching; fastening: *Somebody cut the wire attachment that held the ladder in place.* SYN: tie, bond. **4** affection that binds a person to another person or thing; devotion or loyalty: *The boy had a great attachment to his dog.* SYN: love, regard, fidelity. **5** *Law.* **a** the legal taking of a person or property. **b** the writ authorizing such action.

at|tack (ə tak′), *v., n.* **—*v.t.*** **1** to set upon to hurt; use force or weapons on; begin fighting against (someone): *The dog attacked the cat.* **2** *Figurative.* to talk or write against; set upon with hostile actions or words to injure or discredit: *The candidate angrily attacked his opponent's record as mayor.* SYN: criticize, blame. **3** to go at with vigor; begin to work vigorously on: *The boy attacked his piano practicing. The hungry child attacked his dinner.* **4** to act harmfully on: *Fever attacked the man bitten by insects.*

—*v.i.* to make an attack; begin fighting: *The enemy attacked at dawn.*

—*n.* **1** the act of attacking or the condition of being attacked; assault: *The enemy attack took us by surprise.* **2** a sudden occurrence of something, such as illness, discomfort, or misgivings of conscience: *My teacher had an attack of flu.* **3** the offensive part in any active proceeding or contest. **4** the beginning of vigorous work or action on some task, problem, or other undertaking. [< French *attaquer* < Italian *attaccare* < same root word as *attach*] **—at|tack′a|ble,** *adj.* **—at|tack′er,** *n.*

—*Syn.* *v.t.* **1, 2 Attack, assail, assault** mean to set upon either with physical force or with words. **Attack,** the general word, emphasizes the idea of falling upon a person or enemy without warning, sometimes without cause, or of starting the fighting: *Germany attacked Belgium in 1914.* (*Figurative.*) The candidate attacked his opponent's voting record on environmental problems. **Assail** means to attack with violence and repeated blows or continuous criticism: *The enemy assailed our defense positions. Rip Van Winkle's wife assailed his drinking.* **Assault** means to attack suddenly with furious or brutal force, and suggests contact as in hand-to-hand fighting: *In a rage he assaulted his neighbor with a stick. The mayor complained that he had been unfairly assaulted by those who demanded his immediate resignation.*

attack plane, an airplane armed for low-flying bombing or strafing attacks.

attack politics, a political campaign that attacks the character or reputation of an opponent rather than political issues: *The Helms-Gantt race . . . provides a stark commentary on both the effectiveness—and the hollow core—of the attack politics of the 1990's* (New York Times Magazine).

at|tain (ə tān′), *v.t.* **1** to arrive at; reach (a state or condition) by living, growing, or developing: *Grandfather has attained the age of 80.* **2** to gain by effort; accomplish; win: *The early American patriots attained freedom.* SYN: achieve, acquire, secure, obtain. **3** to reach (a place); arrive at; gain: *By scrambling we attained the top of a hill.* **—*v.i.*** **1** to succeed in coming (to) or getting: *He attained to a position of great influence.* **2** to reach by living, growing, or developing: *Sequoia trees attain to a great height.* [< Old French *ataindre* < Vulgar Latin *attangere* < Latin *attingere* < *ad-* to + *tangere* touch] **—at|tain′er,** *n.*

at|tain|a|bil|i|ty (ə tā′nə bil′ə tē), *n.* the quality of being attainable.

at|tain|a|ble (ə tā′nə bəl), *adj.* that can be reached or achieved: *The office of President is the highest attainable in the United States.* **—at|tain′a|ble|ness,** *n.*

at|tain|der (ə tān′dər), *n.* **1** the loss of property and civil rights as the result of being sentenced to death or being outlawed. **2** *Obsolete.* disgrace; dishonor. [< Old French *ataindre* attain; sense influenced by Old French *taindre* to stain]

at|tain|ment (ə tān′mənt), *n.* **1** the act or process of attaining: *The right to speak freely is one of the necessary means to the attainment of the truth* (Atlantic). **2** accomplishment; ability: *Benjamin Franklin was a man of varied attainments; he was a diplomat, statesman, writer, and inventor.* **3** something attained; acquirement.

at|taint (ə tānt′), *v., n.* **—*v.t.*** **1** to condemn by attainder; condemn. **2** *Figurative.* to disgrace; taint; stain. **3** *Archaic.* to accuse. **4** *Obsolete.* to convict. **—*n.*** **1** disgrace. **2** = attainder. [< Old French *ataint,* past participle of *ataindre* attain; to touch or hit in tilting]

at|taint|ment (ə tānt′mənt), *n.* = attainder.

at|tain|ture (ə tān′chər), *n.* **1** = attainder. **2** a taint; stain; disgrace.

at|tan (ə tan′), *n.* a popular folk dance of Afghanistan in which brightly costumed men and women form large circles and perform lively dances to the music of drums and flutes. [< Pashto *attan*]

at|tap (at′əp), *n.* in the Malay Peninsula: **1** a thatched roof made with palm leaves. **2** thatch made from palm leaves. [< Malay *atap*]

at|ta|pul|gite (at′ə pul′jīt), *n.* a type of clay found in the southeastern United States, used chiefly in refining mineral, vegetable, and animal oils. It is a hydrated magnesium aluminum silicate. [< *Attapulgus,* a town in Georgia, where it is produced + *-ite*[2]]

at|tar (at′ər), *n.* **1** a perfume made from the petals of flowers. **2** = attar of roses. [< Persian *'aṭar* essence < Arabic *'iṭr* perfume]

attar of roses, a fragrant essential oil made from rose petals.

at|tem|per (ə tem′pər), *v.t.* **1** to temper; soften. **2** to modify by admixture; qualify. **3** to adapt. [< Old French *atemprer,* learned borrowing from Latin *attemperāre* < *ad-* to + *temperāre* to temper]

at|tempt (ə tempt′), *v., n.* **—*v.t.*** **1** to make an effort at; try: *to attempt to get better marks. I will attempt a reply to your question.* SYN: undertake, essay, endeavor. See syn. under **try.** **2** to make an effort against; try to take or destroy: *to attempt a man's life.* SYN: attack, assail, assault. **3** *Archaic.* to tempt.

—*n.* **1** a putting forth of effort to accomplish something, especially something difficult or uncertain; effort; endeavor: *He made an attempt to climb the highest mountain in the world. The attempt, and not the deed, Confounds us* (Shakespeare). SYN: trial. **2** an attack: *The assassin made an attempt on the king's life.* SYN: assault. [< Latin *attemptāre* < *ad-* upon + *temptāre* try] **—at|tempt′a|ble,** *adj.* **—at|tempt′er,** *n.*

at|tempt|a|bil|i|ty (ə temp′tə bil′ə tē), *n.* the quality of being attemptable; capability of attempting.

at|tend (ə tend′), *v.t.* **1** to be present at: *Children must attend school.* **2** to wait on; care for; tend: *Nurses attend the sick. His companion . . . attends the Emperor in his royal court* (Shakespeare). SYN: serve. **3** to go with as a result: *Danger attends delay. Success often attends hard work.* See syn. under **accompany.** **4** to go with; accompany as a subordinate: *Noble ladies attended the queen.* **5** *Archaic.* to pay attention to; listen to; heed: *My tale attend* (Scott). **6** *Archaic.* to be ready for; wait for; expect. **—*v.i.*** **1** to direct one's care; give thought; look (to): *a clergyman with a large church to attend to. Please attend to the baggage.* **2** to apply oneself (to): *to attend to one's work.* **3** to be present (at): *to attend at a certain church.* **4** to give attention: *Attend to my story.* **5** to be present in readiness for service (on, upon): *to attend upon the emperor.* **6** *Archaic.* to be a result or consequence; follow (on, upon): *Destruction and misery attend on war.* **7** *Obsolete.* to wait or delay. [< Old French *attendre* < Latin *attendere* (*animum*) apply (the mind) to < *ad-* toward + *tendere* stretch] **—at|tend′er,** *n.*

at|tend|ance (ə ten′dəns), *n.* **1** the act of being present at a place; attending: *Our class had perfect attendance today.* **2** the number of people present; persons attending: *The attendance at church was over 200 last Sunday.* **3** *Obsolete.* a retinue.

dance attendance on, to attend often and with much care; be too polite and obedient to: *In hopes of her favor the young man danced attendance upon the rich widow.*

in attendance, in charge; on duty: *the physician in attendance.*

take attendance, to call the roll: *The teacher takes attendance before class.*

attendance teacher, *U.S.* an official charged with finding and returning truants and other absentee students to school.

at|tend|ant (ə ten′dənt), *n., adj.* **—*n.*** **1** a person who waits on another, such as a servant or follower. SYN: escort, companion. **2** an employee who waits on customers. **3** an accompanying thing or event. SYN: accompaniment. **4** a person who is present.

—*adj.* **1** waiting on another to help or serve: *An attendant nurse is at the sick man's bedside.* SYN: assistant, auxiliary. **2** going with as a result; accompanying: *attendant circumstances. Coughing and sneezing are some of the attendant discomforts of a cold.* SYN: consequent, concomitant. **3** present: *attendant hearers.*

at|tend|ee (ə ten′dē′, -ten′dē), *n.* a person who attends; attender: *Many expected attendees were delayed because of the day-long snowstorm* (New York Times).

at|tent (ə tent′), *adj. Archaic.* attentive: *. . . with an attent ear* (Shakespeare).

at|ten|tat (á tän tá′), *n. French.* a criminal attempt.

at|ten|tion (ə ten′shən), *n., interj.* **—*n.*** **1** the act of attending; heed: *The children paid attention to the teacher's explanation.* **2** the power of attending; notice: *He called my attention to the cat trying to catch the mouse.* **3** care and thought; consideration: *The girl showed her grandmother much attention. Your letter will receive early attention.* **4** a military attitude of readiness; a steady, erect posture prescribed and assumed in readiness for future orders: *The soldier came to attention when the officer addressed him. The private stood at attention during inspection.*

—*interj.* a command to come to attention.

attentions, acts of courtesy or devotion, especially of a suitor: *The pretty girl received many attentions, such as presents of candy and flowers, and invitations to parties.* [< Latin *attentiō, -ōnis* < *attendere* attend]

at|ten|tion|al (ə ten′shə nəl), *adj. Psychology.* having to do with attention as a factor in learning.

attention deficit disorder, a neurological or psychological disorder of children, characterized by excessive restlessness and an inability to concentrate on a single subject or activity; hyperactivity: *The use of Ritalin and other stimulants to treat attention deficit disorder (ADD), commonly called hyperactivity, . . . has been a controversial issue* (Jenny Tesar).

at|ten|tion-get|ting (ə ten′shən get′ing), *adj.* attracting attention; conspicuous: *Wall space was converted to selling space by the use of big blocks of attention-getting color* (Wall Street Journal).

at|ten|tisme (á täɴ tēzm′), *n. French.* a policy of watchfulness and opportunism; wait-and-see position or attitude: *Like many other Indochinese they* [*the Vietnamese*] *chose attentisme .... They would join the side that won in the end* (Time).

at|ten|tiste (á täɴ tēst′), *n. French.* a person who practices attentisme.

at|ten|tive (ə ten′tiv), *adj.* **1** paying attention; observant: *The attentive pupil is most likely to learn.* **SYN:** heedful, mindful. **2** courteous; polite: *The well-mannered girl was attentive to her mother's guests.* **SYN:** considerate, thoughtful. **3** paying the attentions of a lover; courting. —**at|ten′tive|ly**, *adv.* —**at|ten′tive|ness**, *n.*

at|ten|u|a|ble (ə ten′yü ə bəl), *adj.* that can be attenuated.

at|ten|u|ant (ə ten′yü ənt), *adj., n.* —*adj.* attenuating; making thin, as fluids.
—*n.* a medicine that thins the fluids of the body.
[< Latin *attenuāns, -antis,* present participle of *attenuāre* attenuate]

at|ten|u|ate (*v.* ə ten′yü āt; *adj.* ə ten′yü it), *v.,* **-at|ed, -at|ing,** *adj.* —*v.t.* **1** to weaken in force, amount, or value; reduce: *The authority of kings has been attenuated in modern times.* **2** *Bacteriology.* to make (microorganisms or viruses) less virulent: *Former vaccines against anthrax, dating back to the time of Pasteur, were made from attenuated, or weakened, spores of the anthrax germs* (Science News Letter). **3** to make thin or slender: *He was attenuated by hunger.* **4** to make less dense; dilute.
—*v.i.* to become thin or slender: *An earthworm's body alternately attenuates and thickens as it crawls.*
—*adj.* **1** slender; thin. **2** thin in consistency. **3** *Botany.* gradually tapering.
[< Latin *attenuāre* (with English *-ate*[1]) < *ad-* to + *tenuāre* make thin < *tenuis* thin] —**at|ten′u|a′tion**, *n.* —**at|ten′u|a′tor**, *n.*

at|test (ə test′), *v., n.* —*v.t.* **1** to give proof of; certify: *The child's good health attests his mother's care. The high quality of your performance attests your ability.* **SYN:** prove, confirm, manifest. **2** to bear witness to; testify to: *The handwriting expert attested the genuineness of the signature.* **3** to put (a person) on his oath. **4** *British.* to administer the oath of allegiance to (a recruit).
—*v.i.* to bear witness (to); testify (to) the truth or genuineness of anything: *Several witnesses attest to this agreement.*
—*n. Archaic.* evidence; testimony.
[< Latin *attestārī* confirm < *ad-* in addition + *testārī* bear witness < *testis* witness] —**at|test′er, at|tes′tor**, *n.*

at|test|ant (ə tes′tənt), *adj., n.* —*adj.* that attests.
—*n.* a person who attests.

at|tes|ta|tion (at′ə stā′shən), *n.* **1** the act of attesting. **2** proof or evidence. **3** formal testimony.

at|tes|ta|tive (ə tes′tə tiv), *adj.* of the nature of or having to do with attestation.

***at|tic** (at′ik), *n.* **1** the space in a house just below the roof and above the other rooms; garret. **2** *Architecture.* a low story above an entablature or the main cornice of a building. [< French *attique,* learned borrowing from Latin *Atticus* Attic < Greek *Attikós*]

***attic**
definition 1

At|tic (at′ik), *adj., n.* —*adj.* **1a** of Attica, a region of Greece famous in ancient times for its chief city, Athens, and as a center of literature and art. **b** of Athens; Athenian. **2** characterized by simple and refined elegance; classical: *Addison's prose is Attic prose* (Matthew Arnold).
—*n.* **1** a native of Attica. **2** the ancient Greek dialect of Attica, the language of Plato, Sophocles, Euripides, and Pericles.

Attic faith, inviolable faith.

At|ti|cism or **at|ti|cism** (at′ə siz əm), *n.* **1** a style or idiom of Attic Greek. **2** an elegant expression or turn of speech. **3** sympathy with Athens.

At|ti|cist (at′ə sist), *n.* a person who affects Attic style.

At|ti|cize or **at|ti|cize** (at′ə sīz), *v.,* **-cized, -cizing.** —*v.i.* **1** to use Attic usages or idioms. **2** to sympathize with Athens.
—*v.t.* to make conformable with Attic usage.

Attic salt or **wit,** dry, delicate, and pungent wit.

at|tine (at′īn), *adj., n.* —*adj.* of or having to do with a genus of leaf-cutting ants that attack crops.
—*n.* any ant of this genus: *The ants, called attines, inhabit an area extending from Argentina to the southern United States* (Science Journal).
[< New Latin *Atta* the genus name + English *-ine*[1]]

at|tire (ə tīr′), *n., v.,* **-tired, -tir|ing.** —*n.* **1** clothing or dress; array: *The queen wore rich attire to her coronation.* (*Figurative.*) *Earth in her rich attire ...* (Milton). **SYN:** See syn. under **dress. 2** *Heraldry.* the antlers of a stag.
—*v.t.* to clothe or dress; array; adorn: *She was attired in a cloak trimmed with ermine. His shoulders large a mantle did attire* (John Dryden).
[< Old French *atirer* arrange < *a-* to + *tire* row, order < a Germanic word] —**at|tir′er**, *n.*

at|tire|ment (ə tīr′mənt), *n.* dress; attire.

at|ti|tude (at′ə tüd, -tyüd), *n.* **1** a way of thinking, acting, or feeling; feeling, manner, or behavior of a person toward a situation or cause: *As the work became more familiar, his attitude toward school changed from dislike to great enthusiasm.* **2** a position of the body suggesting an action, purpose, emotion, or mental state. Standing, sitting, lying, and stooping are attitudes. *He raised his fists in the attitude of a boxer ready to fight.* **SYN:** posture, pose. **3** the position of an aircraft, spacecraft, or other object in flight, in relation to some reference line or plane, such as the horizon or the horizontal: *In a banking attitude, an airplane dips one of its wings.* **4a** a ballet pose in which the dancer extends one leg backward with knee bent and the corresponding arm raised. **b** any dramatic pose intended to convey an emotion, often humorously exaggerated: *an attitude of mock despair.*
strike an attitude, to pose for effect; assume a pose in a theatrical manner, and not as the natural expression of feeling: *You will find him ... striking pious attitudes at every new object of reverence* (James Gilmour).
[< French *attitude* < Italian *attitudine* < Late Latin *aptitūdō, -inis.* See etym. of doublet **aptitude.**]

at|ti|tu|di|nal (at′ə tü′də nəl, -tyü′-), *adj.* of or having to do with attitude.

at|ti|tu|di|nise (at′ə tü′də nīz, -tyü′-), *v.i.,* **-nised, -nis|ing.** *British.* attitudinize.

at|ti|tu|di|nize (at′ə tü′də nīz, -tyü′-), *v.i.,* **-nized, -niz|ing.** to assume attitudes; pose for effect: (*Figurative.*) *In every line that he wrote Cicero was attitudinizing for posterity* (James Anthony Froude). —**at′ti|tu′di|niz′er**, *n.*

attn., attention.

atto-, *combining form.* one quintillionth (10^{-18}) of a ___: *Attofarad = one quintillionth of a farad.*
[< Danish *atten* eighteen]

at|torn (ə tėrn′), *Law.* —*v.t.* to assign to another; transfer.
—*v.i.* **1** to acknowledge the relation of tenant to a new landlord. **2** to transfer homage and service to a new feudal lord.
[< Old French *atorner* transfer, appoint < *a-* to + *torner* < Latin *tornāre* to turn] —**at|torn′ment**, *n.*

at|tor|ney (ə tėr′nē), *n., pl.* **-neys. 1** = lawyer. *Abbr:* atty. **2** a person who has power to act for another in business or legal matters. **SYN:** agent. **3** *Obsolete.* agent; deputy. [< Old French *atorne,* past participle of *atorner* to assign, attorn]

attorney at law, = lawyer.
▶**Attorney at law** is the term generally used in the United States by lawyers to indicate their professional status, serving as a title after a lawyer's name in writing: *John Smith, Attorney at Law.* It has less use in Great Britain, where the more specific terms **barrister** and **solicitor** (the former designating a lawyer who pleads cases in court, the latter designating one who prepares cases but may plead them only in certain courts) are generally preferred in titles.

attorney general, *pl.* **attorneys general** or **attorney generals.** the chief law officer of a country, state, or province.

Attorney General, the head of the United States Department of Justice and the chief legal adviser of the President. He is a member of the Cabinet. *Abbr:* Atty. Gen.

at|tor|ney-gen|er|al|ship (ə tėr′nē jen′ər əl ship), *n.* the office or term of service as attorney general.

attorney in fact, an attorney authorized to act for his client out of court.

at|tor|ney|ship (ə tėr′nē ship), *n.* the function, status, or skill of an attorney.

at|tract (ə trakt′), *v.t.* **1** to draw to oneself; draw (objects) to or toward itself: *The magnet attracted the iron filings. The school fair attracted a number of visitors. His whistle attracted her attention.* **2** *Figurative.* to be pleasing to; win the attention or liking of: *Bright colors attract children. She has the gift of attracting friends.* **SYN:** allure, fascinate. See syn. under **charm.**
—*v.i.* **1** to possess or exert the power of drawing objects to or toward it: *It is a property of matter to attract.* **2** *Figurative.* to be pleasing or winning: *Her flirtatious manners are intended to attract.*
[< Latin *attractus,* past participle of *attrahere* draw toward < *ad-* to + *trahere* draw] —**attract′er, at|trac′tor**, *n.*

at|tract|a|bil|i|ty (ə trak′tə bil′ə tē), *n.* the quality or fact of being attractable.

at|tract|a|ble (ə trak′tə bəl), *adj.* that can be attracted. —**at|tract′a|ble|ness**, *n.*

at|tract|ant (ə trak′tənt), *n.* a substance or agent having the power to attract or lure insects, animals, or the like: *In some insects, both sexes exude attractants. The male boll weevil, for instance, can attract the female of the species from a distance of 30 feet* (John Barbour).

at|trac|tile (ə trak′təl), *adj.* = attractive.

at|trac|tion (ə trak′shən), *n.* **1** a thing that delights or attracts people: *The elephants were the chief attraction at the circus.* **SYN:** magnet, lure. **2** the act or power of attracting: *The attraction of the bright headlights made the deer stop in the road.* **SYN:** pull, magnetism. **3** *Figurative.* charm; fascination: *Sports have great attraction for most boys. Wealth had no attraction for him.* **SYN:** allurement, appeal. **4** *Physics.* the electric or magnetic force exerted by oppositely charged particles, atoms, or other particles of matter on one another, tending to draw or hold them together, or the gravitational force exerted by one body on another.

attraction sphere, *Biology.* the area around a centrosome, from which the aster rays radiate; centrosphere.

at|trac|tive (ə trak′tiv), *adj.* **1** winning attention and liking; pleasing: *She wore an attractive hat to the party. ... unlike her sister, she was unusually attractive* (Theodore Dreiser). **SYN:** charming, alluring, engaging. **2** attracting: *Magnets have great attractive power for iron filings.* —**at|trac′tive|ly**, *adv.* —**at|trac′tive|ness**, *n.*

attrib., 1a attribute. **b** attributed. **2a** attributive. **b** attributively.

at|trib|ute (*v.* ə trib′yüt; *n.* at′rə byüt), *v.,* **-ut|ed, -ut|ing,** *n.* —*v.t.* **1** to think of as caused by; regard as an effect or product of: *We attribute Edison's success to intelligence and hard work. She attributes her great age to a carefully planned diet.* **2** to think of as belonging or appropriate (to): *We attribute courage to the lion and cunning to the fox. This play is attributed to Shakespeare.*
—*n.* **1** an object considered appropriate to a person, rank, or office; symbol: *The eagle was the attribute of Jupiter.* **2** a quality considered as belonging to a person or thing; characteristic: *Patience is an attribute of a good teacher.* **SYN:** trait, property. **3** an adjective, or any word or phrase used as an adjective. **4** *Logic.* that which may be predicated of a subject. **5** *Obsolete.* honor; reputation.
[< Latin *attribūtus,* past participle of *attribuere* to associate < *ad-* to + *tribuere* assign; (originally) divide among the tribes < *tribus* tribe] —**at|trib′ut|a|ble**, *adj.* —**at|trib′ut|er, at|trib′u|tor**, *n.*
—*Syn. v.t.* **2 Attribute, ascribe** mean to consider something as belonging or due to someone or something, and are often interchangeable. But **attribute** suggests believing something appropriate to a person or thing or belonging to it by nature or right: *We attribute importance to the words of great men.* **Ascribe** suggests guessing or basing a conclusion on evidence and reasoning: *I ascribe your failure to your lack of interest.*

at|tri|bu|tion (at′rə byü′shən), *n.* **1** the act of attributing; ascription. **2** a thing or quality attributed; attribute.

at|trib|u|tive (ə trib′yə tiv), *adj., n.* —*adj.* **1** expressing a quality or attribute. **2** that attributes. **3** of or like an attribute.
—*n.* an attributive word. In the phrase "big brown dog," *big* and *brown* are attributives; in "morning star," *morning* is an attributive. —**at|trib′u|tive|ly**, *adv.* —**at|trib′u|tive|ness**, *n.*
▶**attributive.** An adjective that stands next to its noun is attributive (a *blue* shirt; the church *militant*), as contrasted with a predicate adjective that is related to its noun by a linking verb (The shirt is *blue*).
A noun placed immediately before another noun and serving as a modifier is an attributive noun, as in "*highway* patrol."

at|trite (ə trīt′), *adj.* **1** worn or ground down by friction; attrited. **2** *Theology.* imperfectly contrite.
[< Latin *attrītus,* past participle of *atterere* to rub away < *ad-* to + *terere* rub]

at|trit|ed (ə trī′tid), *adj.* worn down by continued friction.

at|tri|tion (ə trish′ən), *n.* **1** the action or process of rubbing away, or wearing or grinding down, by friction: *Pebbles become smooth by attrition.* **2** *Figurative.* any gradual process of wearing down, especially to exhaust an opponent's energy or resources: *The long war of attrition exhausted the strength of both countries.* **3** *Figurative.* a reduction or weakening in number or force; decline: *The remaining firemen, some 27,000, would be kept on the job, but as they quit, died, retired, or were promoted to engineers, wouldn't be replaced—a process referred to as "attrition"* (Wall Street Journal). **4** an imperfect repentance for sin.

at|tri|tion|al (ə trish′ə nəl), *adj.* having to do with or causing attrition: *The left-handed Miss Stroud [a tennis player] can be awkward to beat, unless she is hustled out of her attritional rhythm* (London Times).

at|tri|tive (ə trī′tiv), *adj.* having to do with or characterized by attrition.

at|tri|tus (ə trī′təs), *n.* matter reduced to particles by attrition. [< Latin *attrītus, -ūs* < *atterere;* see etym. under **attrite**]

at|tune (ə tün′, -tyün′), *v.,* **-tuned, -tun|ing.** *— v.t.* to put in tune; put in accord; tune: *His ears are attuned to the noise of a big city.* **SYN:** harmonize. *— v.i.* to be in tune. **SYN:** adjust.
[< *at-* + *tune,* verb] — **at|tune′ment,** *n.*

atty., attorney.

Atty. Gen., attorney general.

A|tum (ä′tum), *n. Egyptian Mythology.* a form of the sun god Ra who is associated with the closing of the day.

ATV (no periods), all-terrain vehicle.

a|twain (ə twān′), *adv. Archaic.* in or into two parts; in two; asunder.

at|weel (at wēl′), *adv. Scottish.* surely. Also, **'tweel.** [< Scottish *wat weel* (*wot well*), an imperative phrase]

a|tween (ə twēn′), *prep., adv. Archaic or Dialect.* between.

a|twirl (ə twėrl′), *adj.* twirling: *Twelve hundred dancers were atwirl simultaneously* (New Yorker).

a|twitch (ə twich′), *adj.* twitching: *The moment anyone made even a motion..., Rudolf was alert and atwitch with expectation* (New Yorker).

a|twit|ter (ə twit′ər), *adj.* twittering.

a|twixt (ə twikst′), *prep. Archaic.* betwixt; between.

at. wt., atomic weight.

A-type star (ā′tīp′), a star belonging to spectral class A, characterized by strong hydrogen lines in its spectrum. Sirius and Vega are A-type stars.

a|typ|ic (ā tip′ik), *adj.* = atypical.

a|typ|i|cal (ā tip′ə kəl), *adj.* not typical; irregular; abnormal: *Some drugs produce an atypical reaction in very sensitive patients.* — **a|typ′i|cal|ly,** *adv.*

au (ō), *French.* to the; in the; with the. It is a contraction of *à le,* masculine form of *à la,* occurring in some phrases frequently used in English, as *au courant, au revoir.*

Au (no period), gold (chemical element; Latin, *aurum*).

A.U. or **a.u.,** astronomical unit.

A.U., A.u., a.u., Å.U., Å.u., or **å.u.,** angstrom unit.

au|bade (ō bȧd′), *n.* **1** a short instrumental composition in lyric style. **2a** a song or piece to be performed in the open air at dawn. **b** any morning song. [< French *aubade* < Old Provençal *auba, alba* dawn; see etym. under **alba**[1]]

au|berge (ō berzh′), *n. French.* an inn.

au|ber|gine (ō ber zhēn′), *n. French.* eggplant.

au|ber|giste (ō ber zhēst′), *n. French.* an innkeeper.

Au|brey hole (ô′brē), any one of 56 holes surrounding the main stone circle of Stonehenge, in southern England, believed to be the remains of an ancient astronomical calendar for predicting the seasons and eclipses. [< John *Aubrey,* 1626-1697, an antiquarian, who discovered the holes]

au|brie|tia (ō brē′shə), *n.* any plant of a group of dwarf perennials of the mustard family, native to Europe and western Asia, with bright, usually purple flowers. [< New Latin *Aubrietia* the genus name < Claude *Aubriet,* 1651-1743, a French botanical painter]

au|burn (ô′bərn), *n., adj.* reddish-brown. [< Middle French *auburn* < Old French *auborne* < Medieval Latin *alburnus* whitish < Latin *albus* white; apparently confused with *brown*]

Au|bus|son rug or **carpet** (ō bʏ sôɴ′), a kind of French rug woven like tapestry. [< *Aubusson,* a town in central France, where it was originally made]

A.U.C., in the year since the founding of the city (of Rome, in 753 B.C. according to legend); Latin, *ab urbe condita* or *anno urbis conditae.*

Au|ca (ou′kə), *n.* **1** a member of a tribe of South American Indians living chiefly in the Ecuadorian region of the Andes. **2** the Araucanian language of the Aucas.

au con|traire (ō kôɴ trer′), *French.* on the contrary.

au cou|rant (ō kü räɴ′), *French.* **1** well informed on the topics of the day; up-to-date: *Europeans want to be au courant, to know what fiction has critical prestige in America* (New York Times). *The Northwesterner wants enough excitement brought to town to keep him au courant and amused* (Saturday Review). **2** (literally) in the current.

auc|tion (ôk′shən), *n., v. — n.* **1** a public sale in which each thing is sold to the person who offers the most money for it: *Many people at the auction bid on the old furniture.* **2** in card games: **a** the bidding, or the period of the game when the players bid, for the privilege of naming trumps, as in bridge. **b** auction bridge.
— v.t. to sell at an auction: *Her family auctioned the paintings when the artist died.*
auction off, to sell or try to sell by auction: *The stable auctioned off its horses when it went out of business.*
[< Latin *auctiō, -ōnis* < *augēre* to increase]

auction block, the stand or table on which items are placed to be bid upon at an auction.
on the auction block, for disposal or sale to the highest bidder: *On Tuesday, $30 million Ohio bonds will go on the auction block* (Wall Street Journal).

auction bridge, a form of bridge played with 52 cards by four players divided into two partnerships which bid to win a stated minimum of tricks at a given trump suit or at no-trumps, and are credited with as many tricks as they win.

auc|tion|eer (ôk′shə nir′), *n., v. — n.* a person who conducts an auction.
— v.t. to sell at an auction.

auction pinochle, a form of pinochle usually played by three persons, with a fourth acting as dealer. Each player receives fifteen cards from the dealer, and a widow of three cards is auctioned to the highest bidder.

auction pool, a system of betting in which the bets are sold at auction.

auc|tor|i|al (ôk tôr′ē əl), *adj.* of or having to do with an author. [< Latin *auctor* author + *-ial*]

au|cu|ba (ô′kyə bə), *n.* a plant native to eastern Asia, with glossy, leathery green leaves mottled with yellow and red berries, much cultivated for ornament. [< New Latin *Aucuba* < Japanese *aokuba* < *ao* green + *Ki* tree + *ba* leaf]

aud., auditor.

au|da|cious (ô dā′shəs), *adj.* **1** having the courage to take risks; bold; daring: *John Glenn was the audacious pilot of the first U.S. spacecraft.* **SYN:** fearless, adventurous. **2** too bold; impudent: *The audacious boy went to the party without being asked.* — **au|da′cious|ly,** *adv.* — **au|da′cious|ness,** *n.*

au|dac|i|ty (ô das′ə tē), *n., pl.* **-ties. 1** reckless daring; boldness: *The highest trapeze could not daunt the acrobat's audacity.* **SYN:** confidence, intrepidity. **2** too much boldness; impudence: *He had the audacity to go to the party without being invited.* **SYN:** presumption, effrontery. [< Latin *audāx, -ācis* bold < *audēre* to dare]

au|de|mus jur|a nos|tra de|fen|de|re (ô dā′məs jür′ə nōs′trə dā fen′də rā), *Latin.* we dare defend our rights (the motto of Alabama).

au|di|bil|i|ty (ô′də bil′ə tē), *n.* **1** the quality of being audible; distinctness to the hearing: *The phonograph's low audibility made the record hard to hear.* **2** a measure of the intensity of a sound, usually expressed in decibels.

au|di|ble (ô′də bəl), *adj., n. — adj.* that can be heard; loud enough to be heard: *She spoke in such a low voice that her quiet remarks were barely audible.*
— n. American Football. a substitute play or formation called at the scrimmage line: *... standing behind the Baltimore Colts' offensive line, calling audibles to pick up a blitz* (Time).
[< Late Latin *audībilis* < Latin *audīre* hear]
— **au′di|ble|ness,** *n.* — **au′di|bly,** *adv.*

au|di|ence (ô′dē əns), *n.* **1** the people gathered in a place to hear or see: *The audience at the theater enjoyed the play.* **2** any persons within hearing: *A popular television program may have an audience of several million people.* **3** the readers of a book, newspaper, or magazine: *A best-selling book has a large national audience.* **4** a chance to be heard; hearing: *He should have an audience with the committee, for his plan is good.* **5** a formal interview with a person of high rank: *The visiting students were granted an audience with the President.* **6** the act or fact of hearing. [< Old French *audience,* learned borrowing from Latin *audientia* a hearing < *audīre* hear]

audience room, a room for formal hearings or interviews.

au|di|en|ci|a (ô′dē en′tsē ə), *n.* a court of judges appointed in 1527 by Charles I of Spain to govern New Spain. [< Spanish *audiencia* a hearing, audience]

au|di|ent (ô′dē ənt), *adj.* listening.

au|dile (ô′dəl), *adj., n. — adj.* = auditory.
— n. Psychology. a person in whose mind auditory images are predominant, or especially distinct.
[< Latin *audīre* hear + *-ilis* of, like]

au|dim|e|ter (ô dim′ə tər), *n.* an electronic recording device attached to a television set to determine the pattern of a viewer's selection of programs, used in the rating of program popularity.

au|ding (ô′ding), *n. Psychology, Education.* attentive listening to speech sounds and patterns, as opposed to simple hearing. [< Latin *audīre* hear + English *-ing*]

au|di|o (ô′dē ō), *adj., n. — adj.* **1** *Radio, Electronics.* using or involving audio frequencies. **2** *Television.* involving or used in transmitting or receiving sound. An audio problem is a sound problem; a video problem involves the image that is supposed to appear on the screen.
— n. Television, Motion Pictures. sound reproduction: *Some of the audio for this film was distorted.*
[< Latin *audīre* hear]

audio-, *combining form.* **1** of hearing: *Audiology = the science of hearing.*
2 of sound: *Audiophile = a lover of sound.*
[< Latin *audīre* hear]

au|di|o-an|i|ma|tron (ô′dē ō an′ə mə tron), *n.* an audio-animatronic figure; a computer-controlled automaton or robot.

au|di|o-an|i|ma|tron|ic (ô′dē ō an′ə mə tron′ik), *adj.* **1** having to do with audio-animatronics. **2** controlled or operated by audio-animatronics.

au|di|o-an|i|ma|tron|ics (ô′dē ō an′ə mə tron′iks), *n.* **1** a process for making inanimate figures move and talk by means of an electronic computing system. **2** a show or display featuring such animated figures. [< *audio-* + *anima*(tion) + (elec)*tronics*]

audio frequency, the frequency corresponding to audible sound vibrations. The range for human beings is from about 20 to about 20,000 cycles per second. *Abbr:* AF (no periods). — **au′di|o-fre′quen|cy,** *adj.*

au|di|o|gram (ô′dē ə gram), *n.* the record made by an audiometer.

au|di|o-lin|gual (ô′dē ō ling′gwəl), *adj.* of or having to do with language instruction using such techniques and devices as conversation and tape recordings instead of textbooks: *audio-lingual language training.*

au|di|o|log|i|cal (ô′dē ə loj′ə kəl), *adj.* of or having to do with audiology.

au|di|ol|o|gist (ô′dē ol′ə jist), *n.* a person who studies the science of hearing.

au|di|ol|o|gy (ô′dē ol′ə jē), *n.* the science of hearing.

au|di|om|e|ter (ô′dē om′ə tər), *n.* **1** an instrument for measuring keenness and range of hearing. **2** an instrument for measuring the intensity of sound.

au|di|o|met|ric (ô′dē ə met′rik), *adj.* of or having to do with audiometry.

au|di|om|e|trist (ô′dē om′ə trist), *n.* a person who records, or studies the results of such recording of, the power of hearing or the intensity of sounds on an audiometer.

au|di|om|e|try (ô′dē om′ə trē), *n.* the testing of the sense of hearing.

au|di|on (ô′dē ən, -on), *n.* = triode. [(coined by Lee De Forest) < *audi*(o)- + (i)*on*]

au|di|o|phile (ô′dē ə fīl), *n.* a devotee of high-fidelity sound reproduction.

au|di|o|phil|i|a (ô′dē ə fil′ē ə), *n.* enthusiasm for high-fidelity sound and equipment.

au|di|o|phil|i|ac (ô′dē ə fil′ē ak), *n.* = audiophile.

au|di|o|spec|tro|gram (ô′dē ō spek′trə gram), *n.* a record or tracing made by an audiospectrograph.

au|di|o|spec|tro|graph (ô′dē ō spek′trə graf, -gräf), *n.* an instrument for recording sound patterns.

au|di|o|tac|tile (ô′dē ə tak′təl), *adj.* of or involving the senses of hearing and touching: *audiotactile stimuli.*

au|di|o|tape (ô′dē ə tāp′), *n.* a sound tape recording: *The difference between making a copy of an audiotape and a videotape is quite marked* (New Scientist).

au|di|o-vid|e|o (ô′dē ō vid′ē ō), *adj.* having to do with or involving the transmission or reception of both sounds and images.

Pronunciation Key: hat, āge, cãre, fär; let, ēqual, tėrm, it, īce; hot, ōpen, ôrder; oil, out; cup, pu̇t, rüle; child; long; thin; ᴛʜen; zh, measure; ə represents **a** in about, **e** in taken, **i** in pencil, **o** in lemon, **u** in circus.

au|di|o-vis|u|al (ô′dē ō vizh′ü əl), *adj.* having to do with the use of globes, films, recordings, slides, or other devices involving both hearing and sight, especially in teaching: *Audio-visual education . . . overcomes reading limitations . . .* (New York Times). **—au′di|o-vis′u|al|ly,** *adv.*

au|di|o-vis|u|als (ô′dē ō vizh′ü əlz), *n.pl.* audio-visual material or equipment: *The curriculum has begun to draw fire, mainly because of the realistic audio-visuals* (Edward B. Fiske).

au|di|phone (ô′də fōn), *n.* = dentiphone. [American English < Latin *audīre* hear]

au|dit (ô′dit), *v., n.* **—*v.t.*** **1** to examine and check (business accounts) systematically and officially. **2** to attend (a class or course) as a listener without receiving academic credit. **3** make an energy audit of: *"Honeywell," he says, "would audit a building, identify conservation possibilities, install the equipment, and monitor its operation* (Christian Science Monitor). **—*v.i.*** to examine the correctness of a business account: *Auditing is the Government's chief tax enforcement weapon* (Wall Street Journal). [< noun]
—*n.* **1** a systematic and official examination and check of business accounts. **2** a statement of an account that has been examined and checked officially. **3** = energy audit: *Audits to determine the needs of various offices are being initiated* (Tuscaloosa News). **4** *Archaic.* **a** a hearing. **b** a judicial hearing of complaints.
[< Latin *audītus* a hearing < *audīre* hear]

au|di|tion (ô dish′ən), *n., v.* **—*n.*** **1** a hearing to test the ability or suitability of a musician, actor, or other performer. **2** the act of hearing. **3** the power or sense of hearing. **4** an object of hearing; something heard.
—*v.t.* to give (a musician, actor, or performer) a hearing to test ability or suitability for a part.
—*v.i.* to sing, act, or perform in an audition.
[< Latin *audītiō, -ōnis* a hearing < *audīre* hear]

au|di|tive (ô′də tiv), *adj.* = auditory.

au|di|tor (ô′də tər), *n.* **1** a person who examines and checks business accounts. **2** a person who attends the meetings of a class without receiving academic credit. **3** a hearer; listener. **4** a person who listens in a judicial capacity and tries cases brought before him. **—au′di|tor|ship,** *n.*

au|di|to|ri|a (ô′də tôr′ē ə, -tōr′-), *n.* a plural of **auditorium.**

au|di|to|ri|ly (ô′də tôr′ə lē, -tōr′-), *adv.* by the use of hearing; with the sense of hearing.

au|di|to|ri|um (ô′də tôr′ē əm, -tōr′-), *n., pl.* **-to|ri|ums, -to|ri|a.** **1** a large room for an audience in a church, theater, school, or other institution; large hall. **2** a building especially designed for public meetings, lectures, concerts, or other large gatherings. [< Latin *audītōrium* < *audīre* hear]

au|di|to|ry (ô′də tôr′ē, -tōr′-), *adj., n., pl.* **-ries.**
—*adj.* of or having to do with hearing, the sense of hearing, or the organs of hearing: *the auditory nerve.* SYN: acoustic.
—*n.* **1** = audience. **2** = auditorium.
[< Late Latin *audītōrius* < Latin *audīre* hear]

auditory arts, music and the theater.

auditory canal, a duct from the eardrum to the external ear by which sound waves are transmitted from the outer to the inner ear. See picture under **ear**[1].

auditory nerve, a sensory nerve consisting of two fibers or branches, the cochlear, that carries impulses stimulated by sound to the the brain, and the vestibular, that carries impulses in maintaining equilibrium.

au|di|tress (ô′də tris), *n.* a woman auditor.

audit trail, a record of the passage of data in a computer or data processing machine, used especially to trace data from an output back to the original or source items: *the computer's audit trail—the internal monitoring system that can record all significant actions of the users* (New Yorker).

Au|du|bon's caracara (ô′də bonz), a large bird of tropical America, related to the falcons, with a black crest and long, naked legs, feeding largely on carrion, ranging as far north as the southern United States. [< John J. *Audubon,* 1785-1851, an American ornithologist]

Audubon's oriole, a large oriole, found especially in Texas and Mexico, with black head, upper breast, and tail, and yellowish-green back, shoulders, and hind part.

Audubon's warbler, a warbler having a yellow throat and white outer tail feathers, found from western Canada to Guatemala, common in the western United States.

au fait (ō fe′), *French.* **1** well informed; having knowledge (in). **2** highly skilled; expert (in).

Auf|klä|rung (ouf′klār′ùng), *n. German.* **1** enlightenment. **2** a movement in France and elsewhere in the 1700's toward intellectual freedom.

au fond (ō fôN′), *French.* at bottom; fundamentally; essentially.

auf Wie|der|sehen (ouf vē′dər zān′), *German.* good-by for now; until we see each other again.

aug., augmentative.

Aug., August.

Au|ge|an (ô jē′ən), *adj.* **1** of Augeas or resembling his stables. **2** *Figurative.* abominably filthy. **3** *Figurative.* extremely difficult: *The Augean character of the street-club project's job is nowhere more evident than in a place like the Williamsburg section of Brooklyn* (New Yorker).

Augean stables, *Greek Legend.* the stables of Augeas, king of Elis, which sheltered 3,000 oxen and had not been cleaned for 30 years. As the sixth of his twelve labors, Hercules cleaned them in one day by turning the rivers Alpheus and Peneus through them.

au|gend (ô′jend, ô jend′), *n.* a number or quantity to be increased by the addition of another. [< Latin *augendum,* gerund of *augēre* to increase]

au|ger** (ô′gər), *n., v.* **—*n. **1** a tool for boring holes in wood. **2** a large tool for boring holes in the earth, ice, etc.
—*v.t.* to bore or pierce with, or as if with, an auger: *The ridge has been augered on both sides* (Atlantic).
[Old English *nafugār* (originally) a nave borer < *nafu* nave of a wheel + *gār* spear; Middle English *a nauger* taken as *an auger*]

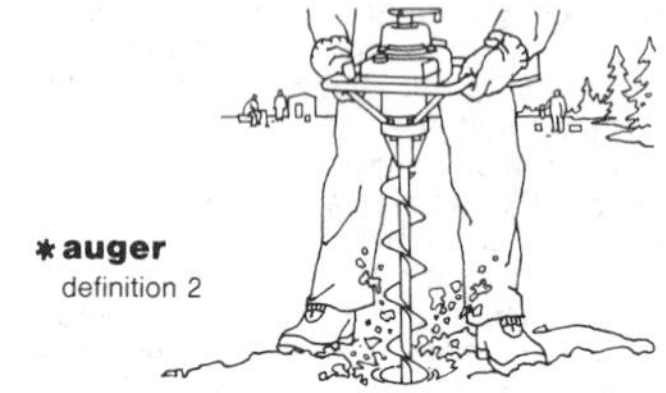
***auger** definition 2

Au|ger effect (ō zhā′), the movement of electrons from the outer to the inner shells of the atom, accompanied by the loss of an electron from the atom, caused by the absorption of energy by the atom. [< Pierre V. *Auger,* born 1899, a French physicist]

Auger electron, an electron emitted by an atom in the Auger effect.

auger shell, **1** a gastropod commonly found in tropical seas, having an elongate, finely tapered shell that suggests an auger. **2** the shell.

Auger shower, secondary rays of electrons and photons, created when a cosmic ray of high energy strikes the atmosphere. [< Pierre V. *Auger;* see etym. under **Auger effect**]

aught[1] (ôt), *n., adv.* **—*n.*** anything whatever: *Unfaith in aught is want of faith in all* (Tennyson).
—*adv.* in any way; to any degree; at all: *Help came too late to avail aught. But none the glittering evil valued aught* (William Morris). Also, **ought.**
[Old English *āwiht* < *ā-* ever + *wiht* anything]

aught[2] (ôt), *n.* zero; cipher; nothing. Also, **naught, ought.** [< *naught; a naught* taken as *an aught*]

aught[3] (ôHt), *n. Scottish.* possession; property. [Old English *æht*]

aught|lins (ôHt′linz), *adv. Scottish.* at all.

au|gite (ô′jīt), *n.* a mineral, a variety of pyroxene having a greenish, brownish, or pure black color, occurring mostly in volcanic rocks. [< Latin *augītes* < Greek *augítēs* an inferior type of turquoise < *augḗ* luster]

au|git|ic (ô jit′ik), *adj.* **1** of or containing augite. **2** resembling augite.

aug|ment (*v.* ôg ment′; *n.* ôg′ment), *v., n.* **—*v.t.*** **1** to make greater in size, number, amount, or degree; enlarge: *The king augmented his power by taking over rights that had belonged to the nobles.* SYN: amplify, swell. See syn. under **increase.** **2** to add an augment to. **—*v.i.*** to become greater; increase; grow; swell: *The sound of traffic augments during the morning rush hour.*
—*n.* **1** a prefix or lengthened vowel marking the past tenses of verbs in Greek and Sanskrit. **2** *Obsolete.* increase; augmentation.
[< Late Latin *augmentāre* < Latin *augmentum* an increase < *augēre* to increase] **—aug|ment′a|ble,** *adj.* **—aug|ment′er, aug|men′tor,** *n.*

aug|men|ta|tion (ôg′men tā′shən), *n.* **1** the act of augmenting or state or condition of being made larger; enlargement or increase: *The power of the nobles declined with the augmentation of the power of the king.* **2** a thing that augments; addition. **3** *Music.* the transformation of a melody by doubling or otherwise proportionately increasing the time values of the original notes.

aug|men|ta|tive (ôg men′tə tiv), *adj., n.* **—*adj.*** **1** serving to augment. **2** *Grammar.* increasing the force of the idea conveyed.
—*n.* an augmentative affix or word.

aug|ment|ed (ôg men′tid), *adj. Music.* increased from the corresponding normal tonic interval by a half tone.

au grat|in (ō grat′ən, grä′tən; *French* ō grà taN′), cooked with a layer of bread crumbs or grated cheese, to make a browned crust; with crumbs. [< French *au gratin* (literally) in the style of browned (meat or other food)]

Augs|burg Confession (ôgz′bėrg; *German* ouks′bùrk), a Protestant statement of faith written by Philipp Melanchthon and approved by Martin Luther in 1530. [< *Augsburg,* a city in Germany]

au|gur (ô′gər), *n., v.* **—*n.*** **1** a high-ranking priest in ancient Rome who foretold future events and gave advice on the course of public business by interpreting such signs and omens as the flight of birds, or thunder and lightning. **2** a prophet; soothsayer; fortuneteller.
—*v.t.* **1** to be a sign or promise of: *The strange mixture of ingenuous lightheartedness and fixed determination, . . . seemed to augur a future that was perplexed and full of danger* (Lytton Strachey). **2** to guess from signs or omens; predict; foretell. SYN: prophesy, prognosticate, forecast.
—*v.i.* to conjecture from signs or omens; predict; foretell; prognosticate.
augur ill, to be a bad sign: *Those stormy clouds augur ill for a picnic.*
augur well, to be a good sign: *. . . a reverential deference, which augured well for the success of his mission* (W. H. Prescott).
[< Latin *augur* (apparently, originally) Increase, Growth (of crops), as personified in ritual service < *augēre* to increase]

au|gu|ral (ô′gyər əl), *adj.* having to do with an augur; affording an omen.

au|gu|ry (ô′gyər ē), *n., pl.* **-ries.** **1** prediction; indication; sign; omen. **2** the art or practice of foretelling events by interpreting such signs and omens as the flight of birds, the appearance of the internal organs of sacrificed animals, and thunder and lightning. **3** the rite of examining the omens. [< Latin *augurium* < *augur* augur]

au|gust (ô gust′), *adj.* inspiring reverence and admiration; majestic; venerable. SYN: imposing, stately, grand, noble. [< Latin *augustus* < unrecorded *augus* increase < *augēre* to increase] **—au|gust′ly,** *adv.* **—au|gust′ness,** *n.*

Au|gust (ô′gəst), *n.* the eighth month of the year. It has 31 days. *Abbr:* Aug. [< Latin *Augustus (Caesar)*]

Au|gus|tan (ô gus′tən), *adj., n.* **—*adj.*** of the Roman emperor Augustus or his reign.
—*n.* a writer during an Augustan age of Latin or English literature.

Augustan age, **1** the period when Latin literature is traditionally held to have reached its highest point, corresponding to the reign of Augustus, 27 B.C. - A.D.14. **2** an age thought of as similar in any national literature (applied especially to that of England in the reign of Anne, in the early 1700's).

au|guste (ô gust′; *French* ô gʏst′), *n.* a clown with white makeup and painted lines on the face, often wearing a long-haired wig. [< French *auguste* (literally) august]

Au|gus|tin|i|an (ô′gə stin′ē ən), *adj., n.* **—*adj.*** of or having to do with Saint Augustine (A.D. 354-430), his teachings, or any of the religious orders named after him.
—*n.* **1** a member of any of the religious orders named after Saint Augustine. **2** a person who follows the teachings of Saint Augustine.

Au|gus|tin|i|an|ism (ô′gə stin′ē ə niz′əm), *n.* the teachings of Saint Augustine, especially on the immediate efficacy of grace and predestination.

Au|gus|tin|ism (ô gus′tə niz əm), *n.* = Augustinianism.

au jus (ō zhʏ′), *French.* served in its own gravy or juice: *roast beef au jus.*

auk (ôk), *n.* a diving sea bird found in arctic regions, with legs set so far back that it stands like a penguin. It has short wings, used chiefly as paddles in swimming, and webbed feet, and a short tail. [< Scandinavian (compare Old Icelandic *ālka*)]

auk|let (ôk′lit), *n.* any one of various small northern Pacific auks.

au|la (ô′lə), *n., pl.* **-las.** a large hall, especially in a cathedral or a university building: *The bishops assembled in the aula of St. Peter's for the first session of the Vatican Council* (Time). [< Latin *aula* hall, court < Greek *aulḗ*]

au lait (ō le′), *French.* with milk.

auld (ôld), *adj. Scottish.* old.

Auld Horn|ie (hôr′nē), *Scottish.* a name for the Devil.

auld lang syne (ôld′ lang sīn′, zīn′), *Scottish.* old times; long ago in one's life.

Auld Lang Syne, an old Scottish song with words reworked by Robert Burns, sung at partings, reunions, and New Year.

au|lic (ô′lik), *adj.* of or having to do with a royal court. [< Latin *aulicus* < Greek *aulikós* < *aulḗ* court, hall]

Aulic Council, one of the two supreme courts of the Holy Roman Empire and the personal council of the emperor from 1501 to 1806.

au|los (ô′los), *n., pl.* **-loi** (-loi). a woodwind instrument of ancient Greece, consisting of a double-reed mouthpiece and one or two pipes. [< Greek *aulós* hollow tube, flute]

AUM (no periods), air-to-underwater missile.

au na|tu|rel (ō nȧ tʏ rel′), *French.* **1** natural; nude. **2** in the plainest or simplest manner.

aune (ōn), *n.* an old French measure of length equal to 45 to 50 inches, used in measuring cloth. [< French *aune* < Old French *alne* ell]

aunt (ant, änt), *n.* **1** a sister of one's father or mother. **2** the wife of one's uncle. [< Old French *aunte* < Latin *amita* father's sister]

Aunt Ed|na (ed′nə), *British.* a conventional person of pedestrian tastes, especially as personifying a typical member of the audience at a play, or the average viewer of a television program.

aunt|ie (an′tē, än′-), *n.* = aunty.

aunt|ly (ant′lē, änt′-), *adj.* of or characteristic of an aunt: *"It is no good your trying to excuse your infamous conduct . . . !" This is the true, auntly note* (Kenneth Tynan).

Aunt Sally, *British.* **1** a game played at fairs, in which sticks are thrown at a pipe in the mouth of the figure of a woman. **2** *Figurative.* a target of criticism; scapegoat: *It [a university] had become an Aunt Sally at which all sides could take pot shots* (London Times).

aunt sally, *British.* any idle amusement.

aunt|y (an′tē, än′-), *n., pl.* **aunt|ies.** *Informal.* a diminutive of **aunt.**

au pair (ō pãr′), **1** on even terms; with exchange of services or benefits, as with board and room (but no salary) given in exchange for tutoring or other service: *Housewives in the community often take girls "au pair" from such home economics schools* (London Times). **2** a girl who works au pair: *"I'd like to appeal to your more experienced readers," she wrote, "for a set of simple rules for au pairs"* (New Yorker). [< French *au pair* on equal terms]

au pied de la let|tre (ō pyā′də lä let′rə), *French.* to the foot of the letter; literally: *It is both uncharitable and unworldly to take the words of politicians au pied de la lettre* (Listener).

au poi|vre (ō pwä′vrə), *French.* in pepper: *steak au poivre.*

au|ra (ôr′ə), *n., pl.* **au|ras, au|rae** (ôr′ē). **1** something supposed to come from a person or thing and surround him or it as an atmosphere: *An aura of holiness enveloped the saint.* **2** a subtle emanation or exhalation from any substance, such as the odor of flowers. **3** a field of ionized air or gas caused by the discharge of electricity from a sharp point. **4** a sensation in which the subject may hear strange sounds, smell a peculiar odor, see lights, or have other warning symptoms of a seizure, especially of an attack of epilepsy. [< Latin *aura* < Greek *aúrā* breeze, breath]

au|ral[1] (ôr′əl), *adj.* **1** of the ear or ears. **2** having to do with hearing; auricular. [< Latin *auris* ear English *-al*[1]] **—au′ral|ly,** *adv.*

au|ral[2] (ôr′əl), *adj.* **1** of an aura or auras. **2** resembling an aura. [< *aura* + English *-al*[1]]

au|ran|ti|a|ceous (ô ran′tē ā′shəs), *adj.* **1a** orangelike. **b** allied to the orange. **2** orange-colored. [< New Latin *aurantium* orange + English *-aceous*]

au|rar (ou′rär, oi′-), *n.* plural of **eyrir,** an Icelandic coin.

au|rate (ôr′āt), *n.* a salt of auric acid.

au|re|a me|di|o|cri|tas (ôr′ē ə mē′dē ok′rə tas), *Latin.* the golden mean (in Horace, *Odes* II.x.5).

au|re|ate (ôr′ē it, -āt), *adj.* **1** golden; gilded. **2** brilliant; splendid. [< Medieval Latin *aureatus* < Latin *aureus* golden < *aurum* gold]

au|re|o|la (ô rē′ə lə), *n.* = aureole.

au|re|ole** (ôr′ē ōl), *n., v.,* **-oled, -ol|ing.** **—*n. **1** a ring of light surrounding a figure or object, especially in religious paintings; halo. **2** a ring of light surrounding the sun, especially during an eclipse; corona. **—*v.t.*** to encircle with, or as if with, a halo. [< Late Latin (Biblical) *aureola* (*corōna*) golden (crown) < *aurum* gold]

***aureole**
definition 1

Au|re|o|my|cin (ôr′ē ō mī′sin), *n. Trademark.* an antibiotic used to check or kill certain bacterial infections and viruses, derived from a microorganism found in the soil; chlortetracycline.

au reste (ō rest′), *French.* for the rest; besides.

au|re|us (ô′rē əs), *n., pl.* **au|re|i** (ô′rē ī). the standard gold coin of the Roman Empire, about the size of a denarius and worth 25 denarii. [< Latin *aureus* (literally) golden]

au re|voir (ō rə vwȧr′), *French.* good-by; till we see each other again.

au|ric (ôr′ik), *adj.* **1** of gold. **2** containing gold, especially with a valence of 3. [< Latin *aurum* gold + English *-ic*]

auric acid, *Chemistry.* a hydroxide of gold, which behaves as a weak acid and forms salts.

au|ri|cle (ôr′ə kəl), *n.* **1** the chamber of the heart that receives the blood from the veins and forces it into a ventricle; the atrium of the heart. The heart of mammals, birds, and reptiles has two auricles; that of fishes has one auricle. **2** the outer part of the ear in animals; pinna. See picture under **ear**[1]. **3** an earlike part; lobe. [< Latin *auricula* (external) ear (diminutive) < *auris* ear]

au|ri|cled (ôr′ə kəld), *adj.* having auricles; auriculate.

au|ric|u|la (ô rik′yə lə), *n.* **1** a primrose, a native of the Swiss Alps, having a bright-yellow flower. It is sometimes called *bear's-ear* from the shape of its leaves. **2** the outer part of the ear; auricle. [< New Latin *auricula* < Latin, ear, auricle]

au|ric|u|lar (ô rik′yə lər), *adj.* **1** having to do with an auricle of the heart. **2** of or near the ear; aural. **3** heard by or addressed to the ear: *auricular confession.* **4** shaped like an ear. **—au|ric′u|lar|ly,** *adv.*

au|ric|u|lars (ô rik′yə lərz), *n.pl.* the tuft of feathers covering the orifice of a bird's ear.

au|ric|u|late (ô rik′yə lit, -lāt), *adj.* **1** having ears, auricles, or earlike parts. **2** ear-shaped. **—au|ric′u|late|ly,** *adv.*

au|ric|u|lat|ed (ô rik′yə lā′tid), *adj.* = auriculate.

au|ric|u lin (ô rik′yə lin), *n.* a hormone produced by the heart that dilates blood vessels, decreases the rate of heart contractions, and stimulates the excretion of sodium in the urine: *A lack of . . . auriculin could play an important role in causing some forms of hypertension* (John H. Laragh). [< Latin *auricul(a)* auricle + English *-in*[2]]

au|ric|u|lo|ven|tric|u|lar (ô rik′yə lō ven trik′yə lər), *adj.* = atrioventricular.

au|rif|er|ous (ô rif′ər əs), *adj.* containing or yielding gold. [< Latin *aurifer* (< *aurum* gold + *ferre* bear) + English *-ous*] **—au|rif′er|ous|ly,** *adv.*

au|ri|form (ôr′ə fôrm), *adj.* ear-shaped; having the form of the external human ear.

Au|ri|ga (ô rī′gə), *n., genitive* **Au|ri|gae.** a large northern constellation between Perseus and Gemini, the Charioteer or Wagoner. Auriga is supposed to represent a charioteer kneeling in his chariot. [< Latin *aurīga* (literally) charioteer < *aureae* bit, bridle + *-iga* driver < *agere* to drive]

Au|ri|gae (ô rī′jē), *n.* genitive of **Auriga.**

Au|rig|na|cian (ôr′ig nā′shən), *adj., n.* **—*adj.*** of or having to do with Upper Paleolithic culture, especially that of the Cro-Magnon man. **—*n.*** an extinct man of the Aurignacian period or culture. [< *Aurignac,* a village in southern France where remains of this culture were found + *-ian*]

au|ri|scope (ôr′ə skōp), *n.* an instrument for examining the ear; otoscope. [< Latin *auris* ear + English *-scope*]

au|rist (ôr′ist), *n.* a doctor who treats diseases of the ear; otologist. [< Latin *auris* ear + English *-ist*]

au|rochs (ôr′oks), *n., pl.* **-rochs.** **1** a bison of Europe, now almost extinct; wisent. **2** an extinct wild ox of Europe; urus. [< German *Auerochs* < Middle High German *ūr-ochse* < *ūr* aurochs + *ochs* ox]

Au|ro|ra (ô rôr′ə, -rōr′-), *n.* the Roman goddess of the dawn, identified with the Greek goddess Eos. [< Latin *Aurōra* (literally) dawn]

au|ro|ra (ô rôr′ə, -rōr′-), *n., pl.* **-ras, -rae** (-rē). **1** the dawn. **2** streamers or bands of light appearing in the sky at night, especially in polar regions. The aurora is a luminous atmospheric phenomenon due to the impact of streams of particles from the sun on upper regions of the earth's atmosphere. **3** *Figurative.* the beginning; early period.

aurora aus|tra|lis (ô strā′lis), the streamers or bands of light appearing in the southern sky at night; southern lights. [< New Latin *aurora australis*]

aurora bo|re|al|is (bôr′ē al′is, -bōr′-; -ā′lis), the streamers or bands of light appearing in the northern sky at night; northern lights. [< New Latin *aurora borealis*]

au|ro|ral (ô rôr′əl, -rōr′-), *adj.* **1** of or like the dawn. **2** of the aurora borealis or the aurora australis. **3** *Figurative.* shining; bright. **—au|ro′ral|ly,** *adv.*

aurora po|lar|is (pō lãr′is), **1** a polar aurora. **2** = aurora borealis. [< New Latin *aurora polaris*]

au|ro|re|an (ô rôr′ē ən, -rōr′-), *adj.* of or like the dawn.

au|rous (ôr′əs), *adj.* **1** of gold. **2** containing gold, especially with a valence of 1. [< Latin *aurum* gold + English *-ous*]

au|rum (ôr′əm), *n. Chemistry.* gold. *Symbol:* Au [< Latin *aurum*]

Aus., **1** Australia. **2** Austria.

AUS (no periods), Army of the United States.

aus|cul|tate (ôs′kəl tāt), *v.t., v.i.,* **-tat|ed, -tat|ing.** to examine by listening to sounds within the human body with a stethoscope to determine the condition of the heart, lungs, or abdominal organs. [< Latin *auscultāre* (with English *ate*[1]) listen] **—aus′cul|ta′tion,** *n.* **—aus′cul|ta′tor,** *n.*

aus|cul|ta|tive (ôs′kəl tā′tiv), *adj.* of or of the nature of auscultation.

aus|cul|ta|to|ry (ô skul′tə tôr′ē, -tōr′-), *adj.* of or having to do with auscultation.

au se|cours (ō sə kür′), *French.* help!

aus|form (ôs′fôrm′), *adj., v.* **—*adj.*** of or designating a class of strong, highly ductile steels made by a process of austenitizing, deformation, and quenching and tempering. **—*v.t., v.i.*** to produce (steel) by the ausform process. [< *aus*(tenitize) + (de)*form*(ation)]

Aus|gleich (ous′glīʜ′), *n. German.* agreement; compromise.

Aus|län|der (ous′len′dər), *n. German.* a foreigner; stranger.

aus|pex (ôs′peks), *n., pl.* **-pi|ces** (-pə sēz). = augur (def. 1). [< Latin *auspex* < *avis* bird + *specere* look at, watch]

aus|pi|cate (ôs′pə kāt), *v.t.,* **-cat|ed, -cat|ing.** **1** to initiate (an undertaking) with a ceremony calculated to ensure good luck. **2** to begin; inaugurate. [< Latin *auspicāre* (with English *-ate*[1]) (literally) take omens < *auspicium* auspice]

aus|pi|ces (ôs′pə siz *for 1;* ôs′pə sēz *for 2*), *n.pl.* **1** helpful influence; approval or support; patronage: *The school fair was held under the auspices of the Parents' Association.* **2** omens; signs: *The ancient Romans used to observe the way birds flew as auspices to guide their actions.* [< Middle French *auspice,* learned borrowing from Latin *auspicium* < *auspex* auspex]

aus|pi|cial (ô spish′əl), *adj.* **1** of or having to do with auspices or augury. **2** = auspicious.

aus|pi|cious (ô spish′əs), *adj.* **1** with signs of success; favorable: *The new boy had an auspicious first day in school.* **SYN:** propitious, promising, hopeful. See syn. under **favorable. 2** prosperous; fortunate. **—aus|pi′cious|ly,** *adv.* **—aus|pi′cious|ness,** *n.*

Aus|sie (ô′sē), *n., adj. Slang.* **1** Australia. **2** Australian.

Aust., **1** Australia. **2** Austria. **3** Austrian.

aus|ten|ite (ôs′tə nīt), *n.* a nonmagnetic solid solution of carbon in an allotropic form of iron. It is a constituent of steel, under certain conditions. [< Sir William Roberts-*Austen,* 1843-1902, an English metallurgist + English *ite*[1]]

aus|ten|it|ic (ôs′tə nit′ik), *adj.* containing sufficient nickel, chromium, or manganese to retain austenite at atmospheric temperatures, therefore producing steel that is usually nonmagnetic and resistant to heat and corrosion.

aus|ten|it|ize (ôs′tə nə tīz), *v.t., v.i.,* **-ized, -iz|ing.** to form austenite by heating (a ferrous alloy).

Aus|ter (ôs′tər), *n. Poetic.* **1** the south wind. **2** the south. [< Latin *auster* south wind]

aus|tere (ô stir′), *adj.* **1** stern in manner or appearance; harsh: *Grandfather was a silent, austere man, very strict with his children.* **SYN:** severe. **2** strict in morals; severe in self-discipline: *Some of the ideas of the Puritans seem too austere to us. To these austere fanatics a holiday was an object of positive disgust* (Macaulay). **SYN:** rigorous, relentless. **3** severely simple: *The tall, plain columns stood against the sky in austere beauty.* **SYN:** unadorned. **4** grave; sober; serious: *. . . austere and grave in deportment* (Longfellow). **5** sour-tasting. [< Latin *austērus* < Greek *austērós,* related to dialectal *aûos* dry] **—aus|tere′ly,** *adv.* **—aus|tere′ness,** *n.*

aus|ter|i|ty (ô ster′ə tē), *n., pl.* **-ties.** **1** sternness in manner or appearance; harshness; strictness; severity. **2** severe simplicity. **3** strict limiting or rationing of food, clothing, fuel, or other commodities, in order to conserve national resources. **austerities,** severe practices, such as going without food or praying all night: *The austerities and blameless purity of Ximenes's life had given him a reputation for sanctity throughout Spain* (W. H. Prescott).

Aus|tin (ôs′tən), *n.* an Austin friar; Augustinian.

Austin friar, a member of a mendicant order (Hermits of Saint Augustine) named for Saint Augustine; an Augustinian.

Austl. or **Austr.,** Australia.

Pronunciation Key: hat, āge, cãre, fär; let, ēqual, tėrm; it, īce; hot, ōpen, ôrder; oil, out; cup, pu̇t, rüle; child; long; thin; ᴛʜen; zh, measure; ə represents **a** in about, **e** in taken, **i** in pencil, **o** in lemon, **u** in circus.

aus|tral[1] (ôs′trəl), *adj.* = southern. [< Latin *austrālis* < *auster* the south wind]

aus|tral[2] (ou sträl′), *n.* the monetary unit of Argentina, equal to 100 centavos. It replaced the peso in 1986. [< American Spanish (Argentina) *austral* < Spanish *austral* southern < Latin *austrālis*]

Aus|tral (ôs′trəl), *adj.* of or having to do with Australia or Australasia.

Austral., **1** Australasia. **2** Australia.

Aus|tral|a|sian (ôs′trə lā′zhən, -shən), *adj., n.* **—*adj.*** of or having to do with Australasia or its people. **—*n.*** a native or inhabitant of Australasia (Australia, Tasmania, New Guinea, New Zealand, and other nearby islands).

Aus|tral|ia antigen (ô strāl′yə), an antigen found in the blood plasma of persons affected with serum hepatitis. It was originally found in a blood sample taken from an Australian aborigine.

Australia Day, an Australian national holiday celebrating the first British settlement of Australia, at Sydney, on January 26, 1788.

Aus|tral|ian (ô strāl′yən), *adj., n.* **—*adj.*** of Australia or its people.
—*n.* **1** a person born or living in Australia. **2** an aboriginal native of Australia. **3** any one of several aboriginal languages of Australia.

Aus|tral|i|a|na (ôs trāl′ē ä′nə, -an′ə, -ā′nə), *n.pl.* **1** a collection of books, documents, facts, or other literary material about Australia, especially its history. **2** a collection of early Australian furniture, textiles, or other handcrafted products. **3** anecdotes, folklore, songs, or other things about Australia or typical of Australia and Australian culture.

Australian ballot, a ballot with the names of all the candidates for election to public office on it. The ballot is marked by the voter in a private booth to guarantee secrecy.

Australian bear, = koala.

Australian crawl, a fast way of swimming by alternate overarm strokes combined with a fast flutter kick.

Aus|tral|ian|ism (ô strāl′yə niz əm), *n.* **1** a word, phrase, or meaning originating, or more widely used in Australian English than in other varieties of English: *"Bail up" meaning "to rob" is an Australianism.* **2** devotion or loyalty to Australia and to its customs and traditions. **3** a custom or trait peculiar to Australia.

Australian nut, the nutlike fruit of the macadamia.

Australian pine, a type of casuarina that has been transplanted to California and grown there for its red wood, which is used in furniture.

Australian red snail, a red freshwater snail of Australia commonly used in aquariums.

Australian rules, a form of football played in Australia since the 1850's, using teams of 18 players each and four goal posts.

Australian terrier, a small terrier with a rough, blue- or silver-black coat and tan markings on the head and legs. The breed originated in Australia.

Aus|tra|li|oid (ô strā′lē oid), *adj., n.* = Australoid.

aus|tra|lite (ôs′trə līt), *n.* a kind of tektite, a rounded lump of natural glass, found in Australia and elsewhere. [of unknown origin]

Aus|tra|loid (ôs′trə loid), *adj., n.* **—*adj.*** of the racial type characterized by the Australian aborigines and certain neighboring peoples.
—*n.* a member of an Australoid people.

Aus|tra|lo|pi|the|cine (ôs′trə lō pith′ə sēn), *n., adj.* **—*n.*** any primate of an extinct genus of the early Pleistocene, whose fossil remains have been found in various parts of the world and especially in South Africa.
—*adj.* of or belonging to this genus.
[< Latin *austrālis* southern + Greek *píthēkos* ape + English *-ine*[1]]

Aus|tra|lo|pi|the|cus (ôs′trə lō pith′ə kəs), *n.* an Australopithecine primate: . . . *another possible human progenitor, Australopithecus, will be determined* (Science News Letter).

Aus|tral|orp (ôs′trə lôrp), *n.* a breed of chicken developed in Australia, and bred primarily for egg production. It is derived from the Orpington. [< *Austral* + *Orp*(ington)]

Aus|tra|sian (ô strā′zhən, -shən), *adj., n.* **—*adj.*** of Austrasia (the eastern kingdom of the Franks) or its people.
—*n.* a native or inhabitant of Austrasia.

Aus|tri|an (ôs′trē ən), *adj., n.* **—*adj.*** of or having to do with Austria or its people.
—*n.* a person born or living in Austria.

Aus|tro-A|si|at|ic (ôs′trō ā′zhē at′ik, -shē-), *adj.* of or having to do with a language family of southeastern Asia related to Austronesian that includes Khmer and Vietnamese.

Aus|tro-Hun|gar|i|an (ôs′trō hung gãr′ē ən), *adj., n.* **—*adj.*** of or having to do with the former dual monarchy or empire of Austria and Hungary.
—*n.* an inhabitant or subject of this monarchy or empire.

Aus|tro-Ma|lay|an (ôs′trō mə lā′ən), *adj.* of or having to do with Australia and the Malay Archipelago.

Aus|tro|ne|sian (ôs′trō nē′zhən, -shən), *adj., n.* **—*adj.*** of Austronesia (the islands of the south and mid-Pacific), its people, or its languages.
—*n.* **1** a native or inhabitant of Austronesia. **2** a probable linguistic family of the Pacific, comprising the Indonesian, Polynesian, and Melanesian languages.

aus|tro|sau|rus (ôs′trō sô′rəs), *n.* a fossil reptile excavated in Queensland, Australia. [< *Austro-* Australian + Greek *saûros* lizard]

aut-, *prefix.* the form of **auto-**[1] before vowels, as in *autacoid, autism.*

au|ta|coid (ô′tə koid), *n.* a hormone or other substance that acts like a hormone. [< *aut-* self + Greek *ákos* remedy + English *-oid*]

au|tar|chic (ô tär′kik), *adj.* **1** of, having to do with, or resembling autarchy. **2** = autarkic.

au|tar|chi|cal (ô tär′kə kəl), *adj.* **1** = autarchic. **2** = autarkic.

au|tar|chy[1] (ô′tär kē), *n., pl.* **-chies**. an absolute or autocratic rule; despotism. [< Greek *autarchiā* autocracy < *aútarchos* an absolute ruler < *autós* self + *archós* leader]

au|tar|chy[2] (ô′tär kē), *n., pl.* **-chies**. = autarky. [< Greek *autárkeia;* see etym. under **autarky**]

au|tar|kic (ô tär′kik), *adj.* of or having to do with autarky; resembling autarky.

au|tar|kist (ô′tär kist), *n., adj.* **—*n.*** a person who advocates autarky. **—*adj.*** of autarky.

au|tar|ky (ô′tär kē), *n., pl.* **-kies**. independence of imports from other countries; economic self-sufficiency. [< Greek *autárkeia* < *autárkēs* self-sufficient < *autós* self + *arkeîn* suffice]

aut Cae|sar aut ni|hil or **nul|lus** (ôt sē′zər ôt nī′hil, nul′əs; out kī′sär out ni′hil, nůl′ůs), *Latin.* either great success or utter failure; either a Caesar or a nobody.

au|te|cious (ô tē′shəs), *adj.* = autoecious.

au|te|cism (ô tē′siz əm), *n.* = autoecism.

au|te|col|o|gy (ô′tə kol′ə jē), *n.* the branch of ecology dealing with the biological relation between a single species, or an individual organism, and its environment.

au|teur (ô tœr′), *n. French.* **1** a motion-picture director whose films have a distinctive personal style. **2** (literally) author.

auth., **1** authentic. **2** author. **3** authorized.

au|then|tic (ô then′tik), *adj.* **1** worthy of trust, belief, or acceptance; reliable: *We heard an authentic account of the wreck, given by one of the ship's officers.* SYN: authoritative. **2** coming from the source stated; not copied; genuine; real: *We saw an authentic letter written by George Washington.* SYN: true. **3** *Music.* **a** designating a cadence in which the final chord of the dominant immediately precedes that of the tonic. **b** designating a church mode whose sounds are comprised within an octave from the keynote. See syn. under **genuine**. [< Late Latin *authenticus* < Greek *authentikós* < *autós* self + *-héntēs* one who acts] **—au|then′ti|cal|ly**, *adv.*

au|then|ti|cal (ô then′tə kəl), *adj.* = authentic.

au|then|ti|cate (ô then′tə kāt), *v.t.,* **-cat|ed, -cat|ing**. **1** to establish the truth of; show to be genuine; prove authentic: *The art dealer authenticated the painting as an original.* SYN: See syn. under **confirm**. **2** to make valid or authoritative; establish the validity of: *The corporation's seal authenticated the contract.* **3** to establish the authorship of. **—au|then′ti|ca′tion**, *n.* **—au|then′ti|ca′tor**, *n.*

au|then|tic|i|ty (ô′then tis′ə tē), *n.* **1** reliability: *The value of the evidence depends on its authenticity.* **2** genuineness: *The lawyer questioned the authenticity of the signature.*

au|thor (ô′thər), *n., v.* **—*n.*** **1** a person who writes books, poems, stories, or articles; writer: *My little brother's favorite author is Dr. Seuss.* **2** the works of an author; an author's publications: *Have you read this author?* **3** a person who creates or begins anything: *Are you the author of this scheme?* SYN: creator, inventor, originator, maker. **4** the person responsible for anything.
—*v.t.* to be the author of; write; compose.
[< Old French *autor,* learned borrowing from Latin *auctor* (literally) one who causes to grow < *augēre* to increase] **—au′thor|less**, *adj.*

au|thor|ess (ô′thər is), *n.* a woman author.

au|tho|ri|al (ô thôr′ē əl, -thōr′-), *adj.* of or having to do with an author. **—au|tho′ri|al|ly**, *adv.*

au|thor|ise (ô′thə rīz), *v.t.,* **-ised, -is|ing**. *British.* authorize.

au|thor|i|tar|i|an (ə thôr′ə tãr′ē ən, -thor′-), *adj., n.* **—*adj.*** favoring obedience to authority instead of individual freedom: *An authoritarian government will often censor newspapers. Authoritarian regimes insist on deciding themselves what is proper for the people to know* (C. L. Sulzberger). SYN: totalitarian. **—*n.*** a person who favors obedience to authority instead of individual freedom.

au|thor|i|tar|i|an|ism (ə thôr′ə tãr′ē ə niz′əm, -thor′-), *n.* the principle of obedience to authority; body of principles underlying authoritarian belief or practice: *The authoritarianism of dictatorship is usually shattered in revolution. The sciences . . . have endeavored to dispossess authoritarianism and to substitute for it direct, confirmable observation* (Bulletin of Atomic Scientists).

au|thor|i|ta|tive (ə thôr′ə tā′tiv, -thor′-), *adj.* **1** having authority; officially ordered; proceeding from a recognized authority: *Authoritative orders came to the ambassador from the president.* SYN: official. **2** of or characterized by authority; commanding: *In authoritative tones the policeman shouted, "Keep back."* SYN: peremptory, imperious. **3** that ought to be believed or obeyed; entitled to obedience or respect; having the authority of expert knowledge: *A doctor's statement concerning the cause of an illness is considered authoritative. We have long desired an authoritative edition of this author's works.* SYN: valid, authentic. **—au|thor′i|ta′tive|ly**, *adv.* **—au|thor′i|ta′tive|ness**, *n.*

au|thor|i|ty (ə thôr′ə tē, -thor′-), *n., pl.* **-ties**. **1** the power to enforce obedience; right to control, command, or make decisions; jurisdiction: *A father has authority over his children. A policeman has the authority to arrest speeding drivers.* **2** a person, body, board, or the like, that has such power, right, or jurisdiction: *The authority came to the door and asked why I wasn't in school.* **3** a source of correct information or wise advice; book or passage regarded as settling a disputed point: *A good dictionary is an authority on the meanings of words.* **4** an expert on some subject; person whose advice or opinion is accepted: *He is an authority on the Revolutionary War. Recognizing all these pitfalls, many authorities . . . insist economists should never make precise predictions* (Newsweek). **5** power over the opinions of others; influence that commands respect and confidence: *the authority of Aristotle.* SYN: prestige. **6** delegated power; authorization: *An appointed official derives his authority from the President.* **7** a judicial opinion that may be cited as a precedent.
the authorities, the officials in control; government of a country, state, or local area: *Who are the proper authorities to give permits to hunt or fish?*
[< Old French *auctorite,* learned borrowing from Latin *auctōritās* < *auctor* author]
—*Syn.*1 Authority, control, influence mean power to direct or act on others. **Authority** often implies legal power, given by a person's position or office, to give commands and enforce obedience: *Teachers have authority over pupils.* **Control** applies to power, given by a person's position, to direct people and things: *Parents should have control over their children.* **Influence** applies to personal power, coming from a person's character, personality, or position, to shape the actions of others: *Some teachers have great influence over young people.*

Au|thor|i|ty (ə thôr′ə tē, -thor′-), *n., pl.* **-ties**. *U.S.* a government body that runs some activity or business on behalf of the public. Authorities provide electricity for housing, develop ports, build turnpikes, and perform other public business functions. *New York Port Authority, Tennessee Valley Authority.*

au|thor|i|za|tion (ô′thər ə zā′shən), *n.* **1** the act or process of giving legal power to; authorizing: *The authorization of policemen to arrest beggars put an end to begging on the streets.* **2** official permission; legal right; sanction; warrant: *Congress gave the President authorization to help underdeveloped countries.*

au|thor|ize (ô′thə rīz), *v.t.,* **-ized, -iz|ing**. **1** to give power or right to: *The principal was authorized to speak for the teachers. The President authorized his ambassador to sign the treaty.* SYN: empower. **2** to make legal; approve; sanction: *Congress authorized the spending of money for a new post office.* SYN: commission. **3** to give authority for; justify: *The dictionary authorizes the two spellings "traveler" and "traveller."* [< Old French *autoriser* < Medieval Latin *auctorizare* < Latin *auctor* author] **—au′thor|iz′er**, *n.*

au|thor|ized (ô′thə rīzd), *adj.* **1** having authority; authoritative. **2** supported or sanctioned by authority.

Authorized Version, the English translation of the Bible published in 1611 during the reign of James I of England (and therefore often called the *King James Version*). *Abbr:* A.V.

author's alteration, a change in the original version of a manuscript, made by an author after the printer has set the manuscript in type.

au|thor|ship (ô′thər ship), *n.* **1** the origin as to author: *What is the authorship of that novel?* **2** the source or cause of anything. **3** the occupation of an author; writing: *The profession of literature, or to speak more plainly, the trade of*

authorship (Samuel Taylor Coleridge).
Auth. Ver., Authorized Version (of the Bible).
au|tism (ô′tiz əm), *n.* a disorder in development that usually begins before the age of four, characterized especially by an inability to relate socially to other people. [< New Latin *autismus* < Greek *autós* self]
au|tist (ô′tist), *n.* a person who tries to escape from reality by indulging in fantasy.
au|tis|tic (ô tis′tik), *adj., n.* **—adj.** of or characterized by autism; lacking interest in or awareness of external reality.
—n. an autistic person, especially a child.
au|to (ô′tō), *n., pl.* **-tos.** = automobile.
auto-[1], *combining form.* **1** self: *Autohypnosis = self-hypnosis.*
2 of or by oneself: *Autobiography = biography of oneself.* Also, **aut-**. [< Greek *autós* self]
auto-[2], *combining form.* automobile; vehicle: *Automaker = automobile maker.* [< *automobile*]
auto., **1** automatic. **2** automotive.
au|to|ag|gres|sive (ô′tō ə gres′iv), *adj.* = autoimmune.
au|to|a|nal|y|sis (ô′tō ə nal′ə sis), *n., pl.* **-ses** (-sēz). **1** psychological analysis of a person by himself. **2** analysis by an autoanalyzer.
au|to|an|a|lyz|er (ô′tō an′ə lī′zər), *n.* an electronic or mechanical device that automatically analyzes a thing.
au|to|an|ti|bod|y (ô′tō an′tē bod′ē), *n., pl.* **-bod-ies.** an antibody that attacks the body's own cells and tissues.
au|to|bahn or **Au|to|bahn** (ô′tō bän′, ou′-), *n., pl.* **-bahns, -bah|nen** (-bä′nən). (in Germany) an express highway; turnpike or expressway. [< German *Autobahn* < *Auto* (for *Automobil* automobile) + *Bahn* highway, road]
au|to|bike (ô′tō bīk), *n. British.* a motorbike.
au|to|bi|og|ra|pher (ô′tə bī og′rə fər, -bi-), *n.* a person who writes the story of his own life.
au|to|bi|o|graph|ic (ô′tə bī′ə graf′ik), *adj.* = autobiographical.
au|to|bi|o|graph|i|cal (ô′tə bī′ə graf′ə kəl), *adj.* **1** having to do with the story of one's own life. **2** telling or writing the story of one's own life: *The novel has about it such a solid air of reality that I originally suspected a sizable element might be autobiographical* (Atlantic). **—au′to|bi′o|graph′i|cal|ly,** *adv.*
au|to|bi|og|ra|phy (ô′tə bī og′rə fē, -bi-), *n., pl.* **-phies. 1** the story of a person's life written by himself. **2** the writing of such an account.
au|to|cade (ô′tō kād), *n.* = motorcade.
au|to|car (ô′tō kär), *n. Rare.* an automobile.
au|to|ca|tal|y|sis (ô′tō kə tal′ə sis), *n. Chemistry.* the catalysis of a reaction by a product of its own making.
au|to|cat|a|lyt|ic (ô′tō kat′ə lit′ik), *adj.* **1** of autocatalysis. **2** resembling autocatalysis.
au|to|ce|phal|ic (ô′tō sə fal′ik), *adj.* = autocephalous.
au|to|ceph|a|lous (ô′tō sef′ə ləs), *adj.* independent of jurisdiction; self-governing, as certain Greek Orthodox churches, bishops, or ministers. [< Late Greek *autoképhalos* (with English *-ous*) < *autós* self + *kephalê* head]
au|toch|thon (ô tok′thən), *n., pl.* **-thons, -thon|es** (-thə nēz). **1** a person sprung from the land he inhabits; a native. **2** one of the native animals or plants of a region. [< Latin *autochthonēs* (plural) < Greek *autóchthōn* sprung from the land itself < *autós* self + *chthṓn* earth]
au|toch|tho|nism (ô tok′thə niz əm), *n.* autochthonous origin or condition.
au|toch|tho|nous (ô tok′thə nəs), *adj.* **1** originating where found; aboriginal; indigenous. **2** belonging to a region; native: *There is no peace treaty giving it* [the East German regime] *legitimation as an autochthonous government in international law* (Uwe W. Kitzinger).
au|toch|tho|ny (ô tok′thə nē), *n.* autochthonous condition.
au|to|cide (ô′tə sīd), *n.* an automobile crash that causes one's own death. [< *auto-*[2] + (sui)*cide*]
au|to|clave (ô′tə klāv), *n., v.,* **-claved, -clav|ing.** **—n. 1** a strong, closed vessel used especially for sterilizing and cooking. It develops superheated steam under pressure. *The autoclave is practically the same as a pressure cooker* (Fred W. Emerson). **2** a heavy vessel for chemical reactions which require high pressure.
—v.t., v.i. to sterilize or cook in an autoclave. [< French *autoclave* (literally) self-locking < Greek *autós* self + Latin *clāvis* key]
au|to|code (ô′tō kōd), *n., v.,* **-cod|ed, -cod|ing.** **—n. 1** a method of programming a digital computer to produce or adapt automatically the code it needs for solving a problem. **2** the resulting code. **3** the program for such a code.
—v.i. to devise such a program or code.
au|to|coid (ô′tə koid), *n.* = autacoid.
au|to|col|li|ma|tion (ô′tō kol′ə mā′shən), *n.* collimation of an optical instrument by the use of a flat mirror in which the objective lens is reflected.
au|to|col|li|ma|tor (ô′tō kol′ə mā′tər), *n.* a type of telescope used in autocollimation.
auto court, *U.S.* **1** a group of cabins providing shelter for automobile travelers. **2** a motel.
au|toc|ra|cy (ô tok′rə sē), *n., pl.* **-cies. 1a** government by a single person having unrestricted power. **b** a country or state that has such a government. **2** absolute authority; unlimited power or influence in any sphere or group of persons. **3** *Obsolete.* independent power. [< Greek *autokráteia* < *autokratês* autocrat]
au|to|crat (ô′tə krat), *n.* **1** a ruler having unrestricted power over his subjects; absolute ruler: *A dictator usually demands the power of an autocrat.* SYN: despot, dictator. **2** a person who uses his power over others in a harsh way: *A policeman should never be an autocrat.* [< Greek *autokratês* < *autós* self + *krátos* power]
au|to|crat|ic (ô′tə krat′ik), *adj.* of or like an autocrat; having absolute power or authority; ruling without checks or limitations: *The coach's autocratic manner made him unpopular among the players on the team.* SYN: despotic, dictatorial. **—au′to|crat′i|cal|ly,** *adv.*
au|to|crat|i|cal (ô′tə krat′ə kəl), *adj.* = autocratic.
au|to|crit|i|cal (ô′tə krit′ə kəl), *adj.* critical of oneself or of one's own work.
au|to|crit|i|cism (ô′tə krit′ə siz əm), *n.* critical analysis and evaluation of oneself or one's achievements: *Believing that the police will send in a bad report to his firm, he makes an autocriticism of his guilt* (Manchester Guardian Weekly).
au|to|cy|cle (ô′tō sī′kəl), *n. Especially British.* a motorcycle.
au|to-da-fé (ô′tō də fā′, ou′-), *n., pl.* **au|tos-da-fé. 1** the public ceremony accompanying the passing of sentence by the Spanish Inquisition. **2** the act of burning a heretic. [< Portuguese *auto da fé* act of the faith]
au|to de fé (ou′tō dā fā′), *Spanish.* auto-da-fé.
au|to|di|dact (ô′tō di dakt′, -dī-), *n.* a self-taught person: *Every American is an autodidact; every American feels himself capable of being the founder of his own religion* (Thornton Wilder).
au|to|di|dac|tic (ô′tō di dak′tik, -dī-), *adj.* = self-taught.
au|to|dom (ô′tō dəm), *n. U.S.* the world of automobile manufacturing and selling: *... autodom's hottest competition since before the war* (Time).
au|to|drome (ô′tō drōm), *n.* a race course for automobiles. [< *auto-*[2] + *-drome*]
au|to|dyne (ô′tə dīn), *adj. Radio.* of or denoting a type of heterodyne reception in which the detector tube serves as oscillator.
au|toe|cious (ô tē′shəs), *adj.* going through all stages of the life cycle on the same host. Some parasitic fungi are autoecious. Also, **autecious.** [< Greek *autós* same + *oikíā* house]
au|toe|cism (ô tē′siz əm), *n.* the fact of being autoecious. Also, **autecism.**
au|to|e|rot|ic (ô′tō ē rot′ik), *adj.* of or having to do with autoeroticism. **—au′to|e|rot′i|cal|ly,** *adv.*
au|to|e|rot|i|cism (ô′tō ē rot′ə siz əm), *n.* sex gratification by one's own body or mind.
au|to|er|o|tism (ô′tō er′ə tiz əm), *n.* = autoeroticism.
au|to|ette (ô′tō et′), *n.* a small, three-wheeled motor vehicle. [< *auto-*[2] + *-ette*]
au|to|fo|cus (ô′tə fō′kəs), *adj., n., v. Photography.* **—adj.** that can focus automatically: *autofocus cameras.*
—n. automatic focusing of a camera lens: *Autofocus ... allows you to concentrate more completely on taking pictures because you're less distracted by setting the lens* (Lou Jacobs, Jr.).
—v.i., v.t. to focus automatically.
au|to|gam|ic (ô′tə gam′ik), *adj. Botany.* characterized by or adapted to autogamy.
au|tog|a|mous (ô tog′ə məs), *adj. Botany.* self-fertilized.
au|tog|a|my (ô tog′ə mē), *n.* **1** *Botany.* self-fertilization; fecundation of the ovules of a flower by its own pollen. **2** *Biology.* the mating of like with like. [< *auto-*[1] + *-gamy*]
au|to|gen|e|sis (ô′tō jen′ə sis), *n. Biology.* spontaneous generation; self-production; abiogenesis.
au|to|ge|net|ic (ô′tō jə net′ik), *adj.* **1** = self-generated. **2** *Biology.* having to do with autogenesis. **—au′to|ge|net′i|cal|ly,** *adv.*
au|tog|e|nous (ô toj′ə nəs), *adj.* **1** produced by or within oneself; self-produced; self-generated. **2** arising in, or derived from, a given body, such as a bacterial vaccine prepared from bacteria present in the patient's own body. [< Greek *autogenês* self-produced (< *autós* self + *-genês* born) + English *-ous*]
au|tog|e|ny (ô toj′ə nē), *n.* = autogenesis.
au|to|gi|ro (ô′tə jī′rō), *n., pl.* **-ros.** a propeller-driven wingless aircraft supported in flight by a large rotor above the fuselage that spins from the air pressure against its blades. Also, **autogyro.** [< Spanish *autogiro* < Greek *autós* self + *gyros* circle]
Au|to|gi|ro (ô′tə jī′rō), *n. Trademark.* autogiro.
au|to|graft (ô′tō graft, -gräft), *n., v.* **—n.** a graft of skin or other tissue taken from the body of the grafted person rather than from another person; autotransplant.
—v.t., v.i. to transplant an autograft.
au|to|graph (ô′tə graf, -gräf), *n., v.* **—n. 1** a person's name written by himself: *Many people collect the autographs of celebrities.* **2** something written in a person's own handwriting, especially the original copy of a manuscript, letter, or other document. SYN: holograph.
—v.t. 1 to write one's name in or on: *The star of the play autographed my program.* **2** to write with one's own hand. [< Late Latin *autographum* < Greek *autógraphon* < *autós* self + *gráphein* write]
au|to|graph|ic (ô′tə graf′ik), *adj.* **1** of or for an autograph. **2** in one's own handwriting. **—au′to|graph′i|cal|ly,** *adv.*
au|to|graph|i|cal (ô′tə graf′ə kəl), *adj.* = autographic.
au|tog|ra|phy (ô tog′rə fē), *n.* **1** autograph writing. **2** autographs collectively. **3** a lithographic process by which writing or drawing is transferred from paper to stone or other reproducing surface.
au|to|gy|ro (ô′tə jī′rō), *n., pl.* **-ros.** = autogiro.
***au|to|harp** (ô′tō härp′), *n.* a type of zither, provided with dampers for the mechanical production of chordal effects.

***autoharp**

au|to|hyp|no|sis (ô′tō hip nō′sis), *n.* self-induced hypnosis or hypnotic state.
au|to|hyp|not|ic (ô′tō hip not′ik), *adj.* of or having to do with autohypnosis.
au|to|hyp|no|tism (ô′tō hip′nə tiz əm), *n.* = autohypnosis.
au|toi|cous (ô toi′kəs), *adj.* having both male and female inflorescence on the same plant, as certain mosses. [< *aut-* + Greek *oíkos* house + *-ous*]
au|to|ig|ni|tion (ô′tō ig nish′ən), *n.* = preignition.
au|to|im|mune (ô′tō i myün′), *adj.* of, having to do with, or caused by autoantibodies: *Another immunological problem under study is "autoimmune disease," a condition in which an individual's tissues may be attacked by his own antibodies* (James P. Hendrix).
au|to|im|mu|ni|ty (ô′tō i myü′nə tē), *n., pl.* **-ties.** the condition in which the body forms autoantibodies; production of antibodies that attack the body's own cells and tissues.
au|to|im|mu|ni|za|tion (ô′tō im′yů nə zā′shən), *n.* = autoimmunity.
au|to|in|fec|tion (ô′tō in fek′shən), *n.* infection from within the organism; self-infection.
au|to|in|oc|u|la|tion (ô′tō i nok′yə lā′shən), *n.* **1** inoculation of a healthy part of a person with a virus or other microorganism from a diseased part of his own body. **2** the spread of infection from its center to other parts of the person.
au|to|in|tox|i|ca|tion (ô′tō in tok′sə kā′shən), *n.* poisoning by or resulting from toxin formed within the body; autotoxemia.
au|to|ist (ô′tō ist), *n.* = motorist.
au|to|ki|ne|sis (ô′tō ki nē′sis), *n.* self-movement; spontaneous motion.
au|to|ki|net|ic (ô′tō ki net′ik), *adj.* self-moving; automatic. [< Greek *autokīnētos* self-moved (< *autós* self + *kīneîn* to move) + English *-ic*]
auto lift, a mechanical device for lifting an automobile to permit examination or repair of the undersides.
au|to|load|er (ô′tō lō′dər), *n. U.S.* a semiautomatic rifle, pistol, or other gun.
au|to|load|ing (ô′tō lō′ding), *adj. U.S.* semiautomatic: *an autoloading firearm.*
au|tol|o|gous (ô tol′ə gəs), *adj.* **1** transplanted from the same person's body: *an autologous graft.* See also **autograft. 2** donated by a person and preserved for his own future use: *autologous blood. Self-donated (autologous) transfusions prevent your contracting an infectious disease, such as AIDS or hepatitis* (Woman's Day). [< *auto-*[1] + Greek *lógos* relation]

Pronunciation Key: hat, āge, cãre, fär; let, ēqual, tėrm; it, īce; hot, ōpen, ôrder; oil, out; cup, pu̇t, rüle; child; long; thin; ᴛʜen; zh, measure; ə represents **a** in about, **e** in taken, **i** in pencil, **o** in lemon, **u** in circus.

Au|tol|y|cus (ô tol′ə kəs), *n. Greek Mythology.* the thieving son of the god Hermes.

au|to|ly|sate (ô′tə lī′sāt, ô tol′ə-), *n.* a product of autolysis.

au|to|ly|sin (ô′tə lī′sin, ô tol′ə-), *n.* a substance, such as an enzyme, capable of breaking down the cells or tissues of an organism within which it is produced, especially after death or in some diseased conditions.

au|tol|y|sis (ô tol′ə sis), *n.* the disintegration of tissue, especially of plant or animal tissue separated from the plant or animal, by the action of enzymes present within its own cells. [< *auto-*[1] + Greek *lýsis* a breaking down]

au|to|lyt|ic (ô′tə lit′ik), *adj.* of or having to do with autolysis.

au|to|lyze (ô′tə līz), *v.*, **-lyzed, -lyz|ing.** *—v.i.* to undergo autolysis. *—v.t.* to cause autolysis.

au|to|mak|er (ô′tō mā′kər), *n.* an automobile manufacturer.

au|to|ma|nip|u|la|tion (ô′tə mə nip′yə lā′shən), *n.* masturbation; autoeroticism.

au|to|mat (ô′tə mat), *n.* a cafeteria in which food is obtained from compartments that can be opened after coins are inserted in slots. [< German *Automat* < Greek *autómatos* automatic]

au|tom|a|ta (ô tom′ə tə), *n.pl.* automatons; a plural of **automaton.**

au|to|mate (ô′tə māt), *v.*, **-mat|ed, -mat|ing.** *—v.t.* to convert to automation; operate by automation: *As steel plants have become more automated, maintenance and adjustments of equipment have become a larger share of the cost of running the mills* (Wall Street Journal). *—v.i.* to make use of automation.
[back formation < *automation*]

au|to|mat|ic (ô′tə mat′ik), *adj., n. —adj.* **1** moving or acting by itself; regulating itself: *an automatic lock, an automatic pump. When you press a button the automatic elevator takes you to the floor you want.* SYN: self-regulating. **2** done without thought or attention; not voluntary: *Breathing and swallowing are usually automatic. His anger was an automatic response to her insult.* **3a** reloading by itself: *an automatic pistol.* **b** of an automatic firearm: *under heavy automatic fire from a rebel ambush* (London Times).
—n. **1** a pistol or other gun that throws out the empty shell and loads a new cartridge by itself. An automatic that is fully self-acting continues to fire until the pressure on the trigger is released. The semiautomatic fires a single shot each time the trigger is pulled. **2** a self-acting machine: *This dishwasher is an automatic.* **3** the position or condition necessary for automatic action: *The record player is on automatic and will shut itself off.*
[< Greek *autómatos* self-acting (< *autós* self + *-matos* thinking, related to *ménos* intention; mind) + English *-ic*] **—au′to|mat′i|cal|ly,** *adv.*
—Syn. adj. **2 Automatic, involuntary** mean not controlled by the will. **Automatic** means done unconsciously due to a natural or habitual reaction to a situation or stimulus: *My automatic response when I see a red light while driving is to brake.* **Involuntary** means done without conscious intention: *I gave an involuntary jump when the door slammed.*

automatic direction finder, a radio receiving set that automatically indicates the direction of the station or stations to which it is tuned, used especially on aircraft.

automatic drive, = automatic transmission.

au|tom|a|tic|i|ty (ô tom′ə tis′ə tē), *n.* the degree of a machine's ability to function automatically. The order of a machine's automaticity is raised each time it is designed to duplicate an additional faculty of man.

automatic pilot, a gyroscopic mechanism designed to keep an aircraft, missile, and the like on a given course and at a given altitude without human assistance; autopilot. In an automatic pilot, gyroscopes, servomechanisms, and other devices make automatic adjustments of the control surfaces to maintain the desired course and attitude, now usually by fixing on a stellar object in combination with radio signals.

automatic pistol, = automatic.

automatic teller, an electronic machine that releases cash, records, deposits, makes change, etc., upon insertion of an identification card and the pressing of appropriate buttons: *Bankers big and small are rushing to install automatic tellers in their branches* (Time).

automatic teller machine, = automatic teller.

automatic transmission or **shift,** any automotive transmission that shifts gears automatically and does not require a clutch. Most types of automatic transmission transmit driving power to the wheels by means of a set of turbine blades which forces oil or other fluid against another set of turbine blades or through a torque converter transmitting power in turn to sets of gears operated by liquid. The flow of liquid is controlled by combinations of valves; automatic drive.

au|to|ma|tion (ô′tə mā′shən), *n.* **1** the use of automatic controls in the operation of machinery. In automation, electronic or mechanical devices do many of the tasks formerly done by people. *Actually automation is based upon the concept of "feedback" or self-regulation of a machine or process. In automation feedback is of paramount concern. The operation is designed in such a manner that information concerning its status at any given point is signaled to a preceding point where corrective action can be taken if necessary* (New York Times). **2** the method of making something, such as a manufacturing process or a production line, operate automatically by the use of built-in or supplementary controls in machinery. [< *autom*(atic) + *-ation*]

au|tom|a|tism (ô tom′ə tiz əm), *n.* **1** action not controlled by the will; involuntary action; automatic action. **2** the quality or condition of being automatic or of acting mechanically only. **3** *Philosophy.* the doctrine that all living creatures, including human beings, are machines, controlled not by consciousness, which exists only as an adjunct, but by physiological necessity. **4** *Physiology.* the act or fact of functioning without an external stimulus, or as the result of an external stimulus but without conscious thought or attention; automatic or involuntary action. **5** *Psychology.* any reflex or thoroughly habitual act performed by a person without his conscious intent. **6** (in surrealism) a method of releasing subconscious images and feelings for artistic expression, by deliberate suspension of conscious mental controls.

au|tom|a|tist (ô tom′ə tist), *n. Philosophy.* a person who holds the doctrine of automatism.

au|tom|a|tize (ô tom′ə tīz), *v.t., v.i.,* **-tized, -tiz|ing. 1** to make or become automatic. **2** = automate. **—au|tom′a|ti|za′tion,** *n.*

au|tom|a|ton (ô tom′ə ton, -tən), *n., pl.* **-tons, -ta** (-tə). **1** a person or animal whose actions are entirely mechanical. **2** a machine or toy that has its motive power concealed so that it appears to move spontaneously: *The man was selling little automatons in the shape of different animals.* **3** any thing able to move itself. [< Greek *autómaton,* neuter of *autómatos;* see etym. under **automatic**]

au|to|mo|bile (*n.* ô′tə mə bēl; ô′tə mə bēl′, -mō′bēl; *adj.* ô′tə mō′bəl, -bēl; *v.* ô′tə mə bēl′, -mō′bēl; ô′tə mə bēl), *n., adj., v.,* **-biled, -bil|ing.** *—n. Especially U.S.* a passenger vehicle on four wheels, run by its own motor especially on streets and roads (in Great Britain, usually called a *motorcar*).
—adj. **1** of or for automobiles: *an automobile engine, an automobile mechanic.* **2** self-propelled.
—v.i. to travel by automobile.
[< French *automobile* < Greek *autós* self + French *mobile* moving, mobile]

au|to|mo|bil|ism (ô′tə mə bē′liz əm, -mō′bə-), *n.* the use of automobiles.

au|to|mo|bil|ist (ô′tə mə bē′list, -mō′bə-), *n. Especially U.S.* a person who uses an automobile; motorist.

au|to|mo|bil|i|ty (ô′tō mō bil′ə tē), *n.* the driving or use of automobiles; automobilism: *"Freedom of Automobility" [is] the slogan of the National Highway Users Conference* (Harper's).

au|to|mor|phic (ô′tə môr′fik), *adj.* characterized by the ascription of one's own attributes to others.[< *auto-*[1] + Greek *morphḗ* form + English *-ic*]

au|to|mo|tive (ô′tə mō′tiv), *adj.* **1** of or having to do with cars, trucks, and other self-propelled vehicles. Automotive engineering deals with the design and construction of motor vehicles. **2** furnishing its own power; moving by itself; self-propelled: *A truck is one type of automotive vehicle.*

au|to|nom|ic (ô′tə nom′ik), *adj.* **1** *Zoology.* of or having to do with the autonomic nervous system. **2** *Botany.* caused by internal stimuli; spontaneous. **3** = autonomous (defs. 1, 2). **—au′to|nom′i|cal|ly,** *adv.*

au|to|nom|i|cal (ô′tə nom′ə kəl), *adj.* = autonomic.

autonomic nervous system, the ganglia and nerves of the nervous system of vertebrates that control involuntary reactions, such as digestive and reproductive processes and breathing.

au|ton|o|mism (ô ton′ə miz′əm), *n.* the principle or policy of autonomy. **—au|ton′o|mist,** *n., adj.*

au|ton|o|mis|tic (ô ton′ə mis′tik), *adj.* = autonomist.

au|ton|o|mous (ô ton′ə məs), *adj.* **1** independent; self-governing: *Many former African colonies have become autonomous nations. The autonomous individual, striving to realize himself and prove his worth, has created all that is great in literature, art, music, science, and technology* (Harper's). **2** of or having to do with an autonomy. **3** *Zoology, Botany.* = autonomic (defs. 1, 2). [< Greek *autónomos* (with English *-ous*) < *autós* self + *nómos* law] **—au|ton′o|mous|ly,** *adv.*

au|ton|o|my (ô ton′ə mē), *n., pl.* **-mies. 1** independence; self-government (contrasted with *heteronomy*): *Algeria achieved autonomy from France in 1962.* **2** a self-governing state or community. [< Greek *autonomíā* < *autónomos* autonomous]

au|to|nym (ô′tə nim), *n.* **1** a real name or one's own name, especially the real name of an author: *Samuel Langhorne Clemens was the autonym of Mark Twain.* **2** a book published under the author's real name. [< *aut-* + dialectal Greek *ónyma* name]

au|to-ox|i|da|tion (ô′tō ok′sə dā′shən), *n.* = autoxidation.

au|to|phag|ic (ô′tə faj′ik), *adj.* of or characterized by autophagy.

au|toph|a|gy (ô tof′ə jē), *n.* the process of breaking down parts of a cell by the cell's own lysosomes. [< *auto-*[1] + Greek *phageîn* eat]

au|to|phyte (ô′tə fīt), *n.* any plant which can manufacture its own food from simple compounds. [< *auto-*[1] + Greek *phytón* plant]

au|to|pi|lot (ô′tō pī′lət), *n.* = automatic pilot.

au|to|pis|ta (ô′tō pis′tə, ou′tō pēs′tä), *n.* (in Spanish-speaking countries) a turnpike or expressway. [< Spanish *autopista*]

au|to|plas|tic (ô′tə plas′tik), *adj.* of or having to do with autoplasty; using autoplasty.

au|to|plas|ty (ô′tə plas′tē), *n.* the act or process of repairing wounds or diseased parts with tissue taken from other parts of the same body. [< *auto-*[1] + Greek *plastós* molded]

au|to|pol|y|ploid (ô′tə pol′ə ploid), *n. Genetics.* a polyploid the chromosomes of which all come from the same species and are identical: *Many garden flowers are autopolyploids.*

au|top|sic (ô top′sik), *adj.* **1** of or having to do with an autopsy or autopsies; post-mortem. **2** = autoptic.

au|top|sist (ô′top sist, -təp-), *n.* a person who makes an autopsy; medical examiner.

au|top|sy (ô′top sē, -təp-), *n., pl.* **-sies,** *v.,* **-sied, -sy|ing.** *—n.* **1** a medical examination of a dead body to find the cause of death or the character and site of the disease of which the person died; post-mortem; necropsy: *The autopsy revealed that the dead man had been poisoned.* **2** *Figurative.* any critical analysis or thorough examination, as of a book or an event.
—v.t. to perform an autopsy upon (a corpse).
[< New Latin *autopsia* < Greek *autopsíā* personal examination < *autós* self + *optós* visible]

au|top|tic (ô top′tik), *adj.* having to do with or based on personal observation. **—au|top′ti|cal|ly,** *adv.*

au|top|ti|cal (ô top′tə kəl), *adj.* = autoptic.

au|to|put (ô′tō püt′, -ou′-), *n.* (in Yugoslavia) a turnpike or expressway. [< Serbo-Croatian *autoput*]

au|to|ra|di|o|gram (ô′tō rā′dē ō gram), *n.* = autoradiograph.

au|to|ra|di|o|graph (ô′tō rā′dē ō graf, -gräf), *n.* a photograph made by autoradiography.

au|to|ra|di|o|graph|ic (ô′tō rā′dē ō graf′ik), *adj.* **1** of an autoradiograph. **2** of autoradiography.

au|to|ra|di|og|ra|phy (ô′tō rā′dē og′rə fē), *n.* the process of recording radioactive particles by their own tracks on photographic film or plates in an electron-sensitive emulsion. This process can be used to discover the constitution of minerals and to locate accurately radioactive atoms in a thin section of tissue or mineral.

au|to|ro|tate (ô′tō rō′tāt), *v.i.,* **-tat|ed, -tat|ing.** to rotate freely without engine power: *If all power fails, any helicopter can autorotate down to a safe landing* (Harper's).

au|to|ro|ta|tion (ô′tō rō tā′shən), *n. Aeronautics.* **1** the free rotation of rotor blades without engine power. **2** an uncontrolled rolling of an aircraft, as in a spin.

au|to|ro|ta|tion|al (ô′tō rō tā′shə nəl), *adj.* = autorotative.

au|to|ro|ta|tive (ô′tō rō′tə tiv), *adj.* having to do with or made by autorotation.

au|to|route (ô′tō rüt′, -rout′; *French* ô tō rüt′), *n.* (in France, Quebec, and other French-speaking areas) a turnpike or expressway. [< French *autoroute* < *auto* automobile + *route* road, route]

au|to|sen|si|tiv|i|ty (ô′tō sen′sə tiv′ə tē), *n.* = autoimmunity.

au|to|sen|si|ti|za|tion (ô′tō sen′sə tə zā′shən), *n.* = autoimmunity.

au|to|sex|ing (ô′tə sek′sing), *n.* the crossbreeding of poultry to identify sex by a difference in color or other easily recognizable genetic character.

au|to|so|mal (ô′tə sō′məl), *adj.* of or having to do with an autosome or autosomes.

au|to|some (ô′tə sōm), *n. Genetics.* any chromosome that is not a sex chromosome. [< *auto-*[1] + Greek *sôma* body]

au|to|spore (ô′tō spôr′, -spōr′), *n.* = daughter cell.

au|to|sta|bil|i|ty (ô′tō stə bil′ə tē), *n. Physics.* the condition of being stable because of a self-acting mechanism, or because of shape, balance, or mode of suspension.

au|to|sta|bi|liz|er (ô′tō stā′bə lī′zər), *n.* a self-acting mechanism which gives autostability to an aircraft or ship.

au|to|stop (ô′tō stop′), *v.,* **-stopped, -stop|ping,** *n. Especially British.* —*v.i.* to hitchhike.
—*n.* hitchhiking.

au|to|stra|da (ou′tō strä′dä), *n., pl.* **-stra|de** (-strä′de), **-stra|das.** (in Italy) a turnpike or expressway. [< Italian *autostrada* < *auto* (for *automobile*) + *strada* street]

au|to|sug|ges|tion (ô′tō səg jes′chən, -sə jes′-), *n.* **1** suggestion to oneself of ideas that produce mental or physiological effects. **2** a technique for improving health or behavior by repetition of a verbal formula.

au|to|sug|ges|tive (ô′tō səg jes′tiv, -sə jes′-), *adj.* arising from autosuggestion.

au|to|ther|a|py (ô′tō ther′ə pē), *n.* **1** a spontaneous cure. **2** = self-treatment.

au|tot|o|miz|er muscle (ô tot′ə mī′zər), the muscle used to bring about autotomy.

au|tot|o|my (ô tot′ə mē), *n.* the act or process of casting off a part of the body by an animal when disturbed or seeking escape. Certain crustaceans will cast off legs by autotomy and some salamanders and lizards cast off tails by the same process. [< *auto-*[1] + Greek *-tomíā* a cutting]

au|to|tox|e|mi|a or **au|to|tox|ae|mi|a** (ô′tō tok-sē′mē ə), *n.* = autointoxication.

au|to|tox|ic (ô′tə tok′sik), *adj.* causing or caused by an autotoxin.

au|to|tox|in (ô′tō tok′sin), *n.* a poison or toxin formed within the body.

au|to|trans|form|er (ô′tō trans fôr′mər), *n.* a transformer in which part of the primary coil serves also as a secondary, or part of the secondary as the primary coil; compensator.

au|to|trans|fu|sion (ô′tō trans fyü′zhən), *n.* a method of returning a patient's blood to his system upon recapturing and processing it after internal bleeding in surgery or because of trauma: *to perform autotransfusion . . . the blood lost is collected, filtered, and processed, and then introduced back into the patient's circulatory system* (Byron T. Scott).

au|to|trans|plant (ô′tō trans′plant, -plänt), *n.* = autograft.

au|to|trans|plan|ta|tion (ô′tō trans′plan tā′-shən), *n.* transplantation of an autograft.

au|to|troph (ô′tə trof), *n.* an organism that can manufacture its own food from inorganic substances, getting its energy either from photosynthesis or from chemosynthesis, as in certain bacteria. [< *auto-*[1] + Greek *trophē* nourishment]

au|to|troph|ic (ô′tə trof′ik), *adj.* of or having to do with an autotroph; providing its own nourishment: *an autotrophic plant.*

au|to|truck (ô′tō truk), *n. Especially U.S.* a motor truck (in Great Britain, usually, *lorry*).

au|to|type (ô′tə tīp), *n., v.,* **-typed, -typ|ing.** —*n.* **1** = facsimile. **2a** an early photographic process for producing permanent prints in a carbon pigment. **b** a print produced by this process.
—*v.t.* to reproduce by the autotype process.

au|to|typ|ic (ô′tə tip′ik), *adj.* of or reproduced by the autotype process; resembling an autotype.

au|to|typ|y (ô′tə tī′pē), *n.* the autotype process.

au|tox|i|da|tion (ô tok′sə dā′shən), *n. Chemistry.* **1** oxidation by direct combination with oxygen, as by exposure to air. **2** an oxidation reaction that takes place only when an additional substance induces the reaction.

au|tre|fois ac|quit (ō tref wä′ à kē′), *Law.* the plea that the defendant had been tried by another court for the same offense and been acquitted; a plea of double jeopardy. [< French *autrefois acquit* formerly acquitted]

au|tres temps, au|tres moeurs (ō trə täɴ′, ō trə mœrs′), *French.* other times, other ways; times change.

au|tumn (ô′təm), *n., adj.* —*n.* **1** the season of the year between summer and winter; fall. **2** *Figurative.* a time of maturity and the beginning of decay: *the autumn of life.*
—*adj.* of autumn; coming in autumn; in autumn: *autumn leaves, autumn flowers, autumn rains.*
[< Latin *autumnus*]

autumn adonis, = pheasant's-eye.

au|tum|nal (ô tum′nəl), *adj.* **1** of autumn; coming in autumn: *autumnal frosts.* **2** *Figurative.* past the prime (of life, vigor, or other condition).

autumnal equinox, the equinox that occurs about September 23.

au|tum|nal|ly (ô tum′nə lē), *adv.* **1** in or during autumn. **2** in an autumnal manner; as in the colors of autumn.

autumn crocus, = colchicum.

au|tun|ite (ô′tə nīt), *n.* a yellow, radioactive mineral of a hydrous phosphate of uranium and calcium, occurring in tabular crystals with a very nearly square outline. [< Autun, a city in France]

aut vi|tam aut cul|pam (ôt vī′təm ôt kul′pəm; out wē′täm out kůl′päm), *Latin.* for life unless guilty of misconduct (applied especially to a professorial or other academic appointment).

Au|ver|gnat (ō ver nyà′), *n. French.* a native or inhabitant of Auvergne (region in central France).

aux (ō), *French.* to the; at the; with the. It is the form taken by the preposition *à* in combination with the plural of the definite article (*les*).

aux., auxiliary.

aux|a|nom|e|ter (ôk′sə nom′ə tər), *n.* an instrument for measuring the rate of growth in plants. [< Greek *auxánein* to increase + English *-meter*]

aux armes (ō zàrm′), *French.* to arms!

aux|e|sis (ôk sē′sis), *n.* **1** *Biology.* the growth of cells by expansion instead of division. **2** *Rhetoric.* the use of a more unusual and high-sounding word for the ordinary and proper word. [< Greek *aúxēsis*]

auxil., auxiliary.

aux|il|i|ar (ôg zil′ē ər), *adj., n. Archaic.* auxiliary.
—**aux|il′i|ar|ly,** *adv.*

aux|il|ia|ry (ôg zil′yər ē, -zil′ər ē; -ē er′ē), *adj., n., pl.* **-ries.** —*adj.* **1** giving help or support; helping; assisting: *Some sailboats have auxiliary engines. The chief sent only auxiliary firemen to put out the fire.* **2** additional; subsidiary: *an auxiliary purpose. The main library has several auxiliary branches.* SYN: subordinate, supplementary. **3** designed to take the place of the normal apparatus should that break down or fail; kept in reserve or as a substitute: *an auxiliary lighting system.* **4** having an engine as well as sails: *an auxiliary schooner.*
—*n.* **1a** a person or thing that helps; aid: *The microscope is a useful auxiliary to the human eye.* SYN: accessory. **b** a group subsidiary to the main body: *a men's club with a ladies' auxiliary.* **2** = auxiliary verb.
auxiliaries, foreign or allied troops that help the army of a nation at war; mercenaries: *The Roman Empire depended largely on auxiliaries for its defense.*
[< Latin *auxiliārius* < *auxilium* aid]

auxiliary language, a language, such as pidgin English or Interlingua, used as a means of communication among persons who do not speak each other's native language.

auxiliary verb, a verb used to form the tenses, moods, or voices of other verbs; helping verb; verbal auxiliary. *Be, can, do, have, may, must, shall,* and *will* are auxiliary verbs. *Examples:* I am going; he *will* go; they *are* lost; they *must* stop.

aux|in (ôk′sin), *n. Botany.* any hormone of a group synthesized in the protoplasm of the young, active parts of plants, which regulates plant growth and development. [< Greek *aúxein* to increase + English *-in*]

aux|o|chrome (ôk′sə krōm), *n. Chemistry.* any group of atoms capable of making a chromogen into a dye or pigment. [< Greek *aúxē* an increase + *chrōma* color]

aux|o|spore (ôk′sə spôr, -spōr), *n.* a reproductive cell of a diatom. [< Greek *aúxē* an increase + English *spore*]

aux|o|troph (ôk′sə trof), *n.* an organism, especially a bacterium or mold, which through genetic recombination cannot grow on a medium on which its parents could grow because of its requirement of substances the medium does not contain. [< Greek *aúxē* an increase + *trophē* nourishment]

aux|o|troph|ic (ôk′sə trof′ik), *adj.* of or having to do with an auxotroph.

av., **1** avenue. **2** average. **3** avoirdupois.

Av., avenue.

A.V. or **AV** (no periods), **1a** atrioventricular. **b** auriculoventricular. **2** Authorized Version (of the Bible).

A/V (no periods) or **a.v.,** ad valorem.

a|va[1] or **a|va′** (ə vä′), *adv. Scottish.* of all; at all.

a|va[2] (ä′və), *n.* = kava. [< Tahitian *ava*]

av|a|da|vat (av′ə də vat′), *n.* = amadavat.

a|vail (ə vāl′), *v., n.* —*v.t.* to be of use or value to; help: *Your greatest efforts will not avail you now. Money will not avail you after you are dead.* SYN: benefit. —*v.i.* to be of use or value; help: *Talk will avail little without work.*
—*n.* help; use; benefit: *Of what avail is crying over spilt milk? I complained at being scolded, but to no avail.* SYN: profit, advantage, usefulness.
avail oneself of, to take advantage of; profit by; make use of; employ: *While traveling in France, he availed himself of the opportunity to learn French.*
[< Old French *a-* to + *vaill-,* stem of *valoir* be worth < Latin *valēre*] —**a|vail′ing|ly,** *adv.*

a|vail|a|bil|i|ty (ə vā′lə bil′ə tē), *n., pl.* **-ties. 1** the quality or condition of being available; capability of being used; being at hand; being ready: *The availability of water power helped make New England a manufacturing center.* **2** a person, object, or facility that is available.

a|vail|a|ble (ə vā′lə bəl), *adj., n.* —*adj.* **1** that can be used: *The saw is not available for the job; Father is using it.* SYN: usable, obtainable, handy. **2** that can be had: *All available tickets were sold.* SYN: accessible. **3** *Law.* valid: *available rights.* **4** *Obsolete.* of avail; beneficial.
—*n.* an available person or thing: *. . . the leading availables for the party's Presidential nomination* (New York Times). —**a|vail′a|ble|ness,** *n.*

a|vail|a|bly (ə vā′lə blē), *adv.* in an available manner; so as to be used or had readily.

av|a|lanche (av′ə lanch, -länch), *n., v.,* **-lanched, -lanch|ing.** —*n.* **1** a large mass of snow and ice, or of dirt and rocks, rapidly sliding or falling down the side of a mountain. **2** *Figurative.* anything like an avalanche: *The reporters asked the governor an avalanche of questions. An avalanche of books fell off the shelf.*
—*v.i.* to move like an avalanche.
[< French *avalanche* < Swiss French *avalantse,* perhaps < unrecorded *labanca,* of a pre-Latin Alpine language]

avalanche diode, a semiconductor in which a certain applied voltage causes electric charges to gain such an influx of energy that they begin a rapid generation of new charge carriers, with a resulting increase in current.

avalanche lily, a delicate, white flower which blooms profusely in high mountain meadows as soon as the snow melts.

***a|vale|ment** (ə val′mənt; *French* à vál mäɴ′), *n.* a method of skiing fast on turns by leaning far back on one's haunches while thrusting the skis all the way forward. [< French *avalement* < *avaler* to swallow < Old French *avaler* go down]

***avalement**

Av|a|lon or **Av|al|lon** (av′ə lon), *n. Celtic Legend.* an ocean island in the west, an earthly paradise to which King Arthur and other heroes were carried after death, and where Morgan le Fay held her court. Also, **Avilion.**

a|vant-cou|ri|er (ə vänt′kėr′ē ər, -kůr′-), *n.* a person who goes in advance, as a herald.
avant-couriers, the advance guard of an army: *Having suffered 2000 of the enemies' horse* (*the avant-couriers of the Turks' army*) *to pass by him* . . . (Richard Knolles).

a|vant-garde (ä′väɴ gàrd′), *n., adj.* —*n.* a group of people, especially in the arts, who are ahead of all others in using or creating new ideas, methods, designs, or styles.
—*adj.* of or having to do with an avant-garde.
[< French *avant-garde* (literally) advance guard. See etym. of doublet **vanguard.**]

a|vant-gard|ism (ä′väɴ gär′diz əm), *n.* the beliefs and practices of the avant-garde; adherence to or disposition toward avant-garde beliefs or methods: *literary avant-gardism.* —**a′vant-gard′-ist,** *n.*

A|var (ä′vär, ä′-), *n.* **1** a member of a Ural-Altaic people prominent in southeastern Europe during the early Middle Ages, now living in the Caucasus. **2** the Caucasian language of this people.

av|a|rice (av′ər is), *n.* too great a desire to acquire money or property; greed for wealth. SYN: avidity, cupidity. [< Old French *avarice,* learned borrowing from Latin *avāritia* < *avārus* greedy]

av|a|ri|cious (av′ə rish′əs), *adj.* greatly desiring money or property; like a miser; greedy for wealth. SYN: covetous. —**av′a|ri′cious|ly,** *adv.* —**av′a|ri′cious|ness,** *n.*

a|vas|cu|lar (ā vas′kyə lər), *adj.* having few or no blood vessels or lymphatics.

a|vast (ə vast′, -väst′), *interj. Nautical.* stop! stay! hold it!: *"Avast there!" shouted the sailor on watch.* [probably < Dutch *houd vast* hold fast!]

av|a|tar (av′ə tär′), *n.* **1a** *Hinduism.* the descent of a god to earth in bodily form; incarnation. **b** one of the ten appearances of Vishnu in human form. **2** *Figurative.* any manifestation in bodily form; embodiment: *He sees himself quite simply as a kind of technological avatar, come for the liberation of mankind* (Time). [< Sanskrit *avatāra* descent < *ava-* down + *tar* pass over]

Pronunciation Key: hat, āge, cãre, fär; let, ēqual, tėrm; it, īce; hot, ōpen, ôrder; oil, out; cup, půt, rüle; child; long; thin; ᴛʜen; zh, measure; ə represents **a** in about, **e** in taken, **i** in pencil, **o** in lemon, **u** in circus.

a|vaunt (ə vônt′, -vänt′), *interj. Archaic.* begone! get out! go away!: *Avaunt, she cried, offensive to my sight!* (Alexander Pope). [< Old French *avant* forward < Latin *abante* < *ab* from + *ante* before]

avdp., avoirdupois.

a|ve (ā′vē, ä′vā), *interj., n.* **—*interj.*** hail! farewell! **—*n.*** a shout of welcome or farewell.
[< Latin *avē*]

A|ve (ā′vē, ä′vā), *n.* **1a** the prayer Ave Maria. **b** a saying of this prayer. **c** the time for saying it. **2** a rosary bead; an Ave Maria. [< *Ave Maria*]

Ave. or **ave.**, Avenue; avenue.

a|ve at|que va|le (ā′vē at′kwē vā′lē; ä′wā ät′-kwe wä′lā), *Latin.* hail and farewell!

a|vec plai|sir (á vek ple zēr′), *French.* with pleasure.

a|vel|lan (ə vel′ən, av′ə lən), *adj. Heraldry.* designating a kind of cross resembling four filberts in their husks, joined at their larger ends. See the diagram under **cross.** [< Latin *Avellānus* of Avella, an Italian town famous for its fruits and nuts]

A|ve Ma|ri|a (ä′vā mə rē′ə, ä′vē), **1a** "Hail Mary," the first words of the Latin form of a prayer of the Roman Catholic Church. **b** this prayer. **c** a saying of this prayer; an Ave. **2** the time for saying it. **3** a rosary bead. [< Latin *avē Maria*]

A|ve Mar|y (ā′vē mãr′ē), = Ave Maria.

av|e|na|ceous (av′ə nā′shəs), *adj.* **1** of or like oats. **2** belonging to the same genus as the oat.
[< Latin *avēnāceus* (with English *-ous*) < *avēna* oats]

a|venge (ə venj′), *v.,* **a|venged, a|veng|ing.** **—*v.t.*** **1** to get revenge for: *to avenge an insult. He vowed to avenge his brother's murder by tracking down the murderer.* SYN: See syn. under **revenge.** **2** to take vengeance on behalf of: *The clan avenged their slain chief.*
—*v.i.* to get revenge: *Thou shalt not avenge* (Leviticus 19:18). SYN: retaliate.
[< Old French *avengier* < *a-* to + *vengier* < Latin *vindicāre* punish < *vindex* champion]
—a|venge′ment *n.*

a|veng|er (ə ven′jər), *n.* a person who avenges a wrong.

a|veng|ing (ə ven′jing), *adj.* that avenges: *. . . an avenging Deity* (Edward Gibbon). **—a|veng′ing|ly,** *adv.*

av|ens (av′inz), *n.* any perennial plant of a genus of the rose family, native to cold and temperate regions and commonly grown as garden flowers; geum. [< Old French *avence;* origin unknown]

av|en|tail or **av|en|tayle** (av′ən tāl), *n.* = ventail.

a|ven|tu|rine or **a|ven|tu|rin** (ə ven′chər in), *n.* **1** a gold-flecked, brownish-colored glass. **2** a variety of quartz containing bright specks of mica or some other mineral. [< French *aventurine* < Italian *avventurina* < *avventura* chance < Latin *adventūra* adventure (from its supposed accidental discovery and its rarity)]

av|e|nue (av′ə nü, -nyü), *n.* **1** *Especially U.S.* a wide street; main street: *The avenues of the city were crowded with shoppers.* SYN: thoroughfare, boulevard. **2** a wide road or walk bordered by trees: *Many people walked down the avenue through the center of the park.* **3** *Figurative.* a way of approach; passage: *Hard work is one avenue to success.* **4** *Especially U.S.* a city thoroughfare, often running at right angles to others, which are usually shorter or narrower, and called *streets. Abbr:* Ave. [< Middle French *avenue,* (originally) feminine past participle of *avenir* arrive < Latin *advenīre* < *ad-* to + *venīre* come]

a|ver[1] (ə vėr′), *v.t.,* **a|verred, a|ver|ring.** **1** to state to be true; assert positively; affirm: *The man averred that he had nothing to do with breaking into the parked car.* SYN: declare, avouch, asseverate. **2** *Law.* to offer to prove or justify; allege.
[< Old French *averer* < Vulgar Latin *advērāre* < Latin *ad-* + *vērus* true] **—a|ver′ra|ble,** *adj.* **—a|ver′ment,** *n.*

a|ver[2] (ā′vər), *n. Scottish.* a beast of burden.
[< Old French *aveir,* noun use of verb < Latin *habēre* to have]

av|er|age (av′rij, -ər ij), *n., adj., v.,* **-aged, -ag|ing.** **—*n.*** **1** the quantity found by dividing the sum of all the quantities by the number of quantities; arithmetic mean. The average of 3 and 5 and 10 is 6 (3 + 5 + 10 = 18; 18 ÷ 3 = 6). **2** a ratio or percentage indicating a record of achievement: *A good hitter has a high batting average in baseball. The best student in the class had an A average.* **3** the usual sort or amount; the generally normal or typical quantity, degree, rate, quality, or kind: *The amount of rain this year has been below average. His mind is above the average.* SYN: standard, norm. **4** *Commerce.* **a** a small charge, paid by a ship for pilotage, towage, or other expenses of coming into port. **b** an expense or loss arising from damage at sea to ship or cargo. **c** the equitable distribution of such expense or loss among all parties interested. **d** any small charge or expense in addition to freight charges, paid by a shipper of goods. *Abbr:* av.
—*adj.* **1** obtained by averaging; being an average: *an average price. The average temperature for the week was 82.* SYN: mean. **2** usual; ordinary: *average intelligence. The average American boy likes sports.* SYN: medium, middling. **3** *Maritime Law.* estimated or assessed on the rules of average.
—*v.t.* **1** to find the average of: *Will you average those numbers for me?* **2** to have as an average; amount on the average to: *The cost of our lunches at school averaged two dollars a week.* **3** to do, get, or yield, on an average: *He averages six hours of work a day. The farmer averaged forty bushels of wheat to the acre.* **4** to divide among several proportionately: *We averaged our gains according to what each put in.*
—*v.i.* to buy (**average up**) or sell (**average down**) increasing quantities of a stock or commodities in order to improve one's position with respect to the mean price paid.
average out, to reach a balance one against the other: *Hot and cold days average out during the year.*
on the average, considered on the basis of the average: *People are kind on the average. He works six hours a day on the average.*
on (upon, or **at) an average,** taking the arithmetic mean or an approximation of this: *The farm produces, on an average, forty bushels of wheat to the acre.*
[< Middle French *avarie* damage to ship or cargo < Italian *avaria,* probably < Arabic *ʽawārīya* goods damaged by seawater (sense developed from "equal distribution of loss")] **—av′er|age|ly,** *adv.* **—av′er|age|ness,** *n.* **—av′er|ag|er,** *n.*

A|ver|nal (ə vėr′nəl), *adj.* of Avernus; of Hades; infernal.

A|ver|nus (ə vėr′nəs), *n. Roman Mythology.* the lower world; Hades.

Av|er|ro|ism (av′ə rō′iz əm), *n.* the philosophy of Averroës (Arab philosopher), chiefly consisting of a pantheistic interpretation of the teachings of Aristotle. **—Av′er|ro′ist,** *n., adj.*

a|verse (ə vėrs′), *adj.* **1** turned away in mind or feeling; having a strong or fixed dislike; opposed; unwilling (to): *Fear made her averse to fighting. I now had several pages of uncommonly fine prose fiction, which I did not feel averse to reading aloud to someone* (New Yorker). SYN: reluctant, loath, disinclined. **2** *Botany.* turned away from the main stem (as distinguished from *adverse*).
[< Latin *āversus,* past participle of *āvertere* avert] **—a|verse′ly,** *adv.* **—a|verse′ness,** *n.*

a|ver|sion (ə vėr′zhən, -shən), *n.* **1** a strong or fixed dislike; antipathy: *She has an aversion to the bitter taste of tea. He has an aversion to stirring up unnecessary national crises* (Time). SYN: distaste, loathing, disgust, repugnance. **2** a thing or person disliked: *Conceit is his special aversion.* **3** unwillingness (to). **4** act of turning away.
▶**aversion.** Either *to* or *for* follows *aversion: He has an aversion to moving fast and working hard. He has an aversion for fried shrimp.*

aversion therapy, *Psychology.* the treatment of addiction, compulsion, or other abnormal psychological condition by causing the patient to develop an aversion to the object responsible for his behavior: *The main kinds of treatment available—aversion therapy by means of electric shocks, . . . membership of Alcoholics Anonymous—are all of the "unlearning" kind* (New Scientist).

a|ver|sive (ə vėr′siv), *adj.* **1** that shows aversion; averse. **2** *Psychology.* tending to avoid.

a|vert (ə vėrt′), *v.t.* **1** to keep from happening; prevent the occurrence of (a disaster or other misfortune); avoid: *The driver averted an accident by a quick turn of the steering wheel.* **2** to turn away; turn aside (the face, eyes, or mind): *She averted her eyes from the wreck.* [< Latin *āvertere* < *ā-* from + *vertere* turn] **—a|vert′er,** *n.* **—a|vert′i|ble, a|vert′a|ble,** *adj.*

A|ver|tin (ə vėr′tin), *n. Trademark.* tribromoethanol.

A|ves (ā′vēz), *n.pl.* the class of warm-blooded vertebrate animals that have wings and feathers. All birds belong to this class. [< Latin *aves,* plural of *avis* bird]

A|ves|ta (ə ves′tə), *n.* the sacred writings of the ancient Zoroastrian religion, parts of which are still used by the Parsees. Also, **Zend-Avesta.** [< Pahlavi *Avistāk.*]

A|ves|tan (ə ves′tən), *n., adj.* **—*n.*** the Iranian language in which the Avesta is written.
—*adj.* of or having to do with the Avesta or the language in which it is written.

avg., average.

av|gas (av′gas′), *n. U.S.* any aviation gasoline.

av|go|lem|o|no (av′gō lem′ə nō), *n.* a Greek soup made with chicken broth, eggs, lemon, and often rice. [< Modern Greek *avgolemono* (literally) egg-lemon]

a|vi|an (ā′vē ən), *adj., n.* **—*adj.*** of or having to do with birds.
—*n.* a bird.
[< Latin *avis* bird + English *-an*]

a|vi|an|ize (ā′vē ə nīz), *v.t.,* **-ized, -iz|ing.** to produce changes in (a microorganism) or prepare (a vaccine) by growing the bacteria or viruses in chicken embryos.

avian leucosis complex, a complex group of apparently related diseases characterized by swelling of the internal organs, and principally affecting adult chickens.

a|vi|a|pho|bi|a (ā′vē ə fō′bē ə), *n.* = aviophobia.

a|vi|a|rist (ā′vē ər ist), *n.* the keeper of an aviary.

a|vi|ar|y (ā′vē er′ē), *n., pl.* **-ar|ies.** a house, enclosure, or large cage for many birds, especially wild birds; birdhouse.
[< Latin *aviārium,* neuter of *aviārius* of birds < *avis* bird]

a|vi|ate (ā′vē āt, av′ē-), *v.i.,* **-at|ed, -at|ing.** to fly in an aircraft. [back formation < *aviation*]

a|vi|a|tion (ā′vē ā′shən, av′ē-), *n.* **1** the art or science of operating and navigating aircraft, especially airplanes: *Pilots of large aircraft are masters of aviation.* **2** the designing and manufacture of aircraft, especially airplanes. **3** aircraft collectively, together with personnel and equipment: *American aviation, European aviation.* [< French *aviation* < Latin *avis* bird]

aviation gasoline, a high-octane gasoline prepared especially for use in aircraft with reciprocating engines.

aviation medicine, the branch of medicine dealing with the problems of man in air flight; aeromedicine.

aviation spirit, *British.* aviation gasoline.

a|vi|a|tor (ā′vē ā′tər, av′ē-), *n.* a person who flies an aircraft; a pilot.

a|vi|a|to|ri|al (ā′vē ə tôr′ē əl, -tōr′-; av′ē-), *adj.* **1** of aviation. **2** of aviators.

a|vi|a|to|ry (ā′vē ə tôr′ē, -tōr′-; av′ē), *adj.* = aviatorial.

a|vi|a|tress (ā′vē ā′tris, av′ē-), *n.* = aviatrix.

a|vi|a|trix (ā′vē ā′triks, av′ē-), *n.* a woman aviator.

av|i|cide (av′ə sīd), *n.* the killing of birds. [< Latin *avis* bird + English *-cide*[2]]

a|vi|cul|tur|al (ā′və kul′chər əl), *adj.* of or having to do with aviculture.

a|vi|cul|ture (ā′və kul′chər), *n.* the raising or keeping of birds. [< Latin *avis* bird + *cultūra* rearing, tending]

a|vi|cul|tur|ist (ā′və kul′chər ist), *n.* a bird fancier.

av|id (av′id), *adj.* extremely eager; greatly desirous; greedy: *The dictator had an avid desire for power. The miser was avid for gold.* SYN: keen, craving, covetous. [< Latin *avidus* < *avēre* desire eagerly] **—av′id|ly,** *adv.*

av|i|din (av′ə din, ə vid′in), *n.* an albumin present in raw egg white which, when eaten by humans or animals, renders the biotin in their systems inactive, causing symptoms of vitamin deficiency. Cooking of the egg removes this effect. [< *avid* + (biot)*in*]

a|vid|i|ty (ə vid′ə tē), *n.* **1** great eagerness: *The hungry boys looked at the pie with avidity. One of the many things that impress the traveler in Japan is the avidity with which the Japanese go on journeys* (Atlantic). **2** greed for wealth; avarice. **3** *Chemistry.* **a** the relative strength of an acid or base, as determined by its degree of dissociation. **b** chemical affinity, as between an antibody and a virus.

a|vi|fau|na (ā′və fô′nə), *n.* the birds of a region.
[< Latin *avis* bird + English *fauna*]

a|vi|fau|nal (ā′və fô′nəl), *adj.* of the avifauna of a region.

a|vi|fau|nist (ā′və fô′nist), *n.* a person who studies avifauna.

av|i|ga|tion (av′ə gā′shən), *n. Rare.* the navigation of aircraft; aviation.

A|vil|ion (ə vil′yən), *n.* = Avalon.

a vin|cu|lo ma|tri|mo|ni|i (ā ving′kyə lō mat′rə-mō′nē ī), *Latin.* from the tie of matrimony (referring to an absolute divorce).

a|vion (á vyôN′), *n. French.* an airplane.

a|vi|on|ic (ā′vē on′ik), *adj.* **1** of or having to do with avionics. **2** for avionics: *avionic equipment.*

a|vi|on|ics (ā′vē on′iks), *n.* the branch of technology having to do with the development and production of electronic devices for use in aviation, rocketry, and astronautics. [< *avi*(ation) + (electr)*onics*]

a|vi|o|pho|bi|a (ā′vē ə fō′bē ə), *n.* fear of flying in an aircraft: *Aviophobia . . . is believed to cost the airline industry up to $1.5 billion a year* (Robert L. DuPont). [< *aviaphobia* < *avia-*(tion) + *phobia*]

a|vir|u|lent (ā vir′yə lənt), *adj.* completely or relatively harmless; not virulent: *avirulent bacteria.*

a|vi|so (ə vī′zō), *n., pl.* **-sos.** **1** a dispatch boat. **2** *Archaic.* a formal notification; a dispatch.
[< Spanish *aviso* < *avisar* < Old French *aviser* advise]

a|vi|ta|min|o|sis (ā vī′tə mə nō′sis), *n.* any illness

caused by a lack of one or more vitamins. [< *a-*[4] without + *vitamin* + *-osis*]

avn., aviation.

A-V node, = atrioventricular node.

av|o|ca|do (av′ə kä′dō, ä′və-), *n., pl.* **-dos.** **1** a tropical fruit shaped like a pear, with a dark-green or purplish skin and a very large seed; alligator pear. Its yellow-green pulp has a nutty flavor and is used in salads and soups. Avocados belong to the same family as the laurel. See picture under **alligator pear**. **2** the tree that it grows on. **3** a dark-green color. [< Mexican Spanish *avocado,* popular form of Spanish *aguacate* < Nahuatl *ahuacatl*]

a|vo|cat (à vô kà′), *n. French.* a lawyer.

av|o|ca|tion (av′ə kā′shən), *n.* **1** something that a person does besides his regular business; minor occupation; hobby: *He is a lawyer by vocation, but writing stories is his avocation.* **2** *Informal.* one's regular occupation, calling, or vocation: *My avocation is in London city* (Dickens). **3** diversion of the attention; distraction. [< Latin *āvocātiō, -ōnis* < *āvocāre* to call away < *ā-* away + *vocāre* to call]

►See **vocation** for usage note.

av|o|ca|tion|al (av′ə kā′shə nəl), *adj.* of or having to do with an avocation. **—av′o|ca′tion|al|ly,** *adv.*

a|voc|a|to|ry (ə vok′ə tôr′ē, -tōr′-), *adj.* calling away or back; recalling.

av|o|cet (av′ə set), *n.* a web-footed wading bird with a long, slender beak that curves upward and with long legs. Also, **avoset.** [< French *avocette* < Venetian Italian *avocetto;* origin uncertain]

A|vo|ga|dro's law (ä′vō gä′drōz), *Chemistry, Physics.* a law stating that equal volumes of different gases, under like conditions of pressure and temperature, contain the same number of molecules. [< Count Amedeo *Avogadro,* 1776-1856, an Italian physicist, who stated it]

Avogadro's number, *Chemistry, Physics.* the number of molecules in one mole of any substance. It is approximately 6.0253×10^{23}.

a|void (ə void′), *v.t.* **1** to keep away from; keep out of the way of: *We avoided driving through large cities on our trip.* **2** to have nothing to do with: *The shy old man avoided his neighbors.* **3** to prevent from occurring: *To avoid an accident in the dark, use a flashlight.* **4** *Law.* to make void; annul. **5** *Obsolete.* to empty. [< Anglo-French *avoider,* Old French *esvuidier* empty, quit < *es-* out (< Latin *ex-*) + *vuidier* < Vulgar Latin *vocitāre* to void, empty] **—a|void′er,** *n.*

—Syn. **1, 2 Avoid, shun** mean to keep out of the way of. **Avoid** suggests trying not to meet someone or something that might be unpleasant: *He always left by the back door to avoid his creditors. The driver skillfully avoided the potholes in the road.* **Shun** suggests feeling strong dislike or disgust for the person or thing avoided: *We are likely to shun people with horrible diseases.*

a|void|a|ble (ə voi′də bəl), *adj.* **1** that can be avoided: *With care the accident would have been avoidable.* **2** *Law.* voidable. **—a|void′a|bly,** *adv.*

a|void|ance (ə voi′dəns), *n.* **1** the act of avoiding; keeping away from: *Her avoidance of old friends caused her to be lonely.* **2** *Law.* the act of making void; invalidation; annulment. **3** a becoming or being vacant: *The avoidance of the office . . . by death* (Sir William Henry Beveridge). **4** *Obsolete.* an emptying out.

avoir., avoirdupois.

av|oir|du|pois (av′ər də poiz′), *n.* **1** = avoirdupois weight. *Abbr:* av., avdp., avoir. **2** *Informal.* a person's weight; heaviness; stoutness. [< Middle French *avoir de pois* < Old French *avoir de peis* goods of weight < Latin *habēre* have, *dē* from, and *pēnsum* weight < *pendere* weigh]

avoirdupois weight, a system of weights based on a pound of 16 ounces:

16 drams = 1 ounce or 28.3495 grams
16 ounces = 1 pound or 0.4536 kilogram
2,000 pounds = 1 ton or 907.18 kilograms

Avoirdupois weight is used chiefly in North America to weigh everything except gems, precious metals, and drugs.

à vo|lon|té (à vô lôɴ tā′), *French.* at will; at pleasure.

av|o|set (av′ə set), *n.* = avocet.

à vo|tre san|té (à vô trə säɴ tā′), *French.* to your health.

a|vouch (ə vouch′), *v.t.* **1** to declare positively to be true; affirm: *What I have said I will avouch, in the presence of the king* (Shakespeare). **2** to vouch for; guarantee: *I can avouch his honesty. The bank avouches all the work of its employees.* **3** to acknowledge; avow: *He has avouched himself as the author of this plan.* [< Old French *avochier* < *a-* to + *vochier* call < Latin *vocāre* call] **—a|vouch′a|ble,** *adj.* **—a|vouch′er,** *n.* **—a|vouch′ment,** *n.*

a|vow (ə vou′), *v.t.* to declare frankly or openly; admit; acknowledge: *He avowed that he could not sing. The critics avowed their disgust for the new taxes with boldness.* [< Old French *avouer* < *a-* to + *vouer* to vow < Vulgar Latin *votāre*] **—a|vow′a|ble,** *adj.* **—a|vow′er,** *n.*

a|vow|al (ə vou′əl), *n.* a frank or open declaration; admission; acknowledgment: *He made a plain avowal of his opinions even though they were unpopular.*

a|vowed (ə voud′), *adj.* frankly or openly declared; admitted: *He is an avowed candidate for the office of mayor.* **—a|vow′ed|ly,** *adv.*

a|vow|ry (ə vou′rē), *n., pl.* **-ries.** *Law.* an avowal of an act.

á vues|tra sa|lud (ä vwes′trä sä lüᴛʜ′), *Spanish.* to your health.

a|vulsed (ə vul′sid), *adj.* with the tissue pulled away, as a wound.

a|vul|sion (ə vul′shən), *n.* **1** the act of pulling or tearing apart or off; forcible separation. **2** a part torn off. **3** *Law.* a sudden removal of land, as by change of a river's course or the action of flood, to another's estate, the land remaining the property of the original owner. [< Latin *āvulsiō, -ōnis* < *āvellere* tear away < *ā-* away + *vellere* tear]

a|vun|cu|lar (ə vung′kyə lər), *adj.* **1** of an uncle. Avuncular families exist among the Hopi Indians of the southwestern United States; in them the mother's brother has more authority than the actual father. **2** like an uncle. [< Latin *avunculus* mother's brother (diminutive) < *avus* grandfather] **—a|vun′cu|lar|ly,** *adv.*

a|vun|cu|lar|i|ty (ə vung′kyə lar′ə tē), *n., pl.* **-ties.** an avuncular manner, gesture, statement, or the like: *The marshal stood up and called with threatening avuncularity for complaints* (Manchester Guardian).

A/W (no periods), **1** actual weight. **2** all water.

a|wa (ə wä′), *adv. Scottish.* away.

a|wa|bi (ä′wä bē), *n. Japanese.* an abalone.

A|wacs or **AWACS** (ā′waks), *n.* an airborne radar system of the U.S. Air Force originally for the early detection of enemy bombers. [< *A*(irborne) *W*(arning) *a*(nd) *C*(ontrol) *S*(ystem)]

a|wait (ə wāt′), *v.t.* **1** to wait for; look forward to: *I shall await your answer to my letter with eagerness. He has awaited your coming for weeks.* SYN: expect. **2** to be ready for; be in store for: *Many pleasures await you on your trip.* **3** *Obsolete.* to watch for; lie in wait for. *—v.i.* to wait. [< Old North French *awaitier* < *a-* for + *waitier* wait < Germanic (compare Old High German *wahtēn.* keep watch)] **—a|wait′er,** *n.*

►See **wait** for usage note.

a|wake (ə wāk′), *v.,* **a|woke** or **a|waked, a|waked** or *(especially British)* **a|wo|ken, a|wak|ing,** *adj.* *—v.i.* **1** to come out of sleep; wake up; arouse: *I awoke from a sound sleep at sunrise.* **2** *Figurative.* to bestir oneself; become vigilant. *—v.t.* **1** to arouse from sleep; waken: *The alarm clock awoke me.* **2** *Figurative.* to stir up: *These words awoke his anger.* *—adj.* **1** roused from sleep; not asleep: *He is always awake early.* **2** *Figurative.* on the alert; watchful: *The explorer was ever awake for the dangers that surrounded him.* SYN: vigilant.

awake to, *Figurative.* to become aware of; realize: *England and France at length awoke to the value of their fisheries* (John Yeats).

[fusion of Old English *āwacian* and *awōc, onwōc,* past tense forms of *awæcnian,* earlier *onwæcnian* awaken. See related etym. at **wake.**]

a|wak|en (ə wā′kən), *v.i.* to wake up; arouse: *The sun was shining when we awakened.* *—v.t.* **1** to arouse from sleep; wake up: *He was awakened late this morning.* **2** *Figurative.* to rouse to activity or awareness; stir: *His plight would awaken compassion in the hardest heart.*

awaken to, *Figurative.* to come to realize: *Her mind has not yet awakened to the danger.*

[Old English *awæcnian, onwæcnian* < *on-* on + *wæcnan* waken, rouse] **—a|wak′en|er,** *n.* **—a|wak′en|ment,** *n.*

a|wak|en|ing (ə wā′kə ning), *n., adj.* waking up.

a|want|ing (ə won′ting, -wôn′-), *adj. Archaic.* wanting; lacking.

a|ward (ə wôrd′), *v., n.* *—v.t.* **1** to give after careful consideration; grant: *A medal was awarded to the best speller in the class.* SYN: assign. **2** to decide upon or settle by law; adjudge: *The court awarded damages of $5,000 to the injured man.* SYN: assign, decree. *—n.* **1** something given as a reward, payment, or the like, after careful consideration; prize: *My dog won the highest award.* SYN: reward. **2** a decision by a judge or arbitrator: *We all thought the award of $5,000 for damages was fair.* [< Anglo-French *awarder,* Old French *esguarder* observe, decide < Vulgar Latin *ex-* from (< Latin) + *wardāre* to guard < Germanic (compare Old Saxon *wardon* watch)] **—a|ward′a|ble,** *adj.*

a|ward|ee (ə wôr dē′, -wôr′dē), *n.* the receiver of an award.

a|ward|er (ə wôr′dər), *n.* the giver of an award.

a|ware (ə wãr′), *adj.* having knowledge; realizing; conscious: *I was too sleepy to be aware how cold it was. She was not aware of her danger.* SYN: See syn. under **conscious.** [Old English *gewær*] **—a|ware′ness,** *n.*

a|wash (ə wosh′, -wôsh′), *adv., adj.* **1** level with the surface of the water; just covered with water: *The beach was awash with the flowing tide.* **2** carried about by water; floating: *The floodwater set everything awash in the cellar.* **3** *Figurative.* filled (with); overflowing: *The music . . . was awash with melancholy* (New Yorker).

a|way (ə wā′), *adv., adj.* *—adv.* **1** from a place; to a distance: *Stay away from the fire.* **2** at a distance; a way off; far: *The sailor went far away from home.* SYN: distant, off. **3** out of one's possession, notice, or use: *He gave his boat away.* **4** out of existence: *The sounds died away.* **5** in another direction; aside: *He turned his car away just in time to avoid an accident.* **6** without stopping; on; continuously: *She worked away at her job.* **7** without delay; at once: *Fire away! Do as I bid, and fly away.* *—adj.* **1** at a distance; far: *His home is miles away.* **2** absent; gone: *My mother is away today.* **3** *Sports.* played on the opponent's grounds, field, or court, rather than on one's own: *to finish the season with two away games.* **4** *Baseball.* out: *A home run with two away in the ninth won the game.*

away back, *Informal.* far back in space or time: *Our candidate is a good man and a fighter from away back.*

away with, take (someone or something) away: *Away with him to the dungeon!*

away with you, you go away: *Away with you! . . . I'll put everybody under an arrest that stays* (Thomas Sheridan).

do away with. See under **do**[1].

where away? See under **where.**

[Old English *on weg* < *on* on + *weg* way]

awe (ô), *n., v.,* **awed, aw|ing.** *—n.* **1** great wonder; a feeling of wonder and reverence inspired by anything of great beauty, sublimity, majesty, or power: *We feel awe when we stand near vast mountains, or when we think of God's power and glory.* **2** fear and reverence; dread mingled with reverence: *When the young lawyer entered the Supreme Court he felt great awe.* **3** *Archaic.* power to inspire fear or respect. *—v.t.* **1** to cause to feel awe; fill with awe: *The majesty of the mountains awed us.* **2** to influence or restrain by awe: *The profound silence awed everyone.*

stand in awe of, to have a profound respect for: *The Prince of Wales, in particular, stood in tremendous awe of his mother* (Lytton Strachey).

[Middle English *aghe* < Scandinavian (compare Old Icelandic *agi*)]

a|wea|ry (ə wir′ē), *adj. Poetic.* weary; tired (of): *am aweary, aweary, I would that I were dead* (Tennyson).

a|weath|er (ə weᴛʜ′ər), *adj., adv.* on or toward the windward (weather) side or direction.

a|weigh (ə wā′), *adj.* just clear of the bottom, and hanging straight down, leaving a ship free to move: *The ship began to move as soon as its anchor was aweigh.*

awe-in|spir|ing (ô′in spīr′ing), *adj.* causing awe; awesome.

►See **awful** for usage note.

awe|less (ô′lis), *adj.* **1** = fearless. **2** = irreverent.

awe|some (ô′səm), *adj.* **1** causing awe: *A great fire is an awesome sight.* **2** showing awe; awed: *awesome admiration.* **3** filling with awe; impressive: *"It was awesome when they announced a staff for their Midwest office that was larger than the number of officers we have in our corporate banking department"* (Business Week). **4** *Informal.* tremendous, spectacular: *The party was really awesome.* **—awe′some|ly,** *adv.* **—awe′some|ness,** *n.*

awe-strick|en (ô′strik′ən), *adj.* filled with awe; awe-struck.

awe-strike (ô′strīk′), *v.t.,* **-struck, -strik|ing.** to strike with awe.

awe-struck (ô′struk′), *adj.* filled with awe: *She was awe-struck by the grandeur of the mountains.*

aw|ful (ô′fəl), *adj., adv.* *—adj.* **1** causing fear; dreadful; terrible: *An awful storm with thunder and lightning came up.* SYN: fearful. **2** *Informal.* very bad, great, ugly, or otherwise unusual: *He is an awful nuisance. His room was in an awful mess.* SYN: appalling, monstrous, shocking. **3** deserving great respect and reverence: *He felt the awful power of God.* SYN: majestic, sublime. **4** filling with awe; impressive: *The mountains rose to awful heights.* SYN: imposing.

Pronunciation Key: hat, āge, cãre, fär; let, ēqual, tėrm; it, īce; hot, ōpen, ôrder; oil, out; cup, pu̇t, rüle; child; long; thin; ᴛʜen; zh, measure; ə represents a in about, e in taken, i in pencil, o in lemon, u in circus.

—*adv. Informal.* very: *He was awful mad.* [Middle English *aghful*] —**aw′ful|ness**, *n.*

▶In formal English **awful** means filling with awe. In familiar and informal English it is a general utility word of disapproval: *awful manners, an awful cold, an awful mistake.* As a result the word is seldom used in careful writing; **awe-inspiring** has taken its place.

aw|ful|ly (ô′flē, -fə lē), *adv.* **1** dreadfully; terribly: *The broken leg hurt awfully.* **2** *Informal.* very: *I'm awfully sorry that I hurt your feelings.*

a|while (ə hwīl′), *adv.* for a short time: *He stayed awhile after dinner to talk. She paused awhile before answering.* [Old English *āne hwīle* (for) a while]

▶**Awhile** is often used as a noun meaning "a short time," as in: *We rested for awhile. I met her on a trip awhile back.* The word was formed by coalescing the article and noun in the phrase *a while,* probably on the analogy of the adverb *awhile.*

a|whirl (ə hwėrl′), *adj.* in a whirl; whirling.

a|wing (ə wing′), *adv., adj.* on the wing.

awk|ward (ôk′wərd), *adj.* **1a** not graceful or skillful in movement or shape; clumsy: *Seals are very awkward on land, but graceful in the water.* **b** not done with grace or skill; unable to do or use with ease or effectiveness: *an awkward drawing of stick figures. His awkward speech made him difficult to understand.* **2** not well suited to use: *The handle of this pitcher has an awkward shape.* SYN: unhandy. **3** not easily managed; difficult to negotiate: *This is an awkward corner to turn.* **4** inconvenient or embarrassing: *an awkward moment. He asked me such an awkward question that I did not know what to reply.* **5** ill at ease; embarrassed: *An awkward manner makes everyone uneasy.* [< obsolete *awk* perverse(ly), in the wrong way < Scandinavian (compare Old Icelandic *ǫfugr*) + English *-ward*] —**awk′ward|ly**, *adv.* —**awk′ward|ness**, *n.*

—*Syn.* **1a Awkward, clumsy, ungainly** mean not graceful. **Awkward** means lacking grace, ease, quickness, and skill: *The girl is still in the awkward age. An awkward girl is no help in the kitchen.* **Clumsy** suggests moving heavily and stiffly: *The clumsy boy bumped into all the furniture.* **Ungainly** means awkward in moving one's body: *He is as ungainly as a newborn calf.*

awkward age, the time of life when one is no longer a child and yet not fully grown up; the beginning of adolescence: *Handling a suddenly grown body and many new problems makes the awkward age an awkward time to go through.*

A.W.L., *Military.* **1** absence with leave. **2** absent with leave.

***awl** (ôl), *n.* a sharp-pointed tool used for making small holes in leather or wood. [Old English *æl*]

***awl**

aw|less (ô′lis), *adj.* = aweless.

awl-shaped (ôl′shāpt′), *adj.* slender and tapering toward the extremity from a broadish base; subulate: *awl-shaped leaves.*

awl|wort (ôl′wėrt′), *n.* a small, stemless water plant of the mustard family, with slender leaves which taper to a point. It is found in Europe, Siberia, and North America.

aw|mous (ô′məs), *n. Scottish.* alms.

awn (ôn), *n.* **1** one of the bristly hairs forming the beard on a head of barley, oats, and other grasses. **2** any similar bristly growth. [Middle English *agun* < Scandinavian (compare Old Icelandic *ǫgn, agnar* chaff)]

awned (ônd), *adj.* having awns.

awn|ing (ô′ning), *n.* a piece of canvas, metal, or other material spread before a door or window or over a porch, deck, or patio. Awnings are used for protection from the sun or rain. [origin uncertain]

awn|inged (ô′ningd), *adj.* fitted with one or more awnings: *an awninged porch.*

awn|less (ôn′lis), *adj.* without awns.

awn|y (ô′nē), *adj.* having awns; bearded.

a|woke (ə wōk′), *v.* a past tense and past participle of **awake:** *I awoke early. My sister has not yet awoke.*

a|wo|ken (ə wō′kən), *v. Especially British.* a past participle of **awake**: *She was awoken by a loud noise.*

AWOL or **A|wol** (ā′wôl, *or pronounced as initials*), *adj., adv., n.* —***adj., adv.*** absent without leave: *to be AWOL for 12 days.*

—***n.*** *Slang, especially U.S.* a person who is absent without leave.

A.W.O.L., AWOL (no periods), or **a.w.o.l.,** *Military, especially U.S.* absent without leave.

a|wry (ə rī′), *adv., adj.* **1** with a twist or turn to one side: *Her hat was blown awry by the wind.* **2** *Figurative.* out of order; wrong: *Our plans have gone awry. The seasons at this time of year are all awry* (New Yorker). [< *a* [1]- on + *wry*]

ax** or **axe** (aks), *n., pl.* **ax|es**, *v.,* **axed, ax|ing.** —n.*** **1** a tool with a flat, sharp blade fastened to a handle, used for chopping, splitting, and shaping wood. **2** a weapon like this; battleax. **3** = ice ax. **4** *U.S. Slang.* a musical instrument.

—***v.t.*** **1** to shape or trim with an ax. **2** *Informal, Figurative.* **a** to discharge (an employee or employees), especially summarily: *Some executives in a merged company question their future and get out before they're axed* (Wall Street Journal). **b** to reduce greatly; make much less: *The budget was axed to keep expenses down. Prices were axed for the holiday sale.*

get the ax, *Informal.* **a** to be discharged: *This department shut down when its members got the ax last week.* **b** to reduce the size of or get rid of in order to reduce in size: *17 chapters will get the ax within four years unless membership rises* (Look).

give the ax, *Informal.* to discharge, dismiss, or spurn: *A growing number of men in the South Pacific are feeling bitter because their girls are now giving them "the ax" and marrying men in the States* (Baltimore Sun).

have an ax to grind, to have a special purpose, usually from a selfish reason, for taking action or being interested: *The habitual French fear that any high-level intimacy between London and Washington means that Britain has an axe to grind at France's expense* (New York Times). [Old English *æx*] —**ax′like′, axe′like′**, *adj.*

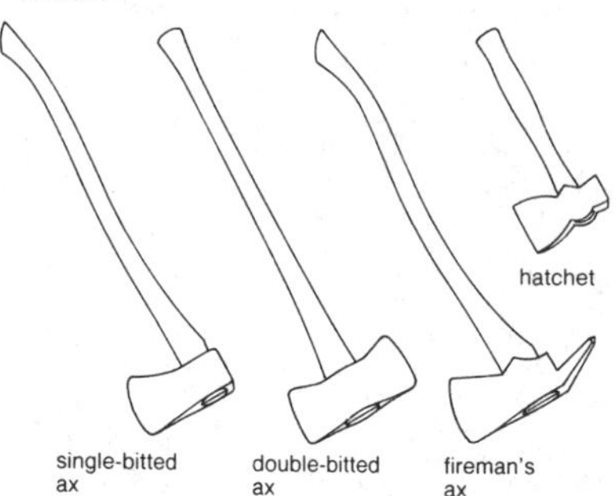

ax., axiom.

axe-grind|er (aks′grīn′dər), *n. Slang.* a person who acts because of a special purpose, usually from a selfish reason.

axe-grind|ing (aks′grīn′ding), *n. Slang.* the action or behavior of an axe-grinder.

axe|head (aks′hed′), *n.* the edged head of an ax.

ax|el (ak′səl), *n.* a jump in figure skating in which the skater leaps from the outside front edge of one skate, takes one and a half turns in the air and lands on the outside back edge of the other skate. [short for *Axel Paulsen,* a skater after whom the jump was named]

axe|man (aks′mən), *n., pl.* **-men.** = axman.

a|xen|ic (ā zen′ik, -zē′nik), *adj.* characterized by an absence of contaminating organisms: *an axenic culture.* [< *a-* [4] without + Greek *xénos* strange, foreign + English *-ic*] —**a|xen′i|cal|ly**, *adv.*

ax|es[1] (ak′siz), *n.* plural of **ax.**

ax|es[2] (ak′sēz), *n.* plural of **axis**[1].

ax-grind|er (aks′grīn′dər), *n.* = axe-grinder.

ax-grind|ing (aks′grīn′ding), *n.* = axe-grinding.

ax|head (aks′hed′), *n.* = axehead.

ax|i|al (ak′sē əl), *adj.* **1** of an axis; forming an axis: *The wheel turns on an axial rod.* **2** along, on, or around an axis.

ax|i|al-flow (ak′sē əl flō′), *adj.* having a fluid flow directed by rotary blades and stators along a line parallel to the axis of rotation: *an axial-flow compressor, an axial-flow turbine.* An axial-flow pump is a high-speed pump used for liquid or for air, especially for pumping air into jet engines.

ax|i|al|ly (ak′sē ə lē), *adv.* in a line with or the direction of the axis; from pole to pole.

axial skeleton, the skeleton of the trunk, head, and tail (distinguished from *appendicular skeleton*).

ax|il (ak′səl), *n.* the angle between the upper side of a leaf or stem and the supporting stem or branch. A bud is usually found in the axil. [< New Latin *axil* < Latin *axilla* armpit]

ax|ile (ak′səl, -sīl), *adj. Botany.* situated in or belonging to an axis, as a placenta in the axis of the ovary.

ax|il|la (ak sil′ə), *n., pl.* **ax|il|lae** (ak sil′ē). **1** = armpit. **2** = axil. **3** the undersurface of a bird's wing. [< Latin *axilla,* related to *āla* armpit, wing]

ax|il|lar (ak′sə lər), *adj., n.* —***adj.*** = axillary.

—***n.*** a long, stiff feather growing from the axilla of a bird.

ax|il|lar|y (ak′sə ler′ē), *adj., n., pl.* **-lar|ies.** —***adj.*** **1** of or near the armpit; alar. **2** in or growing from the axil of a plant; alar: *axillary buds.*

—***n.*** = axillar.

ax|i|nite (ak′sə nīt), *n.* a mineral consisting essentially of an aluminum and calcium borosilicate, commonly occurring in flattened, brown crystals edged like an ax. [< Greek *axinē* ax]

ax|i|o|log|i|cal (ak′sē ə loj′ə kəl), *adj.* of or having to do with axiology. —**ax′i|o|log′i|cal|ly**, *adv.*

ax|i|ol|o|gy (ak′sē ol′ə jē), *n. Philosophy.* the study of the nature, types, criteria, and status of human values. Axiology involves such questions as "What is beautiful?" "What is good?" "What is holy?" [< Greek *áxios* worthy + English *-logy*]

ax|i|om (ak′sē əm), *n.* **1** a statement taken to be true without proof; self-evident truth: *It is an axiom that a whole is greater than any one of its parts. It is an axiom that if equals are added to equals the results will be equal.* **2** a well-established principle, rule, or law: *It is an axiom that medicine should be kept out of the reach of young children.* [< Latin *axiōma* < Greek *axíōma* < *áxios* worthy]

ax|i|o|mat|ic (ak′sē ə mat′ik), *adj.* **1** accepted without proof; self-evident: *It is axiomatic that a whole is greater than any one of its parts.* **2** full of axioms or maxims; aphoristic. —**ax′i|o|mat′i|cal|ly**, *adv.*

ax|i|o|mat|i|cal (ak′sē ə mat′ə kəl), *adj.* = axiomatic.

ax|i|om|a|tize (ak′sē om′ə tīz), *v.t.,* **-tized, -tiz|ing.** to formulate in terms of axioms; state in the form of an axiom or axioms: *to axiomatize a theory.* —**ax′i|om′a|ti|za′tion**, *n.*

axiom of choice, *Mathematics.* an axiom stating that, given a collection of sets that do not overlap, it is possible to form a new set containing one element from each of the sets.

ax|i|on (ak′sē on), *n.* a hypothetical elementary particle having neutral charge and zero spin, and a mass of less than one-thousandth of a proton. [perhaps < Greek *áxios* worthy + English *-on*]

***ax|is**[1] (ak′sis), *n., pl.* **ax|es. 1** a straight line about which an object turns or seems to turn. The axis of the earth is an imaginary line through the North Pole and the South Pole. **2** a central or principal line around which parts are arranged regularly: *The axis of a cone is the straight line joining its apex and the center of its base.* **3** any line used for reference. **4** *Anatomy.* **a** a central or principal structure extending lengthwise and having the parts of the body arranged around it: *The axis of the skeleton is the spinal column.* **b** the second cervical vertebra. **5** *Botany.* **a** the central part or support on which parts are arranged: *The axis of a plant is the stem.* **b** the main stem and root. **6** any of three lines about which any mis-

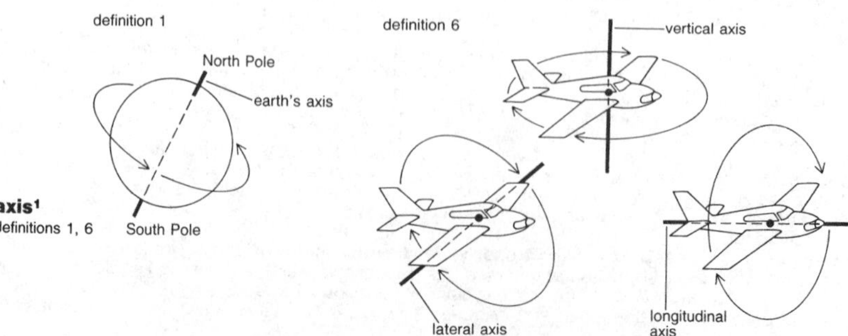

axis[1]
definitions 1, 6

sile, rocket vehicle, or aircraft revolves, one lengthwise in the plane of symmetry, and the other two perpendicular to each other and to the lengthwise axis. **7** in the fine arts and design: **a** an imaginary central line in a composition, referred to for balance of parts or the like. **b** an actual central line in a drawing or other work of art. **8** *Crystallography.* one of three or four imaginary lines assumed in defining the position of the plane faces and classifying the crystal. **9** *Optics.* a straight line drawn through the optical center of a lens, and perpendicular to both its surfaces. **10** *Figurative.* an important line of relation: *the Bonn-Washington axis.*

the Axis, Germany, Italy, Japan, and their allies, during World War II. *The Axis powers . . . simply took over one area after another by threat or use of force without a formal declaration of war* (Bulletin of Atomic Scientists). [< Latin *axis* axle, axis]

ax|is² (ak′sis), *n.,* or **axis deer**, any deer of a genus of Southeast Asia, India, and Ceylon (Sri Lanka) having the body spotted with white; chital. [< Latin *axis;* origin unknown]

axis cylinder, the central portion of a nerve fiber, which is the essential conducting element and a continuation of an axon of the nerve cell.

ax|i|sym|met|ric (ak′sə si met′rik), *adj.* symmetric about the axis: *an axisymmetric conical flow of gases.*

ax|le (ak′səl), *n.* **1** a bar or shaft on which a wheel turns. Some axles turn with the wheel. **2** = axletree. **3** *Obsolete or Poetic.* an axis. [Old English *eaxl* shoulder, crossbar; influenced by Scandinavian (compare Old Icelandic *öxull* axle)]

axle box, **1** the journal box of a rotating axle, as on a railroad car. **2** a bushing which forms the bearing of an axle.

ax|le|tree (ak′səl trē′), *n.* a crossbar connecting two opposite wheels of a cart, wagon, carriage, or other horse-drawn vehicle. The wheels turn on its ends. [probably < Scandinavian (compare Old Icelandic *öxul-trē* < *öxull* axle + *trē* tree, beam)]

ax|man (aks′mən), *n., pl.* **-men**. a man who uses an ax in chopping or fighting. Also, **axeman**.

Ax|min|ster (aks′min stər), *n.,* or **Axminster carpet**, **1** a kind of handmade carpet with a finely tufted, velvetlike pile. **2** a carpet made by machine to imitate it. [< *Axminster,* a town in England, where it was formerly made]

ax|o|lotl (ak′sə lot′əl), *n.* any salamander of several common in lakes and lagoons in Mexico and the Southwestern United States, that usually retain their gills and tadpole form through life. In Mexico they are valued as food. [< Spanish *axolotl* < the Nahuatl name]

ax|om|e|ter (ak som′ə tər), *n.* an optician's measuring device used in determining the optical centers of the lenses and adjusting their positions in relation to the centers of the eyes. [< Greek *áxōn* axis + English *-meter*]

ax|on (ak′son), *n.* the long extension of a nerve cell that carries impulses away from the body of the cell. [< New Latin *axon* < Greek *áxōn* axis]

ax|o|nal (ak′sə nəl), *adj.* = axonic.

ax|one (ak′sōn), *n.* = axon.

ax|on|ic (ak son′ik), *adj.* of or having to do with an axon.

ax|o|plasm (ak′sə plaz′əm), *n.* the protoplasm within an axon.

ax|o|style (ak′sə stīl), *n. Zoology.* a slender skeletal rod in certain protozoans. [< Greek *áxōn* axis + *stylos* pillar, support]

ax|seed (aks′sēd′), *n.* an herb of the pea family native to Europe and naturalized in the eastern United States, having pinkish flowers and ax-shaped seeds.

ax|unge (ak′sunj), *n.* **1** fat or grease, especially of hogs or geese. **2** lard prepared for use in medicine. [< Middle French *axunge* < Latin *axungia* < *axis* axle + *ungere* to grease]

ay¹ (ī), *adv., n.* = aye¹.

ay² (ā), *adv.* always; ever: *"A mother's love lasts forever and ay."* Also, **aye²**. [< Scandinavian (compare Old Icelandic *ei*)]

ay³ (ā), *interj. North English Dialect.* ah! (an exclamation, as of surprise).

ay me! alas! ah me!

a|yah (ä′yə), *n.* a native nurse or lady's maid in India. [< Hindustani *āya* < Portuguese *aia* governess < Latin *avia* grandmother]

a|ya|huas|ca (ä′yə wäs′kə), *n.* a drink that produces hallucinations, made from the roots of a South American vine. [< American Spanish *ayahuasca* < Quechua]

a|ya|tol|lah (ä′yə tōl′ə), *n.* **1** the title of a Shiite Moslem religious teacher of the highest rank, especially in Iran: *The prime force was the bitterness of the mullahs and of their leaders—the ayatollahs—against the Shah's industrializing and modernizing campaign* (Max Lerner). **2** any forceful leader: *America's out-of-touch ayatollah of intolerance* (New York Times Magazine). [< Arabic *āyatollāh* (literally) sign of God]

aye¹ (ī), *adv., n.* —*adv.* = yes: *Aye, aye, sir.*

—*n.* an affirmative answer, vote, or voter: *The ayes won when the vote was taken.* Also, **ay**. [apparently Old English *gī, gīe*]

aye² (ā), *adv.* always; ever. Also, **ay**.

aye-aye (ī′ī′), *n.* a squirrellike lemur of Madagascar. [< French *aye-aye* < Malagasy *aiay*]

a|yin (ä′yin), *n.* the 16th letter of the Hebrew alphabet. [< Hebrew *'ayin* eye]

Ay|ma|ra (ī′mä rä′), *n., pl.* **-ra** or **-ras**. **1** a member of a group of South American Indians of Peru and Bolivia, some of whom developed an advanced pre-Incan civilization. **2** any of a group of South American Indian dialects of Bolivia and Peru, including the language of the Aymara.

Ay|ma|ran (ī′mä rän′), *adj., n.* —*adj.* of the Aymara Indians or their language.

—*n.* the language of the Aymara Indians.

ayre (ãr), *n.* = madrigal (def. 2). [variant of *air*]

Ayr|shire (ãr′shir, -shər), *n., adj.* —*n.* a dairy cow of a breed that is red and white or brown and white, originating in Ayrshire, Scotland.

—*adj.* of or having to do with this breed.

a|yun|ta|mien|to (ä yün′tä myen′tō), *n. Spanish.* in Spain and former Spanish colonies: **1** a municipal council. **2** the building occupied by a municipal government; town hall.

A|yur|ve|da (ä′yər vā′də), *n.* the ancient Hindu system of medicine. [< Sanskrit *āyurvēda* life knowledge]

A|yur|ve|dic or **a|yur|ve|dic** (ä′yər vā′dik), *adj., n.* —*adj.* of or based upon Ayurveda: *Ayurvedic medicine.* —*n.* a practitioner of Ayurveda.

az-, *combining form.* the form of **azo-** before vowels, as in *azide.*

az., azure.

AZ (no periods), Arizona (in postal Zip Code).

az|a|cy|clo|nol (az′ə sī klō′nəl), *n.* a drug used in the treatment of schizophrenia and related conditions. *Formula:* $C_{18}H_{21}NO$

a|zal|ea (ə zāl′yə), *n.* **1** a shrub bearing many showy flowers, growing mainly in eastern North America and in China. Azaleas belong to the heath family, but are usually not evergreen. **2** its flower. **3** any one of various similar plants. [< New Latin *azalea* < Greek *azaléā,* feminine of *azaléos* dry < *ázein* parch (it grows in dry soil)]

a|zan (ä zän′, ə zan′), *n.* the Moslem call to public prayer, proclaimed five times a day by the muezzin (crier) from the minaret of a mosque. [< Arabic, *'adhān* invitation]

A|za|ni|an (ə zā′nē ən), *n., adj.* —*n.* a native or inhabitant of Azania, the African nationalist name of South Africa.

—*adj.* of or having to do with Azania or Azanians.

az|a|role (az′ə rōl), *n.* **1** the slightly acid, pleasantly flavored fruit, about the size of a cherry, of a species of hawthorn of southern Europe. **2** the tree itself. Also, **Neapolitan medlar**. [< French *azerole* < Arabic *az-zu'rūr*]

az|a|thi|o|prine (az′ə thī′ə prēn), *n.* = Imuran.

A|za|zel (ə zā′zəl, az′ə-), *n.* **1** (in the Bible) the evil spirit of the wilderness to whom a scapegoat was sacrificed in the Mosaic ritual of atonement. **2a** (traditionally) the chief of those angels who took wives among the daughters of men. He was taken prisoner by the angels and bound until the Day of Judgment. **b** (in Moslem tradition) one of the jinn. **c** (in *Paradise Lost*) an angel who rebelled with Satan.

a|zed|a|rach (ə zed′ə rak), *n.* **1** the china tree, an East Indian tree cultivated elsewhere for ornament. **2** the cathartic and emetic bark of its root. [< French *azédarac* < Persian *āzād dirakht* "free (noble) tree"]

az|e|la|ic acid (az′ə lā′ik), a crystalline diacid used as a lubricant and formed by the action of nitric acid on oleic acid and castor oil. *Formula:* $C_9H_{16}O_4$ [< *az-* + Greek *élaion* olive oil + *-ic*]

a|ze|o|trope (ə zē′ə trōp), *n. Chemistry.* a mixture of two or more substances which, at a certain proportion and at a certain pressure, boils at a constant temperature and, in distillation or partial evaporation, retains the same composition in the vapor state as in the liquid. Such a mixture, compared to other mixtures of the same substances, exhibits either a minimum or a maximum boiling point. [< *a-* without + Greek *zêin* to boil + *trópos* way, manner]

az|e|o|trop|ic (az′ē ə trop′ik), *adj. Chemistry.* having to do with or resembling an azeotrope.

A|zer|bai|ja|ni or **A|zer|bai|dzha|ni** (ä′zər bī jä′nē), *n.* **1** a native or inhabitant of Azerbaijan, a republic of the U.S.S.R. and a province in northwest Iran. **2** a Turkic language spoken in Azerbaijan.

A|zer|bai|ja|ni|an or **A|zer|bai|dzha|ni|an** (ä′zər bī jä′nē ən), *n.* = Azerbaijani.

az|ide (az′īd, -id; ā′zīd), *n.* any one of various salts of hydrazoic acid, containing the radical $-N_3$.

a|zi|do|thy|mi|dine (az′ī dō thī′mə din, -dēn), *n.* an antiviral drug used in the treatment of AIDS: *While azidothymidine is the first drug shown to benefit AIDS victims, researchers . . . emphasized that it is not a cure* (Science News).

A|zil|ian (ə zil′yən), *adj., n.* —*adj.* of or having to do with a Stone Age culture in transition between the paleolithic and neolithic periods.

—*n.* this culture. Also, **Asilian**.

[< Le Mas d'*Azil,* a region in southern France where remains of the culture were found]

az|i|muth (az′ə məth), *n.* **1** *Astronomy.* the angular distance along the horizon measured from its north point toward the east to the great circle that passes through a celestial body and the zenith and is perpendicular to the horizon: *A star due northeast from the observer has an azimuth of 45 degrees.* **2** an angle constructed in surveying between a north-south line through the observer and a line from the observer to any point on, or projected on, the earth's surface, measured clockwise, from north. [< Middle French *azimut* < Arabic *as-sumūt* the ways < *samt* way]

az|i|muth|al (az′ə muth′əl, az′ə myü′thəl), *adj.* of or in the azimuth; used in taking azimuths. —**az′i|muth′al|ly**, *adv.*

***azimuthal equidistant projection**, a type of map projection centered on a given point in such a way that the distance along a great circle to any other point is represented to scale on a straight line connecting the two points.

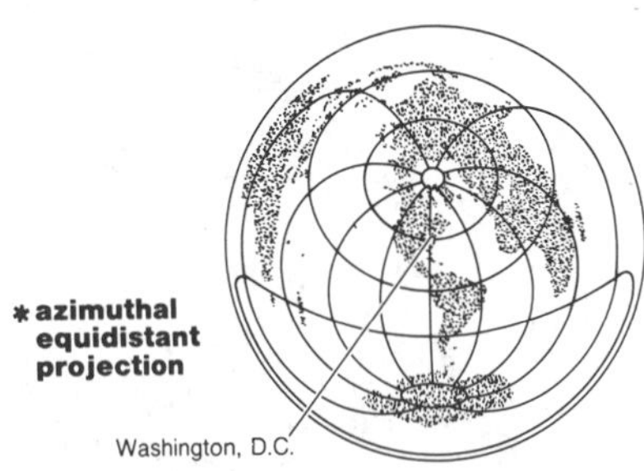

***azimuthal equidistant projection**

projection centered on Washington, D.C.

azimuthal projection, = azimuthal equidistant projection.

azimuth circle, **1** one of the great circles intersecting one another in the zenith and nadir, and cutting the horizon at right angles. **2** a device like a gunsight mounted on a movable ring on a stand which contains a compass. By sighting through the azimuth circle, the navigator can determine the bearing of an object from his craft.

az|in (az′in), *n.* = azine.

az|ine (az′ēn, -in), *n. Chemistry.* **1** any compound of a group of organic compounds containing a ring of six atoms, one or more of which is nitrogen. The number of nitrogen atoms present is denoted by a prefix, as in *diazine, triazine.* **2** any compound of a group of nitrogenous compounds produced from an aldehyde or a ketone and hydrazine.

az|o (az′ō, ā′zō), *adj. Chemistry.* containing the -N:N- group.

azo-, *combining form.* azo; azote; nitrogen, as in *azobenzene.* Also, **az-** before vowels. [< *azote*]

az|o|ben|zene (az′ō ben′zēn, -ben zēn′; ā′zō-), *n.* a yellowish-orange, crystalline compound derived from nitrobenzene, used in making dyes. *Formula:* $C_{12}H_{10}N_2$

azo dyes, a large group of synthetic dyes containing the grouping R-N:N-R, a basic structure of two atoms of nitrogen and two radicals of the benzene or naphthalene series, which can form subsequent, complex structures having a variety of dyeing properties.

A|zo|ic (ə zō′ik), *n., adj.* —*n.* **1** the oldest geological era, when the earth had its very beginning, characterized by the absence of living things. **2** the rocks formed in this era.

—*adj.* of this era or these rocks.

[Greek *ázōos* (< *ā-* without + *zōê* life)]

az|o|im|ide (az′ō im′īd, -id; ā′zō-), *n.* = hydrazoic acid.

az|ole (az′ōl, ə zōl′), *n. Chemistry.* any compound of a group of organic compounds having a ring of five atoms, one or more of which is nitrogen. The number of nitrogen atoms is denoted by a prefix, as in *diazole, triazole.* [< *az-* + *-ole*]

a|zon|al (ā zō′nəl), *adj.* not divided into or distinguished by zones.

a|zon|ic (ā zon′ik), *adj.* not confined to a zone or region; not local.

a|zo|o|sper|mi|a (ā zō′ə spėr′mē ə), *n.* absence

Pronunciation Key: hat, āge, cãre, fär; let, ēqual, tėrm; it, īce; hot, ōpen, ôrder; oil, out; cup, pu̇t, rüle; child; long; thin; ᴛʜen; zh, measure; ə represents **a** in about, **e** in taken, **i** in pencil, **o** in lemon, **u** in circus.

of spermatozoa in the semen. [< Greek *ázōos* lifeless + *spérma* seed]

a|zo|o|sperm|ic (ā zō′ə spėr′mik), *adj.* having no spermatozoa: *azoospermic semen.*

A|zo|re|an (ə zō′rē ən), *adj., n.* **—*adj.*** of or having to do with the Azores.
—*n.* a native or inhabitant of the Azores.

az|ote (az′ōt, ə zōt′), *n.* a former name of nitrogen. [< French *azote* < Late Greek *ázōtos* not to be lived, insupportable < *a-* not + unrecorded *zōtós,* verbal adjective of *zôein* live]

az|oth (az′oth), *n.* in alchemy: **1** mercury, as the assumed first principle of all metals. **2** the universal remedy of Paracelsus. [ultimately < Arabic *az-zā'ūq* the quicksilver]

a|zot|ic (ə zot′ik), *adj.* of or having to do with nitrogen.

az|o|tize (az′ə tīz), *v.t.,* **-tized, -tiz|ing.** = nitrogenize.

a|zo|to|bac|ter (ə zō′tə bak′ter), *n.* any bacterium of a genus of aerobic bacteria, able to fix atmospheric nitrogen for their own use.

az|o|tu|ri|a (az′ō tyůr′ē ə), *n.* an acute, noninfectious disease of horses occurring after enforced idleness and high feeding, and also affecting cattle. The urine is colored deep red or black.

Az|ra|el (az′rē əl), *n.* the angel of death, according to the Koran and in tradition, who takes the soul from the body.

AZT (no periods), *Trademark.* azidothymidine.

Az|tec (az′tek), *n., adj.* **—*n.*** **1** a member of a powerful and highly civilized American Indian people who ruled a large empire in central Mexico from about 1200 A.D. until its conquest by the Spaniards under Cortés in 1521. **2** any member of the nation ruled by this people. **3** their language; Nahautl.
—*adj.* of the Aztecs or their language: *great stones decorated in Aztec art.*

Az|tec|an (az′tek ən), *adj.* Aztec or Nahuatlan.

a|zu|le|jo (ä′thü lā′hō), *n., pl.* **-jos.** a colored tile, often blue, used in Moorish architecture. [< Spanish *azulejo* (diminutive) < *azul* blue]

az|ure (azh′ər, ā′zhər), *n., adj.* **—*n.*** **1** the clear-blue color of the unclouded sky; sky blue. **2** a bright-blue pigment or dye, especially cobalt (blue). **3** *Heraldry.* the blue color in coats of arms, in engraving represented by horizontal lines. **4** *Poetic.* the unclouded vault of heaven.
—adj. blue like the color of the unclouded sky; sky-blue.
[< Old French *l'azur* the azure < Arabic *lāzuward* < Persian *lājward* lapis lazuli]

azure stone, 1 = lapis lazuli. **2** = azurite.

az|u|rite (azh′ů rīt), *n.* **1** a blue copper ore. It is a basic carbonate of copper. *Formula:* $2CuCO_3$-$Cu(OH)_2$ **2** a form of this mineral used as a semiprecious stone.

az|ur|y (azh′ər ē, ā′zhər-), *adj.* **1** = bluish. **2** = blue.

az|y|gous (az′ə gəs), *adj. Anatomy.* not being one of a pair; single, such as a muscle or vein. [< Greek *ázygos* (with English *-ous*) < *a-* without + *zygón* yoke]

az|ym (az′im), *n.* a cake of unleavened bread, such as the bread used at the Jewish Passover. [< Late Latin *azymus* < Greek *ázȳmos* unleavened < *a-* without + *zýmē* leaven]

az|yme (az′īm, -im), *n.* = azym.

Bb

***B¹** or **b** (bē), *n., pl.* **B's** or **Bs, b's** or **bs. 1** the second letter of the English alphabet. There are two *b* 's in *baby.* **2** any sound represented by this letter. **3** as a symbol: **a** the second (of an actual or possible series): *a reservation for bedroom B, a member of Company B in an infantry battalion.* **b** the second best (of its kind or class): *a B motion picture, grade B canned fruit.* **c** a known quantity (used especially in algebraic equations, along with *a, c,* etc.; *x, y,* and *z* most commonly represent unknown quantities). **4** the second highest grade (in schools and colleges): *to get a B in English.* **5** *Music.* **a** the seventh tone in the scale of C major. **b** a symbol representing this tone. **c** a key, string, etc., that produces this tone. **d** the scale or key which has B as its keynote: *a sonata in B.*

***B¹**
definition 5b

B² (bē), *n., pl.* **B's.** anything shaped like the letter B.

b., an abbreviation for the following:
1 *Baseball.* **a** base. **b** baseman.
2 *Music.* bass.
3 born.
4 *Sports.* bowled.
5 breadth.
6 brother (of).
7 *Sports.* bye.

B (no period), **1** bishop, in chess. **2** boron (chemical element). **3** one of the four main groups used to determine blood compatibility in transfusions. A person with B type blood can receive blood of either the B or O group.

B., an abbreviation for the following:
1 bacillus.
2 *Baseball.* **a** base. **b** baseman.
3 *Music.* bass.
4 battery.
5 Bay.
6 Bible.
7 book.
8 British.
9a brother. **b** brotherhood.

B-, *U.S. Air Force.* bomber: *B-17, B-29.*

ba (bä), *n.* the soul, in ancient Egyptian religion. It was represented in art by a birdlike figure and supposed to return to the body sometime after death.

Ba (no period), barium (chemical element).

BA (no periods), Bachelor of Arts (Latin, *Baccalaureus Artium*). Also, **AB** (no periods).

B.A., 1 Also, **A.B.** Bachelor of Arts (Latin, *Baccalaureus Artium*). **2** British Academy. **3** British America.
▶See **A.B.** for usage note.

baa (ba, bä), *n., pl.* **baas,** *v.,* **baaed, baa|ing.** —*n.* the sound a sheep makes; a bleat.
—*v.i.* to make this sound; bleat. [imitative]

Ba|al (bā′əl, bāl), *n., pl.* **Ba|al|im** (bā′ə lim), **Ba|als. 1** the chief god of the Canaanites and Phoenicians. In some places he was the god of fertility; in others, he was the sun god. His cult, which included related deities, was condemned as idolatrous by the Israelites. **2** any one of several local deities among the ancient Semitic peoples.
3 *Figurative.* any false god. [< Hebrew *ba'al* lord]

Ba|al|ish (bā′ə lish, bā′lish), *adj.* **1** of or belonging to Baal. **2** idolatrous.

Ba|al|ism (bā′ə liz əm), *n.* **1** the worship of Baal. **2** gross idolatry. —**Ba′al|ist,** *n.*

Ba|al|ite (bā′ə līt), *n.* = Baalist.

baas (bäs), *n.* master (now especially a form of address an African is required to use to a white man in the Republic of South Africa). [< Afrikaans *baas*]

baas|kap or **baass|kap** (bäs′käp), *n.* the supremacy of the white race in the Republic of South Africa; mastery over the native and colored peoples by white people in the Republic of South Africa. [< Afrikaans *baaskap*]

baaskap or **baasskap apartheid,** = apartheid.

Baa|thism or **Ba'a|thism** (bä′thiz′əm), *n.* the beliefs and principles of a Socialist party of various Arab countries, especially Syria and Iraq.
—**Baa′thist, Ba'a′thist,** *n., adj.*

ba|ba¹ (bä′bə; *French* bȧ bȧ′), *n.* a small, spongy, light cake, made with yeast, and flavored with rum, kirsch, or the like. [< French *baba* < Polish, (originally) old woman]

ba|ba² (bä′bä), *n.* a child or baby, in India. [< Hindustani *bābā* father, probably < Arabic]

ba|ba³ (bä′bä), *n.* a title of respect in Turkey, especially for a noble. [< Turkish *baba* < Arabic *bābā* father]

ba|ba au rhum (bȧbȧ′ō rôm′), *French.* a baba (cake) flavored with rum; rumbaba.

ba|bas|su or **ba|ba|su** (bä′bə sü′), *n.* **1** a Brazilian palm whose hard-shelled nuts yield an oil used in making soap and inexpensive candies.
2 Also, **babassu oil.** the oil. [< Portuguese *babasu,* perhaps < a Tupi word]

Bab|bit's metal (bab′its), *Especially British.* babbitt.

bab|bitt (bab′it), *n., v.* —*n.* an alloy of tin, antimony, copper, and sometimes lead, used especially in bearings to lessen friction; Babbitt metal. Babbitt is whitish in color and usually feels slippery, almost greasy, when it is rubbed.
—*v.t.* to line or furnish (a bearing) with babbitt. [American English < Isaac *Babbitt,* 1799-1862, an American inventor]

Bab|bitt (bab′it), *n.* a smug, self-satisfied businessman, especially one who conforms to middle-class standards of respectability and business success. [< George *Babbitt,* the central character of Sinclair Lewis's novel *Babbitt* (1922)]

Babbitt metal, = babbitt.

bab|bitt|ry or **Bab|bitt|ry** (bab′ə trē), *n.* conformity to middle-class ideas of respectability and business success.

bab|ble (bab′əl), *v.,* **-bled, -bling,** *n.* —*v.i.* **1** to make sounds like a baby: *My baby brother babbles and coos in his crib.* **2** to talk foolishly; prattle: *She babbled on and on about her new dress.* SYN: gabble. **3** to talk too much; chatter. **4** to tell secrets: *He babbled all about the surprise party we had planned.* **5** to make a murmuring sound: *The little brook babbled away just behind our tent.*
—*v.t.* to reveal foolishly: *She babbled our secret.* SYN: blab.
—*n.* **1** talk that cannot be understood: *A confused babble filled the room.* **2** foolish talk. **3** a murmuring sound: *The babble of the brook put me to sleep.*
[imitative of babies' chatter (similar forms are found in many languages)] —**bab′ble|ment,** *n.* —**bab′bling|ly,** *adv.*

bab|bler (bab′lər), *n.* **1** a person or thing that babbles. **2** any of a family of passerine birds with a loud, chattering cry.

Bab|cock test (bab′kok), a test for measuring the amount of butterfat in milk. [< Stephen M. *Babcock,* 1843-1931, an American chemist, who devised it]

babe (bāb), *n.* **1** a baby. **2** *Figurative.* an innocent or inexperienced person; a person who is like a child. SYN: innocent. **3** *U.S. Slang.* a girl or young woman. [an imitative word (originating perhaps in child language)]

babe in the wood or **woods,** a very innocent or inexperienced person; one who has a child's blind trust or lack of experience and hence is likely to become the victim of unscrupulous persons.

Ba|bel (bā′bəl, bab′əl), *n.* **1 Tower of Babel,** a high tower built after the Flood to reach heaven. God punished its builders by changing their language into several new and different languages. Because they could not understand one another, they had to leave the tower unfinished (in the Bible, Genesis 11:1-9). **2** *Figurative.* Also, **babel.** a noise; confusion: *... a babel of fury and shouts* (Harper's). **b** a place of noise and confusion: *When the teacher came back, she found the room a babel.* **3** Babylon. [< Hebrew *bābel* Babel, Babylon]

Ba|bel|ic (bə bel′ik), *adj.* **1** of or having to do with Babel. **2** *Figurative.* Also, **babelic.** of the nature of a Babel; noisily confused: *a Babelic crescendo of confusion.*

Ba|bel|ize (bā′bə līz, bab′ə-), *v.t.,* **-ized, -iz|ing.** to throw into confusion; make unintelligible; confound. —**Ba′bel|i|za′tion,** *n.*

bab|e|si|a|sis (bab′ə zī′ə sis), *n.* = piroplasmosis. [< New Latin *babesiasis* < *Babesia* genus name of the protozoan (variant of *Piroplasma*) that causes the disease (< Victor *Babes,* 1854-1926, a Romanian bacteriologist) + *-iasis*]

Bab|i (bä′bē), *n., adj.* —*n.* **1** = Babism. **2** = Babist. —*adj.* of or having to do with Babism.

bab|i|a|na (bab′ē ā′nə), *n.* a plant of the iris family, having spikes of lilac, red, or yellow flowers. [< New Latin *Babiana* < Dutch *Babianer* < *Babian, Baviaan* baboon (because baboons eat the stems of these plants)]

ba|biche (bä bēsh′), *n. Canadian.* thongs or lacings of rawhide, sinew, or gut, used especially to make snowshoes, snares, and other items of wood and leather exposed to the weather. [< Canadian French *babiche* < an Algonkian word]

ba|bies'-breath (bā′bēz breth′), *n.* **1** a tall plant bearing numerous clusters of small, fragrant, white or pink flowers on branching stalks; gypsophila. Babies'-breath is a member of the pink family and is often grown in rock gardens. **2** any of various other plants bearing somewhat similar flowers, often pink or rose. Also, **baby's-breath.**

ba|bies'-slip|pers (bā′bēz slip′ərz), *n.* = bird's-foot trefoil.

Ba|bin|ski's reflex (bə bin′skēz), a reflex in which the big toe turns up, instead of curling under, when the sole of the foot is stroked. The abnormal reaction usually indicates a brain lesion. [< Joseph F. F. *Babinski,* 1857-1932, a French neurologist born in Poland, who first noted it]

bab|i|ru|sa, bab|i|rous|sa, or **bab|i|rus|sa** (bab′ə rü′sə, bä′bə-), *n.* a wild hog found in the East Indies. The boar has tusks that curve upward and backward from its snout. [< Malay *babi* hog + *rusa* deer]

Bab|ism (bä′biz əm), *n.* the belief and practice of a Persian sect, founded by Mirza Ali Muhammad, 1819-1850, teaching a high morality, recognizing the equality of the sexes, and forbidding polygamy. [< *Bab,* title of the founder (< Persian *bab* gate) + *-ism*] —**Bab′ist,** *n., adj.*

Bab|ite (bä′bīt), *n., adj.* = Babist.

bab|ka (bäb′kə; *Polish* bäb′kä), *n., pl.* **-kas.** a round yeast cake made with raisins or cottage cheese, and spice and often flavored with rum or vanilla. [< Polish *babka* (diminutive) < *baba* baba¹]

ba|boo (bä′bü), *n., pl.* **-boos.** in India: **1** a Hindu title meaning "sir," "Mr.," "gentleman." **2** (in Anglo-Indian use) a native with a smattering of English education. **3** (in Anglo-Indian use) a native clerk who writes English. Also, **babu.** [< Hindustani *bābūsir*]

ba|boo|ism (bä′bü iz əm), *n.* the superficial English culture and imperfect English of baboos. Also, **babuism.**

ba|boon (ba bün′), *n.* **1** a kind of large, fierce monkey with a doglike face and a rather short tail. Baboons live in the rocky hills of Africa and Arabia in large troops. They have large canine teeth, cheek pouches, and naked, leathery flesh on the buttocks, often of a bright color. The chacma, drill, and mandrill are baboons. **2** *Figurative.* someone who is uncouth or vulgar; lout. SYN: oaf. [< Middle English *babewyn* grotesque figure < Old French *babouin* stupid person; (later) ape]

ba|boon|er|y (ba bü′nər ē), *n., pl.* **-er|ies.** baboonish behavior; loutishness.

ba|boon|ish (ba bü′nish), *adj.* **1** like a baboon. **2** characteristic of baboons.

ba|bouche or **ba|boosh** (bä büsh′), *n.* a soft, slipperlike leather shoe with a curling toe and no heel, worn in Iran, North Africa, and surrounding areas. [< French *babouche* < Arabic *bābūsh* < Persian *pāpūsh*]

ba|bu (bä′bü), *n., pl.* **-bus.** = baboo.

ba|bu|ism (bä′bü iz əm), *n.* = babooism.

ba|bul (bä bül′, bä′bül), *n.* **1** any tree of various acacias that yield gum and tannin. **2** the gum,

***B¹**
definition 1

Script letters look like examples of fine penmanship. They appear in many formal uses, such as invitations to social functions.

Bb *Bb*

Handwritten letters, both manuscript or printed (left) and cursive (right), are easy for children to read and to write.

Bb *Bb*

Roman letters have *serifs* (finishing strokes) adapted from the way Roman stonecutters carved their letters. This is *Times Roman* type.

Bb *Bb*

Sans-serif letters are often called *gothic.* They have lines of even width and no serifs. This type face is called *Helvetica.*

Bb *Bb*

Between roman and gothic, some letters have thick and thin lines with slight flares that suggest serifs. This type face is *Optima.*

B

Computer letters can be sensed by machines either from their shapes or from the magnetic ink with which they are printed.

pods, or bark of a babul tree. [< Hindustani *babūl*]

ba|bush|ka or **ba|boush|ka** (bə büsh′kə *for 1;* bä′büsh kə *for 2*), *n.* **1** a woman's scarf or kerchief worn on the head and tied under the chin. **2** a grandmother; baba. [< Russian *babushka* grandmother (diminutive) < *baba*]

ba|by (bā′bē), *n., pl.* **-bies,** *adj., v.,* **-bied, -by|ing.** —*n.* **1a** a very young child, especially one too young to walk or speak; infant: *A hungry baby will usually cry.* **SYN:** nursling. **b** the young of an animal: *a mother cat and her babies.* **2** the youngest of a family or group: *She may be the baby of the group, but she's as smart as any of us.* **3** *Figurative.* a person who acts like a baby; childish person: *Don't be a baby and cry over that little scratch.* **4** *Especially U.S. Slang.* **a** a girl or young woman, especially a sweetheart; babe. **b** any person or thing: *That boxer is a tough baby. Instead of a hundred miles an hour, you bring this baby in at almost twice that* (Harper's). **c** *Figurative.* a plan, idea, or project, which is the chief interest or responsibility of a person or group: *The Air Force, claiming that all pilot instruction is their baby, took over training of Army helicopter pilots from the Army* (Newsweek).
—*adj.* **1** young: *The sheep gave birth to a baby lamb.* (*Figurative.*) *Of course we're having trouble with our prototype . . . Everybody is. This is a baby industry* (Wall Street Journal). **2** *Informal, Figurative.* small for its kind; small: *my baby finger.* **3** of or for a baby: *a baby doctor. Baby shoes are often made of cloth.* **4** like that of a baby; childish: *Of course their motives are not all baby pure* (Manchester Guardian Weekly). **SYN:** babyish, infantile.
—*v.t.* **1** to treat as a baby; pamper: *to baby a spoiled child.* **SYN:** coddle. **2** *U.S. Sports.* to strike or stroke (a ball) gently.
hold the baby, *Especially British.* to carry a burden or responsibility unwillingly: *We're in a no-man's-land between emancipation and equality; we suspect we're also holding the baby* (London Times).
throw out the baby with the bathwater, to discard the essential along with the superfluous because of excessive zeal: *The overly vivid presentation of the truth is no real reason to throw that truth overboard. This is throwing out the baby with the bathwater* (Maclean's).
[Middle English *babi* (diminutive) < *babe* babe]
—**ba′by|like′,** *adj.*

baby act, 1 a babyish or childish act. **2** *Informal.* **a** an excusing or defending of oneself on the ground of legal infancy, inexperience, or the like. **b** a statute releasing a person from liability for such a reason.

baby beef, 1 the beef of a calf one year to 20 months old that has been fattened for slaughtering. **2** the calf so raised or fattened.

Baby Bell, any of the regional telephone companies originally a part of the national American Telephone and Telegraph Company.

baby blue, *Especially U.S.* a soft, light-blue color. —**ba′by-blue′,** *adj.*

baby blue-eyes, or **ba|by-blue-eyes** (bā′bē blü′īz′), *n.* **1** any one of certain North American plants of the waterleaf family having blue flowers. Different species are found in California, Oklahoma, the Northwestern United States, and southwestern Canada. **2** the flower of such a plant.

baby bond, *U.S. Informal.* a U.S. government bond having a face value of $25, $50, or $100.

baby bonus, *Canadian Slang.* family allowance (def. 2).

baby book, 1 *Informal.* a manual or book of advice on the care of infants. **2** a notebook to record a baby's birth, weight, growth, and other interesting facts about its development.

baby boom, a sudden increase in the birth rate of a population.

baby boomer, a child born in a baby boom, especially in the U.S. between 1946 and 1965.

baby buggy or **carriage,** *Especially U.S.* a small carriage with a handle for pushing, designed for a baby to lie in; pram.

***baby bunting,** an infant's warm, hooded outer garment closed at the bottom; bunting.

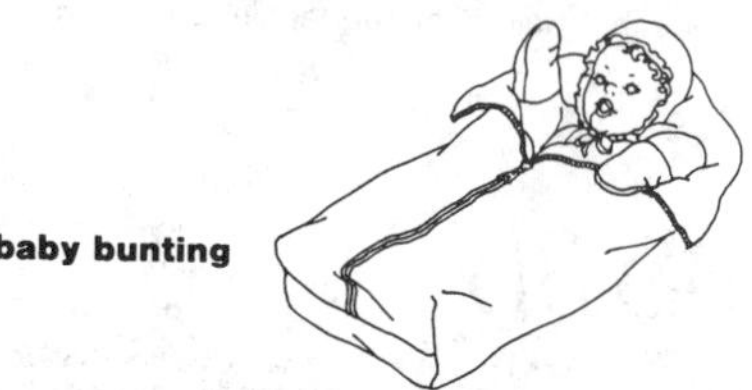

***baby bunting**

ba|by-faced (bā′bē fāst′), *adj.* **1** having a rather round, chubby, youthful-looking face. **2** *Figurative.* suggesting or appearing to have extreme youth and innocence.

baby farm, a place where babies are boarded for pay (used disparagingly).

baby farming, the business carried on by a baby farmer (used disparagingly).

baby food, any of various foods specially prepared for infants, usually by chopping, straining, or blending of ingredients. They are usually characterized as having very little flavor. —**ba′by-food′,** *adj.*

baby grand, a small grand piano.

ba|by|hood (bā′bē hu̇d), *n.* **1** the condition or time of being a baby. **SYN:** infancy. **2** babies as a group.

baby house, = dollhouse.

ba|by|ish (bā′bē ish), *adj.* like a baby; childish; silly. —**ba′by|ish|ly,** *adv.* —**ba′by|ish|ness,** *n.*

ba|by|ism (bā′bē iz əm), *n.* **1** silliness. **2** a babyish act or phrase. **3** *U.S.* = babyhood.

Bab|y|lon (bab′ə lən, -lon), *n.* **1** any great, rich, or wicked city. **2** *Figurative.* any place of exile or bondage. [< *Babylon,* the capital of ancient Babylonia, in SW Asia, on the Euphrates. It was noted for its wealth, power, and magnificence, and for the wickedness of its people.]

Bab|y|lo|ni|an (bab′ə lō′nē ən), *adj., n.* —*adj.* **1** of or having to do with ancient Babylon or Babylonia. **2** *Figurative.* magnificent; luxurious. **3** wicked; immoral.
—*n.* **1** an inhabitant of Babylon or Babylonia: *Many Greek discoveries, such as the Pythagorean theorem . . . , were known long, long before to the Babylonians* (Science). **2** the Semitic language of Babylonia.

Babylonian captivity, 1 the 50-year exile of the Jews in Babylon after Nebuchadnezzar destroyed Jerusalem about 586 B.C. **2** the period during the 1300's when the popes lived at Avignon in France. **3** *Figurative.* any prolonged condition or period of captivity, exile, or forced absence.

Bab|y|lon|ish (bab′ə lō′nish), *adj.* **1** of Babylon. **2** *Figurative.* confused in language.

ba|by-mind (bā′bē mīnd′), *v.i. Especially British.* to baby-sit. —**ba′by-mind′er,** *n.*

ba|by-mind|ing (bā′bē mīn′ding), *n. Especially British.* baby-sitting.

ba|by's-breath (bā′bēz breth′), *n.* = babies'-breath.

ba|by-sit (bā′bē sit′), *v.i.,* **-sat, sit|ting. 1** to take care of a child or children while the parents are away for a while. **2** *Figurative.* to take care of someone or something which is usually otherwise taken care of: *I had to baby-sit for our neighbor's cat while they were on vacation.* [back formation < *baby sitter*]

baby sitter, a person who takes care of a child or children while the parents are away for a while.

ba|by-sit|ting (bā′bē sit′ing), *n.* the action or occupation of a person who baby-sits: *Baby-sitting has become so familiar a concept that it is a shock to realize it is only a generation old* (Harper's).

baby talk, 1 the imperfect speech of infants and very young children. It frequently has *w* for *r* and words like *itty-bitty, itsy-bitsy,* and *dada.* **2** the speech of adults imitating this.

baby tears, a low plant having many tiny green leaves and small, blue flowers, usually a house plant.

baby teeth, the first set of teeth; milk teeth; primary teeth. The twenty baby teeth usually come into place between the ages of six and thirty months.

ba|by-watch (bā′bē woch′, -wôch′), *v.i. Especially British.* to baby-sit. —**ba′by-watch′er,** *n.*

ba|by-watch|ing (bā′bē woch′ing, -wôch′-), *n. Especially British.* baby-sitting.

ba|by|wear (bā′bē wãr′), *n. Especially British.* babies' clothes.

bac|a|la|o (bak′ə lä′ō), *n., pl.* **-la|os.** an important food fish of the West Indies belonging to the same family as the sea basses. [< Spanish *bacalao*]

Ba|car|di (bə kär′dē), *n.* **1** *Trademark.* a brand of rum made in Cuba and Puerto Rico. **2** a cocktail made of Bacardi rum, lime or lemon juice, and sugar or (sometimes) grenadine.

bac|ca (bak′ə), *n., pl.* **bac|cae** (bak′sē). a berry. [< Latin *bacca*]

bac|ca|lau|ré|at (bȧ kȧ lô rȧ ȧ′), *n.* the annual examination for graduation from secondary school in France. [< French *baccalauréat*]

bac|ca|lau|re|ate (bak′ə lôr′ē it), *n., adj.* —*n. U.S.* **1** the degree of bachelor given by a college or university. **2** Also, **baccalaureate sermon.** a sermon or other address delivered to a graduating class at, or the Sunday preceding, commencement.
—*adj.* having to do with the degree of bachelor: *a baccalaureate gown.*
[< Medieval Latin *baccalaureatus* < *baccalaureus* bachelor, humorous variant of *baccalarius* bachelor (because of a supposed derivation from Latin *bacca* berry + *laureus* of laurel)]

bac|ca|rat or **bac|ca|ra** (bak′ə rä, bak′ə rä′), *n.* **1** a French card game in which the rest of the players bet against one who is banker. Its most popular form is *chemin de fer.* **2** fine crystal made at Baccarat, France. [< French *baccara*]

bac|cate (bak′āt), *adj.* **1** berrylike; pulpy: *baccate fruit.* **2** bearing berries; bacciferous. [< unrecorded Latin *baccātus* < *bacca* berry]

Bac|chae (bak′ē), *n.pl.* **1** the women companions of Bacchus. **2** priestesses or women worshipers of Bacchus; bacchantes. **3** the women participants in the Bacchanalia.

bac|cha|nal (bak′ə nəl, -nal), *adj., n.* —*adj.* having to do with Bacchus or his worship.
—*n.* **1** a wild, noisy party; drunken revelry; orgy. **2** a drunken reveler. **3** a worshiper of Bacchus. **Bacchanals,** the Bacchanalia: *Intemperance and excess in the heathen Bacchanals was esteemed an act of religious joy* (George Stanhope).
[< Latin bacchānālis having to do with Bacchus]

bac|cha|nale (bak′ə nəl, -nal), *n.* a ballet or modern dance characterized by portrayal of wild or orgiastic merriment and drunken revelry. [< French *bacchanale* bacchanal]

bac|cha|na|li|a (bak′ə nā′lē ə, -nāl′yə), *n.pl. in form, sing. in use.* a wild, noisy party; drunken revelry; orgy.

Bac|cha|na|li|a (bak′ə nā′lē ə, -nāl′yə), *n.pl. in form, sing. in use.* a wild, noisy party; drunken revelry; orgy.

Bac|cha|na|li|a (bak′ə nā′lē ə, -nāl′yə), *n.pl. in form and use.* a wild, noisy ancient Roman festival in honor of Bacchus.

bac|cha|na|li|an (bak′ə nā′lē ən, -nāl′yən), *adj., n.* —*adj.* **1** having to do with the Bacchanalia. **2** drunken and wildly merry; bacchantic; bacchic.
—*n.* a drunken reveler; bacchant.

Bac|cha|nals (bak′ə nəlz, -nalz), *n.pl. in form and use.* the Bacchanaiia.

bac|chant (bak′ənt), *n., pl.* **bac|chants, bac|chan|tes** (bə kan′tēz), *adj.* —*n.* **1** a priest or man worshiper of Bacchus; bacchanal. **2** a drunken reveler. —*adj.* **1** worshiping Bacchus. **2** given to drunken carousing. **3** wine-loving.
[< Latin *bacchāns, -antis,* present participle of *bacchārī* celebrate the rites of Bacchus]

bac|chan|te (bə kan′tē, bə kant′, bak′ənt), *n.* a priestess or woman worshiper of Bacchus; maenad. [< French *bacchante,* learned borrowing from Latin *bacchāns, -antis* bacchant]

bac|chan|tic (bə kan′tik), *adj.* = bacchanalian.

Bac|chic (bak′ik), *adj.* **1** of Bacchus or his worship. **2** = bacchanalian.

Bac|chus (bak′əs), *n.* **1** *Roman and Greek Mythology.* the god of wine. The Greeks also called him Dionysus. **2** wine or liquor.

bac|cif|er|ous (bak sif′ər əs), *adj.* bearing or producing berries. [< Latin *baccifer* (< *bacca* berry + *ferre* to bear) + English *-ous*]

bac|ci|form (bak′sə fôrm), *adj.* shaped like a berry. [< Latin *bacca* berry + English *-form*]

bac|civ|or|ous (bak siv′ər əs), *adj.* feeding chiefly on berries, as some birds do. [< Latin *bacca* berry + *vorāre* devour + English *-ous*]

bach¹ (bach), *v., n. Informal.* —*v.i.* Also, **bach it.** to live as a bachelor, alone and doing one's own cooking and housekeeping, especially of a man: *At one time, when his wife had a job in Burlington and lived there except for weekends, Teal bached it on the farm* (New Yorker).
—*n.* a bachelor, especially an unmarried man. Also, **batch.** [< *bachelor*]

bach² (bach), *n.* a small country or seaside house, in New Zealand, used on weekends. [< probably < *bach¹*]

bach|e|lor (bach′ə lər, bach′lər), *n.* **1** a man who has not married; unmarried man: *The young bachelor will soon be taking a wife.* **SYN:** celibate. **2** Also, **Bachelor. a** a person who has what is usually the first of the degrees granted by a college or university, especially Bachelor of Arts or Bachelor of Science. Students who complete the undergraduate course of four years in the United States and Canada and three years in England are given the degree of bachelor. **b** the degree itself. **3a** = knight bachelor. **b** (originally) a young knight who served under the banner of another because he was not old enough, or had too few vassals, to display his own banner; bachelor-at-arms. **4** the male of any animal unmated during breeding season, especially one of the young male fur seals which are kept away from the breeding grounds by the older males. **5** *U.S. Dialect.* = crappie. [earlier *bachelor* a young knight < Old French < unrecorded Medieval Latin *baccalaris,* variant of *baccalarius* helper or tenant on a *baccalaria* section of land]

bachelor apartment or **bachelor flat,** an apartment suitable for one person.

bach|e|lor-at-arms (bach′ə lər ət ärmz′, bach′lər-), *n., pl.* **bach|e|lors-at-arms.** a young knight; bachelor.

bachelor chest, a small, low chest of drawers with a folding top for converting it into a table.

bach|e|lor|dom (bach′ə lər dəm, bach′lər-), *n.* the state of being a bachelor.

bachelor girl, *U.S.* an unmarried girl or young woman who lives alone: *... the thirtyish bachelor girl trying to carve out a career in a man's world* (New Yorker).

bach|e|lor|hood (bach′ə lər hu̇d, bach′lər-), *n.* the condition of being a bachelor.

Bachelor of Arts, **1** a degree given by a four-year college or by a university to a person who has completed a course of study meeting the requirements, generally with emphasis on the liberal arts. *Abbr:* A.B., B.A. **2** a person who has this degree.

Bachelor of Science, **1** a degree given by a four-year college or by a university to a person who has completed a course meeting the requirements, generally with emphasis on the sciences. *Abbr:* (*U.S.*) B.S., (*Canadian and British*) B.Sc. **2** a person who has this degree.

bachelor party, a party for men only, given in honor of a bachelor who is about to be married.

***bach|e|lor's-but|ton** (bach′ə lərz but′ən, bach′lərz-), *n.* **1** a plant of the composite family having a small, button-shaped flower of a blue, purple, pink, or white color; cornflower. **2** its flower. **3** = globe amaranth.

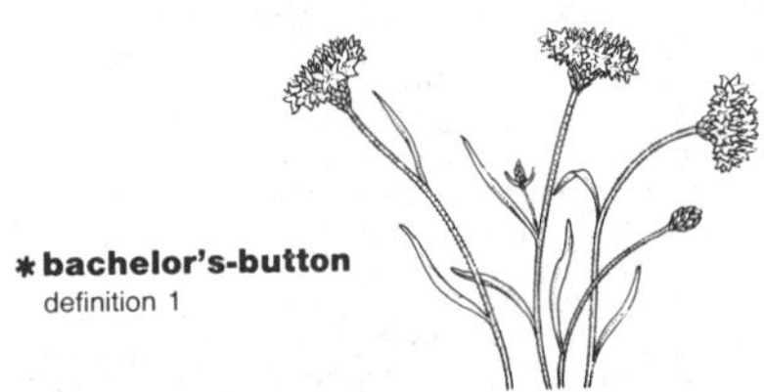

***bachelor's-button**
definition 1

bachelor's or **bachelor hall**, the home of a bachelor, or of one or more men only.

bach|e|lor|ship (bach′ə lər ship, bach′lər-), *n.* **1** the state or condition of being a bachelor. **2** the rank or degree of bachelor. **3** the unmarried state of a man.

bachelor woman, *U.S.* a bachelor girl.

ba|cil|lar (bə sil′ər, bas′ə lər), *adj.* = bacillary.

ba|cil|lar|y (bas′i ler′ē), *adj.* **1a** of or caused by a bacillus. **b** like a bacillus. **2** characterized by bacilli. **3** rod-shaped; bacilliform. [< New Latin *bacillarius* < Late Latin *bacillus*]

bacillary dysentery, a disease caused by a bacillus; shigellosis. It is a form of dysentery.

ba|cil|li (bə sil′ī), *n.* plural of **bacillus**.

ba|cil|li|form (bə sil′ə fôrm), *adj.* rod-shaped.

ba|cil|lus (bə sil′əs), *n., pl.* **-cil|li**. **1** any bacterium. **2** any one of the rod-shaped aerobic bacteria, especially one that forms spores: *the typhoid bacillus.* See picture under **bacteria**. [< Late Latin *bacillus,* variant of Latin *bacillum* (diminutive) < *baculum* rod, staff]

Bacillus Cal|mette-Gué|rin (kȧl met′gā raN′), a strain of attenuated tuberculosis bacilli, used living as a vaccine (BCG vaccine) against tuberculosis. [< Albert *Calmette,* 1863-1933, and Camille *Guérin,* 1872-1961, French bacteriologists, who developed it]

bac|i|tra|cin (bas′ə trā′sin), *n.* an antibiotic obtained from a soil bacillus, effective against various Gram-positive bacteria, used especially in treating skin infections. [< *baci*(llus) + Margaret *Tracy* (patient in whom the germ was isolated)]

back¹ (bak), *n., v., adj.* —*n.* **1a** the part of a person's body opposite to his face or to the front part of his body. It extends from the neck to the end of the backbone. *His sunburned back hurt so much he couldn't turn his head.* **b** the upper part of any animal's body from the neck to the end of the backbone: *The little girl rode on the pony's back.* **2a** the backbone; spine: *He fell off the ladder and broke his back.* **b** the power to act or continue to act: *The back of opposition resistance was broken last week.* **3** the side of anything away from one; the rear, upper, or farther part: *the back of the head, the back of a hill. Put the chair in the back of the room.* **4** the reverse or under side: *the back of a rug, fabric, or coin.* **5** the part of a chair, couch, bench, or the like, which supports the back of a person sitting down: *When the boy tipped, he broke the back of the chair.* **6** that part of a garment which covers the back: *She split her coat up the back.* **7a** a player whose position is behind those players on the line of scrimmage in American football or behind the forwards in soccer, Rugby, and various other games. **b** the position of such a player. **8** the spine or backbone of a book. **9** *Archery.* the surface of a bow, opposite the side facing the string.

—*v.t.* **1** to support or help: *Many of his friends backed his plan.* SYN: aid, uphold, second. **2** to cause to move away from the front: *He backed his car out of the driveway.* **3** to endorse or underwrite: *to back a check. The millionaire backed the costs of the new play.* SYN: countersign. **4** to bet on: *to back a baseball team in the World Series.* **5** to make or be a back for: *Our little farm was backed by woods.* **6** to provide with a back; strengthen or support at the back: *to back satin with heavy crepe, to back a book.*

—*v.i.* **1** to move away from the front: *She backed away from the dog.* **2** to change direction counterclockwise: *The wind backed from west to southwest.* **3** to accumulate and rise: *The water backed onto the floor from the drain.*

—*adj.* **1** opposite the front; away from one: *He was sitting in the back seat of the car.* SYN: rear, hinder. **2** belonging to the past: *Have you read the back issues of this magazine?* **3** due but not yet paid; overdue: *The debtor was overwhelmed with back bills.* **4** in distant or frontier regions: *to live a lonely life in the back country.* SYN: remote, outlying. **5** in a backward direction; coming back; returning: *a back swing.* **6** *Phonetics.* pronounced at the back of the mouth, such as the *o* in *go* is.

back and fill, **a** to trim sails to keep a boat in a channel and floating with the current. The wind alternately fills the sails and spills out of them by a steering maneuver used in combination with handling the sails. *By backing and filling the sails we endeavored to avoid collision with the larger masses* [*of ice*] (James C. Ross). **b** *U.S. Informal, Figurative.* to be undecided; keep changing one's mind; vacillate: *The boar backed and filled as the dogs circled and took nips* (Newsweek).

back down, to give up an attempt or claim; withdraw: *He said he could swim, but he backed down when he got to the lake. The Tamils retorted by a threat of civil war and the Government backed down* (Observer).

back in (or **into**), to gain (something) chiefly by accident, as through the carelessness of others: *When all the other heirs died he backed into a fortune.*

back off, **a** to move back a distance: *Hackworth requests that you back off 1,000 meters to the north* (Harper's). **b** *Figurative.* to withdraw; back down: *The auto industry executives are not willing to back off their predictions of a big gain* (New York Times).

back out (or **out of**), *Informal.* **a** to break a promise: *My uncle promised to take me fishing, but he backed out when Mother said she would go too.* **b** to withdraw from an undertaking: *The village backed out of building a pool when the cost got too high.*

back up, **a** to move backward: *He backed up against the wall.* **b** to cause to move backward: *to back a car up in reverse gear.* **c** *Figurative.* to help or support: *The enthusiasts for reform were backed up by the general public.* **d** to accumulate and rise: *The extent of backing-up which will be effected is indicated by the excess height of the spillway dam* (Science News).

behind one's back, without one's knowing it; secretly: *The cashier of the store stole money behind the owner's back.*

break the back of, to ruin; destroy: *A prolonged strike, the President said, "could well break the back of the present expansion"* (New York Times).

get off one's back, to leave one alone; stop annoying or harassing one: *The only way to get the military off his back will be ... to make the army less important* (Manchester Guardian Weekly).

get one's back up, **a** to make or become angry: *His nagging got my back up. "I'm your brother." "Are you?" I said, beginning to get my back up* (H. Rider Haggard). **b** to be stubborn; resist: *The mule got his back up and refused to move.*

on (or **upon**) **one's back**, **a** sick: *... very feeble, having been for several weeks upon my back* (George Catlin). **b** helpless; prone; prostrate: *They never look up to heaven, till God lays them on their back* (William Gurnall).

put one's back up, **a** to make one angry: *He goes his own way ... if you put his back up* (Sunday Magazine). **b** to be stubborn: *The baby put her back up and would not eat the cereal in spite of mother's coaxing.*

stab in the back, to try to injure in a sly, treacherous manner; slander or betray: *This is the stuff of a good Washington controversy, to be enjoyed in this case even by those stabbed in the back* (London Times).

the back of beyond, *Informal.* ever so far off; some very out-of-the-way place: *If anybody's stomach is going to rebel, it is better to get the rebellion over before launching into the back of beyond* (Peter Fleming).

the back of one's hand, a rebuke or rebuff: *The backs of our hands are only to those intent upon grinding us down* (Patrick Ryan).

turn one's back on, to abandon; forsake: *I have never turned my back on my leader yet* (George Macdonald).

with (or **having**) **one's back to the wall**, unable to escape without fighting; hard-pressed: *After having their back to the wall for half the game, the players on the home team finally rallied and made a good score.*

[Old English *bæc*]

back² (bak), *adv.* **1** to or toward the rear; backward; behind: *Please go back three steps.* SYN: rearward. **2** in or toward the past: *That happened some years back.* SYN: ago. **3** in return: *They paid back what they borrowed.* **4** in the place from which someone or something came: *Put the books back.* **5** in check: *The police held the crowd back. Hold back your temper.* **6** in reserve: *Keep back enough paint to do the door.*

back and forth, first one way and then the other: *Dogs ran back and forth across the field.*

back (or **in back**) **of**, *U.S. Informal.* **a** in the rear of; behind: *The barn is in back of the house.* **b** *Figurative.* supporting; helping: *Once Jerry was back of you, there was nothing halfway about it* (New Yorker). **c** causing: *What's back of his proposal?*

go back on. See under **go¹**.

[Middle English for *aback*]

back³ (bak), *n.* a tub, trough, or vat, especially one used by brewers, dyers, or picklers. [< Dutch *bak* < Old French *bac* ferryboat, basin < Vulgar Latin *baccus* ferryboat]

back|ache (bak′āk′), *n.* a continuous pain in the back.

back-al|ley (bak′al′ē), *adj.* of or having to do with an unpleasant environment or undesirable neighborhood: *back-alley squalor.*

back-and-forth (bak′ən fôrth′, -fōrth′), *adj.* that moves alternately backward and forward; to-and-fro: *a back-and-forth motion.*

back|bar (bak′bär′), *n.* a bar in an open fireplace used to hang a vessel on.

back|bench or **back-bench** (bak′bench′), *n., adj.* —*n.* a rear seat, especially that of a backbencher: *Rumours of revolt on the Government back-benches always make for more excitement* (Punch).

—*adj.* of, having to do with, or designating a backbencher or backbenchers: *Backbench opinion can be decisive not only in matters of legislative detail, but also in times of grave crisis—witness the fall of the Chamberlain government in 1940* (Sunday Times).

back|bench|er or **back-bench|er** (bak′ben′chər), *n.* **1** a member of the British House of Commons who is not one of the leaders of his party: *... for once the back-benchers, the private members who hold no Government or party office, have dominated the business of the House of Commons* (Manchester Guardian Weekly). **2** any person of similar status in a legislature patterned on the British House of Commons.

back|bite (bak′bīt′), *v.t., v.i.,* **-bit**, **-bit|ten** or **-bit**, **-bit|ing**. to speak evil of; slander (an absent person). SYN: defame, malign, revile. —**back′bit′er**, *n.*

back|block|er (bak′blok′ər), *n. Australian.* a resident of the backblocks: *... sitting on his heels over the fire in an attitude peculiar to backblockers* (Ernest W. Harnung).

back|blocks (bak′bloks′), *n.pl. Australian.* country remote from settled areas or from a riverfront.

back|board (bak′bôrd′, -bōrd′), *n., v.* —*n.* **1** *Basketball.* the rectangular or fan-shaped board directly behind the basket, on which the basket is mounted. **2** a board placed at or forming the back of anything, as of a picture, a cart, or a boat. **3** a board held across the back of a person for support and to straighten the spine.

—*v.t.* to subject to the wearing of a backboard.

***back|bone** (bak′bōn′), *n.* **1** the main bone along the middle of the back in man and other mammals, birds, reptiles, amphibians, and fishes; spine; spinal column. The backbone consists of many separate bones, called vertebrae, held together by ligaments. **2** anything like a backbone. The backbone or spine of a book is where the sections or signatures are gathered and glued together and attached to the covers or case. *The backbones of nucleotide chains are separated by a constant distance throughout the length of the molecule* (Isaac Asimov). **3** *Figurative.* the most important part; chief support; basis: *Scientific research is the backbone of modern industrial progress.* SYN: foundation, bedrock. **4** *Figurative.* strength of character; firmness: *A coward lacks the backbone to stand up*

Pronunciation Key: hat, āge, cãre, fär; let, ēqual, tėrm; it, īce; hot, ōpen, ôrder; oil, out; cup, pu̇t, rüle; child; long; thin; ᴛʜen; zh, measure; ə represents **a** in about, **e** in taken, **i** in pencil, **o** in lemon, **u** in circus.

for his beliefs. SYN: fortitude, hardihood. —**back'-bone'less,** *adj.*

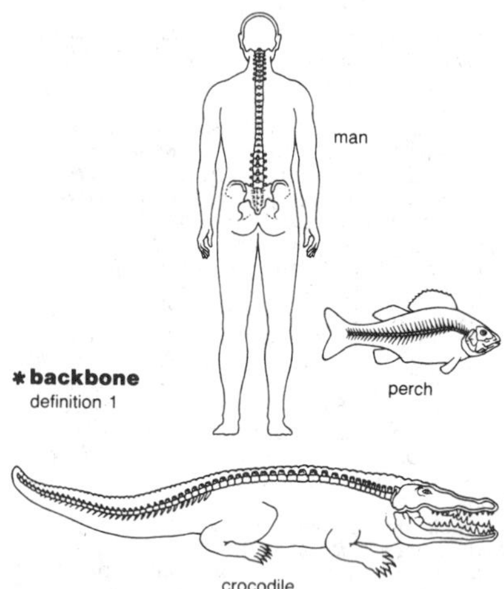

***backbone**
definition 1

back|boned (bak'bōnd'), *adj.* having a backbone.
back|break|er (bak'brā'kər), *n.* **1** a backbreaking task, assignment of work, or other undertaking. **2** a person who works extremely hard.
back|break|ing (bak'brā'king), *adj.* very exhausting or tiring; demanding great effort: *backbreaking work.* —**back'break'ing|ly,** *adv.*
back burner, on the back burner, in a secondary place; set aside or postponed as subordinate: *The first of the High Energy Astronomy Observatory satellites . . . resumed development earlier this year after being put on the back burner by NASA* (Science News).
back|cast (bak'kast', -käst'), *n.* **1** a throw or cast to the rear. **2** the upward and backward motion of the fishing rod, line, and fly or other lure that immediately precedes a cast.
back-chan|nel (bak'chan'əl), *adj., n.* —*adj.* secret; clandestine: *Mr. Kelly had been engaged in back-channel discussions with Lieut.-Col. Oliver North . . . on hostage releases* (Manchester Guardian Weekly).
—*n.* the person or means by which something is carried on secretly.
back|chat (bak'chat'), *n. Informal.* **1a** witty talk; repartee: *the effervescence of Beaumarchais with lines of pinpoint carbonation that bubble wittily with what G. B. Shaw called "retortive backchat"* (Time). **b** impudent or insolent retorts; back talk: *Don't give me any of your backchat.* **2** friendly, informal talk; chit-chat: *too reminiscent of the jaunty backchat of commentators in newsreels* (London Times).
back-check[1] (bak'chek'), *n.; v.* —*n.* the checking of a completed job for errors.
—*v.t.* to check a completed job before giving final approval. [< *back*[2] + *check,* noun]
back-check[2] (bak'chek'), *v.i. Hockey.* to skate back toward one's own goal to cover an opponent's rush. [< *back*[2] + *check,* verb]
back|cloth (bak'klôth', -kloth'), *n. Especially British.* **1** the rear curtain on stage; backdrop. **2** background: (*Figurative.*) *These conflicts were taking place against the backcloth of sweeping social changes* (Manchester Guardian).
back|comb (bak'kōm'), *v.t.* to comb (hair) from the ends toward the scalp to raise it or give it shape; tease.
back country, country that is rural and thinly settled, away from the more developed centers of population; hinterland: *The economic integration of the back country with the national economy is incomplete* (Scientific American).
back-coun|try (bak'kun'trē), *adj.* **1** that is rural and thinly settled: *a back-country region.* **2** of or having to do with a back-country region or the people who live in it: *back-country manners. The back-country accent he uses in addressing farmers is more political than real* (Newsweek).
back|court (bak'kôrt', -kōrt'), *n.* **1** *Tennis.* the part of the court between the service line and the base line. **2** *Basketball.* the half of the court of the defending team.
back|cross (bak'krôs', -kros'), *v., n. Genetics.* —*v.t., v.i.* to cross (a hybrid of the first generation) with either one of its parents.
—*n.* such a cross.
back|date (bak'dāt'), *v.t.,* **-dat|ed, -dat|ing. 1** to put an earlier date on, especially a date that is earlier than the actual date: *. . . indicted for backdating tax returns* (Time). **2** to reckon as from an earlier date: *to backdate the salary increases three months.*
back door, 1 a door in the back of a room or house. **2** *Figurative.* a secret, devious, or irregular means. [*She*] *charged that the Democratic plan was "socialized medicine by the back door"* (New York Times).
back|door (bak'dôr', -dōr'), *adj.* unofficial or irregular; secret; clandestine; devious: *"Backdoor" financing bypasses the appropriations process and draws money direct from the Treasury* (Wall Street Journal).
back|down (bak'doun'), *n. Informal.* a backing down; retreat from a claim, position, or point of view after a challenge: *. . . backdowns, concessions and shifts* (Time).
back|draft (bak'draft', -dräft'), *n.* a draft of air or current of gas going in a direction contrary to normal, as in a furnace.
back|drop (bak'drop'), *n., v.,* **-dropped** or **-dropt, -drop|ping.** —*n.* **1** a curtain at the back of a stage, often painted and used as part of the scenery. **2** background: (*Figurative.*) *The committee also must labor against a backdrop of political pressure points* (New York Times).
—*v.t.* to provide with a backdrop.
backed (bakt), *adj.* provided with a back; having a back, background, or backing (used especially in compounds): *silver-backed.*
back end, *British Informal.* autumn.
back|er (bak'ər), *n.* a person who backs or supports another person, a plan, or an idea: *His friends were backers of the plan.*
back|er-up (bak'ər up'), *n. American Football.* a linebacker.
back|fall (bak'fôl'), *n.* **1** a falling back. **2** that which falls back. **3** a fall or throw on the back in wrestling.
back|fat (bak'fat'), *n.* a layer of fat between the skin and the muscles of an animal.
back-fence (bak'fens'), *adj.* between neighbors; neighborly: *back-fence gossip.*
back|field (bak'fēld'), *n.* **1** the players whose usual position is behind those on the line of scrimmage in American football or behind the forwards in soccer and Rugby, especially the quarterback, the halfbacks, and the fullbacks. **2** the area occupied by these players. **3** the positions of these players: *He is trying out for the backfield.*
back|field|er (bak'fēl'dər), *n.* a person who plays in the backfield.
back|fill (bak'fil'), *v., n.* —*v.t.* to refill (an excavation). —*n.* soil or other material used to backfill.
back|fire (bak'fīr'), *n., v.,* **-fired, -fir|ing.** —*n.* **1** an explosion of gas occurring at the wrong time or in the wrong place in an internal-combustion engine: **a** an explosion in the intake or exhaust, resulting from unburned fuel in the exhaust, or slow-burning fuel in the cylinder causing the new charge to ignite through the open intake valve. **b** an explosion of gas occurring too soon in a cylinder. **2** an explosion coming out of the breech of a firearm. **3** *U.S.* a fire set to check a forest fire or other open fire by controlled burning off of the area in front of the forest fire.
—*v.i.* **1** (of gas) to explode at the wrong time or in the wrong place. **2** to have a result opposite to the expected result: *His scheme backfired, and instead of getting rich he lost all his money.* **3** *U.S.* to use a backfire in fire fighting.
Backfire bomber, or **Backfire,** *n.* a long-range Soviet supersonic bomber that can be refueled in flight. [a Nato code name for this bomber, officially known as the Tupolev V-G]
back|fisch (bäk'fish'), *n. Informal.* a young girl; a half-grown schoolgirl. [< German *Backfisch* (originally) a small fish for baking or frying]
back|flash (bak'flash'), *v.i.* (of a flame consuming combustible gas) to move back through the current of gas and burn at a point nearer the source than is desired.
back flip, a backward somersault, as in fancy diving.
back|flow (bak'flō'), *n.* a moving back or returning to the source.
back formation, a word formed by dropping an ending or beginning from a longer word that itself appears to be derived from the new, shorter word. *Examples: burgle* from *burglar; enthuse* from *enthusiasm; pea* from *pease* taken as plural; *typewrite* from *typewriter.*

***backgammon**
definition 1

***back|gam|mon** (*n.* bak'gam'ən, bak'gam'-; *v.* bak'gam'ən), *n., v.* —*n.* **1** a game for two played on a divided board with 12 spaces on each side. Each player has 15 pieces, which are moved according to the throw of the dice. **2** a victory won in this game before all the opponent's men are in play.
—*v.t.* to defeat at backgammon, especially by means of a gammon or backgammon.
[probably < *back*[1] + *gammon* a game]
back|ground (bak'ground'), *n., v., adj.* —*n.* **1** the part of a picture or scene toward the back: *The cottage stands in the foreground with the mountains in the background.* **2** the part which shows off the chief thing or person; surface upon which things are made or placed: *Her dress had a pattern of pink flowers on a white background.* SYN: setting, base, ground. **3** *Figurative.* earlier conditions or events that help to explain some later condition or event: *This book gives the background of the Revolutionary War.* SYN: backdrop. **4** *Figurative.* one's past experience, knowledge, and training: *His early background included living on a farm.* SYN: groundwork. **5** the accompanying music or sound effects in a play, motion picture, television program or other show.
—*v.t. U.S. Informal.* to provide documentation, color, or subordinate plot material for (a story, play, or other production): *Two books were consulted to background the story* (Birmingham News).
—*adj.* of or having to do with the background or setting of a play, motion picture, or other production: *He composed the background music which we enjoyed.*
in the background, out of sight or not in clear view; obscure: *The shy girl kept in the background. He is the man who really gives the orders, but he is careful always to remain in the background.*
back|ground|er (bak'groun'dər), *n.* **1** *U.S.* a press conference held to explain the background of some event or policy by an official who cannot be identified or quoted directly: *A "backgrounder" permits newspapermen to publish information given them though without attribution to the source* (Drew Pearson). **2** a bulletin explaining the background of some event or policy.
background radiation, the low radiation from cosmic rays and trace amounts of radioactive substances naturally present in the atmosphere, the material of a counter, etc.
back|hand (bak'hand'), *n., adj., adv., v.* —*n.* **1a** a stroke in tennis and other games played with a racket or paddle, made with the back of the hand turned outward and the arm usually held across the body: *His backhand is his most effective stroke.* **b** the use of such strokes, as part of a person's skill in playing. **2** handwriting in which the letters slope to the left.
—*adj.* **1** backhanded. **2** of or characterized by the use of the backhand: *Practice will improve your backhand game.*
—*adv.* with a backhanded stroke or motion.
—*v.t.* **1** to hit or catch backhand. **2** *Slang.* to criticize or snub; rebuff.
back|hand|ed (bak'han'did), *adj., adv.* —*adj.* **1** done or made with the back of the hand turned outward: *a backhanded stroke.* **2** *Figurative.* indirect: *He means to help, even though he offers to in a backhanded way.* **3** *Figurative.* sounding like praise but actually an insult; insincere: *A backhanded compliment is really a criticism.* **4** slanting to the left: *backhanded writing.* **5** awkward; clumsy. **6** with the strands of rope or cable twisted in the reverse of the usual direction.
—*adv.* backhand. —**back'hand'ed|ly,** *adv.* —**back'hand'ed|ness,** *n.*
back|hand|er (bak'han'dər), *n.* **1** a backhanded blow or stroke. **2** an extra glass of wine. **3** *British.* an unofficial commission for some service provided in business, often underhand; bribe.
back|haul (bak'hôl'), *n.* **1** the return trip of a vehicle carrying freight. **2** the freight brought back on such a trip; return freight: *If the ships that ferry materials to Alaska could return south with a backhaul, . . . the northbound freight rates would decrease* (New Yorker).

***backhoe**
definition 2

***back|hoe** (bak'hō'), *n.* **1** a bucketlike shovel at the end of a jointed mechanical arm, mounted on the rear of a tractor to dig out trenches or other small excavations by scooping the dirt toward the tractor. The mechanism is usually run by hydraulic power from the tractor. **2** a tractor equipped with such a mechanism.
back|house (bak'hous'), *n.* **1** *U.S.* an outhouse

behind a main building; privy. 2 *Scottish.* the back room or kitchen of a cottage.

back|ing (bak′ing), *n.* **1a** support or help: *Do I have your backing in my campaign for a stoplight at the school crossing?* SYN: assistance, aid. **b** supporters or helpers. SYN: backers, champions. **2** something placed at the back of anything to support or strengthen it: *This picture will need a firm backing before it can be framed.* SYN: reinforcement. **3** the first 50 yards of older line put on a fishing reel spool, seldom needed in ordinary fishing. **4** *U.S. Informal.* musical accompaniment to a solo instrument.

back|land (bak′land′), *n.* hinterland; back country: *He ... has learned about his country and its people by tramping dusty backlands roads and sleeping in peasant huts* (Time).

back|lash (bak′lash′), *n., v.* **—*n.*** **1** a jarring reaction, striking back, or backward movement in a machine or mechanical device. **2** the movement or play between worn or badly fitting parts. **3** a tangle in the portion of a fishing line still on the reel, caused when the spool continues to unwind line that is not payed out after the lure. **4** *Figurative.* **a** a sudden, adverse reaction usually caused by fear or anger: *His insulting remarks finally brought a sharp backlash of anger from his patient helper.* **b** a reaction of antagonism by one group to the pressure exerted by another group or movement, such as white backlash to the black civil-rights movement.
—*v.t.* to produce a backlash; backfire. **—back′-lash′er,** *n.*

back|less (bak′lis), *adj.* having no back.

back-lift (bak′lift′), *n. Cricket.* the backswing of the bat before a stroke.

back|light (bak′līt′), *v.t.,* **-light|ed** or **-lit, -light-ing.** to light from the rear: *In a day or two after the new moon, we see a narrow crescent in the west after sunset, for the lunar globe is now backlighted by the sun* (Bernhard, Bennett, Rice).

back line, a line drawn across a curling rink six feet from the tee line to mark off the area where a player must begin delivery.

back|list (bak′list′), *n.* a publisher's list of reprinted or previously published books.

back|log (bak′lôg′, -log′), *n., v.,* **-logged, -log-ging.** **—*n.*** **1** *Informal.* **a** a reserve of orders, duties, or commitments that have not yet been filled or carried out: *He is working on the backlog of homework assignments that accumulated while he was sick.* **b** something reserved for use at a later time: *The campers took a backlog of food in case they got lost.* **2** *Especially U.S.* something serving as a basis or support: *His insurance policy was intended as a backlog against illness.* **3** *Especially U.S.* a large log at the back of a wood fire in a fireplace.
—*v.t.* to hold or accumulate as a backlog: *Manufacturers are trying to fill orders backlogged during summer plant closedowns* (Wall Street Journal).

back|lot (bak′lot′), *n.* an outdoor area near a motion-picture studio used for sets: *It could have been filmed as well on the studio backlots as in Africa* (Newsweek).

back|mark|er (bak′mär′kər), *n. British.* one that starts with the worst handicap in a race or match.

back matter, those pages of a book that follow the main text, usually containing such things as the index and bibliography.

back|most (bak′mōst), *adj.* = hindmost.

back number, **1** an old issue of a magazine or newspaper. **2** *Figurative.* an old-fashioned person or out-of-date thing, especially one whose fame has been eclipsed or popularity forgotten.

back-of-the-en|ve|lope (bak′əv ᴛʜə en′və lōp, -än′-), *adj.* quickly and easily determined; not requiring elaborate calculations: *A simple back-of-the-envelope sum illustrates the problem* (New Scientist).

back order, an order received for merchandise not currently available and acknowledged for supplying at a later date.

back-or|der (bak′ôr′dər), *v.t.* to place (merchandise) on back order.

back|out (bak′out′), *n. Informal.* a backing out; withdrawal.

back|pack (bak′pak′), *n., v.* **—*n.*** **1** something made for carrying as a pack on one's back: *a backpack parachute.* **2** anything carried as a pack on one's back: *Three were skin divers with backpacks of scuba gear* (Time).
—*v.t., v.i.* to carry a backpack or inside a backpack: *The three men carried all they had on their backs ..., quite a lot to backpack at such heights* (Maclean's). **—back′pack′er,** *n.*

back-pad|dle (bak′pad′əl), *v.i.,* **-dled, -dling.** to back water. See under **water.**

back|pat (bak′pat′), *v.,* **-pat|ted, -pat|ting,** *n.* **—*v.t., v.i.*** to pat on the back; show approval (of): *... an exercise in backpatting* (Saturday Review).
—*n.* a pat on the back or any similar sign of encouragement or approval: *... the effectiveness of a few verbal backpats* (Newsweek).

back|ped|al (bak′ped′əl), *v.i.,* **-aled, -al|ing** or (*especially British*) **-alled, -al|ling.** *Informal.* **1** to move backward so as to keep away from one's opponent in a boxing match or fight. **2** *Figurative.* to qualify or retreat from an announced policy, program, or endorsement. **3** to press back on the pedals (of a bicycle with a coaster brake) to give a braking action.

back|plate (bak′plāt′), *n.* **1** a plate fastened at or forming the back: *The spindle of a doorknob is held in place by two backplates.* **2** a piece of armor covering the back and fastened to the breastplate with straps.

back play, *Cricket.* a batting stroke made with the bat pulled back toward the wicket.

back pressure, pressure in a direction opposite to normal, such as pressure against the discharge of a cylinder in an exhaust system, or pressure against the flow in any circulation of fluids, as caused by an obstruction.

back|pro|ject (bak′prə jekt), *v.t.* to project (an image) on the back of a translucent screen for viewing from the front.

back projection, the projection of a film on a translucent screen, used as a background for a scene being filmed or photographed.

back|rest (bak′rest′), *n.* **1** anything that supports the back. **2** a support at the back, as on a lathe.

back road, any little-used road, especially one in the country; side road.

back|room (bak′rüm′, -rům′), *n., adj.* **—*n.*** **1** a room in the back of a house, store, etc. **2** *Figurative.* a place of secret or behind-the-scenes influence, planning, or machination: *diplomatic backrooms.* **—*adj.*** done or decided without public knowledge; secret or clandestine: *... a spectacle of machine control and backroom politics* (Time).

backroom boy, *Informal.* anyone who works in secrecy, especially: **a** a politician who negotiates secretly with other politicians. **b** a scientist engaged in secret research.

back|saw (bak′sô′), *n.* a handsaw stiffened by a thick metal band along its back.

back|scat|ter (bak′skat′ər), *n., v. Physics.* **—*n.*** radioactive particles, light waves, or other radiation deflected by any obstacle at an angle of more than 90 degrees. **—*v.t.*** to deflect (radioactive particles, light waves, or other radiation) at an angle of more than 90 degrees.

back|scat|ter|ing (bak′skat′ər ing), *n. Physics.* the deflection of radioactive particles, light waves, or other radiation at an angle of more than 90 degrees.

back|scratch|er (bak′skrach′ər), *n.* **1** *Informal.* a person who engages in backscratching. **2** *Informal.* a flatterer. **3** any device for scratching the back.

back|scratch|ing (bak′skrach′ing), *n. Informal.* the giving and taking of favors for personal advantage: *No law can eliminate backscratching, favoritism ...* (Newsweek).

back seat, **1** a seat in or at the back. **2** *Informal, Figurative.* a place of inferiority or insignificance: *When the discussion turned to local politics, the stranger had to take a back seat.*

back-seat driver (bak′sēt′), *Informal.* **1** a passenger who constantly criticizes or advises the driver of an automobile. **2** *Figurative.* any person who freely criticizes or persistently advises without assuming any responsibility himself.

back|set (bak′set′), *n.* **1** a check to progress; setback: *It would give a backset and might ... endanger their ultimate success* (John C. Calhoun). **2** an eddy or backward-flowing current.

back|sheesh or **back|shish** (bak′shēsh), *n., v.t., v.i.* = baksheesh.

back|shop (bak′shop′), *n.* **1** a private shop next to the main one. **2** the printing shop of a newspaper: *A slowdown in the backshop operations made us late with editions* (Wall Street Journal).

back|side (bak′sīd′), *n.* **1** the back; rear: *The dog ran around to the backside of the shed and hid.* **2** *Informal.* Also, **backsides.** the rump; buttocks: (*Figurative.*) *to be taken to the woodshed of public odium and have his backsides tanned with the leather strap of public contempt* (New York Times). **3** the dark side of the moon.

back|sight (bak′sīt′), *n.* a sight or reading taken in a backward direction or to a previous station in surveying.

back slang, slang in which words are pronounced or written backwards or in some other organization of the letters that is different from their normal form, as in pig Latin. *Example: ynnep* or *ennypay* for *penny.*

back|slap|per (bak′slap′ər), *n. Informal.* a person whose friendly manner is so hearty and effusive as to seem insincere: *Although not a backslapper, he is a highly effective campaigner* (Harper's).

back|slap|ping (bak′slap′ing), *n., adj.* **—*n.*** *Informal.* a too hearty and friendly manner; the practices of a backslapper.
—*adj.* too hearty and friendly: *They are intellectuals and very different from the ... backslapping, vigorous, go-ahead sorts of men* (Newsweek).

back|slide (bak′slīd′), *v.i.,* **-slid, -slid|den** or **-slid, -slid|ing.** to slide back into wrongdoing; gradually return to old habits or practices, especially ones forbidden by a church or by authority; relapse: *So far none of the reformed drinkers has backslid* (Time). **—back′slid′er,** *n.*

back|space (bak′spās′), *v.i.,* **-spaced, -spac|ing.** to move a typewriter carriage backward a fixed space or spaces.

back|spin (bak′spin′), *n.* a rolling motion in reverse to the direction of a ball. It checks or reverses the forward motion of a ball when it strikes a surface.

back|splash (bak′splash′), *n.* a vertical extension at the back of a counter, stove, or other flat working surface to protect the wall behind it; splashback.

back-stab|ber (bak′stab′ər), *n. Informal.* a person who slyly attempts to ruin or damage someone.

back-stab|bing (bak′stab′ing), *n. Informal.* a sly or treacherous attempt to ruin or damage, as by slander or betrayal.

back|stage (bak′stāj′), *adv., adj.* **—*adv.*** **1** in or to that part of a theater which is not seen by the audience; behind a backdrop, in the wings, or in a dressing room; offstage: *The actor went backstage after his part was over.* **2** in, at, or toward the rear of a stage; upstage: *The chorus stood backstage, behind the soloist.*
—*adj.* **1** located or taking place backstage: *The star gave the reporter a backstage interview.* **2** *Figurative.* not known to the general public; secret or confidential: *Backstage negotiations were revealed to the public as soon as the agreement was reached.*

back|stair (bak′stãr′), *adj.* = backstairs.

back stairs, **1** stairs in the back part of a house, used especially for deliveries or by servants. **2** *Figurative.* a private, secret, or underhanded method or course.

back|stairs (bak′stãrz′), *adj.* **1** secret and underhanded: *...backstairs influence and clandestine government* (Edmund Burke). **2** scandalous or defamatory: *a web of backstairs gossip.*

back|stamp (bak′stamp′), *n.* a mark, such as a postmark, stamped on the back of a piece of mail or a trademark stamped on the bottom of earthenware.

back|stay (bak′stā′), *n.* **1** a rope or wire extending aft from the top of a mast to the ship's side and helping to support the mast. **2** a spring, rod, or strap, used for support at the back of various mechanisms or other objects.

back|stitch (bak′stich′), *n., v.* **—*n.*** stitching or a stitch in which the thread doubles back each time on the preceding stitch.
—*v.t., v.i.* to sew with such stitches: *The seam of your dress will be stronger if you backstitch it.*

back|stop (bak′stop′), *n., v.,* **-stopped, -stop-ping.** **—*n.*** **1a** a wall, fence, or screen used in various games, such as baseball and tennis, to keep the ball in the area of play. **b** *Informal.* a player who stops balls in various games, especially a catcher in baseball and cricket. **2** *Informal, Figurative.* anything that supports or reinforces: *... a kind of economic backstop in case a recession sets in* (Wall Street Journal). **3** (in machinery) a part for preventing recoil beyond a designated point.
—*v.i., v.t.* *Informal.* **1** to serve as a backstop: *The ordinary safeguards against the escape of radioactive rays are backstopped by the 5-ft. thick walls of the plant* (Time). **2** *Figurative.* to support; reinforce: *There are a dozen top-rank aides, backstopped in depth by aides of their own, who stand like breakwaters between him and the deluge of his official responsibilities* (New York Times).

back-straight (bak′strāt′), *n. British.* the backstretch of a race track.

back|strap (bak′strap′), *n.* **1** the narrow backpart or spine of a book: *On the backstrap, they cry, "The most important book you will ever read"* (New Yorker). **2** the part of a horse's harness passing along the middle of the back.

back|street (bak′strēt′), *adj.* furtive; clandestine; backstairs: *backstreet intrigue.*

back|stretch (bak′strech′), *n.* the portion of a race track. opposite and parallel to the home stretch, usually farthest from those watching a

---

Pronunciation Key: hat, āge, cãre, fär; let, ēqual, tėrm; it, īce; hot, ōpen, ôrder; oil, out; cup, pu̇t, rüle; child; long; thin; ᴛʜen; zh, measure; ə represents a in about, e in taken, i in pencil, o in lemon, u in circus.

race.

back|stroke (bak'strōk'), *n.* **1** a swimming stroke made by a swimmer lying on his back. **2** a backhanded stroke in tennis and other games played with a racket or paddle. **3** a blow or stroke in return; recoil.

back|swept (bak'swept'), *adj.* = swept-back.

* **back swimmer**, an aquatic, bloodsucking insect that swims on its back, using its long, flattened hind legs in the same fashion as oars.

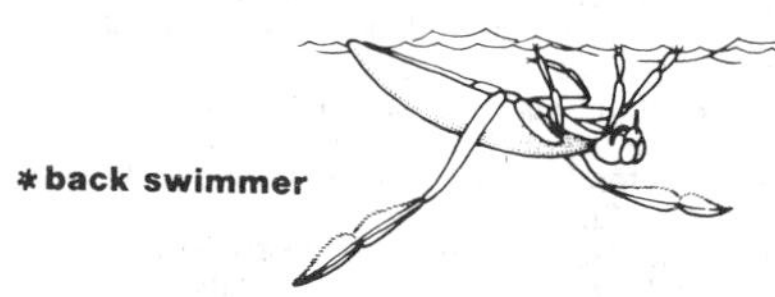

* **back swimmer**

back|swing (bak'swing'), *n.* **1** a preparatory movement of a bat, club, or the like, backward to the position from which it is swung forward. **2** a return to a past attitude, view, manner, etc.: *a backswing of women's fashions.*

back|sword (bak'sôrd', -sōrd'), *n.* **1** a sword with only one cutting edge; broadsword. **2** = singlestick. **3** a fencer with the broadsword or singlestick.

back|sword|man (bak'sôrd'mən, -sōrd'-), *n., pl.* **-men.** a fencer with the backsword or singlestick.

back talk, *Informal.* impudent answers, especially by a younger person or subordinate.

back-to-back (bak'tə bak'), *adj.* **1** placed with backs near or joined: *back-to-back houses.* **2** consecutive: . . . *two 45-minute shows back-to-back* (TV Guide).

back-to-ba|sics (bak'tə bā'siks), *adj. Especially U.S.* characterized by or advocating a return to the essentials or fundamentals: *The back-to-basics movement in education . . . stresses reading, writing, and math in the lower grades* (Edward Alvey, Jr.). *[They] are advocates of a back-to-basics life style that cost them less than $1,500 last year* (Today).

back|track (bak'trak'), *v.i.* **1** to go back over a course or path: *Studies of the Mendenhall Glacier . . . show that since about 1765 the ice has backtracked two miles* (Science News Letter). **2** *Figurative.* to withdraw from an undertaking or position: *He backtracked on the promise he made last week.*

back|up (bak'up'), *n., adj.* **—n. 1** something or someone kept in reserve as a substitute or for assistance: *a backup of troops.* **2** an accumulation: *a backup of traffic. Slow demand for steel is causing a backup along the entire raw material supply channel* (Wall Street Journal).
—adj. 1 kept in readiness or reserve: *The A.E.C. requires a pumping system to keep the reactor cool. If the primary source of power for the pumps fails, a "backup" system must take over to keep the coolant flowing* (Wall Street Journal). **2** complementary; supporting: . . . *our office in Ottawa, staffed by an experienced man with backup staff* (Canada Month).

back|veld (bak'velt'), *n.* a country area in South Africa distant from urban life. [< *back*[1] + Afrikaans *veld* veld]

back vowel, a vowel, as *u,* sounded with the tip of the tongue receded and the back of it raised toward the soft palate.

back|ward (bak'wərd), *adv., adj.* **—adv. 1** toward the back: *He walked backward.* **2** with the back first: *He tumbled over backward.* **3** toward the starting point: *to look backward.* **4** opposite to the usual way: *Can you read backward?* **5** from better to worse: *In some countries living conditions improved; in some they went backward.* **6** toward the past: *He looked backward forty years and talked about his childhood. The lights of memory backward stream* (John Greenleaf Whittier). Also, **backwards.**
—adj. 1 directed toward the back: *She gave him a backward look over her shoulder.* SYN: rearward. **2** with the back first: *a backward fall off a ladder.* **3** directed to or toward the starting point; returning: *a backward movement.* SYN: regressive. **4** done in the reverse way or order: *a backward process.* SYN: retrograde. **5** reaching back into the past: *Far as thy mind thro' backward time can see* (Alexander Pope). **6** slow in development: *Backward children need special help in school.* **7** behind time; late: *This is a backward season; spring is two weeks late.* **8** shy; bashful: *Shake hands with her; don't be backward.* SYN: reluctant.
backward and forward, perfectly; completely: *I hope that from here on the Julliard Opera Theatre will concentrate on works that are less familiar, offering the public a taste of what it does not already know backward and forward* (Winthrop Sargeant).
bend, fall, or **lean over backward,** *Informal.* to make every effort to be accommodating: *Companies whose business is . . . closely interwoven with the military establishment ought to lean over backward so that no suggestion of favoritism . . . could be read into their conduct* (New York Times).
[Middle English *bakward* < *bak* back[2] + *-ward,* Old English *-weard* toward] **—back'ward|ly,** *adv.* **—back'ward|ness,** *n.*
▶**Backward** and **backwards** are used interchangeably as adverbs: *Try doing the work backward. Try doing the work backwards.* Only *backward* is used as an adjective: *He hurried off without a backward glance.*

back|ward|a|tion (bak'wər dā'shən), *n. British Finance.* postponement of the delivery of shares or commodities by the seller with the consent of the buyer, who is usually paid a premium.

back|wards (bak'wərdz), *adv.* = backward.
backwards and forwards. See under **backward.** ▶See **backward** for usage note.

back|wash (bak'wosh', -wôsh'), *n.* **1a** the water thrown back by oars, paddle wheels, a passing ship, or surf against rocks. **b** a backward current of air behind propellers or jet engines. **c** *Surfing.* a stretch of rough water made by cross currents meeting. **2** bad aftereffects; aftermath: *The backwash of war had left his people in extreme privation* (Harper's). **3** a backward place; backwater: *He also depicts it [a State] as a poverty-stricken backwash of ignorance* (New York Times).

back|wa|ter (bak'wôt'ər, -wot'-), *n., v.* **—n. 1** a stretch of water held, pushed, or thrown back. **2** *Figurative.* **a** a backward place: *The village was a backwater of civilization.* **b** a sluggish, stagnant condition or situation: *His job had drifted into a hopeless backwater.* **3** a backward current or swell; backwash.
—v.i. 1 *U.S.* to retreat; withdraw: *The candidate backwatered on several promises when he got into office.* **2** to reverse or halt a boat by reversing the action of the oars or propeller: *The captain backwatered as we approached the dock.* **3** to back water. See under **water.**

back|wind[1] (bak'wind'), *v.t. Nautical.* to blanket (def. 3). [< *back*[2] + *wind*[1]]

back|wind[2] (bak'wīnd'), *v.t.,* **-wound, -wind|ing.** to wind (film in a camera) backward. [< *back*[2] + *wind*[2]]

back|wood (bak'wůd'), *adj.* = backwoods.

back|woods (bak'wůdz'), *n., adj.* **—n. pl. 1** uncleared or wild regions far away from towns: *The trapper lived in the backwoods far from the city's cares.* **2** a remote area; backward place.
—adj. 1 of or in the backwoods: *a narrow, two-track backwoods road.* **2** crude; rough: *You might not guess from his backwoods manners that he is a well-traveled man.*

back|woods|man (bak'wůdz'mən), *n., pl.* **-men. 1** a person who lives in the backwoods. **2** a person whose origin is in the backwoods. **3** *British.* a member of the House of Lords who seldom attends its meetings: *There is no sign of going back to the backwoodsmen. What we are going in for now is progressive government* (London Times).

back|woods|y (bak'wůdz'ē), *adj.* = backwoods.

back|yard (bak'yärd'), *n.,* or **back yard, 1** the yard behind a house or building: *We have a vegetable garden in the backyard and flowers in the front.* **2** *U.S.* any adjoining region or area thought of as one's home grounds: *U.S. steel makers must compete in their own backyard with aggressive producers of aluminum, glass, plastics, cement, and other materials* (Wall Street Journal).

ba|con (bā'kən), *n.* salted and smoked meat from the back and sides of a pig or hog: *Farmers used to cure their own bacon in a smokehouse.*
bring home the bacon, *Informal.* **a** to be successful; win the prize: *The winning horse brought home the bacon to the tune of $100,000.* **b** to earn a living: *Most men who bring home the bacon five days a week relax over the weekend.*
save one's bacon, *Informal.* to escape all bodily harm, damage, and loss: *But as he ran to save his bacon, By hat and wig he was forsaken* (William Combe).
[< Old North French *bacun* < Germanic (compare Middle High German *bache* ham, bacon)]

ba|con|er (bā'kə nər), *n. British.* a pig, especially one raised for bacon.

Ba|co|ni|an (bā kō'nē ən), *adj., n.* **—adj. 1** of Francis Bacon (1561-1626), his written works, or his doctrines. The Baconian method was a method of scientific study by proceeding from particular instances to general principles. **2** of the Baconian theory.
—n. 1 a follower of Francis Bacon's doctrines. **2** a supporter of the Baconian theory.

Baconian theory, the theory that Francis Bacon was the author of Shakespeare's plays.

bact., bacteriology.

bac|te|re|mi|a or **bac|te|rae|mi|a** (bak'tə rē'mē ə), *n.* the presence of bacteria in the bloodstream. [< *bacter*(ia) + *-emia*]

bacteri-, *combining form.* a form of **bacterio-**, as in *bactericide.*

* **bac|te|ri|a** (bak tir'ē ə), *n., pl. of* **bac|te|ri|um.** very tiny and simple plants, so small that they can usually be seen only through a microscope. Certain bacteria cause diseases such as pneumonia and typhoid fever; others do useful things, such as turning cider into vinegar. Bacteria consist of single cells that are rod-shaped, spherical, or spiral, and most kinds have no chlorophyll. Most bacteria multiply by splitting apart, some by forming spores. [< New Latin *bacteria,* plural of *bacterium* < Greek *baktērion* little staff, related to *báktron* stick, rod]

* **bacteria**

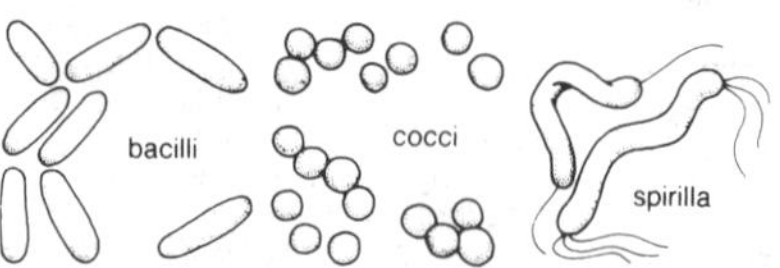

bac|te|ri|al (bak tir'ē əl), *adj.* **1** of or having to do with bacteria: *bacterial life.* **2** resembling bacteria. **3** caused by bacteria: *bacterial diseases.* **—bac-te'ri|al|ly,** *adv.*

bac|te|ric (bak tir'ik), *adj.* = bacterial.

bac|te|ri|cid|al (bak tir'ə sī'dəl), *adj.* destructive to bacteria.

bac|te|ri|cide (bak tir'ə sīd), *n.* any substance that destroys bacteria. [< *bacteri-* + *-cide*[1]]

bac|te|ri|cid|in (bak tir'ə sī'dən), *n.* an antibody that attacks bacteria.

bac|te|ri|form (bak tir'ə fôrm), *adj.* having the form of bacteria.

bac|te|rin (bak'tər in), *n.* a vaccine that is prepared from dead bacteria. [< *bacteria* + *-in*]

bacterio-, *combining form.* bacteria: *Bacteriology = the science of bacteria.* Also, **bacteri-**. [< New Latin *bacterium* bacterium]

bac|te|ri|oid (bak tir'ē oid), *n., adj.* = bacteroid.

bac|te|ri|o|log|ic (bak tir'ē ə loj'ik), *adj.* = bacteriological.

bac|te|ri|o|log|i|cal (bak tir'ē ə loj'ə kəl), *adj.* **1** of or having to do with bacteriology. **2** using bacteria, especially harmful bacteria: *bacteriological warfare.* **—bac|te'ri|o|log'i|cal|ly,** *adv.*

bac|te|ri|ol|o|gist (bak tir'ē ol'ə jist), *n.* a student of bacteriology.

bac|te|ri|ol|o|gy (bak tir'ē ol'ə jē), *n.* the science that deals with bacteria, a branch of biology: *The idea has persisted in bacteriology until very recently that microorganisms are somehow quite different from other plants and animals* (Atlantic).

bac|te|ri|ol|y|sin (bak tir'ē ol'ə sin), *n.* any substance that can destroy bacteria by lysis.

bac|te|ri|ol|y|sis (bak tir'ē ol'ə sis), *n.* **1** the destruction or dissolution of bacteria. **2** the chemical decomposition of solid organic matter in sewage by means of bacteria, without oxygen.

bac|te|ri|o|lyt|ic (bak tir'ē ə lit'ik), *adj.* **1** destructive to bacteria. **2** of or having to do with bacteriolysis.

bac|te|ri|o|phage (bak tir'ē ə fāj), *n.* a virus that destroys various bacteria, normally present especially in the intestines and blood; phage. [< *bacterio-* + Greek *phageîn* eat]

bac|te|ri|o|phag|ic (bak tir'ē ə faj'ik), *adj.* destructive to bacteria: *bacteriophagic viruses.*

bac|te|ri|oph|a|gous (bak tir'ē of'ə gəs), *adj.* = bacteriophagic.

bac|te|ri|oph|a|gy (bak tir'ē of'ə jē), *n.* the destruction of bacteria by a bacteriophage.

bac|te|ri|o|scop|ic (bak tir'ē ə skop'ik), *adj.* of or having to do with bacterioscopy.

bac|te|ri|o|scop|i|cal (bak tir'ē ə skop'ə kəl), *adj.* = bacterioscopic.

bac|te|ri|os|co|pist (bak tir'ē os'kə pist), *n.* a student of bacterioscopy.

bac|te|ri|os|co|py (bak tir'ē os'kə pē), *n.* the study of bacteria by microscope.

bac|te|ri|o|sta|sis (bak tir'ē ə stā'sis), *n.* the arrest of the growth or development of bacteria without killing them. [< *bacterio-* + *stasis*]

bac|te|ri|o|stat (bak tir'ē ə stat), *n.* an agent that arrests the growth or development of bacteria.

bac|te|ri|o|stat|ic (bak tir'ē ə stat'ik), *adj.* arresting the growth or development of bacteria.

bac|te|ri|o|ther|a|py (bak tir'ē ō ther'ə pē), *n.* the treatment of disease by introducing a specific type of bacteria into the system.

bac|te|ri|um (bak tir'ē əm), *n.* singular of **bacteria.** [< New Latin *bacterium;* see etym. under **bacteria**]

bac|ter|ize (bak'tə rīz), *v.t.,* **-ized, iz|ing.** to treat or modify by bacterial action. **—bac'ter|i|za'tion,** *n.*

bac|te|roid (bak'tə roid), *n., adj.* **—n.** a microorganism of bacterial character found in the root

nodules of nitrogen-fixing plants, such as the legumes. *—adj.* resembling or allied to bacteria.
bac|te|roi|dal (bak′tə roi′dəl), *adj.* = bacteroid.
Bac|tri|an (bak′trē ən), *adj.* of or having to do with Bactria, an ancient country in central Asia: *The Bactrian rulers governed northern Afghanistan until the 100's B.C.* (Paul L. Hanna).
Bactrian camel, a camel with two humps, found in central Asia. It has longer hair and is stockier in build than the one-humped Arabian camel or dromedary. See picture under **camel**.
ba|cu|li|form (bə kyü′lə fôrm, bak′yə-), *adj. Biology.* shaped like a rod. [< Latin *baculum* rod]
bac|u|line (bak′yə lin), *adj.* having to do with the rod (for punishing). [< Latin *baculum* rod]
bad[1] (bad), *adj.,* **worse, worst,** *n., adv.* *—adj.* **1** not good; not as it ought to be; inferior: *bad soil. Lincoln often studied in bad light.* **SYN**: poor, inadequate. **2** evil; wicked: *A bad man might hurt a helpless person.* **3** causing harm; harmful: *It is bad for your eyesight to read in a dim light.* **4** not friendly; cross; unpleasant: *He had a bad temper.* **SYN**: offensive, troublesome. **5** unfavorable: *He came at a bad time.* **SYN**: unfortunate. **6** severe: *a bad case of pneumonia. A bad thunderstorm delayed the airplane.* **7** rotten; spoiled: *Don't use that egg; it's bad.* **SYN**: defective. **8** sorry: *I feel bad about losing your baseball.* **SYN**: distressed, regretful, disturbed. **9** sick; ill: *Her cold made her feel bad.* **10** incorrect: *to speak bad French. He made a bad guess.* **SYN**: faulty. **11** worthless: *a bad check.* **12** *Law.* not valid: *a bad claim, a bad plea.* **13** *U.S. Slang.* remarkable; outstanding; very good: *"Bullins is a bad dude. There's no better playwright in the American theater today"* (New Yorker).
—n. something that is bad; bad condition or quality: *One must be willing to take the good with the bad.*
—adv. Informal. badly: *He wanted so bad for it to be right.*
bad off, *Informal.* badly off: *I told him how bad off I was* (A. W. Tourgee).
be in bad, *Informal.* to be in disfavor (with a person over a thing): *I'm in bad with the teacher, because I didn't do my homework.*
go from bad to worse, to grow steadily worse; deteriorate: *During Stalin's long rule, things had gone from bad to worse in the countryside* (Canada Month).
not (or **not half**) **bad**, *Informal.* fairly good: *The teacher thought the idea of a class picnic was not bad.*
not so bad, *Informal.* rather good: *We had bagged three bulls before breakfast, which was not so bad* (W. R. Kennedy).
too bad, something to be regretted; a pity: *Their work is far from being known in a lot of places, which is too bad* (Canada Month).
to the bad, a toward ruin: *He and his muddled affairs soon went to the bad.* **b** in debt; in deficit: *His account is now $100 to the bad.*
[Old English *bædd* (originally) past participle of *ge-bǣdan* to oppress, constrain] —**bad′ness**, *n.*
—Syn. adj. **2 Bad, evil, wicked** mean morally wrong. **Bad**, the common word, is very general, ranging in application from naughtiness to being very corrupt, immoral, vile, etc.: *Lying is a bad habit.* **Evil** means very bad and sometimes suggests threatening great harm: *It is evil for judges to accept bribes.* **Wicked** emphasizes willfully defying and breaking moral laws: *Deliberately leading an evil life is wicked.*
▶ **bad, badly.** Following a linking verb, formal English prefers the predicate adjective *bad,* not the adverb *badly: He feels bad about the news.* Informal speech sometimes uses *badly: He feels badly about the news.* In formal English and informal writing, the adverb *badly* is used to modify verbs: *She sings badly.* But in informal speech *bad* is often used: *She sings bad.*
▶ **badder, baddest.** Though acceptable forms from the 1300's to the 1700's, they have been replaced by *worse, worst* and are now used only in informal or humorous contexts.
bad[2] (bad), *v. Archaic.* bade; a past tense of **bid**.
bad actor, *Slang.* **1** a person or animal that behaves badly. **2** an incorrigible or unscrupulous person.
bad apple, *Slang.* an incorrigibly bad person, especially one who is a corrupting influence: *There are a few bad apples in any crowd.*
bad blood, very unfriendly feeling; hatred: *There was bad blood between Cain and Abel. Bad blood between key lawmakers will keep Congress roiled up for months* (Wall Street Journal).
bad debt, a debt believed or proved to be uncollectable.
bad|de|ley|ite (bad′ə lē īt, bad′lē-), *n.* zirconium dioxide, a principal ore of zirconium. *Formula:* ZrO_2 [< J. *Baddeley,* the discoverer + *-ite*[1]]
bad|der (bad′ər), *adj. Informal.* worse.
▶ See second usage note at **bad**[1].
bad|der|locks (bad′ər loks), *n. Scottish.* an edible, olive-green seaweed, common in the North Sea and elsewhere off the coast of northern Europe. [earlier *Balderlocks,* perhaps < *Balder* a Scandinavian deity + *lock*[2] (from the plant's resemblance to locks of hair)]
bad|dest (bad′əst), *adj. Informal.* worst.
▶ See second usage note at **bad**[1].
bad|die or **bad|dy** (bad′ē), *n., pl.* **-dies.** *Slang.* a villain or one of his accomplices in a movie or television show; badman: (*Figurative.*) *The characters in the Central African drama cannot simply be divided into goodies and baddies* (Manchester Guardian Weekly).
bad|dish (bad′ish), *adj.* rather bad.
bade (bad, bād), *v.* a past tense of **bid** (defs. 1-6): *The captain bade the soldiers march on.*
▶ **Bade** is used chiefly in formal and literary English: *The king bade her remain.*
bad egg, *Slang.* a bad or worthless person.
bad faith, treachery: *How can you tell, except by consulting your own leanings, where bad faith bargaining begins and good faith stops?* (Wall Street Journal).
badge (baj), *n., v.,* **badged, badg|ing.** *—n.* **1a** something worn to show that a person belongs to a certain occupation, school, class, club, or society: *Policemen and firemen wear badges. The Red Cross badge is a red cross on a white background.* **SYN**: insigne. **b** something worn to show achievement or proficiency: *The scout's badge was for bravery.* **2** *Figurative.* a symbol or sign: *Chains are a badge of slavery.* **SYN**: token, emblem.
—v.t. to mark with, or distinguish by, a badge.
[Middle English *bage,* perhaps < Old French *bage* emblem; origin unknown]
badg|er (baj′ər), *n., v.* *—n.* **1** a hairy, gray mammal that feeds at night and digs a hole in the ground to live in. Badgers live in Europe, Asia, and North America and are related to the weasel, but are larger and more heavily built. **2** its hair or fur. **3** in Australia: **a** the wombat. **b** the bandicoot. **4** a soft brush made of badger's hair.
—v.t. to keep on annoying or teasing; bother or question persistently; tease; bait: *That salesman has been badgering my father for two weeks to buy a new car.*
[perhaps related to *badge* (from the white blaze on the animal's forehead)]
Badg|er (baj′ər), *n.* a nickname for a native or inhabitant of Wisconsin.
badger baiting, a former sport in which a badger is put in a barrel or other confined area and one or more dogs are set upon it to drag it out.
Badger State, a nickname for Wisconsin.
bad hat, *Especially British Slang.* a corrupt or worthless person.
ba|di|geon (bə dij′ən), *n.* **1** a mixture of ground stone and plaster for filling up holes in stone for sculpture or masonry. **2** a wash for giving plaster the appearance of stone. [< French *badigeon;* origin unknown]
bad|i|nage (bad′ə näzh′, bad′ə nij), *n., v.,* **-naged, -nag|ing.** *—n.* good-natured joking; banter: *the cheerful exchange of badinage after the match.* **SYN**: raillery, persiflage.
—v.t. to tease; banter.
[< French *badinage* < *badiner* to banter < Middle French *badin* fool, ultimately < Medieval Latin *batare* gape. See related etym. at **bay**[2].]
Bad|lands (bad′landz′), *n.pl.,* or **Bad Lands, 1** the rugged, barren region in southwestern South Dakota and northwestern Nebraska in which erosion has produced unusual land formations. **2** Usually, **badlands.** any similar region.
bad|ly (bad′lē), *adv.* **1** in a bad manner: *She sings badly.* **2** *Informal.* greatly; very much: *He wants to go badly.*
badly off, *Informal.* in a state of poverty, need, or distress: *They were not at all badly off, but the wife had preferred to go out to work* (Esquire).
▶ See first usage note at **bad**[1].
bad|man (bad′man′), *n., pl.* **-men.** *Informal.* **1** any outlaw or criminal; desperado. **2** the villain in a motion picture, play, television show, or other theatrical performance.

***badminton**
definition 1

***bad|min|ton** (bad′min tən), *n.* **1** a game in which either two or four players use light rackets to keep a shuttlecock moving back and forth over a high net. Badminton is somewhat like tennis. **2** *Especially British.* a drink made of dry wine, especially Bordeaux, sugar, and soda water. [< *Badminton,* an estate in Gloucestershire]
bad-mouth (bad′mouth′, -mouŦH′), *v.t. U.S. Slang.* to talk badly about; criticize or malign: *He attacked those who are "bad-mouthing our country all day long, all week long"* (New York Times).
bad news, *U.S. Informal.* a person or thing that brings trouble: *"I knew the kid was bad news first morning I met him ..."* (New Yorker).
bad patch, *British.* a period of bad luck.
bad-tem|pered (bad′tem′pərd), *adj.* having a bad temper; cross; irritable: *The bad-tempered old man was always chasing the children away.* **SYN**: cranky.
bad trip, *Slang.* a frightening experience involving hallucinations and pain, caused by taking a psychedelic drug, especially LSD.
B.A.Ed., Bachelor of Arts in Education.
Bae|de|ker (bā′də kər), *n.* a guidebook for travelers, especially one of a series of guidebooks first issued by Karl Baedeker (1801-1859), a German publisher.
baff (baf), *v., n.* *—v.i. Golf.* to strike the ground with the sole of the club in making a stroke.
—v.t. Scottish. to strike.
—n. **1** *Golf.* the act of baffing. **2** *Scottish.* a blow. [perhaps imitative, or related to Old French *baffe* a blow (with the back of the hand)]
baf|fle (baf′əl), *v.,* **-fled, -fling,** *n.* *—v.t.* **1** to be too hard for (a person) to understand or solve; bewilder: *This puzzle baffles me.* **SYN**: confound, perplex, disconcert. **2** to keep or hold back; hinder; thwart: *The thief baffled pursuit by locking us in before escaping.* **SYN**: foil, balk. See syn. under **frustrate. 3** to control or regulate (the flow of air or other gases, water, sound waves, or electrons) by a baffle. **4** to check; hold back: *If the wind does not baffle us ...* (Frederick Marryat).
—v.i. to struggle without success: *The ship baffled against high winds and finally foundered on the rocks.*
—n. a device for hindering or changing flow, especially of air or other gases, water, sound waves, or electrons. A baffle on a rocket engine can change the direction of the exhaust thus causing a change in direction of the rocket.
[< Scottish *baffull* to dishonor in effigy, probably related to French *bafouer* abuse] —**baf′fle|ment**, *n.* —**baf′fler**, *n.*
baf|fle|gab (baf′əl gab), *n. Informal.* very involved or confusing language; gobbledygook: *financial bafflegab.* [< *baffle* + *gab*]
baf|fle|plate (baf′əl plāt′), *n.* = baffle.
baf|fling (baf′ling), *adj.* **1** puzzling; bewildering: *a baffling problem.* **2** hindering; thwarting: *His duty was obstructed by baffling regulations.* **3** shifting: *baffling winds.* —**baf′fling|ly**, *adv.* —**baf′fling-ness**, *n.*
baf|fy (baf′ē), *n., pl.* **-fies.** *Golf.* a short wooden club with a deeply pitched face, for lofting the ball. [< *baff* + *-y*[2]]
bag (bag), *n., v.,* **bagged, bag|ging.** *—n.* **1a** a container made of paper, cloth, plastic, or leather, that can be pulled together to close at the top: *a flour bag. Fresh vegetables are sometimes sold in plastic bags.* **b** the amount that a bag holds; bagful: *Mother bought a bag of beans.* **2** something like a bag in its use or shape: *Mother calls her purse her bag. Father has a new overnight bag.* **3a** a pouch or sack for game. **b** the game or fish killed or caught at one time by a hunter or fisherman. **4** a base in baseball. **5** *U.S. Slang.* **a** something suited to one's taste or interest: *At one point they were trying to categorize me as a racial satirist, but that's not my bag. Let's say I deal in universal human foibles* (New York Times). **b** a matter or problem: *Malcolm's whole trouble was that he got caught up in that religious bag* (New Yorker). **6a** a sac in an animal's body: *the honey bag of a bee.* **b** an udder. **7** *Slang.* a woman, especially an ugly or old woman (used in an unfriendly or offensive way). **8** the envelope containing the gas of a balloon or dirigible. **9** *U.S. Slang.* **a** an envelope containing a small portion of a narcotic, especially heroin. **b** the portion itself.
—v.t. **1** to cause to swell or bulge: *Loss of sleep bagged his eyes and stooped his shoulders.* **2** to put into a bag or bags: *We bagged the cookies in dozens to sell them.* **3** to kill, trap, or catch in

Pronunciation Key: hat, āge, cãre, fär; let, ēqual, tėrm; it, īce; hot, ōpen, ôrder; oil, out; cup, pu̇t, rüle; child; long; thin; ŦHen; zh, measure; ə represents **a** in about, **e** in taken, **i** in pencil, **o** in lemon, **u** in circus.

hunting: *The hunter bagged many ducks.* **4** *Informal.* **a** to gain; win: *The new Premier's . . . coalition had bagged 174 of 300 parliamentary seats* (Time). **b** to catch, take, or steal: *I bagged the pencil which was lying about.* **5** *British Slang.* to claim first: *Bags I first ride on the bike!*
—*v.i.* **1** to hang loosely: *The boy's pants bag at the knees.* **2** to bulge; swell.
bag and baggage, with all one's belongings; entirely: *Farmers and their families were ordered from their homes and moved eastward, bag and baggage* (Time).
bags, *Informal.* **a** *British.* trousers. **b** plenty; more than enough: *bags of room, bags of time.*
hold the bag, *U.S. Informal.* **a** to take the blame or responsibility for something, unwillingly: *There can be no doubt that dealers are nervous about being left holding the bag, in this instance a bag full of new automobiles* (New York Times). **b** to be empty-handed: *Acquiring a complex of eighteen solvent insurance companies, . . . he systematically drained [them] of assets . . . leaving fifty-three thousand policyholders and scores of creditors holding the bag* (New Yorker).
in the bag, *Informal.* certain of success; sure: *My greatest anxiety now is lest our own supporters should conclude that the election is 'in the bag'* (London Times).
[Middle English *bagge,* probably < Scandinavian (compare Old Icelandic *baggi* pack)] **—bag'like',** *adj.*
—*Syn.* *n.* **1 Bag, sack** mean a container made of paper, cloth, etc., that can be closed at the top. **Bag** is the general word, applying to any such container of suitable size and material: *Fresh vegetables are sometimes sold in plastic bags.* **Sack** applies particularly to a large bag made of coarse cloth: *Mail is carried in sacks, and grain and potatoes are shipped in sacks.* But *sack* is now often used of a heavy paper bag, and in some places of any paper or similar bag: *Put my groceries in a sack.*

B.Ag., Bachelor of Agriculture (Latin, *Baccalaureus Agriculturae*).

Ba|gan|da (bə gan'də), *n., pl.* **-das** or **-da.** a member of the largest tribe of Uganda, living in the central and southern part and consisting mainly of farmers.

ba|gasse (bə gas'), *n.* the pulp of sugar cane after the juice has been extracted, used especially in the manufacture of wallboard and paper and as fuel. [< French *bagasse* < Spanish *bagazo* residue from pressing grapes, olives, etc., ultimately < Latin *bacca* berry]

ba|gat|a|way (bə gat'ə wā), *n. Canadian.* an Indian game from which lacrosse developed. Also, **baggataway.** [< an Algonkian word]

bag|a|telle (bag'ə tel'), *n.* **1** a mere trifle; thing of no importance. **2** a short piece of music, usually in a light style. **3** a game somewhat like billiards, played on a table having a semicircular end with nine holes to hit balls into with a cue. [< French *bagatelle* < Italian *bagattella* (diminutive) < dialectal Italian *baga* berry < Latin *bacca* berry]

ba|gel (bā'gəl), *n.* a hard roll made of raised dough shaped into a ring, simmered in water, and then baked, usually having a slightly shiny surface. Also, **beigel.** [< Yiddish *beygel*]

ba|gel|li|no (bā gə lē'nō), *n. U.S.* a cross between a bagel and a pretzel, usually covered with sesame seeds: *For those who follow the fashions in sidewalk vending, frozen yogurt and bagelinos made their debuts* (Marian Burros). [< *bagel* + *-ino,* as in *bambino*]

bag|ful (bag'fůl), *n., pl.* **-fuls. 1** the amount that a bag holds when filled: *to eat a bagful of peanuts.* **2** an abundant supply; plenty: *The rich tycoon has bagfuls of money.*

bag|gage (bag'ij), *n.* **1** the trunks, bags, or suitcases that a person takes with him when he travels; luggage. **2** the equipment that an army or an exploring party takes with it, such as tents, blankets, dishes, and cooking utensils. **3** *Informal, Figurative.* a burden of beliefs, theories, or characteristics, especially when excessive or superfluous: *His chief political baggage . . . consisted of a violent anti-Americanism* (Atlantic). **4** a young woman (used familiarly or playfully, especially with adjectives such as *artful, cunning, sly, pert, saucy,* or *silly*). [< Old French *bagage* < *bague* pack, bundle, perhaps < Scandinavian (compare Old Icelandic *baggi* bag)]

baggage car, *U.S.* a railroad car for carrying baggage, mailbags, and light freight.

bag|gage|man (bag'ij man'), *n., pl.* **-men.** a man whose business is handling baggage.

bag|gage|mas|ter (bag'ij mas'tər, -mäs'-), *n.* **1** the person in charge of baggage at a railroad station or on a baggage car. **2** the person in charge of baggage on a ship or at a pier. **3** the person in charge of baggage at any other terminus of public transportation.

bag|gat|a|way (bə gat'ə wā), *n.* = bagataway.

bag|ger (bag'ər), *n.* **1** a person or thing that places anything in a bag, such as groceries at a supermarket. **2** a machine which automatically packages a commodity in a bag or wrapper.

bag|gie (bag'ē), *n.* **1** a small bag. **2a** a plastic bag used to store food or to hold trash. **b Baggie.** a trademark for such a bag. **3** *Scottish.* the stomach.

bag|ging (bag'ing), *n.* cloth for making bags, covering bales of cotton, and other packing, usually made of a coarse woven hemp or jute; sacking.

bag|gy (bag'ē), *adj.,* **-gi|er, -gi|est. 1** hanging loosely; baglike: *The clown had baggy trousers.* **2** swelling; bulging: *The baggy sails were full before the wind.* **—bag'gi|ly,** *adv.* **—bag'gi|ness,** *n.*

bag|gys (bag'ēz), *n.pl.* loose-fitting swim trunks worn by surfers.

bag job, *U.S. Slang.* an illegal search by government agents of a suspect's residence to obtain incriminating evidence.

bag|man (bag'mən), *n., pl.* **-men. 1** *U.S. Slang.* a person to whom graft or protection money is given and who, in turn, delivers it to the person for whom it is intended. **2** *U.S.* a postal employee who handles and checks bags of mail. **3** *British.* a traveling salesman.

bagn|io (ban'yō, bän'-), *n., pl.* **-ios. 1** a house of prostitution; brothel. **2** (formerly) a prison for slaves in North Africa and the Near East. [originally, bathhouse < Italian *bagno* < Vulgar Latin *baneum* < Latin *balneum* bath < Greek *balaneîon*]

bag of bones, a very thin person or animal.

bag|pipe** (bag'pīp'), *n., v.,* **-piped, -pip|ing. —*n. Often, **bagpipes,** *pl.* a musical instrument made of a pipe to blow through, a leather bag for air, and four sounding pipes. Air is blown into the bag and pressed by the performer's arm into the sounding pipes, producing shrill tones. Bagpipes are used especially in Scotland and Ireland.
—*v.i.* to play the bagpipe; pipe. **—bag'pip'er,** *n.*

***bagpipe**

bag pudding, a pudding boiled in a bag.

B.Agr., Bachelor of Agriculture (Latin, *Baccalaureus Agriculturae*).

bags (bagz), *n.pl.* See under **bag.**

ba|guette or **ba|guet** (ba get'), *n.* **1a** a gem cut in a narrow, oblong shape. See picture under **gem. b** the shape itself. **2** a small, semicircular molding. **3** Usually, **baguette.** a long, thin, crusty loaf of French bread. [< French *baguette*]

ba|gui|o (bag'ē ō, bä'gē-), *n., pl.* **-gui|os.** a tropical hurricane or cyclone, especially in the Philippines. [< Philippine Spanish *baguio*]

bag|wig (bag'wig'), *n.* a wig worn by men in the 1700's, the back hair of which was enclosed in an ornamental bag.

bag|wom|an (bag'wům'ən), *n., pl.* **-wom|en.** *U.S. Slang.* a woman to whom graft or protection money is given and who, in turn, delivers it to the person for whom it is intended.

bag|worm (bag'wėrm'), *n.* the larva of a moth commonly found throughout the northern United States. When the bagworm hatches, it spins a bag of silk, leaves, and other debris for its protection, and moves around with the bag hanging downward while feeding on leaves of trees and shrubs.

bah (bä), *interj.* an exclamation of scorn, contempt, or impatience.

ba|ha|da (bä hä'də, -ᴛʜə), *n. Southwestern U.S.* bajada.

ba|ha|dur (bə hä'důr), *n.* a great man; distinguished personage (often affixed in Anglo-Indian use as a title to an officer's name). [< Hindustani *bahādur* (literally) hero]

Ba|ha|i (bə hä'ē), *n., adj.* **—*n.*** **1** a believer in Bahaism: *Bahais believe there is only one God, and that He created the world for all men* (Salvatore A. Pelle). **2** = Bahaism.
—*adj.* of or having to do with Bahais or Bahaism.

Ba|ha|ism (bə hä'iz əm), *n.* a religious system, an outgrowth of Babism, founded by Mirza Ali Hussain, 1817-1892, known as Bahaullah. It emphasizes the essential unity of all religions and stresses the practical and ethical elements in religion rather than the speculative. [< Persian *bahā'ī* of splendor + English *-ism*] **—Ba|ha'ist,** *n., adj.*

Ba|ha|mi|an (bə hā'mē ən, -hä'-), *n., adj.* **—*n.*** a native or inhabitant of the Bahamas.
—*adj.* of or having to do with the Bahamas.

Ba|ha|sa In|do|ne|sia (bä hä'sə in'də nē'zhə, -shə), the official language of Indonesia, an adaptation of Malay; Indonesian. [< Malay *bahasa* language < Sanskrit *bhāṣā*]

Bahasa Ma|lay|sia (mə lā'zhə, -shə), the official language of Malaysia, an adaptation of Malay.

Ba|hi|a grass (bə ē'ə), a perennial tropical American pasture grass. [< *Bahía,* a state in Brazil]

Bahia wood, = brazilwood.

Bah|rai|ni or **Bah|rei|ni** (bə rā'nē), *n., adj.* **—*n.*** a native or inhabitant of the Bahrain Islands.
—*adj.* of or having to do with these islands.

baht (bät), *n., pl.* **bahts** or **baht.** the unit of money of Thailand (formerly the *tical*), a coin or note worth about 5 cents. [< Thai *bāt*]

ba|hut (bə hüt'; *French* bå ʏ'), *n.* **1** a large chest especially common in the Middle Ages for holding such items as clothing or linen. **2** an ornamental buffet or cabinet. [< French *bahut*]

Ba|hu|tu (bä hü'tü), *n.* a member of a large Bantu tribe living in central Africa.

ba|hu|vri|hi (bä'hü vrē'hē), *n., pl.* **-his.** a noun or adjective compound whose first element describes a quality possessed by the second, as *hunchback* or *hunchbacked, redhead* or *redheaded.* [< Sanskrit *bahuvrīhi* (literally) much-riced, the word used to exemplify this type of compound]

bai|dar|ka (bī där'kə), *n.* = bidarka.

bai|gnoire (be nwår'), *n.* a theater box on the ground floor. [< French *baignoire* (literally) bathtub < *baigner* to bathe]

bail[1] (bāl), *n., v.* **—*n.*** **1** the guarantee of money necessary to set a person free from arrest until he is to appear for trial: *His lawyer put up bail for the man accused of stealing.* **SYN:** surety, bond. **2** the money or property guaranteed. **3** the person or persons who stand ready to pay the money guaranteed. **SYN:** bailsman, bondsman.
—*v.t.* to obtain the release of (a person under arrest) by guaranteeing to pay bail: *The man's employer bailed him out of jail.*
admit to bail, to grant the privilege of being bailed: *The magistrate may admit him to bail* (Frederic W. Maitland).
bail out, a to supply bail for: *The man accused of stealing was bailed out by his lawyer.* **b** *Figurative.* to help or assist: *I was deeply in debt until my father gave me money and bailed me out.*
go bail for, to supply bail for: *After his second arrest his brother refused to go bail for him.*
[< Anglo-French, Old French, custody, delivery from it < *baillier* possess, hand over < Latin *bajulāre* carry for pay < *bajulus* porter] **—bail'a|ble,** *adj.* **—bail'er,** *n.*

bail[2] (bāl), *n., v.* **—*n.*** **1** the curved handle of a kettle or pail. **2** *U.S. and Australia.* a hooplike support. The bails of a covered wagon hold up the canvas. **—*v.t.*** to provide with a bail or bails.
bail up, (in Australia) **a** to secure: *"Have you bailed up the cows?" "Yes, they're bailed up"* (E. A. Petherick). **b** to hold up: *We were bailed up by an armed man on horseback* (Melbourne Argus). **c** to detain for conversation: *The sundowner bailed up the rancher to ask for food.*
[Middle English *beyl,* probably < Scandinavian (compare Old Icelandic *beygla*)]

bail[3] (bāl), *v., n.* **—*v.t.*** **1** to throw (water) out of a boat, with a pail, a dipper, or any other container: *The fishermen bailed water from their sinking boat.* **2** to dip water from. **—*v.i.*** to remove water from a boat with a bail or other container.
—*n.* a scoop or pail used to throw water out of a boat. Also, *especially British,* **bale.**
bail out, to jump from an airplane or balloon by parachute: *When the airplane caught fire, the pilot bailed out.*
[Middle English *beyle* < Middle French *baille,* ultimately < Latin *bajulus* porter]

bail[4] (bāl), *n.* **1** either of two small wooden bars that form the top of a wicket in the game of cricket. **2** a bar or pole to separate horses standing in an open stable. **3** the wall of the outer court of a feudal castle. **4** the outer court.
bails, *Obsolete.* an outer line of fortifications, formed of stakes; palisade.
[< Old French *baille* barrier < Latin *baculum* stick, staff]

bail bond, the bond or security given as bail.

bail|ee (bā'lē'), *n.* a person to whom goods are committed in bailment.

bail|er (bā'lər), *n.* **1** a person or thing that bails water out. **2** a marine gastropod of the southwestern Pacific whose round shell is used by natives to bail water. **3** Also, **bailer shell.** the melon-shaped shell of this mollusk.

bai|ley (bā'lē), *n., pl.* **-leys.** the external wall enclosing the outer court of a feudal castle, or the outer court itself (now surviving only in such proper names as the *Old Bailey,* the chief criminal court in London); bail. [Middle English variant of *bail*[4]]

Bai|ley bridge (bā′lē), a type of bridge which may be assembled quickly from prefabricated sections of welded steel in lattice pattern, first widely used by the Allies in Europe in World War II. [< Sir Donald C. *Bailey,* born 1901, a British engineer, who designed it]

Bailey's beads, = Baily's beads.

bail|ie (bā′lē), *n.* **1** an official of a Scottish town or city corresponding to an English alderman. **2** *Obsolete.* a bailiff. [< Old French *bailli,* later variant of *baillif* bailiff]

bail|iff (bā′lif), *n.* **1** an officer of a court of law who has charge of jurors and guards prisoners while they are in the courtroom. **2** an assistant to a sheriff. A bailiff executes writs and processes and makes arrests. **3** in England: **a** an overseer or steward of an estate. The bailiff collects rents from the tenants and directs the work of employees for the owner. **b** the chief magistrate in certain towns. **c** the keeper of certain royal castles. [< Old French *baillif* administrative official, deputy, related to *baillir* hand over; govern < *bail* governor, manager < Latin *bajulus* porter]

bail|i|wick (bā′lə wik), *n.* **1** a person's field of knowledge, work, or authority. **2** a district or place over which a bailiff or bailie has authority. [< *bailie* (for *bailiff*) + obsolete *wick* village]

bail|ment (bāl′mənt), *n.* **1** the delivery of goods in trust. **2** the act of bailing an accused person.

bail|or (bā′lər), *n.* a person who delivers goods in trust.

bail|out or **bail-out** (bāl′out′), *n.* **1** the action of bailing out of an aircraft. **2** an emergency rescue or relief, as through financial aid: *It [a country] presumably depends on another bailout by the U.S.* (Time).

bails (bālz), *n.pl.* See under **bail**[4].

bails|man (bālz′mən), *n., pl.* **-men.** a person who gives bail.

Bai|ly's beads (bā′lēz), the last rays of direct sunlight observable before a total eclipse of the sun, broken up by irregularities of the moon's limb, briefly resembling a crescent-shaped string of glittering white gems. Also, **Bailey's beads.** [< Francis *Baily,* 1774-1844, a British astronomer, who first observed the phenomenon]

bain|ite (bā′nīt), *n.* a form of steel produced by decomposition of austenite. It is intermediate in strength between martensite and troostite. [< Edgar C. *Bain,* born 1891, an American metallurgist + *-ite*[1]]

bain-ma|rie (baɴ′mȧ rē′), *n., pl.* **bains-ma|rie** (baɴ′mȧ rē′). a vessel partly filled with heated water, into which a smaller vessel may be placed for gentle cooking or heating. Both the double boiler and the modern restaurant steam table are based on the same principle as the bain-marie. [< French *bain-marie* < Middle French, loan translation of Medieval Latin *balneum Mariae* alchemist's apparatus, (literally) "Mary's bath" (exact allusion uncertain)]

Bai|ram (bī räm′), *n.* either of two Moslem festivals after Ramadan, the first or lesser Bairam lasting three days, and the second or greater Bairam lasting four days and coming 70 days after the first. [< Turkish *bairām* < Persian]

bairn (bãrn), *n. Scottish.* a child. [Old English *bearn,* originally past participle of *beran* bear[1]]

bait (bāt), *n., v.* —*n.* **1** anything, especially food, used to attract fish or other animals so that they may be caught. **2** *Figurative.* a thing used to tempt or attract a person to do something he would not wish to do: *The open purse was a bait for the hungry and homeless young man.* **SYN:** temptation, enticement, allurement. **3a** a meal; food. **b** a halt, especially in a journey, for rest and food.
—*v.t.* **1** to put bait on (a hook) or in (a trap): *The hunter baited his traps.* **2** *Figurative.* to tempt; attract. **SYN:** allure, entice. **3** to set dogs to attack: *Men used to bait bulls for sport.* **4** to attack; torment: *The dogs baited the bear.* **5** *Figurative.* to torment or worry by unkind or annoying remarks: *Only a cruel person would bait a cripple.* **6** *Archaic.* to give food and drink to (a horse or other animal), especially on a journey.
—*v.i.* **1** to take food; feed. **2** *Archaic.* to stop and feed horses; stop and rest: *For evil news rides past, while good news baits* (Milton).
[Middle English *bayte* food < Scandinavian (compare Old Icelandic *beita* cause to bite)]

bait casting, in fishing: **1** the throwing forward of comparatively heavy natural or artificial bait that carries the line out with it. **2** fishing in this manner.

bait|er (bā′tər), *n.* a person who baits or worries something, especially animals; tormentor.

baith (bāth), *adj., pron., conj. Scottish.* both.

bai|za (bī′zə), *n., pl.* **-za** or **-zas.** a copper coin of Oman, worth 1/1000 of a rial. [< Arabic *baiza* < Hindustani *paisā* pice]

baize (bāz), *n.* a thick, coarse woolen or cotton cloth resembling felt, used especially for curtains, table covers, and as a lining. [< French *baies* brown material < Old French *bai* bay[5]]

ba|ja|da (bä hä′də, -ᴛʜə), *n. Southwestern U.S.* **1** a formation of drift extending out from the base of mountains. **2** a desert of hard, sun-baked clay resulting from such a formation. Also, **bahada.** [< Spanish *bajada* descent, slope < *bajar* descend < Vulgar Latin *bassiāre* < Medieval Latin *bassus;* see etym. under **base**[2]]

Ba|jan (bā′jən), *adj., n.* (in Barbados) Barbadian; Bim. [alteration of (Bar)*badian*]

baj|ra (bäj′rə), *n.* (in India) = pearl millet. [< Hindustani *bājrā, bājrī*]

baj|ri or **baj|ree** (bäj′rē), *n.* = bajra.

bake (bāk), *v.,* **baked, bak|ing,** *n.* —*v.t.* **1** to cook (food) by dry heat without exposing it directly to the fire: *My mother is baking a cake in the oven.* **2** to dry or harden by heat: *Bricks and china are baked in a kiln.* **3** to make very warm: *to lie on the beach and be baked by the sun.* **4** *Obsolete.* to harden: *Th' earth When it is bak'd with frost* (Shakespeare).
—*v.i.* **1** to cook foods by dry heat; do the work of baking: *She bakes every Saturday.* **2** to become baked: *Cookies bake quickly. The dirt road became dusty as it baked under the summer sun.*
—*n.* **1** *U.S.* a social gathering at which a meal is served: *Steam for 15 minutes and enjoy the informal fun of a real lobster bake* (New Yorker). **2** the act or process of baking. **3** *Scottish.* a cracker.
[Old English *bacan*]

baked Alaska (bākt), a dessert consisting of ice cream with a meringue, which is baked in a very hot oven just long enough to brown the meringue.

baked-ap|ple (bākt′ap′əl), *n.* = cloudberry.

baked beans, beans boiled and baked, especially with salt meat and seasoning, and often with molasses or in tomato sauce.

bake|house (bāk′hous′), *n.* a building or room to bake in; bakery.

Ba|ke|lite (bā′kə līt), *n. Trademark.* an artificial material used especially to make beads, stems of pipes, umbrella handles, fountain pens, and electric insulators. It is a synthetic resin made by condensing phenols with formaldehyde. [< German *Bakelit* < Leo H. *Baekeland,* 1863-1944, a Belgian-American chemist who invented it + *-ite*[1]]

bake|meat (bāk′mēt′), *n.,* or **baked meat,** *Obsolete.* **1** a dish of baked food, as pastry. **2** a meat pie.

bake-off (bāk′ôf′, -of′), *n.* a public baking contest.

bak|er (bā′kər), *n.* **1** a person who makes or sells bread, pies, cakes, and pastries, especially as a business. **2** *U.S.* a small, portable oven.

Ba|ker-Nunn camera (bā′kər nun′), a large telescopic camera used especially for tracking orbiting earth satellites. [< James Gilbert *Baker* and Joseph *Nunn,* American inventors who designed it]

baker's dozen, thirteen: *We bought a baker's dozen, but ate only twelve rolls and saved the last one for Dad.*

bakers' yeast, a selected strain of yeast, used in baking: *... bakers' yeast is a true ascomycete* (Fred W. Emerson).

bak|er|y (bā′kər ē), *n., pl.* **-er|ies.** a place where bread, pies, cakes, and pastries are made or sold; baker's shop; bakeshop: *We bought a cake at the bakery for dessert.*

bake|shop (bāk′shop′), *n.* a baker's shop; bakery.

bakh|shish (bak′shēsh), *n., v.t., v.i.* = baksheesh.

bak|ing (bā′king), *n.* **1** cooking in dry heat without exposing directly to the fire. **2** drying or hardening by heat: *The mud cracked and crumbled baking in the sun.* **3** the amount baked at one time; batch: *Our last baking of bread turned out dry and hard.*

baking powder, a mixture of soda and cream of tartar, or a similar combination, used instead of yeast to cause biscuits or cakes to rise. When baking powder is moistened, it produces carbon dioxide and thus causes dough to expand.

baking soda, = sodium bicarbonate. *Formula:* $NaHCO_3$

bak|la|va or **bak|la|wa** (bäk′lä vä′), *n.* a dessert made of thin layers of pastry baked with honey, chopped nuts, and other condiments. [< Turkish *baklava*]

bak|sheesh or **bak|shish** (bak′shēsh), *n., v.* —*n.* money given as a tip or a bribe, especially in Egypt, Turkey, India, and other countries, especially of the Near East: *There will be the usual baksheesh for the game warden* (New Yorker).
—*v.t., v.i.* to give baksheesh. Also, **backsheesh, backshish, bakhshish.**
[< Persian *bakhshīsh* gift, present < *bakhshīdan* to give, present]

bak|tun (bäk tün′), *n.* a cycle of 400 years, each of 360 days, in the Mayan calendar.

ba|ku (bä′kü), *n.* **1** a kind of material woven from talipot palm leaves, used especially for women's hats: *Pleated in back, the hat of white baku is trimmed with coffee-colored ribbon* (New York Times). **2** a hat made of this material. [< a native name in the Philippines]

bal., *Commerce.* balance.

BAL (no periods) or **B.A.L.,** British Anti-Lewisite (a substance, originally developed as an antidote for lewisite, now used especially against poisoning by arsenic, bismuth, mercury, or other metallic compounds). *Formula:* $C_3H_8OS_2$

Ba|laam (bā′ləm), *n.* the heathen prophet hired by the Moabite king to curse the Israelites, who instead blessed them after being rebuked by the donkey on which he rode (in the Bible, Numbers 22-24).

bal|a|cla|va (bal′ə klä′və), *n.* **1** a balaclava helmet. **2** a kind of heavy, very warm coat having such a covering as its top part. [< *Balaklava,* a Crimean War battle site]

***balaclava helmet** or **hood,** a woolen covering for the head and shoulders, worn especially by soldiers or sailors in very cold weather.

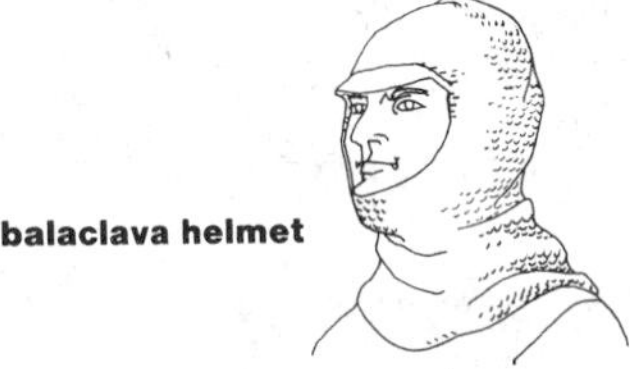

***balaclava helmet**

bal|a|lai|ka (bal′ə lī′kə), *n.* a Russian musical instrument somewhat like a guitar, with a triangular body and usually with three strings. [< Russian *balalajka*]

***bal|ance** (bal′əns), *n., v.,* **-anced, -anc|ing.** —*n.* **1** an instrument for weighing. A common kind of balance consists of a horizontal beam or lever poised to move freely on a central support, with a scale or pan suspended at each end. **SYN:** scale, scales. See picture on the next page at end of entry. **2** the condition of being equal in weight, amount, force, effect, or parts: *Keep the balance between the two sides of the scale.* **SYN:** equilibrium. **3** *Figurative.* comparison of weight, value, importance, or effect; estimate. **4** *Figurative.* proportion in design; harmony: *the balance of space in a Japanese print.* **5** the condition of not falling over in any direction; steady position: *He lost his balance and fell off the ladder.* **SYN:** poise. **6** *Figurative.* all-around development and steadiness of character; poise: *His balance kept him from losing his temper too much.* **SYN:** composure, equanimity. **7** anything that counteracts the effect, weight, or force, of something else: (*Figurative.*) *Demand acts as a balance of supply in the market place.* **SYN:** counterpoise. **8** *Informal.* the part that is left over; remainder: *I will be away for the balance of the week.* **SYN:** rest, surplus. **9a** an equality between the totals of the two sides of an account. **b** the difference between the amount one owes or has withdrawn from an account and the amount one is owed or deposits in an account; the difference between the debit and credit sides of an account: *I have a balance of $20 in the bank.* **c** the sum by which an account is out of balance on either the credit side or debit side. *Abbr:* bal. **10** = balance wheel. **11** greatest weight, amount, or power. **12** a balancing movement in dancing.
—*v.t.* **1** to weigh two things against each other on scales or in one's hands: *He balanced the two rocks in his hands and dropped the heavier one.* **2** to make or be equal to in weight, amount, force, effect, or parts: (*Figurative.*) *A child's exercise and rest should balance each other.* **3** *Figurative.* to compare the value or importance of: *He balanced a trip to the mountains against the chance of a summer job.* **4** to make or be proportionate to. **5** to bring into or keep in a steady condition or position: *Can you balance a coin on its edge?* **SYN:** steady, poise. **6** *Figurative.* to make up for the effect or influence of; counteract: *And weariness was balanced with delight* (William Morris). **SYN:** offset; compensate. **7a** to add up the debit and credit sides of (an account)

Pronunciation Key: hat, āge, cãre, fär; let, ēqual, tėrm; it, īce; hot, ōpen, ôrder; oil, out; cup, pu̇t, rüle; child; long; thin; ᴛʜen; zh, measure; ə represents **a** in about, **e** in taken, **i** in pencil, **o** in lemon, **u** in circus.

to find the difference between their amounts. **b** to make the debit and credit sides of (an account) equal. **c** to settle (an account) by paying an amount due. **8** to approach, bow, and then withdraw from (another couple or group in square dance or reel) in the same pattern of steps.
—*v.i.* **1** to be equal or equivalent in weight, amount, force, effect, or parts; be evenly adjusted: *These scales balance.* **2** to keep a steady condition or position: *to balance on one foot.* **3** to be equal on the debit and credit sides of an account. **4** to hesitate; waver. **5** to approach another couple or group in a square dance or reel with matching steps, bow, and withdraw.
in the balance, with its outcome undecided; uncertain: *The outcome of the baseball game was in the balance until the last inning.*
on balance, taking everything into consideration; in the main: *On balance, there is substantial expectation on Capitol Hill that the railroads will agree to one more delay* (New York Times).
strike a balance, to find the difference between the credit and debit sides of an account: *... not to run long accounts, but to strike clear balances at certain set seasons* (John S. Blackie).
[< Anglo-French *balaunce* scale, Old French *balance* < Late Latin *bilanx, -ancis* (scale) having two plates < Latin *bi-* two + *lanx, lancis* shallow pan] —**bal′ance|a|ble**, *adj.*
► The use of **balance** in the sense of "remainder, rest" (as in *the balance of the program*), although frequently criticized, has been common in America since the latter part of the 1700's.

***balance**
definition 1

Bal|ance (bal′əns), *n.* = Libra.
balance beam, a narrow wooden beam used to perform balancing feats in gymnastics.
bal|anced (bal′ənst), *adj.* **1** stable: *Quiet temperament is the mark of a balanced person.* **2** harmonious; orderly: *a balanced composition.*
balanced diet, a diet having the correct amounts of all kinds of foods necessary for health.
balanced fund, a type of mutual fund that invests in bonds and preferred stocks as well as common stocks.
balanced ticket, *U.S. Politics.* a slate of candidates formed by a political party on the basis of their appeal to the major groups of voters in the electorate.
balance of nature, a balanced condition existing in the animal and plant population of a region when few changes occur in the environment.
balance of payments, the net amount of money when all business between one country and another for a given period of time is balanced, including imports, exports, investments, grants, and tourist expenditures.
balance of power, **1** an even distribution of military and economic power among nations or groups of nations: *The balance-of-power conception of foreign policy ... was to make sure, by whatever means came to hand, that no power became strong enough to dominate the world* (Observer). **2** the ability of a small nation or minority to give a larger nation or group a dominant position by allying itself with the larger: *Yugoslavia holds the balance of power in the Balkans.*
balance of terror, the approximately equal strength of the Communist and Western powers in nuclear weapons: *We insist on maintaining the balance of terror* (*called nuclear deterrence*) (New York Times).
balance of trade, the difference between the value of all the imports and that of all the exports of a country.
bal|anc|er (bal′ən sər), *n.* **1** a person or thing that balances: *Britain has often been the balancer of power in Europe.* **2** a haltere of a dipterous insect. **3** an acrobat. **4** *Electronics.* a device to increase the effectiveness of a direction finder.
balance reef, *Nautical.* a reef in a gaff-rigged sail with the points running from the jaws of the gaff parallel to the boom, so as to reduce the sail to a small triangle.
balance sheet, a written statement showing the profits and losses, the assets and liabilities, and the net worth of a business: *The balance sheet again shows that the company has a sound economy* (News Chronicle).
balance wheel, **1** a wheel for regulating motion. A clock or watch has a balance wheel that controls the movement of the hands by the regularity of its oscillating motion. **2** *Figurative.* anything that is a source of regularity or stability: *The value of cooperatives as balance wheels in agricultural business gives them a significance greater than their relative business volume would indicate* (Joseph G. Knapp).
bal|a|noid (bal′ə noid), *adj.* shaped like an acorn. [< Greek *balanoeidês* < *bálanos* acorn]
bal|as (bal′əs, bā′ləs), *n.*, or **balas ruby**, a delicate rose-red variety of the gem spinel. [< Old French *balais* < Arabic *balakhsh* < Persian *badakhshān* Badakhshan, a district in Persia, where they are found]
bal|a|ta (bal′ə tə), *n.* **1** Also, **balata gum**. the dried gumlike juice of a West Indian and tropical American tree related to the sapodilla, used especially in making gaskets, golf balls, chewing gum, and insulation for wires. It is intermediate in character between caoutchouc and gutta-percha. **2** the tree itself; bully tree. [perhaps < Carib *parata*, the native name]
ba|laus|tine (bə lôs′tin), *n.* **1** the wild pomegranate. **2** the red, roselike flower of the wild pomegranate. [< Latin *balaustium* wild pomegranate flower; see etym. under **baluster**]
bal|bo|a (bal bō′ə), *n., pl.* **-bo|as**. the unit of money of Panama, a silver coin worth about one U.S. dollar. A balboa is equal to 100 centesimos. [< Spanish *balboa* < Vasco N. de *Balboa,* 1475?-1519, a Spanish explorer]
bal|brig|gan (bal brig′ən), *n.* **1** a knitted cotton cloth, used for stockings and underwear. **2** similar woolen cloth.
balbriggans, knitted cotton stockings, underwear, or pajamas: *Balbriggans have been in use overseas longer than any other garment* (New Yorker).
[< *Balbriggan*, a town in Ireland]
bal|co|nied (bal′kə nēd), *adj.* having a balcony or balconies: *a balconied hotel.*
bal|co|ny (bal′kə nē), *n., pl.* **-nies**. **1** an outside projecting platform with an entrance from an upper floor of a building. A balcony is usually enclosed by a balustrade or railing. *The President stood on the balcony waving to the crowd below.* **2** a projecting upper floor in a theater, hall, or church, with seats for part of the audience; gallery: *We saw the play from the balcony.* [< Italian *balcone* < *balco* scaffold < Old High German *balcho* beam. See related etym. at **balk**.]
bald (bôld), *adj.* **1** wholly or partly without hair on the head: *The old man's bald head glistened in the sun.* **SYN**: hairless, glabrous. **2** without its natural covering: *A mountaintop with no trees or grass on it is bald.* **SYN**: naked. **3** *Figurative.* obvious; plainly evident: *The bald truth is that he is lazy.* **4** *Figurative.* bare; plain; unadorned: *a bald translation with no feeling.* **5** having a white spot or blaze on the head, such as some birds or animals have. [Middle English *balled* < *ball* white spot, perhaps < Welsh *bal* having a white spot on the forehead] —**bald′ly**, *adv.* —**bald′ness**, *n.*
bal|dac|chi|no (bal′də kē′nō, bôl′-), *n.* = baldachin. [< Italian *baldacchino*]
bal|da|chin or **bal|da|quin** (bal′də kin, bôl′-), *n.* **1** a structure in the form of a canopy, placed above an altar, throne, or other important focal point of a room. **2a** a canopy of silk or other fabric carried in solemn processions. **b** a similar canopy draped above an altar, dais, or other important focal point of a room. **3** = baudekin. [< French *baldaquin* < Italian *baldacchino* < *Baldacco,* Italian name of Bagdad, where the silk was made]
bald coot, a species of coot common in Europe.
bald cypress, a tall tree of the taxodium family, growing in the southern United States and Mexico; swamp cypress.
bald eagle, a large, powerful North American eagle with white feathers on its head, neck, and tail when adult; American eagle. It is the national emblem of the United States.
Bal|der (bôl′dər), *n.* the Norse god of light, beauty, goodness, wisdom, and peace. Also, **Baldr, Baldur**.
bal|der|dash (bôl′dər dash), *n.* nonsense; foolishness: *I am ashamed to quote such nauseous balderdash* (Macaulay). [origin uncertain]
bald-faced (bôld′fāst′), *adj.* **1** having a white face or white on the face, such as certain animals have: *a bald-faced stag.* **2** *Figurative.* written or spoken without embarrassment; barefaced: *a bald-faced lie.*
bald|head (bôld′hed′), *n.* **1** a person who has a bald head. **2** a breed of pigeon. **3** any one of various birds with a whitish spot on the head.
bald|head|ed (bôld′hed′id), *adj., adv.* —*adj.* having a bald head.
—*adv.* without restraint: *Go into it baldheaded* (James Russell Lowell). —**bald′head′ed|ness**, *n.*
baldheaded brant, = blue goose.
bald|ing (bôl′ding), *adj.* losing the hair on the head; becoming bald.
bald|ish (bôl′dish), *adj.* somewhat bald.
bald|pate (bôld′pāt′), *n.* **1** a person who has a bald head. **2** a wild duck of North America; American widgeon. The male has a white crown and forehead.
bald|pat|ed (bôld′pā′tid), *adj.* = baldheaded. —**bald′pat′ed|ness**, *n.*
Bal|dr (bäl′dər), *n.* = Balder.
bal|dric or **bal|drick** (bôl′drik), *n.* a belt for a sword, horn, or pouch, hung from one shoulder to the opposite side of the body. Also, **baudrick, bawdric**. [origin uncertain; compare Middle High German *balderich* girdle, also a proper name]
bald rush, any leafy-stemmed plant of a genus belonging to the sedge family.
Bal|dur (bôl′dər), *n.* = Balder.
bald wheat, wheat having no beard, or awn.
Bald|win (bôld′win), *n.* a yellowish-red winter variety of apple, once much cultivated in the northeastern United States.
bale[1] (bāl), *n., v.,* **baled, bal|ing**. —*n.* a large bundle of merchandise or material securely wrapped or bound for shipping or storage: *a bale of cotton, a bale of hay.*
—*v.t.* to make into bales; tie in large bundles: *We saw a big machine bale hay.*
[< Flemish *bale* < Old French *balle* round package, perhaps < Old High German *balla*]
—**bal′er**, *n.*
bale[2] (bāl), *n. Archaic.* **1** evil; harm; injury. **2** sorrow; pain; misery; grief. [Old English *balu, bealu*]
bale[3] (bāl), *n. Archaic.* **1** a funeral pyre: *... raise a bale on high* (William Morris). **2** *Scottish.* a signal or beacon fire; balefire. [fusion of Old English *bǣl* and Scandinavian (compare Old Icelandic *bāl* great fire)]
bale[4] (bāl), *n., v.t., v.i.,* **baled, bal|ing**. *Especially British.* bail; scoop. —**bal′er**, *n.*
***ba|leen** (bə lēn′), *n.* horny plates growing downward from the upper jaws or palates of certain whales; whalebone. [< Old French *baleine* < Latin *ballēna,* variant of *ballaena* whale < Greek *phállaina*]

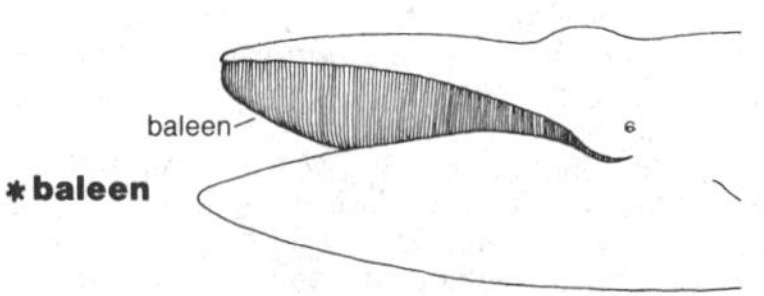

***baleen**

baleen whale, any whale of a group that have an elastic horny substance called baleen or whalebone growing in place of teeth in the upper jaw, such as the right whale, finback, humpback, and gray whale; whalebone whale.
bale|fire (bāl′fīr′), *n. Archaic.* **1** a great fire in the open air; bonfire. **2** a signal fire; bale. **3** the flame of a funeral pyre. [Middle English *bale, bayle* (fire) < Scandinavian (compare Old Icelandic *bāl* flame)]
bale|ful (bāl′fəl), *adj.* **1** very evil or harmful: *The cranky old lady gave the noisy boys a baleful glance.* **SYN**: malignant. **2** full of misfortune; disastrous. [Old English *bealofull* < *bealu* bale[2] + *-full* full] —**bale′ful|ly**, *adv.* —**bale′ful|ness**, *n.*
bale-hook (bāl′hu̇k′), *n.* = baling hook.
baler bag, a large heavy-duty paper bag made to hold smaller bags filled with cement, sugar, flour, or the like.
ba|li (bä′lē), *n.* balibuntal or a material similar to it, used in making hats.
ba|li|bun|tal or **ba|li|bun|tl** (bal′ē bun′təl), *n.* **1** a lightweight, woven straw from the Philippines, used especially for women's hats. **2** a hat made of this material. Also, **ballibuntal, ballibuntl**. [shortened < *Baliuag buntal* < *Baliuag* a town in Luzon + Tagalog *buntál* straw prepared from fibers of the talipot palm]
Ba|li|nese (bä′lə nēz′, -nēs′), *n., pl.* **-nese**, *adj.* —*n.* **1** a native or inhabitant of Bali. **2** the language of Bali.
—*adj.* of Bali, its people, or their language.
baling hook, a steel hook used by stevedores to lift or hold cargo in bales, crates, or boxes; balehook.
ba|lin|ta|wak (bə lin′tə wäk), *n.* the national costume of women in the Philippines, consisting of a long dress with an apron and often a matching kerchief. [< Tagalog *balintawak*]
ba|lis|tra|ri|a (bal′ə strãr′ē ə), *n.* a cross-shaped opening in the wall of a medieval fortress through which a crossbow could be fired. [< Medieval Latin *balistraria* (originally) place of the *ballistra,* Late Latin variant of Latin *ballista* ballista]
balk (bôk), *v., n.* —*v.i.* **1** to stop short and stubbornly refuse to go on: *My horse balked at the fence.* **SYN**: jib, shy. **2** to hesitate or stop (at); avoid; not do: *He balks at every disturbance and*

never finishes his work. SYN: vacillate. **3** *Baseball.* to fail to complete a pitch once started. It is illegal under the rules of baseball for a pitcher to balk.
—*v.t.* **1** to prevent from going on; hinder: *The burglar alarm balked the robber's plans.* SYN: frustrate, foil, baffle. **2** to fail to use; let slip; miss: *If I balk'd this opportunity* (John Dryden).
—*n.* **1** a hindrance, check, or defeat: *This was a balk to them and put a damp to their new projects* (Daniel Defoe). **2** a blunder or mistake. **3** a ridge between furrows; strip left unplowed. **4a** a large beam or timber, especially one that supports the bottom ends of two opposite rafters; a tie beam. **b** any large block or length of timber: *A half-submerged balk of timber wrecked the canoe.* **5** a principal horizontal supporting member of a bridge, especially a temporary bridge built for military use. **6** *Baseball.* a failure of a pitcher to complete a pitch he has started; feint. **7** *Billiards.* **a** any of eight areas set off from the center area of the table by four lines parallel to the ends and sides. **b** that part of a billiard table behind a transverse line at one end from which a player must start play, etc. Also, **baulk**.
[Old English *balca* beam, ridge] —**balk'er**, *n.* —**balk'ing|ly**, *adv.*

Bal|kan (bôl'kən), *adj.* **1** of the people living in the countries of the Balkan Peninsula. **2a** of the Balkan Peninsula. **b** having to do with the countries on the Balkan Peninsula. **3** of the Balkan Mountains.

Bal|kan|ize or **bal|kan|ize** (bôl'kə nīz), *v.t.*, **-ized**, **-iz|ing**. **1** to divide (a region) into small, often hostile, states. **2** *Figurative.* to divide (anything) into small units, especially weak or inefficient units. —**Bal'kan|i|za'tion**, **bal'kan|i|za'tion**, *n.*

balk line, **1** any of the lines on a billiard table marking off the balks. **2** (in track and field events) a line on or across which a contestant may not step without penalty.

balk|y (bô'kē), *adj.*, **balk|i|er**, **balk|i|est**. stopping short and stubbornly refusing to go on; likely to balk: *Mules are balky animals.* SYN: refractory, contrary. —**balk'i|ness**, *n.*

ball[1] (bôl), *n.*, *v.* —*n.* **1** a roundish body thrown, kicked, knocked, or batted about in various games. Different sizes and types of balls are used in golf, tennis, baseball, football, and soccer. *When Dad threw the ball, I dropped it and it rolled under a car.* **2** a game in which some kind of ball is thrown, hit, or kicked, especially baseball. **3a** anything round or roundish: *He bought a ball of string.* **b** something that is somewhat like a ball: *He had a blister on the ball of his foot.* **4** a particular throw or play of a ball in certain games; a ball in motion: *a fast ball, a fly ball.* **5** a baseball pitched too high, too low, or not over the plate, that the batter does not strike at. **6a** a bullet for firearms; a round, solid object to be shot from a gun. **b** a cannon ball. **7** the globe; sphere; the earth: *... round the dark terrestrial ball* (Joseph Addison). **8** the roots of a plant, together with its mass of earth, tied up in a bundle for transplanting.
—*v.i.* to form or gather into a ball.
—*v.t.* to make or form into a ball: *to ball string or yarn.*
ball up, *Slang.* to confuse: *In a situation as balled-up as this, it is not surprising to learn that there would still be knots even if the "historic boundaries" tangle is untied* (Wall Street Journal).
carry the ball, *U.S. Informal.* to take the chief part in pushing or carrying through a plan or activity: *Some good friends are carrying the ball for us* (New Yorker).
have (something) **on the ball**, *Informal.* to be skillful; have ability, alertness, or the like: *The new science teacher has a lot on the ball.*
keep the ball rolling, to keep up an activity by doing one's part: *If they can, they pay a "good-will fee" ... whether they do or not, all work around the place to help keep the ball rolling* (Newsweek).
on the ball, *Slang.* aware of what is going on or needs to be done; alert: *We have to stay on the ball to keep the company satisfied with our vouchers* (Wall Street Journal).
play ball, **a** to begin a ball game or start it again after stopping: *"Let's play ball!" some of the boys shouted as soon as recess began.* **b** *Informal, Figurative.* to get busy; become active: *A worker who doesn't play ball when he is told to finish a job runs the risk of being dismissed.* **c** *U.S. Informal, Figurative.* to work together; cooperate: *Under the ILA system, the union itself did the hiring for shippers at daily "shape-ups," and if a longshoreman refused to play ball he didn't work* (Newsweek).
start the ball rolling, to make a beginning; get started: *I think we should start the ball rolling to get some decent pictures* (London Times).
[probably < Scandinavian (compare Old Icelandic *böllr*)]
—*Syn. n.* **3 Ball, globe** mean something round. **Ball** is the general word for any round or roundish object: *I put melon balls in the salad.* **Globe** applies to anything shaped like a ball, but is used especially of objects which are perfectly round or thought of as being perfectly round: *The light has a glass globe around it.*

ball[2] (bôl), *n.*, *v.* —*n.* **1** a large, formal party with dancing: *The ladies were all dressed in long gowns at the ball.* **2** *Slang.* a very good time: *We'd have had a ball in Hollywood* (New Yorker).
—*v.i. U.S. Slang.* to have a very good time.
[< French *bal* < Old French < *baller* to dance < Late Latin *ballāre* < Greek *ballízein*]

bal|lad (bal'əd), *n.*, *v.* —*n.* **1** a poem that tells a story. Ballads are usually in a simple verse form and tell a popular legend that is passed from one generation to another orally. *The old man sang ballads of the clan's heroes, often to the tune of a folk song.* **2** a simple song: *a charming ballad of the north country.* **3** a sentimental of romantic popular song: *Many of the ballads of mother's day are still popular.* **4** the music for a narrative ballad or folk song: *Many of the old ballads are sung to new words.*
—*v.i.* to write or compose ballads.
[< Old French *ballade* < Old Provençal *balada* (originally) poem for dancing < *balar* to dance < Late Latin *ballāre*] —**bal'lad|er**, *n.*

bal|lade (bə läd', ba-), *n.* **1** a poem typically having three stanzas of eight or ten lines each, followed by an envoy of half the stanza length. The last line of each stanza and of the envoy are the same, and the same rhyme pattern recurs in each stanza. **2** an instrumental composition without a strict formal design, often of a sentimental character and written for the piano or orchestra.
[< French *ballade* ballad (a reborrowing) < Old French; see etym. under **ballad**]

bal|lad|eer (bal'ə dir'), *n.* **1** a singer of ballads. **2** *U.S. Informal.* a singer of popular songs.

bal|lad|ier (bà là dyā'), *n. French.* a singer of ballads.

bal|lad|ist (bal'ə dist), *n.* a writer or composer of ballads.

bal|lad|mon|ger (bal'əd mung'gər, -mong'-), *n.* **1** a dealer in or seller of ballads. **2** an inferior poet; poetaster.

bal|lad|ry (bal'ə drē), *n.* **1a** poetry in the ballad style. **b** ballads collectively. **2** the practice, style, or art of singing ballads.

ballad stanza, a stanza of four lines, rhyming *abcb*, the first and third containing eight syllables each, and the second and fourth six each.

ball and chain, *U.S.* **1** a heavy metal ball and piece of short chain that may be attached to the leg of a prisoner to prevent escape. **2** *Slang.* a spouse (commonly used jocularly by a husband of his wife). **3** any impediment or restraint.

ball-and-claw (bôl'ən klô'), *adj.* = claw-and-ball.

***ball-and-sock|et joint** (bôl'ən sok'it), a flexible joint formed by a ball or knob fitting in a socket, such as the shoulder or hip joint. It permits some motion in every direction.

***ball-and-socket joint**

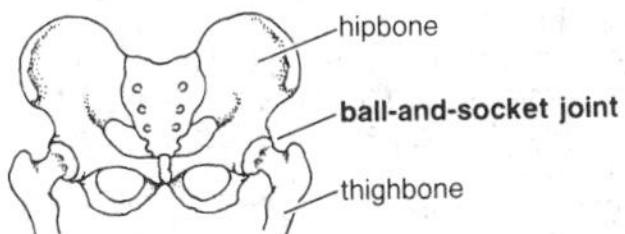

bal|last (bal'əst), *n.*, *v.* —*n.* **1** something heavy carried in the hold of a ship to steady it: *Most ships use seawater as ballast. As the ship takes on cargo, the ballast water is pumped out* (Lionel Casson). **2** bags of sand or other heavy material carried in a balloon or dirigible to steady it or regulate its ascent: *The balloon used sandbags for ballast.* **3** *Figurative.* anything which makes a person or thing steady; stabilizing agent or force: *It wants the ballast of those, whom the world calls moderate men* (Jonathan Swift). **4** gravel or crushed rock used in making the bed for a road or railroad track, or in making concrete. **5** a device to keep an electric current constant, for fluorescent lighting, or other devices, usually consisting of an iron wire mounted in a vacuum tube filled with hydrogen. Its varying resistance counteracts fluctuations of voltage.
—*v.t.* **1** to put ballast in (ships or balloons); furnish or steady with ballast. **2** to put gravel or crushed rock on. **3** *Figurative.* to give stability or steadiness to.
in ballast, (of a ship) with no load other than ballast: *When in ballast the Bywell Castle draws 12 feet aft* (London Daily News).
[< Danish *ballast* < Old Danish *barlast* < *bar* bare + *last* lading] —**bal'last|er**, *n.*

bal|last|ing (bal'ə sting), *n.* **1** the act or process of furnishing with ballast. **2** the material used for ballast.

ballast tank, a compartment in a ship or submarine which may be filled with water or emptied by means of pumps. Ballast tanks help control the vertical movement of submarines.

***ball bearing**, **1** a bearing in which the shaft turns upon a number of freely moving, very smooth metal balls which are contained in a channel around the shaft. Ball bearings are used to lessen friction in machinery and in wheels and axles. **2** one of the metal balls so used.

***ball bearing** definition 1

ball boy, a boy who retrieves tennis balls and supplies them to the players as they are needed, especially in a tournament.

ball carrier, any player who carries the ball in football.

ball clay, = pipe clay.

ball club, *U.S. Informal.* **1** any established baseball, football, soccer, or basketball team, whether amateur or professional. **2** the players, coaches, managers, and other persons associated with such a team, especially a professional team.

ball cock, a valve for regulating the supply of liquid in a tank, cistern, or other container, consisting typically of a valve attached by a lever to a hollow, floating ball and turned off or on by the ball's rise or fall.

bal|le|ri|na (bal'ə rē'nə), *n.*, *pl.* **-nas**. a woman ballet dancer, especially a soloist. [< Italian *ballerina* < *ballare* to dance < Late Latin *ballāre*]

bal|let (bal'ā, ba lā'), *n.* **1** an elaborate dance by a group on a stage. A ballet usually tells a story or expresses a theme through the movements of the dancing and the music, often written especially for it. *Everyone knows the fairy tale of the sleeping beauty which we saw as a ballet.* **2** the style of dancing used in these performances combining graceful, intricate steps, movements, and poses: *to study ballet.* **3** the art of creating or performing ballets. **4** the dancers: *The Royal Ballet will soon perform in our city.* **5** the music for a ballet. [< French *ballet* < Italian *balletto* (diminutive) < *ballo* < *ballare* < Late Latin; see etym. under **ball**[2]]

bal|let blanc (bà le' bläɴ'), *French.* a ballet or scene in a ballet featuring white-skirted ballerinas.

bal|let|ic (ba let'ik), *adj.* of or having to do with ballet. —**bal|let'i|cal|ly**, *adv.*

ballet master, the trainer or director of a ballet.

ballet mistress, a woman ballet master.

bal|let|o|mane (ba let'ə mān), *n.* a person who is very fond of ballets, especially one with considerable knowledge of their music, techniques, and other specific features; ballet enthusiast. [< French *balletomane* < *ballet* + *-mane* < *manie* mania]

bal|let|o|ma|ni|a (ba let'ə mā'nē ə), *n.* devotion to the ballet.

ballet slipper, **1** a type of soft, low-cut, narrow-soled shoe without laces or heel, sometimes padded in the toe, worn for ballet dancing. **2** any one of various women's or girls' shoes patterned on this.

ball|flow|er (bôl'flou'ər), *n.* a round, carved ornament in medieval architecture. It is like a ball within three or four petals of a flower and seen through a quatrefoil or trefoil opening. The entire ornament is usually one of many such balls within a hollow molding.

ball game, **1** a baseball game. **2** any game in which a ball is used. **3** *U.S. Slang.* any situation or activity: *It's a totally different ball game than it was in 1960 ... for mayors in America* (Harper's).

ball|gown (bôl'goun'), *n.* a gown suitable for a ball; evening gown.

bal|li|bun|tal or **bal|li|bun|tl** (bal'ē bun'təl), *n.* = balibuntal.

ball|ing (bô'ling), *n.* **1** the administration of a drug compounded as a bolus or ball, especially to one of the larger animals. **2** the action or process of forming balls in a puddling furnace.

Pronunciation Key: hat, āge, cãre, fär; let, ēqual, tėrm; it, īce; hot, ōpen, ôrder; oil, out; cup, pu̇t, rüle; child; long; thin; ᴛʜen; zh, measure; ə represents a in about, e in taken, i in pencil, o in lemon, u in circus.

***bal|lis|ta** (bə lis′tə), *n., pl.* **-tae** (-tē). a machine used in wars of ancient times to throw stones and other heavy missiles. [< Latin *ballista*, ultimately < Greek *bállein* to throw]

***ballista**

bal|lis|tic (bə lis′tik), *adj.* **1** having to do with the motion or throwing of projectiles: *ballistic qualities.* **2** having to do with the science of ballistics. **—bal|lis′ti|cal|ly,** *adv.*

bal|lis|ti|cian (bal′ə stish′ən), *n.* an expert in or student of ballistics.

ballistic missile, a missile aimed at or before the time of launching. It differs from the type of guided missile, which can be aimed during flight. A ballistic missile is a projectile powered by a rocket engine or engines and is used especially as a long-range weapon of offense. It is propelled through the upward part of a curved trajectory and becomes a free-falling body after the thrust has ended. *The ballistic missile is so named because, like an artillery shell or a stone hurled by the giant slingshot called by the Romans a ballista, it is propelled only over a relatively short time and distance at the beginning of its journey* (Atlantic).

bal|lis|tics (bə lis′tiks), *n.* **1** *sing. in use.* the science that deals with the motion of projectiles, such as bullets, shells, or bombs, and also rockets and missiles after thrust has ended. **2** *pl. in use.* the qualities of a projectile or missile that determine its flight; ballistic qualities.

ballistic trajectory, the curved path followed by a projectile after the propelling force has ended.

bal|lis|tite (bal′ə stīt), *n.* a powerful explosive consisting of nitroglycerin and guncotton. [< Latin *ballista* ballista + English *-ite*[1]]

bal|lis|to|car|di|o|gram (bə lis′tō kär′dē ə gram), *n.* the record of a heart's action taken by a ballistocardiograph.

bal|lis|to|car|di|o|graph (bə lis′tō kär′dē ə graf, -gräf), *n.* an instrument for determining the strength of the heart's contraction, and the amount of blood it pumps, by measuring the body's recoil as blood from the heart is forced into it. [< Latin *ballista* ballista + English *cardiograph*]

bal|lis|to|car|di|o|graph|ic (bə lis′tō kär′dē ə-graf′ik), *adj.* of or having to do with a ballistocardiograph.

bal|lis|to|car|di|og|ra|phy (bə lis′tō kär′dē og′rə fē), *n.* the recording of the heart's action by a ballistocardiograph.

ball|joint (bôl′joint′), *n., adj.* **—*n.*** a ball-and-socket joint.
—*adj.* using or having to do with a ball-and-socket joint: *balljoint suspension.*

ball lightning, a rare kind of lightning shaped like a globe of fire, moving at relatively slow speed, and usually disappearing without a detonation.

ball mill, a crushing and grinding machine that consists principally of a cylinder rotating on its side and containing metal balls or round stones.

ball of fire, *U.S. Slang.* an exceptionally dynamic person; live wire: *He was certainly no ball of fire at those points where leadership was called for* (New Yorker).

bal|lon (bȧ lôN′), *n. French.* **1** the ability of a ballet dancer to give the impression that he remains in the air for a considerable time, as if soaring, during a jump. **2** a large, almost round brandy glass.

bal|lon d'es|sai (bȧ lôN′de se′), *French.* trial balloon.

bal|lo|net (bal′ə net′), *n.* a small bag inside a balloon or airship that holds air or gas to regulate ascent or descent. [< French *ballonnet* (diminutive) < *ballon* balloon]

bal|loon (bə lün′), *n., v., adj.* **—*n.*** **1** an airtight bag filled with heated air or some gas lighter than air so that it will rise and float in air. Some balloons have a basket or container for carrying persons or instruments high up into the air. *A balloon is essentially a body of which the average density is less than that of the surrounding air, and so it rises upwards to the less dense upper atmosphere* (Herz and Tennent). **2** a child's toy made of thin rubber filled with air or some gas lighter than air: *The cat popped the balloon as she caught it with her claws.* **3** a circled or boxed space in a cartoon in which the words of a speaker are written. **4** a large, globular, glass vessel with one or more short necks, used in chemistry. **5** = ballon (def. 2).
—*v.i.* **1a** to swell out like a balloon: *The sails of the boat ballooned in the wind.* **b** to grow or increase rapidly and greatly: *Prices . . . at least aren't ballooning* (Newsweek). **2** to ride in a balloon. **—*v.t.*** **1** to puff (something) out or cause to be inflated like a balloon. **2** to make greater in size, number, etc.: *The present one-story structure is to be "ballooned" to ten stories* (New York Times).
—*adj.* **1** of or having to do with a balloon: *a balloon ascent, balloon performance.* **2** made from or using a balloon: *balloon launched rockets, a balloon satellite.* **3** resembling a balloon, especially in shape: *a balloon explosion.* **4** *Commerce.* having to do with or providing for low periodic payments of a debt followed by a large or greatly inflated final payment: *a balloon note, loan, or mortgage, balloon payments.*
like a lead balloon, without the slightest effect: *His poor joke went over like a lead balloon.*
[< Middle French *ballon* < Italian *pallone* large ball[1]] **—bal|loon′er,** *n.* **—bal|loon′like′,** *adj.*

balloon astronomy, the use of high-altitude balloons equipped with telescopes to obtain photographs of the sun, planets, or other heavenly bodies, and to gather other astronomical data.

balloon barrage, an antiaircraft screen consisting of barrage balloons.

bal|loon|fish (bə lün′fish′), *n., pl.* **-fish|es** or (*collectively*) **-fish** = globefish.

bal|loon|ing (bə lü′ning), *n.* **1** the art of operating a balloon. **2** *Medicine.* the stretching of any cavity of the body by filling it with air. **3** the movement of a spider which rises in the air and floats on its own silk threads with the wind's action.

bal|loon|ist (bə lü′nist), *n.* **1** a person who goes up in a balloon or in balloons. **2** the pilot of a dirigible balloon.

balloon jib, a large, triangular sail of light canvas used by yachts instead of the ordinary jib when winds are light.

balloon platform, a platform, carried aloft by a balloon or balloons, from which rockets are launched.

balloon sail, any one of various large, light sails used by yachts in light breezes, such as the balloon jib.

balloon tire, a large tire containing air under low pressure, for lessening the shock of bumps.

balloon vine, a tropical climbing plant of the soapberry family, with large, three-celled, bladderlike pods.

bal|lot (bal′ət), *n., v.,* **-lot|ed, -lot|ing.** **—*n.*** **1** a piece of paper or other object used in secret voting: *Have you cast your ballot? The ballot is stronger than the bullet* (Abraham Lincoln). **2a** the method of secret voting by means of paper slips, voting machines, or other devices: *The results of a ballot determined the winner of the race for mayor.* **b** the right to vote: *to gain the ballot.* **3** the total number of votes cast. **4** (in New Zealand and certain other countries) the machinery and process of selection for military service; conscription.
—*v.i.* **1** to vote or decide by using ballots: *We will ballot for president of the club.* **2** to select by lot; draw lots (for): *The racers balloted for places by drawing straws.*
—*v.t.* to select by drawing of lots for.
[< Italian *ballotta* little ball for voting < Middle French *ballotte* (diminutive) < *balle* ball[1]]

ballot box, 1 the box into which voters put their ballots after they have voted. **2** the ballot method of secret voting; ballot.
stuff the ballot box, to put fraudulent votes into a ballot box or otherwise fraudulently increase the number of votes: *You could go to jail for stuffing the ballot box* (New Yorker).

bal|lot|té (ba lə tā′), *n., pl.* **-tés** (-tā′). *French.* a tossing movement in ballet in which the dancer raises one leg behind the knee of the other and springs upwards.

bal|lotte|ment (bə lot′mənt), *n.* **1** a method of diagnosing pregnancy, in which, upon a sudden push with the finger on the uterus, the fetus is felt moving away and falling back again. **2** a similar method used in examining floating kidney or other organs. [< French *ballottement* < Middle French *balloter* return a ball < *ballotte* little ball]

ball park or **ball|park** (bôl′pärk′), *n.* **1** a baseball field together with grandstands and bleachers for spectators. **2** *Figurative.* field or area of a particular activity, business, or any other endeavor: *The Smithsonian group searched for rays with energies of about 100 billion electron volts, "an entirely different ballpark," said Dr. Giovanni Fazio of the observatory* (Science News Yearbook).
in the ball park, within acceptable or established limits: *He said it was the lowest cost steel settlement in several years, and said it was "within the ballpark" of this goal* (Wall Street Journal).

ballpark figure, *U.S.* an appropriate estimate within the range of acceptance or credibility: *Around four million viewers . . . a ballpark figure based on Nielsen ratings, and most likely as accurate as police estimates of New Year's Eve crowds in Times Square . . .* (New Yorker).

ball peen hammer, a hammer the head of which has a rounded end opposite its face, used especially by machinists.

ball pen, = ballpoint pen.

ball|play|er (bôl′plā′ər), *n.* **1** a baseball player. **2** a person who plays ball.

ball|point (bôl′point′), *n.,* or **ballpoint pen,** a pen that writes by means of a small metal ball set in its point. The ball turns against a cartridge holding ink in semisolid form and transmits it to the paper against which it is pressed.

ball race, the track, groove, or race in which the balls of a ball bearing run.

ball|room (bôl′rüm′, -rům′), *n.* a large room for dancing.

ballroom dancing, dancing considered appropriate for a ballroom, as the waltz or fox trot.

ball turret, a gun turret in the shape of a ball or hemisphere, designed to project from the fuselage of a bomber, and to house the gunner.

ball-up (bôl′up′), *n. Slang.* a badly tangled situation; mess.

bal|lute (bə lüt′), *n.* a parachute in the form of a balloon, used by a spacecraft when descending through very thin atmosphere, especially during reentry. [blend of *balloon* and (para)*chute*]

ball valve, a valve formed by a ball resting in a concave, circular seat containing an aperture. Pressure of a fluid rising from beneath lifts the ball and opens the aperture. When the pressure is released, the ball drops to close the aperture.

bal|ly (bal′ē), *adj., adv. Slang, originally British, now Rare.* **—*adj.*** confounded (used with no definite meaning, for emphasis or humor).
—*adv.* very. [origin unknown]

bal|ly|hoo (*n.* bal′ē hü; *v.* bal′ē hü, bal′ē hü′), *n., pl.* **-hoos,** *v.,* **-hooed, -hoo|ing.** *Slang.* **—*n.*** **1** noisy advertising; sensational way of attracting attention. **2** uproar; outcry: *The local scandal caused a lot of ballyhoo.*
—*v.t., v.i.* to make exaggerated or false statements; advertise noisily.
[perhaps < *Ballyhooly,* County Cork, Ireland]
—bal′ly|hoo′er, *n.*

bal|ly|rag (bal′ē rag′), *v.t.,* **-ragged, -rag|ging.** = bullyrag.

balm (bäm), *n.* **1** a fragrant, oily, sticky substance obtained from certain kinds of trees, used to heal or to relieve pain; balsam: *Balm flows naturally from some trees.* **2** an ointment or similar preparation that heals or soothes: *Mother spread a creamy balm over her burned hand.* **3** *Figurative.* anything that heals or soothes; healing or soothing influence: *Mother's praise was balm to the little girl's wounded feelings. They laid them down to rest, And so received the balm of sleep* (William Cullen Bryant). SYN: solace, comfort, consolation. **4** a fragrant ointment or oil used in anointing. **5** *Figurative.* sweet odor; fragrance. SYN: aroma, perfume. **6** any one of several fragrant plants of the same family as mint. [< Old French *basme, baume* < Latin *balsamum* < Greek *bálsamon.* See etym. of doublet **balsam.**]

bal|ma|caan (bal′mə kän′), *n.* a short, loose overcoat made originally of rough wool and having raglan sleeves. [< *Balmacaan,* Scotland]

Balm|er series (bäl′mər), a series of radiations emitted by electrons, appearing in the spectra of white stars as bright lines spaced at regularly decreasing intervals from red to violet. [< Johann *Balmer,* 1825-1898, a Swiss physicist]

balm of Gil|e|ad (gil′ē əd), **1a** a fragrant ointment prepared from the resin of certain Asiatic and African evergreen trees; balsam Mecca. **b** any one of the various evergreen trees that yield this resin. **2** a kind of poplar with large, fragrant, resinous buds. **3** the balsam fir. [< *Gilead,* a region in ancient Palestine, where balm was used (Jeremiah 8:22; 46:11)]

Bal|mor|al or **bal|mor|al** (bal môr′əl, -mor′-), *n.* **1** a striped woolen petticoat worn under a looped-up skirt. **2** a shoe or boot that laces up the front. **3** a flat, brimless Scottish cap. [< *Balmoral* Castle in Aberdeen, Scotland]

Bal|mung (bäl′műng), *n.* Siegfried's sword.

balm|y[1] (bä′mē), *adj.,* **balm|i|er, balm|i|est.** **1** mild; gentle: *A balmy breeze blew across the lake.* SYN: soothing, bland, temperate. **2** fragrant: *Balmy heather filled the air.* [< *balm* + *-y*[1]] **—balm′i|ly,** *adv.* **—balm′i|ness,** *n.*

balm|y[2] (bä′mē), *adj.,* **balm|i|er, balm|i|est.** *British Slang.* silly; crazy. [apparently < *balmy*[1], but confused with *barmy* flighty]

bal|ne|al (bal′nē əl), *adj.* of or having to do with a

bath, or with bathing. [< Latin *balneum* bath (< Greek *balaneîon*) + English *-al*[1]]

bal|ne|ol|o|gy (bal′nē ol′ə jē), *n.* the science of bathing, especially in mineral waters, as therapeutic treatment. [< Latin *balneum* bath + English *-logy*]

Ba|lo|chi (bə lō′chē), *n., pl.* **-chi.** = Baluchi.

ba|lo|ney (bə lō′nē), *n., interj.* —*n.* **1** *Slang.* nonsense, especially pretentious nonsense; buncombe. **2** *Informal.* bologna.
—*interj. Slang.* nonsense: *In London, British officials resorted to an Americanism to deny the assertion: "Baloney!"* (Time). Also, **boloney.**
[< *bologna*]

bal|sa (bôl′sə, bäl′-), *n.* **1** a tropical American tree with strong wood which is very light in weight. It belongs to the bombax family. *The wood of the balsa floats better than cork.* **2** its wood, used especially in making rafts or airplane models: *Balsa appeals to model makers because it can be carved so easily.* **3** a raft, especially a raft consisting of two or more floats fastened to a framework. [American English < Spanish *balsa*]

bal|sam (bôl′səm), *n., v.* —*n.* **1a** any one of several fragrant, oily, sticky resins obtained from certain kinds of trees and containing benzoic acid or cinnamic acid: *Balsam is used as a base for good varnish.* **b** balm (def. 1). **2** a balsam-yielding tree, such as the balsam fir of the United States and Canada: *Our Christmas tree was a big balsam.* **3** something that heals or soothes; balm. **4** a garden plant with seed vessels that burst open violently when ripe; garden balsam. It belongs to the same family as the touch-me-not. **5** any one of several compounds, insoluble in water, consisting of resins mixed with volatile oils; oleoresin. **6** any of various transparent, liquid turpentines, especially Canada balsam.
—*v.t.* to treat with balsam.
[< Latin *balsamum.* See etym. of doublet **balm.**]

balsam apple, 1 a vine of the gourd family, with a red or orange fruit. **2** any one of certain allied species.

bal|sa|me|a|ceous (bôl′sə mē ā′shəs, bal′-), *adj.* belonging to a family of tropical trees and shrubs that yield important resinous products, as myrrh, frankincense, or bdellium. [< *balsam* + *-aceous*]

balsam fir, 1a an evergreen tree of North America of the pine family whose resin is used in making varnish and turpentine; balm of Gilead. Balsam firs are much used as Christmas trees. **b** its wood. **2** any one of various other firs.

bal|sam|ic (bôl sam′ik, bal-), *adj.* **1** of the nature of or containing balsam. **2** yielding balsam. —**bal·sam′i|cal|ly,** *adv.*

bal|sa|mif|er|ous (bôl′sə mif′ər əs, bal′-), *adj.* yielding or producing balsam. [< *balsam* + *-ferous*]

bal|sa|mi|na|ceous (bôl′sə mə nā′shəs, bal′-), *adj.* belonging to the same family of plants as the impatiens. [< Middle French *balsamine* (< Greek *balsaminē* balsam plant < *bálsamon*) + English *-aceous*]

balsam Mecca, = balm of Gilead.

balsam of Pe|ru (pə rü′), a resin obtained from a Central and South American tree of the pea family, used in perfumery and in medicine.

balsam of To|lú (tō lü′), a resin obtained from a South American tree of the pea family, used in perfumery, in cough syrups, and in chewing gum.

balsam poplar, a native American poplar having thick, heart-shaped leaves and large buds covered with resin; tacamahac.

balsam spruce, a tall fir of the mountains of the western United States, having blue-green needles; Alpine fir.

balsam tree, any one of various balsam-yielding trees, such as the balsam fir or the balsam poplar of America.

bal|sa|mum (bôl′sə məm, bal′-), *n. Latin.* balsam.

balsam woolly aphid, an aphid of the Northern Hemisphere that is very injurious to fir trees.

bal|sam|y (bôl′sə mē), *adj.* = balsamic.

Balt (bôlt), *n.* a native or inhabitant of the Baltic region.

bal|ter (bôl′tər), *v.t., v.i. Obsolete except Dialect.* to form into masses or lumps; clot; mat. Also, **bolter.** [< Scandinavian (compare Danish *baltre* tumble)]

Bal|tha|sar (bal thā′zər, -thaz′ər), *n.* one of the Three Wise Men, according to legend.

bal|tha|zar (bal thā′zər, -thaz′ər), *n.* a champagne bottle containing 416 ounces, the next to the largest size. [< *Balthazar* (now more commonly *Belshazzar*), ruler of Babylon in the 500's B.C.]

Bal|tic (bôl′tik), *adj., n.* —*adj.* **1** of or having to do with the Baltic Sea: *the Baltic islands, the Baltic coasts.* **2** of or having to do with the Baltic States. **3** of or belonging to the Indo-European languages of the eastern Baltic region, including Lithuanian, Latvian or Lettish, and Old Prussian (now extinct): *Lithuanian and Latvian are the only two languages of any social importance in the Baltic branch* (Henry A. Gleason, Jr.).
—*n.* **1** the Baltic languages. **2** the Indo-European ancestor of these languages, perhaps one member of a Balto-Slavic branch.

Bal|ti|mor|e|an (bôl′tə môr′ē ən, -mōr′-), *n., adj.* —*n.* a native or inhabitant of Baltimore.
—*adj.* of or having to do with Baltimore or its inhabitants.

Bal|ti|more clipper (bôl′tə môr, -mōr), a small clipper built in the 1800's in Baltimore, Maryland.

Baltimore oriole, a North American bird. The male has orange and black feathers and the female has brown and greenish yellow feathers. [earlier *Baltimore bird* (because the male's colors were those of Lord *Baltimore's* livery)]

Bal|to-Slav|ic (bôl′tō slä′vik, -slav′ik), *n.* a grouping of the various Baltic and Slavic languages as one subdivision of Indo-European. It is regarded with skepticism by many modern linguists.

Ba|lu|chi (bə lü′chē), *n., pl.* **-chi. 1** a native or inhabitant of Baluchistan. **2** the language of Baluchistan, of the Iranian branch of the Indo-Iranian subdivision of Indo-European. Also, **Balochi.**

ba|lu|chi|there (bə lü′chə thir), *n.* any one of an extinct genus of very large, hornless mammals with long necks and heads, related to the rhinoceros. [< *Baluchi*(stan), a province of Pakistan + Greek *thērion* beast]

bal|un (bal′ən), *n.* an electrical transmission line for coupling a line that is symmetrically grounded with one that is grounded on only one side. [< *bal*(ance and) *un*(balance)]

***bal|us|ter** (bal′ə stər), *n.* one of the short posts or columns that support the railing of a staircase, balcony, or terrace.
balusters, a balustrade: *He threw the keys over the balusters to the floor below.*
[< Middle French *balustre* < Italian *balaustro* < *balaustra* wild pomegranate flower < Latin *balaustium* < Greek *balaústion* (from the shape)]

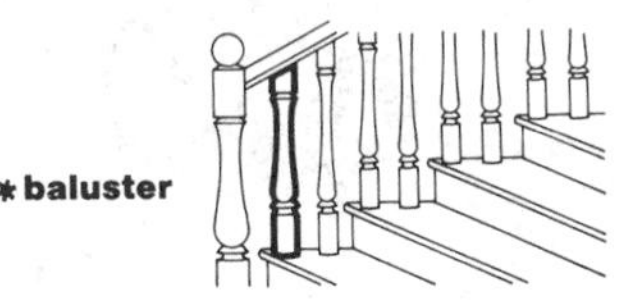

***baluster**

bal|us|trade (bal′ə strād′), *n., v.,* **-trad|ed, -trad·ing.** —*n.* a row of balusters and the railing on them. SYN: banister.
—*v.t.* to provide with a balustrade or balustrades: *. . . each house fortified with a tiny, intimate, balustraded porch* (John Updike).
[< French *balustrade* < Italian *balustrata* < *balaustro;* see etym. under **baluster**]

ba|lut (bä lüt′), *n.* a Philippine dish of duck eggs about to be hatched. The eggs are boiled and served as a delicacy. [< Tagalog *balút*]

Bal|zac|i|an (bal zak′ē ən, bôl-), *adj.* of or having to do with Honoré de Balzac, his many novels, or his style of realistically and minutely detailed and carefully documented writing.

bam[1] (bam), *interj.* (with) a dull thump; bump; slam. [imitative]

bam[2] (bam), *v.,* **bammed, bam|ming,** *n. Slang or Dialect.* —*v.t., v.i.* to bamboozle.
—*n.* a hoax.
[perhaps short for *bamboozle*]

Bam|ba|ra (bäm bä′rä), *n., pl.* **-ra** or **-ras. 1** a member of a Negro people of western Africa. **2** their Mandingo language.

bam|bi|no (bam bē′nō), *n., pl.* **-ni** (-nē) or **-nos. 1a** a baby. **b** a little child: *She needed money for six undernourished bambini* (New Yorker). **2** an image or picture of the infant Jesus. [< Italian *bambino* (diminutive) < *bambo* simple, childish]

bam|boche (bäm bōsh′), *n.* (in Haiti) an informal party. [< French *bamboche*]

bam|boo (bam bü′), *n., pl.* **-boos,** *adj.* —*n.* **1** a woody or treelike grass with a very tall, stiff, hollow stem that has hard, thick joints. Bamboo grows in warm regions. Its stems are used for making canes, fishing poles, furniture, and even houses. The young shoots of some species are used as food. See picture under **grass family. 2** the stem of any of these plants.
—*adj.* of bamboo; made of the stems of this plant: *a bamboo fishing rod.*
[< Dutch *bamboe* < Portuguese *bambu* < Malay]

Bamboo Curtain, an imaginary wall formerly considered a dividing line, separating territory controlled by the Chinese Communists from the non-Communist world.

bamboo telegraph, the means by which news and rumors are quickly spread in countries of the Orient; grapevine. See also **bush telegraph.**

bamboo worm, a reddish annelid with a membranous collar found along the Atlantic coast between North Carolina and the Bay of Fundy.

bam|boo|zle (bam bü′zəl), *v.,* **-zled, -zling.** *Informal.* —*v.t.* **1** to impose upon; cheat; trick: *The boy had been bamboozled out of his cookies by the romping puppy.* **2** to puzzle; perplex: *It had never occurred to them that their high-spirited, self-confident, happy daughter would be bamboozled into muteness by the language of France* (New Yorker).
—*v.i.* to use trickery.
[origin uncertain] —**bam|boo′zle|ment,** *n.* —**bam|boo′zler,** *n.*

bam|bou|la (bam bü′lə), *n.* **1** a primitive drum of Africa and the West Indies. **2** a dance performed to the beat of this drum. [< Creole French *bamboula*]

bam|bu|sa|ceous (bam′byü sā′shəs), *adj.* **1** belonging to a group of grasses comprising the various species of bamboo. **2** resembling the bamboo. [< New Latin *Bambusa* a genus name of the bamboo + English *-aceous*]

ban[1] (ban), *v.,* **banned, ban|ning,** *n.* —*v.t.* **1** to forbid by law or authority; prohibit: *Swimming is banned in this lake.* SYN: interdict, proscribe. **2** to place a ban on; pronounce a curse on. SYN: curse. **3** *Archaic.* to place an ecclesiastical curse upon. **4** *Archaic.* to curse.
—*n.* **1** the forbidding of an act or speech by authority: *The city has a ban on parking cars in this busy street. Opinions which are under the ban of society* (John Stuart Mill). SYN: taboo, prohibition. **2** *Archaic.* a solemn curse by the church. SYN: excommunication, anathema. **3** a sentence of outlawry.
[fusion of Scandinavian (compare Old Icelandic *banna* prohibit, curse) and Old English *bannan* summon, proclaim]

ban[2] (ban), *n.* **1** a public proclamation or edict. **2** in feudal times: **a** the summoning of the (French) king's vassals for war. **b** the whole body of vassals thus assembled, or liable to be summoned. [fusion of Old English *gebann* summons and Old North French *ban* proclamation, jurisdiction < Frankish (compare Old High German *ban*)]

ban[3] (ban), *n.* (formerly) the governor of certain military districts of Hungary, Slavonia, and Croatia. [< Hungarian *bán* < Croatian *bân* < Mongol *bayan* (literally) rich]

ban[4] (bän), *n., pl.* **ba|ni.** a Romanian copper coin, worth 1/100 of a leu. [< Romanian *ban*]

ba|nal (bā′nəl; bə nal′, -näl′; ban′əl), *adj.* not new or interesting; commonplace; trite: *Their conversation was banal, full of uninteresting remarks, such as "nice weather" and "slow traffic today."* SYN: hackneyed. [< French *banal* < Old French < *ban* ban[2], military summons; intermediate sense was "common"] —**ba′nal|ly,** *adv.*

ba|nal|i|ty (bə nal′ə tē), *n., pl.* **-ties. 1** commonplaceness; triteness. **2** a banal statement, idea, or remark.

ba|nal|ize (bā′nə līz, ban′ə-), *v.t.,* **-ized, -iz|ing.** to make banal; reduce to something commonplace or ordinary: *These traits of good character have been banalized by advertising* (Scientific American). —**ba′nal|i|za′tion,** *n.*

ba|nan|a (bə nan′ə), *n., adj.* —*n.* **1** a slightly curved, yellow or red fruit with firm, creamy flesh. Bananas are about five to eight inches long and grow in dense clusters two or three feet long. **2** the plant which bears this fruit, a treelike tropical or subtropical plant, 10 to 25 feet high, with great long leaves. **3** the bland flavor of this fruit. **4** a light cream or straw color. **5** *U.S. Slang.* a dollar.
—*adj.* **bananas,** *U.S. Slang.* crazy; wildly excited: *Whoever said life is just a bowl of cherries is bananas* (Earl Wilson).
[< Spanish or Portuguese *banana;* of East African origin]

banana family, a group of monocotyledonous, tropical herbs, often treelike in size and appearance, having an unbranched stem and a capsule or berry as the fruit. This family includes the banana, plantain, and traveler's-tree.

banana oil, 1 a colorless, inflammable liquid which smells somewhat like bananas, used in making fingernail polish and flavoring extracts and as a solvent. *Formula:* $C_7H_{14}O_2$ **2** *U.S. Slang.* talk that is meant to impress but is obviously foolish or insincere: *pouring on the old banana oil.*

banana quit, any one of a genus of small, tropical American birds, allied to the creepers, that frequent flowering trees and shrubs.

banana republic, any small country, especially in Latin America, that depends for its economy on the export of a single crop or product, such as bananas, coffee, or sugar.

Pronunciation Key: hat, āge, cãre, fär; let, ēqual, tėrm; it, īce; hot, ōpen, ôrder; oil, out; cup, pu̇t, rüle; child; long; thin; ᴛʜen; zh, measure; ə represents **a** in about, **e** in taken, **i** in pencil, **o** in lemon, **u** in circus.

banana split, two or three scoops of ice cream placed on a banana sliced down its length, covered with whipped cream, sweet fruits or sauces, nuts, and other garnishes.

banana water lily, an aquatic plant with yellow flowers, native to the southern United States and Mexico.

ba|nat or **ba|nate** (ban′it), *n.* **1** the territory or jurisdiction of a ban. **2** the term of office of a ban. [< *ban*[3] + *-ate*[3]]

ba|nau|sic (bə nô′sik), *adj.* **1** mechanical: *... alleged that the teaching of music as a manual art was banausic and degrading* (George Grote). **2** practical: *Chief among its many qualities is the author's concern to ask ... certain banausic but highly basic questions about the Greeks* (Sunday Times). **3** materialistic: *Banausic, he called them, banausic, A villainous banausic couple* (Stevie Smith). [< Greek *banausikós* of or for artisans < *bánausos* artisan]

Ban|bur|y tart (ban′bər ē), a tart filled with mincemeat, citrus rind, and raisins. [< *Banbury,* a town in Oxfordshire, England, noted for these tarts]

banc (bangk), *n.* a bench of justice; court.
in banc, in full session with a quorum of the judges present.
[< Anglo-French *banc,* Old French, bank]

ban|ca (bäng′kä), *n.* a kind of dugout or canoe used in the Philippines. [< Philippine Spanish *banca*]

band[1] (band), *n., v.* **—*n.*** **1** a number of persons or animals joined or acting together: *a band of wild dogs. A band of robbers held up the train.* SYN: party, gang, group, crew. See syn. under **company**. **2** a group of musicians playing various instruments together. Bands usually play wind and percussion instruments only and perform chiefly out of doors. *The school band played several marches.* **3** an orchestra that plays popular music, such as for dancing: *a jazz band.* **4** *Western U.S.* a drove or flock of animals; herd.
—*v.t., v.i.* to unite or cause to unite in a group: *The children banded together to buy a present for their teacher.* SYN: confederate, league.
[< Middle French *bande* < Old French, ultimately < Germanic (compare Gothic *bandwa* sign). See related etym. at **banner**.]

band[2] (band), *n., v.* **—*n.*** **1** a thin, flat strip of material for binding, trimming, or some other purpose: *The oak box was strengthened with bands of iron. She wore a band of ribbon in her hair.* **2** a stripe: *The white cup has a gold band.* **3** anything having the shape or appearance of a flat strip: **a** a section considered separately from its surroundings because of some feature: *A band of light rain and showers extended from the Canadian border ... to central Texas* (New York Times). **b** separate section of grooves on a phonograph record. **4** a particular range of wavelengths or frequencies in radio broadcasting. **5** a particular range of wavelengths within a spectrum.
—*v.t.* **1** to put a band on: *Students of birds often band them in order to identify them later.* **2** to mark with stripes.
bands, a collar with two strips hanging down in front, worn as part of certain clerical, legal, or academic costumes.
[< Middle French *bande* < Old French < Germanic (compare Old High German *binta*). See related etym. at **band**[1], **bend**[2].]

band[3] (band), *n.* **1** a moral, spiritual, or legal restraint. **2** *Archaic.* anything with which one's body or limbs are bound; shackle; fetter; chain. [< Scandinavian (compare Old Icelandic *band*)]

band|age (ban′dij), *n., v.,* **-aged, -ag|ing.** **—*n.*** a strip of cloth or other material used in binding up and dressing a wound or injury: *With bandage firm Ulysses' knee they bound* (Alexander Pope).
—*v.t.* to bind, cover, or dress with a bandage: *to bandage a cut finger.*
[< Middle French *bandage* < Old French *bander* to bind < *bande* a strip, band[2]] **—band′ag|er,** *n.*

Band-Aid (band′ād′), *n., adj.* **—*n.*** *Trademark.* a bandage for slight wounds, consisting of a piece of cotton gauze attached to a strip of adhesive tape; adhesive compress.
—*adj.* *U.S.* put together hastily; serving as a stopgap; temporary.

ban|dan|na or **ban|dan|a** (ban dan′ə), *n.* a large, gaily colored cotton kerchief or handkerchief, often worn on the head or neck. [< Hindustani *bāndhnū* way of tying cloth so as to produce designs when dyed]

band|box (band′boks′), *n.* a light, usually cardboard, box to put hats or collars in.

ban|deau (ban dō′, ban′dō), *n., pl.* **ban|deaux** or **ban|deaus** (ban dōz′, ban′dōz). **1** a narrow band worn about the head. **2** any narrow band. **3** a narrow brassiere. [< French *bandeau* < Old French *bandel* strip (diminutive) < *bande*]

band|ed (ban′did), *adj.* **1** having a band or bands. **2** marked with bands; striped.

banded anteater, a squirrellike marsupial of Australia which has no pouch; numbat. It eats ants and termites.

banded rattlesnake, = timber rattlesnake.

band|er (ban′dər), *n.* **1** a device that applies bands. **2** a person who bands, such as one who bands birds for identification.

ban|de|ril|la (bän′dä rēl′yä), *n. Spanish.* a barbed dart with brightly colored streamers attached to its shaft, used in bullfighting: *A banderillero in tight pants and jacket is poised with banderillas high in the air* (New Yorker).

ban|de|ril|le|ro (bän′dä rēl yā′rō), *n., pl.* **-ros.** *Spanish.* an unmounted man who sticks banderillas into the neck and shoulder muscles of a bull in a bullfight.

ban|de|role or **ban|de|rol** (ban′də rōl), *n.* **1** a long, narrow flag with a cleft end, flying from the masthead of ships. **2** a small ornamental streamer. Also, **bannerol**. [< Middle French *banderole* < Italian *banderuola* (diminutive) < *bandiera* banner]

ban|der|snatch (ban′dər snach′), *n.* any very strange and alarming creature: *... a pterodactyl with an eight-foot wingspread and a bandersnatch mien* (New Yorker). [< *Bandersnatch,* a fabulous animal in Lewis Carroll's *Through the Looking-Glass*]

bandh (bänd), *n.* a general stoppage of work and services as a form of protest in India. [< Hindustani *bāndh* stoppage]

***ban|di|coot** (ban′də küt), *n.* **1** a small, burrowing, ratlike marsupial found in Australia and New Guinea. Bandicoots live on insects and carry their young in abdominal pouches. **2** either of two very large, destructive rats of southern Asia and the Near East, about two feet long. [< Telugu *pandi-kokku* (literally) pig rat]

***bandicoot**
definition 1

ban|di|do (ban dē′dō), *n., pl.* **-dos.** a bandit, especially in the southwestern United States and in Central and South America. [< Spanish *bandido*]

band|ing (ban′ding), *n.* **1** material sewn or to be sewn as bands, as on a woman's dress at the cuffs or hem. **2** bands collectively.

ban|dit (ban′dit), *n., pl.* **ban|dits** or **ban|dit|ti.** **1** a highwayman or robber, especially one of a gang. SYN: brigand, desperado. **2a** any outlaw. **b** anyone who uses a position or special advantage to swindle, exploit, or otherwise treat (another) unfairly: *The housing conditions were so horrifying that they ... suspected that they had some of the biggest bandits of all in their midst* (Manchester Guardian Weekly). **3** *Slang.* (in the U.S. Air Force) any enemy aircraft. [< Italian *bandito* an outlaw < *bandire* proclaim; proscribe < Gothic *bandwjan* give a sign]

ban|dit|ry (ban′də trē), *n.* **1** the work of bandits; robbery. **2** bandits.

ban|dit|ti (ban dit′ē), *n.* a plural of **bandit**.

Band|ke|ra|mik (bänt′kā rä′mik), *n.* a kind of banded pottery of the neolithic period in Europe. [< German *Bandkeramik* < *Band* band + *Keramik* pottery]

band|lead|er (band′lē′dər), *n.* the leader of a dance band.

band|mas|ter (band′mas′tər, -mäs′-), *n.* the leader of a band of musicians.

ban|dog (ban′dôg′, -dog′), *n. Rare.* **1** a dog always kept tied or chained up, either as a watchdog or because of its ferocity. **2** a mastiff. **3** a bloodhound. [Middle English *band-doge*]

ban|do|leer or **ban|do|lier** (ban′də lir′), *n.* **1** a broad belt worn over the shoulder and across the breast. Some bandoleers have loops for carrying cartridges; others have small cases for bullets, gunpowder, or fuzes. **2** one of these cases. [< French *bandoulière* < Spanish *bandolera* < *banda* sash, scarf, ultimately < Germanic; see etym. under **band**[1]]

ban|do|line (ban′də lēn, -lin), *n.* a gummy hair dressing to make the hair stay in place. [< French *bandoline,* coined from *bandeau* band[2], ribbon + Latin *linere* to smear]

ban|do|ni|on or **ban|do|ne|on** (ban dō′nē on), *n.* a kind of accordion, with buttons on each side, each button for a single tone. [< Heinrich *Band,* a German musician who invented it in the 1840's + (harm)*oni*(ca) + (accordi)*on*]

ban|dor|a (ban dôr′ə, -dōr′-), *n.* = bandore.

ban|dore (ban dôr′, -dōr′; ban′dôr, -dōr), *n.* an old musical instrument resembling a guitar or lute, with three, four, or six strings. Also, **pandora, pandore.** [probably < Portuguese *bandura* < Late Latin *pandūra* < Greek *pandoúrā* three-stringed lute]

band-pass filter (band′pas′, -päs′), *Electronics.* a filter capable of admitting frequencies within certain limits and of excluding or greatly weakening all others.

bands (bandz), *n.pl.* See under **band**[2].

band saw, a saw in the form of an endless steel belt running over two pulleys.

band shell, *Especially U.S.* an outdoor platform for musical concerts, with a shell-shaped, resonant covering, open at the front.

bands|man (bandz′mən), *n., pl.* **-men.** a member of a band of musicians.

band spectrum, a spectrum consisting of broad bands of molecular origin, each having a sharp edge at its low-frequency end.

band|stand (band′stand′), *n.* an outdoor platform, usually roofed, for band concerts.

band-tailed pigeon (band′tāld′), a wild pigeon of the western United States about the size of a large domestic pigeon, having a black band across the tail.

ban|dur|a (ban dür′ə), *n.* a Russian form of the bandore.

ban|dur|ria (ban dür′yə), *n.* a Spanish form of the bandore.

band|wag|on (band′wag′ən), *n.* **1** a wagon that carries a musical band in a parade. **2** *Informal, Figurative.* a popular, fashionable, or winning group, movement, or trend: *They say the U.S. will have to join the free trade bandwagon or face growing trade discrimination in Europe* (Wall Street Journal).
climb on the bandwagon, *Informal.* to join what appears to be a winning or successful group, movement, or fashion: *Once conservation became popular, everyone climbed on the bandwagon and the ecology movement began to spring up everywhere.*

band|width (band′width′), *n. Electronics.* the range of radio frequencies in a band.

ban|dy (ban′dē), *v.,* **-died, -dy|ing,** *adj., n., pl.* **-dies.** **—*v.t.*** **1** to throw or hit back and forth; toss about: *We bandied the ball from player to player while we waited for the game to start.* **2** to give and take; exchange: *The two angry boys bandied a few blows but never got into a real fight.* **3** to pass from one to another in a group, especially without much thought or concern: *to bandy stories, bandy gossip.*
—*v.i.* to contend; strive; fight.
—*adj.* **1** having a bend or curve outward: *bandy legs.* **2** bandy-legged: *They have their daughters going bandy taking riding lessons* (Atlantic).
—*n.* *Especially British.* **1** Also, **bandy ball.** a form of hockey similar to field hockey but also played on a rink. **2** a curved stick used in this game.
[perhaps < Old French *bander* < *bande* side, group. See related etym. at **band**[1].]

ban|dy-leg|ged (ban′dē leg′id, -legd′), *adj.* having legs that curve outward and back in, like a bow; bowlegged.

bane (bān), *n., v.,* **baned, ban|ing.** **—*n.*** **1** a cause of death, ruin, or harm; curse: *Packs of wolves were the bane of the mountain village.* SYN: scourge. **2** destruction of any kind; ruin; harm. SYN: destruction.
—*v.t.* *Archaic.* to harm, hurt, or poison.
[Old English *bana* murderer]

bane|ber|ry (bān′ber′ē, -bər-), *n., pl.* **-ries.** **1** any one of a genus of herbs of the crowfoot family that have spikes of small, white flowers and clusters of white or red, poisonous berries; cohosh. **2** one of these berries.

bane|ful (bān′fəl), *adj.* **1** causing harm or destruction; injurious: *Air pollution has a baneful effect on trees.* SYN: bad, evil, pernicious. **2** destroying life; deadly: *a baneful poison.* SYN: fatal, lethal. **—bane′ful|ly,** *adv.* **—bane′ful|ness,** *n.*

bang[1] (bang), *n., v., adv., interj.* **—*n.*** **1** a sudden, loud noise: *We heard the bang of a gun.* **2** a violent, noisy blow; thump: *He gave the drum a bang.* **3** *Informal.* a striking result or success. **4** *Informal.* vigor; impetus: *a sales campaign with real bang.* **5** *U.S. Informal.* a thrill; kick: *to get a bang out of flying.*
—*v.i.* **1** to make a sudden, loud noise: *The shutter banged against the side of the house.* **2** to close with a loud noise: *The door banged as it blew shut in a sudden gust of wind.*
—*v.t.* **1** to cause to make a sudden, loud noise; shut with noise; slam: *He banged the door shut.* **2** to hit with violent and noisy blows: *The baby was banging the pan with a spoon.* **3** to handle roughly, and often to mar: *The movers banged the mirror and broke it.*
—*adv.* **1** violently and noisily: *The boy on the bicycle went bang into a telephone pole.* **2** suddenly and loudly: *The balloon blew up bang in my face.* **3** suddenly and abruptly; all at once: *to cut a thing bang off.* **4** directly; squarely; straight:

We live bang on the highway.
—*interj.* **1** imitation of gunfire: *"Bang! Bang!" shouted the boys.* **2** imitation of any sudden, loud noise.
bang up, to damage: *My car was banged up in the accident.*
[probably < Scandinavian (compare Old Icelandic *banga* strike, bang)]

bang[2] (bang), *n., v.* —*n. Usually,* **bangs,** *pl.* a fringe of hair cut short and worn over the forehead: *The little girl wore bangs.*
—*v.t.* **1** to cut squarely across: *She wears her hair banged.* **2** to dock (a horse's tail). [American English < *bang*[1], adverb]

bang[3] (bang), *n.* = bhang.

ban·ga·lore torpedo (bang′gə lôr, -lōr), a metal pipe containing gunpowder or other explosive and having a detonating cap and long fuze. It is pushed forward and exploded to open a path through barbed wire, a mine field, or other obstruction. [< *Bangalore,* a city in India]

bang-bang (bang′bang′), *n.* **1** *U.S. Informal.* noisy and violent shooting or other fighting: . . . *television's bloody bang-bangs* (James Thurber). **2** a type of control system for guided missiles.

bang·board (bang′bôrd′, -bōrd′), *n. U.S.* a piece of additional siding attached to the far side of a wagon, off which ears of corn flung into the wagon by huskers bounce into the vehicle.

bang·er (bang′ər), *n.* **1** a person or thing that bangs. **2** *British Slang.* **a** a sausage: *beer and bangers.* **b** a firecracker. **c** a noisy old car.

bang·kok (bang′kok), *n.* **1** a kind of straw grown in Thailand, used for hats. **2** a hat made from it. [< *Bangkok,* the capital of Thailand]

Ban·gla·desh·i (bäng′glə desh′ē, -dä′shē), *n., pl.* **-desh·is** or **-desh·i,** *adj.* —*n.* a native or inhabitant of Bangladesh (the former province of East Pakistan).
—*adj.* of or having to do with Bangladesh or its people.

ban·gle (bang′gəl), *n.* **1** a small ornament suspended from a bracelet. **2** a bracelet or anklet without a clasp. [< Hindustani *bangrī*]

bang-on (bang′on′), *adj. Especially British Informal.* strikingly accurate or effective.

bangs (bangz), *n.pl.* See under **bang**[2], *n.*

Bang's disease (bangz), = brucellosis.

bang·tail (bang′tāl′), *n. U.S. Slang.* a race horse. [< *bang*[2] + *tail*]

bang-up (bang′up′), *adj. Informal.* strikingly good or effective; first-rate: *He did such a bang-up job that he won a commendation ribbon and was madea captain at 36* (Time).

bang zone, the area covered by a sonic boom; boom carpet.

ba·ni (bä′nē), *n.* plural of **ban**[4].

Ban·ia or **ban·ia** (ban′yə), *n.* = banian (def. 3).

ban·ian (ban′yən), *n.* **1** = banyan. **2** a loose gown, jacket, or shirt of flannel, worn in India. **3** Also, **banya** or **Bania.** a Hindu merchant of a caste that eats no meat. [< Portuguese *banian,* probably < Gujarati *vāniyo* < Sanskrit *vanij* merchant]

ban·ish (ban′ish), *v.t.* **1** to condemn (a person) to leave a country; exile: *England once banished many criminals to Australia.* **2** to force to go away; drive away; expel: *The children banished him from their game because he always cheated.* SYN: dismiss. [< Old French *baniss-,* stem of *banir* proclaim, banish < Frankish (compare Gothic *bandwjan* give a sign)] —**ban′ish·er,** *n.* —**ban′ish·ment,** *n.*
—*Syn.* **1 Banish, exile, deport** mean cause to leave a country. **Banish** means to force a person, by order of authority, to leave his own or a foreign country, permanently or for a stated time: *Napoleon was banished to Elba.* **Exile** means either to compel another to leave his own country or home or voluntarily to remove oneself from either for a protracted period: *The man exiled himself abroad because of his dissatisfaction with the government.* **Deport** usually means to banish a person from a country of which he is not a citizen: *Aliens who have entered the United States illegally may be deported.*

ban·is·ter (ban′ə stər), *n.* **1** = balustrade. **2** one of the supports of a balustrade; baluster. Also, **bannister.**
banisters, the handrail of a staircase, balcony, or terrace, and its row of supports; balustrade: *He held fast by the banisters as he descended the stairs* (Wilkie Collins).
[alteration of *baluster*]

ban·jax (ban′jaks), *v.t. Slang.* to hit, beat, or overcome. [apparently < dialectal Irish *banjax*]

***ban·jo** (ban′jō), *n., pl.* **-jos** or **-joes,** *adj., v.,* **-joed, -jo·ing.** —*n.* a musical instrument having four or five strings, played by plucking the strings with the fingers or a pick. It has a head and neck like a guitar and a body like a tambourine. *Many folksongs were originally played to the plink of the banjo.* —*adj.* shaped like a banjo: *a banjo clock hanging on the wall.* —*v.i.* to play the banjo. [earlier *banjore, banjer;* probably alteration of *bandore*]

***banjo**

ban·jo·ist (ban′jō ist), *n.* a person who plays a banjo.

bank[1] (bangk), *n., v.* —*n.* **1** a long pile or heap: *a bank of clouds. There was a bank of snow over ten feet deep.* SYN: ridge, mound, embankment. **2** the rising ground bordering a river or lake; shore: *He fished from the bank.* **3** a shallow place in a body of water; shoal: *The fishing banks of Newfoundland are famous.* SYN: bar, reef. **4** any steep slope, especially one forming a ravine or hill. **5** the sloping of an airplane to one side, especially when making a turn: *The airplane made a steep bank to avoid the tall building.* **6** in a road or track: **a** the raising of the outside edge of a curve higher than the inside edge: . . . *there is one tight hairpin without sign of bank* (Time). **b** the amount of such slope. **7** *Mining.* **a** the top of a shaft, or the ground level at the top of a shaft: *The cost of ore on the bank is low.* **b** the face worked in a coal mine. **8** the cushion lining the sides and ends of a billiard or pool table.
—*v.t.* **1** to form into a bank; pile up; heap up: *The bulldozer banked the earth into a hill. The tractors banked the snow by the road.* **2** to cause to slope, especially to slope (a roadbed) toward the inside of a curve: *The workmen banked the curves of the express highway so that fast-moving cars would hold the road and not skid.* **3** to make (an airplane) slope to one side, especially when making a turn: *The pilot banked the plane to turn to the airfield.* **4** to cover (a fire) with ashes, or to add fresh fuel and lessen the draft so it will burn slowly: *The guide banked the campfire with ashes for the night.* **5** to raise a ridge or mound about; border with a bank or ridge: *Burning sands, that bank the shrubby vales* (James Thomson). SYN: embank.
—*v.i.* **1** to form banks: *Clouds are banking along the horizon.* **2** to slope to one side, especially when turning an airplane: *Airplanes must bank to approach the airfield. The car banked around the corner.* **3** to slope.
bank up, *British.* to accumulate; collect: . . . *had allowed the traffic to bank up* (London Times).
[probably < Scandinavian (compare Old Icelandic *bakki* ridge)]

bank[2] (bangk), *n., v.* —*n.* **1** a place of business for keeping, lending, exchanging, and issuing money: *A bank pays interest on money deposited as savings.* **2** a small container with a slot through which coins can be dropped to save money: *Mary's father gave her a quarter for her piggy bank.* **3a** any place where reserve supplies are kept. The place where blood is kept for transfusions is called a bank. There are also bone and eye banks. **b** the reserve supply itself: *The blood bank increased after the appeal for blood.* **4** the stock of pieces from which players draw in games such as dominoes. **5** the fund of money in some gambling games out of which the dealer or manager pays his losses. **6** (formerly) the table, counter, or quarters of a money-changer.
—*v.t.* to put (money) in a bank: *My sister banks her salary on payday.*
—*v.i.* **1** to put money in a bank; keep an account with a bank: *My father banks at the County Trust.* **2** to keep a bank; act as a banker: *My son is banking at National City as his first job.* **3** to be in charge of the bank in some gambling games.
bank on, *Informal.* to depend on; be sure of: *I can bank on my brother to help me.*
in the bank, *British Informal.* in deficit; in the red: *Four small discount houses were "in the bank" for a small amount, in spite of moderate help from the authorities* (London Times).
[< Middle French *banque* < Italian *banca* (originally) counter, bench < Germanic (compare Old High German *banch*)]

bank[3] (bangk), *n., v.* —*n.* **1** a row of things: *A bank of switches controlled the plane engines. We saw a bank of machines in the factory.* **2** a row of keys on an organ or typewriter or a row of switches on a panel: *Some organs have two banks of keys. The entire bank of circuit breakers was switched on.* **3a** a row or tier of oars: *The Greeks manned the banks in the Roman galleys.* **b** a bench for rowers in a galley: *The Greek slaves were chained to banks in Roman galleys.* **c** the rowers on such a bench. **4** a section of a newspaper headline set apart from the other sections in the same size and face of type; a deck. —*v.t.* to arrange in rows. [< Old French *banc* bench < Germanic (compare Old High German *banch*)]

bank·a·bil·i·ty (bang′kə bil′ə tē), *n.* the quality or condition of being bankable: *The secret and all-powerful Q Ratings . . . determine a performer's appeal—and ultimately his bankability* (Maclean's).

bank·a·ble (bang′kə bəl), *adj.* **1** that can be converted into cash at or by a bank. **2** certain to produce box-office success and profits: [*He*] *has become a "bankable" superstar, whose commitment to a project means that a film will be made and will be guaranteed a certain success* (New York Times Magazine).

bank acceptance, a draft or bill of exchange drawn on a bank and acknowledged as valid by that bank; banker's acceptance.

bank account, the money in a bank that can be withdrawn by a depositor; a checking, savings, or other account with a bank.

bank annuities, *British.* government funded debts, usually consols.

bank barn, *U.S.* a barn with two floors built on the side of a hill so that both floors have entrances at a ground level.

bank bill, 1 a check drawn by one bank on another; banker's bill; bank draft. **2** *Especially U.S.* a bank note.

bank·book (bangk′bu̇k′), *n.* book that records a person's account at a bank; passbook.

bank call, *U.S.* a periodic demand by the state or federal government for sworn statements giving the financial condition of banks as of a certain date.

bank card, a credit card issued by a bank: *Most bank cards cost consumers nothing—provided they pay their bills at the bank within 30 days* (Time).

bank check, an order issued on or by a bank to pay a designated amount.

bank discount, a charge equivalent to the interest due on the total amount of a loan until maturity, withheld from the borrower at the time a loan is made.

bank draft, = bank bill.

banked[1] (bangkt), *adj.* having banks or raised margins: *a high-banked river.* [< *bank*[1]]

banked[2] (bangkt), *adj.* having a bank or banks, as of oars or organ keys. [< *bank*[3]]

bank·er[1] (bang′kər), *n.* **1** a person or company that manages a bank: *If you have a special checking account or if you've borrowed from a bank to buy a new car, you've dealt with a commercial banker* (New York Times). **2** an officer of a bank. **3** the dealer or manager in a gambling game. [< *bank*[2] + *-er*[2], probably patterned on French *banquier*]

bank·er[2] (bang′kər), *n.* a ship or man in the business of cod fishing on the Newfoundland banks. [< *bank*[1] + *-er*[2]]

bank·er[3] (bang′kər), *n.* a workbench used to dress bricks or stone. [< *bank*[3] + *-er*[2]]

banker's acceptance, = bank acceptance.

banker's bill, = bank bill.

bank examiner, a person assigned by a state or central government to examine bank records.

bank-full (bangk′fu̇l′), *adj.* as full as possible without overspilling.

bank holiday, 1 a day other than Saturday or Sunday on which banks are legally closed; a legal holiday. **2** the period from March 6 to March 13, 1933, during which all banks in the United States were closed by order of the President.

bank indicator, a flight instrument used together with a turn indicator to measure skidding or slipping of an aircraft in a turn. It shows the aircraft's angle of roll about its longitudinal axis.

bank·ing[1] (bang′king), *n.* the business of keeping, lending, exchanging, and issuing money. [< *bank*[2] + *-ing*[1]]

bank·ing[2] (bang′king), *n.* **1** the construction of banks or embankments. **2** a bank or embankment. [< *bank*[1] + *-ing*[1]]

banking account, *British.* a bank account.

bank night, *U.S.* a type of lottery held in motion-picture theaters.

bank note, a promissory note issued by a bank that must be paid on demand; bank bill.

bank paper, 1 any commercial paper acceptable by a bank for discount. **2** any commercial paper endorsed as payable by a bank. **3** the total, or a

Pronunciation Key: hat, āge, cãre, fär; let, ēqual, tėrm; it, īce; hot, ōpen, ôrder; oil, out; cup, pu̇t, rüle; child; long; thin; ᴛʜen; zh, measure; ə represents **a** in about, **e** in taken, **i** in pencil, **o** in lemon, **u** in circus.

part of the total, of bank notes in circulation.

bank rate, 1 the discount rate fixed by a bank or banks for a specified type of notes or other commercial paper. 2 such a rate fixed by a central bank or banking system (in the United States, by the Board of Governors of the Federal Reserve Board).

bank|roll (bangk′rōl′), *n., v.* —*n. Informal.* the amount of money a person has in his possession or readily available.
—*v.t. Slang.* to provide the money for; finance: *... bankroll a new TV quiz show* (Newsweek).
—**bank′roll′er**, *n.*

bank|rupt (bangk′rupt), *adj., v., n.* —*adj.* 1 unable to pay one's debts, especially when declared legally unable to do so: *After his store burned, the shopkeeper was bankrupt.* SYN: insolvent. 2 *Figurative.* at the end of one's resources; destitute: *I find myself bankrupt of hope that the situation can be improved.* SYN: impoverished. 3 *Figurative.* completely lacking in some respect: *The joke was entirely bankrupt of humor.* SYN: poor, deficient.
—*v.t.* to make bankrupt: *Foolish expenditures will bankrupt him.* SYN: impoverish.
—*n.* 1a. a person who is declared by a court of law to be unable to pay his debts and whose property is distributed as far as it will go among the people to whom he owes money. b a person who is unable to pay his debts. 2 a person who is unable to satisfy just claims of any kind made upon him.
[< Middle French *banqueroute* < Italian *banca rotta; banca* bank, and *rotta,* feminine past participle of *rompere* to break < Latin *rumpere*]

bank|rupt|cy (bangk′rupt sē, -rəp-), *n., pl.* **-cies.** 1 bankrupt condition: *When his business failed he went into bankruptcy.* 2 *Figurative.* utter wreck, ruin, or loss (of any good quality): *A general bankruptcy of reputation in both parties* (Edmund Burke).

bank shot, 1 a shot in billiards or pool in which the cue ball is bounced off the cushion to hit the object ball. 2 a shot in basketball in which the player tries to bounce the ball off the backboard into the basket.

***bank|si|a** (bangk′sē ə), *n.* any shrub or tree of a genus of widely growing Australian evergreens, having hard, dry leaves and yellow flowers in close cylindrical heads. [< New Latin *Banksia* < Sir Joseph *Banks,* 1743-1820, a British botanist]

***banksia**

bank statement, 1 a tabular statement of one's deposits and withdrawals sent to a person periodically by the bank. 2 a statement of the assets and liabilities of a bank or banks.

bank swallow, a small swallow of eastern and central North America that nests in a deep hole which it digs in a bank; sand martin. It has a brown back, and a white chest marked with a brownish band.

ban|lieue or **ban|lieu** (ban′lyü; *French* bäɴ lyœ′), *n.* an outlying district or suburb. [< French *banlieue* < Medieval Latin *banleuca*]

ban|ner (ban′ər), *n., adj., v.* —*n.* 1 a flag: *The banners of many countries fly outside the headquarters of the United Nations.* (*Figurative.*) *The crusaders fought under the banner of Christ.* (*Figurative.*) *The patriots unfurled the banner of freedom.* SYN: ensign, standard, pennant. 2 a piece of cloth with some design or words on it, attached by its upper edge to a pole or staff: *Our Boy Scout troop has a banner which we carry in parades.* 3 a newspaper headline extending across the top of a page.
—*adj.* leading or outstanding; foremost: *... a banner year for sales and earnings* (Wall Street Journal).
—*v.t. Informal.* to print as news under a banner: *His newspaper bannered a point-blank refutation ... by an influential diplomat* (Time).
[< Old North French *banere,* Old French *banniere* < Gothic *bandwa* sign. See related etym. at **band**[1].]

ban|nered (ban′ərd), *adj.* 1 furnished with or displaying a banner or banners. 2 displayed on a banner of a coat of arms.

ban|ner|et[1] (ban′ər it), *n. Historical.* 1 a knight able and entitled to bring a company of vassals into battle under his own banner. 2 a former rank of knighthood, usually awarded for valor in battle. [< Old French *baneret* < *banere* banner + *-et* < Latin *-ātus* -ate[1]]

ban|ner|et[2] or **ban|ner|ette** (ban′ə ret′), *n.* a small banner. [< Old French *banerette* (diminutive) < *banere,* and *baniere* banner]

ban|ner|line (ban′ər līn′), *n., v.,* **-lined, -lin|ing.** —*n.* a banner of a newspaper.
—*v.t. Informal.* to banner.

ban|ner|man (ban′ər mən), *n., pl.,* **-men.** 1 a standardbearer; ensign. 2 a member of one of the eight divisions of the Manchu army.

ban|ner|ol (ban′ə rōl), *n.* = banderole.

***ban|ner|stone** (ban′ər stōn′), *n.* a prehistoric stone artifact shaped like a small two-edged ax with an axial perforation, found only in eastern North America.

***bannerstone** 

ban|nis|ter (ban′ə stər), *n.* = banister.

ban|nock (ban′ək), *n.* a flat, round or oval cake, usually unleavened, made of oatmeal or barley flour, eaten in Scotland, northern England, and northern Canada. [Old English *bannuc* bit, piece]

Ban|nock (ban′ək), *n., pl.* **-nock** or **-nocks.** 1 a member of a Shoshonean tribe found chiefly in southern Idaho. 2 the language of this tribe.

banns (banz), *n.pl.* a notice given three separate times in church or some other public place, such as the newspaper, that a certain man and woman are to be married. Also, **bans.** [earlier *banes,* plural of variant of *ban*[2]]

banque d'af|faires (bäɴk dȧ fãr′), *pl.* **banques d'af|faires** (bäɴk dȧ fãr′). *French.* a bank that engages in industrial and commercial investment and management of securities; merchant bank.

ban|quet (bang′kwit), *n., v.,* **-quet|ed, -quet|ing.** —*n.* a formal dinner, often with speeches, prepared for a special occasion and usually for many people; feast: *We went to the wedding banquet.* SYN: See syn. under **feast.**
—*v.t.* to give a banquet or banquets to; provide a banquet for: *The mayor banqueted the famous visitor.* SYN: feast, regale.
—*v.i.* to take part in a banquet.
[< Middle French *banquet* < Italian *banchetto* (diminutive) < *banco* bench around eating tables]
—**ban′quet|er**, *n.*

ban|quette (bang ket′), *n.* 1 a ledge, step, or other platform along the inside of a parapet or trench for soldiers to stand on when firing. 2 an upholstered bench, especially one built against the wall in a restaurant: *I always have the same table, one at the banquette against the wall ... I like a banquette because I don't like to get knocked around in the middle of the room* (New Yorker). 3 a shelf or ledge, as at the back of a buffet. 4 *Southern U.S.* a sidewalk. [< Middle French *banquette* < Italian *banchetta* (diminutive) < *banca* bench, shelf]

Ban|quo (bang′kwō), *n.* a character in Shakespeare's play *Macbeth.* Banquo is murdered by order of Macbeth, but his ghost causes Macbeth to reveal his guilt.

bans (banz), *n.pl.* = banns.

ban|shee or **ban|shie** (ban′shē, ban shē′), *n.* a female spirit in Irish and Scottish folk belief, whose wail is supposed to mean that there will soon be a death in the family. [< Irish *bean sīdhe* woman of the fairies]

bant (bant), *v.i.* to diet to reduce weight by Bantingism. [< *Bantingism*]

ban|tam (ban′təm), *n., adj.* —*n.* 1 Often, **Bantam.** a small-sized kind of chicken. The roosters are often spirited fighters. 2 *Figurative.* a small person who is fond of fighting. 3 (formerly) a jeep. 4 striped brownish pebbles found in the gravel of diamond mines.
—*adj.* 1 light in weight; small. 2 *Figurative.* laughably aggressive.
[< *Bantam,* a town in Java, where this chicken is supposed to have originated]

ban|tam|weight (ban′təm wāt′), *n., adj.* —*n.* a boxer who weighs between 113 and 118 pounds.
—*adj.* very light or small of its kind; miniature: *A bantamweight, 17-inch TV set, so light householders can carry it from room to room* (Wall Street Journal).

ban|teng (ban′teng), *n.* a wild ox of southern and southeastern Asia, domesticated to farm labor. Also, **bantin.** [< a native word]

ban|ter (ban′tər), *n., v.* —*n.* playful teasing; joking: *There was much banter going on at the party.* SYN: raillery, pleasantry.
—*v.t.* to tease playfully; make fun of.
—*v.i.* to talk in a joking way: *Father enjoys bantering with his children.*
[origin uncertain] —**ban′ter|er**, *n.* —**ban′ter|ing|ly**, *adv.*

Ban|thine (ban′thēn), *n. Trademark.* methantheline.

ban|tin (ban′tin), *n.* = banteng.

Ban|ting|ism (ban′ting iz əm), *n.* a method of reducing weight by avoiding fat, starch, and sugar in food. [< William *Banting,* 1797-1878, a London cabinetmaker, who advocated the method]

bant|ling (bant′ling), *n.* a young child; brat: *... their base-born bantlings* (Connoisseur). [perhaps < German *Bänkling* bastard < *Bank* bench]

Ban|tu (ban′tü), *n., pl.* **-tu** or **-tus,** *adj.* —*n.* 1 a member of a large group of Negro tribes living in central and southern Africa, including the Zulus, Xosas, Basutos, Swazis, and Bechuanas. 2 any one of the languages of these tribes, comprising a linguistic family, notable for the great use of prefixes in inflection.
—*adj.* of these tribes or their languages: *Bantu nations extend from the Swahili of Zanzibar ... south to the many tribes of South Africa* (E. H. L. Schwarz).
[< Zulu *abantu* men]

Ban|tu|stan (ban′tü stan), *n.* 1 any one of several regions in the Republic of South Africa designated as separate states to be inhabited and governed by the Bantu. 2 the policy aiming at this.

ban|ty (ban′tē), *n., pl.* **-ties,** *adj. U.S. Dialect.* bantam.

banx|ring (bangks′ring), *n.* a squirrellike, East Indian animal that feeds on insects. [< a Javanese word]

ban|ya (ban′yə), *n.* = banian.

ban|yan (ban′yən), *n.* a fig tree of India, Burma, and other parts of Asia, whose branches have hanging roots that grow down to the ground and start new trunks. One tree may cover several acres. The banyan tree belongs to the mulberry family. Also, **banian.**
[apparently from one such tree under which the *banians* built a pagoda]

ban|zai (bän′zī′), *interj.* 1 a Japanese greeting or patriotic cheer. It means "May you live ten thousand years!" 2 the cry of Japanese soldiers in a banzai attack.

banzai attack or **charge**, a fanatic and suicidal assault, usually on a strongly entrenched position, by massed Japanese troops yelling "Banzai."

ba|o|bab (bā′ō bab, bä′-), *n.* a tall tropical tree of Africa, India, and Australia, with a very thick trunk and an edible, oblong, gourdlike, woolly fruit (monkey bread). The strong fibers of its bark are used especially for making rope, paper, and cloth. The baobab tree belongs to the bombax family. [< New Latin *bahobab,* perhaps < an African language]

bap (bap), *n. Scottish.* a roll or small loaf of bread of various shapes. [origin unknown]

Bap. or **Bapt.**, Baptist.

bap|tis|i|a (bap tiz′ē ə, -tizh′-), *n.* = wild indigo. [< New Latin *Baptisia* < Greek *báptisis* a dipping (from its use as a dye)]

bap|tism (bap′tiz əm), *n.* 1 the act of dipping a person into water or sprinkling water on him, as a sign of the washing away of sin and of admission into the Christian church. 2 *Figurative.* any experience that tests a person or initiates him into a new kind of life: *Iraq, Thailand, and Austria had their TV baptisms* (Newsweek).

bap|tis|mal (bap tiz′məl), *adj.* of or having to do with baptism; used in baptism: *a baptismal ceremony.* —**bap|tis′mal|ly**, *adv.*

baptismal name, the personal or given name; Christian name.

baptism of fire, 1 the first time that a soldier is exposed to enemy fire. 2 *Figurative.* any severe trial or test; ordeal: *The traffic policeman's first day of work was a baptism of fire.* 3 the grace of baptism; baptism by gift of the Holy Ghost (in the Bible, Matthew 3:11). 4 martyrdom.

Bap|tist (bap′tist), *n., adj.* —*n.* 1 a member of a Christian church that believes in baptizing by dipping the whole person into water. Baptists belong to the Protestant denominations which assert that baptism can be administered only upon a personal profession of Christian faith (thus not to infants). 2 Often, **baptist.** a person who baptizes.
—*adj.* of or having to do with the Baptists.

the Baptist, John the Baptist (in the Bible, Matthew 3:1).

bap|tis|ter|y (bap′tə stər ē, -strē), *n., pl.* **-ter|ies.** 1 a place where baptism is performed. A baptistery may be a part of a church or a separate building. 2 a tank in Baptist churches for immersing those being baptized. [< Latin *baptistērium* (originally) bathing place < Greek *baptistērion* < *baptizein* bathe, baptize]

bap|tis|try (bap′tə strē), *n., pl.* **-tries.** = baptistery.

bap|tize (bap tīz′, bap′tīz), *v.,* **-tized, -tiz|ing.** —*v.t.* 1 to dip (a person) into water or sprinkle with water, as a sign of the washing away of sin and of admission into the Christian church: *The*

minister baptized the child in church on Sunday. **2** to give a first name to (a person) at baptism; christen: *The baby was baptized William.* **3** *Figurative.* to give a name to; name: *The space capsules were each baptized by their own crews.* **4** to purify; cleanse: *Sorrow had baptized her* (Oliver Wendell Holmes). **5** *Figurative.* to introduce or initiate: *The flights of Glenn and Gargarin baptized the world into the age of man in space.*
—*v.i.* to administer baptism.
[< Old French *baptiser,* learned borrowing from Latin *baptizāre* < Greek *baptízein* dip, bathe < *báptein* dip] —**bap|tiz′er,** *n.*

ba|pu (bä′pü), *n.* (in India) father: *Mahatma Gandhi ... [was] one of the few men Nehru ever listened to. He came to call Gandhi Bapu* (Newsweek). [< Hindustani *bapu*]

bar¹ (bär), *n., v.,* **barred, bar|ring,** *prep.* —*n.* **1** an evenly shaped piece of some solid, longer than it is wide or thick: *There is a bar of soap on the sink. I ate a chocolate bar at lunch.* **2** a pole or rod put across a door, gate, window, or across any opening, to fasten or shut off something: *Let down the pasture bars for the cows to come in. The windows of the prison have iron bars.* **3a** *Figurative.* anything that blocks the way or prevents progress: *His bad temper was a bar to making friends.* **SYN**: barrier, obstacle, obstruction. **b** a long ridge of sand or gravel, especially one lying across the mouth of a river or harbor, which obstructs navigation; sand bar: *A bar of sand kept boats out of the harbor.* **4** a band of color; stripe: *There is a dark bar of clouds across the setting sun.* **SYN**: strip. **5** *Music.* **a** a unit of rhythm. The regular accent falls on the first note of each bar. **b** the dividing line between two such units on a musical staff. A bar marks off measures. **c** = double bar. **6a** a counter where drinks, usually alcoholic, and sometimes food, are served to customers: *a cocktail bar. We stood at a snack bar and had a soda.* **b** a building or room containing such a counter, especially a barroom or tavern: *The men walked into the bar.* **7** a counter at which certain goods are sold: *a gift bar, a record bar.* **8a** the profession of a lawyer: *After college, he decided to enter the bar. He left the bar for a career in teaching.* **b** the whole group of practicing lawyers: *Judges are chosen from the bar.* **9a** a court of law: *to try a case at the bar.* **SYN**: tribunal. **b** the place where a prisoner stands in a court of law: *The convicted thief stood at the bar to be sentenced by the judge.* **10** the railing around the place where lawyers sit in a law court. **11** *Figurative.* anything like a court of law; any place of judgment: *The bar of public opinion condemns dishonest people.* **SYN**: tribunal. **12** an ingot of precious metal: *bars of gold.* **13** (in lacemaking) a connecting thread; bride. **14** *Law.* **a** a plea or objection sufficient to stop or defeat an action or claim. **b** the stopping of an action or claim. **15** *Heraldry.* an ordinary formed by two parallel lines drawn horizontally across the shield and including not more than a fifth of its surface. **16** See **bars.**
—*v.t.* **1** to put bars across; fasten or shut off with a bar: *He bars the doors every night.* **2** to block; obstruct: *Fallen trees bar the road.* **3** to keep out; exclude or forbid: *Dogs are barred from that store. All talking is barred in the library. Father barred our use of the car tonight.* **SYN**: prohibit. **4** to mark with stripes or bands of color: *Some hawks have barred feathers.* **5** to shut up or confine by or as if by bars: *The writer barred himself in his study.*
—*prep.* except; excluding: *He is the best student, bar none.*
admit to the bar, *U.S.* to give authority to practice law: *After passing his law examinations, he was admitted to the bar.* Also, *British,* **call to the bar.**
[< Old French *barre* < Vulgar Latin *barra* thick ends of bushes]

bar² (bär), *n. U.S.* a mosquito net. [American English < Louisiana French *baire*]

bar³ (bär), *n. Physics.* the unit of pressure equivalent to 1 million dynes per square centimeter in the centimeter-gram-second system. [< Greek *báros* weight]

bar., **1a** barometer. **b** barometric. **2** barrel.

Bar., **1** barrister. **2** Baruch.

BAR (no periods), Browning Automatic Rifle.

Ba|rab|bas (bə rab′əs, bar′ə bəs), *n.* the prisoner whose release the people demanded when Pilate offered to free Jesus (in the Bible, Matthew 27: 16-21; Mark 15:6-11; Luke 23:18-25; John 18:39-40).

bar|ad (bar′ad), *n.* = microbar. [< Greek *báros* weight; patterned on English *farad*]

ba|ra|ka (bä rä′kä, bə räk′ə), *n.* a quality of divine power in Moslem belief, bestowed upon a person or thing: *Baraka ... makes it lucky just to kiss his garments and gives him special title to spiritual (as well as temporal) leadership of his people* (Time). [< Arabic *barakah* (literally) blessing]

bar-and-grill (bär′ənd gril′), *n. U.S.* an establishment where both alcoholic drinks and grilled meats and other foods are served.

ba|ra|sin|gha (bä′rə sing′gə), *n.* any of several species of East Indian deer. [< Hindustani *bārasiṅghā* (literally) having twelve horns]

bar|a|the|a (bar′ə thē′ə), *n.* a fine-textured cloth composed of silk and wool. Also, **barrathea.** [origin unknown]

***barb¹** (bärb), *n., v.* —*n.* **1** a point sticking out and curving backward from the main point of an arrow or fishhook: *The barb of the hook stuck in my finger.* **2** *Figurative.* something that wounds or stings: *the stinging barb of sarcasm.* **3** *Zoology.* **a** one of the hairlike branches on the shaft of a bird's feather. **b** a projection on the tip of a quill of some porcupines. **4** a long, thin growth hanging from the mouth; barbel: *the barbs of a catfish.* **5** *Botany.* a hair terminating in a hook or hooks. **6** part of a medieval woman's headdress, still often worn by nuns, consisting of a piece of white linen passed over or under the chin. **7** a woman's lace neckband or scarf. **8** *Obsolete.* the beard of a man.
—*v.t.* to furnish with barbs: *to barb a hook. (Figurative.) In anger he barbed his reply.*
[< Old French *barbe* < Latin *barba* beard]
—**barb′less,** *adj.*

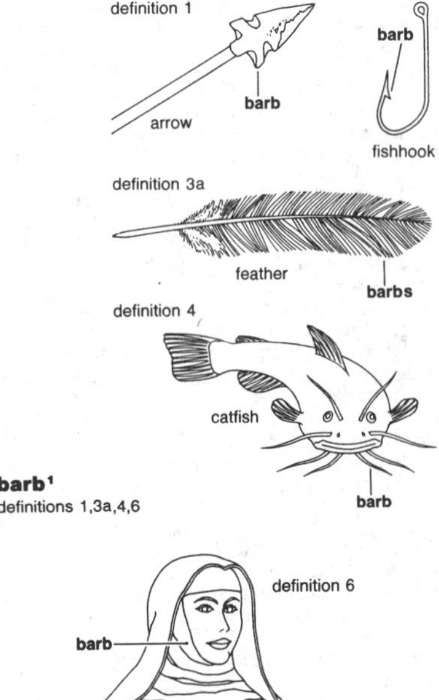

***barb¹**
definitions 1,3a,4,6

barb² (bärb), *n.* **1** a kind of horse that has great speed, endurance, and gentleness. It was introduced into Spain from the Barbary States by the Moors. **2** any bird of a breed of domestic pigeons allied to the carrier pigeons, having a short, broad beak. [< French *barbe* < Italian *barbero* < Latin *barbarus* barbarian, also Berber]

Bar|ba|di|an (bär bā′dē ən), *adj., n.* —*adj.* of or having to do with the island country of Barbados. —*n.* a native or inhabitant of Barbados.

Bar|ba|dos aloe (bär bā′dōz, bär′bə dōz), a widely cultivated aloe native to the Mediterranean region, with yellow flowers and usually no stem.

Barbados cherry, = acerola.

bar|ba|resque (bär′bə resk′), *adj.* barbarous in style, as forms of art.

Bar|ba|resque (bär′bə resk′), *adj.* of or having to do with Barbary (an old name for North Africa).

bar|bar|i|an (bär bãr′ē ən), *n., adj.* —*n.* **1** a person belonging to a people or a tribe that is not civilized: *Rome was conquered by the barbarians.* **2** a person who rejects or lacks interest in literature or the arts. **3** any foreigner, differing from the speaker or writer in language and customs. In ancient times, a barbarian was successively a person who was not a Greek, a person outside of the Roman Empire untutored in its civilization, or (sometimes) a person who was not a Christian.
—*adj.* **1** not civilized; cruel and coarse: *The children of warring countries are often victims of barbarian treatment.* **2** of barbarians: *barbarian customs.* **3** differing from the speaker or writer in language and customs; foreign.
[< Latin *barbaria* foreign country (< *barbarus* foreigner < Greek *bárbaros* (originally) stammering) + English *-an*]
—*Syn. adj.* **1 Barbarian, barbaric, barbarous** mean not civilized. **Barbarian** suggests the full range of lack of civilization: *The Roman Empire was conquered by barbarian peoples.* **Barbaric** emphasizes the love of show and the lack of refinement and gentleness, that distinguish less highly civilized peoples: *The dress of the tribal chief was barbaric.* **Barbarous,** more than the others, emphasizes the harshness and cruelty of uncivilized peoples: *Torture of prisoners is a barbarous custom.*

bar|bar|i|an|ism (bär bãr′ē ə niz′əm), *n.* the state or condition of being a barbarian.

bar|bar|i|an|ize (bär bãr′ē ə nīz), *v.t.,* **-ized, -izing.** to make barbarian.

bar|bar|ic (bär bar′ik), *adj.* **1** suited to an uncivilized people; like barbarians in a rough and rude way: *The barbaric pressures maintained by the enemy in the Korean camps made strict adherence to the code impossible for many men and inordinately difficult for others* (Atlantic). **SYN**: See syn. under **barbarian. 2** rich or splendid in a crude way: *barbaric color, barbaric music. The Viking hall was decorated in barbaric splendor.* **SYN**: See syn. under **barbarian.** [< Latin *barbaricus* < Greek *barbarikós* < *bárbaros* (originally) stammering] —**bar|bar′i|cal|ly,** *adv.*

bar|ba|rism (bär′bə riz əm), *n.* **1** the condition of uncivilized people: *People who have no form of writing live in barbarism.* **2** a barbarous act, custom, or trait. **3** the use of a word or expression not in accepted use: *Barbarism in conversation is often distracting.* **4** a word or expression not in accepted use, such as "his'n" for "his": *The English Department, he said, offers a bonus of fifteen points to the student who spots and records the greatest number of grammatical errors, ambiguities, redundancies, and barbarisms in the speeches made at the school* (New Yorker). **5** particularly offensive bad manners.

bar|bar|i|ty (bär bar′ə tē), *n., pl.* **-ties. 1a** brutal cruelty; inhumanity: *... barbarity and ignorance had not overspread Scotland* (R. Chapman). **b** a cruel act. **2** barbaric manner or style; gaudy taste: *These two ... men rivalled or exceeded Attila in their wholesale barbarities* (Cardinal Newman).

bar|ba|rize (bär′bə rīz), *v.t., v.i.,* **-rized, -riz|ing.** to make or become barbarous: *... barbarous and barbarizing warfare* (Robert Southey). *The Roman empire was barbarizing rapidly* (Thomas De Quincey). —**bar′ba|ri|za′tion,** *n.*

bar|ba|rous (bär′bər əs), *adj.* **1** not civilized; savage: *Cannibals are barbarous people.* **SYN**: See syn. under **barbarian. 2** savagely cruel; brutal: *Torture of prisoners is a barbarous practice.* **3** rough and rude; coarse; unrefined: *The early fur trappers were more barbarous than the Indians they fought.* **4** not in accepted use: *His barbarous speech included "irregardless" and "he don't."* **5** foreign; alien. **6** (of Greek or Latin) not classical or pure; abounding in barbarisms. [< Latin *barbarus* (with English *-ous*) < Greek *bárbaros* foreign, (originally) stammering] —**bar′ba|rous|ly,** *adv.* —**bar′ba|rous|ness,** *n.*

Bar|ba|ry ape (bär′bər ē), a tailless monkey that lives in North Africa and on the Rock of Gibraltar. It is the only monkey now found in its native state in Europe.

barbary sheep, = aoudad.

bar|bas|co (bär bas′kō), *n.* any one of various tropical American plants used in making fish poisons and insecticides, especially the dioscorea, from which synthetic hormones are made. [< American Spanish *barbasco*]

bar|bate (bär′bāt), *adj.* furnished with small, hairy tufts; bearded: *barbate leaves, a barbate head.* [< Latin *barbātus* < *barba* beard]

bar|be|cue (bär′bə kyü), *n., v.,* **-cued, -cu|ing.** —*n.* **1a** an outdoor meal in which meat or fish is roasted over an open fire: *We had a barbecue of hamburgers on Saturday.* **b** the food at such a meal. **2** a grill or open fireplace for cooking meat, usually over charcoal: *I tripped and fell over the barbecue in the backyard. Rolls or buns fresh from your baker, simmering on a barbecue with either hot dogs or hamburgers, make a tangy, tasty snack that's fast to prepare and fun to eat* (Maclean's). **3** meat roasted over an open fire: *The barbecue sizzled as the sauce was poured over it.* **4** *Originally U.S.* an outdoor feast at which animals are roasted whole. **5** an animal roasted whole. **6** a restaurant serving or featuring barbecued meat.
—*v.t.* **1** to roast (meat) before or over an open fire: *We barbecued several pieces of chicken for*

Pronunciation Key: hat, āge, cãre, fär; let, ēqual, tėrm; it, īce; hot, ōpen, ôrder; oil, out; cup, pu̇t, rüle; child; long; thin; ᴛʜen; zh, measure; ə represents **a** in about, **e** in taken, **i** in pencil, **o** in lemon, **u** in circus.

dinner. **2** to cook (meat or fish) in a highly flavored sauce: *The barbecued spareribs made my tongue burn and eyes water.* **3** to roast (an animal) whole: *to barbecue a steer.* Also, **barbeque**. [< Spanish *barbacoa* barbecue < Arawak (Haiti) *barbakoa* (perhaps) tree house] —**bar′be·cu′er**, *n.*

barbecue sauce, a highly flavored sauce of vinegar or wine, certain vegetables, sugar, and spices.

barbed[1] (bärbd), *adj.* **1** having a barb or barbs: *A fishhook is barbed.* **2** *Figurative.* sharply sarcastic; cutting: *barbed wit. He made a barbed remark which was very unfriendly.* [< *barb*[1] + *-ed*[2]]

barbed[2] (bärbd), *adj. Obsolete.* protected by armor, as a horse. [erroneously for *barded;* see etym. under **bard**[2]]

***barbed wire**, wire with sharp points on it every few inches, used for fences chiefly to pen animals and discourage intruders and, formerly, to protect a military position. Also, **barbwire.**

*** barbed wire**

bar·bei·ro (bär bā′rü), *n.* a large assassin bug of tropical America, which transmits Chagas' disease by its bite. [< Portuguese *barbeiro* (originally) barber]

bar·bel (bär′bəl), *n.* **1** a long, thin, fleshy growth projecting from the mouths or nostrils of some fishes; barb. **2a** a large, European, freshwater fish of the carp family, having four such growths. **b** any one of various related fishes. [< Old French *barbel* < Gallo-Romance *barbellus,* ultimately < Latin *barba* beard]

bar·bell (bär′bel′), *n.,* or **bar bell**, a gymnastic device resembling a dumbbell but with a much longer bar, to which weights may be added, used for lifting exercises.

bar·bel·late (bär′bə lāt), *adj.* having short, stiff hairs, as some composites: *barbellate stems.* [< New Latin *barbella* stiff hair]

bar·be·que (bär′bə kyü), *n., v.t.,* **-qued, -que·ing.** = barbecue.

bar·ber (bär′bər), *n., v.* —*n.* **1** a person whose work is cutting and dressing hair, shaving men, or trimming beards: *The barber used scissors to trim my hair.* **2** = barber-surgeon.
—*v.t. U.S.* to cut the hair of, shave, or trim the beard of.
[< Anglo-French *barbour,* Old French *barbeor* < *barbe* beard < Latin *barba*]

barber college, a school to train barbers.

barber or **barber's pole**, a pole painted spirally with red and white stripes, used as a barber's sign.

bar·ber·ry (bär′ber′ē, -bər-), *n., pl.* **-ries. 1** a low, thorny shrub with small, yellow flowers and sour, red or purple berries. Some species are used for hedges. One species of barberry is often the alternate host of a fungus that produces rust disease in wheat. **2** the berry. [Middle English *barbere* < Medieval Latin *barbaris, berberis*]

barberry family, a group of dicotyledonous shrubs or herbaceous plants including the May apple, barberry, Oregon grape, and blue cohosh. Many of the shrubs in this family are ornamental.

bar·ber·shop (bär′bər shop′), *n., adj.* —*n.* the place where a barber works.
—*adj.* characteristic of, in the style of, or suggesting a barbershop quartet.

barbershop quartet, *U.S.* a male quartet which sings improvised arrangements of popular songs and ballads, especially in close harmony and with exaggerated sentiment.

barber's itch, **1** an infection of the skin on the face or neck, especially a ringworm attacking the bearded areas. **2** = sycosis.

barber's shop, *British.* a barbershop.

bar·ber-sur·geon (bär′bər sėr′jən), *n.* (formerly) a man who was a barber and also practiced surgery and dentistry.

bar·bet (bär′bit), *n.* **1** a small dog with long, curly hair, a variety of poodle. **2** any one of a large family of tropical birds, having a large head, a short, conical bill with tufts of bristles at its base, and brightly colored feathers. [< French *barbet* < Middle French *barbe* beard < Latin *barba*]

bar·bette (bär bet′), *n.* **1** a platform or mound in a fort from which a gun mounted upon it can fire over the wall, rather than through an opening. **2** a fixed turret on a warship, which partially protects a gun or battery of guns. [< French *barbette* < Middle French (diminutive) < *barbe* beard < Latin *barba*]

bar·bi·can (bär′bə kən), *n.* a tower for defense built over a gate to a castle or bridge to a city. [< Old French *barbacane* < Medieval Latin *barbacana*]

bar·bi·cel (bär′bə səl), *n.* one of the very small filaments interlocking the barbules of a feather. [< New Latin *barbicella* (diminutive) < *barbula* barbule]

bar·bie (bär′ bē), *n.* shortened form of barbecue: *Paul Hogan [Australian actor] made "G'day, mate" and "Put another shrimp on the barbie" part of the American vernacular* (New York Magazine).

bar·bi·tal (bär′bə tôl, -tal), *n.* a drug, used as a sedative or to induce sleep, containing barbituric acid, in the form of a white, crystalline powder. *Formula:* $C_8H_{12}N_2O_3$ [< *barbit*(uric) + *-al*[1]]

bar·bi·tone (bär′bə tōn), *n. British.* barbital.

bar·bi·tu·rate (bär bich′ə rāt, -rit; bär′bə tůr′āt, -it; -tyůr′-), *n.* **1** any salt or ester of barbituric acid. **2** any one of a group of drugs derived from barbituric acid. Regular use of barbiturates can cause addiction.

bar·bi·tu·ric acid (bär′bə tůr′ik, -tyůr′-), a colorless, crystalline acid, chiefly used as the basis of sedative and sleep-inducing drugs. *Formula:* $C_4H_4N_2O_3$ [< New Latin (*usnea*) *barbata* bearded (lichen) + English *uric acid*]

Bar·bi·zon (bär′bə zon), *adj.* of or having to do with a French school of naturalistic landscape painting of the middle and latter part of the 1800's that included Corot, Daubigny, and Millet. [< *Barbizon,* a village in France]

bar·bo·tine (bär′bə tin), *n. Ceramics.* slip[3]. [< French *barbotine* < *barboter* dabble]

Bar-B-Q, bar-b-q, or **bar-b-que** (bär′bə kyü), *n. Informal.* barbecue.

barbs (bärbz), *n.pl.* **1** folds of the mucous membrane under the tongue of horses and cattle. **2** the disease caused by their inflammation.

bar·bu·do (bär bü′dō), *n., pl.* **-dos.** any one of several threadfins, especially a small food fish of Florida, the West Indies, and other areas of the Caribbean. [< Spanish *barbudo* bearded]

bar·bule (bär′byül), *n.* **1** a little barb. **2** one of a series of small, pointed processes fringing the barbs of a feather. [< Latin *barbula* (diminutive) < *barba* beard]

barb·wire (bärb′wīr′), *n., v.,* **-wired, -wir·ing.** —*n.* = barbed wire.
—*v.t.* to provide with fencing of barbed wire.

bar car, *U.S.* a railroad passenger car equipped for serving drinks, especially alcoholic drinks, and light food.

bar·ca·role or **bar·ca·rolle** (bär′kə rōl), *n.* **1** a Venetian boat song sung by gondoliers. **2** music imitating such a song, typically with a lilting rhythm. [< French *barcarole* < Italian *barcarola* < *barcarolo* gondolier < *barca* bark[3] < Latin]

B. Arch., Bachelor of Architecture.

bar·chan or **bar·chane** (bär kän′), *n., adj.* —*n.* a dune in the shape of a crescent, the convex side facing the prevailing wind, moved slowly by the wind.
—*adj.* having this shape and character. Also, **barkhan.**
[< a native name in Turkestan]

bar chart, a chart or graph of a comparison of quantities by means of darkened rectangles of various lengths, each of which represents a particular quantity; bar graph.

bar-code (bär′kōd′), *v.,* **-cod·ed, -cod·ing.** = bar code (def. 2).

bar code, **1** a code of lines and numbers for identifying a product in a computerized system of checkout and inventory. The Universal Product Code is a bar code. **2** to furnish with such a code: *The Council of Periodical Distributors Associations has asked mass market publishers to "bar code" their books* (Publishers Weekly).

bard[1] (bärd), *n.* **1** a poet and singer of long ago. Bards sang their own poems to the music of their harps, celebrating heroic deeds and love epics. They were Celtic minstrels known from earliest times to the Middle Ages. **2** any poet or singer, as one participating in the Welsh eisteddfod. [probably < Irish *bárd,* Scottish Gaelic *bàrd*]

bard[2] (bärd), *n., v.* —*n.* Often, **bards.** a protective covering for the breast and flanks of a war horse.
—*v.t.* to furnish with bards.
[< Middle French *barde* < Spanish *barda,* perhaps < Arabic *al-barda'a* the packsaddle]

bard·i·an (bär′dē ən), *adj.* = bardic.

bard·ic (bär′dik), *adj.* of, having to do with, or of the character of a bard or bards.

bard·let (bärd′lit), *n.* **1** a young bard. **2** a petty poet; poetaster.

Bard of Avon, William Shakespeare.

bard·ol·a·ter or **bard·ol·a·tor** (bär dol′ə tər), *n.* a person who reveres Shakespeare; a Shakespeare worshiper or devotee. [(coined by George Bernard Shaw) < *Bard* of Avon + (id)*olater*]

bard·ol·a·try (bär dol′ə trē), *n.* devotion to or worship of Shakespeare.

bard·y (bär′dē), *adj. Scottish.* defiant; impudent. [perhaps < *bard*[1]]

bare[1] (bãr), *adj.,* **bar·er, bar·est,** *v.,* **bared, bar·ing.** —*adj.* **1** without covering; not clothed; naked: *The sun burned his bare shoulders. The top of the hill was bare, but the trees grew part way up its slope.* **2** with the head uncovered; bareheaded. **3** not furnished; empty: *The room was bare of furniture.* **4** plain; unadorned: *The trapper lived in a bare little cabin in the woods.* **5** just enough and no more; mere: *He earns only a bare living by his work.* **6** *Figurative.* not concealed; not disguised; open: *the bare truth of the matter.* **7** much worn; threadbare. —*v.t.* to make bare; uncover; reveal: *to bare one's feelings. The dog bared his teeth.*

go bare, *U.S. Informal.* to practice a profession without carrying liability insurance for malpractice: *Whether or not it's wise for a doctor to go bare . . . , the situation clearly leaves patients in a vulnerable position.* (Consumer Reports).

lay bare, to uncover; expose; reveal: *The police laid bare the plot to rob the bank.*

[Old English *bær*] —**bare′ness,** *n.*

—*Syn. adj.* **1 Bare, nude, naked,** when applied to the human body, mean without clothing. **Bare** suggests that a specified part of the body is unclothed: *The sun burned her bare shoulders.* **Nude** and **naked** usually suggest the absence of all clothing from the body. **Nude** is the more neutral, objective term: *Many famous artists have painted nude models.* **Naked** often suggests an unprotected or a shameless condition: *We were shocked at the sight of naked, starving children. A group of naked boys swam in the river.*

bare[2] (bãr), *v. Archaic.* bore; a past tense of **bear**[2].

bare·back (bãr′bak′), *adv., adj.* without a saddle; on a horse's bare back: *The Indian rode bareback* (adv.). *You can see bareback riders at the circus* (adj.).

bare·backed (bãr′bakt′), *adv., adj.* = bareback.

bare·boat (bãr′bōt′), *adj., n.* —*adj.* calling for the delivery of a ship to the chartering party and transferring all responsibility from the owner to the chartering party for manning, supplying, maintaining, and insuring it: *a bareboat charter.*
—*n.* a ship so transferred.

bare·boned (bãr′bōnd′), *adj.* lean; emaciated.

bare bones, the essentials of something, without any embellishment; the unadorned facts: *These are the bare bones of the policy* (London Times).

bare·bones (bãr′bōnz′), *n., adj.* —*n.* a very skinny person, especially one whose bones can be seen. —*adj.* meager: *a barebones program of education.*

bare·faced (bãr′fāst′), *adj.* **1** *Figurative.* impudent in its obviousness; shameless: *a barefaced lie.* SYN: brazen, audacious. **2** with the face bare. **3** not disguised: (*Figurative.*) *I could with barefaced power sweep him from my sight* (Shakespeare). —**bare′fac′ed·ly,** *adv.* —**bare′fac′ed′ness,** *n.*

bare·fist·ed (bãr′fis′tid), *adj.* **1** without boxing gloves: *a barefisted fight.* **2** *Figurative.* ruthless: *barefisted determination.*

bare·foot (bãr′fůt′), *adj., adv.* without shoes and stockings on: *The barefoot child played in the puddles* (*adj.*). *If you go barefoot, watch out for broken glass* (*adv.*).

barefoot doctor, an agricultural worker in China who has been trained to serve as a part-time medical auxiliary.

bare·foot·ed (bãr′fůt′id), *adj., adv.* = barefoot.

ba·rège or **ba·rege** (bə räzh′), *n.* a light, silky dress fabric resembling gauze. [< French *barège* < *Barège,* France]

bare·hand·ed (bãr′han′did), *adj., adv.* **1** without any covering on the hands: *a barehanded catch.* **2** *Figurative.* with no aid but one's own hands: *For seven years, almost barehanded he kept Owen Glendower at bay on the Welsh border* (Atlantic).

bare·head·ed (bãr′hed′id), *adj., adv.* wearing nothing on the head: *to stand bareheaded in respect at the side of a grave* (*adv.*). *In some churches it is not proper for a woman to be bareheaded* (*adj.*). —**bare′head′ed·ness,** *n.*

bare-kneed (bãr′nēd′), *adj.* with the knees uncovered.

bare-knuck·le (bãr′nuk′əl), *adj.* **1** without boxing gloves: *John L. Sullivan was a famous bare-knuckle fighter and world heavyweight boxing champion* (Lyall Smith). **2** *Figurative.* in which quarter is neither asked nor given: *He . . . developed his talent for bare-knuckle politics* (Time).

bare·leg·ged (bãr′leg′id, -legd′), *adj., adv.* without stockings on.

bare·ly (bãr′lē), *adv.* **1** with nothing to spare; only just; scarcely: *He has barely enough money to live on.* SYN: See syn. under **hardly. 2** poorly; scantily: *The hospital room was furnished barely but neatly.* **3** *Figurative.* plainly; openly: *The facts are presented barely, without any comments.*

bare·sark (bãr′särk), *n., adv.* —*n.* = berserker.
—*adv.* without armor: *. . . one of the best films thus far of the brave new underworld of the skin-diver, where the actors are all baresark* (Time). [variant of *berserk,* taken as *bare* + *sark* shirt]

barf (bärf), *v.i. U.S. Slang.* to vomit.

bar·fly (bär′flī′), *n., pl.* **-flies.** *U.S. Slang.* a person who frequents barrooms, especially one who drinks excessively.

bar|gain (bär′gən), *n., v.* —*n.* **1** an agreement to trade or exchange; deal: *The boys made a bargain to exchange baseball gloves.* **SYN:** contract; compact. **2** a good trade or exchange, especially something offered for sale cheap or bought cheap: *This hat is a bargain at $3.* **3** any arrangement or deal considered as either advantageous or unprofitable or otherwise unfavorable: *That old car is a bad bargain at any price.*
—*v.i.* **1** to try to get good terms; try to make a good deal: *For ten minutes she stood bargaining with the farmer for his vegetables.* **SYN:** haggle. **2** to make a bargain; come to terms: *A merchant bargained for it, and carried it off* (Joseph Addison). —*v.t.* **1** to try to get good terms for: *He bargained the trader down to a very good price.* **2** to reach an advantageous agreement, especially by giving some guarantee: *He tried to bargain his boy out of trouble with the neighbors. I'll bargain he keeps his promise.* **3** to trade: *Stealing only bargains one trouble for another.*
bargain for (or **on**), to be ready for; expect: *He hadn't bargained for rain and had left his umbrella at home.*
in (or **into**) **the bargain**, besides; also: *This dress shrank and it faded in the bargain.*
strike a bargain, to make a bargain; reach an agreement: *They finally struck a bargain: his mitt for two baseballs and a bat.*
[< Old French *bargaine*]

bargain basement, a section of a department store, especially a floor below the street level, where relatively inexpensive goods are sold.

bar|gain-base|ment (bär′gən bās′mənt), *adj. Especially U.S.* greatly reduced in price; cheap: *bargain-basement prices.*

bargain counter, **1** any table, stall, counter, or section where goods are sold at reduced prices. **2** *Figurative.* any place where things or ideas are freely exchanged.

bar|gain|ee (bär′gə nē′), *n. Law.* the recipient in a bargain.

bar|gain|er (bär′gə nər), *n.* a person who bargains or stipulates.

bargain hunter, a person who watches for bargains: *Auctions, with their well-known magnetism for chronic bargain hunters* (New Yorker).

bar|gain|ing (bär′gə ning), *n., adj.* —*n.* **1** the act or process of coming to an agreement. **2** discussion or debate for the purpose of reaching an agreement: *Bargaining between management and the labor union broke down.* —*adj.* having to do with negotiating a bargain: *a bargaining agent.*

bargaining chip, an advantage held by any of the parties in a negotiation: *Bargaining from strength calls for arms programs that can serve as bargaining chips to trade for concessions that the other side might not otherwise make* (New York Times Magazine).

bar|gain|or (bär′gə nər), *n. Law.* a person who contracts to sell and convey property to another by bargain or sale.

***barge** (bärj), *n., v.,* **barged, barg|ing.** —*n.* **1** a large, strongly built, flat-bottomed boat for carrying freight: *The oil barge was towed from Syracuse to Buffalo on the Erie Canal.* **2** a large boat used for excursions, pageants, and special occasions: *the royal barge.* **3** a large motorboat or rowboat used by the officer commanding a flagship; launch. **4** *Especially British.* a houseboat. **5** *Archaic.* a small seagoing vessel. **6** *U.S. Obsolete.* a large carriage.
—*v.i.* **1** to move clumsily like a barge: *He barged into the table and knocked the lamp over.* **2** *Informal.* to push oneself rudely; intrude: *Don't barge in where you're not wanted.*
—*v.t.* to carry by barge.
[< Old French *barge* < Medieval Latin *barga*, variant of Latin *barca;* see etym. under **bark**[2]]

barge|board (bärj′bôrd′, -bōrd′), *n.* a board placed flat along or under the overhanging, sloping edge of a gable roof, usually covering a rafter and often ornamented.

barge couple, one of the two rafters that support the barge course or overhanging portion at the end of a gable roof.

barge course, **1** the part of a gable roof projecting beyond the end wall. **2** the range of shingles or tiles along the sloping edges of a gable roof.

barge dog, = schipperke.

bar|gee (bär jē′), *n. Especially British.* a bargeman.

bar|gel|lo (bär jel′ō), *n., pl.* **-loes,** *v.,* **-loed, -lo|ing.** —*n.* an upright stitch used in needlework to produce patterns in zigzag or oblique lines: *The store also sells material for bargello, an Italian geometric pattern* (Melody Cornett).
—*v.i., v.t.* to use this stitch; make such stitches on canvas: *To demonstrate his find, he ... pulled out a canvas that was in the midst of being bargelloed* (Harper's).
[< *Bargello*, a museum in Florence, Italy containing much work of Andrea della Robbia, noted for its highly decorative borders]

barge|man (bärj′mən), *n., pl.* **-men.** a man who works on a barge.

barge|mas|ter (bärj′mas′tər, -mäs′-), *n.* the master or owner of a barge.

barge pole, a long pole for propelling a barge.
touch with a barge pole, *Informal.* to have anything to do with: *If he tries to leave me this funny old place ... I wouldn't touch it with a barge pole* (Mary A. Ward).

bar|ghest (bär′gest), *n. Scottish.* a goblin, fabled to portend *imminent* death or misfortune. [origin unknown]

bar|girl (bär′gėrl′), *n. U.S. Informal.* **1** a waitress in a barroom. **2** a girl or woman who frequents barrooms, especially one who is promiscuous.

bar graph, = bar chart.

bar|hop (bär′hop′), *n., v.,* **-hopped, -hop|ping.** *U.S.* —*n. Informal.* a waitress in a bar: *Blonde barhops in cowboy boots* (Wall Street Journal).
—*v.i. Slang.* to move from bar to bar and continue to drink. —**bar′hop′per,** *n.*

bar|i|a|tri|cian (bar′ē ə trish′ən), *n.* a doctor who specializes in bariatrics.

bar|i|at|rics (bar′ē at′riks), *n.* the branch of medicine dealing with the treatment of overweight people. [< Greek *báros* weight + English *-iatrics* (*as in geriatrics, pediatrics*)]

bar|ic[1] (bar′ik), *adj. Rare.* of or having to do with barium.

bar|ic[2] (bar′ik), *adj.* of or having to do with weight, especially weight of the air as indicated by a barometer; barometric. [< Greek *báros* weight + English *-ic*]

bar|ie (bar′ē; *French* bȧ rē′), *n.* a former unit of gaseous pressure, equal to one dyne per square centimeter. [< French *barie* < Greek *bareîa*, feminine of *barýs* heavy]

ba|ril|la (bə ril′ə), *n.* **1** either of two saltworts grown especially in Spain, Sicily, and the Canary Islands. **2** an impure alkali produced by burning these and allied plants, formerly used in the manufacture of soap, glass, etc. [< Spanish *barrilla* impure soda]

bar|ish (bãr′ish), *adj.* somewhat bare.

barit., baritone.

bar|ite (bãr′īt), *n.* barium sulfate in its natural form, as a mineral found in many parts of the world; heavy spar. It is a principal ore of barium. Also, **barytes.** [alteration of *barytes*]

bar|i|ton|al (bar′ə tō′nəl), *adj.* of or characteristic of a baritone: *a rich baritonal voice.*

***barge**
definitions 1, 2, 3, 4

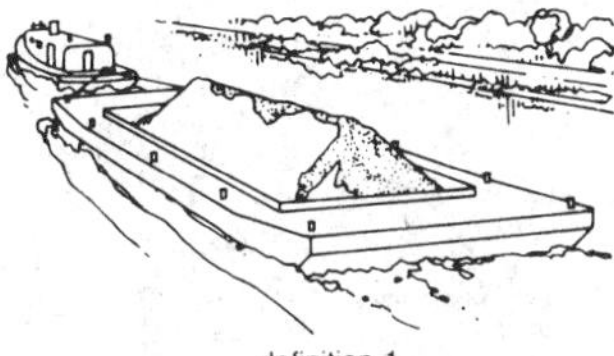
definition 1

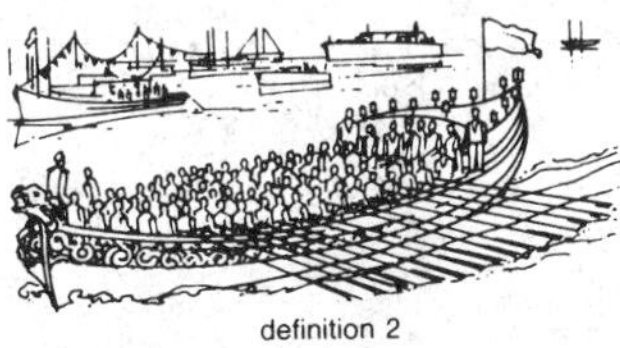
definition 2

definition 3

definition 4

bar|i|tone (bar′ə tōn), *n., adj.* —*n.* **1a** the male voice between tenor and bass: *A baritone is lower than tenor but higher than bass.* **b** a singer with such a voice: *The baritone was the star of the show.* **c** a part in music for such a voice or for an instrument of similar range: *Who will sing the baritone?* **2** a brass-wind musical instrument in B♭, that has the quality or range of this voice. See picture under **French horn.**
—*adj.* of or for a baritone. Also, *British,* **barytone.**
[< Italian *baritono*, learned borrowing from Greek *barýtonos* deep-sounding, baritone]

baritone horn, = baritone (instrument).

***bar|i|um** (bãr′ē əm), *n.* a soft, silvery-white, metallic chemical element, found abundantly combined with other elements, especially in the minerals barite and witherite. Barium compounds are used in making pigments, safety matches, and radio tubes. [alteration of *baryta*, patterned on *sodium*]

***barium**

symbol	atomic number	atomic weight	oxidation state
Ba	56	137.34	2

barium carbonate, a poisonous compound occurring as a mineral, witherite, or prepared synthetically. It is used in the manufacture of optical glass, paints, enamels, and dyes, and as a rat poison. *Formula:* $BaCO_3$

barium hydroxide, a poisonous, extremely alkaline white powder, or colorless crystals, used in refining animal and vegetable oils and beet sugar, in motor oil detergents, and as a water softener. *Formula:* $Ba(OH)_2 \cdot 8H_2O$

barium sulfate, a compound occurring as a mineral, barite, or prepared synthetically. It is used in fluoroscopic examination of the gastrointestinal tract. *Formula:* $BaSO_4$

barium titanate, a crystalline compound of barium, titanium, and oxygen highly sensitive to even very slight changes of pressure, temperature, or electrical field. It is used in condensers, in apparatus for the electronic reception of sound, in electronic computers, and in switching devices in telephone systems. *Formula:* $BaTiO_3$

***bark**[1] (bärk), *n., v.* —*n.* **1** the tough, outside covering of the trunk, branches, and roots of trees and shrubs: *The boys carved their initials in the bark of the tree.* **2** = tanbark (def. 1). **3** cinchona; Peruvian bark.
—*v.t.* **1** to strip the bark from (a tree or other plant). **2** *Figurative.* to scrape the skin from (shins or knuckles): *I fell down the steps and barked my shins.* **3** to cut out a ring of bark from around (a tree) in order to kill it; girdle. **4** to cover with or as if with bark. **5** to tan (hides or skins) with tanbark.
[< Scandinavian (compare Old Icelandic *börkr*)]
—**bark′less,** *adj.*

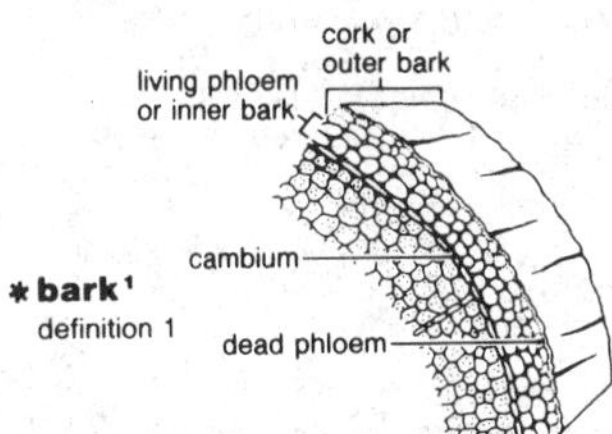

***bark**[1]
definition 1

bark[2] (bärk), *n., v.* —*n.* **1** the short, sharp sound that a dog makes: *The dog's bark frightened the baby.* **SYN:** yelp, bay. **2** a sound like this, especially one that is short, sharp, and repeated; crack: *the bark of a fox;* (*Figurative.*) *the bark of a gun.* **3** *Informal, Figurative.* a cough. [< verb]
—*v.i.* **1** to make this sound or one like it: *The dog barked.* (*Figurative.*) *Rifles barked from behind every tree.* **2** *Informal, Figurative.* to cough. **3** *U.S. Informal, Figurative.* to call out at the entrance of a cheap show, store, or other attraction, to draw customers.
—*v.t. Figurative.* to shout sharply; speak gruffly: *The policemen barked out their orders to the mob.*
[Old English *beorcan*]

***bark**[3] (bärk), *n.* **1** a ship with three masts, square-rigged on the first two masts and fore-and-aft-rigged on the other. **2** *Archaic.* a boat; ship. Also, **barque.** [< Middle French *barque* < Old French

Pronunciation Key: hat, āge, cãre, fär; let, ēqual, tėrm; it, īce; hot, ōpen, ôrder; oil, out; cup, pu̇t, rüle; child; long; thin; ᴛʜen; zh, measure; ə represents **a** in about, **e** in taken, **i** in pencil, **o** in lemon, **u** in circus.

< Old Provençal *barca* < Latin, probably ultimately < Greek *bâris* flat-bottomed Egyptian boat]

***bark^{3}** definition 1

bark beetle, any one of a family of beetles which damage trees, especially pines, firs, and other conifers, by burrowing through the bark to lay eggs; engraver beetle. The fungus that causes Dutch elm disease is transmitted by a beetle of this group.

bark cloth, any of various cloths made from tree bark, such as the tapa: *Bark cloth ... is derived from the inner bark of certain trees whose fibres cross each other at right angles, as do the warp and weft of true cloth* (Melville J. Herskovits).

bar|keep (bär′kēp′), *n., v.*, **-kept, -keep|ing.** *—n. U.S.* a barkeeper.
—v.i. British. to tend a bar.

bar|keep|er (bär′kē′pər), *n.* **1** a person who owns or manages a bar where alcoholic drinks are sold. **2** a man who serves alcoholic drinks to customers at a bar; bartender.

bar|ken|tine or **bar|kan|tine** (bär′kən tēn), *n.* a three-masted ship with the foremast square-rigged and the other masts fore-and-aft-rigged. Also, **barquentine, barquantine.** [< *bark^{3}*, patterned on *brigantine*]

bark|er^{1} (bär′kər), *n.* **1** a person or thing that barks: *That puppy is a noisy barker.* **2** *Figurative.* a person who stands in front of a store, show, or other attraction, urging people to go in.

bark|er^{2} (bär′kər), *n.* **1** a person or implement that strips bark from trees. **2** a machine used for removing bark from wood that is to be made into pulp for paper.

bark grafting, grafting of the bud or branch inserted between the bark and the wood.

bar|khan (bär kän′), *n., adj.* = barchan.

Bark|hau|sen effect (bärk′hou′zən), a series of small, abrupt jumps in the magnetization of iron or other ferromagnetic substances occurring as the magnetizing force is smoothly increased or decreased, considered to be due to atomic reorientation. [< Heinrich *Barkhausen*, 1881-1956, a German physicist, who described it]

bark|ing deer (bär′king), = muntjac.

bark|y (bär′kē), *adj.*, **bark|i|er, bark|i|est.** **1** consisting of or covered with bark. **2** of the nature of bark.

Bar|le|duc (bär′lə dük), *n.* a kind of currant preserve with no seeds, and with some of the currants retaining their shape. [< *Bar-le-Duc*, a town in France where it is made]

bar|ley^{1} (bär′lē), *n.* **1** the seed or grain of a cereal grass that has compact spikes of flowers. Each spike has from one to three smaller spikes at each joint. Barley grows in cool climates and is used for food and for making malt. **2** the plant yielding this grain. The barley plant is a widely cultivated annual. [Old English *bærlīc*, equivalent of *bere* bear^{3}; suffix *-līc* of uncertain meaning]

bar|ley^{2} or **bar|ly** (bär′lē), *interj. Scottish and Dialect.* a cry used by children in certain games when a temporary stop is desired. [perhaps < *parley*]

barley beef, *British.* beef fattened on barley and other concentrated foods.

bar|ley-bree (bär′lē brē′), *n. Scottish.* **1** strong ale. **2** whiskey.

bar|ley|corn (bär′lē kôrn′), *n.* **1a** a grain of barley. **b** the barley plant. **2** a unit of linear measure, about one third of an inch.

Bar|ley|corn (bär′lē kôrn′), *n.* **John, 1** a name for intoxicating liquor; alcoholic beverages. **2** a humorous personification of barley as the grain from which various beers and whiskeys are obtained.

barley water, a soothing drink made by boiling pearl barley in water, formerly often given to invalids.

bar lift, a ski lift consisting of an endless cable supporting steel bars, which skiers grasp to be drawn up a slope.

bar|low (bär′lō), *n.*, or **barlow knife**, *U.S.* a small jackknife having one blade. [< a proper name]

Bar|low's disease (bär′lōz), = infantile scurvy. [< Thomas *Barlow*, 1845-1945, an English physician]

barm (bärm), *n.* a foamy yeast that forms on malt liquors while they are fermenting. [Old English *beorma*]

bar magnet, a permanent magnet in the shape of a bar or rod.

bar|maid (bär′mād′), *n.* a woman who serves alcoholic drinks to customers at a bar.

bar|man (bär′mən), *n., pl.* **-men.** = barkeeper.

Bar|me|cid|al (bär′mə sī′dəl), *adj.* like a Barmecide feast; unreal; sham; illusory.

Bar|me|cide (bär′mə sīd), *n.* **1** a Persian prince at Baghdad, in the *Arabian Nights*, who asked a beggar to join him in a feast, but served no food, although pretending to partake of a delicious repast. **2** *Figurative.* one who offers illusory benefits.

Barmecide feast, **1** a pretended feast with empty dishes. **2** an empty pretense of hospitality, generosity, or other kindnesses or benefits. [< *Barmecide*]

bar mitz|vah (bär mits′və), **1** the ceremony or celebration held when a Jewish boy becomes thirteen years old to affirm that he has reached the age of religious responsibility: *The boy's family and friends attended his bar mitzvah.* **2** the boy himself: *The bar mitzvah read from the Torah.* **3** to make (a boy) a bar mitzvah: *I'd just been bar mitzvahed ...* (Irvin Feld). [< Hebrew *bar miṣwah* son of the commandment]

barm|y (bär′mē), *adj.*, **barm|i|er, barm|i|est.** **1** full of barm; fermenting; frothing. **2** *British Slang, Figurative.* silly; crazy; flighty. **—barm′i|ness,** *n.*

barn (bärn), *n.* **1** a building for storing hay, grain, straw, or other farm produce and for sheltering cows, horses, and farm machinery: *Dairy farms have milking barns where the cows are brought inside to be milked.* **2** *U.S.* a large building for housing subway cars and buses and also for doing light maintenance work on them; garage; depot. **3** *Informal.* any place considered to resemble a barn, such as a huge, drafty room; place of general discomfort and emptiness. **4** a unit of measure used in nuclear physics, equal to 10^{-24} square centimeter. It is the smallest square area thus far designated as a unit of measure. [Middle English *bern* < Old English *berern, bereern* < *bere* barley^{1} + *ærn* storeroom] **—barn′-like′,** *adj.*

Bar|na|bas (bär′nə bəs), *n.* a Christian apostle who was a companion of Paul (in the Bible, Acts 11:24).

***bar|na|cle^{1}** (bär′nə kəl), *n.* **1** a small saltwater animal with a shell, that attaches itself to something under water. Man sees barnacles especially on rocks and timbers of wharves exposed at low tide or on ship bottoms raised out of the water. Barnacles are crustaceans. **2** *Figurative.* a person who clings stubbornly, especially a follower who will not be dismissed or shaken off. **3** = barnacle goose. [origin uncertain; perhaps < Breton *bernic* kind of shellfish]

***barnacle^{1}** definition 1

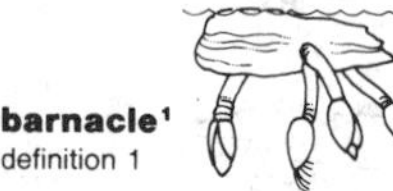

goose barnacles on wood

rock barnacle

bar|na|cle^{2} (bär′nə kəl), *n.* Often, **barnacles.** an instrument consisting of two branches joined by a hinge, placed on the nose of a horse to restrain him, as when he is being shod.
barnacles, *British Informal.* spectacles: *No woman above sixteen ever did ... seam without barnacles* (Scott).
[perhaps < Old French *bernicles* < *bernac* bit for the nose of an unruly horse]

bar|na|cled (bär′nə kəld), *adj.* covered with barnacles or barnacle shells.

barnacle goose, a wild goose similar to and allied to the black brant, which breeds on arctic coasts and islands.

bar|na|cles (bär′nə kəlz), *n.pl.* See under **barnacle^{2}**.

Bar|nard's Star (bär′nərdz), a star of the tenth magnitude that has the largest known proper motion and is the second closest star to the sun after Alpha Centauri. It is in the constellation Ophiuchus. [< E. E. *Barnard*, 1857-1923, an American astronomer, who discovered the star in 1916]

barn burner, or **barn|burn|er** (bärn′bėr′nər), *n. U.S. Slang.* a noteworthy condition, situation, or event.

barn dance, *U.S.* **1** an informal party for square dancing, formerly often held in a barn. **2** a lively square dance resembling a polka.

barn-door skate (bärn′dôr′, -dōr′), a large, flat fish of Atlantic waters, with a squarish body and long, pointed tail. It is related to the ray.

bar|ney (bär′nē), *n. British Slang.* a quarrel; disturbance; row.

barn owl, a common owl of North America and most other parts of the world, having long legs, a heart-shaped face, and small eyes. It often lives in barns or deserted buildings, where it feeds on mice and rats.

barn raising, *U.S.* a gathering of neighbors to build a barn.

barn|storm (bärn′stôrm′), *U.S. Informal.* **—v.i.** **1** to travel from one small town or country district to another, acting in plays, making political speeches, or, sometimes, giving lectures or concerts: *The Whigs barnstormed to victory, shouting the slogan "Tippecanoe and Tyler, too"* (Hugh R. Fraser). **2** to earn one's living as an aviator traveling about, especially during the 1920's, stunt flying at country fairs, selling short flights, and giving occasional instruction.
—v.t. to act in plays, make speeches, or, sometimes, give lectures or concerts in (small towns and country districts). **—barn′storm′er,** *n.*

barn swallow, a swallow that usually nests in barns. It has a reddish breast and a long, forked tail.

barn|y (bär′nē), *adj.* of or like a barn: *... the barny vastness of our City Center* (New Yorker).

barn|yard (bärn′yärd′), *n., adj.* **—n.** a yard around or next to a barn for livestock, often fenced: *The horses were let out in the barnyard while we cleaned their stalls.*
—adj. **1** of or having to do with a barnyard: *barnyard fowl.* **2** befitting a barnyard; indecent; smutty: *barnyard humor.*

barnyard golf, *Informal.* horseshoes (the game).

barnyard grass, an annual grass that is a destructive weed of rice fields; jungle rice.

barnyard millet, a cultivated form of barnyard grass, used chiefly as hay.

baro-, *combining form.* pressure, especially atmospheric pressure: *Barometer = a measure for atmospheric pressure.* [< Greek *báros* weight]

bar|o|cep|tor (bar′ə sep′tər), *n.* = baroreceptor.

bar|o|clin|ic (bar′ə klin′ik), *adj.* (of the atmosphere) having surfaces of equal pressure and surfaces of equal density not in coincidence. [< *baro-* + Greek *klínein* to slope + English *-ic*]

bar|o|clin|ic|i|ty (bar′ə klə nis′ə tē), *n. Meteorology.* an atmospheric condition in which surfaces of equal pressure and equal density do not coincide: *Extratropical cyclones are observed to form in the zone of middle-latitude westerlies, characterized by pronounced baroclinicity* (Arnt Eliassen).

ba|ro|co|co (bə rō′kə kō′), *adj.* grotesquely elaborate. [blend of *baroque* and *rococo*]

bar|o|cy|clo|nom|e|ter (bar′ə sī′klə nom′ə tər), *n.* an aneroid barometer for detecting and following a storm, especially a tropical cyclone, at a distance of several hundred miles. [< *baro-* + *cyclone* + *meter*]

bar|o|gram (bar′ə gram), *n.* a record made by a barograph or similar instrument. [< *baro-* + *gram*]

bar|o|graph (bar′ə graf, -gräf), *n.* an instrument that automatically records changes in air pressure, especially an aneroid barometer with a stylus, which traces a record on a moving drum. [< *baro-* + *graph*]

bar|o|graph|ic (bar′ə graf′ik), *adj.* of or having to do with a barograph; furnished by a barograph: *barographic records.*

ba|rom|e|ter (bə rom′ə tər), *n.* **1** an instrument for measuring the pressure of the atmosphere, used in determining height above sea level and in predicting probable changes in the weather. *Abbr:* bar. **2** *Figurative.* something that indicates changes: *Newspapers are often called barometers of public opinion.* [< *baro-* + *-meter*]

bar|o|met|ric (bar′ə met′rik), *adj.* **1** of a barometer. **2** indicated by a barometer: *Low barometric pressure is a sign of a possible storm.* **—bar′o|met′ri|cal|ly,** *adv.*

bar|o|met|ri|cal (bar′ə met′rə kəl), *adj.* = barometric.

barometric depression, a cyclone.

barometric slope, the direction and rate of fall of atmospheric pressure between two weather stations or two isobaric lines, in Great Britain and the United States commonly expressed in units each representing a fall of .01 inch of mercury per 60 nautical miles.

ba|rom|e|try (bə rom′ə trē), *n.* the art or science of barometric measurement or observation. [< *baro-* + *-metry*]

bar|on (bar′ən), *n.* **1** a nobleman of the lowest hereditary rank. In Great Britain, a baron ranks next below a viscount and has "Lord" before his name instead of "Baron." In other European countries "Baron" is used before his name. **2** an English nobleman during the Middle Ages who held his lands directly from the king; baron by tenure. **3** the title indicating a baron's rank.
4 *Figurative.* a powerful industrialist, financier, or merchant: *a beef baron. The financial markets of Wall Street were once controlled by the barons of industry.* **5** a very choice cut of beef, consisting of both loins, especially the forward part of

both loins, left uncut at the backbone; baron of beef. [< Old French *baron* < *ber* military leader, probably from unrecorded Frankish *baro* king's man]

bar|on|age (bar′ə nij), *n.* **1** all barons. **2** the rank or title of a baron. **3** the nobility; peerage.

bar|o|ness (bar′ə nis), *n.* **1** the wife or widow of a baron. **2** a lady whose rank is equal to that of a baron.

bar|on|et (bar′ə nit), *n.* **1** a man in Great Britain ranking next below a baron and next above a knight, except a Knight of the Garter. A baronet does not belong to the nobility, but his title is a hereditary one. He has "Sir" before his name and "Bart." after it. *Example:* Sir Thomas Beecham, Bart. **2** the title indicating this rank. *Abbr:* Bart.

▶See **Sir** for usage note.

bar|on|et|age (bar′ə nə tij), *n.* **1** the rank or position of a baronet. **2** the body of baronets collectively.

bar|on|et|cy (bar′ə nit sē), *n., pl.* **-cies. 1** the rank or position of a baronet. **2** the document indicating this.

ba|rong (bä rông′, -rong′), *n.* a heavy-backed, cleaverlike knife used by the Moros. [< Sulu (Malayan language) *barong*]

barong ta|ga|log (tä gä′log, tag′ə-), a shirt made of porously woven material and usually elaborately embroidered, worn by men in the Philippines.

ba|ro|ni|al (bə rō′nē əl), *adj.* **1** of a baron or barons: *He gave her a family ring with the baronial crest on it.* **2** suitable for a baron; splendid, stately, and grand: *a baronial castle.* **3** designating a square style of envelope.

ba|ronne (bå rôn′), *n. French.* a baroness.

baron of beef, = baron (def. 5).

bar|o|ny (bar′ə nē), *n., pl.* **-nies. 1** the lands of a baron. **2** the rank or title of a baron. **3** a division of a county in Ireland. [< Old French *baronie* < *baron* baron]

ba|roque (bə rōk′, -rok′), *adj., n.* **—*adj.* 1a** having to do with a style of art and architecture characterized by the use of curved forms and lavish ornamentation. Baroque architecture prevailed in Europe from about 1550 to the late 1700's. **b** having to do with a style of music characterized by complex rhythms and melodic ornamentation: *baroque opera.* **c** = rococo. **2** tastelessly odd; fantastic; grotesque: *baroque development of ladies' fashion.* **3** irregular in shape: *baroque pearls.*

—*n.* 1 the baroque style. **2** architecture or other work in this style.

[< French *baroque* < Portuguese *barroco* a rough pearl] **—ba|roque′ly**, *adv.*

bar|o|re|cep|tor (bar′ə ri sep′tər), *n.* a cell or group of cells sensitive to pressure, such as blood pressure. Also, **baroceptor**.

bar|o|scope (bar′ə skōp), *n.* an instrument for showing changes in the pressure or density of the air without measuring its absolute weight.

bar|o|scop|ic (bar′ə skop′ik), *adj.* having to do with or indicated by a baroscope.

bar|o|scop|i|cal (bar′ə skop′ə kəl), *adj.* = baroscopic.

bar|o|trau|ma (bar′trô′mə), *n.* , *pl.* **-ma|ta** (-mə-tə). injury to the body due to a change in atmospheric or water pressure. [< *baro-* + *trauma*]

bar|o|trop|ic (bar′ə trop′ik), *adj.* (of the atmosphere) having surfaces of equal pressure and surfaces of equal density in coincidence. [< *baro-* + Greek *trópos* a turning + English *-ic*]

ba|rot|ro|py (bə rot′rə pē), *n. Meteorology.* an atmospheric condition in which surfaces of equal pressure and equal density coincide; condition of zero baroclinicity.

ba|rouche (bə rüsh′), *n.* a four-wheeled carriage with a driver's seat, two double passenger seats facing each other, and a folding top. [< German *Barutsche* < Italian *baroccio* < Vulgar Latin *birotium* two-wheeled cart < Late Latin *birotus* < Latin *bi-* two + *rota* wheel]

bar pin, a breastpin or brooch having a long, barlike ornament often set with jewels.

barque (bärk), *n.* **1** a boat; ship. **2** a ship with three masts. Also, **bark**.

bar|quen|tine or **bar|quan|tine** (bär′kən tēn), *n.* = barkentine.

bar|ra|ble (bär′ə bəl), *adj.* that can be barred.

bar|rack¹ (bar′ək), *n., v.t., v.i.* = barracks.

bar|rack² (bar′ək), *British and Australian.* **—*v.i.*** to express decided opinions vociferously; applaud or jeer. **—*v.t.*** to shout for or against (players or a team). [alteration of Australian slang *barracking* banter] **—bar′rack|er**, *n.*

bar|racks (bar′ks), *n., v.* **—*n. pl. or sing.* 1** a building or group of buildings for soldiers to live in, usually in a fort or military camp: *The barracks were plain wooden buildings with long rows of beds inside.* **2** a large, plain building, or group of huts, especially within a common enclosure, in which many people live: *The old manor house was a regular barracks of a place.*

—*v.t.* to provide barracks for; locate in barracks.

—*v.i.* to lodge in barracks.

[< French *baraque* < Middle French < Italian *baracca* < Spanish *barraca*, probably < *barro* clay < Vulgar Latin *barrum*]

▶**Barracks** appears with either a singular or a plural verb: *John wrote that his barracks was a lively place. The barracks were inspected daily.*

barracks bag, a large bag of heavy cloth with a drawstring at the top, used by soldiers to carry their extra clothing and personal possessions from place to place; duffel bag.

bar|ra|coon (bar′ə kün′), *n.* a shed, set of sheds, or open enclosure formerly used to confine slaves or convicts temporarily. [< Spanish *barracón* (augmentative) < *barraca* barrack¹]

bar|ra|cou|ta (bar′ə kü′tə), *n., pl.* **-ta** or **-tas**. = barracuda.

*** bar|ra|cu|da** (bar′ə kü′də), *n., pl.* **-da** or **-das**. any one of several fish of tropical and subtropical seas that look like pike and have spiny fins. The great barracuda may grow to more than 5½ feet in length and sometimes attacks man in the seas around the West Indies. It has never been known to attack man in the Pacific. [< American Spanish *barracuda;* origin uncertain]

*** barracuda**

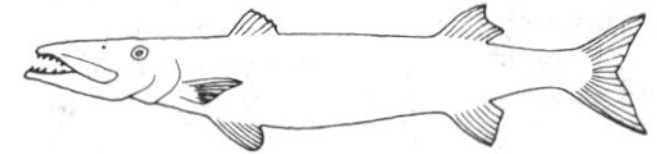

bar|rage (bə räzh′ *for n. 1, 2, v.; especially British* bar′äzh *for n. 1, 2, v.;* bär′ij *for n. 3*), *n., v.,* **-raged, -rag|ing. —*n.* 1** a barrier of artillery fire to check the enemy or to protect one's own soldiers in advancing or retreating. **2** *Figurative.* a large number of words, blows, or other forms of attack, coming quickly one after the other: *The reporters kept up a barrage of questions for half an hour.* **3** an artificial bar in a river; dam: *A barrage is going up on the Tigris to divert its flood waters from Baghdad into Wadi Tharthar, a 200-mile depression* (Newsweek).

—*v.t., v.i.* to fire at with artillery; subject to a barrage.

[< French *barrage* < *barrer* obstruct < *barre* bar¹]

barrage balloon, a balloon fastened with a rope or cable so that it can float at a certain height and sometimes support a net. Barrage balloons were used in World Wars I and II to force aircraft to maintain altitudes too high for accurate bombing. Their fabric is self-sealing if bullets puncture it.

bar|ra|mun|da (bar′ə mun′də), *n., pl.* **-da** or **-das**. a large, freshwater, edible lungfish of Australia; ceratodus. [< a native name]

bar|ra|mun|di (bar′ə mun′dē), *n., pl.* **-di, -dis**, or **-dies**. = barramunda.

bar|ran|ca (bə rang′kə), *n. Southwestern U.S.* **1** a deep ravine or gorge with very steep sides. **2** a bank or bluff with very steep sides. [American English < Spanish *barranca, barranco;* origin uncertain]

bar|ran|co (bə rang′kō), *n., pl.* **-cos**. = barranca.

bar|ra|the|a (bar′ə thē′ə), *n.* = barathea.

bar|ra|tor or **bar|ra|ter** (bar′ə tər), *n.* a person who commits barratry. [< Anglo-French *baratour*, Old French *barateor* < *barater* deceive; origin uncertain]

bar|ra|trous (bar′ə trəs), *adj.* constituting or amounting to barratry: *No act can be barratrous to which the owners have . . . been consenting parties* (Joseph Arnould). **—bar′ra|trous|ly**, *adv.* **—bar′ra|trous|ness**, *n.*

bar|ra|try (bar′ə trē), *n., pl.* **-tries. 1** fraud or gross negligence of a ship's officer, or seaman, against the ship's owners, insurers, or other interested parties. **2** the act or practice of stirring up lawsuits or quarrels. **3** the purchase or sale of ecclesiastical positions or state offices. [< Old French *baraterie* < *barater* cheat, deceive. See related etym. at **barter**.]

Barr body (bär), a piece of chromosomal material in the nuclear membrane of female cells which stains darkly and is the remnant of one of the two female chromosomes (X chromosomes); sex chromatin. [< Murray *Barr*, born 1908, a Canadian anatomist, who discovered these bodies in 1949]

barre (bär), *n.* the rail by which ballet dancers support themselves when practicing. [< French *barre*]

barred (bärd), *adj.* **1** having bars: *a barred window.* **2** marked with stripes: *a chicken with barred feathers.* **3** not permitted; prohibited: *The use of radios is barred in libraries.*

barred owl, a large, grayish-brown owl, with striped feathers on the breast. It lives especially in thickly wooded areas of eastern North America.

barred spiral, *Astronomy.* any one of a class of spiral nebulae characterized by a straight, luminous bar extending through the nucleus with spiral whorls extending from its ends.

bar|rel (bar′əl), *n., v.,* **-reled, -rel|ing** or (*especially British*) **-relled, -rel|ling. —*n.* 1** a container with a round, flat top and bottom and sides that curve out slightly. Barrels are usually made of boards held together by hoops or of cardboard reinforced with metal hoops at the tops and bottoms. SYN: cask. **2a** the amount that a barrel can hold: *They picked a barrel of apples.* **b** a unit of measure for liquids and dry things. Its exact amount is not the same for all commodities, and is often fixed by law. In the United States the barrel for most dry things has 7,056 cubic inches or 115.62 liters; for most liquids, 31½ gallons or 119.24 liters; for petroleum, 42 gallons or 158.98 liters. *Abbr:* bbl. **3** any container, case, or part shaped somewhat like a barrel: *the barrel of a drum.* **4** the metal tube of a gun. The bullet or shell is discharged through the barrel. **5** the chamber of a pump in which the piston works. **6** the cylindrical box containing the mainspring of a watch or clock. **7** the quill of a feather; calamus. **8** a revolving cylinder or drum around which a chain or rope is wound, such as that on a capstan or windlass. **9** the vibrating portion of a bell between the top and the lower, thickened part. **10** the part in which the ink of a fountain pen or ballpoint pen or the lead of a mechanical pencil is enclosed. **11** the housing of a photographic lens, especially a telephoto lens. **12** the central portion of the body of a horse, mule, cow, or other four-legged domestic animal. **13** *Informal.* a great deal; much: *a barrel of fun, to eat a barrel of cookies.*

—*v.t.* to put in barrels: *We plan to barrel the cider next Wednesday.*

—*v.i.* *U.S. Slang.* to move with great speed: *The new law . . . cracks down on motorists, especially those who terrorize pedestrians by barrelling around corners* (New Yorker).

over a barrel, *Informal.* in a defenseless position; in distress: *He had his competitors over a barrel.*

scrape the (or **bottom of the**) **barrel**, to use up one's last resources: *This can run into money just when you've scraped the barrel to pay for the car* (Punch).

[< Old French *baril;* origin uncertain]

bar|rel|age (bar′ə lij), *n.* the amount contained in a barrel or barrels.

barrel cactus, a very large, spiny, spherical cactus of Mexico and the southwestern United States.

barrel chair, an upholstered chair with a relatively high, deep, curved back resembling a barrel with part of the front and sides cut away.

bar|rel-chest|ed (bar′əl ches′tid), *adj.* having a round, broad chest: *In his fifties, ham-fisted and barrel-chested, George is the UMW district man in Sequatchie Valley* (Harper's).

*** barrel distortion**, *Optics.* a distortion produced by a lens causing the sides of a square to appear somewhat rounded, resembling those of a barrel.

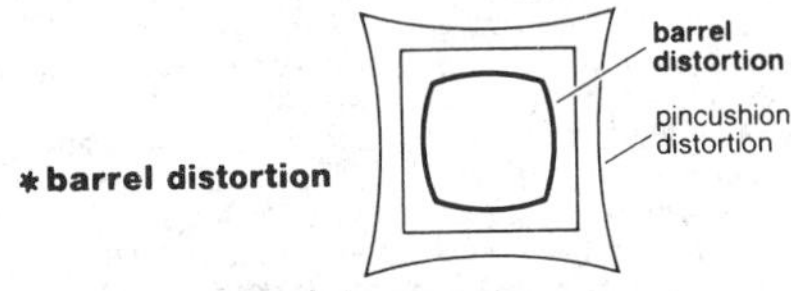

*** barrel distortion**

bar|reled (bar′əld), *adj.* **1** having a barrel or barrels: *a double-barreled gun.* **2** contained in barrels: *barreled beer.*

bar|rel|ful (bar′əl fu̇l), *n.* the amount a barrel can hold.

bar|rel|head (bar′əl hed′), *n.* the top of a barrel.

bar|rel|house (bar′əl hous′), *n. U.S.* **1** jazz with a strong tempo, especially as played by piano, drums, and brasses. **2** (formerly) a low-class drinking saloon.

bar|relled (bar′əld), *adj. Especially British.* barreled.

barrel organ, = hand organ.

barrel roll, a complete revolution of a flying aircraft around its longitudinal axis, following a spiral path in a horizontal direction.

Pronunciation Key: hat, āge, cãre, fär; let, ēqual, tėrm; it, īce; hot, ōpen, ôrder; oil, out; cup, pu̇t, rüle; child; long; thin; ᴛʜen; zh, measure; ə represents a in about, e in taken, i in pencil, o in lemon, u in circus.

***barrel vault**, a vault with a simple, semicylindrical roof, used especially in Roman and Romanesque architecture.

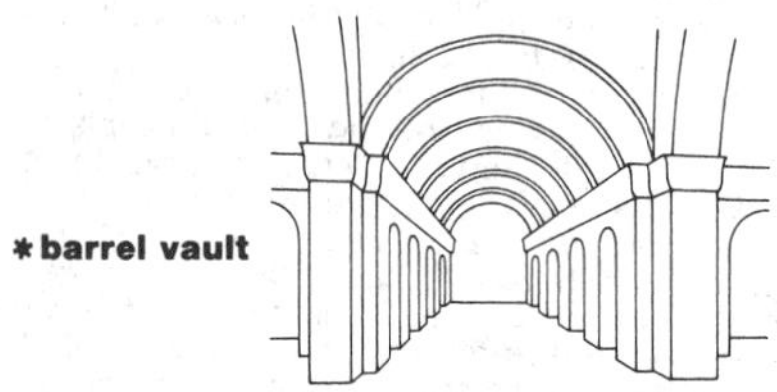

***barrel vault**

bar·ren (bar′ən), *adj., n.* **—*adj.*** **1** not producing anything: *A sandy desert is barren.* SYN: unproductive. **2** not able to bear offspring, yield fruit or seeds; infertile: *Exposure to radioactivity may make animals and plants barren.* SYN: sterile. **3** *Figurative.* without interest; unattractive; dull: *The speech was dry and barren, full of unconnected facts and figures.* **4** *Figurative.* of no advantage; fruitless; unprofitable: *the barren victories of modern war. A barren and unrepaid attachment, a wasted affection* (J. B. Mozley). SYN: unproductive, sterile. **5** *Figurative.* unresponsive: *Will themselves laugh, to set on some quantity of barren Spectators to laugh too* (Shakespeare).
—*n.* a stretch of barren land.
barrens, *U.S. and Canada.* an area of level land, more or less unproductive, poorly forested, and generally having sandy soil: *Ridge faces and summits are scarred by numerous . . . barrens* (Roderick Peattie).
[< Old French *barain* (used of barren land) perhaps < a Germanic word] **—bar′ren·ly,** *adv.* **—bar′ren·ness,** *n.*

Barren Ground caribou, a caribou that inhabits the tundra of northern Alaska and Canada.

bar·ret (bar′it), *n.* a small cap, especially a biretta. [< French *barrette*]

bar·rette (bə ret′, bä-), *n.* a pin with a clasp, used by women and girls for holding the hair in place. [< French *barrette* (diminutive) < *barre* bar[1]]

bar·ri·a·da (bär′rē ä′ᴛʜä), *n. Spanish.* a city quarter, especially a slum inhabited by poor migrants from the country.

bar·ri·cade (bar′ə kād′, bar′ə kād), *n., v.,* **-cad·ed, -cad·ing.** **—*n.*** **1** a rough, hastily made barrier for defense: *The soldiers cut down trees to make a barricade across the road.* SYN: fortification, rampart. **2** *Figurative.* any barrier or obstruction. SYN: block, obstacle, impediment.
—*v.t.* **1** to block or obstruct with a barricade: *The soldiers barricaded the road with fallen trees.* **2** to shut in or out with, or as if with, a barricade.
[< French *barricade* < Provençal *barricada* < *barrica* barrel < *barril* (barrels of earth were the first barricades)] **—bar′ri·cad′er,** *n.*

bar·ri·ca·do (bar′ə kā′dō), *n., pl.* **-does,** *v.t.,* **-doed, -do·ing.** = barricade.

bar·ri·er (bar′ē ər), *n., v.* **—*n.*** **1** something that stands in the way; something stopping progress or preventing approach; obstacle: *A dam is a barrier holding back water.* (*Figurative.*) *Lack of water was a barrier to settling much of New Mexico.* SYN: bar, hindrance. **2** something that separates or keeps apart: *The Isthmus of Panama forms a barrier between the Atlantic and Pacific oceans.* **3** a starting gate in horse racing.
—*v.t.* to shut in or off by a barrier. SYN: barricade.
barriers, *Historical.* the palisades enclosing the ground where a tournament was held; lists: *At length the barriers were opened, and five knights advanced slowly into the area* (Scott).
[< Anglo-French *barrere,* Old French *barriere* < *barre* bar[1]]

barrier beach, a long, thin sand ridge built by the action of waves near a shore.

barrier reef, a long line of rocks or coral reef parallel to the mainland and separated from it by a deep lagoon. The Great Barrier Reef of Australia is more than 1,250 miles long.

bar·ring (bär′ing), *prep.* **1** not including; excepting; except: *Nobody else knows, barring you and me.* **2** except in the event of: *Barring a delay, the train will reach Chicago at noon.*

bar·ri·o (bär′rē ō), *n., pl.* **-ri·os.** **1** in Spanish-speaking countries: **a** a district of a city or town. **b** a local administrative unit approximating a township in the United States. **c** a suburb of a town or city. **2** *U.S.* a section of a large city in which the population is predominantly Spanish-speaking. [< Spanish *barrio* < Arabic *barrī* exterior]

bar·ris·ter (bar′ə stər), *n.* a lawyer in England who can plead in any court. [< *bar*[1]; apparently patterned on *chorister*]
►See the usage note under **advocate.**

bar·room (bär′rüm′, -rům′), *n. Especially U.S.* a room with a bar for the sale of alcoholic drinks; taproom.

barroom plant, = aspidistra.

bar·row[1] (bar′ō), *n., v.* **—*n.*** **1** = wheelbarrow. **2** *British.* a two-wheeled handcart: *We bought fresh oranges and clusters of rich purple grapes from the barrows on Piccadilly* (Atlantic). **3** a frame with two short handles at each end, such as a stretcher has, used for carrying a load. **4** the contents of any of these.
—*v.t.* to carry in a barrow.
[Middle English *barewe,* unrecorded Old English *bearwe*]

bar·row[2] (bar′ō), *n.* a mound of earth or stones over an ancient grave; tumulus. [Middle English *barewe,* Old English *beorg*]

bar·row[3] (bar′ō), *n.* a castrated male pig. [Middle English *barewe,* Old English *bearg*]

barrow boy, *British.* a man or boy who sells from a barrow in the street.

bar·row·man (bar′ō mən), *n., pl.* **-men.** *British.* a costermonger.

bar·ru·let (bar′ə lit, -yə-), *n. Heraldry.* a diminutive of the bar, usually one-fourth of its width. [a diminutive form of an assumed French *barrule* (diminutive) < *barre* bar[1]]

bar·ry (bär′ē), *adj. Heraldry.* (of the field) divided into bars. [< Anglo-French *barré* < Old French *barre* bar]

bars (bärz), *n.pl.* **1** the upper, toothless part of the gums of a horse, to which the bit is fitted. **2** the part of a horse's bit that fits crosswise in the animal's mouth. **3** either of the recurved ends of the wall of a horse's hoof where they curve in to the sole.

bar·shoe (bär′shü′), *n.* a horseshoe with a flat iron plate extending across the rear to protect the frog of the horse's hoof.

bar sinister, a diagonal bar on a coat of arms wrongly supposed to indicate illegitimate descent.

bar·stool (bär′stül′), *n.* any of various, usually high and often cushioned, stools used at a bar.

Bart., baronet.

bar·tend (bär′tend′), *v.i. U.S. Informal.* to tend a bar; work as a bartender.

bar·tend·er (bär′ten′dər), *n.* a man who serves alcoholic drinks to customers at a bar; barkeeper.

bar·ter (bär′tər), *v., n.* **—*v.t.*** to exchange (one kind of goods or services for another): *The Indians bartered furs for beads and guns.* (*Figurative.*) *The citizens bartered their freedom for protection against raids.*
—*v.i.* to trade by exchanging one kind of goods or services for other goods or services without using money: *By offering their services as guides, the Indians were able to barter for blankets and knives.*
—*n.* **1** the act of trading by exchanging goods: *Nations sometimes trade by barter instead of paying money for the things they need.* **2** exchange. **3** something bartered.
barter away, to give away without an equal return, and especially dishonorably or unwisely: *to barter away one's soul for wealth.*
[< Old French *barater* cheat, deceive. See related etym. under **barratry.**] **—bar′ter·er,** *n.*

Barth·i·an (bär′tē ən, -thē-), *adj.* of or having to do with the Swiss theologian Karl Barth (1886-1968) or with Barthianism.

Barth·i·an·ism (bär′tē ə niz əm, -thē-), *n.* the theological doctrines of Karl Barth, associated with the Protestant movement of neoorthodoxy.

Bar·tho·lin gland (bär tō′lin), either of a pair of small, oval glands, one on each side of the base of the vagina, that secrete mucus. [< Caspar *Bartholin,* 1655-1738, a Danish anatomist, who discovered them]

Bar·thol·o·mew (bär thol′ə myü), *n.* **Saint,** one of the Twelve Apostles.

bar·ti·zan (bär′tə zən, bär′tə zan′), *n.* a small, overhanging turret on a wall or tower. [apparently a variant of *bratticing* < *brattice;* used by Sir Walter Scott]

bar·ti·zaned (bär′tə zənd), *adj.* furnished with a bartizan or bartizans.

Bart·lett pear (bärt′lit), a large, juicy kind of yellow pear, native to England, introduced and widely distributed in the United States by Enoch Bartlett.

bar·ton (bär′tən), *n. British.* **1** a farmyard. **2** a demesne farm. [Old English *bere-tūn* enclosure < *bere* barley + *tūn* enclosure, yard]

bar·to·ni·a (bär tō′nē ə), *n.* any one of several large-flowered, prickly plants of western North America. **1** any one of various American herbaceous plants of the gentian family, with small, yellowish flowers. [< New Latin *Bartonia* < Benjamin S. *Barton,* 1766-1815, an American naturalist]

Bar·uch (bär′ək), *n.* **1** the secretary and friend of Jeremiah (in the Bible, Jeremiah 32:12-14; 36:4-32). **2a** a book of the Old Testament Apocrypha supposedly written by him. *Abbr:* Bar. **b** either of two books of revelation attributed to him.

bar·wood (bär′wůd′), *n.* a red dyewood from a tree of the pea family, of western Africa.

bar·y·cen·ter (bar′ə sen′tər), *n.* the center of gravity.

bar·y·cen·tric (bar′ə sen′trik), *adj.* of or having to do with the center of gravity. [< Greek *barýs* heavy + *kéntron* center + English *-ic*]

bar·y·on (bar′ē on), *n.* any of a class of heavy elementary particles that includes the proton, neutron, and hyperons. [< Greek *barýs* heavy + English *-on,* as in *ion*]

bar·y·on·ic (bar′ē on′ik), *adj.* of or having to do with baryons.

baryon number, *Nuclear Physics.* a quantum number equal to the number of baryons minus the number of antibaryons. The baryon number remains the same throughout any reaction.

bar·y·sphere (bar′ə sfir), *n.* = centrosphere (def. 2).

ba·ry·ta (bə rī′tə), *n.* **1** a whitish powder, barium oxide, used in the manufacture of glass and of barium salts; heavy earth. *Formula:* BaO **2** *Obsolete.* = barium. [a New Latin form of *barytes*]

ba·ry·tes (bə rī′tēz), *n.* = barite. [< Greek *barytēs* weight < *barys* heavy]

ba·ryt·ic (bə rit′ik), *adj.* having to do with, formed of, or containing baryta.

bar·y·ton (bar′ə ton), *n.* **1** a viola da gamba having a set of extra sympathetic strings. **2** = euphonium.
[< German *Baryton* < Italian *baritono;* see etym. under **baritone**]

bar·y·tone[1] (bar′ə tōn), *n., adj. British.* baritone.

bar·y·tone[2] (bar′ə tōn), *adj., n.* in Greek grammar: **—*adj.*** not having the acute accent on the last syllable.
—*n.* a barytone word.
[< Late Latin *barytonus* < Greek *barýtonos* < *barýs* heavy, bass + *tónos* pitch, tone]

B.A.S. or **B.A.Sc.,** **1** Bachelor of Agricultural Science. **2** Bachelor of Applied Science.

bas·al (bā′səl), *adj.* **1** fundamental; basic: *Young children learn to read from basal readers.* **2** of the base; at the base; forming the base: *a skyscraper built on basal rock.* **3** *Physiology.* **a** of or designating the minimum level at which vital activity of an organism continues (a state of rest). **b** of an amount sufficient to maintain this level. **4** *Botany.* located at or growing from the base of a plant. **5** of or inducing an unconscious state preparatory to supplemental anesthetization. **—bas′al·ly,** *adv.*

basal cell, any of a variety of cells situated on the layer of the epithelium.

basal metabolic rate, the measure of basal metabolism.

basal metabolism, the amount of energy used by an animal or plant at rest, used as a standard for comparing metabolism under varying conditions. The basal metabolism for a man 30 years old is between 1,400 and 1,500 calories per day.

ba·salt (bə sôlt′, bas′ôlt), *n.* **1** a hard, dark-colored rock of volcanic origin. It often occurs in a form resembling a group of columns. **2** = basalt ware. [< Late Latin *basaltes,* alteration of Latin *basanītēs* a very hard stone, touchstone < Greek *basanītēs* < *básanos* touchstone, test]

basalt glass, a kind of black basalt having a resinous luster and brittle texture; tachylyte.

ba·sal·tic (bə sôl′tik), *adj.* **1** of or having to do with basalt: *basaltic lava.* **2** like basalt.

ba·sal·ti·form (bə sôl′tə fôrm), *adj.* having the form of basalt; columnar.

ba·sal·toid (bə sôl′toid), *adj.* resembling basalt.

basalt ware, a black, unglazed stoneware having a dull gloss, designed by Josiah Wedgwood.

bas·an (baz′ən), *n.* sheepskin tanned in bark, such as oak bark or larch bark, used especially for bookbinding; basil. [< French *basane*]

bas·a·nite (bas′ə nīt), *n.* a black, siliceous rock; touchstone. [< Latin *basanītēs;* see etym. under **basalt**]

bas bleu (bä blœ′), *French.* a bluestocking.

bas·cule (bas′kyül), *n.* a device that works like a seesaw, counterbalancing heavy moving parts with weights.
[< French *bascule* seesaw < *bacul* < *battre* to bump + *cul* the buttocks]

***bascule bridge,** a drawbridge that tilts up to open by pivoting on a horizontal shaft and is counterbalanced by a weight.

***bascule bridge**

base[1] (bās), *n., v.,* **based, bas·ing,** *adj.* **—*n.*** **1** the part on which anything stands or rests; underlying support; bottom: *This big machine rests on a wide steel base. We camped at the base of the mountain.* **2** *Figurative.* the thing or part on which something depends; basis; foundation: *a sound base for reform, a clear base for action. The new law to increase spending for schools was a good base for building more schools.* **3** the most important element of anything; essential part: *Most canned dog food has a meat base. This paint has an oil base.* **4** the place that is a station or goal in certain games, such as baseball or hide-and-seek: *His home run doesn't count because he failed to touch third base.* **5** a starting place; headquarters: *The base for our hike up the mountain was a campground beside a brook. The Red Cross established a base to distribute supplies to flood victims in the area.* **6a** a chemical compound that reacts with an acid to form a salt. Bases are bitter to the taste, have a soapy feel, and turn red litmus paper blue in water solution. Bases yield ions composed of hydrogen and oxygen in which hydrogen is replaceable by an acid radical. The pH value of a base is more than 7. Sodium hydroxide and calcium hydroxide are common bases. **b** any ionic or molecular substance which can take on a proton. **c** any molecule or ion that has available an unshared pair of electrons. **7a** the part of a column on which the shaft stands. See picture under **Corinthian**. **b** the part at the bottom of a wall or monument, especially when treated as a distinct feature. **c** the lowest division of any structure. **8a** the part of an organ of an animal or plant nearest its point of attachment. **b** the point of attachment. **9** the line or surface on which a geometrical figure is supposed to rest. Any side of a triangle can be its base. **10** *Mathematics.* **a** the number that is a definite starting point for a system of numbers. 10 is the base of the decimal system of arithmetic. **b** the aggregate of the vectors or functions in terms of which other vectors or functions are to be given as sums. **11** *Genetics.* any of the four chemical compounds, adenine, cytosine, guanine, and thymine (or uracil) that are present in nucleic acid and combine in various ways to form the genetic code. **12** *Surveying.* a line used as a starting point; base line. **13** *Heraldry.* the lower part of an escutcheon (specifically, the width of a bar separated from the bottom by a horizontal line). **14** *Grammar.* the form of a word to which prefixes or suffixes are attached; root; stem; theme: *In English, the imperative form is the base, or simple, form of the verb* (Paul Roberts).

—*v.t.* **1** to set up and keep going; establish; found: *His large business was based on good service. The movie . . . claims to be based on classical legends* (New Yorker). **2** to make or form a base or foundation for: *The builders based girders for the tall building on deep concrete foundations.* **3** to station: *The Coast Guard bases rescue units along the ocean shores.*

—*adj.* **1** that forms a base: *a base color.* **2** that serves as a base: *a base camp, a base price.*

load the bases, (in baseball) to put runners on all three bases: *With the bases loaded a home run could have saved the team from defeat.*

off base, a *U.S. Informal.* incorrect; wrong: *His criticism is off base.* **b** (in military use) out of bounds: *The soldier was arrested for being off base after the curfew.*

touch base with, *U.S. Informal.* to have communication with; contact: *[He] quickly outraged White House staffers by choosing his top assistants without touching base with the President* (Time).

[< Old French *basse* < Latin *basis* < Greek *básis.* See etym. of doublet **basis.**]

—*Syn. n.* **1, 2 Base, basis, foundation** mean the part on which anything stands for support. **Base,** though chiefly used literally, is also used figuratively to emphasize the support it gives to larger things: *The new charter was welcomed as a base on which to build needed reforms.* **Basis,** chiefly used figuratively, emphasizes how essential the support is: *The basis of her opinion is something she read in the paper.* **Foundation,** used literally and figuratively, emphasizes the firmness and solidness of the base or basis: *His honesty and willingness to work are the foundation of his success.*

base[2] (bās), *adj.,* **bas|er, bas|est,** *n.* —*adj.* **1** selfish and cowardly; morally low or mean: *To betray a friend is a base action.* **2** having little value when compared with something else; inferior: *Iron and steel are base metals but gold and silver are precious metals.* **3a** of inferior quality; poor; shabby: *The cheapest and basest imitation which can escape detection* (John Ruskin). **b** fit for an inferior person or thing; menial; unworthy: *No needed service is to be looked upon as base.* SYN: degrading. **4** *Archaic.* **a** of humble birth or origin. SYN: plebeian. **b** illegitimate. **5** debased; counterfeit: *base coin.* **6** not classical or refined, as language. **7** deep or grave in sound; bass. **8** (in English law) held or holding by such service as a villein owed to his lord: *a base estate, a base tenant.* **9** *Archaic.* of small height; low.

—*n.* the lowest male voice; bass.

[< Middle French *bas* < Old French < Medieval Latin *bassus* low, Late Latin, thick, fat. See etym. of doublet **basso.**] —**base′ly,** *adv.* —**base′ness,** *n.*

—*Syn. adj.* **1 Base, vile, low** mean morally inferior and contemptible. **Base** means reduced to a low moral state, without honor or without moral standards, usually by selfishness or cowardliness: *Betraying a friend for a reward is base.* **Vile** means evil and without moral standards or decency: *In the slums of some cities even small children learn vile language.* **Low** means without a sense of decency or of what is honorable: *To steal from the collection plate in church or from a blind beggar is low.*

base|ball (bās′bôl′), *n.* **1** a game played with bat and ball by two teams of nine players each on a field with four bases arranged as a diamond. A player making a complete circuit of the bases, under the rules, scores a run. The two teams alternately field and bat in each of the (usually) nine innings. The team with the larger number of runs wins. **2** the ball used in this game. [American English < *base ball* (an earlier game)]

base|board (bās′bôrd′, -bōrd′), *n.* **1** *U.S.* a line of boards around the walls of a room, next to the floor. In Great Britain it is called a *skirting board,* or *skirting.* **2** a board at or forming the base of anything.

base|born (bās′bôrn′), *adj.* **1** born of slaves, peasants, or other humble parents. SYN: plebeian. **2** born of parents not married to each other; illegitimate. **3** of base origin or nature.

base box, a unit of measure for tin plate equivalent to an area of 31,360 square inches.

base bullion, a base metal with appreciable amounts of a precious metal or metals.

base|burn|er (bās′bėr′nər), *n. U.S.* a furnace, stove, or water heater fed automatically either from a hopper or a gas line as the fuel at its base is consumed.

base|court (bās′kôrt′, -kōrt′), *n.* the lower or outer court of a castle, occupied by the servants.

based (bāst), *adj.* having a base: *broad-based.*

base exchange, 1 = ion exchange. **2** (in the U.S. Air Force) = Post Exchange.

base hit, a successful hitting of the baseball by a batter so that he gets at least to first base without the help of a defensive error and without forcing out one of his teammates.

base hospital, a military hospital at some place distant from the area of active operations.

base|less (bās′lis), *adj.* without foundation; groundless: *A rumor is baseless if it is not supported by facts.* SYN: unfounded. —**base′less|ly,** *adv.* —**base′less|ness,** *n.*

base level, the theoretical limit to which a stream tends to erode its valley, as the level of the sea or of a lake.

base line, or **base|line** (bās′līn′), *n.* **1** a line used as a base, from which operations are carried on, or on which they depend or rest. **2a** *Baseball.* the unmarked lane or path between one base and the next. A player must keep to it while remaining between bases. **b** *Tennis.* the line at either end of the court parallel to the net: *He began to net his returns and overdrive the base line* (Time). **3** *Surveying.* any precisely determined line forming a side of a triangle, so that when the adjacent angles are measured, the relative position of the third vertex is determined.

bas|el|la|ceous (bas′ə lā′shəs), *adj.* belonging to a small family of tropical, (usually) climbing, herbaceous plants, including the Madeira vine. [< New Latin *Basella* the typical genus + English *-aceous*]

base load, that quantity of electrical power that a power plant or power system must deliver in order to satisfy ordinary or minimum needs.

base|man (bās′mən), *n., pl.* **-men.** a baseball player guarding first, second, or third base: *The runner got caught between the third baseman and the catcher.*

base|ment (bās′mənt), *n.* **1** the lowest story of a building, partly or wholly below ground: *Many basements flooded when the river overflowed.* SYN: cellar. **2** the lowest division of the wall of a building or the lowest part above ground of a building as a whole. **3** = basement complex.

basement complex, *Geology.* a deposit of chiefly metamorphic and igneous rocks under the stratified rocks of any region.

basement membrane, *Anatomy.* a thin, delicate layer or membrane under the epithelium.

basement rock, *Geology.* the dense underlying rock of a basement complex.

base metal, 1 any metal inferior to or less costly than a precious metal, such as tin, lead, copper, and zinc. **2** the chief metallic element in an alloy. **3** any metal that is cut, welded, or plated.

ba|sen|ji (bə sen′jē), *n., pl.* **-jis.** a small, reddish, terrierlike hunting dog native to Africa, distinguished by its inability to bark. It has recently been introduced into the United States as a pet. [< a native name]

base on balls, *Baseball.* a base allowed to a batter after the pitcher has thrown four balls; walk.

base pair, *Genetics.* two bases, either adenine and thymine, or guanine and cytosine, which pair off in the replication of DNA.

base pay, a rate of pay established for a particular job, to which may be added certain increases for length of service, changes in the cost of living, and other benefits.

base period, *Commerce.* a period of normal or average business activity, used as a basis of comparison for calculating an increase or decline in prices, wages, taxes, and other statistical data for any given year: *It cost the typical family $11.04 last month to buy goods and services that cost $10 in the base period* (New York Times).

base|plate (bās′plāt′), *n.* **1** any flat piece that serves as a foundation or support: *a TV camera baseplate.* **2** = bedplate.

base runner, *Baseball.* a player on the team at bat who is on base or running between two bases.

bas|es[1] (bā′siz), *n.* plural of **base[1].**

ba|ses[2] (bā′sēz), *n.* plural of **basis.**

base surge, a cloud of small, highly radioactive drops of water that moves outward in the atmosphere from the point immediately above an underwater nuclear explosion.

bash (bash), *v., n. Informal.* —*v.t., v.i.* **1** to strike with a smashing blow; hit very hard. **2** to set upon vigorously with hostile words, arguments, or abuse; assail: *The premier knew he could "win votes by bashing Brits," now that Canada was a multi-ethnic society* (Tom McArthur).

—*n.* **1** a smashing blow: *a bash in the face.* **2** a big party or meal; blowout: *He was already planning a big bash . . . in the Savoy Grill the night before he sailed for home* (John O'Hara).

have a bash (at), *British Slang.* to give a try; attempt: *You've got to do it yourself but I'll have a bash with you* (Listener). [perhaps < Danish *baske* to beat, strike] —**bash′er,** *n.*

ba|sha (bä′shə), *n.* (in India) a bamboo hut with a thatched roof: *"Malaria" means chills and fever and sweating in bashas* (James Phinney Baxter). [< Assamese]

ba|shaw (bə shô′), *n.* **1** an important person, especially one who is haughty and imperious; grandee. **2** = pasha. [< Turkish (formerly, in Arabic letters) *bāshā.* See etym. of doublet **pasha.**]

bash|ful (bash′fəl), *adj.* **1** uneasy in the presence of strangers; easily embarrassed; shy: *The little girl was too bashful to greet us.* SYN: timid, coy, diffident. See syn. under **shy.** **2** of or like that of a bashful person: *a bashful smile.* [< *bash* (short for *abash*) + *-ful*] —**bash′ful|ly,** *adv.* —**bash′ful-ness,** *n.*

bash|i|ba|zouk or **bash|i-ba|zouk** (bash′ē bə-zük′), *n. Historical.* a mercenary soldier belonging to the irregular mounted troops of the Turkish Army, noted for lawlessness and cruelty. [< Turkish *basi-bozuk* one whose headdress is awry]

ba|sho (bä′shō), *n., pl.* **ba|sho.** a fifteen-match tournament in sumo wrestling. [< Japanese *basho* matches, tournaments]

ba|sic (bā′sik), *adj., n.* —*adj.* **1** forming the basis or base; fundamental: *Addition, subtraction, multiplication, and division are the basic processes of arithmetic.* SYN: essential. **2** being a basis or starting point: *a basic scale of pay.* **3** *Chemistry.* **a** of or being a base; alkaline. **b** having the base in excess; having more than one equivalent of the base for each equivalent of acid. **4** containing less than about 52 per cent of silica in rock.

—*n.* **1** an essential part; fundamental principle, rule, or other factor: *the basics of flying.* **2** *U.S. Slang.* = basic training. —**ba′si|cal|ly,** *adv.*

Ba|sic[1] (bā′sik), *n.* = Basic English.

BASIC or **Basic[2]**, *n.* a computer language made up of a blend of simple English and elementary algebra, used to introduce students to programming. [< *B*(eginners) *A*(ll-purpose) *S*(ymbolic) *I*(nstruction) *C*(ode)]

basic anhydride, the oxide of a metal.

basic crop or **commodity,** *U.S.* any crop essential to the economy, especially one receiving high Federal price support.

basic dress, a woman's dress of simple design

Pronunciation Key: hat, āge, cãre, fär; let, ēqual, tėrm; it, īce; hot, ōpen, ôrder; oil, out; cup, pu̇t, rüle; child; long; thin; ᴛʜen; zh, measure; ə represents **a** in about, **e** in taken, **i** in pencil, **o** in lemon, **u** in circus.

and in a single color, that may be adapted to use on various occasions by adding suitable accessories.

Basic English, a system to simplify English devised by Charles K. Ogden, utilizing a vocabulary of 850 words and a confined grammatical system, intended for use as an international auxiliary language and in teaching English to foreigners.

ba|sic|i|ty (bə sis′ə tē), *n. Chemistry.* **1** the quality or condition of being a base. **2** the power of an acid to combine with bases, dependent on the number of atoms of hydrogen contained in the acid, which are replaceable by a metal.

basic pay, = base pay.

basic process, a process of manufacturing steel or other ferrous metal, in which the furnace is lined and the charge is supplemented with lime, magnesite, dolomite, basic slag, or other basic substance by which the phosphorus in the pig iron is absorbed.

basic research, research into the fundamental nature, structure, and properties of anything, especially research aimed at solving theoretical problems with no immediate practical applications in mind.

basic science, that part of science which is concerned solely or primarily with basic research.

basic slag, *Metallurgy.* a slag in which the ratio of bases to acids is comparatively high. It is produced during the basic process of manufacturing steel, and is itself an important medium in this process. It is also a phosphate fertilizer of considerable agricultural value.

basic training, the schooling in military fundamentals of recruits in the armed forces, carried out over a period of two to four months.

basic wage, = base pay.

ba|sid|i|a (bə sid′ē ə), *n.* plural of **basidium**.

ba|sid|i|al (bə sid′ē əl), *adj.* of or having a basidium or basidia.

ba|sid|i|o|my|cete (bə sid′ē ō mī sēt′), *n.* any plant of a large class of fungi that includes smuts, rusts, mushrooms, and puffballs. The basidiomycetes are characterized by the formation of spores on a basidium. [< *basidium* + Greek *mýkēs, -ētos* fungus]

ba|sid|i|o|my|ce|tous (bə sid′ē ō mī sē′təs), *adj.* of or belonging to the basidiomycetes.

ba|sid|i|o|spore (bə sid′ē ə spôr′, -spōr′), *n.* one of the spores produced on a basidium.

ba|sid|i|um (bə sid′ē əm), *n., pl.* **-i|a** (-ē ə). *Botany.* a small, club-shaped structure on basidiomycetes, generally the swollen terminal cell of a hypha, which produces spores, usually four, at the tips of minute stalks. [< New Latin *basidium* < Greek *básis* + *-idion,* a diminutive suffix]

ba|si|fixed (bā′sə fikst), *adj. Botany.* attached by the base or lower end. [< Latin *basis* base[1] + English *fixed*]

bas|il[1] (baz′əl), *n.* a sweet-smelling plant used in cooking; sweet basil. Basil is a tropical plant of the same family as the mint, and is added to soups, salads, meats, and other dishes to give a pleasant, spicy flavor. [< Old French *basile,* learned borrowing from Late Latin *basilicum* < Greek *basilikón* (*phytón*) royal (plant). See related etym. at **basilic**.]

bas|il[2] (baz′əl), *n.* = basan.

bas|i|lar (bas′ə lər), *adj.* of or situated at the base, especially the base of the skull.

bas|i|lar|y (bas′ə ler′ē), *adj.* = basilar.

Ba|sil|i|an (bə sil′ē ən), *adj.* of or having to do with Saint Basil (330?-379?), a Greek father of the Christian church.

ba|sil|ic (bə sil′ik), *adj.* **1** of or having to do with a basilica; resembling a basilica. **2** of or having to do with a large vein on the inner side of the upper arm. **3** royal; sovereign. [< Latin *basilicus* < Greek *basilikós* kingly]

***ba|sil|i|ca** (bə sil′ə kə), *n.* **1** an oblong hall with a row of columns at each side, separating the high main portion from the side aisles, and a structure in the shape of a half circle at one end, sometimes at both ends. The ancient Romans used such buildings for law courts and public meetings. **2a** an early Christian church built in this form, with an apse at the east end. **b** any building of oblong plan, especially one having a high central portion. **3** (in the Roman Catholic Church) a title conferred by the Pope on a church, giving it certain rights and privileges. [< Latin *basilica* < Greek (*stoá*) *basilikḗ* royal (portico) < *basilikós* royal < *basileús* king]

ba|sil|i|cal (bə sil′ə kəl), *adj.* = basilic.

ba|sil|i|can (bə sil′ə kən), *adj.* basilic; of a basilica.

bas|i|lisk (bas′ə lisk, baz′-), *n., adj.* **—*n.*** **1** (in ancient and medieval legend) a reptile whose breath and look were thought to be fatal; cockatrice. It was supposed to be somewhat like a lizard, to have a black-and-yellow skin and fiery red eyes, and to be hatched by a serpent from an egg laid by a rooster. **2** a tropical American lizard with a crest along its head and back, which it can raise and lower. Basilisks are related to the iguanas.
—*adj.* like that of the legendary basilisk; fiery; blazing: (*Figurative.*) *basilisk wrath,* (*Figurative.*) *a basilisk eye.*
[< Latin *basiliscus* < Greek *basilískos* kind of serpent (diminutive) < *basileús* king]

ba|sin (bā′sən), *n.* **1** a wide, shallow dish for holding liquids; bowl. **2** the amount that a basin can hold: *They have wasted more than a basin of water already.* **3** a shallow area containing water: *Part of the harbor is a yacht basin.* **4** all the land drained by a river and the streams that flow into it; river basin: *The Mississippi basin extends from the Appalachian Mountains to the Rocky Mountains.* **5** a depression where the rivers have no outlets. [< Old French *bacin* < Late Latin *baccīnum* < unrecorded *bacca* vessel, bowl] **—ba′sin|like′**, *adj.*

ba|sined (bā′sənd), *adj.* enclosed in a basin.

bas|i|net (bas′ə nit), *n.* a kind of steel helmet common in the 1200's and 1300's that covered the back and sides of the neck. Also, **basnet**. [< Old French *bacinet* (diminutive) < *bacin* basin]

bas|ing point (bā′sing), a manufacturing or shipping center chosen as the base of a system of graduated prices or freight rates, regardless of actual shipping costs or similar factors.

basin range, a type of mountain range formed by the faulting and tilting of a block of strata.

ba|si|on (bā′sē ən), *n.* the middle of the anterior border of the foramen magnum of the skull. [< New Latin *basion* (diminutive) < Greek *básis* basis]

ba|sip|e|tal (bā sip′ə təl), *adj. Botany.* developing from the apex downward toward the base during growth. [< Latin *basis* basis + *petere* to seek + English *-al*[1]]

ba|sis (bā′sis), *n., pl.* **ba|ses**. **1** the part on which anything stands for essential support; fundamental principle; foundation: *The basis of their friendship was a common interest in sports. We judge a worker on the basis of his performance.* **SYN:** support. See also syn. under **base**[1]. **2** the main part; base: *The basis of his business is making watches but he also sells jewelry. The money he got from his father was the basis for a new business.* **SYN:** groundwork, footing. **3** the principal ingredient: *The basis of this medicine is an oil.* [< Latin *basis* < Greek *básis* thing to step or stand on < *baínein* to go, step. See etym. of doublet **base**[1].]
►The plural of **basis** is pronounced bā′sēz, while **base** takes a regular *-s* plural: bā′siz.

bask (bask, bäsk), *v.i.* **1** to warm oneself pleasantly: *The cat basks in the warm sunshine.* **2** *Figurative.* to feel great pleasure: *He basked in the love of his family.* **SYN:** luxuriate. **—*v.t.*** to warm pleasantly: *We basked ourselves on the sunny beach.* [Middle English *basken*] **—bask′er,** *n.*

Bas|ker|ville (bas′kər vil), *n.* any one of various styles of printing type based on those designed by John Baskerville (1706-1775), an English printer and type designer.

***basilica**
definition 1

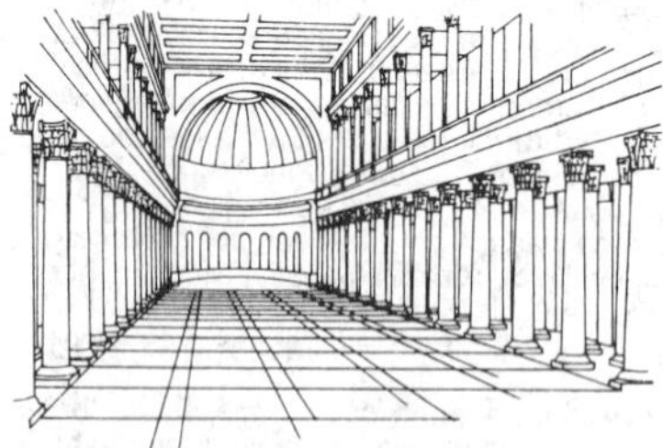

bas|ket (bas′kit, bäs′-), *n., v.* **—*n.*** **1** a container made of twigs, grasses, fibers, strips of wood, or the like, woven together or made of plastic to imitate this: *Mother keeps the laundry in a clothes basket.* **2** the amount that a basket holds: *We ate a basket of peaches.* **3** anything that looks like or is shaped like a basket: *This metal wastepaper basket is dented.* **4** the structure beneath a balloon for carrying passengers, ballast, or material of any sort. **5a** a ring with a net shaped like a basket, but open at the bottom, used as a goal in basketball. **b** a score made in basketball by tossing the ball through this ring with a net. **6** = basket hilt. **7** the ring on a ski pole to keep it from sinking into deep snow. **8** a section of an agreement, or especially a diplomatic declaration, into which the parties to the negotiations include a variety of related proposals: *The 'basket' dealing with cooperation in the field of economics, science, technology and the environment was the least controversial* (John C. Garnett, *Annual Register*).
—*v.t.* to put in a basket: *to basket fruit for the market.*
[origin uncertain] **—bas′ket|like′**, *adj.*

bas|ket|ball (bas′kit bôl′, bäs′-), *n.* **1** a game played with a large, round ball between two teams of five players each. The players try to toss the ball through a ring into a net shaped like a basket but open at the bottom. The ball is dribbled, or thrown from player to player. **2** the ball used in this game.

basket case, **1** a person who has lost both arms and both legs. **2** *U.S. Informal.* a person who has had a mental breakdown; nervous wreck: *There are various degrees of mental illness and a person needn't be a basket case before he decides he should talk things over with a professional* (Ann Landers).

basket cell, one of a layer of tiny, star-shaped cells in the cerebellum whose axons develop terminal branches in a basketlike pattern.

basket chair, a type of wicker chair.

basket cloth, any fabric woven in imitation of the plaiting of a basket.

***bas|ket|fish** (bas′kit fish′, bäs′-), *n., pl.* **-fish|es** or (*collectively*) **-fish**. any one of various small sea animals somewhat resembling a starfish, with slender rays divided into many branches which frequently interlace so as to give a basketlike appearance; basketstar.

***basketfish**
***basket flower**
***basket hilt**

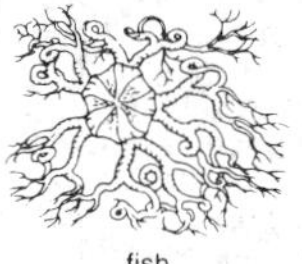
fish

flower

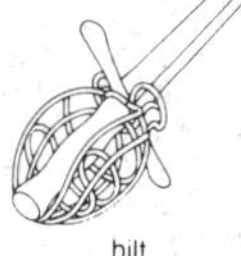
hilt

***basket flower**, an annual plant of the composite family, native to the southwestern United States, having involucres in the form of a basket.

bas|ket|ful (bas′kit fu̇l, bäs′-), *n., pl.* **-fuls**. as much as a basket can hold.

***basket hilt**, a sword hilt of strips of steel curved into basket shape to protect the hand.

Basket Makers, any one of several North American Indian cultures of the southwestern United States that preceded the Pueblo.

basket meeting, *U.S.* a religious meeting held in the form of a picnic.

bas|ket-of-gold (bas′kit əv gōld′, bäs′-), *n.* a perennial plant of the mustard family with yellow flowers and grayish foliage.

bas|ket|ry (bas′kə trē, bäs′-), *n.* **1** the art of making baskets. **2** basketwork; baskets.

bas|ket|star (bas′kit stär′, bäs′-), *n.* = basketfish.

basket weave, a weave in cloth that looks like the interlaced weave used in making baskets.

basket willow, = osier (def. 1).

bas|ket|work (bas′kit wėrk′, bäs′-), *n.* **1** work woven like a basket; wickerwork. **2** the art or occupation of making baskets.

bask|ing shark (bas′king, bäs′-), a large shark, harmless to man, which often floats on the surface of the water to bask in the sun. It ranges in length from about 15 to as much as 40 feet at maturity, and is found in the Northern Hemisphere from arctic waters as far south as Portugal, Virginia, and California.

bas mitz|vah (bäs mits′və), **1** a confirmation ceremony held in a Reform or Conservative synagogue when a Jewish girl becomes thirteen years old, corresponding to the bar mitzvah for boys. **2** the girl herself. Also, **bath mitzvah, bat mitzvah.** [< Hebrew *bath miṣwah* daughter of the commandment]

bas|net (bas′nit), *n.* = basinet.

ba|son (bā′sən), *n.* a wide, shallow bowl used in religious services; basin.

ba|so|phil (bā′sə fil), *n.* **1** a cell, especially a white blood cell, that stains readily with a basic dye. **2** a white blood cell having basophilic granules in the cytoplasm.

ba|so|phile (bā′sə fīl, -fil), *n.* = basophil.

ba|so|phil|i|a (bā′sə fil′ē ə), *n.* **1** an excessive number of basophils in the blood. **2** the presence of basophilic red blood cells in leukemia, lead poisoning, and certain other conditions. [< *basic* + Greek *philíā* a tendency < *phileîn* to love]

ba|so|phil|ic (bā′sə fil′ik), *adj.* staining readily with a basic dye: *basophilic blood cells.*

ba|soph|i|lous (bā sof′ə ləs), *adj.* = basophilic.

Basque (bask), *n., adj.* **—*n.*** **1** one of an ancient people inhabiting the western Pyrenees, in southern France and northern Spain, differing in origin from other Europeans.

2 the language of this people. It is an agglutinative language supposed to derive from that of the ancient Iberians, and is related to no other language now spoken in Europe.
—*adj.* of or having to do with the Basques or their language.
[< French *basque* < Latin *Vascones* people of the Pyrenees]

basque (bask), *n.* **1** a woman's close-fitting bodice that extends below the waist. **2** the continuation of a bodice, forming a kind of short skirt. [probably < *Basque*]

bas-re|lief (bä′ri lēf′, bas′-; bä′ri lēf, bas′-), *n.* carving or sculpture in which the figures stand out only slightly from the background; low relief. Also **basso-relievo**. [< French *bas-relief* < Italian *basso-rilievo*]

***bass**[1] (bās), *n., pl.* **bass|es**, *adj. Music.* —*n.* **1** the lowest male voice: *His bass could be heard booming out of the shower.* **2** a singer with such a voice; basso: *The opera star is a fine bass.* **3** a part in music for such a voice, or for a corresponding instrument: *Who will sing the bass?* **4a** an instrument playing such a part: *Most small orchestras have a string bass.* **b** the low tones of an instrument. *Abbr:* b.
—*adj.* **1** having a deep, low sound: *a bass note.* **2a** for the lowest part in music. **b** that can sing such a part.
[alteration of *base*[2], influenced by Italian *basso* bass]

***bass**[1]
definition 4a

double bass　　electric guitar bass

bass[2] (bas), *n., pl.* **bass|es** or (*collectively*) **bass. 1** a North American fish with spiny fins. Bass live in fresh water or in the ocean and most kinds are used for food, as the black bass, striped bass, calico bass, sea bass, and rock bass. **2** any one of various other fishes belonging to the perch family.
[Middle English *bace,* variant of *barse* perch, Old English *bærs*]

bass[3] (bas), *n.* **1** = basswood. **2** *Botany.* bast; phloem. [< *bast*[1]]

bas|sa|risk (bas′ə risk), *n.* = cacomistle. [< New Latin *Bassariscus* the genus name < Greek *bassaris* fox]

bass-bar (bās′bär′), *n.* an oblong wooden bar running lengthwise within instruments of the violin class, designed to strengthen them against the pressure of the bridge and the tension of the strings.

bass-bar|i|tone (bās′bar′ə tōn), *n.* **1** a male voice with a timbre more resembling that of a bass than of a baritone although its range does not include the lowest bass tones. **2** a person having such a voice.

***bass clef** (bās), a symbol in music showing that the pitch of the notes on a staff is below middle C; F clef.

***bass clef**

bass drum (bās), a large drum that makes a deep, low tone, of no fixed pitch, when struck on one or both of its heads. It is the largest drum now used and is played with its two drumheads usually in a perpendicular position. See picture under **drum**[1].

bas|set[1] (bas′it), *n.,* or **basset hound,** a dog with short legs and a long body. It is built somewhat like a dachshund, but larger and heavier, and has large ears that hang down. Bassets are used in hunting or kept as pets. [< Middle French *basset* < Old French (diminutive adjective) < *bas* low, base[2]]

bas|set[2] (bas′it), *n., v.* —*n.* the edge of a stratum of rock or ore showing at the surface of the ground; outcrop.
—*v.i.* to crop out at the surface of strata.
[perhaps < French *basset* a low stool. See related etym. at **basset**[1].]

bas|set[3] (bas′it), *n.* a card game somewhat resembling faro, invented in Venice, popular throughout Europe during the 1700's. [< Italian *bassetta* (diminutive) < *basso* low, base[2]]

basse-taille (bäs tī′), *n.* an almost transparent enamel laid in thin coats over a design engraved in metal. [< French *basse-taille* < *basse* low + *taille* a cutting; because the design is a bas-relief]

basset horn, an alto clarinet in F, of somewhat greater compass than the ordinary clarinet and slightly bent at top and bottom. It has been replaced by the clarinet in E flat.

basset hound, = basset[1].

bass fiddle (bās), *Informal.* a double bass.

bass horn (bās), **1** = tuba. **2** a wind instrument devised in the 1700's as an improvement on the serpent.

bas|si|net (bas′ə net′, bas′ə net), *n.* **1** a basketlike cradle for a baby, usually with a hood over one end. **2** a child's perambulator of a similar shape. [< French *bassinet* (diminutive) < *bassin* basin]

bass|ist (bā′sist), *n.* **1** the player of a bass part or a bass instrument. **2** = basso.

bas|so (bas′ō; *Italian* bäs′sō), *n., pl.* **bas|sos**; *Italian* **bas|si** (bäs′sē). **1** a singer with a bass voice. **2** the bass part. [< Italian *basso* < Medieval Latin *bassus.* See etym. of doublet **base**[2].]

basso can|tan|te (kən tän′tē; *Italian* kän tän′tā), *pl.* **bassi can|tan|ti** (kän tän′tē). a high bass voice, suitable for solo singing. [< Italian *basso cantante; cantante* singing < *cantare* sing < Latin *cantare*]

basso con|tin|u|o (kən tin′yü ō), *pl.* **basso con|tin|u|os.** *Music.* thorough bass. [< Italian *basso continuo; continuo* continuous < Latin *continuus;* see etym. under **continue**]

bas|so da cam|e|ra (bas′ō də kam′ə rə), a contrabass reduced in size and power but not in compass, and thus adapted to small rooms. [< Italian *basso da camera* (literally) chamber bass]

***bas|soon** (bə sün′, ba-), *n.* **1** a deep-toned wind instrument with a doubled wooden body and a curved metal pipe to which a double reed is attached. The bassoon belongs to the same class as the oboe. **2** a stop in a reed pipe of an organ, having a quality of tone similar to that of the bassoon. [< French *basson* < Italian *bassone* < *basso* basso]

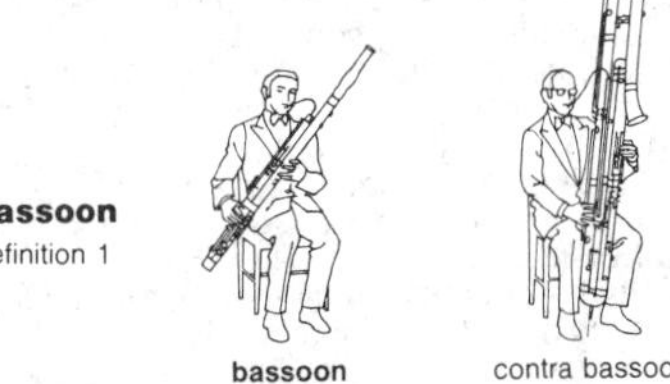

***bassoon**
definition 1

bassoon　　contra bassoon

bas|soon|ist (bə sü′nist, ba-), *n.* a person who plays the bassoon.

basso pro|fon|do (prə fon′dō), *pl.* **basso pro|fon|dos. 1** a deep bass voice having a compass of about two octaves above C below the bass staff. **2** a singer having such a voice. [< Italian *basso profondo; profondo* < Latin *profundus*]

basso pro|fun|do (prə fun′dō), *pl.* **basso pro|fun|dos.** = basso profondo.

bas|so-re|lie|vo (bas′ō ri lē′vō), *n., pl.* **-vos.** = bas-relief. [< Italian *basso-rilievo* bas-relief]

bass reflex (bās), **1** an opening at the front of a loudspeaker cabinet that permits sounds from the back to escape so as to reinforce or improve the reproduction of bass tones. **2** a speaker equipped with such an opening.

bass staff (bās), a musical staff indicating the bass clef.

bass viol (bās), **1** = double bass. **2** = viola da gamba (def. 1).

bass|wood (bas′wu̇d′), *n.* **1a** any one of several trees having a fine straight-grained hardwood, that grow to a considerable height in their native temperate regions; American linden tree; bass; whitewood. **b** its wood. **2** *Dialect.* the tulip tree. [American English < *bass*[3] + *wood*]

basswood family, a family of dicotyledonous trees and shrubs, mostly tropical but including the lindens.

bast[1] (bast), *n.* **1** the inner layer of the bark of trees that contains cells for carrying sap; phloem. **2** the tough fiber in the inner bark of certain trees, used especially in making rope and matting. [Old English *bæst*]

bast[2] (bast), *n.* (in Iran) the right or privilege of political sanctuary.

bas|tard (bas′tərd), *n., adj.* —*n.* **1** a child whose parents are not legally married to each other; illegitimate child. **2** *Figurative.* anything inferior or not genuine, especially anything of bad or spurious origin. **3** *Slang.* an especially unpleasant, disliked, and usually unscrupulous, person.
—*adj.* **1** born of parents who are not married to each other; illegitimate. **2** *Figurative.* not genuine; inferior: *Such poems by such poets should remove misconceptions about light verse as a kind of bastard poetry* (Atlantic). **SYN:** counterfeit, debased, adulterated, corrupt. **3** irregular or unusual in shape, size, style, or the like: *a bastard wheel.* **4** somewhat resembling, but not identical with (used in this sense especially in plant and animal names): *bastard mahogany.*
[< Old French *bastard* < (*fils de*) *bast* (son of) a packsaddle; *bast,* perhaps < Gothic *bansti* barn (hence, baseborn offspring)] —**bas′tard|ly,** *adj.*

Bas|tard (bas′tərd), *n.* (in South Africa) a mulatto; Griqua. [< obsolete Afrikaans *Bastaard* (now *Baster*)]

bastard file, a file of a grade between smooth and rough.

bas|tard|ize (bas′tər dīz), *v.,* **-ized, -iz|ing.** —*v.t.* **1** to make degenerate; debase: *Spanish craft has been bastardized by generations of artisans who each added their own elaborations* (Wall Street Journal). **2** to declare or pronounce to be a bastard.
—*v.i.* to become degenerate; deteriorate. —**bas′tard|i|za′tion,** *n.*

bastard title, = half title (def. 1).

bastard turtle, a kind of sea turtle found in the coastal waters of North America; ridley.

bastard type, a font of type cast on a body smaller or larger than the usual body.

bastard wing, = alula.

bas|tard|y (bas′tər dē), *n., pl.* **-tard|ies.** = illegitimacy.

baste[1] (bāst), *v.t.,* **bast|ed, bast|ing.** to drip or pour melted fat or butter on (meat or fowl) while roasting: *The cook basted the turkey to keep it from drying out and to improve its flavor.* [< Old North French *basser* to moisten] —**bast′er,** *n.*

baste[2] (bāst), *v.t.,* **bast|ed, bast|ing.** to sew with long, loose stitches in order to hold the cloth for further work or until final sewing: *to baste a hem in place, baste a dress.* [< Old North French *bastir* < Frankish (compare Old High German *bestan* sew with bast)] —**bast′er,** *n.*

baste[3] (bāst), *v.t.,* **bast|ed, bast|ing.** to beat soundly; thrash. **SYN:** cudgel, punish. [probably < Scandinavian (compare Old Icelandic *beysta*)]

Bas|tille (bas tēl′), *n.* an old fort in Paris used as a prison, especially for enemies of the king. A mob captured it on July 14, 1789, at the beginning of the French Revolution, and later destroyed it.

bas|tille or **bas|tile** (bas tēl′), *n.* **1** a prison, especially an oppressive one. **2** any prison, jail, or other place of detention. [< Middle French *bastille,* alteration of Old French *bastide* < Old Provençal *bastida* wooden siege tower < *bastir* build < Late Latin *bastīre*]

Bastille Day, July 14, a French national holiday commemorating the capture of the Bastille. It corresponds to Independence Day (July 4) in the United States.

bas|ti|nade (bas′tə nād′), *n., v.t.,* **-nad|ed, -nad|ing.** = bastinado.

bas|ti|na|do (bas′tə nā′dō), *n., pl.* **-does,** *v.,* **-doed, -do|ing.** —*n.* **1a** a beating with a stick, especially on the soles of the feet. **b** such a beating, or a beating of the upper thighs and buttocks, or both, as a kind of punishment, still used in parts of Asia. **2** a stick; cudgel: *They did this … without riots of protest or direct coercion of the bastinado or bayonet* (Time).
—*v.t.* to beat or flog with a stick, especially on the soles of the feet.
[< Spanish *bastonada* < *bastón* stick < Late Latin *bastum*]

bast|ing (bās′ting), *n.* **1** the moistening of meat while roasting, with drippings or other liquid. **2** the liquid used.

bast|ings (bās′tingz), *n.pl.* **1** long, loose stitches to hold cloth in place until the final sewing. **2** the threads used for these.

***bastion**
definition 1

***bas|tion** (bas′chən, -tē ən), *n.* **1** a part of a fortification that sticks out so that the defenders can fire at attackers from as many angles as possible. **2** *Figurative.* a stronghold; center of defense:

Pronunciation Key: hat, āge, cãre, fär; let, ēqual, tėrm; it, īce; hot, ōpen, ôrder; oil, out; cup, pu̇t, rüle; child; long; thin; ᴛʜen; zh, measure; ə represents **a** in about, **e** in taken, **i** in pencil, **o** in lemon, **u** in circus.

. . . *a bastion of free world democracy* (Newsweek). SYN: defense, fortification. [< Middle French *bastion,* variant of *bastillon* (diminutive) < *bastille* bastille]

bas|tioned (bas′chənd, -tē ənd), *adj.* provided with or defended by bastions.

bast|na|site or **bast|nae|site** (bast′nə sīt), *n.* an ore, a carbonate fluoride of cerium. *Formula:* $CeFCO_3$ [< French *bastnaesite* < *Bastnäs,* Sweden, where it is mined]

Ba|su|to (bə sü′tō), *n., pl.* **-to** or **-tos,** *adj.* **—*n.*** a member of the Bantu tribe inhabiting Lesotho (the former Basutoland) and the western border of Natal; Sotho: *Those Basutos now dwell among their mountain fastnesses, with only a swathe of fertile soil left to them after their last disastrous war against the Boers* (C. C. Spencer).
—*adj.* of or having to do with the Basuto.
[< Bantu *Ba-sotho,* plural]

bat¹ (bat), *n., v.,* **bat|ted, bat|ting.** **—*n.*** **1a** a stout wooden stick or club, used to hit the ball in baseball, cricket, and similar games: *The hitter swung the bat and hit a home run.* **b** a racket used in certain games, such as tennis. **c** *U.S. Informal.* a jockey's whip. **2a** the act of batting. **b** a turn at batting: *Who goes to bat first?* **c** a batter or batsman. **3** *Informal.* a stroke; blow. **4** *U.S. Slang.* a wild time; spree. **5** Also, **batt. a** a sheet of cotton wadding, often used for filling quilts; batting. **b** a felted mass of fur, or of hair and wool, used in making hats. **c** a flexible sheet of fiberglass and rock wool, used for insulation. **6** a lump or other piece of certain substances, such as brick, plaster, or clay, especially a flat disk used for various purposes in ceramics. **7** *Dialect and Slang.* rate of stroke or speed; pace.
—*v.i.* *Baseball.* **1** to strike, or strike at, the ball with a bat: *The new pitcher also bats well.* **2** to be at bat; take one's turn as a batter.
—*v.t.* to hit with a bat; hit: *The kitten batted the balloon with its paws.*
at bat, *U.S.* in position to bat; having a turn at batting: *Our side is at bat.*
bat around, a *Slang.* to go from place to place without any definite purpose; move according to the whim of the moment: *His parents gave him a shiny 1920 Buick to bat around in* (New Yorker). **b** *U.S., Slang.* to discuss (something) freely and more or less at random: *to bat a topic around.*
bat in, *Baseball.* to hit the ball so that a player can score: *to bat in a man from second, to bat in the winning run.*
bat out, *U.S. Slang.* to create quickly and more or less casually: *to bat out an outline of a story in two hours.*
carry one's bat, *Cricket.* to be not out when the other ten wickets of an innings have fallen: *The team made its runs in less than two hours and carried out its bats.*
go to bat for, *Informal.* to support the cause of: *You need a really important figure to go to bat for you* (New Yorker).
off one's own bat, *Informal.* on one's own initiative; without help from others; single-handedly: . . . *initiating off his own bat such enterprises as the famous Broadway Translations* (Saturday Review).
right off the bat, *Informal.* without hesitation or deliberation; immediately; quickly: *He made two sales right off the bat.*
take out one's bat, *Cricket.* to be not out at the end of the innings.
[Middle English *batte* cudgel, Old English *batt*]

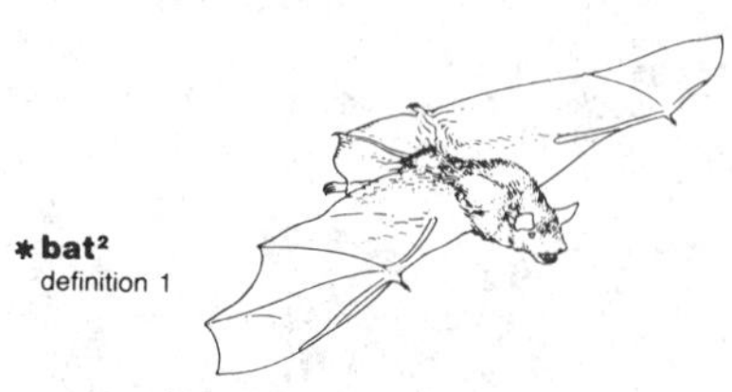

***bat²**
definition 1

***bat²** (bat), *n.* **1** a flying mammal with a body like that of a mouse and wings made of thin skin that are supported by the long, slim bones of the forelimbs; chiropter. Bats fly at night and most eat insects, but some live on fruit and a few suck the blood of other mammals. There are over 1000 species, with bodies varying in size from one and a half inches to twelve inches. **2** a type of bomb with wings, which may be released from an aircraft to glide to its target, guided by radar.
bats in the belfry, *Slang.* **a** the condition of being insane: *The sahib had bats in his belfry, and must be humoured* (Blackwood's Magazine). **b** oddness or unpredictability in behavior: *It's a case of bats in his belfry on that one subject* (R. D. Saunders).
blind as a bat, *Informal.* completely blind; totally unable to see: *He felt blind as a bat without his glasses.*
like a bat out of hell, *Slang.* with great speed; recklessly: *to drive like a bat out of hell.*
[alteration of Middle English *bakke,* perhaps < Scandinavian (compare Danish *-bakke*)] **—bat′-like′,** *adj.*

Pronunciation Key: hat, āge, cãre, fär; let, ēqual, tėrm; it, īce; hot, ōpen, ôrder; oil, out; cup, pu̇t, rüle; child; long; thin; ᴛʜen; zh, measure; ə represents **a** in about, **e** in taken, **i** in pencil, **o** in lemon, **u** in circus.

bat³ (bat), *v.t.,* **bat|ted, bat|ting.** *Informal.* to move (the eyelids) quickly; wink (the eyes), especially from surprise or emotion: *The rock nearly hit him, but he didn't bat an eye. . . . don't you bat your eyes to please none of 'em* (Joel Chandler Harris). [variant of *bate* flutter, beat the wings < Old French *batre* strike]

bat⁴ (bät), *n.* = baht.

bat., **1** battalion. **2** battery.

Ba|ta|vi|an (bə tā′vē ən), *adj., n.* **—*adj.*** **1** of the Netherlands; Dutch. **2** of Batavia (now Djakarta).
—*n.* **1** a native or inhabitant of the Netherlands; Dutchman. **2** a native or inhabitant of Batavia (now Djakarta).

bat boy, *U.S.* a young man who takes care of the bats of a baseball team, especially during a game.

batch¹ (bach), *n., v.* **—*n.*** **1** the quantity of anything made as one lot or set: *Our second batch of candy was better than the first.* SYN: lot, installment. **2** a number of persons or things put together or treated together; set: *He caught a big batch of fish. The A.E.C. will not yet divulge which countries have been chosen to send the first batch of students to this school* (Wall Street Journal). **3a** the quantity of bread, cookies, or rolls made at one baking: *All of the baker's first batch burned.* **b** the quantity of dough to be used for one baking.
—*v.t.* **1** to collect or assemble in a batch or batches. **2** to measure out for mixing, as cement and gravel for making concrete.
[Middle English *bacche* < Old English *bacan* bake]

batch² (bach), *n., v.i.* = bach¹.

batch processing, data processing in which all related operations are grouped in a batch before any of them is executed.

bate¹ (bāt), *v.,* **bat|ed, bat|ing.** **—*v.t.*** to deduct; lessen; hold back. SYN: abate.
—*v.i.* *Obsolete* or *Dialect.* to decrease, especially in size, amount, or force.
with bated breath, holding the breath in great fear, wonder, or interest: *The boys listened to the sailor's story with bated breath.*
[shortened form of *abate*]

bate² (bāt), *v.i.,* **bat|ed, bat|ing.** to beat the wings impatiently or attempt to take flight, as of a falcon or hawk; flutter: *Cressida recognized the point and wanted to take the air, but I checked her. She bated in fury* (New Yorker). [older variant of *bat³*]

bate³ (bāt), *v.,* **bat|ed, bat|ing,** *n. British Dialect.*
—*v.i.* to contend; quarrel.
—*n.* contention; strife; debate.
[shortened form of *debate*]

bate⁴ (bāt), *n., v.,* **bat|ed, bat|ing.** **—*n.*** a solution of dung or other alkaline substance used to soften hides in tanning.
—*v.t.* to soften (hides) by soaking in such a solution.
[Probably < Scandinavian (compare Swedish *beta* to soak, tan)]

bat-eared (bat′ird′), *adj.* **1** having upright ears with rounded tips, somewhat like those of a bat: *a bat-eared foxhound.* **2** *U.S. Informal.* (of a person) having such ears.

***ba|teau** (ba tō′), *n., pl.* **-teaux** (-tōz′). a light riverboat with a flat bottom and tapering ends, used in Canada and Louisiana. Also, **batteau.** [American English < French *bateau,* perhaps ultimately < Old English *bāt* boat]

***bateau**

bateau neck or **neckline,** a high neckline on a sweater, dress, or blouse, the line of the fabric being almost straight across from shoulder to shoulder; boat neck or neckline.

bate|leur (bat lœr′), *n.* a species of eagle found in South Africa, having extremely short tail feathers. [< French *bateleur*]

Bates|i|an mimicry (bāt′sē ən), protective mimicry. [< Henry Walter *Bates,* 1825-1892, an English naturalist + *-ian*]

bat|fish (bat′fish′), *n., pl.* **-fish|es** or (*collectively*) **-fish. 1** any one of a family of fishes shaped somewhat like a bat, especially one of a species found in the Atlantic along the coast of the southern United States; sea bat. **2** = sting ray.

bat|fowl (bat′foul′), *v.i.* to catch birds at night by dazing them with a light, and knocking them down or netting them. [< *bat¹* + *fowl,* verb] **—bat′fowl′er,** *n.*

bath¹ (bath, bäth), *n., pl.* **baths** (baᴛʜz, bäᴛʜz), *v.* **—*n.*** **1** the act of washing, dipping, or soaking the body, especially for cleansing: *He took a hot bath.* **2** water in a tub for a bath: *Your bath is ready.* **3a** a tub for bathing; bathtub: *a full-length bath.* **b** a room for bathing; bathroom: *We bought a house with three bedrooms and two baths.* **4** a building containing facilities for bathing: *a public bath, a Turkish bath.* **5** Often, **baths.** (in ancient times, especially in Rome) an elaborate establishment used for bathing and also for various forms of exercise and recreation; thermae. **6** Often, **baths.** a place or resort with baths for medical treatment, especially in water containing minerals. **7a** liquid in which something is washed or dipped: *a bath for developing photographic film.* **b** the container holding the liquid. **8a** a device for modifying and regulating the temperature of something by interposing sand, water, oil, or other insulating substance between the fire and the vessel to be heated. **b** the receptacle containing the insulating substance. **9** *Metallurgy.* the mass of molten metal in a furnace.
—*v.t., v.i.* *British.* to bathe; wash or immerse in a bath.
take a bath, *U.S. Slang.* to suffer a setback: *the scion of a family that had become wealthy in the silk-dyeing industry in Paterson, but took a bath in the Depression* (Time).
[Old English *bæth*] **—bath′less,** *adj.*

bath² (bath), *n.* either of two ancient Hebrew units of liquid measure, estimated to have been equal to about 7.5 and 9.5 U.S. gallons. [< Hebrew *bath*]

Bath brick, a preparation of fine sand containing much silica, molded in the form of a brick, for cleaning and polishing metal. [< *Bath,* England]

Bath or **bath bun,** *British.* a sweet roll made of yeast dough, usually glazed with sugar or covered with candied fruit. [< *Bath,* England]

Bath or **bath chair,** a wheel chair for invalids, sometimes one with a hood. [< *Bath,* England]

bathe (bāᴛʜ), *v.,* **bathed, bath|ing,** *n.* **—*v.i.*** **1** to take a bath: *Some boys don't like to bathe regularly.* **2** *Especially British.* to go swimming; go into a river, lake, or ocean, for pleasure or to get cool. **3** *Figurative.* to bask; be immersed.
—*v.t.* **1** to give a bath to: *He is bathing his dog.* SYN: lave. **2** to apply water to; wash or moisten with any liquid: *Bathe your feet if they are so tired. The doctor told her to bathe her eyes with the lotion.* SYN: wet. **3** *Figurative.* to cover or surround: *a field bathed in sunlight.* SYN: suffuse.
—*n.* *Especially British.* a bath or swim: *His wife suddenly said she wanted to have a bathe at the little bay* (Cape Times).
[Old English *bathian*] **—bath′er,** *n.*

ba|thet|ic (bə thet′ik), *adj.* showing bathos; characterized by bathos: *The whole enterprise winds up with a dishevelled, richly bathetic funeral scene* (New Yorker). **—ba|thet′i|cal|ly,** *adv.*

bath|house (bath′hous′, bäth′-), *n.* **1a** a building containing dressing rooms for swimmers. **b** a small structure for dressing in, on, or near a beach; cabaña. **2** a building fitted for bathing.

bath|i|nette (bath′ə net′, bäth′-), *n.* a small folding bathtub covered with a rubberized fabric and used for bathing and dressing infants.

bath|ing beauty (bā′ᴛʜing), **1** a participant in a beauty contest among young women in bathing suits. **2** any very attractive young woman.

bathing cap, a rubber cap for covering the head while swimming.

bathing costume, *British.* a bathing suit.

bathing drawers, *British, Obsolete.* a bathing suit.

bathing dress, *British.* a bathing suit.

bathing machine, a covered vehicle which can be run out into the water and used as a dressing room for a bather.

bathing suit, a garment worn for swimming.

bath mat, a mat for use on a bathroom floor or in a bathtub.

bath mitz|vah (bäth mits′və), = bas mitzvah.

bath|o|chrome (bath′ə krōm), *n.* a group of atoms or a radical which, when introduced into an organic compound, causes its absorption spectrum to shift toward the red. [< Greek *báthos* depth + *chrôma* color (because red is "downward" on the spectrum)]

bath|o|chro|mic (bath′ə krō′mik), *adj.* of or having to do with a bathochrome.

bath|o|lite (bath′ə līt), *n.* = batholith.

bath|o|lith (bath′ə lith), *n.* a great mass of granite or other igneous rock intruded below the surface, commonly along the axis of a mountain range, and sometimes exposed by erosion. [< Greek *báthos* depth + *líthos* stone]

bath|o|lith|ic (bath′ə lith′ik), *adj.* having to do with or resembling a batholith.

bath|o|lit|ic (bath′ə lit′ik), *adj.* = batholithic.

Bath Oliver, *British.* an unsweetened digestive biscuit. [< William *Oliver,* 1695-1764, a physician of Bath, England, who supposedly invented it]

ba|thom|e|ter (bə thom′ə tər), *n.* an instrument to determine the depth of water.

bat|horse (bat′hôrs′, bä′hôrs′), *n.* a horse for carrying baggage, especially as once used in the British Army. [< *bat* packsaddle + *horse*]

ba|thos (bā′thos), *n.* **1** ludicrous descent from the elevated to the commonplace in speech or writing. *Example:* "The exile came back to his home, crippled, unfriended, and hatless." *Some American newspapers found room on page one for long stories full of bathos and penny-a-line Freudian theory* (Atlantic). **SYN**: anticlimax. **2** strained or insincere pathos. [< Greek *báthos* depth]

bath|robe (bath′rōb′, bäth′-), *n.* a long, loose garment worn to and from a bath or when resting or lounging.

bath|room (bath′rüm′, -rům′; bäth′-), *n.* **1** a room fitted out for taking baths, and now usually equipped with a sink and a toilet. **2** a room containing a toilet.

baths (baᴛʜz, bäᴛʜz), *n.pl.* See under **bath**[1] (*n.* defs. 5, 6).

bath salts, any of various compounds, especially a scented mixture of sea salts and borax, by which the water of a bath is softened and made fragrant.

Bath|she|ba (bath shē′bə, bath′shə-), *n.* the mother of Solomon. King David married her after sending her first husband, Uriah, to his death in combat (in the Bible, II Samuel 11:3-27).

bath sponge, a sponge used for bathing.

Bath or **bath stone**, a building stone quarried from oolitic formations. [< *Bath,* England]

bath towel, a large, usually thick, towel made of terry cloth for use after bathing.

bath|tub (bath′tub′, bäth′-), *n.* a tub to bathe in, especially one permanently fixed in a bathroom.

bathtub gin, *U.S. Slang.* any homemade gin, especially during the period of national prohibition.

bath|wa|ter (bath′wôt′ər, -wot′-; bäth′-), *n.* water for a bath.

bath|y|al (bath′ē əl), *adj.* of or having to do with the deeper levels of the ocean, especially depths of approximately 600 to 6000 feet. [< Greek *bathýs* deep + English *-al*[1]]

ba|thyb|ic (bə thib′ik), *adj.* living in deep water: *bathybic plankton.* [< Greek *bathýs* deep + *bíos* life + English *-ic*]

bath|y|gram (bath′ə gram), *n.* a graphic record of water depth obtained from an echo sounder. [< Greek *bathýs* deep + English *-gram*[1]]

bath|y|met|ric (bath′ə met′rik), *adj.* having to do with bathymetry.

ba|thym|e|try (bə thim′ə trē), *n.* **1** the science of depth measurement, especially of the sea. **2** the study of the vertical distribution of animal life in the sea. [< Greek *bathýs* deep + English *-metry*]

bath|y|pe|lag|ic (bath′ə pə laj′ik), *adj.* of or having to do with the depths of the sea. [< Greek *bathýs* deep + *pélagos* the sea + English *-ic*]

bath|y|pho|tom|e|ter (bath′ə fō tom′ə tər), *n.* an instrument for measuring the intensity of light in the sea, especially at a relatively deep level. [< Greek *bathýs* deep + English *photometer*]

bath|y|pi|tom|e|ter (bath′ə pi tom′ə tər), *n.* an instrument for measuring the temperature, depth, and rate of movement of a marine current. [< Greek *bathýs* deep + English *Pitot* (tube) + *-meter*]

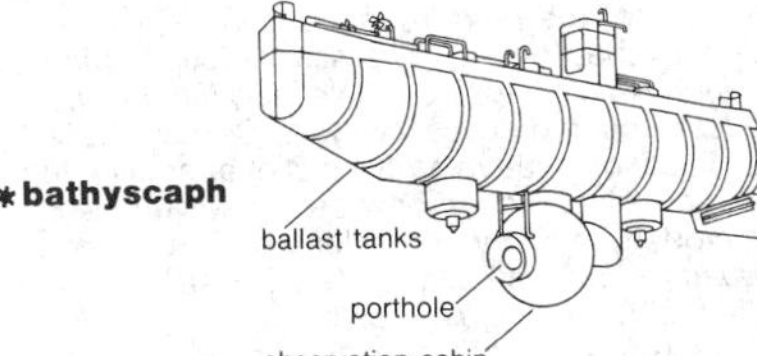

***bathyscaph**

***bath|y|scaph** or **bath|y|scaphe** (bath′ə skaf), *n.* a diving craft consisting of a round steel chamber attached to a hull that can be navigated underwater to explore the depths of the sea: *The bathyscaph's basic idea is to imitate underwater the free-flying balloon of the air* (Manchester Guardian). [< Greek *bathýs* deep + *skáphē* a bowl, tub]

bath|y|sphere (bath′ə sfir), *n.* a watertight steel ball with observation windows, lowered by cables from a ship, formerly used to study the depths of the sea and deep-sea life. [< Greek *bathýs* deep + English *sphere*]

bath|y|ther|mo|graph (bath′ə thėr′mə graf, -gräf), *n.* an instrument for measuring the temperature of the sea, especially at a deep level. [< Greek *bathýs* deep + *thérmē* heat + English *-graph*]

ba|tik (bə tēk′, bat′ik), *n., adj., v.* —*n.* **1** the art and method of making designs on cloth by dyeing only part at a time, the rest being protected by a removable coating of wax. **2** a cloth dyed in this way. **3** a design formed in this way. **4** a design, consisting of a medley of colors, characteristic of or patterned on that of this art.
—*adj.* **1** made by batik; made of batik. **2** like batik; brightly or gaily colored.
—*v.t.* to dye by batik. Also, **battik**.
[< Javanese *mbatik* writing, drawing]

bat|ing (bā′ting), *prep. Archaic.* leaving out of account; excepting; except. [present participle of *bate*[1]]

ba|tiste (bə tēst′), *n.* a fine, thin cloth made of cotton, rayon, or wool. It has the same texture as cambric but is differently finished. [< French *batiste* < Middle French *baptiste* < *Baptiste* of Cambrai, the alleged first maker]

bat|man (bat′mən), *n., pl.* **-men**. *British.* an enlisted man assigned to act as an officer's orderly. [< *bat* packsaddle + *man*]

bat mitz|vah (bät mits′və), = bas mitzvah.

***ba|ton** (ba ton′, bə-), *n.* **1** the light stick or wand used by the leader of an orchestra, chorus, or band to indicate the beat and direct the performance: *As the conductor lowered the baton the band began to play.* **2** a staff or stick used as a mark of office or authority: *a marshal's baton.* **3** a light, hollow metal rod twirled rapidly by a drum major or majorette as a showy display. **4** the light stick passed from runner to runner in a relay race. Each member of the team carries it for part of the race, passing it on to the next runner as he completes his part of a race. **5** *Heraldry.* (in England) a sign of illegitimacy. It is a truncheon with the ends cut off so as not to reach the edges of the shield, placed diagonally on a coat of arms, its upper end on the bearer's left. [< Middle French *baton* < Old French *baston,* ultimately < Late Latin *bastum* stout staff]

baton gun, a weapon shaped somewhat like a baton, designed to shoot bullets made of hard rubber and used especially in riot control.

ba|ton|ist (ba ton′ist, bə-), *n.* the conductor of an orchestra or band.

ba|tra|chi|an (bə trā′kē ən), *adj., n.* —*adj.* **1** of or having to do with the division of vertebrate animals consisting of tailless amphibians, typified by the frogs and toads. **2** like frogs and toads. **3** of frogs and toads.
—*n.* a tailless amphibian: *Frogs and toads are batrachians.*
[< New Latin *Batrachia* < Greek *batrácheia* (*zôia*) froglike (animals) < *bátrachos* frog]

bat|ra|choid (bat′rə koid), *adj.* froglike. [< Greek *bátrachos* frog + English *-oid*]

bat ray, = sting ray.

bats (bats), *adj. Slang.* batty; crazy: *Every time I go some place, it's who are you going with, ... when did you do the dishes last, etc., it's driving me bats* (Newsweek).

bats|man (bats′mən), *n., pl.* **-men**. *British.* the player whose turn it is to bat in cricket; batter.

bats|man|ship (bats′mən ship), *n. British.* the batsman's art; the art of batting at cricket; batting performance.

Bat|swa|na (bat swä′nə, bät′-), *n., pl.* **-na** or **-nas**. a member of the native people of Botswana; Bechuana; Tswana.

batt (bat), *n.* = bat[1] (def. 5).

batt., **1** battalion. **2** battery.

bat|tail|ous (bat′ə ləs), *adj. Archaic.* warlike. [< Old French *battailleus* < *bataille* battle]

bat|ta|lia (bə tāl′yə), *n. Archaic.* **1** order of battle; battle array. **2** a large body of men in battle array or on the march; a marshaled force. **3** the main body or center of an army. [< Italian *battaglia* < Late Latin *battālia* fencing exercises; see etym. under **battalion**]

bat|tal|ion (bə tal′yən), *n.* **1** a tactical unit made up of a headquarters and two or more companies, batteries, or similar organizations. It may be part of a regiment, but separate battalions exist that are administrative as well as tactical units. **2** any large division of an army organized to act together. *Abbr:* bn. **3** an army. **4** any large group organized to work together: *A battalion of volunteers helped to rescue the flood victims.*
battalions, a large number: *battalions of teachers. The soldier-settlers ... came to plant battalions of coffee trees* (Manchester Guardian Weekly).
[< Middle French *bataillon* < Italian *battaglione* < *battaglia* troop < Late Latin *battālia* fencing exercises < Latin *battuere* strike]

bat|teau (ba tō′), *n., pl.* **-teaux** (-tōz′). = bateau.

bat|tel (bat′əl), *v.i.* (at Oxford and Durham universities) to have a college account for board and provisions. [perhaps < obsolete *battle* receive nourishment] —**bat′tel|er**, *n.*

bat|tels (bat′əlz), *n.pl.* at Oxford and Durham universities: **1** college accounts for board and provisions. **2** all one's college accounts.

batte|ment (bat′mənt; *French* bȧt mäɴ′), *n. Ballet.* a movement or pose in which one leg is lifted either high or low. [< French *battement* < *battre* to beat]

bat|ten[1] (bat′ən), *n., v.* —*n.* **1** a strip of wood nailed over the adjoining edges of parallel boards of a door, wall, etc., to strengthen them or cover the cracks. **2** a board used for flooring, usually 6 or more feet long, 7 inches wide, and 2½ inches thick. Battens may be found in barns, and in some early American houses. **3** a narrow strip of wood used in any of various ways on shipboard, such as to protect a mast or spar, to keep a sail flat, or to fasten tarpaulins over hatchways: *The sailors nailed battens over the hatches to hold the covers during the storm.*
—*v.t.* to strengthen or cover with battens.
batten down, to fasten down with or as if with strips of wood: *to batten down the hatches before a storm.*
[variant of *baton*]

bat|ten[2] (bat′ən), *v.i.* **1** to grow fat; thrive: *The cattle battened on the plentiful fodder.* (*Figurative.*) *Melancholy sceptics ... who batten on the hideous facts in history* (Emerson). **SYN**: prosper. **2** to feed greedily; glut oneself. —*v.t. Obsolete.* to feed to advantage; fatten up; fatten.
[< Scandinavian (compare Old Icelandic *batna* improve)] —**bat′ten|er**, *n.*

bat|ten[3] (bat′ən), *n.* a movable bar or arm in a loom which strikes in or closes the weft. [< French *battant* < Old French *batre*]

bat|ter[1] (bat′ər), *v., n.* —*v.t.* **1** to strike with repeated blows so as to bruise, break, or get out of shape; pound: *The fireman battered the door down with a heavy ax.* (*Figurative.*) *Blizzards battered Britain for the third day* (Wall Street Journal). **2** to damage by hard use: *The books were old and battered.*
—*v.i.* to inflict repeated blows; pound: *to batter away at a door.*
—*n. Printing.* **1** a damaged place on the face of printing type or a stereotype plate. **2** a blur or defect in a sheet produced by bruised type. **3** the damaged type.
[probably < Old French *batre* beat < Latin *battuere* strike] —**bat′ter|er**, *n.*

bat|ter[2] (bat′ər), *n., v.* —*n.* a thick liquid mixture of flour, milk, and eggs that becomes solid when cooked. Cakes, pancakes, and muffins are made from batter. A batter may always be poured, as distinguished from *dough.*
—*v.t.* to make into a batter.
[perhaps < Old French *bature* a beating < *batre;* see etym. under **batter**[1]]

bat|ter[3] (bat′ər), *n.* the player whose turn it is to bat in baseball, cricket, and similar games. Also, *British,* **batsman**. [< *bat*[1] + *-er*[1]]

bat|ter[4] (bat′ər), *v., n.* —*v.i., v.t.* to slant gradually backward from the base, as a retaining wall.

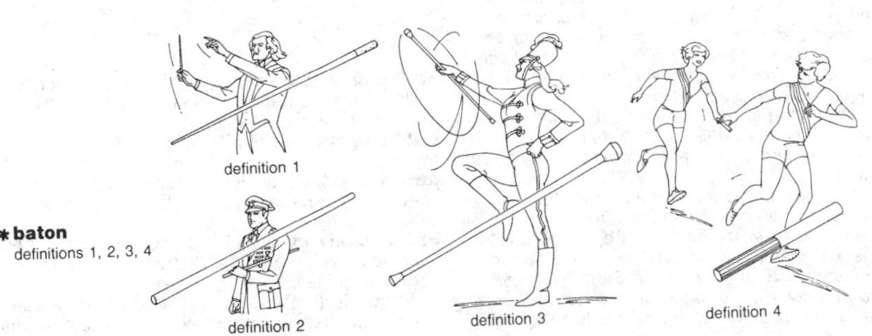

definition 1

definition 2

definition 3

definition 4

***baton**
definitions 1, 2, 3, 4

—*n.* a decrease in thickness of a wall from base to top, made by slanting the outer face. [perhaps < Old French *abatre* to beat down < Latin *battuere* to beat]

batter board, one of the boards fastened horizontally to posts near the corners of an excavation to which strings are stretched to mark the outlines of the wall or building.

bat|ter|cake (bat′ər kāk′), *n.* a pancake; griddlecake.

bat|tered child syndrome (bat′ərd), a condition of severe bruises or other injuries in small children who have been repeatedly beaten or otherwise mistreated by their parents or guardians.

bat|ter|ie (bat′ər ē; *French* bȧ trē′), *n. Ballet.* a movement in which the dancer beats the calves or feet together during a leap. [< French *batterie* < *battre* to beat]

battering ram, **1** a heavy beam used in ancient and medieval warfare for battering down walls and gates. Some battering rams had an iron piece in the shape of a ram's head mounted on a frame at one end. **2a** any heavy object used to break down a door or wall. **b** *Figurative.* anything similar in purpose or effect.

batter's box, *Baseball.* a rectangle marked off in white on either side of the plate, in which a batter must stand while at bat.

bat|ter|y (bat′ər ē, bat′rē), *n., pl.* **-ter|ies.** **1a** a container holding materials that produce electricity by chemical action; a single electric cell: *Most flashlights work on two batteries.* **b** a set of two or more electric cells that produce electric current: *The car won't start because the battery is dead.* **2** *Figurative.* any set of similar or connected things: *The President spoke before a battery of television cameras. If you want this job, you will have to take a battery of tests.* **3** a set of similar pieces of equipment such as mounted guns, searchlights, or mortars, used as a unit: *Four artillery batteries began firing on the enemy.* **4a** a platform or fortification equipped with two or more pieces of artillery. **b** a military unit of artillery, usually commanded by a captain and comprising four pieces of artillery together with the soldiers who serve them. A battery corresponds to a company or troop in other branches of the army. **5** the armament (or any part of it) of a warship: *a main battery of 8-inch guns.* **6** *Baseball.* the pitcher and catcher together. **7** a group of closely arranged cages for raising chicks or chickens in a minimum of space. **8** *Law.* an unlawful beating of another person or any threatening touch to his clothes or body. **9** (collectively) the percussion instruments of an orchestra. [< Middle French *batterie* < Old French *baterie* a battering, a rampart < *batre* beat < Latin *battuere* strike]

bat|tik (bat′ik), *n., adj., v.t.* = batik.

bat|ting (bat′ing), *n.* **1** the action or manner of using or striking with a bat. **2** cotton or wool pressed into thin layers, used to line comforters or quilts.

batting average, **1** a decimal fraction indicating a baseball or cricket player's record as a batter: *A baseball player who is at bat five times and makes two hits has a batting average of .400.* **2** *Informal, Figurative.* the level of success maintained by someone in any activity: *We found out that the batting average was high enough on completing station-to-station calls to make it cheaper always to call station-to-station* (Wall Street Journal).

batting eye, *Baseball.* the keenness of sight and speed of reflex required to be a good batter.

batting order, the order in which the members of a baseball or cricket team take their turns at bat.

bat|tle[1] (bat′əl), *n., v.,* **-tled, -tling.** —*n.* **1a** a fight between opposing armies, navies, air forces, or any combination of these; combat: *The battle for the island lasted six months.* **b** hostilities between nations; fighting or warfare: *The soldier received his wounds in battle.* **SYN:** combat. **2** a fight between two persons or animals; single combat; duel: *The badger and the dog had a ferocious battle in the woods.* **3** any fight or contest: (*Figurative.*) *The candidates fought a battle of words during the campaign.* **SYN:** strife, conflict, struggle. **4** *Archaic.* a battalion.
—*v.i.* to take part in a battle; fight; struggle; contend: *The hunter battled with the attacking wolves.* (*Figurative.*) *It takes courage to battle for justice.*
—*v.t.* to give battle to; fight against: *The swimmer had to battle a strong current.*
give battle to or **do battle (with** or **over)**, to engage in a conflict; fight: *Shall we give battle to the imperialists or not?* (Daniel Defoe). *They are also preparing to do battle over the budget cuts and tuition fees* (Manchester Guardian Weekly).
join battle, to begin to fight: *And there went out the king of Sodom, and the king of Gomorrah, . . . and they joined battle with them in the vale of Siddim* (Genesis 14:8).
[< Old French *bataille* battle, arrayed troops < Late Latin *battālia* fencing exercises < *battuere* strike] —**bat′tler**, *n.*
—*Syn. n.* **1a Battle, action, engagement** mean a fight between armed forces. **Battle** applies to a fight between large forces, such as armies or navies, lasting some time: *The battle for Guadalcanal lasted six months.* **Action** applies to a lively offensive or defensive part of a battle or campaign: *The Normandy landing was a daring action.* **Engagement** emphasizes the meeting of forces, large or small, in combat: *The engagement in Leyte Gulf weakened the Japanese Navy.*

bat|tle[2] (bat′əl), *v.t.,* **-tled, -tling.** *Poetic.* to furnish with battlements [< Old French *bataillier* < *bastailles* battlements < *bastille* bastille]

battle array, **1** the order of troops, war vessels, or planes arranged for battle. **2** *Archaic.* the armor and equipment for battle.

bat|tle-ax or **bat|tle-axe** (bat′əl aks′), *n., pl.* **-ax|es.** **1** an ax with a broad blade, formerly used as a weapon in battle. The battle-ax was a weapon of medieval times. **2** *Slang.* a woman of formidable appearance and temper, especially one who loudly and vigorously asserts her views.

battle cruiser, a large, fast warship, having relatively light armor for its size, intended to combine the speed of a cruiser with the firepower of a battleship. The last battle cruisers were built before World War II.

battle cry, **1** a shout of soldiers rushing into or engaged in battle. **2** *Figurative.* a motto or slogan in any contest: *The battle cry of the campaign for mayor was "Down with Corruption."*

bat|tle|dore (bat′əl dôr′, -dōr′), *n., v.,* **-dored, -dor|ing.** —*n.* **1** a paddle or small racket used to hit a shuttlecock back and forth in the game of battledore and shuttlecock. **2** the game itself, played by two persons.
—*v.t., v.i. Rare.* to drive, toss, or fly to and fro. [Middle English *batyldoure* bat[1] (for washing) perhaps < Old Provençal *batedor* a beater < Latin *battuere* strike]

battledore and shuttlecock, an old game played by two persons, somewhat resembling badminton.

battle dress, a military uniform for use in combat.

battle fatigue, a neurosis resulting from sustained emotional tension and fear, suffered typically by combatant soldiers, and marked by extreme exhaustion; combat fatigue.

bat|tle|field (bat′əl fēld′), *n.* the place where a battle is fought or has been fought.

bat|tle|front (bat′əl frunt′), *n.* a place where actual fighting between two armies takes place; front.

bat|tle|ground (bat′əl ground′), *n.* = battlefield.

battle group, *U.S.* any of the five units of a pentomic army division, usually made up of five companies.

battle jacket, **1** a waist-length woolen jacket forming part of a military uniform. **2** any similar jacket.

battle line, = line of battle.

***bat|tle|ment** (bat′əl mənt), *n.* **1** a low wall for defense at the top of a tower or wall, having solid parts alternating with lower parts or openings. Soldiers stood on a platform behind the wall and shot through the openings. **2** a wall built like this for ornament. [probably < Old French *batailles* < *bastiller* fortify < *bastille* bastille]

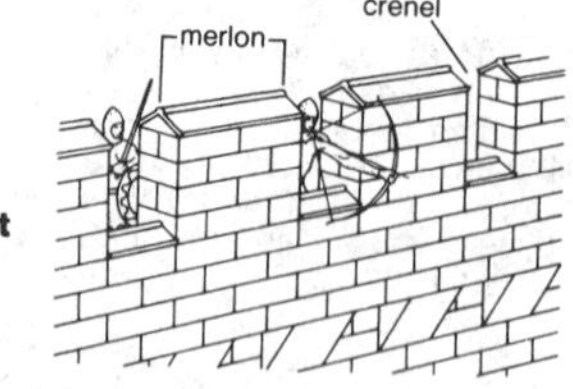

***battlement**
definition 1

bat|tle|ment|ed (bat′əl men′tid), *adj.* furnished with or surmounted by battlements: *the battlemented ramparts of a city.*

bat|tle|plane (bat′əl plān′), *n.* a combat aircraft; warplane.

battle royal, *pl.* **battles royal.** **1** a fight in which several persons take part; riot; free-for-all. **2** a long, hard fight.

bat|tle-scarred (bat′əl skärd′), *adj.* **1** injured or damaged during a battle. **2** showing the effects of many battles.

***bat|tle|ship** (bat′əl ship′), *n.* a very large warship having the heaviest armor and the most powerful guns. The last battleships were built during World War II.

***battleship**

battleship gray, a bluish-gray color.

bat|tle|some (bat′əl səm), *adj.* given to fighting; quarrelsome.

battle station, the assigned position to be taken in a time of combat or emergency, especially by a member of the crew of a naval vessel or military aircraft.

bat|tle|wag|on (bat′əl wag′ən), *n. U.S. Slang.* a battleship.

bat|tle|wise (bat′əl wīz′), *adj.* seasoned or skillful in battle: *The battlewise Chinese coxswain kept his head, stayed out of the line of fire* (Time). [< *battle* + *wise*[1]]

bat|tle-wor|thy (bat′əl wėr′ᴛʜē), *adj.* suitable for use in combat: *battle-worthy tanks.*

bat|tue (ba tü′, -tyü′; *French* bȧ ty′), *n.* **1a** the driving of game from cover toward the hunters. **b** a hunt where this is done. **c** the game thus driven from cover. **2** any wholesale slaughter. [< French *battue* a beating < *battre* beat < Middle French *batterie* battery]

bat|ture (ba tyür′), *n. U.S.* an alluvial elevation of the bed of a river, especially one of those parts of the Mississippi river bed that are dry or submerged according to the season: *The trees that grow out on the batture . . . are half covered with water* (New Yorker). [< French *batture* shoal < *battre* to beat]

bat|ty (bat′ē), *adj.,* **-ti|er, -ti|est.** **1** *U.S. Slang.* crazy; queer. **2** of or resembling a bat or bats. [< *bat*[2] + *-y*[1]]

bat|wing (bat′wing′), *adj.* resembling the wing or wings of a bat: *a batwing cape, a batwing collar.*

batwing sleeve, a long sleeve cut deep at the armhole of a dress.

ba|tyl alcohol (bā′təl), an alcohol found in the liver of sharks and certain other fish, and in yellow bone marrow. It has been used in the experimental treatment of radiation cancer. *Batyl alcohol promises to become a prized material for possible protection against atomic radiation* (Science News Letter). *Formula:* $C_{21}H_{44}O_3$ [< German *Batyl* (*Alkohol*) < New Latin *Batis* a genus of fish + German *-yl* -yl]

bau|bee (bô bē′, bô′bē), *n.* = bawbee.

bau|ble (bô′bəl), *n.* **1** a showy trifle having no real value; gewgaw: *Useless toys and trinkets are baubles.* **SYN:** gimcrack, knickknack. **2** *Historical.* a baton surmounted by a head (often that of a fool with asses' ears), carried by a court jester as a mock emblem of office. [< Old French *babel, baubel* child's toy]

Bau|cis (bô′sis), *n. Greek Mythology.* a poor old woman of Phrygia. She and her husband, Philemon, were the only persons hospitable to Zeus and Hermes when they came to the earth in disguise, and were rewarded by the gods, when old, by being turned into trees which were to stand beside each other forever.

baud (bôd), *n.* a unit of speed in transmitting information, equal to one bit, dot, pulse, or other unit element per second. [< J. M. E. *Baudot*, 1845-1903, a French inventor of a telegraphic code system]

bau|de|kin (bô′də kin), *n.* a rich brocade; baldachin. [< Old French *baudekin* < Medieval Latin *baldakinus* < Italian *baldacchino;* see etym. under **baldachin**]

bau|drons (bô′drənz), *n. Scottish.* a cat's name, like bruin for the bear. [origin uncertain]

Bau|haus (bou′hous′), *n.* a school founded in 1919 by Walter Gropius at Weimar, Germany, and later located successively at Dessau, Berlin, and Chicago, to develop a functional architecture based on a correlation between creative design and modern industry and science. [< German *Bauhaus* < *bauen* build + *Haus* house]

baulk (bôk), *v.i., v.t., n.* = balk.

Bau|mé (bō mā′), *adj.* denoting or calibrated in accordance with a scale first used by Antoine Baumé on his hydrometer, widely used in industrial chemistry to measure the specific gravity of liquids. *Abbr:* Bé. [< Antoine *Baumé*, 1728-1804, a French chemist]

baum marten (boum), **1** the dark-brown fur of the pine marten or the beech marten. **2** the pine marten of Europe. [< German *Baum* tree]

bau|son (bô′sən), *n. Archaic.* a badger. [< Anglo-French *bauçant* (in Old French, white-faced, spotted)]

bau|sond (bô′sənd), *adj. Dialect.* (of animals)

having a white patch on the forehead, or a white stripe down the face. [< Old French *bauçand, bauçant*]

baux|ite (bôk′sīt, bō′zīt), *n.* a claylike mineral from which aluminum is obtained. It consists chiefly of aluminum hydroxide but contains some iron and silica. It is used in making alum, firebricks, and abrasives. *Formula:* $Al_2O_3 \cdot 2H_2O$ [< French *bauxite* < Les *Beaux* or *Baux,* in southern France]

Bav., Bavarian.

ba|var|dage (bȧ vȧr dȧzh′), *n. French.* chatter; prattle.

Ba|var|i|an (bə vãr′ē ən), *adj., n.* **—*adj.*** of or having to do with Bavaria, its people, or the form of German spoken in that region.
—*n.* 1 a native or inhabitant of Bavaria. **2** the German dialect spoken in Bavaria and adjoining portions of southern Germany and Austria.

Bavarian cream, a dessert consisting of whipped gelatin, variously flavored, and whipped cream. [< *Bavaria,* Germany]

baw|bee (bô bē′, bô′bē), *n. Scottish.* a halfpenny. Also, **baubee.** [probably < a mintmaster, the laird of Sille*bawby*]

baw|cock (bô′kok), *n. Dialect.* a fine fellow (in jest or contempt). [< French *beau coq* fine cock]

bawd (bôd), *n.* **1** a person, especially a woman, who keeps a brothel. **2** any woman who acts as a pander; procuress. **3** a prostitute. [< Old North French *baud,* earlier *bald* bold, gay < Frankish (compare Old High German *bald*)]

bawd|ry (bô′drē), *n.* **1** obscenity; lewdness. **2** *Archaic.* the practice or occupation of a bawd. **3** *Obsolete.* unchastity; fornication.

bawd|y (bô′dē), *adj.,* **bawd|i|er, bawd|i|est,** *n.* **—*adj.*** not decent; lewd; obscene. **SYN:** indecent, unchaste.
—*n.* lewdness; bawdry. **—bawd′i|ly,** *adv.* **—bawd′i|ness,** *n.*

bawd|y|house (bô′dē hous′), *n.* = brothel.

bawl (bôl), *v., n.* **—*v.i.* 1** to shout or cry out at the top of one's voice: *The lost calf was bawling for its mother.* **SYN:** yell, clamor, bellow. **2** to weep loudly. **SYN:** wail.
—*v.t.* 1 to utter with bawling; shout at the top of one's voice. **2** to seek buyers by crying out the nature or price of (one's wares), as a peddler or hawker.
—*n.* 1 a shout at the top of one's voice. **2** a loud crying.
bawl out, *U.S. Informal.* to scold loudly; reprimand: *He bawled out his sister for denting his bicycle.*
[probably < Medieval Latin *baulare* bark]
—bawl′er, *n.*

baw|ley (bô′lē), *n. British.* a small sailboat rigged like a cutter, used for fishing on the coasts of Kent and Essex. [origin unknown]

baw|tie or **baw|ty** (bô′tē), *n., pl.* **-ties.** *Scottish.* **1** a dog, especially a large one. **2** a hare.

bax|ter (bak′stər), *n. Scottish.* a baker (originally, a woman baker). [Old English *bæcestre,* feminine of *bæcere* baker < *bacan* bake]

***bay**[1] (bā), *n.* **1** a part of a sea or lake extending into the land. A bay is usually smaller than a gulf and larger than a cove. *The Bay of Biscay is part of the Atlantic Ocean on the coast of France and Spain. Abbr:* b. **2** an indentation in a range of hills; level space partly surrounded by hills. **3** *U.S.* a tract of prairie or open land extending into woods and partly surrounded by them. [< Old French *baie* < Late Latin *baia;* perhaps of Iberian origin]

bay[2] (bā), *n., v.* **—*n.*** a long, deep barking, especially of a large dog: *The hunters heard the distant bay of the hounds.*
—*v.i.* to bark with long, deep sounds, as a hound or mastiff: *Dogs sometimes bay at the moon.*
—*v.t.* 1 to bark at; assail with barking: *I had rather be a dog, and bay the moon, Than such a Roman* (Shakespeare). **2** to give forth, utter, or express by baying. **3** to pursue with barking like a pack of hounds. **4a** to bring to bay: *The boar broke and the dogs bayed him. He broke again and the dogs bayed him again* (Newsweek). **b** to hold at bay.
bring to bay, to put in a position from which escape is impossible; force to stand and fight: *After a long chase the dogs brought the stag to bay at the edge of a cliff. The police brought the robbers to bay in a deserted house.*
hold (or **keep**) **at bay,** to hold off or away; resist successfully: *The stag held the hounds at bay. Aspirin kept the fever at bay.*
stand at bay, to stand and fight when escape is impossible: *The stag stood at bay against the hounds on the edge of the cliff.*
[< Old French *abai* barking < *abayer* (perhaps imitative)]

bay[3] (bā), *n.* **1a** a space or division of a wall or building between columns, pillars, buttresses, or the like. **b** = bay window. **c** a space, usually with a window or set of windows in it, projecting out from a wall. **d** a window space between two mullions; light. **2** a separate place for a specified purpose: *a loading bay.* **3a** a compartment in an airplane intended for some particular use, especially one for carrying bombs; bomb bay. **b** any portion of the interior of an aircraft fuselage between bulkheads or other structural members. **c** the space between struts on the wings of a biplane. **4** a place in a barn for storing hay or grain. **5** a stall or other compartment: *a horse bay.* **6** = sick bay. [< Old French *baee* < *baer* or *beër* stand open < Medieval Latin *batare*]

bay[4] (bā), *adj., n.* **—*adj.*** reddish-brown: *a bay horse.*
—*n.* 1 a reddish-brown horse with black mane and tail: *I'll put my money on the bobtailed nag, Somebody bet on the bay* (Stephen Foster). **2** a reddish brown: *a horse with a coat of bay.*
[< Old French *bai* < Latin *badius* reddish brown]

bay[5] (bā), *n.* **1** any one of various small, evergreen trees or shrubs with smooth, shiny leaves; sweet bay: **a** the laurel of southern Europe. Dried bay leaves are used for flavoring food. **b** a magnolia of North America, having round, fragrant, white flowers. **2** the West Indian bayberry.
bays, a the laurel wreath worn by poets or victors: *Civil wars will not allow bays to the conqueror's brow* (Abraham Cowley). **b** *Figurative.* honor; renown; fame: *I seek to blast no scholar's bays* (Robert Lloyd).
[< Old French *baie* berry, seed < Latin *bāca*]

bay[6] (bā), *n., v.* **—*n*** . a dam or embankment to retain water or divert its course.
—*v.t.* to retain or obstruct (water) with a bay or dam. [origin uncertain]

ba|ya (bī′yə), *n.* a weaverbird of India and Sri Lanka (Ceylon) that builds a hanging flask-shaped nest with a long tubular entrance. [< Hindustani *bayā*]

ba|ya|deer (bä′yə dir′), *adj., n.* = bayadere.

ba|ya|dere (bä′yə dãr′), *adj., n.* **—*adj.*** having brilliantly colored stripes running across the material: *bayadere cloth.*
—*n.* any cloth having such stripes.
[< French *bayadère* (originally) dancing girl < Portuguese *bailadeira* < *bailar* to dance < Late Latin *ballāre*]

bay antler, the second branch of a stag's horn, next above the brow antler; bez antler.

bay|ard (bā′ərd), *n., adj. Archaic.* **—*n.* 1** a bay horse. **2** a kind of mock-heroic allusive name for any horse, especially for a proverbial horse who was both blind and bold. **—*adj.*** of a bay color; bay: *a bayard horse.* [< Old French *baiard* a red-brown horse < *bai* bay[4]]

Bay|ard (bā′ərd; *French* bȧ yȧr′), *n.* **1** a man of heroic courage, chivalrous spirit, and unstained honor. **2** the horse with magical powers ridden by Rinaldo, knight of Charlemagne and hero of old French romances. [def. 1 < Pierre Terrail, Seigneur de *Bayard,* about 1473-1524, the heroic French "knight without fear and without reproach"; def. 2 < *bayard*]

bay|ber|ry (bā′ber′ē, -bər-), *n., pl.* **-ries. 1** a North American shrub with clusters of grayish-white berries coated with wax. The leaves of the shrub are aromatic, and candles made from the wax of the berries burn with a pleasant fragrance. The bayberry belongs to the same genus as the wax myrtle. **2** one of the berries. **3** a West Indian tree whose leaves yield an aromatic oil used in the preparation of bay rum. [American English < *bay*[5] + *berry*]

bay-breast|ed warbler (bā′bres′tid), an American warbler, the breast and crown of which (especially in the male) are bay or chestnut in color.

Bay|er process (bā′ər), a process for extracting alumina from bauxite, by mixing the ore with hot sodium hydroxide. [< Karl Joseph *Bayer,* a German chemist of the 1800's]

Bayes|i|an (bā′zē ən), *adj.* of or having to do with a statistical theory or method by which probabilities can be reassessed or revised in the light of new information. [< Thomas *Bayes,* 1702-1761, an English mathematician]

Ba|yeux Tapestry (bā yü′; *French* bȧ yœ′), a long strip of linen (actually not a tapestry) on which are embroidered representations of events leading up to the Norman Conquest of England. It was probably made in the 1100's. According to tradition it was done for Bishop Odo of Bayeux by the wife of William the Conqueror. [< *Bayeux,* a town in northern France, where it is preserved]

bay|gall (bā′gôl′), *n. U.S.* an area of swampland having a dense growth of bay trees and inkberry. [American English < *bay*[5] + *gall* (because of the bitter flavor of inkberries)]

bay|head (bā′hed′), *n.* the head or upper part of a bay.

bay ice, a mass or formation of ice occurring in a bay or other sheltered body of water in an arctic region, undisturbed by winds or currents and therefore having a relatively smooth or unbroken surface.

bay leaf, the leaf of the laurel or bay of southern Europe, used after drying as an herb to add flavor to soups, stews, and other cooked food.

bay lynx, = bobcat.

bay|man (bā′mən), *n., pl.* **-men. 1** a person who lives on a bay. **2** a person who earns his living on a bay, especially (in British Honduras) a cutter of baywood or mahogany.

bay|o|net (bā′ə nit, -net; bā′ə net′), *n., v.,* **-net|ed, -net|ing.** **—*n.* 1** a blade for piercing or stabbing, attached to the muzzle of a rifle, musket, etc. A bayonet is like a heavy dagger and may be detached and used as a separate hand weapon. **2** a pin or rod which fits into a socket or slot in a machine by means of which a subordinate part or auxiliary attachment may be engaged with the

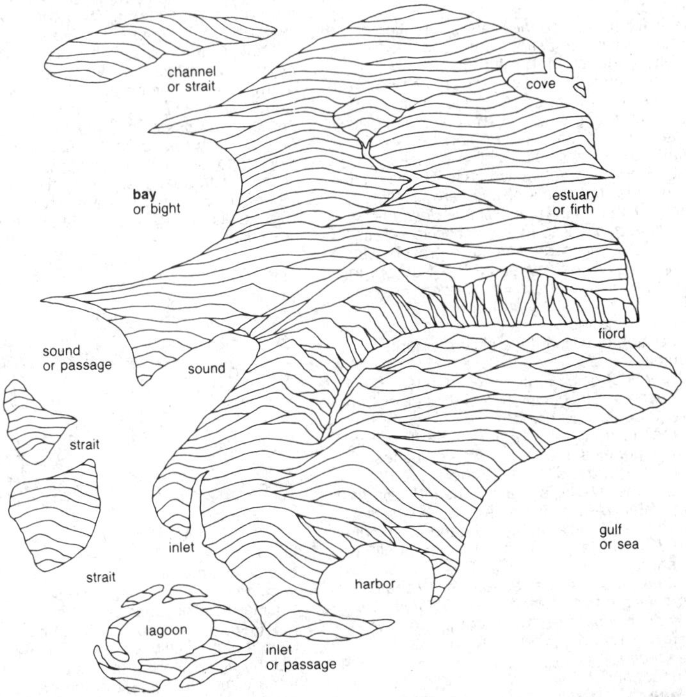

***bay**[1]
definition 1

Pronunciation Key: hat, āge, cãre, fär; let, ēqual, tėrm; it, īce; hot, ōpen, ôrder; oil, out; cup, pu̇t, rüle; child; long; thin; ᴛʜen; zh, measure; ə represents **a** in about, **e** in taken, **i** in pencil, **o** in lemon, **u** in circus.

machine.
—*v.t.* **1** to pierce or stab with a bayonet: *After ammunition ran out the troops bayoneted their way into the fort.* **2** to drive by threatening with a bayonet fixed in place on a gun; coerce (by military force). —*v.i.* to use a bayonet.
[< French *baïonette,* probably < *Bayonne,* France, as a possible place of origin]

bay|ou (bī′ü, bī′ō), *n., pl.* **-ous.** *U.S.* a marshy inlet or outlet of a lake, river, or gulf in the south central United States. The water in a bayou flows sluggishly and may even become stagnant. [American English < Louisiana French *bayou* < Choctaw *bayuk* creek]

bay rum, a fragrant liquid used as a soothing lotion for the skin, originally made by distilling rum or a rum mash in which the leaves of the West Indian bayberry had been steeped. It is now usually made of oil from bay leaves.

bays (bāz), *n.pl.* See under **bay**[5].

bay salt, coarse-grained salt, especially salt obtained by evaporation of sea water; solar salt.

Bay State, a nickname for the State of Massachusetts.

Bay Street, **1** a street in the financial district of Toronto, Canada. **2** *Figurative.* the financial interests or financiers of Canada.

bay tree, the laurel of southern Europe; bay.

***bay window,** **1** a window or set of windows projecting from a wall to form an alcove or small space in a room. A bay window ordinarily begins at or near ground level (as distinguished from an *oriel,* which projects from an upper story).
2 *Slang, Figurative.* a large projecting abdomen.

***bay window**
definition 1

bay|wood (bā′wu̇d′), *n.* a coarse, light kind of mahogany from the vicinity of the Gulf of Campeche, Mexico. [< the *Bay* of Campeche]

ba|zaar or **ba|zar** (bə zär′), *n.* **1** a street or streets full of small shops and booths in Oriental countries: *They came, mingling unobtrusively in the dusty crowds and confusion of Kabul's bazaars and streets* (Newsweek). **2** a place for the sale of many kinds of goods. **3** a sale of things contributed by various people, held for some charity or other purpose. [< Persian *bāzār*]

ba|zaa|ri (bə zä′rē), *n.* an Iranian merchant or shop owner: *The bazaaris usually rented land from the religious foundations and made the foundations big gifts* (New Yorker). [< Persian *bāzārī* < *bāzār* bazaar]

ba|zoo (bə zü′), *n. U.S. Slang.* **1** the mouth.
2 boastful talk. [perhaps < Dutch *bazuin* trumpet]

ba|zoo|ka (bə zü′kə), *n.* a portable gun for firing small rockets, especially against tanks. In its original form it consisted of an open-ended, three-inch tube about five feet long. [American English < name of a trombonelike instrument invented and named by comedian Bob Burns]

BB (bē′bē′), *n.* **1** a standard size of shot, approximately .18 of an inch in diameter. **2** a shot of this size used in a shotgun for large birds, such as wild geese, and especially in an air rifle; BB shot.

B battery, *Radio, especially U.S.* an electric battery connected to the plate lead and to the filament of the electron tube so that the electrons can flow through the tube.

BBC (no periods) or **B.B.C.,** British Broadcasting Corporation.

BB gun, an air rifle. Also, **beebee gun.**

bbl., barrel or barrels.

BB shot, BB.

b.c., bass clarinet.

BC (no periods), before Christ.

B.C., **1** *U.S.* Bachelor of Chemistry. **2** bass clarinet. **3** before Christ. B.C. is used for times before the birth of Christ and always appears after the figure for the year. A.D. is used for times after the birth of Christ and now usually appears before the figure for a specific year. 350 B.C. is 100 years earlier than 250 B.C. From 20 B.C. to A.D. 50 is 70 years. **4** British Columbia.

BCD (no periods), binary coded decimal.

B.C.E., *U.S.* **1** Bachelor of Chemical Engineering.
2 Bachelor of Civil Engineering. **3** before the Christian Era.

B cell, or **B-cell** (bē′sel′), *n.* a type of lymphocyte that produces antibodies, characterized by many fingerlike protrusions on its surface: *Both the B-cells and T-cells recirculate through the body and continually monitor for the presence of potential attackers* (Time). [< *B*(ursa of Fabricius, organ in chickens where the cell was first found)]

BCG (no periods), Bacillus Calmette-Guérin.

bch., bunch.

B.C.L., Bachelor of Civil Law.

B complex, the group of B-complex vitamins; vitamin B complex.

B-complex vitamins, vitamins of the vitamin-B group, including thiamin, niacin, and riboflavin.

B.C.S., Bachelor of Chemical Science.

BCS theory, a theory which explains superconductivity as caused by an interaction between pairs of electrons of opposite momentum and spin and the crystal lattice structure of a solid material. [< the initials of J. *B*ardeen, L. N. *C*ooper, and J. R. *S*chrieffer, American physicists who formulated the theory in 1957]

bd., **1** board. **2** bond. **3** bound. **4** bundle.

b/d, **1** *Bookkeeping.* brought down. **2** barrels per day.

B.D., **1** Bachelor of Divinity. **2** bills discounted.

B/D, **1** bank draft. **2** bills discounted.

bdel|li|um (del′ē əm, -yəm), *n.* **1** a fragrant gum resin, similar to myrrh but weaker, used in medicine and perfumery. **2** any of the plants from which it comes. **3** an unknown precious substance mentioned in the Bible in Genesis 2:12 and Numbers 11:7, considered by various commentators to be a pearl, a carbuncle, a crystal, amber, or a resin. [< Latin *bdellium* < Greek *bdéllion* gum resin < Semitic (compare Hebrew *bədḥōlaḥ*)]

bd. ft., board foot or board feet.

bdl., bundle.

bds., **1** (bound in) boards. **2** bundles.

B.D.S., Bachelor of Dental Surgery.

be (bē), *v.i., present indicative sing.* **am, are, is,** *pl.* **are,** *past indicative sing.* **was, were, was,** *pl.* **were,** *present subjunctive* **be,** *past subjunctive* **were,** *past participle* **been,** *present participle* **being. 1** to have reality; exist; live: *To be or not to be ...* (Shakespeare). *Veterans of the American Revolution are no more.* SYN: subsist. **2** to take place; happen: *His birthday was last week.* SYN: occur. **3** to remain; continue: *He will be here all year.* SYN: stay, abide. **4** to equal; represent: *Let "x" be the unknown quantity.* **5** *Be* is used as a linking verb between a subject and a predicate: *He was the secretary* (predicate noun). *She is sick* (predicate adjective). **6** *Be* is used as an auxiliary verb with: **a** the present participle of another verb to form the progressive tense: *I am asking. He was asking. You will be asking.* **b** the past participle of transitive verbs to form the passive voice: *I am asked. You will be asked. They will be punished. He was asked.* **7** *Be* is used to express future time, duty, intention, and possibility: *He will be here all year. She tries to be good. No shelter was to be seen.* **8** *Be* is used with the past participles of some intransitive verbs to form the perfect tense: *The sun is set.*

be gone. See under **gone.**

be off, **a** to go away; leave quickly: *I'm off now.* **b** to have lessened in quality, etc.: *Johnson was sadly off form and finished last* (London Times).

be that as it may, in spite of what may be; regardless; anyhow: *Be that as it may, business obviously flourishes in Corsica and Portugal* (Sunday Times).

far be it from, outside the plan or intention of: *Far be it from me to criticize the boss's work.*

let be, to not touch; not disturb (a person or thing); not meddle with: *Oh, sick am I to see you, will you never let me be?* (A. E. Housman).

so be it, let it take place; even so: *As it ... ever shall be. So be it* (Salisbury Primer).

[Middle English *been,* Old English *bēon*]

►For the use of the objective case of personal pronouns after the forms of this verb, see **me.**

be-, *prefix.* **1** thoroughly; all around: *Bespatter = spatter thoroughly.* **2** to make; cause to seem: *Belittle = cause to seem little.* **3** to provide with: *Bespangle = provide with spangles.* **4** at; on; to; for; about; against: *Bewail = wail about.*
[Old English *be-,* unstressed form of *bī* by]

b.e., bill of exchange.

Be (no period), beryllium (chemical element).

Bé., Baumé.

B E (no periods) or **B/E,** bill of exchange.

B.E., **1** Bachelor of Education. **2** Bachelor of Engineering. **3** Bank of England.

beach (bēch), *n., v.* —*n.* **1a** an almost flat shore of sand or pebbles over which water washes when high. SYN: strand, coast. **b** the shore of a lake or large river. **c** any area of sand next to a body of water used by swimmers. **2** *Especially British.* the seashore, whether of sand or shingle.
—*v.t., v.i.* to run (a boat or ship) ashore; pull up on the shore.

on the beach, **a** *Nautical.* ashore; not aboard: *The crew was on the beach while the ship was in dry dock.* **b** *Figurative.* without a job; out of work: *He's been on the beach for weeks and he's flat broke.*
[origin uncertain]

beach bag, a canvas or plastic bag with a handle, for carrying things, such as a bathing suit and towel, to a beach.

beach ball, a large, inflated plastic or rubber ball, to play with at a beach.

beach|boy (bēch′boi′), *n.* a young man who works at a beach, especially as an attendant or swimming instructor.

beach buggy, = dune buggy.

beach bunny, *Slang.* a girl who is often at the beach, especially in the company of a surfer.

beach|comb (bēch′kōm′), *v.i.* to live as a beachcomber.

beach|comb|er (bēch′kō′mər), *n.* **1** a vagrant or loafer, especially on the islands of the Pacific.
2 *U.S.* a long wave which rolls in from the ocean upon the beach; breaker; comber.

beach crab, = sand crab.

beach flea, a small crustacean found on saltwater beaches that leaps like a flea; sand hopper; sand flea.

beach|front (bēch′frunt′), *adj., n.* —*adj.* very near to or adjoining a beach. —*n.* a beachfront area; land that is near to or on a beach.

beach grass, any one of various tall, strongly-rooted grasses growing on sandy shores, such as the marram grass.

beach|head (bēch′hed′), *n.* **1** the first position established by an invading army on an enemy beach or shore, especially as part of a larger operation to make possible the landing of troops and supplies. **2** *Figurative.* any preliminary foothold: *The enormous beachheads American capital has made in recent years in numerous countries may result in some benefits* (New York Times).

beach-la-mar (bēch′lə mär′), *n.* bêche-de-mer, a hybrid language largely based on English, used in Melanesia.

beach|less (bēch′lis), *adj.* without a beach.

beach|mas|ter (bēch′mas′tər, -mäs′-), *n.* an officer in charge of the landing of troops or the unloading of supplies on a beachhead.

beach plum, **1** a wild plum common on the northeastern coast of the United States. It belongs to the rose family. **2** its purple or crimson, acid fruit, used in making preserves and jelly.

beach ridge, a large mound of beach deposits behind a beach, heaped up by the action of waves.

beach sein|ing (sā′ning), the use of a long seine which is drawn in a circle around a school of fish and then hauled onto the beach or a platform; drag seining.

beach|side (bēch′sīd′), *adj., n.* = beachfront.

beach umbrella, a large umbrella fitted with a pole for use at a bathing beach.

beach wagon, *U.S.* = station wagon.

beach|wear (bēch′wãr′), *n.* bathing suits, shorts, shirts, robes, or other apparel for wearing at a beach.

beach|y (bē′chē), *adj.* covered with loose pebbles; shingly.

***bea|con** (bē′kən), *n., v.* —*n.* **1** a light or fire used as a signal to guide or warn: *The fire on the hill was a beacon to Highlanders that the British were coming.* **2** a marker, signal light, or radio beams that guides aircraft and ships, especially through fog and storm: *The pilot flew safely through the fog guided by a radio beacon.* **3** a tall tower for a signal; lighthouse: *The boys climbed the beacon to see far out to sea.*
4 any thing or person that is a guiding or warning signal: *The city lights were a beacon to approaching airplanes.* (*Figurative.*) *Washington and Madison were beacons for their times.*
—*v.t.* **1** to give light to; guide; warn. **2** to supply or mark with beacons. —*v.i.* **1** to shine brightly, like a beacon. **2** to serve as a beacon.
[Old English *bēacen.* See related etym. at **beckon.**]

***beacon**
definitions 2,3

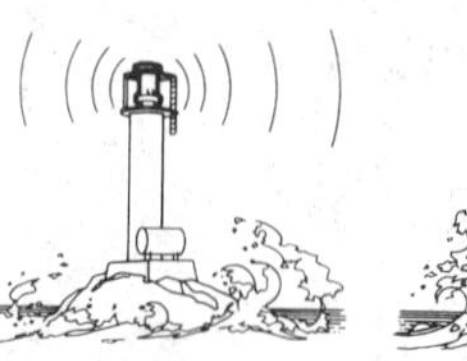

foghorn

lighthouse

bea|con|age (bē′kə nij), *n.* **1** a system of beacons. **2** a charge for its maintenance.

bea|con|ry (bē′kən rē), *n.* the science of making or using radio or radar beacons.

bead (bēd), *n., v.* —*n.* **1** a small ball or bit of glass, metal, plastic, or other material, with a hole through it, so that it can be strung on a thread with others like it to form a necklace or bracelet, or sewn on various fabrics as ornaments: *The Indian belt was covered with a design made of colored beads.* **2** any small, round object like a drop or bubble: *Beads of sweat covered his forehead.* **3a** a bubble in spirits, sparkling wines, or carbonated soft drinks. **b** the foam or head on beer or ale. **4** a piece of metal at the front end of a gun barrel to aim by; sight. **5a** a narrow, rounded molding, usually semicircular or nearly circular in section; beading. **b** any long, narrow strip approximately semicircular in section. **6** a globular ornament, especially one of a series in a line or row. **7** *Chemistry.* a globule of borax or other flux covered with a bit of the mineral to be analyzed, which is heated in a blowpipe flame as a test for the presence of metals. **8** the droplet of the pure metal produced by cupellation in assaying for a precious metal. **9** the flangelike part of an automobile or other pneumatic tire which engages the rim of the wheel.

–***v.t.*** **1a** to put or form beads on: *His forehead was beaded with sweat.* **b** to ornament with beads. **2** to string like beads: (*Figurative.*) *The lights of houses beaded the shore.* –***v.i.*** to form a bead or beads (used especially of liquids): *Eight to ten drops of this chemical per gallon of spray keep it from "beading" and help it to spread out in an even film* (New York Times).

beads, a a string of beads: *She dropped her beads, and several pearls were lost.* **b** a string of beads for keeping count in saying prayers; rosary: [*The*] *beads* [*are*] *so put together that every set of ten smaller ones for the "Hail Marys" is parted by a larger bead, to tell when the "Our Father" must be recited* (Daniel Rock). **c** *Astronomy.* Baily's beads: *The beads vanish almost at once, and their disappearance marks the beginning of totality* (Wasley S. Krogdahl).

draw (or **take**) **a bead on,** to aim a gun at; take aim at: (*Figurative.*) *Columnist Art Buchwald ... drew a bead last week on a familiar target:* [*the*] *White House news secretary* (Newsweek).

say (or **tell** or **count**) **one's beads,** to say prayers, using a rosary: *All the people said their beads in a general silence* (Gilbert Burnet).

[Middle English *bede* prayer, rosary bead, Old English *bed* prayer] –**bead′like′,** *adj.*

bead|ed (bē′did), *adj.* **1** trimmed with beads; having beads. **2** like beads.

beaded lizard, a poisonous lizard of Mexico and Central America closely related to the Gila monster.

bead|house (bēd′hous′), *n.* a poorhouse or other charitable establishment in which the inmates were required or expected to pray for those who had founded or who supported it. Also, **bedehouse.**

bead|ing (bē′ding), *n.* **1** a trimming made of beads threaded into patterns; beadwork. **2** a narrow lace or openwork trimming through which ribbon may be run. **3** a pattern or edge of small beads on woodwork, silver or other metal, and plaster; beadwork. **4** a narrow, rounded molding. **5** a preparation for causing liquor to hang in drops about the glass when poured out.

bea|dle (bē′dəl), *n.* **1a** minor parish officer in the Church of England whose duties include keeping order and waiting on the clergy. In former times if a person went to sleep in church, the beadle woke him up. **b** a person having somewhat similar duties in certain other churches and some synagogues. **2** Also, **bedel** (at Oxford), **bedell** (at Cambridge). an English university official with various functions, chief of which is that of macebearer for academic processions. **3** *Obsolete.* a crier or messenger of a court. [Middle English *bedel* < Old North French < a Frankish word]

bea|dle|dom (bē′dəl dəm), *n.* stupid officiousness (from the frequent portrayal in literature of beadles, especially church beadles, as pompous and meddlesome).

bead lightning, = chain lightning (def. 1).

bead|roll (bēd′rōl′), *n.* **1** a list of deceased persons in the Roman Catholic Church, to be prayed for. **2** a list or string of names. Also, **bederoll.**

bead-ru|by (bēd′rü′bē), *n., pl.* **-bies.** a plant of the lily family found in wooded parts of Canada and the northern United States, bearing small, white flowers and pale-red berries suggestive of beads by their shape and arrangement on the stem of the plant; false lily of the valley.

beads (bēdz), *n.pl.* See under **bead.**

beads|man (bēdz′mən), *n., pl.* **-men. 1a** *Archaic.* a person who says prayers, especially one who does so for another or others, and who is paid to do so. **b** *British.* the inmate of a beadhouse. **2** *Scottish.* a public almsman or licensed beggar. Also, **bedesman.**

beads|wom|an (bēdz′wu̇m′ən), *n., pl.* **-wom|en. 1** a woman who prays for a benefactor. **2** an almswoman. Also, **bedeswoman.**

bead|work (bēd′wėrk′), *n.* **1** ornamental work made of or with beads. **2** beading (def. 3).

bead|y (bē′dē), *adj.,* **bead|i|er, bead|i|est. 1** small, round, and shiny; beadlike: *The mouse has beady eyes.* **2** trimmed or ornamented with beads; beaded. **3** full of bubbles; having a bead or beads; frothy: *a glass of ginger ale, all beady and cold.* –**bead′i|ly,** *adv.*

bead|y-eyed (bē′dē īd′), *adj.* having eyes which resemble beads; especially sharp and penetrating; acutely vigilant.

bea|gle (bē′gəl), *n., v.,* **-gled, -gling.** –***n.*** a small hound with smooth hair, short legs, and drooping ears, and bred for hunting small game.

–***v.i.*** **1a** to follow beagles or other small hounds on foot in pursuit of small game. **b** to run over a prescribed course as if doing this. **2** *U.S. Slang.* to pry into or about something, such as a beagle is supposed to do.

[Middle English *begle;* origin uncertain]

bea|gler (bē′glər), *n.* a person who hunts with beagles.

bea|gling (bē′gling), *n.* the sport of running on foot after, or as if after, a beagle in hunting small game.

***beak**[1] (bēk), *n.* **1** the bill of a bird, especially one that is strong and hooked and useful in striking or tearing. Eagles, hawks, and parrots have beaks. SYN: nib. **2** a similar part in certain other animals. Turtles and octopuses have beaks. SYN: proboscis. **3** *Slang.* the human nose, especially when somewhat pointed or hooked. SYN: hooknose. **4** anything shaped like a beak, such as a projection at the prow of an ancient warship, or the spout of a pitcher or jug. **5** a sharp, projecting process, or prolonged tip in some plants, such as in the seeds of the crane's-bill. **6** *Architecture.* a small, overhanging fillet with a channel behind it, forming a drip from which rain water will fall. [< Old French *bec* < Latin *beccus* < a Gaulish word] –**beak′like′,** *adj.*

***beak**[1]
definitions 1, 2, 4, 5, 6

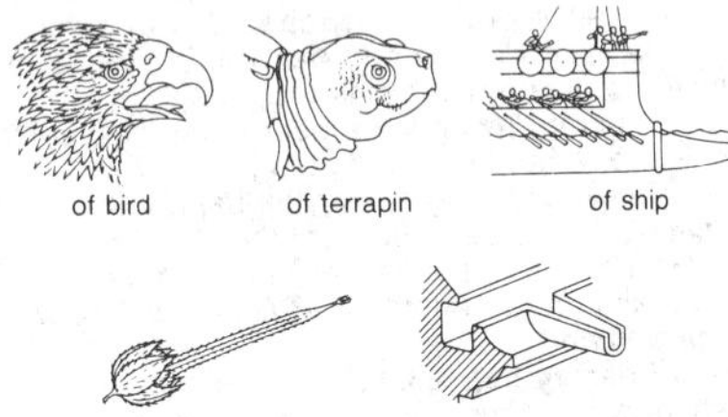

beak[2] (bēk), *n. British Slang.* **1** a magistrate. **2** (originally at Eton, now used generally) a schoolmaster, especially a headmaster. [earlier *beck;* origin unknown]

beaked (bēkt), *adj.* **1** having a beak, or something resembling a beak. **2** shaped like a beak; hooked.

beaked parsley, = chervil.

beaked whale, a whale having an extended, pointed head in the shape of a beak, and very few teeth on each jaw, limited chiefly to the Northern Hemisphere.

beak|er (bē′kər), *n.* **1** a large cup or drinking glass with a wide mouth: *a full beaker of wine.* SYN: goblet. **2** a thin glass or metal cup used especially in laboratories. A beaker has a flat bottom, no handle, and often a small lip for pouring. **3** the contents of a beaker. **4** a small, bell-shaped clay container which some prehistoric tribes of the Bronze Age buried with their dead. [< Scandinavian (compare Old Icelandic *bikarr*) < Vulgar Latin *bicārium* wine cup; spelling influenced by *beak*[1]. See etym. of doublet **pitcher.**]

Beak|er (bē′kər), *adj.* of or having to do with the Beaker Folk: *Beaker pottery, the Beaker culture.*

Beaker Folk or **People,** a prehistoric group of European people before the Bronze Age whose significant artifact was pottery in the shape of a bell or beaker.

beak|ful (bēk′fu̇l), *n., pl.* **-fuls.** as much as a beak can hold: *The bird flew off with a beakful of grass.*

beak|i|ron (bēk′ī′ərn), *n.* **1** the horn or tapering end of an anvil. **2** an anvil with such a horn. [earlier *bickern* < French *bigorne* < Latin *bicornis* two-horned < *bi-* two + *cornū* horn]

be-all and end-all (bē′ôl′ənd end′ôl′), the whole or essence of anything: *Victories ... are not the be-all and end-all of the* [*Olympic*] *Games* (London Times).

beam (bēm), *n., v.* –***n.*** **1** a large, long piece of timber, ready for use in building: *The beams supporting the roof and the sides were all that was left of the house after the fire.* **2** a similar piece of iron, steel, stone, reinforced concrete, or other heavy material used in building. **3** any of the main horizontal supports of a building or ship: *The beams cracked and the top floor caved in.* **4a** the crosswise bar of a balance which supports the scales or pans. **b** the balance itself. **5** a ray or stream of light, heat, or other radiation: *a beam of electrons. The beam from the flashlight shone on a kitten.* **6** *Figurative.* a bright look or smile: *There was a beam from ear to ear on her happy face.* SYN: glow, radiance. **7** a radio or radar signal directed in a straight line, used to guide aircraft or ships: *The pilot rode the beam and landed the airplane safely in the fog.* **8a** the widest part of a ship: *The freighter has a thirty-foot beam.* **b** the side of a ship or the sideward direction at right angles to the keel, especially with reference to wind, sea, or another vessel. The weather beam is the side toward the wind. **9a** the part of a plow by which it is pulled. **b** the straight part or shank of an anchor. **10** a lever often used on a steam engine to transmit the motion of the piston rod to the crankshaft. **11** either of two wooden rollers in a loom, one for warp before weaving, the other for finished cloth. **12** the main stem of a deer's horn which bears the branches or antlers. **13** *Slang, Figurative.* the hips or buttocks: *broad in the beam.*

–***v.t.*** **1** to send out (beams or rays of light); emit in rays: *Mother beamed the flashlight in the corner and saw a mouse.* **2a** to aim; direct: *Microphones were ... beamed at the jury box* (New York Times). *... advertisers' attempts to beam their messages to smaller, but higher-income, audiences* (Wall Street Journal). **b** to direct (a broadcast): *A program was beamed at Russia.*

–***v.i.*** **1** to shine radiantly. **2** *Figurative.* (of a person) to look or smile brightly: *Her face beamed with delight.*

fly (or **ride**) **the beam,** to pilot an aircraft by a radio beam: *The flyer homed in on the radio source and then flew the beam until he reached his home base.*

off the beam, a (of an aircraft) deviating from the right course indicated by a radio beam: *The inexperienced pilot flew the plane so badly that it was off the beam most of the time.* **b** *Informal, Figurative.* (of a person or idea) on the wrong track; mistaken: *He is a good speaker, but his ideas are off the beam.*

on the beam, a (of an aircraft) on the right course as indicated by a radio beam: *The plane began to drift off course but very soon got back on the beam.* **b** *Informal, Figurative.* just right: *His answer was on the beam.*

on the starboard (or **port**) **beam,** at a right angle to the keel of a ship on the starboard (or port) side: *The lookout cried out: "Land on the starboard beam!"*

[Old English *bēam* tree, piece of wood, ray]

– ***Syn.*** *n.* **5 Beam, ray** mean a line of light. **Beam** applies to a shaft, long and with some width, coming from something that gives out light: *The beam from the flashlight showed a kitten.* **Ray** applies to a thin line of light, usually thought of as radiating, or coming out like the spokes of a wheel, from something bright: *There was not a ray of moonlight in the forest.*

beam compass, an instrument consisting of a beam with sliding sockets that carry points, for describing large circles and for laying off distances.

beamed (bēmd), *adj.* furnished with beams, or as if with beams.

beam-ends (bēm′endz′), *n.pl.* the ends of a ship's beams.

on one's beam-ends, a (of a ship) almost capsizing: *... a number of large river craft ... on their beam-ends for want of water* (Jedidiah Morse). **b** *Figurative.* in desperate financial condition: *London symphony orchestras ... are on their beam-ends for want of adequate subsidy* (London Times).

beam|er (bē′mər), *n.* **1** a person or thing that beams. **2** *Cricket.* a ball aimed high by the bowler.

beam house, the area in a tannery where the hides undergo the final preparations for tanning.

beam|ing (bē′ming), *adj.* **1** shining; bright. SYN: gleaming, luminous. **2** looking or smiling brightly; cheerful. SYN: radiant. –**beam′ing|ly,** *adv.*

beam|ish (bē′mish), *adj.* tending to beam with good cheer; beaming: *Come to my arms, my beamish boy!* (Lewis Carroll). –**beam′ish|ly,** *adv.*

beam-pow|er tube (bēm′pou′ər), a kind of vacuum tube for increasing power, in which the electrons flowing to the anode (plate) are focused into a beam which causes secondary electrons to be turned back.

beam rider, a guided missile which follows an

Pronunciation Key: hat, āge, cãre, fär; let, ēqual, tėrm; it, īce; hot, ōpen, ôrder; oil, out; cup, pu̇t, rüle; child; long; thin; ᴛʜen; zh, measure; ə represents a in about, e in taken, i in pencil, o in lemon, u in circus.

electronic beam.

beam-rid|ing (bēm′rī′ding), *n., adj.* **—*n.*** a method of guiding a missile by an electronic beam.
—*adj.* following an electronic beam.

beam sea, waves rolling directly against a ship's side, at or nearly at a right angle to its keel.

beams|man (bēmz′mən), *n., pl.* **-men.** a man who works in a beam house.

beam-split|ter (bēm′split′ər), *n.* **1a** a prismatic device on a camera lens which separates light into the three primary colors. **b** a camera equipped with such a device, used for color photography. **2** a device which breaks up a beam of light as it emerges from the eyepiece of an optical instrument, such as a microscope.

beam|ster (bēm′stər), *n.* a workman who scrapes the last bits of flesh and hair roots from the hide in leather processing.

beam tetrode, *British.* a beam-power tube.

beam transmission, transmission of radio signals reflected into a beam for direction to a particular destination or destinations.

beam valve, *British.* a beam-power tube.

beam weapon, = directed-energy weapon.

beam|width (bēm′width′, -witth′), *n.* the angular width of a radio or radar beam.

beam wind, a wind which strikes a ship or aircraft at right angles to its length.

beam|y (bē′mē), *adj.,* **beam|i|er, beam|i|est. 1** like a beam; massive. **2** (of a ship) broad in the beam. **3** *Figurative.* beaming; radiant: *Bending her beamy eyes in thankfulness* (Shelley). **4** possessing full-grown horns; antlered: *Thou mayst . . . beamy stags in toils engage* (John Dryden). **—beam′i|ness,** *n.*

bean (bēn), *n., v.* **—*n.* 1** a smooth, somewhat flat seed used as a vegetable. Lima beans, kidney beans, and navy beans are three different varieties of beans. **2** the long pod containing such seeds. The green or yellow pods of some varieties, together with the seeds, are also used as a vegetable. **3** the plant that beans grow on. It is a member of the pea family. The varieties are often classified as garden or snap beans (grown for their edible pods), such as the string bean; and field or shell beans (grown for their edible seeds), such as the kidney bean and navy bean. **4** any seed shaped somewhat like a bean. Coffee beans are seeds of the coffee plant. **5** *Slang.* the head. **6** *Slang.* a piece of money: *He doesn't have a bean to his name.*
—*v.t.* *Slang.* to hit (someone) on the head, especially with a thrown object: *He has beaned as many as four batters in one game* (Newsweek).
beans, *Informal.* **a** the smallest amount: *She doesn't care beans about the water boy since the captain of the football team asked her for a date.* **b** something of little value: *That ring is beans compared with the crown jewels.*
full of beans, *U.S. Slang.* in high spirits; lively; active: *We start off—oh, full of beans—and then we stop* (Josephine Elder).
spill the beans, *U.S. Informal.* to reveal a secret; divulge something confidential; confess: *On his way to the F.B.I. headquarters here from his arrest, he had offered to "spill the beans"* (New York Times).
[Old English *bēan*] **—bean′like′,** *adj.*

bean|bag (bēn′bag′), *n.* **1** a small bag partly filled with dried beans, used to toss in play. **2** Also, **beanbag chair.** a chair filled with pellets which takes the shape of the person sitting in it.

bean|ball (bēn′bôl′), *n., v. Baseball Slang.* **—*n.*** a ball thrown by the pitcher purposely at or near the batter's head.
—*v.t., v.i.* to throw a beanball or beanballs. **—bean′ball′er,** *n.*

bean beetle, = Mexican bean beetle.

bean blight, a disease caused by bacteria which attack the stem, leaf, pod, and seed of the bean plant and turn them brown.

bean cake, a compressed cake of beans from which the oil has been removed.

bean caper, a small tree, native to the countries of the eastern Mediterranean, with fleshy leaves and flower buds which are used as capers.

bean count, *U.S. Informal.* a tally or reckoning by numbers; statistical analysis: *The Pentagon's bean count . . . ignores French and Spanish forces because these do not come under direct NATO command* (Time). **—bean counting.**

bean counter, *U.S. Informal.* someone who compiles statistical records or accounts, as of business or sales.

bean curd, a soft cheese made by coagulating the milk of soybeans, eaten originally in the Far East, but now in many soups and other dishes of Western cooking.

bean|er|y (bē′nər ē), *n., pl.* **-er|ies.** *U.S. Slang.* a cheap restaurant.

bean family, a former grouping of plants now classified as a subgroup of the pea family.

bean|feast (bēn′fēst′), *n. British.* **1** an annual dinner given by employers to their workers. **2** any festive occasion; feast: *I have never enjoyed such an emotional beanfeast* (Punch). [< *bean* + *feast;* probably because beans were served on such occasions]

bean|fest (bēn′fest′), *n. British.* beanfeast.

bean|ie (bē′nē), *n.* a small skullcap, usually for schoolboys and other children but sometimes worn by male college freshmen. Also, **beany.**

bean meal, meal made from beans.

bean|o[1] (bē′nō), *n., pl.* **bean|os.** = bingo. [American English, probably < *bean,* patterned on *keno*]

bean|o[2] (bē′nō), *n., pl.* **bean|os.** *British Slang.* a noisy frolic or spree. [short for *beanfeast*]

bean|pole (bēn′pōl′), *n.* **1** a pole stuck in the ground for bean vines to climb on as they grow. **2** *Slang, Figurative.* a tall, thin person.

bean|shoot|er (bēn′shü′tər), *n.* a slender, metal tube for shooting beans or other small missiles by blowing.

bean|stalk (bēn′stôk′), *n.* the stem of a bean plant.

bean tree, any one of various trees having beanlike pods, such as the carob or catalpa.

bean|y (bē′nē), *adj., n., pl.* **bean|ies. —*adj.* 1** having the flavor of beans. **2** full of beans.
—*n.* = beanie.

***bear**[1] (bãr), *n., pl.* **bears** or (*collectively*) **bear,** *v., adj.* **—*n.* 1** a large, heavy mammal with thick, coarse fur and a very short tail. A bear walks flat on the soles of its feet. The black bear, brown bear, grizzly bear, and polar bear are four kinds of bears. Bears are carnivorous or omnivorous. See picture below. **2** any one of several animals more or less similar to the bear, especially in appearance and habits, such as the koala of Australia. **3** *Figurative.* a gruff or surly person. **4a** a speculator who sells short, hoping to lower prices on the stock market, in order to buy cheap. **b** a person who expects stock prices to decline. **5** a portable machine to punch holes in iron plates.
—*v.t.* to operate as or like a bear in (stocks, commodities, or other financial trading).
—*adj.* of or resembling a financial bear; influenced by speculative bears: *a bear market.*
be a bear for, to have the will, strength, or courage, to take on or endure: *That fighter is a bear for punishment.*
have a bear by the tail, have something unwieldy or beyond control: *I foresee a wage-price spiral and once that starts you have a bear by the tail* (Wall Street Journal).
loaded for bear, *U.S. Slang.* ready for action, especially for a fight.
[Old English *bera*] **—bear′like′,** *adj.*

bear[2] (bãr), *v.,* **bore** or (*Archaic*) **bare, borne** or **born, bear|ing. —*v.t.* 1** to hold up or support: *The ice is too thin to bear your weight.* SYN: sustain. **2** to put up with: *She can't bear the noise.* SYN: tolerate, brook. **3** to undergo; experience; suffer: *He cannot bear any more pain.* **4a** to take from one place to another; carry: *It takes two men to bear that stone. He was borne senseless from the lists* (Sir Walter Scott). *A voice was borne upon the wind.* SYN: transport, convey, bring. **b** to move by force; drive: *How the rushing waves Bear all before them* (William Cullen Bryant). **5** to bring forth; produce; yield: *This tree bears fine apples.* **6** to give birth to; have (offspring): *to bear a child. He was born on May 15.* **7** *Figurative.* to act in a certain way; behave; conduct: *The President bore himself with great dignity.* **8** to bring forward; give: *to bear someone company, bear a hand. A person who saw an accident can bear witness to what happened.* SYN: render. **9** *Figurative.* to hold in the mind; hold: *She bears a grudge against her friend.* SYN: cherish, harbor, entertain. **10** to have as an identification or characteristic: *He bears the name of John, the title of earl, and a reputation for learning.* SYN: possess. **11** *Archaic.* to have as a duty, right, privilege, or power: *The king bears sway over the empire.* SYN: exercise. **12** *Figurative.* to take on oneself as a duty; assume; be answerable for: *to bear the cost, bear the responsibility.* **13** *Figurative.* to allow; permit: *The motives of the best actions will not bear too strict an inquiry* (Jonathan Swift).
—*v.i.* 1 to bring forth fruit or the like: *That tree is too young to bear.* SYN: produce. **2** to press; push: *to bear heavily on a cane.* SYN: thrust. **3** to move; go: *When you reach the top of the hill, bear to your right.* SYN: tend. **4** to lie; be situated: *The land bore due north of the ship.*
bear a hand. See under **hand.**
bear arms. See under **arms.**
bear away, *Nautical.* to change the course of a ship more away from the wind: *The voyagers . . . bore away for France* (Francis Parkman).
bear down, a to press down; use pressure: *The dead weight . . . bore it down* (Tennyson). **b** *Figurative.* to make a straining effort; exert oneself: *You'll have to bear down if you expect to pass the exam.*
bear down on, a to put pressure on; lean on: *Don't bear down so hard on your pencil.* (*Figurative.*) *The father bore down so hard on his son that the boy rebelled.* **b** *Figurative.* to put all one's efforts on; try hard: *He bore down on his homework and got it done on time.* **c** to move toward; approach: *The hunters bore down on the wounded animal.*
bear in mind. See under **mind**[1].
bear on, a to have an effect on; have something to do with: *His story does not bear on the question. This legislation bears on the interests of labor.* **b** to be or move in a given direction: *Carried by strong winds, the Pilgrims' ship bore on for the New World.*
bear out, to back up; support, prove; confirm: *The facts bear out his claim.*
bear up, to keep one's courage; not lose hope or faith; remain faithful to: *The policemen bore up to their duty in the face of the mob.*
bear with, to put up with; be patient with: *Please bear with me while I ask some questions.*
bring to bear. See under **bring.**
[Old English *beran*]
—*Syn.* *v.t.* **3 Bear, endure, stand** mean to undergo something hard to take. **Bear,** the general word, suggests only being able to hold up: *He is bearing his grief very well.* **Endure** means to bear hardship or misfortune for a long time without giving in: *The pioneers endured many hardships in settling the West.* **Stand** is the informal word used interchangeably with *bear,* but it suggests bearing stubbornly and bravely: *He can stand more pain than anyone else I know.*
►See **borne** for usage note.

Bear (bãr), *n.* **1** either of two northern constellations, the Little Bear (Ursa Minor) or the Great Bear (Ursa Major). **2** a cub scout of the third highest rank. Bears are nine years old.

bear|a|ble (bãr′ə bəl), *adj.* that can be endured: *With a headache the noise was not bearable.* SYN: supportable, tolerable. **—bear′a|ble|ness,** *n.* **—bear′a|bly,** *adv.*

bear animalcule, a tardigrade organism; water bear.

bear|bait|ing (bãr′bā′ting), *n.* the sport of setting dogs to fight a chained bear, now forbidden by law.

bear|ber|ry (bãr′ber′ē, -bər-), *n., pl.* **-ries. 1** a trailing, evergreen shrub of the heath family, having small, bright-red berries and astringent leaves. **2** a similar shrub having black berries; Alpine bearberry. **3** any one of various other plants, especially a kind of holly growing in the southern United States.

bear|cat (bãr′kat′), *n.,* or **bear cat, 1** *Slang.* a lively, energetic person. **2** = panda. **3** = binturong.

beard (bird), *n., v.* **—*n.* 1** the hair growing on a man's face, especially on his chin and cheeks. **2** something resembling or suggesting this. The chin tuft of a goat is a beard; so are the stiff hairs around the beak of a bird. **3** *U.S. Slang.* a person who wears a beard: *Every middle-aged beard and his brother are out picketing for peace*

***bear**[1]
definition 1

these days (Time). **4** the hairs on the heads of plants like oats, barley, and wheat; awns. **5** a plushlike growth on parts of certain flowers, as on certain varieties of iris. **6** *Printing.* the slanting area of a printing type from the face to the shoulder. **7** *Obsolete.* the barb of an arrow or fishhook.

—*v.t.* **1** to face boldly; defy: *The hero dared to beard the lion in his den. Two noncommissioned officers appeared to beard him in his house one day, declaring he had insulted their rank* (Edmund Wilson). SYN: confront. **2** to take by the beard.

[Old English *beard*] —**beard′like′**, *adj.*

beard|ed (bir′did), *adj.* **1** having a beard: *a bearded man.* **2** having bristlelike appendages; awned: *bearded wheat.*

bearded tit, = reedling.

bearded vulture, = lammergeier.

beard|less (bird′lis), *adj.* **1** without a beard. **2** youthful or immature. SYN: young, callow. **3** *Botany.* without beard or awn: *beardless wheat.* —**beard′less|ness**, *n.*

beard lichen or **moss**, a grayish-green lichen which grows on trees and hangs downward so as to give the appearance of a beard.

beard|tongue (bird′tung′), *n.* a penstemon, a plant of the figwort family.

bear|er (bãr′ər), *n., adj.* —*n.* **1** a person or thing that carries or brings: *The messenger was a bearer of good news, a victory!* **2** a person who holds or presents a check, draft, or note for payment: *Please pay the bearer the sum of ten dollars.* **3** a tree or plant that produces fruit or flowers: *This apple tree is a good bearer.* **4** the holder of a rank or office. **5** = pallbearer.

—*adj. Finance.* negotiable by the bearer: *bearer securities.*

bear garden, **1** *Historical.* a place for baiting bears and other rough sports. **2** a place where there is much noise and confusion.

bear grass, **1** any one of various yuccas of the southern and western United States, having grasslike foliage. **2** any one of various plants of the western United States, having somewhat similar foliage, as a species of the camass of Oregon.

bear hug, **1** a crushing grasp of its victim by the forelegs of a bear. **2** a wrestling hold patterned on this, in which pressure is steadily applied to force the air out of the lungs. **3** *Figurative.* any rough or powerful embrace: *The two friends greeted each other with bear hugs and much boisterous laughter.*

bear|ing (bãr′ing), *n.* **1** way of standing, sitting, walking, or behaving; manner: *A general should have a military bearing.* SYN: deportment, behavior, demeanor. **2** connection in thought or meaning; relation: *His foolish question has no bearing on the problem.* SYN: reference. **3** part of a machine on or in which another part moves. A bearing supports the moving part and reduces friction by turning with the motion. **4** a supporting part, such as in a structure. **5a** the act, power, or time of producing or bringing forth: *a tree past bearing.* **b** that which is produced; fruit; crop. **6** power of sustaining; supporting; endurance: *Considering the government of England as totally without morality, and insolent beyond bearing* (Thomas Jefferson). SYN: toleration. **7** *Heraldry.* a single device on a coat of arms; charge.

bearings, position in relation to other things; direction: *Having no compass, the sailor got his bearings from the stars.*

lose one's bearings, to go astray: *They lost their bearings in a violent snowstorm.*

—*Syn.* **1 Bearing, carriage** mean manner of carrying oneself. **Bearing** applies to a person's manner of managing his whole body, including his gestures, mannerisms, posture, the way he holds his head, and the way he walks and sits: *the regal bearing of the king.* **Carriage** applies only to a person's way of holding his head and body when he stands and walks: *He was thin and tall, with an awkward, slouching carriage.*

bearing metal, any one of various alloys used for bearings, such as babbitt.

bearing rein, the rein by which the head of a horse is held up; checkrein.

bear|ish (bãr′ish), *adj.* **1** like a bear in manner or temper; rough or surly. **2** aiming at or tending to lower prices in the stock market or other financial market. **3** *Figurative.* not hopeful or confident; pessimistic: *He is now bearish on the whole F-104G program* (New York Times). —**bear′ish|ly**, *adv.* —**bear′ish|ness**, *n.*

bear-lead (bãr′lēd′), *v.t.*, **-led** (-led), **-lead|ing.** *British.* to lead or conduct as if by a chain; compel to follow: *The Establishment, bear-led by the Hearst Press, had decided that this turbulent man . . . must, by any hook or crook, go* (Listener). [back formation < *bear leader*]

bear leader, **1** (formerly) a traveling tutor (with allusion to his leading his young, wealthy charges as if they were trained bears). **2** *British.* one who bear-leads; a forceful leader or guide: *At last it became clear that they [the Socialists] had to get out or submit to having the Communist minority as bear leader* (London Times).

bear market, a market in which more traders on a stock exchange want to sell than to buy, with the result that prices of stocks fall.

bé|ar|naise sauce (bėr′nāz, bā′ər-; bā′ər nāz′), a sauce made from or in the fashion of hollandaise sauce, but flavored especially with tarragon, chervil, and shallots, served with grilled meat or fish. [< French *béarnaise*, feminine of *béarnais* of Béarn, a region in France]

bear's-breech (bãrz′brēch′), *n.* = acanthus.

bear's-ear (bãrz′ir′), *n.* = auricula.

bear's-foot (bãrz′fůt′), *n.* a common name for various plants, such as a medicinal species of hellebore and the lady's-mantle.

bear's head mushroom, an edible mushroom found in clumps on the trunks of trees.

***bear|skin** (bãr′skin′), *n.* **1a** the skin of a bear with the fur on it. **b** a rug, blanket, or the like, made from this. **2** a tall, black fur cap worn by some soldiers and drum majors, especially in the British Army. The bearskin is part of the dress uniform of the household troops of the British sovereign. **3** a shaggy kind of woolen cloth used for overcoats.

***bearskin**
definition 2

bear|wood (bãr′wůd′), *n.* cascara, a kind of buckthorn.

beast (bēst), *n.* **1a** any four-footed animal. Lions, bears, cows, and horses are beasts. **b** any animal except man: *Both man and beast fled before the flames of the forest fire.* SYN: See syn. under **animal**. **2** *Figurative.* **a** a coarse, dirty, or brutal person; brute: *Oh you beast, Oh faithless Coward, oh dishonest wretch* (Shakespeare). **b** a human being considered to resemble an animal in lack of self-control, etc.: *Till Morn' sends stagg'ring Home a Drunken Beast* (Sir Richard Steele). [< Old French *beste*, learned borrowing from Latin *bēstia* wild beast] —**beast′like′**, *adj.*

beast epic, a long narrative poem in which the characters are animals who act like people: *Two of the best-known beast epics are the Story of Reynard the Fox and Chicken Little* (Burton Rascoe).

beast|ie (bēs′tē), *n. Informal, originally Scottish.* a small animal, as a mouse: *Wee, sleekit, cowrin', tim'rous beastie* (Robert Burns).

beast|ly (bēst′lē), *adj.*, **-li|er**, **-li|est**, *adv.* —*adj.* **1** like a beast; coarse, dirty, or brutal; vile: *The beastly behavior of the savages frightened their prisoners.* **2** *Informal.* very bad or irritating; unpleasant; disgusting: *I have a beastly headache.* —*adv. Informal.* very; unpleasantly: *Don't be so beastly inquisitive.* —**beast′li|ness**, *n.*

beast of burden, an animal used for carrying or pulling heavy loads.

beast of prey, an animal that kills other animals for food.

beat (bēt), *v.*, **beat**, **beat|en** or **beat**, **beat|ing**, *n., adj.* —*v.t.* **1** to strike again and again; strike; whip; thrash: *The cruel rider beat his horse.* **2** to drive by blows; force by blows: *The explorer beat his way through the thick undergrowth with his long knife.* **3** to dash or strike against, as water or wind. **4** to get the better of; defeat; overcome: *Their team beat ours by a huge score.* SYN: vanquish, conquer. **5** *Informal.* to baffle: *This problem beats me.* **6** *Informal.* to cheat; swindle: *My partner beat me out of my share of the profits.* **7** to make flat; shape with a hammer; forge: *The jeweler beat gold into thin strips with a hammer.* **8** to make flat by much walking; tread (a path): *The children beat a path through the meadow.* **9** to mix by stirring or striking with a fork, spoon, or other utensil: *Mother beats eggs for a cake.* **10** to move up and down; flap: *The bird beat its wings.* **11a** to mark (time) with drumsticks or by tapping with the hands, fingers, or feet. **b** to sound (a signal) on a drum: *to beat a tattoo.* **12** to show (a unit of time or accent in music) by a stroke of the hand, foot, or baton. **13** to go through in a hunt or search: *The men beat the woods in search of the lost child.* **14** to outdo; surpass; excel: *Nothing beats sailing as a sport.*

—*v.i.* **1** to strike repeatedly; pound: *The boy beat so hard on the door that the glass broke.* **2** to throb: *Her heart beats fast with joy.* SYN: pulsate. **3** to make a sound by being struck: *The drums beat loudly.* **4** to move against the wind by a zigzag course; make way by tacking against the wind: *The sailboat beat along the coast.* **5** *Informal.* to win: *I hope you'll beat.* **6** *Physics.* to make a beat (def. 6).

—*n.* **1** a stroke or blow made again and again: *the beat of waves on a beach. We heard the beat of the drum.* **2** a throb: *The doctor listened to the beat of the sick man's heart.* SYN: pulsation. **3** the basic unit of time or accent in music, usually indicated in the time signature: *A waltz has three beats to a measure. The ballet dancer never missed a beat.* **4** a stroke of the hand, foot, or baton, showing a musical beat. **5a** a regular round or route taken by a policeman or watchman: *The policeman knew all of the shopkeepers and residents on his beat.* **5b** a source of news, such as a city hall or police headquarters, regularly assigned to a reporter. **6** *Physics.* the regular pulsation arising from the interference of simultaneous sound waves, radio waves, or electric currents which have slightly different frequencies. **7** *Slang.* a beatnik: *If he is like the beats in disliking the shams and affectations of American middle-class life . . . he is cut off from the beats by this intelligence of his and the shams and affectations of the beats are included in his satire* (Manchester Guardian). **8** *Informal.* a person, thing, or event that wins. **9** *U.S. Journalism.* the securing and publishing of news ahead of one's competitors.

—*adj.* **1** *U.S. Informal.* worn out; tired; exhausted: *Quite beat and very much vexed* (Dickens). **2** *U.S. Informal.* overcome by astonishment; taken aback. **3** *Slang.* of or characteristic of a beatnik or beatniks: *beat poetry.*

beat about, to search around; try to discover something: *I am always beating about in my thoughts for something that may turn to the benefit of my dear country* (Manchester Guardian).

beat (all) hollow, to beat completely: *This Scotch phenomenon . . . Beats Alexander hollow* (Robert Southey).

beat around (or **about**) **the bush**. See under **bush**[1].

beat back, to force or push back: *The policemen beat back the rioting mob.*

beat down, *Informal.* **a** to force to set a lower price: *Though the customer tried hard to beat him down, the shopkeeper's price remained firm.* **b** to force down (a price), as by argument or haggling: *It [usury] beats down the price of land* (Francis Bacon).

beat it, *U.S. Slang.* to go away: *When things aren't going well, he'll just beat it* (Time).

beat off, to drive away (from) by blows; drive or force back: *He beat off the savage dog.*

beat out, **a** to communicate by beats: *He . . . heard the hammer of his heart beating out a reply* (Graham Greene). **b** to keep time with (music or rhythm): *The children's feet were busy beating out the tune.* **c** *Informal.* to write or compose quickly and deliberately: *The reporter beat out a story in time for the morning edition.*

beats, the alternation of small waves with large ones produced by winds over a body of water: *If the two sets [of waves] are approaching from approximately the same angle, the result is a series of beats, or alternation of several small waves with several larger ones* (Robert M. Garrels).

beat up, *Slang.* to thrash soundly: *The boy's friends beat up the bully who tried to take away his candy.*

off (or **out of**) **one's beat**, **a** not at one's regular work: *The watchman is off his beat on Sundays.* **b** *Informal.* not in one's sphere of knowledge or concern: *Africa and America lay somewhere out of their beat* (Thomas Carlyle).

on (the) beat, **a** on the rhythm being played: *The orchestra was not on beat and everything sounded jumbled up.* **b** at the same time as the rhythm being played: *The singer didn't come in on beat; so the pianist started the song over.*

see (or **hear**) **the beat of**, *Especially U.S. Dialect.* to see or hear a person, thing, or event that surpasses or excels: *I never saw the beat of him for elegance* (O. Henry).

[Old English *bēatan*] —**beat′a|ble**, *adj.*

—*Syn. v.t.* **1 Beat, hit, pound** mean to strike. **Beat** means to strike again and again, but does not suggest how hard nor with what: *He beat a* *complicated rhythm on the drums.* **Hit** means to strike a single blow with force and aim: *The batter hit the ball.* **Pound** means to hit hard again and again with the fist or something heavy: *The child pounded the floor with a hammer.*

beat-beat (bēt′bēt′), *n. Aerospace.* dovap.

beat|en (bē′tən), *adj., v.* —*adj.* **1** struck repeatedly; whipped: *The beaten dog crawled to his master's feet.* **2a** much walked on or traveled: *The children wore a beaten path across the grass.* **b** *Figurative.* *. . . subjects out of the beaten line of the reading and thought of their day* (Matthew Arnold). **3** defeated; vanquished; overcome: *The losers were a badly beaten team.* **4** exhausted. **5** shaped by blows of a hammer: *a bowl made of beaten silver.* **6** made light by beating or whipping: *beaten egg whites.*
—*v.* a past participle of **beat:** *Our team was beaten in football on Saturday.*

beaten biscuit, *U.S.* a kind of biscuit made of flour, milk, shortening, and salt, the dough for which is pounded vigorously for a considerable time.

beat|er (bē′tər), *n.* **1** a person or thing that beats: *Mother used an old rug beater to clean the carpet on the clothes line.* **2** a man hired to rouse game during a hunt. **3** a device or utensil for beating or whipping eggs, cream, potatoes, or other foods: *an electric beater.* **4** (in papermaking) a large oval-shaped vat equipped with many bars which rub and press the cellulose fibers of wood into pulp.

beat generation, beatniks as a group.

be|a|tif|ic (bē′ə tif′ik), *adj.* **1** showing very great happiness; exaltedly happy; blissful: *The saint had a beatific smile.* **2** making blessed; blessing or making happy: *a beatific vision.* [< Late Latin *beātificus* < Latin *beātus* happy + *facere* make]
—**be′a|tif′i|cal|ly**, *adv.*

be|a|tif|i|cal (bē′ə tif′ə kəl), *adj.* = beatific.

be|at|i|fi|ca|tion (bē at′ə fə kā′shən), *n.* **1** the act of making blessed. **2** the state of being made blessed. **3** the declaration by a decree of the Pope that a dead person is among the blessed in heaven, and deserves religious honor. Beatification is often a prelude to canonization.

be|at|i|fy (bē at′ə fī), *v.t.,* **-fied, -fy|ing.** **1** to make supremely happy; bless. **2** to declare (a dead person) by a decree of the Pope to be among the blessed in heaven and to deserve religious honor. The person beatified is thereafter entitled "Blessed." [< Late Latin *beātificāre* < *beātificus;* see etym. under **beatific**]

beat|ing (bē′ting), *n.* **1** the act of one that beats; a striking. **2** punishment by blows; whipping; thrashing. **3** the state of being beaten; defeat. **4** a throbbing.
take a beating, a to suffer great physical punishment; be thrashed: *The young boxer took a terrible beating before the referee finally stopped the fight.* **b** *Figurative.* to incur a loss, especially to lose heavily: *Rails also took a severe beating, falling 5.49 points* (Wall Street Journal).

be|at|i|tude (bē at′ə tüd, -tyüd), *n.* **1** supreme happiness; bliss. **2** a blessing. **3 the Beatitudes,** the eight verses in the Sermon on the Mount which begin with "Blessed," as "Blessed are the poor in spirit." Matthew 5:3-12. [< Latin *beātitūdo* state of blessedness < *beātus* happy]

beat man, a newspaper reporter who regularly covers a particular news source.

beat|ness (bēt′nis), *n. Slang.* the quality or condition of being a beatnik.

beat|nik (bēt′nik), *n.* a young person in the 1950's, who rejected middle-class conventions and accepted standards characterized by adopting unusual dress, speech, and other conventions of Bohemianism. [< *beat,* adjective + *-nik*]

Be|a|trice (bē′ə tris), *n.* **1** a Florentine woman, Beatrice Portinari (1266-1290) whom Dante idealized and immortalized in the *Divine Comedy.* **2** (in Shakespeare's *Much Ado About Nothing*) a caustic young woman who engages in clever repartee with Benedick, whom she eventually marries.

beats (bēts), *n. pl.* See under **beat**.

beat|ster (bēt′stər), *n. U.S.* a beatnik.

beat-up (bēt′up′), *adj. Informal.* in very bad condition; showing evidence of hard use: *He drives an old beat-up jalopy.*

beau (bō), *n., pl.* **beaus** or **beaux** (bōz). **1** a young man courting a young woman; suitor or lover. SYN: sweetheart, swain. **2** a man who pays much attention to the way he dresses and to the fashion of his clothes; dandy. SYN: fop, dude. [< French *beau* a dandy < Old French *bel* good < Latin *bellus* fine]
▶**Beaux** is the more formal plural form; ordinarily, use *beaus.*

Beau Brum|mell (bō brum′əl), a dandy; fop (from the name of a famous English dandy of the early 1800's).

∗**Beau|fort scale** (bō′fərt), a scale of wind velocities, ranging from 0 (calm) to 17 (hurricane), used in weather maps and other meteorological work. See picture below. [< Sir Francis *Beaufort,* 1774-1857, a British admiral, who devised it]

beau geste (bō zhest′), *pl.* **beaux gestes** (bō zhest′). *French.* **1** a graceful or kindly act. **2** a pretense of kindness or unselfishness merely for effect.

beau greg|o|ry (bō′greg′ə rē), a tropical marine fish with a bright blue head and a yellow tail. It is a variety of remora.

beau i|de|al (bō′ī dē′əl, ī dēl′), *pl.* **beau i|de|als** (bō′ī dē′əlz, ī dēlz′). **1** the perfect type of excellence or beauty; highest ideal; model. **2** beauty, in its ideal perfection. [< French *beau idéal,* the "beautiful" as an abstract idea]

beau|ish (bō′ish), *adj.* after the manner of a beau; foppish; dandified.

Beau|jo|lais (bō′zhō lā′), *n.* a type of light Burgundy wine, usually red. [< *Beaujolais,* a region in eastern France]

beau monde (bō mond′; *French* bō mônd′), *pl.* **beaux mondes** (bō mond′; *French* bō mônd′). fashionable society. [< French *beau monde* (literally) fine world]

beau|mon|tage (bō mon′tij), *n.* a composition of various mixtures used for hiding cracks and holes in wood and metal work. [perhaps < Elie de *Beaumont,* 1798-1851, a French geologist + English *-age*]

beau sa|breur (bō sȧ brœr′), *pl.* **beaux sabreurs** (bō sȧ brœr′). *French.* **1** a spirited fighter or champion. **2** (literally) handsome swordsman.

beaut (byüt), *n. Slang.* something remarkable or outstanding; a beauty (often used ironically): *His black eye was a beaut.*

beau|te|ous (byü′tē əs), *adj.* = beautiful.
—**beau′te|ous|ly**, *adv.* —**beau′te|ous|ness**, *n.*

beau|ti|cian (byü tish′ən), *n.* a specialist in the use of cosmetics and in the care of the hair and skin, especially one who operates or is employed in a beauty shop.

beau|ti|fi|ca|tion (byü′tə fə kā′shən), *n.* a making or becoming beautiful or more beautiful; beautifying: *Color is perhaps the most universally applicable medium of beautification* (Matthew Luckiesh).

beau|ti|ful (byü′tə fəl), *adj., n.* —*adj.* very pleasing to see or hear; delighting the mind or senses: *The sky is a beautiful blue on a clear day. Great composers have written beautiful music we like to hear again and again.*
—*n.* **the beautiful**, that which has beauty, especially people or things that are beautiful: *The young, the beautiful, the brave* (Byron). *Because I love the beautiful I must Love pleasure chiefly* (Elizabeth Barrett Browning).
—**beau′ti|ful|ly**, *adv.* —**beau′ti|ful|ness**, *n.*
—*Syn. adj.* **Beautiful, lovely, handsome** mean pleasing the senses or mind. **Beautiful** suggests delighting the senses by excellence and harmony, and often also giving great pleasure to the mind by an inner goodness: *Looking at a beautiful painting always gives one satisfaction.* **Lovely** suggests appealing to the emotions and giving delight to the heart as well as to the senses and mind: *Her lovely smile shows a sweet disposition.* **Handsome** means pleasing to look at because well formed, well proportioned, etc.: *That is a handsome phonograph. Beautiful* and *lovely* are usually not applied to men.
▶In modern informal use **beautiful** is often applied to anything that a person likes very much: *to have a beautiful time. Soup of the evening, Beautiful soup!* (Lewis Carroll).

Beautiful People, *Informal.* the fashionable people of high society and the arts who set the trend in beauty and elegance.

beau|ti|fy (byü′tə fī), *v.,* **-fied, -fy|ing.** —*v.t.* to make beautiful; make more beautiful; embellish: *Flowers beautify a room.* SYN: adorn, decorate, ornament. —*v.i.* to become or grow beautiful or more beautiful. —**beau′ti|fi′er**, *n.*

beau|til|i|ty (byü til′ə tē), *n.* the qualities of beauty and usefulness or purpose combined in the design of a building, a piece of furniture, or some other object or structure. [blend of *beauty* and *utility*]

beau|ty (byü′tē), *n., pl.* **-ties.** **1** good looks: *The young lady has beauty as well as great wit and charm.* **2** the quality that continues to please in flowers, pictures, music, and other fine things: *There is beauty in a fine painting.* SYN: loveliness. **3** something beautiful: *Flowers are a part of the beauties of nature.* SYN: embellishment, ornament, grace. **4** a beautiful woman: *Many colonial women were great beauties in their day.* **5** *Informal.* something remarkable or outstanding (often used ironically): *My headache was a beauty.* **6** *Informal.* an attractive or advantageous characteristic or feature: *For the winner, arbitration has the added beauty of being final in the great majority of cases* (Time). **7** *Nuclear Physics.* the property of mass of a bottom quark: *In a search for a name for the unique quantum property of this quark, "beauty" and "bottom" were suggested, so that the upsilon may be composed of a beauty and an anti-beauty quark* (Lawrence W. Jones). [Middle English *beaute* < Old French *belte,* ultimately < Latin *bellus* fine, handsome]

beauty bush, a Chinese ornamental shrub with delicate pink flowers.

beauty contest, a contest among young women to decide who is the most beautiful.

beauty shop, parlor, or **salon,** *U.S.* a place where women have their hair, skin, and fingernails cared for.

beauty sleep, *Informal.* **1** the first two or three hours of sleep before midnight (in allusion to the belief that they are the most beneficial). **2** any short nap.

beauty spot, **1** a small, black patch worn on the face to show off the whiteness of the skin. **2** a mole or other small spot on the skin. **3** any place or natural feature of especial beauty.

beaux (bōz; *French* bō), *n.* beaus; a plural of **beau**.

beaux-arts (bō zȧr′), *n.pl. French.* the fine arts, especially painting, sculpture, and music.

beaux-es|prits (bō′zes prē′), *n. French.* plural of **bel-esprit**.

bea|ver[1] (bē′vər), *n., v.* —*n.* **1** an animal with soft fur, a broad, flat tail, and feet adapted to swimming or walking. Beavers are rodents and live both in water and on land and build dams across streams. With their large incisor teeth they cut down trees and eat the bark. Beavers are noted for their skill in constructing mud and wood lodges and dams. **2** its soft, brown fur: *Mother has a coat trimmed with beaver.* **3** a man's high, silk hat, formerly made of beaver fur. **4** a heavy, felted woolen cloth, used especially for overcoats. **5** *Slang.* **a** a beard. **b** a man who has a beard.
—*v.i. British.* Usually, **beaver away.** to work like a beaver; work hard: *The British delegations at Geneva and New York have been extremely active, beavering away to get a solution* (New Scientist).
work like a beaver, to work hard: *Mr. Baldwin . . . has worked like a beaver since he assumed the management of the mine* (R. W. Raymond). [Old English *beofor*] —**bea′ver|like′**, *adj.*

bea|ver[2] (bē′vər), *n.* **1** the movable lower part of the front of a helmet, protecting the chin and mouth. **2** the movable front part of a helmet; visor. It is hinged to swing upward. [< Old French *baviere* child's bib < *bave* child's babble; saliva < Vulgar Latin *baba*]

Bea|ver (bē′vər), *n.* a nickname for a native or inhabitant of Oregon.

bea|ver|board (bē′vər bôrd′, -bōrd′), *n.* **1** a lightweight material somewhat like very thick, strong cardboard, used for ceilings, partitions, and other building needs. **2 Beaverboard.** a trademark for this material.

bea|ver|ette (bē′və ret′), *n.* an imitation beaver fur.

Beaver State, a nickname for Oregon.

∗Beaufort scale

Beaufort Number	Name	Miles per Hour	Kilometers per Hour	Effect on Land
0	Calm	less than 1	less than 1	Calm; smoke rises vertically.
1	Light Air	1–3	1–5	Weather vanes inactive; smoke drifts with air.
2	Light Breeze	4–7	6–11	Weather vanes active; wind felt on face; leaves rustle.
3	Gentle Breeze	8–12	12–19	Leaves and small twigs move; light flags extend.
4	Moderate Breeze	13–18	20–28	Small branches sway; dust and loose paper blow about.
5	Fresh Breeze	19–24	29–38	Small trees sway; waves break on inland waters.
6	Strong Breeze	25–31	39–49	Large branches sway; umbrellas difficult to use.
7	Moderate Gale	32–38	50–61	Whole trees sway; difficult to walk against wind.
8	Fresh Gale	39–46	62–74	Twigs broken off trees; walking against wind very difficult.
9	Strong Gale	47–54	75–88	Slight damage to buildings; shingles blown off roof.
10	Whole Gale	55–63	89–102	Trees uprooted; considerable damage to buildings.
11	Storm	64–73	103–117	Widespread damage; very rare occurrence.
12-17	Hurricane	74 and above	117 or more	Violent destruction.

beaver tree, = sweet bay (def. 1).

be|bee|rine (bə bir′ēn, -in), *n.* a substance resembling quinine, yielded by the bark and seeds of the greenheart, used as a tonic and a febrifuge. *Formula:* $C_{36}H_{38}N_2O_6$ [< *bebeer*(u) + *-ine*[2]]

be|bee|ru (bə bir′ü), *n.* = greenheart. Also, **bibiru.** [apparently < the native name in Guiana]

be|bop (bē′bop′), *n.* a style of jazz popular during the late 1940's and early 1950's, characterized by unusual rhythms, dissonance, much improvisation, and, frequently, by the singing of meaningless syllables; bop. [imitative]

be|calm (bi käm′, -kälm′), *v.t.* **1** to prevent from moving by lack of wind. **2** to make calm or still; assuage; soothe.

be|calmed (bi kämd′, -kälmd′), *adj.* **1** kept from moving because there is no wind: *The sailboat lay becalmed on the lake.* **2** made calm; calm. SYN: still, quiet, tranquil.

be|came (bi kām′), *v.* past tense of **become:** *The seed became a plant.*

be|cause (bi kôz′), *conj., adv.* **—*conj.*** for the reason that; since: *Boys play ball because it's fun. Because we were late, we ran the whole way home.*
—*adv.* **because of,** by reason of; on account of: *The game was called off because of the rain.*
[Middle English *bi cause* by (the) cause]
▶**Because** introduces a subordinate clause that gives the reason for the main clause: *Because we were afraid of the dark, we avoided the cellar. Since* and *as* can be used in such clauses, but they are less definite, and are more characteristic of informal speech than of writing. *For,* which also introduces clauses of reason, is a more formal word.

bec|ca|fi|co (bek′ə fē′kō), *n., pl.* **-cos.** any one of various small European birds, especially a variety of warbler, much esteemed in Italy as food in the autumn when it is fat from summer eating. [< Italian *beccafico* (literally) fig pecker < *beccare* peck + *fico* fig]

bé|cha|mel (bā′shä mel′), *n.,* or **béchamel sauce,** a kind of creamy, white sauce, made of flour, butter, and rich milk, to which egg yolk, lemon juice, and sometimes parsley, and mushrooms are added. It is sometimes also written on menus and in cookbooks as *sauce à la béchamel* or *Sauce Béchamelle.* [< Louis de *Béchamel,* steward of Louis XIV's household, by whose chef it was invented]

be|chance (bi chans′, -chäns′), *v.,* **-chanced, -chanc|ing.** **—*v.i.*** to happen.
—*v.t.* to happen to; befall.

bêche-de-mer (besh′də mãr′), *n.* **1** a sea cucumber; trepang. **2** Also, **beach-la-mar.** a hybrid language developed chiefly through bartering and based largely on English. It is used throughout most of the Southwest Pacific area. [< French *bêche-de-mer,* alteration of Portuguese *bicho do mar* sea slug]

Bech|u|an|a (bech′ů ä′nə, bek′yů-), *n., pl.* **-an|a** or **-an|as.** a member of a Bantu tribe living in Botswana (the former British protectorate of Bechuanaland) in southern Africa. [< Bantu *Betşwana*]

beck[1] (bek), *n., v.* **—*n.*** **1** a motion of the head or hand meant as a call or command. SYN: gesture. **2** *Especially Scottish.* an inclination of the head; bow; nod.
—*v.i., v.t.* **1** to signal by, or as if by, nodding the head or waving the hand; beckon to. SYN: beckon. **2** *British.* to imitate the mating call of a game bird in order to lure it into shooting range.
at one's beck and call, subject to one's slightest wish; obliged or ready to obey all one's orders or desires: *An errand boy is at the beck and call of his boss.*
[short for *beckon*]

beck[2] (bek), *n.* (in northern England) a brook or stream, especially one with a stony bed or rugged course. [< Scandinavian (compare Old Icelandic *bekkr*)]

beck|et (bek′it), *n. Nautical.* **1** a simple contrivance for holding loose things in place, fastening the sheets of sails, or the like, usually consisting of a loop of rope with a knot on one end and an eye at the other. **2** = grommet (def. 2). [origin uncertain]

becket bend, = sheet bend.

beck|on (bek′ən), *v., n.* **—*v.i., v.t.*** to signal (to a person) by a motion of the head or hand: *The guide beckoned us to follow him.* SYN: gesture, summon.
—*n.* a signaling gesture.
[Old English *bēcnan* < *bēacen* a sign, beacon] **—beck′on|er,** *n.* **—beck′on|ing|ly,** *adv.*
▶**beckon.** The idiom is *beckon to,* not *beckon at: The tall man beckoned to her.*

be|cloud (bi kloud′), *v.t.* **1** to hide by a cloud or clouds: *a room beclouded with steam.* SYN: cloud, overshadow. **2** to make obscure; darken; hide: *These fine words ... becloud unpleasant facts* (George Eliot). SYN: dim, obfuscate, bedim.

be|come (bi kum′), *v.,* **-came, -come, -com|ing.** **—*v.i.*** **1** to come to be; grow to be: *When the sun goes down it becomes colder. He became wiser as he got older.* **2** *Obsolete.* to come about; come to pass; happen.
—*v.t.* **1** to seem proper or fitting for; be suitable for: *It does not become young children to question a teacher's decision.* SYN: befit. **2** to look well on; suit; befit in appearance: *A white dress becomes the girl with long dark hair.*
become of, to happen to; be the fate of: *What has become of the box of candy? What will become of her old toys?*
[Old English *becuman* happen, come about < *be-* be- + *cuman* come]
▶**Become** is one of the common linking verbs: *At his words she became more angry.*

be|com|ing (bi kum′ing), *adj., n.* **—*adj.*** **1** fitting; suitable or appropriate: *Spitting is not becoming to a gentleman.* SYN: seemly. See syn. under **fitting.** **2** pleasant to look at; attractive: *Women in hair curlers are hardly becoming.*
—*n.* *Philosophy.* **1** a coming into existence. **2** a change from one state to another. **—be|com′ing|ly,** *adv.* **—be|com′ing|ness,** *n.*

bec|que|rel (bek′ə rel′, bek rel′), *n.* the international unit of radioactivity, equal to one disintegration per second. It is intended to replace the curie. *Among the SI's* [*Système International*] *derived units with special names are those for ... radioactivity* (*the becquerel, or spontaneous nuclear transitions per second*) *and absorbed dose of radiation* (*the gray, or joules per kilogram*) (Scientific American). [< Antoine H. *Becquerel,* 1852-1908, a French physicist]

Becquerel rays, the invisible rays given off by radium, uranium, and other radioactive substances. This term has been replaced by the more specific terms, *alpha rays, beta rays,* and *gamma rays.* [< Antoine H. *Becquerel,* 1852-1908, a French physicist, who first reported them]

bed (bed), *n., v.,* **bed|ded, bed|ding.** **—*n.*** **1a** anything to sleep or rest on. A bed usually consists of a mattress raised upon a support and covered with sheets and blankets. **b** a bedstead: *a maple bed.* **2** any place where people or animals sleep or rest: *The cat made his bed by the fireplace. Ulysses heaped a bed of leaves* (William Cullen Bryant). **3** a flat base on which anything rests; foundation: *They set the pole in a bed of concrete.* **4** the ground under a body of water: *The bed of the river was muddy.* **5a** a piece of ground to grow plants in; garden: *We planted the bed along the front walk with daffodils.* **b** the plants growing in it: *a bed of tulips.* **6** *Geology.* a layer; stratum: *The miners struck a bed of coal deep in the earth.* **7** the level surface in a printing press on which the form of type is laid. **8a** the lower surface of a brick, stone, slate, or tile fastened in place in a foundation or other structure, such as a wall or roof. **b** either of the horizontal surfaces of such a brick, stone, slate, or tile. **c** the layer of mortar or cement in which such a brick, stone, slate, or tile is set. **9** the layer of broken stone, gravel, or other loose material, upon which the ties of a railroad are laid. **10** the flesh surrounding the base of the claw of an animal.
—*v.t.* **1** to provide with a bed; put to bed: *The farmer bedded his horse in the barn.* **2** to fix or set in a permanent position; embed. **3** to plant in a garden bed: *to bed out seedlings. These tulips should be bedded in rich soil.* **4** to lay flat or in order. **5** to go to bed with.
—*v.i.* **1** to go to bed; retire for the night: *The cave where I bedded ...* (Thomas Hood). **2** to form a compact layer.
bed down, a to make or arrange a sleeping place for: *He bedded the horse down with straw.* **b** to go to bed; lie down for the night: *The great herd had bedded down* (Elisha Mulford).
get up on the wrong side of the bed, to be irritable or bad-tempered: *She got up on the wrong side of the bed and wouldn't speak to anyone all day.*
make one's bed, to take a decisive step of which the consequences are to be accepted: *She made her bed when she quit school to go to work; now let her lie in it.*
put to bed, a to prepare (a child, sick person, or animal) for sleeping: *The doctor ordered that she be put to bed very early.* **b** *Journalism, Slang.* to prepare (a newspaper or magazine edition) to go to press: *Most of the staff didn't go home until the special edition was put to bed.*
take to one's bed, to stay in bed because of sickness or weakness: *By and by he took to his bed* (Harper's).
[Old English *bedd*] **—bed′da|ble,** *adj.* **—bed′-less,** *adj.*

B.Ed., Bachelor of Education.

be|dab|ble (bi dab′əl), *v.t.,* **-bled, -bling.** to spatter all over or make dirty with something, especially something liquid.

be|damn (bi dam′), *v.t.* to invoke or inflict with a curse.

bed and board, 1 a place for sleep and meals. **2** the facilities and privileges of a home: *She has left his bed and board and is suing for divorce.*

be|dark|en (bi där′kən), *v.t.* to darken completely.

be|dash (bi dash′), *v.t.* to dash with water or other liquid; cover with dashes of water, mud, paint, or other liquid.

be|daub (bi dôb′), *v.t.* **1** to smear with something dirty or sticky. SYN: plaster. **2** to ornament in a gaudy or showy way. SYN: bedizen.

be|daze (bi dāz′), *v.t.,* **-dazed, -daz|ing.** to daze completely; stupefy; bewilder. **—be|daze′ment,** *n.*

be|daz|zle (bi daz′əl), *v.t.,* **-zled, -zling.** to dazzle completely; confuse by dazzling. **—be|daz′zle-ment,** *n.*

bed|bound (bed′bound′), *adj.* = bedridden.

***bed|bug** (bed′bug′), *n.* a small, flat, wingless, reddish-brown, blood-sucking insect found in houses and especially in beds; cimex. Its bite is painful.

***bedbug**

bed|cham|ber (bed′chām′bər), *n.* = bedroom.

bed|clothes (bed′klōz′, -klōᴛʜz′), *n.pl.* sheets, blankets, quilts, pillows, and sometimes bedspreads and other coverings.

bed|cov|er (bed′kuv′ər), *n.* bedspread; coverlet. **bedcovers,** bedclothes: *Suddenly, rapidly, he flung back the bedcovers and leaped out* (New Yorker).

bed|cov|er|ing (bed′kuv′ər ing), *n.* = bedclothes.

bed|der (bed′ər), *n.* **1** a plant suitable for being grown in a flower bed. **2** the lower stone in a mill for expressing oil from seeds, fruits, etc. **3** *Southern U.S.* a farmer who works the soil of bottom land. **4** *British.* a woman who makes up the beds at a college or university dormitory.

bed|ding (bed′ing), *n., adj.* **—*n.*** **1a** sheets, blankets, quilts, and sometimes bedspreads and other coverings: *All of the bedding fell to the floor during the pillow fight.* **b** mattresses, pillows, sleeping bags, bedrolls, and sometimes springs. **2** material for beds: *Straw is used as bedding for cows and horses.* **3** a foundation; bottom layer. **4** *Geology.* arrangement of rocks or other strata in beds or layers; stratification. **5** the planting of flowers in beds for decoration.
—*adj.* suitable for being grown in decorative garden beds: *bedding varieties of petunias.*

bedding plane, *Geology.* the surface between successive layers of a formation of stratified rocks; plane of stratification.

bedding roll, = bedroll.

bede (bēd), *n. Obsolete.* a prayer. [Middle English *bede* prayer, rosary bead; see etym. under **bead**]

be|deck (bi dek′), *v.t.* to deck out; adorn; decorate: *The hero was bedecked with medals.* SYN: embellish, trim, garnish.

bed|e|gar or **bed|e|guar** (bed′ə gär), *n.* spongy excrescence or gall produced on rosebushes, especially on the sweetbrier, by various gallflies. [< French *bédegar, bédeguar* < Persian *bādāwar*]

bede|house (bēd′hous′), *n.* = beadhouse.

be|del or **be|dell** (bē′dəl), *n.* a beadle.

bede|roll (bēd′rōl′), *n.* = beadroll.

bedes|man (bēdz′mən), *n., pl.* **-men.** = beadsman.

bedes|wom|an (bēdz′wům′ən), *n., pl.* **-wom|en.** = beadswoman.

be|dev|il (bi dev′əl), *v.t.,* **-iled, -il|ing** or (*especially British*) **-illed, -il|ling.** **1** to trouble greatly; drive frantic; torment: *Biting flies bedeviled the horses.* SYN: worry, bother. **2** to confuse completely; muddle: *The accountant was bedeviled in a mass of figures.* SYN: confound. **3** to put under a spell; bewitch. **4** to change so as to spoil or corrupt. **—be|dev′il|ler,** *n.* **—be|dev′il|ment,** *n.*

be|dew (bi dü′, -dyü′), *v.t.* to wet with dew or drops like dew: *Tears bedewed her cheeks.*

bed|fast (bed′fast′, -fäst′), *adj.* confined to bed; bedridden.

bed|fel|low (bed′fel′ō), *n.* **1** a sharer of one's bed. **2** *Figurative.* an associate: *Politics makes strange bedfellows.*

Bed|ford cord (bed′fərd), a heavy cloth ribbed like corduroy, used especially for riding breeches. [< *Bedford,* a town in England]

bed|gown (bed′goun′), *n.* **1** a nightgown. **2** *Brit-*

Pronunciation Key: hat, āge, cãre, fär; let, ēqual, tėrm; it, īce; hot, ōpen, ôrder; oil, out; cup, půt, rüle; child; long; thin; ᴛʜen; zh, measure; ə represents a in about, e in taken, i in pencil, o in lemon, u in circus.

ish Dialect. a loose jacket worn by women of the working class.

bed|head (bed′hed′), *n.* the upper end of a bed.

Be|dias|ite (bə dī′sīt, -zīt), *n.* tektite found in Texas. [< *Bedias,* a town in Texas + *-ite*[1]]

be|dight (bi dīt′), *v.,* **-dight, -dight** or **-dight|ed, -dight|ing,** *adj. Archaic.* —*v.t.* to adorn; array.
—*adj.* adorned; arrayed.

be|dim (bi dim′), *v.t.,* **-dimmed, -dim|ming.** to make dim; darken; obscure. **SYN**: becloud, overcast.

Bed|i|vere (bed′ə vir), *n.* **Sir,** *Arthurian Legend.* the faithful Knight of the Round Table who brought the dying Arthur to the barge that carried him to Avalon.

be|di|zen (bi dī′zən, -diz′ən), *v.t.* to dress or ornament with showy finery. **SYN**: bedaub. [< *be-* + *dizen*] —**be|di′zen|ment,** *n.*

bed jacket, a jacket of lightweight material, often quilted, worn over a nightgown or pajamas, usually when sitting up in bed.

bed|lam (bed′ləm), *n., adj.* —*n.* **1a** noisy confusion; uproar: *When our team won, there was bedlam in the gym.* **SYN**: Babel. **b** a scene of such confusion. **SYN**: pandemonium. **2** *Archaic.* an insane asylum; madhouse. **3** *Obsolete.* a lunatic; madman.
—*adj. Archaic.* of or fit for a madhouse; mad.
[Middle English *bedlem,* alteration of Saint Mary of *Bethlehem,* hospital for the insane in London]

bed|lam|ite (bed′lə mīt), *n.* an insane person; madman.

bed linen, sheets and pillowcases for a bed.

Bed|ling|ton terrier (bed′ling tən), any one of a breed of medium-sized terriers with rough, woolly fur, typically bluish- or grayish-brown in color. As most terriers are, Bedlingtons are noted for their gameness. [< *Bedlington,* a town in England]

bed|load (bed′lōd′), *n. Geology.* **1** bits of rock, soil, or other detritus, carried along the bottom of a river or stream by the current. **2** coarse particles, such as sand, carried along the ground by the wind.

bed|mak|er (bed′mā′kər), *n.* a person who makes the beds and sweeps the college rooms at Oxford and Cambridge.

bed|mate (bed′māt′), *n.* = bedfellow.

bed molding, 1 a molding, or a series of moldings, on or directly under a cornice, between the corona of the cornice and the frieze of the entablature. **2** any molding beneath a projection.

bed of roses, 1 a situation of luxurious ease. **2** an easy and highly agreeable position.

Bed|ou|in (bed′ů in), *n., pl.* **-ins** or **-in,** *adj.* —*n.* **1** a member of certain tribes of wandering Arabs who live in the deserts of Arabia, Syria, and northern Africa. **2** *Figurative.* any wanderer or nomad.
—*adj.* of the Bedouins; nomadic. Also, **Beduin.**
[< Old French *beduin* < Arabic *badawīy* desert dweller]

Bed|ou|in|ism (bed′ů ə niz′əm), *n.* **1** the Bedouin way of life. **2** *Figurative.* any nomadic or vagabond way of life.

bed|pan (bed′pan′), *n.* **1** a shallow pan used as a toilet by sick people in bed. **2** a pan filled with hot coals for warming a bed; warming pan. [American English < Dutch *bedpanne*]

bed|plate (bed′plāt′), *n.* a flat piece of metal serving as the foundation or support for a machine, stove, or the like.

bed|post (bed′pōst′), *n.* an upright support at a corner of the framework of a bed.
between you and me and the bedpost, in all confidence or secrecy: *Between you and me and the bedpost, young master's quarrelled with old master* (Edward G. Bulwer-Lytton).

be|drab|ble (bi drab′əl), *v.t.,* **-bled, -bling.** to make drabbled, or wet and dirty; bedraggle.

be|drag|gle (bi drag′əl), *v.t.,* **-gled, -gling.** to make limp and soiled by dragging through dirt or moisture. —**be|drag′gle|ment,** *n.*

be|drag|gled (bi drag′əld), *adj.* **1** wet and hanging limp: *When she came in out of the rain she tried to comb her bedraggled hair.* **2** soiled by being dragged in the dirt.

bed|rail (bed′rāl′), *n.* **1** one of the two side pieces of the frame of a bedstead. **2** a rail pulled above the side pieces, as in a hospital bed, to keep a person from falling out of bed.

be|drench (bi drench′), *v.t.* to drench completely; soak.

bed rest, 1 rest taken in bed, especially by a patient. **2** an apparatus for supporting patients in bed.

bed|rid (bed′rid′), *adj.* **1** = bedridden. **2** *Figurative.* worn out; decrepit: *... bedrid in his faculties* (William Hazlitt). **SYN**: impotent. [Old English *bedreda, -rida* (originally) bed rider]

bed|rid|den (bed′rid′ən), *adj.* compelled to stay in bed, usually for a long time, because of sickness or weakness: *a bedridden invalid.*

bed|rock (bed′rok′), *n., adj.* —*n.* **1** the solid rock beneath the soil and looser rocks. **2** *Figurative.* a firm foundation. **3** *Figurative.* the lowest level; bottom: *Demands on resources by the Government and all public authorities should be kept to absolute bedrock* (London Times). **4** *Figurative.* underlying principle: *Honesty was the bedrock of his personal life.*
—*adj.* basic; fundamental.

bed|roll (bed′rōl′), *n.* blankets or a sleeping bag that can be rolled up and tied for carrying.

bed|room (bed′rüm′, -rům′), *n., adj.* —*n.* a room to sleep in.
—*adj.* **1** *U.S.* of or belonging to a bedroom suburb; inhabited by persons who work in the city: *bedroom communities, a bedroom town.* **2** dealing with sexual relationships: *a bedroom comedy.* **3** sexually appealing or stimulating: *bedroom eyes.*

bedroom suburb, *U.S.* a suburb inhabited by persons who work all day in the city and spend only the night at home.

bed|sheet (bed′shēt′), *n.* a sheet for a bed.

bed|side (bed′sīd′), *n., adj.* —*n.* the side of a bed: *The nurse sat by the sick woman's bedside.*
—*adj.* **1** with the sick; attending the sick: *Young doctors need bedside practice.* **2** for a person in bed: *a bedside lamp.* **3** for light reading before sleep: *a bedside book.*

bedside manner, 1 the deportment of a doctor at the bedside of a patient: *The ordinary notion is that a good bedside manner consists of suavity carried to the verge of civility* (British Medical Journal). **2** a smoothly winning or persuasive manner: *A rotund intellectual of 48, with a disarming editorial bedside manner ...* (Newsweek).

bed-sit (bed′sit′), *n., v.* —*n. British Informal.* a bed-sitter.
—*v.i.* to occupy a bed-sitter.

bed-sit|ter (bed′sit′ər), *n. British.* a single room combining bedroom and sitting room.

bed-sit|ting room (bed′sit′ing), *British.* a bed-sitter.

bed|sore (bed′sôr′, -sōr′), *n.* a sore caused by lying too long in the same position. People bedridden by old age or chronic illness are particularly subject to bedsores.

bed|space (bed′spās′), *n.* beds or space for beds in a hotel, hospital, dormitory, or the like: *an acute shortage of hospital bedspace.*

bed|spread (bed′spred′), *n.* a cover for a bed that is spread over the blankets to protect them and make the bed look neater. **SYN**: coverlet.

bed|spring (bed′spring′), *n., adj.* —*n.* **1** a set of springs forming part of a bed and supporting the mattress. **2** one of these springs (usually coiled).
—*adj.* like the coils of a bedspring: *a bedspring antenna.*

bed|stead (bed′sted, -stid), *n.* the wooden or metal framework of a bed, that supports the springs and mattress.

bed|stone (bed′stōn′), *n.* the lower stone of a pair of millstones, upon which the upper stone rotates.

bed|straw (bed′strô′), *n.* a small plant of the madder family with clusters of white or yellow flowers. Its fragrant stems and leaves were formerly dried and used as straw for beds.

bed|tick (bed′tik′), *n.* the cloth covering of a box spring or mattress.

bed|time (bed′tīm′), *n., adj.* —*n.* the time to go to bed: *His regular bedtime is nine o'clock.*
—*adj.* suitable or usual just before going to bed for the night: *a bedtime snack.*

bedtime story, 1 a story, such as a fairy tale, told at bedtime to a child or children. **2** any nice but incredible report, news, etc.

Bed|u (bed′ů), *n., pl.* **Bed|u,** *adj. British.* Bedouin.

Bed|u|in (bed′ů in), *n., adj.* = Bedouin.

bed|ward (bed′wərd), *adv.* toward bed; in the direction of bed.

bed|wards (bed′wərdz), *adv.* = bedward.

bed-wet|ter (bed′wet′ər), *n.* a person, especially a child, who habitually urinates in bed.

bed-wet|ting (bed′wet′ing), *n.* habitual urination in bed; enuresis.

***bee**[1] (bē), *n.* **1** an insect with four wings and a hairy body, that produces wax to make honeycombs and gathers nectar and pollen from flowers to make honey. There are several kinds. Honeybees live in large, permanent, highly organized communities, containing a queen, many workers, and drones. Only the queen and workers have stings. **2** any one of various related insects, such as bumblebees and carpenter bees. There are over 20,000 species of bees in the world. Their hairy bodies distinguish them from wasps, to which they are related. Wild bees show various gradations from elaborately organized colonies to solitary nests. **3** *U.S.* a gathering for work or amusement: *a sewing bee, a husking bee. The teacher let us have a spelling bee in class today.*

have a bee in one's bonnet (or **one's head**), **a** to think of one thing only; be overenthusiastic about one thing: *When he has a bee in his bonnet, he won't consider anything else.* **b** to have some secret idea: *College presidents have perpetual bees in their bonnets, and that gets them into the habit of speaking a lot* (James B. Conant). **c** to be slightly crazy: *John Hunter, notwithstanding he had a bee in his bonnet, was a really great man* (Thomas De Quincey).

put the bee on, *Especially U.S. Slang.* to try to get money from; borrow from: *You don't have to tell me why you don't put the bee on your brother* (Saul Bellow).

the bee's knees, *Slang.* the most outstanding or excellent person or thing; the tops; something special: *"I know Ari. He's the bee's knees"* (Time).
[Old English *bēo*]

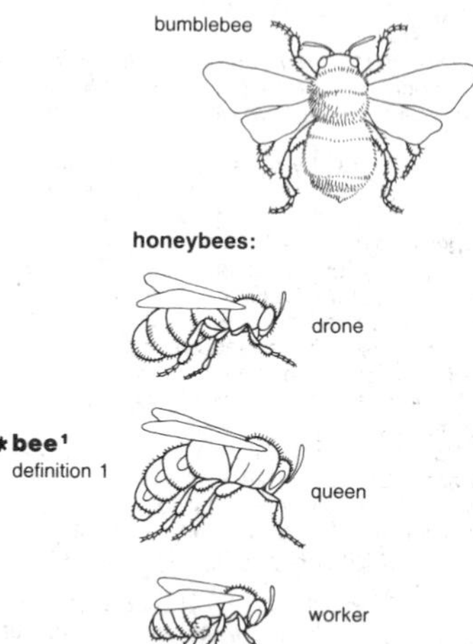

bee[2] (bē), *n. Nautical.* a ring, or a piece of hardwood, bolted to the side of a bowsprit and used to reeve stays through; bee block. [Old English *bēah,* or *bēag* ring]

B.E.E., *U.S.* Bachelor of Electrical Engineering.

bee balm, any one of various perennial plants of North America belonging to the mint family, such as the Oswego tea. Certain varieties have red or lavender blossoms that are very attractive to bees, especially bumblebees, and also to hummingbirds.

bee|bee gun (bē′bē), an air rifle; BB gun.

bee beetle, a blister beetle whose larvae (bee wolf) infest beehives.

bee bird, a small, spotted flycatcher that catches bees.

bee block, *Nautical.* bee².

bee|bread (bē′bred′), *n.* a brownish, bitter substance consisting of pollen, or pollen mixed with honey, used by bees as food, especially for their larvae or young.

beech (bēch), *n., pl.* **beech|es** or **beech** *for 1, adj.* —*n.* **1** a tree with smooth, gray bark and glossy leaves. It bears a sweet nut that is good to eat. Beech trees are found in the Northern Hemisphere. **2** its wood.
—*adj.* of the tree or its wood; made of beech.
[Old English *bōece,* or *bēce*]

beech|drops (bēch′drops′), *n.* **1** a low, annual North American plant without green foliage, that is parasitic upon the roots of the beech. **2** = squawroot.

beech|en (bē′chən), *adj.* **1** made of the wood of the beech. **2** of or having to do with the beech or its wood.

beech family, a group of deciduous trees and shrubs, growing mostly in temperate regions, including the beeches, the oaks, and the chestnuts.

beech marten, the stone marten, a weasellike animal of Europe.

beech|mast (bēch′mast′, -mäst′), *n.* beechnuts, especially when they are lying on the ground.

beech|nut (bēch′nut′), *n.* the small, triangular nut of the beech tree. Beechnuts are good to eat.

beech|wood (bēch′wůd′), *n.* the wood of a beech tree.

beech|y (bē′chē), *adj.* **1** of or having to do with the beech. **2** abounding in beeches.

bee eater, any one of a family of insect-eating birds, native to Europe and Asia, having bright plumage and a slender bill.

***beef** (bēf), *n., pl.* **beeves** *for 2,* **beefs** *for 5, v.* —*n.* **1** meat from a steer, cow, or bull: *Mother had some beef ground up for hamburgers.* See picture across on next page. **2** a steer, cow, or bull when full-grown and fattened for food: *The*

cattleman drove the beeves into the corral. **3** *Informal, Figurative.* strength; muscle; brawn: *The crew is lacking in beef.* **SYN:** muscularity. **4** *Figurative.* weight; heaviness. **5** *Slang.* a complaint; grievance.
– ***v.i.*** *Slang.* to complain: *They began to whine and beef about seeing museums* (New Yorker).
– ***v.t.*** to fatten or slaughter (a steer) for food.
beef up, *Slang.* **a** to make greater; enlarge: *The company plans to beef up benefits to retired workers.* **b** to increase the power of; strengthen: *to beef up an engine.*
[< Old French *boef* beef, ox < Latin *bōs, bovis* ox] – **beef′less**, *adj.*

beef|a|lo (bē′fə lō), *n., pl.* **-loes** or **-los.** *U.S.* any one of a breed of beef cattle developed by interbreeding Herefords and Charolaises with buffaloes. [blend of *beef* and *buffalo*]

beef bacon, salted and smoked beef cut from the rib plate, somewhat resembling bacon in flavor and appearance.

beef|burg|er (bēf′bėr′gər), *n.* = hamburger.

beef|cake (bēf′kāk′), *n. Slang.* photography or photographs emphasizing virile male figures. [patterned after *cheesecake*]

beef cattle, cattle raised for meat.

beef|eat|er (bēf′ē′tər), *n.* **1** Also, **Beefeater. a** a yeoman of the English royal guard. **b** a warder, or special guard, of the Tower of London. **2** an eater of beef: *a nation of beefeaters.* **3** *Figurative.* a stout, well-fed man.

beef|er (bē′fər), *n. Slang.* a complaining person.

beef extract, an extract of beef or beef juices, used to make broth, or as an ingredient of a sauce or gravy.

beef|ing (bē′fing), *n.* = biffin.

bee flower, any one of various flowers or flowering plants, such as the orchid, violet, larkspur, mint, snapdragon, and pea, which attract bees by their fragrant odors and by petals of colors other than red (to which bees are color-blind).

bee fly, any one of a family of flies, many of which look like bees. Members of some species live as parasites in beehives.

Beef|mas|ter (bēf′mas′tər), *n. Trademark.* any of a breed of hardy cattle of the western United States, raised chiefly for beef by crossbreeding Brahmas, shorthorns, and Herefords.

beef|steak (bēf′stāk′), *n.* a slice of beef for broiling or frying.

beefsteak mushroom or **fungus**, = liver fungus.

beef Stro|ga|noff (strô′gə nôf), pieces of beef cooked in butter with chopped onions and mushrooms, to which sour cream and seasonings are added to produce the sauce in which it is served. [< French *boeuf (à la) Stroganoff* < Russian *Stroganov*, an aristocratic surname]

beef tea, a strong beef broth made by soaking and heating beef in water, then straining and seasoning the liquid.

beef-wit|ted (bēf′wit′id), *adj.* stupid.

beef|wood (bēf′wu̇d′), *n.* **1** = casuarina. **2** the close-grained, reddish wood of the casuarina, used for ornamental woodwork and cabinets.

beef|y (bē′fē), *adj.,* **beef|i|er, beef|i|est. 1** *Figurative.* strong, solid, and heavy: *a beefy wrestler.* **2** like beef: *a beefy taste.* – **beef′i|ness**, *n.*

bee glue, = propolis.

bee gum, *Southwestern and Western U.S.* **1** a hollowed gum tree which houses a swarm of bees. **2** a beehive made from such a tree or a section of it.

bee|hive** (bē′hīv′), *n., adj.* – ***n. **1** a hive or house for bees; hive. A beehive was formerly often made of coils of straw stacked one upon the other in the shape of a dome, but is now usually a rectangular box. **2** *Figurative.* a busy, swarming place: *On the day of the sale the department store was a beehive of shoppers looking for bargains.* **3** a woman's hair style having the shape of a conical, coiled beehive.
– ***adj.*** having the top dome-shaped like the traditional beehive: *a beehive oven.*

***beehive** definition 1

coiled

standard

beehive hairdo, = beehive (def. 3).

Beehive State, a nickname for Utah.

beehive tomb, a dome-shaped subterranean tomb of the Mycenaean age in Greece, consisting of a dromos cut into a hillside and ending in a circular chamber.

bee|house (bē′hous′), *n.* = apiary.

bee hummingbird, the smallest known bird in the world, a variety of hummingbird found in Cuba, growing to a length of two inches.

beek (bēk), *v., n. Scottish.* – ***v.i.*** = bask.
– ***v.t.*** = warm.
– ***n.*** a warming or basking.
[origin unknown]

bee|keep|er (bē′kē′pər), *n.* a person who raises bees for their honey; apiarist.

bee|keep|ing (bē′kē′ping), *n.* = apiculture.

bee killer, **1** a digger wasp that stores bees and winged ants in its nest for use as food; bee wolf. **2** = robber fly.

bee|line (bē′līn′), *n., v.,* **-lined, -lin|ing.** – ***n.*** the straightest way between two places, like the flight of a bee to its hive: *The ball sailed on a beeline, straight for the window.*
– ***v.i.*** to move, run, fly, etc., in or as if in a beeline: *Just before the storm broke we beelined for home.*
make a beeline for, *Informal.* to hurry or race directly toward: *The little brothers and sisters made a beeline for the gingerbread men* (Atlantic).

bee louse, a tiny, wingless fly, which lives as a parasite on bees.

Be|el|ze|bub (bē el′zə bub), *n.* **1** the Devil; Satan (in the Bible, Matthew 12:24-27; Mark 3:22; Luke 11:15-19). **2** a devil. **3** a fallen angel next to Satan in power, in Milton's poem *Paradise Lost.*

bee martin, *U.S.* the kingbird.

bee|mas|ter (bē′mas′tər, -mäs′-), *n.* = beekeeper.

bee moth, any one of several species of moths that lay their eggs in beehives. The larvae feed on the honeycomb built by the bees.

been (bin, ben; *especially British* bēn; *see note below*), *v.* the past participle of **be**: *He has been ill. Where have you been? The books have been read by every girl in the room.*
► In origin (bin) is the unstressed and (bēn) the stressed form and some British speakers still employ both forms in this fashion. Today, however, most speakers of British English use (bēn) in all positions and most Americans similarly employ (bin).

bee orchid or **bee orchis**, a European orchid noted for the resemblance of part of its flower to a bee.

beep (bēp), *n., v.* – ***n.*** **1** a sharp, short sound issued as a signal in broadcasting or by a radio direction-finding apparatus: *Did the beeps from the Soviet moon awaken the American people to the realities of the scientific age?* (Bulletin of Atomic Scientists). **2** any sharp, short sound, such as the sound of an automobile horn.
– ***v.t., v.i.*** to make or cause (something) to make sharp, short sounds: *to beep a horn. The first Russian moon rose beeping into the sky* (New Scientist).
[imitative] – **beep′er**, *n.*

bee plant, the cleome, figwort, or any one of various other plants to which bees are attracted as a source of nectar.

beer[1] (bir), *n.* **1** an alcoholic drink made from malted barley flavored with hops: *a glass of yellow beer with a head of white foam.* **2** a soft drink made from roots, barks, or plants, such as ginger beer or root beer. **3** a glass, bottle, can, or other container of beer: *to drink a cool beer.* [Old English *bēor*]

beer[2] (bir), *n. British.* a division of a warp in weaving, consisting of a specified number of threads: *a beer of 40 threads.* [variant of *bier*]

beer and skittles, material comforts and pleasures; enjoyment.

beer bust, *U.S. Slang.* a party at which beer is the main beverage.

beer garden, a garden or enclosed yard where beer is sold and served at tables.

beer|hall (bir′hôl′), *n.* a place where beer is sold and drunk.

beer|house (bir′hous′), *n.* a place where malt liquors are sold; alehouse.

beer|y (bir′ē), *adj.,* **beer|i|er, beer|i|est. 1** of beer: *a beery odor.* **2** caused by or influenced by beer: *beery good humor.* **3** like beer: *a beery drink.* **4** full of beer: *a beery old tramp.* – **beer′i|ly**, *adv.* – **beer′i|ness**, *n.*

bee smoker, a beekeeper's apparatus for producing and driving smoke into a hive to stupefy the bees while the honeycomb is being removed.

beest|ings (bēs′tingz), *n.pl.* the first milk from a cow after it has given birth to a calf; colostrum. Also, **biestings.** [Old English *bȳsting* < *bēost*]

bees|wax (bēz′waks′), *n., v.* – ***n.*** the wax given out by bees, from which they make their honeycomb: *Mother used a polish of beeswax to rub the furniture.*
– ***v.t., v.i.*** to rub, polish, or treat with beeswax.

bees|wing (bēz′wing′), *n.* **1** a thin film that forms in some old wines. **2** an old wine that has such a film.

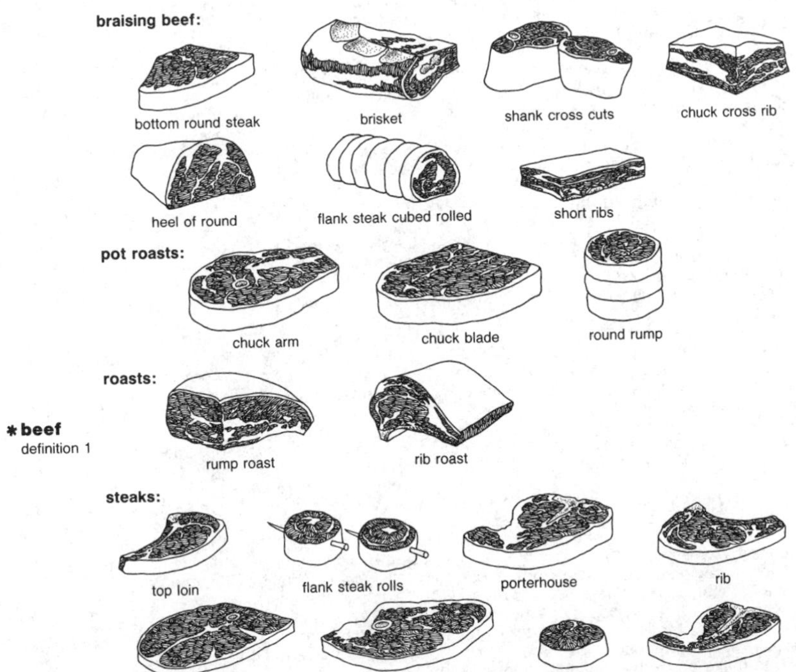

***beef** definition 1

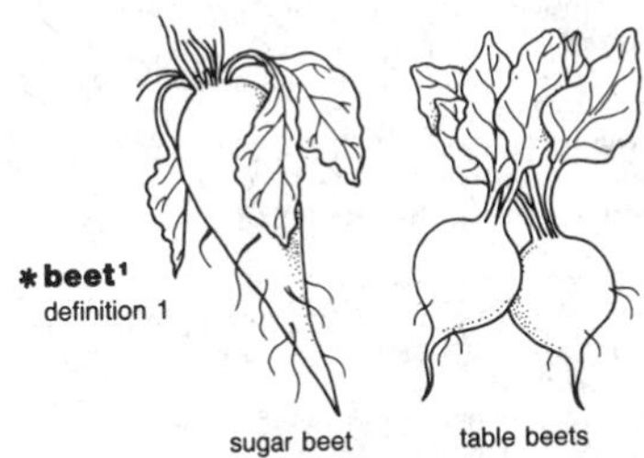

***beet[1]** definition 1

***beet[1]** (bēt), *n.* **1** a plant grown for its thick, fleshy root. The leaves are sometimes eaten as greens.

Pronunciation Key: hat, āge, cãre, fär; let, ēqual, tėrm; it, īce; hot, ōpen, ôrder; **oi**l, **ou**t; cup, pu̇t, rüle; **ch**ild; lo**ng**; **th**in; ᴛʜen; **zh**, measure; ə represents **a** in about, **e** in taken, **i** in pencil, **o** in lemon, **u** in circus.

Beets are biennial plants that belong to the goosefoot family. **2** its root. Red beets are often eaten as a vegetable. Sugar is made from some kinds of white beets. [Old English *bēte* < Latin *bēta*] —**beet′like′**, *adj.*

beet[2] (bēt), *v.t. Dialect.* **1** = repair. **2a** = kindle (a fire). **b** = replenish (a fire). [Old English *bētan*]

beet-faced (bēt′fāst′), *adj.* ruddy; florid.

Bee|tho|ve|ni|an (bā′tō vē′nē ən), *adj., n.* —*adj.* of or having to do with Ludwig van Beethoven or his music: *The tight rein on which Dr. Klemperer held the first movement ... brought out a symphonic force and integrity of an almost Beethovenian cast* (London Times).
—*n.* an expert in or skilled performer of Beethoven's music.

***bee|tle**[1] (bē′təl), *n., v.,* **-tled, -tling.** —*n.* **1** an insect that has two hard, shiny cases that cover its wings when at rest. There are over 250,000 species of beetles, which vary in size from that of a pinhead to nearly that of a man's fist. **2** any insect resembling a beetle, such as the cockroach.
—*v.i. Informal.* to move quickly; scurry: *His eyes beetled across the page* (New Yorker).
[Middle English *betylle,* Old English *bitula.* See related etym. at **bite.**] —**bee′tle|like′,** *adj.*

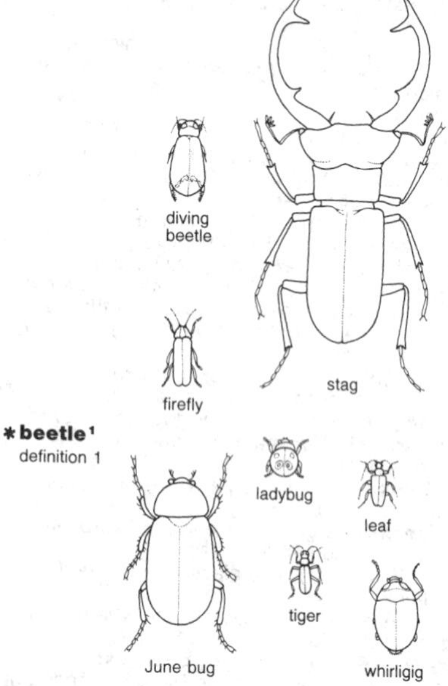

***beetle**[1]
definition 1

bee|tle[2] (bē′təl), *n., v.,* **-tled, -tling.** —*n.* **1** a heavy wooden mallet for ramming, crushing, or smoothing; a maul. **2** *Especially British.* a wooden household utensil for beating or mashing. **3** a machine for finishing linen or cotton cloth by hammering it.
—*v.t.* **1** to pound with a beetle. **2** to finish (cloth) by means of a beetling machine.
[Old English *bīetel* < *bēatan* beat]

bee|tle[3] (bē′təl), *v.,* **-tled, -tling,** *adj.* —*v.i.* to project or overhang: *Great cliffs beetled above the narrow path.*
—*adj.* projecting or overhanging.
[apparently a back formation by Shakespeare < *beetle-browed*]

beet leafhopper, a small, leaping insect that feeds on leaves of sugar beets and spreads a virus disease of sugar beets.

bee|tle-browed (bē′təl broud′), *adj.* **1** having projecting or overhanging eyebrows. **2** *Figurative.* scowling; sullen. [Middle English *bitel-browed; bitel* related to **beetle**[1]]

bee|tle|head (bē′təl hed′), *n.* a stupid person; blockhead. [< *beetle*[2] + *head*]

bee|tle-head|ed (bē′təl hed′id), *adj.* stupid; blockheaded.

bee|tle|weed (bē′təl wēd′), *n.* = galax.

bee|tling (bēt′ling), *adj.* sticking out; projecting; overhanging: *the beetling edge of a cliff, thick, beetling eyebrows.*

bee tree, 1 a hollow tree in which bees hive. **2** the American linden or basswood, whose flowers have much nectar and attract bees.

beet|root (bēt′rüt′, -rut′), *n. Especially British.* a beet, especially the red beet when used as a vegetable.

beet sugar, sugar made from the roots of sugar beets.

beeve (bēv), *n.* a singular of **beeves** (plural of **beef,** def. 2).

beeves (bēvz), *n.* plural of **beef** (def. 2): *Beeves are shipped from the ranch to the city.*

bee wolf, 1 the larva of the bee beetle. **2** = bee killer (def. 1).

beez|er (bē′zər), *n. Slang.* a nose. [origin unknown]

bef., before.

B.E.F., British Expeditionary Force or Forces.

be|fall (bi fôl′), *v.,* **-fell, -fall|en, -fall|ing.** —*v.t.* to happen to: *Be careful that no harm befalls you.* **SYN**: betide.
—*v.i.* **1** to happen: *And so it befell that they often quarrelled and wrangled* (Charles Kingsley). **SYN**: occur, chance. **2** *Archaic.* to fall or come (to) by right.
[Old English *befeallan*]

be|fall|en (bi fô′lən), *v.* the past participle of **befall**: *An accident must have befallen them.*

be|feath|er (bi feᴛʜ′ər), *v.t.* to deck with feathers.

be|fell (bi fel′), *v.* the past tense of **befall**: *Evil befell the knight upon his lonely trip.*

be|fit (bi fit′), *v.t.,* **-fit|ted, -fit|ting.** to be suitable for; be proper for; suit: *She wore a fancy dress to the picnic, which did not befit the occasion at all.* **SYN**: fit, match.

be|fit|ting (bi fit′ing), *adj.* suitable; proper; seemly: *A good thrashing is befitting punishment for a bully.* **SYN**: appropriate, becoming. —**be|fit′ting|ly,** *adv.*

be|flag (bi flag′), *v.t.,* **-flagged, -flag|ging.** to set with flags: *Every public building will be beflagged* (New York Times).

be|fog (bi fog′, -fôg′), *v.t.,* **-fogged, -fog|ging. 1** to surround with fog; make foggy. **2** *Figurative.* to make obscure; confuse; bewilder: *The wine and wassail ... befogged his senses* (Washington Irving).

be|fool (bi fül′), *v.t.* **1** to fool; deceive; dupe. **SYN**: trick, hoodwink, hoax, delude. **2a** to treat as a fool. **b** to call (someone) "fool."

be|fore (bi fôr′, -fōr′), *prep., adv., conj.* —*prep.* **1** earlier than: *Come before we close at five o'clock.* **2** in front of; ahead of: *Do not splash in the puddles when you walk before me.* **3** rather than; sooner than: *I will starve before giving in.* **4** in the presence or sight of: *to perform before an audience.* **5** in front of in time; in the future: *A happy future lies before you.*
—*adv.* **1** earlier; sooner: *Come at five o'clock, not before.* **2** in front; ahead: *The scout went before to see if the trail was safe.* **3** until now; in the past; previously: *I didn't know that before. You were never late before.*
—*conj.* **1** previously to the time when: *I would like to talk to her before she goes.* **2** rather than; sooner than: *I will starve before I give in.*
[Old English *beforan* < *be* by + *foran* before]

be|fore-and-af|ter (bi fôr′ən af′tər; -fōr′-; -äf′-), *adj.* showing, or designed to show, a marked contrast or change in appearance, especially to illustrate the beneficial effects of a product: *before-and-after photographs, before-and-after ads.*

be|fore|hand (bi fôr′hand′, -fōr′-), *adv., adj.* ahead of time; in advance: *Get everything ready beforehand* (adv.). *Are you not a little beforehand with this request for payment?* (adj.)

be|fore-tax (bi fôr′taks′, -fōr′-), *adj.* gained or received before taxes, especially income taxes, are paid: *before-tax profits, before-tax income.*

be|fore|time (bi fôr′tīm′, -fōr′-), *adv. Archaic.* formerly; previously.

be|foul (bi foul′), *v.t.* **1** to make dirty; cover with filth: (*Figurative.*) *By association with the gangsters he befouled his own nest.* **SYN**: soil, pollute, defile, sully. **2** to entangle: *The rope was befouled by weeds and sticks.* —**be|foul′ment,** *n.*

be|friend (bi frend′), *v.t.* to act as a friend to; help: *The policeman befriended the lost boy.* —**be|friend′er,** *n.* —**be|friend′ment,** *n.*

be|fringe (bi frinj′), *v.t.,* **-fringed, -fring|ing.** to adorn with or as if with a fringe.

be|frogged (bi frogd′, -frôgd′), *adj.* ornamented with frogs; frogged: *He was marching through the streets of Antwerp, wearing ... the sort of fantastically befrogged uniform affected by Hussars and lion tamers* (New Yorker).

be|fud|dle (bi fud′əl), *v.t.,* **-dled, -dling. 1** to stupefy; confuse; muddle: *I was befuddled and lost my way in the confusion.* **2** to make stupid with alcoholic drink. —**be|fud′dle|ment,** *n.*

be|fur (bi fėr′), *v.t.,* **-furred, -fur|ring.** to supply or deck out with a fur or furs: *We should plan to allocate $2000 a year to keep being fashionably befurred* (Atlantic).

beg[1] (beg), *v.,* **begged, beg|ging.** —*v.i.* **1** to ask help or charity: *The crippled old man lived by begging.* **2** to make entreaty; petition: *The prisoner begged for mercy.*
—*v.t.* **1** to ask for (food, money, clothes, lodging, or help) as a charity: *The tramp begged his meals.* **2** to ask as a favor; ask earnestly or humbly: *He begged his mother to forgive him.* **3** to ask formally and courteously: *I beg your pardon.*
beg off, to make an excuse for not being able to keep a promise: *He had promised to come but he begged off because of a headache.*
beg the question. See under **question.**
go begging, to find no one who will accept: *His proposals for needed reforms went begging.*
[Middle English *beggen* < Anglo-French *begger;* see etym. under **beggar**]
—*Syn. v.t.* **2 Beg, implore, beseech** mean to ask earnestly. **Beg,** the commonest word, means to ask earnestly or humbly and can be used in all contexts: *The children were begging a ride on the pony.* **Implore,** a more formal word, adds to *beg* the idea of pleading with warm feeling and great humility: *We implored him not to ruin his life by doing anything so foolish.* **Beseech,** still more formal, suggests greater earnestness or humility than *beg: She besought the governor to pardon her son.*

beg[2] (beg, bāg), *n.* = bey.

be|gad (bi gad′), *interj.* a mild oath or emphatic expletive (now chiefly in humorous use). [for *by God*]

be|gan (bi gan′), *v.* past tense of **begin**: *Snow began to fall early in the evening.*

be|gat (bi gat′), *v. Archaic.* begot; a past tense of **beget.**

be|gats (bi gats′), *n.pl. Slang.* descendants: *... a long, geometric progression of begats* (Time).

be|gem (bi jem′), *v.t.,* **-gemmed, -gem|ming.** to adorn with or as if with gems.

be|get (bi get′), *v.t.,* **-got** or (*Archaic*) **-gat, -got|ten** or **-got, -get|ting. 1** to become the father of. **SYN**: procreate. **2** *Figurative.* to cause to be; produce: *Hate begets hate and love begets love.* **SYN**: generate. [Old English *begitan*] —**be|get′ter,** *n.*

beg|gar (beg′ər), *n., v.* —*n.* **1** a person who lives by begging; mendicant: *A hungry old beggar asked everyone on the street for money to buy a cup of coffee.* **2** a very poor person; pauper: *the beggars who live down near the tracks.* **3** a fellow: *My dog is a friendly little beggar.*
—*v.t.* **1** to bring to poverty: *Your reckless spending will beggar your father.* **SYN**: impoverish, ruin. **2** to go beyond; outdo: *The grandeur of Niagara Falls beggars description.* **SYN**: exhaust.
[probably < Anglo-French *begger* < Old French *begard* < Middle Dutch *beggaert* mendicant monk]

beg|gar|dom (beg′ər dəm), *n.* **1** the class or fraternity of beggars. **2** very great poverty.

beg|gar|hood (beg′ər hůd), *n.* **1** the condition of a beggar. **2** beggars collectively; beggardom.

beg|gar-lice (beg′ər līs′), *n.pl. or sing.* = beggar's-lice.

beg|gar|ly (beg′ər lē), *adj.* **1** fit for a beggar; poor: (*Figurative.*) *He possesses only the most beggarly education.* **SYN**: shabby, sorry. **2** mean; sordid. —**beg′gar|li|ness,** *n.*

beg|gar-my-neigh|bor (beg′ər mī nā′bər), *n., adj. Especially British.* —*n.* a children's card game that is won when a player captures all his opponent's cards.
—*adj.* of or having to do with profits derived from or gained by the losses of another: *beggar-my-neighbor protectionism. It is clear that reducing ... aid is just as beggar-my-neighbour a policy as raising tariffs* (London Times).

beg|gar's-but|ton (beg′ərz but′ən), *n.* = burdock (a weed).

beg|gar's-lice (beg′ərz līs′), *n.pl.* **1** (*pl. in use*) the burs or prickly seeds of various plants, that stick to clothes. **2** (*pl. or sing. in use*) any one of several weeds of the borage family on which such burs or seeds grow.

beg|gar's-ticks (beg′ərz tiks′), *n.* **1** any one of several plants of the pea family. **2** = beggar's-lice.

beg|gar-ticks (beg′ər tiks′), *n.pl. or sing.* = beggar's-lice.

beg|gar|weed (beg′ər wēd′), *n.* **1** knotweed, various tickseeds, or any one of several other weeds that grow in poor soil. **2** a forage plant of the pea family, grown in the southern United States.

beg|gar|y (beg′ər ē), *n., pl.* **-gar|ies.** very great poverty; state or condition of a beggar: *to live in beggary, be reduced to beggary.*

beg|ging bowl (beg′ing), **1** a bowl for collecting food, used especially by mendicant priests in countries of Asia: *Buddhist monks ... paddled from house to house with their begging bowls* (New York Times). **2** *Figurative.* a request or appeal for help: *We have come here not to hold out a begging bowl but to hold out to Midlands industry a magnificent opportunity of developing in the Northeast* (Manchester Guardian).

Beg|hard (beg′ərd, bə gärd′), *n.* a member of a religious association of laymen of the 1200's and 1300's in the Low Countries and France. They were known in France as *Beguins.* [< Medieval Latin *beghardus,* probably < Middle Dutch *beggaert* mendicant monk]

be|gin (bi gin′), *v.,* **-gan, -gun, -gin|ning.** —*v.i.* **1** to do the first part; make a start: *When shall*

we begin? **2** to come into being: *The club began two years ago.* SYN: originate, arise. **3** to be near; come near: *Your big brother's suit won't even begin to fit you.* SYN: approach.
—v.t. **1** to do the first part of; start: *I began reading the book yesterday.* **2** to bring into being: *Two brothers began the club two years ago.* SYN: originate, create.
[Old English *beginnan*]
— Syn. v.i., v.t. **1 Begin, commence, start** mean to get something going. **Begin** is the general word: *We will begin work soon.* **Commence** is formal and applies particularly to beginning a formal action: *The dedication ceremonies will commence at two o'clock.* **Start** emphasizes taking the first step in doing something, setting about doing it: *At last they have started building that hotel.*
▶**Begin** is followed by *at* when the meaning is "start from" a definite place: *Let us begin at the third chapter.* It is followed by *on* or *upon* when the meaning is "set to work at": *We must begin on the government survey tomorrow.* When the meaning is "take first in an order of succession," the idiom is *begin with: We always begin with the hardest problems.*

be|gin|ner (bi gin′ər), *n.* **1** a person who is doing something for the first time; person who lacks skill and experience: *You skate well for a beginner.* SYN: amateur, novice. **2** a person who begins anything.

beginner's luck, the good fortune that sometimes allows a novice to outdo an expert, as in fishing or in certain games.

be|gin|ning (bi gin′ing), *n., adj.* *—n.* **1** a start: *The new clerk has made a good beginning.* SYN: commencement, inception, onset, initiation. **2** the time when anything begins: *In the beginning God created the heaven and the earth* (Genesis 1:1). SYN: outset. **3** the first part: *I have enjoyed this book from beginning to end.* **4** the first cause; source; origin: *The idea of the airplane had its beginning with study of the flight of birds. Thy true . . . Beginning and Father is in Heaven* (Thomas Carlyle). SYN: genesis.
—adj. that begins: *Easy words are in the beginning lesson of the spelling book.* SYN: incipient, inceptive.

be|gird (bi gėrd′), *v.t.*, **-girt** or **-gird|ed, -gird|ing.** **1** to bind with a band; gird about. **2** to enclose; encompass. [Old English *begyrdan*]

be|girt (bi gėrt′), *adj., v.* *—adj.* surrounded; encircled.
—v. a past tense and a past participle of **begird**.

be|glam|our or **be|glam|or** (bi glam′ər), *v.t.* **1** to charm or captivate with glamour; infatuate; bedazzle: *Beglamoured by sheer novelty, he tends to overrate some of the works which he describes* (Punch). **2** to invest with glamour: *. . . the vanquished symbols that beglamoured centuries gone by* (Newsweek).

be|gloom (bi glüm′), *v.t.* to fill with gloom: *. . . melancholy begloomed his mind* (John Corry).

be|gob (bi gob′), *interj.* an Irish oath; begad: *Begob, Joe, I don't think even you know as much as that* (Frank O'Connor). [altered pronunciation of *by God*]

be|gog|gled (bi gog′əld), *adj.* equipped with or wearing goggles; goggled.

be|gone (bi gôn′, -gon′), *interj., v.i.* go away; depart: *"Begone!" said the prince* (interj.). *The prince bade him begone* (v.).

be|go|nia (bi gōn′yə, -gō′nē ə), *n.* any one of a family of tropical plants often grown for their large, fleshy, richly colored leaves and waxy flowers. [< New Latin *Begonia* < Michel *Bégon,* 1638-1710, a French patron of botany]

be|gor|ra (bi gôr′ə), *interj.* an Irish oath; begad: *No one handles a camera with more aplomb . . . , and no one, begorra, cares less about what he trains it on* (New Yorker). [alteration of *by God*]

be|got (bi got′), *v.* a past tense and a past participle of **beget:** *He begot a son.*

be|got|ten (bi got′ən), *v.* a past participle of **beget:** *He has begotten two sons.*

be|grime (bi grīm′), *v.t.*, **-grimed, -grim|ing.** to blacken or soil with soot, grease, or dirt; make dirty.

be|grimed (bi grīmd′), *adj.* made grimy; soiled and dirty.

be|grudge (bi gruj′), *v.t.*, **-grudged, -grudg|ing.** **1** to give or allow (something) unwillingly; grudge: *Most parents begrudge allowance spent wastefully. She is so stingy that she begrudges her dog a bone.* **2** to envy (someone) the possession of: *The neighbors begrudge us our swimming pool.* **3** to grumble at; show dissatisfaction with. **—be|grudg′ing|ly**, *adv.*

be|guile (bi gīl′), *v.t.*, **-guiled, -guil|ing. 1** to trick or mislead (a person); deceive; cheat: *His flattery beguiled me into thinking he was my friend.* SYN: delude. **2** to take away from deceitfully or cunningly. *Let no man beguile you of your reward* (Colossians 2:18). **3** to win the attention of; entertain; amuse: *The old sailor beguiled the boys with stories about his life at sea.* SYN: divert. **4** to while away (time) pleasantly: *He read a book to beguile the hours on the long airplane trip.* SYN: See syn. under **while**. **—be|guile′ment**, *n.* **—be|guil′er**, *n.*

be|guil|ing (bi gī′ling), *adj.* **1** deceiving. **2** entertaining; amusing. **—be|guil′ing|ly**, *adv.*

bé|guin (bā gaɴ′), *n. French.* **1** flirtation. **2a** an infatuation: *David shyly confesses his béguin for her* (Perelman). **b** the object of the infatuation.

Beg|uin (beg′in), *n.* = Beghard.

beg|uin|age (beg′ə nij; *French* bā gē nȧzh′), *n.* a community of Beguines. [< French *béguinage*]

be|guine (bə gēn′), *n.* **1** a dance resembling the rumba, originally from Martinique. **2** the music to which a beguine is danced. [< French *béguin* flirtation]

Be|guine (beg′ēn), *n.* a member of a community of Roman Catholic women devoted to a religious and charitable way of life that began in Belgium in the 1100's and came to an end in the 1500's. [< Middle French *béguine* < Old French *beguine* < stem *beg-* in Middle Dutch *beggaert* mendicant]

be|gum (beg′əm, bē′gəm), *n.* a queen, princess, or lady of high rank in Moslem countries. [< Hindustani *begam*]

be|gun (bi gun′), *v.* the past participle of **begin:** *It has begun to rain.*

be|half (bi haf′, -häf′), *n.* side, interest, or favor: *His friends will act in his behalf.*
in behalf of, in the interest of; for: *He worked in behalf of the community chest. I am speaking in behalf of my friend.*
on behalf of, a in the interest of; for: *. . . a publicity photograph on behalf of a charity called the Tolstoy Foundation* (Peter Maas). **b** as a representative of: *The lawyer spoke convincingly on behalf of his client.*
[Old English *be healfe* (*him*) by (his) side]

Be|ha|ri (bə hä′rē), *n.* = Bihari.

be|hat|ted (bi hat′id), *adj.* wearing a hat.

be|have (bi hāv′), *v.*, **-haved, -hav|ing.** *—v.i.* **1** to manage, handle, or conduct oneself; act: *The dog does not behave well in the house. The ship behaves well even in rough water.* SYN: do. **2** to act properly; do what is right: *Did you behave today? "Behave, or I'll take you home," said his mother.* **3** to act or react to a stimulus, environment, or other outside force; act in any relation: *Water behaves in different ways when it is heated and when it is frozen.* SYN: work, operate.
—v.t. **1** to conduct or comport (oneself): *The rowdy boys were poorly behaved in public.* **2** to conduct (oneself) well or properly: *The little boy behaved himself in school.*
[< *be-* + *have*]

be|hav|ior (bi hāv′yər), *n.* **1** manner of behaving; way of acting; conduct; actions; acts: *His sullen behavior showed that he was angry. The boat's behavior was perfect on the trial trip.* SYN: See syn. under **conduct**. **2** manners; deportment: *behavior that is forced and artificial.* SYN: demeanor, bearing. **3a** the manner in which a living organism or a physical substance acts under specified circumstances, or in relation to other things. **b** the observable responses of persons or animals considered as subject matter for psychological study: *Behavior is chiefly learned, the result of group and cultural experiences* (Ogburn and Nimkoff). Also, *British,* **behaviour**.

be|hav|ior|al (bi hāv′yər əl), *adj.* of or having to do with behavior: *behavioral patterns.* **—be|hav′ior|al|ly**, *adv.*

be|hav|ior|al|ism (bē hāv′yə rə liz′əm), *n.* the principles and methods of behavioral science. **—be|hav′ior|al|ist**, *n.*

behavioral science, any one of various social sciences, such as sociology and psychology, dealing with human behavior, especially in a scientific or objective way.

behavioral scientist, a person who is trained or skilled in one or more of the behavioral sciences.

be|hav|ior|ism (bi hāv′yə riz əm), *n.* **1** the doctrine that the objective acts of persons and animals are the chief or only subject matter of scientific psychology. **2** = behavior. **—be|hav′ior|ist**, *n., adj.*

be|hav|ior|is|tic (bi hāv′yə ris′tik), *adj.* of or having to do with behaviorists or behaviorism. **—be|hav′ior|is′ti|cal|ly**, *adv.*

behavior modification, the modification of habits and patterns of behavior by psychological methods such as behavior therapy, reinforcement therapy, and aversion therapy: *Unlike Freudian psychoanalysis, which probes into the life history of the individual . . . behavior modification seeks to change responses and symptoms at the time they occur* (Austin E. Grigg).

behavior therapy, a form of psychological therapy in which a patient is conditioned to replace old habits or patterns of behavior with new ones. Compare **aversion therapy**. *The scientists, convinced of the errors of Freud, maintain that therapies based on conditioning and learning theory—grouped under the umbrella term "behaviour therapy"—are much more effective and practical than in-depth, "arty" therapy which lays bare the patient's soul* (New Scientist).

be|hav|iour (bi hāv′yər), *n. British.* behavior.

be|head (bi hed′), *v.t.* to cut off the head of; decapitate. [Middle English *bihefden*]

be|head|al (bi hed′əl), *n* a beheading.

be|held (bi held′), *v.* the past tense and past participle of **behold:** *The men in the little boat beheld the approaching storm with fear.*

be|he|moth (bi hē′məth, bē′ə-), *n.* **1** a huge and powerful animal mentioned in the Bible. It may have been the hippopotamus. Job 40:15-24. **2** *Figurative.* **a** any large and strong animal. **b** anything very large and powerful. [< Hebrew *bəhēmōth,* plural of *bəhēmāh* beast]

be|he|moth|i|an (bi hē′məth ē ən, bē′ə moth′yən), *adj.* resembling a behemoth; enormous.

be|hest (bi hest′), *n.* **1** a command; order: *I am ready to act at your behest. To fall before her feet at her behest* (Spenser). SYN: injunction. **2** request; bidding; invitation: *At the behest of the James Joyce Society, one of Joyce's three sisters . . . paid a visit to New York from her home in Dublin* (New Yorker). [Middle English *biheste* command, Old English *bihǣs* promise]

be|hind (bi hīnd′), *prep., adv., adj., n.* *—prep.* **1** at the back of; in the rear of: *Stand behind me. The child hid behind the door.* **2** at or on the far side of: *A beautiful valley lies behind the hill.* **3** *Figurative.* in support of; supporting: *His friends are behind him.* **4** *Figurative.* concealed by: *Treachery lurked behind the spy's smooth manners.* **5** later than; after: *The milkman is behind his usual time today.* **6** remaining after: (*Figurative.*) *The dead man left a family behind him.* **7** inferior to; less advanced than: *The boy who was sick is behind the others in his class.*
—adv. **1** at the back; toward the back; in the rear: *The dog's tail hung down behind.* **2** farther back: *The rest of the hikers are still behind.* **3** in reserve: *More supplies are behind.* **4** not on time; slow; late: *The train is behind today.*
—adj. **1** coming after; following: *You must watch the cars behind.* **2** late in payments, work, or other obligations.
—n. Informal. the rump: *. . . one good kick in the behind* (New Yorker).
[Old English *behindan*]
— Syn. prep. **1 Behind, after** express a relation in which one thing is thought of as to the rear of another. **Behind** refers chiefly to position in space and usually implies a definite and usually close interval: *The broom is behind the door. We walked behind the others.* **After** suggests moving in succession or being in a definite order: *We followed after them. They entered the hall one after the other.*

be|hind|hand (bi hīnd′hand′), *adj., adv.* **1** behind time; late: *He handed his assignment in behindhand.* **2** behind others in progress; backward; slow: *He is behindhand in his schoolwork.* **3** in debt; in arrears: *They are behindhand with their rent.*

be|hind-the-scenes (bi hīnd′ᴛʜə sēnz′), *adj.,* not public; private; secret: *Much could be accomplished in the desegregation field by quiet, behind-the-scenes work* (Atlantic).

be|hold (bi hōld′), *v.*, **-held, -hold|ing**, *interj.* *—v.t.* to look at; see; observe: *They got up early to behold the sunrise. Watching the first man land on the moon we beheld a sight never before seen by man.*
—interj. look; take notice: *Behold! the king! The magician reached into his hat, and behold! he pulled out a rabbit!*
[Old English *bihaldan* hold, keep, observe]

be|hold|en (bi hōl′dən), *adj.* under personal obligation for favors or services; in debt: *I am much beholden to you for your help.*

be|hold|er (bi hōl′dər), *n.* an onlooker; spectator.

be|hold|ing (bi hōl′ding), *adj.* = beholden.

be|hoof (bi hüf′), *n.* advantage; benefit: *The father toiled for his children's behoof.* [Old English *behōf,* used in *behōf-līc* useful]

be|hoove (bi hüv′), *v.*, **-hooved, -hoov|ing.** *—v.t.* **1** to be necessary for: *It behooves you to work hard if you want to keep this job.* **2** to be proper for: *It behooves a child to obey his parents.*
—v.i. to be incumbent, proper, or due.
[Old English *behōfian* have use for, need of]

be|hoove|ful (bi hüv′fəl), *adj. Archaic.* useful; ex-

Pronunciation Key: hat, āge, cãre, fär; let, ēqual, tėrm; it, īce; hot, ōpen, ôrder; oil, out; cup, pu̇t, rüle; child; long; thin; ᴛʜen; zh, measure; ə represents a in about, e in taken, i in pencil, o in lemon, u in circus.

pedient; advantageous; necessary.

be|hove (bi hōv′), *v.t., v.i.,* **-hoved, -hov|ing.** *Especially British.* behoove.

be|hove|ful (bi hōv′fəl), *adj. Especially British, Archaic.* behooveful.

beige (bāzh), *adj., n.* —*adj.* pale-brown; light brownish-gray: *a beige dress.*
—*n.* **1** a pale brown. **2** a lightweight woolen dress fabric (originally beige in color). [< French *beige,* earlier *baige* < Old French *bege* of the natural color (of wool), perhaps < Italian *bambagia* cotton]

bei|gel (bā′gəl), *n.* = bagel.

bei|gnet (bā nyā′), *n. French.* a fritter.

bein (bēn), *adj. Especially Scottish.* **1** well-provided. **2** well-to-do. [origin unknown]

be-in (bē′in′), *n.* a gathering of people to socialize, especially in a public place: *The be-in in Central Park, New York, swelled to about 10,000 before nightfall* (London Times).

be|ing (bē′ing), *v., n., adj.* —*v.* the present participle of **be**: *The dog is being fed.*
—*n.* **1** a person; living creature: *Men, women, and children are human beings. Some modern weapons can destroy every being in a large city.* SYN: individual, entity. **2** life; existence: *The world came into being long ago.* SYN: actuality. **3** nature; constitution: *Artists throw their whole being into their work.* SYN: essence. **4** *Philosophy.* **a** that which is actual and complete as both concept and body in space or time: *to worship God, as the Supreme Being.* **b** that which exists as a logically flawless concept within a given epistemology, such as beauty and truth as Platonic archetypes. **c** a state or condition of fully realized potentialities; end point of the process of becoming.
—*adj.* existing; present: *All is well, for the time being.* SYN: existent, actual.

Be|ja (bā′jə), *n. sing. and pl.* **1** a nomadic tribe of Hamitic people living in the region between the Nile and the Red Sea. **2** a member of this tribe. **3** the language of this tribe.

be|ja|bers (bē jā′bərz), *interj., n.* an oath, exclamation, or expression indicating annoyance, anger, surprise, or the like: *This time, bejabers, they have dealt me ten winners* (John Dickson Carr). [altered pronunciation of *by Jesus*]

be|ja|sus (bē jā′zəs), *interj., n.* = bejesus.

be|jeaned (bi jēnd′), *adj.* wearing jeans.

bej|el (bej′əl), *n.* a disease similar to yaws, occurring chiefly in Syria and other countries of the eastern Mediterranean. [< Arabic *bajlah*]

be|je|sus (bē jē′zəs), *interj., n.* = bejabers.

be|jew|el (bi jü′əl), *v.t.,* **-eled, -el|ing** or (*especially British*) **-elled, -el|ling.** to adorn with or as if with jewels: *The sky is bejeweled with stars.*

bé|ké (bā′kā), *n. French Creole.* a white settler: *Martinique still has its white aristocracy, the békés* (London Times).

be|knave (bi nāv′), *v.t.,* **-knaved, -knav|ing.** to call a person a knave.

bel (bel), *n. Physics.* a unit for measuring the difference in intensity level of sounds, equal to ten decibels. [< Alexander Graham *Bell,* 1847-1922, an American physicist and inventor]

Bel (bāl), *n.* the Babylonian god of creation. [< Latin *Bēlus* Baal]

be|la|bor (bi lā′bər), *v.t.* **1** to beat vigorously; thrash: *The rider belabored his tired horse with a stick.* SYN: buffet, pummel. **2** *Figurative.* to set upon with too much talk or advice: *Rip Van Winkle's wife belabored him for being lazy.*

be|la|bour (bi lā′bər), *v.t. Especially British.* belabor.

Bel and the Dragon (bāl), a book of the Old Testament Apocrypha, included in the canon of the Greek and Roman Catholic Bibles as part of Daniel.

be|lat|ed (bi lā′tid), *adj.* **1** happening late; coming late or too late; delayed: *belated thanks. Your belated letter has arrived at last.* **2** overtaken by the darkness of the night: *The belated travelers lost their way after sunset.* —**be|lat′ed|ly,** *adv.* —**be|lat′ed|ness,** *n.*

be|laud (bi lôd′), *v.t.* to laud highly; bepraise: *[He] was belauded by the universal American press* (Edgar Allan Poe).

be|lay (bi lā′), *v.,* **-layed, -lay|ing,** *n.* —*v.t., v.i.* **1** *Nautical.* to fasten (a rope) by winding it around a pin or cleat. **2** to make a belay.
—*n.* a turn or fastening of a rope, such as around a projection of rock, to aid in mountain climbing.
belay that! or **belay there!** *Informal.* stop that! hold on there! enough! *"Belay that and listen!" the first mate shouted.*
[Middle English *beleggen,* Old English *belecgan* to cover]

be|lay|ing pin (bi lā′ing), a pin in a rail of a ship around which ropes can be wound and fastened.

bel can|to (bel kän′tō), singing characterized by full, rich, broad, and flexible tone, especially an Italian singing style (developed in the 1600's and 1700's) tending to passages displaying the singer's technical skills and other ornamentation. [< Italian *bel canto* (literally) fine singing]

belch (belch), *v., n.* —*v.i.* **1** to throw out gas from the stomach through the mouth; eructate. **2** to throw out or shoot forth contents violently: *cannon belching at the enemy.* —*v.t.* to throw out with force: *The volcano belched fire and ashes.*
—*n.* **1** a belching. **2** the substance or thing belched.
[Old English *bealcian,* or *belcettan*] —**belch′er,** *n.*

bel|dam (bel′dəm), *n.* **1** an old woman. **2** an ugly old woman; hag; witch. **3** *Obsolete.* a grandmother. [< *bel-* grand (< Old French *belle* fair) + *dame* mother < Old French *dame* lady]

bel|dame (bel′dəm, -dām′), *n.* = beldam.

be|lea|guer (bi lē′gər), *v.t.* **1** to surround with troops; besiege: *British troops under Cornwallis were beleaguered at Yorktown by patriot forces.* **2** *Figurative.* to surround; beset: *The President is beleaguered by problems.* [< Dutch *belegeren;* influenced by *leger* camp] —**be|lea′guer|er,** *n.* —**be|lea′guer|ment,** *n.*

bel|em|nite (bel′əm nīt), *n.* **1** a dart-shaped fossil now recognized as the shell of an extinct mollusk allied to the cuttlefish; thunderstone. **2** the animal itself. [< Greek *bélemnon* dart + English *-ite*[1]]

bel|em|noid (bel′əm noid), *n., adj.* —*n.* any mollusk of a suborder of extinct cephalopods having two gills, including the belemnite. —*adj.* dart-shaped. [< Greek *bélemnon* dart + English *-oid*]

bel-es|prit (bel′es prē′), *n., pl.* **beaux-es|prits.** *French.* a person of genius or brilliant wit: *The world thought me a beauty and a bel-esprit* (Margaret Edgeworth).

bel|fried (bel′frēd), *adj.* having a belfry.

bel|fry (bel′frē), *n., pl.* **-fries. 1** a tower for a bell or bells, usually attached to a church or other building: *The belfry was toppled by high winds in the storm.* **2** a space in a tower in which a bell or bells may be hung: *Pigeons are always roosting in the belfry.* [Middle English *belfray, berfrey* < Old North French *berfrei* < Frankish (compare Old High German *bervrit* portable shelter < *beran* carry)]

Belg., 1 Belgian. 2 Belgium.

bel|ga (bel′gə), *n.* a Belgian unit of money used from 1926 to 1945, restricted to use in foreign exchange, and valued at five Belgian francs. [< Latin *Belga,* feminine of *Belgus* Belgian]

Bel|gae (bel′jē), *n.pl.* an ancient Celtic people of northern Gaul.

Bel|gian (bel′jən), *n., adj.* —*n.* **1** a person born or living in Belgium. **2** any one of a breed of large, heavy draft horses with a huge body and a chestnut or bay-colored coat.
—*adj.* of Belgium or its people.

Belgian hare, a large, reddish-brown, domestic rabbit.

Belgian Mal|i|nois (mal ə nwä′), a breed of sheep dog with a short-haired coat and longer hair along the back of the hind legs.

Belgian sheepdog, any dog of a breed having a black coat and formerly used to herd sheep.

Belgian Ter|vuren (tėr′vėrn), a breed of sheep dog that holds its ears stiffly erect and has a long tail.

Bel|gic (bel′jik), *adj., n.* —*adj.* **1** of or having to do with the Belgae. **2** of or having to do with the Netherlands. **3** = Belgian.
—*n.* the Gaulish language used by the Belgae.

Belgo-, *combining form.* Belgian and ___: *the Belgo-German frontier = the Belgian and German frontier.*

Bel|gra|vi|a (bel grā′vē ə), *n.* rich and fashionable people; high society (from the name of a fashionable section in London).

Bel|gra|vi|an (bel grā′vē ən), *adj., n.* —*adj.* **1** of or having to do with Belgravia, a fashionable section of the western part of London. **2** *Figurative.* **a** aristocratic. **b** fashionable.
—*n.* **1** a person who lives in Belgravia. **2** *Figurative.* **a** an aristocrat. **b** a member of high society.

Be|li|al (bē′lē əl, bēl′yəl), *n.* **1** the Devil; Satan, especially as the personification of evil; the Antichrist. **2** a fallen angel in Milton's poem *Paradise Lost.*

be|lie (bi lī′), *v.t.,* **-lied, -ly|ing. 1** to give a false idea of; misrepresent: *Her frown belied her usual good nature.* SYN: contradict, controvert. **2** to show to be false; prove to be mistaken. SYN: disprove, refute. **3** to fail to come up to; disappoint: *He stole again, and so belied our hopes.* SYN: betray. [Old English *belēogan* < *be-* be- + *lēogan* lie[1]] —**be|li′er,** *n.*

be|lief (bi lēf′), *n.* **1** what is held to be true or real; thing believed; opinion: *Even after Columbus it was once a common belief that the earth was flat.* **2** acceptance as true or real: *His belief in ghosts makes him afraid of the dark.* **3** confidence in any person or thing; faith; trust: *The judge expressed his belief in the boy's honesty.* SYN: reliance. **4** religious faith; creed: *Most children follow the belief of their parents.* [Middle English *bileve,* earlier *bileafe*]
—*Syn.* **1 Belief, conviction** mean what is held true. **Belief** is the general word, implying acceptance with or without certainty: *It was once a common belief that the earth is flat.* **Conviction** implies that the belief is unshakable and undoubting: *It is my conviction that they are innocent.*

be|liev|a|bil|i|ty (bi lē′və bil′ə tē), *n.* the quality of being believable; credibility.

be|liev|a|ble (bi lē′və bəl), *adj.* that can be believed; credible. —**be|liev′a|ble|ness,** *n.*

be|liev|a|bly (bi lē′və blē), *adv.* credibly.

be|lieve (bi lēv′), *v.,* **-lieved, -liev|ing.** —*v.t.* **1** to think (something) is true or real: *We all believe that the earth is round.* **2** to think (somebody) tells the truth: *My friends believe me.* **3** to think; suppose: *By the looks of the dark sky I believe we are going to have a storm soon.*
—*v.i.* **1a** to have faith (in a person or thing); trust: *We believe in our friends.* **b** to think of something as true or existing; be convinced of the actual existence, occurrence, validity, or truth of something: *I believe in charity. She believes in miracles.* **2** to have religious belief. **3** to exercise faith: *Be not afraid, only believe* (Mark 5:36). **4** to think; suppose.
make believe, to pretend: *We will make believe that there are fairies in the world* (Charles Kingsley).
[Middle English *bileven*] —**be|liev′er,** *n.* —**be|liev′ing|ly,** *adv.*

be|like (bi līk′), *adv. Archaic.* very likely; probably; perhaps: *Things that I know not of belike to thee are dear* (William Wordsworth).

Be|li|sha beacon (bə lī′shə), *British.* a post with a reddish-yellow globe or light marking a crossing place for pedestrians. [< Leslie Hore-*Belisha,* 1898-1957, who introduced it in 1934 while Minister of Transport]

be|lit|tle (bi lit′əl), *v.t.,* **-tled, -tling. 1** to make seem little or unimportant; make less important; make little of; speak slightingly of: *Jealous people belittled the explorer's great discoveries.* SYN: depreciate; disparage. **2** *Archaic.* to cause to appear little; make small by comparison; dwarf.
—**be|lit′tle|ment,** *n.* —**be|lit′tler,** *n.* —**be|lit′tling|ly,** *adv.*

be|live (bi līv′), *adv. Scottish.* **1** quickly; eagerly. **2** soon. [Middle English *bilive, bi live* by life, with life]

Be|li|ze|an (bə lē′zē ən), *adj.* of or having to do with Belize (British Honduras), a country in Central America, independent since 1981.

bell[1] (bel), *n., v., adj.,* —*n.* **1** a hollow metal cup that makes a musical sound when struck by a clapper or hammer. Typically, a bell has a flaring rim and is struck by a clapper suspended from the center of the interior. **2** anything that makes a ringing sound as a signal: *Did I hear the bell at the front door?* **3** the stroke or sound of a bell: *Our teacher dismissed us five minutes before the bell.* **4a** the stroke of a bell used on shipboard to indicate a half hour of time. 1 bell = 12:30, 4:30, or 8:30; 2 bells = 1:00, 5:00, or 9:00; and so on up to 8 bells = 4:00, 8:00, or 12:00. **b** the period of a half hour indicated. **5** anything shaped like a bell. The flaring end of a funnel or of a musical wind instrument is a bell. The shape of the bell affects the resonance, power, and tonal quality of wind instruments. **6** a bell-shaped cover, usually of metal, to keep food warm or moist. **7** *Botany.* **a** a corolla shaped like a bell. **b** the strobile, cone, or catkin containing the seed of the hop. **8** the umbrella of a jellyfish.
—*v.t.* **1** to put a bell on; furnish with a bell: *We belled the sheep.* **2** to cause to swell or bulge out like a bell. —*v.i.* **1** to swell out like a bell; flare. **2** to make the sound of a bell; toll.
—*adj.* shaped like a bell: *bell sleeves.*
bells, *Informal.* bell-bottom trousers: *Wives ... slipped into their striped bells, and pulled sweaters over their torsi* (Donald Barthelme).
bell the cat. See under **cat.**
ring a bell, *Informal.* to evoke a response, as of the memory or of enthusiasm: *That old song rings a bell with his parents.*
ring the bell, *Informal.* to score a hit; be a big success: *A pretty dress is sure to ring the bell with any little girl* (New Yorker).
saved by the bell, *Informal.* saved from trouble by a chance piece of luck (from the former practice which allowed a count against a fallen boxer to be interrupted by the bell signaling the end of a round): *Any report that the party chairman was "saved by the bell" is inaccurate* (Sunday Times).
with bells on, *U.S. Informal.* fully arrayed or prepared; readily; eagerly: *He's an honored guest at the Indianapolis 500, the Phoenix Rodeo, ... to name just a few events he attends with bells on*

(New Yorker).
[Old English *belle*] —**bell′-like′**, *adj.*

bell² (bel), *v., n.* —*v.i., v.t.* to bellow; roar; cry.
—*n.* the cry of a deer at rutting time.
[Old English *bellan* roar]

∗**bel|la|don|na** (bel′ə don′ə), *n.* **1a** a poisonous plant of Europe and Asia, with black berries and red, bell-shaped flowers; deadly nightshade. **b** the leaves and roots of this plant, from which a drug is obtained. **2** the drug made from this plant; atropine. It relaxes muscles and relieves pain and is used to reduce spasms and to dilate the pupils of the eyes. [< Italian *bella donna* fair lady; *bella* < feminine of Latin *bellus; donna* < Latin *domina*]

∗**belladonna** definition 1a

belladonna lily, = amaryllis.

bel|lar|mine (bel′ər mēn, -min), *n.* a large, globular stoneware jug with a narrow neck, decorated with the face of a bearded man, originally designed as a caricature of Cardinal Bellarmine (1542-1621).

Bel|la|trix (be lā′triks), *n.* a bright star in the constellation Orion. [< Latin *bellātrix* female warrior]

bell|bird (bel′bėrd′), *n.* any one of several birds with a clear, bell-like call, especially: **a** a black-winged cotinga, found in the area between Trinidad and the northern part of Brazil. **b** *U.S. Dialect.* = wood thrush. **c** a honey eater of New Zealand.

bell-bot|tom (bel′bot′əm), *adj.* with the bottom of the legs flared: *bell-bottom trousers.*

bell-bot|tomed (bel′bot′əmd), *adj.* = bell-bottom.

bell-bot|toms (bel′bot′əmz), *n.pl.* bell-bottom trousers.

bell|boy (bel′boi′), *n.* a man or boy whose work is carrying baggage and doing errands for the guests of a hotel or club; bellhop: *We tipped the bellboy after he took the bags to our room.*

bell buoy, a warning buoy with a bell hung so as to ring when the buoy is rocked by the waves. See picture under **buoy**.

bell captain, the person in charge of a group of bellboys.

bell cot, or **bell|cot** (bel′kot′), *n.* = bell cote.

bell cote, or **bell|cote** (bel′kōt′), *n. Architecture.* a small structure designed to contain one or more bells, which are often carried upon brackets projecting from a wall.

bell crank, a right-angled lever for communicating motion, as from one bell wire to another lying at right angles to it.

bell curve, *Statistics.* a bell-shaped curve; normal curve.

belle (bel), *n.* **1** a beautiful woman or girl. **2** the prettiest or most admired woman or girl: *She was the belle of the ball.* [< French *belle* < feminine of adjective *beau* beautiful]

belled (beld), *adj.* having a bell or bells.

Bel|leek (bə lēk′), *n., or* **Belleek ware**, a kind of very thin, almost transparent porcelain with an opalescent glaze, made in decorative shapes. [< *Belleek*, a town in Northern Ireland, where it is made]

belle é|poque (bel ā pok′), *French.* **1** the period at the turn of the century (from 1880 to 1905): *In the book, their pure cubism of the belle époque seems intact, as if exhumed in a perfect state* (New Yorker). **2** (literally) beautiful epoch.

Bel|ler|o|phon (bə ler′ə fon), *n. Greek Legend.* a hero who killed the chimera, a dreadful monster, with the help of the winged horse Pegasus.

belles-let|tres (bel′let′rə), *n.pl.* **1** the finer forms of literature, especially poetry or essays. Fiction and other types of imaginative literature are sometimes also meant by the term, but never writing which is explicitly educational or informational. **2** literature as a fine art. [< French *belles-lettres* fine letters, as a parallel to *beaux-arts* fine arts]

bel|let|rism or **bel|let|trism** (bel′let′riz′əm), *n.* devotion to belles-lettres. —**bel′let′rist, bel′let′trist**, *n.*

bel|le|tris|tic (bel′le tris′tik), *adj.* **1** of or having to do with belles-lettres. **2** in the manner or style of belles-lettres.

bell|flow|er (bel′flou′ər), *n.* = campanula.

bellflower family, a widely distributed group of dicotyledonous plants, mainly herbs but including shrubs and small trees. The family includes many ornamentals with usually blue flowers, such as the rampion, harebell, and Canterbury bell.

bell glass, = bell jar.

bell|hang|er (bel′hang′ər), *n.* a person whose business it is to put up and repair bells, wires attached to bells, and the like.

bell|hop (bel′hop′), *n. U.S.* = bellboy.

bel|li|cose (bel′ə kōs), *adj.* fond of fighting and quarreling; inclined to war; warlike: *There have been disturbances from time to time, but these are put down largely to the bellicose and rapacious nature of the . . . tribes in the frontier areas* (London Times). **SYN:** belligerent, combative, contentious, pugnacious, quarrelsome. [< Latin *bellicōsus* < *bellicus* of war < *bellum* war] —**bel′li|cose′ly**, *adv.*

bel|li|cos|i|ty (bel′ə kos′ə tē), *n.* bellicose quality or attitude; quarrelsomeness.

bel|lied (bel′ēd), *adj.* **1** having a belly, especially a big belly (used chiefly in combination): *bellied like a beast, big-bellied.* **2** blown or puffed out: *a bellied bottle, bellied sails.*

bel|lig|er|ence (bə lij′ər əns), *n.* **1** a belligerent attitude; being warlike; fondness for fighting. **2** the act of fighting;being at war.

bel|lig|er|en|cy (bə lij′ər ən sē), *n.* **1** the position or status of a belligerent. **2** pugnacious and stubborn hostility; belligerence. **3** warfare.

bel|lig|er|ent (bə lij′ər ənt), *adj., n.* —*adj.* **1** fond of fighting; tending or inclined to war; warlike: *Some young boys are very belligerent when they first find the use of their fists.* (*Figurative.*) *The defiant child spoke in a most belligerent voice.* **SYN:** hostile, pugnacious. **2** at war; engaged in war; fighting: *Great Britain and Germany were belligerent powers in 1941.* **3** having to do with nations or persons at war.
—*n.* **1** a nation, state, or its citizens at war: *France and Germany were belligerents in World War II. Command of the air, which was formerly the result of a slow attrition of one of the belligerents, can no longer be won according to the standards of 1939-45* (Bulletin of Atomic Scientists). **2** a person engaged in fighting with another person.
[< Latin *belligerāns, -antis,* present participle of *belligerāre* wage war < *bellum* war + *gerere* wage] —**bel|lig′er|ent|ly**, *adv.*

bel|lip|o|tent (bə lip′ə tənt), *adj.* mighty in war. [< Latin *bellipotēns, -entis* < *bellum* war + *potēns* potent]

bell jar, a bell-shaped container or cover made of glass, used in laboratories to cover objects which require protection from variations of the atmosphere, dust, or moisture, or to hold gases in chemical operations; bell glass.

bell-ly|ra (bel′lī′rə), *n.* a kind of portable glockenspiel, consisting of metal bars on a lyre-shaped frame.

bell|man (bel′mən), *n., pl.* **-men.** a man who rings a bell, especially a town crier.

bell metal, a variety of bronze, an alloy consisting typically of three or four parts of copper to one of tin, from which bells are made.

bell-mouthed (bel′mouᴛʜd′, -moutht′), *adj.* having a mouth or opening that flares out like a bell.

Bel|lo|na (bə lō′nə), *n.* a Roman goddess of war, the sister or wife of Mars.

bel|low (bel′ō), *v., n.* —*v.i.* **1** to make a loud, deep noise; roar as a bull does when excited or enraged: *The cows were bellowing in the barn from hunger.* **2** to shout loudly, with anger, or with pain: *He bellowed in pain when the hammer came down on his finger.* **SYN:** See syn. under **cry**.
—*v.t.* to shout in a loud and deep voice; roar: *to bellow an order.*
—*n.* **1** a loud, deep noise; roar: *the bellow of an angry voice.* **2** any noise made by bellowing: *We have lost the bellow of mighty steam engines.*
[Middle English *belwen,* perhaps, Old English *belegian*] —**bel′low|er**, *n.*

∗**bel|lows** (bel′ōz, -əs), *n. sing. or pl.* **1** an instrument for producing a strong current of air, used for blowing fires or sounding an organ or accordion. A bellows consists of an air chamber which expands when air enters through a valve and a nozzle through which air is forced out in a stream when the air chamber is compressed. **2** the folding part of some cameras, behind the lens. **3** *Figurative.* the lungs. [Middle English *belwes,* Old English *belg* bag. See related etym. at **belly**.]

∗**bellows** definitions 1, 2

hand bellows

bellows

bellows camera

bellows pocket, a patch pocket made with box pleats to give room for expansion.

bell pepper, the bell-shaped fruit of the sweet pepper, used for pickling and as a vegetable.

bell|pull (bel′pu̇l′), *n.* a handle for pulling a bell attached by a wire or cord.

bell-push (bel′pu̇sh′), *n. British.* a push button for a doorbell or the like.

bell ringer, **1** a person whose business it is to ring a bell, as of a church. **2** a performer with musical bells. **3** a device or mechanism for ringing a bell or bells.

bell ringing, the art or practice of a bell ringer.

bells (belz), *n.pl.* See under **bell¹**.

bell-shaped (bel′shāpt′), *adj.* shaped like a bell, or like a cup flaring more or less at the rim.

∗**bell-shaped curve**, *Statistics.* a curve representing a symmetrical frequency distribution; normal curve.

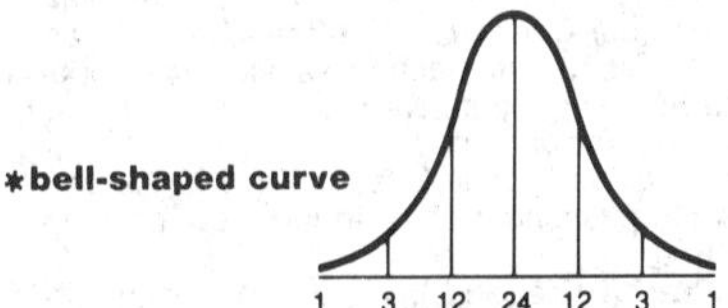

∗**bell-shaped curve**

bells of Ireland, a hardy annual plant with whitish flowers having enlarged, bell-shaped, chartreuse green calyxes.

Bell's palsy (belz), paralysis of the facial muscles. [< Sir Charles *Bell*, 1774-1842, a Scottish physiologist]

bell tent, a conical-shaped tent.

bell tower, a tower built to contain a bell or bells.

bell turret, a turret containing a bell chamber, and usually crowned with a spire or other ornamental feature.

bell|weth|er (bel′weᴛʜ′ər), *n.* **1** a male sheep (wether) that leads the flock, wearing a bell. **2** *Figurative.* a chief or leader, especially of people or groups thought of as resembling sheep in lack of intelligence, foresight, or plan: *You bellwether of the mob . . .* (Robert Southey). **3** *Figurative.* any person or thing that sets a standard or pattern for a group: *Steel production is the bellwether of American industry.*

bell|wort (bel′wėrt′), *n.* **1** = bellflower. **2** *U.S.* any of certain North American lilies, having yellow, bell-shaped flowers.

bel|ly (bel′ē), *n., pl.* **-lies**, *v.,* **-lied, -ly|ing.** —*n.* **1** the lower part of the human body, which contains the stomach and intestines; abdomen: *The scout crept along the ground on his belly.* **2** the under part of an animal's body: *The tramp kicked the dog in the belly.* **3** the stomach: *Green apples give an awful ache in the belly.* **4** *Figurative.* the appetite for food: *His belly ached for a good steak. A coward doesn't have much of a belly for fighting.* **5** the bulging part of anything, or the hollow in it: *the belly of a ship, the belly of a pot.* **6** a hollow in a surface, as the part of a sail filled with wind. **7** the thick portion of a muscle (as distinguished from its tendinous portion). **8** the upper or front, slightly bulging surface of the sounding box on musical instruments of the violin class. **9** the front, inner, or lower surface of anything (as distinguished from the top or back). **10** *Archery.* the surface of a bow facing the string.
—*v.i.* **1** to swell out; bulge: *The ship's sails bellied in the wind.* **2** to move on one's belly; crawl: *For the weary battalions of Marines bellying through the chunks of rubble, progress was slow and costly in lives* (Time).
—*v.t.* to cause to swell out: *But could see the fair west wind belly the homeward sail* (James Russell Lowell).
belly in, to bellyland: *With a dead radio, wing flaps and wheels stuck and the air-speed indicator out . . . there was nothing to do but belly in* (Time).
belly up to, *Especially U.S. Slang.* to move straight toward (something); go directly to: *They bellied up to a bar at the seaman's Cultural Center, the social hub of the city* (San Francisco Chronicle).
[Middle English *bely*, Old English *bælig* bag, skin. See related etym. at **bellows**.]

bel|ly|ache (bel′ē āk′), *n., v.,* **-ached, -ach|ing.** *Informal.* —*n.* **1** a pain in the abdomen; stomachache. **2** *Figurative.* a reason for complaining; grievance.

Pronunciation Key: hat, āge, cãre, fär; let, ēqual, tėrm; it, īce; hot, ōpen, ôrder; oil, out; cup, pu̇t, rüle; child; long; thin; ᴛʜen; zh, measure; ə represents **a** in about, **e** in taken, **i** in pencil, **o** in lemon, **u** in circus.

—*v.i. Figurative.* to complain or grumble, especially persistently and about relatively unimportant things.
—**bel′ly·ach′er**, *n.*
bel·ly·band (bel′ē band′), *n.* a strap around an animal's body to keep a saddle, harness, or pack in place.
belly board, a small surfboard for riding the waves on one's belly.
bel·ly·but·ton (bel′ē but′ən), *n. Informal.* navel.
belly dance, an Oriental dance that makes much use of abdominal movements; danse du ventre.
bel·ly-dance (bel′ē dans′, -däns′), *v.i.*, **-danced, -danc·ing.** to perform a belly dance.
belly dancer, a performer of belly dances.
bel·ly·flop (bel′ē flop′), *v.*, **-flopped, -flop·ping,** *n., adv. Slang.* bellywhop.
bel·ly·flop·per (bel′ē flop′ər), *n.* = bellywhopper.
bel·ly·ful (bel′ē fu̇l), *n., pl.* **-fuls.** *Informal.* **1** as much as fills the stomach or satisfies the appetite. **2** *Figurative.* an excessive quantity, especially of something unpleasant.
bel·ly·hold (bel′ē hōld′), *n.* the hold for cargo beneath the passenger cabin in the fuselage of an aircraft.
bel·ly·land (bel′ē land′), *v.i., v.t.* to land an airplane with landing gear retracted, sliding on the bottom of the fuselage.
belly laugh or **laughter**, *Informal.* a hearty, unrestrained fit of laughter.
belly tank, a detachable, auxiliary fuel tank, carried usually beneath the fuselage of an aircraft.
bel·ly·whop (bel′ē hwop′), *v.i.*, **-whopped, -whop·ping,** *n., adv. U.S. Slang.* —*v.i.* **1** to ride on a sled in a prone position with the stomach downward. **2** to strike the water with the chest, or with the chest and abdomen, in diving.
—*n.* a ride or dive taken in this manner.
—*adv.* by bellywhopping; on the belly; in a prone position: *to dive bellywhop.* —**bel′ly·whop′per**, *v., n., adv.*
bel·o·man·cy (bel′ə man′sē), *n.* divination by means of arrows. [<Greek *bélos* arrow, dart + *manteíā* divination]
be·long (bi lông′, -long′), *v.i.* **1** to have one's or its proper place: *That book belongs on the top shelf.* **2** *Figurative.* to be accepted as part of a particular social group: . . . *the world of old Protestant New Yorkers who were well-to-do, if not, "belonged" through their family connections* (Edmund Wilson).
belong to, a to be the property of: *That coat belongs to me.* **b** to be a part of; be connected with: *That top belongs to this box. Grief has a natural Eloquence belonging to it* (Joseph Addison). **c** to be a member of: *She belongs to the Girl Scouts. He belongs to a large family.*
[Middle English *belongen* <*be-* be- + *longen* belong]
be·long·ing (bi lông′ing, -long′-), *n.* a being part of a group; identification with others; close association: *He vacillated neurotically between a need for popularity and belonging, on the one hand, and independence and isolation on the other* (New Statesman). —**be·long′ing·ness**, *n.*
be·long·ings (bi lông′ingz, -long′-), *n.pl.* things that belong to a person; possessions; goods.
Bel·o·rus·sian (bel′ə rush′ən, byel′-), *adj., n.* = Byelorussian.
be·lote (bə lōt′), *n.* a French card game. [<French *belote*]
be·lov·ed (bi luv′id, -luvd′), *adj., n.* —*adj.* dearly loved; dear: *her beloved children.*
—*n.* a person who is loved; darling: *His sweetheart is his beloved.*
be·low (bi lō′), *adv., prep.* —*adv.* **1** in or to a lower place: *From the airplane we could see the fields below.* **2a** on the lower side or on the bottom: *leaves dark above and light below.* **b** on a lower floor or deck; downstairs: *The sailor went below.* **3** in or from a direction thought of as lower; downstream: *There is good fishing below.* **4** after or later on a page or in a book or article: See the note below. **5** *Figurative.* lower in rank or power: *A sergeant is below a captain. The appeal reversed the decisions of the courts below.* **6** below zero: *The temperature is five below today.* **7a** in hell. **b** on the earth.
—*prep.* **1** lower than; under: *The cellar is below the living room.* SYN: See syn. under **under. 2** *Figurative.* less than; lower in rank or degree than: *It is four degrees below freezing.* **3** too low to be worthy of; unworthy of: *The cheat is below contempt.* [<*be-* + *low*]
be·low·decks (bi lō′deks), *adj., adv.* under the deck; in or into the cabin or hold of a ship: *Nobody is allowed belowdecks without a special permit* (New Yorker). *The "Forrestal" limped toward the Philippines with belowdecks fires raging* (Time).
be·low·ground (bi lō′ground′), *adj., adv.* underground: *a belowground explosion* (adj.); *working belowground in a mine* (adv.).
be·low·stairs (bi lō′stärz′), *adj., adv.* in or on a lower floor or level, especially beneath the main living quarters of a house; downstairs: *Servants were said to live belowstairs in England.*
be·low-the-line (bi lōᴛʜə līn′), *adj.* indicating an out-of-the-ordinary revenue or expense: *a below-the-line expenditure on aid.*
Bel Pa·e·se (bel pä ā′ze), *Trademark.* a kind of ripened, soft, Italian cheese.
Bel·shaz·zar (bel shaz′ər), *n.* the last king of Babylon, at whose feast the hand wrote upon the wall (in the Bible, Daniel 5).
belt (belt), *n., v.* —*n.* **1** a strip of leather, cloth, or the like, fastened around the waist to hold in or support clothes or weapons worn on the body: *He buckled his belt to hold up his pants.* **2** any broad strip or band: *A belt of trees grew between the two fields.* **3** a region having distinctive characteristics; zone: *The cotton belt is the region where mostly cotton is grown.* **4a** an endless band that transfers motion from one wheel or pulley to another: *A belt connected to the motor moves the fan in an automobile.* **b** a similar band used for conveying objects or materials in a factory, or the like. **5** *Slang.* **a** a blow. **b** a drink, especially of some alcoholic beverage. **c** a feeling of great pleasure, amusement, etc.: *But all the fans got a big belt out of the Brooklyn triumph* . . . (New York Times). **6** a series of armor plates running along the water line of a ship. **7** a strait.
—*v.t.* **1** to put a belt around: *She belted her dress.* **2** to fasten on with a belt: *He belted his sword.* **3** to surround or mark with a circle or zone of any kind: *He [the beaver] makes incisions round them [trees], or . . . belts them with his teeth* (Washington Irving). **4** to beat with a belt: *The cruel master belted his dog.* **5** *Slang.* to hit (anything) suddenly and hard: *He belted the ball completely out of sight.*
—*v.i. Slang.* to move very fast; hurry; rush: *He sees himself these days as a getaway sort of person, belting off from his Cromwell flat in an Alfa Romeo* (Sunday Times).
below the belt, a foul; unfair: *The cartoons against [him] are shocking—not as political depictions, but by their below-the-belt viciousness* (Time). **b** foully; unfairly: *to hit a person below the belt.*
belt down, *Slang.* to drink (alcoholic liquor): *"Study hard for what? So I can ride the bar car to Darien every night belting down doubles?"* (New Yorker).
belt out, *Slang.* to sing or play forcefully: *Standing there . . . with her feet apart, belting out . . . Porter's "Get Out of Town"* (Saturday Review).
belt up, *British Slang.* to stop talking; keep quiet: *He is so anxious to tell you which . . . what . . . and who . . . that, free speech or not, one soon wishes he would belt up* (Manchester Guardian).
tighten one's belt, to be or become more thrifty: *The drought continued and farm families tightened their belts.*
under one's belt, *Slang.* well in one's possession: *With his doctorate under his belt, the teacher went to Washington* (New York Times).
[Old English *belt,* ultimately <Latin *balteus*]
—**belt′er**, *n.* —**belt′less**, *adj.*
Bel·tane (bel′tān), *n.* **1** (in Scotland) May 1, in the Old Style calendar. **2** an ancient Celtic anniversary celebration on May Day, at which great bonfires were kindled, especially in Scotland. [<Scottish Gaelic *bealltainn* May Day, the May festival]
belt conveyor, = conveyor (def. 2).
belt drive, **1** the transmission of power from one shaft to another by means of an endless belt passing around a pulley on each shaft. **2** the endless belt and pulleys used in doing this.
belt·ed (bel′tid), *adj.* **1** having or wearing a belt. **2** wearing a special belt as a sign of honor. **3** marked by a belt or band, as of a distinctive color. **4** fastened on by means of a belt: *a belted sword.*
belt·ed-bi·as tire (bel′tid bī′əs), an automobile tire with a belt of cord fabric or metal beneath the tread and above the plies crisscrossing the tire diagonally to the center line of the tread. Also, **bias-belted tire.**
belted kingfisher, an American kingfisher with a dull-blue body above, white below, a crested head and a bluish belt on the breast.
Bel·ti·an (bel′tē ən), *adj.* of or having to do with a section of Proterozoic rocks found in northwestern North America: *There are . . . places where destruction by metamorphism could not have taken place, as in the Beltian rocks of Montana* (Robert M. Garrels). [<Little *Belt* Mountains, Montana]
belt·ing (bel′ting), *n.* **1** material for making belts. **2** belts collectively. **3** *Slang.* a beating.
belt line, *U.S.* a railroad, bus line, road, or the like, that makes a circuit around or almost around a city or special area.
belt·line (belt′līn′), *n.* = waistline.
belt sander, a machine for sanding in which the sandpaper or emery cloth is in the form of an endless belt that revolves between two pulleys.
belt-tight·en·ing (belt′tī′tə ning), *n., adj. Especially U.S.* —*n.* a forced reduction of expenditures.
—*adj.* designed to reduce expenses; economizing: *belt-tightening layoffs.*
belt·way (belt′wā′), *n.* **1** a highway that goes around a city or special area. **2 the Beltway.** Washington, D.C., considered as the seat of the U.S. government and all of the people concerned with the functioning of the government: *There's a life beyond the Beltway, a whole country out there* . . . (Rolling Stone).
beltway bandit, *U.S. Slang.* a consultant or expert, often a former government employee, hired by a corporation to help secure government contracts. [<*beltway* that circles Washington, D.C., seat of the U.S. government]
be·lu·ga (bə lü′gə), *n., pl.* **-ga** or **-gas. 1** a large, white sturgeon of the Black Sea and the Caspian Sea, valued as a source of caviar. **2** Also, **beluga whale.** a small, white whale of the arctic seas, once hunted for its oil and skin; white whale. [<Russian *beluga, belukha* <*belyj* white]
bel·ve·dere (bel′və dir, bel′və dir′), *n.* **1** a structure from which a fine view may be had, especially a top story that is open on one or more sides. **2** a cigar more tapered and slightly shorter than a corona. [<Italian *belvedere* fine view <*bello* handsome (<Latin *bellus*) + *vedere* sight <Latin *vidēre* to see]
bel·ve·dered (bel′və dird, bel′və dird′), *adj.* having a belvedere.
be·ma (bē′mə), *n., pl.* **-ma·ta** (-mə tə). **1** (in ancient Greece) a stage or platform on which a speaker stood to address an assembly. **2** (in Eastern churches) the area, raised and enclosed, between the apse and the nave, including the altar; the sanctuary or chancel. [<Greek *bêma* step, rostrum]
be·maul (bi môl′), *v.t.* to maul severely.
be·maze (bi māz′), *v.t.*, **-mazed, -maz·ing.** to daze; bewilder.
Bem·bo (bem′bō), *n.* a printing type of the old style, based on those designed by the Italian printer Francesco Griffo in the late 1400's. [<Cardinal Pietro *Bembo,* the secretary to Pope Leo X]
be·mean (bi mēn′), *v.t.* to make mean or base; lower in dignity; abase.
be·med·aled (bi med′əld), *adj.* covered with medals; wearing many medals.
be·mire (bi mīr′), *v.t.*, **-mired, -mir·ing. 1** to make dirty with mud. **2** to sink or stick in mud.
be·mist (bi mist′), *v.t.* to cover or surround with mist; befog; obscure.
be·moan (bi mōn′), *v.t.* to moan about or weep for; bewail. —*v.i.* to mourn; lament; grieve.
be·mock (bi mok′, -môk′), *v.t.* to mock; mock at.
be·moil (bi moil′), *v.t. British Dialect.* to befoul with mud or dirt.
be·mud·dle (bi mud′əl), *v.t.*, **-dled, -dling.** to muddle completely.
be·muse (bi myüz′), *v.t.*, **-mused, -mus·ing.** to make utterly confused; bewilder; stupefy. —**bemuse′ment**, *n.*
be·mused (bi myüzd′), *adj.* **1** confused; bewildered; stupefied: *The old man was bemused by the rush and hustle of modern life.* **2** absorbed in thought or daydreaming: *The shepherd sat bemused in the summer sun.* —**be·mus′ed·ly**, *adv.*
ben[1] (ben), *adv., prep., adj., n. Scottish and Dialect.* —*adv.* within.
—*prep.* in or into the inner part of (a house).
—*adj.* inner; interior.
—*n.* the inner room of a cottage, especially the inner one of two rooms (the outer being the *but*). [Middle English *ben,* related to Old English *binnan* inside]
ben[2] (ben), *n.* **1** an Asiatic tree whose winged seed yields an oil used in perfumery and as a lubricant. **2** the seed itself. [<Arabic *ban*]
ben[3] (ben), *n.* a mountain peak (used chiefly in the names of Scottish mountains): *Ben Lomond.* [<Scottish Gaelic *beann*]
ben[4] (ben), *n. Hebrew.* son; son of: *David Ben-Gurion, first premier of Israel; Judah Ben Hur, hero of a novel by Lew Wallace.*
Ben·a·dryl (ben′ə drəl), *n. Trademark.* a synthetic drug used to relieve allergies such as hay fever.
be·name (bi nām′), *v.t.*, **-named** or **-nempt** or **nempt·ed, -nam·ing.** *Archaic.* to name; call; describe as.
Bence-Jones protein (bens′jōnz′), an abnormal globulin found in the urine of persons having multiple myeloma. [<Henry *Bence-Jones,* 1843-1873, an English physician, who first described it]
bench (bench), *n., v.* —*n.* **1** a long seat, usually of wood or stone. A bench may be with or without a back. *Many people sat in the sun on park benches.* **2** a strong, heavy table used by a carpenter, or by any worker with tools and materials;

workbench: *My father painted a chair on his bench in the cellar.* **3a** position as a judge: *He was appointed to the bench last year.* **b** the judge or group of judges sitting in a law court: *The bench read the sentence to the prisoner.* **c** the seat where judges sit in a law court. **d** a law court. **4** *Sports.* **a** the place, usually a long seat, where those members of a team sit who are not actually taking part in a game. **b** the substitute or reserve players of a team collectively: *a team with a good bench.* **5** a seat or thwart in a boat. **6** a seat where persons sit side by side in some official capacity. **7** *U.S.* a raised, level tract of land resembling a terrace, lying either above the bed of a stream on a valley slope, or between a sea or lake and neighboring mountains, and generally marking the outcrop of a new seam or stratum of rock; benchland. See picture under **valley**. **8a** a platform on which dogs stand for exhibition at a dog show. **b** a dog show. See also **bench show**. **9** *Mining.* a layer or strip (of coal, ore, etc.) worked separately.
—***v.t.*** **1** *Sports.* **a** to exclude from play, especially as punishment: *The football player was benched for failing to follow rules.* **b** to take (a player) out of a game: *Don Barrows, the powerful fullback, and a 245-pound tackle, Paul Tully, . . . were benched with injuries* (New York Times). **2** to furnish with benches. **3** to assign a seat on a bench, especially one of honor. **4** to exhibit (a dog) on a platform at a show.
—***v.i.*** *Rare.* to sit on a seat of justice.
on the bench, sitting in a law court as a judge: *Judge Burke . . . has been practicing law for 28 years, on the bench four years* (Time). **a** held out of the game; sitting among the substitute players: *The rookie complained that the coach kept him mostly on the bench.*
[Old English *benc*]

bench clamp, **hook**, or **stop**, a vise or other device on a workbench for holding work steady, or for forcing parts together.

bench dog, a dog exhibited at or competing in dog shows.

bench|er (ben′chər), *n.* **1** in England: **a** one of the senior members governing a society of English lawyers and law students called an Inn of Court. **b** *Informal.* a member of the House of Commons. **2** a person who sits on a bench, such as an oarsman.

bench jockey, *U.S. Slang.* **1** a baseball player who seeks to disconcert members of the opposing team or the umpires by verbal harassing from the bench. **2** anyone who harasses or criticizes sharply from the sidelines.

bench|land (bench′land′, -lənd), *n.* = bench (def. 7).

bench-leg|ged (bench′leg′id, -legd′), *adj.* having the forelegs wide apart: *The Indians' little bench-legged ponies were no match for them* (Andy Adams).

bench mark, **1** *Surveying.* a mark made on a rock, post, or other landmark, and used as a starting point or guide in a line of levels for the determination of altitudes. **2** *Figurative.* anything that is taken as, or serves as, a point of reference.

bench scientist, a scientist who works in a laboratory; research scientist: *There is no longer any talk of 'wasting your education' or 'prostituting your science' if you prefer not to be a bench scientist* (Science Journal).

bench show, an exhibition of animals, especially dogs, at which awards are made for physical merit judged on a standard scale of points (distinguished from *field trial,* which evaluates hunting or herding skill or obedience).

bench table, a low stone seat on the inside of walls, around the bases of pillars, in churches, cloisters, and the like.

bench-ter|race (bench′ter′is), *v.t.,* **-raced, -racing.** to terrace (a steep slope) so as to arrest erosion.

bench warmer, *U.S. Informal.* a member of an athletic team who sits on the sideline and is seldom called upon to play.

bench warrant, a written order from a judge or law court to arrest a person.

bend[1] (bend), *v.,* **bent** or (*Archaic*) **bend|ed**, **bend|ing**, *n.* —***v.i.*** **1** to be crooked; curve: *The branch began to bend as I climbed along it.* SYN: turn, twist, warp, crook. **2** to stoop; bow: *She bent down and picked up a stone.* SYN: incline. **3** *Figurative.* to submit: *I bend to God's will.* **4** *Figurative.* to move in a certain direction; turn or incline in any direction: *Thoughts bend toward home as evening approaches. And now the land . . . Bent southward suddenly* (Henry Wadsworth Longfellow). **5** *Figurative.* to direct one's energies; apply oneself: *Bending to our oars, we reached shore before the storm broke.*
—***v.t.*** **1** to force out of a straight line; make crooked; curve: *The strong man bent the iron bar as if it were rubber.* SYN: turn, twist, crook. **2** *Figurative.* to force to submit; cause to bow or yield: *The spirit of the rebels could not be bent.* **3** *Figurative.* to turn or move in a certain direction; direct: *She bent her mind to the new work. He bent his steps toward home.* SYN: apply. **4** to tie or fasten (a sail, rope, cable, or anchor). **5** to bring (a bow or the like) into tension by a string. **6** *Especially British.* to pervert from the right purpose or use: *. . . to "bend" evidence in an effort to obtain a conviction* (London Times).
—***n.*** **1** a part that is not straight; curve; turn: *There is a sharp bend in the road here.* SYN: crook, angle, twist. **2** a stoop; bow: *Her head moved forward in a quick bend.* **3** *Nautical.* a knot for tying two ropes together or tying a rope to something else.
bend over backward. See under **backward**.
bends, the wales of a ship; the thick planks in a ship's side below the waterways: *She is to be caulked, her bends blacked and painted* (Horatio Nelson).
on the bend, *British Slang.* on a drinking spree: *I'd to promise to give up being on the bend, though, and I'm a bloke that keeps his word* (Punch).
round the bend, *British Slang.* crazy: *Everybody was vastly entertained, except for a few poor Treasury officials who must have been driven half round the bend* (Manchester Guardian Weekly).
the bends, *U.S. Informal.* = caisson disease.
[Old English *bendan* tighten (a bow)] —**bend′a|ble**, *adj.*
►**Bend** is not used of things or materials that are limp, such as cloth or thin paper, which are *folded,* but only of that which has some rigidity, such as cardboard or a card, wood, or metal, or of rigid things having joints, such as the arm or the backbone.

bend[2] (bend), *n.* **1** *Heraldry.* a diagonal band on a coat of arms; an ordinary consisting of two parallel lines drawn from the dexter chief (upper right) to the sinister base (lower left) of the shield. **2** a shape or size in which hides are tanned into leather, forming half of a butt. [Old English *bend* a band; merged in Middle English with Old North French *bende* band[2]]

Ben Da|vis (dā′vis), **1** a yellow, red-striped variety of winter apple known for its keeping qualities, but now little grown because of its lack of flavor. **2** the tree it grows on.

ben|day or **Ben|day** (ben′dā′), *adj.* involving or using a technique in photoengraving of adding a variety of tones, shading, or mottled effects to line drawings by the use of screens with dots set in varying degrees of density. [American English < *Ben*(jamin) *Day,* 1838-1916, an American printer, who developed it]

bend|ed (ben′did), *adj., v.* —***adj.*** bent: *on bended knee.* **a** *Archaic.* bent; a past tense and a past participle of **bend**[1].

bend|er (ben′dər), *n.* **1** a person or thing that bends. **2** *U.S. Slang.* a drinking spree. **3** *Baseball.* a curve. **4** *Obsolete British Slang.* a sixpence.

Ben|der Gestalt test (ben′dər), *Psychology.* a test to determine the perceptual ability of children, consisting of a series of drawings which the children are asked to copy.

bend|ing moment (bend′ing), the moment tending to produce curvature in a beam.

bend|let (bend′lət), *n. Heraldry.* a narrow bend.

bends (bendz), *n.pl.* See under **bend**[1].

bend sinister, *Heraldry.* an ordinary drawn in the opposite direction to a bend (that is, from the sinister chief to the dexter base). It is one of the marks of bastardy.

bene[1] (bēn), *n. Archaic.* a prayer or petition. [Old English *bēn*]

ben|e[2] (ben′e), *n.* a wild boar of New Guinea.

be|neath (bi nēth′), *adv., prep.* —***adv.*** **1** in a lower place; below: *As we flew over the mountains we could see that there were snowy peaks beneath.* **2** on the lower side or on the bottom; underneath: *leaves dark above and light beneath.* **3** lower in rank or power: *The officers heard grumbling in the ranks beneath.* **4** later in a book or article: *See the explanation beneath.*
—***prep.*** **1** to or in a lower place than; below; under; covered by: *His head kept slipping beneath the water. The dog sat beneath the tree.* SYN: See syn. under **under**. **2** immediately under: *The cellar runs beneath the rafters of the first floor.* **3** at the foot of: *a house built beneath a tall cliff.* **4** unworthy of; below the dignity of: *A traitor is so low that he is beneath contempt. I would consider it beneath me to sell an old family secret* (Saul Bellow). **5** *Figurative.* lower than in rank, dignity, or office; inferior to; below: *beneath the angels. A sergeant is beneath a captain.* **6** *Figurative.* under the weight, pressure, or influence of: *to sink beneath a burden of responsibility.*
[Old English *beneothan* < *be-* be- + *neothan* below]

ben|e|dic|i|te (ben′ə dis′ə tē), *interj., n.* —***interj.*** a Latin word which means *Bless you!* or *Bless us!* or *Bless me!*
—***n.*** the invocation of a blessing, especially grace before meals.
[< Latin *benedīcite,* second person plural imperative of *benedīcere* bless < *bene* well + *dīcere* speak of]

Ben|e|dic|i|te (ben′ə dis′ə tē), *n.* **1** the canticle or hymn beginning "Benedicite, omnia opera Domini" ("O all ye works of the Lord, bless ye the Lord"). **2** a musical setting of this.

ben|e|dick (ben′ə dik), *n.* = benedict.

Ben|e|dick (ben′ə dik), *n.* (in Shakespeare's *Much Ado About Nothing*) a young man determined to remain a bachelor, who nevertheless falls in love and marries Beatrice.

ben|e|dict (ben′ə dikt), *n.* **1** a recently married man, especially one who was a bachelor for a long time. **2** a married man. [variant of *benedick*]

ben|e|dic|tine (ben′ə dik′tēn), *n.* a sweet, aromatic liqueur, first made by the Benedictines in France about the 1500's.

Ben|e|dic|tine (ben′ə dik′tin, -tēn, -tīn), *n., adj.* —***n.*** a monk or nun following the rules of the order founded by Saint Benedict about 530 A.D., known for its scholarly efforts in literature and the arts.
—***adj.*** of Saint Benedict, or his order.
[< French *bénédictin,* learned borrowing from Medieval Latin *benedictinus* < *Benedictus* Saint Benedict]

Benedictine rule, a set of rules for a plan of life, used in monasteries of the order established by Saint Benedict.

ben|e|dic|tion (ben′ə dik′shən), *n.* **1a** the asking of God's blessing at the end of a religious service: *The priest stood before the couple and gave the benediction at the end of the marriage ceremony.* **b** the form or ritual of this invocation. **2a** blessing or a blessing: *The old man's benediction was a comfort to followers.* **b** an expression of thanks; grace. **c** the advantage received or given by blessing; mercy. [< Latin *benedictiō, -ōnis* < *benedīcere* praise < *bene* well + *dīcere* speak of. See etym. of doublet **benison.**]

Ben|e|dic|tion (ben′ə dik′shən), *n.* in the Roman Catholic Church: **1** one of several ritual blessings, especially of the Blessed Sacrament, in which the priest officiating makes the sign of the cross over the people with the vessel (monstrance) containing the Eucharist. **2** the consecrating of an abbot or abbess. **3** the ceremony of consecrating certain things, such as a church, bell, or religious garment.

ben|e|dic|tion|al (ben′ə dik′shə nəl), *adj.* = benedictive.

ben|e|dic|tive (ben′ə dik′tiv), *adj.* serving to bless; conveying a blessing.

ben|e|dic|to|ry (ben′ə dik′tər ē), *adj.* of or having to do with the utterance of benediction.

Benedict's solution, a chemical solution used to test for the amount of dextrose in the urine.

Ben|e|dic|tus (ben′ə dik′təs), *n.* **1** a short hymn or canticle beginning "Benedictus qui venit in nomine Domini" ("Blessed is He that cometh in the name of the Lord"), taken from Psalm 118:26 and Matthew 21:9. **2** a canticle or hymn beginning "Benedictus Dominus Deus Israel" ("Blessed be the Lord God of Israel"). Luke 1:68. **3** a musical setting for either of these, that for the first being sometimes connected with the Sanctus. [< Latin *benedictus* blessed]

ben|e|fac|tion (ben′ə fak′shən), *n.* **1** a doing good; kindly or generous action; beneficence. **2** a gift for charity; help given for any good purpose. [< Latin *benefactiō, -ōnis* < *bene facere* do good to]

ben|e|fac|tor (ben′ə fak′tər, ben′ə fak′-), *n.* **1a** a person who has given money or kindly help: *Many members of rich families have become benefactors of hospitals, colleges, orchestras, and other organizations or societies that need help.* **b** a patron. **2** a person who makes a benefaction to a charitable or religious institution.

ben|e|fac|tress (ben′ə fak′tris, ben′ə fak′-), *n.* a woman benefactor.

ben|e|fac|trix (ben′ə fak′triks, ben′ə fak′-), *n., pl.* **ben|e|fac|trix|es**, **ben|e|fac|tri|ces** (ben′ə fak′trə sēz). a woman benefactor; benefactress.

be|nef|ic (bə nef′ik), *adj.* kindly; beneficent; benign. [< Latin *beneficus*]

ben|e|fice (ben′ə fis), *n., v.,* **-ficed, -fic|ing.** —***n.*** **1a** a permanent office or position in the church, consisting of a sacred duty and the income that

---

Pronunciation Key: hat, āge, cãre, fär; let, ēqual, tėrm; it, īce; hot, ōpen, ôrder; oil, out; cup, pu̇t, rüle; child; long; thin; ᴛʜen; zh, measure; ə represents **a** in about, **e** in taken, **i** in pencil, **o** in lemon, **u** in circus.

goes with it; a living. **b** the income or endowment. **2** land granted in feudal tenure; fief.
—*v.t.* to invest with a benefice.
[< Old French *benefice,* learned borrowing from Latin *beneficium* kindness, promotion < *beneficus* obliging, kind < *bene facere* do good to]

be|nef|i|cence (bə nef′ə səns), *n.* **1** the practice of doing good; kindness. **2** a kindly act; gift. [< Latin *beneficentia* < variant stem of *beneficus;* see etym. under **benefice**]

be|nef|i|cent (bə nef′ə sənt), *adj.* **1** doing good; kind: *a beneficent person, beneficent acts.* SYN: benign, benevolent. **2** having good results; giving benefits. —**be|nef′i|cent|ly,** *adv.*

ben|e|fi|cial (ben′ə fish′əl), *adj.* **1** producing good; favorable; helpful: *Sunshine is beneficial to plants.* SYN: advantageous, serviceable, profitable. **2** *Law.* having or conferring the right to the use or benefit, as of property. —**ben′e|fi′cial|ly,** *adv.* —**ben′e|fi′cial|ness,** *n.*

ben|e|fi|ci|ar|y (ben′ə fish′ē er′ē, -fish′ər-), *n., pl.* **-ar|ies,** *adj.* —*n.* **1** any person or thing that receives benefit: *All the children of the neighborhood are beneficiaries of the new playground.* **2** *Law.* **a** a person who receives (or is named to receive) money or property from an insurance policy, a will, or the like. **b** a person for whose benefit a trust exists. **3** a person possessed of a benefice or church living.
—*adj.* **1** having to do with the holding of land by feudal tenure; feudatory. **2** having to do with the holding of an ecclesiastical benefice.

ben|e|fi|ci|ate (ben′ə fish′ē āt), *v.t.,* **-at|ed, -at|ing.** to remove impurities from (an ore) and prepare for smelting or other processes; refine. —**ben′e|fi′ci|a′tion,** *n.*

ben|e|fit (ben′ə fit), *n., v.,* **-fit |ed, -fit|ing.** —*n.* **1** anything which is for the good of a person or thing; advantage: *Good roads are of great benefit to travelers. World peace would be of great benefit to mankind.* SYN: profit, help, good. See syn. under **advantage.** **2** money paid to a sick or disabled person by an insurance company, government agency, or the like. **3** a performance at the theater, a game, or other public attraction, to raise money for a worthy cause: *Last Saturday evening, at the Second Avenue Theatre, the Yiddish Theatrical Alliance staged its annual benefit for aged, infirm, and indigent members* (New Yorker). **4** *Archaic.* a kind deed; act of kindness; favor; gift. **5** *Rare.* financial profit; gain.
—*v.t.* to do good to; be good for: *Rest will benefit a sick person.* —*v.i.* to receive good; get advantage; profit: *He benefited from the medicine. His grades would benefit from more study.*
benefit of the doubt, a favorable judgment when proof of blame or guilt is inconclusive: *Give him the benefit of the doubt, at least until all the evidence is in.*
[Middle English *benfet* < Anglo-French < Latin *benefactum* good deed < *bene* well + *factum,* neuter past participle of *facere* do] —**ben′e|fit′er,** *n.*

benefit of clergy, 1 (formerly) the privilege of being tried in church courts instead of secular courts. **2** the services and rites or approval of the church.

benefit society or **association,** an association which administers a fund to which subscribing members make small, regular payments and from which monetary assistance is made available in times of illness, old age, or other need.

Ben|e|lux (ben′ə luks), *n.* an economic union of Belgium, the Netherlands, and Luxembourg, that was organized in 1948 and is now part of the European Common Market.

be|nempt (bi nempt′), *v., adj. Archaic.* —*v.* benamed; a past tense and a past participle of **bename.** —*adj.* named.

be|net (bi net′), *v.t.,* **-net|ted, -net|ting.** to enclose in or as if in a net; ensnare.

be|ne va|le (ben′ē vā′lē; be′ne wä′lā), *Latin.* farewell.

be|nev|o|lence (bə nev′ə ləns), *n.* **1** desire to promote the happiness of others; good will; kindly feeling: *The judge's benevolence was the wonder and relief of many a frightened offender.* SYN: kindness, generosity. **2** an act of kindness; something good that is done; generous gift: *The wealthy merchant gave a large benevolence to the local hospital.* **3** (formerly) a forced loan to an English king. It is now illegal.

be|nev|o|lent (bə nev′ə lənt), *adj.* having the desire to promote the happiness of others; intended to do good; kindly; charitable: *Giving money to help the Red Cross is a benevolent act.* SYN: generous, bountiful, philanthropic. [< Latin *benevolēns, -entis* < *bene* well + *volēns, -entis,* present participle of *velle* wish] —**be|nev′o|lent|ly,** *adv.*

Beng., 1 Bengal. **2** Bengali.

Ben|gal (ben′gôl, beng′-; -gəl), *adj.* of or from Bengal: *a Bengal tiger.*

Ben|ga|lese (ben′gə lēz′, -lēs′; beng′-), *n., pl.* **-lese,** *adj.* —*n.* a native or inhabitant of Bengal. —*adj.* of Bengal, its people, or their language.

Bengal fire, = Bengal light.

Ben|ga|li (ben gô′lē, beng-), *adj., n., pl.* **-lis** *for 1, no pl. for 2.* —*adj.* of Bengal, its people, or their language.
—*n.* **1** a native of Bengal. **2** the Indic language of Bengal, a modern Indo-European language.

ben|ga|line (beng′gə lēn, beng′gə lēn′), *n.* a corded cloth of silk, rayon, or cotton mixed with worsted, similar to poplin. [< French *bengaline*]

Bengal light, a kind of firework producing a steady, vivid, blue-colored light, used in theatricals and for signals; Bengal fire.

be|night (bi nīt′), *v.t.* **1** to involve in intellectual or moral darkness: *The Aristotelian astronomy benighted science almost completely for 1,800 years* (Scientific American). **2** to overtake by the darkness of night: *The tourists were benighted in a forest* (Thomas De Quincey). [< *be-* + *night*] —**be|night′ment,** *n.*

be|night|ed (bi nī′tid), *adj.* **1** not knowing right from wrong; ignorant; unenlightened. **2** overtaken by darkness. —**be|night′ed|ly,** *adv.* —**be|night′ed|ness,** *n.*

be|nign (bi nīn′), *adj.* **1** having a kind disposition; gracious: *The benign old lady had a warm smile.* SYN: benevolent. **2** showing or indicating kindly feeling; gentle: *a benign countenance.* **3** not dangerous to health; not malignant: *A benign swelling or tumor can usually be cured.* **4a** mild: *Hawaii has a benign climate.* SYN: salutary. **b** favorable; propitious: *the benign influence of the planets.* [Old French *benigne,* learned borrowing from Latin *benignus* good-natured < *bene* well + *-gnus* born] —**be|nign′ly,** *adv.*

be|nig|nan|cy (bi nig′nən sē), *n.* benignant quality or manner.

be|nig|nant (bi nig′nənt), *adj.* **1** having or showing a kindly feeling toward others; benevolent: *The benignant king tried to gain the good will of his subjects.* SYN: gracious. **2** having a good effect; beneficial. SYN: favorable. **3** (of tumors and other growths) benign; not malignant. —**be|nig′nant|ly,** *adv.*

be|nig|ni|ty (bi nig′nə tē), *n., pl.* **-ties. 1** kindly feeling; kindliness; graciousness. **2** a kind act; favor.

ben|i|son (ben′ə zən, -sən), *n.* a blessing; benediction: *Will the benisons of trade incline the Soviet ... to peaceful living?* (Christian Science Monitor). [< Old French *beneisson,* learned borrowing from Latin *benedictiō, -ōnis* < *bene* well + *dīcere* say. See etym. of doublet **benediction.**]

ben|ja|min (ben′jə mən), *n.* **1** the resin benzoin. **2** = benjamin tree. [< earlier *benjoin* benzoin; influenced by *Benjamin*]

Ben|ja|min (ben′jə mən), *n.* **1** the youngest and, next to Joseph, favorite son of Jacob (in the Bible, Genesis 42:4 and 44:20). **2** one of the twelve tribes of Israel. **3** *Figurative.* any youngest and dearly loved child. **4** *U.S.* = benjamin tree.

benjamin bush, *U.S.* = spicebush.

benjamin tree, 1 the tree from which benzoin is obtained, a native of Sumatra, Borneo, etc. **2** a North American shrub which has an aromatic, stimulant, tonic bark, and berries yielding an oil of similar properties; the spicebush.

ben|most (ben′mōst, -məst), *adj. Scottish.* innermost.

ben|ne (ben′ē), *n.* the plant sesame. Its seeds are used in cooking and yield an oil used in soap manufacture and cooking. [American English < Malay *bĕne* grain, seed]

ben|net (ben′it), *n.* **1** any plant of the species of avens. **2** = herb bennet. [< Old French (*herbe*) *beneïte,* learned borrowing from Medieval Latin (*herba*) *benedicta* blessed (herb)]

Ben|ning|ton (ben′ing tən), *n.,* or **Bennington ware,** an American earthenware with a lustrous brown glaze applied in mottled or streaked patterns, made in Bennington, Vermont.

Benn|ism (ben′iz əm), *n. British.* the policy of extending state ownership and intervention in private industry: *Desperate problems beset Labour ... the problem of Bennism, petrified industry, rampant trades unionism, and splitting in two* (Manchester Guardian Weekly). [< Anthony Wedgwood *Benn,* born 1925, British Labour party leader + *-ism*]

ben|ny (ben′ē), *n., pl.* **-nies. 1** *U.S. Slang.* a Benzedrine pill (amphetamine sulfate): *Traffic authorities ... agree that this* [*traffic death*] *is a likely result when drivers dose themselves with bennies to stay awake* (Time). **2** *U.S. Slang.* a derby hat. **3** *Slang.* a particular type of overcoat.

be|no (bē′nō), *n.* (in the Philippines) = aguardiente. [< Spanish *vino* wine]

bent[1] (bent), *v., adj., n.* —*v.* a past tense and a past participle of **bend**[1]: *He bent the wire.*
—*adj.* **1** not straight; crooked; curved: *The farmer's back was bent from years of toil.* **2** *Figurative.* strongly inclined; determined: *He is bent on being a doctor.* SYN: resolute, resolved, set. **3** on one's way; bound: *homeward bent.* **4** *British Slang.* **a** dishonest; crooked: *a bent policeman.* **b** not normal; perverted: *a bent mind.*
—*n.* **1** *Figurative.* a natural inclination; tendency: *He has a decided bent for drawing.* SYN: penchant, bias. **2a** limit of capacity; degree of endurance (now used only in the Shakespearean phrase *to the top of one's bent*). **b** the degree of curve or tension of a bow. **3** curved form or condition. **4** section of a framework consisting of posts connected by ties and braces.
[< the verb *bend*]

bent[2] (bent), *n.* **1** = bent grass. **2** any stiff or wiry grass that grows on sandy or waste land. **3** a stalk of such grass or of bent grass. **4** *Archaic.* a heath; moor. [Old English *beonet-*]

bent grass, redtop or a similar grass, much used as a lawn grass in temperate regions.

ben|thal (ben′thəl), *n., adj.* —*n.* the bottom of the sea or other bodies of water.
—*adj.* of the benthos; having to do with the bottom of the sea or other bodies of water.
[< Greek *bénthos* depth + English *-al*[1]]

Ben|tham|ism (ben′thə miz əm), *n.* the utilitarian doctrines of Jeremy Bentham.

Ben|tham|ite (ben′thə mīt, -tə-), *n., adj.* —*n.* a follower of Benthamism.
—*adj.* having to do with or favoring Benthamism: *The underlying and dominant assumption of Labor policy is Benthamite—the concepts of ... the efficient public servant, the doing of good to the greatest number* (Harper's).

ben|thic (ben′thik), *adj.* of the benthos: *Both benthic and pelagic organisms occurred to a depth of 10,710 metres* (New Scientist). [< Greek *bénthos* depth + English *-ic*]

ben|tho|al (ben thō′əl), *adj.* = benthonic.

ben|tho|graph (ben′thə graf, -gräf), *n.* a device for taking photographs of the bottom of the sea. [< Greek *bénthos* depth + English *-graph*]

ben|thon|ic (ben thon′ik), *adj.* living on the bottom of large bodies of water.

ben|thos (ben′thos), *n.* **1** the bottom of the ocean. **2** the animals and plants that are fixed to or crawl upon the bottom of large bodies of water. [< Greek *bénthos* depth (of the sea)]

ben|tho|scope (ben′thə skōp), *n.* a spherical diving apparatus capable of descending to great depths, used to study undersea life and resources. [< Greek *bénthos* depth]

ben|to (ben′tō), *n. Japanese.* a workingman's lunch of cold fish and rice.

ben|ton|ite (ben′tə nīt), *n.* a soft, absorbent, chemically inert clay formed from the alteration of volcanic ash. [American English < Fort *Benton,* Montana, where it is found + English *-ite*[1]]

ben|ton|it|ic (ben′tə nit′ik), *adj.* of or containing bentonite.

ben tro|va|to (ben trō vä′tō), *Italian.* well designed or contrived.

bent|wood (bent′wu̇d′), *n., adj.* —*n.* wood in rods, bars, or other shapes that is bent, while softened by steam, into various forms, especially for use in making boats and furniture.
—*adj.* made of such wood: *bentwood furniture.*

be|numb (bi num′), *v.t.* **1** to make numb: *My fingers were benumbed by the cold.* SYN: numb. **2** to stupefy; deaden: *She was benumbed with grief at the death of her pet dog. A pen in his hand ... benumbs all his faculties* (Samuel Johnson). SYN: paralyze. [Old English *benumen,* past participle of *beniman* deprive < *be-* + *niman* take] —**be|numb′ing|ly,** *adv.*

be|numbed (bi numd′), *adj.* made numb.

benz-, *combining form.* a form of **benzo-,** as in *benzpyrene.*

ben|zal|de|hyde (ben zal′də hīd), *n.* a colorless, aromatic liquid obtained from the natural oil of bitter almonds or other oils, or produced artificially, used in the manufacture of dyes and perfumes and as a flavoring agent. *Formula:* C_7H_6O

Ben|ze|drine (ben′zə drēn, -drin; ben zed′rin), *n. Trademark.* amphetamine, a drug that causes wakefulness. *Formula:* $C_9H_{13}N$ [< *benz*(ene) + (eph)*edrine*]

ben|zene (ben′zēn, ben zēn′), *n.* a colorless liquid that vaporizes and is set on fire easily, obtained chiefly from coal tar; benzol. It is used for removing grease in motor fuels and in making dyes and synthetic rubber. *Formula:* C_6H_6 [< German *Benzin* < *Benzoe* benzoin]

benzene hex|a|chlo|ride (hek′sə klôr′īd, -id; -klōr′-), a compound of benzene and chlorine, widely used as an insecticide. *Formula:* $C_6H_6Cl_6$

***benzene ring** or **nucleus, 1** a hexagonal arrangement of six carbon atoms bonded together by identical bonds, with each carbon atom also bonded to a hydrogen atom. This structure is found in benzene and many other compounds derived from benzene, in which one or more of the hydrogen atoms may be replaced by other atoms or radicals to form various derivatives. **2** the graphic representation of a molecule of benzene, in the form of a hexagon with a carbon atom united with a hydrogen atom at each of its corners. See diagram under **molecule**.

***benzene ring**
definitions 1, 2

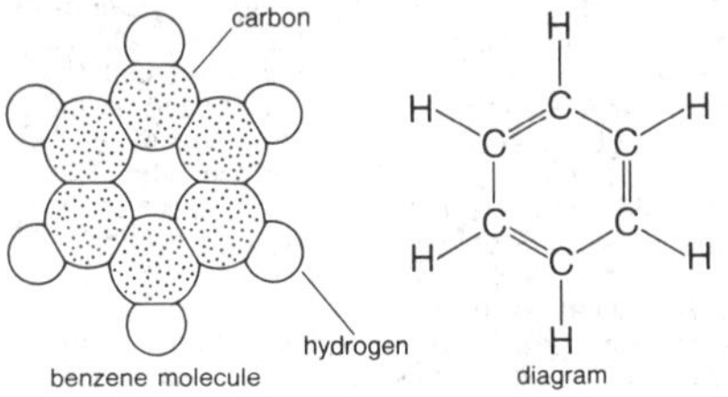

benzene series, a series of compounds of carbon and hydrogen having the general formula C_nH_{2n-6}.

ben|ze|noid (ben′zə noid), *adj.* derived from or related to benzene. [< *benzen*(e) + *-oid*]

ben|zi|din (ben′zə din), *n.* = benzidine.

ben|zi|dine (ben′zə dēn, -din), *n.* a base derived from benzene, used in the preparation of various dyes and as a reagent. *Formula:* $C_{12}H_{12}N_2$ [< *benz-* + *-id* + *-ine*²]

ben|zin (ben′zin), *n.* = benzine.

ben|zine (ben′zēn, ben zēn′), *n.* **1** a colorless liquid that vaporizes and is set on fire easily, a liquid mixture of hydrocarbons obtained in distilling petroleum. It is used in cleaning and dyeing, and as a motor fuel. **2** = benzene. [< German *Benzin*]

benzo-, *combining form.* of or having to do with benzene or benzoic acid, as *benzonitrile, benzopyrene.* Also, **benz-**.

ben|zo|ate (ben′zō āt, -it), *n.* a salt or ester of benzoic acid.

benzoate of soda, a white, crystalline or powdery salt of benzoic acid, used in medicine and to preserve foods; sodium benzoate. *Formula:* C_6H_5COONa

ben|zo|caine (ben′zō kān), *n.* an anesthetic compound used in certain dusting powders and ointments, and also internally, to abate pain from ulcers of the stomach. *Formula:* $C_9H_{11}NO_2$ [< *benzo-* + (co)*caine*]

ben|zo|ic (ben zō′ik), *adj.* of or obtained from benzoin.

benzoic acid, a white, crystalline acid occurring especially in benzoin and cranberries, used in medicine as an antiseptic, and to preserve foods. *Formula:* C_6H_5COOH

ben|zo|in (ben′zō in, ben zō′-; ben′zo in), *n.* **1** a dry, brittle resin with a fragrant odor, obtained by cutting the bark of certain species of trees of Java, Laos, Sumatra, and Thailand. Benzoin is used chiefly in cosmetics, perfumes, and incense, and has long been an ingredient in cough medicine and other medicinal application. **2** a crystalline compound somewhat like camphor, derived from benzaldehyde, used medicinally and in the synthesis of organic compounds. *Formula:* $C_{14}H_{12}O_2$ **3** any one of a small genus of aromatic shrubs and trees of the laurel family, found in North America and Asia, such as the spicebush. [< French *benjoin* < Spanish *benjuí* or Portuguese *beijoim* < Arabic *lubān jāwī* incense of Java]

ben|zol (ben′zōl, -zol), *n.* **1** = benzene. **2** a liquid hydrocarbon obtained from coal tar, containing about 70 per cent of benzene and 20 to 30 per cent of toluene, used in making dyes. [< German *Benzol*]

ben|zole (ben′zōl), *n.* = benzol.

ben|zo|ni|trile (ben′zō nī′trəl, -trīl, -trēl), *n.* a transparent, colorless oil having an almondlike odor, obtained from benzoic acid. It is used in the synthesis of organic compounds, in dyes, and as a solvent for vinyl resins. *Formula:* C_7H_5N

ben|zo|phe|none (ben′zō fē′nōn, -fə nōn′), *n.* a crystalline ketone obtained by distilling calcium benzoate. *Formula:* $C_{13}H_{10}O$ [< *benzo-* + (di)*phen*(yl) (ket)*one*]

ben|zo|py|rene (ben′zō pī′rēn), *n.* = benzpyrene.

ben|zo|qui|none (ben′zō kwi nōn′), *n.* = quinone.

ben|zo|sul|fi|mide (ben′zō sul′fə mīd), *n.* = saccharin.

ben|zo|yl (ben′zō əl), *n.* a univalent radical, C_6H_5CO-, present in benzoic acid and its derivatives. [< German *Benzoyl*]

benz|py|rene (benz′pī′rēn), *n.* a pale-yellow, crystalline hydrocarbon found in cigarette smoke and in the air of industrial areas, which causes cancer in rats and mice and may cause it in humans. *Formula:* $C_{20}H_{12}$

ben|zyl (ben′zəl), *n.* a univalent radical occurring in toluene derivatives. *Formula:* $C_6H_5CH_2$- [< *benz*(ene) + *-yl*]

benzyl benzoate, a colorless, aromatic, volatile oil used to relieve spasms, and in treatment of hypertension and of certain skin infections. *Formula:* $C_{14}H_{12}O_2$

Be|o|wulf (bā′ə wu̇lf), *n.* **1** an Old English heroic poem in alliterative verse, of unknown authorship. It is the oldest epic surviving in English and was probably composed in England about 700 A.D. **2** the hero of this poem.

be|paint (bi pānt′), *v.t.* **1** to paint over. **2** to bedaub with paint. **3** to color as if with paint.

be|plumed (bi plümd′), *adj.* covered or decorated with plumes.

be|pow|der (bi pou′dər), *v.t.* to powder over.

be|praise (bi prāz′), *v.t.*, **-praised, -prais|ing.** to praise greatly; praise too much.

be|puff (bi puf′), *v.t.* **1** to puff, blow out, or swell: *a bepuffed and distorted appearance.* **2** *Figurative.* to praise extravagantly.

be|puz|zle (bi puz′əl), *v.t.*, **-zled, -zling.** to puzzle greatly; perplex. —**be|puz′zle|ment,** *n.*

be|queath (bi kwēꟻʜ′, -kwēth′), *v.t.* **1a** to give or leave by means of a will when one dies: *The farmer bequeathed his farm to his son.* **SYN**: devise. **b** *Figurative:* *One age bequeaths its knowledge to the next.* **SYN**: transmit. **2** *Archaic.* to commit; commend; entrust. [Old English *becwethan* say; give by will < *be-* to, for + *cwethan* say] —**be|queath′a|ble,** *adj.* —**be|queath′er,** *n.* —**be|queath′ment,** *n.*

be|queath|al (bi kwē′ꟻʜəl), *n.* the act of bequeathing; bequest.

be|quest (bi kwest′), *n.* **1** something bequeathed; a legacy: *When the invalid died, he left a bequest of ten thousand dollars to the hospital he had stayed in.* **2** the act of bequeathing. [Middle English *biqueste* < *bi-* to, for + Old English *cwiss* a saying]

be|rat (bə rät′), *n. Turkish.* official rights or privileges issued by a ruler to a person.

be|rate (bi rāt′), *v.t.*, **-rat|ed, -rat|ing.** to scold sharply; upbraid: *The neighbor berated the boys for teasing her cat.* **SYN**: chide, reprimand. [< *be-* + *rate*², verb]

Ber|ber (bėr′bər), *n., adj.* —*n.* **1** a member of a group of Moslem tribes living in northern Africa, west of Egypt. **2** their language, one of the Hamitic languages. **3** any one of the aboriginal inhabitants of North Africa (Barbary), from whom the modern Berbers are descended.
—*adj.* of or having to do with the Berbers or their language.

ber|be|ri|da|ceous (bėr′bər ə dā′shəs), *adj.* belonging to the barberry family or resembling a member of it. [< New Latin *Berberidaceae* the family (< *Berberis, -idis* the typical genus < Medieval Latin *berberis* barberry) + English *-ous*]

ber|ber|in (bėr′bər in), *n.* = berberine.

ber|ber|ine (bėr′bə rēn, -bər in), *n.* a yellow, crystalline alkaloid obtained from the barberry and various other plants. It has a bitter taste and has been used against fever and malaria and externally as a dressing for ulcers. *Formula:* $C_{20}H_{19}NO_5$ [< Medieval Latin *berberis* barberry + English *-ine*²]

berberine tree, an African tree that yields a yellow dye containing berberine.

ber|ceuse (ber sœz′), *n., pl.* **-ceuses** (-sœz′). *French.* **1** a lullaby. **2** *Music.* a vocal or instrumental composition having the tender, soothing qualities of a lullaby.

Ber|cy (ber sē′), *n.*, or **Bercy sauce**, a creamy white sauce made from meat stock with shallots, white wine, lemon juice, and parsley. [< *Bercy,* a district of Paris, France]

ber|dache (bər dash′), *n.* a North American Indian man who dresses and behaves like a woman. [< French *bardache* < Arabic *bardaj* slave]

be|reave (bi rēv′), *v.t.*, **-reaved** or **-reft, -reav|ing. 1** to leave desolate and alone; deprive: *The children were bereaved by the death of their father.* **2** to deprive ruthlessly; rob: *The lost hikers were bereft of hope when the rescue plane did not see them.* **SYN**: strip, dispossess. **3** *Obsolete.* to remove by violence. [Old English *berēafian* < *be-* away + *rēafian* rob] —**be|reav′er,** *n.*
► **Bereaved** and **bereft** are ordinarily not interchangeable. *Bereaved* is used chiefly when the loss is that of a beloved person by death: *the bereaved parents.* In most other situations, *bereft* is used: *bereft of hope.*

be|reave|ment (bi rēv′mənt), *n.* **1** loss of a relative or friend by death. **2** a bereaved condition; great loss: *The bereavement of the widowed Queen lasted for several years.* **3** act of bereaving.

be|reft (bi reft′), *adj., v.* —*adj.* deprived: *Bereft of hope and friends, the old man led a lonely life.*
—*v.* bereaved; a past tense and a past participle of **bereave**: *He was bereft by the loss of his son.*
► See **bereave** for usage note.

Ber|e|ni|ce's Hair or **Locks** (ber′ə nī′siz), the northern constellation Coma Berenices. [< *Berenice,* an Egyptian queen, famed for her beautiful hair]

***be|ret** (bə rā′, ber′ā), *n.* a soft, round cap of wool or felt cloth or yarn, with no visor. Berets are usually somewhat flat and were originally worn especially in parts of France and Spain. [< French *béret* < Vulgar Latin *birrittum* (diminutive) < Late Latin *birrus* cape with a hood]

***beret**

be|ret|ta (bə ret′ə), *n.* = biretta.

berg (bėrg), *n.* **1** an iceberg: *glittering bergs of ice* (Tennyson). **2** (in South Africa) a mountain.

ber|gall (bėr′gôl), *n.* the cunner fish, a small fish of the Atlantic allied to the wrasses. Also, **burgall.** [origin unknown]

ber|ga|mot¹ (bėr′gə mot), *n.* **1a** a pear-shaped variety of orange grown in southern Italy, California, and the Gulf States. The bergamot belongs to the rue family. **b** the tree on which it grows. **c** an oil obtained from the rind of the fruit, used in perfumes. **2** any one of various plants of the mint family, especially one which yields an oil whose odor resembles essence of bergamot. [< *Bergamo,* a town in Italy]

ber|ga|mot² (bėr′gə mot), *n.* a winter variety of pear with a fine flavor. [< French *bergamote* < Italian *bergamotta* < Turkish *beg armudi* prince's pear < *beg* prince, bey + *armud* pear + *-i,* a possessive suffix]

ber|gere or **ber|gère** (bėr′zher, ber zher′), *n.* a kind of upholstered armchair with a high back and sides. [< French *bergère* shepherdess]

ber|ge|rette (bėr′zhə ret, ber zhə ret′), *n.* a kind of French pastoral song or dance, popular especially from the 1500's into the 1700's. [< French *bergerette* (diminutive) < *bergère* shepherdess]

Ber|ger rhythm (bėr′gər), = alpha rhythm. [< Hans *Berger,* 1873-1941, a German psychiatrist who first recorded it]

Berg|fall (berk′fäl), *n. German.* an avalanche of rock or stone.

Berg|mann's rule (bėrg′mənz), *Ecology.* the principle that warm-blooded animals living in cold climates tend to be larger in size than related animals living in warm climates. [< Carl *Bergmann,* a German biologist of the 1800's]

berg|mehl (berk′māl), *n.* a fine, meallike geological deposit, consisting almost entirely of the siliceous cell walls of certain infusoria; rock meal. Bergmehl has been eaten in times of great scarcity. [< German *Bergmehl* (literally) mountain meal]

berg|schrund (berk′shrůnt), *n.* a deep crevasse, or a series of crevasses, at or near the head of a mountain glacier. See picture under **glacier.** [< German *Bergschrund* (literally) mountain fissure]

Berg|so|ni|an (bėrg sō′nē ən), *adj., n.* —*adj.* of or characteristic of the philosophy of Henri Bergson.
—*n.* a person who supports or believes in Bergsonism.

Berg|son|ism (bėrg′sə niz əm), *n.* the philosophy of Henri Bergson, that conceives of the universe as a constantly changing expression of "creative evolution" under the impulse of an *élan vital* (driving life force), with duration as the basic means of expression and the ultimate objective reality.

berg|stock (bėrg′stok′), *n.* = alpenstock. [< German *Bergstock*]

berg wind, a hot, arid wind blowing from the interior to the coast of South Africa.

be|rhyme (bi rīm′), *v.t.*, **-rhymed, -rhym|ing. 1** to make rhymes about. **2** to mention in rhyme. **3** to lampoon. Also, **berime.**

be|rib|boned (bi rib′ənd), *adj.* decorated with many ribbons or medals: *beribboned and bejeweled guests.*

ber|i|ber|i (ber′ē ber′ē), *n.* a disease affecting the nervous system, accompanied by muscular paralysis, weakness, extreme loss of weight, pain, and swelling. It is caused by a lack of vitamin B_1 (thiamine) in the diet, and is common in those parts of Asia where polished rice comprises the principal item of diet. [< Singhalese *beri* weakness]

ber|i|ber|ic (ber′ē ber′ik), *adj.* **1** suffering from beriberi. **2** having to do with or like beriberi.

Pronunciation Key: hat, āge, cãre, fär; let, ēqual, tėrm; it, īce; hot, ōpen, ôrder; oil, out; cup, pu̇t, rüle; child; long; thin; ꟻʜen; zh, measure; ə represents **a** in about, **e** in taken, **i** in pencil, **o** in lemon, **u** in circus.

be|rime (bi rīm′), *v.t.*, **-rimed, -rim|ing.** = berhyme.

be|ringed (bi ringd′), *adj.* wearing rings.

Ber|ing Standard Time (bir′ing, bãr′-), the standard time in the western portion of Alaska, three hours behind Pacific Standard Time.

be|rith mi|lah (bə rēt′mē′lə; brit′, bris′), *Judaism.* the covenant or ceremony of circumcision, performed on a male child on the eighth day after his birth. [< Hebrew *bərīth mīlāh*]

Berke|le|ian (bėr klē′ən; *British* bär klē′ən), *adj., n.* —*adj.* of George Berkeley or his philosophy of extreme idealism.
—*n.* a follower of the philosophy of Berkeley.

Berke|le|ian|ism (bėr klē′ə niz əm; *British* bär-klē′ə niz əm), *n.* the philosophy held by George Berkeley, who claimed that material things existed only if perceived by the mind.

Berke|ley|ism (bėr′klē iz əm; *British* bär′klē iz-əm), *n.* = Berkeleianism.

***berke|li|um** (bėr′klē əm, bėr kē′lē əm), *n.* a radioactive, metallic, chemical element produced artificially from americium, curium, or plutonium. [< *Berkeley,* California, site of the University of California, where it was discovered in 1949]

***berkelium**

symbol	atomic number	mass number	oxidation state
Bk	97	247	4, 3

Berk|shire (bėrk′shir, -shər; *British* bärk′shir, -shər), *n.* any of a breed of black, medium-sized hogs, having white markings.

ber|lin (bər lin′, bėr′lin), *n.* **1a** a four-wheeled, covered carriage with two inside seats and a platform in the rear for footmen. **b** a closed automobile with a glass partition separating the driver's seat from the rear seat. **2** Also, **Berlin.** a soft, woolen yarn; Berlin wool. **3** a kind of knitted glove. **4** a dance resembling the polka. [< French *berline* < Berlin, Germany, where it first became popular]

ber|line or **Ber|line** (bər lin′; *French* ber lēn′), *n.* a berlin; a four-wheeled carriage.

Ber|lin|er (bər lin′ər), *n.* an inhabitant of East or West Berlin in Germany.

Berlin wool, a fine dyed wool used for knitting, tapestry, and the like.

ber|lock or **ber|loque dermatitis** (bėr′lok), a drop-shaped discoloration of the skin that may result from the use of perfumes or cosmetics containing ethereal oil. [< French *berloque* locket, charm (because of the shape)]

berm or **berme** (bėrm), *n.* **1** a narrow space or ledge. **2** the deposit of material, especially sand or small rocks, at the top of a beach. It is usually a nearly horizontal surface but may be of varying width according to seasonal wave action. **3** *U.S.* the bank of a canal opposite the towing path. **4** *U.S.* the shoulder of a road. **5** (in a fortification) a space between the moat and the base of the parapet. [< French *berme* < Middle Dutch]

Ber|mu|da cedar (bər myü′də), a kind of juniper native to Bermuda, with hard, reddish-brown, aromatic wood.

Bermuda grass, a creeping perennial grass that resists drought, valued for lawns and pasture, especially in the southern United States.

Ber|mu|dan (bər myü′dən), *adj., n.* = Bermudian.

Bermuda onion, a large mild onion, grown in Bermuda, Texas, and California.

Bermuda rig, = Marconi rig.

Ber|mu|das (bər myü′dəz), *n.pl. Informal.* = Bermuda shorts.

Bermuda shorts, short trousers that end an inch or two above the knee.

Bermuda skirt, a skirt of approximately the same length as Bermuda shorts.

Bermuda Triangle, an area of the North Atlantic in which disappearances of airplanes and ships have been popularly attributed to mysterious forces; Devil's Triangle: *There have been about half a dozen successful books on the Bermuda Triangle, some of them going high in the best-seller lists* (Listener). [so called from the triangle formed by the points between Florida, Bermuda, and Puerto Rico comprising this area]

Ber|mu|di|an (bər myü′dē ən), *adj., n.* —*adj.* of or having to do with the Bermudas or their inhabitants. —*n.* a native or inhabitant of the Bermudas.

Ber|nard|ine (bėr′nər din, -dēn), *adj., n.* —*adj.* **1** of or having to do with Saint Bernard, 1090-1153, abbot of Clairvaux, the most distinguished member of the Cistercian order and regarded as its second founder. **2** of or having to do with the Cistercians. —*n.* a Cistercian monk or nun.

Ber|nese (bėr nēz′, -nēs′), *adj., n., pl.* **-nese.** —*adj.* of or having to do with Bern (or Berne), the capital of Switzerland, or the canton in which it is located: *the Bernese cantonal government.* —*n.* a native or inhabitant of Bern (or Berne).

Bernese mountain dog, any one of a breed of large, hardy dogs found in the Bernese mountain region. They have long, silky black hair with white and brown markings.

Ber|noul|li's principle, law, or **theorem** (bėr-nü′lēz), **1** *Physics.* the principle that the total energy per unit of mass in the streamline flow of a moving fluid is constant, being the sum of the potential energy, the kinetic energy, and the energy due to pressure. The faster the fluid flows, the less the pressure, and vice versa. **2** *Statistics.* the principle that as the number of random trials of an event increases, the probability of the event's occurrence increases proportionately. [(def. 1) < Daniel *Bernoulli,* 1700-1782, a Swiss mathematician, who formulated it; (def. 2) < Jacob *Bernoulli,* 1654-1705, a Swiss mathematician, who formulated it]

be|robed (bi rōbd′), *adj.* wearing a robe.

ber|ret|ta (bə ret′ə), *n.* = biretta.

ber|ried (ber′ēd), *adj.* **1** having berries. **2** in the form of berries; baccate. **3** (of lobsters, crabs, or other crustaceans) having eggs or spawn.

ber|ry (ber′ē), *n., pl.* **-ries,** *v.,* **-ried, -ry|ing.** —*n.* **1a** any small, juicy fruit with many seeds instead of a stone. Strawberries, raspberries, and gooseberries are berries. **b** a simple fruit having a skin or rind surrounding one or more seeds in a fleshy pulp. Botanists classify grapes, tomatoes, currants, and bananas as berries. See picture under **fruit. 2** a dry seed or kernel of grain or other plants: *Coffee is made from the berries of the coffee plant.* **3** a single egg of a lobster or fish. **4** *U.S. Slang.* a dollar. —*v.i.* **1** to gather or pick berries: *Our fingers got blue berrying for blueberries.* **2** to bear or produce berries.
in berry, (of lobsters and crabs) carrying developing eggs: *Females in berry do not appear to forage* (New Scientist).
[Old English *berie*] —**ber′ry|like′,** *adj.*

ber|sa|glie|re (ber′səl yãr′ē), *n., pl.,* **-glie|ri** (-yãr′ē). a rifleman or sharpshooter in the Italian army. [< Italian *bersagliere* sharpshooter < *bersaglio* a mark]

ber|seem (bər sēm′), *n.* an Egyptian clover cultivated for forage. [< Arabic *birsīm* clover]

ber|serk (bėr′sėrk, bėr sėrk′), *adj., n.* —*adj.* **1** of unsound mind; mad; insane: . . . *the stigma of the mental patient as a violent person berserk in hospital corridors* (Saturday Review). **2** violently angry. —*n.* a berserker.
go berserk or **run berserk,** to be carried away by madness or wild fury; become violently angry: *The sick dog went berserk and tried to bite everyone in its way.*
[back formation < *berserker*]

ber|serk|er (bėr′sėr kər), *n.* **1** *Scandinavian Legend.* one of a class of fierce Norse warriors who fought on the battlefield with such wild fury that they needed no armor. **2** *Figurative.* anyone so carried away by excitement or rage. [< Scandinavian (compare Old Icelandic *berserkr* wild warrior; (literally) "bear-shirt")]

berth (bėrth), *n., v.* —*n.* **1** a place to sleep on a ship, train, or airplane: *Most of the steamship's crew were settled in their berths for the night.* SYN: bunk. **2** a ship's place at anchor or at a wharf: *The huge freighter was eased into her berth by several tugboats.* SYN: slip. **3** a place for a ship to anchor conveniently or safely. SYN: mooring. **4** the space necessary for safety or convenience between a ship and other ships or the shore, rocks, or other obstructions; sea room. **5** a space in a ship in which a number of officers or men eat and live. **6** *Figurative.* a position; job: *My brother has a berth as lifeguard for the summer.* SYN: post, billet. **7** *Figurative.* a position or place (in a contest, on a program, or the like): *Argentina clinched a berth in the second round of the . . . Davis cup* (New York Times).
—*v.t.* to place in or assign to a berth; provide with a berth or berths.
—*v.i.* to have or occupy a berth: *During strikes, large liners often berth without tugs.*
give a wide berth, to keep well away from: *Give her a wide berth when she is angry.*
[perhaps < *bear*[2]]

ber|tha (bėr′thə), *n.* a woman's wide collar, usually of lace, that often extends over the shoulders. [< French *berthe* < *Berthe* or *Bertha,* mother of Charlemagne, known for her modesty]

Ber|tha (bėr′thə), *n.* = Big Bertha.

berth|age (bėr′thij), *n.* accommodation for berthing a vessel.

Ber|thon boat (bėr′thon), a kind of collapsible boat. [< Edward *Berthon,* 1813-1899, an English clergyman, who invented it]

ber|til|lon|age (bėr′tə lon′ij), *n.* application of the Bertillon system.

Ber|til|lon system (bėr′tə lon), a system of identifying persons, especially criminals, by a record of individual measurements and physical peculiarities. Fingerprinting has now almost entirely replaced it. [< Alphonse *Bertillon,* 1853-1914, a French criminologist, who devised it]

ber|trand|ite (bėr′trən dīt), *n.* a mineral, a hydrous silicate of beryllium, occurring in brilliant, transparent, colorless crystals. *Formula:* $H_2Be_4Si_2O_9$ [< French *bertrandite* < E. *Bertrand,* a French mineralogist of the 1800's + *-ite*[1]]

ber|yl (ber′əl), *n.* a very hard mineral, usually green or blue-green, used as a gem and as the source of beryllium. Beryl is a translucent or opaque silicate of beryllium and aluminum. The emerald and aquamarine are transparent varieties of beryl. *Formula:* $Be_3Al_2Si_6O_{18}$ [< Latin *bēryllus* < Greek *bḗryllos,* ultimately < Sanskrit *vaidūrya* cat's-eye]

be|ryl|li|a (bə ril′ē ə), *n.* the oxide of beryllium, a white powder having high electrical resistance and thermal conductivity, used as a ceramic material, and also in transistors, high-temperature reactors, and as an additive to glass and plastics. [< New Latin *beryllia* < *beryllium*]

ber|yl|line (ber′ə lin, -līn), *adj.* like beryl; of a yellow-green color; sea-green.

be|ryl|li|o|sis (bə ril′ē ō′sis), *n.* chronic inflammation of the lungs caused especially by the breathing of beryllium dust.

***be|ryl|li|um** (bə ril′ē əm), *n.* a hard, light, metallic chemical element found in various minerals; glucinum. Beryllium is used in various alloys and in controlling the speed of neutrons in atomic reactors. [< New Latin *beryllium* < Latin *bēryllus;* see etym. under **beryl**]

***beryllium**

symbol	atomic number	atomic weight	oxidation state
Be	4	9.0122	2

beryllium copper, an alloy composed mainly of copper with approximately 2 per cent of beryllium and 2 to 3 per cent nickel or cobalt. It has many uses because of its strength, hardness, electrical conductivity, and resistance to corrosion.

Bes (bes), *n. Egyptian Mythology.* the god of good omen and pleasure, with the power to protect against witchcraft.

be|scat|ter (bi skat′ər), *v.t.* **1** to scatter over something. **2** to bestrew, as with things scattered; besprinkle.

be|screen (bi skrēn′), *v.t.* to cover or hide with or as if with a screen.

be|seech (bi sēch′), *v.t.,* **-sought** or **-seeched, -seech|ing. 1** to ask earnestly; implore (a person): *I beseech you to listen to me.* SYN: supplicate, pray. **2** to beg eagerly for (a thing); entreat: *I beseech your worship's pardon* (Shakespeare). SYN: See syn. under **beg.** [Middle English *bisechen* < *bi-* thoroughly + *sechen* seek]
—**be|seech′er,** *n.* —**be|seech′ing|ly,** *adv.* —**be-seech′ment,** *n.*

be|seem (bi sēm′), *Archaic. v.t.* to seem proper for; befit; suit: *I have already laughed more than beseems my cloth* (Nathaniel Hawthorne). SYN: become.
—*v.i.* to seem proper or fitting.
[Middle English *bisemen* < *bi-* (intensive) + *semen* seem] —**be|seem′ing|ly,** *adv.*

be|seen (bi sēn′), *v. obsolete past participle of obsolete "besee."* **1** seen. **2** clad; arrayed. **3** experienced; skilled. [Old English *besēon*]

be|set (bi set′), *v.t.,* **-set, -set|ting. 1a** to attack from all sides; attack: *We were beset by mosquitoes in the swamp.* SYN: harass, besiege. **b** to surround; hem in: *beset by the crowd.* (*Figurative.*) *In the darkness he was so beset by fear he was unable to move.* SYN: enclose, encompass. **2** to set with decorative objects; stud round: *Her bracelet was beset with pearls.* [Old English *besettan* < *be-* around + *settan* set] —**be|set′ment,** *n.*

be|set|ting (bi set′ing), *adj.* habitually attacking: *A besetting problem of the young foreign student . . . in New York is loneliness* (Harper's).

be|show (bi shō′), *n.* a dark food fish of the west coast of North America that has spiny fins; coalfish; sablefish. [American English < Wakashan (American Indian) *bishowk*]

be|shrew (bi shrü′), *v.t. Archaic.* to call down evil upon; curse (used as a mild exclamation). [Middle English *beshrewen* < *be-* + *shrewen* to curse]

be|side (bi sīd′), *prep., adv.* —*prep.* **1** by the side of; close to; near: *Grass grows beside the fence.* SYN: adjoining. **2** in addition to; over and above; besides: *Other men beside ourselves were helping.* **3** compared with: *The wolf seems tame beside the tiger.* SYN: alongside. **4** away from; aside from; not related to: *That question is beside the point and shows that you were not listening.* **5** except; other than; besides: . . . *the American novelists whom, "beside myself," he considered great* (Atlantic).
—*adv.* = besides.

beside oneself, out of one's senses; greatly excited with some emotion; upset: *He was beside himself with worry over his lost dog.*
[Old English *bi sīdan* by (the) side]

be|sides (bi sīdz′), *adv., prep.* **—*adv.*** **1** more than that; also; moreover: *He didn't want to fight; besides, he had come to see the game.* SYN: too, furthermore, further. **2** in addition: *We tried two other ways besides.* SYN: likewise. **3** otherwise; else: *He is ignorant of politics, whatever he may know besides.*
—*prep.* **1** in addition to; over and above; beside: *Others came to the school picnic besides our own class.* SYN: beyond. **2** other than; except: *Her mother spoke of no one besides her daughter.* SYN: save.
[Middle English *besides* < *besiden* beside + adverbial genitive *-s*]

be|siege (bi sēj′), *v.t.,* **-sieged, -sieg|ing. 1** to try for a long time to take (a place) by armed force; surround and try to capture: *For ten years the Greeks besieged the city of Troy.* SYN: beleaguer, invest. **2** *Figurative.* to crowd around: *Hundreds of admirers besieged the famous astronaut.* SYN: surround. **3** *Figurative.* to overwhelm with requests or questions: *During the flood the Red Cross was besieged with calls for help.* SYN: assail, beset. **—be|siege′ment,** *n.* **—be|sieg′er,** *n.* **—be|sieg′ing|ly,** *adv.*

B. ès L., *French.* Bachelier ès Lettres (Bachelor of Letters).

be|slob|ber (bi slob′ər), *v.t.* to slobber over.

be|slub|ber (bi slub′ər), *v.t.* to bedabble; bedaub; besmear.

be|smear (bi smir′), *v.t.* **1** to smear over; bedaub. **2** *Figurative.* to sully; defile.

be|smirch (bi smėrch′), *v.t.* **1** to make dirty; soil. **2** *Figurative.* to sully; dim the luster of: *His dishonesty has besmirched his family's good name.* **—be|smirch′er,** *n.*

be|smoke (bi smōk′), *v.t.,* **-smoked, -smok|ing. 1** to fill with smoke; make smoky. **2** to blacken with smoke.

be|som[1] (bē′zəm), *n., v.* **—*n.*** **1a** a broom made of twigs. **b** *Dialect.* any broom. **2** a plant used for a besom, such as the common broom (the shrub) of Europe.
—*v.t.* to sweep, as with a broom.
[Old English *besema* bundle of twigs, for cleansing or punishment]

be|som[2] (bē′zəm, biz′əm), *n. Scottish.* a low, worthless woman. [perhaps Old English *bysen*]

be|sot (bi sot′), *v.t.,* **be|sot|ted, be|sot|ting. 1** to make foolish. **2** to stupefy. **3** to intoxicate: (*Figurative.*) *Robbins is besot by rhythm, visual and bodily rhythms as well as auditory* (Agnes De Mille).

be|sot|ted (bi sot′id), *adj.* **1** foolish; infatuated. **2** stupefied. **3** intoxicated. **—be|sot′ted|ly,** *adv.* **—be|sot′ted|ness,** *n.*

be|sought (bi sôt′), *v.t.* a past tense and a past participle of **beseech:** *She besought the doctor to stop the pain.*

be|spake (bi spāk′), *v.t. Archaic.* bespoke; a past tense of **bespeak.**

be|span|gle (bi spang′gəl), *v.t.,* **-gled, -gling.** to adorn with spangles or anything like them.

be|spat|ter (bi spat′ər), *v.t.* **1** to spatter all over: *Plaques inlaid with gold and bespattered with rubies* (Observer). **2** to soil by spattering. **3** to slander. **—be|spat′ter|er,** *n.*

be|speak (bi spēk′), *v.t.,* **-spoke** or (*Archaic*) **-spake, -spo|ken** or **-spoke, -speak|ing. 1** to ask for in advance; order; reserve: *We have already bespoken two tickets for the new play.* **2a** to be a sign of; show; indicate: *The neat appearance of her room bespeaks care.* **b** to show in advance; point toward (some future event): *Circumstances that bespeak war and danger* (Nathaniel Hawthorne). SYN: forebode, presage. **3** *Archaic.* to speak to; address: *My gentle lord, bespeak these nobles fair* (Christopher Marlowe).
[Old English *besprecan* < *be-* about + *sprecan* speak]

be|speck|le (bi spek′əl), *v.t.,* **-led, -ling.** to mark with speckles.

be|spec|ta|cled (bi spek′tə kəld), *adj.* wearing glasses.

be|spell (bi spel′), *v.t.,* **-spelled, -spell|ing.** to cast a spell on; bewitch.

be|spoke (bi spōk′), *v., adj., n.* **—*v.*** a past tense and a past participle of **bespeak:** *We bespoke our tickets early.*
—*adj.* *British.* made to order: *a bespoke overcoat.* **—*n.*** *British.* a bespoke article of clothing: . . . *a collection of bargain bespokes* (Punch).

be|spo|ken (bi spō′kən), *v.* a past participle of **bespeak:** *Several rooms in the hotel have been bespoken for the President.*

be|spread (bi spred′), *v.t.,* **-spread, -spread|ing.** to spread thickly over.

be|sprent (bi sprent′), *adj. Archaic.* sprinkled all over; besprinkled: *What gentle ghost, besprent with April dew Hails me so solemnly?* (Ben Jonson). [Middle English *bespreynt,* past participle of *besprengen,* Old English *besprengan* < *be-* on + *sprengan* sprinkle]

be|sprin|kle (bi spring′kəl), *v.t.,* **-kled, -kling. 1** to sprinkle all over with something: *The walls were besprinkled with holy water* (Edward Gibbon). **2** *Figurative:* . . . *sloping banks besprinkled with pleasant villas* (Charles Dickens).

B. ès S., *French.* Bachelier ès Sciences (Bachelor of Sciences).

Bes|sa|ra|bi|an (bes′ə rā′bē ən), *adj., n.* **—*adj.*** of Bessarabia or its people.
—*n.* a native or inhabitant of Bessarabia.

Bes|sel function (bes′əl), *Mathematics.* any of a group of transcendental functions which are introduced by a differential equation, used especially in mathematical physics to represent quantities such as temperature, current density, and magnetic field strength as functions of space coordinates. [< Friedrich W. *Bessel,* 1784-1846, a German astronomer]

Bes|se|mer (bes′ə mər), *n.* = Bessemer steel.

Bessemer converter, a large container for making molten iron into steel by the Bessemer process.

bes|se|mer|ize (bes′ə mə rīz), *v.t.,* **-ized, -iz|ing.** to treat by the Bessemer process.

Bessemer process, a method of making steel by forcing a blast of air through molten iron in order to burn out carbon and other impurities. [< Sir Henry *Bessemer,* 1813-1898, an English engineer, who invented it]

Bessemer steel, steel made by the Bessemer process.

best (best), *adj., superlative of* **good,** *adv., n., v.* **—*adj.*** **1** most good, excellent, or useful: *the best way to do anything. Her work is good; my work is better; but his is best. He is the best student in the class.* **2** largest: *Teachers spend the best part of the day at school.* SYN: greatest, most. **3** chief: *our best hope. It is the best of all trades to make songs And the second best to sing them* (Hilaire Belloc).
—*adv.*, *superlative of* **well**[1]. **1** in the most excellent way; most thoroughly: *Who reads best?* **2** in or to the highest degree: *I like this book best. He said it that knew it best* (Francis Bacon).
—*n.* **1** the person or thing that is best: *Most parents want the best for their children. He is the best in the class. To seek out the best through the whole Union* (Thomas Jefferson). **2** the most that is possible; utmost: *I did my best to finish the work on time.* **3** best clothes: *dressed in their Sunday best.* **4** the greatest part: *the best of three games.*
—*v.t.* *Informal.* to outdo; defeat; outwit: *The wrestler was quickly bested by the stronger man.*
(all) for the best, not so bad as it seems: *I hope all's for the best* (Shakespeare).
as best one can, to the best of one's ability: *Places east of that Eden must look out for themselves as best they can* (Manchester Guardian Weekly).
at best, under the most favorable circumstances: *Summer is at best very short.*
at one's best, a in one's best health or spirits: *At his best he's still a rather dull fellow.* **b** at the peak of one's ability, strength, etc.: *Most athletes are at their best during their early manhood.*
get the best of, to defeat: *The lawyer easily got the best of his opponent in the debate.*
had best, will be wise to; should; ought to: *You had best leave before the storm breaks.*
have the best of, to have or win the advantage in: *The lawyer certainly had the best of the argument.*
make the best of, to do as well as possible with: *Try to make the best of a bad job.*
one's level best, *Informal.* as well as one can do; one's very best: *He has done his level best to improve things* (Harper's).
to the best of, with as much as possible of: *She . . . will always serve you . . . to the best of her ability* (Charlotte Brontë).
with the best, as well as anyone: *He can play tennis with the best.*
[Old English *betst*]

be|stain (bi stān′), *v.t.* to mark with stains.

be|star (bi stär′), *v.t.,* **-starred, -star|ring.** to adorn with or as if with stars.

best-ball match (best′bôl′), a golf match between two partners, with a ball to each of the four players. At every hole the lowest score in each pair counts to decide the match.

best bower, the joker in certain card games.

best boy, the assistant of the lighting supervisor on a motion-picture or television set; gaffer's assistant.

be|stead[1] (bi sted′), *v.t.,* **-stead|ed, -stead|ed** or **-stead, -stead|ing.** *Archaic.* to be of help to; assist. SYN: serve, avail. [< *be-* + *stead,* verb]

be|stead[2] (bi sted′), *adj.* **1** placed; situated; circumstanced. **2** beset (by dangers, fears, or hazards). [Middle English *bestad* < *be-* + *stad* placed < Scandinavian (compare Old Icelandic *staddr*)]

best|er (bes′tər), *n.* a hybrid sturgeon developed in the Soviet Union for its ability to spawn in its home grounds instead of migrating upstream. [< *be*luga + *ster*let]

best girl, a favorite girl friend.

bes|tial (bes′chəl, best′yəl), *adj.* **1a** like a beast; beastly; brutish. SYN: base, brutal, depraved, vile. **b** sensual; obscene. SYN: gross, coarse, carnal. **2** of beasts: *the bestial signs of the zodiac.* [< Latin *bēstiālis* < *bēstia* beast] **—bes′tial|ly,** *adv.*

bes|ti|al|i|ty (bes′chē al′ə tē, -tē-), *n., pl.* **-ties. 1** bestial conduct or character. SYN: brutality, irrationality, loathsomeness, depravity. **2** unrestricted indulgence; lust; sensuality. **3** a bestial act or practice.

bes|tial|ize (bes′chə līz, best′yə-), *v.t.,* **-ized, -iz|ing.** to make bestial; brutalize; debase. **—bes′tial|i|za′tion,** *n.*

bes|ti|ar|ist (bes′tē ər ist), *n.* the author of a bestiary.

bes|ti|ar|y (bes′tē er′ē), *n., pl.* **-ar|ies.** a treatise on beasts or animals, such as those written in the Middle Ages, with allegorical and moralistic stories about animals. [< Medieval Latin *bestiarium* menagerie, neuter of Latin adjective *bēstiārius* of beasts < *bēstia* beast]

bes|ti|cul|ture (bes′ti kul′chər), *n.* the industries based upon exploitation of native animal life; hunting, trapping, and fishing, collectively. [< Latin *bēstia* beast + English *culture*]

best-in-show (best′in shō′), *n.* the animal that wins the highest prize in a dog show, cat show, or other animal competition.

be|stir (bi stėr′), *v.t.,* **-stirred, -stir|ring.** to rouse to action; stir up; exert: *The cat was napping in the sun, hardly able to bestir itself for its dinner.* SYN: arouse, activate.

best man, the chief attendant of the bridegroom at a wedding.

best|ness (best′nis), *n.* the quality of being best.

be|stow (bi stō′), *v.t.* **1** to give (something) as a gift; give: *Education bestows many benefits. The President bestowed a medal on the hero.* SYN: present, confer. **2** to make use of; apply. **3** to give in marriage. **4** *Archaic.* to put safely; store. **5** *Archaic.* to find quarters for; lodge: *Sir, can you tell, where he bestows himself* (Shakespeare).
[Middle English *bistowen* < *bi-* + *stowen* to put]
—be|stow′a|ble, *adj.* **—be|stow′er,** *n.* **—be|stow′ment,** *n.*

be|stow|al (bi stō′əl), *n.* the act of bestowing: *the bestowal of his daughter in marriage.*

be|strad|dle (bi strad′əl), *v.t.,* **-dled, -dling.** to bestride; straddle.

be|streak (bi strēk′), *v.t.* to mark with streaks.

be|strew (bi strü′), *v.t.,* **-strewed, -strewed** or **-strewn, -strew|ing. 1** to strew (a surface) with things; scatter; sprinkle: *Little children bestrewed the path with flowers.* **2** to strew or scatter (things) about. **3** to lie scattered over (a surface): *Papers bestrewed the park.* [Old English *bistrēowian*]

be|strewn (bi strün′), *adj., v.* **—*adj.*** scattered about: *a daisy-bestrewn lawn.*
—*v.* bestrewed; a past participle of **bestrew.**

be|strid (bi strid′), *v.* a past tense and a past participle of **bestride.**

be|strid|den (bi strid′ən), *v.* a past participle of **bestride:** *The knight has bestridden the horse.*

be|stride (bi strīd′), *v.t.,* **-strode** or **-strid, -strid|den** or **-strid, -strid|ing. 1** to get on, sit on, or stand over (something) with one leg on each side; straddle. You can bestride a horse, a chair, or a fence. **2** to stand over (something) with one leg on each side; straddle over: (*Figurative.*) *Why man, he doth bestride the narrow world Like a Colossus* (Shakespeare). SYN: bestraddle. **3** to stride across; step over. [Old English *bestrīdan*]

be|strode (bi strōd′), *v.* a past tense of **bestride:** *The knight bestrode his horse.*

be|strow (bi strō′), *v.t.,* **-strowed, -strowed** or **-strewn, -strow|ing.** *Archaic.* to bestrew.

best seller, 1 anything, especially a book, that has a very large sale. **2** the author of a best-selling book.

best-sell|er|dom (best′sel′ər dəm), *n. Informal.* **1** the authors, musicians, etc., who have produced best sellers, as a group. **2** a position within this group: . . . *even Ernest Hemingway reached best-sellerdom fairly late* (Harper's).

best-sell|ing (best′sel′ing), *adj.* that is a best seller: *the best-selling novel of the year.*

be|stud (bi stud′), *v.t.,* **-stud|ded, -stud|ding.** to

Pronunciation Key: hat, āge, cãre, fär; let, ēqual, tėrm; it, īce; hot, ōpen, ôrder; oil, out; cup, pu̇t, rüle; child; long; thin; ᴛʜen; zh, measure; ə represents **a** in about, **e** in taken, **i** in pencil, **o** in lemon, **u** in circus.

stud over; dot: *a bracelet bestudded with jewels.*
bet[1] (bet), *v.,* **bet** or **bet|ted, bet|ting,** *n.* **—*v.t.*** **1a** to promise (money or a certain thing) to another if he is right and you are wrong: *I'll bet a dollar he's late.* **SYN:** stake, gamble. **b** to promise to pay (someone) money or a certain thing if he is right and you are wrong: *I bet him he could not outrun me.* **2** to be very sure: *I bet you are wrong about that.* **—*v.i.*** to make a bet; lay a wager: *Which horse did he bet on?*
—*n.* **1** a promise to give some money or a certain thing to another if he is right and you are wrong; wager: *He made a bet that he would win the race.* **2** the money or thing promised: *I won; so he lost his bet* (his nickel). **3** a thing to bet on: *That horse may be a good bet or bad bet.* **4** *Figurative.* a choice or alternative: *Taking the shortcut home is your safest bet. The best bet on a rainy day is to remain indoors.* **5** *Figurative.* definite opinion; certainty: *My bet is that the hangups and heartaches of today are the same ones we've had since Romeo wooed Juliet* (David McReynolds).
you bet, *Informal.* certainly: *Are you going? You bet!*
[origin uncertain]
bet[2] (bet), *adv.* the obsolete form of **better**, the comparative of **well**.
bet., between.
***be|ta** (bā′tə, bē′-), *n.* **1** the second letter of the Greek alphabet, corresponding to English *B, b.* **2** the second of a series. **3** the second brightest star of a constellation. **4** one of several possible positions of atoms or groups of atoms which are substituted in a chemical compound. [< Latin *bēta* < Greek *bêta*]

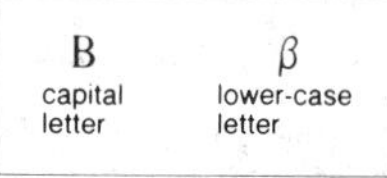

***beta** definition 1

be|ta-ad|ren|er|gic blocking agent (bā′tə-ad′rə nėr′jik, bē′-), = beta-blocker.
be|ta-block|er (bā′tə blok′ər, bē′-), *n.* a beta-blocking agent or drug: *A majority of the treated men got a "beta-blocker," a kind of drug known to reduce the incidence of sudden death in heart-attack patients* (New York Times).
be|ta-block|ing (bā′tə blok′ing, bē′-), *adj.* of or designating a drug that relieves stress on the heart by preventing absorption of adrenalin in the heart cells and blood vessels.
be|ta-car|o|tene (bā′tə kar′ə tēn, bē′-), *n.* an isomer of carotene, one molecule of which is capable of yielding two molecules of vitamin A.
be|ta|cism (bā′tə siz əm, bē′-), *n.* the confusion or interchange of a *b-* sound with a *v-* sound. [< *beta* + *-cism,* as in *lambdacism*]
beta cloth, a fabric made from a very fine, nonflammable glass fiber, used especially for making space suits. [< *Beta,* a trademark for glass fiber]
beta decay, *Physics.* the disintegration of a radioactive substance with the emission of beta particles. The emission of a beta particle changes the atomic number by plus or minus one, with no change in mass number, and consequent transformation into a new kind of atom.
beta emitter, a radioactive substance which gives off beta rays.
be|ta|eu|caine (bā′tə yü kān′, bē′-), *n.* eucaine.
beta gauge, an instrument that measures the thickness of paper, cloth, rolled steel, or other substance, by measuring the absorption of beta rays in the substance being measured.
beta globulin, one of the fractions of globulin, containing enzymes and hormones.
be|ta|in (bē′tə in), *n.* = betaine.
be|ta|ine (bē′tə ēn, -in), *n.* a nonpoisonous, sweetish, crystalline alkaloid obtained chiefly from the sugar beet, used in medicine. *Formula:* $C_5H_{11}NO_2$ [< Latin *bēta* beet + English *-ine*[2]]
be|take (bi tāk′), *v.t.,* **-took, -tak|en, -tak|ing.**
betake oneself, a to try doing; apply oneself: *He betook himself to study.* **b** to go: *So off he betook him the way that he came* (Leigh Hunt).
be|tak|en (bi tā′kən), *v.* past participle of **betake:** *He has betaken himself away.*
be|ta|naph|thol (bā′tə naf′thōl, -thol; -nap′-; bē′-), *n.* a white, crystalline compound used as an antiseptic. *Formula:* $C_{10}H_8O$
beta particle, *Physics.* an electron or positron released by the nucleus of a radioactive substance in the process of disintegration.
beta rays or **beta radiation,** a stream of beta particles.
beta rhythm, the pattern of electrical oscillations in the brain while a person is awake, recorded by an electroencephalograph.
beta test, a series of group intelligence tests, using pictures and simple symbols, given by the U.S. Army in World War I to soldiers who could not read and write English.
be|ta|tron (bā′tə tron, bē′-), *n.* a particle accelerator that greatly increases the speed of electrons by a changing magnetic field. [< *beta* + *-tron*]
beta wave, = beta rhythm.
be|tel (bē′təl), *n.* **1** a climbing pepper plant of the East Indies. People in Asia chew its leaves. **2** its leaf. **3** a preparation made by boiling the seed of the betel nut and then rolling it in the leaf of the betel vine smeared with quicklime. [< Portuguese *betel,* earlier *vitele* < Malayalam *veṭṭila*]
Be|tel|geuse or **Be|tel|geux** (bē′təl jüz, bet′əl-jœz), *n.* a giant, red star, the principal star in the constellation Orion. [< French *Bételgeuse,* perhaps < Arabic *baitu ljawzā′* house of the twins (that is Gemini)]
***betel nut,** the orange-colored nut of the betel palm; areca nut: *Many persons chew betel nuts, which color the lips red and the teeth black* (Virginia Thompson).

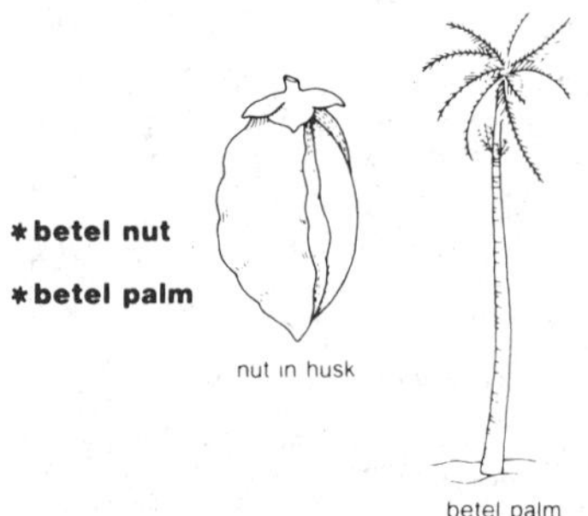

***betel nut**
***betel palm**

***betel palm,** a tall, tropical Asiatic palm which bears the betel nut.
bête noire or **bête noir** (bāt′nwär′), *pl.* **bêtes noires** (bāt′nwär′). a thing or person especially dreaded or detested; bugbear: *Mathematics is my bête noire. The bête noire at the Biennale [the Venice biennial festival] has always been the danger of commercialism* (Saturday Review). [< French *bête noire* black beast]
beth (beth), *n.* the second letter of the Hebrew alphabet. [< Hebrew *bēth* (literally) house]
be|thank|it (bi thang′kit), *n. Scottish.* grace after meat.
Beth Din (beth′dēn′), *Hebrew.* a rabbinical court.
beth|el (beth′əl), *n.* **1** a holy place (in the Bible, Genesis 28:16-22). **2** a church or chapel for seamen. **3** *British.* a chapel or meeting house for any nonconformist Protestant sect. [< Hebrew *bēth-′ēl* house of God]
Be|thes|da (bə thez′də), *n.* **1** a pool in ancient Jerusalem whose waters had curative powers (in the Bible, John 5:2-4). **2** *Figurative.* any source of healing or spiritual comfort. **3** a chapel.
be|think (bi thingk′), *v.,* **-thought, -think|ing.**
—*v.i.* *Archaic.* to deliberate; consider.
—*v.t.* **bethink oneself of, a** to think about; consider; reflect on: *I should bethink myself of the need to study.* **b** to remember: *You should bethink yourself of your duty to them.*
[Old English *bethencan*]
Beth|le|hem (beth′lē əm, -lə hem), *n. Archaic.* a lunatic asylum. [< the Hospital of St. Mary of *Bethlehem,* an asylum in London in the 1400's]
be|thought (bi thôt′), *v.* past tense and past participle of **bethink:** *I bethought myself of my work.*
be|thumb (bi thum′), *v.t.* to thumb all over; mark (books) by thumbing.
be|thump (bi thump′), *v.t.* to thump soundly.
be|tide (bi tīd′), *v.,* **-tid|ed, -tid|ing.** **—*v.t.*** to happen to: *Woe betide him if he dares defy the teacher. Woe betide you if you betray us.* **—*v.i.*** to happen; befall: *No matter what betides, the family will hold together.* [Middle English *betiden* < *be-* + *tiden* happen, Old English *tīdan*]
be|time (bi tīm′), *adv. Archaic or Dialect.* in good time; early. [Middle English *bi time* by time]
be|times (bi tīmz′), *adv. Archaic.* **1** early: *He rose betimes in the morning.* **2a** before it is too late: *It is wise, therefore, to come back betimes, or never* (Nathaniel Hawthorne). **b** in a short time; soon. [Middle English *betime* by (the) right time + adverbial genitive *-s*]
bê|tise (be tēz′), *n. French.* **1** silliness; stupidity. **2** a foolish act.
be|tjak (be′chäk), *n.* (in Indonesia) a pedicab. [< Indonesian *betjak*]
be|to|ken (bi tō′kən), *v.t.* to be a sign or token of; indicate; show: *His smile betokens his satisfaction. The dark clouds betoken a storm.* **SYN:** reveal, exhibit, presage, portend. **—be|to′ken|er,** *n.*
bet|o|ny (bet′ə nē), *n., pl.* **-nies, 1** a plant of Europe and Asia Minor, of the mint family, with spikes of purple flowers, formerly used medicinally and in dyeing. **2** any one of several similar plants. [< Old French *betoine,* learned borrowing from Latin *betōnica* < *Vettōnēs,* a Gaulish tribe]
be|took (bi tůk′), *v.* past tense of **betake:** *He betook himself home as soon as school was out.*
be|toss (bi tôs′, -tos′), *v.t.* to toss about.
be|tray (bi trā′), *v.t.* **1** to give away to the enemy; hand over or expose to the power of the enemy by treachery or disloyalty: *The traitor betrayed his country.* **2** to be unfaithful to; let down: *She betrayed her friends by breaking her promise.* **3** to give away (a secret entrusted to one): *to betray a friend's confidence.* **4** to disclose unintentionally: *The child's eyes betrayed her fear of the big dog.* **5** to show signs of; reveal: *The boy's wet shoes betrayed the fact that he had walked through puddles. His mistakes betrayed his lack of education.* **SYN:** exhibit, evince. **6** to lead into error; mislead; deceive: *He was betrayed by his own enthusiasm.* **7** to seduce and desert. [Middle English *bitraien* < *bi-* + *traien* < Old French *traïr,* ultimately < Latin *trādere* hand over] **—be|tray′er,** *n.*
be|tray|al (bi trā′əl), *n.* the act of betraying or condition of being betrayed; violation of trust or confidence: *His statement was a betrayal of his ignorance on the subject.*
be|trim (bi trim′), *v.t.,* **-trimmed, -trim|ming.** to trim up; deck out; bedeck.
be|troth (bi trōᴛʜ′, -trôth′), *v.t.* **1** to promise in marriage; engage: *He betrothed his daughter to a rich man.* **SYN:** affiance. **2** *Archaic.* to pledge to marry. [Middle English *betrouthen* < *be-* + *trewthe,* Old English *trēowth* a pledge]
be|troth|al (bi trō′ᴛʜəl, -trô′thəl), *n.* a promise in marriage; engagement: *Softly the youth and the maiden repeated the words of betrothal* (Longfellow).
be|trothed (bi trōᴛʜd′, -trôtht′), *n., adj.* **—*n.*** a person engaged to be married: *The knight's betrothed was a lovely princess.* **SYN:** fiancé, fiancée.
—*adj.* engaged to be married; affianced: *James and Sue are now betrothed.*
be|troth|ment (bi′trōᴛʜ′mənt, -trôth′-), *n.* = betrothal.
bet|sy-bug (bet′sē bug′), *n.* a passalid beetle.
bet|ta (bet′ə), *n.* the fighting fish. [< New Latin *Betta* the genus name]
bet|ted (bet′id), *v.* bet; a past tense and a past participle of **bet**[1].
bet|ter[1] (bet′ər), *adj., comparative of* **good,** *adv., v., n.* **—*adj.*** **1a** more good, excellent, or useful than another: *He left for a better job. He does better work than his brother. Better times are at hand.* **b** of superior quality: *Man's better nature triumphed then* (William Cullen Bryant). **2** improved in health; less sick: *The sick child is better today.* **3** larger; greater: *Four days is the better part of a week. The hungry boy ate the better part of a loaf.*
—*adv.*, *comparative of* **well**[1]. **1** in a more excellent way: *Try to read better next time. The plays of Shakespeare were better acted, better edited, and better known than they had ever been* (Macaulay). **2** in a higher degree; more completely: *I know my old friend better than I know anyone else.* **3** more: *It is better than a mile to town.*
—*v.t.* **1** to make better; improve: *We can better that work by being more careful next time.* **SYN:** ameliorate. See syn. under **improve. 2** to do better than; surpass: *The other class cannot better our grades.*
—*v.i.* to become better; improve: *The situation has bettered since yesterday.*
—*n.* a person or thing that is better: *Which is the better of these two dresses? Take the better of the two roads.*
better off, in a better condition: *He is better off now that he has a new job.*
better oneself, to improve one's position, condition, or circumstances: *She left to better herself, and obtained the position of a nurse* (Frederick Marryat).
betters, one's superiors: *Listen to the advice of your elders and betters.*
for better for worse, accepting the possibility of good and bad happenings: *Him and Anne have now resolved to take one another for better for worse* (Dickens).
for the better, toward improvement or recovery: *The sick man took a turn for the better.*
get (or **have**) **the better of,** to be superior to; defeat: *The tortoise got the better of the hare. Sometimes the Medes had the better of the Lydians* (Thomas Stanley).
go one better, to do better than; outstrip; excel: *He tried to go us one better by bidding twice as much as we did for the antique.*
had better, ought to; should: *I had better go before it rains.*
no better than she should be, of doubtful virtue: *You ought to dismiss the new maid if she is no better than she should be.*

think better of, a to think over and change one's mind about; have second thoughts about: *In the morning you will think better of your decision to go on such a long hike.* **b** to form a better opinion of (a person): *I think better of him for his present conduct.*
[Old English *betera*] —**bet′ter|er**, *n.*

bet|ter² (bet′ər), *n.* a person who bets. Also, **bettor**. [< *bet*¹ + *-er*¹]

better half, *Informal.* a wife.

bet|ter-known (bet′ər nōn′), *adj.* very well known; quite familiar: *He numbers among his better-known customers Marshall Field & Co.* (Wall Street Journal).

bet|ter|ment (bet′ər mənt), *n.* the act or process of making better; improvement: *Doctors work for the betterment of their patients' health.*
betterments, *U.S.* an improvement of lands, buildings, or other property, otherwise than by mere repairing.

bet|ter|most (bet′ər mōst), *adj. Dialect.* best: *Men, after their fashion, as well as women, distinguish the bettermost, and aid him to succeed* (George Meredith).

bet|ter|ness (bet′ər nis), *n.* the quality or condition of being better.

bet|ter-off (bet′ər ôf′, -of′), *adj.* better-to-do: *the better-off members of society.*

bet|ters (bet′ərz), *n.pl.* See under **better**¹.

bet|ter-to-do (bet′ər tü dü′), *adj.* above the well-to-do; more prosperous: *the better-to-do section of town.*

bet|ting (bet′ing), *n., adj.* —*n.* **1** the act of making a wager or bet: *Betting was very fashionable in the 18th century.* **2** the placing or accepting of wagers or bets as a business.
—*adj.* of, having to do with, or for the making of wagers or bets: *betting laws, a betting table.*
betting shop, *British.* a licensed establishment for off-track betting.

bet|tor (bet′ər), *n.* a person who bets; better.

bet|ty (bet′ē), *n., pl.* **-ties. 1** = Betty lamp. **2** a baked pudding made of pieces of toast or bread, fruit, and sweetening; brown Betty: *apple betty.* [probably < *Betty,* a nickname of *Elizabeth*]

***Betty lamp**, a kind of very simple oil lamp.

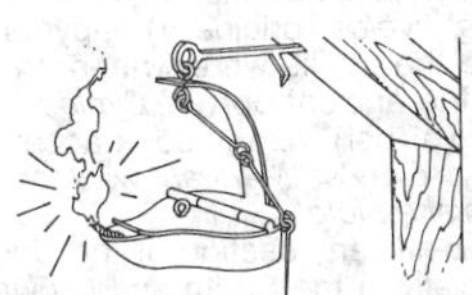
***Betty lamp**

bet|u|la|ceous (bech′ə lā′shəs), *adj.* belonging to the family of trees and shrubs that includes the birch, alder, and hazelnut. [< Latin *betula* birch tree + English *-aceous*]

be|tur|baned (bi tėr′bənd), *adj.* turbaned; wearing a turban.

be|tween (bi twēn′), *prep., adv.* —*prep.* **1** in the space or time separating two points, objects, or places: *Many cities lie between New York and Chicago. There is a distance of ten feet between the two trees. Come some time between three and four o'clock.* **2** in the range or part separating: *shades between pink and red. She earned between ten and twelve dollars.* **3** from one to the other of; joining; connecting: *a link between two parts, the bond between father and son.* **4** having to do with: *Will there be a fight between the two boys?* **5** in regard to one or the other of: *We must choose between the two books.* **6** by the joint action of: *They caught twelve fish between them.* **7** in the combined possession of: *They own the property between them.*
—*adv.* in the space or time separating two points, objects, or places; in an intermediate position or relation: *We could not see the moon, for a cloud came between.*
between ourselves, in confidence: *I wanted to ask a question just between ourselves.*
between you and me, as a secret; confidentially: *This I tell you between you and me; don't tell anyone else.*
in between, a in the middle: *He either studies very hard or not at all, never anything in between.* **b** in the midst of; among: *In between the rows of corn there was a scarecrow. In between the recipes is a running commentary on life in small-town and rural New England* (Harper's).
[Old English *betwēonum* and *betwēon,* both < *be-* by + *twā* two]
▶ See **among** for usage note.
▶ **between you and me.** Prepositions regularly take the objective case of pronouns. When only one pronoun is used, this case is invariably employed: *of him, for me, to her.* But when two pronouns follow, less educated speakers often use the nominative case of the second, and sometimes of both: *between you and I, to her (she) and I.* Standard English requires *between you and me, to her and me.*
▶ **between each.** Sentences like *Melons were planted between each row of corn* are occasionally condemned as being illogical. *Between each row and the next* is accurate but stiff; *between the rows* is both natural and clear.

be|tween|brain (bi twēn′brān′), *n. Anatomy.* = diencephalon.

between maid or **girl**, *British.* a maid servant who assists both the cook and the housemaid; tweeny.

be|tween|ness (bi twēn′nis), *n.* the condition or fact of being intermediate or between.

be|tween|times (bi twēn′tīmz), *adv.* at intervals; betweenwhiles: *Rehearsals went on all evening, with coffee served betweentimes.*

be|tween|whiles (bi twēn′hwīlz), *adv.* at intervals.

be|twixt (bi twikst′), *prep., adv.* = between.
betwixt and between, in the middle; neither one nor the other: *... a betwixt-and-between property, large enough to support a modest planter but not nearly large enough to support a high-living member of the gentry* (New Yorker).
[Old English *betweox*]

Beu|lah (byü′lə), *n.* **1** the land of Israel (in the Bible, Isaiah 62:4). **2** a land of rest and peace; the borderland between earth and heaven.

beurre fon|du (bœr fôɴ dy′), *French.* melted butter.

beurre ma|nié (bœr mȧ nyā′), *French.* a blend of butter and flour, used to thicken sauces.

beurre noir (bœr nwȧr′), *French.* browned butter.

Bev or **bev** (bev), *n.* a billion electron volts, used as a measure of energy in nuclear physics. [< *b*(illion) *e*(lectron) *v*(olts)]

Bev., billion electron volts.

BeV., *British.* billion electron volts.

bev|a|tron (bev′ə tron), *n.* a particle accelerator in which protons are accelerated to velocities of a billion or more electron volts. [< *bev* + *a*(tom) + *-tron*]

bev|el (bev′əl), *n., v.,* **-eled, -el|ing** or (*especially British*) **-elled, -el|ling,** *adj.* —*n.* **1** a sloping edge or surface. There is often a bevel on the frame of a picture, on a mirror, or on a piece of plate glass. **2** any angle except a right angle. **3** an instrument or tool for drawing or measuring angles. A bevel is also used for adjusting the surface of work to a particular angle. It consists of a flat rule with a movable arm pivoted at one end.
—*v.t.* to cut a square edge to a sloping edge; make slope: *to bevel plate glass for French windows. The edges of the board have been beveled with a plane.*
—*v.i.* to slope; slant.
—*adj.* slanting; oblique.
[< Middle French *beveau*] —**bev′el|er**, *especially British,* **bev′el|ler**, *n.*

bevel edge, the oblique edge of a chisel or similar tool.

bevel gear, **1** a wheel with teeth projecting from a conical surface, which engages the teeth of a similar wheel, having its axis set at an angle. **2** the larger of these wheels (the smaller being usually referred to as the pinion).

bevel square, a try square whose blade can be adjusted to any angle and held there by a screw.

bev|er|age (bev′ər ij, bev′rij), *n.* a liquid used or prepared for drinking. Milk, tea, coffee, beer, and wine are beverages. **SYN:** drink. [< Old French *bevrage* < *bevre* to drink < Latin *bibere*]

bev|y (bev′ē), *n., pl.* **bev|ies. 1** any small group: *the whole bevy of renegades* (Macaulay). **2a** a small group of women or girls: *a bevy of pretty girls.* **b** a flock of birds: *a bevy of larks or quail.* [origin uncertain]

be|wail (bi wāl′), *v.t.* to mourn for; weep for; complain of; bemoan: *The little girl was bewailing the loss of her doll.* **SYN:** lament. —*v.i.* to wail; mourn. **SYN:** lament. —**be|wail′er**, *n.* —**be|wail′ing|ly**, *adv.* —**be|wail′ment**, *n.*

be|ware (bi wãr′), *v.i., v.t.,* **-wared, -war|ing.** to be on your guard against; be careful: *Beware! danger is here. You must beware of swimming in a strong current. Beware the fury of a patient man* (John Dryden). **SYN:** heed. [< imperative phrase *be ware*]
▶ **Beware** is a formal word for "be careful." It is followed by *of* or by *lest, how,* or *that ... not,* introducing a subordinate clause: *Beware of the sharpers at the fair. They were told to beware lest they wake him. We must beware how we approach him. Beware that you do not anger him.* *Beware* is sometimes followed directly by its object: *Beware the dog.*

be|weep (bi wēp′), *v.t.,* **-wept, -weep|ing. 1** to weep over or for. **2** to wet with tears.

be|wept (bi wept′), *v.* the past tense and the past participle of **beweep**.

be|wet (bi wet′), *v.,* **-wet|ted, -wet|ting,** *adj.* —*v.t.* = wet.
—*adj.* wetted.

be|whisk|ered (bi hwis′kərd), *adj.* **1** having whiskers: *a splendidly bewhiskered old man.* **2** *Figurative.* very old and (usually) deserving to be given up: *the bewhiskered notion that the common toad causes warts.*

Bew|ick's wren (byü′iks), a wren with a white-edged tail and a white line over its eyes, found from southern Canada to Mexico. [< Thomas *Bewick,* 1753-1828, an English wood engraver and illustrator of birds]

be|wigged (bi wigd′), *adj.* wearing a wig: *a bewigged doll, bewigged fashion models.*

be|wil|der (bi wil′dər), *v.t.* **1** to confuse completely; puzzle; perplex: *The little girl was bewildered by the crowds. The maze of corridors in the office building bewildered her. To choose one from so many able contestants bewildered the judge.* **SYN:** confound, disconcert. See syn. under **puzzle**. **2** *Archaic.* to cause to lose one's way or bearings. [< *be-* + *wilder* lead astray] —**be|wil′der|ing|ly**, *adv.*

be|wil|dered (bi wil′dərd), *adj.* confused completely; puzzled; perplexed. —**be|wil′dered|ly**, *adv.*

be|wil|der|ment (bi wil′dər mənt), *n.* **1** a bewildered condition; complete confusion; perplexity: *In this bright promise for steel ... some steelmakers confess a little bewilderment, and most admit to being pleasantly surprised* (Wall Street Journal). **2** a bewildering maze or tangle.

be|witch (bi wich′), *v.t.* **1** to put under a spell; use magic on: *The wicked fairy bewitched the princess and made her fall into a long sleep.* **2** *Figurative.* to charm; fascinate; enchant; delight: *Our pretty little cousin bewitched us all.* **SYN:** captivate. —**be|witch′er**, *n.* —**be|witch′ment**, *n.*

be|witched (bi wicht′), *adj.* **1** under the influence of magic. **2** *Figurative.* charmed; delighted; fascinated.

be|witch|er|y (bi wich′ər ē), *n., pl.* **-er|ies. 1** the fact or power of bewitching. **2** a charm; spell.

be|witch|ing (bi wich′ing), *adj.* fascinating; captivating; enchanting: *She has a bewitching smile.* —**be|witch′ing|ly**, *adv.*

be|wray (bi rā′), *v.t. Archaic.* **1** to reveal; make known. **2** to betray; expose. [Middle English *bewreien* < *be-* be- + *wreien,* Old English *wrēgan* accuse]

be|write (bi rīt′), *v.t.,* **-wrote, -writ|ten, -writ|ing.** to write about: *I have probably been more bewritten and belied than any man since Byron* (Algernon Charles Swinburne).

bey (bā), *n., pl.* **beys. 1** the governor of a Turkish province or district before Turkey became a republic. **2** (formerly) a title of respect for persons of rank in Turkey, Egypt, or other countries under the influence of Turkey. **3** (formerly) a native ruler of Tunis. [< Turkish *bey*]

bey|lic or **bey|lik** (bā′lik), *n.* the district ruled by a bey. [< Turkish *beylik*]

be|yond (bi yond′), *prep., adv., n.* —*prep.* **1** on or to the farther side of: *He lives beyond the sea.* **2** farther on than: *The school is beyond the last house.* **3** later than; past: *They stayed beyond the time set.* **4** out of the reach, range, or understanding of: *The dying man was beyond the help of a doctor. The meaning of this story is beyond him.* **SYN:** past. **5** more than; exceeding: *The price of the suit was beyond what he could pay. The trip was beyond all we had hoped.* **SYN:** above. **6** in addition to; besides: *I will do nothing beyond the job given me.* **SYN:** outside.
—*adv.* farther away; at a distance: *Your ball did not fall here; look beyond for it. Beyond were the hills.* **SYN:** yonder.
—*n.* an experience or life that lies outside present experience or life.
the back of beyond. See under **back**¹.
the (great) beyond, a life after death: *Each is longing for the Great Beyond, which attests our immortality* (Edward G. Bulwer-Lytton). **b** anything which lies on the other side or farther away: *Young Columbus dreamed of crossing the ocean someday to the great beyond.*
[Old English *begeondan* < *be* by + *geondan* beyond] —**be|yond′ness**, *n.*

bez|ant (bez′ənt, bə zant′), *n.* **1** Also, **byzant.** **a** a gold coin of the Byzantine emperors, widely used in medieval Europe. **b** a Byzantine silver coin. **2** a flat disk used in architectural ornament, usually in a series. **3** *Heraldry.* a small circle or gold roundel, representing the coin, signifying the bearer had been in the Crusades. Also, **bezzant.** [< Old French *bezant* < Latin *Bȳzantius* Byzantine < Greek *Byzántios*]

bez antler (bez, bāz), = bay antler. [< Old

Pronunciation Key: hat, āge, cãre, fär; let, ēqual, tėrm; it, īce; hot, ōpen, ôrder; **oil**, **out**; cup, pu̇t, rüle; **child**; lo**ng**; **th**in; **ᴛʜ**en; **zh**, measure; **ə** represents **a** in about, **e** in taken, **i** in pencil, **o** in lemon, **u** in circus.

French *bes-* twice; inferior (< Latin *bis-* twice) + English *antler*]

be|zazz (bə zaz′), *n. Slang.* pep: *A young man on the way up tries hard to make other people notice him. He's brash, he's bombastic, he's got bezazz* (Maclean's). [variant form of *pizazz*]

bez|el (bez′əl), *n., v.,* **-eled, -el|ing** or (*especially British*) **-elled, -el|ling.** —*n.* **1** a slope or sloping edge, especially of a chisel or other cutting tool. **2** the sloping sides or faces of a cut gem, especially those of the upper half. **3** the grooved ring or rim that holds a gem or a watch crystal in its setting.
—*v.t.* to grind or cut to an edge.
[< Old French *bizel*]

be|zique (bə zēk′), *n.* **1** a card game somewhat like pinochle, using 64, 96, or 128 cards. **2** the combination of the queen of spades and jack of diamonds in this game. [< French *bésigue*]

Be|zirk (bə tsirk′), *n., pl.* **-zir|ke** (-tsir′kə). *German.* a district, especially an administrative district.

be|zoar (bē′zôr, -zōr), *n.* a concretion found in the stomach or intestines of some animals, especially ruminants, once thought to be an antidote to poisons. [< Middle French *bézoard* < Arabic *bāzahr* < Persian *pādzahr* antidote]

be|zo|ni|an (bə zō′nē ən), *n.* **1** a knave; rascal. **2** a raw recruit. [< Italian *bisogno* (literally) a lack, need + English *-ian*]

bez point, = bez antler.

bez|zant (bez′ənt, bə zant′), *n.* = bezant.

bf., *Printing.* boldface.

b.f., **1** *Printing.* boldface. **2** brought forward.

B.F.A., Bachelor of Fine Arts.

B.F.C., *U.S.* Bureau of Foreign Commerce.

bg., bag or bags.

B.G., **1** Brigadier General. **2** British Guiana.

B-girl (bē′gėrl′), *n. U.S. Slang.* a woman employed by a bar to encourage male customers to buy drinks, usually receiving a percentage of the price from the owner. [< *B*(ar) girl]

bgs., bags.

bh., *Baseball.* base hits.

B.H., British Honduras.

Bha|ga|vad-Gi|ta (bug′ə vəd gē′tä), *n.* a Sanskrit philosophical dialogue of about A.D. 1 in which Krishna (Bhagavat) is identified with the Supreme Being, and expounds the duties and customs that are basic to Hinduism. [< Sanskrit *Bhagavadgītā* (literally) song of the blessed one]

bhak|ta (buk′tə), *n. Hinduism.* a person who possesses or practices bhakti. [< Sanskrit *bhakta*]

bhak|ti (buk′tē), *n. Hinduism.* religious devotion or piety: [*The*] *mystics of India believed that a man might be saved by bhakti, by self-annihilating devotion to a friendly god. Karma and bhakti are the two poles of Indian religious thought* (T. R. Glover). [< Sanskrit *bhakti* a share]

bhang (bang), *n.* **1** a variety of hemp grown in India. **2** a preparation of dried hemp leaves and seedcases smoked or eaten as a narcotic and intoxicant in India. Also, **bang.** [ultimately < Sanskrit *bhaṅgā* hemp; a drink made from it]

bhan|gi (bung′gē), *n.* an untouchable in India whose traditional occupation is scavenging. [< Hindustani *bhaṅgī* (literally) a person who uses bhang]

bhar|al (bėr′əl), *n.* a mountain sheep of northern India and Tibet related to the goat; blue sheep. [< Hindustani *bharal*]

Bhar|a|ta Nat|yam (bur′ə tə nät′yəm), a style of Hindu dance, including pantomime and song, that originated as a form of religious ceremony.

BHC (no periods), benzene hexachloride.

bhees|tie, bhees|ty, or **bhis|tie** (bēs′tē), *n., pl.* **-ties.** a servant in India who carries water for use in the home. [< Hindustani *bhistī* < Persian *bihishtī* (literally) one from *bihisht* paradise]

bhik|ku (bik′ü), *n., pl.* **-kus.** a mendicant Buddhist monk. [< Pali *bhikku* < Sanskrit *bhikshu* beggar]

Bhil (bēl), *n.* a member of a primitive hill people of central India. [< Hindustani *Bhīl* < Sanskrit *Bhilla*]

Bhoo|dan or **bhoo|dan** (bü dän′), *n.* a movement in India for redistributing land by gifts of individual holdings to village groups. [< Hindustani *bhūdān* (literally) land gift]

B horizon, the layer of soil beneath the A horizon, in which insoluble iron oxides and clay minerals are deposited.

Bho|ti|a or **Bho|ti|ya** (bō′tē ä), *n.* **1** a member of the ethnic group that comprises the majority of Tibetans. **2** a native of Bhutan or southern Tibet. **3** any one of various Sino-Tibetan languages spoken in Bhutan, Nepal, Sikkim, and surrounding areas. [< Sanskrit *Bhoṭīya* Tibetan]

b.hp., brake horsepower.

Bhu|tan|ese (bü′tə nēz′, -nēs′), *n., pl.* **-ese,** *adj.*
—*n.* a native or inhabitant of Bhutan.
—*adj.* of Bhutan or its people.

Bhu|ti|a (bü′tē ä), *n.* = Bhotia.

bi-, *prefix.* **1a** twice a ___: *Biannual = twice a year.* **b** once every two ___: *Bimonthly = once every two months.*
2 doubly ___: *Bipinnate = doubly pinnate.*
3 two ___s: *Bisect = divide into two parts. Bicuspid = two points* (of teeth).
4 having two ___: *Biped = having two feet.* Also, sometimes **bin-** before vowels.
[< Latin *bi-* < *bis* twice]

Bi (no period), bismuth (chemical element).

bi (bī), *adj. Slang.* attracted to both sexes; bisexual.

BIA (no periods), Bureau of Indian Affairs.

bi|a|cu|mi|nate (bī′ə kyü′mə nit, -nāt), *adj. Botany.* having two diverging points.

Bi|af|ran (bē äf′rən), *adj., n.* —*adj.* of or having to do with Biafra, the eastern region of Nigeria, or its people.
—*n.* a native or inhabitant of Biafra.

bia|ly (byä′lē), *n., pl.* **bia|lys** or **bia|ly.** *U.S.* a kind of flat roll topped with chopped onions. [short for Yiddish *bialistoker* of Byalistok, a city in Poland where this roll was made]

bi|an|gu|lar (bī ang′gyə lər), *adj.* having two angles.

bi|an|nu|al (bī an′yü əl), *adj.* occurring twice a year: *Our school nurse recommends a biannual visit to the dentist.* —**bi|an′nu|al|ly,** *adv.*

▶ **biannual, biennial.** *Biannual* means occurring twice a year; it differs from the more common *semiannual* in not necessarily implying a six months' interval: *The biannual examinations are held in May and October. Biennial* means occurring once in two years, or lasting two years: *At one time the legislature held biennial sessions. Foxgloves and hollyhocks are biennial plants.*

bi|an|nu|late (bī an′yə lit, -lāt), *adj. Zoology.* displaying two encircling rings, or ringlike bands, generally having some color.

bi|as (bī′əs), *n., pl.* **-as|es,** *adj., adv., v.,* **-ased, -as|ing** or (*especially British*) **-assed, -as|sing.**
—*n.* **1** a slanting or oblique line: *Cloth is cut on the bias when it is cut diagonally across the weave.* **2** *Figurative.* an opinion before there is a reason for it; leaning of the mind; prejudice: *An umpire should have no bias in favor of either side.* SYN: inclination, bent, partiality. See syn. under **prejudice.** **3** *Statistics.* the tendency of a sample to be unrepresentative of all cases involved in a particular study. **4a** the lopsided shape of a ball used in bowls, that makes it swerve when rolled. **b** the weight or force that makes it swerve. **c** the curved course taken by the ball. **5** the direct-current voltage supplied to the grid circuit of an electronic tube.
—*adj.* slanting across the weave; oblique; diagonal: *Trim with bias bands.*
—*adv.* **1** obliquely to the direction of weaving; diagonally: *The skirt is bias cut.* **2** *Figurative.* off the straight; awry; wrong.
—*v.t.* **1** to give a slanted opinion to; influence, usually unfairly; prejudice: *The judge tried not to let his feelings bias his judgment.* SYN: incline.
2 to apply a direct-current voltage to.
on the bias, diagonally across the weave: *cloth cut on the bias.*
[< Old French *biais* slant]

bi|as-belt|ed tire (bī′əs bel′tid), belted-bias tire.

bi|ased (bī′əst), *adj.* **1** favoring one side too much; prejudiced: *a biased opinion. A mother is usually biased where her children are concerned.* **2** *Mathematics.* having expectation value different from the true value.

bias tire, an automobile tire with the cord fabric or metal running diagonally to the center line of the tread. Each ply is added so that its cords run at an angle opposite to the angle of the cords below it.

bi|ath|lete (bī ath′lēt), *n.* a person who competes in a biathlon.

bi|ath|lon (bī ath′lon), *n.* an Olympic contest combining a cross-country ski race with rifle marksmanship. [< *bi-* two + Greek *áthlon* contest. Compare etym. under **athlete.**]

bi|au|ric|u|lar (bī′ô rik′yə lər), *adj. Anatomy.* **1** having two auricles; biauriculate. **2** of the two ears.

bi|au|ric|u|late (bī′ô rik′yə lit, -lāt), *adj.* having two auricles or earlike projections.

bi|ax|i|al (bī ak′sē əl), *adj.* having two axes: *a biaxial crystal.* —**bi|ax′i|al|ly,** *adv.*

bi|ax|i|al|i|ty (bī ak′sē al′ə tē), *n.* biaxial quality or character.

bib (bib), *n., v.,* **bibbed, bib|bing.** —*n.* **1** a cloth or piece of plastic or paper worn under the chin to protect clothing while eating. Babies wear bibs for most meals while adults wear bibs for meals of lobster or corn on the cob. **2** a part of an apron or overalls above the waist. **3** anything suggesting a bib by its purpose, shape, or position.
—*v.t., v.i.* to drink; keep on drinking; tipple.
[Middle English *bibben* to drink, perhaps < Latin *bibere*] —**bib′less,** *adj.* —**bib′like′,** *adj.*

Bib., **1** Bible. **2** Biblical.

bi|ba|cious (bi bā′shəs, bī-), *adj.* addicted to drinking; bibulous. [< Latin *bibāx, bibācis* (with English *-ous*) < *bibere* drink]

bib and tucker, *Informal.* clothes.

bi|ba|sic (bī bā′sik), *adj. Chemistry.* = dibasic. [< *bi-* + *basic*]

bi|ba|tion (bi bā′shən, bī-), *n.* **1** the act of drinking. **2** a drink.

bibb (bib), *n. Nautical.* a bracket of timber bolted to a projection on a masthead to support the trestletree. [< *bibbe,* older form of *bib,* which it resembles]

bib|ber (bib′ər), *n.* a habitual drinker of alcoholic liquor; tippler.

Bibb lettuce, a highly perishable kind of lettuce, with dark green leaves growing in tiny, loose clusters. [< J. *Bibb,* an American farmer, who developed it in the 1800's]

bib|cock (bib′kok′), *n.* a faucet having a nozzle bent downward.

bi|be|lot (bib′lō; *French* bē blō′), *n.* a small object valued for its beauty, rarity, or interest: *a rare collection of curios, and bibelots of all kinds.* [< French *bibelot*]

bi|bi|ru (bə bir′ü), *n.* = bebeeru.

bib|i|to|ry (bib′ə tôr′ē, -tōr′-), *adj.* having to do with drinking, especially to excess. [< New Latin *bibitorius* < Latin *bibere* to drink]

bi-bi|va|lent (bī′bī vā′lənt, bī biv′ə-), *adj.* separating into two ions, each having a valence of 2: *a bi-bivalent electrolyte.*

Bibl. or **bibl.,** **1** Biblical. **2** bibliographical.

Bi|ble (bī′bəl), *n.* **1a** the book of sacred writings of the Christian religion; the Old Testament and the New Testament: *One English book, and one only, where ... perfect plainness of speech is allied with perfect nobleness; and that book is the Bible* (Matthew Arnold). **b** a copy of the Scriptures. **c** a particular edition or copy of the Scriptures: *the Gutenberg Bible.* **2** the form of the Old Testament accepted by the Jews. **3** the book of the sacred writings of any religion. The Koran is the Bible of the Moslems. **4** *Figurative.* any book accepted as an authority; bible. [< Old French *bible,* learned borrowing from Medieval Latin *biblia* < Greek *biblía* books < *biblíon* (diminutive) < *bíblos, býblos* (originally) papyrus, probably because the books were written on papyrus brought from the ancient port of *Byblos*]

bi|ble (bī′bəl), *n.* any book accepted as an authority: *Gray's "Manual" was for many years the botanist's bible.*

Bible belt, any section of the United States, especially in the South and Midwest, where fundamentalist religion prevails. [coined by H. L. Mencken, 1880-1956, American writer and critic]

bible paper, a very thin, tough, and durable, opaque paper used for books in which bulk needs to be reduced, such as Bibles and prayer books; India paper.

Bi|ble-punch|er (bī′bəl pun′chər), *n. Slang.* = Bible-thumper.

Bi|ble-thump|er (bī′bəl thum′pər), *n. Slang.* a Christian who follows the teachings of the Bible strictly and zealously or preaches fanatically from a Biblical text.

Bib|li|cal or **bib|li|cal** (bib′lə kəl), *adj.* **1** of the Bible; having to do with the Bible: *We read the Biblical story of Adam and Eve.* **2** according to the Bible: *Biblical history.* **3** in the Bible: *a Biblical reference to Solomon.* —**Bib′li|cal|ly, bib′li|cal|ly,** *adv.*

Biblical Latin, the form of Latin current in Western Europe at the beginning of the Middle Ages and used in the translation of the Bible.

Bib|li|cism (bib′lə siz əm), *n.* **1** strict or literal adherence to the Bible. **2** a Biblical archaism, such as "these twain." —**Bib′li|cist,** *n.*

biblio-, *combining form.* **1** book or books: *Bibliophile = a lover of books.*
2 the Bible: *Bibliolatry = excessive reverence for the letter of the Bible.*
[< Greek *biblíon* a book]

bib|li|o|clast (bib′lē ə klast), *n.* a person who deliberately destroys books. [< *biblio-* + Greek *klas-,* stem of *klân* to break]

bib|li|o|film (bib′lē ə film′), *n. U.S.* a microfilm used to make photographs of pages of books, manuscripts, or art.

bibliog., bibliography.

bib|li|o|gen|e|sis (bib′lē ō jen′ə sis), *n.* the act or process of creating books or literature.

bib|li|og|nost (bib′lē og nost′), *n.* an expert in bibliography. [< *biblio-* + Greek *gnōstēs* one who knows]

bib|li|o|graph (bib′lē ə graf, -gräf), *n., v.* —*n. U.S.* a bibliographer.
—*v.t.* to provide a bibliography for.

bib|li|og|ra|pher (bib′lē og′rə fər), *n.* **1** the compiler of a bibliography. **2** an expert in bibliography.

bib|li|o|graph|ic (bib′lē ə graf′ik), *adj.* = bibliographical.

bib|li|o|graph|i|cal (bib′lē ə graf′ə kəl), *adj.* of or having to do with bibliography. —**bib′li|o|graph′i|cal|ly,** *adv.*

bib|li|og|ra|phy (bib′lē og′rə fē), *n., pl.* **-phies. 1** a list of the books or articles consulted or referred to by an author in the preparation of an article or book. **2** a list of books or articles about a particular subject or person: *a bibliography of cookery.* **3** a list of books or articles by a certain author. *Abbr:* bibliog. **4** the study of the authorship, editions, dates, and the like, of books, manuscripts, articles, or other printed matter. [< Greek *bibliographíā* < *biblíon* book + *gráphein* write]

bib|li|o|klept (bib′lē ə klept), *n.* a person who steals books. [< *biblio-* + Greek *kléptēs* thief]

bib|li|ol|a|ter (bib′lē ol′ə tər), *n.* **1** a person who believes every word of the Bible as literal fact. **2** a worshiper of books. [< *biblio-* + *-later*]

bib|li|ol|a|trist (bib′lē ol′ə trist), *n.* a worshiper of books; bibliolater.

bib|li|ol|a|trous (bib′lē ol′ə trəs), *adj.* worshiping books.

bib|li|ol|a|try (bib′lē ol′ə trē), *n.* **1** excessive reverence for the letter of the Bible. **2** worship of books. [< *biblio-* + *-latry*]

bib|li|ol|o|gist (bib′lē ol′ə jist), *n.* an expert in bibliology.

bib|li|ol|o|gy (bib′lē ol′ə jē), *n.* **1** Biblical literature or doctrine. **2** = bibliography.

bib|li|o|man|cy (bib′lē ə man′sē), *n., pl.* **-cies.** soothsaying by means of a passage chosen at random in a book. [< *biblio-* + Greek *manteíā* divination]

bib|li|o|mane (bib′lē ə mān), *n.* = bibliomaniac. [< French *bibliomane* (< Greek *biblíon* book) + *-mane* < *manie* mania]

bib|li|o|ma|ni|a (bib′lē ə mā′nē ə), *n.* a craze for collecting books, especially rare and curious ones.

bib|li|o|ma|ni|ac (bib′lē ə mā′nē ak), *n.* a person who has a craze for collecting books.

bib|li|o|ma|ni|a|cal (bib′lē ə mə nī′ə kəl), *adj.* having a craze for collecting books.

bib|li|o|peg|ic (bib′lē ə pej′ik), *adj.* of or having to do with bookbinding as a fine art.

bib|li|op|e|gist (bib′lē op′ə jist), *n.* = bookbinder.

bib|li|op|e|gy (bib′lē op′ə jē), *n.* bookbinding as a fine art. [< Greek *biblíon* book + *pēgnýnai* to fasten]

bib|li|o|phil (bib′lē ə fil), *n.* = bibliophile.

bib|li|o|phile (bib′lē ə fīl, -fil), *n.* a lover of books, especially one who likes to collect books. [< French *bibliophile* < Greek *biblíon* book + *phílos* friend]

bib|li|o|phil|ic (bib′lē ə fil′ik), *adj.* of bibliophiles.

bib|li|oph|i|lism (bib′lē of′ə liz əm), *n.* the tastes or practices of a bibliophile; love of books.

bib|li|oph|i|lis|tic (bib′lē of′ə lis′tik), *adj.* of a bibliophile; loving books.

bib|li|oph|i|ly (bib′lē of′ə lē), *n.* love of books; bibliophilism.

bib|li|o|phobe (bib′lē ə fōb), *n.* a person who hates books.

bib|li|o|pho|bi|a (bib′lē ə fō′bē ə), *n.* a dread or hatred of books.

bib|li|o|pole (bib′lē ə pōl), *n.* a bookseller, especially one who deals in rare and curious books. [< Latin *bibliopōla,* ultimately < Greek *biblíon* book + *pōleîn* sell]

bib|li|o|pol|ic (bib′lē ə pol′ik), *adj.* of or belonging to booksellers.

bib|li|o|pol|i|cal (bib′lē ə pol′ə kəl), *adj.* = bibliopolic.

bib|li|op|o|lism (bib′lē op′ə liz əm), *n.* the principles or trade of bookselling. —**bib′li|op′o|list,** *n.*

bib|li|o|taph (bib′lē ə taf, -täf), *n.* a person who hides or buries books, or keeps them away from use in closed or locked cases. [< French *bibliotaphe* < Greek *biblíon* book + *táphos* tomb]

bib|li|o|taph|ic (bib′lē ə taf′ik), *adj.* of a bibliotaph.

bib|li|o|the|ca (bib′lē ə thē′kə), *n.* **1** a library; collection of books. **2** a bibliographer's catalogue. **3** *Obsolete.* the Bible. [< Latin *bibliothēca* < Greek *bibliothḗkē* bookcase; library < *biblíon* book + *thḗkē* receptacle]

bib|li|o|the|cal (bib′lē ə thē′kəl), *adj.* belonging to a library.

bib|li|oth|e|car|i|an (bib′lē oth′ə kãr′ē ən), *adj.* of or having to do with a bibliothecary or librarian.

bib|li|oth|e|car|y (bib′lē oth′ə ker′ē), *n., pl.* **-ries.** = librarian. [< Latin *bibliothēcārius*]

bib|li|o|thèque (bē blē ō tek′), *n. French.* **1** a library. **2** a bookcase.

bib|li|o|ther|a|py (bib′lē ə ther′ə pē), *n.* reading as a means of promoting emotional growth and health; the therapeutic use of books.

Bib|list (bib′list, bī′blist), *n.* **1** a person who regards the Bible as the sole rule of faith. **2** a Biblical scholar.

bib|u|los|i|ty (bib′yə los′ə tē), *n.* addiction to drink; tippling.

bib|u|lous (bib′yə ləs), *adj.* **1a** fond of drinking alcoholic liquor; addicted to drink. **b** = drunk. **2** absorbent of moisture. [< Latin *bibulus* (with English *-ous*) < *bibere* drink] —**bib′u|lous|ly,** *adv.* —**bib′u|lous|ness,** *n.*

bi|cam|er|al (bī kam′ər əl), *adj.* having two legislative chambers. The Congress of the United States is bicameral; it has both the Senate and the House of Representatives. [< *bi-* two + Latin *camera* chamber (< Greek *kamárā*)]

bi|cam|er|al|ism (bī kam′ər əl iz′əm), *n.* the foundation or institution of a bicameral legislature.

bi|cam|er|al|ist (bī kam′ər əl ist), *n.* an advocate of a bicameral legislature.

bi|cam|er|ist (bī kam′ər ist), *n.* = bicameralist.

bi|cap|su|lar (bī kap′syə lər), *adj. Botany.* **1** having two capsules. **2** having a capsule which has two cells.

bi|carb (bī′kärb, bī kärb′), *n. Slang.* sodium bicarbonate.

bi|car|bo|nate (bī kär′bə nit, -nāt), *n.* **1** a salt of carbonic acid formed by neutralizing one hydrogen ion. **2** = sodium bicarbonate.

bicarbonate of soda, = sodium bicarbonate.

bi|car|pel|lar|y (bī kär′pə ler′ē), *adj. Botany.* having two carpels: *a bicarpellary pistil.*

bi|cau|date (bī kô′dāt), *adj. Zoology.* having two taillike appendages.

bice (bīs), *n.* **1** either of two kinds of paint (one blue, the other green), both native carbonates of copper. **2** a shade of blue, duller than azure. [< Old French *bis* brownish-gray]

bi|cen|te|nar|y (bī sen′tə ner′ē, bī′sen ten′ər-; *especially British* bī′sen tē′nər ē), *adj., n., pl.* **-nar|ies.** —*adj., n.* bicentennial.

bi|cen|ten|ni|al (bī′sen ten′ē əl), *adj., n.* —*adj.* **1** having to do with a period of 200 years or a 200th anniversary. **2** recurring every 200 years. —*n.* **1** a 200th anniversary. **2** a celebration of a 200th anniversary.

bi|ceph|a|lous (bī sef′ə ləs), *adj.* having two heads. [< *bi-* + *cephalous*]

bi|ceps (bī′seps), *n.* **1** any muscle having two heads or origins: **a** the large muscle in the front part of the upper arm, which bends the forearm. If you move your fist up to your shoulder, the biceps will stick out. See picture under **arm**[1]. **b** the corresponding large muscle in the back of the thigh. See picture under **leg. 2** *Informal.* strength or muscular development; muscles, especially of the arms: *What biceps that boy has!* [< Latin *biceps* two-headed < *bi-* two + *caput* head]

▶**Biceps** is singular in its strict technical use, but is popularly thought of and used as both a plural and a collective noun.

bich|ir (bich′ər), *n.* a large African fish, found chiefly in the Nile. [< a native name]

bi|chlo|rid (bī klôr′id, -klōr′-), *n.* = bichloride.

bi|chlo|ride (bī klôr′īd, -id; -klōr′-), *n.* **1** a compound containing two atoms of chlorine combined with another element or radical; dichloride. **2** = bichloride of mercury.

bichloride of mercury, an extremely poisonous, white substance, used in taxidermy and in dyeing, and formerly used in solution as an antiseptic and treatment in medicine; mercuric chloride; corrosive sublimate. *Formula*: $HgCl_2$

bi|chon fri|se (bē′shôn fri zā′), a small lively dog with a thick, loosely curled coat of solid white, or white with patches of gray, orange, or pale yellow. [< French *bichon frisé,* literally, curly lap dog]

bi|chro|mate (bī krō′māt), *n., v.,* **-mat|ed, -mat|ing.** —*n.* = dichromate. —*v.t.* to treat with a bichromate.

bi|chrome (bī′krōm), *adj.* = bicolored.

bi|cil|i|ate (bī sil′ē it), *adj.* having two cilia.

bi|cip|i|tal (bī sip′ə təl), *adj.* **1** having two heads or origins, as a muscle. **2** having to do with a biceps (muscle). [< Latin *biceps, -cipitis* (see etym. under **biceps**) + English *-al*[1]]

bi|cir|cu|lar (bī sėr′kyə lər), *adj.* composed of or resembling two circles.

bick|er[1] (bik′ər), *v., n.* —*v.i.* **1** to take part in a petty, noisy quarrel; squabble: *The children bickered through the long, hot afternoon.* SYN: fight, argue. **2** to babble; patter: *Streamlets . . . bicker'd thro' the sunny glade* (James Thomson). **3** to flash; flicker. —*n.* **1** a petty, noisy quarrel. **2** a babble; patter. [Middle English *bikeren*] —**bick′er|er,** *n.*

bick|er[2] (bik′ər), *n. Scottish.* a wooden bowl. [variant of *beaker*]

bick|er|ing (bik′ər ing), *n.* **1** wordy sparring or wrangling: *eternal bickering over German unification* (New York Times). **2** a skirmish.

Bi|col (bi kōl′), *n.* = Bikol.

bi|col|or (bī′kul′ər), *adj., n.* —*adj.* having two colors; bicolored. —*n.* a two-colored blossom.

bi|col|ored (bī′kul′ərd), *adj.* having two colors.

bi|col|our (bī′kul′ər), *adj., n. British.* = bicolor.

bi|com|po|nent (bī′kəm pō′nənt), *adj., n.* —*adj.* having two chemical components, such as polyamide and polyester, embedded in each filament of a synthetic fiber. —*n.* a bicomponent fiber.

bi|con|cave (bī kon′kāv, -kong′-; bī′kon kāv′), *adj.* concave on both sides.

bi|con|ic (bī kon′ik), *adj.* having the form of two cones placed base to base.

bi|con|ju|gate (bī kon′jù git), *adj. Botany.* twice conjugate.

bi|con|stit|u|ent (bī′kən stich′ù ənt), *adj., n.* = bicomponent.

bi|con|vex (bī kon′veks, bī′kon veks′), *adj.* convex on both sides.

bi|corn (bī′kôrn), *adj.* having two horns or hornlike parts; crescent-shaped. [< Latin *bicornis* < *bi-* two + *cornū* horn]

bi|corne (bī′kôrn), *n.* a hat having a brim with two corners or points.

bi|cor|nu|ate (bī kôr′nyù it), *adj.* = bicorn.

bi|cor|po|ral (bī kôr′pər əl), *adj.* having two bodies.

bi|cor|po|re|al (bī′kôr pôr′ē əl, -pōr′-), *adj.* = bicorporal.

bi|cron (bī′kron, bik′ron), *n. Physics.* one billionth of a meter. [< *bi(llion)* + *(mi)cron*]

bi|cul|tur|al (bī kul′chər əl), *adj.* having or blending two distinct cultures: *. . . the bicultural nature of the Canadian state* (Canadian Forum). —**bi|cul′tur|al|ly,** *adv.*

bi|cul|tur|al|ism (bī kul′chər ə liz′əm), *n.* **1** the principle or policy of political union between two cultures on a bicultural or bilingual basis. **2** the practice or support of such a policy. **3** the quality or state of being bicultural.

bi|cus|pid (bī kus′pid), *n., adj.* —*n.* a double-pointed tooth that tears and grinds food; premolar. Adult human beings have eight bicuspids. —*adj.* having two points or cusps. [< *bi-* two + Latin *cuspis, -idis* point]

bi|cus|pi|dal (bī kus′pə dəl), *adj.* = bicuspid.

bi|cus|pid|ate (bī kus′pə dāt), *adj., n.* = bicuspid.

bicuspid valve, the valve of the heart between the left auricle and left ventricle; mitral valve.

∗**bi|cy|cle** (bī′sə kəl, -sik′əl), *n., v.,* **-cled, -cling.** —*n.* a metal frame on two wheels, one behind the other, that supports a rider. The rider sits on a seat and steers with handles attached to the front wheel. On an ordinary bicycle the rear wheel is turned by a chain connected to pedals; on a motor bicycle the chain is attached to an engine. —*v.i.* to ride a bicycle. [< *bi-* two + Greek *kýklos* circle, wheel]

▶**bicycle, bike.** Informal speech often uses the shortened form *bike.*

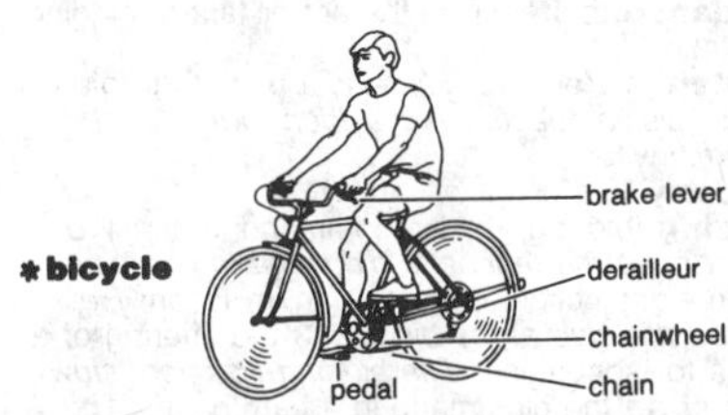

∗**bicycle**

bicycle motocross, a sport of racing stripped-down bicycles with knobby tires over indoor or outdoor tracks featuring dirt mounds, tight turns, and the like.

bi|cy|cler (bī′sə klər, -sik′lər), *n.* = bicyclist.

bi|cy|clic[1] (bī sī′klik, -sik′lik), *adj.* **1** consisting of or having two circles. **2** *Botany.* in two whorls: *bicyclic stamens.* **3** *Chemistry.* containing two rings of atoms in the molecule: *bicyclic alcohol.* [< *bi-* two + Greek *kýklos* circle, wheel + English *-ic*]

bi|cyc|lic[2] (bī sik′lik, bī′sə klik), *adj.* of or having to do with bicycles.

bi|cy|cli|cal (bī sī′klə kəl, -sik′lə-), *adj.* bicyclic; consisting of two circles.

bi|cy|clist (bī′sə klist, -sik′list), *n.* a person who rides a bicycle.

bid (bid), *v.,* **bade, bid,** or (*Archaic*) **bad, bid|den** or **bid, bid|ding,** *n.* —*v.t.* **1** to tell (someone) what to do or where to go; command; instruct; direct: *Do as the law bids. The judge bid the witness sit down.* SYN: order. **2** to say; tell (a greeting or the like); wish: *His friends bade him good-by.* **3** (*past tense and past participle* **bid**) **a** to offer to pay (a certain price): *She bid five dollars for the table. He then bid seven dollars.* **b** to offer to charge a certain price: *The builder bid $1,000 to repair the porch.* SYN: proffer, tender. **4** to proclaim; declare: *He bade defiance to them all.* **5** (*past tense and past participle* **bid**) to state as the number of tricks or points one proposes to make or to win in a hand of a card

---

Pronunciation Key: hat, āge, cãre, fär; let, ēqual, tėrm; it, īce; hot, ōpen, ôrder; oil, out; cup, pùt, rüle; child; long; thin; ᴛʜen; zh, measure; ə represents **a** in about, **e** in taken, **i** in pencil, **o** in lemon, **u** in circus.

game. 6 *Archaic.* to invite: *I made a feast; I bad him come* (Tennyson). —*v.i.* to make an offer; offer a price: *to bid at an auction.*
—*n.* 1 the action of bidding: **a** an offer to pay a certain price: *She made a bid of seven dollars on the table.* **b** an offer to charge a certain price: *The painter made a bid of $100 to paint the room.* 2 the amount offered or stated: *Her bid was seven dollars. The painter's bid was too high.* **3a** the amount bid in a card game. **b** the turn of a player to bid: *Whose bid is it?* 4 *U.S. Informal.* an invitation: *She has three bids to the prom.* 5 an attempt to get or achieve: *She made a bid for our sympathy by saying she was lonely.*
bid fair, to seem likely; have a good chance: *The plan bids fair to succeed.*
bid for, to try to secure, obtain, or win: *Several companies will bid for the contract. The candidate is bidding for votes.*
bid in, to buy at auction to keep for the owner: *The costly books ... were bid in at the sale of 1878* (Joseph F. Daly).
bid up, to raise the price of by bidding more: *They bade them up until they reached 10,000 livres* (John H. Burton).
[Middle English *bidden,* Old English *biddan* ask for, influenced in sense by *bēden* < *bēodan* command, proclaim] —**bid′der,** *n.*
▶In the sense "command," now somewhat archaic, **bid** in the active voice usually takes an infinitive without *to: You bade me forget what is unforgettable.* With the passive *to* is used: *They were bidden to assemble.*
▶See **bade** for another usage note.

b.i.d., (take) twice a day (Latin, *bis in die;* used in doctors' prescriptions).

bid and asked prices, (in stock market quotations) the highest price bid and the lowest price asked for securities that are not actively traded.

bi|dar|ka (bī där′kə), *n.* a portable boat made of skins stretched on a frame, used by the Eskimos of Alaska; baidarka. [American English < Russian *bajdarka*]

bi|dar|kee (bī där′kē), *n.* = bidarka.

bid-ask prices (bid′ask′, -äsk′), = bid and asked prices.

bid|da|bil|i|ty (bid′ə bil′ə tē), *n.* obedience; docility.

bid|da|ble (bid′ə bəl), *adj.* 1 doing what is ordered; obedient; docile. 2 strong enough to justify a bid in a card game.

bid|dance (bid′əns), *n.* the act or fact of bidding; invitation.

bid|den (bid′ən), *v., adj.* —*v.* a past participle of **bid:** *Twelve guests were bidden to the feast.*
—*adj.* invited.

bid|der|y (bid′ər ē), *n.* = bidri.

bid|ding (bid′ing), *n.* 1 a command; order: *We must heed the teacher's bidding.* SYN: direction, charge, injunction, behest. 2 an invitation: *He joined the club at my bidding.* 3 the offering of a price for something: *The bidding was very slow at first.* **4a** the bids made in a card game: *The bidding was erratic.* **b** the stage of the game when they are made.
at the bidding of, by command of; in obedience to: *Whatever Godwine did he did at the bidding of his lord* (Edward Freeman).
do one's bidding, to obey one: *The soldier did the captain's bidding without question.*

bidding block, 1 = auction block. 2 any market or place of selling to the highest bidder.

bidding prayer, *British.* (in the Church of England) an invitation to prayer used at special services in the universities, at assize sermons, on state occasions, and in certain other services. The bidding prayer now comes at the beginning of the service.

bid|dy[1] (bid′ē), *n., pl.* **-dies.** 1 *Slang.* a woman, especially one who is fussy, gossipy, eccentric, or immoral (used in an unfriendly way). 2 Often, **Biddy.** a woman servant. [< *Biddy,* a familiar form of the name *Bridget*]

bid|dy[2] (bid′ē), *n., pl.* **-dies.** a hen. [origin uncertain]

bide (bīd), *v.,* **bode** or **bid|ed** or **bade, bid|ed, bid|ing.** —*v.i.* 1 to remain or continue in some state or action; wait; abide: *Bide here a bit.* 2 *Archaic.* to dwell; reside. —*v.t.* 1 *Archaic.* to put up with; bear; endure; suffer. 2 to face; withstand.
bide one's time. See under **time.**
[Old English *bīdan*]

bi|dent (bī′dənt), *n.* a two-pronged instrument. [< Latin *bidēns, -entis* with two teeth < *bi-* two + *dēns* tooth]

bi|den|tate (bī den′tāt), *adj.* having two teeth or toothlike processes.

bi|det (bi det′, -dā′), *n.* 1 a shallow porcelain bowl, usually with a nozzle and running water, used to bathe the genital and anal areas. 2 a small horse. [< French *bidet,* apparently < Old French *bider* to trot]

bi|di|a|lec|tal (bī dī′ə lek′təl), *adj.* using or able to use two dialects of a language: *The public schools continue to vacillate between the old line, "Talk American, boy, American," and the more cosmopolitan line, "Are our er um Black students ahh bilingual or um bidialectal?"* (New York Times Book Review).

bi|dig|i|tate (bī dij′ə tāt), *adj.* having two digits.

bi|di|men|sion|al (bī′də men′shə nəl), *adj.* having or exhibiting two dimensions.

bid|ing (bī′ding), *n. Archaic.* 1 an awaiting; expectation. 2 a stay; residence; dwelling.

bi|di|rec|tion|al (bī′də rek′shə nəl), *adj.* operating in two directions: *a bidirectional microphone.*

bi|di|rec|tion|al|i|ty (bī′də rek′shə nal′ə tē), *n.* the quality or state of being bidirectional: *the bidirectionality of electronic switches.*

bi|don (bē dôɴ′), *n. French.* a vessel, fitted with a cap, for carrying liquids, now especially a metal container for gasoline.

bi|don|ville (bē dôɴ vēl′), *n. French.* a slum composed of makeshift shanties, often built largely of metal from gasoline containers (bidons) cut and hammered into sheets.

bid|ri or **bid|ree** (bid′rē), *n.* 1 an alloy, especially of copper, lead, and zinc, used as a ground for inlaying with gold or silver, and for making various articles. 2 work or ware of this kind. Also, **biddery.** [< Hindustani *bidrī*]

bid whist, a form of whist in which the highest bidder names trump.

∗**Bie|der|mei|er** (bē′dər mī′ər), *adj.* of or having to do with a style of furniture which evolved in Germany from the Empire style during the mid-1800's. [< Gottlieb *Biedermeier,* an imaginary character popularized in Germany in the mid-1800's as the author of unsophisticated poems]

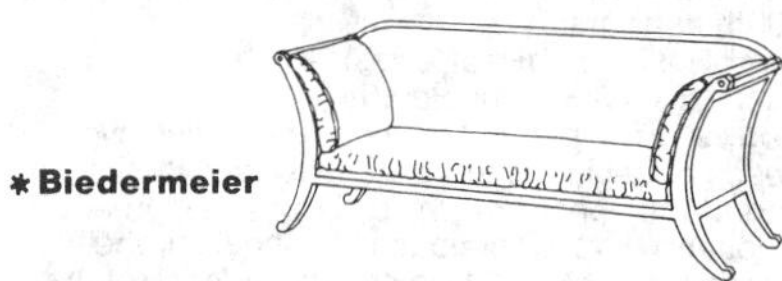
∗**Biedermeier**

bield (bēld), *n., v.t. Scottish Dialect.* shelter: *Better a wee bush than nae bield* (Robert Burns). [Old English *bieldo* courage, boldness]

Bie|lid (bē′lid), *n. Astronomy.* an Andromedid. [< Wilhelm von *Biela,* 1782-1856, an Austrian astronomer]

bi|en|ni|al (bī en′ē əl), *adj., n.* —*adj.* 1 (of plants) requiring two years to reach full development; germinating in one year or growing season and flowering, producing fruit, and dying in the next year or growing season. 2 occurring every two years.
—*n.* 1 a plant that lives two years or seasons. Carrots and onions are biennials. 2 an event that occurs every two years.
[< Latin *biennium* biennium + English *-al*[1]] —**bi-en′ni|al|ly,** *adv.*
▶See **biannual** for usage note.

bi|en|ni|um (bī en′ē əm), *n., pl.* **-en|ni|a** (-en′ē ə). a two-year period. [< Latin *biennium* < *bi-* two + *annus* year]

bien-pen|sant (byaɴ päɴ säɴ′), *adj., n. French.* —*adj.* 1 orthodox; holding conventional or conservative opinions: *... the gray, bien-pensant, judicious members of the Establishment* (New York Review of Books). 2 (literally) right-thinking.
—*n.* an orthodox or conservative person.

bien|ve|nu (byaɴ və ɴʏ′), *n. French.* welcome; admission to membership.

bien vu (byaɴ vʏ), *French.* well thought of; highly regarded.

bier (bir), *n.* 1 a movable stand or framework on which a coffin or dead body is placed before burial. 2 such a stand together with the coffin. 3 a tomb; sepulcher. [Old English *bēr.* See related etym. at **bear**[2].]

bier|kel|ler (bēr′kel′ər), *n.* = bierstube. [< German *Bier* beer + *Keller* cellar]

bier|stu|be or **Bier|stu|be** (bēr′shtü′bə, -stü′-), *n., pl.* **-bes** or **-ben.** a German or German-style tavern where chiefly beer is served. [< German *Bierstube* < *Bier* beer + *Stube* room]

biest|ings (bēs′tingz), *n.pl.* = beestings.

bi|face (bī′fās′), *n.* a primitive hand tool of shaped stone (usually flint) having two plane surfaces.

bi|fa|cial (bī fā′shəl), *adj.* 1 having two faces or fronts. 2 *Botany.* having the opposite faces unlike; dorsiventral. —**bi|fa′cial|ly,** *adv.*

bi|fanged (bī′fangd′), *adj.* having two roots or fangs.

bi|far|i|ous (bī fãr′ē əs), *adj.* 1 *Botany, Zoology.* pointing in two ways; in two opposite rows. 2 twofold; double. [< Latin *bifārius* (with English *-ous*) twofold, ultimately < *bi-* two + *fās* utterance] —**bi|far′i|ous|ly,** *adv.*

bif|er|ous (bif ′ər əs), *adj. Botany.* bearing fruit or flowers twice in one year. [< Latin *bifer* bearing twice + English *-ous*]

biff (bif), *n., v.t. Slang.* hit, slap, or whack.

bif|fin (bif′in), *n.* a variety of red cooking apple, cultivated in England, especially in the county of Norfolk. [< dialectal form of *beef* (because of its deep-red color)]

bi|fid (bī′fid), *adj.* divided into two parts by a cleft; forked. [< Latin *bifidus* < *bi-* two + *findere* to cleave] —**bi′fid|ly,** *adv.*

bi|fid|i|ty (bī fid′ə tē), *n.* the quality of being divided into two parts by a cleft.

bi|fi|lar (bī fī′lər), *adj., n.* —*adj.* having two threads. —*n.* a form of micrometer in which measurements are made by means of two very fine filaments or threads. —**bi|fi′lar|ly,** *adv.*

bi|flag|el|late (bī flaj′ə lāt), *adj.* having two whiplike appendages (flagella), as certain protozoans.

bi|flex (bī′fleks), *adj.* 1 bent in two places. 2 bent in two directions.

∗**bi|fo|cal** (bī fō′kəl, bī′fō′-), *adj., n.* —*adj.* having two focuses. The lenses of bifocal glasses have two sections of different focal lengths, the upper part for distant vision, the lower for close vision.
—*n.* a bifocal lens.
bifocals, a pair of glasses having bifocal lenses.

∗**bifocals**

bi|fold (bī′fōld′), *adj.* = twofold.

bi|fo|li|ate (bī fō′lē it, -āt), *adj.* having two leaves.

bi|fo|li|o|late (bī fō′lē ə lāt, bī′fə lī′-), *adj.* having two leaflets: *a bifoliolate compound leaf.*

bi|fo|rate (bī fôr′āt, -fōr′-), *adj.* having two perforations. [< *bi-* two + Latin *forātus* pierced]

bi|forked (bī′fôrkt′), *adj.* = bifurcate.

bi|form (bī′fôrm′), *adj.* having or combining two forms: *A centaur is biform.* [< Latin *bifōrmis* < *bi-* two + *fōrma* shape]

bi|formed (bī′fôrmd′), *adj.* = biform.

bi|front (bī′frunt′), *adj.* having two fronts or faces. [< Latin *bifrōns, bifrontis* < *bi-* two + *frōns* forehead, front]

Bif|rost (biv′rost, bēf′-), *n. Scandinavian Mythology.* the rainbow bridge used by the gods to travel between heaven (Asgard) and earth (Midgard). [< Old Icelandic *bifrōst*]

bi|fur|cate (*v.* bī′fər kāt, bī fėr′-; *adj.* bī′fər kāt, bī fėr′kit), *v.,* **-cat|ed, -cat|ing,** *adj.* —*v.t., v.i.* to divide into two branches.
—*adj.* divided into two branches; forked.
[< Medieval Latin *bifurcatus* two-forked < Latin *bifurcus* < *bi-* two + *furca* fork] —**bi′fur|cate|ly,** *adv.* —**bi′fur|ca′tion,** *n.*

bi|fur|cat|ed (bī′fər kā′tid, bī fėr′-), *adj.* = bifurcate.

big[1] (big), *adj.,* **big|ger, big|gest,** *adv., n.* —*adj.* 1 great in amount or size; large: *a big room, a big book. Making automobiles is a big business. Elephants are bigger than mice.* SYN: huge, extensive, immense. See syn. under **great.** 2 grown up: *A big girl does not like to play baby games.* 3 *Informal, Figurative.* **a** important; great: *The election of a President is big news.* **b** of high position or standing: *The President is a big man.* **4a** full; loud: *He has a big voice.* **b** filled; teeming: *His eye being big with tears* (Shakespeare). **c** *Figurative.* generous; noble: *His uncle had a big heart and gave him many things.* SYN: magnanimous, liberal. 5 boastful; pompous: *The bully was full of big talk.* 6 pregnant: *big with child.* 7 *Obsolete.* stout; mighty.
—*adv. Informal.* 1 boastfully: *He talks big.* 2 prosperously: *Things are going big.*
—*n.* a thing or person that is big: *This interdependence of bigs and littles is the basis of American manufacturing progress* (Newsweek).
[Middle English *big;* origin uncertain] —**big′ly,** *adv.*

big[2] (big), *n.* = bigg (a kind of barley).

big[3] (big), *v.t. Scottish.* to build. Also, **bigg.** [< Scandinavian (compare Old Icelandic *byggja*)]

big|a|mist (big′ə mist), *n.* a person married to more than one person at one time.

big|a|mous (big′ə məs), *adj.* 1 guilty of bigamy; involved in bigamy. 2 involving bigamy. —**big′a-mous|ly,** *adv.*

big|a|my (big′ə mē), *n., pl.* **-mies.** 1 the practice or condition of having two wives or two husbands at the same time. Bigamy is unlawful in most countries. 2 *Law.* the crime of having two wives or two husbands at the same time. [< Medieval Latin *bigamia,* alteration of Latin *digamia* < Greek *di-* two + *gámos* marriage]

big apple, a dance in quick tempo, popular in the 1930's.

Big Apple, a nickname for New York City.

big|a|rade orange (big′ə räd), = sour orange. [< French *bigarrade* < *bigarré* mottled]

big|a|roon (big′ə rün′), *n.* = bigarreau.

big|ar|reau (big′ə rō′, big′ə rō), *n.* a variety of large, heart-shaped cherry with sweet flavor and firm flesh, yellowish on one side and red on the other. [< Middle French *bigarreau* < *bigarré* mottled]

big bang theory, a theory which maintains that the universe originated in a cosmic explosion of hydrogen, which became condensed into the galaxies.

big beat, *Slang.* = rock'n'roll. —**big-beat′**, *adj.*

Big Ben, **1** a huge bell in the clock tower of the Parliament building in London. **2** *Informal.* the clock itself.

Big Bertha, *Informal.* **1** a long-range gun used by the Germans to fire on Paris in World War I. **2** a powerful cannon. **3** anything having a relatively large size or great range, as certain cameras. Also, **Bertha**. [< *Bertha* Krupp, 1886-1957, owner of the Krupp Steel Works at Essen, Germany, during World War I]

Big Board, *U.S. Informal.* **1** the board on which prices are quoted of the stocks listed on the New York Stock Exchange. **2** the New York Stock Exchange.

big-boned (big′bōnd′), *adj.* having large bones; broadly built: *Spectators saw a handsome man, tall, big-boned, inclined to spareness* (Atlantic).

big boy, *Informal.* an important person, especially one in big business: ... *the big boys on Wall Street* (Wall Street Journal).

big brother, **1** an elder brother. **2** a person who takes the role of an elder brother in befriending someone younger.

Big Brother, **1** the unseen dictator in George Orwell's satiric novel *1984*, who keeps his people under constant surveillance and subjection. **2** a person or government resembling him in the practice of surveillance and tyranny.

Big Broth|er|ism (bruᴛʜ′ər iz′əm), practices characteristic of Big Brother, especially rigid government surveillance or censorship of the communications media.

Big Brotherly, having to do with or characteristic of Big Brother.

big bucks, *U.S. Slang,* a large amount of money: *"That [tourism] is our big industry. Four hundred thousand jobs. That is big bucks"* (New York Times).

big business, *U.S.* **1** very large business and industrial organizations, taken collectively as one large, powerful group: *We demand that big business give the people a square deal* (Theodore Roosevelt). **2** any enterprise involving considerable sums of money: *Today sports is big business* (New York Times).

big C, *Informal.* cancer.

big cheese, *Slang.* an important or high-ranking person: *The dame that's the big cheese at Intourist tried to give me a hard time* (New Yorker).

big-cit|y (big′sit′ē), *adj. U.S. Informal.* metropolitan.

big deal, *U.S. Slang.* an important or impressive person, thing, or activity (often used ironically): ... *the local boy knocking out the big deal from the East* (Atlantic).

big dipper, *British.* a revolving wheel with seats on the rim, at a fun fair.

Big Dipper, the group of seven bright stars in the constellation Ursa Major, thought of as being arranged in the shape of a dipper. The group is also called the *Wagon, Wagoner,* or *Plow,* and (in Great Britain) *Charles's Wain* or *the Wain.* See picture under **constellation**.

big dress, a loose-fitting dress made in the style of the Big Look; droop..

bi|gem|o|ny (bī′jem′ə nē), *n.* political domination by two states: *Bigemony ... generally refers to the condominium exercised by the two superpowers, but inside the Nato camp, too, there are signs of a bigemony of sorts emerging, based on a Bonn-Washington axis* (David Rudnick). [< *bi-* two + (he)*gemony*]

big end, the lower part of an automobile engine's connecting rod at its point of attachment to the crankpin.

Big-end|i|an (big′en′dē ən), *n.* **1** (in Swift's *Gulliver's Travels)* a member of the heretical religious party in Lilliput which maintained that eggs should be broken at the big end. **2** *Figurative.* a disputer about trifles.

bi|ge|ner (bī′jə nər), *n. Botany.* a cross between two species of different genera.

bi|ge|ner|ic (bī′jə ner′ik), *adj. Botany.* having the characters of two different genera.

big|eye (big′ī′), *n.* any one of a small family of bottom-dwelling fishes of tropical seas, having very large eyes, small scales, and a bright red color.

big-eyed (big′īd′), *adj.* **1** having big eyes. **2** with the eyes wide open, especially with interest, amazement, or wonder.

bigeye tuna, a widely distributed tuna closely related to the bluefin and yellowfin, and important as a food fish.

bigg[1] (big), *n. Scottish.* barley, especially a hardy species bearing four rows of grain in an ear, cultivated in northern Europe. Also, **big**. [< Scandinavian (compare Old Icelandic *bygg*)]

bigg[2] (big), *v.t. Scottish.* big (to build).

big game, **1** the larger animals, such as elephants, tigers, and lions, hunted by sportsmen. **2** *Informal, Figurative.* very important objectives: *The district attorney disregarded the petty criminals; he was after big game: the leader of the gang.*

big|ge|ty (big′ə tē), *adj. U.S. Slang.* conceited; cocky. Also, **bigotty, bigoty**.

big|gie (big′ē), *n. U.S. Slang.* an important person or thing: *"I'm right on the fringe of a biggie, R. B. I'm just waiting for it to jell"* (New Yorker).

big|gin[1] (big′in), *n.* **1** *British Dialect.* a child's cap. **2** *British Dialect.* a nightcap. **3** a cap or hood. **4** the coif of a sergeant-at-law. [< French *béguin*]

big|gin[2] (big′in), *n.* a kind of drip coffeepot, usually made of earthenware. [< a proper name]

big|gin[3] (big′in), *n. Scottish.* bigging.

big|ging (big′in), *n. Scottish.* **1** a building. **2** an outbuilding as distinguished from a house. [Middle English *biggen* build]

big|gish (big′ish), *adj.* somewhat big.

big|gi|ty (big′ə tē), *adj. U.S. Slang.* = biggety.

big gun, *U.S. Slang.* an important person or thing.

big|head (big′hed′), *n.* **1a** a disease of sheep characterized by swelling of the tissues of the head, caused by the eating of certain plants and subsequent exposure to sunlight. **b** infectious sinusitis of turkeys. **2** Also, **big head**. *Informal.* **a** a swelled head; arrogance; conceit. **b** a conceited person; braggart.

big|head|ed (big′hed′id), *adj.* arrogant; conceited.

big-heart|ed (big′här′tid), *adj.* kindly; generous; charitable: *a big-hearted gesture.* —**big′-heart′ed|ly**, *adv.* —**big′-heart′ed|ness**, *n.*

big|horn (big′hôrn′), *n., pl.* **-horns** or **-horn**. any one of three kinds of sheep: **a** a wild, grayish-brown sheep of the Rocky Mountains having large, curving horns; Rocky Mountain sheep. It is pale buff in the hot southern mountains. **b** the white mountain sheep of Alaska and western Yukon; Dall sheep. **c** the dark-brown to black mountain sheep of south-central Yukon to central British Columbia; stone sheep.

big house, *U.S. Slang.* = penitentiary.

bight (bīt), *n., v.* —*n.* **1** a long curve in a coastline, the shore of a river, or a range of mountains. **2** a bay formed by this curve. See picture under **bay**[1]. **3a** a loop of rope. **b** the slack of rope between the fastened ends. **4** a bend; angle; corner. —*v.t.* to fasten with the bight of a rope. [Old English *byht*]

big jaw, actinomycosis of cattle and swine.

big labor, *U.S.* very large labor unions, taken collectively.

big league, **1** a major league in baseball or other sport. **2** Often, **big leagues**, *U.S. Informal, Figurative.* the top levels of public affairs, industry, science, or the like, characterized by high professional skill and acumen, large rewards, and stiff competition.

big-league (big′lēg′), *adj.* **1** of or having to do with a major league in any sport. **2** *U.S. Informal, Figurative.* demanding high professional skill; top-level: *The man the big-league hospital can't afford to be without is the heart surgeon* (Harper's).

big-lea|guer (big′lē′gər), *n.* **1** *U.S.* a major-league baseball player. **2** *Figurative.* a person who belongs at the top of his business or profession.

big lie, a large and often obvious untruth reiterated until it is believed, especially as a tactic of demagoguery or an element of propaganda.

big liver disease, a form of lymphomatosis characterized by enlargement of the liver.

Big Look, a fashion in women's clothes characterized by loose, broad, voluminous designs.

Big Mac, *U.S. Informal.* a corporation established in 1975 by New York State to provide funding of New York City bonds during its fiscal crisis.

big|mouth (big′mouth′), *n. Slang.* a very talkative person, especially one who gossips or boasts too much.

big|mouthed (big′mouᴛʜd′, -moutht′), *adj. Slang.* very or excessively talkative; garrulous.

big music, that part of Scottish music that includes warlike or sad songs called pibrochs.

big name, *U.S. Informal.* a well-known or established person or thing.

big-name (big′nām′), *adj. U.S. Informal.* well-known; established.

big|ness (big′nis), *n.* size; magnitude; bulk (large or small).

big noise, *Slang.* a person of importance; bigwig.

big|no|ni|a (big nō′nē ə), *n.* a vine with clusters of large, orange-red flowers shaped like trumpets, found chiefly in warm climates. [< New Latin *Bignonia* < Abbé *Bignon,* librarian to Louis XIV]

big|no|ni|a|ceous (big nō′nē ā′shəs), *adj.* belonging to the bignonia family.

***bignonia family**, a group of plants with showy, trumpet-shaped flowers. The bignonia, trumpet creeper, and catalpa belong to this family of largely tropical plants.

***bignonia family**

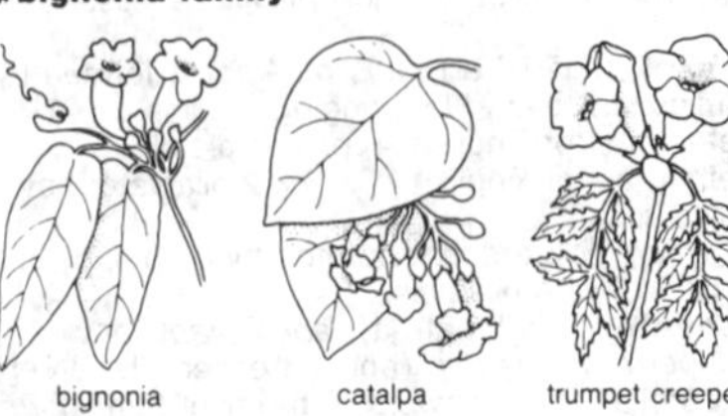

big|ot (big′ət), *n.* an intolerant, prejudiced person; bigoted person: *In philosophy and religion the bigots of all parties are generally the most positive* (Isaac Watts). SYN: dogmatist. [< Middle French *bigot;* origin uncertain]

big|ot|ed (big′ə tid), *adj.* holding fast to an opinion, belief, party, church, or other position, without reason and not tolerating other views; intolerant; prejudiced: *Most bigoted people are ignorant of what they are against.* SYN: biased, narrow-minded. —**big′ot|ed|ly**, *adv.*

big|ot|ry (big′ə trē), *n., pl.* **-ries**. bigoted conduct or attitude; intolerance; prejudice.

big|ot|ty or **big|o|ty** (big′ə tē), *adj. U.S. Slang.* = biggety.

big-scale (big′skāl′), *adj.* large-scale.

big science, scientific and technological research involving large capital investment.

big shot, *Slang.* an important person: *a little man aching to be a big shot* (Time). —**big′-shot′**, *adj.*

big sister, **1** an elder sister. **2** a girl or woman who befriends someone younger than herself.

big stick, military or, sometimes, economic power wielded by a government as a means of coercion: *Speak softly, but carry a big stick* (Theodore Roosevelt).

big-tick|et (big′tik′it), *adj. U.S. Slang.* high-priced; expensive.

big time, *Slang.* the top level, especially in the arts, sports, public affairs, industry, or the theater. —**big′-time′**, *adj.*

big-tim|er (big′tī′mər), *n. Slang.* a person who is in the big time.

big top, *Informal.* **1** the largest tent of a circus. **2** *Informal.* the circus. **3** the canvas covering the main tent of a circus where the principal acts are shown.

big tree, **1** = giant sequoia. **2** = redwood.

big wheel, *U.S. Slang.* an influential or otherwise important person, especially in a particular activity or industry.

big|wig (big′wig′), *n. Informal.* an important person.

Bi|ha|ri (bi hä′rē), *n., adj.* —*n.* **1** a native or inhabitant of Bihar (state in northeastern India). **2** the Indic language of Bihar. —*adj.* of or having to do with Bihar, its people, or their language. Also, **Behari**.

bi|hour|ly (bī our′lē), *adj., adv.* every two hours; once every two hours.

bi|jou (bē′zhü), *n., pl.* **-joux** (-zhüz), *adj.* —*n.* **1** a jewel or trinket. **2** something small and fine. —*adj.* small and fine: *We have this bijou oval track, a miniature of the real thing* (Punch). [< Middle French *bijou* < Breton *bizou*]

bi|jou|te|rie (bi zhü′tər ē), *n.* jewelry, trinkets, and curios, collectively. [< French *bijouterie*]

bi|ju|gate (bī′jů gāt, bī jü′-), *adj.* having two pairs of leaflets. [< *bi-* two + Latin *jugātus* yoked]

bi|ju|gous (bī′jů gəs), *adj.* = bijugate.

bike[1] (bīk), *n., v.,* **biked, bik|ing**. *Informal.* —*n.* **1** a bicycle. **2** a motorcycle. —*v.i.* to ride a bicycle or a motorcycle. [short for *bicycle*]

bike[2] (bīk), *n. Scottish.* **1** a nest of wasps, hornets, or wild bees. **2** *Figurative.* a swarm; crowd.

bik|er (bī′kər), *n.* **1** *Informal.* a bicycle rider. **2** *U.S.* a motorcycle rider, especially one belonging to a motorcycle gang.

bike|way (bīk′wā′), *n. U.S.* a road on which only bicycles are permitted.

bi|ki|ni (bi kē′nē), *n.* a very scant bathing suit in two pieces for women and girls. [< French, < *Bikini,* an atoll in the Marshall Islands, site of atomic and hydrogen bomb tests (perhaps be-

---

Pronunciation Key: hat, āge, cãre, fär; let, ēqual, tėrm; it, īce; hot, ōpen, ôrder; oil, out; cup, půt, rüle; child; long; thin; ᴛʜen; zh, measure; ə represents **a** in about, **e** in taken, **i** in pencil, **o** in lemon, **u** in circus.

cause of the briefness of native dress in this area)]

Bi|ki|ni|an (bi kē′nē ən), *n.* a native or inhabitant of the Bikini Atoll in the Marshall islands.

bi|ki|nied (bi kē′nēd), *adj.* wearing a bikini: *bikinied sunbathers.*

Bi|kol (bi kōl′), *n.* a member of a Christian Malayan group living in the Philippines. Also, **Bicol**.

bi|la|bi|al (bī lā′bē əl), *adj., n.* —*adj.* **1** formed by both lips; articulated by bringing the lips close together, as for English *w*, or completely together, as for English *p, b, m.* **2** bilabiate; having two lips.
—*n. Phonetics.* a sound formed by both lips. *B, p, m,* and *w* are bilabials.

***bi|la|bi|ate** (bī lā′bē āt, -it), *adj. Botany.* having an upper and lower lip (applied especially to certain corollas, as in flowers of the mint family).

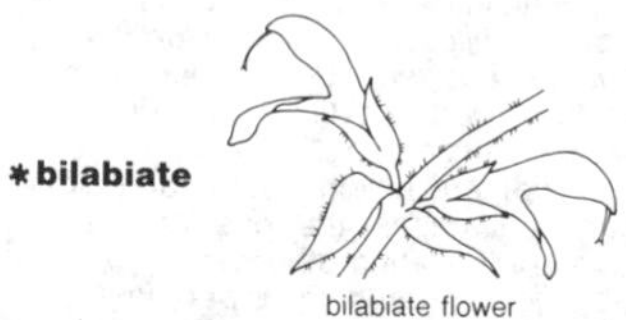
***bilabiate**
bilabiate flower

bi|lam|i|nar (bī lam′ə nər), *adj.* having two laminae, thin plates, or layers.

bi|lam|i|nate (bī lam′ə nāt, -nit), *adj.* = bilaminar.

bil|an|der (bil′ən dər, bī′lən-), *n.* a small merchant ship with two masts, formerly used on canals and along the coast in the Netherlands. [< Dutch *bijlander*]

bi|lat|er|al (bī lat′ər əl), *adj., n.* —*adj.* **1** having two symmetrical sides. **2** on two sides. **3** binding both sides or parties; reciprocal: *The two nations signed a bilateral trade agreement.* **4** of or having to do with two or both sides.
—*n.* a conference or discussion involving only two sides. —**bi|lat′er|al|ly**, *adv.* —**bi|lat′er|al|ness**, *n.*

bi|lat|er|al|ism (bī lat′ər ə liz′əm), *n.* a policy or controlling principle of reciprocity, such as in trade between two nations.

bilateral symmetry, *Zoology.* a condition in which like parts are arranged in two halves, so that each half is the counterpart of the other, divisible in one plane only.

bil|ber|ry (bil′ber′ē, -bər-), *n., pl.* **-ries. 1a** a small, edible, bluish-black berry, much like a blueberry; whortleberry. **b** the shrub that it grows on. It belongs to the heath family. **2** any one of various related plants. [apparently < Scandinavian (compare Danish *böllebær*); influenced by English *berry*]

bil|bo¹ (bil′bō), *n., pl.* **-boes.** Usually, **bilboes.** a long, iron bar fastened down at one end by a lock, and with sliding shackles. Bilboes were formerly used to confine the ankles of prisoners. [perhaps < *Bilbao,* a city in Spain]

bil|bo² (bil′bō), *n., pl.* **-boes.** *Archaic.* a slender sword or rapier noted for the temper of its blade. [< *Bilbao,* a city in Spain, famous for its steel]

Bil|dungs|ro|man (bil′dùngs rō män′), *n. German.* **1** a novel whose theme is the growth and development of its hero. **2** (literally) education novel.

bile (bīl), *n.* **1** a bitter, greenish-yellow liquid secreted by the liver and stored in the gall bladder; gall. It aids digestion in the small intestine by neutralizing acids and emulsifying fats. **2** *Figurative.* ill humor; anger; bitterness of feeling; peevishness: ... *sentences that stir my bile* (James K. Stephen). [< French *bile,* learned borrowing from Latin *bīlis*]

bile acid, any one of the closely related acids found in bile, commonly in combination with glycine and taurine, a part of the large group of steroids.

bi|lec|tion (bī lek′shən), *n.* = bolection.

bile duct, an excretory duct of the liver and gall bladder.

bile pigment, one of the coloring substances in bile, such as bilirubin and biliverdin.

bile salt, **1** any one of the sodium salts of the bile acids, important in emulsifying fats and stimulating the liver. **2** a powder of salts from the gall of cattle, used as a laxative and stimulant of the liver.

bile|stone (bīl′stōn′), *n.* = gallstone.

bilge (bilj), *n., v.,* **bilged, bilg|ing.** —*n.* **1a** the bottom of a ship's hull. **b** the lowest part of a ship's hold. **c** bilge water. **2** the widest part of a barrel. **3** *Informal, Figurative.* nonsense; rubbish.
—*v.t.* to break in (the bottom of a ship).
—*v.i.* **1** to be broken in or spring a leak in the bilge. **2** to bulge; swell out.

bilge out, *U.S. Slang.* to flunk out: *He bilged out of Annapolis and had to fight his way back in* (New Yorker). [variant of *bulge*]

bilge block, one of the blocks supporting the bilge of a vessel under construction or in dry dock.

bilge board, a kind of centerboard lowered vertically into the water from the bilge of a ship to keep it steady on its course.

bilged (biljd), *adj.* having a large bilge; broad-bottomed: *a dirty little bilged coastal steamer.*

bilge keel or **piece**, either of a pair of keellike projections fastened lengthwise at the turn of a ship's bilge, one to each side, to decrease rolling.

bilge pump, a pump for removing bilge water.

bilge water, the dirty water that collects in the bottom of a ship's hold.

bilg|y (bil′jē), *adj.,* **bilg|i|er, bilg|i|est.** like, especially smelling like, bilge water.

bil|har|zi|a (bil här′zē ə), *n.pl.* a group of flatworms parasitic in the veins or the pelvic region and urinary organs of human beings, especially in Egypt and other parts of Africa. [< New Latin *Bilharzia* < Theodor M. *Bilharz,* 1825-1862, a German parasitologist]

bil|har|zi|a|sis (bil′här zī′ə sis), *n.* a disease caused by bilharzia; schistosomiasis.

bil|i|ar|y (bil′ē er′ē), *adj.* **1a** of bile. **b** carrying bile: *a biliary duct.* **2** caused by trouble with the bile; bilious. [< French *biliaire* < New Latin *biliaris* < Latin *bīlis* bile]

bi|lim|bi (bi lim′bē), *n.* **1** an evergreen tree of India yielding a juice considered by the natives to be a cure for skin diseases. **2** the edible, acid berries borne by this tree. [< a native word]

bi|lim|bing (bi lim′bing), *n.* = bilimbi.

bi|lin|e|ar (bī lin′ē ər), *adj.* of or involving two lines.

bi|lin|gual (bī ling′gwəl), *adj., n.* —*adj.* **1** able to speak another language as well or almost as well as one's own; knowing two languages. **2** containing or written in two languages: *a bilingual dictionary.* **3** using or involving two languages: *bilingual education.*
—*n.* a bilingual person; bilinguist.
[< Latin *bilinguis* speaking two languages (< *bi-* two + *lingua* language) + English *-al¹*] —**bi|lin′gual|ly**, *adv.*

bi|lin|gual|ism (bī ling′gwə liz əm), *n.* the ability to speak two languages equally or almost equally well.

bi|lin|gual|i|ty (bī′ling gwal′ə tē), *n.* = bilingualism.

bi|lin|guist (bī ling′gwist), *n.* a person who speaks two languages equally or almost equally well.

bil|ious (bil′yəs), *adj.* **1** suffering from or caused by some trouble with the bile or the liver: *a bilious attack.* **2** *Figurative.* peevish; cross; bad-tempered: *a bilious person. He looked at his work with a bilious eye.* **3** having to do with bile. [< Latin *bīliōsus* < *bīlis* bile] —**bil′ious|ly**, *adv.* —**bil′ious|ness**, *n.*

bil|i|ru|bin (bil′ə rü′bin), *n.* the reddish-yellow pigment normally found in bile. [< Latin *bīlis* bile + *ruber* red + English *-in*]

bi|lit|er|al (bī lit′ər əl), *adj., n.* —*adj.* **1** having two letters. **2** using combinations of two letters, especially in cryptography: *a biliteral code, a biliteral cipher.*
—*n.* a word, root, or syllable formed of two letters.

bi|lit|er|al|ism (bī lit′ər ə liz′əm), *n.* the use of biliteral roots.

bil|i|ver|din (bil′ə vėr′din), *n.* a green pigment found in the bile of herbivorous animals and artificially produced by the oxidation of bilirubin. [< Latin *bīlis* bile + *viridis* green + English *-in*]

bilk (bilk), *v., n.* —*v.t.* **1** to cheat; defraud: *The purported racket that bilked insurance companies of $100,000* (New York Times). **2** to avoid payment of (a debt). **3** to evade; escape from. **4** to balk or spoil an opponent's score in cribbage.
—*n.* **1** a person who avoids paying his bills; a petty swindler; a cheat. **2** a fraud; deception. [origin uncertain] —**bilk′er**, *n.*

bill¹ (bil), *n., v.* —*n.* **1** a statement of money owed for work done or things supplied: *The garage sent us a bill for repairing our car. The store sends out bills monthly.* SYN: invoice, account. **2** *U.S.* a piece of paper money; bank note: *Dad had several dollar bills in his wallet.* **3** a written or printed public notice, such as an advertisement, poster, or handbill: *Post no bills on this fence.* SYN: placard, circular, bulletin. **4** a written or printed statement; list of items. See **bill of fare. 5a** a theater program. **b** the entertainment in a theater. **6** a proposed law presented to a lawmaking body for its approval: *The bill for new taxes will be voted on by the Senate today.* **7** = bill of exchange. **8** *Law.* a written request or complaint presented to a court. **9** *Obsolete.* a written petition or request, especially to a person in authority. **10** *Obsolete.* a written document; a note or memorandum of any kind (originally sealed).
—*v.t.* **1** *U.S.* to send a statement of money owed to: *The drugstore bills us on the first of each month.* **2** *U.S.* to enter in a bill; charge in a bill: *In this store charge accounts are billed regularly.* **3** to announce by bills or public notice: *Many interesting television programs are billed for next week.* **4** to post bills in or on: *The town was thoroughly billed by agents of the circus last week.* **5** to list on a theatrical program. **6** *U.S.* to enter in a waybill; book: *The grain was billed to St. Louis.*

fill the bill, *Informal.* to satisfy requirements: *I don't think I ever saw a word used that ... filled the bill so well as this word "experimentally" will do for us* (W. H. Smith).

foot the bill, *Informal.* to pay or settle the bill: *If our plan succeeded, the landlord was to foot the bill* (Francis A. Durivage).
[< Medieval Latin *billa,* variant of *bulla* document < Latin, amulet] —**bill′a|ble**, *adj.* —**bill′er**, *n.*

bill² (bil), *n., v.* —*n.* **1** the horny part of the jaws of a bird; beak: *the bill of a pigeon or a duck.* **2** anything shaped somewhat like a bird's bill: *the bill of a turtle.*
—*v.i.* **1** to join beaks; touch bills: *We saw two doves billing on the roof.* **2** *Figurative.* to show affection; caress in fondness.

bill and coo, to kiss and talk softly, as pigeons touch bills and coo: *Jenny and Jessamy ... billing and cooing in an arbour* (Thackeray).
[Old English *bile*]

bill³ (bil), *n.* **1** an old military weapon consisting of a spear with a hook-shaped blade and a spike at the back; halberd. **2** a tool for pruning or cutting wood or lopping trees or hedges; billhook. **3** = billman. **4** the point of the fluke of an anchor. [Old English *bill* sword]

bill⁴ (bil), *n.* the booming cry of the bittern: *When first the bittern's hollow bill was heard* (Wordsworth). [probably < *bell²*]

bil|la|bong (bil′ə bong), *n.* in Australia: **1** a branch of a river flowing away from the main stream. **2** a backwater or stagnant pool. [< native Australian name < *billa* river + *bung* dead]

bill|ber|gi|a (bil bėr′jē ə), *n.* a tropical American plant related to the pineapple, having stiff leaves and colorful flowers. [< New Latin *Billbergia* < J. G. *Billberg,* 1772-1844, a Swedish botanist]

bill|board¹ (bil′bôrd′, -bōrd′), *n.* a signboard, usually outdoors, on which to display advertisements or post notices. [< *bill¹* + *board*]

bill|board² (bil′bôrd′, -bōrd′), *n.* a ledge projecting from the side of a ship near the bow, as a rest for the bill of an anchor. [< *bill³* + *board*]

bill broker, a person who negotiates the discount of bills of exchange.

bill|bug (bil′bug′), *n.* any weevil, especially one of the family of the snout beetles.

billed (bild), *adj.* having a bill or beak (usually as part of a compound): *a short-billed bird.*

bil|let¹ (bil′it), *n., v.,* **-let|ed, -let|ing.** —*n.* **1** a written order to provide board and lodging for a soldier. **2** a place where a soldier is lodged. SYN: lodging, station. **3** a job; situation; position. SYN: post, appointment. **4** *Archaic.* a place assigned, as to each of the crew of a man-of-war for slinging his hammock. **5** *Archaic.* a short letter or note.
—*v.t.* **1** to assign to quarters by billet: *Soldiers were billeted in all houses of the village.* SYN: quarter. **2** to provide quarters for; lodge: *The farmer billeted five hired men during the harvest season.*
—*v.i.* to have quarters.
[< Old French *billette,* alteration of *bullette* certificate, ultimately < Latin *bulla* amulet]

bil|let² (bil′it), *n.* **1** a thick stick of wood, especially one for fuel. **2** a short bar of iron or steel. **3** an architectural ornament shaped like a wooden billet or a short cylinder, used, especially in medieval styles, in horizontal strings or series along a molding. **4** in saddlery: **a** a strap which enters a buckle. **b** a pocket or loop that receives the end of a buckled strap. [< Old French *billette* (diminutive) < *bille* log, tree trunk]

bil|let-doux (bil′ē dü′, -ā-), *n., pl.* **bil|lets-doux** (-düz′). a love letter. [< French *billet doux* (literally) sweet note]

bil|let|ed (bil′ə tid), *adj.* **1** (of wood) cut into billets. **2** (of iron or steel) molded into billets. **3** *Architecture.* decorated with billets.

bil|let|er or **bil|le|tor** (bil′ə tər), *n.* a person who provides quarters or lodging for soldiers.

bill|fish (bil′fish′), *n., pl.* **-fish|es** or (*collectively*) **-fish.** any one of several fishes with a long beak or snout, such as the gar or the spearfish.

bill|fold (bil′fōld′), *n. U.S.* a folding pocketbook for carrying paper money, cards, and important papers; wallet.

bill|head (bil′hed′), *n.* **1** a sheet of paper with a name and business address printed at the top and a blank space below for adding a bill. **2** the name and business address printed at the top of such a sheet of paper.

bill|hook (bil′hu̇k′), *n.* a tool for cutting or pruning, having a curved blade with a hooked end.

bil|liard (bil′yərd), *adj., n.* **—*adj.*** of or for billiards: *a billiard table.*
—*n.* **1** a point made in billiards by successively striking the two other balls with the cue ball. **2** *U.S. Informal.* a carom.

billiard ball, a ball used in billiards, originally made of ivory but now usually made of a hard, heavy plastic compound.

bil|liard|ist (bil′yər dist), *n.* a billiard player.

***bil|liards** (bil′yərdz), *n.* **1** a game played with billiard balls on a special table with a raised, cushioned edge. A long stick (cue) is used to hit the balls. **2** any one of several related games, especially pocket billiards or pool. [< Middle French *billard* (diminutive) < Old French *bille* log, trunk]

***billiards**
definition 1

bill|ing (bil′ing), *n.* **1a** the order in which the names of performers or acts are listed in a playbill or similar advertisement. **b** the position in such a listing: *top billing.* **2** the total amount billed to customers or clients for goods or services, usually within a specified period.

billing machine, a business machine combining functions of a typewriter and a calculating machine, used for making out bills and keeping records.

bil|lings|gate (bil′ingz gāt′; *especially British* bil′ingz git), *n.* vulgar, abusive language. [< *Billingsgate*, a fish market in London, where abusive language was common]

bil|lion (bil′yən), *n., adj.* **1** (in the U.S., Canada, and France) one thousand millions; 1,000,000,000. **2** (in Great Britain and Germany) one million millions; 1,000,000,000,000. [< French *billion* < *bi-* two (that is, to the second power) + (mi)*llion*]
▶In recent years **billion** has been increasingly used in Great Britain in the sense of one thousand millions, probably due to the influence of American usage.

bil|lion|aire (bil′yə nãr′), *n.* **1** an extremely wealthy person who has a billion or more dollars, francs, marks, pounds, or the like. **2** any very wealthy person. [American English]

bil|lionth (bil′yənth), *adj., n.* **—*adj.*** **1** coming last in a series of a billion. **2** being one of a billion equal parts. **—*n.*** **1** the billionth member of a series. **2** one of a billion equal parts.

Bill|jim (bil′jim′), *n.* (in Australia) a nickname for the average Australian.

bill|man (bil′mən), *n., pl.* **-men.** **1** a soldier armed with a bill. **2** a laborer using a billhook or bill.

bill of adventure, a bill stating that a merchant is handling goods on behalf of another whose risk it is.

bill of attainder, an act of a lawmaking body that deprives a specific person or persons of property and civil rights, without benefit of judicial trial, because of a sentence of death or outlawry. Such acts are forbidden by the Constitution of the United States.

bill of credit, (in U.S. history) a paper issued by a state, and based on its own credit, to be circulated as money, forbidden by the Constitution.

bill of entry, a written account of goods entered at a custom house, whether imported or intended for export.

bill of exceptions, a list of persons appealing against a judge's decision in certain Scottish courts.

bill of exchange, a written order to a person, bank, or firm to pay a stated sum of money to a specified person; a draft.

bill of fare, a menu.

bill of goods, a list of the goods sold, with the price for each item in a shipment of merchandise.
sell a bill of goods, *Slang.* to mislead or seek to mislead by a specious or false argument, set of facts, or other deception: *I don't mean that these staff members were selling their members a bill of goods about the labor movement* (Harper's).

bill of health, a certificate stating whether or not there are infectious diseases on a ship or in a port. A bill of health is given to a captain when his ship sails.
clean bill of health, a a bill of health certifying total absence of infection. **b** *Informal, Figurative.* a good or favorable report, based on the past record or qualifications of a person or thing: *Service stations selling a single brand of petrol will be given a clean bill of health by the commission* (London Times).

bill of indictment, a detailed written statement presented to a grand jury formally accusing a person of a crime.

bill of lading, a written receipt or contract given by a ship, railroad, express agency, or other carrier, showing a list of goods delivered to it for transportation; waybill.

bill of mortality, *British.* an official return of the births and deaths within a district; weekly bill.

bill of particulars, **1** a written statement giving the demands and claims made by one side of a lawsuit. **2** a detailed statement.

bill of rights, **1** a statement of the fundamental rights belonging to the citizens of a country. **2** any statement of rights or privileges granted to or claimed by a group or class of people.

Bill of Rights, **1** the first ten amendments to the Constitution of the United States, adopted on December 15, 1791, which include a declaration of fundamental rights held by U.S. citizens. **2** an English statute passed in 1689 which confirmed the rights and liberties of English subjects, and settled the succession of the crown in William of Orange and Mary.

bill of sale, a written statement transferring ownership of something from the seller to the buyer.

bill of sight, a record of goods imported, the exact nature of which is not known by the merchant.

bil|lon (bil′ən), *n.* **1** an alloy of gold or silver with much copper or tin. **2** a coin made of such an alloy. [< Old French *billon* (originally) ingot]

bil|low (bil′ō), *n., v.* **—*n.*** **1** a great swelling wave or surge of the sea: *The billows of the Atlantic dash high on the rocks during a storm.* **2** any great wave or swelling mass of smoke, flame, sound, or the like: *Billows of smoke were belching from the chimney.* SYN: undulation.
—*v.i.* **1** to rise or roll in big waves; surge: *The wind made the lake waters billow onto the beach.* **2** to swell out; bulge: *The sheets on the line billow in the wind.* SYN: undulate.
[< Scandinavian (compare Old Icelandic *bylgja*)]

bil|lowed (bil′ōd), *adj.* puffed up or out; fluffy: *a billowed skirt.*

bil|low|y (bil′ō ē), *adj.*, **-low|i|er, -low|i|est.** **1** rising or rolling in big waves. **2** swelling out; bulging. **—bil′low|i|ness,** *n.*

bill|post|er (bil′pōs′tər), *n.* a worker who puts up advertisements or notices in public places.

bill|post|ing (bil′pōs′ting), *n.* the posting of advertisements or notices in public places.

bill|stick|er (bil′stik′ər), *n.* = billposter.

bill|stick|ing (bil′stik′ing), *n.* = billposting.

bil|ly[1] (bil′ē), *n., pl.* **-lies.** **1** *U.S.* a policeman's club or stick; nightstick; truncheon. **2** any stick or club. **3** a billy goat. **4** Also, **billycan. a** (in Australia) a kettle, can, or pot for making tea or for cooking. **b** (in industrial Britain) a can with a lid and handle for carrying tea. [< *Billy*, nickname for William]

bil|ly[2] (bil′ē), *n., pl.* **-lies.** *Scottish.* a companion. [origin obscure]

bil|ly|boy (bil′ē boi′), *n. British.* a flat-bottomed barge especially built for river navigation. [origin uncertain]

bil|ly|can (bil′ē kan′), *n.* = billy[1] (def. 4).

billy cart, (in Australia) any cart, often a box on wheels, used by children to ride or coast on.

billy club, *U.S.* a policeman's club; billy.

bil|ly|cock (bil′ē kok′), *n. British Informal.* a derby hat; bowler. [< *bully-cocked* worn acock, as by a bully[1]]

billy goat, *Informal.* a male goat.

bil|ly-o or **bil|ly-oh** (bil′ē ō′), *n. British Slang.*
like billy-o or **like billy-oh**, at full force; vigorously: *to shout like billy-o.*
[origin unknown]

bi|lo|bate (bī lō′bāt), *adj.* having or divided into two lobes: *a bilobate leaf.*

bi|lo|bat|ed (bī lō′bā tid), *adj.* = bilobate.

bi|lobed (bī lōbd′), *adj.* = bilobate.

bi|lob|u|lar (bī lob′yə lər), *adj.* having two small lobes.

bi|lo|ca|tion (bī′lō kā′shən), *n.* being in two places at the same time.

bi|loc|u|lar (bī lok′yə lər), *adj.* having two locules, chambers, or cells.

bi|loc|u|late (bī lok′yə lit, -lāt), *adj.* = bilocular.

Bi|lox|i (bə lok′sē), *n.* a member of a tribe of Siouan Indians.

bil|sted (bil′sted), *n.* the sweet gum tree. [American English; origin unknown]

bil|tong (bil′tong), *n.* (in South Africa) strips of lean meat (of antelope, buffalo, etc.) dried in the sun. [< Afrikaans *biltong* < *bil* buttock + *tong* tongue]

bim (bim), *n. U.S. Slang.* **1** a woman. **2** an undignified woman: *a beery old bim.* [short for bimbo]

Bim (bim), *n.* (in Barbados) an informal name for a Barbadian.

bi|mah (bē′mə), *n.* = almemar. [< Yiddish *bime* < Russian *bima* bema < Greek *bêma* step]

bim|a|nal (bim′ə nəl, bī mā′-), *adj.* = bimanous.

bi|mane (bī′mān), *n.* a two-handed animal.

bim|a|nous (bim′ə nəs, bī mā′-), *adj. Zoology.* having two hands. [< New Latin *bimanus* (with English *-ous*) < Latin *bi-* two + *manus* hand]

bi|man|u|al (bī man′yu̇ əl), *adj.* involving the use of both hands. **—bi|man′u|al|ly,** *adv.*

bim|ba|shi (bim bä′shē), *n.* **1** a Turkish military captain or commander. **2** (in colonial Egypt) an English officer in the service of the Khedive. [< Turkish *binbaşi* (literally) head of a thousand]

bim|bo (bim′bō), *n., pl.* **-bos** or **-boes**, *adj. Slang.* **—*n.*** **1** a stupid or ineffectual person. **2** a man or boy; fellow (used disparagingly). **3** = bim. **—*adj.*** of, for, or by bimbos; stupid; unintelligent: *The era of the big three networks and . . . "bimbo programming" is passing* (Desmond Smith). [< Italian *bimbo* baby, related to *bambino*]

bi|men|sal (bī men′səl), *adj.* happening once in two months; bimonthly.

bi|mes|tri|al (bī mes′trē əl), *adj.* **1** lasting for two months. **2** happening every two months; bimonthly. [< Latin *bimēstris* (< *bi-* two + *mēnsis* month) + English *-al*[1]]

bi|met|al (bī met′əl), *n., adj.* **—*n.*** something consisting of two different metals: [*In*] *this bimetal . . . the copper is inseparably bonded to the steel* (Science News Letter). **—*adj.*** = bimetallic.

bi|me|tal|lic (bī′mə tal′ik), *adj.* **1** of or having to do with two different metals. **2** of bimetallism; based on bimetallism.

bimetallic strip, two metals with different rates of expansion, fastened in a strip, used to control or measure temperature, as in an oven.

bi|met|al|lism (bī met′ə liz əm), *n.* the use of two metals, especially gold and silver, as the basis of the money system of a nation. The amount in weight of each metal necessary to make coins having the same money value is fixed by law.
—bi|met′al|list, *n.*

bi|mil|len|ni|al (bī′mə len′ē əl), *adj., n.* **—*adj.*** of or having to do with a bimillennium.
—*n.* = bimillennium.

bi|mil|len|ni|um (bī′mə len′ē əm), *n., pl.* **-len|ni|ums, -len|ni|a** (-len′ē ə). a period of 2,000 years.

bi|mo|dal (bī mō′dəl), *adj. Statistics.* having two modes: *a bimodal distribution.*

bi|mo|dal|i|ty (bī′mō dal′ə tē), *n.* the fact or quality of being bimodal.

bi|mo|lec|u|lar (bī′mə lek′yə lər), *adj.* having to do with or formed from two molecules.

bi|month|ly (bī munth′lē), *adj., adv., n., pl.* **-lies.**
—*adj.* **1** happening or appearing once every two months: *A bimonthly magazine is issued six times a year.* **2** happening or appearing twice a month; semimonthly: *The bimonthly meetings are on the first and third Wednesdays of each month.*
—*adv.* **1** once every two months: *The magazine is issued bimonthly.* **2** twice a month; semimonthly: *The meetings are held bimonthly.*
—*n.* a magazine or other periodical that is published once every two months.

bi|morph (bī′môrf), *n.*, or **bimorph cell**, a rigid structure of two quartz or other crystals cemented together, and caused to bend when a potential makes one crystal expand and the other contract. A bimorph is used to activate loudspeakers and various electronic devices. [< *bi-* two + Greek *morphē* form]

bin (bin), *n., v.,* **binned, bin|ning.** **—*n.*** **1** a box or enclosed place for holding or storing grain, coal, or similar things: *The baker emptied several bags of flour into a bin.* SYN: crib. **2** *British.* a dustbin (ashcan). **3** *Slang.* = loony bin.
—*v.t.* to place or store in a bin.
[Old English *binn* manger]

bin-, *prefix.* form of **bi-** before vowels, as in *binal.*

bi|nal (bī′nəl), *adj.* twin; double; twofold.

bi|na|ry (bī′nər ē), *adj., n., pl.* **-ries.** **—*adj.*** consisting of two; involving two: *a binary number.*
—*n.* **1** a set of two things; pair. **2** = binary star.
[< Late Latin *bīnārius* < Latin *bīnī* two at a time]

binary arithmetic, = binary notation.

binary coded decimal, a system of coding numbers in binary units used in programming computers and in higher mathematics. Each decimal digit is represented by four binary digits. *Example:* 234 is represented in binary coded decimal by 0010 0011 0100.

Pronunciation Key: hat, āge, cãre, fär; let, ēqual, tėrm; it, īce; hot, ōpen, ôrder; oil, out; cup, pu̇t, rüle; child; long; thin; ᴛʜen; zh, measure; ə represents a in about, e in taken, i in pencil, o in lemon, u in circus.

binary color, a color, such as orange, violet, or green, made by mixing two primary colors; secondary color.
binary compound, *Chemistry.* a compound of two elements, or of an element and a radical, or of two radicals.
binary digit, **1** either of the digits 0 or 1 used in binary notation. **2** = bit[4].
binary fission, the division or splitting of a cell, especially a protozoan, into two equal parts.
binary form, *Music.* a movement based upon two subjects or one divided into two distinct or contrasted main sections.
binary granite, a variety of granite composed of quartz and feldspar; aplite.
***binary notation**, a system of counting (arithmetical notation) using only two symbols, 0 and 1, rather than the ordinary ten symbols, 0 to 9. Each digit (place value) is therefore written as 0 or 1 or some combination of 0 and 1.

***binary notation**

binary scale or base 2:	decimal scale or base 10:
1	1
10	2
11	3
100	4
101	5
110	6
111	7
1000	8
1001	9
1010	10

binary opposition, *Linguistics.* a distinguishing or significant contrast between two speech components: *The existence of such a binary opposition as n:ng in English is proved by the use of such different pairs of words as kin and king . . . winning and winging. Clearly n and ng . . . are two phonemes in English* (Simeon Potter).
binary scale, = binary notation.
binary star, a pair of stars that revolve around a common center of gravity. Approximately 40,000 binary stars are now known.
binary system, **1** = binary notation. **2** = binary star. **3** any chemical, mechanical, or electronic system having or based on two components.
***bi|nate**[1] (bī′nāt), *adj.* growing in pairs; double. [< New Latin *binatus* < Latin *bīnī* two at a time]

***binate**[1] binate leaves

bi|nate[2] (bī′nāt), *v.i.*, **-nat|ed, -nat|ing.** to say two Masses on the same day. [< Late Latin *bīnatim* doubly] —**bi|na′tion**, *n.*
bi|na|tion|al (bī nash′ə nəl, -nash′nəl), *adj.* of or dealing with two nations, their cultures, languages, policies, or other features.
bi|na|tion|al|ism (bī nash′ə nə liz′əm, -nash′nə-), *n.* the principle or policy of keeping a country bicultural and bilingual; biculturalism.
bin|au|ral (bin ôr′əl, bīn-), *adj.* **1** having to do with or using two speakers, or sources of sound reproduction or transmission, to give a three-dimensional auditory effect; stereophonic: *binaural broadcasting, binaural recording.* **2** of or for both ears: *a binaural stethoscope.* **3** having two ears. [< Latin *bīnī* double + English *aural*[2]] —**bin|au′ral|ly**, *adv.*
bind (bīnd), *v.*, **bound, bind|ing,** *n.* —*v.t.* **1** to tie together; hold together; fasten: *She bound the package with a tight rope. The packing case was bound with metal tape. The prisoners were bound in chains.* SYN: connect, attach. **2** to cause to stick together: *Tar will bind gravel or cinders.* **3** to fasten (sheets of paper) into a cover; put a cover on (a book): *Those loose pages were bound into a small book.* **4** to hold by some force; restrain: *Vines are binding the flowers and choking their growth.* (*Figurative.*) *The vow that binds too strictly snaps itself* (Tennyson). **5** *Figurative.* to hold by a promise, love, duty, or law; oblige: *A doctor is in duty bound to help the sick.* SYN: obligate, constrain. **6** to put under legal obligation: *Parents are bound to send their children to school. He was bound over to keep the peace.* **7** to put under legal obligation to serve as an apprentice: *I have bound him out to be a shoemaker* (Sir Richard Steele). **8** to make (a bargain, contract, or other arrangement) final so that it must be carried out: *A ten dollar deposit bound the bargain.* **9** to put a bandage on: *The nurse will bind up your cut.* **10** to put a band or wreath around; gird; encircle: *a fillet binds her hair* (Alexander Pope). **11** to put a border or edge on to strengthen or ornament: *She bound the sleeves of her dress with red ribbon.* **12** = constipate.
—*v.i.* **1a** to stick together: *The gravel and cinders will not bind without tar.* **b** to become stuck fast; jam: *The piston will bind without oil.* **2** to compel morally or legally; have compelling force: *A contract always binds.* **3** *British Slang.* to complain.
—*n.* **1** anything that binds or ties; band; tie. **2** *Music.* a tie; slur. **3** a twining or climbing plant stem. **4** *Especially U.S. Informal.* a difficult situation; dilemma; predicament: *They are anxious to avoid an embarrassing and awkward bind* (Wall Street Journal).
bind oneself to, to agree to (something); establish an association with: *A landed proprietor may bind himself to a future payment* (Thomas Chalmers).
[Old English *bindan*]
bind|er (bīn′dər), *n.* **1** a person who binds books. **2** anything that ties or holds together: *Tar is used as a binder on some gravel roads.* **3** a cover for a loose-leaf notebook. **4** a machine that cuts stalks of grain and ties them in bundles. **5** *U.S.* a written agreement or amount of money given as a pledge to carry out some obligation. **6** the inner wrapper of a cigar, used to hold the filler in shape.
binder or **binder's twine**, a strong cord with a rough surface.
bind|er|y (bīn′dər ē, -drē), *n., pl.* **-er|ies.** a place where books are bound; bookbindery. [American English < *bind* + *-ery*]
bind|ing (bīn′ding), *n., adj.* —*n.* **1** the covering of a book. **2** a strip protecting or ornamenting an edge. Binding is used on the seams of dresses. **3** the set of fastenings on a ski, usually consisting of a metal piece into which the toe slips, a strap, and a spring that grasps the heel. **4** a band of masonry and brickwork.
—*adj.* **1** that binds, fastens, or connects. **2** *Figurative.* having force or power to hold to a promise, duty, or law; obligatory. A contract is a binding agreement. **3** constricting; astringent; styptic. —**bind′ing|ly**, *adv.* —**bind′ing|ness**, *n.*
binding energy, the energy necessary to break a molecule, atom, or nucleus into its smaller component parts.
bin|dle (bin′dəl), *n. U.S. Slang.* a bundle of clothing, toilet articles, or other possessions, usually tied to a stick which a hobo carries over his shoulder. [perhaps < *bundle*]
bin|dle|stiff (bin′dəl stif′), *n. U.S. Slang.* = hobo. [American English < *bindle*]
bind|weed (bīnd′wēd′), *n.* a plant with long stems that twine around fences, trees, or other plants. It belongs to the morning-glory family.
bine (bīn), *n.* **1** a twining, slender stem of a climbing plant, especially of the hop. **2** any bindweed. **3** = woodbine (defs. 1, 3). **4** any one of several varieties of the hop. [< *bind*, noun]
Bi|net-Si|mon test or **scale** (bi nā′sī′mən), an individual intelligence test first published in 1905 and subsequently revised, used in schools, the armed forces, and other institutions, for determining the mental age of children or adults by means of their performance of tasks and answers to questions. [< Alfred *Binet*, 1857-1911, and Théodore *Simon*, 1873-1964, French psychologists, who devised it]
Bi|net test or **scale** (bi nā′), = Binet-Simon test.
bing[1] (bing), *n., v., adv., interj.* —*n.* a sharp, ringing sound. —*v.i.* to make such a sound. —*adv.* with such a sound. —*interj.* the sound itself. [imitative]
bing[2] (bing), *n. North English Dialect.* a heap or pile. [< Scandinavian (compare Old Icelandic *bingr*)]
binge (binj), *n. Informal.* **1** a heavy drinking bout; drunken spree. **2** a bout or spree of indulging in anything. [< dialectal *binge* to soak]
bin|gle (bing′gəl), *n. Baseball Slang.* = base hit.
bin|go (bing′gō), *n., interj.* —*n.* a game in which each player covers the numbers on his card as they are called out. The player who is first to cover a column of numbers is the winner. Bingo is a game of chance derived from lotto, similar to keno, played for money or prizes.
—*interj. Slang.* an exclamation indicating suddenness or a sharp impact: *Bingo! . . . what a wallop* (Time).
[American English; origin uncertain]
bin|i|o|dide (bin ī′ə dīd, bīn-; -did), *n.* a compound containing two atoms of iodine with another element or radical. [< *bin-* + *iodide*]
bi|nit (bī′nit), *n.* = binary digit. [< *bin*(ary dig)*it*]
bin|man (bin′mən), *n., pl.* **-men.** *British.* a garbage or refuse collector; dustman.
***bin|na|cle** (bin′ə kəl), *n.* a box or stand that contains a ship's compass. The binnacle is placed near the helm. [alteration of *bittacle* < Spanish *bitácula*, or Portuguese *bitácola*, learned borrowings from Latin *habitāculum* dwelling place < *habitāre* dwell]

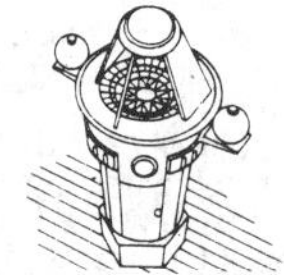
***binnacle**

bin|o|cle (bin′ə kəl), *n.* a telescope or field glass for both eyes; binoculars; opera glasses. [< French *binocle* < Latin *bīnī* two at a time + *oculī* eyes]
bi|noc|u|lar (bə nok′yə lər, bī-), *adj., n.* —*adj.* **1** for both eyes at once: *a binocular microscope.* **2** using both eyes at once: *Most animals have binocular vision.* —*n.* any binocular instrument. [< New Latin *binoculus* a kind of double telescope (< Latin *bīnī* two at a time + *oculī* eyes) + English *-ar*] —**bin|oc′u|lar|ly**, *adv.*
bin|oc|u|lar|i|ty (bə nok′yə lar′ə tē, bī-), *n.* the simultaneous use of both eyes.
bi|noc|u|lars (bə nok′yə lərz, bī-), *n.pl.* a double telescope joined as a unit for use with both eyes at once. Field glasses and opera glasses are binoculars.
bi|no|mi|al (bī nō′mē əl), *n., adj.* —*n.* **1** an expression in algebra consisting of two terms. $8a + 2b$ is a binomial. **2** the scientific name of a plant or animal, consisting of two terms. *Homo sapiens* is a binomial. The first term indicates the genus and the second the species.
—*adj.* **1** consisting of two terms. **2** consisting of two names. **3** having to do with binomials.
[< New Latin *binomium*, neuter of Late Latin *binōmius* having two names (< Latin *bi-* two + *nōmen* name) + English *-al*[1]] —**bi|no′mi|al|ly**, *adv.*
binomial distribution, a distribution discovered in the 1600's, giving the statistical probability of any particular number of recurrences of one of two possible results, such as heads or tails, in a given number of trials, each trial offering equal chances.
bi|no|mi|al|ism (bī nō′mē ə liz′əm), *n. Zoology, Botany.* the binomial method of nomenclature.
binomial nomenclature, the system of classifying plants and animals by two names: their genus and species.
binomial theorem, the algebraic theorem, invented by Sir Isaac Newton, for raising a binomial to any power. *Example:* $(a + b)^2 = a^2 + 2ab + b^2$.
bi|nom|i|nal (bī nom′ə nəl), *adj.* having or using two names, as of genus and species in scientific nomenclature.
bint (bint), *n. British Slang.* a girl or woman. [< Arabic *bint* daughter]
bin|tu|rong (bin′tyə rong), *n.* a civet with a prehensile tail, found in southern Asia; bearcat. [< Malay *binturong*]
bi|nu|cle|ar (bī nü′klē ər, -nyü′-), *adj.* = binucleate.
bi|nu|cle|ate (bī nü′klē it, -āt; -nyü′-), *adj.* having two nuclei, as a cell.
bi|nu|cle|at|ed (bī nü′klē ā′tid, -nyü′-), *adj.* = binucleate.
bi|o (bī′ō), *n., pl.* **bi|os.** *Informal.* biography.
bio-, *combining form.* **1** life; living things: *Biology = science of life or living things.* **2** biological: *Biochemistry = biological chemistry.* [< Greek *bíos* life, way of life]
bi|o|ac|tive (bī′ō ak′tiv), *adj.* having an effect on living matter: *Inorganic mercury is converted to the bioactive, methylated form by fungi and bacteria in natural aerated waterways* (Science News).
bi|o-aer|a|tion (bī′ō ãr ā′shən), *n.* the purification of sewage by aeration in the presence of certain bacteria.
bi|o|as|say (bī′ō ə sā′, -as′ā), *n., v.* —*n.* the determination of the strength of a drug by comparing its effects on a test animal, such as a rat, with those of a standard preparation. —*v.t.* to determine (the strength of a drug) by bioassay.
bi|o|as|tro|nau|tic (bī′ō as′trə nô′tik), *adj.* having to do with bioastronautics.
bi|o|as|tro|nau|tics (bī′ō as′trə nô′tiks), *n.* the science that deals with the biological aspects of travel in outer space.
bi|o|a|vail|a|bil|i|ty (bī′ō ə vā′lə bil′ə tē), *n.* the efficacy of a drug at the site of disease or malfunction in the body: *Researchers have been giving a lot of attention lately to what they call bioavailability—how much of the original drug administered is delivered undiminished or unchanged to*

the site of the body where it is needed (London Sunday Times).

bi|o|bib|li|o|graph|i|cal (bī′ō bib′lē ə graf′ə kəl), *adj.* of or having to do with biobibliography.

bi|o|bib|li|og|ra|phy (bī′ō bib′lē og′rə fē), *n., pl.* **-phies.** a bibliography of the life and writings of an author, or of his literary interests.

bi|o|blast (bī′ō blast), *n. Biology.* **1** a formative cell. **2** a hypothetical unit of protoplasm practically equivalent to a biophore. [< *bio-* + Greek *blastós* germ, sprout]

bi|o|blas|tic (bī′ō blas′tik), *adj.* of or having to do with bioblasts.

bi|o|cat|a|lyst (bī′ō kat′ə list), *n.* a substance which produces a chemical reaction in a living body, such as a coenzyme, vitamin, or hormone.

bi|o|cat|a|lyt|ic (bī′ō kat′ə lit′ik), *adj.* having to do with or caused by biocatalysts.

bi|o|cel|late (bī os′ə lāt, bī′ō sel′it), *adj.* marked with two small, eyelike spots, as a butterfly's wings. [< *bi-* two + *ocellate*]

bi|o|ce|nose (bī′ō sē′nōs), *n.* the interrelationship among organisms that inhabit a specific geographical area and their relationship to that environment. [< New Latin *biocenosis* < Greek *bíos* life + *koínōsis* a sharing < *koinós* common]

bi|o|cen|tric (bī′ō sen′trik), *adj.* centering in life; regarding or treating life as a central fact.

bi|o|chem|i|cal (bī′ō kem′ə kəl), *adj., n.* —*adj.* of or having to do with biochemistry.
—*n.* a biochemical substance. —**bi′o|chem′i|cal|ly,** *adv.*

biochemical oxygen demand, a measure of the amount of oxygen used by bacteria to decompose organic matter in waste water. *Abbr:* BOD

bi|o|chem|ist (bī′ō kem′ist), *n.* an expert in biochemistry.

bi|o|chem|is|try (bī′ō kem′ə strē), *n.* **1** the science that deals with the chemical processes of living animals and plants; biological chemistry. **2** biochemical composition or characteristics: *The virus has developed the capacity to change its biochemistry* (New York Times Magazine).

bi|o|chip (bī′ō chip′), *n.* a microcircuit whose components consist of organic molecules instead of electronic circuits: *Some molecules that could be used are so small that a three-dimensional biochip occupying 1 cubic centimeter (0.06 cubic inch) could be crowded with an astonishing million billion molecular switches* (Arthur Fisher).

bi|o|ci|dal (bī′ə sī′dəl), *adj.* destroying life or living things: *biocidal radiation.*

bi|o|cide (bī′ə sīd), *n.* **1** any substance poisonous to life, such as a pesticide. **2** destruction of life or living things.

bi|o|cli|mat|ic (bī′ō klī mat′ik), *adj.* of or having to do with bioclimatology.

bi|o|cli|ma|tol|o|gy (bī′ō klī′mə tol′ə jē), *n.* the science that deals with the effects of climate on human beings, animals, and plants.

bi|o|com|pat|i|bil|i|ty (bī′ō kəm pat′ə bil′ə tē), *n.* the condition of being biocompatible.

bi|o|com|pat|i|ble (bī′ō kəm pat′ə bəl), *adj.* biologically compatible, especially so as not to cause immunological rejection.

bi|o|con|ver|sion (bī′ō kən vėr′zhən, -shən), *n.* the conversion of biological waste, garbage, and plant material into energy, fertilizer, and other useful products.

bi|o|cy|ber|net|ics (bī′ō sī′bər net′iks), *n.* the study of automatic control and communication in living systems.

bi|o|de|grad|a|bil|i|ty (bī′ō di grā də bil′ə tē), *n.* biodegradable quality or condition.

bi|o|de|grad|a|ble (bī′ō di grā′də bəl), *adj.* that is susceptible of being decomposed, especially by bacterial action: *biodegradable detergents.*

bi|o|de|grade (bī′ō di grād′), *v.t.,* **-grad|ed, -grad|ing.** to break down (a detergent or other substance), especially by bacterial action. —**bi′o|deg′ra|da′tion,** *n.*

bi|o|dy|nam|ic (bī′ō dī nam′ik, -di-), *adj.* of or having to do with biodynamics.

bi|o|dy|nam|i|cal (bī′ō dī nam′ə kəl, -di-), *adj.* = biodynamic.

bi|o|dy|nam|ics (bī′ō dī nam′iks, -di-), *n.* the biological study of vital force or energy, or of the action of living organisms.

bi|o|dyne (bī′ə dīn), *n.* a substance, similar in effect to a hormone, which is produced by an injured cell to aid its recovery by promoting respiration, growth, and reproduction. [< *bio-* + Greek *dýnamis* power]

bi|o|e|col|o|gy (bī′ō ē kol′ə jē), *n.* the branch of ecology dealing with plant and animal interrelationships.

bi|o|e|lec|tric (bī′ō i lek′trik), *adj.* of or having to do with bioelectricity.

bi|o|e|lec|tri|cal (bī′ō i lek′trə kəl), *adj.* = bioelectric.

bi|o|e|lec|tric|i|ty (bī′ō i lek′tris′ə tē, -ē′ek-), *n.* electricity which originates in living matter.

bi|o|e|lec|tro|gen|e|sis (bī′ō i lek′trō jen′ə sis), *n.* production of electrical energy by an organism.

bi|o|e|lec|tron|ics (bī′ō i lek tron′iks), *n.* **1** the application of electronics to the study and control of biological functions and processes. **2** the application of the biological sciences to the study and development of electronic systems or processes, as in the creation of biochips: *Bioelectronics incorporates the development of functional neuronal interfaces which permit contiguity between neural tissue and . . . computing technology* (Christopher R. Lowe).

bi|o|en|er|get|ics (bī′ō en ər jet′iks), *n.* the biological study of energy in living systems.

bi|o|en|er|gy (bī′ō en′ər jē), *n.* energy obtained from biomass.

bi|o|en|gi|neer (bī′ō en′jə nir′), *n.* a person who specializes in bioengineering.

bi|o|en|gi|neer|ing (bī′ō en′jə nir′ing), *n.* the application of various principles of engineering to the study and control of biological processes, structures, and products; biomedical engineering.

bi|o|eth|ics (bī′ō eth′iks), *n.* the study of the ethical problems involved in biological research, such as the ethics of genetic engineering.

bi|o|fa|ci|es (bī′ō fā′shē ēz), *n.* the sum of the fossil deposits of animal life in a stratum of rock, silt, or ice. [< *bio-* + Latin *faciēs* forms]

bi|o|feed|back (bī′ō fēd′bak), *n.* **1** a method of monitoring one's own brain waves by the use of a portable electroencephalograph, especially for the purpose of controlling the alpha rhythm. **2** a similar method used to monitor and control one's own blood pressure, heart rate, blood flow, muscle tensions, and the like.

bi|o|fla|vo|noid (bī′ō flā′və noid), *n.* any one of a complex of substances, present in citrus fruits and other plant foods, that promote capillary resistance to hemorrhaging; vitamin P.

biog., **1** biographer. **2** biographical. **3** biography.

bi|o|gas (bī′ō gas′), *n.* a mixture of methane and carbon dioxide produced by bacterial action on organic waste matter, used as a form of fuel.

bi|o|gen (bī′ə jən), *n.* a hypothetical molecule of protein, at one time thought to be the basic cellular constituent of living substance.

bi|o|gen|e|sis (bī′ō jen′ə sis), *n.* **1** the theory that living things can be produced only by other living things. **2** the genesis or production of living things from other living things. **3** the history of the evolution of living organisms. [(coined in 1870 by Thomas Huxley) < *bio-* life + *genesis*]

bi|o|ge|net|ic (bī′ō jə net′ik), *adj.* of or having to do with biogenesis. —**bi′o|ge|net′i|cal|ly,** *adv.*

bi|o|ge|net|i|cal (bī′ō jə net′ə kəl), *adj.* = biogenetic.

bi|o|gen|ic (bī′ō jen′ik), *adj.* produced by living organisms, as certain marine sediments.

bi|og|e|nous (bī oj′ə nəs), *adj. Biology.* **1** coming from living things. **2** giving life.

bi|og|e|ny (bī oj′ə nē), *n.* = biogenesis.

bi|o|ge|o|chem|i|cal (bī′ō jē′ō kem′ə kəl), *adj.* of or having to do with biogeochemistry.

bi|o|ge|o|chem|is|try (bī′ō jē′ō kem′ə strē), *n.* the study of the effect of the earth's chemical composition upon living things.

bi|o|ge|og|ra|pher (bī′ō jē og′rə fər), *n.* a person who studies biogeography.

bi|o|ge|o|graph|ic (bī′ō jē′ə graf′ik), *adj.* = biogeographical.

bi|o|ge|o|graph|i|cal (bī′ō jē′ə graf′ə kəl), *adj.* of or having to do with biogeography.

bi|o|ge|og|ra|phy (bī′ō jē og′rə fē), *n.* the science of the distribution of animals and plants.

bi|o|graph[1] (bī′ə graf, -gräf), *v.t.* = biographize. [back formation < *biographer*]

bi|o|graph[2] (bī′ə graf, -gräf), *n.* an early form of movie projector. [< *bio-* + (cinemato)*graph*]

bi|og|ra|phee (bī og′rə fē′, bi-), *n.* the subject of a biography.

bi|og|ra|pher (bī og′rə fər, bi-), *n.* a person who writes someone's biography.

bi|o|graph|ic (bī′ə graf′ik), *adj.* = biographical.

bi|o|graph|i|cal (bī′ə graf′ə kəl), *adj.* **1** of a person's life: *biographical details.* **2** of or having to do with biography. —**bi′o|graph′i|cal|ly,** *adv.*

bi|og|ra|phize (bī og′rə fīz, bi-), *v.t.,* **-phized, -phiz|ing.** to write a biography of (a person).

bi|og|ra|phy (bī og′rə fē, bi-), *n., pl.* **-phies.** **1** the written story of a person's life: *After reading a biography of Lincoln he was able to tell many stories about the President.* **2** *Figurative: Don MacKinnon . . . knew the biography of every piece of ground in the area* (Maclean's). **3** part of literature which consists of biographies: *Read . . . nothing but biography, for that is life without theory* (Benjamin Disraeli). [< Late Greek *biographiā* < *bíos* life + *gráphein* write]

bi|o|haz|ard (bī′ō haz′ərd), *n.* any danger or peril resulting from biological research.

bi|o|herm (bī′ō hėrm), *n.* a rock formation mainly built up by marine organisms, such as coral, overlaid or enclosed by another rock. [< *bio-* + Greek *hérma* sunken rock]

bi|o|in|stru|men|ta|tion (bī′ō in′strə men tā′shən), *n.* the use of biosensors and other instruments for recording and transmitting data on the bodily changes of persons or animals.

biol., **1** biological. **2** biologist. **3** biology.

bi|o|log|ic (bī′ə loj′ik), *adj., n.* = biological.

bi|o|log|i|cal (bī′ə loj′ə kəl), *adj., n.* —*adj.* **1** of plant and animal life; connected with the processes of life: *biological science.* **2** having to do with biology: *a biological laboratory.* **3** for use in or prepared by a biological laboratory: *biological serums.* **4** involving the use of living organisms, such as disease germs or viruses, against an enemy: *biological weapons.*
—*n.* a drug or other product prepared from living organisms. —**bi′o|log′i|cal|ly,** *adv.*

biological clock, a mechanism in plants and animals which controls the rhythm of functions and activities, such as photosynthesis in a plant.

biological control, the reduction of plant or insect pests by parasitic organisms or animals, such as the control of mosquitoes by birds.

biological engineering, the artificial selection of different strains of a plant or animal species to improve the structure, function, or yield of an organism, especially a plant or animal of agricultural importance.

biological half-life, the time required for a substance deposited in a living organism, tissue, or organ to lose half its initial value through elimination by biological processes.

biological warfare, warfare in which disease germs and other harmful organisms are used against persons, animals, or crops; germ warfare.

bi|ol|o|gism (bī ol′ə jiz əm), *n.* **1** a doctrine insisting upon the interpretation of all human experience from the biological point of view or by biological methods. **2** support of such a doctrine.

bi|ol|o|gist (bī ol′ə jist), *n.* a person who studies biology.

bi|ol|o|gize (bī ol′ə jīz), *v.i., v.t.,* **-gized, -giz|ing.** **1** to study biologically. **2** *Obsolete.* to hypnotize.

bi|ol|o|gy (bī ol′ə jē), *n.* **1** the science of living things; study of plant and animal life. Specialists in biology study the origin, structure, functioning, activities, and distribution of plant and animal life. Botany, zoology, and ecology are branches of biology. *Abbr:* biol. **2** the plant and animal life of a particular area or region. **3** the biological facts about a plant or animal. [< *bio-* + *-logy*]

bi|o|lu|mi|nes|cence (bī′ō lü′mə nes′əns), *n.* phosphorescence or other emission of light by living organisms. Organisms with this property include fireflies, jellyfish, and some mushrooms.

bi|o|lu|mi|nes|cent (bī′ō lü′mə nes′ənt), *adj.* showing bioluminescence; phosphorescent.

bi|ol|y|sis (bī ol′ə sis), *n.* the dissolution of a living being; death.

bi|o|lyt|ic (bī′ə lit′ik), *adj.* **1** of or having to do with biolysis. **2** resembling biolysis.

bi|o|mag|ni|fi|ca|tion (bī′ō mag′nə fə kā′shən), *n.* the increase in the concentration of toxic chemicals with each new link in the food chain.

bi|o|mag|ni|fy (bī′ō mag′nə fī), *v.i.,* **-fied, -fy|ing.** to undergo biomagnification.

bi|o|mass (bī′ō mas′), *n.* **1** the total mass or weight of living material in a unit of area. **2** plant material or vegetation, especially as a source of fuel or energy.

bi|o|math|e|ma|ti|cian (bī′ō math′ə mə tish′ən), *n.* a specialist in the mathematical study of biological processes, especially the simulation of such processes by mathematical models.

bi|o|math|e|mat|ics (bī′ō math′ə mat′iks), *n.* the application of mathematical principles to biological or medical studies.

bi|ome (bī′ōm), *n.* a natural community of plants and animals, its composition being largely controlled by climatic conditions. [< Greek *bíos* life + *-ōma* group]

bi|o|me|chan|i|cal (bī′ō mə kan′ə kəl), *adj.* of or having to do with biomechanics.

bi|o|me|chan|ics (bī′ō mə kan′iks), *n.* science that deals with the effects of forces on the living organism, especially forces applied to the skeleton by gravity and the system of muscles.

bi|o|med|i|cal (bī′ō med′ə kəl), *adj.* **1** of or having to do with both biology and medicine. **2** of or having to do with biomedicine.

biomedical engineering, = bioengineering.

bi|o|med|i|cine (bī′ō med′ə sən), *n.* the biological and medical study of human tolerance to environmental stresses, especially in space travel.

bi|o|me|te|or|ol|o|gy (bī′ō mē′tē ə rol′ə jē), *n.* = bioclimatology.

bi|o|met|ric (bī′ə met′rik), *adj.* of or having to do with biometry. —**bi′o|met′ri|cal|ly,** *adv.*

Pronunciation Key: hat, āge, cãre, fär; let, ēqual, tėrm; it, īce; hot, ōpen, ôrder; oil, out; cup, pu̇t, rüle; child; long; thin; ᴛʜen; zh, measure; ə represents **a** in about, **e** in taken, **i** in pencil, **o** in lemon, **u** in circus.

bi|o|met|ri|cal (bī′ə met′rə kəl), *adj.* = biometric.
bi|o|me|tri|cian (bī′ə mə trish′ən), *n.* a person who studies biometrics.
bi|o|met|rics (bī′ə met′riks), *n.* the branch of biology that deals with living things by measurements and statistics.
bi|om|e|trist (bī om′ə trist), *n.* = biometrician.
bi|om|e|try (bī om′ə trē), *n.* **1** the measurement of life; calculation of the average duration and probable expectation of human life. **2** = biometrics. [< *bio-* + *-metry*]
bi|o|mol|e|cule (bī′ō mol′ə kyül), *n.* a hypothetical molecule of living matter; the smallest quantity of matter exhibiting life.
bi|o|morph (bī′ō môrf′), *n.* (in art) a lifelike form.
bi|o|mor|phic (bī′ō môr′fik), *adj.* representing or suggesting living forms: *biomorphic sculptures.*
bi|o|morph|ism (bī′ō môrf′iz əm), *n.* a representation of living forms in art.
bi|on|ic (bī on′ik), *adj.* **1** of or having to do with bionics. **2** consisting of electronic or mechanical parts that enhance anatomical structures to produce extraordinary powers: *a "bionic grip".* **3** *Figurative.* having extraordinary ability. —**bi|on′i|cal|ly,** *adv.*
bi|on|i|cist (bī on′ə sist), *n.* a person who studies bionics.
bi|on|ics (bī on′iks), *n.* the study of the anatomy and physiology of animals as a basis for new or improved electronic devices or methods: *Much of the emphasis in bionics has been on sense organs and nervous systems* (New Scientist). [< *bio*(logy) + (electro)*nics*]
bi|o|nom|ic (bī′ə nom′ik), *adj.* of or having to do with bionomics. —**bi′o|nom′i|cal|ly,** *adv.*
bi|o|nom|i|cal (bī′ə nom′ə kəl), *adj.* = bionomic.
bi|o|nom|ics (bī′ə nom′iks), *n.* = ecology. [< *bio-* + (eco)*nomics*]
bi|on|o|mist (bī on′ə mist), *n.* a person who studies bionomics (ecology).
bi|on|o|my (bī on′ə mē), *n.* the science of the laws of life or of living functions. [< *bio-* + Greek *nómos* law]
bi|o-or|gan|ic (bī′ō ôr gan′ik), *adj.* of or having to do with the organic chemical composition of living things: *bio-organic molecules.*
bi|o|pack (bī′ō pak′), *n.* a compact package designed to supply everything needed to support a living organism during space flight.
bi|o|phil elements (bī′ō fil), carbon, nitrogen, oxygen, and phosphorus, the basic chemical elements of living matter.
bi|o|phore or **bi|o|phor** (bī′ə fôr, -fōr), *n.* a formerly supposed minute unit of living protoplasm, capable of growth and reproduction.
bi|o|phys|i|cal (bī′ō fiz′ə kəl), *adj.* of or having to do with biophysics.
bi|o|phys|i|cist (bī′ō fiz′ə sist), *n.* a person who studies biophysics.
bi|o|phys|ics (bī′ō fiz′iks), *n.* the branch of biology which applies the laws of physics to explain the phenomena of biology.
bi|o|pic (bī′ō pik′), *n. Informal.* a filmed account of a person's life; motion-picture biography.
bi|o|plasm (bī′ō plaz əm), *n. Biology.* **1** living matter; protoplasm. **2** = bioplasma. [< *bio-* + Greek *plásma* anything formed]
bi|o|plas|ma (bī′ō plaz′mə), *n.* a hypothetical energy field that according to Soviet parapsychology surrounds all living things. [< Russian *bioplasma*]
bi|o|plas|mic (bī′ō plaz′mik), *adj.* consisting of or having to do with bioplasm.
bi|o|plast (bī′ō plast), *n. Biology.* a particle of bioplasm. [< *bio-* + *-plast*]
bi|o|plas|tic (bī′ō plas′tik), *adj.* having to do with or of the nature of a bioplast.
bi|o|pol|y|mer (bī′ō pol′i mər), *n.* a biological polymer, such as a nucleic acid or a protein.
bi|o|proc|ess (bī′ō pros′es), *n.,* or **bioprocess technology,** = biotechnology (def. 1).
bi|op|sic (bī op′sik), *adj.* of or having to do with a biopsy.
bi|op|sy (bī′op sē), *n., pl.* **-sies. 1** the surgical removal of tissue from a living body for examination and diagnosis. **2** the medical examination of this tissue. [< *bio-* + Greek *ópsis* a viewing]
bi|o|psy|chic (bī′ō sī′kik), *adj.* having to do with both life and mind; involving biological and psychological phenomena.
bi|o|psy|cho|log|i|cal (bī′ō sī′kə loj′ə kəl), *adj.* of or having to do with biopsychology.
bi|o|psy|chol|o|gist (bī′ō sī kol′ə jist), *n.* a person who studies biopsychology.
bi|o|psy|chol|o|gy (bī′ō sī kol′ə jē), *n.* the branch of psychology which deals with mental processes in terms of biological principles; psychobiology.
bi|o|re|gion (bī′ō rē′jən), *n.* a place or area as defined by the biological systems in it. —**bi′o|re′gion|al,** *adj.* —**bi′o|re′gion|al|ly,** *adv.*
bi|o|re|gion|al|ism (bī′ō rē′jə nə liz′əm), *n.* activity in behalf of the preservation of a bioregion. —**bi′o|re′gion|al|ist,** *n., adj.*
bi|o|rhe|ol|o|gy (bī′ō rē ol′ə jē), *n.* the study of the flow and deformation of blood, mucus, and other fluids in plants and animals.
bi|o|rhythm (bī′ō riᴛʜ′əm), *n.* rhythmical or cyclic changes occurring in the functions or activities of organs and organisms.
bi|o|rhyth|mic (bī′ō riᴛʜ′mik), *adj.* of or having to do with biorhythm.
bi|os (bī′os), *n.* **1** all animal and plant life. **2** a substance in yeast essential to its growth. [< Greek *bíos* life]
bi|o|sat|el|lite (bī′ō sat′ə līt), *n.* an artificial satellite that can carry a man or animal.
bi|o|sci|ence (bī′ō sī′əns), *n.* **1** any one of the life sciences, especially those dealing with biological phenomena outside the earth. **2** the life sciences collectively.
bi|o|sci|en|tif|ic (bī′ō sī ən tif′ik), *adj.* of or relating to bioscience.
bi|o|sci|en|tist (bī′ō sī′ən tist), *n.* a person who studies bioscience.
bi|o|scope (bī′ə skōp), *n.* **1** an early form of motion-picture projector. **2** a motion-picture theater.
bi|o|scop|ic (bī′ə skop′ik), *adj.* **1** of or having to do with bioscopy. **2** of or having to do with a bioscope.
bi|os|co|py (bī os′kə pē), *n., pl.* **-pies.** an examination of a body to determine if life exists.
bi|o|sen|sor (bī′ō sen′sər, -sôr), *n.* **1** any one of various devices for recording and transmitting data about physiological changes and other life processes. **2** any one of an animal's nerve endings or sense organs.
bi|o|so|cial (bī′ō sō′shəl), *adj.* of or having to do with the interaction of biological and social forces in human or animal life.
bi|o|so|ci|ol|o|gy (bī′ō sō′sē ol′ə jē, -shē-), *n.* the study of society as biological processes.
bi|o|spe|le|ol|o|gy (bī′ō spē′lē ol′ə jē), *n.* the scientific study of organisms living in caves.
bi|o|sphere (bī′ə sfir), *n.* the region surrounding the earth that can support life, including parts of the lithosphere, hydrosphere, and atmosphere.
bi|o|spher|ic (bī′ō sfer′ik), *adj.* of or characteristic of the biosphere: *biospheric contamination.*
bi|o|stat|ic (bī′ō stat′ik), *adj.* of structure in relation to function. —**bi′o|stat′i|cal|ly,** *adv.*
bi|o|stat|i|cal (bī′ō stat′ə kəl), *adj.* = biostatic.
bi|o|stat|ics (bī′ō stat′iks), *n.* the study of the structure of organisms in relation to functions.
bi|o|stat|is|ti|cian (bī′ō stat′ə stish′ən), *n.* a person who compiles or specializes in biostatistics.
bi|o|sta|tis|tics (bī′ō stə tis′tiks), *n.pl.* = vital statistics.
bi|o|strome (bī′ə strōm), *n. Geology.* a laterally formed layer of sedentary organic remains. [< *bio-* + Greek *strôma* anything laid out flat]
bi|o|syn|the|sis (bī′ō sin′thə sis), *n.* **1** formation of a chemical compound by a plant or animal. **2** the manufacture of a biochemical compound.
bi|o|syn|the|size (bī′ō sin′thə sīz), *v.t.,* **-sized, -siz|ing.** to synthesize by biological or biochemical methods.
bi|o|syn|thet|ic (bī′ō sin thet′ik), *adj.* having to do with biosynthesis. —**bi′o|syn|thet′i|cal|ly,** *adv.*
bi|o|sys|tem|at|ics (bī′ō sis′tə mat′iks), *n.* the classification of biological species on the basis of genetic and ecological studies. It is an experimental form of taxonomy.
bi|o|ta (bī ō′tə), *n.* the animal and plant life of a given region or period; fauna and flora. [< New Latin *biota* < Greek *biotē* life < *bioûn* to live]
bi|o|tech|ni|cal (bī′ō tek′nə kəl), *adj.* of or having to do with biotechnics.
bi|o|tech|nics (bī′ō tek′niks), *n.* the application of biological facts and principles to technology.
bi|o|tech|nol|o|gy (bī′ō tek nol′ə jē), *n.* **1** the use of microorganisms as catalytic agents to produce useful materials or aid in industrial processes. **2** the application of technological facts and principles to biological science, such as in bioengineering.
bi|o|tel|e|met|ric (bī′ō tel′ə met′rik), *adj.* of or used in biotelemetry.
bi|o|te|lem|e|try (bī′ō tə lem′ə trē), *n.* the monitoring of the vital functions of a person or animal and the transmission of the data to a distant point, as from a spacecraft to earth.
bi|o|ther|a|py (bī′ō ther′ə pē), *n.* the use of medicines that consist of, derive from, or are produced by living things, such as yeast, vaccines, or gastric juice, in the treatment of disease.
bi|ot|ic (bī ot′ik), *adj.* **1** of or having to do with life or living things; live; vital. **2** interdependent: *plants and animals in biotic association.* [< Late Latin *bioticus* < Greek *biōtikós* related to life; lively < *biônai,* aorist of *bioûn* to live] —**bi|ot′i|cal|ly,** *adv.*
biotic potential, the capacity of living things to survive in an unfavorable environment.
bi|o|tin (bī′ə tin), *n.* a crystalline, water-soluble acid in the vitamin B family, found in liver, eggs, yeast, and other foods, and necessary for healthy blood circulation and growth. It was formerly called *vitamin H. Formula:* $C_{10}H_{16}N_2O_3S$ [< Greek *bíotos* life, means of life + English *-in*]
bi|o|tite (bī′ə tīt), *n.* a black or dark-green mica, a silicate of aluminum and iron with magnesium and potassium, occurring in igneous rocks. [< *J.B. Biot,* 1774-1862, a French mineralogist]
bi|o|tit|ic (bī′ə tit′ik), *adj.* of or resembling biotite.
bi|o|tope (bī′ə tōp), *n.* a region uniform in environmental conditions and in its distribution of animal life. [< *bio-* + Greek *tópos* region]
bi|o|tox|ic (bī′ō tok′sik), *adj.* of or having to do with poisons produced by animals and plants.
bi|o|tox|ic|i|ty (bī′ō tok sis′ə tē), *n.* poisonousness to animals and plants.
bi|o|tox|in (bī′ō tok′sən), *n.* a biotoxic substance.
bi|o|tron (bī′ə tron), *n.* a structure or laboratory apparatus in which climatic conditions can be strictly controlled for use in plant and animal studies. [< *bio-* + *-tron,* as in *cyclotron*]
bi|o|type (bī′ə tīp), *n.* a race or group of organisms having the same genetic constitution.
bi|o|typ|ic (bī′ə tip′ik), *adj.* of or having to do with a biotype; resembling a biotype.
bi|o|ty|pol|o|gy (bī′ō tī pol′ə jē), *n.* the classification of organisms according to physical differences.
bi|pack (bī′pak′), *n.* a pack of two films or plates in color photography, each sensitive to a different color, superimposed and exposed simultaneously.
bi|pa|ren|tal (bī′pə ren′təl), *adj.* of both parents; from both parents: *biparental inheritance.*
bi|pa|ri|e|tal (bī′pə rī′ə təl), *adj.* having to do with or joining both parietal bones.
bip|a|rous (bip′ər əs), *adj.* **1** (of certain animals) bringing forth two at a birth. **2** (of certain flower clusters) having two branches or axes. [< *bi-* two + Latin *parere* to produce + English *-ous*]
bi|par|ti|san (bī pär′tə zən), *adj.* of or supported by two political parties: *a bipartisan foreign policy supported by both Republicans and Democrats.*
bi|par|ti|san|ism (bī pär′tə zə niz′əm), *n.* **1** bipartisan action, condition, or quality. **2** a doctrine or policy of support by two political parties.
bi|par|ti|san|ship (bī pär′tə zən ship), *n.* support by two political parties.
***bi|par|tite** (bī pär′tīt), *adj.* **1** having to do with two peoples, nations, or other groups: *a bipartite treaty between the United States and Canada.* **2** having two parts: *A clam has a bipartite shell.* **3** *Botany.* divided into two parts nearly to the base: *a bipartite leaf.* [< Latin *bipartītus* < *bi-* two + *partīre* divide] —**bi|par′tite|ly,** *adv.*

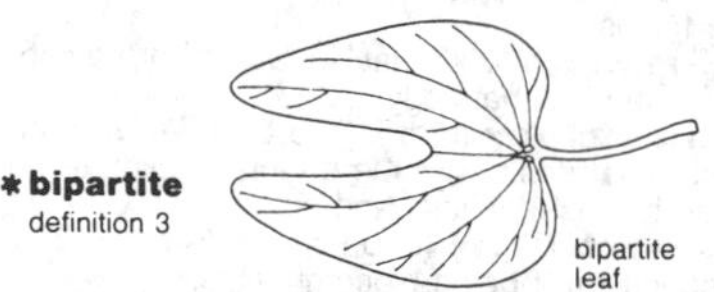

***bipartite** definition 3

bi|par|ti|tion (bī′pär tish′ən), *n.* division into two parts.
bi|par|ty (bī′pär′tē), *adj.* combining two different groups, especially political or religious groups.
bi|pec|ti|nat|ed (bī pek′tə nā′tid), *adj.* formed on both sides like the teeth of a comb.
bi|ped (bī′ped), *n., adj.* —*n.* an animal having two feet. Birds and men are bipeds. —*adj.* having two feet. [< Latin *bipēs, bipedis* < *bi-* two + *pēs, pedis* foot]
bi|pe|dal (bī′pə dəl, bip′-), *adj.* = biped. —**bi′pe|dal|ly,** *adv.*
bi|pe|dal|ism (bī′pe də liz əm), *n.* the condition of having or moving on two feet only.
bi|pet|al|ous (bī pet′ə ləs), *adj.* having two petals; dipetalous.
bi|phas|ic (bī fā′zik), *adj.* **1** having two phases: *a biphasic electrical system.* **2** *Medicine.* developing in two phases: *a biphasic reaction.*
bi|phen|yl (bī fen′əl, -fē′nəl), *n.* a colorless, crystalline hydrocarbon consisting of two phenyl groups, used in organic synthesis; diphenyl. *Formula:* $C_6H_5 \cdot C_6H_5$
bi|pin|nar|i|a (bī′pi nãr′ē ə), *n.* the larval stage of many starfish, in which the larva swims freely by means of cilia. [< New Latin *bipinnaria* < *bi-* two + Latin *pinna* feather]
***bi|pin|nate** (bī pin′āt), *adj.* doubly pinnate. A leaf with leaflets on each side of a stalk is pinnate. A pinnate leaf with pinnate leaflets is bipinnate. —**bi|pin′nate|ly,** *adv.*

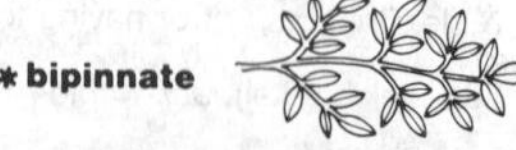
***bipinnate**
bipinnate leaves

bi|pin|nat|ed (bī pin′ā tid), *adj.* = bipinnate.
***bi|plane** (bī′plān′), *n.* an airplane having two

wings on each side of the fuselage, one above the other.

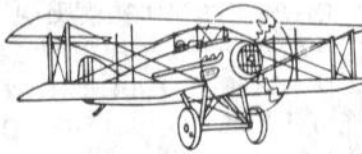

∗biplane

bi|pod (bī′pod), *n.* a two-legged support. [< *bi-* two + Greek *poús, podós* foot]

bi|po|lar (bī pō′lər), *adj.* **1** having two poles. **2** of or found in both polar regions. **3** *Figurative.* having or showing two opposite principles, sets of values, or opinions; antithetical. **4** *Anatomy.* (of nerve cells) having two fibrous processes.

bipolar disorder, a mental disorder characterized by alternating periods of mania and depression; manic-depressive psychosis: *Bipolar disorder . . . is marked by extreme mood swings and by alternating episodes of depression and intense activity* (Lewis L. Judd).

bi|po|lar|i|ty (bī′pō lar′ə tē), *n.* bipolar quality or state.

bi|po|lar|ize (bī pō′lə rīz), *v.t.,* **-ized, -iz|ing.** to divide into two opposing factions: *. . . to bipolarize the world with competing political ideologies* (Science News Letter). —**bi|po′lar|i|za′tion,** *n.*

bi|prism (bī′priz′əm), *n.* a prism which forms in cross section a triangle having two equal acute angles and one very obtuse angle, used to split a beam of light to obtain two images from a single source.

bi|pro|pel|lant (bī′prə pel′ənt), *adj.* having as fuel two liquids, each in a separate tank, which form a combustible mixture when combined, such as liquid oxygen and alcohol.

bi|py|ram|i|dal (bī′pə ram′ə dəl), *adj.* having the form of two pyramids set base to base: *a bipyramidal crystal.*

bi|quad|rate (bī kwod′rāt, -rit), *n. Mathematics.* the fourth power; the square of the square.

bi|quad|rat|ic (bī′kwod rat′ik), *adj., n.* —*adj.* of or containing a fourth power in mathematics; quartic. —*n.* **1** the fourth power of a number. **2** = biquadratic equation.

biquadratic equation, an algebraic equation with one unknown quantity, of which the highest power contained in the equation is the fourth.

bi|quar|ter|ly (bī kwôr′tər lē), *adj., adv.* **1** twice in every three months. **2** once in every two quarters; semiannually.

bi|qui|na|ry (bī kwī′nər ē), *adj.* of or having to do with a scale of arithmetical notation in which the base is alternately 2 and 5, used in some digital computers: *the biquinary code.*

bi|ra|cial (bī rā′shəl), *adj.* of or having to do with two races: *biracial problems.*

bi|ra|di|al (bī rā′dē əl), *adj.* having both a bilateral and a radial arrangement of its parts, as ctenophores: *biradial symmetry.* —**bi|ra′di|al|ly,** *adv.*

bi|ra|di|ate (bī rā′dē āt), *adj.* having two rays.

bi|ra|di|at|ed (bī rā′dē ā′tid), *adj.* = biradiate.

bi|ra|mose (bī rā′mōs), *adj.* = biramous.

bi|ra|mous (bī rā′məs), *adj. Zoology.* having or consisting of two branches.

birch (bėrch), *n., pl.* **birch|es** *for 1 and 3, adj., v.* —*n.* **1** a slender, hardy tree with a smooth bark that peels off in thin layers. Birches belong to the birch family. **2** its hard, close-grained wood, often used in making furniture. **3** a bundle of birch twigs or a birch stick, used for whipping.
—*adj.* of or having to do with birch; birchen.
—*v.t.* to whip with a birch or the like; flog.
[Old English *bierce*]

birch|bark (bėrch′bärk′), *n.* the bark of a birch tree. Some Indians used a certain kind of birchbark and pitch to cover the framework of their canoes.

birch|en (bėr′chən), *adj.* **1** of a birch tree. **2** made of birchwood. **3** having to do with the birch used in punishing.

Birch|er (bėr′chər), *n.* a member of the John Birch Society, an ultraconservative American political organization founded in 1958.

birch family, a group of dicotyledonous trees and shrubs having simple, alternate leaves and monoecious flowers, and bearing a one-seeded nutlet as the fruit. The family includes the birch, alder, and hazel.

Birch|ism (bėr′chiz əm), *n.* the principles and practices of Birchers; extreme conservatism in politics.

Birch|ist (bėr′chist), *adj., n.* = Birchite.

Birch|ite (bėr′chīt), *adj., n.* —*adj.* of or having to do with the John Birch Society. —*n.* = Bircher.

birch partridge, = ruffed grouse.

birch|wood (bėrch′wu̇d′), *n.* **1** the wood of the birch. **2** a woods or forest of birches.

bird (bėrd), *n., v.* —*n.* **1** an animal that has wings, feathers, two legs, and a beak or bill. Birds have backbones, are warm-blooded, and lay eggs. Most birds can fly. **2** a bird hunted for sport; game bird. **3** = shuttlecock. **4** *Slang, Figurative.* a person: *He's an odd bird.* **5** *Slang.* **a** a ballistic or guided missile; rocket. **b** *Slang.* an aircraft or spacecraft. **6** = clay pigeon. **7** *Slang.* a sound of ridicule blown through the lips. **8** *British Slang.* a prison sentence; time served in prison. **9** *U.S. Slang.* the eagle as an insigne of military rank. **10** *British Slang.* an attractive girl or young woman. **11** *Archaic.* the young of any fowl.
—*v.i.* **1** to watch wild birds; act as a bird watcher. **2** to catch or shoot birds.

bird in (the) hand, something certain because one already has it. *A bird in the hand is worth two in the bush* means something certain is better than something uncertain.

eat like a bird, to be a small eater; eat little or only a small amount of food: *She is thin and nervous, and eats like a bird.*

for the birds, *Slang.* of no worth; without value or importance: *His few crumbs of kindness were strictly for the birds* (Punch).

get the bird, **a** to be booed or hissed from the stage by the audience: *To "get the big bird" is occasionally a compliment to the actor's power of representing villainy* (The Graphic). **b** to be dismissed derisively: *This situation . . . can only lead to your catching later trains . . . and getting the bird . . . at the office* (Punch).

kill two birds with one stone, to accomplish two things with one action: *He thinks to kill two birds with one stone, and satisfy two arguments with one answer* (Thomas Hobbes).

the birds and the bees, the basic facts about sex and reproduction: *A young couple's bafflement about the birds and the bees . . . had some funny moments* (New Yorker).
[Old English *bridd* young fowl]

bird band, *U.S.* a band put on a bird's leg to identify it for study of its range.

bird|band|er (bėrd′ban′dər), *n. U.S.* a person who puts bird bands on birds.

bird|band|ing (bėrd′ban′ding), *n. U.S.* the putting of bird bands on birds.

bird|bath (bėrd′bath′, -bäth′), *n.* a shallow basin raised off the ground and filled with water for birds to bathe in or drink.

bird|brain (bėrd′brān′), *n. Slang.* a foolish, shallow person.

bird-brained (bėrd′brānd′), *adj. Slang.* that is a birdbrain; foolish.

bird cage or **bird|cage** (bėrd′kāj′), *n.* **1** a cage for small birds such as canaries or parakeets. **2** *Slang.* a device for throwing dice, similar to a bird cage. **3** *U.S. Slang.* the congested airspace of an airport or air terminal.

bird call, **1** the sound that a bird makes: *the bird calls of dawn.* **2** a sound imitating that which a bird makes. **3** an instrument for imitating the call of a bird in order to attract or decoy them.

bird cherry, a wild cherry of Europe.

bird dog, *U.S.* **1** a dog trained to find birds or bring back birds shot by a hunter. **2** *Informal.* a person who bird-dogs.

bird-dog (bėrd′dôg′), *v.t.,* **-dogged, -dogging.** *U.S. Informal.* **1** to hunt or inquire closely and carefully into or about (some problem). **2** to seek out and prepare or arrange (an investment, customers, a business opportunity, or the like).

bird|er (bėr′dər), *n.* **1** a person who breeds birds. **2** = bird watcher.

bird flower, any one of several plants, such as the red columbine, fuchsia or hibiscus, having colorful flowers which are pollinated by birds.

bird-foot (bėrd′fu̇t′), *n.* = bird's-foot.

bird grass, **1** a forage and lawn grass introduced into North America from Europe. **2** the knotgrass.

bird hawk, = chicken hawk.

bird|house (bėrd′hous′), *n.* **1** a small box with a roof and one or more openings, raised off the ground for birds to nest in. **2** = aviary.

bird|ie (bėr′dē), *n., v.,* **-bird|ied, bird|y|ing.** —*n.* **1** a little bird. **2** a score of one stroke less than par for any hole on a golf course. **3** = shuttlecock. —*v.t.* to score a birdie on (a hole).

bird|ing (bėrd′ing), *n.* **1** the activity of a bird watcher. **2** = fowling.

bird|life (bėrd′līf′), *n.* **1** the birds of a region: *It [the place] was rich in birdlife, from the myrtle warblers . . . to the swifts* (Atlantic) **2** birds in their natural state: *[His] hobby is photographing birdlife* (New York Times).

bird|like (bėrd′līk′), *adj.* resembling a bird.

bird|lime (bėrd′līm′), *n., v.,* **-limed, -lim|ing.** —*n.* a sticky substance smeared on twigs to catch small birds that light on it. It is often made from the inner bark of holly or from the juice of the banyan tree.
—*v.t.* to smear or catch with or as if with birdlime; lime.

bird|ling (bėrd′ling), *n.* a baby bird.

bird|louse, = biting louse.

bird|man (bėrd′man′, -mən), *n., pl.* **-men.** **1** *Informal.* = aviator: *Getting to airports a good deal . . . I decided to become an intrepid birdman* (New Yorker). **2** a person who catches, sells, or trains birds, as a fowler. **3** = ornithologist. **4** a person who stuffs birds; taxidermist.

bird|nest (bėrd′nest′), *v.i.* to search for birds' nests; bird's-nest.

bird of Minerva, the owl (as a symbol of wisdom).

∗bird of paradise, a bird of New Guinea noted for its magnificent plumage.

∗bird of paradise

∗bird-of-paradise

∗bird-of-par|a|dise (bėrd′əv par′ə dīs), *n.* a small plant of South Africa with orange and blue flowers and banana-shaped leaves, somewhat resembling birds of paradise on the wing, grown also in California and Florida.

bird of passage, **1** a bird that flies from one region to another as the seasons change; migratory bird. **2** *Informal.* a person who roams from place to place.

bird of peace, the dove (with reference to the story of Noah).

bird of prey, any one of a group of birds including eagles, hawks, owls, and vultures, that hunt animals and eat their flesh.

bird pepper, a kind of strong red pepper, bearing small berries.

bird ring, *British.* a bird band.

bird ringer, *British.* a birdbander.

bird|seed (bėrd′sēd′), *n.* **1** a mixture of small seeds often fed to caged birds. **2** seed put outside for wild birds.

bird's-eye (bėrdz′ī′), *adj., n.* —*adj.* **1** seen from above or from a distance: *a bird's-eye view of the city from an airplane.* **2** general or brief: *a bird's-eye view of a problem.* **3** having markings somewhat like birds' eyes.
—*n.* **1a** a cotton cloth having markings somewhat like birds' eyes. **b** a weave resembling birds' eyes. **2** any one of various plants with small, round, bright-colored flowers: *A primrose is a bird's-eye.*

bird's-eye maple, a maple wood full of little knotty spots, used in making furniture.

bird's-foot (bėrdz′fu̇t′), *n.* **1** any one of certain plants of the pea family, whose pods are jointed and bent in like claws. **2** any one of various plants whose leaves, flowers, or pods suggest the foot of a bird. Also, **bird-foot.**

bird's-foot fern, **1** a small, tropical American fern whose foliage suggests a bird's foot. **2** a fern of the Pacific Coast.

∗bird's-foot star, an echinoderm related to the starfish.

∗bird's-foot star

∗bird's-foot violet

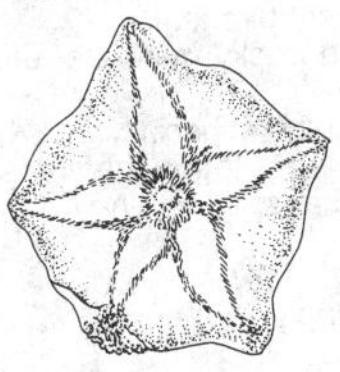

echinoderm

violet

bird's-foot trefoil, a native European and Asian perennial plant of the pea family, whose pods suggest claws; babies'-slippers.

∗bird's-foot violet, a common violet of the eastern United States, having divided leaves which suggest a bird's foot and large, pansylike flowers.

bird shot, a small size of lead shot, used in shooting birds.

bird's-nest (bėrdz′nest′), *n., v.* —*n.* the nest of certain swifts of southeastern Asia, composed mainly of a substance secreted by the salivary glands, used in China as an ingredient for soup. —*v.i.* to search for or collect birds' nests, or their

---

Pronunciation Key: hat, āge, cãre, fär; let, ēqual, tėrm; it, īce; hot, ōpen, ôrder; **oi**l, **ou**t; cup, pu̇t, rüle; **ch**ild; lo**ng**; **th**in; **ᴛʜ**en; **zh**, measure; **ə** represents **a** in about, **e** in taken, **i** in pencil, **o** in lemon, **u** in circus.

contents, as a hobby; birdnest.

bird's-nest fungus, any one of a group of fungi whose peridia resemble small nests of eggs.

bird's-nest moss, = resurrection plant (def. 1).

birds of a feather, people of the same kind: *birds of a feather flock together.*

bird|song (bėrd′sông′, -song′), *n.* **1** the song of a bird. **2** the singing of birds: *birdsong at morning* (Robert Louis Stevenson).

bird spider, any one of a group of very large South American spiders, some of which live in trees and catch small birds for food.

bird strike, a collision between an aircraft and a flock of birds.

bird walk, a stroll or walk in search of birds, especially by a bird watcher.

bird-watch (bėrd′woch′, -wôch′), *v.i.* to watch wild birds; bird.

bird watcher, **1** a person who observes and classifies wild birds in their natural environment. **2** *U.S. Slang.* a newsman or a person who spends much time near missile test centers to observe launchings.

bird watching, the activity of a bird watcher; birding.

bird-wit|ted (bėrd′wit′əd), *adj.* = bird-brained.

bird|wom|an (bėrd′wům′ən), *n., pl.* **-wom|en.** a woman aviator; an aviatrix.

bird|y (bėr′dē), *adj.,* **bird|i|er, bird|i|est. 1** resembling or suggesting a bird: *Pauline made birdy, disapproving vibrations with her head* (New Yorker). **2** having or filled with birds: *Jake [a dog] . . . has an eye and nose for the birdy spots* (Newsweek).

bi|re|frin|gence (bī′ri frin′jəns), *n.* double refraction. [< *bi-* two + *refringence*]

bi|re|frin|gent (bī′ri frin′jənt), *adj.* characterized by birefringence.

***bi|reme** (bī′rēm), *n.* a ship with two rows of oars on each side, one above the other, much used on the Mediterranean in ancient times. [< Latin *birēmis* < *bi-* two + *rēmus* oar]

***bireme**

***bi|ret|ta** (bə ret′ə), *n.* a stiff, square cap with three, or sometimes four, upright, projecting pieces, worn by Roman Catholic or Episcopal clergymen on certain occasions. A priest's biretta is black, a bishop's purple, a cardinal's red. Also, **beretta, berretta.** [< Italian *berretta* < Vulgar Latin *birritta* (diminutive) < Late Latin *birrus; see* etym. under **beret**]

***biretta**

birk (bėrk), *n. Scottish.* birch.

birk|en (bėr′kən), *adj. Scottish.* birchen.

birk|ie (bėr′kē), *n. Scottish.* a cocky man; a strutting fellow. [origin uncertain]

birl (bėrl), *v.t., v.i.* to spin rapidly, especially (among lumberjacks) to revolve a log in the water while standing on it. [perhaps < *birr,* influenced by *whirl*]

birle (bėrl), *v.,* **birled, birl|ing.** *Scottish.* **—*v.t.*** **1** to pour out (drink). **2** to supply with drink.
—*v.i.* to carouse.
[Old English *byrelian* < *byrele* one who pours]

birl|ing (bėr′ling), *n.* **1** the act of spinning rapidly. **2** = logrolling (def. 2).

bir|linn (bir′lin), *n.* a large rowboat, or barge, rowed by a number of oarsmen in the Hebrides. [< Gaelic *birlinn*]

bi|ro (bī′rō), *n. British.* **1** a ballpoint pen: *Out comes the erasing, paraphrasing editorial biro . . .* (Listener). **2 Biro,** the trademark of a particular kind of ballpoint pen.

bi|ro|ta|tion (bī′rō tā′shən), *n.* = mutarotation.

birr[1] (bėr), *n., v.,* **birred, birr|ing.** *Scottish.* **—*n.*** **1** the force of the wind or of a moving body; momentum. **2** vigor; might. **3** a whirring sound.
—*v.i.* to make a whirring noise; move with a whirring sound.
[< Scandinavian (compare Old Icelandic *byrr* favoring wind)]

birr[2] (bir), *n., pl.* **birr** or **birrs.** the monetary unit of Ethiopia, divided into 100 cents. It replaced the Ethiopian dollar in 1976.

birse (bėrs; *Scottish* birs), *n.* **1** a bristle or bunch of bristles. **2** *Figurative.* temper; rage; anger. [Old English *byrst* bristle]

birth (bėrth), *n., adj., v.* **—*n.*** **1** the act of coming into life; being born: *the birth of a baby. At birth, most babies weigh between 6 and 8 pounds.* SYN: nativity. **2** the bearing of young; childbirth: *Twins are born at one birth.* **3** *Figurative.* a beginning; origin: *the birth of a nation, the land of our birth.* SYN: origination, commencement, start. **4** the act or process of bringing forth: *the birth of a plan. We saw the birth of space travel when the first astronauts were sent into outer space.* **5** natural inheritance: *a musician by birth.* **6a** descent; family: *a man of Spanish birth. The king was a man of noble birth.* SYN: parentage, extraction. **b** noble family or descent: *He is a man of birth and breeding.* **7** that which is born; offspring; young.
—*adj.* related by birth or blood, not by adoption or the like; biological: *Parent Finders was started . . . to help adoptees find their birth relatives* (Maclean's).
—*v.t.* to give birth to. **—*v.i.*** to bear offspring.
give birth to, a to bring forth; bear: *The dog gave birth to four puppies.* **b** to be the origin or cause of: *The scientist's experiments gave birth to a new drug.*
[Middle English *byrthe* < Scandinavian (compare Old Swedish *byrth*)]

birth canal, the canal leading from the uterus through which the young of most mammals pass to be born.

birth certificate, an authorized copy of a registrar's form giving the essential facts about a person's birth.

birth|coat (bėrth′kōt′), *n.* the coat of certain animals before their first shedding.

birth control, the control of births or of childbearing by deliberate measures to control or prevent conception; contraception.

birth|day (bėrth′dā′), *n.* **1a** the day on which a person was born. **b** *Figurative.* the day on which something began: *July 4, 1776, was the birthday of the United States.* **2** the yearly return of the day on which a person was born, or on which something began: *Tomorrow is my birthday.*

birthday honours, *British.* the titles of honor conferred by the King or Queen on each anniversary of his or her birthday.

birthday suit, *Informal.* one's skin; the condition or state of being without clothes.

birth|less (bėrth′lis), *adj.* **1** mean; common. **2** fruitless; unprofitable. **3** lacking the advantages of high birth.

birth|mark (bėrth′märk′), *n.* a spot or mark on the skin that was there at birth; nevus.

birth|night (bėrth′nīt′), *n.* **1** the night of the day of one's birth. **2** the night of a birthday.

birth pangs, **1** the pains of childbirth. **2** *Figurative: the frustration and birth pangs of a new project.*

birth|place (bėrth′plās′), *n.* **1** the place where a person was born. **2** *Figurative: Philadelphia is the birthplace of the United States.*

birth rate, the relationship of the number of births in a year to the total population or to some other stated number; natality.

birth|right (bėrth′rīt′), *n.* the rights belonging to a person because he is the oldest son, or because he was born in a certain country, or because of any other fact about his birth: *According to the Bible story, when Esau sold his birthright to his younger brother Jacob, he forfeited all claim to property of his father Isaac.*

birth|root (bėrth′rüt′, -růt′), *n.* the purple trillium, whose astringent roots were reputed to hasten childbirth.

birth|stone (bėrth′stōn′), *n.* a gem associated with a certain month of the year. A birthstone is often supposed to bring good luck when worn by a person born in its month. Each month has a different birthstone.

birth trauma, the anxiety which a child experiences as a result of being born, considered in psychoanalytic theory as a possible source of neuroses in later life.

birth|wort (bėrth′wėrt′), *n.* any one of various woody vines of the birthwort family growing especially in South America. Their roots are used to treat snakebite and for other medicinal purposes.

birthwort family, a group of dicotyledonous, chiefly tropical herbs and woody vines, having luridly colored flowers which often smell like carrion. The family includes the birthwort, Dutchman's-pipe, and wild ginger.

bis (bis), *adv.* **1** twice. **2** *Music.* a direction to repeat a phrase or passage. **3** encore; again. [< French, or Italian *bis* twice < Latin *bis* twice]

Bi|sa|yan (bi sä′yən), *n.* = Visayan.

bis|cuit (bis′kit), *n., pl.* **-cuits** or **-cuit,** *adj.* **—*n.*** **1** *U.S.* **a** a soft bread dough baked in small, round shapes. Biscuits are soft cakes, raised with baking powder, soda, or yeast. **b** one of these cakes. **2** *Especially British.* **a** a crisp, dry bread baked in thin, hard, flat cakes. **b** a cracker. **c** a cookie. **3** pottery after the first baking and before glazing; bisque. **4** a pale brown; tan. **5** *British Slang.* a square, brown mattress. **6** a piece of plastic placed between two stampers in making a phonograph record. **—*adj.*** pale-brown.
take the biscuit, *British.* to win first prize; take the cake: *. . . French cheddar really does take the biscuit* (Sunday Times).
[< Old French *bescuit* < *bes* twice (< Latin *bis*) + *cuit,* past participle of *cuire* to cook < Vulgar Latin *cocere* < Latin *coquere* to cook]

biscuit beetle, a small, brown beetle which feeds on hard biscuit. It also feeds on stored provisions, tobacco, and drugs, and often infests drugstores.

biscuit gla|cé (gla sā′), a rich ice cream with powdered macaroons sprinkled over the top, and usually served in small paper cases. [< French *biscuit glacé*]

biscuit gun, an instrument for giving colored light signals to an aircraft on take-off or landing, used in air traffic control; light gun.

biscuit root, *U.S.* the camass of North America or any one of certain other similar edible herbs.

biscuit tortoni, = biscuit glacé.

bise (bēz), *n.* a dry, cold north or northeast wind in southeastern France, Switzerland, and neighboring regions. [< French *bise,* apparently < Germanic (compare Old High German *bīsa*)]

bi|sect (bī sekt′, bī′sekt), *v.t.* **1** to divide into two parts: *Bisect the apple as well as you can.* **2** to divide into two equal parts: *You can bisect a 90 degree angle into two 45 degree angles.* **—*v.i.*** to divide in two; bifurcate; fork. [< *bi-* two + Latin *sectus,* past participle of *secāre* cut]

bi|sec|tion (bī sek′shən), *n.* **1** the act of bisecting: *the bisection of an angle.* **2** the place of bisecting. **3** one of two equal parts.

bi|sec|tion|al (bī sek′shə nəl), *adj.* the nature of or having to do with bisection. **—bi|sec′tion|al|ly,** *adv.*

bi|sec|tor (bī sek′tər, bī′sek′-), *n.* **1** a line that bisects either an angle or another line. **2** anything that bisects.

bi|sec|trix (bī sek′triks, bī′sek′-), *n., pl.* **bi|sec|tri|ces** (bī′sek trī′sēz). **1** = bisector. **2** a line which bisects the angle of the optic axes in a biaxial crystal.

bi|seg|ment (bī seg′mənt), *n.* one of the segments of a bisected line or angle.

bi|sen|so|ry (bī sen′sər ē), *adj.* affecting two senses: *bisensory hallucination.*

bi|se|ri|al (bī sir′ē əl), *adj.* **1** arranged in two series, especially in two related series. **2** of or having to do with two series.

bi|ser|rate (bī ser′āt, -it), *adj.* **1** *Botany.* doubly serrate. A biserrate leaf is notched like a saw, with each notch also notched. **2** *Zoology.* serrate on both sides: *a biserrate antenna.*

bi|se|tose (bī sē′tōs), *adj. Zoology, Botany.* having two bristles or bristlelike appendages. [< *bi-* two + *setose*]

bi|sex|u|al (bī sek′shů əl), *adj., n.* **—*adj.*** **1** of or having to do with both sexes. **2** combining both male and female organs in one individual animal or plant; hermaphroditic. **3** attracted to both sexes.
—*n.* **1** an animal or plant that is bisexual. **2** an individual attracted to both sexes. **—bi|sex′u|al|ly,** *adv.*

bi|sex|u|al|ism (bī sek′shů ə liz′əm), *n.* = bisexuality.

bi|sex|u|al|i|ty (bī′sek shů al′ə tē), *n.* bisexual quality or condition.

bish|op (bish′əp), *n., v.,* **-oped, -op|ing. —*n.*** **1** a clergyman of high rank who is the head of a church district or diocese: *No Bishop, no King* (attributed to James I of England). **2** a spiritual overseer; an officer of the early Christian church: *the Shepherd and Bishop of your souls* (I Peter 2:25). **3** the layman in charge of a congregation (ward) in the Mormon Church. **4** one of the pieces in the game of chess. A bishop can move only diagonally. See picture under **chess**[1]. **5** a hot drink of oranges or lemons, sugar, and wine, especially mulled and spiced port or other red wine. **6** *U.S.* (in the 1800's) a woman's bustle.
—*v.t.* to name (someone) a bishop.
—*v.i.* to act as bishop.
[Old English *bisceop* < Vulgar Latin *ebiscopus,* variant of Latin *episcopus* bishop, overseer < Greek *episkopos* overseer < *epi-* over + *skopós* watcher]

bish|op|ess (bish′əp is), *n.* the wife of a bishop.

bish|op|ric (bish′əp rik), *n.* **1** the church district under the charge of a bishop; diocese; see. **2** the position, office, or rank of bishop. **3** (in the Mormon Church) a bishop and his two counselors who share administrative duties in the ward. [Old English *bisceoprīce* < *bisceop* bishop + *rīce* domain]

bish|op's-cap (bish′əps kap′), *n.* a plant of the saxifrage family whose seed capsule suggests a bishop's miter; miterwort.

bishop sleeve, a wide, full sleeve, gathered in at the wrist.

bish|op's-weed (bish′əps wēd′), *n.* **1** any one of several plants of the parsley family native to the Mediterranean region, bearing umbels with very large outer petals. **2** a white, spring-flowering plant of the parsley family with medicinal properties.

bis|il|i|ac (bi sil′ē ak), *adj.* relating to both iliac bones, especially to their crests. [< Latin *bis* twice + English *iliac*]

bisk (bisk), *n.* = bisque[1].

Bis|marck herring (biz′märk), fillet of salted herring prepared in vinegar, wine, and spices, and served with raw onion and lemon slices.

Bis|marck|i|an (biz mär′kē ən), *adj.* having to do with or resembling the political ideas or the policies of Otto von Bismarck.

bis|mil|lah (bis mil′ə), *interj.* in the name of Allah or God, a common Moslem exclamation: *Has our pedicab even grazed another vehicle? Just say "bismillah" once and we are safe* (Atlantic). [< Arabic *bism illāh*]

bis|mite (biz′mīt, bis′-), *n.* a principal ore of bismuth, occurring as a yellow, powdery earth. *Formula:* Bi_2O_3 [< *bism*(uth) + *-ite*[1]]

*****bis|muth** (biz′məth), *n.* a brittle, reddish-white, metallic chemical element which occurs in nature as a free metal and in various ores. Some of its compounds are used in medicine and in alloys because of its low melting point. [< earlier German *Bismuth* (now *Wismut*)]

*****bismuth**

symbol	atomic number	atomic weight	oxidation state
Bi	83	208.980	3, 5

bis|muth|al (biz′mə thəl), *adj.* of or containing bismuth.

bis|mu|thic (biz′mə thik, biz myü′-; -muth′ik), *adj.* **1** of bismuth. **2** containing bismuth, especially with a valence of 5.

bis|muth|in|ite (biz muth′ə nīt), *n.* a principal ore of bismuth occurring as lead-gray lustrous crystals or masses; native sulfide of bismuth. *Formula:* Bi_2S_3

bis|muth|ous (biz′mə thəs), *adj.* containing bismuth, especially with a valence of 3.

bis|na|ga (bis nä′gə), *n.* **1** a globular, spiny cactus. **2** any one of various thorny barrel cactuses. [< Spanish *biznaga* wild carrot]

bi|so|ci|a|tion (bī sō′sē ā′shən, -shē-), *n.* an associating of two unrelated or disparate meanings, arguments, ideas, or the like, especially in literature and art.

bi|so|ci|a|tive (bī sō′shē ā′tiv), *adj.* of or characterized by bisociation.

*****bi|son** (bī′sən, -zən), *n., pl.* **-son.** **1** a wild ox of North America, the male of which has a big, shaggy head and strong front legs; buffalo. Bison have a large hump and short, thick, curved horns. *... the enormous herds of bison on which the entire material existence of the Indians depended* (Science News Letter). **2** the wild ox of Europe, slightly larger than the American bison; aurochs. It is now almost extinct. [< Latin *bisōn, bisontis* < Germanic (compare Old High German *wisunt*)]

*****bison** definition 1

bi|so|nant (bī sō′nənt), *adj.* having two sounds. [< *bi-* + *sonant*]

bi|son|tine (bī′sən tīn, -tin; -zən-), *adj.* having to do with or like the bison: *The general aspect of the yak is distinctly bisontine* (Edward Balfour). [< Latin *bisōn, bisontis* bison + English *-ine*]

bisque[1] (bisk), *n.* **1** a rich, thick soup made of cooked shellfish or, sometimes, of birds, rabbits, or other game. **2** a smooth, creamy soup, made of strained tomatoes, asparagus, or other vegetables. **3** ice cream containing powdered macaroons or crushed nuts. Also, **bisk.** [< French *bisque* a soup]

bisque[2] (bisk), *n.* **1a** pottery after the first baking and before glazing; biscuit. **b** a variety of unglazed white porcelain used for statuettes. **2** a pale-brown color; biscuit. [< *biscuit*]

bisque[3] (bisk), *n.* one point, one stroke, or one extra turn to play, allowed to a competitor in tennis, golf, or other games, taken whenever he sees fit in the course of a match. [< French *bisque*]

bis|sex|tile (bi sek′stəl, -stīl), *adj., n.* **—*adj.*** containing or designating the extra day of leap year. February is the bissextile month; February 29 is the bissextile day.
—*n.* = leap year.
[< Late Latin *bissextilis* < Latin *bissextus* (*diēs*) intercalary day of the Julian calendar (the extra day was added after the *sixth* day, doubling it, before the calends of March)]

bis|sey nut (bis′ē), = kola nut. [*bissey* < a native name in western Africa]

bis|son (bis′ən), *adj. Obsolete.* blind; purblind. [Old English *bisene*]

bi|sta|ble (bī stā′bəl), *adj.* remaining indefinitely in either of two stable states: *The basic electronic components of a computer are "bistable;" that is, they have an intrinsically binary character* (New Yorker).

bi|state (bī′stāt′), *adj.* of or between two states: *A bistate agreement made in 1785 gave Virginians fishing rights in its* [*Maryland's*] *waters* (E. M. Lynn).

bi|stat|ic radar (bī stat′ik), a radar system based on two widely separated locations, one for transmitting signals to a body in outer space, another for receiving them as they reflect back to earth.

bi|stel|ic (bī stel′ik), *adj. Botany.* having two steles.

bis|ter or **bis|tre** (bis′tər), *n.* **1** a dark-brown coloring matter made from the soot of certain woods. **2** a dark-brown color. [< French *bistre,* perhaps < *bis* dark gray]

bis|tered or **bis|tred** (bis′tərd), *adj.* browned, as with bister.

bis|tort (bis′tôrt), *n.* a European plant with a large, twisted root, which is sometimes used in medicine as an astringent; snakeweed. [< Medieval Latin (*herba*) *bistorta* < Latin *bis-* twice + *torta,* feminine past participle of *torquēre* twist]

bis|tou|ry (bis′tər ē), *n., pl.* **-ries.** a small, narrow surgical knife with a pointed blade for making incisions. [< French *bistouri*]

bis|tro (bis′trō; *French* bēs trō′), *n., pl.* **-tros.** **1** (in France) a small, modest, neighborhood wineshop and restaurant: *The postman went to Boutet, who kept a bistro—the social club and gathering place of the neighborhood* (New Yorker). **2** *Informal.* any bar or night club. [< French (Parisian slang) *bistro* pub]

bi|sul|cate (bī sul′kāt), *adj.* **1** having two grooves. **2** *Zoology.* = cloven-hoofed. [< *bi-* two + *sulcate*]

bi|sul|fate or **bi|sul|phate** (bī sul′fāt), *n.* a salt of sulfuric acid formed by neutralizing one hydrogen ion.

bi|sul|fid or **bi|sul|phid** (bī sul′fid), *n.* = disulfide.

bi|sul|fide or **bi|sul|phide** (bī sul′fīd, -fid), *n.* = disulfide.

bi|sul|fite or **bi|sul|phite** (bī sul′fīt), *n.* a salt of sulfurous acid containing the univalent group $-HSO_3$.

bi|sym|met|ric (bī′si met′rik), *adj.* = bisymmetrical.

bi|sym|met|ri|cal (bī′si met′rə kəl), *adj.* bilaterally symmetrical; zygomorphic. — **bi′sym|met′ri|cal|ly,** *adv.*

bi|sym|me|try (bī sim′ə trē), *n.* the correspondence of right and left parts; bilateral symmetry.

bit[1] (bit), *n.* **1** a small piece: *bits of broken glass, a bit of string. A pebble is a bit of rock.* **SYN:** fragment, morsel, portion, particle, speck. **2** a small amount: *a bit of work to do.* **3** *Informal.* a short time: *Stay a bit.* **4** *U.S. Informal.* 12½ cents. The term occurs chiefly in the expressions *two bits* (a quarter), *four bits* (a half dollar), and *six bits* (seventy-five cents). **5** *British Informal.* any one of various coins, especially a three-penny bit. **6** *U.S. Slang.* **a** a bit part; small part in a play or motion picture. **b** a piece of stage business; a routine: *... they went conspicuously into the "Gee, boss, you were great!" bit* (New York Times). **c** any typical or standard style, practice, or act: *I'm wearing the uniform: the button-down shirt, the V-neck, the stay-presseds, the penny loafers, the whole bit* (New Yorker).

a bit, a a little; slightly: *I am a bit tired.* **b** somewhat: *The boy who hung around so much became a bit of a nuisance to the workmen.*

a bit much, excessively inconvenient or inconsiderate: *That hand-pulled, open lift in a sort of black chimney at the back, where you go in connection with registered baggage, is a bit much for anyone straight from shiny, continental stations* (Punch).

a bit of all right, *British Informal.* something or someone heartily approved: *This beef is a bit of all right, ma'am* (H. G. Wells).

a bit of one's mind, a person's frank, and usually unfavorable, opinion: *He had given the house what was called a "bit of his mind" on the subject* (London Times).

bit by bit, little by little: *... this sort of bit-by-bit reform, going on for six hundred years* (Edward Freeman).

bits and pieces, stray or small articles; odds and ends: *Our garage is filled with bits and pieces of lumber we've collected over the years.*

do one's bit, to do one's share: *Each person did his bit toward getting the meal on the table.*

every bit, entirely; quite: *The university's social function is every bit as important as its intellectual one* (Manchester Guardian Weekly).

not a bit, not at all: *He is not a bit the worse for his ordeal.*

not a bit of it, not at all; not likely: *But not a bit of it, for Oxford came back with a shattering try* (London Times).

[Old English *bita* piece bitten off < *bītan* to bite]

bit[2] (bit), *v.* the past tense and a past participle of **bite**: *The strong trap bit the leg of the fox.*
► See **bite** for usage note.

*****bit[3]** (bit), *n., v.,* **bit|ted, bit|ting.** **—*n.*** **1** a tool for boring or drilling that fits into a handle called a brace or into an electric drill. **2** the biting or cutting part of a tool. **3** the part of a bridle that goes in a horse's mouth. A bit acts as a control, together with the connecting parts, such as the rings to which the reins are attached. **4** anything that curbs or restrains. **5** the part of a key that goes into a lock and makes it turn.
—*v.t.* **1** to put a bit in the mouth of (a horse); accustom to the bit; bridle. **2** *Figurative.* to curb; restrain. **3** to make a bit on (a key).

champ at the bit, a to be restless or impatient, as from lack of activity or from suppression: *He ... was champing at the bit and acted like a caged lion, so eager was he to get back to work on a less restricted basis* (Wall Street Journal). **b** (of a horse) to work the bit between the teeth impatiently.

take the bit in one's teeth, a to move ahead or act on one's own; refuse to accept guidance or control: *The way he had of taking the bit in his teeth offended his employer.* **b** (of horses) to become unmanageable: *His horse took the bit in his teeth and made off through the brush.*

[Old English *bite* a bite < *bītan* to bite]

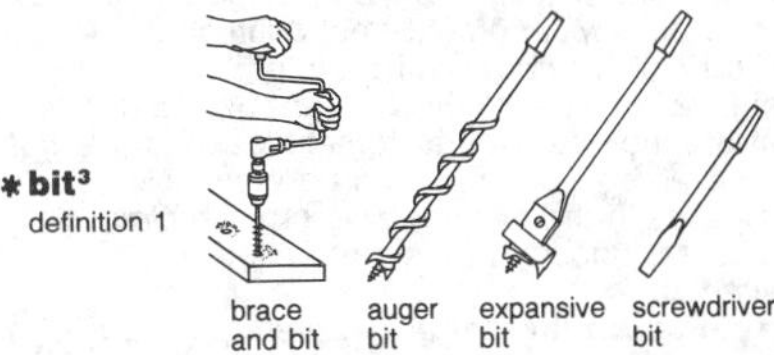

*****bit[3]** definition 1

bit[4] (bit), *n.* the basic unit of information in a digital computing system, expressed in binary notation so as to specify a choice between two possibilities, such as yes or no, off or on, etc. [< *bi*(nary) (digi)*t*]

bi|tan|gent (bī tan′jənt), *adj., n. Geometry.* **—*adj.*** touching a curved line or surface at two different points: *a bitangent line or plane.*
—*n.* a straight line which is tangent to a curve at two different points; a double tangent.

bi|tar|trate (bī tär′trāt), *n. Chemistry.* a salt of tartaric acid, which contains the univalent radical $-C_4H_5O_6$; an acid tartrate. [< *bi-* two + *tartrate*]

bit|brace (bit′brās′), *n.* = bitstock.

bitch[1] (bich), *n., v.* **—*n.*** **1** a female dog, wolf, or fox. **2** *Slang.* **a** a lewd woman. **b** a spiteful, ill-tempered woman. **3** *Slang.* = complaint.
—*v.t.* *Slang.* to spoil; bungle.
—*v.i.* *Slang.* = complain.
[Old English *bicce*]

bitch[2] (bich), *n.* a primitive form of lamp used in Alaska. [origin uncertain]

bitch|er|y (bich′ə rē), *n. Slang.* bitchy quality; spitefulness.

bitch goddess, material success (viewed as an object of base worship).

bitch|y (bich′ē), *adj.,* **bitch|i|er, bitch|i|est.** *Slang.* spiteful and ill-tempered. — **bitch′i|ly,** *adv.* — **bitch′i|ness,** *n.*

bite (bīt), *v.,* **bit, bit|ten** or **bit, bit|ing,** *n.* **—*v.t.*** **1** to seize, cut into, or cut off with the teeth: *She bit the apple. That nervous boy bites his nails.* **SYN:** chew, gnaw, nibble. **2** to wound with teeth, fangs, or a sting: *My dog never bites children. A mosquito bit me.* **3** to cause a sharp, smarting pain to: *His fingers are bitten by frost.* **4** to take a tight hold on; grip: *The wheels bite the rails. The jaws of a vise bite the wood they hold.* **5** to cut; pierce: *The sword bit the knight's helmet.*

Pronunciation Key: hat, āge, cãre, fär; let, ēqual, tėrm; it, īce; hot, ōpen, ôrder; oil, out; cup, pu̇t, rüle; child; long; thin; ᴛʜen; zh, measure; ə represents **a** in about, **e** in taken, **i** in pencil, **o** in lemon, **u** in circus.

6 to eat into or corrode: *Acid bites metal.* 7 *Informal, Figurative.* to deceive; take in (now only in the passive): *We were certainly bitten when we bought that old car.*
—*v.i.* 1 to cause injury by biting: *My dog never bites.* 2 to nip; snap: *a dog biting at fleas.* 3 to press the teeth (into or on). 4 to take a bait; be caught: *The fish are biting well today.* 5 *Figurative.* to be taken in; be tricked: *With a dozen or more trade fairs round the world, the British are not biting—whether it is called a festival or not* (Manchester Guardian Weekly). 6 *Informal.* to bother; annoy: *What's biting you?*
—*n.* 1 the act of biting; a cut or hold with the teeth; nip: *The dog gave a bite or two at the bone.* 2 a piece bitten off; bit of food; mouthful: *Eat the whole apple, not just a bite.* 3 a light meal; snack: *Have a bite with me now or you'll get hungry later.* 4 a wound made by biting or stinging: *The man soon recovered from the snake's bite.* 5 a sharp, smarting pain: *We felt the bite of the cold wind.* 6 *Figurative.* a cutting or wounding quality; sharpness: *the bite of his sarcasm. The style already has polish and bite enough to hold the reader fairly fast* (Punch). SYN: trenchancy. 7 a tight hold or grip: *the bite of a vise, the bite of an engine's wheels on the rails.* 8 the action of acid eating into a metal: *The bite of the acid makes the engraving.* 9 the manner in which the opposing teeth in the upper and lower jaws meet; occlusion. 10 *U.S. Slang, Figurative.* the amount of money taken from a total: *The local tax took a large bite out of his salary.*
bite back, to restrain (speech) by biting the lips: *Hot and strong was the reply which rose to Robert's lips, but he bit it back* (J. H. Riddell).
bite off more than one can chew, to undertake too much; be too ambitious: *Young lawyer Comerford . . . bit off more than he could chew. . . . He could not make good when called on for proof* (Hartford Courant).
bite the hand that feeds one. See under **hand.**
put the bite on, *U.S. Slang.* to borrow, or seek to borrow, money from: *There are several families trying to live at a standard above their income—and putting the bite on acquaintances to make ends meet* (Wall Street Journal).
[Old English *bītan*] —**bite'a|ble,** *adj.*
▶In place of the older, standard past participle **bitten,** the newer **bit** is sometimes used (*He got bit by a dog*). *Bit* may even be preferable sometimes, as in the monosyllabic proverb *Once bit, twice shy,* though this is often quoted as *Once bitten, ...*

bi|tem|po|ral (bī tem'pər əl, -tem'prəl), *adj.* of or having to do with the two temporal bones of the brain.

bit|er (bī'tər), *n.* a person or animal that bites.

bite-size (bīt'sīz'), *adj.* very small: *a bite-size sandwich, a bite-size boy.*

bite-sized (bīt'sīzd'), *adj.* = bite-size.

bite|wing (bīt'wing'), *n.* a kind of X-ray film used by dentists, with a fin which the teeth close on to keep it in place.

bit|ing (bī'ting), *adj.* 1 sharp; cutting: *Dress warmly before you go out in that biting wind.* 2 *Figurative.* sarcastic; sneering; bitter: *Biting remarks hurt people's feelings.* SYN: caustic. —**bit'ing|ly,** *adv.* —**bit'ing|ness,** *n.*

biting louse, any one of an order of wingless lice that feed upon the hair, feathers, and outer skin of birds, rodents, and other warm-blooded animals; bird louse.

biting midge, = punkie.

bi|ton|al (bī tō'nəl), *adj.* composed in or exhibiting two musical tonalities: *bitonal pieces in remotely related keys for . . . characters who had a dual nature* (Atlantic).

bi|to|nal|i|ty (bī'tō nal'ə tē), *n., pl.* **-ties.** the use of two musical tonalities at the same time.

bit part, a small part in a play, movie, or other performance.

bit player, a person who has a bit part.

bit|stock (bit'stok'), *n.* the handle for holding and turning a bit in drilling or boring holes; a brace.

bit|sy (bits'ē), *adj. Informal.* very small; itsy-bitsy.

bitt (bit), *n., v.* —*n.* a strong wooden or metal post on a ship's deck, usually one of a pair, to which ropes or cables are fastened.
—*v.t.* to put (a rope or cable) around the bitts.
[variant of *bit*[3]]

bit|te (bit'ə), *interj. German.* 1 please. 2 what was that again, please? 3 you're very welcome; think nothing of it.

bit|ten (bit'ən), *v.* a past participle of **bite:** *Finish the apple, now that you have bitten into it.*
▶See **bite** for usage note.

bit|ter[1] (bit'ər), *adj., adv., n., v.* —*adj.* 1 having a sharp, harsh, unpleasant taste: *Brussels sprouts are often bitter.* SYN: acrid. 2 *Figurative.* causing pain or grief; hard to admit or bear: *a bitter defeat. Failure is bitter. The death of his father was a bitter loss.* SYN: painful, distressing, grievous. 3 *Figurative.* harsh or cutting: *a bitter remark, bitter enemies.* SYN: caustic, acrimonious, virulent. 4 sharp or severe: *a bitter wound,* (*Figurative.*) *a bitter quarrel.* SYN: stinging. 5 *Figurative.* showing pain or grief: *The lost child shed bitter tears.* 6 very cold: *The bitter winter killed our apple tree.*
—*adv.* bitterly: *a bitter cold day.*
—*n.* 1 that which is bitter; bitterness: *You must take the bitter with the sweet.* 2 a bitter medicine or draught; bitters. 3 a bitter taste or flavor. 4 *Especially British.* dark, bitter beer.
—*v.t.* to make bitter; embitter.
[Old English *biter.* See related etym. at **bite.**]
—**bit'ter|ly,** *adv.* —**bit'ter|ness,** *n.*

bit|ter[2] (bit'ər), *n. Nautical.* a turn of a cable round the bitts. [< *bitt*]

bitter almond, 1 a variety of almond producing extremely bitter nuts. 2 these nuts, from which an oil is derived.

bitter apple, the colocynth, a plant of the gourd family grown for its orangelike fruit.

bitter bark, any one of various trees whose bark is bitter and has medicinal properties, as the cascara in the United States.

bitter brush, = antelope brush.

bitter buttons, = tansy (def. 1).

bitter cassava, a cassava, the source of tapioca, whose roots contain a bitter acid which is removed by grinding and washing to make them edible.

bitter cress, any one of a genus of plants of the mustard family, bearing white or purple flowers.

bitter dock, a European dock with small, greenish or purplish flowers and a rough stem, that is found throughout the United States and southern Canada, growing especially along roadsides and in other waste places; broadleaf dock.

bitter end[1], 1 the very end; last extremity: *We will fight to the bitter end. His insulting behavior was the bitter end.* 2 death.

bitter end[2], the inboard end of a cable or rope on a ship riding at anchor. [< *bitt* + *-er*[2]]

bit|ter-end (bit'ər end'), *adj.* = stubborn.

bit|ter-end|er (bit'ər en'dər), *n.* a very persistent, unyielding person: *There are strong resisters in both political parties, as was evidenced by the bitter-enders at both the presidential conventions* (Atlantic).

bit|ter|ish (bit'ər ish), *adj.* somewhat bitter.

bit|ter|ling (bit'ər ling), *n.* a small, carplike freshwater fish of central Europe. [< German *Bitterling* < *bitter* bitter + *-ling* -ling]

bit|tern[1] (bit'ərn), *n.* a wading bird that lives in marshes and has a peculiar booming cry. It is a small kind of heron. [< Old French *butor,* apparently ultimately < Latin *būtiō* + *taurus* bull]

bit|tern[2] (bit'ərn), *n.* the bitter liquid remaining after salt has crystallized out of seawater or brine. [< *bitter*[1]]

bit|ter|nut (bit'ər nut'), *n.* a species of hickory that grows in swamps and moist woods and bears thin-shelled nuts with a bitter kernel. The bitternut belongs to the walnut family.

bitter orange, = sour orange.

bitter pill, anything that is hard to accept.

bitter pit, a disease of apples and other tree-growing fruit, characterized by small discolorations in the skin and flesh of the fruit.

bitter principle, a strongly bitter substance usually obtained from plants, and generally not of definite chemical composition.

bit|ter|root (bit'ər rüt', -rut'), *n.* a small plant with thick, edible roots and showy, pink or white flowers, found in the northern Rocky Mountains. It belongs to the purslane family. Bitterroot is the state flower of Montana.

bitter rot, a disease of apples, pears, grapes, and other fruits, caused by a fungus related to the group that causes anthracnose.

bit|ters (bit'ərz), *n.pl.* 1 a liquid in which a bitter herb, bark, or root has been steeped. Bitters are used to flavor certain cocktails or foods, and sometimes as medicine. 2 a bitter, dark beer. 3 bitter medicines generally, such as quinine.

bit|ter|sweet (bit'ər swēt'), *n., adj.* —*n.* 1 a climbing plant with purple, blue, or white flowers and small, poisonous, scarlet berries; woody nightshade. It belongs to the nightshade family. 2 a climbing shrub of North America with greenish flowers and orange seed cases that open and show red seeds; false bittersweet. It belongs to the staff-tree family. 3 sweetness and bitterness mixed: (*Figurative.*) *'Tis something like Love, a kinde of bittersweet* (Owen Feltham). 4 Chinese red.
—*adj.* 1 sweet and bitter mixed: *bittersweet chocolate.* 2 *Figurative.* pleasant and painful at once: *The movie had a bittersweet ending which left her uncertain whether to laugh or cry. It awakes all the fountains of bittersweet memory* (George Brimley). —**bit'ter|sweet'ness,** *n.*

bit|ter|weed (bit'ər wēd'), *n.* ragweed, horseweed, or any one of various other plants containing a bitter principle.

bit|ter|wort (bit'ər wėrt'), *n.* any one of various species of gentian.

bit|tock (bit'ək), *n. Scottish.* a little bit.

bit|ty (bit'ē), *adj.,* **-ti|er, -ti|est.** 1 very small; tiny: *A little bitty incentive won't do* (Harper's). 2 consisting of bits and pieces; disconnected; fragmentary: *Conversation was bitty and irresolute* (Punch). —**bit'ti|ness,** *n.*

bi|tu|mas|tic (bə tü mas'tik, -tyü-; bich'u̇-), *adj.* of or designating an asphaltic substance used for coating metal structures to protect them from corrosion. [< *Bitumastic,* a trademark for this substance]

bi|tu|men (bə tü'mən, -tyü'-; bich'u̇-), *n.* 1 any one of a number of minerals that will burn, such as asphalt, petroleum, and naphtha. 2 a pigment used in oil painting, made of asphalt ground in a drying oil, which gives a rich brown, transparent surface. [< Latin *bitūmen, -inis*]

bi|tu|mi|nize (bə tü'mə nīz, -tyü'-), *v.t.,* **-nized, -niz|ing.** 1 to convert into bitumen. 2 to treat with bitumen. —**bi|tu'mi|ni|za'tion,** *n.*

bi|tu|mi|noid (bə tü'mə noid, -tyü'-), *adj.* 1 like bitumen. 2 containing bitumen.

bi|tu|mi|nous (bə tü'mə nəs, -tyü'-), *adj.* 1 containing or made with bitumen. 2 like bitumen.

bituminous coal, coal that burns with much smoke and a yellow flame; soft coal; black coal. The volatile matter in bituminous coal constitutes more than 18 per cent.

bituminous sand = tar sand.

bi|typ|ic (bī tip'ik), *adj.* consisting of two types only (of a genus containing but two species).

bi|une (bī yün'), *adj.* = biunial.

bi|u|ni|al (bī yü'nē əl), *adj.* having or consisting of two combined in one. [< *bi-* two + Latin *ūnus* one + English *-ial*]

bi|u|rate (bī yu̇r'āt), *n. Chemistry.* an acid salt of uric acid. [< *bi-* + *uric* (acid) + *-ate*[2]]

bi|u|ret (bī'yu̇ ret', bī yu̇r'et), *n. Chemistry.* a compound formed by heating urea. *Formula:* $C_2H_3O_2N_3 \cdot H_2O$

biuret test, the red or reddish-violet color which is produced when sodium hydroxide and a dilute solution of copper sulfate are added to a solution containing a protein.

bi|va|lence (bī vā'ləns, biv'ə-), *n.* bivalent quality or condition.

bi|va|len|cy (bī vā'lən sē, biv'ə-), *n.* = bivalence.

bi|va|lent (bī vā'lənt, biv'ə-), *adj., n.* —*adj.* 1a having a valence of 2; divalent. b having two valences, as bismuth. 2 double (applied to a pair of homologous chromosomes when united in synapsis).
—*n.* a bivalent pair of chromosomes.
[< *bi-* two + Latin *valēns, -entis,* present participle of *valēre* be worth]

***bi|valve** (bī'valv'), *n., adj.* —*n.* 1 any mollusk whose shell consists of two parts hinged together so that it will open and shut like a book; lamellibranch; pelecypod. Oysters and clams are bivalves. 2 a seed capsule that splits in two halves, such as a pod of a pea.
—*adj.* having two parts hinged together.

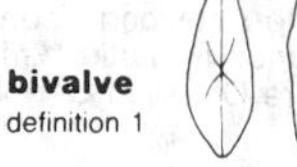

***bivalve** definition 1

bi|valved (bī'valvd'), *adj.* = bivalvular.

bi|val|vu|lar (bī val'vyə lər), *adj.* 1 having two valves. 2 of or having to do with bivalves.

bi|var|i|ate (bī vãr'ē it), *adj.* involving two variates.

biv|ou|ac (biv'u̇ ak, biv'wak), *n., v.,* **-acked, -ack|ing.** —*n.* 1 an outdoor camp usually without tents or with very small tents: *The soldiers made a bivouac for the night in the field.* SYN: encampment. 2 the site of such an encampment.
—*v.i.* to camp outdoors usually without tents or with very small tents: *They bivouacked there until morning.* SYN: encamp.
[< French *bivouac,* probably < Low German *bīwake* < *bī* by + *wake* watch]

biv|ou|ack|er (biv'u̇ ak'ər, biv'wak-), *n.* a person who bivouacs.

bi|wa (bē'wä), *n.* a Japanese stringed instrument resembling a lute. [< Japanese *biwa*]

bi|week|ly (bī wēk'lē), *adj., adv., n., pl.* **-lies.**
—*adj.* 1 happening or appearing once every two weeks: *The magazine is a biweekly publication.* 2 happening or appearing twice a week; semiweekly: *The teachers have biweekly conferences on Mondays and Fridays.*
—*adv.* 1 once every two weeks: *The group meets biweekly.* 2 twice a week; semiweekly.
—*n.* a newspaper or magazine published biweekly.

bi|year|ly (bī yir′lē), *adj., adv.* —*adj.* **1** happening twice a year: *The grandchildren make a biyearly visit to their grandparents.* **2** every two years: *Some comets have a biyearly orbit of the sun.* SYN: biannual. —*adv.* twice a year: *Many businesses pay taxes biyearly.* SYN: biannually.

biz (biz), *n. Slang.* business. [compare use of *buzz* in **buzz word**]

bi|zarre (bi zär′), *adj.* strikingly odd or queer in appearance or style; fantastic; grotesque: *The frost made bizarre patterns on the windowpanes.* [< French *bizarre* < Spanish *bizarro* brave < Basque *bizar* beard] —**bi|zarre′ly**, *adv.*

bi|zar|re|rie (bē zá rə rē′), *n. French.* bizarre quality.

B.J., Bachelor of Journalism.

bk., **1** bank. **2** bark. **3** block. **4** book.

Bk (no period), berkelium (chemical element).

Bk., **1** Bank. **2** Book.

bkg., banking.

bkkpg., bookkeeping.

bkpt., bankrupt.

bks., **1** barracks. **2** books.

bkt., **1** basket. **2** bracket.

bkts., baskets.

bl., **1** bale **2** barrel. **3** black.

b.l., **1** bill of lading. **2** breechloading.

B/L, bill of lading.

B.L., *U.S.* Bachelor of Laws.

B.L.A., Bachelor of Liberal Arts.

blab (blab), *v.,* **blabbed**, **blab|bing**, *n. Informal.* —*v.t., v.i.* to tell (secrets); talk too much. SYN: tattle.
—*n.* **1** babbling talk; chatter. **2** a person who blabs; telltale; tattler. [Middle English *blabbe*]

blab|ber (blab′ər), *v., n.* —*v.t., v.i.* to blab; talk idly.
—*n.* **1** a person who blabs. **2** foolish talk.

blab|ber|mouth (blab′ər mouth′), *n. Slang.* a person who talks indiscreetly or too much.

black (blak), *adj., n. v.* —*adj.* **1** having the color of coal or soot; opposite of white; reflecting little or no light: *Black ink spilled over the picture so that it disappeared.* **2** without any light; very dark: *The room was black as night.* **3** dirty; filthy: *His hands were black with soot.* SYN: soiled, grimy, sooty. **4** *Figurative.* **a** gloomy; dismal: *This has been a black day.* **b** complete and unrelieved: *black despair.* **5** *Figurative.* angry; sullen: *She gave her brother a black look.* SYN: lowering, frowning, threatening. **6** *Figurative.* evil; wicked: *a black lie. Witches were supposed to practice black magic.* SYN: sinister, deadly, baneful. **7** *Figurative.* having a dark skin. SYN: swarthy, dusky. **8** Also, **Black.** **a** of or having to do with blacks. **b** resembling blacks. **9** wearing black or dark clothing: *black canons.* **10** *Figurative.* disastrous: *Black tidings—blacker never came to New England* (Nathaniel Hawthorne). SYN: sad, calamitous. **11** *British.* boycotted or banned by a labor union: *black work, to declare a company's goods black.*
—*n.* **1** the color of coal or soot; the opposite of white: *The black shows up against the white.* **2** a black paint, dye, or pigment. **3** Also, **Black.** **a** a person belonging to any of the black races of Africa, characterized by brown or black skin, coarse, woolly hair, and a broad, flat nose. **b** a member of any other dark-skinned people. **c** a person having some black ancestors (subject to precise definition by law in certain states and countries). **4** black clothes, especially when worn as a sign of mourning. **5a** the squares or other shapes colored black on a checker, chess, or backgammon board. **b** the black or colored pieces used in checkers, chess, or backgammon. **c** the player moving the black or colored pieces.
—*v.t.* **1** to make black; put a black color on: *The children blacked the door with their fingermarks.* **2** to put blacking on (shoes or a stove). **3** *British.* to boycott or ban, especially in protest against the hiring of nonunion workers (blacklegs).
—*v.i.* to become black.
black out, **a** to become temporarily blind or unconscious: *The pain was so intense that he blacked out for several minutes.* **b** to darken completely: *to black out the stage. He blacked out in a blot Thy brief life's pleasantness* (Elizabeth Barrett Browning). **c** to suppress; withhold: *The general blacked out all news of the battle. The Russian censor . . . blacks out all matter that is displeasing to the government* (Charles George Gordon). **d** to exclude from television reception: *All New England was blacked out for the title fight.*
in the black, showing no loss, and usually a profit (entered in black ink in account books): *J & L managed to stay in the black in July* (Wall Street Journal).
[Old English *blæc*]
▶**Black**, meaning Negro, was formerly seldom used in American English in formal writing and speech except when referring contemptuously to Negroes. In the mid-1960's, however, *black* began to gain currency, but this time on a respectable level, as ethnic groups promoted labels with such slogans as "Black is Beautiful." Now black is widely used in referring to the ethnic group and its enterprises and organizations (black capitalism, black power, Black Muslim), but is still considered in some quarters, particularly among older blacks and whites, as somewhat contemptuous.

black alder, a holly of eastern North America bearing scarlet berries that remain after the fall of the leaves; winterberry; deciduous holly.

black|a|moor (blak′ə mu̇r), *n.* **1** a dark-skinned person. **2** a black, especially an African black. [variant of *black Moor*]

black-and-blue (blak′ən blü′), *adj.* discolored from a bruise.

Black and Tan, **1** the constabulary troops sent by the British government in 1920-21 to Ireland to put down the rebellion against the British. **2** a member of these troops.

black and tan terrier, a former name of the Manchester terrier.

black and white, **1** writing or print: *I asked him to put his promise down in black and white.* **2** a picture or sketch using only black and white.

black-and-white (blak′ən hwīt′), *adj.* **1** being, done, or appearing in black and white: *a black-and-white picture.* **2a** divided into opposed, unmixed extremes as good and evil, truth and falsity. **b** evaluating in terms of such extremes: *black-and-white answers to complex problems* (Atlantic).

black|arm disease (blak′ärm′), a bacterial disease of the cotton plant, characterized by long, dark lesions on the stem.

black art, evil magic; black magic; necromancy.

black ash, a North American species of ash.

black-a-viced (blak′ə vīst′), *adj. Dialect.* black-a-vised.

black-a-vised (blak′ə vīzd′, -vīst′), *adj. Dialect.* dark-complexioned; swarthy. [< *black* + French *à-vis* to face (as in *vis-à-vis*)]

black|back (blak′bak′), *n.* = winter flounder.

black-back (blak′bak′), *n.* = black-backed gull.

black-backed gull (blak′bakt′), either of two gulls of the Atlantic coasts of Europe and North America, having backs and upper wing surfaces of a dark slate color.

black-bag job (blak′bag′), *U.S. Informal.* a burglary by a law enforcement agent to obtain information.

black|ball (blak′bôl′), *v., n.* —*v.t.* **1** to vote against; reject as a candidate for membership: *One member of the club blackballed him, so he could not become a member.* **2** to exclude from society; ostracize; taboo: *The community blackballed the family when the father went to prison.*
—*n.* **1** a vote against a person or thing. **2** a black ball used to express such a vote. —**black′ball′er**, *n.*

black|band (blak′band′), *n.* an iron ore containing a large proportion of carbon and resembling coal, such as chalybite or siderite.

black bass, any one of various game fishes of eastern and central North America that live in fresh water, such as the largemouth bass.

black bean, **1a** the edible, black seed of any of various bean plants, especially several varieties grown in South America. **b** the plant it grows on. **2a** = lablab. **b** = Egyptian bean.

black bear, **1** the common species of North American bear, growing about 5 feet long. The color of its dense fur varies between black, brown, gray, and white. See picture under **bear**[1]. **2** an Asiatic bear, smaller than the American variety, having a large, white, crescent-shaped mark on the chest.

black beetle, = oriental cockroach.

black-bel|lied plover (blak′bel′ēd), a gray, black, and white plover that breeds in the arctic regions of North America and Siberia; oxeye. It is the largest plover of North America.

black belt, **1** a section in a city or region where there are more blacks than white people (often used disparagingly). **2** Also, **Black Belt.** a strip of very rich black soil in Alabama and Mississippi. **3a** the highest order in judo and karate. **b** a person admitted to this order. **c** the black sash awarded to such a person.

black|ber|ry (blak′ber′ē, -bər-), *n., pl.* **-ries**, *v.,* **-ried**, **-ry|ing**. —*n.* **1** a small, black or dark-purple fruit of certain bushes and vines. Blackberries are sweet and juicy. **2** the thorny bush or vine that it grows on. The blackberry belongs to the rose family.
—*v.i.* to gather blackberries.
[Old English *blaceberie*]

blackberry lily, a garden perennial of the iris family, with orange, lilylike flowers spotted with red, and clusters of black seeds that suggest blackberries.

black bile, (in ancient and medieval physiology) the one of the four humors, thought to cause melancholy.

black-billed cuckoo (blak′bild′), a North American cuckoo with a black bill, which builds its own nest and hatches its own eggs.

black bindweed, **1** a twining, perennial European vine bearing red berries. **2** a twining herb of the buckwheat family, native to Europe and found in America as a troublesome weed.

black birch, any one of several North American species of birch, especially the sweet birch.

black|bird (blak′bėrd′), *n.* **1** any one of various American birds so named because the male is mostly black. The cowbird, purple grackle, and red-winged blackbird are blackbirds. Blackbirds are related to the orioles. **2** the common European thrush, with a black body and orange bill. **3** *Figurative.* a black or other dark-skinned person seized for forced labor or slavery.

black|bird|er (blak′bėr′dər), *n.* **1** a person who kidnapped blacks or other dark-skinned people for slavery. **2** a ship used to transport slaves.

black|bird|ing (blak′bėr′ding), *n.* the kidnapping of blacks or other dark-skinned people for slavery.

black blizzard, *U.S. Dialect.* a dust storm.

black|board (blak′bôrd′, -bōrd′), *n.* a dark, smooth piece of slate, glass, or painted wood on which to write or draw with chalk.

blackboard jungle, **1** a school in which a condition of disorder and lawlessness exists. **2** the condition itself. [< *The Blackboard Jungle,* a novel about such a school by Evan Hunter, born 1926, an American writer]

black body, or **black|bod|y** (blak′bod′ē), *n.* a theoretical surface or body capable of completely absorbing all the radiation falling on it. The energy radiated per second by each unit area of a perfect black body is proportional solely to the fourth power of its absolute temperature.

black book, a book containing the names of persons to be criticized or punished.
be in one's black book, to have incurred one's displeasure; be out of one's favor: *This unfortunate youth is so deep in your black book* (James Payn).

black bottom, *U.S.* a spirited solo dance popular especially in the 1920's.

black bourse, *British.* = black market.

black box, *Informal.* **1** any self-contained electronic device in an aircraft as a complete unit. A black box may be used for controlling a mechanism or process, for obtaining and recording data, and for automatic landing. **2** a similar unit to detect nuclear explosions, to help enforce a nuclear test ban treaty, or to detect earthquakes. **3** any unknown system, especially one considered solely in terms of input and output without an understanding of its workings: *The computer—for many purposes—may be thought of as a black box* (Atlantic).

black|boy (blak′boi′), *n.* = grass tree.

black brant, a brownish black wild goose of North America.

black bread, a heavy, coarse, dark rye bread.

black-browed (blak′broud′), *adj.* menacing; scowling.

black|buck (blak′buk′), *n.* a medium-sized antelope common in India, black with white underneath.

Black|burn|i|an warbler (blak bėr′nē ən), a North American warbler, the adult male of which has an orange-yellow and black head and neck and an orange-yellow breast. [< a proper name]

black|butt (blak′but′), *n.* a species of eucalyptus cut for timber in Australia.

black cancer, = melanoma.

black canon, an Augustinian canon, so called from his black habit.

black|cap (blak′kap′), *n.* **1** *U.S.* **a** a black raspberry occurring wild in many parts of the United States, and also cultivated in several varieties. **b** its fruit. **2** any one of various birds that have the top of the head black, such as the European warbler or the chickadee. **3** *British.* the black skullcap put on by a judge sentencing someone to death.

black capitalism, *U.S.* the ownership and management of businesses by blacks, especially with government support.

black-capped chickadee (blak′kapt′), the common chickadee of North America.

black-capped vireo, a vireo of the southern, central, and southwestern United States, having black feathers on the top and sides of its head.

black cattle, *British.* cattle raised for beef, regardless of color, distinguished from dairy cattle.

Black Cayuga, = Cayuga duck.

black chaser, = blacksnake.

black cherry, an American wild cherry whose

Pronunciation Key: hat, āge, cãre, fär; let, ēqual, tėrm; it, īce; hot, ōpen, ôrder; oil, out; cup, pu̇t, rüle; child; long; thin; ᴛʜen; zh, measure; ə represents **a** in about, **e** in taken, **i** in pencil, **o** in lemon, **u** in circus.

light, hard, strong, reddish wood is used for cabinetwork, interior finishing, and other woodworking.

black coal, = bituminous coal.

black-coat (blak′kōt′), *adj. British.* white-collar.

black-coat·ed (blak′kō′tid), *adj. British.* black-coat.

black·cock (blak′kok′), *n.* the male of the black grouse; heath cock.

black code, any of the various state laws that regulated the activities of blacks in the South after the Civil War, used generally to restrict the rights of blacks by circumscribing their right to hold office and vote, forbidding ownership of land or the bearing of arms, and curtailing other civil rights.

black coffee, coffee without cream or milk.

black cohosh, a North American medicinal plant of the crowfoot family.

black comedy, a type of comedy characterized by bizarrely or morbidly humorous plots and situations.

black cotton soil, a very thick, dark soil found in the Deccan of southern India.

black cottonwood, **1** a cottonwood of the northwestern United States. **2** a tree of the willow family found in swampy ground in the southern and eastern United States.

Black Country, the smoky, industrialized Midland area of England.

black crappie, = calico bass.

black-crowned night heron (blak′kround′), a heron common in most of the temperate regions, active chiefly at night.

black currant, a European currant with yellow-flowered racemes and black fruit, used in jams, jellies, and wine, though not good to eat raw.

black·damp (blak′damp′), *n.* = chokedamp.

Black Death, the bubonic plague that spread through Europe in the 1300's and destroyed one-fourth of its population.

black diamond, **1** = coal. **2** = carbonado[1].

black disease, an acute, generally fatal disease of sheep caused by toxins from a bacterium which multiplies in the liver as a result of initial damage by the common liver fluke.

black dog, *Slang.* bad humor; the blues.

black draft or **draught**, a purgative medicine consisting of an infusion of senna, fennel, and magnesium sulfate.

black duck, a very common duck of eastern and central North America, having uniformly dark coloration.

black·en (blak′ən), *v.*, **-ened, -en·ing.** *—v.t.* **1** to make black: *Soot blackened the snow.* SYN: darken. **2** to speak evil of: *She blackened his character with false gossip.* SYN: slander, defame. *—v.i.* to become black: *The sky blackened and soon it began to rain.* SYN: darken. **—black′en·er**, *n.*

Black English, any one of various dialects of English spoken by blacks, especially in the United States: *"Black English" is . . . remarkably rich in nuances* (Time).

black·er (blak′ər), *n.* a person who blacks or blackens.

black eye, **1** a bruise around an eye. **2** *Informal.* **a** a severe blow or rebuff: *The insult gave his pride a black eye.* **b** a cause of disgrace or discredit. **c** disgrace or discredit: *When they [surveys] are as far apart as these two studies, market testing gets a black eye* (Wall Street Journal).

black-eyed (blak′īd′), *adj.* **1** having eyes with a black or blackish-brown iris: *a black-eyed brunette.* **2** having an eye blackened or bruised.

black-eyed pea, the brownish seed of the cowpea, much used as food in the southern part of the United States.

∗**black-eyed Su·san** (sü′zən), a yellow daisy with a black or dark center. It is a member of the composite family and is the state flower of Maryland.

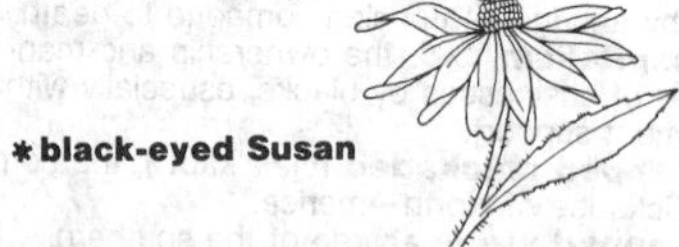

∗**black-eyed Susan**

black·face (blak′fās′), *n., adj. —n.* **1a** a black minstrel, or an actor made up as a black. **b** the makeup for black parts in a show. **c** a show in which the actors are blacks or persons made up as blacks. **2** *Informal.* = boldface. **3** *British.* a hardy kind of sheep with a dark face.
—adj. of or in blackface; having to do with blackface.

black·faced (blak′fāst′), *adj.* **1** having a black or blackened face. **2** gloomy; dispirited; dejected.

Blackface Highland, *U.S.* Scottish Blackface.

black fast, a nonobligatory fast of the Roman Catholic Church in which the evening meal is restricted to bread and water.

Black·feet (blak′fēt′), *n.pl. or sing.* Blackfoot, a tribe of American Indians.

black·fel·low (blak′fel′ō), *n.* a member of any native tribe of Australia.

black fever, = typhus.

black·fin (blak′fin′), *n., pl.* **-fins** or (*collectively*) **-fin. 1** a whitefish of Lake Michigan. **2** any one of certain other whitefishes.

black·fish (blak′fish′), *n., pl.* **-fish·es** or (*collectively*) **-fish. 1** any one of various dark-colored fishes, such as the sea bass or the tautog. **2a** a small, dolphinlike black whale; pilot whale. **b** = killer whale. **3** a small, edible, freshwater fish of Alaska and Siberia. It is able to survive below freezing water temperatures for a certain amount of time. **4** a salmon after spawning.

black flag, **1** the pirate's flag; Jolly Roger; black-jack. It usually had a white skull and crossbones on it. **2** a flag of black cloth hoisted to show that a person condemned to death has been executed.

black-flag (blak′flag′), *v.t.*, **-flagged, -flag·ging.** (in car races) to signal (a car or driver) to leave the course by waving a black flag: *Chief Steward Harlan Fengler had warned drivers that any car spraying oil would be "black-flagged" instantly* (Time).

black fly, **1** a small fly with a black body, found in most parts of the world. The female can inflict a very painful bite. **2** a minute insect that attacks citrus fruit trees.

Black·foot (blak′fu̇t′), *n., pl.* **-feet** or **-foot** *for 1, adj. —n.* **1** a member of a tribe of American Indians that formerly lived in the northwestern United States and southern Canada and now live on reservations in Montana and Alberta, Canada. The Blackfoot speak an Algonkian language. **2** the Algonkian language of the Blackfoot Indians of North America.
—adj. of or having to do with the Blackfoot or their language.
[American English; translation of the Algonkian tribal name *Siksika,* believed to refer to their moccasins]

black-foot·ed ferret (blak′fu̇t′id), a weasel of the western United States, with a brown body and black feet.

black fox, a variety of red fox with a black fur.

Black Friar, **1** a Dominican friar, so called from the black mantle worn by the order. **2** = Black Monk.

Black·fri·ars (blak′frī′ərz), *n.* a locality in the center of London, southwest of St. Paul's.

Black Friday, **1** any Friday when some calamity happens, such as September 24, 1869, and September 19, 1873, dates of financial crises in the United States. **2** Good Friday (so called because on that day the vestments of the clergy are black).

black frost, a very hard frost; killing frost (from the fact that some of the green vegetation is turned black or dark by it).

black game, *British.* black grouse. The male is called *blackcock,* and the female, *gray hen.*

black glass, an opaque glass containing manganese iron.

black gold, *U.S. Informal.* **1** = petroleum; oil. **2** = rubber.

black gram, = urd (a bean of India).

black grass, **1** a species of foxtail grass. **2** a species of rush growing in salt marshes in the United States.

black grouse, a large grouse of Europe and Asia; heathbird. The male is black with white markings and a curled tail. The female is smaller and is brown and gray.

black·guard (blag′ärd, -ərd), *n., v. —n.* a low, contemptible man; scoundrel.
—v.t. to abuse with vile language; revile.
—v.i. to behave like a blackguard.
[< *black guard* (originally) household menials, black with dirt and soot]

black·guard·ism (blag′är diz əm, -ər-), *n.* **1** blackguardly conduct; ruffianism. **2** blackguardly language.

black·guard·ly (blag′ärd lē, -ərd-), *adj., adv.* of or like a blackguard.

black guillemot, a guillemot of both the American and European coasts of the North Atlantic, mostly black in its summer plumage, with red feet.

black gum, a large North American tree, a tupelo, bearing long-stemmed, dark-blue berries; black tupelo; pepperidge.

Black Hand, **1** *U.S.* a secret society organized to commit blackmail and crimes of violence. **2** an anarchistic society in Spain, broken up in 1883.
[American English; translation of Spanish *mano negra* and Italian *mano nera*]

black haw, **1** a North American shrub of the honeysuckle family, having large clusters (cymes) of white flowers and a bright blue-black fruit (drupe); stagbush. **2** a similar shrub, the sheepberry.

black·head (blak′hed′), *n.* **1** a small, black-tipped lump of dead cells and oil plugging a pore of the skin; comedo. **2** any of various birds that have a black head. **3** Often, **blackhead disease.** an acute infectious disease of the intestines and liver of turkeys, chickens, and other fowl, caused by a protozoan parasite.

black-head·ed grosbeak (blak′hed′id), a grosbeak of western North America.

black-headed gull, any one of several gulls with a black head, such as the laughing gull.

black·heart (blak′härt′), *n.* **1** a disease of plants, especially of potatoes and certain trees, characterized by a blackening of the internal tissues. **2** a variety of cherry whose sweet, somewhat heart-shaped fruit has a blackish skin.

black-heart·ed (blak′här′tid), *adj.* wicked; evil.

black heat, a stage in the heating of metals, especially iron or steel, just below red heat.

black hellebore, = Christmas rose.

black henbane, = henbane.

black hole, **1** a hypothetical hole in outer space into which energy and stars and other heavenly matter collapse and disappear: *If the theory can be believed, the final outcome of this process in nature is a "black hole" in space into which matter can be said to have vanished, leaving, however, all its gravitational effects behind* (Tom Alexander). **2** a place of punishment; a dungeon (from Black Hole of Calcutta, where English prisoners were held in 1756).

black horehound, an ill-smelling European plant of the mint family, found in waste land.

black humor, a morbid or bizarre form of humor, especially in novels and plays: *Some writers, of course, take up black humor for just one novel* (Time).

black humorist, a writer of black humor.

black ice, very smooth ice that is hard to see or that looks black at certain angles.

black·ing (blak′ing), *n.* a black polish used on shoes and stoves.

black ink, *U.S.* financial gain; profit.

black·ish (blak′ish), *adj.* somewhat black. **—black′ish·ly**, *adv.*

black ivory, (formerly) blacks as an article of traffic for slave traders in Africa.

black·jack (blak′jak′), *n., v. —n.* **1** a club with a flexible handle, used as a weapon. **2** the black flag of a pirate; Jolly Roger. **3** a small oak of the eastern United States that has a bark that is almost black. **4** a card game in which the players draw cards face down from the dealer, trying for a score of not more than 21 points; the game of twenty-one. **5** caramel or burnt sugar used for coloring spirits, vinegar, and coffee. **6** native zinc sulfide; sphalerite; zinc blende. **7** *Archaic.* a large drinking cup or jug, formerly made of leather: *. . . his nose doth show How oft the blackjack to his lips doth go* (old song).
—v.t. **1** to hit (a person) with a blackjack. **2** to coerce.

black knight, *U.S. Finance.* a company that makes a tender offer to forcibly gain control of another company.

black knot, a destructive disease of fruit trees, characterized by large, black, knot-like growths on the branches, caused by a fungus.

black·land (blak′land′, -lənd), *n.* a tract of dark-colored land, found in parts of the southern United States, especially in Texas.

black lark, a large Eurasian lark, the male of which is entirely black.

black lead, graphite, a soft, black form of carbon; graphite. It is used for lead in pencils, for lubricating machinery, and as a polish. SYN: plumbago.

black·leg (blak′leg′), *n., v.*, **-legged, -leg·ging.** *—n.* **1** *Informal.* a swindler. **2** *British.* a worker who takes a striker's job; strikebreaker; scab. **3** an infectious, usually fatal disease of cattle and sheep, caused by a bacterium and characterized by gaseous swelling of the muscles, especially on the upper parts of the legs. **4** a destructive disease of cabbage plants, in which the stems shrink and become black, causing the plant to die.
—v.i. British. to act as a blackleg or strikebreaker: *The International Union of Electricity . . . had to accept GE's first and only offer when many of its members blacklegged* (Manchester Guardian Weekly).

black lemur, = macaco[2].

∗**black letter** The World Book Dictionary
definition 1

∗**black letter**, **1** a printing type with thick, heavy lines resembling old German manuscript writing. **2** any other heavy-faced type.

black-let·ter (blak′let′ər), *adj.* **1** printed in black letter: *black-letter headlines.* **2** inauspicious: *a black-letter day.*

black-let|tered (blak′let′ərd), *adj.* printed in black letter.

black light, a kind of ultraviolet light imperceptible to the human eye, used to take photographs at night and to give a fluorescent effect.

black liquor, the leftover liquid from wood chips treated by the sulfite process.

black|list (blak′list′), *n., v.* **—*n.*** a list of persons, corporations, or groups who are believed to deserve punishment, blame, or suspicion. Persons or groups on a blacklist are usually boycotted or cut off from membership, affiliation, or employment. *That store keeps a blacklist of persons who do not pay their bills.*
—*v.t.* to put on a blacklist: *If a [baseball] player attempted to "jump" his reserve clause by joining another team without a release, he would be blacklisted by member clubs* (Richard E. Day).

black locust, a medium-sized, handsome shade tree of the pea family, widely-grown in the United States, and bearing fragrant flowers.

black lung, a form of pneumoconiosis which affects coal miners: *"Black lung" is caused by the inhalation of fine particles of coal dust* (Atlantic).

black|ly (blak′lē), *adv.* **1** dismally; gloomily. **2** angrily; sullenly. **3** evilly; wickedly.

black Magellanic cloud, *Astronomy.* the Coalsack.

black magic, magic performed with the aid of evil spirits; sorcery; witchcraft.

black|mail (blak′māl′), *n., v.* **—*n.*** **1** an attempt to obtain (money, a promise, or other gain) from a person by threatening to tell something that will disgrace him or someone dear to him. **2** the threat of such an attempt. **3** a sum of money or something of value obtained by such an attempt. **4** the action of forcing anyone into doing something by the use of threats: *They must be given a guarantee against "blackmail" by the nuclear Powers* (Manchester Guardian Weekly). **5** (in former times) money paid to outlaw bands, for protection against plunder, by farmers and small landowners along the Scottish and English borders.
—*v.t.* **1** to get or try to get blackmail from. **2** to force into doing something by the use of threats.
[< *black* + *mail* rent, tribute, coin < Old French *maille* < *mail, medaille* coin, medal] **—black′mail′er,** *n.*

blackmail picketing, picketing by a union to which a majority of the affected workers do not belong: *Blackmail picketing is aimed at compelling recognition of a union or organizing a nonunion plant* (Wall Street Journal).

black mangrove, blackwood, a small tree of the seacoast marshes of the West Indies and southern Florida.

Black Ma|ri|a (mə rī′ə), *Informal.* a police patrol wagon used to carry prisoners to and from jail.

black mark, a mark of criticism or punishment made against a person. **SYN:** demerit.

black market, **1** the selling of goods or currency at unlawful prices or in unlawful quantities. **2** the place where such selling is done or the organization that does it.

black-mar|ket (blak′mär′kit), *adj., v.* **—*adj.*** of or having to do with a black market: *black-market prices.*
—*v.i.* to operate a black market.
—*v.t.* to sell (goods) on the black market.

black mar|ket|eer (mär′kə tir′), a person who deals on the black market.

black-mar|ket|eer (blak′mär′kə tir′), *v.i., v.t.* = black-market.

black marketer, = black marketeer.

black marlin, a marlin of Pacific waters.

Black Mass, a ceremony burlesquing the Mass of Christian worship, supposed to have been performed by worshipers of Satan.

black measles, a severe type of measles, marked by hemorrhages under the skin.

black medic, a plant of the pea family, having yellow flowers and black pods.

black mica, = biotite.

black mold, a mold or fungus having black spores suspended as dust particles in the air.

Black Monday, the day after Easter; Easter Monday.

black money, *U.S. Slang.* income not reported to the government for tax purposes because of its illegal source.

Black Monk, a Benedictine monk, so called from the black costume.

black moss, a flowering plant in the southern United States and the West Indies, of the pineapple family, that hangs from trunks and branches of live oaks; long moss; Spanish moss.

Black Muslim, *U.S.* a member of the Nation of Islam, a black American sect preaching a form of Moslemism, black racial superiority, and total segregation between blacks and whites.

black mustard, one of the two species of mustard (the other being the *white mustard*) commonly grown in Europe and America for their seeds, used for seasoning and in medicine.

black nationalism, the principles and beliefs of black nationalists.

black nationalist, a member of any one of various black groups, such as the Black Muslims, who wish to establish a social structure independent of the influence of white people.

black|ness (blak′nis), *n.* **1** the quality or condition of being black; black color; darkness: *the blackness of night.* **2** *Figurative.* wickedness. **3** the distinctive qualities or characteristics of black people; negritude: *The call for black studies is the product of Negroes' new pride in their race, a new awareness of their blackness* (New York Times). **4** = black humor.

black nightshade, a weed with white flowers, poisonous black berries, and leaves that have a poisonous juice. It belongs to the nightshade family.

black oak, **1** a North American oak with dark bark, common in the eastern United States; quercitron. **2** its wood.

black|out (blak′out′), *n.* **1a** the action of turning off or concealing all the lights of a city or other area as a protection against an air raid. **b** the condition of having no electricity as the result of a power failure: *Excessive use of air conditioners can cause a blackout.* **2a** a temporary blindness or loss of consciousness resulting from lack of oxygen supply to the brain. **b** a temporary failure of memory. **3a** a failure in radio reception due to jamming or to disturbances in the atmosphere or ionosphere. **b** the withholding of a particular television program, especially a sports event from a specified area, usually so as to assure good local attendance. **4** the withholding of information usually printed or broadcast: . . . *rival newspapers were observing a police request for a news blackout* (Newsweek). **5a** a turning off of all the lights on the stage of a theater. **b** a skit of the type usually ending with a blackout.

Black Panther, *U.S.* a member of a militant black organization seeking to achieve power and equality for blacks by radical means.

black pepper, **1** a seasoning with a hot, sharp taste, made by grinding the dried berries of a woody vine of the pepper family grown in tropical Asia. **2** the vine itself.

black plate, steel or iron in thin sheets to be plated with tin or an alloy of tin and lead.

black point, a fungous and bacterial disease of cereals, that causes the embryo to darken.

black|poll (blak′pōl′), *n.,* or **blackpoll warbler**, a North American warbler. The top of the adult male's head is black.

Black Pope, an informal name for the head of the Society of Jesus (Jesuits), in reference to his authoritative position and the black soutane he wears.

black poplar, a poplar native to temperate Asia and central and southern Europe, planted elsewhere. The familiar Lombardy poplar is one variety.

black pot, **1** a coarse Danish crockery ware exposed to dense smoke in baking as a substitute for glazing. **2** = blood pudding.

black powder, ordinary gunpowder, distinguished from smokeless powder.

Black Power, power of collective action among blacks to achieve equality: *Black Power means that black people have to politically get together to organize themselves so that they can speak from a position of power and strength* (Stokely Carmichael).

black pudding, = blood pudding.

Black|pud|li|an (blak pud′lē ən), *adj., n.* **—*adj.*** of or belonging to Blackpool, a city in northwestern England.
—*n.* a native or inhabitant of Blackpool.
[< *Black*(pool) + (Liver)*pudlian*]

black quarter, = anthrax.

black race, the black or Negro race.

black racer, a blacksnake of the eastern United States.

black raspberry, = blackcap (def. 1).

black rat, a species of rat, darker and somewhat smaller than the common brown rat. One kind of black rat is called the *roof rat.*

Black Rod, **1** In full, **Gentleman Usher of the Black Rod**. the officer responsible for maintaining order in administrative matters in the House of Lords, whose symbol of authority is a black rod. **2** an usher (or sergeant at arms) in certain legislatures of the Commonwealth.

black|root (blak′rüt′, -rut′), *n.* = Culver's root.

black rot, **1** any one of several diseases of cultivated plants, such as the sweet potato, apple, or grape. Fungi produce dark-brown spots in diseased plants. **2** the fungus that causes any one of these diseases.

black rust, **1** a disease of the leaves and stems of wheat and other cereals and grasses. **2** a fungus with dark-colored spores that causes it.

black scissorbill, = black skimmer.

black shank, a fungous disease of tobacco that causes the rotting of roots and stems.

black sheep, a worthless member of a respectable family; scoundrel.

Black Shirt, **1** (formerly) a member of the Italian Fascist party. They wore black shirts as part of their uniform. **2** a member of any similar fascist organization, especially one using black shirts.

black skimmer, the skimmer of North America, black on the upper part and white underneath.

black|smith (blak′smith′), *n.* **1** a person who makes things out of iron by heating it in a forge and hammering it into shape on an anvil. Blacksmiths can mend tools and shoe horses. **2** a man who makes and fits horseshoes. [with reference to "black" metals, e.g., iron]

black|smith|ing (blak′smith′ing), *n.* the practice or business of a blacksmith.

black|snake (blak′snāk′), *n.* **1a** a harmless black or dark-colored snake of North America, having smooth scales, and sometimes attaining a length of 6 feet. **b** a similar black, harmless snake, that has slightly ridged (keeled) and polished scales with white edges; pilot snake; mountain blacksnake. **2** *U.S.* a long, heavy whip made of braided leather, used especially by mule drivers.

black snakeroot, = cohosh.

black spot, **1** any one of various plant diseases caused by fungi or by bacteria and characterized by black spots. **2** *British.* a place where trouble or difficulty occurs or is likely to occur, such as a dangerous part of a road or an area of economic depression. **3** an area in South Africa inhabited by blacks in midst of land inhabited by whites.

black spruce, **1** a North American evergreen tree of the pine family with persistent cones and dark-green needles. **2** its light, soft wood.

black squall, a squall of wind accompanied by a dark cloud.

black squirrel, any variety of the gray squirrel or of the fox squirrel, having black fur.

black|stem (blak′stem′), *n.* any one of various fungous diseases attacking the stems of plants and causing them to turn dark.

black stem rust, the telial stage of stem rust.

black stork, a shiny black-brown stork with white underparts, found in Europe and Asia.

black|strap (blak′strap′), *n.,* or **blackstrap molasses**, a very thick, dark molasses.

black studies, *U.S.* college, university, or high school courses of black history and culture.

black sumac, = dwarf sumac.

black swallower, a deep-sea fish that can swallow other and larger fish whole by distending its stomach.

black swallowtail, an American butterfly, black with yellow spots.

black swan, an Australian swan, black except for a bar of white on each wing, and a whitebanded scarlet bill.

black|tail (blak′tāl′), *n.* = mule deer.

black-tailed deer (blak′tāld′), a variety of the mule deer of the northwestern United States and British Columbia.

black tea, tea which has been allowed to wither and ferment in the air before roasting.

black|thorn (blak′thôrn′), *n.* **1** a thorny European shrub that has white flowers and very small, dark-purple fruit. Blackthorn belongs to the rose family. The fruit, and sometimes the shrub itself, is called *sloe.* **2** a walking stick or club made from the stem of this shrub. **3** any one of various American hawthorns.

black tie, **1** a black bow tie such as is worn with a dinner jacket or tuxedo. **2** evening dress that includes a black bow tie and dinner jacket or tuxedo.

black-tie (blak′tī′), *adj.* of or having to do with a formal affair at which a black tie is worn: *The dinner was a black-tie affair.*

black|tongue (blak′tung′), *n.* a disease of dogs characterized by ulcers of the mouth, inflammation of the digestive tract, and blotches on the skin. It is caused by a nutritional deficiency, similar to pellagra.

black|top (blak′top′), *n., v.,* **-topped, -top|ping.** **—*n.*** **1** asphalt mixed with crushed rock used as a pavement for highways, roads, and other surfaces. **2** a surface covered with this substance.
—*v.t.* to surface or pave (a road) with blacktop.

black tupelo, = black gum.

black velvet, an alcoholic drink composed of

Pronunciation Key: hat, āge, cãre, fär; let, ēqual, tėrm; it, īce; hot, ōpen, ôrder; oil, out; cup, pu̇t, rüle; child; long; thin; ᴛʜen; zh, measure; ə represents **a** in about, **e** in taken, **i** in pencil, **o** in lemon, **u** in circus.

champagne and stout in equal parts.

black vomit, 1a a dark matter, consisting mainly of altered blood, vomited in the last stage of some cases of yellow fever. **b** the act of expelling this substance. **2** = yellow fever.

black vulture, a vulture of the Southern United States and of Central and South America, smaller than the turkey vulture.

black wages, *British.* wages higher than those provided for by a labor union contract, paid to attract nonunion workers because of a shortage of labor.

Black|wall hitch (blak′wôl′), a kind of hitch, single or double, used for attaching a rope to a hook. [< a proper name]

black walnut, 1 a tall North American tree, valued for its dark-brown wood and its round, oily, edible nuts. **2** its nut. **3** its wood, often used for furniture, woodwork, and gunstocks. It is heavy, hard, and strong, is easily worked, and takes a high polish.

Black Watch, 1 a body of Scottish Highlanders organized in 1725 to maintain order in the Highlands and later incorporated (1751) into the British Army as a regiment. **2** a tartan, or plaid, in the pattern worn by members of this regiment.

black|wa|ter fever (blak′wôt′ər, -wot′-), a severe type of malaria, chiefly tropical, characterized by bloody urine.

black|weed (blak′wēd′), *n.* the common ragweed.

black whale, = blackfish.

***black widow,** a poisonous, small spider with a glossy black body, the female of which has a reddish mark in the shape of an hourglass on its underside.

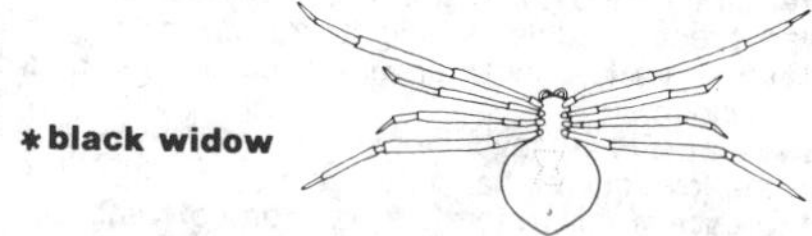

***black widow**

black willow, a willow with rough, dark bark, used mainly in making boxes, crates, furniture, cabinetwork, caskets, and artificial limbs.

black|wood (blak′wu̇d′), *n.* **1** the wood of a large leguminous tree of the East Indies. **2** the wood of an acacia tree, the most valuable timber tree of Australia, noted for its hardness and durability. **3** the black mangrove, in the West Indies and southern Florida, a small tree of seacoast marshes, with very heavy, hard, and dark-brown or nearly black wood.

black|work (blak′wėrk′), *n.* iron forged or wrought by blacksmiths, not filed, burnished, or otherwise made bright.

black|y (blak′ē), *n., pl.* **black|ies.** *Informal.* any black bird or animal.

blad[1] (blad, bläd), *v.t.,* **blad|ded, blad|ding.** *Scottish.* to slap; strike; beat; maltreat; spoil. [probably imitative]

blad[2] (blad, bläd), *n. Scottish.* **1** a piece; a fragment. **2** a large piece or lump. [perhaps < *blad*[1]]

blad|der (blad′ər), *n.* **1** a soft, thin bag in the body that receives urine from the kidneys; urinary bladder. See picture under **kidney. 2** anything like this. A football has a hollow rubber bladder that can be blown up with air. **3** any similar sac in animals or plants, especially: **a** a hollow sac on various plants, as bladderworts and certain seaweeds. **b** the inflated pericarp of some plants. [Old English *blǣdre*]

bladder campion, a campion with an inflated calyx; cowbell.

bladder fern, any one of a number of ferns having sporangia in the shape of bladders.

blad|der|fish (blad′ər fish′), *n., pl.* **-fish|es** or (*collectively*) **-fish.** = globefish.

bladder ket|mi|a (ket′mē ə), an African annual of the mallow family, having a bladderlike calyx, now a weed in North America.

blad|der|nose (blad′ər nōz′), *n.* = hooded seal.

blad|der|nut (blad′ər nut′), *n.* **1** the fruit of any one of a genus of shrubs or small trees, contained in bladderlike pods. **2** any one of these plants, especially a species of eastern North America.

blad|der|weed (blad′ər wēd′), *n.* a seaweed having air bladders in the fronds.

bladder worm, the larva of a tapeworm in its encysted stage; a cysticercus.

blad|der|wort (blad′ər wėrt′), *n.* any one of a family of insect-eating marsh or water plants with yellow or purple flowers. Some varieties float on water by means of small bags or bladders filled with air on their weak stems and their leaves; others grow in mud.

***bladderwort family,** a widely distributed group of dicotyledonous herbs which grow in water or wet places and have small bladders or other structures with which they catch insects. The family includes the bladderwort and butterwort.

***bladderwort family**

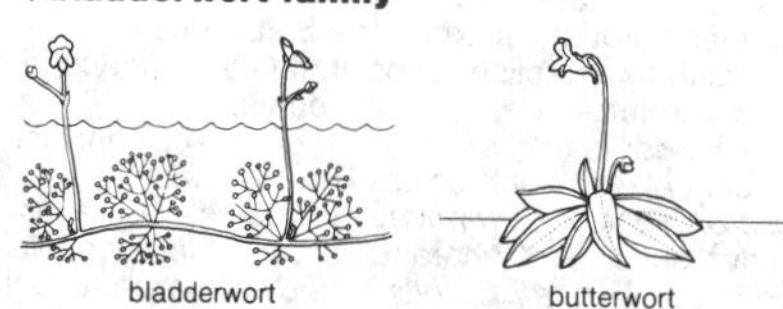

blad|der|wrack (blad′ər rak′), *n.* a seaweed, so named from the floating vesicles in its fronds.

blad|der|y (blad′ər ē), *adj.* **1** thin, inflated, and hollow. **2** having bladders.

blade (blād), *n., v.,* **blad|ed, blad|ing.** —*n.* **1** the cutting part of anything like a knife or sword: *A razor should have a sharp blade.* **2** a sword. **3** a swordsman: *a reckless blade.* **4** a smart or dashing fellow; gallant: *He considers himself quite a blade.* **5a** a leaf of grass. **b** the flat, wide part of a leaf; leaf. **6** the flat, wide part of anything. An oar or paddle has a blade at one end of the shaft. **7a** the wide, flat part of a bone: *the shoulder blade.* **b** a cut of meat from this part. **8** the front, flat part of the tongue, directly behind and around the tip or apex. **9** a roller skate that has wheels arranged in a single line under the shoe: *More like ice skates than the clunky wheels of roller rinks past, the blades are faster and more maneuverable* (Time).
—*v.i.* **1** to come into blade; produce blades. **2** to skate on blades: *Blading is the bright new hope for future growth in sporting-goods sales* (Time).
blades, *Southern U.S.* the leaves of corn, much used as fodder: *Where we breakfasted, the landlord . . . gave our horses some blades* (John Palmer).
[Old English *blæd*] —**blade′like′,** *adj.*

blade angle, the acute angle between the chord of a blade of a propeller or rotor and a plane perpendicular to the axis of rotation.

blade|bone (blād′bōn′), *n.* the shoulder blade or scapula.

blad|ed (blā′did), *adj.* having a blade or blades.

blade|less (blād′lis), *adj.* without a blade.

blad|er (blā′ dər), *n.* a person who skates using blades: *"Every weekend it's a battle between the cyclists and the bladers"* (Time)

blades (blādz), *n.pl.* See under **blade.**

blade|work (blād′wėrk′), *n. Especially British.* the way oars are used in rowing.

blae (blā, blē), *adj. Dialect.* blackish-blue; livid. [< Scandinavian (as in Old Icelandic *blār* dark blue)]

blae|ber|ry (blā′ber′ē, -bər-; blē′-), *n., pl.* **-ries.** *Scottish.* the bilberry. [Middle English *blabery*]

blague (bläg), *n. French.* pretentious falsehood, often as a jest; humbug.

blah (blä), *n., adj. Slang.* —*n.* nonsense. —*adj.* dull; uninteresting: *a blah novel.*
the blahs, a feeling of depression or discomfort: *a mild case of the morning blahs* (Time). [imitative]

blain (blān), *n.* an inflamed swelling or sore on the skin. [Old English *blegen*]

blam|a|ble (blā′mə bəl), *adj.* deserving blame; faulty; blameworthy. **SYN:** guilty, culpable. —**blam′a|ble|ness,** *n.* —**blam′a|bly,** *adv.*

blame (blām), *v.,* **blamed, blam|ing,** *n.* —*v.t.* **1a** to hold (a person or thing) responsible for something bad or wrong: *The cabdriver blamed the fog for his accident.* **SYN:** accuse. **b** to place responsibility for (something bad or wrong) on a person or thing: *They blamed the accident on me.* **SYN:** accuse. **2** to find fault with: *The coach will not blame us if we do our best. Who could blame her for having left such a wretched home?*
—*n.* **1** responsibility for something bad or wrong: *Carelessness deserves the blame for many accidents.* **SYN:** guilt. **2** a finding fault; reproof: *I have done my best; neither praise nor blame can affect me now.* **SYN:** censure, condemnation, reproach. **3** *Archaic.* blameworthiness; fault: *. . . holy and without blame* (Ephesians 1:4).
be to blame, to deserve to be blamed; be responsible: *Each said somebody else was to blame. You are not to blame for his shortcomings.*
[< Old French *blasmer* < Vulgar Latin *blastēmāre,* alteration of Latin *blasphēmāre.* See etym. of doublet **blaspheme.**] —**blam′er,** *n.*
—***Syn.*** *v.t.* **2 Blame, censure, reproach** mean to find fault with. **Blame,** the least formal word, means to find fault with someone for doing something wrong: *The principal blamed him for his frequent absence from school.* **Censure,** less personal, adds to *blame* the idea of expressing disapproval, often publicly: *The Congress censured one of its members for his excessive absence from the Capitol.* **Reproach** adds to *blame* the idea of expressing one's feelings of displeasure or resentment, sometimes unjustly: *I reproached them for their ingratitude.*

blame|a|ble (blā′mə bəl), *adj.* = blamable.

blamed (blāmd), *adj., adv. U.S. Dialect.* —*adj.* confounded: *Where is that blamed cat?* —*adv.* confoundedly; excessively: *Well, it's blamed mean—that's all* (Mark Twain).

blame|ful (blām′fəl), *adj.* **1** deserving blame. **2** blaming others too much. —**blame′ful|ly,** *adv.* —**blame′ful|ness,** *n.*

blame|less (blām′lis), *adj.* that cannot be blamed; free from fault: *The saint lived a blameless life.* **SYN:** faultless, guiltless, unimpeachable. See syn. under **innocent.** —**blame′less|ly,** *adv.* —**blame′less|ness,** *n.*

blame|wor|thi|ness (blām′wėr′ᴛʜē nis), *n.* the quality of being blameworthy; blamableness: *Blame I can bear, though not blameworthiness* (Robert Browning).

blame|wor|thy (blām′wėr′ᴛʜē), *adj.* deserving blame; faulty; culpable: *a blameworthy act.*

blanc fixe (blän fēks′), *French.* barium sulfate.

blanch[1] (blanch, blänch), *v., adj.* —*v.t.* **1** to make white; bleach: *The cook blanched some almonds by soaking off their skins in boiling water. After we blanched the dirty old pennies in acid, they shone like new. Old age blanched his hair.* See syn. under **whiten. 2** to make pale (especially with fear or hunger): *Fear blanched her lips.* See syn. under **whiten. 3** to whiten or prevent from becoming green by excluding the light, as from the stems. We blanch celery by keeping out the light. **4** *Cookery.* to boil briefly and then chill (vegetables or other food). **5** to tin (metal).
—*v.i.* to turn white; become pale; lose color: *The boy blanched with fear when he saw the bear coming.* —*adj. Heraldry.* white; argent.
blanch over, *British.* to present in a flattering light; whitewash: *. . . howsoever you mince it and blanch it over* (Arthur Dent).
[< Old French *blanchir* < *blanc* white < Germanic (compare Old High German *blanch* bright)]

blanch[2] (blanch, blänch), *v.t.* to turn aside; turn back. [variant of *blench*]

blanch|er[1] (blan′chər, blän′-), *n.* a person or thing that blanches or whitens.

blanch|er[2] (blan′chər, blän′-), *n.* **1** a person who starts or balks at anything. **2** a person stationed to turn game in some direction. **3** *Obsolete.* a person who turns aside or causes to turn aside; a perverter.

blanc|mange (blə mänzh′, -mänzh′), *n.* a sweet dessert made of milk boiled and thickened with gelatin, cornstarch, or the like, flavored, and cooled in a mold. [< Old French *blancmanger* (literally) white food]

blan|co (blang′kō), *n., pl.* **-cos,** *v.,* **-coed, -co|ing.** *British.* —*n.* a white or khaki substance used to polish belts, boots, or other leather articles.
—*v.t.* to polish with this substance: *Peter, in the intervals of blancoing his cricket pads,* [*was*] *with Susan* (Manchester Guardian Weekly).
[< *Blanco,* a trademark for such a substance]

bland (bland), *adj.* **1** gentle; soothing; balmy: *a bland summer breeze.* **2** smoothly agreeable and polite: *The friendly salesman had a bland smile.* **SYN:** smooth, affable, urbane. **3** mild; not irritating: *a bland diet of milk, fish, and eggs, with no roughage. Baby food has a bland taste.* [< Latin *blandus* soft]

blan|dil|o|quence (blan dil′ə kwəns), *n.* smooth speech; agreeable or flattering language: *His blandiloquence charmed, but did not convince us.* [< Latin *blandiloquentia* < *blandiloquēns* speaking smoothly < *blandus* smooth, suave + *loquēns, -entis,* present participle of *loquī* speak]

blan|dish (blan′dish), *v.t., v.i.* to persuade by gentle ways; coax; flatter: *She blandished him out of his black mood.* **SYN:** cajole, wheedle, blarney. [< Old French *blandiss-,* stem of *blandir* < Latin *blandīrī* flatter < *blandus* soft, smooth] —**blan′dish|er,** *n.* —**blan′dish|ment,** *n.*

blank (blangk), *n., adj., v.* —*n.* **1** a space left empty or to be filled in: *Leave a blank if you can't answer the question.* **2** *Especially U.S.* a paper with spaces to be filled in: *Fill out this application blank and return it at once.* **3** *Figurative.* an empty or vacant place; a void: *When he read the hard questions, his mind became a complete blank.* **4** a dash marking an empty space for something omitted, such as a letter or word: *The task of filling in the blanks I'd rather leave to you* (W. S. Gilbert). **5** a cartridge containing gunpowder but no bullet or shot. **6** a piece of metal prepared to be stamped or filed into a coin, key, or the like. **7** the white spot in the center of a target; bull's-eye. **8** anything aimed at like a target; objective. **9** a lottery ticket that does not win a prize.
—*adj.* **1** not written or printed on; unused: *sheets of blank paper.* **2** with spaces left to be filled in: *a blank check. Here is a blank form for you to fill in and return.* **3** empty; vacant: *a blank space, a blank mind.* **SYN:** void, bare. See syn. under

empty. 4 without interest or meaning; dull: *There was a blank look on his face.* **5** complete; entire; utter: *a look of blank stupidity.* **6** lacking some usual feature: *a blank cartridge.* **7** without openings; having no variety: *a blank wall.* **8** not finished in detail; uncut: *a blank key.* **9** *Obsolete.* white; pale: *Blank as death in marble* (Tennyson).
—***v.t.* 1** (in games) to keep (an opponent) from scoring. **2** to stamp or cut from a piece of metal: *Spoons and forks are blanked from sheet or strip* (London Times).
blank out, a to hide or obscure; cover over; blot out: *His name had been blanked out.* **b** to become obscured or blotted out: *The television screen blanked out. Her mind blanked out as she fell and lost consciousness.*
draw a blank, to end a fruitless attempt; be unsuccessful in one's efforts: *I drew a blank at least half the time* (Bernard DeVoto).
in blank, prepared with blank spaces, as a form: *A note endorsed in blank is like one payable to bearer* (James Kent).
[< Old French *blanc* white, shining; see etym. under **blanch**[1]] —**blank'ly,** *adv.* —**blank'ness,** *n.*

blank|book (blangk'bu̇k'), *n. U.S.* a book of blank pages or forms for accounts or memorandums.

blank cartridge, a cartridge containing no bullet or shot.

blank check, 1 a signed check that allows the bearer to write in the amount. **2** *Informal, Figurative.* permission to do as a person pleases; carte blanche.

blank endorsement, an endorsement by a simple signature, which makes a check, note, or the like, payable to the bearer.

blan|ket (blang'kit), *n., v., adj.* —***n.*** a soft covering knitted or woven from wool, cotton, nylon, or other material, used to keep people or animals warm: *The campers wrapped themselves in blankets and slept near the fire.* (*Figurative.*) *A blanket of snow covered the ground.*
—***v.t.* 1** to cover with a blanket or as if with a blanket: (*Figurative.*) *The snow blanketed the ground.* **2** to toss in a blanket, as a rough punishment or game. **3** to pass close to windward of (a sailboat or sailing vessel) so as to take the wind out of its sails: *Both skippers are also skilled at the sly tactics of dodging blanketing [by] faking new tacks* (Time). **4** to hinder, obscure, or silence (radio signals) by interference from a more powerful transmitter.
—***adj.*** covering several or all: *a blanket guarantee to repair defects of any kind.*
[< Old French *blankete* < *blanc* white. See related etym. at **blank.**]

blanket cylinder, the roller in an offset printing press that receives the inked impression from the plate cylinder and transfers it to paper. It is covered with rubber.

blan|ket|flow|er (blang'kit flou'ər), *n.* = gaillardia.

blan|ket|ing (blang'kə ting), *n.* material for blankets.

blanket policy, a contract of insurance applied to a class of property rather than to any particular property, in which the risk assumed shifts and varies as different articles or things in the class are brought within the terms of the contract.

***blanket stitch,** a buttonhole stitch with the stitches widely spaced on the edge of cloth too thick to be hemmed. A blanket stitch is also variously spaced for decorative purposes.

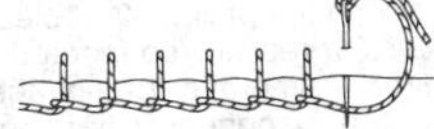
***blanket stitch**

blan|ke|ty-blank (blang'kə tē blangk'), *adj. U.S. Slang.* cursed; confounded (used as a mild or humorous replacement). [reduplication of *blank,* a dash marking a space for an omitted curse]

blank verse, 1 unrhymed poetry having five iambic feet in each line: *Shakespeare's "Julius Caesar" is written in blank verse.* **2** any unrhymed verse: *Walt Whitman wrote most of his poetry in blank verse.*

blan|quette (blän ket'), *n. French.* a stew or fricassee made with a white sauce.

blan|quil|lo (bläng kēl'yō, -kē'yō), *n., pl.* **-los** or (*collectively*) **-lo.** an edible fish of the West Indies or of the coast of southern California. [< American Spanish *blanquillo* (diminutive) < Spanish *blanco* white]

blare (blãr), *v.,* **blared, blar|ing,** *n.* —***v.i.*** to make a loud, harsh sound: *The trumpets blared, announcing the king's arrival at the tournament.*
—***v.t.*** to utter harshly or loudly; bellow.
—***n.* 1** a loud, harsh sound like that of a trumpet: *During the traffic jam the blare of car horns was deafening.* **2** brilliance of color; glare.
[probably imitative. Compare Middle Dutch *blaren.*]

bla|ri|na (blə rī'nə), *n.,* or **blarina shrew,** any one of a genus of short-tailed shrews native to North America. [< New Latin *Blarina* the genus name, perhaps < *Blair,* Nebraska, a typical locality where found]

blar|ney (blär'nē), *n., v.,* **-neyed, -ney|ing.** —***n.*** flattering or coaxing talk: *I want none of your blarney!* —***v.t., v.i.*** to flatter; coax.
[< *Blarney Stone*] —**blar'ney|er,** *n.*

Blarney Stone, a stone built into a castle near Cork, Ireland. Anyone who kissed it is supposed to become skillful in flattering and coaxing people.

bla|sé (blä zā', blä'zā), *adj.* tired of pleasures; bored.
[< French *blasé,* past participle of *blaser* exhaust with pleasure]

blas|pheme (blas fēm'), *v.,* **-phemed, -phem|ing.**
—***v.t.* 1** to speak about (God or sacred things) with abuse or contempt: *Thou didst blaspheme God and the king* (I Kings 21:10). **SYN:** profane. **2** to curse; revile; abuse: *They blaspheme the muse* (Tennyson). —***v.i.*** to speak irreverently or sacrilegiously; utter blasphemy: *Do you think it smart to mock at all the things that are sacred to God and man? Do you think it is smart to blaspheme?* (James T. Farrell).
[< Old French *blasfemer,* learned borrowing from Latin *blasphēmāre* < Greek *blasphēmeîn,* ultimately < *blas-* false + *phēmē* speech. See etym. of doublet **blame.**] —**blas|phem'er,** *n.*

blas|phe|mous (blas'fə məs), *adj.* speaking or writing about God or sacred things with abuse or contempt: *blasphemous language.* **SYN:** irreverent, impious, profane, sacrilegious. —**blas'phe|mous|ly,** *adv.* —**blas'phe|mous|ness,** *n.*

blas|phe|my (blas'fə mē), *n., pl.* **-mies. 1** abuse of or contempt for God or sacred things. **SYN:** profanity. **2** *Judaism.* **a** cursing or reviling God. (In the Bible, Leviticus 24:16). **b** pronouncing the ineffable name of God. **3** any speech or action contemptuous of something deemed sacred: *He was well punished for his blasphemy against learning* (Francis Bacon). **SYN:** contempt, irreverence.

blast (blast, bläst), *n., v.* —***n.* 1** a strong, sudden rush of wind or air: *We bundled up against the icy blasts of winter.* **2a** the blowing of a trumpet, horn, or whistle: *His blast on the bugle made his cheeks bulge.* **b** the sound made by blowing a trumpet, horn, or whistle: *A warning blast on the bugle aroused the camp.* **3a** a strong current of air used in smelting, especially iron. **b** a stream of air forced from the mouth, a bellows, or a nozzle: *The dentist gave my tooth a blast to dry the filling.* **4** a charge of dynamite, gunpowder, or other explosive that blows up rocks, earth, or minerals: *The miners set a large blast of powder in the rocks.* **5a** a blasting; explosion: *The blast of the cannon can be seen across the harbor.* **SYN:** detonation. **b** the wave of high-pressure air that spreads out from an explosion: *Most of the damage was due to blast.* **6** *Figurative.* **a** a cause of witherering, blight, or ruin: *Resistless as the blasts of pestilence* (Samuel Johnson). **b** a strong attack or outburst of criticism: *... the high court's blast at confessions last June* (New York Times). **7** *Informal.* a powerful, explosive hit: *... Howard's 420-foot blast into the left-centerfield bleachers* (New York Times). **8** *Slang.* a big, noisy party; bash: *Carnival in Rio is the wildest, the biggest, the craziest mass blast in the world* (Time).
—***v.t.* 1** to blow up (rocks, earth, or minerals) with dynamite, gunpowder or other explosive: *The old building was blasted.* **2a** to cause to wither; blight; destroy: *disease has blasted our grapes.* (*Figurative.*) *His conviction for theft blasted his reputation.* **SYN:** shrivel, ruin. **b** to force air into or against: *The workmen blasted the stone with sand to clean the building.* **3a** to blow (a trumpet, horn, or whistle): *The driver blasted his horn in the traffic jam.* **SYN:** sound. **b** *Figurative.* to criticize severely; denounce: *He could blast politicians, especially Republicans* (Saturday Review). **4** to throw or launch with explosive force: *A Titan 2 rocket blasted him into space yesterday* (New York Times).
—***v.i.* 1** to be blighted; wither; shrivel up. **2** to blow up rocks or earth with dynamite, gunpowder, or some other explosive. **3** to fly or shoot with explosive force: *Walker's speed was 3,818 m.p.h., ... as he blasted upward into blackness* (Time).
blast off, a *Informal.* to take off into flight propelled by rockets: *The spacecraft will be carefully checked before it blasts off.* **b** *Slang.* to get out; go away; scram: *Either you play ball or you blast off.*
in blast, in operation: *Four or five furnaces ... are in blast* (Jedidiah Morse).
out of blast, not in operation; shut down: *The day when yonder furnaces are out of blast will be the day of your ruin* (Harriet Martineau).
[Old English *blǣst*] —**blast'er,** *n.*

blast-, *combining form.* the form of **blasto-** before vowels.

blast area, the area within which casualties are to be expected and immediate damage is suffered due to the force of an explosion.

blast|ed (blas'tid, bläs'-), *adj.* **1** withered, blighted, or ruined: *a hillside blasted by forest fires.* **2** damned; cursed.

blas|te|ma (blas tē'mə), *n., pl.* **-ma|ta** (-mə tə). **1** the formative substance of a germinating ovum. **2** the initial point of growth from which an organ or part is developed. [< Greek *blástēma* sprout < *blastánein* to sprout]

blas|tem|ic (blas tem'ik, -tē'mik), *adj.* **1** of a blastema. **2** resembling a blastema.

blast furnace, a furnace in which ores are smelted, by forcing a strong current of air into the furnace from the bottom to make a very great heat. It is used especially to produce pig iron from iron ore.

blas|tie (blas'tē, bläs'-), *n. Scottish.* a dwarf. [< *blast* shrivel up + *-ie*]

blast|ing (blas'ting, bläs'-), *n.* **1** a blast; blight. **2a** the operation of blowing rocks to pieces. **b** the result or material product of blowing up rocks.

blasting cap, a detonator.

blast|ment (blast'mənt, bläst'-), *n.* a blasting; blast or blight.

blasto-, *combining form.* connection with or relation to a bud, germ, or early embryonic stage: *Blastodisk = a germinal disk. Blastogenesis = reproduction by budding.* Also, **blast-** before vowels. [< Greek *blastós* sprout, shoot]

blas|to|chyle (blas'tə kīl), *n. Embryology.* the liquid which fills the blastocoel, or cavity of the blastula. [< *blasto-* + *chyle*]

blas|to|coel, blas|to|coele, or **blas|to|cele** (blas'tə sēl), *n.* the central cavity of a blastula; segmentation cavity. See picture under **embryo.**

blas|to|cyst (blas'tə sist), *n.* **1** = germinal vesicle. **2** = blastula.

blas|to|derm (blas'tə dėrm), *n.* the layer of cells formed by the growth of a fertilized egg. It later divides into three layers, from which all parts of the new animal are formed. [< *blasto-* + Greek *dérma* skin]

blas|to|der|mic (blas'tə dėr'mik), *adj.* of or having to do with the blastoderm.

blas|to|disk or **blas|to|disc** (blas'tə disk), *n.* a disklike aggregation of formative protoplasm at one pole of the yolk of a fertilized egg, containing the nucleus; germinal disk.

blast|off (blast'ôf', -of'; bläst'-), *n.* a launching or taking off into rocket-propelled flight: *The astronauts suffered no injury during blastoff and reentry.*

blas|to|gen|e|sis (blas'tə jen'ə sis), *n.* **1** reproduction by gemmation or budding. **2** the theory of the transmission of inherited characters by germ plasm.

blas|to|gen|ic (blas'tə jen'ik), *adj.* of or having to do with blastogenesis.

blas|to|mere (blas'tə mir), *n.* any one of the cells or segments into which an ovum or fertilized egg first divides. [< *blasto-* + Greek *méros* part]

blas|to|mer|ic (blas'tə mer'ik), *adj.* **1** of or having to do with a blastomere. **2** resembling a blastomere.

blas|to|my|cete (blas'tə mī sēt'), *n.* one of the blastomycetes. [< Greek *blastós* germ, sprout + *mýkēs, mýkētos* fungus]

blas|to|my|ce|tes (blas'tə mī sē'tēs), *n.pl.* a heterogeneous group of yeastlike fungi occurring as parasites on or in man and some of the lower animals.

blas|to|my|ce|tic (blas'tə mī sē'tik), *adj.* having to do with or due to blastomycetes.

blastomycetic dermatitis, a form of blastomycosis localized as an inflammation of the skin caused by the presence of blastomycetes.

blas|to|my|ce|tous (blas'tə mī sē'təs), *adj.* = blastomycetic.

blas|to|my|co|sis (blas'tō mī kō'sis), *n.* a chronic disease of man or animals, especially poultry, caused by a yeastlike fungus, sometimes systemic, sometimes attacking the skin, the mouth, the lungs, or the liver, spleen, and kidneys. [< *blasto-* + *mycosis*]

blas|to|po|ral (blas'tə pôr'əl, -pōr'-), *adj.* of or having to do with a blastopore.

blas|to|pore (blas'tə pôr, -pōr), *n.* the external

Pronunciation Key: hat, āge, cãre, fär; let, ēqual, tėrm; it, īce; hot, ōpen, ôrder; **oi**l, **ou**t; cup, pu̇t, rüle; **ch**ild; lo**ng**; **th**in; **ᴛʜ**en; **zh**, measure; **ə** represents **a** in about, **e** in taken, **i** in pencil, **o** in lemon, **u** in circus.

opening of the cavity (archenteron) of a gastrula. See picture under **embryo**.

blas|to|por|ic (blas′tə pôr′ik, -por′-), *adj.* of or having to do with a blastopore.

blas|to|sphere (blas′tə sfir), *n.* **1** = blastula. **2** (specifically) the hollow spherical blastoderm of mammals, formed after gastrulation.

blas|tous (blas′təs), *adj.* of or having to do with a germ or bud. [< *blast-* + *-ous*]

blast|proof (blast′prüf′, bläst′-), *adj.* designed to withstand the effects of explosions.

blast screen, a concrete shield for protecting members of a ground crew against the exhaust blast of jet aircraft taking off.

blast shelter, a blastproof shelter.

blas|tu|la (blas′chə lə), *n., pl.* **-las**, **-lae** (-lē). an early stage in the development of an embryo of an animal, after the fertilization and cleavage of the ovum. It usually consists of a sac or hollow sphere formed by a single layer of cells. See picture under **embryo**. [< New Latin *blastula* (diminutive) < Greek *blastós* sprout, germ]

blas|tu|lar (blas′chə lər), *adj.* **1** having to do with a blastula. **2** resembling a blastula.

blas|tu|la|tion (blas′chə lā′shən), *n.* formation of the blastula.

blast wave, a wave of air at increased pressure, caused by an explosion and radiating from it, followed by a wave of decreased pressure.

blat[1] (blat), *v.,* **blat|ted, blat|ting.** *Informal.* **—*v.i.*** to cry like a calf or sheep; bleat: *This bullheaded monster [the Diesel train engine], whose blatting horn has replaced the romantic wail of the whistle* (Newsweek). **—*v.t.*** to say loudly and foolishly; blurt out. [American English; variant of *bleat*]

blat[2] (blät), *n. Russian Slang.* unethical solicitation; bribery; graft.

bla|tan|cy (blā′tən sē), *n., pl.* **-cies.** noisy or unpleasant intrusion; blatant quality: *Viewers object to the blatancy of some television commercials.*

bla|tant (blā′tənt), *adj.* **1** offensively loud or noisy; loudmouthed: *a blatant fool.* SYN: clamorous, bellowing. **2** showy, especially in dress or manner: *blatant prosperity.* SYN: gaudy. **3** obvious; flagrant: *a blatant lie, a blatant disregard of others.* [(coined by Spenser) apparently < Latin *blatīre* babble] **—bla′tant|ly,** *adv.*

blate (blāt), *adj. Scottish.* **1** bashful. **2** backward. [compare Old English *blāt* pale]

blath|er (blaᴛʜ′ər), *n., v.* **—*n.*** foolish talk; nonsense. **—*v.i., v.t.*** to talk or utter foolishly; talk nonsense. Also, **blether, blither.** [< Scandinavian (compare Old Icelandic *bladhr*)]

blath|er|skite (blaᴛʜ′ər skīt), *n.* **1** *Informal.* a blustering person who talks much and says little. **2** = ruddy duck.

blat|ter (blat′ər), *v., n.* **—*v.t.*** to utter volubly. **—*v.i.*** **1** to speak volubly: *The girls blattered endlessly.* **2** = clatter. **—*n.*** **1** a volley of clattering words. **2** a rattling or clattering noise. [< Latin *blaterāre* talk foolishly]

blau|bok or **blauw|bok** (blou′bok′), *n., pl.* **-bok** or **-boks. 1** a large, bluish South African antelope, now extinct. **2** any one of various small South African antelopes. [< Afrikaans *blauwbok* < Dutch < *blauw* blue + *bok* buck, goat]

blaw (blô), *v.t., v.i. Scottish.* to blow.

blax|ploi|ta|tion (blaks′ploi tā′shən), *n. U.S.* the production of films and plays with black actors for black audiences: *For every blaxploitation movie, 10 white-exploitation movies of cheap thrills of violence . . . are made and exhibited in, I venture, far more theaters and drive-ins than black films* (Psychology Today). [blend of *black* and *exploitation*, patterned on *sexploitation*]

blaze[1] (blāz), *n., v.,* **blazed, blaz|ing. —*n.*** **1** a bright flame or fire; mass of flame: *The scout could see the blaze of the campfires across the river.* SYN: conflagration. See syn. under **flame. 2** a glow of brightness; intense light; glare: *the blaze of the noon sun.* SYN: brilliance. **3** a bright display: *The tulips made a blaze of color in the garden.* **4** *Figurative.* a sudden or violent outburst of feeling or passion: *a blaze of temper.*

—*v.i.* **1** to burn with a bright flame; be on fire: *A fire was blazing in the fireplace.* **2** to show bright color or lights: *On New Year's Eve the big house blazed with lights.* **3** to make a bright display: *Mighty names have blazed upon the world and passed away* (William Cullen Bryant). **4** *Figurative.* to burst out in anger or excitement: *She blazed up at the insult.*

—*v.t.* **1** to cause to shine forth; shed: *The Father . . . on the Son blazed forth unclouded deity* (Milton). **2** to cause to blaze up.

blaze away, *Informal.* **a** to fire a gun or the like continuously: *We . . . blazed away at the lions* (David Livingstone). **b** to work or talk with enthusiasm: *Gomez blazed away with five perfect innings* (New York Times).

go to blazes, *Slang.* go to the devil: *He told the annoying salesman to go to blazes.*

like blazes, *Slang.* furiously; impetuously: *The horse . . . went like blazes* (Thomas De Quincey).

the blazes, *Slang.* the deuce; the devil: *What the blazes is in the wind now?* (Dickens).

[Old English *blæse*]

blaze[2] (blāz), *n., v.,* **blazed, blaz|ing. —*n.*** **1** a mark made on a tree by chipping off a piece of bark, to indicate a trail or boundary in a forest. **2** a white mark on the face of a horse, cow, ox, or other domestic animal.

—*v.t.* **1** to mark (a tree, trail, or boundary) with a blaze or by making blazes. **2** *Figurative.* to pioneer or prepare (a way): *The astronauts are blazing new roads in the conquest of space.*

[perhaps < Low German *Bläse*]

blaze[3] (blāz), *v.t.,* **blazed, blaz|ing. 1** to make known; proclaim. SYN: divulge, publish. **2** *Obsolete.* to blow, as with a musical instrument. [< Scandinavian (compare Old Icelandic *blāsa*)]

blaz|er (blā′zər), *n.* **1** a distinctively colored or decorated jacket. Blazers are sometimes worn as part of the uniform of a team or school. **2** anything which blazes or shines. **3** *U.S.* a small cooking apparatus.

blaz|ing (blā′zing), *adj.* **1** flaming; fiery: *the sight of the blazing dwellings.* (*Figurative.*) *She fixed a glance blazing with rage and scorn on the driver.* **2** shining; bright-colored; glaring: *a blazing sun upon a fierce August day.* **—blaz′ing|ly,** *adv.*

blazing star, 1 any one of several wild plants having showy clusters of flowers. They grow mainly on prairies and meadows in the eastern and midwestern United States. The button snakeroot is one kind. **2** *Archaic.* the brilliant center of admiration; cynosure. **3** *Obsolete.* a comet.

bla|zon (blā′zən), *v., n.* **—*v.t.*** **1** to make known; proclaim: *Big posters blazoned the wonders of the coming circus.* **2** to decorate, especially with designs, names, or colors; adorn: *The bottom of the valley was a bed of glorious grass, blazoned with flowers* (R. Taylor). **3a** to describe or paint (a coat of arms). **b** to inscribe with some ornament: *What matter whose the hillside grave, or whose the blazoned stone* (John Greenleaf Whittier). **4** to display; show: *And blazon o'er the door their names in brass* (Byron).

—*n.* **1** a coat of arms, or a shield with a coat of arms on it. **2** a description or painting of a coat of arms; blazonry. **3** a display; show: *But this eternal blazon must not be* (Shakespeare).

[< Old French *blason* shield] **—bla′zon|er,** *n.* **—bla′zon|ment,** *n.*

bla|zon|ry (blā′zən rē), *n., pl.* **-ries. 1** a bright decoration or display: (*Figurative.*) *The eternal blazonry of nature* (Harriet Beecher Stowe). **2** a coat of arms. **3** a description or painting of a coat of arms.

BLC (no periods), *Aerodynamics.* boundary layer control.

bldg., building.

bldgs., buildings.

bleach (blēch), *v., n.* **—*v.t.*** **1** to whiten by exposing to sunlight or by using chemicals: *We bleached the linen napkins in the wash. Bleached bones lay on the hot sands of the desert.* SYN: See syn. under **whiten. 2** to remove some of the color of; lighten: *The sun had bleached her hair.* **—*v.i.*** to become white; turn pale; lose color: *White sheets bleaching on the hedge* (Shakespeare). SYN: blanch.

—*n.* **1** any chemical used in bleaching: *Laundries often use bleach to whiten shirts.* **2** the act or process of bleaching. **3** the whiteness produced by bleaching.

[Old English *blǣcean.* See related etym. at **bleak.**] **—bleach′a|ble,** *adj.* **—bleach′er,** *n.*

bleach|er|ite (blē′chə rīt), *n. U.S.* a spectator in the bleachers at a sports event.

bleach|ers (blē′chərz), *n.pl.* **1** rows or tiers of low-priced seats, usually not covered by a roof, at an outdoor sports event. **2** the occupants of the section of a stadium, ballpark, or the like, containing these seats. [< *bleach* (from the appearance of such unprotected seats)]

bleach|er|y (blē′chər ē), *n., pl.* **-er|ies.** a place where bleaching is done.

bleach|ing powder (blē′ching), **1** a white powder used for bleaching and disinfecting, made by treating slaked lime with chlorine; chlorinated lime; chloride of lime. **2** any powder for bleaching.

bleak[1] (blēk), *adj.* **1** swept by winds; bare: *The rocky peaks of high mountains are bleak.* SYN: desolate. **2** chilly; cold: *The bleak winter wind made him shiver.* SYN: raw. **3** *Figurative.* cheerless and depressing; dismal: *A prisoner's life is bleak. Lonely and ill, the old woman faced a bleak future.* SYN: dreary. [Middle English *bleke* pale; origin uncertain] **—bleak′ly,** *adv.* **—bleak′ness,** *n.*

bleak[2] (blēk), *n.* a small European freshwater fish of the carp family. [Middle English *bleke,* perhaps < Scandinavian (compare Old Icelandic *bleikja*)]

bleak|ish (blē′kish), *adj.* somewhat bleak.

blear (blir), *adj., v., n.* **—*adj.*** **1** (of the eyes) dim, especially from water or tears. SYN: filmy, misty. **2** indistinct; dim; blurred.

—*v.t.* **1** to dim (the eyes), especially with tears: *The old dog's eyes were bleared by age.* **2** to make dim; blur.

—*n.* a blur; dimness or mistiness: *a blear in the eyes.*

[Middle English *blere;* origin uncertain]

blear-eyed (blir′īd′), *adj.* = bleary-eyed.

blear|y (blir′ē), *adj.,* **blear|i|er, blear|i|est. 1** dim: *Her eyes were bleary with weeping.* **2** indistinct in outline; blurred. **—blear′i|ly,** *adv.* **—blear′i|ness,** *n.*

blear|y-eyed (blir′ē īd′), *adj.* **1** having eyes dim, especially with water or tears. **2** = short-sighted.

bleat (blēt), *n., v.* **—*n.*** **1** the cry made by a sheep, goat, or calf: *The shepherd heard the bleat of the lost lamb over the hill.* **2** a sound like this: *The victim gave a bleat of terror.* [< verb]

—*v.i.* **1** to make the cry of a sheep, goat, or calf: *The lamb bleats for its mother.* **2** to make a sound like this: *The frightened child bleated in terror.* **3** *Figurative.* to complain foolishly or feebly; whine: *Stop bleating about your problems and get to work.*

—*v.t.* to utter with a bleat: *. . . an old half-witted sheep which bleats articulate monotony* (James K. Stephen).

[Old English *blǣtan*] **—bleat′er,** *n.*

bleat|y (blē′tē), *adj.,* **bleat|i|er, bleat|i|est.** bleating; whining: *a bleaty tenor.*

bleb (bleb), *n.* **1** a blister. **2** a bubble. [apparently imitative of the sound of making a bubble with the lips]

bleb|by (bleb′ē), *adj.* full of blebs.

bled[1] (bled), *v.* the past tense and past participle of **bleed:** *The cut bled for ten minutes.*

bled[2] (bled), *n.* a rural district in certain countries of northern Africa. [apparently < Arabic *balda*]

blee (blē), *n. Archaic.* color; complexion. [Old English *blēo*]

bleed (blēd), *v.,* **bled, bleed|ing,** *n.* **—*v.i.*** **1** to lose blood: *He is bleeding from a cut.* **2** to suffer wounds or death; shed one's blood: *He fought and bled for his country.* **3** to lose sap or juice from a surface that has been cut or scratched: *Trees bleed if they are pruned when the sap is rising in the spring.* **4** *Figurative.* to feel pity, sorrow, or grief (for): *My heart bleeds for the poor little orphan.* **5a** (of printed text, illustrations, or decorations) to extend into the margin of the page. **b** to print or trim pages so that this occurs. **6** (of a dye) to run or become diffused when wetted: *When I washed the madras scarf, the dyes bled into each other.*

—*v.t.* **1** to take blood from: *Doctors used to bleed sick people.* **2** to take sap or juice from. **3** *Informal.* to get money away from by extortion. **4** to design or print (text, illustrations, or decorations) so that they leave no margin. **5a** to drain slowly: *to bleed the fluid from a hydraulic brake system.* **b** to drain fluid slowly from: *to bleed a hydraulic brake system.*

—*n.* **1a** any illustration or type area that has no margin. **b** the paper or printed matter trimmed off. **2** a valve or tap; bleeder valve.

bleed white, to use up or take away all of the power, strength, or money of: *England . . . bled herself white in the Hundred Years' War in a futile attempt to keep French territory under the crown* (New York Times).

[Old English *blēdan,* related to *blōd* blood]

bleed|er (blē′dər), *n.* **1** a person who bleeds excessively when injured, because the blood fails to clot; hemophiliac. **2** = bleeder valve. **3** *Electronics.* a resistor connected across a power source to improve the voltage regulation. **4** *Slang.* **a** a sponger. **b** a scoundrel. **c** a wretch: *some poor bleeder.*

bleeder valve, a valve or tap to allow excess fluid, especially fluid under pressure, to be drawn off.

bleed|ing (blē′ding), *adj., n.* **—*adj.*** **1** losing or emitting blood or sap. **2** deeply compassionate or anguished. **3** *British Slang.* cursed; confounded (now usually a profane intensive): *a bleeding error.*

—*n.* **1** hemorrhage: *He applied a tourniquet to stop the bleeding.* **2** bloodletting.

bleeding heart, 1 a common garden plant of the same family as the Dutchman's-breeches, that has drooping clusters of red, pink, or creamy-white, heart-shaped flowers. See picture under **fumitory family. 2** *Slang.* a person given to insincere, exaggerated, or professional display of pity, sorrow, or sympathy: *I want to make sure that the remarks which follow will not be mistaken for the complaints of a bleeding heart* (Harper's).

bleed|ing-heart pigeon (blē′ding härt′), a pigeon, native to the Philippines, whose underparts are white except for a splash of red resembling a wound.

bleep (blēp), *n., v.* **—*n.*** short, high-pitched sound emitted as a signal or to obliterate undesirable words in a broadcast; beep. **—*v.i.*** to emit such a sound. [imitative] **—bleep′er,** *n.*

blel|lum (blel′əm), *n. Scottish.* a blabber.

blem|ish (blem′ish), *n., v.* **—*n.* 1** a physical defect; stain, spot, or scar: *A bad burn improperly treated may leave a blemish on a person's skin.* **2** something that mars completeness or perfection; imperfection; flaw: *These blemishes of smudged printing have been removed in the new edition.* (*Figurative.*) *... if they find some stain or blemish in a name of note* (Alfred Tennyson). SYN: fault. [< verb]
—*v.t.* 1 to stain, spot, or scar. SYN: deface, disfigure. **2** to injure or mar the completeness or perfection of: (*Figurative.*) *One bad deed can blemish a good reputation.* SYN: damage, tarnish, sully.
[< Old French *blemiss-,* stem of *blesmir* harm, make pale, livid] **—blem′ish|er,** *n.* **—blem′ish-less,** *adj.* **—blem′ish|ment,** *n.*

blench[1] (blench), *v.i.* to draw back; shrink away: *I blench and withdraw ...* (Ralph Waldo Emerson). SYN: flinch, quail. **—*v.t.*** to avoid. [apparently Old English *blencan* deceive] **—blench′er,** *n.*

blench[2] (blench), *v.i.* to turn white or pale; blanch: *He blenched with terror.* **—*v.t.*** to make white or pale. [variant of *blanch*[1]]

blend (blend), *v.,* **blend|ed** or (*Archaic*) **blent, blend|ing,** *n.* **—*v.t.* 1** to mix together; mix so thoroughly that the things mixed cannot be distinguished or separated: *Blend the butter and the sugar before adding the other ingredients of the cake.* SYN: combine. See syn. under **mix. 2** to make by mixing several kinds together: *Experts blend teas to suit the water in different areas. Her manner was smoothly blended of graciousness and condescension.*
—*v.i.* 1 to become mixed (with something else) so thoroughly that the things mixed cannot be distinguished or separated: *Even if you mix oil and water, they will not blend.* **2** to shade into each other, little by little; merge: *The colors of the rainbow blend into one another.* **3** to go well together; harmonize: *Brown and gold blend well.*
—*n.* 1 a thorough mixture: *His nature is a perfect blend of liveliness, generosity, and good humor.* **2** a mixture made by blending: *This coffee is a blend of three varieties.* **3** a gradual merging of one thing with another (usually of colors or sounds); shading: *the blend of sky blue into sea blue in the distance, the blend of the woodwinds into the final theme of the strings.* **4** *Linguistics.* a word made by combining two words, often with a syllable in common; portmanteau word. EXAMPLES: *Motel* is a blend of *motor* and *hotel. Smog* is a blend of *smoke* and *fog.* **5** a combination of consonant sounds represented by two or more letters, such as *bl* or *nd* in *blend;* consonant cluster. **6** *U.S.* = blended whiskey.
[Old English *blendan* mix]

blende (blend), *n.* **1** = sphalerite. **2** any one of certain other minerals, especially zinc sulfides, having a resinlike luster. [< German *Blende* < *blenden* to blind, deceive (because its yield is disappointing)]

blended whiskey, *U.S.* a whiskey consisting of not less than 20 per cent of straight whiskey and not more than 80 per cent of neutral spirits.

blend|er (blen′dər), *n.* a person or thing that blends: *a tea blender, a paint blender, a food blender.*

blend|ing inheritance (blen′ding), *n.* the combination of the characteristics of both parents as a result of crossbreeding.

blen|dor (blen′dər), *n.* a device for chopping up and mixing something thoroughly.

Blen|heim spaniel (blen′əm), a variety of English toy spaniel with a short nose and a white coat marked with red. [< *Blenheim* Palace, the Duke of Marlborough's house, Oxfordshire, England]

blen|ni|oid (blen′ē oid), *adj.* **1** like a blenny. **2** of or having to do with the blennies. [< *blenny* + *-oid*]

blen|nor|rhe|a or **blen|nor|rhoe|a** (blen′ə rē′ə), *n.* **1** an excessive secretion and discharge of mucus. **2** = gonorrhea. [< New Latin *blennorrhea* < Greek *blénnos* slime + *rhoiā* a flow < *rheîn* to flow]

blen|ny (blen′ē), *n., pl.* **-nies** or (*collectively*) **-ny.** any one of various small, saltwater fishes with a slender, tapering body. [< Latin *blennius* < Greek *blénnos* slime]

blent (blent), *v. Archaic.* blended; a past tense and a past participle of **blend.**

blephar- or **blepharo-,** *combining form.* **1** eyelid, as in *blepharitis.* **2** flagellum or cilium, as in *blepharoplast.* [< Greek *blépharon* eyelid]

bleph|a|rism (blef′ə riz əm), *n.* continual and involuntary winking or twitching of the eyelids.

bleph|a|rit|ic (blef′ə rit′ik), *adj.* inflamed: *blepharitic eyelids.*

bleph|a|ri|tis (blef′ə rī′tis), *n.* inflammation of the eyelids.

bleph|a|ro|plast (blef′ər ə plast), *n.* a specialized granule of protoplasm in a cell from which a flagellum or cilium arises.

bleph|a|ro|spasm (blef′ər ə spaz′əm), *n.* excessive and involuntary winking.

bles|bok (bles′bok′), *n.* a large South African antelope having a white spot on the face. [< Afrikaans *blesbok* < Dutch *bles* blaze[2] + *bok* he-goat, buck]

bles|buck (bles′buk′), *n.* = blesbok.

bless (bles), *v.t.,* **blessed** or **blest, bless|ing. 1a** to consecrate (a thing) by a religious rite, formula, or prayer: *The bishop blessed the new church.* **b** to make holy or sacred: *And God blessed the seventh day, and sanctified it* (Genesis 2:3). SYN: sanctify, hallow. **2** to ask God's favor for; commend to God's favor or protection: *Bless these little children.* **3** to wish good to; feel grateful to: *I bless him for his kindness.* **4** to make happy or fortunate: *May this country always be blessed with freedom.* **5** to call holy; praise; glorify; adore: *Bless the Lord, O my soul.* SYN: extol. **6** to guard or protect from evil: *Heaven bless this house.* **7** to make the sign of the cross over: *Mrs. Lonigan drew some rosary beads out of her apron pocket, ... blessed herself with it and commenced whispering her rosary* (James T. Farrell).
bless me, an exclamation of surprise: *Bless me! Sir, there's no room for a question* (Sir Richard Steele).
bless you (him, us, etc.), God bless you (him, us, etc.): *The Colonel might have said "Bless you, my children," in the tenderest tones* (John Ruskin).
[Old English *blētsian, blēdsian* consecrate (that is, with blood), related to *blōd* blood] **—bless′er,** *n.*

bless|ed (bles′id; *especially poetic* blest), *adj., n.* **—*adj.* 1** holy; sacred: *the blessed Trinity.* SYN: consecrated. **2** bringing joy; joyful: *the blessed rain following a drought.* **3** happy; fortunate: *Blessed are the pure in heart* (Matthew 5:8). **4** enjoying the favor of heaven; beatified. **5** *Informal.* a euphemism for "cursed"; confounded: *I can't get this blessed car to start.* SYN: annoying.
—*n.* the Blessed, (in the Roman Catholic Church) a person or persons beatified by a decree of the Pope (a title characterizing one adjudged worthy of veneration but not canonized, although often preceding canonization): *The men, in their togas, reminded one of saints; ... they "recalled irresistibly the conventional pictures of evangelical piety that represented the Blessed walking in the vales of Paradise"* (New Yorker).
—bless′ed|ly, *adv.* **—bless′ed|ness,** *n.*

blessed event, *Informal.* **1** the birth of a child. **2** the child itself.

Blessed Sacrament, the Eucharist; Holy Communion.

Blessed Virgin, the Virgin Mary.

bless|ing (bles′ing), *n.* **1** a prayer asking God to show His favor; benediction: *A church service is often concluded with a blessing.* SYN: invocation, benison. **2** a giving of God's favor. **3** a brief prayer of thanks said before or sometimes after a meal. **4** a wish for happiness or success: *When he left home, he received his father's blessing. Blessings on thee, little man* (John Greenleaf Whittier). **5** anything that makes one happy or contented; benefit: *the blessings of nature. A good temper is a great blessing.* SYN: favor, gift, boon. **6** consent or approval: *The marriage had the blessing of the parents of the bride and groom. The court would have to give its final blessing and the bankruptcy would be ended* (Wall Street Journal). SYN: sanction.
a blessing in disguise, a bad thing that turns out to be good in the end: *His sudden illness was a blessing in disguise, for it kept him from going to the theater which burned down that evening.*

blest (blest), *v., adj.* **—*v.*** blessed; a past tense and a past participle of **bless:** *He was blest with good health.*
—*adj.* blessed.

bleth|er (bleᴛʜ′ər), *n., v.i., v.t.* = blather.

blet|ting (blet′ing), *n.* the slow, internal decay that takes place in apples, pears, and some other fruits after they are stored. [< French *blettir* to become overripe + English *-ing*[1]]

bleu cheese (blü), = blue cheese. [< French *bleu* blue]

bleu-de-roi (blœ′dərwȧ′), *n. Ceramics.* the ultramarine blue of Sèvres porcelain. [< French *bleu-de-roi* (literally) king's blue]

blew (blü), *v.* the past tense of **blow**[2] and **blow**[3]: *All night long the wind blew.*

blew|its (blü′its), *n.* an edible, bluish-purple mushroom. [probably the same as *bluets,* plural of *bluet*]

blight (blīt), *n., v.* **—*n.* 1** a disease that causes plants to wither and die. Blights are caused by bacteria, fungi, and viruses and destroy the tissues of the plant. *The apple crop was wiped out by blight.* **2** the bacterium, fungus, or virus that causes such a disease. **3** *Figurative.* anything that withers hopes or causes destruction or ruin: *His father's bankruptcy was a blight on the boy's hopes for an education.* **4** *Figurative.* dilapidation; deterioration; decay: *urban blight.*
—*v.t.* 1 to cause to wither and die: *Mildew blighted the June roses.* **2** *Figurative.* to destroy; ruin: *Rain blighted our hopes for a picnic.*
—*v.i.* to be blighted; suffer from blight.
[origin uncertain] **—blight′ing|ly,** *adv.*

blight|ed (blī′tid), *adj.* afflicted with blight; blasted: *A blighted spring makes a barren year* (Samuel Johnson). (*Figurative.*) *A blighted area is a district of a city that is on the way toward becoming a slum* (Emory S. Bogardus).

blight|er (blī′tər), *n.* **1** a person or thing that blights. **2** *British Slang.* **a** a contemptible man; scoundrel: *One day the District Attorney will bring the smug blighter to book for some of his questionable devices* (Listener). **b** any man; fellow: *the lucky little blighter!*

blight|y or **Blight|y** (blī′tē), *n. British Slang.* **1** England; home (used originally by soldiers on foreign service). **2** a wound that sends a soldier home. [< Hindustani *bilāyatī* foreign, European < Arabic *wilāyat* province, government]

blim|ey (blī′mē), *interj. British Cockney Slang.* an exclamation of surprise; cor! [< *God blind me*]

***blimp**[1] (blimp), *n. Informal.* **1** a small, nonrigid, dirigible airship. **2** any dirigible. **3** a soundproof cover on a motion-picture camera. It prevents the camera's noise from reaching the sound track. [apparently < (British) Type *B limp,* designation for "limp dirigible" in early experiments]

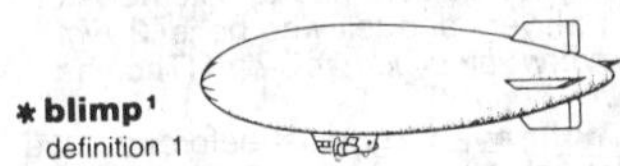

***blimp**[1]
definition 1

Blimp or **blimp**[2] (blimp), *n.* a pompous and complacent ultraconservative person: [*They*] *are silent because they're afraid of looking reactionary, like the blimps who turned out to be wrong about Van Gogh or Cézanne* (Punch). [< Colonel *Blimp,* a character in a British newspaper cartoon, created by David Low, 1891-1963]

Blimp|ish or **blimp|ish** (blim′pish), *adj.* characteristic of a Blimp; pompously ultraconservative.

blind (blīnd), *adj., adv., v., n.* **—*adj.* 1** not able to see: *The blind man needed help to cross the street.* SYN: sightless. **2a** hard to see; hidden: *There is a blind curve on the highway.* **b** hard to trace, read, or follow: *a blind trail.* **3** without the use of sight: *In his blind fumbling in the dark room, he knocked over the lamp.* **4** *Figurative.* without thought, judgment, or good sense: *The angry boy was in a blind rage. When he didn't know he made a blind guess.* SYN: heedless, reckless. **5** with only one opening: *They walked down a blind street and had to turn around and go back.* **6** without an opening: *a blind wall.* **7** of or for blind persons. **8** made without previous knowledge: *a blind purchase.* **9** abortive: *a blind bud.* **10.** *Slang.* drunk: *It makes a pig of you when you get blind* (James T. Farrell).
—*adv.* by means of instruments instead of the eyes: *reading from instruments that make it possible for pilots to fly blind.*
—*v.t.* 1 to make unable to see: *The bright lights blinded me for a moment.* **2** to make difficult to see; conceal: *Clouds blinded the stars from my view.* **3** *Figurative.* to take away the power to understand or judge: *His prejudices blinded him.*
—*n.* 1a something that keeps out light or hinders sight. A window shade or shutter is a blind. **b** = blinder (def. 1). **2** *Figurative.* anything that conceals an action or purpose: *Asking to see how fast his friend's bicycle would go was a blind to get to use it.* SYN: pretext, pretense. **3** a hiding place for a hunter: *When he hunts ducks, he hides behind a blind of twigs, grass, and leaves.* SYN: ambush.
blind to, unable to understand, perceive, or appreciate: *She is blind to his faults.*
[Old English *blind*] **—blind′ing|ly,** *adv.* **—blind′ly,** *adv.* **—blind′ness,** *n.*

blind|age (blīn′dij), *n.* a screen or other structure to protect men in a trench. [< *blind,* noun + *-age*]

Pronunciation Key: hat, āge, cãre, fär; let, ēqual, tėrm; it, īce; hot, ōpen, ôrder; **oi**l, **ou**t; cup, pu̇t, rüle; **ch**ild; lo**ng**; **th**in; ᴛʜen; **zh**, measure; ə represents **a** in about, **e** in taken, **i** in pencil, **o** in lemon, **u** in circus.

blind alley, 1 a passageway closed at one end. SYN: cul-de-sac. 2 *Figurative.* **a** a situation or position that leads nowhere; impasse: *a conversational blind alley.* **b** an employment offering no chance for progress or improvement.

blind date 1 a date between two persons of opposite sex who have not previously met, arranged by someone else. 2 either of the two persons.

blind|er (blīn′dər), *n.* 1 a leather flap on a horse's bridle to keep it from seeing sidewise; blinker; blind. 2 *British Slang.* a dazzling performance.

blind|fish (blīnd′fish′), *n., pl.* **-fish|es** or (*collectively*) **-fish.** a fish that lives in the underground streams of caves, and has rudimentary eyes, useless for vision.

blind flying, = instrument flying.

blind|fold (blīnd′fōld′), *v., adj., adv., n.* **—*v.t.*** 1 to cover the eyes of: *The robbers blindfolded and bound their victim.* 2 to cover (the eyes) with a cloth, etc.: *They blindfolded my eyes for a week after the operation.* 3 *Figurative.* to darken the understanding or judgment of: *Prejudice blindfolds the mind.*
—*adj.*, *adv.* 1 with the eyes covered or as if covered: *"I am going to bring a plane down practically blindfold," he said* (New Yorker). *I was made ... to play ten games simultaneously and blindfold against the junior chess club* (Punch). 2 *Figurative.* reckless; heedless: *With blindfold fury she begins to forage* (Shakespeare).
—*n.* a cloth or other thing for covering the eyes. [Middle English *blindfellen* < *blind* + *fellen* strike down; influenced by English *fold*]

blind gut, = cecum.

blind landing, *Especially British.* = instrument landing.

blind|man's buff (blīnd′manz′ buf′), 1 a game in which a blindfolded person tries to catch one of several other players and tell who he is. 2 *Figurative: Government by blindman's-buff* (Thomas Carlyle). [*buff* < *buffet*]

blindman's holiday, twilight just before the evening lights are lighted, when it is too dark to work, read, or the like.

blind pig, *U.S. Slang.* a place where intoxicating liquors are sold contrary to law.

blind side, 1 the weak or unguarded side of a person or thing. 2 *Rugby.* the portion of the field opposite the referee in scrummage.

blind snake, a small, burrowing snake that feeds on worms and insect larvae.

blind spot, 1 a point on the retina that is not sensitive to light. The optic nerve enters the eye there. See picture under **eye**. 2 *Figurative.* a matter on which a person does not know that he is prejudiced or poorly informed: *Grammar is his blind spot.* 3 an area of poor radio or television reception. 4 an area of poor visibility: *There is a blind spot where the road dips.*

blind staggers, 1 = staggers. See under **stagger**. 2 *U.S. Slang.* extreme drunkenness.

blind|sto|ry (blīnd′stôr′ē, -stōr′-), *n., pl.* **-ries.** a story without windows or other major openings, especially a triforium with no exterior windows.

blind tiger, *U.S. Slang.* = speakeasy.

blind trust, 1 a trust fund into which a person places his financial holdings to be managed by others while he is engaged in a position such as a government appointment in which his business interests might conflict with his duties. 2 a trust established to conceal the identity of the person or persons whose property is held in trust.

blind|worm (blīnd′wėrm′), *n.* a small lizard of Europe, western Asia, and Algeria, with a limbless, snakelike body and very tiny eyes, popularly supposed to be sightless but actually able to see; slowworm.

bling|er (bling′gər), *n. U.S. Slang.* whopper: *one blinger of a headache.* [origin uncertain]

blin|i (blin′ē), *n., pl.* **blin|is** or **blin|i.** a very light, thin, small pancake, served with sour cream, or caviar, smoked salmon, or other delicacy. Also, **bliny.** [< Russian *bliny* pancakes]

blink (blingk), *v., n.* **—*v.i.*** 1 to look with the eyes opening and shutting: *She blinked at the sudden light.* 2 to close the eyes and then open them again quickly; wink: *We blink every few seconds.* 3 to shine with an unsteady light: *A lantern blinked through the darkness.* SYN: twinkle. 4 *Figurative.* to look with indifference (at): *We blink at faults in those we love.*
—*v.t.* 1 *Figurative.* to shut the eyes to; look with indifference at; ignore: *You cannot blink the fact that time slips by.* SYN: evade. 2 to blind: *The sun is blinking my eyes.* 3 to shut (the eyes) for a moment; wink: *The average person blinks his eyes 25 times a minute* (Science News Letter).
—*n.* 1 a winking; a wink: *Several blinks will sometimes get a cinder out of the eye.* 2 a sudden flash of light; gleam: *The blink of the beacon could be seen for miles.* 3 the time taken by a glance: *The cat caught the mouse in a blink of an eye.* 4 *Scottish.* a glance; glimpse: *I wish my master were living to get a blink o't* (Sir Walter Scott). 5 a brightness above the horizon caused by the reflection of light from masses of ice.
on the blink, *Informal.* not working properly; not working: *I can't hear the news since my radio went on the blink.*
[Middle English *blinken, blenken* elude, Old English *blencan* deceive]

blink|er (bling′kər), *n., v.* **—*n.*** 1 a warning signal with flashing lights. 2 a blinder for a horse. 3 *Slang.* **a** an eye; peeper. **b** = black eye.
—*v.t.* *Informal.* to make unable to see or understand; restrict the vision of: *to blinker a horse.*
blinkers, = goggles.

blink|ered (bling′kərd), *adj.* having a restricted outlook; narrow-minded.

blink|ing (bling′king), *adj.* 1 that blinks. 2 *British Slang.* confounded; blooming: *a blinking fool.* **—blink′ing|ly**, *adv.*

blink microscope, an instrument through which two photographs may be viewed in rapid alternation to check the alteration in position or movement of a star, comet, or other heavenly body.

blintze or **blintz** (blints), *n.* a thin, rolled pancake filled with some soft food, such as a soft cheese, jam, or fruit. [< Yiddish *blints* < Ukrainian *blynci*]

blin|y (blin′ē), *n., pl.* **blin|ies** or **blin|y.** = blini.

blip (blip), *n., v.,* **blipped, blip|ping.** **—*n.*** 1 a small spot or dot of light by which a radar or similar apparatus indicates on its screen the location of an object within its range. 2 a sharp, short sound; bleep.
—*v.i.* to appear as or produce a blip. **—*v.t.*** 1 to hit lightly; tap. 2 *U.S.* to replace (a censored word or expression) with a blip, as on a videotape. [imitative]

bliss (blis), *n., v.* **—*n.*** 1 great happiness; perfect joy: *What bliss it is to plunge into the cool waves on a hot day.* SYN: delight, ecstasy, rapture. See syn. under **happiness**. 2 the joy of heaven; blessedness: *... deprived of everlasting bliss* (Christopher Marlowe).
—*v.t.* bliss out, *U.S. Slang.* to fill with bliss; enrapture: *His Peninsula neighbors are too blissed out on tranquillity to know or care what he does for a living* (Town and Country).
[Old English *bliss, blīths* < *blīthe* blithe]

bliss|ful (blis′fəl), *adj.* supremely happy; joyful: *We have blissful memories of a summer vacation.* SYN: delightful, ecstatic, enraptured. **—bliss′ful|ly**, *adv.* **—bliss′ful|ness**, *n.*

blis|ter (blis′tər), *n., v.* **—*n.*** 1 a little baglike place in the skin filled with watery matter. Blisters are often caused by burns or rubbing. *My new shoes have made blisters on my heels.* SYN: vesicle, bleb. 2 a similar swelling on the surface of a plant, on metal, on the surface of painted wood, or in glass. 3 a bulge on the fuselage of an aircraft, often of transparent material, for an observer, navigator, or gunner. 4 a bulging structure built onto the hull of a ship for protection against torpedoes. 5 *Medicine.* anything applied to raise a blister; vesicatory.
—*v.t.* 1 to raise a blister or blisters on: *Sunburn has blistered my back.* 2 *Figurative.* to attack with sharp words. **—*v.i.*** to become covered with blisters; have blisters: *People often blister when they get sunburned.*
[< Old French *blestre* tumor, lump, probably < Scandinavian (compare Old Icelandic *blāstr* swelling)]

blister beetle, any one of various beetles which are dried and powdered for use in raising blisters on the skin in medical treatment, especially the Spanish fly or cantharis.

blister copper, impure copper having a black, blistered surface, obtained during smelting just before the final refining operation.

blis|tered (blis′tərd), *adj.* 1 having blisters: *blistered paint.* 2 ornamented with puffs; puffed.

blister figure, an irregular pattern in such woods as mahogany, satinwood, and elm, caused by the abnormal growth of annual rings.

blister gas, a gas that blisters the skin, used in chemical warfare.

blis|ter|ing (blis′tər ing), *adj.* 1 causing or capable of causing blisters. 2 very hot: **a** sweltering: *blistering heat.* **b** *Figurative.* angry: *a blistering condemnation.* **c** *Figurative.* violent. 3 *Figurative.* very fast: *... this year's blistering production pace* (Wall Street Journal). **—blis′ter|ing|ly**, *adv.*

blister pack, a strong, transparent plastic package, usually mounted on a cardboard backing and designed to fit and show its content while protecting it from damage, dirt, and pilfering.

blister rust, a fungus disease of pine trees.

blis|ter|y (blis′tər ē), *adj.* that blisters; characterized by blisters.

B.Lit., Bachelor of Literature (Latin, *Baccalaureus Litterarum*).

blithe (blīᴛʜ, blīth), *adj.* 1 happy and cheerful; gay: *Hail to thee, blithe spirit! Bird thou never wert* (Shelley). *Blithe would her brother's acceptance be* (Tennyson). SYN: joyous, merry, glad, pleased. 2 heedless. [Old English *blīthe* joyous] **—blithe′ly**, *adv.* **—blithe′ness**, *n.*

blithe|ful (blīᴛʜ′fəl, blīth′-), *adj. Archaic.* blithesome.

blith|er (bliᴛʜ′ər), *n., v.i., v.t.* = blather.

blith|er|ing (bliᴛʜ′ər ing), *adj.* senselessly talkative; babbling.

blithe|some (blīᴛʜ′səm, blīth′-), *adj.* blithe: *On blithesome frolics bent* (James Thomson). SYN: gay, cheerful, happy. **—blithe′some|ly**, *adv.* **—blithe′some|ness**, *n.*

B.Litt., Bachelor of Literature (Latin, *Baccalaureus Litterarum*).

blitz (blits), *n., v., adj.* **—*n.*** 1 = blitzkrieg. 2 a sudden, violent attack using many airplanes and tanks. 3 any sudden, violent attack. 4 *Football Slang.* the defensive tactic of blitzing or red-dogging.
—*v.t.* 1 to attack or overcome by a blitz. 2 *Football Slang.* to pursue and harass (the passer); red-dog. **—*v.i.*** *Football Slang.* = red-dog.
—*adj.* 1 of or having to do with a blitz. 2 swift and aggressive: *... blitz telephone operations to sell stocks* (Time). **—blitz′er**, *n.*

blitz|krieg (blits′krēg′), *n., v.* **—*n.*** 1 warfare in which the offensive is very rapid, violent, and hard to resist. 2 *Figurative.* any sudden, violent attack; blitz. **—*v.t.*** *Informal.* to attack by or as if by blitzkrieg; blitz. [< German *Blitzkrieg* lightning war]

bliz|zard (bliz′ərd), *n.* 1 a blinding snowstorm with a very strong wind and extreme cold. 2 any severe, widespread snowstorm lasting for some time. 3 a similar storm of wind-blown sand or dust. 4 *Figurative.* a severe attack: *caught in a blizzard of criticism.* [American English; variant of dialectal English *blizzer* something sudden, sharp, especially a blow, shot, or choking, or *blizz* violent rainstorm]

bliz|zard|ly (bliz′ərd lē), *adj.* like or characteristic of a blizzard.

bliz|zard|y (bliz′ər dē), *adj.* 1 like a blizzard. 2 in which many blizzards occur: *a blizzardy winter.*

blk., 1 black. 2 block.

B.LL., Bachelor of Laws (Latin, *Baccalaureus Legum*).

bloat (blōt), *v., n.* **—*v.t.*** 1 to swell up; puff up: *Overeating will bloat your stomach.* SYN: inflate, swell. 2 to preserve (herring) by slightly salting and partially smoking.
—*v.i.* to become bloated; swell.
—*n.* 1 a disorder in cattle, sheep, and goats characterized by a swelling of the stomach (rumen) as a result of an accumulation of gases. It is caused by eating green forage, especially legumes, too rapidly, by eating moist feed that ferments, or by changing feed when extremely hungry. 2 *U.S. Informal, Figurative.* wasteful or needless expansion of staff, expenditures, procedures, or the like: *... authorized by Congress to check ... for bureaucratic bloat* (New York Times).
[Middle English *blout* soft with moisture, probably < Scandinavian (compare Old Icelandic *blautr* soft, pulpy)]

bloat|ed (blō′tid), *adj.* 1 swollen and puffy: *the bloated face of a rubber doll.* 2 *Figurative.* pampered; puffed up. 3 *Figurative.* inflated; too great: *... put an end to these bloated armaments* (Benjamin Disraeli). 4 cured as a bloater: *a bloated herring.*

bloat|er (blō′tər), *n.* 1 a herring preserved by slightly salting and partially smoking, softer and less dry than a kipper. 2 a small cisco of the Great Lakes.

blob (blob), *n., v.,* **blobbed, blob|bing.** **—*n.*** 1 a small, soft drop; sticky lump; bubble: *Blobs of wax covered the candlestick.* 2 a splash or daub of color: *a blob of crimson.* 3 something that has no distinct or definite shape: *He imposes on the reader great blobs of incoherent personal emotion* (Alfred Kazin). 4 *Slang.* an insignificant person: *But the people who are supposed to be on our side are just blobs* (New Yorker).
—*v.t.* to smear; splotch: *to blob paint on the wall.*
[perhaps imitative]

bloc (blok), *n.* 1 a group of persons, companies, or nations combined for a purpose: *The farm bloc in Congress is a group from different political parties that favors laws to help farmers.* 2 a group of peoples or nations having common interests: *Poland and East Germany are a part of the eastern European bloc.* [< French *bloc* block, section]

*** block** (blok), *n., v.* **—*n.*** 1a a solid piece of wood, stone, metal, ice, or other material. A block usually has one or more flat sides. *The Pyramids are made of blocks of stone.* **b** a similar, small piece of wood, stone, plastic, or rubber used (usually in sets) as a toy for children: *alphabet blocks. Build*

a house with your blocks. **2** *Figurative.* **a** anything or any group of persons that keeps something from being done; obstruction; hindrance: *A block in traffic kept our car from moving on.* **b** an inability to do or learn a specified thing: *to have a mental block about spelling.* **3** *U.S. and Canada.* **a** a space in a city or town enclosed by streets. **b** the length of one side of a block in a city or town: *Walk one block east to the next street.* **4a** a number of buildings close together. **b** a large, single building consisting of a number of stores or shops, each with its separate entrance to the street. **5** a group of things of the same kind: *a block of ten tickets for a play.* **6** a short section of railroad track between two signals by which trains are spaced. **7** a support for the neck of a person being beheaded: *... a short sharp shock from a cheap and chippy chopper on a big black block* (W. S. Gilbert). **8** a platform where things are put up for sale at an auction. **9** a pulley or pulleys in a holder with a hook, eye, or strap by which it may be attached. Pulleys are used with a rope, belt, or chain, especially to transmit power and change the direction of motion. **10** a mold on which something is shaped or placed to make it keep in shape: *a block for a hat.* **11** a piece of wood, metal, or other material engraved for printing. **12** *Slang.* a person's head. **13** = blockhead. **14** *Medicine.* an obstruction of a normal function, as in the passage of nerve or muscular impulses. **15** *Sports.* an impeding action directed at an opponent: *The football player threw a block that knocked the ball-carrier out of bounds.* **16** the support under the keel of a ship in drydock. **17** *Geology.* a faulting in blocklike sections; block faulting. *Abbr:* bk.
—***v.t.*** **1a** to fill up so as to prevent passage or progress: *The country roads were blocked with snow.* SYN: bar, blockade. **b** *Figurative.* to put things in the way of; hinder; obstruct: *Mother's illness blocked my plans for her birthday party.* **2** to mount on a block. **3** to shape with a mold: *Felt hats are blocked.* **4** *Sports.* to hinder (an opponent or his play). **5** *Medicine.* to prevent normal function of (a nerve or muscular impulse), especially by the injection of an anesthetic. **6** to prevent or postpone the passage of (a bill) in a legislature. **7** *Cricket.* to stop (a ball) with the bat, simply to protect the wicket, without trying to hit for runs. **8a** to manage or control the exchange of (local and foreign currencies) by government order, to prevent the development of an adverse balance of trade. **b** to prohibit the use of (funds) for a given period of time, as during a war.
—***v.i.*** to act in opposition to an opponent, as in baseball, boxing, and football.
block in (or **out**), to plan or sketch roughly without filling in the details; outline: *The artist blocked in parts of a portrait. The committee blocked out its plan.*
block off, to close off: *to block off a street to traffic.*
blocks, a pair of supports against which a sprinter braces his feet at the start of a race: *In the final, Wilma came off the blocks a split second behind the field* (Time).
block up, a to fill up so as to prevent passage, progress, or vision: *The landslide blocked up the riverbed.* **b** to raise on blocks: *to block up the chassis of the truck.*
go to the block, a to go to have one's head cut off: *King Henry VIII caused two of his wives to go to the block.* **b** to be for sale at an auction: *Several museums tried to buy the famous painting when it went to the block.*
knock (someone's) block off, *Informal.* to thrash; pummel: *"If I catch the thief who stole my ball," the boy said, "I'll knock his block off."*
on the block, up for sale or auction: *His collection of paintings will go on the block tomorrow. Within 48 hours the competing evening Telegram broke the first story that the Star was on the block* (Time).
[Middle English *blok,* perhaps < Old French *bloc* piece of wood] —**block'like'**, *adj.*

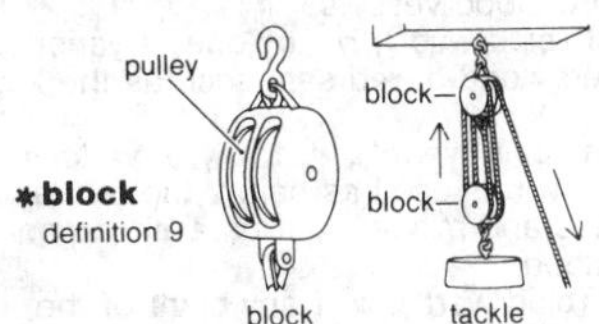

***block**
definition 9

block|ade (blo kād'), *n., v.,* **-ad|ed, -ad|ing.** —***n.*** **1** control of who or what goes into or out of a place, especially by police or by an army or navy: *Ships of the Union navy formed a blockade of southern ports in the Civil War to prevent foreign trade with Europe. After the earthquake police set up a blockade into town to prevent looting.* SYN: See syn. under **siege**. **2** a navy, an army, or a police force used to blockade a place. **3** *Figurative.* anything that blocks up or obstructs: *Sawhorses were used as a blockade to hold back the crowd.*
—***v.t.*** **1** to put under blockade: *The firemen blockaded the area where the fire was raging.* **2** *Figurative.* to block up; obstruct: *His strong argument blockaded any change in the plan.*
run the blockade, to sneak into or out of a port that is being blockaded: *The "Sumter" ... succeeded in running the blockade of the mouth of the Mississippi* (Harper's).
[< *block* (verb) + French *-ade,* ultimately < Latin *-āta,* feminine participial ending] —**block|ad'er**, *n.*
block|ade-run|ner (blo kād'run'ər), *n.* **1** a ship that tries to make a run into or out of a port that is being blockaded. **2** the owner, captain, or one of the crew of such a vessel.
block|age (blok'ij), *n.* an obstruction.
block and tackle, a combination of pulleys and ropes to lift or pull something.
block association, *U.S.* an organization formed by residents of a city block or other small area to protect and promote their interests.
block booking, the renting or selling of motion pictures, or magazines in groups without permitting the exhibitor or retailer to make a selection.
block|bust|er (blok'bus'tər), *n.* **1** a very destructive aerial bomb that weighs two or more tons. **2** *Informal, Figurative.* anything very large, forceful, or overwhelming. **3** *U.S.* a real-estate dealer who engages in blockbusting. **4** a motion picture produced at lavish cost. **5** a highly promoted best-selling book, especially a novel: *Big conglomerate money is what enables the hard-cover houses to pay out big advances for the potential blockbusters that they hope will allow them to hit the paperback-rights bonanzas* (New Yorker).
block|bust|ing (blok'bus'ting), *n., adj.* —***n.*** *U.S.* the practice by some real-estate dealers of causing residents of a block to sell their homes or property at low prices by claiming the present or prospective entry into the neighborhood of persons of another race, religion, or nationality.
—***adj.*** *Informal.* very forceful; overwhelming: *a blockbusting performance.*
block capital, an upper-case block letter.
block club or **organization**, *U.S.* a group of city dwellers organized to improve conditions in the block in which they live and often to protect it from criminal elements.
***block diagram**, **1** a three-dimensional perspective drawing, especially one representing a geological or topographic feature. **2** a drawing of any device, instrument, or system in which the parts are represented by rectangular or boxlike figures.

***block diagram**
definitions 1, 2

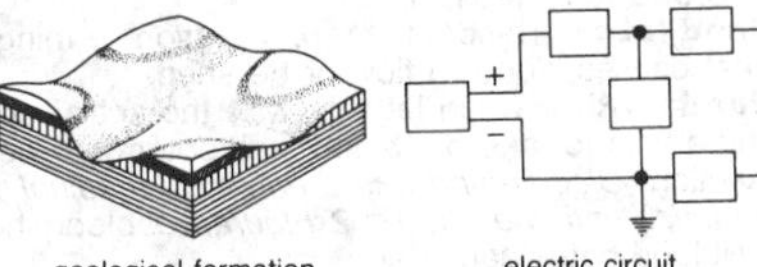

geological formation
electric circuit

blocked (blokt), *adj.* **1** obstructed, hindered, or held in check: *a blocked kick. Blocked pesetas are Spanish funds whose exchange into dollars or other currency is prohibited by the Spanish government* (Wall Street Journal). **2** shaped on or with a block. **3** furnished with blocks.
block|er (blok'ər), *n.* **1** a person or thing that blocks. **2** a player who blocks an opponent or a play, especially in football. **3** a drug or chemical that inhibits the action of a substance or part of the body: *Methadone was dispensed ... nationwide as a chemical blocker and antagonist of heroin* (Byron T. Scott).
block|front (blok'frunt'), *n.* **1** the frontage of a block: *The structure occupies the blockfront between 235th and 236th Streets* (New York Times). **2** a type of chest or desk front having three vertical sections, the center one sunk between the slightly raised ones on each side.
block grant, a fixed grant of money given by the government to local communities instead of separate grants for specific projects: *The H.U.D. office has turned down Hempstead's application for a community block grant* (New York Times).
block|head (blok'hed'), *n.* a stupid person; fool; dunce: *No man but a blockhead ever wrote, except for money* (Samuel Johnson).
block|head|ed (blok'hed'id), *adj.* dull and foolish; stupid. —**block'head'ed|ly**, *adv.* —**block'head'ed|ness**, *n.*
***block|house** (blok'hous'), *n.* **1** a small fort or building with loopholes to shoot from. Blockhouses were made with hewn timbers, often with a projecting upper story. **2** a somewhat similar, smaller structure made of reinforced concrete, used in modern warfare. **3** a structure for protection against blast, heat, or radiation during the firing of a rocket, missile, or nuclear weapon.

***blockhouse**
definition 1

block|ing capacitor or **condenser** (blok'ing), a capacitor designed to stop the flow of direct current or low-frequency alternating current without impeding high-frequency alternating current.
block|ish (blok'ish), *adj.* very dull or stupid. —**block'ish|ly**, *adv.* —**block'ish|ness**, *n.*
block lava, *Geology.* slaglike lava.
***block letter**, **1** a letter or type without serifs or hairlines. **2** = capital letter. **3** a letter carved on a block of wood.

***block letter**
definition 1

THE WORLD BOOK DICTIONARY

block lettering, block letters.
block line, a line over pulleys.
block organization, = block club.
block party, *U.S.* a party held on the street by residents of a block or neighborhood, especially to raise funds for a local organization.
block plane, a small plane used to smooth the ends of boards across the grain.
block print, a picture or design produced by block printing.
block-print|ed (blok'prin'tid), *adj.* printed by means of carved or engraved blocks of wood or other material: *In 868, the Chinese produced the Diamond Sutra, the world's first block-printed book* (Eugene Boardman).
block printing, a printing from engraved or carved blocks of wood or other material. It is used chiefly for textiles and greeting cards.
block programming, radio or television programming that retains the interest of a type of listener or viewer by grouping all programs with similar appeal in the same period of the day.
block release, (in Great Britain) periodic release of a worker from employment to allow him to attend courses at a technical school.
blocks (bloks), *n.pl.* See under **block**.
block|ship (blok'ship'), *n.* a ship used to block a harbor, canal, or other waterway.
block signal, a signal to show whether a short section of railroad track ahead has a train on it.
block system, a system of dividing a railroad track into short sections with signals to warn a train when the section ahead is not clear.
block tin, commercial tin cast into molds.
block or **bloc vote**, **1a** votes cast by proxy and equivalent to the number of persons represented. **b** vote by a group having a common interest. **2** system of voting in which such votes are cast.
block|y (blok'ē), *adj.,* **block|i|er, block|i|est.** **1** like a block; chunky; solid: *a blocky pony.* **2** having patches of light and shade. —**block'i|ly**, *adv.* —**block'i|ness**, *n.*
bloke (blōk), *n. British Slang.* man; fellow. [origin unknown]
blol|ly (blol'ē), *n., pl.* **-lies.** a shrub or small tree, of Florida and the West Indies, bearing oval leaves and bright-red, fleshy fruit. [short for *loblolly*]
blond (blond), *adj., n.* —***adj.*** **1** light in color: *blond hair.* SYN: flaxen. **2** having yellow or light-brown hair, blue or gray eyes, and fair skin: *a blond boy.* SYN: fair. **3** (of wood) very light in color: *blond oak furniture.*
—***n.*** a person having yellow or light-brown hair, blue or gray eyes, and fair skin. A man or boy of this sort is usually referred to as a *blond,* a woman or girl as a *blonde.*
[< Old French *blonde* (feminine) probably < a Germanic word] —**blond'ness**, *n.*
blonde (blond), *adj., n., v.,* **blond|ed, blond|ing.** —***adj.*** = blond. —***n.*** **1** a woman or girl who is blond. **2** Also, **blonde lace.** a silk lace, originally unbleached, now bleached white or dyed black. —***v.t.*** to dye blond; blondine. —**blonde'ness**, *n.*
blond|ine (blon'dēn), *v.,* **-ined, -in|ing,** *n., adj.* *U.S.* —***v.t.*** to dye (hair) blond; bleach; blonde. —***n.*** a preparation for making hair blond; bleach. —***adj.*** bleached: *blondine hair.*

Pronunciation Key: hat, āge, cãre, fär; let, ēqual, tėrm; it, īce; hot, ōpen, ôrder; oil, out; cup, pu̇t, rüle; child; long; thin; ᴛʜen; zh, measure; ə represents a in about, e in taken, i in pencil, o in lemon, u in circus.

blond|ish (blon′dish), *adj.* somewhat or nearly blond or blonde.

blond|ism (blon′diz əm), *n.* the condition of being blond.

blood (blud), *n., v.* —*n.* **1** the liquid in the veins, arteries, and capillaries of vertebrates; the red liquid that flows from a cut. Blood is circulated by the heart, carrying oxygen and digested food to all parts of the body and carrying away waste materials. Although it normally looks red, the blood of humans and most other vertebrates actually consists of a pale-yellow plasma and semisolid, red and white blood cells and platelets. **2** the corresponding liquid in animals other than vertebrates. The blood of most insects looks yellowish or greenish. **3** *Figurative.* relationship by descent from a common ancestor; family; parentage; descent: *Love of the sea runs in his blood. We be of one blood ...* (Rudyard Kipling). **SYN**: race, stock. **4** *Figurative.* high lineage, especially royal lineage: *a prince of the blood.* **5** a man of dash and spirit. **SYN**: rake, dandy. **6** bloodshed: *I have nothing to offer but blood, toil, tears, and sweat* (Sir Winston Churchill). **7** *Figurative.* ancestry known or registered as good; pure or thoroughbred breeding; pedigree: *Nothing like blood, sir, in hosses, dawgs and men* (Thackeray). **8** passion; temper: *When his blood was up he said many things he later regretted.* **9** = lifeblood. **10** persons; people: *We need fresh blood in the company.* **11** a commercial classification of wool fibers by fineness, measured according to the number of fibers per inch. **12** the one of the four humors thought in ancient and medieval physiology to cause cheerfulness.
—*v.t.* **1** to give (hounds or other animals used in hunting) a preliminary taste, smell, or sight of blood. **2** *Figurative.* to give (anyone, especially military troops) their first experience.
blood is thicker than water, relatives are closer than friends: *His needy cousins asked him for help, reminding him that blood is thicker than water.*
curdle one's (or **the**) **blood**, to frighten very much; horrify; terrify: *The piercing scream curdled his blood.*
draw blood, to inflict damage or pain: *The fighting in Ireland has always drawn much blood among families.*
get (**extract**, etc.) **blood from a stone** (or **from stones**), to achieve the impossible: *The court has no machinery that I know of for extracting blood from stones* (Observer).
have (a person's) **blood on one's head**, to carry the responsibility or guilt of a person's death, hardship, bad luck, or the like: *And whosoever shall be with thee in the house, his blood shall be on our head, if any hand be upon him* (Joshua 2:19).
in cold blood, **a** without feeling; cruelly: *... the taking away of human life in cold blood* (Edward A. Freeman). **b** on purpose; deliberately: *The bandits shot down three men in cold blood.*
make one's blood boil (**run cold**, **stir**, etc.), to excite one with anger, fright, passion, etc: *The sight of the driver beating his horse made the kind old man's blood boil.*
shed blood, to destroy life; kill: *The thoughts of shedding human blood for my deliverance were very terrible to me* (Daniel Defoe).
[Old English *blōd*] —**blood′like′**, *adj.*

blood-and-guts (blud′ən guts′), *adj. Informal.* **1** savage; ruthless: *blood-and-guts antagonism.* **2** lurid: *a blood-and-guts thriller.*

blood and iron, military force as distinguished from diplomacy, especially as the policy advocated by Bismarck. [translation of German *Blut und Eisen*]

blood and thunder, sensational or violent melodrama.

blood-and-thun|der (blud′ən thun′dər), *adj.* violently melodramatic.

blood bank, **1** a place for storage of blood to be used in transfusions. **2** the blood kept in storage.

blood bath, a wholesale killing of people; massacre.

blood blister, a blister with blood in it.

blood-brain barrier (blud′brān′), *Medicine.* a barrier in the central nervous system that prevents chemicals injected into blood vessels from entering the brain.

blood brother, **1** a brother by birth; real brother. **2** a person who goes through a ceremony of mixing some of his blood with another person's.

blood brotherhood, the relationship between blood brothers.

blood cancer, = leukemia.

blood cell, a corpuscle or a platelet contained in blood.

blood chit, a piece of cloth carried by members of the U.S. Air Force on which is inscribed in several languages a promise to reward in gold anyone who helps an airman to escape capture.

blood count, a count of the number of red and white blood cells and the amount of hemoglobin in a sample of a person's blood to see if it is normal.

blood|cur|dling (blud′kėr′dling), *adj.* terrifying; horrible: *a bloodcurdling shriek. He told a bloodcurdling story about a haunted house.* —**blood′cur′dling|ly**, *adv.*

blood|ed (blud′id), *adj.* **1** coming from good stock; of good breed or pedigree: *Many race horses are blooded stallions.* **SYN**: thoroughbred. **2** having a certain kind of blood: *Snakes are considered cold-blooded; lions are warm-blooded.*

blood feud, a very bitter feud marked by bloodshed: *A blood feud could be handed down from generation to generation* (New Yorker).

blood|fin (blud′fin′), *n.* a South American fish having red fins, often kept in aquariums.

blood|flow|er (blud′flou′ər), *n.* any of a group of South African plants of the amaryllis family, with showy red flowers.

blood fluke, = schistosome.

blood group, any one of the groups into which human blood may be divided on the basis of the presence or absence of certain substances that cause red cells to clump together; blood type. Blood groups are important in blood transfusions.

blood grouping, blood typing.

blood|guilt (blud′gilt′), *n.* **1** guilt of bloodshed. **2** responsibility for the murder or death of a person.

blood|guilt|y (blud′gil′tē), *adj.* guilty of murder or bloodshed. —**blood′guilt′i|ness**, *n.*

blood heat, the normal temperature at which the blood keeps the human body; 98.6 degrees Fahrenheit.

blood|hound (blud′hound′), *n., v.* —*n.* **1** a large, powerful dog with a keen sense of smell. Bloodhounds are used to track fugitives or find people who are lost. Though commonly described as fierce and vicious, bloodhounds actually are relatively gentle and placid. **2** *Slang, Figurative.* a detective: *... a nationwide manhunt led by a ruminative bloodhound from the FBI* (Newsweek).
—*v.t., v.i.* to track, hunt, or pursue as a bloodhound does: *The FBI did not slip up on its ... trail of bloodhounding* (New Scientist).

blood|less (blud′lis), *adj.* **1** without bloodshed: *By surrounding the city the enemy achieved a bloodless victory.* **2** without enough blood; pale: *a bloodless face.* **SYN**: anemic. **3** *Figurative.* without energy; spiritless: *... thou bloodless remnant of that royal blood* (Shakespeare). **SYN**: lifeless. **4** *Figurative.* cold-hearted; cruel: *bloodless charity.* **SYN**: unfeeling. —**blood′less|ly**, *adv.* —**blood′less|ness**, *n.*

blood|let|ter (blud′let′ər), *n.* a person or thing that causes blood to flow or be shed.

blood|let|ting (blud′let′ing), *n.* **1** the act of opening a vein to take out blood; phlebotomy; venesection: *Bloodletting was a universal medical practice until the 1800's.* **2** *Figurative.* bloodshed or blood bath; slaughter.

blood|line (blud′līn′), *n.* **1** the series of ancestors in a pedigree. **2** pedigree, family, or strain (applied especially to animals).

blood lust, lust for murder; bloodthirst.

blood meal, dried animal blood, used as feed for animals and as fertilizer.

blood|mo|bile (blud′mə bēl), *n.* a bus or other motor vehicle, with medical equipment and staff, that permits people to donate blood without going to a hospital or clinic.

blood money, **1** in medieval times: **a** money paid to have somebody killed. **b** money paid to the relatives of a person who has been killed. **c** money paid to obtain security from vengeance. **2** (in modern times) money gained at the cost of another person's life, freedom, or welfare, especially as a reward for giving up a criminal to justice.

blood orange, any one of various varieties of orange having deep-red pulp.

blood plasma, the pale-yellow liquid part of blood, often placed in blood banks for use in transfusions.

blood platelet, any one of the colorless, round or oval disks found in the blood of vertebrates, smaller than red corpuscles, and important in coagulation; thrombocyte; platelet.

blood poisoning, a diseased condition of blood caused usually by bacteria in the circulating blood; toxemia or septicemia.

blood pressure, the pressure of the blood against the inner walls of the blood vessels. Blood pressure varies with the strength of the heartbeat, exertion, excitement, health, and age.

blood pudding, a kind of sausage made with blood and suet (and sometimes also flour or meal); black pudding; blood sausage.

blood purge, the murdering within a short period of a party's or state's undesirable elements, especially in a fascist or totalitarian country.

blood-red (blud′red′), *adj.* red like blood.

blood relation or **relative**, a person related to another by birth.

blood revenge, **1** the custom, especially in Biblical times, of avenging murder by causing the victim's nearest relative to seek out and kill the murderer. **2** = vendetta.

blood|root (blud′rüt′, -ru̇t′), *n.* **1** a common wild plant of North America that has a red root, red sap, and a white flower that blooms in early spring. It belongs to the poppy family. The sap extracted from its root was formerly used in medicine as a stimulant, expectorant, and emetic. The plant is also called *red puccoon, bloodwort, redroot, turmeric,* and *sanguinaria.* **2** *Rare.* the tormentil.

blood royal, royal family.

blood sausage, = blood pudding.

blood serum, the clear, pale-yellow, watery part of blood that separates from clotting blood.

blood|shed (blud′shed′), *n.* the shedding of blood; slaughter: *There are no battles in war without bloodshed.*

blood|shed|ding (blud′shed′ing), *n.* bloodshed; shedding of blood.

blood|shot (blud′shot′), *adj.* (of the eyes) red and sore from inflamed blood vessels: *A cinder in his eye made it bloodshot.* [earlier *bloodshotten* < *blood* + *shotten* suffused with, earlier past participle of *shoot*]

blood sport, any sport involving the killing of animals, such as bullfighting.

blood|stain (blud′stān′), *n., v.* —*n.* a stain left by blood.
—*v.t.* to stain with blood.

blood|stained (blud′stānd′), *adj.* **1** stained with blood: *His handkerchief was bloodstained from using it on a scratch.* **2** *Figurative.* guilty of murder or bloodshed: *a bloodstained conscience.*

blood|stanch (blud′stanch′), *n.* = fleabane.

blood|stock (blud′stok′), *n.* thoroughbred animals, especially horses.

blood|stone (blud′stōn′), *n.* **1** a semiprecious green variety of quartz with specks of red jasper scattered through it; heliotrope. **2** an oxide of iron, red or metallic; hematite.

blood|stream (blud′strēm′), *n.* the blood as it flows through the body.

blood|suck|er (blud′suk′ər), *n.* **1** a leech or other animal that sucks blood. **2** *Figurative.* **a** a person who gets all he can from others in any way he can; sponger. **b** an extortioner.

blood|suck|ing (blud′suk′ing), *adj., n.* —*adj.* **1** that sucks blood. **2** *Figurative.* extorting.
—*n.* **1** the sucking of blood. **2** *Figurative.* extortion.

blood sugar, glucose in the blood, the presence of which in excessive quantities is a sign of diabetes.

blood sweat, a red, oily substance that flows through the pores of the hippopotamus and covers its skin when it becomes excited.

blood test, an examination of a sample of a person's blood, especially to determine the type of blood or diagnose disease or a harmful physical condition.

blood|thirst (blud′thėrst′), *n.* eagerness for bloodshed.

blood|thirst|y (blud′thėrs′tē), *adj.* eager for bloodshed; cruel and murderous: *a bloodthirsty pirate. The Lord will abhor both the bloodthirsty and deceitful man* (Book of Common Prayer). —**blood′thirst′i|ly**, *adv.* —**blood′thirst′i|ness**, *n.*

blood transfusion, the injection of blood from one person or animal into another: *He had a blood transfusion after the operation.*

blood type, = blood group.

blood-type (blud′tīp′), *v.t.*, **-typed**, **-typ|ing.** to classify (the blood) according to type or (persons) according to blood group.

blood vengeance, = blood revenge.

blood vessel, any tube in the body through which the blood circulates. Arteries, veins, and capillaries are blood vessels.

blood|wood (blud′wu̇d′), *n.* any one of various trees with red wood or red sap, such as the logwood.

blood|worm (blud′wėrm′), *n.* **1** any of various soft, reddish worms used as bait. **2** the red larva of certain flies and midges. **3** a parasitic organism in the blood.

blood|wort (blud′wėrt′), *n.* **1** any plant of the bloodwort family. **2** any one of several other plants with red roots, stems, or leaves, such as the bloodroot, dock, and hawkweed. [Middle English *blodwurt* < *blod* blood + *wurt* wort[2]]

bloodwort family, a small group of monocotyledonous, perennial, herbaceous plants, most species of which have red roots, such as the North American redroot.

blood|y (blud′ē), *adj.,* **blood|i|er**, **blood|i|est**, *v.,*

blood|ied, blood|y|ing, *adv.* — *adj.* **1** covered with blood; bleeding: *He got a bloody nose in the fight.* **2** stained with blood: *His shirt was bloody down the front.* **SYN**: gory. **3** accompanied by much killing; with much bloodshed: *It was a bloody battle.* **SYN**: sanguinary. **4** *Figurative.* eager for bloodshed; bloodthirsty; cruel: *a foul and bloody deed. The Lord will abhor the bloody and deceitful man* (Psalms 5:6). **SYN**: murderous. **5** having the color of blood: *The bloody Sun, at noon, Right up above the mast did stand* (Samuel Taylor Coleridge). **6** *British Slang.* cursed; confounded (see note below): *He's a bloody fool.* **SYN**: damned.
— ***v.t.*** **1** to cause to bleed: *He bloodied his nose in the fall.* **2** to stain with blood: *His pants leg was torn and bloodied when he fell. The sword which was drawn* (*not bloodied, I hope*) *in this unlucky quarrel* (Robert Southey).
— ***adv.*** *British Slang.* very (see note below): *Do what he says? Not bloody likely!*
[Old English *blōdig*] — **blood′i|ly,** *adv.* — **blood′i|ness,** *n.*
▶ In England, **bloody** in the sense of *adj.,* def. 6, and *adv.* was long considered unpardonably vulgar. The ban against its use has now been much relaxed, though it is still avoided in many circles and in mixed company.

Bloody Mary, *U.S.* a mixed alcoholic drink consisting of tomato juice, vodka or gin, lemon or lime juice, and various seasonings.

blood|y-mind|ed (blud′ē mīn′did), *adj.* **1** *Especially British Slang.* perversely stubborn or contrary; bullheaded: *He's too bloody-minded to cooperate willingly.* **2** = bloodthirsty. — **blood′y-mind′ed|ness,** *n.*

bloody murder, = blue murder.

bloody shirt, *U.S.* something used to stir people to vengeance.

bloo|ey (blü′ē), *adj. U.S. Slang.* out of order; askew: *His compass must've gone blooey …* (New Yorker). [imitative]

bloom¹ (blüm), *v., n.* — *v.i.* **1** to have flowers; open into flowers; blossom: *Many plants bloom in the spring. When lilacs last in the dooryard bloom'd* (Walt Whitman). **2** *Figurative.* to be in the condition or time of greatest health, vigor, or beauty; flourish: *Life bloomed with happiness and hope* (Thomas Carlyle). **3** to become marred with a cloudy or milky appearance: *Glossy paint tends to bloom in humid weather.*
— ***v.t.*** **1** to cause to flourish or bring into bloom: (*Figurative.*) *Barr'd clouds bloom the soft-dying day* (Keats). **2** to mar with a cloudy or milky appearance: *The humidity bloomed the paint and dimmed its luster.*
— ***n.*** **1** a flower; blossom. **2** flowers collectively. **3** the condition or time of flowering: *violets in bloom.* **4** the condition or time of greatest health, vigor, or beauty: *She was in the bloom of youth.* **SYN**: freshness, prime. **5** a glow of health or beauty: *the bloom of health and happiness.* **SYN**: flush. **6** a coating like fine powder on some fruits and leaves. There is bloom on grapes and plums. **7a** any of various similar surface coatings: *the bloom on new coins.* **b** *Figurative:* [*Charm is*] *a sort of bloom on a woman* (James M. Barrie). **8** a cloudy or milky appearance on a film of varnish, paint, or the like. **9** *Zoology.* a dense mass of very small, aquatic organisms, such as plankton, easily visible to the eye.
[Middle English *blom* < Scandinavian (compare Old Icelandic *blōm*)] — **bloom′er,** *n.*

bloom² (blüm), *n.* **1** a thick bar of iron or steel with rounded corners, rolled or hammered from an ingot and left for further rolling when required for use. **2** an unmelted, spongy mass of wrought iron from the puddling furnace or forge. **3** an ingot of steel shaped into a block with a cross-sectional area greater than 36 square inches. **4** the first bar produced in the rolling of an aluminum ingot. [Old English *blōma* lump]

***bloom|er¹** (blü′mər), *n.* a style of female attire in the mid-1800's consisting of long, loose trousers gathered closely around the ankles, and worn with a short skirt. [American English < Amelia J. *Bloomer,* 1818-1894, an American social reformer, who advocated bloomers in a magazine she published]

***bloomer¹**
***bloomers**
definition 1

bloom|er² (blü′mər), *n. Slang, Especially British.* a blunder; mistake. [perhaps abbreviation of "a *bloom*(ing) *er*(ror)"]

***bloom|ers** (blü′mərz), *n.pl.* **1** loose trousers, gathered at the knee, formerly worn by women and girls for physical training, sports, and the like. **2** underwear made like these. [< *bloomer*¹]

bloom|er|y (blü′mər ē), *n., pl.* **-er|ies.** a furnace and forge for making blooms, especially one where the wrought iron is obtained directly from the ore by a crude, primitive process. [< *bloom*² + *-ery*]

bloom|ing (blü′ming), *adj.* **1** having flowers; blossoming: *blooming shrubs.* **SYN**: efflorescent. **2** *Figurative.* flourishing: *In the blooming bull market of the past half dozen years, stock oysters have brought many executives immense profits* (Wall Street Journal). **3** *British Slang.* (as an intensive only) confounded: *a blooming idiot, not a blooming chance. When 'Omer smote 'is bloomin' lyre* (Rudyard Kipling). — **bloom′ing|ly,** *adv.*

blooming mill, a rolling mill which reduces steel ingots into blooms, in preparation for further treatment.

Blooms|bur|y (blümz′bėr ē, -brē), *adj.* of or having to do with a literary and intellectual circle formed in the Bloomsbury section of London about 1905 and lasting to about 1930: *Real luster derived from England's … Bloomsbury group: Lytton Strachey, Virginia Woolf, John Maynard Keynes, E. M. Forster, Clive Bell* (Atlantic).

bloom|y (blü′mē), *adj.,* **bloom|i|er, bloom|i|est.** having the surface covered with bloom, as a plum.

bloop (blüp), *n., v. Slang.* — ***n.*** = blooper.
— ***v.t., v.i.*** *Baseball.* to make or hit (a blooper).

bloop|er (blü′pər), *n. Slang.* **1** a very foolish mistake; boner. **2** *Baseball.* a fly which falls beyond the normal positions of the infielders and short of those of the outfielders.

blos|som (blos′əm), *n., v.* — ***n.*** **1** a flower, especially of a plant that produces fruit: *apple blossoms.* **2** the condition or time of flowering: *The cherry trees are in blossom.* **3** *British Slang.* a woman (used ironically).
— ***v.i.*** **1** to have flowers; open into flowers: *All the orchards blossom in spring.* **SYN**: bloom, flower. **2** *Figurative.* to open out; develop: *She blossomed into a beautiful girl. Her musical talent blossomed early.*
[Old English *blōstma*] — **blos′som|less,** *adj.*

blos|som|y (blos′ə mē), *adj.* full of blossoms: *a blossomy valley.*

blot¹ (blot), *n., v.,* **blot|ted, blot|ting.** — ***n.*** **1** a spot of ink or stain of any kind: *A blot of ink stained his shirt.* **SYN**: smudge. **2** *Figurative.* a spot upon one's character or reputation; blemish; disgrace: *The failure was a blot on his good record.* **SYN**: fault.
— ***v.t.*** **1** to make blots on; stain; spot: *Dripping paint blotted his shirt in two places.* **SYN**: blotch, smear, soil. **2** to dry (ink or other liquid) with paper that soaks it up: *Mother blotted up the milk before it ran all over the table.* **3** *Figurative.* to blemish; disgrace. **SYN**: sully, dishonor.
— ***v.i.*** **1** to make a blot or blots: *This pen blots.* **2** to become blotted: *Soft paper tends to blot.*
blot on the escutcheon, a disgrace to honor or reputation: *His crime was a blot on the family escutcheon.*
blot out, a to cover up entirely; hide: *He blotted out the mistake with ink.* **b** *Figurative.* to wipe out; destroy; obliterate: *When the storm brought down all the electric lines, the lights were blotted out. … as the Persian monarchy had been blotted out by Alexander* (James Bryce).
[Middle English *blot;* origin uncertain] — **blot′less,** *adj.* — **blot′like′,** *adj.*

blot² (blot), *n.* **1** an exposed piece in backgammon. **2** any exposed or weak point. [perhaps < Dutch *bloot* exposed]

blotch (bloch), *n., v.* — ***n.*** **1** a large, irregular spot or stain: *large blotches of vivid color.* **2** a place where the skin is red or broken out: *The fever made her face break out in blotches.*
— ***v.t.*** to cover or mark with blotches or stains. [perhaps a blend of *blot* and *botch*]

blotch|y (bloch′ē), *adj.,* **blotch|i|er, blotch|i|est.** having blotches.

blot|ter (blot′ər), *n.* **1** a piece of blotting paper. **2** a book for recording happenings or transactions. A police station blotter is a record of arrests made by policemen.

blot|tesque (blot esk′), *adj.* executed with heavy, blotlike touches, as painting. [< *blot*¹ + (grot)*esque*]

blot|ting paper (blot′ing), a soft, absorbent paper used to dry writing by soaking up ink.

blot|to (blot′ō), *adj. Slang.* very drunk. [perhaps < *blot*¹]

blouse (blous, blouz), *n., v.,* **bloused, blous|ing.** — ***n.*** **1** a loose or fitted upper garment worn by women and children as a part of their outer clothing: *She wore a white silk blouse with a blue skirt.* **2** a loosely fitting garment for the upper part of the body. Sailors wear blouses as part of their uniform. **3** a short, fitted coat, worn as part of a military uniform. **4** a kind of smock reaching to the knees, formerly much worn by European peasants and workmen to protect their clothes.
— ***v.i.*** to project or hang loosely, as a blouse above the belt.
[< French *blouse;* origin uncertain] — **blouse′-like′,** *adj.*

bloused (bloust, blouzd), *adj.* **1** made or fitted like a blouse. **2** wearing a blouse.

***blou|son** (blü′zon; *French* blü zôN′), *n.* **1** a blouse gathered at or below the waist by means of a drawstring or elastic, producing a billowy fullness above. **2** a dress, in one or two pieces, having this effect. [< French *blouson* < *blouse* blouse]

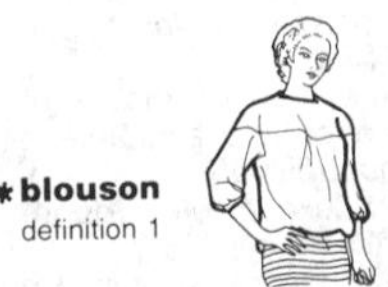

***blouson**
definition 1

blous|y (blou′zē), *adj.,* **blous|i|er, blous|i|est.** = blowzy.

blow¹ (blō), *n.* **1** a hard hit; knock; stroke: *The boxer struck his opponent a blow that knocked him down.* **2** a sudden happening that causes misfortune or loss; severe shock: *His mother's death was a great blow to him.* **SYN**: calamity, disaster, misfortune. **3** a sudden attack or assault: *The army struck a swift blow at the enemy.*
at one blow, by one act or effort: *What it is at one blow to be deserted by a lovely and fascinating creature* (Dickens).
come to blows, to start fighting: *After a few harsh words the two boys came to blows.*
strike a blow, a to hit: *to strike a blow in self-defense.* **b** to cause a setback; inflict harm: *Syria strikes a blow at itself* (Manchester Guardian Weekly). **c** to make an effort to accomplish; advance the cause of: *to strike a blow for freedom.*
[Middle English *blaw*]
— ***Syn.*** **1 Blow, stroke** mean a sudden hard hit. **Blow** emphasizes its force, violence, and heaviness: *She got a blow on the head.* **Stroke** emphasizes the sharpness and precision of a hit or its unexpectedness: *His scar was made by a sword stroke across the face.*

blow² (blō), *v.,* **blew, blown, blow|ing,** *n.* — ***v.i.*** **1** to send forth a strong current of air: *Blow on the fire or it will go out.* **2** to move rapidly or with power; move in a current: *The wind blows in gusts.* **3** to be driven or carried by a current of air; move before the wind: *Dust blew across the road.* **4** to make a sound by a current of air or steam: *The whistle blows at noon. Blow, ye bright angels, on your golden trumpets* (Longfellow). **SYN**: sound. **5** to be out of breath. **SYN**: pant, puff. **6** *Informal, Figurative.* to boast; brag. **7** to melt: *A short circuit caused the fuse to blow.* **8** to spout a column of hot, moist air from the blowholes, before taking in fresh air: *"There she blows!" was the sailor's cry when he spotted the whale.* **9** *Slang.* to go away. **10** *Slang, Figurative.* **a** to explode: *Something was bound to blow in that tense situation.* **b** to get very angry; blow up.
— ***v.t.*** **1** to drive or carry by a current of air: *The wind blew the curtains. She blew a kiss to her mother.* **2** to force a current of air into, through, or against: *to blow the fire into flame. He blew a whiff from his pipe.* **3** to empty or clear by forcing air through: *The mechanic blew the gas line in our car.* **4a** to form or shape by air: *to blow glass.* **b** to swell with air: *to blow bubbles.* **SYN**: inflate. **c** *Figurative.* to puff up: *blown with pride.* **5** to cause to make a sound by a current of air or steam: *Blow the whistle.* **6** to break by an explosion; blow up, open, etc.: *The dynamite blew the wall to bits.* **SYN**: shatter. **7** to melt: *A short circuit will blow a fuse.* **8** to allow (steam or the like) to escape forcibly with a blowing noise. **9** to cause to pant; put out of breath: *He blew his horse by riding him hard.* **10** (of insects) to lay eggs in: *Some flies blow fruit.* **11** *Figurative.* to publish or spread (news, rumors, or the like): *A rumour wildly blown about* (Tennyson). **12** *U.S. Slang, Figurative.* **a** to spend (money) recklessly.

Pronunciation Key: hat, āge, cãre, fär; let, ēqual, tėrm; it, īce; hot, ōpen, ôrder; **oil, out;** cup, pu̇t, rüle; **ch**ild; lo**ng; th**in; **ᴛʜ**en; **zh,** measure; **ə** represents **a** in about, **e** in taken, **i** in pencil, **o** in lemon, **u** in circus.

SYN: squander. **b** to spend money on (oneself or another): *I'll blow you to dinner tonight.* **SYN:** treat. **13** *Slang.* **a** to make a mess of; botch; muff: *The golfer blew a two-foot putt. The actress blew her lines.* **b** to waste or throw away: *The baseball club blew a three-run lead.*
14 *Slang.* to play (a musical instrument): *"Oscar blows fine piano," said Kenton* (New Yorker).
15 *Slang.* to smoke (marijuana).
—*n.* **1** the act or fact of forcing air upon, into, through, or against something; blast; blowing. **2** a gale of wind: *Last night's big blow brought down several trees.* **3** a blowing of a wind instrument; blast. **4** *Figurative.* a boast; boasting. **5a** a single operation, or blast, converting a quantity of iron into steel by the Bessemer process. **b** the time during which a blast is continued. **c** the quantity of steel involved or made in a single operation.
blow away, *U.S. Slang.* to kill or destroy: *Like a pack of wolves ... they are looking for somebody to blow away* (Time).
blow hot and cold, to alternate from a favorable opinion to an unfavorable one; be changeable: *He blows hot and cold about his job.*
blow in, *Slang.* to appear unexpectedly; drop in: *He blew in on his way to Chicago.*
blow into, *Slang.* to appear unexpectedly in: *He blew into town.*
blow off, a to get rid of (steam, energy, or the like) noisily or violently: *... blowing off their superfluous energy in singing and shouting* (Christian Commonwealth). **b** (of steam or the like) to escape noisily or violently: *Carburetted gas ... is liable to blow off and endanger the lives of hundreds of persons* (W. S. Jevons). **c** *Figurative.* to use up energy, especially excess energy: *He blew off a lot of steam about excess taxes.*
blow on, *British Informal.* to penalize: *the umpires blew on one player, and from the resulting 40-yard penalty Neville scored the winning goal* (London Times).
blow one's mind. See under **mind**[1].
blow out, a to put out or be put out by a current of air: *He blew out the candle. The candle blew out.* **b** to suffer a blowout: *The worn tire blew out.* **c** to have or cause a blowout in: *The impact blew out both front tires.*
blow over, a to pass by or over; cease; subside: *The storm has blown over.* **b** *Figurative.* to be forgotten: *In time the scandal blew over.*
blow up, a to explode: *The ammunition ship blew up and sank when it hit the rocks.* **b** to fill with air; inflate: *to blow up a bicycle tire.* **c** *Informal.* to lose one's temper; become very angry: *The harassed commuter suddenly blew up and began to scream at the conductor.* **d** to become stronger; arise: *A storm blew up suddenly.* **e** to enlarge (a photograph): *By blowing up the picture, he could point out many details.*
[Old English *blāwan*]
►The past tense and past participle form **blowed,** found occasionally in standard use in Early Modern English, is today confined to slang or nonstandard dialects. It survives in northeastern New England and in the South, and in Great Britain in exclamations such as *Well, I'm blowed* or *I'll be blowed.*

blow[3] (blō), *n., v.,* **blew, blown, blow|ing.** **—*n.*** **1** a state of blossoming; bloom. **2** a display of blossoms. **—*v.i.*** to blossom; bloom.
[Old English *blōwan*]

blow|back (blō′bak′), *n.* **1** a backward draft or air current. **2** escape of gases formed during the firing of a weapon to the rear and under pressure. **3** the recoil of a bolt in a firearm.

blow|ball (blō′bôl′), *n.* the downy head of the dandelion or salsify.

blow|by (blō′bī′), *n.* leakage of fuel, vapor, or pressure, between the piston and cylinder of an automobile.

blow-by-blow (blō′bī blō′), *adj.* described minutely; including every detail: *The newspapers gave a blow-by-blow account of the trial.*

blow|down (blō′doun′), *n.* rupture of a cooling pipe in a nuclear reactor, especially in a power plant: *In nuclear parlance, "blowdown" is synonymous with catastrophe, as it signifies loss of coolant with the nuclear reactor continuing to produce heat with nothing to carry it away* (New Scientist).

blow-dry (blō′drī′), *v.,* **-dried, -dry|ing,** *n., pl.* **-dries.** **—*v.t.*** **1** to dry or style (hair) with a blow dryer. **2** to blow-dry the hair of. **—*n.*** the act or process of blow-drying the hair.

blow dryer, a portable electric blower for drying and styling the hair: *Using a blow dryer has become a unisex morning ritual. The results are natural and uncontrived—though not unstyled* (Consumer Reports).

blow|er (blō′ər), *n.* **1** a person or thing that blows: *a glass blower.* **2** a fan or other machine for forcing air into a building, furnace, mine, or other enclosed area. **3** *British Slang.* telephone.

blow|fish (blō′fish′), *n., pl.* **-fish|es** or (*collectively*) **-fish.** **1** a puffer or other fish that can inflate its body. **2** *U.S. Dialect.* = walleyed pike.

blow|fly (blō′flī′), *n., pl.* **-flies.** any one of various two-winged flies that deposit their eggs on meat or in wounds or fruit.

***blow|gun** (blō′gun′), *n.* **1** a tube through which a person blows arrows, darts, or other missiles; blowpipe. **2** = peashooter. Also, **blowtube.**

***blowgun**
definition 1

blow|hard (blō′härd′), *n., adj. Slang.* **—*n.*** a noisy boaster; braggart.
—*adj.* noisily bragging: *...* a blowhard rookie (Time).

blow|hole (blō′hōl′), *n.* **1** a hole for breathing, in the top of the head of whales, porpoises, and dolphins. **2** a hole in the ice to which whales, seals, and walruses come to breathe. **3** a hole through which air or gas escapes or can escape. **4** a defect in a metal casting due to a bubble of air or gas. **5** a defect; flaw.

blow|ing (blō′ing), *n.* **1** the act of one that blows. **2** a disturbance occurring when trapped gas or steam escapes from molten metal. **3** a defect in china. **4** hard breathing.

blow|lamp (blō′lamp′), *n. British.* blowtorch.

blow|mo|bile (blō′mə bēl), *n. U.S.* a propeller-driven vehicle mounted on skis. [< *blow*[2] + (auto)*mobile*]

blow molding, a process for forming hollow articles of plastic or similar materials in which the plastic is placed inside a mold and forced outward against the mold by compressed air.

blown[1] (blōn), *adj., v.* **—*adj.*** **1** out of breath; exhausted: *a blown horse.* **2** tainted by flies; tainted; stale; flyblown. **3** shaped by blowing: *blown glass.* **4** (of cattle, sheep, and other ruminants) having the stomach distended by gorging green food; bloated.
—*v.* the past participle of **blow**[2]: *The wind has blown itself out.*

blown[2] (blōn), *v., adj.* **—*v.*** the past participle of **blow**[3]. **—*adj.*** in bloom; fully opened.

blown-up (blōn′up′), *adj.* **1** enlarged: *The reporter had blown-up copies of the photographs.* **2** inflated: *a blown-up expense account.* **3** destroyed by a blast: *blown-up bridges.*

blow|off (blō′ôf′, -of′), *n.* **1** a blowing off. **2** an apparatus that blows off steam. **3** *Informal, Figurative.* a sudden outburst of anger, pent-up emotion, or the like. **4** *Slang, Figurative.* a boaster.

blow|out (blō′out′), *n.* **1** the bursting of an automobile tire, and of the inner tube, if any. **2** a sudden or violent escape of air, steam, or other gas or liquid under pressure. **3** the melting of an electric fuse by a sudden overload in a circuit or line, causing a power failure. **4** a hollow caused by wind erosion. **5** *Slang.* a big party or meal.

blow|pipe (blō′pīp′), *n.* **1** a tube for blowing air or gas into a flame to increase the heat. **2** a blowgun. **3** a long, metal tube used in glass blowing to blow molten glass into the desired shape, form, or size; blowtube. **4** *Medicine.* an instrument for blowing air or gas or cleaning a cavity. **5** a wooden pipe through which a player blows air into the leather bag of a bagpipe.

blow-proof (blō′prüf′), *adj.* that will not blow out; resistant to blowouts: *blow-proof tires.*

blow snake, = hognose snake.

blows|y (blou′zē), *adj.,* **blows|i|er, blows|i|est.** = blowzy. **—blows′i|ly,** *adv.* **—blows′i|ness,** *n.*

***blow|torch** (blō′tôrch′), *n.* **1** a small, portable torch that shoots out a very hot flame. A blowtorch is used to melt lead or solder, thaw frozen pipes, and burn off paint. **2** *U.S. Slang.* **a** an airplane having a jet engine. **b** a jet engine.

***blowtorch**
definition 1

blow|tube (blō′tüb′, -tyüb′), *n.* **1** = blowpipe (def. 3). **2** = blowgun.

blow|up (blō′up′), *n.* **1** an explosion. **2** *Informal, Figurative.* **a** an outburst of anger. **b** a quarrel. **3a** an enlargement of a photograph. **b** an expanded version: *The film is ... a blowup of a television show* (New Yorker). **4** bankruptcy.

blow|y (blō′ē), *adj.,* **blow|i|er, blow|i|est.** windy: *a blowy day.* **—blow′i|ness,** *n.*

blowze (blouz), *n.* **1** *British Dialect.* a fat, red-faced, and coarse-looking or untidy woman. **2** *British Dialect.* a blowzy condition. [origin unknown]

blowzed (blouzd), *adj.* = blowzy.

blowz|y (blou′zē), *adj.,* **blowz|i|er, blowz|i|est.** **1** lacking neatness; untidy; disheveled: *blowzy hair.* **SYN:** unkempt, frowzy, slatternly, slovenly. **2** red-faced and coarse-looking. Also, **blowsy, blousy.** [< *blowze* + *-y*[1]] **—blowz′i|ly,** *adv.* **—blowz′i|ness,** *n.*

bls., **1** bales. **2** barrels.

B.L.S., Bachelor of Library Science.

blub (blub), *v.i., v.t.,* **blubbed, blub|bing.** = blubber.

blub|ber (blub′ər), *n., v., adj.* **—*n.*** **1** the fat of whales and some other sea animals. Blubber lies under the skin and over the muscles. The oil obtained from whale blubber was formerly burned in lamps. **2** excess fat on the body. **3** noisy weeping.
—*v.i.* to weep noisily; sob: *He blubbered like a great schoolboy who had been whipped* (Tobias Smollett). **—*v.t.*** **1** to utter with tears; sob (forth or out): *He blubbered out an apology.* **2** to disfigure or swell with crying: *How blubbered is that pretty face* (Matthew Prior).
—*adj.* swollen; protruding; thick: *blubber lips.*
[Middle English *bluber;* imitative] **—blub′ber|er,** *n.* **—blub′ber|ing|ly,** *adv.* **—blub′ber|like′,** *adj.*

blub|ber|head|ed (blub′ər hed′id), *adj. Slang.* thick-headed; stupid; dull.

blub|ber-lipped (blub′ər lipt′), *adj.* having a swollen or thick, protruding lip or lips.

blub|ber|y (blub′ər ē), *adj.* **1** like blubber: *blubbery lips.* **2** containing blubber; fat.

***blu|cher** (blü′chər, -kər), *n.* **1** a shoe whose tongue and front part are one piece of leather. **2** a strong, leather half boot or high shoe of any of various styles. [< Gebhard von *Blücher,* 1742-1819, a Prussian general]

***blucher**
definition 1

bludge (bluj), *v.,* **bludged, bludg|ing,** *n. Australian Slang.* **—*v.i.*** to avoid work or one's share of work. **—*n.*** an easy job. [back formation < *bludger*]

bludg|eon (bluj′ən), *n., v.* **—*n.*** a short, heavy club. **—*v.t.*** **1** to strike with a bludgeon. **2** to bully or threaten: *There seems to be a prevailing notion that the buying public can be blasted, blathered, or bludgeoned into buying anything any time the manufacturers so desire* (Newsweek).
[origin unknown] **—bludg′eon|er,** *n.*

bludg|eon|eer (bluj′ə nir′), *n.* a person who uses, or is armed with, a bludgeon; bludgeoner.

bludg|er (bluj′ər), *n. Australian Slang.* an idle or good-for-nothing person. [short for *bludgeoner*]

blue (blü), *n., adj.,* **blu|er, blu|est,** *v.,* **blued, blu|ing** or **blue|ing.** **—*n.*** **1** the color of the clear sky in daylight. Blue is one of the primary colors. It lies in the color spectrum between green and violet. **2** a lighter or darker shade of this color: *the dark blue of the Mediterranean Sea.* **3** something having this color: **a** blue coloring matter, dye, or pigment: *The paint needs more blue in it.* **b** a blue object or material. **c** = bluing. **4** a member of a company, team, crew, army, etc., having blue as its distinctive color. **5** a bluestocking: *the company of village literati and village blues* (Washington Irving). **6** *Informal.* a blue ribbon: *The sheep, best entry in its class at the fair, won a blue.* **7** = bluefish. **8** any one of various small, bright blue butterflies that can fly with great speed. **9** Also, **Blue.** *British.* a person who has represented Oxford or Cambridge at sport: *a rowing Blue.*
—*adj.* **1** having the color of the clear sky in daylight or any tone of this color. **2** having a dull-bluish color; livid: *His hands were blue from cold.* **3** *Figurative.* sad; discouraged; gloomy: *I felt blue when I failed.* **SYN:** depressed, despondent, dejected, low-spirited, dismayed. **4** *Figurative.* cheerless; dismal; dispiriting: *The future looks rather blue.* **5** strict in morals or religion; puritanical. **6** somewhat improper; indecent: *a blue joke, a blue movie.* **7** of or in the style of the blues: *Reed pipes wailed ... Louis Armstrong blue notes* (Time). **8** *Informal, Figurative.* great or extreme: *a blue funk.*

—*v.t.* **1** to make blue. **2** to use bluing on. **3** *British Slang.* to squander: *His father blued the family fortunes* (Punch).
into the blue, into the remote distance; out of sight and knowledge: *to disappear into the blue.*
out of the blue, completely unexpectedly: *Suddenly, out of the blue, two Deputies . . . announced that they would switch their votes* (Time).
the blue, a the sky: *Lightning struck from the blue.* **b** the sea: *Many ships sail the blue.*
the blue and the gray, (in the U.S. Civil War) soldiers of the Union and Confederate armies respectively: *Under the sod and the dew, . . . Love and tears for the Blue, Tears and love for the Gray* (Francis M. Finch).
(the) blues. See under **blues.**
[< Old French *bleu* < Frankish (compare Old High German *blao*)] —**blue′ly,** *adv.* —**blue′ness,** *n.*

Blue Andalusian, any chicken of a Mediterranean breed of domestic fowl, resembling the Leghorn.

blue asbestos, = crocidolite.

blue baby, an infant born with a bluish skin, or cyanosis, caused by a defective heart: *The lack of oxygen in the blood results in the blue color and other difficulties of the "blue babies"* (Science News Letter).

blue|back salmon (blü′bak′), = sockeye salmon.

blue bear, a bear with dense, whitish-blue fur and a brown snout, found especially in Alaska; glacier bear.

Blue|beard (blü′bird′), *n.* **1** a legendary man who murdered six of his wives and hid their bodies in a room which he forbade anyone to enter. **2** any man who marries women and murders them.

blue beech, = American hornbeam.

blue|bell (blü′bel′), *n.* any one of various plants with blue flowers shaped like bells, such as the harebell or bluebell of Scotland. All bluebells are native to the Old World, but many now grow also in America. The bluebell belongs to the bellflower family.

blue|bells (blü′belz′), *n.* the lungwort of North America.

blue|ber|ry (blü′ber′ē, -bər-), *n., pl.* **-ries,** *v.,* **-ried, -ry|ing.** —*n.* **1** a small, sweet, blue berry which tastes much like the huckleberry but has smaller seeds. **2** the shrub that it grows on. Blueberries belong to the heath family.
—*v.i.* to search for or gather blueberries.

blue|bill (blü′bil′), *n.* a scaup duck.

blue|bird (blü′bėrd′), *n.* a small songbird of North America. The male usually has a bright-blue back and wings and a chestnut-brown breast. Bluebirds are related to the robin and the thrush.

Blue Bird, *n.* a member of the youngest group of Camp Fire Girls, for girls six, seven, and eight years old.

blue-black (blü′blak′), *n., adj.* very dark blue.

blue blood, 1 aristocratic descent. **2** a person of aristocratic descent: aristocrat.
▶**Blue blood** is a translation of the Spanish *sangre azul,* applied to some of the oldest and proudest families of Castile, who claimed never to have intermarried with Moorish, Jewish, or other non-Castilian peoples. The expression probably originated in the blueness of the veins of such people as compared with those of a darker skin.

blue-blood|ed (blü′blud′id), *adj.* = aristocratic.

blue|bon|net (blü′bon′it), *n.* **1** a plant of the pea family with blue flowers resembling sweet peas. The bluebonnet is the state flower of Texas. **2** = bachelor's-button. **3** a wide, flat cap made of blue woolen cloth, formerly in general use in Scotland. **4** Also, **Blue Bonnet.** a person wearing such a cap; Scot.

blue book, 1a a directory that lists socially prominent people. **b** any pamphlet, book, or other publication listing important corporations, persons, or other leaders, within an industry or area: *a . . . blue book of American industry* (Wall Street Journal). **2** *U.S.* a booklet with a blue paper cover, used for writing answers to examinations. **3** (formerly) an official list of United States government officials. **4** any one of various other official governmental publications, issued in blue covers.

Blue Book, 1 the official list of diplomatic representatives accredited to the United States government, issued monthly by the Department of State. **2** a British official publication.

blue|bot|tle (blü′bot′əl), *n.* **1a** a large blowfly that has a blue or green abdomen and a hairy body. **b** any one of various similar flies. **2** the bachelor's-button. **3** any one of certain other blue-flowered plants, such as various campanulas and squills.

blue box, an electronic device that generates telephone dialing tones, used fraudulently to make direct long-distance calls undetected by the telephone billing apparatus: *[He] was convicted by a federal jury here on felony charges of cheating a telephone company by using "blue boxes" to make illegal overseas calls* (Wall Street Journal).

blue|buck (blü′buk′), *n.* = blaubok.

blue|cap (blü′kap′), *n.* **1** = bluebonnet. **2** a Scot. **3** any one of various blue flowers. **4** a bluish titmouse.

blue catfish, a very large fork-tailed catfish of a blue color, found in the Mississippi River Valley.

blue cheese, a kind of cheese containing streaks of blue mold. Also, **bleu cheese.**

blue chip, 1 a flat, blue disk, used as a counter, usually of the highest value, in poker and certain other gambling games. **2a** a stock issued by a well-established corporation having substantial assets, usually high-priced and considered especially safe for investment. **b** *Figurative: Religion like many other things is blooming in America; it is a blue chip* (Harper's).

blue-chip (blü′chip′), *adj.* **1** of or having to do with a blue chip: *blue-chip investments, blue-chip stocks.* **2** *Figurative: a blue-chip corporation.*

blue|coat (blü′kōt′), *n.* **1** *U.S.* a policeman. **2** *U.S.* a soldier in the Union Army in the Civil War.

blue cohosh, a North American medicinal herb of the barberry family.

blue-col|lar (blü′kol′ər), *adj.* of or having to do with industrial or factory work or workers, or with unskilled or skilled manual labor: *There has been a steady increase in the number of white-collar workers relative to blue-collar factory workers* (Wall Street Journal).

blue comb, a disease of poultry similar to Bright's disease in man, characterized by cyanosis of the comb and wattles; monocytosis.

blue copper, = azurite.

blue crab, the most common edible crab of eastern North America.

Blue Cross, *U.S.* an organization by which individuals and families may obtain hospitalization insurance.

blue curls, 1 any one of various low-growing, annual plants of the mint family, having blue, pink, or occasionally white flowers, the stamens of which have long, curved filaments. **2** = selfheal.

blue devils, 1 low spirits; the blues. **2a** = delirium tremens. **b** horrible things imagined during delirium tremens.

blue dun, a fisherman's artificial fly having a blue body and gray hackle, wings, and tail.

blue earth, blue ground; kimberlite.

blue-eyed (blü′īd′), *adj.* **1** having eyes with a blue iris. **2** *British Informal.* treated preferentially; favorite: *In the troubled days it is exporters who are the blue-eyed boys* (Sunday Times).

blue-eyed grass, a grasslike plant of the iris family with delicate blue flowers.

blue|fin (blü′fin′), *n.* a large tuna.

blue|fish (blü′fish′), *n., pl.* **-fish|es** or (*collectively*) **-fish. 1** a saltwater food fish, bluish or greenish above and silvery below, related to the mackerel. Bluefish live in the Atlantic Ocean from Nova Scotia to the southern tip of South America. Some also live in the Indian Ocean, the Mediterranean Sea, and the Pacific Ocean around Australia. **2** any of several other bluish fishes: **a** a weakfish of the Pacific coast. **b** a small, edible fish of the coast of California. **c** the saury.

blue flag, a kind of iris that has blue flowers.

blue fox, 1 an arctic fox whose fur is bluish-gray or black throughout the year. **2** any one of certain other arctic foxes, whose fur is bluish in summer only. **3** the bluish fur of any of these foxes. **4** any imitation of this fur.

blue galaxy, a heavenly body outside of our own galaxy that is brighter than a quasar.

blue gas, = water gas.

blue|gill (blü′gil′), *n.* a large, edible sunfish of the Mississippi Valley.

blue goose, a North American wild goose having grayish-blue feathers.

blue grama, the most common species of grama, a pasture grass of the Great Plains and the western United States.

blue|grass (blü′gras′, -gräs′), *n.* **1** a grass with bluish-green stems, especially Kentucky bluegrass. Bluegrass is valuable for pasturage, hay, and lawns. **2** *U.S.* a style of country music that originated in rural areas of the South, characterized by simplicity and folksiness and the use of string instruments, especially the banjo.

Bluegrass State, a nickname for the state of Kentucky.

blue-green (blü′grēn′), *adj.* about halfway between blue and green.

blue-green algae, a class of algae with a bluish pigment. Some species have only one cell; in others, the cells form strands. Their cells lack a distinct nucleus. Blue-green algae are classified as bacteria.

blue grosbeak, a large, purplish-blue grosbeak of the southern and western United States and northern Mexico.

blue ground, the rock in which diamonds are found. It is decomposed brecciated rock, found in volcanic pipes in South Africa, Kentucky, and elsewhere; kimberlite; blue earth.

blue grouse, the dusky grouse of western America.

blue gum, a eucalyptus.

blue-head|ed vireo (blü′hed′id), a vireo of northern and eastern North America with a bluish-gray head and white rings around its eyes.

blue|hearts (blü′härts′), *n.pl. or sing.* an American perennial plant of the figwort family, having deep-purple flowers.

blue helmet, 1 the blue-colored helmet worn by members of the United Nations military force. **2** a member of this force.

blue|ing (blü′ing), *n.* = bluing.

blue|ish (blü′ish), *adj.* = bluish.

blue|jack (blü′jak′), *n.* **1** a small oak of the southern United States. **2** = blue vitriol.

blue|jack|et (blü′jak′it), *n.* a sailor in the United States or British navy.

blue jay, a noisy, chattering eastern North American bird with a crest, and blue feathers on its back. [American English < *blue* + *jay*]

blue jeans, or **blue|jeans** (blü′jēnz′), *n.pl. U.S.* jeans of blue cotton twill or denim; levis: *all our girls in blue jeans and pony tails* (Harper's).

blue john, *U.S. Dialect.* skim milk.

blue law, any very strict law regulating personal conduct. Laws prohibiting dancing or going to the theater on Sunday are blue laws.

blue line, either of two blue-colored lines in ice hockey, drawn between the center of the rink and each goal.

Blue Lodge, the basic organization of Freemasonry, in which members earn the three degrees required to become a Master Mason.

blue marlin, a large marlin of temperate Atlantic waters, much valued as a game fish.

blue mass, a drug made by rubbing metallic mercury with confection of roses and other ingredients.

blue mold, any one of various bluish or greenish molds, usually of the same genus as that which yields penicillin. Bluish molds occur on bread and greenish molds in cheese.

blue Monday, *Informal.* the day of returning to work after a weekend, supposedly a dismal day.

Blue Monday, the Monday preceding Lent.

blue moon, a time that seldom if ever comes.
once in a blue moon, once in an indefinitely long period; very rarely: *And when, by some mischance, once in a blue moon, the bell does ring, how startled we are* (London Times).

blue murder, *Slang.* something very difficult, trying, or disastrous; bloody murder.
like blue murder, at a terrific pace; at top speed: *They were off down the road like blue murder* (London Evening News).
yell (scream or **cry) blue murder,** to make an extravagant outcry; shout or lament loudly and emotionally: *Periodically to demand "stern measures" while at the same time yelling blue murder about civil liberties being infringed by the necessary sternness is . . . hypocritical* (London Times).

blue|nose (blü′nōz′), *n. Informal.* a very proper, strait-laced person.

Blue|nose (blü′nōz′), *n. Informal.* a native or inhabitant of Nova Scotia.

blue|nosed (blü′nōzd′), *adj.* **1** having a blue nose. **2** *Informal, Figurative.* very proper; puritanical: *Is any regular mechanism of censorship bound to be a more or less coarse, bluenosed narrowly prejudicial process?* (Newsweek).

blue note, a note between the usual notes in jazz, especially a third or seventh note played or sung a quarter or a half tone flat, characteristic of the blues.

blue ointment, an ointment composed of metallic mercury disseminated through lard and suet.

blue palmetto, a fan palm growing in low regions in the southeastern United States and in the West Indies.

blue pencil, 1 a pencil (traditionally blue) used to make corrections, deletions, or other changes in editing a manuscript: *Most people imagine that an editor's life consists in sitting in an armchair wielding a blue pencil* (Science News). **2** a correction, deletion, or other change made with or as if with a blue pencil: (*Figurative.*) *In desperation, the five-man Commission accepted the blue pencil of the censor* (Bulletin of Atomic Scientists).

Pronunciation Key: hat, āge, cãre, fär; let, ēqual, tėrm; it, īce; hot, ōpen, ôrder; oil, out; cup, pu̇t, rüle; child; long; thin; ᴛʜen; zh, measure; ə represents **a** in about, **e** in taken, **i** in pencil, **o** in lemon, **u** in circus.

blue-pen|cil (blü′pen′səl), *v.t.,* **-ciled, -cil|ing** or (*especially British*) **-cilled, -cil|ling. 1** to change, cut down, or cross out with a pencil: *He blue-pencilled false quantities in Latin verse* (G. Cannan). **2** to edit or censor.

blue peter, a blue flag with a white square in the center, raised as a signal to recall crews and to announce that the ship is about to sail. [< *blue repeater,* the original name]

blue pike, = walleyed pike.

blue pill, a pill made from blue mass.

blue plate, *U.S.* **1** a plate divided by ridges into compartments, to hold a whole main course, such as meat, vegetables, and other food. **2** the food so served, especially as an item on a menu.

blue|point (blü′point′), *n. U.S.* a small oyster from the south shore of Long Island, usually eaten raw. [American English < *Blue Point,* Long Island]

blue point, a variety of Siamese cat having a bluish-white body and blue points (ears, face, feet, and tail).

blue|print (blü′print′), *n., v.* —*n.* **1** a photographic print that shows white outlines on a blue background or blue outlines on a white background. The process of making blueprints is used especially to copy original drawings of building plans, mechanical drawings, and maps. **2a** a detailed plan for doing anything: (*Figurative.*) *a blueprint for future peace.* **b** any pattern or model; template: *The implanted liver cells had blueprints for antibodies. ... Antibody mechanisms of the mice were then able to make antibodies from the blueprints* (Science News Letter).
—*v.t.* **1** to make a blueprint of. **2** to make detailed plans for. —**blue′print′er,** *n.*

blue racer, a dark-blue, harmless variety of the blacksnake found in the central United States.

blue ribbon, 1 a ribbon of a blue color awarded to one that wins first prize in a contest. **2** the first prize; highest honor; greatest distinction: *The prize sheep won a blue ribbon for best entry in its class at the fair.* **3** a badge of a temperance society.

blue-rib|bon (blü′rib′ən), *adj.* **1** specially selected on the basis of education or other qualifications: *a blue-ribbon jury.* **2** comprised of the best or most prominent members of a group: *a blue-ribbon committee.*

blues (blüz), *n.pl.* **1** a slow, melancholy song with jazz rhythm. It is usually in a major key but with the third and seventh (the blue notes) flatted optionally. Blues originated among American Negroes. **2** any composition arranged or performed in this fashion.
the blues, *Informal.* low spirits; melancholy: *A rainy day always gives me the blues.*
[American English; short for *blue devils*] —**blues′-like′,** *adj.*

blue shark, a large shark of tropical and temperate oceans, one of the commonest of those considered dangerous to man.

blue sheep, = bharal.

Blue Shield, *U.S.* an organization by which individuals and families may obtain surgery insurance to supplement payment of hospitalization costs offered by Blue Cross.

blue-sky (blü′skī′), *adj. U.S. Informal.* **1a** worthless; unsound: *a blue-sky stock.* **b** preventing the sale of worthless stocks and bonds: *blue-sky legislation, blue-sky regulations.* **2** *Figurative.* not practical or concrete; theoretical; visionary: *blue-sky research projects.* [probably in allusion to the unclouded faith of the credulous buyer]

blues|man (blüz′man′, -mən), *n., pl.* **-men.** a musician who plays the blues: *He is a jazz equivalent of modern Negro bluesmen* (Sunday Times).

blue star, 1 a very bright, hot star whose light is largely of a blue color. **2** = blue galaxy.

blue|stem (blü′stem′), *n.* any one of various perennial grasses having long, blue leaves and pairs or clusters of spikes, cultivated especially in western North America for pasture.

blue|stock|ing (blü′stok′ing), *n.* a woman who displays great interest in intellectual or literary subjects: *She is a veritable bluestocking; her nose always stuck in a book and her interests devoid of womanly pursuits.* [< the nickname "*Blue Stocking* Society" applied to a group of men and women who used to meet in London about 1750 to discuss literature, often in informal dress, one prominent male member substituting blue worsted stockings for the conventional black silk]

blue|stock|ing|ism (blü′stok′ing iz əm), *n.* female learning or pedantry.

blue|stone (blü′stōn′), *n.* **1** a bluish sandstone. **2** = blue vitriol.

blue streak, *U.S. Informal.* **1** a person or thing thought of as resembling a streak of lightning in speed. **2** rapidly: *to talk a blue streak.*
like a blue streak, very fast, effectively, etc.: *He can read like a blue streak.*

blues|y (blü′zē), *adj.* characteristic or suggestive of the blues: *bluesy music.*

blu|et (blü′it), *n.* **1** a small wild flower of North America with tiny pale bluish flowers that blooms from April to midsummer; innocence; quaker-lady. The bluet is a member of the madder family. **2** = bachelor's-button. [< French *bluet, bleuet* (diminutive) < *bleu* blue]

blue thistle, = blueweed.

blue|throat (blü′thrōt′), *n.* a redstart of northern Europe and Asia, having a bright blue spot on the throat.

blue|tick (blü′tik′), *n. U.S.* a hound with a blue-flecked white coat, used for hunting boars.

blue tit, a Eurasian titmouse with a yellow breast and cobalt-blue crown, wings, and tail.

blue tongue, a virus disease of sheep, somewhat similar to foot-and-mouth disease. It originated in South Africa.

blue vitriol, a poisonous, blue, crystalline compound of copper and sulfuric acid, used in dyeing and printing, in electric batteries, and in sprays to destroy insects and fungi; copper sulfate; cupric sulfate; bluestone. *Formula:* $CuSO_4 \cdot 5H_2O$

blue wav|ey (wāv′ē), = blue goose.

blue|weed (blü′wēd′), *n.* a prickly weed of the borage family, having showy, blue flowers, originally European but now naturalized in the United States; viper's bugloss.

blue whale, a blue-gray whale with yellowish underparts, sometimes growing to over 95 feet in length; sulphur-bottom. It is the largest living animal. *The largest dinosaur, along with an elephant and a man, could stand on a blue whale with plenty of room to spare* (Raymond M. Gilmore).

blue-winged teal (blü′wingd′), a small, wild, North American duck having patches of dull-blue feathers on the wings.

blue|wood (blü′wu̇d′), *n.* a shrub or small tree of the buckthorn family, of the southwestern United States and northern Mexico, which often forms dense thickets or chaparral.

blue|y (blü′ē), *n.* (in Australia) a bushman's bundle, the outside wrapper of which is generally a blue blanket.

bluff[1] (bluf), *n., adj.* —*n.* a high, steep bank or cliff, especially one on the shore of a sea, lake, or river: *Standing at the edge of the bluff she could see the waves crashing below.* See picture under **valley.**
—*adj.* **1** rising with a straight, broad front: *The coast of England rose in a bluff headland out of the sea.* **SYN**: steep. **2** *Figurative.* good-naturedly blunt, frank, or plain-spoken; rough and hearty. **SYN**: unceremonious. See syn. under **blunt.**
[American English; perhaps < obsolete Dutch *blaf* broad] —**bluff′ly,** *adv.* —**bluff′ness,** *n.*

bluff[2] (bluf), *n., v.* —*n.* **1a** confidence of action or speech put on to deceive or mislead others. We say it is a bluff when a person lets others think that he knows more than he really does, that he has more money than he really has, or that the holds better playing cards than he really holds. **b** (in card games, especially poker) a bet, especially a large bet, made on a weak hand to fool players with better hands into believing that they will lose if they stay in the game. **2** a threat that cannot be carried out: *The bully's attempt to scare us is merely a bluff.* **3** the act of bluffing. **4** a person who bluffs; a bluffer.
—*v.t.* **1** to deceive by a show of confidence; fool: *By using logs for cannons the general bluffed the enemy so successfully that they retreated from their attack.* **2** to frighten with a threat that cannot be carried out: *He bluffed the robber with a toy gun.*
—*v.i.* to put on a show of strength or confidence in order to deceive others: *No one knew whether they were bluffing* (Newsweek).
call (one's) bluff, a to ask for proof or for action when pretense is suspected: *General Motors, Ford, and Chrysler still are convinced* [*the*] *strike threat is a bluff and they seemed determined to call it* (Wall Street Journal). **b** (in poker and other card games) to stay in the game in the face of a bluff by matching a bet and demanding a show of cards: *With such a poor hand, I couldn't afford to call his bluff.*
[American English; perhaps < Middle Dutch *bluffen* take a trick at cards] —**bluff′er,** *n.*

blu|ing (blü′ing), *n.* a blue liquid or powder put in water when laundering clothes. It keeps white clothes from turning yellow. Also, **blueing.**
[American English for earlier Engish *blue,* noun]

blu|ish (blü′ish), *adj.* somewhat blue. Also, **blueish.** —**blu′ish|ness,** *n.*

blun|der (blun′dər), *n., v.* —*n.* a stupid or careless mistake; bungle: *Misspelling the title of a book is a silly blunder to make in a book report.* [< verb]
—*v.i.* **1** to make a stupid or careless mistake: *Someone blundered in sending you to the wrong address.* **2** to move clumsily, as if blind; stumble; flounder: *The injured boy blundered through the woods. We had blundered into the carriage entrance* (Hawthorne).
—*v.t.* **1** to do clumsily or wrongly; mismanage grossly; bungle: *He completely blundered his assignment.* **2** to say or reveal clumsily, stupidly, or thoughtlessly; blurt out: *She blundered her thanks.*
[Middle English *blondren* mix up; origin uncertain] —**blun′der|er,** *n.*

∗**blun|der|buss** (blun′dər bus), *n.* **1** a short gun with a wide muzzle and large bore, formerly used to shoot balls or slugs a very short distance without exact aim. **2** a person who blunders, especially habitually. [alteration of Dutch *donderbus* < *donder* thunder + *bus* gun]

∗**blunderbuss**
definition 1

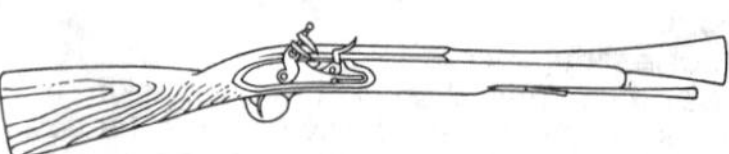

blun|der|head (blun′dər hed′), *n.* a blundering, stupid person.

blun|der|ing (blun′dər ing), *adj.* bungling; clumsy. —**blun′der|ing|ly,** *adv.*

blunge (blunj), *v.t.,* **blunged, blung|ing.** to mix (clay, powdered flint, etc.) with water. [perhaps a blend of *plunge* and *blend*]

blung|er (blun′jər), *n.* **1** an apparatus for mixing (blunging) clay or the like. **2** a person who uses such an apparatus.

blunt (blunt), *adj., v.* —*adj.* **1** without a sharp edge or point: *He sharpened the blunt knife.* **SYN**: See syn. under **dull. 2** *Figurative.* saying what one thinks very frankly, without trying to be tactful; outspoken; frank: *He thinks that blunt speech proves he is honest.* **3** *Figurative.* slow in perceiving or understanding: *blunt feelings, blunt faculties.* **SYN**: insensitive, obtuse.
—*v.t.* to make less sharp; make less keen: *He blunted his knife on the stone.* (*Figurative.*) *Grief has blunted his senses.*
—*v.i.* to become blunt. **SYN**: dull.
[Middle English *blunt* dull of sight; origin uncertain] —**blunt′ly,** *adv.* —**blunt′ness,** *n.*
—*Syn. adj.* **2 Blunt, bluff, curt** mean abrupt in speaking or manner. **Blunt** often emphasizes speaking plainly and frankly in open disregard of the feelings of others and simple good manners: *The chairman's blunt and tactless reply caused resentment.* **Bluff** suggests a frank and rough manner of speaking and acting combined with heartiness and genuineness: *Everyone likes the bluff policeman on the beat.* **Curt** means rudely abrupt and brief: *A curt nod was the only notice he gave that he knew she was there.*

blur (blėr), *v.,* **blurred, blur|ring,** *n.* —*v.t.* **1** to make less clear in form or outline: *Mist blurred the hills.* **2** to dim (the sight, perception, judgment, or other senses): *Tears blurred my eyes.* **3** to smear; smudge: *He blurred the picture by touching it before the paint was dry.*
—*v.i.* to become dim or indistinct: *Her eyes blurred with tears.*
—*n.* **1** a blurred condition; dimness: *The blur in his vision was caused by old age.* **2** a thing seen dimly or indistinctly: *His face was just a blur until I put on my glasses.* **3** a smear; smudge: *The letter had many blots and blurs.* **4** *Figurative.* a blot or stain on one's character or reputation.
[perhaps a variant of *blear*]

blurb (blėrb), *n., v. Informal.* —*n.* a brief advertisement or description full of high praise, especially on the jacket of a book, album, or other packaged item for sale: *The blurb says ... this is not a book for the scholar* (Punch).
—*v.t.* to call to the attention of the public with blurbs.
[American English; supposedly coined in 1907 by Gelett Burgess, 1866-1951, an American humorist]

blur|red|ly (blėr′id lē), *adv.* in a blurred manner; dimly.

blur|red|ness (blėr′id nis), *n.* blurriness.

blur|ry (blėr′ē), *adj.,* **-ri|er, -ri|est. 1** dim; indistinct: *The hills were a blurry outline in the dusk.* **2** full of smears and smudges: *a blurry copy.* —**blur′ri|ness,** *n.*

blurt (blėrt), *v., n.* —*v.t.* to say suddenly or without thinking: *In his anger he blurted out the secret.*
—*v.i.* to speak in blurts; speak thoughtlessly.
—*n.* a blurting out of something; an abrupt or impulsive utterance.
[imitative]

blush (blush), *v., n.* —*v.i.* **1** to become red in the face because of shame, confusion, or excitement: *The little girl was so shy that she blushed*

every time she was spoken to. **2** *Figurative.* to be ashamed: *I blushed at my friend's bad manners and loud talk.* **3** to be or become red or rosy.
—***v.t.*** **1** to make rosy; redden. **2** to express or show by blushing: *She blushed a shy apology.*
—***n.*** **1** a reddening of the face caused by shame, confusion, or excitement: *a youthful blush.* **2** a rosy color or glow: *The blush of dawn showed in the east.* SYN: flush.
at first blush, on first glance; at first thought: *At first blush, he thought the job would be easy.*
[Old English *blyscan* redden, shine] —**blush′·ing·ly**, *adv.*

blush·er (blush′ər), *n.* **1** a person or thing that blushes. **2** a cosmetic to give the cheeks a rosy color. It is similar to, or contains, rouge.

blush·ful (blush′fəl), *adj.* **1** modest; bashful. **2** rosy in color.

blush·less (blush′lis), *adj.* without a blush; unblushing; shameless.

blush wine, a table wine slightly paler and drier than a rosé.

blus·ter (blus′tər), *v., n.* —***v.i.*** **1** to storm noisily blow violently: *The wind blustered around the corner of the house.* **2** *Figurative.* to talk noisily and violently: *He was very excited and angry and blustered for a while.*
—***v.t.*** **1** to do or say noisily and violently. **2** to make, get, force, or drive by blustering; bully: (*Figurative.*) *to bluster one's way out of a difficulty.*
—***n.*** **1** a stormy blowing: *the bluster of the wind and rain.* SYN: turbulence. **2** a noisy and stormy commotion. SYN: turbulence. **3** *Figurative.* noisy and violent talk with empty threats or protests: *angry bluster. He impresses no one by his bluster.* SYN: boisterousness.
[Middle English *blusteren,* perhaps < Low German *blüstern* blow violently] —**blus′ter·er**, *n.* —**blus′ter·ing·ly**, *adv.*

blus·ter·ous (blus′tər əs), *adj.* = blustery.

blus·ter·y (blus′tər ē), *adj.* blustering.

Blut·wurst (blüt′vůrst′; *Anglicized* blüt′wėrst), *n. German.* blood sausage.

blvd., boulevard.

B lymphocyte, = B cell.

b.m., board measure.

B.M., **1** Bachelor of Medicine. **2** Bachelor of Music. **3** British Museum.

B.M.E., **1** Bachelor of Mechanical Engineering. **2** Bachelor of Mining Engineering. **3** Bachelor of Music Education.

B.Met., Bachelor of Metallurgy.

BMEWS (bē′myüz), *n.* Ballistic Missile Early Warning System.

B.M.O.C., *U.S. College Slang,* big man on campus.

BMR (no periods) or **B.M.R.**, basal metabolic rate.

B.Mus., Bachelor of Music (Latin, *Baccalaureus Musicae).*

B.Mus.Ed., Bachelor of Music Education.

BMX (no periods), bicycle motocross.

Bn., **1** baron. **2** battalion.

B.N., bank note.

BNA or **B.N.A. Act**, British North America Act, the act of Parliament that in 1867 created the Dominion of Canada and that serves as Canada's constitution.

B'nai B'rith (bə nā′ brith′, bə rēth′), a Jewish fraternal society founded in New York in 1843. [< Hebrew *bənē bərīth* sons of the covenant]

bnk., bank.

bo[1] (bō), *interj.* an exclamation used to startle; boo. [imitative]

bo[2] (bō), *n. U.S. Slang.* a hobo. [< *hobo*]

b.o., **1** branch office. **2** buyer's option.

B.O., **1** body odor. **2** box office.

B/O or **b/o** (no periods), *Bookkeeping.* brought over.

***bo·a** (bō′ə), *n., pl.* **bo·as. 1** any one of various snakes which are not poisonous, but kill their prey by squeezing it in their coils. Most boas are found in tropical regions and are very large, ranging between 10 and 30 feet in length. Anacondas, pythons, and boa constrictors are boas. **2** a long scarf made of fur or feathers, worn around a woman's neck.
[< Latin *boa* a type of serpent]

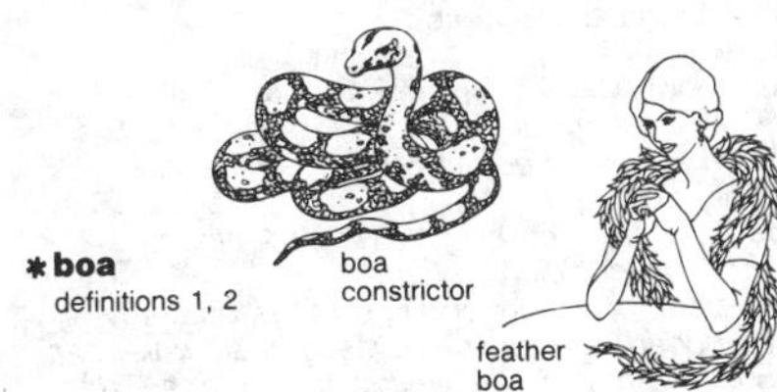

***boa**
definitions 1, 2

bo·a·bab (bō′ə bab), *n.* = baobab.

boa constrictor, a large boa of the tropical parts of America.

Bo·a·ner·ges (bō ə nėr′jēz), *n., pl.* **Bo·a·ner·ges** or **Bo·a·ner·ges·es. 1** a Biblical interpretation of the name given by Christ to the disciples James and John. Mark 3:17. **2** a loud, vociferous preacher or orator.
[< Greek *boanērgés*]

boar (bôr, bōr), *n.* **1** a male pig or hog. **2** a wild pig or hog.
[Old English *bār*]

board (bôrd, bōrd), *n., v.* —***n.*** **1** a broad, thin piece of wood for use in building: *We used boards 10 inches wide and 3 feet long for shelves in a new bookcase.* **2** a flat piece of wood or other material used for some special purpose: *an ironing board, a drawing board, a bulletin board.* **3** the tablet or frame on which pieces are moved in some games: *a chess board.* **4a** = pasteboard. **b** one of a pair of stiff pasteboard rectangles, covered with cloth, paper, or other material, used in making the covers of a hard-bound book. **5** a group of persons managing something; council: *a school board. He is one of six members on the board of directors.* **6** a table to serve food on; table. **7** food served on a table: *a simple board of meat and potatoes.* **8** meals provided for pay, as at a boarding house: *Mrs. Jones gives room and board in her rooming house.* **9a** the side of a ship. **b** the distance of course traversed by a ship when tacking; tack. **10** a border; edge.
—***v.t.*** **1** to cover or enclose with boards: *to board the floors of a house. The firemen boarded the windows of the burned-out building.* **2** to give regular meals, or room and meals, for pay: *We cannot lodge and board a dozen or fourteen Gentlewomen* (Shakespeare). **3** to place where board is supplied: *While his wife was sick, he boarded his son in town. He boards his horse with a farmer.* **4** to get on (a ship, train, bus, or airplane): *We board the bus at the corner every day.* **5** to come alongside of or against (a ship), usually in order to attack: *They grappled the pirate ship, boarded it, and fought hand to hand.* **6** to body-check (a player) in ice hockey.
—***v.i.*** **1** to get regular meals, or room and meals, for pay: *You will have to board elsewhere.* **2** to sail in a zigzag course against the wind; tack.
bet across the board, *Slang.* to bet that a selected horse or dog will win, place, or show in a race: *He felt the horse had equal chances of coming in first, second, or third, so he bet across the board.*
board on board, side by side: *The ships sailed board on board.*
by the board, over the ship's side; overboard: *During the storm, some of the equipment on deck fell by the board.*
go by the board, a to fall over the side of a ship: *Her rattling shrouds, all sheathed in ice, With the masts, went by the board* (Longfellow). **b** *Figurative.* to be given up, neglected, or ignored: *Formalities went by the board.*
on board, a on a ship, train, bus, or airplane: *When everybody was on board, the ship sailed. Half a dozen . . . guards and three private detectives were on board the train when it left Boston* (New York Times). **b** alongside of: *There were several ships on board each other.* **c** part of a group: *Many assistants were on board the President's staff.*
sweep the board (or **boards**), **sweep the boards clean**, to win all the awards, prizes, etc., in a contest or competition: *The Australian coaches and swimmers swept the board through a combination of scientific preparation and hard training* (London Times).
the boards, a the stage of a theater: *He was brought out by his father on the boards of Old Drury* (Dickens). **b** *Basketball.* the backboards: *He's strong under the boards.* **c** the wooden guard fence surrounding a hockey rink: *As he skated to reach the puck, he was checked and fell against the boards.*
tread the boards, to be an actor or actress; play a part in a play: . . . *one of the most honest actors that ever trod the boards* (Fortnightly Review).
[Old English *bord* plank and *bord* side (of a ship)]

board·er (bôr′dər, bōr′-), *n.* **1** a person who pays for meals, or for room and meals, at another's house. **2** one of the men assigned to go on board an enemy ship: *The boarders fought their way to the bridge.* **3** a pupil residing in a boarding school.

boarder baby, *U.S.* an infant or young child who is kept indefinitely in a hospital because the parents are not able or legally permitted to assume custody: *A good example of a boarder baby would be a child born addicted to drugs as a result of [the] mother's addiction* (New York Times).

board foot, *pl.* **board feet**. a unit of measure equal to one foot square and one inch thick; 144 cubic inches or .00236 cubic meter. It is used for measuring logs and lumber. *Abbr:* bd. ft.

board game, any game, such as checkers or chess, played on a board. Monopoly is a board game with real-estate property plotted on a board.

board·ing (bôr′ding, bōr′-), *n.* **1** boards. **2** a structure made of boards. **3** the act of entering a ship, especially by force.

boarding house, or **board·ing·house** (bôr′ding hous′, bōr′-), *n.* a house where meals, or rooms and meals, are provided for pay.

boarding party, a group of seamen who seize or try to seize a ship by boarding it at sea.

boarding school, a school with buildings where the pupils live during the school term.

board lot, the unit of trading on an exchange: *On the N.Y. Stock Exchange 100 shares is a board lot of an active stock.*

board measure, the system for measuring logs and lumber. The unit is the board foot. *Abbr:* b.m.

board of education, *U.S.* a board charged with the supervision of public schools in a state, county, district, city, or town; school board.

board of elections, *U.S.* a board consisting of representatives of the two major parties, appointed by local authorities to supervise elections.

board of estimate, *U.S.* a board charged with estimating and managing a city's budget, usually made up of the mayor, council president, and controller of the city.

board of health, *U.S.* the department of a state or local government in charge of public health.

board of trade, **1** an association of businessmen to protect, regulate, and advance their interests. **2** an association of businessmen to provide a free market in commodities, especially grains.

Board of Trade, the department of the British government concerned with commerce and industry.

board room, **1** the room in which a board of directors meets. **2** a room in a brokerage office for posting the lastest prices of securities.

board rule, a scale for determining the board feet of a piece of lumber, without calculation.

boards (bôrdz, bōrdz), *n.pl.* See under **board**.

board school, a locally administered school in Britain prior to the introduction of state schools.

board·wag·es (bôrd′wā′jiz, bōrd′-), *n.pl.* payment made to domestic servants in lieu of board.

board·walk (bôrd′wôk′, bōrd′-), *n.* **1** a wide sidewalk, usually made of boards, near the water at a shore resort: *The boardwalk at Atlantic City is a famous promenade.* **2** any sidewalk made of boards.

board·y (bôr′dē, bōr′-), *adj.,* **board·i·er, board·i·est.** *Informal.* stiff.

boar·fish (bôr′fish′, bōr′-), *n., pl.* **-fish·es** or (*collectively*) **-fish**. any one of several fishes with a projecting, hoglike snout.

boar·hound (bôr′hound′, bōr′-), *n.* a large dog used for hunting wild boars, such as a Great Dane.

boar·ish (bôr′ish, bōr′-), *adj.* = swinish. **-boar′·ish·ly**, *adv.* —**boar′ish·ness**, *n.*

boart (bôrt, bōrt), *n.* = bort.

boast[1] (bōst), *v., n.* —***v.i.*** **1** to speak too highly of oneself or what one owns or knows; brag: *It is unpleasant to hear one boast about his own abilities, achievements, or possessions.* **2** to be proud.
—***v.t.*** **1** to brag about. SYN: vaunt. **2** *Figurative.* to have (something) to be proud of: *Our town boasts a new high school.*
—***n.*** **1** a statement speaking too highly of oneself or what one owns or knows; boasting words; bragging: *I don't believe his boast that he can run faster than I can.* **2** something to be proud of: *The medal he won at the swimming meet was his boast. Let independence be our boast* (Joseph Hopkinson).
[Middle English *bosten;* origin uncertain]
—**boast′ing·ly**, *adv.*
—*Syn. v.i.* **1 Boast, brag** mean to praise oneself. **Boast** means to talk too much about something one has done or about one's possessions, family, etc., even though there may be some reason to be proud: *She boasts about her grades in school.* **Brag** always suggests showing off and exaggerating: *He is always bragging about what he can do with a car.*

boast[2] (bōst), *v.t. Sculpture.* to shape roughly before putting in the details.
[origin uncertain]

boast[3] (bōst), *v., n. Court Tennis, Rackets.* —***v.t., v.i.*** to hit (the ball) against either of the sidewalls.
—***n.*** a boasted stroke or ball.
[perhaps < French *bosse* place where a ball hits the wall < Old French *boce* hump, boss[2]]

boast·er[1] (bōs′tər), *n.* a person who boasts; braggart.

boast·er[2] (bōs′tər), *n.* a broad-faced chisel, used especially in sculpturing.

Pronunciation Key: hat, āge, cãre, fär; let, ēqual, tėrm; it, īce; hot, ōpen, ôrder; oil, out; cup, pu̇t, rüle; child; long; thin; ᴛʜen; zh, measure; ə represents a in about, e in taken, i in pencil, o in lemon, u in circus.

boast|ful (bōst′fəl), *adj.* **1** speaking too well about oneself; boasting: *a boastful story.* SYN: bragging. **2** fond of boasting: *It is hard to listen very long to a boastful person.* SYN: braggart. —**boast′ful|ly**, *adv.* —**boast′ful|ness**, *n.*

boat (bōt), *n., v.* —*n.* **1** a small, open vessel for traveling on water, such as a motorboat, a sailboat, or a rowboat: *A little stream best fits a little boat* (Robert Herrick). *Just messing about in boats* (Kenneth Grahame). SYN: craft. **2** a large vessel, such as a steamboat or ocean liner; ship. **3** a dish shaped somewhat like a boat for gravy or sauce.
—*v.i.* to go in a boat; travel by boat: *The sightseers went boating on the river.* —*v.t.* **1** to put or carry in a boat: *Ceasing to row, they boated the oars.* **2** to catch and haul (a fish, especially a game fish) into a boat.
burn one's boats, to cut off all chances of retreat: *The . . . leaders have burnt their boats and are certain they will be arrested before the weekend* (Manchester Guardian Weekly).
in the same boat, in the same position or condition; taking the same chances: *Realizing that all independents were in the same boat, [they held] a luncheon meeting to discuss mutual problems* (Wall Street Journal).
miss the boat, *Informal.* to miss an opportunity; lose one's chances: *The buyer missed the boat and never got the house when he offered too low a bid.*
rock the boat, *Informal.* to disturb or upset the way things are: *They will seldom rock the boat or annoy the mayor or board of aldermen with unusual budget requests* (Harper's).
[Old English *bāt*] —**boat′like′**, *adj.*
▶See **ship** for usage note.

boat|a|ble (bō′tə bəl), *adj.* navigable by boat: *The canal will be boatable* (New Yorker).

boat|age (bō′tij), *n.* **1** carriage by boat. **2** a charge made for carriage by boat.

boat|bill (bōt′bil′), *n.* a tropical American bird related to the heron.

boat|build|er (bōt′bil′dər), *n.* a person who designs or constructs boats.

boat|build|ing (bōt′bil′ding), *n.* **1** the designing or building of boats. **2** the art of designing or building boats.

boa|tel (bō tel′), *n. U.S.* a waterside hotel, such as one at a marina, with docks for use by boat owners. Also, **botel**. [blend of *boat* and *hotel*]

boat|er (bō′tər), *n.* **1** a person who boats. **2** a stiff straw hat with a flat crown and brim.

boat hook, a metal hook on a pole, used for pulling or pushing a boat or raft, or for fishing things out of the water.

boat|house (bōt′hous′), *n.* a house or shed for sheltering a boat or boats.

boat|ing (bō′ting), *n.* the action of going by boat, as rowing or sailing, especially for recreation.

boat|load (bōt′lōd′), *n.* **1** as much or as many as a boat can hold. **2** the load that a boat carries.

boat|man (bōt′mən), *n., pl.* **-men**. **1** a man who rents out boats or takes care of them. **2** a man who rows or sails boats for pay. **3** a man who works on a boat.

boat|man|ship (bōt′mən ship), *n.* skill in managing a boat.

boat neck or **neckline**, = bateau neck.

boat people, refugees who emigrate in small boats for any country that will let them in: *The unexpected arrival of the Cuban "boat people"* . . . (Dennis A. Williams). *The total number of Haitian boat people in the United States was estimated at . . . 35,000 by year's end* (Richard C. Schroeder).

boat spike, the largest type of nail, about 15 inches long.

boat|swain (bō′sən; *rarely* bōt′swān′), *n.* **1** a ship's officer in charge of the anchors, ropes, and rigging. He directs some of the work of the crew. Also, **bo's'n**, **bosun**. **2** = tropic bird. [Old English *bātswegen* < *bāt* boat + *-swegen* swain]

***boatswain's chair**, a short, flat board attached at the ends to a bridle of rope, by which it can be hoisted, serving as a seat for a seaman working where there is no foothold; bosun's chair.

***boatswain's chair**

boat|tail (bōt′tāl′), *n., adj.* —*n.* **1** the cylindrical, tapering tail or rear section of a bullet, missile, or other projectile. **2** = boat-tailed grackle.
—*adj.* = boat-tailed.

boat-tailed (bōt′tāld′), *adj.* tapering to the rear, as the hind part of a boat: *a boat-tailed projectile, boat-tailed design.*

boat-tailed grackle, a large grackle with a long, broad tail, of the southern United States and Mexico.

boat train, a railroad train which makes connections with a ship.

boat|yard (bōt′yärd′), *n.* an establishment that repairs, stores, and builds boats.

Bo|az (bō′az), *n.* the husband of Ruth and an ancestor of David (in the Bible, Ruth 2-4).

bob[1] (bob), *v.,* **bobbed, bob|bing**, *n.* —*v.t.* to cause to move up and down, or to and fro, with short, quick motions: *The pigeon bobbed its head as it picked up crumbs.* SYN: jerk.
—*v.i.* **1** to move the body or head with a bobbing motion: *He bobbed suddenly and avoided the blow.* **2** to try to catch with the teeth something floating or hanging: *One game at the party was to bob for apples in a bowl of water.*
—*n.* a short, quick motion up and down, or to and fro, especially of the head. SYN: jerk.
bob up, to appear suddenly or unexpectedly: *It was this committee that kept bobbing up all spring, conducting what Lerner called "the campaign without a candidate"* (Harper's).
[origin uncertain]

bob[2] (bob), *n., v.,* **bobbed, bob|bing**. —*n.* **1** a child's or woman's haircut that is fairly short all around the head. **2** a horse's docked tail. **3** a knob or knot of something, such as hair. **4** a weight on the end of a plumb line; plummet. **5** a float for a fishing line. **6a** = bobsled. **b** = bob skate. **7** a term for certain kinds of changes in bell ringing.
—*v.t.* **1** to cut (hair) short. **2** to dock (an animal's tail).
—*v.i.* to fish using a bob.
[Middle English *bobbe* bunch; origin uncertain]

bob[3] (bob), *n., pl.* **bob**. *British Slang.* a shilling. [origin uncertain]

bob[4] (bob), *n., v.,* **bobbed, bob|bing**. —*n.* a light rap; tap.
—*v.t.* to rap lightly; tap.
[Middle English *bobben;* origin uncertain]

bob[5] (bob), *v.,* **bobbed, bob|bing**, *n. British Dialect.* —*v.t.* **1** to delude; trick; cheat: *You shall not bob us out of our melody* (Shakespeare). **2** to get by trickery. **3** to mock; deride.
—*n.* **1** a trick. **2** a mock; taunt.
[Middle English *bobben* < Old French *bober*]

bobbed (bobd), *adj.* **1** cut in a bob: *bobbed hair.* **2** docked: *a horse with a bobbed tail.* **3** furnished with a bob.

bob|ber (bob′ər), *n.* **1** a person or thing that bobs. **2** a fishing bob. **3** a person who rides a bobsled or is an enthusiast of bobsledding as a sport.

bob|ber|y (bob′ər ē), *n., pl.* **-ber|ies**. (in India) a noisy disturbance; row. [Anglo-Indian; probably < Hindi *Bāp re!* O father! (used for surprise or grief)]

bob|bin (bob′ən), *n.* **1** a reel or spool for holding thread, yarn, and the like. Bobbins are used in spinning, weaving, machine sewing, and making lace. **2** a reel around which wire is coiled in electrical instruments. [< Middle French *bobine*]

bob|bi|net (bob′ə net′), *n.* a cotton netting or lace made by machines. [< *bobbin* + *net*[1]]

bobbin lace, a lace made by winding and knotting threads around a special kind of bobbin stuck in a pillow according to a certain design; pillow lace.

bob|ble (bob′əl), *v.,* **-bled, -bling**, *n.* —*v.i.* **1** to move with a continual bobbing. **2** *Slang.* to blunder; fumble: *Sometimes, in his earnestness, he bobbled a bit* (Newsweek).
—*v.t. Slang.* to fumble (a ball): *The fielder bobbled an easy grounder.*
—*n.* **1** the movement of agitated water. **2** *Slang.* a blunder; fumble.
[probably < *bob*[1]]

bob|by (bob′ē), *n., pl.* **-bies**. *British Informal.* a policeman: . . . *some overworked bobby was already on his way* (Geoffrey Household). [< nickname for Sir *Robert* Peel, 1788-1850, who founded the London police force]

bob|by-daz|zler (bob′ē daz′lər), *n. British Dialect.* something striking or flashy: *His new tie is a bobby-dazzler.*

bobby pin, a metal hairpin whose prongs close on and hold tightly to the hair. Bobby pins are used especially in setting curls or waves. [< *bob*[2] (from its use in bobbed hair)]

bob|by|socks or **bob|by|sox** (bob′ē soks′), *n.pl.* socks reaching just above the ankle, worn especially by young girls. [< *bob*[2] + *socks* (from their being cut short)]

bob|by|sox|er (bob′ē sok′sər), *n.* an adolescent girl, especially one in the 1940's who wore bobbysocks and enthusiastically followed every new fad. [< *bobbysox*]

bob|cat (bob′kat′), *n.* **1** the wildcat or lynx of North America; bay lynx. See picture under **lynx**. **2** **Bobcat**, a cub scout of the beginning rank, who has not yet achieved the rank of Wolf.

bo|bèche (bô besh′), *n. French.* a disk or shallow cup with a hole in it, placed about a candle at the base to catch melted wax.

bob|o|link (bob′ə lingk), *n.* a common North American songbird that lives in fields and meadows and has a call that sounds like its name. It belongs to the same family as the blackbirds. Also called *reedbird* (in the Middle West) and *ricebird* (in the South). [American English; earlier *bob-o-Lincoln;* imitative]

bob skate, a skate with two runners.

***bob|sled** (bob′sled′), *n., v.,* **-sled|ded, -sled|ding**.
—*n.* **1** a long sled with two sets of runners and a continuous seat. It has a steering wheel and brakes. **2** two short sleds fastened together by a plank. **3** either of the short sleds.
—*v.i.* to ride on a bobsled. —**bob′sled′der**, *n.*

***bobsled**
definition 1

bob|sled|ding (bob′sled′ing), *n.* the act or sport of riding on a bobsled.

bob|sleigh (bob′slā′), *n., v.i.,* **-sleighed, -sleigh|ing**. = bobsled.

bob|stay (bob′stā′), *n.* a rope or chain to hold a bowsprit down.

Bob's your uncle (bobz), *British Informal.* you know the rest; that's all there is to it.

bob|tail (bob′tāl′), *n., adj., v.* —*n.* **1** a short tail, or a tail cut short. **2** an animal having such a tail.
—*adj.* **1** having such a tail. **2** *Figurative.* cut short or incomplete: *Chances favor a "bobtail" bill wrapping up pet schemes* (Wall Street Journal).
—*v.t.* **1** to cut short the tail of. **2** *Figurative.* to cut short sometimes, so as to make incomplete.

bob|tailed (bob′tāld′), *adj.* **1** having a bobtail. **2** *Figurative.* cut short; curtailed.

bobtailed disease, *U.S.* = alkali disease.

bob veal, veal from an immature calf.

bob|white (bob′hwīt′), *n.* an American quail that has a grayish body with brown and white markings. Its call is supposed to sound somewhat like its name.

bo|cac|cio (bə kä′chō), *n., pl.* **-cios** or (*collectively*) **-cio**. a large, edible California rockfish. [alteration of Italian *boccaccia* big, ugly mouth < *bocca* mouth < Latin *bucca* cheek]

bo|cage (bō käzh′), *n.* **1** woodland; boscage. **2** a background of foliage, trees, or other vegetation, supporting earthenware or ceramic figures. [< French *bocage* < Old French *boscage;* see etym. under **boscage**]

bo|cal (bō kal′, bō′kəl), *n.* the mouthpiece of a brass musical instrument. [< French *bocal*]

boc|ce (bôt′chā), *n. Italian.* boccie.

boc|cie (boch′ē; *Italian* bôt′chā), *n.* an Italian form of the game of bowls, played outdoors on a narrow, enclosed court. [< Italian *bocce*, plural of *boccia* ball]

Boche or **boche** (bosh, bôsh), *n. Unfriendly Use.* **1** a German soldier. **2** any German. [< French army slang *boche* < *tête de boche* blockhead, earlier *tête de caboche* < *caboche* skull]

bock beer, or **bock** (bok), *n.* a strong, dark-colored, rather sweet beer, usually brewed in the winter for use in the spring. [American English < German *Bock, Bockbier,* short for *Eimbock Bier* beer of *Eimbock*, or *Einbeck*, Hanover, Germany]

bo|cor (bō kôr′), *n. Haitian Creole.* a sorcerer or medicine man.

bod (bod), *n. British Slang.* a person; fellow; chap. [apparently short for *body*]

BOD (no periods) or **B.O.D.**, **1** biochemical oxygen demand. **2** biological oxygen demand.

bo|da|cious (bō dā′shəs), *adj. U.S. Slang.* reckless. [blend of *bold* and *audacious*] —**bo|da′cious|ly**, *adv.* —**bo|da′cious|ness**, *n.*

bo|dark (bō′därk′), *n.* = bodock.

bode[1] (bōd), *v.t., v.i.,* **bod|ed, bod|ing**. to be a sign (of); indicate beforehand; foreshadow: *The rumble of thunder boded rain.* SYN: portend, betoken, presage.
bode ill, to be a bad sign: *The dark clouds boded ill for our picnic plans.*
bode well, to be a good sign: *His good study habits boded well for his success in school. I can see nothing that bodes well to the Church Establishment: I fear its days are numbered* (Richard Whately).
[Old English *bodian* announce, foretell < *boda* messenger]

bode[2] (bōd), *v.* past tense and obsolete past participle of **bide**.

bode|ful (bōd′fəl), *adj.* boding; ominous.
bo|de|ga (bō dē′gə; *Spanish* bō ᴛʜā′gä), *n.* in Spanish-speaking communities: **1** a wineshop or cellar. **2** a retail store, especially a grocery store or a kind of general store. [< Spanish *bodega* < Latin *apothēca* storehouse; see etym. under **apothecary**]
bode|ment (bōd′mənt), *n. Archaic.* **1** an omen. **2** a foreboding. **3** a prediction.
Bo|de's law (bō′dəz), *Astronomy.* an arithmetical approximation of the relative mean distances of the planets from the sun, obtained by adding 4 to the series 0, 3, 6, 12, 24, 48, 96, 192, and 384. The law applies to all the planets except Neptune and Pluto. [< Johann E. *Bode,* 1747-1826, a German astronomer]
bodg|ie (boj′ē), *n., pl.* **-ies**. *Australian Slang.* one of a gang of rowdy and rebellious boys or young men.
bo|dhi (bō′dē), *n. Buddhism.* knowledge; enlightenment. [< Sanskrit *bodhi*]
bo|dhi|satt|va (bō′dē sät′və), *n. Buddhism.* a person who by virtue of his exemplary conduct, spiritual wisdom, and compassion is considered likely to become, in a future incarnation, a Buddha, or savior of mankind. [< Sanskrit *bodhisattva*]
bodhi tree, = bo tree.
bod|ice (bod′is), *n.* **1** the close-fitting upper part of a dress. **2** a wide girdle worn over a dress and laced up the front: *Some European peasant women used to wear bodices.* **3** *Obsolete.* a corset; stays. [variant plural of *body* upper part of a dress]
-bodied, *combining form.* having a ____body: *Heavy-bodied = having a heavy body.*
bod|i|less (bod′ē lis), *adj.* without a body: *Spirits are bodiless.* SYN: incorporeal, disembodied.
bod|i|ly (bod′ə lē), *adj., adv.* —*adj.* **1** of the body; in the body; physical: *bodily pain. Athletes have bodily strength.* **2** having a body or bodies; corporeal; material: *a bodily substance.*
—*adv.* **1** in person; in the flesh: *The man we thought dead walked bodily into the room.* **2** as a whole; all together; entirely: *The audience rose bodily to cheer the hero.*
bod|ing (bō′ding), *n., adj.* —*n.* a premonition; omen; portent: *a boding of disaster.*
—*adj.* portending; ominous: *listening to the boding cry of the tree toad* (Washington Irving).
[Old English *bodung* < *bodian* announce < *boda* messenger] —**bod′ing|ly**, *adv.*
***bod|kin** (bod′kin), *n.* **1** a large, blunt needle, used for drawing tape or cord through a hem, loops, etc. **2** a long hairpin. **3** a pointed tool for making holes in cloth, etc. **4** *Printing.* a tool for picking out letters in correcting type which has been set. **5** a small dagger or other short, pointed weapon; stiletto. [Middle English *boydekyn* dagger; origin unknown]

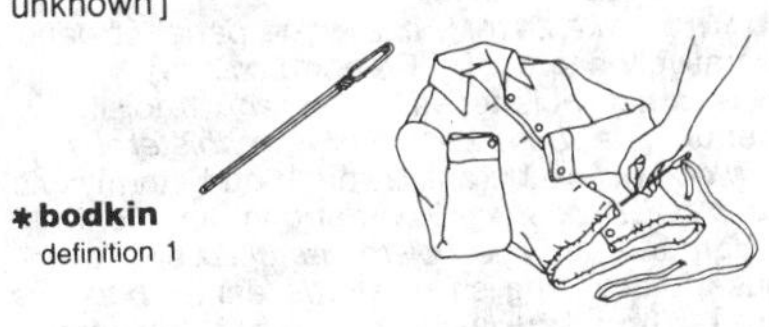
***bodkin**
definition 1

Bod|lei|an (bod lē′ən, bod′lē-), *n., adj.* —*n.* the Oxford University Library.
—*adj.* of or having to do with this library.
[< Sir Thomas *Bodley,* 1545-1613, who restored and refounded the Library in its present form + *-ian*]
bo|dock (bō′dok), *n. U.S.* the Osage orange. [< French *bois d'arc*]
Bo|do|ni (bə dō′nē), *n.* a modern style of type based on the designs of the celebrated Italian printer Giambattista Bodoni (1740-1813).
Bodoni Book, a lightweight style of printing type with a reduced contrast between thick and thin lines that reflects the letter design of Bodoni type.
bod|y (bod′ē), *n., pl.* **bod|ies**, *v.,* **bod|ied**, **bod|y·ing**. —*n.* **1** the whole material or physical part of a person, animal, or plant: *This boy has a strong, healthy body.* **2** the main part of an animal from which other parts, such as the head, limbs, or tail, stick out: *The dog rolled over and scratched its body on the grass.* SYN: torso. **3** the main part of anything, such as the nave of a church, the hull of a ship, or the part of a vehicle that holds the passengers or the load. **4** the fuselage of an aircraft. **5a** the main part of a speech or document, minus the introduction, appendix, or the like: *the body of a will.* **b** the part of a news story following and enlarging on the lead. **6** a group of persons or things considered together: *a body of laws, a body of soldiers. A large body of children sang in the school program. Congress is the lawmaking body of our government.* SYN: aggregate, corpus. **7** *Informal or Dialect.* a person: *She is a good-natured body.* **8** a dead person or animal; corpse. **9** a portion of matter; mass: *A lake is a body of water. The moon, the sun, and the stars are heavenly bodies.* **10** substantial quality; substance; matter; density: *wine or cloth of good body. Thick soup has more body than thin soup.* SYN: bulk. **11** that part of a garment which covers the trunk above the waist. **12** *Printing.* the base on which a letter or face is cut or cast; the breadth of the shank, which is the same throughout the font: *an 8-point face on a 9-point body.* **13** *Law.* a corporation, technically regarded as a person; body corporate. **14** *Obsolete.* a geometric figure of three dimensions; a solid.
—*v.t.* **1** to provide with a body; embody. **2** to give substance or density to: *The most important application of these new clay compounds is ... to 'body' lubricating oils* (Science News). **3** = body forth (see idiom below).
body forth, **a** to give a real form to: *The committee bodied forth its findings in an official report.* **b** to be a sign of; represent; typify: *Both as egoist and as patriot M. de Lesseps bodies forth the age* (Spectator).
in a body, as a unit; in a group; all together: *The old management was swept out of office, virtually in a body* (Canadian Saturday Night).
keep body and soul together, to keep barely alive: *The poor farmer's stock of food was barely enough to keep body and soul together through the long winter.*
over one's dead body, *Informal.* against one's determined opposition: *Harold Wilson is on record as saying that grammar schools will be abolished "over my dead body"* (Manchester Guardian Weekly).
[Old English *bodig*]
body blow, **1** a blow to the body, in boxing or fighting. **2** a serious setback.
body build, or **bod|y-build** (bod′ē bild′), *n.* bodily structure, build, or physique.
body burden, radioactive or other toxic material absorbed in an individual's system: *Lead ... has always been one of the "body burdens" that all of us carry around with us, because it settles in our bones* (Edith Iglauer).
body cavity, the central cavity of the body, as distinguished from special cavities or those of particular organs.
body cell, a somatic cell.
bod|y-cen|tered (bod′ē sen′tərd), *adj. Crystallography.* having cubic crystals with atoms at each corner and in the center of the cube of a crystalline structure.
body check, a defensive play, especially in ice hockey, in which a player attempts to throw the carrier of the puck off stride by bumping him with his body.
bod|y-check (bod′ē chek′), *v.t., v.i.* to check or block with the body, especially in ice hockey.
body clock, an internal mechanism which is thought to regulate the rhythm or cycle of the body's normal activities. Swift transition through several time zones during jet flight disturbs the body clock.
body color, **1** a pigment possessing body or a high degree of consistency, substance, and covering power. **2** a color rendered opaque by an admixture of white pigment.
body corporate, = corporation.
body count, **1** a daily count of the dead bodies on the battlefield as the basis of estimating enemy casualties. **2** any count or tally of individuals.
body English, *U.S. Informal.* motions of the body reflecting the desire of a spectator or player to cause a ball, contestant, or the like, to move in a certain way.
bod|y|guard (bod′ē gärd′), *n.* **1** a man or men who guard a person: *A bodyguard accompanies the President when he travels.* **2** a retinue; escort.
body jewel, an ornament worn on the body instead of on clothing.
body language, the unconscious gestures of the body as a form of communication: *Body language, it's now believed, carries as much information as spoken or written speech—perhaps more* (Barbara Ford).
bod|y|less (bod′ē lis), *adj.* = bodiless.
bod|y|line bowling (bod′ē līn′), *Cricket.* fast bowling directed persistently to the batsman's leg side.
body louse, a species of louse that infests the bodies and clothing of humans and lays its eggs in folds and seams of clothing.
body paint, a paint or cosmetic for decorating parts of the body with designs or figures.
body politic, a people forming a political group with an organized government.
body press, a wrestling hold in which the weight of the body is used to pin an opponent on his back.
body shirt, a tight-fitting shirt or blouse.
body slam, a wrestling throw in which the opponent is lifted and then flung down.
body snatcher, a person who steals corpses from graves, especially for the purpose of dissection. SYN: ghoul.
body stocking, a lightweight, tight-fitting, one-piece undergarment for women that covers most of the body, similar to a leotard.
bod|y|suit (bod′ē süt′), *n.* a tight-fitting, one-piece garment covering the trunk of the body.
bod|y-surf (bod′ē sėrf′), *v.i.* to ride on the crest of a wave without a surfboard.
body surfer, a person who trains for surfboard riding by body-surfing.
body type, *Printing.* the type used for printing the main text of a book or the like.
body wave, a seismic wave that travels through the earth in every direction from its origin.
bod|y|work (bod′ē wėrk′), *n.* **1** the part of a vehicle that holds the passengers or the load; body. **2** work done on the body: *The damaged car needed a lot of bodywork.*
Boe|o|tian (bē ō′shən), *adj., n.* —*adj.* **1** of or having to do with Boeotia (district in ancient Greece) or its people: *Hesiod was a Boeotian farmer.* **2** *Figurative.* dull; stupid (from the ancient tradition that natives of Boeotia were lacking in normal good sense).
—*n.* **1** a native of Boeotia. **2** *Figurative.* a stupid person; dullard.
Boer (bôr, bōr, bůr), *n., adj.* —*n.* a person of Dutch descent living in South Africa.
—*adj.* of or having to do with the Boers. Also, **Boor**.
[< Dutch *boer* farmer]
Boer War, a war between Great Britain and the Boers of South Africa, lasting from 1899 to 1902.
boff (bof), *n. U.S. Slang.* a boffo.
bof|fin (bof′ən), *n. British Slang.* a scientist, designer, or engineer, especially one thought of as dealing chiefly with the theoretical aspects of a problem or field. [origin unknown]
bof|fo (bof′ō), *adj., n., pl.* **-foes** or **-fos**. *U.S. Slang.* —*adj.* **1** funny; hilarious: *boffo jokes.* **2** popular or successful: *a boffo movie.*
—*n.* **1** a very hearty laugh. **2** that which evokes a very hearty laugh; a gag or joke. **3** a very successful musical comedy or other light dramatic performance.
[origin unknown]
bof|fo|la (bo fō′lə), *n. U.S. Slang.* a boffo.
Bo|fors gun (bō′fôrz; *Swedish* bü fôrs′), an automatic weapon of Swedish origin with twin 40-millimeter barrels [< *Bofors* Armament Works, Sweden]
bog (bog, bôg), *n., v.,* **bogged**, **bog|ging**. —*n.* a piece of soft, wet, spongy ground; marsh; swamp. A bog consists chiefly of decayed or decaying moss and other vegetable matter, too soft to bear the weight of any heavy body on its surface. SYN: fen, morass.
—*v.t., v.i.* to sink or get stuck in a bog: *He became bogged in the swamp and had to be rescued.* SYN: mire.
bog down, to sink in or get stuck so that one cannot get out without help: *He bogged down in the middle of his speech because his notes were jumbled.*
[< Irish, Scottish Gaelic *bog* soft]
bo|gan (bō′gən), *n. Especially Canadian.* (in the Maritime Provinces) a backwater or stagnant branch of a river or stream. [< Algonkian *pokelogan*]
bog asphodel, either of two plants of the lily family, one native to the eastern United States and the other to Europe, found in swampy places.
bog bean, = buck bean.
bog|ber|ry (bog′ber′ē, -bər-; bôg′-), *n., pl.* **-ries**. = European cranberry.
bo|gey[1] (bō′gē; *also* bůg′ē *for 1*), *n., pl.* **-geys**, *v.* —*n.* **1** bogy; a goblin: *the bogeys of the dark.* **2a** a score of one stroke over par for any hole on a golf course. **b** a score in golf that players try to equal; par. **3** *Slang.* an unidentified aircraft.
—*v.t. Golf.* to play (a hole) in par plus one stroke.
[variant of *bogy*]
bo|gey[2] (bō′gē), *n., pl.* **-geys**. bogie; a pivoted frame.
bo|gey|man (bō′gē man′, bůg′ē-), *n., pl.* **-men**. a frightening imaginary creature; bogy; goblin: (*Figurative.*) *The bogeymen of speculation and excess credit ... have caused some shuddering in the stock market* (Newsweek).

Pronunciation Key: hat, āge, cãre, fär; let, ēqual, tėrm; it, īce; hot, ōpen, ôrder; oil, out; cup, půt, rüle; child; long; thin; ᴛʜen; zh, measure; ə represents a in about, e in taken, i in pencil, o in lemon, u in circus.

bog|gish (bog′ish, bôg′-), *adj.* marshy; swampy.

bog|gle¹ (bog′əl), *v.*, **-gled, -gling,** *n.* — ***v.i.*** **1** to hold back; raise difficulties or objections; hesitate: *Father boggled at the suggestion at first, but finally agreed to do the job.* **SYN:** waver, shrink, demur. **2** to be overwhelmed with wonder, shock, or the like: *His mind boggled at the thought of inheriting a million dollars.* **3** = blunder. **4** to jump with fright; shy.
— ***v.t.*** **1** to bungle; botch: *He boggled his first attempt at carpentry.* **2** to overwhelm with wonder, shock, or the like: *The vastness of the universe boggles the imagination.*
— ***n.*** **1** a blunder; bungle; botch. **2** the act of boggling.
[probably < *bogle*] — **bog′gler,** *n.* — **bog′gling|ly,** *adv.*

bog|gle² (bog′əl), *n.* = bogle.

bog|gy (bog′ē, bôg′-), *adj.*, **-gi|er, -gi|est. 1** soft and wet like a bog; marshy; swampy: *boggy ground.* **2** full of bogs. — **bog′gi|ness,** *n.*

bog|head coal, or **bog|head** (bog′hed′, bôg′-), *n.* a kind of coal used for the manufacture of paraffin and oils: *Boghead coal differs from cannel in being brown and in consisting largely of algal material* (Fenton and Fenton). [< *Boghead,* Scotland]

bog|hole (bog′hōl, bôg′-), *n.* a sink, hole, or depression with a bottom of soft, spongy, or liquid consistency.

bo|gie¹ (bō′gē; *also* bu̇g′ē *for 1*), *n.* **1** = bogy¹ (def. 1). **2** *Slang.* bogey.

***bo|gie²** (bō′gē), *n.* **1** the assembly of the four rear wheels of a six-wheeled truck. **2** a pivoted frame or truck with two or more pairs of wheels supporting either the front of a locomotive or one end of a railroad car. **3** *British.* a low, strong, four-wheeled truck or cart. Also, **bogey, bogy.** [a dialectal word; origin unknown]

***bogie²** definition 2

bog iron ore, a loose, porous variety of limonite found in bogs or water.

bo|gle (bō′gəl), *n.* a bogy or a specter. [< Scottish *bogill*]

bog manganese, an amorphous mineral, of which the principal ingredient is manganese oxide; wad.

bog moss, = sphagnum.

bog myrtle, = sweet gale.

bog oak, ancient oak preserved and blackened in the peat of a bog.

Bog|o|mil (bog′ə mil), *n.* a member of a heretical Bulgarian sect which arose about the year 1000 and whose main tenet was that God had two sons, Satan and Christ. [< *Bogomilu,* a priest who founded the sect]

bog orchid, a low-growing European orchid with small flowers, found in bogs.

bog ore, = bog iron ore.

bog spavin, a distention of the capsule of the hock joint in horses.

bog spruce, = black spruce.

bog trotter, an Irish peasant.

bo|gus (bō′gəs), *adj., n.* — ***adj.*** *U.S.* not genuine; counterfeit; sham: *The man was arrested when he handed the cashier a bogus ten dollar bill.*
— ***n.*** *Printing.* type that is set to duplicate advertising matter received in completed matrix form, as a requirement of some labor unions: *Bogus is not intended to be used, but it makes work for union members* (Time). [American English, originally an apparatus for making counterfeit money; origin uncertain] — **bo′gus|ness,** *n.*

bog wood, = bog oak.

bo|gy¹ (bō′gē, bu̇g′ē), *n., pl.* **-gies. 1** an evil spirit; goblin: *He mistook the shadow for a bogy in the dark.* **2** *Figurative.* a person or thing that is feared without reason; bugbear; bugaboo: *Socialism is the bogy of many capitalists.* Also, **bogey, bogie, bogle.** [probably < obsolete *bog* bugbear]

bo|gy² (bō′gē), *n., pl.* **-gies.** = bogie².

bo|gy|man (bō′gē man′, bu̇g′ē-), *n., pl.* **-men.** = bogy¹.

bo|hea (bō hē′), *n.* an inferior black China tea (originally the name of one of the finest kinds). [< dialectal Chinese pronunciation of *Wu-i,* hills in north Fukien, China, where originally grown]

Bo|he|mi|a or **bo|he|mi|a** (bō hē′mē ə, -hēm′yə), *n.* **1** an unconventional, carefree existence. **2** a place where painters, writers, and other artists, live in an unconventional, carefree way.

Bo|he|mi|an (bō hē′mē ən, -hēm′yən), *adj., n.*
— ***adj.*** **1** of Bohemia (in Czechoslovakia), its people, or their language. **2** Also, **bohemian.** carefree and unconventional: *the Bohemian life of an artists' colony.*
— ***n.*** **1** a person born or living in Bohemia; Czech. **2** the language of Bohemia; Czech. **3** Also, **bohemian.** a painter, writer, or other artist who lives an unconventional, carefree existence: *He was rather more of a dedicated Bohemian than a dedicated poet.* **4** a gypsy (because the first gypsies in France were thought to come from Bohemia).

Bohemian Brethren, a pre-Reformation Christian association, denying the apostolic succession, formed in 1467. It formed the core of the Moravian Church.

Bohemian garnet, = pyrope.

Bohemian glass, richly colored ornamental glassware made in Bohemia.

bo|he|mi|an|ism or **Bo|he|mi|an|ism** (bō hē′mē ə niz′əm, -hēm′yə niz′-), *n.* a carefree, unconventional way of living.

Bohemian waxwing, a waxwing of the remote forests of Canada and the northern United States, somewhat larger and grayer than the cedar waxwing.

bo|hor (bō′hôr), *n.* a variety of reedbuck native to western Africa. Only the male has horns, which are relatively short. [< a native name in western Africa]

Bohr magneton (bôr, bōr), **1** the intrinsic magnetic moment (magnetism) of an electron in the direction of an applied magnetic field. **2** the unit of magnetic moment for electrons. [< Niels *Bohr,* 1885-1962, a Danish physicist]

Bohr theory, a theory of the structure of atoms proposed by Niels Bohr, stating that electrons revolve around a nucleus in certain orbits of constant energy only. When an electron jumps to another orbit of less energy, energy is either radiated or absorbed.

bo|hunk (bō′hungk), *n. U.S. and Canadian Slang.* **1** a low, rough fellow. **2** an unskilled worker from southeastern or east central Europe (used in an unfriendly way). [perhaps < *Bo*(hemian) + *Hung*(arian)]

boil¹ (boil), *v., n.* — ***v.i.*** **1** to bubble up and give off steam or vapor: *Water boils when heated to 212 degrees Fahrenheit.* **2a** to have its contents boil: *The pot is boiling.* **b** to be subjected to the heating or cooking effects of boiling fluid: *The eggs are boiling.* **3** *Figurative.* to be very excited; be stirred up: *He boiled with anger.* **4** to move violently: *The stormy sea is boiling.*
— ***v.t.*** **1** to cause (a liquid) to boil: *Boil some water for tea.* **2** to cook by boiling or by heating in boiling water: *We boil eggs four minutes. Boil the mixture until it begins to thicken.* **3** to cleanse or sterilize by boiling: *to boil drinking water.* **4** to prepare by boiling and evaporation: *to boil sugar.*
— ***n.*** **1** a boiling. **2** a boiling condition: *Bring the mixture to a boil.* (*Figurative.*) *His anger came to a boil.*

boil away, to evaporate in boiling: *The water began to boil away.*

boil down, a to make less by boiling: *Boil down the sauce to half the amount.* **b** *Figurative.* to shorten by getting rid of unimportant parts: *The notes for his report were so long that the chairman asked him to boil them down to a simple list of important facts.* **c** *Informal, Figurative.* to amount to when briefly stated: *His long, wordy refusal all boils down to this—"You can't go."*

boil over, a to come to the boiling point and overflow: *This pot of milk is boiling over.* **b** *Figurative.* to show excitement or anger: *Father boiled over at my rude remarks, but mother calmed things down again. The political frenzy was now boiling over* (James A. Froude).

come to a boil, to reach the boiling point: *The water won't come to a boil unless you turn up the flame.*

on the boil, in a state of excitement or agitation: *France's student rebels are on the boil again* (New Scientist).

[< Old French *boillir* < Latin *bullīre* seethe < *bulla* a bubble] — **boil′a|ble,** *adj.*

— ***Syn.*** *v.i.* **3 Boil, simmer, seethe,** figuratively used, mean to be emotionally excited. **Boil** suggests being so stirred up by emotion, usually anger, that one's feelings and, often, blood are thought of as bubbling and giving off steam: *Resentment was boiling in my breast.* **Simmer** suggests less intense emotion or greater control, so that one's feelings are just below the boiling point: *I was simmering with laughter.* **Seethe** suggests being violently stirred up, so that a person's mind or feelings or a group of people is thought of as boiling and foaming: *The people seethed with discontent.*

► A past participle **boilt** occurs in nonstandard use. It occurs frequently in several of the Middle Atlantic States and to a lesser extent also in the South.

boil² (boil), *n.* a painful, red swelling on the skin, formed by pus around a hard core; furuncle. Boils are often caused by infection. [Old English *bȳle*]

boiled dinner (boild), a dinner of meat and vegetables, especially potatoes and cabbage, boiled together.

boiled oil, linseed oil prepared for use in painting.

boiled shirt, *U.S.* a white dress shirt with a starched bosom.

boiled sweet, *British.* hard candy.

boil|er (boi′lər), *n.* **1** a tank for making steam to heat buildings or drive engines. **2** a tank for heating and holding hot water. **3** a container for heating liquids.

boiler iron, = boilerplate.

boil|er|mak|er (boi′lər mā′kər), *n.* **1** a person who makes boilers. **2** a drink of whiskey followed by beer as a chaser.

boil|er|plate (boi′lər plāt′), *n.,* or **boiler plate, 1** steel rolled in the form of flat plates, from ¼ to ½ inch in thickness, used especially for making boilers, tanks, and ships; boiler iron. **2** *U.S.* a full-size model of a spacecraft, used in ground and flight tests. **3** *U.S.* articles to be used as filler, especially in a rural newspaper, sent by some central agency on electrotypes or stereotypes. **4** *U.S.* any syndicated material used as filler. **5** = boilermaker (def. 2).

boiler room, 1 a room containing a boiler or boilers. **2** *U.S. Slang.* an establishment that engages in the sale of unlisted and highly speculative securities by solicitation over the telephone.

boiler shop, *U.S. Slang.* a boiler room.

boiler suit, *British Informal.* coveralls.

boil|er|y (boi′lər ē), *n., pl.* **-er|ies. 1** a place or establishment for boiling. **2** an apparatus for boiling.

boil|ing point (boi′ling), **1** the temperature at which a liquid boils. The boiling point of water at sea level is 212 degrees Fahrenheit or 100 degrees centigrade (Celsius). *Abbr:* b.p. **2** *Figurative: In countries with long-standing intergroup problems ... tensions reach the boiling point more easily than they do elsewhere* (Scientific American).

boiling water reactor, a nuclear reactor which has its fissionable material immersed in water, heat being dissipated by conversion of water to steam.

boil-off (boil′ôf′, -of′), *n.* loss of liquid fuel in a rocket by vaporization.

bois (bwä), *n. French.* **1** a wood; a tract of woodland. **2** wood or timber.

bois brû|lé (bwä′ brü lā′; *French* bwä bry lā′), *Canadian.* a half-breed Indian; métis. [< Canadian French *bois brûlé* (literally) charred wood]

bois d'arc (bō′därk′), *n., pl.* **bois d'arcs** or **bois d'arc.** = Osage orange.

boi|se|rie (bwä zə rē′), *n.* a wood panel or panels decoratively carved. [< French *boiserie*]

bois|ter|ous (bois′tər əs, -trəs), *adj.* **1** noisily cheerful: *The room was filled with boisterous laughter.* **SYN:** exuberant. **2** rough and stormy; violent: *a boisterous wind.* **SYN:** strong, turbulent. **3** rough and noisy: *a boisterous child.* **SYN:** clamorous. [Middle English *boistrous,* earlier *boistous* rough] — **bois′ter|ous|ly,** *adv.* — **bois′ter|ous|ness,** *n.*

boîte (bwȧt), *n. French.* cabaret.

Bok|mål (bu̇k′môl′), *n.* the older of the two official languages of Norway; Riksmål. The other official language is *Nynorsk.* [< Norwegian *Bokmål* < *bok* book + *mål* language, speech]

bo|ko (bō′kō), *n. British Slang.* the nose. [origin unknown]

Bol., Bolivia.

***bo|la** (bō′lə), *n., pl.* **-las** (-ləz). a weapon consisting of stone or metal balls tied at the ends of a long cord. South American cowboys throw it so that it winds around and entangles the animal aimed at. Also, **bolas.** [< Spanish *bola* ball < Latin *bulla* bubble]

***bola**

bo|lar (bō′lər), *adj.* **1** of or having to do with bole or clay. **2** having the nature of bole or clay.

bo|las (bō′ləs), *n., pl.* **-las** (-ləz), **-las|es** (-lə siz). = bola.

bolas spider, a variety of spider that spins a single line of silk with a drop of sticky silk at the end instead of spinning a web.

bola tie, an ornamental clasp attached to a length of cord with decorative tips, worn in place of a necktie. [< *bola* (because of the resemblance)]

bold (bōld), *adj., n.* —*adj.* **1** without fear; brave; daring: *Lancelot was a bold knight.* **SYN**: fearless, courageous. **2** showing courage; requiring courage: *a bold plan. Climbing the steep mountain was a bold act.* **3** too free in manner; impudent: *The bold little boy made faces at us as we passed.* **4a** sharp and clear to the eye; striking: *bold handwriting. The mountains stood in bold outline against the sky.* **SYN**: definite, pronounced, stark, free, clear. **b** *Figurative.* vigorous: *a bold imagination.* **5** steep; abrupt: *Bold cliffs overlooked the sea.* **6** *Printing.* bold-faced. **7** *Obsolete.* confident.
—*n. Printing.* boldface.
make bold, to take the liberty; dare; presume; venture: *Nothing, I make bold to say, can be more improbable* (William Gladstone).
[Old English *bald, beald*] —**bold′ly**, *adv.* —**bold′ness**, *n.*
—*Syn. adj.* **3 Bold, brazen, forward** mean too free in manner. **Bold** suggests lacking proper shame and modesty: *They were disconcerted by the girl's bold stare.* **Brazen** also means shameless but defiantly and insolently so: *He is brazen about being expelled.* **Forward** suggests being too sure of oneself, too disrespectul of others, too pert in pushing oneself forward: *His forward manner in the presence of older people made a very poor impression.*

***bold|face** (bōld′fās′), *n., adj.* —*n. Printing.* a heavy type that stands out clearly. Boldface has a thick face that prints blacker than ordinary type. *Abbr:* bf. —*adj.* = bold-faced.

***boldface**
The World Book Dictionary

bold-faced (bōld′fāst′), *adj.* **1** impudent; brazen: *a bold-faced lie.* **2a** (of type) having a thick face. **b** (of letters or words) printed in boldface.

bole¹ (bōl), *n.* the stem or trunk of a tree. [< Scandinavian (compare Old Icelandic *bolr*)]

bole² (bōl), *n.* any one of several fine-grained, heavy clays, usually of a red, yellow, or brown color, used as pigments. [Middle English *bol* < Late Latin *bōlus* bolus]

bo|lec|tion (bō lek′shən), *n. Architecture.* a type of molding or combination of moldings that projects beyond the surface or surfaces which it decorates, used especially to cover the joint between surfaces of different levels. Also, **bilection**. [origin unknown]

***bo|le|ro** (bə lãr′ō; *Spanish* bō lā′rō), *n., pl.* **-ros**. **1** a lively Spanish dance in triple time. **2** the music for it. **3** a short, loose jacket coming barely to the waist. [< Spanish *bolero* < *bola* ball¹ (from the whirling motion of the dance)]

***bolero**
definition 3

bo|le|tus (bō lē′təs), *n.* any one of a genus of mushrooms, having the under surface of the top (pileus) full of tubes, or pores, which are easily separable from the top and from each other. The boletus has no gills. [< Latin *bōlētus* mushroom]

bo|lide (bō′līd, -lid), *n.* a large meteor, usually one that explodes and falls to earth in the form of meteorites. [< French *bolide,* learned borrowing from Latin *bolis, -idis* large meteor < Greek *bolis* missile < *bállein* throw]

bo|li|var (bol′ə vər; *Spanish* bō lē′vär), *n., pl.* **bol|i-vars, bol|i|va|res** (bō′lē vä′rās). the unit of money of Venezuela, a silver coin equal to 100 centimos. [< American Spanish *bolívar* < Simón *Bolívar*]

bo|liv|i|a (bə liv′ē ə), *n.* a soft, woolen cloth somewhat like plush. [< *Bolivia,* the country]

Bo|liv|i|an (bə liv′ē ən), *adj., n.* —*adj.* of or having to do with Bolivia or its people.
—*n.* a native or inhabitant of Bolivia.

bo|li|via|no (bō lē′vyä′nō), *n., pl.* **-nos**. the former unit of money of Bolivia, replaced in 1963 by the peso boliviano. [< American Spanish *boliviano* < *Bolivia*]

bol|ix (bol′iks), *v.t., n.* = bollix.

boll (bōl), *n.* the rounded seed pod of a plant, especially that of cotton or flax. [Old English *bolla* round vessel]

Bol|land|ist (bol′ən dist), *n.* any one of a series of Jesuit editors, beginning with Jean Bolland (1596-1665), engaged in the publication of the *Acta Sanctorum* (lives of the saints).

***bol|lard** (bol′ərd), *n.* **1** a wooden or iron post on a ship or dock for fastening hawsers. **2** *British.* a wooden, concrete, or steel post serving to keep cars out of an area. [perhaps < *bole*¹ + Old French *-ard,* an augmentative suffix]

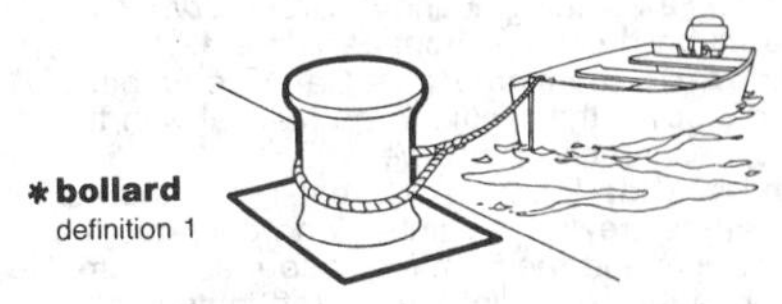

***bollard**
definition 1

bol|lix (bol′iks), *v., n.* —*v.t. U.S. Informal.* to snarl or muddle (up); confuse.
—*n.* a confused state of affairs; muddle: [*He*] *commented on the bollixes that may result from interservice conflicts* (Harper's). Also, **bolix**. [probably a respelling; Old English *beallucas* round objects; testicles]

boll rot, a fungous disease of cotton.

boll weevil, a small beetle with a long snout whose larva is hatched in and does great damage to young cotton bolls; snout beetle.

boll|worm (bōl′wėrm′), *n.* **1** a moth larva which feeds on seeds of the cotton plant and on cotton bolls. **2** a moth larva which feeds on ears of green corn, cotton bolls, and parts of other plants; the corn earworm.

bo|lo (bō′lō), *n., pl.* **-los**. a long, heavy knife, used in the Philippine Islands. It has a single edge and is somewhat like a machete. [< Spanish (Philippines) *bolo*]

bo|lo|gna (bə lō′nē, -nə), *n.* a large, lightly smoked sausage, usually made of beef, veal, and pork. [< *Bologna,* a city in Italy]

Bologna or **bologna sausage**, = bologna.

Bo|lo|gnese (bō′lə nēz′, -nēs′), *adj., n., pl.* **-gnese**. —*adj.* of or having to do with Bologna or its people. —*n.* a native or inhabitant of Bologna.

bo|lo|graph (bō′lə graf, -gräf), *n.* an automatic record of the indications made by a bolometer. [< Greek *bolē* ray]

bo|lo|graph|ic (bō′lə graf′ik), *adj.* of or having to do with a bolograph.

bo|log|ra|phy (bō log′rə fē), *n.* the recording of bolometric measurements.

bo|lo|man (bō′lō man′, -mən), *n., pl.* **-men**. a Filipino fighter or guerrilla armed with a bolo.

bo|lom|e|ter (bō lom′ə tər), *n.* an instrument for measuring the intensity of radiant energy, especially of feeble radiation. [< Greek *bolē* ray]

bo|lo|met|ric (bō′lə met′rik), *adj.* of or indicated by a bolometer.

bo|lo|ney (bə lō′nē), *n. British.* baloney.

bo|lo punch (bō′lō), *Boxing.* a powerful uppercut brought from the rear of the body. [probably < *bolo*]

Bol|she|vik (bōl′shə vik, bol′-), *n., pl.* **Bol|she-viks, Bol|she|vi|ki** (bōl′shə vē′kē, bol′-), *adj.*
—*n.* **1** a member of a radical political party in Russia that seized power in November, 1917. The Bolsheviks became the Communist Party in March, 1918. **2** a member of any Communist Party. **3** Also, **bolshevik**. *Figurative.* any extreme radical.
—*adj.* **1** of the Bolsheviks or Bolshevism. **2** Also, **bolshevik**. *Figurative.* extremely radical.
[< Russian *bol'shevik* < *bol'shij* greater (because of their temporary majority within the Russian Social Democratic Party in 1903)]

Bol|she|vism (bōl′shə viz əm, bol′-), *n.* **1** the doctrines and methods of the Bolsheviks. **2** Also, **bolshevism**. *Figurative.* extreme radicalism.

Bol|she|vist or **bol|she|vist** (bōl′shə vist, bol′-), *n., adj.* = Bolshevik.

Bol|she|vis|tic (bōl′shə vis′tik, bol′-), *adj.* **1** of or like Bolsheviks or Bolshevism. **2** Also, **bolshevistic**. *Figurative.* extremely radical. —**Bol′she|vis′ti|cal|ly, bol′she|vis′ti|cal|ly**, *adv.*

Bol|she|vize or **bol|she|vize** (bōl′shə vīz, bol′-), *v.t., v.i.,* **-vized, -viz|ing**. to make or become Bolshevistic. —**Bol′she|vi|za′tion, bol′she|vi|za′tion**, *n.*

Bol|shie or **Bol|shy** (bōl′shē, bol′-), *n., pl.* **-shies**, *adj. Slang.* —*n.* a Bolshevik.
—*adj.* **1** = Bolshevik: *"Fellow workers" is too Bolshy a term these days* (John Ciardi). **2** *British.* Often, **bolshie** or **bolshy**. *Figurative.* rebellious; rowdy: *There was a long-haired, and some people thought bolshy youth ... who suddenly asked me what I thought the most important thing in life was* (Christopher Layton).

bol|son (bōl′sən, bōl sōn′), *n.* a broad, shallow desert basin draining into a central, shallow lake or sink, especially such a basin surrounded by mountains in the southwestern United States and Mexico. [American English < American Spanish *bolsón* < Spanish *bolsa* purse, bag]

bol|ster (bōl′stər), *n., v.* —*n.* **1** a long, firmly stuffed pillow for a bed or used as a back on a couch. **2** a cushion or pad. **3** *Architecture.* a rounded projection, especially a horizontal element used on top of a post or column to lengthen the bearing surface.
—*v.t.* **1** to support with a bolster. **2** to keep from falling; support; prop (up): *The walls of the church are bolstered up with buttresses.* (*Figurative.*) *Her sympathy bolstered his courage.* (*Figurative.*) *I have done everything in my power to bolster up the credit of the government* (Duke of Wellington).
[Old English *bolster*] —**bol′ster|er**, *n.*

***bolt¹** (bōlt), *n., v., adv.* —*n.* **1** a metal rod with a head at one end and a screw thread for a nut at the other. Bolts are used to fasten things together or hold them in place. **2a** a sliding fastening for a door or gate, especially a bar slid or dropped into place in a bracket: *The farmer slides the bolt in place to keep the gate from swinging.* **b** a similar sliding bar on certain firearms which ejects a used cartridge case, pushes a new cartridge into firing position, and closes the breech. **3** the part of a lock moved by a key: *As I stood behind the door I heard Mother's key slide into the bolt.* **4** a short arrow with a thick head; quarrel. Bolts were shot from crossbows. **5** a discharge of lightning: *It came like a bolt from the sky.* **SYN**: thunderbolt. **6** a sudden start; a running away: *The rabbit saw the man and made a bolt for safety.* **7a** a roll of cloth (in the United States usually 40 yards). **b** a roll of wallpaper. **8** *U.S.* a refusal to support one's political party or its candidates.
—*v.t.* **1** to fasten with a bolt: *Bolt the doors.* **2** to eat hastily; swallow (food) quickly without chewing: *The hungry dog bolted his food.* **3** to blurt out; say hastily. **4** *U.S.* to break away from (one's political party); refuse to support (a party or its candidates): *Several delegates to the convention are expected to bolt the party ticket.* **5** to make up (cloth or wallpaper) into bolts.
—*v.i.* **1** to dash off; run away: *The horse bolted at the sight of the car.* **2** *U.S.* to break away from or refuse to support one's political party or its candidates. **3** to move suddenly or swiftly; dart: *In therefore he bolted and ... turned the key* (Thomas De Quincey). **SYN**: rush, spring. **4** to go to seed very quickly, or become so tall or rank as to be unusable for food: *Some kinds of lettuce bolt in hot weather.*
—*adv.* with one bolt or rush; directly.
bolt from the blue, a sudden, unexpected happening; surprise: *The news of the attack on Pearl Harbor came as a bolt from the blue.*
bolt upright, stiff and straight: *Awakened by the noise of the crash, he sat bolt upright in bed.*
shoot one's bolt, to do as much or as well as one can; expend all one's available resources: *What can they forsee that we don't know about? It's no use asking the producers concerned; they've shot their bolt* (New Scientist).
[Old English *bolt* crossbow arrow] —**bolt′less**, *adj.*

***bolt¹**
definitions 1, 2a, 2b

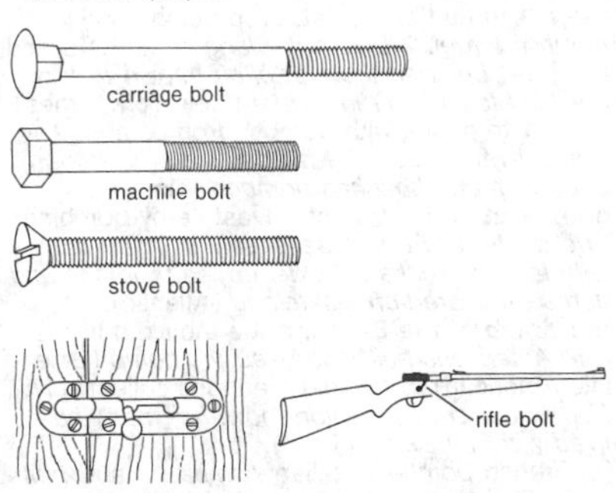

bolt² (bōlt), *v.t.* **1** to sift through a cloth or sieve. Flour is bolted to remove the bran. **2** *Figurative.* to examine by sifting; search into carefully; separate. [< Old French *buleter*]

bolt action, an action on the breech of a gun that consists of a manually operated sliding bolt with a projecting handle. The bolt is pulled back

Pronunciation Key: hat, āge, cãre, fär; let, ēqual, tėrm; it, īce; hot, ōpen, ôrder; oil, out; cup, pu̇t, rüle; child; long; thin; ᴛʜen; zh, measure; ə represents **a** in about, **e** in taken, **i** in pencil, **o** in lemon, **u** in circus.

after each shot to eject the shell and pushed forward to reload.

bolt|er[1] (bōl′tər), *n.* **1** a horse that runs away. **2** *U.S.* a person who breaks away from or refuses to support his political party or its candidates. [< *bolt*[1] + *-er*[1]]

bolt|er[2] (bōl′tər), *n.* a cloth, sieve, or machine used for sifting flour or meal. [< *bolt*[2] + *-er*[1]]

bol|ter[3] (bōl′tər), *v.t., v.i.* = balter.

bolt|head (bōlt′hed′), *n.* **1** the head of a bolt. **2** (formerly) a round or oval matrass.

bolt-hole (bōlt′hōl′), *n.* = loophole.

bolt|ing cloth (bōl′ting), **1** cloth, as of linen or silk, for bolting or sifting meal. **2** the silk to which the stencil is applied in silk-screen printing.

bol|to|ni|a (bōl tō′nē ə), *n.* any one of a genus of perennial plants native to North America and eastern Asia, having white or purplish flowers with yellow centers. [< New Latin *Boltonia* < James *Bolton,* an English botanist in the 1700's]

bolt|rope (bōlt′rōp′), *n.* a rope sewed around the edges of canvas sails to give them shape, prevent ripping, and permit easier attachment to yards.

Boltz|mann constant (bōlts′mən; *German* bôlts′män′), a constant in physics equal to 1.38×10^{-16} ergs per molecule per degree, a fundamental constant in the kinetic theory of gases; molecular gas constant. [< Ludwig *Boltzmann,* 1844-1906, an Austrian physicist, who worked it out]

Boltzmann distribution, an equation that expresses the distribution of energies for a collection of particles at a fixed temperature, based on the Boltzmann constant.

bo|lus (bō′ləs), *n.* **1** a medicine in the form of a large, roundish pill that can be swallowed, used especially in veterinary medicine. **2** a lump of chewed food, ready to be swallowed: *great boluses of spiced mutton ...* (Rudyard Kipling). **3** any small, rounded mass. [< New Latin *bolus* < Late Latin *bōlus* lump (especially of medicated clay) < Greek *bôlos* lump]

bo|ma (bō′mə), *n.* in central Africa: **1** a stockade erected as protection against wild animals. **2** a blind or hiding place for a hunter. **3** the administrative headquarters of a district commissioner. [< Swahili *boma*]

Bo|marc (bō′märk), *n. U.S.* a winged ground-to-air, antiaircraft missile, guided from the ground by radar.

bomb (bom), *n., v.* **—*n.*** **1** a container filled with an explosive. A bomb is exploded by a fuze or by the force with which it hits something or by a time mechanism. Bombs may be filled with a chemical substance and are sometimes dropped from aircraft. **2** any similar explosive device: *a tear gas bomb.* **3** a container filled with an insecticide, paint, cosmetic, or other liquid under pressure that comes out as spray or foam; aerosol bomb. **4** *Figurative.* a sudden, unexpected happening; disturbing surprise. **5** *U.S. Slang.* a failure; flop: *The show was a bomb and closed after three performances.* **6** *British Slang.* a great deal of money; a fortune: *"A bright boy like you. You could make a bomb"* (Punch). **7** *American Football Slang.* a long pass: *[He] has learned the proper way to catch "the bomb"—the high pass* (Time). **8** *Geology.* a great mass of lava thrown out of a volcano.

—*v.t.* **1** to hurl bombs at; drop bombs on: *to bomb a target.* **2** *Baseball Slang.* to hit hard and far: *[He] bombed the first pitch thrown to him to left field for a two-run homer* (New York Times).

—*v.i.* **1** to attack with bombs; drop bombs. **2** *U.S. Slang.* to fail; flop: *... Philadelphia, where many another road show has bombed* (Time).

bomb out, to destroy or devastate by bombing: *The center of Berlin was largely bombed out, with jagged blocks of undestroyed buildings and acres of cleared-off wasteland* (Atlantic).

the bomb or **the Bomb, a** the atomic bomb: *The Americans built and used the bomb* (Scientific American). **b** nuclear weapons collectively: *For a quarter of a century now, he [man] has lived with the Bomb* (Time).

[< French *bombe* < Italian *bomba* < Latin *bombus* a booming sound < Greek *bómbos*]

—bomb′like′, *adj.*

bom|ba|ca|ceous (bom′bə kā′shəs), *adj.* of or having to do with plants of the bombax family. [< New Latin *Bombacaceae* bombax family (< *Bombax* the typical genus) + English *-ous*]

bom|ba|chas (bōm bä′chəs), *n.pl.* the wide, baggy trousers worn by gauchos. [< American Spanish *bombachas*]

bom|bard (*v.* bom bärd′; *n.* bom′bärd), *v., n.* **—*v.t.*** **1** to attack with heavy fire of shot and shell from big guns or rockets: *Artillery bombarded the enemy lines.* **SYN**: shell. **2** to drop bombs on; bomb: *Aircraft bombarded the factories and destroyed them.* **3** *Figurative.* to keep attacking vigorously: *She bombarded me with one question after another.* **SYN**: assail. **4a** to strike (the nucleus of an atom) with a stream of fast-moving particles to change the structure of the nucleus. **b** to cause (particles) to strike a substance. [< noun]

—*n.* **1** the earliest kind of cannon, throwing a stone ball or very large shot. **2** a small warship armed with mortars for throwing bombs; bomb ketch. **3** = bombardon.

[< Middle French *bombarde* cannon < Latin *bombus* a booming sound < Greek *bómbos*]

—bom|bard′er, *n.* **—bom|bard′ment**, *n.*

bom|barde (bom bärd′), *n.* **1** a powerful bass reed stop on the organ. **2** the manual with that stop. [< French *bombarde*]

bom|bar|dier (bom′bə dir′, -bər-), *n.* **1** the member of the crew of a bomber who operates the bombsight and the bomb-release mechanism. He controls the course of the aircraft in its final approach to the target. **2** *British.* a noncommissioned officer in the British artillery. **3** *Obsolete.* an artilleryman. [< Middle French *bombardier* < *bombarde* cannon, bombard]

bombardier beetle, any one of various ground beetles which discharge a small cloud of irritating vapor with an audible sound when in danger.

bom|bar|don (bom′bər dən, bom bär′-), *n.* **1** an old, deep-toned wind instrument, of the oboe or bassoon family. **2** a similar quality of organ stop. **3** a bass tuba. [< Italian *bombardone* (augmentative) < *bombardo* a bombard]

bom|ba|sine (bom′bə zēn′, bom′bə zēn), *n.* = bombazine.

bom|bast (bom′bast), *n., adj.* **—*n.*** **1a** showy or high-flown language that is without much meaning: *A few plain facts are better than a lot of bombast.* **b** overstatement; tall talk. **2** cotton wool used to stuff or pad garments.

—*adj.* = bombastic.

[< Old French *bombace,* learned borrowing from Medieval Latin *bombax* cotton < Medieval Greek *bómbax, -akos* cotton wadding, variant of *bámbax* cotton < Greek *bómbȳx, -ȳkos* silkworm (cocoon), silk]

bom|bas|tic (bom bas′tik), *adj.* using many showy or high-flown words with too little thought: *a bombastic speech.* **SYN**: high-sounding, turgid, inflated. **—bom|bas′ti|cal|ly**, *adv.*

bom|bas|ti|cal (bom bas′tə kəl), *adj.* = bombastic.

bom|bax family (bom′baks), a group of dicotyledonous, tropical trees having a dry or fleshy fruit containing seeds which, in various species, are enveloped by a silky down or fiber. The family includes the silk-cotton tree, balsa, baobab, and sour gourd. [< New Latin *Bombax* a typical genus of this family < Medieval Latin *bombax* cotton; see etym. under **bombast**]

Bom|bay duck (bom′bā, bom bā′), a small fish, salted and dried, served as a condiment or relish with curries. [< *Bombay,* a city in India]

bom|ba|zine (bom′bə zēn′, bom′bə zēn), *n.* a twilled or corded cloth made of silk and wool or of cotton and wool, often dyed black. [< Middle French *bombasin* < Italian *bombagino* made of cotton, ultimately < Medieval Greek *bámbax* cotton; see etym. under **bombast**]

bomb bay, a compartment in the fuselage of a bomber in which bombs are carried and from which they are dropped.

bombe (bônb), *n. French.* a melon-shaped or round mold filled with ice cream.

bom|bé (bôn bā′), *adj. French.* rounded; curved outward: *a bombé commode.*

bombed (bomd), *adj. Especially U.S. Slang.* stupefied by alcohol or (sometimes) narcotics; completely intoxicated.

bomb|er (bom′ər), *n.* **1** an airplane used to drop bombs on the enemy: *The bombers flew over the enemy city releasing bombs that set many targets afire.* **2** a person who throws or drops bombs or who sets explosive charges as acts of sabotage or vandalism.

bom|bil|la (bom bēl′yə), *n.* a small tube with a perforated bulb at one end, used in South America for drinking maté. [< American Spanish *bombilla*]

bom|bi|nate (bom′bə nāt), *v.i.,* **-nat|ed, -nat|ing.** to hum; buzz. [< unrecorded Latin *bombināre* (+ English *-ate*[1]), doubtful variant of *bombitāre* < *bombus* a booming or humming sound] **—bom′bi|na′tion**, *n.*

bomb|ing run (bom′ing), = bomb run.

bomb ketch, a small, ketch-rigged vessel armed with mortars.

bomb|let (bom′lit), *n.* a small bomb.

bomb line, a line drawn on an aerial map to distinguish the position of friendly ground forces from that of the enemy.

bomb|load (bom′lōd′), *n.* the load of bombs carried by a bomber or other aircraft.

bom|bo|ra (bom bô′rə), *n. Australian.* a dangerous offshore surf breaking over a reef. [< a native word]

bomb|proof (bom′prüf′), *adj., n.* **—*adj.*** strong enough to be safe from the effects of bombs and shells.

—*n.* a bombproof shelter.

bomb rack, a latching device for holding bombs in a bomb bay.

bomb run, **1** the flight course of a bombing airplane over a target area just before the release of bombs. **2** the action of flying this course.

bomb|shell (bom′shel′), *n.* **1** a bomb (def. 1). **2** *Figurative.* a sudden, unexpected event or person; disturbing surprise: *The news of his quitting school was a bombshell in a family where everyone had gone to college.*

bomb|sight (bom′sīt′), *n.* an instrument for determining the point in the flight of a bomber at which releasing a bomb will cause it to fall on the target. A bombsight for bombing from high altitudes is a complex instrument which correlates optical sighting with various data on air speed and altitude.

bom|by|cid (bom′bə sid), *n., adj.* **—*n.*** any one of a family of moths formerly including the silkworm moth and various other moths, but now usually restricted by entomologists to the silkworm moth.

—*adj.* of or belonging to the bombycids.

[< New Latin *Bombycidae* the family name < Latin *bombyx* < Greek *bómbȳx, -ȳkos* silkworm]

bo|moh (bō′mō), *n.* a Malaysian medicine man. [< Malay]

Bon (bon), *n.* a Buddhist festival held July 13-16 in Japan, when lanterns are hung to guide returning souls of the dead to their graves and houses; Feast of Lanterns. [< Japanese *bon*]

bo|na|ci (bō′nä sē′), *n.* any fish of several groupers found in the waters around Florida and the West Indies. Also, **bonasi.** [< American Spanish *bonasí*]

bo|na fide (bō′nə fīd′; bon′ə fīd′; bō′nə fī′dē), **1** in good faith; without deceit or fraud. **2** done in good faith; genuine: *a bona fide offer.* [< Latin *bonā fidē*]

► **Bona fide**, a Latin adjective plus noun, both in the ablative case, has come to be used in English as an adverb or attributive adjective: *undertaken bona fide, a bona fide contract.* **Bona fides**, nominative case in Latin, is used only as a substantive and, as in Latin, is construed as a singular: *His bona fides is yet to be demonstrated.*

bo|na fi|des (bō′nə fī′dēz), proof of good faith, proper authority, sincere feeling, or genuine confidence; credentials or references. [< Latin *bona fidēs*] ► See **bona fide** for usage note.

bon a|mi (bôn nä mē′), *French* (*masculine use*). **1** a good friend. **2** a sweetheart.

bo|nang (bō nang′), *n.* a Javanese musical instrument consisting of gongs attached in a row to a wooden frame, and played by striking with the hands or with special mallets. [< a Javanese word]

bo|nan|za (bə nan′zə), *n.* **1** a rich mass of ore in a mine. **2** *Figurative: The oil found on the old farmer's land was a bonanza to him.* [American English < American Spanish *bonanza* a rich lode < Spanish, fair weather, prosperity < Latin *bonus* good]

Bo|na|parte's gull (bō′nə pärts), a small gull of the coasts and large lakes of Canada and the United States. It has a dark-gray head and red legs and feet. [< C. L. J. L. *Bonaparte,* 1803-1857, an American ornithologist]

Bo|na|part|ism (bō′nə pär′tiz əm), *n.* **1** the policy or political system of Napoleon Bonaparte, especially as exercised in similar ways by any dictatorial military figure acting in matters of state. **2** devotion to the Bonaparte family or its dynastic claims. **—Bo′na|part′ist**, *n.*

bon ap|pé|tit (bôn nap ə tē′), *French.* **1** good eating! **2** (literally) good appetite!

bo|na|si (bō′nä sē′), *n.* = bonaci.

bon|bon (bon′bon′), *n.* **1** a piece of candy, usually soft and often having a fancy shape. Bonbons have a coating of creamy sugar or chocolate and a filling of jelly, nuts, or the like. **2** any confection made of sugar. **3** a cracker that explodes. [< French *bonbon* < *bon* good]

bon|bon|nière (bôn bô nyer′), *n. French.* **1** a candy box. **2** a person or establishment that makes or sells candy.

bonce (bons), *n. British Slang.* the head: *to get a bash on the bonce.* [< dialectal English *bonce* a large marble]

bond[1] (bond), *n., v.* **—*n.*** **1a** anything that binds or fastens, such as a rope, cord, or other band: *The strong bonds of rope snapped one by one as the heavy canvas cover tore away in the raging wind.* **b** *Figurative: There is a bond of affection between the two sisters. Speech being the great bond that holds society together ...* (John Locke). **2** a certificate issued by a government or private company which promises to pay back with interest the money borrowed from the buyer of the certificate: *The city issued bonds to raise money for putting in new sewers.* **3a** a written

agreement by which a person says he will pay a certain sum of money if he does not perform certain duties properly: *The messenger had signed a bond to cover his job of carrying money for the bank.* **b** the sum of money put up as security. **4** any agreement or binding engagement: *Is it so nominated in the bond?* (Shakespeare). **5** a person who acts as surety for another. **6** the condition of goods placed in special warehouses until the taxes or duties are paid. **7** a way of arranging bricks or stones, or boards, to bind them together. **8** a brick, stone, or board that binds together. **9a** a substance that binds together the other ingredients of a mixture; binder: *Cement is the bond in concrete.* **b** any substance that binds two things together: *The floor tiles were fastened over the old flooring with a bond of linoleum cement.* **10** the condition of sticking together or holding fast: *Heat sealed the bond on the plastic wrapping over the meat.* **11** *Chemistry.* a unit of force by means of which atoms or groups of atoms are combined or joined together in a molecule, equivalent to that of one hydrogen atom, and often represented in formulas by a dash (—) or a dot (·). A chemical bond usually consists of a pair of shared electrons. The valence of an element or radical is indicated by the number of its bonds. **12** = bond paper.
—v.t. **1** to provide a bond against financial loss for: *to bond an employee. An insurance company has bonded the city treasurer for one million dollars.* **2** to bind together: *He bonded the tiles to the floor with cement.* **3** *Figurative.* to connect by strong emotional or social ties: *He was bonded immediately after birth to 13 relatives* (Lucinda Franks). **4** to arrange (bricks, etc.) so as to lock or bind them together. **5a** to issue bonds on; mortgage: *to bond a railroad.* **b** to convert into bonds: *to bond a debt.*
—v.i. **1** to hold together so as to give solidity, as bricks in a wall: *Concrete bonds to steel by shrinkage and natural adhesion.* **2** *Figurative.* to establish strong emotional or social ties with another or others.
bonds, a shackles; chains; fetters; manacles: *the bonds of slavery.* **b** *Archaic.* imprisonment; confinement: *... to endure Exile, or ignominy, or bonds, or pain* (Milton).
in bond, stored in a bonded warehouse: *A merchant may not wish to sell immediately the goods he imports, he is therefore permitted to place them in bond* (Henry Fawcett).
[variant of *band*[3] a fetter]—**bond′a|ble,** *adj.*
—Syn. n. **1 Bond, tie,** used figuratively, mean something that joins people together. **Bond** applies particularly to a connection that brings two people or a group so closely together that they may be considered as one: *The members of the club are joined by bonds of fellowship.* **Tie** may be used interchangeably with *bond,* but applies particularly to a connection, based on a sense of social obligation, that keeps together people who still remain individuals, and sometimes pulls them together against their personal wishes: *family ties. When he went away, he severed all ties with his old life.*

bond[2] (bond), *n., adj.* —*n. Archaic.* a serf.
—adj. in slavery; not free: *... whether we be bond or free* (I Corinthians 12:13).
[Old English *bonda* husbandman; later, serf < Scandinavian (compare Old Icelandic *bōndi* landholder, dweller)]

bond|age (bon′dij), *n.* **1** lack of freedom; slavery; servitude: *to love bondage more than liberty* (Milton). SYN: serfdom. **2** the condition of being under some power or influence: (*Figurative.*) *A drunkard is in bondage to alcohol.* SYN: captivity, subjugation. [< Medieval Latin *bondagium* < Middle English *bond* a serf]

bond|ed (bon′did), *adj.* **1** secured by bonds: *a bonded debt.* **2** put in a warehouse until taxes are paid: *Whiskey and tobacco are usually bonded goods.*

bonded warehouse, a warehouse where bonded goods are held.

bonded whiskey, *U.S.* whiskey that has been stored in barrels under bond for four or more years before being bottled.

bond|er (bon′dər), *n.* **1** a binding stone or brick. **2** a person who puts goods into bond or owns goods in bond. **3** anything that holds two or more things together.

bond|er|ize (bon′də rīz), *v.t.,* **-ized, -iz|ing.** to put a protective coating on iron, steel, zinc, cadmium, or aluminum surfaces. [< *Bonderized,* a trademark]

bond|hold|er (bond′hōl′dər), *n.* a person who owns a bond or bonds issued by a government or company; a creditor as distinguished from an owner (stockholder).

bon|dieu|se|rie (bôn dyü′zə rē′), *n.* religious art work or artistry of inferior quality. [< French *bondieuserie* < *bon Dieu* good God]

bond|maid (bond′mād′), *n.* a girl or woman slave.

bond|man (bond′mən), *n., pl.* **-men. 1** a slave. **2** a person who belonged with the land and was sold with it in the Middle Ages; serf; villein.

bond paper, paper of superior manufacture, especially paper with a high rag content.

bond servant, 1 a servant who must work for a period without pay. **2** a slave.

bond|slave (bond′slāv′), *n.* a person who is in bondage or slavery.

bonds|man (bondz′mən), *n., pl.* **-men. 1** a person who becomes responsible for another by giving a bond. **2** a bondman.

bond|stone (bond′stōn′), *n.* a stone extending through or partly through a wall, serving as a bond.

bon|duc (bon′duk), *n.* a tropical shrub of the pea family with hard, gray seeds called "nicker nuts," which are used as beads; nicker. [< French *bonduc* < Arabic *bunduq*]

bond|wom|an (bond′wu̇m′ən), *n., pl.* **-wom|en.** a woman bondman.

***bone** (bōn), *n., v.,* **boned, bon|ing,** *adj., adv.* —*n.* **1** one of the pieces of the skeleton of an animal with a backbone: *the bones of the hand, a beef bone for soup.* **2** the hard substance of which bones are made. It consists of animal matter, ossein, and carbonate and phosphate of lime in varying proportions. **3** something like bone. Ivory is sometimes called bone. **4** any article manufactured of bone, ivory, or whalebone, especially a strip of whalebone used to stiffen garments. **5** a pale beige.
—v.t. **1** to take bones out of: *We boned the fish before eating it.* **2** to stiffen (garments) by putting in strips of whalebone, steel, or other springy material. *—v.i.* **1** to apply oneself diligently or determinedly. **2** *Slang.* to study hard.
—adj. pale-beige.
—adv. completely; totally; utterly: *a Europe weary, bone weary, of the wars* (Wall Street Journal).
bones, a *U.S. Slang.* dice: *On the board he whirled a pair of bones* (John Skelton). **b** wooden clappers used in keeping time to music, especially as an accompaniment to a banjo or similar instrument: *Amateur negro melodists ... thumbed the banjo and rattled the bones* (London Times). **c** (*sing. in use*) an end man in a minstrel show, sometimes called "Mr. Bones"; a performer on the bones: *A single row of negro minstrels seated on chairs ... while at the end* [*is*] *Bones* (Saturday Review). **d** skeleton: *nothing but skin and bones.* **e** bodily frame; body; person: *Night hangs upon mine eyes, my bones would rest* (Shakespeare).
bone up on, to become familiar with: *to bone up on medieval art.*
feel (or **feel it**) **in one's bones,** to have a sure intuition of (something); feel certain about (something): *I felt in my bones no good could come of it* (J. H. Beadle).
have a bone to pick, to have cause for argument or complaint.
make no bones about, *Informal.* to show no hesitation about; acknowledge readily: *The town's teenagers make no bones about their displeasure with the curfew* (Parade).
near the bone, a very exacting or mean: *The captain's unreasonably stern ideas of discipline were too near the bone and the crew rebelled.* **b** almost obscene: *The story was very near the bone and most embarrassing.*
throw a bone, to grant a concession so as to soothe or quiet: *He was also quick to throw a bone in the workers' direction, ordering the minimum wage ... doubled immediately* (Time).
to the bone, a so as to strike the bone: *He cut his finger to the bone.* **b** *Figurative.* to the limit: *He slashed his expenditures to the bone, living like a pauper.*
[Old English *bān*]—**bone′less,** *adj.* —**bone′less|ly,** *adv.* —**bone′like′,** *adj.*

***bone**
definition 1
shapes of bones:
flat: rib
long: femur
irregular: vertebra
sesamoid: patella
short: carpal

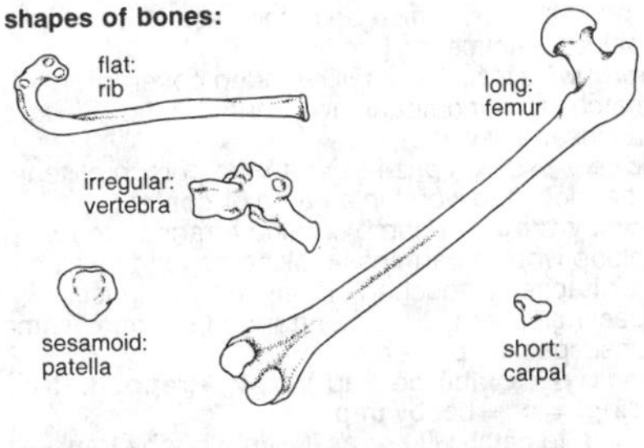

bone ash, phosphate of lime.

bone|black (bōn′blak′), *n.,* or **bone black,** a black powder made by carbonizing bones in closed containers. It is used to remove color from liquids and as a coloring matter.

bone cell, = osteoblast.

bone china, a type of strong, translucent chinaware made of clay mixed with bone ash.

bone conduction, the conduction of sound waves to the auditory nerves of the cochlea via the bony part of the head.

boned (bōnd), *adj.* **1** having a certain kind of bones: *Healthy livestock is usually larger boned than the sickly animals.* **2** with the bones removed: *boned fish ready to fry and eat.*

-boned, *combining form.* **1** having a certain kind of bones: *Big-boned = having big bones.* **2** furnished or stiffened with bone, especially whalebone: *a well-boned corset = a corset well stiffened with whalebone.*

bone-dry (bōn′drī′), *adj.* very dry.

bone fat, fatty matter, of soft, semisolid consistency, extracted from bones by melting or by the use of solvents, used as fertilizer.

bone|fish (bōn′fish′), *n., pl.* **-fish|es** or (*collectively*) **-fish.** any one of various game fishes found principally in southern and tropical waters.

bone|head (bōn′hed′), *n., adj. Informal.* —*n.* a stupid person; blockhead.
—adj. stupid; foolish.

bone|head|ed (bōn′hed′id), *adj. Informal.* stupid. —**bone′head′ed|ness,** *n.*

bone meal, the coarser siftings of crushed or ground bones, used as fertilizer or added to feed for animals.

bone of contention, the cause of a dispute; matter of controversy.

bone oil, a very dark, thick oil obtained by the dry distillation of bones.

bone porcelain, = bone china.

bon|er (bō′nər), *n. Slang.* a foolish mistake; stupid error; blunder; blooper.

bone|set (bōn′set′), *n.* any plant of a genus of plants of the composite family with flat clusters of white, rose, or purple flowers; thoroughwort.

boneset tea, *U.S.* an infusion of boneset leaves used as an old-fashioned tonic.

bone|set|ter (bōn′set′ər), *n.* a person whose work is setting broken bones.

bone shaker, 1 an informal term for an early bicycle. **2** a rough vehicle; rattletrap.

bone spavin, a bony deposit or a growing together of the bones of the hock of a horse.

bone turquoise, = odontolite.

bone yard, *U.S.* **1** *Informal.* **a** a place to which vehicles or pieces of unwanted machinery are sent for breaking up into scrap. **b** any place where unwanted, out-of-date things are kept. **2** *Slang.* a cemetery. **3** the extra playing pieces in some games, especially dominoes.

bon|fire (bon′fīr′), *n.* a large fire built outdoors: *The boys made a bonfire of rubbish and driftwood at the beach picnic.* [earlier *bonefire* a fire to burn bones or, later, corpses]

bong[1] (bông, bong), *n., v.* —*n.* a dull, hollow sound, such as that of a large bell.
—v.i., v.t. to make or express with this sound. [imitative]

bong[2] (bông, bong), *n.* a water pipe for smoking marijuana: *A bong is a long, vertical pipe with a large smoke chamber and a hole that creates a carburetor effect* (New York Times Magazine). [origin unknown]

bon|go[1] (bong′gō), *n., pl.* **-gos.** a kind of small drum played with flattened hands, especially in Latin-American and African music. Bongos usually come in pairs and are held between the knees. See picture under **drum**[1]. [< American Spanish *bongo*]

bon|go[2] (bong′gō), *n., pl.* **-gos.** a large West African antelope having a chestnut-colored body with white stripes. [compare Lingala (African language) *mongu*]

bongo drum, = bongo[1].

bon gré, mal gré (bôɴ′grā mäl′grā), *French.* willingly or not; willy-nilly.

bon|heur-du-jour (bə nėr′dü zhür′; *French* bô nœr dʏ zhür′), *n.* a lady's small desk with drawers, especially popular in the late 1700's and early 1800's. [< French *bonheur du jour* (literally) joy of the day]

bon|ho|mie or **bon|hom|mie** (bon′ə mē′), *n.* good nature; courteous and pleasant ways. [< French *bonhomie* < *bonhomme* good fellow]

bon|ho|mous (bon′ə məs), *adj.* good-natured; pleasant. —**bon′ho|mous|ly,** *adv.*

bon|i|face (bon′ə fās), *n.* **1** the keeper of an inn. **2** the owner of a hotel, restaurant, or other public house. [< *Boniface,* the innkeeper in George Farquhar's play *The Beaux' Stratagem*]

Pronunciation Key: **hat, āge, cãre, fär; let, ēqual, tėrm; it, īce; hot, ōpen, ôrder; oil, out; cup, pu̇t, rüle; child; long; thin; ᴛʜen; zh,** measure; **ə** represents **a** in about, **e** in taken, **i** in pencil, **o** in lemon, **u** in circus.

Bo|nine (bō′nēn), *n. Trademark.* a drug that gives protection against motion sickness. *Formula:* $C_{25}H_{27}ClN_2 \cdot 2HCl$

bo|ni|to (bə nē′tō), *n., pl.* **-tos, -toes,** or (*collectively*) **-to. 1** any fish of a type of saltwater fish with very red, edible flesh, related to the mackerel and the tuna. **2** any one of various related fishes, such as the oceanic bonito or skipjack. [probably < Spanish *bonito* pretty < Latin *bonus* good]

bon jour (bôɴ zhür′), *French.* good morning; good day.

bonk (bongk), *v., n. Slang.* **—*v.t.*** to hit; bop: *Tristessa just bonks her skull and falls headlong* (Jack Kerouac).
—*v.i.* to make a loud, knocking sound: *The steam came cracking and bonking in the radiator* (New Yorker).
—*n.* a loud, hard knock: *to get a bonk on the head.*
[imitative]

bon|kers (bong′kərz), *adj. British Slang.* crazy; mad. [origin unknown]

bon mar|ché (bôɴ mär shā′), *French.* a good bargain.

bon mot (bôɴ mō′), *pl.* **bons mots** (bôɴ mōz′; bôɴ mō′). *French.* a clever saying; witty remark.

bonne (bôn), *n. French.* **1** a maidservant. **2** a child's nurse; nursemaid.

bonne a|mie (bôn á mē′), *French.* the feminine form of **bon ami.**

bonne bouche (bôn büsh′), *French.* a dainty morsel saved for the end of a meal.

bonne foi (bôn fwá′), *French.* good faith.

bonne nuit (bôn nwē′), *French.* good night.

***bon|net** (bon′it), *n., v.* **—*n.* 1** a covering for the head, usually tied under the chin with strings or ribbons, worn by women and children. **2** a cap worn by men and boys in Scotland. **3** a headdress of feathers worn by North American Indians. **4** a cover or cap over part of a machine or object: **a** a cowl for a chimney. **b** *British.* the hood covering the engine of an automobile, truck, etc. **c** a metal plate covering the openings in the valve chambers of a pump. **5** *Nautical.* a piece of canvas laced to the bottom of a sail, especially a jib, to increase the sail area in light winds. **6** a horny area on the tip of the snout of right whales.
—*v.t.* to put a bonnet on.
[< Middle French *bonnet* hat; fabric for hats < Medieval Latin *abonnis* kind of hat]

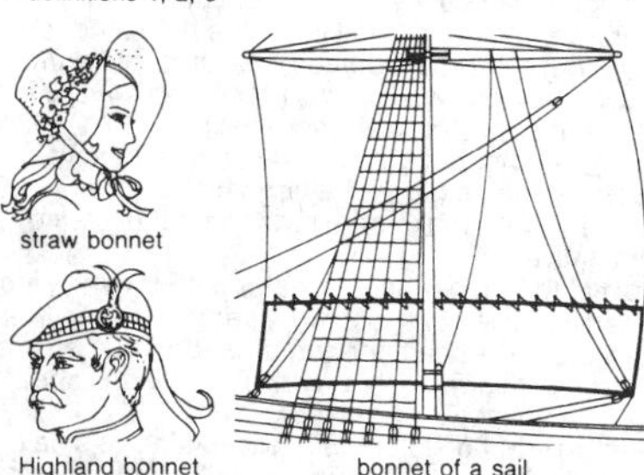
*** bonnet**
definitions 1, 2, 5
straw bonnet
Highland bonnet
bonnet of a sail

bon|net|head (bon′it hed′), *n.* a species of hammerhead shark, abundant on the Atlantic coast of the United States.

bonnet monkey, a monkey of India and Sri Lanka (Ceylon), having a tuft of hair on its head that somewhat resembles a bonnet.

bonnet pepper, a tropical American pepper plant of the nightshade family, from whose fruit a kind of paprika is obtained.

bonnet piece, a gold coin issued by James V of Scotland, so called from the representation of a Scottish bonnet on the king's head.

bon|net rouge (bô ne rüzh′), *pl.* **bon|nets rouges** (bô ne rüzh′). *French.* **1** the red cap worn by the radicals in the French Revolution. **2** a radical;anarchist.

bonnet shark, = shovelhead.

bon|ny or bon|nie (bon′ē), *adj.,* **-ni|er, -ni|est. 1** fair to see; rosy and pretty: *What a bonny baby!* **2** fine; excellent. **3** healthy-looking. **4** gay and cheerful. [Middle English *bonne,* apparently < Old French *bone* (feminine) good < Latin *bonus* good]—**bon′ni|ly,** *adv.* —**bon′ni|ness,** *n.*

bon|ny|clab|ber (bon′ē klab′ər), *n.* **1** = clabber. **2** = cottage cheese. [< Irish, Scottish Gaelic *bainne clabir* milk of the dasher, clapper (unrecorded meaning)]

***bon|sai** (bon′sī), *n., pl.* **bon|sai. 1** a miniature shrub or tree, dwarfed by controlling its root area and its food supply, and used in a dish or pot for decoration. **2** the Japanese art of growing miniature shrubs and trees. [< Japanese *bonsai*]

*** bonsai**
definition 1

bon soir (bôɴ swär′), *French.* good evening; good night.

bon|spiel (bon′spēl, -spəl), *n.* a curling match or tournament. [perhaps < Dutch *bond* contract, alliance + *spel* play]

bon|te|bok (bon′tē bok), *n.* a large South African antelope, closely related to the blesbok, of a reddish color with a white face and rump. [< Afrikaans *bontebok* < *bont* mottled + *bok* goat, buck[1]]

bon ton (bôɴ tôɴ′), *French.* **1** good style; fashion. **2** fashionable society. **3** good breeding.

bont tick (bont), a South African tick with variegated coloring, parasitic on cattle, ostriches, and man. [< Afrikaans *bont* mottled]

bo|nus (bō′nəs), *n.* something extra, given in addition to what is due: *The company gave each worker a vacation bonus.* [< Latin *bonus* good]

bon vi|vant (bôɴ vē väɴ′), *pl.* **bons vi|vants** (bôɴ vē väɴ′). *French.* a person who is fond of good food and luxury.

bon vi|veur (bôɴ vē vœr′), *French.* a person who leads a life of pleasure.

bon voy|age (bon voi äzh′; *French* bôɴ vwá yázh′). good-by; good luck; pleasant trip. [< French]

bon|y (bō′nē), *adj.,* **bon|i|er, bon|i|est. 1** of bone: *the bony structure of the skull* **2** like bone. **3** full of bones: *bony fish.* **4** having big bones that stick out: *the bony hips of a thin horse.* **5** very thin: *bony, old hands.* —**bon′i|ness,** *n.*

bony fish, 1 a fish with a bony rather than cartilaginous skeleton. **2** any one of various bony fishes, especially the menhaden.

bony labyrinth, the bony part of the inner ear.

bonze (bonz), *n.* a Buddhist monk, specifically of Japan but also of China or other countries of the Far East. [< Portuguese *bonzo* < Japanese *bonzō* < Chinese]

bon|zer (bon′zər), *adj. Australian Slang.* excellent; extremely good. [perhaps < *bonanza*]

boo[1] (bü), *n., pl.* **boos,** *interj., v.,* **booed, boo|ing.** **—*n.* , *interj.*** a sound made to show dislike or contempt, or to frighten: *Boos were heard from those who didn't like the concert* (n.). *We were frightened when he jumped out shouting, "Boo!"* (interj.). **—*v.i.*** to make such a sound. **—*v.t.*** to shout "boo" at: *He sang so badly that the audience booed him.* —**boo′er,** *n.*

boo[2] (bü), *n. U.S. Slang.* marijuana. [origin unknown]

boob (büb), *n., v.* **—*n. Slang.* 1** a stupid person; fool; dunce. **2** a blunder; mistake.
—*v.i.* to blunder. [American English < *booby*]

boo|bird (bü′bėrd′), *n. U.S. Slang.* a sports fan who boos members of the team he roots for when they play poorly.

boo|boi|sie (bü bwä zē′), *n. U.S. Slang.* boobs as a class or group: *He [H. L. Mencken] made the American public, which he called the "booboisie," the special target of his criticism* (I. W. Cole). [< *boob* + (bourg)*oisie*]

boo-boo (bü′bü′), *n. U.S. Slang.* a foolish blunder.

boo|book owl (bü′bu̇k, -bük), a small Australian owl of a rusty red color. [imitative]

boob tube, *Slang.* a television set.

boo|by (bü′bē), *n., pl.* **-bies. 1** a stupid person; fool; dunce. **2** Also, **booby gannet.** a kind of large, tropical or subtropical sea bird. Boobies belong to the gannet family. **3** the person or team that does the worst in a contest or game. [probably < Spanish *bobo* fool, sea bird < Latin *balbus* stammering]

booby hatch, 1 a small, wooden cover for a hatchway or companionway on a boat. **2** *Slang.* an insane asylum.

booby prize, a prize given to the person or team that does the worst in a game or contest.

booby trap, 1 a bomb or mine arranged to explode when a harmless-looking object to which it is attached is touched or moved by an unsuspecting person. **2** a trick arranged to annoy some unsuspecting person.

boo|by-trap (bü′bē trap′), *n., v.,* **-trapped, -trapping.** **—*n.*** = booby trap.
—*v.t.* to catch with or as if with a booby trap.

boo|dle (bü′dəl), *n., v.,* **-dled, -dling.** *Slang.* **—*n.* 1** *U.S.* money from bribes; graft. **2** a group of people or things; caboodle, used especially in the phrase *the whole kit and boodle.* **3** counterfeit money. **—*v.t.* , *v.i.*** *U.S.* to bribe; practice bribery. [American English < Dutch *boedel* goods]
—**boo′dler,** *n.*

boo|ga|loo (bü′gə lü′), *n., v. U.S.* **—*n.*** a dance in two-beat rhythm, performed with shuffling feet, swiveling motions, and rotation of shoulders and hips. **—*v.i.*** to dance the boogaloo.
[origin unknown]

boog|ie (bu̇g′ē, bü′gē), *n.* = boogie-woogie.

boogie beat, the rhythm of boogie-woogie.

boog|ie-woog|ie (bu̇g′ē wu̇g′ē, bü′gē wü′gē), *n.* a form of blues played especially on the piano, marked by a repeating bass rhythm under a freely and elaborately varied, syncopated melody. [perhaps < *boogie,* variant of *bogy*[1] jazz musician + a rhyming word]

boo|hoo (bü′hü′), *v.,* **-hooed, -hoo|ing,** *n., pl.* **-hoos,** *interj.* **—*v.i.*** to cry loudly; weep noisily.
—*n.* noisy weeping.
—*interj.* loud crying.

book (bu̇k), *n., v., adj.* **—*n.* 1** written or printed sheets of paper bound together between covers: *She read the first two chapters of her book.* **SYN:** volume. **2** blank sheets bound together: *You can keep a record of what you spend in this book.* **3** a main division of a book: *a poem divided into twelve books. Genesis is the first book of the Old Testament.* **4** anything thought of as containing lessons or instructions: *the book of nature.* **5a** the words of an opera, operetta, or other musical drama or comedy; libretto: *W. S. Gilbert wrote the books of the Gilbert and Sullivan light operas.* **b** the script of a play. **6a** a record of bets, especially on a horse race. **b** *U.S. Informal.* = bookmaker. **7** something fastened together like a book: *a book of tickets, stamps, or checks.* **8** a specified number of tricks forming a set in a card game. **9** a large bundle consisting of 15 double skeins or 30 small skeins of raw silk. *Abbr:* bk.
—*v.t.* 1 to make reservations to get tickets or to engage service: *He has booked passage by air from New York to London.* **SYN:** reserve. **2** to make accommodations for: *to book a passenger from New York to Boston on a plane.* **3** to make engagements for; engage: *The lecturer is booked for every night of the week.* **4a** to enter a charge against (a person) in a police record: *He booked the suspect on a charge of breaking and entering.* **b** to enter, write, or register in a book or list. **SYN:** record.
—*v.i.* to engage passage, a seat, a place, or other accommodation, beforehand: *Sam Weller booked for them all* (Dickens).
—*adj.* 1 of or having to do with books: *a book salesman, the book trade.* **2** according to books; learned from books: *book lore.* **3** shown on books of account: *a book loss of 10 cents a share of stock, a net book profit of $1 million from the sale.*

be in (someone's) **bad books,** be in disfavor with one: *The Arminians . . . at that time were in his bad books* (W. Perry).

book in, a to enter the arrival of an employee in a book: *Wanted young lady, . . . one able to book in* (London Daily Chronicle). **b** to register one's arrival: *In any fleet garage at shift time, at any cashier's cage where the men book in . . .* (New York Times Magazine).

book off, *British.* to record one's going off duty in a book: *Tonight he drives his engine for the last time. Tomorrow he "books off" . . . and the Line knows him no more* (Observer).

books, the complete records of a business: especially records of business accounts: *If you received the note from us, it must be entered in our books* (Maria Edgeworth).

bring to book, a to demand an explanation from: *His employer brought him to book over the missing stock.* **b** to call to account; rebuke: *We shall have to bring him to book about his poor standard of work.* **c** to examine the evidence for; investigate: *By means of these figures we bring the matter, as it were, to book, and eliminate tangible results* (Cassel's Technical Education).

by the book, a by rule; accurately: *He played the game carelessly and not by the book.* **b** with careful attention to prescribed detail: *to work by the book.*

close the books, a to stop entering items in an account book to balance the account, draw up statements, or the like: *The books were closed for the audit.* **b** *Figurative.* to bring anything to an end: *After the criminal's trial and conviction, the district attorney finally closed the books on the case.*

in one's book, *U.S. Informal.* in one's opinion or judgment: *In my book, he's the best writer of fiction now living.*

in one's good books, in favor with one; in one's good opinion: *The new pupil wanted to be in the teacher's good books.*

in the book, on record; known: *He . . . has amassed a total of 46 convictions for almost every con game in the book* (Maclean's).

keep a book, to run a betting system, usually

small and unlawful: *The police raided the house where he was keeping a book.*
keep books, to keep a record of business accounts: *An accountant keeps books for the grocer.*
like a book, with fullness or accuracy; completely: *Good teachers know their students like a book.*
make book, *U.S.* to take bets: *I'll make book on him. If anybody in the world can save* [*it*], *he can* (New Yorker).
one for the book, something exceptional or extraordinary: *Two half brothers in the same race is a rarity; three is one for the book* (New Yorker).
on the books, enrolled on the official list, especially of students or members, or listed as part of a group of patients, clients, customers with charge account privileges, or the like: *She ... continued on the books as an outpatient* (H. Watson).
suit one's book, to be favorable to one's aims: [*She will*] *sell other nations down the river when it suits her book* (Manchester Guardian Weekly).
the book, **a** the Bible: *"Swear," added Enoch sternly, "on the book," And on the book, half-frightened, Miriam swore* (Tennyson). **b** the telephone book: *Give me a call soon; my name is in the book.*
throw the book at, *U.S. Slang.* to punish to the full limit of the law: *The judge threw the book at the man who had slugged a policeman.*
without book, **a** by memory; without reading; without notes: *He ... speaks three or four languages word for word without book* (Shakespeare). **b** without authority: *To show you that I do not speak wholly without book* (John Locke).
[Old English *bōc*] —**book'a|ble**, *adj.*
► **Book** often refers especially to the contents, **volume** to the physical appearance. A *book* may be two or more *volumes.*

book bank, a place where used books are collected and usually sold to raise funds for a charitable cause.

book|bind|er (bůk'bīn'dər), *n.* **1** a person whose work or business is binding books; binder. **2** a binder for preserving loose printed sheets, separate issues of a publication, or the like.

book|bind|er|y (bůk'bīn'dər ē, -drē), *n., pl.* **-er|ies**. *U.S.* an establishment for binding books; bindery.

book|bind|ing (bůk'bīn'ding), *n.* **1** the binding on a book. **2** the act, art, or business of binding books.

book burning, the destruction or removal of books as a means of suppressing or restricting the free exchange of ideas, opinions, and beliefs.

book|case (bůk'kās'), *n.* a piece of furniture with shelves for holding books.

book club, a business organization that supplies certain books regularly to its subscribers, usually at a reduced rate.

book end, a prop or support placed at the end of a row of books to hold them upright.

book|er (bůk'ər), *n.* a person who enters or secures reservations, especially of space for travel, theater seats, rooms in a hotel, or the like.

book fair, **1** a fair at which books are displayed by publishers to promote and sell them or to sell rights to them. **2** a sale or auction of books for some charity or other special purpose. Authors often make personal appearances at such fairs.

book|ie (bůk'ē), *n. Informal.* a bookmaker (def. 1).

book|ing (bůk'ing), *n.* **1a** the action of engaging a seat or place. **b** the issuing of tickets, entitling to a seat or place. **2** the condition of being engaged to do something; engagement to perform, lecture, play, or the like.

booking agent, **1** a person who makes reservations, sells tickets, or the like. **2** a person who obtains engagements, plans schedules, and the like, for singers, musicians, lecturers, or other performers.

booking clerk, *British.* a booking agent.

booking hall, *British.* a place where tickets are sold in a railway station or the like.

booking office, *British.* a ticket office, such as in a railway station or at a theater.

book inventory, an inventory made by a check of books of account instead of by counting stock.

book|ish (bůk'ish), *adj.* **1** fond of reading or studying; studious: *The bookish boy spent many hours reading.* **SYN**: scholarly. **2** knowing books better than real life: *The scholar was a bookish man, lost in the business world.* **SYN**: impractical. **3** stiffly dignified or formal; scholarly in a dull and narrow way; stilted: *His conversation was sprinkled with bookish phrases.* **SYN**: learned, pedantic. **4** of or having to do with books; literary. —**book'ish|ly**, *adv.*

book|ish|ness (bůk'ish nis), *n.* **1** a fondness for books or study; learning. **2** knowledge only from books: *Diderot despised mere bookishness* (John Morley).

book jacket, a removable paper cover for a book, often colorfully illustrated and containing a short description of the book and its author.

book|keep|er (bůk'kē'pər), *n.* a person who keeps a record of business accounts.

book|keep|ing (bůk'kē'ping), *n.* the work of keeping a record of business accounts.

book|learn|ed (bůk'lėr'nid), *adj.* learned in books and not from real life: *a booklearned old recluse.*

book learning, **1** learning acquired by reading; acquaintance with books and literature: *Intelligent as respects book learning, but much deficient in worldly tact* (Hawthorne). **2** *Informal.* schooling.

book|less (bůk'lis), *adj.* **1** without a book or books: *A bookless house isn't a real home.* **2** uneducated; unlearned.

book|let (bůk'lit), *n.* a small book; thin book. Booklets often have paper covers.

book|list (bůk'list'), *n.* a list of books to be read for a particular purpose.

book|lore (bůk'lôr', -lōr'), *n.* book learning.

book louse, a small insect that feeds on the glue and paper of books, cartons, and other things containing paper and glue.

book lung, a breathing organ of some arachnids consisting of small sacs within the abdomen, connected with the outer air by small openings. Within each sac are many layers of tissue containing many blood vessels arranged like the leaves of a book.

book|mak|er (bůk'mā'kər), *n.* **1** a person who makes a business of accepting bets on horse races or other contests at odds fixed by himself. **2** a maker of a book or books; a writer, editor, or manufacturer of books.

book|mak|ing (bůk'mā'king), *n.* **1** the business of taking bets on horse races or other contests, at odds fixed by the taker, distinguished from pari-mutuel betting. **2** the writing, editing, or manufacture of books.

book|man (bůk'mən), *n., pl.* **-men**. **1** a man of letters; scholar; student. **2** *Informal.* a person in the book business; an editor, publisher, or manufacturer of books.

book|mark (bůk'märk'), *n.* **1** a piece of something, such as paper, cloth, or leather, put between the pages of a book to mark the reader's place. **2** = bookplate.

book matches, matches contained in a cardboard folder.

book|mo|bile (bůk'mə bēl), *n.* a bus or truck that serves as a traveling branch of a library. [< *book* + (auto)*mobile*]

book name, *Zoology, Botany.* a name other than the scientific name of an animal or plant, found only in treatises, and not in use as a vernacular name. *Example:* the use of the name paradoxure for an animal of the genus *Paradoxurus.*

book of account, any journal, ledger, or other accounting record of original entry.
books of account (often shortened to **books**), all the bills, checks, contracts, vouchers, and other records, needed to make an audit, or used to record business transactions.

Book of Books, = Bible.

Book of Common Order, the liturgy of the Church of Scotland, taken from the liturgy of the English Church at Geneva. It was introduced in 1562.

Book of Common Prayer, the book containing the doctrine, ordinances, prayers, and services of the Church of England or, with some changes, of the Episcopal Church and other churches of the Anglican Communion.

book of hours, a book of prayers to be recited for each of the canonical hours. Artists were commissioned by many noblemen during the Renaissance to illuminate books of hours.

Book of Mormon, a sacred book of the Church of Jesus Christ of Latter-day Saints, originally published in 1830: *The Book of Mormon tells ... of a band of Israelites who ... fled by boat to the Western Hemisphere* (New York Times).

book of original entry, an account ledger or book containing the first entry of a transaction made by the creditor.

Book of the Dead, a collection of ancient Egyptian religious maxims, and other information, to guide the soul on its journey to the other world.

book|plate (bůk'plāt'), *n.* a label pasted in a book with the owner's name or emblem.

book|rack (bůk'rak'), *n.* **1** a rack for holding an open book. **2** a rack for holding a row of books.

book review, an article about a book, especially a new one, discussing its merits and faults.

book reviewer, a person who reviews books in a publication or on a broadcast by radio or television.

book reviewing, the act or practice of writing book reviews.

books (bůks), *n.pl.* See under **book**.

book scorpion, a small, reddish-brown spider resembling a tailless scorpion, often found in old books and papers.

book|sell|er (bůk'sel'ər), *n.* a person whose business is selling books.

book|sell|ing (bůk'sel'ing), *n.* the business of selling books.

book|shelf (bůk'shelf'), *n., pl.* **-shelves**. a shelf for holding books.

book|shop (bůk'shop'), *n.* = bookstore.

book|stack (bůk'stak'), *n.* a set of bookshelves one above another, as in a library.

book|stall (bůk'stôl'), *n.* **1** a booth or stand where books (sometimes second-hand) are sold. It is often outdoors. **2** a makeshift display of books, as on a table, for sale.

book|stand (bůk'stand'), *n.* **1** a stand for holding an open book, usually a large book, such as a dictionary. **2** a stand or counter for showing books for sale. **3** a place where books are sold.

book|store (bůk'stôr', -stōr'), *n.* a store where books are sold.

book|sy (bůk'sē), *adj.* = bookish.

book|tel|ler (bůk'tel'ər), *n.* a person who records the text of a book on tape or record, which is then reproduced and sold as a talking book.

book token, *British.* a ticket or coupon of a certain value that may be exchanged at a bookstore for a book or books. Book tokens are often given as gifts.

book value, **1** the value of anything as it appears on the account books of the owner. It may be higher or lower than the real or present value. **2** the excess of assets over liabilities, or net worth, such as of a corporation or stock.

book|work (bůk'wėrk'), *n.* **1** the study of books, especially as applied to an academic curriculum. **2** the keeping of books, records, or the like: *The secretary did the bookwork of the business.* **3** the use of books as contrasted with a more active side of an activity: *He found the bookwork harder than the laboratory periods.*

book|worm (bůk'wėrm'), *n.* **1** a person who is very fond of reading and studying; one who is always poring over books. **2** (originally) any insect larva that gnaws the bindings or leaves of books.

book|y (bůk'ē), *adj.*, **book|i|er**, **book|i|est**. = bookish.

Bool|e|an or **Bool|i|an** (bü'lē ən), *adj.* of or having to do with Boolean algebra.

Boolean or **Boolian algebra**, a mathematical system dealing with the relationship between sets, used to solve problems in logic, probability, and engineering. [< George *Boole*, 1815-1864, an English mathematician + *-an*]

boom[1] (büm), *n., v., adj.* —*n.* **1** a long, deep, hollow sound: *The great bell of St. Peter's tolled with a deep boom* (Hawthorne). **SYN**: reverberation. **2** a rumbling or roaring: *the boom of cannon, the boom of big waves.* **3** a buzzing, humming, or droning. **4** = sonic boom. **5** a sudden activity and increase in business, prices, or values of property; rapid growth: *Our town is having such a boom that it is likely to double its size in two years.* **6** a vigorous pushing or urging. **7** *U.S.* an increase in public favor, as of a political candidate, or a vigorous movement in favor of a candidate or cause. **8** the cry of the bittern.
—*v.i.* **1** to make a deep, hollow sound: *The big man's voice boomed out above the rest.* **SYN**: thunder. **2** to make a rumbling, humming, or droning noise. **3** to increase suddenly in activity; grow rapidly: *Business is booming.* **SYN**: flourish.
—*v.t.* **1** to utter with a deep, hollow sound: *The big guns boomed their message.* **2** to push or urge to rapid progress: *The mayor's friends are booming him for senator.*
—*adj.* **1** produced by a boom: *boom prices.* **2** marked by a boom; booming: *boom times.*
[Middle English *bomben* make a resonant sound]

***boom**[2] (büm), *n., v.* —*n.* **1a** a long pole or beam. A boom is used to extend the bottom of a sail or as the lifting and guiding pole of a derrick. **b** a long metal arm for projecting a microphone above the camera angle. **2a** a chain, cable, or line of timbers that keeps logs from floating away. A boom is stretched across a river or around an area of water. **b** an area surrounded by a floating barrier. **3** a logjam or other obstruction to the current of a stream.
—*v.t.* to extend (a sail) with a boom.
—*v.i.* to sail very fast.
lower the boom, *Informal.* to take stern measures; crack down: *He raised the rent on any*

Pronunciation Key: hat, āge, cãre, fär; let, ēqual, tėrm; it, īce; hot, ōpen, ôrder; oil, out; cup, půt, rüle; child; long; thin; ᴛʜen; zh, measure; ə represents **a** in about, **e** in taken, **i** in pencil, **o** in lemon, **u** in circus.

pretext, lowered the boom at the first late payment (Time). [< Dutch *boom* tree, pole]

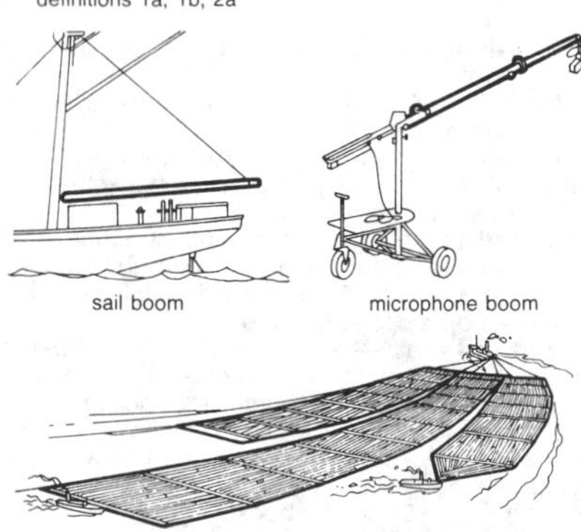

***boom[2]**
definitions 1a, 1b, 2a

boom-and-bust (büm′ən bust′), *n. Informal.* an economic cycle of great prosperity followed by a serious depression.
boom box, a large portable radio, often combined with a cassette player; ghetto blaster: *Advertising trucks equipped with monstrous boom boxes are cruising East German towns blaring rock music interspersed with advertising blurbs* (Time).
boom carpet, the area covered by a sonic boom; bang zone: *The "boom carpet" of a superjet is between fifty and eighty miles wide* (New York Times).
boom·er (bü′mər), *n.* **1** *U.S. Slang.* a roving worker. **2** a person that joins in a sudden increase of activity or rush. **3** = mountain beaver. [apparently < *boom[1]* + *-er[1]*]
boom·er·ang** (bü′mə rang, büm′rang), *n., v.* **—*n. **1a** a curved piece of wood used as a weapon by Australian aborigines and in some other countries. Boomerangs are made of a shape so that when properly thrown they return to the thrower. **b** a similar curved piece of hard wood used by the Hopi Indians of northern Arizona for hunting jack rabbits. **2** *Figurative.* anything that recoils or reacts to harm the doer or user.
—*v.i.* to act as a boomerang: (*Figurative.*) *The evidence one member gave against the gang boomeranged when he was convicted too.*
[< native dialectal word of New South Wales]

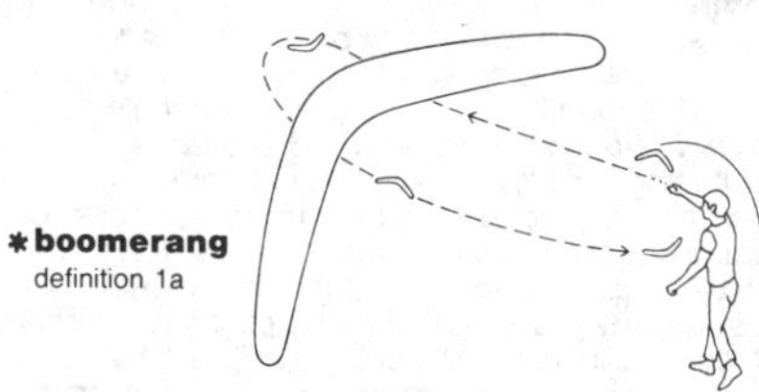
***boomerang**
definition 1a

Boomer State, a nickname for Oklahoma.
boom·ing (bü′ming), *adj.* increasing rapidly in activity; thriving. **—boom′ing·ly**, *adv.*
boom·let (büm′lit), *n.* a small boom, such as on the stock exchange.
boom·slang (büm′slang′), *n.* a poisonous snake of southern Africa. [< Afrikaans < *boom tree* + *slang* snake]
boom town, a town that has grown up suddenly, usually as a result of an increase of economic activity, such as land speculation or mining.
boom·y (bü′mē), *adj.* **1** of a boom. **2** like a boom. **—boom′i·ness**, *n.*
boon[1] (bün), *n.* **1** a great benefit; blessing: *Those warm boots were a boon to me in the cold weather. Sleep is a boon to the weary.* SYN: favor, gift, advantage. **2** *Archaic.* something asked for or granted as a favor. [< Scandinavian (compare Old Icelandic *bōn* petition)]
boon[2] (bün), *adj.* **1** full of cheer; jolly; merry: *The two good friends were boon companions.* SYN: gay, congenial, convivial. **2** kindly; pleasant. [< Old French *bon* good < Latin *bonus*]
boon·docks (bün′doks′), *n.pl. U.S. Slang.* rough backwoods; bush. [apparently < Tagalog *bundók* mountain]
boon·dog·gle (bün′dog′əl), *v.*, **-gled, -gling,** *n.* *U.S. Informal.* **—*v.i.*** to do useless work.
—*n.* a worthless work or product.
[American English; origin uncertain] **—boon′dog′gler,** *n.*
boon·ga·ry (büng′gər ē), *n., pl.* **-ries.** a small, arboreal kangaroo of Queensland, Australia. [< an Australian native name]
boon·ies (bü′nēz), *n.pl.* = boondocks.
boor (bůr), *n.* **1** a very rude, ill-mannered person. SYN: churl, lout. **2** a clumsy person, especially from the country; bumpkin. SYN: rustic, clodhopper. **3** *Obsolete.* a farm laborer; peasant. [< Low German *būr* or Dutch *boer* farmer, bumpkin]
Boor (bür), *n., adj.* = Boer.
boor·ish (bůr′ish), *adj.* like a boor; rude or rustic. SYN: clumsy, unrefined, ill-mannered. **—boor′ish·ly,** *adv.* **—boor′ish·ness,** *n.*
boost (büst), *n., v.* **—*n.*** **1** a push or shove that helps a person in rising or advancing: *Give me a boost over the fence.* **2** an act of promoting or uplifting; encouragement: *His friend's willingness to help him was a big boost to his morale.* **3** an increase, especially in degree, amount, price, or pay: *There has been a boost in prices at the supermarket.* **4** *U.S. Slang.* theft, shoplifting: *a rash of department store boosts.*
—*v.t.* **1** to lift or push from below or behind; raise: *Boost me up the tree and I'll get some apples. Atlas missile . . . boosts the astronaut into space* (Chicago Sun-Times). **2** *Figurative.* to help by speaking well of; promote: *The manufacturers are boosting the new cereal in a series of T.V. ads.* SYN: advance. **3** to make greater; raise; increase: *to boost a person's spirits. The supermarket has boosted its prices.* SYN: improve. **4** to increase the voltage in (an electric circuit). **5** *U.S. Slang.* to steal or shoplift.
—*v.i.* **1** to give a boost to a person or thing. **2** *U.S. Slang.* to steal or shoplift.
[American English; perhaps blend of *boom* and *hoist*]
boost·er (büs′tər), *n.* **1** a person or thing that boosts: (*Figurative.*) *His suggestions offer India a self-starter or booster* (Harper's). **2** an accessory generator or other device interposed in series in a circuit for increasing the voltage in an electric circuit. **3a** any one of various devices for increasing the power or thrust of an engine: *The heavy first stage of the rocket could consist of four . . . solid-propellant boosters* (Time). **b** Also, **booster rocket.** a rocket attached under the tail assembly of a missile or spacecraft to assist in its takeoff, or some phase of its flight: . . . *Saturn, the multi-stage space booster planned for large payloads* (Wall Street Journal). **4** a radio-frequency amplifier between an antenna and a radio or television receiving set. **5** *U.S. Informal, Figurative.* an enthusiastic supporter of a person, group, institution, or idea. **6** *Informal.* = booster shot. **7** *U.S. Slang.* a thief or shoplifter: *Male boosters shove suits inside their trench coats while an accomplice distracts the salesman's eye* (Harper's).
boost·er·ism (büs′tər iz əm), *n.* the attitudes or activities of promoters; enthusiastic boosting of an idea, person, or product.
booster shot, an additional inoculation of a vaccine or serum to continue the effectiveness of a previous inoculation.
booster station, a radio or television installation which picks up, amplifies, and relays signals from the main station.
boost-glide vehicle (büst′glīd′), a vehicle to be launched into space by rockets, but provided with aerodynamic surfaces to permit gliding back to the earth.
boot[1] (büt), *n., v.* **—*n.*** **1a** a covering for the foot and lower part of the leg, usually of leather or rubber (distinguished from *shoe*). **b** *British.* a high-cut shoe that covers the whole foot, including the ankle. **c** a protective covering for part of the hoof and leg of a horse. **2** any sheath or case that resembles or suggests a boot. **3** a kick: *He gave the ball a boot.* **4** *Slang.* a new recruit in training in the U.S. Navy, Marines, or Coast Guard. **5** an old instrument of torture used to crush a person's leg. **6** *British.* **a** a space for baggage in an automobile; trunk. **b** (formerly) space for baggage in a coach. **7** a protecting apron or cover for the driver of an open carriage. **8** a patch put inside an automobile tire to protect its tube from a break or a weak spot in the casing. **9** the box or channel in a reed organ through which the wind is conveyed to the reeds.
—*v.t.* **1** to put boots on; supply with boots: *If Washington could have booted his army, the men might never have stayed at Valley Forge.* **2** to give a kick to: *He booted the empty can off the sidewalk.* **3** to kick (a football or soccer ball). **4** *Informal, Figurative.* to get rid of; dismiss. **5a** *Baseball.* to misplay (the ball). **b** *Slang.* to lose (an opportunity) through clumsiness. **6** to torture with the boot: *Tradition says . . . Granger and his wife were booted* (Sir Walter Scott).
bet your boots, to depend on it; be sure: *You may bet your boots that I'll come to the party.*
die with one's boots on, to die in battle; die fighting for a cause: *If you keep on slinging your six-shooter around . . . , you will . . . die with your boots on* (Joaquin Miller).
have one's heart in one's boots. See under **heart**.
lick the boots of, to flatter; follow or obey slavishly: *Those [candidates] who aren't rich are usually party hacks who got a chance to run after years of licking the boots of party leaders* (New Yorker).
put the boot in, to engage in dangerous play, especially in Rugby: *He put the boot in once too often and was sidelined for the season.*
the boot, *Slang.* dismissal: *There'll be the money to take over the Moat Farm and give that varmint . . . the boot* (H. Rider Haggard).
wipe one's boots on, to treat in an insulting way: *Though he often wiped his boots on a man, he never showed him the more stinging insolence of condescension* (John W. Mackail).
[< Old French *bote*] **—boot′like′,** *adj.*
▶See **shoe** for usage note.
boot[2] (büt), *n., v.* **—*n.*** *Archaic.* profit; use; avail.
—*v.i.* *Archaic.* to be of use or profit; avail: *What boots thy wealth?* (Robert Southey).
—*v.t.* *Obsolete.* to enrich; benefit.
to boot, in addition; besides: *He gave me a compass for my knife and a canteen to boot.*
[Old English *bōt* profit, compensation]
boot[3] (büt), *n.* booty; spoil; plunder. [< *boot[2]*]
boot·black (büt′blak′), *n.* a person whose work is shining shoes and boots.
boot·boy (büt′boi′), *n. British.* a boy hired as a boots.
boot camp, *U.S.* a camp at which Navy, Marine Corps, or Coast Guard recruits are trained.
boot·ed (bü′tid), *adj.* **1** wearing boots; having boots on. **2** covered with a horny, bootlike sheath, as the tarsus of thrushes.
booted and spurred, ready and equipped to take on an adversary.
boot·ee (bü tē′; *especially for 1* bü′tē), *n.* **1** a baby's soft shoe, often knitted. **2** a woman's short boot. Also, **bootie**. [American English < *boot[1]*]
boot·er (bü′tər), *n. Informal.* a football or soccer player. [< *boot[1]* + *-er[1]*]
Bo·ö·tes (bō ō′tēz), *n., genitive* **Bo·ö·tis**. a northern constellation near Ursa Major that includes the star Arcturus. Boötes is sometimes called the Huntsman because it seems to hold the leashes of a constellation called The Hunting Dogs. It is also called the Herdsman because it is thought of as guarding a fold of animals formed by nearby stars. [< Latin *Boōtēs* < Greek *boṓtēs* ox driver < *boûs, boós* ox]
booth (büth), *n., pl.* **booths** (büᴛʜz, büths). **1** a covered stall or similar place where goods are sold or shown at a fair, market, or convention: *The country fair had rows of booths where women sold their pies and cakes and quilts.* **2** a small, enclosed place for a telephone, motion-picture projector, or other device: *I made my telephone call from a hot and stuffy booth at the station.* **3** a small, enclosed place for voting at elections. **4** a partly enclosed space in a restaurant or café, containing a table and seats for a few persons. **5** a temporary shelter made of boards, boughs of trees, or other materials.
[< Scandinavian (compare Old Danish *bōth*)]
boot hill, *U.S.* a cemetery in or near a frontier town of the old West.
boot·ie (bü′tē), *n.* = bootee.
boot·i·kin (bü′tə kin), *n.* **1** a little boot. **2** a kind of soft boot or mitten formerly worn as a cure for the gout. **3** an instrument of torture; the boot.
Bo·ö·tis (bō ō′tis), *n.* genitive of **Boötes**.
boot·jack (büt′jak′), *n.* a device to help in pulling off boots.
boot·lace (büt′lās′), *n. British.* a shoelace for a high shoe or boot.
by one's bootlaces, by solitary effort against great odds: *Starting out penniless, he raised himself by his bootlaces to the ownership of a large factory.*
boot·leg (büt′leg′), *v.*, **-legged, -leg·ging,** *adj., n.* *U.S.* **—*v.t., v.i.*** to sell, transport, or make unlawfully: *bootlegging liquor across the state line.*
—*adj.* sold, transported, or made unlawfully: *bootleg liquor.*
—*n.* goods, especially alcoholic liquor, sold, transported, or made unlawfully.
[American English (from practice of smuggling liquor in boot legs)] **—boot′leg′ger,** *n.*
boot·less[1] (büt′lis), *adj.* without shoes or boots. [< *boot[1]* + *-less*]
boot·less[2] (büt′lis), *adj.* of no benefit or profit; useless: *Doth not Brutus bootless kneel?* (Shakespeare). SYN: unavailing, unsuccessful, fruitless, futile, vain. [< *boot[2]* + *-less*] **—boot′less·ly,** *adv.* **—boot′less·ness,** *n.*
boot·lick (büt′lik′), *Informal.* **—*v.t.*** to curry favor with; toady to.
—*v.i.* to be a toady or slavish flatterer; fawn. **—boot′lick′er,** *n.*
boot·mak·er (büt′mā′kər), *n. British.* a shoemaker.
boots (büts), *n., pl.* **boots**. *British.* a servant, especially in a hotel, who shines shoes and boots and does similar tasks. [< *boot[1]*]

boots and saddles, a cavalry bugle call to mount horses.

boot|strap (büt′strap′), *n., v.* **—*n.*** **1** a loop of leather or cloth at the back of a boot or high shoe by means of which it may be pulled onto the foot. **2** the operation of using a small set of basic instructions in computer programming to develop additional instructions until the complete program is assembled.
—*v.t.* **bootstrap oneself**, to get into or out of something by one's own effort: *Somehow we have to bootstrap ourselves to a thriving export trade* (New Scientist).
by one's bootstraps, by one's own efforts, and usually in the face of great obstacles; without help from others: *It is not hard to imagine what a fraction of this [$25 billion a year] would do for young countries trying to pull themselves up by their bootstraps* (Harper's).

boot-tag (büt′tag′), *n. British.* a bootstrap.

boot training, *U.S. Informal.* **1** the training of recruits in the U.S. Navy, Marine Corps, or Coast Guard. **2** the period of this training.

boot tree, a shaped block put into a boot or a shoe to keep it in shape.

boo|ty (bü′tē), *n., pl.* **-ties**. **1** things taken from the enemy in war; spoils of war. SYN: pillage, loot. See syn. under **plunder**. **2** things seized by violence and robbery; plunder: *The pirates got much booty from the town they raided.* SYN: loot. **3** any valuable thing or things obtained; gains; winnings; prize. [perhaps < Middle Dutch *botye*, or Old French *butin*]

booze (büz), *n., v.,* **boozed, booz|ing.** *Informal.* **—*n.*** **1** any intoxicating liquor. **2** a drinking bout; spree.
—*v.i.* to drink heavily. SYN: tipple, guzzle.
[perhaps < Middle Dutch *būsen* drink heavily]

booz|er (bü′zər), *n.* **1** *Informal.* a person who boozes; heavy drinker. **2** *British Slang.* a place for drinking; pub.

booz|y (bü′zē), *adj.,* **booz|i|er, booz|i|est.** *Informal.* **1** somewhat drunk. **2** often drunk. **—booz′i|ly,** *adv.* **—booz′i|ness,** *n.*

bop[1] (bop), *n., v.,* **bopped, bop|ping.** *Slang.*
—*n.* a blow with the fist, a club, or other weapon.
—*v.t.* to hit (someone); strike.
[imitative] **—bop′per,** *n.*

bop[2] (bop), *n.* = bebop: *Ballroom and Bop for beginners* (Cape Times).

bo|peep (bō pēp′), *n.* = peekaboo.

bop|ster (bop′stər), *n. Slang.* a devotee of bebop.

bor., borough.

bo|ra[1] (bôr′ə, bōr′-), *n.* a violent, dry, cold, north or northeast wind of the Adriatic and its coasts. [< dialectal Italian (Venetian) for *borea* < Latin *boreās* north wind]

bo|ra[2] (bôr′ə, bōr′-), *n.* a ceremony of the aborigines of eastern Australia by which a boy is admitted to the rights of manhood.

bo|rac|ic (bə ras′ik), *adj.* = boric.

bo|ra|cite (bôr′ə sīt, bōr′-), *n.* a mineral, a borate and chloride of magnesium, occurring in translucent to transparent, white or colorless crystals, and remarkable for its pyroelectric properties. *Formula:* $Mg_3B_7O_{13}Cl$ [< *borac*(ic) + *-ite*]

bor|age (bėr′ij, bôr′-, bor′-), *n.* **1** a plant, native to southern Europe, having bright blue or purplish flowers and hairy stems and leaves. It is used in salads, in flavoring beverages, and in medicine. **2** any one of various related or similar plants. [< Anglo-French *burage*, learned borrowing from Medieval Latin *burrago* < Late Latin *burra* coarse wool (because of its hairy foliage)]

borage family, a group of dicotyledonous plants, chiefly herbs of north temperate regions, often having rough and hairy leaves and regular, five-petaled flowers, and usually bearing a fruit consisting of four distinct nutlets. The family includes the borage, bugloss, alkanet, heliotrope, and forget-me-not.

bo|rag|i|na|ceous (bə raj′ə nā′shəs), *adj.* belonging to the borage family. [< New Latin *Boraginaceae* the family name (< *Borago* the genus name < Medieval Latin *burrago;* see etym. under **borage**) + English *-ous*]

bo|ral sheet (bôr′əl, bōr′-), a sheet or shield of boron carbide and aluminum for protection against radiation.

bo|rane (bôr′ān, bōr′-), *n.* any one of various unstable hydrides of boron. [< *bor*(on) + *-ane*]

bo|ras|sus palm (bō ras′əs), = palmyra. [< New Latin *Borassus* the genus name < Greek *bórassos*]

bo|rate (*n.* bôr′āt, -it; bōr′-; *v.* bôr′āt, bōr′-), *n., v.,* **-rat|ed, -rat|ing.** **—*n.*** a salt or ester of boric acid.
—*v.t.* to mix or treat with boric acid or borax.

bo|rax (bôr′aks, -əks; bōr′-), *n.* **1** a white, crystalline powder used as an antiseptic, as a cleansing agent, in fusing metals, and in making heat-resistant glass; sodium borate. Borax has a sweetish, alkaline taste. *Formula:* $Na_2B_4O_7$ **2** *U.S. Slang.* cheap and gaudy furniture. [< Old French *boras*, learned borrowing from Medieval Latin *borax, -acis* < Arabic *būraq*, probably < Persian *būrah*]

borax bead, a bead of fused borax, used especially in chemical analysis.

bor|a|zine (bôr′ə zēn, bōr′-), *n.* a compound of boron, nitrogen, and hydrogen whose physical properties closely resemble those of benzene. *Formula:* $B_3N_3H_6$

bor|a|zon (bôr′ə zon, bōr′-), *n.* **1** a crystalline compound of boron and nitrogen, as hard as diamond and able to withstand higher temperatures. It is the only substance other than diamond capable of scratching diamond. **2 Borazon.** a trademark for this substance. *Formula:* BN [< *bor*(on) + *azo* + *n*(itrogen)]

bor|bo|ryg|mus (bôr bə rig′məs), *n.* the rumbling noise caused by gas within the intestines. [< Greek *borborygmós*]

Bor|deaux (bôr dō′), *n.* **1** a red or white wine made in the region near Bordeaux, France. Red Bordeaux is often called *claret.* **2** Bordeaux mixture. [< *Bordeaux*, a French seaport]

Bordeaux mixture, a liquid mixture of copper sulfate, lime, and water, sprayed on trees and plants to kill fungi and other pests.

bor|del (bôr′dəl), *n.* = bordello. [< Old French *bordel* brothel, cabin < *borde* wooden shack < Germanic (compare Old High German *bord* plank)]

Bor|de|laise sauce (bôr′də lāz′), any one of various rich, highly flavored sauces. [< French *à la Bordelaise* in the Bordeaux style]

bor|del|lo (bôr del′ō), *n., pl.* **-los.** a house of prostitution; brothel. [< Italian *bordello* < Old French *bordel* bordel]

bor|der (bôr′dər), *n., v.* **—*n.*** **1** the side, edge, or boundary of anything, or the part near it: *We pitched our tent on the border of a lake.* (*Figurative.*) *Beyond the rigid border of the science* (James Martineau). SYN: margin, rim. See syn. under **edge**. **2** a line which separates one country, state, or province from another; a frontier: *We crossed the border between France and Belgium.* **3** a strip of ground planted with flowers, shrubs, or other plants, edging a garden, walk, or the like. **4** a strip on the edge of anything for strength or ornament: *Her handkerchief has a blue border.* SYN: edging.
—*v.t.* **1** to form a boundary to; bound: *The Rio Grande borders part of Texas.* **2** to put a border on; edge: *We have bordered our garden with shrubs.* **3** to be situated on the border of; adjoin: *the lands that border the Gulf of Mexico.*
border on (or **upon**), **a** to touch at the edge or boundary; be next to; adjoin: *The estate borders on the river. Canada borders on the United States.* **b** to be close to; verge on; resemble: *His silly behavior borders on the ridiculous.*
the border, a the frontier between the United States and Mexico. **b** the frontier between the United States and Canada.
the Border, the region near the boundary between England and Scotland: *Through all the wide Border his steed was the best* (Scott).
[< Old French *bordure* < *border* to border < *bord* side, boundary < Germanic (compare Old Saxon *bord* side of a ship)] **—bor′der|er,** *n.* **—bor′der|less,** *adj.*

bor|de|reau (bôr də rō′), *n., pl.* **-reaux.** *French.* a memorandum or note, especially a detailed list, as of documents.

bor|dered (bôr′dərd), *adj.* edged; fringed.

bordered pit, *Botany.* a thin, hollow area in the wall of a tracheid around which a thickened cellular growth overhangs.

bor|der|land (bôr′dər land′), *n.* land or area near a border; area forming a border: (*Figurative.*) *the borderland between sleeping and waking.*

bor|der|lights (bôr′dər līts′), *n.pl.* the rows of lights above the scenery in a theater.

bor|der|line (bôr′dər līn′), *n., adj.* **—*n.*** a dividing line or boundary: (*Figurative.*) *the borderline between life and death.* **—*adj.*** **1** on a dividing line or boundary: (*Figurative.*) *He stayed home with a borderline case of mumps but didn't have to go to bed.* **2** *Psychology.* on the line of division between two groups, such as normal and subnormal or adjusted and maladjusted.

border states, any state on or near the Mason-Dixon line in the United States.

Border States, the slave states on the border between the North and the deep South in the United States before the Civil War; Delaware, Maryland, Virginia, Kentucky, and Missouri. Although kinship and the institution of slavery tied them to the South, most of them remained in the Union.

border terrier, any one of a breed of terriers with a slim body and a broad flat head with turned down ears and short whiskers. It comes from the border country of northern England.

bor|dure (bôr′jər), *n.* a heraldic bearing around the outside of a shield, always a fifth of its surface. [earlier form of *border*]

bore[1] (bôr, bōr), *v.,* **bored, bor|ing,** *n.* **—*v.i.*** **1** to make a hole by means of a tool that keeps turning, or by penetrating as a worm does in fruit: *Bore through the handle of that brush so we can hang it up. The men dug the oil well by boring through the ground with huge drills.* SYN: pierce, perforate, drill. **2** to be bored; be suited for boring: *This wood bores easily.* **3** to force a way; push forward.
—*v.t.* **1** to make (a hole or passage) by means of a tool or by pushing through or digging out: *Plumbers bored a hole in the floor to put a radiator pipe through. A mole has bored its way under the hedge.* SYN: pierce, perforate, drill. **2** to bore a hole in; hollow out evenly. **3** to make one's way through (a crowd).
—*n.* **1** a hole made by a revolving tool: *As the drill was stuck in the bore it had to be forced out.* **2** the hollow space inside a pipe, tube, or gun barrel: *He cleaned the bore of his gun.* **3** the distance across the inside of a hole or tube: *A two-inch pipe will slip inside a pipe with a three-inch bore.*
[Old English *borian* pierce]

bore[2] (bôr, bōr), *v.,* **bored, bor|ing,** *n.* **—*v.t.*** to make weary by tiresome talk or by being dull: *His long speech bored me so that it was hard to sit still.* SYN: tire, fatigue.
—*n.* a dull, tiresome person or thing: *It is a bore to have to pick up other people's messes.*
[origin unknown]

bore[3] (bôr, bōr), *v.* the past tense of **bear**[2]: *She bore her duties with concern.*

bore[4] (bôr, bōr), *n.* a sudden tidal wave that rushes up a channel with great force. [Middle English *bare* wave < Scandinavian (compare Old Icelandic *bāra* wave)]

bo|re|al (bôr′ē əl, bōr′-), *adj.* **1** of the north; northern. **2** of the north wind. **3** of Boreas. [< Latin *boreālis* < *Boreās* Boreas < Greek *Boréās*]

bo|re|an (bôr′ē ən, bōr′-), *adj.* = boreal.

Bo|re|as (bôr′ē əs, bōr′-), *n.* **1** *Greek Mythology.* the north wind as a god. **2** the north wind personified. [< Latin *Boreās* < Greek *Boréās*]

bore|cole (bôr′kōl′, bōr′-), *n.* a plant related to the cabbage; kale. [probably < Dutch *boerenkool* peasant's cabbage]

bore|dom (bôr′dəm, bōr′-), *n.* a bored condition; weariness caused by dull, tiresome people or events; ennui. SYN: tedium.

bore|hole (bôr′hōl′, bōr′-), *n.* a hole drilled into the surface of the earth to provide samples, such as of the minerals or water, available at specified depths.

bor|er (bôr′ər, bōr′-), *n.* **1** any one of various insects or larvae that bore, especially into wood or fruit. **2** any one of various mollusks, especially the shipworms, that bore, especially through wood. **3** a tool for boring holes.

bore|scope (bôr′skōp, bōr′-), *n.* an instrument like a periscope, inserted into an enclosed hollow space, such as an ancient tomb, for viewing the inside and recording data about it: . . . *technicians lowering borescope into nuclear reactor* (New York Times). [< *bore*[1], noun + *-scope*]

bore|some (bôr′səm, bōr′-), *adj.* boring; dull; tiresome.

Bor|gian (bôr′jən), *adj.* characteristic of the Borgias of medieval Italy; involving intrigue and treachery: *a Borgian plot.*

bo|ric (bôr′ik, bōr′-), *adj.* of or containing boron; boracic.

boric acid, **1** a white, crystalline substance used as a mild antiseptic, in making cement, glass, and soap, and to preserve food. Boric acid occurs in nature or is made from borax. *Formula:* H_3BO_3 **2** any one of several other acids which contain boron.

bo|ride (bôr′īd, bōr′-), *n.* a compound of boron with a metallic element or radical.

bor|ing[1] (bôr′ing, bōr′-), *n., adj.* **—*n.*** **1** the act of piercing or perforating with a rotating tool. **2** the hole thus made.
—*adj.* that bores or perforates.
borings, the chips or dust produced in boring.

bor|ing[2] (bôr′ing, bōr′-), *adj.* dull; tiresome. **—bor′ing|ly,** *adv.* **—bor′ing|ness,** *n.*

born (bôrn), *adj., v.* **—*adj.*** **1** brought into life; brought forth: *A baby born on Sunday is supposed to be lucky.* **2** thought up; conceived. **3** by birth; by nature: *Most good ballplayers are born athletes.*
—*v.* a past participle of **bear**[2]: *He was born on*

Pronunciation Key: hat, āge, cãre, fär; let, ēqual, tėrm; it, īce; hot, ōpen, ôrder; oil, out; cup, pu̇t, rüle; child; long; thin; ᴛʜen; zh, measure; ə represents **a** in about, **e** in taken, **i** in pencil, **o** in lemon, **u** in circus.

December 30, 1900. Abbr: b.
be born again, to be converted; become regenerate in spirit and character: *Except a man be born again, he cannot see the kingdom of God* (John 3:3).
▶ See **borne** for usage note.
born-a|gain (bôrn′ə gen′), *adj. U.S.* believing in personal conversion as a way to salvation through Christ; evangelical: *Graham said, "There is nothing too hard for the Lord to accomplish" and Carter, a born-again Baptist, "can take comfort in that"* (Durham Morning Herald).
borne (bôrn, bōrn), *v.* a past participle of **bear**[2]: *I have borne it as long as I can. She has borne three children.*
▶ **borne.** In the sense "give birth to," the very commonly used passive voice form is *borne* when not followed by *by: She had borne five children.*
bor|né (bôr nā′), *adj.* bounded; limited; contracted; narrow [< French *borné,* past participle of *borner* to limit]
Bor|ne|an (bôr′nē ən), *adj., n.* **—*adj.*** of or having to do with Borneo or its people.
—*n.* a native or inhabitant of Borneo.
bor|ne|ol (bôr′nē ōl, -ol), *n.* a substance resembling camphor, found in fissures in the trunk of a large tree native to the East Indies; camphol. *Formula:* $C_{10}H_{18}O$
Born|holm disease (bôrn′hōm, bōrn′-), = pleurodynia. [< *Bornholm,* a Danish island in the Baltic where it was first reported]
born|ite (bôr′nīt), *n.* a brittle, reddish-brown sulfide of copper and iron, a valuable ore of copper. *Formula:* Cu_5FeS_4 [< German *Bornit* < Ignatius von *Born,* 1742-91, an Austrian mineralogist]
*** bo|ron** (bôr′on, bōr′-), *n.* a nonmetallic chemical element which occurs only in combination with other elements. It is present in borax. Boron is used in fuels, alloys, and nuclear reactors. Two allotropic forms of this element are known, one a brown, amorphous powder, slightly soluble in water, the other crystalline, and with a luster and hardness inferior only to those of the diamond. [< *bor*(ax) + (carb)*on*]

*** boron**

symbol	atomic number	atomic weight	oxidation state
B	5	10.811	3

boron carbide, an extremely hard, crystalline compound, used in cutting tools. *Formula:* B_4C
boron nitride, a white, crystalline compound of boron and nitrogen, formed in various ways, such as by burning boron in air. *Formula:* BN
bo|ro|sil|i|cate (bôr′ə sil′ə kit, -kāt; bōr′-), *n.* a salt of both boric and silicic acids.
borosilicate glass, a glass containing at least 5 per cent boric oxide, highly resistant to heat and shock, used in making chemical glassware, kitchen utensils, and the like.
bor|ough (bėr′ō), *n.* **1** (in some states of the United States) an incorporated town with certain privileges, smaller than a city. **2** one of the five divisions of New York City. **3** (in Alaska) a district similar to a county. **4** in Great Britain: **a** a town with a municipal corporation and a charter that guarantees the right of local self-government. **b** a district that sends representatives to Parliament. [Old English *burg, burh* fortified buildings]
bor|ough-Eng|lish (bėr′ō ing′glish), *n.* a custom in certain parts of England by which an estate passes to the youngest son, or, if there is no son, to the youngest brother.
bor|ough|mon|ger (bėr′ō mung′gər, -mong′-), *n.* a person who sold or bought parliamentary seats for boroughs in England (frequent in discussions of parliamentary reform before 1832).
bor|row[1] (bor′ō, bôr′-), *v.t.* **1** to get (something) from another person with the understanding that it must be returned: *Can I borrow your book to read at home and then return in a few days?* **2** to take and use as one's own; adopt: *Rome borrowed many ideas from Greece.* **SYN:** appropriate. **3** to take from another language: *The words for the vegetable "squash" and for "canoe" were borrowed from the American Indians.* **4** to take (one) from the digit immediately to the left and add its place value to the digit being subtracted from: *In 46 minus 19, borrow 10 from 40 to add to the 6, making the subtraction in the first digit 9 from 16.* **5** *Dialect.* to lend. **—*v.i.*** **1** to borrow something: *She always borrows from me.* **2** *Golf.* to putt to the left or right of a straight line with the hole in order to compensate for a roll or slant of the green.
borrow trouble. See under **trouble.**
[Old English *borgian* < *borg* pledge] **—bor′row|a|ble,** *adj.* **—bor′row|er,** *n.*
▶ **Borrow** is often followed by *from: I would like to borrow five dollars from you.* It is followed less commonly and more formally by *of: He borrowed a large sum of the bank.*
bor|row[2] (bor′ō, bôr′ō), *n.* **1** a pledge; surety. **2** a tithing or frankpledge. [Old English *borg*]
bor|rowed time (bor′ōd, bôr′-), time beyond what could be normally expected, usually a very limited amount of time: *Both were living on borrowed time, facing deportation* (Newsweek).
bor|row|ing (bor′ō ing, bôr′-), *n.* **1** the act of a person who borrows. **2** a thing borrowed.
borrow pit, *Civil Engineering.* an excavation dug to provide fill at another site.
Bors (bôrs), *n.* **1 Sir,** a nephew of Lancelot and knight of the Round Table, who saw the Holy Grail. **2 Sir,** an illegitimate son of King Arthur. **3** a king of Gaul and uncle of Lancelot.
borsch (bôrsh), *n.* a Russian soup consisting of meat stock, cabbage, and potatoes, or made with beets, and served with sour cream. [< Russian *borshch*]
borsch circuit or **belt,** *U.S. Informal.* resorts in the Catskills where dancers, comedians, singers, and other performers provide entertainment for the guests.
borscht (bôrsht), *n.* borsch consisting mainly of beets and served hot or cold. [< Yiddish *borsht* < Russian *borsch*]
borscht circuit, = borsch circuit.
Bör|se (bœr′zə), *n. German.* stock exchange.
bors|hold|er (bôrs′hōl′dər), *n.* in English history: **1** (originally) the head or chief of a borrow (tithing); a headborough. **2** (later) a petty constable. [Middle English *borgesaldre* head of a borrow (tithing)]
bor|stal (bôr′stəl), *n.* (in Great Britain) a reformatory that stresses vocational training and close supervision of the offenders after their release: *For offenders aged between 14 and 21 there will be three types of institution: borstal, detention centre, and the new young offenders' institution* (London Times). [< *Borstal,* a village in southern England]
bort (bôrt), *n.* coarse or inferior diamonds, or fragments obtained in cutting diamonds, used to make diamond dust. Also, **boart.** [perhaps < Old French *bort, bord* bastard < Latin *burdus* mule]
bortsch (bôrch), *n.* = borsch.
bort|y (bôr′tē), *adj.* of or resembling bort.
bortz (bôrts), *n.* = bort.
bor|zoi (bôr′zoi), *n.* any one of a breed of tall, slender, swift dogs with long, silky hair; Russian wolfhound. The borzoi was developed in Russia for use in chasing hare and other game. [< Russian *borzoj* < (archaic) *borzyj* swift]
bos|cage (bos′kij), *n. Poetic.* a small wood; thicket; shrubbery; grove: *the cool boscages and orangeries of the place* (Thomas Carlyle). [< Old French *boscage* < *bosc* < Frankish (compare Old High German *busk* woods)]
bosch|bok (bosh′bok′), *n.* bushbuck, a rather small South African antelope. [< Afrikaans *boschbok* < Dutch *bosch* woods + *bok* goat, buck]
Bosche (bosh, bôsh), *n.* = Boche.
bosch|vark (bosh′värk′), *n.* the bush pig of South Africa. [< Afrikaans *boschvark* < Dutch *bosch* woods + *varken* pig]
Bose-Ein|stein statistics (bōs′īn′stīn), a statistical theory in quantum mechanics which holds that in the distribution of nuclear particles of a given type any number of identical particles may occupy a particular quantum-mechanical state. [< Satyendra *Bose,* born 1894, an Indian physicist + Albert *Einstein,* 1879-1955, a German-born physicist]
bosh (bosh), *n., interj. Informal.* foolish talk or ideas; nonsense: *He thought the new theories were bosh* (n.). *"Bosh," he responded when asked for an opinion* (interj.). [< Turkish *bos* empty]
bosh shot, *British Dialect and Slang.* an unsuccessful attempt; a miss or bungle.
bo|sie (bō′zē), *n. Australian.* the googly. [shortened from B. J. T. *Bosanquet,* an English cricket player of the early 1900's]
bosk (bosk), *n.* a grove; small wood; thicket. [variant of *busk,* dialectal for *bush*[1]]
bos|ket (bos′kit), *n.* a planting of small trees in a garden, park, or other area; thicket. [< French *bosquet* < Old French < Italian *boschetto* (diminutive) < *bosco* wood]
Bos|kop (bos′kop), *adj.* of or having to do with a type of Stone Age man of southern Africa whose remains were discovered in 1913 at Boskop, in the Transvaal: *The Boskop type skulls . . . strongly recall the Bushman-Hottentot type of South Africa* (Alfred L. Kroeber).
bosk|y (bos′kē), *adj.,* **bosk|i|er, bosk|i|est. 1** having a growth of small trees and bushes; wooded. **2** shady. **—bosk′i|ness,** *n.*
bo's'n (bō′sən), *n.* = boatswain.
Bos|ni|an (boz′nē ən), *adj., n.* **—*adj.*** of or having to do with Bosnia or its people.
—*n.* a native or inhabitant of Bosnia.
bos|om (bůz′əm, bü′zəm), *n., adj., v.* **—*n.*** **1** the upper, front part of the human body; breast. **2** the part of a garment covering the breast: *She wore a flower on the bosom of her dress.* **3** *Figurative.* heart or feelings: *He kept the secret in his bosom.* **4** *Figurative.* the center or inmost part: *He did not mention it even in the bosom of his family.* **5** the enclosure formed by the breast and the arms. **6** *Figurative.* the surface (of the sea, a lake, a river, or the ground).
—*adj.* **1** close and trusted; intimate: *Very dear friends are bosom friends.* **2** of the bosom.
—*v.t.* **1** to cherish; conceal in the bosom. **2** to take to the bosom; embrace.
[Old English *bōsm*]
-bosomed, *combining form.* having a ___ bosom: *Round-bosomed = having a round bosom.*
bos|om|y (bůz′ə mē, bü′zə-), *adj.* having or appearing to have large breasts.
bo|son (bō′son), *n.* any one of a class of particles in quantum mechanics, two or more of which may occupy the same state. Bosons include pi-mesons and photons. [< Satyendranath *Bose,* 1894-1974, an Indian physicist + *-on,* as in *electron*]
boss[1] (bôs, bos), *n., v., adj.* **—*n.*** **1** a person who hires workers or watches over or directs them; foreman, manager, or superintendent: *The boss was always on the job, directing his workers.* **2** any person in charge; chief or master: *Mother is the boss in her kitchen.* **3** a person who controls a political organization, especially a local one: *The local political boss took his orders from city hall.* **4** *U.S.* the head of a unit of the Mafia; capo.
—*v.t.* to be the boss of; direct; control: *Who is bossing this job?* **SYN:** manage.
—*adj.* **1** master; chief. **2** *U.S. Slang.* first-rate; champion.
[American English < Dutch *baas* master, uncle]
boss[2] (bôs, bos), *n., v.* **—*n.*** **1** a raised ornament of silver, ivory, or other material on a flat surface: *The boss on the knight's shield consisted of his coat of arms.* **2** the enlarged part of a shaft on a machine. **3** a protuberance or swelling on the body of an animal or plant. **4** a mass of rock protruding through a stratum of another kind.
—*v.t.* to decorate with ornamental nails, knobs, or studs.
[< Old French *boce, boche* hump]
boss[3] (bôs, bos), *n. U.S.* bossy; a cow or calf.
bos|sa no|va (bäs′ə nō′və), a dance music of Brazil that combines the rhythm of samba with jazz music. [< Portuguese *bossa nova* (literally) new tendency]
boss|dom (bôs′dəm, bos′-), *n.* **1** the sphere of influence of a political boss. **2** the control of politics by bosses.
boss|ism (bôs′iz əm, bos′-), *n. U.S.* control by political bosses.
boss|y[1] (bôs′ē, bos′-), *adj.,* **boss|i|er, boss|i|est.** *Informal.* fond of telling others what to do and how to do it; domineering. [American English < *boss*[1] + *-y*[1]] **—boss′i|ness,** *n.*
boss|y[2] (bôs′ē, bos′-), *adj.* decorated with bosses; projecting as bosses do. [< *boss*[2]]
bos|sy[3] or **bos|sie** (bôs′ē, bos′-), *n., pl.* **-sies.** *Informal.* a familiar name for a cow or calf (used chiefly in calling or soothing). [< dialectal English *borse, boss* young calf]
bos|ton[1] (bôs′tən, bos′-), *n.* a card game resembling whist, but played by four players individually, with two decks of cards. [< French *boston* < *Boston,* Massachusetts, where it was invented by French officers at the time of the Revolutionary War]
bos|ton[2] (bôs′tən, bos′-), *n.* a ballroom dance, a variation of the waltz. [< *Boston,* Massachusetts]
Boston arm, an artificial arm that is battery-powered and activated by electric signals from the amputee's remaining arm or shoulder muscles. [< *Boston,* Massachusetts, where it was developed]
Boston brown bread, a very dark, steamed bread containing corn meal, flour (usually both wheat and rye), molasses, soda, and water or milk, commonly baked in cylindrical loaves.
Boston bull, = Boston terrier.
Boston cream pie, a two-layer cake with whipped-cream or cream filling.
Boston fern, a variety of sword fern having long, drooping fronds, often grown as a house plant.
Bos|to|ni|an (bôs tō′nē ən, bos-), *adj., n.* **—*adj.*** of Boston, Massachusetts.
—*n.* a person born or living in Boston.
Boston ivy, = Japanese ivy.
Boston lettuce, a kind of lettuce that forms relatively loose heads, with slightly yellowish inner leaves.
*** Boston rocker,** a rocking chair of early American style, with a high back of curved spindles

and a curved, solid wooden seat. It is often painted black and stenciled in gilt.

***Boston rocker**

Boston terrier, any one of a breed of small dogs, brindled or black, with white markings and smooth short hair; Boston bull. The breed is the result of crossing an English bulldog with a terrier.

bo|sun (bō′sən), *n.* = boatswain.

bosun's chair, = boatswain's chair.

Bos|well (boz′wel, -wəl), *n.* any author of a biography of a close friend (in allusion to James Boswell and Samuel Johnson).

Bos|well|i|an (boz wel′ē ən), *adj.* of, having to do with, or suggestive of James Boswell (1740-1795) or his biography of Samuel Johnson, which is characterized by great faithfulness and fullness, with minute details of the sayings and doings of its subject.

Bos|well|ize (boz′wə līz), *v.t.*, **-ized, -iz|ing.** to write about in the style or manner of James Boswell: *One can't help regretting that Adams never had the time to Boswellize himself and his era* (New Yorker).

bot (bot), *n.* the larva of a botfly, parasitic in horses, cattle, sheep, and, occasionally, human beings. Also, **bott.** [origin uncertain]

bot., **1** botanical. **2** botanist. **3** botany.

bo|ta (bō′tä), *n. Spanish.* a wineskin.

bo|tan|ic (bə tan′ik), *adj.* = botanical.

bo|tan|i|cal (bə tan′ə kəl), *adj., n.* —*adj.* **1** having to do with plants and plant life. **2** having to do with the study of plants.
—*n.* a drug made from roots, leaves, flowers, or other parts of plants.
[< Late Latin *botanicus* (< Greek *botanikós* < *botánē* plant) + English *-al*[1]] —**bo|tan′i|cal|ly,** *adv.*

botanical garden, a large public garden in which the principal types of plants are cultivated and displayed.

bot|a|nist (bot′ə nist), *n.* a scientist who studies plants.

bot|a|nize (bot′ə nīz), *v.*, **-nized, -niz|ing.** —*v.i.* **1** to study plants in their natural environment. **2** to seek for or collect plants for the purpose of studying and classifying them.
—*v.t.* to explore or examine the plant life of.
—**bot′a|niz′er**, *n.*

bot|a|ny (bot′ə nē), *n., pl.* **-nies. 1** the science of plants; study of plants and plant life. Botany deals with the structure, growth, and classification of plants. It is a branch of biology. **2** the plant life of a particular area: *the botany of Greenland.* **3** botanical facts about a plant or group of plants: *the botany of ferns.* **4** a scientific book about plants and plant life. *Abbr:* bot. [< *botan*(ic) + *-y*[3]]

Botany Bay kino, resin from the eucalyptus tree which protects wood against shipworms and other borers.

Botany wool, a fine wool of the merino type grown in Australia and used in high-quality fabrics. [< *Botany* Bay, Australia, near which it was originally grown]

botch[1] (boch), *v., n.* —*v.t.* **1** to spoil by poor work; bungle: *The careless boy made so many mistakes building his model airplane that he completely botched the job.* **2** to repair clumsily or imperfectly.
—*n.* **1** a poor piece of work. **2** a clumsy patch.
[Middle English *bocchen;* origin uncertain]
—**botch′er**, *n.*

botch[2] (boch), *n. Dialect.* a swelling on the skin, such as a boil, ulcer, or pimple. [Middle English *bocche* < Old North French *boche;* origin uncertain]

botch|er|y (boch′ər ē), *n., pl.* **-er|ies.** a botcher's work; clumsy or awkward workmanship or its result; patchwork.

botch|y (boch′ē), *adj.*, **botch|i|er, botch|i|est.** poorly made or done; botched. —**botch′i|ly**, *adv.*

bote (bōt), *n. sing. or pl.* in old English law: **1a** a privilege or allowance for the repair of buildings, bridges, fences, or other structures. **b** an assessment levied for this. **2** compensation, as for an injury or offense against someone. [Middle English *bote* boot[2]]

bo|tel (bō tel′), *n.* = boatel.

bot|fly (bot′flī′), *n., pl.* **-flies.** a two-winged fly whose larvae are parasites of horses, cattle, sheep, and sometimes man. [< *bot* + *fly*[2]]

both (bōth), *adj., pron., adv., conj.* —*adj.* the two; the one and the other: *Both houses are white.*
—*pron.* the two together: *Both belong to him.*
—*adv.* together or alike; equally: *He fears and hopes both at once.*
—*conj.* together; alike; equally: *He is both strong and healthy.*
[Middle English *bothe,* apparently < Old English *bā thā* both these]
▶ **Both** is used in informal English to emphasize the fact that two persons or places or things are involved in a situation: *The twins were both there.* Strictly speaking, the *both* is redundant, but it gives emphasis.

both|er (boᴛʜ′ər), *n., v., interj.* —*n.* **1** much fuss or worry about small matters; trouble: *What a lot of bother about nothing!* **SYN:** disturbance. **2** a person or thing that causes worry, fuss, or trouble: *A door that will not shut is a bother.* **SYN:** annoyance.
—*v.i.* to take trouble; concern oneself; fuss: *Don't bother about my breakfast; I'll eat what is here.*
—*v.t.* **1** to annoy; irritate: *Hot weather bothers me.* **SYN:** pester, vex. **2** to bewilder; fluster; confuse: *This problem has bothered the experts for many years.*
—*interj. Especially British.* an expression of annoyance: *"Bother Mrs. Harris!" said Betsey Prig ... "I don't believe there's no sich a person"* (Dickens).
[Anglo-Irish; origin uncertain] —**both′er|er**, *n.*

both|er|a|tion (boᴛʜ′ə rā′shən), *n., interj. Informal.* = bother.

both|er|some (boᴛʜ′ər səm), *adj.* causing worry or fuss; troublesome; annoying.

bot|o|gen|in (bot′ə jen′in), *n.* a steroid compound derived from a Mexican variety of yam, used as a source of cortisone. *Formula:* $C_{27}H_{40}O_4$ [origin uncertain]

bot|o|né or **bot|o|née** (bot′ə nā), *adj. Heraldry.* having an ornament of three knobs or other parts, resembling a trefoil. See picture under **cross.** [< Old French *botoné* < *botoner* to bud]

bot|o|ny (bot′ə nē), *adj.* = botoné.

bo tree (bō), the sacred fig tree of India under which the founder of Buddhism is said to have attained the enlightenment which constituted him the Buddha; pipal. The bo tree belongs to the mulberry family. [< Singhalese *bo* < Pali *bodhi* (*taru*) perfect knowledge (tree) < Sanskrit]

bot|ry|oid (bot′rē oid), *adj.* = botryoidal.

bot|ry|oi|dal (bot′rē oi′dəl), *adj.* having the form of a bunch of grapes. [< Greek *botryoeidês* (< *bótrys* grape cluster + *eîdos* form) + English *-al*[1]]
—**bot′ry|oi′dal|ly**, *adv.*

bot|ry|o|my|co|sis (bot′rē ō mī kō′sis), *n.* a disease of horses in which a micrococcus causes the formation of small, fibrous tumors in the lungs and other parts of the horse. [< Greek *bótrys* grape cluster + English *mycosis*]

bot|ry|ose (bot′rē ōs), *adj.* **1** = botryoidal. **2** *Botany.* indeterminate.

bo|try|tis (bə trī′tis), *n.* any one of a genus of fungi which thrive in cool damp weather and attack the buds of flowering plants, causing them to shrivel up and die. [< New Latin *Botrytis* the genus name < Greek *bótrys* grape cluster]

bots (bots), *n.pl.* a disease especially of horses, cattle, sheep, and oxen, caused by infestation of the stomach and intestines with the larvae of botflies. Also, **botts.**

bott (bot), *n.* bot; the larva of a botfly.

bot|te|ga (bōt tā′gä), *n., pl.* **-ghe** (-gā). *Italian.* a studio; workshop.

bot|tine (bo tēn′), *n.* a woman's boot or shoe. [< French *bottine* (diminutive) < *botte* boot]

bot|tle[1] (bot′əl), *n., v.,* **-tled, -tling.** —*n.* **1** a container without handles for holding liquids, usually made of glass. Most bottles have narrow necks which can be closed with stoppers. Some bottles, however, have wide necks; some are closed with caps. *He dropped the bottle and it broke.* **2** the amount that a bottle can hold: *He can drink a whole bottle of soda at one time.*
—*v.t.* **1** to put into bottles: *Many companies bottle perfume.* **2** to hold in; keep back; control.
bottle up, to hold in; keep back; control: *He managed to bottle up his anger.*
crack a bottle, to open a bottle and drink what is in it: *Two gentlemen ... are cracking a bottle together at some inn* (Henry Fielding).
hit the bottle, *Slang.* **a** to drink a great deal of intoxicating liquor: [*She*] *started hitting the bottle at twenty ... Then, through the good offices of Alcoholics Anonymous, she got a grip on herself* (New Yorker). **b** to become intoxicated: *The first time he hit the bottle he became very sick.*
the bottle, *Slang.* intoxicating liquor: *The former alcoholic made up his mind to stay away from the bottle and he succeeded.*
[< Old French *boteille* < Medieval Latin *butticula* (diminutive) < Late Latin *buttis* cask, butt[4]]
—**bot′tle|like′**, *adj.*

bot|tle[2] (bot′əl), *n. British Dialect.* a bundle, such as one of hay or straw. [< Old French *botel* (diminutive) < *botte* cask]

bottle baby, **1** an infant who is bottle-fed rather than breast-fed. **2** *U.S. Slang.* a person who drinks too much alcoholic liquor.

bot|tle|brush (bot′əl brush′), *n.* any one of various plants, such as the mare's-tail or certain horsetails, that look like thin brushes.

bottle club, *U.S.* a private club at which alcoholic drinks are served after the legal closing hours of public bars.

bot|tled gas (bot′əld), butane, propane, or a similar gas liquefied and stored under pressure in portable tanks.

bottled in bond, *U.S.* untaxed during government-supervised storage of bottled whiskey.

bot|tle-feed (bot′əl fēd′), *v.t.*, **-fed** (fed), **-feed|ing.** to feed (a baby or young animal) with a bottle: *Visitors are invited to cuddle newborn calves and bottle-feed kids* (Harper's).

bot|tle|ful (bot′əl fu̇l), *n., pl.* **-fuls.** as much as a bottle will hold.

bottle gentian, = closed gentian.

bottle gourd, a gourd shaped like a flask, dried and used for a cup, bowl, or other container.

bottle green, a very dark green.

bot|tle|head (bot′əl hed′), *n.* = bottle-nosed whale.

bottle imp, a Cartesian devil.

bot|tle|neck (bot′əl nek′), *n., adj., v.* —*n.* **1** the neck of a bottle. **2** a narrow passageway or street. **3** a person, thing, or condition that hinders progress; check. **4** any situation in which progress is hindered: *Heavy traffic caused a bottleneck at the narrow bridge. Labor bottlenecks also are likely to develop in the ... construction and machine tool industries* (New York Times).
—*adj.* like a bottleneck; narrow: *Several highways converged into a bottleneck approach to the airport.*
—*v.t.* to confine in a bottleneck; hinder or delay: *to bottleneck traffic on an approach to a bridge.*
—*v.i.* to be hindered or delayed: *Decisions bottleneck on his desk* (Harper's).

bot|tle|nose (bot′əl nōz′), *n.* = bottle-nosed dolphin.

bot|tle-nosed dolphin (bot′əl nōzd′), a dolphin with a bottle-shaped nose. It grows up to 12 feet long and weighs as much as 800 pounds.

bottle-nosed whale, any one of various small whales, such as the blackfish.

bottle party, *U.S.* a party to which the guests bring their own alcoholic liquor.

bot|tler (bot′lər), *n.* a person or machine that bottles beverages or other liquids.

***bottle tree**, **1** an Australian tree with a short trunk that bulges like a round bottle. Australian aborigines make nets of bottle-tree fibers and drink bottle-tree sap. The bottle tree belongs to the sterculia family. **2** = sour gourd. **3** = baobab.

***bottle tree**
definition 1

bot|tle-wash|er (bot′əl wosh′ər, -wôsh′-), *n. Informal.* a general caretaker; factotum: *Marcovic had been the bodyguard, bottle-washer, and friend of film star Alain Delon* (London Times).

bot|tom (bot′əm), *n., adj., v.* —*n.* **1** the lowest part: *the bottom of the hill. These berries at the bottom of the basket are crushed.* **2** the part on which anything rests; base: *The bottom of that glass is wet.* **3** the ground under water: *Many wrecks lie at the bottom of the sea.* **4** Often, **bottoms,** *pl.* the low land along a river, especially when the river is large and the level area is of considerable extent. **5** a seat: *This chair needs a new bottom.* **6** *Figurative.* basis; foundation; origin: *We will get to the bottom of the mystery.* **SYN:** groundwork, base. **7** the buttocks. **8a** the keel or hull of a ship: *When the ship went over the rock it tore a hole in its bottom and sank.* **b** a ship. **9** the working part of a plow.

Pronunciation Key: hat, āge, cãre, fär; let, ēqual, tėrm; it, īce; hot, ōpen, ôrder; oil, out; cup, pu̇t, rüle; child; long; thin; ᴛʜen; zh, measure; ə represents **a** in about, **e** in taken, **i** in pencil, **o** in lemon, **u** in circus.

—*adj.* **1** lowest or last: *These are bottom prices. I see a robin on the bottom branch of that tree. I have spent my bottom dollar.* **2** *Figurative.* underlying; fundamental. **3a** of, having to do with, or at the bottom: *bottom life in the ocean.* **b** living at or near the bottom: *a bottom fish.*
—*v.t.* **1** to put a seat on. **2** *Figurative.* to get to the bottom of; understand fully. **3** to set upon a foundation; base; rest.
—*v.i.* **1** to rest on a foundation; be based or grounded. **2** to reach the bottom: *The boat has bottomed twice on this shallow stretch.*
at bottom, fundamentally: *He is, at bottom, a good-hearted fellow.*
be at the bottom of, to be the real author, source, or cause of: *Her headache was at the bottom of her grumpy behavior.*
bottom out, to reach the lowest possible part, from which only a rise is possible: *Signs of a bottoming out in the economy are becoming more pronounced* (Wall Street Journal).
bottoms up! *Informal.* drink up! empty your glass: *Matt liked a world of familiar . . . and well-worn refrains; without a touch of apology he gave "Bottoms up" toasts and uttered "See you in the funny papers" good nights* (New Yorker).
get to the bottom of, to discover the underlying source, cause, or significance of: *The British authorities tried to get to the bottom of the Boston Tea Party but the leaders remained unnamed.*
knock the bottom out of, to render invalid; make of no effect; bring to naught: *The rainstorm knocked the bottom out of our camping plans.*
scrape the bottom of the barrel, to use up one's last resources: *New plans must be found for raising money, he said, because "we are scraping the bottom of the barrel right now"* (New York Times).
the bottom falls out (of), to have a collapse (of): *The Toronto Stock market suffered the sharpest decline since the big drop of May, 1962, when the bottom fell out of the New York market* (New York Times).
[Old English *botm*]

bottom dog, *Informal.* an underdog: *The bottom dogs have remained on the bottom, sharing hardly at all in the advances that the income groups above them have made* (New Yorker).

-bottomed, *combining form.* having a ___ bottom: *Flat-bottomed boat = a boat having a flat bottom.*

bottom grass, grass growing in lowlands or bottom lands.

bottom heat, heat supplied to plants beneath their roots by fermenting or decomposing substances placed under them, by means of electricity, or by running flues or pipes under them.

bottom land, the low land along a river.

bot|tom|less (bot′əm lis), *adj.* **1a** without a bottom: *The satellite fell into bottomless space.* **b** *Figurative.* baseless. **2a** very, very deep; so deep that the bottom cannot be reached: *sunk in the bottomless depths of the sea, a bottomless lake in the mountains,* (*Figurative.*) *bottomless stupidity.* **SYN:** abysmal. **b** *Figurative.* unfathomable. **SYN:** immeasurable.

bottomless pit, **1** a pit into which Satan is to be cast for a thousand years (in the Bible, Revelation 20:1-3). **2** hell.

bottom line, *U.S. Informal.* practical result; main or essential point: *The message was guardedly drawn, in spots lawyerly to the point of obscurantism. . . . But the bottom line seemed plain: no deal* (Newsweek).

bot|tom|most (bot′əm mōst), *adj.* farthest down; lowest: *the bottommost layer.*

bot|tom|o|ni|um (bot′ə mō′nē əm), *n. Nuclear Physics.* a hypothetical particle consisting of a bottom quark and its antiparticle: *It was a fortunate thing in that CESR [a particle accelerator] was designed to operate optimally in just the energy range where bottomonium can be made before anyone knew what the mass of bottomonium would be* (Science News). [< *bottom* (quark) + *-onium*, as in *charmonium*]

bottom quark, a quark having three times the mass of a charmed quark: *The upsilon, formed of a bottom quark and a bottom antiquark, is 10 times more massive than the proton* (Walter Sullivan).

bottom round, a cut of meat from the outside of a round of beef.

bot|tom|ry (bot′əm rē), *n., pl.* **-ries.** a contract by which a shipowner mortgages his ship to get money to make a voyage. If the ship is lost, the lender loses the money. [< *bottom* (keel of a) ship, after Dutch *bodemerij*]

bottom yeast, a variety of brewers' yeast which grows at or near the bottom of a brewing vat.

botts (bots), *n.pl.* = bots.

bot|u|li|form (boch′ə lə fôrm), *adj. Botany.* sausage-shaped. [< Latin *botulus* sausage]

bot|u|lin or **bot|u|line** (boch′ə lin), *n.* the toxin formed by botulinus.

bot|u|li|nus (boch′ə lī′nəs), *n.* the bacterium causing botulism. [< New Latin *Botulinus* < Latin *botulus* sausage]

bot|u|lism (boch′ə liz əm), *n.* a poisoning caused by eating food that has been spoiled by the action of certain anaerobic bacteria, especially in foods not properly canned or preserved, as sausages, canned meats, and canned vegetables. It affects the nervous system of both men and animals and is frequently fatal. [< German *Botulismus* < Latin *botulus* sausage (sausages were originally responsible for many cases)]

bot|u|lis|mus (boch′ə liz′məs), *n.* = botulism. [< German *Botulismus*]

***bou|bou** (bü′bü), *n.* a long, shapeless garment worn by men and women in western Africa. Also, **bubu.** [< a native name]

***boubou**

bou|clé (bü klā′), *n., adj.* —*n.* **1** a knitted cloth having a surface with tiny loops and curls. **2** yarn used in making such a surface.
—*adj.* (of cloth) having a rough, knotted surface: *bouclé tweed.*
[< French *bouclé* knotted, corded, buckled over]

bou|din (bü daɴ′), *n. French.* blood pudding.

bou|doir (bü′dwär, -dwôr; bü dwär′, -dwôr′), *n.* a lady's private dressing room or sitting room. [< French *boudoir* (literally) a place to sulk]

bouf|fant (bü fänt′; *French* bü fäɴ′), *adj., n.* —*adj.* puffed out; billowy: *a bouffant skirt, a bouffant hairdo.* —*n.* a woman's puffed-out hairdo: *. . . a lady in the audience who wore a mink jacket and a big bouffant* (Harper's). [< French *bouffant*]

bouf|fante (bü fäɴt′), *adj. French.* bouffant (the feminine form).

bouffe (büf), *adj. French.* comic.

bou|gain|vil|le|a or **bou|gain|vil|lae|a** (bü′gən vil′ē ə), *n.* any one of a genus of tropical American climbing shrubs. The decorative "blossoms" of bougainvillea consist of large, bright-colored leaves (bracts) surrounding very small flowers. Bougainvillea belongs to the four-o'clock family. [< New Latin *Bougainvillaea* the genus name < L. A. de *Bougainville,* 1729-1811, a French navigator and explorer]

bough (bou), *n.* **1** one of the branches of a tree: *The rabbits hid under a pile of boughs cut from the tree.* **SYN:** See syn. under **branch.** **2** a branch cut from a tree, especially one laden with blossoms or fruit: *She held a blossoming bough from the apple tree.* **SYN:** See syn. at **branch.** **3** *Archaic.* the gallows. [Old English *bōg* bough, shoulder]

boughed (boud), *adj.* **1** having boughs. **2** shaded with boughs.

bough|pot (bou′pot′), *n.* **1** a pot or other vessel for holding boughs or flowers for ornament. **2** a flowerpot. **3** a bouquet.

bought[1] (bôt), *v.* the past tense and past participle of **buy**: *We bought apples from the farmer.*

bought[2] (bout), *n.* **1** a bend or curve. **2** a turn or loop, as in a rope; coil: *The dragon-boughts . . . Began to move, seethe, twine, and curl* (Tennyson). **3** *Obsolete.* a fold, as of cloth. [probable variant of *bight,* influenced by *bow*[1]]

bought|en (bô′tən), *adj. U.S. Dialect.* bought; not homemade.
▶**Boughten** is a nonstandard expression.

bough|y (bou′ē), *adj.* having many boughs.

bou|gie (bü′jē, -zhē; *French* bü zhē′), *n.* **1a** a thin, flexible instrument for exploring, dilating, and medicating passages of the body. **b** = suppository. **2** a wax candle. [< French *bougie* wax candle < *Bougie,* Algeria, where wax is exported]

bouil|la|baisse (bül′yə bās′; *French* bü yȧ bes′), *n.* a fish chowder often seasoned with white wine, saffron, and herbs. [< French *bouillabaisse* < Provençal *bouiabaisso* < *boui* to boil + *abaisso* (go) down (from its being brought quickly to a boil and then allowed to simmer down)]

bouil|li (bü yē′), *n. French.* boiled or stewed meat.

bouil|lon (bül′yon, -yən; *French* bü yôɴ′), *n.* **1** a clear, thin soup or broth. **2** a liquid, nutritive medium used for growing cultures of bacteria. [< French *bouillon* < *bouillir* boil[1]]

bouillon cube, bouillon dehydrated and made into a cube.

bouk (bük), *n. Scottish.* the trunk of the body. [Old English *būc*]

bou|lan|ge|rie (bü läɴ zhə rē′), *n. French.* a bakery.

boul|der (bōl′dər), *n.* a large rock, rounded or worn by the action of water or weather. Also, **bowlder.** [Middle English *bulder,* short for *bulderston,* probably < Scandinavian (compare Swedish *bullersten,* perhaps < *bullra* roar + *sten* stone)]

boulder clay, stiff, unlaminated, tenacious clay, especially that of the ice age, often containing boulders.

boul|der|y (bōl′dər ē), *adj.* **1** resembling a boulder. **2** full of boulders.

bou|le[1] (bü′lē), *n.* a legislative or advisory council in ancient Greece. [< Greek *boulḗ*]

boule[2] (bül), *n.* a synthetic ruby, sapphire, or the like, made by the fusion of powdered alumina into a bullet-shaped mass. [< French *boule* ball]

boule[3] (bül), *n.* = buhl.

boul|e|vard (bül′ə värd, bü′lə-), *n.* **1** a broad street or avenue, often planted with trees; wide thoroughfare: *We motored around the city on the boulevards. Boulevards of Paris, where walls once stood to defend the city against attack, are crowded with automobiles, buses, and taxis* (David F. Schoenbrun). *Abbr:* blvd. **2** *U.S. and Canadian Dialect.* a strip of grass between the sidewalk and street. **3** *Obsolete.* **a** the flat top of a rampart. **b** a street on the site of demolished fortifications. [< French *boulevard* (originally) the passageway along a rampart < Middle Low German *bolwerk* < Middle Dutch *bolwerc* bulwark]

bou|le|var|dier (bül vär dyā′), *n. French.* a gay and dashing fellow; man-about-town.

bou|le|ver|se|ment (bül vers mäɴ′), *n. French.* a turning upside down; overthrow; confusion.

boulle (bül), *n.* = buhl.

boul|ter (bōl′tər), *n.* a long fishing line strung with a number of hooks. [a Cornish dialectal form]

boun (boun), *adj., v. Archaic.* —*adj.* **1** ready; prepared. **2** ready or intending to go; bound.
—*v.t.* to make ready; prepare.
—*v.i.* **1** to get ready. **2** to set out; go.
[Middle English *boun,* older form of *bound*[4]]

bounce (bouns), *v.,* **bounced, bounc|ing,** *n.*
—*v.i.* **1** to spring into the air like a ball: *The baby likes to bounce up and down on the bed.* **2** to come and go, especially noisily, angrily, or excitedly; burst or bound: *She bounced out of the room.* **3** to leap; spring. **4** *Informal.* (of a check) to be refused by the bank on which it is drawn, for lack of funds in the account of the person who signed it: *She had no money and her check bounced when I went to cash it.* **5** *Obsolete.* to knock loudly. —*v.t.* **1** to cause to spring into the air: *Bounce the ball to me.* **2** to relay or reflect (a signal or message) by a communications satellite. **3** *Slang.* to throw out; eject. **4** *Slang.* to discharge from work or employment. **5** *Obsolete.* to thump; knock; bang.
—*n.* **1** a springing back; bound; bouncing: *I caught the ball on the first bounce.* **SYN:** rebound. **2** a sudden spring or leap. **3** a boasting; a bragging: *The whole story is a bounce of his own* (Thomas De Quincey). **4** *Informal.* ability to recover; energy; spirit: *He is as full of bounce as ever, despite his troubles.* **SYN:** resilience. **5** a heavy blow or thump. **6** *Slang.* discharge from work or employment: *Had you ever thought . . . of giving her the bounce yourself?* (O. Henry).
bounce back, to begin anew, especially with vigor or enthusiasm: *He bounced back after his failure and made a fortune.*
[Middle English *bunsen.* Compare Dutch *bonzen* thump.]

bounce|back (bouns′bak′), *n.* a bouncing back to a former position.

bounc|er (boun′sər), *n.* **1** a person or thing that bounces. **2** anything very large of its kind. **3** *Informal.* a person who boasts or brags. **4** *Slang.* a strong man hired by a night club, hotel, or the like, to throw out disorderly persons. **5** *British Informal.* a thumping lie; a whopper.

bounc|ing (boun′sing), *adj.* **1** that bounces: *a bouncing ball.* **2** big and strong. **3** vigorous; healthy: *a bouncing baby boy.* —**bounc′ing|ly,** *adv.*

bouncing Bet or **Bess**, a European plant of the pink family naturalized in the United States, growing wild by roadsides, etc., and having white or pink, often double flowers. It is a species of soapwort.

bounc|ing-pin indicator (boun′sing pin′), an apparatus for measuring the intensity of the detonation taking place in a cylinder of an internal-combustion engine, used especially in testing fuels.

bounc|y (boun′sē), *adj.,* **bounc|i|er, bounc|i|est.** *Informal.* **1a** that bounces; bouncing. **b** full of bounces: *a bouncy ride.* **c** springy: *a bouncy diving board.* **2a** having a bouncing rhythm or tempo: *a bouncy piece of music.* **b** lively; quick: *a bouncy style.* **3a** energetic; vivacious; ebullient: *. . . a plump, bouncy man wearing a flowered tie*

(New Yorker). **b** cocky: *a bouncy manner.* —**bounc′i|ly**, *adv.* —**bounc′i|ness**, *n.*

bound[1] (bound), *adj., v.* —*adj.* **1** under some obligation; obliged: *I feel bound by my promise. It is better to love than to hate, to question than to accept, to be free than to be bound* (Mardi Valgemae). **2** certain; sure: *Everyone is bound to make a mistake sooner or later. If you continue trying, you are bound to find the answer.* **3** *U.S. Informal.* with one's mind firmly made up; determined; resolved: *He was bound to spend all of his savings, though we did our best to stop him.* **4** put in covers: *a bound book.* **5** tied fast; fastened: *bound hands.* **6** held by a chemical bond. **7** constipated.
—*v.* the past tense and past participle of **bind**: *The pirates bound their prisoners with ropes.*
bound up in (or **with**), **a** closely connected with: *A farmer's life is bound up in his work.* **b** very devoted to: *The old friends are completely bound up in each other.*
[shortened < *bounden,* past participle]

bound[2] (bound), *v., n.* —*v.i.* **1** to spring back; bounce; rebound: *The rubber ball bounded from the wall.* **2** to leap or spring lightly along; jump: *Mountain goats can bound from rock to rock.* **3** to leap or spring upward: *to bound into the air.*
—*v.t.* to cause to bound or rebound; bounce.
—*n.* **1** a spring back; a bounce; rebound: *I caught the ball on the first bound.* **2** a leaping or springing lightly along; jump: *The deer's bound over the ice sounded like breaking glass.* **3** a leap or spring upward or onward: *With one bound the deer went into the woods.*
[< French *bondir* leap < Old French, resound < Gallo-Romance *bombītīre* buzz, ultimately < Latin *bombus* a booming sound < Greek *bómbos*]

bound[3] (bound), *n., v.* —*n.* **1** Often, **bounds**, *pl.* a limiting line; boundary; limit: *The king maintained peace and order within the bound of his realm.* (*Figurative.*) *Keep your hopes within bounds.* **SYN**: border, confine. **2** *Mathematics.* a number which a function does not exceed (upper bound) or does not go below (lower bound).
—*v.t.* **1a** to form the boundary of; limit: *Canada bounds the United States on the north. A line of blue hills that bounded the landscape* (Washington Irving). **b** *Figurative: He was forced to bound his desires by reason.* **2** to name the boundaries of: *Can you bound the state of North Carolina?* **3** *Obsolete.* to enclose; contain: *Whose veins bound richer blood than Lady Blanch* (Shakespeare).
—*v.i.* to share a boundary; have its boundary (on): *They bound on us between two and three thousand miles* (Thomas Jefferson). **SYN**: abut, adjoin.
beat the bounds, to tour the limits of a parish, in procession, striking the boundary markers with boughs, as a ceremony calling attention to the proper boundaries: *Beating the bounds is an old English custom.*
bounds, a land on or near a boundary: *He warned them against trespassing a second time on his bounds.* **b** the area included within boundaries, especially as established by rule, custom, or law: *He kicked the ball out of bounds. This town is out of bounds for the soldiers.*
perambulate the bounds, to make an official inspection of the boundaries of a town, traditionally the jurisdiction of town governments in New England.
[< Old French *bodne* < Medieval Latin *bodina.* See etym. of doublet **bourn**[2].]

bound[4] (bound), *adj.* on the way; going: *I am bound for home. He entered a train bound for Chicago.* [Middle English *boun* < Scandinavian (compare Old Icelandic *būinn,* past participle of *būa* get ready)]

bound|a|ry (boun′dər ē, -drē), *n., pl.* **-ries**. **1a** a limiting line or thing; limit; border: *Lake Superior forms part of the boundary between Canada and the United States.* **b** *Figurative: the boundaries of human thought.* **2** *British.* **a** the limit of a cricket field. **b** a hit to or off the boundary: *His first full scoring strokes were boundaries* (London Times). [< *bound*[3] + *-ary*]

boundary layer, **1** *Physics.* the region next to the surface of a stationary body in which fluid flows at a much slower velocity than elsewhere. **2** *Aerodynamics.* a thin layer of air next to an airfoil of an aircraft in flight, distinguishable from the main airflow by characteristic differences in flow.

boundary rider, a person who rides horseback to inspect and repair fences on a cattle or sheep ranch in Australia or New Zealand.

bound charge, an electrostatic charge which is bound by a charge opposite in polarity to it.

bound|ed (boun′did), *adj. Mathematics.* **1** (of a function) having both an upper bound and a lower bound, always less than some fixed number and also greater than some fixed number. **2** contained within some fixed closed curve. —**bound′ed|ness**, *n.*

bound electron, an electron which is bound to a proton and neutron in certain atoms.

bound|en (boun′dən), *adj.* **1** required; obligatory: *A child's bounden duty is to obey his parents.* **2** under obligation because of favors received; obliged. [past participle of *bind*]

bound|er (boun′dər), *n. Informal.* a rude, vulgar person; upstart; cad. [< *bound*[2]]

bound|er|ish (boun′dər ish), *adj.* of or characteristic of a bounder.

bound|er|ism (boun′də riz əm), *n.* the behavior of a bounder.

bound form, a linguistic form which is part of a larger unit and never occurs alone, such as *-ly* in *coldly.*

bound|less (bound′lis), *adj.* **1** not limited; infinite: *Outer space is boundless.* **2** vast: *the boundless ocean. He has boundless energy.* —**bound′less|ly**, *adv.* —**bound′less|ness**, *n.*

bounds (boundz), *n.pl.* See under **bound**[3].

bound verse, verse that is bound to or based on a metrical pattern. Bound verse is an older and commoner form of verse than free verse.

bound water, water that is a basic part of any substance, so that its removal changes the substance's chemical composition: *In the freeze-drying process ... almost all the water is removed, leaving only about 2.5 per cent of bound water which prevents the protein molecules from breaking down* (New Scientist).

boun|te|ous (boun′tē əs), *adj.* **1** given freely; generous: *The rich man gave bounteous gifts to the poor.* **SYN**: liberal, beneficent, munificent. **2** plentiful; abundant: *Because of the spring rains, the farmers had a bounteous crop.* **SYN**: copious. [alteration of Middle English *bountyvous* < Old French *bontif, -ive* full of goodness < *bonté* goodness, bounty] —**boun′te|ous|ly**, *adv.* —**boun′te|ous|ness**, *n.*

boun|ti|ful (boun′tə fəl), *adj.* **1** giving freely; generous; open-handed: *the help of bountiful friends.* **2** more than enough; plentiful; abundant: *We put in so many plants that we have a bountiful supply of tomatoes.* —**boun′ti|ful|ly**, *adv.* —**boun′ti|ful|ness**, *n.*

boun|ty (boun′tē), *n., pl.* **-ties**, *v.,* **-tied**, **-ty|ing**.
—*n.* **1** whatever is given freely; generous gift. **2** generosity in bestowing gifts: *the bounty of Providence, the bounty of Nature.* **SYN**: liberality, munificence. **3** a reward: *In the early days of the West many states paid a bounty for captured criminals.*
—*v.t.* **1** to give a bounty to. **2** to pay for with a bounty: *The bobcat is often regarded as a predator and is bountied* (New York Times).
—*v.i.* to give out as bounty: *For every pound ... we were bountying out this year we shall get back thirty bob in trade* (Punch).
[< Old French *bonté* < Latin *bonitās* < *bonus* good]

bounty hunter, a person who hunts fugitives from the law or harmful animals to collect the bounty for their capture.

bounty jumper, *U.S.* a person who enlisted as a soldier during the Civil War for the sake of the bounty offered and then deserted.

bou|quet (bō kā′, bü- *for 1;* bü kā′ *for 2 and 3*), *n.* **1** a bunch of flowers; nosegay. **2** the fragrance or aroma that rises from a wine or liqueur and often forms one of its valued characteristics. **3** *Figurative.* praise; compliment: *Chorus and orchestra win full praise, but perhaps the biggest bouquet should be reserved for the engineers* (London Times). [< Middle French *bouquet* < Old North French *bousquet* (diminutive) < Old French *bosc* wood]

bou|quet gar|ni (bō kā′ gär nē′), *pl.* **bou|quets gar|nis** (bō kāz′ gär nē′). herbs, often consisting of parsley, bay leaf, and thyme, wrapped in cheesecloth and put in soups or cooked with roasts and other foods as a flavoring. [< French *bouquet garni* (literally) garnished bouquet]

bou|qui|niste (bü kē nēst′), *n. French.* a dealer in used books.

bour|bon or **Bour|bon**[1] (bėr′bən, bůr′-), *n.* an American whiskey distilled mainly from fermented corn mash. [American English < *Bourbon* County, Kentucky, where originally manufactured]

Bour|bon[2] (bůr′bən; *occasionally* bėr′bən), *n.* **1** a member of the last royal family of France, ruling from 1589 to 1792, from 1814 to 1815, and from 1815 to 1848. Members of the family also ruled in Spain, Sicily, and parts of Italy, especially Naples. The Bourbons were in power in France when the French Revolution began. **2** a person who clings to old ideas and opposes any change; extreme conservative; reactionary. [< *Bourbon* l'Archambault, a town in France]

Bour|bon|ism (bůr′bə niz əm; *occasionally* bėr′bə niz əm), *n.* **1** support of the Bourbons. **2** extreme conservatism in politics; reaction. —**Bour′bon|ist**, *n.*

bour|don (bůr′dən, bôr′-, bōr′-), *n.* **1a** the bass pipe (drone) of a bagpipe. **b** the unvarying sound made by it. **2a** a bass stop in an organ. **b** a similar stop in a harmonium. **3a** the refrain of a song. **b** (formerly) a low undersong or vocal accompaniment to a melody. [< Middle French *bourdon,* Old French, drone (of a bee). See etym. of doublet **burden**[2].]

Bourdon gauge, a device for measuring pressures, consisting of a curved or spiral elastic tube (Bourdon tube) with an oval cross section. The tube tends to straighten under pressure moving a needle on an attached indicator showing the pressure of the fluid, gas, or steam measured in the tube. [< Eugène *Bourdon,* 1808-1884, a French engineer, who invented the gauge]

Bourdon tube, the curved or spiral tube of a Bourdon gauge.

bou|rette (bü ret′), *n.* a fabric with small knots or lumps at intervals over the surface, due to irregularities in the yarn. [< French *bourrette* coarse silk < Old French *bourre* rough cloth]

bourg (bůrg), *n.* **1** a town: *Ye think the rustic cackle of your bourg The murmur of the world!* (Tennyson). **2** a market town. [< Middle French *bourg* < Late Latin *burgus* < Germanic (compare Old High German *burg* small town)]

bour|geois[1] (bůr zhwä′, bůr′zhwä), *n., pl.* **-geois**, *adj.* —*n.* **1** a person of the middle class, such as a merchant or professional person. A bourgeois is traditionally thought of as having a higher social position than a wage earner or farm hand and lower than an aristocrat or person of great wealth. **2** a person who owns property or who is engaged in business or commerce as an owner or partner, in contrast to a proletarian. **3** (originally) a citizen or freeman of a French city or burgh.
—*adj.* **1** of or characteristic of the middle class: *'Bourgeois' ... is an epithet which the riffraff apply to what is respectable and the aristocracy to what is decent* (Anthony Hope). **2a** like the middle class in way of thinking, appearance, or the like; ordinary: *bourgeois attitudes.* **SYN**: common. **b** lacking in dignity or refinement; mean: *bourgeois taste.* **SYN**: common.
the bourgeois, the middle class collectively: *... progressive Hypatia, conscientiously shocking the bourgeois to right and left* (New Statesman).
[< French *bourgeois* < Medieval Latin *burgensis* a town dweller < Late Latin *burgus* bourg. See etym. of doublet **burgess**.]

bour|geois[2] (bər jois′), *n.* a size of type between brevier and long primer; 9 point. [supposedly from the name of a French printer]

bour|geoise (bůr zhwäz′), *n., pl.* **bour|geoises** (bůr zhwäz′), *adj.* feminine of **bourgeois**[1]: *De Baudricourt reminds Poulengey that "she's not a farm wench, she's a bourgeoise"* (Punch).

bour|geoi|sie (bůr′zhwä zē′), *n.* **1** the middle class. **2** people traditionally thought of as being of the middle class; people between the very wealthy class and the working class: *French business matured in an old-fashioned manner and behind the times because it was controlled by the French bourgeoisie with their old habit and privilege of high profits, restricted production, high prices and small salaries* (New York Times). **3** property owners and businessmen as a class, as contrasted with the working class or proletariat. [< French *bourgeoisie* < *bourgeois*]

bour|geoi|si|fy (bůr zhwä′sə fī), *v.t.,* **-fied**, **-fy|ing**. to change to bourgeois characteristics or values; turn bourgeois: *... Castro's Cuba and Mao's China, countries where the popular revolution has not yet become "bourgeoisified"* (Atlantic). —**bour′geoi|si|fi|ca′tion**, *n.*

bour|geon (bėr′jən), *n., v.i., v.t.* = burgeon.

***bourkha**

***bour|kha** (bůr′kä), *n.* a long robe worn by Moslem women, especially in India and Pakistan. It envelops her from the top of her head to the ground except for a veiled opening for the eyes. Also, **burka**. [< Hindustani *burqā* < Arabic *burqu'*]

Pronunciation Key: hat, āge, cãre, fär; let, ēqual, tėrm; it, īce; hot, ōpen, ôrder; oil, out; cup, pu̇t, rüle; child; long; thin; ᴛʜen; zh, measure; ə represents **a** in about, **e** in taken, **i** in pencil, **o** in lemon, **u** in circus.

bourn¹ or **bourne¹** (bôrn, bōrn), *n.* a small stream; brook: . . . *every bosky bourn* (Milton). Also, **burn.** [Old English *burna*]

bourn² or **bourne²** (bôrn, bōrn, bu̇rn), *n.* **1** *Archaic.* a boundary; limit: *The undiscovered country, from whose bourn No traveler returns* (Shakespeare). **2** *Archaic.* a goal; aim. **3** *Obsolete.* a realm; domain. [< Middle French *bourne,* Old French, earlier *bodne.* See etym. of doublet **bound³**.]

bour|rée (bü rā′), *n.* **1** a lively dance, of French origin, in duple time. **2** a musical composition, usually in duple rhythm, in which the character of the dance is represented. It is allied to the gavotte. [< French *bourrée* rustic dance]

bour|re|let (bu̇r rə lā′), *n.* a narrow, smoothly machined band on a shell that lies near the shell's center of gravity and touches the inside of the gun barrel.

bourse (bu̇rs), *n.* an exchange where merchants transact business with one another, especially a stock exchange. [< French *bourse* (originally) purse < Late Latin *bursa*]

Bourse (bu̇rs), *n.* the stock exchange in Paris, and in certain other European cities.

bour|tree (bu̇r′trē), *n. Scottish,* a common European elder tree. [origin uncertain]

bouse¹ (bous, bouz), *v.t.,* **boused, bous|ing.** *Nautical.* to pull up or about with tackle. Also, **bowse.** [origin uncertain]

bouse² (büz, bouz), *n., v.,* **boused, bous|ing.** —*n.* **1** *Informal.* alcoholic liquor; drink; booze. **2** a drinking bout.
—*v.i.* to drink to excess. Also, **bowse.**
[perhaps < Middle Dutch *busen* to booze]

bou|stro|phe|don (büs′trə fē′dən, bous′-), *n., adj.* —*n.* an ancient method of writing in which the lines run alternately from right to left and from left to right, such as in various ancient inscriptions in Egyptian, Greek, and certain other languages.
—*adj.* written in this way.
[< Greek *boustrophēdon* with turning like that of oxen in plowing < *boûs* ox + *stréphein* to turn]

bous|y (bü′zē, bou′-), *adj.* drunk; intoxicated.

bout (bout), *n.* **1** a trial of strength or skill; contest: *Those are the two boxers who will appear in the main bout.* SYN: match. **2** a length of time spent in a particular way; spell: *I have just had a long bout of illness.* **3** a turn; bend. [perhaps variant of *bought* a bending, turn]

bou|tique (bü tēk′), *n.* a small shop that specializes in stylish clothes and accessories: *Much of the excitement in fashion has been generated by the adventurous . . . boutiques of London, Paris, and New York* (New York Times). [< French *boutique* < Greek *apothēkē* storehouse; see etym. under **apothecary**]

boutique farm, a farm that specializes in raising exotic crops and livestock.

boutique farmer, a person who owns or works on a boutique farm.

boutique farming, the act or fact of engaging in the operation of a boutique farm.

bou|ti|quier (bu̇′tē kyā′), *n.* the owner of a boutique. [< French *boutiquier*]

bou|ton|niere or **bou|ton|nière** (bü′tə nyãr′), *n.* a flower or flowers worn in a buttonhole.
[< French *boutonnière* buttonhole < *bouton* button]

bou|var|di|a (bü vär′dē ə), *n.* **1** a tropical American plant of the madder family having clusters of red, yellow, pink, or white flowers, used especially in bridal bouquets. **2** a flower of this plant.
[< New Latin *Bouvardia* < Charles *Bouvard,* superintendent of The Royal Gardens, Paris]

Bou|vier des Flan|dres (bü vyā′ dā fläN′drə), *pl.* **Bou|viers des Flan|dres** (bü vyā′ dā fläN′drə). any one of a breed of working dogs developed in Belgium, having a rough fawn to black coat and standing 23 to 27 inches high. [< French *Bouvier des Flandres* cowherd of Flanders]

***bou|zou|ki** (bü zü′kē), *n., pl.* **-kis.** a stringed instrument resembling a mandolin, capable of producing chords similar in tone to those of a harpsichord, and used especially in folk singing and dancing. [< New Greek *mpouzouki*]

***bouzouki**

bou|zou|ki|a (bü zü′kē ə), *n.* music for the bouzouki. [< New Greek *mpouzoukia*]

bo|var|ism or **bo|var|ysm** (bō′və riz əm), *n.* a romantic outlook on life, especially as typified by Emma Bovary, the main character in Flaubert's *Madame Bovary.*

bo|vid (bō′vid), *adj.,* of or having to do with the family of animals comprising the hollow-horned ruminants, such as oxen, sheep, goats, and antelopes. [< New Latin *Bovidae* the ox family < Latin *bōs, bovis* ox, cow]

bo|vine (bō′vīn), *adj., n.* —*adj.* **1** of an ox or cow. **2** *Figurative.* like an ox or cow; slow; stupid: *She gave me a vacant bovine stare.* **3** *Figurative.* without emotion; stolid: *Her cold nature is bovine. Her placid bovine face gave no response.* **4** belonging to the group of mammals that chew the cud, including domestic cattle, bison, water buffaloes, and the like.
—*n.* **1** an ox or cow. **2** any animal belonging to a group of mammals that chew the cud, including domestic cattle, bison, water buffaloes, and the like. [< Late Latin *bovīnus* < Latin *bōs, bovis* ox, cow] —**bo′vine|ly,** *adv.*

bo|vo|vac|cine (bō′vō vak′sēn, -vak sēn′), *n.* a vaccine used to prevent tuberculosis in cattle.

Bov|ril (bov′rəl), *n. Trademark,* a drink made from a meat extract.

bov|ver (bov′ər), *n. British Slang.* street fighting by a gang or gangs, especially in which heavy, hobnailed boots are used for kicking. [origin unknown]

bow¹ (bou), *v., n.* —*v.i.* **1** to bend the head or body in greeting, respect, worship, or submission: *The people bowed before the king. He smiled, bowed, and extended his hand* (Macaulay). **2** *Figurative.* to give in; submit; yield (to): *The boy bowed to his parents' wishes.* SYN: acquiesce. **3** *Archaic and Dialect.* to bend; curve: (*Figurative.*) *Better bow than break.*
—*v.t.* **1** to bend (the head or body) in greeting, respect, worship, or submission: *The minister bowed his head in prayer.* **2** to show by bowing: *The actors bowed their thanks at the end of the play.* **3** to usher with a bow or bows. **4** to cause to stoop; bend: *The old man was bowed by age.* **5** *Figurative.* to submit; yield: *The king bowed his will to the nobles' demands.* **6** *Archaic and Dialect.* to cause to bend.
—*n.* the act of bending the head or body in greeting, respect, worship, or submission: *She answered his bow with a curtsy.* SYN: nod.
bow and scrape, to be too polite or slavish: *Every time I see the President the band has been playing "Hail to the Chief" and everyone has been bowing and scraping* (Time).
bow down, a to weigh down: *bowed down with care.* **b** to worship: *O come, let us . . . bow down: let us kneel before the Lord our maker* (Psalms 95:6).
bow out, a to withdraw: *[He] . . . bowed out of the picture because he found it difficult to work in location sequences being filmed . . . at altitudes ranging up to 10,000 feet* (New York Times). **b** to usher out: *returning from bowing out Dr. Sneyd with much civility* (H. Martineau).
make one's bow, a to make an entrance: *Making his bow into the ballroom, the Senator was greeted with applause.* **b** to make an initial appearance before the public: *She will make her bow as a singer in a new musical comedy.* **c** to retire from public notice: *After an eventful political career, he finally made his bow at the age of seventy.*
take a bow, to accept praise or applause for something done: *After the dinner, the guest of honor was asked to take a bow.*
[Old English *būgan*]

***bow²**
definitions 1, 2a

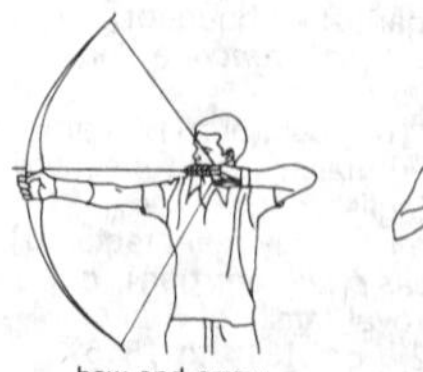

bow and arrow

violin bow

***bow²** (bō), *n., v., adj.* —*n.* **1** a weapon for shooting arrows. A bow usually consists of a strip of flexible wood bent by a string. Modern bows are also made of many strips of wood glued together, or of metal or spun glass. **2a** a slender rod with horsehairs stretched on it for playing a violin, cello, or some other stringed instruments. **b** a single stroke of the bow across a string or strings. **3** a curve; bend: *the bow of a person's lips.* **4a** something curved: *A rainbow is a bow.* **b** something resembling a bow. **5** a looped knot; bowknot: *tie your shoelaces in a bow. She wears a bow of blue ribbon in her hair.* **6** *U.S.* either of two arms fastened by hinges to the outer edges of a pair of spectacles and fitting over the ears. **7** *U.S.* a metal loop or ring forming a handle, such as in a watch, key, or scissors. **8** *Archaic.* = bowman. **9** *Dialect.* = oxbow.
—*v.t.* **1** to play (a violin, cello, or some other stringed instruments) with a bow. **2** to curve; bend: *The branches of the young tree were bowed by the weight of the snow.*
—*v.i.* **1** to have a curved shape; be bent. **2** to use a bow on a violin, cello, or some other stringed instruments.
—*adj.* shaped like a bow; bent; bowed.
[Old English *boga*] —**bow′less,** *adj.* —**bow′like′,** *adj.*

bow³ (bou), *n.* **1** the front part of a ship, boat, or aircraft. SYN: prow, stem. **2** = bow oar.
bows on, with the bow of the vessel turned toward the object considered or in view: *The 'standard type' has equal offensive strength in all directions—whether bows on or broadside* (Westminster Gazette).
on the bow, within 45 degrees of a line directly ahead: *A trawler is steaming into a gale with wind and sea . . . on the bow* (London Times).
[compare Middle Dutch *boegh* shoulder, Danish *bov.* See related etym. at **bough.**]

Bow bells, or **Bow|bells** (bō′belz′), *n.pl.* the bells of Bow Church, in London (St. Mary-le-Bow). Because it is nearly in the center of the City of London, the phrase *within the sound of Bow bells* came to be synonymous with "within the City bounds."

bow chaser (bou), a gun at the bow of a ship, for firing at vessels pursued.

bow compass (bō), a small pair of compasses for drawing small circles or arcs, especially one whose legs are held apart by a curved spring.

Bow|ditch (bou′dich), *n. U.S. Nautical.* a manual of navigation, especially any one of a series of manuals published since 1802. [< Nathaniel *Bowditch,* 1773-1838, an American mathematician and astronomer, who edited the first of these manuals]

bowd|ler|ism (boud′lə riz əm), *n.* the practice of bowdlerizing; bowdlerization.

bowd|ler|ize (boud′lə rīz), *v.t.,* **-ized, -iz|ing.** to remove or alter words or passages in (a book or writing) thought to be improper: *He touches on the perennial subject of "Bawdry" with the resolute masculine statement that rather than bowdlerize such songs he will not deal with them at all* (Newsweek). [< Thomas *Bowdler,* 1754-1825, who published an expurgated edition of Shakespeare in 1818] —**bowd′ler|i|za′tion,** *n.* —**bowd′ler|iz|er,** *n.*

***bow|drill** (bō′dril′), *n.* a tool for drilling, consisting of a small bow, string, and pointed stick. It was used by some primitive people to bore holes in stone, shell, or other hard objects. It can also be used to start a fire by friction when applied to very soft wood.

***bowdrill**

bow|el (bou′əl, boul), *n., v.,* **-eled, -el|ing** or (*especially British*) **-elled, -el|ling.** —*n.* a part of the bowels; intestine. SYN: gut.
—*v.t.* to take out the bowels of; disembowel. SYN: eviscerate.
[< Old French *boel* < Vulgar Latin *botellus* intestine < Latin, little sausage (diminutive) < *botulus* sausage]

bowel movement, 1 the discharge of waste matter from the intestines. **2** the waste matter discharged; excrement.

bow|els (bou′əlz, boulz), *n.pl.* **1** the tube in the body into which food passes from the stomach; intestines. **2** *Informal.* = colon. **3** *Figurative.* the inner part of anything; depths: *Miners dig for coal in the bowels of the earth.* SYN: heart, center. **4** *Archaic, Figurative.* **a** a pity; tender feelings: *bowels of compassion* (I John 3:17). **b** the inner parts as the seat of pity or kindness.

Bow|en's disease (bō′ənz), a precancerous condition of the skin marked by the formation of reddish pustules covered by a horny layer of tissue. [< John T. *Bowen,* 1857-1940, an American dermatologist]

bow|er¹ (bou′ər), *n., v.* —*n.* **1** a shelter of leafy branches. **2** an arbor. **3** a dwelling, especially a rustic abode. **4** *Archaic.* a bedroom.
—*v.t.* to embower; enclose.
[Old English *būr* dwelling] —**bow′er|like′,** *adj.*

bow|er² (bou′ər), *n.* one of the two anchors carried at the bow of a ship. [< *bow³*]

bow|er³ (bou′ər), *n.* the jack of trumps (right

bower) or the other jack of the same color (left bower) in certain card games. The joker is sometimes called best bower. They rank: best bower, right bower, and left bower, above all other cards. [American English < German *Bauer* jack (in cards), peasant]

bow|er[4] (bou′ər), *n.* a person who bows or stoops. [< *bow*[1] + *-er*[1]]

bow|er[5] (bō′ər), *n.* a player on a violin or other stringed instrument played with a bow. [< *bow*[2] + *-er*[1]]

bow|er|bird (bou′ər bėrd′), *n.* any one of a family of birds of Australia and New Guinea, the males of which build bowers decorated to attract the females. [< *bower*[1] + *bird*]

bow|er|maid|en (bou′ər mā′dən), *n. Archaic.* a maid or woman who attends a lady. [< *bower*[1] (bedroom) + *maiden*]

bow|er|y[1] (bou′ər ē), *adj.* **1** like a bower; leafy; shady. **2** containing bowers. [< *bower*[1] + *-y*[1]]

bow|er|y[2] (bou′ər ē), *n., pl.* **-er|ies.** a farm or estate of colonial Dutch settlers of New York: *He had his little bowery, or retreat in the country* (Washington Irving). [American English < Dutch *bouwerij* farm < *bouwer* farmer]

Bow|er|y (bou′ər ē), *n.* **the, 1** a street in New York City, once its theatrical center, that now has cheap stores, amusements, and flophouses, known as the place of derelicts and alcoholics. **2** the part of New York City where this street is located. [< *bowery*[2]]

bow fast, a hawser or chain at the bow to secure a vessel to a wharf.

bow|fin (bō′fin′), *n.* a freshwater fish found chiefly in the rivers of eastern North America; mudfish.

bow-front (bō′frunt′), *adj.* curved outward; bombé: *a bow-front chest.*

bow|grace (bou′grās′), *n.* a fender or bumper, as of rope, old cordage, or oakum, for protecting a ship's bow from floating ice or other obstructions.

bow hand (bō), **1** *Archery.* the hand that holds the bow, usually the left hand. **2** *Music.* the hand that holds the bow of a violin or some other stringed instruments, usually the right hand.

on the bow hand, off the mark; all wrong (perhaps because the bow hand in archery is the left hand, which is usually more awkward than the right): *He shoots wide on the bow hand, and very far from the mark* (Edmund Spenser).

bow|head (bō′hed′), *n.* = arctic right whale.

bow|ie (bou′ē), *n. Scottish.* **1** a tub. **2** a wooden container for milk or porridge. [origin unknown]

bow|ie knife (bō′ē, bü′-), a long, single-edged hunting knife carried in a sheath. A bowie knife has a blade from 10 to 15 inches long, curved near the point. [American English < Colonel James *Bowie,* 1799-1836, American pioneer, the supposed inventor or popularizer]

bow|ing (bō′ing), *n.* **1** the direction of the strokes of the bow in playing the violin, or some other stringed instruments, on music scores commonly marked for downward and upward strokes. **2** the technique of using the bow to produce various effects, as *spiccato* or *saltato.*

bow|ing acquaintance (bou′ing), a slight acquaintance; nodding acquaintance.

bow|knot (bō′not′), *n.* a slipknot such as is made in tying shoelaces; bow. It usually has two loops and two ends, and can be untied by pulling the ends.

bowl[1] (bōl), *n.* **1** a hollow, rounded dish, usually without handles: *Cake batter was in the mixing bowl.* **2** the amount that a bowl can hold; bowlful: *She had a bowl of soup for lunch.* **3** the hollow, rounded part of anything: *The bowl of a pipe holds the tobacco.* **4** a formation or structure shaped like a bowl: *The Yale Bowl is a stadium used for football and other sports.* **5** *Archaic.* **a** a large drinking cup: *Fill high the sparkling bowl* (Thomas Gray). **b** *Figurative.* drinking: *O'er the bowl they communed* (Robert Southey). **c** *Figurative.* drink. [Old English *bolla*] —**bowl′like′**, *adj.*

bowl[2] (bōl), *n., v.* —*n.* **1** a large, heavy ball used in certain games. The balls used in bowls are wooden; those in bowling are made of hard rubber or plastic. **2** a throw or casting of a bowl in modern bowling, ninepins, or bowls. **3** the disk sometimes used in playing skittles. **4** the roller or cylinder in some machines.

—*v.i.* **1** to play the game of bowls or bowling: *The men bowled until their arms were sore.* **2** to roll a bowl, as in the game of bowls. **3** to roll or move along rapidly and smoothly: *The car bowled along on the open highway. We bowled through the little village of Overton* (William Black). **4** to deliver the ball to the batsman in the game of cricket. This must be done without the elbow being bent.

—*v.t.* **1** to roll (a bowl) along the ground toward the jack. **2** to roll or cause (something) to move along rapidly and smoothly: *In the spring the children bowl their hoops.* **3** in cricket: **a** to deliver (a ball) to the batsman. **b** to knock down (a wicket) or knock off (the bails). **c** to put out, or dismiss (a batsman) by knocking down a wicket. **4** to carry or remove in a wheeled vehicle: *The wretched fellow was bowled to hell in the devil's chaise* (Shelley).

bowl down, to knock down: *The contender was bowled down during the first round of the boxing match.*

bowl over, a to knock over: *The force of the wind nearly bowled him over.* **b** *Informal, Figurative.* to make helpless and confused; bewilder; nonplus: *I was bowled over by the bad news.* [< Old French *boule* < Latin *bulla* ball, bubble, knob]

bowl|der (bōl′dər), *n.* = boulder.

bow|leg (bō′leg′), *n.* **1** a leg that curves outward in the middle and back in at its extremities. **2** an outward curve of the legs.

bow|leg|ged (bō′leg′id, -legd′), *adj.* having the legs curved outward toward their middle and back in at the feet: *a bowlegged cowboy.* —**bow′leg′ged|ness**, *n.*

bowl|er[1] (bō′lər), *n.* a person who bowls.

bow|ler[2] (bō′lər), *n.,* or **bowler hat**, *British.* a derby hat. [< John *Bowler,* a London hat manufacturer of the 1800's]

bowl|ful (bōl′fu̇l), *n., pl.* **bowls|ful** or **bowl|fuls.** the amount that a bowl will hold; contents of a bowl: *Give the plant two bowlfuls of water.*

bow light (bou), a lighted lamp at the front end of a ship or boat.

bow|line (bō′lən, -līn), *n.* **1a** a knot used to tie a loop that does not slip. See picture under **knot.**[1] **b** a nonslipping noose or loop. **2** a rope running forward from the edge of a square sail nearest the wind to the bow. It holds the sail steady when sailing into the wind.

on a bowline, close-hauled, so as to sail close to the wind: ... *running in for San Andreas on a bowline* (M. Scott).

bowline knot, = bowline (def. 1a).

bowl|ing (bō′ling), *n.* **1a** a game played indoors, in which balls are rolled down a wooden alley at ten bottle-shaped wooden pins; tenpins. **b** (formerly) = ninepins. **2** the game of bowls. **3** the playing of any of these games.

bowling alley, **1a** a long, narrow lane for bowling; alley. **b** a building having a number of alleys for bowling. **2** a long enclosure for playing at bowls, tenpins, duckpins, or other pin games.

bowling bag, a small bag for carrying a bowling ball, and often shoes and other equipment.

bowling ball, **1** a round, plastic or hard rubber ball with a hole for the bowler's thumb and one or more for the fingers, used in the modern game of bowling. **2** a lopsided or weighted ball used in the game of bowls.

bowling crease, *Cricket.* the line from behind which the bowler pitches the ball.

bowling green, a smooth, flat stretch of grass for playing the game of bowls.

bowling pin, one of the ten pins used in bowling.

bowls (bōlz), *n.pl.* **1** a game played on a lawn (a bowling green) by rolling a slightly lopsided or weighted ball toward a stationary ball (the jack); lawn bowling. **2** a game in which a ball is rolled to knock down bottle-shaped pins; ninepins, tenpins, or skittles; bowling. **3** = skittles. [plural of *bowl*[2]]

bow|man[1] (bō′mən), *n., pl.* **-men.** a soldier armed with bow and arrows; archer: *the Norman bowmen who won the Battle of Hastings.* [< *bow*[2] + *man*]

bow|man[2] (bou′mən), *n., pl.* **-men.** a bow oarsman; man on the bow oar. [< *bow*[3] + *man*]

Bow|man's capsule (bō′mənz), a double-walled, cup-shaped structure around the glomerulus of each nephron of the kidney. It serves as a filter to remove organic wastes, excess inorganic salts, and water. [< William *Bowman,* 1816-1892, an English anatomist]

bow net (bō), a kind of wickerwork trap for catching lobsters and other shellfish.

bow oar (bou), **1** the oar nearest the bow of a boat. **2** the man who pulls this oar.

bow pen (bō), a bow compass with a pen at the end of one leg.

bow pencil (bō), a bow compass with a pencil at the end of one leg.

bow|pot (bou′pot′), *n.* = boughpot.

bow saw (bō), a saw for making curved cuts. It has a flexible blade set in a D-shaped frame, the blade being the straight side of the D: *a one-man bow saw that handles wood up to 13.8 inches thick* (Science News Letter).

bowse[1] (bouz), *v.t.,* **bowsed, bows|ing.** = bouse[1]; haul by means of tackle.

bowse[2] (bouz), *n., v.i.,* **bowsed, bows|ing.** = bouse[2]; booze.

bow|ser (bou′zər), *n.* **1** *British.* a tank truck for refueling aircraft or other vehicles. **2** (in Australia and New Zealand) a gasoline pump. [< *Bowser,* a trademark for a gasoline pump]

bow shock, or **bow|shock** (bou′shok′), *n.* the shock wave caused by the impact of a planet's magnetic field on solar wind: *About 20 minutes before the spacecraft reached its closest distance to Mercury (about 466 miles), there were very clear signs of a bow shock* (Science News).

bow|shot (bō′shot′), *n.* **1** the distance that a bow will shoot an arrow. **2** a shot from a bow.

∗**bow|sprit** (bou′sprit, bō′-), *n.* a pole or spar projecting forward from the bow of a ship. Ropes attached to the bowsprit help to steady sails and masts and hold the jib. [probably < Middle Low German *bōchsprēt*]

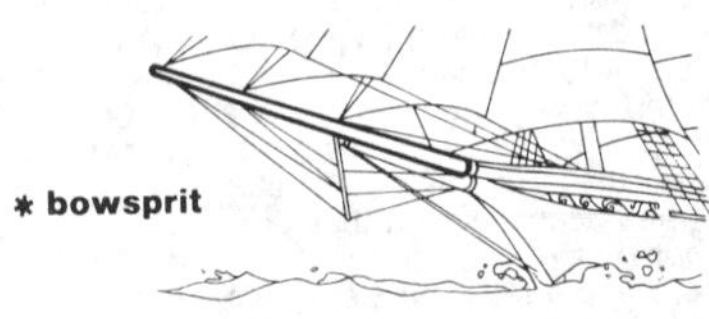

∗ **bowsprit**

Bow Street (bō), **1** a street in central London, the site of a principal police court. **2** the court itself: *to appear on charges at Bow Street.*

Bow Street runner, an officer attached to the court at Bow Street, especially in the early 1800's.

bow|string (bō′string′), *n., v.,* **-stringed** or **-strung, -string|ing.** —*n.* **1** a strong cord stretched from the ends of a bow, pulled back by the archer and then released to send the arrow forward. **2** a cord like this.

—*v.t.* to strangle with a bowstring; garrote.

bowstring hemp, **1** any one of various Asiatic and African perennial herbs of the agave family, whose fibers are used in making bowstrings, cordage, and the like. **2** the fiber itself.

bowstring truss or **girder**, a truss in which a curved beam is held together by a horizontal tie attached to the ends of the beam.

bow thruster, an auxiliary propeller in a ship's bow: *The use of a bow thruster increases a vessel's maneuverability in confined channels and in docking* (New York Times).

bow tie (bō), a small necktie tied in a bow.

bow wave (bou), the wave produced on either side of the bow by a ship or boat in motion.

bow window (bō), **1** a curved bay or oriel window. **2** *Informal.* a potbelly.

bow-win|dowed (bō′win′dōd), *adj.* having a bow window.

bow|wood (bō′wu̇d′), *n.* = Osage orange. Its very strong and elastic wood was much used by Indians for their bows.

bow-wow (bou′wou′), *n., adj., v.* —*n.* **1** the bark of a dog. **2** an imitation of the barking of a dog. **3** a dog (in stories for young children or the like). —*adj. Slang.* barking and overbearing; arrogant: *the bow-wow style of criticism.* —*v.i.* to bark. [imitative]

bow|yang (bō′yang), *n.* (in Australia) a string or cord tied around the bottom of trouser legs to keep the cuffs from dangling.

bow|yer (bō′yər), *n.* **1** a maker of, or dealer in, bows. See also **fletcher.** **2** *Archaic* or *Poetic.* an archer: *His Norman bowyer band* (Scott).

box[1] (boks), *n., v.* —*n.* **1** a container, usually with four stiff sides, a bottom, and a lid, to pack or put things in: *He packed the boxes full of books.* SYN: receptacle, carton. **2** the amount that a box can hold; boxful: *Strawberries at 90 cents a box are too expensive. Mother bought a box of soap.* **3** a small enclosed place in a theater, hall, stadium, grandstand, or race track, with chairs for spectators or audience. **4** an enclosed space in a courtroom for a jury, witnesses, or newspaper reporters: *bringing twelve good men into a [jury] box* (Henry Brougham). **5a** the driver's seat on a coach or carriage. **b** the part of a cart or wagon in which the passengers ride or freight is carried. **6a** a small shelter: *a box for a sentry.* **b** a small hut. **7** anything shaped or used like a box: *Come, children, let us shut up the box and the puppets for our play is played out* (Thackeray). **8** a hollow part that encloses or protects some piece of machinery: *a journal box on a railroad car.* **9** *Baseball.* **a** the place where the pitcher stands to throw the ball; mound. **b** the place where the batter or catcher stands. **c** the place outside the first- or third-base line where a coach stands. **10** a compartment for a horse in a stable or car; box stall: *The horse's box was so large that the horse could walk around in it.* **11** a space in a

Pronunciation Key: hat, āge, cãre, fär; let, ēqual, tėrm; it, īce; hot, ōpen, ôrder; **oi**l, **ou**t; cup, pu̇t, rüle; **ch**ild; lo**ng**; **th**in; ᴛʜen; **zh**, measure; ə represents **a** in about, **e** in taken, **i** in pencil, **o** in lemon, **u** in circus.

newspaper, magazine, or other printed matter, set off by enclosing lines. **12** a receptacle in a post office for a subscriber's mail. **13** *British.* a gift; present: *a Christmas box.* **14** *U.S.* a cavity made in a tree for collecting sap. **15** *British.* a small country house for use while following a sport such as hunting or fishing: *a shooting box.* **16** *Soccer.* an area with special restrictions. Goal kicks are taken from the edge of a small box toward the goal. The penalty area is sometimes also referred to as the *goalkeeper's box.*
—v.t. **1** to pack in a box; put into a box: *The farmers boxed the fruit before shipping it to market.* **2** to furnish or fit with a box, as the journal of an axle. **3** to divide up (space in a theater) into boxes. **4** to box-haul. **5** to make a hole in the trunk of (a tree) to obtain sap. **6** to alter (a building, room, or wall) in shape by surrounding with boards or putting up lath and plaster.
boxes, the occupants of a theater box: *The boxes applauded her.*
box the compass. See under **compass**.
box up (in), to shut in; keep in; confine: *The family was boxed up in a small shed on the hill during the flood.*
in a box, *Informal.* in a difficult situation: *Having accepted two invitations for the same evening, she found herself in a box.*
knock out of the box, *Baseball.* to cause (a pitcher) to be withdrawn by hitting his pitches successfully: *Twitchell was knocked out of the box, and in the seventh inning Richardson took his place* (Chicago Tribune).
the box, *Informal.* television: *At least I'd have been able to listen to the whole game on the radio, or watch it on the box* (Sunday Times).
[Old English *box* < Late Latin *buxis* < Latin *pyxis* < Greek *pýxis*] **—box'like'**, *adj.*

box[2] (boks), *n., v.* **—*n.*** a blow with the open hand or fist, especially on the ear or side of the head: *She met the insolence of Essex with a box on the ear* (John R. Green). **SYN:** cuff, buffet.
—v.t. **1** to strike with such a blow: *I will box your ears if you yell at me again.* **2** to fight (a person) with fists, especially in the sport of boxing.
—v.i. to fight with the fists, especially as a sport: *To box ... was in those days a mere necessity of schoolboy life at public schools* (Thomas De Quincey). **SYN:** spar.
[origin uncertain]

box[3] (boks), *n.* **1** an evergreen shrub or small, bushy tree much used for hedges and borders. It has dark-green leathery leaves. **2** its hard, durable wood; boxwood. [< Latin *buxus* < Greek *pýxos*]

Box and Cox, two persons never out or in together: *He and Lindemann were never reconciled. In Whitehall they performed a Box and Cox act which had a note of sarcastic comedy* (C. P. Snow). [< *Box and Cox*, a farce by J. M. Morton, 1811-1891, an English playwright, in which a room is rented to two men, one of whom works at night and the other by day.]

box bed, **1** a bed boarded in and roofed over so as to resemble a large box. **2** a bed arranged so as to fold up into a box.

box|ber|ry (boks'ber'ē, -bər-), *n., pl.* **-ries**. **1** = wintergreen. **2** = partridgeberry.

box|board (boks'bôrd', -bōrd'), *n.* **1** a pasteboard for making cartons and boxes. **2** a wide piece of lumber suitable for the side of a box.

box calf, calfskin tanned with chrome salts, and having square marks produced by graining.

box camera, a simple camera in the form of a box, which does not fold up. It usually has a fixed focus and a single shutter speed for daylight pictures of about of a second.

box canyon, *U.S.* a narrow canyon or gorge with nearly vertical sides.

***box|car** (boks'kär'), *n.* a railroad freight car enclosed on all sides. Most boxcars are loaded or unloaded through a sliding door on either side.

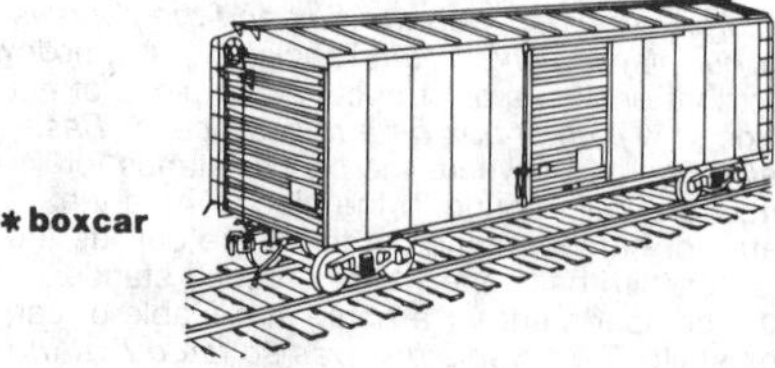
***boxcar**

box cloth, a close-woven cloth for outdoor wear.

box coat, **1** an overcoat with a straight, unfitted back. **2** a heavy, warm overcoat formerly worn by the driver and passengers on a coach.

box elder, a North American maple tree, often grown for ornament. The box elder has compound leaves. These trees have soft wood and the branches break easily.

box|er[1] (bok'sər), *n.* **1** a man who fights with his fists as a sport, usually with padded gloves according to special rules; pugilist. **2** a medium-sized dog with a smooth, brown coat, related to the bulldog and terrier. [< *box*[2] + *-er*[1]]

box|er[2] (bok'sər), *n.* a person or machine that packs things in boxes. [< *box*[1] + *-er*[1]]

Box|er (bok'sər), *n.* a member of a Chinese secret society opposed to foreigners and Christianity. The Boxers rose in arms in 1900 in the northern provinces of China in an effort to expel foreigners from China. They besieged the legations at Peking for two months, but were defeated by an international force of foreign soldiers. [< *boxer*[1], adaptation of Chinese (Peking) *i hê ch'üan* "fists for righteousness and harmony," one of the names]

boxer shorts, or **box|ers** (bok'sərz), *n.pl.* **1** short, loose trousers with an elastic waistband, worn by boxers. **2** similar shorts worn especially as underpants or swimming trunks.

box|es (bok'siz), *n.pl.* See under **box**[1].

box family, a family of tropical or subtropical evergreen trees, shrubs, and herbs with leathery leaves and inconspicuous flowers, several of which, including boxwood and Japanese spurge, are widely grown for ornament.

box|fish (boks'fish'), *n., pl.* **-fish|es** or (*collectively*) **-fish**. = trunkfish.

box|ful (boks'fůl), *n., pl.* **-fuls**. **1** the amount that a box can hold. **2** the contents of a box.

box-haul (boks'hôl'), *v.t.* to veer (a square-rigged ship) round sharply by throwing the yards on the foremast aback and thus turning the ship's head quickly.

box|hold|er (boks'hōl'dər), *n.* a person who owns or rents a box, as in a post office or theater.

box|ing[1] (bok'sing), *n.* the action or sport of fighting with the fists. Boxers usually wear well-padded leather gloves. [< *box*[2] + *ing*[1]]

box|ing[2] (bok'sing), *n.* **1** the material used for boxes. **2** the act or process of putting into or furnishing with a box. **3** a boxlike enclosure; casing. **4** the sides of a window. [< *box*[1] + *ing*[1]]

Boxing Day, (in Great Britain and some parts of the Commonwealth) the first weekday after Christmas; December 26 or 27. It is a legal holiday on which employees, servants, postmen, errand boys, and others who perform personal services, receive Christmas boxes. When it falls on a Saturday or Sunday, the next Monday is celebrated as the legal holiday.

boxing gloves, the padded leather gloves worn when boxing.

box iron, a hollow flatiron heated by an insert of hot metal, no longer used.

box jacket, **1** a loose jacket with fitted shoulders and unfitted back, having a square, boxlike shape. **2** an overcoat of similar design; box coat.

box kite, a tailless kite consisting of two rectangular boxes with open ends, fastened together lengthwise with a space between.

box loom, a loom with more than one shuttle box at either end of the lathe.

box lunch, a ready-made, prepackaged lunch, usually inside a paper box or container.

box|man (boks'mən), *n., pl.* **-men**. **1** a person who weighs the charges for a blast furnace. **2** a person who attends to boxes used in washing coal. **3** a person who fills boxes of any sort.

box office, **1** the office or booth in a theater, hall, or stadium, where tickets of admission are sold. **2** the money taken in at such a place. **3** *Informal.* an entertainer or entertainment capable of attracting audiences and earning money.

box-of|fice (boks'ôf'is, -of'-), *adj. Informal.* **1** with respect to receipts taken in at a box office: *The popular play was an astounding box-office success.* **2** popular and profitable: *This concert isn't box-office.*

box oyster, *U.S.* a large, high-grade oyster, formerly packed in boxes instead of barrels.

box pleat, a double pleat with the cloth folded under at each side.

box|room (boks'rüm', -rům'), *n. British.* a storeroom, especially for boxes, trunks, unwanted furniture, and other household miscellany.

box score, a statistical summary of all the plays of a baseball game arranged in a table by the names of the players.

box seat, a chair or seat in a box at a theater, hall, stadium, grandstand, or race track.

box set, a stage set in which the back and sidewalls are visible to the audience.

box social, a social gathering, usually to raise money, at which boxes of food or gifts are raffled or auctioned: *The Ladies Auxiliary of the 19th Alberta Dragoons held a successful box social and dance* (Edmonton Journal).

box spanner, *Especially British.* a box wrench.

box spring, a set of bedsprings in a boxlike frame with padding over them, covered with ticking or some other firmly woven material.

box stall, a roomy, enclosed compartment for a horse or other large animal in a stable or vehicle; box.

box tail, a tail or rudder used on certain early aircraft and shaped somewhat like a box kite.

box|thorn (boks'thôrn'), *n.* any one of various ornamental shrubs of the nightshade family, some of which are grown for their bright-red or orange berries; matrimony vine.

box toe, **1** a toe in shoes or boots with a stiff, strong lining: *Thermoplastic material ... is used for hard box toes* (Science News Letter). **2** the lining used.

box top, the top part or cover of a packaged product, usually bearing the brand name, used as evidence of purchase by a consumer to obtain a premium: *Buy the merchandise and send the box top off with a coin in return for all sorts of items* (New York Times).

box trap, a trap for catching small animals alive, consisting of an inclined box which drops flat when a baited trigger is disturbed or a box with a flap or flaps that drop down.

***box turtle** or **tortoise**, any one of several species of American land turtles, which can withdraw entirely within their shells and close them by hinges in the lower halves.

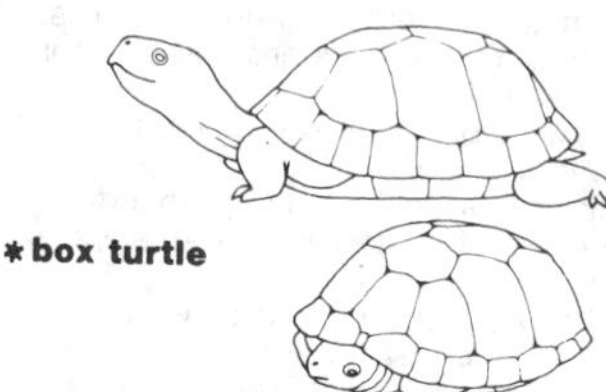
***box turtle**

box wallah, in India: **1** a peddler. **2** a shopkeeper; merchant.

box|wood (boks'wůd'), *n.* **1** the hard, fine-grained wood of the box, much used for wood engraver's blocks, and for musical and mathematical instruments. **2** the tree or shrub itself. **3** any one of various shrubs or trees with a hard, compact wood, such as the flowering dogwood of the United States.

box|work (boks'wėrk'), *n.* a colorful network of calcite crystals, usually found on the ceilings of caves.

box wrench, a kind of wrench which fits completely around the bolthead; socket wrench.

box|y (bok'sē), *adj.,* **box|i|er**, **box|i|est**. **1** shaped like a box; square; squat: *a boxy house.* **2** loose-fitting with straight lines, as a box coat. **—box'i|ness**, *n.*

boy (boi), *n., interj.* **—*n.*** **1** a male child from birth to about eighteen: *... a lad of mettle, a good boy* (Shakespeare). **2a** a young or immature man: *a college boy.* **b** *Informal.* man; fellow. **3** a male servant. **4** a bellboy. **5** *U.S. Slang.* a black male of any age (used in an unfriendly way).
—interj. *Informal.* an exclamation of surprise, dismay, etc.: *Boy! Isn't it hot!*
the boys, **a** the sons of a family: *The boys will be home for Thanksgiving.* **b** *Informal.* a strictly male company: *The card game at the lodge is for the boys only.* **c** *Informal.* political followers; hangers-on: *Machine politicians ... always want someone who will be kind to 'the boys'* (New York Evening Post).
[Middle English *boie* (originally) servant, helper < Old French *embuié* fettered, originally past participle of *embuiier* to fetter]

bo|yar (bō yär', boi'ər), *n.* **1** a member of a former high-ranking order of the Russian aristocracy, abolished by Peter the Great. **2** a member of a former privileged class in Romania: *The government took the estates of the large landowners, or boyars, and sold them in small lots to small farmers* (Alvin Z. Rubinstein). [< Russian *bojarin*]

bo|yard (bō yärd', boi'ərd), *n.* = boyar.

boy|au (bwä yō', boi'ō; *French* bwȧ yō'), *n., pl.* **boy|aux** (bwä yōz', boi'ōz; *French* bwȧ yō'). *Military Science.* **1** a connecting trench. **2** a branch or small gallery of a mine. [< French *boyau* alimentary canal < Old French *boel* bowel]

boy|cott (boi'kot), *v., n.* **—*v.t.*** **1** to join together against and have nothing to do with (a person, business, nation, employer, or any other person or thing) in order to coerce or punish. If people are boycotting someone, they do not associate with him, or buy from or sell to him, and they try to keep others from doing so. **2** to refuse to buy or use (a product or service).
—n. an act of boycotting: *The Amalgamated Clothing Workers ... were ready to press a boycott on Japanese textile goods* (New Yorker).
[< Captain Charles *Boycott*, 1832-1897, an English land agent over Irish tenants, and victim of a famous instance of it when he refused to lower

rents in hard times]—**boy′cot|ter**, *n.*

boy|friend (boi′frend′), *n.*, or **boy friend**, *Informal.* **1** a girl's sweetheart or steady male companion. **2** a male friend.

boy|hood (boi′hůd), *n.* **1** the time or condition of being a boy: *boyhood adventures.* (*Figurative.*) *In the boyhood of the year* (Tennyson). **2** boys as a group: *The boyhood of the nation produces the leaders of the future.*

boy|ish (boi′ish), *adj.* **1** of a boy: *boyish ambitions, the lad's boyish energy.* **2** like a boy: *a boyish young man.* **3** like a boy's: *the girl's boyish hair.* **4** fit for a boy; suitable for a boy: *boyish games.* —**boy′ish|ly**, *adv.* —**boy′ish|ness**, *n.*

Boyle's law (boilz), *Physics, Chemistry.* the law that at any given temperature the volume of a given mass of gas varies inversely with the pressure to which it is subjected. [< Robert *Boyle*, 1627-1691, an Irish scientist and philosopher, who formulated it]

boy|o (boi′ō), *n., pl.* **boy|os**. **1** *Irish Dialect.* a boy; lad. **2** *U.S. Slang.* a man; fellow.

boys (boiz), *n.pl.* See under **boy**.

boy scout, **1** Also, **Boy Scout**. a member of the Boy Scouts. **2** *U.S. Slang, Figurative.* an unrealistic or overly idealistic person: *They are all judge, secular priest, and transcendent boy scout rolled into one* (Commentary).

Boy Scouts, an organization for boys to learn skills and develop manliness and usefulness to others. It was founded in England in 1908 by Lieutenant-General Sir Robert S. S. Baden-Powell.

boy|sen|ber|ry (boi′zən ber′ē), *n., pl.* **-ries**. **1** a purple berry like a blackberry in size and shape, and like a raspberry in flavor. **2** the plant it grows on. It was developed in California from a cross between several kinds of blackberries and a raspberry. The boysenberry belongs to the rose family. [American English < Rudolph *Boysen*, an American botanist, who developed it]

boy's-love (boiz′luv′), *n.* = southernwood.

boy wonder, *U.S. Informal.* a young man of outstanding intelligence and skill.

Boz (boz, bōz), *n.* a pen name of Charles Dickens.

bo|zo (bō′zō), *n., pl.* **-zos**. *U.S. Slang.* a stupid person; boob. [origin unknown]

boz|zet|to (bot set′ō), *n., pl.* **-zet|ti** (-set′ē). a small preliminary sketch or clay model for a large sculpture, painting or casting. [< Italian *bozzetto* (diminutive) < *bozzo* rough stone, sketch]

bp., **1** baptized. **2** birthplace. **3** bishop.

b.p., **1** below proof. **2** boiling point. **3** the public good (Latin, *bonum publicum*).

Bp., Bishop.

B/P (no periods), bills payable.

B.P., **1** before present: *10,000 years B.P.* **2** bills payable. **3** blood pressure. **4** British Pharmacopeia.

B.P.E., *U.S.* Bachelor of Physical Education.

B.Phil., Bachelor of Philosophy.

B-pic|ture (bē′pik′chər), *n.* a motion picture of inferior quality, usually made rapidly and at minimum expense: *Hollywood was apparently rescuing realism from its friends, and burying in B-pictures the stuff of genius* (Harper's).

bpl., birthplace.

b quark, = bottom quark.

br., **1** branch. **2** bronze. **3** brother.

Br (no period), bromine (chemical element).

Br., **1** Britain. **2** British. **3** Brother.

B/R (no periods), **1** Bill of Rights. **2** bills receivable.

B.R., **1** bills receivable. **2** British Railways.

bra (brä), *n.* a brassiere.

braai|vleis (brī′flās′), *n.* (in South Africa) a barbecue. [< Afrikaans *braaivleis* roasted meat < *braai* to roast + *vleis* flesh]

Brab|an|çon (brab′ən son), *n.* a griffon with a smooth coat. Brabançons were developed by crossing the rough-coated griffon with the pug, also a toy dog. [< French *Brabançon* (literally) a native of Brabant, a province of Belgium]

brab|ble (brab′əl), *v.*, **-bled**, **-bling**, *n. Dialect.* —*v.i.* to wrangle; brawl. —*n.* wrangling talk. [origin uncertain; perhaps < Dutch *brabbelen*] —**brab′ble|ment**, *n.*

brac|cate (brak′āt), *adj.* having the shanks and feet covered with feathers: *braccate birds.* [< Latin *braccātus* wearing breeches < *braccae* breeches]

brace (brās), *n., v.*, **braced**, **brac|ing**. —*n.* **1** a thing that holds parts together or in place. An iron rod or a timber used to strengthen a building, a tight bandage for the wrist, and a metal frame to hold the ankle or other parts of the body straight are all braces. SYN: prop, support. **2** the handle for a tool or drill used for boring. See picture under **bit**³. **3** a pair; couple: *a brace of ducks.* **4** either of these signs { }, used to enclose words, figures, staffs in music, or a set in arithmetic. **5** a leather thong which slides up and down the cord of a drum, used to regulate the tension of the skins and thus the pitch. **6a** a rope attached to a yard of a ship and reaching to the deck, used to swing the yard in trimming the sails. **b** a metal bracket fixed to the sternpost of a ship and serving to support the rudder. **7** *U.S. Military Slang.* a position of stiff attention. **8a** = bracer² (def. 2). **b** a state of preparation or defense. [< verb]

—*v.t.* **1** to give strength or firmness to; support: *He braced the roof with four poles.* SYN: prop, reinforce, buttress. **2** to prepare (oneself): *He braced himself for the crash.* **3** to plant firmly; set down rigidly: *He braced his feet and stood ready for the attack.* **4** *Figurative.* to give strength and energy to; refresh: *The mountain air braced us after the long climb.* **5** to increase the tension of; tighten. **6** to trim (yards or sails) by means of braces. **7** *Poetic.* to encompass; gird; clasp; fasten: *The adverse winds in leathern bags he braced* (Alexander Pope). **8** *U.S. Military Slang.* to cause (a cadet or recruit) to come to and hold a position of stiff attention.

—*v.i.* to summon up one's energies.

braces, **a** metal wires used to straighten or prevent crooked teeth: *The braces pulled her teeth in line.* **b** *Especially British.* suspenders: *I'd rather wear braces, only the elastic perishes, so a leather belt's good enough* (Graham Greene).

brace up, *Informal.* to gather one's strength or courage anew: *The candidate braced up after his defeat and decided to run again in the next election.*

[< Old French *bracier* embrace, gird tightly < *brace* the two arms outstretched or embracing < Latin *bracchia*, plural of *bracchium* arm < Greek *brachīōn* upper arm]

brace and bit, a tool for boring, consisting of a drill (the bit) fitted into a handle (the brace). See picture under **bit**³.

braced (brāst), *adj.* **1** strained; strengthened; girt. **2** *Heraldry.* interlaced or linked together. **3** *Obsolete.* contracted.

brace|let (brās′lit), *n.* **1** a band or chain worn for ornament around the wrist or arm. **2** *Informal.* a handcuff. [< Middle French *bracelet* (diminutive) < Old French *bracel*, ultimately < Latin *bracchium* arm < Greek *brachīōn* upper arm]

brace|let|ed (brās′lə tid), *adj.* wearing a bracelet or bracelets.

brace|mate (brās′māt′), *n.* either one of a pair of dogs trained to hunt together.

brac|er¹ (brā′sər), *n.* **1** a person or thing that braces. **2** *U.S. Slang.* a stimulating drink: [*He*] *stepped up to the bar for a bracer* (Time). [< *brace*, verb + *-er*¹]

brac|er² (brā′sər), *n.* **1** (in archery, fencing, etc.) a guard for the wrist. **2** the part of a suit of armor covering the arm. [< Old French *brasseüre* < *bras* arm < Latin *bracchium* arm < Greek *brachīōn* upper arm]

bra|ce|ro (brə sãr′ō), *n. Southwestern U.S.* a Mexican laborer who enters the United States under contract on a legal, temporary basis to work for a specified employer. [American English < American Spanish *bracero*, ultimately < Latin *bracchium* arm < Greek *brachīōn* upper arm]

brace root, = prop root.

brac|es (brā′siz), *n. pl.* See under **brace**.

brach (brach, brak), *n.* a hound bitch. [< Old French *brachet* (diminutive) < *brac* hound < Germanic (compare Old High German *braccho*)]

brach|et (brach′it), *n.* = brach.

bra|chi|a (brā′kē ə, brak′ē-), *n.* plural of **brachium**.

bra|chi|al (brā′kē əl, brak′ē-), *adj.* **1a** of or belonging to the arm: *the brachial artery.* **b** of or belonging to the foreleg, wing, or other forelimb of a vertebrate. **2** armlike: *the brachial appendages of a starfish.* [< Latin *bracchiālis* of the arm < *bracchium* arm < Greek *brachīōn* upper arm]

bra|chi|ate (*adj.* brā′kē it, -āt; brak′ē-; *v.* brā′kē āt, brak′ē-), *adj., v.*, **-at|ed**, **-at|ing**. —*adj.* **1** *Botany.* having widely spreading branches. **2** *Zoology.* having brachia or armlike appendages, as a crinoid.

—*v.i.* to move by swinging from branch to branch with the arms; advance by brachiation: . . . *brachiating from handhold to handhold like chimpanzees in a jungle* (Time).

bra|chi|a|tion (brā′kē ā′shən, brak′ē-), *n.* a movement through a tree, or from tree to tree, by swinging from branch to branch with the arms, as the gibbons and other arboreal monkeys do.

bra|chi|a|tor (brā′kē ā′tər, brak′ē-), *n.* an animal that moves by brachiation.

brach|i|o|pod (brak′ē ə pod, brā′kē-), *n.* any one of a phylum of sea animals characterized by a bivalve shell and, coiled within the shell, a pair of arms covered with cilia for sweeping tiny food organisms into the mouth: *About 350,000 years ago brachiopods, similar to worms, were perhaps the most abundant animals on earth* (Science News Letter). [< New Latin *Brachiopoda* the class name < Greek *brachīōn* upper arm + *poús, podós* foot]

brach|i|o|saur (brak′ē ə sôr), *n.* = brachiosaurus.

brach|i|o|saur|us (brak′ē ə sôr′əs), *n.* any dinosaur of an extinct genus of the late Jurassic: *Brachiosaurus was the largest of all dinosaurs, even though it had a rather short tail. It was 70 feet long and weighed 85 tons* (Samuel P. Welles). [< New Latin *Brachiosaurus* the genus name < Greek *brachīōn* upper arm + *saûros* lizard]

bra|chi|ot|o|my (brā′kē ot′ə mē, brak′ē-), *n., pl.* **-mies**. a surgical operation on or removal of the arm. [< Greek *brachīōn* upper arm + *-tomíā* a cutting]

bra|chis|to|chrone (brə kis′tə krōn), *n. Geometry.* the curve in which a body descending to a given point under an external force will reach another point in the shortest possible time; the curve of quickest descent. [< Greek *bráchistos* shortest (< *brachýs* short) + *chrónos* time]

bra|chi|um (brā′kē əm, brak′ē-), *n., pl.* **-chi|a**. **1** the upper arm, from the shoulder to the elbow. **2** the part of any forelimb that corresponds to it. **3** an armlike part. [< Latin *bracchium* arm < Greek *brachīōn* upper arm]

brach|y|ceph|al (brak′ə sef′əl), *n.* a person with a short, broad head; brachycephalic person.

brach|y|ce|phal|ic (brak′ə sə fal′ik), *adj.* having a short or broad head; having a breadth of skull at least four-fifths as great as the length from front to back: *He is blond, brachycephalic, square-jawed, and deep-chested* (New Yorker).

brach|y|ceph|a|lous (brak′ə sef′ə ləs), *adj.* = brachycephalic.

brach|y|ceph|a|ly (brak′ə sef′ə lē), *n.* the condition of being short-headed or broad-headed. [< Greek *brachýs* short + *kephalḗ* head]

brach|y|dac|tyl|ic (brak′ə dak til′ik), *adj.* having extremely short fingers.

bra|chy|dac|ty|ly (brak′ə dak′tə lē), *n.* an extreme shortness of the fingers. [< Greek *brachýs* short + *dáktylos* finger]

brach|y|dome (brak′ə dōm), *n. Crystallography.* a dome whose planes are parallel to the shorter lateral axis in an orthorhombic system. [< Greek *brachýs* short + Late Latin *dōma* roof]

bra|chyg|ra|phy (brə kig′rə fē), *n.* shorthand; stenography. [< Greek *brachýs* short + English *-graphy*]

bra|chyl|o|gy (brə kil′ə jē), *n.*, pl. **-gies**. **1** conciseness. **2** a condensed form of expression. [< Late Latin *brachylogia*, ultimately < Greek *brachýs* short + *lógos* speech]

bra|chyp|ter|ous (brə kip′tər əs), *adj.* short-winged. [< Greek *brachýs* short + *pterón* wing + English *-ous*]

brach|y|u|ran (brak′ē yůr′ən), *adj., n.* —*adj.* of or belonging to a group of ten-footed crustaceans comprising the common crabs, characterized by a small, short abdomen.

—*n.* a brachyuran crustacean; crab.

[< Greek *brachýs* short + *ourā́* tail + English *-an*]

brach|y|u|rous (brak′ē yůr′əs), *adj.* having a small, short abdomen, as a crab. [see etym. under **brachyuran**]

brac|ing (brā′sing), *adj., n.* —*adj.* giving strength and energy; refreshing: *The mountain air was bracing.* SYN: invigorating.

—*n.* **1** a brace or braces. **2** the action or power of a brace or braces. —**brac′ing|ly**, *adv.* —**brac′ing|ness**, *n.*

brack|en (brak′ən), *n.* **1** a large, coarse fern common on hillsides, in woods, and in boggy areas. **2** a thicket of these ferns. [Middle English *braken*, apparently < Scandinavian (compare Swedish *bräken*)]

***brack|et** (brak′it), *n., v.* —*n.* **1** a flat piece of stone, wood, or metal projecting from a wall as a support for a shelf, statue, or other thing: *When a bracket came loose the shelf crashed to the floor.* **2** such a support most often in the shape of a right triangle. **3** a small shelf supported by brackets. **4** *Architecture.* any member designed to support an overhanging balcony, cornice, or other projecting structure, such as a piece attached to the wall or the end of a beam that extends under the overhanging surface. **5** a gas or electric fixture projecting from a wall. **6a** either of these signs [ ], used to enclose words or figures: *In the article, he used brackets to show which parts expressed his own opinion.* **b** a parenthesis. **c** a brace (def. 4). **7** *Figurative.* any group thought of or mentioned together; class or category: *The old building is occupied by persons in a low income bracket.* **8** *Mathematics.* a straight

Pronunciation Key: hat, āge, cãre, fär; let, ēqual, tėrm; it, īce; hot, ōpen, ôrder; oil, out; cup, pu̇t, rüle; child; long; thin; ᴛʜen; zh, measure; ə represents **a** in about, **e** in taken, **i** in pencil, **o** in lemon, **u** in circus.

line placed over an expression and meaning the same as parentheses around the expression; vinculum. **9** one of the two side pieces of a gun carriage. **10** the (specified) distance between a pair of shots fired, one beyond the target and one short of it, in order to find the range for artillery. **11** a calypso song with nonsense verses.
—*v.t.* **1** to support with a bracket or brackets: *He bracketed the shelves underneath to make them stronger.* **2a** to enclose within brackets: *to bracket a phrase. The teacher bracketed the mistakes in my homework.* (*Figurative.*) *The Calvertson facility ... will soon be bracketed by the Long Island Expressway on the south and the existing Jericho turnpike* (New York Times). **b** to couple with a brace. **3** *Figurative.* to think of or mention together; group in the same class or category: *Poets, artists, and musicians are often bracketed.* **4** to fire two shots, one beyond and one short of (a target) in order to find the range for artillery.
[< Middle French *braguette* codpiece (diminutive) < *brague* breeches < Old Provençal *braga* < Latin *brāca*, ultimately < a Germanic word] **—brack′et|like′**, *adj.*

***bracket**

definition 6a

[ ] The reason for this [the amendment] is...

bracket clock, **1** a clock originally designed to stand on a bracket attached to a wall. **2** a clock designed to stand on a table or shelf.
bracket creep, *Economics.* the condition of being taxed on income at an increasingly higher rate as one's income increases, usually because of inflation: *As "bracket creep" has moved more and more of us into the range of punitive tax rates formerly aimed at the rich, the economy has slowed to a trudge* (New York Post).
bracket fungus, a fungus on the trunks or stumps of trees that grows out horizontally like a rounded bracket. See picture under **fungus**.
brack|et|ing (brak′ə ting), *n. Architecture.* a series of supporting brackets.
brack|ish (brak′ish), *adj.* **1** slightly salty: *Coastal marshes often have brackish water.* **2** *Figurative.* distasteful; unpleasant. SYN: nauseous. [earlier *brack* < Dutch *brak*] **—brack′ish|ness**, *n.*
brac|o|nid (brak′ə nid), *n.* = ichneumon fly. [< New Latin *Braconidae* the family name < Greek *brachýs* short]
***bract** (brakt), *n.* a small leaf growing at the base of a flower or on a flower stalk. [< Latin *bractea*, false spelling of Latin *brattea* thin metal plate]

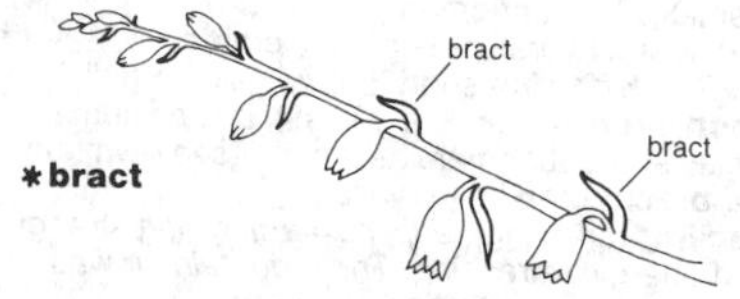

***bract**

brac|te|al (brak′tē əl), *adj.* **1** of a bract. **2** like a bract. **3** being a bract.
brac|te|ate (brak′tē it, -āt), *adj.* having bracts.
bract|ed (brak′tid), *adj.* having bracts.
brac|te|o|late (brak′tē ə lit, -lāt), *adj.* having bractlets. [< Latin *bracteola* a thin gold leaf (diminutive) < *brattea* bract]
brac|te|ole (brak′tē ōl), *n.* = bractlet.
bract|let (brakt′lit), *n.* a small bract situated on a secondary axis, as on a pedicel, or even on a petiole.
brad (brad), *n.* a small, very thin nail with a small head: *The artist fastened the picture in the frame with wire brads.* [variant of *brod* < Scandinavian (compare Old Icelandic *broddr* spike, shaft)]
brad|awl (brad′ôl′), *n.* an awl with a cutting edge for making small holes for brads.
brad|ded (brad′id), *adj.* furnished with brads.
Brad|ford (brad′fərd), *n. Trademark.* any one of a breed of beef cattle developed in the southern United States by crossbreeding Brahmas and Herefords.
Brad|shaw (brad′shô), *n.* a timetable of all passenger trains in Great Britain. [short for *Bradshaw's Railway Guide*, first issued in 1839 and discontinued in 1961]
brad|y|car|di|a (brad′ə kär′dē ə), *n.* abnormally slow heart action. [< Greek *bradýs* slow + *kardiā* heart]
brad|y|car|dic (brad′ə kär′dik), *adj.* of or having to do with bradycardia; characterized by bradycardia.
brad|y|ki|nin (brad′ə kī′nən), *n.* a polypeptide released by blood plasma globulin when acted on by certain enzymes. It stimulates the action of smooth muscle, lowers blood pressure, and is believed to produce some of the signs of inflammation, such as swelling and pain. [< Greek *bradýs* slow + English *kinin*]
brad|y|pod (brad′ə pod), *n.* any animal of the same family as the sloth. [< Greek *bradýpous, -podos* slow-footed < *bradýs* slow + *poús, pódos* foot]
brad|y|seism (brad′ē sī′zəm, -səm), *n.* a slow rise and fall of the earth's crust: *The slow movements, or bradyseisms ... resulted in the formation of continents* (London Daily News). [< Greek *bradýs* slow + *seismós* earthquake]
brad|y|seis|mic (brad′ē sīz′mik, -sīs′-), *adj.* of or marked by bradyseism.
brad|y|seis|mi|cal (brad′ē sīz′mə kəl, -sīs′-), *adj.* = bradyseismic.
brae (brā), *n. Scottish.* the steep bank bounding a river valley; slope; hillside: *Ye banks and braes o' bonnie Doon* (Robert Burns). [Middle English *bra* < Scandinavian (compare Old Icelandic *brā* (eye)brow; (later) brow of a hill)]
brag (brag), *v.,* **bragged**, **brag|ging**, *n., adj.,* **brag|ger**, **brag|gest**. **—*v.i.*** to praise oneself or what one has; boast: *He bragged about his new car.* SYN: vaunt. See syn. under **boast**.
—*v.t.* to boast of: *He brags his service* (Shakespeare). SYN: vaunt. See syn. under **boast**.
—*n.* **1** a boast. **2** boasting talk; boastfulness: *His brag was tiresome to listen to.* **3** a thing that is boasted of: *Beauty is nature's brag* (Milton). **4** a boaster; braggart. **5** a card game similar to poker, played by bluffing and bragging.
—*adj.* **1** that is boasted of; very fine or excellent: *a brag horse.* **2** *Archaic.* boastful; bragging.
[Middle English *braggen*; origin uncertain]
Bra|ge (brä′gə), *n.* = Bragi.
brag|ga|do|ci|o (brag′ə dō′shē ō), *n., pl.* **-ci|os**. **1** a boasting; bragging. **2** a boaster; braggart. [< *Braggadochio*, the name of a boastful character in Spenser's *Faerie Queene*, made up from the word *brag*]
brag|gart (brag′ərt), *n., adj.* **—*n.*** a person who brags; boaster.
—*adj.* bragging; boastful.
[< French *bragard* < *braguer* brag; show off one's breeches < *brague* breeches; see etym. under **bracket**]
brag|gart|ism (brag′ər tiz əm), *n.* the ways of a braggart.
brag|ger (brag′ər), *n.* a person who brags; boaster.
brag|gy (brag′ē), *adj.,* **-gi|er**, **-gi|est**. *U.S. Informal.* bragging; boastful.
brag-hard (brag′härd′), *n. Dialect.* braggart.
Bra|gi (brä′gē), *n. Scandinavian Mythology.* the god of poetry, a son of Odin and the husband of Ithunn.
Brah|ma[1] (brä′mə), *n.* **1** in Hindu theology: **a** the pervading soul of the universe; the essence of being and intelligence; Atman. **b** the god of creation. Brahma is thought of as a trinity (Brahma the Creator, Vishnu the Preserver, and Siva the Destroyer). **c** the creator, one of the gods of this trinity. **2** Brahman, a kind of cattle. [< Sanskrit *bráhman* prayer, worship, the Absolute, the Creator]
brah|ma[1] (brä′mə, brā′-), *n.* Brahman, a kind of cattle. [< *Brahma*[1]]
brah|ma[2] or **Brah|ma**[2] (brä′mə, brā′-), *n.* one of a breed of large chickens with feathered legs and small wings and tail. [< *Brahmaputra*, a river in northeastern India, the supposed place of their origin]
brah|ma|cha|ri (brä′mə chä′rē), *n.* (in Brahmanism) a person who practices brahmacharya; celibate.
brah|ma|char|ya (brä′mə chär′yə), *n.* (in Brahmanism) monklike abstinence or celibacy. [< Sanskrit *brahmacárya* < *bráhman* prayer + *carya* conduct]
Brah|man (brä′mən), *n.* **1** *pl.* **-mans**, **-ma|na** (-mə nə). a member of the priestly caste, the highest caste in India: *According to the Hindu doctrine of transmigration, the more nearly perfect souls are born into the Brahman caste, automatically making it the best* (New Yorker). **2** (in Hindu theology) Brahma, the Creator. **3** a kind of cattle characterized by a large hump (sometimes double) on its shoulders, originally imported from India and related to the zebu. It is often used for crossbreeding with cattle in the United States because it is able to endure considerable dryness and resist ticks and other parasites. Also, **Brahmin**. [< Sanskrit *brāhmana* < *bráhman* prayer, worship]
Brah|ma|na or **brah|ma|na** (brä′mə nə), *n.* (in Sanskrit literature) one of the prose portions of the Vedas, concerned chiefly with dogma and ritual.
Brah|ma|ni or **Brah|ma|nee** (brä′mə nē), *n.* a Brahman woman or girl.
Brah|man|ic (brä man′ik), *adj.* of or having to do with a Brahman or the Brahmans.
Brah|man|i|cal (brä man′ə kəl), *adj.* = Brahmanic. Also, **Brahminical**.
Brah|man|ism (brä′mə niz əm), *n.* the Hindu religious and social system. It is based on caste and a pantheistic, philosophical religion promising a return to and union with Brahma (the universal soul). Also, **Brahminism**.
Brah|man|ist (brä′mə nist), *n.* a believer in Brahmanism. Also, **Brahminist**.
Brah|man|is|tic (brä′mə nis′tik), *adj.* of or having to do with Brahmanism; influenced by Brahmanism: *Later Javanese art is increasingly Brahmanistic* (Alfred L. Kroeber).
Brah|man|y (brä′mə nē), *adj.* **1** having to do with Brahmans or Brahmanism. **2** regarded as sacred by the Hindus.
Brahmany bull, a white Brahman bull.
Brahmany kite, a kitelike bird of prey of India, regarded as sacred by the Hindus.
Brah|min (brä′mən), *n., pl.* **-min**. **1** = Brahman. **2** *Figurative.* a cultured, intellectual person of the upper class: *He comes of the Brahmin caste of New England* (Oliver Wendell Holmes).
Brah|min|ic (brä min′ik), *adj.* **1** = Brahmanic. **2** *Figurative.* having to do with a Brahmin (def. 2).
Brah|min|i|cal (brä min′ə kəl), *adj.* = Brahmanic.
Brah|min|ism (brä′mə niz əm), *n.* **1** = Brahmanism. **2** *Figurative.* intellectuality, especially of a conscious or exclusive sort.
Brah|min|ist (brä′mə nist), *n.* = Brahmanist.
Brah|min|y (brä′mə nē), *adj.* = Brahmany.
Bra|hu|i (brä hü′ə), *n., pl.* **-hu|i**. **1** a Dravidian people of Baluchistan. **2** a member of this people. **3** their language.
braid**[1] (brād), *n., v.* **—*n. **1** a band formed by weaving together three or more strands of hair, ribbon, straw, or the like; plait: *She wore her hair in two long braids.* **2** a narrow band of fabric used to rim or bind clothing: *The general's uniform was trimmed with gold braid.* **3** a band or string for confining the hair: *A chain of gold ye shall not lack nor braid to bind your hair* (Scott).
[< verb]
—*v.t.* **1** to weave or wind together (three or more strands of hair, cord, or the like); intertwine; plait: *She can braid her own hair.* **2** to make by braiding: *to braid rugs.* **3** to trim or bind with braid: *to braid an apron.* **4** to confine (the hair) with a band or ribbon.
—*v.i.* to weave; crisscross: *water braiding downstream. Read it before you go ... to the Caribbean, or braiding through Mexico* (Charles Poore).
[Old English *bregdan*] **—braid′er**, *n.* **—braid′like′**, *adj.*

***braid**[1]
definition 1

braid[2] (brād), *adj. Scottish.* broad.
braid|ed (brā′did), *adj.* **1** woven; intertwined. SYN: plaited, interwoven. **2** trimmed with braid: *The band wore braided jackets.*
braided rug, a rug or mat made by braiding strips of fabric, often rags, and sewing them together in an oval, circular, or rectangular pattern.
braid|ing (brā′ding), *n.* **1** braid used as trimming. **2** anything braided. **3** the act of a person or thing that braids.
brail (brāl), *n., v.* **—*n.*** one of the small ropes fastened to the edge of a sail, especially a fore-and-aft sail, used in drawing the sail up or in.
—*v.t.* to gather or haul in with brails.
[< Old French *braiel* clew line < *braie* guy rope, fastening; earlier, breeches < *brague*; see etym. under **bracket**]
Braille or **braille** (brāl), *n., v.,* **Brailled**, **Braill|ing** or **brailled**, **braill|ing**. **—*n.*** **1** a system of writing and printing for blind people. The letters in Braille are represented by different arrangements of raised points and are read by touching them. **2** the letters themselves.
—*v.t.* to print or type (some piece of writing) in Braille.
[< Louis *Braille*, 1809-1852, a French teacher of the blind, who developed a dot system and published it in 1829]
Braill|er (brā′lər), *n.* a typewriter with six keys for typing in Braille.
Braille|writ|er (brāl′rī′tər), *n.* = Brailler.
brain** (brān), *n., v.* **—*n. **1** the soft mass of nerve cells and nerve fibers enclosed in the skull or head of vertebrate animals. The tissue is a grayish or whitish matter with which we can learn, think, and remember. In man it consists of the cerebrum, cerebellum, pons Varolii, and medulla oblongata. The technical name for the brain is

encephalon. *The human brain is composed of some 10 billion nerve cells, more or less alike, which interact in various ways.* **2** that part of the nervous system of invertebrates corresponding in position or function to the brain of vertebrates. **3** a large electronic system capable of solving complex problems, storing data, examining and analyzing material, and controlling processes with great speed; an electronic brain: *Nearly all large-scale electronic brains are general purpose computers which can be adapted to many specialized applications* (Wall Street Journal). **4** the vital center of control of any system. In simple mechanisms, such as a heating or cooling system, the brain is the thermostat. In more complex mechanisms, such as guided missiles, satellites, and the like, it is a complex of regulatory and guidance controls. *The toughest problem is guidance—keeping the missile on course and giving it a "brain" that will make changes and correct errors* (Newsweek). **5** *Slang.* a very intelligent person. **6** Often, **brains**. *Figurative.* intellectual power; mind; intelligence: *I am a Bear of Very Little Brain* (A. A. Milne).
—*v.t.* **1** to kill by smashing the skull of: *The man brained the snake with a heavy rock.* **2** *Slang.* to hit on the head.
have (something) on the brain, *Informal.* to be extremely interested in or eager about something: *She has ballet on the brain.*
pick the brains of, to extract useful information or material from (someone): *His success in picking the brains of Mr. Onslow of a secret encouraged him* (Edward G. Bulwer-Lytton).
rack (or **beat** or **cudgel**) **one's brains**, to try very hard to think of something: *He racked his brains for his friend's phone number, but he couldn't remember it.*
turn the brain, to make conceited or foolish: *Eminence, though fancied, turns the brain* (Edward Young).
[Old English *brægen*]

***brain**
definition 1

divisions of the brain:

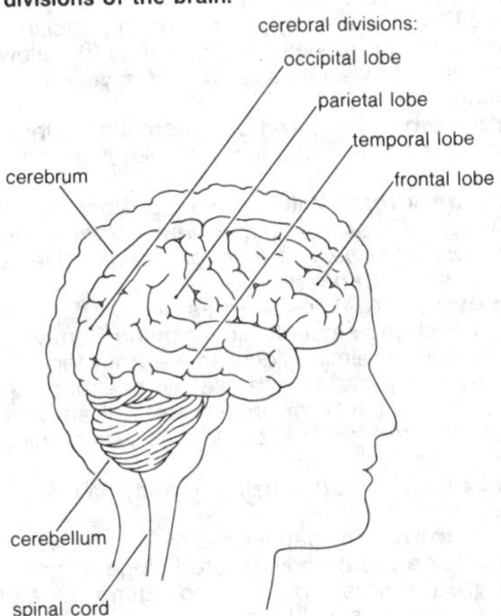

brain section:

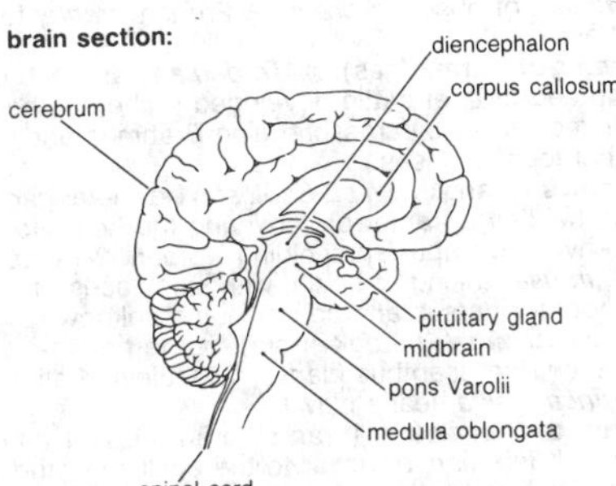

brain bucket, *U.S. Slang.* a crash helmet.
brain|case (brān′kās′), *n.* the cranium, the part of the skull enclosing the brain.
brain cell, a nerve cell in the brain.
brain|child (brān′chīld′), *n., pl.* **-chil|dren**. *Informal.* any idea, invention, or discovery.
brain coral, a reef-forming coral having a grooved surface resembling the convolutions of the brain. See picture under **coral**.
brain dead, showing brain death.
brain death, death of the cerebral cortex, shown by flat tracings on the electroencephalograph; cerebral death: *The Harvard panel urged that death be determined by "brain death" ... even though the heart and other organs may continue to function by artificial means* (New York Times).
brain drain, *Informal.* a shortage of professional or skilled labor caused by the emigration of scientists, technicians, and craftsmen to more favorable labor markets: *Part of the problem ... is that there is a "brain drain" from the farms into the cities where life is better* (Tuscaloosa News).
brain-drain (brān′drān′), *v.i., v.t. Informal.* to emigrate, or be induced to emigrate, to a place with more favorable job opportunities: *[He is] an Englishman brain-drained to the US some 10 years ago* (New Scientist). —**brain′-drain′er**, *n.*
-brained, *combining form.* having a ____brain: *Mad-brained = having a mad brain.*
brain|fag (brān′fag′), *n.* mental exhaustion, as from overwork.
brain fever, cerebrospinal meningitis or encephalitis.
brain|ish (brā′nish), *adj. Archaic or Obsolete.* headstrong; passionate.
brain|less (brān′lis), *adj.* **1** stupid; foolish. **2** without a brain. —**brain′less|ly**, *adv.* —**brain′lessness**, *n.*
brain|pan (brān′pan′), *n.* the part of the skull enclosing the brain; cranium.
brain-pick|ing (brān′pick′ing), *n. U.S. Informal.* the extraction of useful information by repeated questioning: *There's a large number of people to whom the Vice-President turns for sporadic brain-picking* (Wall Street Journal).
brain|pow|er (brān′pou′ər), *n.* **1** the power of the intellect; brains. **2** intellectual power considered as a force or instrument.
brains (brānz), *n.pl.* mind; intelligence. See **brain** *n.,* def. 6.
brain|sick (brān′sik′), *adj.* **1** diseased in the brain or mind; crazy; insane. **2** proceeding from a diseased mind. —**brain′sick′ly**, *adv.* —**brain′sick′ness**, *n.*
brain stem, the base of the human brain lying beneath the cerebrum and the cerebellum, which connects the spinal cord with the forebrain. The brain stem comprises especially the axis, the motor and sensory tracts, and the nuclei of the cranial nerve.
brain|storm (brān′stôrm′), *n., v.* —*n.* **1** *Informal.* a sudden inspiration. **2** a sudden and violent, but temporary, mental disturbance.
—*v.i.* to stimulate the imagination of a group by having its members state every solution of a problem that comes to mind, withholding all criticism until the production of ideas is exhausted.
—*v.t.* **1** to subject (a group or a problem) to brainstorming: *Organized in teams of six ... they brainstormed such questions as how to stimulate creative thinking in the U.S. Navy* (Newsweek). **2** to arrive at (a solution or idea) by brainstorming: *The plant superintendent ... brainstormed a plan to install a conveyor system* (Wall Street Journal). —**brain′storm′er**, *n.*
brains trust, *British.* **1** a public meeting or radio or television program in which experts debate or answer questions submitted to them; panel discussion. **2** brain trust.
brain|teas|er (brān′tē′zər), *n.* a puzzle to test a person's ingenuity; a baffling problem; teaser: *Mathematical brainteasers are an ancient sport* (Scientific American).
brain trust, a group of experts consulted by an administrator or political leader.
brain truster, a member of a brain trust.
brain|wash (brān′wosh′, -wôsh′), *v., n.* —*v.t.* to subject to brainwashing; indoctrinate.
—*n.* the act or process of brainwashing: *the brainwash of war prisoners.* —**brain′wash′er**, *n.*
brain|wash|ing (brān′wosh′ing, -wôsh′-), *n.* a process of systematically, forcibly, and intensively indoctrinating a person to destroy or weaken his beliefs and ideas, so that he becomes willing to accept different or opposite beliefs and ideas.
brain wave, **1** electric current produced by the rhythmic electric fluctuations between the parts of the brain. Brain waves can be recorded by an analyzer or an electroencephalograph. **2** a telepathic vibration supposed to effect transference of thought by other than physical means of communication. **3** *Informal.* a sudden bright idea; brainstorm.
brain|work (brān′wėrk′), *n.* work requiring special use of the brain, as distinguished from manual or mechanical work.
brain|work|er (brān′wėr′kər), *n.* a person who does brainwork.
brain|y (brā′nē), *adj.,* **brain|i|er**, **brain|i|est**. *Informal.* intelligent; clever. —**brain′i|ly**, *adv.* —**brain′i|ness**, *n.*
braise (brāz), *v.t.,* **braised**, **brais|ing**. to brown (meat) quickly in fat and then cook long and slowly in a covered pan with a very little liquid. [< French *braiser* < Old French *braise* hot charcoal < a Germanic word] —**brais′er**, *n.*
***brake¹** (brāk), *n., v.,* **braked**, **brak|ing**. —*n.* **1a** anything used to slow or stop the motion of a wheel or vehicle by pressing or scraping or by rubbing against. The brakes on a railroad train are blocks that press against the wheels. **b** *Figurative.* anything that retards or holds back; restraint; bridle: *The traditional class structure of British society is a powerful ... brake on growth* (Atlantic). **2** a large, high, four-wheeled carriage; break. **3** the handle or lever of a pump. **4** a frame for holding a horse's foot while being shod.
—*v.t.* **1** to slow up or stop by using a brake: *He braked the speeding car and it skidded to a stop.* **2** to use a brake on: *He braked the car in vain; the brakes would not hold.*
—*v.i.* **1** to use a brake or brakes. **2** to be braked; slow up or stop: *The train braked with a screech.* [Middle English *brake*, perhaps < Old French *brac, bras* arm (from the arm's strength being applied to the device)]

***brake¹**
definition 1a

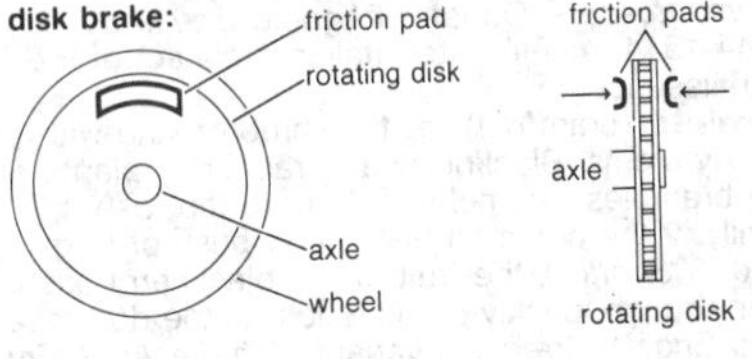

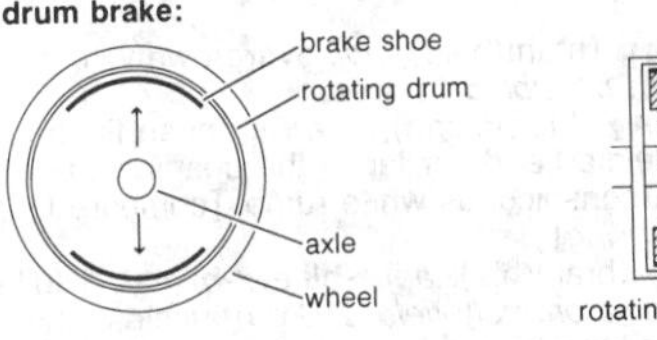

brake² (brāk), *n., v.,* **braked**, **brak|ing**. —*n.* **1** a tool or machine for breaking up flax or hemp into fibers. **2** a baker's machine for kneading or rolling. **3** a heavy harrow for breaking clods.
—*v.t.* to break up (flax or hemp) into fibers.
[< Middle Dutch *braeke*]
brake³ (brāk), *n.* a thick growth of bushes; thicket: *So thick entwined, As one continued brake, the undergrowth Of shrubs and tangling bushes* (Milton). [compare Middle Low German *brake*]
brake⁴ (brāk), *n.* **1** a large, coarse fern; bracken. **2** any of various other ferns of related genera. [probably variant of *bracken*]
brake⁵ (brāk), *v. Archaic.* broke; a past tense of **break¹**: *He took the bread and brake it.*
brake|age (brā′kij), *n.* **1** the action of a brake in stopping a train or rolling vehicle. **2** a brake or brakes. [< *brake¹* + *age*]
brake band, a flexible band which, when tightened against a brake drum, causes friction and resultant braking action.
brake disk, a disk revolving with a wheel, against which pads press to cause friction.
brake drum, a metal cylinder revolving with a wheel or shaft, against which a brake band or shoe is pressed to create the friction necessary for retarding motion.
brake fade, a loss of braking power in a motor vehicle, caused by the expansion of the brake drum from severe or continuous application of the brakes.
brake fluid, the fluid used in a hydraulic brake.
brake horsepower, the net output of horsepower of an engine, turbine, or other source of power, as measured by a band brake or a dynamometer; effective horsepower. *Abbr:* b.hp.
brake lining, a material generally consisting of asbestos combined with other materials, riveted or cemented to a brake band or brake shoe, to increase friction and resist heat.
brake|man (brāk′mən), *n., pl.* **-men**. a man who helps the engineer or conductor of a railroad train usually by coupling and uncoupling cars and by working the brake when a car is rolling free; trainman. Also, *British,* **brakesman**. [American English < *brake¹* + *man*]
brake parachute, = drag parachute.
brake pedal, the pedal by which the driver of an automobile or other vehicle controls the brakes.
brakes (brāks), *n.pl.* the parts, such as drums and shoes, comprising the mechanism used in

Pronunciation Key: hat, āge, cãre, fär; let, ēqual, tėrm; it, īce; hot, ōpen, ôrder; **oi**l, **ou**t; cup, pu̇t, rüle; **ch**ild; lo**ng**; **th**in; **ᴛʜ**en; **zh**, measure; **ə** represents **a** in about, **e** in taken, **i** in pencil, **o** in lemon, **u** in circus.

braking. See **brake**[1] (def. 1a).

brake shoe, a part of a brake mechanism on railroad cars, automobiles, and other vehicles; a shaped metal block which rubs against a wheel, drum, or other surface in motion to provide friction when the brakes are applied.

brakes|man (brāks′mən), *n., pl.* **-men**. *British.* brakeman.

brake-van (brāk′van′), *n. British.* a railway car on a freight train, or a compartment on a passenger train, where the brakes are operated.

brak|ie or **brak|ey** (brā′kē), *n. Informal.* brakeman.

brak|y (brā′kē), *adj.* overgrown with bushes and shrubs.

bra|less (brä′lis), *adj.* not wearing a brassiere.

Bram|ah lock (bram′ə, brä′mə), a form of lock characterized by a series of notched sliding pieces which are moved by the key. [< Joseph *Bramah*, 1748-1814, an English inventor]

Bra|man|tesque (brä′män tesk′), *adj.* of or having to do with Renaissance architecture: *Bramantesque balance and symmetry.* [< Italian *Bramantesco* < Donato d'Agnolo *Bramante*, 1444-1514, a celebrated Italian architect of the Renaissance]

bram|ble (bram′bəl), *n.* **1** a shrub or vine with prickly stems. Blackberry and raspberry plants are brambles. Brambles belong to the rose family. **2** the common blackberry bush of England. **3** *Scottish.* the fruit of the blackberry bush. **4** any rough, prickly shrub, such as the dog rose. [Old English *bræmbel*, variant of *brēmel* < *brōm* broom]

bram|bled (bram′bəld), *adj.* overgrown with brambles: *brambled hedges.*

bram|bling (bram′bling), *n.* a European finch, closely related and similar to the chaffinch, but having a conspicuous white rump. [compare German *Brämling*]

bram|bly (bram′blē), *adj.*, **-bli|er**, **-bli|est**. **1** full of brambles: *a brambly field.* **2** like brambles; prickly: *a brambly bush.*

Bramp|ton stock (bramp′tən), a stock about two feet high that bears fragrant white, pink, red, purple, or yellow blossoms.

bran (bran), *n.* the broken covering of seeds or kernels of grains like wheat and rye, which is separated from the inner part that is made into flour. Bran is used for fodder and in cereal, bread, and other foods. [< Old French *bran, bren*]

Bran (bran), *n.* a Celtic god, son of Llyr (the sea), and legendary king of Britain.

bran|card (brang′kərd), *n.* a litter or stretcher for carrying wounded or sick persons. [< French *brancard* litter < *branche* branch]

***branch** (branch, bränch), *n., v., adj.* —*n.* **1** a part of a tree, shrub, or other plant growing out from the trunk; any woody part of a tree above the ground except the trunk. A bough is a large branch. A twig is a very small branch. **2** *Figurative.* any division that extends like a branch of a tree: **a** a line of family descent. **SYN**: offshoot. **b** a tributary stream: *The Ohio River has two main branches.* **3** *Figurative.* a division; part: *The FBI is a branch of the Justice Department. History is a branch of learning.* **4** *Figurative.* a local office: *a branch of a bank. The main library operates several branches around town.* **5** *Figurative.* a subdivision of a family of languages; a linguistic group. **6** *Especially Southern U.S.* a small stream; a brook.
—*v.i.* **1** to put out branches; spread in branches: *As it grew, the tree near the house branched over the roof.* **SYN**: ramify. **2** to divide into branches: (*Figurative.*) *The road branches at the bottom of the hill.* **SYN**: fork.
—*v.t.* **1** to divide into branches; spread out as branches. **2** to adorn with branches or sprays, as in needlework.
—*adj.* **1** forming a branch. **2** of or having to do with a branch.

branch off, a to go off a main road or route in a different direction; diverge: *The new route branches off to the left.* **b** to divide into branches: *A very early concentration of speech from which these dialects branched off ...* (Max Müller).

branch out, a to put out branches: *Soon after it was planted, the rosebush began to branch out.* **b** to extend business, interests, or activities; undertake fresh activities: *That store used to be a meat market only; now it is branching out into groceries and household supplies.*
[< Old French *branche* < Late Latin *branca* paw]
—**branch′less**, *adj.* —**branch′like′**, *adj.*
—*Syn. n.* **1 Branch, bough, limb** mean a part of a tree growing out from the trunk or from another similar part. **Branch** is the general word, and applies to any of the woody outgrowths, large or small, of a tree or shrub: *The branches waved in the breeze.* **Bough** applies particularly to a main branch, but often is used to suggest any branch covered with blossoms, fruit, etc., especially when it has been cut from the tree: *Those boughs of flowering plum are beautiful on the table.* **Limb** applies to a main or large branch: *The wind broke a whole limb from the tree.*

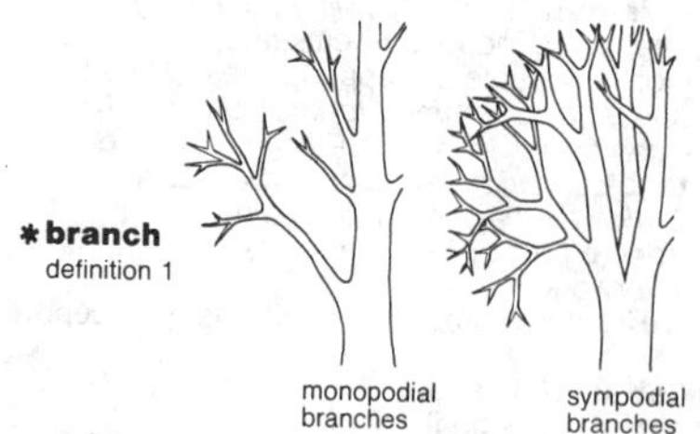

***branch** definition 1

-branched, *combining form.* having ___ branches: *Many-branched trees = trees having many branches.*

branched chain (brancht, bräncht), *Chemistry.* a molecular pattern in which a chain of atoms branches off from another chain.

branch|er (bran′chər, brän′-), *n.* a young hawk or other bird when it first leaves the nest and takes to the branches of trees.

branch herring, = alewife (a sea fish related to the herring).

bran|chi|a[1] (brang′kē ə), *n. Zoology.* **1** a gill. See **branchiae**. **2** a gill-like organ. [< Latin *branchiae* gills < Greek *bránchia*, plural of *bránchion* fin]

bran|chi|a[2] (brang′kē ə), *n.pl. Zoology.* branchiae. [< Greek *bránchia* fins]

bran|chi|ae (brang′kē ē), *n.pl.* **1** the organs of respiration in fishes; gills. **2** the gill-like organs of other animals. [see etym. under **branchia**[1]]

bran|chi|al (brang′kē əl), *adj.* of or resembling branchiae or gills.

bran|chi|ate (brang′kē it, -āt), *adj.* having branchiae or gills.

bran|chi|at|ed (brang′kē ā′tid), *adj.* = branchiate.

bran|chif|er|ous (brang kif′ər əs), *adj.* bearing or having branchiae. [< *branchi*(ae) + *-ferous*]

bran|chi|form (brang′kə fôrm), *adj.* like gills.

branch|ing program (bran′ching, brän′-), a program used in a teaching machine in which the sequence of information and questions is determined by the individual student's answers. If a student answers questions incorrectly, he is directed to a branch of the program with review material that explains his error. If he answers correctly, he may be directed to a branch of more advanced material.

bran|chi|o|pod (brang′kē ə pod), *n.* any crustacean of a subclass of chiefly freshwater crustaceans having an elongated body and numerous pairs of flat, leaflike, thoracic appendages that serve as gills. Water fleas belong to this subclass. The group also includes the anostracans, notostracans, and conchostracans. [< Greek *bránchia* gills + *poús, podós* foot]

bran|chi|os|te|gite (brang′kē os′tə jīt), *n.* a section of the carapace which covers the gills of crustaceans. [< Greek *bránchia* gills + *stégein* cover + English *-ite*[1]]

bran|chi|u|ran (brang′kē yůr′ən), *n.* any one of a group of crustaceans related to the copepods, having sucking mouths, parasitic on marine and freshwater fishes; carp louse; fish louse. [< Greek *bránchia* gills + *ourá* tail + English *-an*[1]]

branch|let (branch′lit, bränch′-), *n.* **1** a little branch. **2** a smaller branch growing from a larger one.

branch water, *Southern U.S.* **1** water from a creek or small river. **2** *Informal.* plain water (not carbonated) used with whiskey to make a highball.

branch|y (bran′chē, brän′-), *adj.* **1** having many branches: ... *the branchy structure of the arterial system* (Bulletin of Atomic Scientists). **2** branching; ramifying.

***brand** (brand), *n., v.* —*n.* **1** a certain kind, grade, or make; the quality or kind (of goods) as indicated by a mark, stamp, or label: *This is not as good a brand of butter as we are used to.* **2** a name or mark that a company uses to distinguish its goods from the goods of others; trademark: *The store doesn't sell that particular brand of coffee.* **3** an iron stamp for burning a mark. **4** a mark made by burning the skin or hide with a brand: *The cattle on this big ranch have a brand which shows who owns them.* **5** *Figurative.* a mark of disgrace: *He could never rid himself of the brand of coward.* **SYN**: stigma, blot, stain. **6** a piece of wood that is burning or partly burned: *By each gun the lighted brand* (Thomas Campbell). **7** *Botany.* **a** a fungous disease in which the leaves and stems of plants appear as if burned. **b** any fungus producing such a disease. **8** *Archaic.* a sword.
—*v.t.* **1** to mark by burning the skin or hide with a hot iron. In former times criminals were often branded. **SYN**: sear. **2** *Figurative.* **a** to put a mark of disgrace on; stigmatize: *He has been branded as a traitor.* **b** to single out: *Her hairstyle brands her as old-fashioned.* **3** *Figurative.* to impress upon: *events branded on one's memory.*
[Old English *brand* (sword) blade; torch]
—**brand′er**, *n.*

***brand** definition 3

branding irons

bran|den|burg (bran′dən bėrg), *n.* an ornament of braid with loops, for fastening a garment; a frog. [probably < the Elector of *Brandenburg*, in whose army they were worn]

brand goose, = brant[1].

bran|died (bran′dēd), *adj.* prepared, mixed, or flavored with brandy.

brand|ing iron (bran′ding), a brand used for branding cattle, horses, or other animals, and sometimes, for putting a mark of ownership on tools and other articles.

brand|i|ron (brand′ī′ərn), *n.* **1** an iron for branding. **2** *Dialect.* a gridiron, andiron, or trivet.

bran|dish (bran′dish), *v., n.* —*v.t.* **1** to wave or shake in a threatening manner; flourish: *The old man brandished his walking stick at the menacing dog.* **2** to shake or flourish about.
—*n.* a threatening shake; flourish: *She answered with a brandish of her umbrella.*
[< Old French *brandiss-*, stem of *brandir* < *brand* sword < Germanic (compare Old High German *brant*)] —**bran′dish|er**, *n.*

brand|ling (brand′ling), *n.* **1** a small, reddish-brown earthworm with rings or bands of yellow, used as bait by anglers. **2** *Dialect.* a young salmon.

brand name, **1** a brand or trademark; trade name. **2** a product bearing a well-known trade name.

brand-new (brand′nü′, -nyü′), *adj.* very new; entirely new: *Dressed in brand-new uniforms, the fliers looked fit despite their long ordeal* (Newsweek). Also, **bran-new**.

bran|dy (bran′dē), *n., pl.* **-dies**, *v.*, **-died**, **-dy|ing**.
—*n.* **1** a strong alcoholic liquor made from wine. **2** a somewhat similar liquor made from fermented fruit juice, as of apples or peaches.
—*v.t.* to mix, flavor, or preserve with brandy.
[< Dutch *brandewijn* < *brandende wijn* burning (that is, distilled) wine]

brandy ball, *British.* a ball of brandy-flavored candy.

brandy mint, *U.S.* peppermint.

brandy snap, a brandy-flavored gingersnap.

bran|gle (brang′gəl), *n., v.*, **-gled**, **-gling**. *Dialect.*
—*n.* a wrangle; squabble.
—*v.i.* to wrangle; squabble.
[variant of obsolete *branle* < French *branler* to shake]

Bran|gus (brang′gəs), *n. Trademark.* any one of a breed of beef cattle developed in the southern United States by crossbreeding Brahmas and Aberdeen Anguses.

branks (brangks), *n.pl. Scottish.* **1** a metal gag or bit, held by a framework covering the head, formerly used to punish scolding women. **2** (*sing. or pl. in use*) a kind of bridle, with sidepieces of wood, for horses and cows. [origin unknown]

brank|ur|sine (brangk ėr′sin), *n.* the bear's-breech; the acanthus plant. [< Medieval Latin *branca ursina* bear's claw]

bran|le or **brans|le** (bran′əl, brän′əl), *n.* **1** an old French folk dance similar to the cotillion. **2** the air or music for this dance. Also, **brawl**. [< Middle French *branle, bransle* < *branler* to shake]

bran-new (bran′nü′, -nyü′), *adj.* = brand-new.

bran|ni|gan (bran′ə gən), *n. U.S. Slang.* a brawl. [probably < the name *Brannigan*]

bran|ny (bran′ē), *adj.* of or like bran.

Brans-Dick|e theory (brans′dik′ē), a theory that predicts a lesser degree of curvature for electromagnetic waves passing through a strong gravitational field than that predicted by Einstein's general theory of relativity; scalar-tensor theory. [< Carl *Brans* and Robert *Dicke*, American physicists]

brant[1] (brant), *n., pl.* **brants** or (*collectively*) **brant**. any one of several small, dark wild geese, which breed in arctic regions and migrate south in the autumn. Also, **brand goose, brant goose, brent.** [origin uncertain]

brant[2] (brant), *adj. Scottish.* brent; steep; smooth.

bran|tail (bran′tāl′), *n. Dialect.* the redstart of Europe.

brant goose, = brant[1].

bran-tub (bran′tub′), *n. British.* a tub full of bran with presents hidden in it to be drawn out at random, as at Christmas festivities.

brash[1] (brash), *adj., n.* —***adj.*** **1** showing lack of respect; impudent; saucy: *a very brash young man. Many are brash, but few are brave* (Harper's). **2** hasty; rash: *a brash act.*
—***n.*** **1** an attack of illness. **2** a rash or eruption. **3** = water brash. **4** a burst of rain and wind.
[origin uncertain] —**brash′ly,** *adv.* —**brash′ness,** *n.*

brash[2] (brash), *n., adj.* —***n.*** **1** a mass of loose, broken rock. **2** fragments of crushed ice drifted together. **3** clippings from hedging and pruning. **4** *British Dialect.* broken or refuse boughs, twigs, etc.
—***adj.*** *U.S. and British Dialect.* easily broken; brittle: *brash timber.*
[perhaps < Old French *breche* < Germanic (compare Old High German *brecha* fracture)]

brash|y (brash′ē), *adj.* broken; crumbly; fragmentary. —**brash′i|ness,** *n.*

bra|sier (brā′zhər), *n.* = brazier[2].

brass (bras, bräs), *n., adj., v.* —***n.*** **1** a metal that is usually a yellowish color and an alloy of copper and zinc, in various proportions, commonly two parts of copper, or a little less, to one of zinc. It can be shaped or drawn. **2** anything made of brass, such as an ornament or dish: *The man polished all the brasses.* **3** *Music.* Also, **brasses. a** musical instruments made of metal and played by blowing into a cup-shaped mouthpiece. The trumpet, trombone, and French horn are brasses. **b** the section of an orchestra or band made up of these instruments (distinguished from the strings, woodwinds, and percussion). **4** *Informal, Figurative.* rude boldness; impudence: *He had the brass to go to the party uninvited.* **SYN:** effrontery, shamelessness.
5 *Slang, Figurative.* **a** military officers of high rank: *Top Pentagon brass are taking the aviation-gasoline restriction seriously* (Newsweek).
b the officers or executives of any business: *police brass, TV network brass.* **6** a memorial plate of brass incised with an effigy, coat of arms, or inscription: *We took rubbings off the old brasses in the church aisles.* **7a** hardness; imperishability. **b** insensibility.
—***adj.*** made of brass; brazen: *brass candlesticks.*
—***v.t.*** to coat with brass by electroplating or otherwise.
brasses, a Music. brass (def. 3). **b** that part of a bearing which fits around the shaft, usually a brass cylinder cut in two or more sections with a lining of babbitt or white metal forming the rubbing surface.
double in brass, *U.S. Slang.* to play two parts; do two jobs; double: *The men are television technicians doubling in brass as an optical expert, a photographer, and a machinist* (Newsweek).
[Old English *bræs*]

brass|age (bras′ij, bräs′-), *n.* a mint charge levied to cover the expense of coining money. [< French *brassage* < Old French *brasser* mix (molten metals), brew < *brais* barley mash]

bras|sard (bras′ärd, brə särd′), *n.* **1** a band worn above the elbow as a badge. **2** armor for the upper part of the arm. [< French *brassard* < *bras* arm]

bras|sart (bras′ərt), *n.* = brassard (def. 2).

brass band, a group of musicians all or most of whom play upon metal (chiefly brass) wind instruments; military band.

brass|bound (bras′bound′, bräs′-), *adj.* **1** *Informal.* **a** keeping strictly to rule; refusing to accept modification; inflexible: *brassbound fanatics; brassbound rigidity.* **b** impudent; brazen: *a brassbound liar.* **2** bound or fitted with brass: *a brassbound box.*

brass-col|lar (bras′kol′ər, bräs′-), *adj. U.S. Informal.* brassbound; inflexible: *His sharecropper father was a brass-collar Democrat out of the old South* (Harper's).

brasse|rie (brås rē′), *n. French.* **1** a saloon or beer garden that also serves food. **2** a brewery.

brass|es (bra′sis, brä′-), *n.pl.* See under **brass.**

brass hat, *Slang.* **1** a high-ranking military officer, especially a general or staff officer. **2** a civilian official in a high position. [because of the gilt insignia on officers' caps]

bras|si|ca (bras′ə kə), *n.* any one of a genus of herbs of the mustard family, including the cabbage, kale, broccoli, turnip, rape, and mustard. [< Latin *brassica* cabbage]

bras|si|ca|ceous (bras′ə kā′shəs), *adj.* **1** belonging to the mustard family, a family of plants including the cabbage, turnip, radish, and cress. **2** cabbagelike. [< Latin *brassica* cabbage + English *-aceous*]

brass|ie (bras′ē, bräs′-), *n., pl.* **brass|ies.** a golf club with a wooden head, on the bottom of which there is a metal plate. It has a loft between that of a driver and a spoon and is used for long shots off the fairway. Also, **brassy.** [< *brass* + *-ie*]

bras|siere or **bras|sière** (brə zir′), *n.* a woman's undergarment worn to support the breasts. [< French *brassière* bodice < *bras* arm]

bras|sin (bras′ən), *n.* a plant hormone that stimulates the division, elongation, and lateral enlargement of plant cells. It was isolated from the pollen of the plant rape. [< *brass*(ica) + *-in*]

brass knuckles, a metal bar or linked rings that fit across the knuckles, used as a weapon.

brass plate, a plate made of brass, indicating the occupant of a building.

brass ring, *U.S. Slang.* a big prize; a chance for riches or success: *"Sure, George is ambitious," one of them says. "When he sees the brass ring coming round, he can't help grabbing for it"* (Saturday Evening Post).

brass rubbing, 1 the art or practice of taking a tracing of effigies or inscriptions on brass objects by rubbing colored wax on paper pressed over the brass plate. **2** an impression made this way.

brass tacks, *Informal.* the actual facts or details.
get (or **come**) **down to brass tacks,** to get down to fundamentals: *After the exchange of a few pleasantries we immediately got down to brass tacks* (Life).

brass|ware (bras′wãr′, bräs′-), *n.* things made of brass.

brass-wind (bras′wind′, bräs′-), *adj.* of or having to do with the brasses or brass winds.

brass winds, metal musical instruments that are played by blowing into a cup-shaped mouthpiece, such as trumpets or trombones. See **brass** (*n.* def. 3a).

brass|y (bras′ē, bräs′-), *adj.,* **brass|i|er, brass|i|est,** *n., pl.* **brass|ies.** —***adj.*** **1** of or covered with brass. **2** like brass: *a brassy green sky.* **3** *Figurative.* loud and harsh: *a brassy voice. The music was somewhat brassy, overpercussive, and generally monotonous* (New Yorker). **4** *Informal, Figurative.* shameless; impudent; brazen: *a brassy manner.*
—***n.*** = brassie. —**brass′i|ly,** *adv.* —**brass′i|ness,** *n.*

brat (brat), *n.* **1a** an unpleasant child. **b** a child. **2** *British.* a check cloth used as an apron or other overgarment, especially of a coarse or makeshift character. **3** *Scottish.* the tough film or skin which forms on porridge, rice pudding, etc. [perhaps special use of Middle English *brat* rag, coarse garment, Old English *bratt* cloak, covering]

bratch|et (brach′it), *n.* **1** = brach. **2** = child (usually contemptuous or familiar). [< French *brachet* (diminutive) < *brac* hound]

brat|tice (brat′is), *n., v.,* **-ticed, -tic|ing.** —***n.*** **1** a partition for ventilation in a mine, usually made of cloth impregnated with creosote, nailed to props erected as needed. **2** *Obsolete.* a temporary breastwork, parapet, or gallery of wood erected on the battlement of a fortress, for use during a siege.
—***v.t.*** **1** to line the sides of (a shaft, or the like) with planking or boarding. **2** to provide with a brattice.
[earlier *bretis* < Old French *bretesce* wooden parapet, perhaps < Medieval Latin *brittisca* foreign, British fortification]

brat|tic|ing (brat′ə sing), *n.* **1** a piece of ornamental openwork, as over a shrine. **2** a brattice or brattices in a mine.

brat|tish (brat′ish), *adj.* like a brat; bratty; impudent. —**brat′tish|ly,** *adv.* —**brat′tish|ness,** *n.*

brat|tish|ing (brat′ə shing), *n.* = bratticing.

brat|tle (brat′əl), *n., v.,* **-tled, -tling.** *Especially Scottish.* —***n.*** a sharp rattling sound: *Thou need na start awa sae hasty wi' bickering brattle!* (Robert Burns).
—***v.i.*** **1** to clatter. **2** to scamper.
[probably imitative]

brat|ty (brat′ē), *adj.,* **-ti|er, -ti|est.** *Informal.* disobedient; impudent; fresh. —**brat′ti|ness,** *n.*

brat|wurst (brät′wėrst′, -vůrst′), *n.* a small, highly seasoned sausage made of ground pork, usually served fried. [< German *Bratwurst*]

braun|ite (brou′nīt), *n.* a brittle, brownish-black mineral, an oxide and silicate of manganese, occurring both crystallized and massive, an ore of manganese. *Formula:* $MnSiO_3$-$3Mn_2O_3$ [< August E. *Braun,* 1809-1856, a German archaeologist + *-ite*[1]]

braun|schwei|ger or **Braun|schwei|ger** (broun′shwī′gər; *German* broun′shvī′gər), *n.* smoked liver sausage. [< German *Braunschweiger* (*wurst*) Brunswick sausage]

bra|va (brä′vä), *interj., n. Italian.* feminine form of **bravo**[1].

bra|va|do (brə vä′dō), *n., pl.* **-does** or **-dos.** a great show of boldness without much real courage or real desire to fight. [< Spanish *bravada* < Italian *bravata,* ultimately < *bravo* brave]

brave (brāv), *adj.,* **brav|er, brav|est,** *n., v.,* **braved, brav|ing.** —***adj.*** **1** without fear; having courage; showing courage: *brave knights. Bravest of all in Fredericktown* (John Greenleaf Whittier). **2** making a fine appearance; showy: *The town fair had a brave display of flags for the Fourth of July.* **SYN:** splendid. **3** *Archaic.* fine; excellent: *brave new world* (Shakespeare). **SYN:** worthy, admirable.
—***n.*** **1** a brave person or persons: *The United States has been called "the land of the free and the home of the brave." None but the brave deserves the fair* (John Dryden). **2** a North American Indian warrior. **3** *Archaic.* a bully; tough. **4** *Archaic.* a boast; bravado; defiance: *A whole life's braves should somehow be made good* (Robert Browning).
—***v.t.*** **1** to meet without fear: *The Pilgrim Fathers braved the perils of the sea and the dangers and hardships of a new life in a new land for the sake of freedom.* **2** to dare; defy: *He braved the king's anger.* **SYN:** challenge. **3** *Obsolete.* to make splendid.
—***v.i.*** *Obsolete.* to boast; vaunt. **SYN:** swagger.
[< Middle French *brave* < Italian *bravo* bold, and < Spanish *bravo* wild < Vulgar Latin *brabus* < Latin *barbarus;* see etym. under **barbarous**]
—**brave′ly,** *adv.* —**brave′ness,** *n.*
—*Syn. adj.* **1 Brave, courageous** mean showing no fear. **Brave** suggests daring, being able to face danger, trouble, or fear boldly and with determination: *The brave girl went into the burning house to save a baby.* **Courageous** suggests being fearless in facing danger, having a strength and firmness of character that makes one able to endure, physically or otherwise, any trial with fortitude and resolution: *The courageous pioneers were not daunted by the perils of the westward journey. The courageous attorney prosecuted the grafters, although his career was threatened.*

brav|er|y (brā′vər ē, brāv′rē), *n., pl.* **-er|ies. 1** a being brave; fearlessness; courage: *The soldier was given a medal for bravery in battle.* **SYN:** boldness, daring, pluck, intrepidity. See syn. under **courage. 2** fine appearance; showy dress; finery: *She came to the party in all the bravery of her new dress and pink ribbons.* **3** ostentation; splendor.

bra|vis|si|mo (brä vēs′sē mō), *interj., n., pl.* **-mos.** superlative of **bravo**[1].

bra|vo[1] (brä′vō), *interj., n., pl.* **-vos.** —***interj.*** well done! fine! excellent!: *Bravo, Heracles, brave words, said he* (Benjamin Jowett).
—***n.*** a cry of "bravo!": *Sophy gave him a dazzling performance, to which he responded with enough bravos to fill a page* (Harper's).
[< Italian *bravo*]

bra|vo[2] (brä′vō, brā′-), *n., pl.* **-voes** or **-vos.** a hired fighter or murderer; daring villain. [< Italian *bravo*]

Bra|vo (brä′vō), *n. U.S.* a code name for the letter *b,* used in transmitting radio messages.

bra|vu|ra (brə vyůr′ə, -vůr′-; *Italian* brä vü′rä), *n., adj.* —***n.*** **1a** a piece of music requiring great skill and spirit in the performer. **b** a show of brilliant performance. **2** a display of daring; dash; spirit.
—***adj.*** **1** technically difficult; elaborate: *a bravura passage for tenor.* **2** capable of performing bravura music: *a bravura singer.*
[< Italian *bravura* bravery, spirit < *bravo* brave]

braw (brô, brä), *adj. Scottish.* **1** making a fine appearance. **2** excellent; fine: *a braw new coat* (Robert Burns). [variant of *brave*]

brawl[1] (brôl), *n., v.* —***n.*** **1** a noisy and disorderly quarrel: *Whatever brawls disturb the street, There should be peace at home* (Isaac Watts). **SYN:** fracas, fray. **2** babble; clamor. [< verb]
—***v.i.*** **1** to quarrel in a noisy and disorderly way; squabble. **2** to make a loud babbling noise: *A wild stream ... came brawling down its bed of rock* (Scott). **3** to raise a clamor or disturbance: *Patriotism ... may brawl and babble yet a little while* (Thomas Carlyle).
—***v.t.*** **1** to wrangle about. **2** to utter clamorously. **3** to drive or force by brawling.
[Middle English *brallen;* origin unknown]
—**brawl′er,** *n.* —**brawl′ing|ly,** *adv.*

brawl[2] (brôl), *n.* = branle. [variant of *branle*]

braw|ly or **braw|lie** (brô′lē), *adv. Scottish.* finely; excellently; well.

brawn (brôn), *n.* **1** firm, strong muscles; muscle. **2** muscular strength: *Football requires brain as*

Pronunciation Key: hat, āge, cãre, fär; let, ēqual, tėrm; it, īce; hot, ōpen, ôrder; oil, out; cup, půt, rüle; child; long; thin; ᴛʜen; zh, measure; ə represents a in about, e in taken, i in pencil, o in lemon, u in circus.

well as brawn. **3** boiled and pickled meat from a boar or hog. **4** headcheese. [< Old French *braon* < Germanic (compare Old High German *brāten* roast)]

brawn|y (brô′nē), *adj.,* **brawn|i|er, brawn|i|est.** strong; muscular: *The muscles of his brawny arms are strong as iron bands* (Longfellow). **SYN:** sinewy, powerful. **—brawn′i|ness,** *n.*

brax|y (brak′sē), *n., pl.* **brax|ies,** *adj.* **—*n.*** **1** an acute, usually fatal disease of young sheep, due to a bacterial infection of the fourth stomach. **2** a sheep having this disease.
—*adj.* affected with braxy.
[probably Old English *bræcsēoc* < *bræc* catarrh + *sēoc* sick]

bray¹ (brā), *n., v.* **—*n.*** **1** the loud, harsh sound made by a donkey: *the defiant bray of a donkey.* **2** any loud, harsh sound: *the bray of trumpets. And with rude crash and jarring bray The rusty bolts withdrawn* (Scott). [< verb]
—*v.i.* **1** to make a loud, harsh sound: *The trumpets brayed.* **2** to utter in a loud, harsh voice.
—*v.t.* to utter or emit with a loud, harsh sound: *The man brayed his orders to the waiter.*
[< Old French *braire* cry out < Gallo-Romance *bragere*] **—bray′er,** *n.*

bray² (brā), *v.t.* **1** to pound or crush into fine bits; grind into a powder (usually in a mortar): *Though thou shouldest bray a fool in a mortar . . . with a pestle, yet will not his foolishness depart from him* (Proverbs 27:22). **2** *Dialect.* to beat. **3** to temper and spread (printing ink). [< Old French *breier* < Frankish (compare Old Saxon *brecan*)]
—bray′er, *n.*

Braz., **1** Brazil. **2** Brazilian.

bra|za (brä′thä, -sä), *n.* a Spanish unit of linear measure, amounting to 5.48 feet in Spain, and 5.68 feet in Argentina. [< Spanish *braza* < *brazo* arm]

braze¹ (brāz), *v.t.,* **brazed, braz|ing. 1** to make of brass; cover or decorate with brass. **2** *Figurative.* to make like brass. [Old English *brasian* < *bræs* brass]

braze² (brāz), *v.,* **brazed, braz|ing,** *n.* **—*v.t.*** to solder with brass or other hard solder that has a high melting point, especially to unite (pieces of brass, steel, or other metal) by intensely heating the parts to be joined and applying zinc or an alloy of copper and zinc.
—*n.* **1** a brazed joint or fitting. **2** a brazing.
[perhaps < French *braser* solder < Old French *braiser* to burn] **—braz′er,** *n.*

bra|zen (brā′zən), *adj., v.* **—*adj.*** **1** *Figurative.* having no shame; shameless; impudent: *The brazen girl told lie after lie.* **SYN:** See syn. under **bold.** **2** *Figurative.* loud and harsh; brassy: *the brazen bellow of a horn.* **3** made of brass: *a brazen helmet.* **4** *Figurative.* like brass in color or strength: *a brazen barrier.*
—*v.t.* to make shameless or impudent.
brazen out (or **through**), **a** to act as if one did not feel ashamed of (something): *To brazen things out only provokes greater suspicion and hostility* (Manchester Guardian). **b** to get out of by acting shamelessly or impudently: *to brazen one's way out of a situation.*
[Old English *bræsen* < *bræs* brass] **—bra′zen|ly,** *adv.* **—bra′zen|ness,** *n.*

bra|zen-faced (brā′zən fāst′), *adj.* with bold, unblushing front; impudent.

brazen sea, a large vessel of brass in Solomon's temple, for the priests to wash in before performing the service of the temple; molten sea (in the Bible, II Kings 25:13, I Kings 7:23-26, II Chronicles 4:2-5).

bra|zier¹ (brā′zhər), *n.* a large metal pan or tray to hold burning charcoal or coal. Braziers are used in some countries for heating rooms. Also, **brasier.** [< Old French *brasier* < *breze* hot coals]

bra|zier² (brā′zhər), *n.* a person who works with brass. Also, **brasier.** [< *braze¹* + *-ier*]

bra|zier|y (brā′zhər ē), *n., pl.* **-zier|ies.** a place where brass is worked.

bra|zil (brə zil′), *n.* **1** = brazilwood. **2** the red dyestuff obtained from brazilwood. **3** (originally) a dyewood obtained from an East Indian tree; sappanwood. [< Spanish *brasil* < Old French *bresil* reddish dye]

bra|zil|e|in (brə zil′ē in), *n.* oxidized brazilin. *Formula:* $C_{16}H_{12}O_5$

Bra|zil|ian (brə zil′yən), *adj., n.* **—*adj.*** of Brazil or its people.
—*n.* a person born or living in Brazil.

braz|i|lin (braz′ə lin), *n.* a coloring matter, dyeing red with bases, yellow with acids, obtained from brazil in the form of yellow crystals which turn orange on exposure to air. *Formula:* $C_{16}H_{14}O_5$

Brazil nut, a large, triangular nut of a tree growing in Brazil. It is good to eat.

Bra|zil-nut tree (brə zil′nut′), a lofty evergreen tree found in large forests in Brazil, that yields the Brazil nut.

bra|zil|wood (brə zil′wůd′), *n.* a large tropical tree of the pea family whose wood was formerly used for making red and purple dyes and is still used for violin bows; Bahia wood; Pernambuco wood.

breach (brēch), *n., v.* **—*n.*** **1** an opening made by breaking down something solid; gap; fissure: *There is a breach in the hedge where I ran through it with my bicycle.* **SYN:** break, fracture, crack, rent. **2** *Figurative.* a breaking or neglect: *For the guard to leave before his replacement comes would be a breach of duty.* **SYN:** infraction, infringement. **3** *Figurative.* a breaking of friendly relations; quarrel: *I do not want . . . to widen the breach between us* (John Wesley). **SYN:** estrangement, alienation. **4a** the breaking of waves on a coast or over a vessel. **b** the waves themselves. **5** a whale's leap clear of the sea. **6** *Obsolete.* an irruption, inroad, or assault. **7** *Obsolete.* **a** a damaged part of the body; an injury. **b** = hernia. **8** *Obsolete.* **a** the physical action of breaking. **b** the fact of being broken; breakage; fracture.
—*v.t.* to break through; make an opening in: *The rushing floodwaters finally breached the dike of sandbags and dirt.*
—*v.i.* to rise or leap clear of the sea: *They saw a whale spouting and breaching* (Charles Kingsley).
stand in the breach, a to take the place of someone missing or unable to act, in an emergency: *By your wise counsel . . . stand in the breaches of your own family* (Jeremy Taylor). **b** *Figurative.* to bear the main weight of an attack: *Moses his chosen stood before him in the breach, to turn away his wrath, lest he should destroy them* (Psalms 106:23).
[Old English *brǣc* a break, breaking]

breach of contract, the breaking of a contract.

breach of faith, a breaking of a promise.

breach of promise, a breaking of a promise, especially a promise to marry.

breach of the peace, a public disturbance.

breach of trust, a violation of duty by an executor, trustee, or other fiduciary.

breach|y (brē′chē), *adj.* apt to break fences and get out of enclosures: *a high-spirited, breachy horse.*

bread (bred), *n., v.* **—*n.*** **1** food made of flour or meal mixed with milk or water and baked. Bread may be made with or without yeast or other leaven and is usually kneaded. *We eat bread and butter. Buy a loaf of bread.* **2** food in general. **3a** means of keeping alive; food; livelihood; sustenance: *How will you earn your daily bread?* **b** *U.S. Slang.* money: *"You owe the government bread to the tune of thirty-eight dollars"* (New Yorker). **4** a piece of bread or wafer used in the Eucharist.
—*v.t.* to cover with breadcrumbs before cooking: *She breaded the chicken before frying it.*
bread buttered on both sides, great good fortune; lucky circumstances: *Wherever Walter goes he is pretty sure to find his bread buttered on both sides* (John G. Lockhart).
break bread, a to eat or share a meal: *The preacher asked him inside and insisted he break bread with his family* (Atlantic). **b** to administer or take Communion: *The worshipers kneeled at the altar rail to break bread.*
cast one's bread upon the waters, to do good with little or no expectation of reward (in allusion to Ecclesiastes 11:1): *A charitable person will cast his bread upon the waters.*
know which side one's bread is buttered on, to know what is to one's advantage: *I know what's what, I know on which side my bread is buttered* (John Ford).
set bread, to mix batter or dough and leave it to rise: *The baker rose early to set bread for the morning baking.*
take the bread out of one's mouth, a to take away a person's livelihood: *You little Prigs, will you offer to take the bread out of my mouth?* (Peter A. Motteux). **b** to take from a person what he is on the very point of enjoying: *Lord Johnny dashed forward to take the bread out of his [Sir Robert Peel's] mouth* (J. W. Croker).
[Old English *brēad*]

bread and butter, 1 bread spread with butter. **2** *Figurative.* things necessary to live; a living; livelihood: *He earns his bread and butter by selling cars.*

bread-and-butter (bred′ən but′ər), *adj.* **1** *Informal.* **a** basic; staple: *Wagner's operas have never . . . been bread-and-butter items of the record companies as have Verdi and Puccini* (Harper's). **b** prosaic; commonplace: *bread-and-butter situation comedy.* **SYN:** mundane. **2** expressing thanks for hospitality: *a bread-and-butter letter.* **3** *Informal.* of or like a boy or girl; adolescent: *bread-and-butter schoolgirls.* **4** controlled by material wants and desires; mercenary: *bread-and-butter schemes.*

bread and cheese, simple fare.

bread and circuses, 1 food and amusements given to people by a government or other ruling power to keep the people content. **2** = welfare. [translation of Latin *pānem et circenses,* a phrase in Juvenal's *Satires*]

bread and scrape, bread having a meager spread of butter.

bread|bas|ket (bred′bas′kit, -bäs′-), *n.* **1** a basket or tray for holding or carrying bread. **2** *Figurative.* a region that is a chief source of grain: *. . . Alentejo, the rich breadbasket province of rolling wheat and cork groves* (Atlantic). **3** *Slang, Figurative.* the stomach. **4** *Slang.* a large aerial bomb containing a cluster of smaller explosive or incendiary bombs.

bread-bin (bred′bin′), *n. British.* breadbox.

bread|board (bred′bôrd′, -bōrd′), *n., v.* **—*n.*** **1** a board on which dough is kneaded. **2** a board on which bread is cut. **3** a board or similar flat surface on which experimental arrangements of any system, such as a system of electronic circuits, can be laid out.
—*v.i., v.t.* to make a breadboard for (an experimental system).

bread|box (bred′boks′), *n.* a box for storing bread, rolls, cake, etc.

bread|crumb or **bread-crumb** (bred′krum′), *n., v.* **—*n.*** **1** a crumb of bread. **2** the soft part of bread. **—*v.t.*** to cover or roll with breadcrumbs.

bread-crust bomb (bred′krust′), a mass of volcanic lava (bomb) having a compact but cracked outer crust and a spongy interior.

***bread|fruit** (bred′früt′), *n.* **1** a large, round, starchy fruit grown in the islands of the Pacific, much used for food. When it is baked it tastes somewhat like bread. **2** the tree that it grows on. It belongs to the mulberry family. **3** some similar fruit, such as the jack.

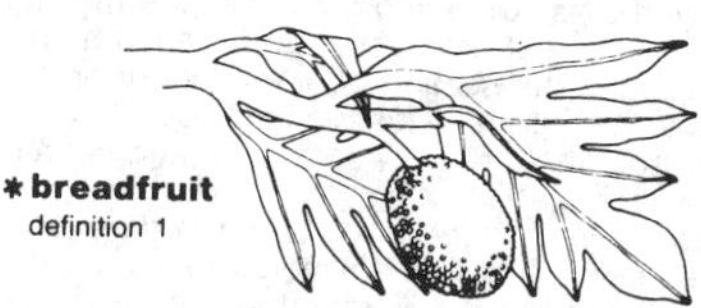

***breadfruit**
definition 1

bread knife, a knife for cutting bread, often having a notched or toothed edge.

bread|less (bred′lis), *adj.* **1** without bread: *a breadless diet.* **2** *Figurative.* without food: *breadless refugees.*

bread line, a line of people waiting to be given food as charity or relief.

bread mold, a black fungus that grows on bread.

bread|nut (bred′nut′), *n.* the nut of a tree of the mulberry family, of Jamaica and Central America, which is roasted or boiled for use as food.

bread|root (bred′rüt′, -rût′), *n.* the starchy, edible root of a plant of the pea family, found in central North America.

bread stick, a long, slender, cylindrical piece of bread dough baked until dry and crisp.

bread|stuff (bred′stuf′), *n.* **1** Also, **breadstuffs.** grain, flour, or meal for making bread. **2** = bread.

breadth (bredth, bretth), *n.* **1** how broad a thing is; distance across; width: *the breadth of the road, the breadth of the ocean. He has traveled the length and breadth of this land.* **2a** a piece of a certain width; a width: *a breadth of cloth.* **b** a measurement for flags equal to 9 inches in width. A four-breadth flag is 36 inches wide. **3** *Figurative.* freedom from narrowness in outlook: *Education and experience breed a breadth of vision and understanding.* **SYN:** latitude, amplitude, liberality. **4** spaciousness; extent: *The breadth of the explorer's travels was greater than that of the journeys of a dozen ordinary men.* **SYN:** scope, range. **5** a broad effect achieved by elimination or minimizing of details in the fine arts. [Middle English *bredethe,* alteration of *brede,* Old English *brǣdu* < *brād* broad]

breadth|ways (bredth′wāz′, bretth′-), *adv.* in the direction of the breadth.

breadth|wise (bredth′wīz′, bretth′-), *adv.* = breadthways.

bread wheat, any wheat commonly used in making bread.

bread|win|ner (bred′win′ər), *n.* **1a** a person who earns a living for himself and those dependent on him: *No fewer than 735,000 moved from the unemployed list to jobs, 452,000 of them married men in the vital family breadwinner category* (Time). **b** a person who earns his bread or living. **2** the tools, art, or craft with which anyone earns his living.

bread|win|ning (bred′win′ing), *n.* **1** the act of earning a living for oneself and one's dependents: *But the increase in female employment has been far greater than the rise in male breadwinning* (Wall Street Journal). **2** a means of earning a living.

break¹ (brāk), *v.,* **broke** or (*Archaic*) **brake, broken** or (*Archaic*) **broke, break|ing,** *n.* **—*v.t.*** **1** to

cause to come to pieces by a blow or pull: *He broke the window with a rock.* **2** to destroy the evenness, wholeness, regularity, or arrangement of: *to break a five-dollar bill, break step, break ranks,* (*Figurative.*) *to break the silence.* **3** to damage, injure, ruin, or destroy: *She broke her watch by winding it too tightly.* (*Figurative.*) *Hard work and long hours broke his health.* **4a** to crack or split the bone of: *to break one's arm, break one's neck.* **b** to rupture or crack the skin or covering of; lacerate: *Jack fell down and broke his crown. The fall bruised me badly but didn't break the skin.* **5** to fail to keep; act against; violate: *to break the Sabbath. He never breaks a promise. People who break the law are punished.* SYN: disobey. **6** to make less; lessen the force of; weaken: *The trees break the wind. The bushes broke his fall from the tree.* **7a** to put an end to; stop: *to break one's fast, break a strike.* **b** to stop for a time; interrupt: *to break a journey, break a schedule, break the boredom of a lonely summer.* **8** to reduce in rank or dismiss: *The captain was broken for neglect of duty.* **9** to escape or become free from: *to break jail. The boat broke its moorings in the storm.* **10** to force open: *to break the enemy's ranks.* **11a** *Figurative.* to train to obey; tame: *to break a colt.* **b** *Figurative.* to train away from a habit: *to break a child of running away.* **12** to go beyond; exceed: *The speed of the new train has broken all records.* **13** to dig or plow (ground), especially for the first time: *The settlers on the prairie worked hard to break ground for the first crops.* **14a** to make known; reveal: *Someone must break the news of the boy's accident to his mother.* **b** to utter (a jest, a sigh, or other expression or noise). **15** *Figurative.* to figure out; decipher; untangle: *to break a code.* **16** to stop the flow of electricity in (a circuit). **17** to ruin financially; make bankrupt. **18** *Figurative.* to alleviate: *Light broke the darkness.* **19** to set aside (a will) by legal action.
—*v.i.* **1** to come apart; crack; burst: *The plate broke when it fell on the floor.* SYN: split, splinter. **2** to force one's way: *The man broke out of prison. The police broke through the crowd.* (*Figurative.*) *Our friendliness finally broke through the newcomer's reserve.* **3** to come suddenly; come as a surprise: *The storm broke within ten minutes. The news broke unexpectedly.* **4a** to change suddenly: *to break into a gallop. The spell of rainy weather has broken.* **b** (of the voice) to crack: *His voice broke with emotion.* **5** *Figurative.* to be crushed; give way: *The dog's heart broke when his master died.* **6** *Figurative.* to become weak; fail: *His health was breaking fast.* **7** *Figurative.* to dawn; appear: *The day is breaking.* **8** to decline suddenly and sharply: *The sick child's fever broke.* **9** (of fish) to jump from the water. **10** to break ranks or fall into disorder, as a band of soldiers. **11** to become bankrupt. **12a** *Baseball.* (of a pitch) to curve or swerve abruptly: *The pitcher threw a ball that broke over the plate.* **b** *Cricket.* (of a delivery) to change direction after striking the ground. **13** *Racing.* to begin running from a starting position: *He breaks fast. In every race he's ever run, he gets out in front* (New Yorker). **14** *Figurative.* to become interrupted or disconnected: *The silence broke when the children came into the library.* **15** (of oil, cream, or other viscous substances) to dissolve; disintegrate. **16** of plants: **a** = bud. **b** to flower too soon. **17** (of boxers) to come out of a clinch. **18** *Linguistics.* to become diphthongal, as certain vowels under certain conditions in Old English.
—*n.* **1** a broken place; gap; crack: *a break in the wall.* **2** the act of breaking; fracture, rupture, or shattering. **3** the act or process of forcing one's way out: *The prisoners made a break for freedom.* **4a** a sudden change: *a break in the weather.* **b** a sudden emergence. **c** *Figurative.* dawn (of day). **5** *Figurative.* a short interruption in work or practice: *a break for coffee at ten. The coach told us to take a break for five minutes.* **6** *Slang.* a chance; opportunity: *Finding that money was a lucky break.* **7a** the act or process of making an electric circuit incomplete. **b** the discontinuance of the current when a circuit is rendered incomplete. **8a** a blank space left between paragraphs, chapters, etc. **b** leaders. **c** marks (. . .) employed in print or writing to indicate abrupt pauses. **9** a sudden, sharp decline, especially in prices. **10** *Prosody.* a pause or interruption; caesura. **11** in pool, billiards, and other similar games: **a** the opening shot that separates the balls. **b** the right to make the first shot. **12** a successful run of points or shots, as in billiards. **13** *Music.* **a** (in jazz playing) a short cadenza, usually about two measures, in which the soloist improvises without accompaniment. **b** the point of separation between the different registers of a voice (as from alto to soprano or from chest tone to head tone) or of a wind instrument. **14** *U.S. Slang.* an awkward remark; mistake in manners: *When a clerk makes a fool break, I don't want to beg his pardon* (George H. Lorimer). **15** *Bowling.* a failure to knock down all the pins with two balls in one frame; error. **16** a large four-wheeled carriage or wagon; brake. **17** a piece of land assigned for a specific purpose, as for grazing, or planting. **18** *Cricket or Baseball.* a sudden curve of the ball: *Four wickets had fallen for eight runs; Goonesena was propelling his leg breaks high into the air and turning them appreciably* (London Times). **19** (of a horse) a change from one gait to another. **20** something abruptly breaking the line or level, such as an irregularity, roughness, or knot.

break away, a to start before the signal: *The excited horse broke away at a gallop.* **b** to escape; pull or run away (from): *The rabbit broke away from the boy's arms. One of the arrested thieves managed to break away.* **c** *Figurative.* to change suddenly: *If people break away from the ordinary methods . . . they must take their chance* (William Black). **d** to go suddenly: *A dappled hart . . . flung aside the boughs and broke away* (Martin F. Tupper).

break back, *Cricket.* (of the ball) to turn in from the off side: *Clean bowled by . . . , the ball apparently breaking back* (London Daily Telegraph).

break down, a to go out of order; fail to work: *The car's engine broke down.* **b** *Figurative.* to become weak or ill; fail suddenly; collapse: *His health broke down.* **c** to cause to collapse; destroy; overcome: *to break down a wall, break down all opposition.* **d** *Figurative.* to begin to cry: *She broke down when she heard the bad news.* **e** *Figurative.* to analyze: *These figures on living expenses must be broken down into food, shelter, education, medical bills, and so on.* **f** to separate or divide into parts, steps, or other smaller units: *to break down a chemical, break down a process or operation.*

break in, a to prepare for work or use; train: *He broke in the new office boy.* **b** to make comfortable by wearing: *to break in a pair of shoes.* **c** to enter by force: *The thieves broke in through the cellar.* **d** *Figurative.* to interrupt: *He broke in with a remark while I was looking at the TV show.*

break into, a to enter by force: *A robber broke into the house.* **b** to begin suddenly: *He broke into a run.* **c** to interrupt: *He broke into their conversation.* **d** *British.* to begin to spend: *to break into a pound note.*

break in upon, to intrude upon or disturb suddenly: *The loud noise broke in upon his thoughts.*

break loose, a to separate from anything; break a connection or relation: *The boat broke loose from its mooring.* **b** to run away; free oneself: *The man broke loose from prison.* **c** *Slang.* to go on a spree: *She broke loose in the store and spent every cent.*

break off, a *Figurative.* to stop suddenly: *He broke off in the middle of his speech to clear his throat.* **b** *Figurative.* to stop being friends: *She broke off with her old classmates when she went away to college.* **c** to detach by breaking: *to break off a twig.*

break out, a (1) to start or spring up suddenly: *A fire broke out in the boiler house. A rash breaks out when he eats strawberries.* (2) to have pimples or a rash on the skin: *The child broke out with measles.* **b** to leave by force; escape: *The thief broke out of jail.* **c** to burst out: *A cry of horror broke out among the spectators when someone yelled "Fire!" The boy broke out in a mixture of fear and rage, 'I Yusef's boy'* (Graham Greene). **d** to open up: *Broke out our chests today, found all our things in good order* (N. Kingsley).

break up, *Informal.* **a** to scatter: *The fog is breaking up.* **b** *Figurative.* to put an end to; stop: *The boy scouts broke up the meeting early.* **c** *Figurative.* to disturb greatly; upset: *The news of his brother's death broke him up.* **d** to overwhelm or be overwhelmed with laughter: *Remember the joke that broke everyone up . . . ?* (Maclean's). *"Can you imagine those yaps hammering on the door? I break up just thinking about it"* (New Yorker). **e** to become separated or divorced: *Mr. and Mrs. Cross broke up, after years of bickering* (New Yorker).

break with, a to stop being friends with: *He broke with me after our fight.* **b** to sever a connection with: *to break with the past.*
[Old English *brecan*]

—*Syn. v.t.* **1 Break, shatter, smash** mean to make something come or go to pieces. **Break** means to divide something into two or more pieces by pulling, hitting, dropping, or striking it: *I broke the handle off a cup.* **Shatter** means to break suddenly into a number of pieces that fly in all directions: *I shattered the cup when I dropped it on the floor.* **Smash** means to break completely to pieces with sudden violence and noise: *I smashed the headlights when I hit the wall.*

break² (brāk), *n.* **1** a carriage skeleton used to break in young horses. **2** = wagonette. [perhaps < *break¹*]

break|a|ble (brā′kə bəl), *adj., n.* —*adj.* that can be broken. —*n.* **breakables,** goods easily broken: *. . . crated breakables being dropped* (Punch).

break|age (brā′kij), *n.* **1** a breaking; break: *The breakage of the girder was due to a fault in the steel.* **2** the amount or quantity of anything broken: *The breakage was excessive.* **3** damage or loss caused by breaking: *a high rate of breakage.* **4** an allowance made for such loss or damage. **5** the pennies or fractions of a penny not paid out to winning parimutuel betters, as at horse races, the payments being to the nearest nickel. **6** the leaving of empty space in stowing a ship's hold.

break|a|way (brāk′ə wā′), *n., adj.* —*n.* **1** the act or condition of separating sharply from a group or pattern. **2** the separation of the shock wave from the fireball of an atomic explosion as it moves ahead. **3** *U.S. Slang.* a stage prop simulating a piece of furniture, crockery, or the like, that breaks easily and harmlessly when struck by or against something **4** a start, as of competitors in a contest, especially a race. **5** in Australia: **a** a stampede of sheep, cattle, or other livestock. **b** an animal which breaks away from a herd or flock.
—*adj. British.* separated from a larger unit; seceded; separatist; independent: *a breakaway political party, a breakaway province.*

break|bone fever (brāk′bōn′), = dengue.

break-bulk (brāk′bulk′), *adj.* packed for breaking into smaller shipments: *break-bulk cargo.*

break dancing, *U.S.* a style of dancing, often competitive, in which the dancers wriggle, spin on their backs, and perform other acrobatics: *They are young street dudes, nearly all of them black . . . and what they are doing is a new style of dancing known as "breaking" or "break dancing"* (New York Daily News).

break|down (brāk′doun′), *n., adj.* —*n.* **1a** failure to work: *Lack of oil caused a breakdown in the motor.* **b** failure; collapse: *. . . the breakdown of the old regime* (Edmund Wilson). **2** loss of health; weakness: *If she keeps on worrying, she will have a nervous breakdown.* **3** separation or division of anything into parts, steps, or other units; analysis: *The breakdown of the 500,000-man military establishment . . . is as follows: 400,000 in the ground forces, 80,000 in the Air Force, and 20,000 in the Navy* (New York Times). **4** chemical decomposition or analysis. **5** a noisy, lively, American dance with stamping and shuffling.
—*adj.* used in repairing a breakdown, specifically on the railroads: *a breakdown crew.*

breakdown voltage, the amount of voltage at which an electrical current is able to pass through the insulating material of a wire or cable.

break|er¹ (brā′kər), *n.* **1** a wave that breaks into foam on the beach or on rocks: *breakers crashing on the beach.* SYN: comber. See syn. under **wave. 2** a person or thing that breaks, crushes, or destroys something: *a breaker of promises, a breaker of hearts.* **3** a machine for breaking things, such as coal, into smaller pieces. **4** = circuit breaker. [< *break¹* + *er¹*]

break|er² (brā′kər), *n.* a small water cask for use in a boat. [alteration of Spanish *barrica* cask]

break-e|ven point (brāk′ē′vən), the point at which gains and losses are equal, especially in a business operation.

break|fast (brek′fəst), *n., v.* —*n.* the first meal of the day. —*v.i.* to eat breakfast: *I like to breakfast alone.* —*v.t.* to provide with breakfast; entertain at breakfast: *The hotel regularly breakfasts 400 people.* [< *break¹* + *fast²*]
—**break′fast|er,** *n.* —**break′fast|less,** *adj.*

breakfast food, *U.S.* cereal, especially dry cereal, eaten at breakfast.

***breakfront**

***break|front** (brāk′frunt′), *n.* a cabinet, desk, bookcase, or the like, with upper shelves or drawers set back, the shelves usually enclosed with glass, so as to break the vertical plane at the front.

Pronunciation Key: hat, āge, cãre, fär; let, ēqual, tėrm; it, īce; hot, ōpen, ôrder; oil, out; cup, pu̇t, rüle; child; long; thin; ᴛʜen; zh, measure; ə represents **a** in about, **e** in taken, **i** in pencil, **o** in lemon, **u** in circus.

break-in (brāk′in′), *n.* breaking and entering; burglary: *The Oceana Seafood Market reported a break-in and theft early today* (New York Times).

break|ing (brā′king), *n.* the process of beating dry flax stalks with mallets or running them through grooved rollers so that the woody part of the stalk will separate into small pieces.

breaking and entering, *Law.* entry by force or guile into a house, business establishment, or other premises, with intent to steal, commit an assault, or the like.

breaking cart, a special type of cart used to train horses for driving in harness; break².

breaking point, the point at which something or someone breaks down under stress: *Other mass commuter facilities are at the breaking point* (New York Times). *It was evident . . . that tension was already near breaking point* (London Times).

break|neck (brāk′nek′), *adj.* likely to cause a broken neck; very risky; dangerous: *The car traveled at breakneck speed.*

break of day, = dawn. SYN: daybreak.

break|off (brāk′ôf′, -of′), *n.* **1** stoppage: *the breakoff of negotiations.* **2** detachment or secession; separation: *the breakoff of Singapore from Malaysia.*

break|out (brāk′out′), *n.* **1** the act or condition of becoming free of or escaping (from): *a breakout from prison.* **2** = breakthrough (def. 1).

break point, **1** = breaking point. **2** any point of division between separate elements or operations. **3** a point in computer programming at which a program may be manually stopped for a check of the progress of the operation. **4** a point won in tennis by the receiving side on the opponent's serve.

break|through (brāk′thrü′), *n.* **1** a military attack that gets through the enemy defensive system into the area in the rear. **2** an achievement or solution of some problem, often of a scientific or technical nature: *The development of the Salk vaccine against polio was a major breakthrough in medical research.* **3** a breaking through opposition or resistance: *The first big breakthrough in the talks occurred yesterday* (London Times).

break|up (brāk′up′), *n.* **1** a scattering; separation: *the breakup of a gang.* SYN: dispersal. **2** a stopping; end: (*Figurative.*) *the breakup of all one's hopes.* SYN: disruption. **3** a collapse; decay. SYN: disintegration. **4** *Informal.* a becoming helpless with grief. **5** *U.S. Slang.* (of an actor) the condition of becoming helpless with laughter.

***break|wa|ter** (brāk′wôt′ər, -wot′-), *n.* a wall or barrier to break the force of waves, especially one to form or protect a harbor; pier.

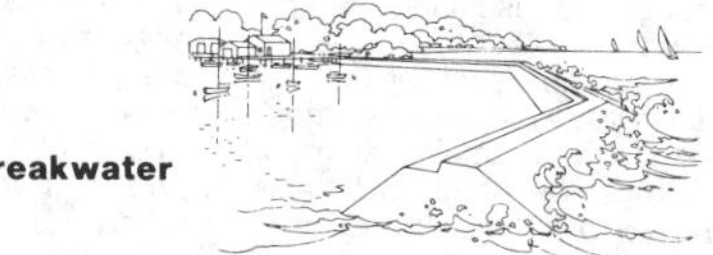
***breakwater**

bream¹ (brēm), *n., pl.* **breams** or (*collectively*) **bream.** **1a** a yellowish fish of the same family as the carp, common in inland European waters. **b** any one of various related fishes that have rather deep bodies. **2** the common freshwater sunfish of the United States. **3** = sea bream. [<Middle French *brême* <Old French *bresme, braisme* <Germanic (compare Old High German *brahsima*)]

bream² (brēm), *v.t. Archaic.* to clean (a ship's bottom) of barnacles, seaweed, or other debris by singeing it to soften the pitch and then scraping. [origin uncertain]

breast (brest), *n., v.* —*n.* **1a** the upper, front part of the human body between the shoulders and the stomach; chest; thorax. **b** the corresponding part in animals. **2a** a gland of females that gives milk; mammary gland. **b** the analogous rudimentary organ in males. **3** *Figurative.* the heart or feelings; emotions: *Pity tore his breast. Music hath charms to soothe a savage breast* (William Congreve). **4** the upper, front part of a coat, dress, or other garment. **5** a thing suggesting the human breast in shape or position; front or forward part: *the breast of the hill.* **6** *Figurative.* a source of nourishment. **7** *Mining.* the face of a working. **8** the forward part of the moldboard of a plow.
—*v.t.* to struggle with; advance against; oppose; face: *He breasted every trouble as it came. The swimmer breasted the waves with powerful strokes.*
—*v.i.* to press on confidently.
beat one's breast, to show grief, regret, or misfortune, in a loud or emotional manner: *Why should we beat our breasts over imaginary injustices when actually there is no real . . . resentment?* (New York Times).
make a clean breast of, to confess completely: *When he was shown proof that he broke the window, he made a clean breast of it.*
[Old English *brēost*]

breast-beat|ing (brest′bē′ting), *n., adj.* —*n.* a loud, and often emotional, public display of grief, regret, or misfortune: *While inquiry into faulty judgment and poor coordination is in order, there is no ground for excessive breast-beating over a "lost opportunity" at Paris* (Wall Street Journal).
—***adj.*** characterized by breast-beating: *breast-beating emotionalism.*

breast|bone (brest′bōn′), *n.* the thin, flat bone in the front of the chest to which the ribs are attached by cartilages; sternum.

breast drill, a portable drill having a plate against which the chest is pressed to provide pressure in drilling.

-breasted, *combining form.* having a ______ breast: *Broad-breasted = having a broad breast.*

breast-fed (brest′fed′), *adj.* (of infants) fed at the mother's breast.

breast-feed (brest′fēd′), *v.t., v.i.,* **-fed, -feed|ing.** to feed at the mother's breast, rather than with a bottle; nurse.

breast-high (brest′hī′), *adj., adv.* as high as the chest.

breast|pin (brest′pin′), *n.* an ornamental pin worn on the breast; brooch.

breast|plate (brest′plāt′), *n.* **1a** a piece of armor worn over the chest: *Smote . . . through breastplate and through breast* (Macaulay). See picture under **armor**. **b** *Figurative: . . . the breastplate of righteousness* (Ephesians 6:14). **2** a strap or straps passing across the breast of a riding horse and attached to the saddle or girths, used only with certain horses or for some special situation. **3** a gold-framed, square vestment of linen and colored thread set with twelve jewels, each betokening one of the tribes of Israel, worn anciently by the high priests of Israel (Exodus 28:15-30). **4** the plate against which the chest is pressed in a breast drill. **5** = plastron.

breast|plow (brest′plou′), *n.* a kind of spade propelled by pressure of the breast on a crossbar, for cutting turf.

breast|rail (brest′rāl′), *n.* **1** the upper rail of a balcony or parapet. **2** a railing in front of a ship's quarterdeck.

breast|stroke (brest′strōk′), *n.* or **breast stroke**, a swimming stroke made by a swimmer face downwards with both arms, extended forward and together swept to the sides and back under water, while the legs make a frog kick.

breast|sum|mer (brest′sum′ər), *n.* a summer or beam placed horizontally over a large opening, such as a shop window, to support the superstructure.

breast wall, = retaining wall.

breast|work (brest′wėrk′), *n.* a low, sometimes hastily built wall for defense; parapet.

breath (breth), *n.* **1** the air drawn into and forced out of the lungs: *The drowning man gasped for a breath.* **2** the act of breathing: *The injured man's breath was labored.* SYN: respiration. **3** the moisture from breathing: *You can see your breath on a very cold day.* **4** the ability to breathe easily: *Running fast made him lose his breath.* **5a** a single drawing in and forcing out of air from the body: *I'll fight to the last breath* (Harriet Beecher Stowe). **b** the air drawn in: *Take a deep breath, and hold it.* **c** the time required for one breath; a moment: *Love that endures for a breath* (Algernon Charles Swinburne). **6** *Figurative.* a slight movement in the air; light breeze: *Not a breath was stirring.* **7** time to breathe freely; respite: *Give me some little breath, some pause, dear Lord* (Shakespeare). SYN: rest, pause. **8** *Figurative.* something said softly; whisper. **9** *Figurative.* a slight trace or suggestion; hint: *the breath of suspicion. This administration has not been marred by one breath of scandal.* SYN: stain, film, taint. **10** = life. SYN: existence. **11** *Phonetics.* forming a sound without motion of the vocal cords, producing such consonants as *h, s, f, p, t, k.* **12** the fragrance given off, especially by flowers; odor; smell: *the breath of spring.* SYN: scent. **13** anything trivial or short-lived: *a dream, a breath, a froth of fleeting joy* (Shakespeare). **14** *Obsolete.* vapor; steam; exhalation.
catch one's breath, a to gasp; pant: *The dogs were catching their breath after the long chase.* **b** to stop for breath; rest: *He took off a few minutes from the game to catch his breath.* **c** to hold one's breath suddenly in emotion: *When the little girl saw the new doll, she caught her breath for joy.*
hold one's breath, to check exhalation: *We all held our breath as we listened for the noise again.*
in the same breath, a at the same time: *She laughed and cried in the same breath.* **b** *Figurative.* in the same category or class: *Many critics consider it sacrilege to mention him [a bullfighter] in the same breath with Manolete, Belmonte, . . . or Paco Camino* (Time).
out of breath, short of breath; breathless: *At the end of the race the winner was out of breath.*
save one's breath, to keep silent: *You might as well save your breath, since no one is listening to you.*
take (or **gather**) **breath**, to rest for a moment; pause to rest or reflect: *The exhausted workers sat down to take breath.*
take the breath (**away**), to make breathless with surprise or shock; dumfound; flabbergast: *But the growth since the war has taken the breath of even experts* (Wall Street Journal).
under (or **below**) **one's breath**, in a whisper: *She was talking under her breath so no one could hear.*
[Old English *brǣth* odor; steam]

breath|a|bil|i|ty (brē′ᴛʜə bil′ə tē), *n.* **1** the condition of being breathable. **2** permeability; porosity: *A new micro-porous vinyl, claimed to have the breathability of ordinary fabrics . . .* (J. Frados).

breath|a|ble (brē′ᴛʜə bəl), *adj.* **1** fit or agreeable to breathe or to be inhaled; respirable. **2** permeable; porous.

breath|a|lyz|er (breth′ə lī′zər), *n.* **1** a device that measures the degree of intoxication of a person by analyzing his breath. Also, *British,* **breathalyser.** **2 Breathalyzer.** a trademark for such a device. Also, *British,* **Breathalyser.**

breathe (brēᴛʜ), *v.,* **breathed, breath|ing.** —***v.i.*** **1a** to draw air into the lungs and force it out; inhale and exhale; respire: *You can breathe through your mouth if your nose is stuffy.* **b** to take up oxygen and give out carbon dioxide, as fish do by means of gills. **2** *Figurative.* to stop for breath; rest: *At last there is time to breathe.* SYN: pause. **3** *Figurative.* to blow lightly or softly: *The air breathes upon us here most sweetly* (Shakespeare). **4** *Figurative.* to be alive; live: *As long as her big brother breathes, no one can hurt her. Breathes there the man with soul so dead* (Scott). SYN: exist. **5** *Figurative.* **a** to give forth breath or sound that can be heard; speak, sing, or the like. **b** to speak softly: *We could not even breathe in the baby's room.* **6** *Phonetics.* to make a sound with the breath and not with the voice. **7** *Figurative.* to send out an odor or vapor; smell: *All Arabia breathes from yonder box* (Alexander Pope).
—***v.t.*** **1a** to draw (air) into the lungs and force (it) out; inhale and exhale: *She wanted to get out of the stuffy room and breathe some fresh air.* **b** to draw into the lungs; inhale: *They had been breathing poisonous fumes.* **2** *Figurative.* to stop to rest after hard work or exercise: *At the top of the hill the rider breathed his horse.* **3** to put out of breath; tire: *That pace will soon breathe you.* **4** *Figurative.* to say softly; whisper; utter: *Don't breathe a word of this to anyone.* **5** to send out from the lungs; exhale: *The dragon breathed fire from its nostrils.* **6** *Figurative.* to send out; give; impart: *Her enthusiasm breathed new life into our club.* SYN: inspire, infuse, inject. **7** *Figurative.* to be alive with; express: *passages which breathe the true spirit of poetry* (Thomas Wright). SYN: manifest, exude. **8** *Phonetics.* to utter with the breath and not with the voice. **9** to give an airing to; exercise briskly: *He had breathed the Proctor's dogs* (Tennyson). **10** to blow into, or cause to sound by the breath. **11** to open and bleed (a vein).
breathe again, to recover from anxiety or pain; be relieved: *Now I breathe again aloft the flood* (Shakespeare).
breathe easy (or **easily**), to feel relieved; be free of anxiety or pain: *Officials will breathe easier if the January orders also are up* (Wall Street Journal).
breathe freely, to be at ease; feel easy: *War was the element in which the Spartan seemed to have breathed most freely* (Connop Thirlwall).
breathe one's last. See under **last¹**.
[Middle English *brethen* <*breth* breath]

breathed (bretht, brēᴛʜd), *adj.* **1** *Phonetics.* uttered with breath as opposed to voice; voiceless; surd. **2** having a certain kind of breath: *short-breathed, deep-breathed.*

breath|er (brē′ᴛʜər), *n.* **1** a short stop for breath; rest: *He had stopped for a few minutes' breather.* SYN: respite, pause. **2** a person or thing that breathes: *I will chide no breather in the world but myself against whom I know most faults* (Shakespeare). **3** *Informal.* a thing that puts a person out of breath. **4** a spell of exercise. **5** a small vent for the release of pressure, fluids, or gas, from an airtight or enclosed space: *the breather of a crankcase.*

breath group, the group or sequence of speech sounds made in one breath.

breath|ing (brē′ᴛʜing), *n., adj.* —*n.* **1** respiration: *the sick man's labored breathing.* **2** a single breath. **3a** the time needed for a single breath; a very short time: *It was there only for the breath-*

ing of a second (Benjamin Disraeli). **b** a pause; rest. **4** a remark; utterance: *Hide not thine ear at my breathing* (Lamentations 3:56). **5** a slight breeze; a soft wind: *The breathings of the lightest air that blows* (William Cowper). **6a** the sound of the letter *h;* aspiration. **b** either of two marks, like single inverted commas, placed above a vowel in Greek to show whether it is aspirated. **7** physical exercise, as stimulating breathing. **8** aspiration; longing.
– ***adj.*** **1** respiring; living. **2** *Figurative.* lifelike: *The portrait was a real breathing likeness.*

breathing hole, **1** a hole in the ice where an aquatic animal, such as a seal, comes up to breathe. **2** a vent for air, such as in a cask.

breathing space, room or time enough to breathe easily; opportunity to rest.

breathing spell, a period of inactivity; time to catch one's breath; opportunity to rest.

breath|less (breth′lis), *adj.* **1** out of breath; breathing with difficulty; panting: *The messenger burst in, so breathless he could hardly speak. Running up stairs very fast made him breathless.* **2** unable to breathe freely because of fear, amazement, interest, or excitement: *The beauty of the scenery left her breathless. The holy time is quiet as a nun Breathless with adoration* (Wordsworth). **3** without breath; lifeless; dead: *The nymphs about the breathless body wait* (John Dryden). **4** without a breeze; motionless: *the breathless air of a hot summer day.* – **breath′less|ly**, *adv.* – **breath′less|ness**, *n.*

breath|tak|ing (breth′tā′king), *adj.* thrilling; exciting: *a breathtaking ride on a runaway horse.* – **breath′tak′ing|ly**, *adv.*

breath-test (breth′test′), *n., v. British.* – ***n.*** a test of intoxication, usually by means of a breathalyzer.
– ***v.t.*** to subject to a breath-test.

breath|y (breth′ē), *adj.* (of the voice or singing) characterized by or interspersed with audible sounds of breathing. – **breath′i|ly**, *adv.* – **breath′i|ness**, *n.*

bre|ba (brā′bə), *n.* the first crop of the common fig, produced on branches made the previous season and maturing in late June or early July. [< Spanish *breva* < Latin *bifera* bearing twice]

brec|ci|a (brech′ē ə, bresh′-), *n.* a rock consisting of angular fragments of older rocks cemented together. [< Italian *breccia* < Germanic (compare Old High German *brehhan* to break)]

brec|ci|at|ed (brech′ē ā′tid, bresh′-), *adj.* having the form of breccia or breccias.

brec|ci|a|tion (brech′ē ā′shən, bresh′-), *n.* brecciated formation.

Brecht|i|an (brek′tē ən), *adj.* of or characteristic of the German playwright Bertolt Brecht, 1898-1956, or his writings: *In play after play ... the Brechtian moment is man selling man* (Time).

breck (brek), *n. British.* a rolling down or heath: *the East Anglian breck.* [perhaps alteration of *break*[1], noun]

bred (bred), *v.* past tense and past participle of **breed**: *He bred cattle for market.*

brede (brēd), *n. Archaic.* anything interwoven, such as embroidery or a braid: *... with brede Of marble men and maidens overwrought* (Keats). [variant of *braid*]

bred-in-the-bone (bred′in ᴛʜə bōn′), *adj.* thoroughly confirmed or established; firmly fixed; deep-rooted.

bree (brē), *n. Scottish.* pot liquor or broth; juice; broo. [Old English *brīw* pottage]

breech (*n.* brēch; *v.* brēch, brich), *n., v.* – ***n.*** **1** the part of a gun behind the barrel. **2** the lower part; back part. **3** the rump; buttocks. **4** the base of a pulley.
– ***v.t.*** **1a** to provide (a gun) with a breech. **b** to secure (a gun) with a breeching. **2** to clothe with breeches. **3** to whip on the breech.
[back formation < *breeches*]

breech baby, a baby presenting at birth the feet or buttocks first, rather than the head.

breech|block (brēch′blok′), *n.* a movable metal block which closes the breech end of the bore or barrel in certain firearms.

breech|cloth (brēch′klôth′, -kloth′), *n.* = loincloth.

breech|clout (brēch′klout′), *n.* = breechcloth; loincloth.

breech delivery, the birth of a child with the feet or buttocks first, rather than the head.

breeched (brēcht), *adj.* wearing breeches.

breech|es (brich′iz), *n. pl.* **1** short, close-fitting trousers fastened just below the knees. **2** = trousers.

wear the breeches, (of a wife) to rule the husband: *... the violent inclination she felt to wear the breeches* (Washington Irving).
[new plural < Middle English *brech* < Old English *brēc* breeches]

***breeches buoy**, a pair of short canvas trousers fastened to a belt or life preserver. A breeches buoy slides along a rope on a pulley and is used to rescue people from sinking ships or to transfer people from one ship to another.

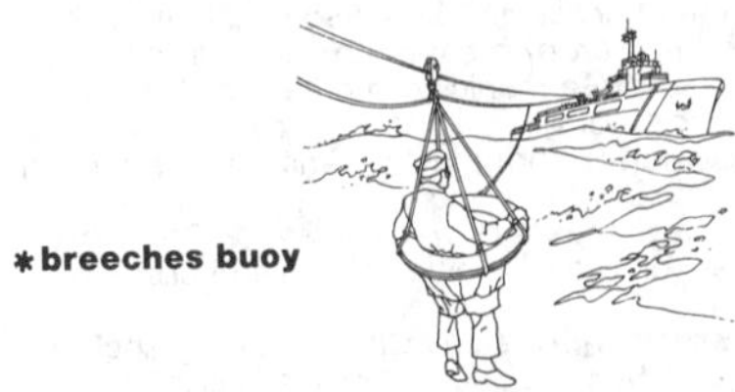

***breeches buoy**

breech|ing (brich′ing, brē′ching), *n.* **1** the part of a harness that passes around a horse's rump, enabling him to push back or hold back a vehicle. **2** a smoke pipe connecting one or more boilers with a chimney. **3** a stout rope which secures a gun to a ship's side and checks recoil. **4** the parts forming the breech of a gun.

breech|less (brēch′lis), *adj.* without breeches.

breech|load|er (brēch′lō′dər), *n.* a breechloading gun.

breech|load|ing (brēch′lō′ding), *adj.* (of guns) loaded from behind the barrel, instead of at the muzzle end.

breed (brēd), *v.,* **bred, breed|ing**, *n.* – ***v.t.*** **1a** to produce (young): *Rabbits breed families rapidly.* **b** to propagate or produce (plants), especially by controlled pollination: *to breed new varieties of corn.* **2a** to raise (especially livestock): *This farmer breeds cattle and hogs for market.* **b** to raise by exercising careful selection of hereditary qualities: *Kentucky has bred fine horses for generations.* **3** *Figurative.* **a** to be the cause of; produce: *Dirt breeds germs. Careless driving breeds accidents.* **SYN**: cause, occasion. **b** to be the native place or source of. **4** to bring up; train: *The captain bred his boy to be a sailor.* **SYN**: educate, school. **5** to convert (nonfissionable material) into fissionable material.
– ***v.i.*** **1** to produce offspring: *to breed from a mare of good stock. Rabbits breed rapidly.* **2** *Figurative.* to come into existence; develop: *Sedition or progress can breed from discontent.* **3** *Dialect.* to be pregnant.
– ***n.*** **1** a group of animals or plants having the same type of ancestors; race; stock: *Jerseys and Guernseys are breeds of cattle. The Norsemen were a hardy breed.* **2** kind; sort; type: *Mountain life produces a strong, tough breed of men.* **3** *U.S. Slang.* (now always offensive in use) a half-breed.

breed in and in, to breed from related parents; inbreed: *They breed in and in ... Marrying their cousins—nay, their aunts and nieces* (Byron).

breed out, to remove (an undesirable trait) through selective breeding: *Cruelty and the fighting instinct have not yet been bred out of the human species* (Wall Street Journal).
[Old English *brēdan*]

breed|er (brē′dər), *n.* **1** a person who breeds animals: *a cattle breeder, a dog breeder.* **2** an animal that produces offspring. **3** *Figurative.* a source; cause: *Great crises are breeders of great events in history.* **4** = breeder reactor.

breeder pile, = breeder reactor.

breeder reactor, a reactor that produces at least as much fissionable material as it uses. In one type of reaction it consumes uranium and produces plutonium.

breed|ing (brē′ding), *n.* **1** the producing of offspring. **SYN**: procreation. **2** the producing of animals or new types of plants, especially to get improved kinds: *Breeding has produced types of wheat which can be grown in the far North.* **SYN**: hybridization. **3** bringing up; training; behavior; manners: *Politeness is a sign of good breeding.* **4** the producing in a reactor of at least as much fissionable material as is used.

breeding ground, **1** a place in which animals, insects, bacteria, or other living things breed, or to which they return to breed. **2** *Figurative.* a place in which anything commonly originates: *Hurricane breeding grounds, the Caribbean and Gulf of Mexico ...* (Science News Letter).

breed of cat, *Informal.* a type of thing; breed; species: *"Football players are a special breed of cat," trainer Mert Prophet had said* (Maclean's).

breeks (brēks), *n. pl. Scottish.* breeches.

breen (brēn), *n.* a brown-tinted green color; brownish green. [blend of *brown* and *green*]

breeze[1] (brēz), *n., v.,* **breezed, breez|ing**. – ***n.*** **1a** a light, gentle wind: *The fair breeze blew, the white foam flew* (Samuel Taylor Coleridge). **b** *Meteorology.* any wind blowing between 4 and 31 miles per hour (on the Beaufort scale, numbers 2 through 6). See also **gale[1]**. **SYN**: See syn. under **wind[1]**. **2** *Informal, Figurative.* anything that is easily done. **3** *British Informal, Figurative.* a disturbance; quarrel: *They had a breeze over the choice of guests.* **4** a rumor; report: *There came a breeze that Spirit Se'guier was near at hand* (Robert Louis Stevenson).
– ***v.i.*** *Informal.* **1** *Figurative.* to move easily or briskly: *She breezed through her homework.* **2** to blow gently, as a breeze. **3** to rise on the breeze, as a noise.
– ***v.t.*** to ride or race (a horse) briskly: *Eddie Arcaro, who breezed Nashua ... will ride him Saturday* (New York Times).

breeze up, to become stronger, as a wind: *The wind breezed up to fifteen knots* (New York Times).

in a breeze, *U.S. Informal.* with little or no strain; easily: *He got the job done in a breeze.*

shoot (or **bat**) **the breeze**, *U.S. Slang.* to talk idly, as to speculate or boast: *They spent all their time sitting around the dock and shooting the breeze* (Saturday Review).
[< Old Spanish and Portuguese *briza* northeast wind] – **breeze′less**, *adj.*

breeze[2] (brēz), *n. Archaic or Dialect.* a gadfly. Also, **brize**. [Old English *briosa*]

breeze[3] (brēz), *n.* small cinders or the ash from a furnace, especially after burning coke. Breeze is used as a filler in mixing concrete. [perhaps < French *braise* < Old French *brese* hot charcoal]

breeze|way (brēz′wā′), *n.* a roofed passage open at the sides between separate buildings, such as a house and a garage.

breez|y (brē′zē), *adj.,* **breez|i|er, breez|i|est.** **1** that has a breeze; with light winds blowing: *a breezy day.* **SYN**: airy. **2** exposed to breezes; swept by the breeze: *a breezy porch.* **SYN**: airy. **3** *Figurative.* brisk; lively; jolly: *a breezy, joking manner.* **SYN**: cheerful, animated. – **breez′i|ly**, *adv.* – **breez′i|ness**, *n.*

breg|ma (breg′mə), *n., pl.* **-ma|ta** (-mə tə). the region of the skull where the sagittal and coronal sutures join. [< Greek *brégma* front of the head]

breg|mat|ic (breg mat′ik), *adj.* having to do with the bregma.

bre|hon (brē′hən, bre′-), *n.* a judge in ancient Ireland. [< Irish *breathamh*]

brehon law, the ancient system of law in Ireland, not entirely superseded by English law among the native Irish until about 1650.

brei (brī), *n. Medicine.* tissue ground to a pulp for study or experimentation: *Extracts of yeast or spleen were as effective as breis made of these tissues* (Bulletin of Atomic Scientists). [< German *Brei* pulp]

breit|schwantz or **breit|schwanz** (brīt′shvänts′), *n.* broadtail (skin). [< German *Breitschwanz* < *breit* broad + *Schwanz* tail]

brek|ker (brek′ər), *n. British Slang.* breakfast.

bre|loque (brə lōk′), *n.* a locket, charm, seal, or other small ornament fastened to a watch chain. [< French *breloque*]

breme (brēm), *adj. Scottish.* **1a** sharp, violent, or stormy, as weather. **b** bleak or windswept, as a place. **c** keen or eager, as a person. **2** *Obsolete.* bright; famous. [Middle English *breme, brim,* Old English *brēme* famous]

brems|strah|lung (brems′shträ′lůng), *n.* electromagnetic radiation produced when a charged particle, such as an electron, moving at great speed, is accelerated or deflected by another charged particle, such as a nucleus, also moving at great speed. [< German *Bremsstrahlung* (literally) brake radiation]

Bren gun, or **Bren** (bren), *n.* a gas-operated machine gun, light and fast, used by the British in World War II. [< *Br*(no), Czechoslovakia, + *En*(field), England, towns where they were manufactured]

brenn|schluss (bren′shlůs′), *n.* burnout in a rocket engine when thrust is terminated. [< German *Brennschluss*]

brent[1] (brent), *n., pl.* **brents** or (*collectively*) **brent.** = brant[1].

brent[2] (brent), *adj. Scottish.* of the forehead: **1** steep; high. **2** unwrinkled; smooth: *your bonny brow was brent* (Robert Burns). Also, **brant**. [Old English *brant*]

br'er or **brer** (brėr, brär), *n. U.S. Dialect.* brother: *Br'er Rabbit and Br'er Fox.*

brere (brir), *n. Dialect.* brier.

bre|telle (brə tel′), *n. Dressmaking.* one of a pair of suspenderlike ornamental bands extending over the shoulders from front to back. [< French *bretelle*]

breth|ren (breᴛʜ′rən), *n. pl.* **1** the fellow members of a church, society, or religious order: *the Brethren ... of the Moravian church in Philadelphia* (Rudyard Kipling). **2** *Archaic.* broth-

Pronunciation Key: hat, āge, cãre, fär; let, ēqual, tėrm; it, īce; hot, ōpen, ôrder; oil, out; cup, půt, rüle; child; long; thin; ᴛʜen; zh, measure; ə represents **a** in about, **e** in taken, **i** in pencil, **o** in lemon, **u** in circus.

ers: *And they said, Thy servants are twelve brethren, the sons of one man* (Genesis 42:13).
► See **brother** for usage note.

Bret|on (bret′ən), *n., adj.* —*n.* **1** a person born or living in Brittany. **2** the language of Brittany. Breton is a Celtic language closely related to Cornish and Welsh.
—*adj.* of or having to do with Brittany, its people, or their language: *Breton fishermen.*
[< Old French *breton* Breton < Latin *Brittō, -ōnis* a Briton]

bret|on (bret′ən), *n.* a shallow-crowned hat with a slightly rolled brim. [< *Breton*]

Breton lace, a netting upon which figures are overlaid with a heavy thread or yarn.

***breve** (brēv), *n.* **1** a curved mark put over a vowel or syllable to show that it is short. **2** a musical note equal to two whole notes. **3** *Law.* a writ or brief. **4** a letter of authority, especially one from a pope. [< Italian *breve* < Latin *brevis* short. See etym. of doublet **brief**.]

***breve**
definition 1

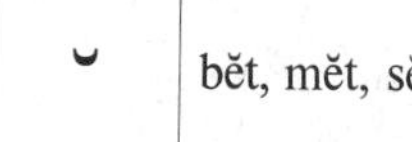

bre|vet (brə vet′; *especially British* brev′it), *n., adj., v.,* **-vet|ted, -vet|ting** or **-vet|ed, -vet|ing.**
—*n.* a commission promoting an army officer to a higher honorary rank without an increase in pay. *Abbr:* bvt.
—*adj.* having or giving rank by a brevet: *In 1783, ["Mad Anthony"] Wayne became a brevet major general, but he retired the same year* (John R. Alden).
—*v.t.* to give rank by a brevet.
[< Middle French *brevet* < Old French *brievet* (diminutive) < *brief* letter, brief]

bre|vi|ar|y (brē′vē er′ē, brev′ē-), *n., pl.* **-ar|ies.** **1** a book of prescribed prayers to be said daily by clergymen of the Roman Catholic Church. **2** any similar book used in some other church. [< Latin *breviārium* summary, (originally) neuter of *breviārius* abridged < *brevis* short]

bre|vier (brə vir′), *n.* a size of type between minion and bourgeois; 8 point. [< Old French *bréviaire,* learned borrowing from Latin *breviārium* breviary (from its use in the printing of breviaries)]

brev|i|ped (brev′ə ped), *adj.* having short feet or legs. [< Latin *brevis* short + *pēs, pedis* foot]

brev|i|pen|nate (brev′ə pen′āt), *adj.* having short wings; brachypterous. [< Latin *brevis* short + *penna* feather + English *-ate*¹]

brev|i|ros|trate (brev′ə ros′trāt), *adj.* having a short bill or beak. [< Latin *brevis* short + *rōstrum* beak + English *-ate*¹]

brev|i|ty (brev′ə tē), *n., pl.* **-ties.** **1** shortness; briefness: *The brevity of the concert disappointed the audience.* **2** shortness in speech or writing; contraction into a few words; conciseness: *Brevity in storytelling makes the story more exciting. Brevity is the soul of wit* (Shakespeare). **SYN**: succinctness, terseness. [< Latin *brevitās* < *brevis* short]

brew (brü), *v., n.* —*v.t.* **1a** to make (beer, ale, or mash) by soaking, boiling, and fermenting malt, hops, or grain: *Many monasteries brewed their own ale in the Middle Ages.* **b** to convert (barley, malt, or grain) into a fermented liquor. **2** to make (a drink) by soaking, boiling, or mixing: *Tea is brewed in boiling water.* **3** *Figurative: The boys whispering in the corner are brewing some mischief.* **SYN**: plan, plot, concoct, contrive.
—*v.i.* **1** to make beer or the like. **2** *Figurative: Dark clouds show that a storm is brewing.* **SYN**: gather, impend.
—*n.* **1** a drink that is brewed: *a good brew of ale.* **SYN**: brewage, concoction. **2** the quantity brewed at one time: *a brew of tea. The last brew of beer was bitter.* **3** the process of brewing.
[Old English *brēowan.* See related etym. at **bread, broth.**]

brew|age (brü′ij), *n.* **1** a beverage that has been brewed; a brew. **2** the process of brewing.

brew|er (brü′ər), *n.* a person who brews beer, ale, or mash: *Brewers use about one-half pound of hops per barrel of beer* (Wall Street Journal).

brewers' grains, the residue left from the grain in the manufacture of beer, used for feeding livestock.

brewers' yeast, a selected strain of yeast used in the brewing of beer.

brew|er|y (brü′ər ē), *n., pl.* **-er|ies.** a place where beer, ale, or mash is brewed.

brew|house (brü′hous′), *n.* = brewery.

brew|ing (brü′ing), *n.* **1** the preparing of a brew. **2** the amount brewed at one time. **3** the occupation of making liquors such as beer and ale.

brew|is (brü′is), *n. Dialect.* **1** a broth, especially of beef and vegetables, sometimes thickened with bread or meal. **2** bread soaked in this. [< Old French *broez* meat-broth soup (diminutive) < *breu, bro* < Germanic (compare Old High German *brod* broth)]

brew|mas|ter (brü′mas′tər, -mäs′-), *n.* a specialist in the art of brewing.

brew|ster (brüs′tər), *n. Obsolete or Scottish.* a brewer (originally female). [Middle English *brewester*]

Brewster angle, *Optics.* the polarizing angle. [< Sir David *Brewster,* 1781-1868, a British physicist, who defined it]

Brew|ster's booby (brü′stərz), a bird with pale gray-brown feathers, a white belly, blue bill, and green feet, found along the Pacific Coast below the Gulf of California. [< William *Brewster,* an American ornithologist of the 1900's]

Brewster's law, *Optics.* the law relating as an equality the index of refraction of a substance and the tangent of the polarizing angle.

Brezh|nev Doctrine (brezh′nef, -nev), the doctrine that the Soviet Union has the right to interfere in the affairs of other Communist countries in defense of Communism. [< Leonid I. *Brezhnev,* born 1906, first secretary of the Soviet Communist Party]

bri|ar¹ (brī′ər), *n.* = brier¹.

bri|ar² (brī′ər), *n.* = brier².

bri|ard (brē ärd′; *French* brē är′), *n.* a large, black or gray sheep dog having a coat of long, wavy hair and a long tail. [< French *Briard*]

Bri|ar|e|an (brī är′ē ən), *adj.* **1** of or having to do with Briareus. **2a** having or seeming to have many hands: *a Briarean grasp of detail.* **b** reaching or grasping in many directions.

Bri|ar|e|us (brī är′ē əs), *n. Greek Legend.* a giant with fifty heads and a hundred hands.

bri|ar|root (brī′ər rüt′, -rüt′), *n.* = brierroot.

bri|ar|wood (brī′ər wu̇d′), *n.* = brierwood.

bri|ar|y (brī′ər ē), *adj.* = briery.

brib|a|bil|i|ty (brī′bə bil′ə tē), *n.* corruptibility; venality.

brib|a|ble (brī′bə bəl), *adj.* open to bribery; corrupt; venal.

bribe (brīb), *n., v.,* **bribed, brib|ing.** —*n.* **1a** money or other reward given or offered to get someone to do something he thinks it is wrong to do: *The thief offered the policemen a bribe to let him go. The chairman accepted a bribe of a thousand dollars for awarding the contract without receiving bids. Shall we now contaminate our fingers with base bribes?* (Shakespeare). **b** a reward for doing something that a person does not want to do: *A child should not need a bribe to obey his parents.* **2** *Obsolete.* a thing stolen or robbed; plunder.
—*v.t.* **1a** to give or offer a bribe to: *A gambler bribed one of the boxers to lose the fight.* **b** to reward (a person) for doing something that he does not want to do: *She bribed the little girl to take a nap by offering cookies.* **2** to clear or open (a way) by means of bribery: *He bribed his way to power.* **3** *Archaic.* to purchase or obtain by bribery.
—*v.i.* to use or practice bribery: *He bribed because he had no power to persuade or convince.*
[< Middle French *bribe* bit of bread given to a beggar] —**brib′er**, *n.*

brib|er|y (brī′bər ē), *n., pl.* **-er|ies.** **1** the giving or offering of a bribe: *The policeman accused the thief of bribery.* **2** the taking of a bribe: *The honest policeman was cleared of bribery.*

bric-a-brac or **bric-à-brac** (brik′ə brak′), *n.* **1** interesting or curious trinkets used as decorations; small ornaments, such as vases, old china, or small statues: *The exaggerated cult of the Victorian, like the Victorian age itself, goes with an obsequious respect for bric-a-brac* (London Times). **2** odds and ends of any sort: *Instead of the automobile's expressing advancement, the story is now one of external bric-a-brac* (Atlantic).
[< French *bric-à-brac*]
► **Bric-a-brac** is a collective noun, not used in the plural (*bric-a-bracs*) or modified by *a: The bric-a-brac showed evidence of her good taste.*

brick (brik), *n., pl.* **bricks** or (*especially collectively for def. 1*) **brick**, *adj., v.* —*n.* **1** a block of clay baked by sun or fire. Bricks are used to build walls or houses and to pave walks. *Everybody knows I can't lay bricks* (Alfred E. Smith). **2** the substance of which these blocks consist: *as hard as brick. Chimneys are usually built of brick or stone.* **3** anything shaped like a brick: *Ice cream is often sold in bricks.* **4** *Informal, Figurative.* a good fellow; one who is generous and dependable. **5** a child's toy block. **6** *Informal, Figurative.* a brickbat; insult or criticism: *It is becoming fashionable to throw bricks at the Post Office* (London Times).
—*adj.* **1** made of bricks: *a brick house.* **2** resembling brick: *a brick color.*
—*v.t.* to build or pave with bricks; cover or fill in with bricks: *He bricked the walk in front of his house.*
brick up, to block up; wall in: *The back entrance to the building was bricked up and a new one installed in front.*
drop a brick, *Slang.* to commit a blunder or indiscretion: *I've got to keep my head shut, or I shall be dropping a brick* (John Galsworthy).
hit the bricks, *U.S. Slang.* to go out on strike: *"Hit the bricks at 12:01 if that's what you want," said Mr. Frank after the vote was completed* (New York Times).
like a brick, *Informal.* with a vengeance; vigorously: *When he heard of the damage his son had done, he landed on him like a brick.*
like a ton of bricks, with great speed and weight: *Before he could defend himself, they were down upon him like a ton of bricks.*
make bricks without straw, to accomplish something without the necessary material (in allusion to Exodus 5:7): *It was not his fault that the R.A.F. was called upon to make so many bricks without straw in the opening stages of the war* (London Times).
[< Middle French *brique* a kind of loaf] —**brick′like′**, *adj.*

brick|bat (brik′bat′), *n., v.,* **-bat|ted, -bat|ting.**
—*n.* **1** a piece of broken brick, especially one used as a missile: *A number of members of the police force received injuries from brickbats hurled by the crowd* (Times of India). **2** *Figurative.* an insult or sharp criticism: *It's not at all unusual for a tax program to draw brickbats* (Wall Street Journal).
—*v.t.* **1** to pelt with brickbats: *The Republican procession was brick-batted* (Boston Journal). **2** *Figurative.* to insult or criticize sharply: *Amis ... wrote his sardonic original with the idea of brickbatting university life* (Newsweek).

brick cheese, a strong, somewhat sweet, brick-shaped American cheese made from whole milk.

brick|earth (brik′ėrth′), *n.* earth or clay suitable for making bricks.

brick|en (brik′ən), *adj.* made of brick.

brick field, *British.* a brickyard.

brick|field|er (brik′fēl′dər), *n.* a hot, dry, northerly gale in Australia.

brick|ie (brik′ē), *n. British Informal.* a person who works with bricks, especially a bricklayer.

brick|kiln (brik′kil′, -kiln′), *n.* a kiln or furnace for baking (firing) bricks.

brick|lay|er (brik′lā′ər), *n.* a person whose work is building with bricks.

bricklayer's hammer, a small hammer that has a striking face and a sharp cross peen, used in dressing brick.

brick|lay|ing (brik′lā′ing), *n.* the act or work of building with bricks.

brick|le (brik′əl), *adj. Dialect.* liable to break; easily broken; fragile; brittle. [Middle English *bruchel*]

brick|mak|er (brik′mā′kər), *n.* a person who makes bricks.

brick|mak|ing (brik′mā′king), *n.* the trade or occupation of making bricks.

brick|ma|son (brik′mā′sən), *n.* a bricklayer; mason.

brick red, a yellowish or brownish red.

brick-red (brik′red′), *adj.* yellowish-red or brownish-red.

brick tea, tea that has been molded into a brick-like mass.

brick|work (brik′wėrk′), *n.* **1** a wall, foundation, or other structure made of bricks. **2** the part of a building made with bricks. **3** = bricklaying.

brick|y (brik′ē), *adj.* **1** like brick in shape or color. **2** consisting or made of bricks.

brick|yard (brik′yärd′), *n.* a place where bricks are made or sold.

bri|cole (bri kōl′, brik′əl), *n.* **1** a shot in billiards in which the cue ball is made to strike a cushion before touching either of the other two balls. **2** *Figurative.* an indirect, unexpected stroke or action. **3** an ancient catapult for throwing stones or bolts. **4** a harness worn by men who have loads to carry or drag. [< French *bricole* catapult < Old Provençal *bricola*]

brid|al (brī′dəl), *adj., n.* —*adj.* of or having to do with a bride or a wedding: *a bridal veil, a bridal bouquet.* **SYN**: nuptial.
—*n.* **1** a wedding. **2** a wedding feast or festival.
[Old English *brȳdealo* wedding feast, (literally) bride ale] —**brid′al|ly**, *adv.*

bridal wreath, a shrub of the rose family having long sprays of small, white flowers that bloom in the spring. It is a kind of spiraea.

bride¹ (brīd), *n.* a woman just married or about to be married: *... as a bride adorned for her husband* (Revelation 21:2). [Old English *brȳd*]

bride² (brīd), *n.* **1** a thread connecting the pattern in lace; a bar. **2** a bonnet string. [< Old French *bride* < Germanic (compare Middle High German *bridel* rein)]

bride·groom (brīd′grüm′, -grům′), *n.* a man just married or about to be married; groom. [alteration of Old English *brȳdguma* < *brȳd* bride + *guma* man; influenced by *groom*]

bride price, a payment made by a prospective husband or his family to the family of the bride: *In tribal societies daughters are as welcome as sons; not only do they till the soil, they bring in dowry, bride price, lobola—there are many names for this payment* (Elspeth Huxley).

brides·maid (brīdz′mād′), *n.* a young woman who attends the bride at a wedding.

brides·man (brīdz′mən), *n., pl.* **-men**. a man who attends the bridegroom at a wedding; groomsman.

bride·well (brīd′wel, -wəl), *n.* a house of correction for vagrants or disorderly persons; jail. [< *Bridewell,* a building formerly used as a prison, at St. *Bride's Well,* London]

***bridge¹** (brij), *n., v.,* **bridged, bridg·ing.** *—n.* **1a** something built that carries a road, railroad, or path across a river, another road, a valley, or other obstruction: *Engineers design bridges of great length and strength to cross the widest rivers.* SYN: viaduct. **b** any structure or part similar in form or use. SYN: viaduct. **c** *Figurative: . . . home leave . . . one of the most helpful bridges between prison and freedom* (London Times). *Mathematics is a bridge between philosophy and science.* **2** a platform above the deck of a ship for the officer in command: *The captain directed the course of his ship from the bridge.* **3a** the upper, bony part of the nose. **b** = pons Varolii. **4** a false tooth or teeth in a mounting fastened to or resting against real teeth. **5** *Music.* **a** a thin, arched piece over which the strings of a violin or other stringed instrument are stretched. **b** a passage in a composition connecting one theme, movement, or other segment, to another. **6** the curved central part of a pair of eyeglasses which rests on the nose. **7** an apparatus for measuring the electrical resistance of a conductor, or its inductance or capacitance. **8** *Especially U.S.* a structure on which signals are placed over a number of parallel railroad tracks; a gantry. **9** a low partition, generally of firebrick, in a furnace. **10** (in billiards, pool, and similar games) a support for the cue, whether a player's hand or a notched wooden or metal piece at the end of a long rod, used to steady the cue when taking a shot. **11** *Astronomy.* a bright filament consisting of luminous cosmic dust across a sunspot. **12** *Chemistry.* an atom or group of atoms connecting another or others, especially within a ring.

—v.t. **1a** to build a road, railroad, or path over a river, another road, a valley, or other obstruction: *The engineers bridged the river.* **b** *Figurative: Politeness will bridge many difficulties.* SYN: surmount. **2** to extend over; span: *A log bridged the brook.*

burn one's bridges, to cut off all chances of retreat: *Having signed the contract, he burned his bridges and could not recover the money he invested.*

cross that (or **a**) **bridge when one comes to it,** to deal with a problem when it arises: *Asked if he would accept a place on the ticket . . . he said "We'll have to cross that bridge when we come to it"* (New York Times).

[Old English *brycg*] **—bridge′a·ble,** *adj.* **—bridge′like′,** *adj.*

bridge² (brij), *n.* a card game for two pairs of players, played with 52 cards, derived from whist. The highest bidder names the trump suit or declares no trumps. Auction bridge and contract bridge are two kinds. [earlier *biritch;* origin uncertain]

bridge·board (brij′bôrd′, -bōrd′), *n.* a notched board at the side of a wooden staircase, supporting the steps.

bridge·build·er (brij′bil′dər), *n.* **1** a person who builds bridges. **2** *Figurative.* a person who tries to resolve differences or reach agreement between opposite groups or different systems: *The experienced diplomat was a bridgebuilder between East and West.*

bridge crane, a crane that moves back and forth on a bridge suspended on overhead rails. It is used in factories and foundries to carry heavy materials from one end of the shop to the other or to load.

bridge deck, **1** a partial deck above the deck of a ship; bridge. **2** the platform of a bridge. **3** any platform serving as a bridge or deck.

bridge·head (brij′hed′), *n.* **1** a position obtained and held by troops within enemy territory, used as a starting point for further attack. **2** *Figurative.* any position taken as a foothold for further advances: *It [the Soviet Union] has extended its ideological expansion steadily and now has bridgeheads to the Americas and Africa* (Time). **3** a fortification protecting the end of a bridge toward the enemy. **4** either end of a bridge.

bridge house, a structure on which the bridge of a ship is located, usually the top of the bridge deck.

bridge lamp, a movable floor lamp, usually with an adjustable arm, originally designed for use at or near a bridge table.

***bridge¹**
definitions 1a, 2, 3a, 5a, 6, 8, 10

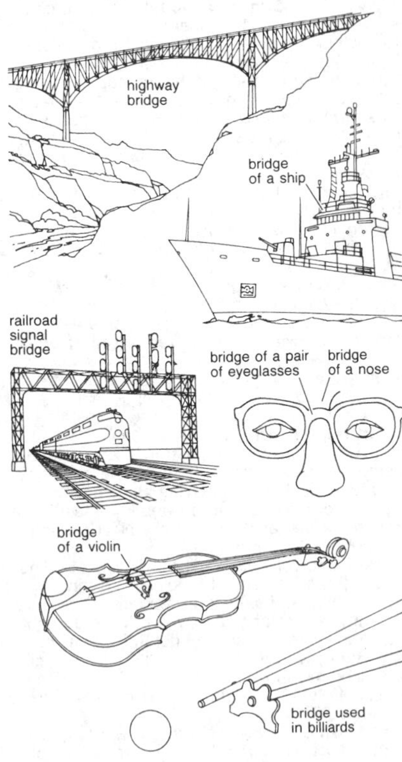

bridge·less (brij′lis), *adj.* without a bridge.

bridge·man (brij′mən), *n., pl.* **-men**. **1** a person whose work is in building bridges. **2** = bridge tender.

bridge of boats, a course or passageway built over a series of moored boats.

bridge table, a light, folding table for playing bridge or other uses.

bridge tender, a person who operates a bridge, especially a drawbridge.

bridge tower, **1** a tower or raised structure of a bridge, for the support of cables, etc. **2** a tower for the defense of a bridge, sometimes erected on the bridge, with the road passing through an archway in its lowest story, sometimes separate from the bridge and defending the approach to it.

bridge-tun·nel (brij′tun′əl), *n.* a causeway consisting of several bridges and underwater tunnels, designed to carry automobile, truck, and train traffic across a large body of water: *A bridge-tunnel [to]span the Chesapeake Bay . . . allowing tourists to drive more than 17 miles across one of the world's greatest estuaries* (Science News Letter).

bridge·work (brij′wėrk′), *n.* false teeth mounted and fastened to or resting against real teeth.

bridg·ing (brij′ing), *n.* braces placed between two beams to strengthen them and to keep them apart.

bridging species, any species of plant on which a parasitic fungus may be trained or adapted to infect species otherwise immune.

bri·dle (brī′dəl), *n., v.,* **-dled, -dling.** *—n.* **1** the part of a harness that fits over a horse's head, used to hold him back or control him. A bridle usually consists of a headstall, bit, and reins. **2** *Figurative.* anything that holds back or controls; curb. SYN: check. **3** a strip, link, or flange on a machine that limits the motion of a part; a guide. **4** the assumption of an attitude of offended dignity: *"Miss Howe" . . . repeated she, with a scornful bridle* (Samuel Richardson). **5** a strong double cable by which a ship may be moored in bad weather. **6** a line or lines attaching a kite to a flying line. **7** an old instrument used to punish or correct scolding women; branks. **8** *Anatomy.* = frenum.

—v.t. **1** to put a bridle on: *He saddled and bridled his horse.* **2** *Figurative.* to hold back; bring under control; check: *Bridle your temper.* SYN: control, curb. *—v.i. Figurative.* to hold the head up high with the chin drawn back to express pride, scorn, or anger: *She bridled when we made fun of her new hat.*

[Old English *brīdel, brigdels* < *bregdan* to braid] **—bri′dler,** *n.* **—bri′dle·less,** *adj.*

bridle hand, the hand which holds the bridle in riding; left hand.

bridle path or **road**, a path suitable for people riding horses.

bridle trail or **way**, = bridle path.

bri·dle-wise (brī′dəl wīz′), *adj.* trained to respond to the pressure of the reins on the neck, instead of a pull on the bit, as a horse.

bri·doon (bri dün′), *n.* a light snaffle bit, with a separate rein, used independently of the curb bit in some military bridles. [< French *bridon* < Old French *bride* bride²]

Brie cheese (brē), a kind of soft, whole-milk, white cheese, ripened by mold, made chiefly in Brie, in northern France.

brief (brēf), *adj., n., v., adv.* **—*adj.*** **1** lasting only a short time; short: *A brief shower fell just before noon.* SYN: fleeting, transitory. See syn. under **short**. **2** using few words: *He sent around a brief announcement of only a few lines. Be as brief as you can, giving just the outline.* SYN: concise, succinct, terse. **3** curt; abrupt.

—n. **1** a short statement; summary. **2a** a statement of the facts and the points of law of a case to be pleaded in court. **b** (in England) an abstract of the facts of a case drawn up by a solicitor for the use of the barrister who acts in court. **3** a writ; summons. **4** a briefing. **5** a letter bearing the papal signet, less formal than a bull. **6** *Informal.* a client; a case at law to plead. **7** *Obsolete.* a letter, especially a circular letter from the authorities of the Church of England licensing a collection for a charity.

—v.t. **1** to give detailed information to; furnish with a brief: *The park ranger briefed the boys on fire prevention. He was briefed by city and county officials on the progress of the joint investigation by their agencies into the cave-in* (New York Times). **2** to make a brief of; summarize: *She made me brief a Shelley ode as though it were a legal argument* (Atlantic). **3** *British.* to retain as a lawyer or counsel. **4** to give a briefing to or instruct as to plans: *The commanding officer briefed the pilots about the rescue mission just before they took off.*

—*adv.* **1** *Archaic.* in short; in a few words: *Brief, they made a monk of me* (Robert Browning). **2** *Poetic.* in or after a brief time.

briefs, short, snug-fitting underpants: *[They] are cut freer than briefs to provide snug support without binding and chafing* (New Yorker).

hold a brief for, to argue for; support; defend: *I hold no brief for cheating. Professor Dowden holds a brief for Shelley; he pleads for Shelley* (Matthew Arnold). *[He] holds little brief for slick and fashionable jargon* (A. J. Vogl).

in brief, in few words; in short: *In brief, it has been an exciting day.*

[< Old French *bref* < Latin *brevis* short. See etym. of doublet **breve**.] **—brief′er,** *n.* **—brief′ly,** *adv.* **—brief′ness,** *n.*

brief bag, = briefcase.

brief·case (brēf′kās′), *n.* a flat bag for carrying loose papers, books, drawings, letters, or other small items. A briefcase has a handle like a suitcase does.

brief·ing (brē′fing), *n.* **1** a summary of detailed information given by an expert to inform or to provide a background: *The President gave the reporters a briefing on the crisis in Africa.* **2** a short summary of the details of a plan about to be undertaken.

brief·less (brēf′lis), *adj.* **1** without a brief. **2** having no clients.

brief of title, an abstract of the documents concerning ownership of a property.

briefs (brēfs), *n.pl.* See under **brief**.

bri·er¹ (brī′ər), *n.* **1** a thorny or prickly plant or bush that has a woody stem. The blackberry, the wild rose, and the dog rose are often called briers. **2** a mass of prickly, thorny bushes; briers collectively. **3** a branch or twig of a brier. Also, **briar**. [Old English *brēr*]

bri·er² (brī′ər), *n.* **1** a white heath tree found in southern Europe. Its root is used in making tobacco pipes. **2** a tobacco pipe made of brierroot. Also, **briar**. [< French *bruyère* heath < Old French, ultimately < a Gaulish word]

bri·er·root (brī′ər rüt′, -růt′), *n.* **1** the woody root of the brier, used in making tobacco pipes. **2** any one of various other woods similarly used. **3** a pipe made of any of these woods. Also, **briar-root**.

Pronunciation Key: hat, āge, cãre, fär; let, ēqual, tėrm; it, īce; hot, ōpen, ôrder; oil, out; cup, půt, rüle; child; long; thin; ᴛʜen; zh, measure; ə represents a in about, e in taken, i in pencil, o in lemon, u in circus.

bri|er|wood (brī′ər wu̇d′), *n.* **1** the wood of brier tree roots, used in making tobacco pipes. **2** any one of various woods of which tobacco pipes are made. **3** a pipe made from such wood. Also, **briarwood.**

bri|er|y (brī′ər ē), *adj.* full of briers; thorny. Also, **briary.**

*** brig¹** (brig), *n.* **1** a ship with two masts and square sails set at right angles across the ship. **2** a prison on a warship. **3** *Slang.* a guardhouse. [short for *brigantine*]

*** brig¹** definition 1

brig² (brig), *n., v.t. Scottish.* bridge.

Brig., **1** brigade. **2** brigadier.

bri|gade (bri gād′), *n., v.,* **-gad|ed, -gad|ing.** —*n.* **1** a part of an army, usually made up of headquarters troops and two or more regiments or battalions, commanded by a brigadier general or a colonel. It is usually part of a division. **2** a large body of troops. **3a** a group of people organized for some purpose: *The fire brigade successfully extinguished the blaze. Production brigades ... were urged instead of the smaller production units of the recovery years* (New York Times). **b** *Figurative: Down the river came brigades of fur-heavy canoes* (Maclean's).
—*v.t.* **1** to form into a brigade. **2** to form (people) as if into a brigade; combine; associate.
[< French *brigade* < Italian *brigata* < *brigare* strive, fight < *briga* strife]

brig|a|dier (brig′ə dir′), *n.* **1** a brigadier general. In the British Army, *brigadier* became the official term in 1928; in the U.S. Army, Air Force, and Marine Corps, *brigadier* is an informal equivalent of *brigadier general.* **2** a noncommissioned officer in certain European armies. **3** an officer in command of a brigade. [< French *brigadier* < *brigade* brigade]

brigadier general, *pl.* **brigadier generals.** a military officer next in rank above a colonel and below a major general. *Abbr:* Brig. Gen.

brig|a|low (brig′ə lō), *n.* (in Australia) any one of several species of acacia, especially one yielding a hard, heavy wood used in building, turnery, and other woodworking. [< a native name]

brig|and (brig′ənd), *n.* **1** a man who robs travelers on the road, especially one of a gang of robbers in mountain or forest regions; robber; bandit: *Brigands demand your money or your life* (Samuel Butler). **2** a person who uses, or is alleged to use, lawless methods to attain his ends. [< Middle French *brigand* (originally) foot soldier < Italian *brigante* a trooper < *brigare* go in troops; strive < *briga* strife]

brig|and|age (brig′ən dij), *n.* **1** robbery; plundering. **2** brigands collectively.

brig|an|dine (brig′ən dēn, -dīn), *n.* a coat of armor made usually of linen or leather, strengthened with metal rings or thin metal pieces. [< Middle French *brigandine* armor for a foot soldier < *brigand* brigand]

*** brig|an|tine** (brig′ən tēn, -tīn), *n.* **1** a ship with two masts. The foremast is square-rigged; the mainmast is fore-and-aft-rigged. **2** = hermaphrodite brig. [< Middle French *brigantin* < Italian *brigantino* < *brigare;* see etym. under **brigand**]

*** brigantine** definition 1

Brig. Gen., brigadier general.

bright (brīt), *adj., adv., n.* —*adj.* **1** giving much light; shining: *The stars are bright, but sunshine is brighter.* **2** very light or clear: *It is a bright day with no clouds.* **3** *Figurative.* clever; quick-witted; intelligent: *a bright answer. A bright girl learns quickly.* SYN: smart. **4** vivid; glowing: *a bright fire. Dandelions are bright yellow.* **5** *Figurative.* lively or cheerful: *a bright smile. Everybody was bright and gay at the party.* SYN: vivacious, animated. **6** likely to turn out well; favorable: *There is a bright outlook for the future.* SYN: promising. **7** famous; glorious: *The knight was a bright example of courage in battle.* **8** physically charming; beautiful: *a bright lady surpassingly fair* (Samuel Taylor Coleridge). **9** clear or luminous to the mental perception: *bright hopes.* **10** sharp; keen; watchful: *to keep a bright lookout.* **11** (of tobacco) flue-cured: *Specially constructed log barns built near the tobacco field are used for the curing of bright tobacco* (Roy Flannagan).
—*adv.* in a bright manner: *The fire shines bright.*
—*n. Poetic.* brightness; brilliance: *in the bright of the moon.*
[Old English *briht, beorht*] —**bright′ly,** *adv.*
—*Syn. adj.* **1 Bright, radiant, brilliant** mean shining. **Bright** is the general word, and applies to anything thought of as giving out or reflecting light: *Her silver earrings are bright.* **Radiant** suggests shining with a light that comes from deep within the thing or person described: *Her face was radiant with happiness.* **Brilliant** means very bright or excessively bright and often suggests sparkling or flashing: *The fountain is brilliant in the sunlight.*

bright|en (brī′tən), *v.i.* **1** to become bright or brighter: *The sky brightened after the storm.* SYN: lighten, clear. **2** *Figurative.* to become happy or cheerful: *Her face brightened as she read the letter.*
—*v.t.* **1** to make bright or brighter: *Flowers brighten the fields in the spring.* **2** *Figurative.* to make happy or cheerful: *Hope brightens our outlook on life.* SYN: cheer, enliven. —**bright′en|er,** *n.*

bright-eyed (brīt′īd′), *adj.* **1** having bright eyes: *a bright-eyed kitten.* **2** dreamy; innocent; starry-eyed: *bright-eyed schemes.*

bright|ish (brī′tish), *adj.* rather bright.

bright-line spectrum (brīt′līn′), a spectrum composed of a pattern of brightly-colored lines on a dark background, having as its source of light a glowing gas that radiates in certain wave-lengths characteristic of the chemical elements in the composition of the gas.

bright|ness (brīt′nis), *n.* **1** the quality of being bright. **2** the intensity of a color, as distinguished from its hue and saturation, especially as classified on a scale ranging from black (zero brightness) to white (maximum brightness); value.

Bright's disease (brīts), a kidney disease characterized by albumin in the urine. [< Richard *Bright,* 1789-1858, a British physician, who first described it]

bright|some (brīt′səm), *adj. Archaic.* bright.

bright|work (brīt′wėrk′), *n.* trim or fixtures of polished, unpainted metal, formerly often brass, now usually chromium, stainless steel, or other bright metal, especially on an automobile or ship: *Even small bits of brightwork, such as chromium windshield wipers or decorations on the dash, can reflect sunlight and cause spots of glare* (Time).

brill (bril), *n., pl.* **brills** or (*collectively*) **brill.** a European flatfish related to the turbot. [origin uncertain]

bril|liance (bril′yəns), *n.* **1** great brightness; radiance; sparkle: *the blue brilliance of southern skies.* SYN: luster, effulgence. **2** *Figurative.* **a** splendor; magnificence: *the brilliance of the royal court.* **b** great ability: *His brilliance as a pianist was known all over the world.* **3** *Music.* clarity and vividness of sound. **4** the presence of enriching overtones and high frequencies in the reproduction of musical sounds by a phonograph or other high-fidelity system.

bril|lian|cy (bril′yən sē), *n.* = brilliance.

bril|liant (bril′yənt), *adj., n.* —*adj.* **1** shining brightly; sparkling: *brilliant jewels, brilliant sunshine.* SYN: glittering, resplendent. See syn. under **bright. 2** *Figurative.* **a** splendid; magnificent: *The famous singer gave a brilliant performance.* **b** having great ability: *He is a brilliant musician.* SYN: accomplished, talented. **c** extremely favorable: *brilliant prospects.* **3** *Music.* clear and vivid in tone. **4** having a striking effect; showy.
—*n.* **1a** a diamond or other gem cut to sparkle brightly. It is typically shaped like two pyramids united at their bases, the top one cut off near the base and the bottom one close to the apex, with many facets on the slopes. See picture under **gem. b** this form of cutting gems. **2** the smallest regular size of type; 3½ point.
[< French *brillant,* present participle of *briller* shine < Italian *brillare* glitter, probably < Latin *bēryllus* beryl] —**bril′liant|ly,** *adv.* —**bril′liant-ness,** *n.*

bril|lian|teer (bril′yən tir′), *v.i.* to cut the facets of a gem into smaller facets so as to increase their brilliance.

bril|lian|tine (bril′yən tēn), *n., v.,* **-tined, -tin|ing.** —*n.* **1** an oily liquid used to make the hair glossy. **2** a glossy cloth of cotton and wool, resembling alpaca.
—*v.t.* to dress (the hair) with brilliantine.
[< French *brillantine* < *brillant;* see etym. under **brilliant**]

Bril|louin zone (brē yə wan′), *Physics.* a polyhedral zone in a crystal lattice, used to define the frequency or energy of wave motion, especially in the study of complex metals and alloys. [< L. *Brillouin,* a French physicist of the 1900's]

Brill's disease (brilz), a mild form of typhus. [< Nathan *Brill,* 1860-1925, an American physician, who first described it]

brim¹ (brim), *n., v.,* **brimmed, brim|ming.** —*n.* **1a** the edge of a cup or bowl; rim: *You have filled my glass to the brim.* **b** *Figurative: Filled to the brim with girlish glee* (William S. Gilbert). **2** the edge or border of anything: *the brim of a basket.* **3** the projecting edge about something: *The hat's wide brim shaded his eyes from the sun.* **4** an edge bordering water; water at the edge: *He drank at the brim of the spring.* **5** *Poetic.* **a** the sea. **b** water in flood.
—*v.i.* **1** to be full to the brim: *The pond is brimming with water after the hard rains.* **2** *Figurative: She was brimming with hope. His voice brimmed with anger.*
—*v.t.* to fill to the brim; fill to overflowing: *As I brimmed the bowl I thought on thee* (Samuel Taylor Coleridge).
brim over, to spill; overflow: *The bustle of the market ... brimmed over into the streets* (Hawthorne).
[Middle English *brimme*] —**brim′ming|ly,** *adv.*

brim² (brim), *n. Southern U.S.* = bream¹ (def. 2).

brim|ful or **brim|full** (brim′fu̇l′), *adj.* full to the brim; full to the very top.

brim|less (brim′lis), *adj.* without a brim.

brimmed (brimd), *adj.* **1** having a brim, as a hat. **2** filled to the brim; brimful.

brim|mer (brim′ər), *n.* a cup, bowl, or the like, filled to the brim.

brim|my (brim′ē), *adj.,* **-mi|er, -mi|est.** having a wide brim; broad-brimmed.

brim|stone (brim′stōn′), *n.* **1** sulfur, especially roll sulfur. **2** a virago; spitfire. [Middle English *brinston* < *brinn-* burn + *stōn* stone; perhaps influenced by *brim*¹]

brimstone butterfly, a common, yellow butterfly in England.

brim|ston|y (brim′stō′nē), *adj.* **1** of brimstone. **2** resembling brimstone.

brin|ded (brin′did), *adj.* = brindled: *Thrice the brinded cat hath mew'd* (Shakespeare). [Middle English *brended.* Probably related to **brand, branded.**]

brin|dle (brin′dəl), *adj., n.* —*adj.* = brindled.
—*n.* **1** a brindled color. **2** a brindled animal.
[< *brindled*]

brin|dled (brin′dəld), *adj.* gray, tan, or tawny with darker streaks and spots. [variant of *brinded*]

brine (brīn), *n., v.,* **brined, brin|ing.** —*n.* **1** very salty water. Some pickles are kept in brine. **2** a salt lake, sea, or ocean. **3** *Especially Poetic.* the sea.
—*v.t.* to treat with brine; pickle.
[Old English *brȳne*]

Bri|nell hardness (bri nel′), the relative hardness of a metal, determined by pressing a steel ball under a given pressure into the substance under test. [< J. A. *Brinell,* 1849-1925, Swedish engineer, who devised the test for it]

Brinell number, a number expressing the hardness of metal, obtained by pressing a steel ball, of standard dimensions and under a given pressure, into the substance under test.

Brinell test, the test for the hardness of metal, determining its Brinell number.

brine pan, a shallow container in which salt is obtained by evaporation.

brine shrimp, a small crustacean found in salt lakes, salt ponds, and the like; anostracan.

bring (bring), *v.t.,* **brought, bring|ing. 1** to come with (some thing or person) from another place; take along to a place or person: *The waiter brought me a clean plate. The bus brought us home.* **2** to cause to come: *What brings you into town today?* **3** to win over to a belief or action; influence; persuade; convince: *The principal was brought to agree with us about our need for a swimming pool.* SYN: induce, lead. **4** to sell for; fetch: *Fresh vegetables bring a high price in the winter.* **5a** to present before a law court: *The driver of the other car brought a charge against us in a lawsuit.* **b** to advance or bring forward (a statement or argument). **6** to cause (a ship, etc.) to come or go into a certain position or direction, chiefly in phrases: *to bring by the board, by the lee, or into the wind.* **7** to cause one to have; procure.
bring about, a to cause to happen; cause: *The flood was brought about by a heavy rain. He ... had borne a chief part in bringing about the marriage* (Macaulay). **b** to cause (a ship) to change from one tack to the other: *The boat was brought about by the wind.*
bring around (or **round**) **a** to restore to consciousness: *When she fainted, they brought her around with smelling salts.* **b** *Figurative.* to win over to a belief or action; convince; persuade: *At first her parents refused to let her go to the party, but she finally brought them around and they let her go.*
bring back, to cause to return (to a place or

state); restore; recover; recall: *The country air brought back her strength. The visit brought back fond memories.*
bring down, **a** to cause to fall to the ground; overthrow: *The guns brought down the ship's mast.* **b** *Figurative*: *to bring down one's enemies.* **c** to cause (punishment, judgments, wrath, or some other consequence) to alight (on or upon); *... to bring down on themselves the hostility of the most powerful maritime State* (London Times). **d** to kill or wound (a flying bird or other animal): *He brought down the partridge with a single shot.* **e** to reduce; lessen; lower (price): *The increased competition brought down prices.*
bring forth, **a** to give birth to; bear: *The trees in the orchard bring forth many apples. Bring forth men-children only* (Shakespeare). **b** to make known something that has been hidden; reveal; show: *He never thought of what the future might bring forth* (Benjamin Jowett).
bring forward, **a** to reveal; show: *The judge ordered the prisoner to be brought forward.* **b** to cite as evidence: *to bring forward proof.* **c** *Accounting, Bookkeeping.* to carry over from one page to another: *to bring a sum forward.*
bring home (to), to make clear, emphatic, or realistic: *to bring home a lesson to a person, to bring a charge home to the actual offender.*
bring in, **a** to introduce or try out: *...there shall be false teachers among you, who privily shall bring in damnable heresies* (II Peter 2:1). **b** to make (money): *A side line of greeting cards brought in a surprising amount.* **c** to report or announce officially; return: *to bring in a verdict.* **d** to cause to flow by drilling: *to bring in an oil well.* **e** to arrest: *It didn't take the police long to bring in the offender.*
bring off, to cause to happen; carry out successfully: *He brought off a good business deal.*
bring on, to cause to happen; cause: *His bad cold brought on pneumonia. These evils ... I myself have brought them on* (Milton).
bring out, **a** to reveal; show: *The truth was brought out at the trial.* **b** to offer to the public. *The company is bringing out a new product.* **c** to introduce (a young lady) formally to society: *She was brought out at a fashionable club last April.*
bring over, to win over to do or believe; convince; persuade: *Try to bring him over to our way of thinking. The house of commons was brought over to second his request* (Oliver Goldsmith).
bring through, to treat successfully through the stages of an illness: *The doctor hopes to be able to bring him through.*
bring to, **a** to restore consciousness: *She fainted when she heard the news, but they finally brought her to.* **b** to stop; check: *The captain brought the ship to.*
bring to bear, **a** to cause to have influence or effect: *Every author has a way of his own in bringing his points to bear* (Laurence Sterne). **b** to bring or point (a gun) so as to aim at: *to bring a gun to bear on a target.*
bring up, **a** to care for in childhood: *Grandmother brought up four children.* **b** to educate or train, especially in behavior or manners: *His good manners showed he was well brought up.* **c** to suggest for action or discussion: *Please bring your plan up at the meeting.* **d** to stop suddenly: *Within seconds a policeman brought his car up at the scene of the accident.* **e** to vomit: *He was so excited he brought up his lunch.* **f** to lead (troops or other groups) to the scene of action: *The sergeant brought up a squad of policemen to control the milling crowd.* **g** to bring into a higher position; elevate; raise; rear: *The cellar wall needs to be brought up several feet.* **h** to bring into the presence of authority: *He was brought up to the court to answer the charge against him.* **i** to bring to anchor or to a standstill: *They let go the other anchor ... and brought the vessel up* (Richard H. Dana).
[Old English *bringan*] **—bring'er,** *n.*
—*Syn.* **1 Bring, fetch** mean to come to a person or place with something. **Bring** means to come from somewhere with something: *I brought some cake home with me.* **Fetch** means to go somewhere else and get something and bring it back: *Please take the car and fetch him.*
▶**Bring, take.** In formal or standard English, *bring* is used when something is being carried toward the speaker or person spoken to: *Bring me that pencil. The waiter brought bread to my table. Take* is used when something is being carried away from the speaker (or in any direction other than toward him): *I took the letter to the Post Office.* This distinction is not generally maintained in informal English, *bring* being often used where formal English would require *take*, as in: *Bring that note to your teacher. I brought the child to school.*
bring|ing-up (bring'ing up'), *n.* **1** care and training given to a child when growing up; upbringing. **2** education; training.

brin|ish (brī'nish), *adj.* somewhat briny; saltish. **2** of the sea. **3** *Figurative.* bitter; nauseous.
brin|jal (brin'jôl), *n.* (in India) the fruit of the eggplant. [< Portuguese *bringella, beringela* < Arabic *bādhinjān*]
brink (bringk), *n.* **a** the edge at the top of a steep place: *the brink of the cliff.* **b** *Figurative*: *His business is on the brink of ruin.* SYN: edge, verge. [Middle English *brinke*, probably < Scandinavian (compare Swedish *brink* descent of a hill)]
brink|man (bringk'mən), *n., pl.* **-men.** a person who practices brinkmanship: *Judging from his record he is more moderate, less of a brinkman* (Maclean's).
brink|man|ship (bringk'mən ship), *n.* **1** the urging or maintaining of a policy to the limits of safety before giving ground. **2** the urging or sustaining of anything to the brink: (*Figurative.*) *The pianissimo of Beethoven's opening spread chord ... was an essay in dynamic brinkmanship on the edge of inaudibility* (London Times). [< *brink* + *-manship*]
brinks|man (bringks'mən), *n., pl.* **-men.** = brinkman.
brinks|man|ship (bringks'mən ship), *n.* = brinkmanship.
brin|y (brī'nē), *adj.,* **brin|i|er, brin|i|est,** *n.* **—*adj.*** of or like brine; very salty: *Too much salt gives a briny taste to food.*
—*n.* the briny, the ocean; the sea: *They dive into the briny ... and disport themselves among sting rays, gaping bass, and other denizens of the sea* (New Yorker). **—brin'i|ness,** *n.*
bri|o (brē'ō), *n. Italian.* **1** liveliness and vigor. **2** heartiness of style: *It's a lot of lighthearted fun, and told with all the brio for which Miss Tracy is justly famous* (Harper's).
bri|oche (brē'ōsh, -osh), *n.* a very light, round roll, raised with yeast, rich in butter and eggs. [< French *brioche*]
bri|o|lette (brē'ə let'), *n.* a pear-shaped diamond, having its entire surface cut with triangular facets. [perhaps < French *briller* to sparkle]
bri|on|y (brī'ə nē), *n., pl.* **-nies.** = bryony.
bri|quette or **bri|quet** (bri ket'), *n., v.,* **-quet|ted, -quet|ting. —*n.*** **1** a molded block of coal dust or charcoal used for fuel. **2** a similar block of some other finely ground material.
—*v.t.* to form (coal dust, charcoal, or other finely ground material) into briquettes: *Broken brick can be milled, briquetted, compacted together with slag and re-used* (New Scientist). [< French *briquette* (diminutive) < *brique* brick]
bri|sance (brē zäns'), *n.* the shattering effect of such high explosives as nitroglycerin and guncotton, largely depending on rate of combustion. [< French *brisance* < *briser* shatter]
bri|sant (brē zän'), *adj.* having a shattering effect: *a brisant explosive.* [< French *brisant*, present participle of *briser* shatter]
brise-brise (brēz'bē'), *n. Especially U.S.* a curtain of net or lace for the lower part of a window. [< French *brise-bise*]
Bri|se|is (brī sē'is), *n. Greek Legend.* a beautiful woman captured by Achilles, as related in Homer's *Iliad.* She was the indirect cause of his feud with Agamemnon.
brise-so|leil (brēz'sō lā'), *n., pl.* **brises-so|leil** (brēz'sō lā') or **brise-so|leils.** *Architecture.* any system of exterior louvers, screens, or the like, in a building, to keep out sun glare while admitting light and air: *Brises-soleil shield vast work and exhibition spaces* (Architectural Record). [< French *brise-soleil* (literally) sun breaker]
brisk (brisk), *adj., v.* **—*adj.*** **1** quick and active; lively: *A brisk walk brings him home from work in ten minutes.* SYN: nimble, spry. **2** keen; sharp: *brisk weather.* **3** agreeably sharp to the taste; effervescent (as opposed to *flat*): *a brisk young wine.* **4** sharp to the taste; keen: *Ginger has a brisk flavor.* **5** strong or violent: *a brisk breeze.*
v.t., v.i. to make or become brisk: *Modestine brisked up her pace* (Robert Louis Stevenson). [perhaps varient of *brusque*] **—brisk'ly,** *adv.* **—brisk'ness,** *n.*
brisk|en (bris'kən). *v.t., v.i.* to make or become brisk.
bris|ket (bris'kit), *n.* **1** the meat from the breast of an animal. **2** the breast of an animal. [Middle English *brusket*; origin uncertain]
bris|ling (bris'ling), *n.* **1** a sardinelkie Norwegian fish packed in oil and used for food. **2** = sprat. [< Norwegian *brisking* sprat]
bris|tle (bris'əl), *n., v.,* **-tled, tling. —*n.*** **1** one of the short, stiff hairs of some animals or plants: *Brushes are often made of the bristles of hogs.* **2** a synthetic substitute for a hog's bristle: *a hairbrush with stiff bristles.*
v.i. **1** to stand up straight: *The dog growled and his hair bristled.* **2** toi have one's hair stand up straight: *The frightened kitten bristled when it saw the dog.* **3** *Figurative.* to show that one is aroused and ready to fight: *The whole country bristled with indignation. Don't bristle at me—I'm trying to help you.* **4** *Figurative.* to be thickly set: *The harbor bristled with boats and ships. His knowledge of arithmetic was so poor that he found algebra bristling with difficulities.*
—*v.t.* **1** to provide or cover with bristles: *Ice ... bristles all the brakes and thorns* (Tennyson). **2** to cause (hair) to stand up: *He would ... bristle up his feathers* (Charles Kingsley). **3** to set thickly with obstrusive objects: *He would bristle all the land with castles* (Edward George Lytton). [Middle English *brustel*, Old English *byrst* bristle] **—bris'tle|like',** *adj.*
bris|tle|cone pine (bris'əl kōn'), an evergreen tree or shrub of the western United States with long, curving prickles on its cones; foxtail pine; hickory pine. Some of these pines are among the oldest living trees.
bris|tled (bris'əld), *adj.* having bristles; bristly.
bris|tle|tail (bris'əl tāl'), *n,* any one of several wingless insects having three long, bristlelike appendages at the end of the abdomen.
bristle worm, any one of various segmented marine annelids, having a pair of parapodia on each segment, found chiefly in mud and sand and in rocky coastal waters.
bris|tly (bris'lē), *adj.,* **-tli|er, -tli|est.** **1** rough with bristles or hair like bristles: *The trapper had a bristly chin after a week in the woods.* **2** like bristles: *bristly hair.* **3** *Figurative.* likely to bristle; aroused or easily roused to resistance: *a bristly temper, a bristly mood.* **—bris'tli|ness,** *n.*
bristly crab, = horse crab.
Bris|tol blue (bris'təl), a deep blue. [< *Bristol*, a city in England]
Bristol board, a fine, smooth cardboard or pasteboard, sometimes glazed.
Bristol fashion, *British.* in good order: *After spring cleaning, all was shipshape and Bristol fashion.*
brit (brit), *n.* **1** *U.S.* the small sea animals upon which whalebone whales subsist. **2** the young of the herring and sprat. **3** ant one of various similar small fishes swimmimg together. **4** the young of various other fish, as the mackerel. [< Cornish dialectal *brit*, perhaps < Cornish *bruit* speckled]
Brit., **1** Britain. **2** Briticism. **3** British.
Bri|tan|ni|a (bri tan'ē ə, -tan'yə), *n.* **1** Britain; Great Britain. **2a** the British Empire. **b** the United Kingdom of Great Britain and Northern Ireland. **3** a woman personifying Britain or the British Empire: *Britannia seated on a penny.* **4** the Latin name for: **a** the island of Great Britain. **b** the ancient Roman colony in Southern England. **5** = Britannia metal. [< Latin *Britannia*]
Britannia or **brittania metal,** a white alloy of tin, copper, and antimony, used in tableware.
Britannia ware, articles made of Britannia metal.
Bri|tan|nic (bri tan'ik), *adj.* of Britain; British: *Her Britannic Majesty.* [< Latin *Britannicus* < *Britannia* Britannia]
britch|es (britch'iz), *n.pl. Informal.* breeches: *By hook or crook an actor can put together a wardrobe: a coat, shirt and a pair of britches* (Show).
too big for one's britches, overestimating oneself: too cocky: *Before the mike and camera, he spoils them with praise; behind the scenes, he boxes their ears when they get too big for their britches* (Time).
Brit|i|cism (brit'ə siz əm), *n.* a word or phrase used especially by the British. *Lift* meaning *elevator* and *petrol* meaning *gasoline* are Briticisms.
▶**Briticism,** though sometimes condemned by purists on the ground that there is no form *Britic* from which a noun in *-ism* might legitimately be derived, is now firmly established. Of the substitutes, only *Britishism* has some currency.
Brit|ish (brit'ish), *adj., n.* **—*adj.*** **1** of Great Britain or its people. **2** of or belonging to ancient Britain or the ancient Britons: *the British warrior queen.* **3** *Obsolete.* of or belonging to Britanny; Breton.
—*n.* **1** *pl. in use.* the people of Great Britain. **2** the English spoken in Great Britain. **3** the language of the ancient Britons. *Abbr:* Brit. [old English *Brittisc* < *Brittas* Britons < a Celtic word] **—Brit'ish|ly,** *adv.* —Brit'ish|ness, *n.*
▶**British** is not now generally applied to the Commonwealth as a whole or to its fully independent member states.
British An|ti-Lew|is|ite (an'tē lü'əsīt), = BAL.
British Columbian, **1** of or having to do with British Columbia, a province in southwestern Canada. **2** a person born or living in British Columbia.
British dollar, = Hong Kong dollar.
British Empire, a former empire consisting of all

Pronunciation Key: hat, āge, cãre, fär; let, ēqual, tėrm; it, īce; hot, ōpen, ôrder; oil, out; cup, pu̇t, rüle; child; long; thin; ᵺen; zh, measure; ə represents **a** in about, **e** in taken, **i** in pencil, **o** in lemon, **u** in circus.

the countries and colonies owing allegiance to the British crown. At its height, in the late 1800's and early 1900's, it was the largest empire in the history of the world. The term now has no official use.

British English, the form of English spoken and written in Great Britain; British.

Brit|ish|er (brit′i shər), *n.* a British subject, especially an Englishman.

Brit|ish|ism (brit′i shiz əm), *n.* **1** the characteristic qualities of the British. **2** a British peculiarity, form of expression, or the like; Briticism.
▶ See **Briticism** for usage note.

British thermal unit, a unit for measuring heat. It is the amount of heat necessary to raise the temperature of a pound of pure water one degree Fahrenheit. *Abbr:* B.T.U., B.t.u., or Btu (no period).

Brit|on (brit′ən), *n.* **1** a native or inhabitant of Great Britain or the former British Empire. **2** one of the early Celtic inhabitants of southern Britain before the Roman conquest of Britain. [alteration of Middle English *Bryton, Breton* < Old French; see etym. under **Breton**]

Brit|rail pass (brit′rāl′), a pass permitting unlimited railroad transportation for a specified period of time on British Railways.

brits|ka (brits′kə), *n.* an open, four-wheeled carriage, widely used in Europe during the early 1800's, with calash top and space for reclining when used for a long journey. Also, **britzka, britzska.** [< Polish *bryczka*]

Brit|ta|ny spaniel (brit′ə nē), any one of a breed of medium-sized hunting dogs resembling a setter and having a thick, flat or wavy coat that is orange and white or liver and white. It is born with a short tail or none. [< *Brittany,* a region in France, where the breed was developed]

brit|tle (brit′əl), *adj., n.* —*adj.* **1** very easily broken; breaking with a snap; apt to break: *Thin glass and ice are brittle.* **SYN**: fragile, frail. **2** of a sharp quality: *disapproval in a brittle tone of voice.* **3** cool and formal; unfriendly: *a brittle manner.* **4** insecure, unstable, or changeable: *The brittle tribute of his praise* (Richard Brinsley Sheridan). **5** *Obsolete.* perishable.
—*n. U.S.* a candy of caramelized sugar and nuts, made in thin, hard sheets, broken into pieces for eating: *peanut brittle.*
[Middle English *britel* < Old English *brēotan* to break] —**brit′tle|ness**, *n.*

brittle silver ore, = stephanite.

brittle star, any one of several sea animals, related to the starfish and so called from the fragility of their slender arms; ophiuran.

brittle willow, = crack willow.

britz|ka or **britz|ska** (brits′kə), *n.* = britska.

Brix (briks), *adj., n.* —*adj.* of, based on, or according to a scale for measuring the density of sugar solutions. On a hydrometer or saccharometer, the degrees Brix represent the percentage by weight of sugar in the solution at a particular temperature.
—*n.* the Brix hydrometer or scale. [< A. F. W. *Brix,* 1798-1890, a German scientist]

bro. or **Bro.**, brother.

broach (brōch), *v., n.,* —*v.t.* **1** to begin to talk about; introduce: *She broached the subject of a picnic to her parents.* **2a** to open by making a hole: *He broached a barrel of cider.* **b** to open up other kinds of containers. **c** to draw (liquor) by piercing a cask. **3** Also, **broach out.** to enlarge and finish (a drilled hole) with a broach. **4** to dress (stone) with a broach. **5** *Obsolete.* to pierce; spit.
—*n.* **1** a pointed tool to make and shape holes; reamer. **2** a sharp-pointed, slender rod on which meat is roasted; a spit. **3** a gimlet used in opening casks. **4** = brooch. **5** a tool for dressing stone, used by masons. **6** a perforation or boring.
broach to, to turn or cause (a ship) to turn broadside on to the wind and sea: *It too often happens that some of the men catch crabs with their oars, and broach the boat to* (Frederick Bedford).
[< Old French *broche* < Vulgar Latin *brocca* pointed tool < Latin *broccus* projecting]
—**broach′er**, *n.*

broad (brôd), *adj., adv., n.* —*adj.* **1** large across; wide: *Many cars can go on that broad new highway.* **SYN**: See syn. under **wide**. **2** having wide range; extensive; vast: *the broad expanse of the ocean. A teacher has broad experience with children.* **SYN**: ample. **3** *Figurative.* not limited or narrow; liberal; tolerant: *The police took a broad view of the boys' prank and did not bring charges against them.* **4** including only the most important parts; general: *Give me the broad outlines of what the speech was about.* **SYN**: main. **5** clear; full: *The theft was made in broad daylight.* **6** plain; plainspoken; frank: *to criticize in broad phrases. He gave his parents broad hints of what he wanted for his birthday.* **7** coarse; not refined: *broad jokes.* **SYN**: gross. **8** uninhibited; free from restraints: *broad mirth.* **9a** markedly dialectal; having local characteristics: *broad Scotch.* **b** characterized by full, strong utterance. **10** pronounced with a wide opening between tongue and palate. The *a* in *father* is broad. **11** indicating pronunciation by using one symbol for each phoneme, disregarding allophones.
—*adv.* **1** in a broad manner; fully; widely: . . . *being in bed but broad awake* (John Wesley). **2** outspokenly; without reserve: *Who can speak broader than he that has no house to put his head in?* (Shakespeare). **3** with a broad accent: *Some Devonshire countrymen speak very broad.*
—*n.* **1** the broad part of anything, especially of a part of the body: *He fell on the broad of his back.* **2** *British.* an extensive stretch of fresh water spreading out from a river: *the Norfolk broads.* **3** *U.S. Slang.* (sometimes regarded as vulgar or offensive) a woman or girl.
[Old English *brād*] —**broad′ly**, *adv.* —**broad′ness**, *n.*

broad arrow, **1** an arrow having a broad head. **2** the sign of British government property.

***broad|ax** or **broad|axe** (brôd′aks′), *n., pl.* **-ax|es.** an ax with a broad blade, such as a battle-ax or an ax for hewing timber.

***broadax**

broad|band or **broad-band** (brôd′band′), *adj.* operating over, or designed for use over, a wide range of frequencies: *broadband radio transmission.*

broad-based (brôd′bāst′), *adj.* built on a broad base; applied to many different areas, interests, ideas, or the like; including a wide range; not limited: *The economy is broad-based and does not rely too much on a single product or a small section of the population* (Manchester Guardian).

broad bean, **1** a smooth, kidney-shaped, laterally flattened, edible seed borne in long pods by an Old World plant of the pea family, used as a vegetable; horse bean; fava bean. **2** the plant it grows on.

broad|bill (brôd′bil′), *n.* **1** the scaup duck, shoveler, spoonbill, or any one of various other birds having a broad bill. **2** = swordfish.

broad-billed (brôd′bild′), *adj.* having a broad bill: *The scaup duck is a broad-billed bird.*

broad|brim (brôd′brim′), *n.* **1** a hat with a very wide brim. **2** *Archaic.* a person who wears such a hat; Quaker; Friend.

broad-brimmed (brôd′brimd′), *adj.* having a broad brim.

broad-brush (brôd′brush′), *adj.* not detailed; sketchy; rough: *Details are lacking, but broad-brush plans call for recruitment of young people from U.N. member countries to "intern" in U.N. agencies* (Time).

broad|cast (brôd′kast′, -käst′), *n., v.,* **-cast** or **-cast|ed, -cast|ing,** *adj., adv.* —*n.* **1** something sent out by radio or television; a radio or television program of speech, music, or the like: *The President's broadcast was televised from Washington, D.C.* **2** a sending out by radio or television: *a nationwide broadcast.* **3a** a scattering or spreading far and wide: *nature's broadcast of seed.* **SYN**: dissemination. **b** the method of sowing by scattering seed broadcast.
—*v.i.* **1** to send out programs by radio or television: *Some stations broadcast 24 hours of the day.* **2** to take part in or supply an item of a radio or television program.
—*v.t.* **1** to send out (a message, news, music, or other program) by radio or television: *The Columbia Broadcasting System . . . broadcast the anniversary ceremonies* (Look). **2** to scatter or spread widely: *to broadcast seed.* **SYN**: strew. **3** *Figurative.* to make generally known or available; disseminate widely: *to broadcast news, ideas, gossip, or scandal.*
—*adj.* **1** sent out by radio or television: *a broadcast appeal for donors.* **2** of or connected with radio broadcasting: *broadcast interests.* **3** scattered or spread widely. **4** widely disseminated; made public: *broadcast accusations, broadcast information.*
—*adv.* **1** so as to reach many radio or television receiving stations or sets in various directions. **2** over a wide surface: *The seed was sown broadcast.*

broad|cast|er (brôd′kas′tər, -käs′-), *n.* **1a** a person or thing that broadcasts. **b** a broadcasting company or station. **2** an apparatus for broadcasting by radio or television.

broad|cast|ing (brôd′kas′ting, -käs′-), *n.* **1** the act of a person or thing that broadcasts over radio or on television. **2** the field or profession of a radio or television broadcaster.

Broad-Church (brôd′chėrch′), *adj.* of or having to do with a party in the Anglican Communion that seeks to avoid rigid definitions of dogma and ritual.

Broad Churchman, an Anglican who favors Broad-Church views and attitudes.

broad|cloth (brôd′klôth′, -kloth′), *n.* **1** a closely woven cotton or silk cloth with a smooth finish, used in making shirts, dresses, and pajamas. **2** a closely woven woolen cloth with a smooth finish, used in making suits, coats, and dresses.

broad|en (brô′dən), *v.i.* to become broad or broader; widen: *The river broadens at its mouth where it meets the sea.*
—*v.t.* to make broad or broader; widen: *to broaden a narrow road.* (*Figurative.*) *Travel can broaden a person's sympathies for people from foreign lands.*

broad gauge, a width between the rails of a railroad, greater than the standard width of 56½ inches.

broad-gauge (brôd′gāj′), *adj.* **1** having railroad tracks more than 56½ inches apart. **2** *Figurative.* broad-minded; liberal: *broad-gauge leadership.* **3** widely ranging: *a broad-gauge economic program.*

broad-gauged (brôd′gājd′), *adj.* = broad-gauge.

broad hatchet, a hatchet with a wide blade.

broad|ish (brô′dish), *adj.* somewhat broad.

broad jump, **1** a jump to cover as much ground as possible. **2** a contest for the longest jump: *He won the broad jump.* Also, **long jump**.

broad-jump (brôd′jump′), *v.i.* to do a broad jump or jumps; long-jump. —*v.t.* to get across (something) by a broad jump or jumps: *He broad-jumped gutters and dodged cars on his way to class* (Harper's). —**broad′-jump′er**, *n.*

broad|leaf or **Broad|leaf** (brôd′lēf′), *n.* any one of various tobaccos with broad leaves, used especially for cigars.

broadleaf dock, = bitter dock.

broadleaf evergreen, an evergreen tree or shrub in which the leaves are broad and flat, rather than needle-shaped, such as the rhododendron or the bull bay. See picture under **deciduous.**

broadleaf plantain, = plantain[2] (def.1).

broadleaf tree, any tree with broad, flat leaves, including all deciduous trees and such evergreen trees as the holly and live oak. Broadleaf trees have flowers that develop into fruits.

broad-leaved (brôd′lēvd′), *adj.* having broad leaves, as the hardwoods.

broad|loom (brôd′lüm′), *adj., n.* —*adj.* woven on a wide loom: *a broadloom carpet.*
—*n.* material woven in this way: *gray broadloom.*

broad-mind|ed (brôd′mīn′did), *adj.* not prejudiced or bigoted; tolerant: *Some of the older people of the town do not share the mayor's broad-minded attitude toward the new businesses coming in.* **SYN**: liberal. —**broad′-mind′ed|ly**, *adv.* —**broad′-mind′ed|ness**, *n.*

broad|piece (brôd′pēs′), *n.* an old English gold coin worth 20 shillings, first issued in 1619 by James I, so called after the introduction, in 1663, of the guinea, which was smaller in diameter but thicker.

broad seal, the official seal of a government, such as of a state or country.

broad|sheet (brôd′shēt′), *n.* = broadside (def. 5).

broad|side (brôd′sīd′), *n., adv.* —*n.* **1** the whole side of a ship above the water. **2a** all the guns that can be fired from one side of a ship. **b** the firing of all these guns at the same time: *The broadside caught the pirates completely by surprise.* **3** *Informal, Figurative.* a violent attack; storm of abuse. **4** a broad surface or side, such as of a house. **5** a large sheet of paper printed on one or both sides: *broadsides announcing a big sale.*
—*adv.* with the side turned: *The ship drifted broadside to the pier.*

broad-spec|trum (brôd′spek′trəm), *adj.* having a wide range of use or application.

broad|sword (brôd′sôrd′, -sōrd′), *n.* a sword with a broad, flat cutting blade.

broad|tail (brôd′tāl′), *n.* **1** the skin of a very young karakul lamb, with flat, wavy hair, or several skins, used to make or trim garments. **2** Also, **broadtail sheep.** a kind of Asiatic sheep having a fat tail.

broad|way (brôd′wā′), *n.* a broad road or highway.

Broad|way (brôd′wā′), *n.* **1** a street running northwest and southeast through New York City. Part of Broadway lies in the main theater district and is gaily lighted. **2** the New York City commercial theater.

broad|ways (brôd′wāz′), *adv.* = breadthways.

broad|wife (brôd′wīf′), *n., pl.* **-wives.** *Southern U.S. History.* a slave's wife whose owner was not the owner of her husband.

broad-winged hawk (brôd′wingd′), a hawk of eastern North America with dark grayish brown upper parts and barred light-brown under parts.

broad|wise (brôd′wīz′), *adv.* = breadthwise.

brob (brob), *n.* a wedge-shaped spike driven in beside an abutting timber to keep it from slipping. [< a dialectal British form]

Brob|ding|nag (brob′ding nag), *n.* the land of giants in Jonathan Swift's *Gulliver's Travels.*

Brob|ding|nag|i|an (brob′ding nag′ē ən), *adj., n.* **—*adj.*** **1** gigantic; huge; enormous. **2** of or like Brobdingnag. **—*n.*** a giant.

bro|cade (brō kād′), *n., v.,* **-cad|ed, -cad|ing.** **—*n.*** an expensive cloth woven with raised designs on it, used for clothing or upholstery: *silk brocade, a velvet brocade vest.*
—*v.t.* to weave or decorate with raised designs. [< Spanish *brocado* < Catalan *brocat* < Italian *broccato* < *brocca* pointed tool < Vulgar Latin; see etym. under **broach**]

bro|cad|ed (brō kā′did), *adj.* **1** woven or worked into a brocade: *Brocaded flowers o'er the gay mantua shine* (John Gay). **2** dressed in brocade. **3** decorated with flowers or other designs in relief: *a brocaded silk.*

bro|cage (brō′kij), *n.* = brokage; brokerage.

broc|ard (brok′ərd, brō′kərd), *n.* a legal or other maxim; canon. [< French *brocard* < *Burkhard,* Bishop of Worms, in the 1000's, who compiled ecclesiastical canons]

Bro|ca's area (brō′kəz), an area of the left hemisphere of the brain, associated with motor aspects of speech. [< Pierre Paul *Broca,* 1824-1880, a French surgeon]

broc|a|tel or **broc|a|telle** (brok′ə tel′), *n.* **1** a cloth with brocade designs woven into it, usually made of silk or rayon and linen, used especially for tapestry and upholstery. **2** a kind of variegated ornamental marble. [< French *brocatelle* < Italian *broccatello* thin gold tinsel (diminutive) < *broccato* brocade]

broc|co|li (brok′ə lē), *n.* **1** a plant having green stems and flower heads. It belongs to the mustard family and is a kind of cauliflower. **2** its tender heads and stems, which are eaten as a vegetable. [< Italian *broccoli,* plural of *broccolo* sprout, (diminutive) < *brocco* stalk, shoot < Latin *broccus* projecting]

broccoli sprouts, = broccoli.

bro|ché (brō shā′), *adj., n.* **—*adj.*** woven with a pattern, like embroidery, on the surface: *broché silk.* **—*n.*** such cloth. [< French *broché,* past participle of *brocher* to stitch, brocade]

bro|chette (brō shet′), *n.* a small spit or skewer used in cooking meat. [< Old French *brochette* (diminutive) < *broche* spit, broach]

bro|chure (brō shůr′), *n.* a pamphlet: *a collection of brochures on vacations abroad.* [< French *brochure* < *brocher* stitch < Old French, to prick < *broche* broach]

brock (brok), *n. Especially Dialect.* **1** a badger: *in the beechwood grey where the brocks were grunting* (John Masefield). **2** a stinker, like a brock (used as an insult). [Old English *broc*]

Brock|en specter (brok′ən), an optical illusion sometimes seen by a mountaineer or aviator between the sun and a bank of fog or cloud, by which he sees himself, or his aircraft, projected on the cloud and apparently greatly enlarged. [< *Brocken,* a mountain in Germany, legendary gathering place of witches]

brock|et (brok′it), *n.* **1** any one of a group of small tropical American deer with straight, unbranched antlers. **2** a male red deer in his second year with his first antlers, which are straight and spikelike. [< Middle French *brocart* stag in its second year < Old French *broc* tine of stag's horn, variant of *broche* broach]

bro|de|rie an|glaise (brô drē′ än glez′), *French.* **1** open embroidery on white linen or cambric, with designs cut out of the foundation material. **2** (literally) English embroidery.

bro|gan (brō′gən), *n.* a strong work shoe made of heavy leather. [< Irish Gaelic *brógan* (diminutive) < *bróg* brogue[2]]

brogue[1] (brōg), *n., v.,* **brogued, brogu|ing.** **—*n.*** **1** an Irish accent or pronunciation of English. **2** a strongly marked pronunciation or accent peculiar to a dialect.
—*v.t.* to say or speak in a brogue: *"You'll see," brogued the guide, and he was . . . plucking my sleeve to draw me* (Punch).
[perhaps < *brogue*[2] in the sense of "the speech of those who call their shoes brogues"]

***brogue[2]** (brōg), *n.* **1** a shoe made for comfort and long wear, often with decorative perforations: *brogues suitable for country wear.* **2** a coarse shoe, commonly of untanned hide, worn, especially formerly, in Ireland and Scotland. **3** = brogan. [< Irish Gaelic *bróg* shoe]

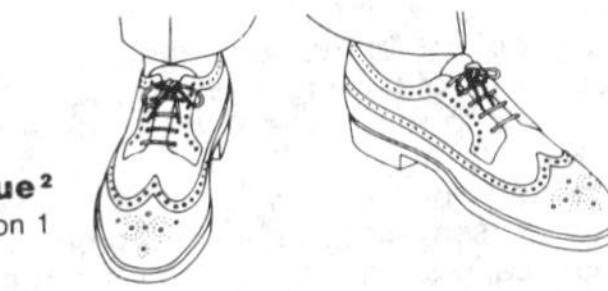

***brogue[2]**
definition 1

brogue[3] (brōg), *n. Scottish.* fraud; trick; cheat. [origin unknown]

broi|der (broi′dər), *v.t. Archaic.* **1** to embroider. **2** *Figurative.* to adorn: *The violet, crocus, and hyacinth, with rich inlay Broider'd the ground* (John Milton). [< Middle French *broder* < Old French *brosder;* influenced by archaic English *broid* braid]

broi|der|y (broi′dər ē), *n., pl.* **-der|ies.** *Archaic.* embroidery.

broil[1] (broil), *v., n.* **—*v.t.*** **1** to cook by putting or holding directly over the fire or heat, or directly under it in a pan; grill: *Flames flared as he broiled meat over a small fire.* **2** to make very hot; scorch: (*Figurative.*) *We turned back, much broiled in the hot sun* (Hawthorne).
—*v.i.* **1** to be or grow very hot: (*Figurative.*) *You will broil in this hot sun.* **2** *Figurative.* to be worked up with anger, impatience, or other emotion: *Her female friends, with envy broiling, beheld her airs and triumph* (Byron).
—*n.* **1** broiled food. **2** a broiling; a very hot state. **3** a state of excitement from emotion: *He was in a broil of indignation.*
[perhaps < Old French *bruiller,* earlier *brusler* to burn]

broil[2] (broil), *n., v.* **—*n.*** an angry quarrel or struggle; brawl: . . . *plunging us in all the broils of the European nations* (Thomas Jefferson). [< verb]
—*v.i.* to quarrel; fight.
[< Middle French *brouiller* to disorder < Old French *broueillier* to mix, soil]

broil|er (broi′lər), *n., adj.* **—*n.*** **1** a pan or rack for broiling: *Mother set the lamb chops on the broiler.* **2** a young chicken, tender enough for broiling. **3** a person or thing that broils. **4** *Informal.* a very hot day; scorcher.
—*adj.* (of poultry) suitable for broiling.

broil|ing (broi′ling), *adj.* scorching; very hot. **—broil′ing|ly,** *adv.*

bro|kage (brō′kij), *n.* = brokerage. Also, **brocage.**

broke[1] (brōk), *v., adj., n.* **—*v.*** **1** past tense of **break:** *The little girl broke her doll.* **2** *Archaic.* a past participle of **break.**
—*adj.* **1** *Slang.* **a** without money. **b** ruined financially; bankrupt: *It took me six weeks and two days to go broke* (Stewart Edward White). **2** *Occasionally.* broken.
—*n.* **go for broke,** *Slang.* to exert all of one's efforts; give everything one has: *Musicians who go for broke by trying to survive in the field of chamber music alone often . . . go broke* (Time).

broke[2] (brōk), *v.i.,* **broked, brok|ing.** to act as a broker. [< *broker*]

bro|ken (brō′kən), *v., adj.* **—*v.*** past participle of **break:** *The window was broken by a ball.*
—*adj.* **1** separated into parts by a break; in pieces; fractured: *a broken cup.* **2** not in working condition; damaged: *a broken watch.* **3** rough; uneven: *broken ground, to speak in a broken voice.* **4** acted against; not kept: *a broken promise.* **5** imperfectly spoken: *The French boy speaks broken English.* **6** *Figurative.* weakened in strength or spirit; tamed; crushed: *broken health, broken by failure. A thoroughly broken resistance seldom recovers.* **7** *Figurative.* interrupted; incomplete; fragmentary: *broken sleep. This broken tale was all we knew* (Byron). **8** bankrupt; ruined: *a broken man.* **9** torn; split; ruptured: *broken skin.* **10** *Obsolete.* dissolved. **—bro′ken|ly,** *adv.* **—bro′ken|ness,** *n.*

bro|ken-backed (brō′kən bakt′), *adj.* **1** having a broken back. **2** hunchbacked. **3** *Figurative.* sagging; uneven; lopsided: *a broken-backed building, a broken-backed mountain.*

broken chord, = arpeggio (def. 1).

bro|ken-down (brō′kən doun′), *adj.* **1** shattered; ruined: *broken-down health.* **2** unfit for use: *a house filled with broken-down furniture, a broken-down shack.*

bro|ken|heart|ed (brō′kən här′tid), *adj.* crushed by sorrow or grief; heartbroken: *a brokenhearted lover.* **—bro′ken|heart′ed|ly,** *adv.*

broken wind, = heaves.

bro|ken-wind|ed (brō′kən win′did), *adj.* **1** (of a horse) breathing with sudden, short efforts; suffering from heaves. **2** (of persons) out of breath.

bro|ker (brō′kər), *n., v.* **—*n.*** **1** a person who buys and sells stocks, bonds, grain, cotton, or other commodities for other people; agent. **2** a person who acts as a middleman in negotiating bargains or contracts. **3** *British.* a second-hand dealer; pawnbroker.
—*v.i.* to act as a broker; engage in brokerage.
—*v.t.* to arrange or negotiate as a broker: *I was trying to broker the deal, and I had a four-o'clock deadline for a $25,000 deposit my client had promised to put up* (New Yorker).
[< Anglo-French *brocour* retailer of wine, tapster, variant of Old French *brocheor* to tap (a keg) < *broche* broach]

bro|ker|age (brō′kər ij), *n.* **1** the business or office of a broker. **2** the money charged by a broker for his services. Also, **brokage, brocage.**

bro|ker-deal|er (brō′kər dē′lər), *n.* a stockbroker who buys and sells securities both for himself and, especially, as an agent for clients.

brok|ing (brō′king), *adj. British.* of or having to do with brokerage.

brol|ga (brol′gə), *n.* a light gray crane of Australia and New Guinea with a bare red patch on its head, noted for its rhythmic strutting and prancing in flocks. [< a native name]

brol|ly (brol′ē), *n., pl.* **-lies.** *British Informal.* umbrella. [alteration of *(um)brella* + *-y*[2]]

bro|ma (brō′mə), *n.* **1** cacao seeds from which all oil has been expressed. **2** *Medicine.* food of any kind that is eaten and not drunk. [< Greek *brôma* food]

bro|mal (brō′məl), *n.* a colorless, oily compound produced by the action of bromine on alcohol, used medicinally. *Formula:* C_2HBr_3O [< German *Bromal* < *Brom* bromine + *Al(kohol)* alcohol]

bro|mate (brō′māt), *n., v.,* **-mat|ed, -mat|ing.** **—*n.*** a salt of bromic acid.
—*v.t.* to treat or combine with bromine; brominate.

brome grass, or **brome** (brōm), *n.* any one of a genus of about 60 kinds of grasses found mainly in the Northern Hemisphere, most of which are bearded, and some of which are coarse weeds, although a few species, such as chess, are cultivated for forage. [< Latin *bromos* oats < Greek *brómos*]

bro|me|li|a (brō mē′lē ə), *n.* = bromeliad.

bro|me|li|a|ceous (brō mē′lē ā′shəs), *adj.* belonging to the family of plants typified by the pineapple. [< New Latin *Bromelia* the typical genus (< Olaf *Bromel,* 1639-1705, a Swedish botanist) + English *-aceous*]

bro|me|li|ad (brō mē′lē ad), *n.* **1** a tropical American plant of the pineapple family, having lance-shaped, spiny leaves and brightly colored flowers. **2** any plant of the pineapple family, such as the billbergia. [< New Latin *Bromelia* (see etym. under **bromeliaceous**) + *-ad* (suffix for names of plants related to a genus)]

bro|me|lin (brō′mə lin), *n.* an enzyme present in pineapple which aids in the hydrolysis of proteins. [< New Latin *Bromelia* + English *-in*]

bro|mic (brō′mik), *adj.* **1** containing bromine, especially with a valence of 5. **2** of bromine.

bromic acid, an acid containing bromine and oxygen, used in making dyes and drugs. *Formula:* $HBrO_3$

bro|mid (brō′mid), *n.* = bromide (def. 1).

bro|mide (brō′mīd), *n.* **1** any compound of bromine with another element or radical, especially potassium bromide. **2** a drug used especially to calm nervousness or cause sleep. **3** *Informal, Figurative.* a commonplace idea; trite remark. **4** *Figurative.* a person whose thoughts and conversation are conventional and commonplace. [< *brom(ine)* + *-ide*]

bro|mid|ic (brō mid′ik), *adj. Informal.* like a bromide; commonplace; trite. SYN: banal.

bro|min (brō′min), *n.* = bromine.

bro|mi|nate (brō′mə nāt), *v.t.,* **-nat|ed, -nat|ing.** to treat or combine with bromine; bromate. **—bro′mi|na′tion,** *n.*

***bro|mine** (brō′mēn, -min), *n.* a dark, brownish-red chemical element. Bromine is a nonmetallic liquid somewhat like chlorine and iodine and gives off an irritating vapor. It is used in antiknock compounds for gasoline, in drugs, and in photography. [< French *brome* bromine (< Greek *brômos* stench) + English *-ine*[2]]

***bromine**

symbol	atomic number	atomic weight	oxidation state
Br	35	79.904	±1, +5

bro|min|ism (brō′mə niz əm), *n.* = bromism.

bro|mism (brō′miz əm), *n.* = a diseased condition

Pronunciation Key: hat, āge, cãre, fär; let, ēqual, tėrm; it, īce; hot, ōpen, ôrder; **oi**l, **ou**t; cup, pu̇t, rüle; **ch**ild; lo**ng**; **th**in; **TH**en; **zh,** measure; **ə** represents **a** in about, **e** in taken, **i** in pencil, **o** in lemon, **u** in circus.

produced by excessive use of bromides, especially of potassium bromide.

bro|mize (brō′mīz), *v.t.*, **-mized**, **-miz|ing.** to treat or combine with bromine.

bro|mo (brō′mō), *n., pl.* **-mos.** a remedy for headache and indigestion, containing sodium bicarbonate. [< *Bromo(-Seltzer)*, trademarked remedy]

bro|mo|form (brō′mə fôrm), *n. Chemistry.* a colorless liquid, analogous to chloroform, used in medicine. *Formula:* $CHBr_3$

bro|moil (brō′moil), *n. Photography.* a print made by a process (**bromoil process**) in which an oil pigment is applied to an image formed by a silver bromide emulsion. [< *brom*(ide) + *oil*]

bro|mol (brō′mol, -mōl), *n.* a white, crystalline substance, a bromine derivative of phenol, used as an antiseptic and disinfectant. *Formula:* $C_6H_3Br_3O$

Brompton cocktail and **mixture** (brom′tən), a preparation of narcotics used to relieve pain and other symptoms of cancer: *The so-called Brompton cocktail, which can include both heroin and cocaine, is valuable in treating nausea* (New York Times). [*Brompton* Chest Hospital, in London, England, where it was apparently first used.]

bronc (brongk), *n. U.S. Slang.* a bronco.

*****bron|chi** (brong′kī), *n., pl. of* **bronchus. 1** the two large, main branches of the windpipe, one going to each lung. **2** the smaller branching tubes in the lungs that divide into bronchioles.

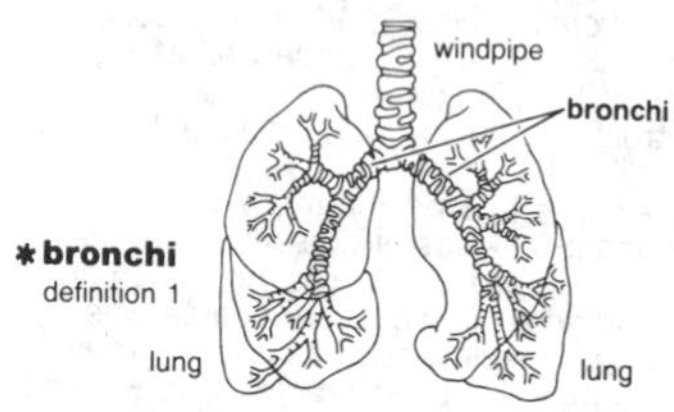

*****bronchi**
definition 1

bron|chi|a (brong′kē ə), *n.pl.* the bronchial tubes, especially the smaller tubes. [< Late Latin *bronchia* < Greek *brónchia* < *brónchos* windpipe]

bron|chi|al (brong′kē əl), *adj.* of or having to do with the bronchi or their many branching tubes.

bronchial asthma, a form of asthma caused by an allergic reaction to some foreign substance in the bronchioles.

bronchial tubes, the bronchi and their branching tubes.

bron|chi|ec|ta|sis (brong′kē ek′tə sis), *n.* enlargement of one or more of the larger bronchial tubes, often with inflammation. [< Greek *brónchos* windpipe + *éktasis* expansion]

bron|chi|ec|tat|ic (brong′kē ek tat′ik), *adj.* of or like bronchiectasis.

bron|chi|o|gen|ic (brong′kē ō jen′ik), *adj.* = bronchogenic.

bron|chi|ole (brong′kē ōl), *n.* a very small branch of the bronchi. [< New Latin *bronchiola* (diminutive) < Latin *bronchus* bronchus]

bron|chi|o|li|tis (brong′kē ō lī′tis), *n.* inflammation of the small bronchial tubes.

bron|chit|ic (brong kit′ik), *adj., n.* **—*adj.* 1** of or having to do with bronchitis. **2** having bronchitis.
—*n.* a person with bronchitis.

bron|chi|tis (brong kī′tis), *n.* inflammation of the mucous membrane that lines the bronchial tubes. A deep cough goes with it. Bronchitis may be acute or chronic. [< New Latin *bronchitis* < Greek *brónchos* windpipe + *-ītis* disease]

bron|cho (brong′kō), *n., pl.* **-chos.** = bronco.

bron|cho|bust|er (brong′kō bus′tər), *n. U.S. Slang.* broncobuster.

bron|cho|cele (brong′kō sēl), *n.* = goiter. [< Greek *bronchokḗlē* throat tumor < *brónchos* windpipe + *kḗlē* tumor]

bron|cho|di|la|tor (brong′kō dī lā′tər, -də-), *n.* a drug or instrument for dilating the bronchial air passages.

bron|cho|gen|ic (brong′kō jen′ik), *adj.* affecting or arising from the bronchi: *bronchogenic carcinoma.*

bron|chog|ra|phy (brong kog′rə fē), *n.* X-ray examination of the bronchial tubes.

bron|cho|pneu|mo|nia (brong′kō nü mōn′yə, -mō′nē ə; -nyü-), *n.* inflammation of the lungs usually beginning with inflammation of the terminal bronchioles. [< Greek *brónchos* windpipe]

bron|cho|scope (brong′kə skōp), *n.* a very thin tube by which a doctor can see into the bronchi, administer treatment, or remove foreign objects or mucus. [< Greek *brónchos* windpipe]

bron|cho|scop|ic (brong′kə skop′ik), *adj.* of or resembling a bronchoscope. **—bron′cho|scop′i-cal|ly,** *adv.*

bron|chos|co|py (brong kos′kə pē), *n.* the use of a bronchoscope.

bron|cho|spasm (brong′kə spaz′əm), *n.* spasm of the bronchial muscles, causing constriction of the bronchi.

bron|cho|tome (brong′kə tōm), *n.* an instrument for use in bronchotomy.

bron|chot|o|my (brong kot′ə mē), *n., pl.* **-mies.** the operation of making an incision in the trachea or windpipe. [< Greek *brónchos* windpipe + *-tomiā* a cutting]

bron|chus (brong′kəs), *n., pl.* **-chi. 1** one of the bronchi. **2** (sometimes) any small bronchial tube. [< New Latin *bronchus* < Late Latin, windpipe < Greek *brónchos*]

bron|co (brong′kō), *n., pl.* **-cos. 1** a wild or partly tamed horse of western North America. **2** = mustang. Also, **broncho.** [American English < American Spanish *bronco* < Spanish, rough (as woods), rude]

bronco bean, = jumping bean.

bron|co|bust|er (brong′kō bus′tər), *n. U.S. Slang.* in the West and Southwest: **1** a person who breaks broncos to the saddle. **2** a cowboy.

bronco grass, a Mediterranean brome grass introduced into California.

bron|to|graph (bron′tə graf, -gräf), *n.* **1** = brontometer. **2** the tracing or record produced by a brontometer. [< Greek *brontḗ* thunder]

bron|tom|e|ter (bron tom′ə tər), *n.* an instrument for recording the phenomena of thunderstorms. [< Greek *brontḗ* thunder + English *-meter*]

bron|to|saur (bron′tə sôr), *n.* = brontosaurus.

bron|to|sau|ri|an (bron′tə sôr′ē ən), *adj.* of or like a brontosaurus; dinosaurian: ... *immense machines with brontosaurian necks* (New Yorker).

*****bron|to|sau|rus** (bron′tə sôr′əs), *n., pl.* **-sau|ri** (-sôr′ī), **-sau|rus|es.** a huge herbivorous dinosaur of all the continents during the Jurassic and Cretaceous periods. Some kinds were as long as sixty feet and as high as fourteen feet. [< New Latin *Brontosaurus* the genus name < Greek *brontḗ* thunder + *saûros* lizard]

*****brontosaurus**

Bronx cheer (brongks), *U.S. Slang.* a sound of derision, made by an explosive expulsion of breath through nearly closed lips; raspberry.

bronze (bronz), *n., adj., v.,* **bronzed, bronz|ing.**
—*n.* 1 a brown metal, an alloy of copper and tin. See also **brass. 2** a similar alloy of copper with zinc or another metal. **3** a statue, medal, or disk made of bronze: *A bronze was given to the boy who won the contest.* **4** the color of bronze; dark yellowish brown or reddish brown: *The lifeguard was a deep bronze.*
—*adj.* 1 made of bronze: *a bronze bell.* **2** dark yellowish-brown or reddish-brown.
—*v.t., v.i.* 1 to make or become bronze in color: *The sailor was bronzed from the sun.* **2** to give a bronzelike surface to. **3a** to harden or make like bronze. **b** *Figurative.* to make hard or unfeeling. [< Middle French *bronze* < Italian *bronzo* bell metal; origin uncertain]

Bronze Age, 1 the prehistoric period after the Stone Age when bronze tools, weapons, and utensils were used. It lasted in different parts of Europe from about 3000 B.C. to about 1000 B.C. and was followed by the Iron Age. **2** Also, **bronze age.** (in classical mythology) the age of Neptune, following the gold and silver ages of Saturn and Jupiter and characterized by violence and warfare.

bronze copper, an American butterfly, the male of which has wings of a coppery brown spotted with black and the female, wings of orange-red with black spots.

bronzed grackle (bronzd), a grackle of Canada and the Mississippi Valley, with black plumage, which on the male is tinted with purple and blue-green around the neck and bronze on the back.

bronze diabetes, = hemochromatosis.

bronze disease, a green, powdery layer of corrosion appearing on bronze artifacts after they are excavated in desert areas and exposed to air and moisture.

bronz|en (bron′zən), *adj.* **1** made of bronze: *a bronzen statue.* **2** resembling bronze: *furniture with bronzen finish.*

bronz|er (bron′zər), *n.* a cream or lotion used to give a bronze or tan color to the skin.

bronze|smith (bronz′smith′), *n.* a man who works with bronze.

Bronze Star, a U.S. military decoration created in 1944, awarded for valor.

Bronze turkey, the largest turkey among the American domestic varieties, weighing up to 50 pounds. Its feathers are dull black, glossed with red and green on the front and bronze in the rear.

bronz|ite (bron′zīt), *n.* a mineral consisting of a ferriferous silicate of magnesium, which is often characterized by a bronzy luster. *Formula:* $(MgFe)SiO_3$

bronz|y (bron′zē), *adj.* **1** tinged with bronze color: *A bronzy cotton with an Oriental print* ... (New Yorker). **2** resembling bronze. **—bronz′i|ness,** *n.*

broo (brü), *n. Scottish.* pot liquor or broth; juice; bree. [perhaps < Old French *breu, brou*]

brooch (brōch, brüch), *n.* an ornamental pin having the point fastened by a catch; broach. Brooches are often made of gold, silver, or with jewels. Originally brooches were worn as a fastening for clothing. [variant of *broach*]

brood (brüd), *n., v., adj.* **—*n.* 1** the young birds hatched at one time in the nest or cared for together: *a brood of chicks.* SYN: hatch. **2** young animals or humans who share the same mother or are cared for by the same person: *That mother and father have a brood of twelve children.* **3** a kind, type, or breed (of animals or things): *a brood of thieves.*
—*v.i.* 1 to sit on eggs in order to hatch them; incubate. Hens and birds brood till the young are hatched. **2** to cover or protect with or as if with the wings. **3** to worry a long time about some one thing: *The boy brooded about his lost dog. Just as theologians worry about the nature of God and physicists worry about the nature of matter, historians brood about the study of man's past* (New York Times). SYN: meditate, ponder.
—*v.t.* 1 to sit on in order to hatch: *Hens and birds brood their eggs till the young hatch out.* SYN: incubate. **2** to dwell on in thought: *For years he brooded vengeance.* **3** *Figurative.* to produce from the mind; evolve by contemplation: ... *to brood those flashes of expression that transcend rhetoric* (Lowell). **4** to protect and cherish, as a bird her young.
—*adj.* kept for breeding.
brood on (or **over**), **a** to keep thinking about: *She brooded over her grievances.* **b** *Figurative.* to hover over; hang close over: *Mists and storms brood over it* (Macaulay).
[Old English *brōd*]

brood|er (brü′dər), *n.* **1** a closed place that can be heated, used especially in raising chicks and other fowl. **2** a person who broods. **3** a hen hatching or ready to hatch eggs.

brood|ing (brü′ding), *adj.* **1** hovering closely around, as a bird over her brood: *lost in a brooding cloud of fog* (Charles Kingsley). **2** dwelling moodily upon a subject of thought. **—brood′ing-ly,** *adv.*

brood mare, a mare kept for breeding.

brood nest, a round area in the center of a bees' nest consisting of cells containing eggs and developing bees. The bees store pollen in cells above and on the sides of the brood nest.

brood|y (brü′dē), *adj.,* **brood|i|er, brood|i|est. 1** brooding: *a broody hen.* **2** inclined to brood as a hen does; moody: *a broody disposition.*
—brood′i|ness, *n.*

brook[1] (brůk), *n.* a small stream. A brook is a natural waterway smaller than a river. SYN: creek, rivulet. [Old English *brōc*]

brook[2] (brůk), *v.t.* to put up with; endure; tolerate: *He will not brook any more of your insults. He can brook nothing that even faintly resembles an opposition* (Wall Street Journal). SYN: abide, suffer. [Old English *brūcan* use]

brook|ite (brůk′īt), *n.* a mineral, titanium oxide, having the same composition as rutile but found in orthorhombic crystals of a brown or yellow color to black. *Formula:* TiO_2 [< H. J. *Brooke,* 1771-1857, an English mineralogist + English *-ite*[1]]

brook lamprey, a freshwater lamprey living in brooks.

brook|let (brůk′lit), *n.* a little brook; streamlet.

brook|lime (brůk′līm′), *n.* **1** a European and Asian plant of the figwort family with small, racemose flowers, growing on the edges of brooks. **2** a related plant of America. **3** = water cress. [Middle English *brok-lemok* < *broc* brook + *lemok,* Old English *hleamoc* the plant's name]

Brook|lyn (brůk′lin), *n. Bowling.* a strike made when a right-handed bowler's ball hits on the left side of the head pin, or when a left-handed bowler's ball hits on the right side of the head pin.

Brook|lyn|ese (brůk′lə nēz′, -nēs′; brůk′lə nēz′, -nēs′), *n.* a type of English pronunciation heard in New York City, especially in the borough of Brooklyn: *The word "adjournment" was misspelled, appearing as "adjoinment." The stockholder quipped: "What's that? Brooklynese?"* (Wall Street Journal).

Brook|lyn|ite (brůk′lə nīt), *n.* a person born or living in Brooklyn, New York.

brook stickleback, a stickleback found in fresh waters from New York to Kansas.

brook trout, 1 a freshwater, speckled game fish

of the eastern part of North America; speckled trout. **2** a north European freshwater trout; the brown trout.

brook|weed (bru̇k′wēd′), *n.* a North American herb of the primrose family, growing in damp places and having small, white flowers; the water pimpernel.

brook|y (bru̇k′ē), *adj.* having many brooks.

broom (brüm, bru̇m), *n., v.* —*n.* **1** a brush with a long handle for sweeping, originally made from twigs of broom: *We swept the broken glass into a pile with a broom.* **2** a bush with slender branches, small leaves, and yellow flowers. It belongs to the pea family. —*v.t.* to sweep with a broom. [Old English *brōm* the plant]

broom|corn (brüm′kôrn′, bru̇m′-), *n.* a tall plant resembling corn, with seed clusters growing on long, stiff stems used for making brooms. Broomcorn is a kind of sorghum.

broomcorn millet, = millet (def. 1).

broom|rape (brüm′rāp′, bru̇m′-), *n.* any one of various parasitic, leafless herbs which live on the roots of broom, furze, clover, and the like. [partial translation of Medieval Latin *rapum genistae* knob or excrescence of broom]

broom|stick (brüm′stik′, bru̇m′-), *n.* the long handle of a broom: *He used a broomstick to push up the window.*

broom|y (brü′mē), *adj.* **1** covered with or abounding in broom. **2** of a broom or besom. **3** like broom or a broom.

bros. or **Bros.**, brothers.

brose (brōz), *n. Scottish.* a dish made by pouring boiling water, broth, milk, or other liquid on oatmeal or sometimes on pease meal. [variant of *browis* broth]

broth (brôth, broth), *n.* **1** a thin soup made from water in which meat, fish, or vegetables have been boiled or simmered: *a bowl of steaming broth.* **2** a medium in which cultures of bacteria are grown. **3** *Irish Dialect.* a fine or outstanding example: *a broth of a boyo* (Newsweek). [Old English *broth*]

broth|el (broth′əl, broŦH′-; brôth′-, brôŦH′-), *n.* a house of prostitution. [Middle English *brothel* abandoned person < Old English *brēothan* go to ruin]

broth|er (bruŦH′ər), *n., pl.* **broth|ers** or (*Archaic*) **breth|ren,** *adj., v.* —*n.* **1a** the son of the same parents. A boy is a brother to the other children of his parents. *He is in a family of four brothers.* **b** the son only of the same mother or father; half brother. **c** a son of one's stepfather or stepmother by a former marriage; stepbrother. **2a** a close friend, companion, or countryman: *my brother Jonathan* (II Samuel 1:26). *We few, we happy few, we band of brothers* (Shakespeare). **b** *U.S.* a soul brother, such as a fellow Negro or one closely identified with Negro interests. **c** a fellowman: *Am I not a man and a brother?* (Josiah Wedgwood). **d** (in the Bible) a kinsman. **3** a male member of the same church, union, or club: *The church party was given by the brothers in the men's club.* **4a** a male member of a religious order who is not a priest: *a lay brother.* **b** a man belonging to a religious order which does not have priests. **5a** a novice preparing for the priesthood. **b** a friar. **6** a member of any of certain Christian sects calling themselves "Brethren." *Abbr:* bro.

—*adj.* being in or of the same profession or calling: *brother officers.*

—*v.t.* to treat or address as brother.

[Old English *brōthor*]

▶ The plural **brethren** is now archaic except in the names of several Protestant denominations, such as the Plymouth Brethren, and to designate fellow members of a church or fraternal organization.

broth|er|hood (bruŦH′ər hu̇d), *n.* **1** the bond between brothers; feeling of brother for brother: *Soldiers who are fighting together often have a strong feeling of brotherhood.* **2a** an association of men with some common aim, characteristic, belief, or profession: *The brotherhood had sent word to its members several days ago to begin the strike at 6* A.M. (New York Times). **b** the members of such an association; persons joined as brothers. **3** the members of certain religious orders collectively.

broth|er-in-law (bruŦH′ər in lô′), *n., pl.* **brothers-in-law.** **1** the brother of one's husband or wife: *She asked her brother-in-law if he could come for his brother's birthday.* **2** the husband of one's sister: *He called his sister to see when his brother-in-law was going fishing.* See picture under **family tree**. **3** the husband of the sister of one's wife or husband.

Brother Jonathan, 1 a nickname, originally applied in derision by British soldiers in the 1700's to an American patriot. **2** the American nation as a whole. **3** a native or inhabitant of the United States.

broth|er|less (bruŦH′ər lis), *adj.* without a brother: *War left her brotherless.*

broth|er|like (bruŦH′ər līk′), *adj.* like a brother.

broth|er|li|ness (bruŦH′ər lē nis), *n.* brotherly affection or sympathy.

broth|er|ly (bruŦH′ər lē), *adj., adv.* —*adj.* **1** of a brother: *brotherly affection. It is a brotherly trait to tease little sisters.* SYN: fraternal. **2** like a brother's; friendly; kindly; affectionate: *brotherly care. The older boy gave the newcomer some brotherly advice.* SYN: fraternal. —*adv.* like a brother.

brougham (brüm; brü′əm, brō′-), *n.* a closed carriage or automobile having an outside seat for the driver. [< Lord *Brougham,* 1778-1868, a British statesman]

brought (brôt), *v.* past tense and past participle of **bring**: *He brought his lunch yesterday. She was brought to school in a car.*

brou|ha|ha (brü′hä hä), *n.* a confused uproar; hullabaloo: *What a buzz there was, what a brouhaha in faculty common rooms* (Saturday Review). [< French (informal) *brouhaha*]

brow (brou), *n.* **1** the part of the face above the eyes; forehead: *a wrinkled brow.* **2** the arch of hair over the eye; eyebrow: *He drew his heavy black brows together in a frown.* **3** the ridge above the eye, on which the eyebrow grows. **4** the edge of a steep place; top of a slope: *His house is on the brow of a hill.* **5** *Poetic.* the seat of the facial expressions, such as joy, sorrow, shame, anxiety, or resolution: *an anxious brow.* **6** *Figurative.* fronting aspect; countenance: *... in his early youth [he had] resisted the brow of military and civil tyranny* (Scott). [earlier meaning was "eyelid"; Old English *brū* eyelash]

brow antler or **tyne,** the first branch or tine of an antler, overhanging the forehead.

brow|beat (brou′bēt′), *v.t.,* **-beat, -beat|en** or **-beat, -beat|ing.** to frighten into doing something by overbearing looks or threats; bully: *Today's browbeaten youngster, in short, may become tomorrow's tyrant in the home* (Newsweek). SYN: intimidate, domineer. —**brow′beat′er,** *n.*

-browed, *combining form.* having a ___brow or brows: *Black-browed = having black brows.*

brown (broun), *n., adj., v.* —*n.* **1** a color like that of toast, potato skins, walnut shells, or coffee; a dark or dusky color, inclining to red or yellow. **2** a pigment or dye having this color. **3** brown cloth or clothing. **4** *British Slang.* a copper penny or halfpenny.

—*adj.* **1** having a color like that of toast, potato skins, walnut shells, or coffee: *Many people have brown hair.* **2** dark-skinned; tanned: *a brown beauty.* **3** of the color brown: *then to the spicy nut-brown ale* (Milton). **4** of or denoting the Malay race. **5** *Figurative.* gloomy; serious.

—*v.t., v.i.* to make or become brown: *Sunbathing browned us. The dahlias browned overnight in the first frost. The cook browned the onions in hot butter.*

brown out, to dim or partially extinguish lights, especially in a city, to conserve power or fuel or to reduce danger of aerial attack: *During the power shortage, the government ordered the electric companies to brown out every night after 10* P.M.

do brown, *Archaic.* to cheat; deceive: *'He goes in rayther raw, Sammy', said Mr. Weller ... 'and he'll come out done so exceedin' brown ...'* (Dickens).

do up brown, *U.S. Informal.* to carry out to the last detail; do perfectly: *The party was done up brown.*

[Old English *brūn*] —**brown′ness,** *n.*

brown algae, a class of multicellular marine algae, generally dark brown to olive green as a result of the presence of a brown pigment as well as chlorophyll. The kelps and gulfweeds are brown algae.

brown bagging, *U.S.* the practice of carrying one's own alcoholic liquor into a restaurant, club, or social function, especially in states where the sale of liquor in public establishments is prohibited. [because such bottled liquor was usually carried in brown paper bags] —**brown bagger.**

brown bat, a common species of bats in the United States, having a brownish color.

brown bear, 1 any bear having brown fur that lives in northern Europe and Asia, and North America, especially Alaska. **2** a variety of the common black bear having brown fur.

brown belt, 1 a rank in judo or karate below the black belt. **2** a person who has attained this rank. **3** the brown sash worn by such a person.

Brown Bess, *Informal.* a flintlock, smoothbore musket used by the British Army throughout the 1700's.

brown betty or **Betty,** a baked pudding made of apples, sugar, and breadcrumbs.

brown body, an intestinal structure in bryozoans believed to function as an excretory organ.

brown bread, 1 a dark, steamed bread containing molasses; Boston brown bread. **2** a bread made of dark flour, such as graham bread or rye bread.

brown bullhead, a dark-brown catfish found from North Dakota to New England and south to Florida.

brown coal, dark-brown coal, often having a woody texture; lignite.

brown creeper, 1 a small creeping shrub of North America that attaches itself to tree trunks and grows up on them. **2** a small, brown-and-white bird of North America with a slender, curved bill and stiffened tail feathers. It is usually seen working its way up the trunks of trees in a spiral path, in search of insects.

browned-off (bround′ôf′, -of′), *adj. Slang.* fed up; exasperated: *Fellow was telling me that he was browned-off with radio serials* (Cape Times).

brown|ette (brou net′), *n.* a brown-haired woman. [< *brown* + *-ette;* patterned after *brunette*]

brown-eyed Su|san (broun′īd′ sü′zən), a composite plant having flowers with a dark center and trilobate leaves. It is a kind of coneflower, like the black-eyed Susan.

brown fat, a tissue containing deposits of fat whose oxidation is a major source of heat in man and animals.

brown-head|ed nuthatch (broun′hed′id), a nuthatch of the southern United States, with bluish-gray upper parts and grayish-white under parts.

brown hyena, a blackish-gray hyena of southern Africa. Its fur is remarkably long and shaggy.

Brown|i|an (brou′nē ən), *adj.* having to do with any person bearing the name of Brown; Brunonian.

Brownian movement or **motion,** *Physics.* a constant, random, irregular motion often observed in very minute particles suspended in a liquid or gas, caused by the impact of surrounding molecules. [< Dr. Robert *Brown,* 1773-1858, a Scottish botanist, who first described it]

brown|ie (brou′nē), *n.* **1** a good-natured elf or fairy, especially one supposed to help secretly at night. **2** a small, flat, sweet chocolate cake, often containing nuts.

Brown|ie (brou′nē), *n.* a member of the youngest age group in the Girl Scouts or Girl Guides.

Brownie point, 1 a point earned by a Brownie for merit or achievement. **2** *Figurative.* credit earned for good behavior: *He'll do well; he wants high Brownie points* (David Boroff).

brown|ing (brou′ning), *n.* a preparation, as of sugar, wine, or spices, for coloring sauces, baking, etc.

Browning automatic rifle, an air-cooled, gas-operated rifle, both automatic and semiautomatic, which loads and fires from a magazine at a maximum rate of 200 to 350 rounds per minute. [< John M. *Browning,* 1855-1926, an American inventor]

Brown|ing|esque (brou′ning esk′), *adj.* of or characteristic of the English poet Robert Browning (1812-1889) or his style: *... Browningesque turns of narrative* (Punch).

brown|ish (brou′nish), *adj.* **1** somewhat brown. **2** tending toward brown.

Brown|ism (brou′niz əm), *n.* an ecclesiastical system and doctrine that formulated the principles of Congregationalism. [< Robert *Browne,* 1550?-1633?, an English Puritan + *-ism*] —**Brown′ist,** *n.*

brown lung, = byssinosis.

brown|out (broun′out′), *n.* a dimming or partial extinguishing of lights, especially in a city, to conserve power or fuel or to reduce danger of aerial attack.

brown patch, a fungus disease that occurs in lawns under conditions of high temperature and humidity.

Brown Power, a slogan used by Mexican Americans, modeled on the term Black Power.

brown race, brown-skinned peoples who live mainly in Polynesia and the Malay Archipelago (a nonscientific grouping).

brown rat, a common rat, having coarse, brown fur, found on ships, in houses, and in buildings virtually everywhere in the world; Norway rat.

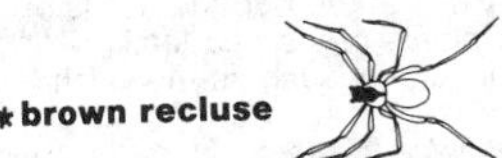

***brown recluse**

***brown recluse,** a small, brown, poisonous spider with a violin-shaped mark on its back.

Pronunciation Key: **h**a**t**, **ā**ge, **c**ã**re**, **f**ä**r**; **l**e**t**, **ē**qual, **t**ė**rm**; **i**t, **ī**ce; **h**o**t**, **ō**pen, **ô**rder; **oil**, **out**; **c**u**p**, **p**u̇**t**, **r**ü**le**; **ch**ild; lo**ng**; **th**in; **ŦH**en; **zh**, measure; **ə** represents **a** in about, **e** in taken, **i** in pencil, **o** in lemon, **u** in circus.

brown rice, rice that is not polished.
brown rot, a disease, especially of apples, peaches, plums, and cherries, in which the fruit becomes soft and brown and a moldlike growth develops, caused by a fungus.
brown shirt, **1** a member of the group of storm troopers that was organized by Adolf Hitler in 1923 and reorganized as a national militia in 1934. **2** any supporter of Hitler; Nazi. [translation of German *Braunhemd* < *braun* brown + *Hemd* shirt]
brown spot, a fungous disease of lawns, in which the leaves and stems of plants develop brownish discolorations, especially under hot and humid conditions.
brown|stone (broun′stōn′), *n.* **1** a reddish-brown sandstone used as a building material. **2** a building, especially a two- or three-story house, with exterior walls built of this sandstone.
brownstone front, **1** a house front made of brownstone. **2** a house with such a front: *Dulcie went up to her room—the third floor back in a West Side brownstone front* (O. Henry).
brown study, a condition of being absorbed in thought; serious reverie.
brown sugar, a sugar that is not refined or only partly refined.
Brown Swiss, any one of a sturdy breed of dairy cattle that originated in Switzerland.
brown-tail moth, or **brown|tail** (broun′tāl′), *n.* a European tussock moth, introduced into eastern North America, whose larvae are very destructive to deciduous trees. It has white wings and, in the female, a brown-tipped abdomen.
brown thrasher, a songbird of eastern North America, with reddish-brown head and back and a white breast speckled with black. It looks somewhat like a thrush, but is closely related to the mockingbird, and sings like it.
brown thrush, = brown thrasher.
brown trout, the common trout of European streams and rivers, also introduced into the United States.
brown widow, a poisonous spider found in Florida that is closely related to the black widow.
brown wren, = house wren.
brown|y (brou′nē), *adj.*, **brown|i|er, brown|i|est.** inclining to brown; brownish.
brow|ridge (brou′rij′), *n.* the supraorbital ridge that overhangs the eye in the skulls of certain apes and hominoids: *the large browridges of the Neanderthal man's skullcap.*
browse (brouz), *v.*, **browsed, brows|ing**, *n.* —*v.i.* **1** to feed on grass or leaves by nibbling and eating here and there; graze: *The sheep browsed in the meadow.* SYN: nibble, crop. **2** *Figurative.* **a** to read here and there in a book or in books: *He browsed reading snatches in a book of poems.* **b** to pass the time looking at books in a library or bookstore: *He spent the afternoon browsing in the bookstores. The lending library is starting off with sixty thousand shiny new volumes, all on open shelves, among which one may browse at will* (New Yorker).
—*v.t.* to feed on (grass, twigs, or leaves); graze.
—*n.* **1** the tender shoots of trees and shrubs; green food for cattle and other livestock: *Certain woody bushes and low trees are being planted to hold the soil and furnish browse for livestock* (Scientific American). **2** the act of browsing.
[< Middle French *brouster* < Old French *brost* bud < Germanic (compare Old Saxon *brustian* to sprout)] —**brows′er**, *n.*
bru|cel|la (brü sel′ə), *n., pl.* **-cel|lae** (-sel′ē), **-cel|las.** any one of the bacteria that cause brucellosis. [< New Latin *Brucella* the genus name; see etym. under **brucellosis**]
bru|cel|lo|sis (brü′sə lō′sis), *n.* a contagious disease affecting cattle, goats, swine, and, to a lesser extent, other animals and man, caused by bacteria, usually infecting the reproductive organs and leading to abortion and sterility; Bang's disease. In persons, it is usually called *undulant fever.* [< New Latin *Brucella* a genus of bacteria (< Sir David *Bruce*, 1855-1931, an Australian pathologist and surgeon) + English *-osis*]
bru|chid (brü′kəd), *adj., n.* —*adj.* of or belonging to a group of weevils that feed on the seeds of vetches and other plants of the pea family.
—*n.* a weevil of this group, such as the vetch bruchid.
[< New Latin *Bruchidae* the family name < Latin *brūchus* a wingless locust < Greek *brouchos*]
bru|cin (brü′sin), *n.* = brucine.
bru|cine (brü′sēn, -sin), *n.* a poisonous alkaloid obtained, with strychnine, from the seeds of the nux vomica and other closely related trees. *Formula:* $C_{23}H_{26}N_2O_4$[< James *Bruce*, 1730-1794, a Scottish explorer + *-ine*[2]]
bru|cite (brü′sīt), *n.* hydrated oxide of magnesia, a source of magnesium, occurring naturally in parts of Quebec, Ontario, and Nevada. *Formula:* $Mg(OH)_2$[< A. *Bruce*, 1777-1818, an American mineralogist + *-ite*[1]]
Brü|cke (brü′kə), *n.* a group of early (1904-1913) expressionist artists in Germany who used thick, pure colors and enclosed them with heavy outlines. [< German *Die Brücke* The Bridge]
Bruck|ne|ri|an (brůk nir′ē ən), *adj.* of or having to do with the Austrian composer Anton Bruckner (1824-1896), his symphonies, or his musical style.
bru|in (brü′ən), *n.* = bear[1] (def. 1). [< Middle Dutch *bruin* brown]
Bru|in (brü′ən), *n.* a name for the bear, originally in the medieval epic of "Reynard the Fox."
bruise (brüz), *n., v.*, **bruised, bruis|ing.** —*n.* **1a** an injury to the body, caused by a fall or blow, that breaks blood vessels without breaking the skin; contusion: *The bruise on my arm turned black and blue.* **b** an injury to the outside of a fruit, vegetable, or plant: *The pear had bruises of ugly dark spots.* **c** *Figurative.* a hurt to the feelings. **2** a dent. [< verb]
—*v.t.* **1a** to injure the outside of: *Though not cut, his knees were bruised when he fell. Rough handling bruised the apples before they could be sold.* **b** *Figurative: Harsh words bruised her feelings.* SYN: injure, hurt. **2** to pound or crush (drugs or food); grind; pulverize: *Oats are bruised for horses.* —*v.i.* to become bruised: *Her flesh bruises easily.*
[fusion of Old English *brȳsan* crush and Middle English *brisen* < Old French *bruisier* break]
bruis|er (brü′zər), *n. Informal.* **1** a prizefighter or boxer. **2a** a bully. **b** a very muscular person: *young jut-jawed bruisers wearing leather coats* (New Yorker).
bruit (brüt), *v., n.* —*v.t.* **1** to spread a report or rumor of: *News of the girl's engagement was bruited about.* **2** to spread the fame of. [< noun]
—*n.* **1** *Archaic.* report; rumor. **2** *Archaic.* noise or din. **3** *Obsolete.* fame.
[< Old French *bruit* < *bruire* roar < Gallo-Romance *brūgere* < *bragare* bray[1] and Latin *rūgīre* roar]
bru|ja (brü′hä), *n., pl.* **-jas.** *Spanish.* a sorceress; witch.
bru|jo (brü′hō), *n., pl.* **-jos.** *Spanish.* a witch doctor; sorcerer.
Bru|maire (brʏ mer′), *n.* the second month (October 22 to November 20) in the calendar instituted in 1793 by the first French republic. [< French *Brumaire* < *brume* brume]
bru|mal (brü′məl), *adj.* wintry. [< Latin *brūmālis* < *brūma*; see etym. under **brume**]
brum|by (brum′bē), *n., pl.* **-bies.** *Australian Slang.* an unbroken horse.
brume (brüm), *n. Rare.* mist; fog: *drifting brume* (Longfellow). [< French *brume* < Latin *brūma* frost, winter < unrecorded form *brevima* (*diēs*) shortest (day) < *brevis* short]
brum|ma|gem (brum′ə jəm), *adj., n. Informal.* —*adj.* cheap and showy; tawdry.
—*n.* anything cheap and showy.
[local form of *Birmingham*, England]
Brum|mie or **Brum|my** (brum′ē), *n., pl.* **-mies**, *adj. British Informal.* —*n.* a native or inhabitant of Birmingham, England.
—*adj.* of or from Birmingham, England.
bru|mous (brü′məs), *adj. Rare.* **1** foggy. **2** brumal.
brunch (brunch), *n.* a meal taken late in the morning and intended to combine breakfast with lunch. [< *br*(eakfast) + (l)*unch*]
brune (brün), *n.* a dark-complexioned girl or woman; brunette. [< French *brune* (feminine) < *brun* brown]
Bru|nei|an (brü nī′ən, -nā-), *n.* a native or inhabitant of Brunei, a small country on the northern coast of Borneo.
bru|nette or **bru|net** (brü net′), *adj., n.* —*adj.* **1** dark-colored: *brunette hair.* **2** having dark-brown or black hair, brown or black eyes, and a dark skin: *a brunette actress.*
—*n.* a person having a dark skin, dark-brown or black hair, and brown or black eyes. A man with this complexion is a brunet; a woman is a brunette. *Many Spanish women are brunettes; many Swedish women are blondes.*
[< French *brunette* (feminine diminutive) < *brun* brown < Late Latin *brūnus* < Germanic (compare Old High German *brūn*)]
Brun|hild (brün′hild), *n. German Legend.* a legendary queen in the *Nibelungenlied*, the wife of King Gunther, for whom she is won by Siegfried. In the Old Norse legend she is a Valkyrie, won by Sigurd for Gunnar. Also, **Brynhild.**
Brun|hil|de strain (brün hil′də), one of the three known types of virus causing polio. The other two are the Lansing and Leon strains. [< *Brunhilde*, a chimpanzee tested with the virus]
bru|ni|zem (brü′nə zem, brü nə zyōm′), *n.* a grassland soil similar to chernozem. [probably irregularly formed < French *brun* brown + *-zem* (as in *chernozem*)]
Brünn|hil|de (brʏn hil′də), *n.* a Valkyrie, in Wagner's *Die Walküre*, cast into a magic sleep by Wotan, from which Siegfried awakens her. See also **Brunhild.**
Bru|no|ni|an (brü nō′nē ən), *adj.* having to do with some person or thing bearing the name of Brown, such as Brown University. [< Medieval Latin *Bruno, -onis* Brown (proper name)]
brunt (brunt), *n.* **1** the main force or violence; hardest part: *The island felt the brunt of the hurricane. The infantry bore the brunt of the battle.* **2** *Obsolete.* an assault; attack. [origin uncertain]
brush[1] (brush), *n., v.* —*n.* **1** a tool for cleaning, sweeping, or scrubbing, or for putting on paint. A brush is made of bristles, hair, or wires set in a stiff back or fastened to a handle. **2** a brushing; a rub with a brush: *He gave his puppy a good brush.* **3** a light touch in passing: *Give the desk a brush with the cloth.* **4** a short, brisk fight or quarrel: *The hunter had a sharp brush with an old bear and her cubs.* SYN: skirmish. **5** the bushy tail of an animal, especially of a fox: *The last we saw of the fox was his brush disappearing into his burrow.* **6a** a piece of carbon or copper used to connect the electricity from the revolving part of an electric motor or generator to the outside circuit. See picture under **generator.** **b** = brush discharge. **7** the art or skill of an artist. **8** *Figurative.* a mild reproof: *I have given them a brush through Colonel Pater* (Duke of Wellington).
—*v.t.* **1** to clean, sweep, scrub, or paint with a brush; use a brush on: *She brushed her hair until it was shiny.* **2** to wipe away; remove: *The child brushed the tears from his eyes.* **3** to touch lightly in passing: *No harm was done—your bumper just brushed our fender.*
—*v.i.* **1** to move quickly. **2** to touch (against) something lightly, as if with a brush: *A man brushed against him in the crowded lobby.*
brush aside (or **away**), to put aside; refuse to consider: *The captain of the ship brushed aside warnings of a hurricane and kept on.*
brush off, *Informal.* **a** to refuse to see or listen to (someone): *The mayor hurried into his office, brushing off the reporters.* **b** to dismiss as unimportant; make light of: *The mayor brushed off the reporter's question with a joke.*
brush up on (or **up**), *Figurative.* to refresh one's knowledge of; review: *He brushed up on fractions before taking the arithmetic test.*
[< Old French *broisse* < Vulgar Latin *bruscia* bunch of new shoots < Latin *bruscum* excrescence on a maple] —**brush′er**, *n.* —**brush′like′**, *adj.*
brush[2] (brush), *n.* **1** *U.S.* branches broken or cut off; brushwood: *After the storm the lawn was littered with brush.* **2** shrubs, bushes, and small trees growing thickly in the woods; brushwood: *They found the snake where it had crawled off into the brush.* **3** *U.S.* thinly settled country; backwoods. [< Old French *brosse*]
brush cut, a short haircut for men and boys, resembling the bristles of a hairbrush.
brush discharge, a brush-shaped, visible discharge around a wire carrying a current of high potential; corona.
brushed (brusht), *adj.* having a nap; napped: *brushed rayon, brushed cotton.*
brush|fire war (brush′fīr′), a war confined to a small area or occurring on a small scale; limited war.
brush-foot|ed butterfly (brush′fůt′id), any one of various butterflies in which the front legs are much reduced; nymphalid.
brush|off (brush′ôf′, -of′), *n. Informal.* a refusal to see or listen; an abrupt dismissal or rebuke: *The reporter got a polite brushoff when he asked the mayor for an appointment. His girl friend is giving him the brushoff.*
brush|stroke (brush′strōk′), *n.* **1** a movement of the brush when applying paint. **2** the method of using brushstrokes in painting.
brush-tongued (brush′tungd′), *adj.* having the tongue set with long papillae, as certain parrots.
brush turkey, **1** a large fowl of eastern Australia. **2** any one of various related birds of New Guinea.
brush|up (brush′up′), *n.* **1** the act of refreshing memory or reviewing something learned, studied, etc.: *As far as I've been able to gather from a hasty brushup on the subject, the Koreans have no ethnological ties with the Chinese* (New Yorker). **2** a smartening or sprucing up: *A matching skirt is packed away until that before-dinner brushup* (New York Times).
brush war, = brushfire war.
brush wheel, **1** a toothless wheel formerly used to turn a similar wheel by means of bristles, cloth, or the like, attached to the circumference. **2** a circular rotary brush used for polishing or cleaning.
brush|wood (brush′wůd′), *n.* = brush[2] (defs. 1 and 2).
brush|work (brush′wėrk′), *n.* **1** an artist's char-

acteristic manner of using a brush in his paintings. **2** a painting done with a brush.

brush|y[1] (brush′ē), *adj.,* **brush|i|er, brush|i|est.** like a brush; rough and shaggy. [< *brush*[1] + *-y*[1]]

brush|y[2] (brush′ē), *adj.,* **brush|i|er, brush|i|est.** covered with bushes, shrubs, or the like. [< *brush*[2] + *-y*[1]]

brusk (brusk), *adj.* = brusque.

brusque (brusk), *adj.* abrupt in manner or speech; blunt: *He was brusque in saying "I don't like it" when he could have said "No, thank you."* SYN: curt, bluff. [< French *brusque* < Italian *brusco* coarse < Late Latin *brūscus,* blend of Latin *ruscum* butcher's broom and Gaulish *brūcos* heather] —**brusque′ly,** *adv.* —**brusque′ness,** *n.*

brus|que|rie (brʏs kə rē′), *n. French.* abruptness; brusqueness.

Brus|sels carpet (brus′əlz), machine-made carpet with a pattern of small loops of yarn having various colors. [< *Brussels,* a city in Belgium]

Brussels griffon, = griffon[2] (def. 1).

Brussels lace, a heavy lace with a very elaborate design.

Brussels sprouts, 1 a plant having many small heads growing along a stalk. It belongs to the mustard family. **2** its heads, which are eaten as a vegetable.

brut (brʏt), *adj. French.* **1** (of wines, especially champagne) not sweet; very dry. **2** (of a gem) roughly shaped but not polished. **3** (literally) rough.

bru|tal (brü′təl), *adj.* **1** like a brute; savagely cruel: *a brutal remark, a brutal attack. The Vikings were brutal in battle.* SYN: inhuman, bestial. See syn. under **cruel. 2** rude and coarse; unrefined. **3** sensual. —**bru′tal|ly,** *adv.*

bru|tal|ism (brü′tə liz əm), *n.* a style of architecture using plain, massive, structural components, usually of concrete. —**bru′tal|ist,** *n., adj.*

bru|tal|i|tar|i|an (brü tal′ə târ′ē ən), *n.* a person who practices or advocates brutality.

bru|tal|i|tar|i|an|ism (brü tal′ə târ′ē ə niz′əm), *n.* the actions and ideas of brutalitarians.

bru|tal|i|ty (brü tal′ə tē), *n., pl.* **-ties. 1** brutal conduct; cruelty; savageness: *The brutality of the punishment shocked the onlookers.* **2** a brutal act: *The punishment was a brutality greater than the crime.* **3** coarse behavior; sensuality.

bru|tal|ize (brü′tə līz), *v.,* **-ized, -iz|ing.** —*v.t.* **1** to make brutal: *War brutalizes many men.* **2** to treat in a brutal or cruel manner.
—*v.i.* to become brutal. —**bru′tal|i|za′tion,** *n.*

brute (brüt), *n., adj.* —*n.* **1** an animal without power to reason: *The ox is a brute but good for hauling heavy loads.* SYN: See syn. under **animal. 2** a stupid, cruel, or coarse person: *The bully was a brute of a boy.* **3** man's animal nature: *Exalt the brute and sink the man* (Robert Burns). **4** *U.S. Dialect.* a bull.
—*adj.* **1** without power to reason: *The very brute animals were charmed to silence* (Washington Irving). **2** of or characteristic of animals as distinguished from man; dull; stupid. **3** cruel or coarse: *The ruffians' brute manners and loud laughter embarrassed everyone in the restaurant.* **4** sensual. **5** unconscious; without feeling: *Man has struggled long against the brute forces of nature.*
[< Old French *brut,* learned borrowing from Latin *brūtus* heavy, dull]

brute|hood (brüt′hu̇d), *n.* the character or condition of a brute.

bru|ti|fy (brü′tə fī), *v.,* **-fied, -fy|ing.** —*v.t.* to make brutish. —*v.i.* to become brutish.

brut|ing (brü′ting), *n.* the process of cutting or shaping diamonds by rubbing one against another. [< *brut* + *-ing*[1]]

brut|ish (brü′tish), *adj.* **1** like a brute; stupid, cruel, or coarse: *The life of [primitive] man is nasty, brutish and short* (Thomas Hobbes). **2** lacking restraint; sensual. —**brut′ish|ly,** *adv.* —**brut′ish|ness,** *n.*

brut|ism (brü′tiz əm), *n.* the condition or behavior of a brute.

brux|ism (bruk′siz əm), *n.* habitual grinding of teeth, especially during sleep: *Bruxism may be the cause of periodontal (gum) disease* (Science News Letter). [< Greek *brýchein* gnash teeth + English *-ism*]

Bryn|hild (brin′hild, brʏn′-), *n. Norse Legend.* the daughter of Odin and one of the Valkyries. See also **Brunhild, Brünnhilde.**

bry|o|log|i|cal (brī′ə loj′ə kəl), *adj.* of or having to do with bryology.

bry|ol|o|gist (brī ol′ə jist), *n.* a person who studies bryology.

bry|ol|o|gy (brī ol′ə jē), *n.* the branch of botany that deals with mosses and liverworts. [< Greek *brýon* tree moss + English *-logy*]

bry|o|ni|a (brī ō′nē ə), *n. Pharmacy.* the root of a species of bryony, a drastic cathartic. [< Latin *bryōnia* bryony]

bry|o|ny (brī′ə nē), *n., pl.* **-nies.** a climbing plant of the gourd family, having small, greenish flowers and red, white, or black berries. The roots of some kinds are used in medicine. [< Latin *bryōnia* < Greek *bryōniā* < *brýein* swell]

bry|o|phyte (brī′ə fīt), *n.* any one of a division of nonflowering plants comprising the true mosses and liverworts. [< New Latin *Bryophyta* < Greek *brýon* tree moss + *phytón* plant < *phýein* grow]

bry|o|phyt|ic (brī′ə fit′ik), *adj.* of or having to do with the bryophytes.

bry|o|zo|an (brī′ə zō′ən), *n., adj.* —*n.* any one of a phylum of minute, mosslike aquatic animals, chiefly saltwater, found mainly in permanent, attached colonies, each individual of which is formed by gemmation (budding) and has a distinct alimentary canal; a polyzoan.
—*adj.* of or belonging to the bryozoans.
[< New Latin *Bryozoa* the class name < Greek *brýon* tree moss + *zôion* animal]

bry|o|zo|on (brī′ə zō′on), *n., pl.* **-zo|a** (-zō′ə). a bryozoan or sea moss. [< Greek *brýon* tree moss + *zôion* animal]

Bryth|on (brith′ən), *n.* **1** a member of a large group of Celts who in ancient times occupied South Britain but were later confined to Wales, Cornwall, and ancient Cumbria. **2** *Obsolete.* a Briton of Wales, Cornwall, or ancient Cumbria. [< Welsh *Brython* < Old Celtic *Britton* a Briton]

Bry|thon|ic (bri thon′ik), *adj., n.* —*adj.* = Cymric.
—*n.* one of the two main divisions of Celtic languages (the other being Goidelic), including Welsh, Cornish, and Breton; Cymric.

b.s., 1 balance sheet. **2** bill of sale.

B.S., Bachelor of Science.

B.S.A., Boy Scouts of America.

B.Sc., Bachelor of Science (Latin, *Baccalaureus Scientiae*).

B scope, a radarscope that shows both the range and direction to an object.

B.S.Ed., Bachelor of Science in Education.

bskt., basket.

B.S.N., Bachelor of Science in Nursing.

BST (no periods) or **B.S.T.,** British Standard Time (introduced about 1968).

Bt. or **Bt** (no period), baronet.

B.T. or **B.Th.,** Bachelor of Theology (Latin, *Baccalaureus Theologiæ).*

B.Th.U., *British.* British thermal unit or units.

Btry., battery.

Btu (no periods), **B.t.u.,** or **B.T.U.,** British thermal unit or units.

bu., 1 bureau. **2** bushel or bushels.

bub (bub), *n.* a childish term for a brother, also used in familiar address to any boy or man. [compare German *Bube* boy]

bu|bal or **bu|bale** (byü′bəl), *n.* a large antelope, a hartebeest, of North Africa and Arabia. [< Latin *būbalus* < Greek *boúbalos* African antelope]

bu|ba|line (byü′bə līn, -lin), *adj.* **1** of or having to do with a genus of antelopes including the bubal, hartebeest, and blesbok. **2** of or like a buffalo.

bub|ble (bub′əl), *n., v.,* **-bled, -bling,** *adj.* —*n.* **1** a thin, round film of liquid enclosing air or gas. When water boils, it is full of bubbles, which come to the top and break. **2** a round space filled with air or gas in a liquid or solid. Sometimes there are bubbles in ice or glass. **3** a quantity of air or gas occluded within a liquid, such as the portion of air left in a spirit level. **4** any spherical or dome-shaped structure, usually transparent: *This area will be shielded by a plastic "bubble" for all-weather dining* (New York Times). **5a** the act or process of bubbling. **b** the sound of bubbling. **6** *Figurative.* a plan or idea that looks good, but soon goes to pieces: *the great South Sea bubble.* **7** *Figurative.* anything lacking firmness, permanence, substance, or reality: *Seeking the bubble reputation Even in the cannon's mouth* (Shakespeare). **8** a bubbletop. **9a** = magnetic bubble. **b** = bubble memory. [< verb]
—*v.i.* **1** to send up or rise in bubbles; have bubbles; make bubbles: *Water bubbled up between the stones.* SYN: effervesce. **2** to make sounds like water boiling; gurgle: *The baby bubbled and cooed.* **3** *Figurative.* to arise or issue like bubbles; overflow (with feeling): *to bubble with joy or laughter. His passion boiled and bubbled* (Thackeray). —*v.t.* **1a** to cause to bubble. **b** to burp (an infant). **2** *Figurative.* to overflow with (feeling): *He is a very cheerful and enthusiastic officer who bubbles energy and good will* (Manchester Guardian Weekly). **3** *Archaic.* to swindle.
—*adj.* unsubstantial; fragile; delusive.
bubble over, a to be very full; overflow: *The water bubbled over on the stove.* **b** to overflow with feeling: *Suzanne fairly bubbles over with high spirits* (London Times). **c** to be very enthusiastic: *The boys bubbled over at the idea of an overnight camping trip.*
[Middle English *bobelen*] —**bub′bling|ly,** *adv.*

bubble and squeak, a traditional English dish of meat and greens fried together, usually consisting of beef and cabbage. [< the sound of its cooking]

bubble bath, a bath covered with soap bubbles, made by adding a liquid or powdery soap preparation to water.

bubble car, = bubbletop car.

bubble chamber, a small vessel filled with a very hot liquid through which charged subatomic particles leave tracks of bubbles. In this way they can be examined and identified. Hydrogen or propane under pressure are the liquids most commonly used. *Occasionally while passing through a bubble chamber a gamma ray creates secondary electrons, which are evident as a string of bubbles* (Scientific American).

bubble gum, a chewing gum that can be blown out through the lips so as to form a large bubble.

bubble memory, a computer memory that has data stored in magnetic bubbles: *Bubble memories might someday achieve densities up to a billion bits per square inch.... If this density is achieved, bubble memories will probably replace most disks and drums and provide much faster access at a comparable cost* (John R. Rice).

bub|bler (bub′lər), *n.* a drinking fountain with a small nozzle from which water bubbles up.

bub|ble|top (bub′əl top′), *n.* **1** a transparent plastic top or canopy, often retractable, on an automobile or airplane; bubble. **2** = bubbletop car.

bubbletop car, an automobile with a bubbletop: *He stood and waved from the rear of his open bubbletop car along ... a winding 33-mile motorcade route* (Newsweek).

bub|bly (bub′lē), *adj.,* **-bli|er, -bli|est,** *n., pl.* **-blies.** —*adj.* **1** full of bubbles; effervescent: *bubbly champagne.* **2** like a bubble. **3** very lively; ebullient: *bubbly dance music.*
—*n. Slang.* champagne: *In some districts of London ... a wine merchant will stock little more than British wines among the beer and spirits, although one can usually find a bottle of 'bubbly' for festive occasions* (Listener).

bubbly jock, *Scottish.* a turkey.

bub|by (bub′ē), *n., pl.* **-bies.** *Informal.* = bub.

bu|bo (byü′bō), *n., pl.* **-boes.** an inflammatory swelling of a lymph gland, especially in the groin or armpits. [< Late Latin *būbō* < Greek *boubôn* swelling in the groin]

bu|bon|ic (byü bon′ik), *adj.* having or characterized by inflammatory swelling of the lymph glands.

bubonic plague, a very dangerous contagious disease, accompanied by high fever, chills, and swelling of the lymph glands. It is usually carried to human beings by fleas from rats or squirrels.

bu|bon|o|cele (byü bon′ə sēl), *n.* inguinal hernia, especially a partial one that extends only far enough to make a small swelling in the groin like a bubo. [< Greek *boubonokḗlē* < *boubôn* groin + *kḗlē* a rupture]

bu|bu (bü′bü), *n.* = boubou.

buc|cal (buk′əl), *adj.* **1** of the cheek. **2** of the sides of the mouth or the mouth. [< Latin *bucca* cheek, mouth + English *-al*[1]]

buc|ca|neer (buk′ə nir′), *n., v.* —*n.* a pirate, especially one who preyed upon Spanish vessels and colonies in the 1600's and 1700's: *... a buccaneer or pirate in the Spanish Main* (John Hill Burton).
—*v.i.* to act as a buccaneer; be a buccaneer: *Wealth, which it was whispered he had acquired by buccaneering* (Washington Irving).
[< French *boucanier* < *boucan* frame for curing meat, perhaps < Arawak (West Indies). The word was later used for French and English hunters, who preserved meat in this way; later on, the word was used for pirates of the same area.]

buc|ca|neer|ish (buk′ə nir′ish), *adj.* like a buccaneer: *From his black beard and buccaneerish sort of look, a sailor would suppose it to be Davy Jones* (Robert Southey).

buc|ci|na|tor (buk′sə nā′tər), *n.* a thin, flat muscle which forms the wall of the cheek, assisting in chewing and also in blowing wind instruments. [< Latin *buccinātor* trumpeter < *buccināre* blow the trumpet < *buccina* hunter's or herder's horn < Greek *bukánē* spiral trumpet]

buc|ci|na|to|ry (buk′sə nə tôr′ē, -tōr′-), *adj.* **1** of or having to do with a trumpeter or trumpeting. **2** of or having to do with a buccinator.

bu|cen|taur[1] (byü sen′tôr), *n.* the state barge in which on Ascension Day the doge of Venice went to wed the Adriatic by dropping a ring into it. [< Italian *bucentoro*]

bu|cen|taur[2] (byü sen′tôr), *n.* a legendary monster, half man and half bull. [< Greek *boûs* ox + *kéntauros* centaur]

Pronunciation Key: hat, āge, câre, fär; let, ēqual, tėrm; it, īce; hot, ōpen, ôrder; oil, out; cup, pu̇t, rüle; child; long; thin; ᴛʜen; zh, measure; ə represents **a** in about, **e** in taken, **i** in pencil, **o** in lemon, **u** in circus.

Bu|ceph|a|lus (byü sef′ə ləs), *n.* **1** the war horse of Alexander the Great. **2** *Humorous.* any riding horse.

Buch|man|ism (buk′mə niz əm), *n.* a religious movement founded in the 1920's that emphasizes a personal rededication to the moral principles of Christianity rather than adherence to the forms or doctrines of ecclesiastical religion; Moral Re-Armament; Oxford Group. [< Frank *Buchman,* 1878-1961, the founder]

Buch|man|ite (buk′mə nīt), *n.* an adherent of Buchmanism.

bu|chu (byü′kyü), *n.* the medicinal, aromatic leaves of several shrubby South African plants. [< a native name]

buck[1] (buk), *n., pl.* **bucks** or (*collectively*) **buck,** *adj.* **—*n.*** **1** a male deer, goat, hare, rabbit, antelope, or sheep (but not applied to a male elk, moose, or red deer). **2** a dashing young man; dandy: *the . . . young buck, driving his own equipage* (Washington Irving). SYN: fop. **3** *Informal.* a man. **4** = buckskin. **—*adj.*** male: *a buck rabbit.* [fusion of Old English *buc* male deer, and *bucca* male goat]

buck[2] (buk), *v., n.* **—*v.i.*** **1** (of horses or mules) to jump into the air with back curved and come down with the front legs stiff: *The cowboy's horse began to buck, but he managed to stay on.* **2** (of an automobile, motor, or other machinery) to run unevenly; jerk, as when the fuel supply is low or the motor is cold. **3a** *Informal, Figurative.* to resist or oppose: *It is useless to buck against fate.* **b** to butt. **4** *Informal.* to talk big; swagger; boast: *He bucks too much about his exploits.*
—*v.t.* **1** to throw or attempt to throw (a rider) by bucking: *The cowboy was bucked by the bronco.* **2a** *Informal, Figurative.* to fight against; resist stubbornly: *He bucked the merger, but to no avail.* **b** to push or hit with the head; butt. **c** to rush at; charge against; work against: *The swimmer bucked the current with strong strokes.* **3** *American Football.* to charge into (the opposing line) with the ball.
—*n.* **1** a throw or attempt to throw (a rider) by bucking. **2** *American Football.* a charge made into the opponent's line with the ball. **3** bragging.
buck for, *Informal.* to strive earnestly for: *I was bucking very strong for the job* (Benjamin I. Hayes).
buck up, *Informal.* **a** to cheer up; be brave or energetic: *Buck up; everything will be all right.* **b** to give fresh courage or energy to: *This has bucked her up something wonderful* (H. G. Wells).
[special use of *buck*[1], (that is, jump like a deer)]

buck[3] (buk), *n. U.S. Slang.* a dollar: *All you . . . do is fool around, when any other man would be trying to make a buck or two* (New Yorker). [origin uncertain]

***buck**[4] (buk), *n.* **1** a sawhorse; sawbuck. **2** *Gymnastics.* a leather-covered frame, usually adjustable in height, used in vaulting exercises. [American English, short for *sawbuck*]

***buck**[4]
definition 2

buck[5] (buk), *n. Poker.* an article placed in a jackpot and taken by the winner, serving to remind him that when the deal passes to him he must order another jackpot.
pass the buck, *Informal.* to shift the responsibility for something, such as blame or work, to someone else: *Congress passed the buck to the President, asked him to recommend specific spots for pruning* [*the budget*] (Newsweek).
[American English, reputedly < *buckhorn* handles of knives, used as counters]

buck[6] (buk), *n., v. Archaic or Dialect.* **—*n.*** **1** lye or suds in which cloth is steeped or boiled to clean and bleach it. **2** a quantity of clothes washed or bleached in lye or suds. [< verb]
—*v.t.* **1** to steep, boil, or wash in lye or suds. **2** to clean by beating in water; wash.
[Middle English *bouken.* Compare Low German *büken.*]

buck[7] (buk), *n. British Dialect.* the body of a cart or wagon. [perhaps Old English *būc* belly]

buck[8] (buk), *v.t.* to pulverize or break into small pieces, as ore. [perhaps < Middle Dutch and Middle Low German *boken* beat]

buck and wing, a rapid clog or tap dance, usually performed by one person.

buck|a|roo (buk′ə rü′, buk′ə rü′), *n., pl.* **-roos.** *U.S.* a cowboy. [American English; alteration of Spanish *vaquero* < *vaca* cow < Latin *vacca*]

buck|ay|ro (bu kãr′ō), *n., pl.* **-ros.** = buckaroo.

buck basket, a basket to carry a washing.

buck bean, a perennial bog herb of the gentian family having racemes of white or pink flowers. [apparently, translation of Flemish *bocksboonen* goat's beans]

buck|ber|ry (buk′ber′ē, -bər-), *n., pl.* **-ries.** a huckleberry of the southern United States, so called because deer feed on it.

***buck|board** (buk′bôrd′, -bōrd′), *n.* an open, four-wheeled carriage having the seat fastened to a platform of long, springy boards instead of a body and springs. [American English < *buck*[7] + *board*[1]]

***buckboard**

buck|een (bu kēn′), *n. Anglo-Irish.* a young man of the poorer gentry or aristocracy, having no profession, and aping the habits of the wealthy. [< *buck*[1] + *-een,* a diminutive suffix < Irish *-ín*]

buck|er (buk′ər), *n.* **1** a horse given to bucking. **2** a person who saws felled trees into logs.

buck|et (buk′it), *n., v.,* **-et|ed, -et|ing.** **—*n.*** **1** a pail made of wood, metal, or plastic. Buckets are used for carrying such things as water, milk, and coal. **2** the amount that a bucket can hold; bucketful: *We poured several buckets of water on the fire.* **3a** a scoop of a dredging machine. **b** one of the scoops or receptacles on an endless-belt conveyor or a water wheel. **c** one of the blades on the rotor of a gas or steam turbine. **d** a cupped vane of a water wheel. **4** the piston of an ordinary simple pump. **5** a leather receptacle for a whip, carbine, or lance: *I put the whip in the bucket and drove steadily on* (George Whyte-Melville). **6** *Slang.* a ship, car, or other conveyance, especially one that is old and slow.
—*v.i.* **1** *Informal.* **a** to move fast: *The old flivver bucketed along at about sixty.* **b** to move jerkily and irregularly. **c** to drive forward hurriedly. **2** to swing the body forward too hurriedly before taking the stroke in rowing. **3** to conduct a bucket shop; act as a bucketeer. **—*v.t.*** **1** to lift or carry in a bucket or buckets. **2** to ride (a horse) hard. **3** to handle (orders to buy or sell stock or other securities) as in a bucket shop. **4** to swing (the body) forward too hurriedly in rowing.
kick the bucket, *Slang.* to die: *I mean in plain English that I am likely to shuffle off long before you kick the bucket* (Atlantic).
[perhaps < Anglo-French *buket* washtub, pail < Old English *būc* vessel, pitcher]

bucket brigade, a line of persons formed to pass buckets of water one to another to put out a fire.

buck|et|eer (buk′ə tir′), *n.* **1** a broker who handles his customers' orders or property fraudulently or irregularly. **2** a person operating a bucket shop.

buck|et|ful (buk′it fu̇l), *n., pl.* **-fuls.** the amount that a bucket can hold.

bucket seat, a small, low, single seat with a rounded back, used especially in sports cars and small airplanes.

bucket shop, **1** an establishment conducted ostensibly for buying and selling stocks or commodities, but really for making bets on the rise and fall of their prices, with no actual buying and selling. **2** a similar establishment that secretly bets against its customers by taking the other side of their trades, or otherwise mishandles their orders or property. [American English; a place where liquors were mixed and sold in *buckets*]

buck|eye (buk′ī′), *n.* **1** a tree or shrub, a type of horse chestnut, with showy flowers, large divided leaves, and large brown seeds, especially a large tree with an ill-smelling bark. **2** its seed. It has a light-brown scar like the partly opened eye of a buck. **3** an American butterfly, which has eye spots on its wings, that occurs throughout the southeastern United States. It feeds in the larval state upon plantain, snapdragon, and figworts.

Buck|eye (buk′ī′), *n.* **1** a nickname for a native or inhabitant of Ohio, where buckeyes are plentiful. **2** a breed of American class chicken that lays brown-shelled eggs.

Buckeye State, a nickname for Ohio.

buck fever, *U.S. Informal.* the nervous excitement felt by an inexperienced hunter when he first sights game.

buck|horn (buk′hôrn′), *n.* the horn of bucks or deer, used especially for making handles for knives and similar implements.

buck|hound (buk′hound′), *n.* any hound used for hunting deer.

buck|ie (buk′ē), *n. Scottish.* **1** the spiral shell of a mollusk. **2** a perverse or refractory person. [origin unknown]

Buck|ing|ham Palace (buk′ing əm), the official London residence of all British sovereigns since 1837.

buck|ish (buk′ish), *adj.* of or resembling a buck or dandy; foppish. **—buck′ish|ly,** *adv.* **—buck′ish|ness,** *n.*

buck-jump (buk′jump′), *n.* a leap like that of a buck or a bucking horse or mule.

buck-jump|er (buk′jum′pər), *n.* a person or animal that makes buck-jumps.

buck-jump|ing (buk′jum′ping), *n.* the act of jumping like a buck or a bucking horse or mule.

buck|le (buk′əl), *n., v.,* **-led, -ling.** **—*n.*** **1** a catch or clasp used to hold together the ends of a belt, strap, or ribbon: *When the buckle broke his belt came loose.* **2** a metal ornament for a shoe: *The Pilgrims wore buckles on their shoes.* **3** a bend, bulge, or wrinkle: *The buckle in the plaster showed the ceiling might fall.* **4** *Obsolete.* a wave or crimp in the hair, especially of a wig.
—*v.t.* **1** to fasten together with a buckle: *He buckled his belt.* **2** to bend out of shape; bulge or wrinkle: *Settling of the house has buckled the plaster.* **—*v.i.*** **1** to bend, bulge, or lose shape, especially under strain or pressure: *The heavy snowfall caused the roof to buckle.* **2** to close with an opponent; grapple; engage: *Each man closely buckled to his antagonist* (David Hume).
buckle down to, to work hard at: *He buckled down to his studies before the test.*
[< Old French *boucle* metal ring (on a shield) < Latin *buccula* cheek strap on a helmet (diminutive) < *bucca* cheek]

buck|ler** (buk′lər), *n., v.* **—*n. **1** a small, round shield used to parry blows or thrusts. **2** *Figurative.* a means of defense; protection; protector: *His faithfulness and truth shall be thy shield and buckler* (Book of Common Prayer).
—*v.t.* to act as a buckler to; shield; defend; protect. [< Old French *boucler* shield < *boucle* metal ring < Latin *buccula;* see etym. under **buckle**]

***buckler**
definition 1

buck|min|ster|ful|ler|ene (buk′min stər fu̇l′ə rēn′), *n. Chemistry.* a highly stable molecule consisting of sixty carbon atoms arranged as interlocking pentagons and hexagons: *Scientists suspect that buckminsterfullerene has unusual properties that could lead to the development of new lubricants and catalysts* (Peter J. Andrews). [< *Buckminster Fuller,* 1895-1983, an American designer who developed the geodesic dome, which this molecule resembles in structure + *-ene*]

buck|o (buk′ō), *n., pl.* **buck|oes.** a person who domineers; a bully. [< *buck*[1]]

buck passer, *U.S. Slang.* a person who avoids responsibility by shifting it to someone else.

buck-pass|ing (buk′pas′ing), *n. U.S. Slang.* the act or practice of avoiding responsibility, blame, or work, by shifting it to someone else.

buck private, *Slang.* a common soldier below the rank of private first class.

buck|ra (buk′rə), *n.* (in the Negro speech of the West Indies and the southern United States) a white man. [American English < Efik (African) *mbakara* white man]

buck|ram (buk′rəm), *n., adj., v.,* **-ramed, -ram|ing.** **—*n.*** **1** a coarse cloth made stiff with glue or something like glue, used especially for stiffening garmets and binding books: *Four rogues in buckram let drive at me* (Shakespeare). **2** *Figurative.* stiffness of manner: *A fine, good-humoured, unaffected lad, no pride or buckram* (Charles Cornwallis). **3** *Obsolete.* a fine linen or cotton fabric.
—*adj.* **1** made of buckram: *. . . his buckram shirt collar* (Byron). **2a** like buckram. **b** *Figurative.* stiff; formal; haughty: *A wondrous buckram style,—the best he* [*Samuel Johnson*] *could get* (Thomas Carlyle).
—*v.t.* **1** to pad or stiffen with buckram: *. . . the starched, buckramed skirts of my female relatives* (George A. Sala). **2** *Figurative.* to make stiff: *His buckramed habit of clerical decorum* (Hawthorne).
[< Old French *bouquerant;* origin uncertain]

buck|saw (buk′sô′), *n.* a saw set in a light frame and held with both hands. [American English, apparently < *buck*[4] (def. 1), with which it was used + *saw*[1]]

buck|shee (buk′shē, buk shē′), *adj. British Slang.* free. [alteration of *baksheesh*]

buck|shot (buk′shot′), *n.* a large lead shot, used to shoot large animals, such as deer. [< *buck*¹ + *shot*]

buck|skin (buk′skin′), *n., adj.* —*n.* **1** a strong, soft leather, yellowish or grayish in color, made from the skins of deer or sheep: *moccasins of buckskin.* **2** the skin of a buck: *a large buckskin stretched for tanning.* **3** *Western U.S.* a horse of the color of buckskin. **4** = Buckskin.
—*adj.* made of buckskin: *buckskin gloves.*
buckskins, clothing made of buckskin.

Buck|skin (buk′skin′), *n.* an American soldier in the Revolutionary War (many of whom wore buckskins).

buckskin cloth, **1** a strong, twilled woolen cloth with a closely cut nap. **2** a cotton cloth with a clear surface and napped back.

buck|tail (buk′tāl′), *n. Angling.* **1** an artificial fly made of long fibers from the tails of deer. **2** any similar artificial fly.

buck|thorn (buk′thôrn′), *n.* **1** a small, thorny tree or shrub with clusters of black berries, each containing two to four tiny seeds. It belongs to the buckthorn family. **2** a low, thorny tree of the sapodilla family with black, cherrylike fruit, that grows in the southern United States. [< *buck*¹ + *thorn*]

buckthorn family, a family of trees and shrubs of wide distribution, including the buckthorn, the jujube, and the ceanothus.

buck|tooth (buk′tüth′), *n., pl.* **-teeth**. a tooth that sticks out beyond the rest. [< *buck*¹ + *tooth*]

buck|toothed (buk′tütht′, -tüŦʜd′), *adj.* having a protruding tooth or teeth.

∗**buck|wheat** (buk′hwēt′), *n.* **1** a plant with black or gray, triangular seeds and fragrant, white flowers. **2** the seeds, used as food for animals or ground into flour. **3** meal, flour, or batter made from buckwheat, popular in the United States as an ingredient in griddlecakes. [Middle English *buck* beech (Old English *bōc*) + English *wheat* (from its beechnut-shaped seeds); perhaps influenced by Middle Low German *bukwete*]

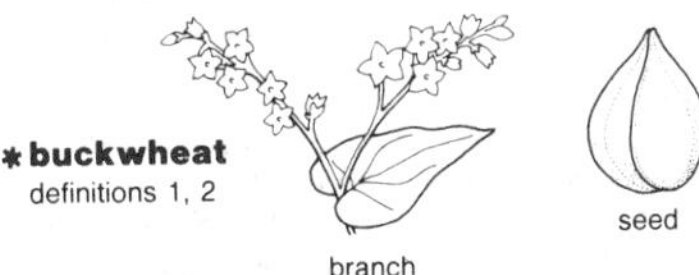

∗**buckwheat** definitions 1, 2

buckwheat family, a group of dicotyledonous herbs, shrubs, and trees, having alternate and usually entire leaves with stipules which form a sheath around the base of the petiole. The family includes the buckwheat and rhubarb, as well as many weedy plants, such as dock and knotgrass.

bu|col|ic (byü kol′ik), *adj., n.* —*adj.* **1** of shepherds; pastoral: *Bucolic poetry is seldom written by shepherds themselves.* **2** rustic; rural: *a bucolic setting, bucolic wit.*
—*n.* **1** a poem about shepherds; eclogue; idyl. **2** *Humorous.* a peasant; countryman.
[< Latin *būcolicus* < Greek *boukolikós* rustic < *boukólos* herdsman < *boûs* cow] —**bu col′i-cal|ly**, *adv.*

bu|col|i|cal (byü kol′ə kəl), *adj.* = bucolic.

bu|crane (byü krān′), *n.* an ornament, often sculptured, representing the skull of an ox. [< Latin *būcrānium* < Greek *boukránion* < *boûs* ox + *kranion* skull]

bu|cra|ni|um (byü krā′nē əm), *n., pl.* **-ni|a** (-nē ə). = bucrane.

∗**bud**¹ (bud), *n., v.,* **bud|ded, bud|ding.** —*n.* **1** a small swelling on a plant that will grow into a flower, leaf, or branch. A bud is a mass of growing tissue. *Buds on the trees are a sign of spring.* **2** a partly opened flower or leaf. **3** *Figurative.* anything in an undeveloped state or beginning stage. **4** *Figurative.* **a** a child or young girl. **b** a young girl introduced into society; debutante. **5** a small swelling or group of cells in certain simple plants or animals that grows into a new organ, a new animal, or a new plant of the same species; gemma: *The buds of new yeast plants grow very quickly.* **6** a minute, bud-shaped part or organ: *a taste bud.*
—*v.i.* **1** to put forth buds: *The rosebush has budded.* **2** *Figurative.* to begin to grow or develop: *That boy is budding into a scientist.* **3** *Figurative.* to be like a bud in youth, beauty, or promise. **4** (of birds) to eat buds.
—*v.t.* **1** to bring into bud; cause to bud. **2** to put forth as buds. **3** to graft a bud from one kind of plant into the stem of (a different kind), as a method of propagating a desired quality or variety. **4** to produce by means of buds.
in bud, in the time or condition of budding: *In spring the pear tree is in bud.*
nip in the bud, to stop at the very beginning; forestall: *The coach nipped the boys' argument in the bud before it really got started.*
[Middle English *budde*] —**bud′der**, *n.* —**bud′like′**, *adj.*

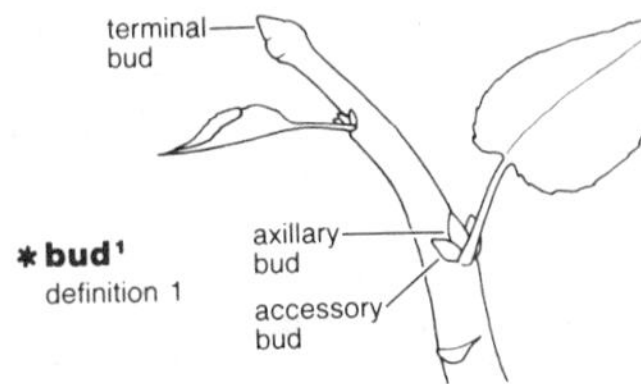

∗**bud**¹ definition 1

bud² (bud), *n. U.S. Informal.* = buddy. [American English, back formation < *buddy*]

Bud|dha (bůd′ə, bü′də), *n.* a title applied to Siddhartha Gautama, 563?-483? B.C., called by his followers Gautama Buddha and regarded as a teacher possessing perfect enlightenment and wisdom. He was the founder of Buddhism. [< Sanskrit *buddha* wise, enlightened]

Bud|dhism (bůd′iz əm, bü′diz-), *n.* a religion based on the teachings of Gautama Buddha that teaches that right living will enable people to attain nirvana, the condition of a soul that does not have to live in a body and is free from all desire and pain. Buddhism developed in the 500's B.C., in northern India and spread over central, southeastern and eastern Asia.

Bud|dhist (bůd′ist, bü′dist), *n., adj.* —*n.* a believer in Buddhism.
—*adj.* having to do with Buddha or Buddhism.

Bud|dhis|tic (bů dis′tik, bü-), *adj.* = Buddhist.

Bud|dhis|ti|cal (bů dis′tə kəl, bü-), *adj.* = Buddhist.

bud|die (bud′ē), *n., pl.* **-dies**. = buddy.

bud|ding (bud′ing), *adj.* in process of development or emergence: (*Figurative.*) *a budding scientist, a budding crisis.*

bud|dle (bud′əl), *n.* a shallow, inclined trough for separating the metal in an ore from the earthy or valueless part by means of running water. [compare German *buddeln* to dig out]

bud|dle|ia (bud lē′ə, bud′lē-), *n.* any plant of a genus of chiefly tropical ornamental shrubs or trees, bearing showy clusters of flowers in many shades and tones of purple, red, yellow, pink, and lavender, as well as white; butterfly bush and summer lilac. [< New Latin *Buddleia* the genus name < Adam *Buddle,* died 1715, an English botanist]

bud|dy (bud′ē), *n., pl.* **-dies**, *v.,* **-died, -dy|ing.** *Informal.* —*n.* **1** a close friend; comrade; pal. **2** a little boy. **3** brother (used as a form of address). Also, **buddie**.
—*v.i.* to be or become close friends: *We were cussing the Germans . . . and now we are buddying with them* (Newsweek).
[perhaps < dialectal English *butty* friend, mate]

bud|dy-bud|dy (bud′ē bud′ē), *adj., n., pl.* **-dies**, *v.,* **-died, -dy|ing.** *Slang.* —*adj.* very friendly; chummy.
—*n.* a close friend; chum.
—*v.i.* to be or act as close friends.

buddy pair, two swimmers of an underwater demolition team assigned an area in which to take depth soundings, locate and describe the types and position of obstacles, and note enemy installations.

buddy system, *U.S.* the pairing of two persons participating in the same activity so that each is responsible for the other's welfare and safety, such as patrolmen on a beat, soldiers on reconnaissance, or children swimming.

budge¹ (buj), *v.,* **budged, budg|ing.** —*v.i.* to move from one's place even a little; stir (usually with negative): *Father wouldn't budge from his chair. The witness would not budge from his first statement.*
—*v.t.* to cause to move (something heavy or inert): *The stone was so heavy that the boy could not budge it.*
[< French *bouger* stir < Vulgar Latin *bullicāre* to boil < Latin *bullāre* to bubble, boil, or < *bulla* a bubble]

budge² (buj), *n., adj.* —*n.* lambskin dressed with the wool outward, formerly much used as a fur for trimming.
—*adj.* **1** trimmed or adorned with budge. **2** *Obsolete.* solemn; pompous.
[Middle English *bugeye,* perhaps variant of *bulge* leather bag < Old French *boulge;* see etym. under **bulge**]

budg|er|i|gar (buj′ər ē gär′), *n.* a small, brightly colored parakeet, native to Australia, popular as a cage bird; shell parakeet. The budgerigar is bright green below, greenish yellow with brownish markings on its upper parts, and with bright-blue cheeks and tail feathers. [< native Australian *budgereegah* < *budgeri* good + *gar* cockatoo]

budg|et (buj′it), *n., v.,* **-et|ed, -et|ing.** —*n.* **1** an estimate of the amount of money to be received and the amounts to be spent for various purposes in a given time. Governments, schools, companies and persons make budgets. *The expenses for the school year are an important part of our city budget.* **2** a plan of procedure based on such an estimate. **3** an allotment of expenditures for various items for a period of time: *She always stays within her budget.* **4** *Figurative.* a stock or collection: *a budget of news.* **5** *Dialect.* **a** a bag, pouch, or wallet. **b** the contents of a bag or wallet.
—*v.t.* **1** to make a plan for spending based on how much you have: *The traveler budgeted his money so enough would be left for his return trip home. Budget your time. He budgeted his allowance so that enough money was left to save for a tent.* **2** to put in a budget; allot: *The school budgeted $5000 a year for building repairs.*
—*v.i.* **1** to draw up or prepare a budget: *She is budgeting for a trip to Europe.* **2** to arrange (for) in a budget.
[< Old French *bougette* (diminutive) < *bouge* bag, earlier *boulge;* see etym. under **bulge**]

budg|et|ar|y (buj′ə ter′ē), *adj.* of a budget: *The budgetary deficit was reaching an all-time high* (Atlantic).

budg|et|eer (buj′ə tir′), *n.* = budgeter.

budg|et|er (buj′ə tər), *n.* a person who makes up a budget.

budget plan, a plan of budgeting income by paying for goods and services in installments.

budg|ie (buj′ē), *n. Informal.* = budgerigar.

bud grafting, a process for growing a different variety of fruit or plant from a given stock by transferring a bud with a little of the woody tissue behind it to a cleft in the bark of the stock.

bud|less (bud′lis), *adj.* without a bud.

bud|let (bud′lit), *n.* a small bud.

bud scale, one of the small, often resinous or hairy, scalelike leaves forming the outside protective covering of the buds of certain woody plants in winter or in the dry season.

bud variation, a variation in the outgrowth of a bud from the ordinary growth of the plant, producing a sport. Many varieties in cultivated plants arise through bud variation.

bud|worm (bud′wėrm′), *n.* any one of various moth larvae destructive to buds. Larvae of the noctuid moth attack the tobacco plant.

bue|nas no|ches (bwā′näs nō′chās), *Spanish.* good evening; good night.

bue|nos di|as (bwā′nōs dē′äs), *Spanish.* good day; good morning.

Buer|ger's disease (bėr′gərz), a circulatory disease characterized by the progressive closing of the smaller blood vessels, especially of the legs and feet, leading to gangrene. [< Leo *Buerger,* 1879-1943, an American physician, who described it]

buff¹ (buf), *n., adj., v.* —*n.* **1a** a strong, soft, dull-yellow leather. Buff was formerly made from the skin of buffalo and is now made from the skin of oxen. **b** a soldier's coat made of this; buffcoat. **2** a dull yellow. **3** a polishing wheel or stick covered with leather. **4** *Informal, Figurative.* bare skin: *to swim in the buff.*
—*adj.* **1** dull-yellow. **2** made of buff leather: *a buff jerkin.*
—*v.t.* **1** to polish with a wheel or stick covered with leather. **2** polish; shine: *He buffs his shoes to make them shine.* **3** to give a fuzzy surface to (leather, etc.) with an abrasive. **4** to stain or dye dull yellow.
the Buffs, certain British regiments, so called because of the color of their facings.
[< French *buffle* < Italian *bufalo* buffalo]

buff² (buf), *n. U.S. Informal.* a fan or devotee (usually qualified): *a model-train buff, a football buff.* [originally, a fire-fighting enthusiast; special use of **buff**¹ (because of the buff-colored uniforms formerly worn by volunteer firemen in New York City)]

buff³ (buf), *v., n.* —*v.t.* to soften or deaden the shock (of), as a buffer does. —*v.i.* to act and sound as a buffer, or as the body which strikes it.
—*n.* **1** = blindman's buff. **2** *Obsolete.* a blow; stroke.
[< Old French *buffe,* imitative of sound made in blowing out puffed-up cheeks]

buf|fa (büf′fä), *n., pl.* **buf|fe** (büf′fā). *Italian.* a woman who sings comic roles in opera or light opera.

buf|fa|lo (buf′ə lō), *n., pl.* **-loes, -los** or (*collectively*) **-lo**, *v.,* **-loed, -lo|ing.** —*n.* **1** the bison of North America, a wild ox with a great shaggy

head, a humped neck, and strong front legs. Herds of buffalo used to graze on the plains of the United States. **2** any one of several kinds of oxen. The tame water buffalo of Asia (especially of India and the Philippines) and the wild Cape buffalo of Africa are two different kinds. **3** *Informal.* (in the United States and Canada) a buffalo robe. **4** = buffalo fish.
— ***v.t.*** *Slang.* **1** to intimidate or overawe: *Don't let them buffalo you into doing something you don't want to do.* **2** to puzzle; mystify: *His maneuvers in the market had his competitors buffaloed.*
[< Italian *bufalo* < dialectal Late Latin *būfalus,* Latin *būbalus* wild ox, African gazelle < Greek *boúbalos* African gazelle]

buffalo berry, **1** the edible, acid, red or yellowish berry of either of two thorny shrubs of western North America. **2** either of these shrubs.

buffalo bird, any one of several starlinglike birds that light on cattle, buffalo, or other animals and pick off ticks or other parasites.

buffalo bug, = carpet beetle.

buffalo bush, = buffalo berry (def. 2).

buffalo chips, *U.S.* pieces of dried dung used for fuel.

buffalo fish, a large, dark-colored freshwater fish having a more or less humped back, found from southern Canada to Guatemala.

buffalo fly or **gnat**, a black fly having a protruding thorax. One kind lives in the lower Mississippi Valley and attacks cattle.

buffalo grass, a short native grass common on the plains of central and western North America where the buffalo used to graze, often used for pasture.

Buffalo Indian, = Plains Indian.

buffalo moth, = carpet beetle.

buffalo nut, **1** the oily nut of a North American shrub, related to sandalwood. **2** the shrub it grows on.

buffalo robe, a cloak, lap robe, or rug made of the skin of the American bison, and dressed with the hair on.

buff|coat (buf′kōt′), *n.* **1** a thick coat of buff, worn in the 1600's especially by soldiers. **2** a person who wears a buffcoat; soldier.

buff|er[1] (buf′ər), *n., v.* — ***n.*** **1** a mechanical device that helps to soften the shock of a blow, especially a device for absorbing the recoil of a gun, or the cushion of springs that helps to prevent shocks reaching one railway car from another. **2** any person or thing that helps to soften the shock of a blow or to balance the effect of opposing forces: (*Figurative.*) *Mother was a buffer between my brother's anger and me.* **3** = buffer solution. **4** = buffer state.
— ***v.t.*** **1** to soften or lessen the impact of, as by means of a buffer. **2** to treat with a buffer solution.
buffers, *British.* a heavy arrangement of timbers and shock-absorbing springs at the end of a railway track or spur: *The engine ran out of control and hit the buffers.*
[< *buff*[3], earlier, to hit so as to give a deadened sound + *-er*[1]]

buff|er[2] (buf′ər), *n.* **1** a stick or pad having a soft cloth or leather surface for polishing. **2** a person who polishes. [< *buff*[1] + *-er*[1]]

buff|er[3] (buf′ər), *n. Slang.* fellow; guy; chap (used especially of an elderly person, generally with a slight degree of contempt): *The old buffer was so blind he didn't see where he was going.* [origin uncertain]

buffer solution, a substance in a solution that makes the degree of acidity (hydrogen ion concentration) resistant to change when an acid or base is added.

buffer state, a small country between two larger countries that are enemies or competitors.

buffer stock, a stockpile of an essential commodity held in reserve to keep its fluctuating price within an agreed range.

buffer zone, **1** a neutral area established as a barrier between two adjoining enemy or rival areas. **2** = buffer state.

buf|fet[1] (buf′it), *n., v.,* **-fet|ed, -fet|ing.** — ***n.*** **1** a blow of the hand or fist. **2** a knock, stroke, or hurt: *The lifeguard withstood the buffets of the waves. ... the vile blows and buffets of the world* (Shakespeare).
— ***v.t.*** **1** to strike with the hand or fist. **2** to knock about, strike, or hurt: *The waves buffeted him.* (*Figurative.*) *Fate buffeted him about from job to job.* **3** to fight or struggle against: *The boat buffeted the heavy waves in the storm. He reached home exhausted from buffeting the storm.*
— ***v.i.*** **1** to deal blows; struggle; contend. **2** to move or advance with a series of efforts or blows.
[< Old French *buffet* (diminutive) < *buffe;* see etym. under **buff**[3] blow] — **buf′fet|er**, *n.*

buf|fet[2] (bů fā′, bu-; *especially British* buf′it), *n.* **1a** a piece of dining-room furniture with a flat top for dishes and with shelves or drawers for holding silver and table linen; sideboard. **b** a cupboard in a recess, for china and glasses. **2** a meal set out in serving dishes on tables or buffets, from which guests serve themselves: *a buffet lunch or supper, a buffet party.* **3** a counter where food and drinks are served. **4** a restaurant or bar with such a counter: *The audience munched ham sandwiches and drank beer and cognac in the buffet before the show and during the intermission* (New Yorker). [< French *buffet* piece of furniture; origin uncertain]

buffet car, a railroad car with a small compartment where light meals are prepared and served.

buff|ing (buf′ing), *n.* (of horses) the striking of the inside of one foot at the quarter with some part of the opposite foot.

buffing wheel, a wheel covered with leather, felt, cloth, or other material, used with emery or other powders in polishing, especially metal; buff wheel.

buf|fle (buf′əl), *n. Obsolete.* a buffalo. [< French *buffle;* see etym. under **buff**[1]]

buf|fle|head (buf′əl hed′), *n.* **1** a small North American duck, related to the goldeneye; butterball. The adult male has a remarkable fullness of feathers on the head. **2** *Figurative.* a blockhead or fool; stupid fellow. [American English < obsolete *buffle* buffalo + *head*]

buf|fo (bü′fō; *Italian* büf′fō), *n., pl.* **-fi** (-fē), *adj.* — ***n.*** a male comic singer, usually a basso, in opera or light opera.
— ***adj.*** comic: *a buffo base, a buffo operatic part.*
[< Italian *buffo*]

buf|foon (bu fün′), *n., v.* — ***n.*** **1** a person who amuses people with tricks, pranks, and jokes; clown: *to act the buffoon.* **2** a person given to undignified or rude joking.
— ***v.i.*** to behave this way.
[< French *bouffon* < Italian *buffone* jester < *buffa* jest < *buffare* blow (out the cheeks)]

buf|foon|er|y (bu fü′nər ē), *n., pl.* **-er|ies.** **1** the tricks, pranks, and jokes of a clown: *We enjoyed the buffoonery at the circus.* **2** undignified or rude joking.

buf|foon|ish (bu fü′nish), *adj.* like or characteristic of a buffoon.

buff stick, a small stick covered with leather or the like, used in polishing.

buff wheel, = buffing wheel.

buff|y (buf′ē), *adj.* buff-colored or approaching buff in color.

buffy coat, the buff-colored layer on the upper surface of a blood clot, from which the red blood corpuscles settled prior to complete coagulation.

bu|fo|ten|in (byü′fə ten′in), *n.* = bufotenine.

bu|fo|ten|ine (byü′fə ten′ēn, -in), *n.* a drug with some of the properties of serotonin, obtained from the skin glands and salivary glands of certain toads, and used experimentally to induce hallucinations. *Formula:* $C_{12}H_{16}N_2O$ [ultimately < Latin *būfo* toad + English *-ine*[2]]

bug[1] (bug), *n., v.,* **bugged, bug|ging.** — ***n.*** **1** a crawling insect with a pointed beak for piercing and sucking. A bug either has no wings or has a front pair of wings thickened at the base. Bedbugs, plant lice, and chinch bugs are true bugs. All true bugs are hemipterous insects. **2** any insect or other animal somewhat like a true bug. Ants, spiders, beetles, and flies are often called bugs. **3** = bedbug. **4** *Informal.* a disease germ: *the flu bug.* **5** *Informal.* a defect in the operation of a machine: *to work the bugs out of a new car.* **6** *Informal.* **a** a person who is very enthusiastic about something: *He is a basketball bug and goes to a lot of games.* **b** great interest; keenness: *the travel bug.* **7** a very small microphone hidden within a room, a telephone, or the like, for overhearing a conversation: [*He*] *sometimes talks into the phone while letting water run into a basin or tapping a pencil against his receiver, though experts find these measures questionable against "bugs"* (Newsweek). **8** *Slang.* a small vehicle, such as a compact car or a lunar rover.
— ***v.t.*** **1** to hide a small microphone within (a room, telephone, or the like) for overhearing a conversation: *The spy bugged enemy headquarters.* **2** *Slang.* to annoy; irritate; pester; trouble: *They tried to bug me with the banging on the bars* (New York Times).
— ***v.i.*** *U.S. Informal.* (of the eyes) to bulge, as with astonishment; bug out: ... *details that really made the subcommitteemen's eyes bug* (New Yorker).
bug off (or **out**), *U.S. Slang.* to run or rush away; depart; retreat: *The regime and its followers thereupon bugged out ... as fast as planes and ships would bear them* (Time).
bug out, *U.S. Informal.* (of the eyes) to bulge or open wide: *The eyes of the little boy bugged out with astonishment when he saw his new bicycle.*
[origin uncertain] — **bug′like′**, *adj.*

bug[2] (bug), *n. Obsolete.* a bugaboo; bogy. [Middle English *bugge;* origin uncertain]

bug|a|boo (bug′ə bü), *n., pl.* **-boos.** an imaginary thing feared; bogy: *In these days children are not scared by tales of witches, ghosts, and other bugaboos.* [< *bug*[2] bogy + *boo*]

Bu|ga|ku (bü gä′kü), *n.* an ancient Japanese court dance: *The slow and stately dancing of Noh shows clearly the influence of one of the oldest Japanese art forms, Bugaku* (Atlantic). [< Japanese *bugaku*]

bug|bane (bug′bān′), *n.* a plant of the north temperate regions whose white flowers have an unpleasant odor that was supposed to repel bedbugs. The bugbane is a perennial herb of the crowfoot family.

bug|bear (bug′bãr′), *n.* **1** a thing feared without reason; bugaboo; bogy. **2** a difficulty, problem, or obstacle: *Out-of-date machinery is the chief bugbear of this old factory.* **3** a pet hate. **4** *Obsolete.* an imaginary being supposed to devour naughty children. [< *bug*[2] bogy + *bear*[1]]

bug boy, *U.S. Slang.* an apprentice jockey.

bug-eyed (bug′īd′), *adj. Slang.* with eyes wide open and bulging, especially with wonder or excitement: *bug-eyed spectators.*

bug|fish (bug′fish′), *n., pl.* **-fish|es** or (*collectively*) **-fish.** *U.S.* the menhaden.

bug|ger (bug′ər), *n., v.* — ***n.*** **1** a contemptible or low person. **2** *Informal.* a chap; fellow. **3** *British Slang.* **a** something troublesome or unpleasant: *That job is a real bugger.* **b** a tinker's damn; a trifle: *He doesn't care a bugger about anything.* **4** a sodomite.
— ***v.t.*** (in British legal use) to commit buggery with.
bugger about, *Slang.* to be unprofitably busy: *to bugger about the house all day.*
bugger off, *Slang.* to go away; get out: *He tells the reporters to bugger off* (Time).
bugger up, *Slang.* to throw into confusion: *The town is being completely buggered up by the invasion of tourists.*
[< Old French *bougre,* earlier *boulgre,* learned borrowing from Late Latin *Bulgarus* a Bulgarian; (originally) Bulgarian heretics of the 1000's]

bug|ger|y (bug′ər ē), *n.* the crime of sodomy (in British legal usage).

***bug|gy**[1] (bug′ē), *n., pl.* **-gies.** **1** (in the U.S.) a light carriage, with or without a top, pulled by one horse and having a single large seat. **2** = baby buggy. **3** (in England) a light, two-wheeled vehicle without a folding top. **4** (in India) a light, two-wheeled carriage with a folding top. [origin uncertain]

***buggy**[1]
definition 1

bug|gy[2] (bug′ē), *adj.,* **-gi|er, -gi|est.** **1** swarming with bugs. **2** *Slang.* crazy; bugs: *You have to think only of the next game ... If you try to think back, you go buggy* (Leonard Koppett). [< *bug*[1] + *-y*[1]]

bug|house (bug′hous′), *n., adj. Slang.* — ***n.*** an asylum for lunatics.
— ***adj.*** crazy; insane.
[< slang *bug* crazy person + *house*]

bu|gle[1] (byü′gəl), *n., v.,* **-gled, -gling.** — ***n.*** **1** a musical instrument like a small trumpet, made of brass or copper, that has no keys or valves. Bugles can play only a few tones within a limited range and have long been used in military forces for sounding calls and orders. Some bugles have been built with valves so that they can play a complete scale. *Blow, bugle, blow, Set the wild echoes flying* (Tennyson). **2** a hunting horn.
— ***v.i.*** to blow a bugle.
— ***v.t.*** to direct or summon by blowing on a bugle.
[Middle English *bugle horn* < *bugle* wild ox < Old French, learned borrowing from Latin *būculus* (diminutive) < *bōs* ox]

bu|gle[2] (byü′gəl), *n.* = bugleweed. [< Old French *bugle;* origin unknown]

bu|gle[3] (byü′gəl), *n.* a long, tubular, glass bead, usually black, used as a trimming on dresses. [perhaps < *bugle*[1] in sense of "tube"]

bugle call, a short melody sounded upon a bugle as a signal or order.

bu|gled (byü′gəld), *adj.* decorated with bugles: *a bugled dress.*

bugle horn, a bugle or hunting horn.

bu|gler (byü′glər), *n.* **1** a person who blows a bugle. **2** a soldier who gives signals with a bugle.

bu|glet (byü′glit), *n.* a small bugle.

bu|gle|weed (byü′gəl wēd′), *n.* **1** any plant of a genus of herbs of the mint family, especially a species bearing spikes of tubular blue flowers; bugle. **2** any plant of another genus of herbs of the mint family, especially a species considered astringent and sedative. **3** = wild indigo.

bu|gloss (byü′glos, -glôs), *n.* any one of several plants of the borage family, especially: **a** an annual European plant, naturalized in the United States, with bristly leaves and stems and blue flowers. **b** a European medicinal herb with rough leaves and stems; anchusa; alkanet. [< Middle French *buglosse,* learned borrowing from Late Latin *būglōssa* (literally) ox-tongue < Greek *boúglōssos* < *boûs* ox + *glôssa* tongue]

bug|out (bug′out′), *n. U.S. Slang.* **1** a running away; flight; retreat; desertion. **2** a person who flees or deserts; deserter.

bugs (bugz), *adj. U.S. Slang.* not of sound mind; senseless; mad.

bug|seed (bug′sēd′), *n.* an annual plant of the goosefoot family, widely distributed over northern temperate regions. Its flat oval seeds suggest bugs.

bug|shah (büg′shə), *n., pl.* **-shahs** or **-shah.** = buqsha.

buhl (bül), *n.* **1** wood inlaid with elaborate patterns of tortoise shell, ivory, brass, white metal, and other materials, used for furniture. **2** furniture or other objects made of buhl. Also, **boulle**. [a Germanized spelling < André C. *Boule,* 1642-1732, a French cabinetmaker]

buhl work, = buhl.

buhr (bėr), *n.* **1** = burr[1] (def. 2). **2** = burr[4].

buhr|stone (bėr′stōn′), *n.* = burrstone.

buik (byük, bük), *n. Scottish.* book.

build (bild), *v.,* **built** or (*Archaic*) **build|ed, build|ing,** *n.* —*v.t.* **1** to make by putting materials together; construct: *Birds build nests. Men build houses, dams, bridges, ships, and machines.* SYN: erect, frame, assemble. **2** *Figurative.* to produce gradually; develop: *to build a business.* **3** *Figurative.* to establish on some foundation; base: *A lawyer builds his case on facts. On God and Godlike men we built our trust* (Tennyson). SYN: found. **4** *Figurative.* to form by art in any way; fashion: *He knew himself to sing, and build the lofty rhyme* (Milton). **5** (in card games) to put together (a sequence of cards) according to number, suit, or other category.
—*v.i.* **1** to practice the art or follow the business of constructing buildings; make a structure: *He builds for a living.* **2** to make nests or the like: *A jackdaw had built in the chimney.* **3** to construct or establish anything. **4** *Figurative.* to accept as a basis for argument, planning, or acting; rely; depend: *We can build on that man's honesty.*
—*n.* **1** the form, style, or manner in which a person or animal is put together; structure: *An elephant has a heavy build.* **2** the shape, lines, or rig; construction: *the build of a ship or vehicle.*
build in, a to build round about; enclose: *When we first came here, the neighborhood was open, but we are now completely built in.* **b** to fill a space by building; block up: *The workers began to build in the hole with bricks.*
build up, a to form gradually; develop: *The firm has built up a wide reputation for fair dealing.* **b** to fill with houses: *The hill overlooking the town has been built up in the last five years.* **c** *Figurative.* to increase or strengthen: *When sick you must rest to build up your health.* **d** *Figurative.* to enhance the image of; make more attractive: *They used publicity to build up their candidate.*
[Old English *byldan* < *bold* dwelling]

build|a|ble (bil′də bəl), *adj.* **1** that can be built: *a buildable spacecraft.* **2** that can be built on: *a buildable site.*

build-down (bild′doun′), *n., v.,* **built-down, build|ing-down.** —*n.* a reduction of nuclear armament by eliminating existing weapons for new ones produced: *Some of the steam went out of . . . the so-called "build-down" scheme for reducing the superpower's nuclear arsenals* (Economist).
—*v.t.* to reduce (armaments) by a build-down: *President Reagan will . . . offer to "build-down" the USA's nuclear weapons when deadlocked strategic arms talks resume* (USA Today).
[patterned on *build-up*]

build|ed (bil′did), *v. Archaic.* built; a past tense and a past participle of **build**.

build|er (bil′dər), *n.* **1** a person or animal that builds. **2** a person whose business is constructing buildings or other structures. **3** an abrasive or filler used with a soap or detergent.

build|er's knot (bil′dərz), = clove hitch.

build|er-up|per (bil′dər up′ər), *n. Informal.* a person or thing that builds up; developer; promoter.

build|ing (bil′ding), *n.* **1** a thing built. Barns, factories, stores, houses, and hotels are all buildings. *All great buildings, after all, express an idea—and . . . the Palace of Westminster is undeniably a great building* (Manchester Guardian Weekly). **2** the business, art, or process of making houses, stores, bridges, ships, and similar things: *The boom in building . . . has resulted in the local land being more valuable now for houses* (London Times). *Abbr:* bldg.
—*Syn.* **1 Building, edifice, structure** mean something constructed. **Building** is the general term and applies to all purposes, sizes, materials, etc.: *From the hill we could see the buildings in the city.* **Edifice**, a more formal word, suggests a large and imposing building: *The cathedral is a handsome edifice.* **Structure** emphasizes the type of construction, as the materials used, arrangement of parts, etc.: *The new library is a fireproof structure.*

building and loan association, = savings and loan association.

building block, **1** a block of concrete, limestone, pressed cinders, or the like (but not a brick) used as a material for foundations, partitions, or walls. **2** any basic material which can be combined to form more complex structures: *Amino acids are the building blocks of protein.*

building code, a group of ordinances regulating the construction remodeling, repairing, and maintenance of a building.

building sickness, = sick building syndrome.

building society, *British.* a savings and loan association.

building stone, stone used in construction, especially for the foundations, walls, and steps of buildings, for the supports of piers and bridges, and for finishing and decorating.

building trades, the group of trades concerned with construction and forming the building industry: *The principal kinds of skilled workers in the building trades include bricklayers, carpenters, ironworkers, painters, plasterers, plumbers, and steam fitters* (W. C. Huntington).

build-up (bild′up′), *n.* **1** an increasing of strength: *a military build-up.* **2** an increase in any quantity or rate: *a build-up of pressure.* **3** *Figurative.* enhancement or promotion, as by the use of publicity: *The play had a big build-up in the press.*

built (bilt), *v.* a past tense and a past participle of **build**: *The bird built a nest. It was built of twigs.*

built-in (bilt′in′), *adj., n.* —*adj.* **1** included in or provided for as part of the plan or design of anything; not movable or removable: *A built-in bookcase is fastened to the wall.* **2** *Figurative.* having as a part of one's nature: *a built-in sense of humor.* **3** included as an integral part: *The U.S. Constitution has built-in checks and balances.*
—*n.* any built-in household fixture: *The kitchen features built-ins for every need—range, oven, refrigerator, freezer* (Wall Street Journal).

built-up (bilt′up′), *adj.* **1** having many houses or other buildings; urban or suburban rather than rural. **2** made up of separate parts or layers put together: *built-up heels, a built-up gun.*

buird|ly (bu̇rd′lē), *adj. Scottish.* burly; stalwart.

bul., bulletin.

***bulb** (bulb), *n., v.* —*n.* **1** a round, underground bud consisting of a small stem covered with thick, fleshy leaves from which certain plants grow. Onions, tulips, and lilies grow from bulbs. **2** any plant that has a bulb or grows from a bulb. The narcissus is a bulb. **3** the thick part of an underground stem resembling a bulb; tuber or corm: *a crocus bulb.* **4** any object with a rounded end or swelling part: *the bulb of a thermometer.* **5** the glass container surrounding the filament of an incandescent lamp or the electrodes of a fluorescent lamp. **6** an electron tube. **7a** = medulla oblongata. **b** a roundish dilation of any cylindrical organ or structure in an animal body. —*v.i.* to swell into a bulb or bulbs. [< Latin *bulbus* < Greek *bolbós*] —**bulb′less,** *adj.* —**bulb′like′,** *adj.*

***bulb**
definitions 1, 3

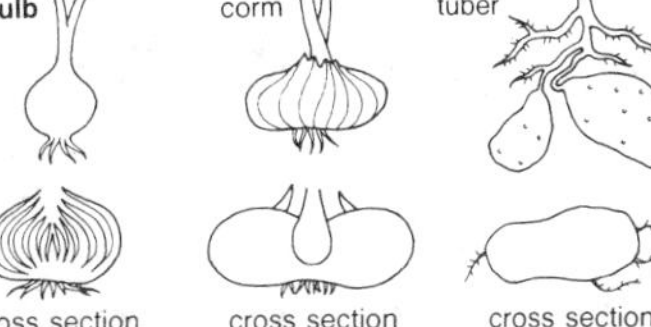

bul|ba|ceous (bul bā′shəs), *adj.* = bulbous. [< Latin *bulbāceus* (with English *-ous*)]

bul|bar (bul′bər), *adj.* having to do with a bulb, especially the medulla oblongata, the bulb of the spinal cord: *Bulbar polio, in which the virus directly invades the medulla* (Marguerite Clark).

bulbed (bulbd), *adj.* having a bulb or bulbs.

bul|bel (bul′bəl), *n.* = bulbil.

bul|bif|er|ous (bul bif′ər əs), *adj.* producing bulbs.

bul|bil (bul′bəl), *n.* **1** an aerial bud with fleshy scales, growing in the leaf axils, as in the tiger lily, or taking the place of flowers, as in the onion. **2** any little bulb or bulblike body. [< New Latin *bulbillus* (diminutive) < Latin *bulbus* bulb]

bulb|let (bulb′lit), *n.* a little bulb; bulbil.

bul|bose (bul′bōs), *adj.* = bulbous.

bul|bo|u|re|thral glands (bul′bō yu̇ rē′thrəl), = Cowper's glands.

bul|bous (bul′bəs), *adj.* **1** shaped like a bulb; rounded and swelling: *The clown had a bulbous red nose.* SYN: protuberant. **2** having bulbs; growing from bulbs: *Daffodils are bulbous plants.* SYN: tuberous. [< Latin *bulbōsus* (with English *-ous*) < *bulbus* bulb] —**bul′bous|ly,** *adv.*

bulb-shaped (bulb′shāpt′), *adj.* having or resembling the shape of a bulb.

bul|bul (bu̇l′bu̇l), *n.* **1** a songbird of southern Africa and Asia, often mentioned in Persian poetry. **2** any one of a family of tropical Old World oscine birds. **3** a singer. [probably through Persian *bulbul* nightingale < Arabic]

Bulg., **1** Bulgaria. **2** Bulgarian.

Bul|gar (bul′gär, bu̇l′-), *n.* = Bulgarian.

Bul|gar|i|an (bul gãr′ē ən, bu̇l-), *adj., n.* —*adj.* of or having to do with Bulgaria, its people, or their language. —*n.* **1** a native or inhabitant of Bulgaria. **2** the Slavic language of Bulgaria.

bulge (bulj), *v.,* **bulged, bulg|ing,** *n.* —*v.i.* to swell outward: *His pockets bulged with candy.* SYN: protrude. —*v.t.* to cause to swell outward: *The candy bulged his pockets.* [< noun]
—*n.* **1** an outward swelling: *When the man leaned against the tent, he made a bulge in the canvas. The force of the water caused a bulge in the dam.* SYN: protuberance, prominence, bump. **2a** the bottom of a ship's hull; bilge. **b** a structure attached outside the hull of a ship to protect it from mines, torpedoes, etc.; a blister. **3** *Figurative.* a temporary increase: *The graph shows a bulge in the birth rate.*
get (or **have**) **the bulge on,** *U.S. Slang.* to get an advantage over; get the better of: *The conductor kicked at what seemed a wholesale business, but the mother had the bulge on him* (Columbus Dispatch).
[< Old French *boulge* (originally) leather bag < Latin *bulga* bag; of Gaulish origin]

bulg|er (bul′jər), *n.* **1** a person or thing that bulges. **2** a driver or brassie with a convex face, formerly used in golf. **3** a stick with a thick head whose back is convex, used in field hockey.

bul|gur (bu̇l′gu̇r), *n.* a Middle Eastern cereal made of cracked wheat. [< Turkish *bulgur*]

bulg|y (bul′jē), *adj.,* **bulg|i|er, bulg|i|est.** having a bulge or bulges; bulging; swollen. —**bulg′i|ness,** *n.*

bu|lim|a|rex|i|a (byü lim′ə rek′sē ə), *n.* a psychological disorder in which a person alternates between an abnormal craving for food and an aversion to it, found especially among young women. [< *bulim*(ia) + *a*(*no*)*rexia*]

bu|lim|i|a (byü lim′ē ə), *n.* a constant and insatiable craving for food. [< New Latin *bulimia* < Greek *boulīmiā* < *boûs* ox + *līmós* hunger]

bu|lim|i|ac (byü lim′ē ak), *adj., n.* = bulimic.

bu|lim|ic (byü lim′ik), *adj., n.* —*adj.* of or having to do with bulimia; voracious.
—*n.* a person affected with bulimia: *Some bulimics employ extreme diets, constant exercise, or laxatives to lose weight* (Science News).

bu|li|my (byü′lə mē), *n.* = bulimia.

bulk[1] (bulk), *n., v., adj.* —*n.* **1a** size; volume: *A vast bulk of gold bullion is stored at Fort Knox.* SYN: magnitude. See syn. under **size**[1]. **b** large size: *An elephant has unforgettable bulk.* SYN: magnitude. See syn. under **size**[1]. **2** the largest part; main mass: *The oceans form the bulk of the earth's surface.* **3a** a ship's hold. **b** the cargo of a ship **4** *Archaic.* the body of a person or other animal: *Bones of some vast bulk that lived and roar'd before man was* (Tennyson). **5** *Obsolete.* a heap or pile.
—*v.i.* **1** to have size; be of importance: *The danger of drought bulks large in a farmer's life.* **2** to grow large; swell: *Numerous small contributions soon bulk up into a considerable sum.* **3** to form or gather into a mass.
—*v.t.* **1** to pile in heaps; put into a bulk or mass. **2** to measure or determine the bulk of. **3** to cause to swell out; stuff.
—*adj.* in large quantities; large-scale: *bulk goods.*
break bulk, a to begin unloading cargo: *The whole cargo can be sampled and sold the moment the steamer breaks bulk.* **b** to remove a portion from a parcel or quantity of goods.
in bulk, a lying loose in heaps, not in packages: *In most markets you can buy fresh fruit in bulk. The ship's cargo of grain was loaded in bulk.* **b** in

Pronunciation Key: hat, āge, cãre, fär; let, ēqual, tėrm; it, īce; hot, ōpen, ôrder; oil, out; cup, pu̇t, rüle; child; long; thin; ᴛʜen; zh, measure; ə represents **a** in about, **e** in taken, **i** in pencil, **o** in lemon, **u** in circus.

large quantities: *Grain goes to the mill in bulk. Goods are sold in that store both in bulk and in separate units.*
[< Scandinavian (compare Old Icelandic *būlki* heap, cargo)]

bulk[2] (bulk), *n.* a structure projecting from the front of a building, such as a stall. [origin uncertain; perhaps < Scandinavian (compare Old Icelandic *bālkr* beam)]

bulk|head (bulk′hed′), *n., v.* **—*n.*** **1a** one of the upright partitions dividing a ship into compartments. **b** a similar partition in the fuselage of an aircraft, to support and stiffen it. **2** a wall or partition built in a tunnel, conduit, or the like, to hold back water, earth, rocks, or air. **3** a boxlike structure covering the top of a staircase or other opening. **4** a horizontal or inclined door leading from the outside of a house to the cellar.
—*v.t.* to build or supply with bulkheads: *Proceeds of the ... bond issue would go for dredging, filling and bulkheading the site* (Wall Street Journal).
[probably < *bulk*[2] + *head*]

bulk|head|ed (bulk′hed′id), *adj.* furnished with or divided off by bulkheads.

bulk mail, (in the postal system of the United States) identical pieces of printed matter sent and paid for in bulk at a special rate.

bulk|y (bul′kē), *adj.*, **bulk|i|er, bulk|i|est. 1** taking up much space; large: *Bulky shipments are often sent in freight cars.* **SYN:** massive, ponderous.
2 hard to handle; clumsy: *She dropped the bulky package of curtain rods twice.* **SYN:** unwieldy.
—bulk′i|ly, *adv.* **—bulk′i|ness**, *n.*

bull[1] (bu̇l), *n., adj., v.* **—*n.*** **1** the full-grown male of cattle. **2** the male of the whale, elephant, seal, walrus, and other large animals. **3** a person whose size or loudness resembles that of a bull. **4a** a person who buys stocks, bonds, or other securities, with the hope of selling later at a higher price. **b** a person who believes that conditions are or will be favorable. **5** *U.S. Slang.* a policeman. **6** *Slang.* foolish talk; bunk; nonsense.
7 = bulldog. **8** *British Slang.* **a** intensive cleaning; polishing. **b** fastidious duties seemingly purposeless. **9** = bull's-eye.
—*adj.* **1** male: *a bull moose.* **2** like that of a bull: **a** large; strong; beefy: *a bull neck.* **b** roaring: *a bull voice.* **3** having to do with or characterized by rising prices, especially in the stock market: *a bull market.*
—*v.t.* **1** to get by force; push: *to bull one's way through a crowded street.* **2** to buy (stocks, bonds, or other securities) with the hope of selling later at a higher price: *Ward bulls his way to fortune* (New York Times Book Review). **3** *British Slang.* to subject to intense cleaning or polishing: *He bulled his boots.*
—*v.i.* to speculate in the stock market.
shoot the bull, *U.S. Slang.* to talk idly, as to speculate or boast: *The purpose of the meeting was to come to a decision, not just to sit around and shoot the bull.*
take the bull by the horns, to deal directly with a difficult or dangerous situation: *Determined to take the bull by the horns ... I stepped forward* (Henry B. Tristram).
[Middle English *bule,* Old English *bula*]

bull[2] (bu̇l), *n.* **1** a formal announcement or official decree from the Pope. **2** a seal affixed to a document, especially the seal used by the Pope; bulla. **3** an official letter or edict. [< Medieval Latin *bulla* document, seal < Latin, bubble, amulet]

bull[3] (bu̇l), *n.* an absurd and amusing mistake in language, especially one that is self-contradictory. *Example:* If you don't receive this letter, write and let me know. [Middle English *bull* a falsehood; origin uncertain]

bull[4] (bu̇l), *n.* a drink consisting of water drawn from a cask that has held spirits. [origin unknown]

bull[5] (bu̇l), *n.* a deck game in which beanbags are thrown onto a numbered, inclined board. [origin unknown]

Bull (bu̇l), *n.* a constellation and the second sign of the zodiac; Taurus.

Bull (bu̇l), *n.* **John**, a name for England or its people.

bull., bulletin.

bul|la (bu̇l′ə, bul′-), *n., pl.* **bul|lae** (bu̇l′ē, bul′-). **1a** a round seal of lead appended to a papal bull, stamped on one side with the name of the Pope and on the other with the heads of Peter and Paul. **b** a similar seal of the Byzantine and Holy Roman emperors. **2a** a vesicle containing watery fluid and causing an elevation of the skin; a blister. **b** a rounded, blisterlike, bony projection, as an inflated portion of the bony external meatus of the ear. **3** a boss, knob, or stud. **4a** a locketlike ornament worn by children in ancient Rome: *Boys wore a lucky charm, called a bulla, around their necks* (Betsy Talbot Blackwell). **b** any round ornament, especially if suspended.
[< Medieval Latin *bulla;* see etym. under **bull**[2]]

bul|lace (bu̇l′is), *n.* **1** a small, Old World species of plum, related to the damson. **2** the tree it grows on. [Middle English *bolace,* perhaps < Old French *beloce* wild plum]

bul|la|ri|um (bu̇ lãr′ē əm, bu-), *n., pl.* **-la|ri|a** (-lãr′ē ə). a collection of papal bulls. [< Medieval Latin *bullarium* < *bulla;* see etym. under **bull**[2]]

bul|late (bu̇l′āt, -it; bul′-), *adj.* having blisterlike projections, as a leaf; blistered or puckered. [< Latin *bulla* bubble + English *-ate*[1]]

bull-bait|ing (bu̇l′bā′ting), *n.* the formerly popular sport of setting dogs to attack a tethered bull.

bull|bat (bu̇l′bat′), *n.* = nighthawk.

bull bay, the evergreen magnolia of the southern United States.

bull|ber|ry (bu̇l′ber′ē), *n., pl.* **-ries**. *U.S.* = buffalo berry.

bull block, a power-driven reel that draws heavy-gauge wire through a die.

bull|boat (bu̇l′bōt′), *n. U.S.* a boat made of hides stretched over a light, wooden framework.

bull brier, *U.S.* any vine of several North American species of smilax, having a thick underground root and prickly, climbing stems.

bull chain, a very heavy chain to which a number of short chains with hooks on one end and dogs on the other are attached, used to draw logs from a millpond up a gangway.

bull|dog (bu̇l′dôg′, -dog′), *n., adj., v.*, **-dogged, -dog|ging.** **—*n.*** **1** a heavily built dog with a large head, very short nose, strong jaw, and short hair. Bulldogs are not large, but they are very muscular and courageous. They were originally bred for bull-baiting. **2** a short-barreled revolver of large caliber. **3** *British Informal.* one of the proctors' attendants at Oxford and Cambridge universities.
4 *British.* a bailiff or sheriff's officer.
—*adj.* like a bulldog's: *bulldog courage, bulldog determination, a bulldog grip.*
—*v.t.* **1** *Western U.S.* to bring (a steer) to the ground by grasping its horns and twisting its neck. **2** to attack like a bulldog.
[< *bull*[1] + *dog*]

bulldog ant, an ant found in Australia and Tasmania, with large jaws and a painful sting. It is believed to be the earliest or most primitive form of ant.

bulldog edition, *U.S.* the earliest edition of a morning newspaper, especially for distant or rural distribution, usually on sale the evening before.

bull|dog|ger (bu̇l′dôg′ər), *n. Western U.S.* a cowboy who trips and throws running steer.

bulldog pickerel, a small species of pike which lives east of the Alleghenies from Massachusetts to Florida. The bulldog pickerel is too small to be an important food or game fish.

bull|doze (bu̇l′dōz′), *v.t.*, **-dozed, -doz|ing. 1** *Informal.* to frighten, sometimes by violence or threats; bully: *The chairman tried to bulldoze the committee into voting for his proposal. When he tried to bulldoze Jordan's Premier, the Premier resigned* (Time). **2a** to move, clear, dig, or level with a bulldozer: *But the houses have been bulldozed down to make this new thoroughfare* (Listener). **b** *Figurative.* to force through or away; railroad: *[He] bulldozed his idea through all opposition* (Maclean's). **3** to flog severely. [apparently < earlier *bulldose* a beating (literally) a dose for a bull]

***bull|doz|er** (bu̇l′dō′zər), *n.* **1a** a powerful tractor with a wide steel blade that pushes rocks, earth, trees, or brush, used especially for grading, road building, and clearing land. **b** the blade. **2** *Informal.* a person who bullies or frightens another, sometimes by violence or threats. **3** *U.S. Slang.* a large pistol.

***bulldozer**
definition 1a

bul|let (bu̇l′it), *n., v.* **—*n.*** **1** a piece of lead, steel, or other metal, shaped to be fired from a pistol, rifle, or other small gun. See picture under **cartridge**. **2** a small, round ball. **3** *Figurative: The alternating gradient synchrotron ... accelerates proton "bullets" to energies of 33,000,000,000 electron volts* (New York Times).
—*v.i.* to go swiftly, like a bullet; shoot: *The ball bulleted past us. The road ... goes bulleting off through the mountains* (Saturday Review).
bite the bullet, to act with courage; submit to something painful without protest or delay: *The former film star added that college administrators should be willing to "bite the bullet" and stand up to demonstrators* (London Times).
[< Middle French *boulette* (diminutive) < *boule* ball[1]]

bul|let|head (bu̇l′it hed′), *n.* **1** a round head. **2** a person with such a head. **3** *Informal.* a pig-headed, obstinate person.

bul|let-head|ed (bu̇l′it hed′id), *adj.* having a round head.

bul|le|tin (bu̇l′ə tən), *n., v.* **—*n.*** **1a** a short statement of news: *Sports bulletins and weather bulletins are published in most newspapers.* **SYN:** report. **b** a statement for the information of the public, especially by an authority: *Doctors issue bulletins about the condition of certain of their well-known patients. Abbr:* bull. **2** a magazine or newspaper appearing regularly: *Our club publishes a bulletin each month.* **3** *Obsolete.* an official certificate.
—*v.t.* to make known by a bulletin: *News of its recovery was bulletined to observatories in the Western Hemisphere* (Scientific American).
[< Middle French *bulletin* < Italian *bulletino* (diminutive) < *bulleta* (diminutive) < Latin *bulla;* see etym. under **bull**[2]]

bulletin board, **1** a board on which notices are posted. **2** a computer service that displays information, messages, and news to subscribers and often allows them to communicate directly with each other: *The best way to tap into the free software market is to belong to a user's group or find the local computer bulletin board* (Washington Post).

bul|let|proof (bu̇l′it prüf′), *adj., v.* **—*adj.*** that will not let bullets through; resistant to bullets: *a bulletproof jacket.* **—*v.t.*** to make bulletproof.

bul|let|wood (bu̇l′it wu̇d′), *n.* **1** the wood of the bully tree. **2** the bully tree.

bull fiddle, *Informal.* = contrabass.

bull fiddler, *Informal.* = contrabassist.

bull|fight (bu̇l′fīt′), *n.* a fight between men and a bull in an arena. Bullfights are popular in Spain, Portugal, Mexico, and parts of South America.

bull|fight|er (bu̇l′fī′tər), *n.* a man who fights a bull in an arena; matador.

bull|fight|ing (bu̇l′fī′ting), *n.* the sport of fighting a bull in an arena: *For more than seven centuries, bullfighting has been Spain's reigning craze and pastime* (Newsweek).

bull|finch[1] (bu̇l′finch′), *n.* **1** a European and Asiatic songbird. The male has a blue and gray back and light-red breast and a short, stout bill. It is related to the grosbeaks. **2** any one of various other related birds, especially any one of various North American gray grosbeaks. [< *bull*[1] (uncertain reference) + *finch*]

bull|finch[2] (bu̇l′finch′), *n.* a hedge too high for a horse to jump in hunting. [origin uncertain]

bull|frog (bu̇l′frog′, -frôg′), *n.* a large frog of North America that makes a loud, croaking noise. [American English < *bull*[1] + *frog* (because of the sound it makes)]

bull|head (bu̇l′hed′), *n.* **1** any one of several American catfishes which have large, broad heads and hornlike growths near their mouths.
2 a stupid fellow; blockhead. **3** a sculpin or miller's-thumb. **4** = golden plover. [< *bull*[1] + *head*]

bull|head|ed (bu̇l′hed′id), *adj.* **1** stupidly stubborn; obstinate; headstrong: *Bullheaded opposition has finally defeated many good plans.* **2** having a large, broad head like a bull's. **—bull′head′ed|ly**, *adv.* **—bull′head′ed|ness**, *n.*

bullhead shark, a small, brown shark of the Pacific and Indian Oceans that feeds on mollusks and is not dangerous to man.

***bull|horn** (bu̇l′hôrn′), *n.* a megaphone or loudspeaker, especially a portable, battery-powered loudspeaker.

***bullhorn**

bullhorn acacia, an acacia native to Mexico that has thorns in pairs like the horns of cattle.

bul|lion (bu̇l′yən), *n.* **1a** uncoined gold or silver in the form of bars or ingots. **b** gold or silver in the mass. **c** coin, plate, or the like, considered only with reference to metallic value. **2** a cordlike trimming made of twisted gold or silver thread. [< Anglo-French *bullion* < Old French *bouillir* to boil; influenced by *billon* debased metal < *bille* stick]

bul|lion|ism (bu̇l′yə niz əm), *n.* the doctrine or system of an exclusively metallic currency, or a metallic currency combined with a convertible paper currency. **—bul′lion|ist**, *n.*

bul|li|rag (bu̇l′ē rag′), *v.t.*, **-ragged, -rag|ging.** = bullyrag.

bull|ish (bu̇l′ish), *adj.* **1** like a bull in manner or temper. **2a** trying to raise prices or tending to raise prices, especially in the stock market: *a* *bullish buyer.* **b** prompted by the expectation that prices will rise: *a bullish market.* **3** hopeful or confident; optimistic: *I'm bullish about next year's business prospects* —**bull′ish|ly**, *adv.* —**bull′ish|ness**, *n.*

bull market, a generally rising market: *Symptoms of the rise of speculative activity have been apparent in the recent bull market* (New York Times).

bull-mas|tiff or **bull|mas|tiff** (bůl′mas′tif, -mäs′-), *n.* a fearless, agile dog with a dense coat, a cross between a bulldog and mastiff.

Bull Moose, **1** a member of the Progressive Party led by Theodore Roosevelt in the presidential election of 1912. **2** the emblem or symbol of this party.

bull|necked (bůl′nekt′), *adj.* having a thick neck: ... *a two-fisted, stocky, bullnecked veteran of 39 years of moving freight* (Newsweek).

bull nettle, a silvery-leaved, prickly weed of the nightshade family.

bull|ock (bůl′ək), *n., v.* —*n.* **1** an ox; steer. **2** a young bull; bull calf.
—*v.t., v.i.* to force (a way) through people or a situation.
[Old English *bulluc* bull calf]

bul|lock's-heart (bůl′əks härt′), *n.* **1** = custard apple. **2** its fruit.

bullock shell, a kind of small, thick pearl oyster, inhabiting tropical America.

Bul|lock's oriole (bůl′əks), an oriole of the western part of North America, with orange and black feathers. [< William *Bullock*, an English naturalist of the 1800's]

bull|ock|y (bůl′ə kē), *n., pl.* **-ock|ies**, *adj. Australian.* —*n.* the driver of a team of bullocks used for hauling.
—*adj.* **1** resembling that of a bullock; oxlike: *bullocky noises.* **2** having to do with driving bullocks or managing cattle.

bul|lous (bůl′əs, bul′-), *adj.* of or characterized by the eruption of large blisters. [< *bulla* + *-ous*]

bull pen, **1** *Baseball.* **a** a place outside the playing limits in which baseball relief pitchers warm up during a game. **b** the relief pitchers on a baseball team: *a strong bull pen.* **2** *Slang.* **a** a temporary prison. **b** a room in a jail or adjoining a court where a number of prisoners are temporarily confined together. **c** a jail of any kind. **3** a pen for a bull or bulls. **4** *U.S. Slang.* any room or section of a building used by unassigned or reserve members of an office force. **5** *U.S. Slang.* the bunk room of a lumber camp.

bull point, *British.* a point scored against an opponent; an advantage: *A bull point for the Lancashire and Midland operators, though not for London, is the new monopoly position within the companies' own areas* (London Times).

bull|pout (bůl′pout′), *n.* = hornpout.

bull-punch|er (bul′pun′chər), *n. Australian.* a driver of bullocks.

bull ring, or **bull|ring** (bůl′ring′), *n.* an arena for bullfights.

bull-roar|er (bůl′rôr′ər, -rōr′-), *n.* a long, thin strip of wood with a cord or thong at one end, by which it is whirled rapidly to make a roaring sound in certain primitive religious rites.

bull|rush (bůl′rush′), *n.* = bulrush.

bull session, **1** *Informal.* **a** a frank, informal discussion about any interesting topic. **b** any rambling discussion. **2** *British Slang.* a period of intense cleaning, polishing, or routine tasks, especially in military use.

bull's-eye or **bulls|eye** (bůlz′ī′), *n.* **1** the center of a target: *The bull's-eye was marked with a large red circle.* **2a** a shot that hits it: *The archer's shot was a perfect bull's-eye.* **b** any act or remark that successfully hits an actual or figurative target: *He scored a bull's-eye in their argument with that witty retort.* **3a** a thick piece of dome-shaped glass fixed in the deck or side of a ship to let in light. **b** *Architecture.* any circular opening for light or air. **4a** a lens shaped like a half-sphere to concentrate light. **b** a small lantern with such a lens in its side. **5** *Especially British.* a kind of candy made in round, hard lumps. **6** *Nautical.* an oval or circular wooden block having a groove around it and a hole in the center through which to reeve a rope.

bull|shot (bůl′shot′), *n. U.S.* an alcoholic drink made with vodka or gin and bouillon.

bull snake, any one of various North American snakes that live on rodents. All are harmless to man.

bull terrier, a strong, active, short-haired dog, white or brindle marked with white, developed from a cross between a bulldog and a terrier.

bull thistle, the common thistle.

bull tongue, *U.S.* a simple form of plow.

bull-tongue (bůl′tung′), *v.t.* **-tongued, -tonguing.** *U.S.* to plow with a bull tongue.

bull trout, **1** = salmon trout. **2** the Dolly Varden trout of the Pacific coast.

bull|whack (bůl′hwak′), *n., v. Western U. S.* —*n.* a whip with a long, heavy lash and a short handle.
—*v.t.* to drive (a team of oxen or other draft animals) with a bullwhack or other whip.

bull|whack|er (bůl′hwak′ər), *n. Western U.S.* **1** the driver of a wagon drawn by a team of oxen or other draft animals. **2** a bullwhack.

bull|whip (bůl′hwip′), *n.* a long, heavy leather whip like those formerly used by drivers of oxen.

bul|ly[1] (bůl′ē), *n., pl.* **-lies**, *v.,* **-lied, -ly|ing**, *adj., interj.* —*n.* **1** a person who teases, frightens, threatens, or hurts others who are not as strong as he is. **2** *Archaic.* a hired ruffian; bravo; bullyboy. **3** *British Dialect.* mate; companion. **4** *Obsolete.* a good friend; fine fellow. **5** *Obsolete.* a sweetheart.
—*v.t.* **1** to frighten (into doing something) by noisy talk or threats: *The older boys bullied him into giving away his candy.* SYN: overawe, intimidate. **2** to be a bully toward.
—*v.i.* to be a bully; be overbearing. SYN: bluster.
—*adj.* **1** *Informal.* very good; excellent. **2** jovial; gallant; spirited. **3** like a bully or ruffian.
—*interj. Informal.* bravo! well done!: *Bully for you!*
[perhaps < Dutch *boel* lover, brother; later influenced by *bull*[1]]

bul|ly[2] (bůl′ē), *n.* = bully beef. [probably < French *bouilli* boiled beef < *bouillir* to boil]

bul|ly[3] (bůl′ē), *n., pl.* **-lies**, *v.,* **-lied, -ly|ing.** *Field Hockey.* —*n.* = bully-off. —*v.t., v.i.* to cross sticks three times and hit (the ball). [origin unknown]

bully beef, canned or pickled beef.

bul|ly|boy (bůl′ē boi′), *n.* a person hired to gain ends by violence or the threat of violence; thug.

bul|ly-off (bul′ē ôf′, -of′), *n. Field Hockey.* **1** the start of play. **2** the crossing of sticks before the ball is played.

bul|ly|rag (bůl′ē rag′), *v.t.,* **-ragged, -rag|ging.** *Informal.* **1** to attack with abusive language; bully; abuse. **2** = tease. Also, **ballyrag, bullirag.**

bully tree, any one of various West Indian and tropical American trees of the sapodilla family, especially the species from which the gum balata is obtained. [origin uncertain]

***bul|rush** (bůl′rush′), *n.* **1** a tall, slender plant that grows in wet places, used in making mats, bottoms of chairs, and the like. The bulrush belongs to the sedge family. **2** *British.* the cattail. **3** *U.S.* any one of several rushes, especially the common rush. **4** the papyrus of Egypt (in the Bible, Exodus 2:3). Also, **bullrush.** [Middle English *bulrysche* < *bule* bole[1] + *rysche*, Old English *rysc* rush]

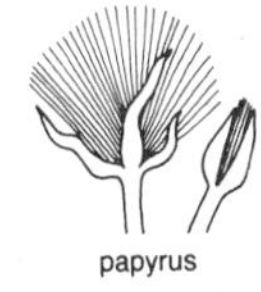

***bulrush** definitions 1, 4

bul|tow (bůl′tō), *n.* a trawl line. [compare Danish *bulletouw* ship ropes]

bul|wark (bůl′wərk), *n., v.* —*n.* **1** a person, thing, or idea that is a defense or a protection: *A free press and free speech are bulwarks of democracy.* SYN: safeguard, support. **2** a wall of earth or other material for defense against an enemy; rampart: *The city was protected by a bulwark and a moat surrounding it.* **3a** a breakwater for protection against the force of the waves. **b** an embankment.
—*v.t.* **1** to defend; protect; shelter: *Friends bulwarked him about from infancy to boyhood* (Robert Browning). **2** to provide with a bulwark or bulwarks.
bulwarks, the side of a ship extending like a fence above the deck.
[Middle English *bulwerk*, apparently < *bole* + *work*, that is, a work made of tree trunks. Compare etym. under **boulevard.**]

bum[1] (bum), *n., v.,* **bummed, bum|ming**, *adj.,* **bum|mer, bum|mest.** *Informal.* —*n.* **1** an idle or good-for-nothing person; loafer. **2** a tramp; hobo. **3** a person who is extremely devoted to a sport, sometimes to the point of seeming to do nothing else but participate in it or follow it: *a tennis bum, a surf bum, a track bum.* **4** a drunken spree: *to go on a bum.* **5** a drunken loafer.
—*v.t.* to get (food, money, or anything else) by sponging on others; beg: *He tried to bum a ride.*
—*v.i.* **1** to loaf around; idle about: *playing pool and bumming with the boys* (O. Henry). **2** to sponge on others; beg. **3** to drink heavily.
—*adj.* **1** of poor quality; worthless: *Every bum novel begins that way* (Robert W. Chambers). **2** sore or lame: *a bum knee.* **3** false; mistaken: *The information he got was a bum steer. The prisoner claimed that he got a bum rap from the court.*
bum (someone) **out**, *U.S. Slang.* to disgust, annoy, or vex: *Most of the bands they get in here are so bad they really bum me out, but these are good* (Atlantic Monthly).
on the bum, a not functioning; out of order: *Our old toaster is on the bum.* **b** living as a bum: *He spent two years on the bum.*
[short for earlier *bummer* loafer < German *Bummler*]

bum[2] (bum), *v.,* **bummed, bum|ming**, *n. Chiefly Dialect.* —*v.i.* to make a humming sound; hum; buzz. —*n.* a humming noise. [imitative]

bum[3] (bum), *n.* = buttocks. [Middle English *bom*; origin unknown]

bum|ber|shoot (bum′bər shüt′), *n.* (used humorously) an umbrella. [humorous alteration of *umbre*(lla)-(para)*chute*]

bum|ble (bum′bəl), *n., v.,* **-bled, -bling.** —*n.* an awkward mistake.
—*v.i.* **1** to act or proceed in a bungling, awkward manner: *[He] bumbles along, a monumental misfit who spends much of his time begging everyone's pardon* (Newsweek). **2** to commit a bumble or bumbles: *He bumbled, contradicted himself and flubbed questions that were thrown at him* (Time).
—*v.t.* to do (something) in an awkward, foolish way; bungle; botch: *to bumble a job.*
[origin uncertain] —**bum′bler**, *n.*

bum|ble|bee (bum′bəl bē′), *n.* a large bee with a thick, hairy body, usually banded with gold; humblebee. Bumblebees make a loud buzzing sound. They live in small colonies often in underground nests or old logs, where they raise their young and store honey. See picture under **bee**[1]. [earlier *bumble* buzz + *bee*]

bum|ble|dom (bum′bəl dəm), *n.* arrogant and incompetent officials, as a group. [< *Bumble*, the pompous beadle in Dickens' *Oliver Twist.* Compare etym. under **bumbling.**]

bum|ble-pup|py (bum′bəl pup′ē), *n.* **1** the game of whist played unscientifically. **2** a game in which a ball slung to a post is struck in opposite directions by two players.

bum|bling (bum′bling). *adj.* **1** marked by or subject to blundering and awkward ways, inept: *The bumbling old porter dropped the luggage.* **2** filled with self-importance; officious. [present participle of *bumble* act with confusion; reinforced by *Bumble*, the beadle in Dickens' *Oliver Twist*] —**bum′bling|ly**, *adv.*

bum|boat (bum′bōt′), *n.* a boat used in peddling small merchandise, fresh fruit, and other provisions to ships in port or lying offshore. [< *bum* buttocks + *boat*]

bu|me|li|a (byü mē′lē ə), *n.* a tree or shrub with a milky juice, a spiny stem, and small white or greenish flowers, native to the West Indies. [< New Latin *Bumelia* the genus name < Latin *būmelia*, a kind of ash tree]

bumf (bumf), *n. British Slang.* **1** toilet paper. **2** worthless paper; trash: *His office pigeonhole has to swallow an enormous volume of bumf* (Punch). Also, **bumph.** [short for *bumfodder* < *bum*[3] + *fodder*]

bum|kin (bum′kin), *n.* = bumpkin[2].

bum|ma|ree (bum′ə rē′), *n. British.* **1** a middleman at the Billingsgate fish market. **2** a porter at the Smithfield meat market.

bum|mer (bum′ər), *n. Slang.* **1** a bum; loafer. **2** a bad experience. **3** a failure; flop: ... *all the films released this summer have been box-office bummers* (New Yorker). **4** during the civil war in the United States, a camp follower or a plundering straggler.

bump (bump), *v., n., adv.* —*v.i.* **1** to push throw, or strike (against something large or solid): *She bumped against the table in the dark. The jostling crowd bumped against the railing in their eagerness to see the race.* SYN: thump, knock. **2** to move by bumping against things: *Our car bumped along the dirt road.* SYN: jolt, jog. **3** *Cricket.* (of a delivery) to rear up off the ground.
—*v.t.* **1** to hit or come against with heavy blows: *That truck bumped our car.* **2** *U.S. Informal, Figurative.* to oust and take the place of (someone), especially on a plane or in a job, as by exercising a higher priority or greater seniority: *Every time there's a layoff at one of the shifts at our mill, the men bump each other according to seniority* (Wall Street Journal). **3** to seize (a person) and thump him against a wall or tree. **4** *British.* (in boat racing) to overtake and touch (the boat ahead).
—*n.* **1** a heavy blow or knock: *The bump*

Pronunciation Key: hat, āge, cãre, fär; let, ēqual, tėrm; it, īce; hot, ōpen, ôrder; oil, out; cup, půt, rüle; child; long; thin; ᴛʜen; zh, measure; ə represents **a** in about, **e** in taken, **i** in pencil, **o** in lemon, **u** in circus.

knocked our car forward a few feet. **2** a swelling caused by a bump: *He has a bump where a baseball hit him on the head.* **3** any swelling or lump: *He tried to avoid the bump in the road.* **4** a jolt or upward thrust of an airplane due to a rising current of air. **5** *Informal.* a displacement or promotion: *a bump to full colonel.* **6** *Phrenology.* **a** a protuberance. **b** the faculty represented by the protuberance. **7** *Slang.* a suggestive thrusting forward of the hips or abdomen, as in a striptease act: *a burlesque dancer's bumps and grinds.*
8 *British.* an overtaking in a boat race with a staggered start marked by contact with the boat in front. **—*adv.*** with a bump: *He went bump down the stairs.*
bump into, *Informal.* to meet by chance; run across: *He hoped to bump into some of his old classmates at the party.*
bump off, *Slang.* to kill: *Dutch was bumped off in Newark by a rival mob* (Time).
bump up, a *Especially British Informal.* to increase suddenly: *to bump up sales.* **b** *U.S. Informal.* to promote: . . . *a former marshal who was bumped up several places to the No. 4 position* (Time).
[imitative]

bump·er (bum′pər), *n., adj., v.* **—*n.*** **1** any device that protects against damage by bumping. **2** a bar or bars of metal across the front and back of a car, bus, or truck, that protects it from being damaged if bumped: *Trucks had been observed moving bumper to bumper, with lights on, in an unprecedentedly large movement . . . southwards* (Manchester Guardian Weekly). **3** a cup or glass filled to the brim: . . . *fill me a bumper, a bumper of claret* (Thomas Love Peacock). **4** *Informal.* something unusually large of its kind: *His crop of potatoes was a bumper.* **5** *Cricket.* a fast ball that rears off the ground, usually short pitched and to the danger of the batsman. **6** a marine fish with a compressed body, common in the West Indies.
—*adj.* unusually large; abundant: *The farmer raised a bumper crop of wheat last year.* SYN: outsize.
—*v.t.* to fill to the brim.

bumper sticker, a sticker bearing a printed slogan for display on an automobile bumper.

bumph (bumf), *n.* = bumf.

bump·kin[1] (bump′kin), *n.* an awkward or simple person from the country: *The more bashful country bumpkins hung sheepishly back* (Washington Irving). SYN: lout, churl, boor, clodhopper. [perhaps < Middle Dutch *bommekyn* little barrel]

bump·kin[2] (bump′kin), *n.* a short beam projecting from a ship, used to extend a sail, secure blocks, or the like. Also, **bumkin.** [probably < Middle Dutch *boomken* little tree]

bump·out (bump′out′), *n. U.S.* an addition that increases the space of a room in an office, apartment, or house without adding significantly to the outside dimension of a structure: *Ambitious bumpouts can be virtually room-size, large enough to be called an addition* (New York Times).

bump·tious (bump′shəs), *adj.* unpleasantly forward or conceited; arrogant and quarrelsome: *Babbitt was a selfish, bumptious, small-souled provincial* (Newsweek). [probably < *bump,* perhaps patterned on obsolete *presumptious*]
—bump′tious·ly, *adv.* **—bump′tious·ness,** *n.*

bump·y (bum′pē), *adj.,* **bump·i·er, bump·i·est.** **1** having bumps; full of bumps: *a bumpy road.* **2** causing bumps; jolty: *a bumpy ride.* **—bump′i·ly,** *adv.* **—bump′i·ness,** *n.*

bum's rush, *Especially U.S. Slang.* **1** a forcible ejection (of a person from a place): *He gave Fredo a firm bum's rush out the door, closing it and bolting it on Fredo's clamorous protests* (New Yorker). **2** *Figurative.* any means used to get rid of someone.

bun[1] (bun), *n.* **1** bread or cake in small shapes. Buns are often slightly sweetened and may contain spice or raisins. **2** hair coiled at the back of the head in a knot suggesting a bun. Also, **bunn.** [Middle English *bunne;* origin uncertain]

bun[2] (bun), *n. Slang.* a drunken condition; enough liquor to get drunk on: *He kept drinking till he got a bun on.* [origin uncertain]

bun[3] (bun), *n.* **1** = squirrel. **2** = rabbit. [related to *bunny*]

Bu·na (bü′nə, byü′-), *n.* **1** *Trademark.* a synthetic rubber made from butadiene, used especially in making automobile tires. Buna S is made by copolymerization of butadiene with styrene. Buna N is produced by the copolymerization of butadiene with acrylonitrile. **2 buna.** this or any similarly produced rubber. [< German *Buna* < *Bu* (tadien) + *Na,* symbol (< *Natrium*) for sodium]

Bun·bur·y (bun′bėr ē, -brē), *v.i.,* **-bur·ied, -bur·y·ing.** to travel for the pleasure of traveling or sightseeing. [< *Bunbury,* an imaginary character used as an excuse to visit in other places in Oscar Wilde's play *The Importance of Being Earnest*]

bunch (bunch), *n., v.* **—*n.*** **1** a group of things of the same kind growing fastened, placed, or thought of together: *a bunch of grapes, a bunch of flowers, a bunch of sheep.* SYN: batch, cluster. See syn. under **bundle. 2** *Informal.* a group of people: *a bunch of thieves. They are a friendly bunch.* SYN: band, gang. **3** *Informal.* any group not necessarily together; lot: *He's got a bunch of cousins.* **4** a swelling; protuberance.
—*v.i.* to come together in one place: *The sheep bunched up in the shed to keep warm.*
—*v.t.* **1** to bring together and make into a bunch: *We have bunched the flowers for you to carry home.* **2** to put in folds; gather: *a dress bunched up on the hips and at the back.*
[Middle English *bunche;* origin uncertain]
—bunch′er, *n.*
▶Formal English limits the use of **bunch** to objects that grow together or can be fastened together: *a bunch of radishes, a bunch of flowers, a bunch of keys.* Informal English, however, clings to the older usage of *bunch,* applying it to a small collection of anything, including people: *A bunch of us meet at the Grill every night.*

bunch·ber·ry (bunch′ber′ē, -bər-), *n., pl.* **-ries.** a low shrub with white flowers and dense clusters of bright-red berries; cornel.

buncher resonator, = klystron.

bunch·flow·er (bunch′flou′ər), *n.* a North American herb of the lily family, having grasslike leaves and a tall stem with a panicle of small, greenish flowers.

bunch grass, any one of various grasses of the Western United States that grow in distinct bunches or tufts.

bunch pink, = sweet william.

bunch·y (bun′chē), *adj.,* **bunch·i·er, bunch·i·est.** **1** having bunches or clusters. **2** growing in bunches. **3** bulging or protuberant. **—bunch′i·ly,** *adv.* **—bunch′i·ness,** *n.*

bun·co (bung′kō), *n., pl.* **-cos,** *v.,* **-coed, -co·ing.** **—*n.*** **1** *Slang.* a swindle, especially one perpetrated by means of cardsharping or some form of confidence trick. **2** a kind of card game.
—*v.t.* *Slang.* to swindle or cheat. Also, **bunko.**
[American English; apparently < American Spanish *banca, -o* a card game]

bun·combe (bung′kəm), *n.* = bunkum.

bunco steerer, *U.S. Slang.* a decoy or shill for a bunco.

bund (bund), *n.* **1** (in the Far East, especially Anglo-Chinese ports) an embankment forming a promenade or thoroughfare along a shore. **2** (in India) an artificial embankment. [< Hindustani *band* < Persian]

Bund (bůnd; *German* bůnt), *n., pl.* **Bün·de** (byn′də). **1** a former organization in the United States of persons with Nazi sympathies, founded in 1936. **2** an association; society; league. [< German *Bund.* See related etym. under **band**[1].]

bun·der (bun′dər), *n. Anglo-Indian.* a landing place; pier; harbor. [< Hindustani *bandar* < Persian]

Bun·des·rat (bůn′dəs rät′), *n.* **1** the upper house of the federal legislature of West Germany or of Austria. **2** the federal council in the legislature of the former German Empire. **3** the federal council or chief executive authority of Switzerland.
[< German *Bundesrat* < *Bund* federation + *Rat* council]

Bun·des·tag (bůn′dəs täk′), *n.* the lower house of the federal legislature of West Germany. [< German *Bundestag* < *Bund* federation + *tagen* to meet, confer]

Bun·des·wehr (bůn′dəs vär′), *n.* the federal defense forces of West Germany. [< German *Bundeswehr* < *Bund* federation + *Wehr* defense]

bun·dle (bun′dəl), *n., v.,* **-dled, -dling. —*n.*** **1** a number of things tied or wrapped together: *a bundle of rags, a bundle of firewood.* **2** a parcel; package: *We sent my uncle a large bundle on his birthday.* **3** a number of things considered together; bunch: *She was a bundle of nerves.* **4** a group of muscle or nerve fibers bound closely together; a fasciculus. **5** *Botany.* an aggregation of cells for conduction and support in the stems and leaves of plants. **6** a measurement of yarn equal to twenty hanks. **7** a quantity of paper consisting of two reams. *Abbr:* bdl. **8** *U.S. Slang.* a sum of money, especially a large sum. **9** *British Slang.* a teen-age gang fight; rumble.
—*v.t.* **1** to tie or wrap together; make into a bundle: *We bundled all our old newspapers and set them out at the curb.* **2** to send in a hurry; hustle: *They bundled me off to the hospital in an ambulance.* **3** to collect; gather (up or together) into a mass.
—*v.i.* **1** to go or leave in a hurry: *They bundled down to town in a cab to catch the next train.*
2 to conduct a courtship, fully dressed, in bed, as couples did in New England in colonial days.
bundle up, to dress warmly: *You should bundle up on cold winter mornings.*
[perhaps < Middle Dutch *bondel*] **—bun′dler,** *n.*
—*Syn.* *n.* **1, 2 Bundle, bunch, parcel** mean something fastened or wrapped together for convenient handling. **Bundle** suggests a number of things of the same or different sizes and shapes bound or wrapped together, often clumsily: *We gave away several bundles of old newspapers and magazines.* **Bunch** suggests a number of things of the same kind bound or fastened together, usually closely and neatly: *I bought a bunch of flowers.* **Parcel** suggests one or more things wrapped and tied neatly for carrying or mailing: *I had too many parcels to carry on the bus.*

bundle of His (his), = atrioventricular bundle. [< Wilhelm *His,* 1863-1934, a Swiss anatomist]

bun·dook (bun′důk), *n. Anglo-Indian.* a rifle. [< Hindustani *bandūq*]

bun·fight (bun′fīt′), *n. Slang.* a brawl.

bung (bung), *n., v.* **—*n.*** **1** a stopper for closing the hole in the side or end of a barrel, keg, or cask: *The bung was pulled out of a long-sealed cask of excellent wine* (Harper's). **2** = bunghole.
—*v.t.* to close (a bunghole) with a stopper.
bung up, a to close with a stopper: *to bung up a bunghole or a cask.* **b** to stop up; choke up: *to bung up one's mouth.* **c** *Slang.* to bruise: *He tripped, fell, and bunged up his arms and knees.*
[probably < Middle Dutch *bonghe*]

bun·ga·loid (bung′gə loid), *adj.* **1** having the appearance or style of a bungalow: *bungaloid hotels.* **2** filled with bungalows: *bungaloid cities.* [< *bungal*(ow) + *-oid*]

bun·ga·low (bung′gə lō), *n.* **1** a small house, usually of one story or a story and a half, with low, sweeping lines. **2** (in India) a one-storied thatched or tiled house, usually having a veranda on one or more sides. [< Hindustani *banglā* (literally) Bengalese]

bun·gee (bun′jē), *n.* a tension device, such as a set of springs, an elastic cable, or a rubber cord, used in aircraft to assist in moving the controls. [origin unknown]

bungee cord, an elastic cord with hooks at both ends, used to hold bulky items in place, as on top of a car or a bike rack.

bung-full (bung′fůl′), *adj.* crammed or stuffed full: *The bag was bung-full and hard to close.*

bung·hole (bung′hōl′), *n.* the hole in the side or end of a barrel, keg, or cask through which it is filled and emptied.

bun·gle (bung′gəl), *v.,* **-gled, -gling,** *n.* **—*v.t.*** **1** to do or make (something) in a clumsy, unskillful way. SYN: botch, boggle, bumble. **2** to spoil by unskillful workmanship: *He tried to make a birdhouse but bungled the job.* **—*v.i.*** to work or act unskillfully or clumsily; blunder.
—*n.* a clumsy, unskillful performance or piece of work.
[imitative]

bun·gler (bung′glər), *n.* a person who bungles.

bun·gle·some (bung′gəl səm), *adj.* bungling; clumsy; unskillful.

bun·gling (bung′gling), *n., adj.* **—*n.*** unskillful or clumsy work or action.
—*adj.* that bungles; showing unskillfulness; clumsy. **—bun′gling·ly,** *adv.*

bun·ion (bun′yən), *n.* a painful, inflamed swelling on the foot, especially on the first joint of the big toe. [origin uncertain]

bunk[1] (bungk), *n., v.* **—*n.*** **1** a narrow bed against a wall like a shelf, often with another bed placed above it: *Sailors sleep in bunks.* **2** any place to sleep. **3** *U.S.* **a** a piece of timber on which logs rest in a logging sled, car, or truck. **b** the sled, car, or truck. **4** a feed trough for cattle.
—*v.i.* **1** to sleep in a bunk; occupy a bunk. **2** to sleep in rough quarters: *We bunked in an old barn.* **3** to share quarters: *You can bunk with me, if you wish.*
—*v.t.* **1** *Informal.* to provide with a place to sleep. **2** *U.S.* to place (logs) on bunks.
[perhaps related to **bank**[1]]

bunk[2] (bungk), *n., v. Slang.* **—*n.*** insincere talk; nonsense; humbug; bunkum: *You're making speeches full of bunk* (New York Times).
—*v.t.* to humbug; delude.
[American English; short for *bunkum,* alteration of *buncombe*]

bunk[3] (bungk), *v., n. British Slang.* **—*v.i.*** to flee. **—*n.*** **do a bunk,** to flee: *When Lennox shows up in a daze, not sure that he hasn't murdered his wife, . . . Marlowe helps him do a bunk to Mexico* (Atlantic). [a dialectal word]

bunk bed, *U.S.* one of a pair of single beds placed one above the other to conserve space.

bunk·er[1] (bung′kər), *n., adj., v.* **—*n.*** **1** a place or bin for coal, especially on a ship: *The reactor in an atomic ship corresponds to the fuel in the bunkers of an ordinary steamship* (New Scientist). **2** a sandy hollow or mound of earth on a golf course, forming an obstacle: *The course, with its many bunkers, and particularly its long, clinging rough, is not suited to [his] game* (London Times). **3** a fortified shelter built partly or entirely below

ground. Bunkers are used as a defensive position in battle. A bunker is often part of a larger fortification. —*adj.* characterized by or adopting a strongly defensive attitude or position in the face of a threat; last-ditch: *a bunker atmosphere, a bunker philosophy. The reactionary regime has already receded into a bunker mentality* (Time).
—*v.t.* **1** to supply (a ship) with coal or other fuel for its operation. **2** to hit (a golf ball) into a bunker. [origin uncertain]

bunk|er² (bung′kər), *n.* = menhaden. [short for *mossbunker*]

bunk|er|age (bung′kər ij), *n.* **1** the act of supplying a ship with fuel. **2** the place where fuel is stored on a ship; a bunker or bunkers.

bunker coal, the coal carried on a ship, especially on a collier, for use as its own fuel.

bunker oil, **1** oil carried on a ship for use as its own fuel. **2** a similar grade and weight of heavy oil used to operate other machinery.

bunker silo, a silo built above ground, usually with wood or concrete sides, and one or both ends may be open.

bunk|house (bungk′hous′), *n.* a rough building with sleeping quarters or bunks, especially one provided for workers: *The men in the lumber camp slept in bunkhouses.* [American English]

bunk|ie or **bunk|y** (bung′kē), *n., pl.* **bunk|ies.** *U.S. Informal.* a roommate; comrade. [< *bunk*¹]

bunk|mate (bungk′māt′), *n. U.S. Informal.* a person who shares a bunk.

bun|ko (bung′kō), *n., pl.* **-kos**, *v.,* **-koed**, **-ko|ing.** = bunco. [American English; variant of *bunco*]

bun|kum (bung′kəm), *n.* insincere talk; nonsense; humbug. Also, **buncombe.** [alteration of *buncombe* < *Buncombe* County, North Carolina, whose congressman in 1819-1821 kept making long-winded and pointless speeches "for Buncombe"]

bunn (bun), *n.* = bun¹.

bun|nia (bun′ya), *n.* Anglo-Indian. a Hindu tradesman. [< Hindustani *baniyā*]

bun|ny (bun′ē), *n., pl.* **-nies. 1** a pet name for a rabbit. **2** *U.S.* a squirrel. **3** *Slang.* a pretty, scantily dressed nightclub waitress, originally one wearing a rabbit costume. [perhaps < Scottish *bun* tail of a hare; origin uncertain]

bunny hug, an American ballroom dance in ragtime rhythm, popular between 1910 and 1930.

Bun|ra|ku (bün rä′kü), *n.* the traditional Japanese puppet theater: *Bunraku . . . originated 300 years ago when the arts of puppetry, recitation, and samisen-playing were combined experimentally* (New York Times). [< Japanese *Bunraku*]

***Bun|sen burner** (bun′sən), a gas burner with a very hot, blue flame, used in laboratories. Air is let in at the base and mixed with gas. [< Robert W. *Bunsen*, 1811-1899, a German chemist, who invented it]

***Bunsen burner**

bunt¹ (bunt), *v., n.* —*v.i.* , *v.t.* **1** to hit (a baseball) lightly so that the ball goes to the ground and rolls only a short distance: *Andy Seminick bunted into a force play* (New York Times). **2** to strike with the head or horns, as a goat does; butt. **3** to push; shove.
—*n.* **1a** the act of bunting a baseball. **b** a baseball that is bunted. **2** a push; shove.
[perhaps variant of *butt*³]—**bunt′er**, *n.*

bunt² (bunt), *n., v.* —*n.* **1** the middle, bellying part of a square sail. **2** the bagging section of a fishing net.
—*v.i.* to swell out or belly, as a sail does.
—*v.t.* **bunt up**, to haul (a sail) up to a yard so that its middle part forms an irregular roll.
[origin uncertain]

bunt³ (bunt), *n.* **1** a disease of wheat in which the center of the kernels is replaced by black, ill-smelling spores, caused by a parasitic fungus; stinking smut. **2** the fungus producing this disease. [origin unknown]

bun|ting¹ (bun′ting), *n.* **1** a thin cloth used for flags. **2** long pieces of cloth having the colors and designs of a flag, used to decorate buildings and streets on holidays and special occasions. **3** a flag, or flags collectively, especially of a ship. **4** a baby's warm, hooded, outer garment closed at the bottom; baby bunting. [perhaps Middle English *bonten* to sift (because the cloth was used for sifting)]

bun|ting² (bun′ting), *n.* any one of several small, usually brightly colored birds with stout bills. The bunting belongs to the same family as the finch. [origin uncertain]

bunt|line (bunt′līn′, -lən), *n.* a rope fastened to the bottom of a sail. It is used to haul the sail up to the yard for furling. [< *bunt*² + *line*¹]

bun|ya-bun|ya (bun′yə bun′yə), *n.* a large evergreen tree of Australia, having strong, durable wood, and bearing edible seeds about two inches long. [< a native Australian name]

Bun|yan (bun′yən), *n.* **Paul**, a giant lumberjack in American folklore with amazing strength, who did marvelous deeds.

Bun|yan|esque (bun′yə nesk′), *adj.* **1** characteristic of or suggesting Paul Bunyan or the tales told about him; of exaggerated proportions; having very large size: *Bunyanesque hyperbole.* **2** characteristic of or suggesting the style, writings, etc., of John Bunyan, 1628-88, the author of *Pilgrim's Progress: a Bunyanesque allegory.*

bun|yip (bun′yip), *n.* **1** a fabulous animal of native Australian tradition, usually described as large and amphibious. **2** an imposter; humbug. [< a native Australian name]

buo|na|ma|no (bwō′nä mä′nō), *n., pl.* **-ni** (-nē). *Italian.* a gratuity; tip.

buon fres|co (bwôn fres′kō), *Art.* painting on wet plaster, as distinguished from secco painting; fresco. [< Italian *buon fresco* (literally) good fresco]

***buoy** (boi, bü′ē), *n., v.* —*n.* **1** a floating object anchored on the water to warn against hidden rocks or shallows, or to show the safe part of a channel. In mooring places, an anchored buoy is often set up, to which a ship, or especially a small boat, may make fast. *The crewmen took heart . . . when they saw the welcome blinking of a buoy lamp* (Harper's). **2** a cork- or plastic-filled belt, ring, jacket, or other buoyant object, used to keep a person afloat in the water; life buoy.
—*v.t.* to furnish with buoys; mark with a buoy.
—*v.i.* to float.
buoy up, a to hold up; keep from sinking: *His life jacket buoyed him up until rescuers came.* **b** *Figurative: Hope buoys him up, even when something goes wrong.*
[probably < Middle Dutch *boeie* < Old French *boie*]

***buoy**
definition 1

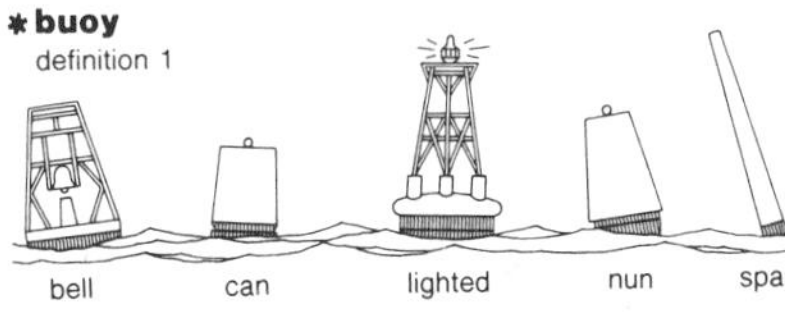

buoy|age (boi′ij, bü′ij), *n.* **1** a series of buoys. **2** buoys collectively. **3** the providing of buoys.

buoy|an|cy (boi′ən sē, bü′yən-), *n.* **1** the power to float: *Wood has more buoyancy than iron.* **2** the power to keep things afloat: *Salt water has greater buoyancy than fresh water.* **3** a body's loss in weight when immersed in a liquid. **4** tendency to rise. **5** *Figurative.* tendency to be hopeful and cheerful; light-heartedness: *Her buoyancy kept us from being downhearted.* **SYN:** cheerfulness, hopefulness.

buoy|ant (boi′ənt, bü′yənt), *adj.* **1** able to float: *Wood and cork are buoyant; iron and lead are not.* **2** able to keep things afloat: *Balloons can float because air is buoyant.* **3** tending to rise: (*Figurative.*) *buoyant hopes, a buoyant stock market.* **4** *Figurative.* cheerful and hopeful; lighthearted: *Children are usually more buoyant than adults.* **SYN:** blithe, jocund, gay. —**buoy′ant|ly**, *adv.*

buoyant mine, a mine that floats on or just below the surface of the water.

bu|pres|tid (byü pres′tid), *n.* any one of a family of beetles, often brilliantly colored, having short, toothed antennae and a long, tapering abdomen. The eggs are laid in the bark of trees and plants, and the larvae are often destructive borers in the wood. [< Latin *būprestis* a poisonous beetle < Greek *boúprēstis*, (literally) ox-sweller < *boûs* ox + *prēthein* cause to swell (because of their fatal effect on cattle who eat them)]

buq|sha (bük′shə), *n., pl.* **-shas** or **-sha.** a unit of money of Yemen, equal to 1/40 of a riyal. Also, **bugshah.** [< Arabic *buqsha*]

bur (bėr), *n., v.,* **burred, bur|ring.** —*n.* **1** a prickly, clinging seedcase or flower of some plants; burr. Burs stick to cloth and fur. *Do roses stick like burs?* (Robert Browning). See picture under **chestnut.** (*Figurative.*) *I am a kind of bur, I shall stick* (Shakespeare). **2** a plant or weed that has burs, especially the burdock; burr. **3** burr; a tool for drilling or cutting.
—*v.t.* to remove burs from; burr.
[probably < Scandinavian (compare Danish *borre* burdock)]—**bur′like′**, *adj.*

bur., bureau.

bu|ra (bü rä′), *n.* = buran.

bu|ran (bü rän′), *n.* a violent northerly wind on the Russian and Siberian steppes, carrying snow or ice particles in winter and laden with dust in summer. [< Russian *buran* < a Turkic (probably Tartar) language]

Bur|ber|ry (bėr′bər ē), *n., pl.* **-ries.** *Trademark.* **1** a kind of waterproof cloth for coats. **2** a coat made of it.

bur|ble (bėr′bəl), *v.,* **-bled, -bling,** *n.* —*v.i.* **1** to make a bubbling noise. **2** to speak in a confused, excited manner.
—*n.* **1** a bubble; bubbling. **2** *Aeronautics.* an induced turbulence of the air around a wing or other airfoil, especially when the airfoil has reached maximum lift. [probably imitative]

burble point, *U.S. Aeronautics.* a point reached in an increasing angle of attack at which a particular airfoil stalls and burble begins.

bur|bly (bėr′blē), *adj.* **1** full of bubbles; bubbly. **2** turbulent.

bur|bot (bėr′bət), *n., pl.* **-bots** or (*collectively*) **-bot.** a freshwater fish related to the cod, having an elongated, slender body, and one barbel on the chin and two on the nose; eelpout. [< Middle French *bourbette*, altered < *barbote* < *barbe* beard < Latin *barba*]

Bur|chell's zebra (bėr′chəlz), = dauw. [< William *Burchell*, an English naturalist of the 1800's]

bur|den¹ (bėr′dən), *n., v.* —*n.* **1** something carried; a load (of things, care, work, duty, or sorrow): *A light burden of cork was loaded on the old mule's back.* (*Figurative.*) *We have to carry each day's burden.* **SYN:** See syn. under **load. 2** a load too heavy to carry easily; heavy load: (*Figurative. His debts are a burden that will ruin him.* **SYN:** weight, encumbrance. **3** the quantity of freight that a ship can carry; weight of a ship's cargo.
—*v.t.* **1** to put a burden on; load: *The mule was burdened with the campers' supplies.* **2** to load too heavily; weigh down; oppress: (*Figurative.*) *The President is burdened with responsibility for decisions which may affect the whole world.*
[Old English *byrthen.* See related etym. at **bear**².]
—**bur′den|less**, *adj.*

bur|den² (bėr′dən), *n.* **1** the main idea or message: *The way to achieve peace was the burden of the President's speech.* **SYN:** gist. **2** a repeated verse in a song; chorus; refrain. **3** *Obsolete.* the bass undersong or accompaniment, especially on a bagpipe; bourdon. [< Old French *bourdon* a humming; the drone of a bagpipe < Medieval Latin *burdo, -onis* pipe. See etym. of doublet **bourdon.**]

burden of proof, the obligation to establish a fact by proof. The responsibility of offering convincing proof rests upon the affirmative side in a debate or the prosecution in a criminal case.

bur|den|some (bėr′dən səm), *adj.* hard to bear; very heavy; oppressive: (*Figurative.*) *The President's many duties are burdensome.* **SYN:** oppressing, onerous. See syn. under **heavy.**
—**bur′den|some|ly**, *adv.* —**bur′den|some|ness**, *n.*

bur|dock (bėr′dok′), *n.* a coarse weed with burs and large, broad leaves. It belongs to the composite family. [< *bur* + *dock*⁴]

bur|eau (byůr′ō), *n., pl.* **-eaus** or **-eaux** (-ōz). **1** an office: *We asked about the airplane fares at the travel bureau.* **2** a division within a government department: *The Bureau of Mines inspects and enforces safety conditions in the mines.* **3** a chest of drawers for clothes; dresser. It often has a mirror. **4** *British.* a desk or writing table with drawers. [< French *bureau* office, desk (originally cloth-covered) < Old French *burel* (diminutive) < *bure* coarse woolen cloth, ultimately < Late Latin *burra* coarse wool]

bu|reauc|ra|cy (byů rok′rə sē), *n., pl.* **-cies. 1** a system of government by groups of officials, each dealing with its own kind of business under the direction of its chief: *Though the Czar was ruler in name, the Government of Russia before the revolution was really a bureaucracy.* **2** the officials running government bureaus: *Every President faces . . . problems that necessarily work their way up through a cumbersome bureaucracy* (Harper's). **3** concentration of power in administrative bureaus: *Capitalism is balanced against the obstinate bureaucracy of Socialism* (New Yorker). **4** too much insistence on rigid routine, resulting in delay in making decisions; red tape: *It was not centrally administered and went with a minimum of bureaucracy and maximum speed* (London Times). [< French *bureaucratie* < *bureau* desk + Greek *-kratiā* rule < *krátos*]
▶The vowel (o) in the second syllable, where (ō) might be expected, is due to the analogy of

Pronunciation Key: hat, āge, cãre, fär; let, ēqual, tėrm; it, īce; hot, ōpen, ôrder; oil, out; cup, pu̇t, rüle; child; long; thin; ᴛʜen; zh, measure; ə represents a in about, e in taken, i in pencil, o in lemon, u in circus.

words like *autocracy* and *democracy.*

bur|eau|crat (byůr′ə krat), *n.* **1** an official in a bureaucracy: *a knowledgeable and experienced bureaucrat. As the old excuses for foreign aid run out, our bureaucrats invent new ones* (Newsweek). **2** a government official who insists on rigid routine. [< French *bureaucrat* < *bureau* bureau; patterned on *bureaucratie* bureaucracy]

bur|eau|crat|ese (byůr′ə krat′ēz′, -ēs′), *n.* bureaucratic jargon; officialese: *In Washington bureaucratese, a "Schedule A man" is one who, while not of Cabinet or subCabinet rank, has an important policy-making function* (Time).

bur|eau|crat|ic (byůr′ə krat′ik), *adj.* **1** having to do with a bureaucracy or a bureaucrat: *Big business, big foundations and big education easily slip into a bureaucratic routine* (Wall Street Journal). **2** arbitrary: *a bureaucratic decision against which appeal is useless.* — **bur′eau|crat′i|cal|ly,** *adv.*

bu|reauc|ra|tism (byů rok′rə tiz əm), *n.* bureaucracy: *The growth of bureaucratism is not confined to government agencies, of course* (Wall Street Journal). — **bu|reauc′ra|tist,** *n.*

bu|reauc|ra|tize (byů rok′rə tīz), *v.t.,* **-tized, -tiz|ing.** to make a bureaucracy of; make bureaucratic: *the great bureaucratized collective that is the modern corporation* (Harper's). — **bu|reauc′-ra|ti|za′tion,** *n.*

***bu|rette** or **bu|ret** (byů ret′), *n.* a graduated glass tube, usually with a tap at the bottom. It is used for accurately measuring small amounts of a liquid or gas. [< Middle French *burette* (diminutive) < *buire* flagon]

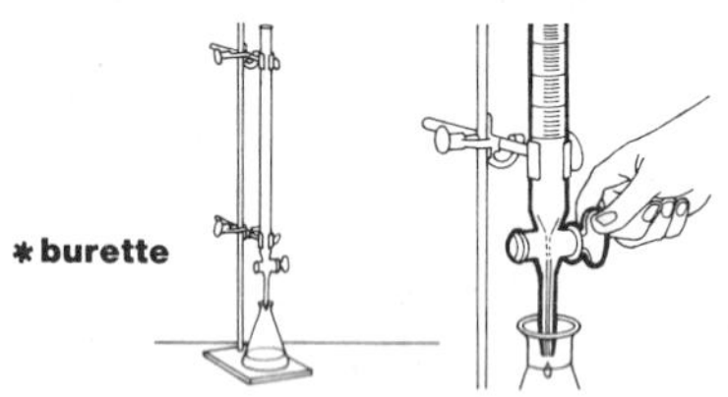

***burette**

burg (bėrg), *n.* **1** *Informal.* a town or city. **2** *Historical.* a fortress or walled town. Also, **burgh, burh.** [variant of *borough*]

burg|age (bėr′gij), *n.* **1** a system of English land tenure whereby townsmen leased their houses and lands from the king or other lord for a certain yearly rent. **2** a system of Scottish land tenure whereby townsmen lease their houses and lands from the crown for the nominal service of watching and warding. [< Anglo-French *bourgage* < *bourg* bourg]

bur|gall (bėr′gôl), *n.* = bergall.

bur|gee (bėr′jē), *n.* **1** a small, swallow-tailed flag or pennant, used in the international code of flag signals and as a distinguishing flag on merchant ships and yachts. **2** a kind of small coal used for burining in the furnaces of engines. [origin uncertain]

bur|geon (bėr′jən), *v., n.* — *v.i.* **1** to bud; grow or shoot forth; sprout. **2** *Figurative.* to grow or develop rapidly; flourish: *New suburbs burgeoned all around the city.*
— ***v.t.*** to shoot out; put forth as buds.
— ***n.*** a bud; sprout. Also, **bourgeon.**
[< Old French *burjon,* apparently < Germanic]

burg|er (bėr′gər), *n.* = hamburger.

-burger, *combining form.* **1** a roll or bun containing a cooked patty of ____: *Fishburger = a roll or bun containing a cooked patty of fish.*
2 a hamburger topped with ____: *Cheeseburger = a hamburger topped with cheese.*
[< (ham)*burger*]

bur|gess (bėr′jis), *n.* **1** a member of the lower house of the colonial legislature in Virginia or Maryland. **2** *British.* a citizen of a borough. **3** (formerly) a representative of a borough, corporate town, or university in the British Parliament. [< Old French *burgeis* < Late Latin *burgēnsis* citizen. See etym. of doublet **bourgeois**[1].]

burgh (bėr′ō *for 1, 3;* bėrg *for 2*), *n.* **1** a chartered town in Scotland. **2** a burg. **3** *Scottish.* borough. [< Scottish variant of *borough*]

burgh|al (bėr′gəl), *adj.* of or having to do with a burgh: *a burghal government.*

burgh|er (bėr′gər), *n.* a citizen of a burgh or town; citizen: *... well-fed burghers in sidewalk cafés sip coffee* (Time).

bur|glar (bėr′glər), *n.* **1** a person who breaks into a house or other building, usually at night, to steal or commit some other crime. **2** a person who breaks into and enters a building at any time. [< Anglo-French *burglour.* Compare Old English *burgbryce* burglary.]

burglar alarm, a mechanical or electrical device that registers an alarm when a door or window is tried or opened or when a painting or other valuable object is tampered with.

bur|glar|i|ous (bėr glãr′ē əs), *adj.* **1** having to do with burglary. **2** like a burglar. — **bur|glar′i|ous|ly,** *adv.*

bur|glar|ize (bėr′glə rīz), *v.t.,* **-ized, -iz|ing.** *U.S. Informal.* to break into (a building) to steal. [American English < *burglar* + *-ize*]

bur|glar|proof (bėr′glər prüf′), *adj.* so strong or safe that burglars cannot break in: *a burglarproof vault.*

bur|glar|y (bėr′glər ē), *n., pl.* **-glar|ies. 1** a breaking into a house or other building, usually at night, to steal or commit some other crime. **2** (under laws of some places) the act of breaking into and entering a building at any time. **3** *Informal.* robbery.

bur|gle (bėr′gəl), *v.t., v.i.,* **-gled, -gling.** *Slang.* to break into (a building) to steal; burglarize. [back formation < *burglar*]

bur|go|mas|ter (bėr′gə mas′tər, -mäs′-), *n.* **1** the mayor of a town in Austria, Belgium, Germany, or the Netherlands. **2** a large, whitish gull of the arctic regions. [< Dutch *burgemeester* < *burg* borough + *meester* master; influenced by English *master*]

bur|go|net (bėr′gə net), *n.* **1** a visored helmet with a movable joint at the neck. **2** a light steel cap, worn especially by pikemen. [< Middle French *bourguignotte* < *Bourgogne* Burgundy]

bur|goo (bər gü′, bėr′gü), *n.* **1** a thick oatmeal gruel or porridge. **2** *U.S.* a soup or stew made with a variety of game, meats, and vegetables, highly seasoned, and used especially at outdoor gatherings in some of the Southern States. [probably < Arabic *burghul* (porridge of) boiled wheat]

bur grass, any of several grasses that grow spiny burs, but that are used as fodder before the burs appear; sandbur.

bur|grave (bėr′grāv′), *n.* formerly, in Germany, Austria, and other German-speaking areas: **1** the governor of a fortified town or castle. **2** the hereditary head of a castle or town and the adjacent domain. [alteration of German *Burggraf* < *Burg* fortified town + *Graf* count[2]]

Bur|gun|di|an (bər gun′dē ən), *adj., n.* — ***adj.*** of Burgundy or its people.
— ***n.*** a person born or living in Burgundy.

Bur|gun|dy (bėr′gən dē), *n., pl.* **-dies. 1** a red or white wine produced in eastern France in the region of Burgundy. Burgundy is full and dry in flavor, usually still, and comes in many varieties. *In 1950 the white Burgundies were better than the red* (Atlantic). **2** any one of certain somewhat similar wines made elsewhere but appropriating the name.

burh (bůrн), *n.* = burg.

bur|i|al (ber′ē əl), *n., adj.* — ***n.*** **1** the act of putting a dead body in a grave, in a tomb, or in the sea; burying; funeral: *The sailor was given a burial at sea.* **SYN:** interment, entombment. **2** a place of burial; a grave (now used chiefly by anthropologists and archaeologists): *the great burials at Ur, the Sutton Hoo burial excavated near Ipswich (England) in 1939.* **SYN:** tomb.
— ***adj.*** having to do with burying: *a burial service.* [Middle English *biriel,* new singular form of *biriels,* Old English *byrgels* burying place]

burial ground, a graveyard; cemetery.

Bur|iat (bůr′yät, bůr yät′), *n.* **1** a member of a Mongol people living in the southeast Soviet Union. **2** the language. Also, **Buryat.** [< Russian *buryat* < a Tartar word]

bur|ied (ber′ēd), *v., adj.* — ***v.*** past tense and past participle of **bury:** *The dog buried his bone. Many nuts were buried under the leaves.*
— ***adj.*** laid, sunk, or concealed under ground: *buried treasure.*

bur|i|er (ber′ē ər), *n.* a person or thing that buries.

***bu|rin** (byůr′in), *n.* **1a** an engraver's pointed steel tool for cutting. **b** a similar tool used by marbleworkers. **2** the style of execution of an engraver. **3** a flint tool of the upper paleolithic period, having a cutting edge somewhat similar to that of an engraver's tool. [< French *burin* < Italian *borino* < Germanic (compare Old High German *bora* borer)]

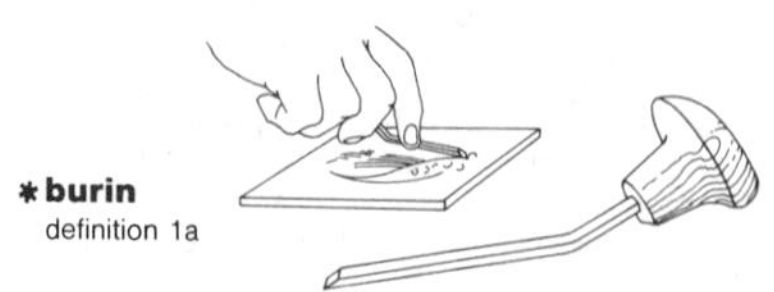

***burin**
definition 1a

bu|ri|on (byůr′ē ən), *n.* a small finch of the southwestern United States. [American English < American Spanish *burrión* sparrow]

bur|ka (bůr′kä), *n.* = bourkha.

burke (bėrk), *v.t.,* **burked, burk|ing. 1** (originally) to murder by suffocating so as to leave no marks on the body, and thus to obtain an unmarked cadaver to sell for dissection. **2** *Figurative.* to hush up; suppress. [< William *Burke,* hanged in 1829 at Edinburgh, for this type of murder]
— **burk′er,** *n.*

Bur|kitt's lymphoma (bėr′kits), a cancer of the lymphatic system, especially common among children in central Africa. [< Dennis *Burkitt,* a British surgeon, who first described it in 1957]

burl (bėrl), *n., v.* — ***n.*** **1** a small knot or lump in wool or cloth. **2a** a large knot or excrescence in certain woods. The most highly prized burls include redwood, myrtle, walnut, cherry, ash, and maple. **b** a veneer made with this wood.
— ***v.t.*** to remove knots from.
[< Old French *bourle* < Vulgar Latin *burrula* (diminutive) < Late Latin *burra* coarse wool]
— **burl′er,** *n.*

bur|lap (bėr′lap), *n., v.,* **-lapped, -lap|ping** or **-laped, -lap|ing.** — ***n.*** a coarse heavy cloth woven with yarns from the fibers of the jute or hemp, used to make bags. A better grade of burlap is used for curtains, wall coverings, upholstery, and clothing. *Then, there is quite an outfit in gold-brown burlap lined with vividly striped cotton* (New Yorker).
— ***v.t.*** to wrap around with burlap: *If the tree is large, it should be dug with a ball and then burlaped* (New York Times).
[origin uncertain]

bur|laps (bėr′laps), *n.* = burlap.

burled (bėrld), *adj.* that has burls.

bur|lesk (bėr lesk′), *n., adj. U.S.* burlesque (vaudeville).

bur|lesque (bėr lesk′), *n., v.,* **-lesqued, -lesqu|ing,** *adj.* — ***n.*** **1a** a story, play, or essay, that treats a serious subject ridiculously, or a trivial subject as if it were important: *Mark Twain's story, "A Connecticut Yankee in King Arthur's Court," is a burlesque of the legends about King Arthur.* **SYN:** parody, take-off, mock-heroic.
b *Figurative.* a ridiculous imitation of something worthy or dignified; mockery: *By taking bribes the judge made a burlesque of his high office.* **2** a kind of vaudeville characterized by coarse, vulgar comedy and dancing.
— ***v.t., v.i.*** to imitate so as to make fun of: *Firbank ... violently burlesqued the esthetic world in which he lived* (Newsweek). **SYN:** caricature, travesty.
— ***adj.*** **1** making people laugh; comically imitative. **SYN:** comical. **2** of or having to do with the kind of vaudeville called burlesque: *a burlesque show.*
[< French *burlesque* < Italian *burlesco* < *burla* jest] — **bur|lesque′ly,** *adv.* — **bur|lesqu′er,** *n.*

bur|let|ta (bėr let′ə), *n.* a comic opera; musical farce. [< Italian *burletta* (diminutive) < *burla* jest]

bur|ley or **Bur|ley** (bėr′lē), *n., pl.* **-leys.** a kind of thin-leaved tobacco grown widely in Kentucky and North Carolina: *Burley is one of the main ingredients in cigaret blends* (Wall Street Journal). [< *Burley,* a proper name]

bur|ly (bėr′lē), *adj.,* **-li|er, -li|est. 1** big and strong; sturdy: *a burly wrestler.* **SYN:** brawny, stout.
2 bluff; rough: *They [Englishmen] are as generous as they are hasty and burly* (Cardinal Newman). [Middle English *burli,* variant of *borlich*]
— **bur′li|ly,** *adv.* — **bur′li|ness,** *n.*

Bur|man (bėr′mən), *n., adj.* = Burmese.

bur marigold, any plant of a genus of composite herbs, whose prickly, seedlike fruits stick to clothing or fur, especially those species bearing showy, yellow flowers, such as the tickseed sunflower; beggar's-lice.

Bur|mese (bėr mēz′, -mēs′), *n., pl.* **-mese,** *adj.*
— ***n.*** **1** a person born or living in Burma. **2** the chief language of Burma, belonging to the Sino-Tibetan family.
— ***adj.*** of Burma, its people, or their official language.

Burmese cat, a cat similar to the Siamese cat but darker in color, having deep-brown fur.

Burmese glass, a type of glassware first made in the early 1880's, in which the surface often was given a dull satin finish by treating it with acid; peach blow glass. It ranges in color from pink to bluish white.

burn[1] (bėrn), *v.,* **burned** or **burnt, burn|ing,** *n.*
— ***v.i.*** **1** to be on fire; be very hot; blaze; glow: *The campfire burned all night.* **SYN:** flame. **2** to be destroyed or suffer death by fire: *The old hotel burned years ago and was never rebuilt.* **3** to be injured, charred, singed, or scorched by fire, heat, or acid: *Your hand will burn if you touch that hot iron.* **4** to feel hot: *The sick man's forehead burns with fever.* **5** *Figurative.* to be very excited or eager: *Our visiting relatives were burning with enthusiasm to tour the city.* **6** *Figurative.* to be inflamed with anger or other strong emotion: *She burned with fury at his unkind remarks about her parents.* **7** to give light: *Lamps were burning in every room.* **8** to sunburn: *My skin burns easily.* **9** *Chemistry.* to undergo combustion; oxidize rapidly. **10** *Nuclear Physics.* to undergo fission or fusion. **11** (of a rocket engine) to

consume fuel after being fired or ignited: *The engine had to burn for more than seven minutes in order to produce a final velocity of 4,128 miles . . . per hour* (Wernher von Braun and Frederick I. Ordway). **12a** (in certain games) to approach the hidden object. **b** *Figurative.* to approach near to the truth. **13** *U.S. Slang.* to die in the electric chair; be electrocuted.
—***v.t.*** **1** to set on fire; cause to burn: *The campers burned all their wood to keep warm.* **SYN:** ignite, fire. **2** to destroy by fire: *She burned her old letters so no one could read them.* **3** to injure, char, singe, or scorch by fire, heat, or acid: *The flame from the candle burned her finger. He burned his hand on the hot iron.* **4** to make by fire, heat, or acid: *His cigar burned a hole in the rug. He burned his initials on the handle.* **5** to give a feeling of heat to: *Too much mustard burns the tongue.* **6** *Figurative.* to inflame with anger or other strong emotion. **7a** to produce, harden, or glaze by fire or heat: *to burn bricks, burn lime.* **b** to use to produce heat: *Our furnace burns oil.* **c** to use to produce energy: *an atomic reactor that burns uranium.* **8** *Chemistry.* to consume or change in chemical form by combining with oxygen; oxidize rapidly: *The body makes energy by burning food.* **9** to sunburn: *The sun burned her arms badly.* **10** to fire or ignite (a rocket engine) so as to produce thrust: *Armstrong had to burn the engines for another 70 seconds to reach a smoother landing site* [*on the moon*] (Wernher von Braun and Frederick I. Ordway). **11** to cauterize. **12** to parch; wither. **13** to put to death by fire: *Anne Williams was burned at the stake.* **14** *U.S. Slang.* to put to death in the electric chair; electrocute.
—***n.*** **1** an injury caused by fire, heat, or acid; burned place: *She got a burn on her hand where she touched the hot pan. These skin-graft experiments, it is hoped, will save thousands of lives lost every year as a result of severe burns* (Newsweek). **2** a sunburn: *Don't lie too long in the sun or you will get a painful burn.* **3a** the firing of a rocket engine to produce thrust: *A "perfect burn" pulled them out of lunar orbit and towards a splashdown in the Pacific* (Manchester Guardian Weekly). **b** the period of firing: *Its retrorockets were fired in a 10-minute "burn" . . . after the satellite had come into the moon's gravitational field* (London Times).
burn away, to burn or be burned: *The coal burns away to nothing.*
burn down, a to burn or be burned to the ground: *Although the house should be burned down, yet the tenant must continue to pay the rent* (L. St. Leonards). **b** to decrease in fuel and heat: *The fire has burnt down to a spark.*
burn in, *Photography.* to allow extra light to darken part of a print.
burn into, a to eat its way into: *The acid has burned into the pan.* **b** *Figurative.* to make an indelible impression on: *The sight of such poverty burned into his soul.*
burn oneself out, to use oneself up physically or mentally; exhaust one's store of energy, ambition, or ideas: *He burned himself out with a life of aimless dissipation.*
burn out, a to destroy by burning: *His store was burned out and he never went back into business. Must you with hot irons burn out both mine eyes?* (Shakespeare). **b** to cease to burn; become extinct: *Don't let the fire burn out.* (*Figurative.*) *His zeal will soon burn itself out.* **c** to burn the inside of: *The warehouse was burned out.* **d** to drive (a person) out by fire: *The poor man was burned out of house and home.* **e** to consume: *During the long race he burned out his brakes.*
burn up, *Informal.* **a** to destroy by fire; go up in flames: *The papers were burned up.* **b** (1) to consume: *This car burns up the gasoline.* (2) to devour: *This car burns up the miles.* **c** *Informal.* to make angry; inflame to anger; enrage: *Your attitude burns me up. The farmers know this and they're burned up about it* (Wall Street Journal). **d** to blaze into life: *The flames suddenly burned up and light filled the room.*
[fusion of Old English *beornan* be on fire, and *bærnan* consume with fire] —**burn'a|ble,** *adj.*
—***Syn.*** *v.i., v.t.* **3 Burn, scorch, sear** mean to injure or be injured by fire, heat, or acid. **Burn** is the general word and suggests any degree of damage, from slight injury to complete destruction: *The toast burned. I burned the toast.* **Scorch** means to burn the surface enough to discolor it, sometimes to damage the texture: *The cigarette scorched the paper. The blouse was scorched because the iron was too hot.* **Sear** suggests burning or scorching the surface by heat or acid enough to dry or seal it, and is applied particularly to burning the tissues of people or animals: *Wounds are seared to cauterize them. She seared the roast to brown it in a Dutch oven.*

▶**burn.** The past tense and past participle of *burn* are either *burned* or *burnt. Burnt* is usual when the participle is used as an adjective: *The partially burnt papers gave them little help in solving the mystery.* Verb: *They hastily burned all the old letters before they left.*

burn[2] (bėrn), *n. Scottish.* a small stream; brook. Also, **bourn, bourne.** [Old English *burna*]
burn bag, a bag used to burn completely discarded documents.
burn|bag (bėrn'bag'), *v.t.,* **-bagged, -bag|ging.** to destroy by burning, especially in a burn bag.
burned-out (bėrnd'out'), *adj.* **1** damaged or destroyed by fire: *a burned-out building.* **2** used up; extinguished: *a burned-out fire, a burned-out light.* **3** *Figurative.* exhausted; burnt-out: *an apathetic, burned-out individual.*
burn|er (bėr'nər), *n.* **1** the part of a lamp, stove, or furnace where the flame is produced. **2** a thing or part that burns or works by heat: *Some stoves are oil burners; others are gas burners.* **3** a person whose work is burning something: *a charcoal burner.* **4** a combustion chamber in a jet engine. **5** a lamp to burn the paint off a surface.
burner drag, the total drag produced by all the parts of a jet engine.
bur|net (bėr'nit), *n.* any plant of a genus of perennial herbs of the rose family, especially a species with tall spikes of white, greenish, or red flowers, whose leaves are used to flavor salads and drinks. [< Old French *burnet* brown, variant of *brunet* brunet]
burn|ing (bėr'ning), *adj.* **1** glowing; hot. **SYN:** fiery, blazing, flaming, incandescent. **2** *Figurative.* vital or urgent: *a burning question.* **SYN:** heated, fervid. **3** *Figurative.* flagrant; outright: *a burning disgrace.* —**burn'ing|ly,** *adv.*
burning bush or **burn|ing-bush** (bėr'ning-bu̇sh'), *n.* **1** any one of various plants whose red flowers, berries, or leaves in autumn suggest the name, as the wahoo. **2** = fraxinella. **3** the bush out of which the angel appeared to Moses. (in the Bible, Exodus 3:2).
burning glass, a convex lens used to produce heat or set fire to a substance by focusing the sun's rays on it.
bur|nish (bėr'nish), *v., n.* —***v.t.*** **1** to make shiny; polish: *to burnish copper or brass.* **SYN:** shine. **2** to make bright and glossy. —***v.i.*** to respond to burnishing. —***n.*** a polish; shine. **SYN:** luster. [< Old French *burniss-*, stem of *burnir* make brown, polish < *brun* brown < Frankish (compare Old High German *brūn*)] —**bur'nish|er,** *n.*
*****bur|noose** or **bur|nous** (bėr nüs', bėr'nüs), *n.* a long woolen cloak with a hood, worn by Moors and Arabs. [< French *burnous* < Arabic *burnus*]

***burnoose**

burn|out (bėrn'out'), *n.* **1** a failure due to burning or extreme heat. **2** *Aerospace.* **a** the extinguishing of the flame in a rocket engine because fuel is exhausted or shut off according to plan. **b** the time at which this event occurs. **c** the point in the rocket's trajectory at which it takes place. **3** *Figurative.* extinction of energy, motivation, or incentive: *Teacher burnout . . . is a psychological condition, produced by stress, that can result in anything from acute loss of will to suicidal tendencies* (Time).
burnout velocity, the velocity of a rocket missile or vehicle at the instant of burnout.
burns (bėrnz), *n.pl. U.S. Slang.* sideburns.
burn|sides or **Burn|sides** (bėrn'sīdz'), *n.pl.* a growth of hair on the cheeks but not on the chin; sideburns, especially when long and heavy; mutton chops. [American English < Ambrose E. *Burnside,* 1824-81, a Union general in the Civil War] ▶See **sideburns** for usage note.
burnt (bėrnt), *v.* a past tense and a past participle of **burn**[1]: *He doesn't like burnt toast.* ▶See **burn**[1] for usage note.
burnt almonds, almonds cased in burnt sugar.
burnt offering, 1 an offering, especially a whole animal, burned on an altar as a sacrifice to a god or gods: *Thou delightest not in burnt offerings* (Book of Common Prayer). **2** anything offered as a sacrifice.
burnt-out (bėrnt'out'), *adj.* exhausted; worn out; dissipated: *The novel's hero . . . is a burnt-out Southern poet who keeps trying to fire up the clinkers of his talent with alcohol* (Time).
burnt sienna, 1 a dark-brown color. **2** a pigment of this color, especially calcined raw sienna.

burnt umber, 1 a reddish-brown or deep-reddish pigment. **2** a reddish-brown color.
burn|up (bėrn'up'), *n.* the consumption of fuel in a nuclear reactor.
burn|y (bėr'nē), *adj.,* **burn|i|er, burn|i|est.** *Informal.* burning; fiery.
bur oak, 1 a hardy North American oak tree whose acorns have large, fringed cups covered with scales. **2** its hard, tough, close-grained wood.
burp (bėrp), *n., v. Informal.* —***n.*** a belch: *A baby's first smiles, unsmiling pediatricians insist, are merely mechanical preludes to burps* (Time).
—***v.i.*** to belch. —***v.t.*** to assist (a baby) in the expulsion of gas from the stomach, as by patting on the back; cause to belch: . . . *patting baby's back while you burp him* (Good Housekeeping). [imitative]
burp gun, an air-cooled submachine gun, used especially by the Germans in World War II.
burr[1] (bėr), *n., v.* —***n.*** **1** = bur. **2** Also, **buhr.** a rough ridge or edge left by a tool, especially on metal or wood after cutting, drilling, or punching it. **3** a tool used especially by engravers and die makers to cut and shape metal. **4** a tool with a head shaped like a bur, used by dentists in drilling. —***v.t.*** **1** = bur. **2** to form a rough ridge or edge on. [variant of *bur*] —**burr'like',** *adj.*
burr[2] (bėr), *n., v.* —***n.*** **1** a rough or guttural pronunciation of *r,* as in Northumberland. **2** a rough or dialectal pronunciation in which *r* sounds are prominent: *a Scottish burr.* **3** a whirring sound.
—***v.i.*** **1** to pronounce *r* roughly. **2** to speak with a rough articulation. **3** to make a whirring sound.
—***v.t.*** to pronounce with a burr: *He burrs his r's.* [probably imitative]
burr[3] (bėr), *n.* **1** a washer placed on the small end of a rivet before the end is swaged down. **2** a disk or blank driven out of a piece of sheet metal by a punch. [Middle English *burrow,* variant of *brough,* perhaps < Scandinavian (compare Old Icelandic *borg* circular enclosure)]
burr[4] (bėr), *n.* **1** = burrstone. **2** a siliceous rock occurring among calcareous or other softer formations. **3** = whetstone. [perhaps < *burr*[1], as being rough textured]
bur|ra sa|hib (bur'ə sä'ib), a title of respect for the head of a family, a chief officer, etc., in India. [< Hindi *barā sāhib* (literally) great master]
bur reed, any one of a genus of perennial aquatic plants with narrow, reedlike leaves and burlike fruits.
burr|fish (bėr'fish'), *n., pl.* **-fish|es** or (*collectively*) **-fish.** = sea porcupine.
bur|ri|to (bėr rē'tō, bu̇r-), *n., pl.* **-tos.** a thick tortilla rolled up with a filling of meat and often cheese: *The drive-in Dairy Queen offers tacos, enchiladas, and burritos along with its standard shakes, burgers, and fries* (New Yorker). [< Mexican Spanish *burrito* (literally) little burro]
*****bur|ro** (bėr'ō, bu̇r'-), *n., pl.* **-ros.** a small donkey used to carry loads or packs in the southwestern United States. [< Spanish *burro* < *borrico* small horse, ultimately < Late Latin *buricus*]

***burro**

bur|row (bėr'ō), *n., v.* —***n.*** **1** a hole dug in the ground by an animal for refuge or shelter. Rabbits and woodchucks live in burrows. **2** *Figurative: The chief advantage of London is that a man is always so near his burrow* (James Boswell).
—***v.i.*** **1** to dig a hole in the ground: *The mole quickly burrowed out of sight.* **SYN:** tunnel. **2** to live in burrows. **3** *Figurative.* to work a way into or under something: *She burrowed under the blankets.* **4** *Figurative.* to hide oneself: *The fugitive burrowed into the alleys and covered passageways.* **5** *Figurative.* to search: *She burrowed in the library for a book about Indian life.*
—***v.t.*** **1** to make burrows in; dig: *Rabbits have burrowed the ground for miles around.* **2** *Figurative.* to hide in or as if in a burrow: *The runaway burrowed himself in the haystack.* **3** to make by burrowing: *dens burrowed in the mountainside.* [Middle English *borowe,* apparently related to Old

Pronunciation Key: hat, āge, cãre, fär; let, ēqual, tėrm; it, īce; hot, ōpen, ôrder; oil, out; cup, pu̇t, rüle; child; long; thin; ᴛʜen; zh, measure; **ə** represents **a** in about, **e** in taken, **i** in pencil, **o** in lemon, **u** in circus.

English *beorg* hill, barrow, burial place, *gebeorg* refuge] —**bur′row|er**, *n.*

bur|ro|weed (bėr′ō wēd′, bůr′-), *n. U.S.* any of various weeds growing in desert regions and considered palatable to burros.

bur|row|ing owl (bėr′ō ing), a long-legged owl of North and South America, that hunts by day as well as by night, and always makes its nest in a hole in the ground; the ground owl.

burr|stone (bėr′stōn′), *n.* **1** a siliceous rock capable of being used for a millstone. **2** a millstone made from this rock. Also, **buhr**, **buhrstone**, **burstone**.

bur|ry¹ (bėr′ē), *adj.*, **-ri|er**, **-ri|est**. full of burs; rough; prickly: *a burry, homespun tweed.* [< *bur* + *-y¹*]

bur|ry² (bėr′ē), *adj.*, **-ri|er**, **-ri|est**. (of speech) characterized by a burr. [< *burr²* + *-y¹*]

***bur|sa** (bėr′sə), *n., pl.* **-sae** (-sē), **-sas**. *Anatomy.* a sac of the body, especially one containing a lubricating fluid that reduces friction between a muscle or tendon and a bone; pouch or cavity. [< Medieval Latin *bursa* bag, purse < Late Latin, variant of *byrsa* hide < Greek *býrsa*. See etym. of doublets **bourse**, **burse**, **purse**.]

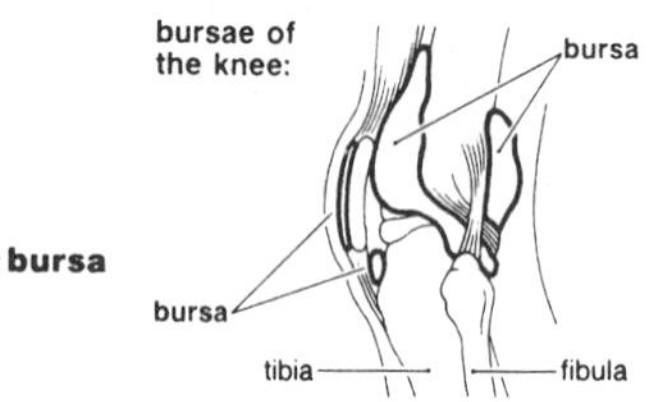

***bursa**

bur|sal (bėr′səl), *adj.* **1** of or having to do with a bursa or bursae. **2** having to do with the public revenue.

bur|sar (bėr′sər, -sär), *n.* **1** a treasurer, especially of a college or university. **2** (in Scotland) a student who holds a bursary. [< Medieval Latin *bursarius* < *bursa;* see etym. under **bursa**]

bur|sar|i|al (bėr sãr′ē əl), *adj.* belonging to a bursar or a bursary.

bur|sa|ry (bėr′sər ē), *n., pl.* **-ries**. **1** the treasury of an institution, especially of a college, university, or monastery. **2** an endowment granted to a student in a university or college; burse.

burse (bėrs), *n.* **1a** a fund or foundation to provide allowances for students. **b** such an allowance. **2** *Roman Catholic Church.* the richly covered receptacle in which the corporal is placed when not in use on the altar. **3** *Obsolete.* an exchange; bourse. [< French *bourse.* See etym. of doublets **bourse**, **bursa**, **purse**.]

bur|seed (bėr′sēd′), *n.* a troublesome European weed, a stickseed, naturalized in the United States.

bur|ser|a|ceous (bėr′sə rā′shəs), *adj.* belonging to a family of plants typified by the torchwood. [< New Latin *Bursera* the typical genus (< Joachim *Burser*, 1593-1649, a German botanist)]

bur|si|form (bėr′sə fôrm), *adj.* shaped like a purse; pouchlike; vesicular. [< Medieval Latin *bursa* pouch, bag + English *-form*]

bur|si|tis (bər sī′tis), *n.* inflammation of a bursa, usually near the shoulder or hip.

burst (bėrst), *v.*, **burst**, **burst|ing**, *n.* —*v.i.* **1** to break open; break out; fly apart suddenly; explode: *The balloon will burst.* SYN: erupt. **2** to go, come, or do by force or suddenly: *He burst into the room without knocking.* **3** to be very full, as if ready to break open: *The barns were bursting with grain.* (*Figurative.*) *At the suggestion of a picnic the class was bursting with enthusiasm.* SYN: teem. **4** *Figurative.* to give way or be about to give way from violent pain or emotion: *to burst into tears.* **5** to open or be opened suddenly or violently: *The trees had burst into bloom. The door burst open.* **6** *Figurative.* to act or change suddenly in a way suggesting a break or explosion: *She burst into loud laughter. He burst into speech.*
—*v.t.* **1** to force open suddenly or violently: *He burst the lock with a hammer.* **2** to cause to break open or into pieces; shatter: *to burst a blood vessel. The prisoner burst his chains.*
—*n.* **1** an outbreak: *There was a burst of laughter when the clown fell down.* SYN: outburst. **2** a sudden and violent issuing forth; sudden opening to view or sight: *a burst of sunlight.* **3** a sudden display of activity or energy: *In a burst of speed, he won the race in the last minute.* SYN: spurt. **4** the act of bursting; split. **5** an explosion of a shell, bomb, or other explosive device. SYN: detonation. **6** a series of shots fired by one pressure on the trigger of an automatic weapon. **7a** a sudden increase in the radiation intensity of ionized particles, such as may be observed in a shower of cosmic rays, or in the trailing particles in an ionization chamber. **b** a sudden, short emission of X rays, gamma rays, and the like, occurring at intervals. **8** *Slang.* a spree; bust.
burst in, a to appear suddenly: *The boys were in the kitchen when the cook burst in and ordered them out.* **b** *Figurative.* to interrupt: *During the debate, a man kept bursting in with questions.*
burst out, to come out with suddenly; exclaim: *"Oh, no!" Jack burst out when the glass fell.*
[Old English *berstan*]

burst|er (bėrs′tər), *n.* **1** one who or that which bursts. **2** a celestial body that is the source of bursts, such as an X-ray burster.

burst|ing charge (bėrs′ting), the charge of explosive which bursts a shell or the like.

bur|stone (bėr′stōn′), *n.* = burrstone.

bur|then (bėr′ᵺən), *n., v.t. Archaic.* burden¹.

bur|ton¹ (bėr′tən), *n.* a light tackle usually having two or three blocks, used for various purposes. [perhaps < *Burton*, a proper name]

bur|ton² (bėr′tən), *n.*
go for a burton, *British Slang.* to be lost or gone; disappear: *Nearly all the handles of the . . . eighteenth-century pink Davenport tea cups went for a burton* (Listener).
[originally, to go for some *Burton* ale or beer; see etym. under **Burtonize**]

Bur|ton|ize (bėr′tə nīz), *v.t.*, **-ized**, **-iz|ing**. to harden (water for brewing) by treatment, especially with gypsum or Epsom salt. [< *Burton*-on-Trent, place in England noted for its superior brewing water and ale + *-ize*]

Bu|ru|shas|ki (bůr′ə shäs′kē), *n.* a language spoken by some of the people in northwestern Kashmir. Its relationship with other languages has not been shown.

bur|weed (bėr′wēd′), *n.* any one of several plants with a burlike fruit, such as the cocklebur.

bur|y (ber′ē), *v.t.*, **bur|ied**, **bur|y|ing**. **1** to put (a dead body) in the earth, in a tomb, or in the sea: *The boys buried the dead bird in the backyard.* SYN: inter, entomb. **2** to perform a funeral service for. **3** to cover up; hide: *The squirrels buried many nuts under the dead leaves.* SYN: conceal, secrete. **4** *Figurative.* **a** to absorb; engross: *She buried herself in an interesting book.* **b** to put or sink (oneself) deeply: *He buried himself in a welter of activities.* **5** *Figurative.* to forget: *He had long ago buried the memory of the accident.* **6** to withdraw or cause to move to obscurity or retirement: *Many well disposed persons . . . are so unfortunate as to be totally buried in the country* (Samuel Johnson). **7** to suffer loss through death: *She had buried two sons.* [Old English *byrgan*]

Bur|yat (bůr′yät, bůr yät′), *n.* = Buriat.

bur|y|ing beetle (ber′ē ing), a beetle that buries small dead animals and birds and lays her eggs in them; sexton beetle.

burying ground, a cemetery or burial ground.

bus (bus), *n., pl.* **bus|es** or **bus|ses**, *v.*, **bused**, **bus|ing** or **bussed**, **bus|sing**. —*n.* **1** a motor vehicle larger than an automobile, with seats to carry passengers, and an entrance usually at the front; omnibus; motorcoach. Buses usually run between fixed stations, along a certain route. **2** *Informal.* an automobile or airplane. **3a** an electric conductor or system of conductors for making a common connection between several circuits and distributing them. **b** = bus bar. **c** a conductor in an electronic computer, used as a path for the transmission of signals from one or more sources to one or more destinations.
—*v.t.* to take by bus: *The city bused the children to school.* —*v.i.* **1** to go by bus: *He buses to work every day.* **2** *U.S.* to work as a busboy.
miss the bus, *Slang.* to lose an opportunity: *The Prime Minister has 'missed the bus' . . . He has thrown away the greatest opportunity ever offered* (London Daily Mail).
[short for *omnibus*]

bus., **1** bushel or bushels. **2** business.

bus bar, an electric conductor in the form of a metal bar or rod, used to carry large or heavy currents or to make a common connection between several circuits. In a generating station, a bus bar collects and distributes the power produced by the generators.

bus|boy (bus′boi′), *n.*, or **bus boy**, a waiter's assistant. He brings bread and butter, fills glasses, and carries off used dishes.

***busby**

***bus|by** (buz′bē), *n., pl.* **-bies**. a tall fur hat with a bag hanging from the top over the right side, worn as part of a dress uniform by hussars and certain other corps in the British Army. [probably < *Busby*, a proper name]

bush¹ (bůsh), *n., v.* —*n.* **1** a woody plant smaller than a tree, often with many separate branches starting from or near the ground. Some bushes are used as hedges; others are grown for their fruit or for ornament. **2a** open forest or wild land: *The explorer went into the bush of Alaska. He came out of the shadow of the bush path and blinked in the sun* (Harper's). **b** the country as opposed to the town. **3a** something resembling a bush, such as unruly hair or feathers: *. . . little streams of soda water irrigated the black bush on his chest* (Graham Greene). **b** *Obsolete.* a fox's tail; brush. **4a** a branch, especially of ivy, hung out as a vintner's sign or as the sign of a tavern. **b** any tavern sign: *Good wine needs no bush* (Old proverb).
—*v.i.* to spread out like a bush; grow thickly: *She stood, Half spied, so thick the roses bushing round About her glowed* (Milton).
—*v.t.* **1** *Informal.* to exhaust utterly: *The trip completely bushed her.* **2** to set (ground) with bushes; cover with bushes. **3** to protect with bushes or brushwood. **4** to smooth (planted land) by means of a bushharrow.
beat around (or **about**) **the bush**, to avoid a direct answer or direct action; not come straight to the point: *Tell me the facts now, and don't beat around the bush. Obliged to be off: Excuse me . . . but no good beating about the bush* (Punch).
beat the bushes (**for**), *Especially U.S.* to search (for), in or as if in remote areas: *to beat the bushes for new customers, to beat the bushes to find a good job.*
go bush, *Australian.* to live a wild life, as in the bush, or as a bushranger: *The English settlers . . . tried to tame them for domestic purposes. But the greater number had already 'gone bush'* (M. Terry).
[Middle English *busch*, variant of *busk* < Scandinavian (compare Old Icelandic *buskr*)]

bush² (bůsh), *n., v. Machinery.* —*n.* = bushing. —*v.t.* to furnish with a bushing; line (a bearing or the like) with metal. [< Middle Dutch *busse* box]

bush baby, = galago.

bush basil, small cultivated form of sweet basil.

bush bean, a variety of nonclimbing bean.

bush-beat|ing (bůsh′bē′ting), *n. U.S. Slang.* a random but thorough search, as for people of talent, dishonesty in government, or other investigative findings.

bush|boy (bůsh′boi′), *n.* **1** = bushman. **2** = Bushman.

bush|buck (bůsh′buk′), *n.* a South African antelope of a reddish or orange color with white stripes. Also, **boschbok**. [< Dutch *bosch-bok*]

bush clover, any lespedeza, allied to the clover, but usually growing erect.

bush|craft (bůsh′kraft′, -kräft′), *n.* knowledge of how to get food and shelter, find one's way or take care of other necessities, in the bush.

bush cranberry, = cranberry tree.

bush dog, **1** = potto. **2** a wild dog of South America.

bushed (bůsht), *adj.* **1** *Informal.* very tired; exhausted: *He kept you right on your toes, and, after an hour and a half, you went out feeling pretty bushed* (Newsweek). **2** lost in the bush. **3** bewildered; at a loss.

***bush|el¹** (bůsh′əl), *n.* **1** a measure for grain, fruit, vegetables, and other dry things. It is equal to 4 pecks or 32 quarts or 35.2383 liters. **2** a container that holds a bushel. **3** the weight of a bushel. *Abbr:* bu. **4** *Informal.* an indefinitely large quantity: *I have a bushel of things to do today.* [< Old French *boissiel* (diminutive) < *boisse* a measure of grain]

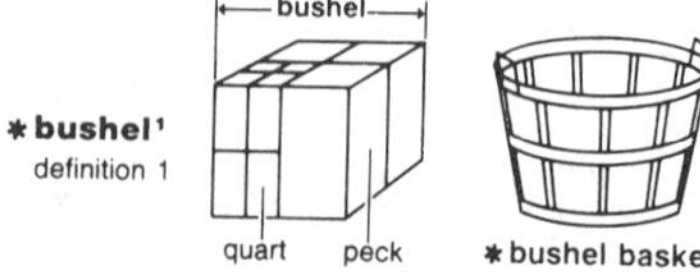

***bushel¹** definition 1 ***bushel basket**

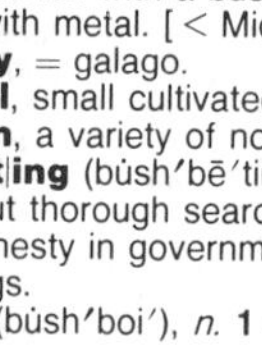

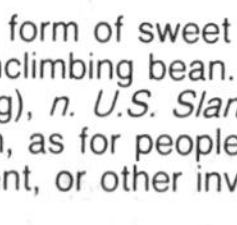

bush|el² (bůsh′əl), *v.t., v.i.*, **-eled**, **-el|ing** or **-elled**, **-el|ling**. *U.S.* to repair or alter (clothing). [American English; perhaps < German *bosseln* work over petty jobs; emboss; cut]

***bushel basket**, a basket that holds a bushel.

bush|el|er or **bush|el|ler** (bůsh′ə lər), *n.* = bushelman.

bush|el|ful (bůsh′əl fůl), *n., pl.* **-fuls**. a quantity of material occupying a bushel.

bush|el|man (bůsh′əl mən), *n., pl.* **-men**. tailor's assistant who repairs garments; busheler.

bush|er (bůsh′ər), *n. U.S. Slang.* **1** a baseball player in a minor league. **2** a beginner, especially a clumsy beginner, at anything.

bush|fire (bůsh′fīr′), *n.* an uncontrolled fire in a

bush, especially the Australian bush.

bush|ham|mer (bu̇sh′ham′ər), *n., v.* **—n.** a hammer with a notched face, used to dress stone. **—v.t.** to dress (stone) with a bushhammer.

bush|har|row (bu̇sh′har′ō), *n.* a frame with bushes or branches attached for covering seed.

***bush hat**, a slouch hat, especially of the type worn by Australian bushmen.

***bush hat**
***bush jacket**

bush honeysuckle, a low shrub native to North America extensively cultivated for its profuse, yellow flowers.

Bu|shi|do or **bu|shi|do** (bü′shē dō′), *n.* the moral code of the knights and warriors of feudal Japan; Japanese chivalry. [< Japanese *bushidō* < *bushi* (Samurai) warrior + *dō* way]

bush|ing (bu̇sh′ing), *n.* **1** a removable metal lining used to protect parts of machinery from wear. **2** a metal lining inserted in a hole, pipe, or other aperture, to reduce its size. **3** a lining for a hole, to insulate one or more wires or other electrical conductors passing through. **4** *Slang.* very high-pressure selling; luring a buyer by offering a bargain price, then hiking the price. [< *bush*[2]]

***bush jacket**, a sports or hunting jacket with shirtlike collar and sleeves, usually having four pockets and a belt; bush shirt.

bush|land (bu̇sh′land′), *n.* wild, uncleared country; bush.

bush lawyer, (in Australia) a glib person claiming to be knowledgeable in law.

bush league, *Slang.* **1** a minor league in baseball. **2** *Figurative.* any insignificant or inexpert group, person, or organization: *There will be far less whistle-stopping and fewer talks with local bosses, now that TV is out of the bush league of politicking* (Time). **—bush′-league′**, *adj.*

bush leaguer, *U.S. Slang.* = busher.

bush|man (bu̇sh′mən), *n., pl.* **-men.** *Australian.* **1** a settler in the Australian bush. **2** a person who knows much about life in the bush.

Bush|man (bu̇sh′mən), *n., pl.* **-men. 1** a member of a tribe of roving hunters of southern Africa. Bushmen formerly lived in all South Africa but now live mainly in and around the Kalahari Desert region. **2** the language of this tribe, consisting of a number of local dialects and related to the Hottentot language.

bush|mas|ter (bu̇sh′mas′tər, -mäs′-), *n.* the largest poisonous snake of tropical America.

Bush Negro, any individual of a people of Surinam (Dutch Guiana) descended from African slaves who escaped from the Dutch into the bush before slavery was abolished in the mid-1800's.

bush pig, a South African wild swine; boschvark.

bush pilot, **1** a pilot who flies a small plane over unsettled country, such as northern Canada and parts of Alaska. **2** a pilot accustomed to flying without benefit of ground-based navigational aids, large airports, or the like: *The bush pilots who fly sportsmen in for the kill make a handsome living* (New Yorker).

bush|rang|er (bu̇sh′rān′jər), *n.* **1** a person who ranges in the bush; woodsman. **2** a criminal hiding in the Australian bush who lives by robbery.

bush|rope (bu̇sh′rōp′), *n.* a tropical creeper tangling trees together.

bush shirt, = bush jacket.

bush sickness, (in bush country, especially New Zealand) an anemic condition of sheep, cattle, and other grazing animals, caused by a lack of certain minerals in the pasture.

bush tea, **1** the leaves of a South African plant of the pea family, dried to make tea. **2** the strong-scented tea made from these leaves.

bush telegraph, the means by which news is quickly spread in wild country; grapevine.

bush tit, a small North American titmouse, noted for building an elaborate pendent nest.

bush|wa or **bush|wah** (bu̇sh′wä), *n. U.S. Slang.* bunk; humbug; nonsense.

bush|whack (bu̇sh′hwak′), *v.i.* to live in or work in the bush or backwoods. **—v.t.** to attack or fight, as a bushwhacker: *Snipers bushwhacked lone Red couriers on the new road to Lhasa* (Time). [< *bush*[1] + *whack*]

bush|whack|er (bu̇sh′hwak′ər), *n.* **1** a person who lives or works in wooded areas. **2** a person who clears out underbrush. **3** a scythe for cutting bushes. **4a** a guerrilla fighter. **b** a guerrilla on the Confederate side in the Civil War.

bush|whack|ing (bu̇sh′hwak′ing), *n.* **1** the act of beating one's way through bushes. **2** fighting from behind bushes, rocks, or from other hiding places; guerrilla warfare.

bush|y (bu̇sh′ē), *adj.,* **bush|i|er, bush|i|est.** **1** spreading out like a bush; growing thickly: *a bushy beard.* **2** overgrown with bushes: *a bushy ravine.* **—bush|i|ly**, *adv.* **—bush′i|ness**, *n.*

bus|ied (biz′ēd), *v.* the past tense and past participle of **busy**.

bus|i|ly (biz′ə lē), *adv.* in a busy manner; actively: *Bees are busily collecting honey in the clover.* **SYN:** diligently, industriously, assiduously, energetically.

busi|ness (biz′nis), *n., adj.* **—n. 1a** a thing that one is busy at; occupation, profession, or trade; work: *A carpenter's business is building.* **SYN:** vocation, job. See syn. under **occupation. b** something to be done or attended to: *the business of the day. Business comes before pleasure.* **2** a matter; affair: *Taking chances is sometimes risky business. I am tired of the whole business.* **3** buying and selling; commercial dealings; trade: *This hardware store does a big business in tools.* **4** a store, factory, or other commercial enterprise: *They sold the bakery business for a million dollars.* **SYN:** concern. **5** the right to act; responsibility: *Other people's business is not your business.* **6** the action in a play as distinct from dialogue; things done to make a play seem realistic: *Stage directions here call for the business of turning away and lighting a cigarette.* **7** *Obsolete.* busyness.

—adj. of or having to do with business.

business as usual, a condition or attitude of overlooking problems or difficulties: *It was almost business as usual in the white outer neighborhoods and the suburbs of Atlanta . . .* (New York Times).

business is business, commerce and profit must override personal feelings: *He refused to extend credit to his friends by saying, "business is business."*

get down to business, to turn or give one's attention to important things; tackle in earnest a task, difficulty, or the like: *After twice taking three puts going out he got down to business . . . and by accurate iron play had 3's out of five holes* (London Times).

have no business, to have no right: *The State has no business to provide more than subsistence benefits* (Listener).

make it one's business, to attend to specifically: *Harriet's parents make it their business to see that she does her homework every evening.*

mean business, *Informal.* to be in earnest; be serious: *When he says he is going to get good marks, he means business. The point would be to convince the Reds we mean business and at the same time assure the world we don't want a general war* (Newsweek).

mind one's own business, to attend to one's own affairs; refrain from meddling with what does not concern one: *I most desire all those critics to mind their own business* (Henry Fielding).

on business, with definite work to do: *No admittance except on business.*

the business, *U.S. Slang.* a roughing up; bad treatment; a punishing, beating, or killing: *His dock gang "got the business" when they balked at paying the tribute* (New York Times).

[Old English *bisignis* care; later, diligence, activity < *bisig* busy + *-nis* -ness]

business agent, a labor union representative who handles all business negotiations between union members and employers.

business card, a businessman's card bearing his name, business address, telephone number, and often the designation of his business or profession.

business college, a school that gives training in shorthand, typing, bookkeeping, and other business subjects.

business cycle, a cycle of business activity usually regarded as passing through the alternating stages of prosperity and recession or depression.

business double, *Bridge.* a double for penalties.

business education, training in subjects useful in business, such as bookkeeping and accounting, banking and commission, business-machine operation, shorthand and typing.

business end, the end that does the important work or is the obvious point from which the purpose is achieved: *the business end of a needle.*

business law, = commercial law.

busi|ness|like (biz′nis līk′), *adj.* having system and method; well-managed; practical: *He runs his store in a businesslike manner.* **—busi′ness|like′-ness**, *n.*

business machine, any machine used in a business office to speed up such operations as keeping records, bookkeeping, and processing data. Computers, duplicators, and data processors are business machines.

busi|ness|man (biz′nis man′), *n., pl.* **-men. 1** a man in business. The manager of a store is a businessman. **2** a man who runs a business: *Some stores in our town are run by local businessmen who live in the town.*

business suit, *Especially U.S.* a man's suit of matching coat and trousers, for everyday wear.

busi|ness|wom|an (biz′nis wu̇m′ən), *n., pl.* **-wom|en. 1** a woman in business. **2** a woman who runs a business: *The owner of our bakery is a good businesswoman.*

bus|ing or **bus|sing** (bus′ing), *n. U.S.* the compulsory transportation by bus of Negro and white students from one school to another to achieve a better racial balance in schools.

busk[1] (busk; *Scottish* bu̇sk), *v.t. Scottish.* to prepare; get ready: *Busk ye, busk ye my bonny, bonny bride* (William Hamilton). [< Scandinavian (compare Old Icelandic *būask* prepare oneself < *būa* make ready). See related etym. at **bound**[4].]

busk[2] (busk), *v.i. British Slang.* to perform as a street musician or entertainer. [origin uncertain]

busk|er (bus′kər), *n. British Slang.* a street musician or entertainer regaling passers-by, theater queues, and the like.

***bus|kin** (bus′kin), *n.* **1** a boot reaching to the calf or knee, worn in olden times. **2** a high shoe with a very thick sole, worn by Greek and Roman actors of tragedies to make them look more impressive. **3** *Figurative.* tragic drama; tragedy. **buskins, a** the stockings worn by a bishop at Mass. **b** a bishop's sandals.

[perhaps alteration of Old French *brousequin* small leather boot; influenced by English *buckskin*]

***buskin**
definition 1

bus|kined (bus′kind), *adj.* **1** shod or covered with buskins. **2** *Figurative.* of or having to do with tragic drama. **3** *Figurative.* lofty or elevated, as language.

bus|load (bus′lōd′), *n.* as many as a bus can hold or carry: *busloads of visitors.*

bus|man (bus′mən), *n., pl.* **-men.** a driver or conductor on a bus.

busman's holiday, a holiday spent in doing what one does at one's daily work: *Max Goberman, the conductor . . . on a Sunday off, some time ago, took a busman's holiday to play all six of the violin sonatas of Handel's Opus 1* (New Yorker).

buss (bus), *v.t., v.i., n. Informal.* kiss: *Eager greeters pumped his hands and bussed his glowing pink cheeks* (Time). *She gave him a big buss* (Newsweek). [probably imitative]

bus|ses (bus′iz), *n.* buses; a plural of **bus**.

bust[1] (bust), *n.* **1** a statue of a person's head, shoulders, and upper part of the chest. **2** the upper, front part of the body. **3** a woman's bosom. [< French *buste* < Italian *busto,* perhaps < Latin *bustum* crematorium, bust]

bust[2] (bust), *v., n.* **—v.i. 1** *Slang.* to burst; break: *Her balloon busted when it hit the light.* **2** *Informal.* to fail financially; become bankrupt.

—v.t. 1 *Slang.* to burst; break: *He busted the glass when he fell.* **2** *Informal.* to bankrupt; ruin. **3** *Informal.* to punch; hit: *I'll bust you one in the nose.* **4** *Informal.* to demote, especially as a punishment: *The corporal was busted to private.* **5** to train to obey; tame: *to bust a bronco.* **6** to break up (a trust) into smaller companies. **7** *Slang.* to arrest or jail: *I have never been busted for pot . . .* (Time).

—n. 1 *Slang.* a burst or break. **2** a punch; hit: *The bully gave him a bust in the nose.* **3** a total failure; bankruptcy: *The peach crop in such states as Georgia, South Carolina, Texas and Illinois appears a bust* (Wall Street Journal). **4** *Informal.* a spree: *He went on a bust.* **5** *Slang.* an arrest.

bust up, a *Informal.* to ruin: *to bust up a party.* **b** *Slang.* to become separated or divorced: *The couple busted up after an argument.*

[American English, variant of *burst*]

▶**Bust** is the slang form of **burst** in the sense of explode or break out. It is informal in the

---

Pronunciation Key: hat, āge, cãre, fär; let, ēqual, tėrm; it, īce; hot, ōpen, ôrder; oil, out; cup, pu̇t, rüle; child; long; thin; ᴛʜen; zh, measure; ə represents **a** in about, **e** in taken, **i** in pencil, **o** in lemon, **u** in circus.

sense of fail financially, but is standard English in *busting a bronco* or *busting a trust.*

bus|tard (bus′tərd), *n.* any one of a family of large game birds related to the plovers, having long legs and a heavy body, found on the dry, open plains of Africa, Europe, Asia, and Australia. [fusion of Old French *bistarde* and *oustarde,* both < Latin *avis tarda* slow bird]

bust|ed (bus′tid), *adj.* **1** *Slang.* broken. **2** *Informal.* ruined; bankrupt.

-busted, *combining form.* having a ——bust: *Full-busted = having a full bust.*

bus|tee (bus′tē), *n.* a slum in India. [< Hindustani *bastī* village; district, quarter]

bust|er (bus′tər), *n.* **1** *U.S.* a person who breaks horses: *a bronco buster.* **2** *Informal.* as a form of address: **a** a small boy. **b** a fellow. **3** *Informal.* something very big, striking, or remarkable of its kind. **4** *Slang.* a dashing fellow. **5** *Informal.* a frolic; spree. **6** *Australian.* a southerly gale.

bus|tic (bus′tik), *n.* a tropical American tree of the sapodilla family, having heavy, hard, dark-brown wood. [origin unknown]

bus|tier (bʏs tyā′, büs-), *n.* a strapless top or dress: *Strapless dresses and tube tops (this year called "the bustier") are giving the bosom a comeback* (Maclean's). [< French *bustier* strapless brassiere < *buste* bust]

bus|tle[1] (bus′əl), *v.,* **-tled, -tling,** *n.* **—*v.i.*** to be noisily busy and in a hurry: *The children bustled to get ready for the party. Let the great world bustle on* (Emerson). **—*v.t.*** to make (someone) hurry or work hard: *The jolly old man bustled them out of the house* (Charles Kingsley).
—*n.* noisy or excited activity; commotion; fuss: *There was a great bustle as the children got ready for the party.* **SYN:** ado. See syn. under **stir.** [perhaps imitative] **—bus′tler,** *n.* **—bus′tling|ly,** *adv.*

***bus|tle**[2] (bus′əl), *n.* **1** (formerly) a pad, cushion, or small wire frame used to puff out the upper back part of a woman's skirt. **2** a fullness at the back of a woman's skirt just below the waist as made by a bow or gathering of material [perhaps special use of *bustle*[1]]

***bustle**[2]
definition 2

bust|up (bust′up′), *n. Slang.* **1** a quarrel. **2** a violent fight.

bust|y (bus′tē), *adj. Informal.* bosomy.

bus|y (biz′ē), *adj.,* **bus|i|er, bus|i|est,** *v.,* **bus|ied, bus|y|ing.** **—*adj.*** **1** having plenty to do; not idle; working; active: *During the sale the clerks were very busy in the store.* **2** full of work or activity: *Main Street is a busy place. Holidays are a busy time.* **3** in use: *I tried to call her up, but her telephone line was busy.* **4** prying into other people's affairs; meddling: *That inquisitive woman is always busy.* **SYN:** meddlesome, officious. **5** over-filled with color, design, or ornament: *a busy wallpaper, a busy pattern.*
—*v.t.* to make busy; keep busy: *The bees busied themselves making honey.* **—*v.i.*** to be busy. [Old English *bysig*]
— *Syn.* *adj.* 1 Busy, industrious, diligent mean actively or attentively occupied. **Busy** means active, or working steadily or at the moment: *He is such a busy man, it is hard to get an appointment with him.* **Industrious** means hard-working by nature or habit: *Bees and ants are industrious workers.* **Diligent** means hard-working at a particular thing, usually something one likes or especially wants to do: *a diligent student. A diligent host attends to the needs of all his guests.*

bus|y|bod|y (biz′ē bod′ē), *n., pl.* **-bod|ies.** a person who pries into the affairs of others; meddler.

bus|y|ness (biz′ē nis), *n.* being busy: *No simple rules work in coping with preschoolers' busyness* (Sidonie M. Gruenberg).

bus|y|work (biz′ē wėrk′), *n.* work assigned or done merely to fill time or to appear to be busy: *It must be discouraging to learn what many have long suspected, that most of this busywork is in vain* (Bulletin of Atomic Scientists).

but[1] (but), *conj., prep., pron., adv., n., v.* **—*conj.*** **1** on the other hand; yet: *You may go, but you must come home at six o'clock. It rained, but I went anyway. Their hopes sank, but their courage did not.* **2** if not; unless; except that: *It never rains but it pours.* **3** other than; otherwise than: *We cannot choose but listen.* **4** except; save: *He is right but for one thing.* **5** that: *I don't doubt but he will come.* **6** that not: *He is not so sick but he can eat.*
—*prep.* **1** with the exception of; except; save: *Father works every day in the week but Sunday.* See syn. under **except.** **2** other than: *No one answered but me.*
—*pron.* who not; which not: *None visit him but are fed.*
—*adv.* **1** no more than; only; merely: *He is but a small boy. He was here but an hour ago. My love she's but a lassie* (Robert Burns). **2** only; not otherwise: *We can but try.* **3** *Informal.* definitely; positively: *Go to it but this instance.*
—*n.* an objection or restriction: *Not so many buts, please.*
—*v.t.* **but me no buts,** offer no excuses or objections: *'I heartily wish I could, but'—'Nay, but me no buts—I have set my heart upon it'* (Scott).
all but. See under **all.**
but that, were it not that: *I should come in but that it is impossible.*
but what, except that; save: *Not but what many changes have been wrought* (George du Maurier). [Old English *būtan* without, unless < *be-* by + *ūtan* outside < *ūt* out]
— *Syn.* *conj.* 1 But and **however** express a contrasting relationship. **But** suggests a simple balance of opposites: *He is sick, but he soon will be well.* **However** implies comparison or contrast: *We have not yet reached a decision; however, our opinion of your plan is favorable.*
▶**but.** Two main clauses connected by *but* are usually separated by a comma. The contrast in idea suggests the use of punctuation even when the clauses are relatively short: *I couldn't see the license number, but it was a New York plate.* Two clauses connected by *however* are regularly separated by a semicolon.

but[2] (but), *n., adj., adv. Scottish.* **—*n.*** an outer room (kitchen) of a cottage, especially the outer of two (the inner being the *ben*).
—*adj.* outside; outer; exterior.
—*adv* . in the outer part of a cottage; outside. [Old English *būtan* outside]

but|a|di|ene (byü′tə dī′ēn, -dī ēn′), *n.* **1** a colorless gas made from alcohol or petroleum by-products, used in making synthetic rubber and as an anesthetic. **2** its isomeric hydrocarbon. *Formula:* C_4H_6 [< *buta*(ne) + *di-*[1] + *-ene*]

bu|tane (byü′tān, byü tān′), *n.* a colorless gas much used as a fuel. Butane is a hydrocarbon of the methane series and is found in two isomeric forms. It is produced in petroleum refining. *Formula:* C_4H_{10} [< *but*(yl) + *-ane*]

bu|ta|nol (byü′tə nōl, -nol), *n.* = butyl alcohol.

bu|ta|none (byü′tə nōn), *n.* an inflammable ketone, used as a solvent, in the manufacture of plastics, and in organic synthesis. *Formula:* C_4H_8O [< *butan*(e) + *-one*]

Bu|ta|zol|i|din (byü′tə zol′ə din), *n. Trademark.* phenylbutazone.

butch (būch), *n., adj.* **—*n.*** **1** Also, **butch haircut.** a haircut resembling but shorter than a crew cut: *His scalp showed clean and white . . . where the sun's rays struck the dark butch of his bent head* (Atlantic). **2** *Slang.* a tough boy or man. **3** *Slang.* a Lesbian who acts as a male.
—*adj.* *Slang.* having the appearance of a male; behaving like a male: *a butch girl.* [< *Butch,* a boy's name]

butch|er (būch′ər), *n., v.* **—*n.*** **1** a person who cuts up and sells meat. **2** a person whose work is killing animals for food. **SYN:** slaughterer. **3** *Figurative.* a brutal killer; murderer: *O pardon me . . . that I am meek and gentle with these butchers* (Shakespeare). **SYN:** slayer. **4** *U.S.* a vender; peddler, especially one who goes through trains selling magazines, candy, food and drink, and notions. **5** *Informal, Figurative.* a person who botches or bungles.
—*v.t.* **1** to kill (animals) for food. **SYN:** slaughter. **2** to kill (people, wild animals, or birds) wholesale, needlessly, or cruelly: *. . . Butchered to make a Roman holiday* (Byron). **SYN:** massacre. **3** *Figurative.* to kill brutally; murder. **SYN:** slay. **4** *Figurative.* to spoil by poor work: *Don't butcher that song by singing off key.* [< Old French *bochier* (originally) one who slaughters and sells he-goats < *boc* he-goat, buck[1] < Germanic (compare Old High German *boc*)] **—butch′er|er,** *n.*

butch|er|bird (būch′ər bėrd′), *n.* any one of various large shrikes that fasten their prey on thorns; northern shrike.

butch|er-block (būch′ər blok′), *adj.* made of or patterned after a butcher's block, traditionally of unpainted laminated wood usually of varying colors: *An upper West Side restaurant . . . features hanging plants, butcher-block tables* (New Yorker).

butcher knife, a very sharp knife for cutting meat.

butch|er|ly (būch′ər lē), *adj., adv.* **—*adj.*** like or befitting a butcher. **—*adv.*** savagely; inhumanly.

butch|er's-broom (būch′ərz brüm′, -brūm′), *n.* a shrubby European evergreen of the lily family, with rigid, branched, and spiny leaflike stems bearing a greenish flower and red berries.

butcher shop, a place where meat is sold; butcher's place of business.

butch|er|y (būch′ər ē), *n., pl.* **-er|ies.** **1** brutal killing; murder in large numbers: *He began boasting of his fights, his cruelties, and his butcheries* (Charles Kingsley). **SYN:** carnage. **2a** = slaughterhouse. **b** = butcher shop. **3** a butcher's work; cutting up and selling meat.

bu|tene (byü′tēn), *n.* any one of the three isomeric forms of butylene. *Formula:* C_4H_8

bu|te|o (byü′tē ō), *n., pl.* **-te|os.** any one of a genus of broad-winged, soaring hawks that includes the red-tailed hawk; buzzard hawk. [< New Latin *Buteo* the genus name < Latin *buteo* hawk]

but|ler (but′lər), *n.* **1** the head male servant in a household, in charge of the pantry and table service. **2** the male servant in charge of the wines and liquors; wine steward. [< Anglo-French *butuiller* cupbearer, variant of Old French *bouteillier* < *bouteille* bottle]

butler's pantry, a small room between the kitchen and dining room, for use by a butler or serving maid.

but|ler|y (but′lər ē), *n., pl.* **-ler|ies.** **1** = butler's pantry. **2** = buttery.

Buts|kel|lism (buts′kə liz′əm), *n. Especially British Politics.* a condition in which political opponents espouse the same or very similar policies. [< R. A. *But*(ler), born 1902, an English Tory politician + Hugh (Gait)*skell,* 1906-1963, an English Labour politician + *-ism*]

butt[1] (but), *n.* **1** the thicker end of a tool, weapon, ham, handle, or shaft: *the butt of a gun.* **2** the end that is left; stub or stump: *The butt of a pipe stuck out from the wall where the sink had been removed.* **3a** *Slang.* = cigarette. **b** the unsmoked end of a cigarette or cigar that has been smoked. **4a** the thicker, hinder part of a hide of an animal. **b** the thick leather made from this. **5** the base of a leafstalk, tree trunk, or the like. **6** *Slang.* = buttocks. [fusion of Middle English *but, bott* (see related etym. at **buttocks**) and Old French *bout* end < Scandinavian (compare Old Icelandic *būtr* block of wood)]

butt[2] (but), *n., v.* **—*n.*** **1** an object of ridicule or scorn: *The new boy's strange speech was the butt of many jokes.* **2** a target, especially one in archery. **3a** a mound of earth or sawdust behind the targets to stop shots on a rifle, archery, or artillery range. **b** a mound on which an archery target is set up. **4** a joint where two boards or timbers meet end to end. **5** a hinge that fits between two surfaces, for example, between a door and the jamb; butt hinge. **6** a small, open shelter for grouse shooting: *Shooting from butts near Inverness, Scotland, he brought down four grouse with one barrel of his twelve-gauge* (Atlantic). **7** *Obsolete.* a goal; boundary. **8** *Obsolete.* an end; aim; object.
—*v.i., v.t.* **1** to join end to end or edge to edge: *to butt two boards.* **2** to cut off the rough ends of (boards or logs).
the butts, a place to practice shooting; target range: *Riflemen were practicing on the butts.* [fusion of Old French *bout* end, and *but* aim, purpose]

butt[3] (but), *v., n.* **—*v.i.*** **1** to push or hit with the head or horns: *A goat butts.* **2** to project; run out; jut (out or into): *One wing of the house butted out as far as the roadway.*
—*v.t.* to strike with the head or horns; push or drive.
—*n.* **1** a push or blow with the head or horns. **2** a thrust with a sword.
butt in, *Slang.* to meddle; interfere; intrude: *The French . . . were incensed at the U.S. for butting in* (New York Times).
[< Old French *bouter,* earlier *boter* thrust < Germanic (compare Old High German *bōzan*)]
—butt′er, *n.*

butt[4] (but), *n.* **1** a large barrel for wine or beer. **SYN:** cask. **2** a variable liquid measure commonly equal to 126 U.S. gallons of wine or 108 U.S. gallons of ale. [< Old French *botte* < Late Latin *butta,* variant of *buttis*]

butt[5] (but), *n.* any one of various flatfishes, such as the sole, fluke, or halibut. [Middle English *butte*]

butte (byüt), *n. Western U.S.* a steep, flat-topped hill standing alone. [American English < French *butte* hill, mound]

butt end, **1** the butt, extremity, or thicker end of a thing. **2** *Figurative.* the concluding part.

but|ter (but′ər), *n., v.* **—*n.*** **1** the solid, yellowish fat separated from cream by churning: *I do like a little bit of butter to my bread* (A. A. Milne). **2** food like butter in looks or use: *peanut butter. Apple butter is made by cooking apples to a thick jam and adding sugar and spices.* **3** any one of certain anhydrous metallic chlorides: *butter of zinc.* **4** *Informal, Figurative.* gross flattery.

— *v.t.* **1** to put butter on or in; spread with butter: *Please butter my bread.* **2** *Informal, Figurative.* to flatter grossly.

butter up, *Informal.* to flatter: *Most corporate executives ... irately reject any suggestion that they try to "butter up" union officials* (Wall Street Journal).

butter would not melt in (one's) mouth, extremely delicate, sweet, or coy; excessively demure: *She smiles and languishes, you'd think that butter would not melt in her mouth* (Thackeray).

[Old English *butere* < Latin *būtȳrum* < Greek *boútȳron*] — **but′ter|less,** *adj.* — **but′ter|like′,** *adj.*

but|ter-and-egg man (but′ər ən eg′), *U.S. Slang.* a middle-class businessman who is, or is thought to be, wealthy and free with his money.

but|ter-and-eggs (but′ər ən egz′), *n.* a common European toadflax having showy yellow-and-orange flowers and growing as a weed in much of North America.

but|ter|ball (but′ər bôl′), *n.* **1** *U.S. Informal.* a small, plump person: *Willie Pastrano was a fat little five-foot butterball* (Time). **2** = bufflehead.

butter bean, 1 a variety of the Lima bean having small, white or brown seeds, grown in the southern United States. **2** a yellow string bean; wax bean.

butter boat, a small dish in which melted butter is served as a sauce.

but|ter|box (but′ər boks′), *n.* = bufflehead (def. 1).

but|ter|bur (but′ər bėr′), *n.* a perennial European composite herb whose large, soft leaves are said to have been used for wrapping butter.

butter clam, a large, edible, burrowing clam of the Pacific Coast of the United States, having a shell with prominent concentric ridges, which was used for money by the California Indians; money shell.

but|ter|cup (but′ər.kup′), *n.* a common plant with bright yellow flowers shaped like cups. The buttercup belongs to the crowfoot family. Its deeply divided leaves resemble a crow's foot.

But|ter|cup (but′ər kup′), *n.* a breed of chicken developed in Sicily for its egg-laying capacity, that has featherless shanks and white earlobes.

but|ter|fat (but′ər fat′), *n.* the fat in milk. It can be made into butter. A certain percentage of butterfat is required by law in each of the various grades of milk and cream.

but|ter-fin|gered (but′ər fing′gərd), *adj. Informal.* apt to let things drop or slip through one's fingers: *The most butter-fingered of incompetents ... had no trouble at all installing the panels* (New Yorker).

but|ter|fin|gers (but′ər fing′gerz), *n. Informal.* **1** a person who drops something that he ought to hold. **2** a careless or clumsy person: *He is unskilled at these games* [*and*] *they call him butterfingers* (Harper's).

but|ter|fish (but′ər fish′), *n., pl.* **-fish|es** or (*collectively*) **-fish.** any one of several small, edible, silvery fishes with slippery skins covered with mucus, oval bodies, and spiny fins, such as the dollarfish, gunnel, and pompano of the Atlantic Coast of North America or a related fish of the northern Pacific Coast.

but|ter|flied (but′ər flīd), *adj.* split and spread apart like the wings of a mounted butterfly: *butterflied steak, a butterflied leg of lamb.*

∗**but|ter|fly** (but′ər flī′), *n., pl.* **-flies,** *adj.* — ***n.*** **1** an insect with a slender body and two pairs of large, usually brightly colored, overlapping wings. Butterflies fly mostly in the daytime. They pass through a larva, or caterpillar, stage, and emerge full-grown from the pupa. See also **moth.** **2** *Figurative.* a person who suggests a butterfly by such characteristics as delicate beauty, bright clothes and flightiness: *Mamma says that she was then the prettiest, silliest, most affected, husband-hunting butterfly she ever remembers* (Mary Russell Mitford). **3** the butterfly stroke.

— ***adj.*** shaped like the outstretched wings of a butterfly: *a butterfly roof, butterfly doors.*

butterflies in the stomach, feelings of nervousness: *When he gets up in front of his audience, he has butterflies in his stomach, no matter how many times he does it* (Time).

[Old English *buterflēoge* < *butere* butter + *flēoge* flying creature]

butterfly bush, = buddleia.

∗**butterfly chair,** a wide-backed easy chair with a canvas support for the body and a metal frame.

butterfly damper, a thin plate of metal which turns on an axis across a pipe so that it controls the amount of the passage left open in the pipe; butterfly valve.

∗**butterfly fish,** any one of several fishes noted for their bright colors or for their broad fins somewhat resembling the wings of the butterfly, especially: **a** any one of a family of small tropical marine fishes. **b** a blenny. **c** = flying gurnard.

butterfly lily, = mariposa lily.

butterfly orchid, a white orchid with red spots, somewhat resembling a butterfly, found in England.

∗**butterfly stroke,** a breaststroke in which both arms are brought out of the water and over the head and drawn back together.

∗**butterfly table,** a small table with drop leaves supported by brackets shaped like a butterfly's wings.

∗**butterfly tail,** an aircraft tail assembly having the stabilizers and elevators set at an acute dihedral, forming a V.

∗**butterfly valve, 1** a valve in a pipe, consisting of a disk turning on its diametral axis, as a damper or the throttle valve in a carburetor for gasoline engines: *The amount of scavenging air is controlled by butterfly valves in the manifold* (New Science). **2** a double clack valve.

butterfly weed, 1 a North American herb of the milkweed family, having orange flowers; pleurisy root. The root has been used medicinally as an emetic and as a cathartic. **2** a perennial herb of the evening-primrose family, bearing spikes of white to scarlet flowers.

butter-head (but′ər hed′), *n.* a type of lettuce that forms a smaller head than crisp lettuce, and has waxy or buttery leaves.

but|ter|ine (but′ə rēn), *n.* an artificial butter; oleomargarine or margarine. [< *butter* + *-ine*[1]]

but|ter|is (but′ər is), *n.* a steel instrument for paring the hoofs of horses. [origin uncertain; perhaps variant of *buttress*]

butter knife, a small knife with a dull edge for cutting and spreading butter at the table.

but|ter|milk (but′ər milk′), *n.* the liquid left after butter has been separated from cream. Milk can also be changed to buttermilk artificially.

butter muslin, *British.* cheesecloth.

but|ter|nut (but′ər nut′), *n.* **1** an oily kind of walnut grown in North America, which is good to eat. **2** a tree with a light-brown, coarse-grained soft wood, that bears butternuts. **3** = souari nut. **4** a brown dye made from butternut husks and bark. **5** the brown color of homespun uniforms worn by Confederate soldiers in the American Civil War. **6** *U.S.* a Confederate sympathizer in the North; Copperhead.

butter print, a stamp for marking out butter.

but|ter|scotch (but′ər skoch′), *n., adj.* — ***n.*** a candy made from brown sugar and butter.

— ***adj.*** flavored with brown sugar and butter: *butterscotch pudding.*

butter tree, any one of various trees whose seeds yield a substance with a resemblance to butter, such as the shea.

but|ter|weed (but′ər wēd′), *n.* any one of various plants with yellow flowers or smooth, soft leaves, especially: **a** = horseweed. **b** one of the ragworts.

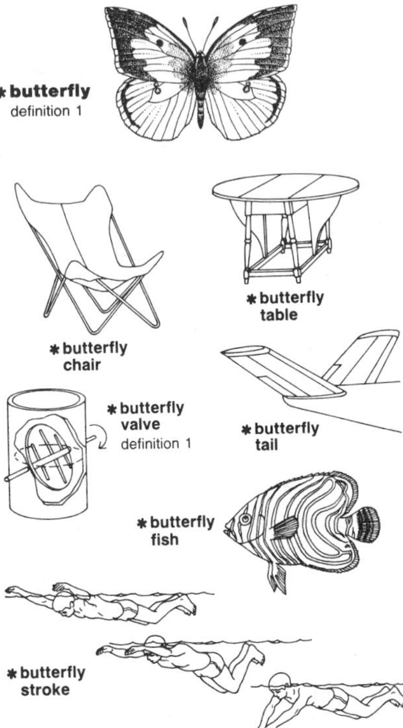

∗**butterfly** definition 1

∗**butterfly table**

∗**butterfly chair**

∗**butterfly valve** definition 1

∗**butterfly tail**

∗**butterfly fish**

∗**butterfly stroke**

but|ter|wort (but′ər wėrt′), *n.* any plant of a genus of small herbs of the bladderwort family, whose yellowish-green, stemless leaves secrete a sticky substance for catching insects.

but|ter|y[1] (but′ər ē), *adj.* **1** like butter. **2** containing or spread with butter: *buttery rolls.* **3** *Figurative.* given to flattery: *buttery manners.* [< *butter* + *-y*[1]] — **but′ter|i|ness,** *n.*

but|ter|y[2] (but′ər ē, but′rē), *n., pl.* **-ter|ies. 1** a room in which the wines, liquors, and provisions of a household are kept; pantry. **2** (in the colleges at Oxford, Cambridge, and Durham universities) a place where liquors, fruits, and other foods are kept for sale to students. [< Old French *boterie* storage place for casks < *botte* butt[4]]

buttery hatch, a half door at the entrance to a buttery, over which provisions are served.

butt hinge, = butt[2] (def. 5).

but|ting (but′ing), *n.* a boundary; limit.

but|tin|sky (but in′skē), *n., pl.* **-skies.** *U.S. Slang.* a person who forces himself in where he is not wanted or needed. [< *butt in* + *-sky,* in imitation of Slavic and Jewish names in *-(in)sky, -(in)ski*]

butt-joint (but′joint′), *n.* a joint made by placing two lengths of wood, steel, or iron end to end, and usually strengthened by short lapping pieces fastened above and below or along the sides.

but|tle (but′əl), *v.i.,* **-tled, -tling.** *U.S. Slang.* to serve as a butler: *Collins buttles for British chain-store magnate Sir Simon Marks* (Newsweek). [back formation < *butler*]

butt|leg|ger (but′leg′ər), *n. U.S.* a person who engages in buttlegging.

butt|leg|ging (but′leg′ing), *n. U.S.* the illegal transportation and sale of cigarettes on which a very low or no cigarette sales tax has been paid. [American English < *butt* cigarette + (boot)*legging*]

but|tock (but′ək), *n.* one of the two protuberances forming the rump. [perhaps Old English *buttuc* end, small piece of land]

but|tocks (but′əks), *n.pl.* **1** the fleshy hind part of the body where the legs join the back; rump. **2** the rounded part of the stern of a ship above the water line.

but|ton[1] (but′ən), *n., v.* — ***n.*** **1** a round, usually flat piece of metal, bone, glass, or plastic fastened on garments to hold them closed or to decorate them. **2** a knob used as a handle or a catch to take hold of, or push, or to turn so that it holds or closes something. **3** a knob or disk pushed or turned to cause something to work: *Push the button of the elevator to make it go up.* **4a** a young or undeveloped mushroom. **b** a bud or other protuberant part of a plant. **5** (in assaying) the metal remaining in the crucible after fusion. **6** a small knob on the end of a fencing foil. **7** a knob formerly on a Chinese official's cap, indicating his rank. **8** the last segment of the rattle on a rattlesnake. **9** *Slang.* the center of the chin, especially in boxing. **10** = badge (def. 2). **11** the fastener on the end of a violin or other string instrument to which the tailpiece holding the strings is anchored.

— ***v.t.*** **1** to fasten buttons of; close with buttons: *Please button my shirt for me.* **2** *Informal, Figurative.* to close (anything) tightly: *I buttoned my mouth and refused to talk.* **3** *Fencing.* to touch with the button of the foil. **4** to furnish with buttons.

— ***v.i.*** to be, or be able to be, fastened with buttons.

buttons, a *Slang.* faculties; intellect: *The poor man hasn't got all his buttons.* **b** *British Informal.* a bellboy or page in a hotel.

button up, *Informal.* to complete satisfactorily: *It took involved bargaining, but* [*they expect*] *to have the deal buttoned up next month* (Newsweek).

on the button, *Slang.* done exactly or precisely: *The timing of each action or revelation is right on the button* (New Yorker).

[< Old French *boton* bud, knob < *bouter* thrust; see etym. under **butt**[3]] — **but′ton|er,** *n.* — **but′ton|less,** *adj.* — **but′ton|less|ness,** *n.* — **but′ton-like′,** *adj.*

but|ton[2] (but′ən), *n.* = tee[2].

but|ton|ball (but′ən bôl′), *n.* **1** = buttonwood (def. 1). **2** = buttonbush.

but|ton|bush (but′ən bu̇sh′), *n.* an American and Asian shrub of the madder family with globular, white or yellow flower heads.

but|ton-down (but′ən doun′), *adj., n.* — ***adj.*** **1** that can be fastened with buttons: *a button-down collar.* **2** furnished with such buttons: *a button-down shirt.*

— ***n.*** a button-down collar or shirt.

Pronunciation Key: hat, āge, cãre, fär; let, ēqual, tėrm; it, īce; hot, ōpen, ôrder; oil, out; cup, pu̇t, rüle; child; long; thin; ᴛʜen; zh, measure; ə represents **a** in about, **e** in taken, **i** in pencil, **o** in lemon, **u** in circus.

but|toned (but′ənd), *adj.* furnished, decorated, or fastened with buttons: *buttoned shoes.*

but|ton|hole (but′ən hōl′), *n., v.,* **-holed, -hol|ing.** —*n.* **1** a hole, slit, or loop through which a button is passed, especially to fasten clothing. **2** *British Informal.* a boutonniere.
—*v.t.* **1** to make buttonholes in. **2** to sew with the stitch used in making buttonholes. **3** to hold in conversation or force to listen, as if holding someone by the buttonholes of his coat: *The judge had a habit of buttonholing his friends and asking their advice* (New Yorker). —**but′ton-hol′er,** *n.*

***buttonhole stitch,** a method of finishing the edge of a buttonhole, or an opening or piece of material, in which the stitches are laid side by side and perpendicular to the edge, each being linked at the edge with the one before it.

***buttonhole stitch**

but|ton|hook (but′ən hu̇k′), *n.* a hook for pulling the buttons, especially of gloves or shoes, through the buttonholes.

button lac, lac melted, dropped into disk forms, and then solidified.

button man, *U.S. Slang.* a low-ranking member of the Mafia or Cosa Nostra; soldier.

but|ton|mold or **but|ton|mould** (but′ən mōld′), *n.* a disk of wood or other material to be covered with cloth to form a button.

button quail, any one of a family of birds that resemble quails but are smaller and lack a hind toe, found in the temperate and tropical parts of the Old World. Button quail are related to the cranes and the bustards.

but|tons (but′ənz), *n.pl.* See under **button**[1].

button snakeroot, any plant of a genus of North American perennial herbs of the composite family, bearing spikes of rose-purple, buttonlike flowers; the blazing star or gayfeather.

button stick, a device for protecting a blouse or jacket while polishing buttons, especially used in the armed forces.

button tree, 1 a low tropical tree with very heavy, hard, compact wood. **2** = buttonwood (def. 1).

but|ton|wood (but′ən wu̇d′), *n.* **1** the sycamore tree of North America. The buttonwood of the Midwest is the largest deciduous tree in the United States. **2** its wood.

but|ton|y (but′ə nē), *adj.* **1** resembling a button. **2** abounding in buttons.

***but|tress** (but′ris), *n., v.* —*n.* **1a** a support built against a wall or building to strengthen it. **b** *Figurative: While I cannot be called a pillar I must be regarded as a buttress of the Church because I support it from outside* (attributed to Viscount Melbourne). SYN: pier. **2** a projecting portion of a hill or mountain resembling the buttresses of a building. **3** a bony process or protuberance, especially a horny growth at the heel of a horse's hoof.
—*v.t.* **1a** to strengthen with a buttress. **b** *Figurative: The pilot buttressed his report of the flight with photographs.* SYN: prop. **2** to conceal by a buttress: *Beside the portal doors, Buttress'd from moonlight, stands he* (Keats).
[< Old French *bouterez* flying buttress, plural < *bouter* thrust against; see etym. under **butt**[3]]

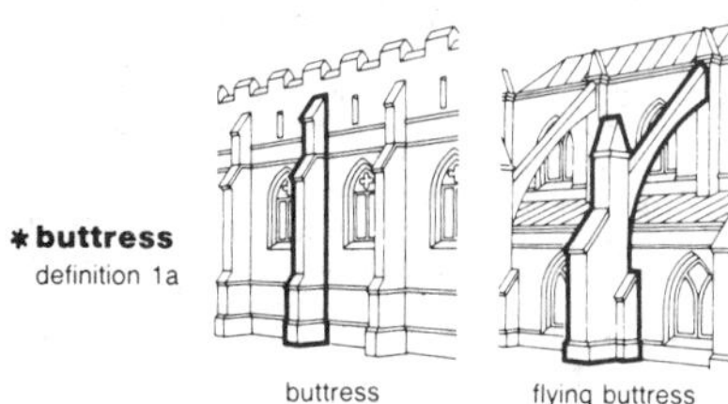

***buttress** definition 1a

but|try (but′rē), *n., pl.* **-tries.** a pantry; buttery.

butt shaft, a blunt or unbarbed arrow.

butt|stock (but′stok′), *n.* the stock behind the breech of a firearm.

butt weld, a weld formed by joining the flattened ends of two pieces of iron or other metal at white heat; a butt-joint made by welding.

butt-weld (but′weld′), *v.t.* to join with a butt weld.

but|ty (but′ē), *n., pl.* **-ties.** *British Informal.* **1** a companion. **2** a labor manager in a mine. [origin unknown]

but|ty-gang (but′ē gang′), *n.* a syndicate sharing the work and profits of a big job.

bu|tut (bu̇ tüt′), *n., pl.* **-tut** or **-tuts.** a unit of money in Gambia, equal to 1/100 of a dalasi. [< the native name in Gambia]

bu|tyl (byü′təl), *n.* a univalent hydrocarbon radical obtained from butane. There are four isomeric univalent radicals. *Butyl is used in the manufacture of automobile inner tubes, electric insulation and mechanical goods* (Wall Street Journal). *Formula:* C_4H_9 [< *but*(yric acid) + *-yl*]

butyl alcohol, any one of four isomeric alcohols derived from butane and used as a solvent for resins, adhesives, and varnishes; butanol. *Formula:* $C_4H_{10}O$

bu|tyl|ate (byü′tə lāt), *v.t.,* **-at|ed, -at|ing.** to introduce a butyl into (a compound).

bu|ty|lene (byü′tə lēn), *n.* a gaseous hydrocarbon of the ethylene series, often used in making synthetic rubber. Butylene is found in three isomeric forms (butenes). *Formula:* C_4H_8 [< *butyl* + *-ene*]

butyl rubber, a synthetic rubber that holds air and gases much better than natural rubber and resists aging, heat, and the effects of gases. Butyl rubber is made by the copolymerization of isobutylene (a gas) with isoprene (a liquid).

bu|tyr|a|ceous (byü′tə rā′shəs), *adj.* of the nature of butter; producing or containing butter. [< Latin *būtȳrum* butter + English *-aceous*]

bu|tyr|al (byü′tə ral), *n.* an acetal of butyraldehyde.

bu|tyr|al|de|hyde (byü′tə ral′də hīd), *n.* an inflammable liquid used especially in making rubber products and synthetic resins. *Formula:* C_4H_8O

bu|tyr|ate (byü′tə rāt), *n.* a salt or ester of butyric acid. [< *butyr*(ic) + *-ate*[2]]

bu|tyr|ic (byü tir′ik), *adj.* **1** of or derived from butyric acid. **2** of or derived from butter. [< Latin *būtȳrum* butter + English *-ic*]

butyric acid, an oily, colorless liquid that has an unpleasant odor. It is formed especially by fermentation in rancid butter and cheese. *Formula:* $C_4H_8O_2$

bu|ty|rin (byü′tər in), *n.* a yellowish, liquid fat found in butter, formed from butyric acid and glycerin. [< *butyr* (ic acid) + *-in*]

bux|a|ceous (buk sā′shəs), *adj.* belonging to the box family of plants. [< New Latin *Buxaceae* the family name (< Latin *buxus* box tree)]

bux|om (buk′səm), *adj.* **1** plump and good to look at; healthy and cheerful: *a hearty buxom lass.* **2** *Archaic.* blithe; lively; gay. **3** *Archaic.* submissive. **4** *Obsolete.* flexible. [Middle English *buhsum* pliant, amenable; (later) jolly, comfortable-looking < Old English *būgan* to bend] —**bux′om|ly,** *adv.* *bux′om|ness, n.*

buy (bī), *v.,* **bought, buy|ing,** *n.* —*v.t.* **1** to get by paying a price, usually in money; purchase: *You can buy a pencil for five cents.* **2** *Figurative.* to get in exchange for something else, or by making some sacrifice: *Enduring friendship can only be bought by unfailing affection.* **3** to bribe: *It was charged that two members of the jury had been bought by the defendant.* **4** to be sufficient to purchase or procure: *Gold cannot buy health.* **5** to redeem (obsolete except in theological use). **6** *U.S. Informal, Figurative.* to accept, especially as valid or feasible: *If you say it's true, I'll buy it.*
—*v.i.* **1** to buy things. **2** to serve as a buyer; be a buyer: *to buy for a retail chain.*
—*n.* **1** *Informal.* a bargain: *That famous old book was a real buy.* **2** *Informal.* a thing bought; purchase. **3** the act of buying.

buy in, a to lay in a stock of: *Many farmers buy in ewes in autumn* (London Times). **b** to buy back one's property at an auction when the bids are not high enough: *An auctioneer, at the moment of non-sale, should be required to state plainly to his audience that an item has been bought in* (Theodore Crombie).

buy into, to obtain an interest or footing in by purchase, as of the shares of a joint-stock company: *Instead of a sponsor buying into a program (he could not buy into a magazine article), the new plan is to sell commercial time only to the advertiser and keep the programs under the control of the broadcasters* (D. B. Lucas).

buy off, a to get rid of (trouble, interference, or any other obstacle) by paying money to: . . . *to buy off the presence of troops by enormous gifts to their captains* (Richard C. Trench). **b** to bribe: *The crook tried to buy off the guard.*

buy out, a to buy all the shares, rights, merchandise, or other holdings of: *to buy out a business, buy a person out.* **b** to relinquish a commitment by payment of money: *He bought himself out of the army.*

buy over, to bribe: *[He] had bought the soldiers over to a man* (M. W. Freer).

buy up, to buy all that one can of or all that is available: *The new owner agreed to buy up all of the old merchandise in the store.*
[Old English *bycgan*] —**buy′a|ble,** *adj.*
—*Syn. v.t.* **1 Buy, purchase** mean to get something by paying a price. **Buy** is the general and informal word: *A person can buy anything in that store if he has the money.* **Purchase,** a somewhat more formal word, suggests buying after careful planning or negotiating or on a large scale: *The bank has purchased some property on which to construct a new building.*
▶**Buy** is used with *from,* not *off of: He bought it from a stranger he met on the street.*

buy-back (bī′bak′), *n., adj.* —*n.* a buying back; repurchase. —*adj.* of or involving a repurchase, especially the repurchase of crude oil by the producer from the government of the country which owns the oil.

buy-down or **buy|down** (bī′doun′), *n. U.S.* a subsidy by a builder or real-estate developer that lowers a buyer's monthly mortgage payments for a specified period.

buy|er (bī′ər), *n.* **1** a person who buys; a purchaser. SYN: customer, patron. **2** a person whose work is buying goods for a department store or other business; purchasing agent.

buyer's market, an economic condition that arises when more goods are offered for sale than people are immediately willing to buy. Prices are usually low in a buyer's market.

buyer's strike, a combined refusal of consumers to buy in protest against high prices.

buy-out or **buy|out** (bī′out′), *n.* the purchase of an entire company or of the entire stock of a product: *a conglomerate buyout.*

buz|ka|shi (büz′kä′shē), *n.,* or **buz kashi,** a sport of Afghanistan, involving competitive riding of horses for the possession of a dead goat: *The players in the game of buz kashi do not form teams. The object of the game is not to prove one group better than another, but to find a champion* (Listener). [< Pashto *buz kashi* (literally) goat snatching]

buzz[1] (buz), *n., v.* —*n.* **1** the humming sound made by flies, mosquitoes, or bees. SYN: drone. **2** the low, confused sound of many people talking quietly: *The buzz of whispers stopped when the teacher entered the room.* **3** a whisper; rumor. **4** *Informal.* a call on the telephone: *Give me a buzz when you get home.* **5** a busy movement; stir; state of activity or excitement. **b** the sound of such activity.
—*v.i.* **1** to make a steady, humming sound; hum loudly: *The radio should be fixed; it buzzes when you turn it on.* **2** to talk with enthusiasm or excitement: *The whole class buzzed with the news of the holiday.* **3** = gossip. **4** (of places) to be filled with the noise of conversation or other low, confused sound. **5** to move busily or fussily about. —*v.t.* **1** to sound in a low, confused way. **2** to utter or express by buzzing. **3** to tell or spread (gossip); whisper. **4** to signal with a buzzer: *The editor buzzed his secretary.* **5** *Informal.* to call (a person) on the telephone. **6** to fly an aircraft very fast and low over (a place or person): *A pilot buzzed our school yesterday.*

buzz about, to move about busily: *The actors buzzed about the stage, getting ready to perform the play.*

buzz off, a *Especially U.S.* to ring off on the telephone: *As soon as I answered the phone, the caller buzzed off.* **b** *Slang.* go away! clear off! *Buzz off, child, and stop bothering the baby.*
[imitative]

buzz[2] (buz), *v.t. British.* to finish to the last drop the contents of (a bottle or other container).

buz|zard[1] (buz′ərd), *n.* **1a** a kind of large, heavy, slow-moving hawk. **b** = buteo. **2** = turkey buzzard. **3** a mean, greedy, or selfish person: *The old buzzard never has a kind word for any of his neighbors.* [< Old French *busart* < *buson,* earlier *buison* < Latin *būteō, -ōnis* kind of hawk]

buz|zard[2] (buz′ərd), *n. Dialect.* any one of various insects that fly by night, such as large moths. [< *buzz* [1]]

buzzard hawk, = buteo.

buzz bomb, a type of jet-propelled, pilotless aircraft; an aerial projectile that can be guided from land to its target, where it explodes; flying bomb; robot bomb; V-1. It was developed by the Germans in World War II.

buzz|er (buz′ər), *n.* **1** an electrical device that makes a buzzing sound as a signal. **2** a thing that buzzes. **3** siren or whistle acting as a signal.

buzz saw, = circular saw.

buzz|wig (buz′wig′), *n.* **1** a large, bushy wig. **2** a person wearing such a wig.

buzz word, a catchword or word used in business jargon: *"Guideline" has become something of a Democratic economists' buzz word* (Time).

b.v., book value.

B.V., **1** Blessed Virgin (Latin, *Beata Virgo)* . **2** farewell (Latin, *bene vale)* .

BVDs (bē′vē′dēz′), *n.* **1** *U.S. Informal.* underwear. **2 B.V.D.s,** *Trademark.* (originally) a kind of one-piece underwear for men.

B.V.M., Blessed Virgin Mary.

bvt., **1** brevet. **2** brevetted.

BW (no periods), biological warfare.

bwa|na (bwä′nə), *n. Swahili.* master; sir.

B.W.I., British West Indies.
BWR (no periods), boiling water reactor.
bx., box.
bxs., boxes.
by (bī), *prep., adv., adj., n.* **—*prep.*** **1a** at the side or edge of; near; beside: *a town by a river. The garden is by the house. Sit by me.* **b** beyond; past: *He walked by the church. She ran right by him.* **2** along; over; through: *He went by the main road.* **3** through the means or use of: *a novel by Dickens. He travels by airplane. The house was destroyed by fire.* SYN: See syn. under **with**. **4** combined with in multiplication or relative dimensions: *a room ten by twenty feet.* **5** in the measure or quantity of: *They sell eggs by the dozen. I pay her by the hour.* **6** as soon as; not later than: *Be here by six o'clock.* **7** in the course of; during: *The sun shines by day.* **8a** according to: *They all work by the rules.* **b** (in oaths) in the presence or with the sanction of: *to swear by all that is holy.* **9** with respect to; in relation to; concerning: *She did well by her seven children.* **10** to the extent of; as the result of comparison: *larger by half. He is taller by a head. He is bigger by far.* **11** taken separately as units or groups in a series: *two by two. Algebra must be mastered step by step.* **12** toward: *The island lies south by east from here.* **13** in imitation of; after (with verbs of *calling* or *naming*): *a rose by any other name would smell as sweet* (Shakespeare).
—*adv.* **1** at hand: *near by.* **2** past: *Julius Caesar lived in days gone by. A car raced by.* **3** aside or away: *She put money by every week to save for a new sewing machine.* **4** *Informal.* at, in, or into another's house when passing: *Please come by and eat with me.*
—*adj.* **1** situated at the side; out of the way. **2** away from the main purpose; secondary; private.
—*n.* bye.
by and by, after a while; before long; soon; shortly: *Summer vacation will come by and by.*
by and large, **a** for the most part; on the whole: *By and large it is a good book.* **b** *Nautical.* to the wind and off it: *They soon find out one another's rate of sailing, by and large* (Fraser's Magazine).
by the by, by the way; incidentally: *By the by, here is the pen you lent me.*
by the way. See under **way**.
[Old English *bī*, unstressed *be*]
by-, *prefix.* **1** secondary; minor; less important: *By-product = a secondary product.*
2 near by: *Bystander = a person standing near by*
3 aside; side: *By-road = side road.*
[Middle English *bi-*, Old English *bī-*]
by-and-by (bī′ən bī′), *n.* the future.
by-bid|der (bī′bid′ər), *n.* a person employed to bid on items at an auction so that the seller may obtain higher prices.
by-blow (bī′blō′), *n.* **1** a side blow; accidental blow. **2** an illegitimate child.
bye (bī), *n., adj.* **—*n.*** **1** the position of a participant in a tournament who is not paired with an opponent, usually in the first round, and advanced to the next round without playing. **2** *Golf.* the holes not played after one player has won. **3** *Cricket.* a run made on a missed ball. Also, **by**.
—*adj.* aside from the main point; incidental.
by the bye, incidentally: *As brother Job says, (who, by the bye . . . began to whine a little under his afflictions) 'Are not my days few?'* (Thomas Jefferson).
go bye-bye, *Informal.* to go out; leave; take a walk or ride (said especially to or by a child): *Let's go bye-bye in Daddy's car. I have to go bye-bye now.*
[variant of the preposition *by*]
bye-bye (bī′bī′), *interj. Informal.* good-by.
bye-byes (bī′bīz′), *n.pl.* = sleep.
by-e|lec|tion (bī′i lek′shən), *n. British.* a special election; election held at a time other than that of the regular elections.
Byel|o|rus|sian (byel′ə rush′ən), *adj., n.* **—*adj.*** of or having to do with Byelorussia, or White Russia.
—*n.* a native or inhabitant of Byelorussia. Also, **Belorussian**.
by-end (bī′end′), *n.* a secondary or incidental aim or object, especially a private end, or secret purpose or design.
By|er|ly Turk (bī′ər lē), one of the three stallions from which all English thoroughbred horses are descended. The other two were the Darley Arabian and the Godolphin Barb. [< Captain *Byerly*, an Englishman, who supposedly brought it from Turkey in the late 1600's]
by|gone (bī′gôn′, -gon′), *adj., n.* **—*adj.*** gone by; past; former; departed: *The ancient Romans lived in bygone days.*
—*n.* **1** something in the past. **2** the past.
let bygones be bygones, to forgive and forget: *The Soviet Union's desire to let bygones be bygones and eliminate all hostility between [it] and its former Yugoslav allies was reiterated* (New York Times).
by|lane (bī′lān′), *n.* a side lane.
by|law (bī′lô′), *n.* **1** a law made by a city, company, club, or other group for the control of its own affairs. **2** a secondary law or rule; not one of the main rules: *Our club has a constitution and bylaws.* **3** *British.* any law made by a local government authority. [< Scandinavian (compare Danish *bylov* municipal law < *by* town + *lov* law); meaning later influenced by *by-*]
by-line (bī′līn′), *n., v.,* **-lined, -lin|ing.** **—*n.*** a line at the beginning of a newspaper or magazine article giving the name of the writer.
—*v.t.* to write and sign one's name to: *to by-line a story.*
by-lin|er (bī′lī′nər), *n.* a writer having a by-line.
by-name (bī′nām′), *n.* **1** a secondary name. **2** = nickname.
by-pass or **by|pass** (bī′pas′, -päs′), *n., v.* **—*n.*** **1** a road, channel, or pipe providing a secondary passage to be used instead of the main passage: *Drivers use the by-pass to skirt the city when there is a lot of traffic.* **2** a pathway or passage made surgically between two or more blood vessels to divert the blood from its normal channels; shunt: *a coronary bypass.* **3** *Electricity.* = shunt.
—*v.t.* **1** to go around: *The new highway bypasses the entire city.* **2** to provide a secondary passage for. **3** to go over the head of (an immediate superior) to a higher authority. **4** to set aside or ignore (regulations or the like) in order to reach a desired objective. **5** to get away from; avoid; escape: *to by-pass a question.* **6** *Military.* = flank.
by-pass condenser, a condenser that furnishes a by-pass for alternating current in a circuit where the impedance is high.
by|past (bī′past′, -päst′), *adj.* = bygone.
by-path (bī′path′, -päth′), *n.* a side path; byway.
by-place (bī′plās′), *n.* an out-of-the-way place or situation.
by-play (bī′plā′), *n.* action that is not part of the main action, especially on the stage.
by-prod|uct (bī′prod′əkt), *n.* **1** something of value produced in making the main product: *Kerosene is a by-product of petroleum refining. The investigations will also include work on fish by-products, such as fish oils and meals* (Science News Letter). **2** a secondary result produced in doing something else.
byre (bīr), *n. British.* a cow barn; shed: *Our onecow byre is hung literally to the rafters with grey bats* (Punch). [Old English *býre*]
byr|nie (bėr′nē), *n.* a coat or shirt of mail; hauberk. [variant of Middle English *brynie*]
by-road (bī′rōd′), *n.* = side road.
By|ron|ic (bī ron′ik), *adj.* **1** of Byron or his poetry: *Byronic rhymes.* **2** like Byron; arrogant, cynical, unconventional, or romantic: *a Byronic attitude to responsibility.* **—By|ron′i|cal|ly**, *adv.*
By|ron|ism (bī′rə niz əm), *n.* **1** the characteristics of Byron or his poetry. **2** imitation of Byron.
bys|sa|ceous (bi sā′shəs), *adj. Botany.* consisting of fine threads or filaments.
bys|sal (bis′əl), *adj.* of or having to do with the byssus of a mollusk.
bys|si (bis′ī), *n.* a plural of **byssus**.
bys|sif|er|ous (bi sif′ər əs), *adj.* having a byssus.
bys|sine (bis′in), *adj.* of or like byssus or fine linen. [< Latin *byssinus*]
bys|si|no|sis (bis′ə nō′sis), *n.* an industrial disease characterized by bronchial inflammation and frequently by an asthmatic condition, resulting from long-continued inhalation of dust in cotton mills; brown lung. [< Late Latin *byssinum* linen + English *-osis*]
bys|sus (bis′əs), *n., pl.* **bys|sus|es** or **bys|si**. **1** a group of tough filaments secreted by a gland of the foot, by which various mussels attach themselves to rocks and other objects. **2a** a kind of yellow flax known to the ancients, especially the ancient Egyptians. **b** a fine and valuable linen fabric made from it. It was this fabric, sometimes mistranslated as cotton or silk, that was generally used by the ancient Egyptians for wrapping their dead in mummification. [< Latin *byssus* < Greek *býssos* flax, apparently < Semitic (compare Hebrew *būṣ*)]
by|stand|er (bī′stan′dər), *n.* a person who stands near or looks on but does not take part; onlooker; spectator: *As an interested bystander I went on a private investigation of the wardrobes under the huge stage* (London Times).
by-street (bī′strēt′), *n.* a side street.
by-talk (bī′tôk′), *n.* small talk; gossip.
byte (bīt), *n.* a unit of eight bits in a computer memory. [< *b* (inar)*y* (digi)*t e*(ight)]
by|way (bī′wā′), *n.* a side path or road; way that is little used.
by|word (bī′wėrd′), *n.* **1** a common saying; proverb. **2** a person or thing that becomes well known as a type of some characteristic. **3** an object of contempt; thing scorned: *His cowardice made him a byword to all who knew him.* **4** a nickname, especially a scornful nickname. **5** a trick of speech; pet phrase. [Old English *bīword*]
by-work (bī′wėrk′), *n.* work done by the way, in intervals of leisure.
by-your-leave (bī′yər lēv′, -yůr′-), *n.* an expression of apology for not having asked permission: *They walked in and sat down without so much as a by-your-leave.*
By|zan|tian (bi zan′shən), *adj., n.* = Byzantine.
Byz|an|tine (biz′ən tēn, -tīn; bi zan′tin), *adj., n.* **—*adj.*** **1** of or like the Byzantine Empire or Byzantium, an ancient city, afterward Constantinople. **2a** having to do with a style of art developed in Byzantium, characterized by emphasis on formal religious symbols, the absence of perspective, and the use of gilding and rich colors. **b** of or like Byzantine architecture. **3** having to do with the Byzantine Empire. **4** of or having to do with the Eastern Church: *the Byzantine rite.* **5** resembling or suggesting the politics of ancient Byzantium; characterized by much scheming and intrigue: *Was French party politics, with its Byzantine maneuvers and its feuding factions, really en route to a transformation?* (New York Times).
—*n.* a native or inhabitant of Byzantium.
[< Latin *Byzantīnus* < *Byzantium,* ancient Greek city, now Istanbul]
***Byzantine architecture**, a style of architecture developed in the Byzantine Empire in the 400's and the centuries immediately following. It is characterized by complex vaulting with domes and other rounded forms, spatial richness, and lavish decoration, usually involving mosaics and mural paintings.

***Byzantine architecture**

Byzantine Empire, the eastern part of the Roman Empire after the division in 395 A.D. It ceased to exist after the fall of its capital, Constantinople, in 1453.
Byz|an|tin|esque (bi zan′tə nesk′), *adj.* fashioned in the Byzantine style.
Byz|an|tin|ism (bi zan′tə niz əm), *n.* **1** the spirit, principles, and methods of the Byzantines. **2** the manifestation of Byzantine characteristics.
Byz|an|tin|ist (biz′ən tē nist, -tī-; bi zan′tə nist), *n.* a person who studies Byzantine art, architecture, literature, and the like.
Byz|an|tin|ize (bi zan′tə nīz), *v.t.,* **-ized, -iz|ing.** to fashion according to Byzantine ideas.
Bz., benzene.
BZ (no periods), a United States Army code name for an incapacitating gas that produces disorientation and hallucination.

***C¹** or **c** (sē), *n., pl.* **C's** or **Cs, c's** or **cs. 1** the third letter of the English alphabet: *There are two c's in cancel.* **2** any sound represented by this letter. **3** as a symbol: **a** the third (of an actual or possible series). **b** third best (of its kind or class): *grade C canned fish.* **c** a known quantity (used especially in algebraic equations along with *a, b,* etc.; *x, y,* and *z* most commonly represent unknown quantities). **4** the third highest grade (in most schools and colleges): *to get a C in history.* **5** *Music.* **a** the first tone in the scale of C major, the natural scale without flats or sharps; the third tone of A minor. **b** the symbol representing this tone. **c** a key, string, etc., that produces this tone. **d** the scale or key which has C as its keynote: *a concerto in C.* **6** the Roman numeral for 100. **7** *U.S. Slang.* **a** a hundred-dollar bill. **b** one hundred dollars.

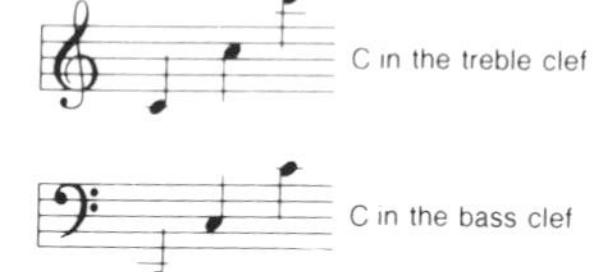

***C¹**
definition 5b

C² (sē), *n., pl.* **C's**. anything shaped like the letter C.
c (no period), **1** centi-. **2** centimeter.
c., an abbreviation or symbol for the following:
1 Also, **ca.** about; approximately (Latin, *circa*).
2 carat.
3 (in baseball) catcher.
4 cathode.
5 center.
6 centimeter.
7 cent or cents.
8 centime.
9 *Mathematics, Physics.* constant.
10 copy.
11 copyright.
12 cubic.
13 cup or cups.
14 curie.
15 *Electricity.* current.
16 cycle.
17 hundredweight (Latin, *centium*).
C (no period), an abbreviation or symbol for:
1 capacitance.
2 *Electricity.* capacity.
3 carbon.
4 Celsius (= centigrade).
5 centigrade: *A rise of 10°C doubles the rate of many chemical reactions* (K. D. Wadsworth).
6 central.
7 *Physics.* (electric) charge.
8 *Mathematics, Physics.* constant.
9 copyright.
10 cytosine.
11 one hundred (Latin, *centum*).
C., an abbreviation for the following:
1 candle.
2 Cape.
3 Catholic.
4 Celsius (= centigrade).
5 center.
6 centigrade: *100°C.*
7 central.
8 century.
9 chapter (Latin, *capitulum*).
10 Church.
11 cirrus (cloud).
12 City.
13 Congress.
14 Conservative (political party).
15 Court.
C¹⁴, carbon 14.

***C¹**
definition 1

ca' (kä, kô), *v., n. Scottish.* —*v.t., v.i.* to call; drive.
—*n.* a call.
Ca (no period), calcium (chemical element).
ca., **1** cathode. **2** centiare or centiares. **3** Also, **c.** about; approximately (Latin, *circa*) : *ca. 1776.*
CA (no periods), **1** California (in postal Zip Code). **2** *Psychology.* chronological age.
C.A., an abbreviation for the following:
1 Central America.
2 Also, **c.a.** chartered accountant.
3 chief accountant.
4 *Psychology.* chronological age.
5 commercial agent.
6 consular agent.
7 controller of accounts.
C/A, **1** capital account. **2** credit account. **3** current account.
Caa|ba (kä′bə), *n.* = Kaaba.
cab¹ (kab), *n., v.,* **cabbed, cab|bing.** —*n.* **1** an automobile that can be hired with driver; taxicab: *My father telephoned for a cab to take him to the airport.* **2a** a carriage that can be hired with driver, usually pulled by one horse: *We rode through the park in an open cab.* **b** a hansom (cab). **3** the covered part of a railroad engine where the engineer and fireman sit: *The engineer invited the boy to sit in the cab with him.* **4** an enclosed seat on a truck, tractor, or other vehicle or machinery, where the driver or operator sits. **5** the glass-enclosed booth of a control tower at an airport.
—*v.i.* to go by cab.
[short for *cabriolet*] —**cab′less,** *adj.*
cab² (kab), *n.* a Hebrew unit of dry measure, equal to about 2 quarts. Also, **kab.** [< Hebrew *qab*]
cab³ (kab), *v.,* **cabbed, cab|bing,** *n. British Slang.* —*v.t.* **1** to pilfer. **2** to crib.
—*n.* a literal translation, or crib.
[short for *cabbage²*]
CAB (no periods) or **C.A.B.,** Civil Aeronautics Board.
ca|ba (kä′bä), *n.* (in the Philippines) a measure of capacity equal to about 1 U.S. bushels. [< Spanish (Philippines) *caba*]
ca|bal (kə bal′), *n., v.,* **-balled, -bal|ling.** —*n.* **1** a small group of people working or plotting in secret; faction: *The cabal of disruptive conspirators ... had no right to be where they were, when, on May 5, they were arrested on the Capitol steps* (New York Times). SYN: junto, clique. **2** a secret scheme of such a group; plot. SYN: intrigue. **3** *Historical.* five ministers of Charles II forming an unpopular faction. Their initials happened to make up the word: *C*lifford, *A*rlington, *B*uckingham, *A*shley, and *L*auderdale.
—*v.i.* to form such a group; conspire: *The barons ... began to cabal against his succession* (Henry Hallam).
[< French *cabale,* learned borrowing from Medieval Latin *cabbala* cabala] —**ca|bal′ler,** *n.*
cab|a|la or **Cab|a|la** (kab′ə lə, kə bä′-), *n.* **1** a system of interpretation of the Scriptures based on the numerical rather than the alphabetical value of the letters of a word, developed in the Middle Ages by certain rabbis. **2** a mystical belief; secret doctrine. Also, **cabbala, kabala, kabbala.**
[< Medieval Latin *cabbala* < Hebrew *qabbālā* tradition]
cab|a|let|ta (kab′ə let′ə; *Italian* kä′bä let′ä), *n.* an operatic song in rondo form with variations imitating the hoofbeats of a cantering horse. [< Italian *cabaletta*]
ca|bal|ic (kə bal′ik), *adj.* of or having to do with the cabala.
cab|a|lism (kab′ə liz əm), *n.* **1** the system of the cabala (def. 1). **2** mystic or occult doctrine; occultism.
cab|a|list¹ (kab′ə list), *n.* a person expert in the cabala or other secret doctrine; a mystic. Also, **kabbalist.** [< *cabal*(a) + *-ist*]
cab|a|list² (kab′ə list), *n.* a secret intriguer or plotter. [< *cabal* + *-ist*]
cab|a|lis|tic (kab′ə lis′tik), *adj.* **1** having a mystical meaning; secret. SYN: occult, mystic. **2** of or suitable for the Jewish cabala. Also, **kabbalistic.**
—**cab′a|lis′ti|cal|ly,** *adv.*
cab|a|lis|ti|cal (kab′ə lis′tə kəl), *adj.* = cabalistic.
cab|al|le|ro (kab′əl yār′ō, -ə lār′-; *Spanish* kä′vä-lyä′rō), *n., pl.* **-ros. 1** in Spain: **a** a gentleman: *Respectable caballeros no longer take their wives or fiancées to such places* (Time). **b** a knight. **2** *Southwestern U.S.* **a** a horseman. **b** an ardent admirer of women or of a particular woman; gallant.
[American English < Spanish *caballero* < Late Latin *caballārius* horseman < Latin *caballus* (inferior) horse. See etym. of doublets **cavalier, chevalier.**]
cab|al|line (kab′ə lin), *adj.* of or having to do with a horse or horses: *the caballine spring* (the spring Hippocrene produced by a stroke of the hoof of Pegasus). [< Latin *caballīnus* < *caballus* horse]
ca|ba|na or **ca|ba|ña** (kə ban′ə, -bä′nə, -bän′yə), *n.* **1** a shelter like a small tent or cabin, used on a beach or near a swimming pool for dressing or to provide shade; bathhouse. **2** a cabin. [American English < Spanish *cabaña* < Late Latin *capanna* hut, (later) tent. See etym. of doublets **cabane, cabin.**]
cabana set, a set of matching short-sleeved jacket and bathing shorts, used as beachwear for men.
ca|bane (kə ban′), *n.* a system of struts for supporting an airplane wing above the fuselage. [< French *cabane* < Late Latin *capanna* hut. See etym. of doublets **cabana, cabin.**]
cab|a|ret (kab′ə rā′, kab′ə rā), *n.* **1a** a restaurant offering singing and dancing as entertainment. **b** the entertainment: *Students in Leipzig were ... putting on a satirical cabaret* (Manchester Guardian Weekly). **2** a set of dishes for coffee or tea and the stand or tray holding them. [American English < French *cabaret,* probably < Middle Dutch *cameret,* ultimately < Latin *camera* vault, arch]
cab|as (kab′ə; *French* kȧ bä′), *n.* a bag of plaited straw, or of silk, leather, or other material, carried by women to hold small purchases, articles for work, or sewing. [< French *cabas* basket, bag < Old Provençal]
cab|bage¹ (kab′ij), *n., v.,* **-baged, -bag|ing.** —*n.* **1a** a plant whose leaves are closely folded into a round head that grows from a short stem. Cabbage belongs to the mustard family. The most common kind is called white cabbage; red and savoy cabbage are two other kinds. See picture under **mustard family. b** its head, eaten either cooked or raw as a vegetable. **2** any one of a number of related plants, such as the Portuguese cabbage and the Chinese cabbage. **3** the large, tender terminal bud of various palm trees, sometimes eaten as a vegetable. **4** *Slang.* paper money; bank notes.
—*v.i.* to form a head like that of a cabbage in growing.
[< Middle French *caboche* head < Picard, variant of Old French *caboce*]
cab|bage² (kab′ij), *n., v.,* **-baged, -bag|ing.** —*n.* **1** pieces of cloth stolen by tailors in the process of cutting out clothes. **2** *British Slang.* a translation, usually literal, of a classical or other work in a foreign language, used dishonestly by schoolboys in preparing their lessons or recitations; crib.
—*v.t.* **1** *Informal.* to appropriate surreptitiously; pilfer: *Someone has cabbaged my pen.* **2** *British Slang.* to crib: *... a speech, which ... had been what schoolboys call 'cabbaged' from some of the forms of oration* (P. Thompson). —*v.i.* to pilfer: *Steelyards ... who cabbaged, giving short weight* (H. Marryat).
[origin unknown]
cabbage bug, = harlequin bug.
cabbage butterfly, a kind of white butterfly whose larvae often damage cabbages.
cab|bage|head (kab′ij hed′), *n.* **1** a head of cabbage. **2** *Informal.* a large, round head. **3** *Informal, Figurative.* a stupid person: *We hear persons whose talents are rather of the solid than the brilliant order spoken of as "cabbageheads"* (Nation). [< *cabbage¹* + *head*]
cabbage looper, the larva of a common noctuid moth. The cabbage looper is pale green with white lateral stripes, and is a serious pest of cabbage and related plants.
cabbage maggot, a root maggot which works upwards into the stems of cauliflower, kale, cabbage, and other vegetables, often killing the plant.
cabbage moth, = diamondback moth.
cabbage palm or **palmetto,** any palm tree whose buds are eaten as a vegetable.

Cc

Script letters look like examples of fine penmanship. They appear in many formal uses, such as invitations to social functions.

Cc Cc

Handwritten letters, both manuscript or printed (left) and cursive (right), are easy for children to read and to write.

Cc Cc

Roman letters have *serifs* (finishing strokes) adapted from the way Roman stonecutters carved their letters. This is *Times Roman* type.

Cc Cc

Sans-serif letters are often called *gothic.* They have lines of even width and no serifs. This type face is called *Helvetica.*

Cc Cc

Between roman and gothic, some letters have thick and thin lines with slight flares that suggest serifs. This type face is *Optima.*

C

Computer letters can be sensed by machines either from their shapes or from the magnetic ink with which they are printed.

cabbage rose, a rose with a large, round, compact flower.
cab·bа·ges and kings (kab′ə jiz), miscellaneous subjects, as of conversation or discussion, in allusion to the lines: " 'The time has come,' the Walrus said, 'To talk of many things: Of shoes—and ships—and sealingwax—Of cabbages—and kings' " from Lewis Carroll's *Through the Looking-Glass.*
cabbage tree, any one of various cabbage palms.
cabbage white, = cabbage butterfly.
cab·bage·worm (kab′ij wėrm′), *n.* any one of various larvae which feed on cabbages, such as the larva of the cabbage white.
cab·bag·y (kab′ə jē), *adj.* of or like a cabbage: *a cabbagy odor.*
cab·ba·la or **Cab·ba·la** (kab′ə lə, kə bä′-), *n.* = cabala.
cab·ble (kab′əl), *v.,* **-bled, -bling.** —*v.t.* to break up into pieces (iron which has been smelted with charcoal, balled, and flattened) before fagoting, fusing, and rolling into bars.
—*v.i.* to cabble iron.
[origin uncertain] —**cab′bler,** *n.*
cab·by or **cab·bie** (kab′ē), *n., pl.* **-bies.** *Informal.* a cabdriver: *The normally tough New York cabbie was so startled he couldn't get the cab started* (Wall Street Journal).
cab·driv·er (kab′drī′vər), *n.* a person who drives a cab, especially a taxicab.
***ca·ber** (kā′bər), *n.* a long, heavy pole or beam tossed as a trial of strength in Scottish Highland games. [< Scottish Gaelic *cabar* pole, rafter]

***caber**

Ca·ber·net (ka ber nā′), *n.* **1** a light, dry red wine made from a black grape originally grown in the Gironde district of France and now also in California and Australia. **2** the grape from which this wine is made.
cab·e·zon (kab′ə zon; *Spanish* kä′bā sōn′), *n.* a surf fish of the Pacific Coast of North America. [American English < Spanish *cabezón* (originally) big-headed < *cabeza* head, ultimately < Latin *caput, -itis*]
ca·bil·do (kə bil′dō), *n., pl.* **-dos.** *Southwestern U.S.* **1** the chapter house of a cathedral church. **2** the chapter itself. **3** the governing council of a town. [< Spanish *cabildo*]
cab·in (kab′ən), *n., v.* —*n.* **1a** a small, roughly built house; hut: *The settlers lived in a cabin in the woods.* SYN: shanty, shack. **b** a small house built for some special purpose; cottage: *a summer cabin, a tourist cabin.* **2a** a private room in a ship. A cabin serves as quarters for an officer or officers, or for a passenger or passengers: *The 500 passengers occupied 300 cabins.* **b** a room on a small boat containing the bunks. **3** the place for passengers in an aircraft: *Only the stewardess can go from the cabin to the cockpit.* **4** the part of a trailer serving as living quarters.
—*v.i.* to live in or as if in a cabin: *Bands of Indians cabined along the borders of the cove* (Francis Parkman).
—*v.t.* **1** to confine within narrow limits; cramp; hamper: *The fact that so many lives have become cabined and confined explains in a measure, I think, the tremendous growth of amateur participation in the arts* (New York Times). **2** to lodge or accommodate in or as if in a cabin.
[< Old French *cabane* < Old Provençal *cabana* < Late Latin *capanna* hut. See etym. of doublets **cabana, cabane.**]
cabin boy, a boy or man whose work is waiting on the officers and passengers on a ship.
cabin class, a class or grade of passenger accommodations on a ship, lower than first class and higher than tourist class.
cabin cruiser, a motorboat with berths, cooking, and other living facilities; cruiser: *I have this twenty-three-foot cabin cruiser that sleeps four* (New Yorker).
cab·i·net (kab′ə nit, kab′nit), *n., adj.* —*n.* **1a** a piece of furniture with shelves or drawers, used to hold articles, such as dishes, linens, jewels, papers, or specimens: *a medicine cabinet, a filing cabinet for letters. Mother keeps her good dishes in the china cabinet.* **b** a case for a radio, television set, phonograph, or other electronic equipment; console. **2** Also, **Cabinet. a** a group of advisers chosen by the head of a nation to help in the government. The Attorney General and the Secretary of Defense are members of the cabinet of the President of the United States. *This will be the second meeting of the Cabinet since Parliament adjourned for the summer recess* (London Times). SYN: ministry. **b** *Archaic.* the private room in which the cabinet members of a state meet for deliberation. **c** *Archaic.* a meeting in such a room. **3** *Archaic.* a small private room; boudoir. **4** *Obsolete.* a little cabin, hut, or cottage. **5** *Obsolete.* a summerhouse or leafy shelter in a garden.
—*adj.* **1** of or having to do with a political cabinet: *a cabinet meeting of government ministers.* **2** private; secret; confidential: *cabinet decisions.* **3** of such beauty, value, or size as to be suited for a private room or for keeping in a case: *a cabinet edition.* **4** of or having to do with a cabinetmaker or cabinetmaking: *cabinet woodwork, cabinet shop.*
[< Middle French *cabinet* < Italian *cabinetto,* or *gabinetto,* perhaps < *gabbia* cage < Latin *cavea*]
cab·i·net·eer (kab′ə nə tir′, kab′nə-), *n.* Also, **Cabineteer.** *Informal.* a cabinet member.
cabinet government or **Cabinet government, 1** control of the government of a country, for example in Great Britain, by a group of the more important ministers of the Cabinet selected by the prime minister who are also all members of Parliament. **2** government by this or a similar system.
cab·i·net·mak·er (kab′ə nit mā′kər, kab′nit-), *n.* a person whose work is making fine furniture and woodwork.
cab·i·net·mak·ing (kab′ə nit mā′king, kab′nit-), *n.* the cabinetmaker's occupation or skill.
cabinet minister, a member of the cabinet of certain countries, such as Great Britain and Canada, or of a province, such as Quebec.
cabinet organ, a small, portable organ, usually a reed organ or harmonium.
cabinet pudding, a kind of spongelike pudding made with bread or cake and dried fruit, eggs, and milk.
cab·i·net·ry (kab′ə nə trē, kab′nə-), *n.* = cabinetwork.
Cabinet system, = cabinet government (def. 1).
cab·i·net-wood (kab′ə nit wůd′, kab′nit-), *n.* wood suitable for cabinetwork, such as oak, walnut, or mahogany.
cab·i·net·work (kab′ə nit wėrk′, kab′nit-), *n.* **1** any beautifully made furniture or woodwork: *The Louis XIV chair is an elaborate specimen of cabinetwork.* **2** the making of such furniture or woodwork.
cabin ship, a passenger ship providing accommodations for only one class of passengers.
***ca·ble** (kā′bəl), *n., v.,* **-bled, -bling.** —*n.* **1** a strong, thick rope, now usually made of wires twisted together: *The truck used a cable to tow the automobile. Large suspension bridges, such as the Golden Gate Bridge in San Francisco, hang supported by steel-wire cables* (Walter R. Williams, Jr.). **2a** the rope or chain by which an anchor is raised and lowered. **b** = cable's length. **3a** an insulated bundle of wires which carries an electric current. Telegraph messages are sent across the ocean by a waterproof, underwater cable. *Current was restored while they were repairing high-tension cables* (London Times). **b** = coaxial cable. **c** a bundle of optical fibers that carries information in the form of extremely rapid pulses of light. **4** a message sent across the ocean by cable; cablegram: *A transoceanic cable arrived from Paris.* **5** an ornament with a design like that of a cable. **6** = cable television: *Seventy percent of Canadian households have access to cable* (Maclean's).
—*v.t.* **1** to tie or fasten with a cable: *A ship was cabled to the pier.* **2** to send (a message) across the ocean by underwater cable: *He cabled the good news about his arrival from Rome.* **3** to send a cablegram to: *The sailor cabled his family from Tokyo.* **4** to provide with a cable or cables.
—*v.i.* **1** to send a message across the ocean by underwater cable; communicate by cable: *We will cable when we arrive.* **2** to provide with a cable or cables.
[< Old North French *cable* < Late Latin *capulum* halter < Latin *capere* take hold of] —**ca′ble·less,** *adj.* —**ca′ble·like′,** *adj.*

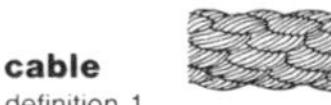
***cable**
definition 1

cable bend, the knot or clinch by which a cable is attached to an anchor.
cable car, a car pulled by a moving cable that is operated by an engine, such as a streetcar or a car on a ski lift; grip car.
cable carrier, a tub or bucket suspended from grooved wheels traveling on a cable, or directly attached to a moving cable, and used to transport sand, minerals, or other heavy materials on a wire ropeway.
ca·ble·cast (kā′bəl kast′, -käst′), *n., v.* —*n.* a telecast by cable television: *Shuey also helped to produce a series of cablecasts to acquaint Kansas voters with the candidates* (National Cable Television Association).
—*v.i.* to telecast by cable television: *Subscription cablecasting of sports events is not permitted within two years of the sports event telecast live* (Mary A.M. Phillips).
ca·ble·cast·ing (kā′bəl kas′ting, -käs′-), *n.* broadcasting by cable TV.
ca·ble·gram (kā′bəl gram), *n.* a message sent across the ocean by underwater cable: *A brief cablegram . . . was Emily's first news that he had survived and was freed* (Chicago Daily News).
ca·ble-laid (kā′bəl lād′), *adj.* made by a counterclockwise twisting of three ropes, each of which has three strands that are twisted clockwise; hawser-laid: *cable-laid rope.*
cable length, = cable's length.
cable molding, *Architecture.* a molding with its surface cut in imitation of the twisting of a rope.
ca·ble·pho·to (kā′bəl fō′tō), *n.* a photograph sent by cable: *Radiophoto and cablephoto service across the Atlantic has long been available* (Wall Street Journal).
cable railway, an apparatus consisting of cars drawn by a continuously moving cable that is between and beneath the rails of a street railroad or suspended between the towers of a ski lift.
ca·ble-read·y (kā′bəl red′ē), *adj.* designed or able to be plugged into a cable television system: *Make sure the VCR is cable-ready and can be hooked up directly to the cable* (Hans Fantel).
cable release, a stiff wire inside a flexible outer casing, that releases the shutter on a camera without the photographer's touching the camera.
cable road, = cable railway.
ca·blese (kā′bə lēz′, -lēs′), *n.* the style of shortening and combining words to reduce the length of messages sent by cable; telegraphese.
cable ship, or **ca·ble·ship** (kā′bəl ship′), *n.* a ship used to lay a submarine cable.
cable's length, a unit of measurement frequently used in sailing directions (720 feet in the United States Navy and about 100 fathoms or 607.56 feet in the British Navy); cable length.
***cable stitch**, a combination of stitches in knitting which produces ridges resembling those of twisted cable.

***cable stitch**

ca·ble-stitch (kā′bəl stich′), *v.t.* to knit (a garment) using a cable stitch.
ca·blet (kā′blit), *n.* a cable-laid rope less than 10 inches in circumference. [< *cable* + *-et*]
cable tank, a strong, watertight tank on a cable ship for holding a coiled section of cable.
cable television, a system for transmitting television programs by coaxial cable to individual subscribers: *Now cable television is a versatile broadband communications system that can provide a subscriber with many more channels than there are programs to fill them* (William T. Knox).
ca·ble-tool (kā′bəl tül′), *adj.* of or having to do with a method of drilling wells, in which the bit is raised and dropped in the bore of the well, rather than revolved.
cable TV, = cable television.
cable walk, *U.S.* a narrow footway along a cable to the top of a tower of a suspension bridge: *Climbing the cable walk of the Brooklyn Bridge to the top of one of its towers . . . is one of the routine jobs which is guaranteed to make photographers slightly nervous* (Literary Digest).
ca·ble·way (kā′bəl wā′), *n.* a conveying apparatus in which a wire cable supports or conveys the moving load: *They have also built a cableway and a suspension footbridge over the Zambezi* (London Times).
cab·man (kab′mən), *n., pl.* **-men.** a man who drives a cab, especially a taxicab.
ca·bob (kə bob′), *n.* = kabob.
ca·boched (kə bosht′), *adj.* = caboshed.

Pronunciation Key: hat, āge, cãre, fär; let, ēqual, tėrm; it, īce; hot, ōpen, ôrder; oil, out; cup, půt, rüle; child; long; thin; ᴛʜen; zh, measure; ə represents a in about, e in taken, i in pencil, o in lemon, u in circus.

ca|bo|chon (kab′ə shon; *French* kȧ bō shôɴ′), *n., adj.* —*n.* **1** a precious stone cut in a convex shape, which is polished without being faceted. See picture under **gem**. **2** the style itself.
—*adj.* cut in convex shape; polished but not faceted: *a cabochon emerald.*
[< French *cabochon* < *caboche* head]

ca|bo|clo (kə bô′klü), *n., pl.* **-clos.** a person descended wholly or in part from the native American Indians of Brazil. [< Portuguese (Brazil) *caboclo* < Tupi]

ca|boo|dle (kə bü′dəl), *n. Slang.* a group of people or things: *At last the whole caboodle is in the air in a great straggling, lacy flock* (Atlantic). [American English < *ca-* (perhaps < *kit*¹) + *boodle*]

ca|boose (kə büs′), *n.* **1** a small car on a freight train in which the conductor and trainmen can work, rest, and sleep. It is usually the last car. *You would be all worn out weeks before the little red caboose behind the 6½ million freight cars came in sight* (Newsweek). **2** a kitchen on the deck of a ship: *A thin cloud of smoke, that arose from the caboose, showed that the crew were already preparing their evening meal* (G. A. McCall). SYN: galley. **3** any similar small deckhouse: *The captain had his quarters in one of the cabooses, under the bridge between the two paddle boxes* (New Yorker). [American English, perhaps < Dutch *kabuyse* ship's supply room, galley]

ca|boshed (kə bosht′), *adj. Heraldry.* full-faced but with no part of the neck showing on the head of an animal. Also, **caboched.** [< past participle of obsolete *caboche* to cut off the head of (a deer) < Old French *caboche* head]

ca|bot (ka bō′), *n.* a dry measure in general use in the island of Jersey, one of the Channel Islands. [< French dialectal *cabot*]

cab|o|tage (kab′ə tij), *n.* **1** navigation between ports along a coast. **2** air transportation within a country by domestic aircraft. **3** the right of air carriers to engage in cabotage. [< French *cabotage* < *caboter* to sail along the coast]

cab rank, *British.* a place where cabs are or can be drawn up for hire; cabstand.

ca|bré (ka brā′), *adj. Heraldry.* capering; rearing on the hind legs, as a horse does. [< Middle French *cabrer* to rear < Spanish *cabra* goat < Latin *capra*]

ca|bret|ta (kə bret′ə), *n.* a durable leather obtained from haired sheep of South America and Africa. [< Spanish, Portuguese *cabra* goat]

ca|bril|la (kə bril′ə), *n.* **1** any one of certain edible serranoid fishes, such as the California rock bass. **2** the red hind or other grouper. [< Spanish *cabrilla* spiny-finned fish (diminutive) < *cabra* goat < Latin *capra*]

cab|ri|ole (kab′rē ōl), *n.* **1** a style of curved leg with an ornamental foot, used especially in Chippendale and Queen Anne furniture. **2** *Ballet.* a leap in which one leg is extended and the other leg is brought up to the first. [< French *cabriole* a leap, variant of *capriole* (because it resembles the foreleg of an animal making a capriole)]

***cab|ri|o|let** (kab′rē ə lā′), *n.* **1** (formerly) an automobile somewhat like a coupé, but having a convertible top. **2a** a light carriage with a folding top, one or two seats, and two wheels, pulled by one horse. **b** a four-wheeled carriage somewhat similar to the victoria. [< French *cabriolet* < *cabrioler* to caper, leap, alteration of obsolete *caprioler* < Italian *capriolare* to capriole (because of its bouncing motion)]

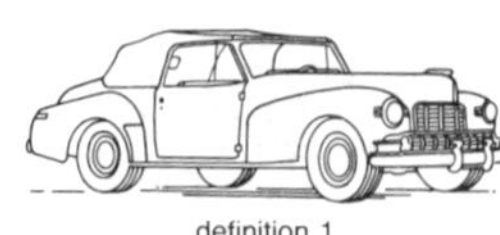

definition 1

***cabriolet**
definitions 1, 2a

definition 2a

cab|rite (kab′rīt), *n.* a lizard with the lower eyelid partly transparent and movable, found in central and southern India. [< New Latin *Cabrita* < Spanish *cabrita* a she-goat < *cabra* goat < Latin *capra*]

cab|stand (kab′stand′), *n.* a place where cabs are or can be drawn up for hire.

cabt., cabinet.

cab tout, *British.* a person whose job is to fetch cabs and help with luggage.

cac|a|fue|go (kak′ə fyü′gō) *n., pl.* **-gos.** *Obsolete.* a bragging, vaporing fellow. [< Latin *cacāre* to excrete + Spanish *fuego* fire]

ca'can|ny (kä kan′ē, kô-), *v., n.* —*v.i. Scottish.* **1** to drive carefully. **2** to go cautiously. **3** to proceed in a leisurely manner.
—*n. British Slang.* deliberate restriction of production on the part of workers: *This feature has not led to slackness or "ca' canny" methods of working, but ... has removed a source of dispute and bitterness* (J. L. Burn).
[< *ca'* call, (literally) drive + *canny*]

ca|ca|o (kə kā′ō, -kä′-), *n., pl.* **-ca|os. 1** the seeds from which cocoa and chocolate are made. They are fermented, then washed to remove the sticky coating, and dried. **2** the tropical American tree that they grow on; chocolate tree. Cacao is a small evergreen tree that belongs to the sterculia family. [< Spanish *cacao* < Nahuatl *cacauatl*]

cacao bean, the seed of the cacao. Also, **cocoa bean.**

cacao butter, a yellowish-white fat expressed from cacao seeds, used especially in making candy, soap, and cosmetics. Also, **cocoa butter.**

cacao powder, the product obtained after pressing out a portion of the cacao butter from roasted and shelled cacao beans and pulverizing the resultant hard mass.

ca|cha|ca (kä chä′sä), *n.* a Brazilian rum distilled from sugar cane. [< Portuguese (Brazil) *cachaça*]

cach|a|lot (kash′ə lot, -lō), *n.* = sperm whale. [< French *cachalot* < Portuguese *cachalote* big-headed fish < *cachola* fat head]

cache (kash), *n., v.,* **cached, cach|ing.** —*n.* **1** a hiding place to store food, supplies, or treasures: *Arctic explorers hide their food in caches in the snow on the outward journey to support them on the way back from their trip.* **2** any hidden place of storage: *Texas Gulf uncovered the cache ... It contains an estimated 60 million tons of high-grade copper, zinc, silver and lead deposits* (New York Times). **3** anything stored or hidden in a cache: *Squirrels make caches of nuts for winter food.*
—*v.t.* to put in a cache; store in hiding; hide: *The bear had cached her cubs in a cave.*
—*v.i.* to keep or stay in concealment; hide oneself.
[< French *cache* < Old French *cacher* hide < Vulgar Latin *coacticāre* press together, ultimately < Latin *cogere* compel]

ca|chec|tic (kə kek′tik), *adj.* having to do with or characterized by cachexia: *All were hopeless, terminal cases of cancer, most of whom were ... emaciated, cachectic, often anemic* (Scientific American).

ca|chec|ti|cal (kə kek′tə kəl), *adj.* = cachectic.

cache|pot (kash′pot′), *n.* a decorative container for holding potted house plants.

ca|chet (ka shā′, kash′ā), *n.* **1** a private seal or stamp, especially of an important or powerful person: *The letter was sealed with the king's cachet.* **2** *Figurative.* a distinguishing mark of quality or genuineness; stamp: *The antique cabinet bore the cachet of a famous colonial craftsman.* **3** a stamped or printed slogan, design, or the like, on mail. **4** a flat capsule or wafer of some digestible material, enclosing a medicine. [< Middle French *cachet* < Old French *cacher* to crowd (together); hide, cache]

ca|chex|i|a (kə kek′sē ə), *n.* a general condition of weakness and emaciation due to a serious chronic disease. [< Late Latin *cachexia* < Greek *kachexiā* < *kakós* bad + *héxis* state < *échein* have, or be in, a certain condition]

ca|chex|y (kə kek′sē), *n.* = cachexia.

cach|in|nate (kak′ə nāt), *v.i.,* **-nat|ed, -nat|ing.** to laugh loudly or immoderately. [< Latin *cachinnāre* (with English *-ate*¹)]

cach|in|na|tion (kak′ə nā′shən), *n.* loud or immoderate laughter: *[He] ruins a gag by anticipating the laughter with his own cachinnations* (Punch).

cach|in|na|to|ry (kak′ə nə tôr′ē, -tōr′-), *adj.* of or having to do with loud or immoderate laughter.

cach|o|long (kash′ə lông), *n.* a variety of opal, usually of a milky-white color. [probably < *Cach,* a Kalmuck word]

ca|chot (kȧ shō′), *n. French.* a dungeon cell, usually subterranean.

ca|chou (kə shü′, ka-), *n.* **1** = catechu. **2** a confection, usually in the form of a pill, used for sweetening the breath; lozenge. [< French *cachou* < Portuguese *cachu* < Malay *kachu.* See etym. of doublet **catechu.**]

ca|chu|cha (kä chü′chä), *n.* **1** a lively Andalusian solo dance in triple time, accompanied by castanets. **2** the music used in the dance. [< Spanish *cachucha*]

ca|cique (kə sēk′), *n.* **1** a native Indian chief or prince, especially in the West Indies and Mexico. **2** any one of certain tropical American orioles having the bill enlarged at the base. **3** a local political boss in Spain, Latin America, and the Philippines, especially one who is able to dominate because of wealth, land owned, or the like. [< Spanish *cacique* < the Arawak (Haiti) name]

ca|ciqu|ism (kə sēk′iz əm), *n.* the exercise of political power by caciques.

cack|le (kak′əl), *n., v.,* **-led, -ling.** —*n.* **1** the shrill, broken sound that a hen makes, especially after laying an egg: *The cackle in the henhouse awoke the farmer.* **2** shrill, harsh, or broken laughter: *Before the comedian finished the joke, there were a few cackles from the audience. It was really a cackle, a prankster's giggle at having pulled a mad trick* (Atlantic). **3** *Figurative.* noisy chatter; silly talk.
—*v.i.* **1** to make a shrill, broken sound, especially after laying an egg: *The hens started to cackle early in the morning.* **2** to laugh in a shrill, harsh, or broken way: *The old man cackled at his own joke.* **3** *Figurative.* = chatter.
—*v.t.* to utter with or express by cackling.
[Middle English *cakelen;* imitative] —**cack′ler,** *n.*

cack|ling goose (kak′ling), a small, dark-colored variety of Canada goose; greaser: *The cackling goose ... nests on the coast and islands of western Alaska, and winters mainly in California* (Joseph J. Hickey).

cac|o|de|mon or **cac|o|dae|mon** (kak′ə dē′mən), *n.* an evil spirit. [< Greek *kakodaímōn* < *kakós* evil + *daímōn* spirit]

cac|o|de|mo|ni|a (kak′ə də mō′nē ə), *n.* **1** possession by an evil spirit. **2** the delusion that one is possessed by an evil spirit. [< New Latin *cacodemonia* < Greek *kakodaímōn;* see etym. under **cacodemon**]

cac|o|dor|ous (kak ō′dər əs), *adj. Rare.* having a bad odor; malodorous. [< Greek *kakós* bad + English *odorous*]

cac|o|dox|y (kak′ə dok′sē), *n., pl.* **-dox|ies.** a false or wrong opinion or opinions, especially in matters of religion; heresy. [< Greek *kakodoxiā* < *kakós* evil + *dóxa* opinion, doctrine]

cac|o|dyl (kak′ə dil), *n.* **1** a univalent radical consisting of arsenic and methyl, having compounds characterized by an offensive smell and highly poisonous vapors. *Formula:* C_2H_6As **2** a poisonous liquid having an offensive smell. *Formula:* $C_4H_{12}As_2$ [< Greek *kakṓdēs* bad-smelling (< *kakós* bad + *ózein* smell) + English *-yl*]

cac|o|dyl|ate (kak′ə dil′āt), *n.* a salt of cacodylic acid.

cac|o|dyl|ic (kak′ə dil′ik), *adj.* of cacodyl.

cacodylic acid, a crystalline, deliquescent compound, odorless and poisonous, used in the making of dyes and perfumes. *Formula:* $(CH_3)_2AsO \cdot OH$

cac|o|ep|y (kak′ō ep′ē, ka kō′ə pē), *n.* bad pronunciation. [< Greek *kakoépeia* faulty language < *kakós* bad + *épos* word]

cac|o|e|thes (kak′ō ē′thēz), *n.* a very strong desire or urge; mania. [< Greek *kakóēthes* < *kakós* bad + *êthos* disposition]

cac|o|gas|tric (kak′ə gas′trik), *adj.* having to do with a disordered stomach. [< Greek *kakós* bad + English *gastric*]

cac|o|gen|e|sis (kak′ə jen′ə sis), *n.* **1** low vitality and infertility in a breed, especially common in mixed breeds. **2** *Medicine.* an abnormal formation or tumor, either congenital or of later development. [< Greek *kakós* bad + *génesis* origin]

cac|o|gen|ic (kak′ə jen′ik), *adj.* = dysgenic.

cac|o|gen|ics (kak′ə jen′iks), *n.* = dysgenics. [< Greek *kakós* bad + English (eu)*genics*]

ca|cog|ra|pher (kə kog′rə fər), *n.* a bad writer or speller.

cac|o|graph|ic (kak′ə graf′ik), *adj.* **1** having to do with bad handwriting. **2** having to do with incorrect spelling.

cac|o|graph|i|cal (kak′ə graf′ə kəl), *adj.* = cacographic.

ca|cog|ra|phy (kə kog′rə fē), *n.* **1** bad handwriting. **2** incorrect spelling. [< Greek *kakós* bad + English *-graphy*]

ca|col|o|gy (kə kol′ə jē), *n.* **1** bad choice of words. **2** faulty diction. **3** bad pronunciation. [< Greek *kakós* bad + English *-logy*]

cac|o|mis|tle (kak′ə mis′əl), *n.* **1** a small, flesh-eating mammal of North America, belonging to the same family as, but smaller than, the raccoon; ringtail; bassarisk. **2** its pelt or fur. [< Mexican Spanish *cacomixtle* < Nahuatl *tlacomiztli* < *tlaco* middle-sized + *miztli* lion]

cac|o|mix|le (kak′ə mis′əl, -mik′səl), *n.* = cacomistle.

cac|o|nym (kak′ə nim), *n.* a name which is in any way undesirable or objectionable; misnomer; barbarism. [< Greek *kakós* bad + dialectal *ónyma* a name]

ca|con|ym|y (kə kon′ə mē), *n.* the use of caconyms; bad or poor terminology.

ca|coon (kə kün′), *n.* a large, flat, tropical bean.

cac|o|phon|ic (kak′ə fon′ik), *adj.* = cacophonous.

ca|coph|o|nist (kə kof′ə nist), *n.* a composer or a lover of music marked by dissonances.

ca|coph|o|nize (kə kof′ə nīz), *v.t.,* **-nized, -niz|ing.** to render cacophonous or ill-sounding: *How should anyone desire to mutilate and cacophonize so musical a name as Clarice?* (M. Collins).

ca|coph|o|nous (kə kof′ə nəs), *adj.* harsh and clashing in sound; dissonant; discordant: *Much of Oskar Kokoschka's painting looks like some mad reflection of his cacophonous name* (Newsweek). —**ca|coph′o|nous|ly,** *adv.*

ca|coph|o|ny (kə kof′ə nē), *n., pl.* **-nies.** harsh, clashing sound; dissonance; discord: *A cacophony of shots, shouts, and screams came through only as a savage sort of overture* (Harper's). [< Greek *kakophōniā* < *kakóphōnos* ill-sounding < *kakós* bad + *phōnē* sound]

cac|o|to|pi|a (kak′ə tō′pē ə), *n.* = kakotopia.

cac|ta|ceous (kak tā′shəs), *adj.* belonging to the cactus family. [< New Latin *Cactaceae* the family name (< Latin *cactus* cactus) + English *-ous*]

cac|to|blas|tis (kak′tə blas′tis), *n.* = cactus moth. [< New Latin *Cactoblastis* the genus name < Latin *cactus* + Greek *blastós* sprout]

cac|toid (kak′toid), *adj. Botany.* resembling the cactus. [< *cact*(us) + *-oid*]

cac|tus (kak′təs), *n., pl.* **-tus|es, -ti** (-tī). a plant with a thick, fleshy stem that usually has spines, but no leaves. Most cactuses grow in very hot, dry regions of America and often have brightly colored flowers. Cactuses range in height from a few inches to more than 50 feet. *Cacti of the American deserts have been transplanted into the corresponding climatic regions of Africa, Australia, and southern Europe, becoming in some places such a nuisance as to be bad weeds* (Fred W. Emerson). [< Latin *cactus* < Greek *káktos* a kind of artichoke, cardoon]
►**Cacti** is the usual plural in scientific writing.

cactus dahlia, any one of various dahlias having showy flowers with long, twisted petals that resemble the flowers of some cactuses.

***cactus family,** a group of dicotyledonous plants found in the dry regions of tropical and subtropical America, including the prickly pear, night-blooming cereus, and saguaro.

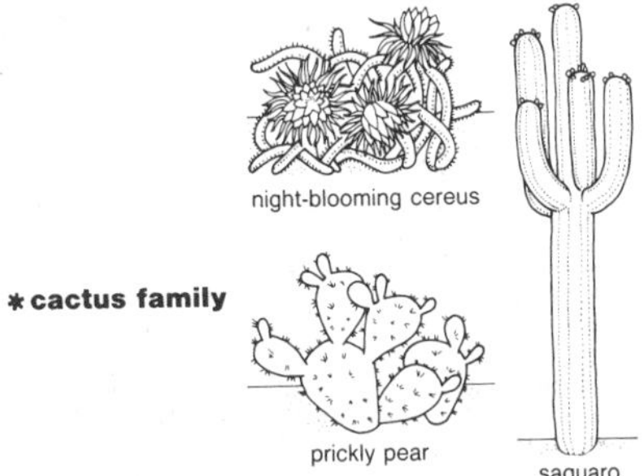

cactus moth, a small, faintly colored moth native to South America, whose larva infests and destroys the prickly pear; cactoblastis.

cactus wren, a large wren with long bill and tail which nests in cactuses in the southwestern United States and in Central America.

ca|cu|men (kə kyü′mən), *n.* the top of anything. [< Latin *cacūmen, -inis* top, peak]

ca|cu|mi|nal (kə kyü′mə nəl), *adj., n. Phonetics.* —*adj.* articulated by drawing the tip of the tongue up and back and placing it near or against the hard palate above the alveoli; retroflex; cerebral. —*n.* a cacuminal consonant.
[< Latin *cacūmen, -inis* top, extreme tip + English *-al*[1]]

cad (kad), *n.* **1** a boy or man who does not act like a gentleman; ill-bred person. SYN: boor, churl. **2** *British.* **a** a hanger-on about a college, ready to do services for the students. **b** a boy or man of the town; townsman (contrasted with *collegian*). **3** *Obsolete British.* a messenger or assistant. **4** *Obsolete British.* the conductor of an omnibus. [< *caddie,* or *cadet*]

CAD (no periods), **1** coronary artery disease. **2** computer-aided design.

ca|dang-ca|dang (kä′däng kä′däng), *n.* a blight of coconut trees common in the Philippines, marked by the discoloration and decay of the palm leaves. [< Spanish (Philippines) *cadang-cadang* < Ilokano]

ca|das|tral (kə das′trəl), *adj.* of or having to do with a cadastre; having reference to the extent, value, and ownership of landed property.
[< French *cadastral* < *cadastre;* see etym. under **cadastre**]

cadastral map, a map indicating the extent and ownership of land.

cadastral survey, 1 a survey of lands for the purposes of a cadastre: *If the government had attempted to allocate the tax it would have needed . . . a detailed cadastral survey* (New Yorker). **2** a survey mapped on a scale sufficient to show the dimensions of every field and other plot of land.

ca|das|tre or **ca|das|ter** (kə das′tər), *n.* a public register of the quantity, value, and ownership of the real property of a region or country, used as a basis for taxation. [< French *cadastre* < Late Latin *capitāstrum* register of poll tax < Latin *caput, -itis* head]

ca|dav|er (kə dav′ər, -dā′vər), *n.* a dead body; corpse.
[< Latin *cadāver* < *cadere* to fall]

ca|dav|er|ic (kə dav′ər ik), *adj.* **1a** of or having to do with dead bodies. **b** characteristic of a corpse. **2** caused by contact with a dead body.
►**Cadaveric** is used more as a technical term than **cadaverous.**

ca|dav|er|ine (kə dav′ə rēn), *n.* a poisonous, colorless, liquid ptomaine yielded by bacterial decomposition of proteins. *Formula:* $C_5H_{14}N_2$ [< *cadaver* + *-ine*[2]]

ca|dav|er|ize (kə dav′ə rīz), *v.t.,* **-ized, -iz|ing.** to make cadaverous or corpselike.

ca|dav|er|ous (kə dav′ər əs), *adj.* **1** pale and ghastly: *a cadaverous expression.* SYN: wan. **2** thin and worn: *[He] is a tall, cadaverous man who walks unevenly* (Time). SYN: haggard. **3** of or like a cadaver. SYN: corpselike. —**ca|dav′er|ous|ly,** *adv.* —**ca|dav′er|ous|ness,** *n.*
►See **cadaveric** for usage note.

cad|die (kad′ē), *n., v.,* **-died, -dy|ing.** —*n.* **1** a person who helps a golf player, especially by carrying golf clubs and finding the ball. **2** *Scottish.* a boy or man who waits about for chance employment as a messenger; an errand boy or messenger. **3** = caddie cart.
—*v.i.* to help a golf player as a caddie: *Nelson was . . . just as much a perfectionist as Hogan from the days they caddied together on the same Texas course* (New York Times). Also, **caddy.**
[< French *cadet* younger brother]

caddie bag, a bag for golf clubs.

caddie cart, 1 a small cart for carrying golf clubs. **2** a small cart for transporting any awkward load, such as groceries or glassware. Also, **caddy cart.**

cad|dis[1] or **cad|dice**[1] (kad′is), *n.* a worsted yarn, braid, or binding, used especially for garters.
[< Old French *cadaz* silk tow, and Middle French *cadis* cheap wool serge]

cad|dis[2] or **cad|dice**[2] (kad′is), *n.* = caddis worm. [origin uncertain]

caddis fly, an insect, somewhat like a moth, that has two pairs of wings and long legs; trichopteran; water moth. Its larva lives under water and forms a case of sand, bits of leaves, or the like, for itself.

cad|dish (kad′ish), *adj.* like a cad; ungentlemanly: *caddish manners.* —**cad′dish|ly,** *adv.* —**cad′dish|ness,** *n.*

caddis worm, the larva of a caddis fly, very important as fish food and used as bait in fishing. Also, **caddis, caddice.**

Cad|do (kad′ō), *n., pl.* **-do** or **-dos. 1** a member of an American Indian tribe of the Caddoan language family. The Caddo, who gave the language family its name, lived in Louisiana, Arkansas, and Texas. **2** the language of this tribe.

Cad|do|an (kad′ō ən), *n.* a family of North American Indian languages, spoken by the Arikara, Pawnee, and Caddo Indians.

cad|dy[1] (kad′ē), *n., pl.* **-dies. 1** a small box, can, or chest, often used to hold tea; tea caddy. **2** any container for holding or storing things: *a tool caddy, a make-up caddy. Compact can caddy keeps cans of frozen juice . . . and soft drinks nearly within fingertip reach* (Science News Letter). [alteration of *catty*[2] < Malay *kati* a small weight]

cad|dy[2] (kad′ē), *n., pl.* **-dies,** *v.i.,* **-died, -dy|ing.** = caddie.

caddy cart, = caddie cart.

caddy spoon, a spoon of special shape for measuring tea out of a caddy.

cade[1] (kād), *n.* a European species of juniper whose wood, when distilled, yields cade oil.
[< French *cade* < Old Provençal < Late Latin *catanum*]

cade[2] (kād), *adj., n.* —*adj.* left by its mother and raised by people: *a cade lamb, a cade colt.*
—*n.* a pet lamb.
[origin unknown]

cade[3] (kād), *n.* a former unit of dry measure for herring or sprats, comprising 500 (or 720) herring or 1,000 sprats.
[< French *cade* barrel < Latin *cadus* large wine vessel]

-cade, *combining form.* procession; formation: *Autocade = procession of automobiles.* [abstracted < *cavalcade*]

ca|delle (kə del′), *n.* the larva or adult of a black beetle that is very destructive to grain. [< French *cadelle*]

ca|dence (kā′dəns), *n., v.,* **-denced, -denc|ing.** —*n.* **1** the measure or beat of music, dancing, or any movement regularly repeating itself; rhythm: *The constant cadence of the surf lulled us to sleep. Wit will shine Through the harsh cadence of a rugged line* (John Dryden). **2** a fall of the voice: *The actor's cadence marked the end of the scene.* **3** a rising and falling sound; modulation: *She speaks with a pleasant cadence. In a strongly stressed language like English it is the end-of-sentence tune that has the greatest significance and it is this final harmony or cadence that changes least* (Simeon Potter). *If my students learned anything, it was from listening to my intonation, not my explanation. Now I teach them to listen for the cadence, and decide their punctuation on that basis* (George P. Faust). **4a** a series of chords bringing part of a piece of music to an end: *He heard the cadence and realized that the concert was almost over.* **b** a melodic strain that brings a section of a musical composition to an end.
—*v.t.* to put into cadence: *Empedocles . . . cadenced his great work on Nature in the same sonorous verse* (John Addington Symonds).
[< French *cadence* < Italian *cadenza* < Vulgar Latin *cadentia* < Latin *cadere* fall. See etym. of doublets **cadenza, chance.**]

ca|denced (kā′dənst), *adj.* having cadence.

ca|den|cy (kā′dən sē), *n., pl.* **-cies. 1** = cadence. **2** the descent of a younger branch from the main line of a family. **3** the state of being a younger son or cadet.

ca|dent (kā′dənt), *adj.* **1** having or displaying cadence. **2** *Archaic.* falling.

ca|den|tial (kā den′shəl), *adj.* of or having to do with cadence.

ca|den|za (kə den′zə), *n.* a flourish or showy passage, often improvised, usually near the end of a section of a piece of music, such as an aria or a movement of a concerto. It precedes the actual cadence. *Miss Curcio treated her cadenza in No. 5 with more freedom than is usual, thus creating the effect of a toccata-like extemporization* (London Times).
[< Italian *cadenza.* See etym. of doublets **cadence, chance.**]

cade oil, a thick, brown oil distilled from the wood of the cade (juniper), used in treating skin ailments.

ca|det (kə det′), *n.* **1a** a young man in training for service as an officer in the army, navy, or air force: *The cadets from West Point will graduate next week.* **b** any person receiving training; trainee: *a nursing cadet, a business cadet.* **2a** a student in a high-school or grade-school military academy. **b** *British.* a student in a college of any one of the armed forces. **3 Cadet,** a member of the Girl Guides from 16 to 21 years old who is training for leadership of the organization. **4** (formerly) a gentleman, usually a younger son, who entered the army to prepare for a commission. **5a** a younger son or brother. **b** the youngest son. **6** *Slang.* = pimp.
[< Middle French *cadet* < Gascon *capdet* < Latin *capitellum* small head, ultimately (diminutive) < *caput, -itis* head]

ca|det|cy (kə det′sē), *n., pl.* **-cies.** = cadetship.

ca|det|ship (kə det′ship), *n.* the rank or position of a cadet.

ca|dette (kə det′), *n.* **1** *New Zealand.* a young woman appointed to a civil-service position after passing a competitive test. **2 Cadette,** a member of the Girl Scouts from 12 through 14 years old, or in the seventh, eighth, or ninth grades. [< *cad*(et) + *-ette*]

cadet teacher, a person, especially one studying to be a teacher, who takes on temporary or part-time teaching assignments either for a living or to gain experience in the field.

cadge (kaj), *v.,* **cadged, cadg|ing.** —*v.t. Informal.* to get (something) by begging shamelessly: *For several years he wandered the streets of New York as a bum, cadging handouts from actors* (New Yorker).
—*v.i.* **1** *Informal.* to beg shamelessly: *I don't believe in cadging off the public* (London Times). **2** *Dialect.* to be a peddler; peddle.
[Middle English *caggen,* or *cachen;* origin uncertain] —**cadg′er,** *n.*

cadg|y (kaj′ē), *adj. Scottish.* **1** cheerful; merry; glad. **2** wanton; lustful; amorous. [origin uncertain]

ca|di (kä′dē, kā′-), *n., pl.* **-dis.** a minor Moslem judge, usually of a town or village. Also, **kadi.**
[< Arabic *qāḍī* judge]

cad|jan (kaj′ən), *n.* **1** the matted coconut-palm

Pronunciation Key: hat, āge, cãre, fär; let, ēqual, tėrm; it, īce; hot, ōpen, ôrder; oil, out; cup, pu̇t, rüle; child; long; thin; ᴛʜen; zh, measure; ə represents **a** in about, **e** in taken, **i** in pencil, **o** in lemon, **u** in circus.

leaves used in southern India for thatch. **2** a section or strip of palm leaf prepared for use as writing material.
[Anglo-Indian < Malay and Javanese *kājāng*]

Cad·me·an (kad mē′ən), *adj.* having to do with Cadmus.

Cadmean victory, a victory involving one's own ruin.

cad·mic (kad′mik), *adj.* of cadmium.

cad·mif·er·ous (kad mif′ər əs), *adj.* containing cadmium.

***cad·mi·um** (kad′mē əm), *n.* a soft, bluish-white chemical element, resembling tin, used in plating, to prevent corrosion, and in making alloys. It is a ductile metal and occurs only in combination with other elements. *Cadmium is produced as a by-product in zinc refining* (Wall Street Journal).
[< New Latin *cadmium* < Latin *cadmīa,* or *cadmēa* zinc ore < Greek *Kadmeiā* (*gê*) Cadmean (earth)]

***cadmium**

symbol	atomic number	atomic weight	oxidation state
Cd	48	112.40	2

cadmium orange, an orange-yellow pigment.

cadmium red, any one of several shades of vivid red characteristic of cadmium sulfide in combination with a selenium compound and sometimes a sulfate of barium.

cadmium sulfide, a bright yellow or orange powder used as a pigment and, because of its sensitivity to light, in such devices as transistors and solar batteries. *Formula:* CdS

cadmium yellow, a lemon-yellow pigment made from cadmium sulfide.

Cad·mus (kad′məs), *n. Greek Legend.* a prince who killed a dragon and sowed its teeth. From these teeth armed men sprang up who fought with each other until only five were left. Cadmus and these five men founded the Greek city of Thebes and introduced the alphabet into Greece.

ca·dre (kä′dər; *in military use* kad′rē), *n.* **1** the staff of officers and enlisted men of a military unit necessary to establish and train a new unit: *Air force and naval cadres reported for duty, and 38 officers and noncoms were in the U.S. for training* (Newsweek). **2** a group of trained men in any activity, especially a group that forms the core of an organization: *What are unions doing to develop cadres of new leadership?* (Harper's). **3** a small cell of trained and zealous revolutionaries, for example of Communists in various Asian countries. **4** a framework or scheme: *The chairman of the board is the highest officer in the company's organizational cadre.*
[< French *cadre* < Italian *quadro* < Latin *quadrum* a square]

ca·dre·man (ka′drē mən), *n., pl.* **-men.** *Military.* a person who belongs to a cadre.

ca·du·ca·ry (kə dü′kər ē, -dyü′-), *adj. Law.* subject to or by way of escheat or lapse. [< Latin *cadūcārius* having to do with *bona cadūca* lapsed possessions]

ca·du·ce·an (kə dü′sē ən, -dyü′-), *adj.* of or having to do with a caduceus.

***ca·du·ce·us** (kə dü′sē əs, -dyü′-), *n., pl.* **-ce·i** (-sē ī). the staff of Mercury, or Hermes, with two snakes twined around it and a pair of wings on top. The caduceus is often used as an emblem of the medical profession. [< Latin *cādūceus,* variant of *cādūceum* < Greek *kērkeion* herald's staff < *kēryx, -ȳkos* a herald]

***caduceus**

ca·du·ci·ty (kə dü′sə tē, -dyü′-), *n.* **1** the infirmity of old age; senility. **2** the tendency to fall away; perishableness.
[< Middle French *caducité* < *caduc,* learned borrowing from Latin *cadūcus* falling < *cadere* to fall]

ca·du·cous (kə dü′kəs, -dyü′-), *adj.* **1** *Botany.* **a** having a tendency to fall. **b** dropping off very early, as the sepals of the poppy, which fall at once on the opening of the flower; fugacious (contrasted with *persistent*). **2** *Zoology.* having to do with organs or parts that fall off naturally when they have served their purpose. **3** fleeting; transitory: *This calamity which I fancied was a part of me . . . was caducous* (Emerson). [< Latin *cadūcus* (with English *-ous*) falling < *cadere* fall]

cae·ca (sē′kə), *n.* plural of **caecum.**

cae·cal (sē′kəl), *adj.* = cecal.

cae·cil·i·an (sē sil′ē ən), *n.* any one of an order of wormlike amphibians having elongated bodies but no legs or tails: *The caecilians look like foot-long earthworms, but actually are relatives of the frogs* (Science News Letter).
[< Latin *caecilia* a blindworm (< *caecus* blind) + English *-an*]

cae·cum (sē′kəm), *n., pl.* **-ca.** = cecum.

cae·no·gen·e·sis (sē′nə jen′ə sis, sen′ə-), *n.* = cenogenesis.

Cae·no·zo·ic (sē′nə zō′ik, sen′ə-), *adj.* = Cenozoic.

Caen or **caen stone** (kän; *French* kăɴ), a soft, cream-colored building stone that hardens with exposure, found near Caen in Normandy, France.

cae·o·ma (sē ō′mə), *n.* a kind of aecium of rust fungi having the spores in chains and lacking a peridium.
[< New Latin *caeoma* < Greek *kaíein* burn (because of its reddish color)]

Caer·phil·ly cheese (kär′fi lē), a creamy, white, mild cheese, originally made in Caerphilly, a town in Wales.

caes·al·pin·i·a·ceous (sez′al pin′ē ā′shəs, ses′-), *adj.* belonging to the senna subfamily of the pea family. [< New Latin *Caesalpiniaceae* the subfamily name. (< Andrea *Cesalpini,* 1519-1603, an Italian botanist) + English *-ous*]

Cae·sar (sē′zər), *n.* **1** the title of the Roman emperors from Augustus to Hadrian, and later of the heir to the throne. **2** an emperor. **3** *Figurative.* a dictator or tyrant. **4** *Figurative.* the temporal monarch as the object of his subjects' obedience; civil power: *Render therefore unto Caesar the things which are Caesar's; and unto God the things that are God's* (Matthew 22:21).
appeal to Caesar, a to appeal to the highest authority: *"Can't she come, Father?" said Percy, adroitly appealing to Caesar* (T. B. Reed). **b** *Politics.* to appeal to the nation in a general election: *If this policy were not accepted as the policy of the Government . . . I should feel it my duty to appeal to Caesar* (Westminster Gazette).
[< Latin *Caesar* < Gaius Julius *Caesar,* 100?-44 B.C., a Roman general and statesman who ruled Rome from 49 to 44 B.C. See etym. of doublets **czar, Kaiser.**]

Cae·sar·dom (sē′zər dəm), *n.* the dominion or dignity of the Caesars: *Charles the Frank . . . transporting the name and the pomp of the Caesardom to the forests of Rhineland* (A. B. Hope).

Cae·sar·e·an or **Cae·sar·i·an** (sē zãr′ē ən), *adj., n.* **—*adj.*** **1** by Caesarean section: *Surgical operations and Caesarian births have been televised in color for the benefit of medical students* (Wall Street Journal). **2** of the Caesars: *the Caesarean succession.* **3** of Julius Caesar: *Caesarean Latin.*
—*n.* **1** = Caesarean section. **2** a follower of Caesarism. Also, **Cesarean, Cesarian.**

Caesarean section or **operation**, an operation by which a baby is removed from the uterus by cutting through the abdominal and uterine walls; hysterotomy. It is performed when delivery cannot take place through the birth canal. This operation is said to have taken place at the birth of Julius Caesar.

Cae·sar·ism (sē′zə riz əm), *n.* absolute government; autocracy: *Rome was tainted with the idea of Caesarism and with the concept of the monolithic centralized imperial government that took over from the Senate* (New Yorker).

Cae·sar·ist (sē′zər ist), *n.* a person who advocates or believes in Caesarism.

Cae·sar·o·pa·pism (sē′zə rō pā′piz əm), *n.* supremacy of the state or secular authority over the church: *The word "Caesaropapism" is shorter than "the doctrine that the King should be head of the Church"* (Punch).

Cae·sar·o·pa·pist (sē′zə rō pā′pist), *n., adj.* **—*n.*** a supporter or advocate of Caesaropapism.
—*adj.* having to do with Caesaropapism.

Caesar salad, a salad of assorted greens, croutons, anchovies, and eggs, served with olive oil, lemon juice, and seasonings.

Caesar weed, a shrubby weed of tropical Asia, Africa, and Central and North America, cultivated for its soft, glossy stem, which is used especially in the making of ropes, fabrics, and hammocks.

cae·si·ous (sē′zē əs), *adj.* bluish-gray. [< Latin *caesius* (with English *-ous*)]

cae·si·um (sē′zē əm), *n.* = cesium.

caes·pi·tose (ses′pə tōs), *adj.* = cespitose.

cae·su·ra (si zhůr′ə, -zyůr′-), *n., pl.* **-su·ras, -su·rae** (-zhůr′ē, -zyůr′-). **1** a pause in a line of verse, generally agreeing with a pause required by the sense. The caesura is the chief pause if there is more than one. In Greek and Latin poetry the caesura regularly falls within a foot, not far from the middle of a line. In English poetry it usually comes near the middle of a line, either within or after a metrical foot. *Example:* "To err is human, / to forgive, divine." *Criticism has concerned itself a good deal with the "caesura" in [Alexander] Pope, believing it possible to explain his verse in terms of a relatively mechanically placed pause* (Whitehall and Hill). **2** *Music.* a pause or break at the end of a phrase or other rhythmic division. Also, **cesura.** [< Latin *caesūra* a cutting < *caedere* to cut]

cae·su·ral (si zhůr′əl, -zyůr′-), *adj.* of or having to do with a caesura.

c.a.f. or **C.A.F.**, **1** cost and freight. **2** cost, assurance and freight.

ca·fard (kə fär′; *French* kȧ fȧr′), *n. French.* an extreme depression, with a feeling of overwhelming fatigue and indifference to duties or surroundings, often suffered by soldiers; the blues.

ca·fe (ka fā′, kə-), *n.* a place to buy and eat a meal; restaurant: *It is a city of balconied houses and a sandy strand bordered with outdoor cafes* (Saturday Review).
[< French *café;* see etym. under **café**]

ca·fé (ka fā′, kə-; *especially for 2* kȧ fā′), *n.* **1** = cafe. **2** *French.* coffee: *It's best of all at breakfast, around eleven of a nippy morning, with your café and croissant* (New Yorker). **3** = barroom. **4** = coffeehouse.
[< French *café* coffee, coffeehouse]

ca·fé au lait (ka fā′ ō lā′, kaf′ē; *especially for 1* kȧ fā′ō le′), **1** *French.* coffee with milk or cream, especially coffee and hot milk in about equal amounts. **2** brownish yellow: *Sometimes our road . . . plunged down into deep, dark gorges, where café au lait torrents rushed by* (New Yorker).

ca·fé chant·ant (kȧ fā′ shäɴ täɴ′), *French.* **1** a cafe in which musical entertainment is provided. **2** (literally) singing cafe.

ca·fé crème (kȧ fā′ krem′), *French.* coffee with cream.

***cafe curtain**, a simple, rectangular window curtain sliding on a rod set across the window frame generally well below the lintel.

***cafe curtain**

ca·fé fil·tre (kȧ fā′ fēl′trə), *French.* coffee prepared from hot water passed through ground coffee with a filter under it.

ca·fé noir (kȧ fā′ nwȧr′), *French.* coffee without milk or cream; black coffee.

café parfait, the original form of parfait, with strong coffee as its flavoring.

café society, the world of fashionable cafes, night clubs, and resorts, especially in which much value is attached to clever, brittle conversation, smart clothes, etc.: *It is to such brave pioneers of old-time Café Society we owe thanks for lifting hair-dyeing into high fashion* (Punch).

caf·e·te·ri·a (kaf′ə tir′ē ə), *n., adj.* **—*n.*** a restaurant where people wait on themselves: *Nowadays Mexican cafeterias look far more like quick-lunch stands than the leisurely neighborhood rendezvous they used to be* (New York Times).
—*adj.* offering a wide assortment of choices: *The chaotic "cafeteria counter" curriculum . . . responds to the difficulty of choosing among conflicting interests by including essentially everything* (Christian Science Monitor).
[American English < Mexican Spanish *cafetería* coffee shop < *café* coffee]

caf·e·to·ri·um (kaf′ə tôr′ē əm, -tōr′-), *n., pl.* **-ums.** a room or hall suitable for use either as a cafeteria or an auditorium. [< *cafe*(teria) + (audi)*torium*]

caff (kaf), *n. British Slang.* coffee house; café.

caf·fè es·pres·so (kaf fe′ es pres′sō), *Italian.* very strong, black coffee, prepared in a machine which forces steam through coffee beans that have been roasted until black.

caf·fe·ic (ka fē′ik, kə-), *adj.* of or having to do with coffee; derived from coffee.

caffeic acid, a yellowish, crystalline, organic acid obtained from coffee. *Formula:* $C_9H_8O_4$

caf·feine or **caf·fein** (kaf′ēn, -ē in), *n.* a slightly bitter, stimulating drug found in coffee and tea. *Formula:* $C_8H_{10}N_4O_2 \cdot H_2O$ [< French *caféine* < *café* coffee]

caf·fe·in·ism (kaf′ē ə niz′əm, kaf′ē niz-), *n.* illness or abnormal condition caused by excessive use of caffeine, or of substances containing it.

caf·fe·ism (kaf′ē iz′əm), *n.* = caffeinism.

caf·fe·ol (kaf′ē ol, -ōl), *n.* an aromatic oil developed in coffee by roasting. [< *caffe*(ine) + *-ol*[2]]

caf·fe·tan·nic (kaf′ə tan′ik), *adj.* having to do with coffee and resembling tannin.

caffetannic acid, a tanninlike substance obtained from coffee.

***caf|tan** (kaf′tən, käf tän′), *n.* **1** a long-sleeved, ankle-length tunic with a girdle, worn under the coat by men, especially in Turkey and Egypt: *Among them were ... mountaineers in caftans of goat hair and Bedouins in red and blue veils of the nomad* (New York Times). Also, **kaftan**. **2** a woman's long, flowing gown, used for lounging or evening wear: *A floor-length caftan and a linen pants set ... were sharply defined in black and white* (Enid Nemy). [< Turkish *kaftan*]

***caftan** definition 1

caf|taned (kaf′tənd, käf′-), *adj.* wearing a caftan.
ca|fu|so (kə fü′zō), *n.* (in Brazil) the child of a Negro and an Indian; sambo. [< Portuguese *cafuso*]
cage (kāj), *n., v.,* **caged, cag|ing.** —*n.* **1** a frame or place closed in with wires, strong iron bars, or wood. Birds and wild animals are kept in cages. **2** a thing shaped or used like a cage: *The bank teller worked in a cage.* **3** *Figurative.* a prison cell or any fenced-in area for prisoners: *The cage ... was a square room of stout iron bars, built in the center of a larger one* (Harper's). **4** the car or closed platform of an elevator, especially in a mine shaft: *A shaft wall crumbled, crushing the cage in which the men were traveling, the reports said* (New York Times). **5** the network and frame forming the goal in ice hockey and similar games. **6** *Basketball.* the basket or net where points are scored. **7** *Baseball.* **a** a place enclosed by a net, for batting practice. **b** a catcher's mask. **8** a steel framework for supporting guns. **9** a sheer or lacy outer dress worn over a slip or a dress.
—*v.t.* **1** to put or keep in a cage: *After the lion was caught, it was caged. First catch, then cage your bird* (old proverb). **2** *Sports.* to put (the ball or puck) into the goal.
[< Old French *cage* < Latin *cavea* coop, cage < *cavus* hollow. See etym. of doublet **cavea.**]
cage antenna, an antenna whose conductor is a set of parallel wires strung between two rings.
cage bird, a bird, such as a parakeet or canary, commonly kept in a cage: *A budgerigar had alighted on the roadside fence ... not, perhaps, the natural setting for a cage bird* (London Times).
cage|ful (kāj′fůl), *n., pl.* **-fuls.** **1** the amount that a cage can hold. **2** the contents of a cage.
cage|like (kāj′līk′), *adj.* resembling a cage.
cage|ling (kāj′ling), *n.* a small bird kept in a cage.
cag|er (kā′jər), *n. U.S. Slang.* a basketball player.
cage|way (kāj′wā′), *n.* **1** the guide ropes, wire, or steel rods for a mine cage. **2** the part of a mine shaft in which the cage is hoisted and lowered.
cage|y (kā′jē), *adj.,* **cag|i|er, cag|i|est.** *Informal.* shrewd and cautious; sharp and wary: *a cagey answer. The cagey fox could not be easily trapped by the farmer.* Also, **cagy.** [American English; origin uncertain] —**cag′i|ly,** *adv.* —**cag′i-ness,** *n.*
cag|y (kā′jē), *adj.,* **cag|i|er, cag|i|est.** = cagey.
ca|hier (kä yā′; *French* kȧ yā′), *n.* **1** a number of leaves of a book or other sheets of paper stacked together, as for binding. **2** a report of proceedings, statement of facts, or the like. [< French *cahier* notebook < Old French *quaier* set of four, ultimately < Latin *quattuor* four. See etym. of doublets **casern, quire**[1].]
Ca|hill (kä′hil, kā′-), *n.* a certain kind of artificial fly used in angling. [< a proper name]
ca|hin|ca root (kə hing′kə), the root of any one of certain shrubs of the madder family, found in tropical America. It has been used in the treatment of snakebite, and as a diuretic. [< Portuguese (Brazil) *cahinca*, probably < Tupi]
ca|hoot (kə hüt′), *n. Slang.*
go cahoots, to go into partnership: *The two friends decided to go cahoots in business by buying a candy store together.*
in cahoots or **cahoot**, in partnership; in league (with), especially as a secret collaborator or accomplice: *Are you willing to work in cahoots with yours truly, until one or the other of us gets tired of the partnership?* (Kirk Munroe).
[American English; origin uncertain; perhaps < French *cahute* cabin]
ca|hot (kä hō′, -ō′), *n.* a ridge of snow which has been heaped up across a road by passing sleighs, leaving a corresponding depression behind; thank-you-ma'am. [American English < Canadian French *cahot* < French, a jolt, jerk]

ca|how (kə hou′), *n.* a petrel native to Bermuda, thought extinct from 1625 until 1951, when they began to be seen again in Bermuda: *The cahow is a rather docile bird, about the size of a pigeon but possessing longer wings* (Science News Letter). [perhaps imitative of its cry]
CAI (no periods), or **C.A.I.**, computer-assisted instruction: *CAI ... can reduce learning time and improve the performance of many students. CAI systems can teach biology, history, foreign languages, mathematics, and numerous other subjects* (George Epstein).
Cai|a|phas (kā′ə fəs, kī′-), *n.* the high priest who presided at the trial of Jesus (in the Bible, Matthew 26:57-66).
caid (kä ēd′), *n.* a rural chieftain in North Africa. [< Arabic *qā'id*]
ca|i|dos (kä ē′dōs), *n. pl.* unpaid or overdue rents or taxes in the Philippines. [< Spanish (Philippines) *caídos* (literally) fallen things < *caer* to fall < Latin *cadere*]
cail|ced|ra (kīl sed′rə), *n.* a tall tree of West Africa, resembling the mahogany. Its wood is used in joiners' work and inlaying, and its bark furnishes a bitter tonic. [ultimately < a native word]
cail|ced|rin (kīl sed′rin), *n.* a resinous compound present to a minute extent in the bark of the cailcedra. [< *cailcedr*(a) + *-in*]
cai|man (kā′mən), *n., pl.* **-mans.** a large crocodilian of tropical America similar to an alligator. Its abdomen is covered by a pair of overlapping, bony plates. Also, **cayman.**
Cain (kān), *n.* **1** the oldest son of Adam and Eve. He killed his brother Abel (in the Bible, Genesis 4:1-17). **2** *Figurative.* a murderer.
raise Cain, *Slang.* to make a great disturbance: *When the teacher left the room, the boys raised Cain.*
cai|na|na (kī nä′nə), *n.* a Brazilian plant of the madder family, whose root has been used by natives as a cure for snakebites; snakeroot. [< Portuguese (Brazil) *cainana*, probably < Tupi]
Cai|no|zo|ic (kī′nə zō′ik), *adj.* = Cenozoic.
***ca|ique** or **ca|ïque** (kä ēk′), *n.* **1** a long, narrow Turkish rowboat, much used on the Bosporus: *A couple of fishermen going by in a caïque stared at them as though they were things in a shopwindow* (New Yorker). **2** a small Mediterranean sailing ship. [< French *caïque* < Italian *caicco* < Turkish *kayik*]

***caique** definition 2

ca|ique|jee (kä ēk′jē), *n.* one of the oarsmen of a caique. [< Turkish *kayikçi*]
ça i|ra (sȧ ē rȧ′), *French.* an early popular song of the French Revolution, having the refrain "ça ira" ("it will go on").
caird (kärd), *n. Scottish.* a traveling tinker; gypsy; tramp; vagrant. [< Scottish Gaelic *ceard* tinker, metalworker < Old Irish *cerd* smith, craftsman]
Cai|rene (kī′rēn, kī rēn′), *n., adj.* —*n.* a native or inhabitant of Cairo, the capital of Egypt.
—*adj.* of or having to do with Cairo.
cairn[1] (kärn), *n.* a pile of stones heaped up as a memorial, tomb, or landmark. [Scottish *carne* < Scottish Gaelic *carn* heap of stones]
cairn[2] (kärn), *n.* = cairn terrier. [< *cairn*[1] (supposedly because of its use to hunt around cairns)]
cairned (kärnd), *adj.* having a cairn.
cairn|gorm (kärn′gôrm), *n.* a yellow or smoky-brown variety of quartz used, especially in Scotland, for brooches, seals, and other ornaments. [< *Cairngorm*, a peak in the Grampians, Scotland; (literally) blue stone < Scottish Gaelic *carn* cairn + *gorm* gray-blue]
Cairn|gorm stone (kärn′gôrm), = cairngorm.
cairn terrier, a small, long-haired working terrier that originated in Scotland; cairn. It has a hard, wiry topcoat and an undercoat of soft fur.
Ca|is|sa (kā is′ə), *n. Humorous Use.* the goddess of chess, an invention of chess players. [< New Latin *Caissa*, an arbitrary formation from English *chess*]
***cais|son** (kā′son, -sən), *n.* **1a** a wagon to carry ammunition, especially artillery shells. **b** a box for ammunition. **2** a watertight box or chamber in which men can work under ground or water, especially to make foundations for buildings or bridges and to dig tunnels. It has an open bottom, the water being kept out by the high air pressure maintained within it. **3** a watertight float used in raising sunken ships: *Huge steel tubes, or caissons, drop to the ocean floor and then powerful air jacks raise the hull above the water surface* (Wall Street Journal). **4** a vessel in the form of a boat used as a floodgate in dikes. **5** *Architecture.* = coffer (def. 2). [< French *caisson* or *casson* < Italian *cassone* < *cassa* < Latin *capsa*]

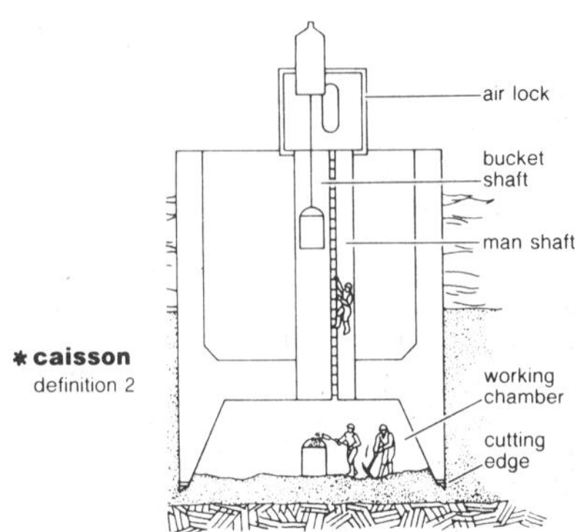

***caisson** definition 2

caisson disease, severe pain, loss of physical control, and asphyxia, caused by changing too suddenly from high air pressure, as in a caisson, to ordinary air pressure; decompression sickness; the bends.
cai|tiff (kā′tif), *n., adj.* —*n. Archaic.* a mean, cowardly person. SYN: coward.
—*adj.* cowardly and mean: *A territory Wherein were bandit earls and caitiff Knights* (Tennyson). SYN: vile.
[< Old North French *caitif*, ultimately < Latin *captīvus* caught. See etym. of doublet **captive.**]
Ca|jan (kā′jən), *n.* = Cajun.
ca|jas (kä′häs), *n.pl. Spanish.* **1** separate insurance and welfare organizations for government employees, factory workers, or laborers, included in a social security system established in 1924 in Chile. The cajas also make loans, operate restaurants, and sell low-cost food and clothing. **2** (literally) chests; boxes.
caj|e|put (kaj′ə pət), *n.* = cajuput (def. 1).
ca|jole (kə jōl′), *v.,* **-joled, -jol|ing.** —*v.t.* to persuade by pleasant words, flattery, or false promises; coax: *He cajoled his friends into deciding in his favor.* —*v.i.* to use cajolery: *Where Mendès whipped men to decision by the scornful lash of his tongue, Fauré seeks to cajole* (Time). SYN: beguile, wheedle. [< French *cajoler*] —**ca|jol′er,** *n.* —**ca|jol′ing|ly,** *adv.*
ca|jole|ment (kə jōl′mənt), *n.* the act of cajoling; cajolery: *Neither official pomposity, threat, or cajolement could blind him* (Maurice Keatinge).
ca|jol|er|y (kə jō′lər ē, -jōl′rē), *n., pl.* **-er|ies.** persuasion by smooth words, flattery, or false promises; coaxing: *The utmost political pressure and personal cajolery were necessary to get Congress to agree to the consummation of "Seward's folly"* (Atlantic). SYN: wheedling, blandishment.
ca|jon (kä hōn′), *n., pl.* **-jo|nes** (-hō′nās). *Southwestern U.S.* a narrow canyon or gorge with vertical sides. [< Spanish *cajón* large box < *caja* box]
Ca|jun (kā′jən), *n. U.S.* a descendant of the French who came to Louisiana from Acadia. [American English, variant pronunciation of *Acadian*]
caj|u|put (kaj′ə pət), *n.* **1** Also, **cajeput.** a small Australian tree or shrub of the myrtle family, whose leaves yield a yellowish, aromatic oil used in medicine as a stimulant and in the treatment of parasitic skin conditions. **2** the oil itself. [< Malay *kayuputeh* < *kayu* tree + *puteh* white]
cake (kāk), *n., v.,* **caked, cak|ing.** —*n.* **1** a baked mixture of flour, sugar, eggs, flavoring, and other things, usually including shortening and baking powder, soda, or yeast: *Mother baked a chocolate cake with white frosting for my birthday.* **2** a flat, thin mass of dough or batter baked or fried on a griddle or in a skillet; pancake or hoecake. SYN: griddlecake. **3** any small, flat, shaped mass of food, such as fish, meat, or corn, browned on both sides in a frying pan or on a griddle: *potato cakes. That restaurant makes good fish cakes.* **4** a shaped mass of solid material: *a cake of ice. She carved a cake of soap into the shape of a dog.* **5** *Scottish.* a thin, hard-baked kind of oaten

Pronunciation Key: hat, āge, cãre, fär; let, ēqual, tėrm; it, īce; hot, ōpen, ôrder; oil, out; cup, pu̇t, rüle; child; long; thin; ᴛʜen; zh, measure; ə represents **a** in about, **e** in taken, **i** in pencil, **o** in lemon, **u** in circus.

bread. 6 *Archaic.* a small loaf of bread. 7 the sum total of the percentages into which something is to be divided; pie: *It shows that the unions are, if anything, more convinced than before of the need and possibility of securing a bigger slice of the cake of economic prosperity for the working populations* (Manchester Guardian Weekly). 8 a chart showing such a division; pie chart.
— ***v.t.*** to form into a solid mass; harden: *Water caked the powder as hard as a stone.* **SYN**: solidify.
— ***v.i.*** to take the form of cake or a flat, compact, hardened mass: *Mud cakes as it dries.* **SYN**: solidify.
a piece of cake, *Informal.* something simple or easy to do or easy to obtain: *As Schirra had predicted it* [*maneuvering in space*] *was "a piece of cake"* (Time).
have one's cake and eat it, to obtain the advantages of two things which contradict each other: *Disarmament in itself is an attempt to have one's cake and eat it, too, to enjoy the advantages of power politics while avoiding their perils* (Bulletin of Atomic Scientists).
take the cake, *Slang.* **a** to win first prize: *Sheriff Moore takes the cake for the first wheat harvesting in Ransom County* (Lisbon (North Dakota) Star). **b** to excel; surpass everyone: *In my book that phony woodcutter takes the cake for the worst villain in literature* (Saturday Review).
[probably < Scandinavian (compare Old Icelandic *kaka*)]

cake-eat|er (kāk′ē′tər), *n. Slang.* a lady's man; playboy.

cake flour, a fine flour made from wheat that is low in gluten content, used in the baking of cakes.

cake ink, a black pigment molded into sticks or cakes for use in drawing and writing; India ink.

cake mix, the dry ingredients for a cake, sold packaged together.

cake mold, a mold in which cakes, such as those of ink, soap, and lac, are formed.

cakes and ale, good things; pleasures of life: *Dost thou think, because thou art virtuous, there shall be no more cakes and ale?* (Shakespeare).

cake|walk (kāk′wôk′), *n., v.* — ***n.*** **1** a dance with prancing high steps that developed from an earlier march or promenade for couples. Dancers used to compete to see who could do the best or most original steps. The winner got a cake. ... *summoning up memories of the cakewalk, the blues, and other musical strains in its past* (New Yorker). **2** a dance modeled on this. **3** *Slang, Figurative.* something easily and certain to be carried out; cinch.
— ***v.i.*** to do a cakewalk: (*Figurative.*) *He cakewalked to a five-game lead in the first set* (New York Times).
[American English, probably < *cake* (the prize) + *walk*] — **cake′walk′er**, *n.*

cak|y (kā′kē), *adj.,* **cak|i|er, cak|i|est. 1** like a cake. **2** formed into a hardened mass.

cal., **1** calendar. **2** caliber. **3** small calorie or calories.

Cal., **1** California. **2** large or great calorie or calories.

cal|a|bar or **cal|a|ber** (kal′ə bər), *n.* **1** the fur of a gray Siberian squirrel. **2** (formerly) the fur of a brown squirrel of Calabria. [apparently < French *Calabre* Calabria, an Italian province]

Cal|a|bar bean (kal′ə bär′), the poisonous seed of a tropical African climbing plant of the pea family, from which the alkaloid physostigmine is obtained. [probably < *Calabar,* a river and its region in Nigeria]

***cal|a|bash** (kal′ə bash), *n.* **1a** a gourdlike fruit whose dried shell is used to make bottles, bowls, drums, rattles, or the like. **b** Also, **calabash tree.** the tropical American tree that it grows on. It belongs to the bignonia family. **2** a bottle, bowl, drum, rattle, or the like, made from such a dried shell: *All hands simply begin, at nightfall, drinking calabashes of the repulsive-looking liquid* (Atlantic). **3a** any one of various gourds, especially those whose necks are used for making tobacco pipes. **b** any one of the vine plants of the gourd family bearing such gourds. **4** a pipe with a large bowl made from a gourd. [< Middle French *calabasse* < Spanish *calabaza,* perhaps ultimately < Persian *kharbuz* melon]

*** calabash**
definitions 3a, 4

cal|a|ba|zil|la (kal′ə bə sēl′yə), *n.* a wild squash of Mexico and the southwestern United States with a fruit whose unripe pulp is used as a substitute for soap. Its exceedingly large root is macerated for use as a medicine. [American English < Mexican Spanish *calabazilla* (diminutive) < Spanish *calabaza;* see etym. under **calabash**]

cal|a|boose (kal′ə büs, kal′ə büs′), *n. Informal.* a jail; prison: *Why, send them to the calaboose, or some of the other places, to be flogged* (Harriet Beecher Stowe). [American English < Spanish *calabozo*]

Ca|la|bri|an (kə lā′brē ən), *adj., n.* — ***adj.*** of or having to do with Calabria (a district in southwestern Italy), its people, or their dialect.
— ***n.*** **1** a native or inhabitant of Calabria. **2** the dialect of Italian spoken in Calabria.

ca|la|di|um (kə lā′dē əm), *n.* any one of a genus of tropical American plants of the arum family, with large colorful leaves. See picture under **arum family.** [< New Latin *Caladium* < Malay *këladi*]

cal|a|man|co (kal′ə mang′kō), *n.* a glossy woolen cloth, checked or brocaded in the warp so that the pattern shows on one side only. [origin uncertain]

cal|a|man|der (kal′ə man′dər, kal′ə man′-), *n.,* or **calamander wood,** the hard, brown-and-black striped wood of an East Indian tree, used for cabinetwork. [perhaps alteration of *Coromandel,* a region in India]

cal|a|mar|y (kal′ə mer′ē), *n., pl.* **-mar|ies.** a squid. [< Latin *calamārius* of a writing reed < *calamus* a reed pen (because the animal's internal shell is pen-shaped)]

ca|lam|i|form (kə lam′ə fôrm), *adj.* having the form of a reed or feather: *a calamiform leaf.* [< Latin *calamus* reed, calamus + English *-form*]

cal|a|mine (kal′ə mīn, -min), *n.* **1** a pink powder made of zinc oxide and ferric oxide, used in lotions to relieve skin irritations or sunburn. **2** (formerly) either of two kinds of zinc ore: **a** a silicate of zinc; hemimorphite. **b** *British.* smithsonite, a carbonate of zinc. [< French *calamine,* learned borrowing from Medieval Latin *calamina,* alteration of Latin *cadmīa* cadmium]

calamine lotion, a soothing preparation containing zinc oxide, used for skin irritations, sunburn, and the like.

cal|a|mint (kal′ə mint), *n.* = savory². [< Old French *calament,* learned borrowing from Medieval Latin *calamentum* < Latin *calaminthē* < Greek *kalaminthē*]

cal|a|mis|trum (kal′ə mis′trəm), *n., pl.* **-tra** (-trə). one of the curved, movable spines on the posterior legs of certain spiders, used to curl and bind the lines of silk coming from the spinnerets. [< New Latin *calamistrum* < Latin, curling iron < *calamus* reed < Greek *kálamos*]

cal|a|mite (kal′ə mīt), *n.* a kind of Carboniferous fossil plant generally regarded as the ancestor of the equisetum. [< New Latin *Calamites* the genus name < Latin *calamus* calamus]

cal|a|mi|te|an (kal′ə mī′tē ən), *adj.* having to do with or belonging to calamites: *the structure of the calamitean stem.*

ca|lam|i|tous (kə lam′ə təs), *adj.* causing calamity; accompanied by calamity; disastrous. **SYN**: dire, grievous. — **ca|lam′i|tous|ly,** *adv.* — **ca|lam′i|tous|ness,** *n.*

ca|lam|i|ty (kə lam′ə tē), *n., pl.* **-ties. 1** a great misfortune, such as a flood, a fire, the loss of one's sight or hearing, or of much money or property; disaster: *The spring floods were a great calamity to the farmers whose crops and homes were ruined.* **SYN**: catastrophe. See syn. under **disaster. 2** serious trouble; misery: *Many people still suffer from the calamity of hunger and poverty. The compensations of calamity are made apparent to the understanding also, after long intervals of time* (Emerson). [< Latin *calamitās*]

calamity howler or **shouter**, *U.S.* a noisy pessimist: [*They*] *were of the stripe of calamity shouters whose occupation is gone unless they can prove that calamity stalks abroad* (Congressional Record).

cal|a|mon|din (kal′ə mon′din), *n.* a small orange with acid juice, native to the Philippines. [< Tagalog *kalamunding*]

cal|a|mus (kal′ə məs), *n., pl.* **-mi** (-mī). **1a** a plant with long, sword-shaped leaves; sweet flag. **b** its fragrant root, used especially in perfumes and medicines: *Steamed and roasted quamash bulb makes a rather acceptable molasses substitute ... and calamus or sweet flag are other choices* (Science News Letter). **2** any one of a group of slender, leafy palms whose long stems furnish rattan, canes, and the like. **3** the quill of a feather; barrel. [< Latin *calamus* < Greek *kálamos* reed]

ca|lan|do (kə lan′dō), *adv., adj. Music.* gradually diminishing in tone and pace. [< Italian *calando,* present participle of *calare* decrease]

ca|lan|dri|a (kə lan′drē ə), *n.* a tank or boiler using heavy water to moderate fission in a nuclear reactor. [< Spanish *calandria* calender, ultimately < Latin *cylindrus* cylinder]

ca|la|scio|ne (kä′lä shō′nā), *n.* a musical instrument of southern Italy, a limited sort of lute or guitar, having two catgut strings tuned a fifth apart, and played with a plectrum. [< Italian *calascione*]

***ca|lash** (kə lash′), *n.* **1** Also, **calèche.** a light, low carriage that usually has a folding top. **2** a folding top or hood. **3** a woman's silk hood or bonnet supported with hoops, worn in the 1700's and 1800's. **4** *Canadian.* (formerly) = calèche. [< French *calèche* < German *Kalesche* < Old Czech *kolesa* wheels, carriage, plural of *kolo* wheel]

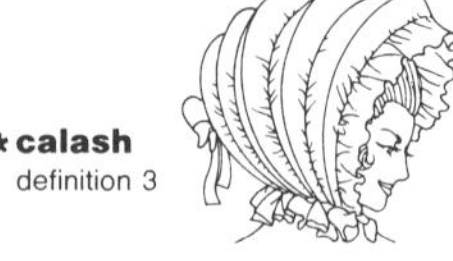
***calash**
definition 3

cal|a|thus (kal′ə thəs), *n., pl.* **-thi** (-thī). a basket shaped like a vase, often a symbol of fruitfulness, especially in ancient sculpture or pottery. [< Latin *calathus* < Greek *kálathos* vase-shaped basket]

cal|a|ver|ite (kal′ə vär′īt), *n.* a telluride of gold, or of gold and silver, bronze-yellow and massive: *Next in importance to native gold as a source of the metal come the gold tellurides, chief of which is calaverite* (W. R. Jones). [American English < *Calaveras* County, California, where first found + *-ite*¹]

cal|ca|ne|um (kal kā′nē əm), *n., pl.* **-ne|a** (-nē ə). = calcaneus.

cal|ca|ne|us (kal kā′nē əs), *n., pl.* **-ne|i** (-nē ī). **1** the bone of the human heel; the outer and largest one of the proximal row of tarsal bones; os calcis. See picture under **foot. 2** the analogous bone in the foot of other vertebrates. [< Late Latin *calcāneus* < Latin (*os*) *calcāneum* (bone) of the heel < *calx, calcis* heel]

cal|car (kal′kär), *n., pl.* **cal|car|i|a** (kal kãr′ē ə). *Biology.* a spur, or a projection resembling a spur. [< Latin *calcar* < *calx, calcis* heel]

cal|ca|rate (kal′kə rāt), *adj.* furnished with a calcar or spur; spurred.

cal|ca|rat|ed (kal′kə rā′tid), *adj.* = calcarate.

cal|car|e|ous (kal kãr′ē əs), *adj.* **1** of or containing lime, calcium carbonate, or limestone: *The rate of deposition of the calcareous sediments formed from Foraminifera shells is faster with warmer water* (Science News Letter). **2** of or containing calcium: *The outer surface of the body* [*of the starfish*] *is covered with hard calcareous plates that provide excellent support and protection for the delicate, soft body parts beneath* (A. M. Winchester). [< Latin *calcārius* (with English *-ous*) < *calx, calcis* lime] — **cal|car′e|ous|ly,** *adv.* — **cal|car′e|ous|ness,** *n.*

cal|ca|rif|er|ous (kal′kə rif′ər əs), *adj. Botany, Zoology.* bearing calcaria or spurs. [< Latin *calcar, -āris* spur + English *-ferous*]

cal|ce|ate (kal′sē āt, -it), *adj.* shod; wearing shoes (used of certain religious orders). [< Latin *calceātus,* past participle of *calceāre* to shoe < *calceus* a shoe < *calx* heel]

calced (kalst), *adj.* = calceate.

cal|ce|i|form (kal′sē ə fôrm, kal sē′-), *adj.* = calceolate.

cal|ce|o|lar|i|a (kal′sē ə lãr′ē ə), *n.* any plant of a tropical American genus of herbs and shrubs of the figwort family, grown for their slipper-shaped flowers; slipperwort. [< New Latin *Calceolaria* < Latin *calceolus* (diminutive) < *calceus* shoe]

cal|ce|o|late (kal′sē ə lit, -lāt), *adj. Botany.* shaped like a shoe or slipper, as the corolla of a calceolaria; calceiform.

cal|ces (kal′sēz), *n.* calxes; a plural of **calx.**

cal|ce|us (kal′sē əs), *n., pl.* **-ce|i** (-sē ī). a kind of shoe worn by ancient Romans, consisting of a sole with straps fastened to the foot and laced around the ankle. Different styles of calcei showed the rank of the wearer. [< Latin *calceus* < *calx* heel]

Cal|chas (kal′kəs), *n. Greek Legend.* the priest of Apollo who accompanied the Greeks in the Trojan War. He was an augur and a seer.

calci-, *combining form.* **1** lime, calcium, or salts of lime or calcium: *Calcification* = *forming or becoming hard like lime.*
2 limestone: *Calcicole* = *growing on limestone.*
[< Latin *calx, calcis* lime]

cal|cic (kal′sik), *adj.* of or derived from lime or calcium.

cal|ci|cole (kal′sə kōl), *adj., n. Botany.* — ***adj.*** growing on limestone or on chalky soil.
— ***n.*** a plant growing on limestone.
[< *calci-* + Latin *colere* inhabit]

cal|cic|o|lous (kal sik′ə ləs), *adj.* = calcicole.

cal|cif|er|ol (kal sif′ə rōl, -rol), *n.* a fat-soluble alcohol, present in fish-liver oils, milk, and eggs, and produced by irradiating ergosterol; vitamin D_2. It prevents rickets. *Formula:* $C_{28}H_{44}O$

cal|cif|er|ous (kal sif′ər əs), *adj.* **1** yielding or containing calcite. **2** forming calcium salts.

cal|cif|ic (kal sif′ik), *adj.* = calciferous.

cal|ci|fi|ca|tion (kal′sə fə kā′shən), *n.* **1a** the process of calcifying, especially hardening of a structure, tissue, or the like, by the deposit of calcium salts. **b** *Figurative.* hardening: *True to his conviction that bigness usually leads to calcification . . .* (Time). **2** a calcified part. **3** the accumulation of calcium in certain soils, especially soils of cool temperate regions where leaching takes place very slowly.

cal|ci|form (kal′sə fôrm), *adj.* having the form of chalk or lime.

cal|ci|fuge (kal′sə fyüj), *n.* a plant which will not grow on limestone: *Most heaths and certain lichens are calcifuges.* [< *calci-* + Latin *fuga* flight < Greek *fugê*]

cal|ci|fy (kal′sə fī), *v.t., v.i.,* **-fied, -fy|ing. 1** to make or become hard or bony by the deposit of calcium salts; convert or be converted into lime: *Cartilage often calcifies in older people.* **2** *Figurative.* to harden: *In recent years, ghetto boundaries have calcified* (New Yorker).

cal|cig|er|ous (kal sij′ər əs), *adj.* producing or containing calcium salts. [< *calci-* + Latin *gerere* to carry, bear + English *-ous*]

cal|ci|mine (kal′sə mīn, -min), *n., v.,* **-mined, -min|ing.** —*n.* a white or colored lime solution containing glue, used as a wash on ceilings and walls. It can be tinted any color.
—*v.t.* to cover with calcimine. Also, **kalsomine.**
[< *calci-* + *-mine,* variant of *-ine*[1]]

cal|ci|nate (kal′sə nāt), *v.t., v.i.,* **-nat|ed, -nat|ing.** = calcine.

cal|ci|na|tion (kal′sə nā′shən), *n.* **1** the act or operation of calcining. **2** anything formed by calcining. **3** the state of being calcined.

cal|ci|na|tor (kal′sə nā′tər), *n.* a furnace or incinerator used to reduce radioactive waste by calcination in order to render it less dangerous and cumbersome when brought out of a nuclear reactor plant, research laboratory, or the like.

cal|cin|a|to|ry (kal sin′ə tôr′ē, -tōr′-; kal′sə nə-), *adj., n., pl.* **-ries.** —*adj.* serving for calcination.
—*n.* a vessel used for calcination.

cal|cine (kal′sīn, -sin), *v.,* **-cined, -cin|ing.** —*v.t.* **1** to burn (something) to ashes or powder: *to calcine bones. It was destroyed by a fire so intense that some of its foundations were calcined into a white powder* (Scientific American). **2** to change to lime by heating: *to calcine limestone.* **3** = oxidize. **4** = frit. —*v.i.* **1** to burn to ashes or powder. **2** to fuse partially. [< Medieval Latin *calcinare* < Late Latin *calcīna* lime, quicklime < Latin *calx, calcis* lime] —**cal′cin|er,** *n.*

cal|ci|no (käl chē′nō), *n.* a disease of silkworms, caused by the development of a vegetable parasite or fungus in the body of the caterpillar. [< Italian *calcino* < Late Latin *calcīnus* of lime < Latin *calx, calcis* lime]

cal|ci|no|sis (kal′sə nō′sis), *n., pl.* **-ses** (-sēz). calcification of the subcutaneous and connective tissues. [< New Latin *calcinosis* < Latin *calcina* lime + *-osis*]

cal|cite (kal′sīt), *n.* a mineral made up chiefly of calcium carbonate. It is the chief substance in limestone, chalk, and marble. *Formula:* $CaCO_3$ [< German *Calcit* < Latin *calx, calcis* lime]

cal|ci|to|nin (kal′sə tō′nən), *n.* a hormone that regulates the level of calcium in body fluids, secreted by the thyroid gland; thyrocalcitonin.

***cal|ci|um** (kal′sē əm), *n.* a soft, silvery-white chemical element. It is a part of limestone, chalk, milk, bones, shells, teeth, and many other things. Calcium is a metal used in alloys and its compounds are used in making plaster, in cooking, and as bleaching agents. *You need calcium in your food to grow strong, healthy bones. In the order of their abundance in the earth's crust, calcium stands fifth among the elements and third among the metals* (W. N. Jones). [< New Latin *calcium* < Latin *calx, calcis* lime]

***calcium**

symbol	atomic number	atomic weight	oxidation state
Ca	20	40.08	2

calcium acetate, a substance derived in large quantity as a by-product in the manufacture of wood alcohol, and employed in making acetone, acetic acid, and the acetates of aluminum and iron used as dyers' mordants. *Formula:* $C_4H_6CaO_4 \cdot H_2O$

calcium arsenate, a white, powdery compound, slightly soluble in water and in dilute acids, used as an insecticide, and extremely poisonous to human beings. *Formula:* $Ca_3(AsO_4)_2$

calcium carbide, a heavy, gray substance that reacts with water to form acetylene gas. *Formula:* CaC_2

calcium carbonate, a compound of calcium occurring in rocks such as marble and limestone, in animal bones, shells, and teeth, and to some extent in plants. It is used in the manufacture of toothpastes, white paint, and cleaning powder. *Formula:* $CaCO_3$

calcium chloride, a compound of calcium and chlorine, used in making artificial ice and spread on roads to settle dust or melt ice. *Formula:* $CaCl_2$

calcium cyanamide or **cyanamid,** a grayish powder obtained by heating calcium carbide to a very high temperature in the presence of dry nitrogen. It is used in fertilizers and for making other nitrogen compounds. *Formula:* $CaCN_2$

calcium fluoride, a white powder occurring naturally as fluorspar and produced synthetically from sodium fluoride and a salt of calcium, used as a flux in metallurgy, in making ceramics, in optical instruments, and electrodes. *Formula:* CaF_2

calcium gluconate, white, odorless powder or granules produced from gluconic acid, used as an antidote for various poisons, and in the treatment of rickets, colic, and allergies. *Formula:* $C_{12}H_{22}CaO_{14} \cdot H_2O$

calcium hydroxide, = slaked lime. *Formula:* $Ca(OH)_2$

calcium light, = limelight.

calcium nitrate, a white crystalline compound used to make matches, explosives, and other chemicals; lime saltpeter; Norwegian saltpeter. *Formula:* $CaNO_3$

calcium oxalate, a white crystalline substance present in plant cells and urine, used in making oxalic acid and various oxalates. *Formula:* CaC_2O_4

calcium oxide, unslaked lime; quicklime; lime[1]. *Formula:* CaO

calcium permanganate, a violet, crystalline salt used as a disinfectant and deodorizer, in sterilizing water, and as an ingredient in liquid rocket fuels. *Formula:* $Ca(MnO_4)_2 \cdot 4H_2O$

calcium phosphate, a compound of calcium and phosphoric acid, used in medicine and in making enamels. It is found in bones and as rock. *Formula:* $Ca_3(PO_4)_2$

calcium sulfate, a white powder found in natural form as gypsum, used in making plaster of Paris and paper and as a polishing powder and in paints. *Formula:* $CaSO_4$

calcium sulfide, a yellow or grayish powder produced by heating calcium sulfate and charcoal, used as a depilatory and in luminous paints. *Formula:* CaS

calcium tungstate, a white powder occurring naturally as scheelite and produced synthetically from calcium chloride and a tungstate of sodium, used in luminous paint, fluorescent lamps, and X-ray photography and treatment. *Formula:* $CaWO_4$

cal|crete (kal′krēt), *n.* a large calcareous mass formed on the sea-bottom by marine animals which cement the sand and other loose material together. [< *cal*(careous) + (con)*crete*]

calc-sin|ter (kalk′sin′tər), *n. Mineralogy.* a hard, crystalline limestone deposited by springs; travertine. [< German *Kalksinter* < *Kalk* lime (< Latin *calx, calcis*) + *Sinter* slag]

calc-spar or **calc|spar** (kalk′spär′), *n. Mineralogy.* calcareous spar or rhombohedral crystallized calcite. [< *calc-,* as in *calc-sinter* + *spar*[3]]

calc-tu|fa (kalk′tü′fə), *n. Mineralogy.* calcareous tufa. [< *calc-,* as in *calc-sinter* + *tufa*]

calc-tuff (kalk′tuf′), *n.* = calc-tufa.

cal|cu|la|bil|i|ty (kal′kyə lə bil′ə tē), *n.* the quality of being calculable.

cal|cu|la|ble (kal′kyə lə bəl), *adj.* **1** that can be calculated: *The connexion of physical causes and effects is known and calculable* (I. Taylor). **2** reliable; dependable. —**cal′cu|la|bly,** *adv.*

cal|cu|late (kal′kyə lāt), *v.,* **-lat|ed, -lat|ing.** —*v.t.* **1** to find out by adding, subtracting, multiplying, or dividing; figure; compute: *We calculated the cost of building a new house.* SYN: reckon, cast. **2** to find out beforehand by any process of reasoning; estimate: *You must calculate all the advantages and disadvantages before coming to a decision.* SYN: ascertain, determine. **3** to suit or adapt to a purpose: *His remarks were calculated to impress us.* **4a** to plan or intend: *He calculates to go next Tuesday.* **b** to suppose; guess: *I calculate it's a good idea.*
—*v.i.* **1** to rely; depend; count (on or upon): *You can calculate on steady advancement if you work hard.* **2** *Informal.* to think; suppose; reckon: *Are you going? I calculate so.* SYN: guess. **3** to make a computation: *Emotional people don't stop to calculate.*
[< Latin *calculāre* (with English *-ate*[1]) < *calculus;* see etym. under **calculus**]

cal|cu|lat|ed (kal′kyə lā′tid), *adj.* **1** determined by computation: *the calculated speed of sound.* **2** planned or intended: *a calculated attempt to deceive.* **3** fitted; suited; apt; likely: *Never had man so many relations so little calculated to inspire confidence* (Robert Southey). —**cal′cu|lat′ed|ly,** *adv.*

cal|cu|lat|ed risk (kal′kyə lā′tid), a possibility of failure or reversal that is accepted as unavoidable in an undertaking: *Several writers have emphasized that any use of atomic energy entails a calculated risk, no less than those features of modern technology that lead to auto accidents and gastric ulcers* (Bulletin of Atomic Scientists).

cal|cu|lat|ing (kal′kyə lā′ting), *adj.* **1** able to calculate; that calculates. **2** shrewd and careful; astute. SYN: clever, cunning. **3** scheming and selfish: *He was calculating and mercenary* (M. Edgeworth). SYN: crafty, wily. —**cal′cu|lat′ing|ly,** *adv.*

calculating machine, a mechanical or electronic device for performing certain calculations, especially mathematical computations; calculator.

cal|cu|la|tion (kal′kyə lā′shən), *n.* **1** the act of adding, subtracting, multiplying, or dividing to find a result; computation: *We made a careful calculation of what the trip would cost us.* **2** the result found by calculating: *Our first calculation was wrong, but the second was correct.* **3** careful thinking; deliberate planning: *The success of the expedition was the result of much calculation. The decision on use of the poliomyelitis vaccine is based on . . . a series of calculations and judgments* (New York Times). SYN: forecast.

cal|cu|la|tion|al (kal′kyə lā′shə nəl), *adj.* of or having to do with calculation.

cal|cu|la|tive (kal′kyə lā′tiv), *adj.* **1** having to do with calculation. **2** tending to be calculating.

cal|cu|la|tor (kal′kyə lā′tər), *n.* **1a** a calculating machine or computer: *The bookkeeper used a desk calculator to help keep the accounts. It will be immediately appreciated that within the calculator proper there is need for considerable storage of information* (Science News). **b** a person who calculates: *Most store clerks are rapid calculators.* **c** a person who operates a calculating machine. **2** a book or set of tables used in calculation.

cal|cu|li (kal′kyə lī), *n.* a plural of **calculus.**
▶See **calculus** for usage note.

cal|cu|li|form (kal′kyə lə fôrm′), *adj.* shaped like a pebble. [< Latin *calculus* pebble]

cal|cu|lous (kal′kyə ləs), *adj.* caused by or containing a calculus (def. 3) or calculi.

cal|cu|lus (kal′kyə ləs), *n., pl.* **-li** or **lus|es. 1** a system of calculation in advanced mathematics, especially a system using algebraic symbols to solve problems dealing with changing quantities: *This calculus is concerned with statistical procedures such as regression and factor analysis* (Scientific American). **2** a method in symbolic logic of arguing from hypotheses by using algebraic symbols and operations. **3** a stone that has formed in the body because of a diseased condition. Gallstones and kidney stones are calculi. [< Latin *calculus* stone used in counting (diminutive) < *calx, calcis* small stone]
▶The plural of **calculus** is *calculi* in the medical and *calculuses* in the mathematical sense.

calculus of variations, a branch of mathematics that studies the maximum and minimum values of functions that depend on a curve or other geometric figure rather than on a number or numbers.

Cal|cut|ta (kal kut′ə), *n.* a sweepstakes by auction pool in which participants bid to win on players in a match or horses in a race that are auctioned off. [probably < *Calcutta,* India]

Cal|cut|tan (kal kut′ən), *n., adj.* —*n.* a native or inhabitant of Calcutta.
—*adj.* of or having to do with Calcutta.

cal|dar|i|um (kal dãr′ē əm), *n., pl.* **-i|a** (-ē ə). the hot room of ancient Roman baths. [< Late Latin *caldārium*]

cal|de|ra (kal dir′ə; *Spanish* käl dā′rä), *n.* a deep, caldronlike cavity on the summit of an extinct volcano. See picture under **volcano.** [< Spanish *caldera* < Late Latin *caldāria* cooking pot, caldron]

cal|dron (kôl′drən), *n.* **1** a large kettle or boiler. **2** *Figurative: When the great caldron of war is seething* (James Russell Lowell). *The place can be a caldron of gales in winter* (Atlantic). Also, **cauldron.** [< Old North French *cauderon* < Late Latin *caldāria* cooking pot < *calidārius* for heating < *calidus* hot < *calēre* be hot]

Ca|leb (kā′ləb), *n.* a Hebrew leader sent as a spy into Canaan (in the Bible, Numbers 13, 14).

Pronunciation Key: hat, āge, cãre, fär; let, ēqual, tėrm; it, īce; hot, ōpen, ôrder; oil, out; cup, pu̇t, rüle; child; long; thin; ᴛʜen; zh, measure; ə represents **a** in about, **e** in taken, **i** in pencil, **o** in lemon, **u** in circus.

✱ca|lèche (kȧ lesh′), *n.* **1** *Canadian.* a light, two-wheeled, one-horse carriage for two passengers, with a seat in front for the driver, now used chiefly for sightseeing in Quebec City and Montreal: *As I reached the splendid square beside the Chateau Frontenac, the calèches, with their shaggy horses and garrulous drivers, were assembling* (Maclean's). **2** = calash (def. 1). [< French *calèche;* see etym. under **calash**]

✱calèche
definition 1

Cal|e|do|ni|a (kal′ə dō′nē ə), *n.* **1** an old name of Scotland: *O Caledonia! stern and wild, Meet nurse for a poetic child!* (Scott). **2** a style of modern printing type, of a lighter weight than Scotch.

Cal|e|do|ni|an (kal′ə dō′nē ən), *adj., n.* —*adj.* **1** of Scotland; Scottish. **2** *Geology.* of or having to do with a system of mountain building of the middle Paleozoic extending from the British Isles to Norway: *Caledonian orogeny.*
—*n.* a native of Scotland; Scotsman.

cal|e|fa|cient (kal′ə fā′shənt), *n., adj.* —*n.* a medical agent which produces warmth or a sense of heat, especially one applied externally, as a mustard plaster.
—*adj.* producing warmth.
[< Latin *calefaciēns, -entis,* present participle of *calefacere* make warm < *calēre* be warm + *facere* make]

cal|e|fac|tion (kal′ə fak′shən), *n.* **1** a making warm; warming; heating. **2** a heated condition. [< Latin *calefactiō, -ōnis* < *calefacere;* see etym. under **calefacient**]

cal|e|fac|tive (kal′ə fak′tiv), *adj.* having the tendency to warm; warming.

cal|e|fac|to|ry (kal′ə fak′tər ē), *adj., n., pl.* **-ries.**
—*adj.* adapted for or tending to warming.
—*n.* a heated room in a monastery where the residents warm themselves.
[< Medieval Latin *calefactōrium* < Latin *calefactōrius* having heating power < *calefacere;* see etym. under **calefacient**]

ca|len|dal (kə len′dəl), *adj.* having to do with the calends: *the most ancient calendal system.*

cal|en|dar (kal′ən dər), *n., adj., v.* —*n.* **1** a table showing the months, weeks, and days of the year. A calendar shows the day of the week on which each day of the month falls. *The calendar shows that Christmas will fall on a Tuesday.* **2** a system by which the beginning, length, and divisions of the year are fixed: *The Julian calendar was established during the reign of Julius Caesar. The calendar, or system of keeping account of time over long intervals, is in most nations involved with the celebration of religious festivals* (John Charles Duncan). **3** a list or schedule; record; register: *The judge proceeded to hear the next case on the calendar.* **4** a schedule of the order in which bills are considered on the floor of a legislative body. **5** *British.* a university or college catalogue, including a list of lectures, examinations, and special events or exercises. **6** a table, arranged chronologically, showing the days dedicated to canonized saints, feasts, vigils, and the like; ecclesiastical calendar: *Though priests may of course conduct rites and ceremonies of a relatively private nature, they are most often in charge of an established calendar of rituals* (Beals and Hoijer). **7** *Obsolete, Figurative.* a guide; directory.
—*adj.* **1** of or by the calendar: *a calendar holiday, a person's calendar age.* **2** of the calendar year: *Calendar 1976 is the date of the United States bicentennial.* **3** of the kind displayed on some wall calendars; tawdry; vulgar: *calendar art.*
—*v.t.* to enter in a calendar or list; register.
[< Anglo-French *calender,* learned borrowing from Latin *calendārium* account book < *calendae* calends (the day bills were due)]

calendar clock, a large clock having dials or other appliances for indicating the days of the week, month, or year, with sometimes the phases of the moon, as well as the hours and minutes.

calendar day, the 24 hours from one midnight to the next midnight.

cal|en|dar|i|al (kal′ən dãr′ē əl), *adj.* of or having to do with a calendar; calendric.

cal|en|dar|i|an (kal′ən dãr′ē ən), *n., adj.* —*n.* a maker of a calendar.
—*adj.* = calendarial: *calendarian festivals.*

cal|en|dar|ist (kə len′dər ist), *n.* = calendarian.

calendar month, one of the 12 parts into which a year is divided; month.

Calendar Wednesday, a procedure or rule in the United States House of Representatives under which every Wednesday each committee may introduce bills not placed on the regular calendar.

calendar year, (according to the Gregorian calendar) a period of 365 days (or in leap year, 366 days) that begins on January 1 and ends on December 31.

cal|en|der[1] (kal′ən dər), *n., v.* —*n.* **1** a machine in which cloth, paper, or similar material is smoothed and glazed by pressing between rollers. **2** *Archaic.* a man whose occupation was to press and glaze cloth, paper, or similar material: *My good friend the calender will lend his horse to go* (William Cowper).
—*v.t.* to make smooth and glossy by pressing in a calender.
[< Middle French *calendre* < Vulgar Latin *colondra,* alteration of Latin *cylindrus* cylinder] —**cal′en|der|er,** *n.*

Cal|en|der or **cal|en|der**[2] (kal′ən dər), *n.* one of a mendicant order of wandering Moslem dervishes, established in the 1300's. [< Persian *qalandar*]

ca|len|dric (kə len′drik), *adj.* having to do with or according to a calendar: *Nor would the study of Aztec calendric manuscripts get many notes as the most bewitching of occupations* (Scientific American).

ca|len|dri|cal (kə len′drə kəl), *adj.* = calendric: *calendrical devices, calendrical calculations.*

cal|en|dry (kal′ən drē), *n., pl.* **-dries.** a place where calenders are used.

cal|ends (kal′əndz), *n.pl.* (*sometimes sing. in use*) the first day of the month in the ancient Roman calendar. Also, **kalends.** [< Latin *calendae* (originally) the proclaiming (of the month's nones), ultimately < *calāre* call out]

ca|len|du|la (kə len′jə lə), *n.* **1** any one of a small genus of composite herbs, with yellow or orange flowers, native to the Mediterranean region but now a common garden flower in many temperate regions of the world. **2** the flower of any one of these herbs, used as medicine. [< New Latin *Calendula* (diminutive) < Latin *calendae* the calends (as if blooming on the first of every month)]

ca|len|du|lin (kə len′jə lən), *n.* a mucilaginous substance obtained from the leaves and flowers of the common marigold.

cal|en|ture (kal′ən chər, -chůr), *n.* any tropical fever accompanied by delirium, especially on board ship: *In this voyage ... I was continually sick, being thrown into a violent calenture by the excessive heat* (Daniel Defoe). [< Middle French *calenture* < Spanish *calentura* < Latin *calēre* be hot]

ca|le|sa (kä lā′sä), *n.* a two-wheeled carriage in the Philippines, resembling a calash. [< Spanish *calesa* < French *calèche* calash]

ca|les|cence (kə les′əns), *n.* growing warmth; increasing heat.

ca|les|cent (kə les′ənt), *adj.* growing warm; increasing in heat. [< Latin *calēscēns, -entis,* present participle of *calēscere* grow warm < *calēre* be warm]

calf[1] (kaf, käf), *n., pl.* **calves** *for 1, 2, 4, 5.* **1** a young cow or bull: *The calf stayed close to its mother in the pasture.* **2** a young elephant, whale, deer, seal, or other large mammal: *The children saw the new seal calves at the zoo.* **3** leather made from the skin of a calf; calfskin: *gloves made of calf.* **4** *Informal.* a clumsy, silly boy or young man. **5** a mass of ice detached from a glacier, iceberg, or floe.
in (or **with**) **calf,** (of a cow) pregnant: *their mares in foal, their cows in calf* (Jonathan Swift).
kill the fatted calf, to prepare a feast to celebrate something or welcome someone; prepare an elaborate welcome: *Go, let the fatted calf be killed* (Abraham Cowley).
[Old English *cealf*]

calf[2] (kaf, käf), *n., pl.* **calves.** the thick, fleshy part of the back of the leg below the knee. [< Scandinavian (compare Old Icelandic *kālfi*)]

calf diphtheria, a usually fatal inflammation of the mouth occurring among calves and other animals. It is a necrotic disease caused by certain anaerobic bacilli.

calf|kill (kaf′kil′, käf′-), *n.* any one of several plants of the heath family, such as the sheep laurel, thought to be poisonous to grazing animals.

calf|less (kaf′lis, käf′-), *adj.* having a thin calf; thin-legged.

calf love, *Informal.* the clumsy, short-lived romantic affection that exists between adolescent boys and girls; puppy love.

calf's-foot jelly (kavz′fůt′, kävz′-), a jellied broth, originally made from the gelatinous meat and tendons of calves' feet.
► The spoken kavz or kävz in this compound is not historically a plural, but an old form of the possessive singular.

calf|skin (kaf′skin′, käf′-), *n.* **1** the skin of a calf. **2** leather made from it.

Cal|gar|i|an (kal gãr′ē ən), *n.* a native or inhabitant of Calgary, a city in southwestern Canada.

Cal|i|ban (kal′ə ban), *n.* **1** the beastlike slave in Shakespeare's play *The Tempest.* **2** a man of degraded, bestial nature.

cal|i|ber (kal′ə bər), *n.* **1a** the inside diameter of the barrel of a rifle, shotgun, or pistol. A .45-caliber revolver has a barrel with an inside diameter of 45/100 of an inch. A 155-mm. rifle has a barrel with an inside diameter of 155 millimeters. **b** the diameter of a bullet or shell fired from a particular gun. **c** the diameter of the bore of a cannon, or other piece of artillery, used as a unit to express its length: *a 40-caliber 12-inch gun.* **d** the internal diameter of a tube or hollow cylinder, such as an artery. **2** *Figurative.* **a** amount of ability or merit: *We have been able to find men of high caliber to fill the vacancies.* **SYN**: capacity, competence. **b** degree of excellence or importance; quality: *We are always trying to improve the caliber of our schools.* **SYN**: grade, standard. Also, **calibre.** [< Middle French *calibre* < Arabic *qālib* a mold]

cal|i|bered (kal′ə bərd), *adj.* having a caliber.

caliber rule, a caliper rule.

cal|i|brate (kal′ə brāt), *v.t.,* **-brat|ed, -brat|ing.** **1** to determine, check, or adjust the scale of (a thermometer, gauge, or other measuring instrument). Calibrating is usually done by comparison with a standard instrument. **2** to find the caliber of. **3** to mark or determine a scale of measure for a thermometer, gauge, or other measuring instrument. —**cal′i|bra′tor,** *n.*

cal|i|bra|tion (kal′ə brā′shən), *n.* **1** the act or process of calibrating: *The melting and boiling points of a large number of substances have been carefully measured and tabulated and these temperatures may now be used in the calibration of any type of thermometer* (Sears and Zemansky). **2** the state or condition of being calibrated. **3** the marks made on a thermometer, gauge, or other measuring instrument as a scale of measure: *The instruments on the dashboard are austere white-on-black, with legible calibrations* (New Yorker).

cal|i|bre (kal′ə bər), *n.* = caliber.

cal|i|ces (kal′ə sēz), *n.* plural of **calix.**

ca|li|che (kä lē′chā), *n.* **1** a crust or formation of calcium carbonate in or on soil in dry regions. **2** a rich surface deposit of sodium nitrate with a varying admixture of sand, or other material, such as is found in parts of Chile. [< American Spanish *caliche* < Spanish, pebble in a brick, ultimately < Latin *calx, calcis* lime]

cal|i|cle (kal′ə kəl), *n.* a cuplike formation or depression, as in corals; calyculus. [< Latin *caliculus* (diminutive) < *calix, -icis* cup]

cal|i|co (kal′ə kō), *n., pl.* **-coes** or **-cos,** *adj.* —*n.* **1** a cotton cloth that usually has colored patterns printed on one side. **2** *British.* unprinted white cotton cloth. **3a** (originally) any cotton cloth from the East, especially from India. **b** (later) any one of various European cotton fabrics.
—*adj.* **1** made of calico: *a calico dress.* **2** spotted in colors: *a calico mare.*
[< *Calicut,* a city in India]

cal|i|co|back (kal′ə kō bak′), *n.* a red-and-black stinkbug that feeds on cabbages and other garden plants; the harlequin bug.

calico ball, a dance where cotton dresses are worn.

calico bass (bas), an edible freshwater fish, marked with a pattern of irregular black blotches, found in central and eastern North America; black crappie.

calico bug, = harlequin bug.

calico bush, flower, or **tree,** = mountain laurel.

calico cat, a domestic cat marked with mottled colors and conspicuous white markings.

calico crab, = lady crab.

calico printer, *British.* a person engaged in printing patterns on calico.

calico printing, the art of impressing designs in color upon cloth.

calico wood, the silver-bell tree of the southern United States, having a soft, compact, light-brown wood.

ca|lic|u|lar (kə lik′yə lər), *adj.* having to do with a calicle; cuplike.

ca|lic|u|late (kə lik′yə lāt), *adj.* having calicles.

ca|lif (kā′lif, kal′if), *n.* = caliph.

Calif., the official abbreviation of California.

cal|if|ate (kal′ə fāt, kā′lə-), *n.* = caliphate.

Cal|i|for|nia black sea bass (kal′ə fôrn′yə, -fôr′nē ə), a jewfish.

California condor or **vulture,** a vulture, the largest land bird of North America, with a bald yellow head and a long hooked beak. It is about 45 to 55 inches long, and has a wingspread of 8 to 11 feet: *The last surviving members of the largest land bird in the nation, the California condor, number 60* (Science News Letter).

California Current, a cold current originating in the northern Pacific Ocean and passing southward and then southwestward along the western coast of North America.
California fuchsia, a fuchsia having scarlet flowers.
California gull, a gull of the Pacific coast.
California hazel, a hazel native to the United States whose nut is of little value.
California laurel, = spice tree.
California maidenhair, a fern similar to the maidenhair, but with fan-shaped pinnules, found in California.
Cal|i|for|nian (kal′ə fôrn′yən, -fôr′nē ən), *adj., n.* —***adj.*** having to do with the state of California. —***n.*** a native or inhabitant of California.
California orange, an orange native to California, which supplies a third of the United States orange crop. Many California oranges are navel oranges.
California poppy, 1 a small herb of the poppy family, having finely divided leaves and orange, yellow, or cream-colored flowers. 2 its flower, the state flower of California.
California quail, a quail with an erect, nodding plume above the forehead, common west of the Rockies.
California red fir, a large, native American fir, valuable for its timber, that has purplish-brown cones when young.
California redwood, = redwood (def. 1a).
California rosebay, = pink rhododendron.
California sea lion, a sea lion that is usually the "trained seal" of circuses.
cal|i|for|nite (kal′ə fôr′nīt), *n.* a mineral, a variety of vesuvianite, resembling jade. [< *Californ(ia)*, where it is found + *-ite*[1]]
***cal|i|for|ni|um** (kal′ə fôr′nē əm), *n.* a radioactive, metallic chemical element, produced artificially from curium, plutonium, or uranium. [< New Latin *Californium* < (the University of) *California*, where it was first produced by nuclear physicists in 1950]

***californium**

symbol	atomic number	mass number	oxidation state
Cf	98	251	3

cal|i|ga (kal′ə gə), *n., pl.* **-gae** (-jē). 1 a military shoe of ancient Rome, the most common form of foot covering of all ranks up to centurion. 2 a bishop's stocking. [< Latin *caliga* shoe, boot]
ca|lig|i|nos|i|ty (kə lij′ə nos′ə tē), *n. Archaic.* mistiness or dimness of sight.
ca|lig|i|nous (kə lij′ə nəs), *adj. Archaic.* dim; murky; dark. [< Latin *cālīginōsus* misty < *cālīgō, -inis* mist, vapor, darkness]
Cal|i|myr|na fig (kal′ə mėr′nə), a variety of Smyrna fig grown in California.
cal|i|ol|o|gy (kal′ē ol′ə jē), *n.* the study of bird nests. [< Greek *kaliá* nest + English *-logy*]
cal|i|pash (kal′ə pash, kal′ə pash′), *n.* the edible, gelatinous, greenish substance found next to the upper shell of certain turtles. Also, **callipash**. [perhaps alteration of *carapace*]
cal|i|pee (kal′ə pē, kal′ə pē′), *n.* the edible, gelatinous, yellowish substance found next to the lower shell of certain turtles. Also, **callipee**. [probably alteration of *calipash*]
cal|i|per (kal′ə pər), *n., v.* —***n.*** 1 diameter; thickness, breadth; caliber: *Both the glazed and unglazed types are made in many calipers for an almost incredibly varied range of applications* (London Times). 2 = calipers. 3 Also, **caliper splint**. a metal support for a broken or deformed leg.
—***v.t.*** to measure with calipers.
—***v.i.*** to use calipers. Also, **calliper**.
[variant of *caliber*]
caliper brake, a brake on the wheel of a bicycle worked with a lever on the handle bars, connected by a cable to small arms that pinch rubber brake shoes against the rim of the wheel.
caliper rule, a rule having a graduated slide with a projecting foot at its end, used as calipers for measuring outside diameters; slide calipers. Also, **caliber rule**.
***cal|i|pers** (kal′ə pərz), *n.pl.* 1 an instrument used to measure the diameter or thickness of some small object. 2 any one of various similar calibrated instruments. Also, **callipers**.

***calipers**

ca|liph (kā′lif, kal′if), *n.* successor of Mohammed, the former title of religious and political heads of some Moslem states. Also, **calif, kalif, khalif, khalifa**. [< Old French *calife* < Arabic *khalīfa* successor]
cal|iph|ate (kal′ə fāt, kā′lə-), *n.* the rank, reign, government, or territory of a caliph. Also, **califate, kalifate, khaleefate, khalifat, khalifate**.
cal|i|sa|ya (kal′ə sā′ə), *n.,* or **calisaya bark**, the bark of cinchona, from which quinine is obtained. [< New Latin *calisaya* the species name, perhaps < a native South American name]
cal|is|then|ic (kal′əs then′ik), *adj.* of calisthenics; serving to promote bodily grace and strength, as muscular exercises do: *[Musical] conductors ... pursue what is possibly the most calisthenic of all callings* (New Yorker). Also, **callisthenic**.
cal|is|then|ics (kal′əs then′iks), *n.* 1 (*pl. in use*) exercises to develop a strong and graceful body. Calisthenics are carried out by moving the body without the use of special equipment. 2 (*sing. in use*) the practice or art of calisthenic exercises. Also, **callisthenics**. [< Greek *kállos* beauty + *sthénos* strength + English *-ics*]
ca|lix (kā′liks, kal′iks), *n., pl.* **ca|li|ces**. 1 a cup, especially a chalice. 2 calyx. [< Latin *calix* cup. See etym. of doublet **chalice**.]
calk[1] (kôk), *v.t.* = caulk. [< Old North French *cauquer* tread, press in < Latin *calcāre* < *calx, calcis* heel] —**calk′er**, *n.*
calk[2] (kôk), *n., v.* —***n.*** 1 a projecting piece on a horseshoe that catches in the ground or ice and prevents slipping. 2 a sharp piece of metal projecting from the heel of a boot such as lumbermen wear, or sometimes on the sole of a shoe, to prevent slipping.
—***v.t.*** 1 to put calks on. 2 to hurt with a calk. [apparently ultimately < Latin *calx, calcis* heel, or *calcar* spur]
calk[3] (kalk), *v.t.* to copy or transfer by tracing. [< French *calquer* < Italian *calcare* press under < Latin *calcāre;* see etym. under **calk**[1]]
calk|in (kô′kin), *n.* a calk on a horseshoe. [apparently ultimately < Latin *calcāneum* heel < *calx, calcis* heel]
call (kôl), *v., n.* —***v.t.*** 1 to say, especially in a loud voice; shout or cry out: *The nurse called the names of the next three patients.* 2a to give a signal to: *The bell called the class to order.* b to attract the attention of, especially by a characteristic sound: *to call a moose.* 3 to rouse; waken: *Call me at seven o'clock.* 4 to command to appear, act, or the like; summon: *He called his dog with a loud whistle. Obey when duty calls you. He called us to help him.* 5 to ask to come; cause to come: *Call a repairman. He called a cab. He called the assembly to order. His case will be called in court tomorrow.* 6 to get; bring: *to call forth a reply,* (*Figurative.*) *call out the best in a person.* (*Figurative.*) *The space age has called into existence a whole new body of scientific and technical words.* 7 to give a name to; name: *to call a person a fool. They called the new baby "John."* SYN: term. 8 to read over aloud: *The teacher called the class roll.* 9 to declare; proclaim; announce: *The head of the union called a strike.* 10 to talk to by telephone; telephone: *Call me at the office.* 11 to consider; estimate: *Everyone called the party a success.* 12a to end; stop: *The ball game was called on account of rain.* b *Sports.* (of an umpire or linesman) to declare a decision in respect to (a pitch, a ball, etc.): *The umpire called the ball foul. He called the runner out at second.* 13a to demand payment of: *The bank called my father's loan.* b to demand for payment: *The company will call its bonds April first.* 14 *U.S. Informal.* to declare or describe in advance; predict: *The stock market "called" every recession and recovery since 1948* (Time). 15 to select for a particular task: *to be called to the ministry.* 16 to demand a show of hands of (a person) in poker: *The gambler called the previous player by making an equal bet.* 17 to describe (a shot one is about to make) by naming an object ball or pocket in billiards or pool, a target in shooting, or any other objective. 18 to chant or shout (instructions) for square dancing: *He called the figures for the dance.* 19 to declare (trumps).
—***v.i.*** 1 to speak, especially in a loud voice; shout or cry: *He called from downstairs.* SYN: yell, shriek, scream. 2 (of a bird or other animal) to make its special noise or cry: *The crows called to each other from the trees around the meadow.* 3 to telephone: *Did anyone call today?* 4 to make a short visit or stop: *Our pastor called yesterday. Eight in the morning on his way to the jetty Scobie called at the bank* (Graham Greene). 5 to demand that hands be shown in a game of poker: *He called for a show of hands.* 6 *Scottish.* to drive.
—***n.*** 1 a loud sound, shout or cry: *I heard the swimmer's call for help.* 2a the special noise or cry a bird or other animal makes: *The call of a moose came from the forest.* b a cry or sound used to attract or decoy birds or animals. c an instrument used to imitate the note of a bird or cry of an animal and thus attract it: *a call for quail.* 3 a signal given by sound: *Army calls are played on the bugle.* 4 an invitation, request, or command; summons: *Every farmer in the neighborhood answered the fireman's call for volunteers. His call was readily obeyed* (Samuel Johnson). 5 a telephone call: *I want to make a call to Chicago.* 6 a short visit or stop: *The doctor made six calls. She had ... made a morning call on Martha Biggs* (Anthony Trollope). 7 a claim or demand: *A busy person has many calls on his time.* 8 a need; occasion: *You have no call to meddle in other people's business.* 9 in finance: a a demand for payment. b a demand that holders present (bonds or other securities) for payment or redemption. 10 a notice requiring actors and stagehands to attend a rehearsal: *The schedule for tomorrow's work arrived with all its facts and figures about the crew call, the set, the ... camera, sound* (London Times). 11 the act of calling. 12 the demand in poker that all hands still active be shown after their players have matched the current bet. 13 an instruction in square dancing which is chanted or shouted. 14 a calling; vocation. 15 the reading aloud of a list; a roll call: *a call of the House of Representatives.* 16 a contractual privilege, usually purchased, entitling its holder to demand and receive certain securities or commodities from its issuer at a specified price and within a given period: *Buying the "call" ... was an accepted and well developed part of the market's prewar mechanism* (Economist). 17 a note or series of notes blown on a hunting horn to encourage the hounds. 18 a player's turn in bridge to make a bid. 19 a player's turn in whist to declare trumps.
call back, a to ask (a person) to return; recall: *Call back the postman.* b to telephone to someone who has called earlier: *Your wife called and said you should call back as soon as you can.* c to take back; retract: *to call back one's words.*
call down, a *Informal.* to scold: *Most people dislike being called down in front of others.* b to invoke from above: *Calling down a blessing on his head* (Tennyson). c to bring about: *To take a liberty called down at once Her Majesty's most crushing disapprobation* (Lytton Strachey).
call for, a to go and get; stop and get: *The cab called for her at the hotel.* b *Figurative.* to need; require: *The recipe calls for two eggs. The crying evil which called for instant remedy* (John Ruskin).
call in, a to summon for advice or consultation: *Mother called in a doctor when I got a high fever.* b to withdraw: *The library calls in books that are damaged.* c to collect as debts: *... on his home farm there is a mortgage that may any day be called in* (J. W. R. Scott).
call in (or **into**) **question**. See under **question.**
call off, a to do away with; cancel: *We called off our trip. We felt that at any moment the manager would call the deal off* (Harper's). b to say or read over aloud in succession: *The teacher called off the names on the roll.* c to order to withdraw: *Call off your dog.*
call on (or **upon**), a to pay a short visit to: *We must call on our new neighbors.* b to appeal to: *He called upon his friends for help.*
call out, a to say in a loud voice; shout: *As he ran off, his mother called out after him to be careful.* b to summon into service or for some special duty or purpose: *The governor called out the National Guard to help with the rescue work during the flood. The union leaders called out the employees on strike.* c *Figurative.* to bring into play; elicit; evoke: *His emotional appeal called out a quick response from the audience.*
call to the bar. See under **bar**[1].
call up, a to bring to mind; bring back: *The old friends called up childhood memories.* b to telephone to: *He called me up at the office.* c to draft into military service: *The army called him up when he finished school.*
on (or **at**) **call**, a prepared to respond to a call to duty; ready or available: *Doctors are expected to be on call day and night.* b subject to payment on demand: *These certificates, in reality, simply represent money borrowed by the Government of the banks, on call* (Nation).
within call, near enough to hear a call: *Mother said to stay within call since supper was almost ready.*
[Old English *ceallian*]

Pronunciation Key: hat, āge, cãre, fär; let, ēqual, tėrm; it, īce; hot, ōpen, ôrder; oil, out; cup, pu̇t, rüle; child; long; thin; ᴛʜen; zh, measure; ə represents a in about, e in taken, i in pencil, o in lemon, u in circus.

—*Syn.* *v.t.* **4, 5 Call, invite, summon** mean to ask or order someone to come. **Call** is the general and informal word: *The principal called the student leaders to his office.* **Invite** means to ask politely, and suggests giving a person a chance to do something he would like to do: *The principal invited the student leaders to come in and talk things over.* **Summon** means to call with authority, and is used especially of a formal calling up to duty or to some formal meeting: *The principal summoned the rebellious students to his office. Summon* often suggests peremptory use of authority: *If I summon you, you must come immediately.*

cal|la (kal′ə), *n.* **1a** a plant with a large, usually white leaf like a petal around a thick spike of small, yellow flowers; Ethiopian lily; calla lily. The calla belongs to the arum family. There are also pink or yellow varieties. See picture under **arum family. b** any of various South African plants of the arum family. **2** a low, perennial North American marsh plant of the arum family having heart-shaped leaves; marsh calla; water arum. [< New Latin *Calla* the typical genus; origin uncertain]

call|a|ble (kô′lə bəl), *adj.* **1** (of a bond or other security) subject to redemption upon a demand for presentation. **2** (of a loan) subject to payment on demand.

calla lily, **1** = calla (def. 1a). **2** its blossom, formed of a white (or pink or yellow) leaf around a yellow spike.

cal|lan (kä′lən), *n.* = callant.

cal|lant (kä′lənt), *n. Scottish.* a lad; youth; stripling. [< dialectal Flemish *Kalant* chap, customer < Old North French *caland,* Old French *chaland* friend]

call|back (kôl′bak′), *n. U.S.* **1** a summoning back of furloughed workers: *. . . large-scale callbacks . . . have bolstered the employment picture* (Wall Street Journal). **2** a second, or an additional, meeting with a customer or client: *It takes four or five callbacks before a deal cooks* (Newsweek). **3** the recall of a product by its manufacturer to correct previously unnoticed defects: *Last month alone, automakers announced at least six callbacks involving more than 180,000 cars and trucks* (Time).

call bell, a small, usually stationary, bell used as a signal to summon an attendant or servant.

call|board (kôl′bôrd′, -bōrd′), *n.* the bulletin board in a theater, on which are posted the hours of rehearsal and other notices.

call box, **1** a telephone located outdoors in a box for use in emergencies or by a policeman reporting to headquarters. **2** *British.* a telephone booth. **3** a callboard in a theater, consisting of a frame or box and usually hung backstage.

call|boy (kôl′boi′), *n.* **1** a bellboy, especially in a hotel or on a ship. **2** a boy who calls actors from their dressing rooms when they are supposed to go on the stage.

call button, a push button or other device for ringing a call bell or sounding an alarm.

call change, a method of bell ringing in which the ringers are told when to ring by a call from the conductor, or by following a written order.

called strike, *Baseball.* a pitch not swung at by the batter but declared a strike by the umpire.

call|ee (kô′lē), *n.* a person who is called or called on.

ca|lle|jón (käl′yā hōn′), *n., pl.,* **-jo|nes** (-hō′nās). *Spanish.* **1** alley; lane. **2** a narrow, fenced-off lane which encircles the arena of a bull ring.

call|er[1] (kô′lər), *n.* **1** a person who makes a short visit: *The doctor said that the patient was now able to receive callers.* **2** a person who calls the steps in a square dance or the like: *Elisha Keeler . . . is one of the nation's best-known square dance callers* (New Yorker). **3** a person who calls. **4** a person who sounds calls: *a bird caller.* **5** a person who calls for a show of the hands in a poker game: *[He] drags down the pot with no callers and shows his hand* (Atlantic). [< *call* + *-er*[1]]

cal|ler[2] (kal′ər, kä′lər), *adj. Scottish.* **1** (of foods) fresh: *Wha'll buy my caller herring?* **2** (of weather, etc.) pleasantly fresh; refreshing. [apparently a variant of obsolete *calver*]

cal|let (kal′it), *n. Dialect.* **1** a lewd woman; trull; strumpet; drab. **2** a scold. [origin uncertain]

call girl, a prostitute who may be summoned by telephone.

cal|lig|ra|pher (kə lig′rə fər), *n.* **1** a person who writes by hand. **2** a person who writes by hand beautifully; penman. **3a** a person who professes the art of elegant penmanship. **b** a professional transcriber of manuscripts.

cal|li|graph|ic (kal′ə graf′ik), *adj.* having to do with calligraphy: *It's primarily calligraphic, made up of quick squiggles and strokes of black pigment on a variedly colored background* (New Yorker). —**cal′li|graph′i|cal|ly,** *adv.*

cal|lig|ra|phist (kə lig′rə fist), *n.* = calligrapher.

***cal|lig|ra|phy** (kə lig′rə fē), *n.* **1** handwriting. **2** beautiful handwriting, particularly in Persian, Chinese, or Japanese characters: *Calligraphy, or the practice of writing as a decorative art, is reckoned a higher accomplishment in China than painting* (New Yorker). **3** abstract art somewhat resembling Oriental calligraphy: *Calligraphy, or expressive draftsmanship for its own sake, is the virtue of Charles Seliger's delicate oils, watercolors and drawings* (New York Times). [< Greek *kalligraphíā* < *kalligráphos* good penman < *kál-los* beauty + *gráphein* write]

***calligraphy**
definition 2

call-in (kôl′in′), *n. U.S.* a radio or television program in which listeners or viewers call the studio by telephone to ask questions, make comments, or the like.

call|ing (kô′ling), *n.* **1** occupation, profession, or trade: *He chose to follow the calling of a teacher, while his brother chose the army as his calling.* SYN: vocation, career, business. **2** an invitation, command, or summons: *the calling of the bells to prayer.* **3** a spiritual or divine summons to a special service or office; call: *He felt an inner calling to be a clergyman. Most galling problem of ministers . . . was a sense of not living up to the calling* (Time).

calling card, a small card with a person's name on it, used when paying a call on someone, in acknowledging or sending gifts, or the like; visiting card.

calling crab, = fiddler crab.

calling hare, = pika. Pikas are called "calling hares" because of the reiterated squeaking cries which they emit while concealed, usually among rocks.

call-in pay (kôl′in′), *U.S.* the payment received by a worker who has not been notified before he reports to work that there is no work available or that he has been put on another shift.

Cal|li|o|pe (kə lī′ə pē), *n. Greek Mythology.* the Muse of eloquence and heroic poetry. [< Latin *Calliopē* < Greek *Kalliópē* < *kállos* beauty + *óps, opós* voice]

***cal|li|o|pe** (kə lī′ə pē, kal′ē ōp), *n.* a musical instrument having a series of steam whistles played by pressing keys on a keyboard. [< *Calliope*]

***calliope**

calliope hummingbird, a hummingbird of the Western United States and Mexico, about three inches long, with a golden-green crown and back and a lilac patch at the throat.

cal|li|op|sis (kal′ē op′sis), *n.* any one of a number of annual species of coreopsis. [< New Latin *calliopsis* < Greek *kállos* beauty + *ôpsis* appearance]

cal|li|pash (kal′ə pash, kal′ə pash′), *n.* = calipash.

cal|li|pee (kal′ə pē, kal′ə pē′), *n.* = calipee.

cal|li|per (kal′ə pər), *v.t., v.i.* = caliper.

cal|li|pers (kal′ə pərz), *n.pl.* = calipers.

cal|li|pyg|i|an (kal′ə pij′ē ən), *adj.* having well-developed or finely shaped buttocks. [< Greek *kallipȳgos* < *kállos* beauty + *pȳgê* buttocks]

cal|li|sec|tion (kal′ə sek′shən), *n.* painless vivisection; the dissection of living animals which have been anesthetized. [< Latin *callus* hard skin + *sectiō, -ōnis* a cutting]

cal|lis|then|ic (kal′əs then′ik), *adj.* = calisthenic.

cal|lis|then|ics (kal′əs then′iks), *n.* = calisthenics.

Cal|lis|to (kə lis′tō), *n.* **1** *Greek Legend.* a nymph whom Hera changed into a bear for being in love with Zeus. When Hera tried to kill the bear, Zeus put it into the sky, where it became Ursa Major. Callisto's son, Arcas, became Ursa Minor. **2** the most distant of the four largest of the twelve satellites of Jupiter.

cal|li|thum|pi|an (kal′ə thum′pē ən), *adj., n. U.S. Dialect.* —*adj.* denoting or having to do with a noisy concert, characterized by beating of tin pans, blowing of horns, shouts, groans, and cat-calls, usually given as a mock serenade.
—*n.* **1** a callithumpian concert; charivari. **2** a person who takes part in a callithumpian concert. [humorous formation < *calli-* (< Greek *kállos* beauty) + *thump* + *-ian*]

call letters, the letters of the alphabet that serve to identify a radio or television station, such as WBBM in Chicago.

call loan, a loan that must be paid back on demand.

call market, the market for call loans.

call money, money borrowed that must be paid back on demand: *Call money is borrowed by brokers and dealers to purchase and carry inventories of securities* (Wall Street Journal).

call note, the call or cry of a bird or other animal to its mate or its young: *. . . the chirping call note of the gecko* (Sir Richard Owen). *The crossbills may also be detected by the sharp "gik, gik, gik" call note, heard among pine trees, spruce firs, larches, or other conifers* (London Times).

call number, a number put on a library book to enable the user to identify and find it.

call-on (kôl′on′, -ôn′), *n. British.* a system of hiring longshoremen in which they line up for possible call by a foreman; shape-up.

cal|lose (kal′ōs), *n.* an amorphous substance, a carbohydrate, found in cell walls. [< Latin *callōsus* callous]

cal|los|i|ty (kə los′ə tē), *n.* **1** *pl.* **-ties.** = callus (def. 1). **2** *no pl.* lack of feeling or sensitivity; hardness of heart.

cal|lous (kal′əs), *adj., v.* —*adj.* **1** having a callus; hard; hardened: *Going barefoot makes the bottoms of your feet callous.* **2** *Figurative.* unfeeling; not sensitive: *Only a callous person can see suffering without trying to relieve it.* SYN: insensible.
—*v.t.* to harden or make callous: *Since Gorki wrote, two wars and a wave of sociological drama have calloused us to squalor* (Punch).
[< Latin *callōsus* < *callus* hard skin] —**cal′lous|ly,** *adv.* —**cal′lous|ness,** *n.*
►The noun **callus** and the adjective **callous,** identically pronounced, are sometimes confused in spelling.

cal|loused (kal′əst), *adj.* made callous; hardened.

call-out (kôl′ out), *n.* a summons into service or for some special duty or purpose: *an emergency crew's response to a call-out; a call-out of the National Guard.*

call-o|ver (kôl′ō′vər), *n. British.* **1** the reading aloud of a roll or list of names; roll call. **2** a calling over or reading aloud of a list of prices, especially betting odds: *He had been quoted at 20 to 1 in the call-over on Monday night, but 100 to 8 was the best price obtainable by midday yesterday* (London Times).

cal|low (kal′ō), *adj., n.* —*adj.* **1** young and inexperienced: *a callow youth. Despite their callow optimism, [his] words are refreshingly sincere and enthusiastic in a business that is too often cynical* (Newsweek). SYN: green. **2** not fully grown or developed; immature: *Like the callow ants, these larvae have an excitatory effect on the workers* (Science News Letter). **3** without feathers sufficiently developed for flight: *a callow bird.* **4** low-lying and liable to flooding.
—*n.* **1** callow land; bottoms. **2** a weak, pale-colored ant or other insect just hatched.
[Old English *calu* bald] —**cal′low|ness,** *n.*

call rate, the rate of interest charged on call loans.

call sign, the set of symbols identifying a radio operator or station or television station; call letters.

call slip, a printed form in a library which is filled out to request a particular book.

call to quarters, *U.S.* a bugle signal sounded fifteen minutes before taps, warning soldiers to go to quarters.

call-up (kôl′up′), *n.* a summoning of persons to duty or training, especially a summoning of men to military duty or training; draft: *In Paris, the*

Government authorized the call-up of 10,000 troops (New York Times). *The call-up of agricultural workers for the forces would be suspended in order to help with the harvest* (London Times).

cal|lus (kal′əs), *n., pl.* **-lus|es**, *v.* —*n.* Also, **callosity.** **1** a hard, thickened place on the skin. **2** a new growth to unite the ends of a broken bone. **3a** a substance that grows over the wounds of plants. **b** the thickening of the substance of the perforated septa (dividing walls) between sieve cells. **c** the thickening formed over the end of a cutting before it sends forth roots. **d** any unusually hard formation in or on a plant.
—*v.i.* to form or develop a callus.
—*v.t.* to form or develop a callus on.
[< Latin *callus*]
▶See **callous** for usage note.

calm (käm, kälm), *adj., n., v.* —*adj.* **1** not stormy or windy; not stirred up; quiet; still: *In fair weather the sea is usually calm.* **SYN:** motionless, smooth, placid. **2** *Figurative.* not excited; peaceful: *Although she was frightened, she answered with a calm voice.*
—*n.* **1** absence of wind or motion; quietness; stillness: *There was a sudden calm as the wind dropped.* **2** *Figurative.* absence of excitement; peacefulness; tranquility: *After the excitement of the birthday party the household settled into its usual calm. Ne'er saw I, never felt a calm so deep* (Wordsworth). **3** *Meteorology.* a condition in which the wind has a velocity of less than 1 mile per hour (on the Beaufort scale, force 0).
—*v.i.* to become calm: *The crying baby soon calmed down. The storm ceased and the sea calmed.*
—*v.t.* to make calm: *Mother calmed the frightened baby.*
[< Old French *calme* < Italian *calma* < Late Latin *cauma* < Greek *kaûma* heat of the day (a time for rest) < *kaíein* to burn] —**calm′ly**, *adv.* —**calm′ness**, *n.*
—*Syn. adj.* **2 Calm, composed, collected** mean not disturbed or excited. **Calm** means being or seeming to be completely undisturbed, showing no sign of being confused or excited: *Mother's calm behavior quieted the frightened boy.* **Composed** means calm as the result of having or having got command over one's thoughts and feelings and, sometimes, an inner peace: *She was composed at the funeral.* **Collected** emphasizes having control over one's actions, thoughts, and feelings, especially at times of danger or disturbance: *He was collected as he led the rescuers.*

cal|ma|tive (kal′mə tiv, kä′mə-), *adj., n.* = sedative.

cal|me|cac (käl′mā käk′), *n.* a special school among the Aztecs that trained outstanding boys and girls for official religious duties. [< Nahuatl *calmecac*]

calm|ing|ly (kä′ming lē, käl′ming-), *adv.* in a way that calms or soothes.

calm|y (kä′mē, käl′mē), *adj. Archaic.* tranquil; peaceful.

cal|o|mel (kal′ə mel, -məl), *n.* a white, tasteless, crystalline powder, a compound of mercury and chlorine, formerly used in medicine as a laxative and now used as a local antiseptic and fungicide; mercurous chloride. *Formula:* Hg_2Cl_2 [< Greek *kalós* beautiful + *mélās* black]

cal|o|res|cence (kal′ə res′əns), *n.* the change of nonluminous heat rays into light rays. [< Latin *calor* heat; patterned on *fluorescence*]

ca|lor|ic (kə lôr′ik, -lor′-), *adj., n.* —*adj.* **1** having to do with heat: *the caloric effect of sunlight.* **2** of or having to do with calories: *the caloric content of grapefruit is very low.*
—*n.* **1** a supposed elastic fluid, to which the phenomena of heat were formerly attributed: *Heat was formerly thought to be an invisible weightless fluid called caloric, which was produced when a substance burned and which could be transmitted by conduction from one body to another* (Sears and Zemansky). **2** *Rare.* heat.
[< French *calorique* < Latin *calor* heat] —**ca|lor′i|cal|ly**, *adv.*

cal|o|ric|i|ty (kal′ə ris′ə tē), *n.* the faculty in warm-blooded animals of developing heat so as to maintain nearly the same temperature at all times.

cal|o|rie or **cal|o|ry** (kal′ər ē), *n., pl.* **-ries.** **1** either of two units for measuring the amount of heat: **a** the quantity of heat needed to raise by one degree centigrade (Celsius) the temperature of a gram of water; small calorie: *Careful experiments show that it takes about 80 calories of heat to melt one gram of ice* (Beauchamp, Mayfield, and West). **b** the quantity of heat needed to raise by one degree centigrade the temperature of a kilogram of water; large calorie: *The large calorie or "kilogram-calorie" is equal to 1000 small calories* (Parks and Steinbach). **2a** a unit of the energy supplied by food. It corresponds to a large calorie. An ounce of sugar will produce about a hundred calories. **b** the quantity of food capable of producing such an amount of energy. [< French *calor,* learned borrowing from Latin, heat < *calēre* be hot]

cal|o|rif|ic (kal′ə rif′ik), *adj.* **1** producing heat. **2** producing food calories; caloric: *Passengers last year downed 83,000 glasses of Irish coffee ... a calorific combination of whiskey, coffee and cream* (Time). **3** *Figurative.* showing feeling or emotion; warm. [< Latin *calōrificus* < *calor, -ōris* heat + *facere* make] —**cal′o|rif′i|cal|ly**, *adv.*

ca|lor|i|fi|ca|tion (kə lôr′ə fə kā′shən, -lor′-), *n.* the production of heat, especially animal heat.

calorific value, the calories or thermal units contained in one unit of a substance, and released when it is burned.

cal|o|ri|gen|ic (kal′ə rə jen′ik), *adj.* = calorific. —**cal′o|ri|gen′i|cal|ly**, *adv.*

cal|o|rim|e|ter (kal′ə rim′ə tər), *n.* an apparatus for measuring the quantity of heat given off by or present in a body, such as the specific heat of different substances or the heat of chemical combination: *The calorimeter consists essentially of two covered metallic cups, one of which is small enough to fit inside the other* (W. N. Jones). [< Latin *calor, -ōris* heat + English *-meter*]

cal|o|ri|met|ric (kal′ər ə met′rik), *adj.* of or having to do with the calorimeter or calorimetry. —**cal′o|ri|met′ri|cal|ly**, *adv.*

cal|o|ri|met|ri|cal (kal′ər ə met′rə kəl), *adj.* = calorimetric.

cal|o|rim|e|trist (kal′ə rim′ə trist), *n.* an expert in calorimetry.

cal|o|rim|e|try (kal′ə rim′ə trē), *n.* **1** the quantitative measurement of heat. **2** studies involving the use of the calorimeter. [< Latin *calor, -ōris* heat]

cal|o|rist (kal′ər ist), *n.* a person who held the view accepted by many scientists of the 1700's that heat is an elastic fluid, which they called caloric. [< *calor*(ic) + *-ist*]

cal|o|ris|tic (kal′ə ris′tik), *adj.* of or having to do with the calorists.

cal|o|riz|ing (kal′ə rī′zing), *n. Metallurgy.* the process of coating the surface of a metal, especially steel, with aluminum, in order to protect it from rust and heat.

cal|o|ry (kal′ər ē), *n., pl.* **-ries.** = calorie.

cal|o|so|ma (kal′ə sō′mə), *n.* any one of a species of ground beetles that feed on the gypsy moth, the brown-tail moth, cutworms, and other injurious insects. [< New Latin *calosoma* < Greek *kalós* beautiful + *sôma* body]

ca|lot (kȧ lō′), *n. French.* a woman's hat, resembling a small, tight-fitting skullcap.

ca|lotte (kə lot′), *n.* a plain skullcap, such as the zucchetto worn by Roman Catholic ecclesiastics. [< French *calotte* < Italian *calotta* < Greek *kalýptrā* headdress < *kalýptein* to cover]

cal|o|type (kal′ə tīp), *n.* **1** a photographic process invented in 1841; talbotype. The pictures were made on paper sensitized with silver iodide. **2** the picture so made. [< Greek *kalós* beautiful + English *type*]

cal|o|yer (kal′ə yər, kə loi′ər), *n.* a monk of the Eastern Church. [< French *caloyer* < Late Greek *kalógeros* venerable < Greek *kalós* fine + *gêras* old age]

calp (kalp), *n.* a dark limestone found in Ireland. [< dialectal Irish *calp*]

cal|pac or **cal|pack** (kal′pak), *n.* a large cap of sheepskin, felt, or wool, worn by Turks and some nearby peoples. Also, **kalpac.** [< Turkish *kalpak*]

cal|pul|lec (kal pu̇l′ek), *n.* the leader of the council of family heads that governed the calpulli. [< Nahuatl *calpullec*]

cal|pul|li (kal pu̇l′ē), *n., pl.* **cal|pul|li.** the primary land-owning unit among the Aztecs. [< Nahuatl *calpulli*]

calque (kalk), *n.* **1** an expression that is a literal translation of a foreign expression; loan translation. *Example:* German *mitleiden* "to sympathize with" is a calque from Latin *compatī,* which, in turn, is a calque from Greek *sympathéin.* **2** a native word or phrase having a new meaning that has been borrowed from an old meaning in a corresponding foreign word. *Example:* English *lip* "liplike part in a plant or animal" is a calque from Latin *labium.* [< French *calque,* literally, a tracing < *calquer* to trace, copy by tracing; see etym. under **calk**[3]]

cal|trop or **cal|trap** (kal′trəp), *n.* Now often **caltrops.** **1** any one of various plants having pointed, spiny flower heads or fruit: **a** = star thistle. **b** any plant of various herbs of South Europe having spiny seeds. **c** = water chestnut or water caltrop. **2** a defensive device against cavalry, consisting of an iron ball with four projecting spikes so arranged that when any three rest on the ground the fourth points upward; crowfoot or crow's-foot. [probably < Old North French *calketrape* < Medieval Latin *calcatrippa* a plant that entangles the feet < Latin *calcā-* step on (< *calcāre* < *calx, calcis* heel) + Old High German *trapo* trap, noose]

ca|lum|ba (kə lum′bə), *n.* the root of an African plant, cultivated also in the East Indies, used in medicine and as a tonic. Also, **columbo.** [< *Colombo,* Sri Lanka (Ceylon), the supposed place of origin]

cal|u|met (kal′yə met, kal′yə met′), *n.* a long, ornamented tobacco pipe smoked by the American Indians in ceremonies as a symbol of peace; peace pipe. [American English < Canadian French *calumet* < Norman-French *calumo* < Late Latin *calamellus* (diminutive) < Latin *calamus* < Greek *kálamos* reed]

ca|lum|ni|ate (kə lum′nē āt), *v.t.,* **-at|ed, -at|ing.** to say false and harmful things about; slander. **SYN:** defame, malign, libel, vilify. [< Latin *calumniārī* (with English *-ate*[1]) < *calumnia* calumny. See etym. of doublet **challenge**, verb.] —**ca|lum′ni|a′tion**, *n.* —**ca|lum′ni|a′tor**, *n.*

ca|lum|ni|a|to|ry (kə lum′nē ə tôr′ē, -tōr′-), *adj.* slanderous; calumnious.

ca|lum|ni|ous (kə lum′nē əs), *adj.* slanderous; defamatory: *a calumnious statement or attack.* —**ca|lum′ni|ous|ly**, *adv.*

cal|um|ny (kal′əm nē), *n., pl.* **-nies.** **1** a false statement made on purpose to do harm to someone; slander: *Calumnies are answered best with silence* (Ben Jonson). *We have seen our friends in other countries ... reduced to an embarrassed and troubled silence before the calumnies of our enemies, ... for they were no longer sure whether these calumnies did not contain some measure of truth* (Atlantic). **SYN:** defamation, libel, vilification. **2** calumniation; slandering. [< Latin *calumnia,* ultimately < *calvī* to trick, deceive. See etym. of doublet **challenge**, noun.]

cal|u|tron (kal′yə tron), *n.* a device for separating isotopes according to their masses, using the principle of a mass spectrograph: *The calutron ... first produced uranium of sufficient purity and quantity for the atomic bomb* (New York Times). [< *Cal*(ifornia) *U*(niversity) (cyclo)*tron,* which was used to build the device]

Cal|va|dos or **cal|va|dos** (kal′və dōs′), *n.* the brandy of Normandy, France, distilled from hard cider: *Calvados is a tart, fiery applejack, stored in small oak vats for periods ranging up to ten years to acquire its distinctive bouquet* (New York Times). [< *Calvados,* a French département]

cal|var|i|a (kal vãr′ē ə), *n.* = calvarium.

cal|va|ri|al (kal vãr′ē əl), *adj.* of or belonging to the calvarium: *One has a calvarial height index ... of 52, or within the range of Cro-Magnon man* (A. L. Kroeber).

cal|va|ri|an (kal vãr′ē ən), *adj.* = calvarial.

cal|var|i|um (kal vãr′ē əm), *n.* the upper, caplike part of the skull; skullcap: *... the calvarium, the top part of the skull, has been found more frequently and in a better state of preservation, than those other more fragile bones* (Melville J. Herskovits). Also, **calvaria.** [< New Latin *calvarium* < Latin *calvāria* skull < *calvus* bald, bare]

Cal|va|ry (kal′vər ē), *n.* the place near ancient Jerusalem where Jesus died on the Cross; Golgotha (in the Bible, Luke 23:33). [< Latin *calvāria* skull < *calvus* bald]

cal|va|ry (kal′vər ē), *n., pl.* **-ries.** **1** a statuary group representing the Crucifixion, usually life-size and placed in the open on a hill, but sometimes smaller and in a chapel: *By the side of the high road ... is one of those calvaries so associated with the landscape of Catholic countries* (Harper's). **2** an experience or period of great personal suffering and hardship. [< *Calvary*]

Calvary cross, *Heraldry.* a cross atop three steps. See picture under **cross.**

calve (kav, käv), *v.,* **calved, calv|ing.** —*v.i.* **1** to give birth to a calf. **2** (of a glacier or iceberg) to detach and throw off a mass of ice.
—*v.t.* **1** to bring forth (a calf). **2** to detach and throw off (a mass of ice): *Icebergs calved from the west Greenland glaciers one summer usually spend their first winter in the vicinity of Melville Bay* (Science News Letter).
[Old English *cealfian* < *cealf* calf]

calves[1] (kavz, kävz), *n.* plural of **calf**[1] (defs. 1, 2, 4, 5).

calves[2] (kavz, kävz), *n.* plural of **calf**[2].

Cal|vin|ism (kal′və niz əm), *n.* **1** the religious teachings of John Calvin (1509-1564) and his followers. Calvin taught that only certain persons, the elect, were chosen by God to be saved, and these could be saved only by God's grace. Calvinism forms the basis for the doctrines and practices of the Huguenots, Puritans, Presbyteri-

Pronunciation Key: hat, āge, cãre, fär; let, ēqual, tėrm; it, īce; hot, ōpen, ôrder; oil, out; cup, pu̇t, rüle; child; long; thin; ᴛʜen; zh, measure; ə represents **a** in about, **e** in taken, **i** in pencil, **o** in lemon, **u** in circus.

ans, and the Reformed churches. **2** belief in or observance of these teachings: *Even Woodrow Wilson, whose stern Calvinism might have found larger rapport with Macaulay, . . . reproved Macaulay for his lucidity of expression* (Jack Valenti). —**Cal′vin·ist**, *n., adj.*

Cal·vin·is·tic (kal′və nis′tik), *adj.* having to do with Calvin or Calvinism. —**Cal′vin·is′ti·cal·ly**, *adv.*

Cal·vin·is·ti·cal (kal′və nis′tik), *adj.* = Calvinistic.

cal·vi·ti·es (kal vish′ē ēz), *n.* baldness. [< Latin *calvitiēs* < *calvus* bald]

calx (kalks), *n., pl.* **calx·es** or **cal·ces.** **1** an ashy substance left after a metal or mineral has been roasted or burned. **2** *Obsolete.* lime or chalk. [< Latin *calx, calcis* lime]

ca·ly·cate (kal′ə kāt), *adj.* provided with a calyx.

ca·ly·ces (kal′ə sēz, kā′lə-), *n.* calyxes; a plural of **calyx.**

ca·lyc·i·form (kə lis′ə fôrm), *adj. Botany.* having the form of a calyx. [< Latin *calyx, -ycis* calyx]

ca·lyc·i·nal (kə lis′ə nəl), *adj.* = calycine.

cal·y·cine (kal′ə sin, -sīn), *adj.* of or like a calyx.

cal·y·cle (kal′ə kəl), *n.* **1** = epicalyx. **2** = calicle. [< Latin *calyculus;* see etym. under **calyculus**]

cal·y·coid (kal′ə koid), *adj.* like a calyx.

cal·y·coid·e·ous (kal′ə koi′dē əs), *adj.* = calycoid.

ca·lyc·u·lar (kə lik′yə lər), *adj.* having to do with a calycle.

ca·lyc·u·late (kə lik′yə lāt), *adj.* having a calycle.

ca·lyc·u·lat·ed (kə lik′yə lā′tid), *adj.* = calyculate.

ca·lyc·u·lus (kə lik′yə ləs), *n., pl.* **-li** (-lī). = calicle. [< Latin *calyculus* (diminutive) < *calyx, -ycis* < Greek *kályx* seed pod]

Cal·y·do·ni·an (kal′ə dō′nē ən), *adj.* of Calydon, an ancient city in Greece.

Calydonian boar hunt, *Greek Legend.* the pursuit of the wild boar which Artemis sent to attack Calydon and which Meleager finally killed.

Ca·lyp·so (kə lip′sō), *n. Greek Legend.* a sea nymph who detained Odysseus on her island for seven years on his way home from the Trojan War.

ca·lyp·so¹ (kə lip′sō), *n., pl.* **-sos,** *adj.* —*n.* **1** a type of improvised song, usually about some matter of current interest, that originated in the British West Indies. It is characterized by jazz influence and rhythmic flexibility. *[The] calypso has been a kind of musical journalism, with such topical titles as The Destruction of Hurricane Janet, The Princess Says No* (Time). **2** a type of folk music played in West Africa, South America, and the Caribbean region.

—*adj.* of or having to do with the style of music to which these songs are sung.

[origin uncertain]

ca·lyp·so² (kə lip′sō), *n., pl.* **-sos.** a small orchid growing in cold bogs or wet woods, and bearing a single flower with crimson petals and sepals (rarely, white) and a whitish sac with purple spots. [< *Calypso*]

ca·lyp·so·ni·an (kal′ip sō′nē ən), *n., adj.* —*n.* a person who improvises and sings calypso songs.

—*adj.* of or having to do with calypso: *It slides into an essentially Negro rhythm: African, spasmodic, and calypsonian* (Atlantic).

ca·lyp·tra (kə lip′trə), *n.* **1** a thick covering on top of the capsule in some mosses, formed by enlargement of the walls of the archegonium. **2** any hoodlike part of a flower or fruit. **3** = root cap. [< New Latin *calyptra* < Greek *kalýptra* headdress, veil < *kalýptein* cover up]

ca·lyp·tro·gen (kə lip′trə jən), *n. Botany.* the layer of the undifferentiated tissue meristem from which the root cap of some plants develops. [< *calyptra* + *-gen*]

***ca·lyx** (kā′liks, kal′iks), *n., pl.* **ca·lyx·es** or **cal·y·ces.** **1** the outer leaves that surround the unopened bud of a flower. The calyx is made up of sepals, either separated or joined in a cup. *In a complete flower the calyx and corolla constitute the perianth or floral envelope* (Heber W. Youngken). **2** *Anatomy, Zoology.* a cuplike structure or organ. Also, **calix.** [< Latin *calyx, -ycis* < Greek *kályx* seed pod, husk]

***calyx**
definition 1
petal
sepal
calyx

cal·za·da (käl sä′ŧʜä, -thä′-), *n. Spanish.* **1** a paved road or highway. **2** (in Latin America) a wide street or avenue.

cal·zone (kal zō′nē, kal zōn′), *n.* a dome-shaped baked pie filled usually with cheese: *I went partway down into the valley and stopped at a pizzeria called the Capri, where I had a calzone* (Alex Shoumatoff). [< Italian]

***cam** (kam), *n.* a noncircular wheel mounted on a shaft that changes a regular circular motion into an irregular circular motion or into a back-and-forth motion. Cams are used to vary the speed of some mechanisms or change the direction of their movement. [perhaps < Dutch *kam* cog]

CAM (no periods), computer-aided manufacture: *In CAM, the final description of the product that the computer decides upon is fed, in computer code, to a machine tool which shapes the finished object* (New Scientist).

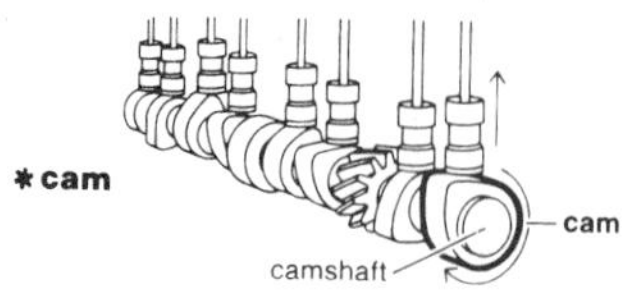

***cam**

CAM., Cambridge.

ca·ma·ïeu (kà mà yœ′), *n. French.* **1** a cameo. **2** a method of painting in monochrome. **3** a monochrome painting.

ca·mail (kə māl′), *n.* a piece of chain mail for protecting the neck and shoulders, especially one attached to the edge of the basinet or some other headpiece. [< French *camail* < Old Provençal *capmalh* < *cap* head (< Latin *caput*) + *malha* mail, armor]

ca·mailed (kə māld′), *adj.* having a camail.

ca·ma·lig (kä mä′lēg), *n.* in the Philippines: **1** a warehouse for storing goods. **2** a small house or cabin. [< Tagalog *kamalig*]

cam·an·cha·ca (kam′ən chä′kə), *n.* a thick mist on the Peruvian and Chilean coasts; garua. [< American Spanish *camanchaca*]

ca·ma·ra·de·rie (kä′mə rä′dər ē), *n.* friendliness and loyalty among comrades; comradeship: *the cheerful camaraderie of school days.* [< French *camaraderie* < *camarade* comrade]

cam·a·ril·la (kam′ə ril′ə; *Spanish* kä′mä rē′lyä), *n.* a group of private advisers; cabal: *The foreign policy of the Empire was shaped by a small camarilla* (Atlantic). SYN: clique, coterie. [< Spanish *camarilla* (diminutive) < *cámara* chamber < Latin *camera* vault]

cam·ass or **cam·as** (kam′əs), *n.* **1** a plant of the lily family growing in western North America, whose sweet, nourishing bulbs were eaten by the Indians: *They gorged on camas bulbs* (Time). **2** = death camass. Also, **quamash.** [American English < Chinook jargon < Nootka *chamass* sweet]

Ca·ma·yu·rá (kä′mə yü rä′), *n.* a member of a primitive tribe of Indians discovered in the 1950's in the jungles of central Brazil.

Camb., Cambridge.

cam·ber (kam′bər), *v., n.* —*v.t., v.i.* to bend or curve upward in the middle; arch slightly.

—*n.* **1** an upward bend or curve in the middle; slight arch. **2** a slightly arching piece of timber. **3** the rise and fall of the curve of an airfoil of an aircraft. **4** a slight inward tilt toward the bottom of the front wheels of an automobile: *As design and materials have improved the camber angle has been decreased until current cars have very little camber* (Purvis and Toboldt). [< Middle French *cambre* bent < Latin *camur* crooked]

Cam·ber·well beauty (kam′bər wel), a kind of butterfly; mourning cloak. [< *Camberwell,* a suburb of London, where it was often seen]

cam·bi·al (kam′bē əl), *adj.* formed of or having to do with cambium: *In the course of the growing season each cell of the cambial sheath gives rise to a radial row of wood cells* (E. W. J. Phillips).

cam·bism (kam′biz əm), *n.* the theory and practice of commercial exchange.

cam·bist (kam′bist), *n.* **1a** a person who deals in bills of exchange. **b** a person who is skilled in the operations of exchanges. **2** a manual giving the equivalent moneys, weights, and measures of various countries. [< French *cambiste* < Italian *cambista* < *cambiare* to exchange < Latin *cambiāre*]

cam·bist·ry (kam′bə strē), *n.* the science or practice of the cambist.

cam·bi·um (kam′bē əm), *n.* a layer of soft growing tissue between the bark and the wood of trees and shrubs. New bark and new wood grow from it. It is the renewal of this growth year after year that produces annual rings. See picture under **bark¹**. [< Medieval Latin *cambiāre* to exchange]

Cam·bo·di·an (kam bō′dē ən), *adj., n.* —*adj.* of or having to do with Cambodia (Kampuchea) or its people.

—*n.* **1** a native or inhabitant of Cambodia. **2** = Khmer (def. 2).

cam·bo·gi·a (kam bō′jē ə), *n. Pharmacy.* = gamboge (def. 1). [< New Latin *cambogia* < *Cambodia,* former name of Kampuchea]

Cam·bri·a (kam′brē ə), *n.* an old name of Wales.

Cam·bri·an (kam′brē ən), *n., adj.* —*n.* **1** the earliest geological period of the Paleozoic era, before the Ordovician. During this period there were large numbers of primitive, invertebrate water animals, such as the trilobites. **2** the rocks formed during this period. **3** = Welshman.

—*adj.* **1** of or having to do with the Cambrian or its rocks: *The Cambrian rocks derive their name from Cambria, the name for Wales, where, a century ago, this division of Paleozoic succession was defined* (Raymond Cecil Moore). **2** = Welsh.

cam·bric (kām′brik), *n.* a fine, thin linen or cotton cloth, similar to nainsook, except for its finish, which is not shiny: *delicate handkerchiefs of white cambric.* [< Flemish *Kameryk,* or French *Cambrai,* a city in Flanders. See etym. of doublet **chambray.**]

cambric tea, a drink made of hot water, milk, and sugar, sometimes flavored with a little tea.

cam·cord·er (kam′kôr dər), *n.* a videocassette recorder combined with a color camera. [< *cam*(era) + (re)*corder*]

came¹ (kām), *v.* past tense of **come:** *He came to school too early this morning.*

came² (kām), *n.* one of the small, grooved bars of lead used for framing the glass in latticework or stained-glass windows. [apparently a variant of earlier *calm* a mold for metal casting]

cam·e·ist (kam′ē ist), *n.* **1** a gem engraver. **2** a person who cuts or carves cameos. **3** a person who is a collector or connoisseur of cameos.

***cam·el** (kam′əl), *n.* **1** a large, four-footed, cud-chewing mammal with one or two humps on its back, a long neck, and cushioned feet. It is used as a beast of burden in the deserts of northern Africa and central Asia because it can go for a long time without drinking water. The Arabian camel, or dromedary, has one hump; the Bactrian camel of Asia has two humps. **2** a watertight tank or drum used, usually in pairs, to raise a ship, barge, or the like, especially a ship that is sunk or aground. [< Latin *camēlus* < Greek *kámēlos* < a Semitic word] —**cam′el·like′**, *adj.*

***camel**
definition 1

Bactrian camel dromedary

cam·el·back (kam′əl bak′), *n., adj., adv.* —*n.* **1** the back of a camel. **2** a compound of reclaimed rubber with a small amount of crude rubber, used especially for retreading or recapping tires. **3** a railroad locomotive on which the cab is placed above the boiler. **4** (in glassmaking) a rounded conveyor on which plates of glass are moved along after annealing.

—*adj., adv.* on the back of a camel: *a camelback rider* (adj.); *to ride camelback* (adv.).

camel bird, = ostrich.

camel cricket, a brownish, wingless, longhorned grasshopper found in caves and in the moist hollows of trees; cave cricket.

cam·el·eer (kam′ə lir′), *n.* **1** a camel driver. **2** a soldier mounted or riding on a camel.

camel gun, a gun, such as a machine gun, made light and short so it can be carried by camel.

cam·el-hair (kam′əl hãr′), *adj.* = camel's-hair.

***ca·mel·lia** (kə mēl′yə, -mē′lē ə), *n.* **1** a shrub or tree with glossy leaves and waxy, white, red, pink, or mottled flowers shaped like roses. The camellia is an evergreen and belongs to the tea family. **2** the flower. [< New Latin *Camellia* the genus name < George *Kamel,* 1661-1706, a missionary to Luzon]

***camellia**
definition 2

camellia red, a bright red, the color of red camellias.

ca·mel·o·pard (kə mel′ə pärd), *n.* the giraffe. The giraffe was given this name because it is formed somewhat like a camel, and is spotted like a leopard. [< Late Latin *camēlopardus* < Latin *camēlopardalis* < Greek *kamēlopárdalis* < *kámēlos* camel + *párdalis* leopard, pard]

Ca·mel·o·pard (kə mel′ə pärd), *n.* a northern constellation between Ursa Major and Cassiopeia; the Giraffe.

Ca·mel·o·par·da·lis (kə mel′ə pär′də lis), *n., genitive* **Ca·mel·o·par·da·lis.** = Camelopard.

Cam·e·lot (kam′ə lot), *n.* **1** a legendary place in Britain where King Arthur had his palace and court: *Turned to towered Camelot* (Tennyson). **2** *Figurative.* a time or place of enchantment and glamour: *those who joined President Kennedy's administration immediately after his inauguration, those who came to Camelot* (Harper's).

cam|el|ry (kam′əl rē), *n., pl.* **-ries**. soldiers mounted on camels.

camel's hair, **1** the hair of a camel, used especially in making cloth and paintbrushes. **2** a cloth made of this hair or something like it. **3** the long hairs from the tail of a squirrel, used to make artists' paintbrushes.

cam|el's-hair (kam′əlz hãr′), *adj.* **1** made of camel's hair, mohair, or some similar fabric. **2** (of artists' paintbrushes) made with camel's hair or the tail hairs of the squirrel.

camel's-hair brush, an artist's paintbrush, made of the long hairs from the tail of a squirrel.

camel's nose, *U.S.* A small part of something large, especially something difficult or unpleasant to deal with: *Even this amount . . . represents merely the camel's nose of the modernization program planned* (Scientific American).

cam|el's-thorn tree (kam′əlz thôrn′), a large, slow-growing tree with very hard wood, common in southern Africa north of the Orange River.

cam|el-thorn (kam′əl thôrn′), *n.* = camel's-thorn tree.

camel walk, a dance resembling the walk of a camel, in vogue in the 1920's.

Cam|em|bert (kam′əm bãr), *n.*, or **Camembert cheese**, a rich, soft, ripened cheese: *Some 200 commercial varieties of cheese are made in France, the most important, in order, being Camembert, Gruyère, Port Salut, and Roquefort* (Science News Letter). [< *Camembert,* a French village near which it was first made]

Ca|me|nae (kə mē′nē), *n.pl. Roman Mythology.* prophetic nymphs of the springs and fountains, in later times identified with the nine Muses.

cam|e|o (kam′ē ō), *n., pl.* **-e|os**, *adj.* **—*n.*** **1** a precious or semiprecious stone carved so that there is a raised design on a background usually of a different color. Agates, other stones with layers, and sometimes shells are used for cameos. **2** an engraving or carving made to resemble this effect. **3a** a very brief but outstanding role or performance in a motion picture, play, or other dramatic performance that highlights a character or event: *There are superb cameos by Dame Edith Evans and Hugh Griffith* (Maclean's). **b** a short but striking literary description highlighting a character, event, object, or trait: *Michael Wall gives us a chilling cameo of hatred on Cyprus* (Manchester Guardian Weekly).

—*adj.* of or like a cameo; short and striking: *a cameo role, a cameo appearance on a show, a cameo portrait or sketch.*

[Italian *cammeo,* perhaps < Arabic *kamkhat* incrustation, coating]

cameo glass, an artistic glass consisting of layers of different colors, the outermost being cut away to leave the design in relief.

cameo incrustation, the art of producing casts of bas-relief within a coating of flint glass.

cameo type, (formerly) a small daguerreotype made to be mounted in a jeweled setting.

cameo ware, pottery with figures in relief on a background of a different color, such as those in Wedgwood ware.

***cam|er|a** (kam′ər ə, kam′rə), *n., pl.* **-er|as** *for 1, 2, and 3b,* **-er|as** or **-er|ae** (-ə rē) *for 3a.* **1** a device for taking photographs or motion pictures, in which film or plates are exposed and the image is formed by means of a lens: *The cinema is a very truthful medium because the camera doesn't let you get away with anything* (New York Times). **2** part of the transmitter which converts images into electronic impulses for television transmitting. **3a** a judge's private office: *The Court of Appeal went into camera to hear an appeal by a father* (London Times). **b** (in Italy, Spain, etc.) a council or legislative chamber. **4** = camera obscura.

in camera, a in a judge's private office: *[She] would sue for the divorce . . . in her native Philadelphia, where divorce hearings can be held in camera* (Time). **b** privately: *I'll tell you the rest in camera.*

[< Latin *camera* vault, arch < Greek *kamárā.* See etym. of doublet **chamber**.]

***camera**
definition 1

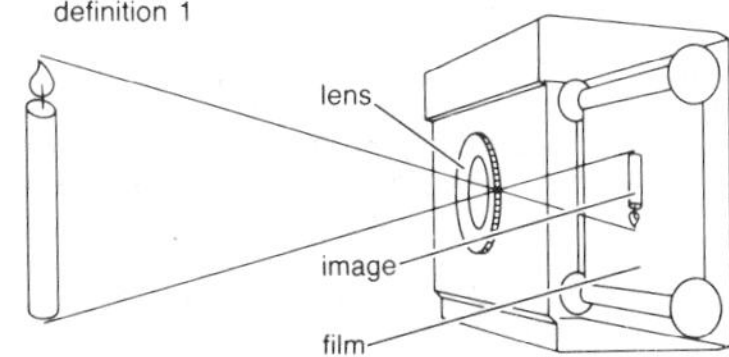

cam|er|al (kam′ər əl), *adj.* **1** of or having to do with a chamber, especially a legislative chamber. **2** of or having to do with public finances or revenue.

cam|er|al|ist (kam′ər ə list), *n.* a person versed in public finance.

cam|er|al|is|tic (kam′ər ə lis′tik), *adj.* having to do with finance and public revenue.

cam|er|al|is|tics (kam′ər ə lis′tiks), *n.* the science of public finance.

camera lu|ci|da (lü′sə də), an optical instrument which may be attached to a microscope, by which the image of an object is projected on a sheet of paper or metal upon which it may be traced. [< New Latin *camera lucida* light chamber < Latin *camera* + *lūcida* light]

cam|er|a|man (kam′ər ə man′, kam′rə-; -mən), *n., pl.* **-men**. a man who operates a camera, especially a motion-picture or television camera.

camera ob|scu|ra (ob skyůr′ə), a box or small chamber in which images of external objects, received through an aperture, are exhibited on a surface arranged to receive them: *The camera obscura is used for sketching large objects, for exhibition purposes, etc. The camera made its first appearance not as an instrument for making pictures, but as the camera obscura or dark chamber, a device that attempted no more than to project an inverted image upon a screen* (Scientific American). [< New Latin *camera obscura* dark chamber < Latin *camera* + *obscura* dark, obscure]

cam|er|a-shy (kam′ər ə shī′), *adj.* nervous or fearful before cameras; afraid of being photographed: *so camera-shy that they think twice before posing for a passport photograph* (New Yorker).

cam|er|ate (kam′ər it, -āt), *adj., n.* **—*adj.*** **1** divided into chambers. **2** belonging to or having to do with an order of Paleozoic crinoids with arched coverings.

—*n.* a camerate crinoid: *In the Early Mississippian Epoch, an almost explosive expansion of the camerates made them the outstanding element in marine invertebrate life* (Raymond C. Moore).

[< Laten *camerātus,* past participle of *camerāre* to vault < *camera* vault, arch]

camera tube, = pickup tube.

cam|er|a|work (kam′ər ə wėrk′), *n.* = photography: *Camerawork with no soundtrack can create many moods—it is a favourite trick of thrillers to create suspense* (Manchester Guardian).

cam|er|ist (kam′ər ist), *n. Informal.* a person who uses a camera; photographer.

cam|er|len|go (kam′ər leng′gō), *n., pl.* **-gos**. = camerlingo.

cam|er|lin|gate (kam′ər ling′git), *n.* the office of camerlingo: *S. Charles . . . absolutely refused the camerlingate, the second and most lucrative dignity in the Roman court* (A. Butler).

cam|er|lin|go (kam′ər ling′gō), *n., pl.* **-gos**. the Pope's chamberlain, chosen from among the cardinals and having charge of the secular interests of the papacy. Also, **camerlengo**. [< Italian *camerlingo* chamberlain < Latin *camera;* see etym. under **camera**]

Cam|er|oo|ni|an (kam′ə rü′nē ən), *adj., n.* **—*adj.*** of or having to do with Cameroon, a country in central Africa, or with the former British trust territory of Cameroons.

—*n.* a native or inhabitant of Cameroon or the former Cameroons.

ca|mik (kä′mik), *n.* a boot made of soft sealskin, used in arctic regions; muckluck. [< Eskimo *kamik*]

cam|i|knick|ers (kam′ə nik′ərz), *n.pl. British.* a woman's undergarment combining a camisole and knickers. [< *cami*(sole) + *knickers*]

Ca|mil|la (kə mil′ə), *n. Roman Legend,* a warrior queen who fought against Aeneas and his followers in Italy.

ca|mi|no re|al (kə mē′nō rā äl′; *Spanish* kä-mē′nō rä äl′), *pl.* **ca|mi|no re|als** (kə mē′nō rā-älz′), *Spanish* **ca|mi|nos re|a|les** (kä mē′nōs rā ä′lās). *Southwestern U.S.* a main highway. [< Spanish *camino real* (literally) royal road]

cam|i|on (kam′ē ən; *French* kȧ myôN′), *n.* **1** a motor truck. **2** a strong cart or wagon; dray. **3** a truck for carrying cannon, military supplies, and the like. [< French *camion* < Middle French *chamion* low cart]

ca|mi|sa (kä mē′sä), *n. Spanish,* **1** a shirt; blouse. **2** a blouse made of piña cloth, white or dyed, embroidered, and with loose sleeves, worn by the native women of the Philippine Islands.

cam|i|sade (kam′ə sād′), *n.* = camisado.

cam|i|sa|do (kam′ə sā′dō), *n., pl.* **-dos**. *Archaic.* an attack by night, originally one in which the soldiers wore shirts over their armor as a means of mutual recognition. [< Spanish *camisada* < *camisa* shirt < Late Latin *camīsia*]

ca|mise (kə mēs′). *n.* a kind of loose shirt or tunic. [< Arabic *qamīs* < Late Latin *camīsia*]

cam|i|sole (kam′ə sōl). *n.* **1** a woman's undergarment that is like the top part of a slip. **2** a loose jacket worn by women as a dressing gown. **3** a kind of jacket with sleeves, once worn by men. **4** a kind of strait jacket with long sleeves which can be tied behind the back. [< French *camisole* < Spanish *camisola* (diminutive) < *camisa* shirt < Late Latin *camīsia*]

cam|let (kam′lit), *n.* **1** a beautiful cloth of silk and wool made in the Orient. **2** a strong, waterproof fabric. **3** a garment of either of these fabrics. [< French *camelot* < Arabic *khamlat* fringed, velvety garment]

cam|le|teen (kam′lə tēn′). *n.* **1** an imitation camlet. **2** a camlet of an inferior kind.

cam|o (kam′ō), *adj., n.* **—*adj.*** having the colors of military camouflage, especially on clothing: *a camo shirt or jacket.* **—*n.*** a garment or other item with a camouflage pattern. [< *camo*(uflage)]

ca|mo|gie (kə mō′gē), *n.* a game similar to field hockey, played by women in Ireland; a form of hurling. [< Irish Gaelic *camóg* the stick used in this game, hurley]

cam|o|mile (kam′ə mīl), *n.* **1** a plant whose daisylike flowers and leaves are sometimes dried and used in medicine. Camomile belongs to the composite family. **2** any one of several allied plants. Also, **chamomile**. [< Late Latin *camomilla,* alteration of Latin *chamaemēlon* < Greek *chamaímēlon* (literally) earth apple < *chamaí* on the ground + *mêlon* apple]

Ca|mor|ra (kəmôr′ə, -mor′-), *n.* a secret society formed in Naples, Italy, about 1820 that developed into a powerful political organization. Later it was associated with blackmail, robbery, and other illegal activities. [< Italian *camorra;* origin uncertain]

ca|mor|ra (kə môr′ə, -mor′-), *n.* a secret society like the Camorra.

Ca|mor|rism (kə môr′iz əm, -mor′-), *n.* the practices of the Camorra. **—Ca|mor′rist**, *n.*

cam|ou|flage** (kam′ə fläzh), *n., v.,* **-flaged**, **-flaging**. **—*n. **1** a disguise or false appearance in order to conceal; protective coloration. The white fur of a polar bear is a natural camouflage; it prevents the bear's being easily seen against the snow. **2a** giving soldiers, weapons, vehicles, planes, or ships a false appearance to conceal them from the enemy. Camouflage may cause an object to blend with its background or to appear to be something different from what it actually is. **b** the materials or other means by which this is done: *The guns were hidden by a camouflage of earth and branches.*

—*v.t.* to give a false appearance to in order to conceal; disguise: *to camouflage a plain sponge cake with frosting. The hunters were camouflaged with branches so that they blended with the trees.* (*Figurative.*) *The boy camouflaged his embarrassment by laughing.* **—*v.i.*** to engage in camouflage; conceal by or as if by camouflage: *We camouflaged in the bushes and no one saw us.* [< French *camouflage* < *camoufler* to disguise < Italian *camuffare*]**—cam′ou|flag′er**, *n.*

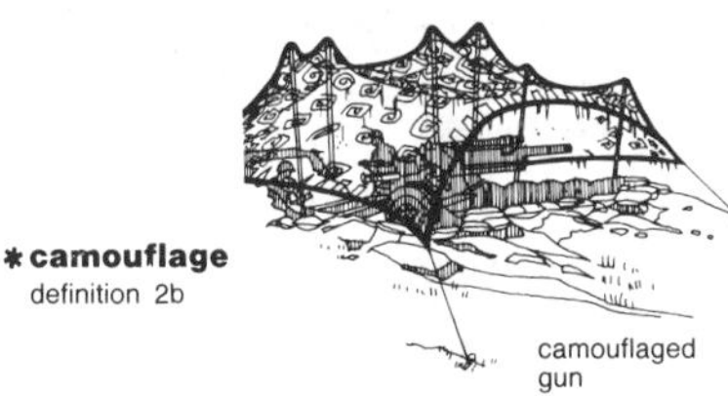

***camouflage**
definition 2b

ca|mou|flet (kȧ mä fle′), *n.* a mine containing a small charge of powder, placed in a wall of earth between the galleries of besieged and besieger to explode and bury, suffocate, or cut off the retreat of the miner on the opposite side. [< French *camouflet* puff of smoke]

cam|ou|fleur (kam′ə flėr), *n.* a person skilled in military camouflage; camouflager. [< French *camoufleur* < *camoufler* to camouflage]

camp[1] (kamp), *n., v.* **—*n.*** **1** a group of tents, huts, or other shelters where people live for a time: *A marching army usually makes camp every night.* **2a** a place where a camp is: *There is a Boy Scout camp at the edge of the lake.* **b** an area where an army sets up temporary shelter. **c** a fortified, usually permanent camp, as one erected by ancient Roman soldiers. **d** a permanent military station. **3** the persons living in a camp: *The camp was awakened by the bugler.* **4** any tent, hut, or other shelter to live in for a

Pronunciation Key: hat, āge, cãre, fär; let, ēqual, tėrm; it, īce; hot, ōpen, ôrder; **oil**, **out**; cup, pu̇t, rüle; **ch**ild; lo**ng**; **th**in; **ᴛʜ**en; **zh**, measure; **ə** represents **a** in about, **e** in taken, **i** in pencil, **o** in lemon, **u** in circus.

time: *Our family lives at an old hunting camp in the woods during the summer.* **5** an outdoor life with very simple shelter; camping. **6** *Figurative.* a group of people who agree or work together or their point of view or beliefs, usually aggressively supported as a doctrine or creed: *The election of a new president divided the voters into two opposing camps. Whether he will rejoin the Soviet "camp" is all but academic, for on every single important international issue he is already on the Soviet side* (Wall Street Journal). **7** *Figurative.* army service; military life: *Sir Edmund Spenser spent his life between camp and court.* **8** *Western U.S.* a town that has sprung up in a mining area.
—*v.i.* **1** to put up tents, huts, or other shelters for a time; make a camp: *The hunters camped by the lake at dark.* **2** to live in a camp for a time: *The Boy Scout troop camped at the foot of the mountain for two weeks.* **3** to live simply, as one does in a tent: *We camped in the empty house until our furniture arrived.*
—*v.t.* to establish in a camp: *to camp troops along a riverside.*
break camp, to pack up tents and equipment: *We broke camp early in the morning to return home.*
camp out, a to live in the open in a tent or camp: *We camped out for a week by the lake.* **b** to spend the night outdoors: *We camped out in the field this night* (George Washington).
in the same camp, in agreement; working together: *Both Britain and Greece—besides being traditionally in the same camp—are members of the Atlantic Alliance* (London Times).
[< French *camp* < Italian *campo* < Latin *campus* field. See etym. of doublets **campo**[1], **campo**[2], **campus**.]

camp[2] (kamp), *n., pl.* **camp**, *adj., v. Slang.* —*n.* anything valued or admired because it is usually considered trivial or outmoded: *Turn-of-the-century postcards are camp; so is ... the 1933 movie King Kong* (Time).
—*adj.* characterized by camp; given to or admiring things usually considered trivial, unsophisticated, or outmoded; campy: *You have camp taste if you can discuss authoritatively the early ... comic books* (Saturday Night).
—*v.t., v.i.* to admire, produce, or fill with camp; be or make campy: *The blurb calls The Day We were Mostly Butterflies "camped up Jane Austenese"* (Punch).
camp it up, to act in a manner considered camp; behave exaggeratedly or affectedly: *He [Tiny Tim] minces and swishes and twitters and flutters and flirts and camps it up* (Maclean's).
[origin uncertain; perhaps special use of *camp*[1]]

cAMP (no periods), cyclic AMP.

cam|pa|gna (käm pän′yə), *n.* **1** level, open country. **2** a military campaign. [< Italian *campagna;* see etym. under **campaign**]

cam|paign (kam pān′), *n., v.* —*n.* **1** a number of connected military operations in a war which are aimed at some special purpose: *The general planned a campaign to capture the enemy's most important city.* **2** *Figurative.* a number of connected activities to do or get something; planned course of action for some special purpose: *Our town had a campaign to raise money for a new hospital.* **3** (in glassmaking and metallurgy) the period of time a furnace remains in operation, from the first firing to the extinguishing of the fire when the refractory brick walls are worn out.
—*v.i.* to take part or serve in a campaign; go on a campaign: (*Figurative.*) *The candidates for mayor campaigned by sending out letters to voters and speaking at public meetings. The old soldier had campaigned in nearly every country in Europe.*
[< French *campagne* open country < Italian *campagna* < Late Latin *campānea* level country < Latin *campus* field. See etym. of doublet **champaign.**] —**cam|paign′er,** *n.*

***campaign hat**, a hat worn in a military campaign, especially a felt hat with a broad brim and four indentations formerly used by the United States Army and Marine Corps.

***campaign hat**

campaign medal or **ribbon**, a medal (or ribbon) awarded to persons who have served in a particular military campaign.

cam|pa|ne|ro (kam′pə när′ō), *n., pl.* **-ros** (-rōz). a South American bellbird. [< Spanish *campanero* < *campana* bell < Late Latin *campāna*]

Cam|pa|ni|an (kam pā′nē ən), *adj., n.* —*adj.* of or having to do with Campania, a region in southern Italy: *The Greeks dominated the whole Campanian coast for the sixth century B.C.* (Harper's). —*n.* an inhabitant of Campania.

cam|pan|i|form (kam pan′ə fôrm), *adj.* bell-shaped. [< Late Latin *campāna* bell + English *-form*]

***cam|pa|ni|le** (kam′pə nē′lē), *n., pl.* **-ni|les, -ni|li** (-nē′lē). a tower built to contain a bell or bells. It may be a separate building. [< Italian *campanile* < *campana* bell < Late Latin *campāna*]

***campanile**

cam|pa|nol|o|ger (kam′pə nol′ə jər), *n.* = campanologist.

cam|pa|no|log|i|cal (kam′pə nə loj′ə kəl), *adj.* having to do with campanology.

cam|pa|nol|o|gist (kam′pə nol′ə jist), *n.* a person skilled in the art of campanology.

cam|pa|nol|o|gy (kam′pə nol′ə jē), *n.* **1** the art or practice of bell ringing. **2** the study of bell founding. [< Late Latin *campāna* bell + English *-logy*]

cam|pan|u|la (kam pan′yə lə), *n.* any of a large genus of plants with bell-shaped, blue, purple, pink, or white flowers, such as the bluebell and Canterbury bell; bellflower. [< Late Latin *campānula* (diminutive) < *campāna* bell]

cam|pan|u|la|ceous (kam pan′yə lā′shəs), *adj.* belonging to the bellflower family.

cam|pan|u|late (kam pan′yə lāt, -lit), *adj.* bell-shaped (applied to parts of plants, especially to the corolla).

camp bed, a light, folding bed or cot.

Camp|bell|ite (kam′bə līt, kam′ə-), *n.* a member of the Disciples of Church, a congregational Christian church founded, 1809, in Pennsylvania by Thomas and Alexander Campbell: *The Campbellites believe that laymen have the right and duty to preach* (Time). [American English < Alexander *Campbell,* 1788-1866, an American clergyman + *-ite*[1]]

camp chair, a lightweight folding chair, often of canvas.

camp|craft (kamp′kraft′, -kräft′), *n.* knowledge about how to camp; skill in living out-of-doors with very simple shelter.

Cam|pea|chy wood (kam pē′chē), = logwood. [< *Campeche,* a state in Mexico]

camp|er (kam′pər), *n.* **1** a person who camps out or lives in a camp. **2** a vehicle, such as a small trailer, or a trailerlike room attached to the bed of a pickup truck, fitted out for camping with bunks, stove, and other facilities.

cam|pe|si|no (käm′pā sē′nō), *n., pl.* **-nos.** *Spanish.* an agricultural worker; farmer; peasant.

cam|pes|tral (kam pes′trəl), *adj.* having to do with or growing in the fields: *... the fantastic head of his own Party, living in secluded campestral concentration in his country house southeast of Paris* (New Yorker). [< Latin *campester, -tris* having to do with a level field (< *campus* field) + English *-al*[1]]

cam|pes|tri|an (kam pes′trē ən), *adj.* = campestral.

cam|pes|trine (kam pes′trin), *adj.* = campestral.

camp|fire (kamp′fīr′), *n.* **1** a fire in a camp for cooking or warmth. **2** a social gathering of soldiers, scouts, or members of a club.

campfire girl, a member of the Camp Fire Girls.

Camp Fire Girls, an organization founded in 1910 to help girls develop good health, character, citizenship, and usefulness to others.

camp follower, **1** a man or woman who follows and attaches to a camp or marching army, without being in military service, especially as a prostitute or peddler. **2** *Figurative.* any person who attaches himself for profit or advantage to a more important person, or to a group, or a cause: *I consider it an intolerable humiliation for any Asian-African country to degrade itself as a camp follower of one or the other side* (New York Times).

camp|ground (kamp′ground′), *n.* **1** a place for camping, now especially a public park with campsites, fireplaces for cooking, and other facilities. **2** a place where a camp meeting is held.

cam|phene (kam′fēn, kam fēn′), *n.* a terpene, solid at ordinary temperatures, used as a substitute for camphor. *Formula:* $C_{10}H_{16}$ [< *camph*(or) + *-ene*]

cam|phine (kam′fēn, kam fēn′), *n.* a purified oil of turpentine, formerly burned in lamps. [< *camph*(or) + *ine*[2]]

cam|phire (kam′fīr), *n.* the henna plant (a faulty translation from the Hebrew in *The Song of Solomon* 1:14, 4:13). [variant of *camphor*]

cam|phol (kam′fol, -fōl), *n.* = borneol.

cam|phol|ic (kam fol′ik, -fō′lik), *adj.* related to or containing camphol.

cam|phor (kam′fər), *n.* **1** a white substance with a strong odor and a bitter taste. Camphor is used in medicine, to protect clothes from moths, and in the manufacture of celluloid. Most camphor is a crystalline substance obtained from the camphor tree. *Formula:* $C_{10}H_{16}O$ **2** any one of various terpene derivatives. [< Medieval Latin *camphora* < Arabic *kāfūr,* ultimately < Malay *kapur*]

cam|pho|ra|ceous (kam′fə rā′shəs), *adj.* of the nature of or resembling camphor.

cam|phor|ate (kam′fə rāt), *v.t.,* **-at|ed, -at|ing.** to impregnate or treat with camphor; add camphor to.

cam|phor|at|ed oil (kam′fə rā tid), a solution of camphor in cottonseed oil, applied as a counterirritant.

camphor ball, a small ball made of camphor, naphthalene, or the like, and used to keep moths from clothing, blankets, and other woolens.

cam|phor|ic (kam fôr′ik, -for′-), *adj.* of or derived from camphor; containing camphor.

camphor ice, *U.S.* a solid preparation of camphor containing also white wax, castor oil, and spermaceti, used as an ointment.

camphor tree, **1** an evergreen tree of the laurel family, found chiefly in Formosa, Japan, and China, from which camphor is obtained. **2** a tree of the East Indies, from which borneol is obtained.

Cam|pi|gnian (kam pin′yən), *adj.* of or having to do with the mesolithic and neolithic remains found at Campigny, a town in France, or their period.

cam|pim|e|ter (kam pim′ə tər), *n.* an apparatus for measuring visual properties, such as the range of color sensitivity of the retina. [< Latin *campus* field + English *-meter*]

cam|pi|met|ri|cal (kam′pə met′rə kəl), *adj.* of or having to do with campimetry.

cam|pim|e|try (kam pim′ə trē), *n.* the measuring of retinal areas with a campimeter.

cam|pi|on (kam′pē ən), *n.* any one of a genus of plants of the pink family, with red, pink, or white flowers. [perhaps < Latin *campus* field]

camp meeting, a religious gathering held outdoors or in a tent, sometimes lasting several days: *They'll all be taken with a very pious streak, to go to camp meeting* (Harriet Beecher Stowe).

cam|po[1] (kam′pō, käm′-), *n., pl.* **-pi** (-pē). (in Italy) a central square in a town: *The genius ... worked with a bad mixture, in the bright light of the campo, among the beggars, in orange-vendors, and the passing gondolas* (New Yorker). [< Italian *campo* (originally) field < Latin *campus.* See etym. of doublets **camp, campo**[2], **campus.**]

cam|po[2] (kam′pō, käm′-), *n., pl.* **-pos.** (in South America) a grassy plain, especially one surrounded by dense forest. [< Spanish, Italian *campo* field, open country < Latin *campus.* See etym. of doublets **camp, campo**[1], **campus.**]

cam|po|de|id (kam pō′dē id), *n., pl.* **-id** or **-ids.** any one of a genus of eyeless insects having three pairs of legs, no wings, and an abdomen in ten segments ending in two long filaments. [< New Latin *Campodea* the genus name < Greek *kampē* caterpillar]

cam|pong (käm pong′, käm′pong), *n.* = kampong.

cam|po|ree (kam′pə rē′), *n.* a gathering or outing by boy scouts or girl scouts of a district: *Scouts helped stress the importance of protecting the nation's ... forests, grasslands, and wildlife. They put up posters, made field trips, and held camporees to aid the effort* (Joseph P. Anderson). [< *camp* + (jamb)*oree*]

cam|po san|to (kam′pō san′tō), *Southwestern U.S.* a cemetery. [< Spanish *campo santo* (literally) holy field]

camp-out (kamp′out′), *n.* an occasion of camping out: *They let some other father take their sons and Scout friends to weekend campouts* (Time).

camp robber, *Canadian Informal.* the Canada jay, so called from its habit of stealing food from camps.

camp|shed (kamp′shed′), *v.,* **-shed|ded, -shed|ding,** *n.* —*v.t.* to face (the bank of a river or side of an embankment) with piles and planks.
—*n.* = campshot.

camp|shed|ding (kamp′shed′ing), *n.* = campshot.

camp|sheet|ing (kamp′shē′ting), *n.* = campshot.
camp|shot (kamp′shot′), *n.* piles or boards to support a riverbank. [origin unknown]
camp|site (kamp′sīt′), *n.* the site of a camp; a place suitable or used for camping.
camp|stool (kamp′stül′), *n.* a lightweight, folding seat.
camp|to|saur (kamp′tə sôr), *n.* one of a group of small (about four yards long), bipedal dinosaurs found in upper Jurassic strata: *This Camptosaur illustrates the generalized ornithopod type from which the later duckbilled dinosaurs evolved* (New Yorker). [< New Latin *Camptosaurus* the genus name < Greek *kamptós* bent + *saûros* lizard]
cam|pus (kam′pəs), *n.* **1** the grounds of a college, university, or school: *The main buildings on a campus usually include classroom buildings, an administration building, a library, a gymnasium, an athletic field and stadium, and dormitories* (John D. Millett). **2** college or university life; the academic world: *Anyone familiar with the campus today knows that many of its problems come from lack of Federal funds* (New York Times). **3** an open field used in ancient Rome for public games, military exercises, etc. [< Latin *campus* field, plain. See etym. of doublets **camp**, **campo**[1], **campo**[2].]
campus school, = laboratory school.
camp|y (kam′pē), *adj.* **camp|i|er, camp|i|est.** *Slang.* appealing to camp taste; charmingly or amusingly trivial, unsophisticated, or outmoded: *"The Decline And Fall of the Entire World As Seen Through The Eyes of Cole Porter Revisited" simmers with campy humor* (Time).
—**camp′i|ly**, *adv.* —**camp′i|ness**, *n.*
cam|pyl|o|drome (kam pil′ə drōm), *adj.* = acrodrome. [< Greek *kampýlos* bent + *drómos* a running < *drameîn* run]
cam|py|lot|ro|pous (kam′pə lot′rə pəs), *adj. Botany.* having the nucellus and its integuments so curved that the micropyle is brought near the hilum of an ovule or seed. [< Greek *kampýlos* curved + *trépein* turn + English *-ous*]
cam|sha|chle (käm shä′ʜəl), *v.t. Scottish.* to twist out of shape; distort; make crooked. [< Gaelic *cam* crooked + English dialectal *shachle* to distort]
cam|shaft (kam′shaft′, -shäft′), *n.* a rod or shaft on which a cam is fastened, such as one in an internal-combustion engine by which the valves of the cylinders are opened and closed.
cam|shell (kam′shel), *n.* (in Orkney and Shetland Islands) cuttlefish bone. [origin unknown]
cam|stone (kam′stōn′), *n.* **1** (in Scotland) a common compact, whitish limestone. **2** a white or bluish-white clay used to whiten hearths, doorsteps, and walls. [origin uncertain]
cam wheel, a wheel, with its axis off center or its circumference not round, that operates as a cam.
cam|wood (kam′wu̇d′), *n.* = barwood.
can[1] (kan), *v., 1st and 3rd person* **can**, *2nd person* **can** *or (Archaic)* **canst;** *past tense* **could**.
—*v. auxiliary.* **1a** to be able to: *He can run fast. You can hear the echo of the mountain stream from our cottage in the woods.* **b** to know how to: *She can sew and cook. He can drive any make of car and overhaul any piece of machinery. You can do the job well if you try.* **2a** to have the right to: *Anyone can cross the street here. Anyone who has a license can drive a car in New York.* **b** to be allowed to; may: *You can take the test again soon.* **3** to feel inclined to: *There are many things I could wish to see otherwise. I could tell you a lot more about the accident.*
—*v.t., v.i. Obsolete.* to know.
[Old English *cann* know, know how, can]
▶**can, may.** The main distinction now is that *can* denotes ability, whereas *may* denotes probability or possibility: *It may be clear tomorrow. He may have been guilty.* In formal usage a distinction is sometimes made between *can* implying ability, and *may* implying permission: *May I go? You may if you wish. He can walk on crutches.* In informal usage this distinction is commonly ignored: *Can I go now? You can if you want to or you can stay.*
can[2] (kan), *n., v.,* **canned, can|ning.** —*n.* **1** a container, usually with a cover or lid and made of thin steel coated with tin: *a paint can, a trash can, a milk can, an oil can.* **2a** the amount that a can holds: *Add three cans of water to make the orange juice.* **b** the contents of a can: *a can of peaches. Mother served a can of beans for lunch.* **3** a drinking cup, especially one made of metal, such as a tankard or stein. **4** *U.S. Slang.* **a** a depth charge. **b** a destroyer: *Two old "cans," terriers of the fleet, had fought a good fight with their traditional verve, skill, and courage* (Atlantic). **5** *U.S. Slang.* **a** a jail; prison. **b** a toilet. **c** the buttocks.
—*v.t.* **1** to put in a can or jar to preserve: *Grandmother is canning fruit.* **2** to seal or enclose (nuclear fuel) in protective metal: *Zirconium is used in atomic plants for canning nuclear fuel elements, because it has the rare property of resisting the bombardment of neutrons* (London Times). **3** *Informal.* to drive (a golf ball) into the hole: *Lunn and Hill improved their positions at once, both approaching close to the hole and canning birdie putts* (London Times). **4** *U.S. Slang.* to dismiss from a job or expel from school; get rid of. **5** *Slang.* to do away with or cease doing (something): *Can the chatter.* **6** *Slang.* to make a recording of; put on a record or tape: *I tried once canning a talk but I found I could not stand the experience of repeating it* (John Ciardi). **7** *British Slang.* to make intoxicated.
carry the can, *Especially British Slang.* to take the blame or responsibility: *When a Cabinet Minister delegates to a civil servant, he carries the can* (David Frost).
in the can, *Informal.* (of motion-picture film) ready to show; completed: *There are already five new full-length motion pictures "in the can" and ready for release* (Newsweek).
[Old English *canne*, probably ultimately < Latin *canna* small vessel]
can., **1** canon. **2** canto.
Can., **1** Canada. **2** Canadian.
Ca|na (kā′nə), *n.* an ancient city in northern Palestine, identified as the scene of Christ's first miracle (in the Bible, John 2:1).
Ca|naan (kā′nən), *n.* **1** a region in Palestine between the Jordan River and the Mediterranean. God promised Canaan to Abraham and his descendants (in the Bible, Genesis 12:1-7). **2** *Figurative.* a land of promise. **3** the fourth of Ham's sons (in the Bible, Genesis 9:18; 10:15-19).
Ca|naan|ite (kā′nə nīt), *n.* **1** an inhabitant of Canaan before its conquest by the Hebrews. **2** the subfamily of Semitic languages that includes ancient Hebrew and Phoenician.
Ca|naan|it|ic (kā′nə nit′ik), *adj., n.* —*adj.* = Canaanitish. —*n.* = Canaanite (def. 2).
Ca|naan|it|ish (kā′nə nī′tish), *adj.* **1** belonging to Canaan (a region in Palestine). **2** of or like a Canaanite.
Canad., Canadian.
Can|a|da balsam (kan′ə də), a sticky, yellow resin obtained from the balsam fir tree. It is used in making lacquers and varnishes, and for mounting objects on glass slides to be examined under a microscope.
Canada Day, July 1, a national holiday in Canada in honor of the establishment of Canada in 1867. It was called Dominion Day until 1982.
Canada fleabane, = horseweed.
Canada goldenrod, the most abundant, widely distributed and typical of American goldenrods, having coarsely toothed, triple-nerved leaves. It sometimes attains a height of eight feet, and often grows in dense masses, monopolizing the soil.
Canada goose, a large, wild goose of North America, having a black head and neck, white throat and cheeks, and a brownish-gray body with gray underparts.
Canada grouse, = spruce grouse.
Canada hemp, a North American plant of the dogbane family; Indian hemp.
Canada jay, a North American bird having black and gray feathers and lacking a crest.
Canada lily, a common wild lily of eastern North America, having nodding yellow or red flowers; meadow lily.
Canada lynx, a North American wildcat with a short, black-tipped tail, larger than a bobcat. See picture under **lynx**.
Canada robin, = cedar waxwing.
Canada spruce grouse, = spruce grouse.
Canada thistle, a prickly European plant, now common as a weed in Canada and the United States. It is an herb of the composite family.
Canada wild rye, a variety of wild rye.
Ca|na|di|an (kə nā′dē ən), *adj., n.* —*adj.* of Canada or its people: *Canadian hospitality.*
—*n.* a person born or living in Canada: *Many Canadians speak both English and French, the country's two official languages.*
Ca|na|di|a|na (kə nā′dē ä′nə, -an′ə, -ā′nə), *n.* **1** a collection of books, documents, facts, or other literary material about Canada, especially its history: *The series of covers and illustrations he has painted for Maclean's since 1944 have been described as a "remarkable piece of Canadiana"* (Barbara Moon). **2** a collection of Canadian furniture, textiles, or other, usually handcrafted, products. **3** anecdotes, folklore, or other things about Canada or typical of Canada or Canadian culture.
Canadian bacon, boneless loin of pork that is smoked and cured.
Canadian English, English as used in Canada, especially by English Canadians.
***Canadian football**, the game of football as played in Canada, resembling both Rugby and American football.

***Canadian football**

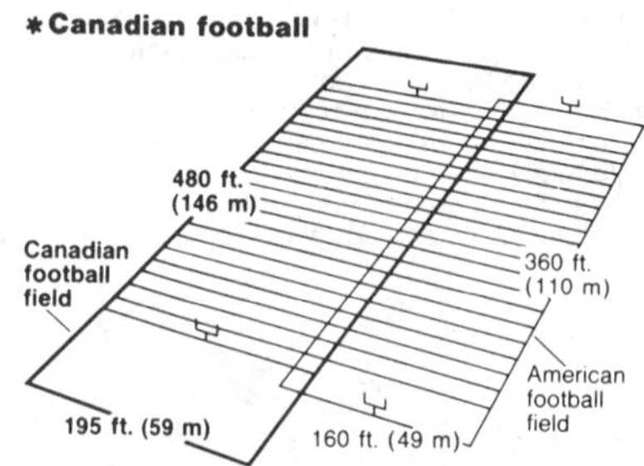

Canadian French, **1** form of French spoken by French-speaking Canadians. **2** French Canadians.
Canadian hemlock, = eastern hemlock.
Ca|na|di|an|ism (kə nā′dē ə niz′əm), *n.* **1** devotion or loyalty to Canada and to its customs and traditions: *The old frictions are withering away under the sun of a broader, wealthier Canadianism* (Maclean's). **2** a word, phrase, or meaning originating or more widely used in Canadian English than in other varieties of English: *He kissed his parents (calling his father "son pere," a Canadianism I have never figured out) and greeted us politely* (New Yorker). **3** a custom or trait peculiar to Canada.
Ca|na|di|an|ize (kə nā′dē ə nīz), *v.t.,* **-ized, -iz|ing.** to make Canadian in habits, customs, or character: *Sir Casimir had become so Canadianized that shortly before his death he remembered little of his mother tongue* (Peter Gzowski).
Canadian Legion, an organization of Canadian ex-servicemen similar to the American Legion. Its official name is Royal Canadian Legion.
Canadian Shield, a vast area of Pre-Cambrian rocks, rich in minerals occupying more than half of Canada from the Arctic Ocean to the Great Lakes, and flanking Hudson Bay in a U-shaped outline; Laurentian Plateau; Laurentian Shield: *A freak of geography, the Canadian Shield discouraged the type of gradual westward expansion that took place in the U.S.* (Wall Street Journal).
Canadian whisky or **whiskey** , a blended whiskey containing a high proportion of rye.
Ca|na|di|en (kȧ nȧ dyaɴ′; *Anglicized* kə nā′dē ən), *n., adj.* —*n.* a Canadian of French descent; French Canadian. —*adj.* of or having to do with Canadians of French descent; characteristic of Canadians of French descent: *Survival of a distinctly Canadien culture depends, finally, on the value that French Canadians place on it* (Maclean's). [< French *Canadien* Canadian]
Ca|na|di|enne (kȧ nȧ dyen′; *Anglicized* kə nā′dē ən), *n.* a French-Canadian girl or woman.
ca|nai|gre (kə nā′gər), *n.* a species of dock of the southwestern United States whose root yields tannin. [American English < American Spanish *cañaigre*]
ca|naille (kə nāl′; *French* kȧ nä′yə), *n.* the lowest class of people; rabble; riffraff. [< French *canaille* < Italian *canaglia* < *cane* dog < Latin *canis*]
ca|nal[1] (kə nal′), *n., v.,* **-nalled, -nal|ling** or **-naled, -nal|ing.** —*n.* **1a** a waterway dug across land for ships or small boats to go through: *More than 5,000 years ago the Chinese were controlling the Yellow River floods with dikes and the Chaldeans were building ziggurats and canals* (New York Times). SYN: watercourse. **b** a man-made ditch to carry water for irrigation. SYN: watercourse. **2a** a tube, duct, or the like, in the body of an animal or plant that carries liquid, air, or food or other solid matter from one part to another. The food that we eat goes through the alimentary canal. SYN: passage. **b** a tube whose chief function is to hold some liquid or gas, especially in the body: *the semicircular canals.* SYN: channel. **3** a long arm of a large body of water. **4** *Obsolete.* any channel of water; watercourse.
—*v.t.* **1** to dig or cut a canal through or across. **2** to furnish with canals.
[< Latin *canālis* trench, pipe < *canna* cane. See etym. of doublets **channel**, **kennel**[2].]
ca|nal[2] (kə nal′), *n.* any one of the long, dark, narrow markings seen on the planet Mars, and now believed by some scientists to be cracks

Pronunciation Key: hat, āge, cãre, fär; let, ēqual, tėrm; it, īce; hot, ōpen, ôrder; oil, out; cup, pu̇t, rüle; child; long; thin; ᴛʜen; zh, measure; ə represents **a** in about, **e** in taken, **i** in pencil, **o** in lemon, **u** in circus.

lined either with some type of plant life or with volcanic sand and dust. [< Italian *canali* channels, as applied to markings on Mars < Latin *canālis* trench]

ca|nal|age (kə nal′ij), *n.* **1** the construction of canals. **2** canals as means of transportation. **3** a charge for the use of a canal.

***canal boat** or **ca|nal|boat** (kə nal′bōt′), *n.* a long, narrow boat used on canals. Canal boats were formerly often pulled along by horses. *The Hendrika-Maria seemed rather stubby, as I suppose a canal boat should* (New Yorker).

***canal boat**

ca|nal-built (kə nal′bilt′), *adj.* built or adapted for use on a canal.

can|a|lic|u|lar (kan′ə lik′yə lər), *adj.* of or having to do with a canaliculus; resembling a canaliculus; minutely tubular: *... the special metamorphoses of the fibres into canalicular, or flattened cylindrical forms* (Francis Bell).

can|a|lic|u|late (kan′ə lik′yə lit, -lāt), *adj. Zoology, Botany.* having one or more longitudinal grooves or hollows; minutely channeled. [< Latin *canāliculātus* < *canāliculus* canaliculus]

can|a|lic|u|lat|ed (kan′ə lik′yə lā′tid), *adj.* = canaliculate: *canaliculated teeth.*

can|a|lic|u|la|tion (kan′ə lik′yə lā′shən), *n. Biology.* a minutely grooved formation; canaliculus.

can|a|lic|u|lus (kan′ə lik′yə ləs), *n., pl.* **-li** (-lī). a small canal or duct in the body. Canaliculi connect the lacunae (small cavities) in the bones. [< Latin *canāliculus* (diminutive) < *canālis* groove, canal]

ca|nal|i|form (kə nal′ə fôrm), *adj.* having the form of a canal or of a tube. [< Latin *canālis* canal + English *-form*]

ca|nal|i|za|tion (kə nal′ə zā′shən, kan′ə lə-), *n.* **1** the act of canalizing: *The joint Franco-German commission met for the first time at the Quai d'Orsay this morning to study plans for the canalization of the Moselle River* (London Times). **2** a system of canals: *the canalization of Holland and Venice.* **3** the draining of wounds by surgical means rather than by the use of tubes.

ca|nal|ize (kə nal′īz, kan′ə līz), *v.,* **-ized, -iz|ing.** — ***v.t.*** **1** to make a canal or canals through: *Hilly countries can be canalized by the construction of locks, tunnels, and bridged aqueducts.* **2** to make into or like a canal. **3** *Figurative.* to lead in a desired direction, so as to control or regulate; channel: *A traditional religion canalizes and routinizes the quest for salvation* (Harper's).
— ***v.i.*** to form new channels, especially of tissue for the passage of blood and other fluid.

ca|nal|ler (kə nal′ər), *n. U.S.* a person who works on canal boats, or who operates a lock or other facility of a canal.

canal lift or **incline**, an elevator or incline formerly used instead of a lock for transferring canal boats from one level to another.

canal rays, the rays of positively charged ions passing through holes in the cathode of a vacuum tube.

ca|nal|side (kə nal′sīd′), *adj.* on or at the side of a canal: *The bullets bit into the canalside dirt 20 feet in front of him* (Newsweek).

can|a|pé (kan′ə pā, -pē), *n.* a cracker or thin piece of toast or bread spread with a seasoned mixture of such appetizers as olives, meats, fish, or cheese, and served as an appetizer: *Canapés are served with cocktails and aperitifs before dinner.* [< French *canapé* couch, sofa; (originally) a couch with curtains of mosquito netting < Old French *canape;* see etym. under **canopy**]

ca|nard (kə närd′), *n., v.* — ***n.*** **1** a false rumor; exaggerated report; hoax: *After World War I, the canard spread that France had even collected rent for the use of trenches on its soil* (Time). **2a** an airplane with its stabilizer and elevators forward of the wing: *So as to secure a reasonable centre of gravity, it* [*the airplane*] *is likely to be of the canard type with its tail organs forward* (New Scientist). **b** the stabilizer and elevators on such an airplane: *SCAT 17 ... has a delta wing and a canard, or balancing surface, at the nose* (Scientific American).
— ***v.i.*** **1** to fly or float about, or circulate as a canard or false report: *certain stories canarding about the hotels.* **2** to imitate or produce the peculiar harsh cry of the duck, as an unskilled player on a wind instrument: *Right before the window ... is a ragged starveling canarding on a clarinet* (Fraser's Magazine).
[< Middle French *canard* duck]

Ca|na|rese (kä′nə rēz′, -rēs′), *n., pl.* **-rese,** *adj.* = Kanarese.

Ca|nar|i|an (kə năr′ē ən), *adj., n.* — ***adj.*** of or having to do with the Canary Islands.
— ***n.*** a native or inhabitant of the Canary Islands.

Ca|nar|ies Current (kə năr′ēz), a cool southward current in the North Atlantic, flowing past Spain, northwestern Africa, and the Canary Islands.

ca|nar|y (kə năr′ē), *n., pl.* **-nar|ies,** *adj.* — ***n.*** **1** Also, **canary bird.** a small songbird, originally from the Canary Islands. The canary belongs to the same family as the finch and is often kept as a pet. The wild bird is greenish, but the domestic bird is usually yellow. **2** a light yellow. **3** a light, sweet, white wine from the Canary Islands. **4** Also, **canaries.** a lively dance, possibly of Spanish origin, especially of the 1500's. **5** *Slang.* a female singer with an orchestra or band: *A brand-new canary trills during dinner and supper in the Maisonette* (New Yorker).
— ***adj.*** light-yellow; canary-colored.
[< French *canarie* < *Canarie* (the chief island of the group) < Spanish *Canaria* < Latin *Canāria* (*īnsula*) (Isle) of Dogs (because of the large dogs found there) < *canis* dog]

canary creeper, a creeper with yellow flowers.

canary grass, any one of several grasses, especially a species native to the Canary Islands whose seed is used as food for pet birds, and the reed canary grass, a species grown in the Northern Hemisphere for use as fodder.

canary seed, the seed of canary grass, used as food for birds; birdseed.

canary stone, a yellow, somewhat rare variety of carnelian.

canary yellow, a light yellow.

ca|nas|ta (kə nas′tə), *n.* **1** a card game similar to rummy, played with two decks of cards plus four jokers. The players try to earn as many points as possible by melding sets of seven or more cards. **2** the set or meld of seven cards in this game: *Seven fours make a canasta score, but a run of four through ten does not count. A seven card set is called a canasta* (Lillian Frankel). [< Spanish *canasta* basket]

ca|nas|ter (kə nas′tər), *n.* a rough kind of tobacco. [< dialectal Spanish *canastra* basket (because it was imported in baskets)]

ca|naut (kə nôt′), *n.* (in India) the side of a tent, or of a canvas enclosure. [Anglo-Indian < Hindustani, or Arabic *ganāt*]

can buoy, a short, broad, cylindrical buoy. See picture under **buoy**.

canc., **1** canceled. **2** cancellation.

can|can (kan′kan′), *n., v.,* **-canned, -can|ning.**
— ***n.*** a gay kind of dance, a form of quadrille, marked by extravagant kicking and leaping.
— ***v.i.*** to dance the cancan: *Nearby a row of hilariously curved hoofers cancanned* (Time).
[< French *cancan,* probably < a childish pronunciation of *canard* duck (from the dance steps that resemble a duck's waddle)]

can|cel (kan′səl), *v.,* **-celed, -cel|ing** or (*especially British*) **-celled, -cel|ling,** *n.* — ***v.t.*** **1a** to put an end to, set aside, or withdraw; do away with; stop: *The teacher canceled his order for the books. She canceled her appointment with the doctor.* **b** to abolish or annul the commitments of (a legal obligation); revoke; rescind: *The decision of the judge canceled the contract.* SYN: nullify. **2** *Figurative.* to make up for; compensate for; balance; neutralize: *The little boy's sweet smile canceled much of his mischief.* **3a** to cross out: *to cancel an ambiguous phrase in a speech.* **b** to mark, stamp, or punch (something) so that it cannot be used again: *The post office cancels the stamps on a letter.* **4** *Mathematics.* **a** to reduce (a fraction) by dividing both the numerator and the denominator by the same quantity. **b** to reduce (an equation) by dividing both members by a common factor. **5** *Printing.* to omit (a page, article, or the like) after it has been set in type or printed. **6** *Music.* to suspend the power of (a sharp or a flat) by inserting the sign of the natural.
— ***v.i.*** *Mathematics.* **1** to reduce a fraction by dividing both the numerator and the denominator by the same quantity. **2** to reduce an equation by dividing both members by a common factor.
— ***n.*** **1a** the act of canceling, erasing, or rescinding: *A cancel of an order is a rare occurrence.* **b** a canceled part. **c** the mark or marks made in canceling a stamp, ticket, or other receipt. **2** *Printing.* **a** the omission of a page, article, or the like, before publication. **b** the omitted part. **c** that which is substituted for the omitted part.
cancel out, a to do away with a plan, commitment, or the like: *Tool orders ... are being let on a month-to-month basis so the company can cancel out at minimum cost if it decides to scrap its program* (Newsweek). **b** to become neutralized: *If all the shells containing electrons are completely filled, the effects cancel out and each atom has a resultant zero magnetic moment* (W. D. Corner).
[< Latin *cancellāre* cross out with latticed lines < *cancellī* crossbars (diminutive) < *cancer,* alteration of *carcer* (originally) network, grating] — **can′cel|a|ble,** *especially British,* **can′cel|la|ble,** *adj.* — **can′cel|er,** *especially British,* **can′cel|ler,** *n.*

can|cel|late (kan′sə lāt), *adj.* resembling latticework; cancellous.

can|cel|lat|ed (kan′sə lā′tid), *adj.* = cancellate.

can|cel|la|tion (kan′sə lā′shən), *n.* **1** a canceling or being canceled; crossing out; striking out: *cancellation of a baseball game because of rain.* **2** marks made when something is canceled or crossed out: *In spite of cancellations and interlineations, the original words can easily be distinguished* (Macaulay). **3** something that is canceled.

can|cel|lous (kan′sə ləs), *adj. Anatomy.* having an open, latticed, or porous, structure; cancellate: *cancellous bone. In flat* (*cancellous*) *bones as of the skull and in the ends of long bones, the interior lacks regular systems and is of more spongy texture* (Tracy I. Storer). [< Latin *cancellī* (see etym. under **cancel**) + English *-ous*]

can|cer (kan′sər), *n., v.* — ***n.*** **1** a very harmful growth in the body; malignant tumor. Cancer tends to spread and destroy the healthy tissues and organs of the body. Cancer is a change in the normal growth of cells, but the causes have not yet been fully determined. *A great many cancers can be cured, but only if properly treated before they have begun to spread or "colonize" in other parts of the body* (Newsweek). **2** any of several diseases characterized by such abnormal growth of cells, such as carcinoma, sarcoma, and leukemia. **3** *Figurative.* an evil or harmful thing that tends to spread: *The increasing use of narcotics is a cancer in modern society. The existence of slums is a cancer in many large cities.*
— ***v.t.*** to corrode or eat (its way) in the manner and with the steadily destructive persistency of a cancer: *The Struldbrug of* [*Jonathan*] *Swift ... was a wreck, a shell, that had been burned hollow and cancered by the fierce furnace of life* (Thomas De Quincey).
[< Latin *cancer* crab, tumor. See etym. of doublets **canker, chancre.**]

Can|cer (kan′sər), *n., genitive* (def. 2) **Can|cri.** **1** the tropic of Cancer. **2** a northern constellation shaped somewhat like a crab. **3** the fourth sign of the zodiac; Crab. The sun enters Cancer about June 21. **4** a person born under the sign of Cancer.

can|cer|ate (kan′sə rāt), *v.i.,* **-at|ed, -at|ing.** to become cancerous.

can|cer|a|tion (kan′sə rā′shən), *n.* a growing cancerous or into a cancer.

can|cered (kan′sərd), *adj.* having cancer.

can|cer|i|za|tion (kan′sər ə zā′shən), *n.* = canceration.

can|cer|o|gen|ic (kan′sər ə jen′ik), *adj.* = carcinogenic.

can|cer|o|pho|bi|a (kan′sər ə fō′bē ə), *n.* fear of contracting cancer.

can|cer|ous (kan′sər əs), *adj.* **1** like cancer: *a cancerous tumor.* **2** having cancer: *a cancerous liver.*

can|cer-root (kan′sər rüt′, -rųt′), *n.* any plant of several herbs without green foliage and parasitic upon the roots of trees, such as the beechdrops.

cancer stick, *Slang.* a cigarette: *Nor for that matter do we stone Florrie Lindley for trafficking in cancer sticks at the corner shop* (London Guardian).

can|cha (kän′chä), *n. American Spanish.* **1** an enclosure for cattle or other herded animals. **2** a court for playing jai alai or handball: *The game is played on a ... cancha, with high walls on three sides* (Edwin Pope). **3** a yard used for cockfights.

can|cio|ne|ro (kän′chō nē′rō), *n., pl.* **-ros.** a medieval anthology of Spanish and Portuguese lyric poetry. [< Spanish *cancionero* < *canción* song]

Can|cri (kang′krī), *n.* genitive of **Cancer** (the constellation).

can|cri|form (kang′krə fôrm), *adj.* **1** = crablike. **2** = cancerous. [< Latin *cancrī,* plural of *cancer* crab; tumor + English *-form*]

can|crine (kang′krin), *adj.* having the appearance or qualities of a crab; crablike: *cancrine verse, which reads the same way backwards and forwards.* [< Latin *cancer* crab + English *-ine*[1]]

can|cri|nite (kang′krə nīt), *n.* a silicate and carbonate mineral containing sodium, calcium, and aluminum, occurring in various volcanic rocks and often bright yellow in color. [< Count *Cancrin,* 1774-1845, a Russian minister of finance + English *-ite*[1]]

can|criv|o|rous (kang kriv′ər əs), *adj.* crab-eating. [< Latin *cancrī,* plural of *cancer* crab + *vorāre* devour + English *-ous*]

can|cri|zans (kang′krə zənz), *adj.* **1** going or moving backward, like a crab. **2** *Music.* designating a canon in which the theme or subject is repeated backward instead of forward. [< Medieval Latin *cancrizans, -antis,* present participle of *cancrizare* go backward like a crab < Latin *cancrī,* plural of *cancer* crab; tumor]

can|croid (kang′kroid), *adj., n.* —*adj.* **1** resembling cancer: *a cancroid tumor.* **2** resembling a crab.
—*n.* a type of skin cancer of comparatively low malignancy.

can|del|a (kan del′ə, -dē′lə), *n.* a unit for measuring the strength or intensity of light, equal to 1/60 of the radiating power of one square centimeter of a black body at the temperature at which platinum solidifies (1772°C.); new candle. It replaced the international candle in 1948, but was not officially adopted in the United States until 1963. [< Latin *candēla* candle]

can|de|la|bra (kan′də lä′brə), *n.* **1** = candelabrum. **2** a plural of **candelabrum**.

* **can|de|la|brum** (kan′də lä′brəm, -lā′-), *n., pl.* **-bra** or **-brums**. an ornamental candlestick with several branches for candles. [< Latin *candēlābrum* < *candēla;* see etym. under **candle**]
▶The plural **candelabra** is sometimes understood as a singular with the plural form, *candelabras.*

* **candelabrum**

can|de|lil|la (kan′də lil′ə), *n.* a shrub of Mexico and southwestern United States which is the source of candelilla wax. [< Mexican Spanish *candelilla* (literally) little candle (diminutive) < Spanish *candela* candle < Latin *candēla*]

candelilla wax, a wax obtained from the candelilla, used industrially for such things as polishes, varnishes, insulation, and phonograph records.

can|dent (kan′dənt), *adj.* **1** softly gleaming: *Memories arise and the old garret is suffused with a candent glow* (New York Times). **2** glowing with heat; at a white heat. [< Latin *candēns, -entis,* present participle of *candēre* glow white with heat]

can|des|cence (kan des′əns), *n.* candescent state; dazzling whiteness or brightness: *the clear candescence of country snow* (Rhoda Broughton).

can|des|cent (kan des′ənt), *adj.* glowing with heat; incandescent. [< Latin *candēscēns, -entis,* present participle of *candēscere* begin to glow < *candēre* glow with heat] —**can|des′cent|ly**, *adv.*

c. & f., cost and freight.

can|did (kan′did), *adj., n.* —*adj.* **1** saying openly what one really thinks; frank and sincere; outspoken: *a candid reply. Please be candid with me. Save me from the candid friend* (George Canning). SYN: truthful, straightforward, open. See syn. under **frank**[1]. **2** fair; impartial: *a candid decision.* SYN: unbiased, just. **3** not posed: *a candid photograph of children playing. Including ... pictures of noted musicians and of audiences, taken mostly in the candid manner, the show is an interesting demonstration of photographic opportunities in the musical world* (New York Times). **4** *Archaic.* pure; stainless; innocent. **5** *Obsolete.* white.
—*n.* an unposed photograph: *The [camera] will ... give you so much photographic fun, so many opportunities for those once-in-a-lifetime candids* (New Yorker).
[< Latin *candidus* white, clear; pure, sincere < *candēre* to shine, glow] —**can′did|ly**, *adv.* —**can′did|ness**, *n.*

can|di|da|cy (kan′də də sē), *n.* the fact or condition of being a candidate: *Please support my candidacy for class president.*

can|di|date (kan′də dāt, -dit), *n.* **1** a person who seeks, or is proposed for, some office or honor: *There are three candidates for president of the club.* **2** a person who is studying for a degree: *a doctoral candidate.* **3** an applicant for a position: *There were twenty candidates for the job.* [< Latin *candidātus* (originally) clothed in white (toga) < *candidus* white; candid]
— ***Syn.*** **1 Candidate, aspirant, nominee** mean a person who seeks office, honor, or the like. **Candidate** applies to someone who is proposed for it, by himself or others: *I think my candidate for mayor has the backing of the majority of our citizens.* **Aspirant** implies that he wants it because he is ambitious or believes himself specially qualified: *One of the aspirants for the governorship does not have a good labor record.* **Nominee** applies to one who contends for it as the chosen representative of a party or group: *The nominee of our party is a man who has devoted his life to public service.*

can|di|date|ship (kan′də dit ship), *n.* = candidacy.

can|di|da|ture (kan′də də chər, -dā′-), *n. British.* candidacy: *At one time his candidature seemed likely to lead to further divisions in the party* (London Times).

candid camera, **1** a small camera with a fast lens for photographing persons unposed, and often unaware that their picture is being taken. **2** any very small camera.

can|di|di|a|sis (kan′də dī′ə sis), *n.* = moniliasis (def. 1). [< New Latin *Candida* the genus name of the fungus causing moniliasis (< Latin *candidus* white) + *-iasis*]

can|died (kan′dēd), *adj.* **1** cooked in sugar; glazed with sugar: *candied sweet potatoes.* **2** *Figurative.* made sweet or agreeable: *candied words of praise.* SYN: honeyed. **3** preserved or encrusted with sugar: *candied ginger. I roamed about in a daze, smelling the popcorn and candied apples* (Atlantic). **4** turned into sugar: *candied honey.* SYN: crystallized.

Can|di|ot (kan′dē ot), *adj., n.* —*adj.* = Cretan. —*n.* = Cretan. [< Italian *Candia* Crete (< Arabic *khandeh*) + French *-ote,* a noun suffix < Latin *-ōta* < Greek *-ōtēs* native of]

Can|di|ote (kan′dē ōt), *adj., n.* = Candiot.

can|dle (kan′dəl), *n., v.,* **-dled, -dling.** —*n.* **1** a stick of wax or tallow with a wick in it, burned to give light: *There are ten candles on his birthday cake. How far that little candle throws its beams* (Shakespeare). **2** anything shaped or used like a candle. Sulfur candles are burned to disinfect rooms. **3** any one of various units used at different times for measuring the intensity of a light: **a** = candela. **b** Also, **international candle**. a former unit equal to the light from five square millimeters of platinum when heated to its melting point (1772°C.). Its light is almost as strong as the light from a standard candle. **c** Also, **standard candle**. an older unit equal to the luminous intensity of a spermaceti candle ⅞ inches long and burning 120 grains each hour.
—*v.t.* to test (eggs) for freshness by holding them in front of a light: *The farmer candled the eggs before he sold them.*
burn the candle at both ends, to use up one's strength and resources rapidly: *You can't burn the candle at both ends, and make anything by it in the long run* (S. Bowles).
hold a candle to, to compare with: *The cake from the bakery did not hold a candle to the one Grandmother made.*
sell by inch of candle, to dispose of an item in an auction by letting it go to the last bid given before a small candle expires: *Selling by inch of candle was an old custom probably adopted from the French.*
worth the candle, worth the cost; worthwhile: *A continued strategy of functional integration in this area raises the question ... whether the game is worth the candle* (Manchester Guardian Weekly).
[Old English *candel* < Latin *candēla* < *candēre* to shine]

candle beam, **1** (in old churches) a beam between the chancel and the nave, on which the rood stood, with candles placed on each side of it. **2** a suspended beam of wood, often with sockets, to support candles.

can|dle|ber|ry (kan′dəl ber′ē), *n., pl.* **-ries.** **1a** = wax myrtle. **b** = bayberry. **2** = candlenut. **3** the fruit of any of these plants.

candle bomb, a small glass bubble filled with water, which when held in the flame of a candle explodes from the force of the steam that is generated.

candle coal, = cannel coal.

candle dipping, the process of manufacturing candles by dipping as distinguished from molding.

can|dle-end (kan′dəl end′), *n.* the remnant of a used candle.

can|dle|fish (kan′dəl fish′), *n., pl.* **-fish|es** or (*collectively*) **-fish.** **1** an edible fish of the west coast of North America, related to the smelt, so oily that when dried it may be burned like a candle. **2** = beshow.

can|dle-foot (kan′dəl fu̇t′), *n.* = foot-candle.

can|dle|hold|er (kan′dəl hōl′dər), *n.* = candlestick.

candle hour, a unit of light equivalent to the energy derived in one hour from the total light flux of a source of light of one candle power.

can|dle|light (kan′dəl līt′), *n.* **1** the light of a candle or candles: *the lamplight or the candlelight, and the fireglow* (London Times). **2** the time when candles are lighted; dusk; twilight; nightfall. **3** artificial light in general.

can|dle|lit (kan′dəl lit′), *adj.* lit by candlelight: *In the glittering, candlelit Hall of Mirrors, 150 guests dined* (Time).

Can|dle|mas (kan′dəl məs), *n.,* or **Candlemas Day**, February 2, a church festival in honor of the purification of the Virgin Mary and the presentation of the infant Jesus in the Temple. It is celebrated with lighted candles. [Old English *candelmæsse* < *candel* candle + *mæsse* Mass]

candle meter, a unit of illumination equivalent to the amount of light from one international candle at a distance of one meter; meter candle; lux.

can|dle|nut (kan′dəl nut′), *n.* **1** the oily nut of a tree of the spurge family, of tropical islands. The kernels are dried and strung together for use as candles. **2** the tree it grows on; kukui.

can|dle|pin (kan′dəl pin′), *n.* one of a set of thin, cylindrical bowling pins.
candlepins, a game of tenpins using these: *Other forms of bowling include ... candlepins, most common in the Boston area* (Wall Street Journal).

candle power, or **can|dle|pow|er** (kan′dəl pou′ər), *n.* **1** the intensity of light, measured in candelas. One candle power is equal to 12.57 lumens. A light having 30 candle power gives approximately 30 times as much light as one candela does. **2** the unit of luminous intensity of the former international candle or older standard candle. *Abbr:* c.p.

can|dler (kan′dlər), *n.* **1** a person who tests eggs for freshness by holding them in front of a light. **2** a candlestick.

can|dle|stick (kan′dəl stik′), *n.* a holder for a candle, to make it stand up straight; candleholder: *I saw seven golden candlesticks* (Revelation 1:12).

can|dle|wick (kan′dəl wik′), *n.* the wick of a candle.

candlewick bedspread, a bedspread, usually of unbleached muslin, into which short, thick bunches of cotton yarns have been hooked in a pattern.

can|dle|wood (kan′dəl wu̇d′), *n.* **1** any resinous wood, splinters of which are burned to give light. **2** any one of several trees which yield such wood, as the ocotillo.

can-do (kan′dü′), *adj. U.S. Informal.* willing and able to get things done: *He comes on as the can-do guy, a style that is very popular around here* (Atlantic).

can|dock (kan′dok), *n.* = water lily. [< *can*[2] + *dock*[4]]

can|dor (kan′dər), *n.* **1** speaking openly what one really thinks; honesty in giving one's view or opinion; frankness and sincerity: *He spared no one's feelings and expressed his views with great candor.* **2** fairness; impartiality: *The team felt cheated and challenged the umpire to prove his candor.* **3** *Obsolete.* freedom from malice; kindliness. **4** *Obsolete.* stainlessness of character; purity. [< Latin *candor* whiteness; sincerity; purity < *candēre* to shine]

can|dour (kan′dər), *n. British.* candor.

CANDU (kan′dü), *n.* the type of nuclear reactor used in Canada. It uses heavy water as both the moderate and the coolant. [< *CAN*(ada) *D*(euterium oxide-)*U*(ranium)]

C & W, country-and-western (music).

can|dy (kan′dē), *n., pl.* **-dies,** *v.,* **-died, -dy|ing,** *adj.* —*n.* **1** sugar or syrup, boiled with water and flavoring, then cooled and made into small pieces for eating: *sugar candy.* Chocolate, butter, milk, nuts, and fruits are often added. SYN: confection. **2** a piece of this: *Take a candy from the box.* SYN: bonbon.
—*v.t.* **1** to turn into sugar; congeal or form into crystals, especially by boiling sugar or syrup. **2** to cook (something) in sugar; preserve by boiling in sugar: *She candied the peaches before canning them.* **3** *Figurative.* to make sweet, agreeable, or palatable; sweeten; sugar over. **4** to cover or incrust with crystals, as of ice: *The cold brook candied with ice* (Shakespeare).
—*v.i.* **1** to turn into candy or become covered with candied sugar. **2** to become crystallized or congealed: *The honey has candied.*
—*adj. Archaic.* flattering; honeyed.
[earlier *sugar candy* < French (*sucre*) *candi* < Italian (*zucchero*) *candito* < Arabic *qandat* sugar < Persian *qand*]

candy bar, a piece of candy, typically bar-shaped, sold as an individually wrapped package.

candy butcher, *U.S.* a vendor or peddler who sells candy and often other small merchandise, on trains, in grandstands at sporting events, and formerly in theaters.

can|dy|floss (kan′dē flôs′), *n. British.* **1** a spun sugar candy; cotton candy. **2** *Figurative.* anything flimsy or insubstantial: *There has been a great*

Pronunciation Key: hat, āge, cãre, fär; let, ēqual, tėrm; it, īce; hot, ōpen, ôrder; oil, out; cup, pu̇t, rüle; child; long; thin; ᴛʜen; zh, measure; ə represents **a** in about, **e** in taken, **i** in pencil, **o** in lemon, **u** in circus.

improvement in the general welfare ... and be hanged to the pundits who write off that improvement as capitalist candyfloss (Sunday Times).

can|dy-pull (kan′dē pu̇l′), *n. U.S.* **1** a social gathering where candy is pulled, or drawn out of its semisolid state after boiling, in order to work it into the desired consistency. **2** a turn at pulling and twisting taffy to make it tough and light-colored.

candy store, *U.S.* a store where candy and other items, such as soft drinks, newspapers, cigarettes, and stationery, are sold.

candy stripe, an alternating narrow stripe of two colors, generally red and white, like that on a stick of peppermint or other hard candy: *In bold flag stripes of blue, red, or brass on white—as well as solid shades and candy stripes ...* (New Yorker).

can|dy-striped (kan′dē strīpt′), *adj.* having or decorated with candy stripes.

candy striper, *Informal.* a young girl who works as a volunteer nurse's aide in a hospital. [because of the candy-striped uniforms worn by such aides]

can|dy|tuft (kan′dē tuft′), *n.* **1** an herb or shrub with pink, white, lavender, or red flowers. The candytuft belongs to the mustard family. **2** its flower. [< *Candia,* Italian name of Crete + *tuft*]

cane (kān), *n., v.,* **caned, can|ing.** —*n.* **1** a slender stick used as an aid in walking; walking stick: *On long walks the old man took along a cane.* **2** a stick used to beat with: *A blow with a cane was an old form of punishment.* **3** a long, jointed stem, such as that of the bamboo. **4** a plant having such stems. Sugar cane, bamboo, and rattan are canes. **5** material made of such stems, used for furniture and chair seats; rattan: *Our porch chairs have cane seats.* **6** any one of various grasses resembling the bamboo, such as the giant cane of the southern United States. **7** the reedlike stem of one of these plants. **8** the main stem of any one of various small fruits, such as the raspberry or blackberry.

—*v.t.* **1** to beat with a cane: *Some schoolmasters used to cane boys when they did not obey.* **2** to make or repair with material made of long, jointed stems: *Mother is having our porch furniture caned.*

[< Old French *canne* < Latin *canna* < Greek *kánna* reed. See etym. of doublet **canna.**]

cane blight, a disease which attacks the canes or branches of small fruits, such as currants or raspberries, caused by various parasitic fungi.

cane borer, any one of various American beetles whose larvae bore in the canes of the raspberry, blackberry, and other plants.

cane|brake (kān′brāk′), *n.* a thicket of cane plants.

canebrake rattlesnake, a rattlesnake of the Atlantic and Gulf coastal plains and in the lower Mississippi Valley.

cane chair, a chair with the seat made of cane strips.

cane field, a field in which sugar cane is grown.

cane fruit, fruit borne by certain plants on canes, chiefly blackberries and raspberries.

cane knife, a large knife, with a wide blade and a sharp barb or hook at the back of the blade, used in cutting sugar cane.

ca|nel|la (kə nel′ə), *n.* the orange-colored inner bark of a West Indian tree, having a cinnamonlike odor and a bitter, pungent taste, used as a tonic and as a condiment. [< Medieval Latin *canella* (diminutive) < Latin *canna* cane, reed]

can|e|phor or **can|e|phore** (kan′ə fôr, -fōr), *n.* = canephora.

ca|neph|o|ra (kə nef′ər ə), *n.* **1** (in ancient Greece) one of the maidens who carried upon their heads baskets containing the sacred objects used at feasts. **2** a representation of one of these, especially in classical architectural sculpture. **3** a caryatid with a basket upon the head. [< Latin *Canēphora* < Greek *kanēphóros* < *káneon* basket (< *kánna* reed) + *phérein* bear, carry]

ca|neph|o|ros or **ca|neph|o|rus** (kə nef′ər əs), *n.* = canephora.

can|er (kā′nər), *n.* a person who canes.

ca|nes|cence (kə nes′əns), *n.* hoariness; dull whiteness: *All colour melts away with the canescence from above. The sky is of a dead milk-white* (R. Burton).

ca|nes|cent (kə nes′ənt), *adj.* **1** becoming grayish or dull white; whitish. **2** *Botany.* having a grayish or hoary pubescence (soft down). [< Latin *cānēscēns, -entis,* present participle of *cānēscere* grow hoary < *cānus* hoary]

cane sugar, sugar made from sugar cane; sucrose.

Ca|nes Ve|na|ti|ci (kā′nēz və nat′ə sī), *genitive* **Ca|num Ve|na|ti|co|rum.** a northern constellation near the Big Dipper; Hunting Dogs.

cane|work (kān′wėrk′), *n.* **1** interwoven or braided strips of cane used to form or fill in the seats or backs of chairs, panels in carriage bodies, and the like. **2** an imitation of braided cane painted upon a carriage panel.

can|field (kan′fēld), *n.* a form of solitaire used in gambling games. [American English, apparently < Richard *Canfield,* 1855-1914, a New York gambler, supposedly the inventor]

can|ful (kan′fu̇l), *n., pl.* **-fuls.** the amount a can will hold.

cangue (kang), *n.* a heavy board formerly worn about the neck as a portable pillory by criminals in China. [< French *cangue* < Portuguese *cango,* perhaps variant of *canga* yoke for oxen]

ca|nic|o|la fever (kə nik′ə lə), a disease of dogs that can be transmitted to man, livestock, and other animals. It is caused by a spirochete and takes the form of a fever and jaundice. [< New Latin (*Leptospira*) *canicola* the spirochete < Latin *canis* dog]

Ca|nic|u|la (kə nik′yə lə), *n.* the Dog Star; Sirius. [< Latin *Canīcula*]

ca|nic|u|lar (kə nik′yə lər), *adj.* **1** of or having to do with either the Dog Star or its rising. **2** of or having to do with the dog days in July and August. [< Latin *canīculāris* of the Dog Star < *Canīcula* the Dog Star (Sirius or Procyon) (originally diminutive) < *canis* dog]

can|i|cule (kan′ə kyül), *n.* = dog days. [< French *canicule* < Latin *canīcula* small dog (diminutive) < *canis* dog]

can|i|kin (kan′ə kin), *n.* = cannikin.

ca|nine (kā′nīn), *adj., n.* —*adj.* **1** of a dog; like a dog: *canine faithfulness.* **2** like that of a dog: *The glutton had a canine appetite.* **3** of or belonging to a group of meat-eating animals including dogs, foxes, and wolves. The coyote is a canine animal.

—*n.* **1** a dog. **2** any animal belonging to a group of meat-eating animals including dogs, foxes, and wolves. **3** a canine tooth; cuspid: *There are incisors for cutting; canines, for tearing; premolars and molars for grinding* (A. M. Winchester).

[< Latin *canīnus* < *canis* dog]

canine tooth, one of the four pointed teeth next to the incisors; cuspid.

ca|nin|i|form (kā nī′nə fôrm, kə nin′ə-), *adj.* shaped like a canine tooth: *The canine and caniniform incisor teeth of this seal function as an extremely efficient saw for cutting through thick and flintly ice* (Scientific American).

can|ions (kan′yənz), *n.pl.* ornamental rolls formerly worn around the lower ends of the legs of breeches. [< Spanish *cañón* tube; canyon]

Ca|nis Major (kā′nis), *genitive* **Ca|nis Ma|jo|ris.** a constellation southeast of Orion that contains Sirius, the brightest of the fixed stars. [< Latin *Canis Major* greater dog]

Canis Ma|jo|ris (mə jō′ris), genitive of **Canis Major.**

Canis Minor, *genitive* **Ca|nis Mi|no|ris.** a constellation east of Orion, separated from Canis Major by the Milky Way. [< Latin *Canis Minor* lesser dog]

Canis Mi|no|ris (mi nō′ris), genitive of **Canis Minor.**

can|is|ter (kan′ə stər), *n.* **1** a small box or can, especially for tea, coffee, flour, or sugar. **2a** a cylinder or shell filled with metal fragments that is shot from a cannon. **b** the metal fragments; case shot. **3** the boxlike part of a gas mask that contains the filtering or chemical substance through which the air is breathed. [< Latin *canistrum* < Greek *kánastron* wicker basket < *káneon* basket < *kánna* reed, cane]

canister shot, = canister (def. 2).

can|ker (kang′kər), *n., v.* —*n.* **1** a spreading sore, especially a canker sore. **2** a fungous disease of plants, especially of fruit trees, that causes slow decay of the bark and tissues: *... as killing as the canker to the rose* (Milton). **3** *Figurative.* anything that causes rot or decay, or destroys by a gradual eating away: *Unemployment is a canker that destroys man's self-respect.* **4** = cankerworm. **5** a disease affecting horses' feet. **6** *Dialect.* the dog rose.

—*v.t., v.i.* to infect or be infected with canker; decay; rot.

[Old English *cancer* < Latin, crab; tumor, gangrene. See etym. of doublets **cancer, chancre.**]

can|ker|ous (kang′kər əs), *adj.* **1** of or like a canker or cankers. **2** causing a canker or cankers; infectious; corroding.

canker rash, a variety of scarlet fever complicated with ulcerations in the throat.

canker root, any one of various plants with astringent or bitter roots, as the goldthread.

canker sore, a small canker of the mouth, especially one inside the lips or cheeks, usually of short duration. Its exact cause is unknown.

can|ker|worm (kang′kər wėrm′), *n.* a caterpillar that eats away the leaves of trees and plants.

can|ker|y (kang′kər ē), *adj.* cankered; decayed.

can|na (kan′ə), *n.* **1** a tropical or subtropical plant with large, pointed leaves and large, red, pink, or yellow flowers. **2** its flower. [< Latin *canna* reed. See etym. of doublet **cane.**]

can|nab|ic (kə nab′ik), *adj.* of or having to do with hemp. [< Latin *cannabis* (< Greek *kánnabis* hemp) + English *-ic*]

can|na|bin (kan′ə bin), *n.* the poisonous resin obtained from the extract of Indian hemp. It is probably the active principle of the drug hashish. [< *cannab*(is) + *-in*]

can|na|bis (kan′ə bis), *n.* **1** the dried flowering tops of the hemp, from which hashish and marijuana are made; bhang. **2** = hemp (the plant). [< Latin *cannabis* hemp < Greek *kánnabis*]

can|na|bism (kan′ə biz əm), *n.* an illness or ill effects due to excessive use of Indian hemp.

canned (kand), *adj.* **1** put in a can; preserved by being put in airtight cans or jars: *canned fruit.* **2** *Slang.* **a** recorded for reproduction; prerecorded on a phonograph record or tape recording: *canned music, canned laughter, a canned commercial. The union understandably keeps urging the use of "live" music and extols its superiority to the canned product* (Harper's). **b** syndicated: *The Detroit Times, which seldom ran anything but canned editorials, now regularly runs two or three editorials a day on local subjects* (Time). **c** stereotyped: *His style is low-key and straight, of the sort that so many people, weary of canned and cautious politicians, find appealing* (Atlantic). **d** discharged; fired. **3** *British Slang.* drunk: *He was canned long before the end of the evening.* [past participle of *can*[2]]

canned heat, a preparation, sold in small cans, which can be lighted and used as a fire for cooking.

can|nel coal, or **can|nel** (kan′əl), *n.* bituminous coal in large lumps that burns with a bright flame. [< *candle* (because of its candlelike flame)]

can|nel|lo|ni (kan′ə lō′nē), *n.pl.* **1** pasta in the shape of thick tubes, usually stuffed with meat or cheese and often served with a sauce. **2** a pastry roll served with a sweetened cream filling and sprinkled with powdered sugar. [< Italian *cannelloni* (augmentative) < *cannello* tube]

can|nel|oid (kan′ə loid), *adj.* resembling cannel coal.

can|ne|lon (kȧn lôɴ′), *n. French.* **1** a hollow roll of puff paste. **2** a roll of minced and seasoned meat or the like, baked or fried.

can|ne|lure (kan′əl yər), *n.* a groove or channel in a surface. [< French *cannelure* < *canneler* to groove, channel]

can|ne|lured (kan′əl yərd), *adj.* grooved; fluted.

can|ne|quin (kan′ə kin), *n.* a white cotton cloth from the East Indies that was popular during the 1700's. [< French *cannequin*]

can|ner (kan′ər), *n.* **1** a person who cans food. **2** *U.S.* **a** an old cow or steer, having meat fit only for canning: *Tough old cows—meat men call them canners and cutters—sold yesterday for over 10 cents a pound here* (Wall Street Journal). **b** a poor grade of beef obtained from such an animal: *The remaining four grades—commercial, utility, cutter and canner—are lacking in fat, tenderness and juices, and usually come from older animals* (Science News Letter).

can|ner|y (kan′ər ē), *n., pl.* **-ner|ies.** a factory where food is canned: *a tuna cannery.*

can|ni|bal (kan′ə bəl), *n., adj.* —*n.* **1** a person who eats human flesh: *Tribes of cannibals once lived on islands in the south Pacific Ocean.* **SYN:** man-eater, anthropophagite. **2** an animal that eats others of its own kind: *Many fishes are cannibals.*

—*adj.* **1** of or having to do with cannibals or cannibalism: *Cannibal ants help control ants that destroy crops.* **2** *Figurative.* like cannibals; bloodthirsty. **SYN:** sanguinary.

[< Spanish *Caníbales,* an old name for the Carib Indians]

can|ni|bal|ic (kan′ə bal′ik), *adj.* = cannibalistic.

can|ni|bal|ise (kan′ə bə līz), *v.t., v.i.,* **-ised, -is|ing.** *Especially British.* cannibalize.

can|ni|bal|ism (kan′ə bə liz′əm), *n.* **1** the act or habit of eating the flesh of one's own kind: *Most animals do not practice cannibalism.* **2** *Figurative.* bloodthirstiness; barbarity.

can|ni|bal|is|tic (kan′ə bə lis′tik), *adj.* of cannibals; characteristic of cannibals: *An animal that consumes members of its own species is termed cannibalistic, and one that eats dead animals is a scavenger* (Tracy I. Storer). —**can′ni|bal|is′ti|cal|ly,** *adv.*

can|ni|bal|ize (kan′ə bə līz), *v.,* **-ized, -iz|ing.** —*v.t.* **1** to take usable parts from (a vehicle, piece of machinery, or the like) to assemble or repair another: *My brother cannibalized a baby carriage to get its wheels for a racing car.* **2a** to eat the flesh of or devour (an animal of the same kind): *The south polar skua is its own predator, cannibalizing chicks in the nests of its skua*

neighbors (Scientific American). **b** *Figurative:* *"Betty's doing a real good job," she said firmly. "We girls have got to stop cannibalizing each other"* (Harper's).
— ***v.i.*** **1** to salvage parts for repair work, or to make repairs by means of salvaged parts. **2** to devour one's own kind; practice cannibalism.
— **can'ni|bal|i|za'tion**, *n.*

can|nie (kan'ē), *adj., adv. Scottish.* canny.

can|ni|kin (kan'ə kin), *n.* a small can or drinking cup: *a cannikin of rum.* Also, **canikin**. [diminutive of *can*[2]; influenced by Middle Dutch *kannekin*]

can|ning (kan'ing), *n.* the preserving of food by sealing it up in airtight cans or jars.

can|non** (kan'ən), *n., pl.* **-nons** or (*collectively*) **-non**, *v.* — ***n. **1** a big gun that is too large to be carried by hand and is fixed to the ground, or mounted on a carriage or in a tank or other vehicle, or on an airplane. Cannons can be raised and lowered to different positions, such as the howitzer used as an artillery piece, or can be set in a fixed position, such as a mortar. The old-fashioned kind of cannon that fired cannonballs was much used during the Civil War and as the principal piece of naval armament until the twentieth century. **2** = cannon bone. **3** *Mechanics.* a hollow, cylindrical piece that revolves or is capable of revolving on and independently of a shaft. **4** the metal loop by which a bell is suspended; ear. **5** *British, Billiards.* = carom. **6** a smooth, round bit for a horse; cannon bit. **7** *U.S. Slang.* a pickpocket: *Like all big sports events, the crowd and its money attract a big turnout of confidence men, touts, bookmakers and cannons* (This Week).
— ***v.i.*** **1** to discharge a cannon. **2** *British, Billiards.* = carom. **3** to come into collison: *to cannon against a tree.*
— ***v.t.*** **1** to attack with cannon; cannonade: *My mother was killed when the Russians cannoned the village* (New Yorker). **2** *British, Billiards.* to cause to carom.
[< Old French *canon* < Italian *cannone* < *canna* tube < Latin *canna* reed, tube, cane]

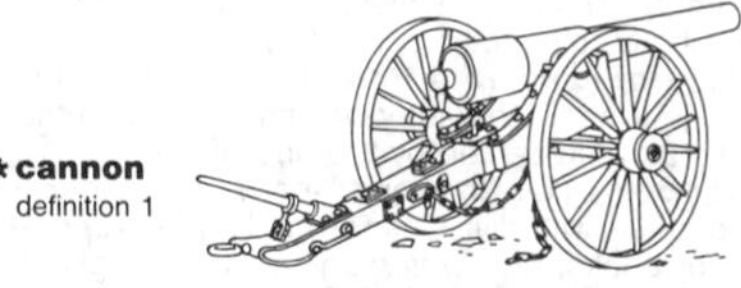

***cannon**
definition 1

can|non|ade (kan'ə nād'), *n., v.,* **-ad|ed, -ad|ing.** — ***n.*** **1** a continued firing of cannon; barrage: *the crash of the cannonade.* **2** *Figurative.* a verbal assault: *a furious political cannonade.*
— ***v.t.*** to attack with or as if with cannons; batter with cannon: *... throwing shells and cannonading the ships* (Robert Beatson). *The Dodgers cannonaded five Yankee hurlers with fourteen hits* (Newsweek).
— ***v.i.*** to discharge cannon; fire large guns: *A Confederate band had struck up a medley of polkas and waltzes in the very midst of the fiercest cannonading* (New Yorker).
[< French *canonnade* < *canon* cannon]

can|non|ball (kan'ən bôl'), *n., adj., v.* — ***n.*** **1** Also, **cannon ball**. a large iron or steel ball formerly fired from cannons. Cannonballs were usually solid. **2** a very fast, straight serve in tennis: *He returned Froehling's cannonball beautifully, breaking him twice in the first set* (New Yorker). **3** *Informal.* anything that moves or travels very fast.
— ***adj.*** *Informal.* very fast: *a cannonball delivery.*
— ***v.i.*** *U.S. Slang.* to travel fast and hard: *The secondary low began cannonballing up the coast, while the Canadian high pushed down into New England* (New York Times).

cannon-ball tree, a South American tree that bears a large, round fruit from whose pulp a sweet drink is made. It is related to the Brazil-nut tree.

cannon bit, a smooth, round bit for a horse; cannon.

cannon bone, the bone between the hock or knee and the fetlock, especially of a horse.

cannon cracker, a large firecracker.

can|non|eer (kan'ə nir'), *n.* an artilleryman; gunner. [< Middle French *canonnier* < *canon* cannon]

can|non|eer|ing (kan'ə nir'ing), *n.* the duties or skill of a cannoneer.

cannon fodder, **1** soldiers considered as expendable war material. **2** *Figurative.* useful material; grist to the mill: *Since civilization began the young and still hopeful have been our cannon fodder when the older ones fail ... to use good sense in their solution of the world's problems* (Wall Street Journal).

Can|non|ism (kan'ən iz'əm), *n. U.S.* excessive or partisan use of the power of the Speaker in the House of Representatives. [< Joseph G. ("Uncle Joe") *Cannon*, Illinois Republican, Speaker of the House from 1903 to 1911 + *-ism*]

cannon metal, a variety of bronze used formerly in making cannon or guns; gun metal.

cannon pinion, the perforated pinion which carries the minute hand and drives the minute wheel of a watch.

can|non|ry (kan'ən rē), *n., pl.* **-ries**. **1** a continued firing of cannon; barrage. **2** heavy weapons; artillery; cannon.

cannon shot, **1** a cannonball or other projectile for a cannon. **2** the range of a cannon.

can|not (kan'ot; ka not', kə-), *v.* can not.
cannot but, cannot do otherwise than: *I cannot but be gratified by the assurance* (Thomas Jefferson).
▶ **cannot, can not.** Usage is divided, but *cannot* is the more common. *Can not* should be used if the negative is to be emphasized.

can|nu|la (kan'yə lə), *n., pl.* **-lae** (-lē). a tubular instrument of any one of several types introduced into a body cavity or tube, especially to permit drainage or irrigation: *During times when experiments are not being carried out on the animal, all electrodes and cannulae can be removed, leaving inconspicuous self-closing and self-healing skin lesions* (Science). Also, **canula**. [< Latin *cannula* (diminutive) < *canna* reed, pipe, cane]

can|nu|lar (kan'yə lər), *adj.* = tubular.

can|nu|late (kan'yə lit, -lāt), *adj.* = cannular.

can|nu|lat|ed (kan'yə lā'tid), *adj.* = cannular.

can|ny (kan'ē), *adj.,* **-ni|er, -ni|est**, *adv.* — ***adj.*** **1** shrewd and cautious in dealing with others: *The canny trader made a large profit by buying goods when they were plentiful and selling them when they became scarce. They may manage to find a way out of their dilemma, for there are some very canny politicians among them* (Newsweek). **2** thrifty: *a canny housewife. Other millions of Americans—more skeptical, perhaps, or cannier in handling their money—evidently have caught on to what is happening* (Harper's). **3** knowing; wise: *a canny lad.* **4** *Scottish.* safe to meddle with; lucky: *Ghosts are not canny.* **5** *Scottish.* quiet; gentle: *a canny little kitten.* **6** *British Dialect.* snug; comfortable; pleasant; cozy: *a canny kitchen.* **7** *Archaic.* skillful; clever.
— ***adv.*** *Scottish.* in a canny manner; carefully; warily; gently.
[apparently < *can*[1]] — **can'ni|ly**, *adv.* — **can'ni|ness**, *n.*

ca|noe** (kə nü'), *n., v.,* **-noed, -noe|ing.** — ***n. a light boat often tapered at both ends, moved with a paddle held in both hands without fixed supports: *The canoe was so light that the Indian could easily carry it.*
— ***v.i.*** to paddle a canoe; go in a canoe: *The trappers canoed to their camp far up the river.*
— ***v.t.*** to transport by canoe.
paddle one's own canoe, to make one's way by one's own exertions: *The members of the Yiewsley (Middlesex) Canoe Club have been making their own craft ... thus improving on the precept that instructs us to paddle our own canoes* (London Times).
[< Spanish *canoa* < Arawak (West Indies) *kanáwa*]

***canoe**

canoe birch, = paper birch.

canoe burial, the custom of depositing corpses in canoes, practiced by some American Indians of the Pacific Northwest.

ca|noe|ist (kə nü'ist), *n.* **1** a person who paddles a canoe. **2** an expert in paddling a canoe.

canoe slalom, a white-water sport in which a canoeist must maneuver his craft through gates similar to a slalom course in skiing.

ca|noe|wood (kə nü'wu̇d'), *n.* the wood of the tulip tree.

can of worms, *U.S. Slang.* a complicated problem or situation; a source of many difficulties: *The whole area of screen acting is probably going to be a big can of worms in the next few years* (Pauline Kael).

can|on[1] (kan'ən), *n.* **1** the rule by which a thing is judged; standard: *Her manners are in keeping with the canons of good taste.* **SYN:** criterion. **2a** the law of a church; body of church law. **b** a rule or law enacted by an ecclesiastical council or other competent authority. **3a** the official list of books of the Bible accepted by the Christian church as genuine and inspired. **b** any recognized set of sacred books. **c** the accepted complete works of an author. **4** an official list of the saints, as in the Roman Catholic and Greek churches. **5** any official list. **6** = Canon. **7** *Music.* a kind of composition, in the style of a fugue, the different voice parts repeating the same melody one after another in strict imitation either at the same or at a different pitch. **8** a large size of type; 48 point. [Old English *canon* < Latin < Greek *kanṓn* rule, (straight) rod]

can|on[2] (kan'ən), *n.* **1** a clergyman belonging to a cathedral or other church having more than one minister: *Sir, it is a great thing to dine with the canons of Christ Church* (Samuel Johnson). **2** a member of a group of Roman Catholic clergymen living according to a certain rule, especially a canon regular. [< Old French *canon* < Late Latin *canonicus* clergyman < Latin, according to rule, canonical < Greek *kannikós* < *kanṓn* rule]

Can|on (kan'ən), *n.* the part of the Mass coming after the offertory and containing the words of the consecration. [< *canon*[1]]

ca|ñon (kan'yən), *n.* = canyon. [American English < Mexican Spanish *cañón* canyon]

can|on|ess (kan'ə nis), *n.* a member of a religious community of women living under a rule, but not taking perpetual vows.

ca|non|ic (kə non'ik), *adj.* = canonical.

ca|non|i|cal (kə non'ə kəl), *adj.* **1** according to church laws: *canonical dress.* **2** in the canon of the Bible: *canonical writings. Thanks to science and invention, our children have the prospect at birth of living to the canonical age of three score and ten* (New Yorker). **3** authorized; accepted; standard: *... challenging all those who may be disinclined to accept his criticism as canonical* (Saturday Review). — **ca|non'i|cal|ly**, *adv.* — **ca-non'i|cal|ness**, *n.*

canonical hours, **1** the seven periods of the day fixed by canon law for prayer and worship. They are matins (and lauds), prime, tierce, sext, nones, vespers, and complin. **2** *British.* the hours between 8 a.m. and 3 p.m., within which a marriage ceremony may take place at a parish church.

canonical letters, letters formerly interchanged by Christian clergymen as testimonials of their faith, for use especially in their travels to distinguish them from heretics when their faith was called into question.

canonical punishments, such punishments as the church may inflict, such as excommunication, degradation, and penance.

ca|non|i|cals (kə non'ə kəlz), *n.pl.* the clothes worn by a clergyman at a church service.

canonical sins, those sins for which, in the early church, capital punishment was inflicted, such as idolatry, murder, adultery, and heresy.

ca|non|i|cate (kə non'ə kāt, -kit), *n.* the position, rank, or dignity of a canon; a canonry.

can|on|ic|i|ty (kan'ə nis'ə tē), *n.* **1** character justifying inclusion, or the fact of inclusion, in a canon, especially the Biblical canon; authenticity. **2** accord with ecclesiastical law; orthodoxy.

ca|non|ics (kə non'iks), *n. Theology.* the study of the formation and authority of the canon of Scripture. [< *canon*[1] + *-ics*]

can|on|ise (kan'ə nīz), *v.t.,* **-ised, -is|ing.** *Especially British.* canonize.

can|on|ist (kan'ə nist), *n.* a person who is skilled in canon law.

can|on|is|tic (kan'ə nis'tik), *adj.* **1** of or belonging to a canonist. **2** concerned with the exposition of canon law.

can|on|is|ti|cal (kan'ə nis'tə kəl), *adj.* **1** having relation to canonistic matters. **2** = canonistic.

can|on|ize (kan'ə nīz), *v.t.,* **-ized, -iz|ing.** **1** to declare formally to be a saint; place in the official list of saints: *Joan of Arc was canonized by the Roman Catholic Chruch in 1920.* **2** *Figurative.* to treat as a saint; glorify. **3** to make or recognize as canonical. **4** = authorize. — **can'on|i|za'tion**, *n.*

canon law, the laws of a church governing ecclesiastical affairs.

canon regular, *pl.* **canons regular**. *Roman Catholic Church.* a member of any one of various institutions made up of regular priests who live in community under a rule: *the Canons Regular of Saint Augustine.*

can|on|ry (kan'ən rē), *n., pl.* **-ries**. **1a** the position or rank of a canon. **b** the benefice of a canon. **2** canons collectively.

can|on|ship (kan'ən ship), *n.* the position, rank, or benefice of a canon; canonry.

ca|noo|dle (kə nü'dəl), *v.i., v.t.,* **-dled, -dling.** *British Slang.* to cuddle amorously. [origin uncertain]

Pronunciation Key: hat, āge, cãre, fär; let, ēqual, tėrm; it, īce; hot, ōpen, ôrder; **oi**l, **ou**t; cup, pu̇t, rüle; **ch**ild; lo**ng**; **th**in; **ᴛʜ**en; **zh**, measure; **ə** represents **a** in about, **e** in taken, **i** in pencil, **o** in lemon, **u** in circus.

can opener, an instrument for opening cans: *The . . . Corporation has designed a can opener with a magnetic lid lifter that prevents the cut-off lids from falling back into the contents of the can* (New York Times).
Ca|no|pic jar or **urn** (kə nō′pik), = Canopic vase.
Canopic vase, **1** a ceremonial vase used in Egypt, chiefly for holding the entrails of embalmed bodies. **2** a vase used to hold the ashes of the dead. [< Latin *Canōpicus* < Greek *Kanopikós* having to do with *Kánōpos* Canopus, a town of ancient Egypt]
Ca|no|pus (kə nō′pəs), *n.* the second brightest star in the sky, in the southern constellation Argo. [< Latin *Canōpus* < Greek *Kánōpos;* see etym. under **Canopic vase**]
can|o|py (kan′ə pē), *n., pl.* **-pies**, *v.,* **-pied**, **-py|ing**. —***n.*** **1** a covering fixed over a bed, throne, or entrance, or carried on poles over a person: *There is a striped canopy over the entrance to the hotel.* **2** a rooflike covering; shelter or shade: *The trees formed a canopy over the old road.* **3** *Figurative.* the sky. **4** the umbrellalike supporting area of a parachute. **5** the sliding cover of the cockpit of a small aircraft: *The plane's canopy, raised at an acute angle from its forward end, loomed over both positions* (New Yorker).
—***v.t.*** to cover with a canopy: *Lofty trees . . . did canopy the herd* (Shakespeare).
[< Old French *canape*, learned borrowing from Medieval Latin *canapēum* < Latin *cōnōpēum* a couch with mosquito curtains < Greek *kōnōpion* (originally) of Canopus]
ca|no|rous (kə nôr′əs, -nōr′-), *adj.* melodious; musical. [< Latin *canōrus* (with English *-ous*) < *canor, -ōris* melody < *canere* sing] —**ca|no′rous|ly**, *adv.* —**ca|no′rous|ness**, *n.*
Ca|nos|sa (kə nos′ə, -nôs′-), *n.*
go to Canossa, to humble oneself; repent (in allusion to the journey of Emperor Henry IV of Germany to Canossa, Italy, to do penance before Pope Gregory VII).
ca|no|tier (kȧ nō tyā′), *n. French.* a hat with a straight brim and flat crown.
can|so d'a|mor (kan′sō də môr′), one of the poetic forms used by the troubadours; love song. [< Provençal *canso d'amor*]
canst (kanst), *v. second person singular present* of **can**[1]. *Archaic.* can (used only with *thou*). "Thou canst" means "you can."
cant[1] (kant), *n., adj., v.* —***n.*** **1** talk that is not sincere; moral or religious statements that many people make, but few really believe or act upon: *Clear your mind of cant* (Samuel Johnson). SYN: hypocrisy. **2** the peculiar language of a special group, using many strange words; argot: *"Jug" is one of the words for "jail" in thieves' cant.* **3** the special language and idiom of a trade, craft, or profession; jargon: *the cant of the psychologists.* **4** stock phrases and expressions fashionable at a particular time or among a group or class of society: *the cant of café society.* **5** a whining manner of speaking, especially as adopted by beggars; whine.
—***adj.*** **1** peculiar to a special language: *cant words of thieves.* **2** used for the sake of fashion; affected: *to borrow a cant phrase.* **3** marked by affected piety; insincere.
—***v.i.*** **1** to use cant; talk in cant. **2** to speak in the manner of a beggar; whine; beg.
—***v.t.*** to use (expressions) merely because they are fashionable; say for fashion's sake: *I have heard the same cant canted about a much finer building* (Macaulay).
[< Latin *cantus* song. See etym. of doublets **canto**, **cantus**.]
cant[2] (kant), *n., v., adj.* —***n.*** **1** a sloping, slanting, or tilted position; lean; inclination: *The ship took on a dangerous cant to starboard.* **2** a sudden pitch or toss which causes a person or thing to overturn or fall. **3** a turning or tilting movement: *Fortune's wheel made suddenly a great cant* (Thomas Carlyle). **4** an oblique line or surface, such as cuts off the corner of a square or a cube or forms the slanting face of a bank, hill, or the like: *up the cant of the rock face.* **5** *Obsolete.* a corner of a building; quoin.
—***v.t.*** **1** to give a slant or slope to; bevel: *He canted the edges of a board.* **2** to put into a slanting position; tip; tilt; incline: *The wind canted the ship to port. The sea broke in upon us, and the canoe being half full, canted her broadside to it* (Archibald Duncan). **3** to pitch or throw with a sudden jerk: *The horse canted his rider into the stream.*
—***v.i.*** **1** to tilt, pitch on one side, or turn over: *The sailboat canted over in the storm. The stone platform collapsed and the building canted over* (L. L. Green). **2** to have a slanting position or direction; slope. **3** to swing away from a course or direction: *The ship canted across the narrow channel and ran aground.*
—***adj.*** **1** having canted corners or edges. **2** tilted from the perpendicular or the horizontal; sloping. [probably < Middle Dutch *cant* < Old French < Vulgar Latin *cantus* corner, edge < Latin, tire of a wheel < Celtic (compare Welsh *cant* rim of a circle)]
cant[3] (kant), *adj. British Dialect.* lively; merry; brisk: *. . . as cant as a kitling* (Evelyn Waugh). [probably a variant of *canty*]
can't (kant, känt), *v.* cannot or can not.
▶**can't, mayn't.** *Can't* almost universally takes the place of the awkward *mayn't: Can't I go now?*
▶**can't help (but)**. In spite of the objection that it involves double negation, *can't* (or *cannot*) *help but* is the established informal usage: *I can't help but feel sorry about it.* In more formal usage this would be: *I cannot* (or *can't*) *help feeling sorry about it* or *I cannot but feel sorry about it.*
Cant., **1** Canterbury. **2** Canticles.
Cantab., of Cambridge (Latin, *Cantabrigiensis*).
cant|a|bank (kan′tə bangk), *n.* a strolling singer. [< Italian *cantambanco* < *cantare* sing + *in* on + *banco* bench]
can|ta|bi|le (kän tä′bē lā), *adj., n. Music.* —***adj.*** in a smooth and flowing style; songlike: *After the interval he turned to virtuosity and romance in various smaller pieces, pouring rich, ripe cantabile tone and eloquent phrasing into Bloch's passionate "Nigun"* (London Times).
—***n.*** **1** cantabile style: *Her clear, pure, soft cantabile was as admirable as her forceful . . . fortissimo in climaxes* (London Times). **2** a musical piece or passage in this style.
[< Italian *cantabile*, learned borrowing from Latin *cantābilis* capable of being sung < *cantāre* sing]
Can|ta|bri|an (kan tā′brē ən), *adj.* of or having to do with the Cantabri, an ancient people of northern Spain, or with Cantabria, the region formerly inhabited by them.
Can|ta|brig|i|an (kan′tə brij′ē ən), *adj., n.* —***adj.*** of Cambridge, England, or Cambridge University.
—***n.*** **1** a native or inhabitant of Cambridge, England. **2** a student or graduate of Cambridge University: *As any middle-aged Cantabrigian might remember it from his student days, Britain's great Cambridge University was a mellow place with a flavor of its own* (Time).
[< Medieval Latin *Cantabrigia* Cantebrig, old name for a section of the present town + English *-an*]
Can|ta|brize (kan′tə brīz), *v.i.,* **-brized**, **-briz|ing.** to imitate or pattern after Cambridge, England, or its University. [< Medieval Latin *Cantabrigia* (see etym. under **Cantabrigian**) + English *-ize*]
can|ta|la (kan tä′lə), *n.* a strong fiber made from the leaves of an agave grown in the Philippines. [< New Latin (*Agave*) *cantala* the name of the plant; origin unknown]
can|ta|lev|er (kan′tə lev′ər, -lē′vər), *n., v.t., v.i.* = cantilever.
can|ta|liv|er (kan′tə liv′ər), *n., v.t., v.i.* = cantilever.
can|ta|loupe or **can|ta|loup** (kan′tə lōp), *n.* a kind of muskmelon with a hard, rough rind and sweet juicy, orange-colored flesh. [< French *cantaloup*, apparently < Italian *Cantalupo*, a papal estate near Rome where the fruit was cultivated]
can|tan|ker|ous (kan tang′kər əs), *adj.* ready to make trouble and oppose anything suggested; ill-natured; quarrelsome: *We have a huge, black, cantankerous Persian tomcat that ruthlessly dominates the house* (Harper's). SYN: crabbed, testy. [alteration of earlier unrecorded *conteckerous* < Middle English *contecker* contentious person < *conteck* strife, quarreling; influenced by *rancorous*] —**can|tan′ker|ous|ly**, *adv.* —**can|tan′ker|ous|ness**, *n.*
can|tar (kan tär′), *n.* = kantar.
can|ta|ta (kən tä′tə), *n.* **1** a musical composition consisting of a story or play which is sung by a chorus and soloists, but not acted. **2** (originally) a narrative in verse set to recitative or alternate recitative and air, for a single voice accompanied by one or more instruments. [< Italian *cantata* < *cantare* sing < Latin *cantāre*]
cantata da camera (dä), *Italian.* **1** a cantata based on a secular subject. **2** (literally) chamber cantata.
cantata da chi|e|sa (kē ā′sə), *Italian.* **1** a cantata based on a sacred subject. **2** (literally) church cantata.
can|ta|te (kan tā′tē), *n.* Psalm 98. [< Latin *cantāte* sing ye, imperative of *cantāre* sing]
can|ta|tri|ce (*Italian* kän′tä trē′chā; *French* kän tȧ trēs′), *n., pl. Italian* **-tri|ci** (-trē′chē), *French* **-trices** (-trēs′). *Italian or French.* a professional female singer.
cant block, a large block used for turning over the body of a whale in stripping off its blubber.
cant board, **1** a sloping or canting board. **2** a division made in the conveyor box of a flour bolter to separate different grades. **3** a board serving to show the plan of the curved side of a carriage in carriage building.
cant body, the portion of a vessel which contains the cant frames.
cant chisel, a large strong chisel having a rib and the ground or slanted edge on one side.
cant dog, = cant hook.
can|teen (kan tēn′), *n.* **1** a small container for carrying water or other drinks: *The thirsty hiker lifted the canteen to his lips, drinking cool sips of water.* SYN: flask. **2** a military store where food, drinks, and other articles are sold to soldiers and sailors. SYN: commissary. **3** a recreation hall for servicemen, especially in a town or city near an army camp or naval base. **4** a store in a school, camp, or factory where food, drinks and other articles are sold or given out: *Cadets had been so disenchanted with the academy's food that the prosperous student canteen made enough money to support 10 student activities* (Wall Street Journal). **5** a box of cooking utensils for use in camp. [< French *cantine* < Italian *cantina* wine cellar, probably (diminutive) < *canto* corner < Vulgar Latin *cantus;* see etym. under **cant**[2]]
can|te hon|do (kän′tā hôn′dō; hôn′dō), *Spanish.* **1** a sad type of flamenco music, originally from Andalusia: *Throat-searing cante hondo wails from every bivouac* (New Yorker). **2** (literally) deep song.
can|te jon|do (kän′tā hôn′dō), = cante hondo.
can|ter[1] (kan′tər), *v., n.* —***v.t., v.i.*** to gallop gently: *He cantered his horse down the road. The horse cantered across the meadow.*
—***n.*** a gentle gallop: *The canter is to the gallop very much what the walk is to the trot* (William Youatt).
[short for *Canterbury gallop*]
cant|er[2] (kan′tər), *n.* **1** a person who cants or whines, especially a professional beggar or vagrant. **2** a person who talks cant. [< *cant*[1] + *-er*[1]]
Can|ter|bur|i|an (kan′tər byůr′ē ən), *adj.* **1** of or having to do with the city of Canterbury, England, the seat of the Anglican archbishop who is also the primate of England. **2** of or having to do with the archiepiscopal see itself, especially with its High-Church character in the 1600's.
Can|ter|bur|i|an|ism (kan′tər byůr′ē ə niz′əm), *n.* the High-Church character of England during the 1600's as represented by the see of Canterbury.
can|ter|bur|y (kan′tər ber′ē, -bər-), *n., pl.* **-bur|ies**. a stand with divisions for holding music, papers, or books. [< *Canterbury*, a city in England]
Canterbury bell or **bells**, a plant with tall stalks of bell-shaped flowers, usually purplish-blue, pink, or white. It is a species of campanula.
Canterbury gallop, a gentle or moderate gallop; canter. [because of the easy pace of pilgrims riding to *Canterbury*]
can|ter|er (kan′tər ər), *n.* a person or thing that canters.
cant frames, the frames or ribs of a ship which are near the extremities, and are canted away from the perpendicular or straight line. See picture under **frame**.
can|thar|i|des (kan thar′ə dēz), *n., pl. of* **cantharis**. a preparation of dried beetles (usually powdered), especially the Spanish fly, used externally as a rubefacient and vesicant (formerly considered an aphrodisiac). [< Latin *cantharides*, plural of *cantharis* cantharis]
can|thar|i|din (kan thar′ə din), *n.* a volatile crystalline compound found in blister beetles; the vesicating principle of cantharides: *A small cantharidin plaster is left on the skin overnight and raises a blister* (Scientific American). *Formula:* $C_{10}H_{12}O_4$
can|thar|i|dism (kan thar′ə diz əm), *n.* an illness due to the use of cantharides.
can|thar|i|dize (kan thar′ə dīz), *v.t.,* **-dized**, **-diz|ing**. to treat with cantharides.
can|tha|ris (kan′thər is), *n., pl.* **-thar|i|des**. the Spanish fly, a blister beetle. [< Latin *cantharis* < Greek *kantharís* kind of beetle]
cant hook, a pole with a movable hook at one end, used to grip and turn over logs; cant dog.
can|thus (kan′thəs), *n., pl.* **-thi** (-thī). the outer or inner angle or corner of the eye, where the upper and lower lids meet. [< Late Latin *canthus* < Greek *kanthós*]
can|ti|cle (kan′tə kəl), *n.* a short song, hymn, or chant used in church services. [< Latin *canticulum* (diminutive) < *canticum* song < *cantus, -ūs* song]
Canticle of Canticles, = Song of Solomon, in the Douay Bible.
Can|ti|cles (kan′tə kəlz), *n.* = Song of Solomon.
can|ti|ga (kan tē′gə), *n., pl.* **-gas**. a short lyric poem composed in the 1200's and 1300's in Spanish or Portuguese and influenced by the Provençal troubadours. [< Spanish and Portuguese *cantiga*]
can|ti|le|na (kan′te lē′nə), *n.* **1** a melodic composition, or a melodious section in a composition,

for instruments: *He allowed his melodic invention to run freely in a soaring, long-drawn cantilena* (London Times). **2** such a composition or section for singing. [< Italian *cantilena* < Latin *cantilēna* old song < *cantillāre* sing low < *cantāre* sing]

can|ti|lev|er (kan′tə lev′ər, -lē′vər), *n., v., adj.* —*n.* a large, projecting bracket or beam that is supported at one end only. A cantilever is usually designed to bear a weight or structure over a space where supports cannot be placed or are not desired, such as for supporting balconies, cornices, and the like. Some aircraft wings are cantilevers.
—*v.t.* to build (something) with cantilevers or a cantilever: *The room in which [he] works is cantilevered out over a sheer cliff* (New Yorker).
—*v.i.* to extend out, as a cantilever does: *In this plan the beam cantilevers out too far for balance.*
—*adj.* formed on the principle of the cantilever or with the use of cantilevers: *Of cantilever construction, four of the five rooms hang out in space with no visible means of support* (Wall Street Journal). Also, **cantalever, cantaliver.** [origin uncertain, but probably < *cant*[2] + *lever*]

***cantilever bridge**, a bridge made of two cantilevers whose projecting ends meet but do not support each other.

***cantilever bridge**

can|til|late (kan′tə lāt), *v.t.*, **-lat|ed, -lat|ing.** to recite with musical tones; to chant, especially to chant with a degree of musical improvisation, as the cantor in a synagogue. [< Latin *cantillāre* (with English *-ate*[1]) < *cantāre* to sing] —**can′til|la′tion**, *n.*

can|ti|na (kan tē′nə), *n. Southwestern U.S.* a saloon. [American English < Spanish *cantina* < Italian, probably (diminutive) < *canto* corner < Vulgar Latin *cantus;* see etym. under **cant**[2]]

cant|ing coin (kan′ting), a triangular wooden block with which a barrel is chocked to keep it from rolling when stowed, as on a ship.

can|ti|no (kan tē′nō), *n., pl.* **-nos.** the treble string of a lute, violin, or some other stringed instruments. [< Italian *cantino* < *cantare* to sing < Latin *cantāre*]

can|tle (kan′təl), *n.* **1** the part of a saddle that sticks up at the back: *The undersides of both pommel and cantle are set with Moghul jade plaques inlaid with gold and bespattered with rubies* (Observer). **2** a section or segment cut out of anything; a part; portion: *The huge cantle which is . . . cut out of the holiday* (Charles Lamb). [< Old French *cantel* < Medieval Latin *cantellus* (diminutive) < Vulgar Latin *cantus;* see etym. under **cant**[2]]

cant|let (kant′lit), *n.* a small cantle; a little piece.

can|to (kan′tō), *n., pl.* **-tos. 1** one of the main divisions of a long poem. A canto of a poem is like a chapter of a novel. *There is only a faintly discernible ghost of grandeur in the fading villa where Byron lived while he was writing the fourth canto of "Childe Harold"* (Newsweek). **2** *Music.* the soprano part; the melody. [< Italian *canto* < Latin *cantus, -ūs* song < *canere* sing. See etym. of doublets **cant**[1], **cantus.**]

canto fer|mo (fėr′mō), = cantus firmus. [< Italian *canto fermo*, translation of Medieval Latin *cantus firmus;* see etym. under **cantus firmus**]

can|ton (kan′tən, -ton; kan ton′), *n., v.* —*n.* **1** a small part or political division of a country, especially: **a** one of the 22 sovereign political units that form the Swiss confederation. **b** one of the judicial units into which a French arrondissement (the largest subdivision of a department) is divided. **2** the upper corner of a flag next to the staff where a special design appears. **3** *Heraldry.* a square division occupying an upper corner of an escutcheon, etc. **4** *Obsolete.* a division or part of anything.
—*v.t.* **1** to allot quarters to or provide quarters for (soldiers). **2** to divide into parts; subdivide: *He cantoned out the country to his men . . .* (Daniel Defoe). **3** *Obsolete.* to separate or sever by division from; cut out from a whole.
[< French *canton* < Italian *cantone* (mountain) region < Vulgar Latin *cantō, -ōnis* < *cantus;* see etym. under **cant**[2]]

Can|ton (kan′tən), *adj.* of or designating articles made or originating in the city of Canton, China: *Canton china, Canton enamel, Canton porcelain.*

can|ton|al (kan′tə nəl), *adj.* of or having to do with a canton or cantons: *cantonal elections, cantonal government.*

can|ton|al|ism (kan′tə nə liz′əm), *n.* the cantonal system of administrative government.

Canton crepe, a soft silk cloth with a crinkled surface.

Can|ton|ese (kan′tə nēz′, -nēs′), *n., pl.* **-ese,** *adj.* —*n.* **1** a person born or living in Canton, China. **2** the Chinese dialect spoken in or near Canton.
—*adj.* of Canton (China), its people, or their dialect.

Canton flannel, a strong cotton cloth that is soft and fleecy on one side.

can|ton|ment (kan ton′mənt, -tōn′-; *especially British* kan tün′mənt), *n.* **1** a place where soldiers live; quarters for soldiers. **2** the act of cantoning. **3** (formerly) a permanent military post in British India. [< French *cantonnement* < *canton;* see etym. under **canton**]

can|tor (kan′tər, -tôr), *n.* **1** the person who chants the prayers in a synagogue and leads the congregation in the worship: *Unlike the choirmaster or organist in a Christian church, the cantor (although not ordained) holds a semisacred office; the prayers he sings are an integral part of the service, and he must be trained in Jewish ritual* (Time). **2** the person who leads the singing of a choir or congregation. [< Latin *cantor* singer < *canere* sing]

can|tor|ate (kan′tər it), *n.* **1** the position or office of a cantor. **2** the period during which one is a cantor. **3** cantors as a group. [< *cantor* + *-ate*[3]]

can|to|ri|al (kan tôr′ē əl, -tōr′-), *adj.* of or having to do with a cantor: *cantorial chants.*

cant purchase, a tackle having one of its blocks secured to the masthead of a whaler and the other to the hook in the blubber of a dead whale alongside. It is used for turning the whale over while it is being stripped or flensed.

can|trip (kan′trip), *n.* **1** a spell or charm of witchcraft; a witch's trick or mischievous device. **2** any playfully mischievous trick. [< earlier Scottish phrase *cast cantrapes* to read spells]

can|tus (kan′təs), *n., pl.* **-tus. 1** a song or melody, especially an ecclesiastical melody. **2** the principal voice. [< Latin *cantus, -ūs* song. See etym. of doublets **cant**[1], **canto.**]

can|tus fir|mus (kan′təs fėr′məs), *Music.* **1** = plain song. **2** a melody held unchanged throughout a composition, above or below which other melodic or contrapuntal parts are added and varied. [< Medieval Latin *cantus firmus* < Latin *cantus, -ūs* song, *firmus* set, fixed]

can|tus pla|nus (kan′təs plā′nəs), = plain song. [< Medieval Latin *cantus planus* < Latin *cantus, -ūs* song, *plānus* plain]

can|ty (kan′tē, kän′-), *adj. Scottish.* **1** showing gladness and cheerfulness: *Then at her door the canty dame would sit, as any linnet gay* (Wordsworth). **2** cheerfully brisk or active; lively. [perhaps < Low German or Dutch *kantig* cheerful]

Ca|nuck (kə nuk′), *n., adj. U.S. Slang and Canadian Informal.* **1** Canadian: *Maybe it'll help some Canucks realize what a great country we have and show them what a fine job can be done in Canada by Canadians* (Maclean's). **2** French Canadian: *La Croix was a thick-set, hook-nosed Canuck* (George Mathewson).
▶In spite of the belief of some writers and speakers, the term *Canuck* is not always considered derogatory. Many Canadians apply it to themselves and do not regard it as unfriendly.

can|u|la (kan′yə lə), *n., pl.* **-lae** (-lē). = cannula.

Ca|num Ve|na|ti|co|rum (kā′nəm və nat′ə kō′rəm), genitive of **Canes Venatici.**

Ca|nute (kə nüt′, -nyüt′), *n.* **1** the ancient English king who, according to legend, showed his courtiers he was not infallible by ordering the tide to stop advancing. **2** a person who tries to hold back an irresistible force or process: *He warned them not to get the reputation of Canutes resisting new techniques of farming* (London Times). —**Ca|nute′like′**, *adj.*

Ca|nut|ism (kə nü′ti zəm, -nyü′-), *n.* the practice of a Canute; any attempt to hold back or reverse change: *[The] proposal to cut bank rate by 2 per cent was . . . not so much conservatism as Canutism* (Manchester Guardian Weekly).

can|vas (kan′vəs), *n., adj., v.,* **-vased, -vas|ing** or **-vassed, -vas|sing.** —*n.* **1** a strong cloth with a coarse weave made of cotton, flax, or hemp, used to make tents, sails, or certain articles of clothing: *The tops of my sneakers are made of canvas.* SYN: sailcloth, tarpaulin. **2** something made of canvas: *The sailors threw the canvas over the hatch and lashed it down.* **3** a sail or sails: *The ship flew all its canvas.* **4** a piece of canvas on which an oil painting is done; a picture painted on canvas; oil painting: *The art gallery purchased several beautiful canvases from the artist.* **5** any coarse, stiffened fabric of wide weave used for working tapestry, as a basis for embroidery or other stitching. **6** the circus. **7a** the covered end of a racing boat. **b** the length of this.
—*adj.* **1** made of canvas: *canvas sails.* **2** having the color or appearance of canvas.
—*v.t., v.i.* to cover, line, or furnish with canvas.
the canvas, the floor of a boxing ring: *The champion knocked his opponent to the canvas in the first round.*
under canvas, a in tents: *The circus was held under canvas in an open field.* **b** with sails spread: *The schooner left the harbor under full canvas.*
[< Old French *canevas,* ultimately < Latin *cannabis* hemp < Greek *kánnabis*]

can|vas|back (kan′vəs bak′), *n., pl.* **-backs** or (*collectively*) **-back.** a large, wild duck of North America. The male has a reddish-brown head and neck and a grayish-white back.

can|vass (kan′vəs), *v., n.* —*v.t.* **1** to go through (a city, district, or other area) asking for votes, orders, or donations: *Salesmen canvassed the whole city for subscriptions to magazines.* **2** *Figurative.* **a** to examine the parts of carefully; inspect: *He canvassed the papers, hunting for notices of jobs.* SYN: scrutinize, study. **b** to discuss: *The city council canvassed the mayor's plan thoroughly.* SYN: debate. **3** to examine and count (the votes cast in an election). **4** *Archaic.* to thrash (a person) in writing; criticize destructively.
—*v.i.* to ask for votes, orders, or donations: *The candidates canvassed right up to election day.*
—*n.* **1** the act or process of asking for votes, orders, or donations: *During a canvass of the neighborhood, we collected $100 for UNICEF.* **2** the personal visiting of homes or stores in a district to sell something. **3** = discussion.
[< obsolete *canvass,* verb, toss (someone) in a canvas; shake out, discuss, solicit < *canvas*]

can|vass|er (kan′və sər), *n.* **1** a person who solicits votes, orders, or donations: *Canvassers of both sides return disheartened by the numbers of citizens they find who say that they do not like party politics* (London Times). **2** a person who examines and counts the votes cast in an election.

can|y (kā′nē), *adj.* **1** made of cane. **2** resembling cane.

can|yon (kan′yən), *n.* a narrow valley with high, steep sides, usually with a stream at the bottom: *The continental slope is often cut with deep canyons . . . carrying streams of sediment-laden water to be deposited at the bottom* (New Scientist). SYN: gorge, ravine. Also, **cañon.** See picture under **valley.** [American English < Mexican Spanish *cañón* narrow passage, apparently alteration of earlier *callón* < Spanish *calle* street < Latin *callis* narrow footpath]

canyon mouse, a long-tailed mouse with pale underparts, found in rocky parts of southwestern North America.

can|zo|na (kän tsō′nä), *n., pl.* **-ni** (-nē). = canzone.

can|zo|ne (kän tsō′nā), *n., pl.* **-ni** (-nē). **1** a variety of Provençal or Italian lyric poetry, closely resembling the madrigal but less strict in style. **2** *Music.* **a** a setting to music of the words of a canzone, for one or more voices. **b** an instrumental piece written in the style of a madrigal. **3** any song; ballad. [< Italian *canzone* < Latin *cantiō, -ōnis* a singing, song < *canere* sing]

can|zo|net (kan′zə net′), *n.* a short, light song. [< Italian *canzonetta* (diminutive) < *canzone;* see etym. under **canzone**]

can|zo|net|ta (kän′tsō net′ä), *n.* = canzonet.

Cao Dai (kou′ dī′), a religious sect, originating and centered in Vietnam, that combines in one faith certain elements of Buddhism, Christianity, Confucianism, Taoism, and the philosophies of Victor Hugo, Sun Yat-sen, and Clemenceau: *The oddest religion in the East, and the one with the most catholic pantheon, is known as Cao Dai* (Time).

Cao Da|ism (kou′ dī′iz əm), the principles and beliefs of Cao Dai. —**Cao Da|ist.**

caou|tchouc (kü′chük, kou chük′; *especially British* kou′chük), *n.* **1** the gummy, thickened juice of various tropical plants of the spurge family, from which rubber is made; crude, natural rubber. **2** pure rubber. [< French *caoutchouc* < Spanish < Quechua *cauchuc* Indian rubber tree]

cap[1] (kap), *n., v.,* **capped, cap|ping.** —*n.* **1** a soft, close-fitting covering for the head, usually having little or no brim, but often with a visor: *Most of the men and boys wore caps while working in the rain.* **2** a special head covering worn to show rank or occupation: *a nurse's cap, a freshman cap.* SYN: hat. **3** = mortarboard (def. 2). **4** anything like a cap, especially: **a** the stopper or

---

Pronunciation Key: hat, āge, cãre, fär; let, ēqual, tėrm; it, īce; hot, ōpen, ôrder; oil, out; cup, pu̇t, rüle; child; long; thin; ᴛʜen; zh, measure; **ə** represents **a** in about, **e** in taken, **i** in pencil, **o** in lemon, **u** in circus.

top for a jar, bottle, tube, or fountain pen: *a bottle cap.* SYN: cover. **b** the top or pileus of a mushroom. **c** the calyptra of a moss. **d** the kneecap. **e** a part of the afterbirth sometimes attached to a baby's head when born. **5** the highest part; top: *the polar cap at the North Pole.* SYN: peak. **6** an upper limit on increases in cost, interest rates, especially of a loan, etc.: *Edward F. King [is] founder of an organization that wants to put a cap on state spending* (Time). **7** a layer of fresh rubber joined to the worn part of a pneumatic tire. **8a** a small amount of explosive in a wrapper or covering: *The boy shoots caps in his toy pistol.* **b** = percussion cap. **9** = capital letter. **10** any one of various sizes of paper, especially writing and wrapping papers: *legal cap, bag cap.* **11** *British.* inclusion in a team: *I made forty-seven against Winchester, but the Captain of Cricket gave the last cap to Lord Camelot's son, Esmé* (Punch). **12** *British.* a contraceptive pessary. **13** *Slang.* a capsule of heroin or other drug. **14** a raised plastic cover, usually with windows and a rear door, that fits over the bed of a pickup truck.
—*v.t.* **1** to put a cap on: *He capped the bottle again after having some root beer.* **2a** to put a top on; cover the top of: *Whipped cream capped the dessert.* **b** to cover at the end; protect the end of: *to cap a rope with tape.* **3** to do or follow up with something as good or better: *Each of the two clowns capped the other's last joke. Oates capped the revelations of Bedloe by charging the Queen herself . . . with knowledge of the plot* (John Richard Green). **4** to form or serve as a cap, covering, or crown to; lie on top of: *. . . the house that caps the corner* (Robert Browning). **5** to take off one's cap to (a person) as a mark of respect: *He and the Proctor capped each other as they met* (Thackeray). **6a** *Scottish.* to confer an academic degree on. **b** *U.S.* to place the white cap of a nurse upon (a nursing school graduate). **7** to complete; crown: *The report caps about five months of searching* (Wall Street Journal). **8** *British.* to award a place on a team to.
—*v.i.* to take off the cap as a mark of respect.
cap in hand, in humble fashion: *Suppose that it went cap in hand to every Government in Europe* (Pall Mall Gazette).
cap the climax. See under **climax**.
set one's cap for or **at,** *Informal.* to try to get (a particular man) for a husband: *That girl is setting her cap at you* (Thackeray).
[Old English *cæppe* < Late Latin *cappa* cap, hood, mantle. See etym. of doublet **cape**[1].]
—cap′less, *adj.* **—cap′like′,** *adj.*

cap[2] (kăp), *n. Scottish.* a wooden bowl or dish, often with two ears or handles, formerly used as a drinking vessel. [alteration of Middle English *cop* cup, Old English *copp*]

cap[3] (kap), *v.t.,* **capped, cap|ping. 1a** *Scottish.* to seize (a vessel) as a prize; capture. **b** to entrap or ensnare. **2** *Obsolete.* to arrest. [probably < Old French *caper* to seize, take < Latin *capere*]

Cap (kap), *n. Informal.* head, chief, or master. [short for *Captain*]

cap., **1** capacity. **2** capitalize. **3** *pl.* **caps.** capital letter.

Cap., **1** capital. **2** chapter (Latin, *capitulum, caput*).

CAP (no periods) or **C.A.P.,** **1** Civil Air Patrol. **2** Common Agricultural Policy (of the European Economic Community or Common Market).

ca|pa (kä′pä), *n.* **1** a round cape, such as used by a bullfighter. **2** a Cuban tobacco of fine quality, especially suited for the outsides or wrappers of the best cigars. [< Spanish *capa* < Late Latin *cappa* cap, hood, mantle]

ca|pa|bil|i|ty (kā′pə bil′ə tē), *n., pl.* **-ties. 1** ability to learn and do; power or fitness; capacity: *As a scientist, he has the capability of doing important research.* SYN: competence; aptitude. **2** the characteristics, components, functions, or susceptibility necessary to do something or maintain a process: *the capability of photographic film to reproduce a light impression.* **3** legal or moral qualifications: *A contract has the capability of binding people to a common purpose.*
capabilities, undeveloped properties; potential uses: *Atomic energy has many unexplored capabilities.*

ca|pa|ble (kā′pə bəl), *adj.* having fitness, power, or ability; able; efficient; competent: *a capable teacher. He did a very capable job and was rewarded with much praise.* SYN: proficient, qualified, fitted. See syn. under **able**.
capable of, a having ability, power, or fitness for: *capable of criticizing music. Some airplanes are capable of going 1000 miles an hour.* **b** open to; ready for: *a statement capable of being misunderstood.*
[< Late Latin *capābilis* < Latin *capere* take, contain] **—ca′pa|ble|ness,** *n.*
►See **able** for usage note.

ca|pa|bly (kā′pə blē), *adv.* in a capable manner; with ability; ably: *a job capably done. The details . . . are . . . freshly conceived and capably handled* (Manchester Examiner).

ca|pa|cious (kə pā′shəs), *adj.* able to hold much; large and roomy; spacious: *a capacious storage closet, a capacious bag.* [< Latin *capāx, -ācis* (with English *-ous*) < *capere* hold] **—ca|pa′cious|ly,** *adv.* **—ca|pa′cious|ness,** *n.*

ca|pac|i|tance (kə pas′ə təns), *n.* **1** the property of a capacitor that determines the amount of electrical charge it can receive and store; capacity. **2a** the ratio of the charge of electricity imparted to a conductor to the resulting potential, commonly expressed in farads. **b** the ratio of the charge of electricity on either of two conductors which have received equal and opposite charges to the resulting difference of potential between them. **3** the ability of a circuit or of a condenser to maintain the flow of alternating electric current. [< *capacit*(y) + *-ance*]

ca|pac|i|tate (kə pas′ə tāt), *v.t.,* **-tat|ed, -tat|ing. 1** to make capable or fit; qualify (for, or to do something). **2** to make legally capable. **3** *Biology.* to induce capacitation in (a sperm).

ca|pac|i|ta|tion (kə pas′ə tā′shən), *n.* **1** a rendering capable. **2** *Biology.* a series of changes that sperms undergo in the uterus before attaining the capacity to penetrate and fertilize an egg: *Capacitation, without which most mammalian eggs cannot be fertilized, is a poorly understood change undergone by spermatozoa* (Scientific American).

ca|pac|i|ta|tor (kə pas′ə tā′tər), *n.* = capacitor.

ca|pac|i|tive (kə pas′ə tiv), *adj.* of or having to do with electrical capacity (capacitance).

capacitive coupler, an apparatus which, by electric fields, joins portions of two radio-frequency circuits.

***ca|pac|i|tor** (kə pas′ə tər), *n.* a device for receiving and storing a charge of electricity; condenser: *A common type is the paper and foil capacitor, in which strips of metal foil form the plates and a sheet of paper impregnated with wax is the dielectric* (Sears and Zemansky).

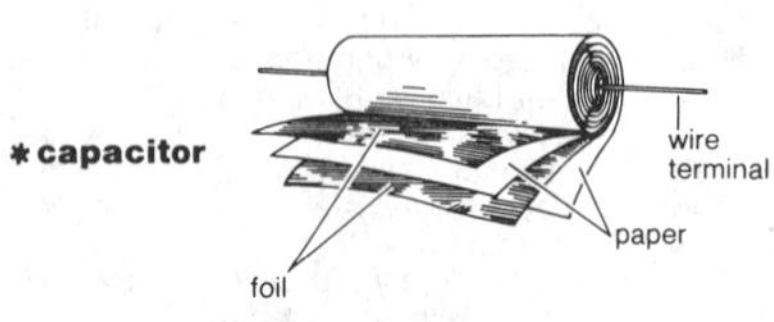

***capacitor**

ca|pac|i|ty (kə pas′ə tē), *n., pl.* **-ties,** *adj.* **—*n.*** **1** the amount of room or space inside; largest amount that can be held by a container: *A gallon can has a capacity of 4 quarts.* SYN: volume. **2a** the ability to receive and hold: *The theater has a seating capacity of 400 people.* **b** the ability to withstand some force or perform some function: *the capacity of a metal for retaining heat.* **c** = capacitance. **3a** the ability to learn or do; mental power or fitness: *Benjamin Franklin had a great capacity for learning. Few people have the capacity to apply the theory of relativity to practical problems.* SYN: competency. **b** the ability to deal with problems, administer work, etc.: *an executive of great capacity. Not the least of the marks of a military genius is his capacity to bend both subordinates and superiors to his plans of action* (Newsweek). **4a** the physical power or ability to produce: *the maximum capacity of a machine. Wilson Dam on the Tennessee River has the greatest generating capacity of any TVA dam* (Russell Lord). **b** a measure of this ability, especially of a battery or other source of electricity. **c** the maximum output: *The electric generators broke down in the summer because they worked beyond capacity.* **5** position or relation: *She is here in the capacity of teacher.* SYN: character. **6** legal power or right; qualification.
—*adj.* that reaches or rises to the utmost capacity: *a capacity crowd.*
[< Latin *capācitās* < *capāx;* see etym. under **capacious**]

cap and bells, a cap trimmed with bells, worn by a jester.

***cap and gown**

***cap and gown,** a flat cap or mortarboard and loose gown, worn by teachers and students on certain occasions, especially when degrees are conferred.

cap-a-pie or **cap-à-pie** (kap′ə pē′), *adv.* from head to foot; completely. [< Old French *cap a pie* < Latin *caput* head, and *pēs, pedis* foot]

ca|par|i|son (kə par′ə sən), *n., v.* **—*n.*** **1** an ornamental covering for a horse. **2** *Figurative.* any rich dress or outfit. SYN: equipment.
—*v.t.* to dress richly: *Gaily caparisoned pedal rickshaws mingle with motor traffic in Dacca* (London Times).
[< Middle French *caparaçon* < Spanish *caparazón,* perhaps < Late Latin *cappa* cape, outer garment]

Cap|com (kap′kom′), *n.* the person at a space flight center who is in charge of maintaining communications with an astronaut during a space flight. [< *Cap*(sule) *com*(municator)]

cape[1] (kāp), *n.* an outer garment, or part of one, without sleeves, worn falling loosely from the shoulders, and often fastened at the neck. [< French *cape* < Spanish *capa,* or *cape* cloak < Late Latin *cappa.* See etym. of doublet **cap**[1].]

cape[2] (kāp), *n.* a point of land extending into the water. *Abbr:* C. SYN: headland, promontory. See picture under **peninsula**. [< Old French *cap* < Old Provençal < Latin *caput* head]

cape[3] (kāp), *n.* = capeskin.

cape[4] (kāp), *v.t.,* **caped, cap|ing.** to excite or distract (the bull) or to draw (it) into a desired position, by fluttering or waving a red cape: *When . . . the picador was set with his lance, Cascabel began to cape the bull over into . . . position* (Barnaby Conrad). [apparently < Spanish *capear* < *capa* cape[1]]

ca|pe|a|dor (kä′pā ä ᴛʜôr′), *n., pl.* **-dors, -do|res** (-ᴛʜō′rās). the person who excites the bull and distracts his attention by using a red cape. [< Spanish *capeador* < *capear* to excite the bull with the cape < *capa* cape[1]]

Cape boy, a South African of mixed descent.

Cape buffalo, a large, fierce, black buffalo of southern Africa. Cape buffalo have horns united at their bases to form a large, bony plate on the front of the head. [< *Cape* of Good Hope, at the tip of South Africa]

Cape canary, a small greenish or greenish-yellow bird of southern Africa with a soft, pleasant buzzing song.

Cape cart, a two-wheeled, hooded vehicle of southern Africa, with two seats, drawn by two or more horses and capable of carrying four people: *The Cape cart . . . is much like an American buggy, but larger and stronger* (E. E. K. Lowndes).

cape chisel, a narrow cold chisel with a gradual taper on both top and bottom of the blade, used for cutting grooves or slots in metal.

***Cape Cod, 1** designating a type of rectangular house consisting of one or one-and-a-half stories and usually having a steep gable roof and a central chimney: *a Cape Cod dwelling, house, or cottage.* **2** this type of house: *The Cape Cod will be available with either two, three or four bedrooms* (New York Times). [< *Cape Cod,* Massachusetts, where this style of cottage originated]

***Cape Cod**
definition 2

Cape Colored, (in South Africa) a person of mixed white and other ancestry: *Alongside the Bantus live 300,000 Indians, most of them shopkeepers and plantation laborers in sugar-growing Natal, and 1,100,000 Cape Colored, i.e., mulattoes, coffee-colored descendants of early Boer settlers* (Time).

Cape cowslip, any one of a large group of plants of the lily family native to southern Africa, having red or yellow flowers on a leafless stem.

Cape crawfish, the spiny lobster of southern Africa.

caped (kāpt), *adj.* **1** having a cape: *Quaintly attired in caped cloak, knee-breeches, and buckled shoes* (Thomas Hardy). **2** wearing a cape.

Cape doctor, (in southern Africa) a strong southeasterly wind: *That rough but benevolent southeast wind, which, owing to its kindly property of sweeping away the germs of disease, is called 'the Cape doctor'* (Annie Martin).

Cape Dutch, 1 South Africans of Dutch extraction. **2** the Dutch spoken in South Africa; Afrikaans: *This . . . language is the 'Cape Dutch' or 'taal,' the servants' language throughout the country, which Boer and Hottentot speak alike* (Beatrice M. Hicks).

Cape glove, a capeskin glove.

Cape gooseberry, 1 a straggling bush, extensively cultivated in southern Africa, which produces a berry resembling the gooseberry. **2** the berry.

Cape hartebeest, a large heartebeest of southern Africa with a reddish-brown coat and white rump patch, that can run very fast.

Cape jasmine, a widely cultivated gardenia native to China, with evergreen leaves and a fragrance similar to that of jasmine. [< *Cape* of Good Hope, at the tip of South Africa, where it was first found]

cape|let[1] (kāp′lit), *n.* a fur piece for women made in the style of a small cape to cover the shoulders. [< *cape*[1] + *-let*]

cap|e|let[2] (kap′ə let), *n.* a wenlike swelling on the heel of a horse's hock, or on the point of the elbow. [< French *capelet,* ultimately < diminutive of Late Latin *cappa* cap[1]]

cap|e|lin (kap′ə lin), *n., pl.* **-lins** or (*collectively*) **-lin.** a small fish of the north Atlantic, used for food and as bait for cod; a kind of smelt. Also, **caplin.** [< French *capelan*]

cap|e|line (cap′ə lin), *n.* **1** a woman's hat that has a soft, usually wide, brim: *... capelines with great wavy brims raised to aureole the face* (New York Times). **2** a surgical bandage which by its arrangement forms a kind of cap or bonnet. **3** a small skullcap of iron worn by archers in the Middle Ages. [< Middle French *capeline* < Italian *capellina* little hat (diminutive) < *cappa* cap, hood < Late Latin *cappa*]

Ca|pel|la (kə pel′ə), *n.* the brightest star in the constellation Auriga, one of the six brightest stars in the sky: *It has been known for several decades that Capella is composed of two giant stars of about equal brightness* (Science News Letter). [< Latin *capella* (diminutive) < *capra* she-goat]

ca|pell|meis|ter (kä pel′mīs′tər), *n.* = Kapellmeister.

ca|per[1] (kā′pər), *v., n.* — ***v.i.*** to leap or jump about playfully: *The court jester capered and danced before the king.* **SYN**: skip, spring, cavort.
— ***n.*** **1** a playful leap or jump: *The boy's caper cost him a twisted ankle.* **SYN**: gambol, prance. **2** *Figurative.* a prank; trick: *The child's Halloween capers made the neighbors laugh.* **3** *Slang.* an illegal or criminal scheme: *He holes up to plan his next caper—the stick-up of the exclusive Tropico Hotel* (Time).
cut a caper (or **capers**), **a** to play or do a trick: *to cut a caper on the straight rope* (Jonathan Swift). **b** to dance, leap, or jump about playfully: *He can dance, though he does not cut capers* (Sir Richard Steele).
[perhaps short for *capriole*] — **ca′per|er,** *n.*

ca|per[2] (kā′pər), *n.* a low, prickly shrub native to the Mediterranean region and growing in southern United States. It is sometimes grown elsewhere in the United States and Canada as a tender annual. *The pungent, slightly bitter flower buds of the caper bush are a timely seasoning because they enhance not only lamb but also many warm-weather foods* (New York Times).
capers, the green flower buds or berries of this shrub, pickled and used for seasoning: *chicken salad sprinkled with capers.*
[back formation < Middle English *caperis,* an assumed plural < Latin *capparis* < Greek *kápparis*]

ca|per[3] (kā′pər), *n.* **1** = privateer. **2** the captain of a privateer. [< Dutch *kaper* < *kapen* seize]

cap|er|cail|lie (kap′ər kāl′yē), *n.* a large grouse of northern Europe; wood grouse. [< Scottish Gaelic *capull coille* great cock (literally, horse) of the wood < *coll* woods]

cap|er|cail|zie (kap′ər kāl′yē, -zē), *n.* = capercaillie.

caper family, a group of dicotyledonous, tropical and subtropical herbs and shrubs, differing from the closely related mustard family in bearing a pod without a partition and kidney-shaped seeds with a coiled embryo. The family includes the caper and cleome.

Ca|per|na|ism (kə pėr′nā iz əm), *n.* the literal interpretation of transubstantiation held by the Capernaites.

Ca|per|na|ite (kə pėr′nā īt), *n.* **1** an inhabitant of Capernaum, a city in ancient Palestine. **2** a believer in transubstantiation, especially one who, from the words of Jesus in Capernaum, adheres to the doctrine of transubstantiation in its literal form (In the Bible, John 6:53-59). [< Latin *Capernaum* (< Greek *Kapharnaoúm*) + *-ite*[1]]

ca|per|some (kā′pər səm), *adj.* given to capering: *I've never seen a cat ... more capersome* (Charles Heavysege).

Cape ruby, a garnet resembling a ruby in color; pyrope.

capes (kāps), *n.pl. Scottish.* **1** grains of corn to which the husk continues to adhere after threshing. **2** grain which is not sufficiently ground. **3** flakes of meal which come from the mill when the grain has not been sufficiently dried. [origin uncertain]

Cape salmon, = geelbec (def. 2).

Cape seal, a fur seal living in waters off the Cape of Good Hope.

cape|skin (kāp′skin′), *n.* **1** a smooth, durable leather made from the skin of lambs or sheep, used in making gloves, jackets, etc.: *Best sellers in gloves are washable capeskins and pigskins* (New York Times). **2** a heavy, durable leather from goats of the Cape district of South Africa, used for gloves.

Ca|pe|tian (kə pē′shən), *adj., n.* — ***adj.*** of or having to do with Hugh Capet or the kings named Capet who reigned over France from 987 to 1328.
— ***n.*** a ruler who belonged to this dynasty.

Cape|to|ni|an (kāp tō′nē ən), *n.* a native or inhabitant of Cape Town, in the Republic of South Africa.

cape|work (kāp′wėrk′), *n.* the practice or art of caping a bull: *Such dazzling displays of capework by the splendidly dressed matadors ...* (New York Times).

cap|ful (kap′fu̇l), *n., pl.* **-fuls.** as much as a cap will contain: *He picked a capful of berries.*

capful of wind, *Nautical.* a light gust of wind.

cap gun, a toy gun that shoots caps.

caph (käf), *n.* = kaph.

ca|pi|as (kā′pē əs, kap′ē-), *n.* a writ ordering an officer to arrest a certain person: *Judge Reynolds issued a capias writ, ordering the arrest of the Ellises for ignoring his order to surrender Hildy* (Newsweek). [< Latin *capiās* you may take]

cap|i|ba|ra (kap′ə bär′ə), *n.* = capybara.

cap|il|la|ceous (kap′ə lā′shəs), *adj.* hairlike or threadlike. [< Latin *capillāceus* (with English *-ous*) hairlike < *capillus* hair (of the head)]

cap|il|la|rim|e|ter (kap′ə lə rim′ə tər), *n.* an instrument for determining the strength of wine or the quality of oil on the principle of capillary attraction.

cap|il|lar|i|ty (kap′ə lar′ə tē), *n.* the raising or lowering of the surface of a liquid which is in contact with a solid of small bore, caused by surface tension, as in a capillary tube.

cap|il|lar|y (kap′ə ler′ē), *n., pl.* **-lar|ies,** *adj.* — ***n.*** **1** a blood vessel with a very slender, hairlike opening. Capillaries join the end of an artery to the beginning of a vein. Most capillaries are so small that only one blood corpuscle can pass through them at a time. **2** = capillary tube.
— ***adj.*** **1** of or in the capillaries. **2** like a hair; very slender.
[< Latin *capillāris* of hair < *capillus* hair]

capillary action, the raising or lowering of the surface of a liquid which is in contact with a solid of small bore, as in a capillary tube, caused by surface tension: *Capillary action is at work when water rises in the soil, kerosene in a lamp wick, and ink in blotting paper* (M. F. Vessel).

capillary attraction, the force that causes a liquid to rise in a small tube or when in contact with a solid. It is this force of adhesion and surface tension that allows a porous substance to soak up a liquid. A plant draws up water from the ground and a paper towel absorbs by means of capillary attraction.

capillary repulsion, the force that causes a liquid to be depressed when in contact with the sides of a narrow tube, as is mercury in a glass tube.

capillary tube, a tube with a very slender, hairlike opening or bore.

ca|pil|li|form (kə pil′ə fôrm), *adj.* in the shape of a hair; hairlike: *capilliform fibers.* [< Latin *capillus* hair + *forma* form]

cap|il|lit|i|um (kap′ə lish′ē əm), *n., pl.* **-lit|i|a** (-lish′ē ə). the tangle of hairlike filaments inside certain spore cases: *The leftover dried network of cytoplasm forms the framework of the sporangium, called the capillitium* (Fred W. Emerson). [< Latin *capillitium* the hair collectively < *capillus* hair]

ca|pi|ta (kap′ə tə), *n. Latin.* plural of **caput.**

cap|i|tal** (kap′ə təl), *n., adj.* — ***n. **1a** the city or town where the government of a country, state, or province is officially located. Washington, D.C., is the capital of the United States. Each state of the United States has a capital. *Rome has a mixture of worn elegance and brusque assurance that marks it instantly as an ancient capital* (New Yorker). **b** the center of some industry, group, or interest: *New York is the financial capital of the world.* **2** any large letter, such as A, B, C, D; capital letter. A capital letter is regularly used at the beginning of a sentence or as the first letter of a proper name. **3** the amount of money or property that a company or a person uses in carrying on a business: *The Smith Company has a capital of $30,000.* **4** a source of power or advantage; resources. **5** national or individual wealth as produced by industry and available for reinvestment in the production of goods. **6** *Accounting.* **a** the net worth of a business after the deduction of taxes and other liabilities. **b** the total investment of owners in a business, often expressed as capital stock. **7a** capitalists as a group, especially as employers: *Capital will benefit particularly from this discovery.* **b** the political and economic interests or claims of this group. **8** the top part of a column or pillar. The capital is often the ornamental part of a column. See picture under **Ionic.**
— ***adj.*** **1** of capital; having to do with capital: *capital assets. Faced with the prospect of better business, the big companies are going ahead with capital expansion plans* (Time). **2** very important; leading: *The invention of the telephone was a capital advance in communication.* **SYN**: marked, momentous. **3** main; chief: *Obedience was formerly considered the capital virtue of a wife.* **SYN**: principal, foremost. **4** of the best kind; first-rate; excellent: *Oak trees give capital shade. The performance is capital, fully as enjoyable as the New York parent company and equally successful in expressing the genial humors of the story* (New York Times). **5** punishable by death: *Murder is a capital crime in many countries.* **6** *Figurative.* fatal; radical; extremely serious: *The candidate fell into the capital error of offending his supporters.* **7** in which the seat of a government is located: *a capital city.*
make capital of, to take advantage of; use to one's advantage: *He made capital of his father's fame to get the job.*
[< Latin *capitālis* pertaining to the head, to life; of first rank < *caput, -itis* head. See etym. of doublets **cattle, chattel.**]
► **Capital, capitol** are often confused because they sound alike and are similar in spelling. *Capital* is either a noun or an adjective, and always has the basic meaning of chief, head, first in its class or in importance. The noun applies particularly to the head city of a country or state and to property, money, goods, and other wealth. *Capitol* is always a noun and applies only to a building, particularly the building in which Congress or a state legislature meets: *There is a dome on the capitol in Sacramento, the capital of California.*

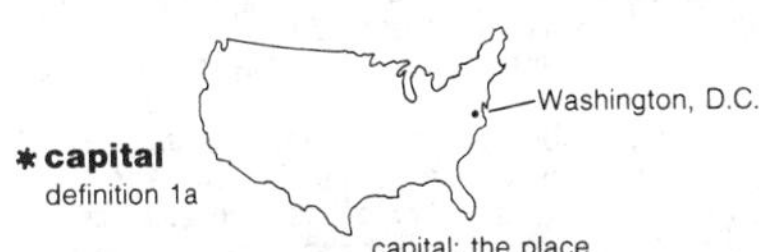

***capital**
definition 1a

capital account, **1** an account of an owner's or shareholder's investments in a business. **2** an account of assets less liabilities, showing the net worth of a business, individual, or foundation on a given date.

capital asset, any asset held or intended for holding by a business, individual, foundation, or government over a considerable period of time, including land, buildings, patents, franchises, and certain types of investments: *It would permit concerns reinvesting in new capital assets to get larger tax deductions on the facilities being retired* (Wall Street Journal).

capital expenditure, **1** an expense incurred by adding to or improving a capital asset. **2** an expenditure made out of capital as distinct from income.

capital gain, a profit derived from the sale of something viewed as part of one's capital, such as from a share of stock sold for more than its original cost: *If you actually managed to sell the item for more than you originally paid for it, that extra gain of selling price over original purchase price would still be taxable only as capital gains* (Wall Street Journal).

capital goods, goods, such as machinery or equipment, that can be used in the production of other goods: *The company's products are also used by such heavy capital goods producers as the farm implement and road building equipment makers* (Wall Street Journal).

capital grant, a grant of money, made usually by a government or foundation, for the acquisition or improvement of capital assets: *Federal approval ... will clear the way for a capital grant ... to acquire land* (New York Times).

cap|i|tal-in|ten|sive (kap′ə təl in ten′siv), *adj.* requiring great expenditure of capital to increase productivity or earnings: *Repeal of the tax credit will crimp the profits of companies in capital-intensive industries* (Time).

capital investment, the total of cash and as-

Pronunciation Key: hat, āge, cãre, fär; let, ēqual, tėrm; it, īce; hot, ōpen, ôrder; oil, out; cup, pu̇t, rüle; child; long; thin; ᴛʜen; zh, measure; ə represents **a** in about, **e** in taken, **i** in pencil, **o** in lemon, **u** in circus.

sets invested in a business enterprise: *Even in the most advanced countries less than one third of capital investment is in factories. Public services, utilities, and housing are the great users of capital investment* (Bulletin of Atomic Scientists).

cap|i|tal|ise (kap′ə tə līz), *v.t., v.i.*, **-ised, -is|ing.** *Especially British.* capitalize.

cap|i|tal|ism (kap′ə tə liz′əm), *n.* **1** an economic system in which private individuals or groups of individuals own land, factories, and other means of production. They compete with one another, using the hired labor of other persons, to produce goods and services for profit: *The characteristic feature of modern capitalism is mass production of goods destined for consumption by the masses* (Newsweek). **2** the concentration of wealth with its power and influence in the hands of a few. **3** a system which favors the existence of capitalists or the concentration of wealth in the hands of a few.

cap|i|tal|ist (kap′ə tə list), *n., adj.* **—n. 1** a person whose money and property are used in carrying on business. **2** a wealthy person. **3** a person who favors or supports capitalism. **—adj. 1** of capitalism or capitalists. **2** favoring capitalism.

cap|i|tal|is|tic (kap′ə tə lis′tik), *adj.* **1** of or having to do with capitalism or capitalists: *capitalistic production.* **2** favoring or supporting capitalism: *capitalistic policies.* **—cap′i|tal|is′ti|cal|ly,** *adv.*

capitalist roader, a communist who, according to Maoist doctrine, seeks to restore or imitate capitalism by emphasizing economic productivity, material incentives for workers, and reliance on foreign experts and technology: *Posters clearly alluding to Mr. Teng had been pasted up accusing him of being a capitalist roader—the term used for Chairman Mao Tse-Tung's enemies during the Cultural Revolution* (New York Times).

cap|i|tal|i|za|tion (kap′ə tə lə zā′shən), *n.* **1** a writing or printing with capital letters. **2** the act of capitalizing or the condition of being capitalized at a certain value. **3a** the amount at which a company is capitalized; capital stock of a business: *Since the first of the year, Pacific has increased its capitalization by $62 million to about $1,690,000,000* (Wall Street Journal). **b** the assigned value of such stock, especially when not fully paid.

cap|i|tal|ize (kap′ə tə līz), *v.*, **-ized, -iz|ing.** **—v.t. 1** to write or print with a capital letter: *He forgot to capitalize the first letter of the name Lincoln.* **2** to set the capital of (a company) at a certain amount. **3** to estimate the value of (an income). **4** *Accounting.* **a** to set up (expenses) as business assets. **b** to turn into capital; use as capital: *The company capitalized its reserve funds.* **5** to provide or furnish with capital. **6** to take advantage of: *She had early realized that she could and should capitalize her looks and charm* (Theodore Dreiser).
—v.i. capitalize on, to take advantage of; use to one's own advantage: *to capitalize on another's mistake.*

capital letter, the large form of a letter; A, B, C, D, and so on, as distinguished from a, b, c, d, and so on; capital. *Abbr:* cap.

capital levy, a direct tax on capital property.

capital loss, a loss deriving from the sale of a capital asset, as from the sale of a share of stock at less than its original cost.

cap|i|tal|ly (kap′ə tə lē), *adv.* **1** very well; excellently: *He acted the part of the butler capitally.* **2** to an important degree; mainly; eminently. **SYN:** principally. **3** in a manner involving a death penalty: *to punish or accuse capitally.*

capital punishment, the death penalty for a crime.

capital ship, any large warship, except an aircraft carrier, especially a battleship or heavy cruiser.

capital stock, the capital used in carrying on a business. It is represented in shares.

capital surplus, the excess of assets over capital and liabilities arising from other than regular operations: *The capital surplus of a corporation may be described as a more or less permanent form of surplus as compared with earned surplus* (Schmidt and Bergstrom).

cap|i|tate (kap′ə tāt), *adj., n.* **—adj. 1** *Botany.* **a** clustered into a head. **b** having a rounded head: *a capitate stigma.* **2** *Anatomy.* having to do with or denoting a bone of the carpus or human wrist, in the center of the distal row of carpal bones. **—n.** *Anatomy.* the capitate bone.
[< Latin *capitātus* < *caput, -itis* head]

cap|i|ta|tion (kap′ə tā′shən), *n.* a tax, fee, or charge of the same amount for every person. [< Late Latin *capitātiō, -ōnis* poll tax < Latin *caput, -itis* head]

capitation grant, a grant of a certain sum for every person who fulfills certain conditions, as to a school for pupils who pass an examination, or to a military company for qualified volunteers.

cap|i|tel|late (kap′ə tel′it), *adj.* **1** *Botany.* growing or terminating in a small head. **2** having a capitellum or capitulum. [< New Latin *capitellatus* < Late Latin *capitellum* small head (diminutive) < Latin *caput, -itis* head]

cap|i|tel|lum (kap′ə tel′əm), *n., pl.* **-tel|la** (-tel′ə). **1** *Anatomy.* the rounded protuberance on the outer surface of the lower end of the humerus, or upper arm. **2** *Zoology.* the portion of the body of a hydroid polyp that bears the tentacles. [< New Latin *capitellum* < Late Latin, small head (diminutive) < Latin *caput, -itis* head]

***Cap|i|tol** (kap′ə təl), *n.* **1** the building at Washington, D.C., in which Congress meets: *The President spoke to both houses of Congress in the Capitol.* **2** Also, **capitol.** the building in which a state legislature meets: *The Governor addressed the Assembly in the Capitol.* **3** the ancient temple of Jupiter on the Capitoline Hill in Rome: *... at Rome ... I sat musing amidst the ruins of the Capitol* (Edward Gibbon). **4** the Capitoline Hill. [< Latin *Capitōlium* temple of Jupiter on the Tarpeian Rock] ► See **capital** for usage note.

***Capitol** definition 1

Capitol: the building

Capitol Hill, 1 the hill in Washington, D.C., on which the United States Capitol stands: *Reporters on Capitol Hill are sensing a new mood that spills across party lines* (Harper's). **2** *Figurative.* the legislative branch of the United States Government; Congress: *This ... will mean better relations between the White House and Capitol Hill* (Wall Street Journal).

Cap|i|to|line (kap′ə tə līn, kə pit′ə-), *n., adj.* **—n.** the Capitoline Hill. **—adj.** having to do with the Capitoline Hill or the Capitol at Rome.

Capitoline Hill, one of the seven hills on which the city of ancient Rome was built.

ca|pit|u|lant (kə pich′ə lənt), *n.* a person who capitulates: *... gaining possession of the fortress which the capitulants held* (Archibald Alison).

ca|pit|u|lar (kə pich′ə lər), *n., adj.* **—n. 1** a person who belongs to an ecclesiastical chapter. **2** an act passed in a chapter; a canon; capitulary. **3** a law of a Frankish sovereign.
—adj. 1 *Botany.* growing in a capitulum or head. **2** *Zoology, Anatomy.* of or having to do with a capitulum. **3** of or having to do with an ecclesiastical chapter.
[< Medieval Latin *capitularis,* adjective < Latin *capitulum* chapter; see etym. under **capitulum**]

ca|pit|u|lar|y (kə pich′ə ler′ē), *adj., n., pl.* **-lar|ies.** **—adj.** of or having to do with a chapter, especially an ecclesiastical chapter.
—n. 1 a member of a chapter. **2** an ordinance or rule, as of an ecclesiastical chapter.
capitularies, the laws of the Frankish rulers.

ca|pit|u|late (kə pich′ə lāt), *v.i.,* **-lat|ed, -lat|ing.** to surrender on certain terms or conditions: *The defenders in the fort capitulated on condition that they be allowed to go away unharmed. I will be conquered; I will not capitulate* (Samuel Johnson). **SYN:** yield. [< Medieval Latin *capitulare* (with English *-ate*[1]) draw up under separate heads, arrange in chapters < Latin *capitulum;* see etym. under **capitulum**] **—ca|pit′u|la′tor,** *n.*

ca|pit|u|la|tion (kə pich′ə lā′shən), *n.* **1** a surrender on certain terms or conditions. **2** an agreement or condition. **3** a statement of the main facts of a subject; summary. **4a** any one of various treaties in which Turkish sultans formerly granted special privileges to citizens of foreign governments, as extraterritorial rights. **b** any one of various similar treaties.

ca|pit|u|la|tion|ism (kə pich′ə lā′shə niz′əm), *n.* **1** the actions of a person who capitulates or is inclined to capitulate. **2** the action or ideology of a Communist charged with retreating from an aggressive anti-Western attitude or policy: *If one did not dare to slight the enemy strategically, one would inevitably commit the error of capitulationism, and if one took heedless and reckless action tactically, one would inevitably commit the error of adventurism* (Manchester Guardian Weekly). **—ca|pit′u|la′tion|ist,** *n.*

ca|pit|u|la|to|ry (kə pich′ə lə tôr′ē, -tōr′-), *adj.* of or having to do with capitulation: *capitulatory rights.*

ca|pit|u|lum (kə pich′ə ləm), *n., pl.* **-la** (-lə). **1** a flower head consisting of a close cluster of sessile flowers, as in red clover or many composite plants. **2** the protuberance of a bone usually fitting into a hollow portion of another bone: *They articulate with the heads, or the capitula, of the ribs* (St. George Mivart). [< Latin *capitulum* (literally) a small head (diminutive) < *caput, -itis* head]

cap|let (kap′lit), *n.* a coated medicinal tablet shaped like a capsule: *The caplet is a solid form of Tylenol pain reliever, which research has proven is the form most preferred by consumers. Unlike tablets, it is specially shaped and coated for easy, comfortable swallowing* (New York Times). [< *cap*(sule) + (tab)*let*]

cap|lin (kap′lin), *n.* = capelin.

cap|lock (kap′lok′), *n.* an old-fashioned muzzleloading gun similar to a flintlock, but with a gunlock in which the hammer strikes a small percussion cap in turn igniting the gunpowder.

Cap'n (kap′ən), *n.* Captain.

cap|no|man|cy (kap′nə man′sē), *n.* divination by means of smoke. [< Greek *kapnós* smoke + *manteĩā*divination]

ca|po[1] (kä′pō), *n., pl.* **-pos.** = capotasto.

cap|o[2] (kap′ō), *n., pl.* **cap|os.** *U.S.* the head of one of the units or branches of the Mafia. [< Italian *capo* head < Latin *caput*]

Ca|po|di|mon|te (kä′pō dē mon′tē), *adj.* of or designating a type of rare porcelain made at Capodimonte, a suburb of Naples, Italy, during the 1700's: *Capodimonte figurines.*

cap of liberty, = liberty cap.

cap of maintenance, a kind of cap of state formerly worn by high personages, and still carried before the sovereign and certain mayors in England, and also represented in heraldry.

Ca|poid (kā′poid, kā′-), *n., adj.* **—n.** a member of a Negroid race that includes the Bushmen and Hottentots. **—adj.** of or belonging to this race. [< *Cape* (of Good Hope) + *-oid*]

ca|pon (kā′pon, -pən), *n., v.* **—n.** a rooster specially raised to be eaten. It is castrated and fattened. **—v.t.** to make a capon of; caponize. [Old English *capūn* < Latin *cāpō, cāpōnis*]

ca|pon|ette (kā′po net′), *n. U.S.* a young male chicken that has acquired the soft and tender flesh of a capon as a result of having its reproductive organs made useless by injection with female hormones. [< *capon* + *-ette*]

cap|o|nier (kap′ə nir′), *n.* a work or covered passage in or across a ditch in a military fortification. [< French *caponnière* < Italian *capponiera* or Spanish *caponera* (literally) coop for capons]

ca|pon|ize (kā′pə nīz), *v.t.,* **-ized, -iz|ing.** to make (a young male chicken) into a capon or caponette: *About four years ago there was a "flurry" of concern about hormone injections used to caponize male chickens* (Wall Street Journal). [< *capon* + *-ize*] **—ca′pon|i|za′tion,** *n.*

cap|o|ral[1] (kap′ə ral′), *n.* a variety of tobacco. [< French *tabac du caporal* corporal's tobacco (as superior to *tabac du soldat* common soldier's tobacco)]

cap|o|ral[2] (kap′ə ral′), *n. Southwestern U.S.* the overseer or foreman of a ranch. [American English < Spanish *caporal* corporal]

cap|o|re|gime (kap′ō ri zhēm′), *n. U.S.* a member of the Mafia below a capo in rank and serving as one of his lieutenants.

ca|pot (kə pot′), *n., v.,* **-pot|ted, -pot|ting.** **—n.** a winning of all the tricks in piquet. **—v.t.** to win all the tricks from in piquet. [< French *capot*]

ca|po|tas|to (kä′pō täs′tō), *n.* a device attached to a fretted musical instrument, such as the guitar, for the purpose of raising the pitch of all the strings at once. [< Italian *capotasto* < *capo* chief, head + *tasto* musical key]

ca|pote (kə pōt′), *n.* **1** a long cloak with a hood. **2** a close-fitting bonnet with strings. [< French *capote* (diminutive) < *cape* cape, garment]

cap|pa (kap′ə), *n., pl.* **cap|pae** (kap′ē). a cloak forming part of a religious habit. [< Italian *cappa* cap, hood < Late Latin]

Cap|pa|do|cian (kap′ə dō′shən), *adj., n.* **—adj.** of or having to do with Cappadocia, an ancient kingdom of eastern Asia Minor.
—n. 1 an inhabitant or native of Cappadocia. **2** the language of ancient Cappadocia.

cap|pa|ri|da|ceous (kap′ər ə dā′shəs), *adj.* belonging to the caper family. [< New Latin *Capparidaceae* the family name (< Latin *capparis* < Greek *kápparis* caper, shrub) + English *-ous*]

cap|pel|let|ti (kap′ə let′ē), *n.pl.* small pieces of pasta stuffed with minced meat or cheese and cooked in broth. [< Italian *cappelletti* (diminutive) < *cappello* hat, ultimately < diminutive of Late Latin *cappa* cap[1]]

cap|per (kap′ər), *n.* **1** a person or device that makes caps or fixes caps in position. **2** *U.S. Slang* **a** a confederate in a gambling game. **b** a dummy bidder at an auction. **3** *U.S. Slang.* an ending or climax: *The capper comes when everyone is gathered to watch Forrest open his presents* (Saturday Review).

cap|pie (kap′ē), *n. Scottish,* a small drinking vessel. [< *cap*[2] + *-ie*]

cap|ping (kap′ing), *n.* **1** the act of a person or thing that caps. **2** that with which something is capped.

cap pistol, a toy pistol that shoots caps.

cap|pu|ci|no (kap′ə chē′nō, käp′ü-), *n.* **1** a drink made by adding foaming hot milk to espresso coffee. **2** a hot chocolate drink laced with rum or brandy. [< Italian *cappucino* Capuchin (from the light brown color of his habit)]

cap|rate (kap′rāt), *n.* a salt or ester of capric acid.

cap|re|o|late (kap′rē ə lāt, kə prē′-), *adj.* **1** *Botany.* having tendrils. **2** *Anatomy.* like tendrils. [< Latin *capreolī* vine tendrils, plural of *capreolus* roebuck (its horns are tendril-shaped) + English *-ate*[1]]

cap|ric acid (kap′rik), a fatty acid found especially in butter and coconut oil and having a faint goatlike odor. *Formula:* $C_{10}H_{20}O_2$ [< Latin *caper, caprī* goat + English *-ic*]

ca|pric|ci|o (kə prē′chē ō; *Italian* kä prēt′chō), *n., pl.* **-ci|os**, *Italian* **-ci** (-chē). **1** a lively piece of music in free, irregular, and often whimsical style. **2** a caper; prank; caprice. [< Italian *capriccio* (literally) a shiver < *capo* head (< Latin *caput*) + *riccio* (originally) hedgehog < Latin *ērīcius.* See etym. of doublet **caprice.**]

ca|pric|ci|o|so (kə prē′chē ō′sō; *Italian* kä′prēt-chō′sō), *adj. Music.* denoting a free, fantastic style (used as a direction). [< Italian *capriccioso* (literally) like a *capriccio;* see etym. under **capriccio**]

ca|price (kə prēs′), *n.* **1** a sudden change of mind without reason; unreasonable notion or desire; whim: *Her decision to wear only blue clothes was pure caprice.* **SYN:** whimsy, humor, fancy. **2** a tendency to change suddenly and without reason: *Public opinion ... has her caprices* (Edmund Burke). **3** = capriccio (def. 1). [< French *caprice* < Italian *capriccio.* See etym. of doublet **capriccio.**]

ca|pri|cious (kə prish′əs, -prē′shəs), *adj.* **1** likely to change suddenly without reason; changeable; fickle: *capricious weather. A spoiled child is often capricious. The capricious star was the despair of every producer.* **2** *Obsolete.* characterized by wit or fancy. **—ca|pri′cious|ly,** *adv.* **—ca|pri′cious-ness,** *n.*

Cap|ri|corn (kap′rə kôrn), *n.* **1** the tropic of Capricorn. **2** a southern constellation shaped somewhat like a goat. **3** the tenth sign of the zodiac. The sun enters Capricorn about December 22. **4** a person born under the sign of Capricorn. [< Latin *Capricornus* < *caper, caprī* goat + *cornū* horn]

Cap|ri|cor|ni (kap′rə kôr′nī), *n.* genitive of **Capricornus.**

Cap|ri|cor|nus (kap′rə kôr′nəs), *n., genitive* **Cap-ri|cor|ni.** = Capricorn.

cap|ri|fi|cate (kap′rə fə kāt), *v.t.,* **-cat|ed, -cat-ing.** to fertilize by caprification.

cap|ri|fi|ca|tion (kap′rə fə kā′shən), *n.* a process designed to secure the pollination of the cultivated fig, which produces only female flowers. It consists in suspending branches of the wild fig (caprifig) in the cultivated trees to provide pollen, which is carried to the female flowers by wasps. [< Latin *caprificus* wild fig + English *-ation*]

cap|ri|fig (kap′rə fig), *n.* a wild fig of the Mediterranean region and southern United States, the male form of the common fig. Its fruit is usually not edible but its pollen, by means of caprification, makes the cultivated fig fruitful. [< Latin *caprificus* wild fig; (literally) goat fig]

cap|ri|fo|li|a|ceous (kap′rə fō′lē ā′shəs), *adj.* belonging to the honeysuckle family. [< Late Latin *caprifolium* honeysuckle, (literally) goat leaf (< Latin *caper, caprī* goat + *folium* leaf) + English *-aceous*]

cap|ri|form (kap′rə fôrm), *adj.* shaped like or resembling a goat. [< Latin *caper, caprī* goat + English *-form*]

cap|rine (kap′rīn, -rin), *adj.* of or like a goat: *... her bleating, caprine voice* (New Yorker). [< Latin *caper, caprī* goat + English *-ine*[1]]

cap|ri|ole (kap′rē ōl), *n., v.,* **-oled, -ol|ing.** **—*n.*** **1** a high leap made by a horse without moving forward. **2** a leap or caper, for example in dancing.
—*v.i.* **1** (of a horse) to make a high leap without moving forward. **2** to leap; caper.
[< obsolete French *capriole* < Italian *capriola* < *capriolare* to caper, ultimately < Latin *caper* goat]

Cap|ri pants (kə prē′), women's tight-fitting trousers, with tapered legs ending just above the ankle, usually worn informally. [< *Capri,* island in the Bay of Naples]

Ca|pris (kə prēz′), *n.pl.* = Capri pants.

ca|pro|ate (kap′rō āt, kə prō′-), *n.* a salt or ester of caproic acid.

cap rock, any one of several types of overlying strata, especially a layer of shale, limestone, or other material lying over and sealing in deposits, especially of petroleum and natural gas: *A cap rock must be practically impermeable to oil or gas* (Gilluly, Waters, and Woodford).

ca|pro|ic acid (kə prō′ik), a fatty acid, used in making esters. *Formula:* $C_6H_{12}O_2$ [< Latin *caper, caprī* goat + English *-ic*]

cap|ro|lac|tam (kap′rō lak′təm), *n.* a white crystalline compound used in making synthetic materials, especially one form of nylon. *Formula:* $C_6H_{11}NO$ [< *capro(ic)* acid + *lactam*]

ca|pryl|ic acid (kə pril′ik), a fatty, colorless acid with a faint but unpleasant odor, found as a glyceride, especially in butter and coconut oil. *Formula:* $C_8H_{16}O_2$

caps., **1** capitalize **2** capital letters.

cap|sa|i|cin (kap sā′ə sin), *n.* a colorless, crystalline substance, the bitter principle of the cayenne pepper, used as an irritant. *Formula:* $C_{18}H_{27}NO_3$ [< *capsicum* + *-in*]

cap screw, a bolt with a thread and no nut that screws into an opening.

Cap|si|an (kap′sē ən), *n., adj.* **—*n.*** a late Paleolithic culture following the Mousterian, typified by flint implements found at Gafsa in western Tunisia: *Microliths are especially characteristic of the Capsian* (Beals and Hoijer). **—*adj.*** of or having to do with this culture. [< *Capsa,* an old name for Gafsa]

cap|si|cum (kap′sə kəm), *n.* **1** any plant of various kinds of herbs and shrubs of the nightshade family, with red or green pods containing seeds that usually have a hot, peppery taste. Green peppers, chilies, and pimentos are pods of different kinds of capsicum. **2** such pods prepared for seasoning or medicine. [< New Latin *Capsicum* the genus name < Latin *capsa* box]

cap|sid[1] (kap′sid), *n.* any one of a family of hemipterous insects that live on the juices of plants and trees, especially a variety that attacks cocoa plants. [< New Latin *Capsidae,* the family name, probably from Greek *kápsis* a gulping down < *káptein* to gulp down]

cap|sid[2] (kap′sid), *n.* a protein coat or shell enveloping the nucleic acid of a virion or virus particle: *The capsid* [*of herpes virus*] *is composed of 162 capsomeres* (Scientific American.). [< Latin *capsa* box + *-id*]

cap|siz|al (kap sī′zəl), *n.* an upset.

cap|size (kap sīz′, kap′sīz), *v.t., v.i.,* **-sized, -siz-ing.** to turn bottom side up; upset; overturn: *The sailboat nearly capsized in the squall, and the rough waves capsized the rowboat.* [origin uncertain]

cap sleeve, a short sleeve or flap, covering only the top of the shoulder.

cap|so|mere (kap′sə mir), *n.* one of the units that make up a capsid: *The capsomeres are packed in a regular pattern to form the shell or "capsid" as an approximate sphere* (New Scientist). [< *caps*(id) + *-mere*]

***cap|stan** (kap′stən), *n.* **1** a machine for lifting or pulling that revolves on an upright shaft or spindle, now usually operated by an engine. Sailors on old ships hoisted the anchor or raised heavy sails by turning the capstan. **2** a small pulley that regulates the passage of tape through a tape recorder. [< Old Provençal *cabestan,* ultimately < Latin *capistrum* halter < *capere* to hold]

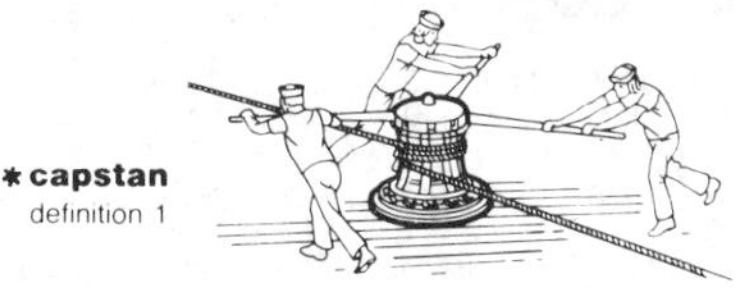

***capstan**
definition 1

capstan bar, a pole used to turn a capstan.

cap|stone (kap′stōn′), *n.* **1** one of the stones along the top of a wall or of some other structure. **2** *Figurative.* a finishing touch; climax: *This was, perhaps, the capstone of his career* (Newsweek).

cap|su|lar (kap′sə lər, -syə-), *adj.* **1** of or having to do with a capsule. **2** formed or shaped like a capsule. **3** in a capsule.

capsular ligament, *Anatomy.* the ligament which surrounds every movable joint, and contains the synovia.

cap|su|late (*v.* kap′sə lāt; *adj.* kap′sə lāt, -lit; -syə-), *v.,* **-lat|ed, -lat|ing,** *adj.* **—*v.t.*** **1** to enclose in a capsule; encapsulate. **2** to make a concise summary of; capsulize.
—*adj.* enclosed in a capsule; formed into a capsule. **—cap′su|la′tion,** *n.*

cap|su|lat|ed (kap′sə lā′tid, -syə-), *adj.* = capsulate: *a capsulate abscess.*

cap|sule (kap′səl, -syül), *n., adj., v.,* **-suled, -sul-ing.** **—*n.*** **1** a small case or covering. Medicine is often given in capsules made of gelatin. **2a** = space capsule: *The Air Force abandoned hope of recovering an instrumented capsule from orbiting Discoverer VII after the capsule failed to separate from the earth satellite* (Wall Street Journal). **b** a section of an aircraft, such as the cockpit, which can be handled or ejected as a unit. **3a** a dry seedcase that opens when ripe. **b** the spore case of mosses and various other lower plants. **4a** a membrane or ligament enclosing some part or organ, as in a sac: *the capsule of the crystalline lens of the eye, the capsule of the hip joint.* **b** either of two white layers of nerve fibers in the cerebrum. **5** a concise summary.
—*adj.* **1** in condensed or abridged form; very short: *a capsule history of Williamsburg.* **2** very small; miniature: *a capsule radio transmitter.* **3** of or having to do with a space capsule: *a capsule communicator.*
—*v.t.* to furnish within or enclose with a capsule: *It will be capsuled in a cylinder six feet in diameter and seven and a half feet in height* (Science News Letter).
[< Latin *capsula* (diminutive) < *capsa* box < *capere* hold]

cap|su|lif|e|rous (kap′sə lif′ər əs), *adj. Biology.* bearing capsules. [< Latin *capsula* (see etym. under **capsule**) + English *-ferous*]

cap|su|lize (kap′sə līz, -syə-), *v.t.,* **-ized, -iz|ing.** to present in a concise or condensed form: *A slogan that ... capsulizes Washington's economic thinking ...* [*is*] *Balance the Budget!* (Birmingham News).

Capt., Captain.

cap|tain (kap′tən), *n., v.* **—*n.*** **1** a head of a group; leader or chief: *Robin Hood was captain of his band.* **2a** the commander of a ship: *The captain refused to leave his sinking ship while there were others on board.* **b** a navy officer ranking next below a rear admiral and next above a commander. He usually commands a warship. **3** an army, air force, or marine officer ranking next below a major and next above a first lieutenant: *The captain led his company in the attack. With the rank of captain, he served as a sieve to filter requests from Air Force commands* (New Yorker). **4** a police or fire department officer, usually ranking next above a lieutenant. **5** a leader of a team in sports: *He is captain of the football team. Abbr:* Capt.
—*v.t.* to lead or command as captain: *He will captain the basketball team next season. John Paul Jones captained the "Bonhomme Richard" in its battle with the "Serapis."*
[< Old French *capitaine,* learned borrowing from Late Latin *capitāneus* commander; prominent chief < Latin *caput, -itis* head. See etym. of doublet **chieftain.**]

cap|tain|cy (kap′tən sē), *n., pl.* **-cies.** **1** the rank, commission, or authority of a captain. **2** an area or district administered by a captain.

captain general, a commander in chief.

cap|tain|less (kap′tən lis), *adj.* without a captain.

captain's biscuit, a ship biscuit of fine quality.

captain's chair, a wooden chair with a low back consisting of upright slats supporting a narrow, contoured backrest.

cap|tain|ship (kap′tən ship), *n.* **1** = captaincy. **2** ability as a captain; leadership.

cap|tan (kap′tan), *n. U.S.* a plant fungicide, sold under various trade names.

cap|ta|tion (kap tā′shən), *n.* the use of artful endeavors or appeals to secure something, especially approval or applause: *... to induce candidates to rely ... less on the arts of political captation* (London Daily News). [< Latin *captātiō, -ōnis* < *captāre* strive to take < *capere* take]

cap|tion (kap′shən), *n., v.* **—*n.*** **1** a title under a picture explaining it or a title at the head of a page, chapter, poem, or the like. **2** a subtitle in motion pictures or on a television screen. **3** the part of a legal document which gives the time, place, or authority for the document.
—*v.t.* to put a caption on: *an effective poem ... captioned 'The Song of the Innuit'* (Science).
[< Latin *captiō, -ōnis* a taking < *capere* take]
—cap′tion|less, *adj.*

cap|tious (kap′shəs), *adj.* **1** hard to please; faultfinding: *The captious might have regarded our journey as a retreat from Sweden, but we veterans regarded it as a surprise attack on Paris* (Atlantic). **SYN:** caviling, carping. **2** apt or designed to entrap or entangle by subtlety: *captious arguments.* [< Latin *captiōsus* < *captiō* a deceiving, a fallacious argument < *capere* catch, take] **—cap′-tious|ly,** *adv.* **—cap′tious|ness,** *n.*

cap|ti|vate (kap′tə vāt), *v.t.,* **-vat|ed, -vat|ing.** **1** to hold captive by beauty or interest; charm; fascinate: *The children were captivated by the story of Peter Pan. The prima donna captivated the audience.* **SYN:** enchant, entrance. **2** *Obsolete.* to capture. [< Late Latin *captīvāre* (with English

Pronunciation Key: hat, āge, cãre, fär; let, ēqual, tėrm; it, īce; hot, ōpen, ôrder; oil, out; cup, pu̇t, rüle; child; long; thin; ᴛʜen; zh, measure; ə represents **a** in about, **e** in taken, **i** in pencil, **o** in lemon, **u** in circus.

-ate[1]) < Latin *captīvus* captive] —**cap′ti|vat′-ing|ly**, *adv.* —**cap′ti|va′tor**, *n.*

cap|ti|va|tion (kap′tə vā′shən), *n.* **1** a captivating or being captivated. **2** *Figurative.* charm; fascination: *the arts which ladies ... employ for captivation* (Jane Austen).

cap|ti|va|tive (kap′tə vā′tiv), *adj.* fitted or tending to captivate.

cap|tive (kap′tiv), *n., adj.* —***n.*** **1** a person or animal captured and held against his will; prisoner: *The pirates took many captives and sold them as slaves.* **2** *Figurative.* a person charmed or enslaved as by beauty or love.
—***adj.*** **1** made a prisoner; held against one's will; confined: *The captive rabbits were shut up in a cage.* **2** *Figurative.* captivated: *The captive spectators sat spellbound before the tightrope walker.* **3** owned and controlled by a parent company for the use of the latter: *This steel company owns and operates a captive coal mine.* **4** of or belonging to a captive.
[< Latin *captīvus* < *capere* take. See etym. of doublet **caitiff.**]

captive audience, a group of persons involuntarily subjected to an advertising appeal or other message.

captive balloon, a balloon secured and controlled by a rope or cable to the ground.

captive bolt, **1** a bolt or rod in a special gun used for stunning animals to be slaughtered. **2** the gun.

captive firing, a ground test of a bolted-down missle or rocket engine.

cap|tiv|i|ty (kap tiv′ə tē), *n., pl.* **-ties.** **1** the condition of being in prison: *Captivity weakened his will to fight.* **SYN:** imprisonment. **2** the condition of being held against one's will: *Some animals cannot bear captivity, and die after a few weeks in a cage.* **SYN:** bondage, servitude, slavery.

Cap|tiv|i|ty (kap tiv′ə tē), *n.* = Babylonian captivity.

cap|tor (kap′tər), *n.* a person who takes or holds a prisoner: *His captors guarded the bear in a garage until the circus people arrived.*

cap|tress (kap′tris), *n.* a female captor.

cap|ture (kap′chər), *v.,* **-tured, -tur|ing,** *n.* —***v.t.*** **1** to make a prisoner of; take by force, skill, or trickery; seize: *We captured butterflies with a net.* **SYN:** apprehend. See syn. under **catch.** **2** to attract and hold; catch and keep: *The magician's tricks captured the boy's attention.* **3** *Nuclear Physics.* (of an atomic nucleus) to cause the capture of (an elementary particle). [< noun]
—***n.*** **1** a person or thing taken in this way: *The first capture of the day was a python for an American zoo. ... was ordered to collect the prisoners and bring them with all his captures to Scapa* (Sunday Times). **2** a capturing or a being captured: *With the capture of the escaped lion everyone in town felt relieved.* **SYN:** seizure, arrest, apprehension. **3** *Nuclear Physics.* the process by which an atomic nucleus absorbs or acquires an additional elementary particle, especially a neutron, often resulting in emission of radiation or fission of the nucleus. **4** retrieval of information stored in a computer memory bank.
[< French *capture,* learned borrowing from Latin *captūra* taking < *capere* take] —**cap′tur|a|ble,** *adj.* —**cap′tur|er,** *n.*

ca|puche (kə püsh′, -püch′), *n.* a long, pointed cowl, such as that worn by the Capuchins. [< French *capuche* < Italian *cappuccio* < *cappa* < Late Latin]

Cap|u|chin (kap′yu̇ chin, -shin), *n.* a Franciscan friar belonging to an order that wears a long, pointed hood or cowl; Friar Minor Capuchin. [< Middle French *capuchin* < Italian *cappuccina* monk wearing a cowl < *cappuccio* cowl, hood; see etym. under **capuche**]

cap|u|chin (kap′yu̇ chin, -shin), *n.* **1** a South American monkey with black hair on its head that looks like a hood; sapajou. **2** a woman's cloak with a hood. [< *Capuchin*]

cap|u|cine (kap′yu̇ sin), *n.* = capuchin (def. 1).

Cap|u|let (kap′yə lit, -let), *n.* a member of Juliet's family in Shakespeare's play *Romeo and Juliet.*

ca|put (kā′pət, kap′ət), *n., pl.* **ca|pi|ta.** *Latin.* head.

ca|put mor|tu|um (kā′pət môr′tyu̇ əm, kap′ət), *Latin.* **1** (formerly) the residuum of chemicals after distillation or sublimation. **2** *Figurative.* any worthless residue.

cap|y|ba|ra (kap′ə bär′ə), *n.* a rodent of South America. It is the world's largest extant rodent, up to 4 feet long and 2 feet high, and has a very short tail. Capybaras are aquatic animals. Also, **capibara.** [< Portuguese *capybara* < the Tupi name]

car (kär), *n.* **1** an automobile: *They made the trip by car. Motorcycles and cars were halted, but buses were able to continue* (London Times). **2a** a railroad vehicle for freight or passengers: *a Pullman car.* **b** any vehicle that runs on rails: *A streetcar is often called a car.* **3** any vehicle that moves on wheels: *A carriage or cart is sometimes called a car.* **4** carload. **5a** the closed platform of a balloon or airship, for carrying passengers or cargo. **b** *U.S.* the cage of an elevator. **6** a chariot: *... the gilded car of Day* (Milton). [< Old North French *carre* < Medieval Latin *carra* < Latin *carrus* four-wheeled cart] —**car′less,** *adj.*
▶In popular use in the United States, *car* now commonly replaces *automobile, auto, motorcar,* and other terms for four-wheeled vehicles with internal-combustion engines. It is not used for trucks, buses, taxis, and other specifically commercial vehicles.

CAR (no periods), Civil Air Regulations.

ca|ra|ba|o (kär′ə bä′ō), *n., pl.* **-ba|os.** the water buffalo of the Philippine Islands, now commonly domesticated. [< Spanish *carabao* < Malay *kĕrbau*]

car|a|bid beetle (kar′ə bid), = ground beetle. [< New Latin *Carabidae,* the family name < Greek *kárabos,* a horned beetle]

car|a|bin (kar′ə bin), *n.* = carbine.

car|a|bine (kar′ə bīn), *n.* = carbine.

car|a|bi|neer or **car|a|bi|nier** (kar′ə bə nir′), *n.* a cavalry soldier armed with a carbine (in former times). Also, **carbineer.** [< French *carabinier*]

ca|ra|bi|ne|ro (kä′rä bi nā′rō), *n., pl.* **-ros.** **1** (in Spain) a carbineer. **2** (in the Philippines) a soldier appointed to prevent smuggling; a custom-house guard or coast guard. [< Spanish *carabinero*]

ca|ra|bi|nie|re (kä′rä bi nye′rē), *n., pl.* **-ri** (-rē). an Italian policeman. [< Italian *carabiniere*]

car|a|cal (kar′ə kal), *n.* a small lynx of Asia and Africa, of a reddish-brown color, having a tuft of long, black hair at the tip of each ear; Persian lynx. [< French *caracal* < Turkish *karakulak* < *kara* black + *kulak* ear]

ca|ra|ca|ra (kär′ə kär′ə), *n.* any one of several vulturelike hawks found in tropical and subtropical America. Audubon's caracara is the national emblem of Mexico. [< Spanish *caracará* < the Tupi (perhaps Brazil) name; probably imitative]

car|ack (kar′ək), *n.* = carrack.

car|a|col (kar′ə kol), *n., v.i.,* **-colled, -col|ling.** = caracole.

car|a|cole (kar′ə kōl), *n., v.,* **-coled, -col|ing.** —***n.*** **1** a half turn to the right or left, made by a horse and rider. **2** one of the turns made by a horse in prancing on a zigzag course. —***v.i.*** to move in a series of half turns; prance from side to side: *Theirs are huge and heartshaped monsters ... glossy black as the black patent leather pumps in which we once caracoled in society's exclusive cotillions* (New Yorker). [< French *caracole* < Spanish *caracol* (originally) spiral shell, snail; of uncertain origin]

car|a|cul (kar′ə kəl), *n.* **1** a type of short, flat, loose, curly fur made from the skin of newborn or very young lambs of a breed of robust, fat-tailed Asian sheep. **2** any sheep of this breed. **3** a name sometimes applied to the skins of young goats. Also **karakul.** [< Turkish *Kara Kul,* a typical name of lakes in Turkestan, (literally) black lake]

ca|rafe (kə raf′, -räf′), *n.* a glass bottle, especially an ornamental one, for holding water, wine, coffee, or the like: *The "snack bars" ... [of Paris] sell hot dogs and hamburgers with carafes of vin ordinaire* (New York Times). [< French *carafe* < Italian *caraffa* < Spanish *garrafa* < Arabic *gharrāf* drinking vessel]

car|a|ga|na (kar′ə gā′nə), *n.* any one of a group of leguminous trees or shrubs native to China and Siberia, having feathery pale-green foliage and yellow flowers appearing in early spring. [< New Latin *Caragana* the genus name < *karaghan,* the Tartar name]

car|a|geen (kar′ə gēn), *n.* = carrageen.

ca|ra|gua|ta (kä′rä guä′tä), *n.* a plant of the pineapple family found in Paraguay and Argentina, which yields a long silky fiber used especially in making cordage and sacks. [< Spanish *caraguata* < Tupi *caraguata* < *caránhe* scratch + *goatágo*]

ca|ram|ba (kä räm′bä), *interj. Spanish.* an exclamation of dismay, anger, or surprise.

car|am|bo|la (kar′əm bō′lə), *n.* **1** the acid fruit of a small East Indian tree. **2** the tree itself. [< Spanish *carambola,* perhaps < Marathi *karambal* < Sanskrit *karmaranga*]

car|a|mel (kar′ə məl, kär′məl), *n., v.,* **-meled, -mel|ing** or (*especially British*) **-melled, -mel|ling.** —***n.*** **1** sugar browned or burned over heat and used for coloring and flavoring food: *Cake frosting and custard are often flavored with caramel.* **2** a small block of chewy candy flavored with this sugar. **3** the color of caramel; any shade of brown.
—***v.t., v.i.*** = caramelize.
[< French *caramel* < obsolete Spanish *caramelo*]

car|a|mel|ise (kar′ə mə līz, kär′mə-), *v.,* **-ised, -is|ing.** *Especially British.* to caramelize.

car|a|mel|ize (kar′ə mə līz, kär′mə-), *v.,* **-ized, -iz|ing.** —***v.t.*** to melt (sugar) over heat so that it turns brown: *Caramelize the sugar in a heavy skillet over low heat, stirring constantly* (Sunset). —***v.i.*** (of sugar) to melt and turn brown.

ca|ran|gid (kə ran′jid), *adj., n.* = carangoid.

ca|ran|goid (kə rang′goid), *adj., n.* —***adj.*** of or having to do with a family of fish having spiny fins and forked tails: *The pompano and cavalla are carangoid fishes.*
—***n.*** any fish of this family.
[< New Latin *Caranx, -angis* the typical genus (< Spanish *caranga*) + English *-oid*]

car|a|pace (kar′ə pās), *n.* **1** a shell or bony covering on the back or part of the back of turtles, armadillos, and crustaceans such as lobsters and crabs. **2a** any hard outer covering: *... the large, rusting carapace of a 1957 Chevrolet* (New Yorker). **b** *Figurative: Behind Baudelaire's carapace is a sensibility always struggling for transcendence* (Saturday Review). [< French *carapace* < Spanish *carapacho*]

ca|ra|pa|cial (kar′ə pā′shəl), *adj.* = carapacic.

ca|ra|pa|cic (kar′ə pā′sik), *adj.* of or having to do with the carapace.

car|at (kar′ət), *n.* **1** a unit of weight for precious stones, equal to gram or 200 milligrams. **2** one 24th part of gold in an alloy: *A gold ring of 18 carats is 18 parts pure gold and 6 parts alloy. Abbr:* kt. Also, **karat.** [< Middle French *carat* < Italian *carato* < Arabic *qīrāṭ* < Greek *kerâtion* carob seed; (originally) the (horn-shaped) pod of the carob tree (diminutive) < *kéras, -ātos* horn]

car|at|age (kar′ə tij), *n.* quantity or weight in carats.

car|a|van (kar′ə van), *n., v.,* **-vaned, -van|ing** or (*especially British*) **-vanned, -van|ning.** —***n.*** **1a** a group of merchants, pilgrims, tourists, or the like, traveling together for safety through difficult or dangerous country: *a caravan of Arab merchants laden with spices and Oriental silks.* **b** any similar group of travelers. **c** the vehicles or beasts of burden used by such a group: *...traveling by caravan, that is, great droves of laden camels* (William Warner). **2a** a closed truck or trailer, or formerly a large, covered wagon, for moving people or goods; van. **b** *British.* a house on wheels; trailer: *Small auto-trailers designed for holidaying—"caravans"—went on the Canadian market* (Maclean's).
—***v.t., v.i.*** to travel or convey by caravan: *Having caravanned all over this continent, he admitted that there is an awful lot of it to love* (London Times).
[< Old French *caravane* < Persian *kārwān*]

car|a|van|eer (kar′ə va nir′), *n.* a person who travels with a caravan in the Orient.

car|a|van|er (kar′ə van′ər), *n.* = caravanner.

car|a|van|ner (kar′ə van′ər), *n.* **1** *British.* a person who travels by or lives in a trailer or house on wheels. **2** a person who travels with a caravan in the East; caravaneer.

car|a|van|ning (kar′ə van′ing), *n. British.* traveling or living in a trailer, especially while on vacation.

caravan park, *British.* a trailer court.

car|a|van|sa|ry (kar′ə van′sər ē), *n., pl.* **-ries.** **1** an inn or hotel in the Orient where caravans stop to rest, usually a large, four-sided building surrounding a spacious court. **2** *Figurative.* any large inn or hotel. [< Persian *kārwānsarāī* < *kārwān* caravan + *sarāī* inn]

car|a|van|se|rai (kar′ə van′sə rī, -rā), *n.* = caravansary.

***car|a|vel** or **car|a|velle** (kar′ə vel), *n.* **1** a small, fast sailing ship of the type used by Columbus and other early navigators, with a broad bow and high stern. **2** any one of various small sailing ships of former times. Also, **carvel.** [< French *caravelle* < Portuguese *caravela* (diminutive) < *cávo* < Late Latin *cārabus* < Late Greek *kârabos* kind of light boat < Greek, horned beetle, crawfish, probably < ancient Macedonian]

***caravel** definition 1

car|a|way (kar′ə wā), *n.* **1** a plant that yields fragrant, spicy seeds, used to flavor bread, rolls, or cakes. It belongs to the parsley family. **2** its seeds. [< Old Spanish *alcarahueya, alcaravea* < Spanish Arabic *al-karawia* < Arabic *al-karāwiyā*]

caraway seeds, the seeds of the caraway.

carb (kärb), *n. Informal.* carburetor.

carb-, *combining form.* carbon: *Carbide = carbon plus a metal.* Also, **carbo-** before consonants. [< *carbon*]

car|bam|ate (kär bam′āt, kär′bə māt), *n.* a salt or ester of carbamic acid. [< *carbam*(ic) + *-ate*²]

car|bam|ic acid (kär bam′ik), an acid occurring only in the form of salts. Its ammonium salt occurs in commercial ammonium carbonate. *Formula:* CH_3NO_2 [< *carb-* + *am*(ide) + *-ic*]

car|ba|mide (kär′bə mīd, -mid; kär bam′īd, -id), *n. Chemistry.* urea.

car|ba|myl (kär′bə mil), *n.* the univalent radical, $-NH_2CO$, of carbamic acid.

car|ban|i|on (kär ban′ī′ən, -on), *n.* an organic anion such as $(NO_2)_3C^-$, occurring as an intermediate in many reactions. [< *carb-* + *anion*]

car|barn (kär′bärn′), *n.* a building for the storage and maintenance of trolley cars, buses, and railroad cars.

car|bar|sone (kär′bər sōn), *n.* a preparation containing arsenic, used to treat amebic dysentery.

car|ba|ryl (kär′bə ril), *n.* a highly toxic compound of methyl carbamate and naphthol, widely used against many types of insect pests.

car|ba|zole (kär′bə zōl), *n.* a crystalline compound derived from anthracene, used in the manufacture of certain dyes. *Formula:* $C_{12}H_9N$ [< *carb-* + *az*(o) + *-ole*]

car|be|cue (kär′bə kyü), *n.* a device for melting down and compacting scrap automobiles.

car|bene (kär′bēn), *n.* an organic radical containing divalent carbon, such as $-CH_2-$ (methylene), occurring as an intermediate in certain reactions.

car|bide (kär′bīd, -bid), *n.* **1** a compound of carbon with another element, usually a metal. **2** = calcium carbide.

car|bine (kär′bīn, -bēn), *n.* **1** a short, light, automatic or semiautomatic rifle of relatively great power but short range. **2** a short-barreled rifle or musket formerly used in the cavalry. Also, **carabin, carabine**. [< French *carabine* a small harquebus < *carabin* cavalryman]

car|bi|neer (kär′bə nir′), *n.* a cavalry soldier armed with a carbine. Also, **carabineer, carabinier**.

car|bi|nol (kär′bə nōl, -nol), *n.* **1** methyl alcohol or methanol. *Formula:* CH_3OH **2** an alcohol derived from it. **3** the univalent radical $-CH_2OH$. [< German *Karbinol* (coined by Hermann Kolbe, 1818-84, a German chemist) < *Karbin* methyl]

carbo-, *combining form.* the form of **carb-** before consonants, as in *carbohydrate.*

car|bo|cy|clic compound (kär′bō sī′klik, -sik′lik), any one of many organic compounds in which all the atoms of the ring are carbon, such as in benzene.

car|bo|hol|ic (kär′bə hol′ik), *n.* a person with a craving for sweets and starches: *To remedy the problem, I have devised a special diet for carboholics . . . which balances the proportion of carbohydrates, protein, and fats* (Neil Solomon). [< *carbo*(hydrate) + (alco)*holic*]

car|bo|hy|drase (kär′bō hī′drās), *n.* any one of a number of enzymes which catalyze the hydrolysis of carbohydrates.

car|bo|hy|drate (kär′bō hī′drāt), *n.* a substance made from carbon dioxide and water by green plants in sunlight. Carbohydrates are made up of carbon, hydrogen, and oxygen. Sugar and starch are carbohydrates. Carbohydrates comprise a major class of foods for animals.

car|bo|late (kär′bə lāt), *n.* a salt of carbolic acid.

car|bo|lat|ed (kär′bə lā′tid), *adj.* containing carbolic acid.

car|bol|fuch|sin (kär′bol fük′sin), *n.* a solution of fuchsin used in staining specimens for microscopic study, in which the staining power of the dye has been enforced by the addition of carbolic acid.

car|bol|ic (kär bol′ik), *adj.* made from carbon or coal tar. [< *carb-* + *-ol*¹ + *-ic*]

carbolic acid, a very poisonous, corrosive, white, crystalline substance obtained from coal tar, used in solution as a disinfectant and antiseptic; phenol. *Formula:* C_6H_5OH

car|bo|lize (kär′bə līz), *v.t.*, **-lized, -liz|ing.** to add carbolic acid to; treat with carbolic acid.

Car|bo|loy (kär′bə loi), *n. Trademark.* an extremely hard alloy containing tungsten, carbon, and cobalt, used in the making of cutting tools.

car|bo|my|cin (kär′bə mī′sin), *n.* an antibiotic used to treat infections caused by Gram-positive bacteria or by organisms which have developed resistance to other antibiotics; Magnamycin. *Formula:* $C_{42}H_{67}NO_{16}$ [< *carbo-* + (strepto)*mycin*]

★**car|bon** (kär′bən), *n.* **1** a very common chemical element which occurs in combination with other elements in all plants and animals. Diamonds and graphite are pure carbon in the form of crystals; coal and charcoal are mostly carbon in uncrystallized form. Carbon is nonmetallic, forms organic compounds in combination with hydrogen, oxygen, nitrogen, and the like, and is manufactured especially as coke or lampblack. Its outstanding characteristic is the ability of its atoms to link with one another in rings or chains, thus giving rise to innumerable complex compounds. **2** a piece of carbon such as is used in batteries or arc lamps. **3** a piece of carbon paper: *The typist put a carbon between the sheets of paper to make two copies of the letter.* **4** a copy made with carbon paper; carbon copy: *The secretary kept a carbon of each letter she typed.* [< French *carbone,* learned borrowing from Latin *carbō, -ōnis* charcoal] —**car′bon|less**, *adj.*

★**carbon**
definition 1

symbol	atomic number	atomic weight	oxidation state
C	6	12.01115	±4, +2

carbon 12, the most common isotope of carbon, now used as the standard for measuring atomic weights. *Symbol:* C^{12}

carbon 13, a stable, heavy isotope of carbon, having a mass number of 13, used as a tracer in physiological studies, especially in cancer research. *Symbol:* C^{13}

carbon 14, a radioactive isotope of carbon produced by the bombardment of nitrogen atoms by neutrons; radiocarbon. Since carbon 14 gives off radioactivity at a uniform rate in all animals and plants that have died, scientists are able to find out the age of many ancient remains of living things, or of geological formations in which organic matter occurs, by measuring the amount of carbon 14 left in them. *Symbol:* C^{14}.

car|bo|na|ceous (kär′bə nā′shəs), *adj.* **1** of or like carbon; containing carbon: *a carbonaceous compound, carbonaceous shale.* **2** like or containing coal, charcoal, or other common forms of carbon.

car|bo|na|do¹ (kär′bə nā′dō), *n., pl.* **-does**. an opaque, dark-colored, massive form of diamond, found chiefly in Brazil and used for drills; black diamond. [< Portuguese *carbonado* (literally) carbonized (from its color)]

car|bo|na|do² (kär′bə nā′dō), *n., pl.* **-does** or **-dos**, *v.*, **-doed, -do|ing.** —*n. Obsolete.* a piece of meat, fish, or poultry scored and then broiled. —*v.t.* **1** *Archaic.* to score and broil. **2** to cut; slash; hack.
[< Spanish *carbonada* thing cooked on the coals < *carbón* charcoal < Latin *carbō, -ōnis*]

carbon arc, **1** a lamp whose light source is an electric arc spanning two carbon electrodes. **2** an arc with a carbon electrode on one or both sides.

Car|bo|na|ri (kär′bō nä′rē), *n.pl., sing.* **-ro** (-rō). an Italian secret society organized early in the 1800's for the purpose of liberating Italy from Austrian domination and forming a republic. [< Italian *Carbonari* (literally) charcoal burners, plural of dialectal *carbonaro* < Latin *carbōnārius* < *carbō, -ōnis* charcoal]

car|bon|ate (*n.* kär′bə nāt, -nit; *v.* kär′bə nāt), *n., v.*, **-at|ed, -at|ing.** —*n.* a salt or ester of carbonic acid, which contains the bivalent group $-CO_3$, such as calcium carbonate, $CaCO_3$.
—*v.t.* **1a** to charge or saturate with carbon dioxide. Soda water is carbonated to make it bubble and fizz. SYN: aerate. **b** to change into a carbonate. **2** to burn to carbon; char; carbonize. —**car′bon|a′tion**, *n.*

car|bon|a|tite (kär′bə nə tīt′), *n.* an intrusive rock that is rich in carbonate, resembling limestone and granite in chemical composition.

carbon bisulfide, = carbon disulfide.

carbon black, a smooth, black pigment of pure carbon, formed by deposits, especially from incomplete burning of natural gas and oil, and used in the manufacture of rubber and printing inks. It is a black soot, finer and purer than lampblack. *Seventy million pounds of carbon black are used in printing newspapers, magazines and books* (Science News Letter).

carbon copy, **1** a copy made with carbon paper. **2** *Figurative.* any person or thing that appears to duplicate another; replica: *He is a carbon copy of his father. They lined up the party behind a program that was virtually a carbon copy of the Christian Democratic platform* (Harper's).

carbon cycle, **1** *Biology.* the circulation of carbon in nature. Plants take in carbon dioxide from the atmosphere and convert it to carbohydrates by photosynthesis; animals eat the plants and release the energy from the carbohydrates by exhaling carbon dioxide, which in turn is taken in by plants. **2** *Physics.* the series of nuclear transformations in incandescent stars that, beginning and ending with a carbon 12 atom, liberate atomic energy and transform hydrogen into helium: *[He] discovered the series of nuclear reactions known as the carbon cycle and thereby offered the first reasonable theory of what makes the stars shine* (Scientific American).

car|bon-date (kär′bən dāt′), *v.t.*, **-dat|ed, -dat|ing.** to determine the age of (a specimen) by carbon dating: *The tools themselves, being stone, could not be carbon-dated* (Science News).

carbon dating, a method of determining the age of an organic, geological, or archaeological specimen by measuring the amount of carbon 14 left in them; radiocarbon dating: *By carbon 14 dating, they determined that the city was first settled about 800 B.C.* (Time).

carbon dioxide, a heavy, colorless, odorless gas, present in the atmosphere or formed when any fuel containing carbon is burned; carbonic-acid gas. The air that is breathed out of an animal's lungs contains carbon dioxide. Plants absorb it from the air and use it to make plant tissue. Carbon dioxide is used in soda water and in fire extinguishers. *Formula:* CO_2

car|bon-di|ox|ide snow, (kär′bən dī ok′sīd), solidified carbon dioxide, used as a refrigerant; dry ice.

carbon disulfide, a colorless liquid, used as a solvent for resins, rubber, and the like, and as an insecticide; carbon bisulfide. *Formula:* CS_2

carbon fiber, a strong, light synthetic fiber used in plastics, made by carbonizing acrylic fiber.

car|bon|ic (kär bon′ik), *adj.* of or containing carbon.

carbonic acid, an acid made when carbon dioxide is dissolved in water. It gives the sharp taste to soda water and occurs in the form of salts, the carbonates. *Formula:* H_2CO_3

car|bon|ic-ac|id gas (kär bon′ik as′id), = carbon dioxide.

carbonic anhydrase, an enzyme, present in the human body, which catalyzes the reaction between water and carbon dioxide.

car|bon|if|er|ous (kär′bə nif′ər əs), *adj.* containing or producing carbon or coal: . . . *the caves of Virginia and Kentucky in the older carboniferous limestone support a rich and diverse fauna of animals* (R. S. Hawes). [< *carbon* + *-ferous*]

Car|bon|if|er|ous (kär′bə nif′ər əs), *n., adj.* —*n.* **1** the geological period of the Paleozoic era including the Pennsylvanian and Mississippian periods. During the Carboniferous, the warm, moist climate produced great forests of tree ferns, horsetail rushes, and conifers, whose remains form the great coal beds. **2** the rocks and coal beds formed during this period.
—*adj.* of or having to do with this period or its rocks: *In the history of the earth, the Carboniferous period was one of the best for the growth of green plants* (Fred W. Emerson).

car|bon|ise (kär′bə nīz), *v.t.*, **-ised, -is|ing.** *Especially British.* to carbonize.

car|bon|ite (kär′bə nīt), *n.* an explosive used in blasting, containing nitroglycerin and various other substances, such as powdered wood and sodium nitrate.

car|bon|i|um ion (kär bō′nē əm), an organic cation, such as $(C_6H_5)_3\,C^+$, occurring as an intermediate in many reactions. [< *carb-* + (amm)*onium*]

car|bon|ize (kär′bə nīz), *v.t.*, **-ized, -iz|ing.** **1** to change into carbon by burning; char: *Pakistan's coal, because of its high content of volatile matter and non-coking properties, is to be carbonized in a low temperature carbonization plant* (London Times). **2** to cover or combine with carbon. —**car′bon|iz′a|ble**, *adj.* —**car′bon|i|za′tion**, *n.* —**car′bon|iz′er**, *n.*

carbon knock, the sound caused by an improper burning of fuel due to accumulated carbon in an internal-combustion engine; knock.

carbon microphone, a microphone in which an electric current passes through a package of carbon grains whose conductivity varies with its degree of compression. The transmitter in a telephone is a carbon microphone.

carbon monoxide, a colorless, odorless, very poisonous gas formed when carbon burns with an insufficient supply of air. It is part of the exhaust gases of automobile engines. *Formula:* CO

car|bon|nade (kär bə näd′), *n.* a Flemish beef stew made with onions, brown sugar, and beer. [< French *carbonnade,* probably < Spanish *carbonada* thing cooked on the coals; see etym. under **carbonado**²]

carbon paper, **1** thin paper having a preparation of carbon or other inky substance on one surface. It is used between sheets of paper to make a copy of what is written or typed on the upper sheet. **2** paper that is used in the carbon process of photography.

carbon process, a photographic process for producing permanent prints in black and white by the use of paper treated with carbon in gelatin.

carbon steel, steel containing varying amounts

of carbon and very small amounts of other alloying elements.

carbon tet·ra·chlo·ride (tet′rə klôr′īd, -id; -klōr′-), a colorless, poisonous liquid that does not burn, often used in fire extinguishers and in cleaning fluids, as a solvent, and in other ways. Its fumes are very dangerous if inhaled. *Formula:* CCl_4

car·bon·yl (kär′bə nil), *n.* **1** a bivalent radical, -CO-, occurring in aldehydes, ketones, and acids. **2** any one of a group of compounds of carbon monoxide united with a metal, such as nickel carbonyl, $Ni(CO)_4$.

car·bon·yl·a·tion (kär′bə nə lā′shən), *n.* the introduction of a carbonyl group into a compound.

carbonyl chloride, = phosgene.

car·bon·yl·ic (kär′bə nil′ik), *adj.* of or containing carbonyl.

car·bo·ra (kär bôr′ə, -bōr′-), *n.* a wood-burrowing worm of Australia which lives between high and low water in a tidal river. [< a native word in Australia]

car·bo·rane (kär′bə rān), *n.* any one of a class of compounds of carbon, boron, and hydrogen useful in the synthesis of polymers and lubricants.
[< *car*(bon) + *bor*(on) + *-ane*]

car·borne (kär′bôrn′, -bōrn′), *adj.* **1** traveling by car: *the carborne public.* **2** carried in a car: *a carborne radio transmitter.*

Car·bo·run·dum (kär′bə run′dəm), *n. Trademark.* an extremely hard compound of carbon and silicon used for grinding, cutting, and polishing. *Formula:* SiC [American English < *carbo*(n) + (co)*rundum*]

car·box·y·he·mo·glo·bin (kär bok′sē hē′mə glō′bən), *n.* the compound formed in the blood when inhaled carbon monoxide combines with hemoglobin: *The increased amount of carboxyhemoglobin restricts the amount of oxygen that the blood can carry* (Science News). [< *carboxy*(l) + *hemoglobin*]

car·box·yl (kär bok′səl), *n.* a univalent radical, -COOH, existing in many organic acids, the hydrogen being replaceable by a basic element or radical, thus forming a salt. [< *carb-* + *ox*(ygen) + *-yl*]

car·box·yl·ase (kär bok′sə lās), *n.* an enzyme, found in yeast, which removes carbon dioxide from the carboxyl group of amino acids.

car·box·yl·ate (*n.* kär bok′sə lāt, -lit; *v.* kär bok′sə lāt), *n., v.,* **-at·ed, -at·ing.** *—n.* a salt or ester of carboxylic acid.
—v.t. to introduce the carboxyl group into (a compound). —**car·box′yl·a′tion,** *n.*

car·box·yl·ic (kär′bok sil′ik), *adj.* of or having to do with carboxyl; resembling carboxyl.

carboxylic acid, any organic acid containing the carboxyl group.

car·boy (kär′boi), *n.* a very large glass bottle, usually enclosed in basketwork or in a wooden box or crate to keep it from being broken. It is chiefly used for holding acids and other corrosive liquids.
[< Persian *qarābah* large flagon]

car·bun·cle (kär′bung kəl), *n.* **1a** a very painful, inflamed swelling under the skin. A carbuncle discharges pus like a boil but is a more deep-seated infection, has several openings, lacks a hard central core, and is more serious in its effects **b** a red spot or pimple. **2a** a smooth, round garnet or other deep-red jewel. **b** a garnet cut to have a convex surface without facets. **3** either of two colors: **a** a brownish red. **b** a deep red.
[< Latin *carbunculus* (diminutive) < *carbō, -ōnis* live coal]

car·bun·cled (kär′bung kəld), *adj.* **1** affected with a carbuncle or carbuncles; spotted; pimpled. **2a** red or shining like a carbuncle or garnet. **b** set or adorned with carbuncles or garnets.

car·bun·cu·lar (kär bung′kyə lər), *adj.* of or having to do with carbuncles.

car·bu·rant (kär′bər ənt, -byər), *n.* a carbon compound, such as gasoline, used for carbureting with air or gas; carburetant.

car·bu·ra·tion (kär′bə rā′shən, -byə-), *n.* the process of charging air with hydrocarbon, such as gasoline, in finely divided liquid form, the resulting gas being burned for the production of energy.

car·bu·ret (kär′bə rāt, -byə ret), *v.,* **-ret·ed, -ret·ing** or (*especially British*) **-ret·ted, -ret·ting,** *n.*
—v.t. **1** to mix (air or gas) with carbon compounds, such as gasoline or benzine; carburize. **2** to combine with carbon.
—n. = carbide.
[< *carb*(on) + *-uret,* a chemical suffix < New Latin *-uretum*] —**car′bu·re′tion,** *n.*

car·bu·ret·ant (kär′bə ret′ənt, -byə-), *n.* = carburant.

***car·bu·re·tor** (kär′bə rā′tər, -byə ret′ər), *n.* a device for sending air through or over a liquid fuel to produce an explosive vapor for ignition in an internal-combustion engine: *A conventional carburetor has two barrels—a design growing more and more obsolete as the frenzied horsepower race continues in the industry at hot-rod proportions* (Wall Street Journal).

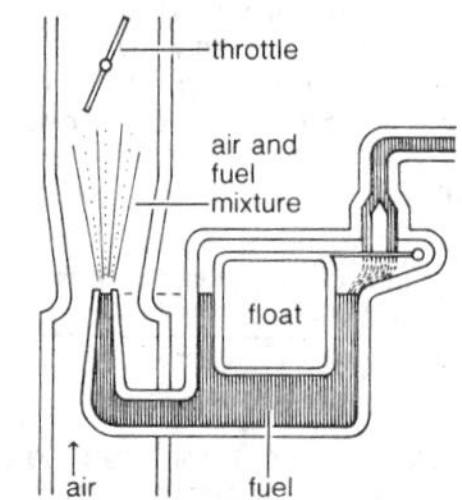

***carburetor**

car·bu·ret·tor (kär′byə ret′ər), *n. British.* carburetor.

car·bu·rize (kär′bə rīz, -byə-), *v.t.,* **-rized, -riz·ing.** **1** to combine (an element or substance) with carbon or a carbon compound, as in the conversion of iron into steel. **2** = carburet. [< French *carbure* carbide + English *-ize*] —**car′bu·ri·za′tion,** *n.* —**car′bu·riz′er,** *n.*

car·byl·a·mine (kär′bəl ə mēn′, -am′in), *n.* any organic cyanide having a nauseating odor and containing the radical—N: C.

car·ca·jou (kär′kə jü, -zhü), *n.* = wolverine. [American English < Canadian French form of the Algonkian (Montagnais) *karkaju*]

car·cake (kär′kāk′), *n.* a small cake baked on a griddle and eaten on Shrove Tuesday in parts of Scotland.
[apparently < Old English *caru* care + Middle English *cake* cake]

car·ca·net (kär′kə net), *n. Archaic.* an ornamental collar, necklace, or headband, of gold or jewels.
[< Middle French *carcan* iron collar]

car card, a kind of advertising poster displayed on buses, trains, and other conveyances.

car·case (kär′kəs), *n., v.t.,* **-cased, -cas·ing.** *Especially British.* carcass.

car·cass (kär′kəs), *n., v.* *—n.* **1a** the dead body of an animal: *Steak is cut from a beef carcass. The numbers of rabbits also fluctuate with the seasons, as can be seen from figures for exports of carcasses and skins* (Fenner and Day). **b** *Informal.* a human body, dead or living (now usually in ridicule or humor). **c** the whole trunk of a butchered animal, after removal of the head, limbs, and offal. **2** the shell or framework of a structure such as a building, ship, or piece of furniture. **3** *Figurative.* the lifeless shell or husk of anything: *The carcass of the sacrament cannot give life; but the soul of it* (Bishop Hall). **4** the inner, corded wall of the casing of a pneumatic tire. **5** a kind of incendiary shell; fireball.
—v.t. to erect or set up (the framework of a building, ship, or other structure).
[< Middle French *carcasse* < Italian *carcassa;* origin uncertain]

car·cel (kär sel′, kär′səl), *n.* a former French unit of illuminating power, based on the light emitted by a standard Carcel lamp.
[< B. G. *Carcel,* a French inventor of the 1800's]

Carcel lamp, a lamp in which the oil is fed to the wick by means of a pump operated by clockwork, used in lighthouses and the like, and for testing illuminating power.

car·ce·plex (kär′sə pleks), *n.* a molecular complex consisting of a large molecule in which a smaller molecule has been chemically trapped: *A carceplex consists of . . . a hollow "prison" molecule and a "guest" molecule trapped inside. These guest molecules . . . exist in a state of matter different from the familiar states represented by solids, liquids, gases and electrically charged plasmas* (New York Times). [< Latin *carcer* prison + English (com)*plex*]

car·char·o·don (kär kar′ə don), *n.* **1** a large man-eating tropical shark with extremely sharp, triangular teeth; great white shark. **2** any one of a number of similar types of extinct fish that reached eighty feet in length. [< New Latin *Carcharodon* the genus name < Greek *karcharódōn* having sharp teeth < *kárcharos* sharp + *odoús, odóntos* teeth]

car·char·o·dont (kär kar′ə dont), *adj.* having sharp, triangular teeth like those of a carcharodon.

car·cin·o·gen (kär sin′ə jən), *n.* any substance or agent that produces or tends to produce cancer: *Malignant growths can be produced experimentally in animals by the use of certain irritating substances called carcinogens* (Newsweek). [< *carcino*(ma) + *-gen*]

car·ci·no·gen·e·sis (kär sin′ə jen′ə sis), *n.* the growth or production of cancer.

car·cin·o·gen·ic (kär sin′ə jen′ik), *adj.* **1** producing or tending to produce cancer: *All the different classes of chemicals we have mentioned have been found to be carcinogenic in animals* (Scientific American). **2** caused by cancer.

car·ci·no·ge·nic·i·ty (kär sin′ə jə nis′ə tē), *n.* the power or tendency to cause or produce cancer.

car·cin·oid (kär′sə noid), *adj., n.* *—adj.* resembling a carcinoma, but usually benign.
—n. a carcinoid tumor: *a feebly malignant tumor called "carcinoid"* (Scientific American).

car·ci·no·ma (kär′sə nō′mə), *n., pl.,* **-mas, -ma·ta** (-mə tə). any one of various cancers of the skin, body organ linings, or glandular tissue: *one has tumours of the endoderm, such as carcinomas of the stomach, intestines and so forth* (E. Dodds).
[< Latin *carcinōma* < Greek *karkínōma* < *karkinoûsthai* to spread crabwise < *karkínos* crab]

car·ci·no·ma·to·sis (kär′sə nō′mə tō′sis), *n.* the condition characterized by the formation of carcinomas (cancers of epithelial origin) in many parts of the body.

car·ci·nom·a·tous (kär′sə nom′ə təs, -nō′mə-), *adj.* characterized by, or of the nature of, carcinoma.

car·ci·no·sar·co·ma (kär′sə nō sär kō′mə), *n., pl.* **-mas, -ma·ta** (-mə tə). a tumor with the characteristics of both carcinoma and sarcoma.

car coat, a short topcoat for casual wear: *We come upon a patch-pocket car coat of caramel beaver, mid-thigh length* (New Yorker).

card[1] (kärd), *n., v.* *—n.* **1** a flat piece of stiff paper, thin cardboard, or plastic, usually small and rectangular. A card is designed to have written or printed matter on it: *a postal card, a membership card.* **2a** a piece of cardboard or paper, often folded, bearing ornamental designs and greetings, sent to persons on special occasions: *a Christmas card, a birthday card.* **b** a rectangular piece of thin pasteboard bearing a person's name, or name, business, and address: *Tradesmen left their cards, and were eager to supply the new household* (Thackeray). **3a** a printed program of events at boxing matches, races, and the like. **b** = scorecard. **4** the series of items forming a program or list. **5** one of a pack of cards, used in playing games; playing card. Cards are typically arranged in four suits (spades, hearts, diamonds, and clubs), of 13 each (two to ten, jack, queen, king, ace). **6** a round piece of paper or pasteboard on which the 32 points of the compass, and usually the degrees of a circle, are marked: *On life's vast ocean diversely we sail, Reason the card, but passion is the gale* (Alexander Pope). **7** *Informal.* an odd, original, or amusing person: *[She] is the wag, the card, the dreadfully cheerful joker* (Punch). **8** a plan or means: *a doubtful card.*
—v.t. **1** to provide with a card or cards. **2** to write or enter on a card or cards; list. **3** to score: *Ike finished the round, carding a flashy 40* (Time). **4** to fix on a card; attach to a card. **5** to attach by means of a card: *His name was carded upon three staterooms* (Edgar Allan Poe).

cards, a a game or games played with a pack of playing cards. **b** playing such games: *Many of the people at the party were busy at cards.*

card up one's sleeve, a plan in reserve; extra help kept back until needed: *There was no question in Western capitals that the Russians had many more cards up their sleeves* (New York Times).

give cards and spades, *U.S. Informal.* to give or concede a generous advantage (in allusion to the scoring in cassino): *The calentura [a tropical fever] can give cards and spades to yellow fever in the game of death* (New York World).

hold all the cards, to have complete control (over): *Ask [him] about politics; he holds all the cards* (New Yorker).

in (or **on**) **the cards,** likely to happen; possible: *It was on the cards [that] Ireland should not belong to France* (John Stuart Mill).

lay (or **put**) **one's cards on the table,** to show what one has or can do; be perfectly frank about something: *Let them [writers] actually lay their cards on the table, so that critics, reviewers, and other serious students of literature can see at a glance what it is they wish to say* (Atlantic).

pack cards with, *Archaic.* to make a cheating arrangement with: *The poor King tried . . . to pack cards with fortune* (Justin H. McCarthy).

play one's cards, to deal or act in a calculating manner to gain an end: *If you play your cards well, the old man will leave you all his money.*

play the _____ card, to use a (specified) tactic to gain an advantage: *He plays the human rights card by noting that violators such as Argentina . . . and Ethiopia were recipients of some $600 millions* (Manchester Guardian Weekly).

show one's cards, to reveal one's plans: *He was a hard-boiled guy, and he had learned his lesson . . . He wasn't going to show his cards to nobody again* (James T. Farrell).

speak by the card, to speak precisely: *I speak by the card in order to avoid entanglement of words* (Benjamin Jowett).

stack the cards, to arrange secretly or unfairly: *In purely economic terms the cards are now stacked heavily in the companies' favor* (Manchester Guardian Weekly). *The way the cards are stacked against a young fellow today, I can't say I approve of early marriages* (Sinclair Lewis).
sure (or **safe, likely**, etc.) **card, a** a certainty or likelihood: *We have one sure card, which is to carry him before Justice Frolick* (Henry Fielding). **b** a person whose action, or the use of whose name, will ensure success: *Consider me a sure card in that line* (John P. Kennedy).
throw up one's cards, to give up: *He . . . threw up his cards and foreswore his game for that time and always* (Thomas Hardy).
[< Middle French *carte,* learned borrowing from Latin *charta.* See etym. of doublet **chart.**]

card[2] (kärd), *n., v.* **—*n.*** **1a** a toothed tool or wire brush used to separate, clean, and straighten the fibers of wool, cotton, flax, or the like, before spinning. **b** = carding machine. **2** a wire brush used to clean the grooves of a metal file. **3** a similar instrument for raising a nap on cloth.
—*v.t.* to clean or comb with such a tool or wire brush, or in a carding machine: *to card wool for spinning.*
[< Old North French *carde,* ultimately < Latin *carduus* thistle < *carrere* to card] **—card′er,** *n.*

Card., cardinal.

car|dam|i|ne (kär dam′ə nē, kär′də mīn), *n.* any one of a genus of plants of the mustard family, including the common lady's-smock or cuckooflower; bitter cress. [< Greek *kardaminē* a cress-like plant < *kárdamon* cress]

car|da|mom or **car|da|mum** (kär′də məm), *n.* **1** the fruit and aromatic seeds of an East Indian herb of the ginger family, used as seasoning and in medicine. It is grown in India, Malaya, and Jamaica. **2** this plant or various related plants whose seeds are used as inferior substitutes. [< Latin *cardamōmum* < Greek *kardámōmon* a spice of *kárdamon* cress + *ámōmon* an Indian spice plant]

car|da|mon (kär′də mən), *n.* = cardamom.

Car|dan joint (kär′dan), = universal joint. [< Jerome *Cardan* (Geronimo Cardano), 1501-1576, an Italian mathematician who invented it]

card|board (kärd′bôrd′, -bōrd′), *n., adj.* **—*n.*** a stiff material made of layers of paper pressed together, used to make cards and boxes; paperboard. **—*adj.*** having the flat, stiff characteristics of a piece of cardboard; two-dimensional; unreal: *a cardboard hero.*

card-car|ri|er (kärd′kar′ē ər), *n.* an official member of an organization: *He aims to push through a constitutional revision disciplining members who follow the Communist line—whether card-carriers or not* (Wall Street Journal).

card-car|ry|ing (kärd′kar′ē ing), *adj.* **1** holding a card which signifies membership in an organization, or which entitles the holder to certain privileges: *the millions of workers who are just card-carrying members and who take no interest in union affairs* (Wall Street Journal). **2** being officially a member (of the organization specified): *A New York actor testified he was a card-carrying Communist in 1946-47* (Wall Street Journal). **3** *Figurative.* being easily identified as (a special type); typical: . . . *a card-carrying representative of the modern condition* (New Yorker); . . . *the card-carrying capitalists of the labor movement* (Harper's).

card|case (kärd′kās′), *n.* a case for carrying visiting cards.

card catalog or **catalogue**, **1** a catalog in the form of a card index for helping people find books in a library, information in a file, or items in a collection, each book or item being entered on a separate card: *Guided by the attendant to a bank of mahogany card catalogue files at one end of the room, he began flicking his way through them knowingly* (New Yorker). **2** any card index: *a card catalog of paintings.*

card|ed (kär′did), *adj.* prepared by a card or carding machine: *carded yarn.*

car|del (kär′dəl), *n.* a barrel or cask formerly used by whalers. [< Dutch *kardeel*]

card file, a collection of systematically arranged cards which contain information: *The Zoo keeps a card file of the complete life history of each animal* (Harper's).

card|hold|er (kärd′hōl′dər), *n.* **1** a person who carries a card signifying his membership in an organization, or entitling him to certain privileges: *Only a cardholder may borrow books from the library.* **2** a person or thing that holds a card: *the cardholder of a stereoscope.*

car|di|a (kär′dē ə), *n.* the orifice which connects the esophagus and the upper part of the stomach. [< Greek *kardiā* heart]

car|di|ac (kär′dē ak), *adj., n.* **—*adj.*** Also, **cardial. 1** of or having to do with the heart: *cardiac disease, cardiac arteries.* **2** having to do with the upper part of the stomach.
—*n.* **1** a person who has heart disease: *I was lucky, and like every other cardiac, I enjoyed talking about my case* (Harper's). **2** a medicine that stimulates the heart. **3** = stomachic.
[< Latin *cardiacus* < Greek *kardiakós* < *kardiā* heart]

car|di|a|cal (kär dī′ə kəl), *adj.* = cardiac.

cardiac arrest, heart failure, especially in a potentially functional heart. Electric shock and drowning cause cardiac arrest.

cardiac asthma, labored breathing due to imperfect action of the heart.

cardiac cycle, **1** a complete pulsation of the heart, including dilation and contraction; heartbeat. **2** the time in which a complete pulsation takes place.

cardiac muscle, the muscle of the heart: *The cardiac muscle develops in a similar way from the mesoderm around the heart, but the cells become striated and connected with one another* (A. M. Winchester).

cardiac neurosis, a group of symptoms associated with physical exertion, especially in soldiers, characterized by short and labored breathing, palpitation, and vertigo, but not the result of heart disease.

car|di|al (kär′dē əl), *adj. Rare.* = cardiac.

car|di|al|gi|a (kär′dē al′jē ə), *n.* **1** any pain in the region near the heart. **2** = heartburn. [< Greek *kardialgiā* < *kardiā* heart, cardiac end of the stomach + *álgos* pain]

car|di|ant (kär′dē ənt), *n.* a drug or other agent that stimulates the heart. [< *cardi(ac)* + (stimul)*ant*]

car|di|gan (kär′də gən), *n.* a knitted jacket or sweater that opens down the front. [< the seventh Earl of *Cardigan,* 1797-1868]

Car|di|gan (kär′də gən), *n.* one of two varieties of Welsh corgi, characterized by a relatively long tail. [< *Cardigan,* county in Wales]

car|di|nal (kär′də nəl), *adj, n.* **—*adj.*** **1** of first importance; chief; principal: *The cardinal value of his plan is that it is simple.* SYN: main. **2** bright, rich red: *a cheerful cardinal sweater.* **3** of or having to do with a cardinal.
—*n.* **1** one of the princes, or high officials, of the Roman Catholic Church, appointed by the Pope and ranking next below him. Cardinals wear red robes and hats. [*He*] *was summoned to Rome to join his fellow cardinals in selecting a successor to the late Pope* (New York Times). **2** a bright, rich red. **3a** a North American songbird; redbird; cardinal grosbeak. The male has bright-red feathers marked with a little gray and black. It is a kind of finch. **b** any one of certain related birds. **4** = cardinal number. **5** a short, hooded cloak, originally scarlet, worn by women.
[< Latin *cardinālis* having to do with a hinge; chief < *cardō, -inis* hinge, turning point, pivot] **—car′di|nal|ly,** *adv.*

car|di|nal|ate (kär′də nə lāt), *n.* **1** the position or rank of a cardinal. **2** the Sacred College of cardinals.

cardinal bird, = cardinal (def. 3a).

cardinal bishop, a member of the highest order of cardinal in the Sacred College of the Roman Catholic Church.

cardinal deacon, a member of the third and lowest order of cardinal in the Sacred College of the Roman Catholic Church.

cardinal fish, any one of a genus of tropical, marine fish, often bright red.

cardinal flower, **1** the large, bright-red flower of an eastern and central North American plant. **2** the plant it grows on, which belongs to the lobelia family.

cardinal grosbeak, = cardinal (def. 3a).

car|di|nal|ic (kär′də nal′ik), *adj.* of or having to do with the office of a cardinal.

car|di|nal|ism (kär′də nə liz′əm), *n.* the system of the College of Cardinals. **—car′di|nal|ist,** *n.*

car|di|nal|i|tial (kär′də nə lish′əl), *adj.* of or having to do with a cardinal or cardinals; having the rank of cardinal. [< Italian *cardinalizio* + English *-al*[1]]

car|di|nal|i|ty (kär′də nal′ə tē), *n.* **1** the condition or property of being expressible in quantity. **2** the size of a mathematical set, without regard to the kinds of elements contained in the set: *Whenever we add one more member to an infinite set we do not get a set of greater cardinality, only one of equal cardinality* (Scientific American).

cardinal number or **numeral**, **1** a number that shows how many are meant. One, two, three, and four are cardinal numbers; first, second, third, and fourth are ordinal numbers. **2** a number that expresses the size of a mathematical set, or how many elements it contains, without regard to the kinds of elements it contains; number that expresses cardinality.
▶**Cardinal numbers** (def. 1), like 3, 10, 246, 9,371, are the numbers used in counting. **Ordinal numbers**, like first, second, and twenty-fourth, indicate order or position in a series.

cardinal points, any one of the four main directions of the compass; north, south, east, west.

cardinal priest, a member of the second order of cardinal in the Sacred College of the Roman Catholic Church.

cardinal red, a bright-red color.

car|di|nal-red (kär′də nəl red′), *adj.* of a bright red (darker than that of a cardinal's dress).

car|di|nal|ship (kär′də nəl ship), *n.* **1** the state of being a cardinal. **2** the rank, office, or term of a cardinal.

cardinal sins, = seven deadly sins.

cardinal virtues, prudence, fortitude, temperance, and justice. They were considered by the ancient philosophers to be the basic qualities of a good character. Faith, hope, and charity, which are known as the theological virtues, are often included with them.

card index, a file of cards referring to separate books, pictures, or other items in a collection, so arranged as to aid in finding items desired; card file; card catalog: [*He*] *and his people have built up a card index with details of every one of the 10,000 people around the church* (Manchester Guardian).

card-in|dex (kärd′in′deks), *v.t.* to list in a card index; make a card for: *We card-indexed every loan and sent receipts to every lender* (New Yorker).

car|di|nes (kär′də nēz), *n.* plural of **cardo.**

card|ing (kär′ding), *n.* the cleaning and straightening of the fibers of wool, cotton, flax, and the like, for spinning.

carding engine, *British.* carding machine.

carding machine, a machine for carding wool, cotton, flax, or the like: *Cotton carding machines 75 years ago used stationary flats to help them disentangle and arrange cotton fibers* (Science News Letter).

cardio-, *combining form.* **1** the heart: *Cardiology = the science of the heart.* **2** the heart and ___: *Cardiovascular = relating to the heart and blood vessels.*
[< Greek *kardiā* heart]

car|di|o|gen|ic (kär′dē ō jen′ik), *adj.* originating in the heart: *These two were among twelve who were in cardiogenic shock* (*almost complete circulatory collapse*), *a condition that carries a forbidding mortality of 80% or more* (Time).

car|di|o|gram (kär′dē ə gram), *n.* = electrocardiogram.

car|di|o|graph (kär′dē ə graf, -gräf), *n.* = electrocardiograph.

car|di|o|graph|ic (kär′dē ə graf′ik), *adj.* = electrocardiographic. **—car′di|o|graph′i|cal|ly,** *adv.*

car|di|og|ra|phy (kär′dē og′rə fē), *n., pl.* **-phies.** = electrocardiography.

car|di|oid (kär′dē oid), *n., adj.* **—*n.*** a mathematical curve shaped rather like a heart, being the path of a point on the circumference of a circle when the circle rolls around a fixed circle of equal size.
—*adj.* having the shape of a heart.
[< Greek *kardioeidēs* heart-shaped < *kardiā* heart + *eîdos* form]

car|di|o|in|hib|i|to|ry (kär′dē ō in hib′ə tôr′ē, -tōr′-), *adj.* tending to stop or to diminish the strength and regularity of the heartbeat. [< Greek *kardiā* heart + English *inhibitory*]

car|di|o|log|i|cal (kär′dē ə loj′ə kəl), *adj.* of or having to do with cardiology.

car|di|ol|o|gist (kär′dē ol′ə jist), *n.* an expert in cardiology: *Cardiologists and surgeons alike have been doubtful that the new blood-vessel operations either add to the heart muscle's blood supply or help the patient* (Harper's).

car|di|ol|o|gy (kär′dē ol′ə jē), *n.* the branch of medicine dealing with the heart and the diagnosis and treatment of its diseases.

car|di|o|meg|a|ly (kär′dē ō meg′ə lē), *n.* a condition in which the heart becomes enlarged due to disease or overuse; hypertrophy of the heart. [< *cardio-* + Greek *mégas, -álou* big]

car|di|o|my|op|a|thy (kär′dē ō mī op′ə thē), *n., pl.* **-thies.** any one of various diseases of the heart muscle, characterized by progressive weakness and enlargement. [< *cardio-* + *myopathy*]

car|di|o|pul|mo|nar|y (kär′dē ō pu̇l′mə ner′ē), *adj.* of or having to do with the heart and lungs.

cardiopulmonary resuscitation, = CPR.

car|di|o|res|pir|a|to|ry (kär′dē ō res′pər ə tôr′ē, -tōr′-), *adj.* of or having to do with the action of both the heart and lungs.

car|di|o|spasm (kär′dē ə spaz′əm), *n.* a spasm

Pronunciation Key: hat, āge, cãre, fär; let, ēqual, tėrm; it, īce; hot, ōpen, ôrder; oil, out; cup, pu̇t, rüle; child; long; thin; ᴛʜen; zh, measure; ə represents **a** in about, **e** in taken, **i** in pencil, **o** in lemon, **u** in circus.

or contraction affecting the cardia and (usually) areas of the stomach and esophagus connected by the cardia.

car|di|o|spas|tic (kär′dē ə spas′tik), *adj.* of or having to do with cardiospasm.

car|di|o|ta|chom|e|ter(kär′dē ō tə kom′ə tər), *n.* an instrument which counts heartbeats and thus indicates their rate, often used during operations to warn of heart stoppage: *The cardiotachometer instantly detects heart stoppage on the operating table seconds before it is recognizable to the surgeon* (Newsweek).

car|di|o|ton|ic (kär′dē ə ton′ik), *adj.* tending to restore or augment the tonus or degree of contraction of the cardiac muscle.
—*n.* a cardiotonic drug.

car|di|o|vas|cu|lar (kär′dē ō vas′kyə lər), *adj.* of or affecting both the heart and the blood vessels, as hardening of the arteries and high blood pressure: *research in cardiovascular diseases.*

car|di|o|ver|sion (kär′dē ō vėr′zhən, -shən), *n.* restoration of normal heartbeat by the use of a cardioverter: *The "cardioversion" room contains devices for administering electric shocks to restore normal rhythm in hearts that have developed dangerous arrhythmias* (Scientific American). [< *cardio-* + Latin *versiō, ōnis* a turning]

car|di|o|ver|ter (kär′dē ō vėr′tər), *n.* a device for restoring normal heartbeat by means of electric shock: *Electric current from the cardioverter being applied directly to a patient's heart by doctors at the National Heart Hospital, London* (London Times). [< *cardio-* + Latin *vertere* to turn]

car|di|tis (kär dī′tis), *n.* inflammation of any part of the heart. [< New Latin *carditis* < Greek *kardiā* heart + *-ītis* disease]

car|do (kär′dō), *n., pl.* **-di|nes.** the basal maxillary joint of an insect. [< Latin *cardo* hinge]

car|dol (kär′dōl, -dol), *n.* an oil found in the shell of the cashew nut which may cause severe allergic reaction, such as blistering: *Her trouble: allergy to cashews, which contain an oil called cardol* (Time). [< New Latin *(Ana)card(ium)* the cashew genus + English *-ol*[2]]

car|don or **car|dón** (kär dōn′), *n.* any one of various giant cactus plants found in dense, forestlike growths along the shores of the Pacific, from lower California to Chile. [< Spanish *cardón* teasel]

car|doon (kär dün′), *n.* an edible, composite plant closely allied to and resembling the artichoke, native to Mediterranean regions. [< French *cardon* < Late Latin *cardō, -ōnis* thistle < *cardus* < Latin *carduus*; see etym. under **card**[2]]

card|play|er (kärd′plā′ər), *n.* a person who plays cards.

card|play|ing (kärd′plā′ing), *n.* the activity of playing a game of cards: *His cardplaying is now limited to occasional bouts of solitaire* (New Yorker).

card punch, a mechanism which transfers data by means of a punched code, to be read by a computer: *Card punch puts the payroll on coded cards, which are ... then run through a machine that prints the pay checks* (Louis N. Ridenour).

card puncher, a person or thing that punches cards, especially in a punched code for a computer.

card reader, a mechanism which transfers coded data from punched cards, usually to magnetic tape, to be used in a computer.

cards (kärdz), *n.pl.* See under **card**[1].

card shark, = cardsharp.

card|sharp (kärd′shärp′), *n.* a person who makes a trade of cheating at cards: *Then he might be ... cheated in a poker game by a cardsharp who used a marked deck of cards* (Charlton Laird).

card|sharp|er (kärd′shär′pər), *n.* = cardsharp.

card|sharp|ing (kärd′shär′ping), *n.* the practice of cheating at cards as a trade.

card table, a light table usually with folding legs, used or intended to be used for playing card games.

car|du|a|ceous (kär′jù ā′shəs), *adj.* of or belonging to a large subgroup of the composite family, including the sunflower, goldenrod, and aster. [< Latin *carduus* thistle + English *aceous*]

card vote, *British.* a method of voting in trade-union meetings by which the vote of each delegate is valued according to the number of his constituents: *The resolution was carried on a card vote* (London Times).

care (kãr), *n., v.,* **cared, car|ing.** —*n.* **1** a troubled state of mind because of fear of what may happen; worry: *Few people are free from care.* **2** serious attention; heed: *A pilot must do his work with great care. Want of care does us more damage than want of knowledge* (Benjamin Franklin). SYN: caution, regard. **3** a cause of anxiety or unrest: *He has always been a care to his mother.* **4** watchful keeping; charge: *under a doctor's care. The little girl was left in her older sister's care.* **5** an object of concern or attention: *the cares of state* (Benjamin Jowett). **6** food, shelter, and protection: *Your child will have the best of care.* **7** liking; regard: *Public spirit ... its essence is care for a common good* (George Eliot). **8** sorrow; grief: *His words infix'd unutterable care Deep in great Hector's soul* (Alexander Pope). **9** *British.* guardianship or protection by local officials: *Where children had to go into care, he appealed to local authorities to put the maximum possible into foster homes* (London Guardian).
—*v.i.* **1** to feel interest; be concerned; *Musicians care about music. One cannot care so much about what has happened in the past and not care what is happening in one's own time* (Edmund Wilson). **2** to like; want; wish: *A cat does not care to be washed.* **3** to be concerned so as to feel or express objection; mind (in negative and conditional constructions): *I don't care what they say.*
—*v.t.* to be concerned (to a specified degree or extent): *I can think of only one element who ... cares a twopenny cuss for the principles or sufferings of humanity in this country* (Manchester Guardian Weekly).
care for, a to be fond of; like: *the boy and his grandfather care very deeply for one another.* **b** to want; wish: *I don't care for any dessert tonight.* **c** to take charge of; attend to: *The nurse will care for him now.* **d** to attend to; provide for: *The widow was cared for by the terms of the will.*
could care less, *U.S. Informal.* not to care at all; be completely indifferent (to): *Mitchum looks as if he could care less what the film is going to do for his career* (Women's Wear Daily).
have a care, to be careful: *Have a care or you will fall.*
in care of, at the address of: *All mail for the governor should be sent in care of the state house.*
take care, to be careful: *Take care to be accurate.*
take care of, a to take charge of; attend to: *A baby sitter is expected to take care of children. My father will take care of this bill.* **b** to watch over; be careful with: *Take care of your money.* **c** to deal with: *Never mind about the owner, I'll take care of him.*
[Old English *caru*] —**car′er**, *n.*
—*Syn. n.* **1 Care, concern, solicitude** mean a troubled, worried, or anxious state of mind. **Care** suggests being burdened with heavy responsibilities or constant worries and fears: *It is care that has made her sick.* **Concern** suggests uneasiness over someone or something one likes or is interested in: *He expressed concern over her health.* **Solicitude** suggests great concern, often together with loving care: *Her friends wait on her with solicitude.*

CARE (kãr), *n.* Cooperative for American Relief to Everywhere (formerly, Europe), Inc., a voluntary nonprofit organization, established after World War II, to send packages of food, clothing, tools, books, etc., to the needy in other countries.

care|cloth (kãr′klôth′, -kloth′), *n.* a cloth held over the heads of a bride and bridegroom during the marriage ceremony as performed in England in the Middle Ages. [origin uncertain]

ca|reen (kə rēn′), *v., n.* —*v.i.* **1a** to lean to one side; tilt; tip: *The ship careened in the strong wind.* **b** to tip or sway sharply (used especially of vehicles, sometimes of persons): *The speeding taxi went careening around the corner.* **2** to heave a ship over on one side for cleaning, painting, or repairing below the water line: *His orders were ... to careen and refit* (Robert Beatson).
—*v.t.* **1a** to heave (a ship) over on one side for cleaning, painting, or repairing below the water line: *Finding a convenient harbor ... he unloaded and careened his vessels* (Washington Irving). **b** to clean or repair (a ship) after placing it in this position: *His sloop could not go to sea without being careened.* **2a** to cause to lean to one side: *The gale careened the sailboat.* **b** to cause (anything, especially a wagon or other vehicle) to tip or sway sharply: *The sliding load careened the wagon at the corner.* [< noun]
—*n.* **1a** the position of a ship when laid on one side for cleaning, painting, or repairs: *When a ship is laid on a careen, everything is taken out of her* (Falconer). **b** the process of careening: *The Duchess began to make ready for a careen* (Will Rogers). **2a** the position of a ship driven on her beam ends by wind, waves, or other violence: *a broadside which laid her on a careen.* **b** a leaning over: *The charm of the camel is not ... in the movement, the noiseless stepping, or the broad careen* (Lew Wallace).
[< Middle French *carène* < Italian (Genoese) *carena* < Latin *carīna* a keel] —**ca|reen′er**, *n.*

ca|reen|age (kə rē′nij), *n.* **1** a place for careening a ship. **2** a charge for careening a ship.

ca|reer (kə rir′), *n., v., adj.* —*n.* **1a** a general course of action or progress through life: *It is interesting to read of the careers of great men and women.* **b** way of living; occupation or profession: *The boy planned to make law his career.* SYN: vocation, calling. **c** notable success or advancement in any particular profession, trade, or the like: *We can offer a career to a young man of energy and integrity.* **2** a run at full speed; going with force; speed: *The boys raced downhill in full career to see who could get to school first.* SYN: flight. **3** *Figurative.* steady and uninterrupted activity; the height of any course of action or process: *in the full career of success* (Macaulay). **4** *Obsolete.* **a** a gallop at full speed; charge. **b** a frisk; gambol. **5** *Obsolete.* **a** a path; way; road. **b** a race course.
—*v.i.* to rush along wildly; dash: *The runaway horse careered through the streets. The little boy was careering about the room.*
—*v.t.* **1** to ride or drive (a horse or vehicle) at full speed: *A Moor is born ... to career the steed* (Washington Irving). **2** to move or gallop swiftly: *The moon was careering the clouds.*
—*adj.* following a certain occupation or profession throughout life: *a career diplomat.*
[< Middle French *carrière* race occurs < Latin *carrus* wagon, cart]

career girl or **woman**, a girl or woman who pursues an occupational career.

ca|reer|ism (kə rir′iz əm), *n.* the methods or practices of a person interested in achieving personal advancement in his career or profession, often without consideration of or for other persons or things: *Where ... could one find a pure passion for learning uncontaminated by snobbery or careerism?* (Harper's). —**ca|reer′ist**, *n.*

ca|reer|man (kə rir′mən), *n., pl.* **-men. 1** a man who pursues a career; professional. **2** a career diplomat.

careers master, a person who gives vocational guidance in a secondary school in Great Britain.

care|free (kãr′frē′), *adj.* without worry; happy; gay: *a carefree attitude, a carefree summer doing what one pleases.* —**care′free′ness**, *n.*

care|ful (kãr′fəl), *adj.* **1** thinking what one says or watching what one does; taking pains; watchful; cautious: *He is careful to tell the truth at all times. I felt just sufficient fear to render me careful* (John Tyndall). *You'll get a good dinner, but be careful of the sweets* (Graham Greene). **2** showing care; done with thought or effort; exact; through: *Arithmetic requires careful work. His drawing was careful.* SYN: painstaking, meticulous, accurate. **3** full of care or concern; attentive to the interests of others; exercising care: *She was careful of the feelings of others. Be careful of the horses, Sam ... don't ride them too fast* (Harriet Beecher Stowe). **4** *Archiac.* anxious; worried: *It is a sight the careful brow might smooth* (Byron). **5** *Archaic.* (of things) fraught with care; attended with sorrow, trouble, or anxiety: *He upon his careful couch hears all around the deep and longdrawn breath of sleep* (Robert Southey).
—**care′ful|ly**, *adv.* —**care′ful|ness**, *n.*
—*Syn.* **1 Careful, cautious, wary** mean watchful in speaking and acting. **Careful** means being observant and giving serious attention and thought to what one is doing, especially to details: *He is a careful driver.* **Cautious** means very careful, looking ahead for possible risks or dangers, and guarding against them by taking no chances: *She is cautious about making promises.* **Wary** emphasizes the idea of being mistrustful and on the alert for danger or trouble: *He is wary of overfriendly people.*

care|giv|er (kãr′giv′ər), *n.* a person who provides care for the very young, sick, or elderly: *... the link between early "attachments" to a primary caregiver and later adaptation at school* (Science News). —**care′giv|ing**, *n., adj.*

care label, a label on a garment or fabric containing cleaning or laundering instructions.

care|less (kãr′lis), *adj.* **1** not thinking what one says or not watching what one does; not taking enough pains; not careful: *That careless boy broke the cup. A careless mistake ruined the experiment.* **2** done without enough thought or effort; not exact or thorough: *careless work.* SYN: headless, inaccurate, negligent. **3** artless; unstudied: *to flop into a chair with careless ease; ... one evening, as he framed the careless rhyme* (James Beattie). **4** not caring or troubling; indifferent: *He has a careless attitude toward his homework, rarely getting it done on time ... careless their merits or their faults to scan* (Oliver Goldsmith); *... careless of mankind* (Tennyson). **5** without worry; happy: *Thus wisely careless, innocently gay, Cheerful he played the trifle, Life, away* (Alexander Pope). SYN: untroubled, gay.
—**care′less|ly**, *adv.* —**care′less|ness**, *n.*
—*Syn.* **1 Careless, unthinking, heedless, thoughtless** mean exhibiting lack of thought, interest, or attention. **Careless** emphasizes being

unconcerned about responsibilities or obligations, and thus offhanded or light-hearted, negligent or lazy: *His attire was disarrayed and careless. She was careless about her duties to her family.* **Unthinking** implies being unreflecting and thus inconsiderate, unwise, or the like: *An unthinking leader has put us in this unfortunate predicament.* **Headless** denotes being inattentive, unobservant, and without proper regard: *Headless of the gathering clouds, he had taken no raincoat nor unbrella. One heedless movement on the ice slope sent him hurtling over the precipice. The boy is utterly heedless of advice.* **Thoughtless** implies lack of forethought and thus being without regard or consideration for others: *His thoughtless conduct got us all into trouble.*

ca|rene (kə rēn′), *n.* a forty days' fast on bread and water, formerly imposed by a bishop, upon clergy or laity, or by an abbot upon monks. [< Medieval Latin *carena*, ultimately < Latin *quadrāgintā* forty; influenced by Latin *carēre* to lack]

ca|ress (kə res′), *n., v.,* **-ressed** or (*Archaic or Poetic*) **-rest, -ress|ing.** **—*n.*** **1** a touch showing affection; tender embrace or kiss: *The little boy was embarrassed by his aunt's caresses.* **2** an expression of public regard or esteem; show of popular favor: *when the gifts and caresses of mankind shall recompense the toils of study* (Samuel Johnson).

—*v.t.* **1a** to touch or stroke affectionately; embrace or kiss tenderly: *The mother caressed her baby. My very hands seem to caress her* (Longfellow). **b** to touch lightly; affect in a soothing manner: *Its prolonged echoes caress the ear* (James Russell Lowell). **2** to treat with kindness; show favor to: *without being much countenanced or caressed by his superiors* (Samuel Johnson).

[< Middle French *caresse* < Italian *carezza* < Latin *cārus* dear] **—ca|ress′a|ble,** *adj.* **—ca|ress′er,** *n.* **—ca|ress′ing|ly,** *adv.*

ca|res|sant (kə res′ənt), *adj. Poetic.* caressing; fondling: *Those tender hands caressant* (Robinson Ellis). [< French *caressant*]

ca|res|sive (kə res′iv), *adj.* **1** habitually caressing. **2** of the nature of a caress: [*He*] *is an ingenious orchestrator whose often unique . . . instrumental combinations give off a moody, feline, caressive air* (Whitney Balliett). **—ca|res′sive|ly,** *adv.*

***car|et**[1] (kȧr′ət), *n.* a mark placed below a line to show where something should be put in, used in writing and in printing. [< Latin *caret* there is lacking]

***caret**[1]

∧ — was / something ∧ missing

car|et[2] (kȧ re′; *Anglicized* kar′ət), *n.* a sea turtle having a mouth shaped like a hawk's beak; hawksbill turtle. [< French *caret*]

care|tak|er (kãr′tā′kər), *n., adj.* **—*n.*** a person who takes care of another person, a place, or a thing, often for the owner or for somebody else: *The caretaker of the house met them, hat in hand* (W. G. Willis).

—*adj.* (of a government or management) carrying on the functions of an office on a temporary basis pending an election, the accession of a new administration, or the like: *caretaker government. For a year* [*he*] *held the premiership in a "caretaker" capacity* (Maclean's).

care|tak|ing (kãr′tā′king), *n.* the work or responsibility of a caretaker, especially keeping someone else's house or grounds in good order.

care|worn (kãr′wôrn′, -wōrn′), *adj.* showing signs of worry; tire or weary from care: *The old woman had a careworn look on her face.*

Car|ey Street (kãr′ē), *British.* a state of bankruptcy: *"Ending up on Carey Street" is still an amusing euphemism for going bankrupt* (London Times). [< the name of a street in London where the Bankruptcy Court was formerly located]

car|fare (kär′fãr′), *n. U.S.* the money paid for riding on a bus or subway, in a taxicab, or other passenger vehicle.

car ferry, 1 a vessel for transporting railroad cars or automobiles across a body of water. **2** an aircraft used to transport automobiles across a body of water: [*He*] *roared out to the airport, put his car on a . . . car ferry, landed at Le Bourget and zipped into Paris in 2 hr. 45 min.* (Time).

car float, a barge for transporting railroad cars.

car|ful (kär′fůl), *n., pl.* **-fuls.** as much as a car holds; enough to fil a car: *a carful of children.*

car|ga|dor (kär′gə dôr, -dōr; *Spanish* kär′gä ᴛʜôr′), *n.* **1** = porter. **2** a man who supervises the loading and driving of pack animals. [< Spanish *cargador* < *cargar* to load; see etym. under **cargo**]

car|go (kär′gō), *n., pl.,* **-goes** *or* **-gos. 1** the load of goods carried by a ship or aircraft; freight: *The freighter had docked to unload a cargo of wheat. Quinquireme of Ninevah . . . rowing home to haven . . . with a cargo of ivory and apes and peacocks* (John Masefield). SYN: lading. **2** a large quantity; load; burden: *When they moved, their chief care was their cargo of books. Of our ten animals, six were intended for riding, and four for carrying cargoes* (Charles Darwin). [< Spanish *cargo* a loading, burden < *cargar* to load, ultimately < Latin *carrus* wagon]

cargo cult, any one of various cults of the South Pacific having as their central idea that ancestors or gods will return bearing huge cargoes of Western goods: *Cargo cults originated in the people's bewilderment at the richness of the Europeans who were then beginning to visit their country* (Kenneth Ingham).

cargo liner, 1 a large aircraft for carrying cargo, especially on a commercial airline. **2** any liner used for carrying cargo, especially one belonging to a shipping line.

car|hop (kär′hop′), *n. U.S.* a waiter or waitress who serves customers in their cars at a drive-in restaurant.

Car|ib (kar′ib), *n.* **1** a member of a group of Indian tribes of northeastern South America. They now live in the Amazon River Valley, the Caribbean islands, and the Guianas. Only a few are left. **2** any Indian speaking a Cariban language. **3** a language family found primarily in northeastern South America, in Guiana, northern Brazil, Venezuela, and parts of Columbia and Peru, and to a lesser extent in Central America and the West Indies. [< Spanish *caribe* < Carib *Galibi* the Caribs]

Car|ib|an (kar′ə bən), *adj., n.* **—*adj.*** denoting or having to do with the Carib language family.

—*n.* the Carib language family.

Car|ib|be|an (kar′ə bē′ən, kə rib′ē-), *adj., n.* **—*adj.*** **1** of or having to do with the Caribbean Sea or the islands in it: *the Caribbean climate, the Caribbean sugarbird.* **2** of or having to do with the Caribs.

—*n. British.* a native or inhabitant of one of the Caribbean islands.

ca|ri|be (kä rē′bā), *n.* = piranha. [< Spanish *caribe* cannibal]

car|i|bou (kar′ə bü), *n., pl.* **-bous** or (*collectively*) **-bou.** a large deer of North America closely related to the reindeer. Caribou are found in wooded and tundra areas of Alaska and Canada, and formerly in Maine. See picture under **antler.** [American English < Canadian French *caribou* < Algonkian *xalibû* (literally) pawer (from the animal's habit of pawing snow to find grass)]

caribou moss, = reindeer moss.

car|i|ca|ceous (kar′ə kā′shəs), *adj.* = papayaceous. [< New Latin *Caricaceae* the family including the papaya (< *Carica* the genus name < Latin *carica* dried fig) + English *-ous*]

car|i|ca|tur|a|ble (kar′ə kə chůr′ə bəl), *adj.* susceptible to an exaggerfated description; easy to caricature . . . *as caricaturable a rich uncle . . . as one would wish to see* (London Times).

car|i|ca|tur|al (kar′ə kə chůr əl, -chər-), *adj.* of the nature of caricature; resembling a caricature: *In radio and television the caricatural conception that a writer is a necessary evil to have around a show has grown too popular* (Newsweek).

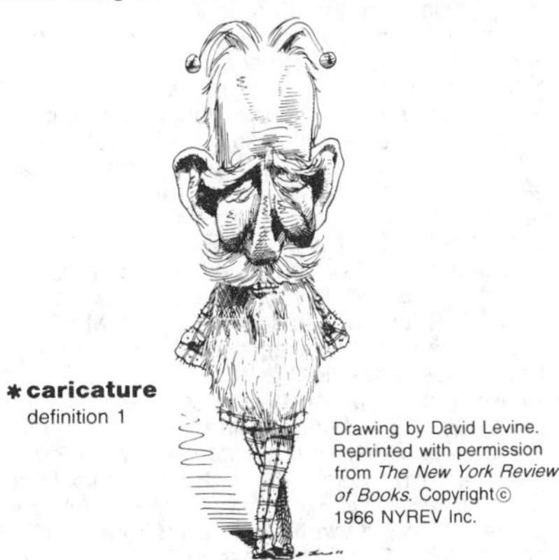

***caricature** definition 1

Drawing by David Levine. Reprinted with permission from *The New York Review of Books.* Copyright© 1966 NYREV Inc.

George Bernard Shaw

car|i|ca|ture** (kar′ə kə chůr, -chər), *n., v.,* **-tured, -tur|ing.** **—*n. **1** a picture, cartoon, description, or the like, that ridiculously exaggerates the peculiarities of a person or the defects of a thing: *Caricatures of celebrities appear daily in the newspapers.* **2** the art of making such pictures, cartoons, or descriptions: *His eye for detail made him a master of caricature. The best portraits are perhaps those in which there is a slight mixture of caricature* (Macaulay). **3** an imitation or rendering of something by ridiculous exaggeration of the flaws and deformities in the original: *He raised his feet high, as if in a caricature of Germans in a movie comedy doing the goose step* (James T. Farrell).

—*v.t.* to make a caricature of: *Uncle Sam is often caricatured as a tall, thin man with chin whiskers, red and white striped pants, a swallow-tailed coat, and a tall, silk hat. The appointed fate of the Renaissance architects, to caricature whatever they imitated* (John Ruskin).

[< French *caricature* < Italian *caricatura* < *caricare* overload, exaggerate < Late Latin *carricāre* to load < Latin *carrus* wagon]

caricature plant, a plant of the acanthus family growing in Indonesia, having curious variegations of the leaves which sometimes look like drawings of grotesque human profiles.

car|i|ca|tur|ist (kar′ə kə chůr′ist, -chər-), *n.* a person who draws, paints, or writes caricatures.

Car|i|com *or* **CARICOM** (kär′ə kom, kãr′-), *n.* a common market established in 1974 by ten countries of the eastern Caribbean: *Haiti and Surinam applied to join Caricom, and diplomatic relations were established between Caricom countries and Cuba* (Philippe Decraene). [< *Cari*(*b*-bean) *com*(munity) or *com*(mon market)]

car|i|cous (kar′ə kəs), *adj.* resembling a fig: *a caricous swelling.* [< Latin *cārica* a kind of dry fig + English *-ous*]

car|ies (kãr′ēz, -ē ēz,), *n.* the decay of the teeth, bones, or tissues: *so much stress on caries prevention rather than good gum health* (Parade). [< Latin *cariēs*]

car|il|lon** (kar′ə lon, -lən; kə ril′yən), *n., v.,* **-lonned, -lon|ning.** **—*n. **1** a set of bells arranged for playing melodies. The bells are played upon with hammers, either by hand or by a keyboard or other mechanism. **2** a melody played on such bells. **3a** a part of an organ imitating the sound of bells. **b** a musical instrument consisting of a set of metal plates arranged horizontally on a frame and played by striking with hammers. **4** a bell tower.

—*v.i.* to play a carillon.

[< French *carillon* < Old French *quarellon* set of four, ultimately < Latin *quattuor* four (because it originally consisted of four bells)]

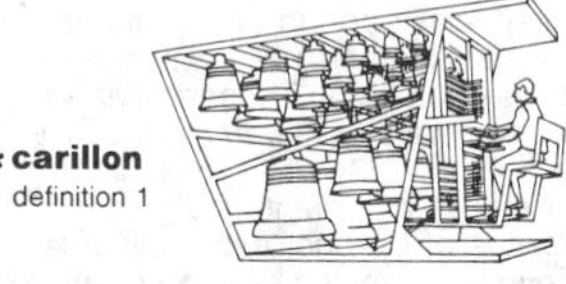

***carillon** definition 1

car|il|lon|er (kə ril′yə nər), *n.* = carillonneur.

car|il|lon|ic bells kar′ə lon ik), an electronic device which duplicates the sound of bells, consisting of small pieces of tuned bell metal struck by a tiny rod, and played from a keyboard like that of a piano. The sound is electronically amplified.

car|il|lon|neur (kar′ə lə nėr′), *n.* a person who plays a carillon. [< French *carillonneur* < *carillon*; see etym. under **carillon**]

ca|ri|na (kə rī′nə), *n., pl.* **-nae** (-nē). **1** *Zoology.* a structure or part having the form of a ridge or keel, such as the middle ridge on the breastbone of most birds. **2** *Botany.* the lower, keel-shaped pair of petals, characteristic of flowers of the pea family. [< Latin *carīna* keel]

Ca|ri|na (kə rī′nə), *n.* one of the four constellations into which the large southern constellation Argo has been divided; the Keel. It contains Canopus, a large, extremely bright star.

ca|ri|nal (kə rī′nəl), *adj.* having to do with or resembling a carina.

car|i|nate (kar′ə nāt), *adj.* shaped like or having a carina, or keel. [< Latin *carīnātus* having a keel < *carīna* keel]

car|i|nat|ed (kar′ə nā′tid), *adj.* = carinate.

car|i|na|tion (kar′ə nā′shən), *n.* a carinate or keellike formation.

ca|rin|i|form (kə rin′ə fôrm), *adj.* shaped like a carina or keel; carinate [< Latin *carīna* keel + English *-form*]

car|i|o|ca (kar′ē ō′kə), *n.* **1a** a dance of South America similar to the samba. **b** music for such a dance. **2 Caricoa,** a native or inhabitant of Rio de Janeiro. [< Brazilian Portuguese *carioca*]

car|i|o|gen|ic (kãr′ē ō jen′ik), *adj.* causing or producing caries: *cariogenic bacteria.*

car|i|ole (kar′ē ōl), *n.* **1a** a small carriage drawn

Pronunciation Key: hat, āge, cãre, fär; let, ēqual, tėrm; it, īce; hot, ōpen, ôrder; oil, out; cup, pu̇t, rüle; child; long; thin; ᴛʜen; zh, measure; ə represents **a** in about, **e** in taken, **i** in pencil, **o** in lemon, **u** in circus.

by one horse, used especially in the 1800's. **b** a covered cart. **2** a light, open sleigh drawn by one or two horses or sometimes by dogs. Also, **carriole**. [< French *carriole,* ultimately < Latin *carrus* wagon]

car|i|os|i|ty (kãr′ē os′ə tē), *n., pl.* **-ties. 1** carious state or condition. **2** a carious formation.

car|i|ous (kãr′ē əs), *adj.* having caries; decayed: *carious teeth.* [< Latin *cariōsus* < *cariēs* decay] —**car′i|ous|ness,** *n.*

car|i|tas (kar′ə tas), *n.* Christian love of one's fellow man; charity. [< Latin *cāritās* dearness, affection]

car|i|ta|tive (kar′ə tā′tiv), *adj.* charitable; benevolent. [< Medieval Latin *cāritātivus* < Latin *cāritās*]

car jockey, *U.S.* a person employed to take cars in and out of a parking lot or garage.

cark (kärk), *n., v.* —*n.* a troubled state of mind; distress (especially in *cark and care*): *The swart mechanic comes to drown his cark and care* (Longfellow).
—*v.t.* to burden with care; harass; vex; trouble.
—*v.i.* to be anxious; fret oneself: *The old man carked about the uncertainties of life.*
[< Anglo-French *karke* < *karkier* to burden < Vulgar Latin *carcāre,* Late Latin *carricāre* to load. See etym. of doublets **charge, carry.**]

cark|ing (kär′king), *adj.* **1** troublesome; worrying: *Some carking care that would not be driven away* (Dickens). **2** of persons: **a** fretting; anxious. **b** toiling. **c** miserly. —**cark′ing|ly,** *adv.*

car knocker, a railroad employee who checks cars for mechanical failure.

carl or **carle** (kärl), *n.* **1** *Archaic.* **a** a peasant; rustic. **b** a serf; bondman. **2** *Scottish.* **a** a boor; churl. **b** a fellow. [< Scandinavian (compare Old Icelandic *karl* man)]

car|let (kär′lit), *n.* a file with a triangular cross section, having two cutting sides and one side smooth, formerly used in making combs. [< French *carrelet* a square file (diminutive) < *carreau* square, file, ultimately < Latin *quadrum* square]

carl-hemp (kärl′hemp′), *n.* the female or pistillate plant of hemp, which is harvested after the male or staminate plant. [< *carl* (from its greater coarseness and robustness, it was supposed to be the male plant)]

car|lin or **car|line**[1] (kär′lin, ker′-), *n. Scottish.* **1** a woman, especially an old one (often implying contempt or disparagement). **2** a witch or one charged with being such. [< Scandinavian (compare Old Icelandic *kerling* < *carl* man, carl + *-ing,* a feminine suffix)]

car|line[2] (kär′lin), *n.* any plant of a genus of thistlelike composites of Europe, especially one species whose involucral scales are so sensitive to moisture (hygroscopic) that they serve as a natural weatherglass. [< French *carline* < Medieval Latin *Carolina* (with reference to Charlemagne, Charles the Great)]

car|line[3] (kär′lin), *n.* = carling.

car|ling (kär′ling), *n.* one of the short fore-and-aft timbers between deck beams in the framework of a ship's deck. [apparently < French *carlingue* mast socket < Scandinavian (compare Old Icelandic *kerling*); see etym. under **carline**[1]]

car|lings (kär′lingz), *n.pl. British.* peas, especially parched peas: *Many persons [in England] eat carlings ... on Carling Sunday* (Elizabeth H. Sechrist).

Carling Sunday, the fifth Sunday in Lent. [apparently < *Care* (Sunday) (originally) the Sunday preceding Good Friday + *-ling*]

carl|ish (kär′lish), *adj. Dialect.* churlish; clownish; vulgar. [< *carl* + *-ish*]

Car|lism (kär′liz əm), *n.* **1** support of the claims to the throne by Don Carlos (1788-1855), pretender to the Spanish throne, or his descendants. **2** support of Charles X of France, following his forced abdication in 1830, and the elder branch of the Bourbons, especially after 1830. —**Car′list,** *n., adj.*

car|load (kär′lōd′), *n.* **1** as much as a car can hold or carry. **2** *U.S.* the minimum weight, as defined by law, of a shipment entitled, on a basis of quantity, to a reduced freight rate. *Abbr:* c.l.

car|load|ings (kär′lō′dingz), *n.pl.* the number of freight cars loaded during a particular period, often used as a measure of manufacturing and commercial activity.

carload lot, *U.S.* a shipment which meets the minimum weight (carload) as defined by law.

car|lot[1] (kär′lot′), *n. U.S.* carload lot. [< *car* + *lot*]

car|lot[2] (kär′lət), *n. Obsolete.* a countryman. [diminutive of *carl*]

Car|lo|vin|gi|an (kär′lə vin′jē ən), *adj., n.* = Carolingian. [< French *Carlovingien* < *carlingian,* influenced by *Merovingian*]

Car|lyl|e|an (kär lī′lē ən), *adj., n.* —*adj.* of or having to do with Thomas Carlyle (1795-1881), a Scottish essayist, historian, and philosopher: *First there is the hero of Wagnerian dimensions, capable of great public service, as Plutarch would have him, but a Carlylean hero forced to breast the wave of ignorance around him* (Atlantic).
—*n.* an admirer or imitator of Thomas Carlyle.

Car|lyl|ese (kär′lī lēz′, -lēs′), *n.* the literary style of Carlyle.

Car|lyl|ism (kär lī′liz əm), *n.* **1** the style of Thomas Carlyle, characterized by conversational and irregular sentences and many metaphors and allusions. **2** the ideas or teachings of Thomas Carlyle, especially his emphasis on men's need of rulers and strong leaders.

car|ma|gnole or **Car|ma|gnole** (kär′mən yōl′; *French* kȧr mȧ nyōl′), *n.* **1** a dance and song popular during the French Revolution. **2a** the costume worn by the French revolutionists after 1792, consisting of black trousers, a short jacket with wide lapels and metal buttons, a scarlet waistcoat, and a red cap. **b** the jacket itself. **3** a soldier of the French Revolution. [< French *carmagnole,* perhaps < *Carmagnola,* a town in Piedmont, Italy]

car|mak|er (kär′mā′kər), *n.* a manufacturer of cars.

car|man (kär′mən), *n., pl.* **-men.** *U.S.* **1** a person who checks and repairs railroad cars in a yard or station. **2** the motorman or conductor of a streetcar. **3** a person who drives a cart.

Car|mel|ite (kär′mə līt), *n.* **1** a mendicant friar of a Roman Catholic religious order founded probably in the 1100's on Mount Carmel in Syria; white friar. **2** a nun of a similar order founded in 1562. **3** a fine woolen material, usually gray or light brown. [< Medieval Latin *Carmelites* (properly) inhabitant of Mount Carmel (where the first colony was founded)]

car|min|a|tive (kär min′ə tiv, kär′mə nā′-), *adj., n.* —*adj.* expelling gas from the stomach and intestines.
—*n.* a medicine that does this: *Peppermint is often used as a carminative.*
[< Latin *carminātus,* past participle of *carmināre* to card (< *carmen, -inis* a wool comb < *carrere* to card) + English *-ive*]

car|mine (kär′mən, -mīn), *n., adj., v.,* **-mined, -min|ing.** —*n.* **1a** a deep red with a tinge of purple. **b** a light crimson. **2** a crimson coloring matter found in cochineal, used to stain microscopic sections and formerly used as a dye.
—*adj.* **1** deep-red with a tinge of purple. **2** light-crimson.
—*v.t.* to make carmine: *She outlined her eyes with black grease pencil and carmined her lips* (Harper's).
[< Medieval Latin *carminium* < Arabic *qirmiz* the kermes insect + Latin *minium* red lead. Compare etym. at **cramoisy, crimson, kermes.**]

car|min|ic (kär min′ik), *adj.* = carmine.

carminic acid, a purplish-brown acid found in the buds of some plants, but most abundantly in the cochineal insect, used in dyeing and photography. *Formula:* $C_{22}H_{20}O_{13}$

car|mi|nite (kär′mə nīt), *n.* an arsenate of iron and lead, occurring in clusters of needles having a carmine color. [< *carmin*(e) + *-ite*[1]]

car|mot (kär′mot), *n.* according to the alchemists, the substance of which the philosophers' stone was supposed to consist. [origin unknown]

Car|na|by Street (kär′nə bē), a street in London, England, noted as a center of new fashions in clothing: *The English Mod or Carnaby Street look ... received great publicity and had a devoted following among the young* (Anne Fogarty).

car|nage (kär′nij), *n.* **1** the slaughter of a great number of people; wholesale killing; butchery: *The battle resulted in frightful carnage. War and all its deeds of carnage must in time be utterly lost* (Walt Whitman). SYN: massacre. **2** *Archaic.* a collection of dead bodies, especially of the slain in a battle; heap of carcasses: *Where those who scorned to fly or yield In one promiscuous carnage lie* (Richard Harris Barham). [< Middle French *carnage* < Italian *carnaggio,* ultimately < Latin *carō, carnis* flesh]

car|nal (kär′nəl), *adj.* **1a** of or connected with the appetites and passions of the body; sensual: *Gluttony and drunkenness have been called carnal vices.* SYN: fleshly, gross. **b** sexual; libidinous: *But that false fruit For other operation first displayed, carnal desire inflaming* (Milton). **2** worldly; not spiritual: *Mirth and pleasantry ... were looked upon as the marks of a carnal mind* (Joseph Addison). SYN: unsanctified, materialistic. **3** *Archaic.* temporal, as opposed to spiritual; secular. [< Latin *carnālis* < *carō, carnis* flesh. See etym. of doublet **charnel.**] —**car′nal|ly,** *adv.*

car|nal|ism (kär′nə liz əm), *n.* = carnality.

car|nal|ist (kär′nə list), *n.* a person given to the indulgence of sensual appetites; an unspiritual person.

car|nal|i|ty (kär nal′ə tē), *n., pl.* **-ties. 1** fleshliness; sensuality. **2** worldliness. **3** a carnal thing, act, or desire.

car|nal|ize (kär′nə līz), *v.t.,* **-ized, -iz|ing.** to make carnal.

carnal knowledge, = sexual intercourse.

car|nall|ite (kär′nə līt), *n.* a hydrous chloride of potassium and magnesium, an important source of potassium. *Formula:* $KMgCl_3 \cdot 6H_2O$ [< Rudolf von *Carnall,* 1804-74, a mining official in Prussia + English *-ite*[1]]

car|nal-mind|ed (kär′nəl mīn′did), *adj.* having a carnal mind; unspiritual. —**car′nal|mind′ed|ness,** *n.*

car|nap|per or **car|nap|er** (kär′nap ər), *n.* a person who steals a car or cars. [< *car* + *-napper,* as in *kidnapper*]

car|nas|si|al (kär nas′ē əl), *adj., n.* —*adj.* of or having to do with certain teeth of carnivorous animals, adapted for tearing flesh (the last upper premolars and the first lower molars of living mammals): *The cats also use the two bladelike carnassial teeth at the back of the jaws like the blades of a pair of scissors for slicing through the meat of the prey once it is killed* (New Biology).
—*n.* a carnassial tooth: *Lastly, having cut off the flesh, those of the bones that are not too large are cracked by the more conical, less bladelike, teeth immediately in front of the carnassials* (R. F. Ewer).
[< Middle French *carnassier* carnivorous, ultimately < Latin *carō, carnis* + English *-al*[1]]

car|na|tion (kär nā′shən), *n., adj.* —*n.* **1a** a red, white, or pink flower with a spicy fragrance, grown in gardens and greenhouses. The state flower of Ohio is a scarlet carnation. **b** the plant of the pink family that it grows on. **2a** Also, **carnation red.** a rosy pink. **b** *Obsolete.* the color of human flesh or skin; flesh. **3** *Rare.* flesh tints in a painting.
—*adj.* rosy-pink.
[< Middle French *carnation* < Italian *carnagione* flesh color < *carne* flesh < Latin *carō, carnis*]

carnation grass, any plant of certain sedges whose leaves resemble those of the carnation.

car|nau|ba (kär nou′bə), *n.* the Brazilian wax palm. [< Portuguese *carnauba* < the Tupi (Brazil) name]

carnauba wax, a wax obtained from the leaves of the carnauba, used as a polish and in plastics and lubricants: *Brazilian carnauba wax is used in America to make high-grade polishes, carbon paper, stencils, phonograph records, electric insulation, special inks and waterproof paper* (Science News Letter).

car|neau (kär nō′), *n., pl.* **-neaux** (-nōz′). any one of a breed of large domestic pigeons raised chiefly for food. Its big squabs are considered a delicacy. [< French *carneau*]

Car|ne|gie unit (kär′nə gē, kär nā′gē), *U.S. Education.* a unit representing a year's study in any high-school subject (120 hours or their equivalent), used as a standard for measuring college entrance requirements: *Colleges also require the traditional fifteen or sixteen Carnegie units* (New York Times). [< the *Carnegie* Foundation for the Advancement of Teaching, which originally defined it]

car|nel|ian (kär nēl′yən), *n.* a red or reddish-brown variety of chalcedony, used in jewelry: *a carnelian ring.* Also, **cornelian.** [alteration of *cornelian;* influenced by Latin *carō, carnis* flesh]

car|ne|ous (kär′nē əs), *adj.* **1** consisting of flesh; fleshy. **2** flesh-colored. [< Late Latin *carneus* (with English *-ous*) < Latin *carō, carnis* flesh]

car|net (kär ne′), *n. French.* **1** an official paper or certificate, such as a passport or a license to camp: *Every motorist must have a carnet or triptyque and insurance certificate in duplicate* (Observer). **2** a notebook. **3** a small book of tickets, checks, or the like.

car|ney[1] (kär′nē), *v.t., v.i.,* **-neyed, -ney|ing,** *n., pl.* **-neys.** = carny[2].

car|ney[2] (kär′nē), *n. Archaic.* a disease of horses, in which the mouth is so furred that they cannot eat. [compare Latin *carō, carnis* flesh]

car|nie or **car|ney**[3] (kär′nē), *n. U.S. Slang.* carny[1].

car|ni|fy (kär′nə fī), *v.,* **-fied, -fy|ing.** —*v.t.* to change or convert into flesh.
—*v.i.* to lose the normal structure and become fleshy, as in the development of a fibrous condition of the lung.
[< Latin *carō, carnis* flesh + English *-fy*] —**car′ni|fi|ca′tion,** *n.*

car|ni|tine (kär′nə tēn), *n.* a substance chemically identical to vitamin B_T, present in animal muscle, and essential in the nutrition of certain insects. *Formula:* $C_7H_{15}NO_3$ *Carnitine occurs in human and other animal muscles, and presumably a normal animal body can ... make its own carnitine* (Newsweek). [< Latin *carō, carnis* flesh + English *-ite*[1] + *-ine*[2]]

car|ni|val (kär′nə vəl), *n.* **1** a place of amusement or a traveling show having merry-go-rounds, games, and side shows. **2** an organized program of events involving a particular sport or institution: *a water carnival, a school carnival.* **3** *Figurative.* feasting and merrymaking; noisy and unrestrained revels; celebration. **SYN:** festival, festivity, revelry. **4** a time of feasting and merrymaking just before Lent. [< Italian *carnevale,* alteration of *carnelevare* a leaving off of (eating) meat < *carne* flesh (< Latin *carō, carnis*) + *levere* remove < Latin *levāre* lift up]

Car|niv|o|ra (kär niv′ər ə), *n. pl.* the large order of flesh-eating mammals: *The Carnivora include mainly terrestrial and climbing animals, but there are several genera of aquatic and semiaquatic mammals in this order* (Ernest P. Walker). [< New Latin *Carnivora* < Latin *carnivora* flesh-eating, feminine of *carnivorus;* see etym. under **carnivorous**]

car|ni|vore (kär′nə vôr, -vōr), *n.* **1** an animal that feeds chiefly on flesh. Carnivores have large, strong teeth with sharp cutting edges. Dogs, cats, lions, tigers, weasels, and the like, are carnivores. **2** a plant that eats insects.

car|ni|vor|e|an lethargy (kär′ni vôr′ē ən), *Biology.* the winter sleep of bears during which the body temperature does not drop much below normal, as it does in hibernation.

***car|niv|o|rous** (kär niv′ər əs), *adj.* **1a** of or having to do with an order of mammals that feed chiefly on flesh. They are characterized especially by large, sharp canine teeth. The order Carnivora includes cats, dogs, lions, tigers, and bears. **b** using other animals as food; feeding chiefly on flesh: *the strong carnivorous eagle* (Elizabeth Barrett Browning). *The carnivorous habits of dogs make them preferable to vegetarian animals such as horses or reindeer* (Gabriele Rabel). **2** having leaves specially adapted to trap small animals, chiefly insects, for use as food. The sundew, pitcher plant, and Venus's-flytrap are carnivorous plants. [< Latin *carnivorus* (with English *-ous*) < *carō, carnis* flesh + *vorāre* devour] —**car|niv′o|rous|ly,** *adv.* —**car|niv′o|rous|ness,** *n.*

***carnivorous**
definition 2

pitcher plant

sundew

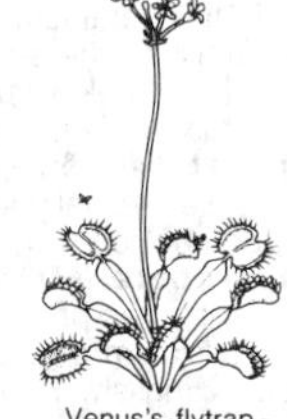

Venus's-flytrap

car|no|sau|ri|an (kär′nə sôr′ē ən), *n.* any one of a group of flesh-eating saurischian dinosaurs of the Jurassic period. [< Latin *carō, carnis* flesh + Greek *saûros* lizard + English *-ian*]

car|nose (kär′nōs, kär nōs′), *adj.* consisting of or resembling flesh; fleshy; pulpy. [< Latin *carō, carnis* flesh + English *-ose*[2]]

Car|not cycle (kär nō′), *Thermodynamics.* a series of operations consisting of isothermal expansion, adiabatic expansion, isothermal compression, and adiabatic compression, which make up the cycle of an ideal heat engine at maximum thermal efficiency. [< Nicolas *Carnot,* 1796-1832, a French physicist]

Carnot engine, a theoretical engine invented to illustrate the Carnot cycle.

car|no|tite (kär′nə tīt), *n.* a yellowish, radioactive mineral found in the western and southwestern United States, a vanadate of potassium, uranium, and other elements. It is a source of uranium, radium, and vanadium. [< Marie Adolphe *Carnot,* 1839-1920, a French inspector-general of mines]

car|ny[1] (kär′nē), *n., pl.* **-nies.** *U.S. Slang.* **1** a carnival (def. 1). **2** a person who works or performs in a carnival: *To the carny, all noncarnies are "people," whose dull lives arouse both pity and scorn* (Time). Also, **carnie, carney.**

car|ny[2] (kär′nē), *v.,* **-nied, -ny|ing,** *n., pl.* **-nies.** —*v.t., v.i. Informal.* to coax; wheedle; cajole. —*n.* insincere praise. Also, **carney.** [origin unknown]

***carob**
definition 2

carob bean

***car|ob** (kar′əb), *n.* **1** an evergreen tree of the pea family grown in the Mediterranean region and occasionally in southern United States; the locust; algarroba. **2** Also, **carob bean.** a long, flat, hornlike pod of this tree, containing hard seeds embedded in pulp; St.-John's-bread. The pods are used as fodder and sometimes as food for people. [< Middle French *caroube* < Arabic *(al-) kharrūbah* (the) bean pods. Compare etym. under **algarroba.**]

ca|roche (kə rōch′, -rōsh′), *n.* a kind of stately or luxurious coach used in the 1600's to convey officials and members of the nobility. [< French *carroche* < Italian *carrozza* < *carro* wagon, car < Latin *carrus*]

car|ol (kar′əl), *n., v.,* **-oled, -ol|ing,** or (*especially British*) **-olled, -ol|ling.** —*n.* **1** a hymn of joy, especially one sung at Christmas. **2** a song of joy: *He heard the birds their morning carols sing* (Wordsworth). **3** in the Middle Ages: **a** a dance done in a ring with accompaniment of song. **b** the accompanying song.
—*v.i.* **1** to sing Christmas carols, especially in a group or chorus: *Several girls in the fifth grade in Rye sent $2 they had collected through caroling* (New York Times). **2** to sing joyously: *The birds carol in the early morning. No more on prancing palfrey borne, He carolled, light as lark at morn* (Scott).
—*v.t.* **1** to sing joyously: *carolling as he went a true-love ballad* (Tennyson). *Still they are carolled and said ... after the singer is dead* (Robert Louis Stevenson). **2** to praise with carols: *The shepherds ... carol her goodness loud in rustic lays* (Milton).
[< Old French *carole* < *caroler* to dance, ultimately < Latin *choraula* alteration of Greek *choraúlēs* flute player accompanying a choral dance < *chorós* dance + *aulós* flute]

Car|o|le|an (kar′ə lē′ən), *adj.* **1** of or having to do with Charles I and II of England. **2** of or designating the period, style of clothing, decoration, or furniture, or state of the arts that prevailed during the reigns of Charles I or II of England.

car|ol|er (kar′ə lər), *n.* a person who carols, especially one who sings Christmas carols: *The carolers were still wandering through the narrow streets of Chelsea this Christmas singing the old hymns in the snow* (New York Times). Also, *especially British,* **caroller.**

Car|o|li|na allspice (kar′ə lī′nə), = strawberry shrub.

Carolina hemlock, a hemlock growing in mountainous regions of the southeastern United States, with dark green needles that extend from all sides of the twig.

Carolina jasmine or **jessamine,** = yellow jasmine.

Carolina locust, a grasshopper with short antennae, of eastern North America.

Carolina parakeet or **paroquet,** a green parakeet with a yellow head that formerly inhabited the central and southeastern United States.

Carolina pink, = pinkroot.

Carolina poplar, **1** = cottonwood (def. 1). **2** a hybrid tree derived from the native cottonwood of America and the black poplar of Europe.

Carolina rail, = sora.

Carolina wren, a wren of the southern United States that often nests in farm buildings: *The Carolina wren measures about 5½ inches long* (Leonard W. Wing).

Car|o|line (kar′ə līn, -lin), *adj.* of or having to do with the reign or period of Charles, especially of Charles I or II of England, or (less frequently) of Charlemagne (Charles the Great), and Charles II of Spain; Carolinian.

Car|o|lin|gi|an (kar′ə lin′jē ən), *adj., n.* —*adj.* of or having to do with the second Frankish dynasty. It ruled in France from A.D. 751 to 987, in Germany from 751 to 911, and in Italy from 774 to 887.
—*n.* a member or one of the sovereigns of the Carolingian family or dynasty. Charlemagne was a Carolingian. Also, **Carlovingian, Carolinian.**
[< Medieval Latin *Carolus* Charles + Germanic *-ing* descendant of + English *-ian*]

Car|o|lin|i|an (kar′ə lin′ē ən), *adj., n.* —*adj.* **1** of North Carolina and South Carolina, or either of them. **2** = Carolingian. **3** = Caroline.
—*n.* a person born or living in North Carolina or South Carolina.

car|ol|ler (kar′ə lər), *n. Especially British.* caroler.

car|o|lus (kar′ə ləs), *n., pl.* **-lus|es, -li** (-lī). **1** an English gold coin struck in the reign of Charles I, originally worth 20 shillings. **2** any one of various coins issued under kings named Charles. [< Medieval Latin *Carolus,* Latinization of Frankish *Karl* Charles]

car|om (kar′əm), *n., v.* —*n.* **1** the act of hitting and bouncing off. **2** a shot in the game of billiards in which the ball struck with the cue hits two balls, one after the other. **3** a similar shot in other games.
—*v.i.* **1** to hit and bounce off: *The car went out of control and caromed off the wall.* **2** to make a carom.
—*v.t.* to cause something to bounce off: *Broadcasters can carom their message-carrying waves off the ionosphere to almost any point on earth* (Wall Street Journal). Also, **carrom.**

caroms, a game in the United States for two or four players, played on a square board. The players try to shoot 24 round counters into pockets at the corners.
[short for *carambole* < French < Spanish *carambola,* perhaps same word as *carambola;* see etym. under **carambola**]

car|o|tene (kar′ə tēn), *n.* **1** a red or yellow, crystalline pigment found in the carrot and other plants, and in animal tissue, and converted by the body into vitamin A. *Formula:* $C_{40}H_{56}$ **2** a carotenoid hydrocarbon. Also, **carotin.** [< Latin *carota* carrot + English *-ene*]

ca|rot|en|oid (kə rot′ə noid), *n., adj.* —*n.* any one of a group of pigments ranging from yellow to dark-red in color, found in various plant and animal tissues. The group includes carotene and certain related alcohols, ketones, and ethers. *In decaying leaves we find considerable amounts of terpenes, in the form of yellow pigments, or carotenoids* (Scientific American).
—*adj.* **1** like carotene. **2** of the carotenoids.

ca|rot|ic (kə rot′ik), *adj.* **1** having to do with or of the nature of stupor: *carotic sleep.* **2** *Rare.* carotid. [< French *carotique* < Greek *karōtikós* stupefying < *karoûn* stupefy; see etym. under **carotid**]

ca|rot|id (kə rot′id), *n., adj.* —*n.* either of two large arteries, one on each side of the neck, that carry blood to the head. See diagram under **circulation.** —*adj.* having to do with or adjoining either or both of these arteries. [< Greek *karōtides* < *karoûn* stupefy < *káros* stupor (a state producible by compression of the carotids)]

ca|rot|i|dal (kə rot′ə dəl), *adj.* = carotid.

car|o|tin (kar′ə tin), *n.* = carotene.

ca|rot|in|oid (kə rot′ə noid), *n., adj.* = carotenoid.

ca|rotte (kȧ rôt′), *n. French.* a roll of tobacco.

ca|rous|al (kə rou′zəl), *n.* **1** a noisy feast or drinking party: *The Germans were celebrated for their hospitality ... and their carousals* (William Butler Yeats). **2** = carrousel.

ca|rouse (kə rouz′), *v.,* **-roused, -rous|ing,** *n.*
—*v.i.* to drink heavily; take part in noisy feasts or merrymaking: *Thomson ... carousing with Lord Hertford and his friends* (Samuel Johnson).
—*v.t. Obsolete.* to drink up; drain.
—*n.* **1** a noisy feast or drinking party; carousal: *What means this revel and carouse?* (Longfellow). **2** *Obsolete.* a whole cup or toast drunk at once: *Quaff the full carouse* (Scott).
[< obsolete adverb *carouse* completely < German (*trink*) *gar aus!* (drink) all up!] —**ca|rous′er,** *n.*

car|ou|sel (kar′ə sel′, -zel′), *n.* **1** = carrousel (def. 1). **2** a circular tray for a slide projector, from which each slide is placed before a lens for viewing and then returned to its slot.

carp[1] (kärp), *v., n.* —*v.i.* to find fault; complain: *We will not carp at this great writer* (Matthew Arnold). *No doubt every psychologist will find something to carp at—a quibble over a definition or a complaint about an omission* (New Scientist).
—*n.* a minor or trivial complaint; cavil: *My only carp was that, on this occasion at least, they seemed to be preaching to the converted* (London Times).
[< Scandinavian (compare Old Danish *karpa* to boast); influenced by Latin *carpere* pluck at; revile] —**carp′er,** *n.*

carp[2] (kärp), *n., pl.* **carps** or (*collectively*) **carp.** **1** a bony, freshwater fish which lives in ponds and slow streams. It feeds mostly on plants and sometimes grows quite large. **2** any one of a group of similar fishes, including goldfish, minnows, chub, and dace. [< Old French *carpe* < Old Provençal *carpa* < Late Latin, probably < Germanic (compare Middle High German *karpe*)] —**carp′like′,** *adj.*

car|pal (kär′pəl), *adj., n.* —*adj.* of or having to do with the carpus or wrist: *carpal bones, a carpal fracture.* —*n.* a bone of the carpus. [< New Latin *carpalis* < Greek *karpós* wrist]

carpal angle, *Ornithology.* the bend of the wing. The length of wing is the distance from the carpal angle to the end of the longest quill feather.

car|pa|le (kär pā′lē), *n. Anatomy.* a bone of the carpus; carpal. [< New Latin *carpale,* neuter of *carpalis* carpal]

carpal joint, *Anatomy.* **1** a joint of the carpus. **2a** the joint between the radius and the carpus in man. **b** a corresponding joint in other vertebrates.

car park, *British.* an open area reserved for the

Pronunciation Key: hat, āge, cãre, fär; let, ēqual, tėrm; it, īce; hot, ōpen, ôrder; oil, out; cup, pu̇t, rüle; child; long; thin; ᴛʜen; zh, measure; ə represents **a** in about, **e** in taken, **i** in pencil, **o** in lemon, **u** in circus.

parking of cars; parking lot.

Car|pa|thi|an (kär pā′thē ən), *adj.* of or having to do with the Carpathian Mountains (a system of mountains in northern Romania and Czechoslovakia).

car|pe di|em (kär′pē dī′em), *Latin.* **1** enjoy today; make the most of the present. **2** (literally) seize the day.

***car|pel** (kär′pəl), *n.* a modified leaf which forms a pistil or part of a pistil of a flower: *The central whorl of floral organs, the pistil or pistils of the flower, is formed of one or more carpels* (Harbaugh and Goodrich). [< New Latin *carpellum* (diminutive) < Greek *karpós* fruit]

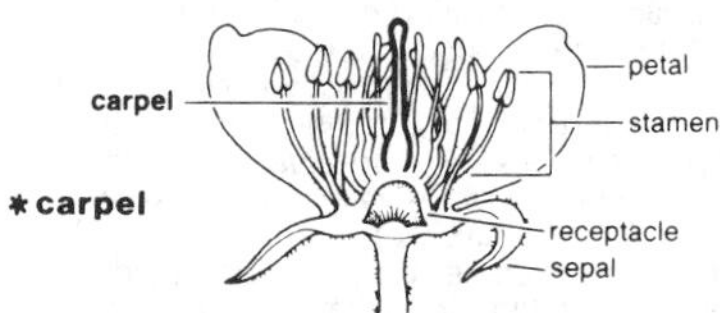

***carpel**

car|pel|lar|y (kär′pə ler′ē), *adj.* of or like a carpel.

car|pel|late (kär′pə lāt), *adj.* having carpels: *The young carpellate cones appear in May or early June as pinkish purple structures arranged . . . laterally along the new growth* (Heber W. Youngken).

car|pen|ter (kär′pən tər), *n., v.* **—*n.*** a person whose work is building and repairing the wooden parts of houses, barns, ships, or similar constructions. The occupation of carpenter and joiner are often combined.
—*v.i.* to do carpenter's work: *He carpentered with more enthusiasm than skill.*
—*v.t.* to make by carpentry: *The next morning he did not enter his study, but carpentered an often-postponed wall-cage for broody hens* (Harper's).
[< Old North French *carpentier* < Late Latin (*artifex*) *carpentārius* carriage maker < Latin *carpentum* two-wheeled carriage]

carpenter ant, a black or brown ant that builds its nest in dead or decaying trees or wooden parts of buildings by chewing out large, irregular holes in the wood.

carpenter bee, any one of a subfamily of solitary bees that make tunnels and compartments in wood for depositing their eggs.

carpenter bird, a redheaded woodpecker of California that cuts holes in dead branches, in which it inserts acorns.

car|pen|ter|ing (kär′pən tər ing), *n.* = carpentry.

carpenter moth, a large moth whose larvae burrow in the solid wood of deciduous trees.

carpenter or **carpenter's scene,** *Theater.* **1** a scene to allow time for elaborate scenery to be set up. **2** the scenery, usually a drop, to conceal most of the stage while such a scene is being set up.

car|pen|ter|worm (kär′pən tər wėrm′), *n.* the larva of the carpenter moth.

car|pen|try (kär′pən trē), *n., pl.* **-tries. 1** the trade or work of a carpenter. **2** something constructed by a carpenter.

car|pet (kär′pit), *n., v., adj.* **—*n.* 1a** a heavy, woven fabric for covering floors and stairs. **b** a covering made of this fabric. Carpets are usually tacked or nailed to the floor; rugs are not. **2** anything like a carpet: (*Figurative.*) *He walked on a carpet of grass.*
—*v.t.* 1 to cover with a carpet: (*Figurative.*) *In the spring, the ground was carpeted with violets; in the fall, the ground was carpeted with leaves.* **2** *Informal.* to summon for the purpose of reprimanding or calling to account: *They had done nothing. Why were they carpeted?* (Henry Cockton).
—*adj.* avoiding danger and exertion; effeminate; stay-at-home: *No carpet soldiers, but hardy troops* (George Rawlinson).
on the carpet, a under consideration or discussion: *a question of importance being on the carpet* (Mason L. Weems). **b** *Informal.* being scolded or rebuked: *He was constantly on the carpet for promising deliveries, blaming others for his failures* (Wall Street Journal). **c** into the presence of a superior to be scolded or rebuked: *The salesman was called on the carpet.*
sweep (or **push**) **under the carpet,** *Informal.* to conceal or ignore (a problem or duty): *What worries me, however, is the attitude that . . . it must always be the moral issue which is swept under the carpet* (Manchester Guardian Weekly).
[< Medieval Latin *carpeta, carpita* thick cloth < Vulgar Latin *carpīre* to pick, card (wool) < Latin *carpere*] **—car′pet|less,** *adj.*

car|pet|bag** (kär′pit bag′), *n., adj., v.,* **-bagged, -bag|ging. —*n. a traveling bag made of carpet: *Our dozen trunks and half-dozen carpetbags, being already packed and labelled* (Hawthorne).
—*adj. U.S.* of or having to do with the practices of a carpetbagger: *a carpetbag reformer.*
—*v.i. U.S.* to travel or act as or resemble a carpetbagger: *Mr. McDuffie carpetbagged from somewhere down into Alabama* (Congressional Record).

***carpetbag**

car|pet|bag|ger (kär′pit bag′ər), *n. U.S.* **1a** a Northerner who went to the South to get political or other advantages during the time of disorganization that followed the American Civil War: *moving in the best circles of carpetbagger society* (Margaret Mitchell). **b** any person who follows a similar course anywhere: *The first Nationalist governor to take over from the Japanese at war's end had arrived with a retinue of carpetbaggers and incompetents* (Time). **c** *Slang.* a fraudulent traveling banker, promoter, or the like, of the early West. **2** a traveler who carries a carpetbag.

car|pet|bag|ger|y (kär′pit bag′ər ē), *n. U.S.* carpetbaggism.

car|pet|bag|gism (kär′pit bag′iz əm), *n. U.S.* **1** the practices or methods of carpetbaggers. **2** government by carpetbaggers.

carpet bed, a garden having dwarf plants of different colors arranged like the pattern of a carpet.

carpet beetle or **bug,** any one of several small beetles whose larvae destroy carpets, other fabrics, and furs; buffalo bug.

car|pet-bomb (kär′pit bom′), *v.t., v.i.* to bomb an area by covering it with bombs as with a carpet; engage in carpet bombing.

carpet bombing, a method of bombing in which an area containing numerous targets is carpeted with bombs.

carpet dance, an informal dance.

carpet grass, a creeping, drought-resistant pasture grass found in the tropics and southern United States, commonly used to cover athletic fields, golf courses, and playgrounds.

car|pet|ing (kär′pə ting), *n.* **1a** a fabric for carpets or other floor coverings: *Wilton carpeting.* **b** carpets: *Matting and carpeting have done much for the stone floor* (Leigh Hunt). **2** a covering that resembles or suggests a carpet: (*Figurative.*) *Next morning there was a carpeting of fresh snow.*

carpet knight, a soldier who is more used to parlors than to battlefields.

carpet rods, rods for holding a stair carpet in place.

carpet shark, a tropical shark of the western Pacific whose spotted back is suggestive of a carpet.

carpet slipper, a slipper made of carpet fabric: *Outside the door two dear old pudgy housemaids are sitting on the floor in white caps, aprons, and carpet slippers, sibilantly gossiping* (Manchester Guardian).

carpet snake, a python of Australia having a variegated skin: *An enormous carpet snake . . . was found to measure 12 feet 6 inches in length* (Glasgow Herald).

carpet sweeper, a wheeled device for cleaning carpets and rugs. When it is pushed back and forth, brushes revolved by the wheels sweep the dust into a container.

car|pet|weed (kär′pit wēd′), *n.* an annual, North American, prostrate weed introduced from tropical America and now common in the central and eastern United States. It forms mats over the ground.

carpetweed family, a family of herbs and grasses, with cymose or solitary flowers and capsular fruit. The carpetweed is representative.

car|phol|o|gy (kär fol′ə jē), *n. Medicine.* a delirious picking at the bedclothes, as in certain fevers; floccillation. [< Greek *karphologia* < *kárphos* bits of wool; straw + *légein* collect]

car|pho|sid|er|ite (kär′fō sid′ə rīt), *n. Mineralogy.* a hydrous iron sulphate, occurring in straw-yellow incrustations. [< Greek *kárphos* straw + *sidērítēs* of iron < *sídēros* iron]

car|pi (kär′pī), *n.* the plural of **carpus.**

carp|ing (kär′ping), *adj., n.* **—*adj.*** that carps; faultfinding; complaining: *that carping spirit in which she had been wont to judge of his actions* (Anthony Trollope). **SYN:** censorious, captious.
—*n.* faultfinding; captious criticism: *showed his age with some more of his crotchety carping* (Newsweek). **—carp′ing|ly,** *adv.*

car|pin|te|ro (kär′pin tār′ō), *n., pl.* **-ros.** any one of various woodpeckers of the western United States. [< Spanish *carpintero* carpenter]

car|pi|tis (kär pī′təs), *n.* an inflammation of the synovial membranes covering the bones of the carpal joint in domestic animals, causing pain, swelling, and lameness. [< New Latin *carpitis* < *carpus* carpus + *-itis* -itis]

carp louse, a branchiuran, parasitic on fish.

car|po|gen|ic (kär′pə jen′ik), *adj.* fruit-producing. [< Greek *karpós* fruit + English *-gen* + *-ic*]

car|po|go|ni|al (kär′pə gō′nē əl), *adj.* of or having to do with a carpogonium.

car|po|go|ni|um (kär′pə gō′nē əm), *n., pl.* **-ni|a** (-ni ə). *Botany.* the single-celled female sex organ of certain algae. Its distal end is prolonged to form a tube which receives the male gamete. [< Greek *karpós* fruit + New Latin *-gonium* < Greek *gónos* offspring]

car|po|lite (kär′pə līt), *n.* a fossil fruit. [< Greek *karpós* fruit + English *-lite*]

car|po|log|i|cal (kär′pə loj′ə kəl), *adj.* of or having to do with carpology.

car|pol|o|gist (kär pol′ə jist), *n.* an expert in or student of carpology.

car|pol|o|gy (kär pol′ə jē), *n.* the branch of botany dealing with fruits. [< Greek *karpós* fruit]

car pool, 1 an arrangement for private transportation in which the responsibility of providing an automobile is rotated among members of a group of automobile owners: *Growing numbers of commuters, as a result, are driving their own cars to work or joining car pools in which members usually take turns in furnishing transportation for fellow commuters* (Wall Street Journal). **2** the members of such a group arrangement.

car|pool or **car-pool** (kär′pül′), *v.i.* to join or take part in a car pool: *In Houston, Texas, five friends and neighbors car-pool daily to their jobs at Shell Oil Company's headquarters* (Woman's Day).

car|poph|a|gous (kär pof′ə gəs), *adj.* fruit-eating. [< Greek *karpophágos* (with English *-ous*) < *karpós* fruit + *phageîn* eat]

car|po|phore (kär′pə fôr, -fōr), *n. Botany.* **1** a slender elongation of the receptacle of a flower, supporting the carpels of some compound fruits, as in the geranium and many plants of the parsley family. **2** the stalk of a sporocarp or spore fruit. [< Greek *karpophóros* fruit-bearing < *karpós* fruit + *phérein* bear]

car|port (kär′pôrt′, -pōrt′), *n.* a shelter for automobiles, usually attached to a house and open on at least one side.

car|po|spore (kär′pə spôr, -spōr), *n. Botany.* one of the spores produced in red algae as a result of fertilization of a carpogonium. [< Greek *karpós* fruit + English *spore*]

carp-suck|er (kärp′suk′ər), *n.* any one of several large, North American, carplike freshwater fishes; buffalo fish.

car|pus (kär′pəs), *n., pl.* **-pi. 1** the wrist. **2** the bones of the wrist. **3** the part in other vertebrates corresponding to this. [< New Latin *carpus* < Greek *karpós* wrist]

car|rack (kar′ək), *n.* a large ship of former times; galleon: *They saw the great carracks from the East, laden deep with pepper and spices, coming into Lisbon and Antwerp* (New Statesman). Also, **carack, carrick.** [< Old French *carraque* < Arabic *qarāqīr,* plural of *qurqūra* large cargo ship < Greek *kérkouros* light fishing vessel]

car|ra|geen or **car|ra|gheen** (kar′ə gēn), *n.* a purplish or reddish-brown, edible seaweed common on North Atlantic coasts, which when dried and bleached is used in making soups and blancmange, and in ointments; Irish moss. [< *Carragheen,* near Waterford, Eire, where it is abundant]

car|ra|gee|nin (kar′ə gē′nin), *n.* the mucilaginous constituent of carrageen that absorbs water readily.

car|ré (kȧ rā′), *n.* a bet made in roulette to take in four numbers in a square, the money being placed on the intersecting lines of the four numbers. [< French *carré,* (originally) past participle of *carrer* to make square < Latin *quadrāre* to square. Compare etym. under **quadrate.**]

car|re|four (kar′ə für′, kar′ə für), *n.* **1** an intersection of crossing roads. **2** a square in a city or village. [< Middle French *quarrefour* < Late Latin *quadrifurcum* < Latin *quadri-* four + *furca* fork]

car|rel or **car|rell** (kar′əl), *n.* a small enclosed place for individual study in a library, usually containing a desk and bookshelves: *Collegians study hard . . . in the 500 carrells of the Firestone Library at Princeton* (Newsweek). [variant of *carol* (in the sense of Medieval Latin *carola* circular enclosure, a monk's study)]

car|ret|a (kär rā′tä), *n. Southwestern U.S.* a rudely built cart having a long bottom frame provided with large rings for ropes that hold the load in place. [< Spanish *carreta* a narrow cart < *carro* car, cart. Compare etym. under **car.**]

car|re|te|la (kä re tā′lä), *n.* a carriage or coach used in the Philippine Islands. [< Spanish *carretela* < *carreta* a narrow cart]

car|ri|a|ble (kar′ē ə bəl), *adj.* capable of being carried. Also, **carryable**.

car|riage (kar′ij; *for 4c also* kar′ē ij), *n.* **1a** a vehicle that moves on wheels. Some carriages are pulled by horses and are used to carry people. Baby carriages are small and light, and may be folded. *... a carriage and four splendid horses* (Thackeray). **b** *British.* a passenger car of a railroad train. **2a** a frame on wheels that supports a gun. **b** a moving part of a machine that supports some other part. **c** the moving part of a typewriter that holds the paper and the roller. **d** the wheels and frame of a vehicle without the body. **3a** the manner in which a person holds his head and body; bearing: *She has a queenly carriage.* SYN: See syn. under **bearing**. **b** *Archaic.* behavior; deportment. **4a** the act of taking persons or goods from one place to another; carrying; transporting: *All carriage to that mountain town has to be done by animals.* SYN: transportation. **b** the conveyance of merchandise; commercial trans port: *refrigerated carriage of fruit and flowers.* SYN: transportation. **c** the cost or price of carrying: *This will be $10 for the gift package plus a charge of 50 cents for carriage.* **5** management; handling; administration: *The carriage of the whole enterprise was in his hands.* **6** *Obsolete, Figurative.* a burden or load. [< Old North French *cariage* < *carier;* see etym. under **carry**]

car|riage|a|ble (kar′ə jə bəl), *adj.* **1** = portable. **2** passable by carriages, as a road.

carriage and pair, a carriage and two horses.

carriage bolt, a bolt once used principally in fastening together parts of a carriage and now having more general uses. The round shaft is square under the head. See picture under **bolt**[1].

carriage clock, an early design of traveling clock with glass sides.

carriage company, people who keep private carriages: *No phrase more elegant and to my taste than that in which people are described as 'seeing a great deal of carriage company'* (Thackeray).

carriage dog, = Dalmatian.

carriage drive, a road for carriages in private grounds, parks, and the like.

carriage forward, *British.* with the cost of shipping not prepaid.

car|riage-free (kar′ij frē′), *adj.* with the cost of shipping prepaid.

carriage house, the building in which a carriage, coach, or other horse-drawn vehicle is housed.

carriage paid, *British.* carriage-free.

carriage trade, wealthy people who are patrons of theaters, expensive restaurants, and stores, so called because they formerly drove in private carriages: *The exclusive store prided itself on its carriage trade.*

car|riage|way (kar′ij wā′), *n. British.* that part of the road intended for vehicular traffic: *All these schemes will give drivers lengths of road exclusively for their use, laid out with dual carriageways* (London Times).

car|rick (kar′ik), *n.* = carrack.

carrick bend, a type of knot used to join cables, hawsers, or heavy ropes.

carrick bitt, one of the bitts or posts which hold a ship's windlass on either side.

Car|rick|ma|cross lace (kar′ik mə krôs′, -kros′), a lace from the vicinity of Carrickmacross in Ireland, consisting of a pattern cut from cambric and applied to net: *She was attired in a bouffant gown of light ivory satin and heirloom Carrickmacross lace* (New York Times).

car|ried (kar′ēd), *adj. Scottish.* rapt in thought; abstracted.

car|ri|er (kar′ē ər), *n.* **1a** a person or thing that carries something. A postman is a mail carrier. A porter is a baggage carrier. **b** a bearer; messenger: *A jungle safari usually has water carriers. Troubadours and peddlers were often carriers of news.* **2** a company that transports goods or people, usually over certain routes and according to fixed schedules. Bus systems, truck companies, airlines, and railroads are carriers. *The carriers say they need to lift rates to offset higher labor, tax and service costs* (Wall Street Journal). **3a** a person or thing that carries or transmits a disease. Carriers are often healthy persons who are immune to a disease, but carry its germs. *The outbreak of typhoid fever was traced to a single carrier.* **b** a person or animal that carries and transmits a recessive gene: *If the carrier bull is mated to a dwarf-free cow, no dwarfs will appear in the first generation, but half of the calves will be carriers* (Time). **4** any rack or carriage for parcels or luggage, such as a bicycle rack for small parcels or a cart for wheeling luggage at an air terminal. **5** = aircraft carrier. **6** = carrier wave. **7** *Chemistry.* a catalytic agent which brings about, or helps in, the transference of an element or group from one compound to another: *Iron can be a carrier of oxygen.* **8** a drain or channel for water or other liquid. **9** a mechanical part or device by which something is carried, moved, or driven. **10** = carrier pigeon. **11 Carrier**, a North American Indian tribe belonging to the Athapascan family, living in British Columbia.

carrier bag, *British.* shopping bag.

car|ri|er-based (kar′ē ər bāst′), *adj.* operating from an aircraft carrier: *carrier-based planes.*

carrier pigeon, **1** a homing pigeon; a pigeon trained to return to its home when released many miles away: *Carrier (homing) pigeons are a domesticated version of pigeons that thrive in city parks, trained to get the message through* (Newsweek). **2** any one of a breed of large, domestic pigeons raised as show birds. The carrier pigeon is descended from the rock dove and has a long, erect body and large wattle.

carrier rocket, a rocket designed to carry or launch something, such as an artificial satellite: *The carrier rocket separated from the cone-shaped satellite once it reached its orbit.*

carrier transmission, a way of sending several telephone conversations, each at a different frequency, on the same pair of wires. Electronic filters at each end of the line sort out the conversations.

carrier wave, a radio wave whose intensity and frequency are varied in order to transmit a signal, usually in broadcasting radio and television programs and sending telephone and telegraph messages.

car|ri|ole (kar′ē ōl), *n.* = cariole.

car|ri|on (kar′ē ən), *n., adj.* —*n.* **1** dead and decaying flesh: *Some crows feed largely on carrion.* **2** *Figurative.* rottenness; filth; garbage.
—*adj.* **1** dead and decaying. **2** feeding on dead and decaying flesh: *a carrion crow.* **3** *Figurative.* rotten; filthy.
[alteration of Middle English *caroine* < Old North French *carogne* < Vulgar Latin *carōnia,* ultimately < Latin *cariēs* decay. See etym. of doublet **crone**.]

carrion crow, **1** the common European crow that feeds on carrion. **2** a black vulture of the southern United States.

car|ritch (kär′ich), *n. Scottish.* a catechism. [back formation < *carritches,* an assumed plural < *catechize*]

car|ri|witch|et (kar′ē wich′it), *n.* **1** a piece of jocularity or facetiousness. **2** = pun. **3** a tricky question; conundrum. Also, **carwitchet**. [origin unknown]

car|roc|cio (kär rôt′chō), *n., pl.* **-ci** (-chē). the car of war, on which the standard was borne into battle, peculiar to the Italian republics of the Middle Ages. [< Italian *carroccio* < Latin *carrus* wagon]

car|rol|lite (kar′ə līt), *n.* a sulfide of copper and cobalt obtained from Carroll County, Maryland.

car|rom (kar′əm), *n., v.i., v.t.* = carom.

car|ro|ma|ta (kär′rō mä′tä), *n.* (in the Philippines) a two-wheeled work cart, usually pulled by one horse or other draft animal. [< Philippine Spanish *carromata* < Italian *carromatto* low, four-wheeled cart < Latin *carrus* (see etym. under **car**) + *mattus* dull]

car|ro|nade (kar′ə nād′), *n.* a short cannon with a large bore, not used now. [< *Carron,* Scotland, where the cannon was first cast]

car|ron oil (kar′ən), a liniment composed of equal parts of linseed oil and lime water, used for burns. [< *Carron* Ironworks, at Stirlingshire, Scotland, where it was much used to treat burns]

car|rot (kar′ət), *n., v.* —*n.* **1** a plant which has a long, tapering, orange-red root. It belongs to the parsley family. **2** its root, which is eaten as a vegetable, either cooked or raw. **3** *Figurative.* a reward or gain, especially one that is tantalizing and hard to attain: *The capital grants ... are a juicy carrot to hang before boards that are contemplating expansion* (New York Times).
—*v.t.* to prepare (fur) for felting by subjecting it to chemical action, usually with mercuric nitrate.
[< Middle French *carotte,* learned borrowing from Latin *carōta*]

carrot and stick, an incentive or reward joined with a threat or risk: *Profit and loss, then, is ... the carrot and stick of industry and commerce. Under capitalism, the carrot is the pleasure of profit, the stick is the pain of loss* (Wall Street Journal).

car|rot|top (kar′ət top′), *n. U.S. Slang.* a person having red hair; redhead.

carrot weed, the ragweed, whose foliage somewhat resembles that of the carrot.

car|rot|y (kar′ə tē), *adj.,* **-rot|i|er, -rot|i|est. 1** like a carrot in color; orange-red: *She was attractive, with ... amazing hair, which could only be described as a carroty, fiery orange colour* (Cape Times). **2** red-haired: *The plainest, oldest, and carrotiest of the three redheaded maids* (C. N. and A. M. Williamson). —**car′rot|i|ness**, *n.*

car|rou|sel (kar′ə sel′, -zel′), *n.* Also, **carousel**. **1** a merry-go-round: *It's within sound of the merry carrousel calliope* (New Yorker). **2** a circular conveyor, as for the delivery of luggage at an airport. **3** a circular tray for a slide projector. **4** Also, **carousal**. *Historical.* a tournament in which companies of knights engaged in various exercises, often including chariot races and other entertainments. [< French *carrousel* < Italian *carosello* < Latin *carrus* wagon]

car|roz|za (kär rôt′tsä), *n., pl.* **-ze** (-tsā). *Italian.* a carriage: *So I went out into the warm Roman night and hired myself a carrozza, one of the four-wheel horse-drawn cabs* (Maclean's).

car|ru|cate (kar′ə kāt), *n.* = carucate.

car|ry (kar′ē), *v.,* **-ried, -ry|ing,** *n., pl.* **-ries.** —*v.t.* **1** to take (a thing or person) from one place to another; transport: *He carried the box into the house. Railroads carry coal from the mines to the factories.* (*Figurative.*) *This story will carry your thoughts back to last winter.* **2a** to bear or have with one, especially as a habit, part of a duty, or the like: *He always carries a little pocketknife. The policeman carries a whistle. The sailor carried a tattoo on his arm.* (*Figurative.*) *The President has to carry many problems.* **b** to be pregnant with: *At this time of year the does are carrying their fawns.* **3a** to hold up; support; sustain: *Rafters carry the weight of the roof.* **b** to give validity to; support (a similar case): *Your case will probably be carried by the judgment in the Florida case of last year.* **4a** to hold (one's body and head) in a certain way: *A trained soldier carries himself well.* **b** to behave or comport (oneself): *She carries herself haughtily.* **5** to capture or win: *Our congressman was elected when he carried all the towns in his district. Our troops carried the enemy's position.* **6** to get (a motion or bill) passed or adopted: *The motion to adjourn the meeting was carried.* **7a** to continue or extend: *to carry a road into the mountains.* (*Figurative*). *He carried his theory to a logical result.* **b** to cause to come or go; drive or impel: *Hard work carried him far.* **c** to go (a distance) or go past (an obstacle), as in golf: *His drive carried the brook.* **d** (of a hunting dog or other animal) to follow (a scent). **8** *Figurative.* to influence greatly; lead: *The speaker carried his audience.* **9** *Figurative.* to have as a property or characteristic; involve: *The expert's judgment carries great weight.* **10** to sing (a melody, theme, or part) with correct pitch: *The children in the chorus can all carry a tune.* **11** to sing or play (a melody, theme, or part): *She will carry the soprano solos. The first violins carry the melody.* **12** *Commerce.* **a** to keep in stock: *This store carries clothing for men.* **b** to keep on the account books of a business. **13** to publish or broadcast: *The evening newspaper carried a review of the new play. Her speech was carried on radio and television.* **14** to transfer (a number) from one place or column in the sum to the next: *A 10 in the 1's column must be carried to the 10's column.* **15** to yield, as a crop: *This land carries a large crop of corn.* **16** to support, as cattle: *a ranch that will carry a thousand head of cattle.* **17** to place (a weapon or standard) in a certain position prescribed by military regulations, especially as part of a command. **18** to support or help bear financially: *The company carried the research project for new anti-pollutants without any subsidy from the government.*
—*v.i.* **1** to act as a bearer. **2** to cover the distance; have the power of throwing or driving: *Our football coach has a voice that carries clear across the field. Sound carries far on a still day. Some guns will carry for miles.* **3** to be passed or adopted: *The motion ... could have carried with the support of five of the six defecting Republicans* (Arthur Krock). **4** to hold the head in a certain way: *This horse carries high.*
—*n.* **1** the range of a gun. **2a** a portage between rivers, lakes, or navigable channels. **b** the place where portage is done. **3** the distance a golf ball travels in the air before bouncing. **4a** a method or position of moving or holding something: *a fireman's carry.* **b** *Military.* the position to which a weapon, standard, or the like, is moved after the command "carry." **5** the act of carrying.

carry all (or **everything**) **before one**, to meet with uninterrupted success; be very successful in spite of opposition: *Some men there be that carry all before 'em* (Robert Wild).

carry away, **a** to arouse strong feeling in; influence beyond reason: *The little girl was so carried*

Pronunciation Key: hat, āge, cãre, fär; let, ēqual, tėrm; it, īce; hot, ōpen, ôrder; oil, out; cup, pu̇t, rüle; child; long; thin; ᴛʜen; zh, measure; ə represents a in about, e in taken, i in pencil, o in lemon, u in circus.

away by the sad story that she began to cry. Woman-kind ... are carried away with everything that is showy (Sir Richard Steele). **b** to cause the death of; kill: *The epidemic carried away a number of people before it was checked.*

carry forward, a to go ahead with; make progress with: *After the death of the store's founder, his sons carried forward the business.* **b** *Bookkeeping.* to reenter (an item or items already entered) on the next or a later page or column of an accounting record: *Present law permits a corporation to carry forward and deduct from its own income the losses sustained in prior years by companies which were merged into it* (Wall Street Journal).

carry off, a to win (a prize or honor): *The champion swimmer carried off two gold medals at the Olympic games.* **b** to succeed with; brave or face out: *Frightened too ... but carrying it off, sir, really like Satan* (Robert Louis Stevenson). **c** to be the death of; kill: *A severe case of pneumonia carried him off.*

carry on, a to do; manage; conduct: *He carried on a successful business.* **b** to keep going; not stop; continue: *We must carry on in our effort to establish world peace. The conversation was carried on* (Jane Austen). **c** to go on with after being stopped: *The director told us to carry on with our work after he finished speaking to us.* **d** *Especially Military.* to continue as before; resume a former situation, position, or duty: *Tomorrow the workaday life of the Fleet begins again, and the word will be, 'Carry on!'* (London Daily Chronicle). **e** *U.S. Informal.* to behave wildly or foolishly: *The small boys carried on at the party.* **f** to flirt or have a love affair: *Lady Carmine's eldest daughter is carrying on with young Thriftless* (G. J. Whyte-Melville).

carry out, to get done; do; accomplish; complete: *He carried out his job well. It seemed to Scobie that life was immeasurably long. Couldn't the test of man have been carried out in fewer years?* (Graham Greene).

carry over, a to have left over or be left over: *The store carried over the previous year's stock of men's hats. ... there appeared in his relation to his group something of the attitude of the older brother, carried over from his relation to his family, and a good deal of the inspired schoolmaster* (Edmund Wilson). **b** to keep until later; continue; extend: *I'll carry your account over the next month.*

carry through, a to get done; do; accomplish; complete: *Most people could not have accomplished the task which it was his destiny to carry through.* **b** to bring through trouble; keep from being discouraged: *Impudence had carried him through before now* (F. C. L. Wraxall).

[< Old North French *carier* < Late Latin *carricāre* < Latin *carrus* wagon, cart. See etym. of doublet **charge, cark.**]

—*Syn. v.t.* **1 Carry, convey, transport** mean to take or bring from one place to another. **Carry,** the general word, suggests holding and moving a person or thing in or with something, such as a vehicle, container, or hands: *The cat carried its kittens away.* **Convey** suggests getting a person or thing to a place by some means or through some channel, and therefore is sometimes used figuratively in the sense of communicate: *Escalators convey people. Language conveys ideas.* **Transport** suggests conveying in a ship, plane, or vehicle: *Trucks transport freight.*

▶ **Carry** in the sense of "escort" (*to carry a girl to a dance*) still survives in the South of the United States, in both popular and cultivated speech.

car|ry|a|ble (kar′ē ə bəl), *adj.* = carriable.

car|ry|all¹ (kar′ē ôl′), *n.* **1** a lightweight, covered, one-horse carriage, for carrying several people. **2** a closed passenger automobile having a bench along each side for passengers. **3** = station wagon. [American English; alteration of *cariole*]

car|ry|all² (kar′ē ôl′), *n.* a large bag, basket, or the like: ... *the straw carryall that always hangs on my arm when I travel in and out of town* (New Yorker). [< *carry* + *all*]

car|ry-back (kar′ē bak′), *n.* **1** the spreading of a portion of an individual's or corporation's profits or losses in the current taxable year over immediately preceding years, in computing federal taxes: *The tax bill provides for ... an increase from six to eight years in the carry-back on losses* (Newsweek). **2** the amount that may legally be so spread: *The Senators specified that third-year carry-back should be available only for up to $50,000 of loss* (Wall Street Journal).

car|ry|cot (kar′ē kot′), *n. British.* a portable crib; bassinet.

car|ry-for|ward (kar′ē fôr′wərd), *n.* **1** the spreading of a portion of an individual's or a corporation's profits or losses in the current taxable year over the years immediately following: *The aircraft company could in four years more than recoup its $35 million purchase price with tax savings from ... loss carry-forward* (Time). **2** the amount that may legally be so spread: *The group is able to add as much as £4,356,071 to its reserves and carry-forward* (New Scientist).

car|ry-home (kar′ē hōm′), *adj. U.S.* (of a package or carton) convenient to carry.

carrying capacity, the largest number of a population of a species the environment can support.

car|ry|ing case (kar′ē ing), a small case or bag for holding a particular object or set of objects, such as a film projector, shaving equipment, or tape recorder.

carrying charge, 1 an interest charge on the balance owed for an installment purchase or loan: *If he owes an installment debt, on which he pays a high rate of interest as carrying charges, he should not make small payments on his debt and put some money in the bank, where it earns a low rate of interest* (E. C. Harwood). **2** the expenses involved in continuing ownership of property or goods: *Carrying charges pay for maintenance, interest, and amortization of the mortgage and other costs* (Wall Street Journal).

car|ry|ing-on (kar′ē ing on′, -ôn′), *n., pl.* **car|ry-ings-on.** *Informal.* conspicuous, frolicsome, or indecorous behavior: *paid no attention to his wife's carryings-on with another man* (Time).

carrying party, a military party detailed to carry or bring up supplies.

carrying place, *U.S.* portage.

carrying trade, the trade or business of conveying goods, especially over sea between different countries.

car|ry-on (kar′ē on′, -ôn′), *adj., n.* —*adj.* small enough to be carried aboard an airplane by a passenger: *Coats and carry-on baggage are stowed in large overhead storage compartments* (Time).

—*n. British Informal.* carrying-on: ... *belligerent family carry-ons* (Manchester Guardian Weekly).

car|ry-out (kar′ē out′), *adj.* of or having to do with food prepared to be eaten out of the premises; take-out: *carry-out chop suey; ... to launch a Chicken Delight carry-out shop* (Time).

car|ry-o|ver (kar′ē ō′vər), *n.* **1** a part left over: *About the only carry-over from the unsuccessful attempt at centralization is that a single officer is in charge of all purchasing* (Wall Street Journal). **2** the portion of a crop, stock, or the like, to be disposed of with the following crop or stock: *She is now faced with a big carry-over and a big new crop coming along* (New York Times). **3** *Bookkeeping.* the item or items carried forward in an accounting record. **4** = carry-forward.

carse (kärs), *n. Scottish.* the low alluvial land along the bank of a river. [perhaps < dialectal *carr* fen, bog]

car seat, 1 an infant's portable seat for use in automobile travel, having adjustable back hooks that attach to the front seat of the automobile. **2** any of the seats in an automobile.

carse deposit, *Geology.* an estuarine deposit made up of clay and silt.

car|sick (kär′sik′), *adj.* nauseated by the motion of traveling in a car, train, or other conveyance.

car|sick|ness (kär′sik′nis), *n.* motion sickness caused by traveling in a car, train, or other conveyance.

cart (kärt), *n., v.* —*n.* **1** a strong vehicle with two wheels, used in farming and for carrying heavy loads. Horses, donkeys, and oxen are often used to pull carts. **2** a light wagon, used to deliver goods or for general business. **3** a small vehicle on wheels, moved by hand: *a grocery cart.* **4** *Obsolete.* a chariot.

—*v.t.* **1** to carry in a cart: *Cart this rubbish away to the dump. We were all carted to the little town* (Thomas De Quincey). **2** to carry or transport laboriously: *He carted two chimpanzees from England to Kenya* (Life). *When his show is over, the artist carts his work home to make room for the next man's* (New Yorker). **3** *Obsolete.* to carry in a cart through the streets, by way of punishment or public exposure: *Democritus ne'er laugh'd so loud, To see Bawds carted through the crowd* (Samuel Butler).

—*v.i.* to work with a cart: *Horses cart better than oxen.*

in the cart, in an unpleasant or difficult situation: *We were simply all over 'em and had 'em in the cart in no time* (Punch).

put the cart before the horse, to reverse the accepted or usual order of things: *The boy put the cart before the horse by starting off dinner with apple pie. ... she puts the overloaded cart of her erudition before the horse of her research* (Theodor Reik).

[< Scandinavian (compare Old Icelandic *kartr*)]

cart|age (kär′tij), *n.* **1** the act of carting or transporting. **2** the cost or price of carting.

carte¹ (kärt), *n.* **1** *Scottish.* a playing car. **2** a bill of fare. **3** *Obsolete.* a map; chart.

cartes, *Scottish.* cardplaying; a game of cards. [< French *carte* card¹]

carte² (kärt), *n.* a position in fencing; quarte. [< French *quarte*]

carte blanche (kärt′ blänsh′; *French* kȧrt′ bläNsh′), *pl.* **cartes blanches** (kärts′ blänsh′; *French* kȧrt′ bläNsh′), freedom to use one's own judgment; full authority: *The law allows a surgeon to operate without permission in order to save life, but no such carte blanche exists merely to save vision* (New York Times). [< French *carte blanche* (literally) white paper]

carte de visite (kȧrt′ də vē zēt′), *French.* **1** a visiting card. **2** a small mounted photograph of a person, formerly used as a calling card: *I have a photograph of him—a carte de visite, taken about the date of the marriage* (New Yorker).

carte du jour (kȧrt′ dY zhür′), *French.* a menu or bill of fare for the day: *When I arrived at my table, I did not even look at the carte du jour* (New Yorker).

car|tel (kär tel′, kär′təl), *n.* **1** a large group of business firms that agree to operate as a monopoly, especially to regulate prices and production: *The methodical Swiss, who think that there is a place for everything, staunchly believe that the place for industry is in cartels* (Time). SYN: syndicate, combine. **2** a written agreement between countries at war for the exchange of prisoners or some other purpose. **3a** a written challenge to a duel. **b** a letter of defiance. **4** Also, **Cartel.** (in France and Belgium) a political group with a common cause or object; a bloc. **5** *Rare.* a paper or card bearing writing or printing. [< Middle French *cartel* < Italian *cartello* little card < Latin *charta*]

car|tel|ism (kär tel′iz əm, kär′tə liz-), *n.* the principles and practices of a business cartel: *The Group has strengthened itself for the vigors of new competition by casting off the remnants of cartelism—long European business' favorite form of capitalism* (Time). —**car|tel′ist,** *n., adj.*

car|te|lize (kär′tə līz, kär tel′īz), *v.t., v.i.,* **-lized, -liz|ing.** to combine or organize into a cartel or cartels: *No Swiss business has been more tightly cartelized than the watch industry* (Time). —**car′te|li|za′tion,** *n.* —**car′te|liz′er,** *n.*

cart|er (kär′tər), *n.* a person whose work is driving a cart or truck.

cartes (kärts), *n.pl.* See under **carte¹**.

Car|te|sian (kär tē′zhən), *adj., n.* —*adj.* of or having to do with René Descartes, 1596-1650, or with his doctrines or methods: *Cartesian logic. On the surface she seemed cold and calculating enough, almost a Cartesian spirit* (Edgar Maass). See also **Cartesianism.** —*n.* a follower of Descartes's doctrines or methods. [< New Latin *Cartesianus* < *Cartesius,* Latinized form of *Descartes*]

Cartesian coordinate, 1 either one of two intersecting lines which determine the position of every point in a plane. **2** any one of three intersecting lines which determine the position of points in space.

Cartesian devil, a philosophical toy consisting of a hollow figure filled with air in the upper part and water in the lower, and often fashioned in the form of a devil. It will rise and fall in a cylinder of water by changes in pressure produced by manipulating a sheet of rubber, or the like, stretched over the top of the cylinder. Pressure on the rubber causes more water to enter the lower part of the figure, compressing the air within and causing the figure to sink; release of the pressure on the rubber causes the figure to rise.

Cartesian diver, = Cartesian devil.

Car|te|sian|ism (kär tē′zhə niz əm), *n.* the philosophical system of Descartes, resting upon his famous axiom *Cogito; ergo sum* (I think; therefore I am), seeking to impart to metaphysics the certainty and precision of mathematics, and stressing a fundamental dualism of thought (mind) and extension (matter).

Cartesian product or **set**, *Mathematics.* the set of all ordered pairs that can be formed by matching each member of one set with each member of a second set in turn.

cart|ful (kärt′fu̇l), *n., pl.* **-fuls.** enough to fill a cart: *a cartful of sand.*

Car|tha|gin|i|an (kär′thə jin′ē ən), *adj., n.* —*adj.* of Carthage.

—*n.* a person who was born or who lived in Carthage.

car|tham|ic acid (kär tham′ik), = carthamin.

car|tha|min (kär′thə min), *n.* a dark red powder derived from the safflower and used as a dye. *Formula:* $C_{21}H_{22}O_{11}$ [< New Latin *Carthamus* a genus of plants including the safflower + English *-in*]

cart horse, a big, strong draft horse.

Car|thu|sian (kär thü′zhən), *n., adj.* —*n.* **1** a

member of an austere monastic order founded by St. Bruno in 1084. **2** a member of the Charterhouse School in England.
—*adj.* of or having to do with the Carthusians. [< Medieval Latin *Cartusianus* < *Cartusia* (now *Chatrousse*), a village near the first monastery of the order]

car|ti|lage (kär′tə lij), *n.* **1** the tough, elastic substance forming parts of the skeleton of vertebrates; gristle. Cartilage is more flexible than bone and not as hard. The external ear consists of cartilage and skin. *Cartilage is ... composed of collagen and mucopolysaccharide, secreted by the cells (chondrocytes) embedded in it* (Sir Herbert Seddon). **2** a part formed of this substance. [< Middle French *cartilage*, learned borrowing from Latin *cartilāgō, -inis*]

cartilage bone, bone substance or a bone that was formed, in the development of the organism, from cartilage.

cartilage cell, = chondrocyte.

car|ti|lag|i|noid (kär′tə laj′ə noid), *adj.* hard and gristly, like cartilage. [< Latin *cartilāgō, -inis* cartilage + English *-oid*]

car|ti|lag|i|nous (kär′tə laj′ə nəs), *adj.* **1** of or like cartilage; gristly. **2** having the skeleton formed mostly of cartilage: *Sturgeons and sharks are cartilaginous fish.* [< Latin *cartilāginōsus*]

cart|load (kärt′lōd′), *n.* as much as a cart can hold or carry.

cart|man (kärt′man′, -mən), *n., pl.* **-men.** a man who drives a cart, truck, or the like; teamster.

car|to|gram (kär′tə gram), *n.* a diagrammatic map which uses different kinds of lines, shadings, and other such techniques, to give information. [< French *cartogramme*]

car|tog|ra|pher (kär tog′rə fər), *n.* a maker of maps or charts: *If a geographer happens to be a cartographer, it is merely a coincidence. Most geographers are not cartographers* (White and Renner).

car|to|graph|ic (kär′tə graf′ik), *adj.* having to do with cartography or cartographers: *Indians have long complained of cartographic aggression by China in mapping these areas as parts of China* (Time). —**car′to|graph′i|cal|ly**, *adv.*

car|to|graph|i|cal (kär′tə graf′ə kəl), *adj.* = cartographic.

car|tog|ra|phy (kär tog′rə fē), *n.* the making or study of maps or charts. [< Medieval Latin *carta* chart, map + English *-graphy*]

car|to|log|i|cal (kär′tə loj′ə kəl), *adj.* **1** of maps or charts. **2** having to do with cartology.

car|tol|o|gy (kär tol′ə jē), *n.* the science of maps and charts.

car|to|man|cy (kär′tə man′sē), *n.* divination by means of playing cards. [< Medieval Latin *carta* card[1] + Greek *manteíā* divination]

car|ton (kär′tən), *n.* **1a** a box made of cardboard or pasteboard: *a candy carton. Pack the books in a large carton. It's his job to pull sealed cartons off the conveyor at random and open them up to see for himself* (Newsweek). **b** the amount that a carton holds: *He could drink a carton of milk at one meal.* **2** a paperlike material that certain insects make from pieces of wood, sometimes with sand added. **3** in rifle practice: **a** a white disk or circle within the bull's-eye of a target. **b** a shot that strikes this. [< French *carton* pasteboard < Italian *cartone* < *carta* paper < Latin *charta* chart. See etym. of doublet **cartoon**.]

car|ton|nage (kär′tə näzh′, kär′tə nij), *n.* **1** the material used to make an Egyptian mummy case, consisting of layers of linen or papyrus solidified with plaster. **2** an Egyptian mummy case. [< French *cartonnage* < *carton* pasteboard + *-age* -age]

car|ton pierre (kär tôɴ′ pyer′), a kind of papier-mâché made to imitate stone or bronze, used for statuary and architectural decorations. [< French *carton-pierre* (literally) cardboard of stone]

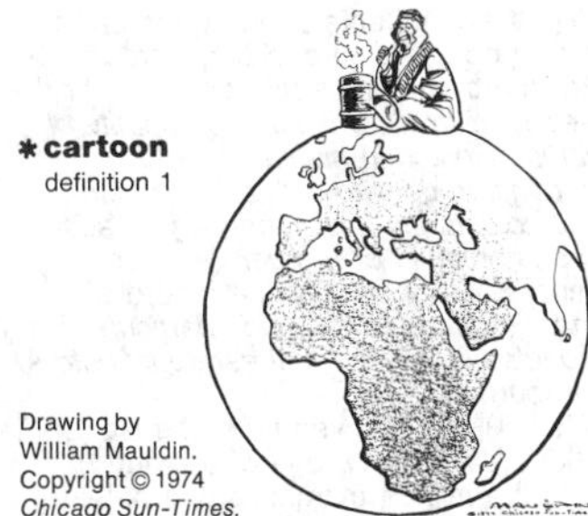

∗cartoon
definition 1

Drawing by William Mauldin. Copyright © 1974 *Chicago Sun-Times.*

∗car|toon (kär tün′), *n., v.* —*n.* **1** a sketch or drawing showing persons, things, or events in an amusing way: *Political cartoons often represent the United States as a tall man with chin whiskers, called Uncle Sam. The arc light was heralded in popular cartoons as an agent that would do away with nighttime crime more effectively than a policeman* (New Yorker). **2** = animated cartoon. **3** = comic strip. **4** a full-size drawing of a design or painting, used as a model for a fresco, mosaic, tapestry, or other medium: *Such famous painters as Peter Rubens and the Van Eycks designed cartoons for Flemish tapestries* (William M. Milliken).
—*v.t.* to make a cartoon of: *Sir Max Beerbohm cartooned many prominent politicians, artists, and writers.*
—*v.i.* to make a cartoon or cartoons: *Mr. Bendix did prewar cartooning against Hitler* (Harper's). [< French *carton* pasteboard (because it is drawn on paper). See etym. of doublet **carton**.]

car|toon|ist (kär tü′nist), *n.* a person who draws cartoons: *Writers don't consider cartoonists writers—because we not only write but draw. Artists don't consider cartoonists artists—because we not only draw but write* (Walt Kelly).

car|top (kär′top′), *adj.* designed to be transported on the roof of an automobile: *a cartop boat.*

∗car|touche or **car|touch** (kär tüsh′), *n.* **1a** an architectural ornament much used in the French and Italian Renaissance styles, consisting usually of an oval or shield-shaped area for an inscription, coat of arms, or the like, surrounded by vines, scrolls, or other curving motifs. **b** an oval or oblong figure designed to enclose the characters of the name of an Egyptian ruler, often used in ancient times as a seal. **c** a scroll-shaped ornament, as on the top of a column. **2a** the part of certain fireworks enclosing the inflammable materials. **b** a cartridge, especially if made of cardboard. **c** a box of or for cartridges. [< French *cartouche* < Italian *cartoccio* paper cylinder or cone < *carta;* see etym. under **carton**]

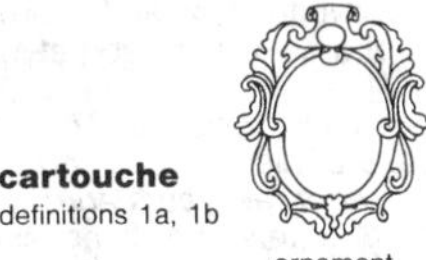

∗cartouche
definitions 1a, 1b

∗car|tridge (kär′trij), *n.* **1a** a case made of metal, plastic, or cardboard for holding gunpowder and a bullet or shot. Cartridges for blank guns do not contain bullets. **b** a case for any explosive charge, especially one to be used for blasting. **2** any one of various containers: *a filter cartridge, an ink cartridge for a fountain pen.* **3** *Photography.* **a** a small container holding a roll of photographic film. **b** a roll of photographic film. **4** a unit holding the needle in the pickup of a phonograph. [alteration of French *cartouche;* see etym. under **cartouche**]

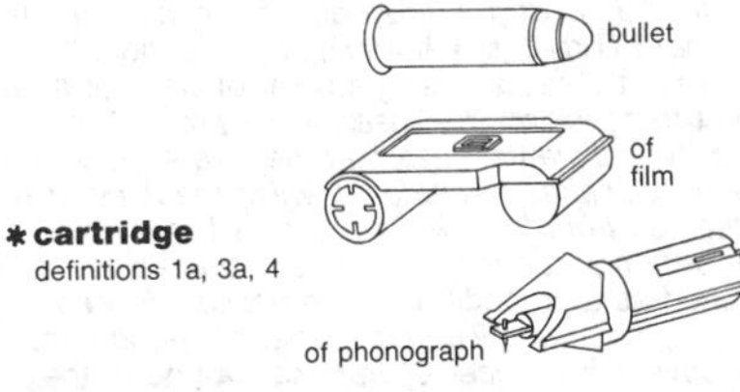

∗cartridge
definitions 1a, 3a, 4

cartridge belt, a belt worn about the waist or over the shoulder, having loops or pockets for cartridges.

cartridge box, a portable case or box of leather, for holding cartridges.

cartridge brass, a highly ductile brass containing about 70 percent copper and 30 percent zinc, used in making cartridge cases and musical instruments.

cartridge case, **1** the tube, closed at one end, which holds the powder and usually the shot or the rear end of the bullet in a cartridge. **2** = cartridge box.

cartridge clip, a metal holder for cartridges, used in some firearms.

cartridge gauge, a gun-metal ring of the required size, with a handle, on which is stamped the size of the cartridge, used to test the diameter of a cartridge.

cartridge paper, **1** a thick, strong paper used originally for making cartridges, and later as drawing paper. **2** a kind of wallpaper.

car|tu|lar|y (kär′chə ler′ē), *n., pl.* **-lar|ies.** = chartulary.

cart|way (kärt′wā′), *n.* a way along which carts may pass, often too rough and narrow for larger vehicles.

cart|wheel (kärt′hwēl′), *n., v.* —*n.* **1** the wheel of a cart. **2** a sideways handspring or somersault. **3** a woman's hat with a very wide brim: *No one has yet figured out a way to see through a cartwheel* (New York Times). **4** *Slang.* a large coin, especially a silver dollar.
—*v.i.* **1** to make a sideways handspring or somersault: *He landed all askew and cartwheeled down the slope for nearly 75 yards* (Time). **2** to move like a rotating wheel: *The flight performance consisted of an airplane cartwheeling from a steep bank.*

cart whip, a horsewhip made with a short, stiff handle and a long lash, used by teamsters.

cart|wright (kärt′rīt′), *n.* a skilled workman who makes carts.

car|ty (kär′tē), *adj.* of the breed and build of a cart horse.

car|u|cage (kar′ə kij), *n.* (formerly, in England) a tax levied on each plow or carucate of land. [< *caruca*(te) + *-age*]

car|u|cate (kar′ə kāt), *n.* (formerly, in England) a measure of land and a unit for assessment, often about 100 acres, but varying, especially according to the nature of the soil. Also, **carrucate.** [< Medieval Latin *carrucata* < *carruca* plow < Latin *carrūca* coach < *carrus* wagon, cart]

car|un|cle (kar′ung kəl, kə rung′-), *n.* **1** a protuberance at or near the point of attachment of a seed. **2** a fleshy process, such as the comb or wattle of a turkey or chicken. [< French *caruncle*, learned borrowing from Latin *caruncula* little piece of flesh < *carō, carnis* flesh]

ca|run|cu|lar (kə rung′kyə lər), *adj.* of or like a caruncle.

ca|run|cu|late (kə rung′kyə lit, -lāt), *adj.* having a caruncle or caruncles.

car|va|crol (kär′və krōl, -krol), *n.* a thick liquid, an isomer of thymol, obtained from various herbs of the mint family, used as a disinfectant and in organic synthesis. *Formula:* $C_{10}H_{14}O$ [< French *carvi* caraway + Latin *ācer, ācris* sharp + English *-ol*[2]]

carve (kärv), *v.,* **carved, carv|ing,** *n.* —*v.t.* **1** to cut into slices or pieces: *Father carves the meat at the table.* (*Figurative.*) *The country was carved into equal districts* (William Stubbs). **2a** to make by cutting; cut: *Statues are carved from marble, stone, or wood.* **SYN:** chisel, sculpture. **b** to decorate with figures or designs cut on the surface: *a carved box. The oak chest was carved with scenes from the Bible.* **c** to cut or engrave (figures or designs) on or into a surface: *They carved their initials on the tree.* **3** *Figurative.* to cut, or make as if by cutting: *He ruthlessly carved himself a financial empire.*
—*v.i.* **1** to cut up and serve meat, or the like, at the table: *They carved at the meal With gloves of steel* (Scott). **2** to make figures or designs by cutting; practice sculpture or engraving: *We carve and paint, or we behold what is carved and painted* (Emerson).
—*n.* treatment by carving; a carving stroke. [Middle English *kerven*, Old English *ceorfan*]

carved (kärvd), *adj.* cut; sculptured; engraved: *carved figurines.*

car|vel (kär′vəl), *n.* = caravel.

car|vel-built (kär′vəl bilt′), *adj.* (of a ship or boat) built with the edges of the planks flush, not overlapping.

carv|en (kär′vən), *adj. Archaic.* carved; decorated by carving; sculptured: *Yon oaken chest, carven with figures* (Longfellow).

carv|er (kär′vər), *n.* **1** a person who carves. **2** a knife for carving meat; carving knife.
carvers, a knife and fork set for carving meat.

carve-up (kärv′up), *n.* a division; partition: *last century's big carve-up of Africa* (Atlantic).

carv|ing (kär′ving), *n., v.* —*n.* **1** carved work; carved decoration: *a wood carving.* **2** the act or art of a person or thing that carves.
—*v.* present participle of **carve**: *Father is carving the meat.*

carving fork, a large fork used to hold meat while it is being carved, usually provided with a guard to prevent cutting the hand if the knife slips.

carving knife, a knife for cutting meat. See picture under **knife**.

car|vone (kär′vōn), *n.* an unsaturated ketone found especially in the oils of spearmint, caraway, and dill and made synthetically. *Formula:* $C_{10}H_{14}O$ [< French *carvi* caraway + English *-one*]

car wash, **1** a business establishment that washes automobiles. **2** the equipment, often automatic, used by such an establishment. **3** the washing of an automobile.

car|witch|et (kär wich′it), *n.* = carriwitchet.

car|y|at|ic (kar′ē at′ik), *adj.* having to do with

caryatids; caryatidal: *the caryatic order of architecture.*

***car|y|at|id** (kar′ē at′id), *n., pl.* **-ids, -i|des** (-ə dēz). a statue of a woman used as a column. In ancient Greek architecture, these figures usually wore long garments hanging in folds that somewhat resembled the fluting of conventional columns. *On Braque's canvas they became as depersonalized as caryatids* (New Yorker). [< Latin *Caryātides* < Greek *Karyâtides* women of Caryae (*Karýai*), a village in Laconia]

***caryatid**

car|y|at|i|dal (kar′ē at′ə dəl), *adj.* **1** of or like a caryatid. **2** supported by caryatids.

car|y|at|i|de|an (kar′ē at′ə dē′ən), *adj.* = caryatidal.

car|y|a|tid|ic (kar′ē ə tid′ik), *adj.* = caryatidal.

car|y|o|phyl|la|ceous (kar′ē ō fə lā′shəs), *adj. Botany.* **1** belonging to the pink family. **2** having five petals with long claws in a tubular calyx, as in the carnation corolla. [< New Latin *Caryophyllaceae* the family name (< Greek *karyóphyllon* the clove pink < *káryon* nut + *phýllon* leaf) (from the dried flower head) + English *-ous*]

car|y|o|phyl|le|ous (kar′ē ə fil′ē əs), *adj.* = caryophyllaceous.

car|y|op|sis (kar′ē op′sis), *n.* a small, dry seed fruit, especially of grasses. A grain of wheat is a caryopsis.
[< New Latin *caryopsis* < Greek *káryon* nut + *ópsis* appearance]

car|y|o|tin (kar′ē ō′tin), *n.* = karyotin.

ca|sa (kä′sə), *n. Southwestern U.S.* a house: *At the Camelback Inn, adobe houses, called casas here, are sprinkled around the grounds and are about as luxuriously appointed as any desert retreat from California to Kuwait* (Saturday Review). [American English < Spanish *casa* < Latin, cabin, hut]

ca|sa|ba (kə sä′bə), *n.,* or **casaba melon,** a kind of winter muskmelon with a yellow rind that belongs to the gourd family. Its flesh is good to eat. Also, **cassaba.** [American English < *Kassaba,* near Smyrna, Turkey, from where it was introduced]

ca|sal (kā′səl), *adj. Grammar.* of or having to do with case.

Ca|sa|no|va (kaz′ə nō′və, kas′-), *n.* a man noted as a lover; lady's man. [< Giovanni Jacopo *Casanova,* 1725-1798, an Italian adventurer famous for his romantic conquests]

ca|saque (kə zak′; *French* kå zåk′), *n.* a loose blouse or jacket for women. [< French *casaque*]

Cas|bah (käz′bä), *n.* **1** the older and native section of Algiers. **2** Also, **casbah.** a similar section of any one of various other cities, especially in North Africa. **3** *Figurative.* anything that resembles the winding, mazelike patterns made by streets in the Casbah: *the Casbah of loft buildings and theatrical hotels surrounding Broadway* (New Yorker).
[< Arabic *qaṣaba* fortress, citadel]

cas|ca|bel (kas′kə bəl), *n.* a projecting part at the rear of the breech of a cannon loaded through the muzzle. [< Spanish *cascabel* small round bell, rattle < Vulgar Latin *cascabus* < Latin *caccabus* cooking pot < Greek *kákkabos*]

cas|cade (kas kād′), *n., v.,* **-cad|ed, -cad|ing.** —*n.* **1a** a small, steep waterfall: *Cascades are often of great height.* **b** *Figurative.* a torrent: *She burst into a cascade of words* (New Yorker). **2** anything like this: **a** loose, descending folds of lace or similar material: *Her dress had a cascade of ruffles down the front.* **b** flowers arranged to fall in a loose, descending manner. **c** a kind of firework simulating a waterfall: *Roman candles, Catherine wheels, and cascades.* **3** a series of pieces of apparatus, such as fluid containers, electric cells, circuits, condensers, electronic tubes, and the like, serving to continue or develop a process. **4** a series of reactions in which one causes or produces another, for example the reactions that occur when one atomic particle displaces other atomic particles from a nucleus with which it has collided. These particles then strike others, causing further displacements at progressively lower energy levels.
—*v.i.* to fall, pour, or flow in a cascade: *The water cascaded off the roof in the thunderstorm. Many new buildings are girdled with safety nets to protect passers-by from cascading bricks and plaster* (Time).
—*v.t.* to cause to fall, pour, or flow in a cascade: **a** to pass through a series of similar pieces of apparatus. **b** to arrange or connect (pieces of apparatus) so that one feeds into the next.
[< French *cascade* < Italian *cascata,* ultimately < Latin *cāsus* a falling < *cadere* to fall]

cascade effect, a series of events in which one causes or produces the next, often intensifying each other.

cas|cal|ho (käs käl′yō), *n., pl.* **-hos.** a deposit of pebbles, gravel, and ferruginous sand that contains diamonds or gold, found especially in Brazil. [< Portuguese *cascalho* (literally) pebble]

cas|car|a (kas kãr′ə), *n.* **1** = cascara buckthorn. **2** = cascara sagrada. [American English; short for *cascara sagrada*]

cascara buckthorn, a shrub or small tree of the northwestern United States; bearwood. It belongs to the buckthorn family and yields cascara sagrada.

cascara sa|gra|da (sə grā′də), **1** a medicine prepared from the dried bark of the cascara buckthorn, used as a laxative. **2** = cascara buckthorn. [< American English < Spanish *cáscara sagrada* (literally) sacred bark; *cáscara* < *cascar* break, shatter; see etym. under **cask**]

cas|ca|ril|la (kas′kə ril′ə), *n.* **1** Also, **cascarilla bark.** the bitter, aromatic bark of a West Indian shrub of the spurge family, used as a tonic and as flavoring in smoking tobacco. **2** the shrub itself. [< Spanish *cascarilla* (diminutive) < *cáscara;* see etym. under **cascara sagrada**]

cas|ca|ron (kas′kə rōn′), *n.* an eggshell filled with confetti, thrown by merrymakers at carnivals, balls, and other festivities. [< Spanish *cascarón*]

cas|co (kas′kō), *n.* **1** the hull of a ship. **2** a flat, almost rectangular boat of the Philippines, used especially as a lighter between ships and shore. [< Spanish *casco* hull of a ship; skull; see etym. under **cask**]

case¹ (kās), *n.* **1a** an example; instance: *The lost books were another case of his carelessness. A case of this kind happened a few years ago.* **b** any special condition of a person or thing; situation; state: *a case of poverty, a case for the teacher to decide.* SYN: event, circumstance. **2** the actual condition; real situation; true state: *He thought he had found the right answer, but that was not the case.* **3a** an instance of a disease or injury: *A case of measles kept him in bed.* **b** a person who is being treated by a doctor; patient: *Hospitals had many cases of polio each summer before a vaccine to prevent it was developed. The doctor was worried about his pneumonia case.* **c** *Informal.* an odd or unusual person: *He was a real case in his younger days.* **4a** a matter for a law court to decide: *The case will be brought before the court tomorrow. Of the unfair-labor-practice cases handled . . . individual workers filed 37% of the 3,522 charges against management* (Time). SYN: lawsuit, cause, action. **b** a statement of facts raising a point of view for a law court to consider: *the case for the prosecution. It was the claimants' case that they were the sole concessionaires of crude oil which the Japanese extracted from their wells* (London Times). SYN: deposition. **c** a case which has been decided and is cited as a precedent: *leading cases.* **5** a convincing argument: *The agent made a good case for buying insurance.* **6** *Grammar.* **a** one of the forms of a noun, pronoun, or adjective used to show its relation to other words. "I" is the nominative case; "me" is the objective case; "my" is the possessive case. **b** the relation shown by such a form: *"I" is in the nominative case.* **c** any group of such forms or relations in a particular language: *Latin has six cases, Greek five.* **d** such forms or relationships considered collectively. **7** *Slang.* a strong attraction or infatuation; crush: *He has quite a case on her.*

get (or **come**) **down to cases,** *Especially U.S.* to come to the point; attend to the facts or the matter at hand: *"Unless we get down to cases soon," he says, "there's a danger that we'll break up before anybody realizes what's involved"* (Maclean's).

get off one's case, *U.S. Slang.* to leave one alone; stop annoying or harassing one: *When pressed about her boyfriends she gets very sarcastic and . . . will say something like "Get off my case"* (New York Post).

in any case, no matter what happens; anyhow: *In any case, you should prepare for the worst.*

in case, if it should happen that; if; supposing: *What would you do in case fire broke out at home?*

in case of, if there should be; in the event of: *In case of fire, walk quietly to the nearest door.*

in no case, under no circumstances; never: *In no case should you panic.*

just in case, in anticipation of some irregularity, mishap, or misfortune; merely as a protective measure: *On that night the village was shaken by a storm and the priest had grumbled mildly at being kept out of bed, but the Roncallis believed in prompt baptism, just in case* (New York Times).
[< Old French *cas,* learned borrowing from Latin *cāsus* a falling, chance < *cadere* fall]
—*Syn.* **1 Case, instance** mean example. **Case** applies to a fact, actual happening, situation, or the like, that is typical of a general kind or class: *The accident was a case of reckless driving.* **Instance** applies to an individual case used to illustrate a general idea or conclusion: *Going through a stop signal is an instance of his recklessness. Our law That wilderness of single instances* (Tennyson). See also the study under **example.**

case² (kās), *n., v.,* **cased, cas|ing.** —*n.* **1** a thing to hold or cover something; container; receptacle: *a typewriter case, a cigarette case.* SYN: holder. **2** a covering; sheath: *Put the knife back in its case.* SYN: casing. **3a** a box; crate: *There is a big case full of books in the hall.* SYN: chest. **b** the amount that a case can hold: *The children drank a case of ginger ale at the party.* **c** a pair; couple; brace: *a case of pistols.* **4** a frame: *The sticky window has swollen in its case.* **5** a tray for holding printing type, with a compartment for each kind of letter. Cases are usually arranged in pairs, capital letters being in the compartments of the upper case and small letters in those of the lower case. **6a** the completed covers prepared for the binding of a book. **b** a protective cover for unbound journals, phonograph records, or the like.
—*v.t.* **1** to put in a case; cover with a case: *He cased the books for shipping.* SYN: enclose, encase. **2** to face (a building) with superior material: *The builders cased the lower story of the building with stone.* **3** *Slang.* to look over carefully; inspect or examine: *The thieves cased the bank before the robbery. Secret Service advance men had thoroughly cased Palm Springs for security* (Time).
[< Old North French *casse* < Latin *capsa* box container < *capere* hold. See etym. of doublet **chase³**.] —**cas′er,** *n.*

case³ (kās), *n.* a cavity in the head of the sperm whale which contains spermaceti and oil. [compare **case²**]

ca|se|ase (kā′sē ās), *n.* a bacterial enzyme which assists the ripening of cheese. [< *case*(in) + *-ase*]

ca|se|ate (kā′sē āt), *v.i.,* **-at|ed, -at|ing.** to undergo caseation. [back formation < *caseation*]

ca|se|a|tion (kā′sē ā′shən), *n.* **1** a disease in which tissues turn into a cheeselike substance. **2** the forming of cheese. [< Latin *cāseus* cheese + English *-ation*]

case|bay (kās′bā′), *n. Carpentry.* **1** any division of a roof (except that adjoining the end wall or gable) comprising two principal rafters with the purlins between them. **2** a corresponding division of a floor, comprising two girders and the intervening joists.

case|book (kās′bu̇k′), *n.* a collection of detailed notes of actual cases in a specific field, such as law, medicine, psychiatry, or social work.

case ending, *Grammar.* the letter or letters, or the sounds they represent, added in inflected languages to the stem of a noun, pronoun, or adjective to indicate its case.

case finding, the finding of people in need of medical treatment, especially for infectious disease.

case fly, = caddis fly.

ca|se|fy (kā′sə fī), *v.t., v.i.,* **-fied, -fy|ing.** to make or become like cheese. [< Latin *cāseus* cheese + English *-fy*]

case|hard|en (kās′här′dən), *v.t.* **1** to harden (iron or steel) on the surface. **2** *Figurative.* to make callous or unfeeling: *At spring training he even had the casehardened and unimpressionable baseball writers babbling most incoherently* (New York Times).

case history, 1 all the facts about a person, or group, that may be useful in deciding what medical or psychiatric treatment, social services, or the like, are needed: *Since the whole personality of an individual is involved in his life-accommodations, in dealing with a specific instance of maladjustment it is necessary to secure a complete case history of the persons concerned* (Emory S. Bogardus). **2** the record of a case: *Kaymarq's case history holds particular lessons for speculative-minded real estate investors* (Wall Street Journal).

ca|se|ic (kā′sē ik), *adj.* derived from cheese.

ca|se|i|din (kā sē′ə dən), *n.* one of a group of substances in the milk of mammals that provide infant immunity against certain infectious diseases. [< Latin *cāseus* cheese + English *-id* + *-in*]

ca|sein (kā′sēn, -sē in), *n.* a protein present in milk, used in making plastics, synthetic fibers, adhesives, and certain kinds of paints. Casein is a conjugated protein containing phosphorus. Cheese is mostly casein. [< Latin *cāseus* cheese

+ English *-in*[2], variant of *-ine*[2]]

ca·se·in·o·gen (kā′sē in′ə jən, kā sē′nə-), *n.* casein in a dissolved, unclotted state. [< *casein*]

case knife, 1 a knife carried in a case; sheath knife. **2** = table knife.

case law, law established by the decisions of actual previous cases: *It is not legal antiquarianism . . . to wish to preserve the best features of the existing customary law, and at the same time to permit its organic development through case law* (London Times).

case·load (kās′lōd′), *n.* the number of cases on the agenda of a court, clinic, or agency, or of any of its staff members: *The board is confronted with a mammoth caseload* (Wall Street Journal).

case·mak·er (kās′mā′kər), *n,* **1** a clothes moth whose larva is a caseworm that spins its case out of pieces of cloth. **2** a person who makes cases or covers for books.

case·mate (kās′māt), *n.* **1** a bombproof chamber in a fort or rampart, with openings from which cannon may be fired: *Every conqueror added a few casemates, a few walls, until it* [*Luxembourg*] *became the strongest of European strongpoints* (Saturday Night). **2** an armoured enclosure protecting guns on a warship. [< Middle French *casemate* < Italian *casamatta* (influenced by *casa* house), earlier *camata,* apparently < Greek *chásmata* openings, plural of *chásma* chasm]

case·mat·ed (kās′mā tid), *adj.* **1** provided with casemates. **2** strongly fortified.

***case·ment** (kās′mənt), *n.* **1** a window which opens on hinges like a door. **2** any window. **3** a casing; covering; frame. [probably < *case*[2] + *-ment*]

***casement**
definition 1

casement cloth, a cotton material designated for curtains.

case·ment·ed (kās′mən tid), *adj,* furnished with casements.

case method, 1 the teaching of a subject by presenting and discussing actual cases or situations: *The education school will utilize the "case method" of teaching used in the Harvard Business School* (New York Times). **2** = case system. **3** case-study method.

case of conscience, a problem or situation in the solution of which morality is concerned: *the determination of cases of conscience* (Jeremy Taylor).

ca·se·o·phile (kā′sē ə fīl′), *n.* a person who is fond of cheese. [< Latin *cāseus* cheese + English *-phile*]

ca·se·ose (kā′sē ōs), *n.* any one of various soluble products formed in the gastric and pancreatic digestion of casein. [< *case*(in) + *-ose*[2]]

ca·se·ous (kā′sē əs), *adj.* of or like cheese; cheesy. [< Latin *cāseus* cheese + English *-ous*]

ca·sern or **ca·serne** (kə zėrn′), *n.* a place for soldiers to live in a fortified town; barracks: *One well-placed missile in each of these casernes* (*camps*) *would destroy most of the tanks, trucks, jeeps and other equipment* (Time). [< French *caserne* (originally) a lodge for four soldiers on watch < Provençal *cazerna* small hut < Vulgar Latin *quaderna* four each < Latin *quaternī* < *quattuor* four. See etym. of doublet **cahier, quire**[1].]

case shot, the small projectiles contained in a case, as the shot or metal fragments in a canister or a shrapnel shell.

case stud·y, 1 a case history, especially of an individual. **2** an analysis of a case history or histories; a study based on exhaustive compilation of actual cases.

case-stud·y method (kās′stud′ē), a method of sociological or educational research that makes use of a group of case studies to reach general conclusions and principles; case method.

case system, the teaching of law by the study of the decisions in actual cases instead of, or in addition to, general textbooks.

ca·se·ta (kä sä′tä), *n. Spanish.* a small house.

case·work (kās′wėrk′), *n.* the work of a caseworker; thorough study of the history, environment, experiences, illnesses, or the like, of an individual or family as a basis for advice, guidance, or treatment.

case·work·er (kās′wėr′kər), *n.* a person trained to collect case histories of individuals or families to help them with advice, guidance, or treatment. Caseworkers are usually employed by psychiatric clinics and social counseling agencies rather than by private physicians, and work mainly with the underprivileged.

case·worm (kās′wėrm′), *n.* an insect larva that builds a case around itself; the caddis worm.

cash[1] (kash), *n., v.* —*n.* **1a** money in the form of coins and bills: *She didn't have enough cash with her to pay for the book, so she wrote a check.* SYN: currency. **b** money or a check paid at the time of buying something: *He paid cash for his new suit instead of charging it and paying later.* **2** *Obsolete.* a chest or box for money.
—*v.t.* **1a** to give cash for: *The bank will cash your check.* **b** to get cash for: *He cashed the check at the store after the bank closed.* **2** (in bridge) to lead or lead to (a card certain to take a trick): *South cashed two more diamonds and the good spade in his hand, . . . to make his contract.* (New York Times).

cash down, ready money: *The dealer reduced the price for cash down.*

cash in, a *Informal.* to change into cash; surrender for cash: *He cashed in his savings bonds at the bank to pay for a new car.* **b** *Informal.* to make a profit: make money: *A leading maker of reactor components said: "We're going to lose our shirts for the next five years. . . . Only those who can hold on will finally cash in"* (Newsweek). **c** *U.S. Slang.* to die: *They hadn't lived together for twenty years when he cashed in* (J. L. Vance).

cash in on, *U.S. Informal.* **a** to make a profit from: *After holding the land till the city needed it, he finally cashed in on his real-estate investments.* **b** to take advantage of; use to advantage: *Other companies are cashing in on the convention interest with promotional campaigns pegged on a political theme* (Wall Street Journal).

in (the) cash, in a good financial position; well-off: *He was not in the cash and had to borrow money from his friends. He bets . . . freely when he is in cash* (Thackeray).
[< French *caisse* money box, coffer < Provençal *caissa* < Vulgar Latin *capsea* box < Latin *capsa.* See related etym. at **case**[2], **chase**[3].]

cash[2] (kash), *n., pl.* **cash. 1** a coin of small value, used especially in China and India. **2** a former Chinese cooper coin with a square hole in it. [< Portuguese *caixa,* earlier *casse,* perhaps < Malayalam *kāshu* small copper coin]

cash·a (kash′ə), *n.* a flannellike fabric, made from a blend of cashmere and wool, and used for women's coats, jackets, and blouses. [probably < *cashmere*]

cash·a·ble (kash′ə bəl), *adj.* that can be cashed: *Vouchers, cashable in food at certified grocery stores, are distributed to strikers* (Wall Street Journal).

cash account, 1 an account of money received, paid, or on hand. **2** a specific amount of credit given by a bank, to a person or business on receipt of a bond for repayment on demand of the amount actually advanced.

cash-and-car·ry (kash′ən kar′ē), *adj.* **1** with immediate payment for goods purchased and without delivery service: *One of the most astonishing postwar business phenomena has been the mushrooming of discount houses, which undersell orthodox retailers by operating on a cash-and-carry basis* (Newsweek). **2** operated on a cash-and-carry basis: *a cash-and-carry market.*

ca·shaw (kə shô′), *n. U.S.* cushaw.

cash bar, *U.S.* a bar at a party or reception at which alcoholic drinks are sold.

cash·book (kash′bu̇k′), *n.* a book in which a record is kept of money received and paid out.

cash·box (kash′boks′), *n.* **1** a box or other container for keeping money: *The proprietor's cashbox had vanished in the confusion of the night* (Manchester Guardian). **2** a treasury: *two thousand dollars added to the club cashbox.*

cash carrier, an automatic device for conveying money received at the counters of a store to the cashier and returning the change.

cash cow, *U.S. Finance.* a regular and reliable source of income or profit: *Karin Lissakers of the Carnegie Endowment quotes a banker in . . . an unguarded moment: "That (unmentioned country) is a cash cow for us. We hope they never repay!"* (Washington Post).

cash credit, = cash account.

cash crop, a crop grown for sale, rather than for consumption on the farm: *Wheat, cotton, and tobacco are cash crops* (John Gunther).

cash customer, a purchaser who pays cash and does not buy on account.

cash discount, 1 the privilege of a purchaser to subtract a percentage from his bill if payment is made within a preestablished period of time: *Cash discounts are commonly offered by sellers to encourage early cash payment* (Schmidt and Bergstrom). **2** the amount subtracted.

cash dividend, a dividend paid in money to a stockholder, rather than in stock or other form: *The regular semiannual cash dividend of 75 cents a share on present stock was also declared* (Wall Street Journal).

cash·ew (kash′ü, kə shü′), *n.* **1** a small, kidney-shaped nut which is good to eat. **2** the tropical American tree that it grows on. The cashew is native especially to Brazil and Central America. [< French *acajou* mahogany < Portuguese (Brazil) *acajú* the fruit < Tupi *acayú* the tree]

cashew apple, the edible, fleshy, pear-shaped receptacle which bears the cashew nut.

***cashew family,** a group of dicotyledonous trees and shrubs most common in the tropics. The family includes plants of economic value, such as the cashew, pistachio, mango, and varnish tree, as well as other varieties, such as the sumacs and poison ivy.

***cashew family**

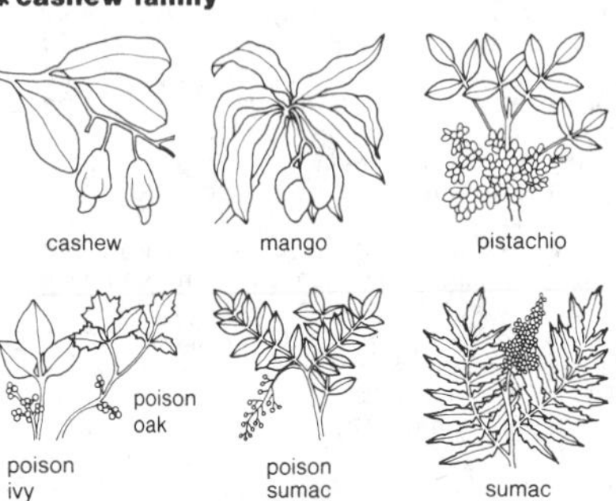

cash flow, a business firm's net income plus depreciation, amortization, and other costs not involving actual payment of money: *Many economists are paying less heed to profits as a measurement than to cash flow* (Time).

cash·ier[1] (ka shir′), *n.* **1** a person in charge of collecting and recording payments in a store or other business establishment. **2** a bank officer who is in charge of the bank's monetary transactions. [< French *caissier* treasurer < *caisse;* see etym. under **cash**[1]]

cash·ier[2] (ka shir′), *v.t.* **1** to dismiss from service; discharge in disgrace: *The dishonest officer was deprived of his rank and cashiered.* **2** to discard; get rid of: *I shall straightway cashier the hunting-frock* (Richard Brinsley Sheridan). [< Dutch *casseren* < Old French *casser, quasser* < Latin *quassāre* break, and ultimately < *cassus* empty]

cashier's check, a check drawn by a bank on its own funds and signed by its cashier.

cash-in (kash′in′), *n. U.S.* the cashing of securities, such as savings bonds: *Cash-ins of Series E bonds seem virtually certain to exceed purchases* (New York Times).

cash·less (kash′lis), *adj.* without cash.

cash machine, = automatic teller.

cash·mere (kash′mir), *n.* **1a** a fine, soft wool, used in making sweaters or coats. The finest cashmere is obtained from a breed of long-haired goats of Asia. **b** = Cashmere shawl. **2** a fine, soft wool from sheep. **3** a fine, soft woolen cloth. [variant of *Kashmir,* India]

cash·me·rette (kash′mi ret′), *n.* a fabric for women's dresses, made with a soft and glossy surface, in imitation of cashmere.

Cashmere goat, any one of a breed of long-haired goats, famous for fine, silky wool. They live in Kashmir and Tibet. Also, **Kashmir goat.**

Cashmere shawl, = Kashmir shawl.

cash on delivery, payment when goods are delivered. *Abbr.* C.O.D.

cash on the barrelhead, *Informal.* ready money for immediate payment: *Many foreign concerns will no longer ship goods to Istanbul without cash on the barrelhead* (Time).

ca·shoo (kə shü′), *n.* = catechu.

cash·point (kash′point′), *n.* an electronic machine from which money can be withdrawn after inserting an identification card and keying in an account number; automatic teller machine.

cash register, a machine which records and shows the amount of a sale. It usually has a drawer to hold money. *Even the familiar cash register is really a highly developed and efficient accounting machine* (Schmidt and Bergstrom).

cash surrender value, the amount of money, out of the total reserve of an insurance policy, that is guaranteed to the insured if he should cancel or surrender the policy before it becomes payable.

cash value, = cash surrender value.

Pronunciation Key: hat, āge, cãre, fär; let, ēqual, tėrm; it, īce; hot, ōpen, ôrder; oil, out; cup, pu̇t, rüle; child; long; thin; ᴛʜen; zh, measure; **ə** represents **a** in about, **e** in taken, **i** in pencil, **o** in lemon, **u** in circus.

cas|i|mire or **cas|i|mere** (kas′ə mir), *n.* = cassimere.

cas|ing (kā′sing), *n.* a covering put around something; case: **a** the heavy body and tread of a pneumatic tire, made of rubber and textile cords; shoe. **b** a frame: *A window fits in a casing.* **c** a steel pipe lining an oil well. **d** an intestine, usually of cattle, hogs, or sheep, cleaned, salted, and used to hold sausage meat. **e** the outside shell of a turbine that directs the flowing fluids against the turbine wheel.

cas|ing|head (kā′sing hed′), *n.* the fitting attached to the top of an oil or gas well.

casinghead gas, natural gas taken at the casinghead of an oil well: *The commission said the liquid fuel content of casinghead gas and its value as residue gas for pipelines is enough to justify expense* (Wall Street Journal).

casinghead gasoline, the gasoline condensed from casinghead gas; natural gasoline.

casing nail, a nail having a flaring head designed to lie flush with the surface into which the nail is driven.

ca|si|no (kə sē′nō), *n., pl.* **-nos**. **1** a building or room for public shows, dancing, and gambling: *If he is a man of substance and leisure he may even be ... gambling in tuxedoed tranquility at the world's biggest casino* (Newsweek). **2** = cassino, a card game. **3** a small country house in Italy; lodge; summer house: *And thus Vasari, together with Vignola (1507-63), designed the Villa Giulia, the country casino of Pope Julius III* (Nikolaus Pevsner). [< Italian *casino* (diminutive) < *casa* house < Latin, cabin]

cask (kask, käsk), *n.* **1** a barrel. A cask may be large or small, and is usually made to hold liquids. **SYN**: keg, tun. **2a** a cask with its contents: *They sell cider at $10 a cask. The Cask of Amontillado* (Edgar Allan Poe). **b** the amount that a cask holds. [< Spanish *casco* skull, helmet, cask; potsherd < *cascar* break, shatter < Latin *quassāre* break. See etym. of doublet **casque**.]

cas|ket (kas′kit, käs′-), *n., v.* — *n.* **1** a coffin: *Members ... mounted guard and stood around the casket* (New York Times). **2** a small box or chest, often fine and beautiful, used to hold jewels, letters, or other valuables. **3** *Figurative.* a receptacle of anything that is valued: *I unlock the casket of memory* (William Hazlitt).
— *v.t.* to place or enclose in or as if in a casket: *the beauties casketed like gems within these walls* (Washington Irving).
[probably alteration of Old French *cassette* small case < Italian *cassetta* < *cassa* case < Latin *capsa;* influenced by obsolete *cask* casket]

cask|ing (kas′king, käs′-), *n.* **1** the filling of casks: *the casking of wine after the vintage.* **2** wine in casks, collectively.

Cas|lon (kaz′lən), *n.* an old-style printing type designed by William Caslon, an English type founder, 1692-1766, or a face imitating his design.

Cas|par|i|an strip (kas pãr′ē ən), *Botany.* a water-resistant strip or band occurring in the radial and end walls of endodermal cells. [< R. *Caspary,* a German botanist of the 1800's + English *-ian*]

Cas|pi|an (kas′pē ən), *adj.* of or having to do with the Caspian Sea or the lands around it: *Caspian plain, Caspian tern.*

Caspian tern, a large tern with a shining black crest and pearl-gray back and wings. The Caspian tern is found along seacoasts throughout the world.

casque (kask), *n.* **1** a piece of armor to cover the head; helmet: *the very casques That did affright the air at Agincourt* (Shakespeare). **2** *Zoology.* any helmetlike structure. The frontal boss or shield of certain birds such as the cassowary is a casque. [< French *casque* cask < Spanish *casco.* See etym. of doublet **cask**.]

casqued (kaskt), *adj.* wearing a casque or casques: *Clothed in a dragon's dress, belted and casqued* (Scott).

cas|quet (kas′kit), *n.* a light and open helmet or casque, without beaver or visor. [< French *casquet* (diminutive) < *casque* cask; see etym. under **casque**]

cas|que|tel (kas′kə tel′), *n.* a small open helmet of a light kind, without beaver or visor, having flexible plates to cover the neck behind. [< *casquet* + Old French *-el,* a diminutive suffix]

cas|quette (kas ket′), *n.* a brimless hat or cap having a visor and resembling a casque. [< French *casquette,* feminine of *casquet;* see etym. under **casquet**]

cas|sa|ba (kə sä′bə), *n.* = casaba.

Cas|san|dra (kə san′drə), *n.* **1** *Greek Legend.* a daughter of King Priam of Troy. Apollo gave her the power to foretell the future, but later in anger punished her by ordering that no one should believe her prophecies. **2** a person who prophesies misfortune, but is not believed.

cas|sa|reep (kas′ə rēp), *n.* the condensed juice of the bitter cassava, used as a seasoning. [< a native Caribbean word]

cas|sa|ta (kə sä′tə), *n.* a fancy Italian ice cream with candied fruit and nuts. [< Italian *cassata*]

cas|sa|tion¹ (ka sā′shən), *n.* the act of making null or void; annulment or reversal. [< Medieval Latin *cassatio, -onis* < Late Latin *cassāre* annul, and < Latin *quassāre* break]

cas|sa|tion² (ka sā′shən), *n.* a small serenade of the 1700's, often performed outdoors: *These pieces are patently street music; like cassations of old, both for and of the open air* (Saturday Review). [< Italian *cassazione;* origin uncertain]

cas|sa|va (kə sä′və), *n.* **1** a tropical plant with starchy roots; manioc. It belongs to the spurge family. **2** a starch made from its roots. Bitter cassava, the source of tapioca, contains in its roots a bitter, inedible acid that is removed by grinding and washing the roots. A variety called sweet cassava may be eaten like potatoes. [< French *cassave* < Spanish *casabe* < Arawak (Haiti) *cacábi*]

Cas|se|grain (kas′ə grān), *n.* a telescope in which the light is reflected back through a hole in the main concave mirror, from a convex mirror placed between the main mirror and its focal point. [< N. *Cassegrain,* a French physician and astronomer of the 1600's, the inventor]

Cas|se|grain|i|an telescope (kas′ə grā′nē ən), = Cassegrain.

Cas|sel brown or **earth** (kas′əl), = Vandyke brown. [< *Cassel* (Kassel), a city in Germany]

cas|se|role (kas′ə rōl), *n.* **1a** a covered baking dish in which food can be both cooked and served. Most casseroles are made of stoneware or glass. **b** food cooked and served in such a dish. Casseroles usually consist of meat, cheese, or vegetables in macaroni, rice, or mashed potatoes, and sauce. *keeps all foods, from spaghetti to stews, casseroles to baked beans, enjoyably warm for hours and hours* (New Yorker). **c** a mold, often of boiled rice, mashed potatoes, or macaroni, filled with meat, cheese, or vegetables. **d** *Especially British.* a saucepan. **2** a small, deep porcelain dish with a handle, used in chemical laboratories for heating substances. [< French *casserole* < Middle French *casse* pan < Late Latin *cattia* trowel, probably < Greek *kyáthion* small cup < *kýathos* cup]

***cas|sette** (ka set′), *n.* **1** a cartridge of photographic roll film, magnetic tape, or typewriter ribbon: *a 35-mm. camera with interchangeable cassettes* (Newsweek); *a mono signal when played on a monophonic cassette recorder* (Saturday Review). **2** a cartridge of videotape to play on a home television set. **3** a case of baked clay, usually round with a flat bottom, in which china and other delicate ware are enclosed while baking; sagger. [< French *cassette* small case < *casse* case²]

***cassette**
definition 1

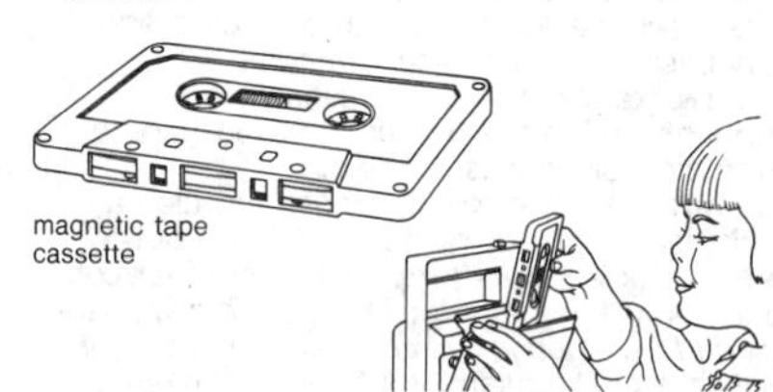

magnetic tape cassette

cas|sia (kash′ə, kas′ē ə), *n.* **1** an inferior kind of cinnamon, made from cassia bark: *Much of our cassia comes from China* (Science News Letter). **2** the tree. It belongs to the laurel family. **3** = cassia bark. **4** a plant yielding leaves and pods that are used in making senna. It belongs to the pea family. **5** the pods or their pulp. [Old English *cassia* < Latin < Greek *kassíā* < Hebrew *qeṣīʻā*]

cassia bark, the bark of a tree of the laurel family of southern China, yielding cassia; Chinese cinnamon.

cassia bud, the bud of the cassia, used as a spice.

cassia oil, a yellow or brownish volatile oil with a strongly sweet taste and an odor like that of cinnamon, obtained from the twigs and leaves of the cassia and used as a flavoring in foods and as an ingredient in perfumes. Also called **oil of cinnamon**.

cassia pod, the pod of the cassia plant, from which sweet cassia pulp is obtained.

cassia pulp, a sweet pulp of cassia pods from which a mild laxative is made.

cas|sid|e|ous (kə sid′ē əs), *adj. Botany.* helmet-shaped; helmetlike. [< Latin *cassis, cassidis* helmet + English *-ous*]

cas|si|mere (kas′ə mir), *n.* a soft, lightweight woolen cloth, sometimes used for men's suits; kerseymere. Also, **casimire, casimere**. [variant of *cashmere*]

cas|si|nette (kas′ə net′), *n.* a lightweight cloth, a modification of cassimere, with the warp of cotton, and the weft of very fine wool, or wool and silk. [perhaps an alteration of *cassimere*]

Cas|si|ni division (ka sē′nē), = Cassini's division.

Cassini's division, a 3,000-mile gap between the bright ring and outer ring of Saturn, appearing through a telescope as a dark band. [< Jean-Dominique *Cassini,* 1625-1712, a French astronomer]

cas|si|no (kə sē′nō), *n.* a card game in which cards in the hand are matched with cards on the table. The ten of diamonds and the two of spades have special counting value. Also, **casino**. [variant of *casino*]

cas|si|o|ber|ry (kas′ē ə ber′ē), *n., pl.* **-ries**. **1** the fruit of any one of certain plants, such as the yaupon or a species of viburnum, both of the southern United States. **2** either of these plants. [*cassio-* (< Middle French *cassine* yaupon < the American Indian native name) + *berry*]

Cas|si|o|pe|ia (kas′ē ə pē′ə), *n., genitive* (def. 2) **Cas|si|o|pe|iae**. **1** *Greek Legend.* the wife of the Ethiopian king Cepheus and mother of Andromeda. **2** a northern constellation near Polaris, thought to resemble Cassiopeia sitting in a chair.

Cas|si|o|pe|iae (kas′ē ə pē′yē), *n.* genitive of **Cassiopeia** (the constellation).

Cassiopeia's Chair, a group of seven stars in the constellation Cassiopeia, which suggests a chair.

cas|sique (kə sēk′), *n.* = cacique.

cas|si|ri (kä′si rē′), *n.* an alcoholic drink made in Guiana from fermented sweet potatoes or cassava juice.

cas|sis (kä sēs′), *n.* **1** the black currant. **2** a cordial made from the black currant, often mixed with vermouth. [< French *cassis*]

cas|sit|e|rite (kə sit′ə rīt), *n.* a dioxide of tin, found pure in nature, the chief source of tin; tinstone. *Formula:* SnO_2 [< Greek *kassíteros* tin + English *-ite¹*]

cas|sock (kas′ək), *n.* **1a** a long outer garment, usually black, worn by a clergyman. **b** a double-breasted coat, usually of black silk and reaching to the hips, worn under the Geneva gown (outer gown) by certain clergymen. **2a** a clergyman: *He had a suspicion of all cassocks* (Thackeray). **b** *Figurative.* the clerical office; the priestly vocation: *He chose the cassock instead of the [military] uniform.* **3** *Obsolete.* a long, loose cloak or coat, worn formerly by soldiers, shepherds, horsemen, and others: *The coarse frieze-cassock of the private soldier* (Scott). [< French *casque* < Italian *casacca*]

cas|socked (kas′əkt), *adj.* wearing a cassock: *cassocked priests.*

cas|so|lette (kas′ə let′), *n.* **1** a container in which perfumes are burned; censer. **2** a box or vessel for holding perfumes, provided with a perforated cover to permit their diffusion. **3** a small casserole. [< French *cassolette* (diminutive) < *cassole* little pan, diminutive < *casse* pan]

cas|so|ne (kə sō′nē), *n., pl.* **-ni** (-nē). a large Italian coffer, especially one for holding a bridal outfit, often elaborately carved and decorated. [< Italian *cassone* (augmentative) < *cassa* chest]

cas|sou|let (ka′sə lā′, -let′), *n.* a casserole of baked beans and meat. [< French *cassoulet* (diminutive) < *cassole* little pan]

cas|so|war|y (kas′ə wer′ē), *n., pl.* **-war|ies**. a large bird of Australia and New Guinea like an ostrich, but smaller. Cassowaries run swiftly but cannot fly. [< Malay (*burong*) *kĕsuari* cassowary (bird)]

cast (kast, käst), *v.,* **cast, cast|ing**, *n., adj.* — *v.t.* **1** to throw, fling, or hurl: *to cast a stone, cast a fishing line or an anchor. The thieves were cast into prison.* **SYN**: See syn. under **throw**. **2** to deposit (a ballot); give (a vote): *Voters cast their ballots for President of the United States in an election held every four years.* **3a** to direct or turn: *He cast a glance of surprise at me.* **b** *Figurative.* to cause to fall: *Coming events cast their shadows before* (Thomas Campbell). *Modern research continually casts new light on old problems.* **4** to throw off; throw away; throw aside: *The snake cast its skin. The horse had cast a shoe* (Thackeray). *The state Cannot with safety cast him* (Shakespeare). **SYN**: lose, shed. **5** to throw up (earth, sand, or the like), especially with a spade or shovel: *The soldiers cast up earthworks.* **6a** to add; calculate. **b** to calculate astrologically: *to cast a horoscope.* **7** to arrange: **a** *Figurative.* to arrange in divisions; put in proper order: *I shall cast what I have to say under two principal heads* (Sir Richard Steele). **b** *Theater.* (1) to assign the various parts of (a play): *The play was well cast.* (2) to select for a part in a play: *The director cast the tall actor as Abe Lin-*

coln in the play. (3) to fill (a part) by assigning an actor to it: *Ophelia has not been cast.* **8a** to shape by pouring or squeezing into a mold to harden. Metal is first melted and then cast. **b** to produce (an object) by running molten metal, plastic, plaster of Paris, or other liquid into a mold: *The sculptor cast his statue in bronze.* **c** to make (type) into a plate for printing, especially a stereotype. **9a** to turn. **b** to turn or wear (a ship). **10** to throw down: **a** to throw on the ground, especially in wrestling. **b** to throw (an animal) on its back or side.

—***v.i.*** **1** to throw. **2** to calculate. **3** (of a sailing ship) to turn from the wind; wear. **4** *Obsolete.* to conjecture as to the future. **5** *Obsolete.* to ponder; deliberate; consider.

—***n.*** **1a** a throw: *With a cast of his hand he sent the pebble far out into the lake.* **b** the distance a thing is thrown: *He was standing less than a stone's cast from the shore.* **c** a stroke of fortune; chance; lot; fate. **2** a toss of a fishing line into the water: *The fisherman made a long cast into the middle of the lake.* **3a** a throw of dice: *I have set my life upon a cast And I will stand the hazard of the die* (Shakespeare). **b** the number of spots showing after a throw of dice. **4a** a plaster mold used to support a broken bone while it is mending: *His broken arm is in a cast.* **b** a thing made by casting; a thing that is molded: *The sculptor made a cast of a bust of Lincoln.* **c** a mold used in casting; mold: *The statuettes are made by pouring bronze into a cast.* **d** a fossil formed by new mineral substances filling the cavity (mold) left in a stone by the dissolution of the original fossil. **5** *Theater.* **a** the actors in a play or motion picture: *The cast will meet at four. The film has a superior cast* (New Yorker). **b** the assignment of the parts in a play to the various actors: *The cast is complete.* **6** *Figurative.* kind; quality: **a** outward form or look; appearance; configuration: *His face had a gloomy cast.* **b** kind; sort; type: *a man of humble cast.* **c** bent; tendency: *The mind that hath any cast towards devotion* (Joseph Addison). **7** a slight squint: *Her eyes ... had odd casts in them* (Sir Richard Steele). **8** a dash: **a** a slight amount of color; tinge: *a white dress with a pink cast.* **b** a bit of some quality or ingredient. **9** the form into which anything is thrown; arrangement. **10** a lift in a conveyance given to a traveler for a part of the way. **11** that which is thrown off or out: **a** the convoluted earth and waste thrown out by an earthworm, or the sand by a lugworm: *These casts, held together by mucus, act directly in creating good soil structure* (Science News Letter). **b** the shed skin of an insect. **12** a reckoning: **a** addition; calculation: *a rapid cast of the figures to estimate the total.* **b** a forecast; conjecture. **13a** that which is cast; the quantity cast. **b** a couple of birds, especially the couple of hawks flown from the hand at one time in falconry. **14** the spreading out of the hounds in various directions to pick up a scent in hunting. **15a** the act of casting or founding. **b** the amount of metal cast at a single time: *an enormous cast of nearly 200 tons.* **c** a resulting kind; type; stamp.

—***adj.*** **1** made by casting. **2** having all the parts allotted in a play or motion picture.

cast about (or **around**), **a** to search or look (for); look around: *The company cast around for a long time until it found a site for its new factory. In 1890, the government, casting about for a replacement for Castle Garden, ... set up Ellis Island as an immigration station* (New Yorker). **b** *Figurative.* to lay plans; scheme; contrive (with an infinitive or a clause): *She cast about to change her shape* (Jonathan Swift). **c** (of dogs or hunters) to spread out and search in different directions, as for a lost scent.

cast aside, **a** to throw or put aside: *to cast aside a stone in the road.* **b** to throw aside from use; discard; dismiss: *to cast aside an old hat.*

cast away, **a** *Figurative.* to abandon: *He cast away the project as useless. Hope is not wholly to be cast away* (Samuel Johnson). **b** to shipwreck: *The small Mexican brig which had been cast away in a southeaster, ... now lay up, high and dry* (Richard Henry Dana).

cast back, **a** to throw the memory back; refer to something past: *Grandfather could cast back and recall the years before radio and television existed.* **b** to return toward some ancestral type or character: *I think there must have been a dreadful misalliance somewhere in our genealogy and that you have cast back to it* (Charlotte Riddell).

cast down, **a** to turn downward; lower: *His head was cast down in shame. Every eye was cast down before him* (Samuel Johnson). **b** to make sad or discouraged: *He was cast down by the sad news.*

cast in, to throw into the bargain: *'Twere worth both Testaments, and cast in the Creed* (John Dryden).

cast loose, **a** to unfasten; separate: *The captain ordered the boat to be cast loose* (Archibald Duncan). **b** *Figurative.* to set adrift; abandon: *an orphan cast loose on a sea of troubles.*

cast off, **a** to let loose; set free; untie: *to cast off a boat from its moorings.* (*Figurative.*) *He cast off the last ties that held him to home.* **b** *Figurative.* to abandon or discard: *He cast off his old friends as soon as he moved into a new neighborhood. It was as if this body had cast him off, disowned him—"I know you not"* (Graham Greene). **c** to make the last row of stitches in knitting: *... to cast off, which is done by knitting two loops and pulling the first made loop over the last* (Plain Knitting). **d** to estimate the space a given amount of copy will occupy when set in a specified style and size of type: *The compositors in your chapel do not cast off their copy well* (Benjamin Franklin).

cast on, to make the first row of stitches on the needles in knitting: *Will you cast on a stocking for me? Cast on 83 stitches* (Fancy Workbasket).

cast out, to drive out forcibly; banish; expel: *His pride had cast him out of Heav'n* (Milton).

cast up, **a** to turn upward; raise (the eyes or head): *His eyes ... cast up to count the peaches on the wall* (George Sala). **b** to find the sum of; add up; calculate: *Did go to cast up how my cash stands* (Samuel Pepys). **c** *Figurative.* to turn up; cause to appear: *Public hearings on Friday failed to cast up any plans which the legislative leadership considered favorable* (New York Times). **d** to throw up; vomit: *The sick bird cast up what it ate.*

[< Scandinavian (compare Old Icelandic *kasta* throw)]

cast|a|ble (kas′tə bəl), *adj.* capable of being cast; suitable for casting.

Cas|ta|li|a (kas tā′lē ə), *n.* **1** a spring on Mount Parnassus, sacred to Apollo and the Muses. **2** anything regarded as a source of poetic inspiration.

Cas|ta|li|an (kas tā′lē ən), *adj.* **1** of or having to do with Castalia. **2** *Figurative.* regarded as a source of poetic inspiration; poetic: *Lips wet with Castalian dews* (William Cowper).

Cas|ta|lie or **Cas|ta|ly** (kas′tə lē), *n., pl.* **-lies.** = Castalia.

cas|ta|ne|ous (kas tā′nē əs), *adj.* chestnut-colored. [< Latin *castaneus* (with English *-ous*) < *castanea;* see etym. under **chestnut**]

***cas|ta|net** (kas′tə net′), *n.* one of a pair of instruments held in the hand and clicked together to beat time for dancing or music. Castanets are made of hard wood or ivory and shaped like small cymbals. *We heard the click of castanets and the butter-pat sound of the rhythmic clapping for the dance* (Atlantic). [< Spanish *castañeta* (diminutive) < *castaña* chestnut < Latin *castanea;* see etym. under **chestnut**]

***castanet**

cast|a|way (kas′tə wā′, käs′-), *adj., n.* —***adj.*** **1** thrown away; cast adrift. **2** outcast; rejected.

—***n.*** **1** a shipwrecked person: *The castaways swam to the island.* **2** an outcast.

cast-by (kast′bī′, käst′-), *n. Scottish.* a person or thing cast aside and neglected; outcast.

caste (kast, käst), *n.* **1a** one of the social classes into which Hindus are divided. By tradition, a Hindu is born into the caste of his father and cannot rise above it. The constitution of the Republic of India forbids such discrimination, especially against the lowest caste, the "untouchables." *My family are Brahmins—the highest Hindu caste* (Junior Scholastic). *Another confusing factor is that in the course of the last two thousand years many of the castes have lost their original characteristics and occupations* (Santha Rama Rau). **b** the system or basis of this division into classes, long maintained among the Hindus: *the stationary institutions of India, especially that of caste* (J. B. Norton). **c** the position which caste confers: *to renounce caste.* **2** an exclusive social group; distinct class: *The priestly caste in ancient Egypt had great power.* **3** *Figurative.* a social system having distinct classes separated by differences in rank, wealth, or position. **4** any one of the specialized classes into which a colony of social insects is divided. The honeybee occurs in three castes: queens, workers, and drones.

lose caste, to lose social rank or position: *a natural fear of losing caste among her neighbors* (Mary R. Mitford). *He [a Hindu] has lost caste for becoming a Christian* (Mary M. Sherwood).

[< Spanish, Portuguese *casta* race < Latin *castus* pure. See etym. of doublet **chaste.**] —**caste′less**, *adj.*

caste|ism (kas′tiz əm, käs′-), *n.* the policy or practice of maintaining castes: *The greatest homage that people could pay Rabindranath Tagore was by rising above parochialism, casteism and sectarianism* (Times of India).

cas|tel|lan (kas′tə lən), *n.* the governor of a castle; chatelain. [< Latin *castellānus* occupant of a stronghold < *castellum* castle. See etym. of doublet **chatelain.**]

cas|tel|lan|ship (kas′tə lən ship), *n.* = castellany.

cas|tel|la|ny (kas′tə lā′nē), *n., pl.* **-nies.** **1** the office or jurisdiction of a castellan. **2** the district belonging to a castle.

cas|tel|lar (kas tel′ər), *adj.* having to do with or belonging to a castle: *ancient castellar dungeons* (Horace Walpole). [< Latin *castellum* (see etym. under **castle**) + English *-ar*]

cas|tel|late (kas′tə lāt), *n.* the district belonging to a castle; castellany. [< Medieval Latin *castellatus* the precinct of a castle < Latin *castellum* castle + *-ātus* -ate[3]]

cas|tel|lat|ed (kas′tə lā′tid), *adj.* **1** built like a castle; having turrets and battlements: *the castellated fortresses of the Scottish border.* **2** having many castles; castled.

cas|tel|la|tion (kas′tə lā′shən), *n.* **1** the building of castles. **2** the furnishing of a house with battlements. **3** a fortified or castellated structure. **4** a battlement.

caste mark, **1** a mark on the forehead indicating the caste to which a Hindu belongs. **2** *Figurative.* any sign of membership in a class or group: *... the socially disabling caste mark of a colored skin* (Harper's).

cast|er (kas′tər, käs′-), *n.* **1** Also, **castor.** **a** a small wheel on a swivel set into the base of a piece of furniture or other heavy object to make it easier to move. **b** a shaker or bottle containing salt, mustard, vinegar, or other seasoning for table use: *a sugar caster.* **c** a stand or rack for such bottles. **2** a person or thing that casts: *The inexperienced caster tangled his fishing line in a tree.* **3** a machine that casts type.

cast house, a steel and concrete building at the base of a blast furnace from which the operation of drawing off molten iron is controlled.

cas|tice (kas′tis), *n.* a person of Portuguese parentage born and living in the East Indies. [< Portuguese *castiço* of good birth < *casta* race; see etym. under **caste**]

cas|ti|gate (kas′tə gāt), *v.t.,* **-gat|ed, -gat|ing.** **1** to criticize or rebuke severely: *I am appalled that one so-called authority could ... castigate thousands of successful, worthwhile programs* (New York Times). **2** to censure, chasten, or punish in order to correct: *Discipline by which they should be castigated for their sins ...* (S. Cox). [< Latin *castīgāre* (with English *-ate*[1]) < *castus* pure] —**cas′ti|ga′tion**, *n.* —**cas′ti|ga′tor**, *n.*

cas|ti|ga|to|ry (kas′tə gə tôr′ē, -tōr′-), *adj.* serving to castigate; corrective; punitive.

Cas|tile (kas tēl′), *n.* = Castile soap.

Castile or **castile soap**, **1** a pure, hard soap made from olive oil and soda. **2** any one of certain similar soaps. Also, **Castile.** [< *Castile,* a Spanish province, where it was originally made]

Cas|til|ian (kas til′yən), *adj., n.* —***adj.*** of Castile, a region in central Spain, its people, or their language.

—***n.*** **1a** = Spanish. **b** = Castilian Spanish. **2** a person born or living in Castile.

Castilian Spanish, Spanish as spoken in Castile, the accepted standard form of the Spanish language.

cast|ing (kas′ting, käs′-), *n.* **1** a thing shaped by being poured into a mold to harden: *The liner's great propellers are bronze castings.* **2** the act or process of shaping things by pouring into a mold, especially metals: *Casting in bronze was practiced in ancient Greece.* **3** the act or process of assigning the parts of a play, motion picture, or the like, to the performers: *Casting trouble was given as the reason for the postponement of the Strauss work* (New York Times). **4a** the cast of an earthworm. **b** a mass of undigested matter ejected from the stomach of a hawk or other bird of prey; pellets. **5** a method of restraining a large animal in a reclining position before administering an anesthetic to it. **6** the act of throwing a fishing line into the water by means of a fishing rod and reel, as in bait casting, fly casting, and spinning.

casting director, a person in charge of the casting in a play, motion picture, or the like.

Pronunciation Key: hat, āge, cãre, fär; let, ēqual, tėrm; it, īce; hot, ōpen, ôrder; **oi**l, **ou**t; cup, pu̇t, rüle; **ch**ild; lo**ng**; **th**in; **ᴛʜ**en; **zh**, measure; **ə** represents **a** in about, **e** in taken, **i** in pencil, **o** in lemon, **u** in circus.

casting table, a table on which molten glass is poured in making plate glass.

casting vote or **voice**, a vote by the presiding officer to decide a question when the votes of an assembly, council, board, or committee are evenly divided.

cast iron, a hard, brittle form of iron made by casting. Cast iron is made by remelting pig iron. It contains carbon and silicon and is used to make automobile engine blocks and the like.

cast-i|ron (kast′ī′ərn, käst′-), *adj.* **1** made of cast iron: *The cast-iron parts of an automobile include the engine block, manifold, and water pump case.* **2** *Figurative.* not yielding; hard; unbending: *cast-iron policies. A cast-iron conservative ... found himself in an embarrassing and awkward role last week* (Time). **3** *Figurative.* hardy; strong: *a cast-iron constitution. His cast-iron stomach could digest almost anything.*

***cas|tle** (kas′əl, käs′-), *n., v.,* **-tled, -tling.** —*n.* **1a** a large building or group of buildings with thick walls, turrets, battlements, and other defenses against attack: *The knight rode over the drawbridge into the castle.* **b** a palace that once had defenses against attack. **c** a large and imposing residence. **d** a pile of any kind, resembling or likened to a castle: *a sand castle, a castle of cards.* **2** *Figurative.* a stronghold or fortress: *Shake not the castles of his pride* (Charles Lamb). *Every man's house is his castle* (Sir Edward Coke). **3** one of the pieces in the game of chess, shaped like a tower; rook. **4** a small, wooden defensive tower, especially one on the back of an elephant. **5** a high structure on the deck of early ships, such as those used in northern Europe in the 1200's and 1300's.
—*v.i.* in chess: **a** to move the king from his own square two squares toward either corner and bring the rook from that corner to the square the king has passed over. **b** (of the king) to be thus moved.
—*v.t.* **1** to place in or as if in a castle: *Some fierce tribe, castled on the mountain peak* (Robert Browning). **2** to move (the king) beyond the castle or rook in chess.
[< Old North French *castel* stronghold < Latin *castellum* castle (diminutive) < *castrum* fort. See etym. of doublet **chateau.**] —**cas′tle|like′**, *adj.*

***castle**
definition 1a

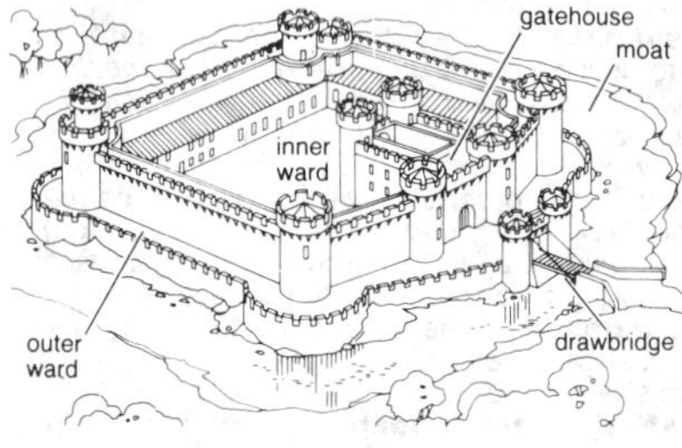

cas|tle-build|er (kas′əl bil′dər, käs′-), *n.* a person given to building castles in the air; a daydreamer.

cas|tle-build|ing (kas′əl bil′ding, käs′-), *n.* the building of castles, especially castles in the air; daydreaming: *The pleasant languor, the dreamy tranquillity, the airy castle-building which in Asia stand in lieu of the vigorous, intensive, passionate life of Europe* (Richard F. Burton).

cas|tled (kas′əld, käs′-), *adj.* **1** having a castle or castles: *a cruise up the castled Rhine* (Time). **2** = castellated.

cas|tle-guard (kas′əl gärd′), *n.* **1** the binding obligation of a feudal tenant to defend his lord's castle when called upon to do so. **2** the tenure of such service. **3** a tax levied in place of this service.

castle in Spain, a daydream; castle in the air.

castle in the air, something imagined but not likely to come true; daydream: *They built castles in the air, and thought to do great wonders* (Sir Thomas North).

Castle walk, a ballroom dance of the early 1900's consisting of one step to each beat. [< Vernon *Castle*, 1887-1918, who created it]

cas|tock (kas′tək), *n. Scottish.* the stalk or stem of a cabbage. [Middle English *calstok* < *cal* kale, cabbage + *stok* stock]

cast|off (kast′ôf′, -of′; käst′-), *adj., n.* —*adj.* thrown away; abandoned; discarded: *castoff clothes.*
—*n.* a person or thing that has been cast off: ... *his everlasting castoffs* (Charles Spurgeon). *Thou shalt be From the city of the free Thyself a castoff* (John Blackie).

cas|tor[1] (kas′tər, käs′-), *n.* = caster (def. 1).

cas|tor[2] (kas′tər, käs′-), *n.* **1** an oily substance with a strong odor, secreted by beavers; castoreum. It is used in making perfume and in medicines. **2a** a hat made of beaver fur. **b** any hat resembling this. **3** a heavy woolen cloth especially used for overcoats. **4** a soft-finished glove leather, usually gray in color. **5** = beaver. [< Latin *castor* < Greek *kástōr* beaver]

Cas|tor (kas′tər, käs′-), *n.* **1** *Greek and Roman Legend.* one of the twin sons of Zeus and Leda. Castor was mortal; his brother, Pollux, was immortal. Castor and Pollux became the constellation Gemini after Castor's death. **2** the fainter of the two bright stars in the constellation Gemini.

Castor and Pollux, **1** the twin sons of Zeus; Dioscuri. **2a** the constellation Gemini. **b** its two brightest stars. **3** double balls of light due to a discharge of atmospheric electricity; St. Elmo's fire.

***castor bean**, *U.S.* **1** the seed of the castor-oil plant. **2** the plant itself.

cas|to|re|um (kas tôr′ē əm, -tōr′-), *n.* the castor of a beaver. [< Latin *castoreum* < Greek *kastóreion* < *kástōr* beaver]

cas|tor|ite (kas′tə rīt, käs′-), *n. Mineralogy.* a variety of petalite, occurring in distinct transparent crystals. [< *Castor* + *-ite*[1] (because it is closely associated with petalite; in reference to the relationship between *Castor and Pollux*)]

castor oil, a thick, yellowish or colorless oil obtained from the beans of a tall, tropical plant, used as a laxative and as a lubricant for machines.

***cas|tor-oil plant** (kas′tər oil′, käs′-), a tall, tropical plant of the spurge family, probably native to Africa, but now widely distributed in all tropical regions. Its seeds yield castor oil.

***castor-oil plant**

plant

fruit

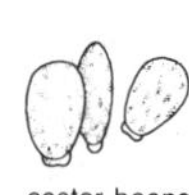
castor beans

castor sugar, a fine, white, powdered sugar.

cas|tra|me|ta|tion (kas′trə mə tā′shən), *n.* the art or science of planning military camp sites. [< French *castramétation* < Latin *castra mētārī* lay out a camp < *castra* camp, *mēta* boundary]

cas|trate (kas′trāt), *v.,* **-trat|ed, -trat|ing,** *n.* —*v.t.* **1a** to remove the male glands of; geld; emasculate. An ox is a castrated bull. **b** to remove the female glands of; spay. **2** *Figurative.* to mutilate or expurgate.
—*n.* a castrated animal or person: *A castrate is more docile than the normal of the species* (Scientific American).
[< Latin *castrāre* (with English *-ate*[1])] —**cas′trat|er**, *n.* —**cas|tra′tion**, *n.*

cas|tra|to (käs trä′tō), *n., pl.* **-ti** (-tē). a male singer who formerly, especially in Italy, was made a eunuch while a boy so that he might retain a soprano or alto voice. [< Italian *castrato* < *castrare* to castrate < Latin *castrāre*]

Cas|tro|ism (kas′trō iz əm), *n.* = Fidelismo.

Cas|tro|ite (kas′trō īt), *n., adj.* = Fidelista.

cas|trum (kas′trəm), *n., pl.* **-tra** (-trə). a Roman military camp. [< Latin *castrum*]

cast steel, steel which is produced by casting or which has undergone fusion.

cast-steel (kast′stēl′, käst′-), *adj.* **1** made of cast steel. **2** resembling cast steel.

cas|u|al (kazh′ů əl), *adj., n.* —*adj.* **1** happening by chance; not planned or expected; accidental: *Our long friendship began with a casual meeting at a party.* **2** without plan or method; careless: *a casual answer. I didn't read the newspaper but gave it only a casual glance. She kissed him perfunctorily on the forehead and he gave her hand a casual caress* (Graham Greene). **3** uncertain; indefinite; indifferent; vague: *Not for a casual period but for a complete lifetime* (George Grote). **4a** informal in manner; offhand: *casual manners. Some people took his casual behavior for rudeness. American sportswear designers know how to design for up-to-date, casual living* (New York Times). **b** designed for informal wear: *We dressed in casual clothes for the picnic.* **c** not to be depended on or considered seriously; unmethodical; haphazard: *He does his work in much too casual a manner.* **5a** occasional or irregular: *He employs casual labor on his farm and then only at harvest time.* **b** *British.* of or denoting persons receiving occasional work or public aid from a place in which they do not permanently reside: *the casual poor.* **6** of or resulting from accidents: *a casual patient. I pointed out that the causes of illnesses are multiple and that a useful diagnosis should take casual factors into account* (Sunday Times). **7** *Obsolete.* uncertain; precarious.
—*n.* **1a** a casual laborer: *The Waterfront Commission has done much to eliminate waterfront casuals who in the past have absorbed much of the waterfront income* (New York Times). **b** *British.* a person occasionally receiving public aid. **2** a soldier awaiting orders, transportation, or the like, at a post or in a unit to which he is not attached or assigned. **3** a casual dress, shoe, or other piece of informal clothing. **4** *Biology.* a plant or animal found outside its native habitat.
[< Latin *cāsuālis* < *cāsus* chance; see etym. under **case**[1]] —**cas′u|al|ly**, *adv.* —**cas′u|al|ness**, *n.*

cas|u|al|ism (kazh′ů ə liz′əm), *n.* **1** a state of things in which chance prevails. **2** the doctrine that all things exist or are governed by chance or accident. —**cas′u|al|ist**, *n.*

casual laborer, a person with no regular job.

cas|u|al|ty (kazh′ů əl tē), *n., pl.* **-ties. 1** a soldier, sailor, or other member of the armed forces who has been wounded, killed, captured, or has fallen ill as a result of enemy action: *The war produced many casualties in both armies. In Israel, every casualty of the war is like a family crisis* (James Reston). **2a** a person injured or killed in an accident or disaster: *If drivers were more careful, there would be fewer casualties on the highways. The earthquake caused many casualties.* **b** *Figurative.* anything destroyed or lost accidentally: *Truth is the first casualty of war* (New York Times). **3** an accident, especially a fatal or a serious one: *a casualty at sea. Several casualties have happened this week, and the bill of mortality is very much increased* (Jonathan Swift). SYN: mishap, disaster. **4** *Scottish.* an incidental charge or payment. **5** chance or accident as the basis of events: *Combinations of skilful genius with happy casualty* (Samuel Johnson).

casual water, an accumulation of water that is not one of the regular hazards of a golf course.

cas|u|a|ri|na (kazh′ů ə rī′nə), *n.* any one of a genus of trees or shrubs, native chiefly to Australia, having long, jointed, whiplike, green branches bearing whorls of small scales at the nodes: *A new township has risen amid the gum trees and casuarinas of the Australian bush* (Economist). [< New Latin *Casuarina* < *casuarius* cassowary (from a fancied resemblance to the feathers of the bird)]

cas|u|ist (kazh′ů ist), *n.* **1** a person who reasons cleverly but falsely, especially in regard to right and wrong. SYN: sophist, quibbler. **2** a person who decides questions of right and wrong in regard to conscience or conduct, applying general moral principles to a particular case: *Who shall decide, when doctors disagree, and soundest casuists doubt, like you and me?* (Alexander Pope). [< French *casuiste* < Latin *cāsus;* see etym. under **case**[1]]

cas|u|is|tic (kazh′ů is′tik), *adj.* **1** of or like casuists; of or using casuistry: *the weedy pool of casuistic argument.* **2** too subtle; sophistical; deceptive: *a casuistic defense.* —**cas′u|is′ti|cal|ly**, *adv.*

cas|u|is|ti|cal (kazh′ů is′tə kəl), *adj.* = casuistic.

cas|u|is|tics (kazh′ů is′tiks), *n.* = casuistry.

cas|u|ist|ry (kazh′ů ə strē), *n., pl.* **-ries. 1** clever but false reasoning, especially in regard to right and wrong: *Casuistry ... destroys, by distinctions and exceptions, all morality, and effaces the essential difference between right and wrong* (Henry St. John, Viscount Bolingbroke). SYN: sophism, sophistry. **2** the act or process of deciding questions of right and wrong in regard to conscience or conduct.

cas|u|la (kas′yə lə), *n.* a priest's vestment; chasuble. [< Late Latin *casula* (originally, diminutive) < Latin *casa* house]

ca|sus (kā′səs), *n. Latin.* **1** a case. **2** an occurrence; matter; occasion.

ca|sus bel|li (kā′səs bel′ī), *Latin.* **1** an occurrence or series of events which is considered a justification for going to war: *A new restraint in reacting to border incidents, such as the shooting down of a plane, that formerly might have been considered a casus belli, ... leads to the hope that the stalemate may keep its precarious stability for a long time* (Bulletin of Atomic Scientists). **2** (literally) a case of war.

cas|well|ite (kaz′wə līt), *n.* an altered form of biotite, occurring as a micaceous mineral of a copper-red color. [< John H. *Caswell*, an American mineralogist of the 1800's + *-ite*[1]]

cat[1] (kat), *n., v.,* **cat|ted, cat|ting.** —*n.* **1a** a small, four-footed, furry mammal, often kept as a pet or for catching mice and rats: *The neighbors took in a stray cat. The mechanism which enables us to experience colour is lacking in cats* (Katharine Tansley). **b** any animal of the group including cats, lions, tigers, and leopards. **c** an animal resembling a cat. **2** *Figurative.* a mean, spiteful woman. **3** the skin or fur of a cat. **4** = catfish. **5** = cat-o'-nine-tails. **6** a tackle for hoisting an anchor. **7** = catboat. **8** in games: **a** *Especially British.* (1) the small, tapered stick struck in playing tipcat. (2) the game of tipcat. (3) *Ob-*

solete. the longer stick used as a bat in tipcat. **b** a ball game not between teams. **9** *Slang.* **a** a jazz admirer or musician; hepcat: *The hottest cats in Bucharest—longhair cats at that—are the combo that makes up the jazz symphony orchestra* (New York Times). **b** any man; fellow; guy: *When Earl and another cat named Onion started to get into the drug thing, nobody really had ... to say much about it* (Harper's).
— ***v.t.*** **1** to hoist (an anchor) and fasten to a beam on the ship's side. **2** to flog with the cat-o'-nine-tails.
— ***v.i.*** *British Slang.* to vomit.
bell the cat, to undertake to do something dangerous: *Who will bell the cat? Clearly the U.N. was in no position to "bell" such a formidable and predatory cat as the Soviet Union* (Wall Street Journal).
cat around, *Slang.* to seek aimlessly for amusement: *Instead of finding a job, he wasted his time catting around.*
let the cat out of the bag, to tell a secret: *It was supposed to be a surprise party, but he said something that let the cat out of the bag.*
put (or **set**) **the cat among the pigeons,** *British Informal.* to pit enemies against each other; set the stage for an inevitable fight: [*He*] *set the cat among the pigeons when he suggested ... that in certain circumstances a sovereign Government would be justified in breaking a contract with an oil concessionary* (Manchester Guardian Weekly).
rain cats and dogs, to pour down rain very hard: *I know Sir John will go, though he was sure it would rain cats and dogs* (Jonathan Swift).
the cat's pajamas (or **whiskers**), *Slang.* something considered outstanding; the most: *If you're a painter, you're ... the cat's pajamas, you are it* (Delmore Schwartz). *"It's a big advantage being English—they think I'm the cat's whiskers"* (London Times).
turn cat in the pan, to change one's views or position, or change sides, for personal advantage: *God saith, 'Cry, cease not', but they turn cat in the pan, and say 'Cease, cry not'* (Thomas Becon).
which way (or **how**) **the cat jumps,** what direction events are taking: *He understood so well which side his bread was buttered, and which way the cat jumped* (Charles Kingsley).
[Old English *catt* (masculine), *catte* (feminine), perhaps < Late Latin *cattus, catta;* both of unknown origin]

cat² (kat), *n.* a caterpillar tractor: *The cats drag the logs to loading points, leaving deep gouges in the scarred earth* (Atlantic).

Cat (cat), *n. Trademark.* = Caterpillar.

cat-, *prefix.* the form of **cata-** before vowels and *h,* as in *category, cathode.*

CAT (no periods), **1** clear air turbulence: *CAT is not the usual turbulence associated with storms, but freakish vertical updrafts and downdrafts that occur without warning at the altitudes used by jets* (Science News). **2** *British.* College of Advanced Technology. **3** computerized axial tomography. See **CAT scan.**

cat., **1** catalogue. **2** catechism.

cata-, *prefix.* **1** down; downward: *Catadromous = descending rivers to spawn* (*as eels*).
2 against: *Catapult = a weapon for hurling darts or missiles against a target.*
3 wrongly; amiss: *Catachresis = misuse* (*of words*). Also, **cat-,** before vowels and *h.*
[< Greek *kata-* < *katá* down, against]

Cat|a|bap|tist (kat'ə bap'tist), *n.* **1** a person who rejects the orthodox doctrine of baptism. **2** = Anabaptist. [< Greek *katabaptistēs* < *katá* down + *baptistēs* baptizer]

ca|tab|a|sis (kə tab'ə sis), *n., pl.* **-ses** (-sēz). a going down. [< Late Latin *catabasis* < Greek *katábasis* < *katabaínein* to go down < *katá* down + *baínein* go]

cat|a|bat|ic (kat'ə bat'ic), *adj.* (especially of a fever or disease) going down or declining in intensity; subsiding.

cat|a|bol|ic (kat'ə bol'ik), *adj.* of or exhibiting catabolism. — **cat'a|bol'i|cal|ly,** *adv.*

ca|tab|o|lism (kə tab'ə liz əm), *n.* the process of breaking down living tissues into simpler substances or waste matter, thereby producing energy: *There are two phases of metabolism; namely, the constructive phase or anabolism, and the destructive phase or catabolism* (Heber W. Youngken). **SYN:** dissimilation. Also, **katabolism.** [< *cata-* + Greek *bolē* a throw (< *bállein* to throw) + English *-ism*]

ca|tab|o|lite (kə tab'ə līt), *n.* a product of catabolism.

cat|a|caus|tic (kat'ə kôs'tik), *adj., n.* in optics:
— ***adj.*** having to do with caustic curves formed by reflected light. — ***n.*** a caustic curve formed by the reflection of the rays of light.
[< *cata-* back, again + Greek *kaustikós* burning, caustic (from the intensity of light and heat produced by the rays striking such a surface)]

cat|a|chre|sis (kat'ə krē'sis), *n., pl.* **-ses** (-sēz). **1** the misuse or strained use of words, as in an inconsistent metaphor. **2** misuse of word elements, changing the form of a word: *As a result of catachresis it* [*the suffix -ish*] *then acquired the meaning 'having the bad qualities of' as in brutish, clownish, and foppish* (Simeon Potter). [< Late Latin *catachrēsis* < Greek *katáchrēsis* misuse, ultimately < *kata-* amiss + *chrêsthai* to use]

cat|a|chres|tic (kat'ə kres'tik), *adj.* having to do with or showing catachresis. — **cat'a|chres'ti|cal|ly,** *adv.*

cat|a|chres|ti|cal (kat'ə kres'tə kəl), *adj.* = catachrestic.

cat|a|clasm (kat'ə klaz əm), *n.* a break or disruption. [< Greek *katáklasma,* ultimately < *kata-* down + *klân* break]

cat|a|cli|nal (kat'ə klī'nəl), *adj. U.S.* descending with the dip of the geological strata (contrasted with *anaclinal*): *a cataclinal valley.* [< *cata-* + Greek *klínein* to incline + English *-al*¹]

cat|a|clysm (kat'ə kliz əm), *n.* **1** a great flood, earthquake, or any sudden, violent change in the earth. **SYN:** calamity. **2** *Figurative.* any violent change or upheaval: *Atomic warfare between nations would be a cataclysm for all mankind. ... a day that has been designated by historians of the Wall Street cataclysm of that year as Black Thursday* (New York Times). [< Latin *cataclysmos* < Greek *kataklysmós* flood, ultimately < *kata-* down + *klýzein* wash]

cat|a|clys|mal (kat'ə kliz'məl), *adj.* = cataclysmic.

cat|a|clys|mic (kat'ə kliz'mik), *adj.* of or like a cataclysm; extremely sudden and violent: (*Figurative.*) *This sudden and cataclysmic shifting of power at the top came as a shock to the audience* (Time). — **cat'a|clys'mi|cal|ly,** *adv.*

cat|a|comb (kat'ə kōm), *n.* Usually, **catacombs.** an underground gallery forming a burial place, especially a network of such galleries with recesses in which to place the dead. [< Late Latin *catacumbae,* plural, probably < phrase *cata* (< Greek *katá*) *tumbās* (< Greek *týmbos*) among the tombs; influenced by *-cumbere* to lie]

cat|a|cous|tics (kat'ə küs'tiks, -kous'-), *n.* the science of reflected sound; cataphonics. [< *cat-* + *acoustics*]

cat|a|di|op|tric (kat'ə dī op'trik), *adj.* involving both reflection and refraction of light: *The Astroscope* [*a telescopic instrument*] *has the same catadioptric lens system astronomers use in their high-powered sky-mapping cameras* (New Yorker).

cat|a|di|op|tri|cal (kat'ə dī op'trə kəl), *adj.* = catadioptric.

cat|a|di|op|trics (kat'ə dī op'triks), *n.* the branch of optics dealing with catadioptric phenomena.

ca|tad|ro|mous (kə tad'rə məs), *adj.* living in fresh water but going to salt water to spawn, as eels. [(coined as opposite to *anadromous*) < *cata-* + Greek *drómos* running + English *-ous*]

***cat|a|falque** (kat'ə falk), *n.* **1** a stand or platform to support a coffin in which a dead person lies. **2** a structure resembling a coffin or tomb, sometimes used at Requiem Masses. **3** a kind of open hearse or funeral car. [< French *catafalque* < Italian *catafalco* scaffold < Vulgar Latin *catafalicum* < Latin *cata-* down + *fala* scaffolding]

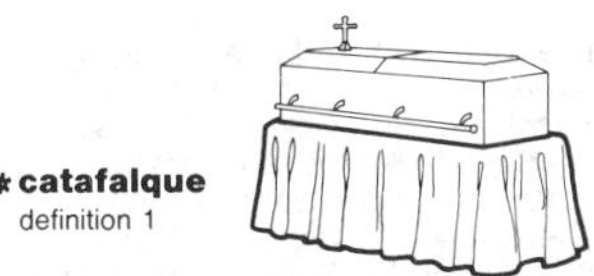
catafalque
definition 1

cat|ag|mat|ic (kat'ag mat'ik), *adj. Medicine.* having the property of consolidating broken parts; promoting the union of fractured bones: *a catagmatic powder, plaster, or medicine.* [< French *catagmatique* < Greek *kátagma, -matos* fracture < *katagnúnai* to break, shatter]

Cat|a|lan (kat'ə lan, -lən), *adj., n.* — ***adj.*** of Catalonia, a region in northeastern Spain, its people, or their language.
— ***n.*** **1** a person born or living in Catalonia. **2** the language spoken in Catalonia. It is a Romance language, closely related to Provençal. *Catalan is for him* [*Pablo Casals*] *the language of deepest intimacy* (New Yorker). Also, **Catalonian.**

cat|a|lase (kat'ə lās), *n.* an enzyme, found in most living cells, which catalyzes the separation of hydrogen peroxide into gaseous oxygen and water. [< *catal*(ysis) + *-ase*]

cat|a|lec|tic (kat'ə lek'tik), *adj.* lacking one or more unstressed syllables in the last foot of a line of verse; incomplete. [< Late Latin *catalēcticus* < Greek *katalēktikós* incomplete, ultimately < *kata-* down + *lēgein* leave off, end]

cat|a|lep|sis (kat'ə lep'sis), *n.* = catalepsy.

cat|a|lep|sy (kat'ə lep'sē), *n.* a condition, usually associated with schizophrenia, in which a person's muscles become more or less rigid, and his arms and legs maintain any position in which they are placed. [< Late Latin *catalēpsia* < Greek *katálēpsis* seizure, ultimately < *kata-* down + *lambánein* take]

cat|a|lep|tic (kat'ə lep'tik), *adj., n.* — ***adj.*** **1** of catalepsy. **2** having catalepsy.
— ***n.*** a person who has catalepsy.

cat|a|lep|ti|form (kat'ə lep'tə fôrm), *adj.* resembling catalepsy.

cat|a|lep|toid (kat'ə lep'toid), *adj.* cataleptiform; resembling catalepsy.

cat|al|lac|tics (kat'ə lak'tiks), *n.* the science of exchanges (formerly used as a designation of political economy or economics). [< Greek *katallassein* to change, exchange (< *kata-* completely + *állassein* to change) + English *-ics*]

cat|a|lo (kat'ə lō), *n., pl.* **-loes** or **-los.** = cattalo.

cat|a|log (kat'ə lôg, -log), *n., v.t., v.i.,* **-loged, -log|ing.** — ***n.*** **1** a list of items in some collection. A catalog either identifies each item very briefly or describes it more fully. A library has a catalog of its books, arranged in alphabetical order. **SYN:** See syn. under **list. 2a** a book or pamphlet containing such a list: *A company sometimes prints a catalog with pictures and prices of the things that it sells.* **b** *U.S.* a volume or booklet issued by a college or university listing rules, courses to be given, faculty, fees, and other descriptions of the institution. In Great Britain a catalog is called a *prospectus* or *calendar.* **3** *Figurative.* any list or series: *a catalog of misfortunes.* **4** = register.
— ***v.t.*** **1** to make a list of: *He cataloged all the insects in his collection.* **2** to put in a catalog: *Birds are cataloged under natural history.*
— ***v.i.*** to make a catalog.
[< Old French *catalogue,* learned borrowing from Late Latin *catalogus* a list < Greek *katálogos,* ultimately < *kata-* completely + *légein* to count]

cat|a|log|er (kat'ə lôg'ər, -log'-), *n.* **1** a person who catalogs, such as a librarian who enters books acquired in a catalog. **2** a person who makes a catalog: *Many of the cases of disappearing stars arise from catalogers recording stars where none existed.*

cat|a|log|ist (kat'ə lôg'ist, -log'-), *n.* a person who catalogs. Also, **cataloguist.**

cat|a|log|ize (kat'ə lôg'īz, -log'-), *v.t.,* **-ized, -iz|ing.** = catalog.

cat|a|logue (kat'ə lôg, -log), *n., v.,* **-logued, -logu|ing.** = catalog. — **cat'a|logu'er,** *n.*

ca|ta|logue rai|son|né (kà tà lôg' re zô nā'), *French.* **1** a systematically arranged catalog of books, paintings, and other articles. **2** (literally) reasoned catalog.

cat|a|logu|ist (kat'ə lôg'ist, -log'-), *n.* = catalogist.

Cat|a|lo|ni|an (kat'ə lō'nē ən), *adj., n.* = Catalan.

ca|tal|pa (kə tal'pə), *n.* a tree of North America, West Indies, and Asia with large, heart-shaped leaves, clusters of bell-shaped flowers, and long pods. It belongs to the bignonia family. See picture under **bignonia family.** [American English < Muskhogean (Creek) *kutuhlpa* winged head (referring to the flowers)]

cat|a|lyse (kat'ə līz), *v.t.,* **-lysed, -lys|ing.** *Especially British.* catalyze. — **cat'a|lys'er,** *n.*

ca|tal|y|sis (kə tal'ə sis), *n., pl.* **-ses** (-sēz). the regulation of a chemical reaction by the presence of a catalyst. [< Greek *katálysis* dissolution, ultimately < *kata-* completely + *lýein* to loose]

cat|a|lyst (kat'ə list), *n.* **1** a substance that causes a chemical reaction while itself remaining practically unchanged: *Catalysts are properly defined as substances that regulate the rate at which chemical reactions proceed. Some catalysts accelerate reactions ... Other catalysts slow reactions. Examples of both types exist ... within the cells and fluids of living organisms, where they are known as enzymes* (Scientific American). **2** *Figurative.* a person or thing that brings about some change or changes, without being directly affected itself: *The talent agent is the catalyst who brings performers and jobs together* (Wall Street Journal). *Job dissatisfaction and severe unemployment are catalysts to violence rather than primary causes* (Morton Salkind). Also, **catalyzer.**

cat|a|lyt|ic (kat'ə lit'ik), *adj., n.* — ***adj.*** **1** of catalysis: *The fuel is self-igniting and is broken down by catalytic action into water* (Newsweek). **2** causing catalysis. **3** *Figurative.* causing change without being directly affected itself: *Nuclear* *physics . . . has exerted a strong catalytic influence on developments in science* (Bulletin of Atomic Scientists). —*n.* a catalyst. —**cat′a|lyt′i|cal|ly**, *adv.*

cat|a|lyt|i|cal (kat′ə lit′ə kəl), *adj.* = catalytic.

catalytic antibody, an enzyme that is designed to speed chemical reactions in certain substances in an organism: *Scientists have designed many catalytic antibodies known also as abzymes* (Science News).

catalytic converter, a device in automobiles which contains a chemical catalyst to oxidize exhaust gases, converting them into harmless products. It has also been used to oxidize smoke exhaust from chimneys.

catalytic cracker, the apparatus or device used for catalytic cracking; cat cracker.

catalytic cracking, a method of breaking down the heavy hydrocarbons in petroleum into lighter ones by the use of alumina-silica mixtures, certain types of clay, or other catalysts. Catalytic cracking produces more gasoline of higher octane than thermal cracking does.

cat|a|lyze (kat′ə līz), *v.t.*, **-lyzed, -lyz|ing.** to act upon by catalysis: *This enzyme catalyzes, or sparks, the transfer of oxygen from hydrogen peroxide or other peroxides to another substance* (Science News Letter). —**cat′a|lyz′er**, *n.*

***cat|a|ma|ran** (kat′ə mə ran′), *n.* **1a** a boat with two hulls side by side joined by crosspieces. **b** a raft made of pieces of wood lashed together. **2** *Informal, Figurative.* a cross, quarrelsome person, especially a woman. [< Tamil *kaṭṭa-maram* (literally) tied tree < *kaṭṭa* a tie, *maram* tree]

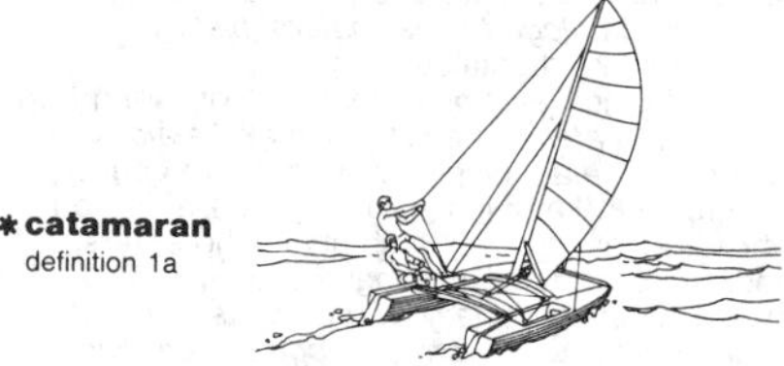
***catamaran**
definition 1a

cat|a|me|ni|a (kat′ə mē′nē ə), *n.* = menstruation. [< New Latin *catamenia* < Greek *katamēnia,* neuter plural of *katamēnios* monthly < phrase *katà mêna* by the month, each month]

cat|a|me|ni|al (kat′ə mē′nē əl), *adj.* = menstrual.

cat|a|mite (kat′ə mīt), *n.* a boy kept for unnatural purposes. [< Latin *Catamītus,* alteration of *Ganymēdēs* < Greek *Ganymḗdēs* Ganymede]

cat|a|mount (kat′ə mount), *n.* **1a** any one of several wild animals of the cat family, especially the cougar. (So called by early settlers in eastern North America.) **b** a wildcat, such as a lynx. **2** = catamountain. [short for *catamountain*]

cat|a|moun|tain (kat′ə moun′tən), *n.* any wild animal of the cat family, such as the European wildcat, leopard, cougar, or lynx. Also, **cat-o′-mountain.** [Middle English *cat of the mountain*]

cat-and-dog (kat′ən dôg′, -dog′), *adj.* full of strife; quarrelsome: *During Franklin D. Roosevelt's Presidency, . . . Wall Street and Washington tended to be on cat-and-dog terms* (New Yorker).

cat-and-mouse (kat′ən mous′), *n.,* or **cat-and-mouse game**, an act or situation in which one person, a group of people, or an animal has another in his power, teasing and harassing him for a time before disposing of him.
play cat-and-mouse, to engage in a cat-and-mouse game: *[He] had hidden in the squalid back alleys of Athens, playing cat-and-mouse with police, while he and his illegal spy ring sent information across the border* (Time).

cat|a|pan (kat′ə pan), *n.* a high official who governed Calabria and Apulia in the south of Italy under the Byzantine emperors. [< Medieval Latin *catapanus,* perhaps < Greek *katepánō* (*tôn axiōmátōn*) (one) placed (over the dignities)]

cat|a|pet|a|lous (kat′ə pet′ə ləs), *adj. Botany.* having the petals united only through their cohesion to the base of a column of united stamens, as in the mallow. [< Greek *katá* each to each + *pétalon* petal + English *-ous*]

cat|a|phon|ic (kat′ə fon′ik), *adj.* having to do with reflected sound. [< Greek *katá* against + *phōnḗ* sound + English *-ic*]

cat|a|phon|ics (kat′ə fon′iks), *n.* = catacoustics.

cat|a|pho|re|sis (kat′ə fə rē′sis), *n. Medicine.* the causing of medicinal substances to pass through or into living tissues in the direction of flow of a positive electric current. [< Greek *katá* down + *phórēsis* a carrying < *phérein* to bear]

cat|a|pho|ret|ic (kat′ə fə ret′ik), *adj.* of cataphoresis; having to do with or resembling cataphoresis.

cat|a|phract (kat′ə frakt), *n.* an ancient defensive armor composed of scales of metal attached to a garment of leather or other material, often covering the whole body. [< Latin *cataphractes* coat of mail < Greek *kataphráktēs,* ultimately < *katá* down + *phrássein* fence in]

cat|a|phyll (kat′ə fil), *n. Botany.* any scalelike leaf which precedes a stage of growth, as the cotyledons of an embryo, or the scales of a bud or rhizome. [< *cata-* + Greek *phýllon* leaf]

cat|a|phyl|lar|y (kat′ə fil′ər ē), *adj.* of the nature of a cataphyll.

cat|a|pla|si|a (kat′ə plā′zhē ə, -zē-), *n.* a form of atrophy involving the regression of tissues to a less developed condition.
[< New Latin *cataplasia* < Greek *kata-* down + *plásis* molding, formation]

cat|a|plasm (kat′ə plaz əm), *n.* a poultice, especially one applied hot. [< Latin *cataplasma* < Greek *katáplasma,* ultimately < *kata-* down + *plássein* to form]

cat|a|plec|tic (kat′ə plek′tik), *adj.* of or having to do with cataplexy.

cat|a|plei|ite (kat′ə plē′īt), *n.* a hydrous silicate of zirconium and sodium, occurring in hexagonal opaque crystals of light yellowish-brown color.
[< Greek *katá* together with + *pleîon* more + English *-ite*[1] (because it occurs along with several other minerals)]

cat|a|plex|y (kat′ə plek′sē), *n.* a loss of muscular power and control without loss of consciousness, usually in an attack of a few seconds only.
[< German *Kataplexie* < Greek *katáplēxis* < *kata-* down + *plḗssein* strike]

***cat|a|pult** (kat′ə pult), *n., v.* —*n.* **1a** a weapon used in ancient times for shooting stones and arrows. **b** *British.* a slingshot: *One afternoon I saw two boys with catapults aiming, as I thought, at a high garden wall* (Cape Times). **2** a device for launching an airplane or missile from a ship's deck, a ramp, or a truck: *Its take-off from a carrier deck will be assisted by a catapult, which might be described as a giant slingshot* (Science News Letter). **3** a device for ejecting a pilot from an aircraft.
—*v.t.* **1** to shoot or launch from a catapult. **2** *Figurative.* to cast suddenly or rapidly; hurl: *He stopped his bicycle so suddenly that he was catapulted over the handle bars. He had been catapulted to fame by winning the International Tchaikovsky Contest in Moscow* (New York Times).
3 *British.* to aim at or hit with a slingshot.
—*v.i. Figurative.* to be catapulted; move suddenly or forcefully: *The frightened cat catapulted from the chair when the big dog came in. Schoolchildren and their nuns catapulted out of classrooms into the streets* (New Yorker).
[< Latin *catapulta* < Greek *katapéltēs,* probably < *kata-* down + *pállein* hurl]

***catapult**
definitions 1a, 2

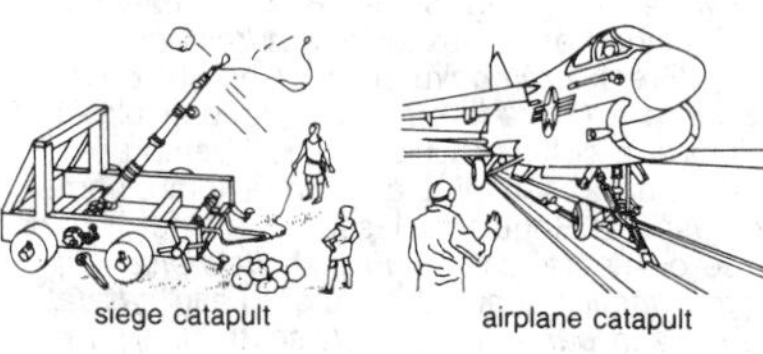
siege catapult airplane catapult

cat|a|pult|ier (kat′ə pəl tir′), *n.* a person who works a catapult.

cat|a|ract (kat′ə rakt), *n.* **1a** a large, steep waterfall: *Venezuela has the world's tallest cataract in Angel Falls, where water drops more than 3,000 feet* (Newsweek). **b** a violent rush or downpour of water; flood: *Cataracts of rain flooded the streets.* (*Figurative.*) *The cataract of the cliff of heaven fell blinding off the brink* (G. K. Chesterton). **SYN:** torrent, deluge. **c** a series of rapids in a river; white water. **2** a disease of the eye in which the lens becomes cloudy, making a person partly or entirely blind: *Cataract robs sight by clouding the lens of the eye so that insufficient light is able to fall on the sensitive retina* (Science News Letter).
[< Latin *catarrhācta* < Greek *katarrhāktēs,* ultimately < *kata-* down + *rhāttein* dash]

cat|a|ract|al (kat′ə rak′təl), *adj.* of or resembling a cataract: *The sea swept . . . with a cataractal fury* (Illustrated London News).

cat|a|rac|tous (kat′ə rak′təs), *adj. Medicine.* affected with cataract: *a cataractous lens.*

ca|tarrh (kə tär′), *n.* **1** an inflamed condition of a mucous membrane, usually that of the nose or throat, causing a discharge of mucus. **2** the mucus that collects in the nose and throat as a result.
[< Middle French *catarrhe,* learned borrowing from Late Latin *catarrhus* < Greek *katárrhous,* ultimately < *kata-* down + *rheîn* to flow]

ca|tarrh|al (kə tär′əl), *adj.* **1** like catarrh.
2 caused by catarrh.

cat|ar|rhine (kat′ə rīn), *adj., n. Zoology.* —*adj.* of or having to do with a superfamily of the order of primates that includes all animals having the nostrils close together, oblique, and directed downwards.
—*n.* a catarrhine monkey or ape.
[< New Latin *Catarrhina* a typical family < Greek *katá* next to + *rhīs, rhīnos* nose]

ca|tarrh|ous (kə tär′əs), *adj.* = catarrhal.

ca|tas|ta|sis (kə tas′tə sis), *n., pl.* **-ses** (-sēz). the height of dramatic action just before the catastrophe. [< Greek *katástasis* settled condition < *katastênai* settle down < *kata-* down + *stênai* to stand]

ca|tas|tro|phe (kə tas′trə fē), *n.* **1a** a sudden, widespread, or extraordinary disaster; a great calamity or misfortune. A big earthquake, flood, or fire is a catastrophe. **SYN:** cataclysm. See syn. under **disaster. b** *Informal, Figurative.* a terrible failure; complete fiasco: *In less tasteful hands, it [the opera La Traviata] might have been a catastrophe* (Harold C. Schonberg). **2** the outcome, especially of a dramatic or literary work; climax; denouement. The catastrophe of a tragedy usually brings death or ruin to the leading character. The catastrophe of a comedy is frequently the marriage of a principal character. **3** a disastrous end; ruin: *Human history becomes more and more a race between education and catastrophe* (H. G. Wells). **4** an event which subverts or overturns the whole order of things: *God reveals his will not by sudden catastrophes and violent revolutions* (Frederic W. Farrar). **5** *Geology.* a sudden and violent change, especially one affecting the earth's surface; cataclysm. [< Greek *katastrophḗ* an overturning, ultimately < *kata-* down + *stréphein* to turn]

catastrophe theory, a system for describing a phenomenon of sudden change in behavior or state by fitting the characteristic attributes into a geometric model consisting of dimensional planes that describe the change in a graph of an umbilic or cuspoid shape: *Catastrophe theory arose from an application of topology, the study of geometric properties of surfaces as they are bent and distorted* (Lynn A. Steen).

cat|a|stroph|ic (kat′ə strof′ik), *adj.* of or caused by a catastrophe; disastrous: *The catastrophic Northeast floods over the week-end took a heavy toll of industry and business* (Wall Street Journal). —**cat′a|stroph′i|cal|ly**, *adv.*

cat|a|stroph|i|cal (kat′ə strof′ə kəl), *adj.* = catastrophic.

ca|tas|tro|phism (kə tas′trə fiz əm), *n.* the theory that certain geological and biological phenomena were caused by catastrophes rather than by continuous and uniform processes.

ca|tas|tro|phist (kə tas′trə fist), *n.* a person who believes in catastrophism.

cat|a|to|ni|a (kat′ə tō′nē ə), *n.* a condition associated with schizophrenia, characterized by mental stupor and muscular rigidity. Catatonia often alternates with sudden outbursts, seizures of panic, or hallucinations. [< *cata-* + Greek *tónos* tone]

cat|a|ton|ic (kat′ə ton′ik), *adj., n.* —*adj.* characterized by catatonia.
—*n.* a person who suffers from catatonia.

Ca|taw|ba (kə tô′bə), *n.* **1a** a light-red grape of North America: *The Catawbas . . . seem to prosper in high, exposed and windy places* (New York Times). **b** a light wine made from it. **2a** a language of the Siouan family originally spoken in South Carolina. **b** the tribe of Indians who spoke this language. [American English < Choctaw *katápa* separated (from other Siouan tribes)]

cat bear, = lesser panda.

cat|bird (kat′bėrd′), *n.* **1** a North American songbird with gray feathers and black on the top of its head. A catbird can make a sound like a cat mewing. It belongs to the same family as the mockingbird. **2** any one of certain Australian birds that make a mewing sound.

catbird seat, *Informal.* a position of power or advantage: *Here, then, was a set of circumstances that put Mr. McDonald in the catbird seat* (Wall Street Journal).

cat block, *Nautical.* a heavy block with a large hook, used in hoisting an anchor to the cathead.

***cat|boat** (kat′bōt′), *n.* a sailboat with one mast set far forward. It has no bowsprit or jib.

***catboat**

cat brier, or **cat|bri|er** (kat′brī′ər), *n. U.S.* greenbrier.

cat burglar, a burglar who enters by skillful feats of climbing.

cat|call (kat′kôl′), *n., v.* —*n.* **1** a shrill cry or whistle to express disapproval. Actors who perform

poorly are sometimes greeted by catcalls from the audience. *The libretto evoked critical catcalls, but the music had a light charm bordering on jazziness* (Time). **2** an instrument which produces such a sound; a whistle.
—***v.i.*** to make catcalls: *Let them catcall and hiss as they will* (George Canning).
—***v.t.*** to attack with catcalls: *He was catcalled at his first performance.*

catch (kach), *v.,* **caught, catch|ing,** *n., adj.* —***v.t.*** **1** to take and hold; seize; capture: *Catch the ball with both hands. The policeman caught the thief. Here, catch hold of the end of the rope.* **2** to entangle or grip: *A nail caught her dress.* **3** to cause to be held or seized accidentally: *She caught her finger in the door.* **4a** to come on suddenly; surprise: *He caught the burglar in the act of opening the safe. Mother caught me just as I was hiding her birthday present.* **b** *Figurative.* to ensnare or entrap: *to catch him in his words* (Mark 12:13). **5** to reach or get to in time: *You have just five minutes to catch your train.* **6** *Figurative.* **a** to take; get: *to catch a breath of fresh air, to catch a movie. Paper catches fire easily.* **b** to grasp or intercept: *to catch the latest news report. The sail caught the breeze. He caught a ride into town with an old friend who was passing by.* **7** *Figurative.* to take or contract, especially by exposure or imitation: *to catch a a cold, to catch the spirit of the occasion.* **8** *Figurative.* **a** to apprehend by the senses or intellect; hear, see, or understand by an effort: *He spoke so rapidly that I didn't catch the meaning of what he said.* **b** to arrest or engage (a sense): *Bright colors catch the baby's eye.* **9** to reach with a blow; hit; strike: *The stone caught him on the leg.* **10** *Figurative.* to check suddenly (one's breath): *She caught her breath in surprise.* **11** to captivate; charm: *She still each method tries to catch me* (Robert Browning).
—***v.i.*** **1** to become hooked or fastened: *My dress caught in the door.* **2** *Figurative.* to become lighted; burn: *Paper catches easily.* **3** to act as a catcher in baseball: *He catches for our school team.* **4** to take proper hold so as to act: *The bolt does not catch.* **5** *Figurative.* to light, as fire; flame up; spread: *His eloquence caught like a flame* (Tennyson).
—***n.*** **1** the act of catching: *Her catch was quick enough to keep the plate from hitting the floor.* **2** a thing that catches: *The catch on that door is broken.* **3** a thing caught: *A dozen fish is a good catch.* **4a** something worth catching. **b** *Informal.* a desirable person to marry because of wealth, position, or other status: *The rich bachelor was the catch of the season.* **5** a scrap or fragment of anything: *He sang catches of songs.* **6** *Figurative.* a choking or stoppage of the breath: *He had a catch in his voice.* **7** *Informal, Figurative.* a hidden or tricky condition in a plan, etc.: *There is a catch to that question.* **8a** a game of throwing and catching a ball: *The children played catch on the lawn.* **b** the act of catching a ball on the fly: *He made a fine catch with one hand.* **c** *Baseball.* = catcher. **9** *Music.* **a** a short song sung by several persons or groups, beginning one after the other. **b** a round for three or more persons in which the words are so arranged as to produce ludicrous effects. **10** the sprouting of a crop in the field.
—***adj.*** **1** getting one's attention; arousing one's interest: *Advertisements often contain catch phrases.* **2** *Figurative.* tricky; deceptive: *a catch question.*

catch at, a to try to catch: *catching at his rein* (William Cowper). **b** to seize eagerly: *to catch at an opportunity, a proposal, etc.*

catch it, *Informal.* to be scolded or punished: *When the boy spilled the milk, he was afraid he would catch it from his mother. We all thought Tom was about to catch it* (Frederick Marryat).

catch on, *Informal.* **a** *U.S.* to get the idea; understand: *The second time the teacher explained the problem, the boy caught on.* **b** to be widely used or accepted; become popular: *That new song caught on quickly.*

catch out, a *Cricket.* to put (a batsman) out by catching the ball: *If a striker is caught out, state the fieldsman's name* (Cricket Manual). **b** *British.* to find out or discover (a person) in a mistake or the like: *The regulations at the docks are so [intricate] that no newcomer could ever hope to catch out an old hand* (Punch).

catch up (with), a to come up even (with a person or thing) while going the same way; overtake: *The dog ran as fast as he could to catch up with the car.* **b** *Figurative.* to come up to date; keep abreast: *I am trying to catch up on my reading. They haven't caught up yet with the latest styles.* **c** to pick up suddenly; snatch; grab: *When flames broke out, she caught up the baby.* **d** *Figurative.* to interrupt and annoy with criticisms or questions; heckle: *You catch me up so very short* (Dickens). **e** to hold up in loops: *Her train was caught up by a ribbon.* **f** *Figurative.* to be or become involved: *There may be parents already caught up in the college panic when they look for a good nursery school* (Saturday Review).
[< Old North French *cachier* chase, hunt < Vulgar Latin *captiāre* < Latin *captāre* try to catch < *capere* take. See etym. of doublet **chase**[1].]
—***Syn.*** *v.t.* **1 Catch, capture** mean to take and hold someone or something. **Catch** suggests overtaking or taking something fleeing or hidden, by force, surprise, or cleverness: *We caught the thief. We caught sight of him. I didn't catch his words.* **Capture** suggests achievement in spite of greater difficulties or obstacles: *After a long chase the police captured the criminal. He captured her heart.*

Catch-22 or **catch-22** (kach′twen′tē tü′), *n., adj. Informal.* —***n.*** a condition intended to deceive or cheat by its hidden complicated or perverted nature, especially in spite of efforts to override such a condition; any paradoxical rule or situation: *. . . the Catch-22 of modern prison life, "a grand hypocrisy in which custodial concerns, administrative exigencies and punishment are all disguised as treatment"* (Atlantic).
—***adj.*** characterized by such a condition or situation: *By organizing for complete military disaster it is possible, on a sort of warped Catch-22 approach, to emerge from war economically prosperous* (New Scientist).
[< *Catch-22,* title of a novel (1961) by Joseph Heller, born 1923, an American writer; from the name given in this novel to an absurdly paradoxical Air Force rule applied to combat pilots]

catch|a|ble (kach′ə bəl), *adj.* that can be caught: *fish raised to a catchable size.*

catch|all (kach′ôl′), *n., adj. U.S.* —***n.*** anything that catches, holds, includes, or covers a variety of odds and ends: *the general catch-all . . . for all the family litter* (Harriet Beecher Stowe). *These demands . . . are merely a catchall for myriad often ill-defined grievances* (Time).
—***adj.*** serving to hold, include, or cover a variety of things: *a catchall Congressional bill full of pork-barrel measures.*

catch-as-catch-can (kach′əz kach′kan′), *adj., n.* —***adj.*** **1** with no holds barred, unrestrained. **2** haphazard; random: *Most of the other kids, in that easygoing atmosphere, took their schooling catch-as-catch-can fashion* (New Yorker).
—***n.*** a style of wrestling in which a wrestler is allowed to hold or take down his opponent below the waist and to use the parts of his own body below the waist to take down his opponent or apply a hold. It is the common style of wrestling in the United States.

catch basin, 1 a receptacle placed beneath the grating or other opening of a sewer to retain matter that might block up the sewer. **2** a reservoir for catching and retaining surface drainage over large areas: *Chemical sprays . . . had to be used with restraint, because of the danger of contaminating the catch basins Bermuda relies on for its drinking water* (New Yorker).

catch crop, a crop grown between the planting of regular crops, when the land would ordinarily lie fallow.

catch-crop|ping (kach′krop′ing), *n.* the practice of growing catch crops.

catch drain, 1 a drain or ditch, especially on a hillside, to catch water. **2** a drain by the side of a canal or conduit to catch the surplus water.

catch|er (kach′ər), *n.* **1** a person or thing that catches something. **2** a baseball player who stands behind the batter to catch balls thrown by the pitcher and not hit by the batter and to tag runners to make a putout at home plate.

catcher boat, a boat with a harpoon gun that accompanies a factory ship and does the actual hunting of whales.

catcher resonator, part of a klystron, or electron tube in an ultrahigh-frequency circuit where bunched electrons are caught and their energy absorbed.

catch|fly (kach′flī′), *n., pl.* **-flies.** a plant of the pink family whose sticky stem and calyx are able to catch small insects.

catch|ing (kach′ing), *adj.* **1** likely to spread from one person to another; contagious; infectious: *Colds are catching. Enthusiasm is catching.* SYN: communicable. **2** *Figurative.* attractive or fascinating: *a catching time. The singer has a catching style.* SYN: captivating.

catch line, 1 a catch phrase or sentence. **2a** a line of type in which a catchword or entry word occurs. **b** a line of type that is shorter than the surrounding lines. **c** a headline inserted on a galley proof for the printer's use and later removed. **3** a phrase or sentence used by a performer to get a laugh.

catch meadow, a meadow irrigated by water from a spring or rivulet on the slope of a hill, especially by catch drains.

catch|ment (kach′mənt), *n.* **1** reservoir for catching water. **2** = drainage. **3** the act of catching.

catchment basin or **area,** a land area, bounded by natural watersheds and usually the sea, where rainfall is drained by a river system.

catch|pen|ny (kach′pen′ē), *adj., n., pl.* **-nies.**
—***adj.*** showy but worthless or useless; made to sell quickly: *the catchpenny lyrics of Tom Dibdin* (Leigh Hunt).
—***n.*** a catchpenny article: *You know already by the title that it is no more than a catchpenny* (Washington Irving).

catch phrase, a phrase which draws, or is intended to draw, attention: *Buber formulates his position in terms of two philosophical catch phrases: I-It and I-Thou* (Time).

catch pit, 1 a pit to catch sediment in drainage water and the like. **2** = catch basin.

catch|pole or **catch|poll** (kach′pōl′), *n.* a bailiff or minor officer employed by a sheriff whose duties formerly included arresting debtors for nonpayment.
[Old English *kaecepol* tax gatherer < Medieval Latin *cacepollus,* probably Latinization of Old North French *cacepol* (literally) chase (or catch) fowl]

catch stitch, a stitch that makes parallel rows of lines like a herringbone design.

Catch-22, See after **catch.**

catch|up (kech′əp, kach′-), *n.* =ketchup.

catch-up (kach′up′), *adj.* helping to overtake or keep up with something: *There was catch-up buying following the strike* (New York Times). *Project Head Start provides catch-up preschool education* (Time).
play catch-up, *U.S.* to try to overtake by unconventional tactics, taking risks, and the like: *There is yet time to develop the requisite technologies . . . rather than playing catch-up as in the case of energy technologies alternative to oil* (Science).

catch|wa|ter (kach′wôt′ər, -wot′-), *n.* a drain to catch surface water; catch drain.

catch|weed (kach′wēd′), *n.* a climbing plant having short, hooked bristles that stick to hedges, clothing, or hides; cleavers.

catch|weight (kach′wāt′), *n. Sports.* **1** the weight of a contestant left to the contestant's option: *to wrestle the best of three falls at catch-weight* (Daily Chronicle). **2** the weight carried by a race horse left to the owner's option.

catch|word (kach′wėrd′), *n.* **1** a word or phrase used again and again for effect; slogan: *"No taxation without representation" was a political catchword during the Revolutionary War. Man is a creature who lives not upon bread alone but principally by catchwords* (Robert Louis Stevenson). **2a** one or other of the words at the top of the page of a dictionary or other reference book to indicate the first and last entries beginning on that page; guide word. **b** *Especially British.* the word at the head of a reference-book article; entry word. **c** the first word of the following page of a book, formerly added in the lower right-hand corner of each page. **3** an actor's or performer's cue, especially of one word.

catch|work (kach′wėrk′), *n.* an artificial watercourse or series of watercourses for irrigating lands lying on the slopes of hills.

catch|y (kach′ē), *adj.,* **catch|i|er, catch|i|est.** *Informal.* **1** easy to remember; attracting attention or interest: *a catchy title for a book. The new musical play has several catchy tunes.* **2** *Figurative.* that is misleading; tricky; deceptive: *The third question on the test was catchy; everyone in the class gave the wrong answer.* **3** occurring irregularly; fitful; spasmodic: *The wind was very catchy.*
—catch′i|ly, *adv.* **—catch′i|ness,** *n.*

cat-claw (kat′klô′), *n.* = cat's-claw.

cat cracker, = catalytic cracker.

cat cracking, = catalytic cracking.

cat distemper, = feline enteritis.

cate (kāt), *n. Archaic.* a delicacy to eat; dainty: *feed on cates* (Shakespeare).
[variant of Middle English *acate* < Old North French *acat* a purchase < *acater* buy; see etym. under **cater**[1]]

cat|e|che|sis (kat′ə kē′sis), *n., pl.* **-ses** (-sēz). oral instruction in religious matters, by question and answer, especially to prepare for baptism or confirmation.
[< Late Latin *catēchēsis* < Greek *katēchēsis* < *katēchein* teach orally]

Pronunciation Key: hat, āge, cãre, fär; let, ēqual, tėrm; it, īce; hot, ōpen, ôrder; oil, out; cup, půt, rüle; child; long; thin; ᴛʜen; zh, measure; ə represents **a** in about, **e** in taken, **i** in pencil, **o** in lemon, **u** in circus.

cat|e|chet|ic (kat′ə ket′ik), *adj.* = catechetical.

cat|e|chet|i|cal (kat′ə ket′ə kəl), *adj.* **1** teaching by questions and answers. **2** like or according to a catechism. —**cat′e|chet′i|cal|ly,** *adv.*

cat|e|chet|ics (kat′ə ket′iks), *n.* the art of catechetical instruction.

cat|e|chin (kat′ə chin, -kin), *n.* a yellow, acid, powdery compound used in tanning and in textile dyeing. *Formula:* $C_{15}H_{14}O_6$ [< *catech*(u) + *-in*]

cat|e|chise (kat′ə kīz), *v.t., v.i.,* **-chised, -chis|ing.** = catechize. —**cat′e|chis′er,** *n.*

cat|e|chism (kat′ə kiz əm), *n.* **1a** a book of questions and answers about religion, used for teaching religious doctrine, especially of a given church: *Each student in Sunday school was handed a catechism.* **b** the series of questions and answers in such a book: *The older Sunday school students knew the catechism by heart.* **2** a set of questions and answers about any subject. **3** *Figurative.* a long or formal set of questions: *Candidates for political office are often given a catechism by the party they belong to. "Yes, Mother," I answer, and we begin an unvarying catechism that ends after ten minutes* (New Yorker). **4** *Obsolete.* catechetical instruction; catechesis. [< Late Latin *catēchismus* < Greek *katēchízein* teach orally; see etym. under **catechize**]

cat|e|chis|mal (kat′ə kiz′məl), *adj.* of or having to do with, a catechism.

cat|e|chist (kat′ə kist), *n.* **1** a person who catechizes, especially a deep and persistent questioner: *The detective was an experienced catechist.* **2** a teacher of religious principles to catechumens.

cat|e|chis|tic (kat′ə kis′tik), *adj.* of a catechist or catechism. —**cat′e|chis′ti|cal|ly,** *adv.*

cat|e|chis|ti|cal (kat′ə kis′tə kəl), *adj.* = catechistic.

cat|e|chize (kat′ə kīz), *v.,* **-chized, -chiz|ing.** —*v.t.* **1** to teach by questions and answers. **2** to question about the elements of religious belief: *He was closely catechized by a commission of members of the consistory* (Christopher Morley). **3** to question closely: *I will catechize the world for him* (Shakespeare). —*v.i.* to teach a catechism. Also, **catechise.** [< Latin *catēchizāre* < Greek *katēchízein* teach orally, variant of *katēchein* < *kata-* thoroughly + *ēchein* to sound] —**cat′e|chi|za′tion,** *n.* —**cat′e|chiz′er,** *n.*

cat|e|chol (kat′ə chōl, -kōl), *n.* = pyrocatechol. [< *catech*(u) + *-ol*[1]]

cat|e|chol|a|mine (kat′ə chōl′ə mēn, -kōl′-), *n.* any one of a class of hormones, such as adrenalin, that acts upon the nerve cells: *Stress liberates certain hormones called catecholamines into the human bloodstream which will promptly raise the blood pressure* (Science News Letter).

cat|e|chu (kat′ə chü, -kyü), *n.* a hard, brown, sticky, brittle substance obtained from certain acacia trees of India and Southeast Asia; cutch. After boiling and hardening for sale it is used in dyeing and tanning and as an astringent in medicine. Also, **cashoo, cachou.** [< New Latin *catechu,* alteration of Malay *kachu*]

cat|e|chu|ic (kat′ə chü′ik, -kyü′-), *adj.* of or having to do with catechu.

cat|e|chu|men (kat′ə kyü′mən), *n.* **1** a person who is being taught the elementary principles of Christianity. SYN: neophyte. **2** a person who is being taught the fundamentals of any field of study. SYN: novice. [< Latin *catēchūmenus* < Greek *katēchoumenos* one being instructed, present passive participle of *katēchein;* see etym. under **catechize**]

cat|e|chu|me|nal (kat′ə kyü′mə nəl), *adj.* having to do with a catechumen.

cat|e|chu|me|nate (kat′ə kyü′mə nāt), *n.* **1** the condition or position of a catechumen. **2** a house for catechumens.

cat|e|chu|men|i|cal (kat′ə kyů men′ə kəl), *adj.* = catechumenal.

cat|e|gor|e|mat|ic (kat′ə gôr′ə mat′ik, -gor′-), *adj. Logic.* capable of being used by itself as a complete term, as a noun or an adjective. [< Greek *katēgórēma, -atos* a predicate + English *-ic*]

cat|e|gor|ic (kat′ə gôr′ik, -gor′-), *adj.* = categorical.

cat|e|gor|i|cal (kat′ə gôr′ə kəl, -gor′-), *adj.* **1a** without conditions or qualifications; positive: *His categorical answer left no doubt about his opinion. All we had from the union was a categorical "no" on all the points we raised* (Wall Street Journal). SYN: absolute, unconditional. **b** explicit; direct: *The ratification of the Ghent treaty ... was in no wise distinct and categorical* (John Motley). **2** of or in a category. —**cat′e|gor′i|cal|ly,** *adv.* —**cat′e|gor′i|cal|ness,** *n.*

categorical imperative, the ethical principle of Immanuel Kant that a person should act only in the way he would will all others to act in the same situation.

categorical syllogism, *Logic.* a syllogism consisting only of categorical propositions, or such as do not involve a condition or hypothesis.

cat|e|gor|ise (kat′ə gə rīz), *v.t.,* **-ised, -is|ing.** *Especially British.* categorize. —**cat′e|gor|is′er,** *n.*

cat|e|gor|ist (kat′ə gər ist), *n.* = categorizer.

cat|e|gor|ize (kat′ə gə rīz), *v.t.,* **-ized, -iz|ing.** to place in a category or categories; classify: *The Dalai Lama of Tibet, visiting India, categorized Europeans as "the red-faced people"* (New Yorker). —**cat′e|gor|i|za′tion,** *n.* —**cat′e|gor|iz′er,** *n.*

cat|e|go|ry (kat′ə gôr′ē, -gōr′-), *n., pl.* **-ries. 1** a group or division in classification; class: *The crabby old man places all people in two categories: those he likes and those he dislikes.* **2** *Logic.* **a** one of the modes or aspects of conception under which the mind, according to Kant, organizes the impressions received from the senses: *The Kantian categories differ from those of Aristotle in being subjective.* **b** one of the fundamental modes or aspects of existence recognized by Aristotle: *Substance, quantity, quality, space, and time are all categories.* [< Late Latin *catēgoria* < Greek *katēgoriā* assertion, ultimately < *kata-* in answer to + *agoreúein* speak < *agorá* assembly]

cat|e|lec|trode (kat′i lek′trōd), *n. Electricity.* = cathode. [< *cat-* + *electrode*]

cat|e|lec|tro|ton|ic (kat′i lek′trə ton′ik), *adj.* having to do with or exhibiting catelectrotonus.

cat|e|lec|trot|o|nus (kat′i lek′trot′ə nəs), *n.* the changed physical and physiological condition in the neighborhood of the cathode when a constant electrical current is passed through a piece of nerve or muscle. [< *cat-* + *electrotonus*]

ca|te|na (kə tē′nə), *n., pl.* **-nae** (-nē). a chain or connected series, especially a commentary or exegesis made up of excerpts from the works of the church fathers. [< Latin *catēna* chain]

ca|te|nac|ci|o (kä′tə nät′chē ō), *n.* a formation in soccer using four defenders in the defensive line, three players in midfield, and three on the attack: *Juventus ... represents the conservative, traditional style known as catenaccio* (Time). [< Italian]

cat|e|nane (kat′ə nān), *n. Chemistry.* a compound of carbon molecules interlocked like the links of a chain, but not chemically bonded together. [< Latin *catēna* chain + English *-ane*]

cat|e|nar|i|an (kat′ə nãr′ē ən), *adj.* = catenary.

cat|e|nar|y (kat′ə ner′ē; *especially British* kə tē′nər ē), *n., pl.* **-nar|ies,** *adj. Mathematics.* —*n.* the curve formed by a heavy, perfectly flexible cord, cable, or the like, hanging freely from two fixed points not in the same vertical line. —*adj.* having to do with or like a catenary. [< Latin *catēnārius* relating to a chain < *catēna* chain]

cat|e|nate (kat′ə nāt), *v.,* **-nat|ed, -nat|ing,** *adj.* —*v.t.* to link like a chain; connect in a series. —*adj.* having the nature or appearance of a chain. [< Latin *catēnāre* (with English *-ate*[1]) < *catēna* chain] —**cat′e|na′tion,** *n.*

cat|e|nat|ed (kat′ə nā′tid), *adj.* = catenate.

ca|ten|u|late (kə ten′yə lāt), *adj.* chainlike in form or appearance. [< Latin *catēnula* small chain (< *catēna* chain) + English *-ate*[1]]

ca|ter[1] (kā′tər), *v.i.* **1** to provide food and supplies, and sometimes service: *He runs a restaurant and also caters for weddings and parties.* SYN: purvey. **2** *Figurative.* to provide what is needed or wanted: *The Children's Palace in Shanghai is a recreation centre catering for children from 7 to 17 years old* (Manchester Guardian Weekly). *The sculptor also won honor in San Mateo, a suburb that caters to split-level executives* (Harper's). —*v.t.* to provide food or supplies for (a party, wedding, or other social function): *to cater an affair.* SYN: purvey. [< earlier *cater* buyer, Middle English *acatour* < Old North French *acateor* < *acater* buy < Vulgar Latin *accaptāre* acquire < Latin *ad-* to + *captāre* seize < *capere* take]

ca|ter[2] (kā′tər), *n. Obsolete or Archaic.* **1** four. **2** the four at cards or dice. [< French *quatre* four]

cat|er|an (kat′ər ən), *n. History.* a member of a band of marauders or fighters in the Scottish Highlands. [< Scottish Gaelic *ceathairne* peasantry, common soldiers]

cat|er-cor|ner (kat′ər kôr′nər), *adj., adv.* = catercornered. Also, **kitty-corner.**

cat|er-cor|nered (kat′ər kôr′nərd), *adj., adv.* —*adj.* diagonal; placed diagonally: *A cater-cornered walk crosses the park.* —*adv.* diagonally: *He walked cater-cornered across the park.* Also, **catty-cornered, kitty-cornered.** [< obsolete *cater* to set or move diagonally (< French *quatre* four) + *cornered*]

ca|ter-cous|in (kā′tər kuz′ən), *n.* **1** any person related in some respect to another: *cater-cousins in politics.* **2** intimate friend; close associate. [< obsolete *cater* four (< French *quatre*) + *cousin*]

ca|ter|er (kā′tər ər), *n.* **1** a person who provides food and supplies, and sometimes service, for parties, weddings, and other social functions. **2** *Figurative.* a person who caters in any way to the requirements of others.

ca|ter|ess (kā′tər is), *n.* a woman caterer.

ca|ter|ing (kā′tər ing), *n.* the providing and serving of food and refreshment for parties, entertainments, and other social functions.

***cat|er|pil|lar** (kat′ər pil′ər), *n.* **1** the larva or wormlike form in which insects such as the butterfly and the moth hatch from the egg. **2a** = caterpillar tractor. **b** any vehicle or machine that moves on endless belts or chains instead of wheels. **3** *Figurative.* a person who preys upon society: *the caterpillars of the commonwealth* (Shakespeare). [< Old North French *catepelose,* Old French *chatepelose* hairy cat < Latin *catta pilōsa*]

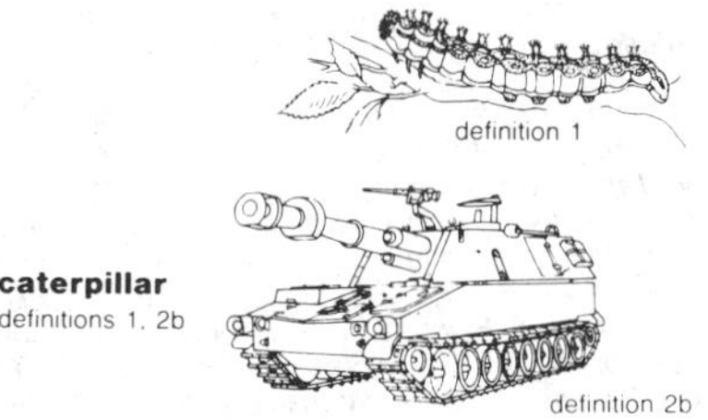
definition 1
***caterpillar** definitions 1, 2b
definition 2b

Cat|er|pil|lar (kat′ər pil′ər), *n. Trademark.* = caterpillar tractor.

caterpillar fungus, a fungus which grows upon the larvae of insects.

caterpillar tractor, a tractor that can travel over very rough ground on its two endless belts.

cat|er|waul (kat′ər wôl), *v., n.* —*v.i.* **1** (of cats) to utter long-drawn, wailing cries, especially in the night; give their characteristic cry at rutting time: *Dread midnight come, the cats 'gan caterwaul* (Jeremy Taylor). **2** *Figurative.* **a** to howl like a cat; screech: *The bagpipes caterwauled.* **b** to quarrel noisily: *Those that are concerned in another's Love and Honour, are ... always caterwauling* (Samuel Butler). —*n.* **1** the characteristic cry of a rutting cat. **2** *Figurative.* any sound, such as music or singing, likened to this; screech: *The lovely caterwaul, Tart solo, sour duet, and general squall,—These are our hymn* (Oliver Wendell Holmes). [Middle English *caterwrawe* < *cater* cat + *wrawe, wawe* wail, howl; perhaps influenced later by *howl, yowl*]

cat|er|waul|ing (kat′ər wô′ling), *n., adj.* —*n.* **1** = caterwaul. **2** *Figurative.* a whining or complaining: *There'll probably be a lot of caterwauling about the guaranteed annual wage* (Wall Street Journal). —*adj.* resembling the characteristic cry of a cat at rutting time.

cat eye, a highly sensitive television system for viewing objects in the dark, used especially in navigation and photographing stars and planets.

cat-eyed (kat′īd′), *adj.* **1** able to see in the dark. **2** having eyes like a cat, especially having an almond shape: *lovely, cat-eyed Yvonne* (Time).

cat|face (kat′fās′), *n.* a partly healed scar left especially by fire on the stem of a tree, or on lumber from it.

cat|fac|ing (kat′fā′sing), *n.* an injury to peaches caused by the punctures of various insects.

cat|fall (kat′fôl′), *n. Nautical.* the rope or tackle by which an anchor is hoisted to the cathead.

cat family, a family of carnivorous mammals including the domestic cat, the lion, tiger, jaguar, and the lynxes.

cat|fight (kat′fīt′), *n.* a quarrel, especially between women, marked by intense acrimony and spite: *The clash between the two queens [was] a catfight on the imperial level* (Punch).

cat|fish (kat′fish′), *n., pl.* **-fish|es** or (*collectively*) **-fish.** any one of several fishes without scales, having long, slender feelers around the mouth that look somewhat like a cat's whiskers. Catfish have sharp spines on the breast. See picture under **barb**[1].

cat-foot (kat′fůt′), *v.i.* to move in a cat-footed manner; go furtively like a cat: *Each night, he stole out of the ward with his knowing and insolent smile and cat-footed into the Rec Hall* (Leo Rosten).

cat-foot|ed (kat′fůt′id), *adj.* **1** having feet like those of a cat; digitigrade, with sharp, retractile claws. **2** soft-footed; noiseless; quiet; stealthy: *"We will meet by and by," the old, cat-footed hunter murmured under his breath as he urged me along the leafy path* (Atlantic).

cat|gut (kat′gut′), *n.* **1** a tough string made from the dried and twisted intestines of sheep or other animals, used to string violins and tennis rackets, and by surgeons for stitching wounds. **2** in humorous or contemptuous use: **a** a violin. **b** stringed instruments. [perhaps alteration of earlier *kit* small violin + *gut*]

Cath., Catholic.

cat-hammed (kat′hamd′), *adj.* having hams or thighs like those of a cat, as certain cattle and horses.

Cath|a|rine wheel (kath′ər in, kath′rin), = Catherine wheel.

Cath|a|rism (kath′ə riz əm), *n.* the doctrine of the Catharists.

Cath|a|rist (kath′ər ist), *n.* **1** a member of any one of various sects aiming at or professing a superior purity. **2** = puritan. [< Medieval Latin *Catharistae,* plural < Greek *katharistaí* pure < *katharízein* purify]

Cath|a|ris|tic (kath′ə ris′tik), *adj.* of or having to do with the Catharists.

cat|harp|ing (kat′härʹping), *n. Nautical.* one of the short ropes or iron cramps used to bind in the shrouds at the masthead, so that the yards may be braced up sharply. [origin uncertain]

ca|thar|sis (kə thär′sis), *n.* **1** a purging. **2** *Figurative.* an emotional purification or relief, especially by vicarious experience such as that provided by drama: *the catharsis of autobiography* (Newsweek). **3** *Psychoanalysis.* = abreaction. Also, **katharsis.** [< Greek *kátharsis* < *kathaírein* purge < *katharós* clean]

ca|thar|tic (kə thär′tik), *n., adj.* **—*n.*** a strong laxative. Epsom salts and castor oil are cathartics. SYN: purgative.

—*adj.* **1** strongly laxative. SYN: purgative. **2** *Figurative.* emotionally purifying: *Tart, cathartic virtue* (Emerson).

ca|thar|ti|cal (kə thär′tə kəl), *adj.* = cathartic.

cat haw, *Dialect.* the fruit of the hawthorn.

Ca|thay (ka thā′), *n. Archaic.* China. [< Medieval Latin *Cathaya;* apparently of Tartar origin]

cat|head (kat′hed′), *n.* a beam on the side of a ship near the bow. The anchor is hoisted and fastened to it.

ca|thec|tic (kə thek′tik), *adj. Psychoanalysis.* of cathexis; having to do with or resembling cathexis: *Cathectic subjects are normally inspirations as well as blind spots* (Alex Comfort).

ca|the|dra (kə thē′drə, kath′ə-), *n., pl.* **-drae** (-drē). **1a** a bishop's throne in a cathedral. **b** the episcopal rank, office, or diocese. **2** a seat of authority. [< Latin *cathedra* < Greek *kathédrā* seat < *kata-* down + *hédrā* seat. See etym. of doublet **chair, chaise.**]

ca|the|dral (kə thē′drəl), *n., adj.* **—*n.*** **1** the official church of a bishop. The bishop of a district or diocese has a throne in the cathedral. **2** a large or important church: *In the vast cathedral* [*Westminster Abbey*] *leave him* (Tennyson).

—*adj.* **1** having a bishop's throne: *cathedral churches.* **2a** of or proceeding from a pope's or bishop's throne; ex cathedra: *the cathedral utterances of Leo XIII.* **b** *Figurative.* of or characteristic of one in office or authority; authoritative; official; pontifical: *The style is too uniformly didactic, cathedral and declamatory* (George Bernard Shaw). **3a** of or like a cathedral: *a cathedral city.* **b** *Figurative.* appropriate to or suggestive of cathedrals: *Here aged trees cathedral walks compose* (Alexander Pope).

[< Late Latin *cathedrālis* of the (bishop's) seat < Greek *kathédrā* seat; see etym. under **cathedra**]

cathedral ceiling, a ceiling with exposed beams through which the sides of a sloping roof are visible: *By day, natural light floods the room from a huge skylight in the peak of the cathedral ceiling* (Good Housekeeping).

ca|the|draled (kə thē′drəld), *adj.* **1** having a cathedral. **2** like a cathedral.

ca|the|dral|esque (kə thē′drə lesk′), *adj.* like a cathedral: *cathedralesque churches.*

cathedral glass, an ornamental glass textured on one side so that it diffuses the light passing through it.

cath|e|drat|ic (kath′ə drat′ik), *adj.* **1** of or having to do with the bishop's cathedra or the episcopal see. **2** pronounced ex cathedra; authoritative. [< Medieval Latin *cathedraticus* < Latin *cathedra;* see etym. under **cathedra**]

ca|thep|sin (kə thep′sin), *n.* any one of a group of proteolytic enzymes that cause autolysis in animal cells and tissues. [< German *Kathepsin* < Greek *kathépsein* to boil down < *kata-* down, thoroughly + *hépsein* to boil]

Cath|e|rine wheel (kath′ər in, kath′rin), **1a** a wheel with spikes projecting from its rim. **b** *Heraldry.* the figure of such a wheel. **2** a firework which revolves like a wheel while burning; pinwheel: [*She*] *arrived at dinner fizzing like a Catherine wheel* (New Yorker). *He throws off ideas like a Catherine wheel* (Newsweek). **3** a circular window with radiating divisions; rose window. **4** (in embroidery) a wheellike combination of stitches radiating from a central point, serving to fill a round space or hole. **5** = cartwheel, a kind of handspring. Also, **Catharine wheel.** [< Saint *Catherine* of Alexandria, condemned to torture on the wheel]

cath|e|ter (kath′ə tər), *n. Medicine.* a slender rigid or flexible tube to be inserted into a passage or cavity of the body. A catheter may be used to remove urine from the bladder. [< Late Latin *cathetēr* < Greek *kathetḗr* < *kathīénai* to let down < *kata-* down + *hīénai* let, send]

cath|e|ter|ism (kath′ə tə riz′əm), *n.* the operation of using a catheter; catheterization. [< Latin *cathetērismus* < Greek *kathetērismós* < *kathetḗr* catheter]

cath|e|ter|ize (kath′ə tə rīz), *v.t.,* **-ized, -iz|ing.** to introduce a catheter into. **—cath′e|ter|i|za′tion,** *n.*

cath|e|tom|e|ter (kath′ə tom′ə tər), *n.* an instrument for measuring vertical distances, especially small differences of level. [< Greek *káthetos* perpendicular + English *-meter*]

cath|e|to|met|ric (kath′ə tə met′rik), *adj.* of or obtained by means of a cathetometer.

ca|thex|is (kə thek′sis), *n. Psychoanalysis.* **1** the libido fixed upon a particular object. **2** the affective value of an object. [< Greek *káthexis* a retention, ultimately < *kata-* back + *échein* to hold]

cath|ode (kath′ōd), *n.* **1** a negatively charged electrode. In an electrolytic cell or electron tube, electrons flow from the cathode to the anode. The filament in most vacuum tubes is a cathode. **2** the positive terminal of a battery or cell that sends out current. The carbon electrode in a dry cell is the cathode. Also, **kathode.** [< Greek *káthodos* a way down < *kata-* down + *hodós* way]

cathode rays, the invisible streams of electrons from the cathode in a vacuum tube. When cathode rays strike a solid substance, they produce X rays.

***cath|ode-ray tube** (kath′ōd rā′), a vacuum tube in which high-speed electrons are produced and passed through electromagnetic fields in the form of a beam. Cathode-ray tubes are used in reproducing images in television receivers, radar sets, and computer terminals.

***cathode-ray tube**

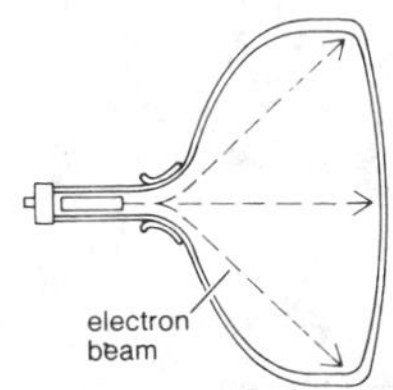

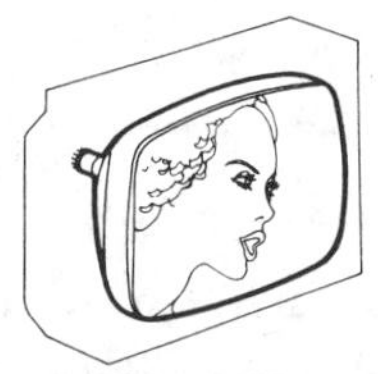

ca|thod|ic (kə thod′ik), *adj.* having to do with or resembling a cathode: *Spectacular results are being achieved with cathodic protection—that is, controlling the flow of electric currents that produce corrosion* (Wall Street Journal).

ca|thod|o|graph (kə thod′ə graf, -gräf), *n.* a photograph taken with cathode rays.

cath|o|dog|ra|phy (kath′ə dog′rə fē), *n.* photography by cathode rays. [< *cathode* + *-graphy*]

ca|thod|o|lu|mi|nes|cence (kə thod′ə lü′mə nes′əns), *n.* a phosphorescent or fluorescent glow excited by the action of cathode rays.

cath|o|lic (kath′ə lik, kath′lik), *adj.* **1a** of interest or use to all people: *Music makes a catholic appeal to all ages, races, and classes of men.* SYN: general. **b** having sympathies with all; broad-minded; liberal: *I bless my stars for a taste so catholic* (Charles Lamb). **c** of the whole Christian Church; ecumenical. SYN: tolerant. **2** including all; universal: *Science is catholic; it knows no frontiers.* SYN: all-inclusive, comprehensive, all-embracing. [< Latin *catholicus* < Greek *katholikós* universal < phrase *kath' hólou* in general < *katá* in respect to + *hólos* whole]

Cath|o|lic (kath′ə lik, kath′lik), *adj., n.* **—*adj.*** **1** of the Christian church governed by the Pope; Roman Catholic: *a Catholic country like France* (Henry Morley). **2** of the ancient, undivided Christian Church, or of its present representatives, including the Anglican, Orthodox, and Roman Catholic Churches: *the Holy Catholic Church.* **3** of, concerned with, or affecting Roman Catholics: *Catholic emancipation.*

—*n.* a member of a Catholic church, especially the Roman Catholic Church.

ca|thol|i|cal|ly (kə thol′ə klē), *adv.* in a catholic manner. Also, **catholicly.**

Catholic Church, = Roman Catholic Church.

Catholic Epistle, one of the General Epistles of the New Testament, not addressed to a particular church.

ca|thol|i|cism (kə thol′ə siz əm), *n.* = catholicity.

Ca|thol|i|cism (kə thol′ə siz əm), *n.* the faith, doctrine, organization, and methods of the Roman Catholic Church.

cath|o|lic|i|ty (kath′ə lis′ə tē), *n., pl.* **-ties. 1** universality; wide prevalence: *the catholicity of an idea.* **2** broad-mindedness; liberalness: *a catholicity of taste in art.*

Cath|o|lic|i|ty (kath′ə lis′ə tē), *n.* = Catholicism.

ca|thol|i|cize (kə thol′ə sīz), *v.t., v.i.,* **-cized, -ciz|ing.** to make or become catholic or universal.

Ca|thol|i|cize (kə thol′ə sīz), *v.t., v.i.,* **-cized, -ciz|ing.** to make or become Catholic. **—Ca|thol′i|ci|za′tion,** *n.*

ca|thol|ic|ly (kə thol′ə klē), *adv.* = catholically.

ca|thol|i|con (kə thol′ə kən), *n.* a universal remedy; cure-all; panacea. [< French *catholicon* < neuter form of Greek *katholikós* universal; see etym. under **catholic**]

ca|thol|i|cos (kə thol′ə kəs, -kos), *n., pl.* **-cos|es, -coi** (-koi). any one of the heads of certain self-governing churches in the Eastern Church, such as the Armenian and Syrian churches. [< Late Greek *katholikós* < Greek *katholikós* universal; see etym. under **catholic**]

Cath|o|my|cin (kath′ə mī′sin), *n. Trademark.* novobiocin, an antibiotic.

cat hop, two cards of the same denomination left in the dealing box for the last turn in faro. [origin uncertain]

cath|o|scope (kath′ə skōp), *n.* an instrument for exhibiting the optical effects of X rays. [< *catho*(de) + *-scope*]

cat|i|on (kat′ī′ən), *n.* **1** a postively charged ion. During electrolysis, cations move toward the negative pole (contrasted with *anion*). **2** an atom or group of atoms having a positive charge. Also, **kation.** [(coined by Faraday) < Greek *katadown* + *ión* going < *iénai* go]

cat|i|on|ic (kat′ī on′ik), *adj.* of or like a cation: *Nearly all of the long-lived fission nuclides are cationic and virtually all soils have an appreciable cation exchange capacity* (Bulletin of Atomic Scientists).

cat|kin (kat′kin), *n.* the soft, downy or scaly, pointed cluster of flowers, having no petals, which grows on the willow, birch, alder, and poplar; ament; cattail. Catkins grow from the apex, have unisexual flowers, and usually drop off after flowering. *The pussy willow develops furry catkins and its twigs are often used as decorations* (E. L. Little). See picture under **alder.** [< *cat* + *kin*]

cat|lad|der (kat′lad′ər), *n.* a scaling ladder used especially for climbing on the sloping roofs of houses.

cat|like (kat′līk′), *adj.* **1** like a cat; stealthy; cattish: *catlike in movement. With lazy, catlike attitudes* (New Yorker). **2** like that of a cat: *catlike eyes.*

cat|ling (kat′ling), *n.* **1** a little cat; kitten. **2** catgut for a violin, lute, or the like. **3** *Rare.* a long, narrow knife used in surgery.

cat|li|nite (kat′lə nīt), *n.* = pipestone. [< George *Catlin,* 1796-1872, an American painter and student of Indian life + *-ite*[1]]

cat man, = cat burglar.

cat|mint (kat′mint′), *n.* = catnip.

cat|nap (kat′nap′), *v.i.,* **-napped, -nap|ping.** to take a cat nap; doze or nap briefly: *He has the true fisherman's capacity to catnap standing up* (Manchester Guardian Weekly). **—cat′nap′per,** *n.*

cat nap, a short nap or doze.

cat|nep (kat′nep), *n.* = catnip.

cat|nip (kat′nip), *n.* a plant with strongly scented leaves that cats like. Catnip has spikes of small, blue or pinkish flowers and belongs to the mint family. [American English < *cat* + *nip,* perhaps variant of *nep* catnip]

ca|toc|tin (kə tok′tin), *n. Geology.* a protruding mass of rock which rises above the general level because of its greater resistance to erosion. [< *Catoctin,* a mountain, creek, and town in Maryland]

cat-o'-moun|tain (kat′ə moun′tən), *n.* = catamountain.

Ca|to|ni|an (kə tō′nē ən), *adj.* of, having to do with, or resembling the Roman statesman Cato the Elder (234 B.C.-149 B.C.) or his great-grandson, the Roman patriot and Stoic philosopher, Cato the Younger (95 B.C.-46 B.C.), both remarkable for the severity of their manners: *Catonian austerity or obstinacy* [< Latin *Catōniānus*]

Ca|ton|ic (kə ton′ik), *adj.* = Catonian.

***cat-o'-nine-tails** (kat′ə nīn′tālz′), *n., pl.* **-tails.** a whip consisting of nine pieces of knotted cord fastened to a handle. It was formerly used as a means of punishment in the navy. [*The captain*] *and his officers held the ship on the sea by the*

Pronunciation Key: hat, āge, cãre, fär; let, ēqual, tėrm; it, īce; hot, ōpen, ôrder; oil, out; cup, pu̇t, rüle; child; long; thin; ᴛʜen; zh, measure; ə represents a in about, e in taken, i in pencil, o in lemon, u in circus.

grace of God and the cat-o'-nine-tails (Scientific American).

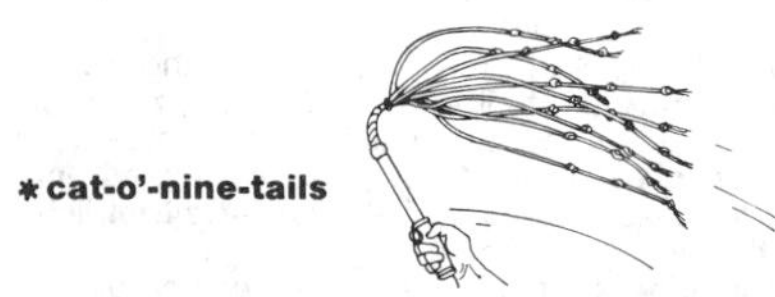

✱cat-o'-nine-tails

ca|top|tric (kə top′trik), *adj., n.* **—*adj.*** of or having to do with the reflection of light or catoptrics. **—*n.*** = catoptrics. **—ca|top′tri|cal|ly,** *adv.*

ca|top|tri|cal (kə top′trə kəl), *adj.* = catoptric.

ca|top|trics (kə top′triks), *n.* the branch of optics dealing with the properties of reflected light, especially light reflected from mirrors or polished surfaces. [< Greek *katoptrikós* pertaining to a *kátoptron* mirror < *kata-* opposite + *op-*, root meaning "see" + *-tron* instrument]

ca|top|tro|man|cy (kə top′trə man′sē), *n.* divination among the ancients by means of a mirror. [< Greek *kátoptron* mirror + *manteíā* divination]

ca|top|tro|man|tic (kə top′trə man′tik), *adj.* having to do with or of the nature of catoptromancy.

ca|tos|to|mid (kə tos′tə mid), *n., adj.* **—*n.*** any one of a family of freshwater cyprinoid fishes comprising the true suckers.
—*adj.* having to do with the catostomids; belonging to this family.
[< New Latin *Catostomidae* the family name < Greek *kátō* down + *stóma* mouth]

ca|tos|to|moid (kə tos′tə moid), *adj., n.* **—*adj.*** **1** resembling a catostomid. **2** belonging to the family of the suckers. **—*n.*** = catostomid.

cat rig, the typical rig of a catboat, consisting of a single mast set well forward, with a large sail extended by a boom and a gaff. There is no jib.

cat-rigged (kat′rigd′), *adj.* rigged like a catboat.

cats and dogs, *U.S. Slang.* **1** worthless shares of stock. **2** worthless or unsalable merchandise.
rain cats and dogs. See under **cat**[1].

CAT scan, 1 an X-ray picture made by computerized axial tomography: *CAT scans depict cross sections or slices of any region of the body as seen looking down through the patient, head to foot* (Irwin J. Polk). **2** = CAT scanner. **3** = CAT scanning.

CAT scanner, a machine that takes X-ray pictures by computerized axial tomography.

CAT scanning, the act or process of taking X-ray pictures by computerized axial tomography.

cat's-claw (kats′klô′), *n.* any one of several prickly shrubs of the Southwestern United States: *The cat's-claw . . . is common in the canyons and on hillsides* (Southern Sierran).

✱cat's cradle, a child's game played with a string looped over the fingers of both hands.

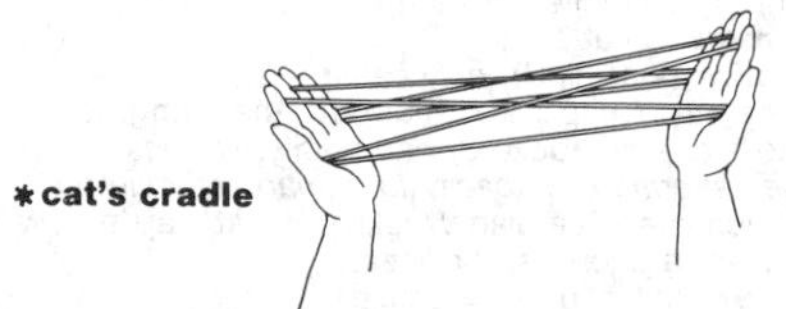

✱cat's cradle

cat-scratch disease or **fever** (kat′skrach′), a disease of humans following a cat scratch, of unknown cause, possibly viral, which affects the lymphatic system.

cat's-eye (kats′ī′), *n.* **1** a semiprecious gem, especially a variety of chrysoberyl, which shows a central streak of reflected light, suggesting the pupil of a cat's eye. **2** a small reflector set in the curb of a road, or in a post, fence, etc., near a road to guide motorists at night. **3** a marble used in the game of marbles, whose markings suggest the eye of a cat.

cat's-foot (kats′fu̇t′), *n.* **1** any of a large genus of composite plants with very small, white, tubular flowers. **2** = ground ivy. **3** mountain cudweed.

cat|skin (kat′skin′), *n.* skin or furry pelt of the cat.

cat|skin|ner (kat′skin′ər), *n.,* or **cat skinner,** *Slang.* an operator of a tractor.

cat's-meat (kats′mēt′), *n.* horsemeat prepared as cat food.

cat's-paw or **cats|paw** (kats′pô′), *n.* **1** a person used by another to do something unpleasant or dangerous (in allusion to the fable of a fox that used the paw of a cat to rake chestnuts out of the fire): *If I could ferret out the cat's-paw, he might lead me to her* (New Yorker). **2** a light breeze that ruffles a small stretch of water. **3** *Nautical.* a hitch or twist in the bight of a rope, forming two eyes through which a toggle may be passed. See picture under **hitch.**

cat's-tail (kats′tāl′), *n.* **1** any one of several plants with parts suggesting the tail of a cat, such as the cattail or certain species of horsetail. **2** = timothy.

cat|stick (kat′stik′), *n.* the stick or bat in certain games, such as tipcat.

cat|sup (kech′əp, kat′səp), *n.* = ketchup.

cat's whisker, = cat whisker.

cat|tail (kat′tāl′), *n.* **1a** a tall marsh plant with flowers in long, round, furry, brown spikes; club grass; flag. **b** any one of various other related plants. **2** = catkin or ament.

cat|ta|lo (kat′ə lō), *n., pl.* **-loes** or **-los.** a hybrid of the bison and the domestic cow. Also, **catalo.** [American English < *catt*(le) + (buff)*alo*]

cat|ter|y (kat′ər ē), *n., pl.* **-ter|ies.** a place for the keeping and breeding of cats.

cat|ti|man|doo (kat′ə man′dü), *n.* a kind of gum obtained in the East Indies from certain species of the spurges. It is used as a cement. [< Telugu *kattimandu*]

cat|tish (kat′ish), *adj.* **1** = catlike. SYN: feline. **2** = catty. **—cat′tish|ly,** *adv.* **—cat′tish|ness,** *n.*

cat|tle (kat′əl), *n.pl.* **1a** animals of the ox family raised for meat, milk, or hides; cows, bulls, steers, heifers, and calves; oxen. **b** (formerly) any farm animals; livestock. **2** *Figurative.* any low, despised people: *Boys and women are . . . cattle of this color* (Shakespeare). **3** *Archaic.* vermin; insects. [< Old North French *catel* < Medieval Latin *capitāle* property, originally neuter of Latin *capitālis.* See etym. of doublet **capital, chattel.**]

cattle cake, *British.* processed food for cattle, in the form of cakes or blocks.

cattle egret, a small, white heron with yellow bill and back, native to the Old World but now found in parts of South America and the Southeastern United States.

cattle feeder, a device for supplying feed in regulated quantities to racks or mangers.

cat|tle-grid (kat′əl grid′), *n. British.* a cattle guard.

cattle grub, a larva of the warble fly.

✱cattle guard, parallel iron bars over a hole near a railroad crossing or pasture entrance to prevent cattle from wandering but letting vehicles pass.

✱cattle guard

cat|tle|lift|er (kat′əl lif′tər), *n. British.* cattle rustler.

cat|tle|man (kat′əl mən), *n., pl.* **-men. 1** a man who raises cattle. **2** a cattle owner.

cattle pen, an enclosure for cattle.

cattle plague, = rinderpest.

cattle run, a wide extent of grazing land.

cattle show, 1 an exhibition of beef and dairy cattle by breeds for prizes, with a view to the promotion of their improvement and increase. In the United States it is usually combined with an agricultural fair. **2** *U.S. Informal.* a public gathering of Presidential candidates running in a primary election campaign: *In a cattle show, national candidates are herded into a ballroom, which then becomes a kind of stockyard-showcase* (William Safire).

cattle stall, an arrangement other than a halter or tie for securing cattle to a rack or manger.

cattle tick, a brown tick, especially of the Southern United States and South America, that carries the protozoan which causes Texas fever; Texas fever tick.

cattle warble, = heel fly.

cat|tle|ya (kat′lē ə), *n.* a highly ornamental epiphytic orchid, native of tropical America from Mexico to Brazil. See picture under **orchid.** [< New Latin *Cattleya* the genus name < William *Cattley,* died 1832, an English collector of plants]

cat|ty[1] (kat′ē), *adj.,* **-ti|er, -ti|est. 1** mean and spiteful: *She made enemies of many of her neighbors with her catty comments.* **2** catlike; cattish. **3** of or connected with cats; interested in cats: *The question of open judging at cat shows has frequently been discussed in catty circles* (F. Simpson). [< *cat* + *-y*[1]] **—cat′ti|ly,** *adv.* **—cat′ti|ness,** *n.*

cat|ty[2] (kat′ē), *n., pl.* **-ties.** an Asian unit of weight varying slightly in different countries, generally equal to about 1⅓ pounds avoirdupois. [< Maylay *kati*]

cat|ty-cor|nered (kat′ē kôr′nərd), *adj., adv.* = cater-cornered.

Ca|tul|li|an (kə tul′ē ən), *adj.* of, having to do with, or characteristic of the Roman lyrical poet Catullus, celebrated for his love poems and the elegance of his style. [< Latin *Catulliānus*]

CATV (no periods), **1** cable TV. **2** community antenna television (a cable television system of television reception using community antenna).

✱cat|walk (kat′wôk′), *n.* a narrow place to walk, on a bridge, near the ceiling of a stage, in or around heavy machinery, or in an airship: *Connected to the boiler room by two catwalks, is the engine room* (New Yorker).

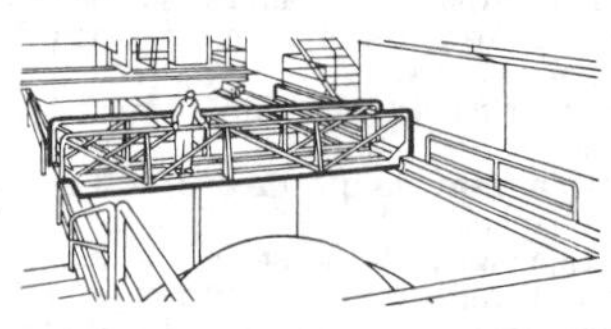

✱catwalk

cat whisker, *Radio.* a very fine, adjustable wire used to make electrical contact with the crystal in a crystal detector. Also, **cat's whisker.**

Cau|ca|sian (kô kā′zhən, -shən; -kazh′ən, -kash′ən), *n., adj.* **—*n.*** **1** a member of the so-called white race, including the chief peoples of Europe, southwestern Asia, northern Africa, the Western Hemisphere, Australia, and New Zealand; Caucasoid. **2** a person born or living in the Caucasus. **—*adj.*** **1** of or having to do with the so-called white race. **2a** of or having to do with the Caucasus or its inhabitants. **b** denoting or having to do with any one of the languages of the Caucasus region, such as Georgian.
[< New Latin *Caucasianus* < the *Caucasus* Mountains (erroneously supposed to be the early home of the European peoples)]

Cau|cas|ic (kô kas′ik), *adj.* Caucasian.

Cau|ca|soid (kô′kə soid), *adj., n.* **—*adj.*** = Caucasian (def. 1). **—*n.*** a member of one of the Caucasian races; Caucasian.

cau|cus (kô′kəs), *n., v.* **—*n.*** **1** *U.S.* a meeting of members or leaders of a political party to make plans, choose candidates, or decide how to vote: *The Craig forces countered with an earlier call for a caucus, and elected their own man* (Time). **2** a similar group in a local council or political party in England. **3** any similar meeting for the private discussion of policy.
—*v.i.* to hold a caucus: *The Public Works Committee caucused privately* (Wall Street Journal).
[American English; probably of Algonkian origin. Compare Virginian *caucauasu* elder.]

cau|dad (kô′dad), *adv. Zoology.* toward the tail or posterior end. [< Latin *cauda* tail + *ad* toward]

cau|dal (kô′dəl), *adj.* **1** of or near the tail; at the posterior end of an animal: *caudal gills of the damsel-fly.* **2** like a tail. [< Latin *cauda* tail + English *-al*[1]] **—cau′dal|ly,** *adv.*

caudal anesthesia, anesthesia produced by means of an injection in the lower part or caudal end of the spine.

caudal fin, a fin located at the hind end of fishes. See picture under **fin.**

cau|date (kô′dāt), *adj.* having a tail. [< Latin *cauda* tail + English *-ate*[1]]

cau|dat|ed (kô′dā tid), *adj.* = caudate.

cau|da|tion (kô dā′shən), *n.* caudate condition.

cau|dex (kô′deks), *n., pl.* **-di|ces** (-də sēz), **-dex|es.** *Botany.* **1** the woody base of a perennial plant, which sends up new herbaceous stems each year in place of the old. **2a** the stem or main axis of a tree. **b** the stem of a palm or a tree fern. [< Latin *caudex, cōdex* trunk of a tree]

cau|di|cle (kô′də kəl), *n. Botany.* the slender, stalklike appendage of the masses of pollen in orchidaceous plants. [< New Latin *caudicula* (diminutive) < Latin *caudex* trunk, stem]

cau|dil|lis|mo (kô′dēl yēz′mō, -dē-; *Spanish* kou′ᴛʜēl yēs′mō, -ᴛʜē-), *n.* the rule of a caudillo.

cau|dil|lo (kô dēl′yō, -dē′-; *Spanish* kou′ᴛʜē′lyō, -yō), *n., pl.* **-los** (-yōz; *Spanish* -lyōs, -yōs). a military leader or dictator in a Spanish-speaking country. [< Spanish *caudillo* < Latin *capitellum* little head; see etym. under **cadet**]

cau|dle (kô′dəl), *n.* a warm drink for sick people, such as wine or ale thickened with gruel or soaked bread, sweetened, and spiced. [< Old North French *caudel* < Medieval Latin *caldellum* (diminutive) < Latin *caldum* hot drink, neuter of *caldus* hot < *calēre* be hot]

caught (kôt), *v.* past tense and past participle of **catch:** *He caught the ball. The mouse was caught in the trap.*
be caught short, to be without something when needed; be unprepared: *Dealers will be forced to stock up in the next three months or risk being caught short in the Christmas buying period* (Wall Street Journal).

caul (kôl), *n.* **1** a portion of the membrane enclosing a child in the womb that is sometimes found clinging to the head at birth. It was supposed to bring good luck and to safeguard against drowning. **2** *Rare.* the great omentum. [perhaps < Old French *cale* a kind of little cap]

cauld (kôld, käld, kôd), *adj., n. Scottish.* cold.

caul|dron (kôl′drən), *n.* = caldron.

cau|les|cent (kô les′ənt), *adj.* having an obvious

stem rising above the ground. [< Latin *caulis* stalk + English *-escent*]

cau|li|cle (kô′lə kəl), *n. Botany.* a small or rudimentary stem (applied to the initial stem in the embryo, to distinguish it from the cotyledons). [< Latin *cauliculus* (diminutive) < *caulis* stalk]

cau|li|flow|er (kô′lə flou′ər, kol′ē-), *n.* **1** a plant having a solid white head with a few leaves around it. It is an annual plant, a species of cole, which belongs, with the cabbage, to the mustard family. **2** its head, which is eaten as a vegetable. [< earlier *cole florie,* half-translation of New Latin *cauliflora* < Latin *caulis* cabbage, cole; stalk + *flōs, flōris* flower]

cauliflower ear, an ear that has been misshapen by injuries received in boxing, or the like.

cau|li|form (kô′lə fôrm), *adj.* having the form of a stem; stemlike. [< Latin *caulis* stalk, stem + English *-form*]

cau|line (kô′lin, -līn), *adj.* **1** of or belonging to a stem. **2** of or growing from the upper part of a stem, as opposed to the basal part. [< Latin *caulis* stalk + English *-ine*[1]]

cau|lis (kô′lis), *n., pl.* **-les** (-lēz). the stalk or stem of a plant, especially an herbaceous plant. [< Latin *caulis*]

caulk (kôk), *v.t.* to fill up (a seam, crack, or joint) so that it will not leak; make watertight. Shipbuilders caulk wooden boats with oakum and tar. Plumbers caulk joints in pipe with lead, string, or a caulking compound. Also, **calk.** [< Old North French *cauquer* tread, press in < Latin *calcāre* < *calx, calcis* heel] —**caulk′er,** *n.*

caulk|age (kô′kij), *n. Nautical.* oakum, cotton fiber, or other material used in caulking the seams of a vessel's planking.

caulk|ing iron (kô′king), a broad-bladed, dull-edged chisel used in driving waterproofing material into seams, cracks, or joints, such as the seams of a wooden vessel.

cau|lo|car|pous (kô′lə kär′pəs), *adj.* bearing fruit repeatedly upon the same stem. [< Greek *kaulós* stalk + *karpós* fruit + English *-ous*]

cau|lome (kô′lōm), *n.* **1** the axis or stem of a plant. **2** a structure morphologically corresponding to it. [< Greek *kaulós* stalk + *-ōma* a growth]

caus., causative.

cau|sa (kô′zə), *n. Latin.* cause.

caus|a|bil|i|ty (kô′zə bil′ə tē), *n.* the capability of being caused.

cau|sa cau|sans (kô′zə kō′zənz), *Latin.* original cause; primary cause: *The apron per se is the causa causans of her ladyship's displeasure* (Punch).

caus|al (kô′zəl), *adj., n.* —*adj.* **1** of a cause; acting as a cause: *one supreme causal God* (Phillips Brooks). **2** having to do with cause and effect: *Hume ... owes his fame to one keen observation ...; that the term cause and effect was loosely ... applied to what we know only as consecutive, not at all as causal* (Emerson). **3** showing a cause or reason. "Because" is a causal conjunction.
—*n.* a word or form that shows cause or reason.

cau|sal|gi|a (kô zal′jē ə), *n.* an intense, burning pain, usually neuralgic. [< Greek *kaûsis* burning heat + *álgos* pain]

cau|sal|i|ty (kô zal′ə tē), *n., pl.* **-ties. 1** the relation of cause and effect; the principle that nothing can happen or exist without a cause: *A belief in causality ... characterizes all valuable minds* (Emerson). **2** causal quality or agency: *Nature has no independent activity, no causality of its own* (Leo H. Grindon).

caus|al|ly (kô′zə lē), *adv.* in a causal manner; by way of cause and effect: *The world of experience must be for intelligence a system of things causally connected* (Robert Adamson).

cau|sa si|ne qua non (kô′zə sī′nē kwä non′), *Latin.* **1** an indispensable cause. **2** (literally) cause without which not.

cau|sa|tion (kô zā′shən), *n.* **1** a causing or being caused: *It sometimes happens that we are punished for our faults by incidents, in the causation of which these faults had no share* (Samuel Taylor Coleridge). **2** whatever produces an effect; a cause or causes: *A serious work, to say nothing of a tragic one, cannot hope to achieve truly high excellence short of an investigation into the whole gamut of causation of which society is a manifest and crucial part* (Arthur Miller). **3** the relation of cause and effect; the principle that nothing can happen or exist without a cause; causality: *historical causation is so endlessly complex* (Bulletin of Atomic Scientists).

caus|a|tion|ism (kô zā′shə niz əm), *n.* the theory or principle or causation. —**caus|a′tion|ist,** *n.*

caus|a|tive (kô′zə tiv), *adj., n.* —*adj.* **1** being a cause; productive (of an effect): *That which is essentially causative of all being must be causative of its own* (Samuel Taylor Coleridge). **SYN:** generative. **2** expressing causation. *Example:* In *enrich, en-* is a causative prefix.
—*n.* a word or form expressing causation.
—**caus′a|tive|ly,** *adv.* —**caus′a|tive|ness,** *n.*

cau|sa|tiv|i|ty (kô′zə tiv′ə tē), *n.* the fact of being causative; causative quality.

cause (kôz), *n., v.,* **caused, caus|ing.** —*n.* **1** a person, thing, or event that makes something happen: *The flood was the cause of much damage.* **2** a reason or occasion for action; ground; motive: *The hero's return was a cause for celebration.* **SYN:** incentive, inducement. See syn. under **reason. 3** good reason; reason enough: *You have no cause to complain. He was angry without cause.* **4** a subject or movement in which many people are interested and to which they give their support: *World peace is the cause she likes to work for.* **5** a matter for a law court to decide; lawsuit. **6** *Figurative.* anything that requires a decision; a matter in dispute: *The cause was decided by vote.*
—*v.t.* to make happen; make do; bring about: *The fire caused much damage. A loud noise caused me to jump.* **SYN:** prompt, induce, effect.
make common cause with, to join efforts with; side with; help and support: *before they made common cause with either French or English* (H. H. Wilson).
show cause, to present a reason or reasons why an order, judgment, or conviction should not be executed or confirmed: [*The judge*] *directed the strikers to show cause why they should not be enjoined from "illegal picketing" of the plant* (Wall Street Journal).
[< Latin *causa.* See etym. of doublet **chose**[2].]
—**caus′a|ble,** *adj.* —**caus′er,** *n.*
—*Syn. n.* **1 Cause, occasion** mean whatever makes something happen. **Cause** applies to a thing, person, situation, action, etc., that brings about an effect sooner or later: *A poor foundation was the cause of the building's collapse.* **Occasion** applies to that which brings forth the effect by giving the opportunity for something to happen: *The earthquake was the occasion of the building's collapse.*

cause cé|lè|bre (kōz sā leb′rə), *pl.* **causes cé|lè|bres** (kōz sā leb′rə), *French.* **1** a famous or notorious case, especially in law: *The trial of the astronomer Galileo for heresy in 1633 has long been a "cause célèbre"* (New York Times). **2** a situation or episode attracting intense and widespread interest. **3** (literally) a celebrated cause.

cause|less (kôz′lis), *adj.* **1** without any known cause; happening by chance. **2** without good reason; not having reason enough: *causeless fear of the dark.* —**cause′less|ly,** *adv.*

cau|se|rie (kō′zə rē′; *French* kōz rē′), *n.* **1** an informal talk or discussion; chat: *His attractive and most vivacious wife, whose conversational impulses have a wonderful way of advancing, instead of interrupting, a causerie* (New York Times). **2** a short, informal written article, as in a periodical. [< French *causerie* < Old French *causer* talk, learned borrowing from Latin *causārī* plead a (legal) cause, dispute < *causa* cause]

cau|seuse (kō zœz′), *n. French.* a small sofa for two persons.

***cause|way** (kôz′wā′), *n., v.* —*n.* **1** a raised road or path, usually built across wet ground or shallow water: *A narrow causeway ran across the bog. The three-lane causeway linking New Orleans with the north shore of Lake Pontchartrain opens to traffic this week* (Newsweek). **2** a main road; highway: *The car followed the causeway over the hills.*
—*v.t.* **1** to provide with a causeway. **2** to pave with cobbles or pebbles: *streets flagged instead of being causewayed* (Scott).
[Middle English *cauce weye* < *cawce, cawcy* causey + *way*]

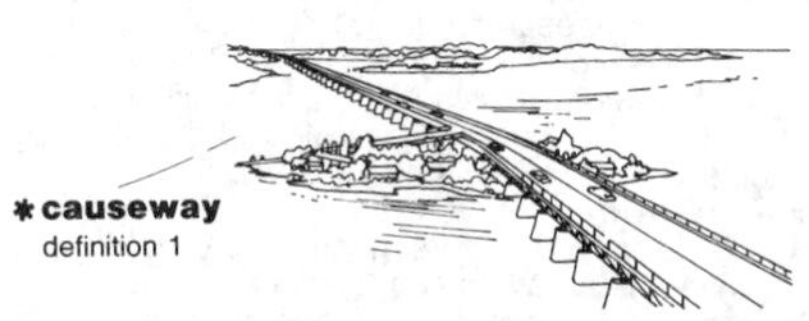

***causeway** definition 1

cau|sey (kô′zē), *n., pl.* **-seys,** *v.* —*n.* = causeway.
—*v.t.* to pave with small stones.
[< Old North French *caucie* < Medieval Latin (*via*) *calciata* paved way, ultimately < Latin *calx, calcis* limestone]

cau|sid|i|cal (kô zid′ə kəl), *adj.* having to do with the pleader or the pleading of legal causes. [< Latin *causidicus* lawyer, pleader (< *causa* cause + *dīcere* say) + English *-al*[1]]

caus|tic (kôs′tik), *adj., n.* —*adj.* **1** that burns or destroys flesh; corrosive. Lye is caustic soda or caustic potash. **2** *Figurative.* very critical or sarcastic; stinging; biting: *The speaker gave a caustic answer to the man who interrupted with a silly question. The coach's caustic remarks made the football players angry.* **SYN:** satirical, mordant, scathing. **3** in optics: **a** of or denoting a curved surface to which are tangent all the rays of light proceeding from a fixed point and reflected or refracted by a curved surface. A caustic surface by reflection is called a *catacaustic* surface; that by refraction a *diacaustic* surface. **b** of or denoting the curve formed by a plane section of such a surface.
—*n.* **1** a substance that burns or destroys flesh; corrosive substance: *My warts were burned away by the caustic put on them.* **2** (in optics) a caustic curve or surface.
[< Latin *causticus* < Greek *kaustikós* < *kaíein* burn] —**caus′ti|cal|ly,** *adv.*

caus|ti|cal (kôs′tə kəl), *adj.* = caustic.

caus|tic|i|ty (kôs tis′ə tē), *n.* **1** caustic quality. **2** a burning, pungent taste. **3** the property of destroying or corroding organic tissue.

caustic potash, = potassium hydroxide.

caustic soda, a brittle, solid, white substance used in medicine, manufacturing, and for cleaning out drains; sodium hydroxide: *Caustic soda is an important raw material in the refinement of bauxite, the ore from which aluminum is extracted* (Wall Street Journal). *Formula:* NaOH

cau|tel (kô′təl), *n. Archaic.* **1** caution or wariness. **2** a precaution. **3** a warning or direction. **4** subtlety; craftiness; wiliness. [< Old French *cautele* < Latin *cautēla* < *cavēre* beware]

cau|te|lous (kô′tə ləs), *adj. Archaic.* **1** cautious or wary: *I have been cautelous in quoting mine authorities* (Scott). **2** crafty.

cau|ter (kô′tər), *n.* a surgical instrument for burning or cauterizing. [< Late Latin *cautēr* < Greek *kautḗr* branding iron < *kaíein* burn]

cau|ter|ant (kô′tər ənt), *n., adj.* —*n.* a caustic or cauterizing substance.
—*adj.* having to do with cautery; that cauterizes; caustic.

cau|ter|ize (kô′tə rīz), *v.t.,* **-ized, -iz|ing. 1** to burn with a hot iron or a caustic substance. Doctors sometimes cauterize wounds to prevent bleeding or infection. **SYN:** sear. **2** *Figurative.* to render insensible; deaden the feelings of: *Custom soon cauterizes human sympathy* (Robert Southey). —**cau′ter|i|za′tion,** *n.*

cau|ter|y (kô′tər ē), *n., pl.* **-ter|ies. 1** an instrument or substance used in cauterizing. **2** a cauterizing. [< Latin *cauterium* < Greek *kautḗrion* branding iron (diminutive) < *kautḗr* < *kaíein* burn]

cau|tion (kô′shən), *n., v.* —*n.* **1** great care; regard for safety; unwillingness to take chances: *Use caution in crossing streets.* **SYN:** prudence, wariness. **2a** a warning: *A sign with "Danger" on it is a caution.* **SYN:** admonition, advice, counsel. **b** *Military.* one or more explanatory words spoken before the word of command in giving an order: *In the order "shoulder arms," "shoulder" is the caution and "arms" the word for command.* **3** *Informal.* a very unusual person or thing: *The way she vamps him is a caution* (Atlantic). **4** *Obsolete.* a precaution.
—*v.t.* to urge to be careful; warn: *The policeman cautioned us against playing in that busy street.* **SYN:** See syn. under **warn.**
[< Old French *caution,* learned borrowing from Latin *cautiō, -ōnis* < *cavēre* beware]

cau|tion|ar|y (kô′shə ner′ē), *adj.* urging to be careful; warning: *This experience had a cautionary effect.*

cautionary town, a town whose control and revenues are granted by a government to a foreign power as security for the payment of a debt or the performance of an obligation. Certain strongholds in the Netherlands, especially the cities of Flushing, Briel, and Rammekens, were thus pledged to the English crown in the time of Elizabeth I.

cau|tion|er (kô′shə nər), *n.* **1** a person who cautions or advises. **2** a person who gives security for another; surety.

caution money, money deposited by students against misconduct, breakage of laboratory equipment, or other property.

cau|tion|ry (kô′shən rē), *n.* (in Scottish law) the act of giving security for another; suretyship.

cau|tious (kô′shəs), *adj.* very careful; taking care to be safe; not taking chances: *A cautious driver never drives his car too fast.* **SYN:** See syn. under **careful.** —**cau′tious|ly,** *adv.* —**cau′tious|ness,** *n.*

cav., **1** cavalier. **2** cavalry. **3** cavity.

Cav., Cavalry: *the 1st U.S. Cav.*

cav|al|cade (kav′əl kād′, kav′əl kād), *n.* **1** a procession of persons riding on horses, in carriages, or in automobiles: *The parade began with*

Pronunciation Key: hat, āge, cãre, fär; let, ēqual, tėrm; it, īce; hot, ōpen, ôrder; oil, out; cup, pu̇t, rüle; child; long; thin; ᴛʜen; zh, measure; ə represents **a** in about, **e** in taken, **i** in pencil, **o** in lemon, **u** in circus.

a cavalcade of city officials riding in big open cars. **2** a series of scenes or events: *a cavalcade of sports.* [< Middle French *cavalcade* < Italian *cavalcata* < *cavalcare* ride horseback < Late Latin *caballicāre* < Latin *caballus* a nag]

cav|a|lier (kav′ə lir′), *n., adj., v.* **—*n.*** **1** a horseman, mounted soldier, or knight: *The cavaliers with sabers drawn charged their horses into the attacking army.* **2a** a courteous gentleman; gallant: *I saw the bud-crowned Spring go forth ... to greet staid ancient cavaliers* (Emerson). **b** a courteous escort for a lady.
—*adj.* **1** careless in manner; free and easy; offhand: *He did not take me seriously and gave a gay, cavalier reply. Very cavalier, indeed, to go out to walk, without waiting to see us* (Maria Edgeworth). **2** proud and scornful; haughty; arrogant: *People were often irritated by his cavalier attitude toward them. This cavalier tone from an unknown person ... did not please me* (Thomas Carlyle). SYN: supercilious, disdainful.
—*v.i.* **1** to play the cavalier: *I must fly from the University forsooth to run a cavaliering* (Thomas Shadwell). **2** to be haughty or domineering: *cavaliering it here over half a dozen persons of distinction* (Samuel Richardson).
—*v.t.* to act as escort or cavalier to (a lady): *from his cavaliering the ladies Percy and Mortimer* (C. Cowden Clarke).
[< Middle French *cavalier* < Italian *cavaliere* knight; horseman < Late Latin *caballārius* < Latin *caballus* a nag. See etym. of doublets **caballero, chevalier.**] **—cav′a|lier′ness,** *n.*

Cav|a|lier (kav′ə lir′), *n., adj.* in English history: **—*n.*** a person who supported Charles I in his struggle with Parliament from 1640 to 1649; Royalist. **—*adj.*** of the Cavaliers; Royalist.

cav|a|lier|ism (kav′ə lir′iz əm), *n.* **1** the practices or principles of cavaliers, especially of the adherents of Charles I of England. **2** an expression characteristic of the Cavalier party.

cav|a|lier|ly (kav′ə lir′lē), *adv., adj.* **—*adv.*** in a cavalier manner; disdainfully: *In some Hollywood quarters the report from Britain was dismissed cavalierly* (New York Times).
—*adj.* characteristic of a cavalier; knightly; haughty.

Cavalier poets, a group of English poets writing during the reign of Charles I, including Herrick, Lovelace, Suckling, and Carew, famous especially for their lyric poetry.

ca|val|la (kə val′ə), *n., pl.* **-la** or **-las. 1** any one of certain carangoid fishes, especially a large mackerellike food fish found off tropical America and north to Cape Cod; crevalle. **2** a variety of Spanish mackerel. [< Portuguese *cavalla* horse mackerel < *cavallo* horse < Latin *caballus* nag]

ca|val|ly (kə val′ē), *n., pl.* **-lies.** = cavalla.

cav|al|ry (kav′əl rē), *n., pl.* **-ries. 1** *Military.* **a** soldiers who fight on horseback; a branch of an army consisting of such troops (now mostly obsolete): *At 19, he went to Mexico where he joined the Mexican Army cavalry for two years to perfect his horsemanship* (Newsweek). **b** soldiers who fight from armored vehicles; a branch of an army in which supplies and soldiers are conveyed by motor vehicles. Animals are employed only occasionally. *Abbr:* Cav. **2** horsemen; horses. **3** *Obsolete.* horsemanship [< Middle French *cavalerie* < Italian *cavalleria* mounted militia; knighthood < *cavaliere* cavalier]

cav|al|ry|man (kav′əl rē mən), *n., pl.* **-men.** a soldier in the cavalry.

ca|vate (kā′vāt), *adj.* hollowed out, as a class of prehistoric dwellings. [< Latin *cavātus,* past participle of *cavāre* hollow out < *cavus* hollow]

cav|a|ti|na (kav′ə tē′nə; *Italian* kä vä tē′nä), *n., pl.* **-ne** (-nā). a short, simple song; melody; air: *A simple melody in an opera is a cavatina.* [< Italian *cavatina*]

cave[1] (kāv), *n., v.,* **caved, cav|ing.** **—*n.*** **1** a hollow space underground, especially one with an opening in the side of a hill or mountain; cavern or den: *He found four caves in the side of Lime Hill. A cave has three zones: the open area just inside the entrance, a twilight region and the perpetually dark interior* (Scientific American). **2** a hollow place of any kind; cavity. **3** = cave-in: *During the earthquake a "cave" had taken place in the drift* (Bret Harte). **4** (in English politics) a cave of Adullam.
—*v.t.* to hollow out; make into a cave: *as if the ground were caved full of hollow galleries* (Holme Lee). **—*v.i.*** to cave in: *He dug his cellar for the new part too near the house ... and it has caved and let one end of the house down* (Thoreau).
cave in, a to fall in; sink: *The weight of the snow caused the roof of the cabin to cave in. Two brothers ... were at work ... dismantling an old pit shaft, when a portion of the sides caved in* (Manchester Guardian). **b** to cause to fall in; smash: *had not the river floods caved in the bank* (Fortescue Cuming). **c** *Informal, Figurative.* to give in; yield; submit: *The Portuguese government finally became weak-kneed and ordered De Carvalho to cave in to the Communist demands* (Atlantic).
[< Old French *cave,* learned borrowing from Latin *cava* hollow (places) < *cavus* hollow]
—cave′like′, *adj.*

ca|ve[2] (kā′vē), *interj., v. British Slang.* **—*interj.*** beware! look out! **—*v.t.*** to be on guard against; beware: *Cave the dog!*
[< Latin *cave,* imperative of *cavēre* beware]

cave[3] (kàv), *n. French.* **1** a wine cellar. **2** a small, intimate cabaret in such a cellar.

ca|ve|a (kā′vē ə), *n., pl.* **-ve|ae** (-vē ē). **1** (in ancient Rome) a cage or den for wild beasts. **2** the auditorium of a Roman theater or amphitheater. [< Latin *cavea.* See etym. of doublet **cage.**]

ca|ve|at (kav′ē ät, -at; kā′vē at), *n.* **1** a legal notice given to a law officer or some legal authority not to do something until the person giving notice can be heard: *He entered a caveat against issuing a patent.* **2** *Figurative.* a warning; admonition; caution: *Although [she] cites these opinions with apparent agreement, this reviewer wants to enter a caveat* (Scientific American). [< Latin *caveat* let him beware]

ca|ve|at emp|tor (kā′vē at emp′tôr), *Latin.* let the buyer beware; you buy at your own risk: *Although subsidy publishing [by vanity presses] is advertised as a useful adjunct to trade publishing—as, indeed, it sometimes is—the dictum of caveat emptor is nowhere more applicable* (Harper's).

ca|ve|a|tor (kā′vē ā′tər), *n.* a person who notifies by means of a caveat.

cave bear, a large extinct bear of the Quaternary geological period, contemporary with man, whose fossil has been found in the caves of Europe.

ca|ve ca|nem (kā′vē kā′nem), *Latin.* beware the dog.

cave cricket, = camel cricket.

cave drawing, one of the specimens of paleolithic pictorial art which have been found in caves in various parts of the world.

cave dweller, 1 a person who lived in a cave in prehistoric times; a cave man. **2** a person who lives in a cave, especially a member of any of those groups in some countries of the Middle East where poverty is extreme.

cave hyena, an extinct hyena whose fossil has been found in many caves of Great Britain along with the bones of other extinct animals.

cave-in (kāv′in′), *n. Informal.* **1** a caving in; collapse: *a tunnel cave-in, the cave-in of a mine.* **2** a place where something has caved in.

cav|el (kav′əl), *n. Nautical.* a wooden cleat or the like to which sheets or other ropes are belayed. [< Old North French *keville,* Old French *cheville,* < Latin *clāvicula* (diminutive) < *clāvis* key]

cave lion, an extinct lion whose fossil has been found in European caves containing the remains of extinct animals.

cave man, 1 a man who lived in a cave in prehistoric times; cave dweller: *The first painter may have been a cave man who stained his fingers with the juices of the berries he was picking and then began to play at making pretty hen tracks on some convenient rocky slab* (Abraham B. Cohen). SYN: troglodyte. **2** *Informal, Figurative.* a rough, crude man: *He was a gorilla in appearance, a cave man in behavior.*

cav|en|dish (kav′ən dish), *n.* a softened and sweetened smoking tobacco pressed into cakes, then flaked or shredded. [< a proper name]

cave of A|dul|lam (ə dul′əm), (in English politics) a secession, or group of people who secede, from a political party on a particular issue (from a speech by John Bright comparing the seceders of the English Liberal Party in 1886 to the followers of David who joined him in the cave of Adullam where David fled to escape King Saul. (In the Bible, I Samuel 22-1, 2).

cave painting, = cave drawing.

cav|er (kā′vər), *n.* a person who explores or studies caves as an avocation; spelunker.

cav|ern (kav′ərn), *n., v.* **—*n.*** a large cave.
—*v.t.* **1** to enclose in or as if in a cavern: *Sickness sits cavern'd in his hollow eye* (Byron). **2** to hollow out; excavate: *The rock was caverned out to make a tunnel.*
[< Middle French *caverne,* learned borrowing from Latin *caverna* < *cavus* hollow]

cav|er|nic|o|lous (kav′ər nik′ə ləs), *adj.* inhabiting caverns; dwelling in caves. [< Latin *caverna* cavern + *colere* to dwell in + English *-ous*]

cav|ern|ous (kav′ər nəs), *adj.* **1a** like a cavern; large and hollow: *a cavernous cellar. This was a cavernous structure that had once been an aquarium* (New Yorker). **b** *Figurative.* deep-set: *cavernous eyes.* **2** characteristic of caverns: *cavernous darkness.* **3** *Figurative.* hollow-sounding; resonant:*a cavernous voice.* **4** full of caverns: *cavernous mountains.* **5** full of cavities or hollows; porous: *Pumice stones are cavernous.*
—cav′ern|ous|ly, *adv.*

cavernous respiration, a hollow respiratory sound sometimes heard over a defective cavity in a lung.

cavernous sinus, a venous sinus of the cranial cavity, lying on the side of the body of the sphenoid bone.

cav|er|nu|lous (kə vėr′nyə ləs), *adj.* full of little cavities or sockets, as those of the gums of the teeth. [< Latin *cavernula* small cavity (< *caverna* cave) + English *-ous*]

cav|es|son (kav′ə sən), *n.* **1** a noseband of iron, leather, or wood, fastened to a headstall or strap to make a horse manageable. **2** a halter with such a noseband. [< French *caveçon*]

ca|vet|to (kə vet′ō; *Italian* kä vāt′tō), *n., pl.* **-vet|ti** (-vet′ē; *Italian* -vāt′tē), **-tos.** a shallow, concave molding, in section usually a simple quarter circle, often used on or under a cornice. [< Italian *cavetto* (diminutive) < *cavo* hollow < Latin *cavus*]

cav|i|ar or **cav|i|are** (kav′ē är, kä′vē-; kav′ē är′), *n.* a salty relish made from the eggs of sturgeon or certain other large fish, eaten as an appetizer: *For a $15 minimum, the proletarian elite ... could eat dinner (caviar, chicken, and ice cream)* (Newsweek).
caviar to the general, unpalatable to those who have not acquired a taste for it; not appreciated by common people: *For the play I remember pleas'd not the million, 'twas caviare to the general: but it was an excellent play* (Shakespeare).
[< French *caviar* < Italian *caviaro* < Turkish *havyar*]

cav|i|corn (kav′ə kôrn), *adj., n. Zoology.* **—*adj.*** having hollow horns.
—*n.* a cow, sheep, goat, etc., with hollow horns.
[< Latin *cavus* hollow + *cornū* horn]

ca|vie (kā′vē), *n. Scottish.* a hencoop. Also, **cavy.** [perhaps < Middle Dutch *kēvie,* ultimately < Latin *cavea* cage, coop < *cavus* hollow]

cav|il (kav′əl), *v.,* **-iled, -il|ing** or (*especially British*) **-illed, -il|ling,** *n.* **—*v.i.*** to find fault without good reason; raise trivial objections; carp: *He cavils about the minor points in the rules of the game. Those who do not value Christianity ... cavil about sects and schisms* (Daniel Webster). SYN: criticize. **—*v.t.*** to find fault with without good reason; raise trivial objections about; carp at: *There are men whose intellectual pride cavils and perverts ... every truth of the revelation of God* (H. E. Manning).
—*n.* **1** a trivial objection; petty criticism: *I must add one cavil: the pot is an eyesore* (New Yorker). **2** the raising of trivial objections; caviling: *His measures were sure to be the subject of perpetual cavil* (John L. Motley). SYN: carping.
[< Old French *caviller,* learned borrowing from Latin *cavillārī* to jeer < *cavilla* a scoffing] **—cav′il|er, cav′il|ler,** *n.*

cav|il|ing (kav′ə ling), *adj.* disposed to find fault; carping; captious: *a caviling logician.* **—cav′il|ing|ly,** *adv.*

cav|il|ling (kav′ə ling), *adj. Especially British.* caviling. **—cav′il|ling|ly,** *adv.*

cav|ing (kā′ving), *n.* = spelunking.

cav|i|tar|y (kav′ə ter′ē), *adj.* **1** having a cavity; hollow. **2** *Medicine.* of or having to do with cavitation.

cav|i|ta|tion (kav′ə tā′shən), *n.* **1** *Physics.* the formation of cavities in a fluid downstream from an object moving in it, as behind the moving blades of a propeller: *Cavitation is produced by high speed propellers and causes heavy erosions in armour plates, a headache for naval engineers* (Gabriele Rabel). **2** *Medicine.* the formation of cavities in any body structure, especially in tuberculous lungs. **3** any one of the cavities thus formed.

cav|i|tied (kav′ə tēd), *adj.* **1** having cavities. **2** having an intestinal cavity.

cav|i|ty (kav′ə tē), *n., pl.* **-ties. 1** a hollow place; hole. Cavities in teeth are caused by decay. SYN: pocket, pit. See syn. under **hole. 2** an enclosed space inside the body: *the abdominal cavity.* [< Old French *cavite* < Late Latin *cavitās* < Latin *cavus* hollow]

cavity resonator, any enclosure in which waves of a given frequency will resonate, especially a metal chamber for reinforcing microwave oscillations: *The cavity resonator ... is used to produce high electric fields to filter signals, to provide circuits in vacuum tubes, and so on* (Scientific American).

cav|i|u|na wood (kav′ē ü′nə), a rosewood obtained from a tall leguminous tree of Brazil. [< Portuguese (Brazil) *cabiuna* < a Tupi word]

ca|vo-ri|lie|vo (kä′vō rē lye′vō), *n., pl.* **-vos.** sculptural relief largely sunk below the surface in which the highest portions are level with the general surface; hollow relief. [< Italian *cavo-rilievo* hollow relief]

ca|vort (kə vôrt′), *v.i. U.S.* to prance about; jump around: *The horses cavorted with excitement.*

The boy cavorted about the field, racing and tumbling. [American English; earlier *cavaut*]

CAVU (no periods), *Aeronautics.* Ceiling and Visibility Unlimited.

ca·vum (kā′vəm), *n., pl.* **-va** (-və). *Anatomy.* the cavity of any organ, such as the heart. [< Latin *cavum* < *cavus* hollow]

ca·vy[1] (kā′vē), *n., pl.* **-vies.** any one of several South American rodents, related to the porcupine. Cavies are short-tailed or tailless and burrow in the ground. The guinea pig is the best known. It is commonly raised as a pet or laboratory animal. [< New Latin *Cavia* the genus name < Carib (Guiana) *cabiai*]

ca·vy[2] (kā′vē), *n., pl.* **-vies.** *Scottish.* cavie.

caw (kô), *n., v.* —*n.* the harsh cry made by a crow or raven. —*v.i.* to make this cry. [imitative]

caw·quaw (kô′kwô), *n.* a porcupine of northern North America whose spines were often used for ornamentation by the Indians. [American English < Algonkian (compare Cree *kaukwa*)]

Cax·ton (kak′stən), *n.* **1** a book printed by William Caxton, the first English printer. **2** a style of printing type in black letters like that used by Caxton.

cay (kā, kē), *n.* a low island; reef; key. [earlier *cayo* < Spanish, shoal, rock. Compare etym. under **key**[2].]

cay·enne (kī en′, kā-), *n.,* or **cayenne pepper, 1** a very hot, biting powder made from the seeds or fruit of two kinds of pepper plant; red pepper. Cayenne is used as a seasoning in cooking and as a gastric stimulant in medicine. **2** either one of the plants from which this powder is obtained. [associated with *Cayenne,* French Guiana, but apparently < Tupi (Brazil) *quiýnha* or *kyýnha*]

cay·man (kā′mən), *n., pl.* **-mans.** any animal of several genera of tropical American reptiles of the alligator family, having the abdomen covered by pairs of overlapping, bony plates: *in search of . . . giant anteaters, two-toed sloths, and fourteen-foot caymans* (New Yorker). Also **caiman.** [< Spanish *caimán,* probably < Carib (Colombia)]

Cay·man·i·an (kā man′ē ən), *adj., n.* —*adj.* of the Cayman Islands, a British colony in the Caribbean Sea, or its people. —*n.* a native or inhabitant of the Cayman Islands.

Ca·yu·ga (kā yü′gə, kī-), *n., pl.* **-ga** or **-gas,** *adj.* —*n.* **1** a member of a tribe of Iroquois Indians formerly living in western New York State. **2** the language of this tribe. —*adj.* of this tribe. [American English < Iroquoian (Cayuga) tribal name *kwĕñiogwĕnh* (literally) the place where locusts were taken out]

Cayuga duck, a duck of a native American breed, noted for egg laying.

Cay·use (kī yüs′), *n., pl.* **-use** or **-us·es.** a member of a tribe of Indians of northeastern Oregon.

cay·use (kī yüs′), *n. Western U.S.* **1** a pony bred by Indians. **2** any pony or horse. [American English < the *Cayuse* Indians, who bred ponies]

ca·zu·e·la de a·ve (kä′thü ā′lä də ä′vā), a thick Chilean soup consisting of chicken, potatoes, corn, rice, onions, and spicy peppers. [< Spanish *cazuela de ave* pan of fowl]

Cb (no period), columbium (chemical element).

CB (no periods), **1** chemical and biological: *CB weapons.* **2** citizens band (radio).

C.B., 1 Bachelor of Surgery (Latin, *Chirurgiae Baccalaureus*). **2** citizens band (radio). **3** *British.* Companion of the Bath.

C battery, an electric battery connected to the grid to regulate the flow of electrons in an electron tube.

CBC (no periods), Canadian Broadcasting Corporation.

C.B.E., Commander of (the Order of) the British Empire.

C.B.er or **CBer** (sē′bē′ər), *n. U.S. Informal.* a person who uses a citizens band radio: *Most C.B.ers start with channel 19, which is the truckers' and motorists' channel and thus is usually pretty active* (Michael Harnwood).

CBI (no periods) or **C.B.I.,** Confederation of British Industry.

CBO (no periods), Congressional Budget Office.

C-bomb (sē′bom′), *n.* cobalt bomb.

CBR (no periods), chemical, biological, radiological (warfare or weapons).

CBS (no periods), Columbia Broadcasting System.

CBW (no periods), chemical and biological warfare.

cc (no periods) or **cc., 1** carbon copy. **2** chapters. **3** cubic centimeter or centimeters.

c.c., 1 carbon copy. **2** cashier's check. **3** cubic centimeter or centimeters.

Cc (no period), cirro-cumulus.

C.C., an abbreviation for the following:
1 cashier's check.
2 chief clerk.
3a city council. **b** city councilor.
4 common councilman.
5 consular clerk.
6 county clerk.

C.C.A., 1 Chief Clerk of the Admiralty. **2** Circuit Court of Appeals.

CCC (no periods), **1** Civilian Conservation Corps. **2** Commodity Credit Corporation.

C.C.C.P., in the Russian alphabet, the initials of the Russian name of the Union of Soviet Socialist Republics.

CCD (no periods), charge-coupled device.

C.C.F. or **CCF** (no periods), Co-operative Commonwealth Federation (a Canadian political party founded in 1933 and largely absorbed in 1961 into the New Democratic Party).

C clef, a symbol in music that shows the position of middle C. It is called the alto clef when placed on the third line of the staff, and the tenor clef when placed on the fourth line of the staff.

ccm (no periods), centimeters.

CCS (no periods), combined chiefs of staff.

CCTV (no periods), closed-circuit television.

CCU (no periods), coronary care unit.

cd., cord or cords.

c.d., cash discount.

Cd (no period), cadmium (chemical element).

CD (no periods) or **C.D., 1** certificate of deposit. **2** civil defense. **3** compact disk: *Because there is no groove in a CD, there are none of the mechanical problems involved in keeping a phonograph needle in a groove* (Suburbia Today).

cd. ft., cord foot or feet.

Cdn., Canadian.

Cdr., commander.

CD-ROM (no periods), compact disk read-only memory (an optical disk used for permanent storage of a large amount of data).

Ce (no period), cerium (chemical element).

C.E., an abbreviation for the following:
1 chemical engineer.
2 Christian Education.
3 Christian Endeavor.
4 Christian Era.
5 Church of England.
6 civil engineer.
7 Common Era.

CEA (no periods), Council of Economic Advisers (an economic advisory board appointed by the President of the United States).

ce·a·no·thus (sē′ə nō′thəs), *n.* any plant of a genus of shrubs of the buckthorn family, many native to the western United States and Canada, and many cultivated for their clusters of blue, pink, or white flowers. [< New Latin *Ceanothus* < Greek *keánōthos* kind of thistle]

cease (sēs), *v.,* **ceased, ceas·ing,** *n.* —*v.i.* **1** to come to an end; stop: *The music ceased suddenly when she turned off the radio.* SYN: discontinue, quit, pause, desist. See syn. under **stop.** **2** *Obsolete.* to become extinct; pass away: *The inhabitants of the villages ceased, they ceased in Israel* (Judges 5:7). —*v.t.* to put an end to; stop: *Cease trying to lift more than you can.* —*n. Obsolete.* cessation.

without cease, without end; incessantly; endlessly: *space . . . extending without cease in all directions* (E. Conder).

[< Old French *cesser,* learned borrowing from Latin *cessāre* to cease from (frequentative) < *cēdere* withdraw]

cease and desist order, *U.S.* an order issued by a government agency or law court to stop some practice or activity regarded as unfair or injurious.

cease-fire (sēs′fīr′), *n.* a halt in military operations, especially for the purpose of discussing peace: *It was more of a cease-fire than a truce* (Harper's).

cease·less (sēs′lis), *adj.* going on all the time; never stopping; continual: *ceaseless effort, the ceaseless roar of the falls.* SYN: incessant, unceasing, perpetual. —**cease′less·ly,** *adv.* —**cease′less·ness,** *n.*

ce·ca (sē′kə), *n.* plural of **cecum.**

ce·cal (sē′kəl), *adj.* **1** of or having to do with the cecum; resembling the cecum: *cecal worms.* **2** ending blindly, like the cecum: *the cecal terminal of a duct.* Also, **caecal.** —**ce′cal·ly,** *adv.*

ce·cec·to·my (sē sek′tə mē), *n., pl.* **-mies.** surgical removal of the cecum. [< *cecum* + *-ectomy*]

ce·ci·form (sē′sə fôrm), *adj.* in the shape of a cecum.

ce·ci·tis (sē sī′təs), *n.* inflammation of the cecum. [< *cec*(um) + *-itis*]

ce·ci·ty (sē′sə tē), *n. Rare.* blindness. [< Latin *caecitās* < *caecus* blind]

ce·cos·to·my (sē kos′tə mē), *n., pl.* **-mies.** the making of an artificial opening into the cecum by surgery. [< *cecum* + Greek *stóma* an opening]

ce·cot·o·my (sē kot′ə mē), *n., pl.* **-mies.** surgical incision into the cecum. [< *cecum* + *-tomy*]

Ce·cro·pi·a moth (sə krō′pē ə), a large silkworm moth of the eastern United States. Its larvae feed on many trees and shrubs. [< New Latin *cecrops* the species name < *Cecrops*]

Ce·crops (sē′krops), *n. Greek Legend.* the founder of Athens and first king of Attica.

ce·cum (sē′kəm), *n., pl.* **-ca.** the first part of the large intestine. It is closed at one end. . . . *an operation becomes necessary to restore the flow of intestinal fluid through the ileum, which joins the large intestine in a kind of pouch called the cecum* (Newsweek). See the diagram of **digestion.** Also, **caecum.** [< New Latin (*intestinum*) *caecum* blind (intestine) < Latin, neuter of *caecus* blind]

CED (no periods), Committee for Economic Development (a U.S. nonprofit research organization for developing national economic policies.

ce·dant ar·ma to·gae (sē′dant är′mə tō′gē), *Latin.* **1** let the military give way to civil authority. **2** (literally) let arms yield to the toga.

ce·dar (sē′dər), *n., adj.* —*n.* **1** an evergreen tree with branches that spread widely, and fragrant, durable, reddish wood. The cedar belongs to the pine family. **2** any one of a number of trees of the cypress family, such as the red cedar. **3** the cryptomeria. **4** any one of a number of tropical trees, mostly of the mahogany family, of the West Indies and Central America. **5** the wood of any of these trees. Cedar is much used for lining clothes closets and making chests, cigar boxes, pencils, and posts. —*adj.* made of cedar. [< Old French *cedre,* learned borrowing from Latin *cedrus* < Greek *kédros* cedar, juniper]

cedar apple, 1 a strangely-shaped mass of tissue on the twigs of live cedar trees. **2** the fungus that forms or produces this mass.

ce·dar·bird (sē′dər bėrd′), *n.* = cedar waxwing.

cedar chest, a chest made of cedar as a protection against moths.

ce·dared (sē′dərd), *adj.* having cedars: *Cedared Lebanon* (Keats).

cedar elm, a valuable American elm tree of the lower Mississippi Valley and Texas. It sometimes attains a height of 80 feet.

ce·darn (sē′dərn), *adj. Poetic.* **1** of or having to do with cedar trees. **2** made of cedar: *The carven cedarn doors* (Tennyson).

cedar of Leb·a·non (leb′ə nən), a tall evergreen tree native to Asia Minor.

cedar rust, 1 a destructive disease caused by a fungus that begins its life cycle on cedar trees and later spreads to apple trees. **2** the fungus that produce this disease.

cedar waxwing, a small North American bird with a crest and small, red markings on its wings; cedarbird.

ce·dar·wood (sē′dər wu̇d′), *n.* **1** the wood of a cedar tree. **2** a woods of cedar.

cede (sēd), *v.t.,* **ced·ed, ced·ing.** to hand over to another; give up; surrender: *Spain ceded the Philippines to the United States. The state was authorized to condemn the island and cede it to the federal authorities in return for ten thousand dollars* (New Yorker). [< Latin *cēdere* yield, withdraw]

ce·dent (sē′dənt), *n.* a person who assigns property to another in Roman and Scottish law. [< Latin *cēdēns, -entis,* present participle of *cēdere* yield, cede]

ce·di (sē′dē), *n., pl.* **-dis.** the basic unit of money in Ghana, a note equal to 100 pesewas. [< Fanti *cedi* (originally) a cowrie]

***ce·dil·la** (sə dil′ə), *n.* a mark somewhat like a comma put under a *c* before *a, o,* or *u* in certain words to show that *c* represents the sound represented by *s. Example:* façade. [< Spanish *cedilla* (diminutive) < *ceda* < Latin *zēta* the letter *z* < Greek *zêta* (because it developed from a form of *z* formerly written after *c* to give it the sound of *s,* in certain Romance languages)]

***cedilla**

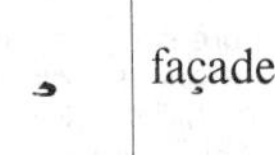

ce·drine (sē′drin), *adj.* of or like cedar. [< Latin *cedrinus* of cedar]

ce·drol (sē′drōl, -drol), *n.* a crystalline compound distilled from the oil of cedarwood, and used in the making of perfumes and disinfectants. *Formula:* $C_{15}H_{26}O$ [< Latin *cedrus* cedar + English *-ol*[2]]

ced·u·la (sej′ə lə; *Spanish* thā′ᴛʜü lä), *n.* **1** a type of security issued by some Spanish American governments. **2** in the Philippines: **a** a personal registration tax certificate: *Watchers from both major party groups checked as voters showed*

Pronunciation Key: hat, āge, cãre, fär; let, ēqual, tėrm; it, īce; hot, ōpen, ôrder; **oi**l, **ou**t; cup, pu̇t, rüle; **ch**ild; lo**ng**; **th**in; ᴛʜen; **zh**, measure; **ə** represents **a** in about, **e** in taken, **i** in pencil, **o** in lemon, **u** in circus.

their cedulas (*identifications*), *put ballots for President, two Vice Presidents, and 52 congressmen in envelopes, and dropped them in ballot boxes* (Newsweek). **b** the tax itself. **3** *Obsolete.* a permit or order issued by the Spanish government. [< Spanish *cédula* schedule]

cee (sē), *n., adj.* —*n.* the letter C.
—*adj.* shaped like the letter C: *Cee springs support the body of the carriage.*

CEEB (no periods) or **C.E.E.B.**, College Entrance Examination Board.

C.E.F., Canadian Expeditionary Force.

cei|ba (sā′bä, -bə; *for 2 also* sī′bə), *n.* **1** any one of a genus of deciduous trees of the bombax family, especially the silk-cotton tree, planted as a shade tree and as a source of kapok. **2** = kapok. [< Spanish *ceiba,* of Arawak (West Indies) origin]

ceil (sēl), *v.t.* **1** to put a ceiling in. **2** to cover the ceiling of. [perhaps < Old French *ciel* canopy; sky < Latin *caelum* heaven] —**ceil′er**, *n.*

cei|lidh (kā′lē), *n. Scottish.* an informal social gathering for storytelling and especially singing. [< Scottish Gaelic *cēilidhe*]

ceil|ing (sē′ling), *n.* **1a** the inside top covering of a room; the surface opposite the floor: *Lying on the couch, he studied the many cracks in the plaster ceiling of the room.* **b** any lining on the interior surface of a structural framework, such as the inside planking of the lower part of a ship. **c** the act or process of lining the roof of a room, especially with plaster or the like: *Ceiling is plasterers' work.* **2** *Aeronautics.* **a** the greatest height to which an aircraft can go under certain conditions; absolute ceiling: *The new jet plane has a ceiling of 100,000 feet.* **b** (also in meterology) the distance between the earth and the lowest clouds: *The weather report said that the ceiling was over 300 feet.* **c** the greatest altitude at which a particular aircraft is able, under standard air conditions, to climb at a rate faster than a specified rate, in the United States and Great Britain 100 feet or about 30 meters per minute; service ceiling. **d** the greatest altitude at which a person can fly without oxygen or other artificial aid. **3a** an upper limit set for prices, wages, rents, and the like; top limit: *Sometimes the government sets a ceiling on food prices. There was a ceiling on the amount the candidate could spend for his election campaign.* **b** a prescribed or natural upper limit for output; maximum: *a farm-production ceiling. Keeping a ceiling on any widespread plant expansions, however, is an acute shortage of the skilled artisans needed to produce pipe organs* (Wall Street Journal).
hit the ceiling, *U.S. Slang.* to become extremely excited or angry: *When the National People's Congress suggested sweeping relaxation of the farm collective program to quiet peasant unrest, Mao hit the ceiling* (Newsweek).
[< *ceil*]

ceil|inged (sē′lingd), *adj.* having a ceiling.
ceilinged off, cut off by a ceiling: *The massive roof of solid oak beams, ceilinged off . . .* (W. Urwick).

ceiling joists, small beams to which the ceiling of a room is attached.

ceiling light, *Meteorology.* a small searchlight used to determine the altitude of the lowest clouds.

ceil|om|e|ter (sē lom′ə tər), *n.* an electronic device for measuring and recording the height of a cloud formation.
[< *ceil*(ing) + *-meter*]

cein|ture (san′chər), *n.* a girdle or belt; cincture. [< French *ceinture* < Latin *cinctūra* girdle]

cel (sel), *n.* a sheet of transparent celluloid on which the drawings of animated cartoons are traced or painted.
[< cel(luloid)]

cel|a|don (sel′ə don), *n.* a pale-green color, much used in porcelain: *A pale-blue iris bends over a shallow celadon vase* (New Yorker). [< French *céladon* < *Céladon,* the sentimental hero of Honoré d'Urfé's romance, *Astrée*]

cel|a|don|ite (sel′ə də nīt), *n.* a green, earthy silicate of iron, magnesium, and potassium. [< *celadon* + *-ite*[1]]

Ce|lae|no (sə lē′nō), *n.* one of the Pleiades.

cel|an|dine (sel′ən dīn), *n.* **1** a plant with yellow flowers, belonging to the poppy family: *The bluebells, lovely as they are, have not submerged the primroses, the anemones, or even the celandines* (London Times). **2** a plant closely related to the buttercup, with yellow flowers and heartshaped leaves; lesser celandine.
[< Old French *celidoine,* learned borrowing from Latin *chelīdonia* < Greek *chelīdónion* < *chelīdṓn, -ónos* swallow[2] (because it appears with the arrival of swallows)]

Cel|a|nese (sel′ə nēz′, sel′ə nēz), *n. Trademark.* an acetate rayon material.

cel|as|tra|ceous (sel′ə strā′shəs), *adj.* belonging to the staff-tree family of plants, that includes the climbing bittersweet, spindle tree, and strawberry bush.
[< New Latin *Celastraceae* the family name (< Greek *kḗlastros* kind of evergreen)]

ce|la|tion (sə lā′shən), *n.* concealment, especially the concealing of pregnancy or delivery of a child. [< Latin *celāre* to conceal + English *-ation*]

cel|a|tive (sel′ə tiv), *adj.* of or having to do with the concealment of an organism from enemies or from its prey.

ce|leb (sə leb′), *n. Slang.* a celebrity: *Big hullabaloo already under way. Celebs. Champagne* (L. A. Sissman).

cel|e|brant (sel′ə brənt), *n.* **1** a person who performs a ceremony or rite. **2** the priest who performs Mass. **3** a person who celebrates; celebrator: *The two men meet at a neighborhood pub . . . before a company of celebrants* (New Yorker).

cel|e|brate (sel′ə brāt), *v.,* **-brat|ed, -brat|ing.**
—*v.t.* **1** to observe (a special time or day) with the proper activities: *We celebrated my birthday with a party and cake and ice cream.* SYN: solemnize. **2** to perform publicly with the proper ceremonies and rites: *The priest celebrates Mass in church.* SYN: solemnize. **3** to make known publicly; proclaim: *The stones themselves would find a voice, to celebrate his praise* (John Wesley). **4** to praise; honor: *His books are celebrated all over the world. He celebrated the surrounding mountains for their number and size and beauty* (Benjamin Jowett). SYN: laud.
—*v.i.* **1** to observe a festival or event with ceremonies or festivities: *On her birthday she was too sick to celebrate.* **2** to perform a religious ceremony, especially Mass. **3** *Informal.* to have a gay time: *When the children saw the snow they celebrated.*
[< Latin *celebrāre* (with English *-ate*[1]) attend in great numbers < *celeber, -bris* thronged, frequented]

cel|e|brat|ed (sel′ə brā′tid), *adj.* much talked about; famous; well-known: *Longfellow was a celebrated poet. He is celebrated, almost everywhere, for his deportment* (Dickens). SYN: noted, renowned, eminent.

cel|e|bra|tion (sel′ə brā′shən), *n.* **1** special services or activities in honor of a particular man, act, time, or day: *A Fourth of July celebration includes a dazzling display of fireworks.* **2** the act of celebrating: *celebration of a birthday.* **3** performance of a solemn ceremony: *the celebration of the Eucharist.*

cel|e|bra|tor (sel′ə brā′tər), *n.* a person who celebrates.

ce|leb|ra|to|ry (sə leb′rə tôr′ē, -tōr′-), *adj.* serving to celebrate; used in or designed for the celebration of an event: *Taking part in the dedication and celebratory services this weekend were world-famous Lutheran churchmen* (Newsweek).

ce|leb|ri|ty (sə leb′rə tē), *n., pl.* **-ties.** **1** a famous person; a person who is well known or much talked about: *Astronauts are celebrities around the world.* SYN: notable. **2** the condition of being well known or much talked about; fame: *His celebrity brought him riches.* SYN: renown, repute.

ce|leb|u|tante (sə leb′yə tänt, -tant), *n.* a young woman who becomes a celebrity on her first appearance in society or in the arts. [< *celeb-*(rity) + (deb)*utante*]

ce|ler|i|ac (sə ler′ē ak), *n.* **1** a variety of celery grown for its edible, turniplike root. **2** the root. [< *celery*]

ce|ler|i|ty (sə ler′ə tē), *n.* swiftness of movement; speed; rapidity: *celerity of flight, celerity of reply. [She] led her Concert Choir . . . with her usual rhythmic celerity and musical understanding* (New York Times). SYN: velocity, haste. [< Latin *celeritās* < *celer* swift]

cel|er|y (sel′ər ē, sel′rē), *n.* **1** a plant having long, crisp stalks with leaves at the top. It belongs to the parsley family. **2** its stalks, which are eaten either raw or cooked as a vegetable. [< French *céleri* < Italian (Lombard) *seleri* < Late Latin *selīnon* < Greek *sélīnon* parsley]

celery cabbage, = Chinese cabbage.

celery salt, a seasoning made from ground celery seed and salt.

***celesta**

***ce|les|ta** (sə les′tə), *n.* a musical instrument with a keyboard, resembling a small upright piano. The tones resemble the tinkle of small bells and are made by hammers hitting steel plates. [< French *célesta* < *céleste* heavenly < Latin *caelestis* < *caelum* heaven]

ce|leste (sə lest′), *adj.* sky-blue. [< French *céleste* heavenly; see etym. under **celesta**]

ce|les|tial (sə les′chəl), *adj., n.* —*adj.* **1** of the sky; having to do with the heavens: *The sun, moon, planets, and stars are celestial bodies. An artificial satellite is a man-made celestial body.* **2** of or belonging to heaven as the place of God and the angels; heavenly; divine: *celestial joy.* SYN: empyreal. **3** very good or beautiful: *Shakespeare's sonnets have a celestial style.*
—*n. Figurative.* an inhabitant of heaven.
[< Old French *celestiel* < Latin *caelestis* heavenly < *caelum* heaven] —**ce|les′tial|ly**, *adv.*

Ce|les|tial (sə les′chəl), *adj., n.* —*adj.* of the Chinese people or the former Chinese Empire; Chinese: *His Celestial Majesty.*
—*n.* (humorously) a native of China; a Chinese: *the country of the Celestials.*

Celestial City, heaven; the New Jerusalem.

Celestial Empire, the Chinese Empire.

***celestial equator**, *Astronomy.* the great circle which divides the celestial sphere into two imaginary equal halves, northern and southern, and represents the intersection of the plane of the earth's equator with the celestial sphere; equinoctial line: *Just as there is a pole of the sky over the earth's pole, so there is a celestial equator that hangs over the terrestrial one* (Bernhard, Bennett, and Rice). See diagram under **celestial pole.**

celestial globe, a globe which shows the position of the heavenly bodies just as an ordinary globe shows the continents, oceans, etc.

ce|les|ti|al|i|ty (sə les′chē al′ə tē), *n.* heavenly quality; heavenliness.

celestial latitude, *Astronomy.* the angular distance of a heavenly body from the nearest point on the ecliptic. It is counted positive or negative according to whether the body is north or south of the ecliptic.

celestial longitude, *Astronomy.* the angular distance eastward from the vernal equinox to the point on the ecliptic which is the foot of a great circle drawn from the pole of the ecliptic to the ecliptic through the body.

celestial mechanics, the branch of mechanics concerned with the motions of natural or man-made celestial bodies under the influence of gravitation: *To place an object in the heavens—to create, in short, a new celestial body revolving about the earth like a small moon and obeying the laws of celestial mechanics—is an event without precedent* (Atlantic).

celestial navigation, a method of navigation in which the geographical position of a ship or aircraft is determined from the position of heavenly bodies by triangulation.

***celestial pole**, *Astronomy.* each of the two points at which the earth's axis, if extended, would touch the celestial sphere.

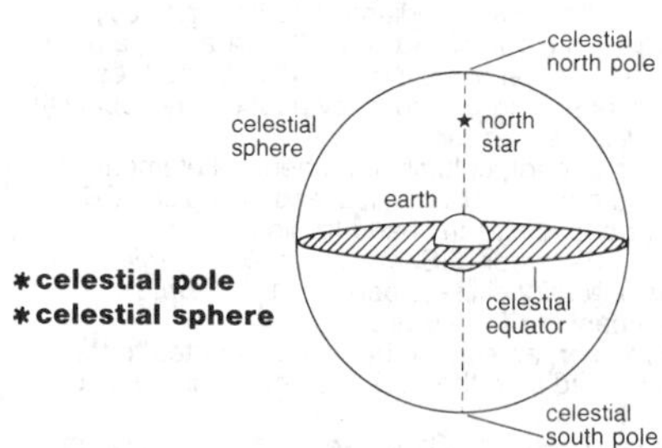

***celestial pole**
***celestial sphere**

***celestial sphere**, the imaginary sphere which appears to enclose the universe. To an observer on the earth, the visible sky forms half of the celestial sphere. *The chief convenience of the celestial sphere is in representing the positions of the stars* (Robert H. Baker).

cel|es|tine (sel′ə stīn, -stin), *n.* = celestite.

cel|es|tite (sel′ə stīt), *n.* a mineral, native strontium sulfate, occurring as white, or sometimes light-blue, crystals. *Formula:* $SrSO_4$ *The sulfate of strontium is known mineralogically as celestite, while that of barium is known as barite* (W. N. Jones). [alteration of *celestine,* perhaps < Italian *celestino* sky-blue (from its color)]

ce|li|ac (sē′lē ak), *adj.* of or having to do with the abdominal cavity. Also, **coeliac.** [< Latin *coeliacus* < Greek *koiliakós* < *koiliā* bowels, belly < *koîlos* hollow]

celiac disease, a chronic digestive disorder, similar to sprue, occurring chiefly in young children, characterized by an intolerance for the wheat protein gluten, and causing diarrhea, swelling of the abdomen, and stunted growth.

cel|i|ba|cy (sel′ə bə sē), *n., pl.* **-cies.** **1** the unmarried state; single life: *Marriage has many pains, but celibacy has no pleasures* (Samuel Johnson). **2** abstention from marriage by a vow: *The celibacy of priests was introduced* *into the English system by Dunstan* (David Hume). **3** abstinence in sexual matters; continence.

cel|i|ba|tar|i|an (sel′ə bə târ′ē ən), *n.* a person who lives as a celibate or favors celibacy.

cel|i|bate (sel′ə bit, -bāt), *n., adj.* **—*n.*** **1** a person who takes a vow not to marry: *Monks and nuns are celibates.* **2** an unmarried person. **3** a person who is abstinent in sexual matters.
—*adj.* **1** unmarried; single: *to exalt the celibate over the wedded life* (Frederick Farrar). **2** under a vow not to marry: *All faiths that have monks and nuns require them to be celibate* (R. Pierce Beaver). **3** abstinent in sexual matters; continent.
[< Latin *caelebs, -ibis* unmarried + English *-ate*¹]

cell** (sel), *n., v.* **—*n. **1a** a small room in a prison, convent, or monastery: *The prisoners lived in their cells but ate in a huge dining hall.* **b** a small monastery or convent, dependent on a larger religious house. **2** any small, hollow place: *Bees store honey in the cells of a honeycomb.* **3** the extremely small, basic unit of living matter of which all plants and animals are made. Most cells consist of protoplasm, have a nucleus near the center, and are enclosed by a very thin membrane. The body has blood cells, nerve cells, and muscle cells. Cells vary in size and shape but are generally microscopic. Plant cells also contain chloroplasts, and many have a prominent vacuole. Some cells, particularly in plants, also have a more rigid cell wall. *A human being contains approximately 50 trillion cells, each of which contains 46 chromosomes* (H. Fernandez-Moran). **4** *Electricity and Chemistry.* a container holding materials which produce electricity by chemical action. A battery consists of one or more cells. The electric cell is made up of two electrodes dipped in an electrolyte. **5** a small group that acts as a political, social, or religious unit for a larger, sometimes revolutionary, organization: *It offered a chart of the Communist chain of command, from the Politburo in the Kremlin down to the local party cell and the front organization* (Newsweek). **6** any enclosed space in an organism or tissue: **a** the sac containing the pollen in an anther. **b** the depression containing a coral polyp. **7** any of the small divisions of an insect's wing formed by the veins. **8** *Aeronautics.* **a** section of a wing structure on one side of the fuselage. **b** a gas-filled section of a balloon or airship. **9** any of the 63 arrangements of raised points in Braille, used to represent the letters of the alphabet, punctuation marks, numerals, etc. The standard cell consists of six raised points arranged in two vertical rows. **10** *Meteorology.* any center of high or low pressure. **11** a small geographical area in which a group of radiotelephones can communicate through a single radio transmitter. **12** a grave: *Each in his narrow cell forever laid* (Thomas Gray).
—*v.i.* to live in a cell, especially a prison cell: *A dictionary buff, a devotee of obscure words, he had been intent on improving his companion's grammar . . . ever since they had celled together at Kansas State Penitentiary* (Truman Capote).
cells, the brain or cells of the brain: *It [the sound] opens all the cells Where Mem'ry slept* (William Cowper).
[< Old French *celle* < Latin *cella* small room]
—cell′-like′, *adj.*

***cell**
definition 3

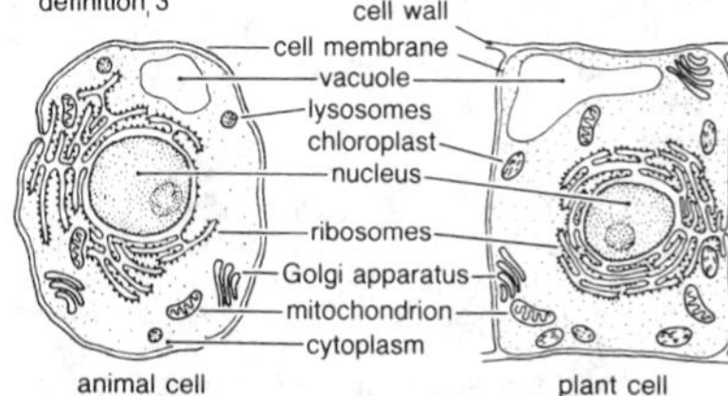

cel|la (sel′ə), *n.* the inner, enclosed section of an ancient Greek or Roman temple, in which was placed the image of the deity, as distinguished from the porticoes. [< Latin *cella*]

cel|lar (sel′ər), *n., v.* **—*n.*** **1** an underground room or rooms, usually under a building and often used for storing food or fuel: *The plumber went down into the cellar to fix the leaky pipe. I came upstairs into the world, for I was born in a cellar* (William Congreve). **2a** such a room for wines: *O conservatism! your pantry is full of meats and your cellar of wines* (Emerson). **b** a supply of wines: *an abundant cellar.* **3** a small, intimate cabaret in France, Germany, and occasionally the United States, usually located in the cellar of a building: *Jazz cellars and cafés in East Berlin are jammed every night* (New Yorker).
—*v.t.* to put into a cellar; store as if in a cellar: *his sympathies . . . cellared in the depths of his mind* (W. S. Mayo).
the cellar, *U.S. Informal, Sports.* the last place in a ranking: *In the last twelve years the team has missed the playoffs eleven times, and has finished in the cellar in the six-team NHL nine times* (Maclean's).
[< Anglo-French *celer,* Old French *cellier* < Latin *cellārium* storeroom < *cella* small room]

cel|lar|age (sel′ər ij), *n.* **1a** space in a cellar. **b** cellars. **2** a charge for storage in a cellar.

cel|lar|er (sel′ər ər), *n.* a person who takes care of a cellar and the food or wines in it, especially in a monastery.

cel|lar|et or **cel|lar|ette** (sel′ə ret′), *n.* a cabinet to hold wine bottles and glasses.

cel|lar|man (sel′ər mən), *n., pl.* **-men.** **1** a man in charge of or employed in a cellar, especially a wine cellar. **2** a wine merchant.

cel|lar|way (sel′ər wā′), *n.* **1** a hatchway or staircase leading into a cellar. **2** a passage through cellars.

cel|late (sel′āt), *adj.* = celled.

cell block, a block or cluster of prison cells.

cell division, *Biology.* the division of a cell into two in the process of reproduction or growth; mitosis or meiosis.

celled (seld), *adj.* having a cell or cells.

cel|lif|u|gal (se lif′yə gəl), *adj. Physiology.* moving away from the body of a cell along one or more of its processes. [< Latin *cella* cell + *fugere* flee + English *-al*¹]

cel|lip|e|tal (se lip′ə təl), *adj. Physiology.* moving toward the body of a cell along one or more of its processes. [< Latin *cella* cell + *petere* seek + English *-al*¹]

cel|list or **'cel|list** (chel′ist), *n.* a person who plays the cello. *Also,* **violoncellist.**

cell|mate (sel′māt′), *n.* a person who shares a cell with another or others.

cell membrane, the thin membrane that forms the outer surface of the protoplasm of a cell; plasma membrane: *It [the cell] consists essentially of a mass of protoplasm, the outer layer of which is somewhat differentiated to form the cell membrane* (Harbaugh and Goodrich). See diagram under **cell.**

cel|lo or **'cel|lo** (chel′ō), *n., pl.* **-los.** a musical instrument like a violin, but much larger and with a lower tone. It is held between the knees while being played and is supported on the floor by a peg or tail pin. Also, **violoncello.** [short for *violoncello*] ▶ The apostrophe, originally indicating that the word was shortened from *violoncello,* is now usually omitted.

cel|lo|bi|ose (sel′ō bī′ōs), *n.* a sugar occurring as the product of the partial hydrolysis of cellulose, used as a reagent in bacteriology. *Formula:* $C_{12}H_{22}O_{11}$

cel|loi|din (sə loi′din), *n.* a pure form of pyroxylin obtained from a solution of collodion, used especially in microscopy in mounting sections on slides. [< *cell*(ulose) + *-oid* + *-in*]

cel|lo|phane (sel′ə fān), *n.* a transparent substance somewhat like paper, made from cellulose. It is used as a wrapping to keep food, candy, tobacco, and other products fresh and clean. [< *cell*(ul)*o*(se) + Greek *phainein* appear]

cell plate, a membranous plate arising in certain plant cells toward the close of cell division due to a thickening of the spindle fibers.

cell theory, the doctrine that the bodies of all animals and plants consist either of a cell or of a number of cells and their products, and that all cells proceed from cells, first formulated by M. J. Schleiden and Theodor Schwann in 1838-1839.

cell therapy or **cellular therapy,** a method of rejuvenation or physical restoration by the injection of suspensions of cells prepared from the organs of embryonic sheep. Cell therapy is not generally accepted by the medical profession and it is not officially permitted in the United States.

cel|lu|ci|dal (sel′yə sī′dəl), *adj. Biology.* that destroys cells. [< Latin *cellula* a little cell + English *-cide*¹ + *-al*¹]

cel|lu|lar (sel′yə lər), *adj.* **1** having to do with cells: *It should be quite clear that microscopic examination of the cellular architecture of the brain substance would give no indication of the cell assembly as a structural unit* (George M. Wyburn). **2** made up of cells: *All animal and plant tissue is cellular.* [< New Latin *cellularis* < Latin *cellula* cellule]

cel|lu|lar|i|ty (sel′yə lar′ə tē), *n.* cellular quality or condition.

cellular phone or **telephone,** a mobile telephone unit, especially in a motor vehicle, capable of extending communication over a wide geographical area by means of low-power radio transmitters linking many smaller areas called cells.

cellular respiration, the process in living cells by which enzymes act on oxygen and the foods in the cells to produce energy. Carbon dioxide is a waste product of cellular respiration.

cel|lu|lase (sel ′yə lās), *n.* an enzyme that hydrolyzes cellulose, found in certain plants and insects. [< *cellul*(ose) + *-ase*]

cel|lu|late (sel′yə lāt), *adj.* having cellular structure.

cel|lu|lat|ed (sel′yə lā′tid), *adj.* = cellulate.

cel|lu|la|tion (sel′yə lā′shən), *n.* cell formation by division.

cel|lule (sel′yül), *n.* a tiny cell. [< Latin *cellula* (diminutive) < *cella* small room]

cel|lu|lif|u|gal (sel′yə lif′yə gəl), *n.* = cellifugal. [< Latin *cellula* cell + *fugere* flee + English *-al*¹]

cel|lu|lip|e|tal (sel′yə lip′ə təl), *adj.* = cellipetal. [< Latin *cellula* cell + *petere* seek + English *-al*¹]

cel|lu|lite (sel′yə līt, -ə lēt), *n.* fatty deposits beneath the skin, forming undesirable dimpling: *American women didn't share their French sisters' concern about cellulite—their word for those orange-peel-like lumps on limbs and posteriors that are so embarrassingly evident at bathing-suit time* (New York Times Book Review). [< French *cellulite* < *cellule* cell]

cel|lu|li|tis (sel′yə lī′tis), *n.* inflammation of cellular tissue. [< Latin *cellula* cell + English *-itis*]

cel|lu|loid (sel′yə loid), *n., adj.* **—*n.*** **1** a hard, transparent substance made from cellulose nitrate and camphor. It catches fire easily. Combs, toilet articles, and camera films are often made of celluloid. *While hot, celluloid can be rolled into sheets or molded into almost any desired shape* (Monroe M. Offner). **2 Celluloid,** a trademark for this substance. **3** motion picture; film: *The work they [Hollywood people] do is to produce on celluloid the dreams they live by* (Harper's).
—*adj.* having to do with motion pictures: *No sooner have the ashes of last season's Broadway bonfires been hauled away than the torches are lit for their celluloid incarnation* (Saturday Review). [American English < *cellul*(ose) + *-oid*]

cel|lu|lose (sel′yə lōs), *n., adj.* **—*n.*** a substance that forms the walls of plant cells; the woody part of trees and plants. Wood, cotton, flax, and hemp are largely cellulose. Cellulose is used to make paper, rayon, plastics, and explosives. *Cellulose, one of the commonest of all components of cell walls, is a carbohydrate closely related to starch* (Fred W. Emerson). *Cellulose is used as a base for 70 per cent of the better plastics on the market today* (Science News Letter). *Formula:* $(C_6H_{10}O_5)_n$ **—*adj.*** containing cells.
[< French *cellulose* < Latin *cellula* cellule]

cellulose acetate, any one of several compounds, insoluble in water, formed from cellulose in the presence of acetic acid. It is used in making textiles, camera films, lacquers, varnishes, and the like.

cellulose acetate butyrate, a cellulose plastic that stands up well under all weather conditions, used in street-light globes, automobile tail-light covers, and outdoor signs.

cellulose nitrate, any of certain esters of nitric acid and cellulose, used in making lacquers and varnishes and explosives; nitrocellulose.

cellulose propionate, an easily molded plastic used in toys, automobile steering wheels, and telephones.

cellulose xanthate, a deep-orange viscous substance formed when cellulose is treated with carbon disulfide, a step in the making of rayon.

cel|lu|lo|sic (sel′yə lō′sik), *n., adj.* **—*n.*** any plastic manufactured from cellulose.
—*adj.* of or like cellulose.

cel|lu|los|i|ty (sel′yə los′ə tē), *n.* the state or property of consisting of cells or of having a cellular structure.

cel|lu|lous (sel′yə ləs), *adj.* **1** full of cells. **2** made of cells.

cell wall, the hard, transparent outer covering of a plant cell, made up mostly of cellulose and surrounding the cell membrane: *The cell wall is generally present in plant cells where it serves to support the cells and the plant as a whole, but in animals it is frequently lacking* (A. M. Winchester).

ce|lom (sē′ləm), *n.* = coelom.

Cel|o|tex (sel′ə teks), *n. Trademark.* a fiberboard made of the fiber of cane.

Cels., Celsius.

Cel|si|us (sel′sē əs), *adj.* of or on the Celsius scale; centigrade: *The unit of temperature is the degree Celsius or Kelvin* (Scientific American). *Abbr:* C., Cels. [< Anders *Celsius,* 1701-44, a Swedish astronomer, who invented it]

***Celsius scale,** the official name of the scale used in centigrade thermometers, in which the

Pronunciation Key: hat, āge, cãre, fär; let, ēqual, tėrm; it, īce; hot, ōpen, ôrder; **oil, out;** cup, pu̇t, rüle; **child;** lo**ng;** **th**in; ᴛʜen; **zh,** measure; **ə** represents **a** in about, **e** in taken, **i** in pencil, **o** in lemon, **u** in circus.

freezing point of water is 0 degrees and the boiling point 100 degrees. *Abbr:* C., Cels.

***Celsius scale**

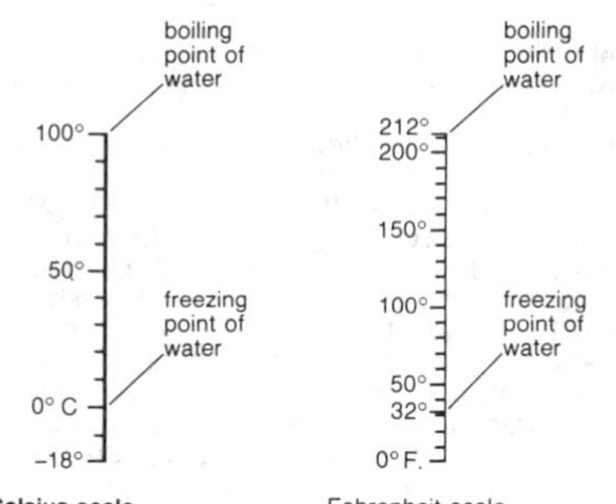

Celsius scale Fahrenheit scale

Celsius thermometer, = centigrade thermometer.

celt (selt), *n.* an implement with chisel-shaped edge, of bronze or stone, but sometimes iron, found among the remains of prehistoric man, apparently having served as a hoe, chisel, ax, and perhaps as an implement of war. [< New Latin *celtes* < Medieval Latin, stone chisel or flintstone < Late Latin *celtis* surgeon's tool (a ghost word originating in misreading of *certē* "certainly" as *celte* in the Vulgate)]

Celt (selt, kelt), *n.* a member of a people to which the Irish, Scottish Highlanders, Welsh, Bretons, and Manx belong. The ancient Gauls and Britons were Celts. Also, **Kelt.** [< Latin *Celtae* the Celts]

Celt., Celtic.

Celt|ic (sel′tik, kel′-), *adj., n.* —***adj.*** of the Celts or their language or customs: *Of the Celtic languages ... only four retain any vitality* (H. A. Gleason).
—***n.*** the group of languages spoken by the Celts, including Irish, Gaelic, Welsh, Breton, and Manx. It is a subdivision of the Indo-European family of languages. Also, **Keltic.**

Celtic cross, a type of cross, common in the work of Celts and later settlers in Celtic parts, having a circle, or concentric circles, at the joint, touching the four projecting arms. See diagram under **cross.**

Cel|ti|cism (sel′tə siz əm), *n.* **1** a Celtic idiom or mode of expression. **2** a Celtic custom. **3** adherence to Celtic manners, speech, and the like.

Cel|ti|cize (sel′tə sīz), *v.t.,* **-cized, -ciz|ing.** to render Celtic.

Cel|tist (sel′tist), *n.* a person who is engaged in or versed in the study of Celtic language and literature.

cel|ti|um (sel′shē əm), *n. Chemistry.* a substance for a time considered to be a new rare-earth element (*at. no.:* 72), later superseded by hafnium, an element of the carbon group (*at. no.:* 72). [< New Latin *celtium* < Latin *Celtae* the Celts]

Cel|to|phil (sel′tə fil), *n.* a person who is fond of the Celts or is devoted to Celtic studies and interests.

Cel|to-Ro|man (sel′tō rō′mən), *adj.* **1** having to do with the mixed population of Celts and Romans in southern and western Europe. **2** having to do with a mixture of Celtic and Latin.

cel|tuce (sel′təs), *n.* a crisp, leafy type of lettuce with an edible stem that combines the flavors of celery and lettuce. [< *cel*(ery) + (let)*tuce*]

cem|bal|ist (sem′bə list, chem′-), *n.* **1** a performer upon a cembalo. **2** the player of the piano in an orchestra.

cem|ba|lo (sem′bə lō, chem′-), *n., pl.* **-los. 1** a harpsichord. **2** a dulcimer. [< Italian *cembalo* < Latin *cymbalum* cymbal < Greek *kýmbalon*]

ce|ment (sə ment′), *n., v.* —***n.*** **1a** a fine, gray powder made by burning a mixture of clay and limestone: *Cement is, in essence, a mixture of the silicates and aluminates of calcium, and is one of the most important of the modern-day silicon-bearing products* (W. N. Jones). **b** this substance mixed with water, sand, and gravel or crushed stone to form concrete, used to make sidewalks, streets, floors, and walls. **c** this substance mixed with water, sand, and lime to form mortar, used to hold stones and bricks together in the walls of buildings. Cement is applied in a soft state and becomes hard like stone. **2** anything applied soft that hardens to make things stick together. See also **rubber cement.**
3 *Figurative.* anything that joins together or unites: *Custom was in the early days the cement of society* (Walter Bagehot). **SYN:** bond. **4a** a substance used to fill cavities in teeth or to fasten fillings into them. **b** = cementum. **5** *Metallurgy.* the powdery substance used during cementation. **6** *Geology.* the groundmass of a clastic rock.
—***v.t.*** **1** to fasten together with cement: *A broken plate can be cemented.* **2** to spread cement over: *The workmen were cementing the sidewalk.* **3** *Figurative.* to join firmly; unite: *The marriage of my son to their daughter cemented the friendship of our two families.*
—***v.i.*** to become joined firmly with cement; stick: (*Figurative.*) *They will ... cement and form one mass with us* (Thomas Jefferson). **SYN:** cohere.
[< Old French *ciment* < Vulgar Latin *cīmentum,* for Latin *caementum* stone chippings < *caedere* to cut] —**ce|ment′er,** *n.* —**ce|ment′like′,** *adj.*

ce|men|tal (sə men′təl), *adj.* of or having to do with cement, as of a tooth.

ce|men|ta|tion (sē′mən tā′shən), *n.* **1a** the action or process of cementing, or producing cohesion. **b** the state of cohesion thus produced.
2 *Metallurgy.* a process in which two substances are heated in contact for the purpose of bringing about a chemical change in one of them, as when iron is heated in powdered charcoal to form steel by chemical combination with the charcoal, or when glass is heated in sand to form some kinds of porcelain.

ce|men|ta|to|ry (sə men′tə tôr′ē, -tōr′-), *adj.* having the quality of uniting firmly.

ce|ment-can anchor (sə ment′kan′), a cylinder-shaped mass of cement with a ring on top, used for anchoring small boats.

cement gland, a gland that secretes the sticky substance by which a barnacle or other cirriped attaches itself to an object.

cement gun, a machine used to apply a mixture of cement, sand, and water under pneumatic pressure, used especially in construction and repair of masonry.

ce|men|tite (sə men′tīt), *n.* a hard, brittle carbide of iron, a constituent of steel. *Formula:* Fe_3C

ce|men|ti|tious (sē′mən tish′əs), *adj.* of the nature of cement.

cement mixer, a machine consisting of a drum mounted on its side and revolved by a motor, used for mixing cement.

ce|men|tum (sə men′təm), *n.* the bony tissue forming the outer crust of the root of a tooth; cement.

cem|e|te|ri|al (sem′ə tir′ē əl), *adj.* belonging or relating to a cemetery.

cem|e|ter|y (sem′ə ter′ē), *n., pl.* **-ter|ies.** a place for burying the dead; graveyard: ... *a flock of mourners dispersing in a desolate cemetery* (Newsweek). **SYN:** necropolis. [< Latin *coemētērium* < Greek *koimētērion* burial place; earlier, sleeping room < *koimân* lull to sleep]

cen., **1** central. **2** century.

cen|a|cle (sen′ə kəl), *n.* **1** a dining room, especially the "upper room" in which the Last Supper was eaten. (In the Bible, Mark 14:15, Luke 22:12). **2** a close social circle; clique; coterie: *Afterwards, the representatives of ... the literary cenacles walked over to the dingy ex-clubhouse* (New Yorker). [< French *cénacle* < Latin *cēnaculum* < *cēna* dinner]

cen|cer|ro (sen ser′ō; *Spanish* then ther′rō), *n., pl.* **-ros.** the leading mule in a pack train. [< Spanish *cencerro* bell worn by the lead animal]

ce|nes|the|sia (sē′nəs thē′zhə, sen′əs-), *n.* = coenesthesia.

ce|nes|the|sis (sē′nəs thē′sis, sen′əs-), *n.* = coenesthesis.

ce|no|bite (sē′nə bīt, sen′ə-), *n.* a member of a religious group living in a monastery or convent. Also, **coenobite.** [< Late Latin *coenobīta* < *coenobium* convent < Late Greek *koinóbion* ultimately < Greek *koinós* common + *bíos* life]

ce|no|bit|ic (sē′nə bit′ik, sen′ə-), *adj.* **1** of or having to do with a cenobite or cenobitism. **2** living in community, as women in a convent.

ce|no|bit|i|cal (sē′nə bit′i kəl), *adj.* = cenobitic.

ce|no|bit|ism (sē′nə bī′tiz əm, sen′ə-), *n.* the state, system, or practices of cenobites.

cen|o|by (sē′nə bē, sen′ə-), *n., pl.* **-bies.** a conventual establishment; a religious community. Also, **coenoby.** [< Late Latin *coenobium;* see etym. under **cenobite**]

ce|no|gen|e|sis (sē′nə jen′ə sis, sen′ə-), *n. Biology.* the stages in the development of an embryo which do not repeat the racial history of its stock, often associated with special embryonic environment. Also, **caenogenesis, kenogenesis.** [< Greek *kainós* new + English *genesis*]
▶ **Cenogenesis** and **palingenesis** represent concepts of embryonic development in vogue in the late 1800's. Their employment by embryologists now is largely restricted to historical contexts.

ce|no|ge|net|ic (sē′nə jə net′ik, sen′ə-), *adj.* of or relating to cenogenesis.

ce|nog|o|nous (si nog′ə nəs), *adj.* (of insects) oviparous at one season of the year and ovoviviparous or viviparous at another. [< Greek *koinós* common + *gónos* generation + English *-ous*]

cen|o|taph (sen′ə taf, -täf), *n.* a monument erected in memory of a person who is buried elsewhere. [< Latin *cenotaphium* < Greek *kenotáphion* < *kenós* empty + *táphos* tomb]

ce|no|te (si nō′tē), *n.* a natural underground reservoir of water; sinkhole. Cenotes typically occur in the limestone of the Yucatán peninsula. [< Spanish *cenote* < Maya *conot*]

Ce|no|zo|ic (sē′nə zō′ik, sen′ə-), *n., adj.* —***n.*** **1** the most recent era of geological history; Age of Mammals. The Cenozoic began about 60 or 70 million years ago, when mammals began to dominate the animal kingdom, and includes the present time. **2** the group of rocks formed during this era.
—***adj.*** of this era or its rocks. Also, **Caenozoic, Cainozoic.**
[< Greek *kainós* new + *zōē* life + English *-ic*]

cense (sens), *v.t.,* **censed, cens|ing.** to burn incense near or in front of; offer incense to; perfume with incense. [Middle English *encens* incense[1]; influenced by *censer*]

***cen|ser** (sen′sər), *n.* a container in which incense is burned, especially during religious ceremonies; thurible. [< Old French *encensier* < *encens* incense[1]]

***censer**

cen|sor (sen′sər), *n., v.* —***n.*** **1** a person who examines books, newspapers and news reports, plays, motion pictures, and letters, and, if necessary, changes or prohibits them to make them acceptable to the government or the organization that employs him: *The novel was banned by the censor as likely to stir up suspicion of the government among the students.* **2** a person who tells others how they ought to behave; a person who exercises supervision over the morals or behavior of others. **SYN:** monitor. **3** a person who likes to find fault; adverse critic. **SYN:** faultfinder. **4** a magistrate in ancient Rome who took the census, supervised the conduct of citizens, and gave out public contracts: *Cato the Censor.* **5** *Psychoanalysis.* the influence of the ego, ego ideal, or superego that tends to exclude unwelcome memories or impulses from the consciousness, unless suitably disguised. **6** an official in some British universities responsible for the studies and conduct of nonboarding students.
—***v.t.*** to examine or change as a censor; take out parts of (news reports, books, letters, plays, or motion pictures): *The foreign government censored the reporter's story of a revolt. Two scenes in the movie were censored for having too much violence.*
[< Latin *cēnsor* < *cēnsēre* appraise] —**cen′sor|a|ble,** *adj.*

cen|sor|ate (sen′sə rit), *n.* a governmental or other body responsible for censorship.

cen|so|ri|al (sen sôr′ē əl, -sōr′-), *adj.* **1** of or having to do with a censor. **2** suitable for a censor; censorious.

cen|so|ri|an (sen sôr′ē ən, -sōr′-), *adj.* of or having to do with a censor; censorial.

cen|so|ri|ous (sen sôr′ē əs, -sōr′-), *adj.* too ready to find fault; severely critical. **SYN:** hypercritical, carping. —**cen|so′ri|ous|ly,** *adv.* —**cen|so′ri|ous|ness,** *n.*

cen|sor|ship (sen′sər ship), *n.* **1** the act or system of censoring: *Censorship of news is common in time of war.* **2** the position or work of a censor. **3** *Psychoanalysis.* the exclusion by the ego, ego ideal, or superego, of unpleasant memories or impulses from consciousness unless suitably disguised.

cen|sur|a|bil|i|ty (sen′shər ə bil′ə tē), *n.* the quality of being censurable.

cen|sur|a|ble (sen′shər ə bəl), *adj.* deserving censure; blamable. —**cen′sur|a|ble|ness,** *n.* —**cen′sur|a|bly,** *adv.*

cen|sure (sen′shər), *n., v.,* **-sured, -sur|ing.** —***n.*** **1** the act of blaming; expression of unfavorable opinion; blame: *Censure is sometimes harder to bear than punishment.* **SYN:** *criticism, disapproval.* **2a** *Archaic.* a judgment. **b** a penalty, as a public rebuke or a suspension from office, especially one imposed on a church official.
—***v.t.*** to express disapproval of; find fault with; blame; criticize: *His employer censured him for neglecting his work.* **SYN:** condemn, reprove. See syn. under **blame.**
—***v.i.*** to give censure or adverse criticism; express disapproval; blame: *Ten censure wrong for one that writes amiss* (Alexander Pope).
[< Latin *cēnsūra* < *cēnsēre* appraise] —**cen′sur|er,** *n.*

cen|sus (sen′səs), *n.* **1** an official count of the

people of a country or district. It is taken to find out the number of people, their age, sex, what they do to make a living, and often many other facts about them. **2** (in Roman history) a registration or count of citizens and their property to determine taxation. [< Latin *cēnsus, -ūs* < *cēnsēre* appraise]

census taker, a person who collects from the residents of a locality data for a census.

census tract, *U.S.* a statistical area, containing an average population of 4000, set up as a unit by the Bureau of the Census for the study of small metropolitan sections: *Four of the census tracts will be in the Watts area; the other four in Avalon* (New York Times).

***cent** (sent), *n.* **1** a coin of the United States and Canada, usually an alloy of copper; penny. 100 cents make one dollar. *Symbol:* ¢. **2** the value of this coin; 1/100 of a dollar. **3** one hundredth part of the basic unit of money in certain other countries. *Abbr:* c., ct. [American English; probably short for Latin *centum* hundred; apparently originated by Gouverneur Morris to designate a coin with the value of 100 of his units of money (each worth 1/1440 of a dollar)]

***cent**
definition 1

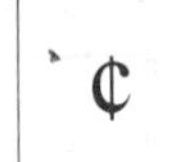

50¢ = fifty cents

cent., an abbreviation for the following:
1 centered.
2 centigrade.
3 centimeter.
4 central.
5 century.

cen|tal (sen′təl), *n.* a weight of 100 pounds. [coined < Latin *centum* hundred; perhaps patterned on *quintal*]

cen|tare (sen′tãr), *n.* = centiare.

***cen|taur** (sen′tôr), *n.* **1** *Greek Legend.* any one of a race of monsters from Thessaly with the head, arms, and chest of a man, and the body and legs of a horse. **2** *Figurative.* a hybrid; double-natured person or thing. **3** an excellent horseback rider. [< Latin *Centaurus* < Greek *Kéntauros*]

***centaur**
definition 1

Cen|taur (sen′tôr), *n.* = Centaurus.

cen|tau|re|a (sen tôr′ē ə), *n.* any one of the genus of composite plants that includes the cornflower and the star thistle. [< New Latin *Centaurea* the genus name < Latin *centaurium* centaury]

Cen|tau|ri (sen tôr′ī), *n.* genitive of **Centaurus.**

Cen|tau|rus (sen tôr′əs), *n., genitive* **Cen|tau|ri.** a Southern constellation containing the third brightest star in the sky, excluding the sun, and faintly resembling a centaur in shape; Centaur. [< Latin *Centaurus* centaur]

cen|tau|ry (sen′tôr ē), *n., pl.* **-ries.** any plant of several Old World herbs of the gentian family, whose medicinal properties were said to have been discovered by Chiron the centaur. [< Latin *centaurium* < Greek *kentaúrion* < *Kéntauros* centaur]

cen|ta|vo (sen tä′vō), *n., pl.* **-vos. 1** a small coin of Bolivia, Colombia, Cuba, the Dominican Republic, Mexico, and the Philippines. 100 centavos make one peso. **2** a coin of Portugal, worth 1/100 of an escudo. **3** a coin of Brazil, worth 1/100 of a cruzado. **4** a coin of Argentina, worth 1/100 of an austral. **5** one hundredth part of the basic unit of money in El Salvador, Nicaragua, Honduras, Guatemala, Peru, and Ecuador. [< American Spanish *centavo* < Spanish < Latin *centum* hundred]

cen|te|nar|i|an (sen′tə nãr′ē ən), *n., adj.* **—*n.*** a person who is 100 years old or more: *As doctors and scientists learn more about the body, people will have a better chance of living to be centenarians.* **—*adj.* 1** 100 years old or more. **2** of 100 years; of a centenary celebration.

cen|te|nar|i|an|ism (sen′tə nãr′ē ə niz′əm), *n.* the condition or fact of being a centenarian.

cen|te|nar|y (sen′tə ner′ē, sen ten′ər-; *especially British* sen tē′nər ē), *n., pl.* **-nar|ies,** *adj.* **—*n.* 1** a 100th anniversary: *1876 was the first centenary of the signing of the Declaration of Independence.* **2** a celebration of the 100th anniversary: *The town was bustling with plans for its centenary.* **3** a period of 100 years; century.
—*adj.* of or having to do with a period of 100 years or a 100th anniversary: *a centenary celebration.*
[< Latin *centēnārius* relating to a hundred < *centum* hundred]

cen|ten|ni|al (sen ten′ē əl, -ten′yəl), *adj., n.* **—*adj.* 1** having to do with the 100th anniversary; of 100 years. **2** 100 years old or more: *centennial pines.*
—*n.* 1 a 100th anniversary: *The town is celebrating its centennial.* **2** a celebration of a 100th anniversary; centenary: *I hope there will be a fair during our centennial.*
[< Latin *centum* hundred; patterned on English *biennial*]**—cen|ten′ni|al|ly,** *adv.*

Centennial State, a nickname for Colorado.

cen|ten|ni|um (sen ten′ē əm), *n., pl.* **-ten|ni|ums, -ten|ni|a** (-ten′ē ə). a period of a hundred years; century. [< Latin *centum* hundred; patterned on English *biennium*]

cen|ter (sen′tər), *n., v., adj.* **—*n.* 1** a point within a circle or sphere equally distant from all points of the circumference or surface: *The bull's-eye is in the center.* **2a** the middle point, place, or part: *the center of a room, the center of equilibrium.* SYN: midst. See syn. under **middle. b** the point, axis, or line around which something turns: *The sun is the center of the solar system.* **3a** *Figurative.* a person, thing, or group in a middle position: *The pictures on loan from the Art Museum were the center of the exhibit.* **b** the main body of an army, as distinct from the two flanks or wings: *Our center has given ground* (Macaulay). **4** *Figurative.* a point toward which people or things go, or from which they come; main point: *New York is one of the centers of world trade.* SYN: hub, core, pivot, focus. **5a** the offensive player who has the position between the guards in the line in football. He begins each scrimmage by passing the ball backward between his legs, usually to the quarterback. **b** a player who starts play in such games as basketball and hockey. **6a** Often, **Center.** the part of certain lawmaking bodies that sits in front of the presiding officer. It is made up of the political groups having moderate opinions. **b** *Figurative.* the persons and parties holding moderate views: *His political views are just left of center.* **7** *Physiology.* a mass of nerve cells closely connected and acting together; nerve center: *the respiratory center, the center of balance.* **8** *Machinery.* **a** a tapered point on either spindle of a lathe or other machine to hold and turn the work. **b** a tapered hole at the end of a shaft or spindle to hold such a point. **9a** the part of a target next to the bull's-eye. **b** a shot, arrow, or dart that hits this part.
—*v.t.* 1 to place in or at the center: *The object glass of a telescope must be accurately centered.* SYN: centralize. **2** *Figurative.* to concentrate, focus, rest: *All his hopes are centered in her.* **3** to mark or provide with a center: *a smooth lawn centered by a pool.* **4a** *American Football.* to pass back (the ball) to begin a play. **b** *Soccer and Hockey.* to cross (the ball or puck) to near the entrance to the goal. **5** to grind or adjust (a lens) so that the optical center is at the geometrical center.
—*v.i.* 1a to gather or collect at a center: *The guests centered around the table.* SYN: converge. **b** *Figurative.* to be concentrated in; rest (on): *All his hopes centered on being promoted.* SYN: focus. **2** to be at a center: *The helicopter centered over the sailor, plucking him from the water.* **3** *Soccer and Hockey.* to cross the ball or puck over to the goalmouth.
—*adj.* of the center; at or comprising the center: *Italy's unstable center parties saw the shape of things to come* (Newsweek). Also, *especially British,* **centre.**

center down, *U.S.* to settle down or concentrate on important matters: *This collective meditation which Friends like my grandmother called a "centering down" was mostly outside our experience* (New Yorker).
[< Old French *centre,* learned borrowing from Latin *centrum* < Greek *kéntron* sharp point]
—cen′ter|less, *adj.*
►**Center around** (or **about**) is used informally to mean "focus upon": *The story centers around* (or *about*) *a robbery.* The formal expression is *center on* or *upon.*

center bit, a carpenter's bit with a sharp point in the center and two cutting wings that turn around the point.

cen|ter|board (sen′tər bôrd′, -bōrd′), *n.* a movable keel of a sailboat. It is lowered through a slot in the bottom of a boat to prevent drifting to leeward. Also, *especially British,* **centreboard.**

center circle, the circle in the center of the playing area of hockey and basketball. The center circle of a basketball court is four feet in diameter.

cen|tered (sen′tərd), *adj.* **1** fixed on a center as a point of support or equilibrium: *a centered arc, a centered position.* **2** being in the center: *Some dictionaries have centered dots between the syllables of entries.* **3** furnished with a center. Also, *especially British,* **centred.**

center field, *Baseball.* **1** the section of the outfield behind second base. **2** the position of the player in this area. *Abbr:* cf.

center fielder, a baseball player whose position is in center field.

cen|ter-fire (sen′tər fīr′), *adj.* **1** (of a cartridge) having the percussion cap or primer in the center of the base, instead of around its rim. **2** (of a gun or pistol) having a firing pin that strikes the cartridge in the center of its base. Also, **central-fire.**

cen|ter|fold (sen′tər fōld′), *n.* an illustrated center spread in a magazine or book that takes up both left- and right-hand pages and sometimes has to be unfolded to be seen in full.

center forward, in soccer, hockey, and, formerly, basketball: **1** a player whose position is in the center of the front line. **2** the position occupied by that player.

center half or **halfback,** in soccer and hockey: **1** a player whose position is in the center of the middle line. **2** the position of that player.

cen|ter-left (sen′tər left′), *adj.* of or having to do with a political coalition involving parties of the center and the left.

cen|ter|line (sen′tər līn′), *n.* **1** a real or imaginary line dividing any plane figure or surface into two symmetrical halves, especially such a line in a mechanical drawing or on the surface of a road or on a playing court or field in a sport. **2** an axis (def. 2).

cen|ter|most (sen′tər mōst), *adj.* nearest the center.

center of buoyancy, a point in a ship or other floating body, corresponding to the center of gravity of the water displaced.

center of curvature, *Geometry.* the center of the circle of curvature.

center of gravity, 1 *Physics.* that point of a body around which its weight is evenly balanced; that point at which the force of gravity acting on the body may be said to be concentrated: *The center of gravity of a child's seesaw is at the center of the board when no one sits on it* (Vera Kistiakowsky). **2** *Figurative.* the point of concentration or focus, especially upon which something rests: *He is almost the center of gravity of the Congress Party* (Time). *Now with the population changes young people are even less at the center of gravity* (Harper's).

***center of mass,** *Physics.* that point in a body which moves as though it bore the entire mass of the body, usually identical with the center of gravity. Many textbooks now use the term *center of mass* instead of *center of gravity. The center of mass is used to calculate the motion of objects due to all kinds of forces, not only gravitational forces* (Vera Kistiakowsky).

***center of mass**

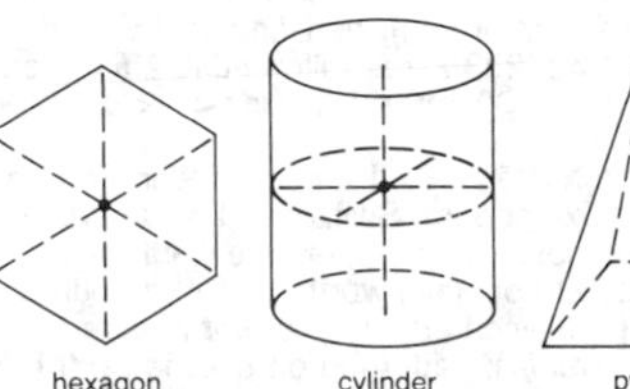

center of oscillation, *Physics.* a point in a pendulum such that, if the whole mass of the pendulum were concentrated there, the time of oscillation would remain unchanged.

center of percussion, (in a moving body) the point where the percussion or stroke is greatest, in which the whole striking force of the body is supposed to be collected.

cen|ter|piece (sen′tər pēs′), *n.* **1** an ornamental piece of glass or lace or an arrangement of flowers for the center of a dining table, buffet, or mantel. **2** any piece which is located in the center of something. **3** the principal or dominant feature (of a policy or program). Also, *especially British,* **centrepiece.**

center punch, a punch with a conical point for marking the center of a hole to be drilled or the center of work to be turned on a lathe.

center rail, a third rail in the form of a rack

Pronunciation Key: hat, āge, cãre, fär; let, ēqual, tėrm; it, īce; hot, ōpen, ôrder; oil, out; cup, pu̇t, rüle; child; long; thin; ᴛʜen; zh, measure; ə represents a in about, e in taken, i in pencil, o in lemon, u in circus.

which engages the cog of a locomotive on a cog railway.

center wheel, the wheel in the center of the frame of a watch or clock whose axis carries the minute hand.

cen|tes|i|mal (sen tes′ə məl), *adj.* **1** hundredth; 100th. **2a** divided into 100ths. **b** relating to division into 100ths. [< Latin *centēsimus* hundredth + English *-al*¹] —**cen|tes′i|mal|ly**, *adv.*

cen|tes|i|mate (sen tes′ə māt), *v.t.*, **-mat|ed**, **-mat|ing**. to take one in every hundred of (soldiers, citizens, or inmates) for punishment, often by execution, as for mutiny or widespread rebellion. [< Latin *centēsimāre* (with English *-ate*¹) < *centēsimus* hundredth] —**cen|tes′i|ma′tion**, *n.*

cen|tes|i|mo (sen tes′ə mō), *n., pl.* **-mos** *for 1, 2, 4;* **-mi** (-mə) *for 3, 5.* **1** a coin of Chile, worth 1/100 of a peso. **2** a coin of Panama, worth 1/100 of a balboa. **3** a unit of money of Italy, worth 1/100 of a lira. Centesimi are used in figuring but not as coins. **4** a coin of Uruguay, worth 1/100 of a peso. **5** a former coin of Italian Somaliland (now Somalia), worth 1/100 of a somalo. [< Italian, Spanish *centésimo*, learned borrowing from Latin *centēsimus* hundredth]

cent|ge|ner (sent′jə nər), *n.* one hundred or any considerable number of representatives of a race, variety, or strain of domesticated animals or cultivated plants, considered as a true sample of the whole. [< Latin *centum* hundred + *genus, generis* kind]

centi-, *combining form.* **1** 100: *Centigrade = 100-degree.* **2** (in the metric system) 1/100 of a unit: *Centimeter = 1/100 of a meter.* [< Latin *centum* hundred]

cen|ti|are (sen′tē âr). *n.* 1/100 of an are; one square meter. *Abbr.* ca. Also, **centare**. [< French *centiare* < *centi-* centi- + *-are* are]

cen|ti|grade (sen′tə grād), *adj.* **1** divided into 100 degrees or equal parts: *The temperature scale used in all scientific work and in common use in many countries is the centigrade scale, in which the fixed points are taken as 0° C and 100° C* (Shortley and Williams). **2** of or according to a centigrade temperature scale; Celsius: *a body temperature of 37 degrees centigrade. Abbr:* C. [< French *centigrade* < Latin *centum* hundred + *gradus* degree]

centigrade thermometer, a thermometer having 0 degrees for the temperature at which water freezes and 100 degrees for the temperature at which water boils; a Celsius thermometer.

cen|ti|gram (sen′tə gram), *n.* a unit of weight in the metric system, equal to 1/100 of a gram. *Abbr.* cg. [< French *centigramme* < *centi-* centi- + *gramme* gram]

cen|ti|gramme (sen′tə gram). *n. Especially British.* centigram.

cen|ti|li|ter (sen′tə lē′tər), *n.* a unit of liquid or dry measure in the metric system, equal to 1/100 of a liter. *abbr.* cl. [< French *centilitre* < *centi* centi- + *litre* liter]

cen|ti|li|tre (sen′tə lē′tər), *n. Especially British.* centiliter.

cen|til|lion (sen til′yən), *n.* **1** (in the U.S. and France) 1 with 303 zeros following it. **2** (in Great Britain) 1 with 600 zeros following it. [< *centi-* + (*mi*)*llion*]

cen|time (sän′tēm), *n.* **1** a coin used in France, Belgium, Luxembourg, Switzerland, and certain other countries. 100 centimes are worth one franc. **2** a coin of Haiti, worth 1/100 of a gourde. *Abbr:* c. [< French *centime* < *cent* hundred (< Latin *centum*); patterned on *décime* tenth]

cen|ti|me|ter (sen′tə mē′tər), *n.* a measure of length in the metric system equal to 1/100 of a meter; 0.3937 inch. See picture under **inch**¹. *Abbr:* cm. [< French *centimètre* < *centi-* centi- + *mètre* meter]

cen|ti|me|ter-can|dle (sen′tə mē′tər kan′dəl), *n.* a unit of illumination equal to one phot.

cen|ti|me|ter-gram-sec|ond (sen′tə mē′tər-gram′sek′ənd), *adj.* having to do with a system of measurement used in scientific calculations in which the centimeter is the unit of length, the gram is the unit of mass, and the second is the unit of time. *Abbr:* c.g.s.

cen|ti|me|tre (sen′tə mē′tər), *n. Especially British.* centimeter.

cen|ti|mil|lion|aire (sen′tə mil′yə nãr′), *n.* a millionaire with a hundred million or more dollars. pounds, or other denomination. [< *centi-* 100 + *millionaire*]

cen|ti|mo (sen′tə mō), *n., pl.* **-mos. 1** a coin of Costa Rica, worth 1/100 of a colon. **2** a coin of Spain, worth 1/100 of a peseta. **3** a coin of Venezuela, worth 1/100 of a bolivar. **4** a coin of Paraguay, worth 1/100 of a guarani. [< Spanish *céntimo* < French *centime* centime]

cen|tip|e|dal (sen tip′ə dəl), *adj.* of or having to do with the centipedes.

***cen|ti|pede** (sen′tə pēd), *n.* a flat, wormlike animal with many pairs of legs; chilopod. The first pair of legs are clawlike and in some cases contain poison glands. The bite of some centipedes is painful. Centipedes vary in length from an inch or so to nearly a foot. *Many desert animals such as centipedes . . . avoid the extreme mid-day heat* (J. L. Cloudsley-Thompson). [< Latin *centipeda* < *centum* hundred + *pēs, pedis* foot]

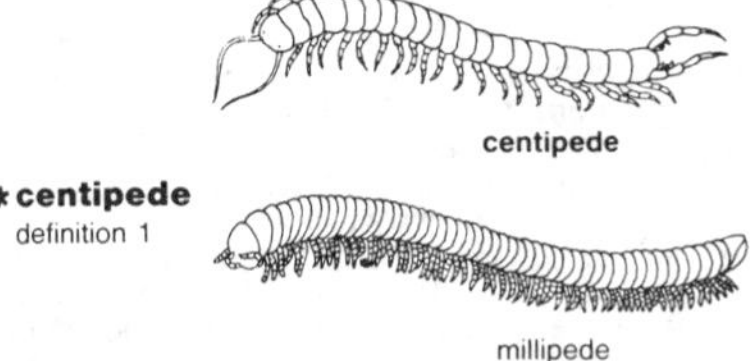

***centipede** definition 1

centipede grass, a creeping grass, originally from China, that resists drought, found in the tropics and the Southern United States. It is used especially to cover athletic fields, golf courses, lawns, and playgrounds.

cen|ti|stere (sen′tə stir), *n.* a unit of volume in the metric system equal to 1/100 of a stere. [< French *centistère* < *centi-* centi- + *-stère* stere]

cen|ti|stoke (sen′tə stōk), *n.* a unit for measuring the kinematic viscosity of a fluid, equal to 1/100 of a stoke. [< *centi-* + *stoke*]

cent mark, the sign ¢; cent sign.

cent|ner (sent′nər), *n.* **1** a European unit of weight corresponding to the hundredweight, fixed at 50 kilograms, or 110.23 pounds avoirdupois, in several countries. **2** (in assaying) one dram. **3** a cental. [< German *Centner* hundredweight < Latin *centēnārius* of a hundred < *centum* hundred]

cen|to (sen′tō), *n., pl.* **-tos. 1** a patchwork composition formed of selected lines or passages from various sources. **2** a collection of any kind; conglomeration; mass. [< Latin *centō* (literally) patchwork garment]

CENTO or **Cento** (sen′tō), Central Treaty Organization (a former alliance of Turkey, Iran, Pakistan, and Great Britain dissolved in 1979).

cen|tra (sen′trə), *n.* a plural of **centrum**.

cen|trad (sen′trad), *adv. Anatomy.* toward the center. [< Latin *centrum* center + *ad* toward]

cen|tral (sen′trəl), *adj., n.* —*adj.* **1** of the center; being or forming the center: *the central mass of the atom. The sun is central in the solar system.* SYN: focal. **2** at the center; near the center: *the quicker central flow in a pipe, the central railroad station. The park is in the central part of the city.* SYN: middle. **3** from the center; head: *The central library sends books to its branches.* **4** equally distant from all points; easy to get to or from: *We shop at a central market.* **5** *Figurative.* main; chief; principal: *What is the central idea in the story?* SYN: dominant. **6** *Anatomy, Physiology.* **a** of or designating the brain and spinal cord as a major division of the nervous system of vertebrates. **b** arising from or affecting these parts of the nervous system: *central anesthesia.* **c** of or having to do with a centrum. **7** *Phonetics.* (of vowels) articulated with the middle of the tongue raised in varying degrees toward the middle of the roof of the mouth, as the American pronunciation of *a* in *sofa;* mixed.
—*n. U.S.* **1** a telephone exchange: *The building was a central for exchanges serving 56,565 telephone lines* (Newsweek). **2** a telephone operator in a central exchange.
[< Latin *centrālis* < *centrum* center] —**cen′tral|ness**, *n.*

Central American, **1** having to do with Central America or its people. **2** a person born or living in Central America.

central bank, a bank which holds the cash reserves of a country's commercial banks, performs numerous monetary services for the government, issues bank notes, and makes funds available to commercial banks. The Federal Reserve Banks of the United States are central banks.

central capability unit, a unit of the British government that reviews policies proposed to the Cabinet by government departments. Its official name is Central Policy Review Staff.

central casting, *U.S.* the casting department of a motion-picture studio.
from central casting, stereotyped: *Halberstam's soldiers are all from central casting* (Time).

central city, a part of a large city or metropolitan area which is the center or core; core city: *The Negro ghettos of the central cities became increasingly crowded* (Richard Harwood).

central dogma, a theory in molecular biology which maintains that only DNA can act as a template or blueprint for the formation of RNA. This theory was considered fundamental until challenged by Teminism.

cen|tral-fire (sen′trəl fīr′), *adj.* = center-fire.

central fissure, = fissure of Rolando.

central force, *Physics.* a force attracting to or repelling from a center.

central heating, the heating of one building or a group of buildings from a single source.

cen|tral|ise (sen′trə līz), *v.t., v.i.,* **-ised, -is|ing**. *Especially British,* centralize.

cen|tral|ism (sen′trə liz əm), *n.* a theory or principle of centralizing control, especially in a government. —**cen′tral|ist**, *n.*

cen|tral|is|tic (sen′trə lis′tik), *adj.* of centralism; having to do with or favoring centralism.

cen|tral|i|ty (sen tral′ə tē), *n.* central position or character: (*Figurative.*) *Clear grasp of ideas, centrality of purpose* (W. M. Rossetti).

cen|tral|i|za|tion (sen′trə lə zā′shən), *n.* **1** the coming or bringing to a center. **2** a gathering together at a center: *Centralization of medical services may prevent waste of effort.* **3** a bringing together under the control of a single authority: *the centralization of government under a dictator.*

cen|tral|ize (sen′trə līz), *v.,* **-ized, -iz|ing**. —*v.t.* **1** to bring to or toward a center; locate in a center. **2** to gather together at a center; concentrate: *The administration of the city schools was centralized during Mayor Jones' term of office.* **3** to bring under the control of a single authority.
—*v.i.* to come together at one center. —**cen′tral|iz′er**, *n.*

cen|tral|ly (sen′trə lē), *adv.* at the center; near the center: *The business district is centrally located.*

central nervous system, the part of the nervous system which in vertebrates consists of the brain and spinal cord; the cerebrospinal system of nerves.

cen|tral|ness (sen′trəl nis), *n,* = centrality.

central processing unit, the processor of a computer or computer system. *Abbr.* CPU (no periods)

Central Standard Time or **Central Time**, the standard time in the central part of the United States and Canada. It is six hours behind Greenwich Time and is calculated by setting noon as the time the sun apparently passes the 90th meridian. *Abbr.* C.S.T., c.s.t.

central tendency, *Statistics.* the number or point best representing or most typical of a particular set of data, near the middle of a normal curve of frequency distribution.

cen|tre (sen′tər), *n., v.t., v.i.,* **-tred, -tring**, *adj. Especially British.* center.

cen|tre|board (sen′tər bôrd′, -bōrd′), *n. Especially British.* centerboard.

cen|tred (sen′tərd), *adj. Especially British.* centered.

cen|tre|piece (sen′tər pēs′). *n. Especially British.* centerpiece.

cen|tric (sen′trik), *adj.* **1** that is in or at the center; central. **2** of or characterized by a center. **3** of or having to do with a nerve center. —**cen′tri|cal|ly**, *adv.*

cen|tri|cal (sen′trə kəl), *adj.* = centric.

cen|tri|cal|i|ty (sen′trə kal′ə tē), *n.* central position; centrality.

cen|tri|cip|i|tal (sen′trə sip′ə təl), *adj.* **1** situated in the middle part of the head. **2** of or having to do with the centriciput.

cen|tric|i|put (sen tris′ə pət), *n.* the middle part of the head, between the sinciput and the occiput. [< Latin *centrum* + *caput* head]

cen|tric|i|ty (sen tris′ə tē), *n.* the state of being centric.

cen|trif|u|gal (sen trif′ə gəl, -yə gəl), *adj., n.* —*adj.* **1** moving away from a center: *The centrifugal tendency is powerfully in operation at the equator, but not at all at the poles* (George B. Airy). **2** making use of or acted upon by centrifugal force, as a pump: *centrifugal separation of uranium isotopes* (Time). **3** *Physiology.* efferent. **4** of plants: **a** developing from the center or apex outward or downward. **b** that turns from the center toward the side of the fruit, as a radicle.
—*n.* **1** a centrifugal machine for separating solids from liquids. **2** the rotating drum or cylinder of such a machine.
[< New Latin *centrifugus* (coined by Newton) (< Latin *centrum* center + *fugere* flee from) + English *-al*¹] —**cen|trif′u|gal|ly**, *adv.*

centrifugal casting, the process of pouring metal into a rapidly rotating mold so that the centrifugal force of the rotation forces the metal against the inner surface of the mold.

***centrifugal force** or **action**, the inertia, or tendency to move in one direction, which causes a body turning around a center to move away from the center. See diagram on next page.

centrigugal inflorescence, flowers opening in descending order from the tip.

cen|trif|u|gal|ize (sen trif′ə gəlīz, -yə-), *v.t.,* **-ized, iz|ing**. to subject to a centrifugal process,

as in a centrifugal machine.
centrifugal pump, a pump in which centrifugal force is generated by means of a fanlike impeller.
cen|trif|u|ga|tion (sen trif′yə gā′shən), *n.* the separation of materials of different densities by centrifugal force: *The insoluble membrane fragments can easily be separated by centrifugation from the soluble matrix material* (Scientific American).
cen|tri|fuge (sen′trə fyüj), *n., v.,* **-fuged, -fug|ing.** —*n.* **1** a machine for separating two substances varying in density, as cream from milk or bacteria from a fluid, by means of centrifugal force; centrifugal machine: *The two solvents are well mixed together and then quickly separated again in a centrifuge which spins them apart* (E. Lester Smith). **2** a similar machine used to test the ability of flight personnel and equipment to withstand gravitational forces.
—*v.t.* **1** to separate with a centrifuge. **2** to rotate in a centrifuge; subject to a centrifugal force. [originally, adjective < French *centrifuge* centrifugal < New Latin *centrifugus;* see etym. under **centrifugal**]
cen|tri|ole (sen′trē ōl), *n.* a minute rod-shaped particle within the centrosome of a cell which organizes the spindle fiber during mitosis: *What sight is more ... instructive than the division of a living cell, when one can see the centrioles take hold of the daughter chromosomes and draw them to opposite sides of the cell?* (New Scientist). See diagram under **meiosis.** [< Latin *centrum* center + *-olus,* a diminutive suffix]
cen|trip|e|tal (sen trip′ə təl), *adj.* **1** moving toward a center. **2** making use of or acted upon by centripetal force. **3** *Physiology.* afferent. **4** of plants: **a** developing inward and upward toward the center. **b** that turns toward the axis of the fruit, as a radicle. [< New Latin *centripetus* (coined by Newton) (< Latin *centrum* center + *petere* seek) + English *-al*[1]] —**cen|trip′e|tal|ly,** *adv.*
***centripetal force**, the force that tends to move things toward the center around which they are turning. The earth's gravity exerts a centripetal force on an orbiting satellite and keeps it from flying off into space.

***centripetal force**

centripetal force

centrifugal force

cen|trism (sen′triz əm), *n.* a moderate position or ideology in politics, midway between left and right.
cen|trist (sen′trist), *n., adj.* —*n.* **1** a member of a moderate political party in one of several countries of continental Europe whose political views are neither radical nor conservative. **2** *U.S.* a moderate in politics; middle-of-the-roader: *A "centrist" in the whole American political spectrum must stand left of center within the Republican Party* (Newsweek).
—*adj.* of the center; moderate in politics: *A broad centrist position has become much more popular than adherence to an uncompromising extreme* (Wall Street Journal).
centro-, *combining form.* center; central; to the center: *Centrosphere = center sphere.* [< Latin *centrum* center]
cen|tro|bar|ic (sen′trə bar′ik), *adj.* of or relating to the center of gravity. [< *centro-* + Greek *báros* weight + English *-ic*]
cen|troid (sen′troid), *n.* **1** the center of mass. **2** *Geometry.* the point of intersection of the medians of a triangle.
cen|tro|lec|i|thal (sen′trə les′ə thəl), *adj.* (of eggs) having the yolk in the center surrounded by a layer of protoplasm. [< *centro-* + Greek *lékithos* yolk + English *-al*[1]]
cen|tro|mere (sen′trə mir), *n.* the point on a chromosome by which it is drawn to the pole during mitosis. [< *centro-* + *-mere*]
cen|tro|some (sen′trə sōm), *n.* a very small body found in the cytoplasm of a cell, containing the centriole. During mitosis it separates into two parts and attracts the divided chromosomes, one group to each part. *In animal cells a centrosome may be seen near the nucleus* (A. M. Winchester). [< *centro-* + *-some*[3]]
cen|tro|som|ic (sen′trə som′ik), *adj.* of or having to do with a centrosome or centrosomes.
cen|tro|sphere (sen′trə sfir), *n.* **1** *Biology.* the mass of protoplasm around a centriole in a centrosome, from which the aster rays radiate; the astrosphere: *When present, the centrosphere takes a conspicuous though probably unimportant part in cell division* (A. Franklin Shull). **2** *Geology.* the central core of the earth.
cen|tro|sym|met|ri|cal (sen′trə si met′rə kəl), *adj.* having symmetry with respect to a point or center.
cen|tro|sym|me|try (sen′trə sim′ə trē), *n.* symmetry with respect to a point or center.
cen|trum (sen′trəm), *n., pl.* **-trums** or **-tra. 1** a central part or center. **2** *Anatomy.* the body of a vertebra. The centrum is the solid part to which a bony arch and processes are attached. *Each vertebra is made up of a spoollike centrum surmounted by a neural arch to house the nerve cord* (Tracy I. Storer). [< Latin *centrum* center]
cent sign, the sign ¢, placed after a number to mean cent or cents.
cents-off (sents′ôf′, -of′), *adj. U.S.* having to do with a form of promotion in which the price of a product is reduced by cents when a shopper presents a coupon with the purchase. The store collects the cents-off coupons and is reimbursed by the manufacturer.
cen|tum language (ken′təm), one of the languages of the western division of Indo-European languages, including Greek, Italic, Celtic, and Germanic. The centum languages are characterized by their use of velar sounds such as represented by *k* in *Kent,* instead of the sibilant sounds found in corresponding words of the satem languages. [< Latin *centum* hundred (because the initial letter of this word in centum languages represents the sound of *c* in *cat,* as distinguished from satem languages in which the initial letter represents the sound of *c* in *cent*)]
cen|tum|vir (sen tum′vər), *n., pl.* **-vi|ri** (-və rī), **-virs.** (in ancient Rome) one of a body of 100 judges (actually 105, 3 from each of 35 tribes) appointed to decide common causes among the people. [< Latin *centum* hundred, *viri* men]
cen|tu|ple (sen′tə pəl, -tyə-), *adj., v.,* **-pled, -pling.** —*adj.* 100 times as much or as many.
—*v.t.* to make 100 times as much or as many; increase a hundredfold.
[< Old French *centuple,* learned borrowing from Late Latin *centuplus* hundredfold, Latin *centuplex*]
cen|tu|pli|cate (*adj., n.* sen tü′plə kit, -kāt; -tyü′-; *v.* sen tü′plə kāt, -tyü′-), *adj., n., v.,* **-cat|ed, -cat|ing.** —*adj.* hundredfold; centuple.
—*n.* one hundred forms or versions; 100 copies.
—*v.t.* to increase 100 times; centuple. —**cen|tu′pli|ca′tion,** *n.*
cen|tu|ply (sen′tə plē, -tyə-), *adv.* in centuple measure or quantity.
cen|tu|ri|al (sen tyůr′ē əl, -tůr′-), *adj.* of or having to do with 100 years. [< Latin *centuriālis* < *centuria* century]
cen|tu|ri|ate (*v.* sen tyůr′ē āt, -tůr-′; *adj.* sen tyůr′ē it, -tůr′-, -āt), *v.,* **-at|ed, -at|ing,** *adj.* —*v.t.* **1** to divide into centuries or hundreds. **2** (in Roman colonization) to divide and assign (land).
—*adj.* centuriated.
[< Latin *centuriāre* (with English *-ate*[1]) < *centuria* century] —**cen|tu′ri|a′tion,** *n.*
cen|tu|ried (sen′chər ēd), *adj.* that has lasted for a century or for centuries; centuries old.
cen|tu|ri|on (sen tyůr′ē ən, -tůr′-), *n.* the commander of about 100 soldiers in the ancient Roman army. [< Latin *centuriō, -ōnis* < *centuria*]
cen|tu|ry (sen′chər ē), *n., pl.* **-ries. 1** each 100 years, counting from some special time, such as the birth of Christ: *the 20th century. For the last three centuries, Western civilization has dedicated a good part of its energies to the invention of machines and the extension of their operations into every corner of life* (New Yorker). **2** a period of 100 years. From 1824 to 1924 is a century. *He lived a century.* **3** a group of 100 people or things; a hundred: *Tribes were subdivided into ten units of 1,000 households and each of these into halves composed of five centuries, each century numbering 100 households* (Beals and Hoijer). **4** *Cricket.* a hundred runs in an innings: *... a boy who ... can be relied on to score a century in most school cricket matches* (London Times). **5** a body of soldiers in the ancient Roman army. Originally, it probably consisted of 100 soldiers. **6** a division of the ancient Roman people for voting. Each century had one vote. **7** *U.S. Slang.* 100 dollars. [< Latin *centuria* a division of a hundred units < *centum* hundred]
►The fifth **century** A.D. ran from the beginning of the year 401 to and including the year 500, the nineteenth century from January 1, 1801, through December 31, 1900. Dates before Christ are similarly reckoned. The first century B.C. runs back from the birth of Christ through 100, the second century from 101 through 200. Popularly, confusion arises because many consider the century changes when the numbers advance from the 99th year to the next hundred, making 2000 the first year of the 21st century rather than 2001, but the century always takes its name from the year completing each hundred-year period.
Cen|tu|ry (sen′chər ē), *n.* a style of printing type.
***century plant**, **1** a large plant with thick leaves, a kind of agave, growing in Mexico and the southwestern United States; American aloe; aloe. It sometimes reaches thirty feet in height and is often wrongly supposed to bloom once every 100 years. **2** any one of a group of desert plants in the agave family.

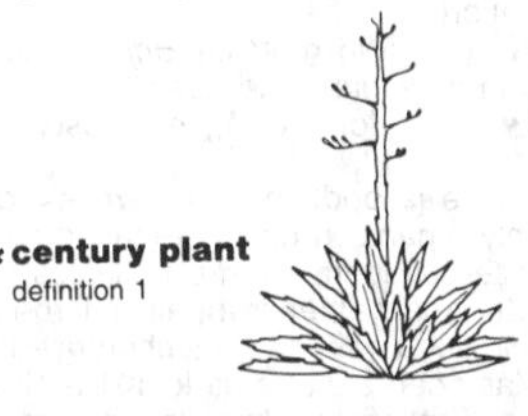
***century plant**
definition 1

Century Schoolbook, a style of modern printing type, often used in textbooks.
CEO (no periods), Chief Executive Officer (of a corporation).
ceol mor (kyôl′ môr′), the classical music of the Scottish Highland bagpipe. [< Gaelic *cèol mór* (literally) great music < *cèol* music + *mór* great]
ceorl (cherl, kyerl), *n.* a freeman of the lowest rank in Anglo-Saxon and medieval England; churl. [Old English *ceorl*]
cepe or **cep** (sēp, sep), *n.* a boletus: *In autumn you can gather here a variety of edible mushrooms, including cepes* (Sunday Times). [< French *cèpe*]
cephal-, *combining form.* the form of **cephalo-** before vowels, as in **cephalic.**
ceph|al|ad (sef′ə lad), *adv. Zoology.* toward the head or anterior end of the body. [< *cephal-* + Latin *ad* toward]
ceph|a|lal|gi|a (sef′ə lal′jē ə), *n.* a headache. [< Latin *cephalalgia* < Greek *kephalḗ* head + *álgos* pain]
ceph|a|las|pid (sef′ə las′pid), *n.* a primitive, ganoid fish found in Devonian strata, having a large plate shaped like a buckler attached to its head. [< Greek *kephalḗ* head + *aspís, -ídos* shield]
ceph|a|late (sef′ə lāt), *adj.* = cephalous.
ce|phal|ic (sə fal′ik), *adj.* **1** of the head. **2** near, on, or in the head. **3** toward the head. [< Latin *cephalicus* < Greek *kephalikós* < *kephalḗ* head]
cephalic index, the ratio of the greatest breadth of the skull to the greatest length from front to back, multiplied by 100. The cephalic index is used in such studies as anthropology and comparative anatomy. *Cro-Magnon skulls are long and narrow with a cephalic index below 75* (Beals and Hoijer).
cephalic vein, a large superficial vein on the front of the arm, running from the elbow to the shoulder.
ceph|a|lin (sef′ə lin), *n.* any one of a group of substances containing phosphorus and resembling lecithin, found in brain tissue. [< *cephal-* + *-in*]
ceph|a|li|za|tion (sef′ə lə zā′shən), *n. Biology.* the degree to which the head is developed and dominates the rest of the body.
cephalo-, *combining form.* **1** head: *Cephalometry = measurement of the head.* **2** head and ___: *Cephalothorax = head and thorax.* Also, **cephal-** before vowels. [< Greek *kephalḗ* head]
ceph|a|lo|car|i|dan (sef′ə lō kar′ə dən), *n.* a recently discovered crustacean, only known living species of a subclass, having a shield around the head characteristic of extinct trilobites. [< *cephalo-* + Greek *kāris, -îdos* shrimp + English *-an*]
ceph|a|lo|cau|dal (sef′ə lō kô′dəl), *adj.* extending from head to tail; having to do with the long axis of the body.
ceph|a|lo|chor|date (sef′ə lō kôr′dāt), *n., adj.* —*n.* any one of a subphylum of semitransparent, fishlike chordate animals having a body pointed at both ends and a notochord running from the body through the indistinct head, but no other skeletal elements. This subphylum comprises the lancelets.
—*adj.* of or belonging to the cephalochordates.
ceph|a|lo|cyst (sef′ə lə sist), *n.* a cyst on the head.
ceph|a|lo|gen|e|sis (sef′ə lō jen′ə sis), *n.* the genesis or development of the head or brain.

Pronunciation Key: hat, āge, cãre, fär; let, ēqual, tėrm; it, īce; hot, ōpen, ôrder; oil, out; cup, půt, rüle; child; long; thin; ᴛʜen; zh, measure; ə represents **a** in about, **e** in taken, **i** in pencil, **o** in lemon, **u** in circus.

ceph|a|lo|ge|net|ic (sef′ə lō jə net′ik), *adj.* having to do with or of the nature of cephalogenesis.

ceph|a|loid (sef′ə loid), *adj. Biology.* shaped like or resembling the head.

ceph|a|lom|e|ter (sef′ə lom′ə tər), *n.* **1** a device for measuring the head, to determine its size and proportions, especially for comparison with those characteristic of a certain sex, race, somatotype, or other distinguishing group. **2** a device for positioning the head precisely, for X-ray measurement or examination.

ceph|a|lo|met|ric (sef′ə lō met′rik), *adj.* having to do with or used in measuring the head.

ceph|a|lom|e|try (sef′ə lom′ə trē), *n.* measurement of the head.

ceph|a|lo|pod (sef′ə lə pod), *n., adj.* **—*n.*** any one of the most highly organized class of marine mollusks, characterized by long, armlike tentacles around the mouth, a large head, a pair of large eyes, a sharp, birdlike beak, and a siphon used in propulsion. Many can expel a dark, inklike fluid out of the siphon. Cuttlefish, squids, octopuses, and nautiluses are cephalopods.
—*adj.* of or belonging to the cephalopods.
[< New Latin *Cephalopoda* < Greek *kephalê* head + *poús, podós* foot]

ceph|a|lop|o|dan (sef′ə lop′ə dən), *n., adj.* = cephalopod.

ceph|a|lop|o|dous (sef′ə lop′ə dəs), *adj.* having to do with or having the characteristics of a cephalopod.

ceph|a|lo|spo|rin (sef′ə lə spôr′in, -spōr′-), *n.* any one of a group of antibiotics chemically related to penicillin, derived from a mold originally found in sewage. [< New Latin *Cephalosporium,* the genus name of the mold < Greek *kephalē* head + *sporá* seed]

ceph|a|lo|tho|rax (sef′ə lō thôr′aks, -thōr′-), *n.* the combined head and thorax of some animals, such as crabs and spiders.

ceph|a|lous (sef′ə ləs), *adj.* having a head; cephalate.

Ce|phe|i (sē′fē ī), *n.* genitive of **Cepheus** (def. 2).

Ceph|e|id (sef′ē id), *n., adj.* **—*n.*** **1** any one of a number of meteors having their radiant in the constellation Cepheus: *The periods of classical Cepheids range from rather over one day to about fifty days* (A. W. Haslett). **2** = Cepheid variable.
—*adj.* having to do with or resembling a Cepheid or a Cepheid variable.
[< *Cepheus* + Latin *-idēs,* a noun suffix]

Cepheid variable, *Astronomy.* any star of a class of variable stars whose changes in brightness recur in a characteristic manner with a relatively short periodicity, and may be due to expansion and contraction.

Ce|phe|us (sē′fē əs, sē′fyüs), *n., genitive* (def. 2) **Ce|phe|i.** **1** *Greek Legend.* an Ethiopian king, husband of Cassiopeia, and father of Andromeda. **2** a northern constellation between Cassiopeia and Draco, near the North Star.

ce|ra|ceous (sə rā′shəs), *adj.* of the nature of wax; waxy.

ce|ram|ic (sə ram′ik), *adj., n.* **—*adj.*** of or having to do with pottery, earthenware, or porcelain, or with making them. Ceramic articles are usually made of fired clay.
—*n.* an article made of pottery, earthenware, or porcelain. Also, **keramic.**
[< Greek *keramikós* < *kéramos* potter's clay, earthen vessel]

ceramic engineering, a branch of engineering concerned with the development, design, and production of heat-resistant, insulating, and other specialized materials mainly for industrial use, such as glass, porcelain, enamels, structural clay products, abrasives, and cements, from nonmetallic minerals.

ce|ram|i|cist (sə ram′ə sist), *n.* **1** an expert in ceramics. **2** a manufacturer of ceramics.

ceramic magnet, a magnet made of ferrite.

ce|ram|ics (sə ram′iks), *n.pl.* **1** (*sing. in use*) the art of making pottery, earthenware, and porcelain: *Ceramics is taught in some colleges.* **2** (*pl. in use*) articles made of pottery, earthenware, or porcelain: *The ceramics in this exhibit were outstanding.*

cer|a|mist (ser′ə mist), *n.* = ceramicist.

ce|ram|o|plas|tic (sə ram′ō plas′tik), *n.* any heat-resistant inorganic plastic made by combining synthetic mica and glass.

ce|rar|gy|rite (sə rär′jə rīt), *n.* native chloride of sliver; horn silver. *Formula:* AgCl [< Greek *kéras* horn + *árgyros* silver + English *-ite*[1]]

ce|ras|tes (sə ras′tēz), *n.* a poisonous snake found in deserts of Africa and of Asia Minor, having a projecting hornlike scale above each eye; horned viper. [< Latin *cerastēs* < Greek *kerástēs* < *kéras* horn]

ce|ras|ti|um (sə ras′tē əm), *n.* a kind of chickweed with horn-shaped capsules. [< New Latin *Cerastium* the genus name < Greek *kerástēs* horned < *kéras* horn]

ce|rate (sir′āt), *n. Medicine.* a firm ointment made of lard or oil mixed with wax or resin. [< Latin *cērātum,* neuter past participle of *cērāre* to wax < *cēra* wax]

ce|rat|ed (sir′ā tid), *adj.* covered with wax; waxed.

cer|a|tin (ser′ə tin), *n.* = keratin.

ce|rat|i|nous (sə rat′ə nəs), *adj.* = keratinous.

cer|a|ti|tis (ser′ə tī′tis), *n. Medicine.* inflammation of the cornea. [< Greek *kéras, -atos* horn; (later) cornea + English *-itis*]

ce|rat|o|dus (sə rat′ə dəs, ser′ə tō′-), *n.* any one of a genus of Australian freshwater lungfishes (a genus so called from the hornlike ridges of the teeth), especially the barramunda. [< New Latin *Ceratodus* < Greek *kéras, -ātos* horn + *odoús* tooth]

cer|a|toid (ser′ə toid), *adj.* **1** horny. **2** shaped like a horn. [< Greek *kerātoeidês* < *kéras, -ātos* horn + *eîdos* form]

cer|a|tops (ser′ə tops), *n.* a plant-eating, Cretaceous dinosaur bearing a horn over each eye. [< New Latin *Ceratops* the genus name < Greek *kéras, -ātos* horn + *ôps* face]

cer|a|top|si|an (ser′ə top′sē ən), *n., adj.* **—*n.*** any one of a group of horned, herbivorous dinosaurs of the Cretaceous period, including the triceratops: *Ceratopsians looked much like rhinoceroses, but many ... were larger* (S. P. Welles).
—*adj.* of or having to do with ceratopsians or the ceratops.

cer|a|top|sid (ser′ə top′sid), *adj., n.* = ceratopsian.

cer|a|to|sau|rus (ser′ə tə sôr′əs), *n.* any one of a group of bipedal dinosaurs of the Jurassic period, about twenty feet in length, and characterized by a large skull bearing a horn. [< New Latin *Ceratosaurus* the genus name < Greek *kéras, -ātos* horn + *saûros* lizard]

ce|rau|no|graph (sə rô′nə graf, -gräf), *n.* an instrument for recording electric disturbances in the atmosphere due to thunderstorms or lightning. [< Greek *keraunós* thunderbolt + English *-graph*]

Cer|be|re|an (sər bir′ē ən), *adj.* relating to or resembling Cerberus.

Cer|ber|us (sėr′bər əs), *n.* **1** *Greek and Roman Mythology.* a dog with three heads that guarded the entrance to Hades. **2** a surly, watchful guard: *... give that Cerberus a sop [bribe]* (William Congreve).

cer|car|i|a (sər kãr′ē ə), *n., pl.* **-i|ae** (-ē ē). a second larval stage of trematode worms, in which the body is usually shaped like a tadpole. [< New Latin *Cercaria* < Greek *kérkos* tail]

cer|car|i|al (sər kãr′ē əl), *adj.* = cercarian.

cer|car|i|an (sər kãr′ē ən), *n., adj.* **—*n.*** a trematode worm or fluke in its second larval stage; cercaria.
—*adj.* having to do with or having the characteristics of a cercaria.

cer|cis (sėr′səs), *n.* = Judas tree. [< *Cercis* the genus name < Greek *kerkis* the Judas tree]

cer|cle (serk′lə), *n. French.* an administrative district, especially one in a French colony or former French colony, such as Mali (a country in western Africa).

cer|cus (sėr′kəs), *n., pl.* **-ci** (-kī). a small sensory appendage of insects, one of a pair extending from the posterior tip of the abdomen. [< New Latin *cercus* < Greek *kérkos* tail]

cere[1] (sir), *n.* a waxy-looking membrane through which the nostrils open near the beak of certain birds, especially birds of prey and parrots. [< Medieval Latin *cera* < Latin *cēra* wax]

cere[2] (sir), *v.t.,* **cered, cer|ing.** to wrap in a cerecloth. [< Latin *cērāre* to wax < *cēra* wax]

ce|re|al (sir′ē əl), *n., adj.* **—*n.*** **1** any grass that produces a grain which is used for food. Wheat, rice, corn, oats, and barley are cereals. Cereals provide the basic food of most of mankind. **2** the grain. **3** any food made from the grain. Oatmeal and cornflakes are breakfast cereals. [< adjective]
—*adj.* of grain; having to do with grain or the grasses producing it: *cereal crops, cereal products.*
[< Latin *Cereālis* having to do with Ceres]

ce|re|al|ist (sir′ē ə list), *n.* an expert in the study of cereals.

cereal leaf beetle, a small leaf beetle that feeds on grain, particularly oats, causing severe damage to crops: *It was feared that a cereal leaf beetle, found to be spreading through grain belt areas in Michigan, Ohio, and Indiana, would develop into a major pest* (Science News Letter).

cer|e|bel|lar (ser′ə bel′ər), *adj.* having to do with or relating to the cerebellum: *The folds of the outer surface elaborate into subfolds deep within the organ; only 15 per cent of the cerebellar cortex can be seen without dissection* (Scientific American).

cer|e|bel|lum (ser′ə bel′əm), *n., pl.* **-bel|lums, -bel|la** (-bel′ə). the part of the brain that controls the coordination of the muscles. It consists of a middle lobe and two lateral lobes and is located below the back part of the cerebrum. *Each side of the cerebellum acts on muscles on the same side of the body* (A. Franklin Shull). See picture under **brain.** [< Medieval Latin *cerebellum* the hindbrain (diminutive) < Latin *cerebrum* brain]

cer|e|bral (ser′ə brəl, sə rē′-), *adj., n.* **—*adj.*** **1** of the brain: *A cerebral concussion may cause a person to faint.* **2** of the cerebrum. **3** *Figurative.* characterized by thought and reason rather than emotion or action; requiring intellectual analysis: *cerebral poetry. Chess is a cerebral game.* **SYN:** mental, rational, logical. **4** *Phonetics.* cacuminal.
—*n.* *Phonetics.* a cacuminal sound.
[< Latin *cerebrum* brain + English *-al*[1]]

cerebral accident, an apoplectic stroke; cerebrovascular accident.

cerebral cortex, the layer of gray matter that covers the cerebrum; cortex: *The largest part of the cerebral cortex is concerned with complex mental processes such as memory, speech, and thought* (H. H. Jasper).

cerebral death, = brain death.

cerebral ganglia, ganglia of the nervous system situated in the head, or a part of the body considered as the head, in many invertebrates.

cerebral hemisphere, either of the two lobes of the cerebrum.

cerebral hemorrhage, bleeding that results from a broken blood vessel in the brain. Blood escapes into the brain and destroys or damages the surrounding tissue, causing the victim to suffer a stroke.

cer|e|bral|ism (ser′ə brə liz′əm), *n.* **1** the belief that consciousness is a function of the brain and may be explained only in this way. **2** *Figurative.* intellectualism, especially abstractionism, in art, music, literature, or the like.

cerebral letters, a class of consonants recognized in Sanskrit and other Indian languages, developed from the dentals by retracting the tongue and applying its tip to the palate.

cer|e|bral|ly (ser′ə brə lē, sə rē′-), *adv.* **1** due to brain damage: *A machine ... will allow cerebrally palsied children to communicate with their teachers* (New Scientist). **2** *Figurative.* in a cerebral manner; intellectually: *Koun talks about the play with insight but not, as he says, "cerebrally"* (London Times).

cerebral palsy, a disabling condition caused by damage to the brain, usually before or at birth. Persons suffering from cerebral palsy have trouble coordinating their muscles and tend to make involuntary jerky movements.

cerebral thrombosis, the formation of a clot, or thrombus, in one of the blood vessels of the brain, causing a stroke.

cerebral vesicles, the three primitive, hollow dilations into which the embryonic brain of vertebrates is divided.

cer|e|brate (ser′ə brāt), *v.i.,* **-brat|ed, -brat|ing.** to use the brain; think. [< Latin *cerebrum* brain + English *-ate*[1]]

cer|e|bra|tion (ser′ə brā′shən), *n.* the action of the brain; mental activity; thinking: *... the deep well of unconscious cerebration* (Henry James). *Only the mechanical part of cerebration is slowly being disclosed* (Saturday Review).

cer|e|bric (ser′ə brik; sə reb′rik, -rē′brik), *adj.* of the brain; having to do with or from the brain.

ce|reb|ri|form (sə reb′rə form), *adj.* having the shape or structure of the brain. [< Latin *cerebrum* brain + English *-form*]

cer|e|bri|tis (ser′ə brī′tis), *n.* inflammation of the cerebrum. [< Latin *cerebrum* brain + English *-itis*]

cer|e|bro|car|di|ac (ser′ə brō kär′dē ak), *adj.* of or affecting both the brain and the heart. [< Latin *cerebrum* brain + English *cardiac*]

cer|e|broid (ser′ə broid, sə rē′-), *adj.* resembling or akin to a brain.

cer|e|bro|path|y (ser′ə brō path′ē, sə rē′-), *n.* hypochondria or other symptoms once associated with overwork of the brain. [< Latin *cerebrum* + English *-pathy*]

cer|e|bro|side (ser′ə brə sīd′), *n.* any one of a class of lipoids found in nerve tissue. [< *cerebrum* + *-ose*[2] + *-ide*]

cer|e|bro|spi|nal (ser′ə brō spī′nəl), *adj.* **1** of or having to do with both the brain and the spinal cord: *a cerebrospinal nerve.* **2** of or designating the part of the nervous system of vertebrates consisting of the brain and the spinal cord, with the cranial and spinal nerves which control voluntary acts. [< Latin *cerebrum* brain + English *spinal*]

cerebrospinal fluid, the clear fluid normally present in the central membrane of the three membranes, the meninges, and enveloping the brain and spinal cord.

cerebrospinal meningitis or **fever,** an infectious, epidemic, febrile bacterial disease, often fatal, characterized by inflammation of the meninges of the brain and spinal cord, and causing headache, constipation, delirium, and, often, small red or purplish spots on the skin; brain fever; spotted fever; epidemic cerebrospinal meningitis.

cer|e|brot|o|my (ser′ə brot′ə mē), *n., pl.* **-mies**. surgical incision into the brain. [< Latin *cerebrum* brain + Greek *-tomíā* a cutting]

cer|e|bro|ton|ic (ser′ə brō ton′ik), *adj., n. Psychiatry.* **—*adj.*** characterized by marked awareness of one's surroundings and withdrawal from physical activity or enjoyment of physical pleasures.

—*n.* a person who exhibits a cerebrotonic condition.

[< Latin *cerebrum* brain + English *tonic*]

cer|e|bro|vas|cu|lar (ser′ə brō vas′kyə lər), *adj.* of or having to do with the blood vessels of the cerebrum: *cerebrovascular diseases.*

cerebrovascular accident, = cerebral accident.

cer|e|bro|vis|cer|al (ser′ə brō vis′ər əl), *adj.* of or having to do with the cerebral and visceral nervous ganglia of mollusks. [< Latin *cerebrum* brain + English *visceral*]

cer|e|brum (ser′ə brəm, sə rē′-), *n., pl.* **-brums, -bra** (-brə). **1** *Anatomy.* **a** the part of the human brain, certain areas of which control particular processes of thought and voluntary muscular movements. It consists of two large lobes (cerebral hemispheres), on the right and on the left. The cerebrum is located above the cerebellum and medulla oblongata and fills nearly the whole cavity of the skull. See picture under **brain**. **b** the anatomically corresponding part of the brain of any vertebrate: *The cerebrum has complex folds in the higher mammals which increase its efficiency* (A. M. Winchester). **2** the brain as a whole (humorously or loosely). [< Latin *cerebrum*]

cere|cloth (sir′klôth′, -kloth′), *n.* **1** waxed cloth. **2** a waxed cloth in which a dead person is wrapped for burial. [earlier *cered cloth* < *cere* to wax, cere]

cered (sird), *adj.* (of birds) having a cere.

cere|ment (sir′mənt), *n.* **1** Often, **cerements**. a cloth or garment in which a dead person is wrapped for burial: *Look at her garments Clinging like cerements* (Thomas Hood). **2** waxed cloth; cerecloth. [< French *cirement* < Latin *cērāre;* see etym. under **cere²**]

cer|e|mo|ni|al (ser′ə mō′nē əl), *adj., n.* **—*adj.*** **1** of or having to do with ceremony: *The emperor's ceremonial costumes were beautiful.* **2** very formal: *The President received his guests in a ceremonial way.*

—*n.* **1** the formal actions proper to an occasion; ritual. Bowing the head and kneeling are ceremonials of religion. **2** a rite or ceremony. **3a** a formality of courtesy or manners. **b** the observance of these in social life. **4** in the Roman Catholic Church: the ordering of religious rites and ceremonies. **5** *Obsolete.* a robe or garment worn on some ceremonial occasion. **—cer′e|mo′ni|al|ly**, *adv.* **—cer′e|mo′ni|al|ness**, *n.*

—*Syn.* *adj.* **1, 2 Ceremonial, ceremonious** differ in meaning and use. **Ceremonial** means having to do with ceremony, and applies to things involving or belonging to ceremonies and formalities of the church, law, polite conduct, fraternities, or other groups or bodies. *Shriners wear ceremonial costumes.* **Ceremonious** means full of ceremony and applies to things done with ceremony or showy formality or to people who pay very strict attention to the details of polite conduct: *ceremonious politeness. The banquet was a ceremonious affair.*

cer|e|mo|ni|al|ism (ser′ə mō′nē ə liz′əm), *n.* **1** adherence to or fondness for ceremonies, for example in religion: *Ceremonialism ... calls on the pageantry of ritual to reinforce belief by dramatizing the deeds of the gods and their place in the universe* (Melville J. Herskovits). **2** ceremonies collectively. **—cer′e|mo′ni|al|ist**, *n.*

cer|e|mo|ni|ous (ser′ə mō′nē əs), *adj.* **1** full of ceremony: *a ceremonious religion. There was a ceremonious unveiling of the statue.* **2** very formal; extremely polite: *a ceremonious welcome.* **SYN:** See syn. under **ceremonial**. **3** adhering to conventional formalities; made in the recognized formal manner: *a ceremonious bow, ceremonious condolences.* **—cer′e|mo′ni|ous|ly**, *adv.* **—cer′e|mo′ni|ous|ness**, *n.*

cer|e|mo|ny (ser′ə mō′nē), *n., pl.* **-nies**. **1** a special form or set of acts to be done on special occasions such as weddings, funerals, graduations, or holidays: *The marriage ceremony was performed in the church. The Sunday morning service, at many of our Protestant churches, exemplifies a ceremony, which may include such rituals as reciting the Lord's prayer, singing prescribed hymns, and performing the sacrament or communion* (Beals and Hoijer). **2** very polite conduct; way of conducting oneself that follows all the rules of polite social behavior: *The old gentleman showed us to the door with a great deal of ceremony.* **3** attention to forms and customs; formality or formalities: *The young prince disliked the traditional ceremony of the court.* **4** an empty form; meaningless formality: *Instead, they put the burden of order onto their children and filled their days with specious rites and ceremonies* (New Yorker). **5** *Obsolete.* an external accessory or symbolic attribute of worship, state, or pomp.

stand on ceremony, to be too polite; be very formal: *He is a hospitable person who does not stand on ceremony and so makes everyone feel at ease in his home.*

[< Latin *caerimōnia* rite]

—*Syn.* **1 Ceremony, rite** mean a set of dignified and usually traditional practices followed on special occasions. **Ceremony** applies to the observances or procedure used on religious, public, or other solemn occasions: *The graduation ceremony was inspiring.* **Rite** applies to a fixed ceremony, in which both the actions and the words are prescribed: *A priest administered the last rites to the dying man.*

Ce|ren|kov counter (chə ren′kôf), a device for detecting and counting the particles in the Cerenkov effect, used especially to study the behavior of high-energy particles, such as cosmic rays and atomic particles. Also, **Cherenkov counter** or **detector**. [< P. A. *Cerenkov,* born 1904, a Soviet physicist, who first observed the Cerenkov effect]

Cerenkov effect or **radiation**, visible radiation produced when electrons or other charged particles pass through a transparent solid or liquid medium faster than the speed of light in the same medium. The blue glow seen in the water of a nuclear reactor is this kind of radiation. Also, **Cherenkov effect** or **radiation**.

Ce|res (sir′ēz), *n.* **1** the Roman goddess of agriculture and the harvest and the mother of Proserpina. The Greeks called her Demeter. **2** the first and largest asteroid to be discovered. [< Latin *Cerēs* Ceres, grain]

ce|re|us (sir′ē əs), *n.* any one of several cactuses, found in the southwestern United States and tropical America, having large tubular flowers. The night-blooming cereus has fragrant flowers that open only at night. [< Latin *cēreus* wax candle < *cēra* wax]

ce|ri|a (sir′ē ə), *n.* a pale-yellow powder, cerium dioxide, a rare earth, used in ceramics and in incandescent gas mantles; cerium oxide. *Formula:* CeO_2[< *cerium*]

ce|ric (sir′ik, ser′-), *adj. Chemistry.* containing cerium, especially with a valence of four: *Its [cerium's] trivalent compounds are called the cerous series and its tetravalent ones the ceric series* (Scientific American).

ce|rif|er|ous (sə rif′ər əs), *adj.* producing wax. [< Latin *cēra* wax + English *-ferous*]

ce|rise (sə rēs′, -rēz′), *adj., n.* **—*adj.*** bright pinkish-red.

—*n.* a bright, pinkish red; cherry.

[< French *cerise.* See etym. of doublet **cherry**.]

ce|rite (sir′īt), *n.* a hydrated silicate of cerium and other metals, one of the chief sources of cerium. [< *cer* (ium) + *-ite¹*]

***ce|ri|um** (sir′ē əm), *n.* a grayish metallic chemical element which occurs only in combination with other elements. It is malleable and ductile and is used in porcelain, glass, and alloys. Cerium is one of the rare-earth metals. [< New Latin *cerium* < *Ceres,* the asteroid]

***cerium**

symbol	atomic number	atomic weight	oxidation state
Ce	58	140.12	3,4

cerium metals, *Chemistry.* a group of closely related rare-earth elements, consisting of cerium, lanthanum, praseodymium, neodymium, promethium, samarium, and europium.

cerium oxide, = ceria.

cer|met (sėr′met), *n.* an alloy of a heat-resistant compound and a metal, used where strength and ability to withstand extremely high temperatures are the primary requirements. Cermets combine the properties of ceramic and metallic materials. *Among the firm's latest products is "cermet," a mixture of ceramics and metals, which is used as a coating liner in combustion chambers and exhaust tubes in jet engines* (Wall Street Journal). [< *cer*(amic) + *met*(al)]

CERN (sėrn), European Council for Nuclear Research (French, *Conseil Européen pour la Recherche Nucléaire)* , an organization of 11 nations centered in Geneva: *CERN ... has been a very successful offspring of UNESCO* (New Scientist).

cer|nu|ous (sėr′nyü əs, -nü-), *adj. Botany.* having the top bent downward; drooping; nodding, as a flower. [< Latin *cernuus* (with English *-ous*) inclined forward]

ce|ro (sir′ō), *n., pl.* **-ros** or (*collectively*) **-ro**. a Spanish mackerel of the Atlantic coast from Cape Cod to Brazil, an important food and game fish; pintado; kingfish; sierra. [< Spanish *sierra* sawfish < Latin *serra* saw]

ce|ro|graph|ic (sir′ə graf′ik, ser′-), *adj.* having to do with cerography.

ce|rog|ra|phist (sə rog′rə fist), *n.* a person skilled in cerography.

ce|rog|ra|phy (sə rog′rə fē), *n.* **1** the art of writing or engraving on wax. **2** encaustic painting. [< Latin *cēra* wax + English *-graphy*]

ce|ro|plas|tic (sir′ə plas′tik, ser′-), *adj.* of or relating to modeling in wax. [< Greek *kēroplastikós* having to do with wax modeling < *kērós* wax + *plastós* molded < *plássein* to mold]

ce|ro|plas|tics (sir′ə plas′tiks, ser′-), *n.* **1** objects modeled in wax. **2** the art of modeling in wax.

ce|rot|ic (sə rot′ik), *adj.* of or derived from beeswax. [< Latin *cērōtum* cerate (< Greek *kērōtē,* ultimately < *kērós* wax) + English *-ic*]

cerotic acid, *Chemistry.* a mixture of two fatty acids found together in beeswax and in carnauba wax. *Formulas:* $C_{26}H_{52}O_2$ and $C_{27}H_{54}O_2$

ce|ro|type (sir′ə tīp, ser′-), *n.* a process of engraving in which a design is cut into a coating of wax on a metal plate, and a printing plate made from it. [< Greek *kērós* wax + English *type*]

ce|rous¹ (sir′əs), *adj. Chemistry.* **1** containing cerium, especially with a valence of three. **2** of cerium. [< *cer* (ium) + *-ous*]

cer|ous² (sir′əs), *adj.* of the nature of or like a cere. [< *cer* (e)¹ + *-ous*]

cert (sėrt), *n. British Slang.* a certain or safe bet. [short for *certain*]

cer|tain (sėr′tən), *adj., n., adv.* **—*adj.*** **1** without a doubt; sure: *It is certain that 2 and 3 do not make 4. I am certain these are the facts. He is certain to change his mind.* **SYN:** See syn. under **sure**. **2** known but not named; some; particular: *certain nations, to a certain degree. A certain person gave our church $1000. Certain of Longfellow's ballads are effective and unforgettable* (Edmund Wilson). **3** settled; fixed: *at a certain hour. He earns a certain amount of money each week.* **4** that can be depended on; reliable: *I have certain information that school will end a day earlier this year.* **SYN:** dependable, trustworthy, unfailing. **5** sure to happen; inevitable: *In this world nothing can be said to be certain but death and taxes* (Benjamin Franklin). **6** *Obsolete.* resolved; steadfast.

—*n.* **for certain**, as a certainty; surely; without a doubt: *He will be here for certain. I hear for certain that Ormond has concluded a peace with the Rebels* (Oliver Cromwell).

—*adv.* *Obsolete.* certainly; of a truth; assuredly: *You will, I am certain-sure, be well pleased* (Robert Southey).

[< Old French *certain* < Vulgar Latin *certānus* < Latin *certus* sure, (originally) past participle of *cernere* decide] **—cer′tain|ness**, *n.*

cer|tain|ly (sėr′tən lē), *adv.* **1** without a doubt; surely: *I will certainly be at the party. "Do you still think the same?" "Certainly."* **2** with certainty; without fail: *He will regret this act as certainly as the sun will rise tomorrow.* **3** admittedly: *Certainly I parked outside your door.*

cer|tain|ty (sėr′tən tē), *n., pl.* **-ties**. **1** freedom from doubt; being certain: *The man's certainty was amusing, for we could all see that he was wrong.* **SYN:** assurance, conviction, certitude. **2** something certain; a sure fact: *The coming of spring and summer is a certainty. Know for a certainty that the Lord your God will no more drive out any of these nations from before you* (Joshua 23:13). [< Anglo-French *certeinte,* Old French *certainete* < *certain* certain]

cer|tes (sėr′tēz), *adv. Archaic.* certainly; in truth. [< Old French *certes* < Gallo-Romance *certās* surely, for Latin *certō,* adverb of *certus* certain]

cer|ti|fi|a|ble (sėr′tə fī′ə bəl), *adj.* **1** able to be certified: *positive and certifiable results.* **2** insane to a degree that justifies legal certification as such: *I shall be certifiable ... when I allow a few newspaper reporters to decide my future for me* (Time). *[He] was a blithering dolt barely this side of being certifiable* (Maclean's). **—cer′ti|fi′a|bly**, *adv.*

cer|tif|i|cate (*n.* sər tif′ə kit; *v.* sər tif′ə kāt), *n., v.,* **-cat|ed, -cat|ing**. **—*n.*** **1** a written or printed statement that may be used as proof of some fact. A birth certificate gives the date and place of a person's birth and the names of his parents. *The vessel was licensed to carry only twenty passengers; but ... the restrictions of the certifi-*

Pronunciation Key: hat, āge, cãre, fär; let, ēqual, tėrm; it, īce; hot, ōpen, ôrder; **oi**l, **ou**t; cup, pu̇t, rüle; **ch**ild; lo**ng**; **th**in; ᴛʜen; **zh**, measure; **ə** represents **a** in about, **e** in taken, **i** in pencil, **o** in lemon, **u** in circus.

cate did not apply to trade between Mediterranean ports (Saturday Review). **2** a written statement of facts or proceedings, usually certified by one court and passed to another: *When the issue is whether a person was absent in the army, this is tried by the certificate of the proper officer, in writing, under his seal* (William Blackstone). **3** paper currency issued by the United States government.
—***v.t.*** **1** to authorize by a certificate; provide with a certificate: *to register and certificate midwives. His Bill would also require that every new boiler plant was certificated according to minimum standards of efficiency* (London Times). **2** to give a certificate stating (a fact): *His good character is adequately certificated.*
[< Medieval Latin *certificatum,* neuter past participle of Late Latin *certificāre* certify]

cer|tif|i|cat|ed airline (sər tif′ə kā′tid), *U.S.* an airline that receives permission from the federal government to use commercial transport planes for scheduled flights.

certificate of deposit, a written acknowledgment by a bank that it has received from the person named a certain sum of money as a deposit. It is negotiable or transferable.

certificate of disability, *U.S.* an official medical certificate stating that a man is no longer able to perform military duties.

certificate of incorporation, a document attesting that a certain corporation has been legally formed, and giving its name, purpose, etc.

certificate of indebtedness, a short-term, negotiable note representing acknowledgment of a debt, especially one issued to cover current government expenses.

certificate of necessity, a certificate issued by an agency of the federal government to a corporation building new plant facilities to produce goods for defense, which permits the corporation to amortize the cost at an accelerated rate; in effect, a tax reduction.

certificate of origin, a document certifying the place of production of a stated commodity, required by the customs authorities in some countries.

certificate of stock, = stock certificate.

cer|ti|fi|ca|tion (sėr′tə fə kā′shən), *n.* **1** the act of certifying or the state of being certified: *the advantages of certification, the certification of teachers.* **2a** a certified statement; certificate: *He hopes to be able to obtain a duplicate of his lost certification.* **b** the writing on the face of a check which certifies it.

cer|tif|i|ca|to|ry (sər tif′ə kə tôr′ē, -tōr′-), *adj.* giving certification.

cer|ti|fied (sėr′tə fīd), *adj.* **1** guaranteed: *certified Grade AA butter.* **2** having a certificate: *a certified teacher.*

certified check, a check whose value is guaranteed by the bank upon whose account it is drawn.

certified mail, *U.S.* a letter or parcel whose delivery is recorded and certified by the postal service, for extra postage. It is designed to insure delivery to the addressee of mail that does not contain valuables, and is cheaper than registered mail.

certified milk, raw or pasteurized milk guaranteed to meet certain official standards.

certified public accountant, *U.S.* an accountant who has fulfilled the legal requirements and been given a state certificate to practice public accounting, and who may use the abbreviation C.P.A. after his name. In Great Britain a *chartered accountant* has an equivalent status.

cer|ti|fy (sėr′tə fī), *v.,* **-fied, -fy|ing.** —***v.t.*** **1** to declare (something) true or correct by an official spoken, written, or printed statement: *This diploma certifies that you have completed high school.* SYN: attest, affirm. **2** to guarantee the quality or value of: *The fire inspector certified the school building as fireproof.* SYN: endorse. **3** to guarantee as certain; attest the reliability of: *The man's employers certified his honesty and reliability.* **4** to make certain; assure; inform reliably: *Lord, let me know ... the number of my days: that I may be certified how long I have to live* (Book of Common Prayer). **5** *U.S.* to guarantee in writing on the face of (a check) that the drawer has sufficient funds in the hands of the bank upon which it is drawn to meet it. **6** to declare (a person) legally insane: *If anybody had predicted back then that we'd be selling at the rate we're selling now, he'd have been certified* (New Yorker).
—***v.i.*** to make a certification; vouch for; give one's testimony (for, to): *... one of the medical men certifying to the insanity of a gentleman* (Alfred Taylor). SYN: testify.
[< Old French *certifier,* learned borrowing from Late Latin *certificāre* < Latin *certus* sure + *facere* make] —**cer′ti|fi|er**, *n.*

cer|ti|o|rar|i (sėr′shē ə rãr′ē, -ī), *n. Law.* an order from a higher law court to a lower court or tribunal, calling for the record of a case for review in the higher court: *a writ of certiorari.* [< Late Latin *certiōrārī* to be informed, certified]

cer|ti|tude (sėr′tə tüd, -tyüd), *n.* the state or quality of feeling certain; certainty; absence of doubt; sureness. [< Late Latin *certitūdō* < Latin *certus* sure; certain]

ce|ru|le|an (sə rü′lē ən), *adj., n.* —***adj.*** sky-blue.
—***n.*** a sky-blue color; cerulean blue.
[< Latin *caeruleus,* variant of *caerulus* dark blue (< *caelum* sky) + English *-an*]

cerulean blue, **1** sky-blue; azure: *... the cerulean blue mosaic-tiled dome* (Newsweek). **2** a cobalt compound used as a pigment by artists and interior decorators, and in ceramics.

cerulean warbler, a warbler of central North America, the male of which has blue and gray upper parts and white underparts.

ce|ru|le|um (sə rü′lē əm), *n.* = cerulean blue (def. 2).

ce|ru|lo|plas|min (sə rü′lə plaz′min), *n.* an enzyme in blood, blue in its purified state, which promotes the oxidation and circulation of copper: *In* Science *for January 18, 1957 (125,117) appeared evidence that ceruloplasmin runs high in serum of schizophrenic patients* (Scientific American). [< Latin *caerulus* dark blue + English *plasm (a)* + *-in*]

ce|ru|men (sə rü′mən), *n.* a waxlike substance in the ears; earwax. [< Medieval Latin *cerumen* < Latin *cēra* wax; probably patterned on Latin *ferumen* glue, solder]

ce|ru|mi|nous (sə rü′mə nəs), *adj.* relating to or containing cerumen.

ce|ruse (sir′üs, si rüs′), *n.* **1** = white lead. **2** a skin cosmetic containing this substance. [< French *céruse,* learned borrowing from Latin *cērussa,* probably < unrecorded Greek *kēroûssa* waxy < Greek *kērós* wax]

ce|rus|site (sir′ə sīt), *n.* a mineral, carbonate of lead, a common ore of lead, found in whitish crystals; white lead. *Formula:* $PbCO_3$ [< Latin *cērussa* ceruse + *-ite*[1]]

cer|ve|lat (ser′və lä′), *n.* a kind of highly seasoned dry sausage, originally made of brains but now usually of young pork salted; saveloy. [< Old French *cervelat* < Italian *cervellata* < *cervello* brain < Latin *cerebellum* cerebellum]

cer|vi|cal (sėr′və kəl), *adj.* **1** of or having to do with the neck or cervix: *cervical vertebrae.* **2** of or having to do with a cervix or necklike part, for example of the uterus. [< Latin *cervīx, -īcis* neck + English *-al*[1]]

cer|vi|ces (sər vī′sēz), *n.* cervixes; a plural of **cervix**.

cer|vi|ci|tis (sėr′və sī′təs), *n.* inflammation of the cervix of the uterus. [< Latin *cervīx, -īcis* neck + English *-itis*]

cer|vi|co|dor|sal (sėr′və kō dôr′səl), *adj.* relating to or affecting both the neck and the back. [< Latin *cervīx* neck + English *dorsal*]

cer|vine (sėr′vīn, -vin), *adj.* **1** of or like a deer. **2** of a deep tawny or fawn color. [< Latin *cervīnus* < *cervus* deer]

Cer-Vit (sėr′vit), *n. Trademark.* an extremely heat-resistant glass made from fused silica.

cer|vix (sėr′viks), *n., pl.* **-vix|es** or **-vi|ces**. **1** the neck, especially the back of the neck. **2** a necklike part of an organ, especially of the uterus or the bladder. **3** a necklike part of a tooth. [< Latin *cervīx, -īcis*]

cer|void (sėr′void), *adj.* like a deer. [< Latin *cervus* deer + English *-oid*]

Ce|sar|e|an or **Ce|sar|i|an** (si zãr′ē ən), *adj., n.* = Caesarean.

ce|sar|e|vitch (si zär′ə vich), *n.* = czarevitch (def.1).

***ce|si|um** (sē′zē əm, sē′sē-), *n.* a soft, silvery metallic chemical element that occurs as a minute part of various minerals. It is one of the alkali metals and is highly electropositive. Scientists use the rate of vibration of cesium atoms as a standard for measuring time. Cesium is also used in photoelectric cells. Also, **caesium**. [< New Latin *caesium,* neuter of Latin *caesius* bluish-gray]

***cesium**

symbol	atomic number	atomic weight	oxidation state
Cs	55	132.905	1

cesium 137, a radioactive isotope of cesium that occurs in fission products and in fallout from nuclear explosions. It has been used in cancer research and therapy. *Cesium 137 is a relatively long-lived radioactive material similar to phosphorus. When taken into the body, it accumulates in the muscles where it can cause a genetic hazard* (Science News Letter).

cesium clock, an atomic clock which measures time by the frequency of the atomic vibrations of the element cesium: *He will match the rate of incoming pulses [from a pulsar] against a cesium clock, an atomic timer that is accurate to one part in 10 trillion* (Time).

ces|pi|tose (ses′pə tōs), *adj.* growing in dense tufts or clumps; turfy. Also, **caespitose**. [< New Latin *caespitosus* < Latin *caespes, -itis* turf]
—**ces′pi|tose′ly**, *adv.*

ces|pi|tous (ses′pə təs), *adj.* = cespitose: *A cespitous or turfy plant has many stems from the same root* (Thomas Martyn).

cess[1] (ses), *n., v. Dialect.* —***n.*** a tax: **a** a rate or tax levied by a local authority: *the parish cess, the church cess.* **b** (in Scotland) the land tax. **c** (in British India) a tax for a specified purpose: *the irrigation cess, the education cess.*
—***v.t.*** to assess.
[short for *assess*]

cess[2] (ses), *n. Anglo-Irish.* luck (only in *bad cess to*): *Sir Lancelot was bad cess to his women* (Atlantic). [perhaps short for *success*]

ces|sa|tion (se sā′shən), *n.* a stopping; a ceasing; discontinuance: *Both armies agreed on a cessation of the fighting. The cessation of conversation caused the hostess to look up.* SYN: stoppage, interruption, suspension. [< Latin *cessātiō, -ōnis* < *cessāre* cease]

ces|sion (sesh′ən), *n.* **1** a handing over to another; ceding; giving up; surrendering: *the cession of territories. If the cession could not be avoided, it was of the utmost importance to secure some advance recognition from the French of the special American interests in Louisiana* (Atlantic). **2** a right, territory, piece of property, or other thing ceded; concession. [< Latin *cessiō, -ōnis* < *cēdere* to yield]

ces|sion|ar|y (sesh′ə ner′ē), *n., pl.* **-ar|ies**. a person to whom something is ceded, assigned, or granted.

cess|pipe (ses′pīp′), *n.* a pipe for carrying off drainage from a cesspool, sink, or the like. [< *cess* (pool) + *pipe*]

cess|pit (ses′pit′), *n.* a pit for refuse: *The drain-pipes were sloping inland toward cesspits* (Manchester Guardian). [< *cess* (pool) + *pit*]

cess|pool (ses′pül′), *n.* **1** a pool or pit for house drains to empty into. Cesspools usually retain solid matter and allow the liquid to escape into the surrounding soil or a drain. *In rural districts or in very small towns the common outdoor toilet or cesspool may be a very dangerous source of pollution of well water* (Beauchamp, Mayfield, and West). **2** *Figurative.* any filthy place or condition: *a cesspool of corruption. The magnitude of the [indictments] suggests a moral cesspool* (Harper's). [perhaps < Italian *cesso* a privy (< Latin *secessus* place of retirement; drain) + English *pool*]

cest (sest), *n. Archaic.* cestus, a belt or girdle.

ces|ta (ses′tə; *Spanish* thās′tä), *n.* **1** a wicker basket or racket worn on the hand to catch and throw the ball in the game of pelota or jai alai. **2** a smooth, hard leather glove worn on each hand by Roman gladiators. [< Spanish *cesta* basket]

c'est-à-dire (se tà dēr′), *French.* that is to say.

c'est la guerre (se là ger′), *French.* **1** that is war; what happens in a war. **2** it can't be helped, as of an inconvenience or discomfort.

c'est la vie (se là vē′), *French.* that is life; that's how life is.

ces|tode (ses′tōd), *n., adj.* —***n.*** any one of a class of parasitic flatworms which, in the adult stage, may infest the intestine of man and various other vertebrates; tapeworm.
—***adj.*** of or belonging to this class.
[< New Latin *Cestoda* < Greek *kestós* girdle]

ces|toid (ses′toid), *adj., n.* —***adj.*** ribbonlike (applied to certain intestinal worms, such as the tapeworm).
—***n.*** = cestode.

c'est se|lon (se sə lôN′), *French.* **1** that depends. **2** (literally) that is according (as).

ces|tui (ses′twē, set′ē), *pron. Law.* he; the person. [< Old French *cestui* that person < Late Latin *ecce istum* behold the one]

ces|tus[1] (ses′təs), *n.* **1** a belt or girdle for the waist, particularly that worn by a bride in ancient times. **2** *Greek and Roman Mythology.* the girdle of Aphrodite, or Venus, supposed to have the power of arousing love. [< Latin *cestus* < Greek *kestós* girdle]

ces|tus[2] (ses′təs), *n.* a covering made of strips of leather, often loaded with metal, worn on the hands and forearms by boxers in ancient times: *The boxers in the mosaic wear the cestus. Their fists, clenched around bars of lead, are wrapped in thongs of hard leather, ... as though they were wearing boxing gloves* (New Yorker). [< Latin *caestus,* apparently < *caedere* to strike]

ce|su|ra (si zhůr′ə, -zyůr′-), *n., pl.* **-su|ras, -su|rae** (-zhůr′ē, -zyůr′-). = caesura.

CETA (sē′tə), *n.* Comprehensive Employment and Training Act (a program of the U.S. government under which state and local governments receive funds for job training and public-service jobs for the unemployed).

Ce|ta|cea (sə tā′shə), *n.pl.* the order of mammals comprising the cetaceans. [< New Latin *Cetacea*]

ce|ta|cean (sə tā′shən), *n., adj.* —***n.*** any one of an order of marine mammals having fishlike, almost hairless bodies, flat, notched tails, and paddle-shaped forelimbs, including whales, dolphins, and porpoises.
—***adj.*** of or belonging to the Cetacea.
[< New Latin *Cetacea* (< Latin *cētus* any large sea animal < Greek *kêtos, kêteos*) + English *-an*]

ce|ta|ceous (sə tā′shəs), *adj.* = cetacean.

ce|tane (sē′tān), *n. Chemistry.* a colorless liquid hydrocarbon of the methane series, originally obtained from sperm-whale oil. *Formula:* $C_{16}H_{34}$
[< Latin *cētus* any large sea animal + English *-ane*]

cetane number or **rating**, a measure of the ability of a diesel fuel oil to ignite spontaneously (ignition quality) expressed as a percentage of cetane (assigned a value of 100) in a test fuel mixture with alpha form of methylnaphthalene (assigned a value of 0). Most diesel engines require fuels with a cetane number of 45 or over.

ce|te|o|sau|rus (sē′tē ə sôr′əs), *n.* a dinosaur of the Jurassic period. [< Greek *kêtos, kêteos* (see etym. under **cetacean**) + *saûros* lizard]

ce|te|ris pa|ri|bus (set′ər is par′ə bəs), *Latin.* other things being equal: *The amount of stridency depends, ceteris paribus, on the rate of air flow* (Robert Krohn).

Ce|ti (sē′tī), *n.* genitive of **Cetus**.

CETI (set′ē), Communication with Extraterrestrial Intelligence: *Work in CETI concentrates on receiving (and possibly exchanging) messages from other civilizations* (Science News). Compare **SETI**.

ce|to|log|i|cal (sē tə loj′ə kəl), *adj.* of or having to do with cetology.

ce|tol|o|gist (sē tol′ə jist), *n.* a person who studies cetology.

ce|tol|o|gy (sē tol′ə jē), *n.* the science of whales.
[< Latin *cētus* large sea animal + English *-logy*]

cet. par., other things being equal (Latin, *ceteris paribus*).

Ce|tus (sē′təs), *n., genitive* **Ce|ti**. a constellation on or near the celestial equator that contains the first variable star discovered, Mira. [< Latin *Cetus* < Greek *Kêtos* the Whale]

cet|yl alcohol (set′əl, sē′təl), a white, crystalline extract of whale oil, used in making perfumes and cosmetics. *Formula:* $C_{16}H_{34}O$ [< Latin *cētus* any large sea animal + English *-yl*]

ce|vap|ci|ci (che väp′chē chē), *n.* a Yugoslavian dish consisting of small, loosely rolled and grilled balls of minced meat. [< Serbo-Croatian *cevapcici*]

ce|vi|tam|ic acid (sē′vī tam′ik, -vi-), = vitamin C.
[< *ce* (for *C* of *vitamin C*) + *vitam*(in) + *-ic*]

Cey|lo|nese (sē′lə nēz′, -nēs′), *adj., n., pl.* **-nese**.
—***adj.*** of Ceylon (Sri Lanka) or its people.
—***n.*** a person born or living in Ceylon (Sri Lanka).

Cey|lon moss (si lon′), an East Indian seaweed, similar to carrageen. It is a red alga and is one of the sources of agar-agar.

cf., **1** calf (of a bookbinding). **2** *Baseball.* **a** center field. **b** center fielder. **3** compare (Latin, *confer*).

Cf (no period), californium (chemical element).

CF (no periods), cystic fibrosis.

C.F., **1** coefficient of friction. **2** cost and freight.

CFA franc, the unit of money of various African countries now or formerly in the French Community, worth 1/50 of a French franc. [abbreviation of *Communauté Financière Africaine* African Financial Community]

c.f.i. or **C.F.I.**, cost, freight, and insurance.

c.f.m. or **cfm** (no periods), cubic feet a minute.

c.f.s., cubic feet a second.

cg. or **cg** (no period), centigram or centigrams.

C.G., **1** center of gravity. **2** Coast Guard. **3** commanding general. **4** consul general.

cgm., centigram or centigrams.

c.g.s. or **C.G.S.** or **cgs** (no periods), centimeter-gram-second (system).

C.G.T. or **CGT** (no periods), **1** either of two major foreign labor organizations: **a** (in France) Confédération Générale du Travail. **b** (in Argentina) Confederación General del Trabajo. **2** (in English) General Confederation of Labor.

ch., **1** chain. **2** chapter. **3** *Chess.* check. **4** child or children. **5** church.

Ch., an abbreviation for the following:
1 chain.
2 champion.
3 chaplain.
4 chapter.
5 *Chess.* check.
6 chief.
7 child or children.
8a China. **b** Chinese.
9 church.

c.h., candle hour.

C.H., **1** clearing house. **2** Companion of Honour. **3** courthouse. **4** custom house.

chab|a|site (kab′ə sīt), *n.* = chabazite.

chab|a|zite (kab′ə zīt), *n.* a colorless or flesh-colored mineral occurring in glassy crystals, composed chiefly of silica, alumina, sodium, and calcium; a zeolite. [earlier *chabazie* (< French < mistaken reading of Greek *chalázie* < *chálaza* hail) + *-ite*[1]]

Cha|blis (shab′lē; *French* shä blē′), *n.* a pale, dry, white Burgundy wine: *In bad years the Sauternes are less sweet, but there's no such thing as "dry Sauternes" (or "sweet Chablis")* (Atlantic). [< French *Chablis* < the town in France near which it is made]

cha|bouk or **cha|buk** (chä′bu̇k), *n.* a long whip used in the Orient to punish people. [< Persian *chābuk*]

Chac (chäk), *n.* any one of the four main Mayan rain gods. Each was identified with a direction and a color.

cha-cha (chä′chä), *n., v.* —***n.*** a ballroom dance with a fast, strongly marked rhythm, originally from Latin America. It is similar to the mambo.
—***v.i.*** to dance the cha-cha.
[short for American Spanish *cha-cha*]

cha-cha-cha (chä′chä′chä′), *n., v.i.* = cha-cha.

cha|cha|la|ca (chä′chə lä′kə, chach′ə-), *n.* any one of various American gallinaceous birds related to the curassow, including one variety found as far north as Texas. [< Spanish *chachalaca* < Nahuatl]

chac|ma (chak′mə), *n.* a large South African baboon. [< a Hottentot word]

cha|conne (shä kôn′), *n.* **1** an old slow dance of Spanish (possibly Moorish or Basque) origin, in 3-4 time, going back to 1591. **2** the music for this dance, which later became a series of variations on a ground bass, used sometimes as a movement of the classical suite. It was frequently used at the end of early operas. [< French *chaconne* < Spanish *chacona,* perhaps < Basque *chacun* pretty]

cha|cun à son goût (shä kœɴ′ nä sôɴ gü′), *French.* everyone to his taste.

chad[1] (chad), *n.* the small round or square piece of tape or paper removed when punching a hole in a punched tape or card: *The presence of chad in the tape would interfere with reliable electrical or photoelectric reading of the paper tape* (Berkeley and Lovett). [origin uncertain]

chad[2] (chad), *n. British.* a young sea bream. [apparently variant of *shad*]

Chad (chad), *n.* any language of a group of Hamitic languages spoken in the Lake Chad area of north central Africa, including Hausa.

Chad|i|an (chad′ē ən), *adj., n.* —***adj.*** of or having to do with Chad, a country in central Africa.
—***n.*** a native or inhabitant of Chad.

chad|less (chad′lis), *adj.* punched, produced, or processed with the chads partly attached to the holes. [< *chad*[1] + *-less*]

chad|or (chud′ər), *n.* = chuddar.

chae|ta (kē′tə), *n., pl.* **-tae** (-tē). *Zoology.* one of the setae, or bristles, on the parapodia of an annelid worm. [< New Latin *chaeta* < Greek *chaítē*]

chae|to|dont (kē′tə dont), *n.* any one of various small or moderate-sized tropical, spiny-finned marine fishes, generally having brilliant coloring, so called on account of their bristlelike teeth. [< Greek *chaítē* a seta + *odoús, odóntos* tooth]

chae|tog|nath (kē′təg nath), *n.* = arrowworm. [< Greek *chaítē* a seta + *gnáthos* jaw]

chae|tog|na|thous (ki tog′nə thəs), *adj.* having to do with or having the characteristics of a chaetognath.

chae|toph|o|rous (ki tof′ər əs), *adj. Zoology.* having chaetae (bristles). [< Greek *chaítē* a seta + English *-phore* + *-ous*]

chae|to|pod (kē′tə pod), *n.* any one of a group of annelid worms, having the body made up of more or less similar segments provided with muscular processes bearing setae. [< Greek *chaítē* a seta + *poús, podós* foot]

chae|top|o|dous (ki top′ə dəs), *adj.* of or resembling the chaetopods.

chafe (chāf), *v.,* **chafed, chaf|ing,** *n.* —***v.t.*** **1** to make sore by rubbing or scraping: *The stiff collar chafed the man's neck.* **2** to rub to make warm: *The mother chafed her child's cold hands.* **3** to wear away by rubbing or scraping. **4** *Figurative.* to make angry or annoyed; irritate; vex: *His big brother's teasing chafed him. Missing such sales chafes retailers* (Wall Street Journal). **SYN:** gall, exasperate. **5** *Obsolete.* to warm; heat.
—***v.i.*** **1** to become worn away by rubbing. **2** to become sore by rubbing. **3** to rub; press or strike with friction: *to chafe at the bit.* **4** *Figurative.* to become angry or annoyed; fret: *He chafed under his big brother's teasing.* **5** (of the sea or waves) to be turbulent; churn.
—***n.*** **1** rubbing; friction. **2** irritation or injury caused by rubbing; abrasion. **3** annoyance; temper. **4** impatience at restraints; sense of frustration.
[< Old French *chaufer* to warm < Vulgar Latin *calfāre,* alteration of Latin *calefacere* < *calēre* be warm + *facere* make]

chaf|er[1] (chā′fər), *n.* any of a group of beetles including the June bugs and scarabs, that usually feed on plants.
[Old English *ceafor*]

chaf|er[2] (chā′fər), *n. Obsolete.* **1** a small portable furnace. **2** a chafing dish.
[< French *chauffoir* < Old French *chaufer* to warm, chafe]

chaf|er[3] (chā′fər), *n.* a synthetic fabric used to protect tires from abrasion, applied to the tire where it meets the rim of the wheel.
[< *chafe* + *-er*[1]]

chaff[1] (chaf, chäf), *n.* **1** the stiff, strawlike bits around the grains of wheat, oats, or rye. Chaff is separated from grain by threshing. **2** hay or straw cut fine for feeding cattle. **3** *Figurative.* worthless stuff; rubbish: *The neighbors' suspicions were chaff of the lowest sort based on gossip and guesswork.* **4** *Botany.* the thin, dry scales or bracts at the base of the florets in the flower heads of many plants. **5** metal foil dropped by aircraft to confuse enemy radar; window. [Old English *ceaf*]

chaff[2] (chaf, chäf), *v., n. Informal.* —***v.t., v.i.*** to make fun of in a good-natured way to one's face; banter: *The boys chaffed the French boy about his mistakes in speaking English.*
—***n.*** good-natured joking about a person to his face; banter: *The French boy did not mind their chaff.*
[origin uncertain]

chaf|fer[1] (chaf′ər), *n., v.* —***n.*** a disputing about a price; bargaining.
—***v.i.*** **1** to dispute about terms or price; bargain. **2** *Figurative.* to deal; discuss terms; bandy or exchange words.
—***v.t.*** **1** to buy and sell; traffic in; exchange; barter. **2** *Figurative.* to exchange or bandy (words).
[Middle English *chaffare* < Old English *cēap* bargain + *faru* journey] —**chaf′fer|er,** *n.*

chaff|er[2] (chaf′ər, chäf′-), *n. Informal.* a person who jokes lightly or banters.
[< *chaff*[2] + *-er*[1]]

chaf|finch (chaf′inch), *n.* a European songbird with a pleasant, short song, often kept as a cage bird. The chaffinch has bright, barred wings. [Old English *ceaf-finc* < *ceaf* chaff[1] + *finc* finch]

chaff|weed (chaf′wēd′, chäf′-), *n.* a low herb of the primrose family.

chaff|y (chaf′ē, chäf′-), *adj.* **1** full of chaff. **2** consisting of chaff. **3** *Figurative.* like chaff; worthless. **4** *Botany.* paleaceous.

chaf|ing dish (chā′fing), **1** a pan with a heater under it, used to cook food at the table or to keep it warm. It usually consists of two pans in a frame over a small alcohol lamp or the like. The upper pan is covered and fits into the lower, in which hot water is put. **2** a vessel to hold burning charcoal or other fuel, for heating anything placed upon it; a portable grate.

chaft (chaft, chäft), *n. Scottish and Northern English Dialect.* the jaw.
chafts, the chaps: . . . *to cry out with open chafts* (Quintin Kennedy).
[perhaps < Scandinavian (compare Old Icelandic *kjaptr* mouth, jaw)]

Cha|ga (chä′gə), *n., pl.* **-ga** or **-gas**. = Chagga.

Cha|gas' disease (chä′gəs, shä′), a form of trypanosomiasis, occurring in South America: *The Triatomas, close relatives of the assassin bugs, spread the trypanosome of Chagas' disease, a serious affliction of man in South America* (Scientific American).
[< Carlos *Chagas,* 1879-1934, a Brazilian physician, who discovered its cause]

Chag|ga (chä′gə), *n., pl.* **-ga** or **-gas**. **1** a member of an African tribe in Tanzania inhabiting the slopes of Mount Kilimanjaro. The Chagga are a tall, agricultural people that produce coffee and cotton for export. **2** their Bantu language.

cha|grin (shə grin′), *n., v.* —***n.*** a feeling of disappointment, failure, or humiliation: *He felt chagrin because he did not pass the test. The impetuous sovereign found, to her chagrin, that there might be disadvantages in being the declared enemy of one of the two great parties in the State* (Lytton Strachey). **SYN:** mortification, vexation.
—***v.t.*** to cause to feel chagrin: *He was chagrined*

by his failure.
[< French *chagrin* grained leather, shagreen (< Turkish *sagri* rump leather); the shift of meaning comes from the idea of being ruffled or because of fusion with Middle French *chagrin* grief, vexation]

chain** (chān), *n., v., adj.* **—*n. **1** a row of links joined together: *an anchor chain, armor made of chain. The dog is fastened to a post by a chain. After a few moments, the Mayor, splendid in full mayoral robes and chain, came out behind them* (New Yorker). **2** a series of things linked together: *a chain of mountains;* (*Figurative.*) *a chain of events.* SYN: sequence, succession, progression. **3** *Figurative.* anything that binds or restrains: *the chains of duty, the chains of love.* SYN: bond, shackle. **4a** a measuring instrument like a chain. A surveyor's chain is 66 feet long; an engineer's chain is 100 feet long. **b** the length of either of these chains, as a linear unit. **5** a number of similar stores, hotels, restaurants, theaters, etc., owned and operated by one person or company: *In many cities, independent luxury markets are the source of the best steak; they don't advertise like the chains, however, and seldom publicly proclaim the astronomical price of the best steak* (Harper's). **6** a number of atoms of the same element linked together like a chain, usually within an organic molecule: *a carbon chain.* **7** *Biology.* a group of organisms, such as bacteria, connected end to end. **8** = chain shot.
—*v.t.* **1** to join together with a chain; fasten with a chain: *The dog was chained to a post. The Bible was chained to the reading desk.* **2** *Figurative.* to bind; restrain; fetter: *to chain enthusiasm with common sense. Work chained him to his desk.* **3** to keep in prison; make a slave of. **4** to restrain with chains; fetter. **5** to measure with a chain.
—*v.i.* to unite or be linked in a chain.
—*adj.* **1** of or like chains. **2** of the nature of chain mail.
chains, a bonds; fetters: *The rebels were brought back in chains.* **b** imprisonment or bondage: *The dictator's enemies had spent many years in chains. Man is born free, and everywhere he is in chains* (Jean Jacques Rousseau).
[< Old French *chaeine* < Latin *catēna*] **—chain′less,** *adj.* **—chain′like′,** *adj.*

***chain**
definition 1

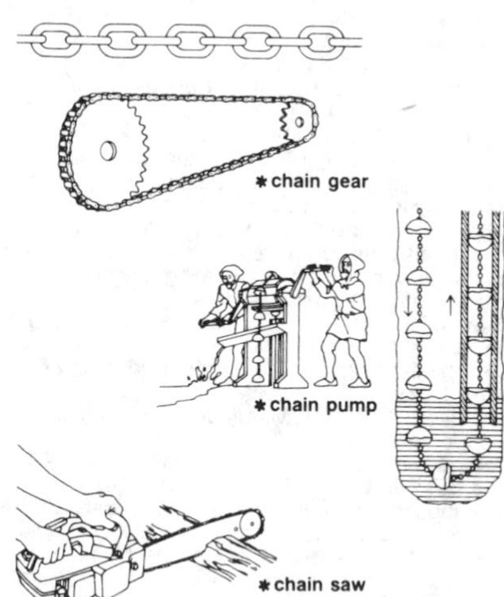
***chain gear**
***chain pump**
***chain saw**

chain|belt (chān′belt′), *n.* a belt made with interlinked metal rings.
chain|break (chān′brāk′), *n.* a commercial or other announcement made during a pause in a network radio or television program or during a station break.
chain bridge, a suspension bridge supported by chains.
chain coupling, an additional coupling for extra safety on railroad freight cars.
chain drive, 1 a mechanism for transmitting power by means of a chain gear. **2** the system using this mechanism.
chain-driv|en (chān′driv′ən), *adj.* driven by means of chain gears.
chai|né (she nā′), *n., pl.* **-nés** (-nā′). *Ballet.* a series of quick turns from one foot to the other, made in moving across the stage. [< French *chaîné* < *chaîner* to chain]
chain fern, a large fern found in the northern hemisphere that bears rows of sori like chains.
chain gang, *U.S.* a gang of convicts, or the like, chained together while at work outdoors or on their way to work: *traditional and less familiar songs based on chain gang, jailhouse, church, backyard, and cemetery* (Saturday Review).
***chain gear,** a gear for transmitting motion by means of an endless chain, especially one in which the chain transmits motion from one sprocket wheel to another.
chain|hoist (chān′hoist′), *n.,* a block and tackle which uses chain instead of rope.
chain|let (chān′lit), *n.* a little chain: *Spurs, and ringing chainlets, sound* (Scott).
chain letter, a letter which each person receiving is asked to copy and send to several others: *With whispers and chain letters they spread the word* (Time).
chain lightning, 1 lightning visible in wavy, zigzag, or broken lines: *I'm goin' there like a streak of chain lightning* (Seba Smith). **2** *U.S. Dialect or Slang.* inferior whiskey: *The worst of lickers ... is called chain lightning, from its terrible ... stunning effect* (Schele De Vere).
chain link fence, a fence of heavy steel wire woven into a lattice and supported by steel posts.
chain lock, 1 a chain attached to a lock, used to fasten a bicycle: *To thwart them* [*thieves*], *careful cyclists favor three chain locks—one locking each wheel to the frame, the third locking the frame to a stout signpost or tree* (Time). **2** a chain used to fasten a door to the jamb from the inside, so that it may be opened only a few inches: *I heard her slide the chain lock off and then the door opened* (Louise Meriwether).
chain locker, a forward compartment below in a ship, where the anchor chains are stored.
chain loom, a loom in which patterns upon a chain control the harnesses, as distinguished from one governed by cams or by a jacquard attachment.
chain mail, a kind of flexible armor used in the Middle Ages, made of metal rings linked together; mail: *Without pay, too, it would have been difficult, if not impossible, for many knights to bear the rapidly rising cost of armor in this period* [*the Renaissance*] *when heavy plate was beginning to replace the simpler chain mail of the crusading era* (Wallace Ferguson).
chain|man (chān′mən), *n., pl.* **-men.** the man who carries the chain in surveying: *Kim ... was to be diligent and enter the Survey of India as a chainman* (Rudyard Kipling).
chain measure, a system of measurement used by surveyors:
7.92 inches = 1 link
100 links in a chain or 66 ft. = 1 chain
10 chains = 1 furlong
80 chains = 1 mile
chain molding, *Architecture.* ornament in the form of links.
chain of command, 1 the line or succession of commanding officers, from superior to subordinate, through which military command is exercised: *The chain of command will then run ostensibly directly from the Joint Chiefs of Staff to the ... European Command* (New York Times). **2** any system of command according to rank; hierarchy: *It offered a chart of the Communist chain of command, from Politburo in the Kremlin down to the local party cell* (Newsweek).
chain of title, a history tracing the successive transfers of ownership of real estate.
chain pickerel, a pickerel of quiet waters in eastern North America, whose sides bear marks resembling links in a chain.
***chain pump** or **lift,** a pump in which water is raised by an endless chain fitted with disks, buckets, or the like.
chain-re|act (chān′rē akt′), *v.i.* to undergo a chain reaction: *The pile was large enough so that it would have been chain-reacting without the control rods* (New York Times Magazine). [back formation < *chain reaction*]
chain-re|act|ing (chān′rē ak′ting), *adj.* (of a substance) that produces a chain reaction.
chain-reacting pile, = reactor.
***chain reaction, 1** a chemical or nuclear process of releasing atomic energy by a series of nuclear fissions that continues automatically once it has been started. When a uranium atom captures a neutron and undergoes fission, the uranium atom separates into two lighter atoms, releasing atomic energy, and emitting more than one neutron, which produce further fissions of the surrounding uranium atoms, the release of more atomic energy, and an increasing supply of neutrons. **2** *Figurative.* any series of events or happenings, each caused by the preceding one or ones: *"This new awareness may well be the end product of a cultural chain reaction set off by the TV industry"* (Sponsor).
chain reactor, = reactor.
chains (chānz), *n.pl.* See under **chain.**
***chain saw,** a saw consisting of an endless chain with a tooth on each link. Chain saws are used in tree surgery, coal mining, and logging. Most chain saws have small, built-in gasoline engines. *I was cutting part of my winter's supply of firewood with a gasoline-operated chain saw* (New Yorker).
chain shot, a projectile (or such projectiles collectively) consisting of two balls or half balls connected by a short chain, formerly used especially in naval artillery.
chain-smoke (chān′smōk′), *v.i., v.t.,* **-smoked, -smok|ing.** to smoke cigarettes or cigars one after another. **—chain′-smok′er,** *n.*
chain stitch, a stitch in sewing, crocheting, or embroidery, in which each stitch makes a loop through which the next stitch is taken. Many industrial bags, such as those containing animal feed, cement, and fertilizer, are closed with chain stitches.
chain-stitch (chān′stich′), *v.t., v.i.* to sew or crochet using a chain stitch.
chain store, one of a group of stores owned and operated by the same person or company. Chain stores carry similar merchandise and are guided by the same policies. *Years ago there was a great to-do about how chain stores would mean the extinction of the small independent grocers, and many were bought out; yet throughout the land today the chains and the independents thrive side by side* (Wall Street Journal).
chain-wale (chān′wāl′, -wəl), *n. Nautical.* = channel². [< *chain* + *wale*]
chain well, = chain locker.
chain|wheel (chān′hwēl′), *n.* a toothed wheel transmitting power through a chain.
chain|work (chān′wėrk′), *n.* work resembling the links of a chain, as in sculpture, armor, and sewing.
chair (chār), *n., v.* **—*n.*** **1** a seat that has a back and, sometimes, arms, usually for one person. **2** a seat of rank, dignity, or authority; throne; bench. **3** *Figurative.* the position or authority of a person who has such a seat: *Professor Smith has the chair of astronomy at this college.* SYN: office. **4** a chairman: *The chair called the meeting to order. All questions are to be addressed to the chair.* **5** a covered chair carried on poles by two men; sedan chair. **6** = electric chair. **7** a metal socket fastened to a railroad tie in which a rail is secured, used especially in Great Britain.
—*v.t.* **1** to conduct as chairman: *to chair a meeting.* **2** to put in a position of authority. SYN: install. **3a** to put or carry in a chair. **b** *British.* to carry high up, as if in a chair: *The winning team chaired their captain.*
get the chair, *U.S. Informal.* to die or be sentenced to die in the electric chair: *Both murderers got the chair.*
take the chair, a to begin a meeting: *When the hour fixed for the meeting to begin arrives, the presiding officer takes the chair ... and directs the secretary to read the minutes of the last meeting* (Henry M. Robert). **b** to preside at a meeting: *The vice-president took the chair when the president was ill. He will also take the chair at a lecture tomorrow on the scientific work of the British-North Greenland expedition* (London Times).
[< Old French *chaiere* < Latin *cathedra* < Greek *kathédrā* seat. See etym. of doublets **chaise, cathedra.**] **—chair′less,** *adj.*
chair|bed (chār′bed′), *n.* a chair having a hinged back that folds down to form part of a bed.

***chain reaction**
definition 1

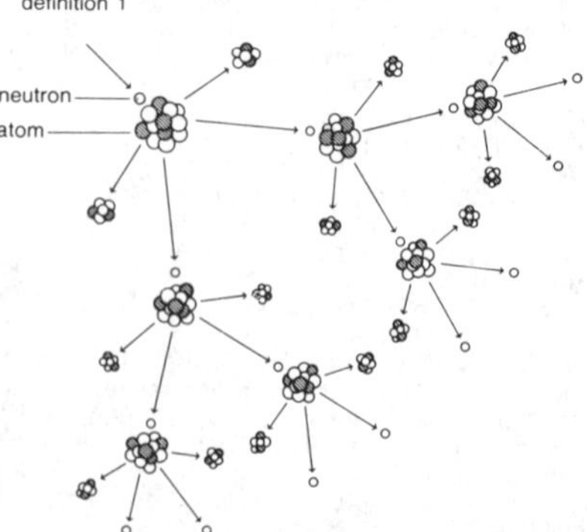

chair|borne (chār′bôrn′, -bōrn′), *adj. Informal.* having to do with the administrative, theoretical, or recreational end of a field or activity; not involved in actual field work, military combat, or the like (used originally of Air Force personnel who were not "airborne"): *a chairborne corporal or sergeant, a chairborne admiral, a chairborne*

mountain climber.
chair|bound (chãr′bound′), *adj.* confined to a chair or wheel chair by a disability: *Although at that time completely chairbound or needing to be lifted bodily I had succeeded in getting down to ... the sea* (Manchester Guardian Weekly).
chair car, *U.S.* **1** a parlor car. **2** a railroad car having individual chairs with adjustable, reclining backs instead of double seats on each side of a central aisle.
chair|la|dy (chãr′lā′dē), *n., pl.* **-dies.** a chairwoman: *a P.T.A. chairlady.*
▶ See **chairwoman** for usage note.
chair lift, a series of chairs suspended from an endless cable for carrying persons, especially skiers, to the top of a slope, or between two points: *Comfortably relaxed and swaying gently in our seats, we were wafted aloft by the chair lift* (Atlantic).
chair|man (chãr′mən), *n., pl.* **-men**, *v.,* **-manned, -man|ning.** —*n.* **1** the person who is in charge of a meeting: *The chairman called the meeting to order.* **2** the person at the head of a committee, board, or other organized body: *The chairman asked the committee if they wished to recess.* **3** a man whose work is carrying or wheeling persons in chairs, sedan chairs, or chairlike conveyances.
—*v.t., v.i.* to conduct or serve as chairman: *He supervised the corporation's financial affairs, chairmanned some of its most important committees* (Time).
▶ See **chairwoman** for usage note.
chair|man|ship (chãr′mən ship), *n.* **1** the position of chairman: *The aim will be to resolve as many issues as possible before the full conference resumes under the chairmanship of Mr. Sandys* (Manchester Guardian). **2** the length of time one is a chairman: *The committee did much work during his chairmanship.*
chair|o|plane (chãr′ə plān), *n.* a kind of merry-go-round with chairs hanging on chains which swing far out when rotated by machinery. [< *chair* + (aer)*oplane*]
chair|per|son (chãr′pėr′sən), *n. U.S.* a person who presides at a meeting; chairman or chairwoman: *Joseph E. Trimble of Oklahoma City University* [*was*] *chairperson of the symposium* (Science News).
▶ See **chairwoman** for usage note.
chair rail, a strip of wood fastened to a wall to prevent the wall from being marked or damaged by the backs of chairs.
chair table, = table chair.
chair|warm|er (chãr′wôr′mər), *n. U.S. Slang.* a person who wastes time at his desk and neglects his duties: *When jaunty Roy W. Johnson moved into the Pentagon ... as boss of the new space program the veteran chairwarmers began to chuckle at his eagerness* (Newsweek).
chair|wom|an (chãr′wu̇m′ən), *n., pl.* **-wom|en.** **1** the woman who presides at or is in charge of a meeting. **2** the woman at the head of a committee.
▶ **chairman, chairwoman.** *Chairman* may quite properly be used for either a man or a woman in charge of a meeting or committee. The forms of address are: *Mr. Chairman, Madame Chairman.*
▶ **chairlady, chairperson, chairwoman.** *Chairlady* is more formal, and less frequent, than *chairwoman;* as forms of address both are preceded by Madame. *Chairperson* was coined to eliminate the reference to the subject's sex, but it is not widely used and is almost never used as a form of address.
chaise (shāz), *n.* **1** a light, open carriage, usually with a folding top, especially a one-horse, two-wheeled carriage for two persons. **2** = post chaise. **3** = chaise longue: *I was lying on the chaise on my back porch* (New Yorker). [< French *chaise,* (originally) variant of *chaire* < Old French *chaiere* chair. See etym. of doublets **chair, cathedra.**]
chaise longue (shāz′ lông′), a chair with a long seat and a back at one end, somewhat like a couch. [< French *chaise longue* long chair; see etym. under **chaise**]
chaise lounge (shāz′ lounj′), = chaise longue.
▶ This form, resulting from a misreading of the spelling *longue,* is avoided by educated speakers.
chaise per|cée (shāz′ per sā′), a chair enclosing a chamber pot or toilet bowl. [< French *chaise percée* pierced chair]
chait|ya (chīt′yə), *n.* a place or an object deserving of worship or reverence in the Buddhist religion. [< Sanskrit *chaitya*]
chak|ra (chuk′rə), *n.* **1** (in India) a disk or circle representing the sun, a cycle of years, and lordliness. **2** a sharp disk-shaped throwing weapon, used especially by the Sikhs: *... an example of the terrible chakra, a disc-shaped weapon, its edges honed to razor sharpness* (New Yorker). [< Sanskrit *cakrā*]
cha|la|za (kə lā′zə), *n., pl.* **-zas, -zae** (-zē). **1** *Zoology.* either of the two membranous twisted strings by which the yolk of a bird's egg is bound to the lining membrane at the ends of the shell and kept near the middle of the albumen. See picture under **egg**[1]. **2** *Botany.* the point on a seed where the integuments diverge from the nucellus: *The three of these nearest the micropyle now gradually disappear and give place to the one nearest the chalaza which is the attachment of the ovule to the scale* (Fred W. Emerson). [< New Latin *chalaza* < Greek *chálaza* hail(stone); a lump like hail]
cha|la|zal (kə lā′zəl), *adj.* of or containing a chalaza.
cha|la|zi|an (kə lā′zē ən), *adj.* **1** of or having to do with a chalaza. **2** like a chalaza.
cha|la|zi|on (kə lā′zē ən), *n. Medicine.* a transparent swelling on the eyelid, due to inflammation. [< Greek *chalázion* (diminutive) < *chálaza* hail(stone)]
cha|la|zi|um (kə lā′zē əm), *n.* = chalazion.
chal|can|thite (kal kan′thīt), *n. Mineralogy.* native copper sulfate or blue vitriol. *Formula:* $CuSO_4 \cdot 5H_2O$ [< Latin *chalcanthum* (< Greek *chálkanthon* solution of blue vitriol < *chalkós* copper + *ánthos* flower) + English *-ite*[1]]
chal|ce|don (kal′sə don), *n.* = checkerspot. [< New Latin *chalcedona,* probably < Latin *chalcēdonius* chalcedony]
Chal|ce|do|ni|an (kal′sə dō′nē ən), *adj.* of or having to do with Chalcedon, an ancient city in Bithynia, or with the fourth ecumenical council held there in A.D. 451.
chal|ce|don|ic (kal′sə don′ik), *adj.* of or like chalcedony.
chal|ced|o|nous (kal sed′ə nəs), *adj.* like chalcedony.
chal|ced|o|ny (kal sed′ə nē, kal′sə dō′-), *n., pl.* **-nies.** a variety of fibrous quartz that has a waxy luster and occurs in various colors and forms. A common kind is grayish or blue. Agate, onyx, carnelian, and jasper are forms of chalcedony. [< Latin *chalcēdonius* < Greek *chalkēdṓn* an unidentified stone (Revelation 21:19)]
Chal|chi|uht|li|cu|e (chäl′chē üt lē′kü ā), *n. Aztec Mythology.* the goddess of running water and wife or sister of the rain god Tlaloc. She was the protectress of newborn children, marriage, and innocent love.
chal|cid (kal′sid), *n.,* or **chalcid fly**, any one of a family of very small, four-winged insects whose larvae live as parasites on other insects. [< New Latin *Chalcides* the genus name < Greek *chalkós* copper (from their color)]
chal|cid|i|an (kal sid′ē ən), *adj., n.* —*adj.* belonging to or having the characteristics of a chalcid.
—*n.* = chalcid.
chalco-, *combining form.* copper; brass: *Chalcograph = an engraving on copper or brass.* [< Greek *chalkós*]
chal|co|cite (kal′kə sīt), *n.* a shiny gray sulfide of copper; native copper sulfide. *Formula:* Cu_2S [earlier *chalcosine* (< Greek *chalkós* copper) + English *-ite*[1]]
chal|co|gen|ide (kal′kə jə nīd, kal koj′ə nīd), *n., adj.* —*n.* a compound formed with any of the elements oxygen, sulfur, selenium, and tellurium (group 6A of the periodic table) and another element or radical.
—*adj.* composed of one or more of the chalcogenides: *chalcogenide glass.*
[< *chalco-* + *-gen* + *-ide*]
chal|co|graph (kal′kə graf, -gräf), *n.* an engraving on copper or brass. —**chal|cog′ra|pher**, *n.*
chal|co|graph|ic (kal′kə graf′ik), *adj.* of or having to do with chalcography.
chal|co|graph|i|cal (kal′kə graf′ə kəl), *adj.* = chalcographic.
chal|cog|ra|phist (kal kog′rə fist), *n.* an engraver on brass or copper; a chalcographer.
chal|cog|ra|phy (kal kog′rə fē), *n.* the art of engraving on copper or brass, as in printing.
chal|co|lite (kal′kə līt), *n.* torbernite, a uranium ore.
chal|co|lith|ic (kal′kə lith′ik), *adj.* of or having to do with the Bronze Age, especially its use of bronze and copper: *These people were of the chalcolithic age, that is to say, they made tools and ornaments of copper* (New Scientist).
chal|co|phil elements, (kal′kə fil), sulfur and zinc, two elements showing a strong affinity for sulfur, commonly found in sulfide ore.
chal|co|py|rite (kal′kə pī′rīt, -pir′īt), *n.* an important copper ore, a yellow sulfide of copper and iron; copper pyrites; fool's gold. *Formula:* $CuFeS_2$
chal|co|stib|ite (kal′kə stib′īt), *n.* a native sulfide of copper and antimony. *Formula:* $CuSbS_2$ [< *chalco-* + *stib*(*ium*) + *-ite*[1]]
Chal|da|ic (kal dā′ik), *adj., n.* = Chaldean.
Chal|de|an (kal dē′ən), *adj., n.* —*adj.* **1** of or having to do with ancient Chaldea, its people, or their language. **2** of or having to do with astrology or magic (because the Chaldeans were renowned as astrologers).
—*n.* **1** a native or inhabitant of Chaldea. The Chaldeans were a Semitic tribe closely related to the Babylonians. **2a** the language of the Chaldeans. **b** Biblical Syriac or Aramaic. **3** an astrologer or a magician.
[< Latin *Chaldaeus* (< Greek *Chaldaîos*) + English *-an*]
Chal|dee (kal dē′, kal′dē), *adj., n.* = Chaldean.
chal|dron (chôl′drən), *n.* any one of various old British dry measures, ranging at different times and places from 32 to 72 imperial bushels, fixed by law after 1878 at 36, not now used. [earlier *chaudern* < Old French *chauderon.* See etym. of doublet **caldron.**]
***cha|let** (sha lā′, shal′ā), *n.* **1** a Swiss house with wide, overhanging eaves. **2** a herdsman's hut or cabin in the Swiss mountains. **3** any house like this. [< Swiss French *chalet,* perhaps ultimately < Latin *casa* hut]

***chalet**
definition 1

chal|ice (chal′is), *n.* **1** a drinking cup or goblet. **2a** the cup that holds the wine used in the Communion service. **b** the wine or portion of the Eucharist contained in it. **3** a flower shaped like a cup. [< Old French *chalice,* learned borrowing from Latin *calix, -icis* cup. See etym. of doublet **calix.**]
chal|iced (chal′ist), *adj.* **1** having a flower shaped like a cup. **2** contained in a chalice.
chal|i|co|sis (kal′ə kō′sis), *n.* a disease of the lungs caused by inhalation of stone particles, as by stonecutters. [< New Latin *chalicosis* < Greek *chalix* pebble + *-ōsis* -osis]
chalk (chôk), *n., v., adj.* —*n.* **1** a soft limestone, made up mostly of very small fossil sea shells. Chalk is white, gray, or yellow and is used for making lime and for writing and drawing. **2a** a white or colored substance like chalk, used for writing or drawing on a blackboard or chalkboard, or for marking: *Colored chalks are useful for complicated diagrams on the blackboard.* **b** a kind of crayon made of chalk. **3** a mark or score made with chalk. **4** a score or record of credit given, especially at an inn, originally made in chalk; credit.
—*v.t.* **1** to mark, write, or draw with chalk: *The teacher chalked the date on the board.* **2** to mix or rub with chalk; whiten with or as if with chalk; blanch. **3** to treat with chalk: *Land poor in lime is regularly chalked.* **4** to score; record.
—*adj.* **1** made of or with chalk: *chalk lime, a chalk drawing.* **2** found in chalk: *a chalk flint.*
by a long chalk, by a very great amount or difference: *Italy is the most popular destination among students "by a long chalk," followed by France and Spain* (London Times).
chalk one up, to gain an advantage: *He chalked one up on his opponent during their first television debate.*
chalk out, to sketch out; plan: *He pursued the course which he had from the first chalked out for himself* (James Grant). *We have now chalked out all the principal outlines of this vast title of the law* (William Blackstone).
chalk up, a to write down; record: *Several important milestones in foreign policy have been passed by this Congress, and they can be chalked up as major accomplishments* (New York Times). **b** to put down as belonging (to): *You learned your lesson the hard way and you can chalk it up to experience.* **c** to score: *His team chalked up ten points.*
[Old English *cealc* < Latin *calx, calcis* lime, limestone] —**chalk′like′**, *adj.*
chalk and cheese, *British.* two persons or things that are complete opposites, especially in quality, value, or appearance: *They are chalk and cheese, these rivals; McMorris the brave grafter, Carew the impulsive dasher* (London Times).
chalk|board (chôk′bôrd′, -bōrd′), *n.* a smooth, hard surface used for writing or drawing on with crayon or chalk. Chalkboards are usually made of pastel-green or yellow composition board.

Pronunciation Key: hat, āge, cãre, fär; let, ēqual, tėrm; it, īce; hot, ōpen, ôrder; oil, out; cup, pu̇t, rüle; **ch**ild; lo**ng**; **th**in; **ᴛʜ**en; **zh**, measure; **ə** represents **a** in about, **e** in taken, **i** in pencil, **o** in lemon, **u** in circus.

chalk line, 1 a line drawn with chalk. **2a** a light cord rubbed with chalk and stretched over a surface to mark a straight line. **b** the line thus made. **walk the chalk line**, to keep in a straight line; submit to strict discipline: *Fellow travelers . . . deny they are Communists, but all of* [*them*] *walk the Communist chalk line* (Time).

chalk|stone (chôk′stōn′), *n. Medicine.* a chalklike concretion in the tissues or small joints of a person affected with gout; tophus.

chalk talk, a lecture illustrated by drawings and diagrams in chalk on a blackboard: *The coaching staff presents the complete game plan for Sunday's battle in a series of chalk talks* (New Yorker).

chalk|y (chô′kē), *adj.*, **chalk|i|er, chalk|i|est. 1** of chalk; containing chalk: *The blackboard eraser was full of chalky dust.* **2** like chalk; white as chalk: *The clown's face was chalky.* **—chalk′i-ness**, *n.*

chal|lah (hä′lə, ʜä′lə), *n., pl.* **chal|lahs, chal|loth** (ʜä lot′). = hallah.

chal|lenge (chal′ənj), *v.*, **-lenged, -leng|ing**, *n.* **—*v.t.*** **1** to call to a game or contest; dare: *The champion swimmer challenged anyone in the world to beat him. Our school challenged the neighboring school's team to a match.* **2** to call to fight: *The knight challenged his rival to a duel. To challenge a person in reply to an insult is no longer customary.* **3** to stop (a person) and question his right to do what he is doing or to be where he is: *When I tried to enter the building, the guard at the door challenged me.* **4** to demand proof before one will accept; call in question; doubt; dispute: *The teacher challenged my statement that rice grows in Oregon.* **5** *Law.* to object to (a juror) or question the admissibility of (evidence or testimony); question (a ruling): *The attorney for the defense challenged the evidence as hearsay.* **6** *U.S.* to object to (a vote) as invalid or (a voter) as not qualified to vote. **7** *Figurative.* **a** to claim or command (effort, interest, or feeling): *Preventing disease is a problem that challenges the attention of the medical profession.* **b** *Archaic.* to claim as one's due; lay claims to. **—*v.i.*** **1** to issue a challenge; call for a fight or contest: *There was also speculation that France planned to challenge for the . . . America's cup* (Douglas Phillips-Bart). **2** *Law.* to make a formal objection to a juror, the admission of evidence, or the like. **3** (of hounds) to bay on finding the scent. **4** *Archaic.* to demand a right; make a claim. [< Old French *chalenger* < Latin *calumniārī* slander < *calumnia.* See etym. of doublet **calumniate.**]

—*n.* **1** a call to a game or contest. Giving a challenge often means that one undertakes to beat everybody else. *The champions accepted our team's challenge.* **2** a call to fight: *His rival accepted the knight's challenge to a duel.* **3** a sudden questioning or calling to answer and explain: *"Who goes there?" is the guard's challenge.* **4** a demand for proof of the truth of a statement; a doubting or questioning of the truth of a statement: *The teacher's challenge of my statement about rice in Oregon led me to read widely about agriculture there.* **5** anything that claims or commands effort, interest, or feeling: *Fractions are a real challenge to him. It is a challenge to archaeology to try to straighten out the conflicting versions of Maya history* (Scientific American). **6** *Law.* an objection made to a juror, a ruling, or the admission of certain evidence or testimony: *The judge upheld the challenge and dismissed the juror from duty.* **7** *U.S.* an objection to a vote as invalid, or to a voter as not qualified to vote. [< Old French *chalenge*, earlier *chalonge* < Latin *calumnia* false accusation. See etym. of doublet **calumny.**] **—chal′lenge|a|ble**, *adj.* **—chal′lenger**, *n.*

challenge grant, a sum of money given in proportion to the amount raised by public contribution, a matching grant.

chal|leng|ing (chal′ən jing), *adj.* **1** that puts one's strength, will, statements, findings, or evidence to a test; exacting; demanding: *He will respond to his most challenging assignment with diligence and resourcefulness* (Newsweek). **2** that excites one's interest or curiosity; tantalizing: *a challenging theory.* **—chal′leng|ing|ly**, *adv.*

chal|lis or **chal|lie** (shal′ē), *n.* a lightweight printed cloth of cotton, wool, or rayon, used for such articles of clothing as blouses, nightgowns, dresses, and robes. [< French *challis* < English *Challis*, a place name]

chal|one (kal′ōn), *n.* an internal secretion that inhibits or reduces the activity of an organ. [< Greek *chalôn*, present participle of *chalân* slacken, let down]

chal|u|meau (shal′yə mō′; *French* shȧ ly mō′), *n. Music.* **1** the lowest register in the clarinet. **2** a shawm. [< French *chalumeau* < Old French *chalemel* < Late Latin *calamellus* a little reed < Latin *calamus* reed. See etym. of doublet **shawm.**]

cha|lutz (hä lüts′), *n., pl.* **cha|lu|tzim** (ʜä′lü-tsēm′). = halutz.

Chal|y|be|an (kal′ə bē′ən, kə lib′ē-), *adj.* of or having to do with the Chalybes, an ancient people of Pontus in Asia Minor, famed as workers in iron and steel: *Chalybean temper'd steel, and frock of mail Adamantean proof* (Milton).

cha|lyb|e|ate (kə lib′ē it, -āt), *adj., n.* **—*adj.*** containing or flavored with salts of iron: *chalybeate mineral water, a chalybeate spring.* **—*n.*** something containing salts of iron, such as a medicine or a spring. [< unrecorded New Latin *chalybeatus* < Latin *chalybēius* < *chalybs* steel < Greek *chálybs, -ybos* < the *Chalybes*, a people of Pontus, noted for their preparation of steel]

chal|y|bite (kal′ə bīt), *n. Mineralogy.* native carbonate of iron; siderite. [< Latin *chalybs* (< Greek *chálybs*) + English *-ite*[1]]

cham (kam), *n. Archaic.* = khan. [< Medieval Latin *cham*]

cha|made (shə mäd′), *n.* a signal by drum or trumpet for a military parley or retreat. [< French *chamade* < Portuguese *chamada* < *chamar* to call < Latin *clamāre*]

cha|mar[1] or **Cha|mar** (chə mär′), *n.* a member of a low caste in India whose traditional occupation is leatherwork. [< Hindustani *chamār* < Sanskrit *carmakāra* leatherworker]

cha|mar[2] (chə mär′), *n.* **1** a fan of feathers or similar material used in the East Indies as one of the insignia of royalty, and also in temples. **2** a swatter for flies. [< Indic (compare Marathi *chamara* the tail of an ox; because of its use as a fly swatter)]

cham|ber (chām′bər), *n., v., adj.* **—*n.*** **1a** a room (in a house): *The children searched each and every chamber of the house for the cat.* **b** a reception room in a palace or similar building: *the audience chamber.* **c** a bedroom: *Upstairs and downstairs and in my lady's chamber* (Nursery Rhyme). **2a** a hall where lawmakers, governors, or judges meet: *the council chamber.* **b** a group of lawmakers: *The Congress of the United States has two chambers, the Senate and the House of Representatives.* **3** a group of people organized for some business purpose: *the local Chamber of Commerce.* SYN: board. **4** an enclosed space in the body of an animal or plant, for example in the brain, eye, or heart, or in a shell. The human heart has four chambers. SYN: cavity. **5** an enclosed space or compartment in some kinds of machinery. The part of a gun that holds the charge is called the chamber. **6** = a chamber pot.

—*v.t.* **1** to provide with a chamber. **2** to form into a chamber or chambers. **3** to place in or as if in a chamber; enclose: *the best blood chambered in his bosom* (Shakespeare).

—*adj.* **1** designed for use in a chamber; suitable for performance in a chamber: *chamber music, a chamber play.* **2** of chamber music; performing chamber music: *Each is a superb musician; as a chamber group they stand unsurpassed* (New Yorker).

chambers, a the office of a lawyer or judge: *The judge met the lawyers for both sides in his chambers.* **b** a set of rooms in a building arranged for living or for offices: *He . . . lived in chambers which had once belonged to his deceased partner* (Dickens).

[< Old French *chambre* < Latin *camera* vault. See etym. of doublet **camera.**]

chamber concert, a concert where chamber music is performed.

chamber counsel, a lawyer advising privately but not in court.

cham|bered (chām′bərd), *adj.* having a chamber or chambers; divided into compartments: *the chambered nautilus.*

cham|ber|er (chām′bər ər), *n. Obsolete.* **1** a chambermaid. **2** a chamberlain. **3** a person who frequents ladies' chambers or society.

cham|ber|lain (chām′bər lin), *n.* **1** a person who manages the household of a king or great noble; steward. **2** a high official of a royal court in Europe: *Lord Chamberlain of the Household.* **3** an official who receives the rents and revenues of a corporation or public office; treasurer: *city chamberlain.* [< Old French *chamberlenc* < Old High German *chamerlinc* < Latin *camera* vault + Germanic *-ling* -ling] **—cham′ber|lain|ship**, *n.*

cham|ber|maid (chām′bər mād′), *n.* a maid who takes care of bedrooms in a house, hotel, or motel.

chamber music, music suited for performance in a room or small hall, such as music for a trio or quartet.

chamber of commerce, a group of business people organized to protect and promote the business interests of a city, state, or country.

Chamber of Deputies, Also, **chamber of deputies**. the lower of the two houses in the Italian legislature and in other parliaments.

chamber of horrors, **1** a room in a waxwork exhibition or museum, containing effigies of noted criminals, instruments of torture, and the like. **2** *Figurative.* any place or group of things arousing horror.

chamber orchestra, a small orchestra, that performs chiefly music of the 1600's and 1700's, which was written for orchestras of a small size.

chamber pot, a portable receptacle, used especially in a bedchamber for urine and slops.

cham|bers (chām′bərz), *n.pl.* See under **chamber.**

Cham|ber|tin (shäɴ ber taɴ′), *n.* a choice French red wine, one of the Burgundies. [< *Chambertin*, a vineyard near Dijon, France]

cham|bran|le (shäɴ bräɴ′lə), *n. Architecture.* a framelike decoration around the sides and top of a door, window, fireplace, or the like. [< French *chambranle;* origin uncertain]

cham|bray (sham′brā), *n.* a soft cotton cloth woven from white (woof) and colored (warp) threads, used for dresses and men's shirts. It is a kind of gingham. [< *Cambrai*, a town in France. See etym. of doublet **cambric.**]

cha|me|le|on (kə mē′lē ən, -mēl′yən), *n.* **1a** a small lizard of the Old World that can change the color of its skin to blend with the surroundings. The chameleon has a long, grasping tail, bulging eyes that move separately, and a long, sticky tongue for catching insects. *If a chameleon is placed so that one end is in sun and the other in shadow, the creature will look like a pair of two-toned sport shoes* (Science News Letter). **b** a related lizard of the New World that can change the color of its skin, such as the American chameleon. **2** *Figurative.* a changeable or fickle person: *He's a chameleon with no opinions of his own.* [< Latin *chamaeleon* < Greek *chamailéōn* (literally) ground lion < *chamaí* on the ground; dwarf + *léōn* lion] **—cha|me′le|on|like′**, *adj.*

Cha|me|le|on (kə mē′lē ən, -mēl′yən), *n., genitive* **Cha|me|le|on|tis**. a southern constellation near Argo.

cha|me|le|on|ic (kə mē′lē on′ik), *adj.* resembling a chameleon.

Cha|me|le|on|tis (kə mē′lē on′tis), *n.* genitive of **Chameleon.**

cham|fer (cham′fər), *n., v.* **—*n.*** a slanting, or sometimes concave, surface made by cutting off an edge or corner equally on both sides, used as decoration on posts or the like, or in making certain types of joints between structural members. **—*v.t.*** **1** to cut off at an edge or corner to make a slanting surface; bevel: *It wasn't a big piece, just the curve neatly chamfered off* (Punch). **2** to make a groove or furrow in: *to chamfer timber or stone.*

[< Middle French *chamfrain* < Old French *chanfraindre* < *chant* edge (< Latin *canthus* cant[2]) + *fraindre* break < Latin *frangere*]

cham|frain (cham′frən), *n.* = chamfron.

cham|fron (cham′frən), *n. Archaic.* armor for the front of a horse's head. [< Old French *chaufrain*, or *chanfrein* < *chafrener* to bring to a stop, ultimately < Latin *caput* head + *frēnum* rein]

cha|mise (shə mēs′), *n.* = chamiso.

cha|mi|so (shə mē′sō), *n.* a shrub found abundantly on the dry coastal ranges and foothills of California. [< American Spanish *chamiso*]

cham|my (sham′ē), *n., pl.* **-mies.** = chamois (leather).

cham|ois (sham′ē), *n., pl.* **-ois**, *v.* **—*n.*** **1** a small, goatlike antelope that lives in the high mountains of Europe and western Asia, known for its agility in climbing steep cliffs: *One can see marmots, wild deer and chamois* (Observer). **2** Also, **chammy, shammy**, or **shammy leather. a** a soft leather made from its skin or from the skin of sheep, goats, or deer. **b** a piece of this, used for cleaning or polishing.

—*v.t.* to prepare (leather) so as to resemble chamois.

[< French *chamois* < Late Latin *camōx, -ōcis*]

chamois skin, the soft, warm leather made from the skin of the chamois. Much sheepskin is sold as chamois skin.

cham|o|mile (kam′ə mīl), *n.* = camomile.

Cha|mor|ro (chä môr′rō), *n., pl.* **-ros**, *adj.* **—*n.*** **1** any one of a people inhabiting Guam and other parts of the Mariana Islands (in the Pacific Ocean east of the Philippines). **2** the Indonesian language of the Chamorros: *Chamorro is the common language of Saipan* (New Yorker).

—*adj.* of or having to do with these people or their language.

champ[1] (champ), *v., n.* **—*v.t.*** **1** to bite and chew noisily. SYN: munch. **2** to work (the bit) between the teeth repeatedly and impatiently: *The race horse champed its bit.* **3** *Scottish.* to crush, mash, or trample.

—*v.i.* to make biting and chewing movements

with the jaws and teeth: *to champ with impatience.*
—*n.* the act of champing. Also, **chomp**.
champ at the bit. See under **bit**[3].
[perhaps imitative]

champ[2] (champ), *n. Informal.* champion (def. 1). [American English, short for *champion*]

cham|pac or **cham|pak** (cham′pak, chum′puk), *n.* an East Indian tree of the magnolia family, bearing fragrant yellow flowers. Guaiol is obtained from its wood. [< Hindustani *campak* < Sanskrit *campaka*]

cham|pa|ca oil (cham′pə kə, chum′-), the oil obtained from the flowers of the champac tree, used in perfumes.

cham|pa|col (cham′pə kōl, -kol), *n.* an alcohol obtained from the wood of the champac; guaiol. [< *champac* + *-ol*[1]]

cham|pagne (sham pān′), *n., adj.* —*n.* **1a** a sparkling, bubbling white wine, sweet or dry, made in Champagne, France. **b** a still wine made in Champagne, France. **c** a wine similar to either of these, made elsewhere. **2** a pale, brownish-yellow color.
—*adj.* pale brownish-yellow: *... a ballerina-length gown of champagne lace* (New York Times).

cham|paign (sham pān′), *n., adj.* —*n.* level, open country; a plain.
—*adj.* level and open.
[< Middle French *champaigne* < Late Latin *campānia.* See etym. of doublet **campaign**.]

cham|pers (sham′pərz), *n. British Slang.* champagne.

cham|per|tor (cham′pər tər), *n. Law.* a person who is guilty of champerty.

cham|per|tous (cham′pər təs), *adj. Law.* of the nature of champerty.

cham|per|ty (cham′pər tē), *n. Law.* an illegal proceeding whereby a party not otherwise interested in a suit aids a plaintiff or defendant for a share of the matter in suit in case of success. [< Anglo-French *champart* sharecropping < Old French *champ* (< Latin *campus* field) + *part* part]

cham|pi|gnon (sham pin′yən; *especially British* cham pin′yən; *French* shäN pē nyôN′), *n.* **1** any edible fungus or mushroom, such as the meadow mushroom: *Madame Ribard, the patronne, had surpassed herself; an omelette aux* [with] *champignons that melted in the mouth* (London Times). **2** (especially in Great Britain) an edible species of mushroom that grows in fairy rings. [< Middle French *champignon*, alteration of Old French *champegneul* < Gallo-Romance *campāniolus* growing in the fields (diminutive) < Late Latin *campānius* campaign]

cham|pi|on (cham′pē ən), *n., adj., v.* —*n.* **1** a person, animal, or thing that wins first place in a game or contest: *He is the swimming champion of our state.* **2** a person who fights or speaks for another; person who defends or supports: (*Figurative.*) *That writer is a great champion of peace.* SYN: protector, supporter, defender. **3** a fighting man; combatant; man of valor: *... in close fight a champion grim* (Scott). **4** anything engaged in a conflict where power will win: *Hot, cold, moist, and dry, four champions fierce, Strive here for mast'ry* (Milton).
—*adj.* first; ahead of all others: *a champion boxer, champion turnips. My sister is the champion talker in our house.*
—*v.t.* **1** to fight for; speak in behalf of; defend; support: (*Figurative.*) *to champion a lost cause. All his life he has championed freedom.* SYN: uphold, back, advocate. **2** *Obsolete.* to challenge to a contest; bid defiance to.
[< Old French *champion* < Late Latin *campiō, -ōnis,* ultimately < Latin *campus* field] —**cham′pi|on|less**, *adj.*
▶The nonstandard pronunciation (cham pēn′) is a survival of a variant once found in standard use.

cham|pi|on|ship (cham′pē ən ship), *n.* **1** the position of a champion; first place: *Our high-school team won the county basketball championship.* **2** a defense; support: *He undertook the championship of our cause.*

champ|le|vé (shamp′lə vā′; *French* shäN lə vā′), *adj., n.* —*adj.* (of enameled work) having the ground cut out or depressed in places to receive the enamel.
—*n.* champlevé work or the process of producing it.
[< French *champlevé*, past participle of *champlever* < *champ* field, ground (< Latin *campus*) + *lever* raise, remove < Latin *levāre*]

Ch'an (chän), *n. Chinese.* **1** Zen. **2** (literally) meditation.

chance (chans, chäns), *n., v.,* **chanced, chancing,** *adj.* —*n.* **1** a favorable time; opportunity: *Now is your chance. The farmer saw a chance to make some money selling some of his woodland.* **2** a likelihood of anything happening; possibility or probability: *With such an early start there is a good chance we will be home before supper. The chances are against snow in July.* **3** fate, fortune, or luck: *Chance led to the finding of gold in California.* **4** a happening; event: *I shall never forget the chance that befell me that day.* **5** a risk; gamble: *He took a big chance when he swam the wide river.* SYN: hazard. **6** a ticket in a raffle or lottery: *She bought two chances in the car raffle at the fair.* **7a** *Baseball.* any defensive fielding play which results in a putout, an assist, or an error. **b** *Cricket.* a possible catch. **8** *Archaic.* a fortuitous, and usually unfortunate, event; mishap; accident.
—*v.i.* **1** to happen by chance; have the fortune; occur; come about: *I chanced to meet an old friend today while walking down the street window shopping.* SYN: befall. See syn. under **happen**.
—*v.t. Informal.* to take the risk of: *Father will not chance driving on the icy roads. He decided to chance one more attempt. ... thereby chancing an outburst of indignation at home and abroad* (London Times). SYN: hazard, venture, gamble.
—*adj.* happening by chance; not expected or planned; accidental; casual: *We were surprised by a chance visit from Grandfather last weekend.* SYN: fortuitous, unexpected.
by any chance, possibly; perhaps: *Do you by any chance have a pen with you?*
by chance, accidentally; without planning: *It was only by chance that I looked down and found the keys you lost.*
chance upon (or **on**), to happen to find or meet: *I chanced upon an old friend when I stopped in the drugstore.*
on the chance, depending on the possibility: *He took the road to the left on the chance that it would lead him to the lake.*
on the off chance, depending on luck: *She went to the department store on the off chance that she would find her mother shopping there.*
stand a chance, to have favorable prospects: *The Ministry ... stand a good chance of seeing themselves reduced to insignificance* (Manchester Examiner).
the chances are, it is likely: *If approved, the chances are that most of the 36 railroads in the Northeast ... will be consolidated* (Newsweek).
[< Old French *cheance* < Vulgar Latin *cadentia* a falling < Latin *cadere* fall. See etym. of doublets **cadence, cadenza**.]

chance|ful (chans′fəl, chäns′-), *adj.* marked by chance; uncertain; perilous; eventful.

chan|cel (chan′səl, chän′-), *n.* the space around the altar of a church, used by the clergy and the choir. It is often separated from the rest of the church by a railing, lattice, or screen. [< Old French *chancel* < Late Latin *cancellus* lattice < Latin *cancellī* grating, bars (from the use of lattices to set off part of the basilica)]

chance|less (chans′lis, chäns′-), *adj. Cricket.* played without giving the fieldsmen a chance to catch the ball: *A chanceless century by Lee ... gave his side a spirited start yesterday* (London Times). —**chance′less|ly**, *adv.*

chan|cel|ler|y (chan′sə lər ē, -slər-; chän′-), *n., pl.* **-ler|ies**. **1** the position or office of a chancellor. **2** the department or office of a chancellor: *Faraway decisions in European and Asiatic chancelleries can have quick effect on the welfare of us and our children* (Newsweek). **3** the building or rooms serving as the office of a chancellor. **4** the building or office of an embassy or legation; chancery: *Anything that threatens to disturb the uneasy status quo in the world oil picture is viewed with grave alarm in the world's chancelleries* (New York Times).

chan|cel|lor (chan′sə lər, -slər; chän′-), *n.* **1** the prime minister or other very high official in Austria and West Germany and formerly in Germany, and many other European countries. **2** *U.S.* the chief judge of a court of chancery or equity in certain states. **3** any one of various high British government officials, especially: **a** the Chancellor of the Exchequer. **b** the Lord Chancellor. **4a** the head or president of some American universities. **b** *British.* the titular head of a British university: *Chancellors are elected for life.* **5** the chief or official secretary of a king, nobleman, or embassy. **6a** an Anglican lay official who handles legal matters for a diocese. **b** a Roman Catholic priest in charge of a diocesan chancery. [< Anglo-French *chanceler*, Old French *chancelier* < Latin *cancellārius* court secretary; (originally) officer stationed at a tribunal < *cancellī* bars (because of the grating behind which he worked)]

Chancellor of the Exchequer, the British cabinet minister responsible for financial affairs.

chan|cel|lor|ship (chan′sə lər ship, -slər-; chän′-), *n.* **1** the position of a chancellor: *He had not reckoned on Thomas, who resigned the chancellorship and took his new archiepiscopal duties seriously* (Newsweek). **2** the term of office of a chancellor.

chan|cel|lor|y (chan′sə lər ē, -slər-; chän′-), *n., pl.* **-lor|ies**. = chancellery.

chance-med|ley (chans′med′lē, chäns′-), *n. Law.* accidental homicide in which some blame is attached to the killer. [< Anglo-French *chance medlée* mixed chance (happening) < Old French *cheance* chance, and *medler* meddle]

chance music, music in which performers introduce random elements into compositions that do not specify all the pitches and rhythms to be followed; aleatoric music.

chanc|er (chan′sər, chän′-), *n. British Slang.* **1** a clumsy, incompetent person. **2** a person who takes any kind of risk, as by speculating, gambling, or lying. [< *chance* + *-er*[1]]

chan|cer|y (chan′sər ē, chän′-), *n., pl.* **-cer|ies**. **1** *Law.* **a** a court of law that deals with cases in which fairness and justice require a settlement not covered by either common law or statute law; court of equity. **b** proceedings in equity; equity. **2** an office where public records are kept; archives. **3a** the office or court of a chancellor; chancellery. **b** the room or building in which this is located; chancellery: *A fire which broke out in the top floor of the chancery building of the British Embassy in Lisbon destroyed the attachés' offices* (London Times). **4** the court of the Lord Chancellor of England, now one of the divisions of the High Court of Justice. **5** *Roman Catholic Church.* the department of a diocese which has the care of official documents. **6** *Wrestling.* a grip on the head.
in chancery, **a** in a helpless position: *He found himself in chancery when the truth came out.* **b** *Law.* (of property, etc.) in a court of equity: *Either party to a cause in chancery shall have the right to an examination of all the witnesses in the case* (Michigan General Statutes). **c** *Boxing.* (of a fighter's head) held, contrary to the rules, between the opponent's arm and body and unable to avoid severe punishment: *I had* [*his*] *head in chancery, and could give it him* (Oliver Wendell Holmes). **d** *Wrestling.* in a headlock or stranglehold.
[variant of *chancellery*]

chanc|ey (chan′sē, chän′-), *adj.,* **chanc|i|er, chanc|i|est**. = chancy.

chan|cre (shang′kər), *n.* an ulcer or sore with a hard base, especially the first lesion of syphilis. [< French *chancre* < Latin *cancer, cancrī* crab. See etym. of doublets **cancer, canker**.]

chan|croid (shang′kroid), *n.* a venereal infection characterized by lesions that resemble chancres but have a soft base and are usually spreading and painful; soft chancre. Chancroid is caused by a specific germ and is not related to syphilis.

chan|crous (shang′krəs), *adj.* of or like a chancre.

chanc|y (chan′sē, chän′-), *adj.,* **chanc|i|er, chanc|i|est**. subject to chance; uncertain; risky: *Acting, which has always been a chancy profession, is more precarious than ever in Hollywood* (New York Times). SYN: untrustworthy. Also, **chancey**. —**chanc′i|ness**, *n.*

chan|da|la (chan′dä′lə), *n.* (in India) an untouchable who has committed a serious crime; criminal. [< Hindustani *chandala* < Sanskrit *candāla*]

***chan|de|lier** (shan′də lir′), *n.* a fixture with branches for lights, usually hanging from the ceiling: *One by one, the 65 crystal chandeliers in the U.S. Capitol had been taken down, disassembled, washed prism by prism, reassembled and rehung* (Time). [< French *chandelier* < Vulgar Latin *candēlārium*, for Latin *candēlābrum* candelabrum]

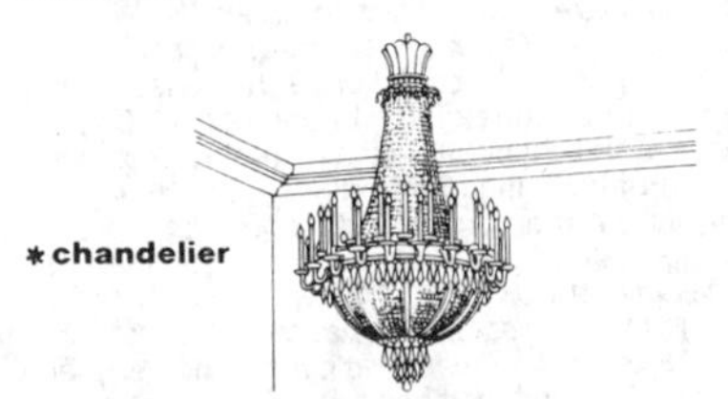
***chandelier**

chan|de|liered (shan′də lird′), *adj.* furnished with a chandelier or chandeliers.

chan|delle (shän del′), *n., v.,* **-delled, -dell|ing.**
—*n.* an abrupt climbing turn in which an airplane is propelled by its own momentum nearly to the point of stalling. —*v.i.* to perform such a turn. [< French *chandelle* (literally) candle; a vertical

Pronunciation Key: hat, āge, cãre, fär; let, ēqual, tėrm; it, īce; hot, ōpen, ôrder; **oil**, **out**; cup, pu̇t, rüle; **ch**ild; lo**ng**; **th**in; **ᴛʜ**en; **zh**, measure; **ə** represents **a** in about, **e** in taken, **i** in pencil, **o** in lemon, **u** in circus.

support or movement]

chan|dler (chan′dlər, chăn′-), *n.* **1** a maker or seller of candles. **2** a dealer in groceries and supplies: *The local fishermen bought their provisions from a ship chandler near the wharf. The corn chandler puts his hat on at five o'clock and goes home* (Punch).
[< Anglo-French *chandeler,* Old French *chandelier* < *chandeile* candle]

Chan|dler's wobble (chan′dlərz), = Chandler wobble.

Chan|dler wobble (chan′dlər), a slight eccentric oscillation of the earth on its axis recurring in cycles which last approximately 14 months: *The Earth's pole undergoes a mutation, the Chandler wobble, . . . whose motion is somehow kept going despite the substantial effects of viscous damping forces* (New Scientist and Science Journal).
[< Seth Carlo *Chandler,* 1846-1913, an American astronomer, who made a study of it]

chan|dler|y (chan′dlər ē, chăn′-), *n., pl.* **-dler|ies.** **1** a storeroom for candles. **2** the warehouse, goods, or business of a chandler.

chan|doo (chan dü′), *n.* opium for smoking.
[< Hindustani *chanḍū*]

chan|fron (chan′frən), *n. Archaic.* chamfron.

chang (chang, chäng), *n.* a thick beer or wine of Tibet made chiefly from barley or rice. [< Tibetan *chaṅ*]

chan|ga (chan′gə), *n.* a mole cricket of South America, Central America, and the southeastern United States: *The changa . . . is the worst insect pest of the sugar crop* (Url Lanham). [< American Spanish *changa*]

change (chānj), *v.,* **changed, chang|ing,** *n.* —*v.t.* **1** to make different; alter; modify: *She changed the room by painting the walls green. Can the Ethiopian change his skin, or the leopard his spots?* (Jeremiah 13:23). **2a** to put (something) in place of another; take in place of; substitute: *to change soiled clothes for clean ones, to change neckties, change handbags, change trains.* **b** to give or receive money of another kind, as foreign or smaller coin, in exchange for: *Can you change a dollar bill for ten dimes? The French traveler wished to change francs into dollars.* **3** to give and take; exchange: *I changed seats with my brother.* **4** to put a clean or fresh covering on: *to change the baby, to change a bed.*
—*v.i.* **1** to become different; alter; vary: *The wind changed from east to west. And every winter change to Spring* (Tennyson). **2** to make an exchange: *We changed from a station wagon to a sedan.* **3** to change one's clothes: *After swimming he went into the cabin and changed.* **4** to transfer from one aircraft, train, or bus to another: *Passengers must change at Chicago for San Francisco.* **5** (of the moon) to pass from one phase to another.
—*n.* **1** a passing from one form or place to a different one; a changing: *a change of scene. The change from flower to fruit is interesting to watch. Vacationing in the country is a pleasant change from city life.* SYN: alteration. **2** a changed condition: *Do you really see any change in his behavior?* SYN: transformation. **3** lack of sameness; variety: *Let me drive for a change.* SYN: diversity. **4** a thing to be used in place of another of the same kind: *She packed two changes of clothing for the trip.* SYN: substitute. **5** money returned to a person when he has given an amount larger than the price of what he buys: *I handed the clerk a quarter for the candy bar, and she gave me fifteen cents in change.* **6** smaller pieces of money given in place of a large piece of money: *Please give me four quarters in change for this dollar bill.* **7** small coins: *He always carries a pocketful of change.* **8** *Music.* modulation. **9** the passage of the moon from one phase to another. **10** *Commerce.* an exchange (originally treated as a contraction of exchange and often written *'change,* especially in the phrase on *'change,* "at the exchange"): *What good, honest, generous men at home, will be wolves and foxes on change!* (Emerson). **11** *Obsolete.* inconstancy; fickleness.

change over, *Informal.* to move to another place or into other circumstances; be shifted or transferred: *He thought of changing over to a different and more suitable job.*

changes, the different ways in which a set of bells can be rung: *To untrained ears, ringing changes sounds like the din of boilermakers at work, but the English love the arithmetical beauty of it all* (Time).

ring the changes, a to ring a set of bells in all its different ways: *The changes are rung on 7, 9 or 11 bells, but in each case 8, 10 and 12 bells respectively are used, the tenor bell remaining the last note of the sequence throughout the composition* (W. W. Starmer). **b** *Figurative.* to do a thing in many different ways; say or wear the same thing in different ways: *I've rung all the changes possible with only two skirts and three sweaters. Ring the changes on great measures and great experiments till it is time to [form] a House* (Benjamin Disraeli).
[< Old French *changier* < Latin *cambiāre* < a Gaulish word]
—*Syn. v.t.* **1,** *v.i.* **1 Change, alter** mean to make or become different. **Change** suggests that the difference is fundamental or complete: *She used to be shy, but has changed since she went to college. Automobiles have greatly changed life in the United States.* **Alter** suggests a less drastic difference, limited to some particular: *to alter the wording of a statement. We can alter the kitchen enough to put in a freezer if we rehang the door. My outlook on life has altered somewhat with the passing of the years.*
►**change,** *v.t.* **2a** When the object is not modified it is usually plural: *to change skirts, change neckties, change trains.* When the object is modified, though only by a possessive, it is usually singular: *I want to change my shirt.*

change|a|bil|i|ty (chān′jə bil′ə tē), *n.* changeable quality or condition: *Yet even this relatively simple aim came into conflict with the changeability of life* (New Yorker). *Changeability, particularly changing into acids, is another characteristic of lipids* (Science News Letter).

change|a|ble (chān′jə bəl), *adj.* **1** that can change; likely to change; varying; fickle: *April weather is changeable.* SYN: inconstant, unstable, variable, mutable, protean. **2** that can be changed; likely to be changed (by others); alterable. **3** having a color or appearance that changes. Silk is called changeable when it shows different colors in different lights. —**change′a|ble|ness,** *n.*

change|a|bly (chān′jə blē), *adv.* in a changeable manner; with constant change or variety.

change|ful (chānj′fəl), *adj.* full of changes; likely to change; changing: *the changeful color of the sky at sunset. . . . fickle as a changeful dream* (Scott). SYN: variable, inconstant. —**change′ful|ly,** *adv.* —**change′ful|ness,** *n.*

change house, *Scottish.* a tavern.

change|less (chānj′lis), *adj.* not changing; not likely to change; constant: *the changeless heat of the desert sun.* SYN: unchanging, steadfast, unvarying, unalterable, immutable. —**change′less|ly,** *adv.* —**change′less|ness,** *n.*

change|ling (chānj′ling), *n.* **1** a child secretly left in place of another: *She may have been . . . a changeling—the adopted daughter of gypsies* (Time). **2** a strange, stupid, or ugly child, supposed to have been left by fairies in place of a child carried off by them. **3** *Archaic.* a person given to change; fickle or inconstant person; waverer; turncoat; renegade. **4** *Archaic.* a half-witted person; idiot; imbecile.
[< *change* + *-ling*]

change|mak|er (chānj′mā′kər), *n.* **1** a machine for releasing small change in various denominations by pressing a lever or key. **2** a person who supplies small change, as at an automat or subway.

change of heart, a change of feeling; conversion: *He had no explanation of what appeared to him to be a complete change of heart on the part of private industry* (Wall Street Journal).

change of life, = menopause.

change of pace, 1 a sudden shift from one type of activity, routine, or habit to another, usually as a form of distraction intended to relieve fatigue or boredom: *After a round of rumbas and cha-chas the band, for a nice change of pace, played a fox trot.* **2** *Baseball.* a pitch thrown to look like a fast ball or fast curve but not really traveling so fast; change-up.

change of venue, a change of the place of a trial.

change|o|ver (chānj′ō′vər), *n.* a thorough change of ownership or control of a business, of products of a factory, or the like: *Earnings may have been affected by greater costs of changeover to new models* (Wall Street Journal).

chang|er (chān′jər), *n.* **1** a person or thing that changes something or makes change. **2** a device in a phonograph record player which automatically releases records from the spindle to the turntable.

change ringing, the art of ringing a peal of bells in regularly varying order, so that all the possible combinations may be made: *For change-ringing purposes, a set of eight bells (called "Major") ranging from treble to tenor are numbered one to eight* (Time).

chang|es (chān′jəz), *n.pl.* See under **change.**

change-up (chānj′up′), *n. Baseball.* a slow pitch delivered with the same motion as a fast pitch, usually following a fast pitch: *The slow ball or change-up is a strategic pitch designed to throw the batter off balance* (New York Times).

chang|ing bag (chānj′ing), a lightproof bag made of dark cloth that serves as a portable darkroom. A photographer puts his hands into the bag to load film into a camera.

changing note or **tone,** a musical note or tone not essential to the harmony, such as a passing tone or a grace note.

changing room, a room used to change one's clothes: *The bath was surrounded by a veranda and changing rooms* (Scientific American).

chang|wat (chăng wät′), *n.* a province in Thailand.
[< Thai *changwat*]

chan|nel[1] (chan′əl), *n., v.,* **-neled, -nel|ing** or (*especially British*) **-nelled, -nel|ling,** *adj.* —*n.* **1** the bed of a stream, river, or other watercourse: *Rivers cut their own channels to the sea.* SYN: race. **2** a body of water joining two larger bodies of water: *The English Channel lies between the North Sea and the Atlantic Ocean.* SYN: strait. See picture under **bay**[1]. **3** the deeper part of a waterway: *There is shallow water on both sides of the channel in this river.* **4** a passage for liquids; groove or canal. The gutter of a street is a channel for water. SYN: duct, conduit. **5** *Figurative.* the means by which something moves or is carried: *The information came through official channels.* SYN: course, passage, avenue, agency. **6** a narrow band of electronic frequencies that carries the programs of a television or radio station. The width of the band depends upon the type of transmission. *The viewer who tunes to an empty channel and waits a long time may see a commercial* (Time). **7** *Figurative.* a course of action; field of activity: *He tried to find a suitable channel for his abilities.* **8** a natural tubular passage for fluids: *One snake, . . . from the size of the poison channel in its fangs, must be very deadly* (Charles Darwin). **9a** a long groove or furrow on a stone or column. **b** a trough-shaped bar of rolled iron or steel, forming in cross section three sides of a rectangle; channel iron. **10** a path or area on a magnetic tape along which sound or video impressions are recorded. **11** a person through whom invisible beings, spirits, or forces supposedly communicate: *J.Z. Knight, the "channel" for Ramtha* (Atlanta Journal/Constitution).
—*v.t.* **1** to form a channel in; wear or cut into a channel; furrow: *The river had channeled its way through the rocks.* **2** to convey through a channel: (*Figurative.*) *Gifts of mind . . . are . . . channelled out to the many through the few* (Cardinal Newman). **3** *Figurative.* to direct into a particular course; concentrate: *Channel all your efforts into this one project, and you will succeed.* **4** to supposedly communicate with (invisible beings, spirits, or forces): *Not all the channeled voices are from outer space* (Time).
—*adj.* having a cross section shaped like this ⊔: *a channel iron.*
[< Old French *chanel* < Latin *canālis.* See etym. of doublets **canal, kennel**[2].] —**chan′nel|er,** *n.*

chan|nel[2] (chan′əl), *n.* a horizontal plank, bolted on edge to the outside of a ship, to which the shrouds are set up to increase their spread. [alteration of *chain-wale*]

channel bass, = red drum.

channel black, = gas black.

channel cat or **catfish,** any one of several species of catfish often found in channels of rivers.

chan|neled (chan′əld), *adj.* **1** having channels or grooves; furrowed; fluted. **2** confined in or directed to or along a channel.

chan|nel|ing (chan′ə ling), *n.* the act or process of supposedly communicating with invisible beings, spirits, or forces: *The extraterrestrials who turn up in the course of channeling . . . appear almost unfailingly wise and benevolent* (Time).

channeling machine a machine for cutting grooves or channels in quarrying stone.

channel iron or **bar,** a flanged bar of rolled iron or steel, shaped so that its cross section forms three sides of a rectangle.

chan|nel|ize (chan′ə līz), *v.t.,* **-ized, -iz|ing.** = channel. —**chan′nel|i|za′tion,** *n.*

chan|nelled (chan′əld), *adj. Especially British.* channeled.

cha|no|yu (chä′nō yü), *n. Japanese.* the ritual of drinking tea.

chan|son (shäɴ sôɴ′), *n. French.* a song.

chan|son d'a|mour (shäɴ sôɴ′ də mür′), *French.* love song.

chan|son de geste (shäɴ sôɴ′ də zhest′), *French.* **1** any Old French epic poem celebrating legendary or historical heroes and events in ancient France, as the *Chanson de Roland.* **2** (literally) epic song.

chan|son de toile (shäɴ sôɴ′ də twäl′), *French.* **1** a short poem written by troubadours in the Middle Ages to accompany needlework, weaving, or dancing. **2** (literally) a sewing song.

chan|son|ette (shäɴ sô net′), *n. French.* a little song.

chan|son|nier (shäɴ sô nyā′), *n. French.* a songwriter or singer, especially of popular songs.

chant (chant, chänt), *n., v.* —*n.* **1** a song; melody; singing: *an Indian war chant.* **2** a short, simple song in which several syllables or words are

sung in one tone. Chants are sometimes used in church services. **3** a psalm, prayer, or other song for chanting. **4** a singsong way of talking. **5** the act of singing or reciting in a monotone, for example in a church service. [probably <verb]
—*v.t.* **1** to sing: *to chant a melody.* **2** to sing to a chant, or in the manner of a chant. A choir chants psalms or prayers. *Heard a carol, mournful, holy, Chanted loudly, chanted lowly* (Tennyson). SYN: intone. **3** *Figurative.* to keep talking about; say over and over again: *The football fans chanted "Go, team, go!"* **4** *Poetic.* to celebrate in song.
—*v.i.* **1** to sing or warble: *How can ye chant, ye little birds!* (Robert Burns). **2** to recite musically; intone a chant or in the style of a chant. **3** *Figurative.* to repeat things monotonously: *He was still chanting away as he disappeared.* **4** (of hounds) to cry; yelp. Also, **chaunt.**
[<Old French *chanter* <Latin *cantāre* sing (frequentative) <*canere* sing]

chan|tage (chan′tij, chän′-; *French* shäɴ tȧzh′), *n.* a blackmailing or being blackmailed. [<French *chantage* <Old French *chanter* to chant]

chan|tant (shäɴ täɴ′; *Anglicized* chan′tənt), *adj.* of a style that is singable; melodious; tuneful. [<French *chantant,* present participle of *chanter* sing]

Chan|te|cler (chan′tə klir′), *n.* any of a breed of American chickens of medium weight with pure-white feathers, that lay brown-shelled eggs.

chant|er (chan′tər, chän′-), *n.* **1** a person who chants or sings; singer; songster. **2a** a person who sings in the choir of a cathedral or the like; chorister. **b** the precentor, or chief singer in the choir; cantor. **3** a priest who sings Masses in a chantry. **4** the pipe with finger holes on which the melody is played on a bagpipe. **5** = hedge sparrow. Also, **chaunter.**

chan|te|relle¹ (shan′tə rel′, chan′-), *n.* a fragrant, reddish-yellow, edible wild mushroom; little goblet. [<French *chanterelle* <New Latin *cantharellus* (diminutive) <Latin *cantharus* drinking cup <Greek *kántharos*]

chan|te|relle² (shäɴ tə rel′), *n. French.* the E (highest) string of the violin. [<French *chanterelle* treble string <Latin *cantāre* to sing]

chan|teur (shäɴ tœr′), *n. French.* a singer.

chan|teuse (shäɴ tœz′), *n. French.* a woman singer.

chant|ey (shan′tē, chan′-), *n., pl.* **-eys.** a song sung by sailors, especially in rhythm with the motions of their work: *May we lift a deep sea chantey such as seamen use at sea?* (Rudyard Kipling). Also, **chanty, shantey, shanty.** [perhaps alteration of French *chanter* to sing]

chan|ti|cleer (chan′tə klir), *n.* a cock; rooster. [<Old French *chantecler* <*chanter* sing + *cler* clear (the name of the cock in *Reynard the Fox*)]

***Chan|til|ly lace** (shan til′ē; *French* shäɴ tē yē′), a French lace, usually black, of a delicate, dull finish, with a net in patterns of six-pointed stars. [<*Chantilly,* a town in northern France, formerly famous for lace manufacturing]

***Chantilly lace**

chant|ress (chan′tris, chän′-), *n.* a female chanter or singer; songstress.

chan|try (chan′trē, chän′-), *n., pl.* **-tries.** **1** a chapel attached to a church, used for the less important services. **2a** an endowment to pay for singing or saying of Masses for a person's soul. **b** a chapel, altar, or part of a church similarly endowed. **c** the priests thus endowed. [<Old French *chanterie* singing <*chanter* to sing, chant]

chant|y (shan′tē, chan′-), *n., pl.* **chant|ies.** = chantey.

Cha|nu|kah (hä′nů kä, ʜä′-), *n.* = Hanukkah.

cha|os (kā′os), *n.* **1a** very great confusion; complete disorder: *The tornado left the town in chaos.* **b** a confused mass or mixture. **2** Also, **Chaos.** the infinite space in which formless matter was thought to have existed before the ordered universe came into existence. **3** *Mathematics, Physics.* random behavior generated within any deterministic system: *The determinism inherent in chaos implies that many random phenomena are more predictable than has been thought. . . . Chaos allows order to be found in such diverse systems as the atmosphere, dripping faucets and the heart* (Scientific American). **4** *Obsolete.* a gaping void; yawning gulf, chasm, or abyss (chiefly from the Vulgate rendering of Luke 16:26). [<Latin *chaos* <Greek *cháos*]

Cha|os (kā′os), *n.* the most ancient of Greek gods, personifying the formless, confused state of matter before the universe existed: *the reign of Chaos and old Night* (Milton).

cha|ot|ic (kā ot′ik), *adj.* very confused; completely disordered: *The town was in a chaotic condition after the flood.* —**cha|ot′i|cal|ly,** *adv.*

chap¹ (chap), *v.,* **chapped, chap|ping,** *n.* —*v.t., v.i.* to crack open; make or become rough: *Cold weather chaps his skin.*
—*n.* a crack in something, especially the skin; place where something is chapped.
[Middle English *chappen* to cut off, chop, break]

chap² (chap), *n.* **1** *Informal.* a fellow; man or boy: *Hello, old chap! Send those other two chaps after us* (Graham Greene). **2** *British. Dialect.* a buyer; customer. [short for *chapman*]

chap³ (chap), *n.* Often, **chaps.** haw; chop: *Till he unseamed him from the nave to the chaps* (Shakespeare). [variant of *chop;* perhaps <*chap¹*, in sense of "bite off"]

Chap. or **chap.,** chapter.

cha|pa|ra|jos (chä′pä rä′hōs), *n.pl.* strong leather trousers without a seat, worn over other trousers by cowboys; chaps. [American English <Mexican Spanish *chaparajos,* variant of *chaparreras*]

cha|pa|re|jos (chä′pä rā′hōs), *n.pl.* = chaparajos.

chap|ar|ral (chap′ə ral′), *n.* a dense, often thorny, thicket of low brushy vegetation, frequently including small evergreen oaks, found in the Southwestern United States. [American English <Spanish *chaparral* <*chaparro* evergreen oak, probably <a Basque word]

chapparral cock, = road runner.

chaparral hen, the female of the road runner or chaparral cock.

chaparral pea, a thorny shrub of the pea family, often growing in dense thickets in the Southwestern United States.

chap|ar|re|ras (shap′ə rer′əs, chap′-), *n.pl.* = chaparajos.

cha|pa|ti (chə pat′ē), *n., pl.* **-pat|ies.** = chapatty.

cha|pat|ty (chə pat′ē), *n., pl.* **-ties.** (in India) a thin, unleavened pancake. [Anglo-Indian <Hindustani *chapātī*]

chap|book (chap′bůk′), *n.* a small book or pamphlet of popular tales, ballads, or the like, formerly sold on the streets. [<*chapmen,* who sold them]

chape (chāp), *n.* the metal edge or trimming reinforcing a scabbard, especially at the point. [<French *chape* cover, cap <Late Latin *cappa* cape]

cha|peau (sha pō′), *n., pl.* **-peaux** or **-peaus** (-pōz′). a hat: *Like calling a hat a chapeau when all you need is something to keep the rain out of your hair* (Newsweek). [<French *chapeau* <Old French *chapel* hat <Vulgar Latin *cappellus* small cape <Late Latin *cappa* cape]

chap|el (chap′əl), *n.* **1** a building for Christian worship, not as large as a church. In earlier times it was consecrated and had an altar; in modern use this is not necessarily so. SYN: oratory. **2** a small place for worship in a larger building: *a hospital chapel.* **3** a room or building for worship in a palace or school. **4** a religious service in a chapel, especially in a school or college: *There is chapel today after classes.* **5** *British.* a house of prayer of a Christian denomination other than the established church, especially of nonconformists. **6** a choir or an orchestra attached to a chapel, court, or musical establishment. **7** an association of journeymen printers for regulating conditions of work among themselves: *I proposed some reasonable alteration in their chapel laws* (Benjamin Franklin). [<Old French *chapele* <Medieval Latin *cappella* originally, the shrine in which was preserved the *cappella* or cloak of Saint Martin of Tours <Late Latin *cappa* cape]

chap|el-mas|ter (chap′əl mas′tər, -mäs′-), *n.* the director of a choir or orchestra, as of a royal chapel.

chapel of ease, a subordinate church for the convenience of distant parishioners.

chap|el|ry (chap′əl rē), *n., pl.* **-ries.** the district assigned to, or the jurisdiction of, a chapel.

chap|er|on or **chap|er|one** (shap′ə rōn), *n., v.,* **-oned, -on|ing.** —*n.* **1** a married woman or an older woman who accompanies a young girl or unmarried woman in public for the sake of good form and protection. SYN: duenna. **2** an older person who is present at a party or other social activity of younger people to see that good taste is observed. **3** a kind of draped turban popular in Europe during the Renaissance.
—*v.t.* to act as chaperon to; escort: *His first expedition into the Sahara was chaperoned . . . by the French army* (Wall Street Journal).
[<Old French *chaperon* hood, protector (diminutive) <*chape* cape <Late Latin *cappa*]

chap|er|on|age (shap′ə rō′nij), *n.* the activities or protection of a chaperon.

chap|fall|en (chop′fô′lən, chap′-), *adj.* dejected, discouraged, or humiliated: *The press applauded, the critics subsided chapfallen* (Time). SYN: dispirited, crestfallen. Also, **chopfallen.**

chap|i|ter (chap′ə tər), *n.* the capital of a column, pillar, or pilaster. [<Old French *chapitre.* See etym. of doublet **chapter.**]

chap|lain (chap′lin), *n.* **1** the clergyman authorized to perform religious functions for a family, royal court, school, unit in the armed forces, prison, or other institution: *Chaplains in the United States armed forces are commissioned officers. But they are called chaplain* (C. B. McDonald). **2** a clergyman or layman authorized to lead religious services in a public assembly, legislative body, or fraternal organization. *Abbr:* Chap. [<Old French *chapelain* <Medieval Latin *cappellanus,* originally, a keeper of the cloak (*cappella*) of Saint Martin; see etym. under **chapel**]
—**chap′lain|ship,** *n.*

chap|lain|cy (chap′lən sē), *n., pl.* **-cies.** the position of a chaplain.

chap|let (chap′lit), *n.* **1** a wreath worn on the head, usually a garland of flowers or leaves, but also of gold, precious stones, or the like; circlet; coronal. **2** a string of beads. **3** in the Roman Catholic Church: **a** a string of beads for keeping count in saying prayers, one third as long as a rosary. **b** the prayers said with such beads. **4** *Architecture.* a narrow molding carved to resemble a string of beads or the like. **5** anything like a chaplet of beads, such as the eggs of a toad. [<Old French *chaplet* (diminutive) <*chapel* headdress; see etym. under **chapeau**]

chap|let|ed (chap′lə tid), *adj.* wearing a wreath on the head: *chapleted nymphs.*

Chap|lin|esque (chap′lə nesk′), *adj.* characteristic or suggestive of the comic acting in silent motion pictures of Charles Chaplin (1889-1977).

chap|man (chap′mən), *n., pl.* **-men. 1** *British.* an itinerant dealer or trader; hawker; peddler. **2** *Archaic.* a man whose business is buying and selling; merchant; trader; dealer. [Old English *cēapman,* earlier *cēapman* <*cēap* trade + *man* man]

cha|pon (shä pôɴ′), *n. French.* a small cube of bread rubbed with garlic, for use in salads.

cha|po|te (chä pō′tā), *n.* **1** a persimmon of Texas and northern Mexico, bearing a black fruit. **2** the fruit. [American English <Mexican Spanish *chapote* <Nahuatl *tzapotl*]

chapped (chapt), *adj.* having chaps; cracked.

chap|pie (chap′ē), *n. Informal.* **1** a fellow, especially a close friend. **2** a little chap: *Ask away, chappie* (New York Times).

chap|ping (chap′ing), *adj.* breaking in short waves; chopping.

chap|py¹ (chap′ē), *adj.,* **-pi|er, -pi|est.** full of chaps or cracks; cleft.

chap|py² (chap′ē), *n., pl.* **-pies.** = chappie.

***chaps¹** (chaps, shaps), *n.pl.* strong leather trousers without a seat, worn over other trousers by cowboys; chaparajos. [short for *chaparajos*]

***chaps¹**

chaps² (chaps), *n.pl.* See under **chap³.**

chap|tal|ize (shap′tə līz), *v.t.,* **-ized, -iz|ing.** to correct or improve the must in making (wine), by neutralizing an excess of acid and adding sugar: *to chaptalize wine.* [<J. A. *Chaptal,* 1756-1832, a French chemist who invented the process + English *-ize*] —**chap′tal|i|za′tion,** *n.*

chap|ter (chap′tər), *n., v.* —*n.* **1** a main division of a book or other writing, usually numbered, dealing with a certain part of the story or subject: *That book is dull until the hero enters in the third chapter. The first chapters of the Biblical book of Genesis tell about the creation of the world.* **2** *Figurative.* anything like a chapter; part; section: *The development of radio is an interesting chapter in modern science.* **3** a local division of an organization, which holds its own meetings; branch of a club, fraternity, society, or the like. **4** *Ecclesiastical.* **a** a regular meeting of the canons of a collegiate or cathedral church, presided over by a dean. **b** the members of such an assembly collectively: *The dean and chapter are . . . the nominal electors of a bishop* (William Blackstone). **c** a general meeting or assembly of the members of a religious or other order. **5** *Roman*

Pronunciation Key: hat, āge, cãre, fär; let, ēqual, tėrm; it, īce; hot, ōpen, ôrder; oil, out; cup, pu̇t, rüle; child; long; thin; ᴛʜen; zh, measure; ə represents a in about, e in taken, i in pencil, o in lemon, u in circus.

Catholic Church. a Biblical passage read as a lesson following the psalms at the canonical hours, at complin, when it follows the hymn, and at matins. **6** *British.* a division of the statute book corresponding to one Act of Parliament, cited with the regnal year: *the fifth Anne, chapter two. Abbr:* ch., chap.
—*v.t.* to divide (a book or other written matter) into chapters; arrange in chapters: *The Bible was chaptered by Cardinal Langton.*
[< Old French *chapitre,* learned borrowing from Latin *capitulum* (diminutive) < *caput, -itis* head. See etym. of doublet **chapiter**.]

chapter and verse, **1** the exact reference to a passage of Scripture. **2** *Figurative.* exact authority (for). **3** *Figurative.* precise information and full detail.

chapter house, **1** the building or rooms where the chapter of a cathedral or monastery holds its meetings: *The monks transact business in their chapter house.* **2** *U.S. and Canada.* the house of a college fraternity or sorority.

chapter of accidents, the unforeseen course of events; a series of unexpected developments.

cha|que|ta (chä kā′tä), *n.* a jacket, especially a heavy one of leather or fabric; worn by cowboys. [American English < Spanish *chaqueta* < Middle French *jaquette* jacket]

char[1] (chär), *v.,* **charred, char|ring,** *n.* —*v.t.* **1** to burn to charcoal or carbon. **2** to burn enough to blacken; scorch: *After the fire a carpenter replaced the charred floor.*
—*v.i.* to become burned to charcoal or carbon.
—*n.* **1** a charred substance. **2** charcoal; boneblack.
[perhaps < *charcoal*]

char[2] (chär), *n., v.,* **charred, char|ring.** *Especially British.* —*n.* **1** a charwoman. **2** an odd job, especially of housework; chore.
—*v.i.* **1** to do housework by the day or hour. **2** to do odd jobs; chare.
—*v.t.* to do (odd jobs).
[Old English *cerr* turn, occasion. Compare etym. under **ajar, chare, chore.**]

char[3] (chär), *n., pl.* **chars** or (*collectively*) **char.** any one of a group of trout with small scales, including the brook or speckled trout, the lake trout, and the common char of Europe. Also, **charr.** [origin unknown]

char[4] (chär), *n. Slang, originally Cockney.* tea. [earlier, *cha.* Compare etym. under **tea.**]

char|a[1] (shar′ə), *n. British Slang.* charabanc: *You can get there in no time, in a bus or a chara* (Manchester Guardian Weekly).

char|a[2] (kar′ə), *n.* any one of a group of submerged, freshwater algae that root in muddy or sandy bottoms by means of rhizoids. [< New Latin *Chara* the genus name < Latin *chara* the name of a plant]

char|a|banc or **char-à-banc** (shar′ə bang, -bangk; *French* shȧ rȧ bäɴ′), *n., pl.* **-bancs** (-bangz, -bangks; *French* -bäɴ′). *British.* **1** a large motorbus used for excursions, having several rows of benches facing forward: *Apart from a few luxurious tourist charabancs, the buses tend to be battered* (Harper's). **2** a large open vehicle drawn by horses, formerly used. [< French *char à bancs* car with benches]

char|a|cid (kar′ə sid), *adj.* of or having to do with characins: *Piranhas belong to the characid fishes.*

char|a|cin (kar′ə sin), *n.* any one of a family of voracious, strong-jawed fishes of Africa or South America: *Some tropical fish that bear their young in eggs are the ... characins and cichlids* (C. L. Hubbs). [< New Latin *Characinidae* the family name < Greek *chárax, -akos* kind of bream]

char|ac|ter (kar′ik tər), *n., v.* —*n.* **1** all qualities or features of anything; kind; sort; nature: *The soil on the prairies is of a different character from that in the mountains. He dislikes people of that character.* **2** moral nature; moral strength or weakness. The special ways in which any person feels, thinks, and acts, considered as good or bad, make up his character. *He has a shallow, changeable character.* **3** moral firmness, self-control, or integrity: *It takes character to endure hardship for very long. The boy has no character whatever.* **4** the estimate formed of a person's qualities; reputation: *to have an infamous character. Her character is unimpeachable.* **5** good qualities, or the reputation of possessing them; good reputation: *He has established his character by his honesty and integrity.* **6a** a distinctive feature; trait; characteristic: *Tell me what one character of liberty the Americans have* (Edmund Burke). **b** a special quality or thing that makes one person, one animal, one plant, one thing, or a group of any kind different from others; trait or characteristic. The size and form of a given breed of dogs and the fragrance of a sweet pea are characters. *The trunk is a character found only in elephants.* **7** position or condition: *The treasurer of the club also serves in the character of secretary.* **8a** a person or animal in a play, poem, story, or book: *The novels of Dickens are filled with amusing characters. Mickey Mouse is a famous cartoon character.* **b** the personality or part assumed by an actor: *As the central character, Christopher Bruce has a nervous energy equally impressive in violent movement or tense repose* (London Times). **9** a person; individual; personality: *a curious character, an interesting character.* **10** *Informal.* a person who attracts attention because he is different or odd: *Merlo is a character. He carries sawdust in his pocket to help his grip* (London Times). **11** a letter, mark, or sign used in writing or printing. A, a, +, —, 1, 2, and 3 are characters. *There are 52 characters in our alphabet, consisting of 26 small letters and 26 capital letters. He felt ... only the dreariness of a man who tries to write an important letter on a damp sheet and finds the characters blur* (Graham Greene). **12a** writing or printing of a certain style: *Books in Gothic character are difficult to read.* **b** the symbols used for writing or printing a particular language, taken collectively. **c** the style of writing of a particular person; hand. **13a** a description of a person's qualities. **b** a literary description of familiar types of people, especially popular in the 1600's; character sketch. **14** a written testimonial, especially from a former employer, describing the qualities and capacities of an employee: *The director had given him a good character.* **15** a distinctive mark or symbol put on anything; a significant symbol; brand. **16** *Archaic.* a system of secret writing; cipher.
—*v.t.* **1** to describe the qualities of; delineate. **2** to represent; portray. **3** to write; inscribe: *the table wherein all my thoughts are visibly charactered and engraved* (Shakespeare). **4** to give a character to; characterize.
in character, as expected; natural or usual; appropriate: *It is not in character for him to be late. ... the answer is clearly in character* (Edward Freeman).
out of character, not as expected; not natural or usual; not appropriate: *It is out of character for small children to sit still for a long time. It is always self-ignorance that leads a man to act out of character* (John Mason).
[< Latin *character* < Greek *charaktêr* instrument for marking; distinctive mark < *charássein* engrave] —**char′ac|ter|less,** *adj.*
—*Syn. n.* **2 Character, personality, individuality** mean the qualities that make a person what he is. **Character** applies to the moral qualities that determine the way a person thinks, feels, and acts in the important matters of life, especially in relation to the principles of right and wrong: *Our pastor is a man of upright character.* **Personality** applies to such personal qualities as voice, bearing, or cordiality, that determine the way he acts in his social and personal relations: *The speaker had a stimulating personality which immediately captured the audience's interest in his otherwise dull topic.* **Individuality** applies to the particular qualities that make a person himself, an individual: *Each human being, however ordinary, begins in early infancy to build an individuality of his own. He has a weak character, but a winning personality, and great individuality.*
► **Character** and **nature** are sometimes used as unnecessary additions to adjectives: *employment of a seasonal character* (*seasonal employment*). *The job is especially fatiguing because of its repetitive nature* (*because it is repetitive*).

character actor, an actor who commonly plays the role of a person with marked unusual or eccentric characteristics.

character assassination, a malevolent attack upon someone's reputation; defamation: *How much did free American reporting of confidential and sometimes irresponsible information ... aid the character assassinations of the McCarthy period?* (Listener).

char|ac|ter|ful (kar′ik tər fəl), *adj.* strongly expressive of character: *It is a challenge to Americans everywhere on their ability in these confused and complicated times to get themselves served by their most scientific and characterful men* (Birmingham Post-Herald).

char|ac|ter|ise (kar′ik tə rīz), *v.t.,* **-ised, -is|ing.** *British.* characterize.

char|ac|ter|is|tic (kar′ik tə ris′tik), *adj, n.* —*adj.* marking off or distinguishing a certain person or thing from others; special; distinctive: *the characteristic stripes of a tiger. Bananas have their own characteristic smell.*
—*n.* **1** a special quality or feature; whatever distinguishes one person or thing from others: *Cheerfulness is a characteristic that we admire in people. An elephant's trunk is its most noticeable characteristic. The number of their legs is a characteristic of insects.* **SYN**: attribute, trait. See syn. under **feature. 2** *Mathematics.* the whole number in a logarithm. *Example:* In the logarithm 2.95424, the characteristic is 2 and the mantissa is .95424. —**char′ac|ter|is′ti|cal|ly,** *adv.*

char|ac|ter|i|za|tion (kar′ik tər ə zā′shən), *n.* **1** a characterizing; description of characteristics or essential features; portrayal in words or in a portrait. **2** the creation of characters in a play, poem, story, book, motion picture, or the like: *The problem of characterization is fundamental to an estimate of Hawley's work* (Harper's). **3a** the way an actor presents or portrays the personality he plays. **b** the personality so presented.

char|ac|ter|ize (kar′ik tə rīz), *v.t.,* **-ized, -iz|ing.** **1** to describe the special qualities or features of (a person or thing); describe: *The story of "Little Red Riding Hood" characterizes the wolf as a cunning and savage beast.* **SYN**: designate, class. **2** to be a characteristic of; distinguish; mark out: *A camel is characterized by the humps on its back and its ability to do without water for several days.* **3** to give character to: *The author characterized his heroine in a few short paragraphs.* —**char′ac|ter|iz′a|ble,** *adj.* —**char′ac|ter|iz′er,** *n.*

character neurosis, *Psychiatry.* any typical or marked characteristic, such as passiveness, aggressiveness, or moodiness, regarded as a form of neurosis.

char|ac|ter|o|log|i|cal (kar′ik tər ə loj′ə kəl), *adj.* of or having to do with characterology: *The patients proved to have one characterological feature in common, namely, that overeating was part of their regular response to stress* (Robert W. White). —**char′ac|ter|o|log′i|cal|ly,** *adv.*

char|ac|ter|ol|o|gy (kar′ik tə rol′ə jē), *n.* the study of character or personality: *Freudian themes ... have given the world a new conception of both infancy and adolescence, and shed much new light upon characterology* (G. Stanley Hall).

character sketch, **1** a literary profile of a person or a type, bringing out notable characteristics. **2** a brief characterization on the stage: *This dandy adaptation of the recent Terence Rattigan play* [*Separate Tables*] *offers some notable character sketches of lonely people at a drab British seaside resort hotel during the off season* (Newsweek).

character study, a representation or description of character in a story, sketch, play, book, motion picture, or the like: *... weakened as a character study by oversimplification and dialogue that is too dramatically weak* (Punch).

character witness, a person who is called upon to give testimony in behalf of the character and reputation of one of the parties in a legal case.

char|ac|ter|y (kar′ik tər ē, -trē), *n., pl.* **-ter|ies.** **1** the use of signs or symbols to express meaning. **2** the characters or symbols collectively.

cha|rade (shə rād′), *n.* **1a** Often, **charades.** a game in which one player acts out a word or phrase or its various parts and the others try to guess what it is. If the word he wants guessed is *penmanship,* the player might act out "pen," "man," and "ship." **b** a word or phrase represented in this game. **2** gestures made for an effect; sham performance or behavior: *Without new life being constantly breathed in, working institutions tend to degenerate into charades* (Harper's). [< French *charade* < Provençal *charrada* a chat, chatter < *charra* to chatter]

cha|ran|go (chə rang′gō), *n., pl.* **-gos.** a small Latin-American guitar with five to ten strings, usually made from the shell of armadillos. [< Spanish *charango*]

char|bon (shär′bən), *n.* = anthrax. [< French *charbon* charcoal, carbon]

Char|bray (shar′brā), *n.* any one of a breed of beef cattle developed in the United States by crossing the Charolaise and the Brahma. [< *Char*(olaise) + *Bra*(hma)]

char|broiled (chär′broild′), *adj.* broiled over charcoal: *charbroiled hamburgers. Some of these items might not be quite as tasty as—well, as a charbroiled prime sirloin* (Atlanta Constitution).

char|coal (chär′kōl′), *n., v.* —*n.* **1** the black, brittle form of carbon made by partly burning wood, bones, or the like in a place from which the air is shut out. Charcoal is used as fuel, in filters, and as a pencil for drawing. It is often specified as wood, vegetable, or animal charcoal, according to the material burned to produce it. **2** a stick, pencil, or crayon of charcoal for drawing. **3** a drawing made with a charcoal stick, pencil, or crayon.
—*v.t.* **1** to mark, write, or blacken with charcoal. **2** to suffocate with the fumes of charcoal.
[Middle English *charcole,* perhaps < *char* to turn, transform + *cole* coal]

charcoal black, a black pigment obtained by pulverizing charcoal, used especially by painters.

charcoal burner, **1** anything in which charcoal

is burned, such as a stove. **2** a person whose work is making charcoal.

char|cu|te|rie (shär kY tə rē′), *n. French.* **1** a store that sells prepared meats and meat dishes. **2** the foods sold at such a store.

char|cu|tier (shär kY tyā′), *n. French.* a person who prepares or sells charcuterie meats.

chard (chärd), *n.* a kind of beet whose large leaves and thickened leafstalks are eaten as a vegetable; Swiss chard. [variant of obsolete *card* < Old French *carde* < Old Provençal *cardo* thistle, artichoke, ultimately < Latin *carduus*]

chare (chãr), *n., v.,* **chared, char|ing.** *British.* **—*n.*** a char; chore: *The maid that milks and does the meanest chare* (Shakespeare).
—*v.i.* to char. **—*v.t. Informal.*** to do (chars). [variant of *char*[2]]

chare|wom|an (chãr′wu̇m′ən), *n., pl.* **-wom|en.** = charwoman.

charge (chärj), *v.,* **charged, charg|ing,** *n.* **—*v.t.*** **1** to ask as a price; put on a price of: *This store charged 75 cents a dozen for eggs. The doctor charges ten dollars for an office call.* **2a** to put down as a debt to be paid: *This store will charge your purchases and let you pay for them later.* **b** to put down as a debt against: *Please charge my account. You will be charged for the labor.* **3** to load or fill: *He charged the old gun with powder and shot. The battery in our car is charged with electricity made by the generator.* **4** to give a task, duty, or responsibility to: *Mother charged me to take good care of my baby sister. The law charges policemen with keeping order.* **5** to give an order or command to; direct: *He charged us to keep the plan secret. The judge charged the jury to arrive at a verdict.* **6** to bring an accusation against; accuse; blame: *The driver was charged with speeding. In all this Job sinned not, not charged God foolishly* (Job 1:22). *Charge an honest woman with picking thy pocket?* (Shakespeare). **7** to rush at with force; attack: *The soldiers charged the enemy.* **8** to attribute (a fault) to a person; lay to one's charge: *The blame should ... be charged on Philip's ministers* (William H. Prescott). **9** to saturate, especially a liquid or a gas, with other matter: *The air may be charged with a sticky dampness.* **10** *Figurative.* to burden mentally; overload: *A fault in the ordinary method of education, is the charging of children's memories with rules and precepts* (John Locke). **11** *Heraldry.* **a** to place (a bearing or charge) on an escutcheon, shield, or other article suitable to bear a coat of arms: *to charge crosses on a field.* **b** to bear upon (an escutcheon, shield, or other article) with a bearing or charge: *to charge a field with crosses.* **12** to level or hold (a weapon) in position for attack.
—*v.i.* **1** to ask a price; demand payment: *This store does not charge for delivery.* **2** to put down the price of a purchase, or have it put down, for later payment: *The dairy will charge for the milk delivered during the month and send a bill at the end of the month. We charge at the service station.* **3** to rush against the enemy; make a sudden attack: *The captain gave the order to charge.* **4a** to deliver a formal instruction or exhortation, as a judge or bishop: *The Bishops one after another began to charge against me* (Cardinal Newman). **b** to bring a charge or accusation: *She wished to get the High Court of Justice to charge on her side.* **5** (of a dog) to crouch with its head resting on its forepaws, on command.
—*n.* **1a** the price asked for or put on something: *The charge for delivery is $3.* **SYN:** See syn. under **price. b** an outlay of money; cost; expense: *a small bodyguard ... armed and mounted at their own charge* (Macaulay). **SYN:** See syn. under **price. 2a** a debt to be paid: *Taxes are a charge on property. The cost of the proceedings will be a charge on the estate.* **b** an entry of something due on the debit side of an account. **3** the amount needed to load or fill something; load. A gun is fired by exploding the charge of powder in the shell. A car is started by drawing out a part of the charge of electricity accumulated in the battery. **4a** a task; duty; responsibility: *I accepted my mother's charge to take good care of my baby sister. Protecting citizens is the charge of the police.* **SYN:** trust. **b** *Figurative.* a heavy load; burden: *I need not be a charge on the old mother* (Thackeray). **5** care; management: *Doctors and nurses have charge of sick people.* **SYN:** custody, superintendence. **6** a person or thing under the care or management of someone: *Sick people are the charges of doctors and nurses.* **7** a parish, church, or congregation committed to the care of a clergyman. **8a** an order; command; direction: *a judge's charge to the jury to arrive at a verdict.* **SYN:** injunction, mandate. **b** the act of accusing or fact of being accused: *He admitted the charge and paid a fine.* **SYN:** indictment, complaint. **9a** an attack; a rush with force: *The charge drove the enemy back. The failure of Pickett's charge ended the Battle of Gettysburg* (F. E. Vandiver). **SYN:** assault, onset. **b** an attack or rush by a large animal. **c** the signal for a military attack: *The pipers on both sides blew their charge* (Scott). **10.** *Physics.* the electrical energy present in an atomic particle: *An electron has a negative charge, a proton a positive charge.* **11** *Heraldry.* a device borne on an escutcheon; bearing.

charge off, a to subtract as a loss: *The store owner charged off money which had been owed him for over three years as bad debts.* **b** to put down as belonging (to): *A bad mistake must be charged off to experience.* **c** *Informal.* to dash away: *The boys charged off to play tag as soon as lunch was over.*

charge oneself with, a to take upon oneself the responsibility of: *She charged herself with the care of her small nephew.* **b** to accuse oneself of: *She charged herself with carelessness in leaving the fire untended.*

charge up, to put down as belonging (to): *I charged it up to inexperience.*

get a charge (from, out of, by, etc.), *Slang.* get pleasure; obtain excitement or a thrill: *The further suspicion arises that he enjoys blasphemous conjunctions, gets a charge out of throwing bishops out of the window* (New Statesman).

in charge, having the care or management; in command: *Who is in charge here? The mate is in charge when the captain leaves the ship.*

in charge of, a having the care or management of: *His uncle is in charge of the book department of the store.* **b** under the care or management of: *The draperies are in charge of another salesman.* **c** in command of: *The corporal was in charge of the patrol.*

[< Old French *chargier* < Late Latin *carricāre* to load < Latin *carrus* wagon. See etym. of doublet **carry.**] **—charge′less,** *adj.*

—*Syn.* *v.t.* **6 Charge, accuse** mean to put blame on a person. **Charge** may suggest blame for some minor wrongdoing, such as breaking a rule, but it commonly suggests a serious offense, such as breaking a law, and making a formal statement before the proper authority: *He was charged with leaving the grounds without permission.* **Accuse** suggests making the charge directly to the person blamed and expressing disapproval, but not necessarily taking him before authority: *They accused me of lying.*

char|gé (shär zhā′), *n.* = chargé d'affaires.

charge|a|bil|i|ty (chär′jə bil′ə tē), *n.* the quality or condition of being chargeable.

charge|a|ble (chär′jə bəl), *adj.* **1** capable of being charged: *The salesman's travel expenses are chargeable to the company.* **2** liable to be charged: *If a person steals he is chargeable with theft.* **3** liable to become a public charge: *employment of the chargeable poor.*

charge account, 1 a system of buying and selling on credit, under which the customer agrees to pay for his purchases when bills are presented. **2** a recorded kept at a store of things bought by a person on credit.

charge conjugation, *Nuclear Physics.* the principle that a positively charged particle must have a negatively charged twin.

charge conservation, = conservation of charge.

charge-cou|pled device (chärj′kup′əld), a semiconductor silicon chip with a dense array of tiny cells in which mobile electric charges can be stored and transferred from cell to cell by the external manipulation of voltages: *Charge-coupled devices can be used in small, sensitive cameras that replace bulky television equipment, or as digital information storage units* (Science News).

charged (chärjd), *adj.* **1** that has been loaded; filled. **2** having an electrical charge: *charged ions.*

char|gé d'af|faires (shär zhā′ də fãr′), *pl.* **char|gés d'af|faires** (shär zhāz′ də fãr′). **1** a diplomatic official in charge of an embassy or legation during the absence of an ambassador, minister, or other diplomat. **2** a diplomatic official of inferior rank, sent to a state to which an ambassador or minister is not appointed. [< French *chargé d'affaires* (literally) entrusted with affairs]

charge|hand (chärj′hand′), *n. British.* a workman in charge of a group of workmen; foreman.

charge nurse, a nurse charged with the supervision of a hospital ward.

charge-off (chärj′ôf′, -of′), *n.* the treatment of bad debts, depreciation, cost of research, or the like, as losses, especially for tax purposes.

charge plate, a small plastic plate stamped with the bearer's identification, formerly used to charge retail purchases in a store.

charg|er[1] (chär′jər), *n.* **1** a horse ridden in war; mount. **2a** a person or thing that charges. **b** a device that gives an electrical charge to storage batteries. [< *charge,* verb + *-er*[1]]

charg|er[2] (chär′jər), *n. Archaic.* **1** a large flat dish, especially a platter for meat: *And she ... said, Give me here John Baptist's head in a charger* (Matthew 14:8). **2** a large vessel for liquids. [Middle English *chargeour,* < unrecorded Old French *chargëoir* < *chargier* to load; charge]

charge-sheet (chärj′shēt′), *n. British.* a police blotter.

charg|ing (chär′jing), *n., adj.* **—*n.*** the act of loading; filling. **—*adj.*** that charges.

✱**char|i|ot** (char′ē ət), *n., v.* **—*n.*** **1** a two-wheeled carriage pulled by horses. The chariot was used in ancient times for fighting, for racing, and in processions. *Nearly 4,000 years ago, the Hittites ... developing the lightest and fastest chariots of the times ... fought at length with Egypt* (Newsweek). **2** a four-wheeled, closed carriage with a single inside seat for two or three persons, used particularly on state occasions in the 1700's. **3** *Figurative.* any stately vehicle; a triumphal car, such as that in which the sun or moon is represented as pursuing their courses. **4** *Slang.* an old, especially large, car. **5** *Obsolete, Figurative.* a vehicle: *He ... maketh the clouds his chariots* (English Book of Common Prayer).
—*v.t.* to carry or convey in a chariot.
—*v.i.* to drive or ride in a chariot.
[< Old French *chariot* < *char* wagon < Latin *carrus*]

✱**chariot**
definition 1

char|i|ot|eer (char′ē ə tir′), *n.* the person who drives a chariot.

Char|i|ot|eer (char′ē ə tir′), *n.* the constellation Auriga.

char|i|ot|ry (char′ē ə trē), *n.* that part of an army which fought from chariots.

char|ism (kar′iz əm), *n.* = charisma.

cha|ris|ma (kə riz′mə), *n., pl.* **-ma|ta** (-mə tə). **1** a personal appeal or power to fascinate and attract others; mysterious power of great personal magnetism or glamour: *the charisma of a popular leader. The magic (or mana, or charisma, or whatever is the fashionable word among sociologists) of a British Prime Minister ... is always less in Britain than the magic of an American President in the U.S.A.* (C. P. Snow). **2** glamour or sex appeal: *Marilyn Monroe's unique charisma* ... (Time). **3** a spiritual gift or grace giving a person the power of prophesying, healing, and other divine gifts. Also, **charism.** [< Greek *chárisma, -atos* < *charízesthai* to favor < *cháris* favor, grace]

char|is|mat|ic (kar′iz mat′ik), *adj., n.* **—*adj.*** **1** having charisma; capable of inspiring great personal allegiance: *After the astonishing news of Hiroshima and Nagasaki, overnight ... scientists became charismatic figures of a new era* (Bulletin of Atomic Scientists). **2** of or having to do with charisma: *India has a dozen leaders whose charismatic appeal falls not so far short of Nehru's* (Encounter).
—*n.* a person possessing, or said to possess, the power of prophesying, healing, or other charismatic gifts: *Charismatics of all churches ... stress a personal relationship to Christ.* **—char′is|mat′i|cal|ly,** *adv.*

char|i|ta|ble (char′ə tə bəl), *adj.* **1** generous in giving help to poor, sick, or helpless people; benevolent and kind: *He was a charitable man who used his wealth to give contributions to the relief of sickness and poverty.* **SYN:** bountiful. **2** of charity; for charity: *The Salvation Army is a charitable organization.* **3** kindly in judging people and their actions; lenient: *Grandfathers are usually charitable toward the mistakes of grandchildren.* **SYN:** tolerant, considerate. [< Old French *charitable* < *charite* charity] **—char′i|ta|ble|ness,** *n.*

char|i|ta|bly (char′ə tə blē), *adv.* in a charitable manner; with charity.

char|i|ty (char′ə tē), *n., pl.* **-ties. 1** generous giving to the poor or to organizations which look after the sick, the poor, and the helpless: *The charity of our citizens enabled the hospital to purchase new beds.* **2** an act or work of charity. **3a** a fund, institution, or organization for helping the sick, the poor, and the helpless: *She gives money regularly to the Salvation Army and to other charities.* **b** that which is given in charity; alms. **4** kindness in judging people's faults: ...

Pronunciation Key: hat, āge, cãre, fär; let, ēqual, tėrm; it, īce; hot, ōpen, ôrder; oil, out; cup, pu̇t, rüle; child; long; thin; ᴛʜen; zh, measure; ə represents **a** in about, **e** in taken, **i** in pencil, **o** in lemon, **u** in circus.

with malice toward none; with charity for all . . . (Abraham Lincoln). **5a** love of one's fellow men: *The Bible says, "And now abideth faith, hope, and charity, and the greatest of these is charity."* **b** God's love to man. **6a** natural affection; love (now especially with some notion of generous or spontaneous goodness). **b** affections; feelings or acts of affection.

cold as charity, a hard and cold; unfeeling: *Cold is thy heart . . . as charity* (Robert Southey). **b** very cold; freezing: *The wind is as cold as charity. We are much more comfortable here* (Anthony Trollope).

[< Old French *charite* < Latin *cāritās* dearness, affection < *cārus* dear]

—Syn. **1, 5a Charity, philanthropy** means having love for one's fellow men and willingness to aid those in need. **Charity** emphasizes personal kindness exhibited to individuals who are poor or suffering: *A charity that many have chosen is the "adoption" of a war orphan in a foreign country and contributing to his care and support.* **Philanthropy** implies the good will directed toward improving the general welfare of one's fellow men. Since the people benefited are not necessarily poor or distressed and since it is frequently carried out on a large scale, it lacks the more personal and sympathetic concept implicit in charity: *The gift of public libraries to many cities was a vastly useful philanthropy.*

charity boy or **girl**, *Archaic.* a child brought up in an institution.

cha|riv|a|ri (shiv′ə rē′, shə riv′-; shär′i vär′ē), *n., pl.* **-ris. 1** a mock serenade made by beating on kettles, pans, and the like; shivaree. **2** a confused, discordant medley of sounds. [< French *charivari*]

char|kha or **char|ka** (chär′kə), *n.* the hand spinning wheel of India, used chiefly for spinning cotton. [< Hindustani *charkhah* < Sanskrit *cakra* wheel]

char|la|dy (chär′lā′dē), *n., pl.* **-dies.** = charwoman.

char|la|tan (shär′lə tən), *n., adj.* **—*n.*** a person who pretends to have more knowledge or skill than he really has; quack. **SYN:** impostor, mountebank.

—*adj.* of or having to do with a charlatan; quack: *Fortunately, 27 of the patients recognized in time that the charlatan treatment was not helping them* (Newsweek).

[< French *charlatan* < Italian *ciarlatano,* apparently < *cerretano* < *Cerreto,* a town in Italy; influenced by *ciarlare* babble]

char|la|tan|ic (shär′lə tan′ik), *adj.* having to do with or like a charlatan; quackish: *charlatanic tricks, a charlatanic boaster.*

char|la|tan|ish (shär′lə tan′ish), *adj.* = charlatanic.

char|la|tan|ism (shär′lə tə niz′əm), *n.* the practices or methods of a charlatan; quackery.

char|la|tan|ry (shär′lə tən rē), *n., pl.* **-ries.** = charlatanism.

Charles's or **Charles' law** (chärl′ziz), *Physics.* the law that at constant pressure the volume of a given mass of gas is directly proportional to the absolute temperature.

[< Jacques A. C. *Charles,* 1746-1823, a French physicist]

Charles's or **Charles' Wain,** *British.* the Big Dipper.

[Old English *Charles Wǣn* Carl's (Charlemagne's) wagon (because of popular confusion between Charlemagne and King Arthur, who was wrongly associated with Arcturus, a name often applied to the Great Bear)]

Charles|ton (chärlz′tən), *n., v.* **—*n.*** a lively ballroom dance popular in the 1920's, usually in 4/4 time and characterized especially by side kicks from the knee. **—*v.i.*** to dance the Charleston. [American English < *Charleston,* the early capital of South Carolina]

char|ley or **char|lie horse** (chär′lē), *Informal.* **1** stiffness, especially of an arm or leg, caused by straining a muscle. **2** a muscle cramp.

Char|lie or **Char|ley** (chär′lē), *n. U.S.* **1** a code name for the letter *c* in transmitting radio messages. **2** *Slang.* a Vietcong soldier; Victor Charlie.

char|lock (chär′lək), *n.* any one of several weeds of the mustard family, often found in grainfields; wild mustard. [Old English *cerlic*]

char|lotte (shär′lət), *n.* a dessert made of cake or bread arranged in a mold and filled with fruit or a cream, custard, or gelatin preparation. [< French *charlotte,* perhaps < a proper name]

charlotte russe (rüs′), a dessert made of a mold of sponge cake filled with whipped cream or custard [< French *charlotte russe* Russian charlotte; allusion uncertain]

charm¹ (chärm), *n., v.* **—*n.* 1** the power of delighting or fascinating; attractiveness: *Our grandmother did not lose her charm for us as she grew older. Her charm lies in her complete naturalness.* **SYN:** allurement. **2** a pleasing quality, feature, or attribute: *the charm of his style.* **3** a small ornament or trinket worn on a bracelet, watch chain, or necklace: *A bunch of charms was attached to her bracelet.* **4a** a word, verse, act, or thing supposed to have magic power to help or harm people; incantation; spell: *Cato knew a charm for setting dislocations.* **b** any object worn or carried about the person to bring luck and avert evil; amulet. **5** *Nuclear Physics.* a quantum unit with the value of + 1 for any quark and -1 for its antiquark: *Charm [is] a quantum number that must be conserved during any interaction among particles* (S.B. Palmer).

—*v.t.* 1 to please greatly; delight; fascinate; captivate: *The boys were charmed by the sailor's stories of adventure.* **2** to act on as if by magic; calm; soothe: *His grandchildren's laughter charmed away the old man's troubles. Music the fiercest grief can charm* (Alexander Pope). *Some men can charm snakes.* **3** to give magic power to; protect as by a charm: *Then charm me that I may be invisible* (Christopher Marlowe). **4** to act upon with or as if with a charm; influence by magic; put a spell on; bewitch: *Some people still believe in charming warts.*

—*v.i.* 1 to attract strongly; delight; be captivating: *Soft is the music that would charm forever* (Wordsworth). **2** to use charms; work magic; cast spells: *Then no planets strike, no fairy tames, or witch hath power to charm* (Shakespeare).

[< Old French *charme* < Latin *carmen* song; enchantment]

—Syn. v.t. **1 Charm, attract, allure** mean to win a person by pleasing. **Charm** emphasizes winning and holding a person's attention and admiration by giving delight: *Her beautiful voice charms everyone.* **Attract** emphasizes drawing attention and liking by being pleasing: *She attracts everyone she meets by her gracious manner.* **Allure** emphasizes attracting a person by appealing to the senses and feelings: *The warm climate, exotic colors, and primitive beauties of Hawaii allure many tourists from the mainland of the United States.*

charm² (chärm), *n.* the blended singing or noise of many birds; blended voices, as of children. [dialectal variant of *cherm* chirm]

charmed (chärmd), *adj.* **1** protected as if by a charm: *The pilot led a charmed life in which he narrowly survived many accidents.* **2** delighted; fascinated; pleased: *Her guests were charmed by their hostess's simple ways.* **SYN:** attracted. **3** enchanged. **SYN:** entranced, bewitched. **4** *Nuclear Physics.* having the characteristics of charm: *a charmed antiquark.*

charmed circle, any very select or exclusive group: *No outsiders broke into the charmed circle of the annual Assembly* (Manchester Guardian Weekly).

charmed quark, a quark having an electric charge of + 2/3 and charm of + 1: *The psi particle is a hadron consisting of a charmed quark and a charmed antiquark* (Scientific American).

charm|er (chär′mər), *n.* **1** a person who charms, delights, or fascinates. **2** a person who overcomes or subdues as if by magic power.

char|meuse (shär mœz′), *n.* a soft satin. [< French *charmeuse* charmer, feminine < *charmer* to charm]

charm|ing (chär′ming), *adj.* **1** very pleasing; delightful; fascinating; attractive: *We saw a charming play. She is a charming hostess.* **SYN:** captivating, enchanting, alluring. **2** using charms; exercising magic power: *the siren's charming song.* **—charm′ing|ly,** *adv.* **—charm′ing|ness,** *n.*

charm|less (chärm′lis), *adj.* without charm; personally unattractive. **—charm′less|ly,** *adv.*

charm|o|ni|um (chär mō′nē əm), *n. Nuclear Physics.* any particle with the characteristics of charm; a charmed particle. [< *charm*¹ (def. 5) + *-onium,* as in *plutonium*]

charm school, a school for training girls to be attractive and graceful.

char|nel (chär′nəl), *n., adj.* **—*n.*** a charnel house or other burial place.

—*adj.* 1 of or used for a charnel. **2** like a charnel; deathlike; ghastly.

[< Old French *charnel* < Latin *carnālis.* See etym. of doublet **carnal.**]

charnel house, any building or place where the bodies or bones of the dead are laid. It was originally a tomb or vault, usually connected with a church.

Cha|ro|lais (shar′ə lāz′), *n.* any one of a breed of large, white or cream-colored beef cattle originally imported from France, and now raised in the United States. [< *Charolais,* a district in France]

Cha|ro|laise (shar′ə lāz′), *n.* = Charolais.

Char|on (kãr′ən), *n.* **1** *Greek Mythology.* the boatman who ferried the spirits of the dead across the rivers Styx and Acheron to Hades. **2** a ferryman. **3** a satellite of Pluto, discovered in 1978: *The total mass of both Pluto and its moon, named Charon, is only 0.0017 of the Earth's mass* (Michael J.S. Belton).

char|pai (chär′pī′), *n.* = charpoy.

char|pie (shär′pē; *French* shȧr pē′), *n.* lint, especially for dressing wounds. [< French *charpie,* feminine past participle of Old French *charpir* pick to pieces < Latin *carpere* pick]

char|poy (chär′poi′), *n.* a common light bed or cot in India: *Gandhi [sat] on a charpoy all day, getting thinner and thinner* (New Yorker). [< Hindustani *chārpāī* < Persian *charār-pāī* four-footed]

char|qui (chär′kē), *n.* jerked beef or other meat. [< Spanish *charqui,* or *-que* < Quechua *charqui*]

charr (chär), *n., pl.* **charrs** or (*collectively*) **charr.** = char (fish).

char|rette (shə ret′, chə-), *n.* a gathering of various groups of people in a community, industry, or other form of organization, to resolve common problems with the assistance of outside experts. [< French (*en*) *charrette* (in a) cart]

char|ro (chär′rō), *n., pl.* **-ros.** *Spanish.* **1** (in Latin America) a cowboy. **2** (originally) a peasant (of Salamanca in Spain).

char|ry (chär′ē), *adj.* of or like charcoal.

chart (chärt), *n., v.* **—*n.* 1a** a map used by sailors to show the coasts, rocks, and shallow places of the sea. The course of a ship is marked on a chart. **SYN:** See syn. under **map. b** an outline map showing special conditions or facts: *The weather chart shows where rain fell over the United States yesterday.* **c** *Obsolete.* any map. **2** a sheet of information arranged in lists, pictures, tables, or diagrams: *Our history book has a chart of the Presidents of the United States.* **3** such a list, table, picture, or diagram. **4** a graphic representation of any variable, such as temperature, pressure, production, or sales.

—*v.t.* 1 to make a map or chart of; show on a chart; map: *The navigator charted the course of the ship. The navigable channels have all been charted.* **2** *Figurative.* to plan in detail: *The explorers charted the expedition with great care.*

the charts, a list of the best-selling or most popular items of a kind, such as recently released records or newly published books: *In popular music, if you're not on the charts every minute of the day, you really feel you're a failure* (Bette Midler).

[< Middle French *charte* < Old French < Latin *charta.* See etym. of dobulet **card¹.**] **—chart′less,** *adj.*

char|ta|ceous (kär tā′shəs), *adj.* of the nature of paper; made of paper; papery.

char|ter (chär′tər), *n., v.* **—*n.* 1** a written grant by a government to a colony, a group of citizens, a university, or a business or a corporation, bestowing the right of organization, with other privileges, and specifying the form of organization: *The proposed new airline must obtain a government charter.* **2** a written order from the authorities of a society, giving to a group of persons the right to organize a new chapter, branch, or lodge. **3a** a document setting forth aims and purposes of a group of nations, organizations, or individuals in a common undertaking: *the Charter of the United Nations.* **b** any document or measure proceeding from or authorized by the sovereign power of a country or state and granting rights or privileges to the people or particular classes of the people: *the second great charter of Roman liberties* (Matthew Arnold). **4** a special right, privilege, or immunity. **5** Also, **charter party. a** a contract for the hiring of a ship, or part of a ship, for a given time or purpose, usually to carry cargo. *Tankers on short-term charter amounted to as much as one-fifth of the total tonnage employed in moving oil* (London Times). **b** the limits or terms of such a contract. **c** a document embodying such a contract. **d** a similar agreement for hiring a plane, bus, or other vehicle. **6** a written document or contract between two parties, especially one dealing with the conveyance of property.

—*v.t.* 1 to give a charter to; grant or establish by charter: *The government chartered the new airline. Early in the reign of Edward III . . . we find the Goldsmiths' Company chartered* (Christopher Barker). **2** to hire (a ship) by charter: *It was impossible to charter a ship for the purpose* (Washington Irving). **3** to hire (a vehicle, airplane, or other conveyance), especially for private use: *The school chartered a bus to take the class to the zoo.*

[< Old French *chartre* < Latin *chartula* a small paper chart < *charta* chart] **—char′ter|able,** *adj.* **—char′ter|er,** *n.* **—char′ter|less,** *adj.*

char|ter|age (chär′tər ij), *n.* the act or practice of chartering ships, vehicles, or other conveyances.

char|tered (chär′tərd), *adj.* **1** founded, privileged, or protected by charter: *The Bank of Canada . . . has proposed an increase in the require re-*

serves of commercial or chartered banks (Wall Street Journal). **2** *Figurative.* privileged; licensed.

chartered accountant, a member of an institute of accountants chartered by the Crown in Great Britain or elsewhere in the Commonwealth of Nations. *Abbr:* C.A., c.a.

charter flight, a plane reserved for a party: *Charter flights, where a whole plane is hired for a party of people, provide the lowest of all international travel costs* (Wall Street Journal).

Char|ter|house (chär′tər hous′), *n., adj.* = Carthusian. [alteration of Anglo-French *chartouse* Carthusian monastery]

charter member, one of the original members of a club, society, or company.

charter party, = charter (def. 5).

chart house, = chart room.

chart|ism (chär′tiz əm), *n. U.S.* the making and study of charts, especially of stock transactions, with a view to predicting future trends.

Chart|ism (chär′tiz əm), *n.* the principles and demands of a reform movement whose members were chiefly workingmen, active in England especially from 1838 to 1848 in extending the vote to workers. [< People's *Chart*(er) + *-ism*] —**Chart′ist**, *n., adj.*

chart|ist (chär′tist), *n.* a person who makes or studies charts, especially of the trading of stocks: *As the market advances, chartists look for more resistance to new highs in the industrial average* (Wall Street Journal).

char|treuse (shär trœz′; *for n. 1 and adj. also* shär trüz′), *n., adj.* —*n.* **1** a light, yellowish green. **2** a green, yellow, or white liqueur first made by the Carthusian monks from aromatic herbs and brandy: *There are a hundred and thirty herbal ingredients in Chartreuse* (New Yorker). **3** a Carthusian monastery. —*adj.* light yellowish-green. [< French *chartreuse* Carthusian < *La Grande Chartreuse* chief monastery of the order]

chart room, a compartment on a ship, where charts and navigating instruments are kept.

char|tu|lar|y (kär′chə ler′ē), *n., pl.* **-lar|ies.** a register of charters, title deeds, and the like, as of a monastery. Also, **cartulary.** [< Medieval Latin *chartularium* repository for charters < Latin *chartula* charter]

char|wom|an (chär′wu̇m′ən), *n., pl.* **-wom|en.** *U.S.* a woman who is hired by the day to clean and scrub homes, offices, and public buildings. Also, **charewoman.** [< *char* [2] + *woman*]

char|y (chãr′ē), *adj.,* **char|i|er, char|i|est. 1** showing caution; careful; wary: *The cat was chary of getting its paws wet. Consumers regardful of their welfare should be equally chary* (Harper's). **2** shy: *A bashful person is chary of strangers.* **3** sparing; stingy: *A jealous person is chary of praising those who do well.* SYN: frugal. [Old English *cearig* sorrowful; later, careful < *caru* care] —**char′i|ly**, *adv.* —**char′i|ness**, *n.*

Cha|ryb|dis (kə rib′dis), *n.* **1** a dangerous whirlpool in the strait between Sicily and Italy, opposite the rock Scylla. **2** *Greek Mythology.* a female monster that sucked down ships.
between Scylla and Charybdis. See **Scylla.**

chase[1] (chās), *v.,* **chased, chas|ing,** *n.* —*v.t.* **1** to run or follow after to catch or kill: *The cat chased the mouse.* **2** to drive; drive away: *The blue jay chased the squirrel from its nest.* **3** to run after; follow; pursue: *The boys chased the ball as it rolled downhill.* **4** to hunt. **5** to put to flight; rout: *Marriage may all those petty tyrants chase* (Alexander Pope). **6** *Informal.* to pursue with attentions; pay excessive court to: *to chase women.* **7** *Informal.* to follow (a strong drink of liquor) with a chaser: . . . *a fellow drinking cognac chased with beer* (New York Times).
—*v.i.* **1** to go in pursuit; follow. **2** *Informal.* to rush; hurry: *Why are you chasing around?* **3** *U.S. Informal.* to pursue girls or women with attentions: *Speed Dash neither smokes, drinks, nor chases* (Erle Stanley Gardner).
—*n.* **1** the act of running after to catch or kill; pursuit: *We watched the children in their chase after butterflies.* **2** hunting as a sport; hunt: *The fox hunter was devoted to the chase.* **3** a hunted animal; quarry: *The chase escaped the hunter.* **4** an open piece of privately owned ground or other place reserved for hunting animals. **5** the right of hunting over a tract of country or of keeping game there.
give chase, to run after; pursue: *The fox gave chase as soon as it spotted the rabbit.*
[< Old French *chacier, cacier.* See etym. of doublet **catch.**]

chase[2] (chās), *v.t.,* **chased, chas|ing.** to decorate (metal) with embossed or engraved work; engrave; carve: . . . *an eight-piece sterling silver tea set, made and chased by hand* (Wall Street Journal). SYN: enchase. [variant of *enchase*]

chase[3] (chās), *n., v.,* **chased, chas|ing.** —*n.* **1** a groove, furrow, or trench cut in a wall, the ground, or other place, for a pipe or other conductor: *The water pipes should be concealed in a chase.* **2** the bore of a gun or the part containing the bore. —*v.t.* to cut grooves in (metal). [< French *chas* (originally) enclosure < Late Latin *capsum* < *capere* take]

chase[4] (chās), *n.* a rectangular metal frame to hold type that is ready to print or make plates from. [< French *châsse,* ultimately < Latin *capsa* box < *capere* take]

chas|er[1] (chā′sər), *n.* **1** a person or thing that chases: *The "File" is based on* [*his*]*experiences as a New York squad-car chaser in the '20s and '30s* (Newsweek). **2** = hunter. **3** a small speedy airplane or ship used to repel and pursue attacking craft. **4** Also, **chase gun.** the gun on the bow or stern of a ship. It is used when chasing, or being chased by, another ship. **5** *Informal.* a drink of water or some other mild beverage taken after a drink of strong liquor. **6** = steeplechaser. [< *chas*(e)[1] + *-er* [1]]

chas|er[2] (chā′sər), *n.* **1** = engraver. **2** a tool for engraving. [< *chas*(e)[2] + *er* [1]]

chas|ing (chā′sing), *n.* **1** the act or work of one who chases metal. **2** the design executed.

chasm (kaz′əm), *n.* **1** a deep opening or crack in the earth; gap. SYN: fissure, cleft, rift. **2** a deep gap or breach in any structure. **3** *Figurative.* a wide difference of feelings or interests between two persons or two groups or a break in the continuity of anything, such as a chain of events or period of time: *The chasm between England and the American colonies grew wider and wider until it finally resulted in the American Revolution. Khrushchev's . . . interview with an American newspaperman reveals a chasm in communication, in mutual understanding, far deeper than the difference between the Russian and English languages* (Wall Street Journal). SYN: gap, gulf, lacuna. [< Latin *chasma* < Greek *chásma*]

chas|mal (kaz′məl), *adj.* of or like a chasm.

chasmed (kaz′əmd), *adj.* having a chasm or chasms: *the chasmed wilderness that is Burma's border with China* (Time).

chas|mic (kaz′mik), *adj.* = chasmal.

chas|mo|gam|ic (kaz′mə gam′ik), *adj.* = chasmogamous.

chas|mog|a|mous (kaz mog′ə məs), *adj.* exhibiting chasmogamy.

chas|mog|a|my (kaz mog′ə mē), *n.* the condition of having flowers that open at maturity for pollination. [< Greek *chásma* opening + *-gamy*]

chas|my (kaz′ə mē), *adj.* **1** having chasms. **2** like a chasm.

chasse (shäs), *n.* a glass or draft of liqueur taken after coffee. [short for French *chasse-café* (literally) chase-coffee]

chas|sé (sha sā′; *U.S. Informal* sa shā′), *n., v.,* **-séd, -sé|ing.** —*n.* (in ballet, quadrilles, or other dance) a gliding step, in which one foot is kept ahead and the other is brought up behind it.
—*v.i.* to perform a chassé. Also, **sashay.**
[< French *chassé* a dance step, (literally) chase]

chasse|pot (shås pō′), *n. French.* a type of breechloading rifle.

chas|seur (shå sœr′), *n. French.* **1** a soldier of a group of cavalry or infantry equipped and trained to move rapidly. **2** a hunter. **3** an attendant or servant dressed in a uniform: *A servant in chasseur's livery entered* (George Eliot).

Chas|sid|ic (ha sid′ik, hä-; ʜä-), *adj.* = Hasidic.

Chas|si|dim (has′i dim, hä′si-; ʜä sē′-), *n., pl. of* **Chas|sid** (has′id, hä′sid; ʜä sēd′). = Hasidim.

Chas|si|dism (has′i diz əm, ʜä′si-), *n.* = Hasidism.

chas|sis (shas′ē, chas′-), *n., pl.* **chas|sis** (shas′ēz, chas′-). **1a** the frame, wheels, and machinery of a motor vehicle that support the body. **b** the working mechanism of an automobile as distinguished from a welded unit of frame and body, as in recent manufacture. **2** the main landing gear that supports the body of an aircraft. **3a** the base or frame for the parts of a radio or television set or other electronic equipment. **b** the parts mounted on this. **4** the frame on which a gun carriage moves backward and forward, as in recoil. **5** *U.S. Slang.* the body. [< French *chassis* < *châsse* frame. See etym. of doublet **sash**[2].]

chaste (chāst), *adj.* **1** morally pure; virtuous: *Chaste as morning dew* (Edward Young). SYN: innocent, continent. **2** *Figurative.* decent; modest. **3** *Figurative.* simple in taste or style; not too much ornamented. SYN: classic. [< Old French *chaste, caste,* learned borrowing from Latin *castus* pure. See etym. of doublet **caste.**]
—**chaste′ly**, *adv.* —**chaste′ness**, *n.*

chas|ten (chā′sən), *v.t.,* **1** to punish to improve; correct; discipline; chastise: *God chastened Job.* **2** *Figurative.* to restrain from excess or crudeness; moderate; temper; subdue. **3** to make chaste or pure; purify; refine. [< obsolete verb *chaste* < Old French *chastier* < Latin *castīgāre* make pure < *castus* pure] —**chas′ten|er**, *n.*

chas|tise (chas tīz′), *v.t.,* **-tised, -tis|ing. 1** to inflict punishment or suffering on to improve; punish: *my father hath chastised you with whips, but I will chastise you with scorpions* (I Kings 12:11). SYN: beat. **2** to criticize or rebuke severely; rebuke: *I have been severely chastised by a gourmet . . . for even mentioning the idea of bacon and trout together* (James A. Beard). SYN: castigate. **3** *Archaic.* to moderate; temper; subdue; chasten. **4** *Archaic.* to purify; refine; correct or revise (a literary work). [related to **chasten;** exact formation unknown] —**chas|tis′a|ble**, *adj.* —**chas|tis′er**, *n.*

chas|tise|ment (chas tīz′mənt, chas′tiz-), *n.* **1** a chastising; punishment: *In what precise manner did God conceive this chastisement and how will He carry it out?* (Newsweek). SYN: beating. **2** a severe criticism or rebuke.

chas|ti|ty (chas′tə tē), *n.* **1** moral purity; virtue: *She . . . would respect all the boarding-school virtues; courage, good sportsmanship, chastity, and honor* (New Yorker). **2** *Figurative.* decency; modesty. **3** *Figurative.* simplicity of style or taste; absence of too much decoration. [< Old French *chastete,* learned borrowing from Latin *castitās* < *castus* chaste, pure]

chastity belt, a beltlike device designed to protect or enforce a woman's chastity.

***chas|u|ble** (chaz′yə bəl, chas′-), *n.* a sleeveless outer vestment worn by the priest at Mass. [< Old French *chasuble* < Late Latin *casubula* < Latin *casa* house]

***chasuble**

chat[1] (chat), *n., v.,* **chat|ted, chat|ting.** —*n.* **1** easy, familiar talk: *The two friends had a pleasant chat about old times.* **2** any one of several birds with a chattering cry, chiefly warblers, including the European whinchat and stonechat, and in North America the yellow-breasted chat. [< verb]
—*v.i.* to talk in an easy familiar way: *My neighbor and I were chatting over the fence after supper.*
chat up, *Especially British Informal.* to talk to informally; have a chat with: *Two* [soldiers] *were chatting up the girls behind the sparkling new counter* (London Times).
[short for *chatter*]

chat[2] (chat), *n. Dialect.* **1** a catkin. **2** a small branch or twig, such as is used for kindling a fire. **3** a bit of stone or other coarse particle. [perhaps < French *chat* cat]

chat|com (chat′kom), *n. U.S. Informal.* an interview program on television or radio that is informal, and usually humorous: *"Late Night" is . . . a chatcom whose mixture of the real and the surreal keeps the viewer agreeably off-balance* (Time). [< *chat*[1] + *com*(edy), patterned on *sitcom*]

châ|teau (sha tō′), *n., pl.* **-teaux** (-tōz′). **1** a large country house in France or elsewhere in Europe. **2** a French castle. [< French *château* < Old French *chastel, castel* < Latin *castellum* castle. See etym. of doublet **castle.**]

Châ|teau (shä tō′), *adj. French.* denoting a wine made from the vineyards of a particular estate or château: *Château d'Yquem, Château Margaux.*

cha|teau|bri|and or **châ|teau|bri|and** (shä tō brē äɴ′), *n.* a choice beefsteak cut from the thickest part of the tenderloin. [< François René de *Châteaubriand,* 1768-1848, French writer and diplomat]

chat|e|lain (shat′ə lān), *n.* = castellan. [< Middle French *châtelain* < Old French *chastelain* < Latin *castellānus.* See etym. of doublet **castellan.**]

chat|e|laine (shat′ə lān), *n.* **1** the mistress or lady of a castle or country house: *As the newest member of this eerie household, Lora had to win her place as chatelaine* (New York Times). **2a** a clasp or chain worn at a woman's waist, to which keys or a purse are fastened. **b** a chain attached to a brooch, or sometimes a watch, worn by women as a lapel ornament. [< French *châtelaine,* originally feminine of *châtelain* chatelain]

Châ|tel|per|ro|ni|an (sha′təl pə rō′nē ən), *adj.* of or having to do with a phase of upper paleolithic culture characterized by the making of curved cutting tools with blunt backs. [< *Châtelperron,* a

Pronunciation Key: hat, āge, cãre, fär; let, ēqual, tėrm; it, īce; hot, ōpen, ôrder; oil, out; cup, pu̇t, rüle; child; long; thin; ᴛʜen; zh, measure;
ə represents a in about, e in taken, i in pencil, o in lemon, u in circus.

place in France where remains of this culture appeared + *-ian*]

cha|toy|ant (shə toi′ənt), *adj., n.* **—*adj.*** (of gems or textiles) having a changeable color or luster, such as a cat's-eye in the dark.
—*n.* a chatoyant stone, such as the cat's-eye.
[< French *chatoyant,* present participle of *chatoyer* shimmer, glisten < *chat* cat]

chat show, *British.* a talk show.

chat|tel (chat′əl), *n.* **1** a piece of property that is not real estate; any movable possession. Furniture, automobiles, and animals are chattels. *May 15 and Oct. 1 are city moving days, and the men who truck household chattels from one place to another tell you that on those dates there's always a sudden lift in broom sales* (New York Times). **2** a slave or bondman. [< Old French *chatel, catel* < Latin *capitāle.* See etym. of doublet **capital, cattle.**]

chat|tel|hood (chat′əl hůd), *n.* the condition or position of a chattel.

chattel interest, an interest in leasehold property.

chattel mortgage, *U.S.* a mortgage on personal property, such as an automobile or furniture.

chattel personal, any movable article of personal property, such as an automobile, furniture, or appliances.

chattel real, an interest or lease in land not amounting to a freehold.

chat|tel|ship (chat′əl ship), *n.* = chattelhood.

chat|ter (chat′ər), *v., n.* **—*v.i.*** **1** to talk constantly in a quick, foolish way about unimportant things: *The children chattered about the circus.* **SYN:** babble, prattle. **2** to make quick, indistinct sounds: *Monkeys chatter. Starlings chatter in the trees on summer evenings.* **SYN:** jabber, gabble. **3** to rattle together: *Cold makes a person's teeth chatter.* **4** (of a cutting tool) to vibrate in cutting, so as to make nicks or notches on the work.
—*v.t.* **1** to utter constantly, rapidly, and foolishly: *to chatter nonsense.* **2** to utter with quick, indistinct sounds: *The monkeys sound as if they were chattering words.* **3** to make rattle together: *Cowering in corners ... gibbering and chattering their teeth* (George A. Sala). **4** (of a cutting tool) to mark (work) with nicks.
—*n.* **1** quick, foolish talk about unimportant things: *The old ladies chattered in the library disturbing everybody. Once it was really true that today's idle chatter in Washington was very likely tomorrow's law* (Wall Street Journal). **2** quick, indistinct sounds: *The chatter of sparrows in the early dawn awoke us.* **3** a sound of rattling together: *the chatter of teeth.*
[imitative] **—chat′ter|ing|ly,** *adv.*

chat|ter|box (chat′ər boks), *n.* a person who chatters all the time.

chat|ter|er (chat′ər ər), *n.* **1** one who chatters. **2a** any one of a family of brightly colored birds related to the flycatchers, of South America and north to Arizona; cotinga. **b** = waxwing.

chatter mark, **1** a mark left on a piece of work by a cutting tool that chatters. **2** one of a series of gouges made on surfaces by the rock fragments held in the lower part of a glacier.

chat|ty[1] (chat′ē), *adj.,* **-ti|er, -ti|est.** **1** fond of friendly, familiar talk about unimportant things: *The chatty old men played checkers and gossiped all afternoon.* **2** having the style or manner of friendly familiar talk: *a chatty article about women's fashions in the newspaper.* [< *chat* + *-y*[1]] **—chat′ti|ly,** *adv.* **—chat′ti|ness,** *n.*

chat|ty[2] (chat′ē), *n., pl.* **-ties.** (in India) an earthen jug for water. [< Hindi *chāṭī*]

cha|tur|an|ga (shä′tůr äng′gä), *n.* an early form of chess played in India in the 500's A.D., and still played in India and Iran under the name shatranj. [< Hindustani *chaturanga* < Sanskrit *catur* four + *anga* limb, member (probably because it was a four-handed game)]

Chau|ce|ri|an (chô sir′ē ən), *adj., n.* **—*adj.*** of or characteristic of Geoffrey Chaucer, the English poet (1340?-1400) or his writings.
—*n.* a student or admirer of Chaucer.

chaud-froid (shō′frwä′), *n.* chicken, game, or the like, prepared hot in a sauce, but served cold with a covering of meat jelly. [< French *chaud-froid* (literally) hot-cold]

chau|dron (chô′drən), *n.* the entrails of an animal, especially as used for food. [< Old French *chaudun*]

chauf|fer (chô′fər, shô′-), *n.* a small, portable furnace or stove; brazier. [alteration of obsolete *chafer;* see etym. under **chafer**[2]]

chauf|feur (shō′fər, shō fėr′), *n., v.* **—*n.*** a person whose work is driving an automobile. A chauffeur is usually the employee of a private person or company. *Experienced chauffeur required by gentleman living near Hayward's Heath, Sussex* (London Times).
—*v.t.* to act as a chauffeur to; drive around: *Sylvie was an ardent moviegoer, and every time our local movie house changed bills, one of us chauffeured her to the nine-o'clock showing* (New Yorker). **—*v.i.*** to act as a chauffeur; drive an automobile for a living.
[< French *chauffeur* stoker < *chauffer* to chafe, heat (the term arose in the days of steam automobiles)]

chauf|feuse (shō fœz′), *n. French.* a woman chauffeur.

chaul|moo|gra or **chaul|mu|gra** (chôl mü′grə), *n.* an East Indian tree whose seeds yield an acrid oil. [< Bengali *cāulmugrā*]

chaulmoogra oil, an acrid oil from the seeds of the chaulmoogra tree, or a related tree, used in treating skin diseases and formerly leprosy.

chaul|moo|gric acid (chôl mü′grik), an acid in chaulmoogra oil. *Formula:* $C_5H_7(CH_2)_{12}\cdot COOH$

chaunt (chônt, chänt), *n., v.t., v.i. Archaic.* chant.

chaunt|er (chôn′tər, chän′-), *n. Archaic.* chanter.

chausses (shōs), *n.pl.* **1** medieval armor, especially mail, worn on the legs and feet. **2** tights formerly worn by men. [< Old French *chausse,* earlier *chauce* < Vulgar Latin *calcia,* for Latin *calceus* shoe, boot < *calx, calcis* heel]

chaus|sure (shō sůr′; *French* shō SYR′), *n.* any foot covering, such as a shoe or slipper. [< Old French *chaucëure* hose and shoes < *chaucier* to shoe < Latin *calceāre* < *calceus* shoe < *calx, calcis* heel]

chau|tau|qua or **Chau|tau|qua** (shə tô′kwə), *n., adj. U.S.* **—*n.*** **1** an assembly for education and entertainment of adults by lectures, concerts, and other cultural activities, originally held at Chautauqua, N.Y.: *Chautauquas sprang up elsewhere in New York and then throughout the United States* (Emory S. Bogardus). **2** an educational meeting conducted on similar lines.
—*adj.* designating a system of home study originating with summer schools held at Chautauqua, or the organization resulting from them.

Chautauqua muskellunge, any one of a variety of muskellunge having savory white flesh and attaining a length of five feet; salmon pike; white pickerel.

chau|tau|quan or **Chau|tau|quan** (shə tô′kwən), *adj., n. U.S.* **—*adj.*** having to do with the Chautauqua institution, system, or assembly, or a chautauqua.
—*n.* a person connected with a chautauqua; chautauqua lecturer or entertainer.

chau|vin (shō′vən), *n.* **1** any person who has a blind and extravagant admiration or enthusiasm for his country's military glory. **2** a name applied to any old soldier of the first French Empire who professed an idolatrous admiration for Napoleon and his achievements. [< French *chauvin* < Nicholas *Chauvin,* an old soldier and enthusiastic admirer of Napoleon I]

chau|vin|ism (shō′və niz əm), *n.* **1** boastful, warlike patriotism; unreasoning enthusiasm for the military glory of one's country; jingoism. **2** *Figurative.* an excessive enthusiasm for one's sex, race, or group: *We have been living in a fool's paradise with respect to suburban chauvinism* (New York Times). *She is above sexual chauvinism and the restricted view that goes with it* (New Yorker). [< French *chauvinisme* < *chauvin* chauvin]

chau|vin|ist (shō′və nist), *n., adj.* **—*n.*** **1** a boastful, warlike person; unreasoning patriot: *The thing is that American art is worth buying. I'm a terrific chauvinist about it* (New Yorker). **SYN:** jingo. **2** *Figurative.* a person excessively enthusiastic about his or her sex, race, or group: *a male chauvinist.* **—*adj.*** = chauvinistic.

chau|vin|is|tic (shō′və nis′tik), *adj.* of chauvinists; characterized by chauvinism: *They [New Yorkers] are nearly as chauvinistic as Texans* (Harper's). *Russia and China blame each other for being "chauvinistic"* (Saturday Review). **SYN:** jingoistic. **—chau′vin|is′ti|cal|ly,** *adv.*

Cha|van|te (shä vän′tā), *n., pl.* **-tes** or **-te.** a member of a tribe of South American Indians maintaining a primitive culture in southwestern Brazil.

Cha|vin (chə vēn′), *adj.* of or having to do with an Andean culture that developed between 900 B.C. and A.D. 500: *Chavin sculpture consisted mostly of fanged human, jaguar, or bird gods created in stone, gold, shell or ceramic* (Sir Herbert Read). [< *Chavin,* a town in central Peru]

chaw (chô), *n., v. Dialect.* **—*n.*** **1** an act of chewing. **2** what is chewed, especially a quid of tobacco. **—*v.t., v.i.*** to chew. [< *chew*]

chay (chā), *n.* **1** the root of an East Indian herb of the madder family from which a red dye similar to madder is obtained. **2** the plant itself. [< Tamil *saya*]

cha|yo|te (chä yō′tā), *n.* **1** a green, furrowed, pear-shaped fruit with a single flat seed, from a tropical American plant of the gourd family, eaten as a vegetable: *A popular squash ... is the chayote ... which is about the size of our own acorn squash* (New York Times). **2** the plant itself. [American English < Mexican Spanish *chayote* < a Nahuatl word]

chaz|an or **chaz|zan** (ʜä′zən, ʜä zän′), *n.* a Jewish cantor. Also, **hazan, hazzan.** [< Hebrew *hazzān* governor, supervisor]

Ch.B., Bachelor of Surgery (Latin, *Chirurgiae Baccalaureus*).

CHD (no periods), coronary heart disease.

Ch.E., **1** chemical engineer. **2** chief engineer.

cheap (chēp), *adj., adv., n.* **—*adj.*** **1** costing little: *Eggs are cheap out in the country.* **2** costing less than it is worth: *Her new sweater will be cheap, because she bought the yarn to knit it herself.* **3** charging low prices: *a cheap market. He bought that suit at a very cheap department store.* **4** *Figurative.* costing little effort; easily obtained: *He thinks that the cheapest way to make friends is to give them presents.* **5** *Figurative.* of little value; not worth respect; common: *cheap entertainment, cheap flattery.* **6** *Informal.* stingy: *cheap customers.* **7** obtainable at a low rate of interest: *The days of cheap money are over.* **8** reduced in value or purchasing power, as money depreciated by inflation: *cheap silver.* **9** *British.* reduced in price for a special occasion or in prescribed circumstances: *cheap fares.*
—*adv.* at a low price; at small cost: *I sold the car cheap to get rid of it.*
—*n.* *Obsolete.* **1** trade. **2** a market place. **3** a price. **4** a bargain. **5** abundance of supply. **6** cheapness.
feel cheap, to feel inferior and ashamed, disconcerted, or embarrassed: *He felt cheap about rushing to get in line before the old lady carrying heavy parcels.*
good cheap, *Archaic.* a good bargain from the buyer's point of view; good market or abundant supply; lowness of price (sometimes used as an adjective or adverb): *Here is very good bread and wine, and good cheap I believe* (George Wheler).
hold cheap, to think little of; despise: *They hold winning cheap in comparison to fair play.*
on the cheap, in a cheap manner; cheaply: *... skiing week-ends on the cheap* (Observer).
[short for Middle English *good cheap* a good bargain; Old English *cēap* price, bargain] **—cheap′ly,** *adv.* **—cheap′ness,** *n.*
—*Syn.* *adj.* **1 Cheap, inexpensive** mean costing little. **Cheap** means low in price, but often is used to express a contemptuous attitude toward the thing and to suggest low quality worth no more or even less than the price: *I won't wear cheap shoes.* **Inexpensive** means not expensive, suggests a quality worth the price or even more, and usually expresses a more impersonal attitude: *This inexpensive car gives good mileage.*

cheap|en (chē′pən), *v.t.* **1** to make cheap; lower the price of: *The flood of imported cars cheapened the cost of cars made here.* **2** *Figurative.* to cause to be thought little of; lower in estimation; vilify. **3** to bargain for; bid for; offer a price for.
—*v.i.* to become cheap: *Frozen cooked fish sticks have cheapened a bit at wholesale lately* (Wall Street Journal). **—cheap′en|er,** *n.*

cheap|ie (chē′pē), *n. Informal.* anything, especially a motion picture, made at little cost: *Most cheapies are made by independent producers who can cut corners because, unlike a big studio, they have no overhead and no expensive stars under contract* (Time).

cheap|ish (chē′pish), *adj.* somewhat cheap.

cheap Jack or **John**, a peddler, usually of bargains, who prices his wares and then discounts them gradually.

cheap|jack or **cheap-Jack** (chēp′jak′), *n., adj. Informal.* **—*n.*** a person who deals in cheap or worthless goods. **—*adj.*** worthless; useless; inferior: *The bathroom lacks towel racks and has a cheapjack shower* (Bernard De Voto).

Cheap|side (chēp′sīd′), *n.* a famous street in London that was a busy market place in medieval times.

cheap shot, *U.S. and Canadian.* **1** *Football.* an unnecessary tackle or block when an opponent is defenseless: *Like most cornerbacks, Parrish is a master of the cheap shot* (Business Week). **2** Figurative: *Porter's article ... contains one omission and two cheap shots which call for a response* (New York Times Magazine).

cheap|skate (chēp′skāt′), *n. Informal.* a person who is very stingy; miserly person.

cheap tripper, *British.* a person who travels at excursion rates; tripper.

cheat (chēt), *v., n.* **—*v.i.*** to play or do business in a way that is not honest; practice deceit; act fraudulently: *He always cheats at cards if he can get away with it.*
—*v.t.* **1** to deceive or trick; swindle; defraud (of or out of): *The peddler cheated the woman out of ten cents.* **SYN:** hoodwink. **2** to beguile (boredom, etc.); pass (the time): *the timeless rhyme, with which the warder cheats the time* (Scott).

—n. **1** a person who is not honest and who does things to deceive or trick others; swindler: *The sly storekeeper was a cheat who added weight to all the vegetables and meat he sold. Corinth . . . was a city of extortioners and cheats* (Frederic Farrar). **SYN:** deceiver, impostor. **2** a fraud; trick or deception. **SYN:** swindle, hoax. **3** *Law.* the obtaining of property from another by deliberate deceit or fraudulent means. **4** a coarse grass or weed; chess. **5** a card game in which the players try to cheat without being discovered but detect the cheating of the other players.
[variant of *escheat*] **—cheat′a|ble,** *adj.*
—cheat′er, *n.*
—Syn. v.i., v.t. **1, 2 Cheat, trick** mean to gain or seek to gain advantage by underhanded means. **Cheat** means to do something dishonest or use misrepresentation: *He cheated me by short-changing me. He cheated to pass the test.* **Trick** emphasizes using a misleading device to deceive and indirectly get what one wants: *The FBI used fake plans to trick the spy.*

cheat|ing (chē′ting), *adj.* that cheats; fraudulent; swindling; deceitful. **—cheat′ing|ly,** *adv.*

che|bec (chi bek′), *n.* = least flycatcher. [American English; probably imitative]

che|cha|co (chi chä′kō, -chak′ō), *n., pl.* **-cos.** = cheechako.

Che|chen (chə chen′), *n., pl.* **-chens** or **-chen. 1** a member of a chiefly Moslem people of the northern Caucasus in the Soviet Union. **2** this people. **3** their Caucasian language.

che|chia or **ché|chia** (shā shyä′), *n.* a fuzzy cylindrical hat, similar to a fez, worn in North Africa by French troops, and in modified versions throughout the world. [< French *chéchia* < Arabic (North Africa) *shāshiya* < *Shāsh,* a town in Persia where the hat was made]

check (chek), *v., n., adj., interj.* **—v.t. 1** to stop suddenly: *The boys checked their steps when they heard the floor squeak under their feet.* **SYN:** See syn. under **stop. 2a** to hold back; control; restrain: *to check a forest fire;* (*Figurative.*) *to check one's anger or a laugh.* **b** to repel or reverse: *to check an enemy attack.* **c** to reprimand. **3** to prove true or right by comparing or examining: *Check your watch with the village clock. Check your answers with mine.* **4** to mark (something examined or compared) with a check: *How many answers did the teacher check as wrong?* **5** to leave or take for safekeeping: *I checked my hat at the door. The hotel checked our baggage.* **6** *U.S.* to send (baggage) on a traveler's ticket to a particular place: *I shall check my bag through to Chicago.* **7** to mark in a pattern of squares or crossing lines. **8** to plant in checkrows. **9** *Chess.* to put (an opponent's king) in immediate danger. A king in this position must be moved or the threatening piece must be blocked off or removed. **10** *Hockey.* to interfere with the advance of (an opponent or the puck) with the body or stick.
—v.i. **1** to be exactly alike when compared, usually with a duplicate or the original: *The two copies check.* **2** to examine something to discover facts or prove true or right: *to check on a statement. Employers like to check on the past experience of applicants.* **SYN:** investigate. **3** *U.S.* to crack or split along crossing lines, as timber or a painted surface. **4** *Chess.* to move so that the opponent's king is in immediate danger. **5** *U.S.* to write a check; draw a check. **6** *Hunting.* (of the hounds) to stop because the scent is lost or in order to make sure of it. **7** *Cards.* to pass one's turn in the betting.
—n. **1** a sudden stop: *The storm warning put a check to our plans for a boat ride.* **SYN:** stoppage. **2** a holding back; control; restraint: *to keep a check on a child.* **3** any person, thing, or event that controls or holds back action. A rein used to prevent a horse from lowering his head is a check. **SYN:** restriction, curb, bridle, obstruction, obstacle, hindrance. **4** a rebuff; repulse; reverse. **5** the act of proving or the condition of being a proof by comparing: *My work will be a check on yours.* **6** a means or guide to ensure truth or rightness. **7** a test or controlled observation, as of a product. **8** a mark (√) to show that something has been examined or compared; check mark. Usually this mark indicates that the thing is true or right. Sometimes, as on examinations, it indicates something false or wrong. *The teacher put a check beside the correct answers.* **9** a ticket or token given in return for a coat, hat, baggage, package, or the like, left for safekeeping, to show ownership or the right to claim again later: *Give your check to the man in the check-room when you want your coat.* **SYN:** tag, coupon. **10** Also, *especially British,* **cheque.** a written order directing a bank to pay money to the person named: *We pay most of our bills by check.* **11** a written statement of the amount owed in a restaurant: *When we finished eating, we asked the waitress for the check.* **12a** a pattern made of squares: *Do you want a check or a stripe for your new dress?* **b** a single one of these squares: *the checks in this dress are big.* **c** a fabric having such a pattern. **13a** *U.S.* a crack; split. **b** imperfection in glass. **14** *Chess.* **a** the position of an opponent's king when it is in immediate danger. A king in this position must be moved or the threatening piece must be blocked off or removed. **b** a move putting the opponent's king in this position: *a series of checks.* **15** *U.S.* a counter used in card games or gambling games, such as a chip in poker or faro. **16** a notch or rabbet by which one stone is fitted to another in masonry. **17** *Ice Hockey.* an interfering with the progress of an opponent or his possession of the puck. **18** a blocking with the body in the game of Rugby.
—adj. **1** used in checking. **2** marked in a pattern of squares.
—interj. **1** *Chess.* a call warning that the opponent's king is in danger and must be moved or protected. **2** *Informal.* OK; all right.
check at, a *Obsolete.* to stop short at: *A true friend should not check at the hazard of a life* (Beaumont and Fletcher). **b** (of the falcon) to forsake the prey and fly after (base) game, especially after some chance bird that crosses the path of flight: *She checked first at one bird, then at the other* (Richard F. Burton).
check in, a to arrive and register at a hotel, motel, or other place where an appointment must be made or kept or where one's presence must be made known: *We checked in and were then shown to our rooms. The salesman checked in at the convention and then went out to dinner.* **b** *Slang.* to die.
check off, to mark, especially on a list, as finished, acceptable, or requiring no further attention: *to check off the items of a bill, to check off the names of applicants.*
check out, a *Especially U.S.* to pay one's bill at a hotel or motel when leaving or otherwise notify a person in charge of a register that one is leaving: *We loaded the car while Father checked out at the desk.* **b** to inspect or examine to see if (something) is in proper order or condition: *The mechanic checked out the plane before take-off.* **c** to prove right or true; substantiate: *to check out a fact or statement.* **d** *Slang.* to die.
check up, *U.S.* to examine or compare to prove true or correct: *If you are not sure, you ought to check up on the facts.*
hand in one's checks, *Slang.* to die: *Beneath this tree lies the body of J. O. who . . . handed in his checks on the 7th December, 1850* (Bret Harte).
in check, a held back; controlled: *He held his temper in check.* **b** *Chess.* (of a king) attacked by an opposing piece: *When your king is attacked by any piece he is said to be in check* (Hardy and Ware).
keep a check on, a to restrain: *One policeman tried to keep a check on the brawling men while the other rushed out for help.* **b** to keep a watch on; keep tabs on: *The [parole] Association is not only concerned with constructive aftercare, but also with the time-consuming task of merely keeping a check on a man's whereabouts* (Observer).
[< Old French *eschequier* < *eschec* a check at chess < Arabic *shāh māta;* see etym. under **checkmate**] **—check′a|ble,** *adj.*
—Syn. v.t. **2a Check, restrain, curb** mean to hold someone or something back. **Check** suggests the use of some means that slows up or stands in the way of action or progress: *Deep mud checked the progress of the march.* **Restrain** suggets use of some force to keep down or within limits or to prevent completely: *A bystander restrained him from jumping off the bridge.* **Curb** suggests use of a control that pulls back suddenly or keeps from acting freely: *His good sense curbed his impulse to hit the man.*
▶See **cheque** for usage note.

check|age (chek′ij), *n.* **1** a checking, as of items in a list. **2** the items checked.

check|book (chek′bůk′), *n.* a book of blank checks on a bank, usually with record stubs or a check register.

checkbook journalism, the payment of large sums of money to public figures for exclusive journalistic interviews.

checked (chekt), *adj.* **1** marked in a pattern of squares; checkered. **2** *Phonetics.* **a** (of a syllable) closed. **b** (of a vowel) occurring in a closed syllable.

check|er¹ (chek′ər), *v., n.* **—v.t. 1** to mark in a pattern of squares of different colors. **2** to mark off with patches different from one another: (*Figurative.*) *The ground under the trees was checkered with sunlight and shade.* **SYN:** variegate, mottle. **3** *Figurative.* to diversify; break up: *checkered with contradictions.* [< noun]
—n. **1a** a pattern of squares of different colors. **b** one of these squares. **2** one of the flat, round pieces used in the game of checkers. **3** = service tree. **4** *Obsolete.* a checkerboard.
[< Old French *eschequier* chessboard < *eschec* a check]

check|er² (chek′ər), *n.* **1** a person who checks, verifies, or inspects. **2** *U.S.* a cashier in a self-service store or market. **3** a person who checks baggage, hats, and coats. [< *check* + *-er¹*]

check|er|ber|ry (chek′ər ber′ē), *n., pl.* **-ries. 1a** the bright-red berry of the American wintergreen plant. **b** the plant. **2** = partridgeberry.

check|er|bloom (chek′ər blüm′), *n.* a wild plant of the mallow family, native to California, also cultivated in gardens.

check|er|board (chek′ər bôrd′, -bōrd′), *n., v.* *—n.* a board marked in a pattern of 64 squares of two alternating colors, used in playing checkers or chess; chessboard.
—v.t. to arrange, divide, or mark off into a pattern resembling a checkerboard.

check|ered (chek′ərd), *adj.* **1** marked in a pattern of squares of different colors: *a checkered tablecloth.* **2** marked in patches. **SYN:** variegated, dappled. **3** *Figurative.* often changing; varied; irregular: *a checkered career.* **SYN:** unstable.

checkered adder, = milk snake.

check|er|ing (chek′ər ing), *n.* the decorative carving on the wooden stock of a sporting rifle.

***check|ers** (chek′ərz), *n.* a game played by two people, each with 12 flat, round pieces to move on a checkerboard. The object of the game is to capture all the opponent's pieces or to prevent them from being able to move. Also, *British,* **chequers, draughts.**

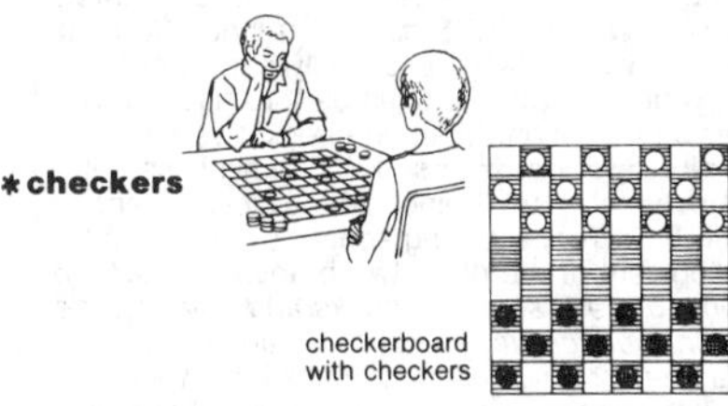
***checkers**

checkerboard with checkers

check|er|spot (chek′ər spot′), *n.* any one of a genus of butterflies that have black wings covered with many yellow spots and are widely distributed throughout the north temperate zone; chalcedon.

checker tree, either of two mountain ash trees; service tree.

check|er|work (chek′ər wėrk′), *n.* **1** work resembling a checkerboard in pattern. **2** *Figurative.* a diversified combination or whole.

check|hook (chek′hůk′), *n.* a hook on a saddle to fasten the end of the checkrein.

check|ing account (chek′ing), a bank account against which bank checks may be drawn at any time.

check|less (chek′lis), *adj.* **1** without check or restraint. **2** not using bank checks as a means of transferring money: *checkless payrolls.*

check line, = checkrein (def. 2).

check list, or **check|list** (chek′list′), *n.* **1** a list of names, titles, jobs, or any other items arranged to form a ready means of reference, comparison, or checking: *The pilot went over the flight check list before take-off.* **2** a list of qualified voters for use at an election.

check mark, = check (*n.* def. 8).

check|mate (chek′māt′), *v.,* **-mat|ed, -mat|ing,** *n., interj.* **—v.t. 1** *Chess.* to put (an opponent's king) in check from which his next move cannot free him, and so win the game. **2** *Figurative.* **a** to defeat completely. **b** to stop, frustrate, or defeat a scheme or act of (an opponent) by a countermove: *The United States and the Soviet Union will checkmate and immobilize each other* (Bulletin of Atomic Scientists). [< noun]
—n. **1** *Chess.* **a** a move that ends the game by putting the opponent's king in check so that he is unable to escape by his next move. **b** the position of the chess pieces when the king is thus attacked. **2** *Figurative.* a complete defeat.
—interj. *Chess.* a declaration that the opposing king is checkmated.
[< Old French *eschec mat* < Arabic *shāh māta* (literally) the king is dead < Persian *shāh* shah, king (in chess)]

check nut, an extra nut screwed on top to prevent slipping; locknut.

check|off (chek′ôf′, -of′), *n. U.S.* **1** an arrangement between a union and an employer by which the employer deducts union dues from wages and turns them over to the union. **2** a choice one can elect by putting a check mark in a designated space, such as the box on the U.S. income-tax form to indicate a desire to contribute to a national campaign fund for political candidates: *According to a sampling of early returns, an average 13% of taxpayers are choosing the checkoff* (Time).

check|out (chek′out′), *n.* **1** an inspection or test, especially of the readiness for performance of something. **2** *U.S.* the checking off of items at a checkout counter.

checkout counter, *U.S.* a counter in a store where a cashier collects payment for merchandise purchased.

check|point (chek′point′), *n.* **1** a place of inspection on a road, at a border, or the like. **2** a landmark used in flying.

check|post (chek′pōst′), *n. Especially British.* checkpoint.

check register, a register to keep a record of the checks written from a checkbook.

check|rein (chek′rān′), *n.* **1** a short rein attached to the saddle or to the harness to keep a horse from lowering its head; bearing rein. **2** a short rein connecting the bit of one of a team of horses to the driving rein of the other; check line. **3** *Figurative.* a means of checking or controlling; restraint; curb: . . . *to apply a tight checkrein on new projects* (Harper's).

check|room (chek′rüm′, -rům′), *n.* a place where coats, hats, baggage, packages, and the like, can be left for safekeeping until called for later.

check|row (chek′rō′), *n., v.* **—*n.*** one of a number of rows of plants, especially corn, which mark the land off into squares for ease in using a cultivator. **—*v.t.*** to plant in checkrows.

checks and balances, **1** *U.S.* limitations set on the powers of any branch of the government, each branch possessing some powers that offset the powers of the other two branches: *Madison planned the system of checks and balances between the legislative, executive, and judicial branches.* **2** any system of limitations whereby contrary forces or powers are kept in balance: [*Man*] *undoes the built-in checks and balances by which nature holds the various species in bounds* (New Yorker).

check|tak|er (chek′tā′kər), *n.* a person who takes tickets.

check-till (chek′til′), *n.* a shop till that records the total received.

check|up (chek′up′), *n.* **1** a careful inspection or examination: *The manager gave the store a final checkup before closing for the night. Can psychiatrists work out a system of routine checkups that will catch a mental skid?* (Maclean's). **2** a thorough physical examination: *The doctor asked the patient to come to his office for a checkup.*

check valve, a valve that allows liquid or gas to flow in one direction but closes shut to stop flow in the opposite direction.

check|weigh (chek′wā′), *v.t.* to check the weight of (containers, loads, or the like): *Scales are being used by an increasing number of banks to checkweigh packages of money to make sure that the bills are all there* (New York Times). **—check′weigh′er**, *n.*

check|weigh|man (chek′wā′mən), *n., pl.* **-men**. a weighman at a mine whose work is to check the weight of the coal or ore, usually in the interest of the miners.

check|writ|er (chek′rī′tər), *n.* a machine for imprinting amounts, account numbers, and other accounting information on blank checks.

ched|dar (ched′ər), *v.t.* (in making Cheddar) to cut (curd) into slabs with sharp steel knives to be flattened for milling. [< *Cheddar*]

Ched|dar or **ched|dar** (ched′ər), *n.*, or **Cheddar cheese**, a kind of hard, white or yellow cheese, made from cow's milk. It was made originally at or near Cheddar, England. American cheese, the ordinary yellow and usually softer cheese made in the United States, is a Cheddar.

chedd|ite (ched′īt, shed′-), *n.* a high explosive used in blasting, consisting typically of potassium chlorate, a nitro compound, and castor oil. [< French *cheddite* < *Chedde*, a town in France, where it was produced]

che|der (ʜā′dər), *n.* = heder.

Che. E., chemical engineer.

chee|cha|ko (chi chä′kō, -chak′ō), *n., pl.* **-kos**. a newcomer; tenderfoot, in Alaska and the Klondike. Also, **chechaco**. [< Chinook jargon]

cheek (chēk), *n., v.* **—*n.*** **1** the side of the face below either eye; the fleshy lateral wall of the mouth. **2** *Figurative.* something suggesting the human cheek in form or position. **3** *Informal.* saucy talk or behavior; shameless boldness; impudence; effrontery: *The new worker had the cheek to tell the foreman how the job should be done. Mr. Wilson is now so full of confidence that he exudes cheek* (New York Times). **4** one of the side pieces of a door or window frame. **5** *Obsolete.* the jaw; jawbone.
—*v.t.* *Informal.* to address cheekily or saucily; speak with cool impudence to; confront boldly.
cheek by jowl, **a** side by side; close together: . . . *a drab huddle of shops crammed cheek by jowl with small factories* (London Times). **b** *Figurative.* close; intimate; familiar: *The general boasted that he was cheek by jowl with the emperor.*
tongue in cheek. See under **tongue**.
turn the other cheek, to submit to insult or injury without protest or retaliation: *We turn the other cheek too much. We ought to put up a bold front and stick to it* (Wall Street Journal).
[Old English *cēce* cheek, jaw]

cheek|bone (chēk′bōn′), *n.* the bone just below either eye; zygomatic bone.

-cheeked, *combining form.* having a ____cheek, or cheeks: *Red-cheeked = having red cheeks.*

cheek|piece (chēk′pēs′), *n.* = cheek strap.

cheek pouch, a fold of skin like a pocket in the cheek of various animals, as gophers and squirrels, used for holding food.

cheek strap, one of the two straps on the side of a bridle. Together they connect the band around the head with the bit; cheekpiece.

cheek tooth, a molar.

cheek|y (chē′kē), *adj.*, **cheek|i|er, cheek|i|est.** **1** *Informal.* saucy; impudent; audacious: *A gentleman as rich as Croesus and apparently as highly regarded in town—risks his local reputation, his business and eventually his hide to save a cheeky American photographer* (New York Times). **SYN:** insolent, presuming. **2** having large sagging cheeks, as a bulldog does. **—cheek′i|ly**, *adv.* **—cheek′i|ness**, *n.*

cheep (chēp), *v., n.* **—*v.i.*** to make a short, sharp sound such as a young bird makes; chirp; peep: *newly hatched chicks constantly cheeping.*
—*v.t.* to utter with a cheeping voice.
—*n.* a short, sharp, sound such as a young bird makes; chirp; peep: (*Figurative.*) *The cheep of the tiller rope running through . . . the well-greased leading blocks* (Michael Scott). [imitative] **—cheep′er**, *n.*

cheer (chir), *n., v., interj.* **—*n.*** **1** a shout of encouragement and support or praise: *the cheers of the crowd in the stadium. Give three cheers for the boys who won the game for us.* **SYN:** acclamation, shouting, applause. **2** good spirits; hope, joy, or gladness; comfort; encouragement: *The warmth of the fire and a good meal brought cheer to our hearts again. You are so sick of late, so far from cheer* (Shakespeare). **SYN:** cheerfulness, gaiety. **3** food; provisions; fare: *Every table was loaded with good cheer* (Macaulay). **4** state of mind; condition of feeling: *His friends encouraged him to be of good cheer.* **SYN:** mood. **5** *Archaic.* the expression of the face; mien.
—*v.t.* **1** to urge on with cheers: *Everyone cheered our team.* **2** to give joy to; make glad; comfort; encourage: *It cheered the old woman to have her young neighbors visit her. Let thy heart cheer thee in the days of thy youth* (Ecclesiastes 11:9). **3** to greet or welcome with cheers: *Many of the audience cheered and applauded this* (Benjamin Jowett). **SYN:** acclaim, applaud.
—*v.i.* **1** to show praise and approval by cheers: *The boys cheered loudly.* **SYN:** acclaim, applaud. **2** *Obsolete.* to be in a specified state of feelings; feel: *How cheer'st thou, Jessica?* (Shakespeare).
—*interj.* **cheers**, a word used in drinking to a person's health.
cheer up, to brighten up; be or make glad; raise one's spirits; comfort: *The sick girl said that our visit cheered her up. Cheer up, perhaps we'll win the next game.*
What cheer? How are you?: *My friend, what cheer?* (Wordsworth).
[Middle English *cheer* expression of the face, face < Old French *chere* < Late Latin *cara* face < Greek *kárā* face, head] **—cheer′ing|ly**, *adv.*
—*Syn.* *v.t.* **1 Cheer, gladden** mean to raise a person's spirits. **Cheer** suggests either making a person feel less downhearted by giving comfort and encouragement (often *cheer up*) or putting him in high spirits by giving pleasure or joy: *The news cheered everyone. Try to cheer him up.* **Gladden** suggests putting a person in good spirits by giving delight and making him feel happy: *Their son's success gladdened both their hearts.*

cheer|er (chir′ər), *n.* **1** a person or thing that gives cheer or gladdens: *the merry cheerer of the heart* (Shakespeare). **2** a person who cheers or applauds: *A dozen pickets . . . milled about the cheerers and jeerers* (New York Times).

cheer|ful (chir′fəl), *adj.* **1** full of cheer; joyful; glad: *She is a smiling, cheerful girl.* **SYN:** gay, cheery, joyous. **2** bringing cheer; pleasant; bright: *This is a cheerful, sunny room.* **3** willing: *When my little brother wants to play he is not a very cheerful helper.* **—cheer′ful|ly**, *adv.* **—cheer′ful|ness**, *n.*

cheer|i|o (chir′ē ō), *interj., n., pl.* **-i|os**. *Especially British Informal.* **1** hello. **2** good-by: *Cheerio, my dear, don't quarrel with bread and butter* (John Galsworthy). **3** hurrah.

cheer|lead|er (chir′lē′dər), *n.* a person who leads a group in organized cheering, especially at high school or college athletic events: *A white-sweater-clad cheerleader tries unsuccessfully to rouse yells from the few hundred spectators* (Wall Street Journal).

cheer|lead|ing (chir′lē′ding), *n.* the function or act of a cheerleader.

cheer|less (chir′lis), *adj.* without joy or comfort; gloomy; dreary: *All's cheerless, dark, and deadly* (Shakespeare). **SYN:** dismal, dull, joyless. **—cheer′less|ly**, *adv.* **—cheer′less|ness**, *n.*

cheer|ly (chir′lē), *adv.* in a way that cheers or enlivens; cheeringly: *Alighting cheerly to inspire The soldier slackening in his fire* (Byron).

cheers (chirz), *interj.* See under **cheer**.

cheer|y (chir′ē), *adj.*, **cheer|i|er, cheer|i|est.** cheerful; pleasant; bright; gay: *a cheery smile. Sunshine and the singing of birds are cheery.* **—cheer′i|ly**, *adv.* **—cheer′i|ness**, *n.*

cheese¹ (chēz), *n.* **1a** a solid food made from the thick part of milk. Cheese is the curd of milk separated from the whey and usually pressed or molded into a shape and covered with a rind. **b** a shaped mass of this food: *a display of cheeses in a store window.* **2** something similar in shape or consistency, such as the fruit of various mallows.
make cheeses, **a** to make a deep curtsey: *The little village maidens made cheeses as the squire passed.* **b** to whirl and sink on outstretched skirts: . . . *spinning round like a schoolgirl when she makes cheeses* (Besant and Rice).
[Old English *cēse* < Latin *cāseus*] **—cheese′like′**, *adj.*

cheese² (chēz), *v.t.*, **cheesed, chees|ing.** *Slang.* to stop; give up; leave off.
cheese it! stop! run away! *"Cheese it!" one of the thieves yelled. "The cops are coming!"*
[perhaps a variant of *cease*]

cheese³ (chēz), *n. Slang.* the right or correct thing; anything good, first-rate in quality, genuine, pleasant, or advantageous. [perhaps < Anglo-Indian (*the real*) *chīz* < Hindustani *chīz* thing < Persian]

cheese|board (chēz′bôrd′, -bōrd′), *n.* **1** a board from which cheese is served: *This includes the main course, all the trimmings and a sweet or selection from the cheeseboard, and a roll and butter* (London Times). **2** the cover of a cheese vat.

cheese|burg|er (chēz′bėr′gər), *n.* a hamburger sandwich with a slice of melted cheese on top of the meat. [< *cheese* + (ham)*burger*]

cheese cake, **1** a kind of cake or pie usually made of cottage cheese or cream cheese, cream, sugar, eggs, and butter, baked together. **2** Also, **cheese|cake** (chēz′kāk′), *n. Slang.* photography or photographs emphasizing attractive feminine figures.

cheese|cloth (chēz′klôth′, -kloth′), *n.* a thin, loosely woven cotton cloth, originally used for wrapping cheese.

cheesed (chēzd), *adj.* Usually, **cheesed off**. *British Slang.* fed up; disgusted: *Seventeen years ago,* [*he*] . . . *got cheesed off with teaching golf to fat ladies in Potter's Bar and departed for New Zealand* (Manchester Guardian Weekly).

cheese hoop, a container lined with cheesecloth in which the curd is pressed and cheese is shaped.

cheese mite, a mite which infests old cheese, flour, and milk.

cheese|mon|ger (chēz′mung′gər, -mong′-), *n.* a person who sells cheese.

cheese|par|ing (chēz′pãr′ing), *n., adj.* **—*n.*** **1** a paring of the rind of cheese. **2** *Figurative.* an object of no value. **3** *Figurative.* niggardly economizing; parsimonious saving.
—*adj.* *Figurative.* niggardly; miserly; parsimonious.

cheese pumpkin, a finely textured pumpkin cultivated especially for commercial canning.

cheese vat, a vat in which the milk used in making cheese is processed to the point where the curd is formed.

chees|y (chē′zē), *adj.*, **chees|i|er, chees|i|est.** **1** of or consisting of cheese: *He had finished licking the cheesy part of a . . . Danish pastry* (New Yorker). **SYN:** caseous. **2** like cheese. **3** *Slang.* of low quality; inferior: *I went to Hartford to a cheesy hotel* (Atlantic). **—chees′i|ness**, *n.*

chee|tah or **chee|ta** (chē′tə), *n.* a flesh-eating, spotted mammal somewhat like a leopard, found in southern Asia and Africa. It belongs to the cat family. Cheetahs run very fast and can be trained to hunt deer and antelope. Also, **chetah**. [< Hindustani *chītā* < Sanskrit *chitraka* < *chitra* speckled]

chef (shef), *n.* **1** a head cook: *the chef of a large restaurant.* **2** any cook. [< French *chef* < Old French *chief* head. See etym. of doublet **chief**.]

chef de ca|bi|net (she′ də kȧ bē nā′), *French.* **1** the chief adviser of a minister. **2** (literally) head of cabinet.

chef de cir|con|scrip|tion (she′ də sir kôɴ skrip-sē ôɴ′), *French.* **1** an administrative head of a French military or colonial district: *Each of the 17 administrative districts of Togo is directed by a chef de circonscription.* **2** (literally) district head.

chef d'é|cole (she′ dā kôl′), *French.* **1** the leading figure or chief proponent of a group of artists or a school of thought. **2** (literally) head of school.

chef de cui|sine (she′ də kwē zēn′), *French.* **1** head cook. **2** (literally) head of the kitchen.

chef de file (she′ də fēl′), *French.* **1** leader: *The last singular literary chef de file was Camus, wastefully killed with his publisher in 1960 in a motor accident* (New Yorker). **2** (literally) head of line.

chef-d'oeu|vre (she dœ′vrə), *n., pl.* **chefs-d'oeu|vre** (she dœ′vrə). *French.* **1** a masterpiece. **2** (literally) chief (piece of) work.

chei|li|tis (kī lī′tis), *n.* inflammation of the lip. [< Greek *cheîlos* lip + English *-itis*]

chei|lo|plas|ty (kī′lə plas′tē), *n.* = chiloplasty.

chei|lo|sis (kī lō′sis), *n.* a disorder associated with riboflavin deficiency in which the lips redden and lesions occur in the angles of the mouth. [< Greek *cheîlos* lip + English *-osis*]

chei|lot|o|my (kī lot′ə mē), *n., pl.* **-mies.** = chilotomy.

chei|ro|man|cy (kī′rə man′sē), *n.* = chiromancy.

chei|ron|o|my (kī ron′ə mē), *n.* = chironomy.

Che|ka (che′kə), *n.* a former commission in the Soviet Union acting as a secret police, charged with protection from counterrevolution. Also, **Tcheka.** [< Russian *Cheka* < *che ka,* names of the initial letters of *Chrezvychainaya Komissiya* Extraordinary Commission, the two main words in its name]

Che|khov|i|an (che kō′vē ən), *adj.* of or characteristic of the Russian writer Anton Pavlovich Chekhov (1860-1904) or his work: . . . *wonderfully timed Chekhovian dialogue* (New York Times).

Che|kist (che′kist), *n.* a member of the Cheka.

che|la[1] (kē′lə), *n. pl.,* **-lae** (-lē). the claw of a lobster, crab, scorpion, or other crustacean. It is like a pincer. [< Latin *chēlē* < Greek *chēlḗ* claw]

che|la[2] (chā′lä), *n.* (in India) a pupil, especially a Buddhist novice studying with a religious teacher: "*We will go in the cool of the evening, chela,*" said the lama (Rudyard Kipling). [< Hindi *chelā* < Pali *cheto* < Sanskrit *cheta* slave, servant]

che|late (kē′lāt), *adj., n., v.,* **-lat|ed, -lat|ing.** —*adj.* having a chela (claw) or chelae. —*n. Chemistry.* an inert complex compound in which two or more metallic ions are simultaneously bound in different positions so as to form two or more rings, or a compound which utilizes residual valences so as to form two or more rings. —*v.t., v.i. Chemistry.* to join or be joined with a metallic ion so as to form a chelate: *Examples of chelated metals in vital processes are . . . magnesium in chlorophyll and iron in haemoglobin* (Science News Letter). [< Greek *chēlḗ claw* + *English -ate*[1]]

che|lat|ing agent (kē′lā ting), any organic compound used to attract metallic ions to itself, forming a stable, inert complex which is soluble in water, used in softening hard water, purifying sewage, and, medically, in eliminating high concentrations of undesirable metallic or radioactive elements in the blood or tissues.

che|la|tion (ki lā′shən), *n.* the process of binding and stabilizing metallic ions by means of a chelating agent.

che|la|tor (ki lā′tər), *n.* a substance that chelates; chelating agent.

che|lic|er|a (kə lis′ər ə), *n., pl.* **-er|ae** (-ə rē). one of the first pair of appendages near the mouth of scorpions and spiders: *The small organs between the pedipalpi, the chelicerae, contain extensions of the mouth that flood the prey with digestive juices and later inbibe it in dissolved form* (Scientific American). [< New Latin *chelicera* < Greek *chēlḗ* claw + *kéras* horn]

che|lif|er|ous (ki lif′ər əs), *adj.* bearing chelae or prehensile claws. [< Greek *chēlḗ* claw + English *-ferous* bearing]

che|li|form (kē′lə fôrm), *adj.* having the form of a chela (claw).

che|li|ped (kē′lə ped, kel′ə-), *n.* one of the pair of limbs, especially of a lobster or crab which bear the chelae. [< Greek *chēlḗ* claw + Latin *pēs, pedis* foot]

Chel|le|an (shel′ē ən), *adj.* = Abbevillian. [< French *Chelléen* < *Chelles,* a locality in France, where remains were found]

Chellean man, a prehistoric man, identified from bones found in 1960 in what is now Tanzania. The bones date back about 500,000 years.

che|loid (kē′loid), *n.* = keloid.

che|lo|ni|an (ki lō′nē ən), *adj., n.* —*adj.* of or having to do with turtles and tortoises. —*n.* a turtle or tortoise. [< New Latin *Chelonia* the order name (< Greek *chelṓnē* tortoise) + English *-an*]

Chel|sea boot (chel′sē), *British.* a boot or shoe with elastic sides. [< *Chelsea,* a section of London where such boots were sold in the 1960's]

Chelsea pensioner, a member of the Chelsea Royal Hospital for old soldiers.

Chelsea ware, articles made of porcelain in Chelsea, England, in the 1700's.

Chel|ten|ham (chelt′nəm), *n.* a style of printing type. [< *Cheltenham,* England]

chem-, *combining form,* the form of **chemo-** before vowels, as in *chemism.*

chem., 1 chemical. 2 chemist. 3 chemistry.

chem|ic (kem′ik), *adj., n. Archaic.* —*adj.* **1** = chemical. **2** of or having to do with alchemy; alchemic. —*n.* chemist. Also, **chymic.** [< New Latin *chymicus,* alteration of Medieval Latin *alchimicus* < *alchimia* alchemy]

chem|i|cal (kem′ə kəl), *adj., n.* —*adj.* **1** of or having to do with chemistry; in chemistry: *a chemical formula. Chemical research has made possible many new products.* **2** made by or used in chemistry: *Chemical apparatus for the laboratory is often made of special glass.* See also **chemical change.** **3** working, operated, or done by using chemicals: *a chemical fire extinguisher. Exhausted gases in a chemical rocket have a high molecular weight* (Science News Letter). —*n.* Often, **chemicals.** any substance that is used in chemistry. Sulfuric acid, bicarbonate of soda, and borax are chemicals.

chemical accelerator, a device similar to a particle accelerator, used to speed up ions and molecules to high energies to investigate chemical reactions on the highest energy level.

chemical balance, = analytical balance.

chemical bomb, a bomb having a chemical agent, especially poison gas, for its main charge.

chemical bomber, a bomber that uses a chemical for fuel, especially a jet bomber using an exotic fuel.

chemical change, a change in which one substance is converted into one or more substances with different properties: *The burning of coal is a process of chemical change in which oxygen in the air unites with carbon from the coal, giving off light and heat.*

chemical culture, = hydroponics.

chemical dynamics, the study of the forces which cause chemical reactions: *Chemical accelerators are probably the most exciting prospect in the future of chemical dynamics* (Richard Wolfgang).

chemical engineer, an expert in chemical engineering.

chemical engineering, the science or profession of using chemistry for industrial purposes.

chem|i|cal|ize (kem′ə kə līz), *v.t.,* **-ized, -iz|ing.** to treat with a chemical or chemicals: *The loaf we buy at the grocer's has been chemicalized, first by the miller and then by the baker* (Atlantic). —**chem′i|cal|i|za′tion,** *n.*

chemical laser, a laser that uses the energy of a chemical reaction instead of electrical energy: *Chemical lasers differ from ordinary lasers in that molecules with abnormally large amounts of energy are produced by particular chemical reactions, not by some external source of radiation* (London Times).

chem|i|cal|ly (kem′ə klē), *adv.* **1** according to chemistry. **2** by chemical processes.

chemically pure, (of an element or compound) having a degree of purity that qualifies it for use in fine chemical work. *Abbr:* C.P.

Chemical Mace, 1 *Trademark.* a spray can for discharging the tear gas Mace. **2** = Mace.

chemical mine, a land mine having a chemical agent, especially poison gas, for its main charge.

chemical warfare, the technique or use of gases, flames, smoke, or any chemical other than explosives as weapons.

chem|i|ga|tion (kem′ə gā′shən), *n.* the irrigation of crops with chemicals, such as fertilizers and pesticides: *Chemigation is usually done with . . . special piping to drip small amounts of chemicals at the base of plants* (Sylvan H. Wittwer). [< *chem-* + (irr)*igation*]

chem|i|ground|wood (kem′ə ground′wu̇d′), *n.* **1** a chemical and mechanical process for converting hardwood into groundwood. **2** wood pulp that has been treated by this process.

chem|i|lu|mi|nes|cence (kem′ə lü′mə nes′əns), *n.* the production of light during a chemical reaction, without a rise in temperature.

chem|i|lu|mi|nes|cent (kem′ə lü′mə nes′ənt), *adj.* producing or produced by chemiluminescence.

che|min de fer (shə maɴ′ də fer′), *French.* **1** a railroad. **2** a modification of baccarat (card game).

che|mise (shə mēz′), *n.* **1** a loose, shirtlike undergarment worn by women and girls; shift. **2** a loosely fitting dress without a belt. **3** a shirtlike outer garment. [Middle English *chemise* smocklike undergarment < Old French < Late Latin *camīsia* shirt; origin uncertain]

chem|i|sette (shem′ə zet′), *n.* **1** a detachable vestee or dickey of lace, muslin, etc., for women; tucker. **2** a sleeveless undershirt or bodice for women. [< French *chemisette* < Old French (diminutive) < *chemise* chemise]

chem|ism (kem′iz əm), *n.* chemical action, operation, activity, or force.

chem|i|sorb (kem′ə sôrb′, zôrb′), *v.t.* to hold by chemisorption. [< *chemi*(cal) + (ad)*sorb*]

chem|i|sorp|tion (kem′ə sôrp′shən, -zôrp′-), *n.* adsorption in which a single layer of molecules is held with great strength to a surface by a chemical bond. [< *chemi*(cal) + (ad)*sorption*]

chem|ist (kem′ist), *n.* **1** a person whose occupation is chemistry or who knows a great deal about it. Chemists investigate chemical compositions, properties, and phenomena, or apply them to uses in industry, medicine, agriculture, or other fields. **2** *British.* a druggist. **3** *Obsolete.* an alchemist. [variant of *alchemist*]

chem|is|try (kem′ə strē). *n., pl.* **-tries. 1** the science that deals with the characteristics of simple substances (elements), the changes that take place when they combine to form other substances, and the laws of their behavior under various conditions. *Abbr:* chem. **2** the application of this to a certain subject: *plant chemistry.* **3a** the chemical composition or characteristics of a substance: *the chemistry of iron.* **b** the chemicals used in a process: *This new photographic paper has its chemistry built in.* **4** *Figurative.* **a** a mixture or synthesis of qualities, emotions, etc.: *Smith and I have the wrong chemistry. He just plain doesn't like me* (Will Sparks) **b** composition; makeup: *the chemistry of a conservative.*

chem|i|type (kem′ə tīp), *n.* a process for taking impressions from an engraving.

chem|my (shem′ē), *n. Informal.* chemin de fer.

chemo-, *combining form,* chemical; by chemical reaction: *Chemosynthesis = chemical synthesis.* Also, **chem-** before vowels. [< *chemical*]

che|mo|au|to|troph (kē′mō ô′tə trof, kem′ō-), *n.* a chemoautotrophic bacterium, protozoan, or other microorganism.

che|mo|au|to|troph|ic (kē′mō ô′tə trof′ik, kem′ ō-), *adj.* providing its own nourishment with energy obtained from chemical oxidations: *chemoautotrophic microorganisms.*

che|mo|cep|tor (kē′mō sep′tər, kem′ō-), *n.* = chemoreceptor.

che|mol|y|sis (ki mol′ə sis), *n.* chemical decomposition or analysis.

che|mo|lyt|ic (kē′mō lit′ik, kem′ō-), *adj.* of or having to do with chemolysis.

che|mo|pal|li|dec|to|my (kē′mō pal′ə dek′tə mē, kem′ō-), *n., pl.* **-mies.** surgery on part of the corpus striatum by the injection of destructive chemicals, used to relieve involuntary muscular tremor, especially in Parkinson's disease. [< *chemo-* + Latin *pallidus* pale + English *-ectomy*]

che|mo|pro|phy|lac|tic (kē′mō prō′fə lak′tik, kem′ō-; -prof′ə-), *adj.* protecting from disease by means of chemical substances or drugs.

che|mo|pro|phy|lax|is (kē′mō prō′fə lak′sis, kem′-ō-; -prof′ə-), *n.* protection from disease, especially a particular disease, by the administering of chemical substances or drugs.

che|mo|re|cep|tion (kē′mō ri sep′shən, kem′ō-), *n.* the physiological reaction to chemical stimulation: *to investigate the relationship between food intake and chemoreception.*

che|mo|re|cep|tor (kē′mō ri sep′tər, kem′ō-), *n.* a nerve ending or sense organ that reacts to chemical stimulation, such as the taste buds in the tongue. [< *chemo-* + *receptor*]

che|mo|sen|so|ry (kē′mō sen′sər ē, kem′ō-), *adj.* of or having a sensory reaction to chemical stimulation: *a chemosensory cell or system, chemosensory acuity.*

chem|os|mo|sis (kēm′oz mō′sis, kem′-; -os-), *n.* a chemical reaction taking place through semipermeable membranes.

chem|os|mot|ic (kēm′oz mot′ik, kem′-; -os-), *adj.*

Pronunciation Key: **hat, āge, cãre, fär; let, ēqual, tėrm; it, īce; hot, ōpen, ôrder; oil, out; cup, pu̇t, rüle; child; long; thin; ᴛʜen; zh,** measure; **ə** represents **a** in about, **e** in taken, **i** in pencil, **o** in lemon, **u** in circus.

of or having to do with chemosmosis: *chemosmotic transport of electrons.*

che|mo|sphere (kē′mə sfir, kem′ə-), *n.* the region of predominant photochemical activity in the outer stratosphere, the mesosphere, and the ionosphere.

che|mo|stat (kē′mə stat′, kem′ə-), *n.* any one of various chemically controlled devices for studying changes in living organisms: *They invented the chemostat . . . for growing bacteria and observing mutations under controlled conditions* (Harper's). [< *chemo-* + *-stat*]

che|mo|ster|i|lant (kē′mō ster′ə lənt, kem′ō-), *n.* a chemical that destroys the ability of an organism, such as an insect, rodent, or certain other pests, to reproduce.

che|mo|ster|i|li|za|tion (kē′mō ster′ə lə zā′shən, kem′ō-), *n.* the use of chemosterilants to control or eliminate harmful insects, rodents, or certain other pests.

che|mo|sur|ger|y (kē′mō sėr′jər ē, kem′ō-), *n., pl.* **-ger|ies.** surgery on cancerous tissue in which chemicals are used to prevent the malignant cells from spreading.

che|mo|syn|the|sis (kē′mō sin′thə sis, kem′ō-), *n.* the formation by cells of carbohydrates from carbon dioxide and water with energy obtained from some chemical reaction, rather than from light as in photosynthesis.

che|mo|syn|thet|ic (kē′mō sin thet′ik, kem′ō-), *adj.* of or using chemosynthesis: *chemosynthetic bacteria.* —**che′mo|syn|thet′i|cal|ly,** *adv.*

che|mo|tac|tic (kē′mō tak′tik), *adj.* of or produced by chemotaxis: *the chemotactic process, a chemotactic response.* —**che′mo|tac′ti|cal|ly,** *adv.*

che|mo|tax|is (kē′mə tak′sis, kem′ə-), *n.* movement of a cell, organism, or part of an organism toward or away from a certain chemical substance. [< *chemo-* + Greek *táxis* arrangement]

che|mo|tax|o|nom|ic (kē′mō tak′sə nom′ik, kem′ō-), *adj.* of or having to do with chemotaxonomy.

che|mo|tax|on|o|my (kē′mō tak son′ə mē, kem′ō-), *n.* the classification of living plant and animal species on the basis of their chemical constituents.

che|mo|ther|a|peu|tic (kē′mō ther′ə pyü′tik, kem′ō-), *adj.* having to do with treatment by chemotherapy. —**che′mo|ther′a|peu′ti|cal|ly,** *adv.*

che|mo|ther|a|peu|tics (kē′mō ther′ə pyü′tiks, kem′ō-), *n.* = chemotherapy.

che|mo|ther|a|pist (kē′mō ther′ə pist, kem′ō-), *n.* a person who studies chemotherapy or treats by chemotherapy.

che|mo|ther|a|py (kē′mō ther′ə pē, kem′ō-), *n.* the treatment of disease and infection by means of chemicals that have a specific toxic effect on the disease, for example the treatment of cancer with chemicals or of bacterial infections with antibiotics.

che|mot|ro|pism (ke mot′rə piz əm), *n.* the tendency of an organism or part of an organism to turn or bend in response to a chemical stimulus.

chem|ur|gic (kem ėr′jik), *adj.* of, having to do with, or produced by chemurgy.

chem|ur|gi|cal (kem ėr′jə kəl), *adj.* = chemurgic.

chem|ur|gist (kem′ėr jist), *n.* a person who studies chemurgy.

chem|ur|gy (kem′ėr jē), *n.* a branch of chemistry that deals with the use of farm and forest products, such as casein and cornstalks, for purposes other than food and clothing: *Finding new uses for the soybean has been one of the achievements of the science of chemurgy* (R. G. Houghtlin). [< *chem*(istry) + Greek *-ourgos* worker]

che|nar (chi när′), *n.* = chinar.

chen|iere (shin′ər ē), *n.* a sandy ridge marked with clusters of gnarled live oaks, found in marshy areas of the United States, especially among the Louisiana bayous. Also, **shinnery.** [< Creole *chênière* < French *chêne* oak tree]

che|nille (shə nēl′), *n.* **1a** a velvety cord of silk, wool, rayon, or cotton, used especially in embroidery and fringe. **b** a fabric woven from this cord, used for bedspreads, rugs, curtains, and the like. **2** a cotton cloth with tufts of soft cotton in designs or allover patterns, giving it a velvety appearance, used for spreads, house robes, etc. [< Old French *chenille* caterpillar < Latin *canīcula* little dog < *canis* dog (from its furry look)]

che|no|pod (kē′nə pod, ken′ə-), *n.* any plant belonging to the goosefoot family. [< New Latin *Chenopodium* the goosefoot genus < Greek *chên, chēnós* goose + *poûs, podós* foot]

che|no|po|di|a|ceous (kē′nə pō′dē ā′shəs, ken′ə-), *adj.* belonging to the goosefoot family. [< New Latin *Chenopodium* (see etym. under **chenopod**) + English *-aceous*]

***che|ong-sam** (che′ong säm′), *n.* a one-piece, close-fitting garment with a high, round collar and slits on either side of the skirt, worn by women in China. [< Cantonese *cheuhng sāam* long dress]

***cheong-sam**

cheque (chek), *n. British.* check (*n.* def. 10).

cheque|book (chek′bu̇k′), *n. British.* checkbook.

cheq|uer (chek′ər), *v., n. British.* checker[1].

cheq|uer|board (chek′ər bôrd′, -bōrd′), *n. British.* checkerboard.

cheq|uers (chek′ərz), *n. British.* checkers.

Cheq|uers (chek′ərz), *n.* the official country residence of the Prime Minister of Great Britain, in Buckinghamshire, northwest of London.

cheq|uing account (chek′ing), *British.* checking account.

cher|chez la femme (sher shā′ lȧ fȧm′), *French.* look for the woman (since a woman must be at the bottom of the matter).

cher|eme (ker′ēm), *n.* a basic signal unit in American Sign Language. [< Greek *cheír* hand + English *-eme* unit of language, as in *phoneme*]

Che|ren|kov counter or **detector** (chə ren′kôf), = Cerenkov counter.

Cherenkov effect or **radiation,** = Cerenkov effect.

ché|ri (she rē′), *n. French.* beloved; darling.

ché|rie (she rē′), *n. French.* feminine of **chéri.**

cher|i|moy|a (cher′ə moi′ə), *n.* **1** a tropical American tree of the custard-apple family native to Peru and cultivated in California and Florida. **2** its pulpy, heart-shaped, edible fruit, of considerable size and having a scaly outer covering. [ultimately < a Quechua word]

cher|ish (cher′ish), *v.t.* **1** to hold dear; treat with tenderness; aid or protect: *A mother cherishes her baby. Cherish those hearts that hate thee* (Shakespeare). **2** *Figurative.* to keep in the mind; cling to: *The old woman cherished the hope of her son's return.* **3** to keep or guard carefully. [< Old French *cheriss-,* stem of *cherir* < *cher* dear < Latin *cārus*] —**cher′ish|a|ble,** *adj.* —**cher′ish|er,** *n.* —**cher′ish|ing|ly,** *adv.*
—*Syn.* **2 Cherish, foster, harbor,** when applied to an idea or feeling, mean to keep it in mind and care for it. **Cherish** implies treasuring it and watching over it with loving care: *to cherish memories of college days, to cherish affection for someone.* **Foster** suggests nourishing an idea or feeling, and helping it to grow: *to foster tolerance, to foster sentiments of patriotism.* **Harbor** suggests letting in an idea or feeling even though it is bad, and brooding over it: *to harbor resentment, to harbor sinister designs.*

cher|no|zem (cher′nə zem, cher nə zyôm′), *n.* a grassland soil having a rich, black upper layer of topsoil and a lower layer of lime. [< Russian *chernozëm* < *chërnyj* black + *zemlja* land, soil]

Cher|o|kee (cher′ə kē, cher′ə kē′), *n., pl.* **-kee** or **-kees. 1** a member of a tribe of Iroquoian Indians, originally of the southern Appalachians, now living mostly in Oklahoma and North Carolina. **2** their language, belonging to the Iroquoian family: *In the mountains was Cherokee, still one of the more important Amerind languages* (Henry A. Gleason). [American English < Cherokee *Tsalagi* or *Tsaragi* < Muskogean (Choctaw) *Chilukki* cave people]

Cherokee rose, an evergreen plant of the rose family with glossy leaflets and fragrant white flowers, which grows wild in the southern part of the United States; the white China rose. It is the state flower of Georgia.

che|root (shə rüt′), *n.* a long, narrow cigar cut off square at both ends. [< French *chéroute* < Tamil *shuruṭṭu* roll]

cherries jubilee or **cherry jubilee,** a dessert of pitted bing cherries flamed in brandy and poured over ice cream.

cher|ry (cher′ē), *n., pl.* **-ries,** *adj.* —*n.* **1** a small, round, juicy fruit, with a stone or pit in it. Cherries are usually a bright red or very dark red and are good to eat. **2** the tree it grows on. The cherry belongs to the rose family. **3** its wood; cherrywood. **4** any fruit bearing some resemblance to the common cherry, or the tree producing it. **5** Also, **cherry red.** a bright red; cerise. **6** *Bowling.* the act of knocking down with the ball only the front pin or pins in an attempt for a spare.
—*adj.* **1** made of the wood of the cherry tree. **2** bright-red: *cherry ribbons.*
[Middle English *chery,* back formation < Old North French *cherise,* an assumed plural < Vulgar Latin *ceresia* < Late Greek *kerasía* cherry tree < Greek *kerasós* cherry (tree). See etym. of doublet **cerise.**] —**cher′ry|like′,** *adj.*

cherry birch, = sweet birch.

cherry blossom soup, a Japanese delicacy with a salty flavor made from pickled cherry blossoms placed in hot water.

cherry bomb, a red firecracker about the size of a large cherry: *A cherry bomb exploded . . . and the big parade began* (New York Times).

cherry brandy, a liqueur of brandy in which cherries have been steeped; kirsch.

cher|ry-col|ored (cher′ē kul′ərd), *adj.* having a clear, bright-red color.

cherry fruit fly, a black fly of the northern United States that infests cherries by laying eggs in the fruit.

cherry laurel, an evergreen shrub of the rose family, having shiny, finely toothed leaves and growing in Europe, Asia, California, and the southern United States. It is not a true laurel.

cherry picker, *U.S.* **1** a crane for picking up logs or other objects out of a heap. **2** a cranelike structure with an elevated platform that can be moved to and away from a launching pad.

cherry pie, 1 a pie made of cherries. **2** the heliotrope.

cherry red, a bright red; cherry.

cherry stone, 1 the pit of a cherry. **2** a small, round quahog, a kind of clam.

cherry tomato, 1 a small red or yellow tomato somewhat like a cherry in size and shape. **2** the plant on which it grows in bunches.

cher|ry|wood (cher′ē wu̇d′), *n.* the reddish wood of the cherry tree, used in cabinetwork: *The shop carries dining tables* (*a large cherrywood one was $250*) (New York Times).

cher|so|nese (kėr′sə nēz, -nēs), *n.* a peninsula. [< Latin *Chersonēsus* < Greek *chersónēsos* peninsula < *chérsos* dry land + *nêsos* island]

chert (chėrt), *n.* a dark, impure mineral containing quartz and hydrated silica, resembling flint but lighter in color. Chert consists of submicroscopic crystals. [origin unknown]

chert|y (chėr′tē), *adj.,* **chert|i|er, chert|i|est.** full of chert; flinty.

***cher|ub** (cher′əb), *n., pl.* **cher|u|bim** *for 1, 2, 5;* **cher|ubs** *for 3, 4.* **1** one of the second highest order of angels. Cherubim rank just below the seraphim, and are distinguished by the faculty of knowledge. **2** a picture or statue of a child with wings or, often, a child's head with wings but no body. **3** a beautiful, innocent, or good child. **4** a person with a chubby, innocent face: *the round-faced rosy cherub before him* (Sir Walter Scott). **5a** a heavenly being with four faces and four wings, described in Ezekiel, chapters 1 and 10. **b** a figure or other representation of such a being, especially as at either end of the mercy seat of the Hebrew Ark of the Covenant (in the Bible, Exodus 25:18-22). [< Latin *cherub* < Greek *cheroúb* < Hebrew *kərūb*]

***cherub**
definition 2

che|ru|bic (chə rü′bik), *adj.* **1** of or like a cherub; angelic: [*He*] *had a round, cherubic face for a man who drove such a formidable machine* (Harper's). **2** innocent; good. **3** chubby. —**che|ru′bi|cal|ly,** *adv.*

cher|u|bim (cher′ə bim, -yu̇-), *n.* **1** a plural of **cherub. 2** (formerly) a cherub. **3** *British.* a provincial name of the barn owl.

cher|vil (chėr′vəl), *n.* **1** an herb of the parsley family, whose fragrant young leaves, roots, and seeds are used to flavor soups, and salads. **2** any one of various related plants. [Old English *cerfille* < Latin *caere folium* < Greek *chairéphyllon* < *chaire-,* of uncertain origin + *phýllon* leaf]

cher|vo|nets (cher vô′nets), *n., pl.* **-von|tsi** (-vôn′tsē). **1** a monetary unit of the Soviet Union before March 1, 1936. It was worth ten gold rubles. **2** a gold coin of this value. [< Russian *chervonec* < dialectal *chervonyj* red < Polish *czerwony*]

Ches|a|peake Bay retriever (ches′ə pēk), any one of a breed of hunting dogs developed in the United States for use in retrieving ducks. It has a thick, oily coat which enables it to work in cold, rough waters.

Chesh|ire (chesh′ər, -ir), *n.* **1** a white, medium-sized breed of hog. **2** = Cheshire cat. [< *Cheshire,* a county in England]

Cheshire cat, 1 the grinning cat in *Alice in Wonderland.* It faded away until only its grin was left. **2** any creature that grins fixedly.
grin like a Cheshire cat, to show the gums and teeth in smiling: *Mr. Newcome says . . . "that woman grins like a Cheshire cat"* (Thackeray).

Cheshire cheese, a hard cheese made from unskimmed cow's milk in the county of Cheshire,

England, either without coloring, white, or colored a carroty red. Some red Cheshire cheese develops a blue veining as it ripens.

Chesh|van (ʜesh′van), *n.* = Heshvan.

∗**chess**[1] (ches), *n.* a game played by two persons each with 16 pieces, which can be moved in different ways on a board marked off into 64 squares of two alternating colors. The pieces are the king, queen, two bishops, two knights, two rooks, and eight pawns. Players make alternate moves, each seeking to checkmate the other's king. [short for Old French *esches,* earlier *eschecs,* plural of *eschec;* see etym. under **check**]

∗**chess**[1]

chessboard with pieces:

pawn, rook, knight, bishop, queen, king, bishop, knight, rook

chess[2] (ches), *n., pl.* **chess** or **chess|es.** one of the crosswise planks which form the road of a pontoon bridge. [Middle English *chess* layer, tier]

chess[3] (ches), *n. U.S.* **1** any one of various brome grasses, especially a plant often growing as a weed in wheat fields; cheat. **2** the darnel, a weed that looks somewhat like rye. [perhaps < *chess*[2]]

chess|board (ches′bôrd′, -bōrd′), *n.* = checkerboard.

chess|man (ches′man′, -mən), *n., pl.* **-men.** one of the pieces used in playing chess.

Ches|sy cat (ches′ē), = Cheshire cat.

ches|sy|lite (ches′ə līt), *n.* azurite, a blue copper ore. [< *Chessy,* a town near Lyons, France + English *-lite*]

∗**chest** (chest), *n.* **1a** the front part of the human body between the neck and the abdomen. It is enclosed by the ribs. **SYN:** thorax. **b** the corresponding part in other animals. **2** a large box with a lid, used for holding things: *a linen chest, a medicine chest, a tool chest.* **3a** a large box or case in which certain commodities, such as tea or sugar, are packed for transport. **b** *Commerce.* a variable measure of quantity for such commodities, now almost confined to tea chests. **4** a piece of furniture with drawers: *Mother put the shirts in my clothes chest.* **5** *Machinery.* a tight container for gas, steam, or other fluid under pressure. **6a** a place in which money is kept; treasury. **b** the money itself.

get (something) **off one's chest,** *Informal.* to express troubling thoughts, knowledge, or feelings and unburden oneself: *This director has accumulated a considerable number of grudges. In his book ... he gets a good many off his chest* (Listener).

play it (or **one's cards**) **close to the chest,** *Informal.* to act cautiously or secretively: *The FBI was either playing it close to the chest or there was not enough evidence for them to proceed* (London Times).

[Old English *cest, cist* < Latin *cista* < Greek *kístē* box]

-chested, *combining form.* having a ___ chest: *Broad-chested = having a broad chest.*

∗**ches|ter|field** (ches′tər fēld), *n.* **1** a single-breasted overcoat with the buttons hidden and a velvet collar: *Among the disputants was a second man in a homburg, who was wearing a slightly seedy chesterfield ...* (New Yorker). **2** *British, Canadian.* a large overstuffed sofa. [< the fourth Earl of *Chesterfield*]

∗**chesterfield**
definition 1

Ches|ter|field|i|an (ches′tər fēl′dē ən), *adj.* of or suggestive of the fourth Earl of Chesterfield (1694-1773) whose letters to his son contain directions as to manners and etiquette.

ches|ter|lite (ches′tər līt), *n.* a variety of potash feldspar, occurring in small white crystals implanted on dolomite. [< *Chester* County, Pennsylvania, where it is found + *-lite*]

Ches|ter|ton|i|an (ches′tər tō′nē ən), *adj.* of or characteristic of the English writer G. K. Chesterton (1874-1936) or his style of writing.

Ches|ter White (ches′tər), a kind of large, white hog believed to have originated in Chester County, Pennsylvania.

chest|ful (chest′fu̇l), *n., pl.* **-fuls.** as much or as many as a chest can hold: *He was awarded a chestful of decorations* (Newsweek).

chest|ni|tsa (chest′ni tsə), *n.* a Serbian Christmas cake containing a silver coin which is supposed to bring good luck to the person who finds it in his piece of cake. [< Serbo-Croatian *česnica*]

chest note, = chest tone.

∗**chestnut**
definitions 2, 4

chestnut:

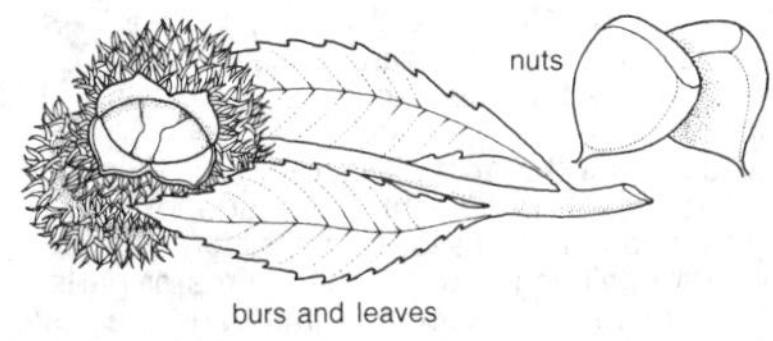

burs and leaves

horse chestnut:

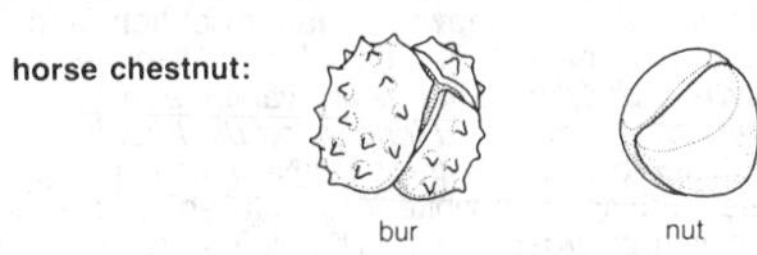

bur nut

∗**chest|nut** (ches′nut, -nət), *n., adj.* —*n.* **1** a large tree that bears nuts in prickly burs. The chestnut belongs to the beech family. **2** the sweet nut of this tree. It is good to eat. **3** the wood of this tree. **4** = horse chestnut. **5** Also, **chestnut brown.** a reddish brown. **6** a reddish-brown horse. **7** the hard knob in the skin of a horse at the inner side of the foreleg. **8** *Informal, Figurative.* a stale joke, story, or piece of music; cliché: *This bouncy cornucopia of musical comedy chestnuts seemed okay for most of the audience* (Wall Street Journal).

—***adj.*** reddish-brown.

pull (someone's) **chestnuts out of the fire,** to help someone out of a difficulty at one's own risk; assume another's burden or hardship: *"More and more I see the big cities turning to the suburbs to pull their chestnuts out of the fire," Mr. Caso declared* (New York Times).

[earlier phrase *chesten nut* < obsolete *chesten* chestnut tree < Old French *chastaigne* < Latin *castanea* < Greek *kastanéā* < *kástana* chestnut; origin uncertain]

chest|nut-backed chickadee (ches′nut bakt′), a kind of chickadee having a brown back, common along the Pacific coast of North America.

chestnut blight, **1** a fungous disease of the chestnut tree: *Forest tree diseases such as the chestnut blight about 20 years ago, can wipe out entire species* (Science News Letter). **2** the fungus that causes it.

chestnut brown, = chestnut; a reddish brown.

chest|nut-sid|ed warbler (ches′nut sī′did), a warbler with a yellow crown and chestnut sides in the spring plumage, found in eastern North America.

chest of drawers, an article of furniture with drawers for clothing, linen, or other items for storage.

chest-on-chest (chest′on chest′, -ôn-), *n.* an article of furniture consisting of two chests with drawers, usually a smaller one on top of a larger one.

chest protector, **1** a warm cover for the chest, as of flannel. **2** a padded piece of equipment worn on the chest especially by baseball catchers and ice hockey goalies.

chest register, the lower range of a voice, especially in singing.

chest-thump|ing (chest′thum′ping), *n.* boasting: *Heaven knows, we've done enough chest-thumping for one ad* (New Yorker).

chest tone, a tone produced in the lower range of the voice.

chest voice, = chest register.

chest|y (ches′tē), *adj.,* **chest|i|er, chest|i|est.** *U.S. Slang.* **1** conceited; self-assertive: *bumbling doctors, madcap crooks, chesty admirals and busty dowagers* (Time). **2** thrusting out the chest; broad-chested. —**chest′i|ly,** *adv.* —**chest′i|ness,** *n.*

che|tah (chē′tə), *n.* = cheetah.

cheth (ʜet, ʜeth, ʜes), *n.* = heth.

chet|nik (chet′nik), *n., pl.* **chet|ni|ci** (chet′ni tsi), **-niks.** a member of a Yugoslav guerrilla force that originated in 1904 and was active in the Balkan Wars in World War I, and against the Nazis during World War II. [< Serbian *chetnik* < *cheta* band]

che|val-de-frise (shə väl′də frēz′), *n., pl.* **chevaux-de-frise. 1** a piece of wood with spikes sticking out, formerly used to hinder the advance of enemy cavalry: *Let us sink in our channel some chevaux-de-frise—And then let 'em come* (Philip Freneau). **2** a row of spikes or broken glass on top of a wall. [< French *cheval-de-frise* (literally) horse of Friesland (because they were first used by Frisians to make up for lack of cavalry)]

che|val glass (shə val′), a tall mirror mounted in a frame so that it swings between its supports. [< French *cheval* (literally) support; horse < Old French < Latin *caballus* a nag]

chev|a|lier (shev′ə lir′), *n.* **1** *Archaic.* a knight: *The Young Chevalier was Charles Edward Stuart, the Young Pretender, grandson of James II of England.* **2** a member of the lowest rank in the Legion of Honor of France. **3** in the French nobility: **a** a noble of the lowest rank. **b** a younger son. **4** a chivalrous man; a lady's cavalier; gallant. [< Old French *chevalier* < Late Latin *caballārius.* See etym. of doublets **caballero, cavalier.**]

chev|al|resque (shev′əl resk′), *adj.* = chivalresque.

che|vaux-de-frise (shə vō′də frēz′), *n.* plural of **cheval-de-frise.**

che|ve|lure (shə və lyr′), *n. French.* **1** the hair of the head; a head of hair. **2** *Obsolete.* a wig.

chev|er|el or **chev|er|il** (chev′ər əl), *n.* = kidskin. [< Old French *chevrel* kid < *chevre* < Latin *capra,* feminine of *caper* goat]

che|vet (shə ve′), *n. Architecture.* the apse, or the termination of the apse, of a church, especially the apsidal end of a church when consisting of a main apse and several (usually five) secondary apses or chapels radiating from it. [< French *chevet* < Medieval Latin *capitium* head (upper end) of church < Latin *caput* head]

Chev|i|ot (chev′ē ət, chē′vē-), *n.* a hardy breed of sheep with heavy bodies and fine, thick-set wool, that originated in the Cheviot Hills, on the

bones of the chest:

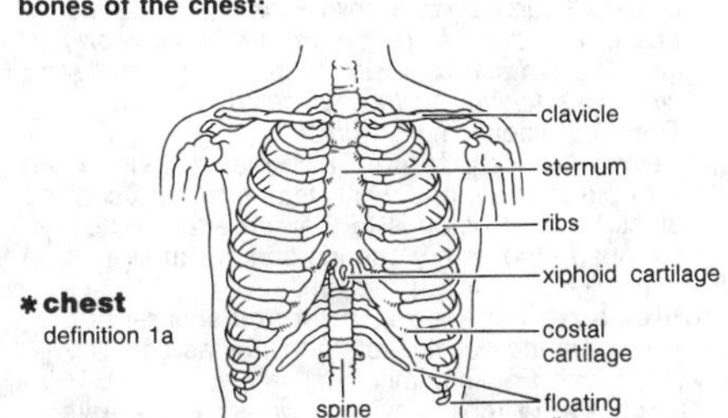

∗**chest**
definition 1a

organs of the chest:

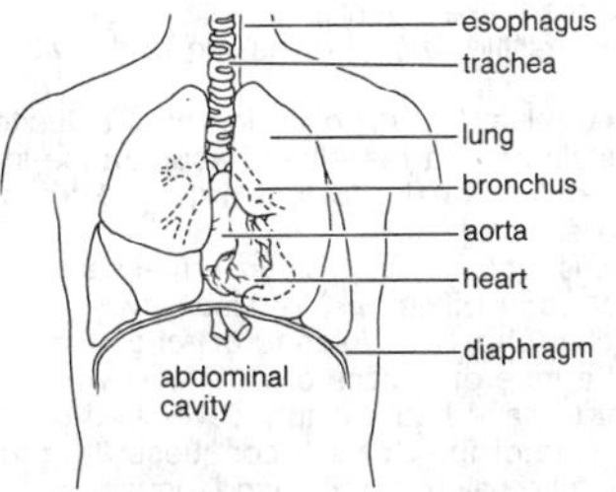

boundary between England and Scotland.
chev|i|ot (shev′ē ət), *n.* **1** a rough, woolen cloth. **2** a cotton cloth like it. [< *Cheviot*]
chev|on (chev′ən), *n.* the meat of a goat. [< French *chèv*(re) goat + English (mutt)*on*]
chè|vre (shev′rə), *n.* a French cheese made from goats' milk. [< French *chèvre* (literally) goat]
***chev|ron** (shev′rən), *n.* **1** a cloth design in the shape of the letter V, either right side up or upside down. It is shaped like ∧ or ∨, worn on the sleeve by noncommissioned officers, policemen, and members of other groups, as an indication of rank, length of service, or wounds in war. **2** a design shaped like the letter V upside down, used in coats of arms and in architecture. [< Middle French *chevron* rafter; later, angled band < *chevre, chievre* goat < Latin *capra* she-goat]

***chevron** definition 1

chevron bone, a V-shaped bone articulating with, and forming an inverted arch beneath, the spinal column of many vertebrates, especially in the caudal region. The series of such bones forms a canal through which blood vessels run.
chev|roned (shev′rənd), *adj.* decorated with chevrons.
chev|ron|wise (shev′rən wīz′), *adv. Heraldry.* in the manner of a chevron; with the lines divided in the direction of a chevron.
chev|ro|tain (shev′rə tān, -tən), *n.* any one of a family of small, hornless, deerlike, cud-chewing animals of Asia and Africa; mouse deer. [< Old French *chevrotain* < *chevrot* kid (diminutive) < *chevre, chievre,* ultimately < Latin *capra* she-goat]
chev|y (chev′ē), *n., pl.* **chev|ies,** *v.,* **chev|ied, chev|y|ing.** —*n.* **1** a hunting cry. **2** a hunt; chase.
—*v.t.* **1** to hunt; chase: *One poor fellow was chevied about among the casks in the storm for about ten minutes* (London Times). **2** to worry.
—*v.i.* to scamper; race. [short for *Chevy Chase,* from the ballad of that name]
chew (chü), *v., n.* —*v.t.* **1** to crush or grind with the teeth; masticate: *He chewed a mouthful of meat but it was too much to swallow.* **2** *Figurative.* to think over (advice, opinions, statements, or anything else); consider.
—*v.i.* **1** to use the jaws and teeth, or toothlike parts, in order to crush or grind something; bite; champ. **2** *Informal.* to chew tobacco. **3** *Figurative.* to think something over; meditate: *When you come to look at it all around, and chew at it and think it over, don't it just* [*outdo*] *anything you ever heard of?* (Mark Twain).
—*n.* **1** the act of chewing: *The puppy left the shredded rag after a good chew.* **2** a bite; the thing chewed; a piece for chewing: *He broke off a good chew of tobacco.*
chew out, *Slang.* to scold severely; reprimand: *The other day I listened to a guy six-foot-four ... chewing out a five-foot-four assistant manager ...* (Robert T. Allen).
chew the fat. See under **fat.**
chew the rag. See under **rag.**
chew up, a to destroy: *Predators kill what is most easily available. ... They don't chew up what can't be replaced* (New Scientist). **b** to consume: *Defense expenditures for military functions ... chew up 41 per cent of the budget* (New York Times).
[Old English *cēowan*] —**chew′a|ble,** *adj.*
chew|er (chü′ər), *n.* **1** a person who chews (gum, tobacco, food). **2** *Figurative.* a person who meditates or studies a problem. **3** a ruminant animal, such as a cow, goat, or sheep.
chew|ing gum (chü′ing), gum for chewing. It is usually chicle that has been sweetened and flavored.
chewing louse, = biting louse.
chew|ings fescue (chü′ingz), a variety of red fescue, which grows in a thick mat of fine leaves and is used for lawns and golf courses.
chewing stick, a piece of fibrous wood with a frayed end, widely used in Asia and Africa for removing bits of food between the teeth: *There is quite an art in using the chewing stick. First the end must be chewed until the brushlike tip is produced. This is then rubbed up and down the surfaces of the teeth* (New Scientist).
che|wink (chē wingk′), *n.* a bird of eastern and central North America whose cry sounds somewhat like its name; towhee. The chewink is a kind of finch. [imitative]
chew|y (chü′ē), *adj.,* **chew|i|er, chew|i|est.** requiring much chewing: *tough chewy meat.*
—**chew′i|ness,** *n.*

Chey|enne (shī en′), *n., pl.* **-enne** or **-ennes.** **1** a member of an Algonkian tribe of American Indians, now living in Montana and Oklahoma. **2** their language. [American English < Siouan (Santee Dakota) *Shahi'yena* people of alien speech]
Cheyne-Stokes breathing or **Cheyne-Stokes respiration** (chān′stōks′), *Medicine.* a type of abnormal breathing found in certain cerebral and cardiac disorders, characterized by alternating periods of heavy, agonized breathing and of temporary suspension of breath. [< John *Cheyne,* 1777-1836, a Scottish physician, and William *Stokes,* 1804-1878, an Irish physician, both of whom described it]
chez (shā), *prep. French.* at the home or establishment of; at: *There was merely time for an hors d'oeuvre—a quick circuit of the suburbs ... followed by an informal dinner party chez Mothersill* (New Yorker).
chf., chief.
chg., *pl.* **chgs.** charge.
chgd., charged.
***chi** (kī), *n.* the 22nd letter of the Greek alphabet, corresponding to the sound represented by *k* and the spelling *ch* in English. [< Greek *chî*]

***chi**

Χ	χ
capital letter	lower-case letter

chi|a (chē′ä), *n.* **1** any one of several species of salvia, of Mexico and the southwestern United States, the seeds of which are used as food and in the preparation of a mucilaginous beverage. **2** the seeds. **3** the beverage. [American English < Mexican Spanish *chía* < a Nahuatl word]
chi|ack (chī′ək), *v.t. Australian Slang.* to jeer at; tease. [probably alteration of *cheek,* verb]
Chi|an (kī′ən), *adj., n.* —*adj.* of or having to do with the Greek island of Chios: *freighted with amber grapes and Chian wine* (Matthew Arnold).
—*n.* a native or inhabitant of Chios.
Chi|an|ti (ki än′tē, -an′-), *n.* **1** a dry, red Italian wine. **2** a similar wine made elsewhere. [< Italian *chianti* < the *Chianti* Mountains, Tuscany, Italy]
chiao (jou), *n., pl.* **chiao.** a Chinese unit of money equal to 1/10 of a yuan. Each chiao is worth ten fen. [< Chinese *chiao*]
chi|a|ro-o|scu|ro (kē är′ō ə skyůr′ō), *n., pl.* **-ros.** = chiaroscuro.
chi|a|ro|scu|rist (kē är′ə skyůr′ist), *n., adj.* —*n.* an artist who draws in chiaroscuro.
—*adj.* executed in chiaroscuro, or by a chiaroscurist.
chi|a|ro|scu|ro (kē är′ə skyůr′ō), *n., pl.* **-ros.** **1** the treatment of the light and shade, or brighter and darker masses, in a picture. **2** a method of painting in which the figures or parts of main interest are strongly lighted and the rest painted in deep shadow, the pattern of light and dark predominating over that of color: *Gentle chiaroscuro, offspring of veiled values and translucent undertones, had long since died behind the prison bars of abstract art* (New Yorker). **3** a sketch in black and white. Also, **clair-obscure.** [< Italian *chiaroscuro* (literally) clear-dark < Latin *clārus* clear + *obscūrus* obscure]
chi|asm (kī′az əm), *n.* = chiasma.
chi|as|ma (kī az′mə), *n., pl.* **-ma|ta** (-mə|tə). **1** *Anatomy.* a crossing or intersecting, especially that of the optic nerve fibers at the base of the brain. **2** the point of interchange of two chromatids during meiosis, resulting in a cross-shaped figure. [< Greek *chíasma* a crossed arrangement < *chiázein* to mark, or arrange, like χ (chi)]
chi|as|mal (kī az′məl), *adj.* of the nature of a chiasma.
chi|as|ma|typ|y (kī az′mə tī′pē), *n.* the theory that chiasmata during meiosis represent points where a crossing over of genetic material has taken place.
chi|as|mic (kī az′mik), *adj.* = chiasmal.
chi|as|mus (kī az′məs), *n., pl.* **-mi** (-mī). a figure of speech in which the order of words in one of two parallel clauses is inverted in the other. *Example:* Die there; there lie. [< Greek *chiasmós* < *chiázein* to mark like χ (chi)]
chi|as|tic (kī as′tik), *adj.* of or having to do with chiasmus.
chi|as|to|lite (kī as′tə līt), *n.* a kind of andalusite whose crystals have a tessellated appearance in cross section. [< Greek *chiastós* arranged crosswise + English *-lite*]
chiaus (chous, choush), *n.* a Turkish messenger, sergeant, or court officer. [< Turkish *çavuş*]
Chib|cha (chib′chə), *n., pl.* **-chas** or **-cha.** **1** a member of a tribe of Indians of Colombia who are thought to have had a highly developed culture at the time of the Spanish conquest. **2** an Indian of any tribe using a Chibchan language. **3** the language of the ancient Chibchas.
Chib|chan (chib′chən), *adj.* **1** of or having to do with a linguistic group of South and Central American Indians. **2** of or having to do with the Chibchas or their culture.
chib|ol (chib′əl), *n.* a spring onion.
chi|bouk, chi|bouque, or **chi|buk** (chi bük′, -bůk′), *n.* a Turkish tobacco pipe with a clay bowl and a very long, wooden stem, sometimes measuring five feet. [< Turkish *çubuk* (literally) tube, small stick]
chic (shēk, shik), *adj.,* **chic|er, chic|est** or **chic-quer, chic|quest,** *n.* —*adj.* up-to-date in fashion; stylish: *... a frothy plot about a silly girl who thinks it very chic to talk in French* (Harper's). ... *a chic gown whipped up by her favorite American designer* (Life).
—*n.* **1** elegant or skillful style: *A traveller* [*in Russia*] *will at once be struck by the absence of chic and by the shapeless nature of women's clothes* (J. V. Davidson-Houston). **2** fashion; vogue: *Historical fiction ..., unhappily, does not have much chic these days* (David Boroff).
[< French *chic,* probably < German *Schick* for *Geschick* dexterity, knack]
Chi|ca|go (shə kô′gō, -kä′-), *n.* a variety of contract bridge in which a rubber consists of four deals. [< *Chicago,* Illinois, where it was introduced]
Chi|ca|go|an (shə kô′gō ən, -kä′-), *n.* a native or inhabitant of Chicago, Illinois.
Chicago brick, a kind of ice cream consisting of layers of caramel and vanilla ice creams with a layer of orange ice in between.
chi|ca|lo|te (chē′kä lō′tā), *n.* any one of several prickly poppies of the southwestern United States and Mexico, especially a white-flowered species and the Mexican poppy. [American English < Mexican Spanish *chicalote* < Nahuatl *chicalotl*]
chi|cane (shi kān′), *n., v.,* **-caned, -can|ing.** —*n.* **1** = chicanery. **2** a hand without trumps, in certain card games. **3** *British.* **a** a raceway, especially a track for automobile racing. **b** a sharp turn on a raceway.
—*v.i.* to use chicanery.
—*v.t.* **1** to get by chicanery. **2** to quibble over.
[< Middle French *chicane* < *chicaner* quibble]
chi|can|er|y (shi kā′nər ē), *n., pl.* **-er|ies.** **1** low trickery; unfair practice; quibbling: *He used chicanery to outwit his partner and take over the business.* SYN: pettifogging. **2** a quibble or subterfuge; trick: *a legal chicanery.* SYN: deception.
Chi|ca|no (chē kä′nō), *n., pl.* **-nos,** *adj.* —*n.* a person living in the United States who was born in Mexico or descends from persons born in Mexico; a Mexican American: *Like the blacks, Mexican Americans who are known as Chicanos, are a varied and diverse people* (Time).
—*adj.* Mexican American: *Chicano farmers, a Chicano organization.*
[< Mexican Spanish (Chihuahua) dialect *Chicano,* alteration of *Mexicano* Mexican]
▶Some speakers and writers believe that *Chicano* is a derogatory term and avoid using it. However, many Mexican Americans apply the name to themselves and do not regard it as unfriendly in any way.
chic|co|ry (chik′ər ē), *n., pl.* **-ries.** = chicory.
chi|cha (chē′chä), *n.* a fermented liquor made from maize, sugar cane, and other plants by certain Indians of South America. [< Spanish *chicha* < a native word]
chi|chi or **chi-chi** (shē′shē′, chē′chē′), *adj., n.* —*adj.* self-consciously or pretentiously ornate so as to be overelegant; elaborately chic; arty: *This small company keeps up a very reasonable standard for its ballets—though they are inclined to be chichi* (New Statesman).
—*n.* affected or pretentious chic; artiness: *The* [*art*] *collector must be in a high tax bracket or he wouldn't be collecting in the first place.* (*This habit, I think is pure chichi*) (Robert M. Coates).
[< French *chichi*]
chick (chik), *n.* **1** a young chicken, especially one that is just hatched: *The little yellow chicks were covered with down and had no feathers yet.* **2** a young bird, especially one still in the egg or only just hatched: *The robin had a nest of three chicks.* **3** *Figurative.* a child: *The child was just a chick, too young to be on the streets.* **4** *Slang.* a girl: *The old subway used to be a very gay time with guys taking out their chicks* (New York Times). [Middle English *chicke*]
chick|a|dee (chik′ə dē), *n.* a small American bird with black, gray, and white feathers and usually a black head. It belongs to the same family as the titmouse, and its cry sounds somewhat like its name. [American English; imitative]
chick|a|ree (chik′ə rē), *n.* the red squirrel of North America or the related Douglas squirrel. [American English; imitative]
Chick|a|saw (chik′ə sô), *n., pl.* **-saw** or **-saws.** **1** a member of a tribe of American Indians, for-

merly of Mississippi, now living in Oklahoma. **2** their Muskhogean language.

chick|ee (chik'ē), *n.* a Seminole Indian dwelling, consisting of a palm-thatched hut with open sides standing on a platform raised about three feet from the ground. [< the Muskhogean name]

chick|en¹ (chik'ən), *n., adj., v.* —*n.* **1** any hen or rooster: *Most of our chickens lay two to three eggs per day.* See picture at **poultry**. **2a** a young hen or rooster; chick: *Our new chickens are too young to lay eggs.* **b** any young bird: *The grouse flew at the fox to protect her chickens.* **3** the flesh of a chicken used for food: *We all ate the crisp fried chicken.* **4** *Figurative.* **a** a young person, especially one who is inexperienced: *He must have been well forward in years—or at all events, as they say, no chicken* (E. Walford). **b** *Slang.* a young woman or girl; chick. **5** *Slang.* **a** *Figurative.* a person who is afraid, especially one who is cowardly: *"You'd think we didn't have fighters or atom bombs. To them we seem like chickens"* (Wall Street Journal). **b** a dare or challenge to do something dangerous as a test of courage, viewed as a game: *The motorists were always playing "chicken." One driver will challenge another by refusing to give way before him* (New Yorker). *The Kenya Opposition party appears to be challenging the Government to a game of chicken* (Manchester Guardian Weekly). **6** *U.S. Slang.* petty discipline; unnecessary duties, especially in the armed forces.
—***adj.*** **1** young; small: *a chicken lobster.* **2** *Slang, Figurative.* afraid of risk; cowardly: *"When they asked me to go along with them, I had to," a gang member explained. "If I didn't go along, they'd know I was chicken and I couldn't live around here any more"* (Newsweek).
—***v.i.*** **chicken out,** *Slang.* to behave in a cowardly manner, especially to refuse a dare: *It is a point of honor not to "chicken out" on anything the gang does* (Newsweek).
(have one's) chickens come home to roost, (have) something bad result from one's own actions; (receive) something asked for or deserved: *That the ... sales should be threatened by a competitor which uses the Swallow wing* [*that he rejected*] *is a somewhat bitter instance of chickens coming home to roost* (New Scientist).
count one's chickens (before they are hatched), to trust or count on something as a certainty before it has actually happened: *Some have been suffering with stuffy, runny noses ... Others* (*although they would not be wise to count their chickens*) *were surprisingly symptom-free* (New York Times).
[Old English *cīcen, cīken*]

chick|en² (chik'ən), *n.* (in India) embroidery. [< Hindustani *chikan* < Persian *chikin* needlework]

chick|en-and-egg (chik'ən ənd eg'), *adj.* involving the dilemma of not knowing which of two things is the cause and which the effect: *The chicken-and-egg argument over slave status and race prejudice—which came first and which caused which ...* (Harper's).

chicken breast, a malformed projection of the breastbone, often associated with rickets; pigeon breast.

chick|en-breast|ed (chik'ən bres'tid), *adj.* having chicken breast.

chicken cac|cia|to|re (kä'chə tō'rē), pieces of chicken cooked in a sauce with tomato paste and wine. [< Italian *cacciatore* < *cacciare* to chase]

chicken cholera, = fowl cholera.

chicken colonel, *U.S. Slang.* a full colonel, whose insigne is an eagle (as distinguished from a lieutenant colonel, whose insigne is a leaf): *"What we got was real pros," says a regular chicken colonel at Phan Rang* (Time).

chicken feed, *Especially U.S. Slang.* **1** a trifling amount of money; small coins. **2** any small undertaking: *The export of U.S. poultry to Europe's Common Market is chicken feed in terms of the total trade* (Wall Street Journal).

chicken fixings, *U.S. Informal.* **1** chicken prepared for eating, as contrasted with less esteemed food. **2** *Figurative.* anything nice or better than usual in the way of food: *We don't have any of your chicken fixings nor little three-cornered handkerchiefs laid out at each plate* (Mary J. Holmes).

chicken hawk, any one of certain hawks that raid poultry yards, such as the sharp-shinned hawk of North America; bird hawk; hen hawk.

chicken hazard, a game with dice.

chick|en-heart|ed (chik'ən här'tid), *adj.* timid; cowardly: *Small thanks to you big, hulking, chicken-hearted men* (Robert Louis Stevenson).

chicken lettuce, lettuce grown by farmers to feed poultry and rabbits.

chick|en-liv|ered (chik'ən liv'ərd), *adj.* timid; cowardly.

chicken louse, any one of several parasitic insects related to bird lice, that infest poultry and pheasants.

chicken mite, a mite that burrows into the skin of fowls, causing loss of vigor and development; chicken tick. Sometimes they infest human beings, causing acariasis. *The common chicken mite ... like the bedbug, sucks the blood of its victims at night and hides in cracks during the day* (Edward A. Chapin).

chicken paprika, chicken spiced with onions and paprika, fried in a pan.

chicken plover, = ruddy turnstone.

chicken pox, a mild, contagious disease of children, accompanied by a rash on the skin; varicella. Chicken pox is a viral disease.

chicken snake, one of several American snakes which eat chickens and eggs; rat snake.

chicken switch, *U.S. Slang.* a switch that releases a rocket with which the pilot of an aborted flight can escape from the aircraft or space vehicle.

chicken thief, *U.S. Informal.* **1** a petty thief; pilferer. **2** a river boat formerly used for small retail trading, so called because its presence encouraged the stealing of chickens and other goods.

chicken tick, = chicken mite.

chicken wire, a light wire netting with mesh of about one inch, used extensively on farms as fence material: *One strip of the mesa was fenced off with chicken wire* (New Yorker).

chick|let (chik'lit), *n. U.S. Slang.* a young woman or girl: *There is some show-stopping* (*if irrelevant*) *footwork by a trio of pretty chicklets* (Time). [< *chick* + *-let*]

chick|ling (chik'ling), *n.,* or **chickling vetch,** a European vetch cultivated for its edible seeds, and also used as a forage plant. [earlier *chicheling* (diminutive) < Middle English *chiche* < Old French; see etym. under **chickpea**]

chick|pea (chik'pē'), *n.* **1** an annual plant of the pea family. Its short, puffy pods contain pealike seeds which are used for food. **2** one of these seeds. [earlier *chich pease,* an assumed plural < *chiche* pea < Old French, alteration of *cice,* learned borrowing from Latin *cicer*]

chick|weed (chik'wēd'), *n.* a common weed with small white flowers. Chickweed belongs to the pink family. The leaves and seeds of many kinds are eaten by birds.

chic|le (chik'əl), *n.,* or **chicle gum,** a tasteless, gummy substance used in making chewing gum. It is the milky juice of the sapodilla tree of tropical America, boiled and kneaded to take out the water. [American English < Mexican Spanish *chicle* < Nahuatl *tzictli*]

chic|ly (shēk'lē, shik'-), *adv.* in a chic manner; stylishly.

chic|ness (shēk'nis, shik'-), *n.* chic quality or condition; elegance; style.

chi|co (chē'kō), *n., pl.* **-cos.** *Western U.S.* the greasewood, a stiff, prickly shrub growing in alkaline regions. [American English; short for Mexican Spanish *chicalote* chicalote]

Chi|com (chī'kəm), *adj., n. U.S.* Chinese Communist.

***chic|o|ry** (chik'ər ē), *n., pl.* **-ries. 1** a plant with blue, pink, or white flowers, whose leaves are used for salad. Chicory belongs to the composite family. **2** a plant of the same genus with bright-blue flowers; succory. **3** its root, roasted and used as a substitute for coffee or for mixing with coffee. **4** *British.* endive. Also, **chiccory.** [< Middle French *cichorée,* learned borrowing from Latin *cichoreum* < Greek *kichóreion* endive]

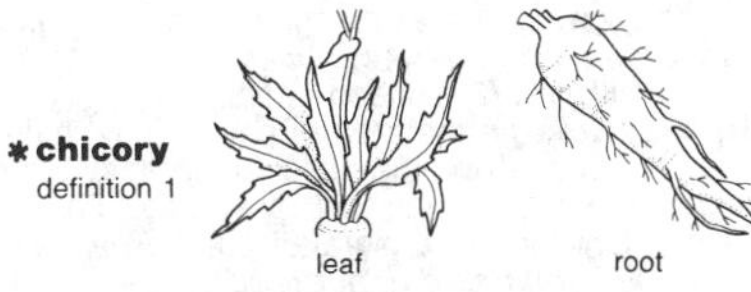

***chicory**
definition 1

chid (chid), *v.* chided; a past tense and a past participle of **chide**: *Only yesterday the foreman chid him for being late. How churlishly I chid Lucetta hence!* (Shakespeare).

chid|den (chid'ən), *v.* chided; a past participle of **chide**: *Vain desire was chidden* (Anthony Munday).

chide (chīd), *v.,* **chid|ed** or **chid, chid|ed, chid,** or **chid|den, chid|ing.** —*v.t.* to find fault with; blame; scold; reproach: *The waitress chided me for knocking my glass on the restaurant floor.* **SYN:** rebuke, reprove, reprimand. See syn. under **scold.**
—*v.i.* to find fault; speak in rebuke: *The old caretaker was always scolding and chiding.* **SYN:** rebuke, reprove, reprimand. See syn. under **scold.**
[Old English *cīdan*] —**chid'er,** *n.* —**chid'ing|ly,** *adv.*

chief (chēf), *n., adj.* —*n.* **1** the head of a group; person highest in rank or authority; leader: *the chief of police.* **2** the head of a tribe or clan: *Sacred chiefs are believed to radiate supernatural power harmful to untitled commoners* (Beals and Hoijer). **3** *Heraldry.* the upper third of an escutcheon.
—***adj.*** **1** at the head; highest in rank or authority; leading: *the state's chief fiscal officer, the embassy's chief secretary, the chief engineer of a building project, the chief officer of an army post.* **2** most important; main; principal: *the chief town in the county. The chief reason for going to school is to learn.* **SYN:** foremost, prime, essential, cardinal. **3** *Archaic.* like a chief; with the manner of a chief.
in chief, at the head; of the highest rank or authority: *commander in chief of the army, editor in chief of a book.*
[< Old French *chief* < Latin *caput, -itis* head. See etym. of doublet **chef.**] —**chief'less,** *adj.*

chief constable, a police chief of a county or an equivalent district, in Great Britain.

chief|dom (chēf'dəm), *n.* the position, dominion, or authority of a chief: *Every Ashanti is by birth a citizen of the chiefdom to which his maternal lineage belongs* (Scientific American).

chief executive, the head of the executive branch of a government or large corporation.

Chief Executive, the President of the United States or the governor of a state.

chief justice, a judge who acts as chairman of a group of judges in a court.

Chief Justice, the presiding justice of the United States Supreme Court. *Abbr:* C.J.

chief|ly (chēf'lē), *adv., adj.* —**adv. 1** for the most part; mainly; mostly: *This vegetable juice is made up chiefly of tomatoes.* **SYN:** essentially. **2** first of all; above all: *We visited Washington chiefly to see the Capitol and the White House.* **SYN:** especially, principally.
—***adj.*** of or proper to a chief: *chiefly status.*

chief magistrate, the highest official or magistrate of a government, such as a country's monarch or president, the governor of a state, or the mayor of a city.

chief master sergeant, a noncommissioned officer in the U.S. Air Force who ranks next above a senior master sergeant.

chief of staff, the senior officer of the staff of a general or admiral.

Chief of Staff, the senior officer of the Army or Air Force of the United States.

chief of state, the formal or ceremonial head of a country or nation, as distinguished from the prime minister or chancellor who heads the government. In the United States, the President is both the chief of state and the Chief Executive.

chief petty officer, the highest grade noncommissioned officer in the U.S. and British navies.

chief|ship (chēf'ship), *n.* **1** the position or authority of a chief. **2** a state ruled by a chief: *The ordinary Briton never gives these native kingdoms, principalities and chiefships a thought* (London Daily News).

chief|tain (chēf'tən), *n.* **1** the chief of a clan or tribe: *a Highland chieftain.* **2** a head of a group; leader: *Labor chieftains kept a discreet silence* (Time). **3** *Poetic.* a military leader; a captain. [< Old French *chevetaine* < Late Latin *capitāneus* < Latin *caput* head. See etym. of doublet **captain.**]

chief|tain|cy (chēf'tən sē), *n., pl.* **-cies.** the position or rank of a chieftain.

chief|tain|ess (chēf'tə nis), *n.* a woman chieftain.

chief|tain|ship (chēf'tən ship), *n.* = chieftaincy.

chiel (chēl), *n. Scottish.* chield.

chield (chēld), *n. Scottish.* **1** a familiar term for a man, especially a young man; lad; fellow; chap. **2** child. [variant of *child*]

Chi'en Lung (chē en' lúng'), of or designating the period of the mid-1700's in Chinese pottery and art work. [< *Ch'ien Lung,* 1711-99, the emperor of China from 1736 to 1796]

chiff|chaff (chif'chaf', -chäf'), *n.* a warbler of Europe with a distinctive call indicated by its name. [imitative]

chif|fon (shi fon', shif'on), *n., adj.* —*n.* a very thin silk, nylon, or rayon fabric, used especially for blouses and evening dresses.
—***adj.*** whipped light and fluffy: *lemon chiffon pie.*
chiffons, laces, ribbons, or finery: *It would stand out well among the fashionable chiffons* (George Eliot).
[< French *chiffon* < *chiffe* rag]

Pronunciation Key: hat, āge, cãre, fär; let, ēqual, tėrm; it, īce; hot, ōpen, ôrder; oil, out; cup, pu̇t, rüle; child; long; thin; ᴛʜen; zh, measure; ə represents **a** in about, **e** in taken, **i** in pencil, **o** in lemon, **u** in circus.

chif|fo|nier (shif′ə nir′), *n.* a high chest of drawers, often having a mirror. [< French *chiffonnier* chest of drawers < *chiffon* chiffon]

chif|fo|robe (shif′ə rōb), *n.* a piece of furniture combining a wardrobe and a chest of drawers: *The chifforobe [is] especially well suited to the storage of men's clothing* (Jean Anne Vincent). [< *chiffo*(nier) + (ward)*robe*]

***chig|ger** (chig′ər), *n.* **1** the larva of certain mites; chigoe; jigger. Chiggers stick to the skin and suck the blood, causing severe itching. *Ticks . . . and their tiny cousins, the chiggers, can make life miserable for outdoorsmen* (Science News Letter). **2** = chigoe (def. 1). [American English; apparently variant of *chigoe*]

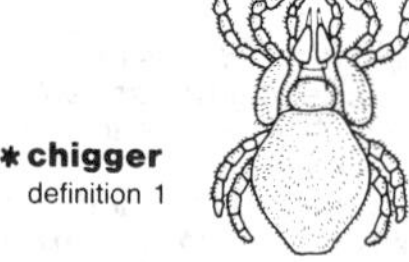

***chigger** definition 1

chi|gnon (shēn′yon; *French* shē nyôN′), *n.* a large knot or roll of hair worn at the back of the head by women: *She had . . . a massive chignon of yellow hair* (Henry James). [< French *chignon* (literally) nape of the neck < Old French *chaignon* < Vulgar Latin *catēniō* < Latin *catēna* chain (referring to the column or "chain" of vertebrae)]

***chig|oe** (chig′ō), *n.* **1** a flea of tropical America, Africa, and India; chigger; jigger. The female burrows under the skin of people and animals, where it causes severe itching and sores. **2** = chigger (def. 1). [< French *chique;* perhaps of West Indian origin]

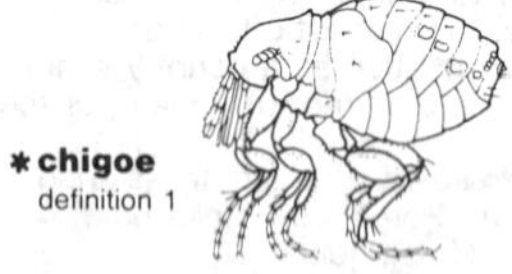

***chigoe** definition 1

chig|re (chig′ər), *n.* = chigoe.

Chi|hua|hua or **chi|hua|hua** (chē wä′wä), *n.* a very small dog of an ancient Mexican breed, usually weighing from one to six pounds. Chihuahuas range in color from solid black, to brown, to solid white and have either a short-haired or long-haired coat. [American English < *Chihuahua,* a state and city in Mexico]

chik|un|gun|ya (chik′ən gun′yə), *n.* a fever similar to dengue, common in Africa and Asia. It is caused by an arborvirus transmitted chiefly by mosquitoes. [< *Chikungunya,* a place in eastern Africa where it was identified]

chil|blain (chil′blān′), *n.* Usually, **chilblains.** an itching sore or redness on the hands or feet caused by exposure to cold: *Chilblains are caused by the defective circulation in the arms and legs, increased softening of the blood-vessel walls, and lessened clotting ability of the blood* (Marguerite Clark). [< *chil*(l) + *blain*]

chil|blained (chil′blānd′), *adj.* affected with chilblains.

child (chīld), *n., pl.* **chil|dren. 1** a young boy or girl: *games for children. The oldest child has a place of honor in most families* (Sidonie M. Gruenberg). *The child is father of the man* (William Wordsworth). **2a** a son or daughter: *children of one father, a mother's love of her child.* SYN: offspring. **b** *Law.* (in matters of inheritance) a legitimate offspring, but sometimes an adopted or illegitimate son or daughter, or a grandchild. **3** a baby; infant: *A six-month-old child cannot talk.* SYN: babe, nursling. **4** *Figurative.* Usually, **children.** a descendant: *the children of Israel.* SYN: progeny. **5** *Figurative.* a person like a child in nearness, affection, interest, or some other personal attribute. **6** an immature person; childish person. **7** *Figurative.* **a** a thing that has been produced by something else, such as a quality or necessity resulting from a force, influence, or need; result; product: *Dreams, Which are the children of an idle brain* (Shakespeare) SYN: issue. **b** a person considered as the product or result of particular agencies, forces, influences, or the like: *a child of nature, children of wrath.* **8** *British Dialect.* a female infant; daughter. **9** Often, **childe.** *Archaic.* a youth of noble birth (used in ballads and poems as a kind of title).
with child, *Archaic.* pregnant: *Such doubts and fears were common to her state, being with child* (Tennyson).
[Old English *cild; children* < Middle English *childer* (< Old English plural *childru*) + *-en,* a plural suffix]

child|bear|ing (chīld′bãr′ing), *n., adj.* —*n.* the act of giving birth to a child or children.
—*adj.* able to bear children: *of childbearing age.*

child|bed (chīld′bed′), *n.* the condition of a woman giving birth to a child; parturition.

childbed fever, an infection of the mucous lining of the uterus occurring after childbirth; puerperal fever.

child|birth (chīld′bėrth′), *n.* the act of giving birth to a child; parturition.

child bride, a very young bride; child wife.

child-care (chīld′kãr′), *adj. U.S.* of or for the care of preschool children, especially of working mothers; day-care: *childcare centers.*

childe (chīld), *n. Archaic.* a youth of noble birth; child: *Childe Roland to the dark tower came* (Robert Browning).

Chil|der|mas (chil′dər məs), *n.* December 28, Holy Innocents' Day. [Old English *cylda mæsse; cylda* of children, *mæsse* Mass]

child guidance, work with children who have emotional or social difficulties by persons trained in such fields as psychology, social work, medicine, and education.

child|hood (chīld′hůd), *n.* **1** the condition of being a child: *The transition line between infancy and childhood is an arbitrary one, which we have set . . . at about the time when the child begins to walk and talk* (Beals and Hoijer). **2** the time during which one is a child.

child|ie (chīl′dē), *n.* little child; dear little child: *"You needn't be so decided, childie," said her father* (Ethel Coxon).

child|ing (chīl′ding), *adj. Archaic.* bearing children.

child|ish (chīl′dish), *adj.* **1** of a child: *sweet childish days* (Wordsworth). **2** like a child; immature: *The little boy will outgrow his childish fear of doctors.* **3** not proper for a grown person; silly; foolish: *Crying for things you can't have is childish.* SYN: weak. [Old English *cildisc* < *cild* child + *-isc* -ish] —**child′ish|ly,** *adv.* —**child′ish|ness,** *n.*
►**Childish, childlike** differ widely in their connotations when applied to adults, though both mean resembling or having the characteristics of a child. *Childish* is derogatory since it emphasizes characteristics which one might be expected to have outgrown. *Pouting when scolded is childish. Childlike,* however, emphasizes such characteristics as innocence, simplicity, and frankness and suggests regret that most adults have lost them: *He has a childlike love for a circus.*

child labor, work done by children in factories or business or otherwise for hire, legally restricted in the United States.

child|less (chīld′lis), *adj.* having no child. —**child′less|ness,** *n.*

child|like (chīld′līk′), *adj.* **1** like a child; innocent; frank; simple: *The old man enjoyed the prank in childlike glee.* SYN: ingenuous, artless. **2** like that or those of a child; characteristic of a child: *a childlike directness of speech.* **3** suitable for a child. —**child′like′ness,** *n.*
►See **childish** for usage note.

child|ly (chīld′lē), *adj.* of or natural to a child or childhood; childish.

child|mind|er (chīld′mīn′dər), *n. British.* **1** a baby sitter. **2** a person who takes care of children at a day nursery or other child-care center.

child|ness (chīld′nis), *n.* **1** the state of being a child. **2** *Obsolete.* childishness; silliness.

child|proof (chīld′prüf′), *adj.* that a child cannot tamper with to endanger himself; safe for children: *a car with childproof locks. Wire fencing with barbed wire would never be childproof. Why come up so far and no farther with chain link [fence], which is childproof?* (London Times).

child psychology, the area of psychology that specializes in studying the actions and attitudes of children, especially in the first six years of life.

chil|dren (chil′drən), *n.* plural of **child**: *The mother took good care of her children.*

chil|dren|ese (chil′drə nēz′, -nēs′), *n. U.S.* a manner or style of talking effectively with children: *Parents have been offered lessons in how to speak "childrenese"* (New York Times).

Children of God, a fundamentalist Christian sect founded in 1968, whose members give up all their worldly goods to the sect, live in communes called colonies, and engage in active proselytizing.

Children of Israel, the Israelites; Hebrews; Jews.

Children's Day, a day of church programs and services devoted to, or conducted by, children.

child's play, something very easy to do: *As man found better means of defending himself, he made lighter and more manageable doors, until today it is literally child's play to open a door* (Scientific American).

child study, the systematic physiological and psychological study of the growth and development of children.

child welfare, the betterment of the conditions of the life of children, especially in poor or needy families, as a social work.

child wife, a very young wife.

chil|e (chil′ē), *n.* = chili.

Chil|e|an (chil′ē ən), *adj., n.* —*adj.* of or having to do with Chile or its people.
—*n.* a native or inhabitant of Chile.

Chil|e|an|ize (chil′ē ə nīz), *v.t.,* **-ized, -iz|ing.** to make Chilean, especially by putting under the control of the Chilean government. —**Chil′e|an|i|za′tion,** *n.*

chil|e con car|ne (chil′ē kon kär′nē), = chili con carne.

chil|e|nite (chil′ə nīt), *n.* a silver-white massive mineral, consisting of bismuth and silver. [< Spanish *Chileno* Chilean + English *-ite*]

Chi|le|no (chē lā′nō), *n. Spanish.* a native or inhabitant of Chile; Chilean.

Chil|e pine (chil′ē), = monkey puzzle.

Chile saltpeter sodium nitrate, found abundantly in Chile, South America. *Formula:* $NaNO_3$

chil|i (chil′ē), *n., pl.* **chil|ies. 1** Also, **chili pepper.** a hot-tasting pod of red pepper, used for seasoning. When reduced to powder, it is called *cayenne.* **2** the plant that it grows on, a tropical American shrub grown in the southern part of the United States. **3** = chili con carne. Also, **chile, chilli.** [< Mexican Spanish *chile* < Nahuatl *chilli*]

chil|i|ad (kil′ē ad), *n.* **1** a group of 1,000 (things); a thousand. **2** a period of 1,000 years: *The scars and dints of centuries, of chiliads of stubborn resistance* (George Macdonald). [< Greek *chīliás, -ádos* < *chīlioi* a thousand]

chil|i|asm (kil′ē az əm), *n.* the doctrine that Christ will return to reign on earth for a millennium. [< Greek *chīliasmós*]

chil|i|ast (kil′ē ast), *n.* a person who believes in chiliasm; millenarian. [< Greek *chīliastês*]

chil|i|as|tic (kil′ē as′tik), *adj.* of or having to do with chiliasm: *The primitive Church . . . for the first two or three centuries was essentially chiliastic* (Contemporary Review).

chil|i con car|ne (chil′ē kon kär′nē), a highly seasoned Mexican dish of chopped meat cooked with red peppers and, usually, kidney beans. Also, **chile con carne.** [American English < American Spanish *chile con carne* chili with meat]

chili dog, *U.S.* chili con carne served on a roll or bun. [patterned after *hot dog*]

chili pepper, = chili (def. 1).

chili sauce, a sauce made of red peppers, tomatoes, onions, and spices, used on meat or fish. Also, **chilli sauce.**

Chil|kat (chil′kat), *n., pl.* **-kat** or **-kats,** *adj.* —*n.* a member of a Tlingit group of Indians living in southeastern Alaska, noted for their brightly-colored blankets and totem poles.
—*adj.* of these Indians.

chill (chil), *n., adj., v.* —*n.* **1** an unpleasant coldness: *to feel a sudden chill. There was a chill in the air.* **2** a sudden coldness of the body, with shivering: *I caught a chill yesterday and today I have a fever.* **3** the condition of feeling cold; shivering. **4** *Figurative.* lack of heartiness; unfriendliness: *There was a chill in his voice.* **5** *Figurative.* a depressing influence; discouraging feeling: *When Pope John XXIII died . . . a chill of uncertainty ran suddenly through the ranks of progressive Roman Catholics* (Maclean's). **6** a metal mold, or a piece of iron in a sand mold, for making chilled castings.
—*adj.* **1** unpleasantly cold: *A chill wind blew across the frozen lake.* **2** feeling the cold; shivering with cold: *They had a fire to warm them when chill* (Mary Shelley). **3** *Figurative.* cold in manner; unfriendly: *The old enemies gave each other a chill greeting.* SYN: unfeeling. **4** *Figurative.* depressing the enthusiasm; discouraging.
—*v.i.* **1** to become cold; feel cold: *His blood chilled as he read the horror story.* **2** to be affected with a sudden chill: (*Figurative.*) *He chilled suddenly at seeing the face of the ghost.* **3** (of metals) to become hard on the surface by cooling rapidly, as cast iron.
—*v.t.* **1** to make cold: *The icy wind chilled us to the bone.* **2** to cool, as in a refrigerator, without freezing: *to chill a salad.* **3** *Figurative.* to depress; dispirit; discourage: *He pleaded with her that [nothing] could chill the ardor of his love for her* (James T. Farrell). **4** to harden (metal, especially cast iron) on the surface by rapid cooling.
chill out, *U.S Slang.* to take it easy; calm down; cool it: *I said angrily, "You messing with my high." "Chill out," he said. "You can't get too deep into this or it will take you out, man"* (Vanity Fair).
take the chill off, to warm up: *Before giving the baby her milk, Mother took the chill off the bottle by heating it in a pan of hot water.*
[Old English *ciele*] —**chill′ness,** *n.*

chilled (child), *adj.* **1** made cold: *chilled milk.* **2** hardened by chilling: *chilled steel.*

chill|er (chil′ər), *n.* **1** a person or thing that chills:

The north wind was a chiller yesterday. **2** *Figurative.* a suspense or horror story or motion picture: *This English chiller . . . is simply too flagrant to be really horrid* (Newsweek).

chill|er-dill|er (chil′ər dil′ər), *n. U.S. Slang.* a suspense or horror story; chiller.

chill factor, = windchill factor.

chil|li (chil′ē), *n., pl.* **-lies.** = chili.

chill|ing (chil′ing), *adj., n.* **—*adj.*** **1** very cold; frigid: *chilling temperatures,* (*Figurative*) *a chilling reception.* **2** *Figurative.* making the blood run cold; frightening; terrifying: *Mary* [*Shelley*] *wrote a chilling tale about a Swiss scientist who learned how to impart life to a homemade man* (New York Times).
—***n.*** the act or fact of making rather cold.
—chill′ing|ly, *adv.*

chilli sauce, = chili sauce.

chill|some (chil′səm), *adj.* chilling; chilly: *It means you can get utterly away from chillsome damps* (Observer).

chill|y (chil′ē), *adj.,* **chill|i|er, chill|i|est,** *adv.* **—*adj.*** **1** unpleasantly cool; rather cold: *It is a rainy, chilly day. You'll feel chilly if you don't wear a coat.* SYN: chill, raw. See syn. under **cold. 2a** affected by a chill or by cold; feeling rather cold. **b** sensitive to cold; easily chilled. **3** *Figurative.* cold in manner; unfriendly: *a chilly greeting. The members of the club gave those with bad manners a chilly reception.*
—***adv.*** in a chill manner. **—chill′i|ly,** *adv.* **—chill′i|ness,** *n.*

chi|log|nath (kī′ləg nath), *n.* a small, segmented, wormlike arthropod that has two pairs of legs apiece for most of its segments; millipede. [< New Latin *Chilognatha* the order name < Greek *cheîlos* lip + *gnáthos* jaw]

chi|log|na|thous (kī log′nə thəs), *adj.* of or having to do with a chilognath, or millipede.

chi|lom|o|nad (kī lom′ə nad), *n.* any one of a genus of one-celled, flagellate organisms noted for their affinity to acids and salts and resistance to certain drugs. [< New Latin *Chilomonas, -adis* the genus name < Greek *cheîlos* lip + *monás, ádos* unit]

chi|lo|plas|ty (kī′lə plas′tē), *n.* plastic surgery of the lip. [< Greek *cheîlos* lip + *plastós* molded]

chi|lo|pod (kī′lə pod), *n.* = centipede. [< New Latin *Chilopoda* the order name < Greek *cheîlos* lip + *poús, podós* foot]

chi|lop|o|dous (kī lop′ə dəs), *adj.* of or having to do with a chilopod, or centipede.

chi|lot|o|my (kī lot′ə mē), *n., pl.* **-mies.** surgical incision into the lip. [< Greek *cheîlos* lip + *-tomiā* a cutting]

Chil|tern Hundreds (chil′tərn), the name of three hundreds (divisions of a county) in Buckinghamshire, England, noted for several nominal or fictitious offices used for a special purpose. A member of Parliament wishing to leave the House applies for the position. By holding it temporarily, he is disqualified from sitting in the House, direct resignation from which is not permissible.
accept (or **apply for**) **the Chiltern Hundreds,** *British.* to resign as a member of Parliament: . . . *a representative of the city of London, in the room of Harvey Combe, Esq. who had accepted the Chiltern Hundreds* (John Evans).
[< *Chiltern* Hills, a range of hills in England]

chi|mae|ra (kə mir′ə, kī-), *n.* **1** any one of a subclass of cartilaginous fishes, having large crushing plates instead of teeth, and a long, slender tail; ratfish: *The chimaera, a relative of the sharks and skates, lives exclusively in very deep waters* (Science News Letter). **2** = chimera. [< Latin *chimaera* chimera]

chim|ar (chim′ər), *n.* = chimere.

chime¹ (chīm), *n., v.,* **chimed, chim|ing.** **—*n.*** **1** a set of bells tuned to the musical scale and played usually by hammers or simple machinery: *We heard the chimes playing in the church.* **2** the music made by a set of tuned bells: *We heard the chime of the church bells.* **3** any sequence of harmonious sounds; music; melody: *the chime of the village clock striking midnight.* **4** *Figurative.* agreement; harmony; accord. **5** = carillon (defs. 1, 3). **6** a set of metal tubes hung vertically from a frame, played by striking with a hammer held in the hand, used in the modern orchestras. **7** an aratus or arrangement for striking a bell or set of bells so as to produce a musical sound.
—***v.i.*** **1** to ring or be rung out musically: *The bells chimed at midnight.* **2** to speak or sing in cadence or singsong. **3** to produce a musical sound from a bell (or the like) by striking it or using other means than ringing. **4** to rhyme; jingle. **5** *Figurative.* to agree; be in harmony (with).
—***v.t.*** **1** to produce by chiming; ring out: *The bells chimed a Christmas carol.* **2** to make musical sounds on (a set of tuned bells). **3** to indicate (the time) by chiming: *The clock chimes midnight.* **4** to bring or drive by chiming; summon by chimes: *The steward chimed us to meals.* **5** to say or utter in cadence or singsong.
chime in, a to break into a conversation, especially to express one's agreement: *I said I would like to go to the circus and my brother chimed in. "He was extremely civil," Wiseman chimed in* (Macaulay). **b** to agree; be in harmony: *Her ideas chimed in beautifully with mine.* **c** to join in harmoniously or in unison: *The softening voices . . . Must chime in to the echo of his revel* (Byron).
[< Old French *cimble,* learned borrowing from Latin *cymbalum* < Greek *kýmbalon* cymbal]

chime² or **chimb** (chīm), *n.* **1** the projecting rim at the ends of a cask, formed by the ends of the staves: *A false deck, which was rough and oily, and cut up in every direction by the chimes of oil-casks* (Richard H. Dana). **2** the staves themselves. Also, **chine.** [related to Old English *cimbing* a joining, juncture]

chim|er¹ (chī′mər), *n.* **1** a person who plays the carillon or chimes. **2** a thing that chimes, such as a clock.

chim|er² (chim′ər, shim′-), *n.* = chimere.

***chi|me|ra** (kə mir′ə, kī-), *n., pl.* **-ras. 1** Also, **Chimera.** *Greek Legend.* a monster with a serpent's tail, a goat's body, and a lion's head, supposed to breathe out fire. It was killed by Bellerophon. **2** *Figurative.* a horrible creature of the imagination; bogy. **3** *Figurative.* an absurd or impossible idea; wild fancy: *The hope of changing lead to gold was a chimera.* **4** a grotesque monster in decorative art, formed of the parts of various animals. **5** *Biology.* an organism consisting of two or more tissues of different genetic composition, produced as a result of mutation in a somatic cell, grafting, etc. Also, **chimaera.** [< Middle French *chimère* < Latin *Chimaera* < Greek *Chímaira* the monster]

***chimera**
definition 1

***chi|mere** (chi mir′, shi-), *n.* a loose outer robe, especially that worn by an Anglican bishop, to which the lawn sleeves are usually attached: *Since* [*the church's*] *founding 105 years ago, seven of its rectors and two assistant rectors have gone on to wear the puffy lawn sleeves of the white chimere* (Newsweek). Also, **chimar, chimer.** [< Medieval Latin (England) *chimera* riding cloak, apparently < Middle French *chamarre* long coat < Spanish *zamarra* shepherd's garment < Arabic *sammūr* the sable. See etym. of doublets **cymar, simar.**]

***chimere**

chi|mère (kī mer′), *n.* = chimera (def. 4.).

chi|mer|ic (kə mer′ik, kī-; -mir′-), *adj.* = chimerical.

chi|mer|i|cal (kə mer′ə kəl, kī- ; -mir′-), *adj.* **1** unreal; imaginary: *Sir, this book . . . is a pretty essay . . . though much of it is chimerical* (Samuel Johnson). SYN: illusory, delusive. **2** wildly fanciful; absurd; impossible: *Don't pay attention to his chimerical schemes for getting rich. While industrialization is highly desirable, it is chimerical to suppose that it alone can cope with India's food and population problem* (Scientific American). SYN: quixotic, fantastic, visionary. **—chi|mer′i|cal|ly,** *adv.*

chim|ney (chim′nē), *n., pl.* **-neys. 1** an upright structure, usually of brick or stone, connected with a fireplace, furnace, or stove to make a draft and carry away smoke: *Her house has two chimneys.* SYN: smokestack. **2** the part of this that rises above the roof: *Only chimneys, masts and ventilator stacks could then be seen* [*above the snow*] (K. D. Wadsworth). **3** a glass tube placed around the flame of a kerosene lamp or candle. See picture under **hurricane lamp. 4** the funnel which carries off smoke or steam from a locomotive engine or the like. SYN: flue¹. **5** a crack or opening in a rock, mountain, volcano, or other natural fissure. SYN: cleft. **6** a steep, very narrow gorge or gully; couloir. **7** *Dialect.* a fireplace or hearth. [< Middle French *cheminée* < Late Latin *camīnāta* < Latin, ovenlike < *caminus* oven, furnace < Greek *kámīnos*] **—chim′ney|less,** *adj.*

chimney cap, 1 a cornice forming the top of a chimney. **2** a rotary device, moved by the wind, which helps the smoke to escape from a chimney by turning the opening away from the wind.

chimney corner, the corner or side of a fireplace; place near the fire.

chim|neyed (chim′nēd), *adj.* having a chimney or chimneys.

chimney money, hearth money; a tax formerly levied in England, the amount depending on the number of chimneys in a house.

chimney piece, *British.* **1** the protective facing, often ornamental as well, around a fireplace and against the chimney; mantelpiece. **2** a shelf or other decoration on the chimney, over a fireplace; mantelshelf: *English families always leave things around, copies of the Tatler or Sketch on the tables, riding crops or gloves on the chimney piece* (Harper's).

chimney place, *U.S.* an open fireplace or hearth.

chimney pot, a pipe of earthenware or metal fitted on top of a chimney to increase the draft and carry off the smoke.

chimney stack, 1 a group of chimneys or flues together. **2** = smokestack.

chimney swallow, 1 the Old World barn swallow. **2** = chimney swift.

chimney sweep, a person whose work is cleaning out chimneys: . . . *a European chimney sweep equipped with the tools of his trade—the dark garments, the tall stovepipe hat, the heavy hempen rope and the worn brushes* (New York Times).

chimney sweeper, 1 = chimney sweep. **2** a long-handled brush for sweeping chimneys.

chimney swift, a bird of North America that often builds its nest in unused chimneys. Chimney swifts are small birds with long, narrow wings and a short tail, somewhat like a swallow.

chimney throat, the narrowest part of a chimney, between the gathering and the flue.

chimp (chimp), *n. Informal.* a chimpanzee: *Some chimps are bright and some are dull, Dr. Nissen has found* (Science News Letter).

chim|pan|zee (chim′pan zē′, chim pan′zē), *n.* a manlike ape of equatorial Africa, smaller than a gorilla, averaging about four and half feet tall. It is probably the most intelligent ape. See picture under **ape.** [< Bantu (West Africa) *kivili-chimpenze* ape]

Chi|mu (chē mü′), *n., pl.* **-mu** or **-mus,** *adj.* **—*n.*** a member of a South American Indian people who lived on the northern coast of Peru until they were conquered by the Incas. The Chimu had a highly developed culture.
—***adj.*** of the Chimu or their civilization.

chin (chin), *n., v.,* **chinned, chin|ning.** **—*n.*** **1** the front of the lower jaw below the mouth: *The motorcycle rider buckled the strap of his helmet under his chin.* **2** the whole lower surface of the face, below the mouth. **3** *Informal.* a chat; gossip; talk.
—***v.t.*** *Informal.* **1** to place (a violin) under the chin, in order to play it. **2** to talk to; gossip to.
—***v.i.*** **1** *Informal.* to chat; gossip. **2** Usually, **chin oneself.** to hang by the hands from an overhead bar and pull up until the chin is even with or above the bar: *I pulled up as though chinning on a sill and swung a leg in* (James Dickey).
keep one's chin up, to bear adversity without flinching or complaining: *The coach told him to keep his chin up since there was still time in which to regain the lead.*
take it on the chin, *Informal.* to take a beating: *A writer should never stop experimenting, . . . and to the extent that he does it in public, expect to take it on the chin* (Saturday Review).
[Old English *cinn*]

Chin., 1 China. **2** Chinese.

chi|na¹ (chī′nə), *n., adj.* **—*n.*** **1** a fine, white pottery made of clay by a special process, first used in China; porcelain. It is baked and glazed at high temperatures to make it very hard and often translucent. Colored designs can be baked into china. *China is made from a still better grade of clay than is used for earthenware* (Monroe M. Offner). **2** dishes, vases, or ornaments made of china. **3** pottery dishes of any kind. Also, **chinaware.**
—***adj.*** **1** of china; made of china or porcelain.

Pronunciation Key: hat, āge, cãre, fär; let, ēqual, tėrm; it, īce; hot, ōpen, ôrder; oil, out; cup, pu̇t, rüle; child; long; thin; ᴛʜen; zh, measure; ə represents **a** in about, **e** in taken, **i** in pencil, **o** in lemon, **u** in circus.

2 made with pottery clay of any kind. [short for earlier *china-ware* ware from China]

chi|na[2] (kī′nə, kē′-), *n.* **1** cinchona bark. **2** any one of various similar barks. [alteration of Spanish *quina* < Quechua (Peru) *kina* cinchona bark. Compare etym. under **quinine.**]

China aster, a composite plant native to China and Japan, closely related to the asters, full-petaled like a chrysanthemum, and widely cultivated in many varieties.

chi|na bark (kī′nə, kē′-), **1** = cinchona. **2** any one of various similar barks. [see etym. under **china[2]**]

chi|na|ber|ry (chī′nə ber′ē) , *n., pl.* **-ries. 1a** a tree of the mahogany family, native to Asia and widely cultivated in warm regions for its clusters of purplish flowers and yellow, berrylike fruits, and for shade; china tree. **b** its fruit. **2** a soapberry, a native of the southern United States, northern Mexico, and the West Indies.

chinaberry tree, = chinaberry.

chi|na blue (chī′nə), a greenish-blue, moderately brilliant color.

china clay, = kaolin.

china closet, a cabinet for storing china.

chi|na|graph pencil (chī′nə graf), a special pencil for writing on china and glassware.

China grass, **1** the fiber of a plant of warm climates used to make grass cloth. **2** the plant itself; ramie.

Chi|na|man (chī′nə mən), *n., pl.* **-men.** *Unfriendly Use.* **1** a native or inhabitant of China; Chinese. **2** a person of Chinese descent.
▶See **Chinese** for usage note.

Chinaman's chance, *Informal.* a slim chance; slight hope: *There's not a Chinaman's chance in the world . . . to bring back a Nationalist government on the mainland* (Wall Street Journal).

China mink, a light-yellow fur obtained from a weasel of China and Japan; Japanese mink.

chi|nam|pa (chi nam′pə), *n.* **1** (in Mexico and South America) a floating mass of filled-in land reclaimed from a pond or swamp by planting with aquatic vegetation. **2** an island of rich, moist earth dredged from a lake bottom by the Aztecs to be used in raising crops. [< Mexican Spanish *chinampa*]

China pink, a frequently cultivated pink native to eastern Asia, bearing rosy, scentless flowers with toothed petals.

Chi|na pob|la|na (chē′nä pôb lä′nä), a Mexican holiday costume consisting of a full red and green skirt decorated with sequins and beads, an embroidered short-sleeved blouse, and a silk shawl. [< Mexican Spanish *china poblana* (literally) girl of the village]

chi|nar (chi när′), *n.,* or **chinar tree**, a variety of the plane tree, especially one of the Middle East. [< Persian *chinār*]

China rose, **1a** the original native type of rose, brought from China to England about 1789, now represented by the common pink monthly rose. It was an ancestor of the tea rose and of many modern cultivated roses. **b** any one of various roses developed from the original China rose. **2** a large shrub of the mallow family, 20 to 30 feet high, with beautiful flowers of pink or white; Chinese hibiscus.

China stone, = petuntse.

China syndrome, a condition in which the radioactive fuel of a nuclear reactor overheats to such a high temperature that the core burns through its protective shield and deep into the earth: *In nuclear slang, "the China syndrome" could theoretically occur if the radioactive core of a nuclear plant were uncovered, allowing the searing heat of the core to melt through the steel pressure vessel, through the concrete bottom of the building, through the earth and "into China"* (New York Times).

Chi|na|town (chī′nə toun′), *n.* the section of a city where Chinese live: *He had emigrated from Britain to Canada in 1908, made a fortune peddling clothes and real estate in the Chinatowns of the Far West* (Newsweek).

chi|na tree (chī′nə), = chinaberry.

chi|na|ware (chī′nə wãr′), *n.* = china[1].

China watcher, a student or observer of contemporary Chinese politics; Pekingologist.

chi|na|wood oil (chī′nə wu̇d′), = tung oil.

chin band, = chin strap.

chin|ca|pin (ching′kə pin), *n.* = chinquapin.

chinch (chinch), *n.* **1** = bedbug. **2** = chinch bug. [< Spanish *chinche* < Latin *cīmex, -icis* bedbug. See etym. of doublet **cimex.**]

Chin|cha (chēn′chə), *n., pl.* **-cha** or **-chas.** a member of an ancient people of Peru who attained a high degree of civilization before they were conquered by the Incas.

chinch bug, a small, usually black-and-white bug that does much damage to wheat, corn, grass, and other cereal plants in dry weather.

chin|che|rin|chee (chin′chə rin′chē), *n.* any plant of a variety of South African bulbous herbs of the lily family, having thin basal leaves, and noted for their showy, white, yellow, or green flowers. Also, **chinkerinchee.** [< a native name]

***chin|chil|la** (chin chil′ə), *n.* **1** a small South American rodent that looks somewhat like a squirrel. **2** its very valuable, soft, bluish-gray fur. **3** a thick woolen fabric woven in small, closely set tufts, used for overcoats. [< Spanish *chinchilla* (diminutive) < *chinche;* see etym. under **chinch**]

***chinchilla**
definition 1

chinchilla cat, a domestic cat with silver-colored hair.

chin-chin (chin′chin′), *n., v.,* **-chinned, -chinning.** *Pidgin English.* **—*n.*** a greeting or parting salutation. **—*v.t.*** to salute or greet.

chin|cho|na (chin chō′nə), *n.* = cinchona.

chin|cough (chin′kôf′, -kof′), *n.* = whooping cough. [earlier *chink cough* < dialectal *chink* to gasp]

chin-deep (chin′dēp′), *adj.* **1** so deep as to reach the chin: *chin-deep in water.* **2** *Figurative.* very deep; deeply immersed in.

chine[1] (chīn), *n., v.,* **chined, chin|ing. —*n.* 1** a backbone; spine. **2** a piece of an animal's backbone with the meat on it, for cooking: *My wife and I dined upon a chine of beef* (Samuel Pepys). **3** a ridge; crest.
—*v.t.* 1 to cut along or across the backbone of. **2** to cut up (a fish).
[< Old French *eschine,* perhaps < Germanic (Old High German *scina* needle, splinter)]

chine[2] (chīn), *n.* = chime or chimb. [variant of *chime[2]*]

chi|né (shē nā′), *adj.* having the warp threads of fabrics so printed in colors as to produce, when woven, a pattern with somewhat distinct outlines: *chiné silk.* [< French *chiné,* past participle of *chiner* color in a particular manner derived from the Chinese < *Chine* China]

Chi|nee (chī nē′), *n. Slang, Unfriendly Use.* a Chinese. [back formation < *Chinese*]
▶See **Chinese** for usage note.

Chi|nese (chī nēz′, -nēs′), *adj., n., pl.* **-nese.**
—*adj.* of China, its people, or their language: *Chinese courtesy, Chinese cooking.*
—*n.* 1 a person born or living in China: *The Chinese are very thoughtful of visitors to their country.* **2** a person of Chinese descent: *Many Chinese try to keep the traditions their ancestors brought to America.* **3** the tonal language of China; any of the large group of dialects spoken in China, of which the Peking dialect, called Mandarin, is regarded as standard: *In Chinese, objects are noted as singular or plural only when the speaker judges the information to be relevant* (Henry A. Gleason).
▶**Chinese** is the standard singular (*a Chinese*) and plural (*the Chinese*). *Chinaman* (or *Chinamen*), *Chinee,* and *Chink* are derogatory terms. *Chinee,* now rare, is a back formation from *Chinese.*

Chinese box, one of a set of boxes, each of which fits within another.

Chinese cabbage, a plant of the mustard family with a loose, lettucelike head and a taste somewhat like that of cabbage, used as a vegetable and in salads; celery cabbage.

Chinese calendar, the ancient lunar calendar formerly used in China, having cycles of 60 years, 12 months in a year, and 29 or 30 days in a month, with an extra month added after each half cycle. The years were counted from 2637 B.C. The Chinese adopted the Gregorian calendar in 1912, the first year of the Chinese Republic, and years are now counted from then.

Chinese checkers, a game resembling checkers, played by two to six persons, using marbles of different colors on a wood board patterned in star shape. The object of the game is to move all one's marbles into the corresponding positions on the opposite side of the board.

Chinese chestnut, a small hybrid chestnut tree that is resistant to chestnut blight.

Chinese Chippendale, Chippendale furniture using Chinese forms and designs.

Chinese cinnamon, = cassia bark.

Chinese goose, any one of a domestic breed of brown goose with a black bill and a yellow stripe on its neck.

Chinese hibiscus, = China rose.

Chinese homer, *Baseball Slang.* a home run made on a hit that travels only a short distance.

Chinese jade, = jadeite.

Chinese lantern, a lantern of thin, colored paper that can be folded up like an accordion, used especially for decoration at dances, outdoor parties, and other festivities; Japanese lantern.

Chinese lantern plant, a ground cherry widely grown for its inflated orange-red calyx, which is used for decoration.

Chinese liver fluke, a liver fluke of China, Japan, Korea, and other areas of Asia, that infests the bile duct and intestines of men and animals through the eating of raw or poorly cooked fish.

Chinese parasol tree, = flame tree.

Chinese pear, = sand pear.

Chinese peony, any one of a group of hybrid peonies that bear double-scented showy flowers which blossom in a wide range of white and rose-colored hues.

Chinese puzzle, something that is very complicated and hard to solve, such as a kind of wooden geometric puzzle with interlocking pieces invented by the Chinese.

Chinese red, an orange-red color.

Chinese restaurant syndrome, a condition characterized by headaches, dizziness, and other symptoms, which appears in some people after eating Chinese food, thought to be a reaction to eating food seasoned with monosodium glutamate.

Chinese scholar tree, = pagoda tree.

Chinese silver grass, an ornamental grass with plumelike flower clusters, used in flower gardens, parks, and other landscaped areas.

Chinese silver pheasant, a type of pheasant whose white upper parts are delicately marked with black lines.

Chinese Wall, **1** = Great Wall of China. **2** Usually, **Chinese wall.** *Figurative.* an impenetrable barrier: *A Chinese wall of the mind and emotions then separates us from the film* (Harper's).

Chinese water deer, = water deer.

Chinese white, white oxide of zinc, a valuable pigment.

Chinese windlass, a differential windlass, with a barrel in two sections of different diameter, which wind or unwind ropes at different speeds when it is revolved.

Chinese wisteria, a woody vine of the pea family with showy racemes usually of purple flowers.

Chinese wood oil, = tung oil.

chin|fest (chin′fest′), *n. U.S. Slang.* a talkfest.

Ch'ing or **Ching** (ching), *n.* the dynasty of the Manchus, from 1644 to 1912. It was the last dynasty of the Chinese Empire. Also, **Ta Ch'ing.**

ching|ma (ching′mä′), *n.* = Indian mallow. [< Chinese (Peking) *ch'ing ma*]

Ching Ming (ching′ming′), a Chinese festival which honors the dead and celebrates the coming of spring. [< Chinese *Ch'ing Ming*]

chink[1] (chingk), *n., v.* **—*n.* 1** a narrow opening; crack; slit: *The chinks between the logs of the cabin let in the wind and snow.* SYN: fissure. **2** *Figurative.* an area of weakness; a vulnerable place; weak side: *The chink in his armor was an inadequate education.*
—*v.t.* to fill up the chinks in: *The trapper chinked the walls of the cabin with mud.*
—*v.i.* to open in cracks or clefts; crack.
[origin uncertain]

chink[2] (chingk), *n., v.* **—*n.* 1** a short, sharp, ringing sound like coins or drinking glasses hitting together. **2** *Informal.* money in the form of coin; ready cash.
—*v.i.* to make a short, sharp, ringing sound like coins or drinking glasses hitting together: *I could hear the spoons chink in the glasses.*
—*v.t.* to cause to make such a sound: *He chinked the coins in his pocket.*

Chink (chingk), *n. U.S. Slang, Unfriendly Use.* Chinese.

chin|ka|pin (ching′kə pin), *n.* = chinquapin.

chin|ke|rin|chee (ching′kə rin′chē), *n.* = chincherinchee.

chink|y (ching′kē), *adj.* full of chinks or fissures.

chin|less (chin′lis), *adj.* **1** without a chin: *a chinless bird.* **2** *Figurative.* without the firmness of character associated with a prominent chin: *Some were powerful giants and others were chinless* (New Yorker).

-chinned, *combining form.* having a ____chin: *Long-chinned = having a long chin.*

chin|ny (chin′ē), *adj.,* **-ni|er, -ni|est. 1** marked by a conspicuous chin: *A face concave and long, with a jaw which divested of flesh would have seemed extravagant; altogether a chinny face* (John Galsworthy). **2** *Informal.* talkative.

chi|no (chē′nō), *n.* a cotton twill or duck fabric having many uses, especially in making trousers. **chinos,** trousers made of this fabric; chino pants: *Joe has such muscles from paddling his surfboard that every time he lifts his arms it pulls his polo shirt out of his chinos* (Ladies' Home Journal). [< American Spanish *chino* a nonwhite halfbreed (referring to the light coffee color)]

chi|noi|se|rie (shē nwäz rē′), *n.* **1** a style of ornate art, decoration, or the like, in, deriving from, or suggesting the Chinese tradition. **2** objects or patterns in this style: *A dress shop hung with cardboard chinoiserie* (Punch). [< French *chinoiserie* < *Chine* China + *-erie* -ery]

Chi|nook (chə nük′, -nu̇k′), *n., pl.* **-nook** or **-nooks. 1** a member of a group of American Indian tribes living along the Columbia River in the northwestern United States, including the Lower Chinook and several extinct tribes classed as Upper Chinook. **2** the language of these Indians. **3** = Chinook jargon. [American English < Salishan *Tsinúk*]

chi|nook (chə nük′, -nu̇k′), *n., adj.* **—*n.* 1** a warm, moist wind blowing from the sea to land in winter and spring in the northwestern United States. **2** a warm, dry wind that comes down the eastern slope of the Rocky Mountains, especially in Montana and Wyoming. **3** = chinook salmon.
—*adj.* of or resembling the type of weather which follows a chinook: *the chinook season, chinook days.* [< *Chinook*]

Chi|nook|an (chə nü′kən, -nu̇k′ən), *adj., n.* **—*adj.*** denoting or having to do with an American Indian linguistic family of the northwestern United States. **—*n.*** an Indian speaking a language of this family; Chinook.

Chinook jargon, a language used in trading in the Pacific Northwest, based on Chinook, with additional elements from French and English, which originated in the dealings of English and American traders with the Indians of that region: *Chinook provided the base for Chinook jargon, a creolized trade language* (Henry A. Gleason).

chinook or **Chinook salmon**, the largest species of Pacific salmon, important as a food fish; quinnat salmon.

chino pants, = chinos.

chi|nos (chē′nōz), *n.pl.* See under **chino**.

chin|qua|pin (ching′kə pin), *n.* **1** a dwarf chestnut tree, with edible nuts, ranging from Maine to Arkansas. **2** a related evergreen tree, grown in California and Oregon, that has a similar nut. **3** the nut of either tree. Also, **chincapin, chinkapin.** [American English; earlier *chincomin*, perhaps < Algonkian (Delaware) *chinqua* large + *min-* a root, seed]

chinquapin perch, = crappie.

chin rest, a device on the top edge of a violin or viola on which the player places the chin to hold the instrument against the shoulder.

chinse (chins), *v.t.,* **chinsed, chins|ing.** *Nautical.* to calk slightly or temporarily. [variant of *chinch*, dialectal form of *chink*[1]]

chin strap, **1a** a band for fastening a hat or cap under the chin. **b** a support for the chin. **2** a strap connecting the throatlatch and noseband of an animal's halter.

chin turret, a turret for a gun located immediately below the nose of a bomber or gunship.

chintz (chints), *n.* **1** a cotton cloth printed in patterns of various colors, and often glazed. **2** a painted or stained calico formerly exported from India. [originally plural, < Hindustani *chhīnt* < Sanskrit *chitra* variegated]

chintz|y (chint′sē), *adj.,* **chintz|i|er, chintz|i|est. 1** of or like chintz. **2** *Slang.* cheap, often in a mean and petty way: *I hate to phone friends and ask if they have these items because it seems so chintzy* (Springfield Leader-Press).

chin-up (chin′up′), *n., adj.* **—*n.*** the exercise of chinning oneself: *They must be able to ... perform five chin-ups and 33 sit-ups* (Time).
—*adj.* keeping one's chin up; maintaining or raising morale: *chin-up courage.*

chin|wag (chin′wag′), *v.,* **-wagged, -wag|ging,** *n. Slang.* **—*v.i.*** to make idle talk; chatter: *chinwagging with other nannies in the park* (Maclean's).
—*n.* chatter: *This was honest-to-goodness, man-to-man chinwag* (Punch).

chi|on|o|dox|a (kī′ə nə dok′sə), *n., pl.* **-dox|as.** any one of several small lilies native to Crete and Asia Minor whose usually blue and white flowers bloom early in spring. [< New Latin *Chionodoxa* the genus name < Greek *chíon* snow + *dóxa* glory]

chip[1] (chip), *n., v.,* **chipped, chip|ping. —*n.* 1** a small, thin piece cut from wood or broken from stone or pottery: *They used the chips of wood to start a fire.* **SYN:** fragment, flake. **2** the place where a small, thin piece has been cut or broken off: *This plate has a chip on the edge.* **3** a small, thin piece of food or candy. Potato chips are fried slices of potato. **4a** a round, flat piece used for counting or to represent money in games: *poker chips.* **SYN:** counter. **b** = bargaining chip: *The President could have used the need for grain as a chip in the ongoing SALT negotiations* (Maclean's). **5a** a strip of wood, palm leaf, or straw, used in making baskets or hats: *hats in chip.* **b** a basket or box made of very thin strips of wood: *Strawberries cost $1 a chip.* **6** a piece of dried dung, used for fuel in some regions: *The trappers made a fire of buffalo chips.* **7** a small piece cut off a diamond. **8** *Figurative.* **a** a worthless or trivial thing: *Basil did not care a chip* (Holme Lee). **b** a dried-up, parched, or tasteless substance: *meat burned to a chip.* **9** *Golf.* = chip shot. **10a** a tiny piece of silicon imprinted or engraved with one or more microcircuits. **b** = microcircuit. [< verb]
—*v.i.* 1 to cut or break off in small, thin pieces; become chipped: *This china chips easily. A poor grade of paint soon chips off.* **SYN:** flake. **2** to make a bet, especially in poker; chip in. **3** *Golf.* to make a chip shot. **—*v.t.* 1** to separate (small pieces) by cutting or breaking: *He chipped off the old paint. They chipped several small pieces of stone from the walls* (Charles Kingsley). **2** to shape by cutting at the surface or edge with an ax or chisel, especially by removing small portions at a time: **a** to make by this method: *The Indians chipped flint arrowheads.* **b** to alter, especially to damage or disfigure, by breaking off pieces: *The vase had been chipped when it fell.* **3** to hew or chop with an ax, adz, or other tool: *The men were chipping and cutting wood.* **4** (of young birds) to break (the shell) when hatching: *Thou isle ... that saw the unfledged eaglet chip his shell* (Byron). **5a** *Golf.* to hit (a ball) with a chip shot. **b** *Tennis and Soccer.* to slice or cut at (a ball); chop. **6** *British Slang.* to make fun of; jeer; chaff. **7** *Obsolete.* to pare (bread) by cutting the crust off.

cash in one's chips, *U.S.* **a** to change (poker chips) into cash: *When the game was over the winner cashed in his chips.* **b** *Slang.* to close or sell a business; retire: *Small businessmen who cannot compete with chain stores are often forced to cash in their chips.* **c** *Slang.* to die: *Two hoodlums cashed in their chips during the shooting.*

chip away at, a to cut away the substance of: *He [the Governor] continued chipping away at the 1,060 measures left behind by the ... Legislature* (New York Times). **b** *Figurative.* weaken; undercut; undermine: *... to chip away at forms of a communal life* (Saturday Review).

chip in, *Informal.* **a** to join with others in giving (money or help): *We all chipped in to buy our teacher a birthday present. Members will chip in so there'll be coffee* (New York Times). **b** to put in (a remark) when others are talking: *[She] ... had little luck with her attempts to chip in, though she contributed some lively asides* (London Times). **c** to add one's stake or bet to a pool, as in poker: *There ain't enough left to chip in on a ten-cent ante* (Bret Harte).

chip off (or **of**) **the old block**, a boy who is much like his father: *Not merely a chip of the old block but the old block itself* (Edmund Burke).

chip on one's shoulder, *Informal.* readiness to quarrel or fight: *The way that dog went about with a chip on his shoulder ... was enough to spoil the sweetest temper* (Harper's).

chips, a *British.* French fried potatoes: *fish and chips.* **b** *Slang.* money: *... better known to gossip columnists as an international party-thrower who is heavy with chips* (Time).

in the chips, *Slang.* wealthy; affluent: *The most pathetic incident is when Duke visits a former crony who is now in the chips* (Wall Street Journal).

let the chips fall where they may, *Informal.* to disregard the consequences, especially of frank speech: *The organization lets the chips fall where they may ... never hesitates to distinguish between hot air and sincerity* (Wall Street Journal).

when the chips are down, when the moment of decision or definite action arrives; in a crisis: *When the chips are down the delegates again will turn to the man who would be the best campaigner and ultimately the best President* (Newsweek).

[Old English *forcippian*]

chip[2] (chip), *n., v.,* **chipped, chip|ping. —*n.*** a short, sharp sound, especially that made by sparrows and certain other birds as their alarm note.
—*v.i.* to make such a sound.
[imitative]

chip[3] (chip), *n.* a trick in wrestling to throw one's opponent. [origin uncertain]

chip|bird (chip′bėrd′), *n.* = chipping sparrow.

chip|board (chip′bôrd′, -bōrd′), *n.,* or **chip board,** a cheap grade of cardboard made of waste paper, pulp, or the like, used especially for making boxes and book covers and for packing books: *In recent years manufacturers have begun to use wood chipboard in furniture* (New Scientist).

Chip|e|wy|an (chip′ə wī′ən), *n.* **1** a member of a small Indian tribe of hunters living in northwestern Canada. **2** the Athapascan language of this tribe.

chip log, a device for measuring a ship's speed, consisting of a cord with carefully spaced knots in it and a chip of wood attached by a harness at the end. The resistance of the chip causes the cord to unreel, the length unreeled in a fixed time indicating the vessel's speed.

chip|muck (chip′muk), *n.* = chipmunk.

chip|munk (chip′mungk), *n.* a small, striped rodent of North America; ground squirrel; chipping squirrel; chippy. It belongs to the same family as the squirrel. Also, **chipmuck.** [American English < Canadian dialect *chitmunk* < Algonkian (probably Ojibwa) *atchitamon* (literally) one who descends trees headlong]

chip|o|la|ta (chip′ə lä′tə), *n., pl.* **-tas. 1** a small, spicy pork sausage. **2** a garnish or stew made with these sausages. [< French *chipolata* < Italian *cipollata* a dish made with onions < *cipolla* onion]

chipped (chipt), *adj.* **1** having small pieces chopped or broken off the edges or surface: *a chipped cup.* **2** (of meat) smoked and cut in very thin slices: *chipped beef.* **3** made of chips or small pieces.

***Chip|pen|dale** (chip′ən dāl), *adj.* in the style of graceful, ornate furniture designed by Thomas Chippendale, or resembling this furniture: *spindle-legged Chippendale tables* (Mary E. Braddon).

***Chippendale**

chip|per[1] (chip′ər), *adj. Informal.* lively and cheerful: *[He] celebrated his 78th birthday, chipper and active despite an occasional feeling that he had "lived past my years"* (Newsweek). **SYN:** sprightly, brisk. [earlier Southern English equivalent of Northern *kipper* frisky; origin uncertain]

chip|per[2] (chip′ər), *n.* a person or thing that chips or cuts: *Logs selected for sawn timber will be passed to the saw mill, where a further chipper is installed* (London Times).

chip|per[3] (chip′ər), *n., v.* **—*n.*** chirping; chatter.
—*v.i.* to chirp or twitter; chatter or babble.
[imitative]

Chip|pe|wa (chip′ə wä, -wā, -wə), *n., pl.* **-wa** or **-was.** = Ojibwa (Indians). [American English; variant of *Ojibwa*]

chip|pie (chip′ē), *n.* = chippy (def. 3).

chipping sparrow, a small sparrow of eastern and central North America; chipbird; chippy.

chipping squirrel, = chipmunk.

chip|py (chip′ē), *n., pl.* **-pies. 1** = chipping sparrow. **2** = chipmunk. **3** *Slang.* **a** a frivolous young girl. **b** a woman of loose morals.

chips (chips), *n.pl.* See under **chip**.

chip shot, *Golf.* a short, lofted approach shot, played near the putting green, especially with wrist motion; chip.

chi|ral (kī′rəl), *adj. Chemistry, Physics.* not superimposable on its mirror image; asymmetric: *a chiral molecule or atom.* [< Greek *cheír, -os* hand + English *-al* (because of the handedness, or tendency toward the right or left, of chiral forms)]

chi|ral|i|ty (kī ral′ə tē), *n. Chemistry, Physics.* the property of being chiral or asymmetric.

chi|ra|ta (chi rä′tə), *n.* **1** a plant belonging to the gentian family, found in northern India. **2** the bitter tonic obtained from this, used like quinine. Also, **chiretta.** [< Hindi *chirāītā*]

chi|ret|ta (chi ret′ə), *n.* = chirata.

Chi-Rho (kī′rō′, kē′-), *n., pl.* **-Rhos.** = XP.

Chir|i|gua|no (chir′ə gwä′nō), *n., pl.* **-no** or **-nos. 1** a member of a South American Indian tribe, living in western Bolivia, and speaking a Tupi-Guarani language. **2** the language of this tribe.

chirk (chėrk), *v., adj.* **—*v.i.*** *Scottish.* **1** to make a strident noise: **a** to grate (or otherwise make a noise with) the teeth. **b** to creak, as a door. **c** to croak. **2** *Archaic.* to chirp; chirrup, as a bird.
—*adj.* *U.S. Informal.* chirky: *She was just as chirk and chipper as a wren* (Harriet Beecher Stowe).

chirk up, *U.S. Informal.* to make or become cheerful; cheer up: *Perhaps Mrs. Kimball would like one herself; it would chirk her up no end* (New Yorker).

[Middle English *chirke* to chirrup; variant of Old English *cearcian* squeak]

chirk|y (chėr′kē), *adj.,* **chirk|i|er, chirk|i|est.** *U.S. Informal.* lively; cheerful: *The score ... is as*

Pronunciation Key: hat, āge, cãre, fär; let, ēqual, tėrm; it, īce; hot, ōpen, ôrder; **oi**l, **ou**t; cup, pu̇t, rüle; **ch**ild; lo**ng**; **th**in; **ᴛʜ**en; **zh**, measure; ə represents **a** in about, **e** in taken, **i** in pencil, **o** in lemon, **u** in circus.

chirky as a summer band concert (New Yorker).

chirm (chėrm), *n., v. Dialect.* —*n.* **1** vocal noise, especially of birds. **2** the mingled din or noise of many birds or voices.
—*v.i.* to chatter or warble, as a bird.
[Old English *cirm*]

chi|rog|no|my (kī rog′nə mē), *n.* the branch of palmistry concerned with judging character from the hand. [< Greek *cheír, -os* hand + *gnômē* judgment]

chi|ro|graph (kī′rə graf, -gräf), *n.* **1** any one of various formally written or signed legal or other documents. **2** a writing executed in duplicate on a single sheet, and then divided, as through letters, or along an indented line, between the copies. **3** a document in one's own handwriting. [< Latin *chirographum* < Greek *cheirógraphon,* neuter of *cheirógraphos* written with the hand < *cheír, -os* hand + *gráphein* write]

chi|rog|ra|pher (kī rog′rə fər), *n.* a person who writes or is skilled at writing by hand.

chi|ro|graph|ic (kī′rə graf′ik), *adj.* of chirography.

chi|ro|graph|i|cal (kī′rə graf′ə kəl), *adj.* = chirographic.

chi|rog|ra|phy (kī rog′rə fē), *n.* style or system of writing; handwriting. [< Greek *cheír, -os* hand + English *-graphy*]

chi|ro|man|cer (kī′rə man′sər), *n.* a person who practices or professes chiromancy.

chi|ro|man|cy (kī′rə man′sē), *n.* fortunetelling or divination by inspection of a person's hands; palmistry. Also, **cheiromancy.** [< Medieval Latin *chiromantia* < Greek *cheirómantis* diviner by palmistry < *cheír, -os* hand + *mántis* prophet < *manteiā* divination]

Chi|ron (kī′ron), *n. Greek Legend.* a wise and kindly centaur, teacher of many Greek heroes. He was famous for his medical skill.

chi|ron|o|mid (kī ron′ə mid), *n.* any one of a group of dipterous insects resembling gnats, often forming large swarms in spring: *Fragile chironomids, delicate as mosquitoes, skated on the surface of the water* (R. W. G. Hingston). [< New Latin *Chironomidae* the family name < Greek *cheironómos* pantomimist]

chi|ron|o|my (kī ron′ə mē), *n.* the art of indicating a melody to a choir by hand motions, used in directing Gregorian chant. Also, **cheironomy.** [< Greek *cheironómos* pantomimist < *cheír, -os* hand + *-nómos* (related to *némein* manage)]

chi|rop|o|dist (kə rop′ə dist, kī-; *see note below*), *n.* a person who removes corns and treats other troubles of the feet; podiatrist. [< Greek *cheír, -os* hand + *poús, podós* foot + English *-ist*]
►The pronunciation (shə rop′ə dist) presumably has arisen because of a mistaken notion that the word is of French origin.

chi|rop|o|dy (kə rop′ə dē, kī-), *n.* the work of a chiropodist; podiatry.

chi|ro|prac|tic (kī′rə prak′tik), *n., adj.* —*n.* **1** the treatment of diseases by manipulating the spine and other body structures. It is based on the theory that many diseases are caused by pressure, especially of the vertebrae, upon nerves.
2 = chiropractor.
—*adj.* having to do with the treatment of diseases by manipulating the spine.
[American English < Greek *cheír, -os* hand + *prāktikós* concerned with practice, ultimately < *prâssein* do, act]

chi|ro|prac|tor (kī′rə prak′tər), *n.* a person who treats diseases by manipulating the spine.

chi|rop|ter (kī rop′tər), *n. Zoology.* any animal of the order of mammals that comprises the bats, having forelimbs modified as wings; a bat. [< New Latin *Chiroptera* < Greek *cheír, -os* hand + *pterón* wing]

chi|rop|ter|an (kī rop′tər ən), *adj., n.* —*adj.* of or having to do with a chiropter.
—*n.* = chiropter; bat.

chi|rop|ter|ous (kī rop′tər əs), *adj.* **1** wing-handed, as a bat. **2** having the characteristics of a chiropter or bat. **3** = chiropteran.

chirp (chėrp), *n., v.* —*n.* **1** the short, sharp sound made by some small birds and insects: *The chirp of a sparrow.* **2** any sound like this: *One by one the ten Superforts touched down, with a chirp of tires* (Time). SYN: cheep.
—*v.i.* **1** to make a chirp: *The crickets chirped outside the house.* SYN: cheep. **2** to make a sound imitative of, or similar to, the chirp of a bird: **a** to make a sound of suction with compressed lips by way of encouragement or greeting; chirrup. **b** *Figurative.* to speak in a manner in some respect like the chirping of birds.
—*v.t.* **1** to utter with a chirp. SYN: cheep. **2** to greet or incite by chirping: *He chirped his horses on.*
[imitative] —**chirp′er.** *n.*

chirp|y (chėr′pē), *adj.,* **chirp|i|er, chirp|i|est.** *Informal.* **1** inclined to chirp. **2** cheerful; lively; enthusiastic. —**chirp′i|ly,** *adv.* —**chirp′i|ness,** *n.*

chirr (chėr), *v., n.* —*v.i.* to make a shrill, trilling sound, somewhat like chirping but more continuous and monotonous: *The grasshoppers chirred in the fields.*
—*n.* a shrill, trilling sound. Also, **churr.**
[imitative]

chir|rup (chir′əp, chėr′-), *v.,* **-ruped, -rup|ing,** *n.* —*v.i., v.t.* to chirp again and again; make a chirping sound, for example to a tame bird or horse. —*n.* the sound of chirruping.
[alteration of *chirp*]

chir|rup|y (chir′ə pē, chėr′-), *adj. Dialect.* chirpy; cheerful.

chi|rur|geon (kī rėr′jən), *n. Archaic.* a surgeon. [alteration of Middle English *cirurgien* < Old French *cirurgien.* See etym. of doublet **surgeon.**]

chi|rur|ger|y (kī rėr′jər ē), *n. Archaic.* surgery.

chi|rur|gic (kī rėr′jik), *adj. Archaic.* surgical.

chi|rur|gi|cal (kī rėr′jə kəl), *adj. Archaic.* surgical.

Chi|san|bop (chiz′ən bop, jē′sən-), *n. Trademark.* a system of calculating arithmetically with the fingers, invented by Sung Jin Pai, a Korean mathematician. It is used especially to teach elementary arithmetic. *With Chisanbop, the fingers are used to count to 99, with larger numbers being carried over by memory or written down* (Maclean's). [< Korean, literally, finger counting]

chis|el (chiz′əl), *n., v.,* **-eled, -el|ing** or (*especially British*) **-elled, -el|ling.** —*n.* a tool with a sharp cutting edge at the end of a strong blade. Chisels are used to cut or shape wood, stone, or metal.
—*v.t.* **1** to cut or shape with a chisel: *The sculptor was at work chiseling a statue.* **2** *Slang, Figurative.* to cheat; get by trickery; defraud: *"Everybody is out to chisel everybody else"* (New Yorker). *A lot of the things we have ... we bought or chiseled out of relatives* (New York Times). —*v.i.* **1** to work with a chisel. **2** *Slang, Figurative.* to use unfair practices; cheat or swindle.
chisel in on, *Informal.* to cut in on; force oneself into: *He won't allow anyone to chisel in on his profits.*
[< Middle French *chisel, cisel* < Old French < Vulgar Latin *cisellum, caesellum* < Latin *caesus* a cutting, past participle of *caedere* cut] —**chis′el|er, chis′el|ler,** *n.* —**chis′el|like′,** *adj.*

chis|eled (chiz′əld), *adj.* **1** cut, shaped, or wrought with a chisel. **2** having clear and sharp outlines, as if cut with a chisel.

chis|elled (chiz′əld), *adj. Especially British.* chiseled: (*Figurative.*) *With chisell'd features clear and sleek ...* (Tennyson).

Chis|holm Trail (chiz′əm), a famous western cattle trail from San Antonio, Texas, to Abilene, Kansas. [American English < Jesse *Chisholm,* about 1808-1868, a half-Cherokee trader]

chi-square test, or **chi-square** (kī′skwãr′), *n. Statistics.* a test devised by Karl Pearson in 1900 to measure how closely the frequency distribution of actual data matches that expected in theory.

chis|te|ra (chis′tə rə; *Spanish* chēs tā′rä), *n.* **1** the wicker racket used in the game of pelota or jai alai: *Chisteras, used for both catching and throwing, add a wicked impetus to the pelota* (Time). **2** the game of pelota or jai alai. [< Spanish *chistera* < Basque *xistera*]

chist|ka (chēst′kə), *n.* a Communist political purge: *The chistka had involved ... as many as 7,000,000 Russians—uncounted numbers of whom disappeared into Siberian slave camps* (Time). [< Russian *chistka* cleaning, purge < *chistit′* to clean]

chit¹ (chit), *n.* **1** a signed note or ticket for a purchase, a meal at a hotel, etc., that is to be paid for later: *Luke sighed and turned to his desk, where the chits had accumulated* (Margery Allingham). **2** a letter or note; memorandum: *The next day I received a chit from Somerset Maugham* (Tallulah Bankhead). Also, **chitty.** [short for *chitty* < Hindi *chiṭṭhī* < Sanskrit *chitra* a spot, mark]

chit² (chit), *n.* **1a** a child. **b** a person considered as no better than a child (now mostly of a girl or young woman): *A little chit of a miller's daughter of eighteen* (Dickens). **2** a saucy, forward girl. [related to **kit(ten)**; origin uncertain]

chit³ (chit), *n., v.,* **chit|ted, chit|ting.** —*n.* a sprout of a seed; a shoot, as of a potato.
—*v.i.* = sprout. [Middle English *chitte*]

chi|tal (chē′təl), *n., pl.* **-tals** or (*collectively*) **-tal.** **1** a deer of southern Asia having a spotted body; axis deer. **2** a venomous water snake of the East Indian seas. [< Hindi *chītal* spotted, a spotted snake, and *chītāl,* a spotted deer, both related to Hindustani *chītā* cheetah. See etym. under **cheetah.**]

chi|tar|ro|ne (kē′tə rō′nā), *n., pl.* **-ni** (-nē). a lute with two necks, similar to the theorbo, but longer. [< Italian *chitarrone* < *chitarra* guitar]

chit-chat (chit′chat′), *n., v.,* **-chat|ted, -chat|ting.** —*n.* **1** friendly, informal talk; chat: *This age group, I found by chit-chat ... is not exclusively preoccupied with dating* (Atlantic). **2** idle talk; gossip.
—*v.i.* to engage in chit-chat: *She soon becomes adept at ordering meals and chit-chatting at parties* (Harper's).
[reduplication of *chat*] —**chit′-chat′ter,** *n.*

chit-chat|ty (chit′chat′ē), *adj.* like chit-chat; gossipy: *... a somewhat nondescript, chit-chatty book* (Scientific American).

chi|tin (kī′tin), *n.* a horny substance forming the hard outer covering of lobsters, crabs, beetles, crickets, and some fungi: *This chitin is a stiff substance rather closely related to cellulose* (Norbert Wiener). [< French *chitine* < Greek *chitṓn* coat of mail, chiton]

chi|tin|ize (kī′tə nīz), *v.t.,* **-ized, -iz|ing.** to make into chitin; harden by deposition of chitin. —**chi′tin|i|za′tion,** *n.*

chi|tin|ous (kī′tə nəs), *adj.* of or like chitin.

chit|lings (chit′lingz), *n.pl.* = chitterlings.

chit|lins (chit′linz), *n.pl.* = chitterlings.

∗**chi|ton** (kī′tən, -ton), *n.* **1** a long, loose garment worn next to the skin by men and women in ancient Greece. **2** *Zoology.* any animal of a class of sluggish marine mollusks that adhere to rocks; amphineuran. They are bilaterally symmetrical and elliptical, with a shell of eight overlapping plates. [< Greek *chitṓn* tunic, coat of mail]

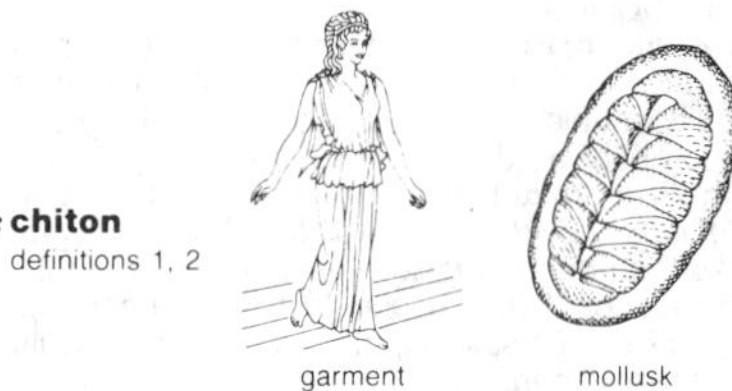

∗**chiton**
definitions 1, 2

chit|tam (chit′əm), *n.* = cascara sagrada.

chit|ter (chit′ər), *v.i.* **1** to twitter; chirp: *the chittering of robins. Rats chitter behind the wainscoting* (Time). **2** *Especially British.* to shiver with cold; tremble. [imitative; probably formed from *chatter*]

chit|ter|lings (chit′ər lingz; *see note below*), *n.pl.* parts of the intestines of pigs, cooked as food, usually deep-fat fried: *The house servants ... had their own feast of hoecakes and yams and chitterlings* (Margaret Mitchell). Also, **chitlings, chitlins.** [Middle English *cheterlingis;* origin uncertain]
►Now in the United States and historically usually written *chitterlings,* especially by those writing about the South. The current pronunciation of those who really eat them is *chit′lingz,* or more often, *chit′linz.*

chit|ty (chit′ē), *n., pl.* **-ties.** a chit; note.

chiv|al|resque (shiv′əl resk′), *adj.* proper or suited to the age of chivalry. [< French *chevaleresque* < *chevalier* chevalier]

chiv|al|ric (shiv′əl rik, shə val′-), *adj.* **1** having to do with chivalry. **2** = chivalrous.

chiv|al|rous (shiv′əl rəs), *adj.* **1a** having the qualities of an ideal knight; brave, courteous, helpful, honorable, and devoted to the service of the weak and oppressed. SYN: considerate, gallant. **b** having to do with the rules of knights in the Middle Ages: *the old feudal and chivalrous spirit of fealty* (Edmund Burke). **c** devoted to the service of the female sex. **2** *Obsolete.* like or characteristic of a medieval knight, especially brave.
[< Old French *chevalrous, chevalreus* < *chevalier* chevalier] —**chiv′al|rous|ly,** *adv.* —**chiv′al|rous|ness,** *n.*

chiv|al|ry (shiv′əl rē), *n.* **1** the qualities of an ideal knight in the Middle Ages. Chivalry includes bravery, honor, courtesy, respect for women, protection of the weak, generosity, and fairness to enemies. *He loved chivalry, Truth and honour, freedom and courtesy* (Chaucer). **2** the rules, customs, and beliefs of knights in the Middle Ages; system of knighthood: *The young man took the vows of chivalry to become a knight.* **3** knights as a group: **a** a group of knights, horsemen, or warriors, especially those conspicuous for gallantry. **b** gallant gentlemen: *And Belgium's capital had gathered then Her Beauty and her Chivalry* (Byron). **4** *Archaic.* the position or character of a knight: **a** bravery or prowess in war. **b** knighthood as a rank or order. [< Old French *chevalerie* < *chevalier* chevalier]

chive (chīv), *n.,* or **chive garlic.** Often **chives.** **1** a plant of the same family as the onion and leek, having a very small bulb. Chives are perennial. See picture under **amaryllis family.** **2** its long, slender leaves, used as a seasoning in soups, salads, stews, and other prepared foods. [Middle English *cive* < Old French, any of several small species of onion < Latin *caepa* onion]

chiv|vy (chiv′ē), *v.,* **-vied, -vy|ing,** *n., pl.* **-vies.** —*v.t.* **1** to chase: *... clients who have just been chivvied abruptly out of their rightful train* (Punch). *She [the ship] came ... with an armada*

of boats and aircraft to chivvy her along (Manchester Guardian Weekly). **2** *Figurative.* to harass, annoy, nag: *In spite of stories of stars being chivvied by . . . hordes of autograph hounds, many of them aren't so pursued* (Saturday Evening Post). *—v.i.* **1** to chevy; scamper. **2** *Figurative.* to worry; nag. *—n.* = chevy.
[variant of *chevy*]

chiv|y (chiv′ē), *v.,* **chiv|ied, chiv|y|ing,** *n., pl.* **chiv|ies.** = chivvy.

Ch. J., Chief Justice.

chlam|y|date (klam′ə dāt), *adj. Zoology.* having a pallium or mantle, as a mollusk. [< Greek *chlamýs, -ydos* chlamys + English *-ate*[1]]

chla|myd|i|a (klə mid′ē ə), *n.* **1** any one of a group of parasitic rickettsias that cause a wide variety of diseases, including trachoma and psittacosis. **2** a venereal disease caused by a species of chlamydia and typically affecting the lymph nodes in the groin; lymphogranuloma. [< *Chlamydia,* the genus name < Greek *chlamýs, -ydos* chlamys]

chlam|y|do|spore (klam′ə də spôr, -spōr), *n.* a thick-walled, dark spore formed by smuts and other fungi. [< Greek *chlamýs, -ydos*]

***chla|mys** (klā′mis, klam′is), *n., pl.* **chla|mys|es, chlam|y|des** (klam′ə dēz). a short cloak, fastened on the shoulder, worn by men in ancient Greece. [< Greek *chlamýs, -ydos* short mantle]

***chlamys**

chlo|an|thite (klō an′thīt), *n.* a native arsenide of nickel, a mineral of white to grayish or black color with a metallic luster. *Formula:* $NiAs_2$ [< Greek *chloanthês* sprouting < *chlón* a young green shoot (because of its color) + English *-ite*[1]]

chlo|as|ma (klō az′mə), *n.* discoloration of the skin in large, yellowish or yellow-brownish spots or patches. [< Greek *chlóasma* greenness < *chloázein* to become green]

Chlo|e or **Chlo|ë** (klō′ē), *n.* a name for a beloved maiden in pastoral literature. [< Greek *Chlóē* (literally) verdure]

chlor-, *combining form.* the form of **chloro-** before vowels, as in *chloric.*

chlor|a|ce|tic acid (klôr′ə sē′tik, -set′ik; klōr′-), = chloroacetic acid.

chlor|ac|ne (klôr ak′nē, klōr-), *n.* a skin eruption resembling acne, caused by exposure to chlorinated hydrocarbons.

chlo|ra|gogue or **chlo|ra|gog cells** (klôr′ə gôg, -gog; klōr′-), the round, yellowish cells covering the exterior of the intestines of some annelids, such as earthworms. [< Greek *chlōrós* greenish-yellow + *agōgós* leading < *ágein* to lead]

chlo|ral (klôr′əl, klōr′-), *n.* **1** a colorless, oily liquid made from chlorine and alcohol, used in making chloral hydrate and DDT. It has a pungent odor. *Formula:* C_2HCl_3O **2** = chloral hydrate. [< French *chloral* < *chlore* chlorine + *alcool* alcohol]

chloral hydrate, a colorless, crystalline drug formerly much used to quiet nervousness and produce sleep. It is a combination of water with chloral. *Chloral hydrate is used in Mickey Finns.*

chlo|ral|ism (klôr′ə liz əm, klōr′-), *n.* **1** the habitual use of chloral hydrate. **2** a diseased condition due to the use of chloral hydrate.

chlo|ral|ize (klôr′ə līz, klōr′-), *v.t.,* **-ized, -iz|ing.** to bring under the influence of or treat with chloral hydrate.

chlor|al|um (klô ral′əm, klō-), *n.* an antiseptic consisting of an aqueous solution of chloride of aluminum. *Formula:* $AlCl_3 \cdot 6H_2O$

chlor|am|bu|cil (klôr am′byə sil, klōr-), *n.* a drug derived from nitrogen mustard, used to arrest the growth of cancerous tissue, especially in Hodgkin's disease. [< *chlor-* + *am*(ine) + *bu*(tyric) + arbitrary suffix *-cil*]

chlor|a|mine (klôr′ə mēn, klōr′-), *n.,* or **chloramine-T,** a white or yellowish crystalline powder derived from toluene, used in solution as a strong antiseptic, especially to cleanse wounds. *Formula:* $C_7H_7O_2NSClNa \cdot 3H_2O$

chlor|am|phen|i|col (klôr′am fen′ə kōl, klōr′-; -kol), *n.* an antibiotic drug used in the treatment of diseases caused by rickettsiae or bacteria, such as Rocky Mountain spotted fever or typhoid fever; Chloromycetin. *Formula:* $C_{11}H_{12}Cl_2N_2O_5$ [< *chlor-* + *am*(ide) + *phe*(nol) + *ni*(tro-) + (gly)*col*]

chlor|an|il (klôr′ə nil, klōr-), *n.* a yellow substance soluble in alcohol and benzene, used as a fungicide in treating seeds and potatoes and as an oxidizing agent in manufacturing dyes. *Formula:* $C_6Cl_4O_2$

chlo|rate (klôr′āt, klōr′-; -it), *n. Chemistry.* a salt of chloric acid, which contains the univalent radical $-ClO_3$

chlorate of potash, = potassium chlorate.

chlor|cy|cli|zine (klôr sī′klə zēn, klōr-), *n.* a white, bitter, odorless, crystalline drug, used as an antihistamine. *Formula:* $C_{18}H_{21}ClN_2$ [< *chlor-* + *cycl-* + *azine*]

chlor|dan (klôr ′dan, klōr′-), *n.* = chlordane.

chlor|dane (klôr′dān, klōr′-), *n.* a liquid insecticide derived from indene. *Formula:* $C_{10}H_6Cl_8$ [< *chlor*(ine) + (in)*dan,* a derivative of *indene*]

chlor|di|az|e|pox|ide (klôr′dī az′ə pok′sīd, klōr′-), *n.* a chemical substance widely used in the form of its hydrochloride as a tranquilizer: *The pills known to relieve mild anxiety are the tranquilizers—chlordiazepoxide* (*Librium*)*, diazepam* (*Valium*)*, and meprobamate* (*Miltown*) (Earl Ubell). *Formula:* $C_{16}H_{14}ClN_3O$ [< *chlor-* + *di-*[1] + *az-* nitrogen + *epoxide*]

chlo|rel|la (klə rel′ə), *n.* one of a genus of single-celled green algae, a potential source of low-cost nutrients. [< New Latin *Chlorella* the genus name < Greek *chlōrós* pale green]

chlo|ren|chy|ma (klə reng′kə mə), *n.* any plant tissue which contains chlorophyll. [< *chlor-* + (par)*enchyma*]

chlor|hy|dric (klôr hī′drik, klōr-), *adj.* = hydrochloric.

chlo|ric (klôr′ik, klōr′-), *adj. Chemistry.* **1** of or having to do with chlorine. **2** containing chlorine, especially with a valence of 5.

chloric acid, a colorless acid which occurs only in water solution and is a strong oxidizing agent. *Formula:* $HClO_3$

chlo|rid (klôr′id, klōr′-), *n.* = chloride.

chlo|ri|date (klôr′ə dāt, klōr′-), *v.t.,* **-dat|ed, -dat|ing. 1** to treat with a chloride. **2** to combine with chlorine; form into a chloride.

chlo|ride (klôr′īd, klōr′-; -id), *n.* **1a** a compound of chlorine with another element or radical. Sodium chloride is a compound of sodium and chlorine. **b** a salt of hydrochloric acid. **2** = chloride of lime.

chloride of lime, a white powder used for bleaching and disinfecting, made by treating slaked lime with chlorine; bleaching powder; chlorinated lime. *Formula:* $CaOCl_2$

chlo|rid|ic (klə rid′ik), *adj.* having to do with or of the nature of a chloride.

chlo|ri|di|za|tion (klôr′ə də zā′shən, klōr′-), *n.* **1** the act or process of chloridizing. **2** the state of being chloridized.

chlo|rid|ize (klôr′ə dīz, klōr′-), *v.t.,* **-ized, -iz|ing. 1** to convert into a chloride, especially to roast (a silver ore) with salt in order to convert the silver into chloride. **2** to treat with a chloride.

chlo|rin (klôr′in, klōr′-), *n.* = chlorine.

chlo|rin|ate (klôr′ə nāt, klōr′-), *v.t.,* **-at|ed, -at|ing. 1** to combine with chlorine. **2** to treat with chlorine: **a** to disinfect or sterilize (water or sewage) by the use of chlorine: *to chlorinate water in a swimming pool.* **b** to treat (gold or silver ore) with chlorine, to extract the precious metal; chloridize. **—chlo′rin|a′tion,** *n.* **—chlo′rin|a′tor,** *n.*

chlo|rin|at|ed hydrocarbon (klôr′ə nā′tid, klōr′-), any one of a class of synthetic pesticides, formed by a chlorine-carbon bond, that are among the most persistent of environmental poisons. Chlorinated hydrocarbons include DDT, aldrin, dieldrin, endrin, chlordane, and lindane.

chlorinated lime, = chloride of lime.

***chlo|rine** (klôr′ēn, -in; klōr′-), *n.* a greenish-yellow, bad-smelling, poisonous gas. It is a chemical element, one of the halogens, which occurs chiefly in combination with sodium as common salt. Chlorine is very irritating to the nose, throat, and lungs. It is used in bleaching and disinfecting, and in making plastics, explosives, and dyes. Also, **chlorin.** [(coined by Sir Humphry Davy) < Greek *chlōrós* pale green, greenish yellow]

***chlorine**

symbol	atomic number	atomic weight	oxidation state
Cl	17	35.453	±1, +3, +5, +7

chlorine dioxide, a yellowish, explosive gas, used especially to bleach flour and paper, and to remove unpleasant tastes and odors from water. *Formula:* ClO_2

chlo|rin|i|ty (klô rin′ə tē, klō-), *n.* quality or degree of being chlorinous: *the chlorinity of water.*

chlo|rin|ous (klôr′ə nəs, klōr′-), *adj.* of or having to do with chlorine: *a chlorinous odor.*

Chlo|ris (klôr′is, klōr′-), *n.* the Greek goddess of springtime and flowers, equivalent to Flora in Roman mythology.

chlo|rite[1] (klôr′īt, klōr′-), *n. Chemistry.* a salt of chlorous acid, which contains the univalent radical $-ClO_2$ [< *chlor*(ous) + *-ite*[2]]

chlo|rite[2] (klôr′īt, klōr′-), *n. Mineralogy.* any one of a group of green hydrous silicates of magnesia and alumina, resembling mica. [adaptation of Greek *chlōrîtis* (*líthos*) a kind of grass-green (stone) < *chlōrós* pale green]

chlo|rit|ic (klə rit′ik), *adj.* having to do with or containing chlorite[2] (mineral).

chlo|ri|tize (klôr′ə tīz, klōr′-), *v.t.,* **-tized, -tiz|ing.** to change (a mineral) in a rock into chlorite. [< *chlorit*(e)[2] + *-ize*] **—chlo′ri|ti|za′tion,** *n.*

chlo|ri|toid (klôr′ə toid, klōr′-), *n.* a mineral, a native silicate of aluminum, ferrous iron, and magnesium, having a dark-green color and occurring usually in brittle laminae. [< *chlorit*(e)[2] + *-oid*]

chlor|mad|i|none (klôr mad′ə nōn, klōr-), *n.* a synthetic hormone similar to progesterone, used as an oral contraceptive. [< *chlor-* + *m*(ethyl) + *a*(cetoxy) + *di-* + connective *-n-* + *-one*]

chloro-, *combining form.* **1** green: *Chlorospinel = a green variety of spinel.* **2** chlorophyll: *Chlorosis = an abnormal lack of chlorophyll.* **3** chlorine: *Chlorobenzene = a compound of chlorine and benzene.* Also, **chlor-** before vowels. [< Greek *chlōrós* pale green]

chlo|ro|a|ce|tic acid (klôr′ō ə sē′tik, -set′ik; klōr′-), a colorless, crystalline acid, used in medicine and in organic synthesis. *Formula:* $C_2H_3ClO_2$ Also, **chloracetic acid.**

chlo|ro|ac|e|to|phe|none (klôr′ō as′ə tō fē nōn′, -ə sē′tō-; klōr′-), *n.* a highly toxic compound derived from acetophenone by chlorination, used as a tear gas; CN. *Formula:* $C_6H_5COCH_2Cl$

chlo|ro|ben|zene (klôr′ō ben′zēn, -ben zēn′; klōr′-), *n.* a colorless, inflammable liquid, formed by combining chlorine with benzene, and used in the manufacture of paints and varnishes, drugs, perfumes, and insecticides. *Formula:* C_6H_5Cl

chlo|ro|cru|or|in (klôr′ō krü′ər in, klōr′-), *n.* a green pigment found in the respiratory tract of certain marine worms, mollusks, and insects. [< *chloro-* + *cruor* + *-in*]

chlo|ro|dyne (klôr′ə dīn, klōr′-), *n.* a powerful anodyne of varying composition, containing morphine, chloroform, hydrochloric acid, extract of Indian hemp, etc. [< *chloro*(form) + (ano)*dyne*]

chlo|ro|flu|o|ro|car|bon (klôr′ə flü′ər ə kär′bən, klōr′-; flůr′ə-), *n.* = Freon.

chlo|ro|flu|o|ro|meth|ane (klôr′ə flü′ər ə-meth′ān, klōr′-; -flůr′ə-), *n.* any one of various fluorinated hydrocarbons combined with methane; one of the Freon gases: *Everyday millions of aerosol cans . . . release chlorofluoromethanes, propellant gases that may be reducing the atmosphere's ozone layer* (Joseph Eigner).

chlo|ro|form (klôr′ə fôrm, klōr′-), *n., v.* *—n.* a colorless liquid with a sharp, sweetish smell and taste. Chloroform evaporates quickly and easily. When its vapor is inhaled, it makes a person unconscious or unable to feel pain. It is also used in making refrigerants, propellants, and plastics and as a solvent to dissolve rubber, resin, wax, and many other substances. Chloroform is usually obtained by treating acetone with chloride of lime. *Queen Victoria gave birth to her eighth child, Prince Leopold, under chloroform* (George Rosen). *Formula:* $CHCl_3$
—v.t. **1a** to make unconscious or unable to feel pain by giving chloroform. **b** to apply chloroform to (a thing); soak with chloroform. **2** to kill with chloroform.
[< French *chloroforme* < *chloro-* chlorine + *formyl* in obsolete sense, "methenyl"]

chlo|ro|form|ist (klôr′ə fôr′mist, klōr′-), *n.* a person who administers chloroform professionally, as to patients.

chlo|ro|gen|ic acid (klôr′ō jen′ik, klōr′-), an acid found in most edible plants, important in plant metabolism. It is the substance that turns apples and other fruits brown after they are peeled and exposed to air. *Formula:* $C_{16}H_{18}O_9$

chlo|ro|hy|drin (klôr′ə hī′drin, klōr′-), *n. Chemistry.* any of a group of organic compounds having both a chlorine atom and a hydroxyl (OH) radical.

chlo|rom|e|ter (klə rom′ə tər), *n.* an instrument or device for estimating percentages of chlorine.

Chlo|ro|my|ce|tin (klôr′ə mī sē′tin, klōr′-), *n. Trademark.* chloramphenicol.

chlo|ro|phane (klôr′ə fān, klōr′-), *n.* a variety of fluorite, which exhibits a bright-green glow when heated. [< *chloro-* + Greek *phaínein* appear]

chlo|ro|phyll or **chlo|ro|phyl** (klôr′ə fil, klōr′-), *n.* the green coloring matter of plants. In the presence of light it makes carbohydrates, such as starch and sugar, from carbon dioxide and water, a process called photosynthesis. Chlorophyll usually occurs in small bodies (chloroplasts) within the cell, and exists in several known forms, all having a porphyrin nucleus containing magnesium and a phytol side chain. Chlorophyll is essential to most plants and thus indirectly to almost all living organisms. It has been used in medicines and as a coloring for waxes and oils. *The spectroscopic examination of chlorophyll shows that it absorbs the light of just those wave lengths which are most effective in photosynthesis* (Fred W. Emerson). [< French *chlorophylle* < Greek *chlōrós* plale green + *phýllon* leaf]

chlo|ro|phyl|la|ceous (klôr′ə fə lā′shəs, klōr′-), *adj.* of the nature of chlorophyll; chlorophyllous.

chlo|ro|phyl|lin (klôr′ə fil′in, klōr′-), *n.* any one of the pigments in chlorophyll.

chlo|ro|phyl|lose (klôr′ə fil′ōs, klōr′-), *adj.* = chlorophyllous.

chlo|ro|phyl|lous (klôr′ə fil′əs, klōr′-), *adj.* having to do with or containing chlorophyll.

chlo|ro|pic|rin (klôr′ō pik′rin, -pī′krin; klōr′-), *n.* a colorless, pungent liquid, used as an insecticide and in chemical warfare. Its vapor causes vomiting. *Formula:* CCl_3NO_2 Also, **chlorpicrin.** [< *chloro-* + *picr*(ic) (acid) + *-in*]

chlo|ro|plast (klôr′ə plast, klōr′-), *n.* a tiny body in the cells of green plants that contains chlorophyll: *The green color of stems is usually due to chloroplasts in the cortical cells just beneath the epidermis* (Fred W. Emerson). See picture under **cell.** [< *chloro-* + *-plast*]

chlo|ro|prene (klôr′ə prēn, klōr′-), *n.* a colorless liquid, synthesized from acetylene and hydrogen chloride, used in the manufacture of synethetic rubber. *Formula:* C_4H_5Cl [< *chloro-* + (iso)*prene*]

chlo|ro|pro|ma|zine (klôr′ə prō′mə zēn, klōr′-), *n.* = chlorpromazine.

chlo|ro|quin (klôr′ə kwin, klōr′-), *n.* = chloroquine.

chlo|ro|quine (klôr′ə kwīn, klōr′-), *n.* a medicine used mainly in the treatment of malarial attacks. [< *chloro-* + *quin*(olin)*e*]

chlo|ro|sis (klə rō′sis), *n.* **1** *Botany.* a condition of plants in which the green parts are blanched or yellow because of inadequate formation of chlorophyll, usually resulting from a lack of iron or magnesium in the soil, or from a lack of light. **2** *Medicine.* a form of anemia affecting girls at or about puberty, characterized by a yellowish-green complexion and irregular menstruation; greensickness. [< New Latin *chlorosis* < *chlor-* + *-osis* condition]

chlo|ro|spi|nel (klôr′ə spi nel′, klōr′-), *n.* a variety of spinel having a grass-green color, which is due to the presence of copper.

chlo|ro|thi|a|zide (klôr′ə thī′ə zīd, klōr′-), *n.* a drug used in the treatment of hypertension and as a diuretic. *Formula:* $C_7H_6ClN_3O_4S_2$ [< *chloro-* + *thiaz*(ol) + *-ide*]

chlo|rot|ic (klə rot′ik), *adj.* **1** of or having to do with chlorosis. **2** having or suffering from chlorosis: *A plant ... shut up in a dark place ... becomes chlorotic; its green color disappears* (Thomas L. Phipson). —**chlo|rot′i|cal|ly,** *adv.*

chlo|rous (klôr′əs, klōr′-), *adj. Chemistry.* **1** of chlorine. **2** containing chlorine, especially with a valence of 3.

chlorous acid, an acid occurring only in solution or in the form of its salts (chlorites). *Formula:* $HClO_2$

chlor|pic|rin (klôr pik′rin, -pī′krin; klōr-), *n.* = chloropicrin.

chlor|pro|ma|zine (klôr prō′mə zēn, klōr-), *n.* a synthetic drug, used as a sedative and antiemetic, especially in the treatment of mental illness; Thorazine: *Chlorpromazine seems to be most effective in suppressing the delusions of paranoid patients and in quieting patients who are restless, hyperactive and over-elated* (Scientific American). *Formula:* $C_{17}H_{19}ClN_2S$ Also, **chloropromazine.** [< *chlor-* + *promazine*]

chlor|pro|pa|mide (klôr prō′pə mīd, klōr-), *n.* a drug given orally for the treatment of mild forms of diabetes. *Formula:* $C_{10}H_{13}ClN_2O_3S$ [< *chlor-* + *prop*(ane) + *amide*]

chlor|tet|ra|cy|cline (klôr tet′rə sī′klin, klōr-), *n.* = Aureomycin.

chm., **1** chairman. **2** checkmate.

chmn. or **chn.,** chairman.

cho|a|no|cyte (kō′ə nə sīt), *n.* one of a layer of flagellated cells on the interior surface of a sponge. [< Greek *choánē* funnel + English *-cyte*]

cho|a|no|flag|el|late (kō′ə nə flaj′ə lāt), *n.* any microbe of a group of flagellates in which a collar of protoplasm encircles the flagellum. [< Greek *choánē* funnel + English *flagellate*]

choc (chok), *n., adj. British Informal.* chocolate: *Take a couple of hours off and curl up with a box of chocs* (Punch).

***chock** (chok), *n., v., adv.* —*n.* **1** a block or wedge, put under a barrel, wheel, or the like, to keep it from rolling, or under something, such as a boat on a ship's deck, to keep it in place: *Put the chocks under the back wheels when I stop.* **2** a block of metal or strong wood having two arms curving inward for a rope or cable to pass through in mooring, anchoring, or towing, usually on the rail or deck of a ship.
—*v.t.* **1** to provide or fasten with chocks; stop with chocks: *Chock the back wheels when I stop.* **2** to put (a boat) on chocks: *to chock a boat on a ship's deck.*
—*adv.* as close or tight as can be; quite: *seized up a great stone, and crowded it chock against the grinding, slipping wheel* (Adeline D. T. Whitney).
[earlier *chuck,* apparently < Old North French *choque* log]

***chock** definition 2

chock-a-block or **chock|a|block** (chok′ə blok′), *adj.* **1** (of tackle) with the blocks drawn close together. **2** *Figurative.* jammed together; crowded; packed: *The museum ... keeps its members happy with a calendar chock-a-block with concerts, poetry readings, art classes and a movie series* (Time).

chock-full (chok′fu̇l′), *adj.* as full as can be; crammed full; stuffed full: *The boy's pockets were chock-full of marbles.* Also, **chuck-full.**

chock|stone (chok′stōn′), *n.* a rock wedged into a fissure on a mountain slope, often used by mountaineers for footholds.

choc|o|late (chôk′lit, chok′-; -ə lit), *n., adj.* —*n.* **1** a substance made by roasting and grinding cacao seeds. Chocolate has a strong, rich flavor and is often sweetened and flavored, as with vanilla. It has much value as food. **2** a drink made of chocolate with hot milk or water and sugar. **3** candy made of chocolate; a piece of candy made of or covered with chocolate. **4** Also, **chocolate brown.** a dark-brown color; the color of chocolate: *cloth varying from deep chocolate to chestnut.*
—*adj.* **1** made of or flavored with chocolate: *chocolate cake.* **2** dark-brown.
[< Mexican Spanish *chocolate* < Nahuatl *chocolatl* (literally) acrid, or sour, water]

choc|o|late-box (chôk′lit boks′, chok′-; -ə lit-), *adj.* decorative in an overly sentimental or elaborate way; pretty-pretty: *chocolate-box art, chocolate-box backdrops.*

chocolate point, a variety of Siamese cat having a cream-colored body and medium-brown points.

chocolate tree, = cacao (def. 2).

choc|o|la|ty or **choc|o|la|tey** (chôk′lə tē, chok′-; -ə lə-), *adj. Informal.* chocolate; like chocolate.

Choc|taw (chok′tô), *n., pl.* **-taw** or **-taws. 1** a member of a tribe of American Indians, now living mostly in Oklahoma. **2** the Muskhogean language of these Indians. **3** *Figurative.* any unknown or difficult language. **4** a fancy figure in skating consisting of a forward stroke on either edge of one skate and then a backward stroke on the opposite edge of the other. [American English < Choctaw *Chahta,* the native name]

cho|ga (chō′gə), *n.* a loose garment with long sleeves like a dressing gown, worn chiefly in Afghanistan. [< Turki *choghā*]

chog|set (chog′set), *n.* = cunner (fish). [< Algonkian (Massachuset) *chohchohkesit* striped, spotted]

chog|yal (chog′yäl), *n.* the title of the ruler of Sikkim, equivalent of maharaja or king.

choice (chois), *n., adj.,* **choic|er, choic|est.** —*n.* **1** the act of choosing; selection: *She was careful in her choice of friends. We had the choice of a house or an apartment. The choice of color, material, and style is all-important in buying a dress.* **2** the power or chance to choose; option: *His father gave him a choice between a radio and a camera. You have no other choice but to leave now.* **3** a person or thing chosen: *each to his choice* (Rudyard Kipling). *This hat is my choice.* **4** a thing among several things to be chosen; alternative: *The store was out of milk and she had no choice but to buy it elsewhere.* **5a** a quantity and variety to choose from: *We found a wide choice of vegetables in the market. There's small choice in rotten apples* (Shakespeare). **b** a well-chosen supply: *They were regaled with choice of food and drink.* **6** the best or finest part; the pick: *These flowers are the choice of my garden.* **7** *Archaic.* discrimination; judgment.
—*adj.* **1** excellent; of fine quality; superior; select: *choice food and wines. The choicest fruit had the highest price. The choice and master spirits of this age* (Shakespeare). *In a sea of folly tossed, my choicest hours of life are lost* (Alexander Pope). **SYN:** exquisite. See syn. under **fine. 2** carefully selected; well-chosen: *choice arguments. Choice word and measured phrase* (Wordsworth). **3** (of beef and veal), being the grade of meat between prime and good. U.S. choice beef looks like prime but contains less fat. **4** *Chiefly Dialect.* **a** showing nice discrimination; fastidious: *a choice taste in food.* **b** careful of one's possessions, etc.; making much: *the latest sailor songs ... which they were very choice of* (Richard Henry Dana).
[< Old French *chois* < Germanic (Old High German *kiosan, cheosan* choose)] —**choice′ly,** *adv.* —**choice′ness.** *n.*
—*Syn. n.* **2, 3, 4. Choice, alternative, preference, option** mean the chance to choose or the thing to be chosen. **Choice,** the general and most informal word, emphasizes freedom in choosing, both in the way one chooses and in the number of possibilities from which to choose: *Take your choice of the puppies.* **Alternative** emphasizes limitation of the possibilities, usually to two but sometimes several, between which one must choose: *You have the alternative of leaving or staying and behaving.* **Preference** emphasizes choosing according to one's own liking: *Which is your preference?* **Option** means a right to choose granted by someone to another; in business use, it means the purchased right to buy or to refrain from buying at the end of a stated period: *The court gave him the option of going to jail or paying a fine. He holds an option to buy the building.*

choir (kwīr), *n., v., adj.* —*n.* **1** the group of singers who sing together and lead the musical part of a church service: *As the choir rose to sing the people joined in, filling the church with the music of the first hymn.* **2** that part of a church set apart for the singers. In cathedrals and certain other churches the choir is that part between the nave and the main altar reserved for the choristers and clergy. **3** any group of singers; chorus: *a choir of carolers.* **4** *Music.* **a** instruments of the same class in an orchestra: *the string choir, the brass choir.* **b** the musicians playing such a class of instruments. **5** a band of dancers, or of dancers and singers (especially in ancient heathen worship). **6** any one of the nine orders of angels.
—*v.i., v.t.* to sing all together at the same time; sing in chorus: *The dreaming Joseph, the rapt shepherds, and the choiring angels form a kind of halo around the central drama* [*of*] *a mother's first sight of her baby* (Time).
—*adj.* belonging to that part of the membership of a religious order which is obligated to perform the daily Divine Office in choir. Also, **quire.**
[< Old French *cuer* < Medieval Latin *chorus* part of a church; body of church singers < Latin. See etym. of doublet **chorus.**]

choir aisle, one of the aisles which flank the choir in a church, often including the passage around the chevet.

choir|boy (kwīr′boi′), *n.* a boy who sings in a choir; chorister: *He looked just like a little choirboy, with his pink face and close-cut, blond hair* (Time).

choir loft, the gallery from which the choir sings in some churches.

choir|man (kwīr′mən), *n., pl.* **-men.** a man who sings in a choir or chorus.

choir|mas|ter (kwīr′mas′tər, -mäs′-), *n.* the leader or director of a choir.

choir organ, one of the principal sections of a large organ, containing stops especially suited for choir accompaniment.

choir stall, any one of the seats built into the chancel of a church or cathedral for the use of singers.

choke (chōk), *v.,* **choked, chok|ing,** *n.* —*v.t.* **1** to stop the breath of (an animal or person) by squeezing the throat or blocking it up; suffocate; stifle: *The smoke from the burning building almost choked the fireman.* **SYN:** throttle. **2** to check or extinguish by cutting off the supply of air; smother: *A bucket of sand will choke a fire.* **3a** to fill up or block; clog: *Sand is choking the river.* **SYN:** fill. **b** to fill chock-full: *Rome was becoming choked with impoverished citizens* (James A. Froude). **4** *Figurative.* to suppress or smother, as a feeling: *She choked her laughter with a cough. ... all pity choked with custom of fell deeds* (Shakespeare). **5** *Figurative.* to check or hinder in growth, progress, or expansion: *to choke the progress of true knowledge with formalities* (John Hill Burton). **SYN:** obstruct. **6** to reduce the supply of air to (an internal-combustion engine) to make a richer fuel mixture, especially in starting. **7** to kill or injure (a plant) by depriving it of air and light or of room to grow. **8** *Sports.* to grip (a bat, club, racket, or stick) at some distance from the end of the handle.
—*v.i.* **1** to be unable to breathe: *He choked when a piece of meat stuck in his throat. I must say ... or choke in silence* (Robert Browning). **SYN:**

gag. **2** to be blocked or congested: (*Figurative.*) *Tho' every channel of the state Should almost choke with golden sand* (Tennyson).
—*n.* **1a** the act of choking: *He gave a few chokes and then got his breath.* **b** the sound of choking: *Men ... who express by grunts and chokes the inexpressible eloquence which is not in them* (Algernon Swinburne). **2** that which chokes or impedes respiration. **3** the valve that reduces the supply of air to an internal-combustion engine. **4** a narrow or constricted part of, as a tube in a chokebore of a shotgun. **5** *Electricity.* choke coil.
choke back, to hold back, control, or suppress: *to choke back a sob or laughter.*
choke down, **a** to swallow against one's inclination; force down: *He choked down the evil-tasting brew.* **b** to choke back: *She choked down her sobs.*
choke off, to put an end to; get rid of; stop: *The break in the water main choked off the city's supply of water.*
choke up, **a** to block up; fill up; clog up: *A traffic jam choked up the highway. Multitudes of fugitives were choking up the bridges* (Macaulay). **b** *Figurative.* to fill with emotion; be or cause to be on the verge of tears: *The audience was choked up by the death of the hero in the last scene of the movie.* **c** *Informal, Figurative.* to feel tense or apprehensive under pressure: *The leading actor was so choked up at curtain time that he missed his first cue.* **d** *Sports.* to grip a bat, club, racket, or stick at some distance from the end of the handle: *Don't choke up on the bat.* [variant of Middle English *cheken*]

choke|ber|ry (chōk′ber′ē), *n., pl.* **-ries. 1** the astringent, berrylike fruit of any plant of a genus of eastern North American shrubs of the rose family. **2** any one of these shrubs: *The chokeberry ... presents a beautiful sight when loaded with its bright scarlet fruit* (C. T. Mohr).

choke|bore (chōk′bôr′, -bōr′), *n.* **1** the bore of a shotgun that narrows toward the muzzle to keep the shot from scattering too widely. **2** a shotgun having such a bore.

choke|cher|ry (chōk′cher′ē), *n., pl.* **-ries. 1** a bitter wild cherry of North America. **2** the tree that it grows on. It belongs to the rose family. See picture under **deciduous**.

choke coil, *Electricity.* a coil of wire around a core of iron or air, used to control alternating currents in an electric circuit.

choke collar, a collar that tightens like a noose, used to control large or poorly behaved dogs.

choke|damp (chōk′damp′), *n.* a heavy, suffocating, nonexplosive gas, mainly carbon dioxide, that gathers in mines, old wells, and other underground caverns; blackdamp.

choke-full (chōk′fu̇l′), *adj.* = chock-full.

choke pear, a kind of pear with a harsh, astringent taste.

choke point, or **choke|point** (chōk′point′), *n.* a narrow route or passageway, especially at sea: *The Soviet access to the open seas passes through a number of choke points (such as the Bosphorus, Gibraltar, and the Greenland-Iceland-United Kingdom gap)* (London Times).

chok|er (chō′kər), *n.* **1** a person or thing that chokes. **2** something that fits tightly around the neck, such as: **a** a necklace. **b** a high collar. **c** a jacket with a high collar. **d** a wide tie.

chok|ey (chō′kē), *n., pl.* **-eys.** = choky[2].

chok|ing (chō′king), *adj., n.* —*adj.* **1** that chokes: *a choking grip.* **2** showing a tendency to choke, as with emotion: *I begged with a choking voice.*
—*n.* an acute obstruction in the esophagus, common in cattle, but affecting all species of domestic animals. —**chok′ing|ly**, *adv.*

choking coil, = choke coil.

chok|y[1] (chō′kē), *adj.,* **chok|i|er, chok|i|est. 1** inclined to choke, especially with emotion. **2** tending to choke: *a choky collar.* SYN: suffocating. **3** having a hoarse, throaty voice: *a choky singer.* [< *chok*(e) + *-y*[1]]

chok|y[2] (chō′kē), *n., pl.* **chok|ies.** *Anglo-Indian.* **1** a station, such as for the collection of customs or tolls, or for palanquin bearers, police, or the like. **2** a jail or lockup. [< Hindustani *chaukī*]

Chol (chōl), *n., pl.* **Chol** or **Cho|les** (chō′lās). a member of a tribe or division of the Maya Indians in southeastern Mexico.

cho|la (chō′lä), *n., pl.* **-las.** a female cholo. [< American Spanish *chola*]

chol|a|gog|ic (kol′ə goj′ik), *adj., n.* —*adj.* promoting the flow of bile. —*n.* = cholagogue.

chol|a|gogue (kol′ə gôg, -gog), *n.* a substance that promotes the flow of bile. [< French *cholagogue* < Greek *cholagōgós* carrying off bile < *cholḗ* bile + *agōgós* leading < *ágein* to lead]

chol|an|gi|o|gram (kol an′jē ə gram), *n.* an X-ray photograph of the bile ducts. [< Greek *cholḗ* bile + *angeîon* vessel + English *-gram*]

chol|an|gi|tis (kol′ən jī′tis), *n.* inflammation of the bile ducts. [< Greek *cholḗ* bile + *angeîon* vessel]

cho|late (kō′lāt, kol′āt), *n.* a salt or ester of cholic acid.

chol|e|cyst (kol′ə sist), *n.* the gall bladder. [< Greek *cholḗ* bile + *kýstis* cyst]

chol|e|cys|tec|to|my (kol′ə sis tek′tə mē), *n., pl.* **-mies.** surgical removal of the gall bladder.

chol|e|cys|ti|tis (kol′ə sis tī′tis), *n.* inflammation of the gall bladder.

chol|e|cys|to|graph|ic (kol′ə sis′tə graf′ik), *adj.* having to do with or produced by means of cholecystography.

chol|e|cys|tog|ra|phy (kol′ə sis tog′rə fē), *n.* X-ray examination of the gall bladder.

chol|e|cys|to|ki|nin (kol′ə sis′tə kī′nin), *n.* the intestinal hormone that causes the gall bladder to contract and empty. [< *cholecyst* + Greek *kīneîn* to move + English *-in*]

chol|e|li|thi|a|sis (kol′ə lə thī′ə sis), *n.* the formation or presence of gallstones. [< Greek *cholḗ* bile + *líthos* stone + English *-iasis*]

cho|lent (chô′lənt, shô′-), *n.* a Jewish dish of slowly stewed or baked meat and vegetables, served on the Sabbath. [< Yiddish *tsholnt, sholnt*]

chol|er (kol′ər), *n.* **1** an irritable disposition; anger; wrath: *His choler sometimes chokes him and he flaunts his outrage like a red tie at an academic banquet* (Wall Street Journal). SYN: irascibility. **2a** (in ancient and medieval physiology) the one of the four humors thought to cause irascibility; yellow bile. **b** bile viewed as a malady or disease; bilious disorder; biliousness: *Let's purge this choler without letting blood* (Shakespeare). [< Late Latin *cholera* bile < Latin, jaundice; see etym. under **cholera**]

chol|er|a (kol′ər ə), *n.* **1a** a painful disease of the stomach and intestines that causes cramps, vomiting, weakness, and diarrhea; Asiatic cholera. Cholera is an acute, infectious, bacterial disease which is endemic in India, frequently epidemic elsewhere, and often causes death. *Cholera is under international quarantine. People who go to Asian countries receive injections of cholera vaccine.* **b** any one of several diseases occurring chiefly in hot weather and causing acute diarrhea, including cholera infantum and cholera morbus. **2** any one of various diseases of animals. **3** *Obsolete.* choler (one of the four humors). [< Latin *cholera* < Greek *choléra* biliousness; jaundice < *cholḗ* bile]

chol|e|ra|ic (kol′ə rā′ik), *adj.* having to do with, or of the nature of, cholera.

cholera in|fan|tum (in fan′təm), any disease of infants that causes severe diarrhea, especially in hot weather. [< New Latin *cholera infantum*]

cholera mor|bus (môr′bəs), any inflammation of the intestines accompanied by diarrhea, fever, and pain. [< New Latin *cholera morbus*]

chol|er|ic (kol′ər ik), *adj.* **1a** having an irritable disposition; easily made angry; hot-tempered: *a choleric old tyrant to his family.* SYN: irascible, irritable. **b** enraged; angry; wrathful: *He was subject to choleric outbursts of temper.* **2** of or having to do with cholera. **3** *Obsolete.* **a** characterized by bile or biliousness; bilious. **b** causing choler or biliousness. —**chol′er|ic|ly**, *adv.*

chol|e|rine (kol′ər in; -ə rēn, -rīn), *n. Medicine.* **1** the early stage of cholera. **2** a mild form of cholera. [< *choler*(a) + *-ine*[1]]

cho|le|sta|sis (kō′lə stā′sis), *n.* a stoppage in the flow of bile. [< Greek *cholḗ* bile + *stásis* a standing, stoppage]

cho|les|ter|ic (kə les′tər ik), *adj. Chemistry, Physics.* having a molecular structure characteristic of compounds containing cholesterol; consisting of a series of layers in which the molecules are arranged in close parallel, vertical lines: *The most prominent application of cholesteric liquid crystals are in thermal mapping of living systems and in color displays of electronic components* (Science News).

cho|les|ter|in (kə les′tər in), *n.* = cholesterol.

cho|les|ter|ol (kə les′tə rōl, -rol), *n.* a white, fatty substance found in the blood and tissues of the body and also in foods such as eggs and meat, especially animal fats. It is important in metabolism. *The accumulation of cholesterol in the blood vessels forms plaques which may eventually restrict the flow of blood* (New York Times). *Formula:* $C_{27}H_{46}O$ [< Greek *cholḗ* bile + *stereós* solid, stiff + English *-ol*[2]]

cho|le|styr|a|mine (kə lə stī′rə mēn, -stir′ə-), *n.* a drug that decreases the synthesis of cholesterol. [< *chole*(sterol) + *styr*(ene) + *amine*]

cho|li (chō′lē), *n., pl.* **-lis.** (in India) a very short jacket for women, covering the bust: *She was wearing a white sari and a white choli, or jacket, the costume of adult Indian women* (New Yorker). [< Hindustani *cholī*]

cho|lic (kō′lik, kol′ik), *adj.* having to do with bile. [< Greek *cholḗ* bile + English *-ic*]

cholic acid, a white, crystalline acid, related to cholesterol, produced from the nitrogenized acids of bile during its decomposition. *Formula:* $C_{24}H_{40}O_5$

cho|line (kō′lēn, -lin; kol′ēn, -in), *n.* a constituent of the vitamin B complex, present in many animal and plant tissues, which prevents accumulation of fat in the liver. Choline is the basic constituent of lecithin. *Formula:* $C_5H_{15}NO_2$ [< Greek *cholḗ* bile + English *-ine*[2]]

cho|lin|er|gic (kō′lə nėr′jik, kol′ə-), *adj.* **1** that is stimulated or caused to act by choline, especially applied to the parasympathetic nerves which liberate acetylcholine at the nerve endings. **2** that stimulates the parasympathetic nerves and the release of acetylcholine: *a cholinergic substance, agent, chemical, or drug.* [< *choline* + Greek *érgon* + English *-ic*]

cho|lin|es|ter|ase (kō′lə nes′tə rās, kol′ə-), *n.* an enzyme which prevents the accumulation of acetylcholine at the nerve endings by stimulating its hydrolysis; acetylcholinesterase: *The enzyme cholinesterase, present in all nerve tissue, performs this essential task by cleaving the acetylcholine molecule into choline and acetic acid* (Scientific American). [< *choline* + *ester* + *-ase*]

cho|li|no|mi|met|ic (kō′lə nō mi met′ik, -mī-), *adj., n.* —*adj.* that mimicks the action of acetylcholine in the nervous system.
—*n.* a cholinomimetic chemical or drug.

chol|la (choi′ə; *Spanish* chō′yä), *n.* any one of certain spiny, treelike cactuses found in the southwestern United States and in Mexico. [American English < Mexican Spanish *cholla* < Spanish, head]

cho|lo (chō′lō), *n., pl.* **-los. 1** a person of mixed Spanish and Indian descent, especially in Bolivia and Peru; mestizo. **2** any half-breed of Spanish America. [< American Spanish *cholo*]

chol|o|lith (kol′ə lith), *n.* = gallstone. [< Greek *cholḗ* bile + *líthos* stone]

chome (chōm), *n.* a group of city blocks forming a subdivision of a section or neighborhood in Tokyo. [< Japanese *chōme*]

chomp (chomp), *v.t., v.i.* = champ[1].

chon (chon), *n., pl.* **chon.** a unit of money in South Korea, equal to 1/100 of a won. [< Korean]

Chon|do|kyo (chon′dō kyō′, -kē′ō), *n.* an indigenous religion of Korea which combines elements of Confucianism, Christianity, and Buddhism; Chontoism. [< Korean *chon do kyo* society of heaven]

chondr- or **chondri-**, *combining form.* **1** lump; grain: *Chondrule* = *a small grain.* **2** cartilage: *Chondroid* = *resembling cartilage.* Also, **chondro-**. [< Greek *chóndros*]

chon|drich|thi|an (kon drik′thē ən), *n.* any one of a class of fishes whose skeletons are formed of cartilage and whose gills are thin and platelike; elasmobranch. Sharks and rays belong to this class. [< Greek *chóndros* cartilage, lump + *ichthys, -ýos* fish]

chon|dri|fy (kon′drə fī), *v.t., v.i.,* **-fied, -fy|ing.** to convert or be converted into cartilage. [< *chondri-* + *-fy*] —**chon′dri|fi|ca′tion**, *n.*

chon|dri|o|some (kon′drē ə sōm), *n. Biology.* any one of the mitochondria, or minute bodies contained in the form of rods, granules, and threads in the cytoplasm of cells. [< Greek *chondríon* small lump (< *chóndros* lump) + English *-some*[3]]

chon|drite (kon′drīt), *n.* a meteorite containing chondrules.

chon|drit|ic (kon drit′ik), *adj.* having the peculiar granulated structure characteristic of a chondrite: *Any theory for the origin of meteorites should try to account for the chondritic stone meteorites* (Scientific American).

chondro-, *combining form.* a form of **chondr-**, as in *chondrocyte.*

chon|dro|cyte (kon′drə sīt), *n.* any one of the cells found in the cavities in cartilage; cartilage cell. [< *chondro-* + *-cyte*]

chon|dro|dite (kon′drə dīt), *n.* a yellow-to-red mineral, a fluosilicate of magnesium, often occurring in granular form in crystalline limestones. [< Greek *chondrṓdēs* granular (< *chóndros* lump) + English *-ite*[1]]

chon|dro|dys|tro|phic (kon′drō dis trō′fik), *adj.* = achondroplastic.

chon|droid (kon′droid), *adj.* resembling cartilage; cartilaginous.

chon|dro|ma (kon drō′mə), *n., pl.* **-mas, -ma|ta** (-mə tə). a tumor resembling cartilage in substance. [< *chondr-* + *-oma*]

chon|dro|sar|co|ma (kon′drō sär kō′mə), *n., pl.* **-mas, -ma|ta** (-mə tə). a sarcoma in or partly consisting of cartilage.

chon|drot|o|my (kon drot′ə mē), *n.,pl.* **-mies.**

Pronunciation Key: hat, āge, cãre, fär; let, ēqual, tėrm; it, īce; hot, ōpen, ôrder; oil, out; cup, pu̇t, rüle; child; long; thin; ᵺen; zh, measure; ə represents a in about, e in taken, i in pencil, o in lemon, u in circus.

surgical incision into a cartilage. [< *chondro-* + *-tomy*]

chon|drule (kon′drül), *n.* a small spheroidal grain of mineral embedded in varying numbers in some meteorites, as in a chondrite: *Most meteorites that are tuffs contain grains, or chondrules, which differ from anything formed on the earth* (Fenton and Fenton). [< *chondr-* + *-ule*]

chon|drus (kon′drəs), *n., pl.* **-dri** (-drī). = chondrule. [< Greek *chóndros* lump; grain]

chon|ta (chon′tə), *n.* any one of various prickly palms with hard, black wood, found especially in Ecuador and Peru and used by Indians for making spears, bows, and arrowheads. [< Quechua *chunta, chonta* hardwood palm]

Chon|to|ism (chon′tō iz əm), *n.* = Chondokyo. [< *Chonto* (alteration of *Chondo*(kyo)) + *-ism*]

choo-choo (chü′chü′), *n., pl.* **-choos**, *v.*, **-chooed**, **-choo|ing**. *U.S. Informal.* **—*n.*** a railroad train: *The American baby calls a train a "choo-choo"* (H. Allen Smith).
—*v.i.* to go by train.
[imitative]

chook (chůk), *n. Australian Informal.* a chicken. [probably imitative]

choose (chüz), *v.*, **chose**, **cho|sen** or (*obsolete*) **chose**, **choos|ing**. **—*v.t.*** **1** to pick out; select from a number: *He chose a book from the library. Choose the cupcake you like best.* **2** to prefer and decide; think fit (to do something): *The cat did not choose to go out in the rain. When I travel, I always choose to regulate my own supper* (Oliver Goldsmith). **3** *Informal.* to desire; wish to have: *Do you choose any refreshment, sir?* (George Colman). **—*v.i.*** **1** to make a choice between things or alternatives; decide on a preference: *You must choose for yourself. He chose wisely.* **2** *Dialect.* to do as one pleases.
cannot choose but, to be forced or obliged to: *Without an argument I cannot choose but agree with you.*
choose up, *U.S. Informal.* to select the opponents in a game or contest: *As the battle heightened, Los Angeles Catholics began choosing up sides* (Time).
pick and choose. See under **pick**[1].
[Old English *cēosan*] **—choos′er**, *n.*
—*Syn.* *v.t.* **1 Choose, select, pick** mean to decide on a choice. **Choose** suggests deciding wisely, whether or not we like: *She chose sensible walking shoes.* **Select** suggests deciding carefully on the one we like best: *I selected black shoes to go with my new suit.* **Pick** suggests deciding on the basis of our personal likes or wishes: *The chairman had picked his best friend as his successor.*

choos|ey (chü′zē), *adj.*, **choos|i|er**, **choos|i|est**. = choosy.

choos|y (chü′zē), *adj.*, **choos|i|er**, **choos|i|est**. *Informal.* particular or fussy: *She was too choosy about what dress to wear and was late to the party. Country bankers have become more choosy in granting loans* (Wall Street Journal). **—choos′i|ly**, *adv.* **—choos′i|ness**, *n.*

chop[1] (chop), *v.*, **chopped**, **chop|ping**, *n.* **—*v.t.*** **1a** to cut by hitting with something sharp: *You can chop wood with an ax.* SYN: See syn. under **cut**[1]. **b** to make by cutting: *to chop a pile of kindling. The explorer chopped his way through the underbrush.* SYN: See syn. under **cut**[1]. **2** to cut into small pieces; mince: *to chop up cabbage for coleslaw.* **3** *Figurative.* to cut down sharply; reduce severely: *to chop costs, chop prices, chop a budget. The proposal ran afoul of a Congress ... reluctant to slash Government income without chopping spending as well* (Time). **4** *Tennis, Baseball, Cricket, etc.* to swing at or hit with a downward stroke. **5** to interrupt repeatedly and rhythmically (as a beam of light or flow of electricity): *The microphone is situated inside the satellite and the influx of gas is chopped by a mechanical shutter so that an alternating signal is obtained, indicating the density of gas* (New Scientist).
—*v.i.* **1a** to make a blow or a series of blows with an ax or similar implement: *We need a block to chop on.* **b** to make quick, short movements; jerk. **2a** *Tennis, Baseball, Cricket, etc.* to swing or hit with a downward stroke: *The boy chopped at the ball with his bat.* **b** to aim a hacking or hewing blow: *He ... chops at it fiercely and hastily* (Charles Kingsley). **3** to go or come suddenly or with violence; break in; pounce: *How have I trembled, lest some passing stranger should chop in between me and the prize* (Scott).
—*n.* **1a** a cutting blow or stroke: *He felled the little tree with one chop of his ax.* **b** an act of chopping. **c** *Boxing.* a sharp downward blow. **2a** a piece chopped off; slice. **b** a slice of meat, especially of lamb, veal, or pork, with a piece of bone. There are rib, loin, and shoulder chops. **3a** a short, irregular, broken motion of waves; choppiness. **b** an area of rough or choppy water. **4** *Obsolete.* a crack; cleft; chap in the skin. [Middle English *choppen*]

chop[2] (chop), *n., v.*, **chopped**, **chop|ping**. **—*n.*** = jaw. **—*v.t.*** **1** to take into the chops and eat; snap up. **2** *Figurative.* to swallow or bolt (words) in hurried reading or speaking.
chops, **a** the jaws or cheeks: *The cat is licking the milk off her chops. His cheekbones and his chops are shattered* (Bayard Taylor). **b** the jaws and intervening space; the cavity of the mouth: *... the nut stowed away in its chops* (Thoreau). **c** the mouth, opening, or entrance, as of an abyss, canyon, valley, or channel: *He runs into a cannon's chops* (Jonathan Swift).
lick one's chops over, *Slang.* to relish or delight in the prospect of (something), as one licking his mouth in anticipation of food; gloat over (something) with anticipation: *The Communists have been licking their chops over the expected collapse of the non-Soviet world* (New York Times).
[apparently variant of *chap*[3]]

chop[3] (chop), *v.*, **chopped**, **chop|ping**. **—*v.i.*** **1a** to change suddenly; shift quickly; veer: *The wind chopped around from west to north. Watch the sails now the wind is chopping.* **b** *Figurative.* to turn with, or like, the wind. **2** to give in exchange: **a** to answer back. **b** *Obsolete.* to barter.
—*v.t.* *Dialect.* to barter.
chop and change, to change one's tactics or ways; make frequent changes; change about: *We hope he knows his own mind this time, and does not intend chopping and changing about again.*
chop logic. See under **logic**.
[short for *chop and change* barter and exchange, apparently variant of obsolete *chap* to bargain. See related etym. at **cheap**.]

chop[4] (chop), *n.* **1** formerly in India, China, etc.: **a** an official stamp, seal, license, or permit. **b** a ship's port clearance, called a *grand chop.* **2** (in the former China trade) a brand on goods to indicate quality or nature, or a class of goods bearing the same such mark.
first (or **second**, etc.) **chop**, *Anglo-Indian and Informal.* first (or second, etc.) rate, position, quality, or the like: *He thinks himself a gentleman of the first chop* (Margaret Bell).
[< Hindustani *chhāp* stamp, brand]

chop-chop (chop′chop′), *adv. Pidgin English.* quickly. [< Chinese (Canton) *kap-kap* hurry]

chop|fall|en (chop′fô′lən), *adj.* = chapfallen.

chop|house (chop′hous′), *n.* a restaurant that makes a specialty of serving chops, steaks, and other cuts of meat. [< *chop*[1], noun + *house*]

chop|in[1] (chop′in), *n.* = chopine.

chop|in[2] (chop′in), *n.* any one of several liquid measures, now largely obsolete, equal to about a pint or a quart. [perhaps < Old French *chopine*]

***cho|pine** (chō pēn′, chop′in), *n.* a shoe with a very thick sole, often of cork, formerly worn by women. [< Spanish *chapín*, perhaps < *chapa* piece of leather, (originally) thin metal plate]

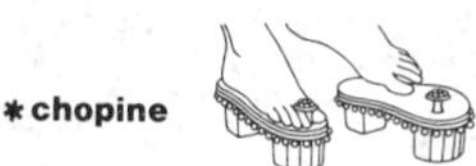
***chopine**

chop|log|ic (chop′loj′ik), *n., adj.* **—*n.*** **1** sophistical or contentious argument; hairsplitting: *Its choplogic ... ordains that a man who kills with a gun may be hanged while a man who kills with a knife may not* (Punch). **2** *Obsolete.* a person who bandies logic: *choplogics and prattlers* (Thomas Newton). **—*adj.*** = choplogical: *a choplogic discussion.* [< *chop*[3] + *logic*]

chop|log|i|cal (chop′loj′ə kəl), *adj.* argumentative; hairsplitting.

chop|per (chop′ər), *n., v.* **—*n.*** **1** a person who chops or cuts into pieces: *a chopper of wood.* **2** a tool or machine for chopping. A short ax and a heavy knife are choppers. **3** *Slang.* a helicopter. **4** any one of several devices for interrupting electrical or wave signals, electrical currents, or beams of light. **5** *Slang.* a large, specially built motorcycle.
—*v.i., v.t.* *Slang.* to fly by helicopter.
choppers, *Slang.* teeth: *Dimples fixed and choppers glistening, he stepped from a special train ... to the plaudits of 3,000 screeching fans* (Newsweek).

chop|ping[1] (chop′ing), *adj.* choppy; jerky.

chop|ping[2] (chop′ing), *adj.* big and vigorous; strapping: *a chopping young child.* [< *chop*[1]]

chopping block, a heavy block of wood to hold something to be chopped, as meat or firewood.

chop|py[1] (chop′ē), *adj.*, **-pi|er**, **-pi|est**. **1** making quick, sharp movements; jerky: *The speaker made nervous, choppy gestures.* **2** moving in short, irregular, broken waves: *The wind made the water choppy. The sea is choppy today.* **3** full of chops or clefts. [< *chop*[1] + *-y*[1]] **—chop′pi|ly**, *adv.* **—chop′pi|ness**, *n.*

chop|py[2] (chop′ē), *adj.*, **-pi|er**, **-pi|est**. **1** changing suddenly; shifting quickly: *A choppy wind tossed the boat about.* SYN: variable. **2** shifting; unstable. SYN: fluctuating. [< *chop*[3] + *-y*[1]]

chop|py[3] (chop′ē), *adj.*, **-pi|er**, **-pi|est**. = chappy.

chops (chops), *n.pl.* See under **chop**[2].

chop shop, *U.S.* a place where stolen cars are disposed of: *Today, the typical thief works for a "chop shop," which dismantles the car and sells the parts* (Emerson Cammack).

***chop|sticks** (chop′stiks′), *n.pl.* a pair of small, slender sticks used by many Orientals to raise food to the mouth. Chopsticks are made usually of wood or ivory and are used especially by the Chinese and Japanese. [< Chinese Pidgin English *chop-chop* quickly + English *stick*[1]]

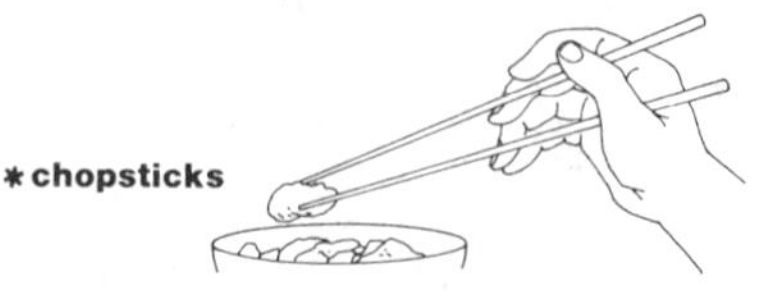
***chopsticks**

chop stroke, a quick downward stroke at a sharp angle to the path of the ball in tennis and other games.

chop su|ey (chop′sü′ē), a dish consisting of fried or stewed chicken, pork, or other meat, and vegetables cut up and cooked together in a sauce. It is usually served with rice and soy sauce. Chop suey contains such vegetables and seasonings as bean sprouts, onions, green peppers, mushrooms, and sesame seeds, fried in oil. *Chop suey, unknown in China, was originated in New York City by an American chef* (Clarke County Democrat). [American English; alteration of Chinese (Canton) *tzap-sui* odds and ends]

cho|rag|ic (kə raj′ik, -rā′jik; kō-, kō-), *adj.* having to do with a choragus.

cho|ra|gus (kə rā′gəs, kō-, kō-), *n., pl.* **-gi** (-jī). **1** the leader of an ancient Greek chorus. **2** *Figurative.* the leader of a chorus or choir or of a band of any kind. [< Latin *chorāgus* < Greek *chorāgós* < *chorós* dance, chorus + *agós* leader < *ágein* to lead]

cho|ral (*adj.* kôr′əl, kōr′-; *n.* kə ral′, -räl′, kôr′əl, kōr′-), *adj., n.* **—*adj.*** **1** of a choir or chorus: *The church choral society meets on Wednesdays.* **2** sung by a choir or chorus: *a choral hymn.* **3** of or having to do with music appropriate for a choir or chorus: *The Saint of Bleeker Street is primarily a choral opera* (Atlantic).
—*n.* = chorale.
[< Medieval Latin *choralis* < Latin *chorus* chorus] **—cho′ral|ly**, *adv.*

cho|rale (kə ral′, -räl′; kôr′əl, kōr′-), *n.* **1** a musical setting of a hymn. **2** a simple hymn sung in unison.

chorale prelude, *Music.* an organ composition based on a chorale.

cho|ral|ist (kôr′ə list, kōr′-), *n.* **1** a person who sings in a chorus or a choir. **2** a composer of choral music.

choral speaking, the recital of poetry or prose by a chorus.

chord**[1] (kôrd), *n., v.* **—*n. a combination of two or more tones of music sounded at the same time in harmony: *We all stood at the playing of the first chords of the hymn.*
—*v.i., v.t.* *Rare.* to accord musically; form a chord; harmonize.
[variant of *cord*, shortened form of *accord*, noun; influenced by *chord*[2]]

***chord**[1]

chord[2] (kôrd), *n.* **1** a straight line connecting two points on a curve. See picture under **angle**. **2a** a structure in an animal body that looks like a string; cord. **b** a tendon. **3** a string of a harp or other musical instrument. **4** *Figurative.* a feeling or emotion: *The stray and hungry puppy touched a tender chord in him.* **5** a main, horizontal part of a bridge truss. **6** *Aeronautics.* **a** the dimension of an airfoil from the leading to the trailing edge. **b** a straight line drawn from the leading to the trailing edge of a cross section of an airfoil. Camber is measured from the chord. [spelling alteration of *cord* < Old French *corde* cord; influenced by Latin *chorda* < Greek *chordḗ* gut, string]

chord|al (kôr′dəl), *adj.* **1** having to do with, or of the nature of, the strings of a musical instrument. **2** *Music.* of or having to do with chords. **3** *Medicine.* relating to the chorda tympani. **—chord′al|ly**, *adv.*

chor|da|mes|o|derm (kôr′də mes′ə dėrm, -mē′sə-), *n. Embryology.* the part of the meso-

derm from which the notochord develops. [< New Latin *chorda* chord² + English *mesoderm*]
Chor|da|ta (kôr′dā′tə), *n.* the phylum of animals comprising the chordates. [< New Latin]
chor|date (kôr′dāt), *n., adj.* —*n.* any animal of a phylum that has a notochord at some stage of development. Chordates include man and all other vertebrates. *Chordates are excelled in mobility only by a few insects* (Beals and Hoijer).
—*adj.* **1** of or belonging to this phylum. **2** having a notochord.
[< New Latin *Chordata* the phylum name < Latin *chorda* chord²]
chord|ed (kôr′did), *adj.* having chords or strings, as a musical instrument.
chord organ, an electric organ with a row of buttons to be pushed by the fingers of the left hand to produce musical chords. The keys of the chord organ are played with the right hand.
chor|do|to|nal (kôr′də tō′nəl), *adj.* responsive to the vibrations or tones of sound. [< Greek *chordê* string + *tónos* tone + English *-al*]
chordotonal organ, a structure especially in insects, spiders, and certain larvae which is capable of sensing small movements by means of sensory cells responsive to sound vibrations.
chore (chôr, chōr), *n.* **1** an odd job; small task: *Feeding his dog was his daily chore.* **2** a difficult or disagreeable thing to do: *She found housekeeping quite a chore. Preparing an income tax return is a chore if you have not kept good records.* [variant of *chare*]
cho|re|a (kô rē′ə, kō-), *n.* **1** a nervous disorder characterized by involuntary twitching of the muscles; St. Vitus's dance. **2** a similar disease affecting dogs and rarely horses, cattle, or pigs. [short for New Latin *chorea Sancti Viti* dance of St. Vitus < Latin *chorēa* dance < Greek *choreiā*]
cho|re|al (kô rē′əl, kō-), *adj.* **1** having to do with, or symptomatic of, chorea. **2** affected with chorea. Also, **choreic**.
chore boy, *U.S.* **1** a boy who does chores. **2** a cook's helper or camp keeper on a ranch or in a lumber camp. **3** *Informal.* errand boy.
cho|re|graph|ic (kôr′ə graf′ik, kōr′-), *adj.* = choreographic.
cho|reg|ra|phy (kə reg′rə fē), *n.* = choreography.
cho|re|ic (kô rē′ik, kō-), *adj.* = choreal.
choreo-, *combining form.* dance; dancing: *Choreodrama = dance drama. Choreomania = a mania for dancing. Choreosymphony = a symphony that includes dancing.* [< Greek *choreiā* dance]
cho|re|o|graph (kôr′ē ə graf, kōr′-; -gräf), *v.t.* to arrange or design dancing for: *The New York City Ballet unveiled ... "Ivesiana," which George Balanchine choreographed to music by the late Charles Ives* (Newsweek). —*v.i.* to do choreography.
[back formation < *choreography*]
cho|re|og|ra|pher (kôr′ē og′rə fər, kōr′-), *n.* a planner or creator of dances in a ballet, motion picture, or musical play: *A musical comedy is the end product of the combined efforts of many people in addition to the cast—author, composer, lyricist, director, choreographer* (New Yorker).
cho|re|o|graph|ic (kôr′ē ə graf′ik, kōr′-), *adj.* having to do with choreography: *Balinese dance is but one portion of the choreographic riches of Indonesia* (Atlantic). Also, **choregraphic**.
cho|re|og|ra|phist (kôr′ē og′rə fist, kōr′-), *n.* = choreographer.
cho|re|og|ra|phy (kôr′ē og′rə fē, kōr′-), *n.* **1a** the art of planning, designing, or arranging the dancing in a ballet, motion picture, or musical play; dance composition. **b** (formerly) any one of various written notations of dancing. **2** the art of ballet or other dancing for the stage; dance compositions, collectively, as a branch of the arts. **3a** a dance composition. **b** the dancing composed and arranged for a stage performance or motion picture. Also, **choregraphy**. [< Greek *choreiā* dance + English *-graphy*]
cho|ri|amb (kôr′ē amb, kōr′-, kor′-), *n.* a classical poetic foot of four syllables, one long, two short, and one long. [< Late Latin *choriambus* < Greek *choriambos* < *choreîos* trochee + *iambos* iamb]
cho|ri|am|bic (kôr′ē am′bik, kōr′-, kor′-), *adj.* consisting of or containing choriambs.
cho|ri|am|bus (kôr′ē am′bəs, kōr′-, kor′-), *n., pl.* **-bi** (-bī), **-bus|es.** = choriamb.
cho|ric (kôr′ik, kōr′-, kor′-), *adj.* of or for a chorus, especially a chorus in an ancient Greek play.
cho|rine (kôr′ēn, kōr′-), *n. U.S.* a chorus girl: [*His*] *choreography has amazing liveliness, and the hoofing chorines are the jolliest bunch of girls in several seasons* (Time).
cho|ri|o|al|lan|to|ic (kôr′ē ō al′ən tō′ik), *adj.* of or belonging to the chorioallantois.
cho|ri|o|al|lan|to|is (kôr′ē ō ə lan′tō is), *n.* a baglike fetal membrane formed by the fused walls of the chorion and the allantois, especially in birds. The chorioallantois of chick embryos is used as a culture medium for viruses and cells.
cho|ri|o|car|ci|no|ma (kôr′ē ō kär′sə nō′mə, kōr′-), *n.* cancer of the chorionic tissue, especially in the placenta during or immediately following pregnancy. [*chorio*(nic) + *carcinoma*]
cho|ri|oid (kôr′ē oid, kōr′-), *adj., n.* = choroid.
cho|ri|o|men|in|gi|tis (kôr′ē ō men′in jī′tis, kōr′-), *n.* inflammation of the membrane enveloping the brain, often due to a viral infection and characterized by the presence of lymphocytes in the cerebrospinal fluid: *lymphocytic choriomeningitis.* [< Greek *chórion* membrane + English *meningitis*]
cho|ri|on (kôr′ē on, kōr′-), *n. Embryology.* the outermost membrane, enclosing the amnion, of the sac which envelops the embryo or fetus of the higher vertebrates, such as mammals, birds, and reptiles. [< Greek *chórion* membrane]
cho|ri|on|ic (kôr′ē on′ik, kōr′-), *adj.* of or having to do with the chorion: *The human placenta is complex, as some living tissues of the uterus disappear and embryonic blood vessels on the chorionic villi are bathed in maternal blood* (Tracy I. Storer).
cho|ri|pet|al|ous (kôr′ə pet′ə ləs, kōr′-), *adj. Botany.* polypetalous. [< Greek *chōri* apart + English *petal* + *-ous*]
cho|ri|phyl|lous (kôr′ə fil′əs, kōr′-), *adj. Botany.* composed of separate leaves or parts, as a perianth. [< Greek *chōri* apart + *phýllon* leaf + English *-ous*]
cho|ri|sep|al|ous (kôr′ə sep′ə ləs, kōr′-), *adj. Botany.* polysepalous. [< Greek *chōri* apart + English *sepal* + *-ous*]
cho|rist (kôr′ist, kōr′-, kor′-), *n.* a member of a chorus or choir.
chor|is|ter (kôr′ə stər, kor′-), *n.* **1** a singer in a choir: *Choristers and dancers pour out from the wings to take their places in the ... set for Scene 2* (Time). **2** = choirboy: *A melody ... sung by the pure voice of a boyish chorister* (George Eliot). **3** the leader of a choir. [< Medieval Latin *chorista* chorister < Latin *chorus;* see etym. under **chorus**]
cho|ri|zo (chə rē′zō), *n., pl.* **-zos.** a Spanish sausage containing pork seasoned with cayenne pepper and reddened with paprika. [< Spanish *chorizo*]
C horizon, the bottom layer of soil, beneath the B horizon, containing a mixture of decomposed rock and unchanged materials from which soil has not yet begun to form.
cho|rog|ra|pher (kə rog′rə fər), *n.* a person who studies chorography.
cho|ro|graph|ic (kôr′ə graf′ik, kōr′-), *adj.* having to do with or relating to the description of a country or district. —**cho′ro|graph′i|cal|ly**, *adv.*
cho|ro|graph|i|cal (kôr′ə graf′ə kəl, kōr′-), *adj.* = chorographic.
cho|rog|ra|phy (kə rog′rə fē), *n.* **1** the science and art of describing or mapping a district. **2** a description or map of a district. **3** the natural configuration and features of a region. [< Latin *chōrographia* < Greek *chōrographíā* description of a country or countries < *chōra* land + *-graphíā* -graphy]
cho|roid (kôr′oid, kōr′-), *adj., n. Anatomy.* —**adj.** **1** like the chorion; membranous. **2** having to do with or designating the choroid membrane or coat.
—*n.* the choroid membrane or coat. Also, **chorioid**.
[< Greek *choroeidês* < *chórion* membrane, chorion + *eîdos* resemblance, shape]
cho|roi|dal (kə roi′dəl), *adj.* = choroid.
cho|roi|di|tis (kôr′oi dī′tis, kōr′-), *n. Medicine.* inflammation of the choroid membrane of the eye. [< *choroid* + *-itis*]
choroid membrane or **coat**, a delicate membrane or coat between the sclerotic coat and the retina of the eyeball. See the diagram of **eye**.
cho|ro|log|ic (kôr′ə loj′ik, kōr′-), *adj.* of or having to do with chorology or geographical distribution: *chorologic phenomena.*
cho|ro|log|i|cal (kôr′ə loj′ə kəl, kōr′-), *adj.* = chorologic.
cho|rol|o|gist (kə rol′ə jist), *n.* a person who studies chorology.
cho|rol|o|gy (kə rol′ə jē), *n.* the science dealing with geographical distribution, especially that of plants and animals. [< Greek *chōra* land + English *-logy*]
chor|ten (chôr′tən), *n.* a Buddhist place or object of worship. [< Tibetan *chorten*]
chor|tle (chôr′təl), *v.,* **-tled, -tling,** *n.* —*v.i., v.t.* to chuckle or snort with glee: *He chortled in his joy* (Lewis Carroll).
—*n.* a gleeful chuckle or snort.
[(coined by Lewis Carroll) a blend of *chuckle* and *snort*] —**chor′tler**, *n.*
cho|rus (kôr′əs, kōr′-), *n., pl.* **-rus|es,** *v.,* **-rused, -rus|ing.** —*n.* **1** a group of singers who sing together, such as a choir: *The local school chorus gave a concert at the town hall. While Heaven's whole chorus sings* (Alexander Pope). **2a** a song sung by many singers together. A chorus is often a part of an oratorio or a scene in an opera. **b** a musical composition written usually in four parts, each part being sung by a number of voices: *The college choir will sing the Hallelujah Chorus in Handel's Messiah.* **3** the repeated part of a song coming after each stanza, in which a chorus or the whole group often joins the solo singer or singers: *Everybody knew the chorus by heart.* SYN: refrain. **4** *Figurative.* a saying by many at the same time; utterance in words or cries: *a chorus of laughter. My question was answered by a chorus of "no's."* **5** *Theater.* **a** (in the modern theater) a group of singers and dancers: *the chorus of a musical comedy.* **b** (in ancient Greek drama) an organized group of singers and dancers under a leader, engaging in dialogue with the actors and commenting on the action on stage. The chorus played an important role in Attic drama. **c** (in English drama) a group or part adapted from Attic tragedy, or (especially in Elizabethan plays) a single person, who speaks the prologue and explains or comments upon the course of events: *Admit me chorus to this history* (Shakespeare). **d** the song, dance, or speech performed by a chorus in any of these senses.
—*v.t.* **1** to sing or utter all the same time: *The audience chorused its approval by loud cheering.* **2a** to sing with a chorus; provide with a chorus: *Let every song be chorused with his name* (Daniel Defoe). **b** *Figurative.* to add an expression, such as of assent to (another's utterances); echo.
—*v.i.* to sing or speak all at the same time: *The birds were chorusing around me.*
in chorus, all together at the same time: *The whole class replied in chorus to the teacher's questions.*
[< Late Latin *chorus* choir < Latin, band of dancers < Greek *chorós* band of dancers, dance. See etym. of doublet **choir**.]
chorus girl, a girl who sings or dances in the chorus of a musical comedy or revue; chorine.
chose[1] (chōz), *v.* **1** the past tense of **choose:** *She chose the red dress. They chose to vote for the other candidate.* **2** *Obsolete.* chosen; a past participle of **choose**.
chose[2] (shōz), *n. Law.* a thing; a piece of personal property.
chose in action, an incorporeal right enforceable by legal action: *money due on a bond is a chose in action* (William Blackstone).
[< Middle French *chose* < Latin *causa* a matter, thing. See etym. of doublet **cause**.]
chose ju|gée (shōz zhʏ zhā′), *French.* **1** a matter that has been decided already. **2** (literally) thing judged.
cho|sen (chō′zən), *v., adj.* —*v.* a past participle of **choose:** *Have you chosen a book from the library?*
—*adj.* **1** picked out; selected from a group: *a carefully chosen target. Six chosen scouts marched at the front of the parade. Your lordship's thoughts are always just, your numbers harmonious, your words chosen, your expressions strong and manly* (John Dryden). **2** *Theology.* elect: *chosen of God, and precious* (I Peter 2:4).
Chosen People, the Israelites (in the Bible, Deuteronomy 14:2).
cho|sis|me (shô zēz′mə), *n.* a form of literary realism current in the 1960's, especially in France, characterized by an emphasis on physical details, such as the exhaustive description or listing of a variety of objects. [< French *chosisme* (literally) thingism < *chose* thing + *-isme* -ism]
cho|ta haz|ri (chō′tə häz′rē), a light refreshment served before breakfast in India. [< Hindi *choṭā hāzrī* little breakfast]
cho|ta peg (chō′tə peg′), a small drink of whiskey served in India: *Audrey insisted on pausing frequently for a chota peg* (New Yorker). [< Hindi *choṭa* little + English *peg* (def. 5)]
chott (shot), *n.* = shott.
chou (shü), *n., pl.* **choux** (shü). *French.* **1** cabbage. **2** an ornamental ribbon tied in a fluffy knot and worn on a dress or hat.
Chou (jō), *n.* a Chinese dynasty ruling from about 1122 B.C. to about 256 B.C., a period notable as the era of the philosophers Confucius, Lao Tzu, and Mencius (Meng-tse).
chou|croute (shü krüt′), *n. French.* sauerkraut: *Returning to the table, I finished my choucroute*

Pronunciation Key: hat, āge, cãre, fär; let, ēqual, tėrm; it, īce; hot, ōpen, ôrder; oil, out; cup, pu̇t, rüle; child; long; thin; ᴛʜen; zh, measure; ə represents a in about, e in taken, i in pencil, o in lemon, u in circus.

almost without noticing how good it was (New Yorker).

chough (chuf), *n.* a European crow, black with red feet and a red beak. [Middle English *choughe* jackdaw; origin uncertain]

chouse[1] (chous), *n., v.,* **choused, chous|ing.** —*n. Archaic.* **1** a cheat; swindler. **2** a person easily cheated; dupe; gull; tool.
—*v.t. Informal.* to cheat; dupe; trick; swindle or defraud: *Bristol stones won't buy stock;* [*he*] *only wants to chouse you* (Frances Burney).
[earlier *chaus* < Turkish *çavus* interpreter (said to allude to a swindle in England by a Turkish agent in 1609)]

chouse[2] (chous), *v.t.,* **choused, chous|ing.** *Western U.S.* to herd (cattle or sheep) too roughly. [origin unknown]

chow[1] (chou), *n.* a Chinese dog of medium size with a short, compact body, large head, a black tongue, and a thick coat of one color, usually brown or black. [< dialectal Chinese, related to Cantonese *kaú* dog]

chow[2] (chou), *n. Slang.* **1** food. **2** the time when food is served. [American English, *chowchow*]

chow[3] (chou, chü), *n. Scottish.* jowl.

chow|chow or **chow-chow** (chou′chou′), *n., adj.* —*n.* **1** a Chinese mixed preserve. **2** mixed pickles or preserves, especially a mixture of sliced or chopped, pickled vegetables in mustard sauce.
—*adj.* **1** miscellaneous; mixed; assorted; diverse. **2** (of water) having short, irregular waves or small whirlpools; broken.
[American English < Chinese pidgin English]

chow chow, = chow[1].

chow|der (chou′dər), *n.* a thick soup, or sometimes a stew, usually made of clams or fish and potatoes, onions, salt pork, milk, and seasonings. Chowder is sometimes made with a vegetable such as corn in place of clams or fish. [American English, apparently < French *chaudière* pot < Late Latin *caldāria* cooking pot < *calidus* hot]

chow|der|head (chou′dər hed′), *n. U.S. Slang.* a fool; oaf; simpleton.

chow|hound (chou′hound′), *n. U.S. Slang.* a glutton. [< *chow*[2] + *hound*]

chow line, *U.S. Informal.* a line of people waiting to be served at a cafeteria, lunch counter, or the like: *Dump your Navy sea bag on your bunk . . . to take your place in the chow line in the galley* (New Yorker).

chow mein (chou′ mān′), a thickened stew of onions, celery, and meat, served with fried noodles. It may also contain bean sprouts, egg, mushrooms, or shrimp. *Chow mein is another one-dish main course that is popular in Chinese restaurants, and chicken chow mein is one of the most often selected of this variety* (Ladies' Home Journal). [American English < Chinese (Canton) *ch'au min* fried noodles]

chow|ry (chou′rē), *n., pl.* **-ries.** a whisk for driving off flies, usually made of a yak's tail, and being in this form an ancient ensign of royalty in the East Indies. [< Hindi *chaunrī*]

Chr., **1** = Christ. **2** Christian.

chre|ma|tis|tic (krē′mə tis′tik), *adj.* having to do with money-making or the acquisition of wealth. [< Greek *chrēmatistikós* < *chrēmatízein* transact business < *chrêma* money]

chre|ma|tis|tics (krē′mə tis′tiks), *n.* the science of wealth; political economy as concerned with the accumulation and management of wealth.

chres|tom|a|thy (kres tom′ə thē), *n., pl.* **-thies.** a collection of literary passages: *a Browning chrestomathy.* [< Greek *chrēstomátheia* < *chrēstós* useful + *máthē* a learning]

chrism (kriz′əm), *n.* **1** consecrated oil, used by some churches in baptism and other sacred rites. **2** a sacramental anointing; the ceremony of confirmation, especially as practiced in the Greek Church. Also, **chrisom.** [Old English *crisma* < Latin *chrisma* < Greek *chrîsma* an anointing, unction < *chríein* anoint. See etym. of doublet **cream.**]

chris|mal (kriz′məl), *adj.* having to do with chrism.

chris|ma|tion (kriz mā′shən), *n.* the application of chrism.

chris|ma|to|ry (kriz′mə tôr′ē, -tōr′-), *n., pl.* **-ries.** the receptacle for the chrism. [< Medieval Latin *chrismatorium* < Latin *chrisma;* see etym. under **chrism**]

chris|mon (kriz′mon), *n.* = Christogram. [< Medieval Latin *chrismon* < Latin *Chris*(tus) Christ + Late Latin *mon*(ogramma) monogram]

chris|om (kriz′əm), *n.* **1** = chrism. **2a** a white robe, garment, or cloth, formerly used to dress a child, especially to cover the head where the baptismal oil was placed, at baptism as a token of innocence. It was later given as an offering at the mother's purification or churching. **b** a child wearing this cloth or robe. **c** an infant; babe; innocent. [variant of *crisme* chrism (in Old English, a chrism cloth)]

chrisom child, a child at about the age for baptism.

Christ (krīst), *n.* **1** Jesus of Nazareth, whose life and teachings are the source of the Christian religion. **2** Also, **the Christ.** the Messiah whose advent was foretold in the Old Testament; the Lord's Anointed: *Then charged he his disciples that they should tell no man that he was Jesus the Christ* (Matthew 16:20). [Old English *Crist* < Latin *Christus* < Greek *Christós* (the) anointed (one) < *chríein* anoint]
▶*Christ* is usually treated as a proper name. It was originally a title given Jesus as embodying the Messianic prophecy.

Christ child, a picture or image of Christ in His childhood.
the Christ child, Christ as a child: *Many a time* [*she*] *spoke of her Christmas tree, and of the marvelous things which the Christ child would lay beneath it* (Mary Howitt).

***christ|cross** (kris′krôs′, -kros′), *n. Archaic.* **1a** the figure or mark of a cross formerly placed in front of the alphabet in hornbooks, etc. **b** the alphabet. **2** the figure or mark of a cross in general; crisscross. [Middle English *cristcross* (literally) Christ's cross (me speed), a formula placed before the alphabet]

***christcross**
definition 1a

christ|cross-row (kris′krôs′rō′), *n. Archaic.* the alphabet (so called from the figure of a cross set before it in hornbooks).

Chris|te e|le|i|son (kris′tē e lā′i son), **1** the words of an invocation in Latin litanies of the Roman Catholic Church, preceded and followed by Kyrie eleison, each of the three petitions being said three times. **2** a musical setting to this prayer. [< Medieval Latin *Christe eleison* (literally) Christ have mercy < Greek *Christé eléēson*]

chris|ten (kris′ən), *v.t.* **1** to give a first name to (a person) at baptism: *The child was christened James. These young ladies—not supposed to have been actually christened by the names applied to them* (Dickens). **2a** to give a name to and dedicate (bells, ships, or other objects): *The new ship was christened before it was launched.* **b** *Informal.* to make the first use of. **3** to baptize as a Christian. **4** to name; give a name to. [Old English *cristnian* make Christian < *cristen* Christian < Latin *christiānus* < Greek *christiānós* one belonging to Christ]

Chris|ten|dom (kris′ən dəm), *n.* **1** Christian countries; the Christian part of the world: *Many of the monarchs of Christendom took part in the Crusades.* **2** all Christians collectively; the church: *Christendom everywhere celebrates Christmas.* **3** *Obsolete.* Christianity. [Old English *cristendōm* < *cristen* Christian + *-dōm* -dom]

chris|ten|ing (kris′ə ning, kris′ning), *n.* baptism; the act or ceremony of baptizing and naming.

Christ|hood (krīst′hůd), *n.* the condition of being the Christ.

Chris|tian (kris′chən), *n., adj.* —*n.* **1** a person who believes in Christ and follows His teachings; person belonging to the religion of Christ: *Christians celebrate Christmas. Every Stoic was a Stoic; but in Christendom where is the Christian?* (Emerson). **2** *Informal.* a decent, respectable, or presentable person: *You must take your passage like a Christian* (Dickens). **3** *Informal and Dialect.* a human being as opposed to an animal: *a fitter food for a horse than a Christian* (Henry Fielding). **4** the principal character of John Bunyan's *Pilgrim's Progress.* **5** *U.S.* one of the Disciples of Christ; Campbellite.
—*adj.* **1** of Christ, His teachings, or His followers: *the Christian faith, Christian worship.* **2** believing in Christ; following His example or teachings; belonging to the religion of Christ: *the Christian church, Christian countries.* **3** of Christians or Christianity: *the Christian God. If thou dost shed one drop of Christian blood* (Shakespeare). **4** showing a gentle, humble, helpful spirit: *Christian kindness. That supply of light, of love, and of resolve, which enriches . . . the Christian soul* (Henry P. Liddon). **5** *Informal.* **a** decent; civilized; respectable: *Every man deserves a Christian burial. Had you been to fight with any Christian weapons* (Scott). **b** human; not animal.
most Christian, a title of the kings of France: *Religious criticism hath made but little progress among the subjects of the most Christian king* (John Brown).
[alteration of earlier *cristen;* see etym. under **christen**]

Christian Brothers, a religious congregation of Roman Catholic laymen, the Brothers of the Christian Schools, founded about 1680 and devoted to the education of the poor.

Christian Church, = Disciples of Christ.

Christian Democrat, a member of any one of several political parties, especially those in western Europe, that advocate a policy of Christian socialism: *The growth of Europe's Christian Democrats—multinational political parties with strong, if paradoxical, Christian and Socialist roots—remains a great postwar political phenomenon* (Newsweek).

Christian Democratic, of or having to do with Christian Democrats.

Christian Era, the time since the date (now considered as having been set from four to eight years too late) assigned to the birth of Christ, in use in all predominantly Christian countries; A.D. is in the Christian Era; B.C. is before it.

Chris|ti|an|i|a turn, or **Chris|ti|an|i|a** (kris′chē an′ē ə, kris′tē-), *n. Skiing.* a skidding turn begun from a crouched position with the skis kept parallel, the body swinging in the desired direction during a spring just sufficient to free the skis from its weight: christie. [< *Christiania,* former name of Oslo, the capital of Norway]

Chris|tian|ise (kris′chə nīz), *v.t.,* **-ised, -is|ing.** *Especially British.* Christianize.

Chris|tian|ism (kris′chə niz əm), *n.* the Christian religious system; Christianity (obsolete except as a nonce word, when Christianity is classed with other -isms).

chris|tian|ite (kris′chə nīt), *n.* a variety of the feldspar anorthite. [< *Christian* Frederik, a prince of Denmark + *-ite*[1]]

Chris|ti|an|i|ty (kris′chē an′ə tē), *n., pl.* **-ties.** **1** the religion taught by Christ and His followers; Christian religion: *The glory of Christianity is the very gap between its teachings of perfection and the struggles of a hopelessly imperfect mankind to reach it* (Newsweek). **2** Christian beliefs or faith; condition of being a Christian; Christian spirit or character: *His Christianity consisted of going to church on Sunday.* **3** all Christians; the Christian part of the world; Christendom: *Christianity recognizes the cross as its symbol.*

Chris|tian|ize (kris′chə nīz), *v.t.,* **-ized, -iz|ing.** to make Christian; convert to Christianity: *Thousands of intelligent Africans, despite the odds against them, have Christianized themselves, educated themselves, civilized themselves* (Atlantic). —**Chris′tian|i|za′tion,** *n.* —**Chris′tian|iz′er,** *n.*

Chris|tian|like (kris′chən līk′), *adj.* befitting or proper to a Christian; showing a Christian spirit.

Chris|tian|ly (kris′chən lē), *adj., adv.* —*adj.* proper to or befitting a Christian.
—*adv.* in a Christian manner; in a way becoming a Christian.

Christian name, a first name; given name: *"John" is the Christian name of "John Smith."*

Christian Science, a religion and system of healing founded by Mary Baker Eddy in 1866. It treats disease by mental and spiritual means, emphasizing the belief that a thorough spiritual understanding of God as the all-powerful source of all that is good and true can destroy sin, sickness, and the like without material aid.

Christian Scientist, a believer in Christian Science; a member of the Church of Christ, Scientist.

Christian socialism, any one of various socialistic theories or systems designed to secure practical adjustments for the benefit of all by the application of the principles of Christianity to the ordinary business of life.

chris|tie or **Chris|tie** (kris′tē), *n., pl.* **-ties,** *v.,* **-tied, -ty|ing.** —*n.* = Christiania turn.
—*v.i.* to make a Christiania turn or turns. Also, **christy.**

Christ Jesus, = Jesus.

Christ|less (krīst′lis), *adj.* without Christ; lacking Christian spirit or faith; unchristian. —**Christ′less|ness,** *n.*

Christ|like (krīst′līk′), *adj.* like Christ; like that of Christ; showing the spirit of Christ: *a Christlike patience* (Thomas Ken). —**Christ′like′ness,** *n.*

Christ|ly (krīst′lē), *adj.* **1** of Christ; Christlike. **2** of or having to do with Jesus Christ. —**Christ′li|ness,** *n.*

Christ|mas (kris′məs), *n.* **1** the yearly celebration of the birth of Christ; December 25; Yule. Christmas is marked by special church services, giving of gifts, and sending of greetings. **2** the religious and festive season before and after Christmas Day; Yule; Yuletide. [Old English *Cristes mæsse* Christ's Mass]

Christ|mas|ber|ry (kris′məs ber′ē), *n., pl.* **-ries.** **1** an evergreen shrub of the rose family found on the Pacific Coast of North America; toyon. **2** the bright red berries of this shrub, often used for Christmas decoration.

Christmas box, *British.* **1** (originally) a box used at Christmas for the presents of money to apprentices, servants, porters, and other helpers.

2 a tip given at Christmas to a servant or employee, or to public servants such as a letter carrier or policeman. 3a a Christmas present. b a box of presents at Christmas.

Christmas cactus, a South American cactus with red flowers, naturally growing on trees for support but commonly grown as a house plant.

Christmas card, an ornamental card sent by way of Christmas greeting.

Christmas carol, a song or hymn sung in celebration of Christmas and especially of the nativity of Christ.

Christmas club, a group of bank accounts into which depositors, wishing to accumulate savings to be used for shopping before Christmas, make weekly deposits throughout the year.

Christmas Day, December 25.

Christmas disease, a form of hemophilia, inherited and transmitted like classical hemophilia, but caused by the deficiency of a different clotting factor of the blood and somewhat less severe than classical hemophilia. [< *Christmas,* the surname of one of the first patients in whom the disease was recognized]

Christmas Eve, the night (often also the day) before Christmas Day, marked by preparations for the Christmas festival.

Christmas fern, an evergreen fern of eastern North America, having simply pinnate fronds: *The Christmas fern, being very firm in texture, is much used in holiday decoration* (Science News Letter).

Christmas flower, 1 = Christmas rose. 2 = poinsettia.

Christmas pudding, *Especially British.* plum pudding served at Christmas dinner.

Christmas rose, a low-growing, European, evergreen plant of the crowfoot family, grown for its white flowers which bloom in winter or early spring; black hellebore.

Christmas seal, an ornamental adhesive stamp offered for sale during the Christmas season.

Christ|mas|sy or **Christ|mas|y** (kris′mə sē), *adj. Informal.* in the spirit of Christmas; suitable for or suggestive of Christmas: *Strands of holly, laden with red berries, embroidered down each side of the inserts and ... around the cuffs are what make it* [*a dress*] *especially Christmassy* (New Yorker).

Christ|mas|tide (kris′məs tīd′), *n.* the Christmas season; Yuletide. It is properly from midnight of December 24 to New Year's Day or, especially in England, to Epiphany. *The door is decorated with a holly wreath at Christmastide, and passers-by seldom give the house a second glance* (Wall Street Journal). [< *Christmas* + *tide*[1] time]

Christ|mas|time (kris′məs tīm′), *n.* the Christmas season: *At Christmastime, there were trees and holly and carols* (Newsweek).

∗**Christmas tree**, 1 an evergreen or artificial tree decorated with lights and ornaments, and often bearing Christmas presents. The Christmas tree now is a regular feature of the Christmas celebration in the United States and several other countries, especially Germany, where it originated. 2 a special valve system used in oil wells. 3 a small standard placed on the map of a plotting board to show the track of an aircraft or of a formation of aircraft.

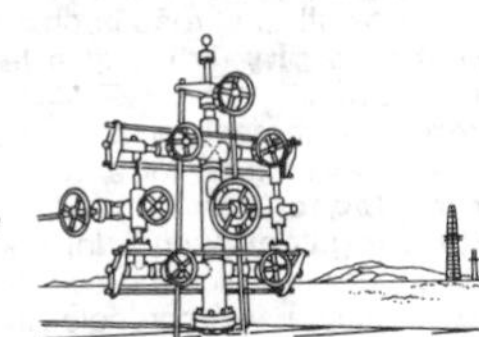

∗**Christmas tree**
definition 2

Chris|to|cen|tric (kris′tə sen′trik), *adj.* having Christ as its center: *Christocentric theology.*

Chris|to|gram (kris′tə gram), *n.* the symbol XP used for Christ's name, especially as a monogram; chrismon. See **XP**.

Chris|tol|a|try (kris tol′ə trē), the worship of Christ. [< *Christ* + Greek *latreíā* worship]

Chris|to|log|i|cal (kris′tə loj′ə kəl), *adj.* having to do with Christology.

Chris|tol|o|gy (kris tol′ə jē), *n.* 1 the study of the life and attributes of Christ. 2 a theory or doctrine concerning Christ.

Christ's-thorn (krīsts′thôrn′), *n.* any one of several Palestinian thorny shrubs or small trees supposed to have formed Christ's crown of thorns, as the common jujube.

chris|ty or **Chris|ty** (kris′tē), *n., pl.* **-ties**, *v.,* **-tied**, **-ty|ing**. = christie.

chrom-, *combining form.* the form of **chromo-** before vowels, as in *chrominance.*

chro|ma (krō′mə), *n.* saturation and hue considered together as a quality of color; the degree of a color's freedom from white, gray, or black: *If you mixed steps of color between a pure red and a neutral gray of the same value, or lightness, you would have a series of chromas* (Faber Birren). [< Greek *chrôma* color]

chro|maf|fin (krō maf′in), *adj.* 1 having an affinity for salts of chromic acid. 2 of or having to do with certain pigmented cells in the medulla of a suprarenal gland: *chromaffin tissue.* [< *chrom*(ium) + Latin *affīnis* akin]

chro|maf|fine (krō maf′ēn, -in), *adj.* = chromaffin.

chro|ma|lize (krō′mə līz), *v.t.,* **-lized**, **-liz|ing**. to metalize with a substance containing chromium.

chromat-, *combining form.* the form of **chromato-** before vowels, as in *chromatin.*

chro|mate (krō′māt), *n., v.,* **-mat|ed**, **-mat|ing**. *Chemistry.* — *n.* a salt or ester of chromic acid, which contains the bivalent radical $-CrO_4$.
— *v.t.* to treat with a chromate.
[< *chrom*(ic) + *-ate*[2]]

chro|mat|ic (krō mat′ik), *adj., n.* — *adj.* 1a of color or colors: *Most paint stores have chromatic charts.* b of or having to do with chroma: *chromatic color.* 2a progressing only by half steps instead of by the regular intervals of the musical scale: *There are twelve chromatic tones.* b having to do with or involving the use of tones which do not belong to a particular key or musical scale. c of tones which are marked with accidentals, are not normal to the scale in which they occur, but do not cause modulation.
— *n. Music.* = accidental.
[< Latin *chrōmaticus* < Greek *chrōmatikós* (in a musical sense) < *chrôma* color] — **chro|mat′i|cal|ly**, *adv.*

chromatic aberration, *Optics.* failure of the different colors of light to meet in one focus when refracted through a convex lens, resulting in a prismatic coloring around the edge of the image; chromatism: *An objective should be as free as possible from chromatic aberration, which causes colors to form around a brilliant object* (Bernhard, Bennett, and Rice).

chro|mat|i|cism (krō mat′ə siz əm), *n.* the use of tones of a chromatic musical scale.

chro|ma|tic|i|ty (krō′mə tis′ə tē), *n.* the state, degree, or quality of being chromatic; chroma.

chro|mat|ic|ness (krō mat′ik nis), *n.* = chromaticity.

chro|mat|ics (krō mat′iks), *n.* 1 the science that deals with colors. 2 the branch of colorimetry dealing with hue and saturation.

∗**chromatic scale**, a musical scale that progresses by half steps within the octave.

∗**chromatic scale**

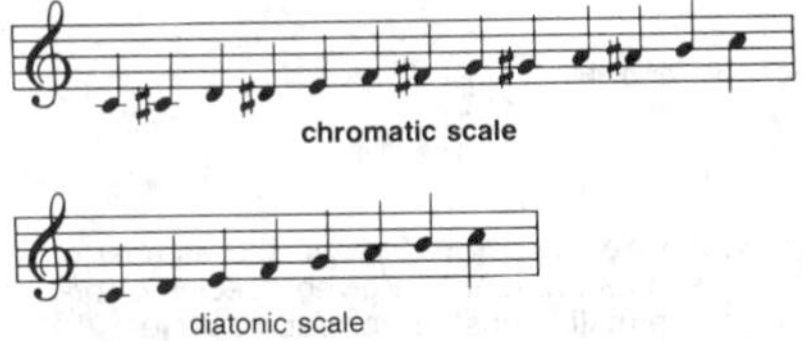

chromatic scale

diatonic scale

chro|ma|tid (krō′mə tid), *n. Biology.* one of the two identical longitudinal halves into which a chromosome divides during cell division, which in turn develops into a complete new chromosome.

chro|ma|tin (krō′mə tin), *n.* 1 a protein substance in the nucleus of an animal or plant cell; chromoplasm. The chromosomes are made up in part of chromatin. It consists of granules or threads of deoxyribonucleic acid and protein, absorbs basic stains readily, and draws together to form chromosomes during mitosis. 2 sex chromatin; Barr body: *A cell component called chromatin is found in the nucleus of female cells but not in that of male cells* (Science News Letter).

chro|ma|tin|ic (krō′mə tin′ik), *adj.* of or having to do with chromatin.

chro|ma|tism (krō′mə tiz əm), *n.* = chromatic aberration.

chro|ma|tist (krō′mə tist), *n.* a person who studies chromatics.

chromato-, *combining form.* 1 color or the pigment producing it: *Chromatology = the science of color.*
2 chromatin: *Chromatolysis* = the disappearance of chromatin. Also, **chromat-** before vowels.
[< Greek *chrôma, -atos* color]

chro|ma|to|gram (krō′mə tə gram), *n.* the pattern of separate sections on the adsorbent in chromatography: *The mushrooms are minced, and after alcohol extraction and evaporation, a chromatogram on filter paper is prepared from the residue* (Science News Letter).

chro|ma|to|graph (krō′mə tə graf, -gräf; krō-mat′ə-), *n., v.* — *n.* an instrument for analyzing mixtures by chromatography. — *v.t.* to analyze or represent by using chromatography.

chro|ma|tog|ra|pher (krō′mə tog′rə fər), *n.* a person skilled in chromatography.

chro|ma|to|graph|ic (krō′mə tə graf′ik), *adj.* having to do with chromatography. — **chro′ma|to|graph′i|cal|ly**, *adv.*

chro|ma|tog|ra|phy (krō′mə tog′rə fē), *n.* the separation and analysis of mixtures of chemical compounds by the use of an adsorbing material, so that the different compounds become adsorbed in separate sections: *The amounts and kinds* [*of amino acids*] *in the stomach juices of the patients and normal persons after fasting were determined by paper-partition chromatography* (Science News Letter).

chro|ma|tol|o|gy (krō′mə tol′ə jē), *n.* the science of colors; chromatics.

chro|ma|tol|y|sis (krō′mə tol′ə sis), *n.* the breakup and destruction of chromatin in a cell nucleus.

chro|ma|to|lyt|ic (krō′mə tə lit′ik), *adj.* having to do with or causing chromatolysis.

chro|ma|to|phore (krō′mə tə fôr, -fōr), *n.* 1 one of the specialized pigment-bearing bodies in the cells of plants, especially of algae, such as a chloroplast or chromoplast. 2 a pigment cell able to produce rapid color change in the skin of certain animals by its contraction or expansion, for example in a cuttlefish or a chameleon.

chro|ma|to|phor|ic (krō′mə tə fôr′ik, -for′-), *adj.* having to do with or containing chromatophores.

chro|ma|to|plasm (krō′mə tə plaz′əm), *n.* the colored portions of protoplasm; the pigment substance of cells.

chro|ma|to|scope (krō′mə tə skōp), *n.* a device for compounding colors by combining light rays of different colors.

chro|ma|trope (krō′mə trōp), *n.* 1 an arrangement in a magic lantern, stereopticon, or other light projector for producing effects similar to those of a kaleidoscope. 2 a device consisting of a disk on which circular arcs of bright colors are so placed that when the disk is revolved rapidly streams of color seem to flow to or from the center. [< Greek *chrôma* color + *tropē* a turning]

chro|ma|type (krō′mə tīp), *n. Photography.* 1 a picture made upon paper sensitized with bichromate of potassium or some other salt of chromium. 2 the process of making such pictures. [< *chromium* + *-type*]

chrome (krōm), *n., v.,* **chromed**, **chrom|ing**. — *n.* 1 = chromium. 2a the name given to several different paint pigments, such as chrome yellow. b *Dyeing.* potassium or sodium dichromate. 3 = chrome steel.
— *v.t.* 1 to cover or plate with chrome: *chromed steel.* 2 *Dyeing.* to treat with a solution of potassium or sodium dichromate.
[< French *chrome* < Greek *chrôma* color (from the brilliant colors of its compounds)]

chrome alum, *Chemistry.* an alum containing trivalent chromium, such as a violet crystalline compound, ammonium chromic sulfate, used as a mordant, or a violet-red crystalline compound, potassium chromic sulfate, also used as a mordant.

chrome green, any one of several green pigments containing chromium, used in paints and dyes and in textile printing. The chrome greens consist chiefly of chromic oxide. *Formula:* Cr_2O_3

chrome iron or **chrome iron ore**, = chromite (def. 1).

chrome leather, leather tanned with salts of chromium.

chrome-plat|ed (krōm′plā′tid), *adj.* 1 covered or ornamented with chrome: *chrome-plated steel.* 2 *Figurative.* garish; lavish: *chrome-plated economy.*

chrome red, any one of several bright-red pigments consisting of basic lead chromate, approximately $PbCrO_4 \cdot PbO$: *A red pigment known as chrome red may be prepared by boiling chrome yellow with a dilute alkali* (W. N. Jones).

chrome steel, a very hard, strong steel containing chromium; chromium steel.

chrome tanning, a method of tanning leather by treating it with a solution of chromium salt, such as potassium dichromate.

chrome yellow, a yellow coloring matter made from neutral lead chromate, or sometimes from zinc chromate or barium chromate, and used in some yellow paints.

chro|mic (krō′mik), *adj. Chemistry.* 1 of chromium. 2 containing chromium, especially with a valence of 3.

chromic acid, an acid occurring only in solutions or in the form of its salts (chromates). *Formula:* H_2CrO_4

chro|mi|dro|sis (krō′mə drō′sis), *n.* the secretion

Pronunciation Key: hat, āge, cãre, fär; let, ēqual, tėrm; it, īce; hot, ōpen, ôrder; oil, out; cup, pu̇t, rüle; child; long; thin; ᴛʜen; zh, measure;
ə represents **a** in about, **e** in taken, **i** in pencil, **o** in lemon, **u** in circus.

of colored sweat. [< Greek *chrôma* color + *hidrōsis* sweat]

chro|mi|nance (krō′mə nəns), *n.* the difference between any color and a reference color of equal light intensity, used as a colorimetric unit in transmitting hue and saturation signals in color television: *Colour information is supplied to the television receiver by a chrominance signal* (New Scientist). [< *chrom-* + (lum)*inance*]

chro|mi|ole (krō′mē ōl), *n.* a small fragment or granule of chromatin: *Each chromomere consists in turn of one or more smaller particles called chromioles* (Heber W. Youngken). [formed as a diminutive of Greek *chrôma* color]

chro|mite (krō′mīt), *n.* **1** a mineral containing iron and chromium, the commercial source of chromium. *Formula:* $FeCr_2O_4$ **2** *Chemistry.* **a** a salt of chromous acid, which contains the univalent radical $-CrO_2$ **b** a salt of chromium, especially one with a valence of 2.

*** chro|mi|um** (krō′mē əm), *n.* a grayish, hard, brittle, metallic chemical element that does not rust or become dull easily when exposed to air; chrome. The element chromium occurs as a plating, as a constituent of stainless steel, and in making dyes and paints. [< French *chrome* chrome + New Latin *-ium,*]

*** chromium**

symbol	atomic number	atomic weight	oxidation state
Cr	24	51.996	6,3,2

chromium steel, = chrome steel.

chro|mo (krō′mō), *n., pl.* **-mos.** a colored picture printed from a series of stones or plates; [American English; short for *chromolithograph*]

chromo-, *combining form.* color; pigmentation: *Chromophore = a color-producing chemical group.* Also, **chrom-** before vowels. [< Greek *chrôma* color]

chro|mo|dy|nam|ic (krō′mō dī nam′ik), *adj.* of or relating to chromodynamics: *The chromodynamic force . . . bind [s] quarks to other quarks* (Science News).

chro|mo|dy|nam|ics (krō′mō dī nam′iks), *n. Nuclear Physics.* the study of the action of forces by which the property of color binds quarks together: *An essential requirement of chromodynamics is that each species of quark possess three aspects called colors, which have to do with the way it combines with other quarks to form a larger particle* (New York Times Magazine).

chro|mo|gen (krō′mə jən), *n.* **1** *Chemistry.* an organic substance that forms a colored compound or becomes a pigment when exposed to air. **2a** a compound (not a dye) having color-forming groups and thus capable of being converted into a dye. **b** a dye derived from naphthalene, producing a brown color in wool when oxidized. **3** the coloring matter of a plant.

chro|mo|gen|ic (krō′mə jen′ik), *adj.* **1** producing color. **2** of chromogen or a chromogen. **3** developing a characteristic color: *chromogenic bacteria.*

chro|mo|gram (krō′mə gram), *n. Photography.* any one of the three negatives taken through differently colored screens, produced in the process of photographing objects in their natural colors.

chro|mo|leu|cite (krō′mō lü′sīt), *n.* a cytoplasmic color granule; chromoplast.

chro|mo|lith|o|graph (krō′mō lith′ə graf, -gräf), *n.* = chromo.

chro|mo|lith|o|graph|ic (krō′mō lith′ə graf′ik), *adj.* of or executed in chromolithography.

chro|mo|li|thog|ra|phy (krō′mō li thog′rə fē), *n.* the art or process of printing pictures in color by a series of stones or plates.

chro|mo|mere (krō′mə mir), *n. Biology.* one of the deeply staining granules or bands on a chromosome, composed of deoxyribonucleic acid. [< *chromo-* + Greek *méros* part]

chro|mon (krō′mon), *n. Nuclear Physics.* a hypothetical constituent of quarks that determines the property of color: *The color of the composite system is determined by preons called chromon; there are four of them, one with the color red, one yellow, one blue, and one colorless* (Scientific American). [< *chrom-* + *-on*]

chro|mo|ne|ma (krō mon′ə mə), *n., pl.* **-ma|ta** (-mə tə). one of the fine filaments, often coiled, of which chromosomes are composed. [< *chromo-* + Greek *nêma* thread, yard]

chro|mo|phil (krō′mə fil), *adj.* **1** having an affinity for color; staining readily. **2** = chromaffin. [< Greek *chrôma* color + *philos* loving]

chro|moph|i|lous (krō mof′ə ləs), *adj.* = chromophil.

chro|mo|phore (krō′mō fôr, -fōr), *n. Chemistry.* a group of atoms which produce the color within the molecules of colored organic compounds.

chro|mo|pho|to|graph (krō′mō fō′tə graf, -gräf), *n.* a photograph in natural color.

chro|mo|pho|to|graph|ic (krō′mō fō′tə graf′ik), *adj.* having to do with chromophotography.

chro|mo|pho|tog|ra|phy (krō′mō fə tog′rə fē), *n.* the production of photographs of objects in their natural colors; color photography.

chro|mo|phyll (krō′mə fil), *n.* a coloring substance in a plant cell (usually excluding chlorophyll): *Chromophyll is a broad term applied to either the yellow or orange pigments found in chromoplastids* (Heber W. Youngken). [< Greek *chrôma* color + *phýllon* leaf]

chro|mo|plasm (krō′mə plaz əm), *n.* = chromatin.

chro|mo|plast (krō′mə plast), *n. Botany.* a yellow or red body in the cytoplasm of a plant cell containing carotenoid coloring matter. The colors of flowers and fruits are largely due to the presence of chromoplasts. [< *chromo-* + Greek *plastós* formed]

chro|mo|plas|tid (krō′mə plas′tid), *n.* = chromoplast.

chro|mo|pro|tein (krō′mə prō′tēn, -tē in), *n.* a conjugated protein containing a pigment that gives color to the compound, such as a hemoglobin or a flavoprotein. [< Greek *chrôma* color + English *protein*]

chro|mo|so|mal (krō′mə sō′məl), *adj.* of or having to do with a chromosome or chromosomes; resembling a chromosome or chromosomes: *Microscopically detectable changes in chromosome structure are called chromosomal mutations or aberrations* (The Effect of Atomic Weapons). **—chro′mo|so′mal|ly,** *adv.*

*** chro|mo|some** (krō′mə sōm), *n.* any one of the rod-shaped bodies found in the nucleus of a cell that appear when the cell divides. Chromosomes are derived from the parents and carry the genes that determine heredity, controlling the development of the organism and determining its nature. They are of a definite number for each species and occur in pairs in most organisms, except in their germ cells. The genetic material in each chromosome is a long polynucleotide strand, usually of deoxyribonucleic acid but sometimes of ribonucleic acid, set in a protein matrix. *The human embryo develops into a person . . . because the material carried in its chromosomes, its constellation of genes, initiates and guides a marvelously coordinated sequence of reactions that leads inevitably, under normal conditions, to the differentiation and growth of a human being* (Atlantic). [< German *Chromosom* < Greek *chrôma* color + *sôma* body]

*** chromosome** 

chromosomes

chromosome number, *Biology.* the number of chromosomes present in a given species of organism, normally constant for each species: *A recount indicates that the human chromosome number ordinarily is 46 (44 autosomes plus 2 sex chromosomes) and not 48 as believed for so long* (Lorus and Margery Milne).

chro|mo|sphere (krō′mə sfir), *n.* **1** a red-hot layer of gas around the sun which can be seen only during a total eclipse. It forms the third of the four layers of the atmosphere of the sun and is over 8,000 miles deep. **2** a similar layer around a star.

chro|mo|spher|ic (krō′mə sfer′ik), *adj.* of or having to do with the chromosphere.

chro|mo|type (krō′mə tīp), *n.* **1** a print in colors, produced by any process, as chromolithography. **2** a photograph in colors.

chro|mo|typ|ic (krō′mə tip′ik), *adj.* of a chromotype or chromotypy; having to do with or characteristic of a chromotype or chromotypy: *chromotypic printing.*

chro|mo|typ|y (krō′mə tī′pē), *n.* any process of printing in colors.

chro|mous (krō′məs), *adj. Chemistry.* **1** of or having to with chromium. **2** containing chromium, especially with a valence of 2.

chro|myl (krō′məl, -mēl), *adj. Chemistry.* containing the bivalent radical $-CrO_2$.

chron-, *combining form.* the form of **chrono-** before vowels, as in *chronic.*

chron., **1** chronological. **2** chronology.

Chron., Chronicles (books of the Old Testament).

chro|nax|ie or **chro|nax|y** (krō′nak sē), *n.* the time required for a constant electric current to activate a nerve cell or other excitable organ, used to detect changes in nervous or muscular responses. [< *chron-* + Greek *axiā* value]

chron|ic (kron′ik), *adj.* **1a** lasting a long time; lingering; long-continued (contrasted with *acute)* : *Rheumatism is often a chronic disease.* **b** having suffered long from an illness or other affliction; continued: *a chronic invalid.* **2** *Figurative.* never stopping; constant; habitual: *a chronic liar, a chronic smoker. My brother is a chronic tease.* **SYN:** continuous, inveterate, confirmed. **3** *Obsolete.* of or relating to time; chronological. [< Middle French *chronique,* learned borrowing from Latin *chronicus* < Greek *chronikós* having to do with time < *chrónos* time] **—chron′ic|al|ly,** *adv.*

chron|i|cal (kron′ə kəl), *adj.* = chronic.

chro|nic|i|ty (krə nis′ə tē), *n.* a chronic condition or state: *the chronicity of a disease.*

chron|i|cle (kron′ə kəl), *n., v.,* **-cled, -cling.** **—*n.*** **1** a record of happenings in the order in which they happened; history; story: *Columbus kept a careful and detailed chronicle of his voyages.* **SYN:** history, annals. **2a** a record; register; narrative; account: *Human history had hitherto always been written . . . as a chronicle of remarkable happenings* (Edmund Wilson). **b** a frequent title of newspapers: *The Daily Chronicle, Weekly Chronicle, the Houston Chronicle.*

—*v.t.* **1** to write the history of; tell the story of: *Many of the old monks chronicled the Crusades. He chronicled the story of a self-made man.* **SYN:** narrate. **2** to put on record; register.

[< Anglo-French *chronicle,* Old French *cronique,* learned borrowing from Late Latin *chronica* < Latin < Greek *chronikā* annals, neuter plural of *chronikós;* see etym. under **chronic**]

chronicle history, an Elizabethan descriptive title for a chronicle play: *The Chronicle History of Henry the Fifth* (Shakespeare).

chronicle play, a play based on historical matter, especially such as is found in the English historical chronicles of Edward Hall and Raphael Holinshed. Shakespeare's *Richard III* is a chronicle play.

chron|i|cler (kron′ə klər), *n.* a writer of a chronicle; a recorder of events; historian: *Plato was not, like Xenophon, a chronicler of facts* (Benjamin Jowett).

Chron|i|cles (kron′ə kəlz), *n.pl.* (*sing. in use*). either of two books of the Old Testament, called I Chronicles and II Chronicles, coming after II Kings. They are called *I Paralipomenon* and *II Paralipomenon* in the Douay Bible.

chronic respiratory disease, a chronic, viral air-sac infection common in domestic chickens.

chrono-, *combining form.* time:*Chronometer = an instrument that measures time.* Also, **chron-** before vowels. [< Greek *chrónos* time]

chron|o|bi|ol|o|gy (kron′ə bī ol′ə jē), *n.* the study of biorhythm: *One of the relationships discovered by chronobiology is that the many rhythms within the human body normally move in a set synchrony with one another* (Philip Hilts). **—chron′o|bi′o|log′i|cal,** *adj.* **—chron′o|bi|ol′o|gist,** *n.*

chron|o|gram (kron′ə gram), *n.* **1** a phrase, sentence, or inscription in which certain letters (usually distinguished by size or otherwise from the rest) express by their numerical values a date or epoch. **2** a record of time, as one made by a chronograph. [< *chrono-* + *-gram*]

chron|o|gram|mat|ic (kron′ə grə mat′ik), *adj.* having to do with or based on a chronogram.

chron|o|graph (kron′ə graf, -gräf), *n.***1** an instrument for measuring very short intervals of time accurately, such as a stop watch. **2** an instrument for recording the exact instant of an astronomical or other occurrence.

chron|o|graph|ic (kron′ə graf′ik), *adj.* of or having to do with a chronograph.

chro|nog|ra|phy (krə nog′rə fē), *n.* the use of the chronograph.

chronol., **1** chronological. **2** chronology.

chro|nol|o|ger (krə nol′ə jər), *n.* = chronologist.

chron|o|log|ic (kron′ə loj′ik), *adj.* = chronological.

chron|o|log|i|cal (kron′ə loj′ə kəl), *adj.* arranged in the order in which the events happened; of or in accordance with chronology: *In telling a story a person usually follows chronological order.* **—chron′o|log′i|cal|ly,** *adv.*

chronological age, *Psychology.* the actual age of a person, used as the divisor of his mental age to determine his IQ.

chro|nol|o|gist (krə nol′ə jist), *n.* an expert in chronology; chronologer.

chro|nol|o|gize (krə nol′ə jīz), *v.t.,* **-gized, -giz|ing.** to arrange chronologically.

chro|nol|o|gy (krə nol′ə jē), *n., pl.* **-gies.** **1** the science of measuring time and of determining the proper order and dates of events. **2** a table or list that gives the exact dates of events arranged in the order in which they happened. **3** a system of arranging time in periods and assigning dates to events; arrangement of the exact dates of events in the order in which they happened: *[He]was then able by a process of interpolation to fit some of the plays of uncertain date in their most likely position in the sequence—and so produce new evidence of their chronology* (C. B. Williams). [< New Latin *chronologia* < Greek *chró nos* time + *-logiā* -logy]

chro|nom|e|ter (krə nom′ə tər), *n.* a clock or watch that keeps very accurate time. A ship's chronometer is used in determining longitude at sea from the time. [< *chrono-* + *-meter*]

chron|o|met|ric (kron′ə met′rik), *adj.* of or having to do with chronometry; relating to the measurement of time. —**chron′o|met′ri|cal|ly**, *adv.*

chron|o|met|ri|cal (kron′ə met′rə kəl), *adj.* = chronometric.

chro|nom|e|try (krə nom′ə trē), *n.* **1** the science or art of accurately measuring time. **2** measurement of time.

chro|non (krō′non), *n.* hypothetical minimal unit of time in quantum physics. [< Greek *chrónos* time + English *on*]

chron|o|pho|to|graph (kron′ə fō′tə graf, -gräf), *n.* **1** one of a series of photographs of a moving object, taken at equal intervals to record the stages of the motion, as stroboscopic photographs. **2** the series itself.

chron|o|pho|tog|ra|phy (kron′ə fə tog′rə fē), *n.* the taking of chronophotographs.

chron|o|scope (kron′ə skōp), *n.* any one of several instruments which measure very small intervals of time accurately. [< *chrono-* + *-scope*]

chron|o|scop|ic (kron′ə skop′ik), *adj.* **1** of or having to do with a chronoscope. **2** that measures duration: *a chronoscopic instrument.*

chron|o|ther|a|py (kron′ə ther′ə pē), *n.* a treatment for insomnia by adjusting the patient's rhythm of sleeping and waking.

chrys|a|lid (kris′ə lid), *n., adj.* —*n.* chrysalis. —*adj.* of or having to do with a chrysalis.

✱chrys|a|lis (kris′ə lis), *n., pl.* **chrys|a|lis|es, chry|sal|i|des** (krə sal′ə dēz). **1** the stage in the development of moths, butterflies, and most other insects between the larva and the adult stage, when the larva lives in a hard case or cocoon; pupa. **2** the case or cocoon. **3** *Figurative.* a stage of development or change. [< Latin *chrȳsalis* golden pupa of a butterfly < Greek *chrȳsallis* < *chrȳsós* gold]

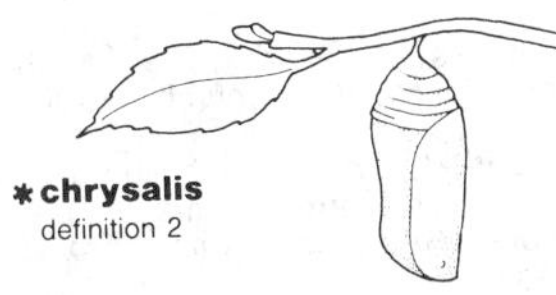

✱chrysalis
definition 2

chrys|an|i|line (krə san′ə lin, -lēn, -līn), *n.* a yellow, crystalline powder obtained as by-product in the manufacture of rosaniline and used chiefly in dyeing leather and silk. *Formula:* $C_{19}H_{15}N_3$ [< Greek *chrȳsós* gold + English *aniline*]

chry|san|the|mum (krə san′thə məm), *n.* **1** any one of several cultivated plants with round flowers of various colors that bloom in the fall. It belongs to the composite family. The different varieties show a great range in the size and form of the flower. **2** its flower. Chrysanthemums have many petals and bloom in many shades, especially in white, yellow, red, and brown. [< Latin *chrȳsanthemum* < Greek *chrȳsánthemon* corn marigold < *chrȳsós* gold + *ánthemon* flower < *ánthos*]

chrys|a|ro|bin (kris′ə rō′bin), *n.* a yellow, crystalline powder derived from Goa powder, used medicinally in the treatment of skin diseases. *Formula:* $C_{15}H_{12}O_3$ [< Greek *chrȳsós* gold + English *ararob*(a) + *-in*]

Chry|se|is (krī sē′is), *n. Greek Legend.* the beautiful young daughter of a priest of Apollo, captured by the Greeks during the Trojan War and given to Agamemnon. The Greeks held her captive until Apollo sent a plague upon their camp.

chrys|el|e|phan|tine (kris′el ə fan′tin, -tīn), *adj.* made of or overlaid with gold and ivory. [< Greek *chrȳselephántinos* < *chrȳsós* gold + *elephántinos* of ivory < *eléphas, -antos* ivory, elephant]

chrys|o-ar|is|toc|ra|cy (kris′ō ar′ə stok′rə sē), *n., pl.* **-cies.** an aristocracy of gold or wealth. [< Greek *chrȳsós* gold + English *aristocracy*]

chrys|o|ber|yl (kris′ə ber′əl), *n.* a yellowish or pale-green mineral consisting of beryllium aluminate, used as a semiprecious stone; cymophane. [< Latin *chrȳsobēryllus* < unrecorded Greek *chrȳsobḗryllos* < *chrȳsós* gold + *bḗryllos* beryl]

chrys|o|chlore (kris′ə klôr, -klōr), *n.* any one of a genus of South African moles, noted for the brilliant metallic luster of their fur. [< New Latin *Chrysochloris* the genus name < Greek *chrȳsós* gold + *chlōrós* green]

chrys|o|col|la (kris′ə kol′ə), *n.* a mineral consisting of a hydrous silicate of copper, varying in color from green to blue. *Formula:* $CuSiO_3 \cdot 2H_2O$ [< Latin *chrȳsocolla* < Greek *chrȳsókolla* solder for gold < *chrȳsós* gold + *kólla* glue]

chrys|oc|ra|cy (krə sok′rə sē), *n.* the rule of gold or wealth; plutocracy. [< Greek *chrȳsós* gold + *krátos* rule]

chrys|o|lite (kris′ə līt), *n.* a yellow or green semiprecious stone; olivine; peridot. Chrysolite is a silicate of magnesium and iron found in lava. *The ancient topaz was the present chrysolite* (Charles W. King). [< Latin *chrȳsolithus* < Greek *chrȳsólithos* a yellow stone < *chrȳsós* gold + *líthos* stone]

chrys|o|mel|id (kris′ə mel′id), *n.* = leaf beetle. [< New Latin *Chrysomelidae* the family name < Greek *chrȳsós* gold + *mēlolónthē* cockchafer]

chrys|o|mo|nad (kris′ə mō′nad), *n.* any one of a large group of infusorians having one or two flagella and no contractile vacuole. [< New Latin *Chrysomonadidae* the family name < Greek *chrȳsós* gold + *monás, -ádos* unit]

chrys|o|prase (kris′ə prāz), *n.* a light-green, semiprecious stone, a variety of chalcedony, with a waxy to pearly luster, used as a gem: *The signet ring of chrysoprase . . . seemed to blaze with hidden fire* (Longfellow). [< Latin *chrȳsoprasus* < Greek *chrȳsóprasos* < *chrȳsós* gold + *práson* leek]

chrys|o|tile (kris′ə tīl), *n. Mineralogy.* a fibrous serpentine. It is the most important type of asbestos. [< Greek *chrȳsós* gold + *tílos* lint, fiber]

chs., chapters.

chtho|ni|an (thō′nē ən), *adj.* living in or under the surface of the earth (used especially of underworld deities): *Hermes stood in the cycle of the chthonian gods, the powers that send up fruits and bounteous blessing from below* (John Leitch). [< Greek *chthónios* of or in the earth (< *chthṓn, chthonós* earth) + English *-an*]

chthon|ic (thon′ik), *adj.* = chthonian.

chthon|o|pha|gi|a (thon′ə fā′jē ə), *n.* an unhealthy desire to eat earth or dirt. [< New Latin *chthonophagia* < Greek *chthṓn* earth + *phageîn* eat]

CHU (no periods), centigrade heat unit (a unit for measuring heat, equal approximately to 1.8 B.t.u.).

chub (chub), *n., pl.* **chubs** or (*collectively*) **chub.** **1** a thick freshwater fish of Europe, related to the carp: *The big chub sleep away the lazy day* (G. C. Davies). **2** any one of several small, freshwater fishes of the central and eastern United States and Canada. They are not related to the European chub. [Middle English *cubbe;* origin unknown]

Chu|bas|co (chü bäs′kō), *n., pl.* **-cos.** a heavy thunderstorm of the west coast of Nicaragua and Costa Rica, occurring especially in May: *the fury of the dreaded Chubasco winds that sometimes come up suddenly from the south* (Sunset). [< American Spanish < Spanish *chubasco* squall < Portuguese *chuvasco* < *chuva* rain < Latin *pluvia*]

chub|by (chub′ē), *adj.,* **-bi|er, -bi|est.** round and plump: *a chubby child. Most babies have chubby cheeks.* —**chub′bi|ly,** *adv.* —**chub′bi|ness,** *n.*

chuck[1] (chuk), *v., n.* —*v.t.* **1** to give a slight blow or tap; pat: *He chucked the baby under the chin.* **2a** to throw or toss: *He chucked the stones into the pond.* **b** to throw out; toss out: *"I do not like chucking money away," he said* (London Times). *It's Tommy this, an' Tommy that, an' "Chuck 'im out, the brute!"* (Rudyard Kipling). **3** *Slang, Figurative.* to quit; give up or abandon: *a wild yearning to chuck it all and take a steamer to Tahiti* (Atlantic). *It would be a tragedy if Mr. [Cecil] King succeeded in reviving the suspicion . . . Chuck it, Cecil* (Punch).
—*n.* **1** a slight blow or tap: *He gave the baby a chuck under the chin.* **2** a throw or toss.
[probably imitative]

chuck[2] (chuk), *n.* **1** any device for holding a tool or piece of work in a machine, especially in a drill or lathe. **2a** a cut of beef between the neck and the shoulder. It includes the first three ribs. **b** a similar cut of lamb or mutton. **3** *Western U.S.* food; provisions: *The outfit consisted of a wagon loaded with chuck* (J. M. Hunter). **4** a boat chock. [variant of *chock*]

chuck[3] (chuk), *n., v.* —*n.* **1** a cluck made by a hen calling chickens, by people calling fowls, or to incite a horse. **2** *Archaic.* a familiar term of endearment, applied to husbands, wives, children, close companions, or other intimates: *Be innocent of the knowledge, dearest chuck, Till thou applaud the deed* (Shakespeare).
—*v.i.* to make a clucking noise like a fowl, or that used in calling fowls.
—*v.t.* to call (together) by making this noise.
[probably imitative]

chuck-a-luck (chuk′ə luk′), *n. U.S.* a gambling game in which bets are placed on the total or combinations shown on three dice rolled in a cage shaped like an hourglass. Also, **chuck-luck.** [< *chuck[1]* + *luck*]

Chuck|chee (chu̇k′chē), *n., pl.* **-chee** or **-chees.** = Chukchi.

Chuck|chi (chu̇k′chē), *n., pl.* **-chi** or **-chis.** = Chukchi.

chuck|er (chuk′ər), *n. U.S. Slang.* a person who throws, especially a baseball pitcher.

chuck-full (chuk′fu̇l′), *adj.* = chock-full.

chuck hole, or **chuck|hole** (chuk′hōl′), *n. U.S.* a deep depression or hole in a street or road: *Can you imagine the jolt when a truck loaded with fifty tons of green logs hits a solidly-frozen chuck hole?* (Wall Street Journal).

chuck|le[1] (chuk′əl), *v.,* **-led, -ling,** *n.* —*v.i.* **1** to laugh to oneself: *Father always chuckles when he reads the funny papers.* **2** *Figurative.* to laugh in an easy, amused manner, with a degree of satisfaction. **3** to cluck, as a fowl does.
—*n.* **1** a soft laugh; quiet laughter. **2** the act or sound of chuckling.
[probably < *chuck[3]*, in an earlier sense "laugh" + *-le* (frequentative)] —**chuck′ler,** *n.* —**chuck′ling|ly,** *adv.*

chuck|le[2] (chuk′əl), *adj.* big and clumsy; blockish (applied contemptuously, especially to the head). [perhaps < *chuck[2]*]

chuck|le|head (chuk′əl hed′), *n. Informal.* **1** a stupid person; dunce. **2** a large or thick head.

chuck|le|head|ed (chuk′əl hed′id), *adj.* thick-headed; dull; stupid. —**chuck′le|head′ed|ness,** *n.*

chuck|ler (chuk′lər), *n.* a member of a caste of tanners or cobblers in India. [< Malayalam *shakkili*]

chuck|le|some (chuk′əl səm), *adj.* causing chuckles: *The humor in this book is chucklesome* (New York Times). *J J is a chucklesome old caution rather than a scoundrel* (Punch). [< *chuckle[1]* + *-some[1]*]

chuck-luck (chuk′luk′), *n.* = chuck-a-luck.

chuck|ly (chuk′lē), *adj.,* **-li|er, -li|est.** chuckling; chucklesome; merry: *Mr. Scott's soothing commentary goes on—now tentative, now chuckly, . . . now a shade coy* (Punch).

✱chuck wagon, *Western U.S.* a wagon that carries food and cooking equipment for cowboys or harvest workers. It is now sometimes a truck. [American English < *chuck[2]* food, *wagon*]

✱chuck wagon

chuck|wal|la (chuk′wol′ə), *n.* a large, brownish lizard of the desert areas of the southwestern United States: *experiments with fur-swathed desert lizards known as chuckwallas to demonstrate an insulating effect against vital heat absorption by cold-blooded animals* (Science News Letter). [American English < Mexican Spanish *chacahuala*]

chuck-will's-wid|ow (chuk′wilz wid′ō), *n.* a goatsucker of the southern United States, like but larger than the whippoorwill, named for its call.

chuck|y (chuk′ē), *n., pl.* **chuck|ies.** *Scottish.* **1** a chicken or other bird. **2** (as a term of endearment) little or dear chuck.

chud|dah (chud′ə), *n.* = chuddar.

chud|dar or **chud|der** (chud′ər), *n.* a rectangular piece of cloth used as a shawl in India and Iran. [< Hindustani *chādar* square of cloth]

chu|fa (chü′fə), *n.* a sedge native to southern Europe, but widely cultivated elsewhere, bearing small, edible tubers. [< Spanish *chufa*]

chuff[1] (chuf), *n., v.,* **chuffed, chuff|ing.** —*n.* a short, explosive sound; chug: *The far-off windy chuff of a shunting train* (D. H. Lawrence).
—*v.i.* to chug: *The vessel . . . stopped here briefly on her way to work; she'll pay a visit to Chicago for a couple of days' open house, and then chuff to home port* (Wall Street Journal). [imitative]

chuff[2] (chuf), *n.* a rustic; boor; clown; churl. [origin unknown]

chuff[3] (chuf), *adj. Obsolete except Dialect.* swollen or puffed out with fat; chubby. [< earlier *chuff* a muzzle, puffy cheek]

chuffed (chuft), *adj. British Slang.* pleased; happy: *Both sides are pretty chuffed with the deal* (London Times). [< earlier dialectal *chuff* pleased; puffed out; see etym. under **chuff[3]**]

chuff|ing (chuf′ing), *n. Aeronautics.* the intermittent burning of the fuel in a rocket engine; chugging.

chuff|y (chuf′ē), *adj.,* **chuff|i|er, chuff|i|est.** **1** fat-cheeked. **2** chubby.

chug (chug), *n., v.,* **chugged, chug|ging.** —*n.* a short, loud burst of sound: *He heard the chug of*

Pronunciation Key: hat, āge, cãre, fär; let, ēqual, tėrm; it, īce; hot, ōpen, ôrder; **oi**l, **ou**t; cup, pu̇t, rüle; **ch**ild; lo**ng**; **th**in; ᴛʜen; **zh**, measure; **ə** represents **a** in about, **e** in taken, **i** in pencil, **o** in lemon, **u** in circus.

a steam engine.
— *v.i.* **1** to make short, loud, explosive sounds, as exhaust gases from an engine cylinder. **2** *Informal.* to go or move with such sounds: *The old truck chugged along.*
[imitative]

chug|a|lug (chug′ə lug), *v.t., v.i.* **-lugged, -lugging.** *U.S. Slang.* to drink (a beverage) in one long swallow: *Every single one of them would fill the tumbler almost to the brim and chugalug it empty without pausing for breath* (Saturday Evening Post). [imitative]

chug-chug (chug′chug′), *n., v.,* **-chugged, -chugging.** = chug.

chug|ging (chug′ing), *n. Aeronautics.* chuffing.

chug hole, or **chug|hole** (chug′hōl′), *n. U.S.* chuck hole.

chu|kar (chə kär′), *n., pl.* **-kars** or (*collectively*) **-kar.** a gray and reddish-brown Asian partridge, common in southeastern Asia and Europe, and now a game bird in the Pacific Northwest. Also, **chukkar.** [< Hindustani *chakor* < Sanskrit *chakora*]

Chuk|chee (chu̇k′chē), *n., pl.* **-chee** or **-chees.** = Chukchi.

Chuk|chi (chu̇k′chē), *n., pl.* **-chi** or **-chis. 1** a member of an aboriginal people inhabiting extreme northeastern Siberia. **2** the Paleosiberian language of these people. Also, **Chuckchi, Chukchee.**

chuk|ka (chuk′ə), *n.* **1** *British.* chukker: *A 60-yarder ... gave Ratanda another goal early in the last chukka to make victory reasonably certain* (London Times). **2** = chukka boot. [variant of *chukker*]

chukka boot, an ankle-high leather boot, similar to that worn for polo: *A traditional two eyelet chukka boot of soft and durable brown mule hide* (New Yorker).

chuk|kar¹ (chə kär′), *n., pl.* **-kars** or (*collectively*) **-kar.** = chukar.

chuk|ker or **chuk|kar²** (chuk′ər), *n.* a period of play in a polo game, usually lasting 7½ minutes: *Between chukkers of the Royal Windsor Polo Cup matches at Windsor Great Park, England, an announcer called for volunteers to replace turf dug up by the ponies' hooves on the rain-soaked field* (Newsweek). [< Hindustani *chakar* a round < Sanskrit *chakra* a wheel]

chu|la (chü′lä), *n., pl.* **-las.** a lively dancing song of Portugal. [< Portuguese *chula*]

chul|lo (chül′yō), *n., pl.* **-los.** a knitted hat with earflaps worn in Bolivia and Peru. [< American Spanish *chullo*]

chum¹ (chum), *n., v.,* **chummed, chum|ming.** *Informal.* — *n.* **1** a very close friend: *Pull yourself together, chum. It's only four hundred years altogether since the thing happened* (Josephine Tey). **2** a roommate (especially in English universities).
— *v.i.* **1** to be on very friendly terms: *The two boys had chummed together since childhood.* **2** to room together (in English universities).
chum up, to strike up a friendship or association: *A ruff ..., in the absence of its own kind, chummed up with a greenshank and followed it everywhere* (London Times).
[short form of *chamber mate, chamber fellow,* and the like.]

chum² (chum), *n., v.,* **chummed, chum|ming.** *U.S.* — *n.* **1** chopped fish, lobsters, or other bait, thrown overboard to attract fish, as in trolling. **2** an important, large, commercial fish whose pinkish flesh is commonly canned in the Pacific Northwest and in Japan; dog salmon; keta.
— *v.i.* to fish with chopped fish or shellfish, as bait.
[origin unknown]

Chu|mash (chü′mash), *n., pl.* **-mash** or **-mash|es. 1** a member of an extinct North American Indian tribe, formerly inhabiting a part of the southern California coast. **2** the Hokan language of this tribe.

chum|mer (chum′ər), *n.* a person who uses chum or throws it overboard in fishing.

chum|my (chum′ē), *adj.,* **-mi|er, -mi|est.** *Informal.* like a chum; very friendly; intimate; sociable: *Stroessner himself was chummy enough with Perón to put his picture and Perón's together on Paraguayan postage stamps* (Time). *He was accused of pushing labor into too chummy a relationship with the factory owners* (Wall Street Journal). [< *chum*¹ + *-y*¹] — **chum′mi|ly,** *adv.* — **chum′mi|ness,** *n.*

chump¹ (chump), *n.* **1** *Informal.* a foolish or stupid person; blockhead. **2** a short, thick block of wood. **3** a thick, blunt end. **4** *Slang.* the head.
off one's chump, *Slang.* off one's head; out of one's senses: *Turner kept jabbering away ... and at first I thought he was off his chump* (New Yorker).
[perhaps nasalized variant of *chop*¹]

chump² (chump), *v.t., v.i.* to champ; munch: *Sir Brian reads his letters and chumps his dry toast* (Thackeray). [variant of *champ*¹]

chum salmon, = chum² (def. 2).

chu|nam (chü nam′), *n.* **1** (in the East Indies) prepared lime, especially a fine kind made from calcined shell and chewed with the areca nut and the betel leaf. **2** a fine plaster for building, capable of receiving a high polish. [< Tamil *chuṇṇam* < Sanskrit *chūrṇa* any powder < *chūrṇ* to pulverize]

chunk¹ (chungk), *n. Informal.* **1** a thick piece or lump: *a chunk of wood.* **2** a stocky animal or person. **3** a strong, stout animal, especially a horse. [perhaps nasalized variant of *chuck*²]

chunk² (chungk), *v.i.* to make a plunging sound, like a paddle in water: *For a time he is on a paddlesteamer—chunking, in the best Kipling tradition* (Punch). [imitative (coined by Rudyard Kipling)]

chunk|ey (chung′kē), *n.* an Indian game of the southeastern United States, played with a stone disk and a pole with a crook at one end, the object being to throw the pole so that its crook comes to rest around the disk. [apparently < a Muskhogean word]

chunk|let (chungk′lit), *n.* a small chunk.

chunk|y (chung′kē), *adj.,* **chunk|i|er, chunk|i|est. 1** like a chunk; short and thick: *He threw a chunky log on the fire.* **2** *Informal.* stocky: *The little boy had a chunky build.* **SYN:** thick-set, stumpy. — **chunk′i|ly,** *adv.* — **chunk′i|ness,** *n.*

chun|nel (chun′əl), *n.* a cross-channel tunnel: *Engineers revived the interest of investors in a chunnel ... under the English Channel, for railroads* (Alzada Comstock). [blend of *channel* and *tunnel*]

chu|ño (chü′nyō), *n.* **1** potatoes frozen by exposure, thawed, and dried, forming the chief vegetable food of Indians of Bolivia and Peru. **2** the floury substance made from these potatoes: *Chuño did not spoil, and the Indians used it instead of wheat to make their bread* (John C. Campbell). Also, **chuñu.** [< Quechua and Aymara *chuñu*]

chun|ter (chun′tər), *v.i. British Dialect or Informal.* **1** to mutter; grumble: *He had been chuntering on for some time before I began to listen* (Manchester Guardian Weekly). **2** to rumble: *[He] chuntered up the hill in his 25-year-old Austin* (M. Parkin). [imitative]

chu|ñu (chü′nyü), *n.* = chuño.

chu|pat|ti (chə pat′ē), *n., pl.* **-tis** or **-ties.** = chapatti.

***chup|pah** (hu̇p′ə, hü pä′), *n., pl.* **chup|pahs, chup|poth** (hu̇p′ōt, hü pōt′). the canopy under which the Jewish wedding ceremony is performed. Also, **huppah, huppa.** [< Hebrew *ḥuppāh*]

***chuppah**

church (chėrch), *n., adj., v.* — *n.* **1** a building for public Christian worship or religious services: *The church was full on Sunday morning. I like the silent church before the service begins, better than any preaching* (Ralph Waldo Emerson). **SYN:** cathedral, chapel. **2** public worship of God in a church: *He is never late for church.* **3a** Usually, **Church.** a group of persons with the same religious beliefs and under the same authority; denomination: *the Methodist Church, the Presbyterian Church.* **SYN:** sect. **b** that portion of the whole body of believers in Christ, or of one denomination of these, which belongs to a particular country, nation, state, or city: *the Established Church of Scotland.* **4** a locally organized unit of a group of Christians for religious services; congregation: *We belong to the First Baptist Church.* **5** Usually, **the Church.** all Christians; the whole body of believers in Christ collectively: *The church is that body of men in whom the Spirit of God dwells as the Source of their excellence* (Frederick W. Robertson). **6** Also, **Church.** the organization of a church; ecclesiastical authority or power as embodied in the clergy and historically constituting one of the three estates: *church and state. The Church was in a very strong position in opposing royal divorces and irregular marriages* (Bertrand Russell). **7** the profession of a clergyman: *He is going into the church as a career.* **8a** any religious body other than Christian; a non-Christian creed or congregation: *the Jewish church.* **b** a building for public worship or religious services of such a body. **SYN:** temple. **9** any building, group, or organization like a church.
— *adj.* of or belonging to church, the church, or a church; ecclesiastical: *church music.*
— *v.t.* **1** to conduct or bring to church, as for a ceremony or service: *The English judges are officially churched in the Easter term.* **2** *U.S.* to bring under church judgment or censure.
[Old English *cirice* < Vulgar Latin *cȳriaca* < Greek *kȳriakón* (*dôma*) the Lord's (house) < *kȳrios* master < *kŷros* power]

church father, one of the fathers or leaders of the early Christian Church.

church|go|er (chėrch′gō′ər), *n.* **1** a person who goes to church regularly: *Everyone in the village but the few churchgoers is on the beach* (New Yorker). **2** *British.* a person who attends services of the Established Church, as contrasted with a Nonconformist, who attends a chapel.

church|go|ing (chėrch′gō′ing), *adj., n.* — *adj.* going to church, especially regularly. — *n.* attendance, especially regular attendance, at church.

church-house (chėrch′hous′), *n.* a building belonging to a church, used for various purposes, such as business or entertainment.

chur|chi|an|i|ty (chėr′chē an′ə tē), *n.* overemphasis on ecclesiastical and denominational matters in Christianity. [< *church* + (Christ)*ianity*]

Church|ill Downs (chėr′chil), a race track in Louisville, Kentucky, where the Kentucky Derby is run annually.

Church|il|li|an (chėr chil′ē ən), *adj.* of, having to do with, or resembling the life, politics, manner, or writing, of Sir Winston Churchill (1874-1965): *Churchillian rhetoric.*

church|ing (chėr′ching), *n.* a ritual, especially in the Anglican Communion, in which a woman makes a public appearance at church to return thanks after childbirth.

church key, *U.S. Slang.* a bottle or can opener, especially of beer.

church|less (chėrch′lis), *adj.* **1** without a church. **2** not attending or belonging to a church. **3** without church sanction.

church|like (chėrch′līk′), *adj.* **1** resembling a church. **2** befitting a church or churchman: *Lancaster ... whose churchlike humours fit not for a crown* (Shakespeare).

church|ly (chėrch′lē), *adj.* **1** of or having to do with a church; ecclesiastical. **2** suitable for a church. — **church′li|ness,** *n.*

church|man (chėrch′mən), *n., pl.* **-men. 1** a clergyman; ecclesiastic. **2** a member of a church, especially one active in church affairs. **3** Also, **Churchman.** a member of the Established Church in a particular country. — **church′manlike′,** *adj.*

church|man|ly (chėrch′mən lē), *adj.* of or befitting a churchman; ecclesiastical.

church|man|ship (chėrch′mən ship), *n.* the position, quality, or action of a churchman.

church militant, the church on earth, as engaged in a warfare with the world, the flesh, and the devil, or the combined powers of temptation and unrighteousness; in distinction from the **church triumphant** in heaven.

church mode, one of the modes in medieval church music.

church-mouse (chėrch′mous′), *n., pl.* **-mice. 1** a mouse supposed to live in a church, where there is nothing for it to eat: *poor as a church-mouse.* **2** *Figurative.* a very poor person: *He told me that before he asked me to marry him. We'd be church-mice, he said, until we'd got the war over and he got busy* (Margery Allingham).

Church of Christ, Scientist, the official name of the Christian Science Church.

Church of England, the church in England that is recognized as a national institution by the government; Anglican Church. It is episcopal and catholic and maintains the apostolic succession. At the Reformation it repudiated the supremacy of the Pope, asserted that of the English sovereign, and incorporated several elements of Protestantism. It has maintained an unbroken organization. *One of the Church of England's most essential doctrines is the apostolic succession, conveyed from one generation of bishops to another from the days of the original church fathers* (New York Times).

Church of God, any one of a large number of independent Christian churches in the United States. The use of this title usually implies fundamentalist or Pentecostal beliefs.

Church of Jesus Christ of Latter-day Saints, the official name of the Mormon Church.

church parade, *British.* the marching of troops to and from a church service.

church-rate (chėrch′rāt′), *n.* a rate or tax raised in England, by resolution of a majority of the parishioners, from the occupiers of land and houses within a parish, for the purpose of maintaining the church and its services. In 1868 an act was passed abolishing compulsory church-rates.

Church Slavic, Old Church Slavic, used in the liturgy of the Eastern Church.

church text, Old English, or black-letter, printing type.

church triumphant, the collective body of saints now glorified in heaven, or in the epoch of their final victory.

church|ward (chėrch′wərd), *adj., adv.* toward church.

church|ward|en (chėrch′wôr′dən), *n.* **1a** a lay official in the Church of England who manages the business, property, and money of a parish church, and legally is the parish representative. **b** a lay official in the Protestant Episcopal Church with similar duties, elected to the vestry. **2** *Informal.* a clay tobacco pipe with a very long stem.

church|wards (chėrch′wərdz), *adv.* = churchward.

church|wom|an (chėrch′wům′ən), *n., pl.* **-wom-en.** a woman member of a church, especially one active in church affairs.

church|y (chėr′chē), *adj.,* **church|i|er, church|i-est.** **1** having to do with or suggestive of a church or the church: *The British House of Lords is as churchy an institution as St. Peter's in Rome* (Time). **2** ardently devoted to a church or to church forms. **—church′i|ness,** *n.*

church|yard (chėrch′yärd′), *n.* the ground around a church. Part of a churchyard is sometimes used as a burial ground.

churl (chėrl), *n.* **1** a rude, surly person. **SYN:** boor. **2** a person of low birth; peasant. **SYN:** rustic, countryman. **3** a person who is stingy in money matters; miser. **SYN:** niggard. **4** a freeman of the lowest rank in Anglo-Saxon and medieval England; ceorl. [Old English *ceorl* freeman (of the lowest rank), man]

churl|ish (chėr′lish), *adj.* **1** rude or surly; bad-tempered: *a churlish reply.* **SYN:** ungracious, boorish, uncivil. **2** stingy; grudging; niggardly; sordid. **SYN:** miserly. **3** (of soil) difficult to work; stiff; hard. **4** *Archaic.* of or relating to a churl; of the rank or position of a churl; rustic; common; vulgar; mean. **—churl′ish|ly,** *adv.* **—churl′ish|ness,** *n.*

∗churn (chėrn), *n., v.* **—*n.*** **1** a container or machine in which butter is made from cream by beating or shaking. This causes the tiny globules of fat to come together in pieces that can be gathered as butter. **2a** a vessel shaped like an old-fashioned upright churn. **b** *British.* a milk can. **3** *Figurative.* a violent stirring or shaking.
—*v.t.* **1** to beat or shake (cream) in a churn: *She made butter by churning the cream.* **SYN:** agitate. **2** to make (butter) by using a churn. **3** *Figurative.* to stir violently; make foamy: *The ship's propeller churned the water.* **SYN:** froth, foam.
—*v.i.* **1** to make butter with a churn: *putting his countess into the dairy to churn and make cheeses* (Macaulay). **2** *Figurative.* **a** to become foamy: *The water churns in the rapids.* **b** to agitate a fluid or mixture, violently. **3** *Figurative.* to move as if beaten or shaken: *The excited crowd churned about the speaker's platform.*
churn out, to produce (writing, music, films, or any other undertaking) in large amounts and without much thought: *I settled to the role of hack, of churning out bits and pieces about absolutely everything* (Punch).
[Old English *cirn*] **—churn′er,** *n.*

∗churn
definition 1

churn|ing (chėr′ning), *n., adj.* **—*n.*** **1a** the stirring and shaking of milk or cream to produce butter. **b** the quantity of butter produced at one time. **2** *Figurative.* a violent agitation of water or anything else. **3** *Commerce.* the practice of inducing an artificial turnover in a particular stock in order to give the appearance of great activity in the stock. Churning is usually illegal and consists of repeatedly selling and buying back the same block of stocks without effecting a change in the price.
—*adj.* that churns.

churr (chėr), *v.i., n.* = chirr.

chur|ras|co (chů räs′kō), *n., pl.* **-cos.** *Spanish, Portuguese.* barbecued beef.

Chur|ri|gue|resque or **chur|ri|gue|resque** (chůr′i gə resk′), *adj.* in or resembling a baroque style of architecture characterized by unconventional use of the classical orders, distortion of forms (as in twisted columns and broken pediments), and lavish ornamentation, especially in stucco. [< José *Churriguera,* 1650-1725, a Spanish architect + *-esque*]

chur|ros (chůr′ōs), *n. Spanish.* deep-fried dough, eaten as a snack in Spain: *You can breakfast on coffee and churros* (London Times).

chute[1] (shüt), *n., v.,* **chut|ed, chut|ing.** **—*n.*** **1** an inclined trough, tube, board, or other channel, for sliding or dropping things to a lower level. There are chutes for carrying mail, soiled clothes, coal, or logs. In England it is often written *shoot.* **2** rapids in a river or a waterfall. **3** a steep slope or sloping passage: *a chute for tobogganing.* **4** Often, **chutes.** *U.S.* a steep slide constructed in an amusement park, down which people can ride in small open cars; chute-the-chute. **5** *U.S.* a narrow passage with high sides through which stock can be moved in single file or can be restrained.
—*v.t.* to cause (an object) to descend by means of a chute: *to chute mail.*
chute the chute (or **chutes**), to take a ride on, or descend, the chute (or chutes), as in an amusement park: *The grand finale ... of the show is the chuting of the chute by big elephants* (London Daily Chronicle).
[apparently a blend of French *chute* fall (of water), and English *shoot*]

chute[2] (shüt), *n., v.,* **chut|ed, chut|ing.** *Informal.* **—*n.*** = parachute. **—*v.i.*** = parachute.

chute-the-chute (shüt′ᴛʜə shüt′), *n. U.S.* chute[1] (def. 4).

chut|ist (shü′tist), *n. Informal.* = parachutist.

chut|nee (chut′nē), *n.* = chutney.

chut|ney (chut′nē), *n., pl.* **-neys.** a spicy sauce or relish made of fruits, herbs, pepper, and other seasoning. [< Hindustani *chaṭnī*]

chutz|pah or **chutz|pa** (ʜůts′pə), *n. Slang.* effrontery; impudence; gall. Also, **hutzpah, hutzpa.** [< Yiddish *khutspe*]

Chu|vash (chü′väsh), *n.* **1** a native of the Chuvash A.S.S.R. of the Soviet Union, one of the largest Turkic groups of European Russia, living in the Volga River Valley. **2** the Turkic language of these people.

chy|la|ceous (kī lā′shəs), *adj.* of or like chyle.

chyle (kīl), *n.* a milky liquid composed of lymph and digested fat, formed from the chyme in the small intestine and carried from there into the veins, chiefly by means of the intestinal lymphatic vessels. [< Late Latin *chȳlus* < Greek *chȳlós* juice, related to *chéîn* pour]

chy|lif|er|ous (kī lif′ər əs), *adj.* conveying chyle.

chy|lif|ic (kī lif′ik), *adj.* forming chyle.

chy|li|fy (kī′lə fī), *v.t., v.i.,* **-fied, -fy|ing.** to convert or be converted into chyle. **—chy′li|fi|ca′-tion,** *n.*

chy|lo|mi|cron (kī′lō mī′kron), *n.* one of the minute particles of emulsified fat, usually about a micron in diameter, found in blood during the digestion of fat. [< *chyle* + *micron*]

chy|lous (kī′ləs), *adj.* **1** of chyle; having to do with or like chyle. **2** full of chyle.

chyme (kīm), *n.* a pulpy mass into which food is changed by the action and secretions of the stomach. Chyme passes from the stomach into the small intestine as a semiliquid acid. [< Latin *chȳmus* < Greek *chȳmós,* related to *chéîn* pour]

chym|ic (kim′ik), *adj., n. Obsolete.* chemic.

chy|mif|er|ous (kī mif′ər əs), *adj.* conveying chyme.

chy|mi|fi|ca|tion (kī′mə fə kā′shən), *n.* the conversion of food into chyme; formation of chyme.

chy|mi|fy (kī′mə fī), *v.t., v.i.,* **-fied, -fy|ing.** to convert or be converted into chyme.

chym|ist (kim′ist), *n. Obsolete.* chemist.

chym|is|try (kim′ə strē), *n. Obsolete.* chemistry.

chy|mo|pa|pa|in (kī′mə pə pā′ən, -pī′ən), *n.* any one of various enzymes that break down proteins into simpler compounds; papain. Chymopapains are obtained from the papaya fruit and leaves. *In numerous orthopedic clinics, ... chymopapain* (*sold in grocery stores as a meat tenderizer*), has been injected directly into prolapsed intervertebral discs. By partially digesting the disc material, the enzyme reduces pressure on nerve roots and thus eliminates pain (Frank F. Mathews). [< *chyme* + *papain*]

chy|mo|tryp|sin (kī′mə trip′sən), *n.* any one of a group of enzymes formed by the action of trypsin on a pancreatic juice, especially useful in the digestion of milk and protein solids: *Measuring amounts of two chemicals in blood, inhibitors of rennin and chymotrypsin, gave an index for response to treatment of leukemia and cancer* (Science News Letter). [< *chyme* + *trypsin*]

chy|mo|tryp|sin|o|gen (kī′mə trip sin′ə jən), *n.* an inactive precursor, or zymogen, of chymotrypsin. It is changed into chymotrypsin by the action of trypsin.

chy|mous (kī′məs), *adj.* having to do with, or of the nature of, chyme.

chy|pre (shē′prə), *n. French.* a perfume made of oils or resins having no alcohol.

Ci (no period), **1** cirrus. **2** curie or curies.

CIA (no periods) or **C.I.A.,** Central Intelligence Agency (an agency of the United States government that deals with matters outside the United States involving national security).

ciao (chou), *interj. Italian.* a familiar salutation at meeting or at parting; hello or good-bye.

ci|bar|i|an (sə bãr′ē ən), *adj. Zoology.* of, having to do with, or characterized by the structure of mouth parts: *a cibarian classification system.* [< Latin *cibārius* of food (< *cibus* food)]

cib|ol (sib′əl), *n.* **1** a type of small-bulbed onion cultivated in Europe. **2** = shallot. [< French *ciboule,* ultimately < Latin *caepa* onion]

∗ci|bo|ri|um (sə bôr′ē əm, -bōr′-), *n., pl.* **-bo|ri|a** (-bôr′ē ə, -bōr′-), **1** a covered container used to hold the consecrated wafers of the Eucharist. **2a** a permanent, dome-shaped canopy over a high altar, usually supported on four columns and shaped like an inverted cup; baldachin. **b** any similar decorative feature, for example over a tomb or statue. [< Late Latin *cibōrium* (altar) canopy (in Latin, cup) < Greek *kibṓrion* cup; seed vessel of the Egyptian water lily]

∗ciborium
definition 1

∗ci|ca|da (sə kā′də, -kä′-), *n., pl.* **-das, -dae** (-dē). a large insect with two pairs of thin, transparent wings. The male makes a shrill sound in hot, dry weather by vibrating membranes on its abdomen. Cicadas are commonly called locusts. The seventeen-year locust of the United States is technically called the periodical cicada. [< Latin *cicāda*]

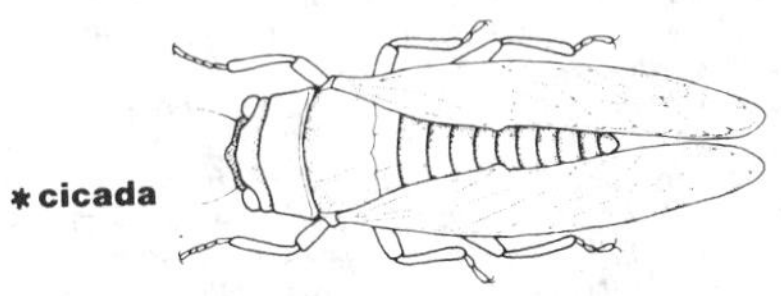

∗cicada

ci|ca|la (si kä′lə), *n., pl.* **-las.** = cicada. [< Italian *cicala* < Latin *cicāla,* variant of *cicāda* cicada]

cic|a|trice (sik′ə tris), *n.* = cicatrix.

cic|a|tri|ces (sik′ə trī′sēz), *n.* plural of **cicatrix.**

cic|a|tri|cial (sik′ə trish′əl), *adj.* having to do with or of the nature of a cicatrix or scar.

cic|a|tri|cle (sik′ə trik′əl), *n.* **1** *Botany.* **a** a small cicatrix. **b** the mark of attachment of leaves to branches. **2** the round, white spot on the surface of the yolk bag of a bird's egg, consisting of the germinal vesicle. [< Latin *cicātrīcula* (diminutive) < *cicātrīx, -īcis* cicatrix, scar]

ci|cat|ri|cose (sə kat′rə kōs), *adj.* full of scars.

cic|a|tric|u|la (sik′ə trik′yə lə), *n., pl.* **-lae** (-lē). **1** a small cicatrix. **2** = cicatricle. [< Latin *cicātrīcula* cicatricle]

cic|a|tric|u|lar (sik′ə trik′yə lər), *adj.* of or belonging to a cicatricula.

cic|a|trise (sik′ə trīz), *v.t., v.i.* **-trised, -tris|ing.** *Especially British.* cicatrize.

cic|a|trix (sik′ə triks, sə kā′-), *n., pl.* **cic|a|tri|ces.** **1** *Medicine.* the new connective tissue which forms when a wound, sore, or ulcer heals; a scar. **2** *Botany.* **a** the scar left on a tree or plant especially by a fallen leaf or branch. **b** the scar on a seed where it was attached to the pod or seed container; hilum. [< Latin *cicātrīx* scar]

cic|a|trize (sik′ə trīz), *v.t., v.i.,* **-trized, -triz|ing.** to heal by forming a scar: (*Figurative.*) *Prior to the discovery of atomic energy, mankind could hope to pass through a sequence of ... bloodlettings and cicatrize its wounds after each of them* (Bulletin of Atomic Scientists). **—cic′a|tri|za′tion,** *n.* **—cic′a|triz′er,** *n.*

cic|e|ly (sis′ə lē), *n., pl.* **-lies.** **1** a perennial herb of the parsley family, such as the sweet cicely, a European plant having white flowers, fragrant, fernlike leaves, and aromatic roots. **2** a similar American species. [perhaps < Latin *seselis* < Greek *séselis* or *séseli* meadow saxifrage]

cic|e|ro|nage (sis′ə rō′nij), *n.* the function or work of a cicerone.

cic|e|ro|ne (sis′ə rō′nē), *n., pl.* **-nes.** a guide for sightseers who explains the antiquities or curiosities of a place. [probably < Italian *cicerone* < Latin *Cicerō, -ōnis* Cicero, a Roman orator (because of the talkativeness of guides)]

Cic|e|ro|ni|an (sis′ə rō′nē ən), *adj.* resembling Cicero's classical literary style; eloquent: *He*

Pronunciation Key: **h**a**t**, **ā**ge, c**ã**re, f**ä**r; l**e**t, **ē**qual, t**ė**rm; **i**t, **ī**ce; h**o**t, **ō**pen, **ô**rder; **oi**l, **ou**t; c**u**p, p**ů**t, r**ü**le; **ch**ild; lo**ng**; **th**in; **ᴛʜ**en; **zh**, measure; **ə** represents **a** in about, **e** in taken, **i** in pencil, **o** in lemon, **u** in circus.

tends to be solemn . . . and Ciceronian when he is making what he regards as a major address before a large audience (New Yorker).

cich|lid (sik′lid), *n., adj.* **—*n.*** any one of a family of tropical freshwater fishes, having spiny fins and resembling a sunfish.
—*adj.* belonging to this family.
[< New Latin *Cichlidae* the family name < Greek *kíchlē* a fish]

cich|loid (sik′loid), *n., adj.* = cichlid.

ci|cho|ri|a|ceous (sə kôr′ē ā′shəs, -kor′-), *adj.* belonging to a group of composite plants including the dandelion, endive, and lettuce. [< New Latin *Cichorāceae* the chicory family (< Latin *cichorium* < Greek *kichórion* chicory)]

ci|cis|be|o (sə sis′bē ō; *Italian* chē′chēz bā′ō), *n., pl.* -be|i (bē ē; *Italian* -bā′ē). **1** (in Italy) a professed gallant and attendant of a married woman. **2** *Archaic.* a bow of silk or ribbon with long hanging ends, attached to a walking stick, the hilt of a sword, or the handle of a fan. [< Italian *cicisbeo;* origin uncertain]

C.I.D., Criminal Investigation Department (of Scotland Yard).

-cide[1], *combining form.* slayer; killer; *Insecticide* = a substance that kills insects. [< Latin *-cīda* killer < *caedere* cut, kill]

-cide[2], *combining form.* (act of) killing: *Patricide* = *killing of* (one's) *father.* [< *-cīdium* a killing < *caedere* cut, kill]

ci|der (sī′dər), *n.* **1** the juice pressed out of apples, used as a drink and in making vinegar and applejack. Before fermentation cider is called *sweet cider,* after fermentation, *hard cider.* **2** the juice pressed from other fruits. Also, *especially British,* **cyder.** [< Old French *sidre,* alteration of Medieval Latin *cizer, cisera,* for Late Latin *sicera* < Greek *sikera* < Hebrew *shēkār* strong drink]

cider gum, = eucalyptus.

cider press, a machine for pressing the juice out of apples.

ci-de|vant (sē′də väɴ′), *adj., n.* **—*adj.*** former; late: *The upper servant in a play like the "Admirable Crichton" . . . puts the ci-devant bosses in their place* (Manchester Guardian Weekly).
—*n.* a former noble or aristocrat: *A ci-devant like Graf Sternberg is glad to act as concierge in his ancient Bohemian family castle* (Listener).
[< French *ci-devant* heretofore, formerly]

Cie., Cie (no period), or **cie.**, company (French *compagnie*).

ciel (sēl), *n.* = ciel blue.

ciel blue, a sky-blue or azure color. [< French *ciel* sky]

C.I.F., CIF (no periods), or **c.i.f.**, cost, insurance, and freight.

***ci|gar** (sə gär′), *n.* a tight roll of cured tobacco leaves for smoking: *Fully 5½ in. long, they are an economical yet satisfying cigar for the discerning smoker* (London Times).
close, but no cigar, *Slang.* not quite enough to succeed or to achieve a desired result: *He has to make up a great deal of ground in the stretch, and more often than not it's close but no cigar* (Audax Minor).
[< Spanish *cigarro* < *cigarra* grasshopper (from a cigar's resembling the insect's body) < Latin *cicāla, cicāda* cicada]

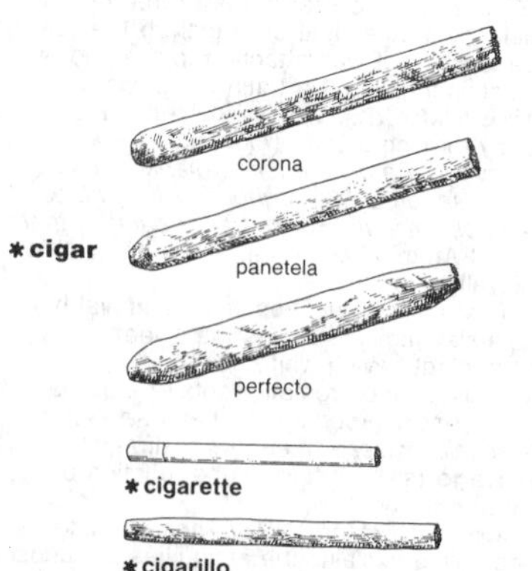

* cigar
* cigarette
* cigarillo

***cig|a|rette** or **cig|a|ret** (sig′ə ret′, sig′ə ret), *n.* a small roll of finely cut tobacco wrapped in a thin sheet of paper for smoking. [< French *cigarette* (diminutive) < *cigare* cigar < Spanish *cigarro*]

cigarette beetle, a widely distributed beetle, destructive to dried tobacco, cigars, and cigarettes.

cigarette girl, a girl or woman who goes from table to table in a nightclub or restaurant selling cigarettes and cigars.

***cig|a|ril|lo** (sig′ə ril′ō), *n., pl.* **-los.** a thin cigar, a little longer than a cigarette: *The cigarillo, a pencil-slim cigar, shorter and usually milder than its big brothers, has won a place in U.S. markets since World War II* (Wall Street Journal). [< Spanish *cigarillo* (diminutive) < *cigarro* cigar]

cigar store, a store specializing in the sale of cigars, cigarettes, and other tobacco products.

ci|gar-store Indian (sə gär′stôr′, -stōr′), = wooden Indian.

cig|gie (sig′ē), *n. Slang.* a cigarette.

ci|gua|te|ra (sē′gwə ter′ə), *n.* **1** a disease caused by eating the poisonous flesh of certain tropical fishes. **2** the substance causing this; ciguatoxin: *The poison ciguatera from tropical marine fishes inhibits an enzyme in heart muscle and other tissues and can cause death in man by asphyxiation* (Science News Letter). [< American Spanish *ciguatera* < Spanish *cigua* sea snail]

ci|gua|tox|in (sē′gwə tok′sən), *n.* a poison that causes ciguatera: *Anticholinesterase action of ciguatoxin has been reported* (Science).

cil|i|a (sil′ē ə), *n. pl. of* ***cillium.*** **1** very small, hairlike parts of leaves, wings, insects, or bits of protoplasm that project from certain kinds of cells. Some microscopic animals use cilia to move themselves or to set up currents in surrounding water. The cilia on the edges of some leaves resemble eyelashes. **2** the eyelashes. [< earlier *cilium* eyelid < Latin *cilium, cilia* plural]

cil|i|ar|y (sil′ē er′ē), *adj.,* **1** of or resembling cilia. **2** of or having to do with certain delicate structures of the eyeball, especially the ciliary muscle and the ciliary process.

ciliary muscle, a delicate muscle around the margin of the lens of the eyeball, a principal agent in the accommodation of the lens. See the diagram of **eye**.

ciliary process, a folded part of the choroid membrane of the eyeball, adjoining the iris.

cil|i|ate (sil′ē it, -āt), *adj., n.* **—*adj.*** provided with cilia.
—*n.* any one of a class of one-celled protozoans having cilia on the surface of the cell. Paramecia are ciliates: *A few ciliates lose their cilia in the adult stage and become anchored on a sort of stem* (White and Renner).

cil|i|at|ed (sil′ē ā′tid), *adj.* = ciliate.

cil|i|a|tion (sil′ē ā′shən), *n.* **1** ciliate state. **2** = cilia.

cil|ice (sil′is), *n.* **1** = hair shirt. **2** = haircloth.
[< Old French *cilice,* learned borrowing from Medieval Latin *cilicium* < Latin *cilicium* covering made of goat's hair < Greek *kilíkion* (originally) from *Kilikía* Cilicia]

Ci|li|cian (sə lish′ən), *adj., n.* **—*adj.*** of or having to do with Cilicia, an ancient country on the southeastern coast of Asia Minor.
—*n.* a native or inhabitant of Cilicia.

cil|i|i|form (sil′ē ə fôrm), *adj.* having the form of cilia; fine and evenly set, as the teeth of certain fish. [< *cilia* + *-form*]

cil|i|o|late (sil′ē ə lāt, -lit), *adj.* having cilia.

cil|i|um (sil′ē əm), *n.* the infrequently used singular of **cilia.** [< Latin *cilium* eyelid]

cim|ar|ron (sim′ə ron), *n. Southwestern U.S.* the bighorn or Rocky Mountain sheep. [< American Spanish *cimarrón* wild, untamed. Compare etym. under **maroon**[2].]

cim|ar|ro|nes (sē′mär rō′nās), *n.pl.* fugitive slaves in the Spanish colonies of America.
[< Spanish *cimarrón* runaway slave]

cim|ba|lom (sim′bə lom; *Hungarian* tsēm′bôlōm), *n.* a large dulcimer, used especially in playing Hungarian gypsy music; zimbalon. [< Hungarian *cimbalom*]

Cim|bri (sim′brī), *n.pl.* the Teutons who invaded Italy in the 100's B.C. [< Latin *Combri*]

Cim|bri|an (sim′brē ən), *adj., n.* **—*adj.*** of or having to do with the Cimbri.
—*n.* one of the Cimbri.

Cim|bric (sim′brik), *adj., n.* **—*adj.*** = Cimbrian.
—*n.* the language of the Cimbri.

ci|mex (sī′meks), *n., pl.* **cim|i|ces** (sim′ə sēz). the bedbug. [< New Latin *Cimex* the genus name < Latin *cīmex, -icis* bedbug. See etym. of doublet **chinch.**]

Cim|me|ri|an (sə mir′ē ən), *n., adj.* **—*n.*** **1** one of a legendary people described by Homer, said to live beyond the ocean in a land of perpetual mists and darkness. **2** a historical people living on the northern shores of the Black Sea, who invaded Asia Minor in the 700's B.C. and were killed or absorbed in little more than a century.
—*adj.* **1** of or belonging to these people. **2** very dark and gloomy: *to plunge a scene into a Cimmerian darkness where there is the slightest excuse . . . is surely to create a momentary sensation, not to lead to a generally valid procedure* (Observer).

C. in C., commander in chief.

CINC (singk), *n.* commander in chief (used especially in combination, as in CINCPOA Commander in Chief, Pacific Ocean Areas).

cinch[1] (sinch), *n., v.* **—*n.*** **1** a strong girth for fastening a saddle or pack on a horse: *The saddle slipped as the cinch snapped under the bucking horse.* **2** *Figurative.* **a** *Informal.* a firm hold or grip. **b** *Slang.* something sure and easy; dead certainty: *It's a cinch to ride a bike once you know how.*
—*v.t.* **1** to fasten on with a cinch; bind firmly; *He bridled the horse, cinched his saddle, mounted and rode away.* **2** *Figurative.* **a** *Informal.* to get a firm hold on. **b** *Slang.* to make certain of: *He cinched a passing grade.*
[American English < Spanish *cincha* < Latin *cinctus* girdle < *cingere* bind]

cinch[2] (sinch), *n.* a card game resembling seven-up. [American English; perhaps extension of *cinch*[1]]

cin|cho|na (sin kō′nə), *n.* **1** an evergreen tree native to the Andes Mountains, now also known in the East Indies, India, and tropical America. It is valuable for its bark. Cinchonas belong to the madder family. **2** its bitter bark, from which quinine and other drugs are obtained; Peruvian bark. Also, **chinchona.** [< New Latin *Chinchona* (named by Linnaeus) < the Countess of *Chinchón* or *Cinchón,* wife of a Spanish viceroy of Peru, who introduced the bark in Europe]

cin|chon|ic (sin kon′ik), *adj.* of or having to do with cinchona.

cin|chon|i|dine (sin kō′nə dēn, -din), *n.* an alkaloid obtained from several species of cinchona, resembling quinine in action, but less powerful. *Formula:* $C_{19}H_{22}ON_2$

cin|cho|nine (sin′kə nēn, -nin), *n.* an alkaloid obtained from species of cinchona or allied plants, resembling quinine in action, but weaker. Its crystals are a different shape from those of cinchonidine and it has a slightly higher melting point. *Formula:* $C_{19}H_{22}ON_2$

cin|cho|nism (sin′kə niz əm), *n.* the disordered condition produced by the excessive use of quinine or cinchona, characterized by ringing in the ears, deafness, and giddiness.

cin|cho|nize (sin′kə nīz), *v.t.,* **-nized, -niz|ing.** **1** to impregnate or treat with quinine. **2** to cause cinchonism in.

cin|cho|phen (sin′kə fən), *n.* a highly toxic synthetic drug, used to relieve fever and pain, especially in gout and rheumatism; Atophan. *Formula:* $C_{16}H_{11}NO_2$ [< *cincho*(nine) + *phen*(yl)]

cinct (singkt), *adj. Archaic.* encircled; surrounded. [< Latin *cinctus,* past participle of *cingere* bind]

cincture (singk′chər), *n., v.,* **-tured, -tur|ing.** **—*n.*** **1** the act or process of girdling, encompassing, or encircling; enclosure. **2a** a belt; girdle: *The stole is wider than the one worn by a priest of the Latin rite and the cincture matches the color of the other vestments* (New York Times). **b** a band, filet, ring, halo, or other encircling object. **3** a surrounding border or belt.
—*v.t.* to encircle; encompass; surround.
[< Latin *cinctūra* a girdle < *cingere* bind, gird]

cin|der (sin′dər), *n., v.* **—*n.*** **1** a small piece of wood or coal that has mostly burned up: *The wind blew a cinder into my eye.* **2** a small piece of coal from which the gaseous or volatile constituents have been burned, but which retains much of the carbon, so that it is capable of further combustion without flame. **3** slag, especially slag produced in making pig iron in the blast furnace. **4** *Geology.* volcanic scoria.
—*v.t.* to burn to a cinder; reduce to cinders.
cinders, a wood or coal partly burned and no longer flaming. Cinders are made up of larger and coarser pieces than ashes are. *When the cinders are hot and glowing, put the meat on the grill.* **b** ashes, especially ashes of coal containing bits of clinker: *the fire is still smoldering beneath the cinders.*
[Old English *sinder,* modern spelling by influence of unrelated Old French *cendre* ash]

cinder block, a rectangular building block of cement and pressed coal cinders, usually hollow. It is used in walls and partitions.

cinder cone, a mass of volcanic cinders accumulated in the shape of a cone, especially at a vent of a volcano.

Cin|der|el|la (sin′də rel′ə), *n.* **1** a girl in a fairy tale who is forced by her cruel stepmother to work very hard, but is rescued by her fairy godmother and married to a prince. **2** *Figurative.* a person or thing whose real worth or beauty is not recognized: *Instrumental and orchestral music had for too long been the Cinderella of Welsh music* (Manchester Guardian Weekly).

Cinderella services, medical and social care provided to the mentally and physically handicapped, the aged, and the chronically ill.

cinder notch, an opening in a blast furnace through which slag runs out.

cin|der|ous (sin′dər əs), *adj.* of or like cinders.

cin|ders (sin′dərs) *n.pl.* See under **cinder**.

cinder track, a track for foot races, with a surface of small cinders.

cin|der|y (sin′dər ē), *adj.* **1** of or like cinders. **2** begrimed with cinders.

cin|e (sin′ə, sin′ē), *adj.* cinematographic; motion-picture: *a cine camera, cine projector, cine film.* [short for *cinema*]

ci|né (si nā′), *adj. French.* cine: *ciné art.*

cin|e|ast or **cin|e|aste** (sin′ē ast), *n.* = cinéaste.

ci|né|aste (sin′ē ast, si nā äst′), *n.* **1** a motion-picture devotee or enthusiast: *[Orson] Welles is considered by many French cinéastes to be the most creative of American directors* (New Yorker). **2** a motion-picture writer or director. [< French *cinéaste* < *ciné* cine + *-aste,* as in *enthousiaste* enthusiast]

cin|e|fluor|o|graph|ic (sin′ə flůr′ə graf′ik, -flü′ər ə-), *adj.* of or having to do with cinefluorography: *Cinefluorographic techniques have enabled the speech therapist to observe the progress of the patient* (Science News Letter).

cin|e|fluo|rog|ra|phy (sin′ə flü rog′rə fē, -flü′ə-rog′-), *n.* the taking of X-ray views by motion picture.

cin|e|ma (sin′ə mə), *n.* **1** a motion picture. **2** a motion-picture theater.
the cinema, motion pictures: *The report submits as "surprising" that 22.5 per cent of those questioned went to the cinema* (London Times).
[short for *cinematograph*]

cin|e|ma|go|er (sin′ə mə gō′ər), *n.* a person who goes often to see motion pictures.

Cin|e|ma|Scope (sin′ə mə skōp), *n. Trademark.* a motion-picture medium in which the use of a special lens on both a standard camera and projector gives the images greater depth when projected on a flat screen about 2½ times as wide as it is high.

cin|e|ma|theque or **cin|é|ma|theque** (sin′ə mə-tek′), *n.* a theater showing experimental or unconventional motion pictures: *Today, almost every major American city boasts at least one "cinematheque" where these pictures, shot on 16 mm film, are constantly on display* (Arthur Knight). [< French *cinémathèque* (literally) film collection, film cabinet; see etym. under **discothèque**]

cin|e|mat|ic (sin′ə mat′ik), *adj.* of or having to do with a motion picture, the art of motion pictures, or a motion-picture theater: *"La Strada" ... reveals the difference between true cinematic feeling and the many kinds of plausible moviemaking ... that try to take its place* (Harper's). **—cin′e-mat′i|cal|ly,** *adv.*

cin|e|mat|ics (sin′ə mat′iks), *n.* cinematic techniques or artistry: *Two thirds of the film's magic is in its cinematics* (New York Times).

cin|e|ma|tize (sin′ə mə tīz), *v.t., v.i.,* **-tized, -tizing. 1** to photograph with a motion-picture camera. **2** to adapt (a play or story) for motion pictures. **—cin′e|ma′ti|za′tion,** *n.*

cin|e|mat|o|graph (sin′ə mat′ə graf, -gräf), *n., v.* **—*n.*** **1** *British.* a machine for projecting motion pictures on a screen. **2** a camera for taking motion pictures.
—*v.t., v.i.* to make a record (of) with a cinematograph. Also, **kinematograph.**
[< French *cinématographe* < Greek *kīnēma, -atos* motion + French *-graphe* -graph]

cin|e|ma|tog|ra|pher (sin′ə mə tog′rə fər), *n.* a person who takes cinematographic pictures.

cin|e|mat|o|graph|ic (sin′ə mat′ə graf′ik), *adj.* of or having to do with a cinematograph or cinematography: *This mute scene, already regarded here as a new cinematographic classic, is the film's climax* (New Yorker). **—cin′e|mat′o|graph′i-cal|ly,** *adv.*

cin|e|mat|o|graph|i|cal (sin′ə mat′ə graf′ə kəl), *adj.* = cinematographic.

cin|e|ma|tog|ra|phy (sin′ə mə tog′rə fē), *n.* the art and science of taking and reproducing motion pictures. Also, **kinematography.**

ci|né|ma vé|ri|té (si nā mä′ vā ri tā′), a type of motion picture or cinematography that conveys documentary realism by filming spontaneous actions with a hand-held camera, editing a minimum of the original footage, and similar techniques. [< French *cinéma-vérité* (literally) cinema truth]

cin|e|mi|crog|ra|phy (sin′ə mī krog′rə fē), *n.* photomicrography in the form of motion pictures.

cin|e|mi|cro|pho|tog|ra|phy (sin′ə mī′krō fə tog′-rə fē), *n.* = cinemicrography.

cin|e|ole or **cin|e|ol** (sin′ē ōl), *n.* a colorless liquid having an odor like that of camphor, occurring in many essential oils, and used medicinally; eucalyptol. *Formula:* $C_{10}H_{18}O$ [< reversal of New Latin *ol(eum) cinae* oil of wormwood]

cin|e|phile (sin′ə fīl), *n.* a lover of motion pictures; movie fan. [< *cine* + *-phile*]

cin|e|plas|ty (sin′ə plas′tē), *n., pl.* **-ties.** surgical connection of muscle in an artificial limb or hand to permit control. [< Greek *kīneîn* move + *plastós* formed]

cin|e|ra|di|o|graph|ic (sin′ə rā′dē ō graf′ik), *adj.* of or having to do with cineradiography.

cin|e|ra|di|og|ra|phy (sin′ə rā′dē og′rə fē), *n.* the producing of X-ray photographs in the form of motion pictures.

Cin|er|am|a (sin′ə ram′ə, -rä′mə), *n. Trademark.* a motion-picture medium that uses three projectors and a large, three-paneled, curved screen to produce the illusion of three dimensions, and a system whereby sound is reproduced from the direction of its original source. [< *cine*(ma) + (pano)*rama*]

cin|e|rar|i|a (sin′ə rãr′ē ə), *n.* **1** any one of several horticultural varieties of a small, composite plant native to the Canary Islands, popular as house plants for their large, heart-shaped leaves and clusters of usually white, red, or purple, daisylike flowers. **2** plural of **cinerarium.** [< New Latin *cineraria,* feminine < Latin *cinerārius* of ashes (from the grayish down under the leaves)]

cin|e|rar|i|um (sin′ə rãr′ē əm), *n., pl.* **-i|a.** a place for keeping the ashes of cremated bodies; funerary urn. [< Latin *cinerārium* cinerary urn < *cinerārius* of ashes < *cinis, -eris* ashes]

cin|e|rar|y (sin′ə rer′ē), *adj.* of or for ashes; used to hold the ashes of a cremated body: *There were also many niches for cinerary urns* (Bayard Taylor).

cin|er|a|tion (sin′ə rā′shən), *n.* the reduction of anything to ashes, as by burning. [< Medieval Latin *cineratus* reduced to ashes (< Latin *cinis, -eris* ashes) + English *-ion*]

cin|er|a|tor (sin′ə rā′tər), *n.* an incinerator; crematory.

ci|ne|re|ous (sə nir′ē əs), *adj.* **1** of the nature of ashes. **2a** of an ashy hue; ash-colored; ash-gray. **b** (in names of birds) having ash-colored feathers: *the cinereous crow, the cinereous eagle.* [< Latin *cinereus* (with English *-ous*) ash-colored < *cinis, -eris* ashes]

cinereous vulture, a large vulture with a bare, pinkish head and black feathers that lives in southern Europe, northwestern Africa, and central Asia.

cin|e|ri|tious (sin′ə rish′əs), *adj.* = cinereous.

cin|e|roent|gen|o|graph|ic (sin′ə rent′gə nə-graf′ik), *adj.* = cineradiographic.

cin|e|roent|gen|og|ra|phy (sin′ə rent′gə nog′-rə fē), *n.* = cineradiography.

ci|né-vé|ri|té (si nā′vā ri tā′), *n.* = cinéma vérité. [< French *ciné-vérité*]

Cin|gha|lese or **Cin|ga|lese** (sin′gə lēz′, -lēs′), *n., pl.* **-lese,** *adj. Especially British.* Singhalese.

cin|gu|lar (sing′gyə lər), *adj.* of or having to do with the cingulum of a tooth: *a cingular cusp.*

cin|gu|late (sing′gyə lit, -lāt), *adj. Zoology.* surrounded by one or more colored bands (used especially in describing the thorax or abdomen of insects). [< Latin *cingulum* cingulum + English *-ate*[1]]

cin|gu|lat|ed (sin′gyə lā′tid), *adj.* = cingulate.

cin|gu|lum (sing′gyə ləm), *n., pl.* **-la** (-lə). **1a** a girdle, now especially one used in connection with surgery. **b** = waist. **2** a girdlelike part: **a** a band or ridge on an animal. **b** a ridge at the base of the crown of a tooth. [< Latin *cingulum* girdle, belt < *cingere* gird]

cin|na|bar (sin′ə bär), *n., adj.* **—*n.*** **1** a reddish or brownish mineral that is the chief source of mercury; native mercuric sulfide. *Formula:* HgS **2** artificial mercuric sulfide, used as a red pigment especially in making paints and dyes; vermilion. **3** a bright-red color; vermilion.
—*adj.* bright-red; vermilion.
[< Latin *cinnabaris* < Greek *kinnábari*]

cin|na|bar|ic (sin′ə bar′ik), *adj.* of or having to do with cinnabar: *cinnabaric sand, cinnabaric medicine.*

cinnabar moth, a large, bright-red moth of Great Britain, having pupae that feed on ragwort.

cin|nam|ate (sin′ə māt, sə nam′āt), *n.* a salt of cinnamic acid.

cin|nam|ic (sə nam′ik, sin′ə mik), *adj.* **1** having to do with or obtained from cinnamon. **2** containing the radical $-C_8H_7$. [< *cinnam*(on) + *-ic*]

cinnamic acid, a white, crystalline acid found especially in storax, various balsams, and cinnamon. *Formula:* $C_9H_8O_2$

cin|na|mon (sin′ə mən), *n., adj.* **—*n.*** **1** a spice made from the dried, reddish-brown inner bark of a laurel tree of the East Indies, Ceylon (Sri Lanka), and Malabar. **2** this bark. **3** the tree itself. **4** any one of several related or similar trees. **5** = cassia bark. **6** a light, reddish brown.
—*adj.* **1** flavored with cinnamon. **2** light reddish-brown: *a cinnamon coat.*
[Middle English *cynamome* < Latin *cinnamōmum* < Greek *kinnámōmon,* or *kinnamon* < the Semitic (compare Hebrew *qinnāmōn*)]

cinnamon bear, the reddish-brown variety of the North American black bear: *The cinnamon bear ... is the compeer of the grizzly in ferocity ... and in everything but size* (Richard Irving Dodge).

cinnamon fern, a large fern with dense, green foliage and cinnamon-colored fronds that bear brown, dustlike spores.

cinnamon stone, any one of various brown or yellow kinds of garnet; essonite; hessonite.

cinnamon teal, a small duck of western North America having a blue patch on the wing, and, in the male, a cinnamon-colored body. It usually migrates south in the winter, often to Mexico.

cin|quain (sing kān′), *n. Rare.* **1** a poem of five lines having respectively two, four, six, eight, and two syllables, a form originated by the American poet, Adelaide Crapsey. *Example:*

These be
Three silent things
The falling snow ... the hour
Before the dawn ... the mouth of one
Just dead.

2 a collection or company of five.
[< French *cinquain* < *cinq;* see etym. under **cinque**]

cinque (singk), *n.* five, especially the five spot in dice and playing cards. [< Old French *cinc,* later cinq < Late Latin *cīnque* < Latin *quīnque* five]

cin|que|cen|tist (ching′kwə chen′tist), *n.* an Italian artist or writer of the cinquecento period.

cin|que|cen|to (ching′kwə chen′tō), *n., adj.* **—*n.*** a term applied in Italy to the 1500's, and to that style of art and architecture which arose about 1500, characterized by a reversion to classical forms: *Titian ... was the last survivor of the great painters of the cinquecento* (William Spalding).
—*adj.* of or having to do with the 1500's.
[< Italian *cinquecento,* short for *mil cinque cento* one thousand five hundred, that is, from 1500]
▶Note that **cinquecento** designates the 16th, not the 15th, century.

***cinque|foil** (singk′foil′), *n.* **1** any one of a genus of plants of the rose family, having small, five-petaled yellow, white, or red flowers and leaves divided into three, five, or more parts. **2** *Architecture.* an ornament made of five connected semicircles or part circles. **3** an ornamental design resembling the leaf of the cinquefoil, such as a bearing in heraldry. [< Latin *quīnquefolium* < *quīnque* five + *folium* leaf]

***cinquefoil** definitions 1, 2

cin|que|pace (sing′kə pās), *n. Obsolete.* an old dance of lively character, characterized by a movement of five steps. [earlier *cinquepas* < French *cinq* five + *pas* paces]

CIO (no periods) or **C.I.O.,** Congress of Industrial Organizations, a group of labor unions organized on a permanent basis in 1938. It merged with the AFL in 1955. The unions in the CIO are organized according to industries (such as the auto workers and the electrical workers); in the AFL they are organized according to crafts (such as the carpenters and the machinists).

ci|on (sī′ən), *n.* = scion.
▶**Cion** is the spelling usual among United States horticulturists.

Ci|pan|go (sə pang′gō), *n.* an island or group of islands east of Asia, first described by Marco Polo and now identified with Japan. Columbus imagined the West Indies to be outlying portions of it. Also, **Zipango, Zipangu, Zumpango.**

ci|pher (sī′fər), *n., v.* **—*n.*** **1** secret writing or code. A cipher transposes the letters of a message according to a set pattern, or replaces the proper letters with substitutes called for in the system used, or combines both methods. *Part of the spy's letter is in cipher.* SYN: cryptograph. **2** something in secret writing or code: *Washington received many ciphers from his spies.* **3** the key to a method of secret writing or code: *Nobody could decode ancient Egyptian writing until a cipher was discovered.* **4** zero; 0. SYN: naught, nought, nil. **5** all Arabic numerals or any Arabic numeral; a number. **6** *Figurative.* a person or thing of no importance; nonentity: *to the lady and lord rather—his lordship being little more than a cipher in the house* (Thackeray). *The impotent estate being reduced to a cipher is as if it had no existence* (Henry Peter Brougham). SYN: nothing. **7** interlaced initials; monogram.
—*v.i.* to do arithmetic; use figures to work arithmetical problems: *She can read, write and cipher.*
—*v.t.* **1a** to work by arithmetic; compute: *The manufacturer ciphered it with his eyes on the ceiling* (Josiah G. Holland). **b** *U.S.: Informal.* to

figure out; calculate; think: *She puzzles her brain to cipher out some scheme for getting it into my hands* (Mark Twain). **2** to express by using characters of any kind, especially in secret writing or code: *He was employed . . . in ciphering and deciphering the letters* (Samuel Johnson). Also, **cypher**. [< Medieval Latin *ciphra* < Arabic *sifr* empty. See etym. of doublet **zero**.] —**ci'pher·a·ble**, *adj.*

cipher alphabet, the conventional letters, numerals, and other signs of a written language, together with the characters or symbols which replace the conventional symbols in any cryptographic system.

ci·pher·er (sī'fər ər), *n.* **1** a person skilled in mathematics. **2** a person skilled in cryptology, especially one whose occupation is putting messages into code.

ci·pher·text (sī'fər tekst'), *n.* a cryptographic text; a text in cipher: *From this it is clear that N in the ciphertext stands for plaintext e* (Time).

cip·o·lin (sip'ə lin), *n.* a kind of marble that shows alternations of various coloring, especially white and green.
[< French *cipolin* < Italian *cipollino* < *cipolla* onion, ultimately < Latin *caepa* onion (because of the alternate-colored layers)]

cip·pus (sip'əs), *n., pl.* **cip·pi** (sip'ī). a low, square or cylindrical pillar of stone, usually bearing an ornamented inscription, used by the ancient Greeks and Romans as a monument marking a grave or sacred place. [< Latin *cippus* post, pillar, stake]

cir. or **circ.**, **1** about (Latin, *circā, circiter,* or *circum*). **2** circular.

cir·ca (sėr'kə), *prep., adv.* about; approximately: *Mohammed was born circa 570* A.D. *Abbr:* ca.
[< Latin *circā* around < *circus* ring, circus]

cir·ca·di·an (sė kā'dē ən), *adj.* of or having to do with a biological or behavioral process that recurs in an innate daily rhythm, such as the 24-hour cycle of sleep and wakefulness in man: *the circadian activity of sparrows.*
[< Latin *circā* around + *diēs* day + English *-an*] —**cir·ca'di·an·ly**, *adv.*

cir·can·ni·an (sėr kan'ē ən), *adj.* of or having to do with a biological or behavioral process that recurs in an innate yearly rhythm, as the annual cycle of hibernation and activity in animals.
[< Latin *circā* around + *annus* year + English *-an*]

cir·can·nu·al (sėr kan'yù əl), *adj.* = circannian.

Cir·cas·sian (sər kash'ən, -ē ən), *adj., n.* —*adj.* of or having to do with a group of tribes of Caucasian race and non-Indo-European language, remarkable for their physical beauty.
—*n.* **1** a native or inhabitant of Circassia, a region in southern Russia on the Black Sea, especially a member of a Circassian tribe. **2** a language of the northern Caucasus.

Circassian walnut, a kind of walnut, native to the Old World, whose wood is used in making furniture.

Cir·ce (sėr'sē), *n.* **1** *Greek Legend.* an enchantress who changed men into beasts. Odysseus withstood her spell and forced her to set free his companions whom she had changed to swine. **2** any enchantress.

Cir·ce·an (sər sē'ən), *adj.* of or resembling the enchantress Circe.

cir·cen·sian (sər sen'shən), *adj.* of or having to do with the Roman circus.
[< Latin *circensis* (< *circus* circus) + English *-an*]

cir·ci·nal (sėr'sə nəl), *adj.* = circinate.

cir·ci·nate (sėr'sə nāt), *adj.* **1** rolled up into a coil; rounded; made circular. **2** *Botany.* coiled from the apex toward the base. The unopened fronds of ferns are circinate.
[< Latin *circinātus* made round, past participle of *circināre* < *circinus* circle < *circus* ring, circus] —**cir'ci·nate'ly**, *adv.*

Cir·ci·ni (sėr'sə nī), *n.* genitive of **Circinus**.

Cir·ci·nus (sėr'sə nəs), *n., genitive* **Circini**. a southern constellation. [< Latin *circinus* pair of compasses]

***cir·cle** (sėr'kəl), *n., v.,* **-cled, -cling**. —*n.* **1** a line every point of which is equally distant from a point within called the center: *The distance across the center of a circle is called the diameter. The circle is . . . the least beautiful of all curves* (John Ruskin). **2** a plane figure bounded by such a line: *He drew a circle by running a pencil around the lid of a jar.* **3** anything shaped like a circle or part of one, such as a halo or a crown: *a circle around the moon. In his dream of hope he grasps already the golden circle* (Samuel Taylor Coleridge). **4** a ring: *We sat in a circle around the campfire. The girls danced in a circle.* **5** = traffic circle. **6** a set of seats in the balcony of a theater. **7** a complete series or course; period; cycle: *A year is a circle of twelve months.* **8** the period of revolution of a heavenly body: *thrice nine days, a full circle of the moon* (George Grote). **9** a group of people held together by the same interests: *the family circle, a circle of friends. I belong to the best social circles in Montreal, in Ottawa and elsewhere* (Pierre Sévigny). **10** a sphere of influence, action, or some other force; range or region: *all around Nature, and inside her circle* (Robert Browning). **11** a situation in which the consequences of a particular circumstance have the effect of intensifying that circumstance: *a vicious circle.* **12** the orbit of a heavenly body. **13** an astronomical or other instrument of which a graduated circle is an essential part. **14** *Logic.* an unsound method of reasoning in which unproved statements are used to prove each other. **15** a set of parts that form a connected whole: *the circle of the sciences.* **16** *Historical.* (in some European countries) an administrative subdivision, especially of a province. **17** *Geography.* **a** a parallel of latitude. **b** a meridian of the terrestrial globe. **18** a sphere; orb: *yon small blue circle, swinging in far ether* (Robert Browning).
—*v.t.* **1** to move in a circle; go around in a circle; revolve around: *The moon circles the earth.* **2** to form a circle around; surround; encircle: *A ring of trees circled the clearing. The imperial metal, circling now thy head* (Shakespeare).
—*v.i.* **1** to move in a circle: *An airplane circles before it lands.* **2** to form a circle: *that proud ring of peers who circled round the king* (Scott).
full circle. See under **full circle**.
square the circle, *Geometry.* to construct a square equal in area to a given circle: *Quadrature of a circle . . . [is] usually called squaring the circle. It is impossible to do this with a straightedge and compass alone* (James and James).
[< Old French *cercle* < Latin *circulus* (diminutive) < *circus* ring, circus] —**cir'cler**, *n.*
—*Syn. n.* **9 Circle, clique** mean a group of people held together by a common tie. **Circle** applies to a group held together around a person or a common interest, cause, or occupation (*literary circles, academic circles*). **Clique** applies to a small, exclusive, sometimes snobbish group, and often expresses an attitude of disapproval on the part of the speaker toward the group: *Every school has its cliques.*

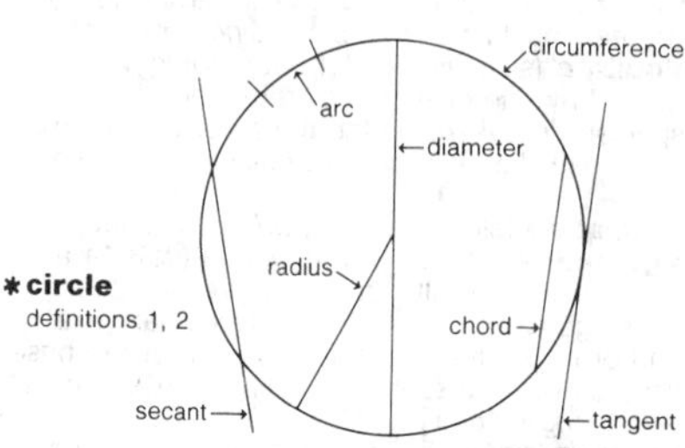

***circle** definitions 1, 2

cir·cled (sėr'kəld), *adj.* **1** surrounded with, or as with, a circle; encircled. **2** marked with a circle or circles. **3** rounded; circular.

circle eight, an evolution in figure skating in which the skater forms an entire circle on one foot and then an adjoining and equal-sized circle on the other foot.

circle graph, a graph that shows the relation of the parts of anything to the whole; pie chart. See picture under **graph**[1].

circle of confusion, *Optics.* a point of light which is imaged as a small circle because of aberration of the photographic lens. The size of the circular image is used to calculate focal sharpness in photography.

circle of curvature, *Geometry.* the circle which serves to measure the curvature of a curve at a given point.

circle of declination, *Astronomy.* a great circle of the sphere, the plane of which is perpendicular to the equator.

circle of fire, = ring of fire.

circle of Hal·ler (häl'ər), *Anatomy.* a circle of connecting arterioles on the sclerotic surrounding the optic nerve. [< Albrecht von *Haller,* 1708-1777, a Swiss physiologist and anatomist]

circle of illumination, *Astronomy.* terminator.

circle of latitude, **1** *Astronomy.* a great circle perpendicular to the plane of the ecliptic, on which celestial latitudes are measured. **2** *Geography.* a parallel of latitude.

circle of least confusion, *Optics.* the minimum diameter of the circle of confusion, in which the image obtained is theoretically in correct focus.

circle of longitude, *Astronomy.* an imaginary great circle through the poles of the earth.

circle of position, a circle on the surface of the earth, having as its center the point on the earth directly beneath a heavenly body and as its radius the distance of the body from the observer's zenith. It is used especially as a means of determining the exact position of an aircraft or vessel.

circle of the sphere, *Astronomy.* a circle described on the sphere of the earth or the heavens. The equator, the ecliptic, the meridians, and the parallels of latitude are all circles of the sphere.

circle of Wil·lis (wil'is), *Anatomy.* a circle formed by several connecting cerebral arteries at the base of the brain. [< Thomas *Willis,* 1621-1675, an English anatomist]

cir·clet (sėr'klit), *n.* **1** a small circle. **2** a round ornament worn on the head, neck, arm, or finger, especially a headband.

cir·cle·wise (sėr'kəl wīz), *adv.* in the manner of a circle.

cir·cling (sėr'kling), *n.* (in the game of marbles) the act of selecting the best location outside the ring for knuckling down.

circling disease, an infectious disease of the brain of cattle, sheep, swine, and less commonly other species of animals and man, caused by a bacterium and characterized by the affected animals' walking in circles.

cir·clip (sėr'klip), *n. British.* a washer in the form of a partial ring. [blend of *circle* and *clip*]

circs (sėrks), *n.pl. British Informal.* circumstances: *In the circs, as the author might have remarked, the bally Sword of Damocles . . . seemed a rusty weapon indeed* (Punch).

***cir·cuit** (sėr'kit), *n., v.* —*n.* **1a** the action of going around; a moving around; a trip around: *The earth takes a year to make its circuit of the sun.* **b** a roundabout course; detour: *They . . . could only advance by long circuits* (Elisha K. Kane). **2a** the route over which a person or group makes repeated journeys at certain times: *Some judges make a circuit, stopping at certain towns along the way to hold court. Some theater companies travel over regular circuits.* SYN: way, course. **b** the persons making such a circuit: *a leading member of the circuit.* **c** the part of the country through which such journeys are made: *The circuit includes Iowa, Kansas, and Nebraska.* **3** the district under the jurisdiction of a circuit court. **4** a territorial division of Methodist churches, served by an itinerant preacher or a group of itinerant preachers: *The Societies in this circuit increase* (John Wesley). **5a** the complete path, or a part of it, over which an electric current flows. A circuit usually includes the generating apparatus. When the path of the current is complete so that the electricity is free to flow, the circuit is a *closed* or *made circuit;* if interrupted at any point, it is an *open* or *broken circuit.* **b** an arrangement of wiring, tubes, transistors, or other electronic components forming electrical connections; hookup. **c** a diagram showing the connections of such an arrangement; hookup. **6a** a number of theaters under the same management and presenting the same shows. **b** a number of places at which performers, speakers, etc., appear regularly or at certain times: *the night club circuit, the lecture circuit.* **c** *U.S.* an association or league of sports teams: *the best club in the circuit.* **7** the distance around any space. **8** the line enclosing any space: *a rude circuit of stones* (George Grote). **9** the space enclosed: *The sound, that fills the circuit of the world around* (Alexander Pope).
—*v.t.* to pass or travel around; make the circuit of: *some . . . comet, circuiting the sun in about eleven years* (Richard Anthony Proctor).
—*v.i.* to go in a circuit; revolve: *the moon as she circuits round the earth* (Richard Anthony Proctor).
[< Latin *circuitus* a going around, variant of *circumitus,* past participle of *circumīre* go around < *circum* around + *īre* go]

***circuit** definition 5

parallel circuit

series circuit

circuit breaker, **1** a switch that automatically interrupts an electric circuit when the current gets too strong: *Circuit breakers can be used in place of fuses* (Wall Street Journal). **2** *U.S. Economics.* a rebate on property tax or income tax granted by a state to certain taxpayers, such as persons over 65, whenever the tax exceeds a specified percentage of income.

circuit court, a court whose judges hold, or used to hold, court first at one place, then at another, in regular sequence through a district.

circuit court of appeals, *U.S.* any one of a

system of nine courts of appeal set up by the Congress in 1891, one for each of the then existing federal judicial circuits. There are now eleven such courts, since 1948 officially designated United States Courts of Appeals.

cir|cu|i|tous (sər kyü′ə təs), *adj.* not direct; roundabout: *We took a circuitous route home to avoid poor roads.* SYN: indirect, devious. —**cir|cu′i|tous|ly**, *adv.* —**cir|cu′i|tous|ness**, *n.*

circuit rider, a preacher who rides from place to place over a circuit to preach. Methodist circuit riders were common in the 1800's. *But while the circuit rider of 1900 was a preacher on horseback, the 1950 circuit rider is a public health worker in an automobile or jeep* (Science News Letter).

cir|cuit|ry (sėr′kə trē), *n., pl.* **-ries. 1** the science of electrical or electronic circuits: *Advances in circuitry ... are providing faster, more efficient, and more compact computer packages* (Vin Zeluff). **2** the wiring, tubes, transistors, printed elements, or other electronic components comprising a circuit: *The complete operation is controlled within the circuitry of the machine* (Wall Street Journal).

cir|cu|i|ty (sər kyü′ə tē), *n., pl.* **-ties. 1** circuitous quality. **2** a roundabout manner of moving or acting: *The correspondence must involve circuities* (Thomas Jefferson).

cir|cu|la|ble (sėr′kyə lə bəl), *adj.* that can be circulated.

cir|cu|lar (sėr′kyə lər), *adj., n.* —*adj.* **1** round like a circle: *The full moon has a circular shape.* SYN: rounded, spherical, orbicular. **2** moving in a circle; going around a circle: *A merry-go-round makes a circular trip.* **3** having to do with a circle, or its mathematical properties: *circular arc, circular function, circular measure.* **4a** sent to each of a number of people: *a circular letter.* **b** affecting or relating to a circle or number of persons: *An old lady ... came from a distant part of the county to pay a circular visit among her relations* (Mrs. Mary Martha Sherwood). **5** roundabout; indirect; circuitous. **6** *Figurative.* happening in a cycle, especially a repetitious cycle: *a circular chain of events.* **7** *Obsolete.* cyclic.
—*n.* a letter, notice, or advertisement sent to each of a number of people.
[< Old French *circulier,* learned borrowing from Latin *circulāris* < *circulus* circle] —**cir′cu|lar|ly**, *adv.* —**cir′cu|lar|ness**, *n.*

circular file, *U.S. Slang.* a wastepaper basket: *A petition to amend the tax law was sent to Governor Carey's office in April but Mr. Bourke said "it probably went into the circular file somewhere"* (New York Times).

circular function, = trigonometric function.

circular inch, a unit of square measure used to measure electric wire, equal to 0.785 square inch.

cir|cu|lar|ise (sėr′kyə lə rīz), *v.t.,* **-ised, -is|ing.** *Especially British.* circularize.

cir|cu|lar|i|ty (sėr′kyə lar′ə tē), *n., pl.* **-ties.** circular shape.

cir|cu|lar|ize (sėr′kyə lə rīz), *v.t.,* **-ized, -iz|ing. 1** to send circulars to: *Minister of Health at the time of the last election, [he] circularized all hospitals about the absent voters arrangements* (London Times). **2** to make circular or round.
—**cir′cu|lar|i|za′tion**, *n.* —**cir′cu|lar|iz′er**, *n.*

circular letter, a form letter, sent to each of a number of people.

circular measure, a system of measure used for angles or their corresponding arcs in a circle; angular measure:
60 seconds = 1 minute
60 minutes = 1 degree
90 degrees = 1 quadrant
4 quadrants or 360 degrees = 1 circle

circular mil, a unit for expressing the area of cross sections of wires, rods, and the like, equivalent to the area of a circle one mil in diameter or 0.000000785 square inch. *Abbr:* c.m.

circular number, *Mathematics.* a number whose powers are expressed by numbers, the last digit in each being the number itself. *Example:* 5 and 6 are circular numbers because $5^2 = 25$, $6^2 = 36$, $5^3 = 125$, $6^3 = 216$, and so on.

circular sailing, sailing along the arc of a great circle.

circular saw, a thin disk with teeth in its edge, turned at high speed by machinery.

circular triangle, a triangle formed by three intersecting circular arcs.

circular velocity, the velocity a body must achieve to remain in orbit around another body; orbital velocity.

cir|cu|late (sėr′kyə lāt), *v.,* **-lat|ed, -lat|ing.** —*v.i.* **1** to go around; pass from place to place or person to person: *Water circulates in the pipes of a building. Money circulates as it goes from person to person. The host and hostess circulated at the party, greeting their guests.* **2** to pass into the hands of readers; be distributed: *A newspaper circulates among the people who read it.* **3a** (of the blood) to flow from the heart through the arteries and veins back to the heart again. **b** (of the lymph) to flow between human tissues and cells. **c** (of other fluids in lower animals and in plants) to flow with a continuous motion. **4** *Mathematics.* (of a decimal) to include a figure or series of figures which is repeated indefinitely. *Example:* 1 ÷ 11 = .090909.
—*v.t.* **1** to send around from person to person or place to place: *The foreman circulated the news of a factory shut-down.* SYN: disseminate, spread. **2** to put into the hands of readers; distribute: *This book has been widely circulated among boys interested in scouting.*
[< Latin *circulāre* (with English *-ate*[1]) < *circulus* circle] —**cir′cu|la′tor**, *n.*

cir|cu|lat|ing capital (sėr′kyə lā′ting), capital which is constantly changing hands or passing from one form into another, such as from goods into money; floating capital.

circulating decimal, a decimal in which a figure or series of figures is repeated indefinitely; repeating decimal; recurring decimal. *Examples:* 1 ÷ 3 = .3333..., 1 ÷ 7 = .142857142857 ...

circulating library, a library whose books can be rented or borrowed.

circulating medium, a medium of exchange; currency.

*** cir|cu|la|tion** (sėr′kyə lā′shən), *n.* **1** a going around; circulating: *Open windows increase the circulation of air in a room.* **2a** the flow of the blood from the heart through the arteries and veins and back to the heart: *The circulation in his arm was cut off with a tourniquet.* **b** the movement of lymph between human tissues and cells. **c** the similar circuit of other fluids in lower animals and in plants. **3** a sending around, as of books and news from person to person or place to place: *Circulation of gossip is vicious.* **4** the number of copies of a book, newspaper, or magazine: *That newspaper has a circulation of 500,000.* **5** a medium of exchange; currency.

cir|cu|la|tive (sėr′kyə lā′tiv), *adj.* tending to circulate or cause circulation.

cir|cu|la|to|ry (sėr′kyə lə tôr′ē, -tōr′-), *adj.* having to do with circulation. Arteries and veins are part of the circulatory system of the human body.

cir|cu|lus in de|fi|ni|en|do (sėr′kyə ləs in di fin′ē en′dō), *Latin.* **1** a circle in defining. **2** a faulty form of definition in which the word or concept to be defined is used to explain the meaning.

circum-, *prefix.* around; on all sides; in a circle: *Circumambulate = to walk around. Circumspect = watchful on all sides.* [< Latin *circum,* originally accusative of *circus* circle, ring]

cir|cum|am|bi|ence (sėr′kəm am′bē əns), *n.* the act or fact of encircling or surrounding.

cir|cum|am|bi|en|cy (sėr′kəm am′bē ən sē), *n.* **1** circumambient quality or condition. **2** that which encompasses; surroundings. **3** a going about; circuitous motion. **4** *Obsolete.* circumambience.

cir|cum|am|bi|ent (sėr′kəm am′bē ənt), *adj.* **1** surrounding; encompassing; encircling: *Her journal ... bears on every page of it the traces of the Baroness and her circumambient influence* (Lytton Strachey). **2** round about; circuitous: *circumambient criticism.* —**cir′cum|am′bi|ent|ly**, *adv.*

cir|cum|am|bu|late (sėr′kəm am′byə lāt), *v.t., v.i.,* **-lat|ed, -lat|ing.** to walk or go about: *If she had had a little less pride she might have gone and circumambulated the Yeobrights' premises ... until she had seen him* (Thomas Hardy). [< Late Latin *circumambulāre* (with English *-ate*[1]) < Latin *circum* around + *ambulāre* walk] —**cir′cum|am′bu|la′tor**, *n.*

★circulation
definition 2a

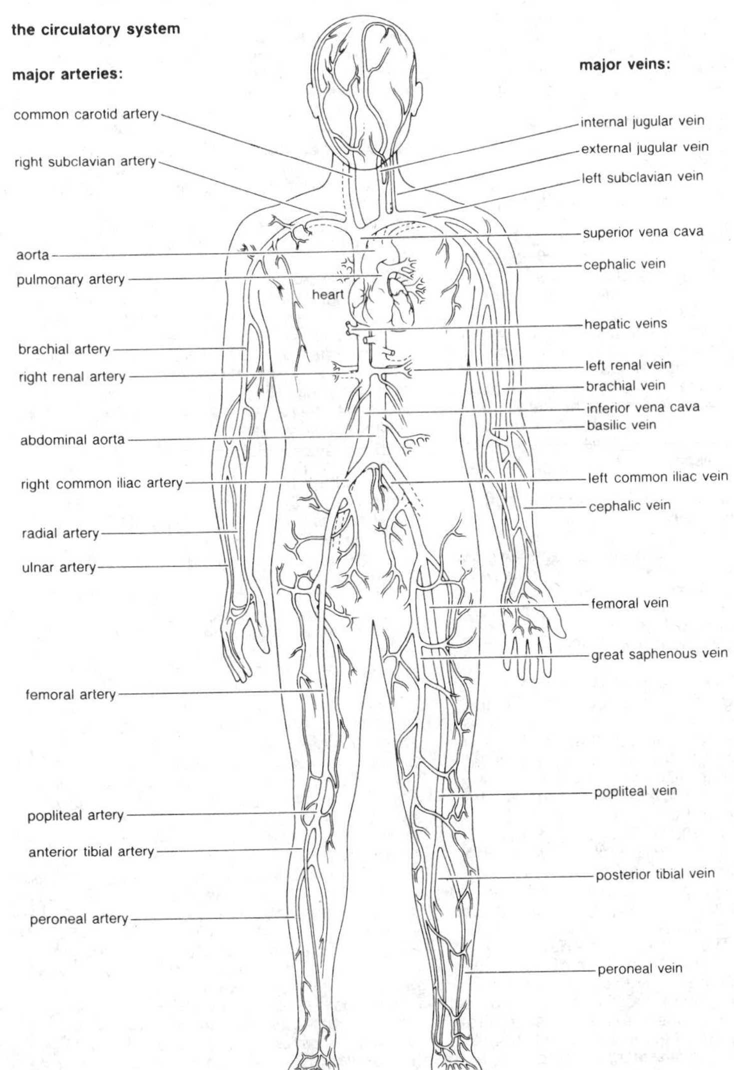

Pronunciation Key: hat, āge, cãre, fär; let, ēqual, tėrm; it, īce; hot, ōpen, ôrder; oil, out; cup, pu̇t, rüle; child; long; thin; ᴛʜen; zh, measure; ə represents a in about, e in taken, i in pencil, o in lemon, u in circus.

cir|cum|am|bu|la|tion (sėr′kəm am′byə lā′shən), *n.* **1** a walking around or about. **2** *Figurative.* an indirect process; a beating about the bush.

cir|cum|am|bu|la|to|ry (sėr′kəm am′byə lə tôr′ē, -tōr′-), *adj.* of or having to do with circumambulation; roundabout.

cir|cum|a|vi|ate (sėr′kəm ā′vē āt, -av′ē-), *v.t.*, **-at|ed, -at|ing.** to fly an aircraft around (something).

cir|cum|ben|di|bus (sėr′kəm ben′də bəs), *n.* a roundabout process or method; twist; turn; circumlocution. [pretended classical derivation < *circum-* + *bend* + Latin ablative plural ending *-ibus*]

cir|cum|cen|ter (sėr′kəm sen′tər), *n.* the center of a circle that is circumscribed around another figure. The circumcenter of a triangle is the center of the circle circumscribed about it.

cir|cum|cise (sėr′kəm sīz), *v.t.*, **-cised, -cis|ing.** **1** to cut off the foreskin of (a male) or the nymphae of (a female), especially for hygienic purposes or as a religious or initiatory rite, as among the Jews, Moslems, and some African and Australian peoples. See also **circumcision. 2** *Figurative.* to cleanse of sin (in the Bible, Jeremiah 4:4).
[< Latin *circumcīsus,* past participle of *circumcīdere* trim around, cut off short < *circum* around + *caedere* cut] — **cir′cum|cis′er,** *n.*

cir|cum|ci|sion (sėr′kəm sizh′ən), *n.* **1a** the act of circumcising. **b** the rite of circumcising. In the Jewish ritual, a boy is circumcised when he is eight days old as a symbol of the covenant which, according to the Bible, God made with Abraham. **2** *Figurative.* spiritual purification (in the Bible, Romans 2:29).
the circumcision, in the Bible: **a** the Jews; the Hebrew nation: *And when Peter was come up to Jerusalem, they that were of the circumcision contended with him* (Acts 11:2). **b** the chosen of God; the spiritually pure: *For we are the circumcision, which worship God in the spirit* (Philippians 3:3).
the Circumcision, a Christian church festival on January 1, commemorating the circumcising of Jesus as prescribed by Jewish law, on the eighth day after his birth: *In our own day the secular features of the opening of the New Year interfere with the observance of the Circumcision* (John J. Tierney).

cir|cum|fer|ence (sər kum′fər əns), *n.* **1** the boundary line of a circle or of certain other surfaces. Every point on the circumference of a circle is at the same distance from the center. The circumference of a sphere is that of a great circle of the sphere. **SYN:** perimeter. See picture under **circle. 2** the distance around: *The circumference of the earth is almost 25,000 miles at the equator.* **SYN:** girth. [< Latin *circumferentia* < *circumferēns, -entis,* present participle of *circumferre* < *circum* around + *ferre* bear]

cir|cum|fer|en|tial (sər kum′fə ren′shəl), *adj.* of a circumference; located at or near the circumference. — **cir|cum′fer|en′tial|ly,** *adv.*

cir|cum|fer|en|tor (sər kum′fə ren′tər), *n.* **1** an instrument formerly used by surveyors for measuring angles, consisting of a flat brass bar with sights at the ends and a compass in the middle, which may be turned over a graduated circle. **2** a wheel of known circumference formerly used for measuring the length of a tire.

cir|cum|flect (sėr′kəm flekt), *v.t.* **1** to bend around. **2** to place a circumflex accent on. [< Latin *circumflectere* < *circum* around + *flectere* bend]

cir|cum|flex (sėr′kəm fleks), *n., adj., v.* — *n.* = circumflex accent.
— *adj.* **1** of or having a circumflex accent. **2** bending or winding around. **3** *Anatomy.* of curved or winding form, like that of certain blood vessels and nerves.
— *v.t.* **1** to write or pronounce with a circumflex accent. **2** to bend or wind around.
[< Latin *circumflexus,* past participle of *circumflectere;* see etym. under **circumflect**]

✱circumflex accent
definitions 1, 2

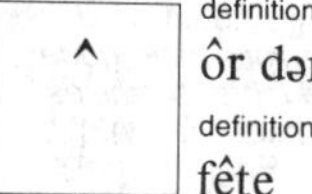

✱circumflex accent, 1 a mark used over *o* in the pronunciations in this book to show that it is pronounced as in *order* (ôr′dər). **2** a mark over a vowel to tell something about its pronunciation, for example in the French word *fête.* The circumflex accent was used in ancient Greek to show a rising and falling pitch.

cir|cum|flex|ion (sėr′kəm flek′shən), *n.* **1** the act of marking or accenting with a circumflex. **2** the act or fact of bending around; circuitous course.

cir|cum|flu|ent (sər kum′flü ənt), *adj.* flowing around; surrounding. [< Latin *circumfluēns, -entis,* present participle of *circumfluere* overflow all around < *circum* around + *fluere* flow]

cir|cum|flu|ous (sər kum′flü əs), *adj.* **1** flowing around or surrounding, as a fluid. **2** surrounded by water. [< Latin *circumfluus* (with English *-ous*) flowing around; surrounded < *circumfluere* overflow all around]

cir|cum|fo|ra|ne|ous (sėr′kəm fə rā′nē əs), *adj.* **1** wandering from market place to market place; vagrant; vagabond. **2** = quack. [< Latin *circumforāneus* (with English *-ous*) < *circum* around + *forum* market place]

cir|cum|fuse (sėr′kəm fyüz′), *v.t.*, **-fused, -fus|ing. 1** to pour or spread around or about. **2** to surround; suffuse. [< Latin *circumfūsus,* past participle of *circumfundere* < *circum* around + *fundere* pour out] — **cir′cum|fu′sion,** *n.*

cir|cum|gy|rate (sėr′kəm jī′rāt), *v.t., v.i.*, **-rat|ed, -rat|ing.** to turn, wheel, or go around. [< Late Latin *circumgȳrāre* (with English *-ate*[1]) < Latin *circum* around + *gȳrāre* turn] — **cir′cum|gy|ra′tion,** *n.*

cir|cum|gy|ra|to|ry (sėr′kəm jī′rə tôr′ē, -tōr′-), *adj.* marked by circumgyration; circumgyrating; revolving.

cir|cum|ja|cence (sėr′kəm jā′səns), *n.* the fact or condition of being circumjacent.

cir|cum|ja|cen|cy (sėr′kəm jā′sən sē), *n.* = circumjacence.

cir|cum|ja|cent (sėr′kəm jā′sənt), *adj.* lying around; surrounding. [< Latin *circumjacēns, -entis,* present participle of *circumjacere* < *circum* around + *jacere* lie]

cir|cum|jo|vi|al (sėr′kəm jō′vē əl), *adj.* **1** revolving about the planet Jupiter. **2** surrounding Jupiter. [< *circum-* + Latin *Jovis* of the planet Jupiter + English *-al*[1]]

cir|cum|lo|cu|tion (sėr′kəm lō kyü′shən), *n.* **1** the use of several or many words instead of one or a few; a roundabout or indirect way of speaking; periphrase: *The witness's account of the accident was so full of circumlocution that it was difficult to understand.* **2** a roundabout expression: *"The wife of your father's brother" is a circumlocution for "Your aunt."* [< Latin *circumlocūtiō, -ōnis* < *circum* around + *locūtiō, -ōnis* a speaking < *loquī* speak]

cir|cum|lo|cu|tion|ize (sėr′kəm lō kyü′shə nīz), *v.*, **-ized, -iz|ing.** — *v.i.* to speak in circumlocution: *A speaker who circumlocutionizes is bound to be dull.*
— *v.t.* to speak of (someone or something) in a roundabout manner.

cir|cum|loc|u|to|ry (sėr′kəm lok′yə tôr′ē, -tōr′-), *adj.* marked by circumlocution; roundabout; periphrastic: *An old man, manager of a shop, was accused in some circumlocutory way of fiddling with the books* (Atlantic).

cir|cum|lu|nar (sėr′kəm lü′nər), *adj.* **1** revolving about the moon: *a man-carrying vehicle on a circumlunar flight—a journey around the moon and back to earth* (United States Air Force Report on the Ballistic Missile). **2** surrounding the moon.

cir|cum|mure (sėr′kəm myůr′), *v.t.*, **-mured, -mur|ing.** to wall about: *a garden circummured with brick* (Shakespeare). [< *circum-* + Late Latin *mūrāre* to wall]

cir|cum|nav|i|ga|ble (sėr′kəm nav′ə gə bəl), *adj.* that can be circumnavigated.

cir|cum|nav|i|gate (sėr′kəm nav′ə gāt), *v.t.*, **-gat|ed, -gat|ing.** to sail around: *Magellan's ship circumnavigated the earth.* [< Latin *circumnāvigāre* (with English *-ate*[1]) < *circum* around + *nāvigāre* sail, navigate] — **cir′cum|nav′i|ga′tion,** *n.* — **cir′cum|nav′i|ga′tor,** *n.*

cir|cum|nu|cle|ar (sėr′kəm nü′klē ər, -nyü′-), *adj.* surrounding a nucleus.

cir|cum|nu|tate (sėr′kəm nü′tāt, -nyü′-), *v.i.*, **-tat|ed, -tat|ing.** (of the growing parts of plants) to bend or move about in a more or less spiral, circular path. — **cir′cum|nu|ta′tion,** *n.*

cir|cum|oc|u|lar (sėr′kəm ok′yə lər), *adj.* situated or extending around the eye or eyes.

cir|cum|or|al (sėr′kəm ôr′əl, -ōr′-), *adj.* situated or extending around the mouth.

cir|cum|po|lar (sėr′kəm pō′lər), *adj.* **1** around the North or South Pole: *circumpolar seas.* **2** revolving around either pole of the heavens without sinking below the horizon: *a circumpolar star. The midnight sun is an example of a circumpolar object* (Robert H. Baker).

cir|cum|po|lar|ize (sėr′kəm pō′lə rīz), *v.t.*, **-ized, -iz|ing.** *Optics.* to rotate the plane of polarization of (light). — **cir′cum|po′lar|i|za′tion,** *n.*

cir|cum|ro|tate (sėr′kəm rō′tāt), *v.i.*, **-tat|ed, -tat|ing.** to rotate like a wheel; make a complete rotation. [< Latin *circumrotāre* (with English *-ate*[1]) < *circum* around + *rotāre* rotate] — **cir′cum|ro|ta′tion,** *n.*

cir|cum|ro|ta|to|ry (sėr′kəm rō′tə tôr′ē, -tōr′-), *adj.* having to do with or marked by a complete rotation.

cir|cum|scis|sile (sėr′kəm sis′əl), *adj.* (of fruits) bursting open by a transverse circular line, so that the upper part comes off like a lid: *The pimpernel, purslane, and monkeypot have circumscissile pods.*

cir|cum|scribe (sėr′kəm skrīb′, sėr′kəm skrīb), *v.t.*, **-scribed, -scrib|ing. 1** to draw a line around; mark the boundaries of; bound: *The horizon circumscribed the sailor's view.* **2** to surround: *the atmosphere circumscribing the earth.* **3** *Figurative.* to put limits on; restrict: *A prisoner's activities are circumscribed.* **SYN:** confine, limit, restrain, abridge. **4a** to draw (a figure) around another figure so as to touch at as many points as possible: *A circle that is circumscribed around a square touches it at four points.* **b** to be so drawn around: *A circle can circumscribe a hexagon.* [< Latin *circumscrībere* (literally) draw a circumference < *circum* around + *scrībere* write] — **cir′cum|scrib′a|ble,** *adj.* — **cir′cum|scrib′er,** *n.*

cir|cum|script (sėr′kəm skript), *adj.* circumscribed; limited. [< Latin *circumscrīptus,* past participle of *circumscrībere* circumscribe]

cir|cum|scrip|tion (sėr′kəm skrip′shən), *n.* **1** the act of circumscribing. **2** the state of being circumscribed. **3** anything that circumscribes or encloses. **4** a circular inscription around a coin, medal, seal, or the like. **5** an outline; boundary. **SYN:** periphery. **6** a circumscribed space or place; district or region of defined limits. **7** *Figurative.* limitation; restriction: *the circumscription of arbitrary power.* **8** *Archaic.* the laying down of the limits of meaning; definition; description. **9** *Rare or Obsolete.* the fact or quality of being confined to definite limits in space, as a property of matter. [< Latin *circumscrīptiō, -ōnis* an encircling < *circumscrībere* circumscribe]

cir|cum|scrip|tive (sėr′kəm skrip′tiv), *adj.* **1** circumscribing. **2** circumscribed or limited. — **cir′cum|scrip′tive|ly,** *adv.*

cir|cum|so|lar (sėr′kəm sō′lər), *adj.* surrounding or revolving about the sun.

cir|cum|spect (sėr′kəm spekt), *adj.* watchful on all sides; cautious or prudent; careful: *His drinking habits have never been exactly circumspect* (Harper's). **SYN:** wary, discreet. [< Latin *circumspectus,* past participle of *circumspicere* look around, consider < *circum* around + *specere* look] — **cir′cum|spect′ly,** *adv.* — **cir′cum|spect′ness,** *n.*

cir|cum|spec|tion (sėr′kəm spek′shən), *n.* **1** circumspect action or conduct; care; caution; prudence. **2** watchful and cautious observation of circumstances or events.

cir|cum|spec|tive (sėr′kəm spek′tiv), *adj.* given to or marked by circumspection; watchful; cautious.

cir|cum|stance (sėr′kəm stans), *n., v.*, **-stanced, -stanc|ing.** — *n.* **1** a condition that accompanies an act or event: *The place, the weather, and other circumstances made the picnic a great success.* **2** a fact or event: *It was a lucky circumstance that she found her money.* **3** unimportant details in a narration; full detail: *The explorer told of his adventure with great circumstance.* **4** conditions that affect a person or thing, taken collectively (singular and without an article): *All are sons of circumstance* (Byron). **5** a detail connected with a fact or event, especially an unessential detail. **6** ceremony; display; formality: *The royal procession advanced with pomp and circumstance.* **7** *Obsolete.* a material adjunct, appendage, appurtenance, matter, or thing belonging.
— *v.t.* **1** to place in specified circumstances; subject to material or other conditions: *They are much better circumstanced than we are.* **2** *Obsolete.* to furnish with details; attach particulars to: *The poet took the matters of fact as they came down to him, and circumstanced them after his own manner* (Joseph Addison). **3** *Obsolete.* to qualify with conditions: *interpositions so guarded and circumstanced* (Samuel Butler).
circumstances, the condition or state of affairs: *A rich person is in good circumstances; a poor person is in bad circumstances. He was forced by circumstances to resign.*
under no circumstances, never; no matter what the conditions are: *Under no circumstances should you reveal the secret of the surprise party we are planning.*
under the circumstances, because of conditions; things being as they are or were: *The tickets to that show were sold out, and under the circumstances there was no choice but to try to get tickets to another show.*
[< Latin *circumstantia* surrounding condition < *circumstāns, -antis,* present participle of *circumstāre* < *circum* around + *stāre* stand]

cir|cum|stan|tial (sėr′kəm stan′shəl), *adj.* **1** depending on or based on circumstances: *The* *usual character of human testimony is substantial truth under circumstantial variety* (William Paley). See also **circumstantial evidence**. SYN: conditional, contingent. **2** not essential; not important; incidental: *Minor details are circumstantial compared with the main fact.* SYN: subsidiary, accidental. **3** giving full and exact details; complete: *a circumstantial report of the accident.* SYN: detailed, minute. —**cir′cum|stan′tial|ly**, *adv.* —**cir′cum|stan′tial|ness**, *n.*

circumstantial evidence, evidence that depends on the accompanying circumstances of a crime. If stolen jewels are found in a man's possession, they are circumstantial evidence that he stole them. If somebody saw him steal them, that would be direct evidence. *He was accused of robbing the house on the circumstantial evidence of being the only person seen entering it that day.*

cir|cum|stan|ti|al|i|ty (sėr′kəm stan′shē al′ə tē), *n., pl.* **-ties. 1** circumstantial quality; attention to details; particularity. **2** a circumstantial matter; a detail.

cir|cum|stan|ti|ate (sėr′kəm stan′shē āt), *v.t.,* **-at|ed, -at|ing.** to give the circumstances of; set forth, narrate, support, or prove with details or particulars: *Defoe ... has so plausibly circumstantiated his false historical records as to make them pass for genuine, even with critics* (Thomas De Quincey). —**cir′cum|stan′ti|a′tion**, *n.*

cir|cum|stel|lar (sėr′kəm stel′ər), *adj.* surrounding or revolving about a star: *circumstellar dust.*

cir|cum|ter|res|tri|al (sėr′kəm tə res′trē əl), *adj.* surrounding or revolving about the earth: *circumterrestrial space, a circumterrestrial satellite.*

cir|cum|val|late (sėr′kəm val′āt), *adj., v.,* **-lat|ed, -lat|ing.** —*adj.* **1** encircled with, or as if with, a rampart, wall, trench, or other defense. **2** *Anatomy.* surrounded by a wall or structure resembling a rampart.
—*v.t.* to encircle with a rampart, wall, trench, or other defense: (*Figurative.*) *The impenetrable barrier of ... self-love that circumvallated his heart* (New Monthly Magazine).
[< Latin *circumvallātus,* past participle of *circumvallāre* < *circum* around + *vallāre* wall in < *vallum* rampart, wall < *vallus* stake] —**cir′cum|val|la′tion**, *n.*

cir|cum|vas|cu|lar (sėr′kəm vas′kyə lər), *adj.* situated or extending around a blood vessel.

cir|cum|vent (sėr′kəm vent′), *v.t.* **1** to get the better of or defeat by trickery: *The dishonest merchant was always trying to circumvent the law. With a commonplace capacity, and with a narrow political education, he intended to circumvent the most profound statesman of his age* (John L. Motley). SYN: outwit, cheat, overreach. **2** to go around: *He took a roundabout route to circumvent the traffic on the main road.* **3** to surround or encompass by hostile stratagem; catch or try to catch in a trap. [< Latin *circumventus,* past participle of *circumvenīre* (literally) surround; get around (someone) < *circum* around + *venīre* come] —**cir′cum|vent′er, cir′cum|ven′tor**, *n.*

cir|cum|ven|tion (sėr′kəm ven′shən), *n.* the act of circumventing.

cir|cum|ven|tive (sėr′kəm ven′tiv), *adj.* inclined to or marked by circumvention.

cir|cum|vo|lant (sər kum′və lənt), *adj.* flying around. [< Latin *circumvolāns, -antis,* present participle of *circumvolāre* < *circum* around + *volāre* fly]

cir|cum|vo|lu|tion (sėr′kəm və lü′shən), *n.* **1a** a rolling, whirling, or turning around an axis or center; revolution; rotation; gyration. **b** a single complete turn, revolution, or rotation. **2a** the winding, rolling, or folding of a thing around something else. **b** a single fold or turn of anything so wound. **3a** winding or moving in a sinuous course. **b** a winding; sinuosity. **4** a roundabout course or procedure.

cir|cum|volve (sėr′kəm volv′), *v.t., v.i.,* **-volved, -volv|ing.** to turn or revolve. [< Latin *circumvolvere* turn or roll (something or oneself) around < *circum* around + *volvere* roll, turn]

cir|cus (sėr′kəs), *n.* **1a** a traveling show of acrobats, clowns, horses, riders, and wild animals: *Circuses usually go on tour during the summer months.* **b** the performers who give the show or the performances they give: *The whole town turned out to see the circus.* **c** the circular area, often covered by a large tent and with tiers of seats for spectators, in which such a performance is given. **2** *Informal, Figurative.* **a** an amusing person or thing. **b** a lively time; noisy disturbance; uproar: *We're going to have a regular circus.* **3** a round, oval, or oblong space with seats around it in rows, each row higher than the one in front of it. Contests among gladiators, chariot races, and other public spectacles took place in circuses in ancient Rome. *Such were the bloody circus' genial laws* (Byron). SYN: amphitheater. **4** *British.* **a** a circular area at a big traffic junction; traffic circle: *Piccadilly Circus.* **b** a circular arrangement of buildings: *Regent Circus.* **5** *Especially British.* a natural amphitheater; rounded hollow: *The party found themselves in a circus of hills* (Benjamin Disraeli). **6** = flying circus. **7** *Obsolete.* a ring; circle. [< Latin *circus* ring. See etym. of doublet **cirque**.]

Cir|cus Max|i|mus (sėr′kəs mak′sə məs), a huge amphitheater in ancient Rome between the Palatine and Aventine Hills. [< Latin *Circus Maximus* largest circus]

cir|cus|y or **cir|cus|sy** (sėr′kə sē), *adj.* resembling or characteristic of a circus: (*Figurative.*) *There is ... something slightly circusy about this proposed parade of American technology* (Wall Street Journal).

ci|ré (sē rā′), *adj., n.* —*adj.* **1** treated with paraffin or wax to give a smooth, lustrous effect: *a ciré fabric.* **2** highly glossy, as if waxed: *A chapeau of ciré silk or straw* (Glasgow Herald).
—*n.* a ciré fabric or other material. [< French *ciré* waxed]

cire-per|due (sir′pər dü′; *French* sēr′per dʏ′), *adj.,* or **cire perdue**, having to do with or designating a process for casting statuary, precision parts, dental work, and other fine work, in metal, by preparing a model with an outer layer of wax, surrounding it with a plaster mold, heating it so as to melt out the wax, and filling the space with molten metal; lost-wax. [< French *cire perdue* lost wax]

cirl bunting (sėrl), a common European bunting. [< New Latin *cirlus* < Italian *cirlo,* perhaps < Italian *zirlo* a whistling (of thrushes)]

cir mil, circular mil.

cirque (sėrk), *n.* **1a** a circular space. **b** *Geology.* a natural amphitheater encircled by heights, especially one in the mountains formed by erosion at the head of a glacier. See picture under **mountain**. **2** a circle, ring, or circlet of any sort. **3** = circus. [< Middle French *cirque,* learned borrowing from Latin *circus.* See etym. of doublet **circus**.]

cir|rate (sir′āt), *adj. Zoology.* furnished with cirri. [< Latin *cirrātus* fringed; originally, curly < *cirrus* a curl]

cir|rho|sis (sə rō′sis), *n.* **1** a chronic disease of the liver characterized by degeneration of liver cells and hardening due to great increase of fibrous tissue on the liver. **2** a similar disease of the kidneys or other organs. [< New Latin *cirrhosis* < Greek *kirrhóein* turn yellow < *kirrhós* orange-yellow (because of the diseased liver's appearance)]

cir|rhot|ic (sə rot′ik), *adj.* **1** having cirrhosis. **2** resembling cirrhosis.

cir|ri (sir′ī), *n.* plural of **cirrus**.

cir|rif|er|ous (sə rif′ər əs), *adj. Zoology.* bearing cirri.

cir|ri|form (sir′ə fôrm), *adj.* formed like a curl or tendril; cirrose: *cirriform clouds.*

cir|rig|er|ous (sə rij′ər əs), *adj.* bearing cirri or a cirrus; cirrate; cirriferous. [< *cirri* + Latin *gerere* to bear + English *-ous*]

cir|ri|grade (sir′ə grād), *adj. Zoology.* moving by means of cirri. [< New Latin *cirrigradus* < Latin *cirrus* a curl + *gradī* to go]

cir|ri|ped (sir′ə ped), *n., adj. Zoology.* —*n.* any animal of a subclass of crustaceans having six, or fewer, pairs of threadlike appendages about the mouth, used in getting food, instead of legs. Cirripeds are parasitic as adults. Barnacles belong to this subclass.
—*adj.* **1** of or having to do with this subclass. **2** having appendages resembling cirri. Also, **cirripede**.
[< New Latin *Cirripeda* the class name < Latin *cirrus* curl + *pēs, pedis* foot]

cir|ri|pede (sir′ə pēd), *n., adj.* = cirriped.

cir|ro-cu|mu|lus or **cir|ro|cu|mu|lus** (sir′ō kyü′myə ləs), *n.* a cloud formation consisting of very small, globular masses of white, fleecy clouds arranged in wavelike rows or groups, occurring at heights of 20,000 feet and above; mackerel sky. *Abbr:* Cc (no period). [< *cirrus* + *cumulus*]

cir|rose (sir′ōs, sə rōs′), *adj.* **1** *Zoology, Botany.* having or resembling a cirrus or cirri. **2** of or resembling cirrus clouds. Also, **cirrous**. [< Latin *cirrus* a curl + English *-ose*]

cir|ro-stra|tive (sir′ō strā′tiv), *adj.* having to do with or resembling a cirro-stratus.

cir|ro-stra|tus or **cir|ro|stra|tus** (sir′ō strā′təs), *n.* a thin, veillike cloud formation of ice crystals occurring at heights of 20,000 feet and above, consisting of a horizontal hazy layer, or in some instances inclined sheets thinning upward into light curls. *Abbr:* Cs (no period). [< *cirrus* + *stratus*]

cir|rous (sir′əs), *adj.* = cirrose.

cir|rus (sir′əs), *n., pl.* **cir|ri. 1** a thin, fleecy white cloud of ice crystals formed very high in the air. It gives the appearance of diverging filaments or wisps, and often resembles curls or locks of hair or wool. See picture under **cloud**. **2** *Zoology.* any one of various slender or filamentary processes or appendages, such as: **a** one of those about the mouth of a barnacle. **b** a barbel of certain fishes. **c** one of the small, armlike processes of a crinoid, growing from the cup-shaped head. **3** a group of hairlike processes on the appendages of certain insects. **4** *Botany.* a tendril. [< Latin *cirrus* curl]

cir|soid (sėr′soid), *adj.* = varicose. [< Greek *kirsós* enlargement of a vein + English *-oid*]

cir|sot|o|my (sər sot′ə mē), *n., pl.* **-mies.** surgical incision into a varicose vein. [< Greek *kirsós* enlargement of a vein + *-tomiā* a cutting]

cis (sis), *adj. Chemistry.* of or having to do with an isomeric compound that has certain atoms on the same side of a plane: *cis configurations.* [< Latin *cis* on this side of]

cis-, *prefix.* **1** on this side of; on the near side of: *Cisatlantic = on this side of the Atlantic.*
2 *Chemistry.* having certain atoms on the same side of a plane: *a cisisomeric compound.*
[< Latin *cis*]

cis|al|pine (sis al′pīn, -pin), *adj.* on the southern side of the Alps. [< Latin *cisalpīnus* < *cis* on this (the Roman) side of + *alpīnus* < *Alpēs, -ium* the Alps]

cis|at|lan|tic (sis′ət lan′tik), *adj.* on this (the speaker's or writer's) side of the Atlantic.

cis|bor|der (sis bôr′dər), *adj.* on this side of the border: *cisborder traffic.*

cis|cau|ca|sian (sis′kô kā′zhən, -shən; -kazh′ən, -kash′-), *adj.* on this (the European) side of the Caucasus Mountains.

cis|co (sis′kō), *n., pl.* **-coes** or **-cos.** *U.S.* any one of certain whitefish of the northern United States, especially of the Great Lakes area; lake herring. [American English; short for *siscowet* < Canadian French *ciscoette,* perhaps < Algonkian (Ojibwa) *siskawit*]

Cish|ti (sish′tē), *n., pl.* **-tis.** a member of the Cishtiya.

Cish|ti|ya (sish′tē yə), *n.* a very influential Moslem order of India, whose members practice mystic contemplation and spiritual confinement to establish union with Allah. [< *Cisht,* a village in Afghanistan, where the founder of the order lived]

cis|lu|nar (sis lü′nər), *adj.* **1** in the moon's vicinity; on this (the earth's) side of the moon: *the path of cislunar rays.* **2** of or having to do with cislunar space: *cislunar phenomena, cislunar probes.*

cislunar space, **1** the space between the earth and the moon, shaped like a frustum and moving like the hand of a clock as the moon revolves about the earth. **2** the space between the earth and the moon's orbit.

cis|mon|tane (sis mon′tān), *adj.* on this (the nearer) side of the mountains, especially on the northern side of the Alps; citramontane. [< Latin *cismontānus* < *cis* on this side of + *mons, montis* mountain]

cis|pa|dane (sis pā′dān, sis′pə-), *adj.* on the near (the Roman) side of the river Po. [< Latin *cis* on this side of + *Padānus* of the *Padus,* the river Po]

cis-pol|y|i|so|prene rubber (sis pol′ē ī′sə-prēn), an artificial rubber prepared from isoprene, used especially to produce heavy truck tires and motor mountings.

cis|pon|tine (sis pon′tin, -tīn), *adj.* on this (the nearer) side of a bridge, especially on the northern side of the Thames in London. [< Latin *cis* on this side of + *pons, pontis* bridge + *-ine*[1]]

cis|rhe|nane (sis rē′nān, sis′rə-), *adj.* on this (the western) side of the river Rhine. [< Latin *cisrhēnānus* < *cis* on this side of + *Rhēnus* Rhine]

cis|sing (sis′ing), *n.* **1** the moistening of wood with beer and rubbing it over with whiting so that the color may adhere. **2** the appearance of small spots on a varnished surface due to grease stains or tiny holes in the wood. [origin unknown]

***cis|soid** (sis′oid), *n., adj. Geometry.* —*n.* a curve originating at one end of the diameter of a circle which has a tangent to the circle at its opposite end, and so constructed that an oblique line from the point of origin intersecting consecutively the circle, the curve, and the tangent will always have equal segments representing the distance from the origin to the intersection with the curve, and the distance from the intersection with the circle to the tangent. See diagram on next page.
—*adj.* contained between the concave sides of two curves which intersect each other.
[< Greek *kissoeidês* like ivy < *kissós* ivy + *eîdos*

Pronunciation Key: hat, āge, cãre, fär; let, ēqual, tėrm; it, īce; hot, ōpen, ôrder; oil, out; cup, pu̇t, rüle; child; long; thin; ᴛʜen; zh, measure; ə represents a in about, e in taken, i in pencil, o in lemon, u in circus.

form (from the curve's resemblance to angles on an ivy leaf)]

cissoid

tangent

★cissoid

cis|sus (sis′əs), *n., pl.* **-sus.** a plant related to the grape, found mostly in the tropics. [< New Latin *Cissus* the genus name < Greek *kissós* ivy]

cis|sy (sis′ē), *n., pl.* **-sies,** *adj.,* **-si|er, -si|est.** *British Informal.* **—*n.*** a sissy: *They set out to prove that London forwards are not cissies* (London Times).
—*adj.* like a sissy; effeminate: *All I can do is get the boy to help with the washing up and to make his bed and tell him it isn't cissy* (Harriet Chare).
[variant of *sissy,* probably influenced by *Cissy,* a form of the name *Cecily*]

cist¹ (sist), *n.* a wicker basket, box, or chest, especially for carrying sacred utensils in ancient Greece and Rome. [< Latin *cista* chest < Greek *kístē* box]

cist² (sist), *n. Archaeology.* a prehistoric burial chamber excavated in rock or formed of stones or hollowed tree trunks, especially a stone coffin formed of slabs placed on edge, and covered on the top by one or more horizontal slabs; cistvaen. [< earlier *kistvaen* < Welsh *cist faen* stone chest]

cis|ta|ceous (sis tā′shəs), *adj.* belonging to a family of plants typified by the rockrose. [< New Latin *Cistaceae* the family name (< Latin *cisthos* a flowering shrub < Greek *kísthos*) + English *-ous*]

Cis|ter|cian (sis tėr′shən), *n., adj.* **—*n.*** a member of a Benedictine order of monks and nuns founded at Cîteaux, France, in 1098.
—*adj.* of or having to do with this order.
[< Medieval Latin *Cistercium* Cîteaux, France, where the order was founded + English *-an*]

Cis|ter|cian|ism (sis tėr′shə niz əm), *n.* the religious system or spirit of the Cistercians.

cis|tern (sis′tərn), *n.* **1** an artificial reservoir for storing water, especially a tank below ground. **2** *Anatomy.* a cavity or vessel in the body, especially any of several spaces in the brain. [< Old French *cisterne* < Latin *cisterna* < *cista* box < Greek *kístē*]

cis|ter|na (sis tėr′nə), *n., pl.* **-nae** (-nē). *Anatomy.* a cistern, as the cisterna magna. [< Latin *cisterna* < *cista* box; see etym. under **cistern**]

cis|ter|nal (sis tėr′nəl), *adj.* of or having to do with a cistern or cisterns.

cisterna mag|na (mag′nə), a large space in the brain enclosed by the arachnoid membrane, cerebellum, and medulla oblongata. [< New Latin *cisterna magna*]

cistern barometer, a barometer in its simplest form, with the bottom end of the tube immersed in a cup of mercury.

cis|tron (sis′tron), *n.* the smallest unit of genetic material producing a phenotypic effect: *Cistrons . . . correspond roughly to the genes of classical genetics. Each cistron controls the structure of a protein* (New Scientist). [< *cis* + *tr*(ans) + *-on* (because of phenotypic comparisons being based on the *cis* and *trans* arrangements of genetic material in the chromosomes)]

cis|tus (sis′təs), *n.* any plant of a genus native to Mediterranean regions, some species of which yield labdanum, while others are cultivated for their flowers; rockrose. [< New Latin *cistus* < Latin *cisthos* < Greek *kísthos*]

cist|vaen (kist′vīn), *n.* a prehistoric stone coffin or burial chamber; a tomb made of slabs of stone; cist. Also, **kistvaen.** [< Welsh *cist faen* stone chest]

cit (sit), *n. Archaic.* a city dweller or tradesman.

cits, *Slang.* civilian clothes; civies: *They were in full dress uniform. Later they were joined by Maj. Judson of the engineers in 'cits'* (Chicago Tribune).
[short for *citizen*]

cit., **1a** citation. **b** cited. **2** citizen.

cit|a|ble (sī′tə bəl), *adj.* = citeable.

cit|a|del (sit′ə dəl, -del), *n.* **1** a fortress, especially one in a city. A citadel serves as a protection and final point of defense, and also to keep the inhabitants in subjection. **2** a strongly fortified place; stronghold. **3** *Figurative.* a strong, safe place; refuge. **4** the heavily plated structure on a warship on which the guns are set. [< Middle French *citadelle* < Italian *cittadella* (diminutive) < *città* city < Latin *cīvitās;* see etym. under **city**]

ci|ta|tion (sī tā′shən), *n.* **1a** a quotation or reference given as an authority for facts or opinions: *It is the beauty and independent worth of the citations, far more than their appropriateness, which have made Johnson's dictionary popular even as a reading-book* (Samuel Taylor Coleridge). **b** the act of citing. **2** honorable mention of a soldier or military unit for bravery in war: [*He*] *holds the Congressional Medal of Honor, nine citations and the highest decorations of the Allied Governments* (Publishers' Weekly). **3** *U.S.* specific mention in an official dispatch. **4** the commendation of a civilian for public service by some official or institution. **5a** a summoning to appear before a law court. **b** the written form for this, or the document containing it. **6** *Obsolete.* enumeration; recital; mention. [< Old French *citation,* learned borrowing from Latin *citātiō, -ōnis* < *citāre;* see etym. under **cite**]

ci|ta|to|ry (sī′tə tôr′ē, -tōr′-), *adj.* citing; summoning; having the force or form of a citation.

cite (sīt), *v.t.,* **cit|ed, cit|ing.** **1** to quote (a passage, book, or author), especially as an authority: *He cited the encyclopedia to prove his statement. The devil can cite Scripture for his purpose* (Shakespeare). **SYN:** See syn. under **quote. 2** to refer to; mention; bring up as an example: *The lawyer cited another case similar to the one being tried.* **3** to give honorable mention to for bravery in war. **4** to commend publicly for service to the community. **5** to summon to appear in a law court. **6** to arouse to action; summon. [< Old French *citer,* learned borrowing from Latin *citāre* summon, excite < *ciēre* set in motion] **—cit′er,** *n.*

cite|a|ble (sī′tə bəl), *adj.* that can be cited. Also, **citable.**

★cith|a|ra (sith′ər ə), *n.* an ancient musical instrument resembling a lyre, with a soundbox of wood and seven to eleven strings. Also, **kithara.** [< Latin *cithara* < Greek *kithára* ancient lyrelike instrument. See etym. of doublets **guitar, zither.**]

★cithara

cith|a|rist (sith′ər ist), *n.* a player on the cithara.

cith|er (sith′ər), *n.* **1** = cittern. **2** = cithara. [< Latin *cithara*]

cith|ern (sith′ərn), *n.* = cittern.

cit|ied (sit′ēd), *adj.* made into or like a city; occupied by a city or cities.

cit|i|fied (sit′ə fīd), *adj. Informal.* **1** having city ways or fashions. **2** of or suggestive of the city: *He had shoes on—and it was only Friday. He even wore a necktie. . . . He had a citified air about him that ate into Tom's vitals* (Mark Twain). Also, **cityfied.**

cit|i|zen (sit′ə zən, -sən), *n.* **1** a person who by birth or by choice is a member of a state or nation which gives him certain rights and which claims his loyalty: *Many immigrants have become citizens of the United States.* **SYN:** national, subject. **2** an inhabitant of a city or town, especially one possessing civic rights, privileges, and freedom. **SYN:** resident. **3a** a person who is not a soldier, policeman, fireman, or, sometimes, a member of the clergy; civilian. **b** (in earlier times) one not a member of the landed nobility or gentry. [< Anglo-French *citisein,* alteration of Old French *citeain* < *cite;* see etym. under **city**]

cit|i|zen|ess (sit′ə zə nis, -sə-), *n.* a woman citizen: *The French Revolution could not have succeeded without the "citizenesses" who encouraged their men and even fought with them in the barricaded streets of Paris* (Theresa Wolfson).

cit|i|zen|ly (sit′ə zən lē, -sən-), *adj.* having to do with or characteristic of a citizen: *citizenly qualities and virtues, to take a citizenly interest in public matters.*

citizen of the world, a person who is interested in the affairs of the whole world; cosmopolitan.

cit|i|zen|ry (sit′ə zən rē, -sən-), *n., pl.* **-ries.** citizens as a group: *The Vigilantes had the open support of the majority of the citizenry* (New Yorker).

citizen's arrest, an arrest made by a citizen who is not a member of a law-enforcing agency. In the United States a citizen has the right to arrest someone whom he sees committing a crime, provided that the person arrested is immediately turned over to the police or other agency of the law.

citizens band, *U.S.* a radio transmitting channel provided by the Federal government for use by private citizens: *Component kits for citizens band radio* [are] *available at varying prices depending on the sets* (Science News Letter).

cit|i|zen|ship (sit′ə zən ship, -sən-), *n.* **1** the duties, rights, and privileges of a citizen. **2** the condition of being a citizen: *Voting is a right of citizenship and obeying the laws is a duty of citizenship.* **3** the conduct or quality of a citizen: *good citizenship.*

Citizenship Day, a day celebrated in the United States on September 17 to honor native-born and naturalized citizens of the United States.

citizenship papers, *U.S.* the documents attesting that a person is a naturalized citizen.

citizen soldier, a civilian who in an emergency serves as a soldier.

cit|ole (sit′ōl, si tōl′), *n.* = cittern. [Middle English *citole* < Old French, apparently alternation of Latin *cithara*]

ci|toy|en (sē twȧ yaN′), *n. French.* a citizen.

ci|toy|enne (sē twȧ yen′), *n. French.* a woman citizen.

cit|ral (sit′rəl), *n.* a strong-smelling, liquid aldehyde present in such oils as that of the lemon and orange, and used as a flavoring and in perfumes. *Formula:* $C_{10}H_{16}O$ [< *citr*(on) + *al*(dehyde)]

cit|ra|mon|tane (sit′rə mon′tān), *adj.* = cismontane. [< Latin *citrā* on this side of + *mons, montis* mountain]

cit|range (sit′rənj), *n.* a hybrid fruit produced by crossing the trifoliate orange and the common sweet orange.

cit|rate (sit′rāt, sī′trāt), *n., v.,* **-rat|ed, -rat|ing.** **—*n.*** a salt or ester of citric acid.
—*v.t.* to add a citrate to.
[< *citr*(ic) + *-ate²*]

cit|re|ous (sit′rē əs), *adj.* lemon-colored; citrine. [< Latin *citreus* (with English *-ous*) having to do with the citrus tree]

cit|ric (sit′rik), *adj.* of or from fruits such as lemons, limes, and oranges. [< Latin *citrus* citron tree + English *-ic*]

citric acid, a white, odorless acid with a sour taste, found especially in the juice of oranges, lemons, limes, and similar fruits. It is used as a flavoring, as a medicine, and in making dyes. *Formula:* $C_6H_8O_7$

citric acid cycle, = Krebs cycle.

cit|ri|cul|ture (sit′rə kul′chər), *n.* the growing of citrus fruits.

cit|ri|cul|tur|ist (sit′rə kul′chər ist), *n.* a person who practices citriculture.

cit|rin (sit′rin), *n. Biochemistry.* vitamin P.

cit|rine (sit′rin), *adj., n.* **—*adj.*** pale-yellow or greenish-yellow; lemon-colored.
—*n.* **1** a pale yellow. **2** a glassy, yellow variety of quartz; false topaz.
[< Old French *citrin* < Latin *citrus* citron tree]

cit|ron (sit′rən), *n.* **1** a pale-yellow fruit, somewhat like a lemon but larger, with less acid and a thicker rind. The citron belongs to the rue family. **2** the shrub or small tree that it grows on. **3** its rind, candied and used in fruit cakes, plum pudding, candies, etc. **4** = citron melon. [< Middle French *citron* < Italian *citrone* < Latin *citrus* citron tree] **—cit′ron|like′,** *adj.*

cit|ron|el|la (sit′rə nel′ə), *n.* **1** Also, **citronella oil.** an oil used in making perfume, soap, and liniment, and for keeping mosquitoes away. **2** a fragrant grass, of southern Asia and Central America, from which this oil is made. [< New Latin *citronella* < French *citronelle,* a plant < Middle French *citron;* see etym. under **citron** (from its citronlike smell)]

cit|ron|el|lal (sit′rə nel′əl), *n.* a mixture of stereoisomeric aldehydes present in many essential oils, used as a flavoring and in making perfume. *Formula:* $C_9H_{17}CHO$

citron melon, *U.S.* a kind of watermelon, bearing a small fruit with firm, white flesh which is used, like the citron, in candied form.

citron wood, **1** the wood of the citron tree. **2** the wood of the sandarac tree.

cit|rous (sit′rəs), *adj.* having to do with fruits such as lemons, grapefruits, limes, and oranges.

cit|ro|vo|rum factor (sit′rə vôr′əm, -vōr′-), a B-vitamin factor of the folic-acid group, important in combating anemia; folinic acid. *Formula:* $C_{20}H_{23}N_7O_7$ [< New Latin *citrovorum* < Latin *citrus* + *vorāre* devour]

cit|rul|line (sit′rə lēn), *n.* an amino acid, originally found in watermelon, that in living organisms is an intermediate between ornithine and arginine. *Formula:* $C_6H_{13}N_3O_3$ [< Medieval Latin *citrullus* watermelon (< Latin *citrus* citron tree)]

cit|rus (sit′rəs), *n., adj.* **—*n.*** **1** any tree bearing lemons, limes, oranges, grapefruit, or similar fruits. Citruses usually grow in warm climates. They are small, often thorny trees and shrubs of a genus of the rue family, bearing pulpy fruit with a (usually) thick, spongy rind. **2** Also, **citrus fruit.** the fruit of such a tree. **—*adj.*** of such trees. Citrus fruits contain much vitamin C. [< Latin *citrus* citron tree]

citrus black fly, a minute insect that attacks and destroys citrus fruit trees by secreting a sticky substance which turns black, causing discoloring and damage to the fruit and leaves.

cits (sits), *n.pl.* See under **cit**.

★**cit|tern** (sit′ərn), *n.* an old instrument somewhat like the guitar, with a flat soundbox, strung with wire strings, and played with a plectrum or quill, much used in the 1500's and 1600's. [blend of *cither* and *gittern*]

★cittern

cit|y (sit′ē), *n., pl.* **cit|ies**, *adj.* —*n.* **1** a large and important town: *The farmers near the city take most of the produce there to sell it.* **SYN:** metropolis. **2** a division of local government in the United States, having a charter from the state that fixes its boundaries and powers. A city is usually governed by a mayor and a board of aldermen, a group of commissioners, or a city manager and a board of councilmen. **SYN:** municipality. **3** a division of local government in Canada of the highest class. **SYN:** municipality. **4** a borough in Great Britain, usually the seat of a bishop, which has been given the rank of "city" by royal authority. **5** the people living in a city: *The city was alarmed by the great fire.* **6** a city-state, such as in ancient Greece and Renaissance Italy. **7** *U.S. Slang.* state, condition, situation, etc., as in *weird city, serious city, fat city. "I get on a talk show, I get talking and whoa! Trouble city!"* (Richard Dreyfuss).
—*adj.* **1** of a city: *City government is more complicated than that of a small town.* **2** in a city: *Many country people find it hard to adjust to city life.*
the City, the business, financial, and judicial district of London: *While the City represents the British way of life, it is not responsible for it, and certainly not in charge of it. Even Whitehall has to tread delicately in this matter* (Punch).
[< Old French *cite,* earlier *citet* < Latin *cīvitās* condition or privilege of citizenship; citizenry; state, city < *cīvis* citizen]

city article, *British.* an article in a newspaper on commercial or financial matters.

cit|y|bil|ly (sit′ē bil′ē), *n., pl.* **-lies.** *U.S. Slang.* **1** a musician who performs country music mostly in large towns or cities. **2** a city-dweller who is a devotee of country music. [< *city* + (hill)*billy*]

city council, the governing body of a city.

city desk, the desk or authority of a city editor.

city edition, the local edition of a metropolitan newspaper, as distinguished from editions designed for the suburbs or other cities.

city editor, 1 *U.S.* the newspaper editor in charge of collecting and editing local news. **2** *British.* the newspaper editor of City news (that is, news of the financial and commercial activities, especially of London).

city fathers, councilmen, aldermen, magistrates, or other leading citizens of a city.

cit|y|fied (sit′ə fīd), *adj.* = citified.

city hall, 1 the headquarters of the officials, bureaus, and other departments of a city government: *The mayor's office is in city hall.* **2** the officials of a municipal government collectively: *You can't fight city hall and win.*

city man or **City man,** *British.* **1** a businessman; financier. **2** a person engaged in business in the City.

city manager, a person hired by a city council to manage the government of a city.

City of Brotherly Love, Philadelphia. [partially a translation of Greek *philadelphiā* brotherly love]

City of David, 1 Jerusalem. **2** Bethlehem.

City of God, heaven.

city of refuge, (in Mosaic law) any one of six cities to which a person who had accidentally slain a human being might flee for refuge.

City of Seven Hills, Rome.

city planner, a person who is in charge of directing the work of city planning; urbanist.

city planning, the planning of the development of a city by proposing the location of buildings, parks, streets, and services, and the type of occupancy to be permitted in various areas.

city room, the room or office of a newspaper assigned to a city editor and his staff.

cit|y|scape (sit′ē skāp), *n.* **1** a view of the scenery of a city: *a stirring cityscape, the asphalt cityscape.* **2** a picture showing a city or a city scene: *The earlier group is made up of near-abstract, transcendental cityscapes, canvases on whose rough surfaces cobwebs of paint cross and recross each other* (New York Times).

city slicker, *U.S.* a man who lives in the city, especially one who is regarded as sly and tricky in a polished, urbane way, especially by a person living in the country: *He went to bed convinced that . . . he had made himself a bundle and had demonstrated how a poor Southern boy could teach the city slickers a lesson* (New Yorker).

cit|y-state (sit′ē stāt′), *n.* an independent state consisting of a city and the territories depending on it. Athens was a city-state in ancient Greece. Florence was a city-state in Renaissance Italy. *At one time, it [Thebes] was the most powerful city-state in all Greece* (Donald W. Bradeen).

cit|y|ward (sit′ē wərd), *adv., adj.* toward the city: *We drove cityward in the morning* (adv.). *We drove in cityward traffic in the morning* (adj.).

cit|y|wards (sit′ē wərdz), *adv.* = cityward.

cit|y|wide (sit′ē wīd′), *adj.* covering an entire city; over all of a city: *a citywide vote.*

civ., 1 civil. **2** civilian.

civ|et (siv′it), *n.* **1** a yellowish substance produced by certain glands near the tail of the civet cat. It has a musky odor and is used in making perfume. **2a** = civet cat. **b** the fur of the civet cat. [< Middle French *civette* < Italian *zibetto* < Arabic *zabād*]

civet cat, 1 a small, spotted mammal of Africa and Asia, having glands that produce civet. Civet cats are carnivorous. **2** any one of certain similar or related animals.

civ|e|tone (siv′ə tōn′), *n.* the ketone that is responsible for the characteristic odor of civet, used in making perfume. *Formula:* $C_{17}H_{30}O$

civ|ic (siv′ik), *adj.* **1** of a city: *My father is interested in civic affairs and will be a candidate for mayor.* **2a** of citizenship: *Every person has some civic duties, such as obeying laws, voting, and paying taxes.* **b** civil; civilian. **3** of citizens. [< Latin *(corona) cīvica* the civic (crown) < *cīvis* citizen] —**civ′i|cal|ly,** *adv.*

civic center, 1 a government-owned auditorium or theater, for use by various groups or organizations in a community. **2** a building or group of buildings, including the city hall, courts, and other government departments, usually located near the center of the city. **3** the headquarters of various departments of city government.

civ|i|cism (siv′ə siz əm), *n.* **1** civic spirit or condition. **2** the principles of civic rights and duties.

civ|ic-mind|ed (siv′ik mīn′did), *adj.* having the interest of the community in mind; concerned with civic matters. —**civ′ic-mind′ed|ness,** *n.*

civ|ics (siv′iks), *n.* the study of the duties, rights, and privileges of citizens. [American English < *civic,* on analogy of *politics*]

civ|ies (siv′ēz), *n.pl. Informal.* civilian clothes (as opposed to military uniform). Also, **civvies.** [< *civilian*]

civ|il (siv′əl), *adj.* **1a** of a citizen or citizens; having to do with citizens: *The government must protect the civil rights of its citizens. Serving as a juror is one of the civil duties of everybody.* **b** of the nature of a citizen: *a civil man, a civil creature.* **2** of or having to do with the government, state, or nation: *Police departments are civil institutions to help and protect local citizens.* **3** occurring among citizens of one community, state, or nation: *High taxes and corruption in government have been the cause of civil strife in much of man's history.* **4** not military, naval, or connected with the church: *The accused soldier was tried in a civil rather than a military court.* See also **civil marriage. 5** polite; courteous; behaving in a civilized way (as a citizen should): *The boy pointed out our road in a civil way. His cool manner this morning was barely civil.* **SYN:** respectful, gracious, affable, urbane. See syn. under **polite. 6** having to do with the private rights of individuals and with the laws protecting these rights. Civil lawsuits deal with such things as contracts, ownership of property, and payment for personal injury. **7** of citizens in their private capacity; personal; individual: *Slaves have no civil liberty* (Edward W. Lane). **8** befitting or becoming a citizen; reasonable: *It was civil, in the Roman sense, to mingle in the amusements of the citizens* (Charles Merivale). **9** marked by or having the organizations that characterize civilized life; enjoying the benefits of civilization; civilized: *as in civil, so in barbarous states* (Robert Southey). **10** (of divisions of time) legally recognized for ordinary purposes: *the civil day of 24 hours, the civil year of 365 days.* **11** of or in accordance with Roman civil law, or civil law derived from it. [< Latin *cīvīlis* proper to a citizen < *cīvis* citizen]

Civil Code, = Code Napoleon.

civil day, = a mean solar day; 24 hours.

civil death, (formerly in English common law) the legal status of a living person who had lost his civil rights by entering a religious order, being banished from the country, or convicted of a serious crime.

civil defense, 1 a civilian emergency program for protecting people and property from such disasters as fires, floods, or enemy attack. **2** an organization responsible for such defense.

civil disobedience, refusal because of one's principles to obey the laws of the country or state, especially by not paying taxes or by refusing to serve in the armed forces.

civil embargo, a restraint placed by a country on its own people and property to prevent vital materials from being shipped to warring nations.

civil engineer, a person whose profession is civil engineering. *Abbr:* C.E.

civil engineering, the planning and directing of the construction of bridges, roads, harbors, canals, dams, and other public works.

ci|vil|ian (sə vil′yən), *n., adj.* —*n.* **1** a person who is not a soldier or sailor or, sometimes, other government official. All men not in the armed forces are civilians. **2** an expert in or student of Roman law or civil law.
—*adj.* of civilians; not military or naval: *Soldiers on leave usually wear civilian clothes.*
▶Policemen and sometimes firemen and other government officials are distinguished from civilians, in addition to members of the army, navy, and air force and, often, members of the clergy.

Civilian Conservation Corps, a federal agency established in 1933 by Congress to provide work for unemployed youth on such projects as reforestation, construction of public parks, and protection from forest fires. It was abolished in 1942. *Abbr:* CCC

ci|vil|ian|ize (sə vil′yə nīz), *v.t.,* **-ized, -iz|ing.** *Military Use.* to render civilian; make (a military body) civilian: *We will civilianize the whole fleet if necessary* (Time).

civ|i|lise (siv′ə līz), *v.t.,* **-lised, -lis|ing.** *Especially British.* civilize. —**civ′i|li|sa′tion,** *n.*

ci|vil|i|ty (sə vil′ə tē), *n., pl.* **-ties. 1** polite behavior; courtesy; consideration: *Thank you for your civility in replying to my letter so promptly.* **SYN:** politeness. **2** an act or expression of politeness or courtesy. **3** *Archaic.* the state of being civilized; freedom from barbarity; civilization. **4** *Archaic.* **a** polite or liberal education; training in the humanities. **b** good breeding; culture; refinement.

civ|i|li|za|tion (siv′ə lə zā′shən), *n.* **1** civilized condition; advanced stage in social development: *A decent provision for the poor is the true test of civilization* (Samuel Johnson). **SYN:** progress, enlightenment. **2** the nations and peoples that have reached advanced stages in social development: *the civilizations of the East and West.* **3** the ways of living of a people or nation: *Chinese civilization differs from ours.* **4** the process of becoming civilized; improvement in culture: *The civilization of a primitive society is a gradual process which takes centuries.* **SYN:** cultivation. **5** the comforts of modern life, especially in the cities: *The survivors of the shipwreck were happy to return at last to civilization.* **6** the act of civilizing.

civ|i|lize (siv′ə līz), *v.t.,* **-lized, -liz|ing. 1** to change from being savage and ignorant to having good laws and customs and knowledge of the arts and sciences; train in culture, science, and art: *The Romans civilized a great part of the world.* **SYN:** enlighten, educate, humanize. **2** to improve in culture and good manners; refine. **SYN:** polish. [apparently < French *civiliser* (with English *-ize*) < Old French *civil,* learned borrowing from Latin *cīvīlis* civil] —**civ′i|liz′a|ble,** *adj.* —**civ′i|liz′er,** *n.*

civ|i|lized (siv′ə līzd), *adj.* **1** advanced in social customs, art, and science: *The ancient Greeks were a civilized people.* **SYN:** enlightened, cultivated, developed. **2** of or having to do with civilized nations or persons. **3** showing culture and good manners; refined: *The author kept his temper and took a civilized attitude toward the critics of his book.* **SYN:** cultured, civil.

civ|i|liz|ing (siv′ə lī′zing), *adj.* that civilizes; promoting civilization.

civil law, 1 the law of a community or state that regulates and protects private rights and is controlled and used by civil courts, not military courts. **2** Roman law as a whole or as applied to citizens of Rome. **3** a system of law based on Roman law, used in France and other Continental countries, and in parts of the United States and Canada, such as Louisiana and Quebec.

civ|il-law (siv′əl lô′), *adj.* having to do with civil law.

civil libertarian, a person who advocates or defends civil liberties.

civil liberty, the right of a person to do and say what he pleases as long as he does not harm anyone else; the freedom of a person to enjoy the rights guaranteed by the laws or constitution

Pronunciation Key: hat, āge, cãre, fär; let, ēqual, tėrm; it, īce; hot, ōpen, ôrder; oil, out; cup, pu̇t, rüle; **ch**ild; lo**ng**; **th**in; **ᴛʜ**en; **zh**, measure; **ə** represents **a** in about, **e** in taken, **i** in pencil, **o** in lemon, **u** in circus.

of a country without any undue restraint or interference by the government.

civil list, **1** *British.* the money voted by Parliament for expenses of the monarch and royal household, and for allowances to other members of the royal family. **2** a similar appropriation in other monarchies.

civ|il|ly (siv′ə lē), *adv.* **1** politely; courteously. **2** according to civil law.

civil marriage, a marriage performed by a government official, not by a clergyman.

civil right|er (rī′tər), *U.S. Informal.* an advocate or champion of civil rights and liberties: *Civil righters were set to boycott schools in protest against de facto segregation* (Time).

civil rightist, *U.S. Informal.* a civil righter: *Particularly disappointing to civil rightists is the fact that voters have rejected fair-housing laws so incisively* (Wall Street Journal).

civil rights, the rights of a citizen, especially those guaranteed to all citizens of the United States, regardless of race, color, or sex, by the Bill of Rights, the 13th, 14th, 15th, 19th, 24th, and 26th amendments to the Constitution, and certain acts of Congress.

civil servant, a member of the civil service.

civil service, the branch of government service concerned with affairs not military, naval, legislative, or judicial. The mint and the diplomatic corps belong to the civil service. Most civilian government workers who are appointed rather than elected are in the civil service.

civil time, mean time reckoned from midnight through the twenty-four hours.

civil twilight, the part of twilight that occurs, for computation purposes, when the sun's center is 6 degrees below the horizon, as distinguished from astronomical twilight, which is longer, lasting until the sun's center is 18 degrees below the horizon.

civil war, war between opposing groups of citizens of one nation: *the Spanish civil war, the civil war in Vietnam.*

Civil War, **1** the war between the northern and southern states of the United States, from 1861 to 1865; War Between the States; War of Secession. **2** the war between the English Parliament and the Royalists, from 1642 to 1646 and from 1648 to 1652.

civil year, = calendar year.

civ|ism (siv′iz əm), *n.* **1** the principles of good citizenship. **2** (originally) devotion to the system established by the French Revolution of 1789. [< French *civisme* < Latin *cīvis* citizen]

civ|vies (siv′ēz), *n.pl. Informal.* civies.

civ|vy (siv′ē) , *n., adj. Informal.* civilian.

Civ|vy Street (siv′ē), *British Slang.* civilian life: *In 1946 young Braithwaite, with five years in the Army Pay Corps behind him, faced Civvy Street on the morrow* (Punch).

C.J., Chief Justice.

ck., *pl.* **cks. 1** cask. **2** check.

cl (no period), centiliter or centiliters.

cl., an abbreviation for the following:
1 centiliter or centiliters.
2 claim.
3 class.
4 classification.
5 clause.
6 clearance.
7 cloth.

c.l., **1** carload. **2** carload lots. **3** *Sports.* center line. **4** civil law.

Cl (no period), chlorine (chemical element).

Cl. **1** clause. **2** clergyman. **3** clerk.

clab|ber (klab′ər), *n., v.* **—*n.*** thick, sour milk; milk curdled naturally; bonnyclabber.
—*v.t., v.i.* to thicken in souring; curdle, as milk does.
[< Irish or Scottish Gaelic *clabar* curds]

clach|an (klähʜ′ən), *n. Scottish and North Irish.* a small village or hamlet in the Highlands or west of Scotland. [< Scottish Gaelic *clachan* < *clach* stone]

clack (klak), *v., n.* **—*v.i.*** **1** to make a short, sharp sound like that of a piece of wood hitting a hard surface or a whip cracking: *The old lady's needles clacked as she knitted. The train clacked over the rails.* **2** to talk noisily; chatter; prate: *He will sit clacking with an old woman for hours* (Macaulay). **3** to cluck or cackle, as a hen does: *The more the white goose laid, It clacked and cackled louder* (Tennyson).
—*v.t.* **1** to cause to clack: *The Australians smacked and clacked their mouths at the sight of his horses and bullocks* (Charles Darwin). **2** to utter chatteringly; reveal by clacking; blab: *What the heart thinketh the tongue clacketh* (Proverb).
—*n.* **1** a short, sharp sound, like that of castanets or pieces of wood striking together: *the clack of a typewriter. We heard the clack of her heels on the sidewalk.* **2** an instrument for making such a noise; rattle. **3** the noise of continuous speech; senseless chatter: *The tread of feet and clack of tongues* (Washington Irving). **4** *Slang.* the tongue: *to hermetically seal up this Mrs. Gentry's clack* (Epes Sargent).
[probably imitative]—**clack′er,** *n.*

clack valve, a check valve to limit flow in one direction, usually a strip of leather reinforced by metal and fastened on one side to form a hinge, used especially in water pumps.

Clac|to|ni|an (klak tō′nē ən), *adj.* of or having to do with the lower paleolithic age in England and Western Europe, in which some of the earliest types of flint tools appear. [< *Clacton*-on-Sea, England, where these tools were first found + *-ian*]

clad[1] (klad), *v.* clothed; a past tense and a past participle of **clothe:** *He was clad all in green.*

clad[2] (klad), *v.,* **clad** or **clad|ded, clad|ding,** *n., adj.* **—*v.t.*** to cover or coat (a metal) with a metal.
—*n.* = clad metal.
—*adj.* consisting of a core of one metal between layers of another metal or of one metal having a coating of another metal: *a clad copper-nickel coin.*
[< *clad*[1]]

clad|ding (klad′ing), *n.* **1** the process of overlaying or coating one metal with another, to give it a corrosion-resisting surface or for other purposes. **2** the overlay or coating applied: *Uranium for use in reactors is given a cladding of zirconium to prevent corrosion and the escape of fission products.*

cla|dis|tic (klə dis′tik), *adj.* having to do with or based on the branching out of ancestral lines of descent in the process of evolution: *a cladistic classification of species.* [< Greek *kládos* sprout, branch + English *-istic,* as in *statistic*]—**cla|dis′ti|cal|ly,** *adv.*

clad metal or **plate,** metal or plate manufactured by cladding.

cla|doc|er|an (klə dos′ər ən), *n., adj.* **—*n.*** any animal of a group of branchiopod crustaceans, found mostly in fresh water, usually having the body completely enclosed in a carapace; water flea.
—*adj.* having to do with or designating a cladoceran.
[< New Latin *Cladocera* the order name < Greek *kládos* sprout + *kéras* horn]

clad|ode (klad′ōd), *n.* = cladophyll.

clad|o|gen|e|sis (clad′ō jen′ə sis), *n. Biology.* the type of evolutionary change resulting from the division or branching out of a species into isolated groups, as distinguished from phyletic or linear descent. [< Greek *kládos* sprout, branch + English *genesis*]

clad|o|ge|net|ic (klad′ō jə net′ik), *adj.* of or having to do with cladogenesis. **—clad′o|ge|net′i|cal|ly,** *adv.*

clad|o|phyll (klad′ə fil), *n. Botany.* a stem assuming the form and function of a leaf, as in asparagus. [< Greek *kládos* young branch + *phýllon* leaf]

claes (klāz), *n.pl. Scottish.* clothes.

claim (klām), *v., n.* **—*v.t.*** **1** to say one has (a right, title, or possession) and demand that others recognize it; assert one's right to: *The prospector claimed the land beyond the river as his.* **2** to demand as one's own or one's right: *Does anyone claim this pencil? He claimed his share of the estate.* SYN: exact. See syn. under **demand.** **3** to say strongly; declare as a fact; maintain: *She claimed that her answer was correct.* **4** to require; call for; deserve: *The new babies claimed all of Mother's attention.* SYN: merit.
—*v.i.* **1** to put forward a claim; assert a right. **2** to assert a belief or an opinion. **3** to occupy land in virtue of a claim.
—*n.* **1a** a demand for something due or alleged to be due; an assertion of a right: *an insurance claim. She makes a claim to the pencil.* **b** a written notice of this: *All claims must be filed within six weeks.* **2** a right or title to something; the right to demand something: *She has a claim on us because she is our mother's sister.* **3** something that is claimed. **4** a piece of public land that a settler or prospector marks out for himself. When the government offers the land for sale, the settler must buy his claim or forfeit it. **5** a declaration of something as a fact: *Careful tests showed claims for the effectiveness of polio vaccine were correct.*
jump a claim, to seize a piece of land already claimed by another: *If such work were not commenced within three days, any other miners might summarily take possession of or jump the claim* (Rolf Boldrewood).
lay claim to, to assert one's right to; claim: *The settler laid claim to the piece of land he occupied. I prevented it being given to any other, by laying claim to it myself* (Frederick Marryat).
[< Old French *claimer, clamer* < Latin *clāmāre* call, proclaim]—**claim′a|ble,** *adj.*

claim|ant (klā′mənt), *n.* a person who makes a claim: *A wise man will . . . know that it is a part of prudence to face every claimant, and pay every just demand on your time, your talents, or your heart* (Emerson).

claim|er (klā′mər), *n.* **1** a person who claims; claimant. **2a** = claiming race. **b** a horse in a claiming race: *a fifteen-hundred-dollar claimer.*

claim|ing race (klā′ming), a race in which any horse entered is open to purchase at a fixed price by any owner entering another horse in the race meeting, and who makes a bid, or claim, before the start of the race.

claim jumper, *U.S.* a person who appropriates a mining claim or the like already taken by another.

Claims Court, = United States Claims Court.

clair|au|di|ence (klãr ô′dē əns), *n.* the power of hearing or knowing about sounds beyond the range of hearing. [< French *clair* clear + English *audience*]

clair|au|di|ent (klãr ô′dē ənt), *adj., n.* **—*adj.*** having the power of hearing or knowing about sounds beyond the range of hearing.
—*n.* a clairaudient person.
[< French *clair* clear + English *audient*]—**clair-au′di|ent|ly** , *adv.*

clair|cole (klãr′kōl), *n.* = clearcole.

clair de lune (kler′ də lʏn′), *French.* **1** moonlight. **2** the color of moonlight, a soft white or pale blue-gray.

clair-ob|scure (klãr′əb skyůr′), *n.* = chiaroscuro.

clair|schach (klãr′shəʜ), *n.* the old Celtic harp, strung with wire. [< Scottish, Irish *clairseach*]

clair|voy|ance (klãr voi′əns), *n.* **1** the supposed power of seeing or knowing about things that are out of sight; second sight. **2** *Figurative.* exceptional insight; keenness of mental perception. [< French *clairvoyance,* noun to *clairvoyant* clairvoyant]

clair|voy|ant (klãr voi′ənt), *adj., n.* **—*adj.*** **1** supposedly having the power of seeing or knowing about things that are out of sight; having second sight. **2** *Figurative.* having exceptional insight.
—*n.* a person who has, or claims to have, the power of seeing or knowing about things that are out of sight: *The clairvoyant claimed to be able to locate lost articles, and to give news of faraway people.* [< French *clairvoyant* < *clair* clear + *voyant,* present participle of *voir* see < Latin *vidēre*]—**clair|voy′ant|ly,** *adv.*

clam[1] (klam), *n., v.,* **clammed, clam|ming.** **—*n.*** **1** a mollusk somewhat like an oyster, with a soft body and a shell in two halves joined by a hinge. Clams burrow in sand along the seashore, or at the edges of rivers and lakes. Many kinds are good to eat. **2** the fleshy portion of one of these mollusks, eaten raw or cooked. **3** *U.S. Figurative.* a close-mouthed or taciturn person: *He is a clam about his business dealings.* **4** = clamshell (def. 2). **5** *U.S. Slang.* a dollar: *I read the check and produced the forty clams necessary to discharge my immediate obligations* (Peter de Vries). **6** *Jazz Slang.* a wrong note: *[Louis] Armstrong's authority was absolute . . . When he did hit a clam, it was a great clam* (Whitney Balliett).
—*v.i.* to go out after clams; dig for clams: *The vacationers were clamming along the seashore.*
clam up, *Informal.* to stop talking; refuse to speak; withhold information: *In meetings with business associates and customers I used to be the silent one. I used to "clam up" when the talk turned to politics or economics* (Wall Street Journal).
happy as a clam, *U.S. Informal.* very happy: *[He] has been happy as a clam in his modest $40,000 home* (Time).
[earlier *clam-shell,* apparently special use of *clam*[2] pair of pincers]—**clam′like′,** *adj.*

clam[2] (klam), *n.* a clamp; a vise.
clams, pincers; forceps; tongs: *The round wire is . . . drawn through . . . clams* (Frederick Britten).
[Old English *clamm* bond, fetter]

clam[3] (klam), *n.* **1** clamminess; cold dampness. **2** *Obsolete.* a soft or plastic mass. [perhaps back formation < *clammy*]

clam[4] (klam), *v.t., v.i.,* **clammed, clam|ming.** = clem.

clam|ant (klā′mənt), *adj.* **1** crying out; clamorous; noisy: *Roberts dropped Rowland's pass when a deliriously clamant crowd rightly thought a try inevitable* (London Times). **2** *Figurative.* crying; urgent: *My appetite was a clamant, instant annoyance* (Robert Louis Stevenson). [< Latin *clāmāns, -antis,* present participle of *clāmāre* cry out]—**clam′ant|ly,** *adv.*

clam|a|to|ri|al (klam′ə tôr′ē əl, -tōr′-), *adj.* of or having to do with a group of perching birds, sometimes with harsh voices, or musical call notes, such as the flycatchers. [< New Latin *Clamatores* the suborder name (< Latin *clāmātōr* clamorer < *clāmāre* cry out) + English *-ial*]

clam|bake (klam′bāk′), *n.* **1a** a picnic where clams are baked or steamed, especially at a beach on hot stones placed in holes and covered with seaweed. A clambake may be an elaborate meal, with much to eat besides clams. **b** this method of cooking clams. **2** *U.S. Slang, Figurative.* any meeting, get-together, or party: *The dissidents left the convention and held their own clambake the next day.* **3** *U.S. Slang.* a bad performance of a television program.

clam|ber (klam′bər), *v., n.* —***v.i., v.t.*** **1** to climb, using both hands and feet; climb awkwardly or with difficulty; scramble: *The boys clambered up the cliff. The men who had fallen were trying to clamber up along bent steel pipes and broken timbers to safety* (New York Times). **2** (of plants) to climb, especially by means of tendrils. **3** *Figurative.* to climb or struggle into a position of eminence; attain with effort.
—***n.*** an awkward or difficult climb.
[Middle English *clambren.* See related etym. at **climb.**] —**clam′ber|er,** *n.*

clam|jam|phrie or **clam|jam|fry** (klam jam′frē), *n. Especially Scottish.* **1** trumpery; rubbish; things of little value. **2** worthless people; rabble; mob; canaille. [origin uncertain]

clam|mer (klam′ər), *n.* a person who gathers or digs clams.

clam|my (klam′ē), *adj.,* **-mi|er, -mi|est.** **1** cold and damp: *A frog is a clammy creature.* **2a** soft, moist, and sticky. **b** (of bread) doughy. **c** (of soil or earth) moist. [Middle English *claymy,* perhaps < *clam* sticky mass] —**clam′mi|ly,** *adv.* —**clam′mi|ness,** *n.*

clam|or¹ (klam′ər), *n., v.* —***n.*** **1a** a loud noise, especially of voices; confused shouting or continual uproar: *The clamor of the milling crowd filled the air.* **b** a shout; cry. **2** *Figurative.* a noisy demand; popular outcry: *The clamor for lower taxes continued year after year.* **3** any loud noise, such as that of animals or musical instruments.
—***v.i.*** **1** to make a loud noise; make a continual uproar; shout. **2** to raise an outcry; demand noisily: *The children were clamoring for candy.*
—***v.t.*** **1** to utter or assert by making a loud noise. **2** *Obsolete.* to disturb with clamor; din. Also, *especially British,* **clamour.**
[< Old French *clamour* < Latin *clāmor* a shout < *clāmāre* cry out] —**clam′or|er,** *n.*

clam|or² (klam′ər), *v.t. Obsolete.* to silence. [perhaps < earlier *clam* the clangor of bells]

clam|or|ous (klam′ər əs), *adj.* **1** loud and noisy; shouting. **SYN:** vociferous, boisterous. **2** *Figurative.* making noisy demands or complaints. **SYN:** importunate. —**clam′or|ous|ly,** *adv.* —**clam′or|ous|ness,** *n.*

clam|our (klam′ər), *n., v.i., v.t. Especially British.* clamor¹. —**clam′our|er,** *n.*

clamp¹** (klamp), *n., v.* —n.*** **1** a brace, band, wedge, or other device for holding things tightly together. A clamp usually has opposite sides or parts which may be screwed or otherwise brought together to hold or compress anything. *He used a clamp to hold the arm on the chair until the glue dried.* **2** a device made of lead, copper, or other soft material to hold objects in a vise without bruising. **3** *Figurative.* any control or restraint: *Many businessmen were pleased ... that strong clamps were placed in internal consumption* (New York Times).
—***v.t.*** **1** to fasten together with a clamp; put in a clamp; strengthen with clamps: *A picture frame must be clamped together while the glue is drying.* **2** to impose forcefully (a control or restraint): *Britain has clamped trade embargoes on Rhodesian tobacco and sugar* (New York Times).
clamp down, *Informal.* to become more strict; put pressure (on): *The police clamped down on speeders.*
[perhaps < Middle Dutch *klampe*]

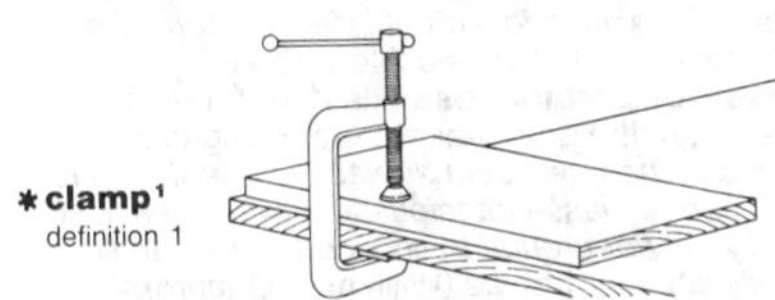

***clamp¹**
definition 1

clamp² (klamp), *v., n. Chiefly Dialect.* —***v.i.*** to tread or stamp heavily and clumsily; clump.
—***n.*** a heavy tread or footstep.
[probably imitative; influenced by *clap, clumsy*]

clamp³ (klamp), *n.* **1** a heap or pile of any one of various materials, especially a pile or stack of bricks built up into a kind of hollow chamber for burning. **2** *British.* a mound of earth or turf lined with straw, in which farm crops are kept during winter: *Most root vegetables in clamps have deteriorated steadily because the protection sufficient in most winters was not so this year* (London Times). [perhaps < Dutch *klamp* heap]

clamp-down or **clamp|down** (klamp′doun′), *n. U.S. Informal.* a strict restriction or prohibition of something, as of gambling.

clamp|er (klam′pər), *n.* **1** a piece of iron with nails or prongs, attached to the sole of a shoe or boot to prevent slipping on ice. **2** *Dialect.* a clamp. **3** a person who clamps.
clampers, *Dialect.* pincers.

clams (klamz), *n.pl.* See under **clam².**

***clam|shell** (klam′shel′), *n.* **1** the shell of a clam. **2** a bucket, box, or the like, hinged like a clamshell, used in dredging and loading; clam.

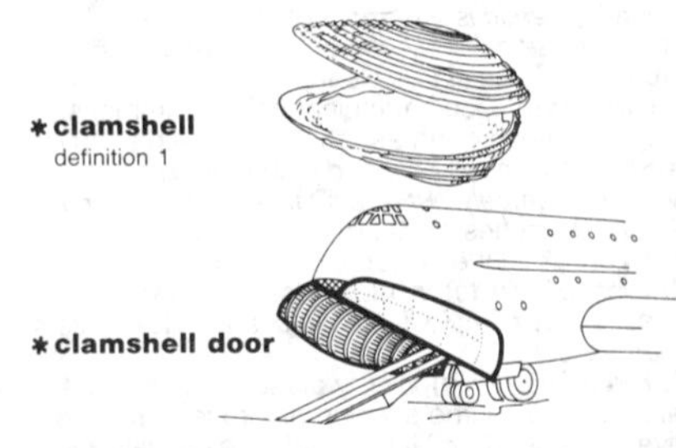

***clamshell**
definition 1

***clamshell door**

***clamshell door,** a door on an aircraft, ship, or truck, used for loading cargo, and consisting of two curved panels that swing apart lengthwise like a clamshell.

clam worm, a burrowing marine worm, a polychaete, commonly used as a bait in saltwater fishing.

clan (klan), *n.* **1** a group of related families that claim to be descended from a common ancestor and have the same surname, especially such a group living together: *a Scottish clan.* **2** a group of people closely joined together by some common interest: *the clan of local political bosses in the state.* **SYN:** fraternity, party, set, lot. **3** *Sociology, Anthropology.* **a** people or families claiming membership in a group by virtue of real or supposed descent through either the female line or the male line from a real or mythical common ancestress, having certain obligations toward one another. **b** *British.* such a group claiming descent from a real or mythical common ancestor through either the male or the female line, similar to but larger than a lineage; sib. [< Scottish Gaelic *clann* family, stock, offspring]

clan|des|tine (klan des′tən, klan′dəs tīn), *adj.* arranged or made in a stealthy or underhanded manner; secret; private; concealed: *The spy's clandestine entry into the country went undetected.* **SYN:** hidden, furtive, covert, surreptitious, underhand. See syn. under **secret.** [< Latin *clandestīnus* < *clam* secretly, related to *cēlāre* hide (something)] —**clan|des′tine|ly,** *adv.* —**clan|des′tine|ness,** *n.*

clan|des|tin|i|ty (klan′des tin′ə tē), *n.* clandestine quality or state; secrecy; privacy.

clang (klang), *n., v.* —***n.*** **1** a loud, harsh, ringing sound like metal being hit: *The clang of the fire bell aroused the town.* **2** the harsh sound of a trumpet. **3** the cry of certain birds, such as cranes or geese.
—***v.i.*** to make a clang: *The fire bells clanged.*
—***v.t.*** **1** to cause to clang: *The firemen clanged the bell on the fire truck as it sped past us.* **2** to strike together with a clang.
[imitative, associated probably with Latin *clangere* resound, ring]

clang|er (klang′ər), *n. British Slang.* a foolish mistake; blunder; clinker: *It speaks of "his record of appalling clangers" and cites many so-called instances of social gaffes* (London Times).

clan|gor (klang′ər, -gər), *n., v.* —***n.*** **1** a continued clanging. **2** a clang.
—***v.i.*** to make a clangor; clang.
[< Latin *clangor* a (ringing) sound < *clangere* clang, resound]

clan|gor|ous (klang′ər əs, -gər-), *adj.* clanging. —**clan′gor|ous|ly,** *adv.*

clan|gour (klang′ər, -gər), *n., v.i. Especially British.* clangor.

clan|ism (klan′iz əm), *n.* clannishness; clanship: *small-town clanism.*

clank (klangk), *n., v.* —***n.*** a sharp, harsh sound like the rattle of a heavy chain: *The clank of heavy machinery filled the factory.*
—***v.i.*** **1** to make a sharp, harsh sound: *The swords clashed and clanked as the men fought one another.* **2** to move with a clanking sound: *The tire chains clanked down the bare highway.*
—***v.t.*** to cause to clank: *The prisoners clanked their chains.*
[probably imitative] —**clank′ing|ly,** *adv.*

clan|like (klan′līk′), *adj.* having the qualities of a clan; clannish.

clan|nish (klan′ish), *adj.* **1** having to do with a clan: *the clannish customs of the Scottish Highlanders.* **SYN:** tribal. **2** closely united; not liking outsiders: *The old settlers were clannish and afraid of their new neighbors.* **SYN:** cliquish. —**clan′nish|ly,** *adv.* —**clan′nish|ness,** *n.*

clan|ship (klan′ship), *n.* **1** association in or as if in clans. **2** attachment to one's clan.

clans|man (klanz′mən), *n., pl.* **-men.** a member of a clan.

clans|wom|an (klanz′wům′ən), *n., pl.* **-wom|en.** a female member of a clan.

clap¹ (klap), *v.,* **clapped, clap|ping,** *n.* —***v.t.*** **1** to strike together loudly: *to clap the cymbals.* **SYN:** beat. **2a** to strike (the hands) together loudly, usually to indicate applause, encouragment, or delight: *The excited audience clapped their hands and stomped for another song from the great singer.* **b** to applaud (a person or performance) by striking the hands together. **3** to strike with a quick blow; slap or pat: *He clapped his friend on the back.* **4** to put or place quickly and effectively: *The police clapped the thief in jail. He clapped spurs to his horse* (Joseph Addison). **SYN:** thrust. **5** (of a bird) to flap (the wings). **6** to make or put together hastily: *to clap together a barn. Was ever match clapped up so suddenly?* (Shakespeare). —***v.i.*** **1** to applaud by striking the hands together: *When the show was over we all clapped. Ladies ... clapped and shouted to the gladiators* (Charles Kingsley). **2** to make a sharp, abrupt sound: *Doors creak and windows clap* (Robert Blair). **3** (of doors, lids, etc.) to close or be closed with a sharp noise.
—***n.*** **1** a sudden noise, such as a single burst of thunder, the sound of the hands struck together, or the sound of a loud slap: *The news ... came upon them like a clap of thunder* (Charles Merivale). **2** a loud, quick blow; slap: *He greeted him with a clap on the shoulder.* **3** the act of clapping the hands, especially in applause; applause: *Dryden and Settle had both placed their happiness in the claps of multitudes* (Samuel Johnson). **4** a contrivance in a mill for striking or shaking the hopper to make the grain move down to the millstones. **5** *Obsolete.* a sudden stroke; a moment of time. **6** *Obsolete.* a sudden mishap.
[Old English *clæppan, clæppettan* to throb]

clap² (klap), *n. Slang.* = gonorrhea. [probably < Middle French *clapoir* bubo; origin uncertain]

clap|board** (klab′ərd; klap′bôrd′, -bōrd′), *n., v., adj.* —n.*** **1** a thin board, thicker along one edge than along the other; weatherboard. Clapboards are used to cover the outer walls of wooden buildings. Each board is made to overlap the one below it somewhat like a shingle but is much longer than a shingle. **2** *British.* (formerly) a small size of split oak, used for barrel staves and wainscoting.
—***v.t.*** to cover with clapboards.
—***adj.*** of or having to do with clapboard: *a clapboard house.*
[partial translation of Low German *klappholt; holt* wood]

***clapboard**
definition 1

clap|board|ing (klab′ər ding; klap′bôr′-, -bōr′-), *n. U.S.* a facing, or other part of a structure, made of clapboards; siding.

clapped-out (klapt′out′), *adj. British Slang.* old and worn out; dilapidated: *This Hercules is a clapped-out propeller driven aircraft* (London Times).

clap|per (klap′ər), *n.* **1** a person or thing that claps. **2** the movable part inside a bell that strikes against and rings the outer part. **3** a device for making noise. **4** *Informal.* a talkative person's tongue.
like the clappers, *British Slang.* very fast: *"He's about eighty miles up now," whispered Futter, "and going like the clappers"* (Punch).

clap|per|board (klap′ə bôrd′, -bōrd′), *n. Especially British.* clapstick.

clapper boy, the person who works the clapstick during the filming of a motion picture.

clapper bridge, *British.* a roughly built bridge, especially of planks or slabs.

clap|per|claw (klap′ər klô′) *v.t. Dialect.* **1** to claw or scratch with the open hand and nails; fight with tooth and nail. **2** *Figurative.* to revile; abuse. [probably < *clapper* (in obsolete, uncertain sense) + *claw*]

clapper rail, a long-billed rail common in the marshes and swamps of the eastern United

---

Pronunciation Key: hat, āge, cãre, fär; let, ēqual, tėrm; it, īce; hot, ōpen, ôrder; oil, out; cup, půt, rüle; child; long; thin; ᴛʜen; zh, measure; ə represents **a** in about, **e** in taken, **i** in pencil, **o** in lemon, **u** in circus.

States.

***clap|stick** (klap′stik′), *n.* a hinged pair of sticks closed with a sharp clap at the start of a motion-picture take to synchronize the picture with the sound track.

***clapstick**

clap|trap (klap′trap′), *n., adj.* **—*n.*** **1** empty talk or an insincere remark made just to get attention or applause: *Everything he said was just claptrap.* **2** a trick or device to catch applause: *Art should be independent of all claptrap* (James McNeill Whistler).
—*adj.* cheap and showy: *Read election speeches and observe how votes are gained by claptrap appeals to senseless prejudices* (Herbert Spencer).
[< *clap* + *trap*]

claque (klak), *n.* **1** a group of persons hired to applaud in a theater. **2** a group that applauds or follows another person for selfish reasons. [< French *claque*, related to *claquer* to clap]

cla|queur (kla kėr′), *n.* a member of a claque: *a hired claqueur, a loyal claqueur.* [< French *claqueur* < *claquer* to clap + *-eur* -or]

clar., clarinet.

clar|a|bel|la (klar′ə bel′ə), *n.* an organ stop which gives soft, sweet tones. [< Latin *clāra*, feminine of *clārus* clear + *bella*, feminine of *bellus* beautiful]

clar|ence (klar′əns), *n.* a closed, four-wheeled carriage with seats for four persons inside, used in the 1800's. [< the Duke of *Clarence*, later William IV]

Clar|en|cieux or **Clar|en|ceux** (klar′ən syü), *n.* (in England) the title of the second king-of-arms, a chief heraldic officer, ranking after Garter King-of-Arms. [< Anglo-French *Clarenceux*, named from *Clarence* (< *Clare*, in Suffolk), a dukedom created for a son of Edward III]

clar|en|don (klar′ən dən), *n.* a style of thick, condensed printing type. [< *Clarendon* Press, Oxford, England]

clar|et (klar′ət), *n., adj.* **—*n.*** **1** a kind of red wine, especially the light, dry red wine made in Bordeaux, France; red Bordeaux. **2** Also, **claret red.** a dark purplish red. **3** *Slang.* blood.
—*adj.* dark purplish-red: *a claret coat.*
[< Old French *claret* light-colored (diminutive) < *cler* clear]

clar|et-col|ored (klar′et kul′ərd), *adj.* having the color of claret (wine).

claret cup, a mixture of iced claret, lemon juice, soda water, various other flavoring ingredients, and sometimes brandy.

claret red, a dark purplish red.

clar|i|fy (klar′ə fī), *v.*, **-fied, -fying.** **—*v. t.*** **1** to make clearer; explain: *The teacher's explanation clarified the difficult instructions.* **SYN:** elucidate. **2** to make clear; purify: *The cook clarified the fat by heating it with a little water and straining it through cloth.*
—*v.i.* to become clear; clear: *His mind suddenly clarified.*
[< Old French *clarifier* glorify, make known, learned borrowing from Late Latin *clarificāre* < Latin *clārus* clear + *facere* make] **—clar′i|fi|ca′tion,** *n.* **—clar′i|fi′er,** *n.*

***clar|i|net** (klar′ə net′), *n.* a woodwind instrument having a tube with a bell-shaped mouth, played by means of holes and keys. A clarinet has a mouthpiece with a single reed and a range of three octaves. *Clarinets make up one section of woodwinds in our band.* Also, **clarionet.** [< French *clarinette* (diminutive) < *clarine* bell, ultimately < Latin *clārus* clear]

***clarinet**

clar|i|net|ist or **clar|i|net|tist** (klar′ə net′ist), *n.* a person who plays a clarinet.

cla|ri|no (klə rē′nō), *n., pl.* **-ni** (-nē), **-nos.** any one of various early trumpets, especially that playing the highest register. [< Italian *clarino*]

clar|i|on (klar′ē ən), *adj., n.,v.* **—*adj.*** clear and shrill: *the clarion sound of the trumpet.*
—*n.* **1** a trumpet with clear, shrill tones. It was formerly much used as a signal in war: *Sound, sound the clarion* (Scott). **2a** the sound made by this trumpet. **b** a similar rousing sound: *the loud clarion of the braying ass* (Alexander Pope).
—*v.i., v.t.* to give forth or emit with a clarion sound: *"Peace is at hand," clarioned the radio and television.* [< Medieval Latin *clario, -onis* trumpet < Latin *clārus* clear]

clarion call, a loud and clear call or summons; a ringing speech or phrase that stirs to action: *[He] sounds no clarion call, and points no direction; it would be entirely out of his family's character if he did* (Manchester Guardian Weekly).

clar|i|o|net (klar′ē ə net′), *n.* = clarinet.

clar|i|ty (klar′ə tē), *n.* clearness; *His writing has great clarity of style.* [< Latin *clāritās* clearness < *clārus* clear]

clark|i|a (klär′kē ə), *n.* any plant of a genus of annual herbs of the evening-primrose family, native to the western United States, especially either of two kinds with showy, purplish flowers. [< New Latin *Clarkia* the genus name < William *Clark*, 1770-1838, an American soldier and explorer]

Clark's crow (klärks), = Clark's nutcracker.

Clark's nutcracker, a bird related to the crow, with light-grayish plumage, its wings and tail marked with black and white, common in the western United States. [< William *Clark*; see etym. under **clarkia**]

cla|ro (klär′ō), *adj., n., pl.* **-ros.** **—*adj.*** made with light-colored tobacco and usually mild: *a claro cigar.* **—*n.*** a mild, light cigar. [< Spanish *claro* light, clear < Latin *clārus* clear]

clart (klärt), *v., n. Scottish.* **—*v.t.*** to smear or spot with something sticky or dirty.
—*n.* a smear or clot of something sticky, dirty, or moist.

clarts, mud or dirt: *brogues caked with clarts.* [origin unknown]

clart|y (klär′tē), *adj.*, **clart|i|er, clart|i|est.** *Scottish.* **1** besmeared with sticky dirt. **2** of the nature of sticky dirt; dirty; nasty. **3** sticky, viscous, or unctuous.

clar|y (klar′ē), *n., pl.* **clar|ies.** **1** a salvia or sage of southern Europe. **2** any one of several closely related plants. [< Middle Frenchy *eclarie*, or < Latin *sclareia* a kind of sage]

clary sage, = clary.

clash (klash), *n., v.* **—*n.*** **1** a loud, harsh sound like that of two things running into each other, of striking metal, or of bells rung together but not in tune: *He heard the clash of cymbals.* **2** *Figurative.* **a** strong disagreement or conflict: *There are many clashes of opinion in that family, for no two of them think alike.* **SYN:** discord. **b** the shock of conflict; collision; hostile encounter. **3** the kind of blow or stroke that yields a clash.
—*v.i.* **1** to make a loud, harsh sound of striking together. **2** to strike together with a clash; come into contact with much violence and noise: *Their swords clashed together.* **3** *Figurative.* **a** to come into conflict: *The two appointments clash because they come at the same time. The two teams clashed in a football game.* **b** to disagree strongly; conflict: *Your feelings and your judgment sometimes clash.* **SYN:** interfere. **4** to go badly together; fail to harmonize: *Those red shoes clash with that orange dress and purple hat.*
—*v.t.* **1** to hit with a clash: *In her haste, she clashed the saucepans against the stove.* **2** to throw, shut, or smash with a clash.
[probably imitative] **—clash′er,** *n.* **—clash′ing|ly,** *adv.*

clasp (klasp, kläsp), *n., v.* **—*n.*** **1** a thing to fasten two parts or pieces together. A buckle on a belt is one kind of clasp. **2** a close hold with the arms: *I was glad to escape the bear's clasp.* **3** a firm grip with the hand: *He gave my hand a warm clasp.* **4** *Military.* **a** a small bar of metal placed across the ribbon of a medal, indicating the battle, area, or other service in which the medal was won. **b** a cluster.
—*v.t.* **1** to fasten together with a clasp: *He clasped the buckles on his boots.* **SYN:** hook. **2** to hold closely with the arms; embrace: *The mother clasped her baby to her breast.* **SYN:** hug. **3** to grip firmly with the hand; grasp: *He clasped a knife in his hand.* **SYN:** clutch. **4a** to take hold of by means of encircling parts; hold closely by closing round. **b** *Chiefly Poetic.* to environ; surround; enfold.
[Middle English *claspen*; origin uncertain]

clasp|er (klas′pər, kläs′-), *n.* **1** a person or thing that clasps. **2** *Botany.* a tendril of a climbing plant which twines round something for support.

claspers, *Zoology.* the appendages of the male of certain fishes and insects, serving to hold the female.

clasp knife, a knife with a blade or blades folding into the handle, especially a large knife with a single blade which, when open, may be secured in place by a catch.

class (klas, kläs), *n., v.* **—*n.*** **1** a group of persons or things alike in some way; kind; sort: *She was of the gracious class of people who are always willing to help those in need.* **SYN:** category. **2** a group of students taught together: *The French class meets in room 202.* **3** a meeting of such a group: *When he was absent he missed a great many classes.* **4** *U.S.* a group of pupils entering a school together and graduating in the same year: *The class of 1980 will graduate in 1980.* **5** a rank of society: *In the Middle Ages, kings and nobles belonged to the upper class, some tradesmen and merchants to the middle class, and peasants to the lower class. The habit of brag runs through all classes, from the Times newspaper . . . down to the boys of Eton* (Emerson). **6** the system of ranks or divisions in society: *prejudices and convictions more impassable than all the mere consequences of class* (Benjamin Disraeli). **SYN:** caste. **7** a high rank in society. **8** a group of military draftees of the same age: *the 1960 class.* **9** grade or quality: *The class of work one does determines his marks in school. First class is the best and most costly way to travel.* **10** *Informal.* high quality; excellence; style: *He has never really shown much class.* **11** *Biology.* a group of animals or plants ranking below a phylum and above an order. Crustaceans and insects are two classes in the phylum of anthropods. Monocotyledons and dicotyledons are two subclasses in the class of angiosperms. **12** *Linguistics.* a group of elements which share some feature: *The class of weak verbs, the class of palatals.* **13** (in British universities) a division of honors candidates according to merit, as a result of examination. **14** *Ecclesiastical.* **a** = classis (def. 1). **b** (in early Methodist societies) a small group of members of a congregation meeting under a leader for religious instruction, etc.
—*v.t.* **1** to put in a class; classify: *He is classed as one of the best baseball players in the league. I have classed artificers, manufacturers, and merchants among the productive laborers* (Adam Smith). *They were popularly classed together* (Macaulay). **SYN:** rank. **2** to assign to a class on a basis of merit or marks gained: *At a second year's examination . . . Tom was not classed at all* (Thackeray). **SYN:** grade.
—*v.i.* to be placed in a class: *those who class as believers* (Horace Bushnell).
the classes, the higher ranks or divisions of society: *He contrasted the classes and the masses.*
[< Middle French *classe*, learned borrowing from Latin *classis* class, collection] **—class′a|ble,** adj.

class., **1** classic. **2** classical. **3a** classification. **b** classified.

class act, a person or thing of very high quality or excellence: *Guest Quarters is the class act. Room service brings breakfast on good china on silver trays* (Forbes).

class action, a legal action brought on behalf of all to whom the case applies: *the right of citizens to bring "class actions" against polluters* (New Yorker).

class|book (klas′bůk′, kläs′-), *n.* **1** *U.S.* a book in which a teacher records the absences and keeps the grades of students. **2** an annual book usually published by the graduating class of a high school or college; yearbook.

class-con|scious (klas′kon′shəs, kläs′-), *adj.* conscious of belonging to a particular social class and of being identified with its interests, often with implication of sharp differentiation from or hostility to other classes: *He attacks . . . the class-conscious feeling of inferiority forced on Communist intellectuals* (New Yorker).

class-con|scious|ness (klas′kon′shəs nis, kläs′-), *n.* the quality or state of being class-conscious: *There is also a subjective orientation to class, or a class-consciousness which leads socially inferior groups to show deference to socially superior groups* (William F. Ogburn).

class day, *U.S.* a day on which the members of a class celebrate their graduation with special ceremonies.

class|er (klas′ər, kläs′-), *n.* = classifier.

class|es[1] (klas′iz, kläs′-), *n.* plural of **class.**

clas|ses[2] (klas′ēz), *n.* plural of **classis.**

clas|sic (klas′ik), *n., adj.* **—*n.*** **1** a book or painting of the highest quality: *"Robinson Crusoe" and Shakespeare's "Hamlet" are classics.* **2** an author or artist of acknowledged excellence, whose works serve as a standard, model, or guide: *Shakespeare is a classic. Dante was the classic of his country* (Benjamin Disraeli). **3** a contest of great importance: *The world series is a baseball classic.* **4** a person who follows classic rules and models: *In matters of form this poet is no romantic, but a classic to the fingertips.* **5** a classic style or article as of clothing. **6** an automobile with a classic design, usually one that was manufactured between 1925 and 1942. **7** a classical scholar; a student of classical literature: *I find that I am a respectable classic* (H. K. White). **—*adj.*** **1** of the highest rank or quality; serving as a standard, model, or guide; excellent; first-class: *a classic author, the classic authority upon all questions of Parliamentary reporting* (Charles Peabody). **2** of the literature, art, and life of ancient Greece and Rome. The classic orders of Greek architecture are the Doric, Ionic, and Corinthian. *The academic elegance, and classic allusion which adorn its columns* (Emerson). **3** like this literature and art; simple and fine in form: *the classic style of Bach's music, the classic design of pyramids.* **4** (of fashion, clothes, and the like) simple in style; likely to remain in style for a long time: *the classic little black dress.* SYN: conservative. **5** famous, as in literature or history; famous; well-known: *classic Alexandria.* **6** conforming to or observing an approved and recognized set of literary, artistic, or other standards: *the classic English essayist.* **7** conforming to what is considered the traditional or common form, and sometimes marked as a supreme example: *Schubert was the classic example of a man of genius who was so devoted to his art that he never managed to live well or adjust to the world* (H. Weinstock). **8** fitting, especially in its effectiveness; efficacious: *a classic reply.*

classics, Often, **the Classics.** the literature of ancient Greece and Rome: *'Tis sixty years . . . since I first ventured to teach Classics* (Frederick E. Gretton).

[< Latin *classicus* pertaining to the highest class (of Romans) < *classis;* see etym. under **class**]

clas|si|cal (klas′ə kəl), *adj.* **1** of or having to do with the literature, art, and life of ancient Greece and Rome: *classical studies. Classical languages include ancient Greek and the Latin of the ancient Romans.* **2** excellent; first-class: *a classical authority.* **3** simple and fine in form: *the classical architecture of colonial Virginia.* **4** *Music.* **a** of high quality and enjoyed especially by serious students of music: *Symphonies and concertos are considered classical music even when they include jazz.* **b** conforming to traditional standards; subordinating content to form. **c** of or having to do with the era of musical classicism, variously dated but roughly between 1750 and 1820, exemplified by Haydn, Mozart, Beethoven, as contrasted with the preceding baroque and the subsequent romantic period. **5** based on the classics: *"Ulysses" is perhaps the best of Tennyson's classical poems.* **6** belonging to an earlier stage or period; being the original or traditional form of something; orthodox and established: *classical physics, classical hemophilia.* **7** denoting or having to do with a course of study or a school in which the emphasis is on broadly cultural rather than technical education. **8** *Ecclesiastical.* of or belonging to a classis: *the ordinances touching classical, provincial, and national synods* (Macaulay). **—clas′si|cal|ly,** *adv.*

classical architecture, 1 any architecture conceived in terms of simplicity and symmetry of structure and plan, restraint and regularity of decoration, and traditional standards of proportion, especially that which uses the orders and other forms of ancient Greek and Roman architecture. **2** the architecture of ancient Greece and Rome. **3** the architecture of any of the revivals of ancient Greek and Roman styles, such as in America in the early and late 1800's.

classical economics, a school of economic thought developed by the Scottish political economist Adam Smith, which held as one of its tenets that, in free competition, each man in pursuit of his own prosperity would so act as to lead to the greatest economic prosperity of all, and hence that the less the government interfered with economic activities the better.

clas|si|cal|ism (klas′ə kə liz′əm), *n.* = classicism. **—clas′si|cal|ist,** *n.*

clas|si|cal|i|ty (klas′ə kal′ə tē), *n., pl.* **-ties. 1** classical quality or style. **2** classical scholarship. **3** an instance or piece of classical learning, art, and the like.

clas|si|cal|ness (klas′ə kəl nis), *n.* = classicality.

classic car, = classic (*n.* def. 6).

clas|si|cism (klas′ə siz əm), *n.* **1a** the principles of the literature or art of ancient Greece and Rome. They include simplicity, regularity, restraint, and interest in form. **b** the following of these principles. **2** knowledge of the literature or art of ancient Greece and Rome; classical scholarship. **3** an idiom or form from Greek or Latin introduced into another language. Also, **classicalism.**

clas|si|cist (klas′ə sist), *n.* **1** a follower of the principles of classicism in literature and art. **2** an expert in the literature of ancient Greece and Rome. **3** a person who urges the study of Greek and Latin.

clas|si|cis|tic (klas′ə sis′tik), *adj.* characterized by classicism.

clas|si|cize (klas′ə sīz), *v.,* **-cized, -ciz|ing.** **—*v.t.*** to make classic.
—*v.i.* to affect or imitate classic style or form.

classic orders, *Architecture.* the Grecian Doric, Ionic, and Corinthian style of columns, and the Roman Tuscan, Doric, Ionic, Corinthian, and Composite style of columns.

classic rock, rock music, especially of the 1960's and 1970's, considered to be the original or traditional form of this music: *a concert of classic rock.*

clas|sics (klas′iks), *n.pl.* See under **classic.**

clas|sif|ic (klə sif′ik), *adj.* **1** distinguishing a class. **2** having to do with classification: *All curators of anthropological museums must recognize the following classific concepts: material, race, geographical areas, social organizations, environment, structure and function, and evolution* (Science). [< Latin *classis* class + *facere* make]

clas|sif|i|cal|ly (klə sif′ə klē), *adv.* with classific force; as one of a class or category.

clas|si|fi|ca|tion (klas′ə fə kā′shən), *n.* **1** the act or process of arranging in classes or groups; a grouping according to some system: *The classification of new books is a difficult job in any library.* **2** the result of classifying; a systematic arrangement in groups or classes: *The classification of books in the library helps you to find the books you want.* **3** *Botany, Zoology.* the arrangement of plants and animals in groups or categories on the basis of ancestral relationship or structure. The categories generally used are (in descending order): phylum (or *division* in botany), class, order, family, genus, and species.

classification yard, a railroad yard with tracks arranged for sorting freight cars.

clas|si|fi|ca|to|ry (klas′ə fə kə tôr′ē, -tōr′-), *adj.* of or having to do with classification.

clas|si|fied (klas′ə fīd), *adj., n.* **—*adj.*** **1** sorted or arranged in classes. A classified telephone directory lists names according to classes of business, services, and professions. **2** (of certain public documents of the United States) having a classification as restricted, confidential, secret, or top secret. **3** *Informal.* secret: *The airplane was on a classified flight.*
—*n.* a classified ad.

classified ad, a small notice, usually on a special page of a newspaper or magazine, stating that something is wanted or is offered, such as a job, an apartment, a car, a pet, or something lost or found; want ad. Classified ads are usually grouped into categories, such as real estate, help wanted, and business opportunities.

clas|si|fi|er (klas′ə fī′ər), *n.* **1** a person who classifies. **2** *Chemistry.* an apparatus used for separating solid particles of different characteristics in a fluid. **3** a machine used for separating crushed ore into various sizes and grades.

clas|si|fy (klas′ə fī), *v.t.,* **-fied, -fy|ing.** to arrange in groups or classes; group according to some method or system: *Employees in the post office classify mail according to the places where it is to go.* SYN: sort, assort. [< Latin *classis* class + English *-fy*] **—clas′si|fi′a|ble,** *adj.*

class inclusion, *Logic.* the relation of one class to a second, where anything which is a member of the first class is also a member of the second. *Example:* "All *roses* are *plants.*"

class interval, *Statistics.* **1** one of the arbitrary groups of equal and convenient size into which the possible values of a variable are often divided. **2** the width of such a group.

clas|sis (klas′is), *n., pl.* **clas|ses. 1** (in certain Reformed churches) a judicatory or directing group of ministers and elders in a district, corresponding to a presbytery in Presbyterian churches. **2** the district formed by the parishes so united. **3** *Obsolete.* a presbytery.
[< Latin *classis* class]

class|ism (klas′iz əm, kläs′-), *n.* discrimination based on class distinctions.

class|less (klas′lis, kläs′-), *adj.* without classes; not divided into social, economic, or other classes: *classless society.* **—class′less|ness,** *n.*

class|man (klas′mən, kläs′-), *n., pl.* **-men.** a member of a class, as in a college or high school (used especially in compounds): *upperclassman, lowerclassman, fourth classman.*

class|mate (klas′māt′, kläs′-), *n.* a member of the same class in school.
[American English; perhaps patterned on *schoolmate*]

class meaning, the meaning common to all members of a form class: *"Houses," "oxen," and "we" have the class meaning of plural.*

class number, the number or number and letter in library cataloging, which shows the class (as literature, history, philosophy, or science) to which a book belongs or the subject it treats.

class|room (klas′rüm′, -rům′; kläs′-), *n.* a room where classes meet; schoolroom.

class struggle, 1 political conflict between opposing classes of the same society. **2** the struggle between capital and labor for power: *[Karl] Marx developed the class struggle idea, namely, that the interests of capitalists and workers are so far apart that they cannot be united* (Emory S. Bogardus).

class war, = class struggle.

class|work (klas′wėrk′), *n.* **1** the schoolwork done by a student in the classroom. **2** the classroom work done jointly by the class and teacher.

class|y (klas′ē, kläs′-), *adj.* **class|i|er, class|i|est.** *Slang.* of high or superior class; stylish; smart.

clas|tic (klas′tik), *adj.* **1** *Biology.* dividing into fragments or separate parts. **2** *Geology.* made up of bits of older rock: *clastic rocks.* **3** composed of a number of separable pieces: *a clastic anatomical model.* [< Greek *klastós* broken (< *klân* break) + English *-ic*]

clath|rate (klath′rāt), *adj., n.* **—*adj.*** **1** *Botany.* resembling a lattice; divided or marked like latticework: *clathrate foliage.* **2** *Chemistry.* formed by or having molecules which are interlaced in a lattice-like geometrical pattern: *Enlarged clathrate crystals, containing argon trapped in a quinol lattice* (Science News Letter).
—*n.* a clathrate crystal or crystalline compound.
[< Latin *clāthrātus* < *clāthrī* lattice < Greek *kleîthron* a bar]

clat|ter (klat′ər), *n., v.* **—*n.*** **1** a confused noise like that of many plates being struck together: *The clatter in the cafeteria made it hard to hear one another talk.* **2** noisy talk; gabble: *the clatter of voices above the noise of the train.*
[< verb]
—*v.i.* **1** to move or fall with confused noise; make a confused noise: *The horse's hoofs clattered over the stones.* **2** to talk fast and noisily; chatter: *The ladies clattered away at their luncheon.* SYN: prattle, babble.
—*v.t.* to cause to rattle or clatter.
[Old English *clatrian*] **—clat′ter|er,** *n.* **—clat′ter|ing|ly,** *adv.*

Claude Lor|rain glass or **mirror** (klôd′lə rān′), a dark or colored, slightly convex mirror for bringing into small compass the features of a landscape, so called from the fancied similarity of its effects to the pictures of Claude Lorrain, 1600-1682, a French landscape painter.

Clau|di|an (klô′dē ən), *adj.* having to do with any one of several distinguished Romans of the name of Claudius, or either of two gentes, one patrician and the other plebeian, of which they were members, especially having to do with the emperors Tiberius, Caligula, Claudius, and Nero, who were members of the patrician gens, or with their period, A.D. 14-68.

clau|di|ca|tion (klô′də kā′shən), *n.* lameness; halting or limping.
[< Latin *claudicātiō, -ōnis* < *claudicāre* to limp < *claudus* lame]

claught (klôHt), *v. Scottish.* a past tense of **cleek.**

claus|al (klô′zəl), *adj.* of or having to do with a clause or clauses.

clause (klôz), *n.* **1** a part of speech having a subject and a verb. It is a group of words forming part of a compound or complex sentence, or sometimes forming by itself a simple sentence. Some linguists define a clause as an utterance occurring with certain intonation patterns. *Example:* In "He came before we left," "He came" is a main or principal clause, and "before we left" is a subordinate clause that depends upon the main clause for completion of its meaning. A main clause can stand alone as a sentence. **2** a single provision of a law, a treaty, or any other written agreement: *There is a clause in our lease that says we may not keep a dog in this building.*
[< Old French *clause,* learned borrowing from Medieval Latin *clausa* < Latin *claudere* close]

Clause|witz|i|an (klou′zə vit′sē ən), *adj.* having to do with or characteristic of Karl von Clausewitz, a Prussian officer and writer on military science, or his theories of warfare: *War has ceased to be, in the Clausewitzian sense, an acceptable extension of international political activity* (Listener).

claus|tral (klôs′trəl), *adj.* **1** of or having to do with a cloister or religious house. **2** like a cloister; savoring of the cloister. [< Medieval Latin *claustralis* < Late Latin *claustrālis* enclosed, enclosing < Latin *claustrum* closed place; bar, bolt, related to *claudere* close]

claustral prior, the chief assistant of an abbot.

claus|tro|pho|bi|a (klôs′trə fō′bē ə), *n.* an abnormal fear of enclosed spaces. [< New Latin *claustrophobia* < Latin *claustrum* closed place + Greek *phóbos* fear]

Pronunciation Key: hat, āge, cãre, fär; let, ēqual, tėrm; it, īce; hot, ōpen, ôrder; oil, out; cup, pu̇t, rüle; child; long; thin; ᴛʜen; zh, measure; ə represents **a** in about, **e** in taken, **i** in pencil, **o** in lemon, **u** in circus.

claus|tro|pho|bic (klôs′trə fō′bik), *adj., n.* —*adj.* of or having to do with claustrophobia.
—*n.* a person who has claustrophobia. —**claus′-tro|pho′bi|cal|ly,** *adv.*

cla|vate (klā′vāt), *adj.* club-shaped: *clavate antennae, a clavate nucleus.*
[< Latin *clāvātus* studded with nails < *clāvus* nail, related to *claudere* close, fasten; meaning influenced by Latin *clāva* club]

cla|vate|ly (klā′vāt lē), *adv.* in the shape of a club.

cla|va|tion (klā vā′shən), *n.* **1** a clavate state. **2** *Anatomy.* an immovable articulation, as the articulation of the teeth in the sockets of the jaw; gomphosis.

cla|ve¹ (klä′vā), *n.* one of a pair of round wooden sticks, each held in one hand, which are struck together as a rhythmic accompaniment in Latin-American music and dancing. [< American Spanish *clave* < Spanish *clave* key < Latin *clāvis*. See etym. of doublet **clef**.]

clave² (klāv), *v. Archaic.* cleaved; a past tense of **cleave²**.

clav|e|cin (klav′ə sin), *n.* = harpsichord.
[< French *clavecin*]

clav|e|cin|ist (klav′ə sə nist), *n.* = harpsichordist.

cla|ver (klā′vər, klä′-), *n., v. Scottish.* —*n.* **1** idle, garrulous talk. **2** an idle story; a piece of idle gossip.
—*v.i.* to talk idly; prate; gossip.
[origin uncertain]

***clav|i|chord** (klav′ə kôrd), *n.* a musical instrument with strings and a keyboard. Its tones are produced by the action of brass pins. The piano developed from it.
[< Medieval Latin *clavichordium* < Latin *clāvis* key + *chorda* string]

*clavichord

clav|i|chord|ist (klav′ə kôr′dist), *n.* a person who plays the clavichord.

clav|i|cle (klav′ə kəl), *n.* = collarbone. [< Middle French *clavicule,* learned borrowing from Latin *clāvicula* bolt (diminutive) < *clāvis* key (reputedly because shaped like ancient window latches)]

clav|i|corn (klav′ə kôrn), *adj., n.* —*adj.* of or having to do with a large number of families of beetles with club-shaped antennae.
—*n.* a clavicorn insect.
[< New Latin *Clavicornes* < Latin *clāva* club + *cornū* horn]

clav|i|cor|nate (klav′ə kôr′nāt), *adj.* = clavicorn.

cla|vic|u|lar (klə vik′yə lər), *adj.* of or having to do with the clavicle or collarbone.

clav|i|cym|bal (klav′ə sim′bəl), *n.* (formerly) a harpsichord. [< Medieval Latin *clavicymbalum* < Latin *clāvis* key + *cymbalum* cymbal]

clav|i|er¹ (klav′ē ər, klə vir′), *n.* **1** the keyboard or set of keys of a piano, organ, or harpsichord. **2** a soundless keyboard used for practice. [< French *clavier* < Old French, key bearer < *clef* key < Latin *clāvis*]

cla|vier² (klə vir′), *n.* a general term for any musical instrument with a keyboard and strings. The harpsichord and piano are two kinds. [< German *Klavier* < French *clavier* keyboard, clavier¹] —**cla-vier′ist,** *n.*

clav|i|form (klav′ə fôrm), *adj.* club-shaped; clavate. [< Latin *clāva* club + English *-form*]

clav|i|lux (klav′ə luks), *n., pl.* **-lux|es.** an instrument used to project patterns of light and color in rhythmic order on a screen; color organ. The motion and combination of forms are supposed to resemble the phrases and themes of music.
[< Latin *clāvis* key + *lūx* light]

***claw** (klô), *n., v.* —*n.* **1a** a sharp, hooked nail on a bird's or animal's foot: *The cat's claws stuck out and scratched my arm.* **b** a similar structure on the feet of insects, crustaceans, etc. **2a** the foot of an animal or bird with such sharp, hooked nails: *The cat held a mouse in its claws.* **b** a pincer of a lobster, crab, scorpion, and various other arthropods; chela: *The meat of lobster claws is good to eat.* **3** anything like a claw. The part of a hammer used for pulling nails is the claw. **4** the hand.
—*v.t.* **1** to scratch, tear, seize, or pull with the claws or hands: *The kitten was clawing the screen door.* **2** to scrape. —*v.i.* to lay hold with the claws or hands; grasp or clutch; scratch.
be (or **have** or **get**) **in one's claws,** to be in one's possession or power: *The artful prosecutor had the other lawyer in his claws and the judge ruled in favor of the State.*
claw back, *British.* to take back or recover (government allowances) by imposing additional taxes: *Above that level, the 15 per cent proposed surcharge evens things out, but not enough to claw back the big concessions* (London Guardian).
get one's claws into, to lay hold of or attack: *The editor got his claws into the opposition in a vicious editorial.*
[Old English *clawu*] —**claw′like′,** *adj.*

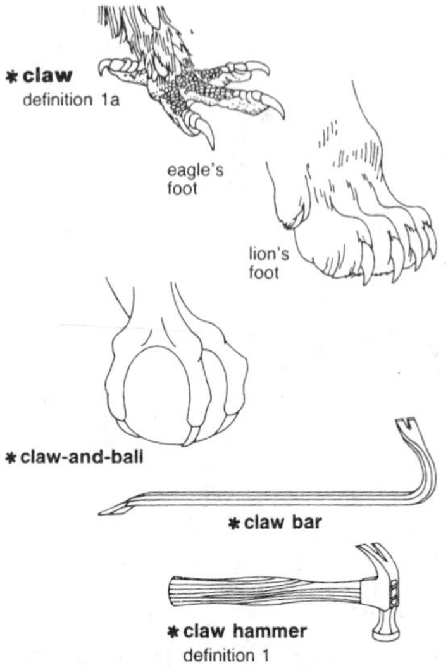

*claw definition 1a
*claw-and-ball
*claw bar
*claw hammer definition 1

***claw-and-ball** (klô′ən bôl′), *adj.* designating a type of furniture foot, or the furniture in which such a foot appears, characterized by the representation of a claw clasping a ball. Also, **ball-and-claw.**

claw-back (klô′bak′), *n. British.* retrieval by the government of money spent on benefits and allowances by imposing additional taxes.

***claw bar,** a lever or crowbar with a bent, bifurcated claw for drawing spikes.

clawed (klôd), *adj.* having claws.

***claw hammer,** **1** a hammer with one end of the head curved like a claw and forked for pulling nails. **2** *U.S. Informal.* a dress coat; swallow-tailed coat.

claw hatchet, a hatchet having one end of the head shaped like a claw and forked.

clay (klā), *n.* **1** a sticky kind of earth that can be easily shaped when wet and hardens when it is dried or baked. Bricks and dishes are made from various kinds of clay. (*Figurative.*) *The pupil is but clay in the hands of his tutor.* **2** earth; moist earth; mire; mud. **3** *Figurative.* **a** the human body (in the Bible, Romans 9:21). **b** earth as the material from which the human body was originally formed. [Old English *clǣg*] —**clay′like′,** *adj.*

clay|bank (klā′bangk′), *n., adj.* —*n.* **1** a bank of clay. **2** the color of a bank of yellowish clay; brownish yellow. —*adj.* having the color of yellowish clay: *a claybank horse.*

clay court, a tennis court with a clay surface: *national clay-court champion.*

clay|ey (klā′ē), *adj.,* **clay|i|er, clay|i|est.** **1** of or like clay. **2** covered or smeared with clay.

clay|ish (klā′ish), *adj.* somewhat clayey.

Clay|ma|tion (klā mā′shən), *n. Trademark.* animation of clay figures filmed in action, especially for use in cartoons and commercials: *The television commercials featured Claymation (clay animation) raisins, dressed in sunglasses, white gloves, and sneakers, who sang and danced* (Bonnie B. Reece).

clay mineral, any one of a group of finely divided, crystalline, hydrous aluminum silicates, found in sedimentary rocks and soils. Clay minerals adsorb large amounts of water.

clay|more (klā′môr, -mōr), *n. Historical.* **1** a heavy, two-edged broadsword formerly used by Scottish Highlanders, once their national weapon. **2** the basket-hilted, often single-edged broadsword of the Highlanders. **3** Also **Claymore.** = claymore mine. [< Scottish Gaelic *claidheamh mor* great sword < Old Irish *claidhebh* sword, *mōr* great]

claymore or **Claymore mine,** an electrically detonated mine that sprays small metal pellets in a wide arch.

clay|pan (klā′pan′), *n.* **1** *U.S.* a layer of clay in the soil. **2** (in Australia) a slight depression or shallow hole in the surface of the ground, having a bottom of clay or silt.

clay pigeon, **1** a saucerlike clay target thrown in the air or released from the trap in trapshooting. **2** *Slang.* a person in a vulnerable position.

clay stone, **1** a concretion found in alluvial clay deposits. **2** = argillite. **3** *Obsolete.* an earthy feldspar.

clay|to|ni|a (klā tō′nē ə), *n.* any plant of a genus of low, rather succulent, chiefly North American, perennial herbs of the purslane family; spring beauty. [< New Latin *Claytonia* the genus name < John *Clayton,* 1693-1773, an American botanist]

C.L.C. or **CLC** (no periods), Canadian Labour Congress.

-cle, *suffix.* **1** little, as in *corpuscle, particle.* **2** other meanings, as in *receptacle, vehicle.*
[< Old French *-cle* < Latin *-culus, -cula, -culum,* or directly < Latin]

clead|ing (klē′ding), *n.* **1** *Scottish.* clothing. **2** *Engineering* and *Architecture.* a covering, casing, or lining, such as the felting put around steam pipes to prevent radiation. [< Scandinavian (compare Old Icelandic *klǣða* clothe) + English *-ing¹*]

clean (klēn), *adj., adv., v.* —*adj.* **1** free from dirt or filth; not soiled or stained: *clean clothes. Soap and water make us clean.* **2** having clean habits: *Cats are clean animals.* **3a** pure or innocent: *a man of good and clean life. The saint had a clean heart.* SYN: virtuous. **b** morally pure or proper; free of obscenity; decent: *a clean joke, a clean show.* **c** *U.S. Slang.* with no criminal record or without guilt: *The suspect claimed that he was clean.* **4** fair; honest: *a clean fight, a clean fighter.* **5a** clear, even, or regular; with no ragged edges: *a clean cut, the clean features of a handsome face.* **b** well-shaped; trim: *an airplane with clean, sleek lines.* **6** complete; entire; total: *to make a clean break with the past.* **7a** free from foreign matter; pure; unmixed: *a seam of good clean coal* (R. Brough Smyth). **b** *U.S. Slang.* without any weapons on one: *The gunman was caught, but by that time he was clean.* **c** *U.S. Slang.* free from the use of narcotics. **d** *U.S. Slang.* without money; penniless. **8** causing little or no radioactive fallout: *a clean nuclear bomb.* **9a** fit for food: *Moslems and Jews do not consider pork a clean meat.* **b** (of persons) free from ceremonial defilement according to Biblical law: *every one that is clean in thy house shall eat of it* (Numbers 18:11). **10** clever; skillful: *a clean performance.* **11a** (of written or typed copy) free from errors or corrections; final; fair. **b** (of printer's proofs) relatively free from corrections or alterations. **12** clear of obstructions; free from rocks or snags: *a clean coast, a clean harbor.* **13** of a ship: **a** having its bottom free of barnacles or other growths or adhesions. **b** having no cargo in its holds; empty: *The ship returned home clean.* **14** *Obsolete.* (of gems) free from anything that dims luster or transparency; clear.
—*adv.* **1** completely; entirely; totally: *The horse jumped clean over the brook.* **2** in a clean manner; cleanly; so as to leave no dirt: *The room must be clean swept.* **3** dexterously; adroitly: *Pope came off clean with Homer* (John Henley).
—*v.t.* **1** to make clean; cleanse: *to clean a room. Washing cleans cloths.* **2** to clear (arable land) of weeds, grass, or trees. **3** to clear (a ship's bottom) of barnacles, shells, or other debris. **4** to remove from (fish or the like) the parts unfit for food.
—*v.i.* **1** to undergo cleaning; admit of being cleaned: *The new rifle cleans easily.* **2** to do cleaning; perform a cleaning process: *Ships go there to clean. I'm going to clean this morning.*
clean out, a to make clean by emptying: *The premises were completely cleaned out. Clean out your desk.* **b** to empty; use up; exhaust: *The boys cleaned out a whole box of cookies. There is a great danger that a man's first life story shall clean him out, so to speak, of his best thoughts* (Oliver Wendell Holmes). **c** *Informal.* to eject (undesirable people) from a place: *I'd go up and clean 'em out* (Stewart Edward White). **d** *Slang.* to deprive of money; rook: *He . . . cleaned me out, but I can go and earn some more* (Dickens).
clean up, a to make clean by removing dirt, rubbish, or other debris: *They were all busy cleaning up the grounds.* **b** to put in order: *On the last day of school the children of the class cleaned up the contents of all the desks, drawers, and chests in the room.* **c** *Informal.* to finish; complete: *I cleaned up all my work.* **d** to free of undesirable persons: *the task of cleaning up New York.* **e** *Slang.* to make money; profit: *We ought to clean up five dollars a thousand on our mill* (Stewart Edward White).
come clean, *Slang.* to confess fully; tell everything; tell the whole truth: *To come clean, after making the trip twice this year, I found the city (N.Y.) exceedingly oppressive* (Manchester Guardian Weekly).
[Old English *clǣne*] —**clean′a|ble,** *adj.* —**clean′-ness,** *n.*

—***Syn.*** *v.t.* **1 Clean, cleanse** mean to make free from dirt or filth. **Clean** means to remove dirt, impurities, or stains, especially from objects: *to clean the windows. The men cleaned the streets.* **Cleanse** is sometimes applied to removing impurities by chemical or other technical processes: *Health experts are trying to cleanse the air in cities. We cleanse wounds.*

clean|a|bil|i|ty (klē′nə bil′ə tē), *n.* the quality of being cleanable; the character of being cleaned, especially repeatedly and well.

clean and jerk, an exercise in weight lifting in which the barbell is lifted from the floor, brought to rest against the chest, and raised above the head: *The clean and jerk is similar* [*to the military press*], *except that the contestant does not have to wait for the referee's signal* (T. K. Cureton, Jr.). —***v.i.*** to execute a clean and jerk. —***v.t.*** to lift (a weight) in this exercise: *The champion cleaned and jerked 464 lb.*

clean-cut (klēn′kut′), *adj.* **1** having clear, sharp outlines: *He has a clean-cut profile.* **2** well-shaped. **3** *Figurative.* clear; definite; distinct: *a clean-cut statement of fact.* **4** *Figurative.* having a neat and wholesome look: *a clean-cut young man.*

clean|er (klē′nər), *n.* **1** a person whose work is keeping buildings, windows, or other objects clean. **2** a tool or machine for cleaning. **3** anything that removes dirt, grease, or stains. **4a** a dry-cleaning establishment. **b** a person who owns or operates a dry-cleaning establishment.

clean-hand|ed (klēn′han′did), *adj.* not guilty of wrongdoing; free from blame. —**clean′-hand′ed-ness**, *n.*

clean hands, freedom from blame, guilt, or wrongdoing: *My Lord Treasurer ... is said to die with the cleanest hands that ever any Lord Treasurer died* (Samuel Pepys).

clean|ing woman (klē′ning), a woman who does house cleaning or cleaning in office buildings; charwoman.

clean-limbed (klēn′limd′), *adj.* having well-shaped limbs; well-proportioned; lithe.

clean-liv|ing (klēn′liv′ing), *adj.* leading a physically and morally clean life; neat and decent in character, habits, or the like.

clean|ly[1] (klen′lē), *adj.*, **-li|er, -li|est. 1a** clean; always, or nearly always, clean: *A cat is a cleanly animal.* **SYN**: neat, tidy. **b** (of personal belongings) habitually kept clean. **SYN**: neat, tidy. **2** *Obsolete.* morally or spiritually clean; pure; innocent [Old English *clǣnlīc*] —**clean′li|ly**, *adv.* —**clean′li-ness**, *n.*

clean|ly[2] (klēn′lē), *adv.* **1** in a clean manner; clearly; neatly; exactly: *The butcher's knife cut cleanly through the meat.* **2** *Obsolete.* ably; cleverly; adroitly; artfully. [Old English *clǣnlīce*]

clean|out (klēn′out′), *n.* **1** the act or process of cleaning out: [*He*] *... said that his cleanout of odd characters, logrollers, and misfits ... would result in a 40 per cent turnover in his department* (Newsweek). **2** an opening in a pipe, chimney, or other conduit to facilitate its cleaning.

clean room, a sterilized and pressurized room for laboratory work or for the manufacture of critical parts for space craft or electronic apparatus.

cleans|a|ble (klen′zə bəl), *adj.* that can be cleansed.

cleanse (klenz), *v.t.*, **cleansed, cleans|ing. 1** to make clean: *to cleanse a wound before bandaging it.* **SYN**: See syn. under **clean. 2** to make pure: *to cleanse the soul.* **SYN**: purify. [Middle English *clensen*, Old English *clǣnsian* < *clǣne* clean]

cleans|er (klen′zər), *n.* **1** a substance that cleans, especially by scouring. Soap and water are good cleansers. Detergents are chemical cleansers. **2** a person or thing that cleanses.

clean-shav|en (klēn′shā′vən), *adj.* with the facial hair or whiskers shaved off.

cleans|ing (klen′zing), *n., adj.* —***n.*** a making clean.
—***adj.*** that cleanses: *a cleansing agent.*

clean|skin (klēn′skin′), *n.* (in Australia) cattle and horses that have never been branded.

clean slate, a record unmarred by discreditable acts or failures: *Once out of prison, he hoped to start life again with a clean slate.*

clean sweep, any sweeping action or change: **a** the elimination of undesirable persons or activities; cleanup: *The insurgent group added that a "clean sweep" of the company's management was needed* (New York Times). **b** a large majority in an election; landslide. **c** the completely satisfactory performance of a ship tested for seaworthiness.

clean-tilled (klēn′tild′), *adj.* grown on land that is kept free from other ground cover: *Cotton, corn, and tobacco are clean-tilled crops, leaving the soil unprotected against the heavy monsoon rains* (White and Renner).

clean|up (klēn′up′), *n.* **1** the act or process of cleaning up, especially of vice, corruption, or illegal activity. **2** *Slang.* a large profit or gain, often acquired in a short period of time: *Few people make a cleanup in the stock market.* **3** *Baseball.* the fourth player to come to bat in any inning.

clear (klir), *adj., v., adv., n.* —***adj.*** **1a** not cloudy, misty, or hazy; bright; light: *a clear day. A clear sky is free of clouds.* **b** bright, lustrous; shining: *clear eyes.* **c** serene; calm: *His brow grew clear as the blue sky above him* (Bulwer-Lytton). **2** easy to see through; transparent: *clear glass.* **3** having a pure, even color: *a clear blue.* **4** easily seen, heard, or understood; not confused; plain; distinct: *a clear voice;* (*Figurative.*) *a clear idea, a clear text. He gave a clear account of the accident.* **SYN**: evident, obvious, manifest, apparent, patent. **5** free from blemishes: *Healthy babies have clear skin.* **6** sure; certain: *It is clear that it is going to rain.* (*Figurative.*) *I am clear in my own mind that I should give up the plan.* **SYN**: positive, confident, convinced. **7** not blocked or obstructed; open: *There is a clear view of the sea from that hill.* **8** not touching; not being caught: *The ship was clear of the iceberg.* **9** *Figurative.* free from blame or guilt; innocent: *a clear conscience. The police thought the man was a thief, but they learned that he was clear.* **10** *Figurative.* free from debts or charges: *He made a clear profit after taking money out to pay taxes and expenses.* **SYN**: net. **11** without limitation; complete: *the clear contrary.* **SYN**: absolute, sheer. **12** (of lumber) free from knots or other imperfections. **13** emptied of contents, cargo or load: *a clear ship.* **14** (of measurement of space or time) without deduction: *a brook seventeen feet clear from side to side.* **15** *U.S.* without admixture, adulteration, or dilution: *clear tea.* **16** *Phonetics.* (of *l*-sounds) not velarized. **17** *Obsolete.* illustrious.

—***v.t.*** **1a** to make clean and free; get clear; make open: *to clear the streets of traffic, clear a room of people. The pioneer cleared the land of trees. He cleared his throat and began to speak.* **b** to free from entangling contact; untangle; disengage: *to clear a fishing line.* **SYN**: extricate. **2a** to remove whatever lessens brightness, transparency, or purity of color from: *to clear a bathroom mirror of steam, clear muddy water by letting the mud settle.* **b** *Figurative.* to make clear to the mind: *He cleared his meaning by further explanation.* **3** to remove in order to leave a space free: *She cleared the dishes from the table.* **4a** to pass by or over without touching: *to clear an iceberg at sea. The horse cleared the fence in a tremendous leap.* **b** to free (a ship or cargo) by meeting requirements on entering or leaving a port. **c** to give authority to or for: *The control tower cleared the airplane for landing.* **5** *Figurative.* **a** to make free from blame or guilt; prove to be innocent: *The jury's verdict of innocence cleared the accused man. ... that will by no means clear the guilty* (Exodus 34:7). **SYN**: vindicate, acquit. **b** to certify as reliable for a position of trust or secrecy: *The scientists were cleared for secret research.* **6** *Figurative.* **a** to settle or pay: *money enough to clear all one's debts.* **b** to free from debt: *to clear an estate.* **7** *Figurative.* to make as profit free from debts or charges; net: *The company cleared a million dollars after taxes last year.* **8** to exchange (checks and bills) and settle accounts between different banks. **9** to empty: *to clear a warehouse.*

—***v.i.*** **1** to become clear or bright: *It rained and then it cleared. So foul a sky clears not without a storm* (Shakespeare). **2** of a ship: **a** to meet all requirements by port authorities on entering or leaving a port. **b** to leave a port after doing this. **3** to settle a business account or certify a check as valid.

—***adv.*** **1** in a clear manner. **2** completely; entirely: *The bullet went clear through the door. He climbed clear to the top.*

—***n.*** **1** a clear space. **2** *Badminton.* a stroke that sends the shuttle in a high arc over the opponent's head so that it will fall into the court behind him. **3** a flour just below the best quality flour and somewhat darker in color. It is used to make special kinds of bread or to mix with rye flour to make rye bread.

clear away, a to remove to leave a space clear: *He cleared away the snow with a shovel.* **b** to disappear; go away: *The fog cleared away.* **c** to clear dishes from a table: *They cleared away the lunch dishes and cleaned up the kitchen.*

clear inwards (or **in**), (of a ship) to comply with port rules and be free to discharge cargo: *The merchant ship began to unload as soon as it finished clearing inwards.*

clear off, a to remove something; clear away: *to clear off the dust from the furniture.* **b** to be off; leave a place clear: *On the sixth it cleared off, and the sun came out bright* (Richard H. Dana). *He asked the noisy boys to clear off.*

clear out, a to make clear by throwing out or emptying: *He cleared out his closet. A considerable ejection of ashes occured, which cleared out the crater* (John Phillips). **b** *Informal.* to go away; leave: *The audience cleared out of the burning theater quickly. Colonel Colden and the Dickenses came one night, ... and cleared out the next day* (George Ticknor). **c** (of a ship) to comply with port rules and be free to leave.

clear outwards, = clear out (def. c).

clear the air. See under **air**[1].

clear up, a to make clear: *You can clear up this mixture by passing it through a filter of carbon.* **b** to become clear: *Stay indoors until the weather clears up.* **c** to put in order by clearing: *to clear up a room.* **d** *Figurative.* to make clear to the mind; explain: *He cleared up the question of his absence by saying that he had been ill.*

in the clear, a between the outside parts; in interior measurement: *a house thirty feet long, and twenty broad, in the clear.* **b** *Figurative.* free of guilt, blame, or suspicion; innocent: *The testimony of the witness puts the suspected thief in the clear.* **c** free from limitations or encumbrances: *The title to his property was in the clear.* **d** in plaintext; not in cipher or code: *Not having enough time to code the message they decided to send it in the clear.*

[< Old French *cler* < Latin *clārus* clear, bright, famous] —**clear′ness**, *n.*

clear|a|ble (klir′ə bəl), *adj.* that can be cleared; able to be put in order.

clear air turbulence, a violent disturbance in air currents, caused by rapid changes of temperature associated with the jet stream. Clear air turbulence is characterized by severe updrafts and downdrafts that affect jet aircraft flying at high altitudes. *Abbr:* CAT (no periods).

clear|ance (klir′əns), *n.* **1** the act of clearing: *Clearance of the theater was quick during the fire.* **2a** a clear space; distance between things that pass by each other without touching: *There was only a foot of clearance between the top of the truck and the roof of the tunnel.* **b** the space between the piston and cylinder head in an engine on dead center. **c** the distance by which the point of a tooth on a gearwheel misses the bottom of the space between teeth on the mating gear. **3** *Figurative.* the act or process of certifying that a person considered for a position of trust is reliable. **4** = clearance sale. **5a** the meeting of requirements to get a ship or cargo free on entering or leaving a port. **b** Also, **clearance papers**, the certificate showing this: *The clearance is the certificate of the customhouse authorities of the last port from which the vessel came that the custom duties have been paid* (Frederick G. D. Bedford). **6** *Banking.* the exchanging of checks and bills and settling of accounts between different banks through a clearing house.

clearance sale, a sale of goods at reduced prices in order to clear away old or superfluous stock.

clear channel, a radio frequency reserved for use by one station.

clear|cole (klir′kōl), *n.* **1** (in painting) a preparation of size put on an absorbent surface to prevent the sinking in of subsequent coats of paint. **2** (in gilding) a coating of size over which gold leaf is to be applied. [< French *clair colle* clear glue]

clear-cut (klir′kut′), *adj.* **1** having clear, sharp outlines: *The handsome actor had clear-cut features ... a cold and clear-cut face* (Tennyson). **SYN**: chiseled, well-defined. **2** *Figurative.* definite; distinct: *Having planned carefully, he had clear-cut ideas about how to do his work.* **SYN**: precise, exact.

clear|er (klir′ər), *n.* **1** a person or thing that clears or renders clear. **2** a tank or reservoir used in condensing salt from brine. **3** a revolving roller with wire brushes which strips cotton, wool, or the like, off the cylinder in a carding machine. **4** a person who passes checks or bills through a clearing house.

clear-eyed (klir′īd′), *adj.* **1** having clear eyes. **2** *Figurative.* having clear, undistorted perception: *These stories are told with the clear-eyed detachment of a mature adult and with an unobtrusive but telling compassion* (Atlantic).

clear-head|ed (klir′hed′id), *adj.* having or showing a clear understanding. —**clear′-head′ed|ly**, *adv.* —**clear′-head′ed|ness**, *n.*

clear|ing (klir′ing), *n.* **1** an open space of cleared land in a forest or in an area of dense undergrowth: *A little beyond Grand river we came to a clearing, and looking into it, saw a handsome house about 500 yards distant* (John Melish).

2 *Banking.* the exchanging of checks and bills and settling of accounts between different banks, usually through a clearing house. **3** the act of a person or thing that clears; brightening, clarifying, or the like.

clearings, *Banking.* the total of the accounts settled in the process of clearing: *A rise in clearings since last month has been reported by the Federal Reserve System.*

clearing bank, any one of a group of large British banks that are members of the London Clearing House: *All the clearing banks except Barclays now issue cheque guarantee cards* (London Times).

clearing house, or **clear|ing|house** (klir′ing-hous′), *n.* **1** a place where banks exchange checks and bills and settle their accounts. Only the balances are paid in cash. **2** any institution of a similar nature in which claims or differences are settled.

clearing nut, a seed of a tree related to the nux vomica, used in the East Indies for clearing muddy water. A seed is rubbed around the inside of a vessel of water, which is then left to settle, all the impurities soon falling to the bottom.

clearing ring, a heavy, jointed, metal ring run down a fishing line to free the line and hook when entangled in an obstacle.

clear|ings (klir′ingz), *n.pl.* See under **clearing.**

clear|ly (klir′lē), *adv.* **1** without obscurity; distinctly: *The top of the mountain rose clearly above us* (John Tyndall). **2** *Figurative.* with full and complete understanding: *There is no choice of words for him who clearly sees the truth* (Emerson). **3** *Figurative.* with clearness and distinctness of expression or exposition; plainly: *Once more; speak clearly, if you speak at all* (Oliver Wendell Holmes). **4** *Figurative.* so as to leave no doubt; manifestly; evidently: *That, by the old constitution, no military authority was lodged in the Parliament, Mr. Hallam has clearly shown* (Macaulay).

clear obscure, = chiaroscuro.

clear|out (klir′out′), *n. British.* the act or process of clearing out; cleanup.

clear-sight|ed (klir′sī′tid), *adj.* **1** able to see clearly. **2** *Figurative.* able to understand or think clearly. **SYN**: discerning, perspicacious. — **clear′-sight′ed|ly**, *adv.* — **clear′-sight′ed|ness**, *n.*

clear|starch (klir′stärch′), *v., n.* — ***v.t., v.i.*** to stiffen with clearstarch.
— ***n.*** a starch, for stiffening clothes, that has been boiled until it is clear.

clear|sto|ry (klir′stôr′ē, -stōr′-), *n., pl.* **-ries.** = clerestory.

clear|way (klir′wā′), *n. British.* **1** a highway on which motor vehicles may not stop or park. **2** a path or passageway.

clear|wing (klir′wing′), *n.* a moth with wings that are mainly transparent and scaleless.

cleat (klēt), *n., v.* — ***n.*** **1** a strip of wood or iron fastened across anything for support or for sure footing: *The gangway had cleats to keep passengers from slipping.* **2** a small, wedge-shaped block fastened to a spar, yard, or the like, for a support, check, or the like. **3** a piece of wood or iron, usually with two arms, used for securing ropes or lines, especially to a flagpole or a dock. **4** a piece of metal, wood, hard rubber, plastic, or stiff leather attached to the sole or heel of a shoe to prevent slipping. **5** the principal set of the cleavage planes found in mining coal.
— ***v.t.*** **1** to fasten to or with a cleat. **2** to furnish with cleats: *Cleated step plates may be screwed to the gunwales of small craft to give crewmen secure footing* (Science News Letter).
[Middle English *cleete* wedge, wedge-shaped piece. See related etym. at **clot.**]

cleav|a|bil|i|ty (klē′və bil′ə tē), *n.* capability of cleavage.

cleav|age (klē′vij), *n.* **1** the act of cleaving or state of being cleft; split; division: (*Figurative.*) *There is little to look upon with pleasure amidst this cleavage of party ties and rending of old associations* (Fortnightly Review). **2a** the way in which something tends to split. **b** *Mineralogy.* the tendency of some minerals to split along definite directions producing an even surface: *Slate and mica show a marked cleavage and can easily be separated into layers.* **3a** *Embryology.* any one of the series of divisions by which the single cell of a fertilized egg develops into the many-celled embryo, or the whole series. **b** *Biology.* = cell division. **4** *Chemistry.* the splitting of a compound into simpler compounds. **5** the cleft between a woman's breasts, as is displayed in a low-cut garment.

cleavage nucleus, *Embryology.* the nucleus which results from the union of the male and female pronuclei, before the division of the egg into two blastomeres.

cleavage spindle, *Embryology.* the karyokinetic spindle of a dividing blastomere, during the early development of the ovum.

cleave[1] (klēv), *v.,* **cleft** or **cleaved** or **clove, cleft** or **cleaved** or **clo|ven, cleav|ing.** — ***v.t.*** **1a** to cut, divide, or split open; hew asunder: *A blow of the whale's tail cleft our boat in two.* **b** to pass through; pierce; penetrate: *The airplane swept across the sky, cleaving the clouds.* **2** to make by cutting: *They cleft a path through the woods.*
— ***v.i.*** **1** to split with a smooth, plane fracture, or in layers; fall asunder. **2** to cut one's way; penetrate; pass.
[Old English *clēofan*] — **cleav′a|ble**, *adj.*

cleave[2] (klēv), *v.i.,* **cleaved** or (*Archaic*) **clave, cleaved, cleav|ing.** to hold fast; cling: *to cleave to an idea. He was so frightened that his tongue cleaved to the roof of his mouth. For I cleaved to a cause that I felt to be pure and true* (Tennyson). [Old English *cleofian*]

cleav|er (klē′vər), *n.* **1** a cutting tool with a heavy blade and a short handle. A butcher uses a cleaver to chop through meat or bone. **2** a prehistoric stone tool with a broad cutting edge. **3** a person who cleaves.

cleav|ers (klē′vərz), *n.sing. and pl.* any one of various climbing plants of the madder family, which adhere by short, hooked bristles to hedges, clothing, or hide. Also, **clivers.** [< *cleave*[2] + *-er*[1] + *-s*[1]]

cleek (klēk), *n., v.,* **claught** or **cleeked, cleek|ing.** — ***n.*** **1** a golf club with a narrow or small head and less slope than a midiron, used for long-distance shots. It may be the "number 1 iron" but it is now usually the "number 4 wood." *It was a day of furious wind by the sea and Mr. Hutchison was stealthily progressing by half cleek shots which kept the ball close to the ground* (Atlantic). **2** *Scottish.* a large hook.
— ***v.t.*** *Scottish.* to seize firmly or suddenly; clutch. Also, **cleik.**
[related to **clutch**]

*****clef** (klef), *n.* a symbol in music indicating the pitch of the notes on a staff. The three clefs are *G* (treble), *F* (bass), and the less commonly used *C* (soprano, alto, or tenor). The forms of the clefs derive ultimately from the shapes of those letters. The staff line where a clef is located is assigned the same pitch as the tone represented by the clef. The tones of the three clefs are the G above middle C, the F below it, and middle C. [< French *clef* < Latin *clāvis* key. See etym. of doublet **clave**[2].]

G clef or treble clef: **F clef or bass clef:**

*** clef**

G middle C F middle C

C clefs:

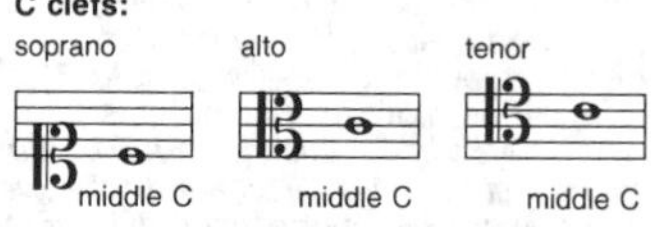

cleft (kleft), *v., adj., n.* — ***v.*** a past tense and a past participle of **cleave**[1]: *His blow cleft the log in two.*
— ***adj.*** **1** split or divided to a certain depth; bifurcate: *a cleft stick.* **2** split into thin pieces. **3** divided into lobes by notches extending halfway, or somewhat further, from the margin to the midrib or to the base: *a cleft leaf.*
— ***n.*** **1** a space or opening made by splitting; crack: *a deep cleft in the rocks.* **SYN**: fissure, crevice, chink, split. **2** a hollow part, such as a dimple: *a cleft on the chin.* **3** a split in the pastern or hoof of a horse.
in a cleft stick. See under **stick**[1].

cleft-graft (kleft′graft′, -gräft′), *v.t.* to engraft (a plant) by cleaving the stock and inserting a cutting.

cleft lip, = harelip.

cleft palate, a narrow opening running lengthwise in the roof of the mouth, caused by failure of the two parts of the palate to join before birth.

cleg (kleg), *n. British.* a gadfly. [Middle English *cleg* < Scandinavian (compare Old Icelandic *kleggi*)]

cleik (klēk), *n., v.t.* = cleek.

cleis|to|gam|ic (klīs′tə gam′ik), *adj.* = cleistogamous.

cleis|tog|a|mous (klīs tog′ə məs), *adj.* having small, self-pollinating flowers that do not open, in addition to regular flowers: *The violet is a cleistogamous plant.*

cleis|tog|a|my (klīs tog′ə mē), *n.* the condition of having small flowers that do not open, but are pollinated from their own anthers in addition to the normal, larger, brightly colored flowers, as in the violet. [< Greek *kleistós* closed + English *-gamy*]

cleith|ral (klī′thrəl), *adj.* having a roof; roofed over: *a cleithral temple.* Also, **clithral.** [< Greek *kleîthron* closing bar + English *-al*[1]]

clem (klem), *v.,* **clemmed, clem|ming.** *British Dialect.* — ***v.t.*** to pinch with hunger, parch with thirst, or benumb with cold.
— ***v.i.*** to suffer from hunger, thirst, or cold. Also, **clam.**
[origin uncertain. Compare Dutch and German *klemmen* pinch.]

clem|a|tis (klem′ə tis), *n.* a climbing vine with clusters of large, white, red, pink, blue, or purple flowers; virgin's-bower. Clematis is a perennial plant which belongs to the crowfoot family. *The clematis seed trails a long feathery plume* (Vernon Quinn). [< Latin *clēmatis* < Greek *klēmatis* a climbing vine < *klêma* vine, branch]

clem|en|cy (klem′ən sē), *n., pl.* **-cies. 1** gentleness in the use of power or authority; mercy or leniency: *The judge showed clemency to the prisoner.* **SYN**: See syn. under **mercy. 2** mildness: *The clemency of the weather allowed them to live outdoors.* [< Latin *clēmentia* calmness, gentleness < *clēmēns, -entis* calm, mild]

clem|ent (klem′ənt), *adj.* **1** merciful toward those in one's power; lenient: *I know you are more clement than vile men, who of their broken debtors take a third* (Shakespeare). **SYN**: kind, compassionate. **2** mild: *Hawaii usually has clement weather.* **SYN**: gentle. — **clem′ent|ly**, *adv.*

clench (klench), *v., n.* — ***v.t.*** **1** to close tightly together: *to clench one's teeth or hand, a clenched fist.* **2** to grasp firmly; grip tightly; clutch: *She clenched my arm in terror.* **3** to clinch (a nail or staple).
— ***n.*** **1** a firm grasp; tight grip: *I felt the clench of his hand on my arm as I began to slip.* **2** a clinch (of a nail or a staple).
[Old English *-clencan,* in *beclencan* hold fast]
— ***Syn.*** *v.t.* **2 Clench, clinch** mean to hold fast or tightly. **Clench** emphasizes holding fast by closing tightly the teeth, lips, etc., or grasping firmly in the fist: *The reporter clenched his pencil in his teeth while he wiped his glasses.* **Clinch** suggests fastening securely: *Clinch the nails to a board.* Figuratively, as in *to clinch an argument,* it means to settle decisively.

clench|er (klen′chər), *n.* **1** a person or thing that clenches. **2** *Figurative.* a decisive argument; clincher.

cle|o|me (klē ō′mē), *n.* any plant of a group of chiefly tropical herbs and shrubs of the caper family, bearing showy flowers. [< New Latin *Cleome;* origin uncertain]

clepe (klēp), *v.t.,* **cleped** or **clept** (also **ycleped** or **yclept**), **clep|ing. 1** *Archaic.* to call by the name of. **2** *Obsolete.* to call; summon. [Old English *cleopian*]

clep|sy|dra (klep′sə drə), *n., pl.* **-dras, -drae** (-drē). a device used by the ancients for measuring time by the flow of water, mercury, or some other liquid, through a small opening. [< Latin *clepsydra* < Greek *klepsýdra* water clock < *kléptein* steal + *hýdōr* water]

clep|to|ma|ni|a (klep′tə mā′nē ə), *n.* = kleptomania.

clep|to|ma|ni|ac (klep′tə mā′nē ak), *n.* = kleptomaniac.

*****clere|sto|ry** (klir′stôr′ē, -stōr′-), *n., pl.* **-ries. 1** the upper part of the wall of a church, having windows in it above the roofs of the aisles. **2** any similar structure, such as a raised section of roof on a building or railroad car, having windows, for lighting or ventilation. Also, **clearstory.** [perhaps < earlier *clere* clear, bright + *story*[2]]

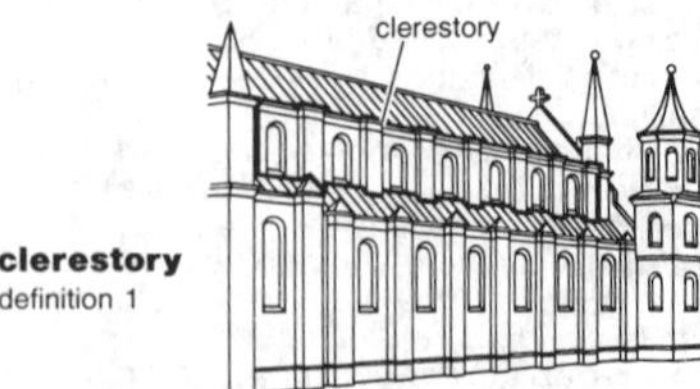

*** clerestory**
definition 1

cler|gy (klėr′jē), *n., pl.* **-gies.** persons ordained for religious work; ministers, pastors or rectors, priests, and rabbis. [< Old French *clergie* < Medieval Latin *clericatus* < Latin *clēricus* cleric]

cler|gy|man (klėr′jē mən), *n., pl.* **-men.** a member of the clergy; minister, pastor or rector, priest, or rabbi: *By a clergyman, I mean one in holy orders* (Sir Richard Steele). **SYN**: cleric, ecclesiastic.

cler|gy|wom|an (klėr′jē wu̇m′ən), *n., pl.* **-wom|en. 1** a woman minister. **2** a woman belonging to a clergyman's household: *From the clergywomen of Windholm down to the charwomen the question was discussed* (Margaret

Wilson Oliphant). 3 *Obsolete.* a woman dedicated to religion, such as a nun.

cler|ic (kler′ik), *n., adj.* **—n. 1** = clergyman. **2** (in the Roman Catholic Church) a man whose head has been partially shaved as a rite preparatory to becoming a priest or monk; clerk.
—adj. of a clergyman or the clergy; clerical.
[< Latin *clēricus* priest. See etym. of doublet **clerk**.]

cler|i|cal (kler′ə kəl), *adj., n.* **—adj. 1** of a clerk or clerks; for clerks: *Keeping records or accounts and typing letters are clerical jobs in an office.* **2** of a clergyman or the clergy: *The minister performed clerical duties in church. The priest wore clerical robes in church.* **3** supporting the power or influence of the clergy in politics.
—n. 1 = clergyman. **2** Also, **Clerical.** a supporter of the power or influence of the clergy in politics.
clericals, the distinctive clothes worn by certain clergymen: *He tucked and pulled nervously at his clericals, and then signaled for silence by clearing his throat* (New Yorker).
[< Late Latin *clēricālis* clerical, priestly < Latin *clēricus* cleric] **—cler′i|cal|ly,** *adv.*

clerical collar, a stiff, white band worn around the neck by clergymen.

cler|i|cal|ism (kler′ə kə liz′əm), *n.* **1a** the power or influence of the clergy in politics: *... the indignities of militarism and clericalism in Spain and Latin America* (Harper's). **b** the support of such power or influence. **2** the principles or practices of clerics or of a clerical party. **—cler′i|cal|ist,** *n.*

cler|i|cal|i|ty (kler′ə kal′ə tē), *n., pl.* **-ties. 1** clerical character or condition. **2** clerical trait or action.

cler|i|cal|ize (kler′ə kə līz), *v.t.,* **-ized, -iz|ing.** to render clerical; exalt the influence of the clergy in: *Socialists accused Catholics of trying to "clericalize" the predominantly Catholic nation* (Newsweek).

cler|i|cals (kler′ə kəlz), *n.pl.* See under **clerical.**

cler|i|ca|ture (kler′ə kə chər), *n.* clerical position or authority.

cler|i|hew (kler′ə hyü), *n.* a humorous jingle in four lines, about a person, supposedly biographical.
Example:
"Sir Christopher Wren
Said 'I'm going to dine with some men.
If anybody calls
Say I'm designing St. Paul's.' "
[< Edmund *Clerihew* Bentley, 1875-1956, an English detective-fiction writer, who devised the form]

cler|i|sy (kler′ə sē), *n.* learned men as a class or group; scholars; literati. [(introduced by Samuel T. Coleridge) < Medieval Latin *clericia* < Latin *clēricus* cleric]

clerk (klėrk; *British* klärk), *n., v.* **—n. 1** *U.S. and Canada.* a person whose work is waiting on customers and selling goods in a store; salesman or saleswoman: *The clerk sold me a dress.* **2** a person whose work is filing records, typing letters, and keeping accounts in an office: *The office clerk filed the letters.* **3** a public official who keeps the records and takes care of routine business in a law court, legislature, town or county government, etc.: *a county clerk, a court clerk.* **4** a layman who has minor church duties. **5a** *Archaic.* a clergyman. **b** = cleric (def. 2). **6** *Archaic.* a person who can read and write; scholar.
—v.i. to work as a clerk: *He clerks in a drugstore after school.*
[partly Old English *clerc, cleric,* and partly < Old French *clerc,* both < Latin *clēricus* < Greek *klērikós* of an allotment < *klêros* the clergy, (originally) a lot, something chosen by lot. See etym. of doublet **cleric.**]

clerk|dom (klėrk′dəm; *British* klärk′dəm), *n.* the condition or fact of being a clerk.

clerk|ish (klėr′kish; *British* klär′kish), *adj.* somewhat like a clerk; suggestive of a clerk, especially in having an unusual interest in small details and, often, a somewhat petty nature: *He is generally a precise, clerkish man, who files the medical articles from the Reader's Digest* (Atlantic).

clerk|ly (klėr′klē; *British* klär′klē), *adj., adv.* **—adj. 1** of or like a clerk; clerkish. **2** of the clergy. **3** *Archaic.* scholarly.
—adv. in the manner of a clerk. **—clerk′li|ness,** *n.*

clerk of the weather, *British.* an imaginary functionary humorously supposed to control the state of the weather.

clerk of the works, a superintendent of the construction of buildings who makes certain that the plans and specifications of the architect are carried out.

clerk regular, *pl.* **clerks regular.** a member of a Roman Catholic religious order who lives in community under a rule but is engaged in active work as a priest. The Jesuits are clerks regular.

clerk|ship (klėrk′ship; *British* klärk′ship), *n.* the position or work of a clerk.

clerk|y (klėr′kē; *British* klär′kē), *adj.* = clerkish.

cle|ro|man|cy (klir′ə man′sē), *n.* divination by throwing dice or lots. [< Medieval Latin *cleromantia* < Greek *klêros* lot + *manteíā* divination]

cle|ruch (klir′ük, -ək), *n.* a citizen in ancient Athens who received an allotment of land in conquered foreign territory, but retained his Athenian citizenship. [< Greek *klēroúchos* < *klêros* lot + *échein* have]

cleth|ra (kleth′rə), *n.* any plant of a group of native American shrubs and trees bearing five-petaled white flowers. [< New Latin *Clethra* the genus name < Greek *klêthra* alder]

cleugh or **cleuch** (klyüн, klüн), *n. Scottish.* a ravine. [< *clough*]

cleve|ite (klē′vīt), *n.* a radioactive, crystallized kind of uraninite from Norway. [< Per T. *Cleve,* 1840-1905, a Swedish chemist + *-ite*[1]]

Cleve|land Bay (klēv′lənd), any one of a breed of sturdy English coach horses. [< *Cleveland,* an area of Yorkshire, England, where it was first bred]

clev|er (klev′ər), *adj.* **1** having a quick mind; bright; intelligent: *She is the cleverest person in our family.* **2** skillful in doing some particular thing: *He is a very clever carpenter.* **SYN:** dexterous, deft, adroit. **3** showing skill or intelligence: *The magician did a clever trick. Her answer to the riddle was clever.* **4** *U.S. Dialect.* good-natured; obliging; amiable. **5** *Dialect.* convenient; agreeable. [Middle English *cliver;* origin uncertain] **—clev′er|ly,** *adv.* **—clev′er|ness,** *n.*
—Syn. 1 Clever, ingenious mean having a quick mind. **Clever** is the general word, and suggests a natural quickness in learning things and skill in using the mind: *He had no training, but was clever enough to become a good salesman.* **Ingenious** means quick to see ways of doing things and skillful in inventing: *Some ingenious person thought of the can opener.*

Clever Dick, *British Slang.* a clever or overly clever person; know-it-all: *Clever Dicks do indeed declare half their income, but the tax man multiplies this by four ...* (Punch).

clev|er|ish (klev′ər ish), *adj.* somewhat clever.

***clev|is** (klev′is), *n.* a U-shaped piece of metal, with a bolt or pin passing through holes at the two ends, for joining a chain or rod to another: *He fastened the handle to the wagon with a clevis.* [perhaps related to **cleave**[1]]

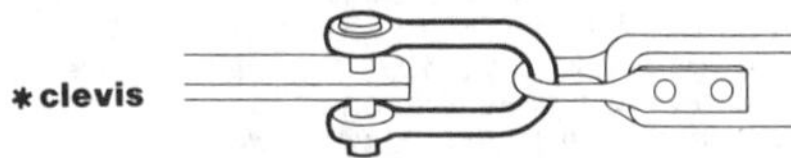

***clevis**

clew (klü), *n., v.* **—n. 1** = clue (def. 1). **2** a ball of thread or yarn. **3** (in ancient legend) a ball of thread unwound to serve as a guide through a labyrinth or maze. **4** *Nautical.* **a** a lower corner of a square sail, or the aftermost lower corner of a fore-and-aft sail. **b** a metal ring fastened there, to which lines are attached; clew iron. **5** the combination of small cords by which a hammock is suspended.
—v.t. 1 *Nautical.* to raise or lower (a sail) by the clews or clew lines. **2** to coil into a ball: *to lie ... clewed up like a hedgehog* (Scott). **3** = clue (def. 1). Also, **clue.**
[Old English *cleowen* ball, conglomeration]

clew iron, a metal ring in the clew of a sail.

clew line, a line attached to the clew of a sail and used in hauling it up to reef.

cli|an|thus (klī an′thəs), *n.* any plant of a genus of shrubs or vines of the pea family, native to Australia and New Zealand and cultivated for their handsome flowers, as the glory-pea. [< New Latin *Clianthus* < Greek *kléos* fame, glory + *ánthos* flower]

cli|ché (klē shā′), *n., adj.* **—n. 1** an expression or idea worn out by long use. "Father Time," "white as snow," and "cheeks like roses" are clichés. *Our complacent cliché is that nervous breakdowns are a prerogative of the rich* (Dwight Macdonald). **SYN:** platitude, commonplace. **2** a trite or overused plot, scene, effect, or the like: *The show tamely follows the musical comedy cliché of a woman voluntarily tied to a scoundrel* (Saturday Review). **SYN:** stereotype. **3** an electrotype or stereotype plate.
—adj. hackneyed; stereotyped: *Heroes standing for greatness in the traditional mold tend to become colorless and cliché* (Daniel J. Boorstin). [< French *cliché,* past participle of *clicher* to stereotype]

cli|chéd (klē shād′), *adj.* representing a cliché or clichés; commonplace; stereotyped: *It [the book] never rests on the clichéd glories of the old sod* (Saturday Review). **SYN:** hackneyed, banal.

click (klik), *n., v.* **—n. 1** a short, sharp sound like that of a key turning in a lock: *With a click of the switch the light went on.* **2** = pawl. **3** *Phonetics.* any one of a class of sounds, found mostly in certain South African languages, produced by withdrawing the tongue with a sucking action from a part of the mouth with which it has been in contact: *Clicks are phonemic in a few languages, but in many more are used in a few special words, as signals to animals, or as exclamatory expressions* (Henry A. Gleason).
—v.i. 1 to make a short, sharp sound: *The key clicked in the lock.* **2** *Slang.* **a** to come to an understanding; be in harmony; agree: *I clicked with him right from the start.* **b** to go well; be effective or successful: *Will this scene of our play click? The writer clicked with his first story.* **c** to become clear to the mind or memory: *Somehow his explanation doesn't click. The name clicked and I suddenly remembered her.*
—v.t. to cause (anything) to make a clicking noise: *The soldier clicked his heels and saluted.*
click off, to register mechanically: *The turnstiles clicked off 158,220 paid visitors* (New York Times). *He clicked off 300,000 miles in a battered 1953 Mercury station wagon* (Time).
clicks, *British.* brief atmospheric disturbances in radio communication: *Repeated clicks interfered with the transmission of the pilot's message.*
[imitative] **—click′er,** *n.*

click beetle, a beetle that makes a click when it springs, as in turning over from its back; snapping beetle; elaterid.

click|et|y-clack (klik′ə tē klak′), *n., v.* **—n.** the sound of clicks and clacks in succession, especially characteristic of railroad cars in motion.
—v.i. to make such a sound.

click|et|y-click (klik′ə tē klik′), *n., v.i.* = clickety-clack.

clicks (kliks), *n.pl.* See under **click.**

cli|ent (klī′ənt), *n.* **1** a person or group for whom a lawyer, certified public accountant, architect, or other professional person or service acts: *The lawyers have a saying that "the man who pleads his own case has a fool for a client"* (George C. Harlan). **2** = customer: *The clients of that fashionable dress shop are very rich.* **3** a person who receives assistance from a social-service agency or similar organization: *a welfare client.* **4** a person who is under the protection or patronage of another; dependent. **5** a poor or humble person in ancient Rome depending on a noble or wealthy man for assistance. **6** = client state. [< Latin *cliēns, -entis* follower of a patron, related to *clīnāre* to lean] **—cli′ent|less,** *adj.*

cli|en|tage (klī′ən tij), *n.* a group of clients, collectively; followers; clientele.

cli|en|tal (klī en′təl, klī′ən-), *adj.* of or having to do with a client or clients.

cli|en|tele (klī′ən tel′), *n.* **1** clients as a group: *a lawyer's clientele.* **2** a body of customers, supporters, or other patrons: *the clientele of a theater.* **3** a body of dependents; a following. **4** number of clients. [< French *clientele,* learned borrowing from Latin *clientēla* the patron-client relationship < *cliēns* client]

cli|ent|ship (klī′ənt ship), *n.* the condition or relation of a client.

client state, a country that is economically or politically dependent on a larger state: *South Africa would gladly allow these black client states to follow what internal policies they liked* (Harper's).

cliff (klif), *n.* a very steep slope of rock or clay: *The cliff overlooks the river fall below.* **SYN:** precipice, bluff. [Old English *clif.* Probably related to **cleave**[1].] **—cliff′like′,** *adj.*

cliff dweller, 1 an Indian in the southwestern United States who lived in prehistoric times in a cave or a house built into a cliff. The cliff dwellers were ancestors of the Pueblo Indians. **2** *Slang.* a person living in a large apartment house; city dweller.

cliff dwelling, a cave or house built into a cliff.

cliff|hang (klif′hang′), *v.i. Slang.* **1** to undergo the suspense of a cliffhanger: *He [Eugene O'Neill] can put a character in a preposterous situation and still make the playgoer cliffhang over the outcome* (Time). **2** to write or produce a cliffhanger.

cliff|hang|er (klif′hang′ər), *n., adj. Slang.* **—n.** a story, play, motion picture, or real situation that depends on unusually strong and sustained suspense for its dramatic interest: *... a script for a Hollywood cliffhanger* (Newsweek).
—adj. suspenseful; cliffhanging: *This episode starts out as a light-hearted doctor and nurse romance ... and ends on a cliffhanger note: "He isn't going to die, is he?"* (Wall Street Journal).

Pronunciation Key: hat, **ā**ge, c**ã**re, f**ä**r; let, **ē**qual, t**ė**rm; it, **ī**ce; hot, **ō**pen, **ô**rder; **oi**l, **ou**t; cup, p**ů**t, r**ü**le; **ch**ild; lo**ng**; **th**in; **ᴛʜ**en; **zh**, measure;
ə represents **a** in about, **e** in taken, **i** in pencil, **o** in lemon, **u** in circus.

cliff|hang|ing (klif′hang′ing), *adj. Slang.* suspenseful: *a cliffhanging contest.*

cliff|side (klif′sīd′), *n.* the side or face of a cliff.

cliff swallow, a North American swallow that builds a bottle-shaped nest of mud, straw, and feathers, and usually fastens it to a cliff or wall.

cliff|y (klif′ē), *adj.* having or formed by cliffs; craggy.

cli|mac|ter|ic (klī mak′tər ik, klī′mak ter′-), *n., adj.* —*n.* **1** a time when some important event occurs, changing the course of things; crucial period: *Italy's climacteric came in 1948, when Signor Alcide de Gasperi was returned as Prime Minister in the first elections since the new Constitution* (Observer). **2** a period of life when the body becomes fundamentally changed, especially the period of the menopause in women or a similar time of change in men.
—***adj.*** of or like a period when some important event or change occurs; crucial: *The Korean War gave China her great opportunity ... to get Russia out of North Korea—an aspect of that climacteric conflict which we in the West all too easily overlooked* (Edward Crankshaw). **SYN**: critical.
[< Latin *clīmactēricus* < Greek *klīmaktērikós* of a critical period < *klīmaktēr* rung of a ladder < *klîmax* ladder < *klī́nein* lean, incline]

cli|mac|ter|i|cal (klī′mak ter′ə kəl), *adj., n.* = climacteric.

cli|mac|tic (klī mak′tik), *adj.* of or forming a climax: *a climactic scene in a play.* —**cli|mac′ti|cal|ly**, *adv.*

cli|mac|ti|cal (klī mak′tə kəl), *adj.* = climactic.

cli|ma|tal (klī′mə təl), *adj.* = climatic.

cli|mate (klī′mit), *n.* **1** the kind of weather a place has over a period of years. Climate includes conditions of heat and cold, moisture and dryness, clearness and cloudiness, wind and calm. *For 50 years or more ... the climate of the Arctic has been warming up* (Time). **2** a region with certain conditions of heat and cold, rainfall, wind, sunlight, and other aspects of weather: *The doctor ordered him to go to a drier climate to relieve his asthma.* **3** *Figurative.* the condition of feeling that exists, especially at some particular time: *The climate of public opinion just before the Revolutionary War was against new British taxes. Some of our progress toward brotherhood is traceable to changes in the economic and educational climate* (Saturday Review). **SYN**: environment, surroundings. [< Latin *clima, -atis* < Greek *klíma; -atos* slope (of the earth) < *klī́nein* to incline]

cli|mat|ic (klī mat′ik), *adj.* of or having to do with climate; climatal: *Given a relatively uniform temperature, rainfall is the most effective climatic agent in soil forming and conditioning* (R. N. Elston). —**cli|mat′i|cal|ly**, *adv.*

cli|mat|i|cal (klī mat′ə kəl), *adj.* = climatic.

climatic year, a year selected for the presentation of data on water supply, precipitation, and the like. The climatic year of the United States Geological Survey extends from October 1 through September 30 of the following year.

cli|ma|ti|za|tion (klī′mə tə zā′shən), *n.* **1** = acclimation. **2** the designing of equipment, as of an aircraft, capable of operating within a range of temperatures under any climatic conditions: *One of the most important space medical problems is the climatization of the cabin* (Hubertus Strughold).

cli|ma|tize (klī′mə tīz), *v.,* **-tized, -tiz|ing.** —***v.t.*** to accustom to a new climate; acclimate: *A plant can climatize itself to new environments.*
—***v.i.*** to become acclimated.

cli|ma|to|log|ic (klī′mə tə loj′ik), *adj.* of climatology: *climatologic science.*

cli|ma|to|log|i|cal (klī′mə tə loj′ə kəl), *adj.* of or having to do with climatology.

cli|ma|tol|o|gist (klī′mə tol′ə jist), *n.* a person who studies climatology: *The climatologist studies the average distribution of weather elements over the earth as well as their relationship ... to the features of the earth's surface* (Neuberger and Stephens).

cli|ma|tol|o|gy (klī′mə tol′ə jē), *n.* the science that deals with climate and climatic conditions.

cli|ma|tom|e|ter (klī′mə tom′ə tər), *n.* an instrument used to detect fluctuations in the conditions of sensible temperature.

cli|mat|o|ther|a|py (klī′mə tō ther′ə pē), *n.* the treatment of disease by means of a favorable climate.

cli|ma|tron (klī′mə tron), *n.* a building or enclosure in which temperature and humidity may be controlled to provide an artificial climate or climates. [< Latin *clima* climate + English *-tron*]

cli|max (klī′maks), *n., v.* —*n.* **1** the highest point of interest; most exciting part: *The climax of his trip to Washington was a visit with the President.* **SYN**: peak, zenith, culmination, acme. **2a** the turning point in a drama, novel, or other literary work. **b** the action or event that determines the outcome. **3** *Rhetoric.* **a** an arrangement of ideas in a rising scale of force and interest. **b** the last or highest of such a figure. **4** *Ecology.* **a** a plant or animal community that is relatively stable, its dominant species having thoroughly adapted themselves to the environment. **b** the stage in which a community achieves or develops such stability. **5** = orgasm. **6** the concluding section of a fugue, which often contains the stretto.
—***v.t., v.i.*** to bring or come to a climax; be the climax (of): *Election to the Presidency climaxed his long career in politics. Agreement on the test-ban treaty climaxed 10 days of negotiations in Moscow* (Wall Street Journal).
cap the climax, to go beyond the limit; surpass expectation or belief: *That fantastic story caps the climax. His conduct in this affair caps the climax of absurdity.*
[< Late Latin *clīmax* < Greek *klîmax* (literally) ladder < *klī́nein* to lean]

climax forest, a forest which comprises a stable and self-perpetuating community of plants and animals.

climb (klīm), *v.,* **climbed** or (*Archaic*) **clomb, climb|ing,** *n.* —***v.i.*** **1** to go up, especially by using the hands or feet, or both; ascend: *The mountaineers climbed for hours.* **2** to go in any direction, especially with the help of the hands: *to climb over a wall.* **3** to rise slowly or with steady effort: (*Figurative.*) *It may take a man many years to climb from poverty to wealth.* **4** to move upward; rise: *Smoke climbed slowly from the chimney. The road climbed gradually through broken country. By noon the sun had climbed high.* (*Figurative.*) *The price of sugar climbed last year.* **5** to grow upward by holding on or twining around: *Vines such as ivy and honeysuckle climb.*
—***v.t.*** **1** to go up by using the hands or feet, or both; ascend: *The old man climbed the stairs slowly. The painter climbed the ladder.* **2** to grow upward on or twine around: *Ivy climbs a wall.*
—***n.*** **1** a climbing; ascent: *Our climb up the mountain took several hours.* **2** a place to be climbed; steep part: *The path ended in a difficult climb.* **3** an upward progression; increase: (*Figurative.*) *The sales chart shows a climb of 30 per cent.*
climb down, **a** to go down, especially by using the hands and feet: *The explorers climbed down a rope which they had dropped from the cliff to the ledge below.* **b** *Informal, Figurative.* to give in; back down; withdraw from an impossible position or unreasonable attitude: *Eventually both the company and the union will have to climb down to reach an agreement.*
[Old English *climban*] —**climb′a|ble**, *adj.*
—***Syn.*** *v.t.* **1 Climb, ascend, mount** mean to go up. **Climb** suggests a need for effort, extra power, or support of some kind: *This car will never climb that hill.* **Ascend** suggests a more steady, stately, and not necessarily effortful movement: *She ascended the steps like a great lady.* **Mount** has the same sense as *ascend,* but it can also mean to get on top of: *He mounted the stepladder, or the horse.*
▶ The past tense **clomb** (klōm), along with other forms like (klim), (klum), and (klüm) survives in the local dialects of certain sections of the United States.

climb|down (klīm′doun′), *n.* the abandonment of a high position taken on some point or question when it has been found untenable or unacceptable.

climb|er (klī′mər), *n.* **1** a person or thing that climbs. **2** *Informal, Figurative.* a person who is always seeking to improve his social status. **3** a climbing plant; vine. **4** = climbing iron.

climb indicator, an instrument that shows the rate of ascent or descent of an aircraft by reacting to changes in barometric pressure.

climb|ing fern (klī′ming), a delicate, decorative North American fern: *The climbing fern is the only native fern that supports itself by climbing low bushes* (New York Times).

climbing fish, a fish that can live out of the water, travel some distance on land, and, reputedly, climb trees; climbing perch; anabas.

climbing iron, one of a pair of frames with spikes, attached to shoes to help in climbing: *Telephone linemen and loggers often wear climbing irons.*

climbing perch, a fish native to Thailand that has prickly spikes on its scales and can crawl on the ground or climb a tree.

climbing rope, a strong rope such as is used in gymnastic or mountain climbing.

climb|out (klīm′out′), *n.* the steep ascent of an aircraft during take-off: *Noise on takeoff will be less offensive because the SST climbout will be steeper and faster* (New York Times).

clime (klīm), *n.* **1** a region or country, especially one having pleasant conditions for living: *Whatever clime the sun's bright circle warms* (Milton). **2** = climate. [< Latin *clīma;* see etym. under **climate**]

cli|mo|graph (klī′mō graf, -gräf), *n.* a graph on which climatic factors are plotted. [< Latin *clima* climate + English *-graph*]

cli|nal (klī′nəl), *adj.* of or having to do with a cline or the study of clines.

cli|na|men (klī nā′mən), *n., pl.* **-nam|i|na** (-nam′ə nə). an inclination; bias. [< Latin *clīnāmen* < *clīnāre* to incline]

cli|nan|dri|um (kli nan′drē əm), *n., pl.* **-dri|a** (-drē ə). a cavity at the apex of the column in orchids in which the anthers rest; androclinium. [< New Latin *clinandrium* < Greek *klī́nē* couch + *anḗr, andrós* male]

clinch (klinch), *v., n.* —***v.t.*** **1a** to fasten (a driven nail or staple or a bolt) firmly by bending over the point that sticks out: *By clinching the nails over the canvas they held the torn sail to the mast.* **SYN**: See syn. under **clench**. **b** to fasten (things) together in this way. **SYN**: See syn. under **clench**. **2** *Figurative.* to fix firmly; settle decisively: *A deposit of five dollars clinched the bargain. The lawyer clinched his case by introducing new evidence.* **3** *Nautical.* to fasten (a rope) by making a half hitch and lashing the end back. **4** = clench.
—***v.i.*** **1a** to grasp one another tightly in boxing or wrestling; grapple: *When the boxers clinched, the crowd booed.* **b** *Informal.* to embrace as lovers. **2** to fasten a driven nail or staple or a bolt by bending the end.
—***n.*** **1** the act of clinching: *The clinch of a few nails held the board fast.* **2a** a tight grasp in boxing or wrestling; close grip: *The referee broke the boxers' clinch.* **b** *Informal.* an embrace by lovers. **3a** a fastening made by bending the end of a driven nail or staple or a bolt. **b** a clinched nail, staple, or bolt, or the bent end of it. **4** *Nautical.* a method of fastening the end of a rope by making a half hitch and lashing the end back. **5** a decisive settlement; confirmation. **6** *Obsolete.* a pun.
[variant of *clench*]

clinch|er (klin′chər), *n.* **1** *Informal.* an argument, statement, or action that is decisive. **2a** a tool for clinching nails, bolts, etc. **b** a nail or bolt used for clinching. **3** a person or thing that clinches. **4** = clincher tire.

clinch|er-built (klin′chər bilt′), *adj.* = clinker-built.

clincher tire, a tire with flanges that fit into grooves in the inner and outer edges of the rim so that the tire is locked in position when inflated.

cline (klīn), *n.* a gradual variation in a particular inherited characteristic found across a series of adjacent populations of a group of related organisms. [< Greek *klī́nein* to slope]

cling (kling), *v.,* **clung, cling|ing,** *n., adj.* —***v.i.*** **1** to stick or hold fast: *A vine clings to its support. Wet clothes cling to the body.* **SYN**: adhere. **2** to grasp; embrace: *The lost child clung to the policeman.* **SYN**: clasp. **3** to keep near: *The clouds cling to the mountains.* **4** *Figurative.* to remain attached or stick (to a plan, doctrine, wish, hope, memory): *He clings to the beliefs of his father.* **5** *Figurative.* to persist in thought or memory: *His mother's last words clung to his memory.* **6** *Obsolete.* to cohere.
—***n.*** **1** the act of clinging. **SYN**: adherence, attachment. **2** = clingstone.
—***adj.*** = clingstone: *a cling peach.*
[Old English *clingan*] —**cling′er**, *n.*

cling|fish (kling′fish′), *n., pl.* **-fish|es** or (*collectively*) **-fish.** any one of a genus of marine fish having a sucking disk on the ventral side by which it attaches itself to objects.

cling|ing (kling′ing), *adj.* that clings; that holds fast. —**cling′ing|ly**, *adv.*

clinging vine, a woman who tends to be dependent on a man or a child who is too dependent upon its mother.

cling peach, = clingstone.

cling|stone (kling′stōn′), *n., adj.* —*n.* **1** a peach, plum, or other fruit whose stone clings to the fleshy part. **2** the stone of such fruit.
—***adj.*** having such a stone.

cling|y (kling′ē), *adj.,* **cling|i|er, cling|i|est.** apt to cling; adhesive.

clin|ic (klin′ik), *n.* **1** a place usually connected with a hospital or medical school where people can receive medical treatment, often free or at low cost. **2** a place for medical treatment or study of certain people or diseases: *a dental clinic. The children's clinic is open during school hours.* **3** the practical instruction of medical students by examining or treating patients in the presence of the students. **4** a place where practical instruction in any subject is given: *a football clinic, a reading clinic.* **5** a class of students receiving medical or practical instruction. [< Latin *clīnicus* physician < Greek *klīnikós* physician who visits bed patients; (literally) of a bed <

klīnē bed < *klīnein* to lean, incline]

clin|i|cal (klin′ə kəl), *adj.* **1** of or having to do with a clinic: *clinical treatment, a clinical center.* **2** used or performed in a sickroom, especially in a hospital: *clinical instruments, a clinical examination.* **3** of or having to do with the study of disease by observation of the patient rather than by experiment, autopsy, etc.: *clinical medicine, a clinical diagnosis. The drug ... is now under clinical tests at several medical centers* (Wall Street Journal). **4** involving the use of laboratory methods and equipment: *clinical pathology, clinical sociology.* **5** *Figurative.* coldly objective or impersonal; detached; dispassionate; unemotional: *a cold clinical tone of voice. ... the intense, almost clinical accuracy with which Hemingway has been able to convey the self's sensations* (Alfred Kazin). **6** *Ecclesiastical.* administered on the sickbed or deathbed: *clinical baptism.*

clin|i|cal|ly (klin′ə klē), *adv.* **1** by clinical methods: *to examine a patient clinically.* **2** *Figurative.* in a clinical manner: *an unfeeling and clinically detailed account.* **3** from a clinical point of view: *He had been pronounced clinically dead.*

clinical psychologist, a person who practices clinical psychology.

clinical psychology, the branch of psychology that deals with the psychological problems and adjustment of individuals by the use of psychological tests and psychotherapy and by research in the diagnosis and treatment of psychological disorders.

clinical thermometer, a thermometer for measuring the temperature of the body.

cli|ni|cian (kli nish′ən), *n.* a physician who practices or teaches clinical medicine.

clin|i|co|path|o|log|i|cal (klin′ə kō path′ə loj′ə-kəl), *adj.* relating both to the symptoms of disease and to the lesions produced by it.

clink¹ (klingk), *n., v.* —*n.* a light, sharp, ringing sound like that of glasses hitting together: *He heard the clink of glass and the clatter of plates as the dishes were being washed.*
—*v.i.* to make a clink. —*v.t.* to cause to clink.
[Middle English *clinken,* perhaps imitative]

clink² (klingk), *n. Informal.* a prison or prison cell; lockup: *When the cops picked him up for vagrancy,* [*he*] *got ten days in the clink* (Time). [apparently < name of a prison in London]

clink³ (klingk), *v.t., v.i. Dialect.* to clinch.

clink-clank (klingk′klangk′), *n., v.* —*n.* a succession of clinking sounds.
—*v.i.* to make such a succession of sounds.

clink|er (kling′kər), *n., v.* —*n.* **1** a large, rough cinder left in a furnace or forge after coal has been burned. **2** a very hard brick. **3** a mass of bricks fused together. **4** the rough, hard waste left after metal is separated from ore by melting; slag. **5** = lava. **6** a substance made in a kiln and reground to make portland cement. **7** *Informal, Figurative.* a bad or stupid mistake, or its result: *Any completely new car is liable to have bugs, particularly at the beginning of a production run, but occasionally the manufacturers produce a real clinker* (Maclean's).
—*v.i.* to form clinkers in burning.
[< Dutch *klinker* < *klinken* to ring (as it does when struck)]

clink|er-built (kling′kər bilt′), *adj.* made of boards or metal plates that overlap one another; lapstreak: *The lifeboat was clinkerbuilt.* Also, **clincher-built.** [< *clink³* + *-er¹* + *built*]

clink|stone (klingk′stōn′), *n.* = phonolite.

clino-, *combining form.* slope; inclination: *Clinometer = instrument for measuring inclination.*
[< New Latin *clino-* < Greek *klīnein* to slope]

cli|no-ax|is (klī′nō ak′sis), *n.* = clinodiagonal.

cli|no|ce|phal|ic (klī′nə sə fal′ik), *adj. Anthropology.* (of skulls) characterized by a saddlelike depression behind the coronal suture.

cli|no|ceph|a|ly (klī′nə sef′ə lē), *n.* a deformity of the skull due to a premature union of the parietal bones with the alisphenoids or with the temporal bones.

cli|no|chlore (klī′nə klôr, -klōr), *n.* a mineral, a variety of chlorite, occurring usually in scaly or granular aggregates, but also in monoclinic crystals.

cli|no|clase (klī′nə klās), *n.* a somewhat translucent arsenate of copper, occurring in dark-green monoclinic crystals. [< *clino-* + *-clase* (as in *orthoclase*)]

cli|no|di|ag|o|nal (klī′nə dī ag′ə nəl), *n.* the diagonal or lateral axis in monoclinic crystals, forming an oblique angle with the vertical axis; clino-axis.

cli|no|graph (klī′nə graf, -gräf), *n.* **1** an apparatus used in mining, etc., for determining the deviation of a boring from the vertical. **2** a device for drawing angles, consisting of two straightedges pivoted together.

cli|nom|e|ter (klī nom′ə tər, kli-), *n.* any one of several instruments for measuring deviation from the horizontal, such as the dip of rock strata or the heeling of a ship.

cli|no|met|ric (klī′nə met′rik), *adj.* **1** having to do with or determined by a clinometer. **2** having to do with oblique crystalline forms, or with solids which have oblique angles between the axes.

cli|no|met|ri|cal (klī′nə met′rə kəl), *adj.* = clinometric.

cli|nom|e|try (klī nom′ə trē, kli-), *n. Geology.* the method or art of measuring the dip of rock strata.

cli|no|stat (klī′nə stat), *n.* a device consisting essentially of a slowly revolving disk on which growing plants are placed, used in studying plant growth to minimize or eliminate the effect of such exterior factors as gravity and light.

clin|quant (kling′kənt), *adj., n.* —*adj.* glittering with gold or silver, or with metallic decorations, etc.; tinseled; spangled.
—*n.* imitation gold leaf; tinsel.
[< French *clinquant,* present participle of obsolete *clinquer* to clink]

Clin|ton (klin′tən), *n., adj. Geology.* —*n.* **1** a phase of the Silurian period in the eastern and central United States. **2** the rock formations or mineral deposits of this epoch.
—*adj.* of or having to do with the mineral deposits, rock formations, or strata of this phase of the Silurian period.
[< *Clinton,* a town in New York, a typical site]

clin|to|ni|a (klin tō′nē ə), *n.* any plant of a small genus of perennial herbs of the lily family, having a few broad, ribbed basal leaves and white or greenish-yellow flowers. [< New Latin *Clintonia* < De Witt *Clinton,* 1769-1828, American statesman]

Cli|o (klī′ō), *n.* **1** *Greek Mythology.* the Muse of history: *Clio ... has a nasty habit of upsetting Grand Designs* (Hans Morgenthau). **2** *pl.* **-os.** *U.S.* a statuette awarded annually for the best production, acting, etc., in television commercials.

cli|o|met|ric (klī′ō met′rik), *adj.* of or having to do with cliometrics. —**cli′o|met′ri|cal|ly,** *adv.*

cli|o|me|tri|cian (klī′ō mə trish′ən), *n.* a specialist in cliometrics.

cli|o|met|rics (klī′ō met′riks), *n.* the use of computers and mathematical methods and measurements in the study of history; mathematical and statistical analysis of historical data: *Cliometrics* [*has*] *made it impossible to write about slavery as a whole without using quantifiable data* (Saturday Review). [< *Clio* + *-metrics,* as in *econometrics*]

clip¹ (klip), *v.,* **clipped, clip|ping,** *n.* —*v.t.* **1** to trim with shears, scissors, or clippers; cut; cut short: *A sheep's fleece is clipped off to get wool. The gardener clips the hedges to keep them straight and level.* SYN: shear, snip. **2** to cut the hair or fleece of; trim: *Our dog is clipped every summer.* **3** to cut out of a newspaper or magazine: *Mother clipped the recipe and pasted it in her book.* **4** *Figurative.* to reduce, decrease, or shorten; curtail: *Because the meeting was running overtime, the agenda had to be clipped.* **5a** to omit syllables of (words) in pronouncing: *... clipping her words in her vehemence* (Mrs. H. Wood). SYN: abbreviate. **b** to shorten by dropping syllables: *The words "quotation" and "taxicab" are often clipped to "quote" and "cab."* SYN: abbreviate. **6** to damage (a coin) by cutting off the edge. **7** *Informal.* to hit or punch sharply: *The boxer clipped his opponent on the jaw.* **8** *Informal.* to swindle or rob, especially by overcharging: *to clip a customer.*
—*v.i.* **1** *Informal.* to move fast; run: *The car clipped down the road at seventy miles an hour.* **2** to cut pieces from a magazine or newspaper. **3** to cut or trim something with shears. **4** *Archaic.* to fly quickly.
—*n.* **1** the act of clipping: *His hair needs a clip around the back of the neck.* **2a** anything clipped off. **b** a clipped word or form: *Shoptalk has many clips—mike for microphone or micrometer* (Porter G. Perrin). **3a** the amount of wool clipped from sheep at one time. **b** the whole season's production of wool: *The efforts ... to enhance the value of the British clip are meeting with considerable success, as the prices realized have risen more than the prices for comparable New Zealand cross-bred wools* (London Times). **4** a piece cut from a reel of film of a motion picture or television program or from a newspaper or magazine: *Clips from the movie itself ... will be presented on video* (New York Times). **5** *Informal.* a fast motion: *The bus passed through the village at quite a clip.* **6** *Informal.* a sharp blow or punch. **7** *Informal.* one time; single occasion: *at one clip.* **clips,** an instrument for clipping; shears: *A bonnier flesh ne'er crossed the clips* (Robert Burns).
[Middle English *clippen,* probably < Scandinavian (compare Old Icelandic *klippa*)]

clip² (klip), *v.,* **clipped, clip|ping,** *n.* —*v.t.* **1** to hold tight; fasten: *The secretary clipped the papers together.* SYN: clasp, grip. **2** to encircle; encompass: *A snake her forehead clips* (Tennyson). **3** to block (a football player who does not have the ball) from behind. It is an illegal play subject to penalty. **4** *Dialect.* to hug; embrace.
—*v.i.* to grip; bite: *The air clipped keen, the night was fanged with frost* (Samuel Taylor Coleridge).
—*n.* **1** a thing used for clipping things together. A clip for papers is often made of a piece of bent wire. **2a** a metal holder for cartridges used in some firearms. **b** the number of rounds this holds. **3** a piece of jewelry fastened by means of a hinged device. **4** a device to hold the bottoms of a bicyclist's trousers closely about the ankles. **5** *Obsolete.* an embrace.
[Old English *clyppan* encircle, embrace]

clip|board (klip′bôrd′, -bōrd′), *n.* a board with a heavy spring clip at one end for holding papers while writing: *Colonel Bruce was propped up on his cot, writing on a clipboard against his knee* (Harper's).

clip-clop (klip′klop′), *n., v.,* **-clopped, -clop|ping,** *adj.* —*n.* a sound having a regular beat similar to that made by a horse's hoofs: *... the clip-clop of students' heels on the cobblestones at dinner time* (Newsweek).
—*v.i.* to walk or run and make the sound of clip-clop: *clip-clopping on high heels ...* (Time).
—*adj.* having or producing the sound of a clip-clop: *clip-clop rhythm.*

clip|e|us (klip′ē əs), *n., pl.* **-e|i** (-ē ī). a large circular shield with a convex outer surface and a concave inner surface, used by the Greeks and Romans. [< Latin *clipeus*]

clip joint, *U.S. Slang.* a store, bar, amusement place, or other place of business, where customers are overcharged or otherwise defrauded.

clip-on (klip′on′, -ôn′), *adj.* designed to be fastened with a clip or clips: *clip-on sunglasses.*

clipped (klipt), *adj.* **1** articulated in a quick, crisp, distinct manner: *the clipped speech of an Englishman.* **2** shortened: *"Ad" is a clipped form of "advertisement." "Bus," "phone," "dorm," and "gym" are clipped words.*
▶**Clipped** words such as *binocs* for binoculars, *sec* for second of time (as in: *Wait a sec while I tie my shoe*), *deli* for delicatessen, or *pres* for president, are frequent in informal usage. Clipped forms are especially common in student jargon; *psych* for psychology, *eco* for economics, *bio* for biology, *phys ed* for physical education.

***clip|per** (klip′ər), *n.* **1** a person who clips or cuts. **2** Often, **clippers.** any one of various tools for cutting, especially scissors or shears: *Barbers use electric hair clippers.* **3** a large sailing ship built and rigged for speed: *Clipper ... a sharp-built vessel whereof the stem and sternpost, especially the former, have a great rake* (Arthur Young). **4** a fast horse. **5** a fast sled for coasting. **6** a large, fast aircraft. **7** an electronic circuit or any part of it that eliminates an undesirable signal. **8** *British Slang.* a first-rate person or thing.

***clipper** definition 3

clipper ship, = clipper (def. 3).

clip|pie (klip′ē), *n. British Slang.* a female conductor on a bus or other public conveyance.

clip|ping (klip′ing), *n., adj.* —*n.* **1** an article, picture, or advertisement cut out of a newspaper or magazine: *The boy brought in a newspaper clipping about the floods.* **2** a piece cut out of or from something else; cutting. **3** the act of cutting with or as if with shears or scissors.
—*adj.* **1** that clips or cuts. **2** that flies or moves fast. **3** *Slang.* excellent; first-rate. —**clip′ping|ly,** *adv.*

clips (klips), *n.pl.* See under **clip¹**.

clip|sheet (klip′shēt′), *n.* a page of news articles, editorials, and other features, printed on one side only for easy clipping and handling. Clipsheets are sent to clients by newspaper syndicates, publicity departments, and the like.

clique (klēk, klik), *n., v.,* **cliqued, cli|quing.** —*n.* a small, exclusive group of people within a larger group: *A few of the girls in the office have a clique that is always holding parties. During World War II he was imprisoned by the Japanese military clique as "a liberal and a pacifist"* (Atlantic). SYN: coterie. See syn. under **circle**.
—*v.i. Informal.* to form or associate in a clique.

Pronunciation Key: hat, āge, cãre, fär; let, ēqual, tėrm; it, īce; hot, ōpen, ôrder; **oil**, **out**; cup, pu̇t, rüle; **ch**ild; lo**ng**; **th**in; **ᴛʜ**en; **zh**, measure; **ə** represents **a** in about, **e** in taken, **i** in pencil, **o** in lemon, **u** in circus.

[< French *clique* < *cliquer* to click]

cli|quey (klē′kē, klik′ē), *adj.* = cliquish. Also, **cliquy.**

cli|quish (klē′kish, klik′ish), *adj.* **1** like a clique: *At the start visitors would drop in, but the gathering was as cliquish as the Mafia and they would soon duck out* (Alistair Cooke). **2** tending to form a clique. **—cli′quish|ly,** *adv.* **—cli′quish|ness,** *n.*

cli|quism (klē′kiz əm, klik′iz-), *n.* cliquish principles or spirit: *those unpleasant elements of cliquism and jealousy which have wrought so much distrust* (Westminster Review).

cli|quy (klē′kē, klik′ē), *adj.* = cliquey.

clish|ma|cla|ver (klish′mə klā′vər), *n., v. Scottish.* **—*n.*** foolish talk; gossip. **—*v.i.*** to gossip. [origin uncertain; probably imitative]

C.Lit., Companions of Literature.

cli|tel|lum (kli tel′əm, klī-), *n.* a glandular swelling around certain sections of an annelid, such as an earthworm, from which a viscous fluid is secreted which forms a cocoon for the eggs. [< New Latin *clitellum* < Latin *clītellae* a packsaddle]

clith|ral (klī′thrəl), *adj.* = cleithral.

clit|o|ral (klit′ər əl, klī′tər-), *adj.* of the clitoris.

clit|o|ris (klit′ər is, klī′tər-), *n.* a small, erectile organ at the forward part of the vulva of the female of most mammals. It is homologous with the penis of the male. [< New Latin *clitoris* < Greek *kleitorís,* perhaps < *kleíein* shut, close in]

cliv|ers (kliv′ərz), *n.sing. and pl.* = cleavers (the plant).

cli|vi|a (klī′vē ə, kliv′ē-), *n.* any plant of a group of African herbs of the amaryllis family noted for its showy flowers: *The color, for which clivia is famed, ranges from orange through orange red to a strong red* (New York Times). [< New Latin *Clivia* the genus name < Lady *Clive,* wife of the third Duke of Northumberland]

clk., 1 clerk. **2** clock.

clo (klō), *n.* a unit for measuring the amount of insulation or warmth provided by a garment: *How well a coat—or any other garment—traps body heat is measured in units called clos* (Elizabeth A. McCullough). [< *clo(thing)*]

clo|a|ca (klō ā′kə), *n., pl.* **-cae** (-sē). **1** *Zoology.* **a** the cavity in the body of birds, reptiles, amphibians, and most fishes, into which the intestinal, urinary, and generative canals open. **b** a similar cavity in certain invertebrates. **2** a sewer. **3** a privy; water closet. **4** *Figurative.* a receptacle of moral filth. [< Latin *cloāca* sewer, perhaps < *cluere* purge]

clo|a|cal (klō ā′kəl), *adj.* having to do with or resembling a cloaca or sewer.

cloak (klōk), *n., v.* **—*n.* 1** a loose outer garment with or without sleeves: *The horseback rider drew his cloak tightly around him in the rain.* **SYN:** mantle. **2** *Figurative.* anything that covers or hides; outward show: *He said mean things about me under the cloak of friendship. Humility is made the cloak of pride* (Robert Southey). **SYN:** mask, disguise, pretense.
—*v.t.* 1 to cover with a cloak: *The peddler cloaked himself and went on in the storm.* **2** *Figurative.* to cover up; conceal; disguise: *to cloak evil deeds under friendly words.* **SYN:** hide. [< Old French *cloque* < Late Latin *clocca* (originally) bell. See etym. of doublets **cloche, clock**[1].]

cloak-and-dag|ger (klōk′ən dag′ər), *adj.* of or having to do with intrigue and adventure, as in certain melodramatic plays and novels, or in espionage or counterintelligence: *As a film, this true story becomes an exciting cloak-and-dagger adventure* (Maclean's).

cloak|room (klōk′rüm′, -rům′), *n.* a room where coats, hats, umbrellas, and parcels can be left for a time; coatroom.

clob|ber (klob′ər), *v., n.* **—*v.t.*** Slang. **1a** to strike or beat heavily: *If a member of one of the ten-man teams happened to clobber a rival with a stick, or send him sprawling on his face, it was all part of the game* (Time). **b** to attack or damage verbally: *The eleven men who had served as chairmen of the FCC had been clobbered unmercifully* (Saturday Review). **2** *Figurative.* to defeat severely: [*He*] *clobbered his last opponent by a 3-to-1 majority* (Maclean's). **3** *British.* to adorn or ornament lavishly: *... cars ... clobbered with chromium plate* (Punch).
—*n.* *British Slang.* **1** clothing: *I wore nothing but the best Italian clobber* (Alex Atkinson). **2** equipment: *... this dear ship, with its whining ventilation, electronic clobber and loud guns* (Punch). [origin uncertain] **—clob′ber|er,** *n.*

clo|chard (klō shär′), *n.* a vagabond; tramp: *Within days the icy streets of Paris were swept clean of the homeless ... clochards—human derelicts who live under the Seine bridges* (Newsweek). [< French *clochard* < *clocher* to limp]

***cloche** (klōsh), *n.* **1** a close-fitting hat for women. **2** a bell-shaped glass cover to protect tender plants. [< French *cloche* bell, ultimately < Late Latin *clocca.* See etym. of doublets **cloak, clock**[1].]

***cloche** definition 1

clock[1] (klok), *n., v.* **—*n.* 1** an instrument for measuring and showing time. A clock is not made to be worn or carried about as a watch is. **SYN:** timepiece. **2** any clocklike device for recording or measuring some activity, such as a time clock, a taximeter, or a speedometer: *He drove a rusted 1955 Ford with 250,000 miles on the clock* (Maclean's). **3** any internal mechanism that regulates the cyclic activities of an organism; biological clock: *Unicellular organisms such as protozoa have clocks* (New Scientist). *The discovery of a circannual clock in hibernators has ... been followed up with investigations of other animals* (Scientific American). **4** a steam or air gauge on a locomotive. **5** *Slang.* **a** a face. **b** a blow (on the face): *He would give the daughter a clock on the jaw* (New Yorker).
—*v.t.* 1 to measure or record the time of; time: *The horse race was clocked to determine whether a record had been broken.* **2** to measure or record (time, distance, number, or amount or rate of output) mechanically: *The racing car clocked 150 m.p.h. Each of these 2N43's* [*transistors*] *have clocked at least 40,000 hours of operating life* (Scientific American).
against the clock, so as to finish in a given time: *It is a race against the clock in which the skier goes straight down* (New Yorker).
around (or **round**) **the clock,** all day and night; without a stop: *Negotiations are continuing around the clock in an effort to avoid a strike* (London Times).
clock in (or **out**) , to register on a time clock the beginning or end of a day's work; punch in or out: *Provided one clocks in at the appointed hour in the morning, and does not clock out earlier than five minutes before the appointed hour at night, one may confidently expect ... a normal pay packet on ... Friday evening* (London Times).
run out the clock, a (in football, basketball, and other timed sports) to use up the time remaining in a game, so as to prevent an opponent from overcoming a lead: *The winning team decided to maintain possession of the ball and run out the clock rather than risk a pass interception.* **b** to go beyond a time limit: *The strike came after the negotiators ran out the clock.*
turn (**set** or **put**) **the clock back,** to move backward; return to an old or out-of-date attitude, condition, or policy: *They were ... seeking to put the clock back, to impose a colonial form of government anew* (London Times).
[< Old North French *cloque* bell or < Middle Dutch *clocke* clock, bell < Late Latin *clocca* bell, probably < Celtic (compare Old Irish *cloc*). See etym. of doublets **cloak, cloche.**]

clock[2] (klok), *n., v.* **—*n.*** an ornamental pattern on the side of a stocking or sock, extending up from the ankle. **—*v.t.*** to embroider with a clock or clocks. [origin uncertain]

clock card, the card in a time clock on which the hours worked by an employee are recorded.

clock|er (klok′ər), *n. Informal.* **1** a timekeeper. **2** a person who secretly times the speed of a horse in trial runs, especially as a means of obtaining information for betting.

clock golf, a variety of golf in which figures numbered from 1 to 12 are placed at equal distances in a circle, in imitation of the dial of a clock, the object of the game being to putt the ball from each of these points into a hole placed anywhere within the circle.

clock|ing (klok′ing), *n.* an amount of time clocked by a timekeeper.

clock|like (klok′līk′), *adj.* like a clock; precise; exact in its regularity: *The annual September rains, which occur with almost clocklike regularity in the northern Midwest, mark the start of the shift from summer to winter weather* (Science News Letter).

clock|mak|er (klok′mā′kər), *n.* a person whose business is making or repairing clocks.

clock radio, a radio with a built-in clock which may be set to turn the radio on or off at any desired time: *The clock radio in the softly shadowed bedroom clicked on at 7:30 sharp* (Time).

clock|vine (klok′vīn′), *n.* any one of a group of chiefly climbing plants of the acanthus family, growing in tropical regions, and having showy, bell-shaped flowers.

clock watch, a watch that strikes the hours, as distinguished from a repeater.

clock watcher, *U.S. Informal.* a person employed in an office or factory who keeps looking at the clock for the time to quit work instead of doing his job; a bad or indifferent worker.

clock|wise (klok′wīz′), *adv., adj.* in the direction in which the hands of a clock move; from left to right: *You must turn the key clockwise to unlock the door* (adv.). *A clockwise turn closes the water faucet* (adj.).

clock|work (klok′wėrk′), *n., adj.* **—*n.* 1** the machinery of a clock: *After the clockwork of the watch was cleaned the watch kept perfect time.* **2** any similar machinery, consisting of gears, wheels, and springs. Toys that move by winding up are run by clockwork.
—*adj.* mechanically regular; automatic: *The clockwork tintinnabulum of rhyme* (William Cowper).
like clockwork, with great regularity and smoothness: *The launching of the rocket went off like clockwork.*

clod (klod), *n.* **1** a small lump of earth or clay; lump: *The horse's hoofs threw up clods of dirt on the muddy road.* **2** earth; soil. **3** *Figurative.* anything earthy or base, as the body of a man in comparison with his soul. **4** *Figurative.* a stupid person; blockhead: *The swindlers stole all of the poor clod's money.* **5** a boor. **6** a cut of beef forming part of the shoulder. **7** *British Slang.* a penny. [Middle English *clodde* clot (of blood), variant of *clotte* clot] **—clod′like′,** *adj.*

clod|dish (klod′ish), *adj.* like a clod; stupid or boorish; uncouth. **SYN:** base. **—clod′dish|ness,** *n.*

clod|dy (klod′ē), *adj.,* **-di|er, -di|est. 1** abounding in clods: *Excessive use of conditioners had caused the soil to become cloddy* (New York Times). **2** clodlike.

clod|hop|per (klod′hop′ər), *n. Informal.* **1** a plowman or farm laborer (used in an unfriendly way). **SYN:** bumpkin, rustic. **2** a clumsy or awkward person; boor; oaf. **SYN:** lout.
clodhoppers, large, heavy shoes: *Purser's shoes* [*are*] *a hybrid breed, between a pair of cast-off slippers and the ploughman's clodhoppers* (E. Howard).

clod|hop|per|ish (klod′hop′ər ish), *adj. Informal.* boorish; oafish.

clod|hop|ping (klod′hop′ing), *adj. Informal.* boorish; oafish: *The clodhopping philistine ... had never heard of little grey cells, fine food, or psychology* (Punch).

clod|pate (klod′pāt′), *n.* a blockhead.

clod|pat|ed (klod′pā′tid), *adj.* stupid; dull; doltish.

clod|poll or **clod|pole** (klod′pōl′), *n.* a blockhead; clodpate.

clo|fi|brate (klō fī′brāt), *n.* a synthetic drug that inhibits the formation of fatty acids and cholesterol in the body: *The blood cholesterol can be effectively lowered by taking daily tablets of a drug called clofibrate* (London Times). *Formula:* $C_{12}H_{15}ClO_3$ [a coined name]

***clog** (klog), *v.,* **clogged, clog|ging,** *n.* **—*v.t.* 1** to fill up; choke up; obstruct: *Grease clogged the drain.* **2** to interfere with; hold back; hinder: *Heavy clothes clogged the swimmer's progress. There will be no massive swoops on scores of men at once* [*by the police*]*, partly because this could clog the courts* (Manchester Guardian Weekly).
—*v.i.* 1 to become filled or choked up: *The expressway always clogs during the rush hour.* **2** to stick together; adhere. **3** to dance by beating a heavy rhythm on the floor with wooden-soled shoes. [< noun]
—*n.* 1 anything that hinders or interferes: *a perpetual clog to public business* (Jonathan Swift). **SYN:** impediment, encumbrance, hindrance. **2** any weight, such as a block of wood or other material, fastened to the leg, neck, or arm of an animal or human being to hinder motion: *The prisoner was forced to wear a clog to prevent his escape.* **3a** a heavy shoe with a thick wooden sole. **b** a lighter shoe with a wooden sole, used in dancing. **4** = clog dance. **5** *Especially Scottish.* a block of wood; log for burning: *the Yule clog.* [Middle English *clogge* a block; origin uncertain]

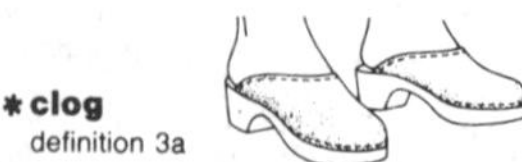

***clog** definition 3a

clog almanac, an early form of almanac or calendar, made by cutting notches and characters on a clog or block, usually of wood.

clog dance, a dance in which the dancer wears clogs to beat time. **—clog dancer. —clog dancing.**

clog|ger (klog′ər), *n.* a person who makes clogs, or the wooden soles for clogs.

clog|gy (klog′ē), *adj.,* **-gi|er, -gi|est.** clogging or apt to clog; adhesive; sticky.

clog|head (klog′hed′), *n.* one of the slender round towers attached to various Irish churches.

cloi|son (kloi′zən), *n.* **1** a partition; dividing band.

2 a fillet used in cloisonné work: *thin bands of gold forming cloisons.* [< French *cloison;* see etym. under **cloisonné**] —**cloi′son|less,** *adj.*

cloi|son|né (kloi′zə nā′), *n., adj.* —*n.* a decorative enamel applied to a metal surface between thin metal strips, fixed on edge, which outline the design and prevent the various colors from running together. After the enamel is fired, the surface is lightly ground and polished. —*adj.* enameled in this way. [< French *cloisonné* partitioned, ultimately < Latin *claudere* to close]

***clois|ter** (klois′tər), *n., v.* —*n.* **1** a covered walk, often along the wall of a building, with a row of pillars on the open side or sides. A cloister is often built around the courtyard of a monastery, church, or college building. **2** a place of religious retirement; convent or monastery. **3** *Figurative.* a quiet place away from the world. **SYN:** retreat.
—*v.t.* **1** to shut away in a cloister or in any quiet place: *He cloistered himself in his study to work.* **2** *Figurative.* to confine or restrain in any way. **SYN:** confine, isolate, sequester. **3** to furnish with a cloister or covered walk.
the cloister, the secluded monastic or conventual life: . . . *a manner which scents of the cloister* (Isaac D'Israeli).
[< Old French *cloistre* < Latin *claustrum* closed place, lock < *claudere* to close]

***cloister**
definition 1

clois|tered (klois′tərd), *adj.* **1** shut away in a quiet place; secluded: *The girls at that boarding school lead a cloistered life.* **2** having a cloister.
cloistered heart, = closed gentian.
clois|ter|er (klois′tər ər), *n.* a monk or nun.
cloister garth, the open court which a cloister surrounds.
clois|tral (klois′trəl), *adj.* **1** of or suitable for a convent or monastery: *a cloistral hush that is completely monastic* (Time). **2** *Figurative.* like a cloister: *cloistral glades.* **3** secluded.
clois|tress (klois′tris), *n. Obsolete.* a nun.
cloke (klōk), *n., v.t.,* **cloked, clok|ing.** *Archaic.* cloak.
clo|ky (klō′kē), *n., adj.* = cloqué.
clomb (klōm), *v. Archaic.* climbed; a past tense and a past participle of **climb.**
clom|i|phene (klom′ə fēn), *n.* a synthetic drug that acts through the pituitary gland to induce ovulation in infertile women. *Formula:* $C_{26}H_{28}ClNO$ [< *c*(h)*lo*(r) + (a)*mi*(ne) + *phene* (< French *phène* benzene)]
clomp (klomp), *v.i.* to walk as with clogs; clamp; clump: *A horse clomped bravely into a Brooklyn subway tunnel* (New Yorker).
clon (klōn, klon), *n.* = clone.
clo|nal (klō′nəl), *adj.* of or like a clone: *clonal roots.* —**clo′nal|ly,** *adv.*
clone (klōn), *n., v.,* **cloned, clon|ing.** —*n.* **1** *Biology.* any group of individuals produced asexually from a single ancestor. **2** *Horticulture.* a group of cultivated plants that have been propagated asexually from a single ancestral plant. **3** a person or thing produced by, or as if by, cloning: **a** an exact duplicate of another; carbon copy: *Both blond and blue-eyed, Mr. Driver and Mr. Haddow agree that they are clones* (Leslie Bennetts). **b** one that acts in a mindless, mechanical fashion; automaton; android; robot: *They suggest the possibility of using clones for work involving radiation or dangerous chemicals, or for fighting wars* (Manchester Guardian Weekly).
—*v.t., v.i.* **1** to reproduce asexually: *Some of the cells given the extra pairs of chromosomes could be "cloned" to give many identical offspring* (New Scientist). **2** to produce an identical copy or copies of (a person or thing) from a model or blueprint: *Since it costs about $2 billion to design and tool up for an all-new plane and engines, most of the new generation will be cloned from present models* (Time).
[< Greek *klōn* twig]
clon|ic (klon′ik), *adj.* having to do with or exhibiting clonus: *Tonic and clonic convulsive movements have been noted . . . in several immature cats* (Science).
clo|nic|i|ty (klə nis′ə tē), *n., pl.* **-ties.** a condition of intermittent spasms.
clonic spasm, = clonus.
clonk (klongk), *n., v.i., v.t.* = clunk.
clo|nus (klō′nəs), *n.* a series of muscular spasms, with partial relaxation intervening. [< New Latin *clonus* < Greek *klónos* turmoil]

cloop (klüp), *n., v.* —*n.* **1** the sound made when a cork is drawn from a bottle. **2** any similar sound. —*v.i.* to make such a sound. [imitative]
cloot (klüt, klʏt), *n. Scottish.* **1** one of the two parts of a cloven hoof. **2** a cloven hoof as a whole. [perhaps < Scandinavian (compare Old Icelandic *klō* claw)]
Cloot (klüt, klʏt), *n. Scottish.* the Devil; Clootie.
cloot|ie (klü′tē, klʏ′-), *n. Scottish.* a little hoof.
Cloot|ie (klü′tē, klʏ′-), *n. Scottish.* the Devil.
clop (klop), *n., v.,* **clopped, clop|ping.** —*n.* a sharp, hard sound such as is made by feet or hoofs: *He could already hear the steady clop of carriages beginning down in the streets* (Barnaby Conrad). —*v.i.* to walk with or make such a sound: *We heard the clopping of spikes on concrete* (New Yorker). [imitative]
clop-clop (klop′klop′), *n., v.,* **-clopped, -clop|ping.** —*n.* a sound of repeated clops. —*v.i.* to walk with or make such a sound.
clo|qué (klō kā′), *n., adj.* —*n.* a fabric with an irregularly raised pattern. —*adj.* having such a pattern. Also, **cloky.** [< French *cloqué* (literally) blistered < *cloquer* to blister]
close¹ (klōz), *v.,* **closed, clos|ing,** *n.* —*v.t.* **1** to bring together or move the parts of, so as to leave no opening; shut: *to close one's eyes, close a book. Close the door.* **2** to stop up; fill; block: *to close a crack in the wall with plaster,* (*Figurative.*) *to close one's mind to new ideas.* **3** to bring together; unite; join: *The troops closed ranks.* **4** to bring to an end; finish: *to close a debate, to close a school, to close a business.* **SYN:** conclude, complete. **5** *Figurative.* to complete (a transaction): *to close the sale of a house. We closed the deal on the new car.* **SYN:** clinch. **6** *Electricity.* to unite the parts of (a circuit) so as to make it complete. **7** *Nautical.* to come close to; come alongside: *The ship closed the tanker to refuel.* **8** *Archaic.* to shut in; bound; surround: *the depth closed me round about* (Jonah 2:5).
—*v.i.* **1** to become shut: *The sleepy child's eyes are closing. The door closed behind him.* **2** to come to an end; finish: *The meeting closed with a speech by the president. School will close early this year. The play closed after ten performances.* **3** to come close: *The men closed around him.* **4** to come together; unite: *The ranks closed. The two divisions closed to form a united front.* **5a** *Figurative.* to come to terms; reach an agreement: *The labor union closed with the company.* **b** to sell for, at the end of a trading period: *That stock closed last night at ten dollars on the stock exchange.* **6** to grapple: *Achilles closes with his hated foe* (Alexander Pope).
—*n.* an end; finish: *the close of day. He spoke at the close of the meeting.*
close down, to shut completely; stop operating: *An industry may close down or move away, leaving hundreds of persons without work* (Donald E. Super).
close in, to come near and shut in on all sides: *The hunters closed in on the bear.*
close out, to sell in order to get rid of: *The store closed out the old models in a special sale.*
close up, a to shut completely; stop up; block: *The windows of the warehouse were closed up with brick.* **b** to bring or come nearer together: . . . *giving the two flanking divisions an opportunity to close up and form a stronger line* (Ulysses S. Grant). **c** to heal: *His wounds were not severe; they closed up quickly.*
[< Old French *clos-,* stem of *clore* to close < Latin *claudere*] —**clos′a|ble,** *adj.*
—*Syn. v.t.* **1 Close, shut** mean to make not open. Although sometimes used interchangeably, **close** is more general in application because both literally and figuratively it emphasizes the idea of making not open, without suggesting the means or way: *Please close the window a little.* **Shut** means to close by pushing or pulling a door, lid, some part, etc., into place across the opening, and therefore puts the emphasis on keeping out or in, literally and figuratively: *Please shut the door.* (*Figurative.*) *We should shut our ears to gossip.*
close² (klōs), *adj.,* **clos|er, clos|est,** *adv., n.* —*adj.* **1** with little space between; near together; near: *These two houses are close. He has close teeth.* **2** fitting tightly; tight; narrow: *She kept a close hold on my arm.* **SYN:** confined. See also **close quarters. 3a** having its parts near together; compact: *a close weave, paper of a close texture.* **SYN:** dense. **b** condensed; concise: *a close and carefully developed paragraph.* **c** viscous. **4** intimate; dear: *The two girls are close friends.* **5a** careful or exact: *a close translation. You need to take closer measurements before ordering the lumber.* **b** *Figurative: There is a close resemblance between the twins.* **c** logical or precise: *a close reasoner.* **6** thorough and, often, strict: *Pay close attention.* **7a** having little fresh air; stuffy: *With the windows shut, the room was hot and close.* **b** hard to breathe: *The air in the cave was very close.* **SYN:** stagnant, oppressive, stifling, sultry. **8** near the surface or short: *a close haircut.* **9** stingy: *A miser is very close with his money.* **SYN:** parsimonious. **10** nearly equal; almost even: *The last game was a close contest.* **11** not fond of talking; keeping quiet about oneself; reserved: *He is very close about his own affairs.* **SYN:** reticent, uncommunicative. **12a** restricted or limited: *a close corporation, a close borough, a close communion.* **b** during which the hunting, trapping, or fishing of certain kinds of game is illegal: *a close season.* **c** hard to get; scarce: *Money is close.* **13a** closely confined; strictly guarded or shut in: *a close prisoner, a close field.* **b** secret or hidden: *in closest confidence.* **14** having all openings covered or drawn together; not open; closed or shut: *a close box, a close carriage.* **15** *Phonetics.* pronounced with some part of the tongue brought near the palate. The vowels in *leap* and *loop* are close vowels. **SYN:** high.
—*adv.* in a close manner; closely; near: *The two farms lie close together. The end of the year is drawing close.*
—*n.* **1** an enclosed place. **2** the grounds around a cathedral or abbey. **3** *Scottish.* an entry or passage leading from the street to a court and the houses within, or to a common stairway of a building.
close on, nearly reaching; almost: *The boat . . . is close on 27 ft. long* (New Scientist).
close to, 1 nearly; almost: *He is close to a master at this* (Norman Mailer). **2** at close range: *Close to, these eyes inspect one with a sense of appraisal rather than curiosity* (Harper's). **3** *Figurative.* friendly or intimate with: *No man was close to Gulbenkian, but a few men were near him* (Time).
[< Old French *clos* < Latin *clausus,* past participle of *claudere* close] —**close′ly,** *adv.* —**close′ness,** *n.*
close air support, air cover given to friendly ground forces, consisting of air attacks on enemy ground forces so close to ground operations as to require detailed coordination between air and friendly ground forces.
close-by (klōs′bī′), *adj.* = nearby.
close call (klōs), *U.S. Informal.* a narrow escape from danger or an accident.
close corporation (klōs), = closed corporation.
close-cropped (klōs′kropt′), *adj.* **1** trimmed or cut short: *close-cropped hair.* **2** wearing the hair cut short; crew-cut: *close-cropped spacemen.*
closed (klōzd), *adj.* **1** fastened up; shut: *a closed door or gate.* **2** enclosed: *a closed carriage, a closed porch.* **3** *Figurative.* not open to new ideas: *a closed mind.* **4** completed: *a closed case.* **5** self-contained; self-sufficient: *a closed system.* **6** restricted: *a closed society, a closed session of the legislature, a closed trade.* **7** *Mathematics.* **a** that starts at a given point and returns to that point: *A sphere is a closed surface or figure.* **b** having the property that the sum or product of an operation is also one of the elements of the operation: *a closed set.* **c** involving a closed set: *a closed operation.*
closed book, 1 something that is not known or understood: *His character, temperament, and state of mind on presentation day are a closed book* (Punch). **2** something that no longer requires consideration; something already solved or accomplished: *The Pakistanis insisted that the Kashmir issue was not a closed book* (London Times).
closed caption, a television caption for the deaf and hard of hearing that is made visible by a special decoding device attached to or built into the television set: *The programs are to be encoded with what are called "closed" captions—subtitles that are invisible on all television sets except those specially equipped to make them appear* (New York Times).
closed captioning, use of closed captions in television programming: *The closed captioning system operates through the imposition of encoded visual subtitles* (The Deaf American).
closed chain, *Chemistry.* an arrangement of atoms in a molecule symbolized in formulas and models by a ring.
closed-cir|cuit (klōzd′sėr′kit), *adj.* denoting or having to do with television or radio transmitted by wire or cable, and not broadcast over the air, but to a certain limited audience, for example in a chain of theaters or a group of classrooms: *Guests can tune in the kitchen . . . by means of a closed-circuit TV, see what the cook is whipping*

Pronunciation Key: hat, āge, cãre, fär; let, ēqual, tėrm; it, īce; hot, ōpen, ôrder; **oi**l, **ou**t; cup, pu̇t, rüle; **ch**ild; lo**ng**; **th**in; ᴛʜen; **zh,** measure; **ə** represents **a** in about, **e** in taken, **i** in pencil, **o** in lemon, **u** in circus.

up for dinner (Time).

closed corporation, a corporation whose stock is held by a few people, often by members of a single family.

closed couplet, a couplet that contains a complete thought and ends with a rhyme.

closed curve, *Mathematics.* a curve which returns into itself, as an oval: *A closed curve divides the plane into two parts (the inside and the outside) and you cannot get from one part to the other without crossing the curve* (Science News Letter).

closed-door (klōzd′dôr′, -dōr′), *adj.* not open to the public; private: *President Eisenhower continued his closed-door huddling with scientists on the touchy missile and satellite topics* (Wall Street Journal).

closed-end (klōzd′end′), *adj.* having to do with or designating a type of investment company whose shares of stock are fixed in number and are sold only on the stock exchange or other recognized market place.

closed gentian, a gentian of eastern North America that blooms in the fall. It has clusters of blue flowers that do not open.

closed loop, *Electronics.* feedback loop.

closed-mind|ed (klōzd′mīn′did), *adj.* having or showing a mind closed to new arguments or ideas; not open-minded. **—closed′-mind′ed|ly,** *adv.* **—closed′-mind′ed|ness,** *n.*

close|down (klōz′doun′), *n.* a stoppage of work in a factory, etc.: *Production was slowed last month, first by strikes and then by a two-week closedown of assembly plants* (Wall Street Journal).

closed primary, *U.S.* a primary in which only recognized party members may vote for candidates of their party.

closed rule, a parliamentary rule under which no amendments to a bill may be made from the floor of a legislature: *Something of great significance may be brought to the floor under what is called a closed rule, which means that . . . the proposal must be voted up or down precisely as it emerged from committee* (Allard Lowenstein).

closed season, any part of the year during which the hunting, trapping, or fishing of certain game is prohibited: *The state imposes a closed season on deer all the year round, but permits an open season all the year round on certain animals that it considers vermin—for example, foxes, possum, weasels, and rats* (New Yorker).

closed sentence, *Mathematics.* a sentence which does not include a variable.

closed shop, **1** a factory or business that employs only members of labor unions, distinguished from a union shop or an open shop. **2** this system of employment.

closed syllable, a syllable that ends in a consonant sound. *Example: can- in candy.*

close-fist|ed (klōs′fis′tid), *adj.* stingy; miserly; penurious. **—close′-fist′ed|ness,** *n.*

close-fit|ting (klōs′fit′ing), *adj.* fitting snugly; tight.

close-grained (klōs′grānd′), *adj.* having a fine, tight grain. Mahogany is a close-grained wood.

close-hand (klōs′hand′), *adj.* at close range; within reach; close: *The spectators . . . slogged up through the slopes for a close-hand look at the world's best skiers* (Time).

close harmony, **1** *Music.* harmony in which the notes making up the chords do not extend beyond one octave; close position. **2** a kind of harmony used by amateur male quartets; barbershop harmony. The four voices are close and use chromatically altered chords. **3** *Figurative.* **a** very near or alike or resembling one another, especially in aim: *The demands of the two groups were in close harmony.* **b** cooperation: *The two scientists worked in close harmony on the project.*

close-hauled (klōs′hôld′), *adj.* having sails set nearly fore-and-aft, for sailing as nearly as possible in the direction from which the wind is blowing.

close-in (klōs′in′), *adj.* **1** in close contact; at close range: *a close-in blast. Fierce close-in fighting raged on for the other positions* (Newsweek). **2** near or adjoining; nearby: *a close-in port, close-in coastal islands.*

close-knit (klōs′nit′), *adj.* firmly united by affection or common interest: *a close-knit family, with its private jokes, sadnesses and reserves* (Punch).

close-lipped (klōs′lipt′), *adj.* = close-mouthed.

close-mouthed (klōs′mouᵺd′, -moutht′), *adj.* not fond of talking; reserved; reticent: *Perhaps no ruling class in the Western world, certainly no ruling class in any democratic society, is as close-mouthed as the British ruling class* (Bulletin of Atomic Scientists). **SYN:** taciturn.

close-or|der drill (klōs′ôr′dər), practice in marching, turning, and formal handling of arms with troops arranged in compact units.

close|out (klōz′out′), *n.* a sale held to close out some or all of the goods handled by a business.

close-packed (klōs′pakt′), *adj.* **1** closely packed; with little or no space between: *close-packed stars.* **2** packed or filled with material: *a close-packed reference book.*

close position, *Music.* a chord arrangement which keeps the parts of the chord within one octave; close harmony.

close quarters, **1** fighting or struggling close together. **2** a place or position with little space: *They live in very close quarters.*

clos|er (klō′zər), *n.* a person or thing that closes.

close reef, the last ordinary reef in a sail, producing the greatest reduction in size.

close-reefed (klōs′rēft′), *adj.* **1** (of a sail) having the last reef taken in. **2** (of a vessel) having the sail or sails so reefed.

close shave, *Informal.* a narrow escape from danger or an accident.

close|stool (klōs′stül′), *n.* a box with a seat and a lid, containing a chamber pot, such as for use in a sickroom.

close support, = close air support.

clos|et (kloz′it), *n., v., adj.* **—*n.*** **1** a small room used for storing clothes or household supplies, such as canned food, china, or linen: *He hung his raincoat in the hall closet. She took fresh sheets out of the linen closet.* **2** a cupboard, especially one for holding china or linen. **SYN:** cabinet. **3** a small, private room for prayer, study, or interviews. **4** the apartment of a king, ruler, or other governmental official, for private consultations or religious meetings. **5** a water closet; toilet.
—*v.t.* **1** to shut up in a private room for a secret talk: *For nearly an hour he had been closeted in a room across the hall with . . . one of his close political associates* (New York Times). **2** to admit to one's private room for secret discussion: *The king asserted that some of the Churchmen whom he had closeted had offered to make large concessions* (Macaulay).
—*adj.* **1a** having to do with a closet; private; secluded; secret: *closet politics. Emily Dickinson was a closet poet.* **b** hidden; covert; secret: *a closet addict . . . the revisionist transmogrification of Dwight D. Eisenhower into a closet dove who would have abandoned the nation's commitments in Southeast Asia and elsewhere* (National Review). **2** designed or suited for private reading or study: *Jeremy Taylor's treatises are in use . . . as well for church service as for closet preparation* (Earl of Shaftesbury). **3** speculative; unpractical; visionary: *a closet thinker.*
[< Old French *closet* (diminutive) < *clos;* see etym. under **close**[2]]

closet drama, a play or type of play suited for reading rather than acting.

close-tongued (klōs′tungd′), *adj.* = close-mouthed.

closet queen, *Slang.* a man who is secretly homosexual.

close-up (klōs′up′), *n., adj.* **—*n.*** **1** a picture taken with a camera at close range: *Close-ups are used in motion pictures or television to give a detailed or intimate view of a scene or character.* **2** a close view.
—*adj.* **1** of or like a close-up. **2** = closein.

close-wo|ven (klōs′wō′vən), *adj.* woven so that the threads are close together.

clos|ing cost (klō′zing), a fee charged to a borrower to cover the cost of arranging a loan.

clos|trid|i|al (klos trid′ē əl), *adj.* of or having to do with clostridia.

clos|trid|i|um (klos trid′ē əm), *n., pl.* **-i|a** (-ē ə). any one of a genus of rod-shaped anaerobic bacteria which produce resistant spores, including the organisms causing botulism and tetanus. [< New Latin *Clostridium* (diminutive) < Greek *klōstêr* spindle]

clo|sure (klō′zhər), *n., v.,* **-sured, -sur|ing.** **—*n.*** **1** the act of closing or shutting. **2** closed condition. **3** a thing that closes. **4** the end; finish; conclusion. **5** the closing of debate in a legislative body or the like; cloture: *The Senate has repeatedly declined to . . . impose closure on the equal rights filibusters* (Arthur Krock). **6** *Mathematics.* a property of an operation on any two members of a set in which the result of the operation is also a member of the set. **7** *Phonetics.* occlusion. **8** *Psychology.* the process by which incomplete figures, ideas, or situations tend to be completed mentally or perceived as complete. **9** *Obsolete.* a thing that encloses or confines; enclosure; cover.
—*v.t., v.i.* to end (a legislative debate); use closure.
[< Old French *closure* < Late Latin *clausūra* a lock, bolt; fortress < Latin *claudere* to close]

clot (klot), *n., v.,* **clot|ted, clot|ting.** **—*n.*** **1** a half-solid lump; thickened mass: *A clot of blood formed in the cut and stopped the bleeding.* **SYN:** coagulation. **2** a rounded mass, lump, or clump: *a clot of soil, gum obtained in clots.* (*Figurative.*) *There were almost a hundred Marines, soldiers, and sailors drawn up into a clot in the street, and they faced a slightly larger clot of Filipinos* (New Yorker). **SYN:** cluster, agglomeration. **3** *British Slang.* a dull fellow; clod: *"The wife's taking cooking lessons—and like a clot I volunteered to try her homework!"* (Cape Times).
—*v.i.* to form into clots; coagulate: *Milk clots when it turns sour. . . . villagers and peasants and workers clotted around loud-speakers and bulletin boards* (Time). **—*v.t.*** to cause to clot; cover with clots; coagulate: *She does not clot her prose with crossword-puzzle words* (Jean Stafford).
[Old English *clott*]

clot|bur (klot′bėr′), *n.* a weed bearing rough burs; cocklebur (def. 1).

cloth (klôth, kloth), *n., pl.* **cloths** (klôᵺz, kloᵺz; klôths, kloths), *adj.* **—*n.*** **1** material made in sheets or webs from wool, cotton, silk, linen, rayon, hair, or other fiber, by weaving, knitting, or rolling and pressing. Cloth is used for clothing, curtains, bedding, and many other purposes. *Essentially the difference between matting and cloth is that the latter is manufactured from fibers that have been spun, while the former consists of intertwined materials of a flat, striplike nature* (Melville J. Herskovits). **SYN:** fabric. **2** a piece of cloth used for a special purpose: *a dust cloth, a polishing cloth, a cloth for the table.* **3** the customary clothing worn by members of a profession or trade. **SYN:** uniform. **4a** the customary clothing worn by the clergy. **b** the profession of a clergyman: *out of respect for his cloth* (Francis Parkman). **5a** the sails of a ship collectively; canvas. **b** *Obsolete.* a sail. **6** *Theater.* a large piece of material used as a backdrop. **7** *Obsolete.* clothing or an article of clothing.
—*adj.* made of cloth.
made out of whole cloth, *Informal.* entirely false or imaginary: *Isn't this entire story . . . made out of whole cloth?* (C. Mathews).
the cloth, clergymen; the clergy: *I could not but wonder at the spartan way of life evidently followed by the young gentlemen who at more normal times occupied the rooms in which I and my colleagues of the cloth were put to live for a week or so* (London Times).
[Middle English *cloth,* Old English *clāth*]

cloth binding, a book binding of cotton cloth, embossed silk, or any plastic impregnated cloth over stiff boards.

cloth|bound (klôth′bound′, kloth′-), *adj.* having a cloth binding: *a clothbound book.*

cloth-cap (klôth′kap′, kloth′-), *adj. British.* of or belonging to the working class: *cloth-cap voters.*

clothe (klōᵺ), *v.t.,* **clothed** or **clad, cloth|ing.** **1** to put clothes on; cover with clothes; dress: *She clothed the child warmly in a heavy sweater and pants.* **2** to provide with clothes: *It costs quite a bit to clothe a family of six.* **3** *Figurative.* to cover: *The sun clothes the earth with light.* **4** *Figurative.* to provide; furnish; equip: *A judge is clothed with the authority of the state.* **5** *Figurative.* to express: *Her ideas are clothed in simple words.* [Middle English *clothen,* Old English *clāthian* < *clāth* cloth]
— *Syn.* 1 Clothe, dress mean to put clothes on. In the reflexive sense, **clothe** requires an object but **dress** does not: *He clothed himself; he dressed (himself).* **Dress** suggests greater concern or care: *I can't go because I haven't time to dress* (that is, dress properly).

cloth-eared (klôth′ird′, kloth′-), *adj. Informal.* having cloth ears; defective in hearing: *The public world is dominated today by the cloth-eared and insensitive noisemongers* (New Scientist).

cloth ears, *Informal.* a defective or tone-deaf sense of hearing.

clothes (klōz, klōᵺz), *n.pl.* **1** covering for a person's body: *She bought a dress, coat, and other clothes.* **SYN:** apparel, clothing, attire, garb, dress, raiment. **2** = bedclothes. [Old English *clāthas,* (originally) plural of *clāth* cloth]

clothes basket, a large basket for holding or carrying clothes or household linen for washing.

clothes|brush (klōz′brush′, klōᵺz′-), *n.* a stiff brush used for freeing clothes from dirt or dust.

clothes hanger, = coat hanger.

clothes|hook (klōz′hu̇k′, klōᵺz′-), *n.* a curved piece of metal, usually attached to a wall, for hanging clothes on: *He walked off camera to the clotheshooks where his wardrobe hung, grabbed a jacket and hurried back* (Maclean's).

clothes|horse (klōz′hôrs′, klōᵺz′-), *n.* **1** a frame to hang clothes on to dry or air them. **2a** *U.S. Slang, Figurative.* a person who places great value on being well dressed, especially one who slavishly follows the latest styles and fashions: *Beau Brummel . . . is usually dismissed as a clotheshorse* (New Yorker). **b** a woman who models clothes;mannequin: *One clotheshorse once had to rush off from a show with her extravagant make-up still on* (New York Times).

clothes|line (klōz′līn′, klōᴛʜz′-), *n.* a rope or wire to hang clothes on to dry or air them.
clothes moth, any one of a family of moths whose larvae are destructive to fabrics or furs.
clothes peg, *Especially British.* a clothespin.
clothes|pin (klōz′pin′, klōᴛʜz′-), *n.* a wooden or plastic clip to hold clothes on a clothesline.
clothes pole, **1** a stick to support a clothesline. **2** a pole supporting a frame and ropes for drying clothes.
clothes|press (klōz′pres′, klōᴛʜz′-), *n.*, or **clothes press**, a chest, cupboard, or closet in which to keep clothes.
clothes tree, an upright pole with branches near the top on which to hang coats and hats.
cloth house, an enclosure of cloth for the cultivation and protection of plants.
cloth|ier (klōᴛʜ′yər, klō′ᴛʜē ər), *n.* **1** a seller or maker of clothing, especially of ready-made clothes. **2** a seller of cloth.
clothier's brush or **teasel**, = fuller's teasel.
cloth|ing (klō′ᴛʜing), *n.* **1** clothes; apparel; dress: *His clothing was soaked in the rain. Many early-American woodsmen wore buckskin clothing.* **2** any covering. **3** = clothing wool.
clothing wool, wool fibers less than 1¼ inches long.
Clo|tho (klō′thō), *n. Greek and Roman Mythology.* one of the three Fates. Clotho spins the thread of life.
cloth of gold, cloth made of gold threads woven with silk or wool threads.
cloth-of-gold (klôth′əv gōld′, kloth′-), *n.* a brilliant orange-yellow species of crocus.
cloth yard, one yard; three feet.
clot|ted cream (klot′id), a cream obtained by scalding or heating milk, which makes it thick or clotted; Devonshire cream.
clot|ty (klot′ē), *adj.*, **-ti|er**, **-ti|est**. **1** full of clots; clotted. **2** tending to clot.
clo|ture (klō′chər), *n.*, *v.*, **-tured**, **-tur|ing**. *U.S.* **—*n.*** a limiting of debate in a legislative body or the like in order to get an immediate vote on the question being discussed; closure: *Northern Democrats and Republicans are sure they have more than 64 votes needed to impose cloture* (Newsweek).
—*v.t.*, *v.i.* to apply cloture (to). Also, **closure**. [< French *clôture* < Vulgar Latin *clausitūra* < Latin *claudere* to close]
clou (klü), *n. French.* **1** the center of attraction; main attraction: *... the clou of the exhibition* (New Yorker). **2** (literally) a nail; stud.

cirrus
cumulus
stratus
nimbus
***cloud**
definition 1

cloud** (kloud), *n.*, *v.* **—*n. **1** a mass of tiny drops of water or ice particles seen floating in the air, usually high above the earth. Clouds may be white, rounded heaps, fleecy sheets or streamers, or dark, almost black, masses. *Usually when it rains, the sky is covered with dark clouds.* **2** a mass of smoke or dust seen in the air: *Dark clouds poured from the factory chimney.* **3** *Figurative.* a great number of things moving close together: *a cloud of birds in flight. A cloud of locusts descended upon the wheat field. Robin Hood's men sent the Sheriff fleeing under a cloud of arrows.* **4** *Figurative.* anything that darkens or dims: *A cloud of disappointment was reflected in his face. They break into our houses under cloud of night* (Scott). **5** *Figurative.* a cause of suspicion or disgrace: *The former convict found it difficult to get a job because a cloud always hung over his reputation.* **6** a dim or unclear patch in something usually clear or transparent; blemish; streak; spot. The dark veins in marble are sometimes called clouds.
—*v.t.* **1** to cover with a cloud or clouds; overshadow; darken: *A mist clouded our view.* **2** *Figurative.* to make obscure; obscure: *the tears which clouded her eyes* (Anthony Trollope). **3** *Figurative.* to make gloomy; darken; dim: *Nothing could cloud his happiness.* **4** *Figurative.* to bring under suspicion or disgrace: *a clouded reputation.* **SYN**: asperse, defame. **5** to streak; spot: *a clouded gem.* **—*v.i.*** **1** to grow or become cloudy: *The sky is clouding over. Her eyes clouded with tears.* **2** *Figurative.* to become gloomy; darken; dim: *His face clouded with anger.*
in the clouds, **a** far above the earth: *The jet plane soared and disappeared in the clouds.* **b** *Figurative.* unrealistic or fanciful; not practical: *The inexperienced planners were completely in the clouds. They ... amuse themselves with phantoms in the clouds* (Samuel Johnson). **c** daydreaming; absent-minded: *He is always up in the clouds; he even forgets to eat.*
under a cloud, **a** under suspicion; in disgrace: *He was under a cloud at court* (Thomas Fuller). **b** in gloom or trouble: *I have known him do great services to gentlemen under a cloud* (Henry Fielding).
[Old English *clūd* rock, hill] **—cloud′like′**, *adj.*
cloud base, the lower surface of a cloud: *When he came out of the cloud base, he was properly lined up for the runway that had been allotted to him by control for his landing* (New Scientist).
cloud belt, **1** a zone around a planet covered by clouds. **2** the belt or ring of clouds itself: *The cloud belts, for which the planet [Jupiter] is famous, will appear in low-powered telescopes as parallel bands stretching across the disc* (Bernhard, Bennett, and Rice).
cloud|ber|ry (kloud′ber′ē, -bər-), *n., pl.* **-ries**. **1** a small, yellow raspberry that grows in northern climates. **2** the plant it grows on.
cloud|burst (kloud′bėrst′), *n.* a sudden, violent rainfall: *The most destructive cloudburst ever known in Grant county ... extended over twelve miles in length ... ; dry gulches were filled and overflowing; the smallest rivulets became roaring torrents* (American Meteorological Journal).
cloud-capped (kloud′kapt′), *adj.* having clouds about its summit; touching the clouds; lofty: *cloud-capped mountains.*
cloud chamber, a large, glass-domed vessel filled with a saturated vapor, especially a vapor of hydrogen and methyl alcohol, through which the paths of individual charged particles, such as protons and electrons, may be observed and photographed and thus be identified: *When cosmic rays traverse a cloud chamber they leave tell-tale tracks with the aid of which important discoveries have been made* (New York Times).
cloud cover, **1** a mass of clouds surrounding a celestial body: *Astronomers had previously estimated that the distance from the top of Venus's cloud cover to the centre of the planet was 3,780 to 3,920 miles* (New Scientist). **2** partial or complete cover of the sky by clouds. **3** *Aeronautics.* the protection from being seen afforded by flying into or behind a cloud.
cloud-cuck|oo-land (kloud′kü′kü land′), *n.* a fanciful or ideal realm; the condition of being away from present-day or practical living: *It is still obvious that many thousands of nonmotorists are living in a cloud-cuckoo-land of the nineteen-twenties* (Punch). [< *Cloud-Cuckoo-Land,* a town built by the birds to separate the gods from mankind, in the comedy *The Birds* (416 B.C.) by Aristophanes]
cloud deck, the upper surface of a cloud: *On schedule it climbed above a high cloud deck and disappeared* (Time).
cloud drift, a body of clouds drifting or floating through the air; cloud rack.
cloud|ed leopard or **tiger** (klou′did), an animal of the cat family that resembles the leopard in size, found chiefly in southeastern Asia. It is arboreal, with a very long tail and fangs, and has a grayish color with dark-brown boxlike markings.
cloud forest, a dense forest in tropical areas that is almost constantly covered by clouds.
cloud|land (kloud′land′), *n.* **1** the region of clouds. **2** *Figurative.* a region of imagination, myth, or unreality.
cloud|less (kloud′lis), *adj.* without a cloud; clear and bright; sunny: *a cloudless sky.* **—cloud′less|ly**, *adv.* **—cloud′less|ness**, *n.*
cloud|let (kloud′lit), *n.* a small cloud.
Cloud Nine, *Slang.* an unreal place; fanciful condition: *I'm no softy ... I'm not up there on Cloud Nine* (Look).
Cloud of Magellan, = Magellanic Cloud.
cloud physics, **1** the physical processes involved in the formation, movement, action, and effects of clouds. **2** the science or study of these processes.
cloud rack, a group of broken clouds driven by the wind.
cloud ring, the cloudy zone of calms and variable winds extending some distance on each side of the equator.
cloud|scape (kloud′skāp), *n.* a picture or a view of the clouds: *There are many pages which merely record what the weather was like, and many more full of those meticulous descriptions of land- and cloudscapes, trees and plants which he delighted to make* (London Times). [< *cloud* + *-scape,* as in *landscape*]
cloud seeder, a person who produces rain by cloud seeding; rainmaker.
cloud seeding, the scattering of particles of silver iodide or certain other chemicals in clouds to produce or increase rain: *Cloud seeding may enable us to divert to the land some of the rain that now falls on the ocean* (Harper's).
cloud|ward (kloud′wərd), *adv.* toward the clouds.
cloud|wards (kloud′wərdz), *adv.* = cloudward.
cloud|y (klou′dē), *adj.*, **cloud|i|er**, **cloud|i|est**. **1** covered with clouds; having clouds in it: *a cloudy sky.* **SYN**: overcast. **2** of or like clouds. **SYN**: nebulous. **3** not clear: *a cloudy liquid. The stream is cloudy with mud.* **SYN**: murky. **4** streaked; spotted: *cloudy marble.* **5** *Figurative.* not carefully thought out; confused; indistinct: *cloudy ideas.* **SYN**: hazy. **6** *Figurative.* not cheerful; gloomy; frowning: *The sulking boy had a cloudy expression.* **SYN**: lowering. **—cloud′i|ly**, *adv.* **—cloud′i|ness**, *n.*
clough (kluf, klou), *n.* a narrow valley; glen. [Old English *clōh* (found in proper names)]
clour (klür), *n., v. Scottish.* **—*n.*** **1** a lump or a dent due to a blow. **2** a blow.
—*v.t.* to strike with a blow that produces a lump or dent.
[origin unknown]
clout (klout), *v., n.* **—*v.t.*** **1** *Informal.* **a** to hit: *The nail bent when he clouted it with the hammer.* **b** to hit with the hand; rap or knock; cuff: *The farmer clouted the cow to get it off his foot.* **2** *Slang.* **a** to hit (a baseball) hard. **b** to score with such a hit: *to clout a double.* **3** *Dialect.* **a** to bandage. **b** to mend; patch.
—*n.* **1** *Informal.* a hit with the hand; rap or knock; cuff: *He gave the boy a clout on the head.* **2** *Slang.* a hard-hit baseball. **3** *Informal.* political force, power, or influence: *The Administration ... will summon all its guile and clout to win passage* (Newsweek). **4a** a white cloth target used in archery. **b** a shot that hits this. **5** *Archaic or Dialect.* **a** a cloth or rag. **b** a piece of cloth or other material for making a patch. **c** a garment. **d** a handkerchief: *... sobbing with his clout in hand* (Jonathan Swift).
clouts, clothes: *A child lay in the crib wrapped in swaddling clouts.*
[Old English *clūt* small piece (of cloth, metal, or the like). See related etym. at **clot**, **cleat**.]
—clout′er, *n.*
clouts (klouts), *n.pl.* See under **clout**.
clove[1] (klōv), *n.* **1** a strong, fragrant spice made from the dried flower buds of a tropical evergreen tree of the myrtle family. **2** the dried flower bud: *Cloves, easily recognized by their characteristic naillike shape, are the dried unopened buds of an evergreen tree* (Science News Letter). **3** the tree. [Middle English *cloue* (apparently misread as *clove*) < Old French *clou* < Latin *clāvus* nail]
clove[2] (klōv), *n.* a small, separate section of a bulb: *a clove of garlic.* [Old English *clufu.* See related etym. at **cleave**[1].]
clove[3] (klōv), *v.* = cleft; a past tense of **cleave**[1].
clove[4] (klōv), *n.* a rocky cleft; ravine; gorge (used in place names, especially in New York). [< Dutch *klove, kloof* cleft]
clove-gil|ly|flow|er (klōv′jil′ē flou′ər), *n.* the clove pink or carnation. [< Old French *clou de gilofre*]
clove hitch, a knot for tying rope around a pole, spar, or other round object; builder's knot. See picture under **hitch**.
clo|ven (klō′vən), *v., adj.* **—*v.*** cleft; a past participle of **cleave**[1].
—*adj.* split; divided into two parts. The hoofs of cows and sheep are cloven.
cloven foot, = cloven hoof.
clo|ven-foot|ed (klō′vən fu̇t′id), *adj.* = cloven-hoofed.
cloven hoof, a hoof divided into two main parts. Cows have cloven hoofs. The Devil is traditionally pictured with cloven hoofs.
clo|ven-hoofed (klō′vən hu̇ft′, -hüft′), *adj.* **1** having cloven hoofs. **2** devilish.
clove pink, a pink with a spicy smell like that of cloves. The carnation is a cultivated variety of clove pink.
clo|ver (klō′vər), *n.* **1** a low plant usually having leaves with three small leaflets and sweet-smelling, rounded heads of small, red, white, yellow, or purple flowers. Clover is grown as food for horses and cattle and to make the soil richer. Clover belongs to the pea family. **2** any similar plant of the pea family, such as sweet clover.

Pronunciation Key: hat, āge, cãre, fär; let, ēqual, tėrm; it, īce; hot, ōpen, ôrder; oil, out; cup, pu̇t, rüle; child; long; thin; ᴛʜen; zh, measure; ə represents **a** in about, **e** in taken, **i** in pencil, **o** in lemon, **u** in circus.

in clover, enjoying a life of pleasure and luxury without work or worry: *He has been sometimes in clover as a traveling tutor, sometimes he has slept and fared hard* (Robert A. Vaughan).
[Old English *clǣfre, clāfre*] —**clo'ver|like'**, *adj.*

***clo|ver|leaf** (klō'vər lēf'), *n., pl.* **-leafs** or **-leaves,** *adj.* —*n.* an intersection of two highways, with one passing over the other, and with a series of curving ramps in the shape of a four-leaf clover that permit traffic to move from one highway to the other without having to cross in front of other traffic.
—*adj.* having the shape of a four-leaf clover: *a cloverleaf container, hot cloverleaf rolls.*

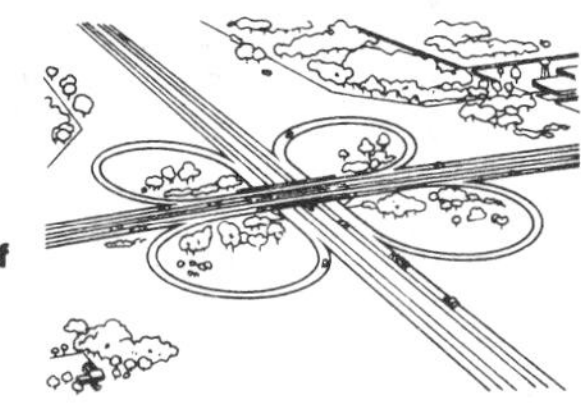

***cloverleaf**

clover worm, a green caterpillar, the larva of an American noctuid moth.

clo|ver|y (klō'vər ē), *adj.* **1** abounding in clover. **2** resembling clover; cloverlike.

Clo|vis (klō'vis), *adj., n.* —*adj.* of, designating, or having to do with an extinct civilization of the Pleistocene in the southwestern United States, centered chiefly in the arid plains of what is now New Mexico, Texas, and Arizona: *Clovis fluted stone points, weapons used by early American man, were found for the first time in direct association with remains of a mammoth in Arizona* (Science News Letter).
—*n.* the Clovis civilization.
[< *Clovis,* a city in New Mexico, the modern site]

clowd|er (klou'dər), *n.* a group (of cats): *That's a fine clowder of cats you have there, Aunt* (New Yorker). [variant of *clutter*]

clown (kloun), *n., v.* —*n.* **1a** a person who makes a business of making people laugh by tricks and jokes; fool or jester. Clowns appear especially at circuses and carnivals and wear funny costumes and make-up. *The clowns at the circus were very funny.* SYN: buffoon. **b** a person who acts like a clown; a joker or comedian: *Who's the clown who put sugar in the saltshaker?* SYN: buffoon. **2** a bad-mannered, awkward person. SYN: boor. **3** a countryman, rustic, or peasant.
—*v.i.* to act like a clown; play tricks and jokes; act silly: *The Twenty-One Club "Gentlemen" clowned through . . . an inning and a half of a softball "contest"* (New York Times).
[origin uncertain]

clown|er|y (klou'nər ē), *n., pl.* **-er|ies. 1** the tricks and jokes of a clown. **2** a clownish act.

clown|ish (klou'nish), *adj.* **1** like a clown; like a clown's: *a clownish appearance, clownish behavior.* **2** boorish; clumsy; rough. —**clown'ish|ly,** *adv.* —**clown'ish|ness,** *n.*

clox|a|cil|lin (klok'sə sil'ən), *n.* a synthetic form of penicillin effective against germs that have developed resistance to natural penicillin. [< *c*(h)*l*(or)- + *ox*(ygen) + *a*(zole) + (peni)*cillin*]

cloy (kloi), *v.t., v.i.* **1** to make or become weary by too much, too sweet, or too rich food: *His appetite was cloyed by all the candy he had eaten.* **2** *Figurative.* to make or become weary by too much of anything pleasant; satiate; surfeit: *These are enough to satisfy, more would cloy* (Thomas Fuller). SYN: pall. [Middle English *acloy, ancloy* drive a nail into < Old French *encloyer* < *en-* in + *clou* nail < Latin *clavus*]

cloy|ing (kloi'ing), *adj.* producing weariness or disgust through surfeit: *I am a great admirer of Massenet, even though the slightly sugary sentimentality of his music can become a little cloying* (New Yorker). —**cloy'ing|ly,** *adv.* —**cloy'ing|ness,** *n.*

cloy|less (kloi'lis), *adj.* that does not cloy: *Sharpen with cloyless sauce his appetite* (Shakespeare).

cloze (klōz), *adj. Education.* of or based upon a method of testing for reading comprehension which measures the ability of a reader to supply words which have been systematically deleted from a reading selection: *the cloze procedure, cloze exercises.* [alteration of *closure* (def. 8)]

C.L.U., Chartered Life Underwriter (of insurance).

***club** (klub), *n., v.,* **clubbed, club|bing,** *adj.* —*n.* **1a** a heavy stick of wood, thicker at one end, used as a weapon: *The farmer used the branch as a club to kill the snake.* SYN: cudgel. **b** *Figurative: Once possessed of the club of the industry-wide strike, he is hardly likely to disarm himself* (Wall Street Journal). **2** a stick or bat used to hit a ball in some games: *golf clubs.* **3** an Indian club. **4** *Nautical.* a light, small spar used to hold a small sail, especially one at the top of a mast of a vessel which is rigged fore and aft. **5a** a group of people joined together for some special purpose: *a tennis club, a canoe club, a nature-study club.* SYN: association, society. **b** the building, rooms, or facilities used by a club; clubhouse or clubroom. **c** a night club: *fashionable clubs and resorts.* **6** a business organization which offers certain benefits to members or subscribers: *a record club, a book club, an investment club.* **7** a group of nations associated in some enterprise or activity: *the NATO club, the Common Market club. . . . to keep Germany partitioned and out of even associate membership in the atomic club* (C. L. Sulzberger). **8** a figure shaped like a trefoil leaf. **9** a playing card with one or more black, trefoil-leaf figures.
—*v.t.* **1** to beat or hit with a club or something similar; knock down with a club: *The boys clubbed the hornets' nest with a long stick. The hikers clubbed the snake to death with their walking sticks.* (*Figurative.*) *They* [*unions*] *have proved by repeated strikes that they could club the city into giving them better contracts* (New York Times). **2** to turn (a rifle) around to use as a club. **3** to gather or form into a club-shaped mass: *He had a few gray hairs plaited and clubbed behind* (Washington Irving). **4** to contribute as one's share toward a common fund or for a certain purpose; make up by contributing jointly: *The alumni of the school clubbed a fund of money for needy students.* **5** to combine into one; join together; unite: *. . . clubbing our books in a common library* (Benjamin Franklin).
—*v.i.* **1** to join together for some special purpose. **2** to contribute to a common fund; share expenses: *The children clubbed together to buy a birthday present for their mother.* **3** to form a club. **4** to gather into a mass.
—*adj.* of or having to do with a club or clubs.
clubs, the suit of playing cards marked with black trefoil-leaf figures: *In this game, clubs are trump.*
[< Scandinavian (compare Old Icelandic *klubba*)]

***club**
definition 8

club|ba|ble or **club|a|ble** (klub'ə bəl), *adj.* fit to be a member of a club; sociable; companionable: *Essentially Wilson was a clubbable man. He loved good company and he loved a good game of golf or bridge* (London Times).

clubbed (klubd), *adj.* club-shaped; thick at the end.

club|ber (klub'ər), *n.* **1** a person who belongs to a club or clubs; clubman. **2** a person who wields a club: [*His*] *reputation as a clubber and as an efficient riot-queller is much more than local* (New York Voice).

club|bish (klub'ish), *adj.* = clubby. —**club'bish-ness,** *n.*

club|by (klub'ē), *adj.* **1** of a clubbable or social nature: *Your natural impulse in the dark is to be clubby* (New Yorker). **2** pervaded by the characteristics of a club: *English literary life is almost too clubby, too narrowly dominated by a set of good companions* (Saturday Review). —**club'bi|ly,** *adv.* —**club'bi|ness,** *n.*

club car, *U.S.* a car of a passenger train equipped with swivel or movable armchairs, frequently also with a buffet or bar.

club chair, a kind of easy chair with thick upholstery, a low back, and upholstered arms.

club collar, a short, close-fitting collar that opens at the front.

club|dom (klub'dəm), *n.* the realm or world of clubs; clubs collectively.

club fighter, a professional boxer of average ability who fights hard and can absorb punishment.

club|foot (klub'fu̇t'), *n., pl.* **-feet. 1** a deformed foot, appearing short and distorted. **2** a deformity of the foot caused by faulty development before birth; talipes. The front part is twisted and appears shortened.

club|foot|ed (klub'fu̇t'id), *adj.* having a clubfoot.

club grass, = cattail (def. 1).

club|hand (klub'hand'), *n.* **1** a deformed hand. **2** a rare deformity of the hand, caused by faulty development before birth.

club|haul (klub'hôl'), *v.t.* to bring (a square-rigged vessel) about when dangerously close to a lee shore or similar peril by dropping the lee anchor, maneuvering the vessel's head into the wind, and cutting the cable as it pays off on the other tack.

club|house (klub'hous'), *n.* a building used by a club: *. . . the clubhouse, a two-story structure that has everything, including a glass front and a handsome dining room* (New Yorker).

club|land (klub'land', -lənd), *n.* the realm of clubs; clubdom: *His spare time was spent in clubland or driving his car in the country* (Punch).

club law, 1 the use of the club to enforce obedience; physical force as contrasted with argument; law or rule of the physically stronger: *Club law . . . may make hypocrites, it can never make converts* (George Bancroft). **2** a rule in the game of loo that when clubs are trumps no player may pass or give up his hand.

club|man (klub'mən), *n., pl.* **-men. 1** a man who belongs to a club or clubs; man who enjoys club activities. **2** a man armed with a club.

club|mo|bile (klub'mə bēl), *n. U.S.* a bus or truck used as a traveling canteen or club to serve soldiers, workers, firemen, or disaster victims. [< *club* + *-mobile,* as in *bookmobile*]

club moss, 1 any one of a group of flowerless plants, related to the ferns and not true mosses, that are either erect or creeping, usually mosslike, and bear club-shaped cones which contain reproductive spores; ground pine; lycopod; lycopodium. Club mosses are often used in Christmas decorations. **2** a huge fossil tree that 300 million years ago grew along with tree ferns in steaming hot swamps and was turned into coal or became petrified.

club|room (klub'rüm', -ru̇m'), *n.* a room for club activities.

club|root (klub'rüt', -ru̇t'), *n.* a disease of cabbages and allied plants caused by a certain slime mold which produces swellings on the roots.

club rush, 1 = bulrush (def. 1). **2** = cattail (def. 1).

clubs (klubz), *n.pl.* See under **club**.

club sandwich, a sandwich, usually of more than one layer, consisting of toast and fillings such as chicken, ham, or bacon with lettuce, tomatoes, and mayonnaise.

club-shaped (klub'shāpt'), *adj.* having the shape of a club; thicker at one end than at the other.

club soda, unflavored carbonated water, used in making mixed drinks.

club sofa, a kind of sofa similar in style to a club chair.

club steak, a small beefsteak cut from the tip of the loin.

club topsail, a large fore-and-aft topsail with its head extended by a light spar and its foot by a club longer than a gaff, so as to permit greater area of sail.

club wheat, a species of wheat characterized by a short, dense head and short, stiff straw: *Club wheats are grown only in the Pacific Coast states* (K. S. Quisenberry).

club|wom|an (klub'wu̇m'ən), *n., pl.* **-wom|en.** a woman who belongs to a club or clubs; woman who enjoys club activities.

cluck (kluk), *n., v.* —*n.* **1** the sound that a hen makes when calling her chickens: *With several motherly clucks the hen rounded up her chicks.* **2** a sound like this. **3** *U.S. Slang, Figurative.* a stupid person; blockhead; fool: *"You are a complete cluck," Susan declared. "So are you," her witty knight countered* (Delmore Schwartz).
—*v.i.* **1** (of a hen) to make a cluck when calling chickens: *The hens began to cluck as we gathered the eggs from their nests.* **2** to make a sound like this: *When Guerin, her jockey, clucked to her, she bounded to the front and won* (New Yorker).
—*v.t.* to call by clucking.
[imitative]

clue (klü), *n., v.,* **clued, clu|ing** or **clue|ing.** —*n.* **1** a fact or object which aids in solving a mystery or problem: *The police could find no fingerprints or other clues to help them in solving the robbery. I hadn't a clue as to how the things should be served . . . I had never seen whale meat in that form* (Edith Iglauer). **2** = clew.
—*v.t.* **1** to indicate (something) by means of a clue. **2** *Informal.* to give a clue to: *A marine won't just tell you something or fill you in; he'll "clue" you* (New York Times).
[variant of *clew*] —**clue'less,** *adj.*

clum|ber (klum'bər), *n.,* or **clumber spaniel,** any one of a breed of hunting dogs having a white coat with orange or yellow markings, short legs and a long, heavy body. It works rather slowly as a hunter, but is easily trained and has a good memory. [< *Clumber,* an estate of the Duke of Newcastle]

clump (klump), *n., v.* —*n.* **1** a small, closely gathered group; cluster: *The boy hid in a clump of trees.* SYN: bunch, clutch[2]. **2** a lump or mass: *a clump of earth.* SYN: clod. **3** *Biology.* a number of bacteria, blood cells, etc., agglutinated together. **4** the sound of heavy, clumsy walking. **5** a thick extra sole on a shoe.
—*v.i.* **1** to walk with a heavy, clumsy, noisy tread: *The weary hiker clumped along in his heavy boots.* **2** to form a clump. **3** *Biology.* to col-

lect into or form clumps.
—*v.t.* **1** to form into a clump; plant in clusters. **2** *Biology.* to cause to collect in clumps: *If red blood cells from one person are mixed with blood plasma of another individual, the cells remain separate in some cases and become clumped, or agglutinated, in others* (Tracy I. Storer).
[probably < Middle Low German *klumpe,* or Middle Dutch *klompe*]

clump|ish (klum′pish), *adj.* somewhat clumpy; heavy and clumsy; lumpish.

clump|y (klum′pē), *adj.,* **clump|i|er, clump|i|est.** **1** full of clumps. **2** like clumps. **3** heavy and clumsy.

clum|sy (klum′zē), *adj.,* **-si|er, -si|est.** **1** awkward in moving; not graceful or skillful: *The clumsy boy bumped into all the furniture.* **SYN**: ungraceful, ungainly. See syn. under **awkward. 2** *Figurative.* awkwardly done; poorly contrived; tactless: *My clumsy reply hurt her feelings.* **3** not well-shaped or well-made: *His rowboat was a clumsy affair made out of old boxes.* **SYN**: unwieldy, inelegant.
[probably Middle English *clumsen* be numb with cold, perhaps < Scandinavian (compare Old Icelandic *klumsa* lock-jawed)] —**clum′si|ly,** *adv.* —**clum′si|ness,** *n.*

clunch (klunch), *n.* **1** any one of certain impure varieties of clay found in England, especially an indurated kind. **2** a soft limestone of England, sometimes used as a building stone. [perhaps < Dutch *klont* lump, clod]

clung (klung), *v.* past tense and past participle of **cling**: *The child clung to her mother. The sticky mud had clung to my fingers.*

Clu|ni|ac (klü′nē ak), *adj.* belonging to the abbey or monastery of Cluny, France.

clunk (klungk), *n., v.* —*n.* **1** a sound like that of a hard object striking the ground; thud; thump: *High and far it* [*the discus*] *spun, then came down with a clunk—on the far side of the little red flag* (Time). **2** *Scottish.* a sound like that made by a cork pulled from a bottle.
—*v.i., v.t.* to make such a sound; strike with a clunk; thump: *... refreshing to find a vehicle on which the doors clunk firmly shut* (Punch). Also, **clonk.**
[imitative]

clunk|er (klung′kər), *n. U.S. Slang.* **1** an old, rickety automobile or other machine; rattletrap. **2** any thing of little value: *His latest book is a clunker.* [< *clunk* + *-er*[1]]

clunk|y (klung′kē), *adj.,* **clunk|i|er, clunk|i|est.** making a heavy, thumping sound; clunking: *clunky shoes.*

***Clu|ny lace** (klü′nē; *French* kly nē′), a kind of lace made of heavy linen or cotton thread, usually with geometrical and wheel designs.

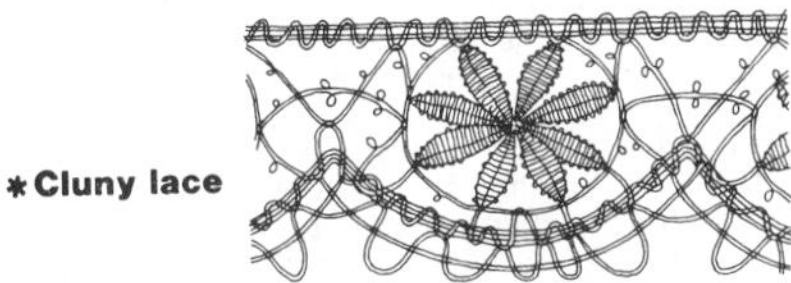
***Cluny lace**

clu|pe|id (klü′pē id), *adj., n.* —*adj.* of or having to do with a family of small, mainly marine fishes, including the herrings, sardines, and shad.
—*n.* a clupeid fish.
[< New Latin *Clupeidae* the family name < *Clupea* the herring genus < Latin *clupea* small river fish]

clu|pe|i|form (klü′pē ə fôrm), *adj.* having the form or appearance of a herring. [< New Latin *Clupea* (see etym. under **clupeid**) + English *-form*]

clu|pe|in (klü′pē in), *n.* a protamine obtained from the roe of herring: *60 mg. of protamine* (*clupein*) *instantaneously neutralize the effect of 100 mg. of heparin* (Beaumont and Dodds). [< New Latin *Clupea* (see etym. under **clupeid**) + English *-in*]

clu|pe|oid (klü′pē oid), *adj., n.* —*adj.* of or like the herrings.
—*n.* a clupeoid fish.
[< New Latin *Clupea* (see etym. under **clupeid**) + English *-oid*]

clu|si|a (klü′shē ə, -sē-), *n.* a tropical American shrub or tree, parasitic in some species: *High up in the forest canopy the large, leathery, dark-green leaves and the showy, rose-colored flowers of clusia mingle with the foliage of the host tree* (Scientific American). [< New Latin *Clusia;* see etym. under **clusiaceous**]

clu|si|a|ceous (klü′sē ā′shəs), *adj.* belonging to a family of tropical trees and shrubs yielding resins, such as gamboge and tacamahac, fruits, such as the mangosteen, and various useful woods. [< New Latin *Clusiaceae* < *Clusia* the typical genus < Charles de Les*cluse,* a French botanist]

clus|ter (klus′tər), *n., v.* —*n.* **1** a number of things of the same kind growing or grouped together: *a cluster of grapes, a little cluster of houses in the valley.* **SYN**: bunch, clump. **2** any group of persons or things: *The citizens appeared in a cluster before the mayor's house.* **SYN**: assemblage. **3** *U.S. Army.* a small metal device placed on the ribbon standing for a medal, to show that the same medal has been awarded again: *an oak-leaf cluster.* **4** *Phonetics.* a sequence of two or more vowel or, especially, consonant sounds. *Str-* in *string* is a consonant cluster. **5** *Astronomy.* a group of stars relatively close to each other and often found to have a common motion in space, especially a globular cluster.
—*v.i.* to be in a bunch; gather in a group: *The girls clustered around their teacher.* **SYN**: assemble, collect, congregate, flock. —*v.t.* **1** to gather into a cluster. **2** to furnish with clusters.
[Old English *cluster, clystre*]

cluster bomb, a bomb that scatters small fragmentation bombs upon impact.

cluster college, any one of a group of small, autonomous, liberal-arts colleges within a university, modeled on those of Oxford and Cambridge: *The University of the Pacific at Stockton, California, has just announced the addition of a third cluster college to its complex* (Saturday Review).

cluster cup, = aecium.

clus|tered (klus′tərd), *adj.* **1** gathered into or forming a cluster: *a clustered column.* **2** furnished or covered with clusters.

cluster fly, a large fly, related to the common housefly, that enters buildings in autumn and clusters especially to windows and walls.

cluster headache, severe headache occurring repeatedly over a period of weeks followed by an interval of relief of several months: *Cluster headaches, unlike migraines, strike with little or no warning, affecting six times as many men as women* (New York Times).

clus|ter-type variable or **Cepheid** (klus′tər-tīp′), any variable star with a period of less than one day.

cluster variable, = cluster-type variable.

clus|ter|y (klus′tər ē), *adj.* having or forming clusters.

***clutch**[1] (kluch), *v., n., adj.* —*v.t.* **1** to grasp tightly; grip firmly: *The girl clutched her doll in her arms.* **SYN**: See syn. under **seize. 2** to seize eagerly; snatch: *The child clutched the marbles and ran away.*
—*v.i.* **1** to seize eagerly; snatch: *A drowning man will clutch at a straw.* (*Figurative.*) *How we clutch at shadows* (Thomas Carlyle). **2** *U.S. Slang, Figurative.* to become tense or anxious.
—*n.* **1** a tight grasp; hold: *He lost his clutch on the rope and fell. The eagle flew away with a rabbit in the clutch of its claws.* **SYN**: grip, clench. **2** Often, **clutches. a** a grasping claw, paw, hand, etc.: *Quick shooting saved the hunter from the bear's clutches.* **b** *Figurative.* control; power: *The thief was in the clutches of the police.* **3** the act of clutching; attempt to seize; snatch. **4a** a device in a machine for connecting or disconnecting the engine or motor that makes the machine go. The clutch of an automobile is used to connect the engine with the transmission or to disconnect it from the transmission. **b** the lever or pedal that operates this device.
—*adj.* **1a** having no handle or strap; designed to be clutched in carrying: *a clutch bag, a clutch purse.* **b** having no fasteners and held closed by clutching: *a clutch coat, a clutch cape.* **2** *U.S. Slang, Figurative.* that can be depended on in a pinch or emergency; crucial or decisive: *a great clutch player.*

in the clutch, *Informal.* at a crucial or decisive moment: *When pressure hits we fall to pieces ...* [*but*] *Barry seems to be at his best in the clutch* (Saturday Evening Post).
[Old English *clyccan* bend, clench]

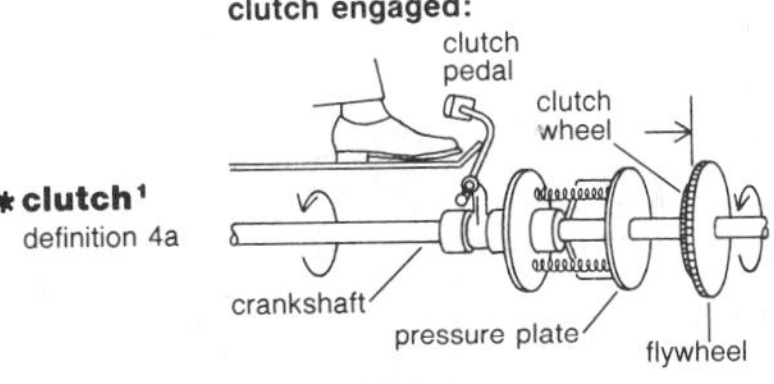

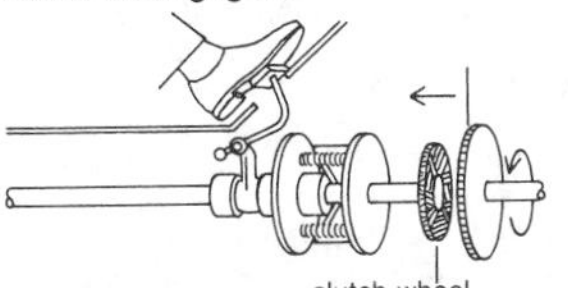

***clutch**[1]
definition 4a

clutch[2] (kluch), *n., v.* —*n.* **1** a nest of eggs: *If a clutch of eggs is lost, it is unusual for a second clutch to be laid* (Scientific American). **2** a brood of chickens. **3** a group of people or things: *It tells a novelettish story about a clutch of Polish resistance workers* (Observer). —*v.t.* to hatch.
[variant of earlier *cletch* < *cleck* hatch < Scandinavian (compare Old Icelandic *klekja* to hatch)]

clut|ter (klut′ər), *n., v.* —*n.* **1** a number of things scattered or left in disorder; litter; confusion: *It was hard to find the lost pen in the clutter of his desk.* **2** a confused noise; loud clatter; hubbub. **3** images of interference on radar: *They will also study "clutter" on radar screens—false signals caused by clouds, rain, patches of warm and cool air, high buildings, and even birds* (London Times).
—*v.t.* **1** to litter with things in confusion: *Her desk was all cluttered with old papers, strings, and other odds and ends.* **2** to throw into mental confusion and disorder: *She cluttered her mind with trivialities.* —*v.i.* **1** to make a confused noise; clatter loudly. **2** to run in crowded and bustling disorder. **3** to run together; collect; crowd.
[apparently a variant of *clotter* < *clot*]

clut|ter|y (klut′ər ē), *adj.* somewhat cluttered or disordered: *We have seen heavy, cluttery pieces* [*of writing*], *with faults clinging to them like barnacles, lifted out of their trouble by the accurate fire of the grammarian* (New Yorker).

Clydes|dale (klīdz′dāl), *n.* a kind of strong draft horse with long, flowing hair below the knee and the hock, popular for pulling wagons in parades. [< *Clydesdale,* Scotland, where they were originally bred]

Clydesdale terrier, any dog of a variety of small Skye terriers.

Clyde|sid|er (klīd′sī′dər), *n.* **1** a person who lives on or near the bank of the river Clyde in Scotland. **2** a member of that segment of the Labour Party in Great Britain whose leaders are associated with Glasgow and the neighboring industrial area.

Clym|e|ne (klim′ə nē), *n. Greek Mythology.* the mother of Atlas and Prometheus.

clyp|e|al (klip′ē əl), *adj.* of or having to do with the clypeus: *the clypeal region.*

clyp|e|ate (klip′ē āt), *adj. Biology.* **1** shaped like a round shield or buckler; clypeiform. **2** having a clypeus: *a clypeate insect.* [< Latin *clipeātus* having a shield < *clipeus* clypeus]

clyp|e|at|ed (klip′ē ā′tid), *adj.* = clypeate.

clyp|e|i|form (klip′ē ə fôrm), *adj.* shaped like a round shield; clypeate. [< Latin *clypeus* round shield + English *-form*]

clyp|e|us (klip′ē əs), *n., pl.* **-e|i** (-ē ī). a shieldlike plate on the front part of the head of an insect, above the mouth. [< Latin *clypeus, clipeus* round shield]

clys|ter (klis′tər), *n.* = enema. [< Latin *clyster* < Greek *klystḗr* liquid for rinsing; a syringe < *klýzein* wash out]

Cly|tem|nes|tra or **Cly|taem|nes|tra** (klī′təm-nes′trə), *n. Greek Legend.* the wife of Agamemnon and half sister of Helen. With her lover Aegisthus, she killed Agamemnon on his return from Troy, and was afterwards slain by her son Orestes.

cm. or **cm** (no period), centimeter or centimeters.

c.m., an abbreviation for the following:
1 church missionary.
2 circular mill.
3 corresponding member.
4 countermarked.

Cm (no period), curium (chemical element).

CM (no periods), **1** command module. **2** Common Market. **3** court-martial.

CMA (no periods), Canadian Medical Association.

Cmdg., commanding.

Cmdr., commander.

C.M.G., Companion of (the Order of) St. Michael and St. George.

cml., commercial.

C.M.T.C., *U.S.* Citizens' Military Training Camp.

CMU (no periods), Canadian Maritime Union.

CN (no periods), **1** chloroacetophenone (a tear gas). **2** credit note.

CND (no periods), Campaign for Nuclear Disarmament.

cne|mis (nē′mis), *n. Anatomy.* the leg from knee to ankle; tibia. [< New Latin *cnemis* < Greek *knēmís* greave, legging < *knḗmē* lower leg]

cni|do|blast (nī′də blast), *n.* the cell in which a nematocyst (a stinging process on a coelenterate) is developed. [< Greek *knídē* nettle + *blastós* germ]

cni|do|cil (nī′də sil), *n.* the external, irritable, cili-

Pronunciation Key: hat, āge, cãre, fär; let, ēqual, tėrm; it, īce; hot, ōpen, ôrder; oil, out; cup, pu̇t, rüle; child; long; thin; ᴛʜen; zh, measure; ə represents **a** in about, **e** in taken, **i** in pencil, **o** in lemon, **u** in circus.

ary process of a cnidoblast: *Each nematocyst is included in an interstitial cell that has been modified as a cnidoblast, on the exterior of which is a triggerlike cnidocil* (Tracy I. Storer). [< *cnido-*(blast) + *cil*(ia)]

CNO (no periods) or **C.N.O.**, Chief of Naval Operations.

C-note (sē′nōt′), *n. Slang.* a hundred-dollar bill. [< *C*[1] + *note*]

CNS (no periods), central nervous system.

co-, *prefix.* a form of **com-**.
1 with; together: *Cooperate = to act with or together.*
2 joint; fellow: *Coauthor = a joint or fellow author.*
3 equally: *Coextensive = equally extensive.*
4 *Mathematics.* complement: *Cosine = sine of the complement (of a given angle or arc).*
[< Latin *co-*, variant of *com-* with < *cum* with]

c/o (no periods) or **c.o.**, **1** carried over. **2** in care of.

Co (no period), cobalt (chemical element).

Co. or **co.**, **1** company. **2** county.

CO (no periods) or **C.O.**, an abbreviation for the following:
1 cash order.
2 Colorado (with postal Zip Code).
3 commanding officer.
4 *Informal.* conscientious objector.

co|ac|er|vate (kō as′ər vāt), *n. Chemistry.* droplets of liquid that form in a lyophilic solution before the precipitation of solid material. [< Latin *coacervātus,* past participle of *coacervāre* to heap up together < *co-* together + *acervāre* heap up < *acervus* heap] —**co′ac|er|va′tion**, *n.*

coach (kōch), *n., v.* —*n.* **1** a large, old-fashioned, closed carriage with seats inside. It was usually pulled by horses. Those which carried passengers along a regular run, with stops for meals and fresh horses, often had seats on top too. **SYN:** stagecoach. **2a** a passenger car of a railroad train; day coach: *The coach seats were filled with commuters on their way home.* **b** a class of passenger accommodations on a commercial aircraft at lower rates than first class. **3** a closed automobile like a sedan. **4** a bus; motor coach: *The coach bumped along the road picking up passengers for Boston.* **5** a person who teaches or trains athletic teams, actors, singers, etc.: *a football coach, a drama coach, a singing coach.* **6** *Baseball.* a person stationed near first or third base to direct base runners and the batter. **7** a private teacher who helps a student prepare for a special test. **SYN:** tutor.
—*v.t.* **1** to train or teach; instruct: *He coaches the football team. She coached me in chess.* **2** to direct (a base runner or a batter) in baseball. **3** to help to prepare for a special test. **4** to carry in a coach.
—*v.i.* **1** to act as a coach: *He coaches at a small college.* **2** *Baseball.* to direct the batter and base runners from a coach's box. **3** to study with or be instructed by a coach. **4** to ride in a coach.
[< Middle French *coche,* ultimately < Hungarian *kocsi* (literally) of *Kocs,* a town in Hungary, where the vehicle originated]

coach-and-four (kōch′ən fôr′, -fōr′), *n.* a coach pulled by four horses: . . . *a coach-and-four would come trundling from a distance, the horses' hoofbeats pounding* (Atlantic).

coach box, the seat occupied by the driver of a coach.

coach|build|er (kōch′bil′dər), *n. British.* a person who designs or builds automobile bodies.

coach|build|ing (kōch′bil′ding), *n. British.* the designing or building of bodies for automobiles.

coach dog, = Dalmatian.

coach|ee (kō′chē), *n. Informal.* a driver of a coach, especially a public coach; coachman.

coach|er (kō′chər), *n.* **1** a baseball coach. **2** = coach horse. **3** *Obsolete.* a coachman.

coach|fel|low (kōch′fel′ō), *n.* **1** either of a pair of coach horses. **2** a close companion; comrade.

coach|ful (kōch′fu̇l), *n., pl.* **-fuls**. as many as a coach will hold.

coach horse, a horse used to draw a coach, especially a heavy harness horse.

coach house, a building or outhouse for a coach or carriage.

coach|ing (kō′ching), *n.* **1** the profession or work of a coach. **2** instruction given by a coach.

coach|load (kōch′lōd′), *n. British.* as much as a coach can hold or carry.

coach|man (kōch′mən), *n., pl.* **-men**. **1** a man who drives a coach or carriage. **2** an artificial fishing fly with white wings, brown hackle, and green body.

coach|man|ship (kōch′mən ship), *n.* the work of a coachman; skill in driving a coach.

coach|whip (kōch′hwip′), *n.* **1** = coachwhip snake. **2** = ocotillo.

coachwhip snake, a harmless snake related to the black snake, having a long, slender body with scales arranged like the braids of a whip.

coach|work (kōch′wėrk′), *n.* the trim and finishing work applied to the body of an automobile.

co|act (kō akt′), *v.t.* to enact together with others. —*v.i.* to act together.

co|ac|tion (kō ak′shən), *n.* compulsion; constraint; coercion. [< Latin *coactiō, -ōnis* a collecting < *cōgere* drive together < *co-* together + *agere* drive, compel]

co-ac|tion (kō ak′shən), *n.* **1** an acting together. **2** *Ecology.* the reciprocal actions or effects of animals and plants: *There are nine kinds of "co-action" possible between weak and strong organisms, ranging from symbiosis, in which there is mutual aid, to a mutual depression or dying together* (Science News Letter).

co|ac|tive (kō ak′tiv), *adj.* coercive; compulsory.

co-ac|tive (kō ak′tiv), *adj.* acting together.

co-ac|tor (kō ak′tər), *n.* a person who acts jointly with another or others.

co|ad|just (kō′ə just′), *v.t.* to adjust mutually, or each to the other. —**co′ad|just′ment**, *n.*

co|ad|ju|tor (kō aj′ə tər, kō′ə jü′-), *n.* **1** a helper; assistant; associate: *Perhaps she was unfortunate in her coadjutors, but, in reality, the responsibility for the failure must lie with [Queen] Victoria herself* (Lytton Strachey). **2** a bishop appointed to assist another bishop, usually having the right to succeed him. [< Old French *coadjuteur,* learned borrowing from Late Latin *coadjūtor* < Latin *co-* with + *adjūtor* helper < *adjuvāre* < *ad-* to, toward + *juvāre* help] —**co|ad′ju|tor-ship**, *n.*

co|ad|ju|tress (kō aj′ə tris), *n.* a woman coadjutor or helper.

co|ad|ju|trix (kō aj′ə triks), *n., pl.* **-ad|ju|tri|ces** (-aj′ə trī′sēz). = coadjutress.

co|ad|ju|van|cy (kō aj′ə vən sē), *n.* assistance; cooperation.

co|ad|ju|vant (kō aj′ə vənt), *adj., n.* —*adj.* assisting; cooperating.
—*n.* **1** a cooperating agent. **2** an ingredient which helps to increase the effect of another ingredient in a medical prescription.

co|ad|u|nate (kō aj′ə nit, -nāt), *adj., v.,* **-nat|ed, -nat|ing**. —*adj.* **1** = united. **2** *Zoology, Botany.* joined together; grown together.
—*v.t.* to make one; unite; combine.
[< Late Latin *coadūnātus,* past participle of *coadūnāre* < *co-* together + *adūnāre* make one < Latin *ad-* together + *ūnus* one. See related etym. at **unite**[1].] —**co|ad′u|na′tion**, *n.*

co|ae|val (kō ē′vəl), *adj.* = coeval.

co|a|gen|cy (kō ā′jən sē), *n., pl.* **-cies**. joint or combined agency.

co|a|gent (kō ā′jənt), *n.* a joint agent; assistant.

co|ag|u|la (kō ag′yə lə), *n.* a plural of **coagulum**.

co|ag|u|la|bil|i|ty (kō ag′yə lə bil′ə tē), *n., pl.* **-ties**. the ability to become coagulated.

co|ag|u|la|ble (kō ag′yə lə bəl), *adj.* that can be coagulated: *Adrenin renders the blood more rapidly coagulable* (Scientific American).

co|ag|u|lant (kō ag′yə lənt), *n.* a substance producing coagulation.

co|ag|u|lase (kō ag′yə lās), *n. Biochemistry.* an enzyme that causes coagulation, produced by certain forms of staphylococci. [< *coagul*(ate) + *-ase*]

co|ag|u|late (*v.* kō ag′yə lāt; *adj.* kō ag′yə lit, -lāt), *v.,* **-lat|ed, -lat|ing**, *adj.* —*v.t., v.i.* **1** to change from liquid to a thickened mass; thicken: *Cooking coagulates the white of egg. Blood from a cut coagulates.* **SYN:** curdle, clot, congeal. **2** *Obsolete.* to form into a solidified cake or mass.
—*adj. Obsolete.* coagulated.
[< Latin *coāgulāre* (with English *-ate*[1]) < *coāgulum* means of curdling < *co-* together + *agere* drive]

co|ag|u|la|tion (kō ag′yə lā′shən), *n.* **1** the act or process of coagulating. If coagulation of the blood does not take place in a cut or wound, the injured person may bleed to death. **2** a coagulated mass; clot.

co|ag|u|la|tive (kō ag′yə lā′tiv), *adj.* tending to coagulate or cause coagulation.

co|ag|u|la|tor (kō ag′yə lā′tər), *n.* a coagulating agent.

co|ag|u|len (kō ag′yə lən), *n.* a concentrated preparation of thrombin or allied substances which causes the clotting of blood and is used to stop hemorrhage. [alteration of *coagulin*]

co|ag|u|lin (kō ag′yə lin), *n.* = precipitin.

co|ag|u|lom|et|er (kō ag′yə lom′ə tər), *n.* an instrument for measuring the rate at which a sample of blood or other fluid coagulates.

co|ag|u|lum (kō ag′yə ləm), *n., pl.* **-la** or **-lums**. a mass of coagulated matter, as of blood; clot. [< Latin *coāgulum* means of curdling; rennet]

Co|a|huil|te|can (kō′ə wēl′tə kən), *n.* an extinct linguistic stock consisting of several languages once spoken among the Indians of the lower Rio Grande in Texas and northeastern Mexico. [< Spanish *coahuilteca* a member of an Indian tribe in Texas and Mexico (< *Coahuila,* a state in Mexico + *azteca* Aztec) + English *-an*]

coak (kōk), *n., v.* —*n.* a projection from a piece of wood or timber fitting into a hole in another piece at their joint, or a cylinder or pin of hard wood or the like set into both pieces, used in ship carpentry.
—*v.t.* to join (wood) by means of a coak or coaks.
[compare French *coche* notch]

coal (kōl), *n., v.* —*n.* **1a** a solid, hard black substance that burns and gives off heat. Coal is composed mostly of carbon. It is formed from partly decayed vegetable matter under great pressure and heat in the earth. Anthracite coal has greater carbonization than bituminous coal because it has been under greater pressure and heat during its formation. Coal is obtained by mining but is not a true mineral. *There are two important kinds of coal: bituminous, or soft, coal, and anthracite, or hard, coal* (Beauchamp, Mayfield, and West). **b** a piece or pieces of this substance for burning: *a bag of coal.* **2** a piece of wood, coal, or other combustible material, burning, partly burned, or all burned; ember: *The big log had burned down to a few glowing coals.* **3** = charcoal.
—*v.t.* **1** to supply with coal: *to coal a ship.* **2** to convert into charcoal; char.
—*v.i.* to be supplied with coal: *The ship stopped just long enough to coal.*
call over the coals, **a** to scold; blame: *He was called over the coals for cheating on the exam.* **b** a scolding; censure: *Your magistrates . . . vastly needed a call over the coals* (H. O. Traill).
carry coals to Newcastle. See under **Newcastle**.
coals, *British.* pieces of coal used for burning: *Turning of trees to coals for fuel, when there is sufficient dead wood, is waste* (Edward Coke).
haul (or **rake**) **over the coals**, to scold; blame: *He [Lenin] threw overboard the Soviet majority, and hauled the Bolsheviks themselves over the coals* (Edmund Wilson).
heap coals of fire on one's head, to make one sorry by returning good for evil: *Therefore if thine enemy hunger, feed him; if he thirst, give him drink: for in so doing thou shalt heap coals of fire on his head* (Romans 12:20).
[Old English *col*]

Coal Age or **coal age**, the Carboniferous period, during which most of the coal deposits were formed: *By the latter part of the Coal Age, this continent had begun to crack up and the pieces to drift apart* (White and Renner).

coal bin, an enclosure for the storage of coal.

coal-black (kōl′blak′), *adj.* black as coal; very black.

coal-box (kōl′boks′), *n. Military Slang.* a low-velocity shell used by the Germans in World War I, to lay quantities of dense, black smoke as a screen.

coal car, *U.S.* **1** an open railroad car designed for carrying coal. **2** a car for carrying coal in a mine or away from it.

coal|er (kō′lər), *n.* **1** a ship, freight car, or railroad, used for carrying or supplying coal. **2** a worker or merchant who supplies coal.

co|a|lesce (kō′ə les′), *v.i.,* **-lesced, -lesc|ing**. **1** to grow together. **SYN:** fuse. **2** to unite into one body, mass, or party; combine: *The thirteen colonies coalesced to form a nation.* **SYN:** consolidate, merge. [< Latin *coalēscere* < *co-* together + *alēscere* grow < *alere* nourish]

co|a|les|cence (kō′ə les′əns), *n.* **1** a growing together. **2** union; combination.

co|a|les|cent (kō′ə les′ənt), *adj., n.* —*adj.* coalescing. —*n.* a person or thing that coalesces.

coal-face (kōl′fās′), *n.* **1** the surface of coal exposed by mining. **2** the place where the coal is being mined.

coal field, or **coal|field** (kōl′fēld′), *n.* a region where beds of coal are found.

coal|fish (kōl′fish′), *n., pl.* **-fish|es** or (*collectively*) **-fish**. **1** = beshow. **2** a pollack.

coal gas, **1a** gas made from coal, used for heating and lighting. **b** coke-oven gas. **2** gas given off by burning coal.

coal heaver, a person who carries or shovels coal.

coal hod, = coal scuttle.

coal|hole (kōl′hōl′), *n.* **1** a trap or hole for receiving coal to be stored in a coal bin. **2** *British.* a coal bin.

coal|house (kōl′hous′), *n.* a building or enclosure for the storage of coal.

coal|i|fi|ca|tion (kō′lə fə kā′shən), *n. Geology.* the formation of a coal bed or seam. [< *coal* + *-fication*]

coal|ing station (kō′ling), a place where ships or trains are supplied with coal.

co|a|li|tion (kō′ə lish′ən), *n.* **1** a union into one mass or body. **SYN:** fusion. **2a** voluntary union or combination, as of parties or principles. **SYN:** league. **b** a temporary alliance, especially of statesmen or political parties, for some special purpose. In wartime several countries may form a coalition against a common enemy. *All the great coalitions, beginning with the Hellenic coalition against Persia in the fifth century B.C., have depended heavily on external pressure for their cohesion* (Harper's). SYN: league. [< Late Latin *coalitiō, -ōnis* < Latin *coalēscere* coalesce]

co|a|li|tion|ist (kō′ə lish′ə nist), *n.* a person who supports a coalition.

co|a|lize (kō′ə līz), *v.t.,* **-lized, -liz|ing.** to join in a coalition. — **co′a|liz′er,** *n.*

coal|man (kōl′mən), *n., pl.* **-men.** a man who sells or delivers coal: *Not much coal left—must ring coalman* (Punch).

coal measures, strata containing coal.

Coal Measures, *Geology.* the upper division of the Pennsylvanian epoch, containing seams of coal with intervening strata of clay, sandstone, or the like.

coal mine, a mine or pit where coal is dug from the earth; colliery.

coal miner, a person who mines coal; collier.

coal mining, the business or work of mining coal.

coal-min|ing (kōl′mī′ning), *adj.* engaged in or connected with mining coal.

coal oil, 1 = kerosene. 2 = petroleum.

coal pit, 1 = coal mine. 2 a place where charcoal is made.

coal plant, a fossil plant found in association with or entering into the composition of coal.

coal pocket, a structure with bunkers and appliances for receiving, storing, and loading coal.

coals (kōlz), *n.pl.* See under **coal.**

Coal|sack (kōl′sak′), *n.* one of two large, dark markings in the Milky Way, due to obscuring clouds of cosmic dust, especially the one near the Southern Cross: ... *studies of the southern Coalsack, the most distinct dark nebula of our Milky Way* (Scientific American).

***coal scuttle,** a bucket for holding or carrying coal; coal hod.

***coal scuttle**

coal tar, a black, sticky substance left after bituminous coal has been distilled to make coal gas. Coal tar is used to make roofing and paving materials. Aniline dyes, flavorings, perfumes, benzene, paraffin, naphtha, and many other products contain substances made from coal tar. *From coal tars came a series of compounds, called aromatic because of their pungent odor, whose structure took the form of ring-shaped molecules* (Scientific American).

coal tit, a European titmouse (bird), with black markings on the head and throat.

co-al|ti|tude (kō al′tə tüd, -tyüd), *n. Astronomy, Surveying.* the complement of the altitude of a heavenly body; its angular distance from the zenith.

coal-whip|per (kōl′hwip′ər), *n. British.* a person or machine that raises coal from the hold of a ship to unload it.

coal|y (kō′lē), *adj.* 1 of or like coal. 2 containing coal.

coal|yard (kōl′yärd′), *n.* a yard in which coal is stored or sold.

co|am|bu|lant (kō am′byə lənt), *adj. Heraldry.* walking side by side: *coambulant deer.*

coam|ing (kō′ming), *n.* 1 a raised edge around a hatch or opening in a deck of a ship or roof to prevent water from running down below: *He swung his thick legs clumsily over the hatch coaming and stood up dizzily, clinging for support to the lifeline at the rail* (Atlantic). 2 one of the pieces of this, especially a fore-and-aft section. [origin uncertain]

Co|an|da effect (kō an′də), the property or tendency of any fluid passing a curved surface to attach itself to the surface; wall-attachment effect. The Coanda effect is important in fluidics and aerodynamics. *A common demonstration of the Coanda effect is seen when a falling jet of water from a tap defies gravity and runs along a spoon or jar just brought into contact with it* (Science Journal). [< Henri Marie *Coanda,* 1885-1972, a French aeronautics engineer and inventor]

co|ap|tate (kō ap′tāt), *v.t.,* **-tat|ed, -tat|ing.** to fit together, as in surgical adjustment of broken bones. [< Latin *coaptāre* (with English *-ate*[1]) < *co-* together + *aptāre* to fit < *aptus* apt, fit]

co|ap|ta|tion (kō′ap tā′shən), *n.* 1 the adaptation or adjustment of parts to one another: ... *the coaptation and union of the elements* (Samuel Taylor Coleridge). 2 *Medicine.* the act of placing the broken ends of a bone in their natural position. 3 *Anatomy.* a kind of gliding articulation of one bone with another, as that of the patella with the femur.

co|arb (kō′ärb), *n.* a person in the Celtic Church who succeeds another in a church office. Also, **comarb.** [< Irish *comharba*]

co|arc|tate (kō ärk′tāt), *adj.* 1 pressed together; compressed; contracted. 2 enclosed in an oval, horny case, and having no external indication of the organs: *a coarctate pupa.* [< Latin *coarctātus,* past participle of *coarctāre* < *co-* together + *arctare* press close < *artus* confined]

co|arc|ta|tion (kō′ärk tā′shən), *n.* 1 pressure; contraction. 2 *Medicine.* the contracting or lessening of the diameter of a canal or vessel: *Babies born with another dangerous heart abnormality—called coarctation of the aorta —also have a better chance for a normal life* (Marguerite Clark).

coarse (kôrs, kōrs), *adj.,* **coars|er, coars|est.** 1 made up of fairly large parts; not fine: *coarse salt, coarse sand.* 2 heavy or rough in looks or texture: *Burlap is a coarse cloth. The old fisherman had coarse, weathered features.* 3 common, poor, or inferior: *coarse food.* 4 not delicate or refined; crude or vulgar: *Many of the frontiersmen had coarse manners.* 5 not refined: *Coarse metals.*
[adjectival use of *course,* noun, meaning "ordinary"] — **coarse′ly,** *adv.* — **coarse′ness,** *n.*
— *Syn.* 4 **Coarse, vulgar** mean not refined in feelings, manners, language, or taste. **Coarse** implies roughness or crudeness: *Many soldiers have to remind themselves when they return home not to use the coarse language of the barracks.* **Vulgar** implies offensive coarseness and often suggests an attitude of distaste and superiority on the part of the speaker: *His vulgar speech and manners show that he is not accustomed to polite society.*

coarse-grained (kôrs′grānd′, kōrs′-), *adj.* 1 having a coarse texture; made up of large, coarse fibers. 2 *Figurative.* not delicate or refined; crude: *a coarse-grained fellow.*

coars|en (kôr′sən, kōr′-), *v.t., v.i.* to make or become coarse: *The actor coarsened his features with make-up to look like a villain. A person's speech and manner may coarsen in bad company.*

coarse wool, wool from such sheep as the blackface, having strong, coarse fibers, used especially in the making of tweeds, carpets, and mattresses.

coast (kōst), *n., v.* — *n.* 1 the land along the sea; seashore: *Many ships were wrecked on that rocky coast. The Roman legions, all from Gallia drawn, are landed on your coast* (Shakespeare). SYN: seaboard, seaside, shore, strand. 2 the region near a coast. 3 a ride or slide down a hill without the use of effort or power. 4 a slope for sliding down a hill on a sled or skis. 5 *Archaic.* the border or boundary of a country.
— *v.i.* 1a to ride or slide down a hill without using effort or power: *You can coast downhill on a sled or a bicycle. He shut off the engine and the car coasted into the driveway.* b (of a missile or space vehicle) to continue forward movement after thrust has ended. 2 to move or advance with little effort or exertion: *He saw by the poor grades he was getting that he could not just coast through school.* 3 to sail from port to port of a coast; go along or near a coast. 4 *Obsolete.* to keep alongside of a moving person. 5 *Obsolete.* to go, pass, or proceed in a roundabout way.
— *v.t.* 1 to sail along or near the coast of; skirt the shore of (a body of water): *coasting the lower lakes with their frail barks* (Washington Irving). 2 to sail from port to port of the coast of (land): *The disabled ship coasted the island, looking for a harbor to make repairs.* 3 *Obsolete.* to keep by the side of (a moving person). 4 *Obsolete.* to go around; pass by.
from coast to coast, from the Atlantic to the Pacific coast; across the continent: *The program was televised from coast to coast. This company has branches from coast to coast.*
the Coast, *U.S. and Canada.* the region lying near the Pacific Ocean: *The family moved from the Midwest to the Coast and settled in San Francisco.*
the coast is clear, no one is in the way; the danger is past: *Is the coast clear? None but friends?* (Oliver Goldsmith).
[< Old French *coste* < Latin *costa* side, rib]

coast|al (kōs′təl), *adj.* of the coast; near or along a coast: *The beacon is an aid to coastal shipping.* — **coast′al|ly,** *adv.*

coastal plain, a flat stretch of land along a coast: *Coastal plains, which characterize every continent to a greater or less degree, represent uplifted sea bottom* (White and Renner).

coast artillery, artillery weapons and equipment used on shore for defense against enemy ships.

coast disease, (in Australia) an anemic disease of sheep caused by a lack of cobalt in the diet.

coast|er (kōs′tər), *n.* 1 a small dish or mat for holding a glass or bottle. A coaster protects surfaces of furniture from moisture. 2 a little tray or stand, sometimes on wheels, on which a glass or bottle is passed around a dining table. 3 a person or thing that coasts. 4 a ship that sails or trades along a coast. 5 a sled or toboggan to coast on. 6 a person who lives near a coast. 7 a low, wheeled frame on which a mechanic lies to work underneath an automobile; cradle. 8 an amusement railway with dips, curves, and bumps.

coaster brake, a brake on the hub of the rear wheel of a bicycle, worked by pushing back on the pedals. It also permits the rear wheel to turn, independent of the driving mechanism.

coast fox, a small, gray fox, weighing about four and a half pounds, found along the coast of southern California.

coast guard, 1a a group of men whose work is preventing smuggling and protecting lives and property along the coast of a country. b a member of any such group. 2 *British.* an organization used as a general police force and defense force, originally to prevent smuggling.

Coast Guard, the government organization whose work is protecting lives and property and preventing smuggling along the coasts of the United States. The Coast Guard also saves lives of persons wrecked at sea and patrols the navigable waterways. It is under the Navy in wartime and under the Department of Transportation in peacetime.

coast|guards|man (kōst′gärdz′mən), *n., pl.* **-men.** a member of a coast guard; coast guard.

Coast|guards|man (kōst′gärdz′mən), *n., pl.* **-men.** *U.S.* a member of the Coast Guard.

coast ice, the belt of ice formed along a coast in high latitudes, and breaking off in summer.

coast|ing trade (kōs′ting), 1 trade carried on by ships between the ports of one country. 2 trade carried on by ships from port to port along the coasts of several countries.

coast|land (kōst′land′), *n.* land along a coast.

coast|line (kōst′līn′), *n.* the outline of a coast.

coast redwood, = redwood (def. 1a).

coast rhododendron, a rhododendron of the western United States, with rose-purple flowers. It is the flower of the State of Washington.

coast-to-coast (kōst′tů kōst′), *adj.* from the Atlantic to the Pacific coast: *In 1951, NBC inaugurated its coast-to-coast television network* (Joseph A. Ryan).

coast|ward (kōst′wərd), *adv., adj.* toward the coast.

coast|wards (kōst′wərdz), *adv.* = coastward.

coast|ways (kōst′wāz′), *adv.* = coastwise.

coast|wise (kōst′wīz′), *adv., adj.* — *adv.* along the coast: *to travel coastwise.*
— *adj.* following the coast: *a coastwise trade.*

coat (kōt), *n., v.* — *n.* 1 an outer garment of cloth, fur, rubber, oilskin, leather, or plastic, with sleeves: *a heavy winter coat. Many office workers wear a coat and a tie.* 2 a natural outer covering: *a dog's coat of hair, the silky coat of a kitten. The skin or rind of a fruit or a seed may be called a coat; so may the bark of a tree or the outside layer of a bulb or an onion.* SYN: integument. 3 a thin layer covering a surface; coating: *a coat of paint.* 4 anything that covers or conceals. 5 *Archaic.* the customary clothing of members of a profession or class.
— *v.t.* 1 to cover with a thin layer: *The floor is coated with varnish. This pill is coated with sugar. Ice coated the roads. The old books were coated with dust.* 2 to provide with a coat.
coats, *Dialect.* petticoats; skirts: *My wife ... hoisted her coats and waded through* (H. Watterson).
cut one's coat to fit (or **according to**) **one's cloth,** *British.* to adapt oneself to circumstances: *Times are changed, and ... we must, to use the homely metaphor, 'cut our coat according to our cloth'* (Homeward Mail).
trail one's coat, to be provocative in one's conduct: [*He*] *seemed to be deliberately trailing his coat when he published the confidential exchanges in Moscow* (Manchester Guardian).
turn one's coat, to change one's party or principles: *Shall I turn my coat, and join the victors?* (James A. Froude).
[Middle English *cote* tunic; coat of mail < Old French; origin uncertain]

coat and skirt, *British.* a two-piece suit for

Pronunciation Key: hat, āge, cãre, fär; let, ēqual, tėrm; it, īce; hot, ōpen, ôrder; oil, out; cup, pu̇t, rüle; child; long; thin; ᴛʜen; zh, measure; ə represents a in about, e in taken, i in pencil, o in lemon, u in circus.

women.

coat card, = court card.

coat dress, a dress buttoned straight down the front like a coat, and usually having coatlike lines.

coat|ed (kō′tid), *adj.* **1** having or covered with a coat or coating. **2** wearing a coat.

coated paper, paper that has been given a glossy, even surface by coating it with clay, used especially for half-tone illustrations.

coat|ee (kō tē′), *n.* a close-fitting coat with short tails, chiefly military.

coat|er (kō′tər), *n.* a person or thing that coats or applies coatings to a product.

coat gene, the viral gene that codes for coat protein: *The second gene is the coat gene. This gene codes for a protein that makes a coat around the gene* (Science News).

coat hanger, a piece of wood, metal, or plastic, to hang a coat, dress, or other garment, curved to fit the shoulders of the garment and having a hook to suspend it; hanger.

***co|a|ti** (kō ä′tē), *n., pl.* **-tis** or (*especially collectively*) **-ti.** a small mammal somewhat like a raccoon, living in the southwestern United States, Mexico, and Central and South America. It has a long body and tail and a flexible snout. *The coati . . . set up their sharp, quick bark* (Richard Henry Dana). [< Tupi (perhaps West Indies) *coati*]

***coati**

co|a|ti|mon|di or **co|a|ti|mun|di** (kō ä′tē-mun′dē), *n., pl.* **-dis** or (*collectively*) **-di.** = coati.

coat|ing (kō′ting), *n.* **1** a layer of any substance spread over a surface: *a coating of paint.* **2** cloth for making coats.

coat|less (kōt′lis), *adj.* **1** without a coat. **2** without a coat of arms.

***coat of arms**, *pl.* **coats of arms**. **1** a shield, or drawing of a shield, with pictures and designs on it, symbolic of family history and distinctions. In the Middle Ages each knight or lord had his own coat of arms. Coats of arms are still used, especially by noble families in Europe. SYN: escutcheon. **2** a somewhat similar device adopted as an emblem of authority by a government, city, or corporation. **3** a coat or tabard embroidered with heraldic arms, worn over armor by medieval knights. [translation of Old French *cote d'armes* light coat, often decorated with heraldic designs, worn over armor by knights in the Middle Ages]

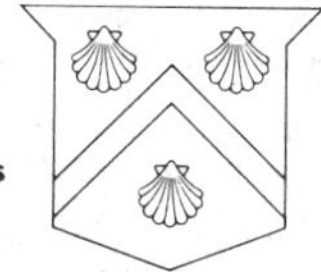
***coat of arms**
definition 1

coat of mail, *pl.* **coats of mail**. a garment made of metal rings or plates, worn as armor; hauberk.

coat protein, a protein that acts as a protective sheath for a virus, making it resistant to antibodies of the host organism: *The putative coat proteins prepared from different clones of one strain . . . supported the view that coat protein is the variant antigen* (Nature).

coat|room (kōt′rüm′, -rům′), *n.* = cloakroom.

coats (kōts), *n.pl.* See under **coat**.

coat|tail (kōt′tāl′), *n., adj.* —*n.* one of a pair of flaps or tails on the lower rear portion of a coat.
—*adj. U.S.* based on the ability of a popular or strong candidate to carry weaker ones along to victory with him: *coattail power, coattail prestige.*

coattails, the tails of a formal coat or jacket: *Then he gave his lapels a determined downward tug, swept back his coattails, and took his place at the piano* (New Yorker).

ride (or **hang** or **climb**) **on** (**another's**) **coattails**, to advance, especially in politics, by means of the popularity or advancement of another, through association with him: *If Connecticut gives the President a respectable victory, . . . Bush is almost sure to ride the Presidential coattails back to Washington* (Newsweek).

coat-trail|ing (kōt′trā′ling), *n., adj. British.* —*n.* provocative conduct; provocation: *The singling out of the Prime Minister [for a vote of censure] is calculated coat-trailing* (London Times).
—*adj.* provoking; provocative: *There is some indignation about a coat-trailing newspaper report that the occasion was being slighted by official disregard* (Manchester Guardian Weekly).

co|au|thor (kō ô′thər), *n., v.* —*n.* a joint author.
—*v.t. Informal.* to write with another or others.

coax (kōks), *v.t.* **1** to persuade by soft words; influence by pleasant ways: *She coaxed her father to let her go to the dance.* SYN: wheedle, cajole, inveigle, entice. **2** to get by coaxing: *The nurse coaxed a smile from the baby.* **3** *Obsolete.* to fool with flattery; take in. **4** *Obsolete.* to fondle; caress. —*v.i.* to use coaxing.
[earlier, to fool, influence, apparently < obsolete *cokes* a fool] —**coax′er**, *n.* —**coax′ing|ly**, *adv.*

co|ax|i|al (kō ak′sē əl), *adj., n.* —*adj.* **1** having a common axis. **2** of or having to do with a coaxial cable; utilizing the principle of the coaxial cable: *a coaxial network.* **3** designed to emit both high- and low-frequency sounds from one point source: *a coaxial speaker.*
—*n.* **1** = coaxial cable. **2** a coaxial speaker in a high-fidelity set: *A coaxial . . . consists of a treble "tweeter" mounted inside—i.e. coaxially with—a larger bass "woofer"* (Atlantic).
[< *co-* + *axi*(s) + *-al*[1]] —**co|ax′i|al|ly**, *adv.*

***coaxial cable**, **1** an electric cable consisting of a tube of insulated conducting materials surrounding an insulated central conductor that has the same axis. The coaxial cable is used for transmitting many telegraph, telephone, and television signals at the same time. It attenuates high frequencies less than ordinary two-wire cable. Coaxial cables work in pairs: one carries signals in one direction, while the other handles signals in the opposite direction. **2** a large cable containing a circular arrangement of single coaxial cables surrounding interstitial wires at the center, all insulated from one another, capable of conducting simultaneously several video circuits and more than 1,500 telephone circuits.

***coaxial cable**
definition 2

cob[1] (kob), *n.* **1** the center part of an ear of corn, on which the kernels grow; a corncob. **2a** a strong horse with short legs. **b** *U.S.* a horse having an affectedly high gait. **3** a male swan: *[He] took pity on a cob and his mate raising four hungry cygnets, and fed them mountains of bread* (New Yorker). **4** *Dialect.* any roundish or lumpy pieces; something round: *a cob of coal, a cob of bread.* **5** a composition of clay, gravel, and straw, used especially in southwestern England for building walls. [Middle English *cobbe* big, stout man; origin uncertain]

cob[2] (kob) *n.* a gull, especially the great black-backed gull. Also, **cobb**. [origin unknown]

co|bae|a (kō bē′ə), *n.* any one of a genus of tropical American plants, especially a vine with pinnate leaves, and large, bell-shaped, purple or white flowers, familiar in cultivation [< New Latin *Cobaea* < Father *Cobo,* a Jesuit missionary and naturalist]

co|bal|a|min (kō′bôl ə min), *n.* = vitamin B_{12}. [< *cobal*(t) + (vit)*amin*]

***co|balt** (kō′bôlt), *n.* **1** a hard, silver-white, metallic chemical element with a pinkish tint. Cobalt is found only in combination with other elements, especially nickel and iron. Cobalt is used in steel for hardness, and in paints and glass for color. *Cobalt, like tungsten, imparts the property of retaining a keen cutting edge to steel even at high temperatures* (White and Renner). **2** = cobalt blue. [< German *Kobalt,* dialectal variant of *Kobold* goblin (because of the belief of miners that this material causes strange things to happen)]

***cobalt**
definition 1

symbol	atomic number	atomic weight	oxidation state
Co	27	58.933	2, 3

cobalt 60, a radioactive isotope of cobalt, produced by bombarding cobalt atoms with neutrons and used as a source of gamma rays in the treatment of cancer.

cobalt 60 bomb, radioactive cobalt enclosed in a lead case, used in the treatment of cancer, and in industry; cobalt bomb.

cobalt bloom, a native hydrated arsenate of cobalt occurring in crystalline and earthy forms.

cobalt blue, **1** a dark-blue coloring matter made from cobalt, especially from an oxide, phosphate, or arsenate of cobalt. Cobalt blue is used in dyeing, paints, and staining glass. **2** the dark-blue color of this pigment.

cobalt bomb, **1** a hydrogen bomb encased in a shell of cobalt instead of steel. It is an extremely dangerous atomic weapon because of the wide dispersal of radioactive cobalt dust. *The cobalt bomb is a fact, but it is a suicide weapon that will not be used to poison the earth and the living things upon it* (Science News Letter). **2** = cobalt 60 bomb.

cobalt green, **1** a bright-green coloring matter derived from zinc oxide and cobalt, used chiefly in paints. **2** the bright-green color of this pigment.

co|bal|tic (kō bôl′tik), *adj.* **1** of cobalt. **2** containing cobalt, especially with a valence of 3.

co|bal|tif|er|ous (kō′bôl tif′ər əs), *adj.* containing or yielding cobalt. [< *cobalt* + *-ferous*]

co|balt|ine (kō′bôl tēn, -tin), *n.* = cobaltite.

co|bal|tite (kō′bôl tīt; kō bôl′-), *n.* a silver-white, brilliant mineral containing cobalt, arsenic, and sulfur. It is an important ore of cobalt. *Formula:* CoAsS

co|bal|tous (kō bôl′təs), *adj.* containing cobalt, especially with a valence of 2.

cobalt yellow, **1** a bright-yellow coloring matter derived from a compound of potassium nitrite, acetic acid, and salt of cobalt, used in dyeing and paints. **2** the bright-yellow color of this pigment.

cobb (kob), *n.* = cob[2].

cob|ber (kob′ər), *n. Australian Slang.* a friend; mate; comrade.

cob|ble[1] (kob′əl), *v.t.,* **-bled**, **-bling**. **1** to mend (shoes); repair; patch. **2** to put together clumsily. [perhaps Middle English *cobbe* lump, big piece]

cob|ble[2] (kob′əl), *n., v.,* **-bled**, **-bling**. —*n.* = cobblestone.
—*v.t.* to pave with cobblestones.

cobbles, coal in lumps about the size of small cobblestones: *Along the dock wharves yesterday I heard that in this nuclear age some of the local tugs have difficulty mustering enough stokers to keep the cobbles flowing into the furnaces* (Cape Times).
[apparently diminutive form of Middle English *cobbe* cobble[1]]

cob|ble[3] (kob′əl), *n.* = coble.

cob|bler (kob′lər), *n.* **1** a person whose work is mending shoes. **2** a clumsy workman; botcher: *Thou cobbler, botching the socks of bombast oratory* (Robert Burns). **3** *U.S.* a fruit pie baked in a deep dish, usually with a crust only on top. **4** an iced drink made of wine, fruit juice, sugar, and crushed ice: *This wonderful invention . . . is called a cobbler. Sherry cobbler, when you name it long; cobbler when you name it short* (Dickens).

cob|bles (kob′əlz), *n.pl.* See under **cobble**[2].

***cob|ble|stone** (kob′əl stōn′), *n.* a naturally rounded stone that was formerly much used in paving; cobble. Smaller stones of the same character are usually called *pebbles,* and larger ones *boulders.*

***cobblestone**

cob|ble|stoned (kob′əl stōnd′), *adj.* paved with cobblestones.

cob|bly (kob′lē), *adj.* **1** shaped like a cobblestone. **2** bumpy, as if paved with cobblestones: *a cobbly road.*

cob|by (kob′ē), *adj.* like a cob (horse): *a team of short-tailed cobby chestnuts.*

cob coal, coal in round lumps.

co|bel|lig|er|ent (kō′bə lij′ər ənt), *n.* a nation or person that helps another in carrying on a war: *The securities jumped up to 22 when the U.S. and Russia were cobelligerents during World War II* (Wall Street Journal).

co|bi|a (kō′bē ə), *n.* = sergeant fish. [origin unknown]

co|ble (kō′bəl, kob′əl), *n.* (in Scotland and in northern England) a type of flat-bottomed rowboat, used especially in fishing. Also, **cobble.** [variant of Old English *cuopl*]

cob meal, *U.S.* a meal made from corn and corncobs ground up: *Cob meal is rapidly replacing corn meal as a mild abrasive in hand soaps.* (Science News Letter).

cob-nosed (kob′nōzd′), *adj. Informal.* having a big, round nose.

cob|nut (kob′nut′), *n.* **1** the nut of certain cultivated varieties of hazel. **2** the tree it grows on.

CO|BOL or **Co|bol** (kō′bôl), *n.* a computer language widely used in business and industry for programing data-processing machines. [< *Co*(mmon) *B*(usiness) *O*(riented) *L*(anguage)]

co|bold (kō′bold, -bōld), *n.* = kobold.

***co|bra** (kō′brə), *n.* **1** a very poisonous snake of southern Asia and Africa. It can make its head and neck look like a hood. The Indian cobra is common in India and adjacent countries, and the king cobra of southeastern Asia is the largest. *Dr. Oliver noted that the baby cobra was capable of inflicting a fatal bite. At birth, the young are equipped with venom sacs and fangs* (New York Times). **2** = mamba. **3** = asp (of Egypt). [short for Portuguese *cobra* (*de capello*) snake (with a hood); *cobra* < Latin *colubra*]

∗cobra definition 1

co|bra de ca|pel|lo (kō′brə dē kə pel′ō), *pl.* **co|bras de ca|pel|lo.** = Indian cobra; spectacled snake. [see etym. under **cobra**]

cobra plant, a species of pitcher plant native to California. Most of the insects caught by this plant are killed.

cob|web (kob′web′), *n., adj., v.,* **-webbed, -web|bing.** —*n.* **1a** the web or net spun by a spider to capture its prey: *The fly was caught in a cobweb spun over a window in the barn.* **b** the stuff it is made of. **c** a single thread spun by a spider. **2** *Figurative.* anything thin and slight or entangling like a spider's web: *The thief had to confess when he was caught in the cobweb of lies that he had spun.* **3** *Figurative.* any musty accumulation or obstruction: *A course in profound thoughts underlying relativity and quantum mechanics* [*would*] *blow away some of the cobwebs which grow in unventilated ivory towers* (Atlantic).
—*adj.* thin; like gauze: *a cobweb veil.* (*Figurative.*) *A cobweb bridge flung from his mind to theirs, an invisible passage* (Edith Wharton).
—*v.t.* to cover or hang with cobwebs.
[Middle English *coppe,* short for Old English *ātorcoppe* spider + *web*]

cob|webbed (kob′webd′), *adj.* **1** covered or hung with cobwebs. **2** musty; stale.

cob|web|ber|y (kob′web′ər ē), *n., pl.* **-ber|ies.** **1** the spinning of cobwebs. **2** a texture of cobwebs.

cob|web|by (kob′web′ē), *adj.* **1** of or like a cobweb. **2** covered with cobwebs.

cob|work (kob′wėrk′), *n.* work consisting of logs laid horizontally with the ends joined so as to form a rectangular or other enclosure, such as in a log house.

co|ca (kō′kə), *n.* **1** a tropical shrub or small tree growing in South America and also in Java and Ceylon (Sri Lanka), whose dried leaves are used to make cocaine and other alkaloids. **2** its dried leaves, often chewed by the natives for their stimulant properties: *The use of coca in Peru . . . is said to have originated with the Incas* (Lindley and Moore). [< Spanish *coca* < Quechua *cuca*]

co|caine or **co|cain** (kō kān′, kō′kān), *n.* a drug used to deaden pain and as a stimulant. It is a narcotic obtained from dried coca leaves. When used in excess, it can cause systemic poisoning. Cocaine is a bitter, crystalline alkaloid. *Formula:* $C_{17}H_{21}NO_{44}$ [< *coca* + *-ine*[2]]

cocaine hydrochloride, a colorless, crystalline powder, the usual form in which cocaine is used in medicine as a local anesthetic. *Formula:* $C_{17}H_{21}NO_4 \cdot HCl$

co|cain|ism (kō kā′niz əm), *n.* a physical and mental disorder produced by the excessive use of cocaine.

co|cain|ize (kō kā′nīz), *v.t.,* **-ized, -iz|ing.** to treat with or affect by cocaine; anesthetize with cocaine. —**co|cain′i|za′tion,** *n.*

co|carde (kô kȧrd′), *n. French.* cockade.

coc|ci (kok′sī), *n.* plural of **coccus.**

coc|cid (kok′sid), *n.* a homopterous insect: *The scale insects and mealy bugs are coccids.* [< New Latin *Coccidae* the family name < Greek *kókkos* berry]

coc|cid|i|a (kok sid′ē ə), *n.* plural of **coccidium.**

coc|cid|i|al (kok sid′ē əl), *adj.* of or caused by coccidia: *Coccidial infections of the intestine are particularly destructive to rabbits and birds* (Hegner and Stiles).

coc|cid|i|oi|dal (kok sid′ē oi′dəl), *adj.* of or having to do with the group of parasitic fungi that cause coccidioidomycosis.

coc|cid|i|oi|do|my|co|sis (kok sid′ē oi′dō mī kō′sis), *n.* a fungous disease of the lungs, particularly affecting persons in dry, dusty areas, caused by inhaled spores; valley fever. [< New Latin *Coccidioides* a genus of parasitic fungi + Greek *mykēs* fungus + English *-osis*]

coc|cid|i|o|sis (kok sid′ē ō′sis), *n.* **1** any one of several diseases caused by protozoan parasites in the intestines, rare in man but comparatively frequent in birds (especially in domestic poultry) and domestic animals. **2** = coccidioidomycosis. [< New Latin *Coccidia* an order of parasites + English *-osis*]

coc|cid|i|o|stat (kok sid′ē ə stat), *n.* a substance that checks the spread of coccidia: *A new coccidiostat* [*is*] *designed to control the poultry disease coccidiosis* (Wall Street Journal). [< *coccidio*(sis) + *-stat*]

coc|cid|i|um (kok sid′ē əm), *n., pl.* **-i|a.** one of the group of protozoan parasites that cause coccidiosis. [< New Latin *Coccidia* the order of parasites]

coc|ci|nel|lid (kok′si nel′id), *n.* = ladybug. [< New Latin *Coccinellidae* the family name < Greek *kókkinos* scarlet < *kókkos* berry]

coc|coid (kok′oid), *adj., n.* —*adj.* of or like a coccus.
—*n.* a coccoid microorganism.

coc|co|lith (kok′ə lith), *n.* any one of the skeletal coverings made of calcite that protect a coccolithophore. In a fossilized state coccoliths form chalk and limestone deposits, such as the White Cliffs of Dover. *Bodies similar to these "coccoliths" were aggregated together into spheroids . . . termed "coccospheres"* (Thomas Huxley). [(coined by Thomas Huxley) < Greek *kókkos* grain + *líthos* stone]

coc|co|lith|o|phore (kok′ə lith′ə fôr, -fōr), *n.* any one of a group of single-celled, golden-brown microorganisms having two whiplike appendages and hard shells composed mostly of calcite. Coccolithophores, along with diatoms, are phytoplankton important to the food chain of the open ocean. [< New Latin *Coccolithophora* the genus name < English *coccolith* + *-phore*]

coc|co|sphere (kok′ə sfir), *n.* **1** a spheroidal mass of coccoliths; skeleton of a coccolithophore. **2** a living coccolithophore. [< Greek *kókkos* grain + *sphaira* globe]

coc|cu|lus in|di|cus (kok′yə ləs in′də kəs), the dried, berrylike fruit of a climbing shrub of the East Indies, containing the bitter, poisonous principle called picrotoxin. [< New Latin *cocculus* little berry (< Greek *kókkos* grain, seed), *indicus* Indian]

coc|cus (kok′əs), *n., pl.* **-ci.** **1** a bacterial cell shaped like a sphere. See picture under **bacteria.** **2** *Botany.* a part of a compound pistil; carpel. **3** = cochineal. [< New Latin *Coccus* a genus of cochineal insects < Greek *kókkos* seed, berry]

coc|cyg|e|al (kok sij′ē əl), *adj.* of or having to do with the coccyx; caudal: *a coccygeal vertebra, muscle, artery, or nerve.* [< Medieval Latin *coccȳgeus* of the coccyx + English *-al*[1]]

coc|cyx (kok′siks), *n., pl.* **coc|cy|ges** (kok sī′jēz). **1** a small, triangular bone forming the lower end of the spinal column in man: *We have a small coccyx as a remnant of our tail vertebrae instead of a urostyle* (A. M. Winchester). **2** a similar part in certain animals and birds. [< Latin *coccyx* < Greek *kókkyx* (originally) a cuckoo (because it is shaped like the cuckoo's bill)]

coch. or **cochl.**, (in a medical prescription) spoonful (Latin, *cochleare*).

co|chair|man (kō chãr′mən), *n., pl.* **-men.** a joint or fellow chairman.

co|cher (kô shā′), *n. French.* a coachman; driver.

Co|chin or **co|chin** (kō′chin, koch′in), *n.,* or **Cochin China**, any chicken of a large breed of domestic fowl originating in Asia that have many feathers on their legs and loose, fluffy plumage. There are buff, white, black, and partridge Cochins.
[< *Cochin China,* a former state in what is now Vietnam]

coch|i|neal (koch′ə nēl′, koch′ə nēl), *n.* a bright-red dye made from the dried bodies of the females of a scale insect that lives on cactus plants of tropical America. It is used for making carmine. [< French *cochenille* < Spanish *cochinilla,* ultimately < Greek *kókkinos* scarlet < *kókkos* seed; berry (gall) of a kind of oak]

cochineal insect, the scale insect from whose dried body cochineal is made: *The pigment extracted from female cochineal insects was already an article of commerce in Mexico when the Spanish arrived there* (B. Nickerson).

Co|chise (kō chēs′, -chēz′), *adj.* of or having to do with an American Indian culture that existed in Arizona and New Mexico in the 8000's B.C.: *There was a well-established hunting tradition in a region previously thought to have been dominated by the Cochise . . . plant-gatherers* (New Scientist). [< *Cochise* county, Arizona]

coch|le|a (kok′lē ə), *n., pl.* **-le|ae** (-lē ē). a spiral-shaped cavity of the inner ear, containing the nerve endings that transmit sound impulses along the auditory nerve: *The cochlea is the structure within which pressures initiated by sound waves are transformed into nerve impulses that ultimately are translated in the brain as sound sensations* (Harbaugh and Goodrich). See picture under **ear**[1]. [< Latin *cochlea* snail (shell) < Greek *kochlías*]

coch|le|ar (kok′lē ər), *adj.* of the cochlea.

coch|le|ate (kok′lē āt), *adj.* shaped like a snail shell; spiral.

coch|le|at|ed (kok′lē ā′tid), *adj.* = cochleate.

cock[1] (kok), *n., v.* —*n.* **1** a male chicken; rooster: *roused by the crowing cock at dawn of day* (Wordsworth). **2** the male of other birds and sometimes other animals: *a turkey cock, a lobster cock.* **3** a faucet used to turn the flow of a liquid or gas on or off; tap: *Water squirted from the hose as he turned the cock at the side of the house.* **4a** the hammer of a gun: *With his firelock nearly at the position of the charge with his thumb upon the cock* (Duke of Wellington). **b** the position of the hammer or firing pin of a gun when it is pulled back ready to fire. **5** = weathercock. **6** *Figurative.* a leader; head; main person: *He was the cock of the school out of doors* (Thackeray). **7** the mark aimed at in the game of curling. **8** *Archaic.* **a** the crowing of a cock in the early morning. **b** the time of its crowing. **9** *Obsolete.* a cockboat.
—*v.t.* to pull back the hammer or firing pin of (a gun), in order to make it ready to fire: *There was a click as the hunter cocked his rifle.*
—*v.i.* to raise or draw back the cock or hammer of a gun.
[Old English *cocc*]

cock[2] (kok), *v., n.* —*v.t.* **1** to turn or stick up, especially as if to defy or inquire: *The little bird cocked his eye at me. The dog cocked his ears when he heard his master's footsteps.* **2a** to set (one's hat) at a jaunty angle on the head: *The sailor cocked his hat on the back of his head.* **b** to turn up the brim of (one's hat).
—*v.i.* **1** to stand or stick up conspicuously: . . . *the little saucy-looking heads cocking up between the old one's ears* (David Livingstone). **2** to swagger; strut; brag: *I'll strut, and cock, and talk as big as wind and froth can make me* (Thomas Southerne).
—*n.* **1** an upward turn or bend of the nose, eye, or ear: *with a knowing cock of his eye to his next neighbor* (Scott). **2a** the turn of a brim of a hat: *a fierce cock to his hat and a shabby genteel air* (Thackeray). **b** a part of the brim of a hat that can be turned up: *The wind being high, he let down the cocks of his hat* (James Boswell).
[apparently < *cock*[1]]

cock[3] (kok), *n., v.* —*n.* a small, cone-shaped pile of hay, dung, or turf in a field.
—*v.t.* to pile in cocks.
[Middle English *cocke;* compare dialectal German *Kocke* heap]

∗cock|ade (ko kād′), *n.* a knot of ribbon or a rosette worn on the hat as a badge: *The only thing that distinguished it from the hats of lesser officers was the color of the cockade on its brim* (New Yorker). Also, *French,* **cocarde.** [alteration of *cockard* < French *cocarde* < *coq* cock[1]]

∗cockade

cock|ad|ed (ko kā′did), *adj.* wearing a cockade.

cock-a-doo|dle (kok′ə dü′dəl), *v.i.,* **-dled, -dling** to crow; cock-a-doodle-doo: *One of those egotistical . . . types who cock-a-doodle a great deal* (New Yorker).

cock-a-doo|dle-doo (kok′ə dü′dəl dü′), *interj., n., v.* —*interj., n.* an imitation of the loud cry of a rooster.
—*v.i.* to make this sound; crow.

cock-a-hoop (kok′ə hüp′), *adj.* **1** boastfully and loudly triumphant; elated; exultant: *He is a cock-a-hoop about his success.* **2** askew; awry: *The film in the projector is all cock-a-hoop.* [origin uncertain]

Cock|aigne (ko kān′), *n.* an imaginary land of luxury and idleness. Also, **Cockayne.** [< Old French *cokaigne* sugar cake]

cock|a|leek|ie (kok′ə lē′kē), *n. Scottish.* a soup made of cock boiled with leeks. Also, **cockie-leekie, cocky-leeky.**

cock|a|lo|rum (kok′ə lôr′əm, -lōr′-), *n.* **1** a self-important little man. **2** boastful talk. [pretended classical derivation from *cock*[1]; perhaps influenced by Dutch *kockeloeren* to crow]

cock|a|ma|mie or **cock|a|ma|my** (kok′ə mā′mē), *adj., n., pl.* **-mies.** *Slang.* —*adj.* foolish, absurd, or nonsensical: *If there are some confus-*

Pronunciation Key: hat, āge, cãre, fär; let, ēqual, tėrm; it, īce; hot, ōpen, ôrder; oil, out; cup, pu̇t, rüle; child; long; thin; ᴛʜen; zh, measure; ə represents **a** in about, **e** in taken, **i** in pencil, **o** in lemon, **u** in circus.

ing or irritating or cockamamy rules of the house . . . these should be explained in advance (Atlantic).
—*n.* something foolish, absurd, or nonsensical: *Arlen characterized the drama as ". . . the most asinine and inept piece of cockamamie that I've seen all year"* (Harper's).
[probably alteration of *decalcomania*]

cock-and-bull story (kok′ən bu̇l′), an absurd, incredible story (from an old fable with two incredible characters, a cock and a bull).

***cock|a|teel** or **cock|a|tiel** (kok′ə tēl′), *n.* a small Australian parrot with a long tail, common as a cage bird. [< Dutch *kakatielje,* perhaps < Portuguese *cacatilho* (diminutive) < *cacatù* cockatoo]

***cockateel**
***cockatoo**
definition 1

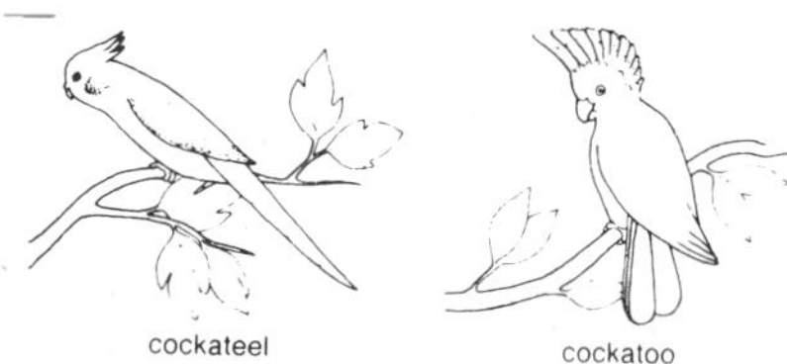
cockateel cockatoo

***cock|a|too** (kok′ə tü′, kok′ə tü), *n., pl.* **-toos.** 1 a large, often brightly colored parrot, especially of Australia and the East Indies. It has a crest of feathers on the head which can be raised or lowered. Cockatoos are noisy but rarely learn to talk. 2 *Australian Slang.* **a** a small farmer; cocky. **b** a person posted as a lookout, especially by criminals. [< Dutch *kaketoe* < Malay *kakatua*]

cock|a|trice (kok′ə tris), *n.* 1 a serpent in old stories whose look was supposed to cause death. The cockatrice was believed to be hatched by a serpent from a cock's egg. It was usually represented as part cock and part serpent. 2 a venomous serpent not now identifiable (in the Bible, Isaiah 14:29). [< Old French *cocatris* (influenced by *coq* cock), ultimately < Latin *calcāre* tread on < *calx, calcis* heel]

Cock|ayne (ko kān′), *n.* = Cockaigne.

cock bead, a bead which is not flush with the general surface, but raised above it in joining wood.

cock|boat (kok′bōt′), *n.* 1 a small rowboat, especially one used as the tender of a ship or larger boat: *It would be more candid . . . to avow our principles explicitly to Russia and France than to come in as a cockboat in the wake of the British man-of-war* (John Quincy Adams). 2 = cockleshell (boat).

cock|chaf|er (kok′chā′fər), *n.* a large European beetle that destroys plants. [< *cock*[1] leader, champion + *chafer*]

cock|crow (kok′krō′), *n.* 1 the crowing of a rooster. 2 the time when roosters begin to crow; dawn.

cock|crow|ing (kok′krō′ing), *n.* = cockcrow.

cocked hat (kokt), 1 a hat with the brim turned up. 2 a hat pointed in front and in back.
knock into a cocked hat, *Informal.* to destroy completely; defeat; ruin: *You can knock all the story books in the world into a cocked hat without shaking an iota of my faith* (Atlantic).

cock|er[1] (kok′ər), *n.* 1 = cocker spaniel. 2 a person who arranges or attends cockfights. [< *cock*[1] (the spaniel was used to hunt woodcock)]

cock|er[2] (kok′ər), *v.t.* to indulge; pamper. [origin uncertain]

cock|er|el (kok′ər əl, kok′rəl), *n.* a young rooster, not more than a year old. [probably a diminutive form of *cock*[1]]

cocker spaniel, any one of a breed of small dogs with long, silky hair and drooping ears; cocker. It is the smallest of the hunting dogs, but is now raised mainly as a show dog and pet.

cock|et (kok′it), *n. British.* 1 a seal of the custom house. 2 a document sealed and delivered by custom-house officers as a warrant that goods have been duly entered and duty on them has been paid. [origin uncertain]

cock|eye (kok′ī′), *n.* an eye that squints or is affected with cross-eye.

cock|eyed (kok′īd′), *adj.* 1 = cross-eyed. 2 *Slang.* tilted or twisted to one side: *Mary's cup, cock-eyed in the saucer, rested by her chair* (New Yorker). 3 *Slang.* foolish; silly: *They did some cock-eyed things, but they had dash and imagination* (Wall Street Journal).

cock feather, the feather standing on top when an arrow is notched on the string.

cock|fight (kok′fīt′), *n.* a fight between roosters or between gamecocks armed with steel spurs.

cock|fight|ing (kok′fī′ting), *n., adj.* —*n.* fighting by roosters or gamecocks for the entertainment of spectators. —*adj.* of or having to do with a cockfight or cockfights.

cock|horse (kok′hôrs′), *n.* = rocking horse.

cock|ie-leek|ie (kok′ē lē′kē), *n.* = cockaleekie.

cock|le[1] (kok′əl), *n., v.,* **-led, -ling.** —*n.* 1a a small, saltwater shellfish that is good to eat. It has a ridged shell in two hinged halves that are somewhat heart-shaped. *Someone passed around a jar of pickled cockles and we ate these with our bitters* (Atlantic). **b** any one of various similar or related mollusks. **c** its heart-shaped shell; cockleshell. 2 a small, light, shallow boat; cockleboat; cockleshell. 3 *U.S.* a small, shell-shaped candy of sugar and flour with a motto rolled up inside. 4 a bulge on the surface; pucker; wrinkle.
—*v.i.* 1 to curl or wrinkle up; pucker: *Paper sometimes cockles when you paste it.* 2 to rise in short, irregular waves; be choppy: *The sea cockled as the wind blew.*
—*v.t.* to cause to curl or wrinkle; crease; pucker.
cockles of one's heart, the inmost part of one's heart or feelings: *Her warm welcome touched her grandfather to the cockles of his heart.*
[< Old French *coquille* < Vulgar Latin *conchīlia* < Latin *conchȳlium* shellfish < Greek *konchȳlion,* ultimately < *kónchē* mussel, conch]

cock|le[2] (kok′əl), *n.* a weed that grows in grainfields, such as the corn cockle, darnel, and cocklebur. [Old English *coccel,* perhaps < unrecorded Latin *cocculus* (diminutive) < Latin *coccum* berry, seed < Greek *kókkos*]

cock|le[3] (kok′əl), *n. Obsolete.* 1 a stove or furnace. 2 a part of a stove or furnace, such as the fire chamber. [origin uncertain]

cock|le|boat (kok′əl bōt′), *n.* a small, light, shallow boat.

cock|le|bur (kok′əl bėr′), *n.* 1 any one of several weeds with rough, heart-shaped, irregular leaves and spiny burs, inside of which are the seeds; clotbur. Cockleburs belong to the composite family. 2 = burdock.

cockle button, = burdock.

cockle hat, a hat adorned with a cockleshell, the badge of a pilgrim.

cock|ler (kok′lər), *n.* a person who gathers or sells cockles or mollusks.

cock|le|shell (kok′əl shel′), *n.* 1 a shell or half of the shell of a cockle. 2a a small, light, shallow boat; cockleboat; cockle. **b** a small rowboat; cockboat: *None but a madman would sail in yon cockleshell with a gale coursing* (Mary E. Braddon).

cock|loft (kok′lôft′, -loft′), *n.* a small attic; garret. [origin uncertain]

cock metal, *U.S.* a soft alloy consisting of various proportions of copper and lead, and sometimes zinc, used especially for faucets.

cock|ney (kok′nē), *n., pl.* **-neys,** *adj.* —*n.* 1a a person born or living in the eastern section of London, who speaks a particular dialect of English. By tradition a cockney is one who was born within the sound of Bow bells. **b** the dialect of cockneys. In the dialect of cockney, words like *lady* and *road* are pronounced as lī′dē and roud, and most sounds represented by "h" are not pronounced. 2 *Obsolete.* **a** a pampered child. **b** a squeamish, affected, or effeminate person.
—*adj.* of or like cockneys or their dialect.
[Middle English *cokeney* city fellow, pampered child, (literally) cock's egg < *cocken* of a cock[1] + *ey* egg, Old English *ǣg*]

cock|ney|dom (kok′nē dəm), *n.* 1 the place in which cockneys live. 2 cockneys collectively.

cock|ney|ese (kok′nē ēz′, -ēs′), *n.* the cockney dialect.

cock|ney|fy (kok′ni fī), *v.,* **-fied, -fy|ing.** —*v.t.* to give cockney qualities to; make cockney. —*v.i.* to become cockney. —**cock′ney|fi|ca′tion,** *n.*

cock|ney|ish (kok′nē ish), *adj.* like a cockney or cockneys.

cock|ney|ism (kok′nē iz əm), *n.* a cockney peculiarity of speech, custom, etc.; cockney quality: *Men . . . had so steeped their brains in London literature as to mistake cockneyism for European culture* (James Russell Lowell).

cock of the rock, or **cock-of-the-rock** (kok′əv ᴛʜə rok′), *n.* a brightly colored South American bird of the same family as the cotinga.

cock of the walk, *Informal.* the master or undisputed leader of any group.

cock of the woods, the northern pileated woodpecker of the United States and Canada: *The redhead . . . is named Dryocopus Pileatus, the Latin name for the Pileated Woodpecker or cock of the woods* (Wall Street Journal).

cock|pad|dle (kok′pad′əl), *n. British.* the lumpfish.

cock|pit (kok′pit′), *n.* 1 the place where the pilot sits in an airplane. See picture under **airplane.** 2 the small, open place in a boat where the pilot or passengers sit. 3 the place where the driver sits in a racing or sport car. 4 an enclosed place for fights between roosters or gamecocks. 5 *Figurative.* the scene of many fights or battles: *Belgium is often called the cockpit of Europe.* 6 the rooms below the deck in warships of former times, used as quarters for junior officers, or as a hospital during battle. 7 *Obsolete.* the pit of a theater.

***cock|roach** (kok′rōch′), *n.* any one of several small, brownish or yellowish insects often found in kitchens and around water pipes. Cockroaches usually come out at night. They have flattened oval bodies and an unpleasant odor. *If the cockroaches Blatta and Periplaneta are subjected to alternating 12-hour periods of light and dark, their activity is largely confined to the latter* (J. L. Cloudsley-Thompson). [alteration of Spanish *cucaracha;* apparently influenced by *cock*[1], *roach*]

***cockroach**

cock robin, a male robin.

cocks|comb (koks′kōm′), *n.* 1 the fleshy, red part on the top of a rooster's head. 2 a pointed cap somewhat like this, worn by a jester or clown. 3 Also, **coxcomb.** a plant with crested or feathery clusters of red, purple, white, or yellow flowers. Cockscomb belongs to the amaranth family and is often grown in gardens. See picture under **angiosperm.** 4 *Obsolete.* a conceited dandy; fool; coxcomb. 5 Also, **coxcomb.** *Obsolete.* the head.

cocks|foot (koks′fu̇t′), *n.* a tall, coarse, perennial grass, native to Europe but widely naturalized, valuable for hay and pasture, having a branched panicle shaped like a cock's foot; orchard grass.

cocks|head (koks′hed′), *n.* an herb of the pea family, closely allied to the sainfoin, growing in Mediterranean regions.

cock|shut (kok′shut′), *n. Dialect.* twilight.

cock|shy (kok′shī′), *n., pl.* **-shies.** 1 the sport of throwing at a target (originally a cock). 2 a throw at a target. 3 the target or object aimed at.

cock|spur (kok′spėr′), *n.* 1 the spur of a cock. 2 a North American hawthorn with long, sharp thorns, sometimes cultivated as an ornamental shrub; cockspur thorn.

cockspur thorn, = cockspur (def. 2).

cock|sure (kok′shu̇r′), *adj., adv.* —*adj.* 1 too sure; overly confident: *In the club car men were crying out their simple, cocksure solutions for the United States of America* (Harper's). 2 perfectly sure; absolutely certain. SYN: confident, positive.
—*adv.* with perfect security or certainty. —**cock′sure′ly,** *adv.* —**cock′sure′ness,** *n.*

cock|swain (kok′sən, -swān′), *n.* = coxswain.

cock|tail (kok′tāl′), *n., adj., v.* —*n.* 1 a chilled alcoholic drink of gin, whiskey, vodka, rum, or brandy mixed with flavorings such as vermouth, fruit juices, sugar, or bitters. 2 an appetizing drink that is not alcoholic, served just before a meal: *a tomato-juice cocktail.* 3 shellfish served in a small glass with a highly seasoned sauce as an appetizer: *a shrimp cocktail.* 4 any mixed fruits, diced and usually served in a glass. 5a a horse with a docked tail. **b** a horse that is not a thoroughbred. 6 a person who considers himself a gentleman, but lacks gentlemanly breeding.
—*adj.* suitable for a cocktail party; semiformal: *a cocktail dress.*
—*v.i.* to drink cocktails: . . . *a cheery bower for cocktailing and dining* (New Yorker).
[American English; origin uncertain]

cocktail hour, the time in the late afternoon or early evening when cocktails are usually served or cocktail parties are held.

cocktail lounge, *U.S.* 1 a room in a hotel or club, furnished with easy chairs, sofas, and tables, where patrons may obtain and drink cocktails. 2 any establishment where drinks are served; bar.

cocktail party, a social gathering held late in the afternoon at which cocktails and other refreshments are served.

cocktail sauce, a highly seasoned sauce, usually with tomato catchup as the chief ingredient, served with shrimp, raw oysters, clams, or other shellfish.

cocktail table, = coffee table.

cock|up (kok′up′), *n.* 1 a distinct turn up at the end or tip. 2 a hat or cap with the brim turned up.

cock-up (kok′up′), *n. British Slang.* a clumsy muddle or mess; confusion: *The Russians have made a proper cock-up of Marx . . .* (Sunday Times).

cock|y[1] (kok′ē), *adj.,* **cock|i|er, cock|i|est.** *Informal.* saucy and conceited; cocksure; arrogant: *That bully is a cocky little fellow.* SYN: swaggering. —**cock′i|ly,** *adv.* —**cock′i|ness,** *n.*

cock|y[2] (kok′ē), *n., pl.* **cock|ies.** *Australian Slang.* a farmer with a small piece of farmland.

cock|y-leek|y (kok′ē lē′kē), *n., pl.* **-leek|ies.** cockaleekie.
cock|y|ol|ly (kok′ē ol′ē), *n.,* or **cockyolly bird,** a pet name for any small bird.
co|co (kō′kō), *n., pl.* **-cos,** *adj.* **—*n.*** **1** = coconut palm. **2** = çoconut.
—*adj.* made of the rind or husk of the coconut: *a coco mat.* Also, **cocoa.**
[< Portuguese *coco* grinning face (because of the resemblance of the shell's base to a monkey face)]
co|coa¹ (kō′kō), *n., adj.* **—*n.*** **1** a powder made by roasting and grinding the seeds of the cacao tree, that tastes much like chocolate. Some of the fat is removed from the seeds. *Most everyone in New England has a box of cocoa in the cupboard.* **2** a drink made of this powder with sugar and milk or water, usually served hot; hot chocolate: *When the Aztec Emperor Montezuma first drank a potation of cocoa with Cortez, the bean was considered so precious that just 100 of them could buy a slave* (Wall Street Journal). **3** the cacao tree. **4** a dull-brown color, lighter than chocolate.
—*adj.* **1** dull-brown: *cocoa-colored draperies.* **2** of or having to do with cocoa: *a cup of hot cocoa-flavored milk.*
[variant of *cacao*]
co|coa² (kō′kō), *n., adj.* = coco.
cocoa bean, = cacao bean.
cocoa butter, a yellowish-white fat obtained from cacao seeds, used especially in making soap and cosmetics; cacao butter.
co|coa|nut (kō′kə nut′, -nət), *n., adj.* = coconut.
co|co|bo|la (kō′kə bō′lə), *n.* = cocobolo.
co|co|bo|lo (kō′kə bō′lō), *n., pl.* **-los.** any one of several dark-colored woods of the West Indies, Central America, and other areas of tropical America, used in cabinetmaking. [< Spanish *cocobolo*]
co|co-de-mer (kō kō′də mãr′), *n.* the large, lobed, edible nut or seed of a very tall palm tree found only in the Seychelles Islands, in the Indian Ocean; double coconut. [< French *coco de mer* sea coconut]
co|con|scious (kō kon′shəs), *adj. Psychology.* in a secondary or dissociated consciousness. **—co-con′scious|ly,** *adv.*
co|con|scious|ness (kō kon′shəs nis), *n. Psychology.* mental phenomena dissociated from, but functioning simultaneously with and aware of, the dominant stream of consciousness; secondary or accompanying consciousness in a divided personality.
co-con|spir|a|tor (kō′kən spir′ə tər), *n.* one of a group of conspirators; a joint conspirator: *He was involved as a co-conspirator, but not as a defendant, in the . . . stock fraud case* (Wall Street Journal).
***co|co|nut** (kō′kə nut′, -nət), *n., adj*—*n.* **1** the large, round, brown, hard-shelled nut of the coconut palm. Coconuts have a white lining that is good to eat and a whitish or clear liquid called coconut milk, used as a drink. The white lining is cut up into shreds and used for cakes, puddings, and pies. **2** the fruit of the coconut palm, containing the nut within a thick, ovoid, fibrous husk: *The coconut yields six commercial products: copra, coconut oil, coconuts, shredded coconut, oil cake, and coir fiber* (Colby and Foster). **3** = coconut palm.
—*adj.* of or made from the fruit of the coconut. Also, **cocoanut.**

*** coconut**
definition 1

coconut crab, a crab of certain Pacific islands, related to the hermit crab but with plates of armor on the rear parts of its body, living in burrows in the ground and feeding chiefly on coconuts; palm crab; purse crab.
coconut milk, the sweet, whitish or clear liquid contained in a coconut.
coconut oil, an oil obtained from the dried meat of coconuts, used mainly in confections and fillings for baked goods, for making soap and candles, and in the reduction of alcohol.
coconut palm, a tall, tropical palm tree on which coconuts grow; coco palm; coco.
coconut shy, *pl.* **coconut shies.** *Especially British.* a cockshy in which coconuts are used as targets.
coconut tree, = coconut palm.
co|coon (kə kün′), *n., v.* **—*n.*** **1** the silky case spun by caterpillars to live in while they are turning into adult insects. Silk is obtained from the cocoons of silkworms: *In the spring a moth came out of the cocoon the caterpillar had spun.* (*Figurative.*) *The mind can weave itself warmly in the cocoon of its own thoughts* (James Russell Lowell). **2** any similar protective covering, such as the egg case of a spider or a plastic covering laid or sprayed over stored machinery.
—*v.t.* to wrap or enclose in a cocoon; encase: (*Figurative. . . . equipment . . . cocooned for storage* (London Times). *The baby was cocooned in blankets beyond recognition* (New Yorker).
[< French *cocon* < *coque* shell, husk]
co|coon|er|y (kə kü′nər ē), *n., pl.* **-er|ies.** a place for raising silkworms: *A cocoonery that will protect a million worms . . .* (Boston Journal of Natural History).
co|coon|ing (kə kü′ning), *n.* a tendency to withdraw into the privacy of one's home, especially during leisure time: *Gandy says his clients are spending a lot more time at home, curled up with good books, good music, and VCR movies. Some refer to this as cocooning* (Christian Science Monitor).
coco palm, = coconut palm.
co|cotte¹ (kō kot′, kə-; *French* kô kôt′), *n.* woman of the demimonde; prostitute. [< French *cocotte*, feminine of *coq* rooster]
co|cotte² (kō kot′, kə-; *French* kô kôt′), *n.* a round pot with a cover and handles; terrine: *There comes from Finland that old reliable iron cocotte, or Dutch oven, . . . whose usefulness remains unimpaired for the . . . braising of a pot roast* (New Yorker). [< French *cocotte* < Middle French *cocasse* a pot, ultimately < Latin *coquere* to cook]
co|co|yam (kō′kō yam′), *n.* the root of the taro or of related plants, somewhat like the root of the potato; eddo: *Asiatic rice, bananas, and cocoyams* [*come*] *from South East Asia* (New Scientist). [< *coco* + *yam*]
co|co|zel|le (kō′kə zel′ē), *n.* a summer squash similar to the zucchini but with light-green to yellow stripes. [perhaps < Italian *cocuzza* gourd]
coc|tile (kok′təl, -tīl), *adj.* made by baking, as a brick. [< Latin *coctilis* < *coquere* cook]
coc|tion (kok′shən), *n.* **1** the process of cooking, especially boiling: *In the sixth boiler the syrup receives its full coction* (Richard Turner). **2** *Obsolete.* digestion. [< Latin *coctiō, -ōnis* < *coquere* cook]
Co|cy|tus (kō sī′təs), *n. Greek Mythology.* the river of wailing, one of the five rivers of Hades.
cod¹ (kod), *n., pl.* **cods** or (*collectively*) **cod.** **1** an important fish used for food, found in the cold parts of the North Atlantic. It is usually about three feet long and weighs from 10 to 25 pounds. *We took more cod than we knew what to do with* (Captain John Smith). **2** any one of various similar and related fishes, such as the Alaska cod, an important fish of the Pacific coast. **3** any one of various similar but unrelated fishes, such as the priestfish. Also, **codfish.** [Middle English *cod;* origin uncertain]
cod² (kod), *n.* **1** = scrotum. **2** *Dialect.* a pod; husk; shell: *He put two cods of chile called long red pepper . . .* (Henry Stubbe). **3** *Obsolete.* a bag. [Old English *codd*]
cod³ (kod), *v.,* **cod|ded, cod|ding,** *n., adj.* **—*v.t.*** *Dialect.* to fool; hoax; tease: *. . . codded him about potatoes that grew on trees* (New Yorker).
—*n.* *British Slang.* a joke, hoax, or parody: *The whole campaign is a cod* (Manchester Guardian).
—*adj.* *British Slang.* of the nature of a cod; mock; burlesque; farcical: *Not all the cod poetry quotations come off* (Punch).
[origin unknown]
COD (no periods), **C.O.D.,** or **c.o.d.,** cash on delivery; collect on delivery.
co|da (kō′də), *n.* **1** a final passage of a musical composition, introduced after the completion of the essential parts, which gives it a definite and satisfactory ending: *The coda concludes the piece with spirit and energy* (European Magazine). **2** an addition to the usual 14 lines of a sonnet, often of 4 lines. **3** a concluding statement, address, or the like. [< Italian *coda* < Latin *cauda* tail]
cod|dle (kod′əl), *v.t.,* **-dled, -dling. 1** to treat tenderly; pamper: *The mother coddled her sick child.* **SYN:** humor, indulge. **2** to cook gently in hot water without boiling: *to coddle an egg.* [variant of *caudle* gruel]—**cod′dler,** *n.*
code (kōd), *n., v.,* **cod|ed, cod|ing.** **—*n.*** **1a** a system of words, letters, figures, or other symbols, used to keep a message short or secret; system of secret writing: *The enemy could not decipher the code in which the general's letter was written.* **b** a system of signals for sending messages, especially by telegraph or flags. The Morse code is used in telegraphy. **c** a system of symbols for representing information in a computer, and the rules for associating them. **2** a collection of the laws of a country arranged in a clear way so that they can be understood and used: *The punishments for robbery and murder are prescribed in the penal code.* **3** any set of rules. A traffic code contains rules for driving. A moral code is made up of the notions of right and wrong conduct held by a person, a group of persons, or a society. **4** = genetic code. **5** *U.S.* **a** lines and numbers printed on a product for identification by an optical scanner: *the code on the cover of a paperback.* **b** = Universal Product Code.
—*v.t.* **1** to change or translate into a code: *The spy coded his message to headquarters. The replies . . . can be coded and transferred to punched cards* (Science News Letter). **2** to enter in code.
code for, to specify the genetic code for (the synthesis of a protein, etc.): *The structural genes that code for this enzyme were identified from research with inbred mouse strains* (Science News).
[< Old French *code* < Latin *cōdex* ledger. See etym. of doublet **codex.**]
code|ball (kōd′bôl′), *n.* either of two games played with a ball six inches in diameter. One resembles handball, the other golf, but only the feet may be used in playing.
code|book (kōd′bu̇k′), *n.,* or **code book,** a book containing the symbols of a code and their meanings, used in coding or decoding messages.
code|break|er (kōd′brā′kər), *n.* a person who deciphers a code or codes.
code clerk, a clerk who codes and decodes messages: *I had been a code clerk in the American Embassy for two years* (James Thurber).
co|dec|li|na|tion (kō′dek lə nā′shən), *n. Astronomy.* the complement of the declination; the angular distance of a heavenly body from the celestial pole; polar distance. [< *co-* + *declination*]
code duello, the etiquette governing the formal duel.
co|de|fend|ant (kō′di fen′dənt), *n.* a joint defendant.
co|deine or **co|dein** (kō′dēn), *n.* a white, crystalline drug obtained from opium and used to relieve pain and coughs, and to cause sleep: *Codeine is similar to morphine in its effect, but it is milder in action* (Monroe M. Offner). *Formula:* $C_{18}H_{21}NO_3 \, H_2O$ [< Greek *kṓdeia* poppy head (< *koîlos* hollow) + English *-ine²*]
code name, a conventional word or name assigned to a secret agent, project, or assignment to avoid identification or detection by enemy intelligence: *Operation Bernhard, the code name the Nazis used for their counterfeiting of some $600 million worth of British bank notes in World War II . . .* (Harper's).
code-name (kod′nām′), *v.t.,* **-named, -nam|ing.** to give a code name to: *At 6:05, Maj. George J. Nelson and his two-men crew will climb into a sleek, needle-nosed B-58 bomber, code-named Hot Point 22* (Wall Street Journal).
Code Na|po|lé|on (kôd′nȧ pô lā ôɴ′), *French.* the body of French civil law promulgated in 1804 by Napoleon I, which still affects laws in parts of Holland, Belgium, Spain, etc., and in the state of Louisiana. Also, **Napoleonic Code.**
Code of Ham|mu|ra|bi (hä′mu̇ rä′bē, ham′u̇-), a collection of laws published by Hammurabi, a king of the first royal dynasty of Babylonia. It placed great stress on the lex talionis, the principle of "an eye for an eye."
Code of Justinian, = Justinian Code.
Code of Manu, the most important legal code of Hinduism, containing detailed commandments and prohibitions for daily living. The Code appeared about 250 B.C. and treats religion as a compulsory social institution.
cod|er (kō′dər), *n.* a person who codes; encoder: *There were . . . off-duty coders, signalmen, telegraphists* (Maclean's).
co|de|ter|mi|na|tion (kō′di tėr′mə nā′shən), *n.* the principle that organized labor should take part in the management of business, especially of big business, and be given a power equal to that of management in such aspects as the formation of policies governing production and welfare benefits: *In Germany there is a system*

Pronunciation Key: hat, āge, cãre, fär; let, ēqual, tėrm; it, īce; hot, ōpen, ôrder; oil, out; cup, pu̇t, rüle; child; long; thin; ᴛʜen; zh, measure; ə represents **a** in about, **e** in taken, **i** in pencil, **o** in lemon, **u** in circus.

known as codetermination where labor leaders do sit on boards of directors (Wall Street Journal).

co|de|ter|mine (kō′di tėr′mən), *v.t.*, **-mined, -min|ing.** to determine mutually, reciprocally, or jointly: *to codetermine policy.*

co|det|ta (kō det′ə; *Italian* kō dāt′tä), *n. Music.* **1** a short coda sometimes used as a transition from one section of a movement to the next. **2** a closing theme in a sonata sometimes occurring at the end of the exposition and then repeated in modified form at the end of the movement. [< Italian *codetta* (diminutive) < *coda* coda]

code word, or **code|word** (kōd′wėrd′), *n.* **1** a seemingly inoffensive word or expression: *Those who advise us that "law and order" is a codeword for racism ...* (National Review). **2** = code name: *He was given a codeword to be passed to the hijackers* (London Times). **3** a group of three letters representing three nucleotides in the genetic code; codon: *Information for the synthesis of protein molecules is stored as a sequence of code words in the DNA* (Stephen L. Wolfe).

▶**Code word** refers to deceptive use to avoid arousing opposition. **Euphemism** applies to use in order to avoid offense.

co|dex (kō′deks), *n., pl.* **co|di|ces.** **1** a manuscript volume, especially one of the Scriptures or of a classical author. **2** *Obsolete.* code. [< Latin *cōdex,* variant of *caudex* tree trunk, block of wood split into flat tablets for writing; book. See etym. of doublet **code.**]

Co|dex Ju|ris Ca|no|ni|ci (kō′deks jůr′is kə non′ə sī), the official statement of canon law by the Roman Catholic Church, made in 1918 and since then effective. [< New Latin *Codex Juris Canonici* Code of Canon Law]

cod|fish (kod′fish′), *n., pl.* **-fish|es** or (*collectively*) **-fish.** = cod[1].

codfish cake, any fried cake made of cod, or cod and mashed potato.

codg|er (koj′ər), *n. Informal.* an odd or peculiar person: *an eccentric old codger.* [apparently variant of *cadger*]

co|di|ces (kō′də sēz, kod′ə-), *n.* plural of **codex.**

cod|i|cil (kod′ə səl), *n.* **1** *Law.* something added to a will to change it, add to it, or explain it: *He had, in a fit of very natural exasperation, revoked the bequest in a codicil* (Dickens). **2** *Figurative.* something added: *We have at present so bitter a codicil to a most severe winter, that Berkeley Square was as much covered with snow this morning as it was two months ago* (Horace Walpole). SYN: supplement, appendix. [< Latin *cōdicillus* a short writing (diminutive) < *cōdex;* see etym. under **codex**]

cod|i|cil|la|ry (kod′ə sil′ər ē), *adj.* of the nature of a codicil.

cod|i|fy (kod′ə fī, kō′də-), *v.t.*, **-fied, -fy|ing.** **1** to arrange (laws) according to a system: *The laws of France began to be codified in 1800 by order of Napoleon I.* **2** to reduce to a general system; systematize: *The attempt to probe into complex issues which cannot reasonably be simplified into a codified answer, may lead to spurious results which are all the more dangerous because of their apparently "scientific" form of presentation* (Anthony H. Richmond). [< *code* + *-fy*] **—cod′i|fi|ca′tion,** *n.* **—cod′i|fi′er,** *n.*

co|di|rec|tor (kō′də rek′tər, -dī-), *n.* joint director.

co|dis|cov|er|er (kō′dis kuv′ər ər), *n.* a joint discoverer.

cod|lin (kod′lin), *n.* = codling[1].

cod|ling[1] (kod′ling), *n.* **1** a small, unripe apple. **2** a kind of long, tapering apple, usually for cooking. [Middle English *querdelyng* apple with a hard core, apparently < French *coeur de lion* (literally) heart of a lion]

cod|ling[2] (kod′ling), *n.* **1** a young or small cod. **2** = hake. [< *cod*[1] + *-ling*]

codling or **codlin moth,** a small moth whose larvae destroy apples, pears, and other fruits.

cod-liv|er oil (kod′liv′ər), oil extracted from the liver of cod or of related species, used in medicine as a source of vitamins A and D.

co|don (kō′don), *n. Genetics.* **1** a sequence of three chemical units or bases forming the arrangement for a specific amino acid in protein synthesis and represented in the genetic code by a three-letter code word: *Codon after codon in the messenger RNA ... adds the attached appropriate amino acid in the right sequence to the growing protein molecule* (New Scientist). **2** the three-letter code word: *Each of the 20 different amino acids ... is represented by one or more three-letter words, or codons* (Scientific American).

cod|piece (kod′pēs′), *n.* a baglike flap at the front of tight-fitting breeches worn by men in the 1400's and 1500's. [< *cod*[2] bag + *piece*]

cods|wal|lop (kodz′wol′əp), *n. British Slang.* nonsense; rubbish: *The trite saying "the game's the thing" is so much codswallop* (LondonTimes). [< phrase *cod's wallop*]

cod war, a prolonged conflict between nations over fishing rights in territorial waters: *For the third time since World War II, Iceland and Britain are near blows in what citizens of both nations call the cod war* (Time).

co|ed or **co-ed** (kō′ed′), *n., adj. U.S. Informal.* **—*n.*** a girl or woman student at a coeducational school. **—*adj.*** = coeducational: *a coed school.* [American English < *coed*(ucational)]

co|ed|u|ca|tion (kō′ej ů kā′shən), *n.* the education of boys and girls or men and women together in the same school or classes.

co|ed|u|ca|tion|al (kō′ej ů kā′shə nəl), *adj.* **1a** educating boys and girls or men and women together in the same school or classes: *a coeducational school.* **b** for both sexes: *The coeducational camp, in which boys and girls enjoy shared activities, is now no rarity* (Sidonie Matsner Gruenberg). **2** having to do with coeducation. **—co′ed|u|ca′tion|al|ly,** *adv.*

co|ed|u|ca|tion|al|ism (kō′ej ů kā′shə nə liz′əm), *n.* **1** the system or practice of coeducation. **2** belief in coeducation.

coef. or **coeff.,** coefficient.

co|ef|fi|cient (kō′ə fish′ənt), *n., adj.* **—*n.*** **1** a number or symbol put with and multiplying another; cofactor. In *3x, 3* is the coefficient of *x,* and *x* is the coefficient of *3;* in *axy, a* is the coefficient of *xy.* **2** *Physics.* a ratio used as a multiplier to calculate the behavior of a substance under different conditions of heat, light, pressure, friction, or other physical conditions. **3** a thing that unites in action with something else in producing an effect or result; cooperating cause. **—*adj.*** cooperating.

coefficient of correlation, *Statistics* = correlation coefficient.

***co|el|a|canth** (sē′lə kanth), *n.* any one of an order of fishes having rounded scales and lobed fins, formerly considered extinct. A coelacanth is similar to the primitive sea vertebrates which gave rise to all land vertebrates. [< New Latin *Coelacanthus* the typical genus < Greek *koîlos* hollow + *ákantha* thorn, spine]

***coelacanth**

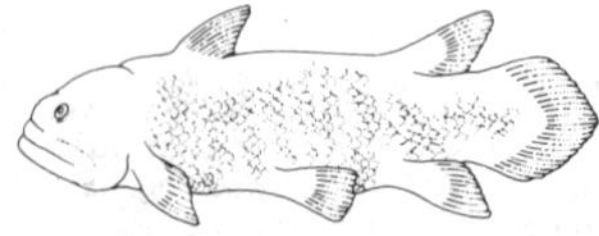

coe|la|can|thine (sē′lə kan′thēn), *adj.* of or having to do with a coelacanth or the coelacanths.

coe|len|ter|ate (si len′tə rāt, -tər it), *n., adj.* **—*n.*** any one of a phylum of aquatic invertebrates with radially symmetrical, saclike bodies and a single internal cavity. Hydras, jellyfish, corals, and sea anemones are coelenterates. **—*adj.*** belonging to this phylum. [< New Latin *Coelenterata* < Greek *koîlos* hollow + *énteron* intestine]

coe|len|ter|on (si len′tə ron), *n., pl.* **-ter|a** (-tər ə). the internal and digestive cavity of a coelenterate. [< New Latin *coelenteron* < Greek *koîlos* hollow + *énteron* intestine]

coe|li|ac (sē′lē ak), *adj.* of or in the abdominal cavity. Also, **celiac.** [< Latin *coeliacus* < Greek *koiliakós* < *koiliā* belly < *koîlos* hollow]

coe|lo|dont (sē′lə dont), *adj., n.* **—*adj.*** having hollow teeth, as certain lizards. **—*n.*** **1** an extinct, woolly mammal, related to the rhinoceros, that lived in the vast prairies of Europe and Asia during the Pleistocene. **2** any animal having hollow teeth. [< Greek *koîlos* hollow + *odoús, odóntos* tooth]

coe|lom (sē′ləm), *n.* the body cavity of most many-celled animals, developed within the mesoderm and different from the intestinal cavity: *A different type of body cavity, the coelom, exists in the starfishes ... and is present in all animals of greater complexity* (Harbaugh and Goodrich). Also, **celom, coeloma, coelome.** [< Greek *koílōma* a cavity < *koîlos* hollow]

coe|lo|ma (si lō′mə), *n., pl.* **-ma|ta** (-mə tə). = coelom.

coe|lo|mate (sē′lə māt), *adj., n.* **—*adj.*** having a coelom: *The earthworm ... is the traditional type with which students begin their study of coelomate animals* (Betty I. Roots). **—*n.*** an animal having a coelom.

coe|lome (sē′lōm), *n.* = coelom.

coe|lom|ic (si lom′ik), *adj.* of or having to do with the coelom: *Circulation is aided by the movements of the coelomic fluid flowing in the cavity which lies between the intestine and the muscle layer* (A. M. Winchester).

coe|lo|stat (sē′lə stat), *n.* a type of telescope in which a reflected image of the sky is made to appear stationary by means of a mirror which revolves slowly by clockwork. [< Latin *coelum, caelum* sky + Greek *statós* standing]

co|emp|tion (kō emp′shən), *n.* **1** the purchase of all of a given commodity in the market, in order to control its price. **2** a form of civil marriage in Roman law consisting in a mutual fictitious sale of the two parties. [< Latin *coemptiō, -ōnis* < *coemere* buy together < *co-* with + *emere* buy]

coe|nen|chy|ma (si neng′kə mə), *n., pl.* **-ma|ta** (-mə tə). the common calcareous tissue uniting the individual polyps or zooids of a compound anthozoan. [< New Latin *coenenchyma* < Greek *koinós* common + *énchyma* infusion]

coe|nen|chy|mal (si neng′kə məl), *adj.* having to do with or of the nature of coenenchyma: *coenenchymal tubes.*

coe|nes|the|sia (sē′nəs thē′zhə, sen′əs-), *n. Psychology.* the total undifferentiated mass of impressions from all organic sensations occurring at the same time, by which one derives a sense of body and body condition. Also, **cenesthesia.** [< Greek *koinós* common + *aísthēsis* sense perception, sensation]

coe|nes|the|sis (sē′nəs thē′sis, sen′əs-), *n.* = coenesthesia.

coe|no|bite (sē′nə bīt, sen′ə-), *n.* = cenobite.

coe|no|bit|ic (sē′nə bit′ik, sen′ə-), *adj.* = cenobitic.

coe|no|bit|i|cal (sē′nə bit′ə kəl, sen′ə-), *adj.* = cenobitical.

coe|no|bit|ism (sē′nə bī tiz′əm, sen′ə-), *n.* = cenobitism.

coe|no|by (sē′nə bē, sen′ə-), *n., pl.* **-bies.** = cenoby.

coe|no|cyte (sē′nə sīt, sen′ə-), *n.* a mass of cytoplasm containing many nuclei enclosed by a single cell wall, as in some green algae and many fungi: *Wall formation does not take place and therefore the fully grown cell, which may be half an inch long, has thousands of nuclei distributed within the cytoplasm, forming a large coenocyte* (Fred W. Emerson). [< Greek *koinós* common + English *-cyte*]

coe|no|cyt|ic (sē′nə sit′ik, sen′ə-), *adj.* of or containing coenocytes: *coenocytic algae.*

coe|no|sarc (sē′nə särk, sen′ə-), *n.* the common soft tissue which unites the individual polyps or zooids of a compound zoophyte, such as coral, and circulates food through the colony. [< Greek *koinós* common + *sárx, sarkós* flesh]

coe|no|sar|cal (sē′nə sär′kəl, sen′ə-), *adj.* having to do with or of the nature of coenosarc.

coe|nure (sē′nyůr), *n.* = coenurus.

coe|nu|rus (si nyůr′əs, -nůr′-), *n.* a stage in the life history of a tapeworm, in which many heads are asexually produced within a single cyst. In the brains of sheep, it causes staggers or gid. [< New Latin *coenurus* < Greek *koinós* common + *ourā́* tail]

co|en|zyme (kō en′zīm), *n.* a lightweight organic substance, usually containing a mineral or vitamin, capable of attaching itself to a specific protein (the apoenzyme) and supplementing it to form an active enzyme system: *A coenzyme is much smaller than an enzyme, ... is not a protein, and is usually resistant to breakdown by heat* (Scientific American).

coenzyme A, a coenzyme important in the metabolism of organic acids in plants and animals: *Coenzyme A is essential to the oxidation of fatty acids* (Scientific American).

coenzyme Q, = ubiquinone.

co|e|qual (kō ē′kwəl), *adj., n.* **—*adj.*** equal in rank, degree, or extent. **—*n.*** a person or thing that is equal to another. **—co|e′qual|ly,** *adv.*

co|e|qual|i|ty (kō′i kwol′ə tē), *n.* the state of being equal in rank, degree, or extent: *He cannot be admitted to coequality, social or political* (London Times).

co|erce (kō ėrs′), *v.t.*, **-erced, -erc|ing.** **1** to compel; force: *The prisoner was coerced into confessing to the crime. The boy was coerced into learning to dance.* SYN: oblige. **2** to control or restrain by force or authority: *The unruly crowd had to be coerced.* SYN: constrain. **3** to effect by compulsion: *to coerce obedience.* SYN: enforce. [< Latin *coercēre* < *co-* together + *arcēre* restrain] **—co|erc′er,** *n.*

co|er|ci|ble (kō ėr′sə bəl), *adj.* **1** that can be coerced. **2** compressible or condensable: *coercible gas.*

co|er|cion (kō ėr′shən), *n.* **1** the use of force; compulsion; constraint: *Dictators rule by coercion. A merger as such involves no necessary connotations of coercion, dominance, or lack of effective competitive pressures* (Wall Street Journal). SYN: restraint, duress. **2** the ability or power to coerce: *the coercion of public opinion.* **3** government by force: *Bills to establish coercion in Ireland were passed in the British Parliament in the 1800's.*

co|er|cion|ist (kō ėr′shə nist), *n.* a person who advocates or supports government by coercion.

co|er|cive (kō ėr′siv), *adj.* **1** using force; serving to coerce; compelling: *He used coercive measures to enforce obedience.* SYN: compulsory, forcing. **2** restraining; constraining: *To Durkheim the essence of group life is that it exercises constraint or coercive power upon the individual* (Ogburn and Nimkoff). —**co|er′cive|ly**, *adv.* —**co|er′cive|ness**, *n.*

coercive force, *Physics.* that intensity of a magnetic field required to reduce to zero the residual magnetism of a substance.

co|er|civ|i|ty (kō′ėr siv′ə tē), *n. Physics.* **1** the property of having coercive force. **2** the degree of coercive force of a substance: *The now widely used ceramic magnets ... have ... high coercivity—a property that gives them very good resistance to demagnetization* (New Scientist).

coes|ite (kō′sīt, -zīt), *n.* a very dense form of silica, occurring naturally in meteoritic or nuclear-bomb craters and produced synthetically by subjecting quartz to very high pressure. [< Loring *Coes*, Jr., born 1915, an American chemist]

co|es|sen|tial (kō′ə sen′shəl), *adj.* having the same essence or nature; united in essence. —**co′es|sen′tial|ly**, *adv.* —**co′es|sen′tial|ness**, *n.*

co|es|sen|ti|al|i|ty (kō′ə sen′shē al′ə tē), *n.* coessential quality or nature.

co|es|tab|lish|ment (kō′ə stab′lish mənt), *n.* joint establishment.

co|e|ta|ne|ous (kō′i tā′nē əs), *adj.* of the same age or duration; contemporary; coeval. [< Latin *coaetāneus* (with English *-ous*) of the same age < *co-* together + *aetās, -ātis* age] —**co′e|ta′ne|ous|ly**, *adv.* —**co′e|ta′ne|ous|ness**, *n.*

co|e|ter|nal (kō′i tėr′nəl), *adj.* equally eternal; existing with another eternally. —**co′e|ter′nal|ly**, *adv.*

co|e|ter|ni|ty (kō′i tėr′nə tē), *n.* coeternal existence or quality; eternal existence with another.

Coeur-d'A|lêne (kėr′də lān′), *n.* a Salishan dialect spoken by certain Indian tribes in the northwestern United States. [< French *coeur d'alêne* (literally) awl heart (from a chief's characterization of a trader)]

co|e|val (kō ē′vəl), *adj., n.* —*adj.* **1** of the same age, date, or duration: ... *an ancient tribe which was coeval with some of the extinct mammals* (James Dwight Dana). **2** = contemporary. —*n.* a contemporary. [< Late Latin *coaevus* (< *co-* equal + *aevum* age) + English *-al*[1]] —**co|e′val|ly**, *adv.*

co|ev|o|lu|tion (kō ev′ə lü′shən), *n. Biology.* evolution of two or more forms or organisms together or in response to one another: *Ultraviolet pigments ... have probably played an important part in the coevolution of flowers with ultraviolet-sensitive insects* (New Scientist).

co|e|volve (kō′i volv′), *v.i.,* **-volved, -volv|ing.** *Biology.* to evolve together or in response to one another: *In the birds of paradise, brilliant colors and long plumes have coevolved with extremely elaborate movements* (Natural History).

co|ex|ec|u|tor (kō′ig zek′yə tər), *n.* a person who is an executor of a will along with another.

co|ex|ec|u|trix (kō′ig zek′yə triks), *n., pl.* **-ex|ec|u|trix|es, -ex|ec|u|tri|ces** (-ig zek′yə trī′sēs). a woman coexecutor.

co|ex|ist (kō′ig zist′), *v.i.* to exist together or at the same time: *Orange trees have coexisting fruit and flowers.*

co|ex|ist|ence (kō′ig zis′təns), *n.* **1** existence together or at the same time. **2** a condition or policy in which two opposing countries or powers coexist without war or direct interference with each other: *peaceful coexistence. Coexistence implies, and indeed necessitates, the total noninterference by any power in the affairs of another* (Time).

co|ex|ist|ent (kō′ig zis′tənt), *adj.* coexisting.

co|ex|tend (kō′ik stend′), *v.t., v.i.* to extend equally or to the same limits.

co|ex|ten|sion (kō′ik sten′shən), *n.* **1** extension over an equal amount of space. **2** extension over exactly the same time.

co|ex|ten|sive (kō′ik sten′siv), *adj.* extending equally; extending over the same space or time. —**co′ex|ten′sive|ly**, *adv.*

co|ex|tinc|tion (kō′ik stingk′shən), *n.* mutual or simultaneous extinction: ... *coexistence is preferable to coextinction* (Bulletin of Atomic Scientists).

co|fac|tor (kō fak′tər), *n.* a joint factor, especially: **1** = coenzyme. **2** one of several factors entering into the same expression in algebra; coefficient.

C. of C., Chamber of Commerce.

coff (kof), *v.t.,* **coft, coff|ing.** *Scottish.* to buy; purchase. [probably < Middle Dutch *coft* bought, or sold]

cof|fee (kôf′ē, kof′-), *n., adj.* —*n.* **1** a dark-brown drink made from the roasted and ground seeds of a tall, tropical tree or shrub. **2** the seeds from which the drink is made; coffee beans. **3** the plant itself. It belongs to the madder family. See picture under **madder family**. **4** the color of coffee; a dark brown, darker than chocolate. **5** a social gathering at which coffee is served.

—*adj.* **1** having the flavor of coffee: *coffee ice cream.* **2** having the color of coffee; dark-brown. **3** at or in which coffee is served: *a coffee party, a coffee club.*

[< Italian *caffè* < Turkish *kahve* < Arabic *qahwah*]

coffee bar, *British.* a coffee shop that specializes in serving caffè espresso; espresso bar.

coffee bean, the seed of the coffee plant. Coffee beans are roasted and ground to make coffee.

coffee berry, the fruit of the coffee tree or shrub, containing coffee beans.

coffee break, a short intermission in the working day, with coffee or other refreshments available: *Washington advocated the coffee break, then* [*in the 1940's*], *as a morale builder—particularly for the defense workers* (Christian Science Monitor).

cof|fee|cake (kôf′ē kāk′, kof′-), *n.* a light, sweetened cake, usually made with yeast, and often with spice, fruit, or nuts, sometimes iced.

coffee cup, a cup for drinking coffee, usually larger than a teacup.

coffee grinder, = coffee mill.

coffee hour, an informal social gathering, often held after a formal meeting, lecture, etc., at which coffee is served.

coffee house, or **cof|fee|house** (kôf′ē hous′, kof′-), *n.* a place where coffee and other refreshments are served. In the 1600's and 1700's, London coffee houses were centers of political and literary conversation, and filled much the same place as modern clubs.

coffee klatch (kläch, kluch), = Kaffeeklatsch.

cof|fee|mak|er (kôf′ē mā′kər, kof′-), *n.,* or **coffee maker**, a utensil for making coffee, as a percolator.

coffee mill, a machine for grinding coffee beans.

coffee nut, **1** the fruit of the Kentucky coffee tree. **2** the tree itself.

cof|fee|pot (kôf′ē pot′, kof′-), *n.,* or **coffee pot**, a container for making or serving coffee.

coffee ring, a coffeecake having the shape of a ring.

coffee shop, a place where coffee, light refreshments, and inexpensive meals are served, especially in a hotel.

coffee spoon, a spoon used to stir coffee, usually smaller than a teaspoon.

coffee stall, a movable structure in which coffee and other light refreshments are sold.

coffee table, any low table for serving coffee and other refreshments. It is often placed in front of a sofa.

cof|fee-ta|ble book (kôf′ē tā′bəl, kof′-), a large, impressive-looking book, richly illustrated but without much substantive text: *Coffee-table books—glossy expensive objects ... often more notable for pictorial than for scholastic value* (London Times).

coffee tree, **1** any plant which bears coffee beans. **2** = Kentucky coffee tree.

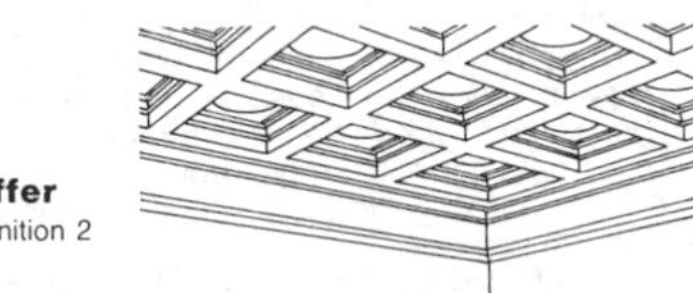

***coffer**
definition 2

***cof|fer** (kôf′ər, kof′-), *n., v.* —*n.* **1** a box, chest, or trunk, especially one used to hold money or other valuable things: *a large ironbound coffer.* SYN: strongbox, safe. **2** an ornamental sunken panel, especially in a ceiling. **3** a canal lock chamber. **4** = cofferdam. **5** = caisson (def. 4).

—*v.t.* **1** to deposit or enclose in or as if in a coffer. **2** to build or ornament with coffers: *a coffered ceiling.*

coffers, a treasury; funds: *Only 30 per cent of the oil revenues goes into the state coffers* (Newsweek).

[< Old French *cofre* < Latin *cophinus* basket < Greek *kóphinos*]

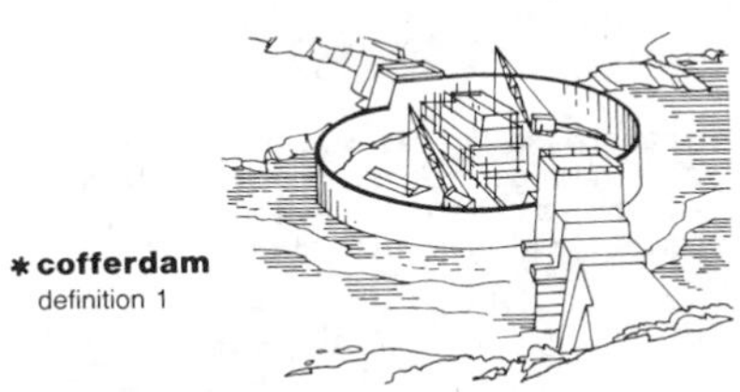

***cofferdam**
definition 1

***cof|fer|dam** (kôf′ər dam′, kof′-), *n.* **1** a temporary dam built in a river, lake, or other body of water, that encloses an underwater area that can be pumped dry for men to build the foundations of a bridge, pier, or the like. **2** chamber used for repairing a ship below the waterline. **3** = caisson (def. 3).

cof|fers (kôf′ərz, kof′-), *n. pl.* See under **coffer**.

cof|fin (kôf′ən, kof′-), *n., v.* —*n.* **1** a box into which a dead person is put to be buried; casket: *His coffin was laid to rest in a deep grave.* **2** the horny part of a horse's hoof containing the coffin bone.

—*v.t.* **1** to put into a coffin. **2** to shut up tightly: *The cards are coffined in their boxes* (Thackeray).

[< Old French *cofin* basket < Latin *cophinus* < Greek *kóphinos*]

coffin bone, the last phalanx in the foot of the horse and related animals, enclosed in the hoof.

coffin corner, *Slang.* a corner of a football field formed by a goal line and a sideline. If a punt is kicked out of bounds there and not over the goal line, the receiving team must resume play at that point.

cof|fin|ite (kôf′ə nīt, kof′-), *n.* a black mineral, silicate of uranium, like coal in appearance, rich in uranium. Formula: $USiO_4$ [< Reuben C. *Coffin*, born 1886, an American geologist]

coffin joint, the joint next above the coffin bone, at the top of the hoof in the horse and related animals.

coffin nail, *Slang.* a cigarette: *He warned me of the havoc wrought by coffin nails on the clockwork of the human body, and he hoped I would never smoke cigarettes* (New Yorker).

cof|fle (kof′əl), *n.* **1** a train of men or beasts fastened together. **2** a gang of slaves chained and driven along together. [< Arabic *qāfilah* caravan, company]

co|fig|ur|a|tive (kō fig′yər ə tiv), *adj. Anthropology.* of or designating a form of society in which each generation or peer group evolves its own values (contrasted with *postfigurative, prefigurative*).

co|found|er (kō foun′dər), *n.* a joint founder: *His grandfather was an older brother of John Jacob Bausch, cofounder of Bausch & Lomb* (New York Times).

C. of S., chief of staff.

coft (koft), *v.* past tense and past participle of **coff**.

cog[1] (kog), *n.* **1** one of a series of teeth on the edge of a cogwheel or gear. A cog transfers motion by locking into the teeth of a similar wheel. *The principle of both clocks and watches is that a number of wheels, locked together by cogs, are forced to turn round* (J. Norman Lockyer). **2** = cogwheel. **3** *Figurative.* a person or thing having a minor but necessary function in the running of any system or organization: *Each ... guerrilla is a cog in a complicated, disciplined command structure* (Time).

slip a cog, to make a mistake: *Many censors' howlers represent nothing more sinister than society's self-protective mechanisms slipping a cog or two* (Manchester Guardian Weekly).

[probably < Scandinavian (compare Swedish *kugge*)]

cog[2] (kog), *n., v.,* **cogged, cog|ging.** *Carpentry.* —*n.* a projection, tenon, or tooth on one piece of wood that fits into a notch on another piece to make a joint.

—*v.t., v.i.* to connect by means of a cog.

[variant of earlier *cock* to secure]

cog[3] (kog), *v.,* **cogged, cog|ging,** *n.* —*v.t.* **1a** to handle (dice) dishonestly. **b** to load (dice) or use (loaded dice). **2** *Obsolete.* to beguile; deceive. **3** *Obsolete.* to wheedle; cajole: *Jesting and frisking ... to cog a laughter from us* (Milton). **4** *Obsolete.* to foist; palm off. —*v.i.* to cheat at dice.

—*n. Obsolete.* a deception; trick; fraud.

[origin uncertain]

cog[4] (kog), *n.* **1** a small boat; cockboat. **2** a type of sailing ship once used in Scandinavia, England, and Holland. It had a clinker-built hull and one large square sail. [Middle English *cogge* < Old French *cogue*]

cog., cognate.

co|gen|cy (kō′jən sē), *n.* forceful quality; power of convincing: *The cogency of his argument helped him win the debate.* SYN: potency, effectiveness, persuasiveness.

co|gen|er|a|tion (kō′jen ə rā′shən), *n.* the production of electric power, heat, and other forms of energy from the same facility: *I propose a special 10 percent tax credit for investments in cogeneration* (Jimmy Carter). —**co|gen′er|a′tor**, *n.*

co|gent (kō′jənt), *adj.* **1** having the power to con-

Pronunciation Key: hat, āge, cãre, fär; let, ēqual, tėrm; it, īce; hot, ōpen, ôrder; oil, out; cup, pu̇t, rüle; child; long; thin; ᴛʜen; zh, measure; ə represents **a** in about, **e** in taken, **i** in pencil, **o** in lemon, **u** in circus.

vince; forceful or convincing: *The lawyer used cogent arguments to persuade the jury that his client was innocent.* SYN: potent, compelling. See syn. under **valid**. **2** constraining; impelling; powerful: *The French Emperor . . . determined to insist in cogent terms* (Alexander Kinglake). [< Latin *cogēns, -entis,* present participle of *cogere* compel < *co-* together + *agere* drive] —**co'gent|ly,** *adv.*

cog|i|ta|ble (koj'ə tə bəl), *adj.* that can be thought; thinkable; conceivable: *. . . something not perceivable by sense, but only cogitable by reason* (John Grote).

cog|i|tate (koj'ə tāt), *v.,* **-tat|ed, -tat|ing.** —*v.i.* to think over; consider with care; ponder; meditate; reflect: *The judge cogitated a long time before making any decision in the case. That lady lay cogitating over the past evening* (Dinah M. Mulock). SYN: deliberate, muse.
—*v.t.* to devise; plan.
[< Latin *cōgitāre* (with English *-ate*[1]) < *co-* (intensive) + *agitāre* consider < *agere* reflect upon] —**cog'i|ta'tor,** *n.*

cog|i|ta|tion (koj'ə tā'shən), *n.* **1a** deep thought; careful consideration; pondering; meditation. **b** the state of being deep in thought. **2** the faculty of thinking or thought. **3** a deep thought; reflection: *They were, at best, vague cogitations jotted down as they came to mind* (Atlantic).

cog|i|ta|tive (koj'ə tā'tiv), *adj.* **1** given to thinking; thoughtful; meditative. **2** having the power of thought: *Belief is more properly an act of the sensitive than of the cogitative parts of our natures* (George H. Lewes). —**cog'i|ta'tive|ly,** *adv.* —**cog'i|ta'tive|ness,** *n.*

co|gi|to er|go sum (koj'ə tō ėr'gō sum'), *Latin.* I think, therefore I am (the basic proposition of Descartes' system of philosophy).

co|gnac or **Co|gnac** (kōn'yak, kon'-), *n.* a brandy of superior quality distilled from wine at or near Cognac, France: *It is the traditionally correct cognac—unchanging in quality—matchless in flavour and aroma* (New Yorker). [< French *cognac* < *Cognac,* a town and region in Charente, France]

cog|nate (kog'nāt), *adj., n.* —*adj.* **1a** related in origin; descended from the same original language. English, Dutch, and German are cognate languages. **b** coming from the same word or root. English *father,* German *Vater,* and Latin *pater* are cognate words. **2** related by family, on either father's or mother's side. SYN: kindred, akin. **3** having a similar nature or quality. SYN: allied, affiliated, alike.
—*n.* **1** a word, language, or thing related to another by having a common source. The German word *Wasser* and the English word *water* are cognates. **2a** *Anthropology.* a person related to another by family; kinsman. **b** a kinsman on the mother's side (distinguished from *agnate*) .
[< Latin *cognātus* of common descent < *co-* together + *gnātus,* past participle of *gnāscī* be born] —**cog'nate|ness,** *n.*

cog|na|tion (kog nā'shən), *n.* cognate relationship or relation; kinship; affinity: *A great danger exists in claiming cognation between two distant peoples from the coincidence of a few words in both languages* (Manley Hopkins).

cog|ni|sance (kog'nə zəns, kon'ə-), *n. Especially British.* cognizance.

cog|ni|tion (kog nish'ən), *n.* **1** the act of knowing; perception; awareness. SYN: sensation. **2** a thing known, perceived, or recognized. **3** (in Scottish law) official notice; cognizance: *The Council appointed a Committee to take cognition of the matter* (James Grant). **4** *Obsolete.* the act or faculty of coming to know; knowledge. [< Latin *cognitiō, -ōnis* < *cognōscere* recognize < *co-* (intensive) + *gnōscere* know]

cog|ni|tion|al (kog nish'ə nəl), *adj.* = cognitive.

cog|ni|tive (kog'nə tiv), *adj.* having to do with cognition; cognizing: *In addition to unusual endowments in terms of cognitive ability, they are by constitution more vigorous and have . . . an exceptional fund of psychic and physical energy* (Scientific American). —**cog'ni|tive|ly,** *adv.*

cognitive therapy, a method of treating mental and emotional problems by trying to change faulty thinking patterns: *cognitive therapy—the exploration of the misperceptions and distortions of thought that cause inappropriate responses* (New York Times).

cog|ni|za|ble (kog'nə zə bəl, kon'ə-), *adj.* **1** that can be known or perceived; recognizable: *No articulate sound is cognizable until the inarticulate sounds which go to make it up have been learned* (Herbert Spencer). **2** within the jurisdiction of a law court. —**cog'ni|za|ble|ness,** *n.* —**cog'ni|za|bly,** *adv.*

cog|ni|zance (kog'nə zəns, kon'ə-), *n.* **1** knowledge obtained by observation or information; perception; awareness: *The shortages in the company's funds came to the cognizance of the treasurer.* SYN: notice, observation. **2** *Law.* **a** an official notice. **b** the right or power to deal with judicially. **c** the hearing or trying of a case in court. **3** jurisdiction; responsibility; charge: *By invasion time, Aldrich, a lieutenant commander, held sway—or had cognizance, as the Navy puts it—over a thousand officers and ten thousand men* (New Yorker). **4a** a device or mark by which a person, company, or group is known or distinguished, such as a crest or coat of arms; badge. **b** *Heraldry.* a device or emblem worn for distinction by all the retainers of a noble house, whether they carried arms or not.
have cognizance of, to be aware of; know by observation or information: *The king had cognizance of plots against him.*
take cognizance of, to take notice of; give attention to; become aware of: *The judge took cognizance of the accused man's ill health in handing down the sentence. The powerful House Rules Committee last week took official cognizance of these criticisms* (Newsweek).
[< Old French *conoissance* < *conoistre* to know < Latin *cognōscere;* see etym. under **cognition**]

cog|ni|zant (kog'nə zənt, kon'ə-), *adj.* **1** having cognizance; aware: *When the doctor was fully cognizant of the patient's serious condition, he acted swiftly to relieve it.* **2** having legal cognizance or jurisdiction.

cog|nize (kog'nīz), *v.t.,* **-nized, -niz|ing.** to take cognizance of; perceive; know. [< Latin *cognōscere;* patterned on *recognize*]

cog|no|men (kog nō'mən), *n.* **1** a surname; family name; last name. **2** a nickname: *"Honest Abe" is a cognomen that carries a far-reaching lesson for leaders everywhere* (Emory S. Bogardus). **3** any name: *I repeated the name* [*Priscilla*] *to myself three or four times . . . this quaint and prim cognomen . . . amalgamated itself with my idea of the girl* (Hawthorne). **4** the third or family name of a person in ancient Rome, for example *Cicero* in *Marcus Tullius Cicero.* [< Latin *cognōmen* < *co-* with + *nōmen* name; influenced by *cognōscere* recognize]

cog|nom|i|nal (kog nom'ə nəl), *adj., n.* —*adj.* **1** having the same name. **2** of or having to do with a cognomen or surname.
—*n. Obsolete.* a namesake.

cog|nosce (kog nos'), *v.t.,* **-nosced, -nosc|ing.** in Scottish law: **1** to investigate judicially. **2** to examine into and declare the legal status of. **3** to pronounce insane. [< Latin *cognōscere;* see etym. under **cognition**]

co|gno|scen|te (kō'nyō shen'tā), *n., pl.* **-ti** (-tē). a person who is well-informed; connoisseur: *Even the cognoscenti cannot agree on the definition and purpose of poetry.* Also, **conoscente.** [< Italian *cognoscente,* learned borrowing from Latin *cognōscēns, -entis,* present participle of *cognōscere;* see etym. under **cognition**]

cog|nos|ci|bil|i|ty (kog nos'ə bil'ə tē), *n.* cognoscible quality; knowableness.

cog|nos|ci|ble (kog nos'ə bəl), *adj., n.* —*adj.* that can be known; knowable; recognizable: *Neither can evil be known, because whatsoever is truly cognoscible is good and true* (Jeremy Taylor).
—*n.* something that can be known.
[< Late Latin *cognoscibilis* < Latin *cognōscere* recognize]

cog|nos|ci|tive (kog nos'ə tiv), *adj.* having the power of knowing; cognitive.

cog|no|vit (kog nō'vit), *n. Law.* a written confession by a defendant that the action or a part of the action against him is just. [< Latin *cognōvit* (*actionem*) he has acknowledged (the action)]

co|gon (kō gōn'), *n.* a tall, coarse grass of the Philippines and neighboring countries, used for thatch. [< Spanish *cogón* < the Tagalog name]

cog|rail (kog'rāl'), *n.* = rack rail.

***cog railway**

***cog railway,** a type of railway for very steep grades, having a rack in connection with the track which a cogged driving wheel on the locomotive engages; rack railway.

***cogwheel**

***cog|wheel** (kog'hwēl'), *n.* a wheel with teeth cut in the rim for transmitting or receiving motion; a gear or gearwheel: *The cogwheels of this watch transmit the power of the spring to the hands.*

co|hab|it (kō hab'it), *v.i.* **1** to live together as husband and wife do (often said of persons not legally married). **2** *Archaic.* to live together. [< Late Latin *cohabitāre* < Latin *co-* with + *habitāre* dwell] —**co|hab'i|ta'tion,** *n.*

co|hab|it|ant (kō hab'ə tənt), *n.* a person who lives together with another or others.

co|heir (kō ãr'), *n.* an heir with another or others.

co|heir|ess (kō ãr'is), *n.* an heiress with another or others.

co|heir|ship (kō ãr'ship), *n.* the fact or condition of being a coheir or coheiress.

Co|hen (kō'ən, kō'ən), *n., pl.* **Co|hens, Co|ha|nim** (kō hä'nim). a Jewish male having certain priestly functions by virtue of descent from Aaron. Also, **Kohen.** [< Hebrew *kōhēn*]

co|here (kō hir'), *v.i.,* **-hered, -her|ing. 1** to stick together; hold together as parts of the same mass or substance: *Brick and mortar cohere.* **2** *Figurative.* to be well connected; be consistent: *The varying details of the witness's story failed to cohere. This means that the sense impressions of the moment are modified by and in some way cohere with the sense impressions of the past* (J. A. V. Butler). [< Latin *cohaerēre* < *co-* together + *haerēre* cling, cleave to]

co|her|ence (kō hir'əns), *n.* **1** *Figurative.* logical connection; consistency; congruity: *The insane man's speech lacked coherence. The laws of brain physiology ultimately depend for their significance, as well as coherence, on mathematical and logical laws* (W. Mays). **2** the act or fact of sticking together; tendency to hold together; cohesion: *the coherence of atoms of the same chemical element.* (*Figurative.*) *The authority of the Church, the coherence of the old social system were lost; and there was no longer any body of thought accepted as more or less authoritative* (Edmund Wilson). **3** harmonious connection of the parts of a discourse.
—*Syn.* **2 Coherence, cohesion** mean the quality or state of sticking together. **Coherence** implies a figurative sticking together and a resulting unity, consistency, or congruity. *Coherence* in an argument implies a logical ordering and clear arrangement of the several points, in a painting the harmonious disposal of the various elements of the design. **Cohesion** ordinarily implies a literal sticking together of the parts of a physical substance: *Surface tension is attributable to the cohesion between the molecules of a liquid.*

co|her|en|cy (kō hir'ən sē), *n., pl.* **-cies.** = coherence.

co|her|ent (kō hir'ənt), *adj.* **1** *Figurative.* logically connected; consistent: *The driver was so upset that he could not give a coherent account of the accident. A coherent sentence is easy to read and clear to understand.* **2** sticking together; holding together: *coherent molecules.* **3** *Physics.* having waves of a similar phase, direction, and amplitude and capable of exhibiting interference: *Lasers . . . form a highly directional and powerful beam of coherent light* (Science News Letter). —**co|her'ent|ly,** *adv.*

co|her|er (kō hir'ər), *n.* a device for detecting radio waves, formerly used instead of vacuum tubes in radios. A coherer consists essentially of a tube containing metal filings or other conducting substances which cohere with a subsequent fall in resistance when struck by a radio wave.

co|he|sion (kō hē'zhən), *n.* **1** a sticking together; tendency to hold together: *Wet sand has more cohesion than dry sand.* (*Figurative.*) *The party lost the election because it lacked cohesion.* SYN: See syn. under **coherence**. **2** *Physics.* attraction between molecules of the same kind: *Drops of water are a result of cohesion.* **3** *Botany.* the congenital union of one part with another. [< Latin *cohaesus,* past participle of *cohaerēre* (see etym. under **cohere**) + English *-ion*]

co|he|sive (kō hē'siv), *adj.* **1** sticking together; tending to hold together: *Magnetized iron filings form a cohesive mass.* (*Figurative.*) *The members of a family are a cohesive unit in our society.* (*Figurative.*) *What is important in determining the work output of an industrial group is whether the group is tight-knit and cohesive enough to be properly called a group* (Science News Letter). **2** causing cohesion: *When a substance is heated, the heat energy causes its molecules to move faster. Eventually, the molecules will move so rapidly that their cohesive forces cannot hold them together* (Louis Marick). —**co|he'sive|ly,** *adv.* —**co|he'sive|ness,** *n.*

co|ho (kō'hō), *n., pl.* **-hoes.** a salmon of the coastal waters and rivers of Alaska and the Pacific Northwest, having deep-red flesh which loses color in canning; coho salmon; silver salmon. [< a native name]

co|ho|ba (kō hō'bə), *n.* a snuff having narcotic properties, made from the seeds of a South American tree similar to the mimosa. [< a native name]

co|ho|bate ((kō′hō bāt), *v.t.*, **-bat|ed, -bat|ing.** *Pharmacology.* to distill again from the same or a similar substance. [< New Latin *cohobare* (with English *-ate*[1]), perhaps < Arabic *ka''aba* to cube]

co|hort (kō′hôrt), *n.* **1** a part of an ancient Roman legion. There were from 300 to 600 soldiers in each cohort, and 10 cohorts in each legion. **2** any group of soldiers: *The Assyrian came down like a wolf on the fold, And his cohorts were gleaming in purple and gold* (Byron). **3** *Figurative.* a group, band, or company: ... *a small cohort of social regenerators* (John Tyndall). **4** *Informal, Figurative.* an associate or follower: *He is one of the cohorts of the local political boss.* [< Latin *cohors, -hortis* a tenth part of a (Roman) legion; any group of persons enclosed together; an enclosure. See etym. of doublet **court**.]

coho salmon, = coho.

co|hosh (kō′hosh, kō hosh′), *n.* any plant of several North American medicinal herbs, especially the black cohosh and the baneberry of the crowfoot family, and the blue cohosh, an herb of the barberry family: *Cohosh yields a drug used to treat St. Vitus's Dance* (Harold N. Moldenke). [American English < an eastern Algonkian language, possibly Massachusetts *kushki* (it is rough)]

co|hune (kō hün′), *n.*, or **cohune palm**, a Central American palm bearing large nuts whose shells are made into ornaments and whose meat yields an oil resembling coconut oil. [< American Spanish *cohune* < an American Indian word]

coif (koif), *n., v.* — ***n.*** **1** = coiffure. **2** a cap or hood that fits closely around the head. **3** a cap worn under a veil by a nun. **4** any one of various caps worn by European women. **5** *Historical.* a metal skullcap, or a leather one under a helmet, worn by a soldier. **6** *British.* **a** a white skullcap formerly worn by sergeants-at-law as a mark of their profession. **b** the position or office of a sergeant-at-law.
— ***v.t.*** **1** to dress, make up, or arrange (the hair). **2a** to provide or cover with a coif or something like a coif: *He would not suffer himself to be coifed, but covered his head with a quilted linen night-cap* (Tobias Smollett). **b** to invest with the coif of a sergeant-at-law.
[< Old French *coife*, apparently < unrecorded Old High German *kuphja*, variant of *chuppha* cap worn under a helmet, probably < *chuph* head]

coiffe (koif), *n., v.t.,* **coiffed, coif|fing.** = coif. [< French *coiffe*]

coif|feur (kwȧ fœr′; *Anglicized* kwä fėr′), *n.* = hairdresser. [< French *coiffeur* < Old French *coiffer* to dress the hair, to coif]

coif|feuse (kwȧ fœz′), *n. French.* a woman hairdresser: *Her wavy, silvery hair always looks as if she has just been to her Fifth Avenue coiffeuse* (Newsweek).

coif|fure (kwä fyůr′; *French* kwȧ fyr′), *n., v.,* **-fured, -fur|ing.** — ***n.*** **1** a style of arranging the hair. **2** a covering for the hair; headdress.
— ***v.t.*** **1** to arrange in a coiffure. **2** to put a coiffure on.
[< Old French *coiffer;* see etym. under **coif**]

coign or **coigne** (koin), *n.* **1** a projecting corner. **2** = coin (def. 3). [variant of *coin*]

coign of vantage, a good location for watching or doing something.

coil[1] (koil), *v., n.* — ***v.t.*** to wind around and around into a pile, a tube, or a curl: *A snake can coil itself up. The wire spring was evenly coiled.* **SYN:** twist, convolute.
— ***v.i.*** **1** to wind oneself around; place or grow around something: *The snake coiled around a branch.* **2** to move in a winding course: *The road coiled upward through the twisting valley.*
— ***n.*** **1** anything that is coiled: *a coil of rope.* **SYN:** convolution. **2** one wind or turn of a coil. **SYN:** twist. **3** a series of connected pipes arranged in a coil or row: *the coils of a radiator.* **4a** wire wound around and around into a spiral for carrying electric current: *an induction coil.* **b** an apparatus consisting of such a wire together with its accessories. **5** a roll of postage stamps. **6** a twist of hair.
[< Old French *coillir* to select, gather < Latin *colligere;* see etym. under **collect**[1]]

coil[2] (koil), *n. Archaic.* commotion; stir; bustle; turmoil.
mortal coil, the bustle or turmoil of human life: *When we have shuffled off this mortal coil* (Shakespeare).
[origin uncertain]

coil|er (koi′lər), *n.* **1** a person or thing that coils. **2** a workman who attends a machine that winds finished products in coils or on bobbins or drums. **3** an apparatus, connected with a carding machine, in textile manufacturing, for receiving the sliver and disposing of it in the form of coils.

coil spring, a spring of spiral shape, as for an automobile, made by winding wire around a center core.

coin (koin), *n., v.* — ***n.*** **1a** a piece of metal, stamped and issued by a government for use as money. Pennies, nickels, dimes, and quarters are United States coins. **b** metal money. A government makes coin by stamping metal. **c** *Slang.* money; cash: *He needs some coin right away.* **2** *Figurative: Bad news from Sheffield is regrettably common coin* (London Times). ... *faith and vision—unfashionable words, worn coin, but real forces* (Listener). **3** Also, **coign, coigne.** *Architecture.* **a** a corner, especially an exterior angle of a wall or building. **b** a cornerstone; quoin. **c** a wedge-shaped stone of an arch. **4** *Printing.* a wedge used for securing type in a chase; quoin.
— ***v.t.*** **1** to make (money) by stamping metal; mint: *The mint coins millions of nickels and dimes each year.* **2** to make (metal) into money; mint: *to coin silver into half dollars.* **3** *Figurative.* to make up; invent: *We often coin new words or phrases to name new products. The word "chortle" was coined by Lewis Carroll.*
— ***v.i.*** **1** to make metal money; mint. **2** *British.* to make counterfeit money: *Coining is a serious offense.*
coin money. See under **money**.
pay (a person) **back in his own coin**, to treat (a person) as he has treated oneself or others: *Since she refused to help me, the next time she asks me for a favor I will refuse, paying her back in her own coin.*
the other side of the coin, the other or reverse aspect; opposite point of view: *A non-union employe will be receiving the same rights ... The other side of the coin is he will be receiving the same restrictions ... as all of the other union members* (Wall Street Journal).
[< Old French *coin* corner < Latin *cuneus* wedge] — **coin′a|ble**, *adj.*

coin|age (koi′nij), *n.* **1a** the making of coins; minting: *The United States mint is in charge of coinage.* **b** the right of coining money. **2** coins; metal money: *He is a collector of foreign coinage.* **SYN:** currency, specie. **3** a system of coins: *The United States has a decimal coinage.* **4** *Figurative.* **a** the act or process of making up; inventing: *Travel in outer space has led to the coinage of many new words.* **b** a word, phrase, etc., invented: *"Transistor" and "laser" are fairly new coinages. The word "Kodak" was a coinage by George Eastman.*

coin box, the receptacle in a coin-operated machine or device, into which the coins are dropped: *Each of the coin-box phones must be changed so that they will take nickels instead of dimes* (Newsweek).

coin changer, = changemaker.

***co|in|cide** (kō′in sīd′), *v.i.,* **-cid|ed, -cid|ing.** **1** to occupy the same place in space. If these triangles △△ were placed one on top of the other, they would coincide. **2** to occupy the same time; occur at the same time: *The working hours of most businesses coincide.* **3** *Figurative.* to be just alike; correspond exactly; agree: *Her answers are correct and coincide with the answers in the book. Her opinion coincides with mine.* **SYN:** concur, harmonize, tally. See syn. under **agree.** [< Medieval Latin *coincidere* < Latin *co-* together + *in* upon + *cadere* fall]

***coincide** definition 1

A B = A + B

co|in|ci|dence (kō in′sə dəns), *n.* **1** the chance occurrence of two things at the same time or place in such a way as to seem remarkable or fitting: *My mother and father were both born on the same day and in the same year; isn't that a coincidence?* **2** *Figurative.* exact correspondence; agreement: *The two authorities were cited for coincidence of opinion.* **3** a coinciding; an occupying the same time or place: *the coincidence of two triangles or circles.*

coincidence counter or **circuit**, *Nuclear Physics.* an assembly of radiation counters, in which a discharge of radiation particles is counted only when all the counters discharge at the same time. It is used especially in finding the exact direction from which radiation is coming.

co|in|ci|dent (kō in′sə dənt), *adj.* **1** happening at the same time; coinciding: *The twins' birthdays are coincident. Ignorance and crime are not cause and effect, they are coincident results of the same cause* (Herbert Spencer). **2** occupying the same place or position. **3** *Figurative.* in exact agreement: *His parents' views are often coincident.* — **co|in′ci|dent|ly**, *adv.*

co|in|ci|den|tal (kō in′sə den′təl), *adj.* **1** showing coincidence; occurring by chance: *I have myself ... noted a considerable number of very striking coincidental dreams* (Notes and Queries). **2** = coincident. — **co|in′ci|den′tal|ly**, *adv.*

coincident indicator, *Economics.* an indicator which tends to move closely with general business, such as employment or industrial production: *The so-called coincident indicators ... are used in measuring recessions and recoveries* (Wall Street Journal).

co|in|di|ca|tion (kō in′də kā′shən), *n.* one of two or more concurrent indications, signs, or symptoms.

coin|er (koi′nər), *n.* **1** a maker; inventor: *Dionysius, a coiner of etymologies* (William Camden). **2** a person who makes coins. **3** a maker of counterfeit coins.

co|in|here (kō′in hir′), *v.i.,* **-hered, -her|ing.** to be included or exist together in the same thing; inhere together.

co|in|her|ence (kō′in hir′əns), *n.* inclusion or existence together in the same thing, such as qualities or activities.

co|in|her|ent (kō′in hir′ənt), *adj.* being included or existing together in the same thing.

co|in|her|it|ance (kō′in her′ə təns), *n.* joint inheritance.

co|in|her|i|tor (kō′in her′ə tər), *n.* a joint heir; coheir.

coin machine, any coin-operated device or machine, as a slot machine: *Organized thugs are successfully moving in on big-city coin-machine operations, especially in the jukebox business and in pinball games* (Time).

coin-op|er|at|ed (koin′op′ə rā′tid), *adj.* put into operation by the insertion of a coin or coins: *Machines which sell candy, cigarettes, and soft drinks, and washing machines in laundromats, are coin-operated.*

coin silver, silver of the standard or legal fineness for making silver coins.

co|in|stan|ta|ne|ous (kō′in stən tā′nē əs), *adj.* happening at the same instant: *A pun, and its recognitory laugh, must be coinstantaneous* (Charles Lamb). — **co′in|stan|ta′ne|ous|ly**, *adv.*

co|in|sur|ance (kō′in shůr′əns), *n.* **1** insurance jointly with another or others. **2** a form of insurance, in which a person taking out insurance on property for less than its full value is regarded as a joint insurer and becomes jointly responsible for losses: *Coinsurance offers a real inducement in that it may provide a reduction in rates ranging from 20% to 70%* (Wall Street Journal).

co|in|sure (kō′in shůr′), *v.t., v.i.,* **-sured, -sur|ing.** to insure jointly with another or others.

Co|in|tel|pro (kō′in tel′prō′), *n.* a program of harassment by the FBI against organizations and individuals considered a threat to national security. [*co*(unter)*intel*(ligence) *pro*(gram)]

Coin|treau (kwän′trō; *French* kwaɴ trō′), *n.* a brand of curaçao, a colorless, orange-flavored liqueur, originally made in France. [< French *Cointreau,* a trademark]

coir (koir), *n.* fiber obtained from the outer husks of coconuts, used especially to make rope and mats. [< Malayalam *kayar* cord]

cois|trel or **cois|tril** (kois′trəl), *n.* **1** *Historical.* a groom who cared for a knight's horses. **2** *Archaic.* a base person; knave: *He's a coward and a coistrel* (Shakespeare). [variant of *custrel*]

co|i|tal (kō′ə təl), *adj.* of or having to do with coitus.

co|i|tion (kō ish′ən), *n.* = coitus. [< Latin *coitiō, -ōnis* < *coīre* < *co-* together + *īre* go]

co|i|tus (kō′ə təs), *n.* = sexual intercourse. [< Latin *coitus* < *coīre;* see etym. under **coition**]

coke[1] (kōk), *n., v.,* **coked, cok|ing.** — ***n.*** the black substance that is left after coal has been heated in a closed oven, from which most of the air has been shut out, until the gases have been removed. Coke is used as a fuel because it burns with much heat and little smoke, and is used in furnaces, and especially for melting metal. *In the carbonization of coal large quantities of coke are produced, totalling about 15 million tons a year* (London Times).
— ***v.t., v.i.*** to change into coke. [perhaps variant of dialectal *colk* core in the sense of "remainder"]

coke[2] (kōk), *n. Slang.* cocaine. [short for *cocaine*]

Coke (kōk), *n. Trademark.* a dark-colored, carbonated soft drink.

coke|fiend (kōk′fēnd′), *n.* = cokehead.

coke|head (kōk′hed′), *n. U.S. Slang.* a cocaine addict.

coke oven, an oven for manufacturing coke.

coke-ov|en gas (kōk′uv′ən), gas obtained when coal is heated in a coke oven, used for heating and formerly for lighting; coal gas.

cok|er|y (kō′kər ē), *n., pl.* **-er|ies.** = coke oven.

Pronunciation Key: hat, āge, cãre, fär; let, ēqual, tėrm; it, īce; hot, ōpen, ôrder; oil, out; cup, pu̇t, rüle; child; long; thin; ᴛʜen; zh, measure; ə represents **a** in about, **e** in taken, **i** in pencil, **o** in lemon, **u** in circus.

cok|ing coal (kōk′ing), bituminous coal of the highest grade, used for making coke: *During . . . carbonization, coking coal fuses and congeals into a solid block of coke* (New Scientist).

col (kol; *French* kôl), *n.* **1** a marked depression in a ridge or mountain chain, usually forming a pass from one slope to the other. **2** *Meteorology.* **a** an area between two anticyclones. **b** the intersection of a trough and a wedge. [< French *col* < Old French, neck < Latin *collum*]

col-, *prefix.* the form of **com-** before *l*, as in *collect.*

col., an abbreviation for the following:
1 collected.
2 collector.
3 college.
4 colonel.
5a colonial. **b** colony.
6a color. **b** colored.
7 column.

Col., an abbreviation for the following:
1 Colombia.
2 Colonel.
3 Colorado (official abbr: *Colo.*).
4 Colossians (a book of the New Testament).

co|la[1] (kō′lə), *n.* = kola. [< New Latin *Cola* the genus name < Temne (Sierra Leone) *kola*]

co|la[2] (kō′lə), *n.* plural of **colon[1]** (def. 2).

co|la[3] (kō′lə), *n.* = colons; a plural of **colon[2]**.

COLA (kō′lə), *n. U.S.* cost of living adjustment: *The last . . . contract included no COLA at all, and as a result the average hourly wage for rubber workers has fallen $1.35 behind that of automobile workers* (Time).

co|la|bor|er (kō lā′bər ər), *n.* a fellow laborer.

***col|an|der** (kul′ən dər, kol′-), *n.* a wire or metal dish full of small holes for draining off liquids from foods. Also, **cullender.** [alteration of Medieval Latin *colatorium* strainer < Latin *cōlāre* to strain < *cōlum* strainer]

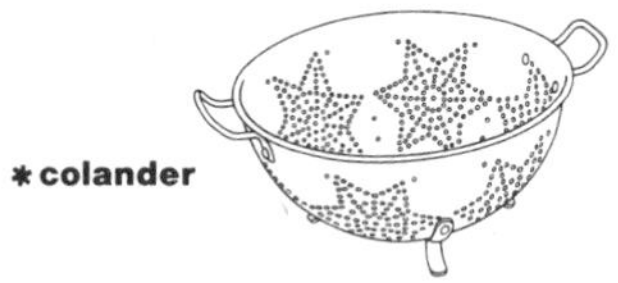
***colander**

cola nut, = kola nut.

co|lat|i|tude (kō lat′ə tüd, -tyüd), *n. Astronomy.* the complement of the latitude; the difference between a given latitude, expressed in degrees, and 90 degrees.

col|can|non (kəl kan′ən, kôl′kan-), *n.* an Irish or Scottish dish consisting of cabbage and potatoes boiled and mashed together and seasoned. [< *col*(e) cabbage; origin uncertain]

col|chi|cine (kol′chə sēn, -sin; -kə-), *n.* a potent alkaloid found in colchicum, and used to treat gout. *Formula:* $C_{22}H_{25}NO_6$ [< *colchic*(um) + *-ine[2]*]

col|chi|cum (kol′chə kəm, -kə-), *n.* **1** any one of a genus of Old World plants of the lily family, with purple or white flowers that resemble crocuses; autumn crocus; meadow saffron. **2** a bitter-tasting medicine for gout and rheumatism obtained from the dried ripe seeds and corms of this plant. [< Latin *colchicum* < Greek *kolchikón* crocuslike plant < *Colchis* (as the home of Medea, from the medicinal or poisonous properties of its roots)]

Col|chis (kol′kis), *n. Greek Legend.* the country where the Golden Fleece was found by Jason and the Argonauts.

col|co|thar (kol′kə thər), *n.* a brownish-red oxide of iron which remains after heating ferrous sulfate, used as a polishing agent and as coloring matter; jewelers' rouge. [< Medieval Latin *colcotar* < Arabic *qolqotār* copperas, perhaps < Greek *chálkanthos* chalcanth]

cold (kōld), *adj., adv., n.* —***adj.*** **1** much less warm than the human body: *Snow and ice are cold.* **2** less warm than usual; having a relatively low temperature; having lost heat: *a lunch of cold chicken. This coffee is cold.* **3** uncomfortable from lack of heat; feeling cold or chilly: *Put a sweater on or you will be complaining that you are cold.* **4** *Figurative.* not kind and cheerful; unfriendly: *The rude boy got a cold greeting.* SYN: aloof. **5** *Figurative.* lacking in feeling, passion, or enthusiasm; indifferent: *The selfish old miser had a cold nature.* SYN: unresponsive, apathetic. **6** *Figurative.* free from personal feeling; unprejudiced: *the cold facts. The judge made a cold evaluation of the evidence.* **7** *Figurative.* depressing; gloomy; chilling: *He had a cold realization that his car was out of gas on the lonely road.* SYN: discouraging, dispiriting. **8** not warmed up; unprepared: *He was sent into the game cold.* **9** faint; weak: *The hunting dogs lost the cold scent of the fox.* **10** far from the object or solution sought (from games such as "I Spy" and "Hide the Thimble"): *You are getting colder all the time.* **11** suggesting coolness. Blue, green, and gray are called cold colors (red and yellow are warm colors). **12a** *Slang.* unconscious: *He was knocked cold by a punch to the jaw.* **b** dead: *The soldier lay cold on the battlefield.*

—***adv.*** *Especially U.S. Informal.* **1** completely; entirely: *The attack was stopped cold. He knows the facts cold.* **2** without warning; suddenly; abruptly: *The bad news hit us cold. He quit the job cold.*

—***n.*** **1a** the condition of being cold; lack of heat or warmth; low temperature; coldness: *The cold in the mountains is easy to bear because the air is usually dry.* **b** cold weather: *The old man, without a coat, stood shivering in the cold.* **2** the sensation or condition produced by a rapid loss of heat from the body: *the mother and infant . . . perishing with cold* (Sir Walter Scott). **3** *Figurative.* a lack of enthusiasm, passion, or feeling: *the bitter cold of human indifference.* **4a** a common sickness that causes running at the nose, sore throat, sneezing, and sometimes chills and fever; common cold; coryza. It is caused by viruses which attack the mucous membranes. *Colds do not strike unless the human body has reached the point where lowered resistance gives the cold virus the green light* (Newsweek). **b** any indisposition of the body caused by exposure to cold, characterized by coughing, hoarseness, sneezing, and other symptoms of the cold caused by virus.

catch (or **take**) **cold**, to become sick with a cold: *Naturally, a mother and father don't begin to worry about their youngster . . . the minute he catches cold* (Sidonie M. Gruenberg).

in cold blood. See under **blood**.

in (or **out in**) **the cold**, all alone; neglected; not taking part: *When the others played games, he was always left out in the cold.*

pour (or **throw** or **dash**) **cold water on**. See under **water**.

[Old English *ceald*] —**cold′ly**, *adv.* —**cold′ness**, *n.*

—***Syn.*** *adj.* **1, 2 Cold, frigid, chilly, cool** mean having a low temperature, especially in comparison with body heat. **Cold**, the general word, means of low temperature, judged by the standard of normal body heat: *A cold wind is blowing.* **Frigid** means intensely cold: *the frigid winters of the Far North.* **Chilly** means cold enough to be uncomfortable and make a person shiver a little: *Without my coat I feel chilly.* **Cool** means neither hot nor cold, but closer to cold: *After the hot day the evening seems cool.*

cold|bar suit (kōld′bär′), an insulated plastic suit for use as a uniform by soldiers in cold and wet climates.

cold-blood|ed (kōld′blud′id), *adj.* **1a** having blood that is about the same temperature as the air or water around the animal. The blood of such animals is colder in the winter than in the summer. Snakes and turtles are cold-blooded; dogs are warm-blooded. **b** feeling the cold because of poor circulation: *The old couple was cold-blooded and kept their house terribly hot.* **2** *Figurative.* lacking in feeling; cruel: *The cold-blooded pirate sold all his captives into slavery.* **3** *Figurative.* without emotion or interest; unimpassioned: *He gave a cold-blooded account of the accident.* —**cold′-blood′ed|ly**, *adv.* —**cold′-blood′ed|ness**, *n.*

cold cash, *Informal.* ready money, as opposed to credit: *These firms get their payment in the form of surplus cotton instead of cold cash* (Wall Street Journal).

cold cathode, a cathode that emits charged particles by such means as photoemission or secondary emission, functioning without the application of heat.

cold chisel, a strong chisel of highly tempered steel for cutting cold metal.

cold comfort, small comfort; something that gives very little encouragement, cheer, or consolation.

cold cream, a creamy, soothing salve for softening or cleansing the skin.

cold cuts, slices of cooked, smoked, or otherwise prepared meat, such as salami, tongue, ham, and bologna, served cold: *Where you find . . . workers who want lunches that give them the quick energy from meat protein and fat you find cold cuts in lunch boxes* (Harper's).

cold desert, **1** a place where it is too cold for most plants to grow. **2** = tundra.

cold-draw (kōld′drô′), *v.t.*, **-drew**, **-drawn**, **-draw|ing.** to draw (a metal) without the use or application of heat: *The new process means that any size of wire can be electroplated with copper in a continuous process, then cold-drawn to desired sizes* (Wall Street Journal).

Cold Duck, *U.S.* an inexpensive mixture of sparkling Burgundy and champagne. [translation of German *Kalte Ente,* alteration of Kalte Ende cold ends (in reference to leftover wines mixed and served at the end of a party)]

cold extrusion, the process of extruding metal through cold plates of a die.

cold-eyed (kōld′īd′), *adj.* **1** having eyes that express or suggest coldness, indifference, or apathy. **2** without emotion or interest; unimpassioned; cool: *He does characteristically look at things two ways, as a susceptible romantic and as a cold-eyed realist always inquiring after facts and causes* (Atlantic).

cold feet, *Informal.* lack of confidence; timidity; fright: *I've got some new clothes now . . . I bought 'em off a tenderfoot with cold feet* (Rex Beach).

have (or **get**) **cold feet**, to lose confidence; become timid: *Lenin leaped at the idea . . . but nobody else wanted to risk it. Mártov himself got cold feet, and it was Lenin who put the scheme through* (Edmund Wilson).

cold fish, *Slang.* a person lacking in warmth, passion, or enthusiasm; an unfriendly individual: *He strikes us as a pretty cold fish . . . ; perhaps he just doesn't see how things look from our point of view* (Manchester Guardian Weekly).

***cold frame**, or **cold|frame** (kōld′frām′), *n.* a frame with a top of glass, plastic, burlap, or the like, and no artificial heat, used out of doors to protect young or tender plants from the cold.

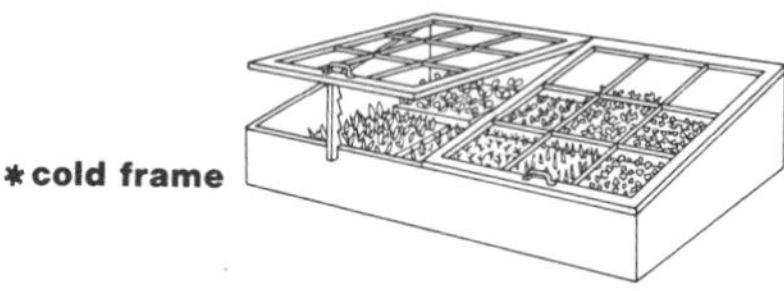
***cold frame**

cold front, the advancing edge of a cold air mass as it overtakes, passes under, and replaces a warmer one: *Tornadoes usually form along a cold front* (James E. Miller). See diagram under **front**.

cold fusion, the fusion of the nuclei of hydrogen atoms at normal temperature, resulting in a release of heat energy, attempted in various experiments, especially one in which an electric current is passed between two electrodes immersed in heavy water at room temperature.

cold-ham|mer (kōld′ham′ər), *v.t.* to hammer (iron or other metal) when cold; shape (a metal) by beating without first applying heat: *Indians living near the rich copper deposits of upper Michigan may have been the first humans to cold-hammer copper into tools* (Beals and Hoijer).

cold heading, riveting with soft iron rivets shaped and closed while cold. It is used on aluminum wing and body surfaces of airplanes.

cold-heart|ed (kōld′här′tid), *adj.* lacking in feeling; unsympathetic; unkind. —**cold′-heart′ed|ly**, *adv.* —**cold′-heart′ed|ness**, *n.*

cold|ish (kōl′dish), *adj.* rather cold; somewhat cold: . . . *a dark misty night, and coldish* (Samuel Richardson).

cold light, light produced below the temperature of incandescence. Phosphorescence and fluorescence are examples of cold light.

cold mold, a method of molding plastics by pressing resin into an unheated mold.

cold moon|er (mü′nər), a person who believes there is no volcanic activity in the moon's core.

cold pack, **1** something cold, such as a folded towel wrung out of cold water, put on the body for medical purposes. **2** a method of canning in which fruits or vegetables are put in jars or cans without cooking and then processed in boiling water or a pressure cooker to ensure sterilization.

cold-pack (kōld′pak′), *v.t.* **1** to put a cold pack on. **2** to can (fruits or vegetables) by cold pack.

cold peace, a lull in a cold war, without any settlement of differences between the opposing nations: *They had been pawns in the cold war and were pawns in the cold peace; their release was a political gesture* (Newsweek).

cold-press (kōld′pres′), *v.t.* **1** to press (metal) without applying heat. **2** to compress or distill without heat: *The highest-grade oils are obtained by pressure alone and are called cold-pressed.*

cold-roll (kōld′rōl′), *v.t.* to roll without applying heat: *to cold-roll steel.*

cold rubber, a tough, synthetic rubber formed at a low temperature: *Cold rubber is . . . produced at a temperature in the neighborhood of 32 degrees Fahrenheit, the freezing point of water* (Science News Letter).

cold-short (kōld′shôrt′), *adj.* brittle when cold: *cold-short iron.*

cold shoulder, *Informal.* deliberately unfriendly or indifferent treatment; neglect.

turn a cold shoulder (to), to act in a deliberately unfriendly or indifferent way: *Pride made him turn a cold shoulder to all offers of help.*

cold-shoul·der (kōld′shōl′dər), *v.t. Informal.* to treat in an unfriendly or indifferent way; turn a cold shoulder to; neglect: *Was this woman's music cold-shouldered, as she thought, because she was a woman?* (Manchester Guardian).

cold-shut (kōld′shut′), *n. Metallurgy.* an imperfection in a casting caused by slow or interrupted pouring of the metal, allowing a surface to congeal before the mold is properly filled.

cold shutdown, a complete stoppage of the activity of a nuclear reactor: *At Three Mile Island . . . technicians continued to ease the damaged reactor to a long-awaited cold shutdown* (Newsweek).

cold snap, a sudden interval of cold weather: *A record November cold snap has literally frozen the shiny red berries off most of the trees here in the Pacific Northwest* (Wall Street Journal).

cold sore, a blister near or on the mouth, caused by a viral infection of the skin and sometimes accompanying a cold or a fever; fever blister or sore: *A cold sore on his lip appeared to be bothering him* (Newsweek).

cold steel, a steel weapon, such as a knife or sword.

cold storage, storage in moist air in a very cold place to preserve such perishable things as foods, furs, flowers, and medicines by slowing the growth of microorganisms and the action of enzymes.

put into cold storage, to set aside for a later time; suspend or postpone for the time being: *The outbreak of the first world war put the Russian ballet into cold storage* (Listener).

cold store, **1** = cold storage. **2** a refrigerating chamber for the cold storage of perishable food.

cold sweat, perspiration accompanied by a chilly feeling, especially as produced by fear or nausea.

cold table, a meal or spread of cold cuts, fish, aspics, salads, etc.

cold turkey, *U.S. Slang.* **1** an exposition of unpleasant facts (usually to an unwilling but helpless listener), sometimes with implied or open threats: *The old man talked cold turkey to his extravagant nephew, hinting that he might disinherit him.* **2** the sudden and complete deprivation of narcotics as a treatment of drug addiction.

cold type, = phototypesetting.

cold war, **1** a prolonged struggle for power between nations or groups of nations, conducted primarily by diplomatic, economic, and psychological rather than by extensive and direct military action: *The present situation is a mixture of peace and war, called cold war* (Wall Street Journal). **2** a condition of hostility between two people or groups.

Cold War, the contest for world leadership that began after World War II between the communist nations headed primarily by the Soviet Union and the nations of the West headed principally by the United States.

Cold Warrior, a statesman or politician who takes an active part in the Cold War.

cold-wa·ter (kōld′wôt′ər, -wot′-), *adj.* having no central facilities for supplying heat or hot water to a tenant or tenants.

cold wave, **1** a period of very cold weather, especially one affecting a large area and regarded as passing from one place to another: *Not every sharp drop in temperature is a cold wave, for to be an authentic one* (*a*) *the thermometer must fall a certain number of degrees within 24 hrs. and* (*b*) *it must drop below a certain fixed minimum* (Finch and Trewartha). **2** a kind of permanent hair waving using a setting solution that does not need to be heated.

cold-weld (kōld′weld′), *v.t., v.i.* to weld without applying heat, as by the use of pressure: *to cold-weld metals.*

cold-work (kōld′wėrk′), *v.t.* to shape or change the form of (a metal or alloy) without applying heat.

cole (kōl), *n.* any one of a genus of plants of the mustard family, including cabbage, cauliflower, kale, and rape; colewort. [Old English *cāl,* variant of *cāwel* <Latin *caulis* cabbage, stalk]

co·lec·to·my (kə lek′tə mē), *n., pl.* **-mies**. the surgical excision of all or part of the colon. [<*co-l*(on)[2] + *-ectomy*]

cole·man·ite (kōl′mə nīt), *n.* a mineral consisting of a hydrated calcium borate, occurring in colorless to white, monoclinic crystals, found in California. Colemanite is the principal natural source of borax. *Formula:* $Ca_2B_6O_{11} \cdot 5H_2O$ [<William T. *Coleman,* 1824-1893, a civic leader of San Francisco + English *-ite*[1]]

co·le·op·ter (kō′lē op′tər, kol′ē-), *n.* a coleopterous insect.

co·le·op·ter·al (kō′lē op′tər əl, kol′ē-), *adj.* having to do with or relating to a coleopterous insect.

co·le·op·ter·an (kō′lē op′tər ən, kol′ē-), *n.* a coleopterous insect; beetle.

co·le·op·ter·ist (kō′lē op′tər ist, kol′ē-), *n.* a naturalist who studies the coleopterous insects.

co·le·op·ter·on (kō′lē op′tə ron, kol′ē-), *n.* a coleopterous insect.

co·le·op·ter·ous (kō′lē op′tər əs, kol′ē-), *adj.* belonging to the largest order of insects, including all insects called beetles, weevils, and fireflies. In this group the front pair of wings is horny, serving to sheathe the second and membranous pair. [<New Latin *Coleoptera* the order name (<Greek *koleópteros* sheath-winged <*koleós* sheath + *pterón* wing) + English *-ous*]

co·le·op·tile (kō′lē op′təl, kol′ē-), *n.* the tubular sheath covering the terminal bud of young grasses for a short time after germination of the grains. [<Greek *koleós* sheath + *ptílon* feather]

co·le·o·rhi·za (kō′lē ə rī′zə, kol′ē-), *n., pl.* **-zae** (-zē). the sheath enveloping the radicle or rudimentary root in the embryo of grasses and certain other plants. The root bursts through the coleorhiza in germination. *There is a well-developed embryonic root enclosed in a special coat, the coleorhiza* (Fred W. Emerson). [<New Latin *coleorhiza* <Greek *koleós* sheath + *rhíza* root]

cole·seed (kōl′sēd′), *n.* **1** = rapeseed. **2** = rape.

cole·slaw (kōl′slô′), *n.* a salad made of finely shredded raw cabbage; slaw. [American English <Dutch *kool sla; kool* <Latin *caulis* cabbage, stalk; *sla,* variant of *salade* salad]

co·le·us (kō′lē əs), *n.* any one of a genus of foliage plants of the mint family, often grown for their showy, colorful leaves: *Take cuttings of fuchsia, geraniums, wax begonias, coleus and others for small house plants this winter* (New York Times).
[<New Latin *Coleus* the genus name <Greek *koleós* sheath]

cole·wort (kōl′wėrt′), *n.* **1** = cole. **2** any kind of cabbage having a loosely packed head of curly leaves: *Kale is a colewort.* [<*cole* + *wort*[2]]

col·ic (kol′ik), *n., adj.* **—*n.*** severe pains in any part of the abdomen, such as the stomach or intestines.
—*adj.* of or having to do with the colon.
[<Late Latin *colicus* <Greek *kōlikós* colicky; having pain of the colon <*kólon* colon]

col·i·cin (kō′lə sən, kol′-), *n.* any of various antibacterial proteins produced by intestinal bacteria: *Colicins are natural antibiotics produced by bacteria to kill competing bacterial species* (Science News).
[<*colic, adj.* + *-in*[2]]

col·ick·y (kol′i kē), *adj.* **1** having colic: *a colicky baby.* **2** of colic.

col·ic·root (kol′ik rüt′, -rut′), *n.* **1** either of two bitter North American perennial herbs of the lily family, having a raceme of yellow or white flowers and a root supposed to be useful in treating colic. **2** any one of various other plants believed capable of relieving colic.

col·ic·weed (kol′ik wēd′), *n. U.S.* **1** = squirrel corn. **2** = Dutchman's-breeches. **3** a small biennial herb of the fumitory family, found in eastern North America.

co·lie (kō′lē), *n.* = coly, any one of a family of small, long-tailed African birds. [<New Latin *Colius* the genus name <Greek *koliós* a green woodpecker]

col·i·form (kol′ə fôrm, kō′lə-), *adj.* of or having to do with the bacilli commonly commensal in the intestines of humans and other vertebrates.
[<Latin *cōlī,* genitive of *cōlon* colon + English *-form*]

co·lin (kol′in), *n.* **1** an American quail, partridge, or bobwhite. **2** a bird of related species. [American English <American Spanish *colín* <Nahuatl *çolin*]

col·i·se·um (kol′ə sē′əm), *n.* a large building or stadium for games, contests, or other sporting events. Also, **colosseum**.
[<Medieval Latin *coliseum,* variant of Latin *colosseum* colosseum]

Col·i·se·um (kol′ə sē′əm), *n.* = Colosseum.

co·li·tis (kō lī′tis, kə-), *n.* inflammation of the colon or other parts of the large intestine, often causing severe pain in the abdomen.
[<New Latin *colitis* <Greek *kólon* colon + *-itis* disease]

coll., an abbreviation for the following:
1 colleague.
2a collect. **b** collection. **c** collector.
3 college.
4 colloquial.

col·lab·o·rate (kə lab′ə rāt), *v.i.,* **-rat·ed, -rat·ing.** **1** to work together, especially in a literary, artistic, or scientific production or project: *The two authors collaborated in writing a history of the United States.* **2** to aid or cooperate with enemies of one's own country: *Some Frenchmen collaborated with the Nazis during World War II.* [<Latin *collabōrāre* (with English *-ate*[1]) <*com-* with + *labōrāre* to work <*labor* work]

col·lab·o·ra·tion (kə lab′ə rā′shən), *n.* **1** the act of working together: *Accommodation is thus a matter of degree and ranges from extremely hostile to extremely cordial collaboration* (Ogburn and Nimkoff). **2** the act of aiding or cooperating with enemies of one's own country.

col·lab·o·ra·tion·ism (kə lab′ə rā′shə niz əm), *n.* advocacy or practice of collaboration with an enemy or occupier of one's own country.

col·lab·o·ra·tion·ist (kə lab′ə rā′shə nist), *n., adj.* **—*n.*** a person who cooperates with or traitorously aids an enemy nation or an occupier of his own country.
—*adj.* of or having to do with a collaborationist or collaborationism.

col·lab·o·ra·tive (kə lab′ə rā′tiv), *adj.* of or resulting from collaboration: *Only an unprecedented collaborative effort can solve the economic problem of low-income countries* (Bulletin of Atomic Scientists). **—col·lab′o·ra′tive·ly**, *adv.*

col·lab·o·ra·tor (kə lab′ə rā′tər), *n.* **1** a person who works with another, especially in literary or scientific work. **2** a person who aids or cooperates with enemies of his own country; collaborationist.

col·lage (kə läzh′), *n., v.,* **-laged, -lag·ing.** **—*n.*** **1** the art of making pictures by pasting on a background such things as parts of photographs and newspapers, fabric, and string. Sometimes paint is added. Collage is used especially in abstract or surrealistic compositions. *It was apparently Picasso—next to children, perhaps, the greatest innovator of them all—who took up collage seriously; and his concern with it . . . is generally believed to have been a part of all the experimenting . . . that so engrossed the early Cubists* (New Yorker). **2** a composition so made: *Jean Arp, whose blandly impish sculpture, paintings, and collages are one of the pleasures of modern art, was looking at a show of his own works* (Newsweek). **3** *Figurative.* anything made of odd parts or pieces; a composite or mixture: *a collage of fabrics, a collage of ideas.*
—*v.t.* to compose in the form of a collage: *The platform is painted and collaged in Rauschenberg's customary manner, with such random objects as a tennis ball, a rubber heel, a shirt sleeve* (New Yorker).
[<Middle French *collage* a gluing <Old French *colle* <Vulgar Latin *colla* <Greek *kólla* glue]

col·la·gen (kol′ə jən), *n.* **1** the protein substance in the fibers of connective tissue, bone, and cartilage of vertebrates. Boiling with water converts collagen to gelatin. **2** a preparation of collagen extracted from calf's skin and purified, used to inject under the skin to smooth out wrinkles, fill in acne scars, and the like: *Collagen has FDA approval, which means that many physicians . . . are becoming experienced in the use of collagen* (Health).
[<French *collagène* <Greek *kólla* glue + French *-gène* -gen]

col·la·gen·ase (kə laj′ə nās), *n.* a pancreatic enzyme able to break down collagen.

collagen disease, any one of several diseases of the skin and joints in which the fibers of the connective tissue are affected: *Several kinds of rheumatism are called collagen diseases.*

col·lag·e·nous (kə laj′ə nəs), *adj.* of or having to do with collagen.

col·lag·ist (kə lä′zhist), *n.* an artist who creates collages.

col·la par·te (kôl′lä pär′tā), *Italian, Music.* with the part; a direction for the accompaniment to follow the tempo of the soloist or leading performer.

col·lap·sar (kə lap′sär), *n.* = black hole (def. 1).
[<*collapse* + *-ar* (as in *quasar, pulsar*)]

col·lapse (kə laps′), *v.,* **-lapsed, -laps·ing,** *n.* **—*v.i.*** **1** to fall in; shrink together suddenly; cave in: *Sticking a pin into the balloon caused it to collapse. The roof collapsed as a result of the fire.* **2** to fold up and become compact: *This telescope collapses to half its size.* **3** *Figurative.* to break down; fail suddenly: *His business collapsed when his health gave out. The labor and management negotiations collapsed after several meetings.* **4** to become deflated: *The patient's lungs collapsed.*
—*v.t.* to fold or push together; cause to collapse; deflate: *to collapse a telescope, collapse a lung.*
—*n.* **1** a falling in; sudden shrinking together: *A heavy flood caused the collapse of the bridge.* **2** *Figurative.* a breakdown; failure: *The depression caused many business collapses.* **3** *Figurative.* physical or nervous exhaustion; prostration: *He sank upon the ground in a collapse of misery* (Cardinal Newman).
[<Latin *collāpsus,* past participle of *collābī* fall in ruins <*com-* completely + *lābī* fall]

col·laps·i·bil·i·ty (kə lap′sə bil′ə tē), *n.* the capa-

Pronunciation Key: hat, āge, cãre, fär; let, ēqual, tėrm; it, īce; hot, ōpen, ôrder; oil, out; cup, pu̇t, rüle; child; long; thin; ᴛʜen; zh, measure; ə represents **a** in about, **e** in taken, **i** in pencil, **o** in lemon, **u** in circus.

bility of collapsing or folding up.

col|laps|i|ble (kə lap′sə bəl), *adj.* made so that it can be folded or pushed together: *a collapsible baby carriage. She put the collapsible card table in the closet.*

collapsible corporation, a corporation intended to be dissolved while still holding a great part of the goods it has produced, thereby evading federal taxes on corporate goods.

col|lar (kol′ər), *n., v.* —*n.* **1** the part of a coat, a dress, a blouse, a shirt, or the like, that makes a band around the neck. **2** a separate band of linen, lace, or other material worn around the neck: *a fur collar.* **3** a leather or metal band put around the neck of a dog or other animal for control, identification, or ornament. **4** a leather roll for a horse's neck to bear the weight of the load he pulls. It is part of the harness. **5** *Zoology.* a colored band, stripe, or other mark around an animal's neck, resembling a collar. **6** a necklace, chain, or band worn around the neck for ornament, or as a badge of rank, office, or livery. **7a** any one of the various kinds of rings, bands, or pipes in machinery, such as one on a rod, shaft, or bearing, to keep it from moving to the side: *The combined weight and stiffness of this new collar keeps the drilling tool in line, assuring a straighter hole and faster drilling* (Wall Street Journal). **b** a short pipe connecting two other pipes. **8** *U.S. Slang.* a capture or arrest: *The Sergeant observed, "There's many a man who made detective on the strength of a good collar in the Sixteenth [Precinct]"* (New Yorker).
—*v.t.* **1** to put a collar on: *Mother collared the dog so we could walk him with a leash.* **2a** to seize by the collar; capture: *The policeman collared the thief after a long chase.* **b** to hold back by talk; buttonhole: *She was collared by some reporters who insisted on an interview.* **c** *Informal.* to lay hold of; take: *Another gentleman comes and collars that glass of punch* (Dickens). **3** *Cookery.* to roll up and tie (meat, fish, etc.) or to cut up and press into a roll.
hot under the collar, *Slang.* irate; furious: *One issue in the last few years . . . made people hot under the collar and ready to trade blows: racial integration* (Harper's).
[< Old French *colier* < Latin *collāre* a band for the neck, collar < *collum* neck] —**col′lar|less**, *adj.* —**col′lar|like′**, *adj.*

col|lar|band (kol′ər band′), *n.* a band to which the collar of a shirt is attached; neckband.

collar beam, a horizontal beam extending between two opposite rafters at some height above their base.

col|lar|bone (kol′ər bōn′), *n.* the bone connecting the breastbone and the shoulder blade; clavicle.

collar button, a stud or button for attaching a collar or collarband to a shirt.

collar cell, a flagellated cell in a sponge or a monad, having a rim or collar around the base of the flagellum to prevent the flagellum from pushing aside food particles.

***col|lard** (kol′ərd), *n.* **1** a form of kale. **2** Usually, **collards**. the fleshy leaves cooked as greens: *In the South no word, as no dish, is better known . . . than collards or greens* (Transactions of the American Philological Association). [alteration of *colewort*]

***collard**
definition 1

col|lared (kol′ərd), *adj.* **1** wearing or having a collar. **2** rolled up and bound with a string, as a piece of meat.

collared dove, = ringdove (def. 2).

collared lemming, a stout-bodied lemming of Greenland and Hudson Bay in Canada. It turns snow-white in winter.

collared lizard, a brightly colored lizard of the Southwestern United States and Mexico, related to the iguana. It sometimes eats other kinds of lizards.

collared peccary, a kind of wild pig, found from South America north to Texas, having a whitish or lightish collar.

col|lar|et or **col|lar|ette** (kol′ə ret′), *n.* a woman's ornamental collar or neckpiece.

***collar of S's** or **SS** or **esses**, an ornamental collar comprising a number of S's, sometimes combined with other figures, long in use in England, having been worn as a badge by adherents of the royal house of Lancaster, and still forming a part of the ceremonial dress of certain officials.

***collar of S's**

col|lar|work (kol′ər wėrk′), *n.* **1** heavy or uphill work, such as compels a horse to press against the collar: *There were still fourteen miles, nearly all collarwork, between that [place] and the baths* (Thomas A. Trollope). **2** *Figurative:* . . . *breaking down in harness, under the severe collarwork of these democratic days* (London Daily News).

collat., collateral.

col|late (kə lāt′, kol′āt), *v.t.,* **-lat|ed, -lat|ing.** **1** to compare carefully in order to note points of agreement and difference: *The scholar visited the chief libraries of Europe to collate manuscripts.* **2a** to arrange in order; put together: *to collate several sets of a manuscript.* **b** *Bookbinding.* to examine and verify the arrangement of (the sheets of a book) before binding. **3** to appoint or institute (a clergyman) by collation to a benefice. [< Latin *collātus,* past participle of *conferre* < *com-* together + *ferre* bring]

col|lat|er|al (kə lat′ər əl), *adj., n.* —*adj.* **1a** aside from the main thing; secondary: *The teacher listed ten books about explorers as collateral reading for the chapter about discovering America.* SYN: indirect. **b** *Figurative.* accompanying; attendant: *We mistake, as is usual, a collateral effect for a cause* (David Hume). **2** side by side; parallel. **3** descended from the same ancestors, but in a different line. Cousins are collateral relatives. **4a** serving to insure fulfillment of a contract or other agreement; confirming; additional: *collateral security.* **b** secured by stocks, bonds, or other property: *a collateral loan.*
—*n.* **1** stocks, bonds, or other property pledged as security for a loan: *The bank will not make a loan without collateral.* **2** a collateral relative.
[< Medieval Latin *collateralis* < *com-* + Latin *laterālis* lateral, having to do with the side < *latus, -eris* side] —**col|lat′er|al|ly**, *adv.*

collateral circulation, circulation of the blood through secondary vessels that have enlarged and branched out, compensating for the failure of a major vein or artery to provide adequate circulation.

collateral damage, the killing of civilians or damaging of nonmilitary structures in the course of conducting bombing raids or other military operations: *Avoidance of collateral damage means "trying not to kill civilians"* (New York Times Magazine).

col|lat|er|al|ize (kə lat′ər ə līz), *v.t.,* **-ized, -iz|ing.** *Commerce.* **1** to use or pledge as collateral: *collateralize a house.* **2** to secure or further secure (a loan) by putting up collateral: *Many banks, now low on loanable funds, are asking that borrowers collateralize some of their loans* (Wall Street Journal).

col|lat|er|al|ly (kə lat′ər ə lē), *adv.* **1** in a collateral manner or position; side by side. **2** *Figurative.* aside from the main course, subject, purpose, etc.; secondarily; indirectly.

col|la|tion (kə lā′shən), *n.* **1a** a collating; careful comparison: *A collation of Emily Dickinson's poems was made to prepare a new edition.* **b** the result of collating. **2** a detailed technical description of a book or manuscript, such as is made by a librarian or bibliographer. **3** the appointment of a clergyman to a benefice, especially in the Church of England by a bishop who is himself the patron or has acquired the patron's rights. **4a** a light meal: *A collation of wine and sweetmeats was prepared* (William Robertson). **b** an entertainment of food and drink. **5** a religious reading and a conference or discussion.

col|la|tive (kə lā′tiv, kol′ā-), *adj.* **1** of or characterized by a collation. **2** presented by collation: *a collative benefice.*

col|la|tor (kə lā′tər, kol′ā-), *n.* a person or machine that collates: *There were new collators that also stapled and stacked automatically* (Dickson Ash).

col|la vo|ce (kôl′lä vō′chā), *Italian.* with the voice; a direction for a singer to follow the tempo of the leading singer.

col|league[1] (kol′ēg), *n.* an associate; fellow worker or fellow member of a profession or organization: *The teacher's colleagues taught his classes while he was ill.* [< Middle French *collègue,* learned borrowing from Latin *collega* one chosen at the same time (as another) < *com-* together + *lēgāre* send or choose as deputy < *lēx, lēgis* contract, law]

col|league[2] (kə lēg′), *v.,* **-leagued, -lea|guing.** —*v.i.* **1** to enter into a league or alliance; combine. **2** = conspire.
—*v.t. Obsolete.* to join in a league or alliance.
[< Old French *colliguer,* learned borrowing from Latin *colligāre* < *com-* together + *ligāre* bind]

col|league|ship (kol′ēg ship), *n.* the state of being a colleague.

col|lect[1] (kə lekt′), *v., adv., adj.* —*v.t.* **1** to bring together; gather together: *We collected sticks of wood to make a fire.* SYN: See syn. under **gather**. **2** to gather together for a set: *Most boys collect stamps at some time or other.* **3** to pick up; take along: *She came over to collect the book she had forgotten. He returned later in the evening to collect his wife.* **4** to ask and receive payment of (bills, debts, dues, or taxes): *The milkman collects money from his customers each month.* **5** *Figurative.* to regain control of: *After the shock he tried to collect himself and his thoughts.* SYN: rally. **6** *Rare.* to infer; conclude: *Many of the laws of Nature . . . may be collected from experiments* (Samuel Butler).
—*v.i.* **1** to come together; assemble: *A crowd soon collects at the scene of an accident.* SYN: See syn. under **gather**. **2** to accumulate: *Junk tends to collect in every household. Dust is collecting under his bed.* **3** to make a collection: *Whether it be books, beer mugs, or antiques, people have an instinct to collect.*
—*adv., adj.* to be paid for at the place of delivery: *to telephone collect* (adv.), *a collect telegram* (adj.).
[< Latin *collectus,* past participle of *colligere* < *com-* together + *legere* gather] —**col|lect′a|ble**, *adj.*

col|lect[2] (kol′ekt), *n.* a short prayer used in certain church services. In Western churches, a collect is said before the Epistle in the Eucharistic service; in Anglican churches, in morning and evening prayer. *Faith, hope, charity, for an increase in which the collect for tomorrow offers petition, rank high among the specifically Christian qualities* (London Times). [< Medieval Latin *collecta* a summary; the assembly (addressed) < Latin, a gathering in (of money, etc.) < *colligere* to collect]

col|lec|ta|ne|a (kol′ek tā′nē ə), *n. pl.* passages collected from various writings; miscellany. [< Latin *collectānea* < *colligere* to collect]

col|lec|tar|i|um (kol′ek târ′ē əm), *n., pl.* **-i|a** (-ē ə). a book, used in medieval times, containing the collects used in the liturgy. [< Medieval Latin *collectarium* < *collecta*; see etym. under **collect**[2]]

col|lect|ed (kə lek′tid), *adj.* **1** brought together; gathered together: *the author's collected works.* SYN: assembled, accumulated. **2** *Figurative.* not confused or disturbed; under control; calm: *The doctor was the most collected person at the scene of the accident.* SYN: composed, self-possessed. See syn. under **calm**. —**col|lect′ed|ly**, *adv.* —**col|lect′ed|ness**, *n.*

col|lect|i|bil|i|ty (kə lek′tə bil′ə tē), *n.* the state of being collectible: *The group said its collection index recorded a new high this month in the collectibility of overdue consumer debts* (Wall Street Journal).

col|lect|i|ble (kə lek′tə bəl), *adj., n.* —*adj.* that can be collected.
—*n.* an object of popular culture that has become rare and unusual enough to be a collector's item: *Chopping boards and a host of other old-time kitchen utensils and accessories of wood and metal have become contemporary "collectibles"* (Atlanta Journal).

col|lect|ing box or **plate** (kə lek′ting), = collection box.

col|lec|tion (kə lek′shən), *n.* **1** the act of bringing together; coming together: *The collection of these stamps took ten years. The collection of a crowd there was unexpected.* **2** a group of things gathered from many places and belonging together: *a collection of proverbs or essays, a collection of minerals. Our library has a large collection of books.* **3** money gathered from people: *A church takes up a collection to help pay its expenses.* **4** a large quantity; mass or heap; accumulation.

collection agency, a bill-collecting agency: *A big Los Angeles store turns unpaid accounts over to collection agencies in 90 days* (Wall Street Journal).

collection box or **plate**, a box, plate, basket, or bag for the collection of money, especially one passed from hand to hand in a church.

collection item, *Banking.* a deposited check, draft, or note which, unlike a cash deposit, is not credited to the account of the depositor until it is paid by the bank against which it is drawn.

col|lec|tive (kə lek′tiv), *adj., n.* —*adj.* of or as a group; taken all together; aggregate: *collective revenues of the government.* **1** of or derived from a number of persons taken or acting together;

common: *the collective wisdom of Congress. The men's club made a collective decision to hold a family picnic during the summer.* **3** formed by collecting. **4** owned, worked, or managed by a group: *collective farming.* SYN: collectivized. **5** *Botany.* resulting from the coalescence of the pistils of several flowers, as the pineapple.
—*n.* **1** a farm, factory, or other organization owned, operated, or managed by a group cooperatively: *There are many collectives in the Soviet Union.* **2** = collective noun. **3** a collective body; aggregate: *Life is here the sum or collective of all moral and spiritual acts* (Samuel Taylor Coleridge). —**col|lec'tive|ness**, *n.*

collective bargaining, negotiation about wages, hours, and other working conditions between workers organized as a group and their employer or employers.

collective behavior, *Sociology.* the behavior of a group of people reacting to a common influence or stimulus. Fads and riots are examples of collective behavior.

collective farm, a farm operated and worked by a group cooperatively. The farm, its buildings, and its machinery may be owned communally by the group, by an institution, or, as in communist countries, by the state. *Students will perfect their vocational training by working directly at industrial enterprises or on collective farms* (Atlantic).

collective fruit, a fruit composed of a cluster of ripened ovaries produced by several flowers, such as the mulberry and pineapple; multiple fruit; compound fruit.

col|lec|tive|ly (kə lek'tiv lē), *adv.* **1** as a group; all together: *Taken collectively, the club members are a pleasant group, though there are a few discontented members.* **2** in a singular form, but with a plural meaning. In the sentence "We caught many fish," *fish* is used collectively.

collective noun, a noun that is singular in form but plural in meaning. *Crowd, people, troop,* and *herd* are collective nouns.
▶**collective nouns.** Whether to use the singular or the plural form of verbs and pronouns with collective nouns depends on the meaning intended. When the collective noun means the group taken as a whole, it takes a singular form of the verb or pronoun: *The committee is planning its work carefully.* When it means the individuals of the group, it takes a plural verb or pronoun: *After the plans are completed, the committee are going to their homes.* Certain nouns, such as *cabinet, company, congress, government, public,* ordinarily singular in the United States, are more commonly treated as plurals in Great Britain.

collective security, the guarantee by a group of countries of the security of each country in the group and the maintenance of peace by collective action against a country attacking any nation in the group: *A great victory for the cause of peace would be the establishment of a collective security system in Europe with the participation of other states too* (New York Times).

collective unconscious, *Psychoanalysis.* those aspects of the unconscious mind which are universal: *The collective unconscious . . . is part of the heritage of the entire human race, and therefore a sort of common pool containing the instincts and some patterns for mental behavior* (Time).

col|lec|ti|vise (kə lek'tə vīz), *v.t.,* **-vised, -vis|ing.** *Especially British.* collectivize. —**col|lec'ti|vi|sa'tion**, *n.*

col|lec|tiv|ism (kə lek'tə viz əm), *n.* a political and economic system in which the means of production of goods and services and the distribution of wealth are controlled by the people as a group or by the government, for example a system such as communism or socialism: *The move toward collectivism, the kolkhozes, industrialization by a five-year plan are all copied from Russian prototypes* (Harper's).

col|lec|tiv|ist (kə lek'tə vist), *n., adj.* —*n.* a person who favors or supports collectivism.
—*adj.* = collectivistic.

col|lec|tiv|is|tic (kə lek'tə vis'tik), *adj.* of collectivism or collectivists: *The collectivistic idea was especially strong among the Inca, the preliterate people of Peru* (Ogburn and Nimkoff).

col|lec|tiv|i|ty (kol'ek tiv'ə tē), *n.* **1** people collectively, especially as forming a community or state. **2** a collective whole; aggregate. SYN: sum, mass. **3** collective state or quality; collectiveness.

col|lec|ti|vi|za|tion (kə lek'tə və zā'shən), *n.* establishment or regulation according to the theories of collectivism: *They are staking the future of their regime on a forced industrial revolution accompanied by the collectivization of agriculture* (Atlantic).

col|lec|ti|vize (kə lek'tə vīz), *v.t.,* **-vized, -viz|ing.** **1** to transfer ownership of from individuals to the state or the people collectively: *The effort to collectivize an economy leads to regimentation, dictatorship from above and eventually the submergence of the individual in a totalitarian state* (New York Times). **2** to make collective; gather into one; combine.

collect on delivery, payment to be collected when goods are delivered. *Abbr:* COD

col|lec|tor (kə lek'tər), *n.* **1** a person who collects: *The stamp collector had several books which held the stamps in his collection.* **2** a thing that collects: *Curtains are dust collectors.* **3** a person hired to collect money owed: *A tax collector brings in money for the government.* **4** a device that collects electrical energy by maintaining contact between moving and stationary parts of a circuit; accumulator. **5** = solar collector. **6** *Obsolete.* a literary compiler.

collector ring, = slip ring.

col|lec|tor|ship (kə lek'tər ship), *n.* **1** the office of a collector. **2** district covered by a collector.

col|lec|tors' or **col|lec|tor's item** (kə lek'tərz), an object rare and unusual enough or close enough to perfection to be suitable for and prized by a collector.

col|leen (kol'ēn, kə lēn'), *n. Irish.* a girl. [< Irish Gaelic *cailīn* (diminutive) < *caile* woman]

col|lege (kol'ij), *n.* **1** a school beyond high school that gives degrees: *After finishing high school, he went to college and then became a teacher.* **2** the academic department of a university for general instruction, as distinguished from the special, professional, or graduate schools: *Between the first and second world wars, Columbia College in New York set the pattern for "general education" in U.S. colleges* (Newsweek). **3** a school for special or professional training, for example in medicine, pharmacy, agriculture, or music, whether as part of a university or independently: *She went to a business college to learn to be a secretary.* **4** a group of persons with the same duties and privileges: *the electoral college. Many large hospitals have a college of surgeons.* **5** the building or group of buildings used by a college. **6a** a separately endowed, self-governing association of scholars within a university (as at Oxford and Cambridge in England), engaged in study and the instruction of students. **b** a similar association not within a university. **7** a secondary school (in France). **8** a community of clergy living together on a foundation for religious service, etc. **9** *Archaic.* a company; crowd; assemblage: *They rode in proud array, thick as the college of the bees in May* (John Dryden). **10** *Archaic.* a course of study or lectures leading to a degree. **11** *British Slang.* a prison. [< Old French *college,* learned borrowing from Latin *collēgium* a fellowship, company < *com-* together + *lēgāre* to contract, appoint < *lēx, lēgis* law]

College Boards, *U.S.* a group of tests covering several fields of aptitude and achievement, given to students applying for admission to a college.

col|lege-bred (kol'ij bred'), *adj.* educated or trained in college: *a college-bred athlete.*

col|lège clas|sique (kô lezh' klȧ sēk'), *pl.* **col|lèges clas|siques** (kô lezh' klȧ sēk'), a Roman Catholic private school in Quebec providing an eight-year course at the high-school and college levels. [< French *collège classique* classical college]

College of Arms, = Heralds' College.

College of Cardinals, = Sacred College.

col|leg|er (kol'i jər), *n.* **1** a student at Eton College, England, supported by the college endowment: *He went to Eton as a colleger and then to Trinity College, Oxford, as a commoner* (London Times). **2** *Obsolete.* a member of a college.

college try, *U.S. Informal.*
give (something) **the college try**, to devote oneself to (something) completely and without restraint: *We are no smarter than the former management but we're going to give it the college try* (Wall Street Journal).

college widow, *U.S. Slang.* a girl or woman living in a college town, who has dated students of several successive classes.

col|le|gi|a (kə lē'jē ə), *n.* plural of **collegium.**

col|le|gi|al (kə lē'jē əl), *adj.* **1** = collegiate. **2** of or having to do with collegiality; associated or sharing as colleagues: *a collegial body, collegial authority.* —**col|le'gi|al|ly**, *adv.*

col|le|gi|al|ism (kə lē'jē ə liz'əm), *n.* the theory of church government maintaining that the church is a voluntary association in which the highest ecclesiastical authority is vested in the whole society, and not in aclerical order or in the state.

col|le|gi|al|i|ty (kə lē'jē al'ə tē), *n., pl.* **-ties.** **1** the association in which the bishops of the Roman Catholic Church and the Pope share collectively the ruling power over the Church. **2** = colleagueship.

col|le|gian (kə lē'jən, -jē ən), *n.* **1** a college student. **2** a member of a college.

col|le|giate (kə lē'jit, -jē it), *adj., n.* —*adj.* **1** of or like a college: *a collegiate library, a collegiate institution.* **2** of or having to do with college students: *collegiate life, collegiate types.* **3** of or having to do with a collegiate church. **4** = collegial (def. 2).
—*n.* = collegiate institute.

collegiate church, **1** a church which has a college or chapter, but not a bishop's see. **2** (in the United States) a church or association of churches administered by several pastors jointly. **3** (in Scotland) a church with two or more pastors of equal rank, especially where one is pastor emeritus and the other his colleague.

collegiate institute, a large high school in some Canadian provinces, required to meet certain standards in regard to its facilities and staff.

col|leg|ing (kol'i jing), *n.* training or education at college.

col|le|gi|um (kə lē'jē əm), *n., pl.* **-gi|a.** **1** a group of officials acting as a ruling body, such as: **a** a group of officials, headed by a commissar, who are in charge of a commissariat in Soviet Russia. **b** an independent and self-governing ecclesiastical body uncontrolled by the state. **2** = collegiate church. [< Medieval Latin *collegium* a self-governing ecclesiastical body < Latin *collēgium;* see etym. under **college**]

col le|gno (kôl lā'nyō), *Italian.* with the wood; a direction in the playing of a violin, cello, etc., to use the back of the bow instead of the hair.

col|lem|bo|la (kə lem'bə lə), *n., pl.* **-la** or **-las.** = springtail. [< New Latin *Collembola* the order name < Greek *kólla* glue + *émbolon* stopper]

col|len|chy|ma (kə leng'kə mə), *n. Botany.* a layer of tissue lying beneath the epidermis, consisting of cells with walls greatly thickened at the angles and generally elongated. It is found in the young stems, petioles, and midribs of leaves of many dicotyledons. [< New Latin *collenchyma* < Greek *kólla* glue + *énchyma* infusion]

col|let (kol'it), *n., v.,* **-let|ed, -let|ing.** —*n.* **1** a ring or collar on a rod or spindle. **2** the small collar which holds the inner end of the hairspring in a watch or clock. **3** the rim or ring in which a jewel is set: *The seal was set in a collet of gold* (Sir Thomas Herbert).
—*v.t.* **1** to set in a collet. **2** to provide with a collet or collar.
[< Old French *collet* (diminutive) < *cou,* earlier *col* neck < Latin *collum*]

col|lide (kə līd'), *v.,* **-lid|ed, -lid|ing.** —*v.i.* **1** to rush against each other; hit or strike hard together; crash: *Two large ships collided in the harbor and sank.* **2** *Figurative.* to clash; conflict: *Their minds were constantly colliding in endless arguments.*
—*v.t.* to cause to collide; bring into collision: *A chemical accelerator at Oak Ridge National Laboratory collides alkali metal atoms with hydrogen atoms to measure the excitation energy of the hydrogen* (Isaac Asimov).
[< Latin *collīdere* < *com-* together + *laedere* injure, strike]

col|lid|er (kə līd' ər), *n.* a particle accelerator used to identify and study subatomic particles by striking together two beams of protons at great speed and energy to cause subatomic particles to be released: *The future holds the exciting prospect of very large . . . colliders* (New Scientist).

col|lie (kol'ē), *n.* a large, intelligent, long-haired dog used for tending sheep and kept as a pet. The breed was developed in Scotland. Also, **colly.** [origin uncertain]

col|lied (kol'ēd), *adj. Archaic.* begrimed; blackened; sooty. [see etym. under **colly**[1]]

col|lier (kol'yər), *n.* **1** a ship for carrying coal. **2** a coal miner. **3** *Obsolete.* a coal dealer. [Middle English *colier* charcoal burner and seller < *col* coal]

col|lier|y (kol'yər ē), *n., pl.* **-lier|ies.** a coal mine and its buildings and equipment.

col|lie|shang|ie (kol'ē shang'ē), *n. Scottish.* a noisy quarrel. [origin uncertain]

col|li|gate (kol'ə gāt), *v.t.,* **-gat|ed, -gat|ing.** **1** to bind together; connect; unite. **2** *Logic.* to bring together or relate (isolated facts) in a recognizable pattern, especially so as to arrive at a general principle. [< Latin *colligāre* (with English *-ate*[1]) < *com-* together + *ligāre* bind]

col|li|ga|tion (kol'ə gā'shən), *n.* **1** conjunction; alliance; union. **2** *Logic.* the bringing together or relating of a number of facts by a suitable general principle or hypothesis.

col|li|mate (kol'ə māt), *v.t.,* **-mat|ed, -mat|ing.** **1** to bring into line; make parallel, as a lens or the rays of light passing through it. SYN: align. **2** to adjust accurately the line of sight of (a surveying instrument, telescope, or other optical instrument): *An instrument with the cross wires*

Pronunciation Key: hat, āge, cãre, fär; let, ēqual, tėrm; it, īce; hot, ōpen, ôrder; oil, out; cup, pu̇t, rüle; child; long; thin; ᴛʜen; zh, measure; ə represents **a** in about, **e** in taken, **i** in pencil, **o** in lemon, **u** in circus.

perfectly adjusted is said to be correctly collimated (J. Norman Lockyer). [< Medieval Latin *"collimare"* (with English *-ate*[1]), a misreading of Latin *collīneāre* < *com-* together + *līneāre* make straight < *līnea* line] —**col′li|ma′tion**, *n.*

col|li|ma|tor (kol′ə mā′tər), *n. Optics.* **1** a small fixed telescope with cross hairs at its focus, used for adjusting the line of sight of other instruments. **2a** the tube with a slit and lens used in the spectroscope to collect the light and throw it upon the prism in parallel rays: *The slit is at the focus of the objective of this telescope, the collimator, so that the rays are parallel as they enter the prism* (Robert H. Baker). **b** the lens itself.

***col|lin|e|ar** (kə lin′ē ər), *adj. Geometry.* lying in the same straight line. [< *col-* + *linear*] —**col|lin′e|ar|ly**, *adv.*

***collinear** — collinear points

col|lin|e|ar|i|ty (kə lin′ē ar′ə tē), *n.* the quality or fact of being collinear.

Col|lins or **col|lins** (kol′ənz), *n.* any one of various mixed drinks made of an alcoholic liquor, carbonated water, sugar, and lemon or lime, and served iced: *a rum collins. A Tom Collins is made with gin.* [supposedly < the proper name of a bartender who invented it]

col|lin|si|a (kə lin′sē ə, -zē-), *n.* any one of a genus of North American annuals of the figwort family, having whorled, parti-colored flowers. [< New Latin *Collinsia* < Zaccheus *Collins,* 1764-1831, an American botanist]

col|li|quate (kol′ə kwāt), *v.t.,* **-quat|ed, -quat|ing.** *Obsolete.* **1** to melt together. **2** to melt; liquefy. [< Medieval Latin *colliquare* (with English *-ate*[1]) < Latin *com-* with + *liquāre* to melt]

col|liq|ua|tive (kə lik′wə tiv), *adj.* **1** melting. **2** *Medicine.* profuse or excessive in flow, so as to cause exhaustion.

col|li|sion (kə lizh′ən), *n.* **1** a violent rushing against; hitting or striking hard together; crash: *His car was badly damaged in the collision.* **2** *Figurative.* clash; conflict: *There was a collision of interests on how to spend the club's money, and some of its members quit.* [< Latin *collīsiō, -ōnis* < *collīdere;* see etym. under **collide**]

collision course, 1 a course taken by an object, especially a ballistic missile, that will cause it to collide with its target. **2** any course that will result in a clash or conflict: *The faint hope is on negotiations, but events are on a collision course* (New York Times).

col|lo|blast (kol′ə blast), *n.* one of the cells on the tentacles of ctenophores that produce secretions helpful in the capture of prey. [< Greek *kólla* glue + *blastós* a sprout]

col|lo|cate (kol′ə kāt), *v.t.,* **-cat|ed, -cat|ing. 1** to place together or side by side: *The older rocks are abruptly collocated* (Sir Roderick Murchison). **2** to put in place; arrange. [< Latin *collocāre* (with English *-ate*[1]) < *com-* together + *locāre* place, put, set < *locus* a place]

col|lo|ca|tion (kol′ə kā′shən), *n.* **1** a placing together or side by side. **2** arrangement or disposition: *the collocation of a word's consonants and vowels.* **3** a combination of words established by usage. *Time and again* and *on the other hand* are frequently used collocations.

col|lo|di|on (kə lō′dē ən), *n.* a gluelike liquid that dries very rapidly and leaves a tough, waterproof, transparent film. Collodion is a solution of nitrocellulose in ether and alcohol. It is used in photography for covering plates with a thin film, and in medicine for coating wounds and burns. *Collodion, the plastic-like material which is widely used for dressing wounds and in other surgical procedures, can be cast into films with pores so small that not even the tiniest virus is able to slip through* (Scientific American). [< Greek *kollṓdēs* gluey, glutinous < *kólla* glue]

collodion cotton, a nitrated cellulose that has less nitration than guncotton, widely used in lacquer and plastic products.

col|lo|di|on|ize (kə lō′dē ə nīz), *v.t.,* **-ized, -iz|ing.** to treat with collodion.

col|lo|di|um (kə lō′dē əm), *n.* = collodion.

col|logue (kə lōg′), *v.i.,* **-logued, -logu|ing. 1** *Dialect.* to plot mischief; conspire; intrigue. **2** *Informal.* to confer privately and confidentially; confabulate. [alteration of earlier *colloque* colloquy, on the analogy of *dialogue, prologue*]

col|loid (kol′oid), *n., v., adj.* —*n.* **1** a substance composed of particles that are extremely small but larger than most molecules (usually ranging from about 0.01 to about 0.001 micron in diameter). The particles in a colloid do not actually dissolve, but remain suspended in a suitable gas, liquid, or solid. Many materials associated with ordinary life, such as soap, most plastics, rubber, and glass, are produced from colloids. Colloids also play an important part in organic functions, such as digestion and excretion. **2** *Medicine.* the colorless or yellowish, transparent, jellylike substance formed in some kinds of tissue degeneration.

—*v.t.* to change (guncotton) into a gelatinous or colloidal substance by treating it with nitroglycerin or other solvents to control the rate of burning.

—*adj.* = colloidal.

[< Greek *kólla* glue + English *-oid*]

col|loi|dal (kə loi′dəl), *adj.* being a colloid; containing a colloid; like a colloid: *colloidal gold or silver.* —**col|loi′dal|ly**, *adv.*

colloidal particles, the fine particles which the ultramicroscope shows to be present in a solution containing a colloid: *The colloidal particles as they are known are too small to be trapped by sieves for recovery* (Science News Letter).

colloid chemistry, the study of particles of one substance distributed through another substance.

col|lop (kol′əp), *n. Dialect.* **1** a slice or lump of meat. **2** *Figurative.* a small slice or piece of anything. **3** a fold of flesh or skin on the body. [Middle English *colope* fried meat (and eggs); later, bacon]

colloq., 1 colloquial. 2 colloquialism. 3 colloquially.

col|lo|qui|a (kə lō′kwē ə), *n.* a plural of **colloquium.**

col|lo|qui|al (kə lō′kwē əl), *adj.* **1** used in common talk; belonging to everyday, familiar talk; informal; conversational: *"The boxer clipped his opponent on the jaw" and "That was a close shave; you nearly ran over the dog!" are colloquial expressions. Abbr:* colloq. **2** of or having to do with colloquy or conversation: *The colloquial wit has always his own radiance reflected on himself* (Samuel Johnson). —**col|lo′qui|al|ly**, *adv.* —**col|lo′qui|al|ness**, *n.*

▶**Colloquial** means conversational, used in speaking. Since the speech of people varies with their education, work, and social status, there are obviously many different types of colloquial English. Since the bulk of conversation is informal, *colloquial* suggests informal rather than formal English. It need not, however, mean the speech of uneducated people, and should be distinguished from slang. As used in many dictionaries, *colloquial* refers to informal cultivated English. In this dictionary, the label *Informal* is preferred to *Colloquial* to avoid confusion.

col|lo|qui|al|ism (kə lō′kwē ə liz′əm), *n.* **1** a colloquial word or phrase. **2** colloquial style or usage: *Their language is ... an actual transcript of the colloquialism of the day* (Samuel Taylor Coleridge).

col|lo|qui|al|i|ty (kə lō′kwē al′ə tē), *n., pl.* **-ties. 1** colloquial quality or style: *He delights in homeliness [and] colloquiality* (Atlantic). **2** a colloquial expression: *We must take care that we are not led ... into mean colloquialities* (Blackwell's Magazine).

col|lo|quist (kol′ə kwist), *n.* a conversationalist; interlocutor.

col|lo|qui|um (kə lō′kwē əm), *n., pl.* **-qui|ums** or **-qui|a. 1** a meeting or conference, especially one of a body of scholars, scientists, or other specialists, on a specified subject or topic: *a physics colloquium.* **2** = seminar. [< Latin *colloquium* conversation]

col|lo|quize (kol′ə kwīz), *v.i.,* **-quized, -quiz|ing.** to take part in a colloquy; converse: *You and I could colloquize to great advantage* (Robert Southey).

col|lo|quy (kol′ə kwē), *n., pl.* **-quies. 1** a talking together; conversation; conference: *For a few moments the Queen spoke in turn to each one of her guests; and during these short uneasy colloquies the aridity of royalty was apt to become painfully evident* (Lytton Strachey). **2** a written dialogue: *Erasmus's Colloquies.* **3** a body in some Reformed churches composed of the pastors and church elders of a district, similar to a presbytery; classis. [< Latin *colloquium* conference, conversation < *colloquī* < *com-* with + *loquī* speak]

col|lo|type (kol′ə tīp), *n., v.,* **-typed, -typ|ing.** —*n.* **1** a photomechanical process of printing in ink from a gelatin plate: *Collotype lends itself admirably to the reproduction of artistic objects in low relief, such as coins, medals, etc.* (H. T. Wood). **2** the plate, or the print made by it.

—*v.t.* to make a collotype of.

[< Greek *kólla* glue + English *type*]

col|lo|typ|ic (kol′ə tip′ik), *adj.* of or having to do with collotype; done by collotype.

col|lo|typ|y (kol′ə tī′pē), *n.* the process of collotyping.

col|low (col′ō), *v.t. Dialect.* to colly (begrime).

col|lude (kə lüd′), *v.i.,* **-lud|ed, -lud|ing.** to act together through a secret understanding; conspire in a fraud. SYN: plot, connive. [< Latin *collūdere* < *com-* with + *lūdere* to play < *lūdus* game] —**col|lud′er**, *n.*

col|lu|sion (kə lü′zhən), *n.* a secret agreement for some wrong or harmful purpose; a secret or crafty understanding for the purpose of trickery or fraud. SYN: conspiracy, connivance. [< Latin *collūsiō, -ōnis* < *collūdere;* see etym. under **collude**]

col|lu|sive (kə lü′siv), *adj.* involving collusion; conspiring to defraud; fraudulent. —**col|lu′sive|ly**, *adv.* —**col|lu′sive|ness**, *n.*

col|lu|vi|um (kə lü′vē əm), *n., pl.* **-vi|a** (-vē ə), **-vi|ums.** loose material deposited at the base of a slope mainly by gravity, as talus. [< Latin *colluvium* < *colluere* wash < *com-* with + *lavāre* wash]

col|ly[1] (kol′ē), *v.,* **-lied, -ly|ing,** *n. Dialect.* —*v.t.* Also, **collow.** to blacken with coal dust or soot; begrime.

—*n.* soot; grime.

[variant of Middle English *colwen* < Old English *col* coal]

col|ly[2] (kol′ē), *n., pl.* **-lies.** = collie.

col|lyr|i|um (kə lir′ē əm), *n., pl.* **-i|a** (-ē ə). an eye salve or eyewash. [< Latin *collyrium* < Greek *kollyrion* poultice, eye salve (diminutive) < *kollyrā* roll of bread]

col|ly|wob|bles (kol′ē wob′əlz), *n. U.S. Slang.* a stomachache; intestinal upset. [humorous formation < *colic* + *wobbles*]

Colo., Colorado (official abbr.).

co|lo|bi|um (kə lō′bē əm), *n., pl.* **-bi|a** (-bē ə). **1** a half-sleeved or sleeveless tunic or robe worn by the clergy of the early church. **2** a similar garment. [< Late Latin *colobium* < Greek *kolóbion* < *kolobós* docked, curtailed]

col|o|bus (kol′ə bəs), *n.* any one of a group of African monkeys distinguished by a rudimentary thumb, cheek pouches, and handsome coloration: *On every tree trunk ... perched the colobus, a little black monkey with a snow-white stole around his neck* (New Yorker). [< New Latin *Colobus* the genus name < Greek *kolobós* docked, curtailed]

col|o|cynth (kol′ə sinth), *n.* **1** a plant of the gourd family, grown especially in southern Asia and Mediterranean regions for its orangelike fruit; bitter apple. **2** the bitter fruit of this plant. **3** the purgative drug prepared from the dried pulp of the fruit; coloquintida. [< Latin *colocynthis* < Greek *kolokynthis* a gourd known for medicinal properties]

colog (no period) or **colog.,** cologarithm.

co|log|a|rithm (kō lôg′ə riᴛʜ əm, -log′-), *n. Mathematics.* the logarithm of the reciprocal of a number. *Example:* log $^1/_5$ = log 1 + colog 5.

co|logne (kə lōn′), *n.* **1** a fragrant liquid, not so strong as perfume; Eau de Cologne. It is used especially as a toilet water. **2** a solid or semisolid form of this substance, such as a stick or a cream. [American English < *Cologne,* Germany, where it was made]

Co|lom|bi|an (kə lum′bē ən), *adj., n.* —*adj.* of or having to do with the South American republic of Colombia.

—*n.* a native or inhabitant of Colombia.

***co|lon**[1] (kō′lən), *n.; pl.* **-lons** *for 1,* **-la** (-lə) *for 2.* **1** a mark (:) of punctuation. Colons are used before explanations, lists, and long quotations to set them off from the rest of the sentence. A colon is also used after the salutation of a business letter. An illustrative sentence or phrase in this dictionary usually has a colon before it. **2** a member or section of a rhythmical period in classical verse, forming a rhythmic unit of from two to six feet with one principal accent or beat. [< Latin *cōlon* < Greek *kôlon* limb; member (of the body or of a sentence); clause]

***colon**[1]

: — definition 1

five main points: first, ...

co|lon[2] (kō′lən), *n., pl.* **-lons, -la** (-lə). the part of the large intestine in which solid waste is accumulated and prepared for elimination from the body. It extends from the cecum to the rectum. See picture at **intestine.** [< Latin *cōlon* < Greek *kólon* part of the large intestine]

co|lon[3] (kō lōn′), *n., pl.* **-lons, -lo|nes** (-lō′nās). **1** the unit of money of Costa Rica, equal to 100 centimos. **2** the unit of money of El Salvador, equal to 100 centavos. [< American Spanish *colón* < *Colón* Columbus]

co|lon[4] (kō lôN′), *n. French.* a French colonial; settler; planter: *To him, the enemy was not France but the land-owning French in Algeria, the colons* (Manchester Guardian).

co|lón (kō lōn′), *n., pl.* **-lo|nes** (-lō′nās). *Spanish.*

colon, the unit of money of Costa Rica or El Salvador.

col|o|nel (kėr′nəl), *n.* an officer ranking next below a brigadier general and next above a lieutenant colonel. A colonel is a commissioned officer. In the United States, the Army, the Air Force, and the Marines all have colonels. ... *the regiment to be commanded by a Colonel and each of the Battalions by a Lieutenant Colonel or Major* (Duke of Wellington). *Abbr:* Col. [earlier *coronel* < Middle French, early variant of *colonel* < Italian *colonnello* commander of a regiment < *colonna* military column < Latin *columna* pillar, post]

▶ **Colonel** is a good example of a spelling that has survived a change of pronunciation. The word, from the French, had two parallel forms, *colonel, coronel,* each pronounced in three syllables. For 175 years the word has been pronounced (kėr′nəl), from the *coronel* form, but only the spelling *colonel* has survived.

Colonel Blimp, an ultraconservative Englishman; Blimp. [< *Colonel Blimp,* a character in a British newspaper cartoon, created by David Low]

Colonel Bo|gey (bō′gē), an imaginary player in golf with an assigned score against which other players must contend. [< *bogey*[1]]

colo|nel|cy (kėr′nəl sē), *n., pl.* **-cies.** the rank, commission, or authority of a colonel.

colo|nel|ship (kėr′nəl ship), *n.* = colonelcy.

co|lo|ni|a (kō lō′nē ä), *n.* (in Mexico) a city district or suburb. [< Spanish *colonia* (literally) colony]

co|lo|ni|al (kə lō′nē əl), *adj., n.* —*adj.* **1a** of or having to do with a colony or colonies: *a colonial governor, colonial policy. Many European countries have lost or given up their colonial possessions since World War II.* **b** practicing colonialism; having colonies: *colonial powers.* **2a** of or having to do with the thirteen British colonies that became the United States of America: *colonial skirmishes with the Indians.* **b** living in one of these colonies: *Paul Revere was a colonial silversmith.* **c** characteristic of or produced in one or several of these colonies: *a colonial costume, colonial furniture.* **3a** *Biology.* forming a colony; consisting of or living as colonies: *colonial wasps.* **b** *Bacteriology.* forming a mass of microorganisms arising from a single cell.

—*n.* a person who lives in a colony: *The colonials are as sensitive to home criticism as the Yankees* (Fraser's Magazine). —**co|lo′ni|al|ly**, *adv.*

colonial bent, a perennial pasture grass that has smaller and shorter red flower clusters than redtop and that grows well in cooler climates. It is used especially in eastern North America to cover golf courses and athletic fields.

co|lo|ni|al|ism (kə lō′nē ə liz′əm), *n.* **1** the policy of a nation that rules or seeks to rule weaker or dependent nations, often with or for economic exploitation: *We condemn colonialism and political subjugation of people in all their forms* (London Times). **2** the condition of being a colony. **3** a colonial idiom, usage, or practice.

co|lo|ni|al|ist (kə lō′nē ə list), *n., adj.* —*n.* a person or nation that favors or practices colonialism. —*adj.* **1** of or having to do with colonialism or colonialists: *the colonialist way of life.* **2** favoring or practicing colonialism: *In the 1800's most European countries were colonialist powers.*

co|lo|ni|al|is|tic (kə lō′nē ə lis′tik), *adj.* = colonialist.

co|lo|ni|al|ize (kə lō′nē ə līz), *v.t.,* **-ized, -iz|ing.** to subject (a country or people) to colonialism.

co|lon|ic (kə lon′ik), *adj.* of, having to do with, or affecting the colon.

Col|o|nies (kol′ə nēz), *n.pl.* **the,** the thirteen British colonies that became the United States of America: New Hampshire, Massachusetts, Rhode Island, Connecticut, New York, New Jersey, Pennsylvania, Delaware, Maryland, Virginia, North Carolina, South Carolina, and Georgia.

col|o|nise (kol′ə nīz), *v.t., v.i.,* **-nised, -nis|ing.** *Especially British.* colonize.

col|o|nist (kol′ə nist), *n.* **1** a person who lives in a colony: *Early colonists in New England suffered much from cold and hunger.* **2** a person who helps to found a colony; settler: *The Roman military colonists remained Roman alike on the Rhine and on the Euphrates* (James A. Froude). **3** an animal or plant found in a region in which it is not indigenous.

col|o|ni|za|tion (kol′ə nə zā′shən), *n.* the establishment of a colony or colonies: *The English, French, Dutch, and Spanish all took part in the colonization of North America.*

col|o|ni|za|tion|ist (kol′ə nə zā′shə nist), *n.* **1** an advocate of colonization. **2** *Historical.* a person in the United States who favored colonization of emancipated slaves and free Negroes, especially in Africa, as the best remedy for the evils and dangers produced by slavery.

col|o|nize (kol′ə nīz), *v.,* **-nized, -niz|ing.** —*v.t.* **1** to establish a colony or colonies in: *The English colonized New England.* **2** to establish (persons) in a colony; settle in a colony. —*v.i.* to form a colony; settle in a colony.

col|o|niz|er (kol′ə nī′zər), *n.* a person or country that colonizes: *Kiliaen Van Rensselaer was one of the leading colonizers of the territory that later became New York* (Ian C. C. Graham).

***col|on|nade** (kol′ə nād′), *n.* a series of columns set the same distance apart. A colonnade usually supports a roof, ceiling, cornice, or the like. [< French *colonnade* < Italian *colonnata* < *colonna* column < Latin *columna*]

***colonnade**

col|on|nad|ed (kol′ə nā′did), *adj.* having a colonnade: *colonnaded halls.*

col|o|ny (kol′ə nē), *n., pl.* **-nies. 1a** a group of people who leave their own country and go to settle in another land, but who still remain citizens of their own country: *The Pilgrim colony came from England to America in 1620.* **b** the settlement made by such a group of people: *The Pilgrims founded a colony at Plymouth, Massachusetts.* **2** a territory distant from the country that governs it: *Hong Kong is a British colony.* SYN: possession, dependency, dominion. **3** *Figurative.* **a** a group of people from one country or occupation living in a certain part of a city: *the Italian colony in Boston. There is a colony of artists in Paris.* **b** the district in which such a group lives: *Greenwich Village in New York is an artists' colony.* **4a** *Biology.* a group of animals or plants of the same kind, living or growing together: *We found two colonies of ants under the steps. Coral grows in colonies.* **b** *Bacteriology.* a mass of microorganisms arising from a single cell, living on or in a solid or partially solid medium: *The petri dish is left in a warm incubator for 24 hours, whereupon numerous bacterial colonies can be seen without magnification* (Fred W. Emerson). [< Latin *colōnia* farm, settlement < *colōnus* cultivator, settler < *colere* cultivate, inhabit]

***col|o|phon** (kol′ə fon, -fən), *n.* **1** a small design or device of a publisher usually placed on the last page of a book, but sometimes on the title page or the spine: *The volume was uninjured and entire from title page to colophon* (Scott). **2** an inscription or a note placed at the end of a book or manuscript, giving the title, the name of the scribe or printer, the date and place of printing, and sometimes the type used. [< Greek *kolophôn* summit, final touch]

***colophon**
definition 1

col|o|pho|ny (kol′ə fō′nē, kə lof′ə-), *n.* = rosin. [< Latin *Colophōnia* (*rēsīna*) Colophonian (resin) < Greek *kolophōnia* (*rhētinē*) < *Kolophôn,* a town in Ionia]

col|o|quin|ti|da (kol′ə kwin′tə də), *n.* = colocynth (def. 3). [< Medieval Latin *coloquintida* < Latin *colocynthis*]

col|or (kul′ər), *n., v.* —*n.* **1a** the sensation produced by the effect of waves of light striking the retina of the eye. Different colors are produced by rays of light having different wave lengths. **b** the appearance of a thing, distinct from form, associated with the effect of particular vibrations of light coming from it; hue. **2** a particular hue or tint; red, yellow, blue, or any combination of them except black, white, or gray. Green is a combination of yellow and blue; purple is a combination of red and blue. *She never wears colors, but always dresses in black or white.* **3** a paint, stain, dye, or pigment: *The color was so thick on the canvas that it began to peel off.* **4a** the coloring of the face; complexion: *His change of color looked very much like fear.* **b** redness of the face; ruddy complexion: *I saw her color beginning to come back* (Dickens). **c** a flush caused by blushing: *A word could bring the color to my cheek* (Tennyson). **5** the skin color of any people or race that is not white: *She is a woman of color* (Robert Louis Stevenson). SYN: duskiness. **6** *Figurative.* an outward appearance; show: *His story has some color of truth. Although he had some color of title, his claim was disallowed.* SYN: semblance. **7** *Figurative.* distinguishing quality; vividness: *The author's gift for description adds color to his stories.* **8** *Figurative.* character; tone: *a horse of a different color. Pendennis ... took his color very readily from his neighbor* (Thackeray). **9** *Figurative. Music.* **a** a quality of tone by which any musical instrument or combination of instruments can be recognized, used especially in orchestration; tone color; timbre: *Every instrument has its peculiar color of sound* (Carl Engel). **b** the quality or style of musical interpretation which may produce an emotional reaction in the listener or audience: *His playing has color and vigor.* **10** *Fine Arts.* **a** the general effect produced by the paints or tints of a picture; coloring; coloration. **b** the suggestion of color by contrasts of light and dark in an engraving or other monochrome. **11** *U.S. Mining, Mineralogy.* a trace or particle of gold or other valuable mineral: *It was hard work, this moving gravel into new piles, ... panning out the residue for the little specks of color* (Pacific Discovery). **12** *Heraldry.* one of the three kinds of tincture (the other two being fur and metal). The heraldic colors are azure, gules, purpure, vert, and sable. Sanguine (murrey) and tenné (tenny) are also used as colors. **13** *Nuclear Physics.* a hypothetical property of quarks by which they combine to form a larger particle (so called by analogy with the primary colors): *When a quark interacts with a gluon, it may change its color* (Sheldon L. Glashow).

—*v.t.* **1** to give color to; put color on; change the color of: *The little boy spent the afternoon coloring pictures with crayons. Who does not know the famous Swan? ... 'Twas colored all by his own hand* (Wordsworth). SYN: paint, dye, stain, tint, tinge. **2** to make red in the face. **3** *Figurative.* to change to give a wrong idea; put in a false light: *The fisherman colored the facts to make his catch seem the biggest of all.* SYN: misrepresent. **4** *Figurative.* to give a distinguishing or vivid quality to: *Love of nature colored all of my grandfather's stories about camping.*

—*v.i.* **1** to become red in the face; blush: *She colors easily when someone mentions her mistakes.* SYN: flush. **2** to take on color; become colored: *His skin had colored and his hair had bleached under the southern skies.* Also, *especially British,* **colour.**

change color, a to turn pale: *Seeing the ghost, he changed color and trembled with fear.* **b** to blush: *The shy little girl changed color when she came into the room to meet the guests.*

colors, a a badge, ribbon, dress, or other decoration worn to show allegiance: *As election day approached, the streets were brightened by the colors of the parties.* **b** *Archaic.* literary embellishments in writings, speeches, etc.: ... *novelists who have more colors in their vocabulary than Turner had on his palette* (George O. Trevelyan).

give (or **lend**) **color to,** to cause to seem true or likely: *In order to give color and probability to the fraud ...* (William Paley).

lose color, to turn pale: *She lost color when we told her about the accident.*

show one's (true) colors, a to show oneself as one really is: *The dictator avoided showing his true colors until he had gained full power.* **b** to declare one's opinions or plans: *Some political candidates prefer not to show their colors when controversial issues are involved.*

the colors, a the flag of a nation, regiment, or group: *Salute the colors.* **b** the ceremony of raising the flag in the morning and lowering it in the evening: *At military school, the day begins with the colors.* **c** the nation represented by the flag, especially its armed forces: *Soldiers and sailors serve the colors.*

with flying colors, successfully; victoriously: *She passed the test with flying colors.*

[< Latin *color* color, hue]

—*Syn. n.* **1a, b Color, hue, shade** mean a sensation produced by the effect of waves of light striking the retina of the eye. **Color** is the general word: *Her dress is the color of grass.* **Hue** is poetic in the general meaning of color. Technically, *hue* means the quality of a color that gives the name, such as red or blue. It is also used to suggest partial alteration of a color: *This pottery is blue with a greenish hue.* **Shade** applies to the darkness and lightness of color: *I like a blue car, but of a lighter shade than navy.* Technically, *shade* refers to the amount of black added to the pure color.

col|or|a|bil|i|ty (kul′ər ə bil′ə tē), *n.* the quality of

Pronunciation Key: hat, āge, cãre, fär; let, ēqual, tėrm; it, īce; hot, ōpen, ôrder; oil, out; cup, pu̇t, rüle; child; long; thin; ᴛʜen; zh, measure; ə represents **a** in about, **e** in taken, **i** in pencil, **o** in lemon, **u** in circus.

being colorable.

col|or|a|ble (kul′ər ə bəl), *adj.* **1** that can be colored. **2** *Figurative.* plausible: *A witness . . . might be held privileged to refuse to answer a question, for the purpose of presenting, at reasonable length, a colorable objection to the propriety of the question* (New York Times). **3** *Figurative.* pretended; deceptive. SYN: covert, feigned, counterfeit. Also, *especially British,* **colourable**. **—col′or|a|ble|ness,** *n.* **—col′or|a|bly,** *adv.*

Col|o|rad|an (kol′ə rad′ən, -rä′dən), *adj., n.* **—*adj.*** of or having to do with the state of Colorado.
—*n.* a person born or living in Colorado.

col|o|rad|o (kol′ə rad′ō, -rä′dō), *adj., n., pl.* **-rad|os.** **—*adj.*** made with medium-colored tobacco and of medium strength: *a colorado cigar.*
—*n.* a cigar of medium color and strength.
[< Spanish *colorado* colored, red, past participle of *colorar* to color < Latin *colōrāre* < *color* color]

Colorado potato beetle or **Colorado beetle,** = potato beetle.

col|or|ant (kul′ər ənt), *n.* a coloring matter, such as a pigment or dye: *The property of a colorant that makes it absorb more of one part of the visible spectrum than another is its chemical constitution* (Deane B. Judd). [< French *colorant,* present participle of *colorer* color < Latin *colōrāre*]

col|or|a|tion (kul′ə rā′shən), *n.* **1** the way in which a person or thing is colored; coloring: *The coloration of a chameleon can change. The tiger's coloration helps conceal the animal in its natural surroundings* (George B. Schaller). **2** coloring as characteristic of a painter or painting. Also, *especially British,* **colouration**.

col|o|ra|tu|ra (kul′ər ə tůr′ə, -tyůr′-), *n., adj.* **—*n.*** **1** ornamental passages in music, such as trills or runs. *Coloratura* is used especially for vocal display. *She can negotiate the trills and arabesques of coloraturas as easily as she trumpets out a stinging dramatic climax* (Time). **2** a soprano who sings such passages. **3** music containing such passages.
—*adj.* **1** suited for singing ornamental passages in music: *a coloratura soprano.* **2** (in vocal music) having ornamental passages.
[< Italian *coloratura* < Late Latin *colōrātūra* full of color < Latin *colōrāre* to color]

col|or|a|ture (kul′ər ə chůr), *n.* = coloratura.

color bar, the denial of social, economic, and political opportunities to some elements of a society on the basis of color: *Perhaps one day I shall hear that some of them, at least, have found employment in a white restaurant, have smashed the color bar by their own skill, their own determination* (Harper's).

col|or|bear|er (kul′ər bãr′ər), *n.* the person who carries the flag or colors; standard-bearer.

col|or-blind (kul′ər blīnd′), *adj.* **1** unable to tell certain colors apart, especially red and green; unable to perceive certain colors or any colors: *Tests on color-blind persons of the type known as "protanopes," who confuse red and green, were particularly interesting when compared with tests on the normal eye* (Science News Letter). **2** *Figurative.* unaware of distinctions or differences; not discriminative: *to be color-blind to facts, color-blind laws.*

color blindness, or **col|or-blind|ness** (kul′ər-blīnd′nis), *n.* a visual inherited defect, consisting of an inability to tell certain colors apart or to perceive certain colors (usually red and green, sometimes blue and yellow).

col|or|cast (kul′ər kast′, -käst′), *n., v.,* **-cast** or **-cast|ed, -cast|ing.** *U.S.* **—*n.*** a television broadcast in color: *NBC showed a satisfying colorcast of the opera "Carmen" to hundreds of invited guests in Manhattan* (Time).
—*v.t.*, *v.i.* to broadcast (a television program) in color: *National Broadcasting Co. announced it would colorcast the Tournament of Roses parade from Pasadena, Calif., New Year's Day* (Wall Street Journal).

col|or-code (kul′ər kōd′), *v.t.,* **-cod|ed, -cod|ing.** to code or key by the use of different colors to denote different items or categories; color-key: *Return envelopes have been color-coded with orange trim for Ontario, green for Quebec* (New York Times).

col|ored (kul′ərd), *adj., v., n.* **—*adj.*** **1** having color; not black or white: *This book has colored pictures.* **2** having a certain kind of color: *a green-colored leaf.* **3** of the black race or any race other than white. **4** (of foliage) of any color but green. **5** *Figurative.* tinged by prejudice, emotion, desire for effect, or the like; biased: *The fisherman gave a highly colored description of the size of the fish he caught.* Also, *especially British,* **coloured**.
—*v.* past tense and past participle of **color:** *He colored the sky blue.*
—*n.* Also, **Colored.** (in South Africa) a Cape Colored.

col|or|er (kul′ər ər), *n.* a person or thing that colors. Also, *especially British,* **colourer**.

col|or|fast (kul′ər fast′, -fäst′), *adj.* dyed so as to retain color without fading, especially in washing: *a shirt made of colorfast material.* **—col′or|fast′ness,** *n.*

col|or-field (kul′ər fēld′), *adj.* of or having to do with a form of abstract art emphasizing color on a smooth surface to produce an effect of chromatic intensity: *Color-field painting . . . drowns the consciousness in rainbow translucences* (Harold Rosenberg).

color film, **1** film for making photographs in color. **2** a motion picture made with film that takes photographs in color.

color filter, a screen of colored glass or other material capable of absorbing a certain frequency of light, used in photography to alter the relative intensity of the light.

col|or|ful (kul′ər fəl), *adj.* **1** having excitement, variety, or interest; picturesque; vivid: *The explorer described his colorful experiences.* **2** full of color: *a colorful dress.* Also, *especially British,* **colourful**. **—col′or|ful|ly,** *adv.* **—col′or|ful|ness,** *n.*

color guard, *U.S.* the honor guard of a military or similar unit that carries or accompanies the flag or colors during ceremonies or reviews.

col|or|if|ic (kul′ə rif′ik), *adj.* **1** producing or giving color: *colorific rays.* **2** of or having to do with color. [< French *colorifique* < Latin *color, -ōris* color, hue + *facere* make]

col|or|im|e|ter (kul′ə rim′ə tər), *n.* **1** any instrument or device for measuring the shade, tint, value, brightness, and purity of a color. **2** a device used in chemical analysis for comparing the color of a liquid with a standard color: *Instruments called colorimeters are used by chemists to determine when two solutions have the same color* (Hardy and Perrin). [< *color* + *-meter*]

col|or|i|met|ric (kul′ər ə met′rik), *adj.* of or having to do with the measurement of color: *colorimetric observations of stars.* **—col′or|i|met′ri|cal|ly,** *adv.*

col|or|i|met|ri|cal (kul′ər ə met′rə kəl), *adj.* = colorimetric.

colorimetric analysis, a method of determining the concentration of a chemical substance by measuring the intensity of its color or of a color produced by it.

col|or|im|e|try (kul′ə rim′ə trē), *n.* measurement or analysis by means of a colorimeter.

color index, *Astronomy.* a measure of the color of a star, determined by the difference between its photographic and its visual magnitude.

col|or|ing (kul′ər ing), *n.* **1** the way in which a person or thing is colored; coloration: *The fisherman had a ruddy coloring.* **2** a substance used to color; pigment. **3** a colored work. **4** *Figurative.* an outward or false appearance: *The story had the coloring of truth, but we knew we could not believe it.* Also, *especially British,* **colouring**.

coloring matter, a substance used to color; pigment.

col|or|ism (kul′ə riz əm), *n.* the style or work of a colorist; coloration.

col|or|ist (kul′ər ist), *n.* **1** an artist who is skillful in painting with colors. **2** a user of color. Also, *especially British,* **colourist**.

col|or|is|tic (kul′ə ris′tik), *adj.* of or having to do with a colorist or with artistic coloring.

col|or|i|za|tion (kul′ə rə zā′shən), *n.* the act or process of making a color photograph or motion picture from black-and-white images by using a computer that is programmed to assign various colors to different shades of black-and-white images: *John Huston . . . denounced the colorization of his classic film, "The Maltese Falcon"* (New York Times).

col|or|ize (kul′ə rīz), *v.t.,* **-ized, -iz|ing.** **1** to make visible the color of (something): *Light has a colorizing effect.* **2** to color. **3** to add color to (black-and-white motion pictures) by the process of colorization: *Supporters of the method claim that colorizing old movies is the only way to get young viewers to watch them* (Philip Wuntch).

col|or-key (kul′ər kē), *v.t.* = color-code.

col|or|less (kul′ər lis), *adj.* **1** without color: *Her face was almost colorless from fright.* SYN: achromatic. **2** without any tinge of red; pallid; pale: *a colorless complexion.* SYN: blanched. **3** *Figurative.* without excitement or variety; not interesting: *a colorless person, a colorless description.* **4** *Figurative,* unbiased, neutral. Also, *especially British,* **colourless**. **—col′or|less|ly,** *adv.* **—col′or|less|ness,** *n.*

color line, the distinction in social, economic, or political privileges drawn between members of different races in certain countries or regions on the basis of skin color.

color man, *U.S.* a radio or television announcer who colors or provides background information: *He [Wally Schirra] also signed on to be Walter Cronkite's color man on CBS's play-by-play coverage of the Apollo space shots* (Esquire).

color organ, = clavilux.

color phase, the coloration at a particular season of an animal whose fur or plumage changes in color according to season, such as the ermine and ptarmigan. Certain animals, such as foxes and hares, have varieties whose color varies according to location, often within a relatively small geographical area.

color photography, photography using color film.

color point, *Heraldry.* an honor point, placed in the upper middle of an escutcheon.

col|ors (kul′ərz), *n. pl.* See under **color**.

color scheme, an arrangement or combination of colors for producing a particular design or effect: *A color scheme which arouses a feeling of warmth . . . is quite suitable for the purpose of a home in which we rest* (Matthew Luckiesh).

color sergeant, a soldier, usually a sergeant, who has charge of the colors of a battalion or regiment.

color slide, a color transparency for the projection of colored images.

color television, television in which images are produced in chromatic colors, not in black and white.

color temperature, *Astronomy.* the temperature at which a black body emits light of the same color as that which is emitted by a given source, especially a heavenly body: *Perhaps the most widely used one-dimensional color scale is that of color temperature for classifying light sources* (Deane B. Judd).

color transparency, a color film made visible by means of light shining through from behind.

Coloss., Colossians (book of the New Testament).

co|los|sal (kə los′əl), *adj.* of huge size; gigantic; vast: *a colossal success. The Empire State Building is a colossal structure.* SYN: immense, enormous, prodigious. **—co|los′sal|ly,** *adv.*

col|os|se|um (kol′ə sē′əm), *n.* = coliseum.

Col|os|se|um (kol′ə sē′əm), *n.* a large amphitheater in Rome, completed in A.D. 80. The Colosseum was built by the emperors Vespasian and Titus for games and contests. Parts of it are still standing. Also, **Coliseum**. [< Latin *colossēum,* neuter of *colossēus* gigantic < *colossus;* see etym. under **colossus**]

Co|los|sian (kə losh′ən), *adj., n.* **—*adj.*** belonging to Colossae, an ancient city of Phrygia, in Asia Minor. **—*n.*** a native or inhabitant of Colossae.

Co|los|sians (kə losh′ənz), *n. pl.* (*sing. in use*). a book of the New Testament, written by the Apostle Paul to the Christian people of Colossae, an ancient city of Asia Minor. Its full title is *The Epistle of Paul the Apostle to the Colossians. Abbr:* Col.

co|los|sus (kə los′əs), *n., pl.* **-los|si** (-los′ī), **-los|sus|es.** **1** a huge statue. **2** *Figurative.* anything huge; a gigantic person or thing: . . . *the post-war emergence of Russia and the United States as the two colossi of world power* (New York Times). [< Latin *colossus* < Greek *kolossós* gigantic (Egyptian) statue]

Colossus of Rhodes, a huge bronze statue of Helios made at Rhodes about 280 B.C. It was placed near the entrance to the harbor and was one of the seven wonders of the ancient world.

co|los|to|my (kə los′tə mē), *n., pl.* **-mies.** the making of an artificial opening into the colon by surgery. [< *colo*(n)[2] + Greek *stóma* opening]

co|los|tral (kə los′trəl), *adj.* of, having to do with, or caused by colostrum: *Foals born from dams which have been immunized or have recovered from natural infection acquire immunity. . . . This colostral immunity gradually wanes, but is usually protective for 6 to 8 months* (New Scientist).

co|los|trum (kə los′trəm), *n.* the thin, yellowish milk secreted by a mammal just before and for a few days after the birth of young. It is especially rich in protein and helps establish both digestion and natural immunity. *Colostrum contains whatever antibodies to disease the mother may previously have developed through having the disease herself* (Science News Letter). [< Latin *colostrum* beestings]

co|lot|o|my (kə lot′ə mē), *n., pl.* **-mies.** a surgical incision into the colon. [< *colo*(n)[2] + *-tomy*]

col|our (kul′ər), *n., v.t., v.i. Especially British.* color.

col|our|way (kul′ər wā′), *n. British.* = color scheme.

col|pi|tis (kol pī′tis), *n.* = vaginitis. [< Greek *kólpos* vagina + English *-itis* inflammation]

col|por|tage (kol′pôr′tij, -pōr′-), *n.* the work done by colporteurs. [< French *colportage* < *colporter* to sell (see etym. under **colporteur**) + *-age* -age]

col|por|teur (kol′pôr′tər, -pōr′-), *n.* **1** a person who travels about and distributes Bibles, religious tracts, and the like. **2** a hawker of books, broadsides, newspapers, or the like. [< French *colporteur* < *colporter* to hawk, carry for sale (on the neck) < Old French *col* neck (< Latin *collum*) + *porter* carry < Latin *portāre*]

colt (kōlt), *n.* **1** a young horse, donkey, zebra, or other member of the same family of animals as the horse, especially a male horse less than four or five years old: *At two years old, the colt, if for harness, may be put to plow or harrow* (John Baxter). **2** *Figurative.* a young or inexperienced person. **3** *Nautical.* the end of a rope used in flogging: *Perry scorned the cat-o'-nine-tails as effeminate. He preferred the "colt," a stout rope with a frayed end* (New Yorker). [Old English *colt*]

Colt (kōlt), *n. Trademark.* **1** an early type of American revolver. **2** any one of various firearms developed by the same maker: *The Colt automatic pistol is a deadly weapon in close fighting* (James Hodgson). [< Samuel *Colt,* 1814-1862, the inventor]

col|ter (kōl′tər), *n.* a sharp blade or disk on a plow to cut the earth ahead of the plowshare. Also, **coulter.** [Old English *culter* knife < Latin, knife, plowshare]

colt|ish (kōl′tish), *adj.* like a colt; lively and frisky: (*Figurative.*) *He is still up to his old coltish tricks, beginning slowly and swerving badly* (New Yorker). **—colt′ish|ly,** *adv.* **—colt′ish|ness,** *n.*

colts|foot (kōlts′fu̇t′), *n., pl.* **-foots.** a plant of the composite family, with yellow flowers and large, heart-shaped leaves which were formerly much used in medicine.

coltsfoot snakeroot, = wild ginger.

colt's-tail (kōlts′tāl′), = horseweed (def. 1).

col|u|brid (kol′yə brid), *adj., n.* **—*adj.*** of or having to do with a family of nonpoisonous snakes having a flattened head and a long, tapering tail. **—*n.*** a snake of this family.

col|u|brine (kol′yə brīn, -brin), *adj.* **1** of or having to do with a snake; like a snake. **2** of or having to do with a family of harmless snakes found throughout the world, including the king snakes and garter snakes: *The colubrine snakes . . . differ in several important particulars from the Viperina* (Timothy Holmes). [< Latin *colubrīnus* < *coluber, -brī* serpent]

co|lu|go (kə lü′gō), *n., pl.* **-gos.** = flying lemur: *Scientists do not classify the flying lemur, or colugo, as a true lemur* (W. M. Mann).

Co|lum|ba (kə lum′bə), *n., genitive* **Co|lum|bae.** a southern constellation near Canis Major. [< Latin *columba* dove]

Co|lum|bae (kə lum′bē), *n.* the genitive of **Columba.**

col|um|bar|i|um (kol′əm bãr′ē əm), *n., pl.* **-i|a** (-ē ə). **1** = dovecote. **2a** an underground vault with recesses in the walls to receive the ashes of the dead: *Of the four atom-bombproof Stockholm shelters, the one under Engelbrekt Church will serve as a columbarium* (Time). **b** one of these recesses. [< Latin *columbārium* (originally) dovecote < *columba* dove]

col|um|bar|y (kol′əm ber′ē), *n., pl.* **-bar|ies.** = dovecote. [< Latin *columbārium;* see etym. under **columbarium**]

Co|lum|bi|a[1] (kə lum′bē ə), *n.* a name for the United States of America. Columbia is often represented as a woman dressed in red, white, and blue. [< New Latin *Columbia* < Christopher *Columbus,* discoverer of the Americas]

Co|lum|bi|a[2] (kə lum′bē ə), *n.* any one of a breed of white-faced sheep raised for wool and meat. [< *Columbia*[1] (the breed was developed in the United States)]

co|lum|bi|ad (kə lum′bē ad), *n.* a heavy cannon with a smooth bore, formerly used in the United States. [< New Latin *Columbia* the United States]

Co|lum|bi|an (kə lum′bē ən), *adj., n.* **—*adj.*** **1** of or having to do with Columbia. **2** of or belonging to America, especially the United States. **3** of or having to do with Christopher Columbus. **—*n.*** a size of printing type (16 point).

co|lum|bic (kə lum′bik), *adj.* containing columbium (niobium), especially with a valence of 5.

col|um|bine[1] (kol′əm bīn), *n.* a plant whose flowers have petals shaped like hollow spurs. Wild columbines have red-and-yellow or blue-and-white flowers. Columbines are a genus of perennials belonging to the crowfoot family. The blue-and-white columbine is the state flower of Colorado; the red-and-yellow flowers are found especially in eastern North America. [< Medieval Latin *columbina* < Late Latin *columbīna* vervain, feminine of Latin *columbīnus* dovelike < *columba* dove]

col|um|bine[2] (kol′əm bīn, -bin), *adj.* **1** of or having to do with a dove; like a dove. **2** *Obsolete.* dove-colored. [< Latin *columbīnus* dovelike < *columba* dove]

Col|um|bine (kol′əm bīn) *n.* a woman character in traditional Italian comedy and in pantomime, the sweetheart of Harlequin.

co|lum|bite (kə lum′bīt), *n.* the native ore of niobium, a black compound containing iron and manganese, and often tantalum. [< *columb*(ium) + *-ite*[1]]

co|lum|bi|um (kə lum′bē əm), *n.* the former name of the chemical element niobium. The name is still used in metallurgy. *Columbium has been used in experimental thermal nuclear reactors* (Wall Street Journal). *Symbol:* Cb (no period). [< New Latin *columbium* < *Columbia*[1] the United States]

co|lum|bo (kə lum′bō), *n., pl.* **-bos.** = calumba.

co|lum|bous (kə lum′bəs), *adj.* containing columbium (niobium), especially with a valence of 3. [< *columb*(ium) + *-ous*]

Co|lum|bus Day (kə lum′bəs), *U.S.* the anniversary of Columbus's discovery of America in 1492, celebrated on October 12 until 1971 and now celebrated on the second Monday in October; Discovery Day. It is a legal holiday throughout the United States.

col|u|mel|la (kol′yə mel′ə), *n., pl.* **-mel|lae** (-mel′ē). **1** a columnlike structure in an animal or plant: *As development proceeds, a dome-shaped wall forms, separating the inner framework, the columella, from the spore-producing portion which surrounds it* (Fred W. Emerson). **2** a little column. [< Latin *columella* (diminutive) < *columna* column]

col|u|mel|lar (kol′yə mel′ər), *adj.* of or having to do with a columella. A columellar lip is the inner lip of a univalve shell.

col|u|mel|li|form (kol′yə mel′ə fôrm), *adj.* shaped like a columella or small pillar.

***col|umn** (kol′əm; *see note below*), *n.* **1a** a slender, upright structure; pillar; post. Columns are usually made of stone, wood, or metal, and are used as supports or ornaments to a building. **b** an upright support consisting essentially of a nearly cylindrical shaft with a base and capital. **c** a similar structure, often of great size, erected alone as a monument: *Trajan's column.* **2** anything that seems slender and upright like a column: *a column of mercury in a tube, the spinal column.* (*Figurative.*) *A column of smoke rose from the fire.* **3** an arrangement of people, especially soldiers, in several short rows one behind another, used especially for marching. **4** a line of ships or aircraft, one behind another. **5** any similar line of persons or things: *A long column of cars followed the procession down the street.* **6a** a narrow division of a page reading from top to bottom, kept separate by lines or by blank spaces. Some newspapers have eight columns on a page. **b** a line or series of letters, figures, or other symbols arranged vertically: *Add the column of figures.* **7a** a part of a newspaper or magazine used for a special subject or written by a special writer: *a financial column, the sports column.* **b** an article appearing in a column. Columns usually carry the name of the writer, and sometimes his picture. **8** *Botany.* an upright cylindrical structure formed by the union of the stamens with the style, as in orchids. *Abbr:* col. [< Latin *columna* column, pillar, post]

▶**column.** The pronunciation (kol′yəm), although generally regarded as substandard, is not uncommon, especially in senses 7a and 7b and as a humorous usage.

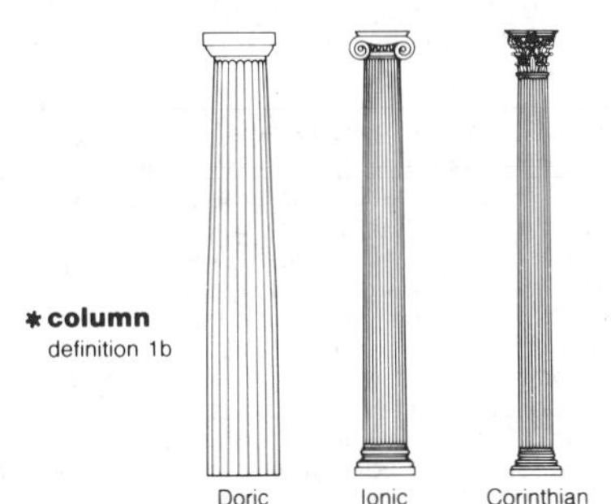

***column** definition 1b

co|lum|na (kə lum′nə), *n., pl.* **-nae** (-nē). *Latin.* **1** a column or pillar. **2** any one of various structures in the human body resembling a column.

co|lum|nar (kə lum′nər), *adj.* **1** like a column: *columnar stalagmites.* **2** of or having to do with a column or columns: *Greek columnar architecture is probably the outcome of the Greek mode of argumentation* (Atlantic). **3** made of columns: *a columnar structure.* **4** written or printed in columns: *Type the lists in columnar form.* **5** (of rocks and crystals) having a columnlike structure; prismatic.

col|umned (kol′əmd), *adj.* **1** having columns: *This columned and voluted pleasure villa* (New Yorker). **2** formed into columns.

co|lum|ni|a|tion (kə lum′nē ā′shən), *n.* **1** the use or arrangement of columns in a building or other structure, especially in relation to the whole design: *The architecture of fenestration and the architecture of columniation are irreconcilable* (Saturday Review of Politics, Literature, Science and Art). **2** the columns used in a structure.

co|lum|ni|form (kə lum′nə fôrm), *adj.* shaped like a column.

col|um|nist (kol′ə mist, -əm nist; *see note below*), *n.* **1** a person who writes a special column in a newspaper or magazine: *The columnists supply light in limited degree* (Harper's). **2** a person who selects and edits the material for such a column.

▶**Columnist** is sometimes pronounced (kol′yə-mist). See note under **column.**

co|lure (kō lu̇r′, kō′lu̇r), *n. Astronomy.* either of two hour circles of the celestial sphere, one passing through the equinoctial points, and the other, 90 degrees away along the ecliptic, through the solstitial points. [< Latin *colūrus* < Greek *kólouros* docktailed < *kólos* cut off + *ourá* tail (because in Greece part of each circle is cut off by the horizon)]

co|ly (kō′lē), *n., pl.* **-lies.** any one of a family of small, long-tailed African birds, which climb about in trees eating berries and fruit. Also, **colie.** [< New Latin *Colius* the genus name < Greek *koliós* a green woodpecker]

col|za (kol′zə), *n.* **1a** any cole, especially rape. **b** the seed of rape; rapeseed. **2** an oil made from these seeds, used as a fuel in lamps, as a lubricant, etc.: . . . *the light of a large swinging colza lamp* (Mary E. Braddon). [< French *colzat* < Dutch *koolzaad* cabbage seed]

colza oil, = colza (def. 2).

com-, *prefix.* with; together; altogether: *Commingle = mingle with one another. Compress = press together.* Also: **co-** before vowels, *h,* and *gn;* **col-** before *l;* **con-** before *n* and other consonants except *b, h, l, m, p, r, w;* **cor-** before *r.* [< Latin *com-* < *cum* with]

com., an abbreviation for the following:
1 comedy.
2 comma.
3a commerce. **b** commercial.
4 common.
5 communication.

Com., an abbreviation for the following:
1 Commander
2a Commission. **b** Commissioner.
3 Committee.
4 Commodore.
5 Commonwealth.
6 Communist.

co|ma[1] (kō′mə), *n., pl.* **-mas.** **1** a prolonged unconsciousness caused by disease, injury, or poison; stupor. **2** *Figurative: Honour, duty, compassion . . . are sentiments never in a state of coma* (William Gladstone). [< Greek *kôma, -atos* deep sleep]

co|ma[2] (kō′mə), *n., pl.* **-mae** (-mē). **1** *Astronomy.* a cloudlike, faintly luminous mass around the nucleus of a comet, consisting of dust particles mixed with frozen water, frozen methane, and frozen ammonia: *The nuclei of the smaller comets are only a mile or so in diameter, but the visible head, or coma, may extend for thousands of miles beyond it* (New Astronomy). **2** *Optics.* the blurred appearance or hazy border surrounding an object viewed through a lens which is not free from spherical aberration: *Coma differs from spherical aberration in that a point object is imaged not as a circle, but as a comet-shaped figure, whence the term coma* (Sears and Zemansky). **3** *Botany.* a tuft of hairs at the end of a seed, or a leafy crown, such as that on a palm tree. [< Latin *coma* < Greek *kómē* hair of the head, mane; trail of light]

Coma Ber|e|ni|ces (ber′ə nī′sēz), *genitive* **Comae Ber|e|ni|ces.** a small northern constellation north of Virgo and between Boötes and Leo; Berenice's Hair. [< Latin *Coma Berenīcēs* (literally) hair of Berenice, daughter of Ptolemy Philadelphus, noted for her beautiful hair]

Co|mae Ber|e|ni|ces (kō′mē ber′e nī′sēz), the genitive of **Coma Berenices.**

co|mak|er (kō mā′kər), *n.* a person who adds his signature on a note to that of the borrower and shares the responsibility for repayment.

co|mal[1] (kō′məl), *adj. Botany.* having to do with or like a coma. [< *coma*[2] + *-al*[1]]

co|mal[2] (kō mäl′), *n., pl.* **-mals, -ma|les** (-mä′lās). a small earthenware grill used in Mexico. [< Mexican Spanish *comal* < Nahuatl *comalli*]

co|man|age (kō man′ij), *v.t.,* **-aged, -ag|ing.** to manage jointly: *The financing will be handled through an investment banking syndicate comanaged by Kuhn, Loeb & Co. and Lehman Brothers* (Wall Street Journal). **—co|man′ag|er,** *n.*

co|man|age|ment (kō man′ij mənt), *n.* = worker participation.

Pronunciation Key: hat, āge, cãre, fär; let, ēqual, tėrm; it, īce; hot, ōpen, ôrder; oil, out; cup, pu̇t, rüle; child; long; thin; ᴛʜen; zh, measure; ə represents **a** in about, **e** in taken, **i** in pencil, **o** in lemon, **u** in circus.

Co|man|che (kə man′chē), *n., pl.* **-ches** or **-che,** *adj.* **—*n.*** **1** a member of a tribe of American Indians that formerly roamed from Nebraska to northern Mexico and now live mainly in Oklahoma. **2** their language, belonging to the Uto-Aztecan family.
—*adj.* of or having to do with this tribe of American Indians.
[American English < Mexican Spanish *Comanche* < Shoshonean (Ute) *kōmánchī* adversary, one who always wants to fight]

Co|man|che|an (kə man′chē ən), *adj., n. U.S., Geology.* **—*adj.*** having to do with or denoting the Lower Cretaceous period or system of rocks in North America; Lower Cretaceous: *In the Gulf region, the Lower Cretaceous is commonly known as the Comanchean Series* (Raymond Cecil Moore).
—*n.* the Comanchean period or system of rocks; Lower Cretaceous.
[< *Comanche,* a town and county in Texas, where remains were found + *-an*]

com|an|che|ro (kom′ən chãr′ō; *Spanish* kō′män-chā′rō), *n., pl.* **-ros.** (formerly, in southwestern U.S.) a person trading with the American Indians. [< Mexican Spanish *comanchero* < *Comanche;* see etym. under **Comanche**]

co|marb (kō′märb), *n.* = coarb.

co|mate[1] (kō māt′), *n.* a companion; fellow; mate. [< *co-* + *mate*[1]]

co|mate[2] (kō′māt), *adj.* **1** *Botany.* comose. **2** hairy; tufted. [< Latin *comātus* having long hair < *coma* hair; see etym. under **coma**[2]]

com|a|tose (kom′ə tōs, kō′mə-), *adj.* **1** in a stupor or coma; unconscious. **2** of or having to do with a coma; like a coma or stupor. **3** drowsy; lethargic. [< Greek *kôma, -atos* deep sleep + English *-ose*] **—com′a|tose′ly,** *adv.*

co|mat|u|lid (kə mach′ə lid, -mat′yə-), *n.* any one of a group of flower-shaped, free-swimming crinoids; feather star. [< New Latin *Comatulidae* the family name < *Comatula* the genus name < Latin *comātula* with neatly curled hair < *comātus;* see etym. under **comate**[2]]

comb[1] (kōm), *n., v.* **—*n.*** **1a** a piece of metal, rubber, plastic, or bone, with teeth, used to arrange or straighten the hair, or to hold it in place: *She ran a comb through her hair to get out the snarls.* **b** = currycomb. **2** anything shaped or used like a comb. One kind of comb cleans and takes out the tangles in wool or flax. **3** the thick, red, fleshy piece on the top of the head of chickens and some other fowls; caruncle. A rooster has a larger comb than a hen. **4** the top of a wave rolling over or breaking. **5** = honeycomb (def. 1).
—*v.t.* **1** to arrange or straighten with a comb: *She combed her hair after coming in from the beach.* **2** to take out the tangles in (wool, flax, etc.) with a comb; card. **3** to curry (a horse). **4** to scrape or rake with an action like that of a comb. **5** to search through; look everywhere in: *We had to comb the whole city before we found our lost dog.*
—*v.i.* (of waves) to roll over or break at the top.
[Old English *comb*] **—comb′less,** *adj.* **—comb′-like′,** *adj.*

comb[2] (küm, kōm), *n.* = combe.

comb., combination.

com|bat (*v., n.* kom′bat, kum′-; *v. also* kəm bat′), *v.,* **-bat|ed, -bat|ing** or (*especially British*) **-bat-ted, -bat|ting,** *n., adj.* **—*v.t.*** **1** to fight against; oppose in battle: *The British and Americans combated French efforts to control North America for 100 years before the American Revolution. Its task was defined as "combatting opponents hostile to the state"* (Hannah Arendt). SYN: engage. **2** *Figurative.* to struggle against; take measures against: *The whole town turned out to combat the fire. All are dedicated to combating alcoholism* (Harper's). *We're all in favor of spending whatever is necessary to combat air pollution* (New York Times).
—*v.i.* to fight or struggle; battle (with or against): (*Figurative.*) *Death seemed combating with life* (Scott).
—*n.* **1** armed fighting between opposing forces; battle: *The soldier was wounded in combat. It* [*the U.S.S. Salu*] *will be armed with guided missiles and is designed for combat against land, air, sea and underwater enemies* (Newsweek). SYN: See syn. under **fight.** **2** a fight, especially between two; duel. **3** *Figurative.* any fight or struggle; conflict; contest: *a combat between two opposing systems of belief.*
—*adj.* of or for combat; having to do with combat: *combat boots, combat troops.*
[< Old French *combattre* < Late Latin *combattuere* < Latin *com-* together with + *battuere* beat] **—com′bat|a|ble,** *adj.*

com|bat|ant (kom′bə tənt, kum′-; kəm bat′ənt), *n., adj.* **—*n.*** one that takes part in combat; fighter: *The chief combatants in World War II were Germany, Italy, and Japan on one side and the United States, Great Britain, France, Russia, and China on the other.*
—*adj.* **1** fighting. **2** ready to fight; fond of fighting; combative. **3** *Military.* trained, equipped, and ready for fighting; actively fighting: *The Navy will be operating 1,005 ships, 411 of them combatant types* (Newsweek).

combat car, *U.S. Army.* any light armored motor vehicle used in combat.

com|bat|er (kom′ba tər, kum′-; kəm bat′ər), *n.* a person who combats; combatant.

combat fatigue, a state of nervous exhaustion that sometimes occurs among soldiers in active combat: *... the picture of psychological disorganization known as "combat fatigue" did not correspond either in its moderate or its extreme form to any recognized or established psychiatric syndrome* (James Phinney Baxter).

com|bat|ive (kəm bat′iv; kom′bə tiv, kum′-), *adj.* ready to fight or oppose; fond of fighting: *A good football team has a combative spirit.* SYN: pugnacious. **—com|bat′ive|ly,** *adv.* **—com|bat′ive-ness,** *n.*

com|ba|tiv|i|ty (kom′bə tiv′ə tē, kum′-), *n.* the quality or character of being combative; disposition to fight; pugnacity: *The judges stopped the bout in the second round and disqualified him for lack of combativity* (New Yorker).

combat neurosis, = shell shock.

com|bat-read|y (kom′bat red′ē, kum′-), *adj.* trained or tested for combat; fully prepared or equipped militarily: *a combat-ready, efficient armed force.*

combat team, a force composed of two or more units of different military branches acting together in battle: *In the line it was not called a regiment but a combat team, for it was composed of the 18th Infantry plus a battalion of field artillery and mobile anti-tank guns* (Ralph Ingersoll).

combat zone, 1 a region in a theater of operations where fighting takes place, extending from the front line to a line or boundary designated by the theater commander. **2** any area where combat takes place or is expected.

combe (küm, kōm), *n.* a deep hollow surrounded on three sides by hills; narrow valley. Also, **comb, coom, coomb.** [Old English *cumb,* probably < Celtic (compare Welsh *cwm*)]

combed yarn (kōmd), yarn made from fibers which have been straightened and separated from short fibers and tangles.

comb|er (kō′mər), *n.* **1** = breaker. **2** a person or thing that combs.

comb-foot|ed spider (kōm′fu̇t′id), any one of certain spiders having movable spines on the posterior legs, used to curl and bind the lines of silk coming from the spinnerets.

comb foundation, a thin sheet of beeswax made to resemble the middle wall of a honeycomb and placed in a hive for the bees to build upon.

comb honey, honey in the comb, or still containing portions of comb; unstrained honey.

com|bin|a|bil|i|ty (kəm bī′nə bil′ə tē), *n.* the fact or condition of being combinable.

com|bi|na|tion (kom′bə nā′shən), *n.* **1** the act or process of combining: *The combination of flour and water makes paste.* **2** the state of being combined; union: *The same images in the same combination* (Samuel Johnson). **3** one whole made by combining two or more different things: *The color purple is a combination of red and blue.* **4a** persons or groups joined together for some common purpose: *The farmers formed a combination to sell their crops at better prices.* SYN: league, combine. **b** *U.S.* an agreement, arrangement, or organization set up especially to secure illegal trading advantages: *a combination in restraint of trade.* SYN: conspiracy. **5a** the series of numbers or letters dialed in opening a combination lock: *Do you know the combination of the safe?* **b** = combination lock: *When the boy had gone he opened his safe again, moving the knob of the combination first left to 32—his age, secondly right to 10—the year of his birth, left again to 65* (Graham Greene). **6** *Mathematics.* **a** the arrangement or arranging of figures, letters, etc., in groups so that each group has a certain number of individuals. **b** the group thus formed. Possible two-letter combinations of *a, b,* and *c* are *ab, ac,* and *bc.* **7** *Chemistry.* **a** the union of substances to form a compound. **b** the resulting product or compound. **8** a suit of underwear having the shirt and drawers in one piece.

com|bi|na|tion|al (kom′bə nā′shə nəl), *adj.* of or having to do with combination.

combination door, a storm door with a panel or panels that can be removed and replaced with screens in the summer.

combination lock, a lock having a movable dial with numbers or letters on it. The lock will not open until the dial has been turned to certain numbers or letters in a certain order and a certain direction.

combination room, one of the common rooms at the University of Cambridge in England: *We returned to the combination room, and took our places for wine* (C. P. Snow).

combination tone, *Physics.* one of the tones generated through aural distortion by the sounding of two tones simultaneously, with a frequency equal to the sum or the difference of the frequencies of the sounded tones.

com|bi|na|tive (kom′bə nā′tiv, kəm bī′nə-), *adj.* **1** tending to combine; combining. **2** having to do with combination. **3** *Phonetics.* taking place through a combination of neighboring sounds. Dissimilation and metathesis are examples of combinative sound changes.

com|bin|a|to|ri|al (kəm bī′nə tôr′ē əl, -tōr′-), *adj.* **1** combinational. **2** of or having to do with combinatorics: *The combinatorial problem here involves 500 vans, 1,000 drivers, 5,000 services, five garages, 16 canteens* (Sunday Times). **—com|bin′a|to′ri|al|ly,** *adv.*

combinatorial analysis, the branch of higher mathematics which deals with analysis by means of combinations, permutations, etc.

combinatorial topology, *Geometry.* the branch of topology which deals with forms reduced to combinations of the simplest geometric figures.

com|bi|na|to|rics (kəm bī′nə tôr′iks, -tōr′-), *n. Mathematics.* the study of the permutations and combinations of elements in finite sets: *A final example of combinatorics can be expressed as a problem in genealogy* (Scientific American).

com|bin|a|to|ry (kəm bī′nə tôr′ē, -tōr′-), *adj.* = combinative.

com|bine (*v. 1, 2* kəm bīn′; *v. 3* kom′bīn; *n. 1* kom′bīn, kəm bīn′; *n. 2, 3* kom′bīn), *v.,* **-bined, -bin|ing,** *n.* **—*v.t.*** **1** to join things, persons, or groups together; unite: *to combine work and play. Our club combined the offices of secretary and treasurer so that one person could do the work of both. A sense of common danger might ... combine them in operations of defense* (James Mill). SYN: associate, ally, mix. See syn. under **join.** **2** to have or show in union or combination: (*Figurative.*) *a position which ... combined ... strength, beauty, and fertility* (Arthur Stanley). **3** to harvest with a combine: *Rains have knocked down the wheat in some fields, made it too moist to combine in others* (Wall Street Journal).
—*v.i.* **1** to unite or join; come together for a common purpose; form a combination: *The great landlords and the financiers had combined against the small bourgeoisie and the workers* (Edmund Wilson). SYN: confederate. **2** to unite to form a chemical compound: *Two atoms of hydrogen combine with one of oxygen to form water.* **3** to harvest with a combine: *Shall we start combining or do we wait until the grain has lost further 1 per cent of moisture?* (London Times).
—*n.* **1** a group of people joined together for some common purpose; combination: *His brother ... became the editor of the Socialist Daily Herald ... owned by the capitalist publishing combine of Odham's* (Maclean's). **2** *U.S.* a machine for harvesting and threshing grain, soybeans, etc. It cuts the stalks and separates the seeds from them as it moves across a field. *The chemical revolution on the farm is as responsible for the farmer's zooming production as his tractor and combine* (Newsweek). **3** an artistic work made up of a combination of painting, collage, and construction: *... the assemblages and combines of Robert Rauschenberg* (New Yorker).
[< Late Latin *combīnāre* < Latin *com-* together + *bīnī* two by two < *bis* twice] **—com|bin′a|ble,** *adj.* **—com|bin′er,** *n.*

com|bined (kəm bīnd′), *adj.* **1** joined together; united. **2** done by groups, persons, or things acting together. **—com|bin′ed|ly,** *adv.*

combined operations, 1 military operations carried on by two or more allies acting together. **2** military operations in which land, sea, and air forces cooperate; amphibious operations: *They* [*the troops*] *cannot land unless, in fact, combined operations are carried out* (Lord Louis Mountbatten).

comb|ing (kō′ming), *n.* the act of a person or thing that combs.
combings, hairs removed by a comb.

combing jacket, a loose jacket worn while dressing the hair: *That was the era when ladies slipped on combing jackets before brushing their long, unpermanented hair* (New Yorker).

combing wool, wool fibers over two inches long.

com|bin|ing form (kəm bī′ning), a form of a word used for combining with other words or other combining forms to make new words. *Examples: Psycho- + analysis = psychoanalysis; Franco- + -phile = Francophile; micro- + -graph = micrograph.* In *psychoanalysis, psycho-* is a combining form meaning "mind"; in *Francophile,*

Franco- is a combining form meaning "French," and *-phile* is a combining form meaning "a person who is fond of"; in *micrograph, micro-* is a combining form meaning "small; microscopic" and *-graph* is a combining form meaning "an instrument that records," or "something drawn or recorded."

combining weight, *Chemistry.* equivalent weight.

com|bite (kom bēt′), *n.* a form of cooperative farm work in Haiti, in which a group of neighbors help another work his field to the accompaniment of drums and singing. [< Haitian Creole *combite*]

comb jelly, = ctenophore.

com|bo (kom′bō), *n., pl.* **-bos.** *U.S. Informal.* **1** a group of musicians playing together regularly, usually smaller than a band or orchestra: *a jazz combo, a four-piece dance combo.* **2** combination: . . . *such desirable combos as lichens and infected pansies* (New Yorker). [short for *combination*]

comb-out (kōm′out′), *n.* **1** a combing or dressing of the hair. **2** the act of combing, searching, or clearing out: (*Figurative.*) *Security forces have already killed or captured about 40 of the infiltrators and the comb-out continues* (Observer).

comb rat, = ctenodactyl. [< the comb-shaped bristles on its hind feet]

com|bre|ta|ceous (kom′brə tā′shəs), *adj.* belonging to a family of tropical shrubs and trees yielding tanning and dyeing materials. [< New Latin *Combretaceae* the family name (< Latin *combrētum* a kind of rush) + English *-ous*]

com|bust (kəm bust′), *v., adj.* **—*v.t.*** to burn up; set ablaze: (*Figurative.*) *All Germany was combusted with great troubles* (Thomas Milles).
—*v.i.* to burn up; flame out; blaze forth: (*Figurative.*) *The government crisis . . . combusted against the looming background of the Common Market negotiations* (New Yorker).
—*adj.* *Astrology.* so near the sun as to be obscured by it: *a combust planet.*
[< Latin *combustus,* past participle of *combūrere;* see etym. under **combustion**]

com|bus|ti|bil|i|ty (kəm bus′tə bil′ə tē), *n.* combustible quality or condition; inflammability.

com|bus|ti|ble (kəm bus′tə bəl), *adj., n.* **—*adj.*** **1** capable of taking fire and burning; easy to burn; burnable: *Gasoline is highly combustible.* SYN: inflammable, flammable. **2** *Figurative.* easily excited; fiery. SYN: excitable.
—*n.* a combustible substance. Wood and coal are combustibles. **—com|bus′ti|ble|ness,** *n.* **—com|bus′ti|bly,** *adv.*

com|bus|tion (kəm bus′chən), *n.* **1** the act or process of burning; consumption or destruction by fire. Many houses are heated by combustion of coal, oil, or gas. *The explosion in the coal mine was caused by the combustion of gases.* **2** *Chemistry.* **a** rapid oxidation accompanied by heat and light, for example, when hydrogen burns in the atmosphere: *The majority of the examples of combustion encountered by the average man are those of the rapid oxidation of easily ignited materials by atmospheric oxygen* (W. N. Jones). **b** chemical combination attended by heat and light. **3** slow oxidation not accompanied by high temperature and light. Food is transformed into energy in an animal body by this type of combustion. **4** *Figurative.* violent excitement; tumult; confusion. SYN: commotion, disorder, hubbub. [< Latin *combustiō, -ōnis* < *combūrere* to burn, ultimately < *com-* completely + *ūrere* to burn]

***combustion chamber**, the chamber in which fuel is burned in an internal-combustion or jet engine, furnace, or rocket.

***combustion chamber**

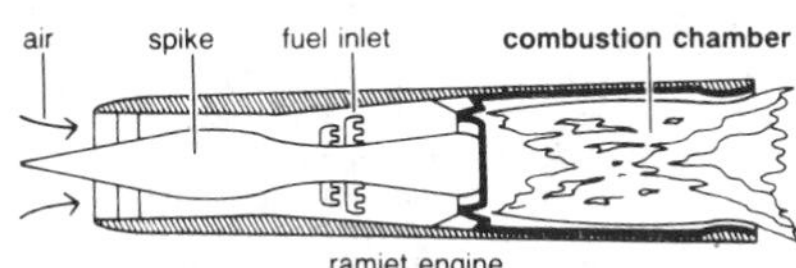

ramjet engine

com|bus|tive (kəm bus′tiv), *adj.* having to do with or characterized by combustion.

com|bus|tor (kəm bus′tər), *n.* the combustion chamber of a jet engine.

Comd., Commander.

comdg., commanding.

Comdr., Commander.

Comdt., Commandant.

come (kum), *v.,* **came, come, com|ing.** **—*v.i.*** **1** to move toward; approach: *Come this way. As soon as the cat came toward me, the dog got up and went away.* **2** to get near; arrive: *The girls will come home tomorrow. The bus comes at noon.* **3** to arrive at in due order or in due course: *We now come to the last problem. The time must come.* **4** to move into view; appear: *The sun comes and goes.* **5** to occur at a certain point or in a certain position: *The index of a book comes at the end.* **6** to reach; extend: *The dress comes to her knees.* **7** to take place; happen; occur: *Snow comes in winter. Life's a pleasant institution; Let us take it as it comes* (William S. Gilbert). **8** to happen (to a person); befall: *All things come alike to all* (Ecclesiastes 9:2). **9** to occur to the mind: *The idea just came to me.* **10** to be derived; issue: *Many English words came originally from the Latin. The noise is coming from the radio next door.* **11** to be born: *That boy comes from a poor family.* SYN: descend. **12** to be caused; result; be due: *You see what comes of meddling.* **13** *Figurative.* to be brought; pass; enter: *to come into fashion, use, or effect; to come to harm.* **14** to reach a desired state: *to churn milk until butter comes.* **15** to become: *The brown paper parcel had "come untied"* (Dickens). **16** to turn out to be: *Her dream came true.* **17** to be obtainable or sold; be available: *This soup comes in a can.* **18** *Imperative.* here! look! stop! behave!: *Come, come, Sikes—we must have civil words* (Dickens). **19** to germinate when sown; grow: *The corn is coming very well.*
—*v.t.* *Informal.* **1** to perform; practice: *He thought to come a trick over his old pal.* **2** to act the part of; play.

come about, a to take place; happen; occur: *Good books come about as the result of hard work.* **b** to turn around; change direction; tack: *A sailboat came about, heading back to the dock.*

come across, a to meet by chance; happen to meet; find: *He came across a rare book.* **b** *Slang.* to hand over; pay: *Come across with the dough!* **c** to reach the audience or the public (originally "across the footlights" was implied): *Magda, dressed as a comedy of manners . . . would probably come across more satisfactorily than it does played as . . . contemporary tragedy* (Westminster Gazette).

come again, *Slang.* what did you say? repeat that, please: *Come again? I can't hear you.*

come along, a to appear: *The party was dull until she came along.* **b** to make progress: *The sick boy seems to be coming along fine.* **c** *Informal.* hurry up; come on: *Come along, children, before it starts raining!*

come around (or **round**), **a** to return to consciousness or health; recover: *The milkman is coming around after his operation and will soon be back at work. She came round so far as to be helped downstairs* (Dickens). **b** *Figurative.* to give in; yield; agree: *His boss came round and gave him the raise.* **c** *Figurative.* to return to a better mood after a fit of bad temper: *He is angry, but he'll soon come around, cheerful as ever.* **d** to turn around; change direction or opinion: *Having reached a dead end, the car came around and headed back to the main road.*

come at, to rush toward; attack: *The man came at the bear with only a knife.*

come back, a to return: *Come back home. The dog ran off, but soon came back for another biscuit.* **b** to return to the memory; come to mind: *The name came back to him.* **c** *U.S. Slang.* to retort; retaliate: *He came back with, "I suppose you think you could do it better!"* **d** *Informal.* to return to a former position or condition: *to come back to normal.*

come between, to divide; separate: *It would be foolish to let a little thing like that come between us.*

come by, a to get; obtain; acquire: *He came by the money honestly.* **b** to pass near: *A large parade came by.*

come down, a to be handed down: *Many fables have come down through the ages.* **b** to lose position, rank, or money: *After the grandfather's death, the family came down in the world.* **c** *British.* to declare oneself; decide: . . . *and have come down . . . in favour of taking this action* (London Times). **d** *U.S. Slang.* to happen; occur: *What's the government doing for all those families; is it telling anybody what really came down there?* (Harper's).

come down on, a *Informal.* to scold; blame: *It's too bad to come down always on you, only because you're such a good fellow* (R. A. King). **b** to attack suddenly: *The treacherous enemy comes down upon a sleeping village* (Paul DuChaillu).

come down with, to become ill with: *He came down with the measles.*

come forward, to offer oneself for work or duty; volunteer: *Courageous people come forward in an emergency.*

come in, a to arrive at its destination: *When did you come in this morning? That horse came in fourth.* **b** to enter: *Come in, please.* **c** to be brought into use or fashion; begin: *A new fashion in hats has come in recently. After the Revolution, Jacobite plots came in* (Macaulay). **d** to reply to a radio operator's call or signal: *"This is Waco 1574 calling Cleveland tower; come in, Cleveland tower."*

come in for, a to get; receive; acquire: *Tornadoes come in for attention in the summer.* **b** to become heir to: *At twenty-one, she will come in for an inheritance.*

come into, a to inherit: *He came into an estate when his uncle died.* **b** to get; receive: *The poor widow came into some money and clothes through friends and relatives.*

come near, to come close to (doing something); almost (do): *I came near forgetting my glasses.*

come off, a to take place; happen; occur: *The rocket launching comes off next week.* **b** to turn out to be: *Their first meeting did not come off as he had expected.* **c** to finish in a certain manner: *to come off with flying colors. Our team came off with a great victory in last week's game.* **d** to result in success; succeed: *For all the effort . . . put into it, "Eugene Onegin" didn't really come off as a moving piece of musical theatre* (Wall Street Journal).

come off it, *Slang.* stop it; don't talk nonsense: *"Oh, come off it," I objected. "Nobody's going to go to all that trouble"* (S. J. Perelman).

come on, a to find or meet by chance: *Moving homeward [Enoch] came on Annie* (Tennyson). **b** *Figurative.* to improve; progress: *She is coming on well and will be out of the hospital next week.* **c** to make an entrance onto the stage: *He comes on in the last act.* **d** to begin: *When will the main feature come on?* **e** *Informal.* hurry up; let's go: *Come on, or we'll be late.* **f** *Informal.* please: *Come on, children, let's have a little quiet. Oh, come on, be serious.* **g** *Especially U.S. Slang.* to make a (specified) impression or effect: *[She] comes on sincere, gazing into eyes, fondly grasping hands* (New York Times). *He is the youngest of the Secretaries, and he comes on as the can-do guy* (Atlantic).

come out, a to be revealed or shown: *The sun came out from behind the clouds. The truth will come out.* **b** to take place in the end; result: *The ball game came out in our favor.* **c** to be offered to the public; be published: *The book will come out next fall.* **d** to put in an appearance: *How many boys came out for baseball?* **e** to declare oneself (in some way): *He has come out for lower taxes.* **f** to turn out to be: *The sum comes out ten.* **g** to make a debut: *Her daughter came out at a fashionable club.*

come out with, a to say; speak: *Come out with it, man! Speak up!* **b** to offer to the public: *The company came out with a new dictionary.*

come over, to take hold of; happen to; befall: (*Figurative.*) *A change has come over him.*

come tardy off, *Archaic.* to fall short: *The work is better overdone than come tardy off* (Leverett).

come through, *U.S.* **a** to be successful; win; succeed: *Clarke was the most relieved man in seven counties when O'Toole came through with that victory in Boston* (Christopher Mathewson). **b** to last through successfully: *He came through the fight without a scratch.* **c** to undergo religious conversion: *Pretty soon it began to look like she was going to come through as Amos Hurd did when he was redeemed* (Gene Porter).

come through with, *Slang.* to hand over; pay: *If he comes through with the money he owes me, we'll be able to leave as planned.*

come to, a to return to consciousness; revive: *He came to slowly after the accident. He had just been all but choked and had that moment come to* (Dickens). **b** *Figurative.* to be equal; amount: *The bill came to $5.* **c** *Nautical.* to stop; anchor: *They resolved . . . to come to, and rest themselves for the night* (Archibald Duncan). **d** *Figurative.* to result in: *If worst comes to worst.*

come up, a to come into being; arise; develop: *The question is not likely to come up.* **b** *British.* to come to a place viewed as higher, especially to a university: *He is coming up to Balliol College next term.*

come up against, to meet suddenly or unexpectedly: *to come up against an obstacle. I have come up against all kinds of censorship* (Clive Goodwin).

come upon, a to meet by chance; find: *We came upon a rabbit in the woods. Out on the road, she came upon a stray dog.* **b** to rush toward or attack: *Suddenly the brush fire came upon them from all sides.*

come up to, to compare with; equal: *His athletic record doesn't come up to the champion's.*

come up with, to produce; improvise: *to come*

up with a solution.
how come, *Informal.* how does (did) it come that: *How come you didn't call me last night?*
where one is coming from, *U.S. Slang.* what one thinks or feels: *The book is a record of what the natives are into, what they have going, . . . where they're coming from, and what's coming down* (New Yorker).
[Middle English *comen,* Old English *cuman*]
— ***Syn.*** *v.i.* **2 Come, arrive** mean to get to a place or point. **Come** emphasizes the movement or progress involved in getting to a place or point: *We came to a conclusion.* **Arrive** emphasizes the idea of reaching an end or goal: *A letter arrived today. We arrived at the airport.*

come-all-ye (kum′ôl yē), *n.* a folk song or ballad of England, Ireland, or Canada. [< *Come all ye,* a frequent first line in such ballads]

come-and-go (kum′ən gō′), *n., adj. Informal.* —***n.*** activity; bustle; comings and goings: *His freedom to choose will lead him to destruction if he retreats before the come-and-go of his time* (Time).
—***adj.*** passing quickly; not lasting or regular: *Come-and-go particles and packets of energy have a merely temporary existence.*

come-at-a|ble (kum at′ə bəl), *adj. Informal.* easily reached or obtained; accessible.

come|back (kum′bak′), *n.* **1** *Informal.* a return to a former condition or position: *Then after his near-fatal auto crash in 1949* [*Ben Hogan*] *made his famous comeback at Merion, Pa., by triumphing in 1950* (New York Times). **2** *U.S. Slang.* a clever answer; sharp reply. **3** *Slang.* a cause for complaining: *He was given a fair trial and had no comeback.*

Com|e|con or **COMECON** (kom′ə kon), *n.* the trade association of Communist countries. [< *Co*(uncil for) *M*(utual) *Econ*(omic) Assistance]

co|me|di|an (kə mē′dē ən), *n.* **1** an actor in comedies; actor of comic parts: *A comedian played the part of the fool.* **2** *Figurative.* a person who amuses others with his funny talk and actions, often acting in a foolish or irresponsible way: *That boy is always playing pranks and is a comedian no one takes seriously.* **3** a writer of comedies. [< Middle French *comédien*]

co|me|dic (kə mē′dik), *adj.* of the nature of comedy; comic: *The play begins casually, with a comedic tone* (Saturday Review). —**co|me′di|cal|ly,** *adv.*

co|mé|die de moeurs (kô mā dē′ də mœrs′), *French.* comedy of manners.

co|mé|die lar|mo|yante (kô mā dē′ lȧr mwȧ-yäɴt′), *French.* larmoyant comedy; comedy of a sentimental or romantic type.

co|me|di|enne (kə mē′dē en′), *n.* an actress in comedies; actress of comic parts. [< French *comédienne,* feminine of *comédien* comedian]

co|mé|die noire (kô mā dē′ nwȧr′), *French.* black comedy.

co|mé|di|et|ta (kə mē′dē et′ə), *n.* **1** a short comedy. **2** a comedy of slight character. [< Italian *commedietta* (diminutive) < *commèdia* comedy]

com|e|dist (kom′ə dist), *n.* a writer of comedies.

com|e|do (kom′ə dō), *n., pl.* **-do|nes** (-dō′nēz), **-dos.** *Medicine.* a blackhead. [< Latin *comedō* glutton, gourmand (in Medieval Latin, worm) < *comedere* devour < *com-* thoroughly + *edere* eat]

come|down (kum′doun′), *n. Informal.* a loss of position, rank, or money which is unexpected: *"It's quite a comedown from being a ten-thousand-dollar-a-year man to this, but I'll come back"* (James T. Farrell).

com|e|dy (kom′ə dē), *n., pl.* **-dies. 1** an amusing play or show having a happy ending: *All comedies are ended by a marriage* (Byron). **2** such plays or shows as a class; branch of drama concerned with such plays: *Restoration dramatists preferred comedy to tragedy.* **3** *Figurative.* an amusing happening; funny incident: *Our picnic in the rain was a comedy of errors and mishaps.* **4a** the comic element of drama or literature, or of life in general: *the human comedy.* **b** a sublime subject treated objectively, regardless of comic or tragic overtones: *Dante's Divine Comedy.* **5** any literary work having a theme suited to comedy or using the methods of comedy. [< Latin *cōmœdia* < Greek *kōmōidiā* < *kōmōidós* actor or singer in a comic chorus < *kômos* merrymaking + *aoidós* singer < *aeídein* sing < *audē* human voice]

comedy drama, a dramatic play containing an element of comedy and usually having a happy ending: *. . . a deft comedy drama, with credible characters and intelligent, crackling dialogue* (New York Times).

comedy of manners, comedy marked by wit and social satire: *The comedy of manners was a type of play that pictured the gay, immoral world of the aristocracy. These plays were Restoration drama at its best* (R. W. Stallman).

come-hith|er (kum′hiTH′ər), *n., adj.* —***n.*** **1** an inviting or persuasive call to a child or animal. **2** *Informal.* an alluring invitation; enticement: *Nancy Reed . . . in whose ballads there is plenty of come-hither* (New Yorker).
—***adj.*** *Informal.* inviting; alluring: *come-hither eyes, a come-hither voice.*

come-late|ly (kum′lāt′lē), *adj.* lately or newly arrived; Johnny-come-lately: *I didn't object to his being come-lately, of course. The naturalized are often the most patriotic* (New Yorker).

come|ly (kum′lē), *adj.,* **-li|er, -li|est. 1** pleasant to look at; attractive: [*She*] *might be rather called comely than beautiful* (John Gay). **SYN:** pretty, handsome. **2** fitting; suitable; proper. **SYN:** decent, becoming, decorous, seemly. [Middle English *cumli,* Old English *cȳmlic* finely made, handsome; spelling influenced by *come*] —**come′li|ness,** *n.*

come-on (kum′on′, -ôn′), *n. Informal.* something offered to attract or allure; enticement; inducement: *The grocery cut the price of milk as a come-on to customers. "In six easy lessons" is an old come-on* (Saturday Review).

come-out|er (kum′ou′tər), *n. U.S.* a person who separates himself from an established organization; a social or political reformer: *If our society is to survive it must provide an atmosphere in which just such misfits and eccentrics and come-outers can flourish* (New York Times).

co|me pri|ma (kō′mā prē′mä), *Italian, Music.* as at first (a direction for the repetition of an effect).

com|er (kum′ər), *n.* **1** a person who comes. **SYN:** visitor, arrival. **2** a person who has recently come. **3** *Informal.* a person who seems likely to succeed or shows promise.

co|me so|pra (kō′mā sō′prä), *Italian, Music.* as above (a direction for the repetition of an effect).

co|mes|ti|ble (kə mes′tə bəl), *n., adj.* —***n.*** Often, **comestibles.** a thing to eat; article of food: *The world's food supply has become only slightly more radioactive since 1945, and in most categories of comestibles there is no slightest threat to health* (Time). [< adjective]
—***adj.*** *Obsolete.* eatable; edible.
[< Late Latin *comestibilis* edible < Latin *comēstus,* variant of *comēsus,* past participle of *comedere* consume < *com-* thoroughly + *edere* eat]

*** com|et** (kom′it), *n.* **1** a bright heavenly body with a starlike center and often with a cloudy tail of light which always points away from the sun. Comets move around the sun like planets, but in an oval course. We can see comets only when they come close to the earth. *The diameters of the heads of comets average 80,000 miles, approximately the size of Jupiter* (Wasley S. Krogdahl). **2** a fancy variety of goldfish. [< Latin *comēta* < Greek *komḗtēs* wearing long hair < *komân* let the hair grow long < *kómē* hair]

***comet**
definition 1

com|e|tar|y (kom′ə ter′ē), *adj.* **1** of or having to do with a comet: *cometary orbits.* **2** like a comet.

co|meth|er (kə meTH′ər), *n. Irish or Informal.* an inviting, persuasive, or controlling influence.
put one's (or **the**) **comether on,** to persuade; influence; coax; wheedle: *We must buy him, or put the comether on him* (Harper's).
[< *come hither*]

co|met|ic (kə met′ik), *adj.* = cometary.

com|et|oid (kom′ə toid), *adj.* like a comet.

comet seeker or **finder,** a telescope of low power but with a wide field, used in searching for comets.

come|up|pance (kum′up′əns), *n. Informal.* one's just deserts: *In his arrogance, he even challenges the British Open champion, and thereby nearly gets his comeuppance* (New Yorker). [< special use of the phrase *come up* + *-ance*]

Com|ex or **com|ex** (kom′əks), *n.* = commodity exchange.

com|fit (kum′fit, kom′-), *n., v.* —***n.*** a piece of candy; sweetmeat; bonbon. —***v.t.*** *Obsolete.* to preserve with sugar; make into a candy.
[< Old French *confit* < Latin *confectus* prepared, past participle of *conficere* < *com-* together + *facere* make]

com|fort (kum′fərt), *v., n.* —***v.t.*** **1** to ease the grief or sorrow of; cheer: *The mother's words of love and help comforted the crying girl.* **2** to give ease to; make comfortable: *The nurse comforted the patient by tidying up his bed.* **3** *Law.* to help; support.
—***n.*** **1a** anything that makes trouble or sorrow easier to bear; consolation: *The news that their missing son was well brought great comfort to his parents.* **b** the feeling of relief or consolation. **2** a person or thing that makes life easier or takes away hardship: *His dog was a great comfort to the lost hunter. Social security is a comfort to retired persons.* **3** a cause or matter of satisfaction; something reassuring: *Knowing that the police would protect him was a comfort to the witness.* **4a** freedom from pain or hardship; ease: *My father makes enough money for us to live in comfort.* **SYN:** See syn. under **ease. b** the conditions which produce or promote such a state: *brought up in comfort and elegance.* **5** *U.S. Dialect.* a comforter for a bed. **6** *Law.* help; support: *Giving aid and comfort to an enemy is called treason.*
[< Old French *conforter* < Late Latin *confortāre* strengthen < Latin *com-* together + *fortis* strong]
— ***Syn.*** *v.t.* **1 Comfort, console** mean to ease sorrow, trouble, or pain. **Comfort** means to ease the grief or sorrow of a person by making him more cheerful and giving him hope or strength: *Neighbors comforted the parents of the injured child.* **Console,** more formal, means to make grief or trouble easier to bear by doing something to lighten it or make the person forget it temporarily: *The pastor tried to console the grieving widow.*

com|fort|a|ble (kumf′tə bəl, kum′fər-), *adj., n.* —***adj.*** **1** giving comfort or ease: *A soft, warm bed is comfortable.* **SYN:** snug, cozy. **2** in comfort; at ease: *The warm fire made him feel comfortable after a cold day outdoors. I feel comfortable about her now that she is with you. Shy people are seldom comfortable speaking to large groups.* **SYN:** easeful, relaxed. **3** easy; tranquil; undisturbed: *a comfortable sleep.* **SYN:** peaceful. **4** *Informal.* enough for one's needs: *He has a comfortable income.* **SYN:** adequate, satisfactory. **5** *Obsolete.* cheerful.
—***n.*** *U.S.* a comforter for a bed. —**com′fort|a|ble|ness,** *n.* —**com′fort|a|bly,** *adv.*

com|fort|er (kum′fər tər), *n.* **1** a person or thing that gives comfort: *The doctor is the best of comforters* (Henry Fielding). **2** *U.S.* a padded or quilted covering for a bed. **3** a long woolen scarf. **4** a rubber nipple put into a baby's mouth to quiet it; pacifier.

Com|fort|er (kum′fər tər), *n.* **the,** the Holy Spirit (in the Bible, John 14:26).

com|fort|ing (kum′fər ting), *adj.* that comforts or consoles; cheering; encouraging: *Let's have a bit of truth, . . . you don't know how tired I am of comforting lies* (Graham Greene). —**com′fort|ing|ly,** *adv.*

com|fort|less (kum′fərt lis), *adj.* **1** bringing no comfort or ease of mind: *comfortless words.* **2** having none of the comforts of life: *a comfortless room.* —**com′fort|less|ly,** *adv.* —**com′fort|less|ness,** *n.*

comfort station, *U.S.* a public lavatory: *At the oil stations are the comfort stations for ladies and for gents* (American Speech).

com|frey (kum′frē), *n., pl.* **-freys.** any of a group of European and Asiatic plants of the borage family, formerly used in treating wounds. [< Old French *confirie,* dialectal variant of *confierge* < Vulgar Latin *cōnfervia,* Latin *cōnferva* a kind of water plant < *cōnfervēre* knit (of bones) < *com-* together + *fervēre* boil (perhaps for its alleged bone-healing properties)]

com|fy (kum′fē), *adj.,* **-fi|er, -fi|est.** *Informal.* comfortable. —**com′fi|ly,** *adv.*

com|ic (kom′ik), *adj., n.* —***adj.*** **1** causing laughter or smiles; amusing; funny: *He developed comic formulas about stupid bridge players* [*and*] *henpecked husbands* (Reporter). **2a** of comedy, as distinct from tragedy: *a comic plot. Punch and Judy are stock comic characters.* **b** acting in or composing comedy: *a comic actor or dramatist.*
—***n.*** **1** = comedian. **2** a comic motion picture, especially an animated cartoon. **3** *Informal.* = comic book.
comics, comic strips; funnies: *The best known hero of the comics is Superman.*
the comic, the amusing or funny side of anything, especially literature, life, or the like: *No two species of writing can differ more widely than the comic and the burlesque* (Henry Fielding).
[< Latin *cōmicus* < Greek *kōmikós* having to do with comedy < *kômos* a merrymaking]

com|i|cal (kom′ə kəl), *adj.* **1** amusing; funny: *a comical scene, a comical performance. The little girl looked comical in her mother's dress and hat.* **SYN:** laughable. **2** *Dialect.* queer; strange; odd. **3** *Obsolete.* of comedy. **4** *Obsolete.* (of style) befitting comedy; trivial; low. —**com′i|cal|ly,** *adv.* —**com′i|cal|ness,** *n.*

com|i|cal|i|ty (kom′ə kal′ə tē), *n., pl.* **-ties. 1** comical quality. **2** something comical.

comic book, a magazine of comic strips.

comic opera, an amusing light opera having some spoken dialogue.

com|ics (kom′iks), *n.pl.* See under **comic.**

comic strip, a group of drawings, sometimes funny, often presenting an adventure or a series of happenings.

Com|in|form (kom′in fôrm), *n.* an international Communist organization intended to coordinate and spread the propaganda of Communist parties throughout the world, formed in 1947 and dissolved in 1956. [< *Com*(munist) *Inform*(ation Bureau); patterned on *Comintern*]

com|ing (kum′ing), *n., adj.* —*n.* **1** a drawing near; approach; arrival: *the coming of summer.* **SYN**: advent. **2** Often, **Coming.** Christ's Second Advent.
—*adj.* **1** approaching; next: *He plans to travel to Europe this coming summer.* **SYN**: forthcoming, impending. **2** *Informal.* on the way to importance or fame: *He is a coming politician.* **SYN**: promising.

com|ing-in (kum′ing in′), *n., pl.* **com|ings-in.** entrance; introduction.

co|min|gle (kə ming′gəl), *v.t., v.i.,* **-gled, -gling.** commingle; mingle together. [< *co-* + *mingle*]

com|ing-out (kum′ing out′), *n.* the act or occasion of making a debut; coming-out party.

coming-out party, a formal party or reception celebrating the introduction of a young woman into the established polite society of a given city or region; debut.

comings and goings, back-and-forth activity; goings on: *With all these comings and goings, it is hardly surprising that politics has become the main determinant of the world's stock markets* (Punch).

Com|in|tern (kom′in tėrn, kom′in tėrn′), *n.* the Third International, an organization founded at Moscow in 1919 to promote Communist revolution in countries outside Russia and dissolved in 1943: *The Comintern had been controlled by the Moscow dictatorship, but outwardly represented the Communist parties of the Soviet Union, Bulgaria, Czechoslovakia, France, Hungary, Italy, Poland and Rumania* (Kenneth Colegrove). Also, **Komintern.** [< Russian *Komintern,* abbreviation of *Kom*(*munisticheskij*) *Intern*(*acional*) Com(munist) Intern(ational)]

com|i|ta|tive (kom′ə tā′tiv), *adj., n. Grammar.*
—*adj.* expressing accompaniment or connection; associative.
—*n.* a comitative case, affix, etc.
[< Latin *comitātus,* past participle of *comitārī* accompany]

com|i|ta|tus (kom′ə tā′təs), *n.* **1** a body of warriors or nobles attached to a king or chieftain. **2** the relationship of such a body to their king or chieftain. [< Latin *comitātus* an escort]

co|mi|ti|a (kə mish′ē ə), *n., pl.* **-ti|a.** a meeting of ancient Roman citizens to pass laws, elect officials, and act upon other public matters. There were many comitia; the one that ended in 27 B.C. was the *Comitia Tributa.* [< Latin *comitia,* plural of *comitium* a meeting place < *com-* together + *itus, -ūs* a going < *īre* go]

co|mi|tial (kə mish′əl), *adj.* of or having to do with the comitia.

co|mi|ti|va (kō′mē tē′vä), *n., pl.* **-ve** (-vā). *Italian.* an organized band of brigands or lawless persons.

com|i|trag|e|dy (kom′ə traj′ə dē), *n., pl.* **-dies.** a tragedy containing an element of comedy: *Through this comitragedy the excuse of "self-defense" was woven like a thread* (Atlantic). [< *comi*(c) + *tragedy*]

com|i|ty (kom′ə tē), *n., pl.* **-ties.** courtesy; civility: *It is the rule of mere comity and courtesy to agree where you can* (Emerson). [< Latin *cōmitās* affability, friendliness < *cōmis* friendly, courteous]

comity of nations, 1 the respect shown by one nation for the laws and customs of another. **2** the nations practicing such respect.

coml. or **coml** (no period), commercial.

comm., 1 commentary. **2** commerce.

Comm., an abbreviation for the following:
1 Commander.
2 Commission.
3 Committee.
4 Commonwealth.

*__com|ma__ (kom′ə), *n.* **1** a mark (,) of punctuation. Commas are used chiefly to show interruptions in the thought or in the structure of a sentence, and to separate the parts of an address or other series of words or numbers. **2** in ancient prosody: **a** a fragment of a colon. **b** the part of a verse in dactylic hexameter that ends or begins with the caesura. **c** the caesura itself. [< Latin *comma* < Greek *kómma* piece cut off < *kóptein* to cut off, strike]

***comma**

definition 1

,

But, he added, ...

Bob, Don, and Jerry

comma bacillus, the comma-shaped bacterium that causes Asiatic cholera.

comma fault, *Grammar.* a comma between related main clauses not connected by a coordinate conjunction; comma splice. *Example:* We were early, hence we waited outside.
► Comma fault should be avoided in formal writing. A semicolon or period may be used instead of the comma.

com|mand (kə mand′, -mänd′), *v., n.* —*v.t.* **1** to give an order to; order; direct: *The captain commanded the soldiers to fire.* **2** to prescribe with authority; ordain; require: *I commanded that the gates should be shut* (Nehemiah 13:19). **3** to be in authority over; have power over; be master of: *The captain commands his ship.* **SYN**: govern, rule. **4** to control by position; rise high above; control strategically; overlook: *The fortress stands on a hill that commands the river.* **5** to be able to have and use: *He cannot command so large a sum of money.* **6** *Figurative.* to deserve and get; force to be given: *Food commands a higher price when it is scarce.* **SYN**: exact. **7** *Obsolete.* to demand with authority.
—*v.i.* **1** to give orders; issue commands: *He was a natural leader, and when he commanded, everyone obeyed.* **2** to have power; exercise authority; rule; control: *Some men are born to command.* **3** to act as commander: *A disaster of war Caesar himself could not have prevented, if he had been there to command* (Shakespeare). **4** to occupy a dominating position; stand overlooking or in control: *a strong built tower, commanding o'er the Loire* (Robert Southey).
—*n.* **1a** an order; direction: *The soldiers obeyed the captain's command.* **SYN**: charge, injunction, mandate. **b** an oral order in prescribed words given to troops, especially at drill. **2** the possession of authority; power; control: *The general is in command of the army.* (*Figurative.*) *High command spake in his eye* (Byron). **3a** the soldiers, ships, or region under a person who has the right to command them: *The captain knew every man in his command.* **b** the position of control or authority: *The general held commands on several fronts during the invasion.* **4** mastery or control by position. **5** outlook (over); range of vision; prospect. **6** ability to have and use; mastery: *An interesting storyteller has a good command of words.* **7** the act of commanding or ordering; bidding. **8a** a pulse, signal, or set of signals initiating one step in the performance of a computer operation. **b** a pulse, signal, or set of signals activating a mechanism or initiating a step or sequence in a spacecraft. **9** *British.* a royal invitation.
at one's command, at one's disposal; available: *Yet has he seldom a guinea at command* (Sir Richard Steele).
[< Old French *comander* < Vulgar Latin *commandāre,* alteration of Latin *commendāre;* see etym. under **commend**]
—*Syn. v.t.* **1 Command, order, direct** mean to tell someone to do something. **Command** means to give an order with authority in a formal way: *The sentry commanded him to halt.* **Order** also means to tell with authority, in a less official and more personal way: *I was ordered to behave.* **Direct** suggests giving instructions rather than a formal order: *She directed me to the bus stop.*

com|mand|a|ble (kə man′də bəl, -män′-), *adj.* that can be commanded.

com|man|dant (kom′ən dant′, -dänt′), *n.* **1** a commander. **2** the officer in command of a fort, naval station, military school, district, or the like. *Abbr:* Comdt. [< French *commandant,* originally present participle of *commander* to command, Old French *comander;* see etym. under **command**]

com|man|dant|ship (kom′ən dant′ship, -dänt′-), *n.* the office or position of a commandant.

command car, *U.S. Army.* a vehicle for use by a commander, equipped with a radio and having a collapsible roof and removable doors.

com|man|deer (kom′ən dir′), *v.t.* **1** to seize (private property) for military or public use: *The policeman commandeered a taxicab to chase the fleeing bank robber. The officers of one of the gold-mining companies were similarly commandeered and assigned to us* (Robert S. S. Baden-Powell). **2** *Informal, Figurative.* to take by force or in a forceful manner: *In a picnic park near Toronto a family had commandeered a table and set their barbecue up beside it* (Maclean's). **3** to force (men) into military service. [< Afrikaans *kommandeer* < French *commander* to command, Old French *comander;* see etym. under **command**]

com|mand|er (kə man′dər, -män′-), *n.* **1** a person who commands; ruler; leader. Anyone who has people or supplies under his control is the commander of them. *The commander of the fleet ordered his ships to attack the pirates.* **SYN**: chief, head. **2a** an officer in charge of an army or part of an army. **b** an officer in charge of a fort, camp, warship, aircraft, or the like: ... *a wartime PT-boat commander* (Newsweek). **3** an officer in the navy, ranking next below a captain and next above a lieutenant commander. *Abbr:* Comdr. **4** a member of high rank in an order of knighthood or a society. **5** a member of high rank in certain medieval military orders, such as the Knights Hospitalers.

commander in chief, *pl.* **commanders in chief. 1** the person who has complete command of the armed forces of a country. The President is the commander in chief in the United States. **2** the officer in command of a major part of an army or navy.

com|mand|er|ship (kə man′dər ship, -män′-), *n.* the office or position of a commander.

com|mand|er|y (kə man′dər ē, -män′-), *n., pl.* **-er|ies. 1** the office or district of a military commander. **2a** the district controlled by a commander in certain medieval orders of knights. **b** a pension or benefice received by the commander of a medieval order. **3** a local branch or lodge in certain secret orders.

command flag, a flag flown on a naval ship to show the title or command of any flag officer on board.

command guidance, a system used in controlling and regulating the flight of a guided missile or other flight-borne object by means of remote electronic pulses or signals: *It is generally assumed in the United States that the Russian intercontinental ballistic missile has command guidance—that is to say it must reply on instructions from the ground reaching it* (Manchester Guardian).

com|mand|ing (kə man′ding, -män′-), *adj.* **1** in command: *a commanding officer, the commanding ship of the fleet.* **2** controlling; powerful: *commanding influences.* **SYN**: compelling. **3** authoritative; impressive: *a commanding voice.* **SYN**: imperious. **4** having a position of control: *a commanding tower.* —**com|mand′ing|ly,** *adv.* —**com|mand′ing|ness,** *n.*

commanding officer, an officer in command, especially a commissioned officer in the armed forces commanding a unit or installation. *Abbr:* CO (no periods).

com|mand|ment (kə mand′mənt, -mänd′-), *n.* **1** one of the ten laws that, according to the Bible, God gave to Moses (in the Bible, Exodus 20:2-17; Deuteronomy 5:6-21). "Thou shalt not kill" is one of the Ten Commandments. **2** any law, order, or direction. **SYN**: mandate, decree, edict. **3** *Obsolete.* the act or fact of commanding; bidding; command.

command module, the unit or section of a spacecraft, which contains the control center, reentry equipment, and living quarters of the astronauts: *The conical-shaped command module is the only portion of the ... spacecraft that returns safely to earth* (William G. Holder). *Abbr:* CM (no periods).

com|man|do or **Com|man|do** (kə man′dō, -män′-), *n., pl.,* **-dos** or **-does. 1** a soldier trained to make brief, daring, surprise raids upon enemy territory. **2** a group of such soldiers. **3** in South Africa: **a** an armed force raised by Portuguese or Dutch settlers against bandits and marauders, or by the Boers against the British. **b** a raid by such a force. [< Afrikaans *kommando,* Dutch, a troop under a commander < Portuguese, a command < *commandar* to command < Vulgar Latin *commandāre;* see etym. under **command**]

command paper, = white paper (def. 2). [because it is technically submitted to the House of Commons on command of the Crown]

command performance, a stage performance, motion picture, or the like, given before royalty by request or order.

command post, *U.S. Army.* the headquarters of a unit and its center of operations in the field.

com|man|dress (kə man′dris, -män′-), *n.* a female commander.

comma splice, = comma fault.

comma tract, a tract of white nerve fibers found within the posterior external column of the spinal cord.

com|meas|ure (kə mezh′ər, -mā′zhər), *v.t.,* **-ured, -ur|ing.** to equal in measure; be coextensive with. —**com|meas′ur|a|ble,** *adj.*

comme ci, comme ça (kôm sē′, kôm sá′), *French.* so-so; passable: *I am very young. My career is since two years. My artistry is comme ci comme ça* (Punch).

com|me|dia dell' ar|te (kôm me′dyä del lär′tā), *Italian.* an old form of comedy, originating in Italy, performed by a company of professional actors representing stock character types but improvising their speeches: *Like burlesque, the Piccolo*

Pronunciation Key: hat, āge, cãre, fär; let, ēqual, tėrm; it, īce; hot, ōpen, ôrder; oil, out; cup, pu̇t, rüle; child; long; thin; ᴛʜen; zh, measure;
ə represents **a** in about, **e** in taken, **i** in pencil, **o** in lemon, **u** in circus.

Teatro is folk theatre, and "The Servant of Two Masters" is in the tradition, somewhat cleaned up and formalized, of the commedia dell' arte (Harper's).

comme il faut (kô mēl fō′), *French.* as it should be; proper: *... dresses all comme il faut with Peter Pan collars* (New Yorker).

com|mel|i|na|ceous (kə mel′ə nā′shəs), *adj.* belonging to the spiderwort family of plants. [< New Latin *Commelinaceae* (< *Commelina* the typical genus < Kaspar, 1667-1731, and Johann, 1629-1698, *Commelin,* Dutch botanists) + English *-ous*]

com|mem|o|ra|ble (kə mem′ə rə bəl), *adj.* worthy of commemoration.

com|mem|o|rate (kə mem′ə rāt), *v.t.,* **-rat|ed, -rat|ing. 1** to honor the memory of: *Christmas commemorates Christ's birth.* **SYN**: observe, celebrate. **2** to preserve the memory of: *Roman emperors built arches to commemorate their victories.* [< Latin *commemorāre* (with English *-ate*[1]) recall, relate < *com-* together + *memorāre* mention, bring to mind < *memor* mindful of, remembering] — **com|mem′o|ra′tor,** *n.*

com|mem|o|ra|tion (kə mem′ə rā′shən), *n.* **1** the act of commemorating. **2** a service or celebration in memory of some person or event: *The Church of England ... set apart days for the commemoration of some who had done and suffered great things for the faith* (Macaulay).
in commemoration of, to honor the memory of: *Memorial Day is observed in commemoration of the soldiers and sailors who died for their country.*

com|mem|o|ra|tion|al (kə mem′ə rā′shə nəl), *adj.* = commemorative.

com|mem|o|ra|tive (kə mem′ə rā′tiv, -ər ə-), *adj., n.* — ***adj.*** preserving or honoring the memory of some person or event: *Commemorative postage stamps are issued to honor a famous person or to celebrate a historical event.*
— ***n.* 1** a commemorative stamp or coin: *The U.N. ... brought its average printing of commemoratives down from four million to two and a quarter million* (New Yorker). **2** anything that commemorates. — **com|mem′o|ra′tive|ly,** *adv.*

com|mem|o|ra|to|ry (kə mem′ər ə tôr′ē, -tōr′-), *adj.* = commemorative.

com|mence (kə mens′), *v.,* **-menced, -menc|ing.** — ***v.i.* 1** to begin; start: *The play will commence at eight o'clock. I have wondered many times what I might do with the money, once I commenced to collect my Social Security* (Peter Smith). **SYN**: See syn. under **begin. 2** *Archaic.* to begin to be; become. **3** *British.* to take a degree at a university.
— ***v.t.*** to begin (an action); enter upon: *A sharp blow of the umpire's whistle commenced play. The injured customer commenced a lawsuit after falling in the store.* **SYN**: See syn. under **begin.**
[< Old French *comencer* < Vulgar Latin *cominitiāre* < Latin *com-* together + *initiāre* begin < *initium* a beginning < *inīre* go in < *in-* in + *īre* go] — **com|menc′er,** *n.*

com|mence|ment (kə mens′mənt), *n.* **1** the act or fact of commencing. **2** time of commencing; beginning; start: *to look forward to the commencement of spring; ... the origin and commencement of this grief* (Shakespeare). **3a** the day during which diplomas or certificates are given by colleges and schools to persons who have completed the required courses of study; day of graduation. **b** the ceremonies on this day; exercises of graduation. **c** the period during which this day falls, in which banquets, class reunions, and other special events are held.

com|mend (kə mend′), *v.t.* **1** to speak well of; praise: *The teacher commended those students who got high grades.* **SYN**: extol. See syn. under **praise. 2** to mention favorably; recommend. **3** to hand over for safekeeping; entrust: *She commended the child to her aunt's care. The dying man commended his soul to God.* **SYN**: commit. **4** *Archaic.* to convey the regards or best wishes of (one person) to another. [< Latin *commendāre* < *com-* + *mandāre* commit, entrust, ultimately < *manum dare* give to the hand] — **com|mend′er,** *n.* — **com|mend′ing|ly,** *adv.*

com|mend|a|ble (kə men′də bəl), *adj.* deserving praise or approval: *Liberality and bounty are exceedingly commendable* (Alban Butler). **SYN**: praiseworthy, laudable. — **com|mend′a|ble|ness,** *n.* — **com|mend′a|bly,** *adv.*

com|men|dam (kə men′dam), *n. Ecclesiastical.* **1** the holding of a benefice by someone in the absence of a regular clergyman. Such a benefice is said to be held *in commendam.* **2** the benefice so held. [< Medieval Latin (*dare*) *in commendam* (give) into (someone's) charge; *commenda* an entrusting < Latin *commendāre;* see etym. under **commend**]

com|men|da|tion (kom′ən dā′shən), *n.* **1** the act of commending; praise; approval: *Good work deserves commendation.* **SYN**: eulogy, encomium. **2** favorable mention; recommendation. **SYN**: approbation. **3** a handing over to another for safekeeping; entrusting.
commendations, *Archaic.* complimentary greetings; respects: *Her uneasiness ... was removed, by the arrival of Whittaker, with her husband's commendations* (Scott).

com|men|da|to|re (kə men′də tôr′ē, -tōr′-), *n.* **1** a member of an Italian chivalric order. **2** a rank conferred by the Italian government upon distinguished citizens. [< Italian *commendatore* < Medieval Latin *commendator* commander < Latin *commendāre;* see etym. under **commend**]

com|mend|a|to|ry (kə men′də tôr′ē, -tōr′-), *adj.* **1** expressing approval; praising. **2** mentioning favorably; recommending. **3a** holding a benefice in commendam. **b** held in commendam.

commendatory prayer, a prayer in the Book of Common Prayer to be used for a person at the point of death, commending his soul to God.

com|men|sal (kə men′səl), *adj., n.* — ***adj.* 1** *Biology.* living in close relationship with another species of animal or plant, sharing food, but not parasitic: *Certain commensal crabs live in the burrows of marine worms, not harming the worms in any way and sometimes receiving benefit from the relationship.* **2** eating together at the same table.
— ***n.* 1** a commensal animal or plant: *When such an association becomes too peaceful, however, so that the host is not harmed at all, we cease to call the animal a parasite, but refer to it as a commensal* (A. M. Winchester). **2** a person who eats with others at the same table; messmate.
[< Medieval Latin *commensalis* < Latin *com-* together + *mēnsālis* belonging to the table < *mēnsa* table] — **com|men′sal|ly,** *adv.*

com|men|sal|ism (kə men′sə liz əm), *n. Biology.* commensal existence or mode of living: *When the animals share a common food supply the association is called commensalism, literally "eating at the same table"* (Scientific American).

com|men|sal|i|ty (kom′en sal′ə tē), *n.* **1** *Biology.* commensalism. **2** the habit of eating together at the same table: *In addition to the changes in the status of the Untouchables [in India], it may be noted that the upper caste observance of teachings regarding commensality ... has weakened, as has the association of caste and occupation* (Ogburn and Nimkoff).

com|men|su|ra|bil|i|ty (kə men′shər ə bil′ə tē, -sər ə-), *n.* the quality of being commensurable.

com|men|su|ra|ble (kə men′shər ə bəl, -sər-), *adj.* **1** measurable by the same standard or scale of values: *Greenness and weight are not commensurable.* **2** corresponding in size, amount, or degree; proportionate: *He was a big man, very tall and of commensurable weight.* [< Late Latin *commēnsūrābilis* < *commēnsūrāre;* see etym. under **commensurate**] — **com|men′su|ra|ble|ness,** *n.* — **com|men′su|ra|bly,** *adv.*

com|men|su|rate (kə men′shər it, -sər-), *adj.* **1** in the proper proportion; proportionate: *The pay should be commensurate with the work. He has sent out over 100 letters in an effort to obtain technical employment commensurate with his background and experience* (Bulletin of Atomic Scientists). **2** of the same size or extent; equal: *The amount he earns and the amount he spends are nearly commensurate. A woman's pay should be commensurate with that of a man who does the same work.* **3** commensurable; measurable by the same set of units: *An ant and an elephant are commensurate, but poetry and business are not.* [< Late Latin *commēnsūrātus,* past participle of *commēnsūrāre* < Latin *com-* together + *mēnsūrāre* to measure < *mēnsūra* a measure] — **com|men′su|rate|ly,** *adv.* — **com|men′su|rate|ness,** *n.*

com|men|su|ra|tion (kə men′shə rā′shən, -sə-), *n.* **1** the act of proportioning or fact of being proportioned; proportion. **2** the measuring of things against or in comparison with each other.

com|ment (kom′ent), *n., v.* — ***n.* 1** a note or remark that explains, praises, or finds fault with a book or other literary work, a person, a concert, or a thing: *The teacher wrote many helpful comments on the pages of the compositions he read. Textbooks often have comments at the bottom of a page or the end of a chapter to explain a difficult part.* **SYN**: annotation, gloss, commentary. **2** a remark; observation: *"I cannot remember a single problem that has been solved by diplomacy" was his somewhat smug comment* (London Times). **SYN**: mention. **3** talk; gossip: *His strange behavior has been causing comment in the neighborhood.* **SYN**: conversation.
— ***v.i.* 1** to make remarks (about persons or things); remark: *Everyone commented on her new hat.* **2** to write notes or remarks that explain, praise, or find fault with a book or other literary work, a person, a concert, or a thing: *In his book, the drama critic commented upon all the plays he had seen.* **3** to talk; gossip.
— ***v.t.*** to make a comment or comments on; annotate; explain: *I asked her to comment her wild talk* (Vladimir Nabokov).
[< Latin *commentum* < *commentus,* past participle of *comminisci* contrive, invent < *com-* thoroughly + *-minīscī* think] — **com′ment|er,** *n.*

com|men|tar|i|al (kom′ən tãr′ē əl), *adj.* relating to or characteristic of commentaries.

com|men|tar|y (kom′ən ter′ē), *n., pl.* **-tar|ies. 1** a series of comments: *a news or sports commentary on radio or television.* (*Figurative.*) *She kept up a running commentary as the club members entered.* **2** a series of notes explaining the hard parts of a book; explanation: *Some Bibles have commentaries at the back that give the reader information and help.* **3** an explanatory essay or treatise: *Many volumes have been written by way of commentary on Dante and his book* (Thomas Carlyle).
commentaries, a record of facts or events; historical records; memoirs: *the Commentaries of Caesar.*

com|men|tate (kom′ən tāt), *v.i., v.t.,* **-tat|ed, -tat|ing.** to write, make, or furnish with comments. [back formation < *commentator*] — **com′men|ta′tion,** *n.*

com|men|ta|tor (kom′ən tā′tər), *n.* **1** a person who reports or comments on news, sporting events, plays, concerts, or other things: *a radio or television commentator.* **2** a writer of comments or annotations; annotator. [< Latin *commentātor* < *commentārī* consider thoroughly (frequentative) < *comminisci;* see etym. under **comment**]

com|men|ta|to|ri|al (kə men′tə tôr′ē əl, -tōr′-), *adj.* of or characteristic of a commentator or commentators.

com|ment vous por|tez-vous? (kô mäɴ′ vü pôr tā vü′), *French.* how do you do?

com|merce (kom′ərs, -ėrs), *n., v.,* **-merced, -merc|ing.** — ***n.* 1a** buying and selling in large amounts between different places; business; trade: *Commerce exists because of the desire of individuals and countries having different goods to exchange their surplus for the surplus of some other people* (Finch and Trewartha). **SYN**: dealings, traffic. See syn. under **trade. b** things, such as ships or messages, that represent such trade: *Saw the heavens fill with commerce, argosies of magic sails* (Tennyson). **2** social dealings: *The old farmer had little commerce with his neighbors.* **3** spiritual communion: *A witch was said to have commerce with the Devil.* **4** = sexual intercourse.
— ***v.i.* 1** *Archaic.* to have social dealings. **2** *Obsolete.* to carry on trade.
[< Middle French *commerce,* learned borrowing from Latin *commercium* trade < *com-* with + *merx, mercis* wares, merchandise]

com|mer|cial (kə mėr′shəl), *adj., n.* — ***adj.* 1** having to do with trade or business: *a store or other commercial establishment, commercial gain. The commercial terminals in Metropolitan New York include the water-front freight terminals of the railroads and the docks and piers of the steamship companies* (Colby and Foster). **2** made to be sold for a profit: *Anything you can buy in a store is a commercial product.* **3** supported by an advertiser or sponsor: *a commercial television program.* **4** engaged in commerce: *New York City is a great commercial center.* **SYN**: mercantile. **5** for business purposes, especially in advertising: *a commercial message on TV.* **6** not perfectly or chemically pure: *commercial silver.* **7** of an average or low quality sufficient only to be sold in large quantity, or at a reduced price, or for use by business, especially to manufacture other products: *commercial diamonds, commercial beef.*
— ***n.* 1** an advertisement on radio or television. **2** *British Informal.* traveling salesman. — **com|mer′cial|ly,** *adv.*

commercial agency, a concern which investigates, for the benefit of its subscribers, the financial standing, reputation, and credit rating of individuals, firms, corporations, and others engaged in business; mercantile agency.

commercial art, art used in business, especially for advertising. Commercial art includes designing, drawing, photography, and other art work.

commercial attaché, an officer attached to an embassy or legation as the business and trade representative of his country.

commercial bank, a bank that renders all or most banking services, as distinguished from savings banks and other specialized banks.

commercial break, = commercial (*n.* def. 1).

commercial fertilizer, a chemically manufactured fertilizer, as distinguished from an organic substance, such as manure: *A commercial fertilizer is considered "complete" if it contains nitrate, phosphate, and potash* (Colby and Foster).

com|mer|cial|ise (kə mėr′shə līz), *v.t.*, **-ised, -is|ing.** *Especially British.* commercialize.

com|mer|cial|ism (kə mėr′shə liz əm), *n.* **1** the methods and spirit of commerce: *Making money is often the only object of commercialism. Since primitive men traded sea shells, commercialism has existed in some form.* **2** the commercial attitude, especially as a dominant characteristic of an age or country: *Commercialism today is infecting even our children, who cry for the cereal their favorite TV hero eats.* **3** a business custom. **4** an expression used in business. — **com|mer′cial|ist,** *n.*

com|mer|cial|is|tic (kə mėr′shə lis′tik), *adj.* of or having to do with commercialism or commerce.

com|mer|ci|al|i|ty (kə mėr′shē al′ə tē), *n.* commercial character or spirit.

com|mer|cial|i|za|tion (kə mėr′shə lə zā′shən), *n.* **1** the act of commercializing. **2** the state of being commercialized: *Commercialization of that American institution—the political convention—this year promises to reach the zenith, or nadir, depending on how you look at it* (Wall Street Journal).

com|mer|cial|ize (kə mėr′shə līz), *v.t.*, **-ized, -iz|ing.** to make a matter of business or trade: *Charging admission to church services would commercialize religion. If we are going to be patrons of art, business reasoned, we must not ... "commercialize" art* (New York Times).

commercial law, the body of principles and rules by which rights and obligations in commercial transactions are determined; business law.

commercial letter of credit, = letter of credit.

commercial paper, any negotiable draft, note, bill, or other instrument of credit given in the course of business.

commercial traveler, = traveling salesman.

com|mère (kom′ãr), *n.* a woman compère. [< French *commère* a gossip, godmother < Late Latin *commāter;* see etym. under **cummer**]

com|mers (kô mers′), *n.* = kommers.

com|mie[1] or **Com|mie** (kom′ē), *n. Informal.* a Communist or Communist sympathizer: *One of Italy's best-known firms recently fired the card-carrying Commie who was its personnel chief* (Newsweek).

com|mie[2] (kom′ē), *n.* a marble in the game of marbles, especially one used as the object of a shot; common playing marble.

com|mi|nate (kom′ə nāt), *v.*, **-nat|ed, -nat|ing.** — *v.t.* to threaten; denounce; anathematize. — *v.i.* to utter threats or anathemas. [< Latin *commināri* (with English *-ate*[1]) < *com-* with + *mināri* threaten, (literally) jut forth, project from < *minae* projections, points (on walls)]

com|mi|na|tion (kom′ə nā′shən), *n.* **1** a threat; denunciation. **2** a recital of divine threats against sinners in the Church of England.

com|min|a|to|ry (kə min′ə tôr′ē, -tōr′-; kom′ə nə-), *adj.* threatening; denunciatory.

com|min|gle (kə ming′gəl), *v.t., v.i.*, **-gled, -gling.** to mingle with one another; blend: *A yell of such terror and woe and wrath, all commingled* (Edward G. Bulwer-Lytton). *As incapable of commingling as oil and water* (John L. Motley). **SYN:** commix. Also, **comingle.** [< *com-* + *mingle*] — **com|min′gle|ment,** *n.*

com|mi|nute (kom′ə nüt, -nyüt), *v.t.*, **-nut|ed, -nut|ing.** to reduce to a powder or small fragments; pulverize. **SYN:** triturate. [< Latin *comminūtus,* past participle of *comminuere* break into pieces < *com-* thoroughly + *minuere* make smaller < *minus* less]

com|mi|nu|ted fracture (kom′ə nü′tid, -nyü′-), a fracture in which a bone is shattered or splintered.

com|mi|nu|tion (kom′ə nü′shən, -nyü′-), *n.* **1** reduction to a powder or small fragments; pulverization. **2** *Surgery.* the fracture of a bone into several pieces.

com|mis (kô mē′), *n. French.* a clerk; deputy: *I began in the kitchen and later became a commis and a waiter* (New Yorker).

com|mis|er|ate (kə miz′ə rāt), *v.t., v.i.*, **-at|ed, -at|ing.** to feel or express sorrow for another's suffering or trouble; pity; sympathize: *Next to the poor farmer, the voter who seems likely to be commiserated with most at this session of Congress is the poor taxpayer* (Newsweek). **SYN:** condole. [< Latin *commiserārī* (with English *-ate*[1]) to pity < *com-* with + *miserārī* to pity, bewail < *miser* wretched] — **com|mis′er|at′ing|ly,** *adv.* — **com|mis′er|a′tor,** *n.*

com|mis|er|a|tion (kə miz′ə rā′shən), *n.* pity; sympathy: *Mutual commiseration was the chief bond of their friendship.* **SYN:** condolence, compassion.

com|mis|er|a|tive (kə miz′ə rā′tiv), *adj.* commiserating; compassionate. — **com|mis′er|a′tive|ly,** *adv.*

com|mis|sar (kom′ə sär), *n.* **1a** (formerly) the head of a government department in the Soviet Union. The title of Commissar or People's Commissar was replaced by *Minister* in 1946. **b** (formerly) a Soviet government official in charge of Communist organization and indoctrination, especially in the army. Army commissars were replaced by political instructors in 1942. **c** any similar government official in Communist countries other than the Soviet Union. **2** a commissary; deputy. [< Russian *komissar* < German *Kommissar* commissioner < Old French *commissaire;* (def. 2) < Old French, learned borrowing from Medieval Latin *commissarius;* see etym. under **commissary**]

com|mis|sar|i|al (kom′ə sãr′ē əl), *adj.* of or having to do with a commissary.

com|mis|sar|i|at (kom′ə sãr′ē at), *n.* **1a** the department of an army that provides food and daily supplies for soldiers. **b** the officers in charge of such a department. **2** a food supply. **3** (formerly) any government department in the Soviet Union. [< French *commissariat* < Medieval Latin *commissarius;* see etym. under **commissary**]

com|mis|sar|y (kom′ə ser′ē), *n., pl.* **-sar|ies. 1** a store handling food and supplies, as in a mining camp, lumber camp, or army camp. **2** an army officer in charge of food and daily supplies for soldiers. **3** a deputy; representative. **SYN:** agent, delegate. **4** *Ecclesiastical.* a representative of a bishop who has jurisdiction in remote parts of a diocese or performs the bishop's duties in his absence. **5** a French police officer ranking next to the mayor and police chief. **6** a commissar in the Soviet Union. [< Medieval Latin *commissarius* < Latin *commissus* entrusted, past participle of *committere;* see etym. under **commit**] — **com′mis|sar′y|ship,** *n.*

commissary general, *pl.* **commissaries general. 1** a chief commissary. **2** the head of an army commissariat.

com|mis|sion (kə mish′ən), *n., v.* — *n.* **1** a written paper giving certain powers, privileges, and duties: *Thomas Jefferson once held a commission as United States minister to France.* **SYN:** warrant, license. **2** a written order giving rank and authority as an officer in the armed forces: *A captain in the United States Army or Navy has a commission signed by the President.* **3** the rank and authority given by such an order: *His commission entitled him to enter the officers' club.* **4** a giving of authority. **5** authority, power, or right given. **6** a thing a person is entrusted to do; errand: *The club gave its president the commission of selecting a place to meet. She was given the commission of establishing a school for native children.* **7** a group of people appointed or elected with authority to do certain things: *The President can appoint a commission to find out why food costs so much.* **8** the act of committing; doing; performance: *People are punished for the commission of crimes.* **9** a percentage of the amount of business done, paid to the agent who does it: *She gets a commission of 10 per cent on all the sales she makes. Abbr.* com.

— *v.t.* **1** to give (a person) the right, power, or duty (to do something); give authority to: *My father commissioned a real estate agent to sell our house. The artist was commissioned to paint a portrait of the President.* **SYN:** license, authorize, empower. **2** to give a commission to. **3** to put into active service; make ready for use: *A new warship is commissioned when it has the officers, sailors, and supplies needed for a sea trip.*

in commission, a in working order; ready for use: *It will take us about a week to put your car in commission.* **b** in service; in use: *Huge jet aircraft have been in commission for several years.* **c** ready for service: *A ship or its commanding officer ready for active service is said to be in commission.*

out of commission, a not in working order; not ready for use: *A flat tire put my bicycle out of commission. We'll have to use your record player; mine is out of commission.* **b** not in service or use: *This machine was old and is now out of commission.* **c** not ready for service: *A ship or its commanding officer or crew retired from active service is said to be out of commission.*

[< Latin *commissiō, -ōnis* < *committere;* see etym. under **commit**]

com|mis|sion|aire (kə mish′ə nãr′), *n.* **1** *Especially British and Canadian.* a person entrusted with small errands or duties, such as that of doorman, messenger, or porter: *I said that I would see her at once and a few moments later the commissionaire brought her to my office* (Maclean's). **2** a retired serviceman or a pensioner, especially in England and on the Continent, who does such work. [< French *commissionnaire*]

com|mis|sion|al (kə mish′ə nəl), *adj.* having to do with a commission.

com|mis|sioned officer (kə mish′ənd), any officer holding the rank of second lieutenant or above in the U.S. Army, Air Force, or Marines, or of ensign or above in the U.S. Navy.

com|mis|sion|er (kə mish′ə nər, -mish′nər), *n.* **1** an official in charge of some department of a government: *a police commissioner. Our county has both a road commissioner and a commissioner of public health.* **2** a member of a commission. **3** one of a group of persons elected or appointed to govern a city or a county.

com|mis|sion|er|ship (kə mish′ə nər ship, -mish′nər-), *n.* **1** the office or position of a commissioner. **2** the district under a commissioner.

commission house, a brokerage firm that buys and sells stocks, securities, or other commercial paper, for others on a commission basis.

commission merchant, a person who buys or sells goods for others who pay him a commission.

***commission pennant,** a long pennant flown on a naval ship to show that the ship is in active service and no officer higher than the commanding officer is on board.

***commission pennant**

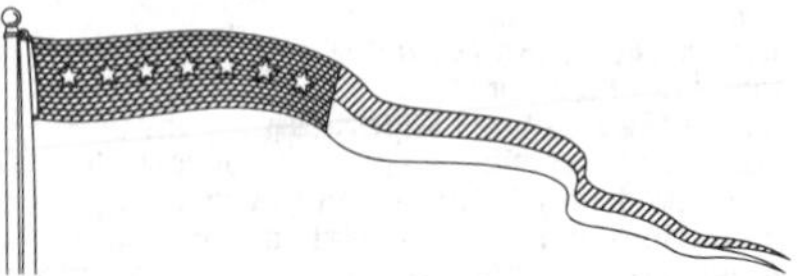

commission plan, a system of municipal government by elected commissioners with legislative, executive, and administrative powers. Each commissioner is the head of a municipal department.

com|mis|su|ral (kə mish′ər əl, kom′ə sůr′-), *adj.* having to do with or of the nature of a commissure (nerve fiber).

com|mis|sure (kom′ə shůr), *n.* **1** *Anatomy.* any one of the nerve fibers connecting corresponding parts of the brain or spinal cord. **2** the line or surface along which two parts touch each other or form a connection; joint; seam; junction. **3** *Botany.* the joint or face by which one carpel coheres with another. [< Latin *commissūra* a joining < *committere;* see etym. under **commit**]

com|mis|sur|ot|o|my (kə mish′ə rot′ə mē), *n., pl.* **-mies.** surgery to relieve obstruction of the mitral valve in certain cases of cardiac constriction. [< *commissure* + *-tomy*]

com|mit (kə mit′), *v.t.*, **-mit|ted, -mit|ting. 1** to do or perform (usually something wrong); perpetrate: *A man who steals commits a crime. Thou shalt not commit adultery* (Exodus 20:14). **2** to hand over for safekeeping; deliver: *The sick man committed himself to a doctor's care. The insane woman was committed to an asylum.* **3** to imprison officially: *The judge committed the thief to prison.* **4** to give over; carry over; transfer: *I will commit the experiences of my early life to writing. Dead people are committed to the grave.* **5** to bind or involve (oneself); pledge: *I have committed myself and must keep my promise. He would not commit himself in any way.* **6** to reveal (one's opinion). **7** to refer (a bill) to a committee for consideration.

commit to memory. See under **memory.**

commit to paper. See under **paper.**

[< Latin *committere* < *com-* with + *mittere* send, put] — **com|mit′ter,** *n.*

— *Syn.* **2 Commit, consign, entrust** mean to hand over a person or thing. **Commit** means to hand over for safekeeping: *The court committed the financial affairs of the orphan to a guardian.* **Consign** suggests formally handing over control of something, usually by signed documents: *His will consigned his share of the bonds to his sister.* **Entrust** means to commit with trust and confidence in the receiver: *I entrusted my door key to my neighbor.*

com|mit|ment (kə mit′mənt), *n.* **1** the act or process of committing. **2** state of being committed. **3a** the act or process of sending to prison or an asylum. **b** an order sending a person to prison or to an asylum. **4** a pledge; promise: *Honest people fulfill their commitments. If we had a wholly Regular army we could meet our present commitments with at least 100,000 fewer men* (London Times). **5** (in parliamentary procedure) the act of referring to a committee for consideration or report; committal. **6a** an agreement to buy or sell stocks, securities, or other commercial paper. **b** a sale or purchase made by such an agreement.

Pronunciation Key: hat, āge, cãre, fär; let, ēqual, tėrm; it, īce; hot, ōpen, ôrder; oil, out; cup, pu̇t, rüle; child; long; thin; ᴛʜen; zh, measure; ə represents **a** in about, **e** in taken, **i** in pencil, **o** in lemon, **u** in circus.

com|mit|ta|ble (kə mit′ə bəl), *adj.* that can be committed. Also, **committible.**

com|mit|tal (kə mit′əl), *n.* the act or process of committing; commitment.

com|mit|tee (kə mit′ē), *n.* **1** a group of persons appointed or elected to do some special thing: *The teacher appointed a committee of five mothers to plan the class picnic. Big decisions at the top are made in committee, and the president must sell the top committee (of which he is a member) on his policies before he can execute them* (Time). *Abbr:* com. **2** *Law.* a person entrusted by a court with the care of a person or estate.
[< Anglo-French *committee* committed, for Middle French *commis,* past participle of *commettre* commit < Latin *committere;* see etym. under **commit**]
►**Committee,** a collective noun, is construed as singular or plural according as the group or the individuals are meant: *The committee meets today at four. The committee get together with difficulty.*

com|mit|tee|man (kə mit′ē mən), *n., pl.* **-men.** a member of a committee.

Committee of Correspondence, any of a number of committees appointed by towns or colonies during the American Revolutionary period to prepare and circulate statements of American grievances and to discuss measures to relieve them.

committee of one, a person who is given an assignment or responsibility usually handled by a committee.

committee of the whole, a committee made up of all the members present of a legislature, club, or other group.

committee room, a room in which a committee holds its meetings.

com|mit|tee|wom|an (kə mit′ē wu̇m′ən), *n., pl.* **-wom|en.** a woman member of a committee.

com|mit|ti|ble (kə mit′ə bəl), *adj.* = committable.

com|mit|tor (kə mit′ôr), *n.* (in British law) a judge, usually the Lord Chancellor, who commits a mentally incompetent person to the care of another.

com|mix (kə miks′), *v.t., v.i.* to mix together; commingle. [back formation < earlier *commixt* < Latin *commixtus,* past participle of *commiscēre* < *com-* together + *-miscēre* to mix]

com|mix|ture (kə miks′chər), *n.* = mixture.

***com|mode** (kə mōd′), *n.* **1** a piece of furniture with drawers for clothing or other items; chest of drawers. SYN: bureau, dresser, chiffonier. **2** a stand in a bedroom to hold a chamber pot, and usually a washbasin, pitcher of water, and soap dish. **3a** a toilet flushed by water; water closet. **b** = closestool. **4** a high headdress of silk or lace worn by women about 1700; fontange. [< Middle French *commode,* learned borrowing from Latin *commodus* convenient, appropriate < *com-* with + *modus* (proper) measure]

***commode** definition 1

com|mod|i|fi|ca|tion (kə mod′ə fə kā′shən), *n.* the turning of works of artistic or cultural value into commodities or articles of trade: *Guilbaut's cultural analysis . . . consists of routine attacks on the commodification and trivialization of art* (New Republic). [< *commodi*(ty) + *-fication*]

com|mo|di|ous (kə mō′dē əs), *adj.* **1** having plenty of room; spacious; roomy: *a commodious suite of rooms.* SYN: ample, large. **2** *Archaic.* convenient; handy: *a commodious location.* [< Medieval Latin *commodiosus* < Latin *commodus;* see etym. under **commode**]—**com|mo′di|ous|ly,** *adv.* —**com|mo′di|ous|ness,** *n.*

com|mod|i|ty (kə mod′ə tē), *n., pl.* **-ties. 1** anything that is bought and sold; article of trade or commerce: *Groceries are commodities. Freight . . . is important on heavy commodities like pig iron, cement, brick, glass, etc.* (Newsweek). **2** anything that is useful, convenient, or serviceable: *The cabin was stocked with all kinds of commodities.* **3** *Obsolete.* usefulness; convenience; advantage. **4** *Obsolete.* a quantity of goods.

commodity exchange, an exchange where staple commodities are bought and sold: *Nearly all the sugar, silk, cotton, hides and metals sold in the U.S. move at prices set on the commodity exchanges of lower Wall Street* (Maclean's).

com|mo|dore (kom′ə dôr, -dōr), *n.* **1** (formerly) an officer in the United States Navy ranking next below a rear admiral and next above a captain. **2** a senior captain in the British Navy in temporary command of a squadron. **3** the flagship of a commodore. **4** the commanding officer of a convoy of naval or merchant marine vessels. **5** the senior captain of a line of merchant ships. **6** a title of honor given to the head of a yacht club or canoe club. [earlier *commandore,* perhaps < Dutch *kommandeur* < French *commandeur*]

com|mon (kom′ən), *adj., n.* —*adj.* **1** belonging equally to all: *The summer cabin is the common property of the three brothers. The two triangles have a common base. Science and medicine form a common front against ignorance and disease.* SYN: joint, united. **2** general; of all; from all; by all; to all: *common knowledge, a common nuisance. By common consent of the class, he was chosen for president.* SYN: popular, universal. See syn. under **general. 3** often met with; usual; familiar: *Snow is common in cold countries.* **4** of the ordinary type or quality; everyday; ordinary: *the business of common life, the common run of mankind. The common man perhaps will always be an abstraction that will attract protestors against the status quo, even if he is rather difficult to single out in real life* (Wall Street Journal). **5** without rank; having no special position: *The common people do most of the work of the world. A common soldier is a private.* **6** below ordinary; having poor quality; inferior: *cloth of a common sort.* **7** coarse; vulgar: *Her speech was very common* (George Macdonald). *He is but the commonest clay* (Byron). **8** belonging to or representative of the entire community; public: *A common council of twelve men governs our city. He sowed a slander in the common ear* (Tennyson). **9** generally or publicly known; notorious: *a common pickpocket, a common liar.* **10** belonging equally to two or more quantities: *a common factor.* See also **common multiple. 11** *Grammar.* See **common case, common gender, common noun, common number. 12** *Prosody.* that can be either long or short: *common syllables.*
—*n.* **1** Also, **commons.** land owned or used by all the people of a town, village, or other community: *Our commons form the last natural reservoirs of wild life left in southern England* (Observer). *Fronting upon the commons . . . were the church, school, and burying ground, together with the home lots of the original settlers* (Finch and Trewartha). **2** that which is common; the commonplace: *to see the miraculous in the common* (Emerson). **3** *Law.* the right to use the land of another, which a man shares with the owner or others, such as the right to fish, pasture animals, or take wood for domestic use: *The tenant farmer had common of pasture on the neighboring farm.* **4** *Ecclesiastical.* Also, **Common. a** the ordinary of the Mass, especially the parts sung. **b** the part of the missal or breviary containing the Masses of all saints who are not assigned special Masses. **c** a form of service used on special festivals. **5** common stock: *additional . . . shares of common will be sold privately* (Wall Street Journal). **6** *Obsolete.* the common people (now only plural).
commons, a the common people; people who are not noblemen: *From the condition of the commons of the shires we turn to a much more intricate subject, the condition of the commons of the boroughs* (William Stubbs). **b** a dining hall or building where food is served to a large group at common tables: *The priests . . . had a College, Society, a Commons, Lodging* (Richard Montagu). **c** the food served: *Berkeley lunched . . . upon a commons of cold beef* (Gentleman's Magazine). **d** food: *however small the commons we ourselves may share* (Walter de la Mare).
in common, equally with another or others; owned, used, or done by both or all: *Although they are twins, the two sisters have few interests in common.*
the Commons, the House of Commons, the lower house of the British or Canadian Parliament: *. . . the Lords endeavoring to insert a clause . . . which . . . the Commons of course rejected* (Hartley Coleridge).
[< Old French *comun* < Latin *commūnis* common, public < *com-* together + *mūnia* duties]
—**com′mon|ness,** *n.*
—*Syn. adj.* **1 Common, mutual** mean belonging equally. **Common** applies regardless of the number involved: *our common heritage, a common purpose, common property.* **Mutual** applies especially when only two are involved: *The two cousins have a mutual dislike.* **3, 4 Common, ordinary** mean usual. **Common** means often met with or usual because shared by many people or things: *Colds are common in winter.* **Ordinary** means in agreement with the normal standards and order of things: *I use ordinary soap for shampoo. . . . measured phrase, above the reach of ordinary men* (Wordsworth).

com|mon|a|ble (kom′ə nə bəl), *adj.* **1** (of land) held in common; subject to general use. **2** (of animals) permitted to pasture on commonland.

com|mon|age (kom′ə nij), *n.* **1** the right to pasture animals on land owned by the town, village, or other community. **2** ownership of land in common. **3** land owned in common: *The Village Board . . . unanimously decided to let the portions of the foreshore commonage . . . for the establishment of bungalows by visitors at a yearly rental of £5* (Cape Times). **4** the common people.

com|mon|al|i|ty (kom′ə nal′ə tē), *n., pl.* **-ties. 1** the common people; commonalty: *Three estates, the clergy, the nobility, and the commonality* (David Hume). **2** common quality or condition; commonness: *the commonality of people's needs and aspirations.*

com|mon|al|ty (kom′ə nəl tē), *n., pl.* **-ties. 1** the common people; persons without rank or title; middle and lower classes of society. **2** people as a group. **3** the members of a corporation. [< Old French *comunalte* < *comunal;* see etym. under **communal**]

common bond, a bond in bricklaying consisting of four to six layers between single header layers; American bond.

common carrier, a company or person whose business is transporting goods or people from one place to another for pay, offering the service to the public generally. Truck lines, railroads, steamboat companies, bus lines, street railways, air transport, and pipelines for natural gas or oil are common carriers.

common case, *Grammar.* a classification of nouns and pronouns identical in form whether used as subject or object. In *The boy is here* and *I met the boy,* the word *boy* is said to be in the common case rather than in the nominative and objective case respectively.

common chord, *Music.* the combination of any tone with its third and fifth, with or without the octave.

common cold, any one of the common viral infections of the respiratory tract which cause running of the nose, sore throat, sneezing, etc.; head cold; coryza.

common council, the lawmaking group of a city, town, or other community.

common councilman, a member of a common council.

common denominator, 1 a common multiple of the denominators of a group of fractions: *12 is a common denominator of 1/2, 2/3, and 3/4, because these fractions can be expressed also as 6/12, 8/12, and 9/12.* **2** a quality, opinion, or other attribute shared by all the persons or things in a group: *As in all one-man collections the invisible common-denominator is the personality of the collector* (New Yorker).

common divisor or **factor,** a number that will divide a group of two or more other numbers without a remainder: *2 is a common divisor of 4, 6, 8, and 10.*

com|mon|er (kom′ə nər), *n.* **1** a person having no special rank or position; a person who does not belong to the nobility or ruling class: *In London, the man in the pub . . . politely argued a princess's right to wed a commoner* (Newsweek). **2** a member of the House of Commons. **3a** (formerly) a student who paid all his expenses at an English university. **b** an undergraduate student who has no scholarship or other college award. **4** a person who has a joint right in commonland; one who enjoys a right of common.

Com|mon|er (kom′ə nər), *n.* a member of the Court of Common Council in London.

Common Era, = Christian Era. *Abbr:* C. E.

common fraction, a fraction expressed as the ratio of two whole numbers. It is written with the numerator above and the denominator below a horizontal or diagonal line.

common gender, *Grammar.* a classification of words that can be of either masculine or feminine gender. The words *parent, child,* and *writer* are said to be of common gender, whereas *father* and *son* are said to be masculine.

com|mon|ize (kom′ə nīz), *v.t.,* **-ized, -iz|ing.** to make common or vulgar.

com|mon|land (kom′ən land′), *n.* land that is used and enjoyed by the public and is not restricted to private ownership; the common of a town, village, or other community: *In many areas of southern England . . . owners of property near commonland are getting really hot about all these heath fires* (Observer).

common law, 1 law based on custom and usage and confirmed by the decisions of judges, as distinct from *statute law.* **2** the law of all countries whose legal systems derive from English law, as distinct from *civil* or *canon law.* **3** law based on the decisions of judges in actual cases; case law.

com|mon-law (kom′ən lô′), *adj.* of or having to do with common law.

common-law marriage, the relationship between a couple who call themselves man and wife, but have not been married by a civil or religious ceremony. Common-law marriage is recognized in some states and not in others.

common lawyer, a person versed in, or practicing, the common law.

common logarithm, *Mathematics.* a logarithm in which 10 is the base.

com|mon|ly (kom′ən lē), *adv.* usually; generally; ordinarily: *Arithmetic is commonly taught in elementary schools.*

common market, an association of countries for promoting free trade among its members by eliminating tariffs, duties, and similar restrictions, with a common tariff for external commerce.

Common Market, a common market originally comprising Belgium, France, Italy, Luxembourg, the Netherlands, and West Germany, established in 1958; European Economic Community. In 1973, Denmark, Ireland, and Great Britain joined the Common Market. *The allure of the continent's Common Market with its promise of one big trading area, accounts for ... freshening interest in European plant sites* (Wall Street Journal).

Common Marketer or **Marketeer**, a member of the Common Market.

common measure, = common time.

common multiple, any number that can be divided by two or more other numbers without a remainder: *12 is a common multiple of 2, 3, 4, and 6.*

common name, = common noun.

common nightshade, = black nightshade.

common noun, *Grammar.* a classification of nouns naming things of a group. *Boy, city,* and *dog* are common nouns. *John, Boston,* and *Rover* are proper nouns.

common number, *Grammar.* a classification of words that are not definitely either singular or plural. *Sheep, politics,* and *fish* are said to have common number because they are either singular or plural.

com|mon-or-gar|den (kom′ən ər gär′dən), *adj. British.* run-of-the-mill; garden-variety: *The "electronic music" ... turned out to be a common-or-garden zither* (London Times).

com|mon|place (kom′ən plās′), *n., adj.* **—*n.*** **1a** an everyday thing: *Forty years ago television was a rare novelty; today it is a commonplace.* **b** anything lacking originality: *Be not content with the commonplace in character any more than with the commonplace in ambition or intellectual attainment* (Atlantic). **2** an ordinary remark: *Talk full of commonplaces about the weather is boring. It is a commonplace that fertile scientific activity results from the posing of the right questions* (Harper's). **3** *Obsolete.* a striking or notable passage cited for reference or use in a commonplace book. **4** *Obsolete.* a commonplace book; a book in which to list references or memoranda.
—*adj.* not new or interesting; everyday; ordinary: *The plots of television movies are often commonplace. Commonplace people dislike tragedy* (John Masefield).
[translation of Latin *locus commūnis,* a translation itself of Greek *koinòs tópos* generally applicable topic] **—com′mon|place′ly**, *adv.* **—com′mon|place′ness**, *n.*
—*Syn.* *adj.* **Commonplace, trite, hackneyed** mean lacking in freshness and interest. **Commonplace** applies to ideas and words so everyday and ordinary that they are dull: *Most movie plots are commonplace.* **Trite** applies to ideas, words, and phrases that once may have been strikingly original and full of meaning, but are now too familiar by overuse and no longer interesting, such as *Necessity is the mother of invention.* **Hackneyed** applies especially to phrases that have been worn out by being used too much and have lost almost all meaning, such as *last but not least, beautiful but dumb.*

commonplace book, a book in which things of special interest are recorded to be remembered or for reference.

common pleas, lawsuits between private individuals that do not involve criminal cases.

common prayer, the prescribed form of liturgy in the Church of England.

common room, *Especially British.* a room for meetings or gatherings, as in universities or inns: *In his common room, he and his senior Fellows discourse ... under the sympathetic gaze of a contemporary portrait of Samuel Johnson* (Newsweek).

com|mons (kom′ənz), *n.pl.* See under **common**.

common school, a public elementary school.

common scold, a woman whose practice of frequent scolding disturbs the peace of the neighborhood: *A common scold is indictable at common law as a nuisance* (Joel Prentiss Bishop).

common sense, good sense in everyday affairs; practical intelligence: *The old farmer didn't have much education but had always gotten along on a lot of common sense. He is hopeful that in the event of another war the world powers may summon enough common sense to avoid mass atomic destruction* (Newsweek).

com|mon-sense (kom′ən sens′), *adj.* having or showing ordinary good sense; sensible; practical: *He was dedicated to the common-sense notion that it was possible to do something about the ridiculous way in which civilized man was stuck in his predicaments* (New Yorker).

com|mon-sen|si|ble (kom′ən sen′sə bəl), *adj. Informal.* common-sense.

com|mon-sen|si|bly (kom′ən sen′sə blē), *adv.* common-sensically.

com|mon-sen|si|cal (kom′ən sen′sə kəl), *adj. Informal.* showing common sense; sensible; practical: *He began to wonder whether historians were possessed of minds any more common-sensical than those Great Minds he had encountered, who had been so credulous* (Josephine Tey). **—com′mon-sen′si|cal|ly**, *adv.*

com|mon-sen|si|cal|i|ty (kom′ən sen′sə kal′ə tē), *n.* the quality of being common-sensical; practical good sense.

common stock, ordinary stock in a company. Common stock has no guaranteed rate of dividend and does not have the privileges of preferred stock.

common tern, a tern rather like a gull but smaller and having a forked tail, white underparts, and a black cap.

common time, *Music.* meter consisting of four quarter notes to the measure; common measure.

common touch, the ability to get along or establish good relations with people from all walks of life.

com|mon|weal (kom′ən wēl′), *n.* **1** the general welfare; public good. **2** *Archaic.* commonwealth. [< *common* + *weal*[1]]

com|mon|wealth (kom′ən welth′), *n.* **1** the people who make up a nation; citizens of a state. **2** a nation in which the people have the right to make the laws; republic: *Brazil, Australia, the United States, and West Germany are commonwealths.* **3** any one of the states of the United States, especially Kentucky, Massachusetts, Pennsylvania, and Virginia. In these four states, Commonwealth is the official title. **4** *Figurative.* a number of persons united by some common interest: *the commonwealth of scholars.* **5** *Obsolete.* public welfare; general good or advantage.

Com|mon|wealth (kom′ən welth′), *n.* the republican government in England under Oliver Cromwell and later his son. It lasted from the execution of Charles I in 1649 to 1660 and included the Protectorate.
the Commonwealth, = Commonwealth of Nations.

Commonwealth Day, May 24, the anniversary of the birthday of Queen Victoria, celebrated as a holiday in parts of the Commonwealth of Nations. It was formerly called *Empire Day* and *Victoria Day.* In Canada it is observed on the Monday before May 24.

Commonwealth of Nations, a group of countries and their dependencies that were formerly under British rule and that are now independent but joined economically to the United Kingdom, including Australia, Bangladesh, Barbados, Botswana, Canada, Cyprus, Fiji, Gambia, Ghana, Guyana, India, Jamaica, Kenya, Lesotho, Malawi, Malaysia, Malta, Mauritius, Nauru, New Zealand, Nigeria, Sierra Leone, Singapore, Sri Lanka, Swaziland, Tanzania, Tonga, Trinidad and Tobago, Uganda, the United Kingdom, Western Samoa, and Zambia.

com|mo|ran|cy (kom′ər ən sē), *n., pl.* **-cies**. an abiding; abode; residence.

com|mo|rant (kom′ər ənt), *adj. Law.* dwelling; ordinary residing. [< Latin *commorāns, -antis,* present participle of *commorārī* to tarry < *com-* with + *morārī* to delay < *mora* delay]

com|mo|tion (kə mō′shən), *n.* **1** bustle or stir; confusion: *the commotion of the market place. That perpetual contest for wealth which keeps the world in commotion* (Samuel Johnson). **SYN**: ferment. **2** public disturbance; rising; tumult: *The crowd's commotion increased with the appearance of the troops.* **SYN**: unrest. **3** violent movement; agitation; turbulence: *the commotion of a storm, commotion of the waves.* **SYN**: turmoil. [< Latin *commōtiō, -ōnis* < *commovēre* < *com-* with + *movēre* move]

com|mo|tion|al (kə mō′shə nəl), *adj.* of or having to do with commotion.

com|move (kə müv′), *v.t.,* **-moved, -mov|ing.** to move violently; agitate; excite: *The air is so commoved by your voice* (George Eliot). [< Old French *commeuv-,* stem of *commouvoir,* < Latin *commovēre* < *com-* with + *movēre* move]

com|mu|nal (kom′yə nəl, kə myü′-), *adj.* **1** of a community; public: *The town swimming pool is communal property.* **2** owned jointly by all; used or participated in by all members of a group or community: *The Plains Indian has both a more plentiful and more regular supply of meat and skins because of the communal buffalo hunt than he could provide by his own unaided efforts* (Beals and Hoijer). **3** of or having to do with the common people. **4** of or having to do with a commune. **—com|mu′nal|ly**, *adv.*

com|mu|nal|ism (kom′yə nə liz′əm, kə myü′nə liz-), *n.* **1** a theory or system of government according to which each commune is self-governing and the state is a federation of communes. **2** the doctrine or practice of communal living, as in a religious community; communism. **—com′mu|nal|ist**, *n.*

com|mu|nal|is|tic (kom′yə nə lis′tik, kə myü′-), *adj.* of or having to do with communalism.

com|mu|nal|i|ty (kom′yə nal′ə tē), *n.* **1** the state or condition of being communal. **2** the feeling of kinship deriving from common purpose or endeavor: ... *the communality of agricultural nations seeking to industrialize themselves ...* (Time).

com|mu|nal|ize (kom′yə nə līz, kə myü′-), *v.t.,* **-ized, -iz|ing.** to make communal; convert into communal property. **—com′mu|nal|i|za′tion**, *n.* **—com′mu|nal|iz′er**, *n.*

com|mu|nard (kom′yə närd), *n.* **1** a communalist. **2** a person who joins or lives in a commune: *Most of the new communards are fleeing what they regard as the constriction, loneliness, materialism and the hypocrisy in straight society* (Time).

Com|mu|nard (kom′yə närd), *n.* a member or adherent of the Commune of Paris in 1871. [< French *Communard* < *Commune* Commune]

com|mune[1] (*v.* kə myün′; *n.* kom′yün), *v.,* **-muned, -mun|ing,** *n.* **—*v.i.*** to talk intimately: *Feasting with the great, communing with the literary* (Washington Irving).
—*n.* an intimate talk; communion.
[< Old French *communer* < *comun;* see etym. under **common**]

com|mune[2] (kom′yün), *n.* **1a** the smallest division for local government in France, Belgium, Italy, and several other European countries. **b** the people or government of a commune. **2** a community or the people comprising it. **3a** a place where a group of people live together communally: [*He*] ... *operates a commune, an apartment where anyone can stay for a night, a week, or as long as he likes* (New York Times). *An abandoned lumber town has been turned into a little commune by a bunch of hippies* (Punch). **b** a group of people living together. **4** (formerly) a unit of local government in Communist China, comprising a group of collective farms organized to carry out planned communal work, including industrial, administrative, and educational projects. **5** (formerly in Russia) the mir. [< Middle French *commune,* alteration of Old French *communge* < Vulgar Latin *commūnia,* neuter plural of Latin *commūnis;* see etym. under **common**]

com|mune[3] (kə myün′), *v.i.,* **-muned, -mun|ing.** to receive Holy Communion. [< Old French *communier* < Late Latin *commūnicāre;* see etym. under **communicate**]

Com|mune (kom′yün), *n.* **the, 1** a revolutionary group that governed Paris from 1792 to 1794. **2** a similar group that governed Paris from March 18 to May 28, 1871.

com|mu|ni|ca|bil|i|ty (kə myü′nə kə bil′ə tē), *n.* the quality of being communicable.

com|mu|ni|ca|ble (kə myü′nə kə bəl), *adj.* **1** that can be transferred or passed along to others: *Scarlet fever is a communicable disease. Ideas are communicable by words. Fear is a communicable emotion.* **2** *Archaic.* talkative; communicative. **—com|mu′ni|ca|ble|ness**, *n.* **—com|mu′ni|ca|bly**, *adv.*

com|mu|ni|cant (kə myü′nə kənt), *n., adj.* **—*n.*** **1a** a person who receives Holy Communion. **b** a regular member of a church. **2** a person who informs or communicates: *The witness refused to reveal the name of his communicant.*
—*adj.* communicating.

com|mu|ni|cate (kə myü′nə kāt), *v.,* **-cat|ed, -cat|ing.** **—*v.t.*** **1** to give (information or news) by speaking or writing; write, telephone, telegraph, etc.: *I asked your sister to communicate my wishes to you. The discovery he made and communicated with his friends* (Jonathan Swift). **2** to pass along; transfer; transmit: *The stove communicated heat to the room. The boy communicated his cold to his classmates.* **3** to administer Holy Communion to.

Pronunciation Key: hat, āge, cãre, fär; let, ēqual, tėrm; it, īce; hot, ōpen, ôrder; oil, out; cup, pu̇t, rüle; child; long; thin; ᴛʜen; zh, measure; **ə** represents **a** in about, **e** in taken, **i** in pencil, **o** in lemon, **u** in circus.

— *v.i.* **1** to give information or news by speaking or writing; send and receive messages; talk, telephone, telegraph, etc.: *We have yet to communicate with the inhabitants of another planet. Deaf people communicate by sign language.* **2** to exchange ideas or thoughts: *A good teacher communicates with his class.* **3** to be connected: *The dining room communicates with the kitchen.* **4** to receive Holy Communion. **5** *Obsolete.* to take part; participate.
[< Latin *commūnicāre* (with English *-ate*[1]) < *commūnis;* see etym. under **common**] — **com-mu′ni|ca′tor**, *n.*
— ***Syn.*** *v.t.* **1, 2 Communicate, impart** mean to pass something along. **Communicate** suggests merely that it becomes the common property of giver and receiver: *He has not communicated his wishes to me.* **Impart** emphasizes giving to another a share of what one has: *A teacher imparts knowledge to his students.*

com|mu|ni|ca|tion (kə myü′nə kā′shən), *n.* **1** a giving of information or news by speaking or writing: *People who are deaf often use sign language as a means of communication. One of the main functions of the arts as communication is to reinforce belief, custom, and values* (Beals and Hoijer). **2** a letter, message, information, or news given: *Your communication came in time to change all my plans.* **3** a means of going from one to the other; passage; connection: *There is no communication between these two rooms.* **4** the act or fact of passing along; transfer. **communications, a** a system of communicating by telephone, telegraph, radio, television, and the like: *A network of communications links all parts of the civilized world.* **b** system of routes or facilities for transporting military supplies, vehicles, and troops: *The enemy bombers tried to break up our line of communications.* **c** the study of giving information and entertainment by talking or writing, by magazine and newspaper, by radio, television, or phonograph records, or other means. Communications includes the study of writing clearly and of transmitting information by artificial satellite: *No universities, even the most communications-minded, give courses in it, and the young writer has to learn by doing* (Saturday Review).

com|mu|ni|ca|tion|al (kə myü′nə kā′shə nəl), *adj.* of or having to do with communication.

communications gap, a failure in communication between different age groups, social classes, etc.: *There is a growing gulf—a widening "communications gap"—between the governors and the governed* (New Scientist).

***communications satellite**, an artificial satellite that relays microwave signals between two points on the earth, such as Telstar; comsat.

***communications satellite**

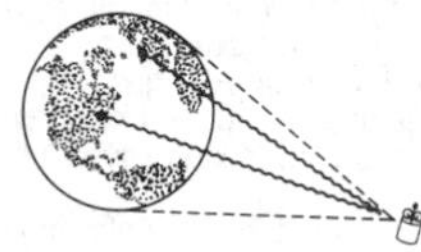

communication theory, the branch of science dealing with the quality and characteristics of transmitted information; information theory.

com|mu|ni|ca|tive (kə myü′nə kā′tiv, -kə-), *adj.* **1** ready to give information; talkative: *Permissive fathers in the group were self-reliant, communicative, persuasive, and efficient* (Newsweek). **2** of or having to do with communication. — **com|mu′ni|ca′tive|ly**, *adv.* — **com|mu′ni|ca′tive|ness**, *n.*

com|mu|ni|ca|to|ry (kə myü′nə kə tôr′ē, -tōr′-), *adj.* of or having to do with communication.

com|mun|ion (kə myün′yən), *n.* **1a** the act of sharing; a having in common; sharing; participation: *The partners had a communion of interests.* **b** the condition of things held in common with others; community; union. **2** exchange of thoughts and feelings; intimate talk; fellowship: *They eat, they drink, and in communion sweet quaff immortality and joy* (Milton). **3** a close spiritual relationship: *To him who in the love of Nature holds communion with her visible forms* (William Cullen Bryant). **4** a group of people having the same religious beliefs. [< Latin *commūniō, -ōnis* < *commūnis;* see etym. under **common**]

Com|mun|ion (kə myün′yən), *n.* **1a** the act of sharing in the Lord's Supper as a part of church worship; Holy Communion; Eucharist. **b** the elements of the Eucharist. **c** an antiphon said or sung during the Communion service. **2** = Communion service.

com|mun|ion|ist (kə myün′yə nist), *n.* **1** a person who has definite beliefs about Holy Communion. **2** = communicant.

communion of saints, the relationship among all members of the same faith; religious fellowship.

Communion service, **1** the celebration of the Lord's Supper. **2** proper order of service for this.

Communion Sunday, any Sunday on which a Communion service is held.

com|mu|ni|qué (kə myü′nə kā′, -myü′nə kā), *n.* an official bulletin, statement, or other communication: *In the countries behind the Iron Curtain even the wording of a communiqué must normally be cleared with Moscow* (Wall Street Journal). [< French *communiqué,* (originally) past participle of *communiquer* < Latin *commūnicāre;* see etym. under **communicate**]

com|mu|nise (kom′yə nīz), *v.t.*, **-nised, -nis|ing.** *Especially British.* to communize.

com|mu|nism (kom′yə niz əm), *n.* **1** a system in which most or all property is owned by the state and is supposed to be shared by all. Communism comes from a philosophy based on the writings of Karl Marx and Friedrich Engels in the 1800's and seeks the overthrow of noncommunist societies in behalf of the laboring class, usually as the result of a series of struggles of class conflict. **2** a political, social, and economic system in which the state, governed by an élite party, controls production, labor, and distribution, and, largely, the social and cultural life and thought of the people: *Communism is expressed in various movements, but Russian sovietism is often referred to as a fair sample. In Communism ownership and control of everything would be in the hands of a small group presumably representing the common people* (Emory S. Bogardus). **3** a social order in which property is held in common by the community or the state; communalism. [< French *communisme* < *commun,* Old French *comun;* see etym. under **common**]
► **Communism** and **socialism** are systems of social organization under which the means of production and distribution of goods are transferred from private hands to the government. The classic difference between the two systems lies in the different means they take to establish themselves: communism emphasizes the impracticability of replacing the existing social order by any means other than armed force or outside intervention; the advocates of socialism seek to establish it by peaceful means, through election and legislation rather than force. The practical differences between the two systems are sometimes varied and great.

Com|mu|nism (kom′yə niz əm), *n.* the political principles and practices of members of a Communist Party, especially of the Communist Party of the Soviet Union.

com|mu|nist (kom′yə nist), *n., adj.* — ***n.*** **1** a person who favors and supports communism. **2** = Communard.
— ***adj.*** = communistic.

Com|mu|nist (kom′yə nist), *n., adj.* — ***n.*** a member of a Communist Party.
— ***adj.*** of or having to do with a Communist Party.

com|mu|nis|tic (kom′yə nis′tik), *adj.* **1** of or having to do with communists or communism. **2** favoring communism.

com|mu|nis|ti|cal (kom′yə nis′tə kəl), *adj.* = communistic. — **com′mu|nis′ti|cal|ly**, *adv.*

Communist International, = Third International.

Communist Party, **1** the single political party in the Soviet Union, originally the left wing of the Social Democratic Party led by Lenin and called the Bolshevik Party, which has controlled the Soviet Union since 1917. *Abbr:* C.P.S.U. **2** a political party anywhere that supports communism.

com|mu|ni|tar|i|an (kə myü′nə tãr′ē ən), *n.* **1** a member of a communistic community. **2** a supporter of communistic principles.

com|mu|ni|ty (kə myü′nə tē), *n., pl.* **-ties**, *adj.* — ***n.*** **1** all the people living in the same place and subject to the same laws; the people of any district or town: *This lake provides water for six communities. Before civilization the size of communities was very small; large numbers of great cities are phenomena of the last hundred years* (Ogburn and Nimkoff). **2** a group of people living together or sharing something in common, such as interests or vocations: *a community of monks, the scientific community.* SYN: fellowship, society, association. **3** ownership together; a sharing together: *community of food supplies, community of ideas.* SYN: partnership. **4** *Figurative.* a group of animals or plants living together; any group of mutually related organisms. SYN: colony. **5** likeness; similarity; identity: *community of interests causes people to work together.* SYN: affinity.
— ***adj.*** **1** of or having to do with a community: *community development.* **2** for or shared by a community: *a community house, a community playground.* **3** owned jointly or in common, especially by a husband and wife.
the community, the public: *To be successful a new product needs the approval of the community.*
[< Old French *communite,* learned borrowing from Latin *commūnitās* < *commūnis;* see etym. under **common**]

community antenna, a television antenna supplying signals to a number of receivers: *Community antennas are usually in cities far away from television stations.... A central antenna picks up the distant signals, amplifies them, and transmits them to subscribers ... by cable* (Wall Street Journal).

community center, a building where the people of a community meet, especially for recreation or social purposes.

community chest, a fund of money given voluntarily by people to support charity and welfare in their community.

community college, a college, often a junior college, that offers courses to nonresident students from the local area.

community property, the property wives and husbands hold together exclusive of property owned before marriage or acquired by either party by bequest, inheritance, or gift.

community singing, organized singing in chorus by a group or gathering of people.

community trust, **1** a private agency for holding and managing the distribution of charitable funds of and for a number of individual agencies, each of which maintains its own identity and character. **2** the funds thus held in trust.

com|mu|nize (kom′yə nīz), *v.t.*, **-nized, -niz|ing.** **1** to make the property of the community: *It is from the true Socialist point of view every bit as important to communize parks and pictures as railways and ploughs* (Pall Mall Gazette). **2** to cause to practice or adopt communism: *Russia and China mean to communize the world* (Bulletin of Atomic Scientists). — **com′mu|ni|za′tion**, *n.*

com|mut|a|bil|i|ty (kə myü′tə bil′ə tē), *n.* the quality of being commutable.

com|mut|a|ble (kə myü′tə bəl), *adj.* that can be commuted; changeable; exchangeable; convertible. — **com|mut′a|ble|ness**, *n.*

com|mu|tate (kom′yə tāt), *v.t.*, **-tat|ed, -tat|ing.** to reverse or regulate the direction of (an electric current) by means of a commutator. [back formation < *commutator*]

com|mu|ta|tion (kom′yə tā′shən), *n.* **1** the changing (of a penalty or obligation) to a less severe one: *The prisoner obtained a commutation of his sentence from death to life imprisonment.* **2a** the substitution of one kind of payment for another. **b** the payment thus made. **3** an exchange; substitution. **4** regular travel to and from work usually by train, bus, or automobile, especially between suburb and downtown and commonly requiring a commutation ticket. **5** a reversal of the direction of an electric current by a commutator. [< Latin *commūtātiō, -ōnis* < *commūtāre;* see etym. under **commute**]

commutation ticket, *U.S.* a ticket sold at a reduced rate, entitling the holder to travel over a given route a certain number of times or during a certain period.

com|mu|ta|tive (kə myü′tə tiv, kom′yə tā′-), *adj.* **1** of or having to do with commutation or exchange. **2** of or having to do with the commutative law, especially in arithmetic and algebra: *a commutative operation.* — **com|mu′ta|tive|ly**, *adv.* — **com|mu′ta|tive|ness**, *n.*

commutative contract, a contract in which each participant gives and receives an equivalent.

commutative law, *Mathematics.* a law stating that the order in which two numbers are added or multiplied is immaterial to the sum or product. *Examples:* $2 + 3$ will give the same sum as $3 + 2$; 2×3 gives the same product as 3×2.

com|mu|ta|tiv|i|ty (kə myü′tə tiv′ə tē), *n. Mathematics.* the property of giving the same result regardless of the order of addition or multiplication.

com|mu|ta|tor (kom′yə tā′tər), *n.* **1** a device for reversing the direction of an electric current in the armature winding of a direct-current generator or motor. **2** a revolving part in a generator or motor that carries the current to or from the brushes: *The commutator is designed so that, no matter how the current in the loop alternates, the commutator segment containing the outward-going current is always against the "out" brush at the proper time* (A. E. Fitzgerald). See picture under **generator**.

com|mute (kə myüt′), *v.*, **-mut|ed, -mut|ing**, *n.*
— ***v.t.*** **1** to change (an obligation or penalty) to an easier one: *The governor commuted the prisoner's sentence of death to one of life imprisonment.* **2** to exchange; substitute; interchange. **3** = commutate.
— ***v.i.*** **1** *U.S.* to travel regularly to and from work usually by train, bus, or automobile, especially

between suburb and downtown: *He commutes to work by bus each morning.* **2** to serve as a substitute; compensate. **3** *Mathematics.* to give the same result in whatever order two numbers are added or multiplied: *In a + b or a×b, a and b commute.* **4** to pay a single sum as an equivalent for a number of successive payments, especially at a reduced price.
—***n.*** *Informal.* a commuting to work; commutation: *The daily commute, . . . exerts a constant drain on their energies* (Wall Street Journal).
[< Latin *commūtāre* < *com-* altogether + *mūtāre* change]

com|mut|er (kə myü′tər), *n., adj.* —***n.*** a person who travels regularly to and from work usually by train, bus, or automobile. —***adj.*** of or for commuters or commuting: *a commuter train.* [American English < *commute* + *-er*[1]]

com|mu|tu|al (kə myü′chü əl), *adj. Poetic.* mutual: *long commutual friendship* (Alexander Pope).

Com|o|ri|an (kom′ər yən), *adj., n.* —***adj.*** of or having to do with Comoros (island country in the Indian Ocean). —***n.*** a native or inhabitant of Comoros.

co|mose (kō′mōs), *adj.* **1** *Botany.* furnished with a coma, or tuft of hair; comate. **2** hairy; tufted. [< Latin *comōsus* having hair or tufts < *coma* hair < Greek *kómē*]

comp[1] (komp), *v.i., v.t., Informal.* to play a jazz accompaniment (to a soloist), especially with irregular rhythmic chords. [short for *accompany*]

comp[2] (komp), *n. Informal.* compositor.

comp[3] (komp), *v., n.* —***v.t.*** to compensate: *The group was flown free from New York . . . is being comped for rooms, meals and beverages* (Esquire). —***n.*** compensation: *I'm still drawing [state] comp, but that doesn't make it* (Newsweek).

comp., an abbreviation for the following:
1a comparative. **b** compare. **c** comparison.
2a compilation. **b** compiled. **c** compiler.
3a compose. **b** composer. **c** composition.
4 compositor. **5** compound. **6** comprising.

com|pact[1] (*adj.* kəm pakt′, kom′pakt; *v.* kəm-pakt′; *n.* kom′pakt), *adj., v., n.* —***adj.*** **1** closely and firmly packed together; closely joined: *The leaves of a cabbage are folded into a compact head.* SYN: solid, dense, firm. **2** having the parts neatly or tightly arranged within a small space; not sprawling or scattered: *a compact community, a compact portable TV set.* **3** *Figurative.* using few words: brief and well organized: *News reporters must learn to write compact sentences.* SYN: terse, pithy, concise. **4** composed or made (of): *It was a tale compact of moon-struck fancy.*
—***v.t.*** to pack closely and firmly together; join closely; compress: *He compacted his clothes in the suitcase by sitting on it.* SYN: consolidate. **2** to make by putting firmly together: *The saleslady compacted a neat package out of all my wife's purchases.* **3** to condense: *to compact several bundles into the space for one.*
—***n.*** **1** = compact car. **2** a small case containing face powder or rouge.
[< Latin *compāctus,* past participle of *compingere* to confine < *com-* together + *pangere* fasten] —**com|pact′er, com|pac′tor,** *n.* —**com|pact′ly,** *adv.* —**com|pact′ness,** *n.*

com|pact[2] (kom′pakt), *n.* an agreement; a contract between parties: *The United Nations is the result of a compact among the great nations of the world.* [< Latin *compactum,* neuter past participle of *compacīscī* < *com-* together + *pacīscī* make an agreement, contract]

compact bone, a structure of the bone consisting of a network of channels (Haversian canals) and the layers of tissue surrounding them.

compact car, a small automobile, designed to cost less to buy, operate, and repair than a standard automobile of larger size.

compact disk or **disc**, **1** a digital disk without grooves whose sounds are picked up by a laser. **2 Compact Disc**, a trademark for such a disk. *Abbr:* CD (no periods).

compact golf, any of various forms of golf played on a small course, including miniature golf.

com|pac|tion (kəm pak′shən), *n.* **1** the act of making compact; compression. **2** the state of being compact. **3** *Geology.* **a** the pressing together of rocks, sediment, or detritus to form a hard mass or stratum: *Eventual compaction of such ooze results in the production of limestone in the form of chalk* (Hegner and Stiles). **b** a mass thus formed.

compact object, any of a class of very dense astronomical bodies, including neutron stars, quasars, and X-ray bursters.

com|pa|dre (kəm pä′drā), *n.* **1** *Spanish.* godfather. **2** *Southwestern U.S.* a close friend.

com|pa|ges (kom pā′jēz), *n.* **1** a complex structure or system. **2** solid or firm structure. [< Latin *compāgēs* < *com-* together + *pag-,* root of *pangere* to fasten, fix]

com|pan|der (kəm pan′dər), *n.* a device used for companding. [< *com*(pressor) + (ex)*pander*]

com|pand|ing (kəm pan′ding), *n.* the process of compressing transmission signals over a communications channel and expanding them on reception: *The terminal also performs important associated functions such as companding . . . a quasi-logarithmic compression of the analogue signal . . . and a corresponding expansion* (Scientific American).

com|pan|ion[1] (kəm pan′yən), *n., v.* —***n.*** **1** one who goes along with or accompanies another; one who shares in what another is doing; comrade: *The twins were companions in work and play.* SYN: associate. **2** a person paid to live or travel with another as a friend and helper. **3** *Figurative.* anything that matches or goes with another in kind, size, and color: *I can't find the companion to this shoe.* **4** a member of the lowest rank of an order of knighthood. **5** *Astronomy.* one of the stars of a double star whose light is fainter than the other: *the faint companion of Sirius.* **6** *Obsolete.* fellow (used contemptuously).
—***v.t.*** to be a companion to; go along with; accompany. —***v.i.*** to associate.
[< Old French *compaignon* < Late Latin *compāniōnem,* accusative of *compāniō* < Latin *com-* together + *pānis* bread] —**com|pan′ion|less,** *adj.*

com|pan|ion[2] (kəm pan′yən), *n.* **1** a hatch or covering over the top of a companionway. **2** = companionway. [< Dutch *kampanje* quarterdeck < Middle Dutch *compaenge* < Old French *compagne* steward's room in a galley < Vulgar Latin *compānia* < Late Latin *compāniō;* see etym. under **companion**[1]]

com|pan|ion|a|bil|i|ty (kəm pan′yə nə bil′ə tē), *n.* = companionableness.

com|pan|ion|a|ble (kəm pan′yə nə bəl), *adj.* pleasant as a companion; sociable; agreeable: *I never found the companion that was so companionable as solitude* (Thoreau). SYN: congenial. —**com|pan′ion|a|ble|ness,** *n.* —**com|pan′ion|a|bly,** *adv.*

com|pan|ion|age (kəm pan′yə nij), *n.* **1** = companionship. **2** a group or list of companions, especially of knights.

com|pan|ion|ate (kəm pan′yə nit), *adj.* of or like companions.

companionate marriage, a proposed form of marriage in which man and wife agree not to have children, and providing for divorce by mutual consent with neither person having any claim on the other.

companion cell, *Botany.* any of the small cells with large nuclei adjacent to and associated with a sieve tube in the phloem of vascular plants.

companion hatch, the covering or hood over a cabin stairway.

companion ladder, *Nautical.* **1** steps or ladder leading to the quarterdeck or poop. **2** steps or ladder leading down from the deck to a cabin.

com|pan|ion|ship (kəm pan′yən ship), *n.* the state or relation of being a companion; fellowship: *Many boys enjoy the companionship of a dog. When others fail him, the wise man looks to the sure companionship of books* (Andrew Lang).

com|pan|ion|way (kəm pan′yən wā′), *n.* **1** stairway from the deck of a ship to the rooms or area below. **2** space where such a stairway is.

com|pa|ny (kum′pə nē), *n., pl.* **-nies,** *adj., v.,* **-nied, -ny|ing.** —***n.*** **1** a group of people: *A great company met the conquering hero. We were a gallant company, riding o'er land and sailing o'er sea* (Byron). **2a** a group of people joined together for some purpose, such as carrying on a business or acting plays: *A band is a company of musicians.* **b** the partners not named in the title of a firm: *John Smith and Company. Abbr:* Co. **c** a medieval trade guild. **3** a gathering of people for social purposes: *She behaves well in company.* **4** a companion or companions: *You are known by the company you keep.* **5** companionship; fellowship: *His dog provided the old man with company during the long winters. I was often in company with a couple of charming women* (Joseph Addison). **6** a guest or guests; visitor or visitors: *company for the weekend. Do you expect company for dinner tonight?* **7a** a military unit made up of two or more platoons, usually commanded by a captain. A battalion in the U.S. Army usually has five companies. *The major led three companies against the enemy.* **b** any body of soldiers. **8** a ship's crew; officers and sailors of a ship: *The ship's company were mustered* (Frederick Marryat). **9** a unit of firemen.
—***adj.*** **1** of or having to do with company: *company manners.* **2a** having to do with a business company: *a company policy, a company reorganization.* **b** having the interests of one's company or one's employers uppermost in mind: *a company man.* **3** owned by a company for use by its employees: *a company store, a company house.*
—***v.i.*** *Archaic.* to keep company; associate: *Those with whom we have here companied through the long years of our earthly sojourn* (H. E. Manning). —***v.t.*** *Archaic.* to accompany: *I am Sir the soldier that did company these three* (Shakespeare).

bear company, to go with; accompany: *His faithful dog shall bear him company* (Alexander Pope).

keep company, **a** to go with; remain with for companionship: *My dog kept me company while you were away.* **b** to go together; associate with as a lover or suitor: *I offered to your sister to keep company* (Dickens).

keep company with, **a** to associate with; accompany: *The gentleman . . . kept company with the wild Prince* (Shakespeare). **b** to associate or go with as a lover or suitor: *My sister Hannah and the young man who was keeping company with her went too* (Sarah Orne Jewett).

part company, **a** to go separate ways: *The friends parted company at the gate.* **b** to have a difference of opinion: *. . . the point at which the scientific man is apt to part company with the theologian* (H. Drummond) **c** to bring an association or relationship to an end: *Mr. Brown [Foreign Secretary] complained "the way this government is run . . . I thought it better that we should part company"* (Annual Register).

[< Old French *compagnie* < *compain* companion[1] < Late Latin *compāniō*]

—***Syn.*** *n.* **1 Company, band, party** mean a group of people brought together in some way. **Company** is the general word: *The chairman led the company in singing.* **Band** applies to a small company sharing a common purpose or lot: *A band of Gypsies is in town.* **Party,** except when used of a political organization, applies to a small company joined for a specific purpose but for only a short time: *A rescue party started up the mountain.*

company officer, *U.S.* a commissioned officer in the Army, Air Force, or Marine Corps, who is not a field officer or a general officer.

company store, a retail store established by a business company for the use of its employees.

company town, a town built by or around a large business company, due to the influx of workers into the area after the building of a factory, offices, etc.: *Kimberley is . . . a company town, and most of its citizens are held together by the common history of De Beers Consolidated Mines, Ltd., the great corporation that was born in Kimberley in 1888* (New Yorker).

company union, **1** a union of workers in one factory, store, or other business establishment, that is not part of a larger union. **2** a union of workers dominated by the employers.

compar., **1** comparative. **2** comparison.

com|pa|ra|bil|i|ty (kom′pər ə bil′ə tē), *n.* the quality of being comparable.

com|pa|ra|ble (kom′pər ə bəl), *adj.* **1** able to be compared (with): *A fire is comparable with the sun; both give light and heat.* **2** fit to be compared (to): *A cave is not comparable to a house for comfort.* —**com′pa|ra|ble|ness,** *n.*

comparable worth, the concept that men and women whose jobs are comparable in skills, training, and responsibility should earn the same pay.

com|pa|ra|bly (kom′pər ə blē), *adv.* in a comparable manner; to a comparable degree: *He was chosen for the mission because no one else was comparably qualified.*

com|par|a|scope (kəm par′ə skōp), *n.* a device attached to a microscope to permit the simultaneous comparison of two slides.

com|par|a|tist (kəm par′ə tist), *n.* a person who studies literature or languages by a comparative method: *Such [morphemic] dictionaries, they claim, would be of immense value and help to comparatists, etymologists, and linguistic analysts* (Simeon Potter). [< *comparat*(ive) + *-ist*]

com|par|a|ti|val (kəm par′ə tī′vəl), *adj. Grammar.* comparative.

com|par|a|tive (kəm par′ə tiv), *adj., n.* —***adj.*** **1** of or having to do with comparison. **2** that compares; involving comparison: *A course in comparative literature emphasizes the differences and similarities among the writings and writers of two or more countries. Comparative anatomy compares the structure of the bodies of different animals.* **3** measured by comparison with something else; not positive or absolute; relative: *Screens give us comparative freedom from flies.* **4** second degree of comparison of an adjective or adverb. *Better* is the comparative form of *good.*
—***n.*** **1** the second degree of comparison of an adjective or adverb. **2** a form or combination of words that shows this degree. *Fairer, better,* and *more slowly* are the comparatives of *fair, good,*

Pronunciation Key: hat, āge, cãre, fär; let, ēqual, tėrm; it, īce; hot, ōpen, ôrder; oil, out; cup, pu̇t, rüle; child; long; thin; ᴛʜen; zh, measure; ə represents **a** in about, **e** in taken, **i** in pencil, **o** in lemon, **u** in circus.

and *slowly.* —**com|par'a|tive|ness**, *n.*

comparative advertising, advertising that unfavorably compares a competitor's product by name: *The advertising community claimed that intense comparative advertising hurts the credibility of all advertising* (Edward Mark Mazze).

comparative linguistics, the study of the history and historical relationship of languages and linguistic forms: *Developed during the nineteenth century primarily in connection with studies of the Indo-European languages, comparative linguistics is generally regarded as possessing a most rigorous methodology* (John B. Carroll).

com|par|a|tive|ly (kəm par′ə tiv lē), *adv.* by comparison; relatively; somewhat: *Mountains are comparatively free from mosquitoes.*

comparative psychology, the psychology of animals; the study of the intelligence, needs, sensory capacities, and characteristic ways of behaving of animals as compared with those of human beings.

comparative religion, the study of various systems of religion by the method of comparing them to each other.

com|par|a|tiv|ist (kəm par′ə tə vist), *n.* = comparatist.

com|pa|ra|tor (kom′pə rā′tər), *n.* an instrument for measuring small differences in parts of machinery or the like by comparing the parts with some standard: *[A] hand comparator for judging surface roughness of mass-produced parts permits metal surfaces to be compared* (Science News Letter).

com|pare (kəm pãr′), *v.*, **-pared, -par|ing,** *n.* —***v.t.*** to find out or point out how persons or things are alike and how they are different: *I compared my answers with the teacher's and found I had made a mistake. He compared the two books to see which one had the better illustrations. Abbr:* cf. **2** to say (something) is like (something else); consider as similar; liken: *The fins of a fish may be compared to the legs of a dog; both are used in moving. Shall I compare thee to a summer's day?* (Shakespeare). **3** to change the form of (an adjective or adverb) to show the comparative and superlative degree; name the positive, comparative, and superlative degrees of. —***v.i.*** to be compared; be considered like or equal: *Artificial light cannot compare with daylight for general use.*

—***n.*** **beyond (past** or **without) compare**, without an equal; most excellent: *Her cakes are beyond compare. "Kwaidan" is a symphony of color and sound that is truly past compare* (Bosley Crowther).

not to be compared with, a very different from: *A table is not to be compared with a vase.* **b** not nearly so good as: *Artificial light is not to be compared with daylight for general use.*

[< French *comparer,* learned borrowing from Latin *comparāre* < *com-* with + *pār* equal] —**com|par′er**, *n.*

▶ **Compare, contrast**. *Compare* is commonly used in two senses: **a** to point out likenesses (used with *to*): *She compared his poetry to a meandering stream.* **b** to examine two or more objects to find both likenesses and differences (used with *with*): *The teacher compared my poem with one of Robert Frost's. Contrast* means to point out differences: *She contrasted her present life of luxury with the poverty of her childhood.*

com|par|i|son (kəm par′ə sən), *n.* **1** the act of comparing; finding the likenesses and the differences: *The teacher's comparison of the heart to a pump helped the students to understand how the heart works.* **SYN**: analogy. **2** likeness; similarity: *There is no comparison between these two cameras; one is much better than the other. The tints are such As may not find comparison on earth* (Shelley). **SYN**: resemblance, similitude. **3** a change in an adjective or adverb to show degrees. The three degrees of comparison are positive, comparative, and superlative. *Example:* cold, colder, coldest; helpful, more helpful, most helpful; good, better, best. **4** a simile: *Good comparisons serve equally to illustrate and to persuade* (Robert Boyle).

by comparison, as compared with something else (implied or thought of); comparatively: *Penrith ... seems here, by comparison, like a metropolis* (Robert Southey).

in comparison with, compared with: *Even a large lake is small in comparison with an ocean. A bear is a friendly beast in comparison with a tiger.*

there is no comparison between them, one is very much better than the other: *Both products cost the same, but there is no comparison between them.*

[< Old French *comparaison* < Latin *comparātiō, -ōnis* < *comparāre;* see etym. under **compare**]

comparison shopper, an employee, especially of a department store, who shops in rival stores to check on the advertising, prices, merchandise, and service of competitors.

comparison spectrum, *Astronomy.* a spectrum formed for comparison, wave length by wave length, with the spectrum under observation.

com|par|sa (kəm pär′sə), *n., pl.* **-sas**. **1** a style of Cuban folk dance and song. **2** a dancing procession in a Cuban carnival. [< American Spanish *comparsa* < Spanish, masquerade]

com|part (kəm pärt′), *v.t.* **1** to divide or mark off into parts; partition: *The interior was comparted by willow screens* (L. H. Morgan). **2** *Architecture.* to lay out according to a plan. [< Old French *compartir* < Late Latin *compartīrī;* see etym. under **compartment**]

com|par|ti|men|to (kəm pär′tə men′tō; *Italian* kôm pär′tē men′tō), *n., pl.* **-ti** (-tē). one of the 20 territorial divisions of modern Italy, each including several provinces. [< Italian *compartimento;* see etym. under **compartment**]

com|part|ment (kəm pärt′mənt), *n., v.* —***n.*** **1** a separate division set off in any enclosed space by walls or partitions. A ship's hold is often built in watertight compartments so that a leak will fill up only one compartment and not the whole ship. *Your pencil box has several compartments for holding different things.* **2** *U.S.* a private room in a Pullman car with sleeping accommodations. **3** *Architecture.* a section of a design that is divided into regular parts, such as one panel of a paneled wall. **4** any part, division, or section, as of a plant or animal or the mind: (*Figurative.*) *She relegated the experience to that compartment she reserved for unpleasant memories.*

—***v.t.*** to separate into compartments; compartmentalize: (*Figurative.*) *The Sunday Mirror ... can be expected to back Labour ... The News of the World and the People are ... less easy to compartment* (Punch).

[< French *compartiment* < Italian *compartimento* < *compartire* divide < Late Latin *compartīrī* < Latin *com-* with + *partīrī* to share < *pars, partis* a portion]

com|part|men|tal (kom′pärt men′təl), *adj.* having or divided into compartments.

com|part|men|tal|i|za|tion (kom′pärt men′tə lə zā′shən), *n.* **1** a dividing into compartments: (*Figurative.*) *Because of a curious compartmentalization of thinking, both of the books ... manage to side-step the really central issue* (Saturday Review). **2** the result of such dividing: (*Figurative.*) *Scientists are now recognizing the undesirability —and impossibility—of continued compartmentalization between science and society* (Bulletin of Atomic Scientists).

com|part|men|tal|ize (kom′pärt men′tə līz), *v.t.*, **-ized, -iz|ing. 1** to arrange in compartments or sections: *Everything is neatly yet automatically compartmentalized by the tray itself* (New Yorker). **2** *Figurative.* to arrange mentally in categories: *The pursuit of science cannot be completely compartmentalized, missiles in one slot and moon shots in another* (Wall Street Journal).

com|part|men|ta|tion (kəm pärt′mən tā′shən), *n.* = compartmentalization.

com|part|ment|ed (kom′pärt men′tid), *adj.* fitted with, or divided into, compartments; compartmentalized: *a compartmented trunk.* (*Figurative.*) *Some forty years ago when I was in the Bureau of Standards, I had my first brush with the stubborn pride of the compartmented mind* (Bulletin of Atomic Scientists).

com|part|ment|iz|er car (kom pärt′mən tī′zər), a boxcar fitted with several rooms or compartments for less than carload shipments.

com|pass** (kum′pəs), *n., v., adj.* —n.*** **1a** an instrument for showing directions, consisting of a needle or compass card that points to the north magnetic pole, which is near the North Pole. **b** an instrument showing direction, consisting of a gyroscope that points to the geographical North Pole. **2** Also, **compasses**. an instrument for drawing circles and measuring distances. A compass consists of two legs hinged together at one end. **3** a boundary; circumference: *A prison is within the compass of its walls.* **4** the space within limits; area; extent; range: (*Figurative.*) *The old sailor had many adventures within the compass of his lifetime.* **SYN**: reach, scope. See syn. under **range. 5** the range of a voice or musical instrument: *You would sound me from my lowest note to the top of my compass* (Shakespeare). *A compass of two octaves is by no means unusual for a speaker who could not possibly sing through that range* (Simeon Potter). **6** *Figurative.* due or proper limits; moderation: *I must keep within compass* (Samuel Richardson). *Within his compass, the pianist was superb.* **7** *Archaic.* a circuit; a going round. **8** *Obsolete.* a circle.

—***v.t.*** **1** to go around; make a circuit of: *The astronaut compassed the earth many times in his space capsule.* **2** to hem in; surround: *The lake is compassed by a ring of mountains.* **3** *Figurative.* to accomplish; obtain; get: *He compassed his goal.* **SYN**: achieve, attain, effect, secure. **4** *Figurative.* to plot; scheme. **SYN**: contrive, machinate. **5** *Figurative.* to grasp with the mind; understand completely: *Strange forebodings of ill ... that cannot be compassed* (Longfellow). **6** *Obsolete.* to bend into a circle; curve.

—***adj.*** circular.

box the compass, a to name the points of the compass in order: *I can raise a perpendicular ... and box the compass* (Frederick Marryat). **b** *Figurative.* to go all the way around and end up where one started: *The wind would regularly box the compass ... in the course of every day* (Richard D. Blackmore).

[< Old French *compas* < *compasser* measure, divide equally < Vulgar Latin *compassāre* measure off < *compassus* equal step < Latin *com-* with + *passus, -ūs* a step, pace] —**com′pass|a|ble**, *adj.*

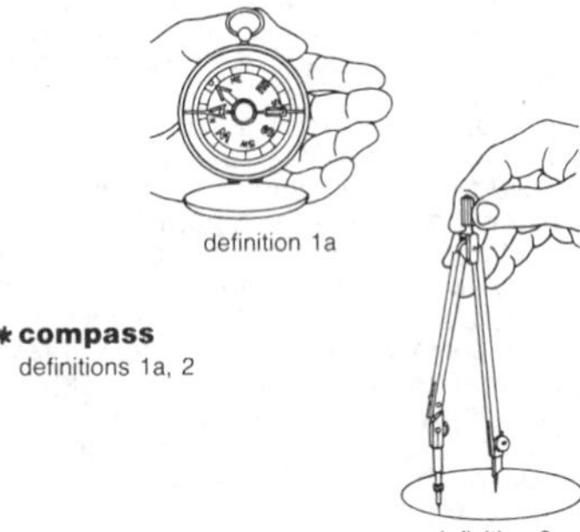

***compass**
definitions 1a, 2

compass card, **1** a circular card set beneath the needle of a compass, showing the 32 points of direction and the degrees of the circle. **2** a similar card attached to a magnetic device that floats in place of the needle and passes under a line drawn over the compass.

com|pass|er (kum′pə sər), *n.* a person who compasses.

com|pass|es (kum′pə siz), *n. pl.* See under **compass** (*n.* def. 2).

compass flower, = compass plant.

com|pas|sion (kəm pash′ən), *n., v.* —***n.*** the feeling for another's sorrow or hardship that leads to help; pity; sympathy: *Compassion for the orphans caused him to give money for their support.* **SYN**: See syn. under **pity**.

—***v.t.*** to have compassion on; pity.

[< Latin *compassiō, -ōnis* < *compatī* suffer with < *com-* with + *patī* suffer]

com|pas|sion|ate (kəm pash′ə nit), *adj.* **1** wishing to help those that suffer; pitying; sympathetic: *The young policeman's compassionate voice calmed the lost child.* **2** (of a transfer, leave, assignment, etc.) given by superiors or sought for the comfort or convenience of a person and not necessarily in the military interest: *While the Admiralty deny that leaves have been cancelled, it was confirmed that a small number of men in the Ocean were recalled from compassionate leave* (London Times). **3** *Obsolete.* pitiable; piteous. —**com|pas′sion|ate|ly**, *adv.* —**com|pas′sion|ate|ness**, *n.*

compass plane, a carpenter's plane with a convex under surface, used for smoothing concave surfaces.

compass plant, any one of various plants whose alternate branches or leaves tend to point north and south. The rosinweed and pilotweed are compass plants.

***compass rose**, a graduated circle, usually marked in degrees, indicating directions and printed or inscribed on a compass card or elsewhere, as on an aeronautical chart.

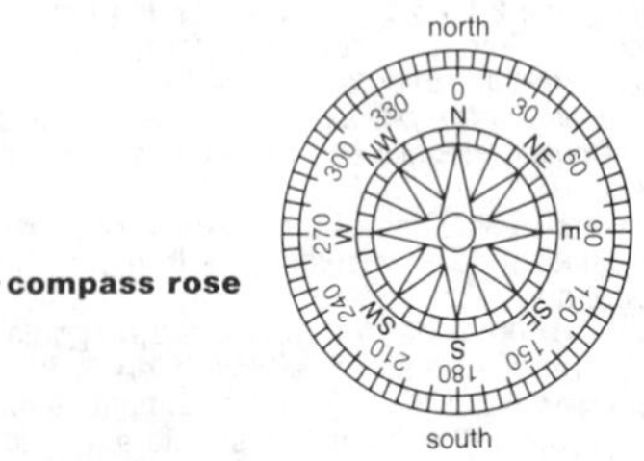

***compass rose**

compass saw, a handsaw with a very narrow, straight blade for cutting curves.

compass termite, an Australian termite that builds its mounds for nesting in such a manner that they invariably face north and south.

com|pat|i|bil|i|ty (kəm pat′ə bil′ə tē), *n.* **1** the ability to exist together; ability to get on well together; agreement; harmony: *Marriages sometimes appear to be wrecked by mere details . . . often, however, these details are but signs of a fundamental lack of compatibility between the two life partners* (Floyd L. Ruch). **2** *Biology.* the ability of transferred or transplanted tissue or cells to function without being rejected: *blood compatibility.* **3** *Botany.* the ability to cross-fertilize or unite with a stock. **4** *Chemistry.* the ability of substances to mix together without impairment of function: *drug compatibility.* **5** the ability of computer software or hardware to be used with different models or systems without adaptation. **6a** the ability to receive color television signals in black and white on conventional television sets. **b** the ability to receive stereophonic sound on a monophonic receiver.

com|pat|i|ble (kəm pat′ə bəl), *adj, n.* —*adj.* **1** able to exist together; that can get on well together; agreeing; in harmony: *Cats and birds are seldom compatible.* SYN: agreeable, congenial, congruous. **2** *Biology.* able to be transferred or transplanted into another's body without being rejected: *compatible blood cells or tissue.* **3** *Botany.* capable of cross-fertilization. **4** *Chemistry.* able to be mixed or combined without interfering with one another: *compatible drugs.* **5** (of computer software or hardware) able to be used with different models or systems without adaptation: *Ideally, all of your "applications" software . . . would be "command compatible" and "file compatible"—they would respond to the same instructions from you, and they would work comfortably with each other's documents* (Stewart Brand). **6a** of or designating a system of television in which color signals can be received in black and white on conventional sets. **b** of or having to do with stereophonic sound that can be received on a monophonic receiver.
—*n.* a computer program or equipment that can be used in different models or systems without adaptation: *The current family of I.B.M. personal computers and compatibles uses an operating system called MSDOS, for Microsoft Disk Operating System* (Peter H. Lewis).
[< Medieval Latin *compatibilis* < Latin *compatī;* see etym. at **compassion**] —**com|pat|i|bly,** *adv.*

com|pa|tri|ot (kəm pā′trē ət; *especially British* kəm pat′rē ət), *n., adj.* —*n.* a fellow countryman: *I look upon all men as my compatriots.*
—*adj.* of the same country. [< Late Latin *compatriōta* < *com-* with + *patriōta* fellow countryman < Greek *patriṓtēs* < *patriá* clan < *patḗr* father]

com|pa|tri|ot|ic (kəm pā′trē ot′ik; *especially British* kəm pat′rē ot′ik), *adj.* of or having to do with compatriots; belonging to the same country.

com|pa|tri|ot|ism (kəm pā′trē ə tiz′əm; *especially British* kəm pat′rē ə tiz′əm), *n.* the position of being compatriots; compatriotic feeling or sympathy.

com|peer (kəm pir′, kom′pir), *n., v.* —*n.* **1** an equal; peer. **2** a companion; comrade. SYN: associate. —*v.t. Obsolete.* to equal; rival.
[< Old French *comper* < Latin *compār* equal to another < *com-* with + *pār* equal]

com|pel (kəm pel′), *v.t.,* **-pelled, -pel|ling. 1** to drive or urge with force; force: *Rain compelled us to stop our ball game. Circumstances compel us to economize.* **2** to bring about by force; command: *A policeman can compel obedience to the law.* **3** to drive or gather together by force. **4** *Obsolete.* to take or get by force. [< Latin *compellere* to force; collect < *com-* together + *pellere* drive] —**com|pel′la|ble,** *adj.* —**com|pel′ler,** *n.*
—*Syn.* **1 Compel, impel** mean to force. **Compel** means force a person to do something one wants or to give in to something: *It is impossible to compel a person to love his fellow men.* **Impel** means force to move forward, but is most often used figuratively to mean drive forward by strong desire or motive or emotion: *His hunger impelled him to beg.*

com|pel|la|tion (kom′pə lā′shən), *n.* **1** the act or mode of addressing a person; form of address. **2** the name or title used in addressing a person; appellation. [< Latin *compellātiō, -ōnis* < *compellāre* accost, call to account < *compellere;* see etym. under **compel**]

com|pel|la|tive (kəm pel′ə tiv), *n.* a term of address; appellation.

com|pel|lent (kəm pel′ənt), *adj.* compelling; constraining.

com|pel|ling (kəm pel′ing), *adj.* **1** that compels; coercive; commanding: *a compelling order, a compelling voice.* **2** *Figurative.* that attracts irresistibly; that holds by force one's interest or attention: *His magnetism was compelling, his personality charming* (New Yorker). **3** strongly convincing or persuasive: *compelling reasons, a compelling testimony.* —**com|pel′ling|ly,** *adv.*

com|pend (kom′pend), *n.* = compendium.

com|pen|di|ous (kəm pen′dē əs), *adj.* brief but comprehensive; concise: *a compendious review of American literature.* SYN: succinct. [< Latin *compendiōsus* < *compendium;* see etym. under **compendium**] —**com|pen′di|ous|ly,** *adv.* —**com|pen′di|ous|ness,** *n.*

com|pen|di|um (kəm pen′dē əm), *n., pl.* **-di|ums, -di|a** (-dē ə). a short summary of the main points or ideas of a larger work; abridgment; condensation. SYN: abstract, précis, epitome. [< Latin *compendium* a shortening; a weighing together < *com-* in addition + *pendere* weigh]

com|pen|sa|ble (kəm pen′sə bəl), *adj.* entitled or entitling to compensation.

com|pen|sate (kom′pən sāt), *v.,* **-sat|ed, -sat|ing.** —*v.t.* **1** to make an equal return to; give an equivalent to: *The hunters compensated the farmer for killing his cow by paying him.* SYN: recompense. **2** to pay: *The company always compensated her for her extra work.* SYN: See syn. under **pay.** **3** *Mechanics.* to adjust so as to offset variations or produce equilibrium; counterbalance: *Watches and clocks are compensated in order to keep the wheels and springs properly balanced.* **4** to stabilize buying power of (money) to meet varying price levels by changing the gold content or equivalent of the monetary unit.
—*v.i.* **1** to balance by equal weight or power; make up (for): *Skill sometimes compensates for lack of strength.* SYN: offset. **2** to make amends: *He left his whole fortune to a children's hospital to compensate for the child his car had crippled.* [< Latin *compēnsāre* (with English *-ate*[1]) balance out < *com-* with + *pēnsāre* weigh < *pendere* weigh out] —**com′pen|sat′ing|ly,** *adv.*

com|pen|sat|ing gear (kom′pən sā′ting), = differential gear.

com|pen|sa|tion (kom′pən sā′shən), *n.* **1** something given to make up for something else; something which makes up for something else: *He gave me a new knife as compensation for the one of mine he lost. American Indians have filed suits against the government demanding compensation for 1.3 billion acres of land* (Newsweek). SYN: recompense. **2** pay: *Equal compensation should be given to men and women for equal work.* **3a** a balancing by equal power, weight, force, or other factors. **b** a means for doing this. **4** *Physiology, Biology.* the increased size or activity of one part (of an organism or organ) to make up for loss or weakness of another: *After one kidney was removed, the other became larger in compensation. The blind man developed especially sharp hearing as a compensation for his loss of sight.* **5** *Psychology.* **a** a behavior which emphasizes some desirable personal trait, feeling, or attitude, in order to conceal an undesirable one: *His hearty manner was a compensation for his feeling of insecurity.* **b** the cancellation of one sensation by another. **6** *Optics.* **a** the equalization of the retardation of two rays of light. **b** = compensator. **7** a compensating or a being compensated.

com|pen|sa|tion|al (kom′pən sā′shə nəl), *adj.* of or having to do with compensation.

com|pen|sa|tive (kom′pən sā′tiv, kəm pen′sə-), *adj.* making amends; compensating.

com|pen|sa|tor (kom′pən sā′tər), *n.* **1** a person or thing that compensates. **2** a device for producing mechanical compensation. **3** *Electricity.* a transformer in which a part of the primary coil is used as a secondary, or a part of the secondary as a primary coil; autotransformer. **4** *Optics.* a plate or combination of prisms for effecting compensation.

com|pen|sa|to|ry (kəm pen′sə tôr′ē, -tōr′-), *adj.* serving to compensate; making amends; compensating: *A civil service employee may get compensatory leave for working overtime.*

com|père (kom′pãr), *n., v.,* **-pèred, -pèr|ing.** —*n.* the host or master of ceremonies conducting a radio or television show. —*v.t.* to serve as compère to; be the host of; guide. —*v.i.* to be a compère. [< French *compère* (earlier) godfather, ultimately < Latin *cum* with + *pater* father]

com|pere (kom′pãr), *n., v.t., v.i.,* **-pered, -per|ing.** = compère.

com|pete (kəm pēt′), *v.i.,* **-pet|ed, -pet|ing. 1** to try hard to win or gain something wanted by others; be rivals; contend: *Blaze was competing against many fine horses for first prize. The rival schools competed for the football trophy.* SYN: See syn. under **contend. 2** to take part (in a contest): *An injury kept him from competing in the final race.* **3** *Commerce.* to strive for preeminence in a market; be in competition: *It is difficult for a small grocery store to compete with a supermarket.* [< Late Latin *competere* strive in common < Latin, coincide, be fit for < *com-* together + *petere* seek, drive toward]

com|pe|tence (kom′pə təns), *n.* **1** the quality or condition of being competent; ability; fitness; capacity: *No one doubted the guide's competence. The madwoman lacked the competence to manage her own affairs.* **2** enough money to provide a comfortable living: *He still thought how fine it would be to take one's ease with a rod by the lake . . . now that his work was behind him and he had his competence* (Atlantic). **3** *Law.* legal power or authority. **4** *Geology.* the ability of a stream to carry and transport solid particles, pebbles, boulders, etc., measured by the size of the largest piece it can move. **5** *Embryology.* the ability of an embryonic tissue to react to various stimuli which can influence its development in particular directions.

com|pe|ten|cy (kom′pə tən sē), *n.* = competence.

com|pe|tent (kom′pə tənt), *adj.* **1** properly qualified; able; fitted: *a competent cook gets high wages. A doctor should be competent to treat many diseases. The girl was so upset she was not competent to decide.* SYN: capable. See syn. under **able. 2** *Law.* legally qualified: *Some states say that persons in a confidential or close blood relationship with the testator are not competent as witnesses* (William T. Dean). **3** rightfully belonging; permissible (to): *It is not competent to the defendant to allege fraud in the plaintiff* (Sir William Blackstone). [< Latin *competēns, -entis,* present participle of *competere* coincide; see etym. under **compete**] —**com′pe|tent|ly,** *adv.* —**com′pe|tent|ness,** *n.*
►See **able** for usage note.

com|pe|ti|tion (kom′pə tish′ən), *n.* **1** the act or state of trying hard to win or gain something wanted by others; rivalry; competing: *There is competition in many games. Competition among business firms for trade increases during a recession.* **2** a contest; match: *She won first place in the dancing competition.* **3** *Biology.* the simultaneous demand by different organisms for food, places for habitation, and other vital factors.

com|pet|i|tive (kəm pet′ə tiv), *adj.* decided by competition; using competition: *Great athletes are noted for their highly competitive spirit. He took the competitive examination for the job of postal clerk.* —**com|pet′i|tive|ly,** *adv.*

com|pet|i|tive|ness (kəm pet′ə tiv nis), *n.* the action of competing; rivalry: *. . . one psychiatrist claims that competitiveness has been a factor in every neurosis she has treated* (Ogburn and Nimkoff).

com|pet|i|tor (kəm pet′ə tər), *n.* a person who tries hard to win or gain something wanted by others; rival: *There are many competitors for the golf championship. He is head and shoulders above his competitors* (London Times).

com|pet|i|to|ry (kəm pet′ə tôr′ē, -tōr′-), *adj.* = competitive.

com|pi|la|tion (kom′pə lā′shən), *n.* **1** the act of compiling: *As a trade magazine editor, I can appreciate the amount of work which went into the compilation of this section* (Newsweek). **2** a book, list, or table that has been compiled.

com|pil|a|to|ry (kəm pī′lə tôr′ē, -tōr′-), *adj.* having to do with a compiler or with compilation.

com|pile (kəm pīl′), *v.t.,* **-piled, -pil|ing. 1** to collect and bring together in one list or account: *Mother compiled a list of the groceries we needed.* **2** to make or form (a book, a report, or an article) out of various materials: *to compile a table of weights and measures. It takes many experts working together to compile an encyclopedia. The scholar compiled a bibliography of the unpublished writings of Emerson.* [< Old French *compiler,* learned borrowing from Latin *compīlāre* steal, (originally) pile up < *com-* together + *pīlāre* press]

com|pil|er (kəm pī′lər), *n.* **1** a person who compiles; one who makes a compilation. **2** a computer program for converting instructions in a compiler language into machine language.

compiler language, a coding system for programming an electronic computer, consisting of ordinary words and word combinations.

com|pi|tal (kom′pə təl), *adj.* **1** *Botany.* **a** (of veins of leaves) intersecting at various angles. **b** (of the sori of ferns) situated at the point of junction of two veins. **2** of or having to do with the crossroads in ancient Rome, where shrines of the domestic gods were placed: *a compital shrine of the time of Caesar.* [< Latin *compitālis* of the crossroads < *compitum* a crossroads < *competere* to coincide; see etym. under **compete**]

com|pla|cence (kəm plā′səns), *n.* **1** = complacency. **2** *Obsolete.* disposition to please; pleasantness; complaisance.

com|pla|cen|cy (kəm plā′sən sē), *n.* **1** the fact or state of being pleased with oneself or what one

Pronunciation Key: hat, āge, cãre, fär; let, ēqual, tėrm; it, īce; hot, ōpen, ôrder; oil, out; cup, pu̇t, rüle; child; long; thin; ᴛʜen; zh, measure; ə represents **a** in about, **e** in taken, **i** in pencil, **o** in lemon, **u** in circus.

has; self-satisfaction: *She solved the puzzle easily and smiled with complacency. ... that entire complacency and satisfaction which beam in the countenances of a new-married couple* (Charles Lamb). **2** contentment: *The old lady's complacency contrasted with the dissatisfied air of her daughter.*

com|pla|cent (kəm plā′sənt), *adj.* pleased or satisfied with oneself or what one has: *The winner's complacent smile annoyed the loser.* **SYN**: smug, self-satisfied. [< Latin *complacēns, -entis,* present participle of *complacēre* be pleasing at the same time < *com-* with + *placēre* to please] —**com|pla′cent|ly**, *adv.*

com|plain (kəm plān′), *v.i., v.t.* **1** to say that something is wrong; find fault: *She complains that the room is cold.* **2** to talk about one's pains or troubles: *She is always complaining that her health is poor. After a sleepless night she complained of a headache.* **3** to make an accusation or charge: *She complained to the police about the barking of her neighbor's dog.* **4** *Dialect.* to suffer; be ailing. **5** *Obsolete.* to lament. [< Old French *complaindre* < Late Latin *complangere* < Latin *com-* + *plangere* to lament] —**com|plain′er**, *n.*

—*Syn.* **1 Complain, grumble** mean to express discontent. **Complain,** the general word, means to express discontent with something: *He is always complaining about the weather.* **Grumble** means to mutter complaints in a bad-tempered way: *Stop grumbling about the food.*

com|plain|ant (kəm plā′nənt), *n.* **1** a person who complains. **2** a person who brings a lawsuit against another; plaintiff: *The complainant accused the defendant of cheating him.*

com|plain|ing (kəm plā′ning), *adj.* expressing or expressive of complaint or discontent: *a complaining tone of voice.* —**com|plain′ing|ly**, *adv.*

com|plaint (kəm plānt′), *n.* **1** the act of complaining; a voicing of dissatisfaction; finding fault: *Her letter is filled with complaints about the food at camp.* **2** an accusation; charge that an offense has been committed: *The judge heard the complaint and ordered an investigation.* **3** a cause for complaining; grievance: *Her main complaint is that she has too much work to do.* **4** an illness; disease: *A cold is a very common complaint.* **SYN**: sickness, ailment, malady. **5** an expression of grief; lamentation; plaint. [< Old French *complainte* < *complaindre;* see etym. under **complain**]

com|plai|sance (kəm plā′zəns, kom′plə zans), *n.* **1** the desire and care to please or defer to the wishes of another; agreeableness. **SYN**: obligingness, courtesy, graciousness, politeness. **2** an act of complaisance. **3** = compliance. [< French *complaisance* < *complaire* acquiesce, learned borrowing from Latin *complacēre;* see etym. under **complacent**]

com|plai|sant (kəm plā′zənt, kom′plə zant), *adj.* **1** inclined to do what is asked; obliging; gracious: *The Prince, who was excessively complaisant, told her the whole story three times over* (Oliver Goldsmith). **SYN**: affable, courteous. **2** = compliant: *She was an old-fashioned wife, entirely complaisant to her husband's will.* **SYN**: yielding, accommodating. [< French *complaisant,* present participle of *complaire* acquiesce < Latin *complacēre;* see etym. under **complacent**] —**complai′sant|ly**, *adv.* —**com|plai′sant|ness**, *n.*

com|pla|nate (kom′plə nit), *adj.* made level; flattened. [< Latin *complānātus,* past participle of *complānāre* make level < *com-* altogether + *plānus* plane]

com|pla|na|tion (kom′plə nā′shən), *n.* **1** a making plane or level; flattening out. **2** *Mathematics.* the reduction of a curved surface to an equivalent plane area.

com|pleat (kəm plēt′), *adj.* = complete.
▶ This archaic spelling is used sometimes for a humorous effect in referring to a person engaged in a particular hobby or pursuit, originally in allusion to *The Compleat Angler,* a celebrated work (1653) by Izaak Walton on the technicalities and the delights of fishing: *In his home workshop, the compleat handyman usually starts out buying a little $25 utility drill to act as a portable sander, buffer and saw* (Time).

com|plect (kəm plekt′), *v.t.* to weave together; interweave. [< Latin *complectī;* see etym. under **complex**]

com|plect|ed (kəm plek′tid), *adj. U.S. Informal.* complexioned.
▶ **Complected** (as in *dark-complected* and *light-complected*), though commonly used, especially in the United States, is not regarded as standard. The standard term is *complexioned.*

com|ple|ment (*n.* kom′plə mənt; *v.* kom′plə ment), *n., v.* —*n.* **1** something that completes or makes perfect: *The teacher considers homework a necessary complement to classroom work. Philosophy is a good complement of scientific studies.* **2** the number required to complete or make perfect: *The ship now had its full complement of men, and no more could be taken on.* **3** full quantity or amount: *He had the usual complement of eyes and ears* (Francis Parkman). **4** a word or group of words completing a predicate. In "The man is good," *good* is a complement. **5** each of two parts which complete each other. **6** *Mathematics.* **a** the amount needed to make an angle or an arc equal to 90 degrees; the angle or arc by which a given angle or arc is less than 90 degrees. **b** those members of a set that do not belong to a subset. *Example:* In the set (1, 2, 3, 4) the complement of subset (2, 4) is (1, 3). **7** *Music.* the interval which added to a given interval completes an octave. **8** *Medicine.* a substance or group of substances found in normal blood serum and protoplasm which combines with antibodies to destroy bacteria and other foreign bodies.
—*v.t.* **1** to supply a lack of any kind; complete: *My fishing poles complement his hooks and lines, so that together we can go fishing. The two brothers complemented each other; one was impulsive and outspoken, the other, cautious and reticent.* **2** *Obsolete.* to praise; commend; flatter.
—*v.i. Obsolete.* to behave with courtesy or ceremony.
[< Latin *complēmentum* < *complēre;* see etym. under **complete**. See etym. of doublet **compliment**.]
—*Syn. v.t.* **1 Complement, supplement** mean to complete. **Complement** means to complete by supplying something that is missing but necessary to make a perfect whole: *The two texts complement each other; what is sketchily dealt with in either one is treated fully in the other.* **Supplement** means to add something to make better or bigger or richer in some way: *Outside reading supplements a person's education.*
▶ **complement, compliment.** *Complement* means something that completes or makes perfect, or a number required to fill (related to *complete*): *She has her full complement of good looks. Compliment* has to do with politeness and praise: *Their progress deserved his compliment.*

com|ple|men|tal (kom′plə men′təl), *adj.* **1** = complementary. **2** *Obsolete.* accomplished. **3** *Obsolete.* formal; ceremonial; ceremonious. —**com′ple|men′tal|ly**, *adv.*

complemental air, = complementary air.

com|ple|men|tar|i|ty (kom′plə men tar′ə tē), *n.* **1** *no pl. Physics.* the principle that physical phenomena may be described in terms of waves, characterized by wave length and frequency, or in terms of the motion of particles, characterized by energy and momentum. **2** *pl.* **-ties.** a complementary relationship: *The contrasts and complementarities of the variations in Opus 109 sound positively choppy* (Igor Stravinsky).

com|ple|men|ta|ry (kom′plə men′tər ē, -trē), *adj.* **1** forming a complement; completing: *The four seasons are complementary parts of the year.* **2** mutually complementing each other's deficiencies.

complementary air, the air which can be drawn into the lungs by an effort after the ordinary inspiration is completed.

complementary angle, either of two angles which together form an angle of 90 degrees: *A 30-degree angle is the complementary angle of a 60-degree angle.* See picture under **angle**.

complementary cell, *Botany.* one of the cells which make up lenticel tissue.

complementary colors, two colors whose reflected lights combine to produce white or gray. Red and green are complementary colors.
▶ The effect of mixing pigments of complementary colors is not the same. Blue and yellow are complementary, but, mixed as paints, they produce green.

complementary distribution, *Linguistics.* the pattern of exclusive occurrence of a member in a pair of speech sounds or other linguistic forms, such as morphemes; complementation. In complementary distribution, either of the two members of any pair will exclude the other member in a particular occurrence because of different environment or context. For example, the two allophones of the phoneme *t* in English, unaspirated *t* as in *still* and aspirated *t* as in *till,* are in complementary distribution, because only the unaspirated form can occur after *s* and only the aspirated form can occur at the beginning of a word. *This important principle, known as complementary distribution, guarantees against error in listing the phonemes of a language; it is the cornerstone of structural phonology* (Joshua Whatmough).

complementary male, (in certain crustaceans and worms) a dwarf male that lives as a parasite upon the ordinary hermaphrodite individuals.

com|ple|men|ta|tion (kom′plə mən tā′shən), *n.* **1** *Mathematics.* an operation to determine the complement of a subset. **2** *Linguistics.* complementary distribution.

complement fixation, *Medicine.* the binding of complement to an antigen-antibody mixture, making it unavailable for subsequent reaction.

com|plete (kəm plēt′), *adj., v.,* **-plet|ed, -plet|ing.** —*adj.* **1** with all the parts; whole; entire: *a complete set of dominoes. We have a complete set of garden tools.* **2** (of a period of time) that has run its full course; whole: *The gardener spent a complete afternoon trimming those two shrubs.* **3** perfect; thorough: *a complete surprise, complete happiness.* **4** finished; done: *My homework is complete.* **5** (of a flower) having all four types of floral organs: sepals, petals, stamens, and pistils. **6** *Archaic.* fully equipped or endowed; accomplished: *a complete gentleman.*
—*v.t.* **1** to make whole or entire; make up the whole number or amount of: *She completed her set of dishes by buying the cups and saucers.* **2** to make perfect or thorough: *The good news completed my happiness.* **3** to get done; end; finish: *The band completed the piece before everyone clapped. By spring they had completed the house and moved in.*
[< Latin *complētus,* past participle of *complēre* finish, fulfill < *com-* up + *-plēre* fill] —**com|plete′ness**, *n.* —**com|plet′er**, *n.*
—*Syn. adj.* **1 Complete, entire** mean with all the parts. **Complete** implies that no part is missing: *I have the complete story now.* **Entire** implies wholeness and unbroken unity: *He gave the entire day to his work, not even taking time for lunch.*

complete fertilizer, any fertilizer including in its composition the elements nitrogen, phosphorus, and potassium.

com|plete|ly (kəm plēt′lē), *adv.* **1** entirely; wholly: *The runner was completely worn out.* **2** thoroughly; perfectly: *The new play was completely delightful.*

complete metamorphosis, metamorphosis in which the insect passes through four separate stages of growth; holometabolism. A butterfly or a moth undergoes complete metamorphosis as embryo, larva, pupa, and imago.

complete protein, a protein that contains every amino acid essential for building blood and tissue. Animal proteins, unlike the proteins in most vegetables, are complete proteins.

***complete quadrilateral**, a plane figure formed by four straight lines (extended) intersecting at six points.

***complete quadrilateral**

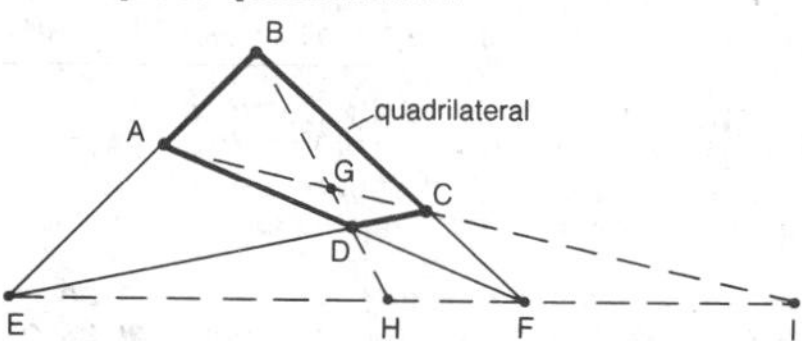

com|ple|tion (kəm plē′shən), *n.* **1** the act of completing; finishing: *After the completion of the job, the workmen went home.* **2** the condition of being completed: *The work is near completion.*

com|ple|tive (kəm plē′tiv), *adj.* serving to complete. —**com|ple′tive|ly**, *adv.*

com|plex (*adj., v.* kəm pleks′, kom′pleks; *n.* kom′pleks), *adj., n., v.* —*adj.* **1** made up of a number of parts: *A watch is a complex device. Hemoglobin is a complex chemical substance in the blood.* **SYN**: composite, compound. **2** hard to understand; complicated: *The instructions for building the radio were so complex we could not follow them.* **SYN**: involved, intricate.
—*n.* **1a** a complicated whole: *The assembly line handled a complex of 200 parts.* **b** a group of related or connected buildings, structures, or units: *The four-building complex will include a library, museum, and an auditorium and planetarium* (New York Times). **2** *Psychology.* an idea or group of repressed ideas associated with a past emotional disturbance so as to influence a person's present behavior to a great or excessive degree: *a complex of inferiority. Complexes are not to be regarded as distinctly abnormal phenomena, since they are a component of every individual's mental life* (Strecker and Ebaugh). **3** a strong prejudice; unreasonable dislike or fear: *She has a complex about snakes.*
—*v.t.* **1** to chelate: *Extra chemicals are sometimes prescribed to complex dissolved iron* (New Scientist). **2** to combine into a complex whole; complicate: *Mere murder got complexed with wile* (Robert Browning).
[< Latin *complexus,* past participle of *complectī* comprise; (literally) embrace < *com-* together + *plectere* twine] —**com|plex′ly**, *adv.* —**com|plex′ness**, *n.*

complex fraction, a fraction having a fraction or mixed number in the numerator, in the denominator, or in both; compound fraction.

com|plex|i|fy (kəm plek′sə fī), *v.t.*, **-fied, -fy|ing.** to make complex or complicated: *There is an underplot . . . which complexifies the incidents* (William Taylor).

com|plex|ion (kəm plek′shən), *n.* **1** the color, quality, and general appearance of the skin, particularly of the face: *The fisherman had a rough complexion from the weather.* **2** *Figurative.* general appearance; nature; character: *The complexion of the war was changed by two great victories.* **3** *Obsolete.* disposition; temperament. **4** *Historical.* the combination of the four humors in certain proportions, believed in medieval times to determine the nature of an animal, plant, or human body. [< Old French *complexion*, learned borrowing from Late Latin *complexiō, -ōnis* physical constitution < Latin, combination, connection < *complexus*; see etym. under **complex**]

com|plex|ion|al (kəm plek′shə nəl), *adj.* of or having to do with complexion, especially of the skin.

com|plex|ioned (kəm plek′shənd), *adj.* having a certain kind of complexion: *dark-complexioned.* ▶See **complected** for usage note.

com|plex|i|ty (kəm plek′sə tē), *n., pl.* **-ties.** **1** complex quality or condition; intricacy: *The complexity of the road map puzzled the lost motorist.* **2** something complex; complication.

✱**complex number**, the sum of a real number and an imaginary number.

✱**complex number** $2+3\sqrt{-1}$

complex sentence, a sentence having one main clause and one or more subordinate clauses. *Example*: When the engineer pulls the cord, the whistle blows.

com|plex|us (kəm plek′səs), *n.* a complex; complicated whole. [< Latin *complexus*; see etym. under **complex**]

complex word, a word consisting either of a free form and a bound form or of two bound forms: *Book is a simple word, books and bookish are complex words, and bookcase is a compound word* (Simeon Potter).

com|pli|a|ble (kəm plī′ə bəl), *adj.* = compliant.

com|pli|a|ble|ness (kəm plī′ə bəl nis), *n.* = compliance.

com|pli|a|bly (kəm plī′ə blē), *adv.* = compliantly.

com|pli|ance (kəm plī′əns), *n.* **1** the act of complying; act of doing as another wishes; act of yielding to a request or command: *A threat of rebellion forced King John to swear compliance with the nobles' provisions of the Magna Charta. I was equally balked by antagonism and compliance* (Emerson). **SYN**: consent, submission. **2** a tendency to yield to others: *Her refusal was all the more surprising in view of her usual compliance.*
in compliance with, complying with; according to: *He sent the package by air mail in compliance with the purchaser's request to send it quickly.*

com|pli|an|cy (kəm plī′ən sē), *n.* = compliance.

com|pli|ant (kəm plī′ənt), *adj.* complying; yielding; obliging: *A compliant person gives in to other people.* **SYN**: acquiescent. See syn. under **obedient** [< *comply* + *-ant*] —**com|pli′antly**, *adv.*

com|pli|ca|cy (kom′plə kə sē), *n., pl.* **-cies.** **1** the quality or state of being complicated. **2** a complicated thing.

com|pli|cate (kom′plə kāt), *v.* **-cat|ed, -cat|ing,** *adj.* —*v.t.* **1** to make hard to understand or to settle; mix up; confuse: *Too many rules complicate a game.* **SYN**: involve. **2** to make worse or more mixed up: *Her constant headaches were complicated by eye trouble.* **3** to entangle.
—*v.i.* to become complicated.
—*adj.* **1** *Botany.* folded upon itself. **2** (of insect's wings) folded lengthwise one or more times. **3** *Archaic.* complicated; complex.
[< Latin *complicāre* (with English *-ate*[1]) < *com-* together + *plicāre* to fold]

com|pli|cat|ed (kom′plə kā′tid), *adj.* hard to understand; involved; complex: *a complicated puzzle, a complicated design, complicated negotiations. Many cookbooks have very complicated directions.* **SYN**: intricate. —**com′pli|cat′ed|ly**, *adv.* —**com′pli|cat′ed|ness**, *n.*

com|pli|ca|tion (kom′plə kā′shən), *n.* **1** a confused state of affairs that is hard to understand or settle: *Such a complication of little rules makes this game hard to learn. His business complications required three lawyers to straighten them out.* **2** something that makes matters harder to untangle or settle; difficulty or problem added to one or more already existing: *Pneumonia was the complication the doctor feared most after the operation.* **3** the act of complicating: *The designer's complication of the diagram with too many details made the plan hard to understand.* **4** an element in a story or play which complicates the plot. **5** *Psychology.* the association of perceptions received through different senses, such as the association of smell and taste in eating food.

com|plice (kom′plis), *n. Archaic.* an accomplice; associate; confederate. [< Old French *complice*; see etym. under **complicity**]

com|plic|i|ty (kəm plis′ə tē), *n., pl.* **-ties.** **1** the state of being an accomplice; partnership in wrongdoing: *Knowingly receiving stolen goods is complicity in theft.* **2** = complexity. [< Middle French *complicité* < Old French *complice* an accomplice, learned borrowing from Late Latin *complex, -plicis* < *complicāre*; see etym. under **complicate**]

com|pli|ment (*n.* kom′plə mənt; *v.* kom′plə ment), *n., v.* —*n.* **1** something good said about one; something said in praise: *to make or pay a compliment. The famous actress was used to hearing many compliments.* **SYN**: commendation, tribute. **2** a courteous act: *The town paid the old artist the compliment of a large audience at his exhibit.* **3** *Dialect.* a complimentary gift; present.
—*v.t.* **1** to pay a compliment to; congratulate: *In awarding the prize, the chairman complimented the winner on his fine exhibit.* **2** to give something to (a person) as a polite attention: *He complimented his mother with an orchid corsage.*
compliments, formal respects, remembrances, or greetings: *In the box of flowers was a card saying "With the compliments of a friend."*
[< French *compliment* < Italian *complimento* < Spanish *cumplimiento* < *cumplir* fulfill, accomplish < Latin *complēre* fill up; see etym. under **complete**. See etym. of doublet **complement**.]
—**com′pli|ment′er**, *n.*
▶See **complement** for usage note.

com|pli|men|tal (kom′plə men′təl), *adj.* of or implying a compliment; complimentary. —**com′pli|men′tal|ly**, *adv.*

com|pli|men|ta|ry (kom′plə men′tər ē, -trē), *adj.* **1** expressing a compliment; praising: *a complimentary remark.* **SYN**: commendatory, laudatory. **2** *U.S.* given free: *The author received two complimentary copies of his new book.* **3** using a compliment or compliments: *He was complimentary about the preparations for the fair.* —**com′pli|men′ta|ri|ly**, *adv.* —**com′pli|men′ta|ri|ness**, *n.*

complimentary close, a polite parting phrase used in closing a letter, as "Sincerely Yours."

com|pli|ments (kom′plə mənts), *n.pl.* See under **compliment**.

com|plin (kom′plin), *n.* **1** the last of the seven canonical hours. **2** the service for it, now usually following vespers. [< Old French *complie* < Latin *complēta* (*hora*) completed hour]

com|pline (kom′plin, -plīn), *n.* = complin.

com|plot (*n.* kom′plot; *v.* kəm plot′), *n., v.,* **-plot|ted, -plot|ting.** *Archaic.* —*n.* a conspiracy; plot: *I know their complot is to have my life* (Shakespeare). —*v.t., v.i.* to plot together. [< French *complot* design, plan < Old French, struggle]

Com|plu|ten|si|an (kom′plü ten′sē ən), *adj.* of or having to do with the earliest complete polyglot Bible, published in the early 1500's in Alcalá de Henares, a town in Spain. [< Latin *Complūtensis* of *Complūtum*, the Latin name of Alcalá de Henares]

com|plu|vi|um (kom plü′vē əm), *n., pl.* **-vi|a** (vē ə). a quadrangular opening in the roof of the atrium in ancient Roman houses toward which the roof sloped and through which the rainwater fell into the impluvium. [< Latin *compluvium* < *compluere* to flow together]

com|ply (kəm plī′), *v.i.*, **-plied, -ply|ing.** **1** to act in agreement with a request or a command: *He complied with the doctor's order that he take a rest. He that complies against his will is of his own opinion still* (Samuel Butler). **SYN**: consent, yield, accede. **2** *Obsolete.* to use compliments; observe courtesies. [< Italian *complire* < Spanish *complir* < Latin *complēre*; see etym. under **complete**] —**com|pli′er**, *n.* —**com|ply′ing|ly**, *adv.*

com|po (kom′pō), *n., pl.* **-pos.** **1** any one of various composite substances, such as stucco, cement, or ornamental plaster; composition. **2** a substitute for ivory in making billiard balls. [short for *composition*]

com|po|né (kəm pō′nā; *French* kôɴ pô nā′), *adj.* = compony.

com|po|nent (kəm pō′nənt), *n., adj.* —*n.* **1** a necessary or essential part; one of the parts that make up a whole: *A chemist can separate a medicine into its components. Because alcohol is a solvent, it is a component of many liquid medicines.* **SYN**: See syn. under **element**. **2** *Physics.* one of the parts of a force, velocity, etc., out of which the whole may be compounded or into which it may be resolved.
—*adj.* that composes; constituent: *Blade and handle are the component parts of a knife.*
[< Latin *compōnēns, -entis*, present participle of *compōnere* compose]

com|po|ny (kəm pō′nē), *adj. Heraldry.* (of a bend) composed of small squares of two alternate tinctures in one row. Also, **componé**. [< Old French *compone*]

com|port[1] (kəm pôrt′, -pōrt′), *v., n.* —*v.t.* to conduct (oneself) in a certain manner; behave: *A judge should comport himself with dignity.*
—*v.i.* to agree (with); suit: *Silliness does not comport with the position of judge.* **SYN**: accord, fit. —*n. Obsolete.* behavior; comportment.
[< French *comporter* < Latin *comportāre* < *com-* together + *portāre* carry]

com|port[2] (kom′pôrt, -pōrt), *n.* a dish for fruit or candy; compote: *A fine pair of Georgian glass comports* (Cape Times). [variant of *compote*]

com|port|ance (kəm pôr′təns, -pōr′-), *n. Obsolete.* comportment.

com|port|ment (kəm pôrt′mənt, -pōrt′-), *n.* behavior; personal bearing. **SYN**: demeanor, deportment.

com|pose (kəm pōz′), *v.*, **-posed, -pos|ing.** —*v.t.* **1** to make up: *The ocean is composed of salt water. Our party was composed of three grown-ups and four children. Water composes nearly 70 per cent of the human body.* **SYN**: form, constitute. **2** to put together; arrange or produce: **a** to create or write (music): *Beethoven composed nine symphonies.* **b** to construct in words; write: *Poe composed mystery stories as well as love poems.* **3** to set (type) to form words and sentences; arrange (words) in type: *to compose the front page of a newspaper.* **4** to arrange the parts of (a painting). **5** to get (oneself) ready; put in a proper state: *After washing the dishes she composed herself to read a book. The witness tried to compose herself to meet the prosecution's embarrassing questions.* **6** to make calm; calm (oneself or one's features): *Stop crying and compose yourself before the doctor gets here.* **SYN**: quiet, relax. **7** to settle; adjust: *to compose a dispute. The players and the coach composed their differences.* **SYN**: reconcile.
—*v.i.* **1a** to write music; be a composer: *The conductor composes only in the morning.* **b** to write books, poems, or other literary works; be an author: *They say he's an excellent poet . . . composing as he goes in the street* (Ben Jonson). **2** to set up type in a printing office.
[< Old French *composer* < *com-* together + *poser* place; influenced in meaning by Latin *compōnere*; see etym. under **component**]

com|posed (kəm pōzd′), *adj.* **1** calm; quiet; self-controlled; tranquil: *The doctor's composed nature calmed his nervous patient.* **SYN**: serene, cool, collected. See syn. under **calm**. **2** *Obsolete.* elaborately or well put together. —**com|pos′ed|ly**, *adv.* —**com|pos′ed|ness**, *n.*

com|pos|er (kəm pō′zər), *n.* **1** a writer of music: *Early composers usually performed their own music* (Grant Fletcher). **2** a person or thing that composes. **3** an author.

com|pos|ing machine (kəm pō′zing), a machine that sets type for printing; typesetter.

composing room, the room or area in which type is set in a printing or typesetting plant.

composing rule, a thin piece of brass or steel fitted to the composing stick, on or against which the type is placed and arranged.

composing stick, a small metal tray in which type is set by hand.

com|pos|ite (kəm poz′it), *adj., n.* —*adj.* **1** made up of various parts; compound: *The photographer made a composite picture by putting together parts of several others.* **2** belonging to the composite family.
—*n.* **1** any composite thing: *English is a composite of many languages.* **SYN**: combination, compound, complex. **2** a composite plant. **3** = composite number. **4** a strong, lightweight, plasticlike material used for building a very light aircraft: *Composites—nonmetallic materials that are built up in thin layers—call for entirely different design, production, testing, and inspection facilities* (Jerry Grey).
[< Latin *compositus*, past participle of *compōnere* < *com-* together + *pōnere* put. See etym. of doublet **compost, compote**.] —**com|pos′ite|ly**, *adv.* —**com|pos′ite|ness**, *n.*

Com|pos|ite (kəm poz′it), *adj. Architecture.* of or designating a columnar order derived by Roman architects from a combination of the Greek

---

Pronunciation Key: hat, āge, cãre, fär; let, ēqual, tėrm; it, īce; hot, ōpen, ôrder; oil, out; cup, pu̇t, rüle; child; long; thin; ᴛʜen; zh, measure; ə represents a in about, e in taken, i in pencil, o in lemon, u in circus.

Corinthian and Ionic styles. The typical Composite capital is decorated with the acanthus leaves of the Corinthian order surmounted by the volutes of the Ionic.

***composite family**, a very large plant family comprising the most highly developed plants, including the daisy, aster, dandelion, marigold, and lettuce. The dicotyledonous plants of this family have a close head of many small flowers, or florets, surrounded by a series of bracts, the whole popularly referred to as the flower.

***composite family**

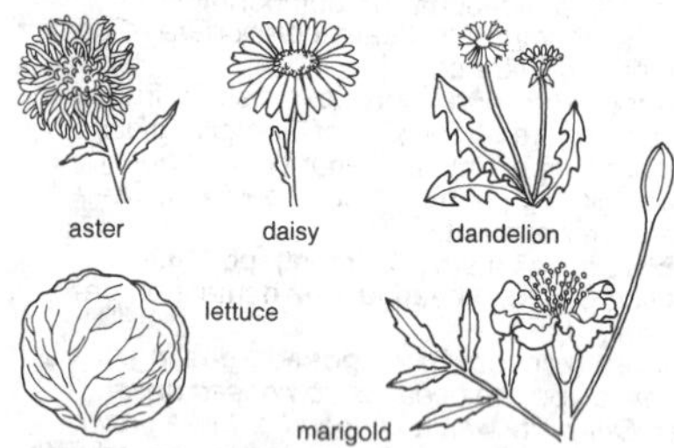

composite number, a number exactly divisible by some whole number other than itself or one. 4, 6, and 9 are composite numbers; 2, 3, 5, and 7 are prime numbers.

composite photograph, a single photograph produced by combining (usually in printing) two or more originally separate ones.

composite portrait, a portrait made by combining various descriptions, especially the portrait or picture of a wanted criminal drawn on the basis of individual features described by identifying witnesses: *A composite portrait of a man with heavy eyebrows, a domed forehead, a flat nose, and a scar on his left cheek* (New Yorker).

composite school, (in Canada) = comprehensive school.

composite track, a sound track made by blending separate records of voice, music, and sound effects. This track is printed with the silent motion picture to make a complete sound and picture print.

com|po|si|tion (kom′pə zish′ən), *n.* **1a** the make-up of anything; what is in it: *The composition of this candy includes sugar, chocolate, and milk.* **SYN**: constitution. **b** the arrangement of anything composed: *This painting has vivid colors but poor composition.* **SYN**: construction, design. **2** a putting together of a whole. Writing sentences, painting pictures, and setting type in printing are all forms of composition. **3** a thing composed. A symphony, poem, or painting is a composition. **4a** a short essay written as a school or college exercise: *I wrote a composition about my dog.* **SYN**: theme. **b** a course in writing: *All students are required to take a year of English composition.* **5** a mixture of substances; compound: *The dentist filled my tooth with a composition that had silver and mercury in it.* **SYN**: blend. **6a** an agreement or compromise; settlement: *A settlement of a debt in which a creditor agrees to accept part of the money owed to him by a debtor is called a composition.* **b** the money thus paid. **7** *Grammar.* the formation of compound words. **8** *Obsolete.* bodily constitution.

com|po|si|tion|al (kom′pə zish′ə nəl), *adj.* of or having to do with composition; suitable for composition: *a compositional exercise.* —**com′po|si′tion|al|ly**, *adv.*

composition B, a very powerful explosive consisting of a mixture of RDX and liquid TNT, that is replacing TNT in artillery shells.

composition board, = wallboard.

composition cloth, a cloth made from long flax, and dressed with a solution that makes it waterproof. It is used for bags, trunk covers, etc.

composition face, = composition plane.

***composition of forces**

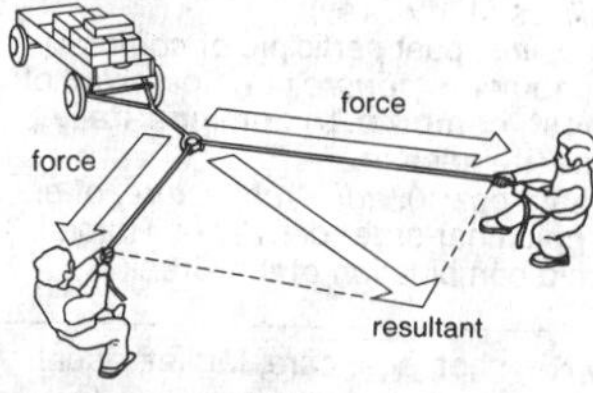

***composition of forces**, *Physics.* the joining or resolution of two or more given forces or vectors (components), acting in the same or different directions, into one force or vector (resultant) having an equivalent effect.

composition plane, *Crystallography.* the common plane or base between the two parts of a twin crystal.

com|pos|i|tive (kəm poz′ə tiv), *adj.* involving composition.

com|pos|i|tor (kəm poz′ə tər), *n.* = typesetter.

com|pos|i|to|ri|al (kəm poz′ə tôr′ē əl, -tōr′-), *adj.* **1** of or having to do with typesetting or compositors. **2** of or having to do with composers.

com|pos men|tis (kom′pəs men′tis), *Law.* of sound mind; sane. [< Latin *compos mentis*]

com|pos|o|graph (kəm pō′zə graf, -gräf), *n.* = composite photograph.

com|pos|si|bil|i|ty (kəm pos′ə bil′ə tē), *n.* coexistent possibility; compatiblity.

com|pos|si|ble (kəm pos′ə bəl), *adj.* possible at the same time with something else; capable of coexisting; compatible.

com|post (kom′pōst), *n., v.* —*n.* **1** a mixture of decaying leaves, manure, and other nutritive matter, for improving and fertilizing soil. **2** a mixture. **SYN**: composition, combination, compound. —*v.t.* **1** to make compost of: *Waste cellophane can be composted ... if small amounts of limestone and fertilizer are used* (Science News Letter). **2** to fertilize with compost.
[< Old French *compost, composte* < Latin *compositus,* past participle of *compōnere.* See etym. of doublet **composite, compote.**]

compost heap or **pile**, a mound of leaves, manure, and other nutritive matter, heaped up for use as compost after its decomposition: *Every morsel, including potato peel and pea shucks, was carried to the compost heap* (Punch).

com|po|sure (kəm pō′zhər), *n.* **1** calmness; quietness; self-control: *When his faithful old dog died, the boy's composure was remarkable. We sit down with great composure and write a letter to ourselves* (Samuel Johnson). **SYN**: serenity, tranquility. **2** *Obsolete.* composition; constitution.

com|po|ta|tion (kom′pə tā′shən), *n.* a drinking together; carouse. [< Latin *compōtātiō, -ōnis* < *com-* together + *pōtāre* drink]

com|po|ta|to|ry (kəm pō′tə tôr′ē, -tōr′-), *adj.* **1** having to do with compotation. **2** addicted to compotation.

com|pote (kom′pōt), *n.* **1** a dish with a supporting stem for fruit or candy. **2** stewed fruit. [< French *compote* < Old French *composte* mixture < Latin *composita,* feminine of *compositus.* See etym. of doublet **composite, compost.**]

com|po|tier (kom′pə tir′; *French* kôN pô tyā′), *n.* = compote (def. 1). [< French *compotier* < *compote* compote]

com|pound[1] (*adj.* kom′pound, kom pound′; *n.* kom′pound; *v.* kom pound′, kəm-), *adj., n., v.* —*adj.* **1** having more than one part: *a compound medicine, a compound molecule.* **SYN**: composite. **2** formed by the joining of two or more grammatical elements: *"Steamship," "horseshoe," and "strawberry" are compound nouns.* See also **compound sentence, compound word. 3** *Zoology.* **a** consisting of an intimate combination of individual animals in a colony, as coral does: *a compound tunicate.* **b** formed of many similar parts: *A cow has a compound stomach.* See also **compound eye. 4** *Botany.* made up of several similar parts combined into a single structure: *a compound umbel.* See also **compound fruit, compound leaf.**
—*n.* **1** something made by combining parts; mixture: *Many medicines are compounds.* **SYN**: composite. **2** a compound noun, verb, etc., such as *freeway, backtrack,* and *lackluster.* **3** a substance formed by chemical combination of two or more substances in definite proportions by weight: *Water is a compound of hydrogen and oxygen.*
—*v.t.* **1** to make up; mix; combine: *The druggist compounded several medicines to fill the prescription.* **2** to settle (a quarrel or debt) by a yielding on both sides: *They finally compounded their differences and shook hands.* **SYN**: compromise. **3** to charge, pay, or increase by compound interest: *Compounding interest payments means paying interest on interest* (New York Times). **4** to add to; increase; multiply: *The rain compounded the troubles of the lost hikers. The challenge to those of us who believe in free institutions is compounded by the steady growth of the Soviet economy* (Atlantic). **5** *Electricity.* to wind the field magnets of (a generator) so that it will be excited by a current flowing through both a shunt and a series coil. **6** *Obsolete.* to make up; constitute; compose. —*v.i.* to settle a quarrel or debt by a yielding on both sides: *He failed ... compounded, and went to America* (Benjamin Franklin). **SYN**: compromise.
[Middle English *compound,* participial adjective < *componen* to compound < Old French *compondre* < Latin *compōnere* < *com-* together + *pōnere* put] —**com|pound′a|ble**, *adj.* —**com|pound′er**, *n.*

com|pound[2] (kom′pound), *n.* an enclosed yard with buildings in it: *A detention camp for prisoners of war is a compound.* [probably < Malay *kampong* enclosure]

Compound B, = corticosterone.

com|pound-com|plex sentence (kom′pound-kom′pleks), *Grammar.* a sentence made up of two or more coordinate independent clauses and one or more dependent clauses. *Example:* At the end the hero dies, and the heroine, who is grief-stricken, swoons.

compound dislocation, a dislocation of a joint accompanied by a wound opening from the body surface.

compound dynamo, *Electricity.* a compound-wound dynamo.

Compound E, = cortisone.

compound engine, an engine in which the mechanical action of the steam or other working fluid is begun in a high-pressure cylinder and ended in a larger, low-pressure cylinder.

***compound eye**, the eye of certain arthropods, composed of many visual units, such as the large lateral eyes of insects. The housefly has a compound eye.

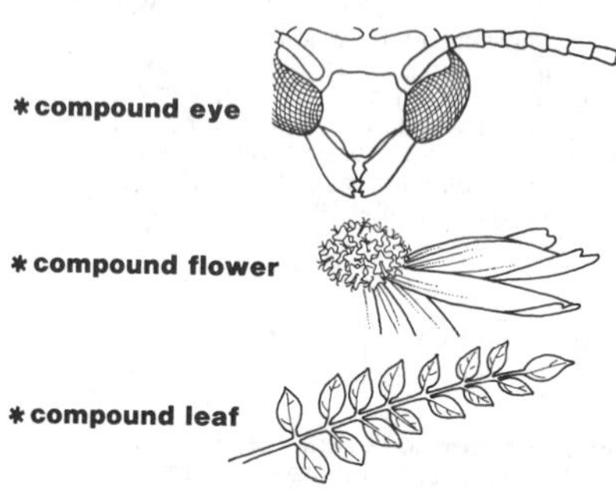

***compound eye**

***compound flower**

***compound leaf**

Compound F, = hydrocortisone.

***compound flower**, *Botany.* the flower head of a composite plant, composed of several small flowers (florets).

compound fraction, = complex fraction.

compound fracture, a fracture in which a broken bone cuts through the flesh and sticks out.

compound fruit, = collective fruit.

com|pound|ing (kom′poun ding), *n.* **1** the act of composing, mixing, or combining: *a sort of compounding between virtue and vice* (Jonathan Swift). **2** the formation of compound words; composition: *rules of compounding.* **3** (in the manufacture of tires) the cleaning and mixing of crude rubber with heat- and wear-resistant materials.

compound interest, interest paid on both the original sum of money borrowed or invested and on the interest added to it: *Many banks pay compound interest on savings.*

***compound leaf**, *Botany.* a leaf composed of two or more leaflets on a common stalk. Clover has compound leaves.

compound lever, a combination of two or more levers used in large weighing and testing machines, usually to decrease the effort.

compound microscope, a microscope having more than one lens, such as one with an eyepiece and an objective.

compound nucleus, *Nuclear Physics.* an excited nucleus resulting from the capture of a neutron by an atomic nucleus and forming an intermediate stage in an induced nuclear reaction.

compound number, a quantity expressed in two or more kinds of units or denominations. *Examples:* 3 ft., 5 in.; 2 hr., 18 min., 40 sec.

compound raceme, *Botany.* an indeterminate inflorescence occurring when a raceme becomes irregularly compound; panicle.

compound sentence, *Grammar.* a sentence made up of two or more main clauses. *Examples:* She liked to walk, but he liked to climb mountains. The wind blew, the rains fell, and the water covered the earth.

compound winding, *Electricity.* the winding of the field magnets of a generator so that it will be excited by a current flowing through both a shunt and a series coil.

compound word, a word made up of two or more words which keep their separate forms. *Steamship* is a compound word made up of the two words *steam* and *ship. Blackbird* and *strawberry* are compound words.

com|pound-wound (kom′pound wound′), *adj.* *Electricity.* (of a generator or a motor) having part of the field-magnet coils in series with the armature circuit and part shunted from it.

com|pra|dor or **com|pra|dore** (kom′prə dôr′), *n.* (formerly in China) a native agent in charge of the native employees in a foreign business house, consulate, etc., and the acting as an intermediary between the foreign agency and the native merchants or officials. [< Portuguese *comprador* buyer < Late Latin *comparātor* < *comparāre* provide < *com-* together + *parāre* furnish]

Com|preg (kom′preg), *n. Trademark.* wood hardened and strengthened by being compressed at high pressure and temperatures after impregnation with resin to prevent swelling or shrinking.

com|pre|hend (kom′pri hend′), *v.t.* **1** to understand the meaning of: *If you know how to use a word correctly, you comprehend it. Man does not yet comprehend the universe.* **SYN:** grasp, perceive. **2** to include; contain: *His report of the accident comprehended all the facts. The Middle West comprehends many farming and industrial areas.* **SYN:** comprise, embrace. See syn. under **include**. [< Latin *comprehendere* < *com-* + *prehendere* seize] —**com′pre|hend′er**, *n.* —**com′pre|hend′ing|ly**, *adv.*

—*Syn.* **1 Comprehend, apprehend** mean to take hold of something mentally. **Comprehend** means to grasp it completely and to understand its meaning fully and perfectly: *He comprehends the principles of an internal-combustion engine.* **Apprehend** means to see something of its meaning but not all its relationships or implications, and therefore to understand it only partly: *He apprehends the word but cannot use it.*

com|pre|hend|i|ble (kom′pri hen′də bəl), *adj.* = comprehensible.

com|pre|hen|si|bil|i|ty (kom′pri hen′sə bil′ə tē), *n.* intelligibility; comprehensible quality: *A combination of brevity and comprehensibility is by no means an easy thing to achieve* (Spectator).

com|pre|hen|si|ble (kom′pri hen′sə bəl), *adj.* that can be comprehended; understandable; intelligible. —**com′pre|hen′si|ble|ness**, *n.*

com|pre|hen|si|bly (kom′pri hen′sə blē), *adv.* understandably; intelligibly.

com|pre|hen|sion (kom′pri hen′shən), *n.* **1** the act or power of understanding; ability to get the meaning: *Arithmetic is beyond the comprehension of a baby. Why she should leave her family is beyond all comprehension.* **SYN:** perception, discernment, conception. **2** the act or fact of including. **3** the quality of being comprehensive; comprehensiveness. **4** *Logic.* the sum of the attributes included in a given term or concept; intension: *"Biped," "feathered," etc., form the comprehension of "chicken."* [< Latin *comprehēnsiō, -ōnis* < *comprehendere;* see etym. under **comprehend**]

com|pre|hen|sive (kom′pri hen′siv), *adj., n.* —*adj.* **1** including much; of large scope or extent: *The month's schoolwork ended with a comprehensive review.* **SYN:** inclusive. **2** able to understand many things fully; comprehending: *Benjamin Franklin had a comprehensive mind.* **SYN:** understanding.
—*n.* **1** a finished layout of an advertisement, complete with details. **2** *British.* comprehensive school. —**com′pre|hen′sive|ly**, *adv.* —**com′pre|hen′sive|ness**, *n.*

comprehensive school, (in Great Britain and Canada) a secondary school with a curriculum designed to meet the needs of a variety of students by offering courses both in general education and in commercial, trade, technical, and other specialized subjects.

com|pres|ence (kəm prez′əns), *n.* presence together: *... the compresence of all these moments in a single experience* (A. S. Pringle-Pattison).

com|press (*v.* kəm pres′; *n.* kom′pres), *v., n.* —*v.t.* to squeeze together; make smaller by pressure; condense: *Cotton is compressed into bales.* (*Figurative.*) *Can you compress the story into a few short sentences?* **SYN:** constrict, compact.
—*n.* **1** a pad of dry or wet cloth applied to a part of the body to prevent bleeding or to lessen inflammation: *Mother put a cold compress on my bruised forehead to reduce the bleeding under the skin.* **2** a machine for compressing cotton into bales.
[< Old French *compresser* < Latin *compressāre* (frequentative) < *comprimere* < *com-* together + *premere* press]

com|pressed (kəm prest′), *adj.* **1** squeezed together; made smaller by pressure; condensed: (*Figurative.*) *When the I.C.B.M. program was accelerated ... it was geared to a timetable so compressed it was viewed as wildly optimistic* (New York Times). **2** *Botany.* flattened along its length. **3** *Zoology.* narrower in the lateral dimension than in the dorsoventral dimension; of greater depth than width: *The flounder has a compressed body.* —**com|press′ed|ly**, *adv.*

compressed air, air that has been put under extra pressure so that it has a great deal of force when released. Compressed air is used to operate certain kinds of brakes, drills, guns, sprayers, and atomizers, and to inflate tires.

com|pressed-air (kəm prest′ãr′), *adj.* utilizing compressed air as a source of power: *a compressed-air drill, gun, or sprayer.*

compressed yeast, yeast pressed and mixed with flour or meal: *Compressed yeast, the other commercial form, contains enough starch and moisture to start fermentation in a short time* (Lewis Hanford Tiffany).

com|press|i|bil|i|ty (kəm pres′ə bil′ə tē), *n.* compressible quality.

com|press|i|ble (kəm pres′ə bəl), *adj.* that can be compressed. —**com|press′i|ble|ness**, *n.*

com|pres|sion (kəm presh′ən), *n.* **1** the act or process of compressing. **2** compressed condition. **3** the reduction in volume of a gas by the application of pressure, especially: **a** (in an internal-combustion engine) the reduction in volume of the explosive mixture, or air in a diesel engine, drawn into the cylinder behind the piston, occurring before spark ignition, or fuel injection, and determining the thermodynamic efficiency of the engine cycle. **b** (in a steam engine) the reduction in volume of the steam left in a cylinder after the exhaust is closed, forming a cushion for the piston at the end of its stroke. **4** *Figurative.* condensed expression or style: *Compression is one pole of Japanese poetry* (Atlantic).

com|pres|sion|al (kəm presh′ə nəl), *adj.* having to do with or producing compression: *a compressional force, compressional energy.*

compressional wave, = compression wave.

compression faucet, a faucet that operates by a screw whose metal disk is faced with a washer that bears against the opening between two chambers to close the faucet.

com|pres|sion|ism (kəm presh′ə niz əm), *n.* a literary style marked by extreme economy in the creation of characters and incidents: *One is compressionism, ... a matter of desperate, boxed-in themes* (London Times). —**com|pres′sion|ist,** *adj.*

compression ratio, the ratio of the volume of the fuel mixture in a cylinder at the beginning of the compression stroke to the volume at the end, used as a measure of an internal-combustion engine's power.

compression wave, *Physics.* a wave in which the particles of a substance move to and fro in the same direction as the motion of the wave, causing the substance to compress: *Sound waves are compression waves.*

com|pres|sive (kəm pres′iv), *adj.* tending to compress; compressing. —**com|pres′sive|ly**, *adv.* —**com|pres′sive|ness**, *n.*

compressive strength, the strength of a material to withstand a load or strain that tends to compress it. Concrete has a compressive strength of 2,000 to 5,000 pounds per square inch.

com|pres|sor (kəm pres′ər), *n.* **1** a person or thing that compresses. **2** *Anatomy.* a muscle which compresses a part. **3** (in surgery) an instrument for compressing a part of the body. **4** a machine for compressing air, gas, or the like. [< Latin *compressor* < *comprimere;* see etym. under **compress**]

com|pres|sure (kəm presh′ər), *n.* the act or process of compressing; compression.

com|pri|ma|ri|o (kom′pri mä′rē ō), *n., pl.* **-os.** the singer of an operatic supporting role. [< Italian *comprimario* < *com-* com- + *primo* first + *-ario* -ary]

com|pris|a|ble (kəm prī′zə bəl), *adj.* that can be comprised.

com|prise (kəm prīz′), *v.t.,* **-prised, -pris|ing.** **1** to be made up of; consist of; include: *The United States comprises 50 states.* **SYN:** contain, comprehend, encompass, embrace, incorporate. See syn. under **include**. **2** to make up; compose; constitute: *Fifty states comprise the United States. The committee is comprised of five members.* [< Old French *compris,* past participle of *comprendre* < Latin *comprehendere;* see etym. under **comprehend**]

com|prize (kəm prīz′), *v.t.,* **-prized, -priz|ing.** = comprise.

com|pro|mise (kom′prə mīz), *v.,* **-mised, -mis|ing,** *n., adj.* —*v.t.* **1** to settle (a quarrel or difference of opinion) by agreeing that each will give up a part of what he demands; come to terms about: *To speak truth, I compromised matters; I served two masters* (Charlotte Brontë). **SYN:** adjust. **2** to put under suspicion; put in danger: *to compromise one's reputation.* **SYN:** endanger, jeopardize, imperil. **3** *Obsolete.* to bind by agreement.
—*v.i.* to make a compromise: *A good politician knows how to compromise.*
—*n.* **1a** a settlement of a quarrel or a difference of opinion by a partial yielding on both sides: *They both wanted the apple; their compromise was to share it.* **SYN:** accommodation, adjustment. **b** adjustment for practical purposes of rival systems, theories, etc., by a partial yielding on both sides: *The essence of politics is compromise* (Macaulay). **2** the result of any such settlement or adjustment: *the Missouri Compromise.* **3** anything halfway between two different things: *A sofa is a compromise between a chair and a bed.* **SYN:** mean, balance. **4** an exposing to danger, suspicion, etc.; an endangering. **SYN:** imperilment.
—*adj.* agreed on by compromise; representing a compromise: *a compromise candidate.*
[< Old French *compromis,* learned borrowing from Latin *comprōmissum,* neuter past participle of *comprōmittere* < *com-* together + *prōmittere* promise] —**com′pro|mis′er**, *n.* —**com′pro|mis′ing|ly**, *adv.*

Comp|sog|na|thus (komp sog′nə thəs), *n.* a very small dinosaur with a big head and large, sharp teeth, distributed throughout the world from the middle Triassic through the Cretaceous. It measured only 2½ feet long, including its tail. [< New Latin *Compsognathus* the genus name < Greek *kompsós* elegant + *gnáthos* jaw]

compt (kount, kompt), *v.t., v.i., n. Archaic.* count[1].

compt., comptroller.

compt|er (koun′tər), *n. Archaic.* a counter (prison for debtors). [old variant of *counter*[3]]

compte ren|du (kôɴt räɴ dʏ′), *French.* **1** a report; official statement: *I find it difficult ... to refrain from quoting here part of the compte rendu in next day's Petit Matin* (New Yorker). **2** *Commerce.* an account rendered.

Comp|tom|e|ter (komp tom′ə tər), *n. Trademark.* a machine that adds, subtracts, divides, and multiplies mechanically.

Comp|ton effect (komp′tən), *Physics.* an increase in the wave length of X rays or gamma rays which occurs when these radiations are scattered on striking an electron. In the collision, kinetic energy is communicated to the electron and the quantum energy of the radiation is reduced. [< Arthur H. *Compton,* 1892-1962, an American physicist, who observed it]

comp|trol|ler (kən trō′lər), *n.* a person employed to look after expenditures and accounts; controller. [variant spelling of *controller,* on analogy of earlier *compter* (now *counter*), *accompt* (now *account*), etc.]

Comptroller General, *pl.* **Comptrollers General** or **Comptroller Generals**. the chief accountant of the United States, head of the General Accounting Office.

Comptroller of the Currency, the chief official of the United States government who oversees the operations of the national banks.

comp|trol|ler|ship (kən trō′lər ship), *n.* the position or rank of a comptroller; controllership.

com|pul|sa|tive (kəm pul′sə tiv), *adj.* = compulsory.

com|pul|sa|to|ry (kəm pul′sə tôr′ē, -tōr′-), *adj. Rare.* compulsory.

com|pul|sion (kəm pul′shən), *n.* **1** the act of compelling; use of force; force: *He can be made to take this medicine only by compulsion. A promise made under compulsion is not binding.* **SYN:** constraint, coercion. **2a** an impulse that is hard to resist: *Wealthy people sometimes feel a compulsion to steal things they can easily afford to buy.* **b** the act itself. [< Late Latin *compulsiō, -ōnis* < Latin *compellere;* see etym. under **compel**]

com|pul|sion|ist (kəm pul′shə nist), *n.* an advocate of some form of compulsion, especially of compulsory military service.

compulsion neurosis, = obsessional neurosis.

com|pul|sive (kəm pul′siv), *adj.* **1** compelling: *She has a compulsive desire to keep her house perfectly neat.* **2** using compulsion: *He gave the boy ahead of him a compulsive push.* **SYN:** coercive. **3** of or having to do with compulsion. —**com|pul′sive|ly**, *adv.* —**com|pul′sive|ness**, *n.*

com|pul|so|ry (kəm pul′sər ē), *adj., n.* —*adj.* **1** compelled; required: *Attendance at school is compulsory for children over seven years of age.* **SYN:** obligatory. **2** compelling; using force.
—*n.* a required demonstration of skill in figure skating, gymnastics, and the like: *All nine judges have placed Miss Linichuk and her partner in first place after the compulsories* (London Times).
—**com|pul′so|ri|ly**, *adv.* —**com|pul′so|ri|ness**, *n.*

compulsory arbitration, arbitration of a dispute between labor and management that is legally binding by government order or previous agreement: *The automatic assurance of compulsory arbitration would encourage one or both parties to neglect their bargaining responsibilities* (John

Pronunciation Key: hat, āge, cãre, fär; let, ēqual, tėrm; it, īce; hot, ōpen, ôrder; oil, out; cup, pu̇t, rüle; child; long; thin; ᴛʜen; zh, measure; ə represents **a** in about, **e** in taken, **i** in pencil, **o** in lemon, **u** in circus.

F. Kennedy).

com|punc|tion (kəm pungk′shən), *n.* **1** uneasiness of the mind because of wrongdoing; pricking of the conscience; regret; remorse: *He had no compunction about having eaten up a whole box of cookies. . . . a remorse and compunction for former sins* (John Donne). **SYN:** contrition. **2** a slight or passing regret; being temporarily sorry: *He threw out the rowdy without compunction.* [< Late Latin *compunctiō, -ōnis* pricking, remorse < Latin *compungere* < *com-* (intensive) + *pungere* to prick] —**com|punc′tion|less,** *adj.*

com|punc|tious (kəm pungk′shəs), *adj.* having or feeling compunction. —**com|punc′tious|ly,** *adv.*

com|pur|ga|tion (kom′pər gā′shən), *n.* **1** a former way of legally clearing a person accused of crime by the oaths of persons testifying to his innocence or veracity. **2** the hearing or vindication of an accused person. [< Late Latin *compurgātiō, -ōnis* < Latin *compurgāre* < *com-* completely + *purgāre* purify, purge]

com|pur|ga|tor (kom′pər gā′tər), *n.* a witness who swears to the innocence or veracity of an accused person.

com|pur|ga|to|ri|al (kəm pėr′gə tôr′ē əl, -tōr′-), *adj.* having to do with compurgation.

com|pur|ga|to|ry (kəm pėr′gə tôr′ē, -tōr′-), *adj.* of or having to do with a compurgator.

com|put|a|bil|i|ty (kəm pyü′tə bil′ə tē), *n.* the quality of being computable; calculability.

com|put|a|ble (kəm pyü′tə bəl), *adj.* that can be computed; calculable.

com|pu|ta|tion (kom′pyə tā′shən), *n.* **1** calculation; reckoning. Addition and subtraction are forms of computation. **2** an amount computed.

com|pu|ta|tion|al (kom′pyə tā′shə nəl), *adj.* of or having to do with computation: *An electronic computer is used for much of the computational work* (New Scientist). —**com′pu|ta′tion|al|ly,** *adv.*

computational linguistics, linguistics studies by the use of computers to process and correlate linguistic data.

com|pu|ta|tive (kəm pyü′tə tiv, kom′pyə tā′-), *adj.* given to computation.

com|pute (kəm pyüt′), *v.,* **-put|ed, -put|ing,** *n.* —*v.t.* to do by arithmetic; calculate; reckon: *Mother computed the cost of our trip.*
—*v.i.* to make a computation; reckon: *His failure to compute correctly resulted in an explosion.*
—*n. Rare.* reckoning; calculation; computation.
[< Latin *computāre* < *com-* (intensive) + *putāre* reckon. See etym. of doublet **count**[1].]

com|put|er (kəm pyü′tər), *n.* **1** a machine which computes, especially an electronic machine that solves complex mathematical problems in a very short time when given certain information: *Computers the size of a matchbox that do the work of a packing case full of normal electronic equipment* (Newsweek). **2** one skilled in computing, or a thing that computes. —**com|put′er|like′,** *adj.*

com|put|er|a|cy (kəm pyü′tər ə sē), *n.* = computer literacy.

computer dating, the arrangement of social dates between single men and women by having a computer match them according to types.

com|put|er-en|hanced (kəm pyü′tər en hanst′, -hänst′), *adj.* (of a photograph) improved in distinctness, clarity or intensity of detail by the use of a computer to control developing.

computer enhancement, the use of computer-enhanced techniques to improve photographic images.

com|put|er|ese (kəm pyü′tə rēz′), *n.* **1** the jargon of people who work with computers: *[He] . . . mixes computerese into his briefings: he talks of "inputs" and "outputs," of "implementing" a policy within a "time frame"* (Time). **2** = computer language: *It can be programmed in English, instead of "computerese"* (Saturday Review).

computer game, a game containing electronic circuitry and computer elements.

computer graphics, the use of computers to produce works of graphics or the graphic arts, as in industrial design and commercial art.

com|put|er|ist (kəm pyü′tə rist), *n.* a person trained or skilled in the use of computers.

com|put|er|i|za|tion (kəm pyü′tər ə zā′shən), *n.* the act or process of computerizing.

com|put|er|ize (kəm pyü′tə rīz), *v.t.,* **-ized, -iz|ing. 1** to adapt to a computer; operate by means of a computer or computers: *to computerize a bookkeeping system.* **2** to install computers in; equip with computers: *to computerize a factory or office.* —**com|put′er|iz′a|ble,** *adj.*

computerized axial tomography, *Medicine.* X-ray photography in which images of an internal part of the body are made by a circling X-ray beam and synthesized by computer into a single cross-sectional view; CAT scanning.

computer language, 1 any system of words and symbols for programming a computer: *Each computer language, such as BASIC, FORTRAN, or COBOL, has its own rules of grammar, conventions, commands, and detailed instructions* (Van Court Hare, Jr.). **2** = machine language.

computer literacy, the ability to understand and use computers.

com|put|er-lit|er|ate (kəm pyü′tər lit′ər it), *adj.* capable of understanding and using computers.

com|put|er|man (kəm pyü′tər mən), *n., pl.* **-men.** = computerist.

computer science, the science of computers, including their design, programming, and operation. —**computer scientist.**

computer virus, a subprogram or routine secretly inserted into a standard computer program or operating system, where it is able to copy itself and from which it may be spread to other programs and computers: *Computer viruses, depending on their instructions, can destroy data, display an unexpected message, make a disk unusable or wreak some other form of havoc* (Philadelphia Inquirer).

com|put|er|y (kəm pyü′tə rē), *n.* **1** the use, manufacture, or operation of computers. **2** computers.

com|put|ing gunsight (kəm pyü′ting), a gunsight, especially one for aircraft machine guns, that automatically calculates for wind, range, and other factors.

computing machine, = computer.

com|put|ist (kəm pyü′tist), *n.* a person who computes or calculates.

com|pu|tor (kəm pyü′tər), *n.* = computer.

com|pu|tus (kom′pyə təs), *n.* **1** a computation. **2** an account. **3** a medieval set of tables for calculating movable dates of the calendar and astronomical occurrences. **4** a calendar. [< Late Latin *computus* < Latin *computāre* compute]

Comr., commissioner.

com|rade (kom′rad; *especially British* kom′rid, kum′-), *n.* **1** a companion and friend: *The two boys were close companions and did everything together.* **2** a person who shares in what another is doing; fellow worker; partner. **3** a fellow member of a union, political party, or other group: *Members of the Communist Party are often called comrades.* **4** = comrade in arms. [< Middle French *camarade* < Spanish *camarada* roommate < Latin *camera* vault < Greek *kamárā*]

comrade in arms, *pl.* **comrades in arms.** a fellow soldier: *Colonel Porfiriev . . . hailed the whole group as "our friends, our comrades in arms who fought fascism!"* (New York Times).

com|rade|ly (kom′rad lē; *especially British* kom′rid lē, kum′-), *adj.* of a comrade; like or befitting a comrade: *With a comradely gesture, he beckoned the refugees to his cabin.* —**com′rade|li|ness,** *n.*

com|rade|ry (kom′rad rē; *especially British* kom′rid rē, kum′-), *n.* = comradeship.

com|rade|ship (kom′rad ship; *especially British* kom′rid ship, kum′-), *n.* **1** the relation of comrades; friendship; fellowship; companionship. **2** the condition of being a comrade.

com|rogue (kom′rōg), *n. Archaic.* a fellow rogue.

com|sat (kom′sat′), *n.* = communications satellite.

Com|so|mol (kom′sə mol), *n.* = Komsomol.

com|stock|er (kum′stok ər, kom′-), *n.* a person who advocates or practices comstockery. [back formation < *comstockery*]

com|stock|er|y (kum′stok ər ē, kom′-), *n.* the carrying to extremes of suppression or censorship of works of literature or art for supposed obscenity. [< Anthony *Comstock,* 1844-1915, an American reformer, + *-ery*]

Com|symp (kom′simp′), *n. U.S. Informal.* a Communist sympathizer.

comte (kôɴt), *n. French.* a count.

com|tesse (kôɴ tes′), *n. French.* a countess.

Com|ti|an (kom′tē ən, kôɴ′-), *adj.* of Auguste Comte or his philosophy of positivism.

Comt|ism (kom′tiz əm, kôɴ′-), *n.* the philosophy of Auguste Comte (1798-1857); positivism. —**Comt′ist,** *adj., n.*

Co|mus (kō′məs), *n. Greek and Roman Mythology.* a young god of revelry.

con[1] (kon), *adv., n.* —*adv.* against: *The two debating teams argued the question pro and con.*
—*n.* a reason against: *The pros and cons of a question are arguments for and against it.*
[short for Latin *contrā* against]

con[2] (kon), *v.t.,* **conned, con|ning. 1** to learn well enough to remember; study: *Hunched at his desk, ceaselessly he conned his books. All his faults observed . . . and conned by rote* (Shakespeare). **2** to examine carefully; pore over: *He . . . stopped to con what he had written before advancing to be greeted by the Speaker* (London Times). **SYN:** peruse. [Middle English *cunnen,* Old English *cunnian* test, examine]

con[3] (kon), *v.,* **conned, con|ning,** *n. Nautical.* —*v.t.* to direct the steering of (a ship): *A local pilot familiar with the harbor steers, or cons, the ship out into deep water* (P. V. H. Weems).
—*n.* **1** the act or process of conning. **2** the station taken by the person who cons. Also, **conn.**
[variant of *cond* < Old French *conduire* lead, guide < Latin *condūcere* to conduct]

con[4] (kon), *adj., v.,* **conned, con|ning.** *Slang.* —*adj.* swindling; duping: *a con game, a con man.* —*v.t.* to swindle; dupe: *I was conned into buying an overpriced used car. I was just wondering how a neurasthenic bookworm had ever conned himself into bouncing through the African bush* (S. J. Perelman).
[American English; for *confidence* (game or man)]

con[5] (kon), *n.* a rap with the knuckles; knock. [compare French *cogner* to strike, thresh]

con[6] (kon), *n. Slang.* a convict.

con[7] (kon), *n. Slang.* consumption; tuberculosis.

con., 1 against (Latin, *contra*). **2** concerto. **3** conclusion. **4** consolidated. **5** *Law.* consort; wife (Latin, *conjunx*).

Con., Consul.

con-, *prefix.* the form of **com-** before *n,* as in *connote,* and before consonants except *b, h, l, m, p, r, w,* as in *concern, conduct.*

CONAD (no periods), Continental Air Defense, a joint command of the three United States services established to defend continental United States against air attack.

con af|fet|to (kôn äf fāt′tō), *Italian, Music.* tenderly and with feeling (used as a direction).

con a|mo|re (kôn ä mō′rā), *Italian.* **1** with love; with tenderness: *He expatiated con amore on the charms of Florence* (Henry James). **2** heartily; with enthusiasm. **3** *Music.* tenderly (used as a direction).

con a|ni|ma (kôn ä′nē mä), *Italian, Music.* with spirit (used as a direction).

co|nar|i|al (kō når′ē əl), *adj.* of or having to do with the conarium.

co|nar|i|um (kō når′ē əm), *n., pl.* **-nar|i|a** (-når′ē ə). = pineal body. [< New Latin *conarium* < Greek *kōnárion* (diminutive) < *kônos* cone (because of its shape)]

co|na|tion (kō nā′shən), *n. Philosophy, Psychology.* the mental faculty or power of striving or effort, whether or not consciously, toward an end and including desire and volition (distinguished from *cognition,* knowing, and *affection,* feeling). [< Latin *cōnātiō, -ōnis* attempt < *cōnārī* to try]

con|a|tive (kon′ə tiv, kō′nə-), *adj.* **1** *Philosophy, Psychology.* having to do with conation or striving. **2** *Grammar.* expressing endeavor.

co|na|tus (kō nā′təs), *n., pl.* **-tus. 1** an effort; endeavor; striving: *. . . a conatus that can find no distinct object to rest upon* (Thomas Chalmers). **2** a force, impulse, or tendency simulating a human effort; nisus. [< Latin *cōnātus, -ūs* < *cōnārī* to try]

con bri|o (kôn brē′ō), *Italian, Music.* vigorously (used as a direction).

conc., 1a concentrate. **b** concentrated. **c** concentration. **2** concerning.

con|cam|er|at|ed (kon kam′ə rā′tid), *adj.* **1** divided into chambers: *a concamerated shell.* **2** *Obsolete.* arched; vaulted. [< Latin *concamerātus,* past participle of *concamerāre* to vault, arch (< *con-* with + *camerāre* to arch) + English *-ed*[2]]

con|cam|er|a|tion (kon kam′ə rā′shən), *n.* **1** concamerated or chambered formation. **2** a chamber or cell.

con|cat|e|nate (kon kat′ə nāt), *v.,* **-nat|ed, -nat|ing,** *adj.* —*v.t.* to unite in a series or chain; link. —*adj.* **1** linked together. **2** *Zoology.* united at the base by ridges, raised lines, etc., especially of rows, spines, or the like. [< Late Latin *concatēnāre* (with English *-ate*[1]) < Latin *com-* together + *catēna* chain] —**con|cat′e|na′tion,** *n.*

***con|cave** (*adj., v.* kon kāv′, kon′kāv, kong′-; *n.* kon′kāv, kong′-), *adj., n., v.,* **-caved, -cav|ing.** —*adj.* **1** hollow and curved like the inside of a circle or sphere; curving in: *The palm of one's hand is slightly concave.* **2** *Obsolete.* hollow.
—*n.* a concave surface or thing: *a shout that tore hell's concave* (Milton).
—*v.t.* to make concave.
[< Old French *concave,* learned borrowing from Latin *concavus* < *com-* (intensive) + *cavus* hollow] —**con|cave′ly,** *adv.* —**con|cave′ness,** *n.*

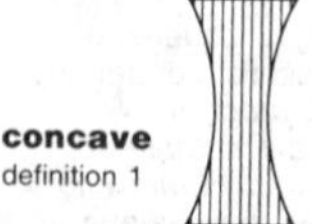

***concave** definition 1

double concave lens

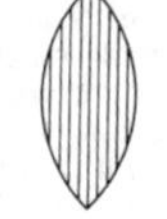

double convex lens

con|cav|i|ty (kon kav′ə tē), *n., pl.* **-ties. 1** concave condition or quality: *The convexity of the [airplane] wing's upper surface and the concavity of its lower aid this alternate gripping and slip-of the air* (Atlantic). **2** a concave surface or thing; hollow.

con|ca|vo-con|cave (kon kā′vō kon kāv′), *adj.* concave on both sides.

con|ca|vo-con|vex (kon kā′vō kon veks′), *adj.* **1** concave on one side and convex on the other: *Some lenses are concavo-convex.* **2** having a greater degree of curvature on the concave face than on the convex face, and so being thinnest in the middle.

con|ceal (kən sēl′), *v.t.* **1** to put or keep out of sight; hide: *He concealed the ball behind his back. . . . the complexity and hard work which real science involves . . . is concealed in popular expositions* (Arthur Beer). **SYN:** See syn. under **hide.** **2** to keep secret: *She concealed her identity by wearing a mask.* **SYN:** shroud, veil, cloak, mask. [< Old French *conceler* < Latin *concēlāre* < *com-* (intensive) + *cēlāre* to hide] —**con|ceal′a|ble,** *adj.* —**con|ceal′er,** *n.*

con|ceal|ment (kən sēl′mənt), *n.* **1** the act of hiding or keeping secret: *The witness's concealment of facts prevented a fair trial.* **2** a being hidden or kept secret. **3** a means or place for hiding: *The tiger lay deep in his concealment of high grass.*

con|cede (kən sēd′), *v.,* **-ced|ed, -ced|ing.** —*v.t.* **1a** to admit as true; acknowledge: *Everyone concedes that 2 and 2 make 4. I conceded that I had made a mistake.* **SYN:** admit. **b** to allow formally for the sake of argument: *Conceding that man is a biological structure, the speaker maintained that he is something more.* **2** to allow (a person) to have; grant; yield: *to concede the game. He conceded us the right to walk through his land.* **SYN:** accord.
—*v.i.* to make a concession.
[< Latin *concēdere* < *com-* (intensive) + *cēdere* yield] —**con|ced′er,** *n.*

con|ced|ed|ly (kən sē′did lē), *adv.* = admittedly.

con|ceit (kən sēt′), *n., v.* —*n.* **1** too much pride in oneself or in one's ability to do things: *In his conceit, the track star thought that no one could outrun him.* **SYN:** vanity. See syn. under **pride. 2** a pleasing fancy; whim. **3** a witty thought or expression, often a far-fetched one; a startling metaphor ingeniously worked out. **4** the use of these in writing: *That . . . liberty of conceit proper to the Poet* (Sir Philip Sidney). **5** favorable opinion; esteem. **6** *Obsolete.* a thought; idea. **7** *Obsolete.* a fancy article; trifle.
—*v.t. Archaic.* **1** to conceive mentally; imagine: *One of two bad ways you must conceit me, Either a coward or a flatterer* (Shakespeare). **2** to have a good opinion of; flatter (oneself). **3** to take a fancy to.
out of conceit with, dissatisfied with: *to be out of conceit with our lot in life* (Cardinal Newman).
[< *conceive,* on the analogy of *deceit*]

con|ceit|ed (kən sē′tid), *adj.* **1** having too high an opinion of oneself or one's ability; vain: *We heard no more of the conceited boy's great strength after he lost the fight.* **SYN:** egotistical, proud, self-satisfied. **2** *Dialect.* full of notions; fanciful; whimsical. **3** *Obsolete.* intelligent; ingenious; clever. —**con|ceit′ed|ly,** *adv.* —**con|ceit′ed|ness,** *n.*

con|ceiv|a|bil|i|ty (kən sē′və bil′ə tē), *n.* the quality or condition of being conceivable.

con|ceiv|a|ble (kən sē′və bəl), *adj.* that can be thought of; imaginable: *We take every conceivable precaution against fire.* —**con|ceiv′a|ble|ness,** *n.* —**con|ceiv′a|bly,** *adv.*

con|ceive (kən sēv′), *v.,* **-ceived, -ceiv|ing.** —*v.t.* **1** to form in the mind; think up: *The Wright brothers conceived the design of the first successful motor-powered plane.* **SYN:** plan, devise, formulate. **2** to form (an opinion); think. **SYN:** See syn. under **imagine. 3** to experience or entertain (a feeling): *He had conceived a dislike . . . for this lady* (Maria Edgeworth). **4** to imagine: *It is difficult to conceive an effect without a cause.* **5** to put into words; express: *The warning was conceived in the plainest language.* **6** to understand; comprehend: *No one could conceive how such a machine could be constructed.* **7** to become pregnant with: *to conceive a child.*
—*v.i.* **1** to have an idea or feeling; think (of): *Young children cannot conceive of life without automobiles and television. We cannot conceive of such a thing happening.* **SYN:** imagine. **2** to become pregnant.
[< Old French *conceiv-,* stem of *conceveir* < Latin *concipere* take in < *com-* altogether + *capere* take] —**con|ceiv′er,** *n.*

con|cel|e|brant (kon sel′ə brənt), *n.* a clergyman who celebrates the Mass jointly with another or others.

con|cel|e|brate (kon sel′ə brāt), *v.t., v.i.,* **-brat|ed, -brat|ing.** to celebrate (Mass) together in the Roman Catholic Church: *The new cardinals had concelebrated Mass in Latin with the Pope at the Basilica's main altar* (Manchester Guardian Weekly). —**con|cel′e|bra′tion,** *n.*

con|cent (kən sent′), *n.* harmony; accord. [< Latin *concentus, -ūs* < *concinere* < *con-* together + *canere* sing, sound]

con|cen|ter (kon sen′tər), *v.t.* to bring or draw to a common center; concentrate; center; focus.
—*v.i.* to meet in a common center; converge to a common center; concentrate. Also, *especially British,* **concentre.** [< French *concentrer* < Latin *com-* with + *centrum* center]

con|cen|trate (kon′sən trāt), *v.,* **-trat|ed, -trat|ing,** *n.* —*v.t.* **1** to bring together in one place: *A magnifying glass can concentrate enough sunlight to scorch paper. Our fire chief concentrated his men on the roof to fight the blaze.* **SYN:** gather, collect, assemble, focus. **2** to make stronger. An acid solution is concentrated when it has very much acid in it. **SYN:** intensify. **3** to remove rock, sand, etc., from (metal or ore).
—*v.i.* **1** to come together in one place. **2** *Figurative.* to pay close attention; focus the mind (on or upon): *He concentrated on his reading so that he would understand the story. He concentrated upon one aspect of the problem to the exclusion of all others.*
—*n.* something that has been concentrated: *Lemon juice with the water removed is a concentrate.*
[< *concenter* + *-ate*[1]] —**con′cen|tra′tor,** *n.*

con|cen|trat|ed (kon′sən trā′tid), *adj.* **1** brought together in one place. **2** (of liquids and solutions) made strong or stronger, especially by removing water: *concentrated orange juice.* —**con′cen|trat′ed|ly,** *adv.* —**con′cen|trat′ed|ness,** *n.*

con|cen|tra|tion (kon′sən trā′shən), *n.* **1** a concentrating or being concentrated: *a concentration of effort, the concentration of ore.* **SYN:** collection, gathering. **2** *Figurative.* close attention: *When he gave the problem his full concentration, he figured out the answer.* **3** the strength of a solution: *The acid solution was of weak concentration because so much water had been added.* **4** a concentrated collection or mass. **5** *Military.* **a** a grouping or assemblage of forces in a small area. **b** the amount of artillery fire directed at a particular target for a limited time.

concentration camp, a camp where political enemies, prisoners of war, and interned foreigners are held.

concentration cell, *Electronics.* a cell whose difference of potential is due to the difference of concentration of the solutions in which the electrodes are immersed.

con|cen|tra|tive (kon′sən trā′tiv), *adj.* tending to concentrate; concentrating. —**con′cen|tra′tive|ness,** *n.*

con|cen|tre (kon sen′tər), *v.t., v.i.,* **-tred, -tring.** *Especially British.* concenter.

***con|cen|tric** (kən sen′trik), *adj.* having the same center: *concentric circles.* —**con|cen′tri|cal|ly,** *adv.*

***concentric**

concentric circles — eccentric circles

con|cen|tri|cal (kən sen′trə kəl), *adj.* = concentric.

con|cen|tric|i|ty (kon′sən tris′ə tē), *n.* the quality or state of being concentric.

con|cept (kon′sept), *n.* a general notion or idea; thought. "Triangle," "animal," and "motion" are concepts. *Einstein said he had always believed that the invention of scientific concepts and the building of theories upon them was one of the great creative properties of the human mind* (Scientific American). **SYN:** conception, construct. [< Latin *conceptus, -ūs* < *concipere;* see etym. under **conceive**]

con|cep|ta|cle (kən sep′tə kəl), *n. Biology.* a cavity producing or enclosing reproductive cells in certain thallophytes. [< Latin *conceptāculum* receptacle (diminutive) < *conceptus, -ūs* conception; see etym. under **concept**]

con|cep|tion (kən sep′shən), *n.* **1** a thought; notion; idea: *His conception of the problem was different from mine. A single feat of daring can alter the whole conception of what is possible* (Graham Greene). **SYN:** impression. **2a** the act of forming an idea or thought: *A scientist has great powers of conception.* **b** the state of being conceived. **3** *Philosophy.* a general notion; concept. **4** a design; plan. **5a** the action or process of conceiving in the womb; a becoming pregnant: *When egg and sperm unite at conception, or fertilization, the fertilized egg contains the full number of chromosomes—twenty-three pairs in the human body* (Sidonie M. Gruenberg). **b** the fact of being conceived. **c** the thing conceived; embryo; fetus.

con|cep|tion|al (kən sep′shə nəl), *adj.* having to do with or of the nature of a conception or idea.

con|cep|tive (kən sep′tiv), *adj.* conceiving; forming conceptions. —**con|cep′tive|ly,** *adv.*

con|cep|tu|al (kən sep′chů əl), *adj.* of or having to do with concepts or general ideas: *Conceptual foresight—the ability to anticipate needs or consequences in a given problem situation* (Science News Letter). —**con|cep′tu|al|ly,** *adv.*

conceptual art, art intended to reflect an idea or concept in the artist's mind during the process of creation; process art: *Kynaston McShine put on a major show of conceptual art at the Museum of Modern Art* (New Yorker).

con|cep|tu|al|ise (kən sep′chů ə līz), *v.t., v.i.,* **-ised, -is|ing.** *Especially British.* conceptualize.

con|cep|tu|al|ism (kən sep′chů ə liz′əm), *n. Philosophy.* **1** the doctrine that universals exist, but only in the mind. **2** the doctrine that the mind can fully form an idea of general and abstract terms such as *plant, horse,* or *blue.*

con|cep|tu|al|ist (kən sep′chů ə list), *n.* **1** an adherent of either of the doctrines of conceptualism. **2** an artist who creates works of conceptual art.

con|cep|tu|al|is|tic (kən sep′chů ə lis′tik), *adj.* having to do with or of the nature of conceptualism.

con|cep|tu|al|i|za|tion (kən sep′chů ə lə zā′shən), *n.* **1** the process of conceptualizing: *With the conceptualization of the unknown into deities and forces, men came to emphasize the unknown as a power and endeavored to placate it* (Ogburn and Nimkoff). **2** = concept.

con|cep|tu|al|ize (kən sep′chů ə līz), *v.,* **-ized, -iz|ing.** —*v.t.* to make or form a concept or concepts of.
—*v.i.* to form concepts or ideas: *The other animals cannot, however, conceptualize to the extent of predicting and altering nature* (Saturday Review).

con|cep|tus (kən sep′təs), *n., pl.* **-tus|es, -ti** (tī). the embryo and surrounding tissue that forms directly after fertilization in highly developed animals. [< Latin *conceptus, -ūs* that which is conceived < *concipere;* see etym. under **conceive**]

con|cern (kən sėrn′), *v., n.* —*v.t.* **1** to have to do with; belong to; interest: *The letter is private and concerns nobody but me.* **SYN:** affect, touch. **2** to make anxious or uneasy; cause to worry; trouble: *Her failing health concerns us very much. The doves settled down on their perch* [*on*] *a very cold day, and she was concerned for them* (William Maxwell). **3** to engage; involve: *Helping to maintain world peace concerns the United Nations.* **SYN:** interest.
—*v.i. Obsolete.* to be of importance.
—*n.* **1** anything that touches or has to do with one's work or one's interest: *The party decorations are my concern; you pay attention to refreshments.* **2** a troubled state of mind; worry; anxiety; uneasiness: *The mother's concern over her sick child kept her awake all night.* **SYN:** See syn. under **care. 3** a business company; firm: *We wrote to two big concerns for their catalogs. The business had been a family concern for more than a century.* **4** relation; reference: *Children have little concern with politics.* **5** *Informal.* a material thing of little importance and difficult to describe exactly; contrivance: *The hackney-coach . . . a great, lumbering square concern* (Dickens).
as concerns, with reference to; about: *As concerns the new traffic rule, we intend to comply with it fully from now on.*
concern oneself, a to take an interest (in); be busy: *Parents cannot help concerning themselves in school affairs.* **b** to be troubled or worried (about); be anxious or uneasy: *The doctor concerned himself about the health of his aging patient.*
of concern, of importance; of interest; of important relation: *Everything we do in life is of concern to our family.*
[< Medieval Latin *concernere* relate to < Late Latin, mingle with, mix < Latin *com-* together + *cernere* distinguish, sift]
▶**Concerned** is used with *in* or *with* to mean taking part or having to do with: *He is concerned in the real estate business. They could not prove he was concerned with the crime.* **Concerned** is used with *for* or *about* to mean worried: *Are you concerned about his escape? Naturally we were concerned for him when we heard of the accident.*

con|cerned (kən sėrnd′), *adj.* **1** troubled; worried; anxious: *He spoke with a grave, concerned look on his face.* **2a** involved, interested, or affected: *All the concerned parties were invited to the reading of the will.* **b** showing concern or interest

Pronunciation Key: **h**a**t**, **ā**ge, **c**ã**re**, **f**ä**r**; **l**e**t**, **ē**qual, **t**ė**rm**; **i**t, **ī**ce; **h**o**t**, **ō**pen, **ô**rder; **oil**, **out**; **c**u**p**, **p**ů**t**, **r**ü**le**; **child**; **long**; **thin**; **ᵺhen**; **zh**, measure;
ə represents **a** in about, **e** in taken, **i** in pencil, **o** in lemon, **u** in circus.

in public affairs: *concerned citizens, a concerned politician. . . . our idealistic, concerned youth* (Time). —**con|cern′ed|ly**, *adv.*

con|cern|ing (kən sėr′ning), *prep.* having to do with; about; regarding; relating to: *The policeman asked many questions concerning the accident. He will make no inquiries concerning you* (Maria Edgeworth). SYN: respecting.

con|cern|ment (kən sėrn′mənt), *n.* **1** importance; weight; moment: *secrets of highest concernment* (Emerson). SYN: interest. **2** worry; anxiety. **3** affair; concern. **4** relation; bearing: *a matter of public concernment.* **5** participation.

con|cert (*n., adj.* kon′sərt; *v.* kən sėrt′), *n., adj., v.* —*n.* **1a** a musical performance in which several musicians or singers take part: *The orchestra gave a concert that lasted two hours.* **b** a musical performance by one musician; recital: *A world-famous pianist gave a concert last night.* **2** a performance by a comedian or other entertainer: *Murphy went on his first major concert tour (he writes all of his own stage material), and one of his performances was . . . shown as a cable television special* (R.E. Allen). **3** agreement; harmony; union: *Is there a perfect European concert?* (London Times). **4** harmony of musical sounds. **5** *Music.* = concerto.
—***adj.*** **1** used in concerts; for concerts: *At the end of the eighteenth century, concert halls as we know them had hardly existed* (Harper's). **2** performing in a concert or concerts: *a concert pianist.*
—***v.t.*** to arrange by agreement; plan or make together: *We began to concert measures for his coming on board with secrecy* (Daniel Defoe).
—***v.i.*** to arrange a matter or act by agreement with someone: *We concerted on the most proper methods for speedily executing the Viceroy's instructions* (Horatio Nelson).
in concert, all together; in agreement: *By acting in concert the little group was able to fight off the wolves.*
[< French *concert* < Italian *concerto* < Latin *concertāre* strive with < *con-* with + *certāre* strive. See etym. of doublet **concerto.**]

con|cer|tan|te (kôn′cher tän′tā), *adj. Music.* giving opportunities for prominent solos by one or more players: *a concertante composition, a concertante part.* [< Italian *concertante*]

con|cert|ed (kən sėr′tid), *adj.* **1** arranged by agreement; planned or made together; combined: *a concerted effort.* **2** *Music.* arranged in parts for several voices or instruments.

con|cert|go|er (kon′sərt gō′ər), *n.* a person who frequently attends concerts.

concert grand, a concert grand piano with sufficient power and brilliancy for use in a large hall or with an orchestra.

con|cer|ti gros|si (kən cher′tēgrō′sē), plural of **concerto grosso.**

con|cer|ti|na (kon′sər tē′nə), *n., adj.* —*n.* a small musical instrument somewhat like an accordion. See picture under **accordion.**
—***adj.*** having folds like the bellows of a concertina: *a hat with concertina pleats.*
[< *concert* + Italian *-ina* -ine[1]]

con|cer|tin|ist (kon′sər tē′nist), *n.* a person who plays on the concertina.

con|cer|ti|no (kôn′cher tē′nō), *n., pl.* **-ni** (-nē). a short concerto. [< Italian *concertino* (diminutive) < *concerto* concerto]

con|cert|ize (kon′sər tīz), *v.,* **-ized, -iz|ing.** —***v.i.*** **1** to give or take part in a concert: *Even after 50 years of concertizing . . . and through the crackling of a bad recording, his elegance, fleetness, playfulness, aptness are astonishing* (Time). **2** to manage a concert or concerts.
—***v.t.*** to perform as or in a concert: *Several famous operatic arias were concertized.*

con|cert|mas|ter (kon′sərt mas′tər, -mäs′-), *n. U.S.* the leader of the strings, usually the first violinist of an orchestra, ranking next to the conductor. [< German *Konzertmeister*]

con|cert|meis|ter (kôn tsert′mīs′tər), *n.* = concertmaster. [< German *Konzertmeister*]

con|cer|to (kən cher′tō), *n., pl.* **-tos, -ti** (-tē). a piece of music to be played by one or more principal instruments, such as a violin or piano, with the accompaniment of an orchestra. It usually has three movements. Also, **concert.** [< Italian *concerto.* See etym. of doublet **concert.**]

con|cer|to gros|so (kən cher′tōgrō′sō), *pl.* **concerti grossi.** a concerto for a small group of soloists and a full orchestra, usually played in four movements. [< Italian *concerto grosso* big concerto]

concert pitch, *Music.* **1** a pitch slightly higher than ordinary pitch, used in tuning instruments for concert use. **2** the pitch as sounded, as distinguished from what is written, used in transposing for certain instruments. **3** *Figurative.* a maximum or optimum state of readiness, conditioning, or activity: *Ole Fols had recently done six furlongs in an amazing 1:08 and was at concert pitch* (New Yorker).

con|ces|sion (kən sesh′ən), *n.* **1** a conceding; granting; yielding: *As a concession, Mother let me stay up an hour longer.* SYN: favor, boon. **2** anything conceded or yielded; admission; acknowledgment: *I have made all the concessions I intend to make.* SYN: allowance. **3** something conceded or granted by a government or controlling authority; grant. Land or privileges given by a government to a business company are called concessions. SYN: franchise. **4** *U.S.* a privilege or space granted or leased for a particular use within specified premises. A circus leases space for concessions selling food and drinks. **5** *Canadian.* **a** (especially in Ontario and Quebec) a subdivision of land in township surveys. **b** = concession road.
concessions, *Canadian.* rural or bush districts: *rely on the concessions for political support.*
[< Latin *concessiō, -ōnis* < *concēdere;* see etym. under **concede**]

con|ces|sion|aire (kən sesh′ə nãr′), *n.* a person, business company, or group, to whom a concession has been granted: *The subcommittee also said proprietors should be responsible for collecting the cabaret tax due from concessionaires* (Wall Street Journal). [< French *concessionnaire*]

con|ces|sion|al (kən sesh′ə nəl), *adj.* of or having to do with a concession or grant: *In Libya we have increased our concessional holdings, and test drilling, as well as geological and geographical survey work, is being carried out* (Economist).

con|ces|sion|ar|y (kən sesh′ə ner′ē), *adj., n., pl.* **-ar|ies.** —***adj.*** having to do with or of the nature of concession. —***n.*** = concessionaire.

con|ces|sion|er (kən sesh′ə nər), *n.* = concessionaire.

con|ces|sion|naire (kôɴ se syô ner′), *n. French.* a concessionaire.

concession road, *Canadian.* a rural road, usually running east and west.

con|ces|sive (kən ses′iv), *adj.* **1** making or implying concession; yielding. **2** *Grammar.* expressing concession. "Though" and "although" are concessive words. —**con|ces′sive|ly,** *adv.*

***conch** (konch, kongk), *n., pl.* **conch|es** (kon′chiz), **conchs** (kongks). **1** a large spiral sea shell. **2** any one of several mollusks of tropical waters with such a shell. **3** the shell which Triton used as a trumpet. **4** Also, **concha.** *Architecture.* **a** the concave surface of a dome. **b** an apse. [< Latin *concha* < Greek *kónchē* mussel, cockle]

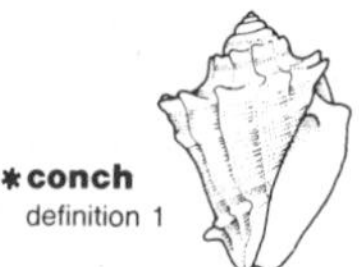

***conch**
definition 1

conch., conchology.

con|cha[1] (kong′kə), *n., pl.* **-chae** (-kē). **1a** the central, hollow part of the external ear. **b** = external ear. **2** a turbinate bone of the nose. **3** *Architecture.* = conch. [< Latin *concha* conch]

con|cha[2] (kon′chə; *Spanish* kôn′chä), *n. Southwestern U.S.* a shell or shell-shaped object, worn especially as an ornament. [< Spanish *concha* < Latin *concha* conch]

conche (konsh; *French* kôɴsh), *n.* a machine for processing chocolate, in which a large cylindrical stone rolling on a stone bed pushes the chocolate back and forth, smoothing off rough edges on the chocolate particles, helping to develop the desired flavor, and blending the entire mass. [< French *conche*]

con|chif|er|ous (kong kif′ər əs), *adj.* having or bearing a shell. [< *conch* + *-ferous*]

con|chi|form (kong′kə fôrm), *adj.* = shaped like a shell. [< *conch* + *-form*]

con|chi|o|lin (kong kī′ə lin), *n.* the organic part of the shells of mollusks, closely allied to keratin. [< Latin *concha* shell + *-ol-* (diminutive) + English *-in*]

Con|cho|bar (kong′kə wər, kon′ůr), *n. Celtic Legend.* a king of Ulster.

con|choid (kong′koid), *n., adj.* —***n.*** *Geometry.* a plane curve such that if a straight line is drawn from a fixed point (the pole) to the curve, the part of the line intercepted between the curve and a fixed straight line (the asymptote) is always equal to a fixed distance. —***adj.*** conchoidal.
[< Greek *konchoeidēs* mussellike < *kónchē* mussel shell + *eîdos* form]

con|choi|dal (kong koi′dəl), *adj. Mineralogy.* having to do with or denoting a fracture having smooth, shell-like convexities and concavities. —**con|choi′dal|ly,** *adv.*

con|cho|log|i|cal (kong′kə loj′ə kəl), *adj.* of or having to do with conchology.

con|chol|o|gist (kong kol′ə jist), *n.* a person who studies conchology.

con|chol|o|gy (kong kol′ə jē), *n.* the branch of zoology that deals with shells and shellfish. [< Greek *kónchē* mussel, conch + English *-logy*]

con|chos|tra|can (kong kos′trə kən), *n.* any one of a group of branchiopod crustaceans having leaflike thoracic appendages and a bivalved carapace enclosing the body. [< New Latin *Conchostraca* (< Greek *kónchē* conch + *óstrakon* shell) + English *-an*]

con|chy (kon′chē, -shē), *n., pl.* **-chies.** *Slang.* a conscientious objector.

con|ci|erge (kon′sē ėrzh′; *French* kôɴ syerzh′), *n.* **1** a doorkeeper. **2** a janitor. **3** *Archaic.* a custodian; warden. [< French *concierge* < Old French *cumcerges* guard, warden]

con|cier|ge|rie (kôɴ syer zhə rē′), *n. French.* the office, room, or lodge of a concierge.

con|cil|i|a|ble (kən sil′ē ə bəl), *adj.* that can be conciliated.

con|cil|i|ar (kən sil′ē ər), *adj.* of or having to do with a council.

con|cil|i|ate (kən sil′ē āt), *v.t.,* **-at|ed, -at|ing.** **1** to win over; soothe: *She conciliated her angry little sister with a candy bar.* SYN: placate, pacify, appease. **2** to gain (good will, regard, favor, etc.) by friendly acts: *The explorers tried to conciliate the natives with bright cloth and beads.* **3** to bring into harmony; reconcile: *Negotiate, conciliate, arbitrate, try as hard as you can for agreement rather than stoppages, because strikes hurt everybody* (London Times). [< Latin *conciliāre* (with English *-ate*[1]) make friendly < *concilium* council < *com-* together + *calāre* call] —**con|cil′i|at′ing|ly,** *adv.* —**con|cil′i|a|tor,** *n.*

con|cil|i|a|tion (kən sil′ē ā′shən), *n.* **1** the act of winning over or soothing; reconciling: *The Roman method of conciliation was, first of all, the most ample toleration of customs, religion, and municipal freedom of the conquered, and then their gradual admission to the privileges of the conqueror* (William E. H. Lecky). **2** the condition of being won over or soothed; being reconciled: *In conciliation, friendliness replaces animosity, and co-operation is established* (Ogburn and Nimkoff).

con|cil|i|a|tive (kən sil′ē ā′tiv), *adj.* = conciliatory.

con|cil|i|a|to|ry (kən sil′ē ə tôr′ē, -tōr′-), *adj.* tending to win over, soothe, or reconcile: *Shaking hands after a fight is a conciliatory gesture.* —**con|cil′i|a|to′ri|ly,** *adv.* —**con|cil′i|a|to′ri|ness,** *n.*

con|cin|ni|ty (kən sin′ə tē), *n., pl.* **-ties.** **1** the skillful and harmonious fitting together of parts, especially in writing; harmony; elegance. **2** an instance of this. [< Latin *concinnitās* < *concinnus* skillfully joined, well-adjusted]

con|cise (kən sīs′), *adj.* expressing much in few words; brief but full of meaning: *The chairman's concise report covered all the subjects briefly.* [< Latin *concīsus,* past participle of *concīdere* < *com-* (intensive) + *caedere* cut] —**con|cise′ly,** *adv.* —**con|cise′ness,** *n.*
—**Syn. Concise, terse, succinct** mean saying much in few words. **Concise,** applying to people or statements, implies that everything unnecessary has been cut out: *He gave a concise report of the meeting.* **Terse,** applying chiefly to statements, implies conciseness that is both pointed and polished: *Lincoln's Gettysburg Address is terse.* **Succinct,** applying to people or statements, implies very compact conciseness: *Winston Churchill's "blood, toil, tears, and sweat" is a succinct description of war.*

con|ci|sion (kən sizh′ən), *n.* **1** the quality or state of being concise; brevity; conciseness: *Because of this new concision of language, however, which amounts to a verbal shorthand . . . .* (New Yorker). **2** a cutting up or off; mutilation.

con|clave (kon′klāv, kong′-), *n.* **1** a private meeting. **2** a private meeting of the cardinals of the Roman Catholic Church for the election of a pope. **3** the rooms where the cardinals meet in private for the election of a pope. **4** = Sacred College. **5** *U.S.* a meeting of men belonging to a fraternal order. **6** *Obsolete.* a private room. [< Latin *conclāve* a room that can be locked < *com-* with + *clāvis* key]

con|clav|ist (kon′klā vist, kong′-), *n.* either of two attendants upon a cardinal in conclave, one a secretary (usually an ecclesiastic) and the other a servant.

con|clude (kən klüd′), *v.,* **-clud|ed, -clud|ing.** —***v.t.*** **1** to bring to an end; finish: *He concluded the meeting by saying "Amen."* SYN: terminate. See syn. under **end.** **2** to reach (certain decisions or opinions) by reasoning; infer: *From the tracks we saw, we concluded that the animal must have been a deer.* **3** to settle; arrange: *The two countries concluded an agreement on trade. After the Revolutionary War the United States and Great Britain concluded a peace treaty.* **4** to decide; resolve: *I concluded not to go.* **5** *Archaic.* to shut up; enclose. **6** *Law.* to restrain; bind. **— *v.i.*** **1** to come to an end; end; finish; close: *The play concluded with a happy ending and the curtain came down.* **SYN**: terminate. See syn. under **end. 2** to come to a decision; decide. **3** to arrive at an opinion or judgment; resolve. [< Latin *conclūdere* < *com-* (intensive) + *claudere* close] **— con|clud′er,** *n.*

— *Syn.* *v.t.* **2 Conclude, infer, deduce** mean to arrive at a decision. **Conclude** implies reaching a sound decision on the basis of the evidence at hand: *From the evidence, we concluded that he was innocent.* **Infer** also suggests using the evidence at hand but does not necessarily imply that the decision is sound: *From his story we inferred that he went unwillingly.* **Deduce** implies an inference based either on good evidence or on some general principle: *Mother deduced from my loss of appetite what had happened to the cookies.*

con|clu|sion (kən klü′zhən), *n.* **1** the final part; end; close: *the conclusion of the story.* **SYN**: termination, finish. **2** the last main division of a speech, an essay, etc., often summing up all the important parts. **3** a decision or opinion reached by reasoning; inference: *He came to the conclusion that he must work harder to succeed. He jumped to a wrong conclusion. More like a fairy tale than the sober conclusions of science* (John Tyndall). **4** a settlement; arrangement: *the conclusion of a peace between two countries.* **SYN**: resolution. **5** a final result; outcome: *to bring work to a good conclusion.* **SYN**: issue, upshot. **6** *Logic.* a proposition deduced by reasoning from previous propositions, especially the last proposition of a syllogism deduced from the first two. **7** *Law.* **a** = estoppel. **b** the closing part of a pleading or deed. **8** *Grammar.* the apodosis of a conditional sentence.

in conclusion, finally; lastly; to conclude: *I will say, in conclusion, that it was an honor to be the speaker at this meeting.*

try conclusions, to take part in a contest: *The Civic Guards ... show little inclination to try conclusions with raiders escaping into Eire* (New Statesman).

[< Latin *conclūsiō, -ōnis* < *conclūdere;* see etym. under **conclude**]

con|clu|sive (kən klü′siv), *adj.* **1** decisive; convincing; final: *a conclusive argument or reply. The evidence against the burglar was conclusive.* **2** *Rare.* occurring at or forming the end. **— con|clu′sive|ly,** *adv.* **— con|clu′sive|ness,** *n.*

con|coct (kon kokt′, kən-), *v.t.* **1** to prepare (food or drink) by mixing a variety of ingredients: *He concocted a drink made of the juices of different fruits and vegetables.* **2** *Figurative.* to make up; devise: *He concocted an excuse to explain why he came late to school.* **SYN**: fabricate, contrive. **3** *Obsolete.* to prepare with heat, as by cooking, boiling, or baking. **4** *Obsolete.* to digest. [< Latin *concoctus,* past participle of *concoquere* digest, ripen; heat together < *com-* together + *coquere* cook] **— con|coct′er, con|coc′tor,** *n.*

con|coc|tion (kon kok′shən, kən-), *n.* **1** the act of concocting: *The concoction of the milk shake took several minutes.* **2** a thing concocted: *He refused to drink the concoction she prepared.* (*Figurative.*) *The story was a concoction from beginning to end.*

con|coc|tive (kon kok′tiv, kən-), *adj.* **1** having to do with concoction. **2** *Obsolete.* having to do with digestion (of food); digestive.

con|col|or (kon′kul′ər), *adj.* **1** of the same color. **2** of one color. [< *con-* + *color*]

con|col|or|ate (kon kul′ə rāt), *adj.* = concolorous.

con|col|or|ous (kon kul′ər əs), *adj.* of uniform color.

con|com|i|tance (kon kom′ə təns, kən-), *n.* **1** existence together; coexistence; accompaniment. **2** an instance of this.

con|com|i|tan|cy (kon kom′ə tən sē, kən-), *n.* = concomitance.

con|com|i|tant (kon kom′ə tənt, kən-), *adj., n.* **— *adj.*** being together; accompanying; attending: *a concomitant result.* **SYN**: concurrent.

— *n.* an accompanying thing, quality, or circumstance; accompaniment: *Disease is a concomitant with poor sanitation.*

[< Latin *concomitāns, -antis,* present participle of *concomitārī* < *com-* together + *comitārī* accompany < *comes, -itis* companion] **— con|com′i|tant|ly,** *adv.*

con|cord (kon′kôrd, kong′-), *n.* **1** agreement; peace; harmony: *concord between friends. No project of theirs could endanger the concord of the empire* (Edmund Burke). **SYN**: accord. **2** *Music.* a harmonious combination of tones sounded together; harmony. **3** = treaty. **SYN**: pact, concordat. **4** an agreement between things: *a concord of sweet sounds.* **5** correspondence of words with respect to number, case, gender, person, or other grammatical feature; agreement. [< Old French *concord,* learned borrowing from Latin *concordia* < *concors, -cordis* of one mind < *com-* together + *cor, cordis* heart]

Con|cord (kong′kərd, kon′kôrd), *n.* = Concord grape.

con|cord|ance (kon kôr′dəns, kən-), *n.* **1** an alphabetical list of the principal words in a book or in the works of an author, with references to the passages in which they occur: *The scholars work on this in a small inner room, equipped with concordances, dictionaries, and all the relevant texts* (New Yorker). **2** concord; agreement; harmony.

con|cord|ant (kon kôr′dənt, kən-), *adj.* agreeing; harmonious. **— con|cord′ant|ly,** *adv.*

con|cor|dat (kon kôr′dat), *n.* **1** an agreement; compact. **SYN**: covenant. **2** a formal agreement between the Pope and a government about church affairs. [< French *concordat,* learned borrowing from Medieval Latin *concordatum* < Latin *concordāre* make harmonious]

Concord coach, *U.S.* a type of stagecoach built for rough roads, used by settlers in the Western frontier. [American English < *Concord,* New Hampshire, where it was first made]

Con|corde (kon′kôrd), *n.* a commercial supersonic aircraft produced jointly by Great Britain and France: *The fourteen Concordes (the French have four and the British five, and five are unsold) have already cost the two governments three billion dollars* (New Yorker).

Concord grape, a large, sweet, bluish-black grape, used especially for making juice and jelly. [American English < *Concord,* Massachusetts, where it was developed]

con|cor|po|rate (*v.* kon kôr′pə rāt; *adj.* kon kôr′pər it), *v.,* **-rat|ed, -rat|ing,** *adj. Rare.* **— *v.t.*** to unite into one body or mass.

— *adj.* united into one body or mass.

[< Latin *concorporāre* (with English *-ate*[1]) < *com-* together + *corporāre* embody < *corpus, -oris* body]

con|cours (kᴏɴ kür′), *n., pl.* **con|cours** (kᴏɴ kür′). *French.* a public contest.

con|course (kon′kôrs, kong′-; -kōrs), *n.* **1** a running, flowing, or coming together: *The fort was built on a wedge of land at the concourse of two rivers.* **SYN**: confluence. **2** a crowd; throng: *The President looked over the vast concourse awaiting his announcement.* **SYN**: assemblage. **3** a place where crowds come, such as a stadium or arena. **4** an open space in a railroad station. **5** a boulevard or driveway. **SYN**: avenue, esplanade. [< Old French *concours* < Latin *concursus, -ūs* < *concurrere* run together < *com-* together + *currere* run]

con|cre|ment (kon′krə mənt), *n.* **1** a growing together. **2** = concretion. [< Latin *concrēmentum* a growing together < *concrēscere;* see etym. under **concrete**]

con|cres|cence (kon kres′əns), *n.* **1** a growing together of parts which originally were separate to form a single part or unit. **SYN**: accrescence, accretion. **2** an increase by the adding of particles. **SYN**: accrescence, accretion. [< Latin *concrēscentia* < *concrēscere;* see etym. under **concrete**]

con|cres|cent (kon kres′ənt), *adj.* growing together.

con|crete (kon′krēt; *especially for v.t. 2, v.i. 1* kon krēt′), *adj., n., v.,* **-cret|ed, -cret|ing. — *adj.*** **1** existing as an actual object, not merely as an idea or as a quality; real: *A painting is concrete; its beauty is not a concrete thing.* **2** not general; specific; particular: *The daisy is a concrete example of a composite flower. The teacher gave concrete examples to show the meaning of faith, hope, and charity.* **3** naming a thing, especially something perceived by the senses: *"Sugar" and "people" are concrete nouns; "sweetness" and "humanity" are abstract nouns.* **4** made of concrete: *a concrete sidewalk.* **5** formed into a mass; solid; hardened. **6** *Obsolete.* grown together.

— *n.* **1** a mixture of cement, sand, gravel, and water that hardens as it dries. Concrete is used for foundations, whole buildings, sidewalks, roads, dams, and bridges. **2** something concrete. **3** a concrete idea or term: *This blending of the concrete and the abstract was the chief characteristic of almost all his researches* (Scientific American).

— *v.t.* **1** to treat, lay, or cover with concrete. **2** to form or mix into a mass; harden into a mass; make solid. **— *v.i.*** **1** to run into a mass; become solid; solidify. **2** to use or apply concrete.

[< Latin *concrētus,* past participle of *concrēscere* < *com-*together + *crēscere*grow] **— con|crete′ly,** *adv.* **— con|crete′ness,** *n.*

concrete block, a gray, rectangular building block of concrete, usually cast with hollow cores.

concrete mixer, = cement mixer.

concrete music, = musique concrète.

concrete number, a number which is connected with something real. *Example:* 4 men + 5 women = 9 persons. The numbers by themselves are *abstract numbers.*

concrete poem, a poem whose text is arranged in shapes and patterns; a combined poem and drawing.

concrete poet, a writer of concrete poems.

concrete poetry, poetry designed to draw attention to its physical appearance by arranging the text in shapes and patterns; concrete poems collectively: *In concrete poetry words are treated as signs, like forms in concrete painting* (London Times).

con|cre|tion (kon krē′shən), *n.* **1** a forming into a mass; a solidifying. **2** a solidified mass; hard formation, especially: **a** a hard morbid formation in the body, such as a gallstone; calculus; stone. **b** a mass formed by aggregation of solid particles, usually around a nucleus, common in certain types of sandstone, shale, and clay.

con|cre|tion|al (kon krē′shə nəl), *adj.* = concretionary.

con|cre|tion|ar|y (kon krē′shə ner′ē), *adj.* **1** formed by concretion. **2** consisting of concreted matter or masses.

con|cret|ism (kon krē′tiz əm), *n.* = concrete poetry.

con|cret|ist (kon krē′tist), *n., adj.* **— *n.*** = concrete poet.

— *adj.* of or having to do with concrete poets or their work: *The concretist movement began simultaneously in Europe and Brazil in the early 1950s* (Time).

con|cre|tive (kon krē′tiv), *adj.* tending to concrete.

con|cret|ize (kon′krə tīz, kon krē′tīz), *v.t., v.i.,* **-ized, -iz|ing.** to make (anything) concrete, definite, or specific; objectify: *The proof of abstraction is concretizing* (John Wesley Powell). **— con|cret′i|za′tion,** *n.*

con|cu|bi|nage (kon kyü′bə nij), *n.* **1** the living together of a man and a concubine. **2** the condition of being a concubine: *Up until fairly recently there was a great deal of selling into concubinage* (Atlantic). [< Middle French *concubinage* < Old French *concubin;* see etym. under **concubine**]

con|cu|bi|nal (kon kyü′bə nəl), *adj.* = concubinary.

con|cu|bi|nar|y (kon kyü′bə ner′ē), *adj., n., pl.* **-nar|ies. — *adj.*** **1** of or having to do with a concubine. **2** living in or sprung from concubinage.

— *n.* a person who lives in concubinage.

con|cu|bine (kong′kyə bīn, kon′-), *n.* **1** a woman who lives with a man without being legally married to him. **2** a wife who has an inferior rank or rights (in countries where polygamy is legal). [< Old French *concubine,* learned borrowing from Latin *concubīna* < *com-* with + *cubāre* to lie, recline]

con|cu|pis|cence (kon kyü′pə səns), *n.* sensual desire; lust.

con|cu|pis|cent (kon kyü′pə sənt), *adj.* eagerly desirous; lustful. [< Latin *concupiscēns, -entis,* present participle of *concupiscere* < *com-* (intensive) + *cupere* desire]

con|cu|pis|ci|ble (kon kyü′pə sə bəl), *adj.* = concupiscent.

con|cur (kən kėr′), *v.i.,* **-curred, -cur|ring. 1a** to be of the same opinion; agree: *The judges all concurred in giving him the prize.* **SYN**: See syn. under **consent. b** to come together; happen at the same time; coincide: *This year two weeks of rain concurred with our vacation.* **2** to work together: *The events of the boy's life concurred to make him what he is.* **SYN**: unite, combine, cooperate. **3** *Obsolete.* to meet. [< Latin *concurrere* < *com-* together + *currere* run] **— con|cur′rer,** *n.*

con|cur|rence (kən kėr′əns), *n.* **1** a having the same opinion; agreement. **SYN**: assent. **2** a happening at the same time. **SYN**: coincidence, juncture. **3** a working together; cooperating. **SYN**: cooperation. **4** *Geometry.* a coming together; a meeting at a point. **5** *Law.* a joint power, authority, or claim. **6** pursuit of the same object; rivalry; competition.

con|cur|ren|cy (kən kėr′ən sē), *n., pl.* **-cies.** = concurrence.

con|cur|rent (kən kėr′ənt), *adj., n.* **— *adj.*** **1** happening at the same time; existing side by side: *The twins had concurrent birthdays.* **2** agreeing; harmonious: *concurrent ideas.* **SYN**: consistent. **3** working together; cooperating. **4** *Law.* having equal authority or jurisdiction; coordinate. **5** coming together; meeting in a point.

— *n.* **1** a concurrent thing or event. **2** a rival claimant; competitor. **— con|cur′rent|ly,** *adv.* **— con|cur′rent|ness,** *n.*

Pronunciation Key: hat, āge, cãre, fär; let, ēqual, tėrm; it, īce; hot, ōpen, ôrder; oil, out; cup, pu̇t, rüle; child; long; thin; ᴛʜen; zh, measure; ə represents a in about, e in taken, i in pencil, o in lemon, u in circus.

concurrent resolution, *U.S.* a resolution passed by the two branches of a legislative assembly, which expresses an opinion but does not have the force of law. A concurrent resolution does not need to be signed by the chief executive.

con|cuss (kən kus′), *v.t.* **1** to shake or shock, as by a blow: *At the very outset he was caught by an avalanche, and was left concussed, frostbitten, snow-blind, and delirious* (Atlantic). **2** = coerce. [< Latin *concussus* < *concutere;* see etym. under **concussion**]

con|cus|sion (kən kush′ən), *n.* **1** a sudden violent shaking; shock: *The concussion caused by the explosion broke many windows. The concussion started jeroboams and nebuchadnezzars of champagne popping in the ... wine cellars* (New Yorker). **2** an injury to the brain or spine from a blow or fall or other shock: *He suffered a severe concussion when he fell off the bicycle. Heads hitting against the ground, knees or helmets accounted for four fatal concussions* (Time). [< Latin *concussiō, -ōnis* < *concutere* shake violently < *com-* (intensive) + *quatere* shake]

concussion grenade, a hand grenade with a light container, designed to injure by concussion rather than fragmentation, so that the thrower need not take cover from his own weapon: *The Americans retaliated with tear gas and concussion grenades which stun but do not kill* (Time).

con|cus|sive (kən kus′iv), *adj.* of or accompanied by concussion.

con|cu|tient (kən kyü′shənt), *adj.* meeting with concussion; colliding with a shock. [< Latin *concutiens, -entis,* present participle of *concutere;* see etym. under **concussion**]

con|cy|clic (kən sī′klik, -sik′lik), *adj. Geometry.* **1** (of a series of points) lying on the circumference of one circle. **2** (of certain quadric surfaces) giving circular sections when cut by the same system of parallel planes. [< *con-* + *cyclic*]

cond., **1** *Music.* conducted. **2** conductivity.

con|demn (kən dem′), *v.t.* **1** to express strong disapproval of: *We condemn cruelty to animals.* **SYN:** denounce, censure. **2** to pronounce guilty of crime or wrong: *The prisoner is sure to be condemned by the jury.* **SYN:** convict. **3** to sentence; doom: *The spy was condemned to death.* **4** to suggest the guilt of; show to be guilty: *His own words condemn him.* **5** to declare not sound or suitable for use: *This bridge has been condemned because it is no longer safe. The milk of the sick cows was condemned.* **6** *U.S.* to take for public use under special provision of the law: *All these streets have been condemned by the city to make room for the new expressway.* **7** *Figurative.* to assign to an unhappy or unpleasant fate or condition: *condemned in business or in arts to drudge* (Alexander Pope). **8** *Figurative.* to declare incurable: *No man considers himself richer because he is condemned by his physician* (John Ruskin). [< Old French *condemner,* learned borrowing from Latin *condemnāre* < *com-* + *damnāre* cause loss to, condemn < *damnum* loss, injury] —**con|dem′na|ble**, *adj.* —**con|demn′er**, *n.* —**con|demn′ing|ly**, *adv.*

con|dem|na|tion (kon′dem nā′shən), *n.* **1** the act of condemning: *the condemnation of an unsafe bridge.* **2** the fact or condition of being condemned: *His condemnation made him an outcast.* **3** a cause or reason for condemning.

con|dem|na|to|ry (kən dem′nə tôr′ē, -tōr′-), *adj.* expressing condemnation; condemning.

con|demned (kən demd′), *adj.* pronounced guilty of a crime or wrong.

con|den|sa|bil|i|ty (kən den′sə bil′ə tē), *n.* the quality of being condensable.

con|den|sate (kən den′sāt), *n. Chemistry.* a product of condensation: *The experts estimated that oil, condensate, gas and sulphur in the underwater coastal areas are worth conservatively about $41,492,650,000* (New York Times). [< Latin *condēnsātus,* past participle of *condēnsāre;* see etym. under **condense**]

con|den|sa|tion (kon′den sā′shən), *n.* **1** the act of condensing: (*Figurative.*) *He* [*Goldsmith*] *was a great and perhaps unequalled master of the arts of selection and condensation* (Macaulay). **2** the state of being condensed. **3** a condensed mass. A cloud is a condensation of water vapor in the atmosphere. **4** the act or process of changing a gas or vapor into a liquid by cooling: *the condensation of steam into water. Condensation begins first on solid surfaces because these get colder than the general mass of air* (Thomas A. Blair). **5** *Chemistry.* a reaction in which two or more molecules unite to form a larger, more dense, and more complex molecule, often with the separation of water or some other simple substance: *the condensation of milk by removing most of the water from it.* **6** *Physics.* **a** an increase in density and pressure in a medium, such as air, due to the passing of a sound wave or other compression wave. **b** the region in which this occurs. **7** *Psychoanalysis.* the process by which images characterized by a common effect are grouped so as to form a single or composite image, as in dreams.

con|den|sa|tion|al (kon′den sā′shə nəl), *adj.* of or belonging to condensation.

condensation nucleus, *Meteorology.* a particle upon which water vapor condenses; nucleus: *Condensation nuclei ... originate chiefly from combustion processes ... and, to a certain extent, from ocean spray* (Neuberger and Stevens).

condensation trail, = contrail.

con|den|sa|tive (kən den′sə tiv), *adj.* tending to condense.

con|den|sa|tor (kon′den sā′tər), *n.* = condenser.

con|dense (kən dens′), *v.,* **-densed**, **-dens|ing**. —*v.t.* **1** to make denser or more compact. **SYN:** compress, contract. **2** to increase the strength of; concentrate: *Light is condensed by means of lenses.* **3** *Figurative.* to put into fewer words; say briefly: *A long story can sometimes be condensed into a few sentences.* **SYN:** reduce, shorten. **4** to change (a gas or vapor) to a liquid. **5** *Chemistry.* to cause to undergo condensation: *Milk is condensed by removing much of the water from it.*
—*v.i.* **1** to become denser or more compact: *Each* [*theory*] *starts from the notion that stars condense from the matter scattered thinly through interstellar space* (W. H. Marshall). **2** to change from a gas or vapor to a liquid. If steam touches cold surfaces, it condenses into water. *If it is cloudy, rainy, or foggy, the water vapor in the air is condensing* (Beauchamp, Mayfield, and West). **3** *Chemistry.* to undergo condensation.
[< Latin *condēnsāre* < *com-* together + *dēnsus* thick] —**con|den′sa|ble**, **con|den′si|ble**, *adj.*

***con|densed** (kən denst′), *adj.* **1** made dense or more dense; highly concentrated; compressed. **2** *Figurative.* expressed briefly: *a condensed version of the novel.* **3** changed from a gas or vapor to a liquid. **4** (of printing type) narrower than usual in proportion to the height. —**con|dens′ed|ly**, *adv.*

***condensed** definition 4 — The World Book Dictionary

condensed milk, a thick, sweetened milk prepared by evaporating some of the water from whole milk and sweetening it.

con|dens|er (kən den′sər), *n.* **1** a person or thing that condenses something. **2** a device for receiving and storing a charge of electricity; capacitor. A condenser generally consists of two conducting surfaces separated by a nonconductor. The current flowing into the condenser accumulates in the nonconductor (the dielectric) as a charge. **3** an apparatus for changing gas or vapor into a liquid. **4** *Optics.* a strong lens or lenses for concentrating light upon a small area. **5** an apparatus for condensing or compressing air.

con|den|ser|y (kən den′sər ē), *n., pl.* **-ser|ies**. a place where condensed milk is produced.

con|den|si|ty (kən den′sə tē), *n.* **1** condensed form or character. **2** conciseness. **3** *Obsolete.* density.

con|de|scend (kon′di send′), *v.i.* **1** to come down willingly or graciously to the level of one's inferiors in rank: *The king condescended to eat with the beggars.* **SYN:** deign, stoop. **2** to grant a favor with a haughty or patronizing attitude: *The colonel's wife finally condescended to visit the sergeant's sick wife.* **3** to stoop or lower oneself: *The policeman would not condescend to taking a bribe.* **4** *Obsolete.* to give one's consent; yield; acquiesce. [< Old French *condescendre,* learned borrowing from Late Latin *condēscendere* < Latin *com-* together + *dēscendere* descend] —**con′de|scend′er**, *n.*

con|de|scend|ence (kon′di sen′dəns), *n.* **1** = condescension. **2** (in Scots law) a specification of particulars of a plaintiff's claim.

con|de|scend|ing (kon′di sen′ding), *adj.* **1** stooping to the level of one's inferiors. **2** haughty or patronizing. —**con′de|scend′ing|ly**, *adv.*

con|de|scen|sion (kon′di sen′shən), *n.* **1a** pleasantness to one's inferiors in rank. **b** an instance of this. **2** a haughty or patronizing attitude. [< Late Latin *condēscēnsiō, -ōnis* < *condēscendere;* see etym. under **condescend**]

con|dign (kən dīn′), *adj.* **1** deserved; adequate; fitting; *condign punishment.* **2** *Archaic.* worthy; deserving. [< Middle French *condigne,* learned borrowing from Latin *condignus* very worthy < *com-* completely + *dignus* worthy]
▶ Because **condign** is so often coupled with *punishment,* it is sometimes misunderstood and used as a synonym for *severe.*

con|di|ment (kon′də mənt), *n.* something used to give flavor and relish to food, such as pepper, mustard, or spices. [< Latin *condīmentum* a spice < *condīre* to pickle or preserve]

con|di|men|tal (kon′də men′təl), *adj.* of or like a condiment or relish; spicy.

con|dis|ci|ple (kon′də sī′pəl), *n.* **1** a fellow disciple. **2** a fellow student. [< *con-* + *disciple*]

con|di|tion (kən dish′ən), *n., v.* —*n.* **1** the state in which a person or thing is: *The condition of his health is poor. The condition of the house is better than when I bought it.* **SYN:** situation, shape. See syn. under **state**. **2** good condition; good health: *People who take part in sports must keep in condition.* **3** fit or satisfactory state for work, market, etc.: *The horse has lost condition. Grain out of condition is unsalable.* **4** social position; rank: *Lincoln's parents were poor settlers of humble condition.* **SYN:** circumstances, station. **5** a thing on which something else depends; thing without which something else cannot be: *Ability and effort are conditions of success.* **SYN:** requirement, prerequisite. **6** something demanded as an essential part of an agreement: *Leases between landlords and tenants usually contain several conditions about the use of the property.* **7** a modifying circumstance; restriction; limitation: *to impose upon those values ... a new condition or restriction* (John Russell Young). **8** *Mathematics.* a requirement that is expressed by an open mathematical sentence. $3 + X = 5$ expresses the condition that a number you are to find, added to 3, must equal 5. **9** *Grammar.* a clause that expresses or contains a condition. **10** *U.S.* **a** a grade in scholarship calling for reexamination or special work before the student passes to the next grade or receives credit for the course. **b** a report of such a grade. **11** *Law.* **a** a provision in a will, contract, or other document, making the force or effect of the document depend upon a future event which may or may not take place. **b** the event itself. **12** *Logic.* a proposition, the truth of which is necessary for the truth of another proposition; antecedent. **13** *Obsolete.* disposition; temper. **14** *Obsolete.* a characteristic; attribute; quality.
—*v.t.* **1** to put in good condition: *Exercise conditions your muscles.* **2a** to train or accustom: *Our ears have become conditioned to noise. His early years had conditioned him ... for self-dependence* (Edmund Wilson). **b** to prepare: *The latest issue of the Building Societies' Gazette ... conditions us for the rise in mortgage rates almost certain to be introduced* (London Times). **c** *Psychology.* to shape the behavior of (a person or animal); accustom; habituate: *Four dogs were conditioned to flex a foreleg to a tone, the* [*stimulus*] *being a shock* (Lawrence E. Cole). **d** to attach (a response) to a new stimulus or (a new response) to a stimulus: *Reflexes were first deliberately conditioned in dogs.* **3** to be a condition of: *Ability and effort condition success.* **4** to subject to a condition; make dependent on: *The gift to the boy was conditioned on his good behavior.* **5** *U.S.* to require reexamination or special work of: *He was conditioned in Latin.* **6** *Commerce.* to test the condition and quality of (a commodity). **7** to make (something) a condition; stipulate: *He only conditioned that the marriage should not take place before his return* (Jane Austen).
—*v.i.* to make conditions; make it a condition.
change one's condition, to marry: *She expected him to say "Jenny, I am going to change my condition"* (Scott).
conditions, a set of circumstances: *Icy roads make for poor driving conditions.*
on condition that, provided that; if: *I will go on condition that you will too.*
[< Old French *condicion,* learned borrowing from Latin *condīciō, -ōnis* agreement < *condīcere* < *com-* together + *dīcere* say]

con|di|tion|al (kən dish′ə nəl), *adj., n.* —*adj.* **1** depending on something else; not absolute; limited. "You may go if the sun shines" is a conditional promise. **2** expressing or containing a condition. "If the sun shines" is a conditional clause. *Conditional statements in the sales agreement limited the use of the land. Conditional renunciation is a different policy* (Manchester Guardian).
—*n. Grammar.* a mood or tense in some languages, such as Spanish and Portuguese, which expresses conditions.

con|di|tion|al|i|ty (kən dish′ə nal′ə tē), *n.* the quality of being conditional.

con|di|tion|al|ly (kən dish′ə nə lē), *adv.* under a condition or conditions: *He accepted the invitation conditionally, until he could check his calendar.*

con|di|tioned (kən dish′ənd), *adj.* **1** put under a condition; subject to certain conditions: *Art is the one corner of human life in which we may take our ease. ... In other places our passions are conditioned and embarrassed* (Henry James). **2** in or having a certain kind of condition. **3** *Psychology.* **a** based on or caused by conditioning: *conditioned behavior.* **b** that evokes a response as a result of conditioning: *a conditioned stimulus.*

conditioned response or **reflex**, *Psychology.* a learned response which results from conditioning.

con|di|tion|er (kən dish′ə nər), *n.* **1** a person or thing that conditions: *Mr. Walz ... taught us the value of running as a conditioner* (New Yorker). **2** a device or substance that maintains or improves the quality of something: *a water conditioner.* **3** = air conditioner. **4** a milling machine for drying damp or musty grains.

con|di|tion|ing (kən dish′ə ning), *n. Psychology.* the process of shaping the behavior of a person or animal by repeated exposure to particular stimuli, with which new responses become habitually associated.

con|do (kon′dō), *n., pl.* **-dos**. *U.S. Informal.* condominium (def. 1): *His North Miami Beach condo would cost him a mere $25 a month* (Newsweek).

con|do|la|to|ry (kən dō′lə tôr′ē, -tōr′-), *adj.* expressing condolence; condoling.

con|dole (kən dōl′), *v.,* **-doled, -dol|ing.** *—v.i.* **1** to express sympathy (with); commiserate: *The widow's friends condoled with her at the funeral.* **2** *Obsolete.* to grieve; lament.
—v.t. Obsolete. to grieve with (another).
[< Latin *condolēre* < *com-* with + *dolēre* grieve, suffer] —**con|dole′ment,** *n.* —**con|dol′er,** *n.* —**con|dol′ing|ly,** *adv.*

con|do|lence (kən dō′ləns), *n.* a condoling; expression of sympathy with a person in grief: *The widow's friends sent her many condolences.*

con do|lo|re (kôn dō lō′rā), *Italian, Music.* sorrowfully (used as a direction).

con|dom (kon′dəm), *n.* a rubber or plastic sheath used by men as a contraceptive or to prevent venereal disease; prophylactic. [origin uncertain]

con|do|min|i|um (kon′də min′ē əm), *n.* **1** *U.S.* **a** an apartment house in which apartments are neither rentals nor cooperatives but are purchased as pieces of real estate and separately valued for property tax purposes. **b** an apartment in such a building. **2** joint control, especially by two or more countries over the government of another country or territory: *Between 1899 and 1956, the Sudan was ruled by a condominium of Egypt and Great Britain.* **3** a country or territory whose government is controlled jointly by two or more others: *The Anglo-Egyptian Sudan was a condominium.* **4** (in Roman law) joint ownership including power of disposal. [< New Latin *condominium* < Latin *com-* with + *dominium* lordship < *dominus* master]

con|don|ance (kən dō′nəns), *n.* = condonation.

con|do|na|tion (kon′dō nā′shən), *n.* the forgiveness of an offense, especially by ignoring or overlooking it.

con|done (kən dōn′), *v.t.,* **-doned, -don|ing. 1** to forgive or overlook: *Good friends will condone each other's faults.* **SYN**: excuse. **2** *Law.* to forgive (a violation of the marriage vow). [< Latin *condōnāre* < *com-* (intensive) + *dōnāre* pardon, give < *dōnum* gift] —**con|done′ment,** *n.* —**con|don′er,** *n.*

con|dor (kon′dər), *n.* **1** a large vulture with a ruffed neck and bare head. Condors live on high mountains in South America and California. **2** a gold coin used in several South American countries, bearing the figure of a condor on one side, and varying in worth from about $1.25 to $9.75. [< Spanish *cóndor* < Quechua *cuntur*]

con|dot|tie|re (kôn′dōt tye′rā), *n., pl.* **-ri** (-rē). **1** a professional captain of mercenary soldiers in Europe during the 1300's and 1400's. **2** a member of a band of mercenaries. [< Italian *condottiere* < *condotto* a mercenary < Latin *conductus;* see etym. under **conduct**]

con|duce (kən düs′, -dyüs′), *v.i.,* **-duced, -duc|ing.** to be favorable (to); lead; contribute: *Darkness and quiet conduce to sleep. As so many viewers report, it* [*a television program*] *probably conduces to a feeling of well-being, and contentment with the status quo* (Sunday Times). [< Latin *condūcere* < *com-* together + *dūcere* lead]

con|du|ci|ble (kən dü′sə bəl, -dyü′-), *adj.* **1** = conducive. **2** advantageous; serviceable; beneficial. —**con|du′ci|ble|ness,** *n.* —**con|du′ci|bly,** *adv.*

con|du|cive (kən dü′siv, -dyü′-), *adj.* favorable or helpful (to): *Exercise and proper eating habits are conducive to good health. Comparing oneself with others is rarely conducive to real happiness* (New York Times). —**con|du′cive|ly,** *adv.* —**con|du′cive|ness,** *n.*

con|duct (*n.* kon′dukt; *v.* kən dukt′), *n., v. —n.* **1** way of acting; behavior: *to win a medal for good conduct. Their conduct was rude and inexcusable.* **2** direction; management; execution: *Conduct of such a large office takes much planning.* **3** leading; guidance. **4** *Obsolete.* an escort; guide.
—v.t. **1** to act in a certain way; behave: *At home he is disorderly, but in company he conducts himself well.* **2** to direct the course of; manage: *Mr. Jones conducts the affairs of a big business.* **SYN**: See syn. under **manage**. **3** to direct (an orchestra, or choir, or the performance of music) as leader: *The overture was conducted by the composer himself.* **4** to accompany and show the way to; guide; lead: *Conduct me to your teacher. He conducted me through the museum.* **SYN**: See syn. under **guide**. **5** to transmit, transfer, or convey (heat, electricity, sound, or other form of energy; be a channel for: *Metal conducts heat and electricity. Those pipes conduct steam to the radiator upstairs.*
—v.i. **1** to act as conductor, especially of an orchestra: *The maestro conducted with his usual brilliance.* **2** to transmit heat, electricity, etc. **3** to lead; be the way; pass. **4** *Rare.* to behave.
[< Latin *conductus,* past participle of *condūcere;* see etym. under **conduce**. See etym. of doublet **conduit**.]
—Syn. n. **1 Conduct, behavior, deportment** mean way of acting. **Conduct** applies to a person's way of acting in general and according to society's principles of right and wrong: *Your conduct is always admirable.* **Behavior** applies to the way of acting before and toward others, especially in a specific situation: *The students' behavior during the trip showed consideration for others.* **Deportment** implies a way of acting according to a conventional code: *He was a model of deportment as a schoolboy.*

con|duct|ance (kən duk′təns), *n.* the power of conducting electricity as affected by the shape, length, or material of the conductor; the ease with which a substance or a solution of it permits the passage of an electrical current. Its unit of measurement is the mho, reciprocal of the ohm.

con|duct|i|bil|i|ty (kən duk′tə bil′ə tē), *n.* the power of conducting heat, electricity, sound or other form of energy.

con|duct|i|ble (kən duk′tə bəl), *adj.* **1** that can conduct heat, electricity, etc. **2** that can be conducted.

con|duc|tion (kən duk′shən), *n.* **1a** the transmission of heat, sound, or other form of energy, by the transferring of energy from one particle to another. Radiators heat the air in a room by conduction. *Conduction is the process by which heat is transferred through matter, without transfer of the matter itself* (Thomas A. Blair). **b** the transmission of electricity by a conductor. **c** = conductivity. **2** a conveying: *the conduction of water through a pipe. The movement of sap in plants is called conduction.* **3** *Physiology.* the transmission of an impulse through muscle or nerve tissue.

con|duc|ti|tious (kon′duk tish′əs), *adj.* hired; serving for hire; open to hire. [< Latin *conductīcius* (with English *-ous*) < *conductus;* see etym. under **conduct**]

con|duc|tive (kən duk′tiv), *adj.* **1** having conductivity. **2** of conduction. —**con|duc′tive|ly,** *adv.*

con|duc|tiv|i|ty (kon′duk tiv′ə tē), *n.* **1** the power of conducting heat, electricity, sound, or other form of energy: *The conductivity of a given material varies with temperature* (Sears and Zemansky). **2** the ability of a given substance to conduct electricity between opposite faces of a one-centimeter cube of the material, measured in reciprocal ohms, or mhos, per centimeter cube. **3** the rate of transfer of heat by conduction between opposite faces of a one-centimeter cube of a substance, having unit temperature difference between opposite faces.

con|duc|tom|e|ter (kon′duk tom′ə tər), *n.* an apparatus for measuring the relative conductivity, especially thermal conductivity, of different materials.

con|duc|to|met|ric (kən duk′tō met′rik), *adj.* of or having to do with the measurement of conductivity; obtained by a conductometer.

con|duc|tom|e|try (kon′duk tom′ə trē), *n.* the measurement of the relative conductivity of different materials, especially by a conductometer.

con|duc|tor (kən duk′tər), *n.* **1** a person who conducts; director; manager: *The successful owner of a business must be an able conductor of business affairs.* **2** the director of an orchestra or chorus. The conductor of an orchestra or chorus trains the performers to work together, selects the music to be used, beats time for the orchestra and conducts rehersals. *The conductor ... a musical interpreter* (New York Times). **3a** the person in charge of a train or a bus and its passengers. The conductor usually collects the tickets or fares from the passengers. **b** a guide or leader; person who is in charge of or guides a group of people traveling together: *the conductor of a tour.* **4** a thing that transmits heat, electricity, light, sound or other form of energy: *Copper is a good conductor of heat and electricity.* **5** = lightning rod. —**con|duc′tor|less,** *adj.*

con|duc|to|ri|al (kon′duk tôr′ē əl, -tōr′-), *adj.* of or having to do with a conductor or conducting: *conductorial techniques.*

con|duc|tor|ship (kən duk′tər ship), *n.* the office or function of a conductor.

con|duc|tress (kən duk′tris), *n.* a woman conductor.

con|duc|tus (kən duk′təs), *n.* a polyphonic form of church music, sung in the 1200's. [< Latin *conductus;* see etym. under **conduct**]

con|du|it (kon′dů it, kon′dit), *n.* **1** a channel or pipe for carrying liquids long distances; aqueduct or canal. **2** a tube or underground passage for electric wires or cables. **3** *Archaic.* a fountain. [< Old French *conduit* < Medieval Latin *conductus* a leading, a pipe < Latin *condūcere* < *com-* together + *dūcere* draw, lead. See etym. of doublet **conduct**.]

con|du|pli|cate (kon dü′plə kit, -dyü′-), *adj.* folded together lengthwise: *a conduplicate leaf in bud.* [< Latin *conduplicātus,* past participle of *conduplicāre* < *com-* together + *duplicāre* to double]

con|du|pli|ca|tion (kon′dü plə kā′shən, -dyü-), *n.* a doubling; repetition.

con|dy|lar (kon′də lər), *adj.* of or having to do with a condyle.

con|dy|larth (kon′də larth), *n.* any one of a group of early Tertiary mammals, believed to be the ancestral stock of the modern ungulates: *The condylarths ... had toes with structures intermediate between claws and hoofs* (Science News Letter). [< New Latin *Condylarthra* the order name < Greek *kóndylos* knuckle + *árthron* joint]

con|dy|larth|rous (kon′də lar′thrəs), *adj.* of or having the characteristics of the condylarths.

***con|dyle** (kon′dəl), *n.* a rounded part that grows out at the end of a bone, articulating with another bone. [< French *condyle,* learned borrowing from Latin *condylus* < Greek *kóndylos* a knuckle]

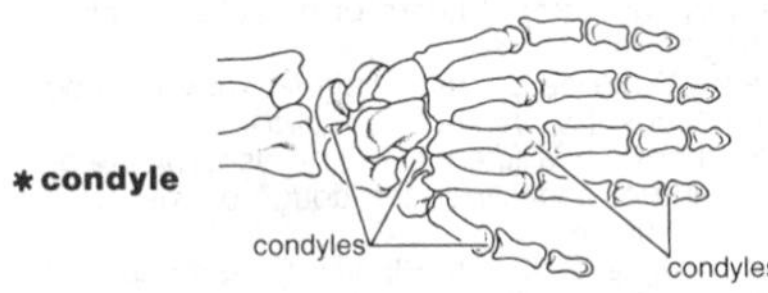

***condyle**

con|dy|loid (kon′də loid), *adj.* having to do with or formed like a condyle.

con|dy|lo|ma (kon′də lō′mə), *n., pl.* **-mas, -ma|ta** (-mə tə). a wartlike growth on the skin, usually near the anus or genitals. [< Latin *condylōma* < Greek *kondýlōma* callous knob < *kóndylos* a knuckle]

con|dy|lom|a|tous (kon′də lom′ə təs, -lō′mə-), *adj.* like a condyloma.

Con|dy's fluid (kon′dēz), a disinfectant made of an aqueous solution of a permanganate. [< Henry Bollman *Condy,* an English physician of the 1800's]

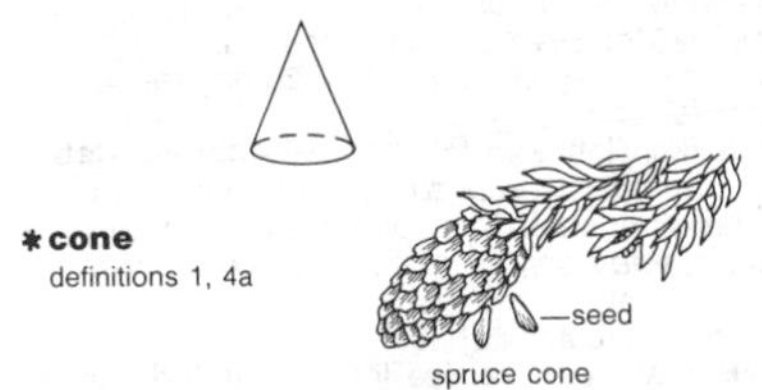

***cone**
definitions 1, 4a

***cone** (kōn), *n., v.,* **coned, con|ing.** *—n.* **1** a solid object that has a flat, round base and narrows to a point at the top. **2** *Geometry.* a surface traced by a moving straight line, one point of which is fixed, the opposite end constantly touching a fixed curve. A cone in which the base is a circle and the vertex lies on the perpendicular to the base at the center is called a *right circular cone.* A cone in which the vertex does not lie on the perpendicular is called an *oblique circular cone.* **3** anything shaped like a cone: *an ice-cream cone. Smoke and lava erupted from Paricutin as the Western Hemisphere's newest volcano rapidly built its cone* (Gordon A. Macdonald). **4a** the part that bears the seeds on pine, cedar, fir, and other evergreen trees; strobile: *Spruces have cones that hang straight downward. Fir trees have cones that stand straight up* (K. A. Armson). **b** a fruit resembling this, such as that of a cycad.

Pronunciation Key: hat, āge, cãre, fär; let, ēqual, tėrm; it, īce; hot, ōpen, ôrder; oil, out; cup, pu̇t, rüle; child; long; thin; ᴛʜen; zh, measure; ə represents **a** in about, **e** in taken, **i** in pencil, **o** in lemon, **u** in circus.

c any inflorescence that resembles a cone, such as that of the hop. **5** one of a group of cone-shaped cells of the retina of the eye that respond to light. The cones are sensitive to the bright light of day; the rods are sensitive to dim light. **6** *Machinery.* any of various cone-shaped parts on a lathe, spinning machine, or firearm.
—***v.t.*** to shape like a cone or part of a cone.
[< Latin *cōnus* < Greek *kônos* cone, pine cone]
—**cone'less**, *adj.*

cone clutch, a friction clutch with a conical surface of contact between the driving and the driven member.

cone|flow|er (kōn'flou'ər), *n.* **1** any one of a genus of plants of the composite family, having showy flowers with a black or dark cone-shaped center and orange-yellow rays. **2** any one of various related plants.

cone-in-cone (kōn'in kōn'), *n. Geology.* a structure of cones packed one inside another, found in certain sedimentary rocks. Individual cones measure from a fraction of an inch to a few feet in height.

cone|let (kōn'lit), *n.* a little cone: *Minor eruptions gradually increased the size of the central conelet* (Scientific American).

cone|like (kōn'līk'), *adj.* having the characteristics of a cone.

Con|el|rad (kon'əl rad), *n.* a system formerly used for broadcasting instructions over radio stations by shifting frequencies, going on and off the air irregularly, while keeping enemy aircraft or guided missiles from utilizing the beams of the station for navigation. [< *Con*(trol) (of) *El*(ectromagnetic) *Rad*(iation)]

cone|nose (kōn'nōz'), *n.* any hemipterous insect of the genera of assassin bugs, which suck the blood of men and animals, such as the kissing bug of the United States.

cone of silence, a cone-shaped extent of space directly over a radio beacon or radar station in which signals are not heard or detected by aircraft flying overhead.

co|ne|pa|tl (kō'ne pä'təl), *n.* (in Mexico) the hog-nosed skunk. [< Nahuatl *conepatl*]

cones (kōnz), *n.* a fine white flour used by bakers for dusting or sprinkling their dough or vessels. [origin unknown]

cone snail, a snail of the Indian Ocean and southwest Pacific Ocean having a poisonous stinger about one-half inch long.

Con|es|to|ga (kon'ə stō'gə), *n., pl.* **-ga** or **-gas**. **1** a member of a tribe of North American Indians of the Iroquoian language family, formerly living in Pennsylvania and Maryland. **2** the language of this tribe.

Conestoga wagon, a covered wagon with broad wheels, used especially by American pioneers for traveling on soft ground or on the prairie. See picture under **covered wagon**. [American English < *Conestoga,* Pennsylvania, where they were first built]

cone wheel, a cone-shaped pulley used to transmit and vary mechanical motion.

co|ney[1] (kō'nē), *n., pl.* **-neys**. = cony.

co|ney[2] (kō'nē), *n. Canadian.* inconnu.

conf., **1** compare (Latin, *confer*). **2** conference. **3** confessor.

con|fab (kon'fab, kən fab'), *n., v.,* **-fabbed, -fabbing**. *Informal (often used humorously).* —***n.*** a confabulating; chat: *The confab lasted an hour and transacted only one item of business* (Wall Street Journal).
—***v.i.*** to confabulate; chat.

con|fab|u|late (kən fab'yə lāt), *v.i.,* **-lat|ed, -lat|ing**. **1** *Informal (often used humorously).* to talk together informally and intimately; chat. **2** *Psychology.* to fabricate experiences. [< Latin *cōnfābulārī* < *com-* together + *fābula* fable] —**con|fab'u|la'tion**, *n.* —**con|fab'u|la'tor**, *n.*

con|fab|u|la|to|ry (kən fab'yə lə tôr'ē, -tōr'-), *adj. Informal.* characterized by confabulation; colloquial.

con|far|re|a|tion (kon far'ē ā'shən), *n.* the highest and most solemn form of marriage among the ancient Romans, marked by the offering of a cake made of spelt. [< Latin *cōnfarreātiō, -ōnis* < *cōnfarreāre* unite in marriage by the offering of bread < *com-* with + *far, farris* grain, spelt]

con|fect (*v.* kən fekt'; *n.* kon'fekt), *v., n.* —***v.t.*** **1** to make up, especially out of various materials: *She has the gift of confecting a story as easily consumed as a soufflé* (Atlantic). SYN: devise, contrive. **2** *Archaic.* to preserve; pickle. **3** *Obsolete.* to compound (a medicine).
—***n.*** *Rare.* a confection.
[< Latin *cōnfectus,* past participle of *cōnficere;* see etym. under **confection**]

con|fec|tion (kən fek'shən), *n.* **1a** a piece of candy or candied fruit. SYN: bonbon, comfit, sweetmeat. **b** any one of various other foods made with sugar, such as jam. **2** a ready-made garment for women's wear, usually elaborate and elegant. **3** a medicine containing various drugs in a soft mass with a sweetening agent such as sugar or honey. **4** the process of compounding or mixing, especially drugs, candy, or preserves. [< Old French *confeccion,* learned borrowing from Latin *cōnfectiō, -ōnis* < *cōnficere* prepare, complete < *com-* with + *facere* make]

con|fec|tion|ar|y (kən fek'shə ner'ē), *n., pl.* **-ar|ies**, *adj.* —***n.*** **1** = confectionery (defs. 2 and 3). **2** a confection; sweetmeat. **3** *Obsolete.* a confectioner.
—***adj.*** **1** of or having to do with confections or the making of them. **2** of or like a confection or candy.

con|fec|tion|er (kən fek'shə nər), *n.* a person who makes or sells candies, ice cream, and cakes.

con|fec|tion|ers' sugar (kən fek'shə nərz), very fine sugar made by grinding granulated sugar. *Symbol:* XXXX.

con|fec|tion|er|y (kən fek'shə ner'ē), *n., pl.* **-er|ies**. **1** candies or sweets; confections. **2** the business of making or selling confections. **3** a place where confections, ice cream, and cakes are made or sold; candy shop.

Confed., Confederate.

con|fed|er|a|cy (kən fed'ər ə sē, -fed'rə sē), *n., pl.* **-cies**. **1** a union of countries or states; group of people joined together for a special purpose; confederation or federation. SYN: league. **2** a conspiracy. **3** the condition or fact of being confederate; alliance.
the Confederacy, the group of eleven Southern states that seceded from the United States in 1860 and 1861; the Confederate States of America: *Progress of* [*Civil*] *War favored the Confederacy in the first months* (John Donald Hicks).

con|fed|er|al (kən fed'ər əl, -fed'rəl), *adj.* of or having to do with a confederation; forming a confederation: ... *the kind of confederal association under law which the nations of the world must ultimately achieve* (Adlai E. Stevenson).

con|fed|er|al|ist (kən fed'ər ə list, -fed'rə-), *n.* **1** a person who believes in confederation; confederationist: *The confederalists look forward to ... the Europe of nation states* (London Times). **2** a member of a confederation.

con|fed|er|ate (*n., adj.* kən fed'ər it, -fed'rit; *v.* kən fed'ə rāt), *n., adj., v.,* **-at|ed, -at|ing**. —***n.*** **1** a person or country joined with another for a special purpose; ally: *The countries of the United Nations are confederates in a search for peace.* **2** an accomplice; partner in crime: *The thief was arrested, but his confederate escaped.* SYN: accessory. See syn. under **accomplice**.
—***adj.*** joined for a special purpose; allied: *Many confederate states in Europe make up the Common Market.*
—***v.t., v.i.*** to join for a special purpose; ally.
[< Late Latin *cōnfoederātus,* past participle of *cōnfoederāre* unite in a league < *com-* together + *foedus, -eris* league < *fīdere* to trust]

Con|fed|er|ate (kən fed'ər it, -fed'rit), *n., adj.* —***n.*** a person who lived in, supported, or fought for the Confederacy.
—***adj.*** of or belonging to the Confederacy: *the Confederate uniform.*

Confederate Memorial Day, a day on which Confederate soldiers who died in the Civil War are commemorated in southern states of the United States; April 26 in Georgia and Florida; last Monday in April in Alabama and Mississippi; May 10 in North Carolina and South Carolina; June 3 in Kentucky, Louisiana, and Tennessee; and the last Monday in May in Virginia. It was the origin of the celebration of Memorial Day in the United States.

Confederate States of America, = the Confederacy.

con|fed|er|a|tion (kən fed'ə rā'shən), *n.* **1** the act of joining together in a league or alliance: *The conference devised a plan for the confederation of the colonies.* **2** the state of being united in a league or alliance. **3** a group of countries, states, etc., joined together for a special purpose; league; confederacy; alliance: *By 1800* B.C., *they* [*the Hittites*] *had established royal rule over a confederation of widely dissimilar peoples* (Newsweek).
Confederation, the union of Ontario, Quebec, Nova Scotia, and New Brunswick in 1867, joined since then by six other Canadian provinces.
the Confederation, the union of the thirteen American states, 1781-89, under the Articles of Confederation.

con|fed|er|a|tion|ist (kən fed'ə rā'shə nist), *n.* a person who favors or supports confederation or a confederation.

con|fed|er|a|tive (kən fed'ə rā'tiv), *adj.* of or having to do with a confederation.

con|fer (kən fėr'), *v.,* **-ferred, -fer|ring**. —***v.i.*** to talk things over; consult together; exchange ideas: *The President often confers with his advisers.* SYN: See syn. under **consult**.
—***v.t.*** **1** to give; bestow: *The President conferred a medal on each of the astronauts.* SYN: award. See syn. under **give**. **2** *Obsolete.* to compare. [< Latin *cōnferre* < *com-* together + *ferre* bring]
—**con|fer'ra|ble**, *adj.* —**con|fer'rer**, *n.*
▶Though *confer* in the sense of "compare" is now obsolete, the abbreviation *cf.* is still in use.

con|fer|ee (kon'fə rē'), *n.* **1** *U.S.* a person who takes part in a conference. **2** a person on whom something is conferred.

con|fer|ence (kon'fər əns, -frəns), *n.* **1** a meeting of interested persons to discuss a particular subject: *A conference was called to discuss getting a playground for the school.* SYN: parley. **2** the act of talking something over; consulting together: *The teacher was in conference with parents after school.* SYN: consultation. **3** a meeting between committees or representatives of the two houses of a legislature to settle differences between them. SYN: council. **4a** a voluntary federation of local churches making up a district, whose representatives convene in an assembly. **b** the district itself. **5** an authorized assembly of clergymen, or of clergymen and laymen, meeting specially or at stated intervals. SYN: congress, convention. **6** an association of the athletic teams of various schools; athletic league. **7** the act of conferring or bestowing.

conference call, a conference over the telephone between a group of people linked by a central switching unit: ... *notified to stand by to come in for a conference call initiated by the White House* (Russell Baker).

conference desk, a desk with an extended top, for use in conferences.

conference table, a large table designed for use at meetings of a committee, staff, or similar body: ... *a long room with a conference table and chairs* (New Yorker). *The Soviet rulers ... held up the vision of a general settlement around a conference table* (Wall Street Journal).

con|fé|ren|cier or **con|fe|ren|cier** (kon'fər ən-sir'; *French* kôɴ fā räɴ syā'), *n.* **1** a lecturer. **2** a moderator. [< French *conférencier*]

con|fer|en|tial (kon'fə ren'shəl), *adj.* of or having to do with a conference.

con|fer|ment (kən fėr'mənt), *n.* = conferral.

con|fer|ral (kən fėr'əl), *n.* a giving; bestowal: *the conferral of degrees at graduation.*

con|fer|ree (kon'fə rē'), *n.* = conferee.

con|fer|ru|mi|nate (kon'fe rü'mə nit), *adj. Botany.* closely adherent, as the cotyledons of the horse chestnut. [< Latin *cōnferrūminātus* soldered together, past participle of *cōnferrūmināre* < *com-* together + *ferrūmināre* to solder]

con|fer|ru|mi|nat|ed (kon'fe rü'mə nā'tid), *adj.* = conferruminate.

con|fer|va (kon fėr'və), *n., pl.* **-vae** (-vē). any freshwater green alga composed of unbranched, many-celled filaments. [< Latin *cōnferva* a kind of water plant; see etym. under **comfrey**]

con|fer|void (kon fėr'void), *adj., n.* —***adj.*** of, having to do with, or like a conferva. —***n.*** a conferva.

con|fess (kən fes'), *v.t.* **1** to acknowledge; admit; own up to: *The fat man confessed his fault, which was a weakness for candy. The thief confessed his crime to the police.* SYN: See syn. under **admit**. **2** to concede; grant: *I confess you are right on one point.* **3** to tell (one's sins) to a priest in order to obtain forgiveness. **4** to hear (a person) tell his sins in order to obtain forgiveness, as a priest does; act as a confessor to. **5** to declare belief in. **6** *Poetic.* to manifest; show. —***v.i.*** **1** to admit one's guilt; own (to): *The thief decided to confess. My brother confessed to eating the cake.* SYN: See syn. under **admit**. **2** to make known one's sins to a priest. **3** to act as a confessor. [< Latin *cōnfessus,* past participle of *cōnfitērī* < *com-* + *fatērī* confess, acknowledge]

con|fes|sant (kən fes'ənt), *n.* a person who confesses; confessor: *The confessant kneels down before the priest sitting on a raised chair above him* (Francis Bacon).

con|fessed (kən fest'), *adj.* acknowledged; admitted: ... *a confessed narcotics user* (Harper's).

con|fess|ed|ly (kən fes'id lē), *adv.* **1** by acknowledgment; admittedly. **2** by personal confession; avowedly.

con|fess|er (kən fes'ər), *n.* a person who confesses or makes confession.

con|fes|sion (kən fesh'ən), *n.* **1** an owning up; acknowledgment; admission: *the confession of a fault or weakness. ... to force from their prisoners the confession of hidden treasure* (Edward Gibbon). **2** admission of guilt: *to make a full confession.* **3a** the telling of one's sins to a priest in order to obtain forgiveness: *Confession is* *good for the soul.* **b** the thing confessed. **4a** the acknowledging of sin or sinfulness, especially as made in liturgical form in public worship. **b** the form used. **5** = confession of faith. **6** a group of believers adhering to the same creed; communion. **7** the tomb, altar, or shrine of a martyr or confessor.

con|fes|sion|al (kən fesh′ə nəl), *n., adj.* **—*n.*** **1** a small booth in which a priest hears confessions. **2** the practice of confessing sins to a priest.
—*adj.* of or having to do with confession. **—con·fes′sion|al|ly,** *adv.*

con|fes|sion|al|ism (kən fesh′ə nə liz′əm), *n.* devotion to the maintenance of a creed or confession of faith within a church.

con|fes|sion|ar|y (kən fesh′ə ner′ē), *adj.* of or having to do with confession.

confession of faith, 1 an acknowledgment of belief. **2** the belief acknowledged; creed.

con|fes|sor (kən fes′ər), *n.* **1** a person who confesses. **2a** a priest who has the authority to hear confessions and to grant absolution. **b** a priest acting as the private spiritual director of a king or other great personage. **3** a person who acknowledges religious belief and adheres to it despite persecution and torture. **4** a person whose life exemplifies sanctity and Christian ideals: *Edward the Confessor.* **—con|fes′sor|ship,** *n.*

con|fet|ti (kən fet′ē; *Italian* kôn fet′tē *for 2*), *n.pl.* **1** bits of colored paper thrown about at carnivals, weddings, or parades. **2** bonbons, or plaster or paper imitations of these, thrown during carnivals in Italy. [< Italian *confetti,* plural of *confetto* sweetmeat, ultimately < Latin *cōnfectus;* see etym. under **confect**]

con|fi|dant (kon′fə dant′, kon′fə dant), *n.* a person trusted with one's secrets or private affairs; close friend.

con|fi|dante (kon′fə dant′, kon′fə dant), *n.* a woman confidant.

con|fide (kən fīd′), *v.,* **-fid|ed, -fid|ing. —*v.t.*** **1** to tell as a secret: *He confided his troubles to his brother.* **2** to give to another to keep safe; hand over: *She confides her baby to the day nursery while she is at work. The collection of dues is confided to the treasurer.*
—*v.i.* **1** to show trust by telling secrets: *The girl confided in no one, but she kept a diary.* **2** to put trust or have faith (in): *Confide in God. You can confide in their good faith. Some other whom they confide in for protection* (Thomas Hobbes).
[< Latin *cōnfīdere* < *com-* completely + *fīdere* trust] **—con|fid′er,** *n.*

con|fi|dence (kon′fə dəns), *n.* **1** firm belief or trust: *We have no confidence in a liar. The leader of the explorers had great confidence in his native guide. With confidence in his Maker, he went to his doom.* **SYN:** faith. **2** a feeling sure or certain; assurance: *with full confidence of victory.* **SYN:** conviction. **3** firm belief in oneself and one's abilities; self-confidence: *Years of experience at his work have given him great confidence.* **4** boldness; too much boldness: *Although he could not swim, he dived into the water with confidence.* **SYN:** presumption. **5** trust that a person will not tell others what is told to him: *The secret was told to me in strict confidence.* **6** a thing told as a secret: *I listened to her confidences for half an hour.* **7** something that gives a feeling of security. **8** *British.* trust, as expressed by a majority vote of the parliament, in the actions and policy of the prime minister and his cabinet: *a vote of confidence.*
in the confidence of, sharing or trusted with the private opinions, plans, or purposes of: *He is in the confidence of several influential government officials.*
take into one's confidence, to share some private matter or matters with; confide matters of importance to: *He took me into his confidence and told me about his latest invention.*
—*Syn.* **3 Confidence, assurance** mean a firm belief in oneself. **Confidence** implies a strong but not haughty belief: *He goes at his work with confidence. The young singer has talent, but lacks confidence.* **Assurance** implies a stronger belief, not always free from arrogance: *He went into the contest with the assurance of a born fighter.*

confidence game, a fraud in which the swindler persuades his victim to trust him, especially with money or valuables.

confidence man, a swindler who persuades his victim to trust him.

confidence trick, *Especially British.* confidence game.

con|fi|dent (kon′fə dənt), *adj., n.* **—*adj.*** **1** firmly believing; certain; sure: *I feel confident that our team will win. The doctor felt confident that his patient would recover.* **SYN:** See syn. under **sure.** **2** sure of oneself and one's abilities: *I, alone, was confident that I would succeed.* **SYN:** assured, sanguine. **3** too bold; too sure: *He has the impudently confident air of inexperience.* **SYN:** presumptuous. **4** *Obsolete.* trustful; confiding.
—*n.* a close, trusted friend; confidant. **—con′fi·dent|ly,** *adv.*

con|fi|den|tial (kon′fə den′shəl), *adj.* **1** spoken or written as a secret: *The spy gave General Washington a confidential report on enemy activity.* **2** showing confidence or trust; confiding: *She spoke in low, confidential tones.* **3** trusted with secret matters: *A confidential secretary should be discreet.* **SYN:** See syn. under **familiar. —con′fi|den′tial|ly,** *adv.* **—con′fi|den′tial|ness,** *n.*

confidential communication, *Law.* a communication which a witness cannot be compelled to disclose, as that of a client to his lawyer or of a person confessing to a priest; privileged communication.

con|fi|den|ti|al|i|ty (kon′fə den′shē al′ə tē), *n.* the quality or state of being confidential.

con|fid|ing (kən fī′ding), *adj.* **1** trustful; trusting. **2** *Obsolete.* trusty; trustworthy. **—con|fid′ing|ly,** *adv.* **—con|fid′ing|ness,** *n.*

con|fig|u|rate (kən fig′yə rāt), *v.t.,* **-rat|ed, -rat|ing.** to give a configuration to; shape; fashion; configure. [< Latin *cōnfigūrāre* (with English *-ate*[1]); see etym. under **configuration**]

con|fig|u|ra|tion (kən fig′yə rā′shən), *n.* **1** the manner of arrangement; form; shape; outline: *Geographers study the configuration of the surface of the earth.* **SYN:** conformation; contour. **2** *Psychology.* = Gestalt. **3** *Astronomy.* **a** the relative position of heavenly bodies, especially of the sun, moon, and planets. **b** any grouping of stars. **4** the relative spatial positions of atoms in a molecule: *In any particular molecule, atom, or nucleus, the constituent particles can usually exist in a variety of configurations* (J. Little). [< Latin *cōnfigūrātiō, -ōnis* < *cōnfigūrāre* form after a pattern < *com-* with + *figūra* a form]

con|fig|u|ra|tion|al (kən fig′yə rā′shə nəl), *adj.* of or having to do with configuration: *A later configurational idea* [*was*] *the use of swept wings with careful fuselage and wing shapings near the kink in the lifting surface* (New Scientist). **—con·fig′u|ra′tion|al|ly,** *adv.*

con|fig|u|ra|tion|ism (kən fig′yə rā′shə niz əm), *n.* = Gestalt psychology. **—con|fig′u|ra′tion|ist,** *n.*

con|fig|u|ra|tive (kən fig′yə rā′tiv, -yər ə-), *adj.* = configurational.

con|fig|ure (kən fig′yər), *v.t.,* **-ured, -ur|ing.** to make or arrange in a certain form: *For some reason, I've always thought of Queen Elizabeth I as being configured along the lines of Edith Sitwell* (New Yorker).

con|fine (*v.* kən fīn′; *n.* kon′fīn), *v.,* **-fined, -fin|ing,** *n.* **—*v.t.*** **1** to keep within limits; restrict: *He confined his reading to biography. He confined himself to two meals a day.* **SYN:** restrain. **2** to keep indoors; shut in: *A cold confined him to the house.* **3** to imprison: *For two years he was confined in the Bastille.* **SYN:** jail.
—*v.i.* *Rare.* to have a common boundary (with); border (on).
[< Middle French *confiner* < Old French *confins;* see the noun]
—*n.* **1** Often, **confines. a** a boundary; border; limit: *These people have never been beyond the confines of their own valley.* **b** a border or frontier. **2** *Obsolete.* **a** a region, territory. **b** a place of confinement. **3** *Archaic.* confinement; limitation.
[< Old French *confins* boundaries, learned borrowing from Medieval Latin *confines,* ultimately < Latin < *com-* together + *fīnis* border] **—con·fin′a|ble,** *adj.* **—con|fine′less,** *adj.* **—con|fin′er,** *n.*

con|fined (kən fīnd′), *adj., n.* **—*adj.*** kept in confinement; shut-in.
—*n.* the confined, shut-in persons: *In visiting the confined, it is best to be brief.*
be confined, to be in childbed: *Mothers today are not confined for long but soon after confinement are up and about.*

con|fin|ed|ly (kən fī′nid lē, -fīnd′lē), *adv.* in a confined or limited manner.

con|fine|ment (kən fīn′mənt), *n.* **1** the act of confining. **2** the fact or state of being confined: *confinement indoors because of a cold.* **3** imprisonment. **4** the period a mother is confined to bed during and after childbirth. [< French *confinement* < Middle French *confiner;* see etym. under **confine,** verb]

con|fines (kon′fīnz), *n.pl.* See under **confine** (*n.* def. 1).

con|fin|ing (kən fī′ning), *adj.* **1** that confines; limiting; restricting. **2** that keeps one confined and steadily busy, without opportunity for change, exercise, relaxation, etc.: *a confining job.* **—con|fin′·ing|ly,** *adv.*

con|firm (kən fėrm′), *v.t.* **1** to prove to be true or correct; make certain: *The rumor that there was flooding was confirmed by a news broadcast.* **2** to make more certain by putting in writing, by consent, or by encouragement: *He sent the written request to confirm his telephone order. The Senate confirmed the treaty.* **SYN:** approve, ratify, sanction. **3** to make firmer; strengthen: *He was confirmed in his opinions by all his friends. A sudden storm confirmed my decision not to leave.* **4** to administer religious confirmation to; admit formally to full communion or membership in a church or synagogue. [< Old French *confermer,* learned borrowing from Latin *cōnfirmāre* < *com-* altogether + *firmāre* strengthen < *firmus* firm, strong] **—con|firm′a|ble,** *adj.* **—con|firm′er,** *n.*
—*Syn.* **1 Confirm, corroborate, substantiate, authenticate** mean to prove to be true or genuine. **Confirm** implies removing all doubt by means of facts or statements that cannot be doubted: *The Mayor confirmed the report that he had resigned.* **Corroborate** implies the strengthening of proof by additional evidence or statements: *Finding the weapon corroborates the police theory.* **Substantiate** implies offering sufficient and solid evidence: *This theory has now been substantiated by the results of many experiments.* **Authenticate** implies the evidence of someone who knows: *Handwriting experts authenticated the will.*
► See **affirm** for usage note.

con|firm|a|bil|i|ty (kən fėr′mə bil′ə tē), *n.* the fact or condition of being confirmable.

con|fir|mand (kon′fər mand′), *n.* a candidate for confirmation: *The bishop lays his hands on the confirmand* (Time). [< Latin *confirmandus* fit to be confirmed < *confirmāre* to confirm]

con|fir|ma|tion (kon′fər mā′shən), *n.* **1** the act or process of making sure by more information or evidence; confirming: *He telephoned the theater for confirmation of the movie's starting time.* **2** a thing that confirms; proof: *Don't believe rumors that lack confirmation.* **3** the action of confirming or ratifying by some additional legal form: *The finding and sentence are subject to confirmation* (London Times). **4a** a Christian ceremony or sacrament in which a baptized person is admitted to full communion or membership in a church. **b** a ceremony held especially in Conservative and Reform synagogues in which young people reaffirm their faith in Judaism and are admitted as adult members of the congregation.

confirmation class, a class of or for young people preparing for religious confirmation.

con|firm|a|tive (kən fėr′mə tiv), *adj.* = confirmatory. **—con|firm′a|tive|ly,** *adv.*

con|firm|a|to|ry (kən fėr′mə tôr′ē, -tōr′-), *adj.* serving to confirm; confirming: *confirmatory experiments.*

con|firmed (kən fėrmd′), *adj.* **1** firmly established; proved: *a confirmed rumor.* **2a** constant or habitual; settled: *a confirmed smoker.* **SYN:** inveterate. **b** permanent; chronic: *a confirmed bachelor, a confirmed invalid.* **3** admitted to the full privileges of a church. **—con|firm′ed|ly,** *adv.* **—con|firm′ed|ness,** *n.*

con|fis|ca|ble (kən fis′kə bəl), *adj.* liable to be confiscated.

con|fis|cat|a|ble (kon′fis kā′tə bəl), *adj.* = confiscable.

con|fis|cate (kon′fis kāt), *v.,* **-cat|ed, -cat|ing,** *adj.* **—*v.t.*** **1** to seize for the public treasury: *The new government confiscated the property of the deposed leaders.* **SYN:** appropriate. **2** to seize by authority; take and keep: *The teacher confiscated the water pistol.* **SYN:** appropriate.
—*adj.* confiscated; forfeited.
[< Latin *cōnfiscāre* (with English *-ate*[1]) seize for the public treasury, (originally) lay away in a chest < *com-* together + *fiscus* public treasury, chest] **—con′fis|ca′tor,** *n.*

con|fis|ca|tion (kon′fis kā′shən), *n.* the act of confiscating; the seizure of private property as forfeited to the public treasury: *the confiscation of wealth.*

con|fis|ca|to|ry (kən fis′kə tôr′ē, -tōr′-), *adj.* **1** of or like confiscation; tending to confiscate: *The British system of income taxation is much like the American, only more extreme, with ... more confiscatory surtaxes* (Wall Street Journal). **2** confiscating.

con|fise|rie (kôN fēz rē′), *n. French.* a confectionery.

con|fit|e|or (kən fit′ē ôr), *n.* a prayer containing a confession of sin. [< Latin *confiteor* I confess]

con|fi|ture (kon′fə chər), *n.* a confection, such as a piece of candy, candied fruit, or jam: *We planned our assault over a yard of bread and*

Pronunciation Key: hat, āge, cãre, fär; let, ēqual, tėrm; it, īce; hot, ōpen, ôrder; oil, out; cup, pu̇t, rüle; child; long; thin; ᴛʜen; zh, measure; ə represents **a** in about, **e** in taken, **i** in pencil, **o** in lemon, **u** in circus.

a pot of confiture (Atlantic). [< Old French *confiture,* learned borrowing from Latin *cōnfectūra* < *cōnficere;* see etym. under **confection**]

con|fla|grant (kən flā′grənt), *adj.* on fire; blazing. [< Latin *cōnflagrāns, -antis,* present participle of *cōnflagrāre;* see etym. under **conflagration**]

con|fla|grate (kon′flə grāt), *v.,* **-grat|ed, -grat|ing.** — ***v.i.*** to catch fire; burst into flame; burn. — ***v.t.*** **1** to burn up. **2** to set ablaze.

con|fla|gra|tion (kon′flə grā′shən), *n.* a big and destructive fire: *A conflagration destroyed the whole neighborhood.* [< Latin *cōnflagrātiō, -ōnis* < *cōnflagrāre* < *com-* (intensive) + *flagrāre* burn]

con|flate (kən flāt′), *v.t.,* **-flat|ed, -flat|ing. 1** to bring or put together; compose of various elements: *... the wide, conflated color vistas Monet drew* (Time). **2** to form (a text, etc.) by the combination of two readings. [< Latin *cōnflāre* (with English *-ate*[1]); see etym. under **conflation**]

con|fla|tion (kən flā′shən), *n.* **1a** a bringing or putting together; composing of various elements. **b** the result of this. **2a** the combining of two variant readings of a text into one. **b** the combined result. [< Latin *cōnflātiō, -ōnis* < *cōnflāre* < *com-* together + *flāre* blow]

con|flict (*n.* kon′flikt; *v.* kən flikt′), *n., v.* — ***n.*** **1** a fight or struggle, especially a long one; battle: *The conflict between Greece and Troy lasted ten years.* **SYN**: strife. See syn. under **fight. 2** *Figurative.* **a** a direct opposition; disagreement; clash: *A conflict of opinion arose over the best way to go on the trip. The recurring conflicts between church and state* (James Froude). **SYN**: discord, contention, dispute, quarrel. **b** a mental or spiritual struggle within a person: *With conflict of contending hopes and fears* (William Cowper).
— ***v.i.*** **1** *Figurative.* to be opposed; clash; differ in thought and action: *The testimony of the two witnesses conflicted on the exact time of the robbery.* **SYN**: disagree. **2** to fight; struggle. **SYN**: contend.
[< Latin *conflictus, -ūs* < *cōnflīgere* < *com-* together + *flīgere* strike]

con|flict|ing (kən flik′ting), *adj.* that conflicts; disagreeing; clashing: (*Figurative.*) *conflicting testimony, conflicting reports.* — **con|flict′ing|ly,** *adv.*

con|flic|tion (kən flik′shən), *n.* the act or fact of conflicting; conflict.

con|flic|tive (kən flik′tiv), *adj.* tending to conflict.

conflict of interest, the actual or potential conflict arising when a person holds an interest in a company doing business with his employer: *The "conflict of interest" statutes bar Government officials who are appointed to their jobs from retaining stock or other interests in a concern that does business with the Federal agency the official works for* (Wall Street Journal).

con|flic|to|ry (kən flik′tə rē), *adj.* conflictive; conflicting: (*Figurative.*) *... holding conflictory opinions as to her temperament* (William H. Gregory).

con|flic|tu|al (kən flik′chủ əl), *adj.* characterized by conflict: (*Figurative.*) *Sublimation is ... an attempt to deal in a socially acceptable way ... with conflictual material struggling for expression* (Saturday Review).

con|flow (kən flō′), *v.i.* to flow together; converge; unite: *The quiet mind, the youthful heart, the racing blood—these conflow to produce wonder* (E. B. White). [< *con-* + *flow*]

con|flu|ence (kon′flủ əns), *n.* **1** a flowing together: *The confluence of those two streams forms a large river.* **2** the place where two or more rivers, streams, or the like, come together: *They pitched camp at the confluence of the two streams. Morainic bands bound the confluence of Malaspina and Marvine glaciers in Alaska* (Scientific American). **3** a body of water produced in this way. **4** *Figurative.* a coming together of people or things. **5** *Figurative.* a throng; assemblage. [< Late Latin *confluentia* < Latin *cōnfluēns, -entis,* present participle of *cōnfluere* < *com-* together + *fluere* flow]

con|flu|ent (kon′flủ ənt), *adj., n.* — ***adj.*** **1** flowing or running together; blending into one: *confluent rivers.* **2** *Medicine.* **a** tending to join or run together: *confluent eruptions of the skin.* **b** characterized by such eruptions.
— ***n.*** **1** a stream which unites and flows with another of nearly equal size. **2** a smaller stream flowing into a larger one.
[< Latin *cōnfluēns, -entis;* see etym. under **confluence**] — **con′flu|ent|ly,** *adv.*

con|flux (kon′fluks), *n.* = confluence. [< Late Latin *cōnfluxus, -ūs* < Latin *cōnfluere;* see etym. under **confluent**]

con|fo|cal (kon fō′kəl), *adj. Mathematics.* having the same focus or foci.

con|form (kən fôrm′), *v., adj.* — ***v.i.*** **1** to act according to law or rule; be in agreement with generally accepted standards of business, law, conduct, or worship: *If you wish to be a member, you must conform to the rules of our club.* **2** to become the same in form; correspond in form or character: *Her dress conformed to the pattern.* **3** *Historical.* to comply with the usages of the Church of England.
— ***v.t.*** **1** to make similar; make like. **2** to bring into conformity; adapt. **SYN**: adjust, accommodate, reconcile.
— ***adj.*** *Obsolete.* **1** consistent; accordant. **2** similar; like.
[< Old French *conformer,* learned borrowing from Latin *cōnfōrmāre* < *com-* with + *fōrmāre* to shape < *forma* a shape]

con|form|a|bil|i|ty (kən fôr′mə bil′ə tē), *n.* the quality or condition of being conformable.

con|form|a|ble (kən fôr′mə bəl), *adj.* **1** = similar. **2** adapted; suited. **SYN**: adjusted. **3** in agreement; harmonious. **SYN**: agreeable. **4** obedient; submissive: *The boy was conformable to his father's wishes.* **SYN**: tractable. **5** *Geology.* (of strata) having the planes of stratification mutually parallel. — **con|form′a|ble|ness,** *n.*

con|form|a|bly (kən fôr′mə blē), *adv.* in a conformable manner.

con|for|mal (kən fôr′məl), *adj.* **1** *Cartography.* having the same scale in all directions at any given point: *The Mercator is a conformal projection; i.e., any very small area, such as a small bay or peninsula, is shown in practically its true shape. Larger areas, however, are distorted both in shape and size* (Finch and Trewartha). **2** *Mathematics.* leaving unchanged the size of all angles. [< Late Latin *cōnfōrmālis* conformable < Latin *com-* with + *fōrmālis* formal]

con|form|ance (kən fôr′məns), *n.* the act of conforming; conformity.

con|for|ma|teur (kon′fôr mə tėr′), *n.* = conformator. [< French *conformateur* < *conformer* conform]

con|for|ma|tion (kon′fôr mā′shən), *n.* **1** the manner in which a thing is formed; structure; form: *the conformation of a flower.* **SYN**: shape. **2** the symmetrical arrangement of the parts of a thing. **3** a conforming; adaptation. **4** *Chemistry.* the geometric shape of a molecule in any of its states.

con|for|ma|tion|al (kon′fôr mā′shə nəl), *adj. Chemistry.* of or having to do with the geometric or three-dimensional shapes assumed by molecules in various states: *a conformational isomer, conformational changes in DNA.*

conformational analysis, the determination of the three-dimensional shapes of molecules whose atoms rotate around one or more bonds, especially for the purpose of correlating the preferred shapes with the physical and chemical properties of the molecules: *Conformational analysis has been invaluable in the synthesis of pharmacological agents, notably steroids and antibiotics of the tetracycline and penicillin families* (Scientific American).

con|for|ma|tor (kon′fôr mā′tər), *n.* an apparatus for determining the conformation of anything.

con|form|er (kən fôr′mər), *n.* **1** a person who conforms or complies with established forms or doctrines: *... conformers to commonplace* (John Stuart Mill). **2** *Chemistry.* a compound whose differing molecular forms are due to conformational variations.

con|form|ism (kən fôr′miz əm), *n.* **1** the principle or policy of conformity; close adherence to established traditions, standards, usages, or the like: *To rob children of their privacy and the chance to be themselves leads them to inhibitions and conformism* (Newsweek). **2** a belief in or insistence on conformity in thought and behavior: *The survey also discloses a rather surprising domesticity and conformism among British undergraduates* (Manchester Guardian).

con|form|ist (kən fôr′mist), *n., adj.* — ***n.*** **1** a person who conforms: *Usually, of course, the child becomes a conformist. The group exerts great pressure to get him to accept its values* (Ogburn and Nimkoff). **2** *Historical.* a person who complies with the usages of the Church of England.
— ***adj.*** of or having to do with conformity or conformism: *The musical programmes especially are dreadfully conformist* (Observer).

con|for|mis|tic (kon′fər mis′tik), *adj.* tending to or practicing conformism; conformist: *The result is that today, in matters of politics, Brazilians are conformistic* (Atlantic). — **con′for|mis′ti|cal|ly,** *adv.*

con|form|i|ty (kən fôr′mə tē), *n., pl.* **-ties. 1** action in agreement with generally accepted standards of business, law, conduct, or worship; fitting oneself and one's actions to the ideas of others; compliance: *A deadly conformity will kill every impulse toward independence and dissent* (Bulletin of Atomic Scientists). **2** likeness; similarity; agreement. **SYN**: correspondence, harmony, congruity, resemblance. **3** obedience; submission. **4a** compliance with the usages of the Church of England. **b** adherence to any legally established or publicly recognized religion. **5** *Obsolete.* a point of resemblance.

con|found (kon found′, kən- *for 1-3, 5-7;* kon′-found′ *for 4*), *v.t.* **1** to confuse; perplex: *The people on the island were frightened and confounded by the violence of the storm. Confusion worse confounded* (Milton). **2** to be unable to tell apart: *The teachers in school confounded the twins until one had to wear glasses.* **3** to surprise and puzzle; disconcert: *He was ... confounded by incessant noise, and crowds, and hurry* (Samuel Johnson). **4** to damn: *Confound your impudence.* **5** *Archaic.* to make uneasy and ashamed; abash: *Silent, and in face confounded long they sate, as strucken mute* (Milton). **6** *Archaic.* to defeat; overthrow. **7** *Obsolete.* to confute. **8** *Obsolete.* to spoil; waste. [< Old French *confondre* < Latin *cōnfundere* < *com-* together + *fundere* pour] — **con|found′er,** *n.*

con|found|ed (kon foun′did, kən-), *adj.* **1** confused; disordered. **2** damned (used as a mild oath). **3** hateful; detestable. — **con|found′ed|ly,** *adv.*

con|found|ing (kən foun′ding), *adj.* that confounds; causing confusion; perplexing: *The noise was so utterly confounding* (Dickens). — **con-found′ing|ly,** *adv.*

con|fra|ter|ni|ty (kon′frə tėr′nə tē), *n., pl.* **-ties.** a group of men united for some purpose or in a profession; brotherhood. **SYN**: guild. [< Medieval Latin *confraternitas* < *confrater;* see etym. under **confrere**]

con|frere (kon′frãr), *n.* a fellow member; colleague: *... our fourth-graders and their confreres in other elementary school grades* (New York Times). [< Old French *confrere* < Medieval Latin *confrater* < Latin *com-* together + *frāter* brother]

con|front (kən frunt′), *v.t.* **1** to meet face to face; stand facing: *Two queer-looking men confronted me as I stepped off the elevator.* **2** to face boldly; oppose: *The little band of settlers, with hands on their rifles, confronted the bandits.* **3** to bring face to face; place before: *We confronted the girl with the dish she had broken. The lawyer confronted the accused man with the forged check.* **4** to compare. [< Old French *confronter,* learned borrowing from Medieval Latin *confrontare* assign limits < Latin *com-* together + *frōns, frontis* forehead] — **con|front′er,** *n.*

con|fron|ta|tion (kon′frun tā′shən), *n.* **1** the act of bringing together, especially for questioning or for comparison: *In the public philosophy, freedom of speech is conceived as the means to a confrontation of opinion* (Atlantic). **2** an open or direct clash; a face-to-face encounter between opponents: *He did not want the present crisis to lead to a confrontation between the United States and the Soviet Union* (London Times). *He had a confrontation with his aloof and unresponsive daughter* (John McCarten).

con|fron|ta|tion|ist (kon′frun tā′shə nist), *adj.* seeking or favoring confrontation: *The confrontationist politicians of our time ... have learned the value not of committing violence but of provoking it* (Richard Hofstadter).

con|front|ment (kən frunt′mənt), *n.* = confrontation.

Con|fu|cian (kən fyü′shən), *adj., n.* — ***adj.*** of or having to do with Confucius, 551?-479 B.C., his teachings, or his followers. — ***n.*** a follower of Confucius or his teachings.

Con|fu|cian|ism (kən fyü′shə niz əm), *n.* the moral teachings of Confucius and his followers. Confucianism teaches that the chief virtues are respect for parents and ancestors, kindliness, faithfulness, intelligence, and proper behavior. — **Con|fu′cian|ist,** *n.*

con fuo|co (kôn fwô′kō), *Italian, Music.* with fire or impetuosity (used as a direction).

con|fus|a|ble (kən fyü′zə bəl), *adj.* **1** that can be confused. **2** liable to be confused.

con|fuse (kən fyüz′), *v.t.,* **-fused, -fus|ing. 1** to throw into disorder; mix up: *He has done more to confuse and mystify the subject than to clear it up* (Thomas Wright). **2** to bewilder; perplex: *So many people talking to me at once confused me.* **SYN**: confound, puzzle. **3** to be unable to tell apart; mistake (one thing for another): *Even their own mother sometimes confused the twins.* **4** to make uneasy and ashamed; embarrass: *Confused by her blunder, she burst into tears and left the room.* **5** *Obsolete.* to rout; discomfit. [< *confused,* adaptation of Old French *confus,* learned borrowing from Latin *cōnfūsus,* past participle of *cōnfundere;* see etym. under **confound**]
— ***Syn.*** **4 Confuse, embarrass, disconcert** mean to disturb a person. **Confuse** means to make a person so uneasy and bewildered that he cannot think clearly or act sensibly: *Honking at a driver who has stalled his car often confuses*

him. **Embarrass** means to make one so uneasy and self-conscious that he cannot talk or act naturally: *Meeting strangers embarrasses me.* **Disconcert** means to disturb so suddenly or badly that for a moment one loses poise and ability to handle the situation: *The unexpected question disconcerted the speaker.*

con|fused (kən fyüzd′), *adj.* **1** mixed up; disordered. **2** bewildered. — **con|fus′ed|ly,** *adv.* — **con|fus′ed|ness,** *n.*

con|fus|ing (kən fyü′zing), *adj.* that confuses; bewildering.

con|fus|ing|ly (kən fyü′zing lē), *adv.* in a confusing manner.

con|fu|sion (kən fyü′zhən), *n.* **1** the act or fact of confusing; mistaking one thing for another: *Words like "believe" and "receive" are a source of confusion in spelling.* **2** a disordered condition of things or of the mind: *The confusion in the room showed that he had packed in a hurry. The confusions created by language deeply affect men's lives* (London Times). **3** tumult: *There was confusion in the busy street after the accident.* **4** failure to distinguish clearly: *A small child's confusion in distinguishing between "left" and "right" is quite natural.* **5** bewilderment: *Today's achievement is only tomorrow's confusion* (William Dean Howells). **6** uneasiness and shame: *Her confusion led to blushes and tears.* **SYN:** embarrassment. **7** a mental disturbance; inability to think clearly: *In her confusion the old woman mistook the stranger for her son.*

con|fu|sion|al (kən fyü′zhə nəl), *adj.* characterized by confusion.

con|fu|ta|tion (kon′fyu̇ tā′shən), *n.* **1** a confuting; disproving: *The lawyer's confutation of the witness's testimony helped him win his case.* **2** a thing that confutes or disproves. [< Latin *cōnfūtātiō, -ōnis* < *cōnfūtāre;* see etym. under **confute**]

con|fu|ta|tive (kən fyü′tə tiv), *adj.* serving to confute.

con|fu|ta|tor (kon′fyu̇ tā′tər), *n.* a person who confutes.

con|fute (kən fyüt′), *v.t.,* **-fut|ed, -fut|ing.** **1** to prove (an argument, testimony, or statement) to be false or incorrect: *The lawyer confuted the testimony of the witness by showing actual photographs of the accident.* **SYN:** disprove, refute. **2** to prove (a person) to be wrong; overcome by argument: *The speaker confuted his opponents by facts and logic.* **3** to bring to naught; make useless; confound. [< Latin *cōnfūtāre* disprove] — **con|fut′a|ble,** *adj.* — **con|fut′er,** *n.*

cong (kong), *n., pl.* **cong.** *Vietnamese.* a measure of land equal to 10 ares or 1000 square meters: *If they [farmers] had seventeen cong, the Front would leave them seven and take ten* (Harper's).

Cong (kong), *n.* = Vietcong.

cong., **a** gallon. **b** congius.

Cong., **1** Congregation. **2a** Congregational. **b** Congregationalist. **3a** Congress. **b** Congressional.

con|ga (kong′gə), *n., pl.* **-gas,** *v.,* **-gaed, -ga|ing.** — *n.* **1** a Cuban ballroom dance in 4/4 time. It is danced by couples or a line of dancers and requires a kick on every fourth beat. **2** the music for this dance.
— *v.i.* to dance the conga.
[< American Spanish (Cuba) *conga*]

conga drum, a long, narrow bass drum struck with the hands. See picture under **drum**[1].

con game, *U.S. Slang.* confidence game.

con|gé (kon′zhā; *French* kôɴ zhā′), *n.* **1** formal departure: *We made our congé briskly* (New Yorker). **2** abrupt dismissal; discharge: *The insolent manager was speedily given his congé.* **3** permission to leave: *You may have your congé any time you like.* **4** a bow or other act of courtesy upon leaving. **5** *Architecture.* a type of molding. Also, **congee.** [< French *congé* < Middle French *congié;* see etym. under **congee**[1]]

con|geal (kən jēl′), *v.t., v.i.* **1** to harden or make solid by cold; freeze: *The river congealed into a solid sheet of ice with the first freeze this winter.* **2** to solidify as if by freezing; thicken; stiffen: *The pudding congealed as it cooled.* (*Figurative.*) *Fear congealed his very blood.* **SYN:** coagulate, jell. [< Old French *congeler,* learned borrowing from Latin *congelāre* < *com-* (intensive) + *gelāre* freeze < *gelū, -ūs* frost, ice] — **con|geal′a|ble,** *adj.* — **con|geal′er,** *n.* — **con|geal′ment,** *n.*

con|gee[1] (kon′jē), *n., v.,* **-geed, -gee|ing.** *Archaic.* — *n.* congé.
— *v.i.* to take one's leave; bow.
[< Middle French *congié* < Old French *cungied* < Latin *commeātus, -ūs* < *commeāre* < *com-* (intensive) + *meāre* go to and fro]

con|gee[2] (kon′jē), *n.* water in which rice has been boiled, used in the diet of invalids and as starch in India. Also, **conjee.** [< Tamil *kañji*]

con|ge|la|tion (kon′jə lā′shən), *n.* **1** the act of congealing or process of being congealed. **2** something congealed; a concretion or crystalline mass; coagulation.

con|ge|ner (kon′jə nər), *n.* **1** a person or thing of the same kind or class as another. **2** a plant or animal of the same genus as another. **3** a congenerous muscle. **4** = congeneric. [< Latin *congener* of the same kind < *com-* together + *genus, -eris* kind, race]

con|ge|ner|ic (kon′jə ner′ik), *adj., n.* — *adj.* **1** of the same kind or genus. **2** of or having to do with a congeneric: *the congeneric content of whiskey.*
— *n.* any incidental or residual substance in an alcoholic liquor, such as a flavoring agent or an impure sediment.

con|gen|er|ous (kən jen′ər əs), *adj.* **1** *Physiology.* having a common function; concurring in the same action, as muscles. **2** = congeneric.

con|gen|ial (kən jēn′yəl), *adj.* **1** having similar tastes and interests; getting on well together: *Congenial companions made the trip pleasant.* **SYN:** kindred, sympathetic. **2** agreeable; suitable: *The boy found mowing the lawn more congenial work than practicing the piano. Solitude is congenial to a studious person.* **SYN:** compatible. [< Latin *com-* together + *geniālis* having to do with generation < *genius* spirit] — **con|gen′ial|ly,** *adv.* — **con|gen′ial|ness,** *n.*

con|ge|ni|al|i|ty (kən jē′nē al′ə tē, -jēn′yal′-), *n.* congenial quality.

con|gen|i|tal (kən jen′ə təl), *adj.* **1** present at birth; inborn. **SYN:** inherent. **2** *Figurative:* *congenital dislikes.* **SYN:** deep-seated. **3** *Medicine.* existing as a result of faulty development, infection, or injury, in the uterus: *The boy is lame because of a congenital defect in his foot.* [< Latin *congenitus* born with (< *com-* with + *genitus* born, past participle of *gignere* beget) + English *-al*[1]] — **con|gen′i|tal|ly,** *adv.*

con|ger (kong′gər), *n.* a large ocean eel that is caught for food along the coasts of Europe. It is also found on the Atlantic coast of America. The conger has no scales and sometimes grows to about 8 feet in length. See picture under **eel.** [< Old French *congre* < Late Latin *congrus* < Latin *conger* < Greek *góngros*]

conger eel, = conger.

con|ge|ries (kon jir′ēz, -ē ēz), *n. sing.* or *pl.* a collection; heap; mass: *The modern urban society ... is itself a congeries of groups often more or less hostile to one another* (Ogburn and Nimkoff). **SYN:** aggregation. [< Latin *congeriēs* heap, pile < *congerere* bring together; see etym. under **congest**]

con|ge|ry (kon jir′ē, kon′jə rē), *n., pl.* **-ries.** = congeries: *The author reveals a congery of opinions* (August Heckscher). [back formation < *congeries*]

con|gest (*v.* kən jest′; *n.* kon′jest), *v., n.* — *v.t.* **1** to fill too full; overcrowd: *Main Street is congested with the traffic of people driving to work each morning. Department stores are often congested before Christmas.* **2** to cause too much blood or mucus to gather in (one part of the body). **3** *Obsolete.* to heap together.
— *v.i.* **1** to become congested. **2** to become too full of blood or mucus. The lungs are congested in pneumonia. *His face congested with anger as the argument grew more heated.*
— *n.* (in Ireland) a tenant living on land whose resources do not adequately support him.
[< Latin *congestus,* past participle of *congerere* bring together < *com-* together + *gerere* carry]

con|ges|tion (kən jes′chən), *n.* **1** an overcrowded or congested condition: *Many drivers were caught in the Sunday traffic congestion and were late getting home.* **2** too much blood or mucus in one part of the body: *Nose drops often relieve nasal congestion.*

con|ges|tive (kən jes′tiv), *adj.* **1** accompanied or produced by congestion: *Congestive heart failure ... gets its name because congestion of the veins is a prominent feature* (Science News Letter). **2** causing congestion.

con|gi|us (kon′jē əs), *n., pl.* **-gi|i** (-jē ī). **1** an ancient Roman unit of liquid measure equal to about 7 pints. **2** *Pharmacy.* a gallon. *Abbr:* C. or cong. [< Latin *congius* < Greek *kónchos* conch, mussel]

con|glo|bate (kon glō′bāt, kong′glə bāt), *adj., v.,* **-bat|ed, -bat|ing.** — *adj.* formed or gathered into a ball; rounded. **SYN:** globular.
— *v.t., v.i.* to form or gather into a ball; unite into a rounded mass.
[< Latin *conglobātus,* past participle of *conglobāre,* ultimately < *com-* together + *globus* ball] — **con′glo|ba′tion,** *n.*

con|globe (kon glōb′), *v.t., v.i.,* **-globed, -glob|ing.** = conglobate.

con|glob|u|late (kən glob′yə lāt), *v.t., v.i.,* **-lat|ed, -lat|ing.** to collect in a rounded mass. [< Latin *conglobulus,* ultimately < *com-* together + *globulus* little ball]

con|glob|u|la|tion (kən glob′yə lā′shən), *n.* **1** the act or process of becoming a round mass. **2** *Figurative.* a mass of various things or persons; mixture; disorganized assortment.

con|glom|er|a|cy (kən glom′ər ə sē), *n.* the formation of business conglomerates.

con|glom|er|ate (*adj., n.* kən glom′ər it; *v.* kən glom′ə rāt), *adj., n., v.,* **-at|ed, -at|ing.** — *adj.* **1** gathered into a rounded mass; clustered. **2** *Figurative.* made up of various parts or materials gathered into a mass: *Any President who does not hold together his party—however conglomerate—is almost sure to fail* (Harper's). **3** of or having to do with a business conglomerate: *a conglomerate enterprise. Many old-line publishers have surrendered their character to become part of a conglomerate empire* (Atlantic). **4** *Geology.* of the nature of or forming a rock made up of pebbles, gravel, or the like, held together by a cementing material.
— *n.* **1** a mass formed of fragments. **2** *Figurative.* a miscellaneous group; conglomeration: *He had organized the committee—a conglomerate of Catholic, Jewish, Protestant, Czech, American, and Swiss relief agencies* (New Yorker). **3** a large corporation made up of many companies that operate in different and often entirely unrelated markets: *Very different companies are coming under combined management through the device of forming conglomerates, which place vast and diverse empires under unified control* (Charles A. Reich). **4** *Geology.* a conglomerate rock.
— *v.t. v.i.* to gather in a rounded mass; collect together. **SYN:** accumulate, cluster.
[< Latin *conglomerātus,* past participle of *conglomerāre* heap together, ultimately < *com-* together + *glomus, -eris* ball of yarn]

con|glom|er|a|teur (kən glom′ə rə tėr′), *n.* the organizer or head of a business conglomerate. [< *conglomerate* + *-eur* (as in *entrepreneur*)]

con|glom|er|at|ic (kən glom′ə rat′ik), *adj.* of the nature or character of a conglomerate.

con|glom|er|a|tion (kən glom′ə rā′shən), *n.* **1** the action of conglomerating or condition of being conglomerated. **2** *Figurative.* a mixed-up mass of various things or persons; mixture: *The stew was a conglomeration of meat and vegetables.*

con|glom|er|a|tor (kən glom′ə rā′tər), *n.* = conglomerateur.

con|glom|er|it|ic (kən glom′ə rit′ik), *adj.* = conglomeratic.

con|glu|ti|nant (kən glü′tə nənt), *adj.* **1** conglutinating. **2** *Medicine.* helping severed parts, especially of a wound, to grow together.

con|glu|ti|nate (kən glü′tə nāt), *v.,* **-nat|ed, -nat|ing,** *adj.* — *v.t., v.i.* to join or become joined as with glue.
— *adj.* conglutinated; cohering. [< Latin *conglūtināre* (with English *-ate*[1]) glue together, ultimately < *com-* together + *glūten, -inis* glue] — **con|glu′ti|na′tion,** *n.*

con|glu|ti|na|tive (kən glü′tə nā′tiv), *adj.* tending to conglutinate.

con|go (kong′gō), *n.* = congou.

Con|go buffalo (kong′gō), a small buffalo of central Africa having upturned horns. It is related to the Cape buffalo.

Congo color or **dye,** any one of a group of direct azo dyes, usually derived from benzidine.

congo eel, **1** *U.S.* an eel-shaped amphibian that has very small, weak legs; congo snake. Congo eels live in swampy regions in the southeastern United States. They grow to 3 feet in length. **2** = eelpout.

Con|go|ese (kong′gō ēz′, -ēs′), *adj., n., pl.* **-ese.** = Congolese.

Con|goid (kong′goid), *n., adj.* = Negroid. [< *Congo,* a region in Africa + *-oid*]

Con|go|lese (kong′gə lēz′, -lēs′), *adj., n., pl.* **-lese.** — *adj.* of or having to do with the Congo region in central Africa, formerly including the French Congo and the Belgian Congo, and now applied chiefly to the Republic of the Congo in west central Africa. — *n.* a native or inhabitant of the Congo region or of the Republic of the Congo. [alteration (with *-ese*) of French *Congolais*]

Congo peacock, a rare peacock discovered in the forests of central Africa in 1937. The male is black with a white tuft of plumes; the female is brown and green.

Congo red, an azo dye which turns blue in the presence of acid and red in the presence of a base, used as a chemical indicator, as a biologi-

Pronunciation Key: hat, āge, cãre, fär; let, ēqual, tėrm; it, īce; hot, ōpen, ôrder; oil, out; cup, pu̇t, rüle; child; long; thin; ᴛʜen; zh, measure; ə represents **a** in about, **e** in taken, **i** in pencil, **o** in lemon, **u** in circus.

cal stain, and in dyeing cotton, wool, and other textiles.

congo snake, = congo eel.

con|gou (kong′gü), *n.* a kind of black tea produced in China. Also, **congo**. [< Chinese (Amoy) *kong-hu* labor (because it has been processed)]

con|grats (kən grats′), *n.pl. Informal.* congratulations: *Many congrats to L.L.L. Golden for properly de-Ivy Leaguing the public relations man* (Saturday Review).

con|grat|u|lant (kən grach′ə lənt), *adj., n.* — ***adj.*** expressing congratulation; congratulating.
— ***n.*** a person who congratulates.

con|grat|u|late (kən grach′ə lāt), *v.t.,* **-lat|ed, -lat|ing. 1** to express pleasure at the happiness or good fortune of (someone); extend good wishes to: *The loser congratulated the winner of the race. We were the first to congratulate the bride and groom.* **SYN**: felicitate. **2** *Obsolete.* to express sympathetic joy or satisfaction at (an event or circumstance). **3** *Obsolete.* to salute; greet. [< Latin *congrātulārī* (with English *-ate*[1]), ultimately < *com-* with + *grātus* pleasing + *-ulus,* a diminutive suffix] — **con|grat′u|la′tor**, *n.*

con|grat|u|la|tion (kən grach′ə lā′shən), *n.* the act of congratulating; wishing a person joy. **SYN**: felicitation.
congratulations, an expression of pleasure at another's happiness or good fortune: *Congratulations on your election victory as new mayor. I thank you for your kind congratulations on my marriage.*

con|grat|u|la|to|ry (kən grach′ə lə tôr′ē, -tōr′-), *adj.* expressing pleasure at another's happiness or good fortune: *a congratulatory note.*

con|gre|gant (kong′grə gənt), *n.* a member of a congregation.

con|gre|gate (*v.* kong′grə gāt; *adj.* kong′grə git, -gāt), *v.,* **-gat|ed, -gat|ing,** *adj.* — ***v.i.*** to come together into a crowd or mass; assemble: *The scouts congregated around the campfire. Bits of steel filings congregated around the magnet.* **SYN**: gather, collect. — ***v.t.*** to bring together into a crowd or mass; assemble: *The church bells rang to congregate the members. The north wind congregates in crowds the floating mountains of the silver clouds* (Shelley). **SYN**: gather, collect.
— ***adj.* 1** gathered together; assembled. **2** collective.
[< Latin *congregāre* (with English *-ate*[1]), ultimately < *com-* together + *grex, gregis* flock, herd, crowd] — **con′gre|ga′tor**, *n.*

con|gre|ga|tion (kong′grə gā′shən), *n.* **1** the act of coming together into a crowd or mass; act of assembling: *the congregation of birds before flying south.* **2** a group of people gathered for religious worship or instruction: *The whole congregation rose to sing a hymn.* **3** a gathering of people or things; assembly: *The congregation of sightseers increased in summer.* **SYN**: company, assemblage. **4** *Roman Catholic Church.* **a** a religious community or order with a common rule with or without solemn vows, devoted to religious or charitable work. **b** a committee of cardinals or other clergymen. **5** all the inhabitants of a settlement, town, or parish in the New England colonies where Congregationalism was established. **6a** (in the Old Testament) the Israelites. **b** (in the New Testament) the Christians. **7** *British.* a general assembly of the qualified members of the faculty of a university.

con|gre|ga|tion|al (kong′grə gā′shə nəl), *adj.* **1** of a congregation; done by a congregation: *congregational singing.* **2** recognizing the governing power of the congregation. — **con′gre|ga′tion|al|ly**, *adv.*

Con|gre|ga|tion|al (kong′grə gā′shə nəl), *adj.* of or having to do with Congregationalism or Congregationalists.

con|gre|ga|tion|al|ism (kong′grə gā′shə nə liz′əm), *n.* a system of church government in which each individual church or congregation governs itself. — **con′gre|ga′tion|al|ist**, *n.*

Con|gre|ga|tion|al|ism (kong′grə gā′shə nə liz′əm), *n.* the principles and system of organization of a Protestant denomination in which each individual church governs itself. — **Con′gre|ga′tion|al|ist**, *n., adj.*

con|gre|ga|tive (kong′grə gā′tiv), *adj.* tending to congregate; congregating. — **con′gre|ga′tive|ness**, *n.*

con|gress (kong′gris), *n.* **1** the lawmaking body of a nation, especially of a republic: *The congress of Chile was composed of a senate and a house of representatives in which each delegate represented 15,000 inhabitants.* **SYN**: legislature, parliament. **2** a formal meeting of representatives of interested groups to discuss some subject: *a writers' congress. Doctors came from all over the world to the medical congress on heart transplants.* **SYN**: conference, convention. **3** a formal meeting or assembly of representatives of various governments to discuss some matter of common interest: *The vogue of congresses began with the big gathering at two places in Westphalia in 1648* (New York Times). **SYN**: council, parley. **4** the act or fact of coming together; meeting; encounter. **5** = sexual intercourse. [< Latin *congressus, -ūs* a coming together < *congredī* meet with < *com-* together + *gradī* to step, walk]

Con|gress (kong′gris), *n.* **1a** the national lawmaking body of the United States, consisting of the Senate and House of Representatives, with members elected from each state: *The Congress shall assemble at least once in every year* (Constitution of the United States). **b** the session of this body. **c** this body serving as a unit for two years: *the 88th Congress.* **2** the lower house of the former Spanish or Portuguese legislature.

congress boot or **gaiter**, a high shoe with a wide strip of elastic in each side.

Congress cap, a white cotton cap worn by members of India's Congress Party: *Congress caps ... [were] worn as a symbol by Nehru and his disciples* (New Yorker).

con|gres|sion (kən gresh′ən), *n. Rare.* a coming together; congress.

con|gres|sion|al (kən gresh′ə nəl), *adj.* of or having to do with a congress. — **con|gres′sion|al|ly**, *adv.*

Con|gres|sion|al (kən gresh′ə nəl), *adj.* of or having to do with the Congress of the United States: *We have gone through one more set of political conventions, another Presidential election, and two Congressional elections* (Saturday Review).

Congressional district, *U.S.* any one of the districts into which a state is divided. Each Congressional district is represented by one member in the House of Representatives.

con|gres|sion|al|ist (kən gresh′ə nə list), *n.* **1** a supporter of a congress. **2** a member of a congressional party.

Congressional Medal of Honor, *U.S.* = Medal of Honor.

con|gress|ist (kong′grə sist), *n.* a member of a congress.

con|gress|man or **Con|gress|man** (kong′gris mən), *n., pl.* **-men.** a member of the United States Congress, especially of the House of Representatives.

con|gress|man-at-large (kong′gris mən ət lärj′), *n., pl.* **con|gress|men-at-large.** *U.S.* a member of the House of Representatives representing an entire state rather than a Congressional district. Congressmen-at-large represent sparsely populated states.

Congress of Industrial Organizations, = CIO.

con|gress|wom|an or **Con|gress|wom|an** (kong′gris wum′ən), *n., pl.* **-wom|en.** a woman member of the United States Congress, especially of the House of Representatives.

con|grue (kən grü′, kong′grü), *v.i.,* **-grued, -gru|ing.** *Obsolete.* to be in accord; agree. [< Latin *congruere* agree]

con|gru|ence (kong′grü əns), *n.* the fact or condition of being congruent: *The congruence we achieved was short-lived. It provides a painless introduction to the concept of numerical congruence formulated by the great German mathematician Carl Friedrich Gauss* (Scientific American).

con|gru|en|cy (kong′grü ən sē), *n.* = congruence.

con|gru|ent (kong′grü ənt), *adj.* **1** *Geometry.* exactly coinciding: *Congruent triangles have the same size and shape.* **2** *Algebra.* producing the same remainder when divided by a given number. **3** in harmony; agreeing. **SYN**: harmonious, accordant, congruous. [< Latin *congruēns, -entis,* present participle of *congruere* agree, correspond with] — **con′gru|ent|ly**, *adv.*

con|gru|i|ty (kən grü′ə tē), *n., pl.* **-ties. 1** *Geometry.* the exact coincidence of lines, angles, figures, etc. **2** the state or quality of being congruous; agreement; harmony. **SYN**: conformity, accordance, correspondence. **3** an instance or point of agreement.

con|gru|ous (kong′grü əs), *adj.* **1** *Geometry.* exactly coinciding. **2** in harmony; agreeing. **SYN**: harmonious, accordant, conformable. **3** fitting; appropriate. [< Latin *congruus* (with English *-ous*) agreeing, fit < *congruere;* see etym. under **congruent**] — **con′gru|ous|ly**, *adv.* — **con′gru|ous|ness**, *n.*

co|ni (kō′nī), *n.* plural of **conus**.

con|ic (kon′ik), *adj., n.* — ***adj.*** = conical.
— ***n.*** = conic section.
[< Greek *kōnikós* < *kônos* cone]

con|i|cal (kon′ə kəl), *adj.* **1** shaped like a cone: *Volcanic mountains are conical.* **2** of a cone. — **con′i|cal|ly**, *adv.* — **con′i|cal|ness**, *n.*

✱**conic projection**, a map projection made by projecting the earth's surface on an imaginary cone which is unrolled to a plane surface.

✱**conic projection**

cone on globe

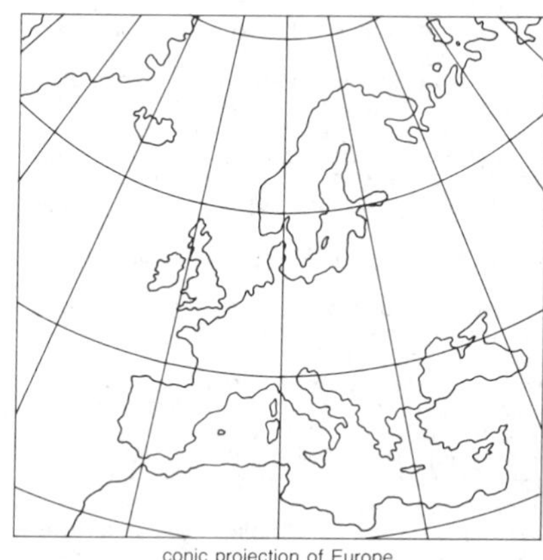

conic projection of Europe

con|ics (kon′iks), *n.* = conic sections.

✱**conic section**, *Geometry.* a curve formed by the intersection of a plane with a right circular cone. Circles, ellipses, parabolas, and hyperbolas are conic sections.
conic sections, the branch of geometry dealing with circles, ellipses, parabolas, and hyperbolas; conics: *One of the main concerns of the early geometers was conic sections* (Scientific American).

✱**conic section**

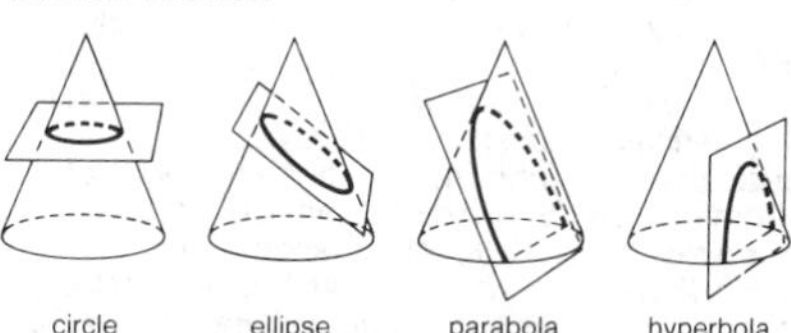

co|nid|i|a (kə nid′ē ə), *n.* plural of **conidium**.

co|nid|i|al (kə nid′ē əl), *adj.* of or like conidia; producing conidia.

co|nid|i|an (kə nid′ē ən), *adj.* = conidial.

co|nid|i|o|phore (kə nid′ē ə fôr, -fōr), *n.* a specialized thread, or hypha, of the mycelium of certain fungi, bearing conidia. [< *conidium* + *-phore*]

co|nid|i|o|spore (kə nid′ē ə spôr, -spōr), *n.* = conidium. [< New Latin *conidium* + English *spore*]

co|nid|i|um (kə nid′ē əm), *n., pl.* **-nid|i|a.** a one-celled, asexual spore produced in certain fungi by abstriction at the end of a conidiophore. [< New Latin *conidium* < Greek *kónis* dust]

co|ni|fer (kō′nə fər, kon′ə-), *n.* any one of a large group of trees and shrubs that bear cones. The pine, fir, spruce, hemlock, larch, and yew are conifers. Most conifers are evergreen. Conifers form an order in the gymnosperm class. [< Latin *cōnifer* cone-bearing < *cōnus* cone + *ferre* to bear]

co|nif|er|in (kə nif′ər in), *n.* a glucoside compound, found in the bark of coniferous trees, from which coniferyl alcohol is derived. *Formula:* $C_{16}H_{22}O_8 \cdot 2H_2O$

co|nif|er|ous (kə nif′ər əs), *adj.* **1** bearing cones. **2** belonging to the conifers. **3** of or characterized chiefly by conifers: *a coniferous forest.* —**co|nif′er|ous|ly,** *adv.*

co|nif|er|yl alcohol (kə nif′ər əl), a derivative of coniferin used in making synthetic vanillin: *Peter Klason ... obtained the first clue to the structure of lignin by his investigation of coniferyl alcohol* (Scientific American).

co|ni|ine (kō′nē ēn, -in), *n.* a violently poisonous, oily liquid alkaloid with a peculiar suffocating odor, present in the poison hemlock. *Formula:* $C_8H_{17}N$ [< New Latin *conium* conium + English *-ine*[2]]

co|nin (kō′nin), *n.* = coniine.

co|nine (kō′nēn), *n.* = coniine.

co|ni|ros|ter (kō′nə ros′tər), *n.* any one of a group of birds with cone-shaped bills, including the finches. [< New Latin *Conirostres* < Latin *cōnus* cone + *rōstrum* beak]

co|ni|ros|tral (kō′nə ros′trəl), *adj.* **1** having a conical bill. **2** belonging to or having to do with the conirosters.

co|ni|um (kō′nē əm), *n.* any one of a group of poisonous plants of the parsley family, such as the poison hemlock. [< New Latin *Conium* the typical genus < Latin *cōnīum* hemlock < Greek *kōneion*]

conj., **1** conjugation. **2a** conjunction. **b** conjunctive.

con|jec|tur|a|ble (kən jek′chər ə bəl), *adj.* that can be conjectured. —**con|jec′tur|a|bly,** *adv.*

con|jec|tur|al (kən jek′chər əl), *adj.* **1** involving a guess; depending on conjecture: *His statement was merely conjectural, not proved.* **SYN:** supposed, hypothetical, theoretical. **2** inclined to conjecture. **SYN:** assumptive. —**con|jec′tur|al|ly,** *adv.*

con|jec|ture (kən jek′chər), *n., v.,* **-tured, -tur|ing.** —*n.* **1** a conclusion reached by guessing; a guess; surmise. **SYN:** supposition. **2** the formation of an opinion admittedly without sufficient evidence for proof; guessing. **3** *Obsolete.* the interpretation of signs, omens, or dreams.
—*v.t.* to guess; surmise: *He conjectured that his stocks would rise on the stock market.* **SYN:** suppose. See syn. under **guess.** —*v.i.* to make a conjecture; guess: *Weather forecasters often have to conjecture about the next day's weather conditions.* **SYN:** suppose. See syn. under **guess.** [< Latin *conjectūra* < *conjicere* discuss, throw together < *com-* together + *jacere* throw] —**con|jec′tur|er,** *n.*

con|jee (kon′jē), *n.* = congee[2].

con|join (kən join′), *v.t.* to join together; unite; combine: *... representatives of a loosely conjoined nation* (Time). **SYN:** associate, connect.
—*v.i.* to become joined together; unite. **SYN:** associate, connect. [< Old French *conjoindre* < Latin *conjungere* < *com-* together + *jungere* join]

con|join|er (kən joi′nər), *n.* a person or thing that conjoins.

con|joint (kən joint′, kon′joint), *adj.* **1** joined together; united; combined. **2** formed by or belonging to two or more in combination; joint. [< Middle French *conjoint,* past participle of *conjoindre;* see etym. under **conjoin**] —**con|joint′ly,** *adv.*

con|ju|bi|lant (kən jü′bə lənt), *adj. Poetic.* rejoicing together. [< Medieval Latin *conjubilans, -antis* < Latin *con-* with + *jubilāre* shout]

con|ju|gal (kon′jə gəl), *adj.* **1** of or having to do with marriage: *conjugal life. The consanguine family tended to disappear ... and the conjugal family became the predominant type* (Ogburn and Nimkoff). **SYN:** matrimonial, nuptial, connubial. **2** of husband and wife: *conjugal love.* [< Latin *conjugālis* < *conjuga* wife < *com-* with + *jugum* yoke] —**con′ju|gal|ly,** *adv.*

con|ju|gal|i|ty (kon′jə gal′ə tē), *n.* the conjugal state; marriage.

con|ju|gant (kon′jə gənt), *n.* a substance or organism that conjugates or takes part in conjugation: *The mercury-antibody conjugant had kept its specificity of reaction* (New Scientist).

con|ju|gate (*v.* kon′jə gāt; *adj., n.* kon′jə git, -gāt), *v.,* **-gat|ed, -gat|ing,** *adj., n.* —*v.t.* **1** *Grammar.* to give the forms of (a verb) according to person, number, tense, mood, and voice: *The past tense of "to be" is conjugated: I was, you were, he was, she was, it was; we were, you were, they were.* **2** to join together; couple. **SYN:** pair, unite. **3** *Chemistry.* to join (a compound) with another or others.
—*v.i.* **1** *Grammar.* to give the conjugation of a verb. **2** *Biology.* to unite in conjugation.
—*adj.* **1** joined together, especially in a pair; coupled. **2** *Botany.* in pairs; coupled. **3** *Grammar.* (of a word) derived from the same root. *Examples:* wise, wisely, wisdom. **4** (of two quantities, axes, points, or other things in mathematical relation) reciprocally related and interchangeable as far as certain properties are concerned. **5** *Chemistry.* **a** expressing the relationship between an acid and a base by the difference of a proton. **b** of or having to do with a ring of carbon atoms linked by alternate single and double bonds.
—*n.* **1** *Grammar.* a word derived from the same root as another. **2** a conjugate axis, point, number, etc. **3** *Biology.* a protozoan taking part in conjugation. **4** *Chemistry.* a compound joined with another or others.
[< Latin *conjugāre* (with English *-ate*[1]) yoke together < *com-* together + *jugum* a yoke]

con|ju|gat|ed protein (kon′jə gā′tid), *Biochemistry.* a compound composed of a simple protein attached to a nonprotein group, as nucleoproteins or glycoproteins.

con|ju|gate solution (kon′jə git), *Chemistry.* a solution of two substances, such as phenol and water, which are in equilibrium at a given temperature.

con|ju|gat|ing tube (kon′jə gā′ting), = conjugation tube.

***con|ju|ga|tion** (kon′jə gā′shən), *n.* **1** *Grammar.* **a** a systematic arrangement of the forms of a verb. **b** a group of verbs having similar forms in such an arrangement. **c** the act of giving the forms of a verb according to such an arrangement. **2a** a joining together; coupling: *a conjugation of favorable circumstances.* **b** the fact or state of being joined; combination: *Society compels men to work in conjugation for the common good of all.* **3** *Biology.* **a** a kind of reproduction in which two one-celled organisms unite temporarily to exchange nuclear material and then separate, for example in various protozoa. **b** the fusion of two outwardly similar cells or of two one-celled organisms for reproduction, during which fertilization occurs, as for example in various algae. *Abbr:* conj.

***conjugation**
definitions 1a, 3b

	singular:	plural:
English		
1st person	I am	we are
2nd person	you are	you are
3rd person	he, she, it is	they are
French		
1st person	je suis	nous sommes
2nd person	tu es	vous êtes
3rd person	il, elle, on est	ils, elles sont
German		
1st person	ich bin	wir sind
2nd person	du bist	ihr seid
3rd person	er, sie, es ist	sie sind
Latin		
1st person	sum	sumus
2nd person	es	estis
3rd person	est	sunt

conjugation of spirogyra

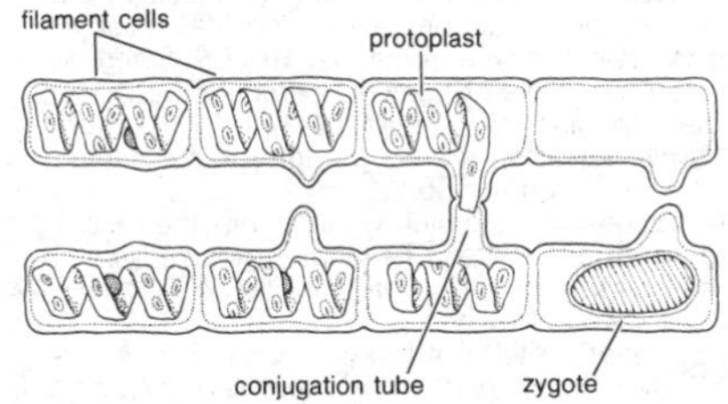

con|ju|ga|tion|al (kon′jə gā′shə nəl), *adj.* of or having to do with conjugation. —**con′ju|ga′tion|al|ly,** *adv.*

conjugation tube, a tube found in certain algae that functions as a bridge between cells to facilitate conjugation.

con|ju|ga|tive (kon′jə gā′tiv), *adj.* having to do with or characterized by conjugation.

con|junct (kən jungkt′, kon′jungkt), *adj., n.* —*adj.* **1** joined together; joint; associated; combined. **SYN:** united, conjoined. **2** formed by conjunction.
—*n.* a person or thing conjoined with another.
[< Latin *conjunctus,* past participle of *conjungere;* see etym. under **conjoin**] —**con|junct′ly,** *adv.*

***con|junc|tion** (kən jungk′shən), *n.* **1** a word that connects words, phrases, clauses, or sentences. *And, but, or, though,* and *if* are conjunctions. **2** the act of joining together; union; connection; combination: *A severe illness in conjunction with hot weather has left the baby very weak.* **SYN:** association. **3** a coming together, especially of events or circumstances: *a happy conjunction of circumstances. It was a strange conjunction—the prim serious young Queen ... and the elderly, cynical Whig* (New Yorker). **4** *Astronomy.* the apparent nearness of two or more heavenly bodies to each other; their appearance in the same region of the heavens: *The moon is in conjunction with the sun when these two bodies have the same celestial longitude* (Robert H. Baker). **5** *Logic, Mathematics.* a sentence or proposition composed of two terms connected by "and." A conjunction such as $a \wedge b$ is true only if *a* is true and *b* is true; if either *a* or *b* is false, the sentence is false. *Abbr:* conj.
▶ **Conjunctions** are used to connect words, phrases, clauses, or sentences. Some conjunctions also serve the double purpose of introducing a clause and connecting it with the rest of the sentence. Conjunctions are classified as follows: **a** *Coordinating:* those that connect words, phrases, or clauses of equal rank, such as *and, but, for, nor, or, so, yet.* **b** *Correlative:* coordinating conjunctions that are used in pairs, such as *both ... and, either ... or, neither ... nor, not only ... but also, whether ... or.* **c** *Subordinating:* those that serve to introduce and to connect subordinate clauses to main clauses, such as *after, although, as, because, before, if, since, when, where, while,* and so on. **d** See also **conjunctive adverbs,** under **conjunctive.**

***conjunction**
definition 5

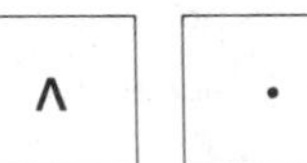

$a \wedge b$ or $a \cdot b$ = a and b

con|junc|tion|al (kən jungk′shə nəl), *adj.* of or having to do with conjunction or conjunctions. —**con|junc′tion|al|ly,** *adv.*

con|junc|ti|va (kon′jungk tī′və), *n., pl.* **-vas, -vae** (-vē). the mucous membrane that covers the front of the eyeball and the inner surface of the eyelids. [< New Latin (*membrana*) *conjunctiva* connecting (membrane) < *conjunctus;* see etym. under **conjunct**]

con|junc|ti|val (kon′jungk tī′vəl), *adj.* **1** of or having to do with the conjunctiva. **2** forming, or formed by, the conjunctiva.

con|junc|tive (kən jungk′tiv), *adj., n.* —*adj.* **1** joining together; connecting; uniting; combining. **SYN:** connective. **2** joined together; joint; united; combined. **SYN:** conjoint. **3a** like a grammatical conjunction; like that of a conjunction. "Then" is a conjunctive adverb. **b** connecting words, phrases, clauses, or sentences in both meaning and construction. "And," "also," and "moreover" are conjunctive conjunctions. **c** = subjunctive.
—*n.* a conjunctive word; conjunction. —**con|junc′tive|ly,** *adv.*
▶ **Conjunctive adverbs** are adverbs that also serve to connect main clauses, thus forming compound sentences. The most common are: *accordingly, also, anyhow, anyway, besides, consequently, furthermore, hence, however, indeed, likewise, moreover, namely, nevertheless, then, therefore.* Before a clause introduced by a conjunctive adverb, a semicolon is usual: *He is extremely conceited; however, he is so charming that people overlook it.*

con|junc|ti|vi|tis (kən jungk′tə vī′tis), *n.* inflammation of the conjunctiva.

con|junc|ture (kən jungk′chər), *n.* **1** a combination of events or circumstances: *This meeting was a conjuncture he had not anticipated.* **2** a critical state of affairs; crisis: *He was faced with a conjuncture in which he must either fight or run.* **3** *Obsolete.* conjunction; combination.

con|ju|ra|tion (kon′jù rā′shən), *n.* **1** the act of invoking by a sacred name; conjuring: *conjuration of spirits.* **2** the practice of magic: *In the fairy tale, the princess was changed into a toad by conjuration.* **SYN:** witchcraft. **3** a magic form of words used in conjuring; magic spell. **SYN:** incantation, invocation. **4** a conjuring trick. **5** *Archaic.* a solemn appeal; entreaty; adjuration.

con|jure (kon′jər, kun′-, *or* kən jùr′ *for v.t. 5, 6, v.i. 4*), *v.,* **-jured, -jur|ing.** —*v.t.* **1** to compel (a spirit, devil, or the like) to appear or disappear by a set form of words: *It is useless to try to conjure spirits or devils unless you believe in them first. Avoid thee, fiend! ... I conjure thee to leave me and begone* (Shakespeare). **2** to affect or influence by or as if by a spell: *The dealer conjured him into buying a more expensive car.* **SYN:** bewitch, enchant. **3** to cause to be or happen by magic or as if by magic. **4** *Figurative.* to cause to appear in the mind: *to conjure a vision.* **5** to

Pronunciation Key: hat, āge, cãre, fär; let, ēqual, tėrm; it, īce; hot, ōpen, ôrder; oil, out; cup, pu̇t, rüle; child; long; thin; ᴛʜen; zh, measure; ə represents **a** in about, **e** in taken, **i** in pencil, **o** in lemon, **u** in circus.

make a solemn appeal to; request earnestly; entreat: *By all that is holy, I conjure you not to betray your country.* SYN: beseech, implore. **6** *Obsolete.* to adjure.

—*v.i.* **1** to summon a devil, spirit, or the like. **2** to practice magic. **3** to perform tricks by very quick, deceiving movements of the hands: *In conjuring, the hands must be quicker than the eyes of the audience.* **4** *Obsolete.* to conspire.

conjure up, a to cause to appear as if by magic: *to conjure up a whole meal in a jiffy. Grandmother conjured up a bag of old-fashioned toys from the attic.* **b** *Figurative.* to cause to appear in the mind: *In her loneliness, her fancy conjured up scenes of happy family life.*

conjure with, to invoke with awe or respect; regard as very important: *If Mr. Sharp succeeds in selling wheat in large quantities, the new minister will indeed become a name to conjure with* (Maclean's).

[< Old French *conjurer,* learned borrowing from Latin *conjūrāre* make a compact (in Late Latin, adjure, exorcise a spirit) < *com-* together + *jūrāre* swear]

con|jur|er or **con|jur|or** (kon′jər ər, kun′-), *n.* **1** a person who performs tricks with quick, deceiving movements of the hands; juggler. **2** a magician; wizard. SYN: sorcerer. **3** a person who solemnly charges or entreats. SYN: adjurer, adjuror.

con|jur|y (kon′jər ē, kun′-), *n., pl.* **-jur|ies.** magic; legerdemain; jugglery.

conk[1] (kongk), *n.* decay in a live tree caused by a fungus. [perhaps < *conch*]

conk[2] (kongk), *v., n. Slang.* —*v.t.* **1** to strike or deal a blow, especially on the head. **2** *U.S. Slang.* to straighten (kinky hair) by rinsing it with lye, using pomade, etc.

—*n.* **1** a blow on the head. **2** the head.

conk out, to cease operation; break down; stall; fail: *The engine conked out after 1,000 miles.* [origin uncertain]

conk|er (kong′kər), *n. British.* a horse chestnut, especially one used in the game of conkers.

conkers, a children's game played in Great Britain, in which each of two players has a conker on a string. They take turns striking each other's conkers until one of the two is broken.

[probably (by alteration) < *conch* + *-er*[2], because the game was originally played with snail shells]

conk|out (kongk′out′), *n. U.S. Informal.* a breakdown: *an engine conkout.*

con man, *Slang.* confidence man.

con|man|ship (kon′mən ship), *n. Slang.* the art or skill of a confidence man: *The Centre of the Action [a novel] is a confessional study of conmanship, in a New York jungle where rat eats rat* (Manchester Guardian Weekly). [< *con*[4] + *-manship*]

con mo|to (kôn mō′tō, kōn), *Italian, Music.* with spirited movement (used as a direction): *To say the least, he conducts con moto. Attending a ... concert is an optical as well as an aural experience* (New Yorker).

conn (kon), *v.t., n.* = con[3].

Conn., Connecticut.

con|nate (kon′āt), *adj.* **1** existing in a person or thing from birth or origin; inborn; congenital. SYN: innate. **2** born, originating, or existing together. SYN: coeval. **3** allied or agreeing in nature; related. SYN: cognate. **4** *Biology.* united into one body: *Connate leaves are united at the base.* [< Latin *connātus,* past participle of *connāscī* < *com-* together with + *nāscī* be born. Compare etym. under **cognate.**] —**con′nate|ly,** *adv.* —**con′nate|ness,** *n.*

connate water, *Geology.* water that becomes permanently entrapped in beds of sediment or rock at the time of deposit.

con|na|tion (kə nā′shən), *n.* connate condition.

con|nat|u|ral (kə nach′ər əl), *adj.* **1** belonging to a person or thing by nature or from birth or origin; inborn; congenital. **2** of the same nature; alike in quality or kind; cognate. —**con|nat′u|ral|ly,** *adv.*

con|nect (kə nekt′), *v.t.* **1** to join (one thing to another); link (two things together); fasten together; unite: *The plumber will have to connect those pipes before we can turn on the water.* **2** to join or unite by telephone or other means of communication: *The operator failed to connect us. I asked her to connect me with the long-distance operator.* **3** to associate; attach; relate: *He feels uncertain when it comes to repairing anything connected with television.* **4** to think of (one thing) with (another); associate in the mind: *We usually connect spring with sunshine and flowers.* **5** to join with others in some business or interest; have any kind of practical relation with: *He is connected with the advertising division of the company. This store is connected with a chain of stores.* **6** to join or link together in an electrical circuit. —*v.i.* **1** to be joined; become connected: *The garage connects with the basement of the house. Connecting with these there is a very small room* (Hawthorne). **2** (of trains, buses, or other public transportation) to run so that passengers can change from one to another without delay: *The afternoon train connects with the ferryboat.* **3** *Sports.* to hit a receiver, a mark, or a ball: *to connect for a 20-yard pass, to connect for a home run.* [< Latin *connectere* < *com-* together + *nectere* to tie] —**con|nect′i|ble, con|nect′a|ble,** *adj.*

▶**Connect** is used with *to, with,* or *by: Now let's connect this wire to that. Be sure this piece connects with the other. The two towns are connected by a railroad. Up* is unnecessary after *connect: He should connect this wire (up) with that.*

con|nect|ed (kə nek′tid), *adj.* **1** joined together; fastened together. **2** joined in orderly sequence: *connected ideas.* **3** having ties and associates: *She is well connected socially.* —**con|nect′ed|ly,** *adv.* —**con|nect′ed|ness,** *n.*

▶**Connected with** and **in connection with** are wordy expressions for *in* or *with: The social life in connection with a fraternity (in a fraternity) will be something you have never experienced before.*

con|nect|er (kə nek′tər), *n.* = connector.

Con|nect|i|cut warbler (kə net′ə kət), a North American warbler with yellow underparts, a gray hood, and a white eye ring.

con|nect|ing rod (kə nek′ting), a bar connecting two or more moving parts in a machine, such as the rod which transmits motion from the piston to the crankshaft in an internal-combustion engine.

con|nec|tion (kə nek′shən), *n.* **1a** the act of connecting; joining together: *The connection of our telephone took several hours. The connection of a coast-to-coast railroad was first completed in 1869.* **b** the condition of being joined together or connected; union: *His connection with our firm has lasted over thirty years.* SYN: junction. **c** a contact between two circuits or electrical wires: *There was a bad connection in the lamp wiring that made the light blink.* **2** a thing that connects; connecting part: *The connection between the radiator and the pipe had become loose.* SYN: bond, tie, link. **3** any kind of practical relation with another thing: *I have no connection with that prank.* **4a** a linking together of words or ideas in proper order; linking of persons or things together: *His last remarks apparently had no connection with the earlier part of his talk.* **b** contextual situation; context. **5** a group of people associated in some way. **6** the scheduled meeting of trains, ships, buses, or airplanes so that passengers can change from one to the other without delay: *The bus arrived late at the airport and we missed our airplane connection.* **7a** a related person; relative: *My sister-in-law is a connection of mine by marriage.* SYN: kin, kinsman. **b** relationship by ties of blood or marriage: *He was by hereditary connection a Cavalier* (Macaulay). **8** a religious sect or denomination: *the Methodist connection.* **9** sexual relations. **10** *U.S. Slang.* a person who sells or supplies narcotics (to addicts): *The junkies ... wait for their "connection" and the heroin he will bring* (Time). Also, *especially British,* **connexion.**

connections, influential, wealthy, or otherwise prominent associates or friends: *I got my summer job through one of my father's connections who knows the owner.*

in connection with, a together with: *The war itself, taken in connection with the bloody feuds that succeeded it ... gave a shock to the civilization of Greece* (Thomas De Quincey). **b** in relation with; in regard to: *He read a biography of George Washington in connection with his study of American history. We may say of Voltaire in connection with history what he said of Corneille in connection with tragedy* (John Morley).

▶See **connected** for usage note.

con|nec|tion|al (kə nek′shə nəl), *adj.* having to do with or like a connection.

con|nec|ti|val (kon′ek tī′vəl), *adj.* of or having to do with a connective.

con|nec|tive (kə nek′tiv), *adj., n.* —*adj.* that connects; having the power of connecting; tending to connect.

—*n.* **1** anything that connects. **2** a word used to connect words, phrases, clauses, and sentences. Conjunctions and relative pronouns are connectives. *A close reasoner and a good writer in general may be known by hispertinent use of connectives* (Samuel Taylor Coleridge). **3** *Botany.* the portion of a stamen which connects the two lobes of the anther. —**con|nec′tive|ly,** *adv.*

connective tissue, tissue that connects, supports, or encloses other tissues and organs in the body, such as fat, bone, and cartilage.

con|nec|tiv|i|ty (kon′ek tiv′ə tē), *n.* **1** *no pl.* the quality or state of being connective. **2** *pl.* **-ties.** linkage; connection: *the connectivities between adjoining pairs of atoms.*

con|nec|tor (kə nek′tər), *n.* **1** a person that connects. **2** a thing that connects: **a** a plug or other device that attaches to an electrical terminal. **b** a covered passageway that connects two buildings. **c** a road that connects two highways.

Con|ne|ma|ra pony (kon′ə mär′ə, -mar′ə), any of a breed of sturdy, gray ponies, originally from the district of Connemara, in County Galway, Ireland. Connemara ponies are good jumpers.

con|ner[1] (kon′ər), *n.* a person who tests or examines; examiner. [Old English *cunnere* < *cunnian* try, test]

con|ner[2] (kon′ər), *n.* a person who cons.

con|nex|ion (kə nek′shən), *n. Especially British.* connection.

con|ning tower (kon′ing), **1** a small tower on the deck of a submarine, used as an entrance and as a place for observation when the submarine is on the surface. **2** an armored control station on the deck of a warship, occupied by the captain during battle. **3** any similar observation tower from which supervision can be carried out: *And you sit up in a conning tower Bossing eight hundred men* (Rudyard Kipling). [*conning,* present participle of *con*[3] direct the steering of (a ship)]

con|nip|tion (kə nip′shən), *n.,* or **conniption fit,** *U.S. Informal.* a fit of hysterical excitement.

conniptions, hysterics: *Here the bard is supposed to have gone into "conniptions" and collapsed* (Troy Daily Times).

[compare dialectal English *canapshus* captious]

con|niv|ance (kə nī′vəns), *n.* **1** the act of conniving; pretended ignorance or secret encouragement of wrongdoing. **2** *Law.* guilty assent to, or knowledge or encouragement of, wrongdoing, without participation in it.

con|niv|an|cy (kə nī′vən sē), *n. Obsolete.* connivance.

con|nive (kə nīv′), *v.i.,* **-nived, -niv|ing. 1** to avoid noticing something wrong; give aid to wrongdoing by not telling of it: *The dishonest sheriff connived at gambling.* **2** to cooperate secretly: *Benedict Arnold connived with the British during the Revolutionary War.* **3** *Biology.* to be connivent. [< Latin *cōnnīvēre* wink (at), shut the eyes < *com-* together + a root *nīv-* press, related to *nictēre,* or *nictāre* wink] —**con|niv′er,** *n.*

con|niv|ence (kə nī′vəns), *n.* = connivance.

con|niv|ent (kə nī′vənt), *adj. Biology.* gradually converging: *The petals of certain flowers and the wings of certain insects are connivent.*

con|nois|seur (kon′ə sėr′), *n.* an expert, especially a critical judge of art or of matters of taste: *He is a connoisseur of antique furniture.* SYN: virtuoso. [< Old French *connoisseur* < *connoistre* know < Latin *cognoscere* become well acquainted with < *co-* (intensive) + *gnoscere* recognize, know]

con|nois|seur|ship (kon′ə sėr′ship), *n.* the role or part of a connoisseur; critical judgment in matters of art or taste.

con|no|tate (kon′ə tāt), *v.t.,* **-tat|ed, -tat|ing.** = connote.

con|no|ta|tion (kon′ə tā′shən), *n.* **1** the act of connoting: *A merger as such involves no necessary connotations of coercion, dominance, or lack of effective competitive pressures* (Wall Street Journal). **2** what is suggested in addition to the simple or literal meaning. *Example:* When Elaine is described in legends about King Arthur as "the lily maid," the connotation is that she was pale blond in coloring, delicate, sweet, and pure. **3** *Logic.* the sum of the attributes contained in a concept or implied by a term; intension.

▶See **denotation** for usage note.

con|no|ta|tive (kon′ə tā′tiv, kə nō′tə-), *adj.* **1** connoting; having connotation. **2** having to do with connotation. —**con′no|ta′tive|ly,** *adv.*

con|note (kə nōt′), *v.t.,* **-not|ed, -not|ing.** to suggest in addition to the simple or literal meaning; mean besides; imply. *Examples: Portly, corpulent,* and *obese* all mean "fleshy"; but *portly* connotes dignity; *corpulent,* bulk; and *obese,* an unpleasant excess of fat. A chubby face connotes ideas of youth, roundness, and pleasant looks. [< Medieval Latin *connotare* < Latin *com-* with + *notāre* to note < *nota* a mark, sign]

con|no|tive (kə nō′tiv), *adj.* = connotative. —**con|no′tive|ly,** *adv.*

con|nu|bi|al (kə nü′bē əl, -nyü′-), *adj.* of or having to do with marriage; conjugal; nuptial; matrimonial. [< Latin *connūbiālis* < *connūbium* marriage < *com-* + *nūbere* marry (said of a woman)] —**con|nu′bi|al|ly,** *adv.*

con|nu|bi|al|i|ty (kə nü′bē al′ə tē, -nyü′-), *n., pl.* **-ties. 1** the connubial state. **2** the practice or right of marrying. **3** an action or thing characteristic of marriage.

co|no|dont (kō′nə dont), *n.* any one of certain minute fossils of a conical, toothlike form, found in Silurian and other rocks, supposed to be the jaws of annelids. [< Greek *kônos* cone + *odoús,* *odóntos* tooth]

co|noid (kō′noid), *adj., n.* **—*adj.*** nearly conical in shape; conoidal. **—*n.*** **1** a geometrical solid formed by the revolution of a conic section about one of its axes. **2** a cone-shaped thing, such as a bullet. [< Greek *kōnoeidês* (orginally) cone-shaped < *kônos* cone + *eîdos* form]

co|noi|dal (kə noi′dəl), *adj.* **1** having to do with or like a conoid. **2** nearly conical in shape.

co|no|scen|te (kō′nō shen′tā), *n.* = cognoscente.

con ot|ta|va (kôn′ ōt tä′vä), *Italian, Music.* with the octave, usually the octave above (a direction added to a melody that is to be played in octaves).

con|quer (kong′kər), *v.t.* **1** to get by fighting; win in war: *The Romans conquered much of the ancient world.* SYN: subjugate. **2** to overcome by force; defeat: *to conquer an enemy.* SYN: vanquish, subdue. See syn. under **defeat**. **3** *Figurative.* to get the better of; overcome: *to conquer a bad habit.* **4** to climb successfully: *Three of the more important peaks had been conquered* (London Daily Chronicle). **—*v.i.*** to be victorious; be the conqueror: *The general said he would conquer or die.* [< Old French *conquerre* < Latin *conquīrere* < *com-* + *quaerere* seek] **—con′quer|a|ble**, *adj.* **—con′quer|ing|ly**, *adv.*

con|quer|ess (kong′kər es), *n.* a woman conqueror.

con|quer|or (kong′kər ər), *n.* a person who conquers; victor. SYN: vanquisher, conquistador.

the Conqueror, William I of England. As Duke of Normandy, he conquered England in the period from 1066 to 1070: *The work of the Conquest was now formally completed; the Conqueror sat in the royal seat of England* (Edward Freeman).

con|quest (kon′kwest, kong′-), *n.* **1** the act of conquering: *the conquest of a country, the conquest of disease. Conquest brings conceit and intolerance* (Havelock Ellis). SYN: triumph. See syn. under **victory**. **2** a thing conquered; land or people conquered: *Troy was the Greeks' hardest conquest.* **3** *Figurative.* a winning of the affections, especially by persuasive courtship: *He addressed himself to the conquest of women* (Edmund Wilson). **4** *Figurative.* a person whose love or favor has been won: *Casanova boasted of his conquests.*

the Conquest, the conquering of England by William the Conqueror, begun in 1066: *... a family of an ancient extraction, even from the time of the Conquest* (Edward Clarendon).
[< Old French *conqueste* < *conquest*, past participle of *conquerre;* see etym. under **conquer**]

conquest state, *Anthropology.* a society based on the conquest and exploitation of weaker groups or classes of people.

con|qui|an (kong′kē ən), *n.* a card game for two, resembling rummy; cooncan. [< Spanish *con quien* with whom]

con|qui|nine (kon′kwi nēn, -nin), *n.* = quinidine.

con|quis|ta|dor (kon kēs′tə dôr, -kwis′-), *n., pl.* **-dors** or **-dores**. **1** a Spanish conqueror in North or South America, especially during the 1500's in Mexico or Peru under Cortes and the Pizarros. **2** = conqueror. [< Spanish *conquistador* < *conquistar* conquer]

Con|rad|i|an (kon rad′ē ən), *adj.* of or characteristic of the novelist Joseph Conrad or his works: *The isolated hero who finds redemption through involvement is a familiar Conradian theme* (Saturday Review).

Con|rail (kon′rāl′), *n. U.S.* Consolidated Rail (Corporation), a private corporation chartered and subsidized by the federal government to operate several northeastern railroads.

con rod, *British Informal.* connecting rod.

cons., **1** consecrated. **2** consonant. **3** constitutional. **4** construction.

Cons., **1** Conservative. **2** Consolidated. **3** Constable. **4** Constitution. **5** Consul. **6** Consulting.

con|san|guine (kon sang′gwin), *adj.* = consanguineous: *a consanguine family like that of the Zuni* (Ogburn and Nimkoff).

con|san|guin|e|al (kon′sang gwin′ē əl), *adj.* = consanguineous.

con|san|guin|e|ous (kon′sang gwin′ē əs), *adj.* descended from the same parent or ancestor; related by blood: *The old lady insisted that she and George Washington were consanguineous.* SYN: akin, kin, kindred, cognate. [< Latin *consanguineus* (with English *-ous*) < *com-* together + *sanguineus* having to do with blood < *sanguis, -inis* blood] **—con′san|guin′e|ous|ly**, *adv.*

con|san|guin|i|ty (kon′sang gwin′ə tē), *n.* **1** relationship by descent from the same parent or ancestor; relationship by blood: *Brothers and cousins are related by ties of consanguinity.* SYN: kinship. **2** *Figurative: The consanguinity of doctrine* (Christopher Cartwright). SYN: kinship.

con|sarn (kən särn′, kon′särn′), *v., adj., adv. U.S. Dialect.* **—*v.t.*** to damn; darn: *Consarn your old skin! is that you?* (C. A. Murray).
—*adj., adv.* consarned: [*He*] *surveyed the results of ... his "consarn fool notion"* (Newsweek).
[< dialectal variant of *concern*]

con|sarned (kən särnd′, kon′särnd′), *adj., adv. U.S. Dialect.* **—*adj.*** darned: *... that consarned old thief* (Kate Wiggin). **—*adv.*** very; darn: *She was so consarned handsome* (Ann S. Stephens).

con|science (kon′shəns), *n.* **1** the sense of right and wrong; ideas and feelings within a person that tell him when he is doing right and warn him of what is wrong: *Let your conscience be your guide. The conscious is aided* (*or tormented*) *by ... the conscience* (William C. Menninger). **2** *Archaic.* the practice of or conformity to what is right; conscientiousness. **3** *Obsolete.* inmost thought; consciousness.

in (all) conscience, **a** reasonably; fairly: *I cannot, in conscience, ask him to do what I would not.* **b** surely; certainly: *Half a dozen fools are, in all conscience, as many as you should require* (Jonathan Swift).
[< Old French *conscience*, learned borrowing from Latin *conscientia* < *conscīre* < *com-* with + *scīre* to know] **—con′science|less**, *adj.*

conscience clause, a clause or article inserted in an act or law which explicitly relieves persons with conscientious or religious scruples from complying with it.

conscience money, money paid by a person whose conscience bothers him because of some dishonesty.

con|science-strick|en (kon′shəns strik′ən), *adj.* suffering from a feeling of having done wrong.

con|sci|en|tious (kon′shē en′shəs), *adj.* **1** careful to do what one knows is right; controlled by conscience: *The foreman is a conscientious worker and knows his duty.* SYN: upright, honorable, righteous, honest. **2** done with care to make it right: *Conscientious work is careful and exact.* SYN: particular, painstaking, scrupulous. **—con′sci|en′tious|ly**, *adv.* **—con′sci|en′tious|ness**, *n.*

conscientious objector, **1** a person whose conscience does not let him take up arms in warfare: *He pledges to support and defend the Constitution, and to bear arms on behalf of the United States, unless he can prove that he is a conscientious objector whose beliefs forbid him to bear arms* (Robert Rienow). **2** a person whose conscience does not let him take an active part in any effort associated with the conduct of war.

con|sci|en|ti|za|tion (kon′shē ən shə zā′shən), *n.* **1** a movement in Latin America to make the uneducated and underprivileged aware of their political rights: *Conscientization ... is spreading throughout the church in Latin America and joining hierarchy and people together in the fight for special justice* (Saturday Review). **2** = consciousness-raising: *The National Council of Churches speaks of "education/conscientization programs"* (Time).

con|scion|a|ble (kon′shə nə bəl), *adj.* according to conscience; just: *The unions didn't propose a specific date for renewing the talks, but said "it is neither constructive nor conscionable to further postpone the task"* (Wall Street Journal). SYN: conscientious, scrupulous, proper. **—con′scion|a|bly**, *adv.*

con|scious (kon′shəs), *adj., n.* **—*adj.*** **1** knowing; having experience; aware: *He was conscious of a sharp pain.* **2** able to feel; awake: *About five minutes after fainting I became conscious again.* **3** known to oneself; felt: *conscious guilt. Talking is more often conscious than breathing is.* **4** meant; intended; intentional: *a conscious lie.* SYN: deliberate. **5** self-conscious; shy; embarrassed: *She was a little conscious in her manner because of her old-fashioned dress.* **6** *Figurative.* knowing or sharing in human actions or secrets. **7** *Obsolete.* knowing something together with another. **8** *Obsolete.* guilty.
—*n.* the conscious, *Psychology.* the group of mental processes of which the individual is aware, in contrast to unconscious mental activity: *They figure in her dreams in forms which imply moral condemnation in the unconscious as well as the conscious, as demons or brutal people* (M. K. Bradby).
[< Latin *conscius* (with English *-ous*) knowing (something) with another < *com-* with + *scīre* know] **—con′scious|ly**, *adv.*
—*Syn.* **1 Conscious, aware** mean knowing that something exists. **Conscious** emphasizes the idea of realizing or knowing in one's mind that one sees, feels, hears, or otherwise senses something, either physically or emotionally: *He was conscious of a great uneasiness among the spectators.* **Aware** emphasizes the idea of merely noticing something one sees, smells, hears, tastes, feels, or is told: *I was aware that someone was talking, but not conscious of what was said.*

con|scious|ness (kon′shəs nis), *n.* **1** the state of being conscious; awareness: *People and animals have consciousness; plants and stones do not.* SYN: cognition, perception. **2** awareness of what is going on about one: *A severe shock often makes a person lose consciousness for a time.* SYN: sensation. **3** all the thoughts and feelings of a person or group of people. Everything of which you are conscious makes up your consciousness. SYN: sense, sensibility. **4** *Philosophy.* the power of the mind, whether rational or not, to be aware of acts, sensations, or emotions. **5** *Psychology.* the mental activity of which the individual is aware, in contrast to unconscious mental activity.

raise one's consciousness, to make one more aware of his or her potential, especially in one's ability to cause political or social change or change in oneself: *The various humiliations to which aging women are subject ... loss of self-esteem, problems of identity. They're in the movie to raise our consciousness* (New Yorker).

con|scious|ness-ex|pand|ing (kon′shəs nis ekspan′ding), *adj.* producing a mental state of extremely intensified awareness or perception; psychedelic: *consciousness-expanding drugs.*

con|scious|ness-rais|ing (kon′shəs nis rā′zing), *n.* a method of making people more aware of their potentials, especially their ability to bring about changes or reforms: *The S.D.S. saw students as in need of education. "Consciousness-raising," they called it* (New York Times).

con|scribe (kən skrīb′), *v.t.*, **-scribed**, **-scrib|ing**. **1** to enlist for military or naval service by conscription. **2** to enlist compulsorily. [< Latin *conscrībere* < *com-* (intensive) + *scrībere* write]

con|script (*v.* kən skript′; *adj., n.* kon′skript), *v., adj., n.* **—*v.t.*** **1** to compel by law to serve in the armed forces; draft. SYN: recruit. **2** to take for government use: *The dictator proposed to conscript the services of both business and labor.* SYN: commandeer.
—*adj.* conscripted; drafted. **—*n.*** a conscripted soldier or sailor. SYN: draftee, recruit.
[< Latin *conscriptus*, past participle of *conscrībere;* see etym. under **conscribe**]

conscript fathers, **1** the senators of ancient Rome. **2** the senators of medieval Venice. **3** the senators or legislators of any nation.

con|scrip|tion (kən skrip′shən), *n.* **1** the compulsory enlistment of men in the armed forces; draft: *In modern times, nations must resort to conscription to get an adequate army* (Ogburn and Nimkoff). **2** the act or system of forcing contributions of money, labor, or other service to the government.

con|scrip|tion|ist (kən skrip′shə nist), *n.* a person who advocates conscription.

con|scrip|tive (kən skrip′tiv), *adj.* involving conscription: *It was possible to make a fair computation of the armies under a conscriptive system* (London Morning Post).

con|se|crate (kon′sə krāt), *v.*,**-crat|ed**, **-crat|ing**, *adj.* **—*v.t.*** **1** to set apart as sacred; make holy: *The new chapel in the church was consecrated by the bishop.* SYN: sanctify. **2** to make an object of veneration or cherished regard; hallow: *Time has consecrated these customs. The brave men, living and dead, who struggled here, have consecrated it* [*Gettysburg Cemetery*] *far above our poor power to add or detract* (Abraham Lincoln). **3** *Figurative.* to set apart for a purpose; dedicate: *A doctor's life is consecrated to keeping people well.* SYN: See syn. under **devote**.
—*adj.* *Archaic.* consecrated.
[< Latin *consecrāre* (with English *-ate*[1]) < *com-* + *sacer, sacrī* sacred] **—con′se|cra′tor**, *n.*

con|se|crat|ed (kon′sə krā′tid), *adj.* set apart as sacred; made holy; hallowed.

con|se|cra|tion (kon′sə krā′shən), *n.* **1** the act of consecrating. **2** the condition of being consecrated. **3** ordination to a sacred office, especially that of bishop.

Con|se|cra|tion (kon′sə krā′shən), *n.* **1** words at Mass which effect the transubstantiation of the elements of bread and wine into the body and blood of Christ. **2** the section of the Mass during which these words are pronounced by the celebrant.

con|se|cra|to|ry (kon′sə krə tôr′ē, -tōr′-), *adj.* serving to consecrate.

con|se|cu|tion (kon′sə kyü′shən), *n.* **1** succession; sequence. **2** a train of reasoning; logical sequence; inference.

con|sec|u|tive (kən sek′yə tiv), *adj.* **1** following one right after another; successive: *Monday, Tuesday, and Wednesday are consecutive days of the week. Four consecutive home runs in one game is a major-league record.* SYN: See syn. under **successive**. **2** made up of parts that follow each other in logical order: *From all the reports, he put together a consecutive account of the ac-*

Pronunciation Key: **hat**, **āge**, **cãre**, **fär**; **let**, **ēqual**, **tėrm**; **it**, **īce**; **hot**, **ōpen**, **ôrder**; **oil**, **out**; **cup**, **pu̇t**, **rüle**; **child**; **long**; **thin**; **ᴛʜen**; **zh**, measure;
ə represents **a** in about, **e** in taken, **i** in pencil, **o** in lemon, **u** in circus.

cident. **3** *Grammar.* expressing consequence or result: *a consecutive clause.* **4** *Music.* having to do with the immediate succession of intervals of the same kind: *consecutive thirds, fifths, or octaves.* [< Middle French *consécutif,* learned borrowing from Medieval Latin *consecutivus* < Latin *consecūtus* following closely, past participle of *consequī* < *com-* (intensive) + *sequī* follow] **—con|sec′u|tive|ly,** *adv.* **—con|sec′u|tive|ness,** *n.*

consecutive points, *Mathematics.* two or more points infinitely close one to another on the same branch of a curve.

con|seil d'é|tat (kôN sā′ dā tá′), *French.* council of state (a French judicial body which investigates complaints of citizens against administrative rules of the government).

con|sen|su|al (kən sen′shü əl), *adj. Law.* made obligatory or binding only by mutual consent: *a consensual contract.* **2** *Physiology.* caused by reflex stimulation, as the contraction of both pupils when light strikes one eye. **3** *Psychology.* of or having to do with reflex action initiated by a distinctly conscious sensation. [< Latin *consensus* consensus + English *-al*[1]] **—con|sen′su|al|ly,** *adv.*

con|sen|sus (kən sen′səs), *n.* **1** agreement in opinion; the opinion of all or most of the people consulted: *Everybody argues so much that we never go anywhere because we can't reach a consensus on where to go. The consensus of the Board was that the park would have to be closed.* **2** general agreement: *I am a democrat and therefore prepared to accept the consensus of opinion in this country on the policy we should follow* (Commentary). [< Latin *consensus, -ūs* < *consentīre;* see etym. under **consent**]

con|sent (kən sent′), *v., n.* **—*v.i.*** **1** to agree; give approval or permission: *My father would not consent to my staying up past 10 p.m.* **2** *Archaic.* to agree in opinion; be of the same mind.
—*n.* **1** agreement; permission; approval: *We have mother's consent to go swimming.* SYN: assent. **2** agreement by a group as to a course of action: *with one consent, by common consent.* **3** *Archaic.* agreement or unity of opinion; unanimity.
[< Old French *consentir* < Latin *consentīre* < *com-* together + *sentīre* feel, think] **—con|sent′er,** *n.*
—*Syn.* *v.i.* **1 Consent, assent, concur** mean to agree. **Consent** means to agree *to* something by approving willingly or by giving in to the wishes of others: *He consented to run for president.* **Assent** means to agree *with* something, by accepting it or expressing approval of it: *He assented to the suggested change in plans.* **Concur,** more formal, means to agree *with* others about something, by having the same opinion: *The majority concurred in the decision to raise the dues.*

con|sen|ta|ne|i|ty (kən sen′tə nē′ə tē), *n.* the quality of being consentaneous.

con|sen|ta|ne|ous (kon′sen tā′nē əs), *adj.* **1** agreeing; accordant; suited. **2** done by common consent; unanimous; concurrent. [< Latin *consentāneus* (with English *-ous*) agreeing < *consentīre;* see etym. under **consent**] **—con′sen|ta′ne|ous|ly,** *adv.* **—con′sen|ta′ne|ous|ness,** *n.*

consent brief, a brief in which all parties agree in an application to a court.

consent decree, *Law.* a decree arrived at with the consent of the contending parties, usually accepted in lieu of a judicial decree, but not binding on the court.

con|sen|tience (kən sen′shəns), *n.* agreement of opinion; accordance.

con|sen|tient (kən sen′shənt), *adj.* **1** agreeing with each other; accordant; unanimous: *a consentient opinion.* **2** acting together to the same end; concurrent: *The council agreed to take consentient action on both projects.*

con|sent|ing (kən sen′ting), *adj.* agreeing together in some action or opinion; of one mind: *consenting adults.* **—con|sent′ing|ly,** *adv.*

consent judgment, *Law.* a judgment arrived at with the consent of the contending parties, commonly a compromise in which the defendant agrees to cease an allegedly illegal practice and the question of his previous guilt or innocence is waived, as in an antitrust prosecution.

consent order, *Law.* an order issued by a court to a defendant enjoining continuation of certain practices, and accepted by the defendant without admission or proof of the illegality of the practices in question.

con|sen|tu|al (kən sen′tü əl), *adj. Law.* done by mutual or common consent: *a consentual act.* [influenced by *consensual*]

con|se|quence (kon′sə kwens, -kwəns), *n.* **1** a result or effect: *The consequence of his fall was a broken leg. If the assassination could trammel up the consequence* (Shakespeare). SYN: outcome, issue. See syn. under **effect. 2** the relation of a result or effect to its cause. **3** a logical result; deduction; inference: *It is no longer a necessary consequence that an object thrown into the air must fall back to earth.* **4** importance: *The loss of her ring is a matter of great consequence to her. This matter is of little consequence.* SYN: moment, weight. See syn. under **importance. 5a** importance in rank or position; distinction: *The manager regarded his clerks as men of little consequence.* **b** assumed importance; consequentiality: *The hostess bustled into the room with an air of great consequence.*
in consequence, as a result; therefore: *Iron is the principal substance contained in the water, which has in consequence a strong, inky taste* (Archibald Geikie).
in consequence of, as a result of; because of: *Our Sun at setting . . . seems sometimes blood-red, in consequence of the absorption of our atmosphere* (Norman Lockyer).
take the consequences, to accept what happens because of one's action: *She did not study for the test, so she had to take the consequences. If he does not conform to their law, he must take the consequences* (Law Times).

con|se|quent** (kon′sə kwent, -kwənt), *adj., n.* **—*adj. **1** resulting; following as an effect; consequential: *His long illness and consequent absence put him far behind in his work.* **2** following as a logical conclusion. **3** logically consistent. **4** *Geology.* having a course determined by the original form or slope of the land: *consequent drainage, a consequent river.*
—*n.* **1** a thing that follows something else; result; effect. **2** a thing or event that follows another (without implication of causal connection). **3** *Logic.* the second part of a conditional proposition. In the statement, "If Richard wants to, he will do it," *he will do it* is a consequent. **4** *Mathematics.* the second term of a ratio. In the ratio 1:4, 4 is the consequent, and 1 the antecedent. **5** *Obsolete.* a result; inference; consequence.
[< Latin *consequēns, -entis,* present participle of *consequī;* see etym. under **consecutive**]

***consequent** definition 4 — 1:4 (antecedent: 1; consequent: 4)

con|se|quen|tial (kon′sə kwen′shəl), *adj.* **1** following as an effect; resulting; consequent. **2** having or showing a high opinion of oneself; self-important; pompous. **3** following as a logical conclusion or inference; resultant. **4** of consequence; important. **—con′se|quen′tial|ly,** *adv.* **—con′se|quen′tial|ness,** *n.*

con|se|quen|ti|al|i|ty (kon′sə kwen′shē al′ə tē), *n.* **1** logical sequence and consistency of thought. **2** self-importance; pomposity. **3** the fact or quality of being consequential.

con|se|quent|ly (kon′sə kwent′lē, -kwənt-), *adv.* as a result; therefore: *He overslept and, consequently, he was late. Most substances suffer contraction from cold, and consequently increase in density* (Archibald Geikie). SYN: See syn. under **therefore.**

con|serv|a|ble (kən sėr′və bəl), *adj.* that can be conserved; preservable.

con|serv|an|cy (kən sėr′vən sē), *n., pl.* **-cies. 1** conservation, as of rivers, forests, or other natural resources. **2** *British.* a commission having jurisdiction over the fisheries, navigation, and general use of a port or river. [alteration of obsolete *conservacy* < Medieval Latin *conservatia*]

con|ser|va|tion (kon′sər vā′shən), *n.* **1** the action of conserving; preservation; protecting from loss or from being used up; avoidance of waste: *the laws of conservation in physics. The conservation of our mineral resources is important because they can never be replenished.* **2** the official protection and care of forests, rivers, and other natural resources: *In recent years, however, the protection and wise use of our natural resources has become so important that the national and state governments spend millions of dollars each year on conservation* (Beauchamp, Mayfield, and West). **3** a forest or other area of natural resource, or a part of it, under public or private protection and care.
►**Conservation,** def. 2, is currently used to mean (1) the complete protection or preservation of wilderness and wildlife, (2) the wise or prudent use of all natural resources, or (3) the careful management of the whole environment, including such factors as waste disposal and urban renewal. These usages are not clearly distinguished and tend to overlap.

con|ser|va|tion|al (kon′sər vā′shə nəl), *adj.* of or having to do with conservation.

con|ser|va|tion|ist (kon′sər vā′shə nist), *n., adj.* **—*n.*** a person who wants to preserve the forests, rivers, and other natural resources of a country: *President Theodore Roosevelt was an ardent forest conservationist.*
—*adj.* of or favoring conservation.

conservation of charge, *Physics.* the principle that the total electric charge of the universe, or of any closed system, remains constant.

conservation of energy, *Physics.* the principle that the total energy of the universe, or of any closed system, remains constant, although it can be changed from one form into another: *Energy can neither be created nor destroyed in all such ordinary reactions. This statement is known as the law of the conservation of energy* (W. Norton Jones, Jr.).

conservation of mass or **matter,** *Physics.* the principle that the total mass of any material system is unchanged by reactions within the system. Thus, in a chemical reaction, matter is neither created nor destroyed but changed from one form of the substance to another.

conservation of momentum, *Physics.* the principle that the total momentum of any system of revolving or colliding bodies remains constant in the absence of outside forces.

conservation of parity, *Physics.* the theory that in strong interactions the behavior of a wave function and that of its mirror image cannot be differentiated in any experiment.

con|serv|a|tism (kən sėr′və tiz əm), *n.* **1** inclination to keep things as they are or were in the past; opposition to change, especially change in traditions: *The conservatism of the Indian peasants is deep-rooted in their social values* (Atlantic). **2** Often, **Conservatism.** the principles and practices of conservative parties, especially of the Conservative Party in Great Britain.

con|serv|a|tive (kən sėr′və tiv), *adj., n.* **—*adj.*** **1** inclined to keep things as they are or were in the past; opposed to change, especially any change in traditions: *"What was good enough for my grandfather is good enough for me" is something that a conservative person might say.* **2** not inclined to take risks; cautious; moderate: *a conservative estimate. This old, reliable company has conservative business methods.* **3** of or belonging to a political party pledged to preserve established traditions and to oppose major changes in national institutions. **4** free from novelties and fads: *It is economical to choose suits of a conservative style.* **5** having the power to preserve from harm or decay; conserving; preserving: *Forces such as those of gravity . . . where the work is not recoverable, are called conservative forces* (Sears and Zemansky).
—*n.* **1** a person who is opposed to change, either by nature or on principle: *The split between the conservatives and the modernists is as wide in Italy as it is elsewhere* (New Yorker). **2** a member of a conservative political party. **3** a means of preserving; preservative. **4** a person who from prejudice or lack of foresight is opposed to true progress. **—con|serv′a|tive|ly,** *adv.* **—con|serv′a|tive|ness,** *n.*

Con|serv|a|tive (kən sėr′və tiv), *adj., n.* **—*adj.*** **1** of or belonging to the Conservative Party in Great Britain or Canada: *Two or three times a year . . . Liberal members of parliament cause painful embarrassment to forty-two Conservative foes* (Maclean's). **2** of or having to do with a modern branch of Judaism regarded as being midway between Orthodox and Reform Judaism: *a Conservative synagogue or temple.*
—*n.* **1** a member of the Conservative Party in Great Britain or Canada. **2** an adherent of the Conservative branch of Judaism.

Conservative Party, 1 a political party in Great Britain that favors existing national institutions or return to some of those recently existing. **2** a similar political party in Canada, now called the Progressive Conservative Party.

con|ser|va|toire (kən sėr′və twär′), *n.* a school for instruction in music; conservatory. [< French *conservatoire*]

con|ser|va|tor (kon′sər vā′tər, kən sėr′və-), *n.* **1** a preserver; guardian: *A conservator, call me, if you please, not a creator or destroyer* (Robert Browning). **2a** a legally appointed guardian. **b** a person or institution appointed by law to take charge of the business or property of one who cannot manage it himself. **3** *British.* a custodian; keeper.

con|ser|va|to|ri|um (kən sėr′və tôr′ē əm, -tōr′-), *n., pl.* **-ri|ums.** a school for instruction in music; conservatory. [< German *Konservatorium*]

con|ser|va|tor|ship (kon′sər vā′tər ship, kən sėr′və-), *n.* **1** *Law.* **a** the position of a conservator in charge of the business or property of others. **b** the condition of being under the charge of a conservator: *Government Savings & Loan Association is the fourth association that has been placed in conservatorship under Maryland's new . . . law* (Wall Street Journal). **2** *British.* the office of conservator.

con|serv|a|to|ry (kən sėr′və tôr′ē, -tōr′-), *n., pl.* **-ries,** *adj.* **—*n.*** **1** a school for instruction in music. **2** a greenhouse or glass-enclosed room for growing and displaying plants and flowers. **3** *Obsolete.* a storehouse; repository.
—*adj.* having the quality of preserving from loss, decay, or injury; adapted to conserve; preservative.
[< Late Latin *conservatorius* (adjective) < Latin *conservāre;* see etym. under **conserve**]

con|serve (*v.* kən sėrv′; *n.* kon′sėrv, kən sėrv′), *v.,* **-served, -serv|ing,** *n.* **—*v.t.*** **1a** to keep from harm or decay; keep from loss or from being used up; preserve: *Try to conserve your strength for the end of the race.* **SYN**: guard, save. **b** *Physics.* to keep (the amount or property of any substance) constant: *Recent evidence seems to confirm that leptons are conserved* (Stuart B. Palmer). **2** to preserve (fruit) in sugar, often as jam: *to conserve grapes.*
—*n.* **1** Often, **conserves.** fruit preserved in sugar, often as jam. **2** a candy or confection preserved in sugar.
[< Old French *conserver* < Latin *conservāre* < *com-* with + *servāre* to preserve] **—con|serv′er,** *n.*

con|sid|er (kən sid′ər), *v.t.* **1** to think about in order to decide; deliberate: *Before you dash off an answer, take time to consider the problem.* **2** to think to be; regard as; look upon as: *I consider him a very able student. We consider Shakespeare a great poet.* **SYN**: deem, judge. **3** to think; believe; suppose: *I consider her to have behaved badly.* **4** to be thoughtful of (others and their feelings); show consideration for: *A kind person considers the feelings of others.* **SYN**: respect. **5** to allow for; take into account: *This watch runs very well, if you consider how old it is.* **6** to think highly of; esteem. **SYN**: regard. **7** *Archaic.* to look at carefully. **8** *Obsolete.* to recompense; remunerate. **9** *Obsolete.* to estimate; reckon. **—*v.i.*** to think carefully; reflect: *He considered fully before accepting the offer.* **SYN**: deliberate, ponder. [< Old French *considerer,* learned borrowing from Latin *consīderāre* look at closely (perhaps as in augury) < *com-* + *sīdus, -eris* star] **—con|sid′er|er,** *n.*
—*Syn.* *v.t.* **1 Consider, study, weigh** mean to think about something in order to decide. **Consider** means to think something over, to give it some careful thought before making a decision about it: *I considered going to college.* **Study** means to think out, to consider with serious attention to details: *He studied ways to support himself.* **Weigh** means to balance in the mind, to consider carefully both or all sides of an idea or action: *I weighed the idea of going to the local college.*

con|sid|er|a|ble (kən sid′ər ə bəl), *adj., n., adv.*
—*adj.* **1** worth thinking about; of consequence; important: *The mayor is a considerable person in his town. Being a school principal is a considerable responsibility.* **SYN**: great. **2** worthy of consideration because of its extent, size, or proportions; rather large: *The Panama Canal was a considerable engineering job.* **SYN**: sizable. **3** in large quantity; not a little; much: *He made a considerable sum of money in real estate.* **SYN**: goodly.
—*n.* **1** *U.S. Informal.* a great deal; not a little; much: *I reckon he earned considerable during his lifetime.* **2** *Obsolete.* a thing to be considered.
—*adv.* *Dialect.* considerably; rather: *He was considerable thirsty. I've thought about it considerable.*
► **considerable, considerably.** In speech there is a tendency not to distinguish between the adverb *considerably* and the adjective *considerable.* In formal and informal writing the distinction is observed: *The teacher's explanation helped them considerably* (modifies verb *helped*). *The teacher's explanation was of considerable help to them* (modifies noun *help*).
► In the informal speech of the United States *considerable* is sometimes used as a noun: *He has done considerable to improve the service.* Educated speakers, however, avoid this use.

con|sid|er|a|bly (kən sid′ər ə blē), *adv.* a good deal; much: *The boy was considerably older than he looked.*
► See **considerable** for usage note.

con|sid|er|ance (kən sid′ər əns), *n. Obsolete.* consideration.

con|sid|er|ate (kən sid′ər it), *adj.* **1** thoughtful of others and their feelings: *A considerate neighbor brought the old woman food when she was sick in bed. Was I more considerate of you and your comfort?* (Jane Austen). **SYN**: attentive. See syn. under **thoughtful. 2** (of things) marked by careful thought; well-considered; deliberate: *The proposal was given a considerate examination.* **3** *Archaic.* (of persons) thoughtful; prudent. **—con|sid′er|ate|ly,** *adv.* **—con|sid′er|ate|ness,** *n.*

con|sid|er|a|tion (kən sid′ə rā′shən), *n.* **1** the act or process of considering; act of thinking about in order to decide: *Before writing your answers please give careful consideration to the questions on the test.* **SYN**: attention, deliberation, reflection. **2** something thought of as a reason; something to be kept in mind: *Price and quality are two considerations in buying anything. Take one consideration with another—A policeman's lot is not a happy one* (William S. Gilbert). **3** thoughtfulness for others and their feelings; regard; respect: *Playing the radio loud at night shows a lack of consideration for the neighbors.* **4** money paid; any payment: *Dishonest people will do anything for a consideration.* **SYN**: compensation, recompense, remuneration. **5** *Law.* something given or done as a recompense or equivalent by one person in return for something given or done by another, without which no contract is binding. **6** claim to attention; importance; esteem: *William Faulkner is an author worthy of consideration.* **SYN**: consequence.
in consideration of (or **for**), **a** because of: *In consideration of his wife's health, he moved to a milder climate.* **b** in return for: *The lady gave the boy tickets to the ball game in consideration for his helpfulness.*
on no consideration, not at all; never: *On no consideration would he give his consent.*
take into consideration, to take into account; make allowance for: *The judge took the boy's age into consideration.*
under consideration, being thought about: *His request for a higher salary is under consideration. The bids for the bridge construction are under consideration.*

con|sid|ered (kən sid′ərd), *adj.* **1** carefully thought out: *This is the judge's considered opinion.* **2** honored; respected: *an old and highly considered public servant.*

con|sid|er|ing (kən sid′ər ing), *prep., adv.*
—*prep.* taking into account; making allowance for: *Considering his age, the little boy reads very well.*
—*adv.* *Informal.* taking everything into account: *He does very well, considering.* **—con|sid′er|ing|ly,** *adv.*

con|sign (kən sīn′), *v.t.* **1** to hand over formally; deliver: *The thief was consigned to prison.* **SYN**: entrust. See syn. under **commit. 2** to hand over to another for care or custody: *The parents consigned the child to its grandmother's care while they were away.* **SYN**: entrust. See syn. under **commit. 3a** to send; transmit: *We will consign the goods to him by express.* **SYN**: deliver. **b** to send goods to (an agent, etc.) for sale or custody. **4** to set apart; assign: *The room was consigned to the salesmen for a conference.* **5** to send away; banish; relegate: *The discredited politician was consigned to a remote post. His ideas were consigned to oblivion.* **6** *Obsolete.* to mark with the sign of the cross, as in baptism; confirm.
—*v.i.* *Obsolete.* to yield; submit. [< Middle French *consigner,* learned borrowing from Latin *consignāre* furnish with a seal < *com-* with + *signum* seal] **—con|sign′a|ble,** *adj.* **—con′sig|na′tion,** *n.*

con|sign|ee (kon′sī nē′, -si-), *n.* a person or company to whom goods are consigned: *Shippers and consignees are cutting distribution costs by routing freight* (Newsweek).

con|sign|er (kən sī′nər), *n.* = consignor.

con|sign|ment (kən sīn′mənt), *n.* **1** the act of consigning: *The President ordered consignment of food and clothing to the flooded area.* **2** something consigned, especially a shipment sent to a person or company for safekeeping or sale.
on consignment, consigned to a person or company with the understanding that the goods will not be paid for until sold: *Not only that, but the firms are offering them on consignment* (Wall Street Journal).

con|sign|or (kən sī′nər; kon′sī nôr′, -si-), *n.* a person or company that consigns goods to another.

con|sil|i|ence (kən sil′ē əns), *n.* a coming together; coincidence; concurrence.

con|sil|i|ent (kən sil′ē ənt), *adj.* coming together or agreeing; coinciding; concurring. [< Latin *com-* with + *salīre* leap + English *-ent*]

con|sil|i|um (kən sil′ē əm), *n. Latin.* consultation: *The injection is not administered until ... after a second consilium with a second vascular cardiologist* (Harper's).

con|sist (kən sist′), *v.i.* **1** to be made up; be formed: *A week consists of seven days. A chair consists of a seat with a back, supported by four legs.* **SYN**: comprise. **2** to be in harmony; agree. **3** *Archaic.* to exist or be capable of existing together. **4** *Archaic.* to hold together; subsist.
consist in, to be contained in; be made up of: *He believes that happiness consists in being easily pleased or satisfied.*
[< Latin *consistere* remain, exist < *com-* + *sistere* to stand, place < *stāre* to stand]

con|sist|ence (kən sis′təns), *n.* = consistency.

con|sist|en|cy (kən sis′tən sē), *n., pl.* **-cies.** **1a** degree of firmness or stiffness: *Frosting for a cake must be of the right consistency to spread easily without dripping.* **b** *Figurative.* quality; condition: *Their friendship was of lasting consistency.* **2a** firmness; stiffness: *The frosting retained its consistency.* **b** *Figurative.* substance; solidity: *The rumor persisted, daily acquiring consistency.* **3** a keeping to the same principles and habits: *consistency of purpose. He showed no consistency when he did excellent work the first part of the year and very poor work after that. A foolish consistency is the hobgoblin of little minds* (Emerson). **4** agreement or harmony among the parts or elements of a thing; accordance: *His courteous behavior is in consistency with his gentle character.* **SYN**: uniformity, regularity. **5** *Obsolete.* a dense or thick substance.

con|sist|ent (kən sis′tənt), *adj.* **1** keeping to the same principles and habits: *What a consistent person says or does today agrees with what he said or did yesterday.* **2** harmonious; in agreement; in accord: *Driving very fast on a rainy night is not consistent with safety. Too much noise is not consistent with comfort.* **SYN**: consonant, compatible. **3** *Mathematics.* having at least one common solution, as of two or more equations or inequalities. **4** *Rare.* holding together firmly; solid; cohering. **—con|sist′ent|ly,** *adv.*

con|sis|to|ri|al (kon′sis tôr′ē əl, -tōr′-), *adj.* of or having to do with a consistory.

con|sis|to|ry (kən sis′tər ē), *n., pl.* **-ries.** **1** a court of clergymen to decide church matters, such as a senate of cardinals presided over by the pope in the Roman Catholic Church, a diocesan court in the Church of England presided over by the bishop, or a governing board in some Reformed churches corresponding to the session of the Presbyterian Church; church council. **2** the meeting of a church council or court. **3** the place where it meets. **4** a council of 32nd-degree Freemasons. **5** *Historical or Poetic.* a meeting of councilors, especially that of the Roman emperors or of the Olympian deities. **6** *Obsolete.* a council chamber. [< Old North French *consistorie,* learned borrowing from Latin *consistōrium* place of assembly < *consistere;* see etym. under **consist**]

con|so|ci|ate (*adj., n.* kən sō′shē it, -āt; *v.* kən-sō′shē āt), *adj., n., v.,* **-at|ed, -at|ing.** **—*adj.*** associated together.
—*n.* an associate; companion; partner.
—*v.t., v.i.* to join in a consociation.
[< Latin *consociātus,* past participle of *consociāre* < *com-* together + *sociāre* join as a fellow < *socius* fellow; one sharing]

con|so|ci|a|tion (kən sō′sē ā′shən, -shē-), *n.* **1** intimate association of persons or things; fellowship. **2** a confederation or union of churches, especially Congregational churches.

con|so|ci|a|tion|al (kən sō′sē ā′shə nəl, -shē-), *adj.* of or having to do with consociation.

con|so|ci|a|tion|ism (kən sō′sē ā′shə niz əm, -shē-), *n.* the principle or practice of the consociation of churches.

con|sol (kon′sol, kən sol′), *n.* singular of **consols.**

consol., consolidated.

con|so|la|tion (kon′sə lā′shən), *n., adj.* **—*n.*** **1** the act of consoling or the state of being consoled; comfort: *He met with cold consolation* (Robert Southey). **SYN**: solace, cheer. **2** a comforting person, thing, or event: *This is the consolation on which we rest in the darkness of the future* (Emerson).
—*adj.* between losers in an earlier round of a tournament; for a consolation prize: *a consolation game or match.*
consolation prize, 1 a prize given to a person or team that does not win but demonstrates worthiness in a contest, or that wins in matches among previously defeated contestants: *a dialectical consolation prize for virtue otherwise unrewarded* (Sydney Morning Herald). **2** *U.S.* a prize given to the person or team making the lowest score, as a consolation.

con|sol|a|to|ry (kən sol′ə tôr′ē, -tōr′-), *adj.* consoling; comforting: *a savage reaction against ... bombastic and consolatory falsehoods* (Atlantic).

con|sole[1] (kən sōl′), *v.t.,* **-soled, -sol|ing.** to ease the grief or sorrow of; comfort: *The policeman consoled the lost child by speaking kindly to him and giving him some candy.* **SYN**: soothe, cheer, solace. See syn. under **comfort.** [< Middle

Pronunciation Key: hat, āge, cãre, fär; let, ēqual, tėrm; it, īce; hot, ōpen, ôrder; oil, out; cup, pu̇t, rüle; child; long; thin; ᴛʜen; zh, measure; ə represents **a** in about, **e** in taken, **i** in pencil, **o** in lemon, **u** in circus.

French *consoler,* learned borrowing from Latin *cōnsōlārī* < *com-* (intensive) + *sōlārī* soothe] —**con|sol'a|ble**, *adj.* —**con|sol'er**, *n.*

con|sole[2] (kon'sōl), *n.* **1** the part of an organ containing the keyboard, stops, and pedals. **2** a panel, usually of buttons, switches, and dials, used to control electrical or electronic equipment in a computer, automobile, missile, or other device. **3** a radio, television, or phonograph cabinet made to stand on the floor. **4** a vertical, or upright, piano larger than a spinet, standing 39 to 41 inches high: *Consoles, by and large, have actions that more closely approximate the feel of a grand. The console's longer strings are supposed to produce a better base, and its larger sounding board, of course, gives it tonal superiority* (New Yorker). **5** any cabinet used to house a machine, piece of equipment, or the like: *The ... Medical Gas Monitor is a complete, mobile console* (Science). **6** *Architecture.* a heavy, ornamental bracket, especially one more or less in the shape of a scroll, for supporting a cornice or bust. **7** = console table. [< French *console* beam, support]

con|sole table (kon'sōl), a narrow table, usually placed against a wall or under a mirror.

con|so|lette (kon'sə let'), *n.* a small console: *rich, full tone in an amazingly compact consolette* (New Yorker).

con|sol|i|date (kən sol'ə dāt), *v.,* **-dat|ed, -dat|ing,** *adj.* —*v.t.* **1** to combine into one; unite: *The small farms were bought by a seed company and consolidated for greater efficiency. Many country schools have been consolidated.* **SYN**: join, merge, amalgamate. **2** to make solid or firm; solidify: *In the seventeenth century Luther's literary language was further consolidated by professional grammarians* (Simeon Potter). **3** to make secure; strengthen: *The Romans consolidated their conquest of Britain by building a wall to keep out the raiding Scots. The presidential candidate consolidated his reputation by winning several primary elections.*
—*v.i.* **1** to unite; combine; merge: *The three banks consolidated and formed a single, large bank.* **2** to become solid or firm.
—*adj.* consolidated.
[< Latin *cōnsolidāre* (with English *-ate*[1]) make solid < *com-* + *solidus* solid]

con|sol|i|dat|ed (kən sol'ə dā'tid), *adj.* united; combined: *consolidated efforts.*

Consolidated Fund, the fund of the British government from which permanent expenditures are paid, such as interest on the national debt, royal annuities, and the salaries of judges, as distinguished from expenditures voted annually by Parliament.

consolidated school, a school for pupils from several school districts.

con|sol|i|da|tion (kən sol'ə dā'shən), *n.* **1** the act of consolidating or condition of being consolidated, especially: **a** a making firm or strong; strengthening: *The consolidation of marble did not fall out at random* (John Woodward). **b** a combining or unifying: *A consolidation of the family's resources made his trip possible.* **2** a combination of two or more corporations in which a new corporation is formed and the original corporations are dissolved or dormant; business merger. **3** a period of relatively small price moves in the stock market, usually coming immediately after or before a substantial advance in prices.

con|sol|i|da|tor (kən sol'ə dā'tər), *n.* a person or thing that consolidates.

con|sol|ing (kən sō'ling), *adj.* that consoles; comforting: *a consoling thought.* —**con|sol'ing|ly**, *adv.*

con|sols (kon'solz, kən solz'), *n.pl.* bonds of the government of Great Britain. [short for *consolidated annuities*]

con|som|mé (kon'sə mā'), *n.* a clear soup made by boiling meat in water. [< French *consommé* (literally) consumed, finished (in the sense of extracted)]

con|so|nance (kon'sə nəns), *n.* **1** agreement; accordance: *There was a consonance of opinion among the members of the jury.* **SYN**: harmony, congruity, concord. **2** harmony of sounds. **3** *Music.* a combination of tones sounded together, as of a note and its fifth, that is agreeable to the ear. **4** *Physics.* = resonance.

con|so|nan|cy (kon'sə nən sē), *n.* = consonance.

con|so|nant (kon'sə nənt), *n., adj.* —*n.* **1** any letter in the alphabet that is not a vowel. All the letters that are not vowels (in English, *b, c, d, f, g, h, j, k, l, m, n, p, q, r, s, t, v, w, x, y, z*) are consonants. **2** any speech sound represented by such a letter or a combination of letters. The two consonants of *ship* are spelled by the letters *sh* and *p.* A consonant is formed by completely or partially stopping the stream of breath with the tongue, teeth, or lips. *Abbr:* cons.
—*adj.* **1** in agreement; in accord; harmonious: *His action is consonant with his beliefs.* **SYN**: congruous, accordant, consistent. **2** harmonious in tone or sound: *Poe's love poems have many consonant lines such as, "The sweet Lenore hath gone before, with Hope that flew beside."* **3** = consonantal. **4** *Physics.* = resonant.
[< Latin *cōnsonāns, -antis,* present participle of *cōnsonāre* < *com-* together + *sonāre* to sound < *sonus* a sound] —**con'so|nant|ly**, *adv.*

con|so|nan|tal (kon'sə nan'təl), *adj.* **1** having to do with a consonant or its sound. **2** of or like a consonant.

con|so|nant|ism (kon'sə nən tiz'əm), *n.* the system of consonants of a particular language.

consonant shift, *Linguistics.* the regular change in consonantal sounds that took place in the development of the Germanic languages, as set forth in Grimm's Law.

con sor|di|no (kôn sôr dē'nō), *Italian, Music.* with the mute (used as a direction).

con|sort[1] (*n.* kon'sôrt; *v.* kən sôrt'), *n., v.* —*n.* **1** a husband or wife. The wife of a reigning king is called a queen consort. The husband of a reigning queen is sometimes called a prince consort or king consort. **SYN**: spouse. **2** a ship accompanying another: *The crews of "Card" and consorts had eaten Christmas dinner in Casablanca before sailing* (Atlantic). **SYN**: escort. **3** an associate; companion.
—*v.i.* **1** to keep company; associate: *He got a bad name consorting with a rough gang of men. Men consort in camp and town, But the poet dwells alone* (Emerson). **2** to agree; accord. **SYN**: harmonize.
—*v.t.* **1** to associate; link. **2** *Obsolete.* to accompany; escort; attend: *Sweet health and fair desires consort your grace* (Shakespeare).
[< Middle French *consort,* learned borrowing from Latin *consors, -sortis* sharer < *com-* with + *sors, sortis* lot]

con|sort[2] (kon'sôrt), *n. Obsolete.* **1** an association; assembly; company: ... *five or six boats in a consort* (Richard Hakluyt). **2** agreement; concord. **3a** harmony; accord: *Choice instruments ... in sweet melodious consort joined* (Richard D. Blackmore). **b** harmonious music. **c** a number of musicians playing or singing together. **d** a concert. [probably variant of *concert*]

con|sor|ti|um (kən sôr'shē əm), *n., pl.* **-ti|a** (-shē ə). **1** *Law.* **a** a partnership; association. **SYN**: coalition. **b** union by marriage. **2a** an agreement among bankers of several nations to give financial aid to another nation, or to finance a project which would be too large for any one of them individually. **b** a group, association, or the like, formed by this or a similar agreement: *Iranian oil is now produced by an international consortium of eight companies* (Newsweek). [< Latin *consortium* partnership < *consors;* see etym. under **consort**[1]]

con|spe|cies (kon spē'shiz), *n., pl.* **-cies**. **1** a species of the same genus as other species. **2** a subspecies or variety.

con|spe|cif|ic (kon'spi sif'ik), *adj.* of the same species.

con|spec|tus (kən spek'təs), *n.* **1** a general or comprehensive view: *It [chess] was a conspectus of life itself, with the illusion of power over life* (Joseph Cross). **2** a short summary or outline of a subject; résumé; digest. [< Latin *cōnspectus, -ūs* < *cōnspicere* < *com-* with + *specere* look]

con|spi|cu|i|ty (kon'spi kyü'ə tē), *n.* conspicuousness: *He stands in lone conspicuity, as if he had no earthly connections* (Charles Stanford).

con|spic|u|ous (kən spik'yü əs), *adj.* **1** easily seen; clearly visible: *A traffic sign should be placed where it is conspicuous.* **SYN**: noticeable. See syn. under **prominent. 2** attracting notice; worthy of notice; remarkable: *an actress of conspicuous charm. Abraham Lincoln is a conspicuous example of a poor boy who succeeded.* **SYN**: striking, manifest, notable, noteworthy, eminent. **3** ostentatious; pretentious: *conspicuous waste, conspicuous consumers.* [< Latin *cōnspicuus* (with English *-ous*) visible < *cōnspicere;* see etym. under **conspectus**] —**con|spic'u|ous|ly**, *adv.* —**con|spic'u|ous|ness**, *n.*

conspicuous consumption, *Economics.* the ostentatious purchase or display of luxuries to enhance one's status in society.

con|spir|a|cy (kən spir'ə sē), *n., pl.* **-cies**. **1** the act of conspiring; secret planning to do something unlawful or wrong: *The leaders of the conspiracy against the government were caught and punished. Society everywhere is in conspiracy against the manhood of every one of its members* (Emerson). **2** a combination of persons for an evil or unlawful purpose; plot or intrigue: *And they were more than forty which had made this conspiracy [to kill Paul]* (Acts 23:13). **3** *Law.* an agreement by two or more persons to act unlawfully. **4** *Archaic.* harmonious action or effort.

conspiracy of silence, a conspiring to keep something wrong, damaging, or unlawful from being divulged: *There has been a conspiracy of silence over one aspect of the Cyprus crisis* (Manchester Guardian).

con|spir|ant (kən spīr'ənt), *adj.* conspiring.

con|spi|ra|tion (kon'spə rā'shən), *n.* **1** joint action or effort. **2** *Obsolete.* conspiracy.

con|spir|a|tive (kən spir'ə tiv), *adj.* involving conspiracy; conspiratorial: *conspirative manner.*

con|spir|a|tor (kən spir'ə tər), *n.* a person who conspires; one who joins in a plot: *A group of conspirators planned to kill the dictator.* **SYN**: plotter.

con|spir|a|to|ri|al (kən spir'ə tôr'ē əl, -tōr'-), *adj.* having to do with conspiracy or conspirators: *The need to keep secrets was concentrated on the inner circle of the conspiratorial band.* —**con|spir'a|to'ri|al|ly**, *adv.*

con|spir|a|to|ry (kən spir'ə tôr'ē, -tōr'-), *adj.* = conspiratorial.

con|spir|a|tress (kən spir'ə tris), *n.* a woman conspirator.

con|spire (kən spīr'), *v.,* **-spired, -spir|ing.** —*v.i.* **1** to plan secretly with others to do something unlawful or wrong; plot: *The two men conspired to steal the jewels and then sell them to a jeweler in another country.* **SYN**: See syn. under **plot**. **2** to act together; contribute jointly: *All things conspired to make her birthday a happy one.* **SYN**: concur, cooperate, combine.
—*v.t.* to plot (something evil or unlawful).
[< Old French *conspirer,* learned borrowing from Latin *cōnspīrāre* < *com-* together + *spīrāre* breathe] —**con|spir'er**, *n.* —**con|spir'ing|ly**, *adv.*

con spi|ri|to (kôn spē'rē tō), *Italian, Music.* with spirit (used as a direction).

con|spue (kən spyü'), *v.t.,* **-spued, -spu|ing.** to spit upon in contempt; assail publicly with demonstrations of contempt. [< Latin *conspuere* < *com-* with + *spuere* spit]

const., **1** constable. **2** *Mathematics.* constant. **3** constitution.

Const., **1** Constable. **2** Constantinople. **3** Constitution.

con|sta|ble (kon'stə bəl, kun'-), *n.* **1** a police officer, especially in a township, district, or rural area of the United States. **2** *British.* policeman: *The troopers [of the Royal Canadian Mounted Police] are called constables* (E. R. Adair). **3** a chief officer of a household, court, or army, especially in the Middle Ages. **4** the keeper of a royal fortress or castle. [< Old French *conestable* < Late Latin *comes stabulī* count of the stable; (later) chief household officer] —**con'sta|ble|ship**, *n.*

con|stab|u|lar (kən stab'yə lər), *adj.* of or belonging to a constable.

con|stab|u|lar|y (kən stab'yə ler'ē), *n., pl.* **-lar|ies,** *adj.* —*n.* **1** the constables of a district or country. **2** a police force organized like an army; state police. **3** a district under a constable.
—*adj.* having to do with constables; consisting of constables; having the functions of constables: *a poorly trained constabulary force of South Koreans.*

con|stan|cy (kon'stən sē), *n., pl.* **-cies**. **1** firmness in belief or feeling; determination; steadfastness: *We admire the constancy of Columbus in looking for a new route to India.* **SYN**: resolution, endurance. **2** faithfulness; loyalty: *A constancy of friendship which won him a host of devoted adherents* (John Richard Green). **SYN**: fidelity. **3** the condition of being always the same; absence of change: *Physiological constancy is the first biological commandment* (Scientific American). **SYN**: uniformity, regularity. **4** something permanent, especially a permanent job.

con|stant (kon'stənt), *adj., n.* —*adj.* **1** never stopping; incessant: *Three days of constant rain made the field muddy.* **SYN**: ceaseless, continuous, perpetual. **2** continually happening; repeated often or again and again: *A clock makes a constant ticking sound.* **SYN**: persistent, unremitting. **3** always the same; not changing: *If you walk due north, your direction is constant. I am constant as the northern star* (Shakespeare). *Some philosophers believe that human nature is constant.* **SYN**: unchangeable, steady, uniform, invariable. **4** faithful; loyal; steadfast: *A constant friend helps you when you need help.* **SYN**: stanch, true, trusty. See syn. under **faithful**. **5** firm in mind or purpose; resolute: *He was constant and single-minded in his resolve to better the human race.* **6** *Mathematics, Physics.* retaining the same value; remaining the same in quantity, size, or other dimension: *a constant force.* **7** *Obsolete.* certain; confident.
—*n.* **1** a thing that is always the same; value or quantity that does not change: *Birth and death and the changes of season are natural constants. The speed of light is an important constant in physics.* **2** *Mathematics.* a quantity assumed to be invariable throughout a given calculation or discussion. **3** *Physics.* a numerical

quantity expressing a relation or value, as of a physical property of a substance, that remains unchanged under certain conditions: *The velocity C of electromagnetic waves in free space is probably the most important fundamental constant known to modern physics* (W. C. Vaughan). [< Latin *constāns, -antis,* present participle of *constāre* stand firm < *com-* (intensive) + *stāre* stand]

con|stan|tan (kon′stən tan), *n.* an alloy consisting of copper and nickel, usually in the proportions of 60 per cent copper and 40 per cent nickel, used for electrical resistance heating and thermocouples. [< *constant*]

Con|stan|ti|a (kən stan′shē ə), *n.* Often, **constantia.** a red or white wine of South Africa: *I have some of the finest old Constantia wine ... that ever was tasted* (Jane Austen). [< *Constantia* vineyards, near Cape Town, South Africa]

Con|stan|tin|i|an (kon′stən tin′ē ən), *adj.* of or having to do with Constantine the Great or his reign.

Con|stan|ti|no|pol|i|tan (kon stan′tə nə pol′ə tən), *adj.* of or having to do with Constantinople (ancient Byzantium) or with the Eastern Empire or Church; Byzantine: *The Constantinopolitan Greek patriarchate.* [< Late Latin *Constantīnopolītānus* < *Constantīnopolis* Constantinople]

Constantinopolitan Creed, = Nicene Creed (def. 2).

con|stant-lev|el balloon (kon′stənt lev′əl), a balloon launched to float at fixed altitudes and transmit atmospheric data by radio.

con|stant|ly (kon′stənt lē), *adv.* **1** always; without change: *He is constantly late.* **2** without stopping: *If a clock is kept wound it runs constantly. The girls chattered constantly.* **3** often; again and again: *He has to be reminded constantly to pay attention.*

con|stant-speed propeller (kon′stənt spēd′), an aircraft engine with a propeller that automatically maintains a uniform number of revolutions per minute under all conditions of flight.

con|state (kən stāt′), *v.t.,* **-stat|ed, -stat|ing.** to establish; ascertain; state positively. [< French *constater* < Latin *constat* it is certain, third person singular of *constāre* stand firm; see etym. under **constant**]

con|sta|tive (kən stā′tiv), *adj. Grammar, Philosophy.* stating or asserting a wish, command, or plan, not its actual performance. "I hope to go" is a constative utterance; "I am going" is a performative utterance.

con|stel|late (kon′stə lāt), *v.t., v.i.,* **-lat|ed, -lat|ing.** to cluster together as stars in a constellation.

***con|stel|la|tion** (kon′stə lā′shən), *n.* **1a** a group of stars, usually having a geometric shape within a definite region of the sky. Constellations are often named after mythological figures. *The Big Dipper is the easiest constellation to locate. Why did no one teach me the constellations when I was a child?* (Thomas Carlyle). **b** *Figurative: a constellation of scholars at a convention.* **2** a division of the heavens occupied by a group of stars. **3** (in astrology) the grouping or relative positions of the stars, thought to influence events, especially their position at the time of a person's birth. **4a** *Psychology.* a complex group of related feelings and ideas. **b** *Figurative: There comes a constellation of changes that mark passage over the brink into deep sleep* (Scientific American). [< Late Latin *constellātiō, -ōnis* < *constellātus* starred, ultimately < Latin *com-* with + *stella* star]

***constellation**
definition 1a

Little Dipper
North Star
Ursa Minor or Little Bear
Big Dipper
Ursa Major or Great Bear

con|stel|la|to|ry (kən stel′ə tôr′ē, -tōr′-), *adj.* having to do with or like a constellation.

con|ster|nate (kon′stər nāt), *v.t.,* **-nat|ed, -nat|ing.** to amaze and terrify; dismay.

con|ster|na|tion (kon′stər nā′shən), *n.* great dismay; paralyzing terror: *To our consternation the train rushed on toward the burning bridge.* **SYN:** fright. See syn. under **dismay.** [< Latin *consternātiō, -ōnis* < *consternāre* terrify, variant of *consternere* lay low, spread, cover over < *com-* (intensive) + *sternere* strew]

con|sti|pate (kon′stə pāt), *v.t.,* **-pat|ed, -pat|ing. 1** to cause constipation in: *It is a bad practice to get the habit of using cathartics, or laxatives, whenever you are constipated* (Beauchamp, Mayfield, and West). **SYN:** bind. **2** *Obsolete.* to crowd or pack closely together; condense. [< Latin *cōnstīpāre* (with English *-ate*[1]) < *com-* together + *stīpāre* press, stuff. See etym. of doublet **costive.**]

con|sti|pa|tion (kon′stə pā′shən), *n.* **1** a condition in which it is difficult to empty the bowels: *There was a time when almost any disorder—indigestion, a cold, an upset stomach, fatigue, headache—was promptly blamed on the villain constipation* (Sidonie M. Gruenberg). **2** *Obsolete.* condensation; compression.

con|stit|u|en|cy (kən stich′ü ən sē), *n., pl.* **-cies. 1** the voters in a district; constituents: *The congressman was reelected to office by his constituency.* **2** this district: *His constituency is composed of farmers and cattlemen.* **3** a group of supporters or customers; clientele: *That brokerage has a wealthy constituency.*

con|stit|u|ent (kən stich′ü ənt), *adj., n.* —*adj.* **1** forming a necessary part; making up: *Flour, liquid, salt, and yeast are constituent parts of bread.* **SYN:** component. **2** appointing; electing: *The school board is the constituent body for the high school.* **3** having the power to make or change a political constitution: *a constituent assembly.*
—*n.* **1** a necessary part of a whole; component: *Sugar is the main constituent of candy.* **SYN:** See syn. under **element. 2a** a voter: *A congressman receives many letters from his constituents.* **b** a person who lives in a certain constituency. **3** *Linguistics.* one of two or more elements into which a word or group of words can be analyzed: *The immediate constituents of 'Poor John ran away' are the two forms 'poor John' and 'ran away;' ... the constituents of 'poor John' are the morphemes 'poor' and 'John'* (Leonard Bloomfield). [< Latin *constituēns, -entis,* present participle of *constituere;* see etym. under **constitute**] —**con|stit′u|ent|ly,** *adv.*

con|sti|tute (kon′stə tüt, -tyüt), *v.t.,* **-tut|ed, -tut|ing. 1** to make up; form: *Seven days constitute a week.* **SYN:** compose, comprise. **2** to set up; establish: *Schools are constituted by law to teach boys and girls. The Salvation Army constituted a relief station for the victims of the fire.* **SYN:** found. **3** to enact: *Laws are constituted to protect individual rights and property.* **4** to give legal form to. **5** to appoint; elect: *The group constituted one member its leader.* **6** *Obsolete.* to set or place. [< Latin *constitūtus,* past participle of *constituere* < *com-* (intensive) + *statuere* set up]

con|sti|tu|tion (kon′stə tü′shən, -tyü′-), *n.* **1** the way in which a person or thing is organized; nature; make-up: *A person with a good constitution is strong and healthy. We may know the chemicals that constitute the human body, but we do not yet know the constitution of life.* **SYN:** composition, organization, structure. **2a** the fundamental principles according to which a nation, state, or group is governed: *The United States has a written constitution. One of the first steps in group organization is to outline a constitution and bylaws.* **b** a document stating these principles. **SYN:** charter. **3** the act of appointing, making, or forming. **4** a setting up; establishment. **SYN:** institution. **5** a law, decree, or established custom. **the Constitution,** the written set of fundamental principles by which the United States is governed. It was first drawn up in 1787, ratified in 1788, and put into effect in 1789. Since then 26 amendments have been added to it.

con|sti|tu|tion|al (kon′stə tü′shə nəl, -tyü′-), *adj., n.* —*adj.* **1** of or in the constitution of a person or thing; essential: *A constitutional weakness makes him catch a cold easily.* **SYN:** inherent, basic. **2a** of or according to the constitution of a nation, state, or group: *a citizen's constitutional rights. Slavery was abolished by a constitutional amendment in 1865. The Supreme Court must decide whether this law is constitutional.* **b** having the power of, or existing by virtue of and subject to, a constitution: *We have constitutional governments in the United States.* **3** adhering to or supporting a constitution: *a constitutional party.* **4** for one's health: *constitutional exercise, a constitutional walk.*
—*n.* a walk taken for the health: *After Sunday dinner Grandfather always takes his constitutional.*

constitutional convention, a convention held to write or to amend the constitution of a nation or state.

con|sti|tu|tion|al|ism (kon′stə tü′shə nə liz′əm, -tyü′-), *n.* **1** the principles of constitutional government. **2** adherence to these principles. **3** a constitutional system of government. —**con′sti|tu′tion|al|ist,** *n.*

con|sti|tu|tion|al|i|ty (kon′stə tü′shə nal′ə tē, -tyü′-), *n.* accordance with the constitution of a nation, state, or group; being constitutional: *The constitutionality of freedom of speech has been upheld in the courts many times.*

con|sti|tu|tion|al|ize (kon′stə tü′shə nə līz, -tyü′-), *v.t.,* **-ized, -iz|ing.** to make constitutional: *He was opposed to factions or formal groupings which would inevitably constitutionalize and impose their own majority rules* (London Times).

con|sti|tu|tion|al|ly (kon′stə tü′shə nə lē, -tyü′-), *adv.* **1** in or by constitution; naturally: *The fat boy is constitutionally unable to run fast.* **2** according to a constitution: *an action constitutionally illegal.*

constitutional monarchy, a monarchy in which the ruler has only those powers given to him by the constitution and laws of the nation: *They* [*the Hittites*] *evolved a pioneering constitutional monarchy; their kings had to answer to a council of nobles* (Newsweek).

Constitution State, a nickname for Connecticut.

con|sti|tu|tive (kon′stə tü′tiv, -tyü′-), *adj.* **1** having the power to establish or enact; instituting. **2** making up or forming a thing; constituent. **3** making a thing what it is; essential. **4** (of an enzyme) present in the cell under all conditions, not formed in answer to the presence of its substrate. —**con′sti|tu′tive|ly,** *adv.*

con|sti|tu|tor (kon′stə tü′tər, -tyü′-), *n.* a person or thing that constitutes: *Elocution is only an assistant, but not a constitutor of eloquence* (Oliver Goldsmith).

constr., construction.

con|strain (kən strān′), *v.t.* **1** to force; compel; oblige: *The principal was constrained to punish the rude boy.* **SYN:** coerce. **2** to confine; imprison: *The wild animal was bound and constrained.* **SYN:** restrict. **3** to restrain; repress: *to constrain a cough during a concert.* **SYN:** suppress. **4** to force or produce by straining: *to constrain a nervous laugh.* **SYN:** strain. **5** *Obsolete.* to compress; contract. **SYN:** constrict. [< Old French *constreindre* < Latin *constringere* < *com-* together + *stringere* pull tightly] —**con|strain′a|ble,** *adj.*

con|strained (kən strānd′), *adj.* **1** forced. **2** restrained; stiff; unnatural: *a constrained smile.* —**con|strain′ed|ly,** *adv.*

con|strain|er (kən strā′nər), *n.* a person who constrains.

con|straint (kən strānt′), *n.* **1** restraint; restriction; limitation: *The proposed legislation is not the best that the city can do, even within the existing political and financial constraints* (New York Times). *Thro' long imprisonment and hard constraint* (Edmund Spenser). **2** force; compulsion: *He appeared in court only under constraint of law.* **SYN:** coercion. **3** a holding back of natural feelings; forced or unnatural manner; embarrassed awkwardness: *We felt a little constraint with the new teacher for the first day or so.* **4** confinement. [< Old French *constreinte,* past participle of *constreindre;* see etym. under **constrain**]

con|strict (kən strikt′), *v.t.* to draw together; contract; compress: *A rubber band can constrict what it encircles. A tourniquet stops the flow of blood by constricting the blood vessels.* [< Latin *constrictus,* past participle of *constringere;* see etym. under **constrain**]

con|stric|tion (kən strik′shən), *n.* **1** the act of drawing together; compression; contraction. **2** a feeling of tightness; constricted condition: *He coughed and complained of a constriction in his chest.* **3** a constricted part. **4** something that constricts.

con|stric|tive (kən strik′tiv), *adj.* drawing together; contracting; compressing. —**con|stric′tive|ly,** *adv.*

con|stric|tor (kən strik′tər), *n.* **1** any snake that kills its prey by squeezing it with its coils. The boa, anaconda, and python are constrictors. **2** a person or thing that constricts: *It has turned out to be an extraordinarily powerful bloodvessel constrictor* (Harper's). **3** a muscle that constricts or narrows a part of the body: *the constrictors of the eyelids.*

con|stringe (kən strinj′), *v.t.,* **-stringed, -string|ing.** to cause to contract; compress; constrict. [< Latin *constringere;* see etym. under **constrain**]

con|strin|gen|cy (kən strin′jən sē), *n.* the quality of being constringent.

con|strin|gent (kən strin′jənt), *adj.* causing constriction; constringing.

con|stru|a|bil|i|ty (kən strü′ə bil′ə tē), *n.* capability of being construed.

con|struct (*v.* kən strukt′; *n.* kon′strukt), *v.t.* **1** to put together; fit together; build; frame: *to con-*

Pronunciation Key: hat, āge, cãre, fär; let, ēqual, tėrm; it, īce; hot, ōpen, ôrder; oil, out; cup, pu̇t, rüle; child; long; thin; ᴛʜen; zh, measure; ə represents **a** in about, **e** in taken, **i** in pencil, **o** in lemon, **u** in circus.

struct the plot of a story. The explorers constructed a raft of logs fastened with tough vines. The ancient Greek temples were constructed mathematically. **SYN**: devise. See. sym. under **make**. **2** to draw (a geometrical figure) so as to fulfill given conditions.
—*n.* **1** an idea or theory resulting from a synthesis of impressions, learned facts, or study, and usually represented in an abstract name; concept: *Freedom, gravity, ego, and electron are constructs.* **2** *Linguistics.* a grammatical construction.
[< Latin *constructus,* past participle of *construere* < *com-* up + *struere* pile, erect] —**con|struct′er,** *n.*

con|struct|i|ble (kən struk′tə bəl), *adj.* that can be constructed.

con|struc|tion (kən struk′shən), *n.* **1** the act of constructing; building: *Construction of the bridge took nearly a month. Construction is not limited to man; beavers have mastered both the science and the art.* **2** the way in which a thing is constructed: *Cracks and leaks are signs of poor construction in a house.* **3** a thing built or put together; structure: *The doll's house was a construction of wood and cardboard.* **SYN**: building. **4** the arrangement or relation of words in a sentence, clause, phrase, or other unit. *Astern* (*a-* + *stern*) is a morphological construction; *toward the stern* is a syntactic construction. *Petrarch ... indulged his fancy by deliberately reviving Latin words and constructions* (H. A. Potter). **5** meaning; interpretation: *He put an unfair construction on what she said because he dislikes her.* **SYN**: explanation. **6** *Art.* a work of constructivism.

con|struc|tion|al (kən struk′shə nəl), *adj.* having to do with construction; structural. —**con|struc′tion|al|ly,** *adv.*

con|struc|tion|ism (kən struck′shə niz əm), *n.* = constructivism.

con|struc|tion|ist (kən struk′shə nist), *n.* **1** a person who gives a certain interpretation to laws, a constitution, or other document: *a strict or loose constructionist.* **2** = constructivist.

construction paper, a heavy paper available in various colors, used for crayon drawings, cutouts, paste-ups, and other display.

con|struc|tive (kən struk′tiv), *adj.* **1** tending to construct; building up; helpful: *During the experiment the teacher gave some constructive suggestions that prevented accidents.* **SYN**: formative, shaping. **2** having to do with construction; structural. **3** not directly expressed; deduced by interpretation; inferred: *constructive malice.* **SYN**: inferential, imputed. —**con|struc′tive|ly,** *adv.* —**con|struc′tive|ness,** *n.*

constructive fraud, fraud based on a deceptive act or statement which leads the victim to a wrong assumption or conclusion: *Constructive fraud includes acts or words that tend to mislead others, as when a man sells his automobile without telling the purchaser that the car will run only a few miles without stalling* (F. E. Inbau).

constructive interference, *Physics.* the condition of the crests of two waves reaching a point at the same time so that they reinforce one another.

con|struc|tiv|ism (kən struk′tə viz əm), *n.* a movement in modern art, originally in painting and later in sculpture and architecture, calling for the use of materials such as glass, wood, paper, and wire, instead of paints, crayons, and the like, and emphasizing the role of art as an instrument for construction. Art in constructivism is typically geometric, massive, and three-dimensional.

con|struc|tiv|ist (kən struk′tə vist), *adj., n.* —*adj.* of or having to do with constructivism; like constructivism: *an architect by profession, and the creator of a huge and rambling piece of constructivist sculpture* (New Yorker).
—*n.* a constructivist painter, sculptor, architect, etc.: *In Moscow, Malevich also was soon experimenting in nonrepresentational painting, with a geometry influenced by cubism, in a course parallel to that of the constructivists, Gabo and Pevsner, in sculpture and in architecture* (Atlantic).

con|struc|tor (kən struk′tər), *n.* a person who constructs; builder.

con|strue (kən strü′; *especially British* kon′strü), *v.,* **-strued, -stru|ing,** *n.* —*v.t.* **1** to show the meaning of; explain; interpret: *Different lawyers may construe the same law differently.* **SYN**: expound. **2** to put a particular interpretation on: *His inability to hold a job can only be construed as indifference.* **SYN**: understand, take. **3** *Grammar.* **a** to analyze the arrangement or relation of words in (a sentence, clause, phrase, or other unit). **b** to combine (words) syntactically: *In Latin some prepositions are construed with the dative case.* **4** = translate. **SYN**: render.
—*v.i.* **1** to analyze grammatical relationships. **2** to admit of grammatical analysis or interpretation.
—*n.* a construing of a sentence, passage, or the like, especially as an exercise in studying a foreign language; translation.
[< Latin *construere;* see etym. under **construct**] —**con|stru′a|ble,** *adj.* —**con|stru′er,** *n.*

con|sub|stan|tial (kon′səb stan′shəl), *adj.* of one and the same substance, essence, or nature. —**con′sub|stan′tial|ly,** *adv.*

con|sub|stan|ti|al|i|ty (kon′səb stan′shē al′ə tē), *n.* identity of substance, especially of the three Persons of the Trinity.

con|sub|stan|ti|ate (kon′səb stan′shē āt), *v.,* **-at|ed, -at|ing.** —*v.i.* **1** to profess the doctrine of consubstantiation. **2** to become united in one common substance or nature.
—*v.t.* to unite in one common substance or nature.

con|sub|stan|ti|a|tion (kon′səb stan′shē ā′shən), *n.* **1** the substantial union of the body and blood of Christ with the bread and wine of the Eucharist. **2** the doctrine that this union occurs.

con|sue|tude (kon′swə tüd, -tyüd), *n.* **1** custom recognized as having legal force. **2** custom; usage; habit. [< Latin *consuētūdo, -inis* < *consuēscere* to accustom < *com-* (intensive) + *suēscere* become accustomed]

con|sue|tu|di|nar|y (kon′swə tü′də ner′ē, -tyü′-), *adj.* = customary.

con|sul (kon′səl), *n.* **1** an official appointed by a government to live in a foreign city. A consul looks after the business interests of his own country and protects citizens of his country who are traveling or living there. **2** either of the two chief magistrates of the ancient Roman republic. **3** one of the three chief magistrates of the French republic from 1799 to 1804. [< Latin *cōnsul* (probably originally) one who consults the senate]

con|su|lar (kon′sə lər), *adj.* **1** of or belonging to a consul: *The ambassadorial conversations will go beyond the consular discussion* (Newsweek). **2** serving as a consul; having the duties of a consul: *the consular representative of the United States at Liverpool.*

consular agent, an official acting as a consul at a place of little commercial importance.

con|su|late (kon′sə lit), *n.* **1** the official residence or the offices of a consul: *The Canadian consulate in New York is on Fifth Avenue.* **2** the duties, authority, and position of a consul. **3** the term of office of a consul. **4** Often, **Consulate.** government by consuls. France was governed by a consulate from 1799 to 1804.

consulate general, *pl.* **consulates general.** the official residence, offices, or jurisdiction of a consul general.

consul general, *pl.* **consuls general.** a consul of the highest rank. He is stationed at an important place or has authority over several other consuls.

con|sul|ship (kon′səl ship), *n.* **1** the duties, authority, and position of a consul. **2** a consul's term of office.

con|sult (*v.* kən sult′; *n.* kon′sult, kən sult′), *v., n.* —*v.t.* **1** to seek information or advice from; refer to: *Consult a dictionary for the meaning of a word. The boy's mother consulted his teacher to learn why his grades were poor.* **2** to take into consideration; have regard for: *A good ruler consults the interests and feelings of his people.* **3** *Obsolete.* to plan; devise; contrive.
—*v.i.* to exchange ideas; talk things over; confer: *He consulted with his lawyer before signing the contract.*
—*n.* consultation.
[< Latin *cōnsultāre* (frequentative) < *cōnsulere* take counsel, consult] —**con|sult′a|ble,** *adj.*
—*Syn. v.i.* **Consult, confer** mean to talk something over with someone in order to make a decision. **Consult** means to talk over something of importance with another or others who are in a position to give wise advice: *She decided to consult with her attorney before buying the property.* **Confer** means to exchange ideas, opinions, or information with another, usually as an equal: *The manager conferred with the committee of employees.*

con|sult|an|cy (kən sul′tən sē), *n., pl.* **-cies.** the work or business of a consultant: *a complete consultancy service to firms who may be faced with increasing development and marketing difficulties* (The Economist).

con|sult|ant (kən sul′tənt), *n.* **1** a person who gives professional or technical advice. **2** a person who consults another.

con|sult|ant|ship (kən sul′tənt ship), *n.* **1** the position of a consultant: *The consultantship ... would not preclude "acceptance of employment elsewhere"* (New York Times). **2** the term of service of a consultant: *It would not be adequate to let* [*his*] *consultantship expire ... on June 30* (Bulletin of Atomic Scientists).

con|sul|ta|tion (kon′səl tā′shən), *n.* **1** the act of consulting; seeking information or advice. **SYN**: deliberation. **2** a meeting to exchange ideas and talk things over: *The three doctors held a consultation to determine the best way to cure the child.* **SYN**: conference.

con|sult|a|tive (kən sul′tə tiv), *adj.* of or having to do with consultation; advisory; deliberative. *a consultative committee.*

con|sult|a|to|ry (kən sul′tə tôr′ē, -tōr′-), *adj.* advisory; consultative.

con|sult|er (kən sul′tər), *n.* a person who consults, or asks counsel or information.

con|sult|ing (kən sul′ting), *adj.* **1** that consults or asks advice. **2** employed in giving professional advice: *a consulting physician, a consulting engineer.*

consulting room, **1** a room in which consultations are held. **2** the room in which a physician examines his patients.

con|sul|tive (kən sul′tiv), *adj.* = consultative.

con|sul|tor (kən sul′tər), *n.* **1** a person who consults; consulter. **2** one of a number of Roman Catholic priests, each representing a diocese, appointed to act as official advisors to a bishop.

con|sum|a|ble (kən sü′mə bəl), *adj., n.* —*adj.* that can be consumed: *to cut down on heavy construction that adds wages but doesn't produce consumable goods until a later date* (Wall Street Journal).
—*n.* a consumable thing.

con|sume (kən süm′), *v.,* **-sumed, -sum|ing.** —*v.t.* **1** to use up; spend: *A student consumes much of his time in studying. He consumed almost all the money he earned last summer.* **SYN**: expend, exhaust. **2** to eat or drink up; devour: *We will each consume at least two sandwiches on our hike.* **3** to destroy; burn up: *A huge fire consumed the entire forest.* **4** *Figurative.* to waste: *Telephoning when you should be studying consumes valuable time.* **SYN**: squander, spend.
—*v.i.* to waste away; be destroyed.
consumed with, absorbed by (curiosity, envy, interest, or other feeling); filled with: *He was consumed with a great interest in stamp collecting. The poor people at the time of the French Revolution were consumed with hatred for the aristocrats.*
[< Latin *cōnsūmere* < *com-* (intensive) + *sūmere* take up]

con|sum|ed|ly (kən sü′mid lē), *adv.* very much; too much: *I long consumedly to see my own country once more.* **SYN**: extremely, hugely.

con|sum|er (kən sü′mər), *n.* **1** a person who uses food, clothing, or anything grown or made by producers: *A low price for wheat should reduce the price of flour for the consumer. Freight means nothing to any consumer of sardines or German toys* (Newsweek). **2** a person or thing that uses up, makes away with, or destroys.

consumer credit, credit given to the consumer while he is in possession and use of an article which he has bought on credit or on an installment plan: *Consumer credit is ... indispensable for the distribution of the more expensive items in the mass-production-mass-consumption equation which underlies the American standard of living* (Harper's).

consumer or **consumers' goods,** *Economics.* goods produced or used to satisfy human wants directly, such as clothing or food.

con|sum|er|ism (kən sü′mə riz əm), *n.* **1** a movement to protect the consumer from unsafe or defectively manufactured products, from misleading labeling, packaging, or promotion practices, and to protect the environment from undue harm: *"Consumerism" involves ... new concepts of corporate responsibility, including protection of the safety and health of citizens and a meaningful choice for consumers in the products they buy* (Ralph Nader). **2** concentration on producing and distributing goods for a market which must constantly be enlarged: *"Consumerism" ... is leading to ... excessive concentration on saleable products, rather than on healthy and happy living* (Julian Huxley). —**con|sum′er|ist,** *n.*

consumer price index, an index compiled by the Bureau of Labor Statistics of the prices paid by consumers for certain specified goods and services in a number of cities during a given month, compared with average prices paid during a specified base period: *The Labor Department announced that the cost of living dropped a tenth of a point on the consumer price index in December* (Time).

consumers' or **consumer cooperative,** *U.S.* a type of rural or suburban cooperative that purchases goods and services mainly for the use of its members: *Consumers' cooperatives market such products as groceries, oil, and gasoline.*

con|sum|er|ship (kən sü′mər ship), *n.* **1** the art or practice of buying: *When salesmanship was local and unscientific, consumership was an ad-*

venturous activity, involving a more or less frivolous exercise of power (New Yorker). **2** ability at buying. **3** consumers as a group.

con|sum|ing (kən sü′ming), *adj.* engrossing; absorbing: *a consuming interest in chess.* **—con·sum′ing|ly,** *adv.*

con|sum|mate (*v.* kon′sə māt; *adj.* kən sum′it), *v.,* **-mat|ed, -mat|ing,** *adj.* **—*v.t.*** **1** to bring to completion; realize; fulfill: *His ambition was consummated when he won the prize.* SYN: accomplish, achieve. **2** to fulfill (the marriage union) with the first act of sexual intercourse. **3** *Obsolete.* to make perfect; perfect.
—*v.i.* to fulfill or perfect itself.
—*adj.* **1** in the highest degree; complete; perfect: *The paintings of great artists show consummate skill.* SYN: supreme, utmost. **2** accomplished; supremely qualified: *a consummate artist. He is a consummate politician who leads by persuasion* (Time).
[< Latin *cōnsummāre* (with English *-ate*[1]) to complete < *com-* (intensive) + *summa* highest degree, total] **—con|sum′mate|ly,** *adv.*

con|sum|mate|ness (kən sum′it nis), *n.* perfection: *consummateness of skill.*

con|sum|ma|tion (kon′sə mā′shən), *n.* completion; fulfillment: *Winning first prize was the consummation of his ambition.*

con|sum|ma|tive (kon′sə mā′tiv), *adj.* able, serving, or tending to consummate.

con|sum|ma|tor (kon′sə mā′tər), *n.* a person that consummates.

con|sum|ma|to|ry (kən sum′ə tôr′ē, -tōr′-), *adj.* that consummates; fulfilling; satisfying: *A consummatory act, such as flight at an alarm call . . . is elicited readily if the animal has not recently made the response* (S. A. Barnett).

con|sump|tion (kən sump′shən), *n.* **1** the act of consuming; using up; use: *We took along some food for our consumption on the trip. The science of economics deals with the production, distribution and consumption of wealth.* **2** the amount used up: *Our consumption of fuel oil increases in cold weather.* **3** a disease that destroys part of the body, especially the lungs; tuberculosis. [< Latin *cōnsumptiō, -ōnis* < *cōnsūmere;* see etym. under **consume**]

consumption goods, = consumer goods.

con|sump|tive (kən sump′tiv), *adj., n.* **—*adj.*** **1** having or likely to have tuberculosis of the lungs. **2** of tuberculosis of the lungs. **3** tending to consume; destructive; wasteful: (*Figurative.*) *To manage such a thing as this in letters was a thing too tedious and consumptive* (Andrew Marvell).
—*n.* a person who has tuberculosis of the lungs.
—con|sump′tive|ly, *adv.* **—con|sump′tive|ness,** *n.*

cont., an abbreviation for the following:
1 containing.
2 contents.
3a continent. **b** continental.
4a continue. **b** continued.
5 contra.
6 contract.
7 control.

con|tact (kon′takt), *n., adj., adv., interj., v.* **—*n.*** **1** the condition of touching; touching together: *To bring fire into contact with gasoline may cause an explosion. A magnet will draw iron filings into contact with it.* SYN: touch. **2a** the condition of being in communication with: *The control tower lost radio contact with the airplane pilot.* **b** a connection: *In college he made contacts with students from many states.* **c** a useful business or social connection: *The insurance salesman tried to make contacts with wealthy people. She has a useful contact in an advertising agency.* **d** a person serving as a liaison: *the chief contact . . . between [atomic scientists] and the army administrators* (Bulletin of Atomic Scientists). **3a** a connection between two conductors of electricity through which a current passes. **b** a device or part for producing such a connection: *The electric light went out when the wire broke off at the contact.* **4** *Medicine.* **a** exposure to a contagious disease. **b** a person who has been exposed to a contagious disease. **5** *Geology.* the surface of the boundary between adjacent rocks. **6** = contact lens.
—*adj.* **1** received on touching: *a contact burn.* **2** occurring on touching: *a contact burst.*
—*adv.* *Aeronautics.* within sight of land or water: *to fly contact.*
—*interj.* *Aeronautics.* the ignition switch is on and the propeller can be turned.
—*v.t.* **1** *Informal.* to get in touch with: *Mother is ill! Contact the doctor immediately!* **2** to put or bring into contact; cause to touch: *An electric arc is struck by contacting the electrodes.*
—*v.i.* to be in contact; establish contact: *If the exposed wires contact, we shall have a short circuit.*
[< Latin *contāctus, -ūs* a touching < *contingere* < *com-* with + *tangere* touch] **—con′tact|less,** *adj.*

contact breaker, a device for automatically breaking, or breaking and making, an electrical circuit.

contact catalysis, catalysis at the surface of a solid catalyst. Contact catalysis takes place when hydrogen and oxygen combine at the surface of powdered platinum to make water.

contact flight, *Aeronautics.* a flight in which land or water is kept in sight as a basis for navigation.

contact flying, *Aeronautics.* navigation by observation of landfalls or water navigation aids, such as buoys.

contact inhibition, *Biology.* cessation of cell division when the surface of one cell comes into contact with the surface of another cell.

contact lens, a very small, thin, plastic lens fitted on the front of the eyeball. It is held in place by the fluid of the eye. Contact lenses take the place of eyeglasses.

contact man, a person serving as a liaison; contact.

contact metamorphism, *Geology.* metamorphism caused by the heat of hot igneous rocks; local metamorphism.

con|tac|tor (kon′tak tər), *n.* = contact breaker.

contact print, a photographic print made by placing the negative in direct contact with sensitized paper or other sensitized surface over a light.

con|tac|tu|al (kon tak′chü əl), *adj.* of or having to do with contact: *Poison ivy is a contactual irritant.* **—con|tac′tu|al|ly,** *adv.*

contact visit, a prison visit during which a prisoner is permitted to have physical contact with his visitors: *Following the ruling Spenkelink was allowed contact visits with his 67-year-old mother . . . and his fiancee* (New York Post).

contact visiting, the act or practice of making a contact visit.

con|ta|gi|a (kən tā′jē ə), *n.* plural of **contagium.**

con|ta|gion (kən tā′jən), *n.* **1** the spreading of disease by direct or indirect contact: *Contagion is hard to prevent in crowded areas.* **2** a disease spread in this way; contagious disease: *The contagion ran all through the dormitories.* **3** the means by which disease is spread. **4** *Figurative.* the spreading of any influence from one person to another: *At the cry of "Fire!" a contagion of fear swept through the audience, causing a panic.* **5** evil influence; moral corruption: *Her mother feared the contagion of drugs.* **6** *Obsolete.* a poison. [< Latin *contāgiō, -ōnis* a touching, related to *contingere;* see etym. under **contact**]

con|ta|gious (kən tā′jəs), *adj.* **1** spreading by direct or indirect contact; catching: *Scarlet fever is a contagious disease. Colds are contagious.* **2** causing contagious disease. SYN: pestilential. **3** *Figurative.* easily spreading from one to another: *Yawning is often contagious.* **—con|ta′gious|ly,** *adv.* **—con|ta′gious|ness,** *n.*

contagious abortion, Bang's disease; brucellosis in cattle.

contagious magic, magic based on the belief that things once in contact continue to act on each other after the contact is broken.

con|ta|gi|um (kən tā′jē əm), *n., pl.* **-gi|a.** = contagion.

con|tain (kən tān′), *v.t.* **1** to have within itself; hold as contents; include: *My purse contains money. A library contains books. Books contain information.* **2** to be capable of holding: *This pitcher will contain a quart of milk.* **3** to be equal to: *A pound contains 16 ounces.* SYN: comprise. **4** to control; hold back; restrain (one's feelings): *She could not contain her anger when he kicked her dog.* **5** *Military.* to control or restrain (enemy forces) by stopping, holding, or surrounding: *The British fleet under Admiral Nelson contained Napoleon's ships at Trafalgar.* **6** to be capable of being divided by (a number) without a remainder: *12 contains 2, 3, 4, and 6.* **—*v.i.*** to restrain oneself or one's feelings: *He could contain no longer, but hasting home, invaded his territories, and professed open war* (Robert Burton). [< Old French *contenir* < Latin *continēre* < *com-* together + *tenēre* hold] **—con|tain′a|ble,** *adj.*
—*Syn.* *v.t.* **1, 2 Contain, hold, accommodate** mean to have within itself or be capable of having and keeping. **Contain** emphasizes the idea of actually having something within itself as contents or parts: *The house contains five rooms. The new edition contains several maps and charts.* **Hold,** although often used interchangeably with *contain,* suggests being capable of containing: *This carton holds one dozen eggs. A paper bag won't hold water.* **Accommodate** means to hold conveniently or comfortably: *Most hotel rooms accommodate two people. The new garage accommodates fifty cars.*

con|tain|er (kən tā′nər), *n.* **1** a box, can, jar, or carton used to hold or contain something. A pitcher is a container. **2** the amount that a container can hold. **3** a person or thing that contains; holder.

container board, a thin but strong board, processed from wood fibers, for making paper cartons or boxes.

container car, a railroad flatcar or gondola freight car fitted to carry large metal containers, used for transportation of drugs, medical supplies, chemicals, and other material in bulk shipments.

con|tain|er|ize (kən tā′nə rīz), *v.t.,* **-ized, -iz|ing.** to ship (cargo) in very large, separate containers. **—con|tain′er|iz′a|ble,** *adj.* **—con|tain′er|i|za′tion,** *n.*

***container ship,** a ship specially designed to carry containerized cargo.

***container ship**

container shipping, the shipping of cargo in very large, separate containers.

con|tain|ment (kən tān′mənt), *n.* **1** the act or fact of containing: *. . . the only known method of containment is with a strong magnetic field* (Richard A. Ferrell). **2** the confinement of an unfriendly political or military force within existing geographical boundaries.

con|ta|ki|on (kən tä′kē on; *Greek* kôn tä′kyôn), *n.* = kontakion.

con|tam|i|nant (kən tam′ə nənt), *n.* a thing that contaminates or spreads contamination: *to seal off the surface from grease and other contaminants* (New Scientist). SYN: pollutant.

con|tam|i|nate (*v.* kən tam′ə nāt; *adj.* kən tam′ə nāt, -nit), *v.,* **-nat|ed, -nat|ing,** *adj.* **—*v.t.*** to make impure by contact; defile; pollute: *Filth from the swarming flies contaminated the milk. Drinking water is contaminated when sewage seeps into the water supply.* SYN: taint, infect, sully.
—*adj.* *Archaic.* contaminated; defiled; sullied.
[< Latin *contāmināre* (with English *-ate*[1]) < *contāmen, -inis* contamination < *com-* + *tag-,* root of *tangere* touch]

con|tam|i|na|tion (kən tam′ə nā′shən), *n.* **1** a contaminating or being contaminated; pollution: *Milk should be kept covered to avoid contamination.* SYN: taint, defilement. **2** a thing that contaminates; an impurity.

con|tam|i|na|tive (kən tam′ə nā′tiv), *adj.* tending to defile; causing contamination.

con|tam|i|na|tor (kən tam′ə nā′tər), *n.* a person or thing that contaminates.

con|tan|go (kən tang′gō), *n., pl.* **-gos.** *British.* the premium paid to postpone payment for a stock to a later date. [coined < *continue*]

contd., continued.

con|te[1] (kōn′tā), *n. Italian.* a count.

conte[2] (kônt), *n., pl.* **contes** (kônts; *French* kônt). a short story or tale, especially of extraordinary and highly imaginative events: *a complete, even a poetic, understanding of the ironic conte* (London Times). [< French *conte* < *conter* narrate]

con|temn (kən tem′), *v.t.* to treat with contempt; value very little; despise; scorn: *The brave soldier contemned the heavy odds against him.* SYN: disdain, slight. [< Latin *contemnere* < *com-* (intensive) + *temnere* disdain]

con|temn|er or **con|tem|nor** (kən tem′ər, -tem′nər), *n.* a person who contemns.

con|tem|per (kən tem′pər), *v.t. Rare.* to temper; blend; modify; adjust. [< Latin *contemperāre* < *com-* with + *temperāre* temper]

con|tem|pla|ble (kən tem′plə bəl), *adj.* that can be contemplated.

con|tem|plate (kon′təm plāt), *v.,* **-plat|ed, -plat|ing.** **—*v.t.*** **1** to think about for a long time; study carefully: *I will contemplate your proposal. The old man contemplated the past with a feeling of longing and regret.* SYN: ponder. **2** to look at for a long time; gaze at: *The afternoon raced by as he contemplated the waves at the seashore.* SYN:

Pronunciation Key: hat, āge, cãre, fär; let, ēqual, tėrm; it, īce; hot, ōpen, ôrder; oil, out; cup, pu̇t, rüle; child; long; thin; ᴛʜen; zh, measure; ə represents **a** in about, **e** in taken, **i** in pencil, **o** in lemon, **u** in circus.

survey, regard. **3** to have in mind; consider, intend, or expect: *She is contemplating a trip to Europe.* **SYN**: consider, plan.

— ***v.i.*** to be absorbed in contemplation; meditate: *All day he did nothing but contemplate.* **SYN**: muse, reflect, think.

[< Latin *contemplārī* (with English *-ate*[1]) survey, observe (an augury) < *com-* + *templum* (originally) a restricted area marked off for the taking of auguries] — **con′tem|pla′tor**, *n.*

con|tem|pla|tion (kon′tәm plā′shәn), *n.* **1** the act of looking at or thinking about something for a long time: *From contemplation one can become wise* (A. Edward Newton). **2** deep thought; meditation: *He was sunk in contemplation and did not hear the doorbell.* **SYN**: reverie, musing. **3** expectation or intention: *We are buying tents and other equipment in contemplation of a camping trip this summer.* **SYN**: prospect.

con|tem|pla|tive (kon′tәm plā′tiv, kәn tem′plә-), *adj., n.* — ***adj.*** **1** deeply thoughtful; meditative: *After the play, he sat in a contemplative mood. Scholars enjoy a contemplative life.* **SYN**: pensive, reflective. **2** devoted to religious meditation, prayer, or study: *The monks lived a quiet, contemplative life in the monastery.*

— ***n.*** a person who leads a contemplative life, especially a monk or a nun: *We reserve our admiration, on the whole, not for talkers or dreamers or contemplatives, but for those ... who deliver tangible benefits to mankind* (Harper's). **SYN**: thinker. — **con′tem|pla′tive|ly**, *adv.* — **con′tem|pla′tive|ness**, *n.*

con|tem|po|ra|ne|i|ty (kәn tem′pәr ә nē′ә tē), *n.* the state or fact of being contemporaneous; contemporaneousness: *The Israelis surprised me principally by the variety of their work and the contemporaneity of their outlook* (New Yorker).

con|tem|po|ra|ne|ous (kәn tem′pә rā′nē әs), *adj.* belonging to the same period of time; contemporary: *The lives of Thomas Jefferson and John Adams were contemporaneous. The development of the airplane was contemporaneous with that of the automobile.* **SYN**: coeval. [< Latin *contemporāneus* (with English *-ous*) < *com-* with + *tempus, -oris* time] — **con|tem′po|ra′ne|ous|ly**, *adv.* — **con|tem′po|ra′ne|ous|ness**, *n.*

con|tem|po|rar|y (kәn tem′pә rer′ē), *adj., n., pl.* **-rar|ies**. — ***adj.*** **1** belonging to the same period of time: *The telephone and the phonograph were contemporary inventions. Bach and Handel were contemporary composers.* **SYN**: coexistent. **2** of the same age or date: *A neighbouring wood, born with himself, he sees, And loves his old contemporary trees* (Abraham Cowley). **SYN**: coeval, connate. **3** of or having to do with the present time; modern: *Our teacher reads the books of many contemporary authors to us.*

— ***n.*** **1** a person who belongs to the same period of time: *Abraham Lincoln and Robert E. Lee were contemporaries. We all tend to seek the society of our contemporaries.* **SYN**: coeval. **2** a person or thing of the same age or date.

[< *con-* together + Latin *temporārius* belonging to the time, timely < *tempus, -oris* time] — **con|tem′po|rar′i|ly**, *adv.* — **con|tem′po|rar′i|ness**, *n.*

Con|tem|po|rar|y (kәn tem′pә rer′ē), *adj., n.*

— ***adj.*** of or designating a style of furniture or architecture marked by streamlined and functional design.

— ***n.*** this style.

con|tem|po|rize (kәn tem′pә rīz), *v.*, **-rized**, **-riz|ing**. — ***v.t.*** to make contemporary: *Mr. Carlyle has this power of contemporizing himself with bygone times* (James Russell Lowell).

— ***v.i.*** to become contemporary.

con|tempt (kәn tempt′), *n.* **1** the feeling that a person or act is mean and low; despising; scorn: *Most people feel contempt for a cheat.* **SYN**: disdain. See syn. under **scorn**. **2** the condition of being scorned or despised; disgrace: *A traitor is held in contempt.* **3** disobedience to or open disrespect for the rules or decisions of a law court or a lawmaking body. A person can be fined or imprisoned for contempt. See also **contempt of court**. [< Latin *contemptus, -ūs* < *contemnere;* see etym. under **contemn**]

con|tempt|i|bil|i|ty (kәn temp′tә bil′ә tē), *n.* **1** the quality or state of being contemptible; contemptibleness. **2** *Obsolete.* contemptuousness.

con|tempt|i|ble (kәn temp′tә bәl), *adj.* **1** deserving contempt or scorn; held in contempt; mean; low: *a contemptible lie. Cowards and cheats are contemptible people.* **SYN**: worthless, despicable. **2** *Obsolete.* full of contempt; scornful. — **con|tempt′i|ble|ness**, *n.* — **con|tempt′i|bly**, *adv.*

▶ See **contemptuous** for usage note.

contempt of court, disobedience to or open disrespect for the rules or decisions of a law court; contempt.

con|temp|tu|ous (kәn temp′chu̇ әs), *adj.* showing contempt; scornful: *a contemptuous toss of the head. The police dog gave the kitten a contemptuous look.* **SYN**: disdainful. — **con|temp′tu|ous|ly**, *adv.* — **con|temp′tu|ous|ness**, *n.*

▶ **Contemptuous** and **contemptible** are sometimes confused. The distinction will be clear if one observes that in *contemptible* the suffix *-ible* means "deserving."

con|tend (kәn tend′), *v.i.* **1** to work hard against difficulties; fight; struggle: *The first settlers in America had to contend with unfriendly Indians, sickness, and lack of food. Farmers in the 1930's had to contend against drought and dust.* **SYN**: cope, wrestle, combat, battle. **2** to take part in a contest; compete; vie: *Five runners were contending in the first race. Billows wild contend, with angry roar* (Harriet Beecher Stowe). **3** to argue; dispute: *The sisters contended about silly trifles.* **SYN**: wrangle. — ***v.t.*** **1** to declare to be true: *Columbus contended that the earth was round.* **SYN**: affirm, assert, maintain. **2** *Obsolete.* to contest; dispute (an object): *When Carthage shall contend the world with Rome* (John Dryden). [< Latin *contendere* exert oneself, strain, strive < *com-* (intensive) + *tendere* stretch]

— ***Syn.*** *v.i.* **2 Contend, compete** mean to take part in a contest for something. **Contend** suggests struggling against opposition: *Our football team is contending for the championship.* **Compete** emphasizes the rivalry involved and the prize to be won: *Two boys are competing for the cup.*

con|tend|er (kәn ten′dәr), *n.* a person who contends; combatant; rival; competitor: *a contender for the boxing championship, the leading contenders in the electoral race.*

con|tent[1] (kon′tent), *n.* **1** Often, **contents**. what is contained in anything; all things inside: *An old chair, a desk, and a bed were the only contents of the room. No man understands a deep book until he has seen and lived at least part of its contents* (Ezra Pound). **2** what is written in a book or said in a speech; facts and ideas stated; meaning: *I didn't understand the content of his speech. The great mass of literature ... is valued because of its intellectual content* (Thomas H. Huxley). **3** the amount contained; volume: *The content of these apple boxes is below standard requirements.* **4** the power of containing; capacity: *The content of the gas tank of this car is 17 gallons.* **5** the amount of a certain substance contained in anything: *the sulfur content of petroleum. Cottage cheese has a high protein content.* **6** size; extent; area, especially the amount of cubic space taken up: *The usual scrub pail has a content of about two and one half gallons.* **7** the subject matter or range of any field of study: *the content of our mathematics course.* [< Latin *contentum,* neuter past participle of *continēre;* see etym. under **contain**]

▶ **content, contents.** *Content* is the more abstract: *the content of the course,* and is used when specifying the amount of an ingredient: *the moisture content. Contents* is the more concrete: *the contents of the box.*

con|tent[2] (kәn tent′), *v., adj., n.* — ***v.t.*** to make easy in mind; satisfy; please: *Will it content you if I let you have the candy tomorrow? Nothing contents that grumbling man.* **SYN**: gratify, appease. See syn. under **satisfy**.

— ***adj.*** **1** satisfied; pleased; easy in mind; contented: *Will you be content to wait till tomorrow? Be well content as the years wear through* (Algernon Charles Swinburne). **2** willing; ready: *He is content to live and let live. I am not content to accept poor workmanship.* **3** *British.* voting in the affirmative; assenting.

— ***n.*** **1** contentment; satisfaction; ease of mind: *The cat lay stretched out beside the fire in sleepy content.* **SYN**: gratification. **2** *British.* **a** an affirmative vote in the House of Lords. **b** a member that votes affirmatively. **3** *Obsolete.* a source of contentment.

content oneself, to be contented: *He contented himself with winning third prize. Most men when they should labour, content themselves to complain* (Samuel Johnson).

cry content with, to be satisfied with: *It is notable that most of the old hands in turf strategy have cried content with their various horses* (London Daily Mail).

to one's heart's content. See under **heart**.

[< Medieval Latin *contentare* < Latin *continēre;* see etym. under **contain**]

con|tent-ad|dress|a|ble (kon′tәnt ә dres′ә bәl), *adj.* having to do with or designating a type of computer memory to which access is determined by presenting to it any word contained in the data being sought: *At the heart of this computer is an associative or content-addressable memory* (New Scientist).

content analysis, an analysis of the content of a newspaper, book, speech, or other communication, obtained by counting the relative frequencies of certain selected elements, such as semantic categories, ideas, or grammatical forms: *Content analysis has been especially adopted by the sociologist ... It is essentially a device for achieving ... objectivity in the analysis of documentary evidence* (Anthony H. Richmond).

con|tent|ed (kәn ten′tid), *adj.* satisfied; pleased; easy in mind: *A contented person is happy with what he has. When men are employed they are best contented* (Benjamin Franklin). — **con|tent′ed|ly**, *adv.* — **con|tent′ed|ness**, *n.*

con|ten|tion (kәn ten′shәn), *n.* **1** a statement or point that one has argued for; statement maintained as true: *Columbus's contention that the earth was round turned out to be correct.* **2** an arguing; disputing; quarreling: *There was some contention about choosing a captain for the baseball team.* **3** an argument; dispute; quarrel. **SYN**: disagreement, wrangle, altercation. **4** a struggle; contest: *The rival teams were in contention for the championship.* **SYN**: competition. [< Latin *contentiō, -ōnis* < *contendere;* see etym. under **contend**]

con|ten|tious (kәn ten′shәs), *adj.* **1** fond of arguing; given to disputing; quarrelsome: *A contentious person argues and disputes about trifles.* **SYN**: disputatious, captious, pugnacious. **2** characterized by contention: *a contentious campaign, contentious issues, contentious boldness.* **3** *Law.* of or having to do with differences between contending parties. — **con|ten′tious|ly**, *adv.* — **con|ten′tious|ness**, *n.*

con|tent|ment (kәn tent′mәnt), *n.* **1** satisfaction; being pleased; ease of mind; happiness: *The noblest mind the best contentment has* (Edmund Spenser). **SYN**: contentedness. **2** *Archaic.* the act of satisfying or the state of being satisfied.

con|tents (kon′tents), *n.pl.* **1** what is contained in anything; all things inside. **2** what is written in a book; what is said in a speech: *The table of contents of a book or magazine contains a list of chapter headings, titles, etc.*

▶ See **content**[1] for usage note.

con|ter|mi|nal (kәn tėr′mә nәl), *adj.* = conterminous.

con|ter|mi|nous (kәn tėr′mә nәs), *adj.* **1** having a common boundary; bordering; meeting at their ends: *Defending the side of Germany conterminous to France* (William E. H. Lecky). **SYN**: contiguous. **2** having the same boundaries or limits; coextensive in space, time, etc.: *The terms of office of the President and his chief advisor were conterminous.* Also, **coterminous**. [< Latin *conterminus* (with English *-ous*) < *com-* with + *terminus* boundary] — **con|ter′mi|nous|ly**, *adv.*

— **con|ter′mi|nous|ness**, *n.*

con|tes|sa (kôn tās′sä), *n., pl.* **-se** (-sā). *Italian.* a countess.

con|test (*n.* kon′test; *v.* kәn test′), *n., v.* — ***n.*** **1** a trial of skill to see which can win. A game or race is a contest. **SYN**: competition. **2** a fight or struggle: *The contest between France and England for North America ended in victory for England. What mighty contests rise from trivial things* (John Dryden). **SYN**: conflict, strife, contention. **3** an argument; dispute. **SYN**: controversy, disagreement. [< the verb]

— ***v.t.*** **1** to fight for; struggle for: *The soldiers contested every inch of ground. The blackbirds contested one another for nesting territory.* **2** to argue against; dispute about: *The lawyer contested the claim, and tried to prove that it was false.* **SYN**: challenge. **3** to call in question; controvert: *to contest an election or a will.* — ***v.i.*** to try to win.

[< Middle French *contester,* learned borrowing from Latin *contestārī* call to witness < *com-* (intensive) + *testis* witness] — **con|test′a|ble**, *adj.*

— **con|test′er**, *n.*

con|test|ant (kәn tes′tәnt), *n.* **1** a person who contests; a person who takes part in a contest: *The brothers were contestants in the race.* **2** a person who contests election returns, a will, a judgment, or other decision or question.

con|tes|ta|tion (kon′tes tā′shәn), *n.* **1** the act of contesting; contention. **2** disputation; controversy; conflict. **3** competition; rivalry.

con|test|ee (kon′tes tē′), *n.* *U.S.* a candidate whose election is contested by another.

con|text (kon′tekst), *n.* **1** the parts directly before and after a word or sentence that influence its meaning. You can often tell the meaning of a word from its context. **2** *Figurative.* the immediate environment; attendant circumstances or conditions; background: *The negotiations ... should ... be regarded within the context of this new situation* (New York Times). [< Latin *contextus, -ūs* < *contexere* < *com-* together + *texere* weave]

con|tex|tu|al (kәn teks′chu̇ әl), *adj.* **1** having to do with the context; depending on the context: *The contextual meaning of a word is the special meaning it has in a sentence.* **2** having to do with earlier conditions or events that help to explain something. **—con|tex′tu|al|ly,** *adv.*

con|tex|tu|al|ism (kən teks′chü ə liz əm), *n.* **1** *Philosophy.* the doctrine that statements or ideas have no useful meaning outside the context in which they appear. **2** *Architecture.* the principle that a structure should fit naturally into its surroundings. **—con|tex′tu|al|ist,** *n.*

con|tex|tu|al|ize (kən teks′chü ə līz), *v.t.,* **-ized, -iz|ing.** to place in context, especially one that is appropriate: *An album so well contextualized that it stands solidly on its own as a fabulous musical experience* (Saturday Review).

con|tex|ture (kən teks′chər), *n.* **1** a weaving together or a being woven together; texture. **2** something woven together; fabric. **3** *Figurative.* the make-up and arrangement of the parts of a thing; structure: *View his whole life; 'tis nothing but a cunning contexture of dark arts and unequitable subterfuges* (Laurence Sterne).

con|tig|na|tion (kon′tig nā′shən), *n. Archaic.* **1a** joining together of beams, boards, etc. **b** the way in which they are joined together. **2** a floor or stage; framework. [< Latin *contignātiō, -ōnis* < *contignāre* join with beams or sticks < *com-* with + *tignum* building material]

con|ti|gu|i|ty (kon′tə gyü′ə tē), *n., pl.* **-ties. 1** a being very close together; nearness: *The contiguity of the house and garage was a convenience in bad weather.* **SYN:** proximity, adjacency. **2** contact: *The candidate's contiguity with the common people served him well.* **3** a continuous mass; unbroken stretch: *contiguity of mountain scenery.*

con|tig|u|ous (kən tig′yü əs), *adj.* **1** in actual contact; touching: *A fence showed where the two farms were contiguous.* **2** *Geometry.* adjoining: *Two contiguous angles are next to each other.* **3** very close together; near; neighboring. [< Latin *contiguus* (with English *-ous*) < *com-* + *tag-,* root of *tangere* touch. See related etym. at **contingent, contagion, contact.**] **—con|tig′u|ous|ly,** *adv.* **—con|tig′u|ous|ness,** *n.*

con|ti|nence (kon′tə nəns), *n.* **1** control of one's actions and feelings; self-restraint; moderation: *The ancient Greeks advised continence in all things.* **SYN:** self-control. **2** self-restraint or complete abstinence in sexual matters; chastity.

con|ti|nen|cy (kon′tə nən sē), *n., pl.* **-cies.** = continence.

con|ti|nent¹ (kon′tə nənt), *n., adj.* **—*n.*** **1** one of the seven great masses of land on the earth. The continents are North America, South America, Europe, Africa, Asia, Australia, and Antarctica. *The deep oceans and the continents are different in their geological structure* (Gaskell and Hill). **2** the mainland of any maritime country, as distinguished from islands or peninsulas. **3** an area of mountains or plateau on the moon. It appears as a light-colored surface. *Over the lunar "continents" (or uplands) the gamma-ray intensity is 1.15 to 1.2 times higher than over the lunar maria* (New Scientist).
—*adj.* *Obsolete.* continuous; connected.
the Continent, the mainland of Europe, as distinguished from the British Isles: *A policy of detente with east Europe ... would allow for a settlement of the basic issues dividing the Continent* (London Times).
[< Latin *continēns, -entis,* short for *terra continēns* continuous land; see etym. at **continent²**]

con|ti|nent² (kon′tə nənt), *adj., n.* **—*adj.*** **1** having control of one's actions and feelings; using self-restraint; temperate: *a continent, persisting, immovable person* (Emerson). **2** characterized by self-restraint or complete abstinence in sexual matters; chaste: *My past life Hath been as continent, as chaste, as true, As I am now unhappy* (Shakespeare). **3** *Obsolete.* capable of holding; capacious. **4** *Obsolete.* restraining; restrictive.
—*n.* *Archaic.* **1** a thing that holds or contains; vessel. **2** something that comprises or sums up; epitome. [< Latin *continēns, -entis,* present participle of *continēre;* see etym. under **contain**] **—con′ti|nent|ly,** *adv.*

con|ti|nen|tal (kon′tə nen′təl), *adj., n.* **—*adj.*** **1a** of or belonging to a continent or mainland: *continental China. They are all deliverable almost anywhere in the continental United States* (New York Times). **b** characteristic of a continent; like that of a continent: *A branched crack that encircles the globe ... divides continental crust on one side from oceanic crust on the other* (Science Journal). **2a** having the range of a continent; *a continental missile.* **b** serving continental flights or aircraft: *continental airport.*
—*n.* **1** an inhabitant of a continent. **2** a piece of American paper money issued by the Continental Congress during the American Revolution, considered almost worthless by the time the war was over. **3** = continental stitch.
give a continental, *Informal.* to care at all: *He didn't give a continental for anybody* (Mark Twain).
not worth a continental, *Informal.* worthless: *That clock you sold me ain't worth a continental* (New York Knickerbocker).

Con|ti|nen|tal (kon′tə nen′təl), *adj., n.* **—*adj.*** **1** belonging to or characteristic of the mainland of Europe; of or like that of the Continent: *Continental customs differ from those of England.* **2** of or having to do with the American colonies at the time of the American Revolution: *the Continental army.* See also **Continental Congress.**
—*n.* **1** a person living on the Continent; European. **2** a soldier of the American army during the American Revolution.

continental bed, *Canadian.* a bed without a headboard or footboard.

continental block, a block of the earth's crust consisting of a continent and its continental shelf; continental mass: *Forces in the ocean floor slowly move to squeeze the sediment and cement it against the continental block* (Science News Letter).

Continental breakfast, a light breakfast, usually of buttered rolls or toast with coffee.

Continental Celtic, Gaulish, as opposed to the Celtic language of the British Isles.

continental code, a modification of the Morse code in which eleven letters differ; continental Morse code; international code.

Continental Congress, 1 either of two legislative assemblies of the American colonies from 1774 to 1781. The Second Continental Congress adopted the Declaration of Independence in 1776. **2** the American legislative assembly under the Articles of Confederation, from 1781 to 1789.

Continental Divide, 1 the ridge in western North America which separates streams flowing toward the Pacific from those flowing toward the Atlantic or the Arctic; Great Divide. The Rocky Mountains form a major part of the Continental Divide. **2** Often, **continental divide.** the line that separates streams flowing to opposite sides of any continent.

***continental drift,** *Geology.* the slow movement of the earth's land masses, thought to be caused by pressure that shifts them over the underlying molten material: *A softening or a heating-up [of] Earth could possibly provide the elusive mechanism for continental drift* (New Scientist).

***continental drift**

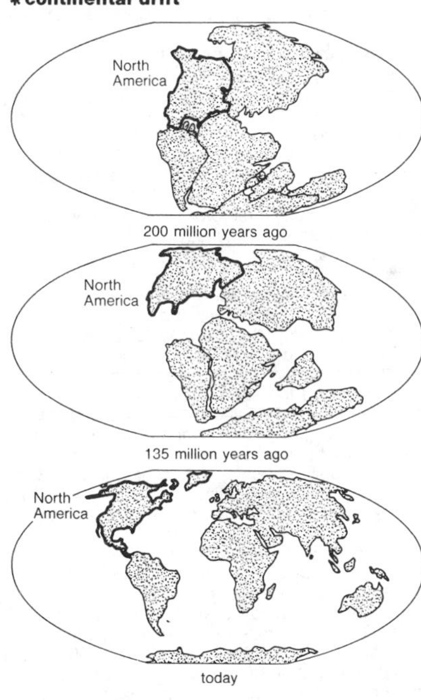

200 million years ago

135 million years ago

today

continental glacier, a sheet of ice that covers a large part of a continent, such as that which covers Greenland.

continental island, an island that is part of a continent, usually separated from it by a stretch of water: *The hills and plateaus of the continental shelf ... project above sea level and constitute the continental islands, such as Nantucket ... and Long Island* (White and Renner).

con|ti|nen|tal|ism (kon′tə nen′tə liz əm), *n.* **1** an expression, opinion, procedure, or other mannerism characteristic of the Continent (of Europe): *It was all a part of the new continentalism* (Punch). **2** the characteristics of a continental land mass as distinguished from those of maritime areas: *Inland, it fades rapidly as the shoreline is left behind and the forces of continentalism are encountered* (White and Renner).

con|ti|nen|tal|ist (kon′tə nen′tə list), *n.* an advocate of cooperation, union, or mutual aid between nations of the same continent especially the Continent (of Europe)

con|ti|nen|tal|i|ty (kon′tə nen tal′ə tē), *n.* **1** the condition of being continental: *Russia may be regarded as the epitome of continentality* (White and Renner). **2** *Meteorology.* the characteristics possessed by a continental climate: *He lays stress on the distribution of land and water within the zones; climate is greatly affected by continentality and oceanity* (Nature).

con|ti|nen|tal|ize (kon′tə nen′tə līz), *v.t.,* **-ized, -iz|ing.** to make continental; extend over a continent or the Continent: *In the Rio treaty we formally continentalized the defensive aspects of the Monroe Doctrine* (Harper's). **—con′ti|nen′tal|i|za′tion,** *n.*

con|ti|nen|tal|ly (kon′tə nen′tə lē), *adv.* **1** in a continental manner, in relation to a continent. **2** *Figurative.* with a wide view; broadly: *They are the men who think continentally* (Alexander Hamilton).

continental mass, = continental block.

continental Morse code, = continental code.

continental platform, the solid platform of a continent, including the continental terrace and surrounded by the ocean basins: *Many river channels, notably those of the Congo and Indus, continue right into the ocean as steep-walled canyons that cut across the continental platform* (New York Times).

continental shelf, the relatively shallow portion of seabed bordering most continents, usually not more than 100 fathoms deep, and ending in a slope which descends steeply to deeper water.

continental slope, the slope beyond a continental shelf.

continental stitch, a firm and durable needlepoint stitch used to fill in background.

continental terrace, the continental shelf and the continental slope together: *The continental terrace ... at its seaward edge ... pitches steeply into the deep ocean basin* (Scientific American).

con|tin|gence (kən tin′jəns), *n.* **1** a touching; contact. **2** = contingency.

con|tin|gen|cy (kən tin′jən sē), *n., pl.* **-cies. 1** a happening or event depending on something that is uncertain; possibility: *The explorer carried supplies for every contingency.* **2** an accidental happening; uncertain event; chance: *Football players seldom think of injury as a contingency while they are playing.* **3** uncertainty of occurrence; dependence on chance. **4** *Philosophy.* **a** the mode of existence, or of coming to pass, which does not involve necessity. **b** a happening by chance or free will. **5** something incidental to something else.

contingency fund, a fund or appropriation reserved for contingencies: *The budget includes a $500 million defense contingency fund, to be spent as the President sees fit* (Time).

contingency table, a statistical table showing the frequency distribution of groups classified according to two (or more) characteristics.

con|tin|gent (kən tin′jənt), *n., adj.* **—*n.*** **1** a share of soldiers, laborers, or other persons furnished to a force from different sources: *The United States sent a large contingent of troops to Europe in World War II.* **2** a group that is a part of a larger group: *The New York contingent had seats together at the national convention.* **3** something accidental or unexpected. **4** a portion or share assigned; allotment: *The young heir's contingent of the estate was smaller than he had hoped for.*
—*adj.* **1** depending on something uncertain; conditional: *Our plans for a picnic are contingent upon fair weather.* **2** liable to happen or not to happen; possible; uncertain: *The traveler set aside five dollars a day for contingent expenses.* **3** happening by chance; accidental; unexpected: *If they had no contingent meeting, he determined to plan one.* **4** *Logic.* accidentally existing or true; not existing or occurring through necessity: *All statements about "human nature" are contingent upon the meaning of "human" and "nature."* **5** *Law.* dependent on events or circumstances that may occur. **6** *Accounting.* depending on or for use in the event of unforeseeable or uncertain circumstances: *a contingent fund.*
[< Latin *contingēns, -entis* touching (on the sides), present participle of *contingere;* see etym. under **contact**] **—con|tin′gent|ly,** *adv.* **—con|tin′gent|ness,** *n.*

contingent liability, a potential liability, such as

Pronunciation Key: hat, āge, cãre, fär; let, ēqual, tėrm; it, īce; hot, ōpen, ôrder; **oi**l, **ou**t; cup, pu̇t, rüle; **ch**ild; lo**ng**; **th**in; **ᴛʜ**en; **zh,** measure; **ə** represents **a** in about, **e** in taken, **i** in pencil, **o** in lemon, **u** in circus.

that accepted by the comaker of a note.

con|tin|u|a (kən tin′yů ə), *n.* plural of **continuum**.

con|tin|u|al (kən tin′yů əl), *adj.* **1** never stopping: *the continual wash of the tides.* **2** repeated many times; very frequent: *No one likes continual interruptions while reading.* —**con|tin′u|al|ness**, *n.*

▶**Continual** and **continuous** are not exact synonyms. *Continual* emphasizes recurrence at regular or frequent intervals: *Dancing requires continual practice. Continuous* means extending uninterruptedly in space or time: *a continuous procession of cars.*

con|tin|u|al|ly (kən tin′yů ə lē), *adv.* **1** always; without stopping: *A doctor is continually on call.* **2** again and again; very frequently: *She is continually losing things.*

con|tin|u|ance (kən tin′yů əns), *n.* **1** a continuing; going on: *There was a continuance of work in spite of the cold weather.* SYN: lasting. **2** the act of remaining; stay: *His continuance in school depends on his health. A public official is paid during his continuance in office.* **3** the time during which anything lasts; duration. **4** a continuation; sequel: *the continuance of a story.* **5** adjournment or postponement of legal proceedings until a future time. [< Old French *continuance* < *continuant,* present participle of *continuer* continue, learned borrowing from Latin *continuāre*]

con|tin|u|ant (kən tin′yů ənt), *n. Phonetics.* a prolongable sound, especially a consonant, such as *f* or *z.*

con|tin|u|ate (kən tin′yů it, -āt), *adj. Obsolete.* continuous; uninterrupted; lasting.

con|tin|u|a|tion (kən tin′yů ā′shən), *n.* **1** the act of going on with a thing after stopping; a beginning again: *Continuation of my work was hard after I had been ill for a month.* SYN: resumption. **2** anything by which a thing is continued; added part: *The continuation of the story will appear in next month's magazine.* SYN: sequel, supplement. **3** the act or fact of not stopping. **4** *British.* (on the stock exchange) the carrying over of an account until the next settling day.

continuation school, **1** a school for people who have left elementary school or high school to go to work. It is held in the evening or during special hours in the day. **2** (in Ontario, Canada) a small secondary school.

con|tin|u|a|tive (kən tin′yů ā′tiv), *adj., n.* —*adj.* **1** tending or serving to continue. **2** *Grammar.* expressing continuance of a thought.
—*n.* **1** something continuative. **2** *Grammar.* a continuative word or expression: *A dependent clause is a continuative.* —**con|tin′u|a′tive|ly**, *adv.* —**con|tin′u|a′tive|ness**, *n.*

con|tin|u|a|tor (kən tin′yů ā′tər), *n.* a person who continues something.

con|tin|ue (kən tin′yü), *v.,* **-tin|ued, -tin|u|ing.** —*v.i.* **1** to go on; keep up; keep on; not stop: *The road continues for miles. The rain continued all day.* SYN: extend. **2** to go on after stopping: *The class begged the teacher to continue with the reading.* SYN: resume. **3** to last; endure: *The king's reign continued for 20 years.* SYN: persist. See syn. under **last**. **4** to stay; remain: *The children must continue in school till the end of June.* **5** to remain in a certain way: *He continues happy. Greece continues to be an important country with respect to merchant shipping.*
—*v.t.* **1** to go on with; keep on; keep up: *We continued our efforts to raise money for the hospital.* SYN: prolong. **2** to extend in space: *The farmer continued his fence from the pasture to the highway.* **3** to take up; carry on; go on with after stopping; begin again: *He ate lunch and then continued his work. The story will be continued in next month's magazine.* SYN: resume, renew. **4** to cause to last; prolong; maintain: *She continued the family tradition by going to law school.* **5** to cause to stay; retain: *The people continued the president in office for another term.* **6** to put off until a later time; postpone; adjourn: *The judge continued the case until next month.*
[< Old French *continuer,* learned borrowing from Latin *continuāre* < *continuus* < *continēre* hold together; see etym. under **contain**] —**con|tin′u|a|ble**, *adj.*

con|tin|ued fraction (kən tin′yüd), a fraction whose numerator is a whole number and whose denominator is a whole number plus a fraction which has a denominator composed of a whole number plus a fraction, and so on.

con|tin|u|ing (kən tin′yů ing), *adj.* **1** persistent; continuous: *Continuing population growth places a premium on capital* (Wall Street Journal). **2** enduring: *For here have we no continuing city* (Hebrews 13:14).

con|ti|nu|i|ty (kon′tə nü′ə tē, -nyü′-), *n., pl.* **-ties.** **1** the condition or quality of being continuous: *The continuity of his story was broken when the telephone rang. Unfortunately, no questions from the audience broke the continuity of his harangue.* **2** a continuous or connected whole; unbroken series: *a continuity of misfortunes. The continuity of the movie was broken when the power failed.* **3** a detailed plan for a motion picture; scenario: *Keaton wrote the story and continuity of "The General," directed it, cut it, and . . . played the leading role* (New Yorker). **4a** any connecting comments or announcements between the parts of a radio or television program. **b** a script for the spoken portion of such a program. **5** *Mathematics.* the property of a line, curve, or the like that extends without a break or irregularity. **a** the property of a continuous function.

continuity girl or **clerk**, an assistant in a motion-picture studio who keeps a record of the filmed scenes to maintain continuity between takes.

continuity man, a person who writes continuity for a radio or television program.

con|tin|u|o (kən tin′yů ō, -tin ů′ō), *n. Music.* a bass part extending throughout a piece, with written figures indicating the intended harmony; thorough bass: *Purists may complain that the continuo, played by harpsichord, cello and double bass, is too heavy* (Maclean's). [< Italian *continuo* < Latin *continuus* continuous; see etym. under **continue**]

con|tin|u|ous (kən tin′yů əs), *adj.* without a stop; connected; unbroken; uninterrupted: *a continuous line of cars, a continuous sound. The radio had been making continuous statements along these lines* (London Times). SYN: ceaseless, incessant, perpetual. —**con|tin′u|ous|ly**, *adv.* —**con|tin′u|ous|ness**, *n.*

▶See **continual** for usage note.

continuous function, *Mathematics, Statistics.* a function which changes systematically in value as the value of the function's independent variable is changed.

continuous kiln, a long kiln in which small rail cars or a conveyor carry brick or other ware through a tunnel to the point of highest temperature at the center; tunnel kiln.

continuous miner, a machine that automatically digs and loads coal.

continuous phase, the medium in which the particles (the disperse phase) of a colloid are distributed.

continuous spectrum, a spectrum whose source emits light of every wavelength in a continuous band. Spectra from incandescent bodies and molten metal, are often continuous.

continuous voyage, *International Law.* a voyage interrupted by stoppages at ports, yet regarded as a single voyage in reference to its purpose, such as the consignment of contraband of war.

continuous wave, a radio or radar wave whose oscillations occur in a regular, uninterrupted pattern, at a constant amplitude and frequency.

con|tin|u|um (kən tin′yů əm), *n., pl.* **-tin|u|a.** **1** a continuous quantity, series, or whole: *the largest and most isolated continuum of preagricultural people in the world* [*the Australian aborigines*] (Atlantic). **2** a thing that remains the same; any characteristic having a continued existence and observable to be the same among a group or series having limitless variations. **3** a continuous whole or other quantitative concept of which the parts are indistinguishable except by reference to something outside of itself, especially the four dimensional space-time continuum within which it is possible to "identify" or "locate" events only by reference to three spatial coordinates and the temporal coordinate (the fourth dimension).
[< Latin *continuum,* neuter of *continuus* uninterrupted; see etym. under **continue**]

con|to (kon′tō; *Portuguese* kōn′tü), *n., pl.* **-tos.** **1** a Portuguese or Brazilian monetary unit, formerly worth 1,000,000 reis, now worth 1,000 escudos in Portugal or 1,000 cruzeiros in Brazil. **2** (in Portugal) a million. [< Portuguese *conto* < Latin *computus, -ūs* a calculation, something computed]

con|toid (kon′toid), *n., adj. Phonetics.* —*n.* any sound having a consonantlike character: *A contoid . . . is a sound involving clearly audible turbulence of the air stream at one point or another in the vocal tract, or else a complete interruption of the air stream* (Charles F. Hockett).
—*adj.* having a consonantlike character: *contoid articulation.*
[< *con*(sonan)*t* + *-oid*]

con|tor|ni|ate (kən tôr′nē it), *adj., n. Numismatics.* —*adj.* having a bordering furrow within the edge.
—*n.* one of a group of Roman medals or coinlike pieces of copper or bronze having a furrow on each side within the edge, and bearing on one side a head and on the other side devices relating to the public games or spectacles, in connection with which these pieces are supposed to have been issued, probably first in the 300's A.D.
[< French *contorniate* < Italian *contorniato* < *contorno* contour, outline]

con|tort (kən tôrt′), *v.t.* to twist or bend out of shape; distort: *The clown contorted his face.*
[< Latin *contortus,* past participle of *contorquēre* < *com-* (intensive) + *torquēre* twist]

con|tor|tion (kən tôr′shən), *n.* **1** a twisting out of shape; distorting: (*Figurative.*) *Such contortions of facts cannot be excused.* **2** twisted condition; distorted form or shape: *The acrobat went through various contortions.*

con|tor|tion|ate (kən tôr′shə nit), *adj.* marked by contortion; twisting.

con|tor|tion|ist (kən tôr′shə nist), *n.* a person who can twist or bend his body into odd and unnatural positions.

con|tor|tive (kən tôr′tiv), *adj.* tending to or characterized by contortion.

con|tour (kon′tůr), *n., adj., v.* —*n.* **1** the outline of a figure: *The contour of the Atlantic coast of America is very irregular.* SYN: See syn. under **outline**. **2** the line that defines or bounds anything: *the subtle melodic contour of late-eighteenth-century music* (New Yorker). **3** = contour line. **4** *Phonetics.* a sequence of different levels of pitch or stress: *Intonation contours are not, of course, phonemes, but morphemes* (H. A. Gleason, Jr.).
—*adj.* **1** showing the outline, especially of hills, valleys, and other topographical features: *a contour interval on a topographic map.* **2** following natural ridges and furrows in plowing to avoid erosion: *contour rows.* See also **contour plowing**. **3** shaped to fit the contour of a particular object: *a contour chair, contour sheets.*
—*v.t.* **1** to make an outline or contour of. **2** to build (a road, trestle, building, or the like) according to a contour. **3** to mark with contour lines.
[< French *contour* < Italian *contorno* < *contornare* encircle, ultimately < Latin *com-* with + *tornus* a turning lathe < Greek *tórnos*]

con|tour-chas|ing (kon′tůr chā′sing), *n.* low-altitude flying that follows closely the contour of the terrain below: *Military aircraft are being designed for contour-chasing to defeat radar defences* (New Scientist).

contour couch, a couch in a spacecraft, that fits closely the form of the occupant, to support and protect the body under extreme pressures.

contour feathers, the outer feathers which determine the contour of a bird's body.

contour interval, difference in height, measured vertically, between the contour lines on a map. Intervals are usually regular and uniform, as every 100, 500, or 1000 feet.

contour line, a line on a map, showing height above or below sea level. All points on a contour line have the same elevation.

***contour map**, a map showing heights at regular intervals above sea level by means of contour lines.

***contour map**

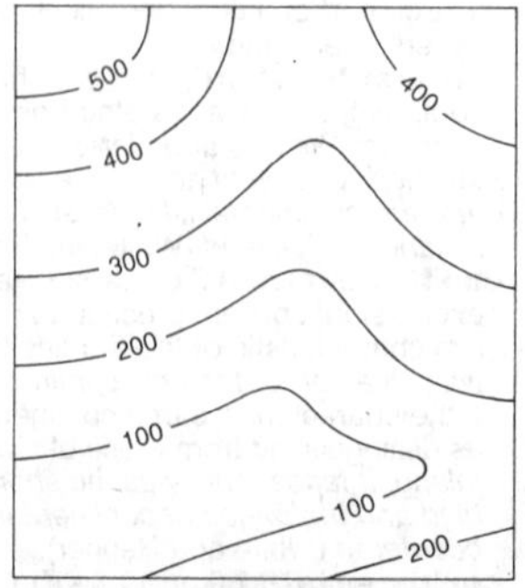

contour map

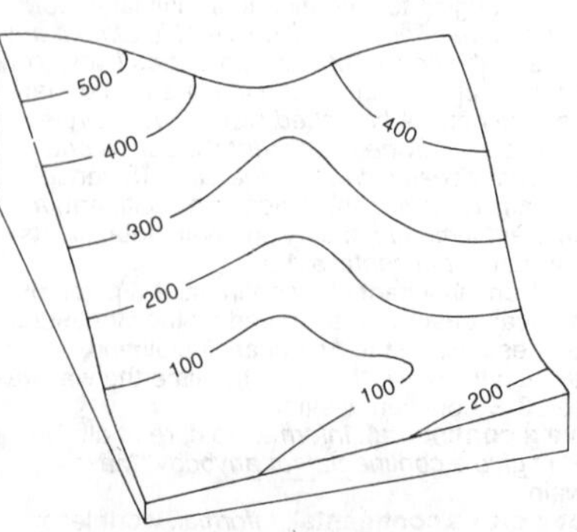

block diagram of map area

***contour plowing**, plowing that follows the contours of land, crosswise to its slope.

***contour plowing**

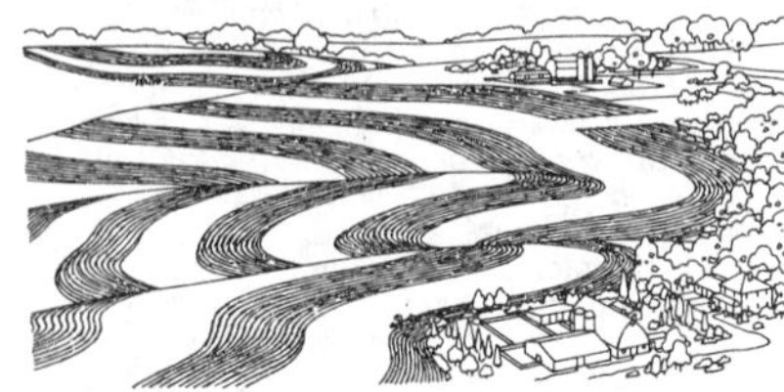

contr., **1a** contract. **b** contracted. **2** contraction. **3** contractor. **4** contralto. **5** contrary. **6** control.

con|tra¹ (kon′trə), *n.* the opposite side or column of an account, especially the right-hand or credit side, in which the liabilities appear. [< Latin *contrā* against]

con|tra² or **Con|tra** (kon′trə), *n., pl.* **-tras.** a member of the rebel military forces that oppose the Sandinistas in Nicaragua. [< American Spanish *contra*, short for *contrarevolucionario* counterrevolutionary]

contra-, *prefix.* in opposition; against: *Contradistinction = distinction by opposition or contrast.* [< Latin *contrā-* < *contrā* against]

con|tra|band (kon′trə band), *n., adj.* **—*n.*** **1** goods imported or exported contrary to law; smuggled goods: *Customs officials went through each bag looking for contraband.* **2** trading contrary to law; smuggling. **3** = contraband of war. **4** *U.S.* a Negro slave who escaped to or was brought within the Union lines during the Civil War.

—*adj.* against the law; prohibited; forbidden: *The sale of stolen goods is contraband in the United States. A small but steady trickle of ... contraband arms was being smuggled across its territory* (Newsweek).

[< Spanish *contrabando* < earlier Italian < *contra-* against + *bando* < Medieval Latin *bannum* ban < a Germanic word]

con|tra|band|ist (kon′trə ban′dist), *n.* a person engaged in contraband trade; smuggler.

contraband of war, goods supplied by neutral nations to countries at war with one another, which either warring country has the right to seize. Ammunition is always contraband of war.

con|tra|bass (kon′trə bās′), *n., adj.* **—*n.*** **1** the lowest bass voice or instrument. **2** a large stringed instrument shaped like a cello and having a very low bass tone; double bass.

—*adj.* sounding an octave lower than the normal bass.

con|tra|bass|ist (kon′trə bā′sist), *n.* a person who plays the contrabass.

con|tra|bas|so (kon′trə bä′sō), *n., pl.* **-sos.** = contrabass.

contra bassoon, or **con|tra|bas|soon** (kon′trə bə sün′), *n.*, a large bassoon, an octave lower in range than the ordinary bassoon; double bassoon: *The additions [to the classic orchestra] today used by the moderns are piccolos, English horns, contra bassoons* (John Philip Sousa). See the picture under **bassoon.**

con|tra|cept (kon′trə sept′), *v.t.* to prevent from being conceived in the womb. [back formation < *contraception*]

con|tra|cep|tion (kon′trə sep′shən), *n.* the use of any method, drug, or device to prevent conception or pregnancy.

con|tra|cep|tive (kon′trə sep′tiv), *adj., n.* **—*adj.*** of or for contraception.

—*n.* a means or device for preventing conception or pregnancy: *an oral contraceptive.*

con|tra|clock|wise (kon′trə klok′wīz′), *adv., adj.* = couterclockwise.

con|tract (*v.t. 1-4, 6, v.i. 1* kən trakt′; *v.t. 5, v.i. 2* kon′trakt or kən trakt′, *n.* kon′trakt), *v., n.* **—*v.t.*** **1** to draw together; make narrow; knit: *Wrinkling your forehead contracts your brows.* **SYN:** condense, reduce, diminish, lessen. **2** to make smaller; shrink; shorten: *to contract a muscle. (Figurative.) By moving into smaller quarters he hopes shortly to contract his expenses.* **SYN:** shrivel. **3** to shorten (a word, syllable, or phrase) by omitting some of the letters or sounds: *In talking we often contract "do not" to "don't."* **4** to bring on oneself; get; form: *Bad habits are easy to contract. His hoarseness and coughing showed that he had contracted a cold. He contracted debts by buying things he could not afford.* **SYN:** incur, acquire. **5** to make, settle, or establish by contract. **6** *Rare.* to betroth; affiance.

—*v.i.* **1** to become shorter or smaller; shrink; *Wood fibers contract in hot water. Earthworms can contract.* **2** to make a contract; agree by contract: *the baker contracted for a load of flour. The builder contracted to build the new highway for a very high price.*

—*n.* **1** mutual agreement. In a contract two or more people agree to do or not to do certain things. **SYN:** pact, compact, bargain. **2a** a written agreement that can be enforced by law. **b** the branch of law dealing with such agreements. **3a** a formal agreement for marriage; betrothal. **b** the act by which two persons take each other in marriage. *Marriage is, first of all, a contract which ... as with all contracts ... must be governed by justice* (Newsweek). **4a** one variety of the game of bridge; contract bridge. **b** the winning declaration in the auction at contract bridge. **c** the number of tricks named by the declarer at contract bridge. **5** *Slang.* an assignment to kill someone for pay: *Some policemen believe that a West End mobster named "Lucky" has put a contract out for Savard* (MacLean's).

contract in, *British.* to arrange or agree to come under certain conditions (of a contract, bill, or agreement): *the Trade Union Bill will provide that members of a trade union wishing to contribute to political funds shall contract in* (London Daily Express).

contract out (of), *British.* to arrange or agree not to come under certain conditions (of a contract, bill, or agreement): *The Cotton Import (Review) Committee recommended that cotton spinners should be allowed to contract out of trading with the commission* (London Times).

[< Old French *contract*, learned borrowing from Latin *contractus, -ūs* agreement < *contrahere* draw together < *com-* together + *trahere* draw]

—con|tract′i|ble, con|tract′a|ble, *adj.*

con|tract|ant (kən trak′tənt), *n.* a party to a contract.

contract bridge, a variety of bridge played by two opposing pairs of players. The highest bidder can score toward a game only as many tricks as he promised to make in his bid.

contract carrier, a person or company whose business is conveying goods or people under individual contracts made with certain customers only: *Many truckers are contract carriers.*

con|tract|ed (kən trak′tid), *adj.* **1** drawn together; made narrow; shortened; made smaller; shrunken: *He sat in a somewhat contracted position* (G. T. Lloyd). *(Figurative) A very contracted summary of the voluminous records* (James Mill). **2** *Figurative.* narrow-minded: *A prejudiced person has a contracted point of view.* **—con|tract′ed|ly,** *adv.* **—con|tract′ed|ness,** *n.*

contracted foot, an abnormal contraction of the hoof wall of a horse's foot.

contracted tendon, a shortening of the flexor tendons of a horse, either congenital or due to injury.

con|tract|i|bil|i|ty (kən trak′tə bil′ə tē), *n.* the quality of being contractible.

con|trac|tile (kən trak′təl), *adj.* **1** capable of contracting: *Muscle is contractile tissue.* **2** producing contraction: *Cooling is a contractile force.*

contractile vacuole, a vacuole in one-celled organisms, especially protozoans, that collects water and soluble waste fluids and at regular intervals forces them out by contracting. The process is the only way the organism can control its water content.

con|trac|til|i|ty (kon′trak til′ə tē), *n.* the ability to contract: *If gelation is prevented ... protoplasmic contractility is lost and the cell becomes immobile* (Scientific American).

con|trac|tion (kən trak′shən), *n.* **1** the act or process of contracting: *Cold causes the contraction of liquids, gases, and solids; heat causes expansion. (Figurative.) He talks of making more contractions of his expense* (Samuel Johnson). **2** the condition of being contracted: *The contraction of mercury by cold makes it go down in thermometers. (Figurative.) the contraction of credit, characteristic of a commercial crisis* (John Stuart Mill). **3** something contracted; a shortened form: *"Can't" is a contraction of "cannot."* **4** *Anatomy.* the shortening and thickening of tissue whereby a muscle pulls, compresses, constricts, or otherwise moves some part of the body. **5** a restriction; limitation.

con|trac|tion|al (kən trak′shə nəl), *adj.* serving or tending to contract.

con|trac|tive (kən trak′tiv), *adj.* **1** of or producing contraction. **2** capable of contracting.

contract labor, labor or laborers supplied by contract, especially when imported from one country to another under agreement to work for a particular employer.

contract miner, a coal miner who is paid according to the amount of coal he delivers instead of on a time basis.

con|trac|tor (kon′trak tər, kən trak′- *for 1;* kən-trak′tər *for 2, 3*), *n.* **1** a person who agrees to furnish materials or to do a piece of work for a certain price: *a building contractor.* **2** a thing that contracts. **3** a muscle that draws together some part or parts of the body.

con|trac|tu|al (kən trak′chü əl), *adj.* **1** of or having to do with a contract. **2** having the nature of a contract: *A teacher has no contractual obligation to entertain students.* **—con|trac′tu|al|ly,** *adv.*

con|trac|ture (kən trak′chər), *n. Medicine.* a permanent shortening of a muscle: *There was time out for a long hospital siege, to straighten out the contractures in Anne's one knee* (Time).

con|tra|cy|cli|cal (kon′trə sī′klə kəl, -sik′lə-), *adj.* designed or serving to offset fluctuations or cycles of inflation and recession in business.

con|tra|dance (kon′trə dans′, -däns′), *n.* = contredanse.

con|tra|dict (kon′trə dikt′), *v.t.* **1** to say that (a statement) is not true; deny: *He contradicted the rumor that he was moving to another town.* **SYN:** impugn, dispute. See syn. under **deny.** **2** to say the opposite of what (a person) has said: *It is rude to contradict a guest.* **SYN:** impugn, dispute. See syn. under **deny.** **3** to be contrary to; disagree with; go counter to: *Your story and your brother's story contradict each other. The sayings "He who hesitates is lost" and "Look before you leap" seem to contradict each other.* **4** *Obsolete.* to speak against; oppose. [< Latin *contrādictus*, past participle of *contrādīcere*, earlier *contrā dīcere* say in opposition] **—con′tra|dict′a|ble,** *adj.* **—con′tra|dic′tor, con′tra|dict′er,** *n.*

con|tra|dic|tion (kon′trə dik′shən), *n.* **1** the act of denying what has been said; saying the opposite: *The expert spoke without fear of contradiction by his listeners.* **2** a statement or act that contradicts another; denial: *His complete contradiction was published the next day.* **3** a contrary condition; disagreement; opposition: *Death is such a strange contradiction to life* (George Moore). **4** an inconsistency: *Your attitude is in contradiction to your character.* **5** a person characterized by contradictory qualities: *You are a contradiction of good sense and foolish vanity.*

contradiction in terms, a statement or phrase which is self-contradictory: *A virtuous tyrant is a contradiction in terms* (Benjamin Jowett).

con|tra|dic|tious (kon′trə dik′shəs), *adj.* inclined to be contradictory; disputatious. [< *contradicti(on)* + *ous*] **—con′tra|dic′tious|ly,** *adv.* **—con′tra|dic′tious|ness,** *n.*

con|tra|dic|tive (kon′trə dik′tiv), *adj.* = contradictory. **—con|tra|dic′tive|ly,** *adv.*

con|tra|dic|to|ri|ly (kon′trə dik′tər ə lē, -trə-), *adv.* **1** in a way that contradicts or involves contradiction; in contradictory terms. **2** *Logic.* with contradictory opposition.

con|tra|dic|to|ry (kon′trə dik′tər ē, -trē), *adj., n., pl.* **—ries.** **—*adj.*** **1** in disagreement; contradicting; contrary; saying the opposite: *First reports of the election were so contradictory we could not tell who won.* **SYN:** inconsistent, irreconcilable. **2** inclined to contradict: *Her contradictory nature leads her into petty quarrels.* **SYN:** disputatious, argumentative. **3** *Logic.* having the quality or character of a contradiction.

—*n.* *Logic.* **1** a proposition so related to a second that either must be false if the other is true. **2** a term that exactly negates another, such as *tall* and *not tall.* **—con′tra|dic′to|ri|ness,** *n.*

con|tra|dis|tinc|tion (kon′trə dis tingk′shən), *n.* distinction by opposition or contrast: *Today we cross the continent in airplanes in contradistinction to the slow covered wagons of our ancestors.*

con|tra|dis|tinc|tive (kon′trə dis tingk′tiv), *adj., n.* **—*adj.*** characterized by contradistinction; serving to contradistinguish.

—*n.* a contradistinctive word or form. **—con′tra-dis|tinc′tive|ly,** *adv.*

con|tra|dis|tin|guish (kon′trə dis ting′gwish), *v.t.* to distinguish by contrasting opposite qualities.

con|tra|fa|got|to (kôn trä fä gôt′tō), *n., pl.* **-ti** (-tē). *Italian.* contra bassoon.

con|trail (kon′trāl), *n.* the smokelike trail of water droplets or ice crystals that sometimes forms in the wake of an aircraft flying at a high altitude; vapor trail. [< *con*(densation) + *trail*]

con|tra|in|di|cant (kon′trə in′də kənt), *adj., n.* **—*adj.*** indicating that a certain medical treatment ordinarily prescribed is not advisable.

—*n.* = contraindication.

con|tra|in|di|cate (kon′trə in′də kāt), *v.t.*, **-cat|ed, -cat|ing.** to indicate (a certain treatment) as being inadvisable: *A weak heart contraindicates shock therapy.*

con|tra|in|di|ca|tion (kon′trə in′də kā′shən), *n.* a condition indicating that a certain medical treatment, used under ordinary circumstances, is inadvisable.

Pronunciation Key: hat, āge, cãre, fär; let, ēqual, tėrm; it, īce; hot, ōpen, ôrder; **oi**l, **ou**t; cup, pu̇t, rüle; **ch**ild; lo**ng**; **th**in; **ᴛʜ**en; **zh**, measure; **ə** represents **a** in about, **e** in taken, **i** in pencil, **o** in lemon, **u** in circus.

con·tra·in·dic·a·tive (kon′trə in dik′ə tiv), *adj.* = contraindicant.

con·tra·lat·er·al (kon′trə lat′ər əl), *adj.* that is on the opposite side: *the contralateral ear.*

con·tral·to (kən tral′tō), *n., pl.* **-tos,** *adj.* **—*n.*** **1** the lowest woman's voice, lower in range than mezzo-soprano; alto. **2** a singer with such a voice. **3** a part to be sung by such a voice. **4** the highest male voice; alto; countertenor.
—*adj.* of or for a contralto.
[< Italian *contralto* < *contra-* counter to (< Latin) + *alto* high < Latin *altus* high]

con·tra·na·tant (kon′trə nā′tənt), *adj.* swimming against the current: *contranatant migrations of fish.*

con·tra·nat·u·ral (kon′trə nach′ər əl), *adj.* contrary to what is natural.

con·tra·oc·tave (kon′trə ok′tāv), *n.* the 16-foot octave of the organ, or the octave in other instruments corresponding to this.

con·tra·plex (kon′trə pleks), *adj.* denoting or having to do with a system of telegraphy for sending two messages simultaneously over the same wire in opposite directions. [< *contra-* + *-plex* (as in *multiplex*)]

con·tra·po·si·tion (kon′trə pə zish′ən), *n.* a placing over against; opposite position; contrast.

con·tra·pos·i·tive (kon′trə poz′ə tiv), *adj.* of or produced by contraposition.

con·trap·pos·to (kon′trə pos′tō), *n.* the crossing of limbs and contrasting of masses in the composition of a painting or sculpture. [< Italian *contrapposto,* noun use of past participle of *contraporre* to oppose < Latin *contrāpōnere* to set opposite < *contrā* against + *pōnere* to set, place]

con·tra·prop (kon′trə prop′), *n. Aeronautics.* a device consisting of two propellers, mounted coaxially, one behind the other, turning in opposite directions.

con·trap·tion (kən trap′shən), *n. Informal.* a device or gadget; contrivance: *Yankee inventors were famous for their contraptions.* [American English, perhaps < *contrive,* on analogy of *conception;* perhaps influenced by *trap*]

con·tra·pun·tal (kon′trə pun′təl), *adj. Music.* **1** of or having to do with counterpoint. **2** according to the rules of counterpoint: *Jazz musicians are using learned contrapuntal dissonances, and learned composers are using jazz* (New York Times). **3** = polyphonic.
[< Italian *contrappunto* counterpoint (< Medieval Latin *(punctum) contrāpunctum* (point, or note) against note) + English *-al*[1]] **—con′tra·pun′tal·ly,** *adv.*

con·tra·pun·tal·ist (kon′trə pun′tə list), *n.* = contrapuntist.

con·tra·pun·tist (kon′trə pun′tist), *n.* a person skilled in the rules and practice of counterpoint.

con·trar·i·an (kən trãr′ē ən), *n. U.S.* a contrary person, especially a stock speculator who does not follow the popular trends in buying and selling stock.

con·tra·ri·e·ty (kon′trə rī′ə tē), *n., pl.* **-ties. 1** the state or quality of being contrary; extreme opposition: *The contrariety of the points of view represented seemed to underscore the difficulty of getting a satisfactory formula* (Wall Street Journal). SYN: contrariness, repugnancy. **2** something contrary; contrary fact or statement. SYN: inconsistency, disagreement, discrepancy.

con·trar·i·ous (kən trãr′ē əs), *adj.* full of opposition; contrary; perverse; adverse; unfavorable. **—con·trar′i·ous·ly,** *adv.* **—con·trar′i·ous·ness,** *n.*

con·tra·ri·wise (kon′trer ē wīz′; *also for 3* kən trãr′-), *adv.* **1** in the opposite way or direction. **2** on the contrary. **3** perversely; contrarily.

con·tra·ro·tate (kon′trə rō′tāt), *v.i.,* **-tat·ed, -tat·ing. 1** to revolve in opposite directions: *The coaxially mounted propeller blades contrarotated.* **2** to rotate in a direction opposite to that of another rotation: *The animal's hind legs contrarotated in falling, so that it landed on its feet.* **—con′tra·ro·ta′tion,** *n.*

con·tra·ry (kon′trer ē; *also for adj. 5* kən trãr′-), *adj., n., pl.* **-ries,** *adv.* **—*adj.*** **1** opposed; opposite; completely different: *My sister's taste in dresses is contrary to my own.* SYN: See syn. under **opposite. 2** opposite in direction or position. SYN: counter. **3** being the opposite one of two: *The players on the contrary side now took their places.* **4** unfavorable: *a contrary wind.* SYN: adverse. **5** opposing others; stubborn; perverse: *a contrary attitude. The contrary boy sneered at what was suggested and refused to do it.* SYN: obstinate, antagonistic, hostile. **6** *Logic.* of or of the nature of a contrary.
—*n.* **1** the opposite: *After promising to stay and clean up, he did the contrary and walked out.* **2** *Logic.* **a** a proposition so related to a second that both may be false, but both cannot be true. *All cows are black* is the contrary of *no cows are black.* **b** one of two terms which are extreme opposites in the same class, as *black* and *white.*
—*adv.* in opposition; contrarily.
by contraries, contrary to expectation: *In the Commonwealth I would (by contraries) execute all things* (Shakespeare).
on the contrary, exactly opposite to what has been said: *He is not stingy; on the contrary, no one could be more generous. Nothing, on the contrary, could be more natural* (Jane Austen).
to the contrary, with the opposite effect: *The next debater, in rebuttal, spoke to the contrary.*
[< Anglo-French *contrarie* < Latin *contrārius* < *contrā* against] **—con′tra·ri·ly,** *adv.* **—con′tra·ri·ness,** *n.*

contrary motion, *Music.* two contrapuntal parts sounding together and moving in opposite directions, one descending in pitch while the other rises.

con·tra·sea·son·al (kon′trə sē′zə nəl), *adj.* contrary to that which is seasonal; out of character with the season: *They [eggs] have taken a contraseasonal drop in price because of surplus supplies* (New York Times). **—con′tra·sea′son·al·ly,** *adv.*

con·trast (*n.* kon′trast; *v.* kən trast′), *n., v.* **—*n.*** **1** a great difference; difference: *Anyone can see the contrast between black and white. There is a great contrast between life now and life a hundred years ago.* SYN: unlikeness, antithesis, distinction. **2** a person, thing, or event that shows differences when put side by side with another: *Black hair is a sharp contrast to a light skin.* **3** (in the arts) the putting close together of varied forms or colors to heighten their effect, and the effect of the whole composition by comparison.
—*v.t.* **1** to place (two things) side by side to show their differences: *Contrast birds with fishes. Golf is less strenuous, contrasted with tennis.* SYN: oppose, differentiate, distinguish. **2** to put close together to heighten an effect by emphasizing differences: *The fiery orator contrasted the idle rich with the toiling working classes.*
—*v.i.* **1** to show differences when compared or put side by side: *The black and the gold contrast well in that design.* **2** to form a contrast: *The strained language of his speeches contrasts oddly with the ease and naturalness of his letters.*
[< French *contraste* < Italian *contrasto* < *contrastare* withstand, resist < Vulgar Latin *contrāstāre* < Latin *contrā-* against + *stāre* stand] **—con·trast′a·ble,** *adj.* **—con·trast′ing·ly,** *adv.*
▶See **compare** for usage note.

con·tra·stim·u·lant (kon′trə stim′yə lənt), *n., adj.* **—*n.*** **1** a medicine that tends to offset the effects of a stimulant. **2** a depressant or sedative.
—*adj.* offsetting a stimulant: *contrastimulant effects.*

con·tras·tive (kən tras′tiv), *adj.* showing a contrast: *Contrastive studies are the more revealing when we choose languages remote from each other and spoken by people of widely divergent cultures* (Beals and Hoijer).

con·trast·y (kon′tras tē), *adj.* having very marked contrast between light and dark areas of a photograph with few intermediate tones.

con·tra·ten·or (kon′trə ten′ər), *n.* = countertenor.

con·trate wheel (kon′trāt), (in watchmaking) a wheel with teeth set at right angles to its plane. [< Latin *contrā* against + English *-ate*]

con·tra·val·la·tion (kon′trə və lā′shən), *n.* a line or network of small fortifications, breastworks, or other fortification, erected around an area or fortress by attackers for protection. [< French *contrevallation* < *contre-* opposite, contra- + Latin *vallātiō, -ōnis* entrenchment, vallation]

con·tra·vene (kon′trə vēn′), *v.t.,* **-vened, -ven·ing. 1** to conflict with; oppose: *A dictatorship contravenes the liberty of individuals.* **2** to contradict; oppose in argument; deny. **3** to act in defiance of; violate: *The British Government made it clear . . . that the Paris agreements in no way contravened the treaty* (London Times). SYN: transgress, infringe. [< Middle French *contravenir,* learned borrowing from Late Latin *contrāvenīre* oppose < Latin *contrā-* against + *venīre* come] **—con′tra·ven′er,** *n.*

con·tra·ven·tion (kon′trə ven′shən), *n.* **1** conflict; opposition. **2** = contradiction. **3** violation; infringement: *switching off a machine which he alleged was being operated in contravention of an agreement on starting and stopping times* (London Times). SYN: transgression.

con·tra·yer·va (kon′trə yėr′və), *n.* the root of a tropical American plant of the mulberry family, used as a stimulant and tonic, and formerly as an antidote to snakebite. [< Spanish *contrayerba* < *contra-* against + *yerba* herb]

con·tre·danse (kôN trə däNs′), *n.* **1** a dance in which the partners stand in two opposite lines facing each other; country-dance. **2** the music written for such a dance, in 2-4 or 6-8 time. Also, **contradance.** [< French *contredanse* < English *country-dance; country* confused with French *contre* against]

cont. rem., *Medicine.* let the remedy be continued (Latin, *continuetur remedium*).

con·tre·temps (kôN trə täN′), *n., pl.* **-temps** (-täNz′; *French* - täN′). an unlucky accident; embarrassing or awkward happening: *In this little contretemps there is perhaps more confusion than basic controversy* (Wall Street Journal). [< French *contre-temps*]

contrib., **1** contribution. **2** contributor.

con·trib·ute (kən trib′yůt), *v.,* **-ut·ed, -ut·ing.** **—*v.t.*** **1** to give (money, help, or other support) along with others; furnish as a share: *Each worker contributed a dollar to the Red Cross. Everyone was asked to contribute suggestions for the party.* **2** to write (articles, stories, or poems) or to make (drawings) for a newspaper or magazine or for a book with more than one author: *He asked him to contribute a bi-weekly article on European affairs* (Edmund Wilson).
—*v.i.* to give or make a contribution: *Will you contribute to the Red Cross?*
contribute to, to help bring about: *A poor diet contributed to the child's bad health. Honesty and hard work contribute to success and to happiness.*
[< Latin *contribūtus,* past participle of *contribuere* bring together, collect < *com-* together + *tribuere* bestow, assign, (originally) divide among the tribes < *tribus* tribe] **—con·trib′ut·a·ble,** *adj.*

con·tri·bu·tion (kon′trə byü′shən), *n.* **1** the act of contributing; giving money or help along with others: *She felt that contribution to the church was a duty and a pleasure. To be happy ourselves is a most effectual contribution to the happiness of others* (Sir John Lubbock). **2** the money or help contributed; gift: *Her contribution to the picnic was a basket of apples. The money came from world-wide contributions* (Newsweek). **3** something written or drawn for a newspaper or magazine or for a book with more than one author. **4** a tax; levy.

con·trib·u·tive (kən trib′yə tiv), *adj.* helping to bring about; contributing: *Exercise taken in open air is . . . contributive to health* (Richard J. Sullivan). **—con·trib′u·tive·ly,** *adv.* **—con·trib′u·tive·ness,** *n.*

con·trib·u·tor (kən trib′yə tər), *n.* **1** a person or thing that contributes: *Of more general interest than the debt were the newly revealed Democratic contributors of the past three months* (Baltimore Sun). **2** a person who writes articles, stories, poems, or makes drawings for a newspaper or magazine, or writes for a book with more than one author.

con·trib·u·tor·ship (kən trib′yə tər ship), *n.* the position of a contributor.

con·trib·u·to·ry (kən trib′yə tôr′ē, -tōr′-), *adj., n., pl.* **-ries. —*adj.*** **1** helping to bring about; contributing: *The workman's own carelessness was a contributory cause of the accident.* **2** having to do with or of the nature of contribution.
—*n.* a person or thing that contributes.

contributory negligence, *Law.* negligence on the part of an injured person, which has contributed or led to the injury: *Under the contributory negligence rule, the victim of an accident can obtain no damages at all if the jury or judge is persuaded that he was in any way responsible for the accident* (New York Times).

con·trite (kən trīt′, kon′trīt), *adj.* **1** broken in spirit by a sense of guilt; penitent: *The boy felt contrite after he had hit his little sister. . . . an humble and a contrite heart* (Rudyard Kipling). SYN: repentant, sorrowful, humbled. **2** showing deep regret and sorrow: *He wrote an apology in contrite words.* [< Latin *contrītus* crushed, past participle of *conterere* to grind < *com-* (intensive) + *terere* rub, grind] **—con·trite′ly,** *adv.* **—con·trite′ness,** *n.*

con·tri·tion (kən trish′ən), *n.* **1** sorrow for one's sins or guilt; being contrite; repentance. SYN: penitence. **2** deep regret.

con·triv·ance (kən trī′vəns), *n.* **1** a thing invented; mechanical device: *The can opener is a handy contrivance.* SYN: invention, gadget, contraption. **2** the act or manner of contriving: *By careful contrivance he repaired the old clock and made it go.* **3** the power or ability of contriving; inventive capacity. SYN: ingenuity. **4** a plan; scheme: *The party was merely a contrivance to bring the unfriendly family together.* SYN: stratagem, tactic.

con·trive (kən trīv′), *v.,* **-trived, -triv·ing. —*v.t.*** **1** to plan with cleverness or skill; invent; design: *The inventor contrived a new kind of engine with fewer moving parts.* SYN: devise. **2** to plan; scheme; plot: *The outlaws contrived a robbery of the train.* SYN: hatch, frame, concoct. **3** to manage: *I will contrive to be there by ten o'clock.* **4** (in writing) to bring about; effect by manipulation of the plot: *The scriptwriter contrived a*

happy ending by having the heroine escape at the last minute. SYN: hatch, frame, concoct.
—*v.i.* to form schemes or designs; plan. [< Old French *controver* < *con-* (< Latin *com-*) + *trover* find < Latin *turbāre* stir up < *turba* commotion]
—**con|triv′a|ble**, *adj.* —**con|triv′er**, *n.*

con|trived (kən trīvd′), *adj.* produced by contrivance; characterized by artifice or craft; not natural; artificial: *The other announcers . . . indulged in the usual synthetic hoopla and contrived excitement* (New York Times). —**con|triv′ed|ly**, *adv.*

con|trol (kən trōl′), *v.*, **-trolled**, **-trol|ling**, *n.* —*v.t.* **1** to have power or authority over; direct: *A captain controls his ship and its crew.* SYN: command, rule, govern. **2** to hold back; keep down; restrain: *She was so upset by the accident that she couldn't control her tears.* SYN: repress. **3** to regulate: *Prices and wages have been controlled by the government from time to time.* **4** to check or verify (an experiment, effect, testimony, or other unknown) by some standard of comparison or by independent investigation. **5** *Accounting.* to check, verify, or regulate (expenditures, accounts, or other statements of finance).
—*n.* **1** power to direct or guide; authority; direction: *A child is under its parents' control.* SYN: regulation, management. See syn. under **authority**. **2** a holding back; a keeping down; restraint: *He lost control of his temper. The essential requirements of a disease organism which is to be used for the control of vermin* (Fenner and Day). **3** a means of restraint; check: *The President's power to veto is a control over the legislation passed by Congress.* **4** a device that controls a machine: *The control of our furnace can be operated from the kitchen.* **5** an individual or group serving as a standard of comparison for testing the results of an experiment performed on a similar individual or group. **6** a spirit that directs a medium in spiritualism: *At this mediumistic proving ground, [she] became host, or hostess, to a garrulous "control," who gave his name as Uvani* (New Yorker). **7** (in motor racing) any part of the course for which the time is not counted, such as a repair stop or a stretch of the course in a city or town.
controls, the instruments and devices by which an aircraft, locomotive, or car is operated: *The pilot sat at the controls ready to take off.*
[< Middle French *contrôler* < Old French *contreroller* < *contrerolle* a register copy < *contre* against (< Latin *contrā*) + *rolle* roll < Latin *rotula* (diminutive) < *rota* wheel] —**con|trol′less**, *adj.* —**con|trol′ling|ly**, *adv.* —**con|trol′ment**, *n.*

control board, = control panel.

control booth, a radio or television control room.

control center, a headquarters for the control of a complex field of activities: *a control center responsible for all air traffic control over Britain.*

control column, a control stick with a wheel at the top which is turned to operate the ailerons of an aircraft.

control electrode, an electrode to control a flow of current, as in a vacuum tube or transistor.

control experiment, an experiment to test or verify the results of another experiment. The method is to duplicate the experiment in every way except for changing one condition or variable in order to determine the effect of the change.

control grid, a control electrode in a vacuum tube, usually a screen or coil of fine wire, used to regulate the current between the cathode and the anode; grid.

control group, a group which serves as a standard of comparison for testing the results of a scientific experiment on an equivalent experimental group.

con|trol|la|bil|i|ty (kən trō′lə bil′ə tē), *n.* the quality of being controllable.

con|trol|la|ble (kən trō′lə bəl), *adj.* that can be controlled; capable of being checked or restrained.

con|trol|la|ble-pitch propeller (kən trō′lə bəl-pich′), a propeller having its blades so mounted that their angle can be changed at will while it is in motion.

con|trolled fusion (kən trōld′), the regulation and retardation of nuclear fusion in order to make available for use the energy released: *The big problem in controlled fusion is to reach the necessary high temperature (millions of degrees) without melting or vaporizing the walls of the container* (Time).

controlled substance, *U.S.* a drug or other chemical substance whose possession and use is restricted by law, especially a narcotic: *Lasco [was] convicted at 17 of aggravated assault, breaking and entering, and possession of controlled substances* (New York Post).

con|trol|ler (kən trō′lər), *n.* **1** a person employed to supervise expenditures or to manage financial affairs; comptroller: *The mayor directed the city controller to examine the expenses of the fire department.* **2** a person who controls, directs, or restrains. **3** a device that controls or regulates the speed, motion, power, etc., of a machine; governor. **4** the person who dispatches aircraft.
—**con|trol′ler|ship**, *n.*

con|trol|ling account (kən trō′ling), *Accounting.* one of the accounts in the general ledger which are summations of subsidiary, more detailed accounts.

controlling interest, **1** ownership of a majority of the shares of capital stock in a corporation. **2** the owner or owners of a majority of such stock.

control panel, a panel containing the instruments, switches, gauges, or other devices, for the management and control of a complex mechanism, such as an aircraft, an electronic computer, or a guidance system: *At zero, a finger pressed a red button in a control panel, and the missile, rising slowly and majestically, started on history's second Atlas flight* (Time).

control point, **1** a point or feature used for purposes of reference or orientation, as a landmark in navigation: *The geodesist . . . establishes what are called geodetic control points, locations he has pinned down . . . as a guide for plotting all other locations and computing all distances* (Life). **2** a position or station used for control and regulation of traffic: *Studies by Stanford's Engineering Division . . . suggest that pictures of trains moving at 60 miles an hour can be flashed to the appropriate control point in a matter of seconds* (New Scientist).

control post, a post or station equipped with instruments, such as seismographs, for the detection and recording of nuclear tests.

control rod, **1** a mechanism containing fuel, neutron-absorbing material, or other matter, used in a nuclear reactor to control the rate of a chain reaction: *Rare earths can be used in control rods for nuclear reactors* (Science News Letter). **2** a rod for transmitting movements from the controls in the cockpit to the rudder, aileron, or other movable controlling surface of an aircraft.

control room, **1** a soundproof room or booth in the studio of a radio or television broadcasting station, from which the director and technicians control the transmission of a program: *A TV control room under the auditorium houses the director, who monitors the lecture, relaying the closeups on to screens suspended from the roof of the auditorium* (David Lutyens). **2** a room equipped with instruments for directing a particular operation, as the activation of a nuclear reactor or the launching of a rocket: *The 2,000-ton structure and its dial-filled control room are expected to be peering into space by October* (Newsweek).

con|trols (kən trōlz′), *n.pl.* See under **control**.

control stick, a lever that controls the direction of an airplane's movement.

control surface, any movable airfoil, such as a rudder, elevator, or aileron, used to guide or control an aircraft in flight.

control system, **1** *Aeronautics.* a system of controls that regulates the attitude of a vehicle in flight. **2** a body of agreements for the international control of nuclear weapons. **3** the segment of an electronic computer which forwards instructions and supervises their execution. **4** any coordinated system providing control, such as the assembly including the control rods in a nuclear reactor.

control tape, a paper or plastic tape bearing coded instructions in the form of perforations, used to guide the operation of numerically-controlled machine tools.

control tower, an observation tower at an airfield for controlling the traffic of aircraft taking off and landing, the movement of ground vehicles on or near landing strips, and, sometimes, local air traffic in flight.

control unit, the part of a digital computer that transmits instructions from the memory unit to the arithmetic unit.

con|tro|ver|sial (kon′trə vėr′shəl, -sē əl), *adj.* **1** of controversy; having to do with controversy: *controversial writing.* **2** open to controversy; debatable; disputed: *Federal aid to education is a controversial subject.* SYN: questionable. **3** fond of controversy; argumentative: *He is eager to be controversial on any subject under the sun.* SYN: disputatious. —**con′tro|ver′sial|ly**, *adv.*

con|tro|ver|sial|ist (kon′trə vėr′shə list), *n.* a person who takes part in or is skilled in controversy.

con|tro|ver|sial|i|ty (kon′trə vėr′shal′ə tē, -sē al′-), *n.* controversial action or behavior: *Today's conformity is more than anything else the retreat from controversiality* (Atlantic).

con|tro|ver|sy (kon′trə vėr′sē), *n., pl.* **-sies**. **1** the act of arguing a question about which differences of opinion exist; debate; dispute: *The controversy between the company and the union ended after the strike was settled.* SYN: disputation. See syn. under **argument**. **2** a quarrel; wrangle. SYN: contention, altercation, disagreement. [< Late Latin *contrōversia* < *contrōvertere* to invert < Latin *contrā-* against + *vertere* turn]

con|tro|vert (kon′trə vėrt, kon′trə vėrt′), *v.t.* **1** to dispute, deny, or oppose: *The statement of the last witness controverts the evidence of the first two. He built up a case against the burly Welshman that could not be controverted* (Time). **2** to dispute about; discuss; debate. —**con′tro|vert′er**, *n.*

con|tro|vert|i|ble (kon′trə vėr′tə bəl), *adj.* that can be controverted; debatable. —**con′tro|vert′i-bly**, *adv.*

con|tro|vert|ist (kon′trə vėr′tist), *n.* a controversialist.

con|tu|ma|cious (kon′tü mā′shəs, -tyü-), *adj.* stubbornly rebellious; obstinately disobedient. SYN: headstrong, perverse, willful. —**con′tu|ma′cious|ly**, *adv.* —**con′tu|ma′cious|ness**, *n.*

con|tu|mac|i|ty (kon′tü mas′ə tē, -tyü-), *n., pl.* **-ties**. stubborn rebelliousness; obstinate disobedience.

con|tu|ma|cy (kon′tü mə sē, -tyü-; kən tü′-, -tyü′-), *n., pl.* **-cies**. stubborn resistance to authority; obstinate disobedience: *The members of the class were mulcted in the sum of ten shillings each, for contumacy* (New Yorker). SYN: willfulness, stubbornness. [< Latin *contumācia* arrogance < *contumax, -ācis* insolent < *com-* (intensive) + *tumēre* swell up]

con|tu|me|li|ous (kon′tü mē′lē əs, -tyü-), *adj.* contemptuously insolent; insulting: *. . . curving a contumelious lip, Gorgonised me from head to foot With a stony British stare* (Tennyson). SYN: abusive. —**con′tu|me′li|ous|ly**, *adv.* —**con′tu-me′li|ous|ness**, *n.*

con|tu|me|ly (kon′tü mə lē, -tyü-; -mē′-; kən tü′-, -tyü′-), *n., pl.* **-lies**. **1** insulting words or actions; humiliating treatment; insolent contempt: *The nobles treated the peasants with contumely. These people are willing to face the contempt of the Northern radicals . . . and the contumely and threats of our own Southern reactionaries* (William Faulkner). SYN: abuse, rudeness, scorn. **2** a humiliating insult: *The pedlars find satisfaction for all contumelies in making good bargains* (Hawthorne). [< Latin *contumēlia* abuse, (originally) insolent action < *com-* (intensive) + *tumēre* swell up. Compare etym. under **contumacy**.]

con|tuse (kən tüz′, -tyüz′), *v.t.*, **-tused**, **-tus|ing**. to injure without breaking the skin; bruise: *The face streamed with sweat, and the eyeballs were contused* (Graham Greene). [< Latin *contūsus*, past participle of *contundere* < *com-* (intensive) + *tundere* pound]

con|tu|sion (kən tü′zhən, -tyü′-), *n.* **1** an injury without breaking the skin; a bruise: *The victim's contusions did not require [his] hospitalization.* **2** the action of bruising or condition of being bruised: *His feelings, if not his body, received serious contusion.*

con|tu|sive (kən tü′siv, -tyü′-), *adj.* of or producing a contusion; bruising.

co|nun|drum (kə nun′drəm), *n., pl.* **-drums**, **-dra** (-drə). **1** a riddle whose answer involves a pun or play on words. *Examples:* "When is a door not a door? When it's ajar." "What has four eyes but can't see? The Mississippi." **2** any puzzling problem: *the dreary record of how all the attempts to solve the conundra of inter-war diplomacy ended in failure* (Punch). [origin unknown]

con|ur|ban (kon′ėr′bən), *adj.* of or characteristic of a conurbation: *the conurban traffic problem* (London Times). [back formation < *conurbation;* influenced by *urban*]

con|ur|ba|tion (kon′ėr bā′shən), *n.* a close grouping of urban communities around an urban center: *All told, more than 40% of the British population lives in seven monstrous conurbations, surrounding London, Birmingham, Manchester, Leeds, Liverpool, Newcastle, and Glasgow* (Time). [< *con-* + Latin *urbs* city + English *-ation*]

co|nus (kō′nəs), *n., pl.* **co|ni**. **1** a conical structure or organ in an animal; infundibulum. **2** = conus arteriosus. [< Latin *cōnus* cone]

conus ar|ter|i|o|sus (är tir′ē ō′səs), *pl.* **coni ar-ter|i|o|si** (är tir′ē ō′sī). **1** the elongated conical ventricle of the heart in some lower vertebrates. **2** a conical structure in the upper left portion of the right ventricle in man, supplying the pulmonary artery. [< New Latin *conus arteriosus* < Latin *cōnus* cone, *artēriōsus* arterial]

Pronunciation Key: hat, āge, cãre, fär; let, ēqual, tėrm; it, īce; hot, ōpen, ôrder; oil, out; cup, pu̇t, rüle; child; long; thin; ᴛʜen; zh, measure;
ə represents **a** in about, **e** in taken, **i** in pencil, **o** in lemon, **u** in circus.

conv., an abbreviation for the following:
1 convent.
2 convention.
3 conventional.
4 convertible.

con|va|lesce (kon′və les′), *v.i.*, **-lesced, -lesc|ing.** to recover health and strength after illness; make progress toward health: *She convalesced at home for three weeks after her operation.* [< Latin *convalēscere* < *com-* (intensive) + *valēscere* grow strong < *valēre* be strong]

con|va|les|cence (kon′və les′əns), *n.* **1** a gradual recovery of health and strength after illness: *After the operation, his convalescence was quick and complete.* **2** the time during which one is convalescing: *The doctor prescribed a three-week convalescence in bed.*

con|va|les|cent (kon′və les′ənt), *adj., n.* **—*adj.*** **1** recovering health and strength after illness; convalescing. **2** of or having to do with convalescence or convalescents: *a convalescent home.*
—*n.* a person recovering after illness: *Grandmother is in a home for convalescents until she is well enough to keep house again.*

con|val|lar|i|a|ceous (kon′və lãr′ē ā′shəs), *adj.* belonging to a group of plants of the lily family, typified by the lily of the valley. [< New Latin *Convallariaceae* the family name (< *Convallaria* the typical genus < Late Latin (*līlium*) *convallium* (lily) of the valleys) + English *-ous*]

con|vect (kən vekt′), *v.t., v.i.* to transfer, circulate, or provide heat or a heated fluid by convection. [back formation < *convection*]

con|vec|tion (kən vek′shən), *n.* **1** the transfer of heat from one place to another by the movement of heated particles of a gas or liquid: *If you hold your hand in the hot air rising from a hot air register, your hand is heated by convection* (John R. Pierce). **2** the act of conveying; conveyance. [< Latin *convectiō, -ōnis* < *convehere* < *com-* together + *vehere* carry]

con|vec|tion|al (kən vek′shə nəl), *adj.* having to do with or characterized by convection. **—con-vec′tion|al|ly,** *adv.*

convection current, the circulation of a gas or fluid produced by the tendency of a warm mass to rise and a cold mass to descend.

con|vec|tive (kən vek′tiv), *adj.* **1** having to do with or resulting from convection. **2** capable of conveying; transporting. **—con|vec′tive|ly,** *adv.*

con|vec|tor (kən vek′tər), *n.* any means or device for heating by convection: *Convectors and baseboard heating units are tested by taking temperature readings from 20 different spots inside the . . . room* (Wall Street Journal).

con|ve|nance (kon′və näns; *French* kôɴ və-näɴs′), *n.* suitability; propriety.
convenances, proprieties: *He [doesn't] regard, in his heart, forms and ceremonies and times and seasons very much, whatever the covenances may lead him to do* (J. W. R. Scott).
[< French *convenance* < Old French *convenir* agree; see etym. under **convene**]

con|vene (kən vēn′), *v.,* **-vened, -ven|ing.** **—*v.i.*** to meet for some purpose; gather in one place; assemble: *Congress convenes at least once a year.* **SYN:** congregate, collect.
—*v.t.* **1** to call together (members of an organization, etc.): *Any member may convene our club in an emergency.* **SYN:** convoke. **2** to summon to appear, as before a tribunal or a judicial officer.
[< Old French *convenir* < Latin *convenīre* agree, suit; assemble < *com-* together + *venīre* come] **—con|ven′a|ble,** *adj.* **—con|ven′er, con|ve′nor,** *n.*

con|ven|ience (kən vēn′yəns), *n.* **1** the fact or quality of being convenient: *The convenience of buying meat already wrapped in packages increased its sale.* **2** comfort; advantage; accommodation: *Many towns have camping places for the convenience of tourists. Many stores have a delivery service for the convenience of shoppers.* **3** anything handy or easy to use; a thing that saves trouble or work: *We find our folding table a great convenience.* **4** an opportune occasion; opportunity. **5** *British.* lavatory; bathroom.
at one's convenience, under conditions or at a time one finds convenient or advantageous: *Come by to pick me up at your convenience. Write at your convenience.*

convenience flag, = flag of convenience.

convenience food, prepared and packaged food that can be stored and served at one's convenience, such as canned food, frozen food, and cake mix: *TV dinners and frozen desserts are convenience foods.*

con|ven|ien|cy (kən vēn′yən sē), *n., pl.* **-cies.** = convenience.

con|ven|ient (kən vēn′yənt), *adj.* **1** saving trouble; well arranged; easy to use; handy; suitable: *to use a convenient tool, take a convenient bus, live in a convenient house.* **2** easily done; not troublesome: *Will it be convenient for you to bring your lunch to school?* **3** within easy reach; easily accessible; handy: *to meet at a convenient place. And then he [a bird] drank a dew from a convenient grass* (Emily Dickinson). **4** *Obsolete.* suitable; appropriate; proper.
convenient to, *Informal.* near: *a house convenient to the markets.*
[< Latin *conveniēns, -entis,* present participle of *convenīre* agree; see etym. under **convene**]
—con|ven′ient|ly, *adv.*

con|vent[1] (kon′vent), *n.* **1** a group of nuns or other persons dedicated to a religious life, living together according to fixed rules and under religious vows. A convent is in the charge of a superior. **2** the building or buildings in which they live. **SYN:** cloister, abbey. [< Anglo-French *covent,* Old French *convent* < Latin *conventus, -ūs* assembly < *convenīre;* see etym. under **convene**]
▶**Convent** formerly meant a community of monks, friars, or nuns, but is now used chiefly of nuns.

con|vent[2] (kon vent′), *v.t., v.i. Obsolete.* to convene. [< Latin *conventus,* past participle of *convenīre;* see etym. under **convene**]

con|ven|ti|cle (kən ven′tə kəl), *n.* **1** a secret or unauthorized meeting, especially for religious worship. **2** a secret religious meeting or assembly of certain Protestants who dissented from the doctrines and forms of the Church of England during the 1500's and 1600's. **3** the place of such a meeting. **4** *Obsolete.* an assembly or meeting. [< Latin *conventiculum* (diminutive) < *conventus, -ūs* assembly < *convenīre;* see etym. under **convene**] **—con|ven′ti|cler,** *n.*

con|ven|tic|u|lar (kon′ven tik′yə lər), *adj.* of or having to do with a conventicle.

con|ven|tion (kən ven′shən), *n.* **1** a meeting arranged for some particular purpose; gathering; assembly: *The Democratic and Republican parties hold conventions every four years to choose candidates for President. Businessmen attend conventions to learn of new developments and products. In a nation of joiners, the convention has become an American social institution* (Newsweek). **SYN:** conference. **2** the delegates to a meeting or assembly. **3** general agreement; common consent; custom: *Convention now permits short hair for women.* **4** a custom or practice approved by general agreement; rule based on common consent: *Using the right hand to shake hands is a convention.* **SYN:** usage, etiquette. **5** an agreement signed by two or more countries about matters less important than those in a treaty. **SYN:** compact. **6** (in the arts) a procedure or detail not taken literally, but accepted by the beholder, reader, or listener as fitting: *It is a convention in the theater that asides are not heard by persons on the stage with the speaker.* **7** an agreement made between opposing military commanders, especially for a truce or cease-fire. **8** (in card playing) a play or bid conveying a special meaning by custom. **9** the calling together of an assembly; convening. [< Latin *conventiō, -ōnis* < *convenīre;* see etym. under **convene**]

con|ven|tion|al (kən ven′shə nəl), *adj.* **1a** depending on conventions; customary: *"Good morning" is a conventional greeting.* **b** of the usual type or design; commonly used or seen: *conventional furniture, a conventional gearshift, conventional aircraft.* **SYN:** See syn. under **formal.** **2a** acting or behaving according to commonly accepted or approved ways: *The people living next door are quiet, conventional people.* **b** conforming to accepted, artificial standards of conduct or taste; formal; not spontaneous: *the conventional phraseology with which English preaching had been so long encumbered* (Arthur P. Stanley). **SYN:** artificial. See syn. under **formal.** **3** (in the arts) following custom and traditional models; formal: *The ode and the sonnet are conventional forms of English poetry. Flowers and leaves are used in a conventional design without any attempt to make them look real.* **4** *Law.* established by contract: *conventional estates.* **5** of or having to do with a convention or assembly. **—con|ven′-tion|al|ly,** *adv.*

con|ven|tion|al|ise (kən ven′shə nə līz), *v.t.,* **-ised, -is|ing.** *Especially British.* conventionalize.

con|ven|tion|al|ism (kən ven′shə nə liz′əm), *n.* **1** tendency to follow conventional usages; adherence to custom. **2** something conventional; a formal usage, word, or phrase. **—con|ven′tion|al|ist,** *n.*

con|ven|tion|al|i|ty (kən ven′shə nal′ə tē), *n., pl.* **-ties.** **1** conventional quality or character: *the conventionality of modern life.* **2** conventional behavior; adherence to custom: *Conventionality requires people to wear clothes in public.* **3** a conventional custom, practice, or rule: *the conventionalities of an institution. Dwellers in great capitals are abject slaves of the conventionalities* (Pall Mall Gazette).

con|ven|tion|al|ize (kən ven′shə nə līz), *v.t.,* **-ized, -iz|ing.** **1** to make conventional; treat conventionally. **2** to design or draw according to customary patterns rather than nature: *The Acanthus leaf, conventionalized, is well liked by architects, painters, and designers* (Bernice G. Chambers). **—con|ven′tion|al|i|za′tion,** *n.*

conventional loan, *U.S.* a mortgage loan that is not insured by a government agency.

conventional wisdom, the generally accepted attitude or opinion; popular belief: *The conventional wisdom about starting newspapers in New York City is that it can't be done* (New Yorker).

con|ven|tion|eer (kən ven′shə nir′), *n., v.* **—*n.*** a person attending a convention; conventioner: *The 5,000 well-brushed, neatly tailored conventioneers . . . turned out for the annual convention of Kiwanis International* (Time).
—*v.i.* to attend a convention: *The conventioneering store men swapped ideas and . . . ways of capturing and caring for new executives* (Wall Street Journal).

con|ven|tion|er (kən ven′shə nər), *n.* a conventioneer.

con|ven|tu|al (kən ven′chů əl), *adj., n.* **—*adj.*** of or like a convent; belonging to or characteristic of a convent: *conventual dress, conventual reverence.*
—*n.* a member of a convent. **—con|ven′tu|al|ly,** *adv.*

Con|ven|tu|al (kən ven′chů əl), *n.* a member of a branch of the Franciscan friars which lives under a rule less austere from that of the others, permitting, for example, the ownership of property in common.

conventual prior, the superior of a monastery smaller than an abbey.

***con|verge** (kən vėrj′), *v.,* **-verged, -verg|ing.**
—*v.i.* **1** to tend to meet in a point: *The sides of a road seem to converge in the distance.* **2** to turn toward each other: *If you look at the end of your nose, your eyes converge.* **3** *Figurative.* to come together; center: *A large group converged on the city hall. The attention of all the audience converged on the screen as soon as the motion picture started.*
—*v.t.* to cause to converge: *A lens thicker in the middle tends to converge parallel rays* (Shortley and Williams).
[< Late Latin *convergere* < Latin *com-* together + *vergere* incline] **—con|verg′ing|ly,** *adv.*

***converge**
definition 1

con|ver|gence (kən vėr′jəns), *n.* **1** the act or process of converging; tendency to meet in one point. **2** the point of converging. **3** the turning inward of the eyes in focusing on something very close to them. **4** *Meteorology.* the converging of air into a particular region. **5** *Biology.* the tendency in animals or plants not closely related to develop similar characteristics when living under the same conditions. **6** *Anthropology.* the development of similarities between cultures due to similar conditions of environment.

con|ver|gen|cy (kən vėr′jən sē), *n., pl.* **-cies.** = convergence.

con|ver|gent (kən vėr′jənt), *adj.* formed by convergence; converging: *convergent lines.*

convergent evolution, the appearance of similar characteristics in animals or plants not closely related to one another.

convergent squint or **strabismus**, a squint in which both eyes are turned inward toward the nose; cross-eye.

con|verg|er (kən vėr′jər), *n.* **1** a person or thing that converges. **2** *Psychology.* a person who excels in close logical reasoning: *The classical converger is a cool, analytical person with a "rational, unimaginative" approach to problems, and is probably a physical scientist* (New Scientist and Science Journal).

con|verg|ing lens (kən vėr′jing), a lens which increases the convergence of a beam of light.

con|vers|a|ble (kən vėr′sə bəl), *adj.* **1** easy or pleasant to talk to. **SYN:** sociable, communicative, affable. **2** fond of talking. **3** having to do with or proper for social intercourse. **—con|vers′a|ble-ness,** *n.* **—con|vers′a|bly,** *adv.*

con|ver|sance (kən vėr′səns, kon′vər-), *n.* the state or quality of being conversant.

con|ver|san|cy (kən vėr′sən sē, kon′vər-), *n.* = conversance.

con|ver|sant (kən vėr′sənt, kon′vər-), *adj.*

1 familiar by use or study; acquainted: *The conductor is conversant with all of the instruments of the orchestra. Students who play football are conversant with the rules of the game.* **SYN**: skilled, proficient, versed. **2** on terms of familiarity (with); intimately associated: *The boy became conversant with the policemen in his neighborhood.* **3** *Obsolete.* accustomed to live or spend time in a certain place. – **con|ver'sant|ly**, *adv.*

con|ver|sa|tion (kon'vər sā'shən), *n.* **1** friendly talk; exchange of thoughts by talking informally together: *Many people say that conversation in a fast-moving world is becoming a lost art.* **2** a talk; a meeting for the purpose of informal talk: *The professor invited his students to his home for a conversation.* **3** an informal meeting of representatives of two or more governments, often preliminary to a formal conference. **4** sexual intercourse or intimacy: *In law, adultery is called criminal conversation.* **5** *Archaic.* the way a person conducts himself; behavior. **6** *Obsolete.* dealing with other people; familiar association. **7** *Obsolete.* familiar acquaintance from using or studying; a being conversant.

make conversation, to converse for the sake of conversing; engage in small talk: *She liked to drop in on her neighbors to make conversation.*

con|ver|sa|tion|al (kon'vər sā'shə nəl), *adj.* **1** of or having to do with conversation. **2** fond of conversation; good at conversation. **3** characteristic of conversation; familiar and informal: *Many poems by Robert Frost are written in a conversational style.* – **con'ver|sa'tion|al|ly**, *adv.*

con|ver|sa|tion|al|ist (kon'vər sā'shə nə list), *n.* a person who is fond of or who is good at conversation.

con|ver|sa|tion|ist (kon'vər sā'shə nist), *n.* = conversationalist.

conversation piece, **1** anything that attracts attention and forms a topic for conversation, especially a rare or unusual object. **2** a kind of genre painting representing a group of figures.

conversation pit, *U.S.* a sunken or recessed area in or near a living room for conversing or entertaining.

con|ver|sa|zi|o|ne (kon'vər sä'tsē ō'nē; *Italian* kôn'ver sä tsyō'nā), *n., pl.* **-o|nes** (-ō'niz), *Italian* **-o|ni** (-ō'nē). *Italian.* a social meeting for conversation on literary, artistic, or scientific topics: *the conversazione held annually in May by the Royal Society* (A. W. Haslett).

con|verse[1] (*v.* kən vėrs'; *n.* kon'vėrs), *v.*, **-versed, -vers|ing,** *n.* – ***v.i.*** **1** to talk together in an informal way; engage in conversation. **SYN**: chat. **2** to hold spiritual communion (with): *and there converse with nature* (James Thomson). **3** *Obsolete.* to consort; keep company (with).
– ***n.*** **1** conversation; discourse; talk: *In like manner as he enjoyed the converse of learned men so also did he take pleasure in the study of eminent writers* (Atlantic). **2** spiritual intercourse; communion: *Like the ships upon the sea which hold an hour's converse* (Alexander Smith).
[< Old French *converser,* learned borrowing from Latin *conversārī* live with, dwell in < *convertere* to change < *com-* around + *vertere* turn] – **con-vers'er**, *n.*

con|verse[2] (*adj.* kən vėrs', kon'vėrs; *n.* kon'-vėrs), *adj., n.* – ***adj.*** **1** opposite or contrary in direction or action: *A converse wind slowed down the airplane.* **2** reversed in order; turned about: *The converse order of the alphabet is from "z" to "a."*
– ***n.*** **1** a thing, especially a statement, that is turned around, opposite, or contrary to something else: *"Honest but poor" is the converse of "Poor but honest."* **2** *Logic.* a proposition obtained from another proposition as the result of conversion.
[< Latin *conversus* turned around, past participle of *convertere;* see etym. under **converse**[1]]

con|verse|ly (kən vėrs'lē, kon'vėrs-), *adv.* if turned the other way around: *Six is more than five; conversely, five is less than six.*

con|vers|i|ble (kən vėr'sə bəl), *adj.* = conversable.

con|ver|sion (kən vėr'zhən, -shən), *n.* **1** the act or process of converting; a changing or turning; change: *Heat causes the conversion of water into steam. Scientists are working on the conversion of salt water into fresh water.* **2** the change from one belief to another or from lack of belief to faith; change from one religion, political party, or other group founded upon belief to another: *Ordinarily we identify conversion with rapid changes of religious conviction, but the same process may occur in other areas of experience* (Ogburn and Nimkoff). **3** an exchange for an equivalent: *the conversion of feet into inches or pounds into dollars.* **4** *Law.* **a** the act of taking and using unlawfully: *Taking over, using, or selling another person's property without his permission is conversion.* **b** a change in the nature of property, such as from real to personal: *the conversion of land into money by selling it.* **5** in football or Rugby: **a** a kick, pass, or run, to score a point or points after a touchdown. **b** one or two extra points scored after a touchdown: *Cole's conversion made it 9-8 and thus the game was wide open again* (Sunday Times). **6** *Mathematics.* a change of a number or quantity into another denomination; reduction. **7** *Logic.* the transposition of subject and predicate in a proposition: *The proposition "no good man is unhappy" gives us by conversion "no unhappy man is good."* **8** the exchanging of an issue of public securities, bonds, or stocks for another, usually carrying a lower rate of interest. **9** *Psychiatry.* the development of physical symptoms of illness as a relief from a repressed mental conflict, with the symptoms acting as symbols of the mental conflict.

con|ver|sion|al (kən vėr'zhə nəl, -shə-), *adj.* of or having to do with conversion.

con|ver|sion|ar|y (kən vėr'zhə ner'ē, -shə-), *adj.* = conversional.

conversion hysteria, *Psychiatry.* hysteria brought on by anxiety or mental conflict, in which repressed wishes or desires are suddenly released by the development of physical symptoms, such as temporary blindness or paralysis, and which produce a characteristic calm and tranquillity.

conversion steel, semifinished steel, usually ingots, obtained from one mill and taken to another to be reworked into a desired finish or shape.

con|vert (*v.* kən vėrt'; *n.* kon'vėrt), *v., n.* – ***v.t.*** **1a** to turn (something) to another purpose; change in form, character, or function; transform: *The generators at the dam convert water power into electricity. These machines convert cotton into cloth. One last effort converted defeat into victory.* **SYN**: turn. See syn. under **transform**. **b** to apply to a use different from that of the original; adapt: *The large mansion was converted into an apartment house. The owner converted the coal furnace into one using oil.* **2** to cause to change from one belief to another or from lack of belief to faith; change from one religion, political party, or other group founded upon belief to another: *French and Spanish missionaries converted some American Indians to the Christian religion.* **SYN**: proselyte, proselytize. **3** *Law.* **a** to take and use unlawfully: *The dishonest treasurer converted the club's money to his own use.* **b** to change (property) from real to personal or personal to real. **4** to turn the other way around; invert; transpose. **5** to exchange for an equivalent: *He converted his dollars into pounds upon arriving in London.* **6** to exchange (a bond or other security) for another type of security, such as common stock. **7** *Obsolete.* to change in position or direction.
– ***v.i.*** **1** to be converted; change: *He converted to his wife's religion when he married her.* **2** (in football or Rugby) to score a conversion: *He converted after all three touchdowns last Saturday.*
– ***n.*** a person who has been converted to a new religion, political party, or other group founded upon belief.
[< Latin *convertere* < *com-* around + *vertere* turn]

con|vert|a|plane (kən vėr'tə plān'), *n.* = convertiplane.

con|vert|er (kən vėr'tər), *n.* **1** a person or thing that converts. **2** a person who makes converts. **3** a person who converts raw textile fabrics into finished products by dyeing or bleaching. **4** a rotating device for changing alternating current into direct current or the reverse. **5** a device in a radio or television receiver for changing from one range of frequency to another. **6** a device which automatically changes one form of computer signal or information into another: *an analog-to-digital converter.* **7** = converter reactor. **8** = Bessemer converter.

converter reactor, a nuclear reactor which converts nonfissionable material to fissionable material.

con|vert|i|bil|i|ty (kən vėr'tə bil'ə tē), *n.* **1** the quality of being convertible: *Trade was freed, and the pound was brought close to convertibility* (Atlantic). **2** the right or freedom to exchange the currency of one country for that of another: *Convertibility greatly facilitates international trade and investment* (Wall Street Journal).

✱**con|vert|i|ble** (kən vėr'tə bəl), *adj., n.* – ***adj.*** **1** that can be converted; capable of being turned into something else or exchanged: *Wood is convertible into paper. A dollar bill is convertible into ten dimes.* **2** (of an automobile) having a top that can be folded down. **3** (of securities) that can be exchanged for others of the same value: *Convertible bonds were firm both Friday and all week* (Wall Street Journal).
– ***n.*** an automobile with a folding top.
convertibles, **a** interchangeable things or terms; equivalents: *to make truths and tales convertibles* (John Stephens). **b** bonds, debentures, preferred stock, or other securities which may be exchanged for common stocks or other securities of equal value, as specified by the terms of their issue: *Convertibles showed gains in more active trading, while ... some foreign bonds declined* (Wall Street Journal).
– **con|vert'i|ble|ness**, *n.* – **con|vert'i|bly**, *adv.*

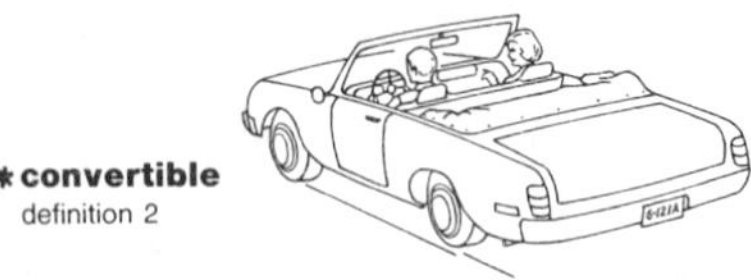

✱**convertible**
definition 2

convertible sofa, a sofa that can be unfolded into a bed, usually with a spring and mattress.

con|vert|i|plane (kən vėr'tə plān'), *n.* an aircraft that operates like a conventional airplane in level flight, but which takes off and lands like a helicopter: *A convertiplane with a helicopter rotor above the fuselage powered by small jet units at the tip of each blade ... was made public* (Science News Letter). Also, **convertaplane**. [< *converti-*(ble) + (air)*plane*]

con|vert|ite (kon'vər tīt), *n. Archaic.* a convert.

con|ver|tor (kən vėr'tər), *n.* = converter.

✱**con|vex** (*adj.* kon veks', kən-; *n.* kon'veks), *adj., n.* – ***adj.*** curved out, like the outside of a circle or sphere; curving out: *The lens of an automobile headlight is convex on the outside. The crystal of a watch is slightly convex. The back of a spoon is a convex mirror* (Beauchamp, Mayfield and West).
– ***n.*** a convex surface, structure, or part.
[< Latin *convexus* vaulted, arched, probably < *com-* around + an unrecorded root *vac-* to bend, related to *vacillāre* totter, sway] – **con|vex'ly**, *adv.* – **con|vex'ness**, *n.*

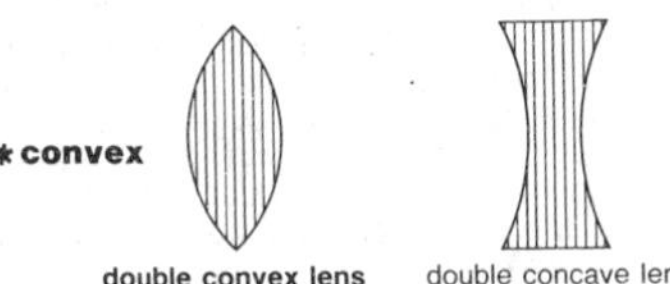

✱**convex**

double convex lens double concave lens

con|vex|i|ty (kən vek'sə tē), *n., pl.* **-ties**. **1** a convex quality or condition. **2** a convex surface or thing.

con|vex|o-con|cave (kən vek'sō kon kāv'), *adj.* convex on one side and concave on the other. In a convexo-concave lens, the convex face has the greater curvature, thus making the lens thickest in the middle. See picture under **lens**.

con|vex|o-con|vex (kən vek'sō kon veks'), *adj.* convex on both sides.

con|vex|o-plane (kən vek'sō plān'), *adj.* convex on one side and flat on the other.

con|vey (kən vā'), *v.t.* **1** to take from one place to another; carry; transport; bear: *A bus conveyed the passengers from the city to the airport.* **SYN**: See syn. under **carry**. **2** to transmit; conduct: *A wire conveys an electric current.* **3** *Figurative.* to make known; communicate; express: *Do the author's words convey any meaning to you? The word "hearth" conveys a feeling of warmth and comfort.* **4** to transfer ownership of (property); hand over; give: *The old farmer conveyed his farm to his son.* **5** *Archaic.* to steal (euphemistic usage). **6** *Obsolete.* to carry off secretly; make away with. **7** *Obsolete.* to conduct or manage with secrecy or craft. [< Old French *conveier* < Vulgar Latin *conviāre* < Latin *com-* with + *via* road. See etym. of doublet **convoy**, verb.] – **con|vey'a|ble**, *adj.*

con|vey|ance (kən vā'əns), *n.* **1** the act of carrying; transmission; transportation: *Freighters engage in the conveyance of goods from one port to another.* **2** a thing that carries people or goods; vehicle; carriage: *Railroad trains and buses are public conveyances.* **3** *Figurative.* communication: *Books are for the conveyance of ideas.* **4** *Law.* **a** a transfer of ownership: *The lease was the first conveyance since 1901* (New York Times). **b** the document showing such a transfer; deed.

con|vey|anc|er (kən vā'ən sər), *n.* a lawyer who searches the title and prepares the deed for a transfer of ownership.

Pronunciation Key: hat, āge, cãre, fär; let, ēqual, tėrm; it, īce; hot, ōpen, ôrder; oil, out; cup, pu̇t, rüle; child; long; thin; ᴛʜen; zh, measure; ə represents **a** in about, **e** in taken, **i** in pencil, **o** in lemon, **u** in circus.

con|vey|anc|ing (kən vā′ən sing), *n. Law.* the preparation of a deed for the transfer of ownership.

con|vey|er (kən vā′ər), *n.* = conveyor.

***con|vey|or** (kən vā′ər), *n.* **1** a person or thing that conveys. **2** a mechanical device that carries things from one place to another, especially by means of a moving, endless belt or chain: *It's his job to pull sealed cartons off the conveyor and open them up to see for himself* (Newsweek). **3** a person who transfers property; conveyancer.

***conveyor** definition 2

conveyor belt, an endless belt that carries things, especially large quantities of material, from place to place. See also **belt** (defs. 4a and b).

con|vey|or|ize (kən vā′ə rīz), *v.t.*, **-ized, -iz|ing.** to provide or carry out with a conveyor.

con|vict (*v., adj.* kən vikt′; *n.* kon′vikt), *v., n., adj.* —*v.t.* **1** to prove or declare guilty, especially after trial before a jury or judge: *The jury convicted the accused man of theft and arson.* **2** *Figurative.* to impress with a sense of guilt: *a person convicted of sin.*
—*n.* **1** a person convicted by a court. **2** a person serving a prison sentence for some crime.
—*adj. Archaic.* convicted.
[< Latin *convictus,* past participle of *convincere;* see etym. under **convince**]

con|vic|tion (kən vik′shən), *n.* **1** the act of proving or declaring guilty: *The trial resulted in the conviction of the guilty man.* **2** the state of being proved or declared guilty: *The thief's conviction meant two years in prison.* **3** the act of convincing (a person). **4** *Figurative.* the state of being convinced. **5** *Figurative.* firm belief: *It was President Lincoln's conviction that the Union must be preserved. We must renew the convictions from which our public morality springs* (Atlantic). SYN: certainty, assurance. See syn. under **belief.** **6** *Figurative.* the fact or condition of being convinced of (one's) sin.

con|vic|tion|al (kən vik′shə nəl), *adj.* of or having to do with conviction or firm belief.

con|vict|ism (kon′vik tiz əm), *n.* **1** the system of transporting convicts to penal settlements. **2** convicts collectively.

con|vic|tive (kən vik′tiv), *adj.* capable of convicting or convincing.

con|vince (kən vins′), *v.t.*, **-vinced, -vinc|ing.** **1** to make (a person) feel sure; cause to believe; persuade firmly: *The mistakes you made convinced me you had not studied your lesson. The buyer was convinced of the salesman's integrity. He convinced the policeman that the parking meter was out of order.* SYN: See syn. under **persuade.** **2** *Obsolete.* to prove or find guilty; convict. **3** *Obsolete.* to refute; disprove. **4** *Obsolete.* to overcome; conquer; overpower. **5** *Obsolete.* to demonstrate; prove. [< Latin *convincere* < *com-* (intensive) + *vincere* overcome] —**con|vince′ment,** *n.* —**con|vinc′er,** *n.*
► **Convince** is followed by the object plus *of* and a noun, or by a *that* clause: *I shall easily convince you of his innocence. You will soon be convinced that I am right.* In less formal but increasingly common usage, it is followed by the object plus an infinitive: *We convinced her to stay. He could not be convinced to let the people go.*

con|vin|ci|ble (kən vin′sə bəl), *adj.* that can be convinced.

con|vinc|ing (kən vin′sing), *adj.* that convinces: *a convincing argument.* SYN: persuasive, cogent. —**con|vinc′ing|ly,** *adv.* —**con|vinc′ing|ness,** *n.*

con|vive (kon′vīv; *French* kôn vēv′), *n.* a drinking or eating companion: *A favored guest ... has been guzzling lobster while his convives made do with haddock and gravy soup* (New Yorker). [< French *convive*]

con|viv|i|al (kən viv′ē əl), *adj.* **1** fond of eating and drinking with friends; sociable; jovial: *A gregarious man, he enjoyed the companionship of a large number of convivial friends* (New Yorker). **2** of or suitable for a feast or banquet; festive; gay. [< Latin *convīviālis* < *convīvium* feast < *com-* with + *vīvere* live] —**con|viv′i|al|ly,** *adv.*

con|viv|i|al|ist (kən viv′ē ə list), *n.* a convivial person.

con|viv|i|al|i|ty (kən viv′ē al′ə tē), *n., pl.* **-ties.** **1** fondness for eating and drinking with friends; good fellowship: *Conviviality is an asset for a lawyer anywhere* (Harper's). **2** eating and drinking with friends; festivity.

con|viv|i|um (kən viv′ē əm), *n., pl.* **-viv|i|a** (-viv′ē ə). a festive celebration; feast; party. [< Latin *convīvium;* see etym. under **convivial**]

con|vo|ca|tion (kon′və kā′shən), *n.* **1** a calling together; an assembling by a summons. **2** an assembly; a number of persons met in answer to a summons: *A convocation of clergymen passed a resolution condemning violence.* **3** an assembly of students and teachers at a college commencement. **4a** an assembly of graduates of certain British universities to discuss or advise on educational matters connected with their universities. **b** a meeting of these graduates.

con|vo|ca|tion|al (kon′və kā′shə nəl), *adj.* of or of the nature of a convocation.

con|vo|ca|tor (kon′və kā′tər), *n.* a person who convokes an assembly; a member of a convocation.

con|voke (kən vōk′), *v.t.*, **-voked, -vok|ing.** to call together; summon to assemble. [< Middle French *convoquer,* learned borrowing from Latin *convocāre* < *com-* together + *vocāre* call] —**con|vok′er,** *n.*

con|vo|lute (kon′və lüt), *adj., v.*, **-lut|ed -lut|ing.** —*adj.* rolled up into a spiral shape with one part over another; coiled: *The leaves in a bud of the cherry tree are convolute. The whorls of certain sea shells are convolute.*
—*v.t., v.i.* to coil up; form into a coiled or twisted shape; twist.
[< Latin *convolūtus,* past participle of *convolvere;* see etym. under **convolve**] —**con′vo|lute′ly,** *adv.*

con|vo|lut|ed (kon′və lü′tid), *adj.* having convolutions; coiled; twisted: *The inner ear or labyrinth ... consists of tiny convoluted channels in the bone* (Simeon Potter).

***con|vo|lu|tion** (kon′və lü′shən), *n.* **1** a coiling, winding, or twisting together: *the convolutions of a snake slithering through the grass.* **2** a coil; winding; twist. **3** an irregular fold or ridge on the surface of the brain: *the convolutions of the cerebral hemispheres.*

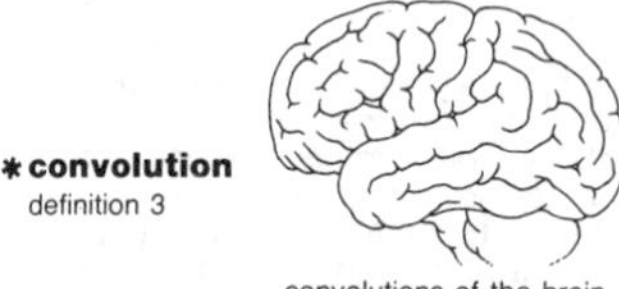
***convolution** definition 3
convolutions of the brain

con|vo|lu|tion|al (kon′və lü′shə nəl), *adj.* = convolutionary.

con|vo|lu|tion|ar|y (kon′və lü′shə ner′ē), *adj.* of or having to do with a convolution or convolutions, especially of the brain.

con|volve (kən volv′), *v.*, **-volved, -volv|ing.** —*v.t.* to roll or wind together; coil; twist.
—*v.i.* to form convolutions.
[< Latin *convolvere* < *com-* together + *volvere* roll] —**con|volve′ment,** *n.*

con|vol|vu|la|ceous (kən vol′vyə lā′shəs), *adj.* belonging to the morning-glory family. [< New Latin *Convolvulaceae* the family name (< Latin *convolvulus;* see etym. under **convolvulus**) + English *-ous*]

***con|vol|vu|lus** (kən vol′vyə ləs), *n., pl.* **-lus|es, -li** (-lī). any one of a group of plants (usually vines) of the same family as the morning-glory, with slender, twining stems, and flowers shaped like trumpets; bindweed. [< Latin *convolvulus* bindweed (diminutive) < *convolvere* roll around (because of its twining stems); see etym. under **convolve**]

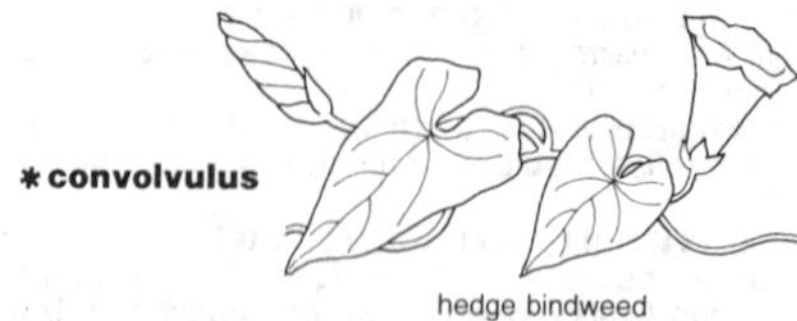
***convolvulus**
hedge bindweed

con|voy (*v.* kən voi′, kon′voi; *n.* kon′voi), *v., n.* —*v.t.* **1** to go with in order to protect; escort: *Warships convoy unarmed merchant ships during time of war.* **2** *Archaic.* to guide; conduct: *Many of the company had bespoken a will-o'-the-wisp to convoy them home* (Hawthorne).
—*n.* **1** a convoying; protection: *The gold was moved from the truck to the bank's vault under convoy of armed guards.* SYN: escort. **2** the warships, soldiers, or others that convoy; protecting escort. **3** a ship, fleet, supplies, or other valuable material that is convoyed: *The convoy reached harbor with all its troops and stores intact. But the cruiser was again ordered to shepherd another convoy* (Newsweek). **4** *Obsolete.* a conducting medium; channel; way.
[< Middle French *convoyer* < Old French *conveier.* See etym. of doublet **convey.**]

con|vul|sant (kən vul′sənt), *adj., n.* —*adj.* that produces convulsions: *A number of reports have appeared suggesting the tranquilizer may have convulsant effects* (Science News Letter).
—*n.* a convulsant drug, agent, etc.

con|vulse (kən vuls′), *v.t.*, **-vulsed, -vuls|ing.** **1** to shake violently: *An earthquake convulsed the island, damaging many of the buildings.* SYN: agitate. **2** to cause violent disturbance in: *His face was convulsed with rage.* **3** to throw into convulsions; shake with muscular spasms: *The sick child was convulsed before the doctor came.* **4** to throw into fits of laughter; cause to shake with laughter: *The clown convulsed the audience with his funny acts.* [< Latin *convulsus,* past participle of *convellere* to tear violently < *com-* (intensive) + *vellere* to tear away]

con|vul|sion (kən vul′shən), *n.* **1** Often, **convulsions.** violent, involuntary contracting of the muscles; spasm: *The sick child's convulsions frightened his mother.* **2** a fit of laughter. **3** *Figurative.* a violent disturbance: *An earthquake is a convulsion of the earth. The country was undergoing a political convulsion.* SYN: tumult, agitation, perturbation.

con|vul|sion|ar|y (kən vul′shə ner′ē), *adj., n., pl.* **-ar|ies.** —*adj.* having to do with, of the nature of, or affected with convulsions.
—*n.* a person who tends to have convulsions, especially as a manifestation of religious or other hysteria.

con|vul|sive (kən vul′siv), *adj.* **1** violently disturbing. **2** having convulsions. **3** producing convulsions. —**con|vul′sive|ly,** *adv.* —**con|vul′sive|ness,** *n.*

co|ny (kō′nē, kun′ē), *n., pl.* **-nies.** **1** rabbit fur. Cony is used to make or trim coats. **2** = rabbit. **3** a small, rabbitlike rodent; pika. **4** a small, rodentlike animal with hoofs; hyrax (in the Bible, Leviticus 11:5). **5** any one of various marine fishes, especially the rock hind. **6** *Obsolete.* a dupe; gull. Also, **coney.** [< Old French *conil* < Latin *cunīculus* rabbit < an Iberian word]

coo (kü), *n., v.*, **cooed, coo|ing,** *interj.* —*n.* **1** the soft, murmuring sound made by doves or pigeons. **2** a sound like this.
—*v.i.* **1** to make a soft, murmuring sound. **2** to murmur softly; speak in a soft, loving manner: *The mother cooed over her baby.*
—*v.t.* to utter or express by cooing.
—*interj. British Informal.* an exclamation indicating astonishment or disbelief.
[imitative] —**coo′er,** *n.* —**coo′ing|ly,** *adv.*

cooch (küch), *n. U.S. Slang.* a solo dance characterized by highly stylized and uninhibited movements. Also, **cootch.** [perhaps < (hootchy)-*kootch*(y)]

coo|ee (kü′ē), *n., pl.* **-ees,** *interj., v.*, **-eed, -ee|ing.** —*n., interj.* **1** a long, shrill signal call of the Australian aborigines, adopted by Australian colonists. **2** *U.S.* a high, repeated, fast call used by farmers to call hogs.
—*v.i.* to make this call.
[imitative]

coo|ey (kü′ē), *n., pl.* **-eys,** *interj., v.i.*, **-eyed, -ey|ing.** = cooee.

coof (küf), *n. Scottish.* a dull, lifeless fellow.

cook¹ (ku̇k), *v., n.* —*v.t.* **1** to prepare (food) by using heat. We use coal, wood, gas, oil, and electricity for cooking. Boiling, frying, broiling, roasting, and baking are forms of cooking. **2** to apply heat or fire to. **3** *Informal.* to subject to atomic radiation, especially by means of a nuclear reactor: *thorium ... can be converted into the fuel U-233 by cooking it in a pile* (Atlantic). **4** *Informal, Figurative.* to tamper with; falsify; doctor.
—*v.i.* **1** to prepare food for eating; act or work as cook: *He cooked in lumber camps for twenty years.* **2** to undergo cooking; be cooked: *Let the meat cook slowly. The dumplings cooked too long.* **3** *Informal, Figurative.* to happen; take place: *We asked Mr. Randall what was cooking in the dance world* (New Yorker). **4** *U.S. Slang.* to act or play with spirit and excitement; work very well: *Ray Fransen is on the drums, and he makes everything cook. It is the best band we have heard yet* (New Yorker).
[< noun]
—*n.* a person who cooks.
cook up, *Informal.* **a** to make up or prepare: *White House foreign policy ... has a brain trust cooking up a new approach to foreign aid* (Wall Street Journal). **b** *Figurative.* to prepare falsely: *He cooked up an excuse for being late. Negroes were arrested on the roads and herded into jails on cooked-up charges* (Time).
[Old English *cōc,* ultimately < Latin *cocus,* variant of *coquus* < *coquere* to cook]

cook² (ku̇k, kük), *v.i. Scottish.* to disappear suddenly. [origin uncertain]

cook|book (ku̇k′bu̇k′), *n.* a book of directions for cooking various kinds of food; book of recipes.
cook|er (ku̇k′ər), *n.* **1a** an apparatus, appliance, or container to cook things in: *a steam cooker.* **b** *British.* stove: *At last an inexpensive cooker with all the luxuries, plus sensational new features* (Sunday Times). **2** *Especially British.* any variety of fruit or vegetable especially suitable for cooking.
cook|er|y (ku̇k′ər ē), *n., pl.* **-er|ies. 1** the art or occupation of cooking: *Besides television, their major diversion is . . . cookery* (Wall Street Journal). **2** a place for cooking.
cookery book, *Especially British.* a cookbook.
cook-gen|er|al (ku̇k′jen′ər əl, -jen′rəl), *n., pl.* **cooks-gen|er|al.** *British.* a servant whose duties include cooking and general housework.
cook|house (ku̇k′hous′), *n.* a room or place for cooking: *the cookhouse that served 3,300 meals a day* (Newsweek).
cook|ie (ku̇k′ē), *n.* **1** a small, flat, sweet cake. **2** *Scottish.* a plain bun. **3** *Slang.* **a** a person, especially a man, of a specified character: *a smart cookie, a tough cookie. "Wish I was as shrewd a cookie as Paul Newman"* (Robert Redford). **b** a familiar form of address for a girl: *Hi, cookie!* **4** *U.S. Cowboy Slang.* a cook who prepares the food and rides the range with a chuck wagon.
that's how (or **the way**) **the cookie crumbles,** *Especially U.S. Informal.* that is the way it is; that is how things are: *He charged in against the dragon relying on God to help him, and if He didn't, well, that's the way the cookie crumbles* (Harper's).
[American English <Dutch *koekje* little cake]
cookie cutter, a mold having sharp edges, for cutting rolled-out dough into a desired shape.
cook|ie-cut|ter (ku̇k′ē kut′ər), *adj. U.S. Informal.* cast from the same mold; identical in form, nature, or character: *At Bush headquarters . . . there are so many beautiful blond cookie-cutter interns it looks like the student union at Princeton* (Vanity Fair).
cookie jar, 1 a jar for storing cookies. **2** *U.S. Informal.* such a jar used as a hiding place for savings: *Digging into their cookie jars . . . to buy instruments and uniforms* (Time).
cookie pusher, *U.S. Slang.* a person who spends an inordinate amount of time at social events at the expense of his work.
cookie sheet, a flat piece of metal, usually with a lip in front, used for baking cookies or biscuits and for warming food in an oven.
cook|ing (ku̇k′ing), *n.* the art of preparing foods for the table, usually by heating them until they are changed in flavor, tenderness, appearance, and chemical composition. Cooking develops flavor, and makes many foods more attractive in appearance.
cook|out (ku̇k′out′), *n.* a meal cooked and eaten outdoors.
cook|shop (ku̇k′shop′), *n.* a place where food is cooked and sold; small restaurant.
Cook's tour (ku̇ks), **1** a hasty and superficial tour; quick sightseeing trip: *Around the World in 80 Days—A Cook's tour [is] derived from the fantasy by Jules Verne* (New Yorker). **2** any cursory survey or examination: *The term's course might involve, not a Cook's tour, but a concentrated study of . . . some focal problem or issue* (Listener).
[<Thomas *Cook,* 1808-1892, the founder of a famous British tourist agency]
cook|stove (ku̇k′stōv′), *n.* a stove for cooking.
cook|top (ku̇k′top′), *n.* a flat metal or ceramic plate embedded with individual heating elements for cooking utensils.
cook|ware (ku̇k′wãr′), *n.* articles used in cooking, such as bowls, pans, and spoons.
cook|y (ku̇k′ē), *n., pl.* **cook|ies.** = cookie.
cool (kül), *adj., adv., n., v.* —*adj.* **1** somewhat cold; agreeably cold; more cold than hot: *a cool, cloudy day. The cool night bathes the world as with a river* (Emerson). **SYN:** See syn. under **cold. 2** allowing or giving a cool feeling: *a cool, thin dress for summer wear. Under the cool shade of a sycamore* (Shakespeare). **3** *Figurative.* not excited; calm; unemotional: *Everyone kept cool when paper in the wastebasket caught fire. While she wept, and I strove to be cool* (Tennyson). **SYN:** dispassionate. **4** *Figurative.* having little enthusiasm or interest; not cordial: *My former friend gave me a cool greeting. The Liberals' reception of the moves has remained cool* (London Times). **SYN:** indifferent, lukewarm. **5** *Figurative.* bold or impudent in a calm way: *In a cool tone the student told the teacher that her test was unfair.* **SYN:** audacious, outrageous. **6** *Informal.* without exaggeration; no less than: *He said he had made a cool million dollars trading in stocks.* **7** *Slang.* admirable; excellent. **8** (of colors) blue, green, or gray: *The cool colors are those between violet and green with a maximum coolness near a greenish blue* (Matthew Luckiesh). **9** not contaminated by radioactivity. **10** *Slang, Figurative.* characterized by a sophisticated, unemotional, and relaxed style, rendition, or technique: *Cool jazz shows a marked influence of classical music.*
—*adv. Slang.* in a cool way; coolly: *Charlotte says, "I just can't come on cool—I don't know why"* (Maclean's).
—*n.* **1** something cool; a cool part, place, or time: *in the cool of the evening.* **2** a moderate temperature; coolness. **3** *Slang, Figurative.* calm restraint; presence of mind: *I thought nothing could shock me any more. I maintained my cool* (Saturday Review). *The Mexican-American kept his cool in his own ghetto* (Time). *Sorry if I blew my cool, but it builds up and I have to let go sometimes* (New Yorker). **SYN:** self-control.
—*v.t.* **1** to make cool; give a feeling of coolness to: *Ice cools water. He was cooled by the shade of the apple tree.* **2** *Figurative.* to cause to lose enthusiasm or zeal; make less ardent; moderate: *Losing every bet cooled his interest in gambling.*
—*v.i.* **1** to become cool: *The ground cools off when the sun goes down.* **2** *Figurative.* to lose enthusiasm or zeal; become less ardent; become moderate: *His interest in flying cooled after he cracked up his plane. What makes her decide to give him up . . . is not his cooling off nor his being already married* (Saturday Review). **3** *Figurative.* to resume an ordinary mental balance after showing a fit of temper: *Don't talk to him now; wait until he cools down. It took him a while to cool off after the quarrel.*
cool it, *Slang.* **a** to calm down: *Simmer down! Cool it!* **b** to take it easy; relax: *I cooled it at a table for a while* (Time). **c** to loosen up; be carefree: *The boys . . . want to go out and cool it with the neighbor's daughters* (New York Times).
cool one's heels. See under **heel**[1].
cool out, a to relax (a race horse) after a race or exercise by leading him gently about. **b** to become relaxed in this manner: *The trainer said that he "will wait to see how the filly cools out before deciding on her next race"* (New York Times).
play it cool, *Slang.* to act unemotionally; affect complete reserve or detachment: *Contemporary realists play it too cool for words like confidence and sympathy, but, almost reluctantly, they seem to be . . . in touch with life* (Time).
[Old English *cōl.* See related etym. at **cold.**]
coo|la|bah or **coo|li|bah** (kü′lə bä), *n.* a kind of Australian eucalyptus, often found near water.
[<a native Australian name]
cool|ant (kü′lənt), *n.* a cooling substance, used to reduce heat in machinery: *Purified water under high pressure formed the primary coolant which extracted the heat from the thermal reactor* (London Times).
cool|er (kü′lər), *n.* **1** anything that cools. **2** a container that cools foods or drinks, or keeps them cool. **3** a cooling medicine or agent; refrigerant. **4** *U.S. Slang.* a prison or jail: *"Well, Mister, into the cooler," the cop said* (New Yorker).
Coo|ley's anemia (kü′lēz), = thalassemia.
[<Thomas Benton *Cooley,* 1871-1945, an American pediatrician]
cool-head|ed (kül′hed′id), *adj.* not easily excited; calm. —**cool′-head′ed|ly,** *adv.* —**cool′-head′ed|ness,** *n.*
Coo|lidge tube (kü′lij), a tube for the generation of X rays by means of a cathode consisting of a spiral of tungsten heated to incandescence.
[<William D. *Coolidge,* 1873-1975, an American physical chemist, who invented it]
coo|lie (kü′lē), *n., pl.* **-lies,** *adj.* —*n.* **1** an unskilled laborer in India or China: *In 1924 he was evicted and fled Peking disguised as a coolie* (Newsweek). **2** a laborer who does hard work for very little pay.
—*adj.* like that worn by a coolie: *a coolie hat or suit.* Also, **cooly.**
[<Hindustani *qūlī,* probably <Tamil *kūli* hired (servant), to hire]
cool|ing-off (kü′ling ôf′, -of′), *adj., n.* —*adj.* arranged or decreed for the purpose of calming down the parties in a quarrel or dispute and preparing for reasonable negotiations: *A "cooling-off" clause specified that a 30-day no-strike period should follow* (Wall Street Journal).
—*n.* a cooling-off interval or period: *Some international diplomatic initiative may produce a cooling-off* (William Beecher).
cooling tower, a structure in which waste steam or water from power plants is cooled for reuse: *The designer of a large cooling tower must . . . know what the temperature of the water will be when it enters the tower and what temperature it should be when it leaves the tower* (Scientific American).
cool|ish (kü′lish), *adj.* rather cool.
cool|ly (kül′lē), *adv.* **1** in a cool condition; with coolness. **2** *Figurative.* without emotion, excitement, or haste; calmly; collectedly. **3** *Figurative.* without fervor, enthusiasm, or friendly warmth; with an air of indifference. **4** *Figurative.* with calm and unabashed assurance.
cool|ness (kül′nis), *n.* **1** the condition of being or feeling cool; cool quality or sensation. **2** *Figurative.* freedom from excitement; calmness: *Only [his] coolness and tact averted a conflict* (John Richard Green). **3** *Figurative.* lack of fervor or enthusiasm; absence of warmth or cordiality. **4** *Figurative.* calm and unabashed assurance.
coolth (külth), *n.* the state of being cool; coolness: *Other electronically active solids convert heat to electricity . . . and still others change electricity to coolth* (Harper's).
coo|ly (kü′lē), *n., pl.* **-lies.** = coolie.
coom[1] (küm, kōm), *n.* = combe.
coom[2] (küm), *n. Scottish.* **1** soot. **2** grease from axles or bearings. [Middle English *colm;* origin uncertain]
coomb (küm, kōm), *n.* = combe.
coon (kün), *n.* **1** = raccoon. **2** a member of the Whig Party in the United States from 1838 to 1844, when the raccoon was the party emblem.
coon's age, *U.S. Informal.* a long time: *We had not seen the amount of cash mentioned as lost, in a coon's age* (J. J. Hooper).
[American English, short for *raccoon*]
coon bear, = giant panda.
coon|can (kün′kan′), *n.* = conquian.
coon|hound (kün′hound′), *n. U.S.* a dog especially good at hunting raccoons.
***coon|skin** (kün′skin′), *n., adj.* —*n.* the skin of a raccoon, used for making caps, coats, mittens, or boots: *Because of the paucity of coonskins, he's using Australian rabbit, skunk, and even silver fox* (Wall Street Journal).
—*adj.* made of coonskin: *a coonskin coat.*

***coonskin**

coon|tie (kün′tē), *n.* **1** any one of various tropical American plants from whose roots and stems a starch called arrowroot is obtained. **2** flour made from this starch. [American English <Muskhogean *kunti* arrowroot flour]
coon|y (kü′nē), *adj.,* **coon|i|er, coon|i|est.** *Slang.* wary and clever; shrewd. [<*coon* + *-y*[1]]
coop[1] (küp, ku̇p), *n., v.* —*n.* **1** a small cage or pen for chickens, rabbits, and other small animals. **2** *Figurative.* a narrow, confined place. **3** *Slang, Figurative.* a prison.
—*v.t.* **1** to keep in a coop. **2** *Figurative.* to confine, especially in a very small space; cage: *The children were cooped up indoors by the rain.*
—*v.i. U.S. Slang.* to sleep in a parked police car while on patrol duty: *Small wonder that there was "cooping," or sleeping on the job; there simply wasn't much work to be done at 4:00* A.M. (Harper's).
fly the coop, *Slang.* to escape: *Jabez had hunted over the place . . . as soon as he discovered that Barbie and me had flown the coop* (R. A. Watson).
[Middle English *coupe* basket, perhaps variant of Old English *cȳpe* basket, ultimately <Latin *cūpa* cask]
co|op[2] or **co-op** (kō′op, kō op′), *n. Informal.* a cooperative store, apartment house, or apartment.
coop. or **co-op., 1** cooperation. **2** cooperative (store, society, or apartment).
coop|er (kü′pər, ku̇p′ər), *n., v.* —*n.* a man who makes and repairs wooden containers, such as barrels, casks, tubs, and, sometimes, crates.
—*v.t.* to make or repair (barrels, casks, tubs, or crates).
—*v.i.* to work as a cooper.
[perhaps <Middle Dutch *kūper* <Latin *cūpārius* <*cūpa* cask]
coop|er|age (kü′pər ij, ku̇p′ər-), *n.* **1** the work done by a cooper; business of a cooper. **2** the price paid for a cooper's work. **3** a shop where such work or business is done.
co|op|er|ant (kō op′ər ənt), *adj., n.* —*adj.* working together; cooperating.
—*n.* a cooperating agent.
co|op|er|ate (kō op′ə rāt), *v.i.,* **-at|ed, -at|ing. 1** to work together; unite in producing a result: *The children cooperated with their teachers in*

Pronunciation Key: hat, āge, cãre, fär; let, ēqual, tėrm; it, īce; hot, ōpen, ôrder; oil, out; cup, pu̇t, rüle; child; long; thin; ᴛʜen; zh, measure; ə represents a in about, e in taken, i in pencil, o in lemon, u in circus.

keeping their classrooms neat. **2** to practice economic cooperation. [< Late Latin *cooperārī* (with English *-ate*[1]) < Latin *com-* together + *operārī* to work < *opera* work < *opus, -eris*]

co|op|er|a|tion (kō op′ə rā′shən), *n.* **1** the act of working together; united effort or labor: *Cooperation can accomplish many things which no individual could do alone. But cooperation with others to achieve a common good is also strongly satisfying to personality* (Ogburn and Nimkoff). **2** *Economics.* the combination of persons for purposes of production, purchase, or distribution for their joint benefit. **3** *Biology.* the mutually beneficial activity of organisms living together.

co|op|er|a|tion|ist (kō op′ə rā′shə nist), *n.* a person who practices or advocates cooperation.

co|op|er|a|tive (kō op′rə tiv, -op′ə rā′-), *adj., n.* —*adj.* **1** wanting or willing to work with others: *Most of the pupils were helpful and cooperative.* **2** of or having to do with cooperation: *The process results from cooperative research by experts in four fields.* **3** of or having to do with a store, apartment, or other property or organization in which profits and losses are shared by members. —*n.* **1** = cooperative store. **2** a union of farmers for buying and selling their produce at the best price. **3** an organization in which the profits and losses are shared by all members. **4a** an apartment house owned and operated by the tenants. In a cooperative, apartments are sold to individual owners, who share the operating costs of the building. **b** an apartment in such a building. —**co|op′er|a|tive|ly**, *adv.* —**co|op′er|a|tive-ness**, *n.*

cooperative bank, = savings and loan association.

cooperative store, a store where merchandise is sold to members who share in the profits and losses according to the amounts they buy.

co|op|er|a|tor (kō op′ə rā′tər), *n.* **1** a person who cooperates. **2** a member of a cooperative society.

Coop|er pair (kü′pər, kůp′ər), a pair of electrons with equal and opposite momentum and spin which, according to the BCS theory of super-conductivity, attract each other and combine through an interaction involving the lattice of positive ions. [< Leon N. *Cooper,* born 1930, an American physicist]

Coop|er's hawk (kü′pərz, kůp′ərz), an American hawk colored like the sharp-shinned hawk but larger. [< William *Cooper,* died 1864, an American naturalist]

co-opt (kō opt′), *v.t.* **1** to elect (a new member) into a body by joint action or by the votes of the existing members: *He was co-opted into the Soviet War College to give history lectures* (New York Times). **2a** to take over; secure for oneself; adopt: *What it means is that rock has been co-opted by high culture, forced to adopt its standards* (New Yorker). **b** to commandeer: *Jack McNally co-opting the cars to carry the President's household staff to Arlington* (Atlantic). —*v.i.* to choose or elect new members: *the establishment of area health boards having an elected membership with powers to co-opt* (London Times). [< Latin *cooptāre* < *com-* together with + *optāre* choose, elect]

co-op|tate (kō op′tāt), *v.t.,* **-tat|ed, -tat|ing.** = co-opt.

co-op|ta|tion (kō′op tā′shən), *n.* election to membership by the votes of the existing members; a co-opting.

co-op|ta|tive (kō op′tə tiv), *adj.* of or chosen by co-optation.

co-op|tion (kō op′shən), *n.* = co-optation.

co|or|di|nal or **co-or|di|nal** (kō ôr′də nəl), *adj. Biology.* belonging to the same order or family.

***co|or|di|nate** (*v.* kō ôr′də nāt; *adj., n.* kō ôr′də nit, -nāt), *v.,* **-nat|ed, -nat|ing,** *adj., n.* —*v.t.* **1** to arrange in proper order; put in proper relation; adjust; harmonize: *A swimmer should coordinate the movements of his arms and legs. A symphonic conductor coordinates the playing of the instruments in his orchestra.* **2** to make coordinate; make equal in importance. —*v.i.* **1** to become coordinate. **2** to be arranged in the proper order or relation; form a system. **3** to act together harmoniously: *If your muscles don't coordinate as you walk, you will trip or fall down.* —*adj.* **1a** equal in importance; of equal rank: *The chief of police has power coordinate with or next to the local judge.* **b** of equal grammatical importance. In the phrase "a cold, windy day," "cold" and "windy" are coordinate adjectives. **2** made up of coordinate parts. **3** joining words, phrases, or clauses of equal grammatical importance. See also **coordinating conjunction**. **4** *Mathematics.* having to do with or involving the use of coordinates. **5** *Chemistry.* in which one atom shares two electrons with another atom: *a coordinate bond.* **6** *U.S.* in which men and women attend separate colleges: *Harvard University, with Harvard College chiefly for men and Radcliffe College for women, is a coordinate university.* —*n.* **1** a coordinate person or thing; an equal: *Citizens are coordinates in a court of law.* **2** *Mathematics.* any of two or more numbers that define the position of a point, line, plane, or system with regard to a frame of reference, such as a fixed figure or system of lines. **coordinates**, clothing matched in color, fabric, or style to produce a harmonious effect in combination: *. . . there's striped and plain coordinates and Him and Her outfits for brothers and sisters* (Punch). [< Latin Latin *coordinātus,* past participle of *coordināre* < Latin *com-* with *ordināre* set in order, regulate < *ordo, -inis* arrangement, order, series] —**co|or′di|nate|ly**, *adv.* —**co|or′di|nate-ness**, *n.* —**co|or′di|na′tor**, *n.*

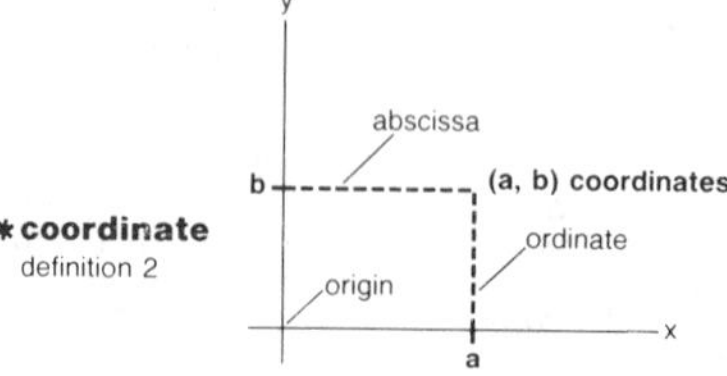

***coordinate**
definition 2

coordinate clause, a clause, especially a main clause, equal in grammatical importance to another clause in the same sentence: *A compound sentence has two or more coordinate clauses.*

coordinate conjunction, = coordinating conjunction.

coordinate geometry, = analytic geometry.

co|or|di|nat|ing conjunction (cō ôr′də nā′ting), a conjunction that connects words, phrases, or clauses of equal rank. *"And" and "but" are coordinating conjunctions.*

co|or|di|na|tion (kō ôr′də nā′shən), *n.* **1** harmonious adjustment or working together: *Poor coordination in his hands made his drawing crude. Lack of coordination and leadership in nonmilitary defense efforts* (New York Times). **2** arrangement in proper order or proper relation: *An outline often helps in the coordination of ideas.* **3** a putting or being put into the same order or rank. **4** *Chemistry.* **a** the formation of coordinate bonds. **b** the group or number of atoms bound to the central atom by coordinate bonds.

co|or|di|na|tive (kō ôr′də nā′tiv), *adj.* coordinating.

Coos (küs), *n.* any one of several American Indian languages of the Penutian group.

coot (küt), *n.* **1** a wading and swimming bird somewhat like a duck, with short wings and webbed feet. **2** a large, black duck of northern regions and seas; scoter. **3** *Informal.* a fool; simpleton. [Middle English *cote*]

cootch (küch), *n. U.S. Slang.* cooch.

coot|ie (kü′tē) , *n.* **1** *Slang.* a louse; body louse. **2** a children's game played by rolling a die to determine who will complete a stylized drawing of a louse. [origin unknown]

co|own|er (kō ō′nər), *n.* a joint owner.

co|own|er|ship (kō ō′nər ship), *n.* joint ownership; copartnership: *Needed in our industrial relations is a great increase in coownership and participation by the workers* (Punch).

cop[1] (kop), *n. Informal.* a policeman. [probably short for *copper*[2] policeman < *cop*[2]]

cop[2] (kop), *v.,* **copped, cop|ping,** *n. Slang.* —*v.t.* **1** to capture; catch; nab: *It is clear that the U.S. has copped the prize for the first lap at least* (Newsweek). **2** to steal. —*n. British.* a capture; catch; acquisition: *a fair cop.*

cop it, *British.* to catch it; be hurt or punished: *Snowdon will cop it from one of those corgis if he's not careful* (Sunday Times).

cop out, *Slang.* **a** to back out; refuse to become involved: *It isn't only the young who are copping out of the political system but also their elders* (James Reston). **b** to avoid or escape (as work or problems); give up; quit: *Actresses who played career girls, like Crawford, could cop out in their roles by getting pregnant* (Pauline Kael). **c** Also, **cop a plea.** to plead guilty to the lesser of two or more charges. **d** to receive a smaller penalty by such a plea: *If he pleads guilty to grand larceny, he can cop out for only five to ten years* (Time). [perhaps < Old French *caper* seize; compare Old English *coppian* steal, pillage]

cop[3] (kop), *n.* **1a** a cone-shaped ball of thread or yarn wound on a spindle in a spinning machine. **b** a tube on which silk is wound in given lengths. **2** *Obsolete.* the top or crest of anything. [Old English *copp* top, summit]

cop., **1** copper. **2** copyrighted.

Cop., Coptic.

co|pa|cet|ic (kō′pə set′ik, -sē′tik), *adj. U.S. Slang.* very good; all right: *"All set," he said to someone. "Everything is copacetic. I'm fixed up with Irma"* (John O'Hara). [origin unknown]

co|pai|ba (kō pā′bə, -pī′-), *n.* an aromatic oleoresin obtained from various South American trees of the pea family, used in varnish and formerly used as a medicine for chronic inflammations of the mucous membranes. [< Brazilian Portuguese *copayva* < Tupi (Brazil) *cupauba*]

co|pain (kô paɴ′), *n. French.* close friend; companion; chum.

co|pal (kō′pəl, -pal), *n.* a hard, lustrous resin from various tropical and subtropical trees, used chiefly in making varnish. [< Mexican Spanish *copal* < Nahuatl *copalli* incense]

co|palm (kō′päm), *n.* **1** a fragrant, yellowish balsam that exudes from the sweet gum. **2** the sweet gum. [origin uncertain]

co|par|ce|nar|y (kō pär′sə ner′ē; *especially British* kō pär′sə nər ē), *n., pl.* **-ries.** **1** joint share in an inheritance; joint heirship. **2** copartnership; joint ownership.

co|par|ce|ner (kō pär′sə nər), *n.* a coheir or coheiress. [< *co-* + *parcener*]

co|part|ner (kō pärt′nər), *n.* **1** a person who shares or takes part with others in any enterprise, office, business, or common interest; fellow partner; associate. **2** an accomplice: *his copartner in crime.*

co|part|ner|ship (kō part′nər ship), *n.* **1** the relation of copartners; possession of a joint share in an enterprise, business, or interest; partnership: *to form a copartnership in business. It is sometimes said that copartnership by bringing the interests of capital and labour more closely together will do away with their old antagonism* (London Times). **2** a company or association of copartners.

cope[1] (kōp), *v.,* **coped, cop|ing.** —*v.i.* **1** to fight with some degree of success; struggle and not fail; get on successfully (with): *Mother could not cope with all the housework and two sick children. Computers will help government cope with workloads which are beginning to overwhelm some offices* (Newsweek). **2** *Archaic.* to have to do (with). **3** *Obsolete.* to come to blows. —*v.t. Obsolete.* to meet in contest. [< Old French *coper, couper* strike < *coup* a blow, coup[1]]

cope[2] (kōp), *n., v.,* **coped, cop|ing.** —*n.* **1** a long cape worn by priests during certain religious rites. **2** anything like a cope; a cloaklike covering, such as a canopy, a high arched roof, or the sky. **3** vertex; height. **4** *Architecture.* = coping. **5** *Metallurgy.* the top half of a flask that fits above a drag and is used in casting and contains the sprue. —*v.t.* **1** to cover with a cope or something like a cope. **2** to provide with a coping or something like a coping: *The mounds . . . were . . . coped and defended with limestone slabs* (Elisha K. Kane). [< Medieval Latin *capa* cloak, variant of Late Latin *cappa* hood]

cope[3] (kōp), *v.t.,* **coped, cop|ing.** to shape (a structural member) to fit another, as at a joint. [< French *coper* cut < Old French; see etym. under **coup** [1]]

co|peck (kō′pek), *n.* = kopeck.

Co|pe|han (kō pā′hən), *n., adj.* —*n.* a linguistic stock of North American Indians in California; Wintu. —*adj.* of or belonging to this stock.

cope|mate (kōp′māt′), *n. Obsolete.* **1** an adversary; antagonist. **2** a partner; associate; companion; comrade. [< *cope*[1] + *mate*[1]]

co|pen|ha|gen blue (kō′pən hā′gən), a medium shade of blue containing some gray. [< *Copenhagen,* Denmark]

cope of heaven, the overarching canopy or vault of heaven.

co|pe|pod (kō′pə pod), *adj., n.* —*adj.* of or having to do with a group of tiny crustaceans found in both fresh and salt water and important as fish food. —*n.* a copepod crustacean. [< New Latin *Copepoda* the order name < Greek *kōpē* oar, handle + *poús, podós* foot]

co|pep|o|dous (kō pep′ə dəs), *adj.* belonging to or characteristic of copepods.

cop|er (kō′pər), *n. British.* a dealer, especially a horse dealer. [< *cop*(e) + *-er*[1]]

Co|per|ni|can (kə pėr′nə kən), *adj.* of or having to do with Copernicus or his system of astronomy.

Copernican system, a system of astronomy based on the now accepted theory developed by Nicolaus Copernicus, 1473-1543, that the earth rotates on its axis and that the planets revolve around the sun: *In the Copernican system the sun was stationary at the center* (Robert H. Baker).

copes|mate (kōps′māt′), *n. Obsolete.* copemate.

cope|stone (kōp′stōn′), *n.* **1a** the top stone of a wall or building. **b** a stone used for or in a coping. **2** *Figurative.* the finishing touch; climax. **SYN:** crown, completion. [< *cope*² + *stone;* influenced by *cop*³ top]

cop|i|a|ble (kop′ē ə bəl), *adj.* that can be copied.

cop|i|er (kop′ē ər), *n.* **1** a person who copies; imitator. **2** a person who makes written copies; transcriber; copyist: *He supposed it [the text] to be corrupted by the copiers* (Samuel Johnson). **3** = copying machine.

co|pi|lot (kō′pī′lət), *n.* the assistant or second pilot in an aircraft.

cop|ing (kō′ping), *n.* the top layer of a brick or stone wall. It is usually built with a slope to shed water. [< *cop*(e)² + *-ing*¹]

coping saw, a narrow saw in a U-shaped frame, used to cut curves.

co|pi|ous (kō′pē əs), *adj.* **1** more than enough; plentiful; abundant: *copious tears. There was a copious supply of wheat in the grain elevators.* **SYN:** overflowing, ample. **2a** containing much matter; full of information. **b** containing many words; profuse; diffuse. **3** *Obsolete.* having or yielding an abundant supply. [< Latin *cōpiōsus* < *cōpia* plenty < *cōpis* well supplied < *co-* with + *ops* resources] —**co′pi|ous|ly,** *adv.* —**co′pi|ous|ness,** *n.*

co|pla|nar (kō plā′nər), *adj. Mathematics.* (of points, lines, figures) situated in the same plane. A circle is a set of coplanar points.

co|pla|nar|i|ty (kō′plā nar′ə tē), *n.* the quality or fact of being coplanar.

co|pol|y|mer (kō pol′i mər), *n. Chemistry.* a compound formed by the polymerization of unlike compounds, each of which usually is able to polymerize alone.

co|pol|y|mer|ize (kō pol′i mə rīz), *v.t., v.i.,* **-ized, -iz|ing.** *Chemistry.* to polymerize two or more unlike substances; change or be changed by a reaction in which two or more unlike molecules, each of which usually is able to polymerize alone, polymerize to form a complex molecule: *Styrene-butadiene rubber is made by copolymerizing styrene and butadiene* (James S. Fritz). —**co|pol′y|mer|i|za′tion,** *n.*

cop-out (kop′out′), *n. Slang.* **1** a backing out or quitting; an avoidance, evasion, or escape: *Addiction is a kind of "cop-out." Without heroin, there would be pain and uncertainty* (Atlantic). *"That was no strategy," one of them observed bitterly, "that was a cop-out"* (New York Times). **2** a person who backs out or quits: *The "flower children" have my vote as the cop-outs of the decade* (Time). **3** a plea of guilty to the lesser of several charges: *One goal is to do away with the need for a lengthy trial by producing a fast guilty plea—a "cop-out"* (Time).

copped (kopt), *adj.* rising to a point; cone-shaped: *copped hills.* [< *cop*³ + *-ed*²]

***cop|per**¹ (kop′ər), *n., v., adj.* —*n.* **1** a tough, reddish-brown, metallic chemical element which occurs in various ores. Copper resists rust and is easily shaped into thin sheets or fine wire. It is an excellent conductor of heat and electricity. *On account of its high electrical conductivity, copper finds its greatest utilization in the electrical industry* (W. R. Jones). **2** something made of copper. **3** a coin made of copper or bronze, especially a penny. **4** a large boiler or caldron, originally made of copper but now usually of other materials. **5** a reddish-brown color like that of polished copper. **6** any one of various small butterflies with copper-colored wings, that can fly at great speed.
—*v.t.* **1** to cover or coat with copper. **2** *U.S.* (in the game of faro) to lay a copper coin or other token upon (a card) to indicate that the player bets against that card; bet against.
—*adj.* **1** of copper: *a copper kettle.* **2** reddish-brown; copper-colored: *She had copper hair.*
coppers, the large boilers or cooking vessels on shipboard: *What can you expect from officers who boil their 'taters in the ship's coppers?* (Frederick Marryat).
[Old English *coper* < Latin *cuprum* copper, for earlier *aes Cyprium* metal of Cyprus]

***copper**¹
definition 1

symbol	atomic number	atomic weight	oxidation state
Cu	29	63.54	2,1

cop|per² (kop′ər), *n. Slang.* a policeman. [probably < *cop*² + *-er*¹]

Copper Age, the prehistoric period after the Stone Age in which implements of copper were first produced: *Bronze ... was not sufficiently superior to copper to enable the Bronze Age to greatly surpass the Copper Age* (White and Renner).

copper arsenite, = Scheele's green.

cop|per|as (kop′ər əs), *n.* a compound of iron and sulfur which occurs in light-green crystals, used in making ink, in dyeing, in medicine as a disinfectant, in purifying water, and in photography; green vitriol. Copperas is a hydrated sulfate of iron. *Formula:* $FeSO_4 \cdot 7H_2O$ [< Old French *couperose,* perhaps < unrecorded Medieval Latin (*aqua*) *cuprosa* (water) of copper < Latin *cuprum;* see etym. under **copper**¹]

copper beech, a cultivated variety of the beech tree of southern and central Europe, having purplish leaves.

copper chloride, 1 = cupric chloride. **2** = cuprous chloride.

copper color, a lustrous, reddish-brown color.

cop|per-col|ored (kop′ər kul′ərd), *adj.* of a lustrous, reddish-brown color: *a copper-colored sky at sunset.*

copper cyanide, a poisonous, white or greenish powder used in electroplating. *Formula:* CuCN

copper glance, = chalcocite.

cop|per|head (kop′ər hed′), *n.* a poisonous snake of eastern North America; redeye. It has a copper-colored head and is related to the water moccasin and the rattlesnake. Copperheads grow to be about three feet long. *Copperheads have pretty copper-colored bands of irregular shape on their slender, graceful bodies that make them beautiful snakes* (A. M. Winchester).

Cop|per|head (kop′ər hed′), *n. U.S.* a person in the North who sympathized with the South during the Civil War.

cop|per|ish (kop′ər ish), *adj.* like copper; coppery.

copper naph|then|ate (naf′thə nāt, -nit), a greenish solid containing about 5 to 10 per cent copper, used in making wood preservatives and germicidal paint.

copper nickel, = niccolite.

copper oxide, 1 = cupric oxide. **2** = cuprous oxide.

***cop|per|plate** (kop′ər plāt′), *n.* **1** a thin, flat piece of copper on which a design, writing, or the like, is engraved or etched. **2** an engraving, picture, or print made from a copperplate. **3** the copperplate printing or engraving process. **4** Often, **Copperplate.** a style of cursive writing popular in Europe and America during the 1700's, characterized by lines of varying thickness; English Round Hand.

***copperplate**
definition 4

The World Book Dictionary

copper pyrites, = chalcopyrite.

cop|pers (kop′ərz), *n.pl.* See under **copper**¹.

cop|per|smith (kop′ər smith′), *n.* **1** a person who makes things out of copper. **2** a bird, the crimson-breasted barbet of India, that utters a gong-like cry.

copper sulfate, a poisonous, blue crystalline substance produced from copper, used as a dye, chemical reagent, preservative, etc.; blue vitriol. *Copper sulfate is effective only against algae, and does not injure fish if used at a low enough concentration* (New York Times). *Formula:* $CuSO_4 \cdot 5H_2O$

cop|per|worm (kop′ər wėrm′), *n.* a shipworm.

cop|per|y (kop′ər ē), *adj.* **1** of or containing copper. **2** like copper: *a coppery sky at sunset.*

cop|pice (kop′is), *n., v.,* **-piced, -pic|ing.** *Especially British.* copse. [Middle English *copys* < Old French *coupeïz* cut-over forest < *couper* to cut]

cop|ple (kop′əl), *n. Dialect.* a crest on a bird's head. [diminutive of *cop*³ top]

cop|ple|crown (kop′əl kroun′), *n. Dialect.* **1** a tuft of feathers on a bird's head. **2** a crested fowl.

cop|ple-crowned (kop′əl kround′), *adj.* crested; peaked.

cop|ra or **cop|rah** (kop′rə, kō′prə), *n.* the dried meat of coconuts. Coconut oil is obtained from copra. [< Portuguese *copra* < Malayalam *koppara*]

cop|re|mi|a or **cop|rae|mi|a** (kop rē′mē ə), *n.* blood poisoning due to absorption of fecal matter. [< Greek *kópros* dung + English *-emia*]

cop|re|mic or **cop|rae|mic** (kop rē′mik, -rem′ik), *adj.* having copremia.

co-pro|duce (kō′prə düs′, -dyüs′), *v.t.,* **-duced, -duc|ing.** to produce (a motion picture, play, or other dramatic production) jointly: *His son coproduced with David B. Graham the bill of three one-act plays* (New York Times). —**co′-pro|duc′er,** *n.*

co|prod|uct (kō′prod′əkt), *n.* something produced along with something else; by-product. [< *co-* + *product*]

co-pro|duc|tion (kō′prə duk′shən), *n.* **1** a motion picture, play, or other dramatic production that is jointly produced. **2** the act or process of jointly producing such a work of art.

cop|ro|lite (kop′rə līt), *n.* a stony, roundish fossil, the petrified excrement of an animal. [< Greek *kópros* dung + English *-lite*]

cop|ro|log|i|cal (kop′rə loj′ə kəl), *adj.* of coprology; scatological.

cop|rol|o|gy (kop rol′ə jē), *n.* **1** a gathering of excrement or filth. **2** obscenity in literature or art; scatology. [< Greek *kópros* dung + English *-logy*]

cop|roph|a|gous (kop rof′ə gəs), *adj.* feeding on dung, as certain beetles. [< Greek *kópros* dung + *phageîn* eat + English *-ous*]

cop|roph|a|gy (kop rof′ə gē), *n.* the condition of being coprophagous.

cop|ro|phil|i|a (kop′rə fil′ē ə), *n. Psychology.* an abnormal interest in excrement. [< Greek *kópros* dung + English *-philia*]

cop|ro|phil|ic (kop′rə fil′ik), *adj.* **1** of or having to do with coprophilia. **2** *Botany.* growing on dung.

co|pro|pri|e|tor (kō′prə prī′ə tər), *n.* a joint proprietor; coowner.

co-pros|per|i|ty (kō′pros per′ə tē), *n.* economic prosperity achieved through partnership or cooperation between countries, as by forming a common market.

cop|ro|zo|ic (kop′rə zō′ik), *adj.* living on dung; coprophagous: *The coprozoic insects ... are attracted to caves by the large stores of guano* (R. S. Hawes). [< Greek *kópros* dung + English *zoic*]

cops-and-rob|bers (kops′ənd rob′ərz), *n.* **1** a children's game in which players enact the pursuit and capture of outlaws by policemen: *to play cops-and-robbers.* **2** a story, motion picture, or television program, resembling this game: *"Doulos—The Finger Man" is cops-and-robbers à la française* (New Yorker).

copse (kops), *n., v.,* **copsed, cops|ing.** —*n.* a thicket of small trees, bushes, or shrubs: *The dog flushed six quail from the copse.* **SYN:** grove, bosk, boscage, brushwood, underwood.
—*v.t.* to cut or trim (trees or shrubs), so as to provide or preserve a copse.
—*v.i.* to form a copse; grow up again from roots or stumps after being cut down. Also, *especially British,* **coppice.**
[variant of *coppice*]

copse|wood (kops′wu̇d′), *n.* **1** the low trees and underwood of a copse. **2** *Obsolete.* a copse.

Copt (kopt), *n.* **1** a native of Egypt descended from the ancient Egyptians. **2** a member of the Coptic Church. [< New Latin *Coptus* < Arabic *Qubt* the Copts < Coptic *Gyptios* an Egyptian < Greek *Aigýptios*]

Copt., Coptic.

cop|ter (kop′tər), *n., v.i., v.t. Informal.* helicopter: *The copter flew forward and spawned a whole new generation of aircraft in America* (Newsweek). *At week's end he coptered out to Gettysburg* (Time).

Cop|tic (kop′tik), *adj., n.* —*adj.* **1** of or having to do with the Copts or the language of the Copts: *the Coptic version of the New Testament.* **2** of or having to do with the Coptic Church: *Coptic rituals.*
—*n.* a Hamitic language formerly spoken by the Copts. It is now used only in the ritual of the Coptic Church.

Coptic Church, the national Christian church of Egypt and formerly of Ethiopia: *The Coptic Church in Egypt ... has been an independent Monophysite Church since the fifth century* (London Times).

cop|u|la (kop′yə lə), *n., pl.* **-las, -lae** (-lē). **1** *Grammar.* a linking verb, often some form of *be. Example:* John *is* a boy. **2** *Anatomy.* a connecting bone, cartilage, etc. **3** a connection; link. **4** *Logic.* the relation or link between the subject and the predicate of a proposition. [< Latin *cōpula* bond < *co-* together + *apere* fasten. See etym. of doublet **couple.**]
▶ A **copula** (linking verb) is used chiefly as a link between the subject of a sentence and a predicate noun or adjective: *His father is a lawyer. She will be beautiful. The grass became greener.* In these sentences *is, will be,* and *became* are the copulas. Many verbs with full meanings of their own (such as *taste, feel, act, look*) can also be used as copulas: *The butter tastes rancid. She felt sad. He acts old. This looks excellent.*

cop|u|lar (kop′yə lər), *adj.* having to do with or of the nature of a copula.

cop|u|late (kop′yə lāt), *v.i.,* **-lat|ed, -lat|ing.** to engage in sexual intercourse. [< Latin *cōpulāre* join, unite (with English *-ate*¹) < *cōpula;* see

Pronunciation Key: hat, āge, cãre, fär; let, ēqual, tėrm; it, īce; hot, ōpen, ôrder; oil, out; cup, pu̇t, rüle; child; long; thin; ᴛʜen; zh, measure; ə represents **a** in about, **e** in taken, **i** in pencil, **o** in lemon, **u** in circus.

etym. under **copula**]

cop|u|la|tion (kop′yə lā′shən), *n.* **1** = sexual intercourse. **2** a joining together; coupling.

cop|u|la|tive (kop′yə lā′tiv, -lə-), *adj., n.* **—*adj.*** **1** serving to couple or connect. **2** *Grammar.* **a** serving to connect words or clauses of equal rank: *"And" is a copulative conjunction.* **b** of the nature of a copula: *"Be" is a copulative verb.* **3** *Logic.* involving connection of the subject and predicate of a proposition.
—*n.* a copulative conjunction or copulative (linking) verb. **—cop′u|la′tive|ly,** *adv.*

cop|u|la|to|ry (kop′yə lə tôr′ē, -tōr′-), *adj.* = copulative.

cop|y (kop′ē), *n., pl.* **cop|ies,** *v.,* **cop|ied, cop|y|ing.** **—*n.*** **1** a thing made to be just like another; a thing made on the pattern or model of another. A written page, a picture, a dress, or a piece of furniture can be an exact copy of another. **SYN:** duplicate, reproduction, imitation, transcript, counterpart, facsimile, replica. **2** a thing to be followed as a pattern or model: *This is the copy you are to imitate.* **3** an example of penmanship to be copied. **4** one of a number of books, newspapers, magazines, or pictures made at the same printing: *Please get six copies of today's newspaper.* **5** written material ready to be set up in print in a newspaper, magazine, or book: *advertising copy, good copy for a magazine feature.*
—*v.t.* **1a** to make a copy of: *Copy this page. She copied my hat. Copy out the figures.* **b** to reproduce or represent (an object) in a picture or on some surface, such as wax or stone: *The potters copied his ugly face on their stone jugs* (Emerson). **2** to be a copy of; follow as an example; imitate: *The little boy copied his father's way of walking.* **—*v.i.*** **1** to make a copy or copies; work by imitation: *No painter who is worth a straw will ever copy* (John Ruskin). **2** to be a copy or an imitation: *No person of independent mind will copy consciously, but many copy unconsciously. Many colors copy poorly on an office photocopying machine.*
hold copy, to act as a copyholder: *He held copy before he was promoted to copy editor.*
[< Old French *copie* < Medieval Latin *copia* transcript < Latin *cōpia* plenty; see etym. under **copious**]
—*Syn.* *v.t.* **1a Copy, imitate** mean to try to make something like another by following a pattern or model. **Copy** suggests trying to follow the original as closely and exactly as possible: *He copied a page of a book.* **Imitate** suggests following it less slavishly: *Sometimes a teacher asks a class to imitate something written by a great author. He could imitate all the great comedians of his generation.*

cop|y|book (kop′ē bu̇k′), *n., adj.* **—*n.*** **1** a book with models of handwriting to be copied in learning to write. **2** a book for or containing copies especially of documents, correspondence, or accounts.
—*adj.* commonplace; conventional; ordinary: *He was no copybook hero.*
blot one's copybook, *British Informal.* to spoil one's record or chances by a mistake, especially by an indiscretion: *"Of course," one steward said, "it is possible to blot your copybook and be blackballed"* (Enid Nemy).

copy boy, a boy who takes copy from one desk to another and runs errands for the staff in the offices of a newspaper or magazine.

copy cat, *U.S. Slang.* a person who has no originality but has to copy the appearance, speech, dress, or behavior of others.

cop|y|cat (kop′ē kat′), *n., v.,* **-cat|ted, -cat|ting.** *U.S. Slang.* **—*n.*** = copy cat. **—*v.t.*** to copy in the manner of a copy cat: *shoddy goods copycatted from U.S. or other foreign manufacturers* (Time). **—*v.i.*** to copy or imitate others.

copy desk, the desk in a newspaper office where news stories and articles are edited and prepared for typesetting.

copy editor, an editor who corrects and prepares material for typesetting and printing; copyreader.

cop|y|hold (kop′ē hōld′), *n.* formerly in English law: **1** ownership of land proved by a copy of the roll of a manorial court. **2** land held in this way.

cop|y|hold|er (kop′ē hōl′dər), *n.* **1a** a person who reads manuscript aloud to a proofreader. **b** a device for holding copy, such as that used by a compositor in setting up type. **2** (formerly in English law) a person who owned land by copyhold.

cop|y|ing ink (kop′ē ing), an ink suitable for making originals from which copies are to be made in a copying press.

copying machine, any machine that makes copies of written, typed, printed, or drawn material quickly and cheaply, especially a photocopier and, sometimes, a duplicator.

copying press, 1 a machine for taking, by pressure, copies of originals made with copying ink. **2** a thin, unsized paper used in making copies in a copying press.

copying ribbon, a ribbon prepared with copying ink, for use in a typewriter when the copy is to be duplicated.

cop|y|ist (kop′ē ist), *n.* **1** a person who makes written copies. **SYN:** transcriber. **2** a person who copies; imitator: *copyists who can market cheap versions of their gowns within weeks after the fall showings* (Time).

copy of verses, *British.* a short composition in verse, usually one set as a school exercise.

cop|y|read (kop′ē rēd′), *v.t.,* **-read** (-red′), **-read|ing.** to read and edit (manuscript copy), especially for typesetting and printing: *She worked night after night addressing campaign literature and copyreading speeches* (Time).

cop|y|read|er (kop′ē rē′dər), *n.* a person who reads and edits copy for a newspaper or book.

cop|y|right** (kop′ē rīt′), *n., v., adj.* **—*n. the exclusive right to publish or sell and otherwise control a book, play, poem, picture, piece of music, or other original work that can be reproduced by printing, playing, or stamping, granted by a government for a certain number of years (in the United States until 1978, it was 28 years, renewable for another 28; after December 1977, the term of copyright is the lifetime of the author plus 50 years). *Abbr:* c.
—*v.t.* to protect (a literary, musical, or artistic work) by getting a copyright.
—*adj.* protected or secured by copyright: *a copyright song.* **—cop′y|right′a|ble,** *adj.*

***copyright**

©1963 Field Enterprises, Inc.

symbol

cop|y|right|er (kop′ē rī′tər), *n.* a person who copyrights a book, picture, or other literary, musical, or artistic work.

cop|y|writ|er (kop′ē rī′tər), *n.* a writer of copy, especially for advertising.

cop|y|writ|ing (kop′ē rī′ting), *n.* the work of a copywriter: *Brower rose through the copywriting end of the ad business* [*and*] *is still a phrasemaker at heart* (Time).

coq au vin (kôk′ōvaɴ′), *French.* chicken prepared by browning it in butter and cooking it with wine.

coq feather (kok; *French* kôk), the feather of a rooster, or a similar feather, used for trimming women's hats. [< French *coq* cock]

coque (kok; *French* kôk), *n.* a loop, knot, or bow of ribbon for trimming. [< French *coque*]

coque|li|cot (kōk′li kō), *n.* **1** the common European corn poppy. **2** its color, a bright orange-red; poppy red. [< French *coquelicot*]

co|quet[1] (kō ket′), *v.,* **-quet|ted, -quet|ting,** *adj.* **—*v.i.*** **1** to act as a coquette; flirt (with). **2** *Figurative.* to trifle or toy (with) a matter or proposal. **SYN:** dally. **—*adj.*** like a coquette; coquettish. [< French *coqueter* < *coquet;* see etym. under **coquet**[2]]

co|quet[2] (kō ket′), *n. Obsolete.* a male flirt. [< French *coquet* < Old French (diminutive) < *coq* cock (because of the similarity of gait and mannerisms)]

co|quet|ry (kō′kə trē, kō ket′rē), *n., pl.* **-ries.** **1** the behavior or arts of a coquette; flirting: *She did not seek to hide the weaknesses in her character, of which the most important was coquetry* (Atlantic). **SYN:** flirtation. **2** *Figurative.* a toying with proposals, political parties, or any other matters, without seriously supporting or considering them; trifling: *There was a good deal of political coquetry in the patriotic independence of ... Wentworth* (Benjamin Disraeli).

co|quette (kō ket′), *n., v.,* **-quet|ted, -quet|ting.** **—*n.*** a woman who tries to attract men merely to please her vanity; flirt.
—*v.i.* to practice coquetry; flirt or toy (with). [< French *coquette,* feminine of *coquet;* see etym. under **coquet**[2]]

co|quet|tish (kō ket′ish), *adj.* **1** of a coquette. **2** like a coquette or a coquette's: *The pretty girl winked and gave him a coquettish smile.* **—co|quet′tish|ly,** *adv.* **—co|quet′tish|ness,** *n.*

co|quil|la nut (kō kēl′yə, -kē′yə), the fruit or nut of a Brazilian palm whose thick, hard shell is much used for carving or turning out objects on a lathe. [< Spanish *coquillo,* or Portuguese *coquilho* (diminutive) < *coco* coconut]

co|quille (kō kil′, -kēl′), *n.* **1** a shell, or a dish in the form of a shell, in which seafood is served. **2** food served in such a shell or dish. [< French *coquille* shell; see etym. under **cockle**[1]]

co|qui|na (kō kē′nə), *n.* **1** a soft, porous, whitish limestone composed of fragments of sea shells and corals: *Coquina is used in Florida and the West Indies as a building material.* **2** a small clam of many shades of color found on the surface of beaches, used especially for making a soup. [< Spanish *coquina* shellfish, cockle]

co|qui|to (kō kē′tō), *n.,* or **coquito palm,** a palm of Chile, whose sap is boiled to make sweet syrup. [< Spanish *coquito* (diminutive) < *coco* coconut]

cor[1] (kôr), *interj. British Slang.* an exclamation of surprise, annoyance, or the like. [altered pronunciation of *God*]

cor[2] (kôr, kōr), *n. Music.* **1** = cor anglais. **2** = mellophone. [< French *cor* horn]

cor-, *prefix.* the form of **com-** before *r,* as in *correct.*

cor., an abbreviation for the following:
1 corner.
2 cornet.
3 coroner.
4 corpus.
5a corrected. **b** correction.
6 correlative.
7a correspondence. **b** correspondent. **c** corresponding.

Cor., 1 Corinthians. **2** coroner.

cor|a|ci|i|form (kôr′ə sī′ə fôrm, kor′-), *adj.* of or having to do with an order of birds that includes the kingfishers, hornbills, motmots, bee eaters, rollers, and hoopoes. [< New Latin *Coraciiformes* the order < Greek *kórax, -akos* raven + English *-form*]

***cor|a|cle** (kôr′ə kəl, kor′-), *n.* a small, light boat made by covering a wooden frame with wicker or grass and a waterproof material such as pitch or animal skin. A coracle looks somewhat like a basket. It originated in ancient England and is still used in Wales and Ireland, especially for inland fishing. *In wicker-framed coracles planked with hides they voyaged even to the Hebrides* (Atlantic). [< Welsh *corwgl* < *corwg* any round body]

***coracle**

cor|a|coid (kôr′ə koid, kor′-), *n., adj. Anatomy.* **—*n.*** **1** a bone between the shoulder blade and the breastbone in birds and certain reptiles. **2** a bony process extending from the shoulder blade to or toward the breastbone in mammals.
—*adj.* of this bone or bony process.
[< New Latin *coracoides* < Greek *korakoeidês* ravenlike < *kórax, -akos* crow, raven + *eîdos* form]

***coral**
definition 1b

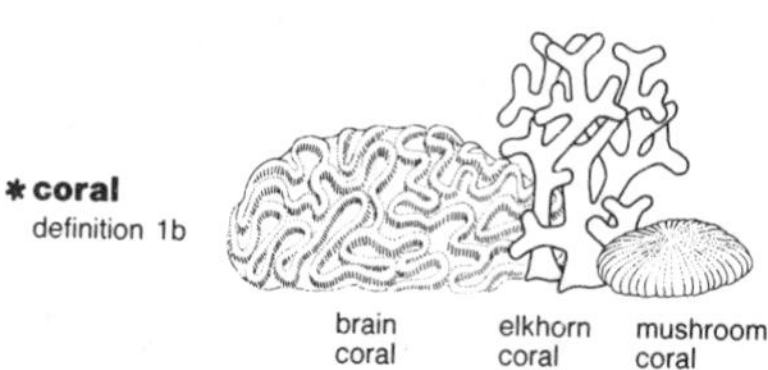

cor|al** (kôr′əl, kor′-), *n., adj.* **—*n. **1a** a stony, often brightly colored substance consisting of skeletons of certain kinds of tiny sea animals called polyps, which usually live in colonies in warm seas. Coral is mainly calcium carbonate. Reefs and small islands consisting of coral are common in the South Seas, the Caribbean, and Bermuda. Coral is often used for jewelry. *Coral grows in tropical areas in shallow water, and in the Pacific and Indian Oceans there are many coral atolls that are ringlike islands, enclosing a lagoon* (Gaskell and Hill). **b** any of the skeletons forming this substance. **2** the little sea animal (a polyp) which makes coral and often forms large, branching or rounded colonies by budding. It is mostly stomach and mouth. **3a** a piece of coral, especially red or pink coral, made into jewelry. **b** a toy made of polished coral, or of glass, bone, or the like, given to infants as a teething ring. **4** a deep pink or red; coral red: *His barefoot soldiers ... tramping the snow to coral where they trod* (James Russell Lowell). **5** the roe or unfertilized eggs of the lobster, that turn red when boiled. **6** = coral snake.
—*adj.* **1** made of coral: *a coral necklace.* **2** resembling coral, especially in color; deep-pink or red; coral-red: *Forth from her coral lips such folly broke* (William Congreve). **3** producing coral: *the coral polyps.* **4** marked by the presence of coral: *the coral seas.*

[< Old French *coral* < Latin *corallum* < Greek *korállion*]

cor·al·bells (kôr′əl belz′, kor′-), *n.pl.* a widely cultivated plant of the saxifrage family, native to Arizona and New Mexico, having bright red flowers shaped like bells.

cor·al·ber·ry (kôr′əl ber′ē, kor′-), *n., pl.* **-ries.** a North American shrub of the honeysuckle family, bearing clusters of coral-red berries in the axils of the leaves.

cor·aled (kôr′əld, kor′-), *adj.* abounding in coral.

coral honeysuckle, = trumpet honeysuckle.

co·ral·la (kə ral′ə), *n.* plural of **corallum.**

cor·alled (kôr′əld, kor′-), *adj. Especially British.* coraled.

cor·al·lif·er·ous (kôr′ə lif′ər əs, kor′-), *adj.* containing or bearing coral.

cor·al·lig·er·ous (kôr′ə lij′ər əs, kor′-), *adj.* = coralliferous.

coral limestone, stone made of fossil coral.

cor·al·line (kôr′ə lin, -līn; kor′-), *adj., n.* —*adj.* **1** consisting of or containing coral. **2** like coral in shape or color.
—*n.* **1** a coral or any similar animal: *Then the ebbing waters reveal a sea floor enamelled with the rose of encrusting corallines* (New Yorker). **2** any of a family of red algae whose fronds contain lime.

cor·al·lite (kôr′ə līt, kor′-), *n.* **1** a fossil coral. **2** the coral skeleton of a polyp.

cor·al·loid (kôr′ə loid, kor′-), *adj.* resembling or formed like coral.

cor·al·loi·dal (kôr′ə loi′dəl, kor′-), *adj.* = coralloid.

co·ral·lum (kə ral′əm), *n., pl.* **-la.** the calcareous skeleton of a compound coral, consisting of individual corallites.

coral pink, a yellowish-pink color.

coral red, a yellowish-pink or yellowish-red color.

coral reef, a reef consisting mainly of coral: *Coral reefs are built up from the bottom in tropical areas by two different groups of coelenterates, aided by a number of other lime-depositing organisms* (A. Franklin Shull).

coral snake, a small, very poisonous American snake whose body is banded with alternating rings of various colors, especially red, yellow, and black. It belongs to the same family as the cobra and is found in the southern United States, Mexico, Central America, and tropical South America.

co·ram ju·di·ce (kō′ram jü′də sē), *Latin.* before a judge having proper jurisdiction.

co·ram no·bis (kō′ram nō′bis), *Latin.* **1** *Law.* issued to order a review of a case involving an alleged error of fact: *The United States Court of Appeals granted a writ of error coram nobis to a man who had already served four years for mail theft* (New York Times). **2** (literally) before us.

co·ram po·pu·lo (kō′ram pop′yə lō), *Latin.* before the people; in public.

cor an·glais (kôr′ äN glā′, kōr′), = English horn. [< French *cor anglais;* see etym. under **English horn**]

co·ran·to (kə ran′tō, -rän′-), *n., pl.* **-tos** or **-toes.** = courante.

cor·ban (kôr′ban, kôr bän′), *n.* a sacrificial gift made to God among the ancient Jews, especially in fulfillment of a vow. [< Hebrew *qorbān*]

cor·beil (kôr′bel), *n. Architecture.* a sculptured ornament shaped like a basket of flowers, fruit, etc. [< Old French *corbeille* basket < Late Latin *corbicula* (diminutive) < Latin *corbis* basket]

cor·beille (kôr′bel; *French* kôr be′yə), *n.* = corbeil.

***cor·bel** (kôr′bəl), *n., v.,* **-beled, -bel·ing** or (*especially British*) **-belled, -bel·ling.** —*n.* **1** a bracket of stone, wood, or other material, on the side of a wall. It helps to support a projecting ledge above. **2** a short timber placed so as to support a girder, beam, or the like, or to give it a larger bearing.
—*v.t.* to furnish with or support by a corbel or corbels.
[< Old French *corbel* (diminutive) < *corb* raven < Latin *corvus* raven]

***corbel**
definition 1

cor·bel·ing (kôr′bə ling), *n.* **1a** the use or arrangement of corbels in building. **b** corbels. **2** a system of masonry in which each course of stones or bricks projects beyond the one below.

cor·bel·ling (kôr′bə ling), *n. Especially British.* corbeling.

cor·bie (kôr′bē), *n. Scottish.* a raven or crow. [alteration of Middle English *corbin* < Old French, (diminutive) < *corb* raven < Latin *corvus*]

corbie gable, a gable made with corbiesteps.

cor·bie·step (kôr′bē step′), *n. Architecture.* one of a series of steps sometimes used instead of a straight slope on the top of a gable wall.

cor·bi·na (kôr bē′nə), *n., pl.* **-nas. 1** any one of several croakers, especially a bronze-colored game fish of the North and South American coasts. **2** a dark-backed weakfish with spotted sides. Also, **corvina.** [< Spanish *corvina* a name for several blackish fishes < Latin *corvīnus* ravenlike]

***cord** (kôrd), *n., v.* —*n.* **1** a thick string; very thin rope: *He tied the package with a cord.* **2** something resembling a cord. **3** an insulated cable with fittings, used to connect an electrical appliance, such as an iron or a lamp, to a socket. **4** a nerve, tendon, or other structure in an animal body that is somewhat like a cord; chord. The spinal cord is in the backbone. The vocal cords are in the throat. **5a** a ridge or ridged pattern on cloth. **b** a cloth with such ridges on it, especially corduroy. **6** *Figurative.* any influence that binds, draws, or restrains: *The very sight of the island had relaxed the cords of discipline* (Robert Louis Stevenson). **7a** a measure of cut wood equal to 128 cubic feet or 3.625 cubic meters. A pile of wood 4 feet wide, 4 feet high, and 8 feet long is a cord. *Abbr:* cd. **b** the amount of wood in a pile of these dimensions: *a cord of oak.* **8** a hangman's rope: *the stake and the cord* (John Morley). **9** an imperfection in glass which appears as long strings of different composition from the main body of the glass.
—*v.t.* **1** to fasten or tie with a cord or cords: *He corded the bundle of rags to carry it easily.* **2** to provide with a cord or cords: *The window sashes need to be corded.* **3** to pile (wood) in cords: *They* [*trees*] *should be cut and corded before spring* (Emerson).
cords, trousers made of corduroy: *our sprightly gentleman in the scarlet jacket and white cords* (Theodore Hook).
[< Old French *corde* < Latin *chorda* < Greek *chordḗ* gut. Compare etym. under **chord**[2]]
—**cord′er,** *n.* —**cord′like′,** *adj.*

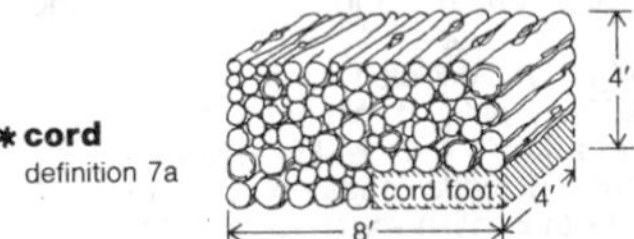

***cord**
definition 7a

cord·age (kôr′dij), *n.* **1** cords or ropes: *Most of the cordage on a sailing ship is in its rigging.* **2** a quantity of wood measured in cords.

cor·date (kôr′dāt), *adj.* heart-shaped: *a cordate petal, cordate shells.* [< New Latin *cordatus* < Latin *cordātus* wise < *cor, cordis* heart] —**cor′date·ly,** *adv.*

cord·ed (kôr′did), *adj.* **1** having ridges on it; ribbed: *Corduroy is a corded cloth.* **2** resembling cord; pulled tight; stringy: *corded muscles.* **3** fastened with a cord; bound with cords: *corded bundles of newspaper.* **4** made of cords; furnished with cords: *a corded rope, corded Venetian blinds.* **5** cut and piled in cords: *corded wood.*

Cor·del·ia (kôr dēl′yə), *n.* the loyal, youngest daughter of King Lear in Shakespeare's tragedy *King Lear.*

Cor·de·lier (kôr′də lir′), *n.* a Franciscan friar (from the knotted cord worn as a girdle by the order). [< French *cordelier* < Old French *cordeler* < *cordele* (diminutive) < *corde;* see etym. under **cord**]

cor·delle (kôr del′, kor′del), *n., v.,* **-delled, -del·ling.** *U.S. and Canada.* —*n.* a towline.
—*v.t.* to tow a canoe, etc., with a cordelle. [< French *cordelle* (diminutive) < Old French *corde;* see etym. under **cord**]

cord foot, a measure of cut wood equal to ⅛ of a cord, or 16 cubic feet, or .45 cubic meter. *Abbr:* cd. ft.

cord·grass (kôrd′gras′, -gräs′), *n.* a perennial grass with long, tough leaves, growing in wet areas, especially saline marshes.

cor·dial (kôr′jəl), *adj., n.* —*adj.* **1** warm and friendly in manner; hearty: *His friends gave him a cordial welcome.* **2** sincere; heartfelt; genuine: *She has a cordial abhorrence of anything false or artificial.* **3** strengthening; stimulating. SYN: restorative, reviving, cheering. **4** *Obsolete.* of or belonging to the heart.
—*n.* **1** a food, drink, or medicine that strengthens or stimulates: (*Figurative.*) *Death, thou'rt a cordial old and rare: Look how compounded, with what care!* (Sidney Lanier). **2** = liqueur.
[< Medieval Latin *cordialis* having to do with the heart < Latin *cor, cordis* heart] —**cor′dial·ly,** *adv.* —**cor′dial·ness,** *n.*

cor·dial·i·ty (kôr jal′ə tē, kôr′jē al′-), *n., pl.* **-ties.** cordial quality; cordial feeling; sincerity; heartiness; warm friendliness: *The cordiality of his welcome made me feel at home.* SYN: warmth.

cor·di·a pul·mo·na·li·a (kôr′dē ə pùl′mə nal′ē ə), plural of **cor pulmonale.**

cor·di·er·ite (kôr′dē ə rīt), *n.* = iolite. [< Pierre L. A. *Cordier,* 1777-1861, a French geologist + *-ite*[1]]

cor·di·form (kôr′də fôrm), *adj.* heart-shaped. [< Latin *cor, cordis* heart + English *-form*]

cor·dil·le·ra (kôr′dəl yãr′ə, kôr dil′ər-), *n.* **1** a system of mountain ranges; chain of mountains. **2** Often, **Cordilleras. a** the main mountain system of a continent: *The Cordilleras of the Andes or of western North America.* **b** the system of mountain ranges extending from Alaska to Cape Horn. [American English < Spanish *cordillera,* ultimately < Latin *chorda* rope; see etym. under **cord**]

cor·dil·le·ran (kôr′dəl yãr′ən, kôr dil′ər-), *adj.* **1** of the cordilleras. **2** in the cordilleras.

cord·ing (kôr′ding), *n.* **1** the act or work of a person or thing that cords. **2** an arrangement of cord on or around something. **3** a kind of embroidery similar to couching in which the stitches are vertical and close together. **4** the cords or ribs of a corded fabric.

cord·ite (kôr′dīt), *n.* a smokeless gunpowder composed of nitroglycerin, guncotton, and petrolatum formed into cordlike lengths. [< *cord* + *-ite*[1] (because of its stringlike appearance)]

cord·less (kôrd′lis), *adj.* without a cord, especially without an electric cable: *A cordless electric clock that works off a battery* (Science News Letter).

cor·do·ba (kôr′də bə; *Spanish* kôr′ᴛʜō vä), *n.* **1** the unit of money of Nicaragua, equal to 100 centavos: *The International Monetary Fund has agreed to a change in the par value of the Nicaraguan cordoba from five to seven a United States dollar* (London Times). **2** a silver coin of this value. [< American Spanish *córdoba* < Francisco Fernández de *Córdoba,* 1475?-1526, a Spanish explorer]

cor·don (kôr′dən), *n., v.* —*n.* **1** a line or circle of soldiers, policemen, forts, warships, or others acting to enclose or guard a place: *A cordon of troops surrounded the burned-out area of the city.* (*Figurative.*) *Foreigners who have been excluded by the strictest cordon ever drawn* (W. F. Stevenson). **2** a cord, braid, or ribbon worn as an ornament or as a badge of honor. **3** *Architecture.* = stringcourse.
—*v.t.* to enclose or cut off with a cordon: *The palace was cordoned by tanks and troops* (Wall Street Journal). *A thousand constables cordoned off the riot area* (Harper's).
[< Old French *cordon* ribbon < *corde;* see etym. under **cord**]

cor·don bleu (kôr dôN blœ′), *pl.* **cor·dons bleus** (kôr dôN blœ′). **1** a blue ribbon worn by members of the highest order of the French monarchy under the Bourbons. **2** a person entitled to wear the cordon bleu. **3** some similar high distinction. **4** any person of great distinction in his field: [*He is*] *a cordon bleu of more than thirty-eight years' experience ... in professional cooking* (New York Times). [< French *cordon bleu*]

cor·don sa·ni·taire (kôr dôN′ sȧ nē ter′), *pl.* **cordons sa·ni·taires** (kôr dôN′ sȧ nē ter′). **1** a line of guards about an infected district to control communication: *the cordon sanitaire which was established along the Rhine to prevent the spread of disease by displaced persons* (James Phinney Baxter). **2** = buffer zone. **3** *Figurative.* any buffer: *There is and can be no cordon sanitaire against the spread of ideas* (Manchester Guardian Weekly). [< French *cordon sanitaire* (literally) sanitary cordon]

cor·dot·o·my (kôr dot′ə mē), *n., pl.* **-mies.** surgical incision into the spinal cord, especially to alleviate severe chronic pain. [< (spinal) *cord* + *-tomy*]

cor·do·van (kôr′də vən, kôr dō′-), *adj., n.* —*adj.* or having to do with a kind of soft leather originally made at Córdoba, Spain.
—*n.* **1** a kind of soft, fine-grained leather. **2** a shoe made from this leather.
[< Spanish *cordobán* < *Córdoba,* Spain]

Cor·do·van (kôr′də vən, kôr dō′-), *adj., n.* —*adj.* of or having to do with Córdoba, Spain.
—*n.* a native or inhabitant of Córdoba.
[< Spanish *cordobano*]

cords (kôrdz), *n.pl.* See under **cord.**

cor·du·roy (kôr′də roi, kôr′də roi′), *n., adj., v.* —*n.* **1** a thick cotton or rayon cloth with close, velvetlike ridges. **2** a suit or garment made of this.
—*adj.* **1** made of corduroy: *a corduroy skirt.*

Pronunciation Key: hat, āge, cãre, fär; let, ēqual, tėrm; it, īce; hot, ōpen, ôrder; oil, out; cup, pu̇t, rüle; child; long; thin; ᴛʜen; zh, measure; ə represents **a** in about, **e** in taken, **i** in pencil, **o** in lemon, **u** in circus.

2 built of logs laid together crosswise, as a road. —*v.t.* **1** to build (a road or bridge) of logs laid together crosswise. **2** to cross (a swamp) with a road or bridge so made.
corduroys, corduroy trousers: *nothing but a pair of corduroys between him and the horse's back* (Geoffrey Gambado).
[< *cord* + obsolete *duroy* a kind of woolen cloth]

***corduroy road,** a road made of logs laid crosswise, usually across low, wet land.

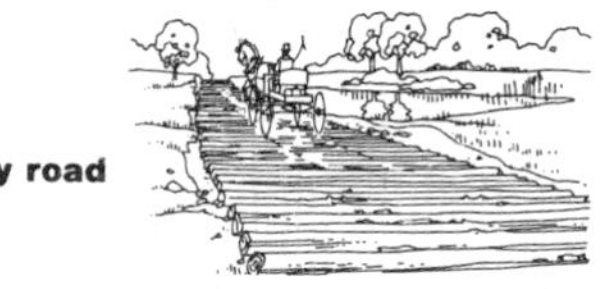

***corduroy road**

cord|wain (kôrd′wān), *n. Archaic.* cordovan leather. [< Anglo-French *cordewan,* Old French *cordouan* < Spanish *cordobán;* see etym. under **cordovan**]

cord|wain|er (kôrd′wā nər), *n. Archaic.* a shoemaker.

cord|wood (kôrd′wu̇d′), *n.* **1** wood sold by the cord. **2** firewood piled in cords. **3** wood cut in four-foot lengths. **4** timber or trees suitable only for firewood.

cord|y (kôr′dē), *adj.* of or like cord.

***core[1]** (kôr, kōr), *n., v.,* **cored, cor|ing,** *adj.* —*n.* **1** the hard, central part, containing the seeds, of fruits like apples and pears: *After eating the apple he threw the core away.* **2** *Figurative.* the central or most important part: *the core of an argument. That boy is honest to the core. The Moslem community on the north side of the Tyne is more compact, consisting of a core of some sixty families* (Anthony H. Richmond). SYN: essence, kernel, nucleus. **3** the heart: *The desertion of his dog had touched him to the core* (Edward Bulwer-Lytton). **4** *Electricity.* **a** a bar of soft iron, bundle of iron wires, or the like, forming the center of an electromagnet, induction coil, etc., and serving to increase and concentrate the induced magnetic field. **b** the conducting wire and its insulation in a subterranean or submarine cable. **5** *Metallurgy.* an inner mold made of sand and other ingredients filling the space to be left hollow in a casting. **6a** the heartwood of a tree. **b** the lumber from this wood, usually soft and inexpensive, used as a base for veneers. **7** the central strand of a rope around which other strands are woven. **8** a cylindrical portion of rock or other material extracted from the center of a mass by cutting or drilling. **9** *Chemistry.* the nucleus of an atom and the inner shells of electrons. **10** *Geology.* the central portion of the earth, lying below the mantle. **11** *Physics.* the part of a nuclear reactor containing fissionable material. **12** *Electronics.* a magnetic core. —*v.t.* to take out the core of: *The cook cored the apples.*
—*adj.* central; basic: *Deterring such an attack has been the core reason for NATO's existence* (Time). *The Fed decided the core questions of regulating the money supply* (New Yorker).
[Middle English *core;* origin uncertain]

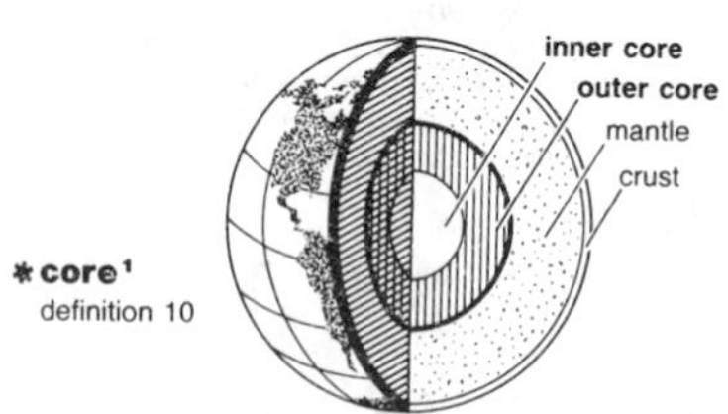

***core[1]**
definition 10

core[2] (kôr, kōr), *n.* **1** a body of people; company. **2** the company of players in a curling match. [an English spelling of French *corps* body]

CORE (no periods) or **C.O.R.E.,** Congress of Racial Equality.

core city, = central city.

core curriculum, a program of studies in which a number of courses are subordinated to and unified by a central subject or theme.

core-drill (kôr′dril′, kōr′-), *v.t.* to drill so as to remove a core intact.

co|re|la|tion (kō′ri lā′shən), *n.* = correlation.

co|rel|a|tive (kō rel′ə tiv), *adj., n.* = correlative.

co|re|li|gion|ist (kō′ri lij′ə nist), *n.* a follower of the same religion. Also, **correligionist.**

core melt, the melting of the core of a nuclear reactor; meltdown.

core memory, = magnetic-core memory.

co|re|op|sis (kôr′ē op′sis, kōr′-), *n.* **1** any plant of a group of the composite family, including several species cultivated for their yellow, red-and-yellow, or reddish flowers shaped like daisies; tickseed. **2** the flower. [< New Latin *coreopsis* < Greek *kóris* bedbug + *ôpsis* appearance (from the shape of the seed)]

core|piece (kôr′pēs′, kōr′-), *n.* a central strand around which other strands are twisted in a hawser-laid rope; core.

cor|er (kôr′ər, kōr′-), *n.* **1** an instrument for removing the cores from fruit. **2** a core-drilling machine; device for removing cores especially of rock and earth: *The research vessel Atlantis surveyed the deep-sea bottom* [*with*] *a . . . corer which takes samples of the sea bed 40 to 60 feet thick* (Scientific American).

cor|e|sis (kôr′ə sēz, kōr′-), *n.pl. Botany.* dark-red, broad, disk-shaped bodies, found beneath the epicarp of grapes. [< Greek *kóris* bedbug (from the resemblance in size and shape)]

co|re|spond|en|cy (kō′ri spon′dən sē; kôr′ə-, kor′-), *n.* **1** the act of being a corespondent. **2** the state of being a corespondent.

co|re|spond|ent (kō′ri spon′dənt; kôr′ə-, kor′-), *n. Law.* a person accused of adultery with a husband or wife who is being sued for divorce.

core tool, a paleolithic tool, such as a biface, made by removing splinters or flakes from a lump of stone.

core tube, a tube inserted into the ground to extract a core of rock or other material.

core wall, a wall or structure of waterproof material in the interior of a dam, dike, or causeway largely constructed of porous material such as earth or sand.

corf (kôrf), *n., pl.* **corves. 1** *British.* **a** a tub, truck, or car used in carrying ore or coal or other mineral to the surface of a mine. **b** a large, strong basket formerly so used. **2** *Obsolete.* a basket. [< Middle Dutch *korf,* ultimately < Latin *corbis* basket]

Cor|fam (kôr′fam), *n. Trademark.* a strong, lightweight, porous plastic that resembles leather, used especially in shoe manufacture.

Cor|fi|ote (kôr′fē ōt), *n.* a native or inhabitant of the island of Corfu, in the Ionian Islands off the west coast of Greece.

cor|gi (kôr′gē), *n.* = Welsh corgi.

co|ri|a (kôr′ē ə, kōr′-), *n.* plural of **corium.**

co|ri|a|ceous (kôr′ē ā′shəs, kōr′-), *adj.* **1** like leather; tough. **2** made of leather. [< Late Latin *coriāceus* (with English *-ous*) < Latin *corium* leather, skin]

co|ri|al (kō′rē äl′), *n.* (in Guiana) a dugout canoe with pointed ends. [< Spanish *corial,* probably < Arawak *kuljara*]

co|ri|an|der (kôr′ē an′dər, kōr′-), *n.* **1** an herb of the parsley family, with a disagreeable odor but bearing aromatic fruits. **2** its seedlike fruit. The oil from the seeds is used as flavoring in cooking and candy making and in medicine as a stimulant and carminative. [< Old French *coriandre,* learned borrowing from Latin *coriandrum* < Greek *koríandron,* variant of *koríannon*]

co|rinne (kə rin′), *n.* a hummingbird with a long, lancelike bill and very brilliant coloration. [< French *corinne*]

cornice
frieze
architrave
entablature
capital
flutes
column
shaft
base
stylobate
stereobate

***Corinthian**
definition 2

***Co|rin|thi|an** (kə rin′thē ən), *adj., n.* —*adj.* **1** of the Greek city of Corinth or its people. **2** of or having to do with the most elaborate style of Greek architecture. The Corinthian column typically has a tall, slender, fluted shaft, a molded base, and a bell-shaped capital adorned with acanthus leaves. **3** ornate; overbrilliant: *a Corinthian literary style.* **4** resembling the immoral manners of ancient Corinth; elegant and dissipated. SYN: profligate.
—*n.* **1** a person born or living in Corinth. **2a** a wealthy sportsman, especially, in the United States, a yachtsman. **b** a man of fashion about town. **3** *Obsolete.* a gay, immoral, shameless man.

Corinthian raisin, = currant (def. 1).

Co|rin|thi|ans (kə rin′thē ənz), *n.pl.* (*sing. in use*). either of two books of the New Testament, I Corinthians and II Corinthians, consisting of letters written by the Apostle Paul to the Christians of Corinth. *Abbr:* Cor.

Cor|i|o|la|nus (kôr′ē ə lā′nəs, kor′-), *n.* a historical tragedy by Shakespeare based on the life of Gaius Marcius Coriolanus, a Roman general of the 400's B.C., who was banished from Rome and later led an army of Volscians in an unsuccessful attack on it.

Cor|i|o|lis acceleration (kôr′ē ō′lis, kor′-), the deflection or acceleration caused by the Coriolis force: *The Coriolis acceleration will impel the missile to deviate from a great circle trajectory* (Kenneth F. Gantz).

Coriolis effect, 1 = Coriolis force. **2** = Coriolis acceleration.

Coriolis force, *Physics, Meteorology.* a force, resulting from the rotation of the earth, that deflects other bodies or forces in motion, especially those above the earth, by causing them to veer to the right in the Northern Hemisphere, or to the left in the Southern Hemisphere: *More recently it has been suggested that the Coriolis forces consequent on the earth's rotation could be measured and used to determine latitude* (G. V. T. Mathews). [< Gaspard G. *Coriolis,* 1792-1843, a French mathematician, who analyzed it]

co-ri|par|i|an (kō′ri pãr′ē ən, -rī-), *n.* any one, especially a country or person, having rights to the use of a river jointly with another.

co|ri|um (kôr′ē əm, kōr′-), *n., pl.* **-ri|a. 1** the innermost layer of the skin; the true skin as distinguished from the cuticle; the dermis as distinguished from the epidermis. **2** the basal end of the forewing of certain insects. [< Latin *corium* leather, skin, hide]

co|rix|id (kə rik′sid), *n.* = water boatman. [< New Latin *Corixidae* the family name < Greek *kóris* bedbug]

cork (kôrk), *n., v., adj.* —*n.* **1a** the light, thick outer bark of the cork oak. Cork is used for bottle stoppers, floats for fishing lines, inner soles of shoes, fillings for some kinds of life preservers, insulation, and some floor coverings. **b** the tree itself. **2** a shaped piece of cork: *the cork of a bottle.* **3** any stopper for a bottle or flask, made of rubber, glass, or plastic. SYN: stopple. **4** *Botany.* an outer bark of woody plants serving as a protective covering for the underlying tissues: *When cells of older portions of the stem become impregnated with suberin, the resulting tissue is known as cork, a material which also serves for protection* (Harbaugh and Goodrich). See picture under **bark[1]**.
—*v.t.* **1** to stop up with or as if with a cork: *Fill and cork these bottles. His private papers were kept corked up for years.* SYN: stopple. **2** to confine; restrain; check: *He managed to cork up his feelings while his guests were in the room.* **3** to provide or fit with cork or a cork: *to cork a float.* **4** to blacken with burnt cork.
—*adj.* made of or with cork.
[< Spanish *alcorque* cork slipper < Arabic *alqurq* < Latin *quercus* oak tree]

cork|age (kôr′kij), *n.* a charge made by a restaurant or hotel for serving wine brought or sent in by a client.

cork black, = Spanish black.

cork|board (kôrk′bôrd′, -bōrd), *n.* a strawboard or cardboard in which ground cork is mixed with pulp. It is light, elastic, and useful as an insulator against heat and noise.

cork cambium, = phellogen.

corked (kôrkt), *adj.* **1** provided or stopped with a cork. **2** tasting of the cork; spoiled by a poor cork: *corked wine.* **3** blackened with burnt cork.

cork elm, = rock elm.

cork|er (kôr′kər), *n.* **1** a person or thing that corks. **2** *Slang.* **a** a person or thing of surpassing quality or size. **b** something that clinches a discussion or settles a question. **c** something very striking or astonishing, such as a monstrous lie: *The story he told was a corker.*

cork|ing (kôr′king), *adj., adv., interj.* —*adj.* **1** that corks: *a corking machine.* **2** *Slang.* excellent; outstanding; fine: *That was a corking record you made in the 50-yard dash.*
—*adv.* remarkably; unusually: *a corking good show.* —*interj. Slang.* excellent! fine!

cor|kir (kôr′kər), *n.* a kind of lichen furnishing a red dye. [Scottish < Gaelic *corcur*]

cork jacket, a jacket made partly of cork, or lined with cork, to support a person in the water.

cork oak, the oak tree, of the Mediterranean area, from which cork is obtained.

cork|screw (kôrk′skrü′), *n., adj., v.,* —*n.* a tool

used to pull corks out of bottles. Corkscrews usually consist of a sharp-pointed steel spiral and a handle. *Nothing spoils the act of a man trying to play the ... host like a corkscrew that disembowels the cork and drops the shattered remains into the bottle* (Newsweek).
— *adj.* shaped like a corkscrew; spiral: *corkscrew curls.*
— *v.t. Informal.* **1** to cause to move or advance in a spiral or zigzag course: [*The horses*] *have to be corkscrewed into our diminutive stables* (Augustus Jessop). **2** to make (one's way) in a spiral or zigzag course: *Mr. Bantam corkscrewed his way through the crowd* (Dickens).
— *v.i. Informal.* to proceed in a spiral or zigzag course: *She's on her way down, corkscrewing crazily through the sky with a whiplash motion* (New York Times).

cork tile, a tile made from tree bark and used for flooring.

cork tree, = cork oak.

cork|wood (kôrk′wu̇d′), *n.* **1** the light, porous wood of any one of various trees, especially of the balsa. **2** any one of several trees yielding such wood, especially a large shrub that grows in the swamps of the southeastern United States.

cork|y (kôr′kē), *adj.,* **cork|i|er, cork|i|est.** **1** *Informal.* of or resembling cork: **a** corklike: *shoes with corky soles, floats with corky buoyancy.* **b** *Figurative.* trifling, frivolous, or buoyant: *They felt so corky it was hard to keep them down* (Oliver Wendell Holmes). **2** tasting of the cork; corked: *corky wine.* — **cork′i|ness,** *n.*

corm (kôrm), *n.* a fleshy, bulblike, underground stem of certain plants, such as the crocus and gladiolus, that produces leaves and buds on the upper surface and roots on the lower. A corm has smaller and thinner leaves than a bulb and it consists mostly of stem tissue. See picture under **bulb.** [< New Latin *cormus* < Greek *kormós* stripped tree trunk < *keírein* to shear]

cor|mel (kôr′məl), *n.* a small corm, especially one growing out of another corm. [< *corm* + *-el* (a diminutive suffix, as in *kernel*)]

cor|mo|phyte (kôr′mə fīt), *n. Botany.* any plant of a former primary division of the vegetable kingdom, comprising all plants with foliage and an axis differentiated into stem and root. [< Greek *kormós* tree trunk, stem + English *-phyte*]

cor|mo|rant (kôr′mər ənt), *n., adj.* — *n.* **1** a very large sea bird that has a pouch under its beak for holding captured fish. Cormorants are found in almost every part of the world. Some species grow to about three feet long. They have dark plumage, a long hooked beak, and webbed feet and are supposed to be greedy. Tame cormorants are used in Asia to catch fish. **2** *Figurative.* a greedy person.
— *adj.* greedy. **SYN:** rapacious. [alteration of Old French *cormaran,* earlier *cormareng* < *corp* raven (< Latin *corvus*) + *marenc* of the sea < Latin *mare*]

***corn[1]**
definition 1

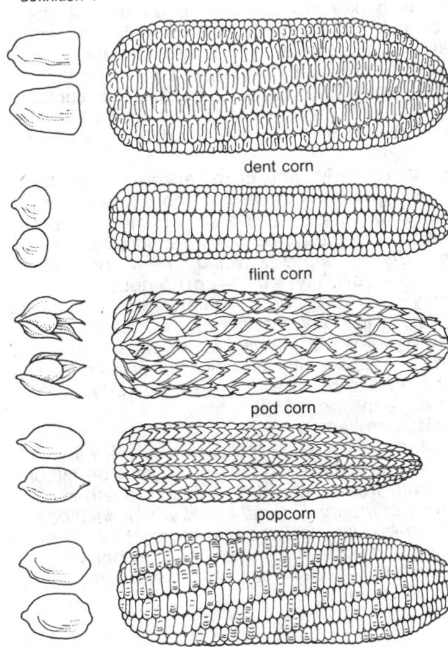
dent corn
flint corn
pod corn
popcorn
sweet corn

***corn[1]** (kôrn), *n., v.* — *n.* **1** a kind of grain that grows on large ears; maize; Indian corn. **2** the plant, a species of cereal grass, that it grows on. **3** = sweet corn. **4** any small, hard seed or grain, especially of wheat, barley, or oats, but also of other plants such as the apple, grape, and pepper; kernel. **5** *British.* grain in general, especially wheat: *During the war, the British government urgently asked the Americans for some thousands of bushels of "corn" to feed liberated populations* (Holiday). **6** *Scottish and Irish.* oats. **7** any small, hard particle, as of sand or salt. **8** *Skiing.* snow having the consistency of grain or granules; corn snow. **9** *U.S. Informal.* = corn whiskey. **10** *Slang.* something trite, outdated, or sentimental: *The lyrics ... contain just the right proportions of imagination, sentimentality, and corn* (Time).
— *v.t.* **1** to preserve (meat) with strong salt water or with dry salt: *to corn beef.* **2** to feed (an animal) with corn or grain: *There is nothing like corning the horse before the journey* (Scott). **3** to plant with corn or grain. **4** to form into grains, as gunpowder; granulate.
[Old English *corn* a seed; a grain (of sand, etc.)]
— **corn′like′,** *adj.*

corn[2] (kôrn), *n.* a hardening of the skin, usually on a toe, caused by pressure or rubbing and often very painful. [< Old French *corn* horn < Latin *cornū*]

Corn., **1** Cornish. **2** Cornwall.

cor|na|ceous (kôr nā′shəs), *adj.* belonging to the dogwood family. [< New Latin *Cornaceae* the order name (< Latin *cornus* cornel) + English *-ous*]

corn aphis, an American aphid that lives by feeding on sugar cane, Indian corn, and other grains; corn leaf aphid.

corn|ball (kôrn′bôl′), *n., adj. U.S. Slang.* — *n.* **1** a sentimental or unsophisticated person: *Several cornballs in the group, afflicted with ingrown scruples, made ineffectual protest* (New Yorker). **2** something trite, banal, or of poor quality.
— *adj.* characterized by triteness or sentimentality: *cornball escape fiction.*
[American English < *corn*[1] something trite + *-ball,* as in *screwball*]

corn|bells (kôrn′belz′), *n.* a bell-shaped fungus which sometimes grows in grainfields.

Corn Belt, *U.S.* an area in the Middle West where corn is grown extensively. Nebraska, Iowa, Illinois, and Indiana are included in the Corn Belt.

corn binder, a harvesting machine for cutting, gathering, and binding together stalks of corn; corn harvester.

corn borer, the larva of a small moth, a serious insect pest in the United States and elsewhere that destroys corn and other plants; European corn borer.

corn bran, the external coating of the kernel of maize, separated by grinding and bolting, used as food for cattle.

corn bread, bread made of corn meal used either instead of flour or in combination with it.

corn cake, *U.S.* a flat cake made with simple corn-meal batter; johnnycake; hoecake.

corn chip, *U.S.* a thin, crisp chip or flake of fried corn meal, eaten as a snack.

corn|cob (kôrn′kob′), *n.* **1** the central, woody part of an ear of corn, on which the kernels grow in rows; cob. **2** Also, **corncob pipe.** a tobacco pipe with a bowl hollowed out of a piece of dried corncob, often polished on the outside.

corn cockle, a weed of the pink family with red or white flowers and black, poisonous seeds, that grows in grainfields.

corn-col|ored (kôrn′kul′ərd), *adj.* light-yellow.

corn cracker, **1** *U.S. Dialect.* a poor white of the southeastern United States; cracker (used in an unfriendly way). **2** = corn crake.

corn crake, a bird of the same family as the rail, common in meadows and grainfields in Europe.

corn|crib (kôrn′krib′), *n.* a bin or small, ventilated building for storing unshelled corn.

corn dance, a ceremonial dance or festival held by American Indians in connection with the harvesting or planting of maize.

corn dodger, *U.S.* a small cake of baked, fried, or boiled corn bread; dodger.

cor|ne|a (kôr′nē ə), *n.* the transparent outside coat of the eyeball. The cornea covers the iris and pupil. *Light enters the eye through a transparent curved shell called the cornea, the space immediately behind which is filled with a liquid called the aqueous humor* (Shortley and Williams). See the diagram under **eye.** [< Medieval Latin *cornea* (*tela*) horny (web) < Latin *cornū* horn]

cor|ne|al (kôr′nē əl), *adj.* of or having to do with the cornea: *Corneal grafting, for example, allows a man suffering from an opaque cornea to see again by replacing it with* [*a*] *healthy cornea* (New Scientist).

corn earworm, a large moth larva that eats cotton bolls and ears of corn; bollworm.

corned (kôrnd), *adj.* preserved with strong salt water or dry salt: *corned beef, corned pork.*

cor|ne|i|tis (kôr′nē ī′tis), *n.* inflammation of the cornea. [< *corne*(a) + *-itis*]

cor|nel (kôr′nəl), *n.* **1** (in Europe) a shrub or small tree of the dogwood family with yellow flowers and edible red berries. **2** (in North America) the flowering dogwood. **3** = bunchberry. [< German *Kornel*(*kirsche*) < Medieval Latin *cornolium,* ultimately < Latin *cornus*]

cor|nel|ian[1] (kôr nēl′yən), *n.* = carnelian.

cor|nel|ian[2] (kôr nēl′yən), *adj.* of or resembling the cornel.

cornelian cherry, a shrub or small tree of the dogwood family, native to southern Europe and the Orient, grown for its clusters of yellow flowers and inch-long, edible berries.

cor|ne|ole (kôr′nē ōl), *n.* the anterior transparent part of each of the segments of the compound eye of insects. [< New Latin *corneola,* diminutive of *cornea* cornea]

cor|ne|ous (kôr′nē əs), *adj.* horny; hornlike. [< Latin *corneus* horny (with English *-ous*) < *cornū, -ūs* horn]

cor|ner (kôr′nər), *n., adj., v.* — *n.* **1** the place where two lines or surfaces meet: *the corners of the mouth, the corner of a room.* **2** the space between two lines or surfaces near where they meet; angle: *He was whipped and told to stand in the corner.* **3** the place where two streets meet: *There is a traffic light at the corner. They were to meet on the corner of Franklin and 39th Street.* **SYN:** intersection. **4** a piece of material to protect or decorate a corner: *The leather pocketbook has gold corners.* **5** a secret place; place away from crowds: *a corner in which to work. The money was hidden in odd corners all over the house.* **SYN:** nook, niche, recess. **6** a place that is far away; extremity: *People have searched in all corners of the world for gold.* **7** any small part, portion, or spot; region; quarter: *I turned and tried each corner of my bed, to find if sleep were there* (John Dryden). **8** *Figurative.* a difficult position; place from which escape is impossible: *His enemies had driven him into a corner.* **9a** the angle of a boxing ring in which a boxer rests between the rounds. **b** a boxer's cornerman. **c** *Figurative.* a side in any contest: *Maybe it'll give* [*him*] *confidence to have somebody in his corner* (Saul Bellow). **10** a buying up of large amounts of some stock or commodity to raise its price: *a corner in cotton. Moonshiners ... until now have had a corner on the corn whisky market* (Wall Street Journal). **11** *U.S.* an exclusive possession or control; monopoly: *Most of them have coldly calculated that the Democrats ... have a corner on the Negro vote* (Atlantic).
— *adj.* **1** at or on a corner: *a corner house.* **2** for a corner: *a corner cupboard.* **3** for making corners: *a corner chisel.*
— *v.t.* **1** to put in a corner; drive into a corner: *cornered in the coziest nook of all* (Robert Browning). **2** *Figurative.* to force into a difficult position; drive into a place from which escape is impossible: *The police cornered the thief in the alley. This question cornered him.* **3** to provide with corners: *The walls are cornered with stone.* **4** to buy up large amounts of (a stock or commodity) to raise its price: *Some speculators have tried to corner wheat.*
— *v.i.* **1a** to round sharp corners at relatively high speeds without sway: *This heavy make of car corners more safely than any of the other lighter cars we tried.* **b** to drive a car around a sharp corner: *It also rolls somewhat, but the driver who is prepared to ignore this can corner quite fast* (Observer). **2** *U.S.* to form a corner; be situated at a corner: *a pew cornering on one of the side aisles* (Hawthorne). **3** to form a corner in a stock or commodity: *These speculators are forming a syndicate in order to corner.*
around the corner, in the near future; soon to happen, be achieved, or acquired: *Computers that think ... are only just around the corner* (Manchester Guardian Weekly).
cut corners, **a** to shorten the way by going across corners: *The boys ran off to school, cutting corners to avoid being late.* **b** to save money, effort, time, labor, or material: *When the manufacturer cut corners by using cheap materials, he lost his market. Employers have tightened up, cut corners, installed more labor-saving machinery* (New York Times).
paint oneself into a corner, to get into a situation from which one cannot extricate oneself: *When better authors than I am find themselves unable to cope with the problem of a married hero, I'm not going to paint myself into that corner again* (Erle Stanley Gardner).
the four corners of the earth, the farthest regions of the earth: *The Moslem pilgrims come to*

Mecca from the four corners of the earth.
turn the corner, to pass the worst or most dangerous point: *Economic experts believe that we have now turned the corner.*
[< Anglo-French *corner,* Old French *cornere* < *corn* horn, ultimately < Latin *cornū*] —**cor′ner|er**, *n.*

cor|ner|back (kôr′nər bak′), *n. American Football.* a defensive player in the position of halfback.

cor|nered (kôr′nərd), *adj.* **1** without hope of escape or relief: *A cornered animal will fight.* **2** having a corner or corners: *four-cornered.*

cor|ner|ing (kôr′nər ing), *n.* **1** the ability to make sharp turns, as of a sports car. **2** the making of a sharp turn. **3** *Surfing.* the act of shooting across a wave at an angle to the shoreline. **4** the act of buying up something to raise its price.

corner kick, a kick in soccer from the nearest corner of the field made by an offensive player when a ball last touched by a defensive player goes over his own goal line.

cor|ner|man (kôr′nər man′), *n., pl.* **-men. 1** a man who assists a boxer between the rounds of a fight. **2** the end man in a minstrel show. **3** a forward in basketball. **4** = cornerback.

cor|ner|piece (kor′nər pēs′), *n.* a casting, guard, cap, or similar piece used for strengthening, protecting, or decorating the corner of anything: *the cornerpieces of a book.*

cor|ner|stone (kôr′nər stōn′), *n.* **1** a stone at the corner of two walls that holds them together. **2** such a stone built into the corner of a building as its formal beginning. The laying of a cornerstone is often accompanied by ceremonies. **3** *Figurative.* something of fundamental importance; foundation; basis: *The cornerstone of most religions is belief in God.*

corner tree, *U.S.* a tree which marks the corner of a surveyed tract.

cor|ner|ways (kôr′nər wāz′), *adv.* = cornerwise.

cor|ner|wise (kôr′nər wīz′), *adv.* **1** with the corner in front; so as to form a corner. **2** from corner to corner; diagonally: *Squares meet one another cornerwise* (Hawthorne).

cor|net¹ (kôr net′; *also for 2* kôr′nit), *n.* **1** a musical wind instrument like a trumpet but having a wider bore. It is usually made of brass and has three valves that control the notes. The tone of a cornet is more singing than that of a trumpet. **2a** a piece of paper rolled into a cone and twisted at one end, used to hold candy, nuts, or the like. **b** a pastry shell shaped like a cone, often filled with whipped cream. **c** *British.* a wafer shaped like a cone for holding ice cream; ice-cream cone. [< Old French *cornet* (diminutive) < *corn* < Latin *cornū* horn]

cor|net² (kôr′nit, kôr net′), *n.* **1** a large, spreading, white cap worn by Sisters of Charity. **2** formerly: **a** an officer in a British cavalry troop who carried the flag. **b** a troop of British cavalry. **3** *Nautical.* a pennant used as a signal. [< French *cornette* (diminutive) < *corne;* see etym. under **corner**]

cor|net-à-pis|tons (kôr′nit ə pis′tənz), *n., pl.* **cor|nets-à-pis|tons** (kôr′nits ə pis′tənz). a cornet (the name used to distinguish the modern musical instrument from one having no pistons). [< French *cornet-à-pistons* cornet with pistons]

cor|net|cy (kôr′nit sē), *n., pl.* **-cies.** the rank or position of a cornet in a troop of cavalry

cor|net|tist or **cor|net|ist** (kôr net′ist), *n.* a musician who plays a cornet.

cor|net|to (kôr net′ō), *n., pl.* **-net|ti** (-net′ē). = zinke. [< Italian *cornetto*]

cor|ne|um (kôr′nē əm), *n.* = stratum corneum.

corn-fed (kôrn′fed′), *adj.* **1** fed on corn or other grain: *prime corn-fed hogs.* **2** *Informal, Figurative.* well-fed; stout.

corn|field (kôrn′fēld′), *n.* a field in which corn is grown.

corn|flakes (kôrn′flāks′), *n.pl.* a dry, ready-to-eat breakfast cereal, made of corn in the form of crisp flakes.

corn flour, **1** flour made from corn. **2** *British.* cornstarch.

corn|flow|er (kôrn′flou′ər), *n.* **1** a plant usually with blue, pink, white, or purple flowers; bachelor's-button; bluebottle; bluebonnet. **2** = corn cockle.

corn harvester, = corn binder.

corn-hog ratio (kôrn′hog′), the ratio of the market price of hogs weighing 100 pounds to the cost of one bushel of corn: *The corn-hog ratio [is] a rough measure of the profit margin in raising pigs* (Wall Street Journal).

corn|husk (kôrn′husk′), *n.* the husk of coarse leaves enclosing an ear of corn.

Corn|husk|er (kôrn′husk′ər), *n.* a nickname for a native or inhabitant of Nebraska.

Cornhusker State, a nickname for Nebraska.

corn|husk|ing (kôrn′hus′king), *n. U.S.* husking.

cor|ni (kôr′nē), *n.* plural of **corno.**

***cor|nice** (kôr′nis), *n., v.,* **-niced, -nic|ing.** —*n.* **1a** an ornamental molding that projects along the top of a wall, pillar, or side of a building. **b** the top part of an entablature, resting on and projecting over the frieze. **2** a molding, usually of wood or plaster, around the walls of a room just below the ceiling. **3** any one of various other ornamental moldings, as for concealing a curtain rod or otherwise decorating the top of a window. **4** an overhanging mass of ice and snow at the edge of a mountain ridge.
—*v.t.* to build or finish with a cornice.
[< French *corniche* < Italian *cornice* < Greek *korōnís* something bent]

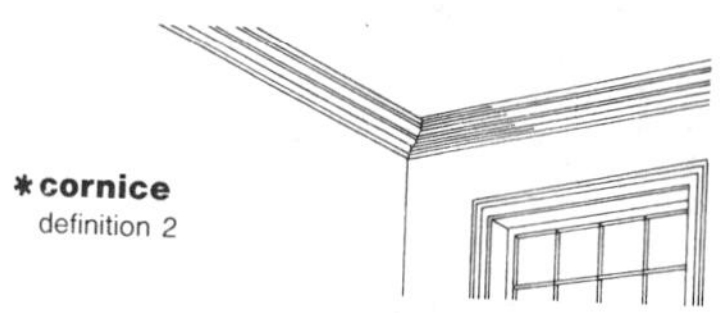
***cornice**
definition 2

cor|niche (kôr′nish, kôr nēsh′), *n.,* or **corniche road**, a road running along the edge of a mountainside. [< French *corniche;* see etym. under **cornice**]

cor|ni|cle (kôr′nə kəl), *n.* **1** any small, hornlike organ or process, as one of the projections or antennae of a snail or an insect. **2** one of two hornlike, tubular organs on the back of an aphid, from which a waxy fluid is secreted; siphuncle. [< Latin *corniculum* little horn; see etym. under **corniculate**]

cor|nic|u|late (kôr nik′yə lāt, -lit), *adj.* having pointed projections like horns; horned. [< Latin *corniculātus* < *corniculum* little horn (diminutive) < *cornū* horn]

Cor|nif|er|ous (kôr nif′ər əs), *adj. Geology.* of or having to do with a portion of the Devonian system containing hornstone. [< Latin *cornifer* horn-bearing + English *-ous*]

cor|ni|fy (kôr′nə fī), *v.t.,* **-fied, -fy|ing.** to make or convert into horn or a horny substance; make chitinous. [< Latin *cornū* horn + English *-fy*]

Cor|nish (kôr′nish), *adj., n.* —*adj.* of or having to do with the English county of Cornwall, its people, their former Celtic language, or their present dialect.
—*n.* **1** a Celtic language spoken in Cornwall until the late 1700's. **2** the modern English dialect spoken in Cornwall. **3** any one of a breed of large, heavy chickens raised mainly for meat. They are originally from England and have unfeathered shanks and a yellow skin.

Cor|nish|man (kôr′nish mən), *n., pl.* **-men.** a native or inhabitant of Cornwall, in southwestern England.

corn|land (kôrn′land′), *n.* land suitable for the cultivation of corn.

corn law, *Historical.* a law regulating trade in grain, especially its import and export.

corn leaf aphid, = corn aphis.

corn lily, any one of a group of South African plants of the iris family.

corn liquor, = corn whiskey.

corn|loft (kôrn′lôft′, -loft′), *n.* a loft for storing corn; granary.

corn meal, **1a** a meal made by grinding up dry corn; Indian meal. **b** a meal made of other grain. **2** *Scottish.* oatmeal.

cor|no (kôr′nō), *n., pl.* **-ni.** *Italian.* **1** a horn. **2** the French horn.

corn oil, a vegetable oil made from whole-grain corn and used chiefly in cooking and salads: *Corn oil can help control blood cholesterol levels* (Science News Letter).

corn oyster, a fritter containing Indian corn cut from the cob, in appearance somewhat like a fried oyster.

corn picker, a machine that picks ears of corn from standing stalks and strips the husks from them.

corn pith, the pith of the stalk of Indian corn, used in the manufacture of paper and formerly at the back of armor of warships to prevent water from entering shot holes.

corn pone, in the southern United States: **1** a simple kind of corn bread, usually made without milk or eggs. **2** a flat loaf of such bread, shaped by hand.

corn-pone (kôrn′pōn′), *adj.* like a bumpkin; rustic: *a little old corn-pone Congressman* (Harper's).

corn popper, a utensil, such as a long-handled, covered pan of woven wire, in which popcorn is popped.

corn poppy, the common field poppy of Europe, having bright red flowers; coquelicot.

corn rose, **1** = corn poppy. **2** = corn cockle.

corn|row (kôrn′rō′), *v.t., v.i. U.S. Dialect.* to arrange hair into flat braids or pigtails.

corn salad, any one of various plants used for salad, sometimes found growing wild in grain-fields.

corn shock, a conical stack of cornstalks cut and set up on end together in a field.

corn silk, the glossy threads or styles at the end of an ear of corn.

corn sirup, = corn syrup.

corn smut, **1** a disease in growing corn produced by a fungus that fills the grains with black, sootlike, powdery spores. **2** this fungus, once used medicinally.

corn snake, a large, harmless rat snake, common in the southern United States, where it is found in cornfields and granaries.

corn snow, *Skiing.* snow having the consistency of grains or granules as a result of alternate melting and freezing.

corn|stalk (kôrn′stôk′), *n.* a stalk of Indian corn.

corn|starch (kôrn′stärch′), *n.* a starchy white flour made from corn, used to thicken puddings, custard, gravies, and other foods.

corn sugar, a sugar made from cornstarch.

corn syrup, a syrup made from cornstarch; a kind of glucose. Also, **corn sirup**.

cor|nu (kôr′nyü), *n., pl.* **-nu|a** (-nyü ə). *Anatomy.* a horn or hornlike part or process. [< Latin *cornū* horn]

cor|nu|al (kôr′nyu̇ əl), *adj. Anatomy.* of a cornu or cornua; hornlike.

***cor|nu|co|pi|a** (kôr′nə kō′pē ə, -nyu̇-), *n.* **1** a horn-shaped container represented in art as overflowing with fruit, vegetables, and flowers; horn of plenty. It is the symbol of fruitfulness and plenty. Originally it represented the horn of the goat Amalthaea, which suckled the infant Zeus. **2** any horn-shaped container or ornament. Cornucopias are hung on Christmas trees. **3** *Figurative.* an overflowing supply; abundance. [< Late Latin *cornūcōpia,* for Latin *cornū cōpiae* horn of plenty; see etym. under **copious**]

***cornucopia**
definition 1

cor|nu|co|pi|an (kôr′nə kō′pē ən, -nyu̇-), *adj.* like a cornucopia; overflowingly abundant or productive: *Comfortable, air-conditioned homes, cornucopian supermarkets* (London Times).

cor|nu|co|pi|ate (kôr′nə kō′pē it, -nyu̇-), *adj.* having the shape of a cornucopia, as certain shells.

cor|nus (kôr′nəs), *n.* = cornel. [< Latin *cornus*]

cor|nute (kôr nyüt′, -nüt′), *adj., v.,* **-nut|ed, -nut|ing.** —*adj.* cornuted.
—*v.t. Archaic.* to make a cuckold of.
[< Latin *cornūtus* horned < *cornū* horn]

cor|nut|ed (kôr nyü′tid, -nü′-), *adj.* **1** horn-shaped. **2** having horns or hornlike projections. **3** *Archaic.* cuckolded.

cor|nu|to (kôr nyü′tō, -nü′-), *n., pl.* **-tos.** *Archaic.* a cuckold. [< Italian *cornuto* (literally) horned < Latin *cornūtus;* see etym. under **cornute**]

corn|wall|ite (kôrn′wô līt), *n.* a green, amorphous arsenite of copper, resembling malachite. [< *Cornwall,* England, where it is found + *ite¹*]

corn whiskey, *U.S.* whiskey distilled from corn; corn liquor.

corn|y¹ (kôr′nē), *adj.,* **corn|i|er, corn|i|est. 1a** of or having to do with corn. **b** abounding in corn. **2** *Informal.* trite, outdated, or sentimental: *corny jokes, corny music. He uses the corniest lines, ones that no one else would dare to try* (Newsweek). —**corn′i|ly**, *adv.* —**corn′i|ness**, *n.*

corn|y² (kôr′nē), *adj.,* **corn|i|er, corn|i|est.** having or having to do with corns on the feet.

cor|o|dy (kôr′ə dē, kor′-), *n., pl.* **-dies. 1** an allowance, especially of provisions for maintenance. **2** the right to receive this. Also, **corrody.** [< Medieval Latin *corrōdium*]

coroll., corollary.

***co|rol|la** (kə rol′ə), *n.* the petals of a flower. The petals which make up the corolla may be either separate from each other or fused together. *The corolla is the inner floral envelope, usually delicate in texture, and showing more or less brilliant colors and combinations of color* (Heber W. Youngken). [< Latin *corolla* garland (diminutive) < *corōna* crown]

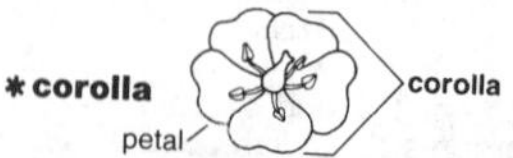

***corolla**

cor|ol|la|ceous (kôr′ə lā′shəs, kor′-), *adj. Botany.* having to do with or resembling a corolla.

cor|ol|lar (kôr′ə lər, kor′-), *adj.* = corollaceous.

cor|ol|lar|y (kôr′ə ler′ē, kor′-; *especially British* kə-rol′ər ē), *n., pl.* **-lar|ies**, *adj.* **—*n.*** **1** a natural consequence or result: *Destruction and suffering are corollaries of war.* **2** an inference; deduction. **3** something proved by inference from something else already proved.
—*adj.* of the nature of a corollary.
[< Late Latin *corollārium* (in Latin, money paid for a gift) < *corolla;* see etym. under **corolla**]

cor|ol|late (kôr′ə lāt, kor′-), *adj. Botany.* **1** having a corolla. **2** resembling a corolla.

cor|ol|lif|er|ous (kôr′ə lif′ər əs, kor′-), *adj.* having or producing a corolla: *corolliferous flowers.*

co|ro|na (kə rō′nə), *n., pl.* **-nas, -nae** (-nē). **1a** a ring of light seen around the sun, moon, or other luminous body. It is usually colored and is caused by diffraction produced by thin clouds or mist. **b** a halo of light around the sun, seen only during an eclipse or with a coronagraph. **2a** a crownlike part, such as the top of the head or the crown of a tooth. **b** *Botany.* a crownlike appendage on the inner side of the corolla in some flowers, such as the daffodil. **c** *Zoology.* the ciliated, retractile area at the anterior end of a rotifer. **3** *Architecture.* the main, projecting element of a cornice. **4** a discharge of electricity, often visible, that occurs at the surface of a conductor or between two terminals; brush discharge. **5** a long, untapered cigar, usually one of superior quality: *Subtle attempts are being made to convince women that a man with a giant corona in his mouth is a sight both gracious and graceful* (Punch). See picture under **cigar.** [< Latin *corōna* < Greek *korōnē. See etym. of doublet* ***crown.***]

Corona Aus|tra|lis (ô strā′lis), *genitive* **Coronae Australis.** a southern constellation near Sagittarius; the Southern Crown. [< Latin *Corōna austrālis* Southern Crown]

Corona Bo|re|al|is (bôr′ē al′is, bōr′-; -ā′lis), *genitive* **Coronae Borealis.** a northern constellation between Hercules and Boötes; the Northern Crown. [< Latin *Corōna boreālis* the Northern Crown]

cor|o|nach (kôr′ə nəʜ, kor′-), *n. Scottish and Irish.* a song or lamentation for the dead; dirge. [< Gaelic *corronach* dirge; (literally) general shout < *comh-* together + *ranach* roaring]

Co|ro|nae Australis (kə rō′nē), genitive of **Corona Australis.**

Coronae Borealis, genitive of **Corona Borealis.**

co|ro|na|graph (kə rō′nə graf, -gräf), *n.* a telescope equipped with a disk that blacks out most of the sun, used for observing the sun's corona at any time. Also, **coronograph.**

cor|o|nal (*n.* kôr′ə nəl, kor′-; *adj.* kə rō′nəl, kôr′ə-, kor′ə-), *n., adj.* **—*n.*** **1** a crown or coronet. **2** a garland.
—*adj.* **1** of or having to do with a crown or corona. **2** *Anatomy.* designating, adjoining, or paralleling the coronal suture. **3** *Phonetics.* articulated by the blade of the tongue.

co|ro|nal|ly (kə rō′nə lē; kôr′ə nə lē, kor′-), *adv.* in the manner of a crown or corona.

coronal suture, *Anatomy.* a suture extending across the skull between the frontal bone and the parietal bones.

cor|o|nar|y (kôr′ə ner′ē, kor′-), *adj., n., pl.* **-ar|ies.**
—*adj.* **1a** of or having to do with either of the two arteries that supply blood to the muscular tissue of the heart. **b** encircling (a part or organ) like a crown, as certain blood vessels do. **2** having to do with or resembling a crown.
—*n.* = coronary thrombosis.
[< Latin *corōnārius* encircling < *corōna* crown, wreath; see etym. under **corona**]

coronary artery, either of the two arteries that supply blood to the muscular tissue of the heart. See diagram under **heart.**

coronary artery disease, a progressive narrowing or blockage of the coronary arteries by deposits of fatty material; atherosclerosis of the coronary arteries. *Abbr:* CAD (no periods).

coronary cushion, a thickened ring of tissue encircling the upper part of the hoof in horses and allied animals. The coronary cushion secretes the horny material that constitutes the wall of the hoof.

coronary occlusion, = coronary thrombosis.

coronary thrombosis, the stopping up of a coronary artery or one of its branches by a blood clot; coronary occlusion. Coronary thrombosis sometimes results in a fatal blocking of blood to the heart muscles.

cor|o|nate (kôr′ə nāt, kor′-; -nit), *adj. Botany.* having a corona or a crownlike part.

cor|o|nat|ed (kôr′ə nā′tid, kor′-), *adj.* = coronate.

cor|o|na|tion (kôr′ə nā′shən, kor′-), *n.* the ceremony of crowning a king, queen, or emperor.

coronation oath, the oath taken by a sovereign at his or her coronation.

cor|o|ner (kôr′ə nər, kor′-), *n.* an official of a local government who investigates any death not clearly due to natural causes. He may be assisted by a jury to determine the cause of death. [< Anglo-French *corouner* officer of the crown < *coroune;* see etym. under **crown**] **—cor′o|ner|ship,** *n.*

coroner's inquest, an investigation of the cause of a person's death, held by a coroner, usually with the aid of a jury. The verdict of the jury is not conclusive, but if crime is involved, it may be the basis for a criminal prosecution.

coroner's jury, a group of persons chosen to witness a coroner's investigation and to determine the cause of any death not clearly due to natural causes.

cor|o|net (kôr′ə net′, kor′-; *especially British* kôr′ə nit, kor′-), *n.* **1** a small crown worn as a mark of high rank: *A king wears a crown; princes and nobles wear coronets.* **2** a circle of gold, jewels, or flowers worn around the head as an ornament. SYN: chaplet, coronal, circlet. **3** the lowest part of the pastern of a horse, just above the hoof. [< Old French *coronet* (diminutive) < *corone* crown < Latin *corōna;* see etym. under **crown**]

cor|o|net|ed or **cor|o|net|ted** (kôr′ə net′id, kor′-; *especially British* kôr′ə net′id, kor′-), *adj.* adorned with a coronet.

co|ro|ni|form (kə rō′nə fôrm), *adj.* having the form of a crown; crown-shaped.

co|ro|ni|um (kə rō′nē əm), *n.* a hypothetical gaseous element formerly assumed to explain a characteristic green line in the spectrum of the sun's corona, now known to be formed by certain highly ionized chemical elements. [< New Latin *coronium* < Latin *corōna* crown]

co|ro|no|graph (kə rō′nə graf, -gräf), *n.* = coronagraph.

cor|o|noid (kôr′ə noid, kor′-), *adj.* **1** shaped like the beak of a crow. **2** of or denoting any of various bony processes of this shape, as one on the lower jaw.
[< Greek *korṓnē* crow + English *-oid*]

Corp. or **corp.,** **1** corporal. **2** corporation.

cor|po|ra (kôr′pər ə), *n.* plural of **corpus.**

corpora al|la|ta (ə lā′tə), plural of **corpus allatum.**

corpora cal|lo|sa (kə lō′sə), plural of **corpus callosum.**

corpora car|di|a|ca (kär dī′ə kə), plural of **corpus cardiacum.**

cor|po|ral[1] (kôr′pər əl, -prəl), *adj.* **1** of or having to do with the body: *Spanking someone is corporal punishment. I would I had that corporal soundness now* (Shakespeare). SYN: bodily, physical. **2** personal: *corporal possession.* **3** *Obsolete.* corporeal. [< Latin *corporālis* < *corpus, corporis* body] **—cor′po|ral|ly,** *adv.*

cor|po|ral[2] (kôr′pər əl, -prəl), *n.* **1** the lowest non-commissioned officer in the U.S. Army, ranking next below a sergeant and next above a private first class. He usually commands a squad. *Abbr:* Cpl., Corp. **2** a noncommissioned officer of similar rank in the U.S. Marine Corps. **3** a former petty officer in the British Navy having police duties under the master-at-arms. [< French *corporal,* former variant of *caporal* < Italian *caporale* < *capo* head < Latin *caput*] **—cor′po|ral|ship,** *n.*

cor|po|ral[3] (kôr′pər əl, -prəl), *n.* a fine cloth, usually of linen, on which the consecrated elements are placed during the celebration of the Eucharist. [< Medieval Latin *corporalis* (*palla*) body (cloth); see etym. under **corporal[1]**]

cor|po|ral|i|ty (kor′pə ral′ə tē), *n.* the state or quality of having a material or corporeal existence; materiality.

corporal oath, an oath ratified by physically touching a sacred object, especially the Bible, as distinguished from a merely verbal oath. [translation of Medieval Latin *corporale juramentum*]

corporal punishment, punishment inflicted on the body, originally including flogging and branding. In law, corporal punishment includes imprisonment and death.

corporal's guard, **1** a detachment of troops directed by a corporal. **2** a small body of followers or supporters.

corpora lu|te|a (lü′tē ə), plural of **corpus luteum.**

corpora stri|a|ta (strī ā′tə), plural of **corpus striatum.**

cor|po|rate (kôr′pər it, -prit), *adj.* **1** forming a corporation; incorporated: *Most car manufacturers are corporate companies. At that time [the firm] was liquidated as a corporate entity, but no change was made in its operation* (Wall Street Journal). **2** of a corporation: *corporate property, corporate responsibility.* **3** united; combined: *The corporate will of the majority prevailed. The group had a corporate identity.* [< Latin *corporātus,* past participle of *corporāre* form into a body < *corpus, -oris* body]

cor|po|rate|ly (kôr′pər it lē, -prit-), *adv.* **1** in a corporate capacity. **2** *Obsolete.* in the body; bodily.

corporate raider, a person or company that makes a tender offer or starts a proxy fight to gain forcible control of a corporation.

corporate state, **1** a state viewed as a vast, impersonal corporation concerned only with increasing its size and power: *Until the corporate state becomes a people's state there will be no peace* (Time). . . . *a single monolith of power—the corporate state* (Charles A. Reich). **2** = corporative state.

cor|po|ra|tion (kôr′pə rā′shən), *n.* **1** a group of persons who obtain a charter giving them as a group certain legal rights and privileges. A corporation can buy and sell, own property, manufacture and ship products, and bring lawsuits, as if its members were a single person. *Abbr:* Corp. **2** a group of persons with authority to act as a single person. The governing body of a college and the mayor and aldermen of a city are corporations. **3** a corporate body in a corporative state, composed of members representing employers and employees, that regiments specific activities in a given economic sphere. **4** *Slang.* the abdomen, especially when large and prominent.

Cor|po|ra|tion (kôr′pə rā′shən), *n. British.* the municipal authorities of a city or town.

cor|po|ra|tism (kôr′pə rə tiz′əm), *n.* = corporativism. **—cor′po|ra|tist,** *n.*

cor|po|ra|tive (kôr′pə rā′tiv), *adj.* having to do with or consisting of a corporation.

corporative state, a state in which the chief economic activities, such as banking and the principal industries, are each controlled through one corporate body, composed in turn of representatives from the various corporations: *the Italian corporative state under Mussolini.*

cor|po|ra|tiv|ism (kôr′pə rā′tə viz′əm), *n.* the theory or system of a corporative state: *The dangers of a producer-dominated economy tending to degenerate into syndicalism or corporativism outweigh the risks of an economy resting on consumer preference* (London Times). **—cor′po|ra′tiv|ist,** *n.*

cor|po|ra|tor (kôr′pə rā′tər), *n.* a member of a corporation.

cor|po|re|al (kôr pôr′ē əl, -pōr′-), *adj.* **1** of or for the body; bodily: *Food and water are corporeal nourishment.* SYN: physical, corporal. **2** material; tangible: *Land, trees, and money are corporeal things.* SYN: concrete. [< Latin *corporeus* belonging to the body (< *corpus, -oris* body) + English *-al[1]*] **—cor|po′re|al|ly,** *adv.* **—cor|po′re|al|ness,** *n.*

cor|po|re|al|i|ty (kôr pôr′ē al′ə tē, -pōr′-), *n.* the quality or state of being corporeal; bodily form or nature; materiality.

cor|po|re|i|ty (kôr′pə rē′ə tē), *n.* **1** the quality of being, or having, a material body. **2** material or physical nature.
[< Medieval Latin *corporeitas* < Latin *corporeus;* see etym. under **corporeal**]

cor|po|sant (kôr′pə zant), *n.* = St. Elmo's fire. [< Portuguese *corpo santo* (literally) holy body < Latin *corpus* body; *sanctum* holy]

corps (kôr, kōr), *n., pl.* **corps** (kôrz, kōrz). **1** a group of soldiers trained for special military service: *the medical corps, the signal corps.* **2** a tactical military unit usually made up of two or more divisions plus supporting troops, usually commanded by a lieutenant general. It is smaller than an army. **3** a group of people with special training, organized for working together: *A large hospital has a corps of nurses. She is very likely the most accomplished first-aider in the Corps* (New Yorker). **4** a students' social club (in Europe). **5** *Obsolete.* a corpse. [short for French *corps d'armée* army corps < Old French *corps* < Latin *corpus* body. See etym. of doublets **corpse, corpus, corse.**]

corps area, one of the nine areas into which the United States was formerly divided for purposes of military administration, now superseded by six areas called service commands.

corps de bal|let (kôr′də ba lā′), a group of ballet dancers, especially those members of a company other than the soloists. [< French]

corps d'é|lite (kôr′ dā lēt′), *French.* **1** a body of picked or élite troops: *The Highland Regiments were not, as had been falsely asserted, a corps d'élite* (Punch). **2** *Figurative: You cannot have true "student nurses" training to be your corps d'élite on a "pair of hands" basis* (London Times).

corpse (kôrps), *n.* **1** the dead body of a human being, or sometimes, of an animal: *The limp and lifeless corpse of the accident victim lay in the street.* SYN: cadaver, ashes, remains. **2** *Figurative: The corpse of the committee had a last, fruitless meeting.* **3** *Obsolete.* a living body. [< Old

---

Pronunciation Key: hat, āge, cãre, fär; let, ēqual, tėrm; it, īce; hot, ōpen, ôrder; oil, out; cup, pu̇t, rüle; child; long; thin; ᴛʜen; zh, measure; ə represents a in about, e in taken, i in pencil, o in lemon, u in circus.

French *corps, cors* < Latin *corpus* body. See etym. of doublets **corps, corpus, corse.**]

corpse candle, the ignis fatuus or will-o'-the wisp; corpse light.

corpse light, = corpse candle.

corpse plant, = Indian pipe.

corps|man (kôr′mən, kōr′-), *n., pl.* **-men. 1** *U.S. Navy.* an enlisted man who performs medical or related duties in a ship's dispensary, a base hospital, or a combat unit of the Marine Corps. **2** *U.S. Army.* a member of a medical battalion assigned to a combat unit and charged with administering to and evacuating the wounded. **3** a member of any corps. **4** = Peace Corpsman.

cor|pu|lence (kôr′pyə ləns), *n.* fatness; stoutness; obesity.

cor|pu|len|cy (kôr′pyə lən sē), *n.* = corpulence.

cor|pu|lent (kôr′pyə lənt), *adj.* large or bulky of body; fat; stout; fleshy: (*Figurative.*) *The body politic seems to him fatally corpulent, awash in its own lard* (Saturday Review). **SYN**: portly, obese. [< Latin *corpulentus* < *corpus, -oris* body] — **cor′pu|lent|ly**, *adv.*

cor pul|mo|na|le (kôr′ pu̇l′mə nal′ē), *pl.* **cordia pulmonalia.** a heart disorder, especially enlargement of the right ventricle, caused by disease of the lungs or of the pulmonary blood vessels. [< New Latin *cor pulmonale* pulmonary heart]

cor|pus (kôr′pəs), *n., pl.* **-po|ra. 1** a complete collection of writings on some subject or of some period, or of laws, or other matter: *Cases cover only a small fraction of the corpus of customary laws* (London Times). **2** a collection of stocks, bonds, or other holdings, forming the principal of a trust fund or estate, as opposed to the interest or income. **3** the whole body; material substance of anything. **4** *Anatomy.* any one of various bodies, masses, or parts of special character or function. **5** a body, especially the dead body of a person or animal. [< Latin *corpus* body. See etym. of doublet **corps, corpse, corse.**]

corpus al|la|tum (ə lā′təm), *pl.* **corpora allata.** *Zoology.* a gland lying behind the brain of an insect, secreting hormones that are involved in molting and metamorphosis. [< New Latin *corpus allatum* applied body]

corpus cal|lo|sum (kə lō′səm), *pl.* **corpora callosa.** the transverse band of nerve fibers connecting the cerebral hemispheres in man and other mammals: ... *the functions of the corpus callosum, that immense band of fibres, nearly 200 million in number, which connected the two cerebral hemispheres* (London Times). See diagram under **brain.** [< New Latin *corpus callosum* callous body]

corpus car|di|a|cum (kär dī′ə kəm), *pl.* **corpora cardiaca.** *Zoology.* either of a pair of organs lying at the back of the head of an insect, functioning with the corpus allatum and the prothoracic glands. [< New Latin *corpus cardiacum* cardiac body]

Cor|pus Chris|ti (kôr′pəs kris′tē), a feast of the Roman Catholic Church in honor of the Eucharist, held on the first Thursday after Trinity Sunday. [< Latin *corpus Christī* body of Christ]

***cor|pus|cle** (kôr′pə səl, -pus əl), *n.* **1** any of the cells that form a large part of blood and lymph. Red corpuscles carry oxygen from the lungs to various parts of the body and remove carbon dioxide; some white corpuscles destroy disease germs. **2** certain parts of the nervous system, such as skin nerve endings, that respond to pressure. **3** a very small particle: *Until about the middle of the 17th century, it was generally believed that light consisted of a stream of corpuscles* (Sears and Zemansky). [< Latin *corpusculum* (diminutive) < *corpus, -oris* body]

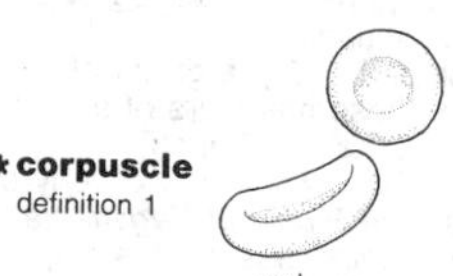

***corpuscle**
definition 1

cor|pus|cu|lar (kôr pus′kyə lər), *adj.* of corpuscles; consisting of corpuscles; like that of corpuscles: *That spring the sun emitted a series of unusually strong and well-defined corpuscular clouds* (Scientific American). **SYN**: cellular.

cor|pus|cu|lar|i|an (kôr pus′kyə lãr′ē ən), *adj., n.* — ***adj.*** having to do with corpuscles or with the corpuscular philosophy.
— ***n.*** a person who favors or believes in the corpuscular philosophy.

corpuscular philosophy, the doctrine of atoms considered as a general explanation of the phenomena of the world, especially this doctrine as advocated by Robert Boyle in the 1600's.

corpuscular theory, *Physics.* the theory that light is propagated as particles: *The photoelectric effect and the Compton effect, then, both seem to demand a return to a corpuscular theory of light* (Sears and Zemansky).

cor|pus|cule (kôr pus′kyül), *n.* = corpuscle.

corpus de|lic|ti (di lik′tī), **1** the body of a murdered person, serving as concrete evidence that a crime has been committed. **2** the actual facts that prove a crime or offense against the law has been committed: *The armies of investigators here and abroad ... have scarcely finished a preliminary examination of the corpus delicti* (Harper's). [< Latin *corpus dēlictī* body of the crime]

corpus ju|ris (ju̇r′is), a complete collection of laws, as of a state or district. [< Latin *corpus jūris* body of law]

corpus lu|te|um (lü′tē əm), *pl.* **corpora lutea. 1** a yellow endocrine mass formed in the ovary when a Graafian follicle (sac containing ova) breaks up in pregnancy or menstruation. In pregnancy, the corpus luteum produces progesterone. **2** an extract of the corpus luteum of a cow or a hog, used in the treatment of ovarian disorders. [< New Latin *corpus luteum* yellow body]

corpus stri|a|tum (strī ā′təm), *pl.* **corpora striata.** either of two bodies of nerve fibers in the brain, each forming part of the undersurface of a cerebral hemisphere. [< New Latin *corpus striatum* striate body]

corpus vit|re|um (vit′rē əm), the vitreous humor of the eye.

corr., an abbreviation for the following:
1a corrected. **b** correction.
2a correspondence. **b** correspondent. **c** corresponding.
3 corrugated.
4 corruption.

cor|rade (kə rād′), *v.t., v.i.* **-rad|ed, -rad|ing.** *Geology.* to wear down by corrasion. [< Latin *corrādere* < *com-* together + *rādere* scrape]

cor|ral** (kə ral′), *n., v.,* **-ralled, -ral|ling.** — ***n. **1** a pen for horses, cattle, and other animals. **2** a circular camp formed by wagons for defense against attack.
— ***v.t.*** **1** to drive into or keep in a corral: *The cowhands corralled the herd of wild ponies.* **2** *Figurative.* to hem in; surround; capture: *After a long chase the boys finally corralled the runaway dog. The reporters corralled the candidate and asked him for a statement.* **3** to form (wagons) into a circular camp for defensive purposes. [< Spanish *corral* < *corro* ring. See etym. of doublet **crawl**[2].]

***corral**
definition 1

cor|ra|sion (kə rā′zhən), *n. Geology.* the scraping away of rock by the action of rock fragments moved by wind or water: *All scraping, grinding and scouring, sometimes called abrasion and corrasion, are weathering processes* (Finch and Trewartha). [< Latin *corrādere* scrape together (see etym. under **corrade**) on the analogy of *abrasion*]

cor|ra|sive (kə rā′siv), *adj. Geology.* of or characterized by corrasion.

cor|rect (kə rekt′), *adj., v.* — ***adj.*** **1** free from mistakes or faults; true; right: *He gave the correct answer.* **2** agreeing with a good standard of taste; proper: *correct manners, correct dress.*
— ***v.t.*** **1** to change to what is right; remove mistakes or faults from: *Correct any wrong spellings that you find. His near-sightedness was corrected by properly fitted glasses.* **SYN**: amend. **2** to point out or mark the mistakes in, so that they can be made right: *The teacher corrected our tests and returned them to us. The brash youngster did not hesitate to correct his elders in public.* **3** to adjust to agree with some standard: *to correct the reading of a barometer.* **4** to punish; set right by punishing; find fault with to improve: *The mother corrected her child for misbehaving.* **SYN**: discipline, chastise, reprove. **5** to counteract or neutralize (something hurtful or undesirable); overcome: *Medicine can sometimes correct stomach trouble.* **SYN**: remedy, cure.
— ***v.i.*** to make a correction or corrections; make up for a deviation or error: *He corrected desperately as the car bounced into a ditch* (New Yorker). *Brokers said* [*that*] *the market "corrected" after its runup the previous days* (Wall Street Journal). *It is possible to transfer genetic information from one type of cell, thereby correcting for a genetic deficiency in that cell* (Science News).
[< Latin *correctus,* past participle of *corrigere* make straight < *com-* (intensive) + *regere* to direct] — **cor|rect′a|ble, cor|rect′i|ble,** *adj.* — **cor|rect′ing|ly,** *adv.* — **cor|rect′ly,** *adv.* — **cor|rect′ness,** *n.*
— ***Syn.*** *adj.* **1 Correct, accurate, exact** mean without error or mistake. **Correct** adds nothing to that basic meaning: *correct answers, a correct statement, correct reasoning.* **Accurate** emphasizes the careful effort to make something agree exactly with the facts or a model: *an accurate account of the accident, an accurate drawing of the Capitol, accurate observations of wild life.* **Exact** emphasizes the complete agreement in every detail with the facts or a model: *His painting is an exact copy of the original.*

cor|rect|ed (kə rek′tid), *adj.* made free from mistakes or faults: *a corrected test paper.* **SYN**: emended, rectified.

corrected time, the time taken by a racing yacht to sail over a course after any adjustments, as for handicapping.

cor|rec|tion (kə rek′shən), *n.* **1** the act or process of correcting or setting right; amendment: *The correction of all my mistakes took nearly an hour.* **2** something put in place of an error or mistake; emendation: *Write in your corrections neatly.* **3** punishment; rebuke; scolding. A prison is sometimes called a house of correction. **SYN**: chastisement. **4** an amount added or subtracted to correct a result: *He made a correction for the thickness of the lens.* **5** the counteracting or neutralizing of harmful or unpleasant effects, for example of a medicine.

cor|rec|tion|al (kə rek′shə nəl), *adj.* of or having to do with correction; corrective: *a correctional institution for young delinquents.* — **cor|rec′tion|al|ly,** *adv.*

cor|rect|i|tude (kə rek′tə tüd, -tyüd), *n.* correctness of conduct or behavior: *Like his father and grandfather he had an eye for correctitude in dress and decorations* (London Times). [< *correct,* on analogy of *rectitude*]

cor|rec|tive (kə rek′tiv), *adj., n.* — ***adj.*** tending to correct; setting right; making better: *Corrective exercises will make weak muscles strong.* **SYN**: remedial.
— ***n.*** something that corrects or tends to correct: *Penalties are correctives of immoral conduct. A corrective for overacidity is an alkaline substance.* **SYN**: remedy. — **cor|rec′tive|ly,** *adv.*

cor|rec|tor (kə rek′tər), *n.* a person or thing that corrects.

cor|reg|i|dor (kə rej′ə dôr; *Spanish* kôr rā′hē-ᵺôr′), *n., pl.* **-dores** (-dôrz; *Spanish* -ᵺō′rās). **1** the chief magistrate of a Spanish town. **2** formerly in the American colonies of Spain: **a** a magistrate having jurisdiction of certain special cases prescribed by law. **b** the chief officer of a corregimiento. [< Spanish *corregidor* (literally) a corrector < *corregir* to correct < Latin *corrigere*]

cor|reg|i|mi|en|to (kə rej′ə mē en′tō; *Spanish* kôr-rā′hē myen′tō), *n., pl.* **-tos** (-tōz; *Spanish* -tōs). (formerly) a geographical division of a province in an American colony of Spain; the district of a corregidor. [< Spanish *corregimiento* < *corregir* to correct < Latin *corrigere*]

cor|re|late (kôr′ə lāt, kor′-), *v.,* **-lat|ed, -lat|ing,** *adj., n.* — ***v.t.*** **1** to put in relation; show the connection or relation between: *Try to correlate your knowledge of history with your knowledge of geography.* **2** *Biology.* to show (structures or characteristics in animals and plants) to be closely or mutually related: *Parasitism ... is often found to be correlated with ... disappearance of structures* (Humphrey D. Rolleston).
— ***v.i.*** to be related one to the other; have a mutual relation: *The diameter and circumference of a circle correlate.*
— ***adj.*** *Rare.* mutually related; correlated.
— ***n.*** either of two related things, especially when one implies the other.
[< *cor-* together + *relate*]

cor|re|lat|ed (kôr′ə lā′tid, kor′-), *adj.* related one to another.

cor|re|la|tion (kôr′ə lā′shən, kor′-), *n.* **1** the mutual relation of two or more things: *There is a close correlation between climate and crops.* **SYN**: interdependence. **2** the act or process of correlating. **SYN**: connection. **3** the condition of being correlated. **4a** *Biology.* similarity of relationship between different structures or characteristics in an animal or plant. **b** *Physiology.* mutual relation, as between organs or functions. **5** *Statistics.* the relationship between two or more variables, such as intelligence and vocabulary. Also, **corelation.**

cor|re|la|tion|al (kôr′ə lā′shə nəl, kor′-), *adj.* having to do with or using correlation.

correlation coefficient, *Statistics.* a measure of the relationship or interdependence of two variables; coefficient of correlation. Variables perfectly correlated positively (that is, the existence of one entailing the existence of the other) having a correlation coefficient of 1, those not correlated at all of 0, and those perfectly correlated negatively (that is, the existence of one entailing the nonexistence of the other) of -1. *Symbol:* r.

correlation ratio, *Statistics.* a measure of the correlation between two sets of variables whose correlation cannot be plotted as a straight line.

cor|rel|a|tive (kə rel′ə tiv), *adj., n.* —*adj.* **1** having a mutual relation; so related that each implies the other: *A free community with correlative rights and duties belonging to every citizen* (George Grote). **2** having a mutual relation and commonly used together. Conjunctions used in pairs, such as "either ... or" and "both ... and," are correlative words. **3** *Biology.* showing correlation.
—*n.* **1** either of two things having a mutual relation and commonly used together. **2** either of a pair of correlative words. **3** *Biology.* a structure or characteristic in correlation with another. Also, **corelative.** —**cor|rel′a|tive|ly,** *adv.* —**cor|rel′a|tive|ness,** *n.*

correlative terms, *Grammar.* a pair of words implying a relation between the objects they denote. *Examples:* parent and child, doctor and patient, man and wife.

cor|rel|a|tiv|i|ty (kə rel′ə tiv′ə tē), *n.* correlative quality; interconnection.

cor|re|lig|ion|ist (kôr′i lij′ə nist, kor′-), *n.* = coreligionist.

cor|re|spond (kôr′ə spond′, kor′-), *v.i.* **1** to agree; be in harmony: *The promise and the performance do not correspond. Her white hat and shoes correspond with her white dress.* **SYN**: harmonize, match, suit, accord. See syn. under **agree. 2** to be similar: *The fins of a fish correspond to the wings of a bird.* **SYN**: parallel. **3** to exchange letters; write letters to each other: *Will you correspond with me while I am away?* **SYN**: communicate, write. [< Medieval Latin *correspondere* < Latin *com-* together, with + *rēspondēre* to answer, respond]

cor|re|spond|ence (kôr′ə spon′dəns, kor′-), *n.* **1** agreement; harmony: *Your account of the accident has little correspondence with the story the other driver told.* **SYN**: accord. **2** resemblance in structure or function; similarity: *There is a correspondence of form in the skeletons of a lion and a tiger.* **SYN**: analogy, likeness. **3** exchange of letters; letter writing: *The boy kept up a correspondence with his friend from camp.* **4** letters: *Keep the correspondence about our vacation in a folder where we won't lose it. Your business will gain the prestige of correctly spelled, precisely written, accurate correspondence* (Newsweek). **5** letters contributed to a newspaper, magazine, or other publication. **6** *Mathematics.* a matching of the members of one set of objects with the members of a second set of objects.

correspondence course, a set of lessons in a certain subject given by a correspondence school.

correspondence school, a school that gives lessons by mail. Instructions, explanations, and questions are sent to the student, who returns his written answers for correction or approval.

cor|re|spond|en|cy (kôr′ə spon′dən sē, kor′-), *n.* *Archaic.* correspondence.

cor|re|spond|ent (kôr′ə spon′dənt, kor′-), *n., adj.* —*n.* **1a** a person who exchanges letters with another: *My mother and her sister have been regular correspondents for years, writing to each other weekly.* **b** a person who contributes letters to a newspaper, magazine, or other publication. **c** a person employed by a newspaper, magazine, or radio or television network to send news from a particular place: *a White House correspondent. The "New York Times" has correspondents in Great Britain, France, Germany, the Soviet Union, and other countries.* **2** a person or company that has regular business with another in a distant place: *This bank has correspondents in all the large cities of the world.* **3** a thing that corresponds to something else; correlative.
—*adj.* corresponding; analogous; matching: *correspondent ideas, anatomically correspondent parts.* **SYN**: congruous, conformable, suitable. —**cor′re|spond′ent|ly,** *adv.*

cor|re|spond|ing (kôr′ə spon′ding, kor′-), *adj.* **1** that corresponds or answers to another; parallel; matching: *The man's attack was met by the dog's corresponding counterattack. The triangles are similar; therefore their corresponding sides are proportional. Her shyness was met by a corresponding hesitation.* **2** that corresponds by letters; in charge of correspondence: *a corresponding secretary.* —**cor′re|spond′ing|ly,** *adv.*

corresponding member, a member of a society living at a distance, who corresponds with the society on its special subject, but generally has no deliberative voice in its administration.

cor|re|spon|sive (kôr′ə spon′siv, kor′-), *adj. Rare.* corresponding; correspondent; answering.

cor|ri|da (kôr rē′ᴛʜä), *n.* a bullfight. [< Spanish *corrida* a running, ultimately < Latin *currere* run]

cor|ri|do (kôr rē′ᴛʜō), *n., pl.* **-dos.** *Spanish.* a Mexican folk song telling of a fight against oppression or other injustice.

cor|ri|dor (kôr′ə dər, -dôr; kor′-), *n.* **1a** a long hallway; a passage in a large building into which rooms open; passageway; hall: *Most classrooms and apartments open out onto corridors.* **b** *British.* the aisle on the side of a railroad car giving access to the compartments. **c** *Figurative.* a narrow passageway through any medium: *corridors of light, the corridor of years. The brain has corridors surpassing material place* (Emily Dickinson). **2** a narrow strip of land connecting two parts of a country or an inland country with a seaport. [< French *corridor* < Italian *corridore* < *correre* run < Latin *currere*]

corridors of power, the centers of political authority or influence.

cor|rie (kôr′ē, kor′-), *n. Scottish.* a more or less circular hollow on a mountainside; cirque. [< Scottish Gaelic *coire* (literally) cauldron]

Cor|rie|dale (kôr′ē dāl, kor′-), *n.* a breed of sheep developed in New Zealand and Australia, raised for wool and meat. [< *Corriedale,* a region in New Zealand]

cor|ri|gen|dum (kôr′ə jen′dəm, kor′-), *n., pl.* **-da** (-də). an error in a book, manuscript, or other written matter, to be corrected.
corrigenda, a list of errors inserted in a book, manuscript, or other written matter, with the corrections: *There are ... five and a half pages of corrigenda* (Law Times).
[< Latin *corrigendum* (thing) to be corrected < *corrigere;* see etym. under **correct**]

cor|ri|gi|bil|i|ty (kôr′ə jə bil′ə tē, kor′-), *n.* the character or state of being corrigible.

cor|ri|gi|ble (kôr′ə jə bəl, kor′-), *adj.* **1** capable of being corrected: *a corrigible error.* **SYN**: rectifiable. **2** yielding to correction; willing to be corrected: *The child was lively and mischievous, but corrigible.* [< Medieval Latin *corrigibilis* < Latin *corrigere;* see etym. under **correct**] —**cor′ri|gi|bly,** *adv.*

cor|ri|val (kə rī′vəl), *n., adj.* —*n.* a rival; competitor.
—*adj.* rivaling each other; rival.
[< Latin *corrīvālis* < *com-* (intensive) + *rīvālis* a rival]

cor|rob|o|rant (kə rob′ər ənt), *adj., n.* —*adj.* strengthening; invigorating (used especially of medicinal agents).
—*n.* **1** a strengthening or invigorating agent, as a tonic. **2** a corroborative fact or statement.

cor|rob|o|rate (kə rob′ə rāt), *v.t.,* **-rat|ed, -rat|ing.** to make more certain; confirm; support: *Witnesses corroborated the policeman's statement.* **SYN**: substantiate, verify, uphold, endorse. See syn. under **confirm.** [< Latin *corrōborāre* strengthen (with English *-ate*[1]) < *com-* (intensive) + *rōborāre* strengthen < *rōbus, -oris* oak tree] —**cor|rob′o|ra′tor,** *n.*

cor|rob|o|ra|tion (kə rob′ə rā′shən), *n.* **1** confirmation by additional proof. **2** something that corroborates; additional proof; confirmation: *His sticky face and hands were corroboration of his mother's suspicion that he had been eating jam.*

cor|rob|o|ra|tive (kə rob′ə rā′tiv, -ər ə-), *adj., n.* —*adj.* making more certain; corroborating; confirming: *corroborative experimental evidence.*
—*n. Medicine.* = corroborant. —**cor|rob′o|ra′tive|ly,** *adv.*

cor|rob|o|ra|to|ry (kə rob′ər ə tôr′ē, -tōr′-), *adj.* = corroborative.

cor|rob|o|ree (kə rob′ər ē), *n.* **1** a native celebration of the Australian aborigines, consisting of dancing and singing, held at night by moonlight or a bush fire. **2** *Especially Australian.* any large or noisy gathering; disturbance; uproar: *By the time he's finished with his first lesson, he'll wish he was back with the boys at the local corroboree* (Punch). [< the Australian (Port Jackson dialect) name]

cor|rode (kə rōd′), *v.,* **-rod|ed, -rod|ing.** —*v.t.* **1a** to wear or eat away gradually by or as if by chemical action: *Moist air corrodes iron. Rust had corroded the steel rails.* **b** *Obsolete.* to erode. **2** *Figurative.* to wear away; deteriorate: *Should jealousy its venom once diffuse, corroding every thought* (James Thomson). **SYN**: gnaw, consume.
—*v.i.* to become corroded; undergo corrosion: *Acid caused the pipes to corrode.* **SYN**: rust, decay.
[< Latin *corrōdere* < *com-* (intensive) + *rōdere* gnaw] —**cor|rod′er,** *n.* —**cor|rod′i|ble,** *adj.*

cor|rod|ed (kə rō′did), *adj.* eaten away.

cor|rod|ent (kə rō′dənt), *n.* a corrosive agent.

cor|ro|dy (kôr′ə dē, kor′-), *n., pl.* **-dies.** = corody.

cor|ro|si|ble (kə rō′sə bəl), *adj.* = corrodible.

cor|ro|sion (kə rō′zhən), *n.* **1** the process of corroding. **2** a corroded condition. **3** a product of corroding, such as rust. [< Late Latin *corrōsiō, -ōnis* < Latin *corrōdere;* see etym. under **corrode**]

cor|ro|sive (kə rō′siv), *adj., n.* —*adj.* **1** eating away gradually; tending to corrode: *acids and other corrosive materials.* **SYN**: caustic, mordant. **2** *Figurative.* wearing to the mind or feelings; fretting: *the corrosive effect of constant anxiety.*
—*n.* a substance that corrodes: *Most acids are corrosives.* **SYN**: mordant. —**cor|ro′sive|ly,** *adv.* —**cor|ro′sive|ness,** *n.*

corrosive sublimate, = bichloride of mercury.

cor|ru|gate (*v.* kôr′ə gāt, -yə-; kor′-; *adj.* kôr′ə git, -gāt, -yə-; kor′-), *v.,* **-gat|ed, -gat|ing,** *adj.* —*v.t.* to bend or shape (a surface or a thin sheet of material) into wavy folds or ridges; wrinkle; furrow.
—*v.i.* to become corrugated.
—*adj.* contracted into folds or wrinkles; wrinkled; furrowed.
[< Latin *corrugāre* (with English *-ate*[1]) < *com-* (intensive) + *rūga* wrinkle]

cor|ru|gat|ed (kôr′ə gā′tid, -yə-; kor′-), *adj.* bent or shaped into a row of wavelike ridges: *The carton was made of corrugated cardboard.*

corrugated iron, sheet iron or steel, commonly galvanized, shaped into wavelike ridges for increased strength, used for walls, roofs, and other construction purposes.

corrugated paper, paper or cardboard that is bent into a row of wavelike ridges, used as a protective wrapping for packages or their contents.

cor|ru|ga|tion (kôr′ə gā′shən, -yə-; kor′-), *n.* **1** the act of corrugating. **2** the state of being corrugated; contraction into wrinkles, folds, or ridges. **3** one of a series of wavy folds or ridges; wrinkle; furrow.

cor|ru|ga|tor (kôr′ə gā′tər, kor′-), *n.* **1** *Anatomy.* a muscle that causes the skin to contract into wrinkles, especially one of two small muscles which contract the brow in the action of frowning. **2** a machine that corrugates paper or cardboard.

cor|rupt (kə rupt′), *adj., v.* —*adj.* **1** morally bad; evil; wicked: *a corrupt man, corrupt desires. The thief led a corrupt life.* **2** influenced by bribes; dishonest: *a corrupt judge.* **SYN**: venal. **3** changed in meaning or form, or deviating from the standard (of language usage or of manuscript reading): *"Sparrowgrass" is a corrupt spelling of "asparagus." The corrupt manuscript was full of errors made in copying from the original.* **4** *Archaic.* rotten; decayed. **SYN**: spoiled, tainted, putrid, vitiated.
—*v.t.* **1** to make evil or wicked: *Bad company may corrupt a good boy.* **SYN**: debase, deprave. **2** to bribe: *That policeman cannot be corrupted.* **SYN**: demoralize. **3** to change in meaning or form or deviate from the standard of language usage or of a reading of a manuscript: *Careless scholars corrupted the original manuscript.* **4** to cause to rot; make putrid; infect; taint. **SYN**: pollute, contaminate. **5** *Archaic.* to spoil; mar.
—*v.i.* **1** to become corrupt or corrupted; become debased. **2** to become putrid; undergo decomposition; rot; decay. **SYN**: putrefy.
[< Latin *corruptus,* past participle of *corrumpere* < *com-* (intensive) + *rumpere* break] —**cor|rupt′er, cor|rup′tor,** *n.* —**cor|rupt′ly,** *adv.* —**cor|rupt′ness,** *n.*
—*Syn. adj.* **1 Corrupt, depraved** mean made morally bad. **Corrupt** implies loss of an earlier soundness or purity: *The Medical Board took away the license of the doctor because of his corrupt practices.* **Depraved** implies a complete deterioration of morals or taste: *This murder was committed by a depraved criminal.*

cor|rupt|i|bil|i|ty (kə rup′tə bil′ə tē), *n.* corruptible quality; willingness to be bribed.

cor|rupt|i|ble (kə rup′tə bəl), *adj.* **1** that can be corrupted; open to bribery or corrupt practices. **2** liable to be corrupted; perishable. **SYN**: mortal. —**cor|rupt′i|ble|ness,** *n.* —**cor|rupt′i|bly,** *adv.*

cor|rup|tion (kə rup′shən), *n.* **1a** the act of making, or the process of being made, evil or wicked: *the corruption of an honest man.* **SYN**: debasement. **b** evil conduct; wickedness: *... corruption never has been compulsory* (Robinson Jeffers). **SYN**: baseness, depravity. **c** a corrupting influence; thing that causes corruption. **2** bribery; dishonesty: *The police force must be kept free from corruption. For many years protests over corruption failed to dim his popularity with the voters* (Newsweek). **3** a corrupt practice; an instance of perversion or impurity. **4a** a changing in meaning or form or a deviating from the standard of language usage or of a reading of a manuscript: *the corruption of a translated passage or*

Pronunciation Key: hat, āge, cãre, fär; let, ēqual, tėrm; it, īce; hot, ōpen, ôrder; **oi**l, **ou**t; cup, pu̇t, rüle; **ch**ild; lo**ng**; **th**in; **ᴛʜ**en; **zh**, measure; ə represents **a** in about, **e** in taken, **i** in pencil, **o** in lemon, **u** in circus.

text, the corruption of a dialect by the influence of tourism and television. **b** an instance of this; a corrupt form of a word: *"Nite" is a slang corruption of "night."* **5** rot; decay.

cor|rup|tion|ist (kə rup′shə nist), *n.* a supporter or practicer of corruption, especially in the administration of public affairs.

corruption of blood, (in English law) the effect of an attainder for treason or felony on a person, whereby he and his descendants could neither inherit nor bequeath an estate, rank, or title. It was abolished in 1870.

cor|rup|tive (kə rup′tiv), *adj.* tending to corrupt; causing corruption.

corrupt practices acts, *U.S.* laws or legislation designed to curb unethical election or electoral campaign practices, such as purchasing votes, tampering with voting machines, and using unlimited funds or funds from illegal sources to influence the outcome of an election. These acts have been modeled after the Federal Corrupt Practices Act of 1925.

cor|sac (kôr′sak), *n.* a species of fox of a yellowish color, found in central and southern Asia. [< Russian *korsak*]

cor|sage (kôr säzh′), *n.* **1** a bouquet to be worn on the waist or shoulder of a woman's dress. **2** the upper part of a woman's dress. [< Old French *corsage* < *cors* bust, body; see etym. under **corse**]

cor|sair (kôr′sãr), *n.* **1** a pirate. **2** the ship of a pirate. **3** a privateer, especially a Saracen or Turkish privateer of the Barbary Coast. [< French *corsaire* < Italian *corsaro* < Medieval Latin *cursarius* runner < Latin *cursus, -ūs* a race, journey < *currere* to run]

cor|sak (kôr′sak), *n.* = corsac.

corse (kôrs), *n. Archaic.* a corpse. [< Old French *cors* < Latin *corpus* body. See etym. of doublets **corps, corpse, corpus.**]

corse|let (kôrs′lit *for 1;* kôr′sə let′ *for 2*), *n.* **1** armor for the upper part of the body. Also, **corslet. 2** a woman's undergarment somewhat like a corset, but usually not boned. Also, **corselette.** [< Old French *corselet* (diminutive) < *cors* body; see etym. under **corse**]

cor|se|lette (kôr′sə let′), *n.* = corselet (def. 2).

cor|set (kôr′sit), *n., v. —n.* **1** Often, **corsets.** a woman's close-fitting undergarment, worn about the waist and hips to support or shape the body. A corset is usually made of elasticized material, stiffened with bone or boning, provided with garters, and fastened with a zipper or laces. **SYN:** stays. **2** *Obsolete.* a close-fitting outer garment, especially a laced bodice.

—v.t. to fit a corset on; dress in a corset.

[< Old French *corset* (diminutive) < *cors* body; see etym. under **corse**]

corset cover, a woman's undergarment, a kind of bodice, usually sleeveless, for wearing over a corset.

cor|set|ed (kôr′sə tid), *adj.* wearing a corset.

cor|se|tiere (kôr′sə tir′), *n.* a person who makes, sells, or fits corsets, girdles, and other foundation garments. [< French *corsetière,* feminine of *corsetier* corset maker]

cor|set|ry (kôr′sit rē), *n.* **1** corsets, girdles, and foundation garments collectively. **2** the making or fitting of corsets, girdles, and other foundation garments.

Cor|si|can (kôr′sə kən), *adj., n. —adj.* of or having to do with Corsica, its people, or their dialect. *—n.* **1** a native or inhabitant of Corsica. **2** an Italian dialect spoken in Corsica.

cors|let (kôrs′lit), *n.* = corselet (def. 1).

cor|tege or **cor|tège** (kôr tāzh′, -tezh′), *n.* **1** a procession: *a funeral cortege.* **2** a group of followers or attendants; retinue: *When the final procession was formed, orders were given that ... he should be included in the diplomatic cortege* (Lytton Strachey). [< French *cortège* < Italian *corteggio* < *corte* court]

Cor|tes (kôr′tiz, -tās), *n.* the national legislature of Spain or the national assembly of Portugal. [< Spanish, Portuguese *Cortes,* plural of *corte* court < Medieval Latin *cortis*]

cor|tex (kôr′teks), *n., pl.* **-ti|ces. 1a** the layer of gray matter that covers most of the surface of the brain; cerebral cortex. **b** the outer layer of an internal organ: *the cortex of the kidney.* **c** the adrenal cortex: *The cortex, properly stimulated, secretes hormones that control many activities of the body, including growth and reproduction* (Time). **2a** that part of the tissue of the roots and stems of plants which in trees becomes the bark. The cortex in all higher plants lies outside the vascular tissue and inside the epidermis. **b** an outer layer of cells (in certain algae, fungi, and lichens). **3a** the bark of a tree. **b** the rind of a fruit. [< Latin *cortex, -icis* bark]

cor|ti|cal (kôr′tə kəl), *adj.* **1a** of or having to do with the cortex, especially of the brain or kidneys. **b** caused by or involving some condition or function of the cortex of the brain: *cortical paralysis.* **2** consisting of cortex; belonging to the cortex or external part of some member or organ of a plant. The bark of a tree or the rind of a fruit is cortical tissue. **—cor′ti|cal|ly,** *adv.*

cor|ti|cate (kôr′tə kit, -kāt), *adj.* having a cortex; covered with bark. [< Latin *corticātus* < *cortex, -icis* bark]

cor|ti|cat|ed (kôr′tə kā′tid), *adj.* = corticate.

cor|ti|ces (kôr′tə sēz), *n.* plural of **cortex.**

cor|ti|coid (kôr′tə koid), *n., adj.* = corticosteroid.

cor|ti|cole (kôr′tə kōl), *adj.* living or growing on bark, as certain lichens. [< Latin *cortex, -icis* bark + *colere* inhabit]

cor|tic|o|lous (kôr tik′ə ləs), *adj.* = corticole.

cor|ti|cose (kôr′tə kōs), *adj.* **1** of or like cortex; resembling bark in structure. **2** having a cortex; corticate.

cor|ti|co|ster|oid (kôr′tə kō ster′oid), *n., adj. —n.* any one of a group of steroids, many of them hormones, produced by the adrenal cortex, such as corticosterone, which play an important part in metabolism and the ability of the body to withstand stress.

—adj. of or having to do with corticosteroids.

cor|ti|cos|te|rone (kôr′tə kos′tə rōn), *n.* **1** a corticosteroid which breaks down proteins and helps to prevent infections. *Formula:* $C_{21}H_{30}O_4$ **2** this substance produced synthetically and used in the treatment of a variety of conditions. [< Latin *cortex, -icis* bark + English *ster*(ol) + *-one*]

cor|ti|co|troph|in (kôr′tə kō trof′in), *n.* = corticotropin.

cor|ti|co|trop|ic (kôr′tə kō trop′ik), *adj.* **1** stimulating the activity of a cortex. **2** =adrenocorticotropic.

cor|ti|co|trop|in (kôr′tə kō trop′in), *n.* an adrenocorticotropic extract from animal pituitary glands, used especially in treating rheumatic conditions; ACTH.

cor|ti|cous (kôr′tə kəs), *adj.* = corticose.

cor|ti|le (kôr tē′lā), *n. Italian.* **1** a small court enclosed by the divisions of a building. **2** any area, court, or courtyard.

cor|tin (kôr′tin), *n.* an extract of the adrenal cortex containing cortisone and other hormones.

cor|ti|sol (kôr′tə sōl), *n.* = hydrocortisone.

cor|ti|sone (kôr′tə zōn), *n.* a steroid hormone obtained from the cortex of the adrenal glands or produced synthetically, used in the treatment of arthritis and other ailments: *Cortisone, first famous for relief of crippling, painful arthritis, shows promise of becoming a speedy remedy for ... facial paralysis* (Science News Letter). *Formula:* $C_{21}H_{28}O_5$ [< (dehydro)*corti*(co)*s*(ter)*one,* the chemical name]

co|run|dum (kə run′dəm), *n.* an extremely hard mineral consisting of aluminum oxide. The dark-colored variety is used for polishing and grinding. Transparent varieties are sapphires, rubies, and Oriental topazes. *Formula:* Al_2O_3 [< Tamil *kurundam* or Telugu *kuruvindam* < Sanskrit *kuruvinda* ruby]

co|rus|cant (kə rus′kənt), *adj.* glittering; sparkling; gleaming.

cor|us|cate (kôr′ə skāt, kor′-), *v.i.,* **-cat|ed, -cat|ing.** to give off flashes of light; sparkle; glitter; flash. **SYN:** scintillate. [< Latin *coruscāre* (with English *-ate*[1]) < *coruscus* glittering, vibrating]

cor|us|ca|tion (kôr′ə skā′shən, kor′-), *n.* **1** a flash of light; sparkle. **2** a flashing; sparkling.

cor|vée (kôr vā′), *n.* **1** unpaid or partly unpaid labor imposed by authorities on the residents of a district, for example on roads. **2** *Historical.* unpaid work done by a peasant for his feudal lord. [< Old French *corvee, corovee* < Late Latin *corrogāta* contribution; its collection < Latin *corrogāre* < *com-* together + *rogāre* ask]

corves (kôrvz), *n.* plural of **corf.**

cor|vette or **cor|vet** (kôr vet′), *n.* **1** (formerly) a warship with sails and only one tier of guns. A corvette was smaller than a frigate. **2** a gunboat used against submarines and as an escort in convoy work. The corvette is a light, fast, highly maneuverable warship of the destroyer class. [< Old French *corvette, corvot,* probably < Middle Dutch *korver,* perhaps < Latin *corbīta* ship of burden, fast transport < *corbis* basket (reputedly used as a signal on the masthead)]

Cor|vi (kôr′vī), *n.* genitive of **Corvus.**

cor|vi|na (kôr vē′nə), *n.* = corbina.

cor|vine (kôr′vīn, -vin), *adj.* **1** of or like a crow. **2** belonging to or having to do with a family of birds including crows, magpies, and jays. [< Latin *corvīnus* ravenlike < *corvus* raven]

Cor|vus (kôr′vəs), *n., genitive* **Cor|vi.** a small southern constellation near Virgo; the Crow or Raven. [< Latin *Corvus*]

Cor|y|bant (kôr′ə bant, kor′-), *n., pl.* **Cor|y|ban|tes** (kôr′ə ban′tēz, kor′-), **Cor|y|bants. 1** any one of the attendants of the ancient goddess Cybele of Asia Minor, who followed her over the mountains by torchlight with wild music and dancing. **2** one of the priests of Cybele who conducted her worship with similar frenzied rites. [< Old French *Corybant,* learned borrowing from Latin *Corybantes* priests of Cybele < Greek *Korýbās, -antos*]

Cor|y|ban|tic (kôr′ə ban′tik, kor′-), *adj.* **1** of the Corybantes. **2** resembling the Corybantes or their rites.

cor|y|bant|ism (kôr′ə ban′tiz əm, kor′-), *n.* a sort of frenzy in which a sick person has fantastic visions.

co|ryd|al|is (kə rid′ə lis), *n.* any plant of a group of herbs of the fumitory family, bearing racemes of spurred yellow, white, or purplish flowers. [< New Latin *Corydalis* < Greek *korydallís,* variant of *korydallós* the crested lark < *kórys, -ythos* helmet]

***cor|ymb** (kôr′imb, -im; kor′-), *n. Botany.* a flat-topped cluster of flowers in which the outer flowers blossom first. Cherry blossoms and candytuft are corymbs. Small flowers on short stems grow from a longer, central stem to form a round cluster, rather flat on top. [< New Latin *corymb* < Latin *corymbus* cluster of fruit or flowers < Greek *kórymbos* top, cluster (of fruit)] **—cor′ymb|like′,** *adj.*

***corymb**

cor|ym|bif|er|ous (kôr′im bif′ər əs, kor′-), *adj.* bearing corymbs. [< Latin *corymbifer* + English *-ous*]

co|rym|bose (kə rim′bōs), *adj.* **1** growing in corymbs. **2** of or like a corymb. **—co|rym′bose|ly,** *adv.*

co|rym|bous (kə rim′bəs), *adj.* consisting of corymbs.

cor|y|phae|us (kôr′ə fē′əs, kor′-), *n., pl.* **-phae|i** (-fē′ī). **1** the person who leads the chorus of an opera or any singing group. **2** the leader of the chorus in the ancient Greek drama. **3** *Figurative.* the chief or leader, especially of a party or sect: *a coryphaeus of modern skepticism.* [< Latin *coryphaeus* < Greek *koryphaîos* leader of the chorus, chief party leader (in the drama) < *koryphḗ* head, top < *kórys* helmet]

cor|y|phée (kôr′ə fā′, kor′-), *n.* **1** a ballet dancer who dances in small ensembles, ranking just below a soloist, but above the corps de ballet. **2** any ballet dancer. [< French *coryphée* < Latin *coryphaeus;* see etym. under **coryphaeus**]

cor|y|phene (kôr′ə fēn), *n.* = dolphin (def. 2). [< New Latin *Coryphaena* the genus name < Greek *koryphaina* dolphin < *koryphḗ* head, top]

co|ry|za (kə rī′zə), *n.* **1** = head cold. **2** an infectious bacterial disease of poultry, affecting the upper air passages and eyes. [< Late Latin *coryza* < Greek *kóryza* catarrh]

co|ry|zal (kə rī′zəl), *adj.* of or having to do with coryza: *coryzal symptoms.*

co|ry|za|vi|rus (kə rī′zə vī′rəs), *n.* any one of a group of viruses associated with the common cold.

cos (kos, kôs), *n.,* or **cos lettuce,** = romaine. [< Greek *Côs,* an island in the Aegean, from which it was introduced]

cos (no period), cosine.

cos., **1** companies. **2** counties.

COS or **c.o.s.,** cash on shipment.

Co|sa Nos|tra (kō′zə nōs′trə, nos′-), a secret society of criminals operating in the United States and identified with the Mafia. [< Italian *cosa nostra* our thing]

co|saque (kō zak′), *n.* = cracker (def. 4). [< French *Cosaque* Cossack]

cosec (no period), cosecant.

co|se|cant (kō sē′kənt, -kant), *n. Trigonometry.* **1** the ratio of the length of the hypotenuse of a right triangle to the length of the side opposite an acute angle. **2** the secant of the complement of a given angle or arc. *Abbr:* csc, cosec (no period).

co|seis|mal (kō sīz′məl, -sīs′-), *adj., n. —adj.* having to do with or denoting a line, curve, zone, etc., connecting or comprising points on the earth's surface where an earthquake wave arrives simultaneously.

—n. a coseismal line or curve.

co|seis|mic (kō sīz′mik, -sīs′-), *adj.* = coseismal.

co|sey (kō′zē), *adj.,* **-si|er, -si|est,** *n., pl.* **-seys,** *v.,* **-seyed, -sey|ing.** = cozy.

cosh (kosh), *n., v. British Slang. —n.* a short, weighted club, blackjack, or the like, used as a weapon.

—v.t. to beat or strike with a cosh.

[perhaps < Romany *kosh* stick]

cosh|er (kosh′ər), *v.t.* to treat with fondness;

pamper. —*v.i.* to live at the expense of others. [< Irish *coisir* a feast, entertainment] —**cosh′er|er**, *n.*

co|sie (kō′zē), *adj.*, **-si|er**, **-si|est**, *n., pl.* **-sies**, *v.*, **-sied**, **-sie|ing**. = cozy.

co|si fan tut|te (kō sē′ fän tüt′tā), *Italian.* so do they (women) all; they all do it.

co-sign (kō sīn′), *v.t.* to act as cosignatory of. —**co|sign′er**, *n.*

co|sig|na|to|ry (kō sig′nə tôr′ē, -tōr′-), *n., pl.* **-ries**, *adj.* —*n.* a person who signs a document, treaty, contract, or loan along with another or others.

—*adj.* signing along with another or others.

co|si|ly (kō′zə lē), *adv.* = cozily.

co|sine (kō′sīn), *n. Trigonometry.* **1** the ratio of the length of the side next to an acute angle of a right triangle to the length of the hypotenuse. In a right triangle, with hypotenuse BC, the cosine of angle ACB is $\frac{AC}{BC}$, the cosine of angle ABC is $\frac{AB}{BC}$. **2** the sine of the complement of a given angle or arc. *Abbr:* cos (no period). [< New Latin *cosinus* < *co-* + Medieval Latin *sinus* sine[1]]

co|si|ness (kō′zē nis), *n.* = coziness.

Cos|ma|tesque (koz′mə tesk′), *adj.* of, like, or having to do with Cosmati work.

Cos|ma|ti work (koz mä′tē), a style of architectural decoration characterized by the use of mosaics. [< *Cosmati,* a family of architects and sculptors, who lived in Rome in the 1200's]

cos|met|ic (koz met′ik), *n., adj., v.,* **-met|icked**, **-met|ick|ing**. —*n.* **1** a preparation for beautifying the skin, hair, or nails. Powder, rouge, lipstick, and face creams are cosmetics. **2** *Figurative.* anything that covers up blemishes or defects: *Preference for the term "quick entry" over the scorned catchword "no-knock" provides glaring evidence of the way in which Government currently uses words as cosmetics . . .* (New York Times).

—*adj.* **1** beautifying to the skin, hair, or nails: *a cosmetic cream for the face.* **2** having to do with cosmetics. **3** *Figurative.* of or for covering up blemishes or defects: *Landscaping of our buildings . . . can be no more than a cosmetic device* (David Rockefeller).

—*v.t.* to treat with cosmetics: *Coarsely cosmeticked, her face looks like* [*an aerial*] *photograph of Utah* (Time).

[< Greek *kosmētikós* skilled in arranging, relating to order, adornment < *kósmos* order, universe]

—**cos|met′i|cal|ly**, *adv.*

cos|me|ti|cian (koz′mə tish′ən), *n.* **1** a person skilled in making or applying cosmetics. SYN: beautician. **2** a seller of cosmetics.

cos|met|i|cize (koz met′ə sīz), *v.t.*, **-cized**, **-ciz|ing**. to treat with cosmetics; make more attractive; beautify.

cosmetic surgery, plastic surgery for improving the outer appearance of parts of the body, especially the face.

cos|me|tize (koz′mə tīz), *v.t.*, **-tized**, **-tiz|ing**. = cosmeticize.

cos|me|tol|o|gist (koz′mə tol′ə jist), *n.* an expert in cosmetology; beautician.

cos|me|tol|o|gy (koz′mə tol′ə jē), *n.* the study or art of applying and sometimes of making cosmetics; work of a beautician.

cos|mic (koz′mik), *adj.* **1** having to do with the whole universe: *Cosmic forces produce stars and meteors.* SYN: universal, macrocosmic. **2** belonging to the material universe, especially as distinguished from the earth. **3** vast: *a cosmic explosion.* **4** *Rare.* orderly or harmonious. [< Greek *kosmikós* < *kósmos* order, world, universe]

cos|mi|cal (koz′mə kəl), *adj.* **1** = cosmic. **2** of or having to do with cosmism. **3** occurring at or near sunrise. —**cos′mi|cal|ly**, *adv.*

cosmic dust, fine particles of matter in outer space, often forming clouds.

cosmic noise, = galactic noise.

cosmic radiation, radiation consisting of cosmic rays.

cosmic rays, rays of very short wave lengths and very great penetration that come to the earth from beyond the earth's atmosphere, especially from the sun and from interstellar space. Cosmic rays consist of high-energy particles which collide with the atomic nuclei of the earth's atmosphere, producing secondary particles, such as the mesons observed at ground level. *Some studies indicate that cosmic rays may have energies up to 30 billion electron volts in space, much larger than the radiation from the biggest existing atom smasher* (Wall Street Journal).

cosmic speed, the speed required to overcome the gravity and atmospheric resistance of the earth. At a speed of five miles per second a vehicle may be put into orbit about the earth. At a speed of seven miles per second it may escape the pull of the earth and enter interplanetary space.

cosmic year, the time it takes the sun to complete one revolution about the center of the Milky Way, estimated at 200,000,000 solar years.

cos|mism (koz′miz əm), *n.* the theory which explains the cosmos or universe solely according to the methods of positive science. —**cos′mist**, *n.*

cosmo-, *combining form.* **1** world; universe, as in *cosmology, cosmochemistry.*
2 cosmic rays, as in *cosmogenic.*
3 outer space; space travel, as in *cosmonautics.*
[< Greek *kósmos* world]

cos|mo|chem|is|try (koz′mə kem′ə strē), *n.* the science dealing with the chemistry of heavenly bodies and of the universe as a whole.

cos|mo|drome (koz′mə drōm′), *n.* a Soviet launching site for spacecraft. [< Russian *kosmodrom* < *kosmo-* cosmo- + *-drom* -drome]

cos|mo|gen|ic (koz′mə jen′ik), *adj.* originating from cosmic rays: *cosmogenic isotopes of helium.*

cos|mog|o|nal (koz mog′ə nəl), *adj.* = cosmogonic.

cos|mo|gon|ic (koz′mə gon′ik), *adj.* of or having to do with cosmogony.

cos|mo|gon|i|cal (koz′mə gon′ə kəl), *adj.* = cosmogonic.

cos|mog|o|nist (koz mog′ə nist), *n.* an expert in or student of cosmogony: *By now we cosmogonists are ready to admit that our earth is an insignificant part of the universe* (Atlantic).

cos|mog|o|ny (koz mog′ə nē), *n.* **1** *no pl.* the origin of the universe. **2** *pl.* **-nies**. a theory, system, or account of its origin: *The first crude steps could now be taken toward a cosmology describing the world at large, and toward a cosmogony accounting for the evolution of its parts* (Scientific American). [< Greek *kosmogoniā* < *kósmos* world + *gónos* birth]

cos|mog|ra|pher (koz mog′rə fər), *n.* a person who studies cosmography.

cos|mo|graph|ic (koz′mə graf′ik), *adj.* of or having to do with cosmography.

cos|mo|graph|i|cal (koz′mə graf′ə kəl), *adj.* = cosmographic.

cos|mog|ra|phy (koz mog′rə fē), *n.* **1** the science that deals with the general appearance and structure of the universe. Cosmography includes astronomy, geography, and geology. **2** *pl.* **-phies**. a description of the general features of the earth or the universe. [< Greek *kosmographiā* < *kósmos* world + *graphiā* drawing, delineation < *gráphein* draw, write]

Cos|mo|line (koz′mə lēn), *n. Trademark.* a heavy grade of petrolatum, used to prevent rust, especially on new or stored firearms.

cos|mo|line (koz′mə lēn), *v.t.*, **-lined**, **-lin|ing**. to preserve with Cosmoline. [< *Cosmoline*]

cos|mo|log|ic (koz′mə loj′ik), *adj.* = cosmological.

cos|mo|log|i|cal (koz′mə loj′ə kəl), *adj.* of or having to do with cosmology: *cosmological speculations.* —**cos′mo|log′i|cal|ly**, *adv.*

cos|mol|o|gist (koz mol′ə jist), *n.* a person who studies cosmology.

cos|mol|o|gy (koz mol′ə jē), *n.* the science or theory of the universe as a whole, its parts, and laws: *Cosmology is the study of the general nature of the universe in space and time—what it is now, what it was in the past and what it is likely to be in the future* (Scientific American).

cos|mo|naut (koz′mə nôt), *n.* an astronaut, especially a Soviet astronaut.
[< Russian *kosmonavt* < *kosmo-* cosmo- + *-navt* < Greek *naútēs* sailor]

▶**cosmonaut, astronaut.** In the United States *cosmonaut* is used only in reference to Soviet space travelers; in Great Britain, *astronaut* and *cosmonaut* are used interchangeably for either Americans or Russians.

cos|mo|nau|tic (koz′mə nô′tik), *adj.* = astronautic.

cos|mo|nau|tics (koz′mə nô′tiks), *n.* = astronautics.

cos|mo|nette (koz′mə net′), *n.* a woman cosmonaut.

cos|mop|o|lis (koz mop′ə lis), *n.* a center of and for people of all the world, their ideas, art, and other cultural affairs; a cosmopolitan city: *The banker is boasting that he will make his beloved city by the bay into an international cosmopolis* (Wall Street Journal). [< *cosmo*(politan) + (metro)*polis*]

cos|mo|pol|i|tan (koz′mə pol′ə tən), *adj., n.*
—*adj.* **1** belonging to all parts of the world; not limited to any one country or its inhabitants; widely spread: *Music is one of the most cosmopolitan of the arts.* SYN: universal, international. **2** free from national or local prejudices; feeling at home in any part of the world: *Diplomats and world travelers are usually cosmopolitan people. The artist's tastes were not provincial but cosmopolitan.* SYN: urbane. **3** having to do with or characteristic of a cosmopolite. SYN: worldly, mundane. **4** widely distributed over the earth: *Certain plants and animals are cosmopolitan in their range.*

—*n.* a person who feels at home in any part of the world; cosmopolitan person or thing; cosmopolite. —**cos′mo|pol′i|tan|ly**, *adv.*

cos|mo|pol|i|tan|ism (koz′mə pol′ə tə niz′əm), *n.* **1** cosmopolitan character or quality. **2** the belief that men are citizens of the world rather than of a single nation or area, having its theoretical basis in Stoic philosophy.

cos|mo|pol|i|tan|ize (koz′mə pol′ə tə nīz), *v.t.*, **-ized**, **-iz|ing**. to make cosmopolitan.

cos|mop|o|lite (koz mop′ə līt), *n.* **1** a cosmopolitan person: *All sorts of cosmopolites and notabilities stopped over, summered, wintered there* (Atlantic). **2** an animal or a plant found in all or many parts of the world. [< Greek *kosmopolítēs* < *kósmos* world + *polítēs* citizen < *pólis* city]

cos|mop|o|lit|ism (koz mop′ə lī tiz′əm), *n.* = cosmopolitanism (def. 1).

cos|mo|ram|a (koz′mə ram′ə, -rä′mə), *n.* a peep show containing characteristic views of all parts of the world, seen through a lens by means of mirrors. [< *cosmo-* + (pano)*rama*]

cos|mo|ram|ic (koz′mə ram′ik, -rä′mik), *adj.* belonging to, or of the nature of, a cosmorama.

cos|mos (koz′məs, -mos), *n.* **1a** the universe thought of as an orderly, harmonious system: *Einstein was convinced that the cosmos is an orderly, continuous unity* (Time). SYN: macrocosm. **b** any complete, harmonious system. SYN: world. **2** order; harmony. **3** a tall, tropical American plant with showy flowers of many colors, that blooms in the fall or late summer. It belongs to the composite family. The cosmos has finely divided leaves and chiefly white, pink, purplish-red, or orange flowers. [< New Latin *cosmus* < Greek *kósmos* order, world, universe]

cos|mo|sphere (koz′mə sfir), *n.* an apparatus to show the position of the earth with respect to fixed stars.

cos|mo|the|ism (koz′mə thē′iz əm), *n.* = pantheism.

cos|mo|tron (koz′mə tron), *n.* a nuclear accelerator at Brookhaven National Laboratory, Upton, New York, designed to produce protons with energy of over two billion electron volts: *The cosmotron . . . thus achieved energies of 2.2 billion volts in June by speeding up protons to 177,000 miles a second* (Science News Letter). [< *cosmo-* + *-tron*]

COSPAR or **Co|spar** (kō′spär), *n.* the Committee on Space Research (an organization established in 1958 for promoting international cooperation on space research).

co-spon|sor (kō spon′sər), *n., v.* —*n.* a joint sponsor.

—*v.t.* to support or sign (legislation, a charity, or other undertaking) as co-sponsor: *. . . a resolution, initiated by the United States and co-sponsored by twenty other countries* (New York Times).

coss (kōs), *n.* = kos.

Cos|sack (kos′ak, -ək), *n.* **1** one of a Slavic people living on the steppes in the southwestern Soviet Union in Europe, noted as horsemen and cavalrymen, especially in czarist Russia. **2** a winter-hardy variety of alfalfa that does not resist wilt. [< Russian *kazak* < Turkic, free man]

Cossack asparagus, the starchy roots of cattails, eaten by the Cossacks of Russia.

Cossack post, *Military.* a group of four men on outguard duty, usually a noncommissioned officer and three privates.

cos|set (kos′it), *n., v.,* **-set|ed**, **-set|ing**. —*n.* a pet, especially a pet lamb.

—*v.t.* to treat as a pet; pamper: *He had been cosseted by his grandparents all during his childhood.* SYN: fondle, caress, pet, indulge, coddle. [perhaps < unrecorded Old English *cossettan* to kiss; compare *cossetung* kissing]

cos|sette (kos′ət, ko set′), *n.* a thin slice, especially of sugar beet, cut in the manufacturing process. [< French *cossette* (diminutive) < *cosse* pod, husk]

cost (kôst, kost), *n., v.,* **cost**, **cost|ing**. —*n.* **1** the price paid or other amount demanded: *The cost of this watch was $10. Paper costs represent over 25 per cent of the average printing job* (Time). SYN: charge, outlay, expense, expenditure. See syn. under **price**. **2** *Figurative.* a loss or sacrifice: *The poor fox escaped from the trap at the cost of a leg. The cost in lives was estimated at 214.* SYN: detriment. **3** outlay or expenditure of time, labor, trouble, or effort.

—*v.t.* **1** to be obtained at the price of; require:

Pronunciation Key: hat, āge, cãre, fär; let, ēqual, tėrm; it, īce; hot, ōpen, ôrder; oil, out; cup, pu̇t, rüle; child; long; thin; ᴛʜen; zh, measure; ə represents a in about, e in taken, i in pencil, o in lemon, u in circus.

The watch cost him $10. **2** *Figurative.* **a** to cause the loss or sacrifice of (something valuable) or the consequence of (something painful or unpleasant): *His carelessness cost him his job. His refusal to testify cost him a month in jail.* **b** to involve an outlay or expenditure of (time, trouble, effort or labor): *The school play had cost much time and effort. It cost me a month to organize the Community Chest drive.* **3** *Especially British.* to estimate or fix the cost of (an article or piece of work).

— ***v.i.*** *Especially British.* to fix or estimate cost, especially cost of producing goods: *Clerk wanted, able to cost.*

at all costs or **at any cost**, regardless of expense; by all means; no matter what must be done: *We had to catch the next boat at all costs, or lose our last chance to escape.*

costs, the expenses of a lawsuit or case in court, whether fixed by law or granted by the court, especially: **a** those expenses which the law or the court awards to the successful party and against the losing party in a case: *That man was found guilty and had to pay a $1000 fine and $50 costs.* **b** the fees paid or payable by a client to his attorney. **c** fees paid or payable to the court, such as the filing fee.

[< Old French *cost* < *couster* < Latin *constāre* < *com-* with + *stāre* stand] — **cost′less**, *adj.*

cos|ta (kos′tə), *n., pl.* **-tae. 1** *Anatomy.* a rib. **2** *Botany.* a rib or primary vein; a midrib of a leaf or frond. **3** a riblike part, as the anterior vein of an insect's wing or a ridge of a shell. [< Latin *costa*]

cost accountant, an accountant who specializes in cost accounting.

cost accounting, 1 any system of accounting that explains total cost by allocating and summarizing the individual costs of raw materials, labor, use of buildings, and other direct and indirect costs. **2** the keeping of accounts for this purpose.

cos|tae (kos′tē), *n.* plural of **costa.**

cos|tal (kos′təl), *adj.* **1** *Anatomy.* of or in the region of a rib or the ribs. **2** bearing ribs. [< Late Latin *costālis* < Latin *costa* rib]

Cos|ta|no|an (kos tä′nō ən), *n.* a linguistic stock of North American Indians in California.

co-star (*n.* kō′stär; *v.* kō stär′, kō′stär), *n., v.,* **-starred, -star|ring.** — ***n.*** a leading actor, singer, or other performer who appears with another star in the same production: *He got along fine with his co-star, Margaret Leighton* (Life).

— ***v.i.*** to appear as a co-star (with): *He will probably co-star with Sir Laurence Olivier in ... Jean Anouilh's new play, "Becket"* (Saturday Review).

— ***v.t.*** to present as a co-star or as co-stars: *The film co-starred two famous actors.*

cos|tard (kos′tərd, kôs′-), *n.* **1** a variety of large English apple. **2** *Archaic.* (humorously) the head. [(originally) a ribbed apple; probably < Old French *coste* rib (< Latin *costa*) + *-art,* a suffix forming masculine names]

Cos|ta Ri|can (kos′tə rē′kən, kôs′-, kōs′-), **1** of or having to do with Costa Rica or its people. **2** a native or inhabitant of Costa Rica.

cos|tate (kos′tāt), *adj.* **1** having a rib or ribs. **2** *Botany.* having one or more primary longitudinal veins or ribs, as a leaf. [< Latin *costātus* < *costa* rib]

cost-ben|e|fit (kôst′ben′ə fit, kost′-), *adj.* of, having to do with, or denoting an analysis or estimate of cost-effectiveness: *cost-benefit accountancy.*

cost-ef|fec|tive (kôst′ə fek′tiv, kost′-), *adj.* effective in terms of the relation of cost to anticipated benefits: *cost-effective spending.*

cost-ef|fec|tive|ness (kôst′ə fek′tiv nis, kost′-), *n.* the effectiveness of an operation or system in terms of the relation of its cost to the benefit anticipated from it: *In these days, cost-effectiveness has inevitably become the governing principle in all military estimates* (London Times).

cost-ef|fi|cien|cy (kôst′ə fish′ən sē, kost′-), *n.* = cost-effectiveness.

cost-ef|fi|cient (kôst′ə fish′ənt, kost′-), *adj.* = cost-effective.

cos|ter (kos′tər, kôs′-), *n.* = costermonger.

cos|ter|mon|ger (kos′tər mung′gər, kôs′-), *n.* a person who sells fruit, vegetables, fish, or other produce or merchandise from a handcart or stand in the street. [earlier *costardmonger* < *costard* + *monger* dealer, trader]

cost inflation, = cost push.

cost|ing (kos′ting), *n. Especially British.* cost accounting.

cos|tive (kos′tiv, kôs′-), *adj.* **1a** = constipated. **b** producing constipation: *a costive medicine or food.* **2** *Figurative.* slow in action. **3** *Figurative.* niggardly; stingy. **4** *Obsolete.* uncommunicative. [< Old French *costive* < Latin *constīpātus,* past participle of *constīpāre.* See etym. of doublet **constipate.**] — **cos′tive|ly**, *adv.* — **cos′tive|ness**, *n.*

cost|ly (kôst′lē, kost′-), *adj.,* **-li|er, -li|est. 1** of great value: *The queen had costly jewels.* **SYN:** precious, valuable, sumptuous, rich. **2** costing much: (*Figurative.*) *He made a costly mistake and had to do his work over at great expense of time.* **SYN:** dear. See syn. under **expensive.**

— **cost′li|ness**, *n.*

cost|mar|y (kost′mãr′ē, kôst′-), *n., pl.* **-mar|ies.** a perennial plant of the composite family, with fragrant leaves, used especially as a potherb and in salads. [Old English *cost* + Middle English (*Saint*) *Mary; cost* < Latin *costos* < Greek *kóstos* a spicy root, probably < Sanskrit *kuṣṭha*]

costo-, *combining form.* rib, as in *costoclavicular.* [< Latin *costa*]

cos|to|cla|vic|u|lar (kos′tō klə vik′yə lər), *adj.* of or affecting both the ribs and the collarbone (clavicle).

cost of living, the average price paid for food, rent, clothing, transportation, and other necessities by a person or family within a given period, and the amount of time and labor needed to obtain them.

cost-of-liv|ing index (kôst′əv liv′ing, kost′-), a comparative rating of the cost of living, especially that made annually by the United States Bureau of Labor Statistics: *The cost-of-living index ... reflects price changes for goods and services families of wage earners and clerical workers buy in cities* (Wall Street Journal).

cos|to|scap|u|lar (kos′tō skap′yə lər), *adj.* of or affecting both the ribs and the shoulder blade (scapula).

cost plus, an arrangement or contract under which the selling price is based on the cost of production plus an agreed profit: *Companies were spurred into war production by tax advantages on plant and equipment, by guaranteed profits under a system of cost plus* (Harper's).

cost-plus (kôst′plus′, kost′-), *adj.* of or having to do with cost plus: *Contracts for the units are on a cost-plus basis now ... and call only for straighttime labor costs* (Wall Street Journal).

cost push, *Economics.* an inflationary upsurge due to a sharp increase in production costs: *Price rises result from the cost push* (Wall Street Journal).

cos|trel (kos′trəl), *n.* a bottle of leather, earthenware, or wood, having an ear or ears by which it can be suspended, as from the waist. [< Old French *costerel,* perhaps (diminutive) < *costier* that which hangs by the side < *coste* side, rib < Latin *costa*]

costs (kôsts, kosts), *n.pl.* See under **cost.**

cost sheet, a statement showing the expense of any undertaking.

cos|tum|bris|ta (kos′təm bris′tə), *n., pl.* **-tas,** *adj.* — ***n.*** (in Spanish-speaking countries) a writer whose works portray the folkways of a region or locality.

— ***adj.*** of or characteristic of costumbristas. [< Spanish *costumbrista* < *costumbre* custom + *-ista* -ist]

cos|tume (*n.* kos′tüm, -tyüm; *v.* kos tüm′, -tyüm′), *n., v.,* **-tumed, -tum|ing.** — ***n.*** **1** dress; outer clothing; style of dress, including the way the hair is worn, kind of jewelry worn, and the like: *The clown wore a funny costume. The kimono is part of the national costume of Japan. Archeologists and historians will not quarrel much with the weapons and the costumes of the period* (Newsweek). **SYN:** garb, attire, apparel, raiment. **2** dress belonging to another time or place, such as is worn on the stage or at masquerades: *The actors wore colonial costumes of breeches, long coats, and powdered wigs.* **3** fashion or style of dress appropriate to an occasion or season: *hunting costume.* **SYN:** livery. **4** a complete set of outer garments: *a street costume. She wore ... the same odds-and-ends costume, and there was the same loose pile of nondescript hair* (New Yorker). **SYN:** outfit.

— ***v.t.*** to provide a costume or costumes for; dress: *One guest was costumed in Oriental style.* **SYN:** clothe, garb, attire.

[< French *costume* < Italian, fashion, habit, custom < Vulgar Latin *cōnsuētūmen.* See etym. of doublet **custom.**]

costume ball, a fancy-dress ball; a party for dancing in which costumes are worn.

costume jewelry, inexpensive imitation jewelry, usually showy or colorful: *Costume jewelry is of two types: the pieces used as a functional or ornamental part of the dress, ... and those pieces purchased separately for a particular costume* (Bernice G. Chambers).

cos|tum|er (kos′tü mər, -tyü-; kos tü′mər, -tyü′-), *n.* **1** a person who makes, sells, or rents costumes. **2** *U.S.* an upright pole on which to hang hats and coats; clothes tree.

cos|tum|er|y (kos tü′mər ē, -tyü′-), *n., pl.* **-er|ies. 1** costumes collectively: *native costumery.* **2** the art or practice of designing costumes.

cos|tum|ey (kos′tü mē, -tyü-), *adj. U.S.* of or like a costume or costumes; overly elaborate or affected: *costumey clothes.*

cos|tum|i|er (kos tü′mē ər, -tyü′-), *n.* = costumer.

cost unit, an amount produced, such as a ton of steel or a cubic yard of gravel, whose cost of production is used as a standard measure of production costs in a company or industry.

cost|wise (kost′wīz′), *adv.* with respect to costs: *When ... the business is no longer competitive, costwise and pricewise, it loses the market* (Wall Street Journal).

co|sy (kō′zē), *adj.,* **-si|er, -si|est,** *n., pl.* **-sies,** *v.,* **-sied, -sy|ing.** = cozy.

cot[1] (kot), *n.* **1** a narrow, light bed. A cot is sometimes made of canvas stretched on a frame that folds together. **2** *British.* a child's crib. **3** *Nautical.* a bed or hammock of canvas suspended from beams. [Anglo-Indian *cot* < Hindustani *khāṭ.* Compare Sanskrit *khaṭvā.*]

cot[2] (kot), *n.* **1** = cottage. **SYN:** hut, lodge, chalet. **2** = cote[1]. **3** a case or protective covering, such as a fingerstall; sheath. [Old English *cot.* See related etym. at **cote**[1].]

cot (no period), cotangent.

co|tan|gent (kō tan′jənt), *n. Trigonometry.* **1** the ratio of the length of the adjacent side (not the hypotenuse) of an acute angle in a right triangle to the length of the opposite side. **2** the tangent of the complement of a given angle or arc. *Abbr:* cot, ctn (no period).

co|tan|gen|tial (kō′tan jen′shəl), *adj.* having the same tangent.

cot death, *British.* crib death: *Breast-feeding could prevent cot death in very young babies, the report says* (London Times).

cote[1] (kōt), *n.* **1** a shelter or shed for small animals or birds. **2** *Dialect.* a cottage. [Old English *cote.* See related etym. at **cot**[2].]

cote[2] (kōt), *v.t.,* **cot|ed, cot|ing.** *Obsolete.* to pass by; go beyond; outstrip; surpass.

co|teau (kō tō′), *n., pl.* **-teaux** (-tōz′). in the northwestern United States: **1** an upland. **2** a broad, flat-topped ridge of moderate elevation. [< French *coteau*]

cote-har|die (kōt′här′dē), *n.* a close-fitting garment with long sleeves, worn by men and women in the late Middle Ages. It was usually buttoned all the way down the front, the men's version reaching to the middle of the thigh and belted, and the women's full-length. [< Old French *cote-hardie* < *cote* tunic + *hardie* bold]

cô|te|lette (kōt let′), *n. French.* a cutlet.

cô|te|line (kō′tə lēn′), *n.* a kind of white, usually corded, muslin. [< French *côteline* < *côtelé* ribbed < *côte* rib < Old French *coste* side, rib < Latin *costa*]

co|tem|po|ra|ne|ous (kō tem′pə rā′nē əs), *adj.* = contemporaneous.

co|tem|po|rar|y (kō tem′pə rer′ē), *adj.* = contemporary.

co|ten|an|cy (kō ten′ən sē), *n., pl.* **-cies.** joint tenancy.

co|ten|ant (kō ten′ənt), *n.* one of two or more tenants of the same place; joint tenant.

co|ten|ure (kō ten′yər), *n.* tenure with another; joint tenure.

co|te|rie (kō′tər ē), *n.* a set or circle of close acquaintances; group of people who often meet socially. **SYN:** clique, ring. [< French *coterie,* in Middle French, an association of tenant farmers holding land in common from the same owner < Old French *cotier* cotter < *cote* hut < Middle Dutch *kote*]

co|ter|mi|nous (kō tėr′mə nəs), *adj.* = conterminous. — **co|ter′mi|nous|ly**, *adv.*

co|thurn (kō′thėrn, kō thėrn′), *n.* = cothurnus.

co|thur|nus (kō thėr′nəs), *n., pl.* **-ni** (-nī). **1** a thick-soled half boot worn by tragic actors in the ancient Athenian drama; buskin. **2** *Figurative.* the manner or style of ancient tragedy. [< Latin *cothurnus* < Greek *kóthornos*]

co|tid|al (kō tī′dəl), *adj.* of or having to do with the coincidence in time of tidal phenomena: *A cotidal line on a map connects all those places at which high tide occurs at the same time.*

co|til|lion (kō til′yən), *n.* **1** any large, formal party for dancing. **2** any one of several dances, chiefly of French origin, consisting of a variety of steps and figures, especially: **a** a dance for four or more couples, with complicated steps and much changing of partners, led by one couple; german. Favors and prizes are often given. **b** an early French social dance for couples. **c** any quadrille. **3** a piece of music for any of these dances. [< French *cotillon* (originally) petticoat (diminutive) < *cotte* < Old French *cote* coat]

co|til|lon (kô tē yôN′), *n. French.* a cotillion.

co|tin|ga (kō ting′gə), *n.* any one of a group of brightly colored tropical American birds, such as the cock of the rock. [< French *cotinga* < Tupi]

co|to|ne|as|ter (kə tō′nē as′tər), *n.* any plant of an Old World group of shrubs, sometimes trailing, of the rose family. [< New Latin *Cotoneaster* < Latin *cotōnea* quince + Greek *astēr* star]

cot|quean (kot′kwēn′), *n. Obsolete.* **1a** the housewife of a cot or hut. **b** a coarse, vulgar, or scolding woman. **2** a man who busies himself with household affairs. [< *cot*[2] + *quean*]

co|trus|tee (kō′trus tē′), *n.* a joint trustee.

Cots|wold (kots′wōld, -wəld), *n.* a breed of large sheep with long wool, developed in the Cotswolds (hills in southwestern England).

cot|ta (kot′ə), *n.* **1** = surplice. **2** a short surplice with short sleeves or none, worn chiefly by choristers. [< Medieval Latin *cotta*, perhaps < Old French *cote* coat]

cot|ta|bus (kot′ə bəs), *n.* an ancient Greek game of throwing wine from a drinking cup into a vessel so as to strike it in a particular manner. [< Latin *cottabus* < Greek *kóttabos*]

cot|tage (kot′ij), *n.* **1** any small house. Farm workers and villagers often lived in cottages. **2** a small house in the country or suburbs. **3** a house at a summer resort. **4** a small, separate dwelling unit at a hospital, hotel, school, or other institution. **5** = cottage orné. [Middle English *cotage* < *cot*[2] + *-age* -age. Compare Old French *cotage* type of land tenure.]

–***Syn.*** **1 Cottage, cabin** mean a small house. **Cottage**, the general word, once applied only to a small, simple house lived in by poor people, but now applies to any small and simple house: *I live in a garden cottage.* **Cabin** applies to a small, roughly built house: *He lives in a cabin in the woods.*

cottage bonnet, a woman's bonnet of a shape fashionable in the first half of the 1800's and seen in early portraits of Queen Victoria.

cottage cheese, a soft, white cheese made from the curds of sour milk; Dutch cheese.

cottage china, English pottery of a cheap sort, especially table utensils decorated with small bouquets and the like.

cot|taged (kot′ijd), *adj.* studded with cottages: *the cottaged hills of a lakeside resort.*

cottage fried potatoes or **cottage fries** = home fries.

cottage hospital, **1** *British.* a small hospital, in a cottage or house, without a resident medical staff, used by the residents of a local community. **2** a hospital made up of a number of detached cottages or similar buildings.

cottage industry, **1** a system of production in the Industrial Revolution where workers made or worked on products, such as clothes, usually at home, for a merchant who paid them for their work. **2** any present-day industry that uses this system of producing goods: *Mr. Nanda in his report to Congress does not believe that cottage industries can either reduce unemployment or satisfy normal consumer demands* (London Times).

cottage loaf, *British.* a loaf of bread formed of two rounded masses of dough, the smaller stuck on top of the larger.

cottage or|né (ôr nā′), a house in the country or suburbs designed for picturesque or romantic effect. [< French *orné* ornate]

cottage piano, a small upright piano.

cottage pudding, plain cake covered with a sweet sauce, especially chocolate sauce.

cot|tag|er (kot′i jər), *n.* **1** a person who lives in a cottage, especially: **a** one of the laboring population in rural districts: *The natural dyestuffs used by these Indian cottagers aren't completely colorfast* (New Yorker). **b** *U.S.* a person who lives in a cottage at a summer resort. **2** *Scottish.* a cotter or cottar.

cottage tulip, any one of various tall-growing, midseason, single-flowered tulips that usually bloom in May.

cot|tage|y (kot′ə jē), *adj.* of or suitable for a cottage.

cot|ter[1] (kot′ər), *n.* **1** a locking device consisting of a pin, key, wedge, or bolt, usually flat in section and tapered, inserted into a hole or through a slot to hold such things as small parts of machinery or wheels in place. **2** = cotter pin. [origin uncertain]

cot|ter[2] or **cot|tar** (kot′ər), *n.* **1** *Scottish.* a peasant who works for a farmer and is allowed to use a small cottage and a plot of land; cottager. **2** (in Irish history) = cottier (def. 2). [< Medieval Latin *cotarius* < *cota* cot[2] < Old English *cot*]

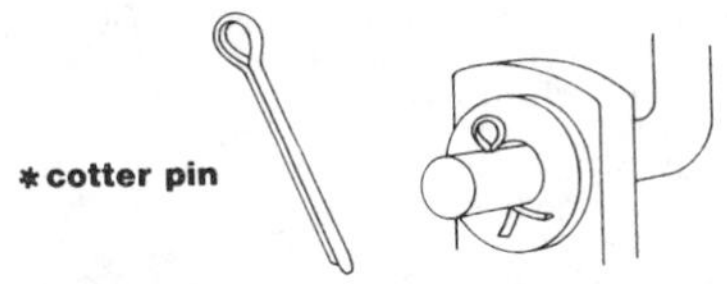

∗cotter pin

∗cotter pin, a split pin inserted through a slot to hold small parts of machinery, wheels, or other parts together. The ends are bent to keep it in its slot.

cot|ti|er (kot′ē ər), *n.* **1** *Especially British.* a person who lives in a cottage; cottager. **2** (formerly) an Irish peasant who rented land directly from its owner, the amount of rent being fixed by public competition. [< Old French *cottier* < *cote* cot; see etym. under **coterie**]

cot|to|lene (kot′ə lēn), *n.* a preparation of cottonseed oil, used as a shortening in cookery. [< *cott*(on) + *-ol*[2] + *-ene*]

cot|ton (kot′ən), *n., adj., v.* —*n.* **1** the soft, white fibers in a fluffy mass around the seeds of a plant, widely used especially in making fabrics or thread. **2a** the tall plant that produces these fibers. It belongs to the mallow family. *Doubtless the seeds of the wild ancestors of cotton were scattered somewhat like those of milkweed* (Fred W. Emerson). See picture under **mallow family**. **b** a crop of such plants. **3** thread made of cotton fibers. **4a** cloth made of cotton thread. **b** a garment made of this: *dressed in a striped cotton.* **5** any downy substance resembling cotton fibers, growing on other plants such as the silk-cotton tree.

—***adj.*** made of cotton: *She bought two cotton dresses.*

—***v.i.*** **1** *Informal.* **a** to take a liking (to): *to cotton to an idea. A girl must cotton to somebody* (Anthony Trollope). **b** to get on together; agree; harmonize. **c** to make friends; fraternize: *Gradually all cottoned together, and plunged into conversation* (Fraser's Magazine). **2** *Obsolete.* to prosper; succeed.

cotton on (to), *Informal.* to understand; catch on: *The children have cottoned on to the underlying principle of mutual action* (Punch). *The next time round I had cottoned on* (New Yorker).

[< Old French *coton* < Italian *cotone* < Arabic *quṭn*] —**cot′ton|like′**, *adj.*

cotton batting, soft, fluffy cotton pressed into thin layers for use especially as a swab or to dress wounds; absorbent cotton.

Cotton Belt, a region in the southern United States, especially Alabama, Georgia, and Mississippi, where cotton is grown extensively.

cotton cake, a mass of cottonseed after the oil has been pressed out, used as feed for livestock.

cotton candy, a light, fluffy form of candy, made by spinning melted sugar.

cotton flannel, a soft, cotton fabric napped on one side, used for babies' clothing, pajamas, and shirts.

cotton gin, a machine for separating fibers of cotton from the seeds; gin.

cotton grass, any plant of a group of sedges whose spikes resemble tufts of cotton: *The scientists . . . condemn, with experimental evidence, the farmers' practice of burning the heather to give the sheep succulent young shoots of cotton grass* (New Scientist).

cotton gum, = tupelo.

cot|ton|mouth (kot′ən mouth′), *n.* = water moccasin. [American English (its open mouth is whitish in appearance)]

cotton picker, **1** a machine that picks ripe cotton in the field. **2** a person who picks cotton by hand.

cot|ton-pick|ing (kot′ən pik′ing), *adj., adv. U.S. Slang.* —***adj.*** **1** lowly; worthless. **2** (as an intensive only) confounded: *Whoever said that if you build a better mousetrap the world will beat a path to your door was out of his cotton-picking mind* (Time). —***adv.*** very.

cotton rat, a small rat, native to the southern United States, found in the lowlands, especially in cotton fields.

cot|ton|seed (kot′ən sēd′), *n., pl.* **-seeds** or (*collectively*) **-seed.** the seed of cotton. It is used for making cottonseed oil, fertilizer, and cattle feed.

cottonseed meal, cottonseed ground after the oil has been expressed, used as feed and as a fertilizer.

cottonseed oil, an oil pressed from cottonseed, used especially for cooking and for making soap: *Cottonseed oil goes to refineries for purification and then to finished products plants, mainly for the production of shortenings, margarine and salad oil* (Wall Street Journal).

cotton stainer, a red bug that stains cotton in the boll.

Cotton State, a nickname for Alabama.

cot|ton|tail (kot′ən tāl′), *n.*, or **cottontail rabbit**, the common North American wild rabbit with a fluffy, white tail.

cotton thistle, a tall, stout thistle with white, cottony down on stems and leaves, found in the south of England and naturalized in the United States in New England.

cotton waste, refuse yarn from the manufacture of cotton, used especially for cleaning machinery and packing axle boxes.

cot|ton|weed (kot′ən wēd′), *n.* any one of various plants whose downy leaves suggest cotton, such as the pearly everlasting.

cot|ton|wood (kot′ən wu̇d′), *n.* **1** a kind of American poplar tree with tufts that look like cotton on its small seeds: *But now, windbreaks of growing trees, especially of cottonwoods, shelter many of the homes on these same far-flung plains* (Fred W. Emerson). **2** the soft wood of this tree.

cotton wool, **1** raw cotton, before or after picking. **2** *British.* absorbent cotton.

cotton worm, the destructive larva of a noctuid moth that attacks the leaves of the cotton plant.

cot|ton|y (kot′ə nē), *adj.* **1** covered with a down or nap resembling cotton. **2** of cotton. **3** like cotton; soft; fluffy; downy: *cottony clouds.*

cot|ton|y-cush|ion scale (kot′ə nē ku̇sh′ən), a scale insect that attacks fruit trees, especially citrus trees.

cot|y|le (kot′ə lē), *n., pl.* **-lae** (-lē). *Anatomy, Zoology.* **1** a cuplike cavity. **2** = acetabulum (def. 2). [< Latin *cotyla* hollow vessel < Greek *kotýlē*]

∗cot|y|le|don (kot′ə lē′dən), *n.* the first leaf, or one of the first pair of leaves, growing from a seed; the embryo leaf in the seed of a plant; seed leaf. The number of cotyledons in the seed serves as an important basis of classification of angiosperms into monocotyledons, with one cotyledon, and dicotyledons, with two. [< New Latin *cotyledon* (introduced by Linnaeus) < Latin < Greek *kotylēdṓn* cup-shaped hollow < *kotýlē* small vessel, cup, hollow]

∗cotyledon

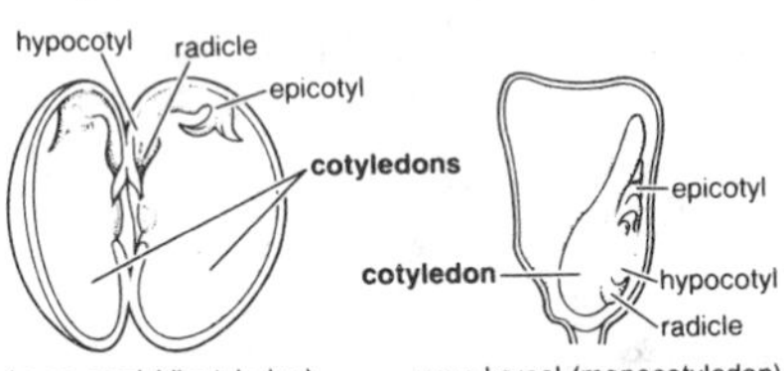

cot|y|le|don|ar (kot′ə lē′də nər), *adj.* = cotyledonary.

cot|y|le|don|ar|y (kot′ə lē′də ner′ē), *adj.* having, or of the nature of, cotyledons.

cot|y|le|don|ous (kot′ə lē′də nəs), *adj.* having cotyledons.

co|tyl|i|form (kō til′ə fôrm), *adj.* shaped like a cup, with a tube at the base.

cot|y|loid (kot′ə loid), *adj.* shaped like a cup, as the socket of the thighbone.

cot|y|lo|saur (kot′ə lə sôr), *n.* a primitive, short-legged reptile of the late Paleozoic, considered to be a link between the early amphibians and various reptiles, including dinosaurs. [< New Latin *Cotylosauria* the order name < Greek *kotýlē* cup, hollow + *saûros* lizard]

Co|tys (kō′tis), *n. Greek Mythology.* a Thracian goddess whose festival, the Cotyttia, was celebrated with licentious revelry.

Co|tyt|ti|a (kō tit′ē ə), *n. Greek Mythology.* a festival in honor of Cotys.

couch[1] (kouch), *n., v.* —***n.*** **1** a long seat, usually upholstered and having a back and arms; sofa: *Over against one wall was a black leather couch—not a davenport, not a settee, but simply a battered old leather couch* (Robert Traver). **SYN:** divan, lounge. **2** a bed or other structure made to sleep or rest on: *Oft when on my couch I lie in vacant or in pensive mood* (Wordsworth). **3** any place for sleep or rest: *The deer sprang up from its grassy couch.* **4a** the burrow of an otter. **b** *Obsolete.* the den or lair of a wild animal. **5** the frame on which barley is spread to be malted. **6** a coat of paint, varnish, or other material.

—***v.t.*** **1** to lay on a couch. **2a** to put in words; express: *His thoughts were couched in beautiful language.* **b** to express obscurely. **3** to lower into a level position ready to attack: *The knights couched their lances and prepared to charge.* **SYN:** lower. **4** to lower (the head or other part of the body); bring down. **5** (in embroidery) to overlay with heavy thread in a pattern, fastened down at equal intervals by fine stitches. **6** *Archaic.* to lay down; cause to lie down; put to bed: *The Hind . . . then couched herself securely by her side* (John Dryden). **7** *Obsolete.* to put (things) horizontally or in layers. **8** *Obsolete.* to lodge; hide; conceal. **9** *Medicine, Obsolete.* **a** to remove (a cataract) by displacing the opaque crystalline lens below the axis of vision. **b** to treat (a per-

Pronunciation Key: hat, āge, cãre, fär; let, ēqual, tėrm; it, īce; hot, ōpen, ôrder; **oi**l, **ou**t; cup, pu̇t, rüle; **ch**ild; lo**ng**; **th**in; **ᴛʜ**en; **zh**, measure; **ə** represents **a** in about, **e** in taken, **i** in pencil, **o** in lemon, **u** in circus.

son) for cataract in this way.

—*v.i.* **1** to lie down on a couch. SYN: recline. **2** to lie hidden ready to attack; lurk: *Bertram ... couches in the brake and fern, hiding his face* (Scott). SYN: crouch. **3** to stoop down; cringe. SYN: cower. **4** to lie in a bed or heap for decomposition or fermentation: *oak leaves crouching as compost.* **5** *Archaic.* to lie at rest; recline; repose: *The peasantry ... couch upon beds of straw* (Harriet Martineau). **6** *Obsolete.* to lie down or together.

[< Old French *couche* < *coucher* lay in place < Latin *collocāre* < *com-* together + *locāre* to place < *locus* a place]—**couch′er**, *n.* —**couch′like′**, *adj.*

couch² (kouch), *n.* = couch grass.

couch|ant (kou′chənt), *adj.* **1** *Heraldry.* represented as lying down, but with the head raised: *The shield had a lion couchant.* **2** lying down; couching (especially of an animal): *a couchant doe.* [< French *couchant*, present participle of Old French *coucher*, see etym. under **couch¹**]

cou|chee (kü′shā, kü shā′), *n.* **1** a reception held about bedtime, as by a king. **2** an evening reception. [< French *couché*, variant of *coucher* a reclining < Old French; see etym. under **couch¹**]

couch|ette (kou chet′), *n.* **1** a European railroad car in which the seats can be converted into berths for sleeping. **2** a seat or berth in such a car. [< French *couchette* (diminutive) < *couche* couch]

couch grass, any one of several coarse, weedlike grasses that spread very rapidly by creeping stems, especially the quack, quitch, or witch grass, a troublesome European weed common in North America.

couch|ing (kou′ching), *n.* **1** a kind of embroidery in which heavy thread is laid on a fabric in a pattern and fastened at equal intervals with fine stitches of another thread. **2** work embroidered like this.

couch potato, *U.S. Informal.* a person who spends much time watching television or videotapes: *Couch potatoes, as their name implies, are happiest when vegetating "all eyes" in front of Television* (Jack Mingo).

couch|y (kou′chē), *adj.* **1** full of or infested with couch grass. **2** of the nature of or resembling couch grass.

Cou|é|ism (kü ā′iz əm), *n.* a system of autosuggestion, used especially in the 1920's to improve one's mental outlook and health.
[< Émile *Coué*, 1857-1926, a French psychologist, who advocated it + *-ism*]

*** cou|gar** (kü′gər), *n.* a large, slender animal of the cat family. The cougar is a flesh-eating mammal with a grayish- or tawny-brown coat, and a black muzzle, found wild in many parts of North and South America; panther; mountain lion; puma; catamount; painter. [< French *couguar* (probably influenced by *jaguar*), ultimately < Tupi (Brazil) *guazuara*]

*** cougar**

cough (kôf, kof), *v., n.* —*v.i.* **1a** to force air from the lungs with sudden effort and noise: *Her cold made her cough. He coughed to clear his throat.* **b** *Figurative: A mortar coughs in the night and shells explode* (New York Times). **2** *Slang, Figurative.* to confess: *Inspector Rowley came back and said 'Has he coughed yet?'* (London Times).

—*v.t.* **1** to bring up (blood) by coughing. **2** to bring into any condition by coughing: *to cough one's life away.*

—*n.* **1a** an act of coughing: *His constant cough annoyed the speaker.* **b** the sound or a sound of coughing: *The hunter's cough scared the deer. (Figurative.) the cough of an automobile engine.* **2** the condition or symptom of repeated coughing. This condition indicates obstruction, irritation, or inflammation of the respiratory passages. *She has a bad cough.*

cough down, to silence (a speaker) by pretending to cough in order to drown his voice: *If he will make long speeches, he must be coughed down* (New Monthly Magazine).

cough up, a to expel from the throat by coughing: *He coughed up the candy that was stuck in his throat.* **b** *Figurative: Corporations will cough up a billion more in taxes this fiscal year* (Wall Street Journal).

[Middle English *coghen*, related to Old English *cohhetan*]—**cough′er**, *n.*

cough drop, a small tablet containing medicine to relieve coughs or hoarseness.

cough|ing (kôf′ing, kof′-), *n.* a forcing of air from the lungs with sudden effort or noise.

cough syrup, a sweet, thick liquid containing medicine to relieve coughing.

could (kůd), *v.* the past tense of **can¹**: *Years ago she could sing beautifully.* [Middle English *coude*, Old English *cūthe*; the *l* was inserted on the analogy of *should, would*]

▶**could, might.** *Could*, the past of *can*, and *might*, originally the past of *may*, are now used chiefly to convey a shade of doubt, or a slight degree of possibility: *It might be all right for her, but it isn't for me. Perhaps I could write a poem, but I doubt it.*

could|n't (kůd′ənt), could not.

couldst (kůdst), *v. Archaic and Poetic.* second person singular of **could**. "Thou couldst" means "You could."

cou|lee (kü′lē), *n.* **1** *Western U.S. and Canada.* a deep ravine or gulch that is usually dry in summer. **2** a stream of lava. [< Middle French *coulée* < Old French *couler* flow, glide < Latin *cōlāre* to strain < *cōlum* strainer, colander]

cou|leur de rose (kü lœr′ də rōz′), *French.* **1** rose color. **2** rose-colored. **3** *Figurative.* in a rosy aspect; hopefully.

cou|lisse (kü lēs′), *n.* **1** a groove or channel in which a sluice gate or movable partition slides. **2** *Theater.* **a** one of the side scenes of a stage. **b** the space between them; the wings. **c** a groove through which scenery may be slid. [< Old French *coulisse*, noun use of past participle of *couler* glide; see etym. under **coulee**]

cou|loir (kü lwär′), *n.* a steep gorge or gully on the side of a mountain. [< Old French *couloir* passage, (literally) a slide, glide < *couler*, see etym. under **coulee**]

cou|lomb (kü lom′), *n.* the unit of electric charge in the meter-kilogram-second system. It is equal to the quantity of electricity furnished by a current of one ampere in one second. *The coulomb is chosen to be a unit of convenient size in working with electric currents* (Shortley and Williams). [< Charles A. de *Coulomb*, 1736–1806, a French physicist]

cou|lomb|ic (kü lom′ik), *adj.* of or based on Coulomb's law: *coulombic attraction.*

Coulomb's law, the principle that the electrostatic attraction or repulsion between electrically charged bodies is directly proportional to the product of the electric charges on each body, and inversely proportional to the square of the distance between the bodies. [< C. A. de *Coulomb*]

cou|lom|e|ter (kü lom′ə tər), *n.* = voltameter. [< *coulomb* + *-meter*]

cou|lo|met|ric (kü′lə met′rik), *adj.* of or having to do with coulometry.

cou|lom|e|try (kü lom′ə trē), *n.* a method used in microanalysis to determine quantities in solution by measuring the amount of electricity required to effect electrochemical deposition or other chemical change in the dissolved material.

coul|ter (kōl′tər), *n.* = colter.

cou|ma|rin (kü′mər in), *n.* a crystalline substance with an aromatic odor, found in sweet clover, sweet woodruff, tonka beans, and other plants, used in flavoring and in perfumes. *Formula:* $C_9H_6O_2$ [< French *coumarine* < *coumarou*; see etym. under **coumarou**]

cou|ma|rone (kü′mə rōn), *n.* a resinous compound used in paints and varnishes, and in the preparation of rubber goods. *Formula:* C_8H_6O [< *coumar*(in) + *-one*]

cou|ma|rou (kü′mə rü′), *n.* **1** the tonka bean tree. **2** its seeds. [< French *coumarou* < Tupi *cumarú* an aromatic tree]

coun|cil (koun′səl), *n.* **1** a group of people called together to give advice and to discuss or settle questions: *till their fate is finally determined in a general council of the victorious warriors* (J. D. Hunter). SYN: conference, meeting, assembly. **2a** a group of persons elected by the people to make laws for and manage a city or town: *a town council, city council.* SYN: legislature. **b** *Especially British.* the local chief administrative authority of a corporate town or city: *a borough council.* **3** a body of delegates from labor unions or local organizations: *a community council.* **4a** a body of persons appointed to assist a chief executive in an administrative, advisory, or legislative capacity: *The governor is assisted by an executive council of six members.* **b** a high government body, sometimes honorary: *the British Privy Council.* **5** any body of delegates or representatives. **6** the deliberation or consultation that takes place in a council or meeting. **7** an ecclesiastical assembly called to consider or decide on matters of doctrine, discipline, or the like: *the Council of Nicaea, the Vatican Council.* **8** (in the New Testament) the Jewish Sanhedrin or a similar group, or one of the meetings of such a group. [< Old French *concile*, learned borrowing from Latin *concilium* < *com-* together + *calāre* call]

▶**council, counsel.** *Council* is always a noun: *They called together a council* (group) *of the town's industrial leaders. Counsel* may be a noun or a verb: *She could always be counted on for good counsel* (advice). *Each side tried to get him as its counsel* (adviser). *I do not like to counsel* (advise) *you on that point.*

council board, **1** the board or table around which a council holds its sessions; council table. **2** a council in session.

council estate, *British.* a group of council houses.

council fire, the fire lighted by North American Indians when in council.

council flat, *British.* an apartment in an apartment house that was built by a town or district council.

council house, **1** a house in which a council meets, especially one used by North American Indians when in council: *an Iroquois council house.* **2** *British.* **a** a house built by a town or district council, usually as part of a housing project. **b** a town hall.

coun|cil|lor (koun′sə lər, -slər), *n.* Especially British. councilor.

coun|cil|lor|ship (koun′sə lər ship, -slər-), *n. Especially British.* councilorship.

coun|cil|man (koun′səl mən), *n., pl.* **-men. 1** a member of the council of a city or town. **2** = councilor.

coun|cil-man|ag|er plan (koun′səl man′ ə jər), a system of municipal government in which a manager appointed and assisted by the city council is in charge of the city administration.

coun|cil|man|ic (koun′səl man′ik), *adj.* of or like a councilman.

council of ministers, the body of advisers to the chief executive or head of government in any of various countries: *The most significant switch occurred in Hungary's Council of Ministers (cabinet)* (B. M. Gwertzman).

Council of Trent, a council held at Trent, Italy, at various times from 1545 to 1563. It condemned Reformation doctrines, formulated many of the present doctrines of the Roman Catholic Church, and initiated many reforms.

council of war, **1** a conference of army or navy officers with a commanding officer, usually to discuss an emergency. **2** *Figurative.* any conference to decide on a plan of action.

coun|ci|lor (koun′sə lər, -slər), *n.* a member of a council. Also, *especially British*, **councillor**.

coun|ci|lor|ship (koun′sə lər ship, -slər-), *n.* the office or position of councilor. Also, *especially British*, **councillorship**.

council school, *British.* a school provided and maintained by a town or county council, now called a *county school.*

council table, = council board.

coun|sel (koun′səl), *n., v.,* **-seled, -sel|ing** or (*especially British*) **-selled, -sel|ling.** —*n.* **1** the act of exchanging ideas; act of talking things over: *Each member benefited from the frequent counsel of the committee.* SYN: consultation, deliberation. **2** carefully considered advice: *A wise person gives good counsel. The lawyer's counsel was that we avoid a lawsuit.* SYN: recommendation, opinion. See syn. under **advice**. **3a** a lawyer or group of lawyers: *Each side of a case in court has its own counsel. The defendant's counsel objected.* **b** a person or persons who give advice about the law. **4** deliberate purpose; design; plan; scheme: *The counsel to extend the park limits was approved.* **5** *Archaic.* wisdom; prudence: *With him is wisdom and strength, he hath counsel and understanding* (Job 12:13). **6** *Obsolete.* a private or secret purpose, design, or opinion.

—*v.t.* **1** to give (a person) advice; advise: *The father counseled his son to stay in school and learn enough to earn a living. The judge counseled the attorney to proceed with caution.* **2** to recommend: *He counseled immediate action. The doctor counseled operating at once to save the boy's life.*

—*v.i.* **1** to exchange ideas; consult together; deliberate: *The Senate committee counseled far into the night.* **2** to give or offer counsel or advice: *So counseled he and both together went into the thickest wood* (Milton).

keep one's own counsel, to keep still about one's ideas and plans; not tell one's secrets: *William kept his own counsel so well that not a hint of his intention got abroad* (Macaulay).

take counsel, to exchange ideas; talk things over; consult together: *He took counsel with his friends as to what he should do. Then from that day forth they took counsel together for to put him to death* (John 11:53).

[< Old French *conseil* < Latin *consilium* counsel, deliberation < *consulere* consult, (originally) con-

voke, gather < *com-* together + an unrecorded root *sel-* take]
► See **council** for usage note.
coun|sel|ee (koun′sə lē′), *n.* a person who receives counsel.
coun|sel|ing (koun′sə ling), *n.* the practice or services of a professional counselor; guidance.
coun|sel|lor (koun′sə lər, -slər), *n. Especially British.* counselor.
coun|sel|lor|ship (koun′sə lər ship, -slər-), *n. Especially British.* counselorship.
coun|se|lor (koun′sə lər, -slər), *n.* **1** a person who gives advice; adviser: *The priest was the village counselor.* **2** = lawyer. **3** an adviser, especially on legal matters, of an embassy, legation, or the like. **4** an instructor or leader in a summer camp.
coun|se|lor|ship (koun′sə lər ship, -slər-), *n.* the office of counselor.
count¹ (kount), *v., n.* — ***v.t.*** **1a** to name numbers in order up to: *Wait till I count ten.* **SYN**: enumerate. **b** to add up; find the number of: *We counted the books and found there were fifty.* **c** to reckon by more complex methods of computation; calculate: *to count one's profits.* **2** to include in counting; take into account: *There will be ten guests, not counting the family. Let's not count that practice game.* **3** to think of as; consider: *I count myself fortunate in having good health. Must we count Life a curse and not a blessing?* (Robert Browning). **SYN**: regard, esteem. **4** *Obsolete.* to ascribe; impute.
— ***v.i.*** **1a** to name numbers in order: *to count by tens to one hundred. The child can count from one to ten.* **b** to find out how many individual objects are in a collection: *While I'm cataloguing the books I'll also count.* **c** to reckon; calculate: *He can read, write, and count. There we acquired the ability to count in units, tens, and hundreds* (R. C. Orford). **2** to be included in counting; be taken into account: *Your first trial is only for practice; it won't count.* **3** *Figurative.* to have an influence; be of value: *Every vote counts in an election. Every penny counts. A novel which counts as a classic.* **4** to depend; rely (on, upon): *We count on your help.* **5** to be in number; amount to: *The army counts two million.* **6** *Obsolete.* to take account (of).
— ***n.*** **1** an adding up; a finding out how many: *The count showed that 5,000 votes had been cast.* **SYN**: calculation, reckoning. **2** the total number; amount: *a full count of years. The exact count was 5,170 votes.* **3** *Law.* each charge in a formal accusation: *The thief was found guilty on all four counts.* **4** ten seconds counted to give a fallen boxer time to get up before he is declared the loser. **5** *Baseball.* the number of balls and strikes called on a batter. The count "1 and 2" means that there has been one ball and two strikes. **6** *Bowling.* the number of pins knocked down by the first ball in a frame, used for adding to a spare in the previous frame. **7** an accounting. **8a** a standard of fineness of yarn for many textile fibers, based on the length of the yarn in relation to a fixed weight, usually the number of hanks to a pound. **b** a standard of the fineness of a fabric, usually the number of cross threads to the inch. **9** *Archaic.* regard; notice; note.
count for, to amount to; be worth: *That idea does not count for much.*
count in, *Informal.* to include: *Count me in on the list for the picnic. "Well, George, if the boys are sending flowers, count me in"* (Saturday Review).
count off, to divide into equal groups by counting: *For the spelling bee, you may count off from the left.*
count out, a to fail to consider or include: *If you go skiing, count me out.* **b** to declare (a fallen boxer) the loser when he fails to rise after 10 seconds have been counted: *He is down on the canvas and the referee is shouting in his ear. He is being counted out* (David Soutar). **c** *Informal.* to defeat (a candidate) by fraudulent miscount of, or failure to count, the ballots: *Mr. Frazier ... was elected representative, taking his seat at the same time that his stepfather, Governor Harris, was counted out by the Overton faction* (H. F. O'Beirne). **d** to defeat: *The UAW leader has never been counted out in a major contract fight* (Newsweek).
[< Old North French *cunter,* Old French *conter* < Latin *computāre* < *com-* (intensive) + *putāre* reckon. See etym. of doublet **compute.**]
count² (kount), *n.* a European nobleman equal in rank to an English earl. [< Anglo-French *counte,* Old French *conte* < Latin *comes, -itis* companion, (later) attendant of the emperor < *com-* with + *īre* go]
count|a|ble (koun′tə bəl), *adj., n.* — ***adj.*** **1** that can be counted: *Stars are countable by the million.* **2** *Mathematics.* denumerable: [*Georg*] *Cantor called countable those infinite sets that can be written as a sequence X1, X2, X3 ...* (Scientific American). **3** *Grammar.* that can take the plural form and follow a cardinal number. *Boy* is a countable noun (*one boy, two boys*); *butter* and *yellow* are not countable.
— ***n.*** a countable noun.
count|down (kount′doun′), *n.* **1** the period of time for preparation before the launching of a missile or rocket, or before the start of any other operation or undertaking. **2** the calling out of the passing minutes or seconds of this period as they pass: *They began the countdown required before launching a 1,000-mile Regulus-type missile* (Time). **3** a counting in reverse to mark the passage of time, or the preparations taken, before the start of an operation or undertaking: *Southeastern Conference football teams begin countdowns ... today as 8 of the 10 open the 1971 season Saturday* (Tuscaloosa News).
coun|te|nance (koun′tə nəns), *n., v.,* **-nanced, -nanc|ing.** — ***n.*** **1** the expression of the face: *His angry countenance showed how he felt.* **SYN**: visage. See syn. under **face. 2** the face; features: *The actor had a handsome and distinguished countenance.* **SYN**: visage. See syn. under **face.** **3** approval, support, or encouragement: *They gave countenance to our plan, but no active help.* **SYN**: favor. **4** calmness; composure; confidence. **5** *Obsolete.* bearing; behavior; conduct.
— ***v.t.*** to approve, support, or encourage: *Mothers do not countenance all that fathers and sons find exciting or fun. I will not countenance such a plan. We extend friendship to both but we do not extend friendship to the point of countenancing aggression by either* (Wall Street Journal). **SYN**: favor, sanction.
keep one's countenance, a to be calm; not show feeling: *She kept her countenance and made no semblance of sorrow* (Thomas Malory). **b** to keep from smiling or laughing: *It was as much as I could do to keep my countenance at the figure he made* (William Chetwood).
lose countenance, to get excited: *Though he was subjected to severe provocation, he did not lose countenance.*
out of countenance, a into a state of confusion or embarrassment: *The table spread ... for a noble breakfast ... that put me out of countenance, so much and so good* (Samuel Pepys). **b** so as to put into such a state: *to stare out of countenance.*
[< Old French *contenance,* learned borrowing from Medieval Latin *continentia* demeanor < Latin, self-control < *continēre;* see etym. under **contain**] — **coun′te|nanc|er,** *n.*
count|er¹ (koun′tər), *n.* **1a** a long table in a store, restaurant, or bank on which money is counted out, or across which goods, food, or drinks are given to customers. **b** a banker's or money-changer's table. **c** any similar long, narrow surface, such as that on which certain work is done in a kitchen. **2** a thing used for counting. Round, flat disks are often used as counters to keep score in card games. **3a** an imitation coin. **b** any coin.
over the counter, through a broker's office instead of a regular exchange: *This includes some stock distributed through trading on exchanges, but the total is made up largely of stock distributed over the counter in companies "going public" for the first time* (Wall Street Journal).
under the counter, in an underhanded manner; without authorization; clandestinely: *The Metropolitan Opera House was crammed with people eager to shed $50 at the box office or $100 under the counter* (Manchester Guardian Weekly).
[< Anglo-French *counteour,* Old French *conteour* < *conter;* see etym. under **count¹**]
count|er² (koun′tər), *n.* **1** a person who counts. **2** a thing that counts, such as an apparatus for keeping count of revolutions or strokes of a piston. [< *count¹* + *-er¹*]
coun|ter³ (koun′tər), *adv., adj., v., n.* — ***adv.*** **1** in the opposite direction; in the reverse direction. **2** opposed; contrary: *He acted counter to his promise. That wild idea runs counter to common sense.*
— ***adj.*** opposite; contrary: *Your plans are counter to ours.*
— ***v.t.*** **1** to oppose; go or act counter to: *She did not like our plan; so she countered it with one of her own.* **SYN**: contradict. **2** to meet or answer (a move, blow, proposal, statement, or challenge) by another in return: *He ducked and countered a left to the jaw. The West sought to counter the Red thrust, strengthening its NATO and other alliances* (Newsweek).
— ***v.i.*** **1** to make a move or take a stand against some person, action, etc., especially by making an opposing statement: *In the debate the other team countered very weakly with a poorly prepared argument.* **2** to give a blow in boxing while receiving or blocking an opponent's blow: *Instead of countering on the head the blow may be aimed at the ribs.* **3** *Obsolete.* to engage in contest; argue in opposition; dispute (against or with).
— ***n.*** **1** that which is opposite or contrary to something else: *The counter to Communism was to show that there was a better way of life for people under a free democracy* (London Times). **2** in boxing: **a** a blow given while receiving or blocking an opponent's blow: *Fontinato's swift right counter opened a ... cut under Richard's left eye* (Newsweek). **b** the act of delivering such a blow. **3** a circular parry in fencing: *Counters are named according to the engagement from which the parry is made* (W. H. Pollock). **4** any play in football in which the action goes one way and the ball carrier goes another way. **5** a stiff piece of leather inside the back of a shoe or boot around the heel. **6** the part of a ship's stern from the water line to the end of the curved part. **7** the part of a horse's breast between the shoulders and under the neck. **8** the depressed part of the face of a type, coin, medal, or the like.
[< Old French *countre* facing, opposite (to) < Latin *contrā* against]
counter-, *combining form.* **1** in opposition to; against: *Counteract = to act against.*
2 in return: *Counterattack = an attack in return.*
3 corresponding: *Counterpart = a corresponding part.*
[see etym. under **counter³**]
coun|ter|act (koun′tər akt′), *v.t.* to act against; hinder or defeat by contrary action: *to counteract a fever with aspirin, counteract adverse publicity. A hot bath and a hot drink will sometimes counteract chills.* **SYN**: counterbalance. — **coun′ter|ac′tion,** *n.*
coun|ter|act|ant (koun′tər ak′tənt), *n.* a counteracting force or agency; counteragent.
coun|ter|ac|tive (koun′tər ak′tiv), *adj., n.* — ***adj.*** tending to counteract.
— ***n.*** something that counteracts.
coun|ter|a|gent (koun′tər ā′jənt), *n.* a counteracting force or agency; counteractant.
coun|ter|ap|peal (koun′tər ə pēl′), *n.* an appeal made to a court of law in opposition to an appeal made by an adversary.
coun|ter|ap|proach (koun′tər ə prōch′), *n.* a work of fortification constructed by the besieged outside the permanent fortifications, to hinder the approaches of the besiegers or to attack their lines and trenches.
coun|ter|ar|gu|ment (koun′tər är′gyə mənt), *n.* an argument in opposition to another; rebuttal.
coun|ter|at|tack (koun′tər ə tak′), *n., v.* — ***n.*** an attack made to counteract another attack.
— ***v.t., v.i.*** to make an attack in return.
coun|ter|at|trac|tion (koun′tər ə trak′shən), *n.* **1** an attraction of an opposite character. **2** an attraction counter to another attraction: *When the crowds deserted her booth for the one opposite, she put up a sign "Free coffee" as a counterattraction.*
coun|ter|bal|ance (*n.* koun′tər bal′əns; *v.* koun′tər bal′əns), *n., v.,* **-anced, -anc|ing.** — ***n.*** **1** a weight balancing another weight; counterpoise. **2** *Figurative: Her husband's cool judgment was a counterbalance to her impulsiveness.*
— ***v.t., v.i.*** **1** to act as a counterbalance (to); counterpoise: *It is not possible to adjust the filling of a balloon so that it will exactly counterbalance a known load at a given altitude* (Herz and Tennent). **2** *Figurative: By studying hard, he was able to counterbalance his difficulty with arithmetic.* **SYN**: counteract, countervail. — **coun′ter|bal′anc|er,** *n.*
coun|ter|blast (koun′tər blast′, -bläst′), *n.* a blast in opposition to another blast.
coun|ter|blow (koun′tər blō′), *n.* a blow struck in return for another; counter.
coun|ter|bore (*v.* koun′tər bôr′, -bōr′; *n.* koun′tər bôr′, -bōr′), *v.,* **-bored, -bor|ing,** *n.* — ***v.t.*** **1** to bore out (a cylindrical hole) for a certain distance so as to form a flat-bottomed enlargement for receiving the head of a screw or the like. **2** to form a counterbore or counterbores in.
— ***n.*** **1** an enlargement of a hole made by counterboring. See picture under **countersink. 2** a tool for counterboring a hole.
coun|ter|brace (koun′tər brās′), *n., v.,* **-braced, -brac|ing.** — ***n.*** a brace that transmits a strain in an opposite direction from a main brace.
— ***v.t.*** to brace in opposite directions.
coun|ter|change (koun′tər chānj′), *v.t.,* **-changed, -chang|ing. 1** to change to the opposite; cause to exchange as places or qualities. **SYN**: transpose. **2a** to alternate; diversify. **b** *Heraldry.* to interchange or reverse (the tinctures of

---

a bearing on a field of two tinctures), so that color comes against metal, and metal against color.

coun|ter|charge (*n.* koun′tər chärj′; *v.* koun′tər-chärj′), *n., v.,* **-charged, -charg|ing.** —*n.* **1** an opposing charge; a charge made by an accused person against his accuser: *A countercharge of libel was made by the opposing counsel.* **2** *Military.* a charge made against an enemy that has charged.
—*v.t.* **1** to bring a charge against (an accuser): *Saudi Arabia countercharged that Britain sought to federate its Arabian coastal protectorates* (Newsweek). **2** *Military.* to charge in return.

coun|ter|check (koun′tər chek′), *n., v.* —*n.* **1** something that restrains or opposes; obstacle. **2** a check made upon a check; double check for verification.
—*v.t.* **1** to restrain or oppose by some obstacle. **2** to make a second check of; check again: *Before taking off the pilot counterchecked the course his copilot had charted.*

counter check, a check which a depositor can obtain at his bank to make a withdrawal.

coun|ter|claim (*n.* koun′tər klām′; *v.* koun′tər-klām′), *n., v.* —*n.* an opposing claim; claim made by a person to offset a claim made against him.
—*v.t.* to ask for as a counterclaim.
—*v.i.* to ask for or make a counterclaim.

coun|ter|claim|ant (koun′tər klā′mənt), *n.* a person who makes a counterclaim.

coun|ter|clock|wise (koun′tər klok′wīz′), *adv., adj.* in the direction opposite to that in which the hands of a clock go: *They danced counterclockwise around the maypole* (adv.). *The dance involved a counterclockwise movement around a central point* (adj.).

coun|ter|coup (koun′tər kü′), *n., pl.* **-coups** (-küz′). a coup which offsets or reverses a previous coup.

coun|ter|cul|tur|al (koun′tər kul′chər əl), *adj.* of or characterizing the counterculture.

coun|ter|cul|ture (koun′tər kul′chər), *n.* the special culture made up of people, especially young people, who oppose the traditional standards and customs of their society: *When their own children desert to the "counterculture" and in effect become strangers, Middle Americans say in bewilderment, "Either we neglected them or we spoiled them"* (Time).

coun|ter|cul|tur|ist (koun′tər kul′chər ist), *n.* a person who belongs to the counterculture.

coun|ter|cur|rent (koun′tər kėr′ənt), *n., adv.* —*n.* a current in the opposite direction; an opposing current.
—*adv.* in an opposing manner; contrary: *His ideas run countercurrent to those of his party.*

coun|ter|cy|cli|cal (koun′tər sī′klə kəl, -sik′lə-), *adj.* = contracyclical.

coun|ter|dem|on|strate (koun′tər dem′ən strāt), *v.i.,* **-strat|ed, -strat|ing.** to engage in a counter-demonstration.

coun|ter|dem|on|stra|tion (koun′tər dem′ən-strā′shən), *n.* a demonstration intended to offset the effect of a preceding demonstration.

coun|ter|drive (koun′tər drīv′), *n.* a drive or military offensive designed to counteract another drive.

coun|ter|es|pi|o|nage (koun′tər es′pē ə nij, -näzh′), *n.* measures taken to prevent or confuse enemy espionage.

coun|ter|ex|am|ple (koun′tər eg zam′pəl, -zäm′-), *n.* an example or instance that contradicts a theory, generalization, or argument.

coun|ter|feit (koun′tər fit), *adj., v., n.* —*adj.* **1** not genuine; sham: *a counterfeit coin, counterfeit stamps. Counterfeit jewels are made of paste.* **SYN:** spurious, forged, fraudulent. See syn. under **false. 2** pretended; dissembled: *an arrogant counterfeit rascal* (Shakespeare). **SYN:** feigned, simulated.
—*v.t.* **1** to copy (money, pictures, or handwriting) in order to deceive; forge: *He was sent to prison for counterfeiting five-dollar bills.* **2** to resemble closely: *a sleep so deep as to counterfeit death.* **3** to pretend; dissemble: *She counterfeited interest to be polite.*
—*v.i.* **1** to make counterfeits, as of money. **2** to practice deceit; use pretense: *Are you not mad indeed, or do you but counterfeit?* (Shakespeare).
—*n.* **1** something copied and passed as genuine; forgery: *This ten-dollar bill looks genuine, but it is a counterfeit. This chest, though made to look like an antique, is plainly a counterfeit.* **2** *Archaic.* **a** a copy. **b** an image; likeness; portrait: *What find I here? Fair Portia's counterfeit* (Shakespeare). **3** *Obsolete.* an impostor.
[< Old French *contrefait* imitated, past participle of *contrefaire* < *contre-* against (< Latin *contrā-*) + *faire* make < Latin *facere*]

coun|ter|feit|er (koun′tər fit′ər), *n.* **1** a person who copies or imitates, especially one who illegally makes copies of current bank notes or coins. **2** a person who assumes a false appearance or makes false pretenses.

coun|ter|flow (koun′tər flō′), *n.* a flow in an opposite direction; an opposing flow.

coun|ter|foil (koun′tər foil′), *n.* a part of a check, receipt, or the like, kept as a record; stub. [< *counter-* + *foil*[2] leaf]

coun|ter|force (koun′tər fôrs′, -fōrs′), *n.* a force acting in opposition to another; contrary, opposing, or resisting force: *The counterforce to the body's efforts is provided by the body-weight* (New Scientist).

coun|ter|fort (koun′tər fôrt′, -fōrt′), *n.* **1** a buttress or projecting piece of masonry strengthening a wall. **2** a spur of a mountain or mountain chain.

coun|ter|glow (koun′tər glō′), *n. Astronomy.* a patch of extremely faint light seen in the heavens near the apparent path of the sun (ecliptic) at a point exactly opposite to the sun; Gegenschein.

coun|ter|guard (koun′tər gärd′), *n.* a small, detached rampart in front of a bastion or the like, to protect it from being breached.

coun|ter|in|sur|gen|cy (koun′tər in sėr′jən sē), *n.* military action against guerrillas or other insurgents.

coun|ter|in|sur|gent (koun′tər in sėr′jənt), *n., adj.* —*n.* a person who engages in counterinsurgency.
—*adj.* of or having to do with counterinsurgency.

coun|ter|in|tel|li|gence (koun′tər in tel′ə jəns), *n.* the system or activity of counteracting the intelligence or spy activities of an enemy. Counterintelligence is generally carried on by a specially designated section of an army.

coun|ter|in|tu|i|tive (koun′tər in tü′ə tiv, -tyü′-), *adj.* running counter to intuition; not consistent with what one perceives intuitively: *Complex systems are counterintuitive. They behave in ways opposite to what most people expect* (Jay W. Forrester).

coun|ter|ir|ri|tant (koun′tər ir′ə tənt), *n.* **1** a medical application or agent used to produce irritation of the surface of the body, in order to counteract inflammation, irritation, or pain of deeper parts. **2** anything that serves a similar purpose: (*Figurative.*) *She afforded him no counterirritant* (George Eliot).

coun|ter|ir|ri|ta|tion (koun′tər ir′ə tā′shən), *n.* irritation artificially produced in order to counteract the action of disease or pain: *A mustard plaster produces counterirritation.*

coun|ter|man (koun′tər man′), *n., pl.* **-men.** a person who serves or works at a counter in a lunchroom or store.

coun|ter|mand (*v.* koun′tər mand′, -mänd′; *n.* koun′tər mand, -mänd), *v., n.* —*v.t.* **1** to withdraw or cancel (an order or command). **SYN:** revoke, stop, rescind, annul, void. **2** to recall or stop by a contrary order; order back.
—*n.* a command, order, or the like, revoking a previous one.
[< Old French *contremander* < *contre-* against (< Latin *contrā-*) + Latin *mandāre* to order]

coun|ter|march (koun′tər märch′), *n., v.* —*n.* **1** a march in the opposite direction; a march back. **2** a movement by which a marching group reverses its direction of march.
—*v.i.* **1** to march in the opposite direction; march back. **2** to execute a countermarch.
—*v.t.* to order or cause (a marching group) to countermarch.

coun|ter|mark (*n.* koun′tər märk′; *v.* koun′tər-märk′), *n., v.* —*n.* **1** an additional mark placed on something previously marked, as for greater security. **2** an artificial cavity made in the teeth of horses to disguise their age.
—*v.t.* to add a countermark to.

coun|ter|meas|ure (koun′tər mezh′ər, -mā′zhər), *n.* a measure or step to offset another; countermove.

coun|ter|mel|o|dy (koun′tər mel′ə dē), *n., pl.* **-dies.** an added or accompanying melody; counterpoint.

coun|ter|mine (*n.* koun′tər mīn′; *v.* koun′tər-mīn′), *n., v.,* **-mined, -min|ing.** —*n.* **1** a submarine mine intended to set off enemy mines prematurely. **2** an excavation dug by defenders of a fortress to intercept the excavation or mine dug by the besiegers. **3** *Figurative.* = counterplot.
—*v.i.* to make or place countermines.
—*v.t.* **1** to make or place countermines against; oppose or defeat by a countermine: *Captain Walker dropped depth charges which countermined a German torpedo as it was about to strike his ship* (Sunday Times). **2** *Figurative.* counterwork: *When sadness dejects me, ... I countermine it with another sadness* (John Donne).

coun|ter|mis|sile (koun′tər mis′əl), *n.* a missile designed to intercept and destroy another missile; anti-missile missile: *To determine the oncoming warhead's target and to launch a countermissile to destroy the warhead it is necessary to predict the trajectory of the enemy missile with great accuracy* (New York Herald Tribune).

coun|ter|move (koun′tər müv′), *n.* a contrary move; a move in opposition to another move.

coun|ter|move|ment (koun′tər müv′mənt), *n.* a movement in opposition to another.

coun|ter|mure (koun′tər myür), *n.* a wall raised within or behind another wall as a reserve defense. [< French *contre-mur* < *contre-* against (< Latin *contrā-*) + *mur* wall < Latin *mūrus*]

coun|ter|of|fen|sive (koun′tər ə fen′siv), *n.* an aggressive attack by a defending force against an attacking force.

coun|ter|of|fer (koun′tər of′ər), *n.* an offer or proposal calculated to surpass or offset another: *Salary offers and union counteroffers have highlighted the meetings* (Wall Street Journal).

coun|ter|pane (koun′tər pān′), *n.* an outer covering for a bed; bedspread. **SYN:** coverlet, quilt. [alteration of *counterpoint*[2]; influenced by *pane* coverlet]

coun|ter|part (koun′tər pärt′), *n.* **1** a person or thing closely resembling another: *She is the counterpart of her twin sister.* **SYN:** double, parallel. **2** a person or thing that complements or corresponds to another: *Night is the counterpart of day.* **3** a copy; duplicate. **SYN:** facsimile.

counterpart fund, a fund consisting of local currency deposited in a foreign country to the American government, in return for the dollars it is granted by the United States in foreign aid. Counterpart funds are usually spent within the aided countries to stimulate their economic recovery.

coun|ter|plan (koun′tər plan′), *n.* a plan to replace or defeat another plan.

coun|ter|plea (koun′tər plē′), *n. Law.* the reply of the plaintiff to the defendant's plea.

coun|ter|plot (koun′tər plot′), *n., v.,* **-plot|ted, -plot|ting.** —*n.* a plot to defeat another plot.
—*v.i.* to plot in opposition.
—*v.t.* to plot against (a plot or plotter).

coun|ter|point[1] (koun′tər point′), *n., v.* —*n.* **1** a melody added to another as an accompaniment. **2** the art of adding melodies to a given melody according to fixed rules. **3** the style of musical composition resulting from the way in which more or less individual melodies are combined according to fixed rules. **4** = polyphony. **5** a style of literary or dramatic composition which uses a number of themes running counter to one another, usually at different levels and from shifting points of view. **6** *Figurative.* any offsetting point or element; contrast: *Their white robes ... were a counterpoint to the predominant black of diplomats* (New York Times).
—*v.t.* to stress by the use of counterpoint or contrasts.
[< Middle French *contrepoint*]

coun|ter|point[2] (koun′tər point′), *n. Obsolete.* a coverlet for a bed; a counterpane. [< Old French *contrepointe,* earlier *cuiltepointe* a quilt stitched through < Latin *culcita puncta*]

coun|ter|poise (koun′tər poiz′), *n., v.,* **-poised, -pois|ing.** —*n.* **1** a weight balancing another weight; counterbalancing weight. **2** *Figurative.* any equal or opposing power or force. **3** the condition of being in balance; equilibrium: (*Figurative.*) *The ... two styles of mind ... are ever in counterpoise* (Emerson).
—*v.t.* to act as a counterpoise to; offset; counterbalance: (*Figurative.*) *A weakness which may counterpoise this merit* (Henry Fielding). **SYN:** compensate.
[< Old French *countrepeis* < *contre-* against (< Latin *contrā-*) + *peis* weight < Latin *pensum* < *pendere* weigh]

coun|ter|poi|son (koun′tər poi′zən), *n.* a poison used to counteract another poison; an antidote.

coun|ter|pres|sure (koun′tər presh′ər), *n.* an opposing pressure or force; counterforce.

coun|ter|pro|duc|tive (koun′tər prə duk′tiv), *adj.* producing results opposite to the desired or expected results: [*Terrorists*] *can only be moved to reconsider the role of violence if they are convinced it is tactically counterproductive* (Time).

coun|ter|prop|a|gan|da (koun′tər prop′ə gan′-də), *n.* propaganda designed to meet the threat of an idea with one favorable to the government.

coun|ter|pro|pos|al (koun′tər prə pō′zəl), *n.* a contrary proposal; counteroffer.

coun|ter|punch (koun′tər punch′), *n., v.* —*n.* a punch in return for another; counterblow.
—*v.i.* to deliver a counterpunch: *When psychoanalysis was first becoming the rage, James Thurber counterpunched with a delicious essay ... called "Leave Your Mind Alone"* (Wall Street Journal). —**coun′ter|punch′er,** *n.*

coun|ter|re|ac|tion (koun′tər rē ak′shən), *n.* a reaction following upon or opposing another reaction: *The Friday rebound ... was generally described as a counterreaction to the abnormal* *declines Thursday* (Wall Street Journal).

coun|ter|ref|or|ma|tion (koun′tər ref′ər mā′-shən), *n.* a reform movement opposed to a previous reform movement.

Counter Reformation, the reform movement within the Roman Catholic Church during the 1500's and early 1600's, designed to counter the effects of the Protestant Reformation.

coun|ter|rev|o|lu|tion (koun′tər rev′ə lü′shən), *n.* a revolution against a government established by a previous revolution.

coun|ter|rev|o|lu|tion|ar|y (koun′tər rev′ə lü′shə-ner′ē), *adj., n., pl.* **-ar|ies.** **—*adj.*** having to do with or of the nature of a counterrevolution.
—*n.* a person who takes part in or advocates a counterrevolution.

coun|ter|rev|o|lu|tion|ist (koun′tər rev′ə lü′shə-nist), *n.* a person who takes part in or advocates a counterrevolution.

coun|ter|ro|tate (koun′tər rō′tāt), *v.i.,* **-tat|ed, -tat|ing.** **1** to contrarotate: *counterrotating propellers.* **2** to rotate counterclockwise: *Cyclones counterrotate in the Northern Hemisphere.*
—coun′ter|ro|ta′tion, *n.*

coun|ter|scarp (koun′tər skärp′), *n.* the outer slope or wall of a moat or ditch in a fortification. [< French *contrescarpe*]

coun|ter|shad|ing (koun′tər shā′ding), *n. Zoology.* protective coloring characterized by the relatively darker coloration of an animal's exposed parts and lighter coloration of its shaded parts: *Countershading protects caterpillars against birds* (Scientific American).

coun|ter|shaft (koun′tər shaft′, -shäft′), *n.* a shaft that transmits motion from the main shaft to the working part of a machine.

coun|ter|sign (koun′tər sīn′), *n., v.* **—*n.*** **1a** a sign or signal used in reply to another sign. **b** *Military.* a password given in answer to the challenge of a sentinel: *The soldier had to give the countersign before he could pass the sentry.* **SYN:** watchword. **2** a signature added to another signature to confirm it. **SYN:** countersignature.
—*v.t.* **1** to sign (something already signed by another) to confirm it: *The check was signed by the treasurer and countersigned by the president.* **2** *Figurative: As to dictionaries, the Dean* [*Swift*] *writes of them, as if he supposed their contents were countersigned beyond the stars* (Fitzedward Hall).
[< French *contresigne*]

coun|ter|sig|na|ture (koun′tər sig′nə chər), *n.* **1** the act of countersigning. **2** a signature added to another person's signature to confirm it.

✱coun|ter|sink (koun′tər singk′), *v.,* **-sunk** (-sungk′), **-sink|ing,** *n.* **—*v.t.*** **1** to enlarge the upper part of (a hole) to make room for the head of a screw or bolt. **2** to sink the head of (a screw or bolt) into such a hole so that it is even with or below the surface.
—*n.* **1** a tool for countersinking holes. **2** a countersunk hole.

✱countersink
definition 2

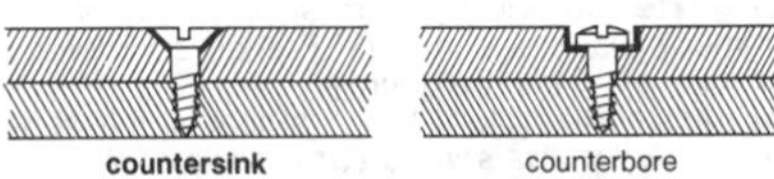

countersink counterbore

coun|ter|spy (koun′tər spī′), *n., pl.* **-spies.** a spy who works to uncover or oppose the activities of enemy spies, often by posing as one of them: *The diplomat, the first secretary of the Soviet embassy, engaged in espionage for nearly two years with an Australian woman who in reality was an Australian counterspy* (Wall Street Journal).

coun|ter|stroke (koun′tər strōk′), *n.* a stroke or blow given in return.

coun|ter|sub|ject (koun′tər sub′jikt), *n.* a melody composed in counterpoint to the subject and, in fugue, beginning usually with the entry of the second voice with the answer.

coun|ter|ten|or (koun′tər ten′ər), *n.* **1** an adult male voice, often falsetto, that is higher than the tenor and lower than the soprano or treble. **2** a singer who has such a voice. **3** a part for such a voice.

coun|ter|ter|ror|ism (koun′tər ter′ə riz əm), *n.* terrorism in reaction to or retaliation for some previous act of terrorism: *There is a fear that Communist terrorism will provoke rightist counterterrorism* (New York Times). **—coun′ter|ter′-ror|ist,** *n.*

coun|ter|thrust (koun′tər thrust′), *n.* a thrust made in opposition or return.

coun|ter|type (koun′tər tīp′), *n.* **1** an opposite type; a logical opposite. **2** a parallel type in another sphere; parallel.

coun|ter|vail (koun′tər vāl′, koun′tər vāl′), *v.t.* **1** to make up for; compensate; offset. **2** *Figurative.* to avail against; have force or be of effect against; counteract. **3** *Obsolete.* to be of equal force in opposition to. [< Anglo-French *countrevaloir* < *countre-* against (< Latin *contrā-*) + *valoir* < Latin *valēre* be of worth, be strong]

coun|ter|view (koun′tər vyü′), *n. Obsolete.* **1** a view from opposite sides or in opposite directions. **2** the position of two persons or things fronting each other.

coun|ter|vi|o|lence (koun′tər vī′ə ləns), *n.* violence in reaction to or retaliation for some violent act: *The violence ... exemplified by lynchings and other unlawful injuries, has provoked counterviolence in many quarters* (Earl Warren).

coun|ter|weigh (koun′tər wā′), *v.i.* to act as a counterpoise or equivalent weight (with or against). **—*v.t.*** to counterbalance; counterpoise.

coun|ter|weight (koun′tər wāt′), *n.* a weight that balances another weight; counterpoise.

coun|ter|weight|ed (koun′tər wā′tid), *adj.* having a counterweight.

coun|ter|word (koun′tər wėrd′), *n.,* or **counter word,** a word used widely and popularly without reference to its exact meaning, such as *terrific, wonderful, divine, ghastly,* or *classic.*

coun|ter|work (*n.* koun′tər wėrk′; *v.* koun′tər-wėrk′), *n., v.* **—*n.*** **1** a work in opposition to another work; opposing work or action. **2** any fortification erected to oppose or offset that of the enemy.
—*v.i.* to work in opposition.
—*v.t.* to work in opposition to; hinder or frustrate by contrary operations. **—coun′ter|work′er,** *n.*

count|ess (koun′tis), *n.* **1** the wife or widow of a count or an earl. **2** a lady whose rank is equal to that of a count or an earl. [< Old French *contesse* < Medieval Latin *comitissa,* feminine of Latin *comes, -itis;* see etym. under **count**[2]]

counting house, or **count|ing|house** (koun′-ting hous′), *n.* a building or office used for keeping accounts and doing business.

counting number, any whole number except 0. The next counting number after 99 is 100.

counting room, a room or office used as a counting house.

count|less (kount′lis), *adj.* too many to count; very many; innumerable: *the countless sands of the seashore, the countless stars.*

count noun, a noun which may form a plural. Count nouns usually refer to something countable and can be preceded by the articles *a* or *an.* Concrete nouns are usually count nouns. *Examples:* book, animal, dream.

count palatine, *Historical.* **1** (in Germany) a count who exercised supreme jurisdiction in his fief or province. **2** (originally) a count at the palace of the Holy Roman Empire, with high judicial authority.

coun|tri|fied (kun′trē fīd), *adj.* **1** looking or acting like a person from the country; rustic. **2** like the country; rural. **3** suitable for the country or rural living; rustic: *It is a pretty, slightly countrified bedroom pattern* (New Yorker). Also, **country-fied.** **—coun′tri|fied′ness,** *n.*

coun|try (kun′trē), *n., pl.* **-tries,** *adj.* **—*n.*** **1** land, region, or district: *The country around the mining town was rough and hilly.* **2a** all the land of a nation: *He came from France, a country across the sea.* **b** the people of a nation: *The whole country turned out to celebrate the holiday.* **c** the public, especially as a body of voters: *The country votes for a new President once every four years.* **3** the land where a person was born or where he is a citizen; native land: *The United States is his country. The people had no love for their country or for their king* (Macaulay). **4** land outside of cities and towns; rural district: *He likes the farms and fields of the country better than the tall buildings and busy streets of the city.* **5** a tract of land having more or less definite boundaries, especially natural boundaries, and inhabited by people of the same race, blood, or speech: *the country of the Macgregors* (Scott). **6** *Law.* a jury representing a person's neighbors or fellow countrymen, originally a jury chosen from the neighborhood (hundred): *for his trial put himself upon the country* (Homersham Cox). **7** *U.S. Informal.* country music: *The album is a blend of pure country, blues, rhythm and blues, and rock 'n' roll* (Saturday Review).
—*adj.* **1** of the country; in the country; rural: *He likes hearty country food and fresh country air.* **SYN:** rustic. **2** characteristic of the country: *country manners, country wit.* **SYN:** unpolished. **3** *Dialect.* of a particular country; of one's own country; native.

across (the) country, more or less directly from one point to another without regard to roads, railroad lines, etc.: *He was directed to hasten thither across the country* (Macaulay).

appeal (or **go**) **to the country,** *Especially British.* to hold a general election: *The Prime Minister, because his Government has been defeated on a major issue in the House of Commons, ... considers that the time has come for appealing to the country* (Sunday Times).
[< Old French *contree* < Vulgar Latin *contrāta* (*regiō*) (region) lying opposite < Latin *contrā* against]

coun|try-and-west|ern (kun′trē ən wes′tərn), *n.* a stylized form of country music, especially of the western United States, usually played with electric guitars.

country club, a club in the country near a city or suburb. It has a clubhouse and arrangements for outdoor sports. *His country club ... was billed on the tournament programs as the most beautiful in the world* (New Yorker).

country cousin, a countrified relative, often pleased but confused by things in the city.

country damage, damage to cotton, coffee, or other agricultural commodities, due to improper handling after shipment.

coun|try-dance (kun′trē dans′, -däns′), *n.* a dance of rural (or native) English origin in which partners face each other in two long lines; contredanse: *The Virginia reel is a country-dance. The term "square dance" is the American equivalent of the English "country-dance"* (London Times).

coun|try|fied (kun′trē fīd), *adj.* = countrified.

coun|try|folk (kun′trē fōk′), *n.pl.* people who live in the country.

country gentleman, a gentleman who lives on his estate in the country.

country house, a home in the country.

coun|try|like (kun′trē līk′), *adj., adv.* **—*adj.*** rural; rustic.
—*adv.* rurally; rustically.

coun|try|man (kun′trē mən), *n., pl.* **-men.** **1a** a man of one's own country: *Soldiers protect their countrymen.* **SYN:** compatriot. **b** a native or inhabitant of a particular region. **2** a man who lives in the country. **SYN:** rustic.

country mile, *Especially U.S. Informal.* a long way; very far: *You hit it like that and it'll go a country mile!* (Newsweek).

country music, **1** folk music, especially of the rural areas of the southern United States, played with the guitar, banjo, and other stringed instruments: *Today's rock* [*is*] *an outgrowth of rhythm and blues and country music* (Winthrop Sargeant). **2** = country-and-western.

coun|try|peo|ple (kun′trē pē′pəl), *n.pl.* **1** men and women living in the country. **2** *Obsolete.* compatriots.

country rock, **1** *Mining, Geology.* **a** the rock adjacent to a lode, vein of ore, or dike. **b** rock enclosing igneous material in any form. **2** a blend of country music and rock'n'roll.

coun|try|seat (kun′trē sēt′), *n.* a residence or estate in the country, especially a fine one; country house.

coun|try|side (kun′trē sīd′), *n.* **1** a rural district; country: *The countryside was bursting with the colors of spring.* **2a** a certain section of the country. **b** its people: *All the countryside is sure to be at the fair.*

country store, a store situated out in the country, usually carrying a varied assortment of goods.

coun|try|wide (kun′trē wīd′), *adj.* = nationwide.

coun|try|wom|an (kun′trē wům′ən), *n., pl.* **-wom|en.** **1** a woman of one's own country. **2** a woman who lives in the country.

count|ship (kount′ship), *n.* **1** the title or rank of a count. **2** the territory owned by or under the control of a count.

coun|ty[1] (koun′tē), *n., pl.* **-ties.** **1** one of the districts into which a state of the United States (except Louisiana and Alaska) is divided for purposes of local government. These purposes may include taxes, courts, public works and maintenance, education, and health regulation. The county is the political unit next below the state. *Abbr:* Co. **2** one of the districts into which Great Britain and Ireland are divided for administrative, judicial, and political purposes. The counties were formed as a result of historical events. **3** one of the larger divisions of land for administrative purposes in certain British Commonwealth countries. **4** the people of a county: *The county voted the measure down.* **5** the officials of a county. **6** the land of a county. **7** *Obsolete.* the domain or territory of a count. [< Anglo-French *counté* < *counte,* Old French *conte; see etym.* under **count**[2]]

coun|ty[2] (koun′tē), *n., pl.* **-ties.** *Obsolete.* count[2] (title). [< Anglo-French *counte,* Old French

Pronunciation Key: hat, āge, cãre, fär; let, ēqual, tėrm; it, īce; hot, ōpen, ôrder; oil, out; cup, pu̇t, rüle; child; long; thin; ᴛʜen; zh, measure;
ə represents **a** in about, **e** in taken, **i** in pencil, **o** in lemon, **u** in circus.

conte; see etym. under **count**²]

county agent, *U.S.* a government official who advises farmers and communities on agricultural matters.

county borough, (in England) a borough with a certain number of inhabitants (100,000 since 1958) which is administratively independent of the county in which it is situated.

county commissioner, *U.S.* (in some states) an officer elected to have administrative supervision over various county interests.

county council, (in England) the representative governing body of an administrative county, consisting of aldermen and councillors.

county court, **1** in the United States: **a** (in some states) an administrative body of a county. **b** *Law.* a court of justice with jurisdiction, usually, over one county. **2** in England: **a** a local civil court of justice, chiefly for the recovery of small debts. **b** *Historical.* a court held by the sheriff of a county for judicial or administrative purposes.

county fair, a fair, usually held once a year, at which the products of a county are displayed and competitions are held for first prizes in each product.

county farm, (formerly) a farm supported by a county, on which poor people were allowed to live and work.

county palatine, the land or jurisdiction of a count palatine.

county school, *British.* a school supported by a local community; council school.

county seat or **town**, the town or city where the government of a county is located.

coup¹ (kü), *n., pl.* **coups** (küz). **1** a sudden, brilliant action; unexpected, clever move; master stroke. **2** = coup d'état. **3** the act or practice by some American Indians, especially Plains Indians, of touching a live opponent with a stick (coup stick) in battle and moving on without killing him, as a feat of bravery.

count coup, to be the first among Indian warriors to touch an enemy with a coup stick: *Warriors who counted coups wore eagle feathers as signs of their courage.*

[< Old French *coup* < Late Latin *colpus* < Latin *colaphus* < Greek *kólaphos* a blow, slap]

coup² (kōp, küp), *v.i.* **1** *Scottish.* to upset, overturn, or tilt. **2** *Obsolete.* to strike; come to blows. —*v.t. Scottish.* **1** to upset; tilt. **2** to empty out. [perhaps variant of *cope*¹]

coup de fou|dre (kü' də fü'drə), *pl.* **coups de fou|dre** (kü' də fü'drə). *French.* **1** love at first sight. **2** a startling or shocking event. **3** (literally) thunderclap.

coup de grâce (kü' də gräs'), *pl.* **coups de grâce** (kü' də gräs'). **1** an action that gives a merciful death to a suffering animal or person, especially a shot to assure the instant death of a person who has been shot by a firing squad or the like. **2** *Figurative.* a finishing stroke: *If this is so, we are but one step and a half from a weapon which may well give the coup de grâce to the whole human race* (Norbert Wiener). [< French *coup de grâce* (literally) stroke of grace; see etym. under **coup**¹]

coup de main (kü' də maɴ'), *pl.* **coups de main** (kü' də maɴ'). **1** a sudden, unexpected attack with force, especially by an army. **2** *Figurative.* any sudden, forceful action. [< French *coup de main* (literally) stroke of hand; see etym. under **coup**¹]

coup de maî|tre (kü' də me'trə), *French.* a master stroke.

coup de poing (kü' də pwaɴ'), *pl.* **coups de poing** (kü' də pwaɴ'). a paleolithic core tool or hand ax. [< French *coup de poing* (literally) a blow with the fist]

coup de reins (kü' də raɴ'), *French.* **1** (in spearfishing) a quick dive in which the diver bends from the waist, snaps his legs straight into the air, and dives toward the fish. **2** (literally) a stroke in the back.

coup de so|leil (kü' də sô le'yə), *French.* sunstroke.

coup d'es|sai (kü' de se'), *French.* **1** an experimental piece; trial. **2** (literally) stroke of attempt.

coup d'é|tat (kü' dā tä'), *pl.* **coups d'é|tat** (kü' dā tä'), **coup d'é|tats** (kü' dā täz'). a sudden and decisive act in politics, usually bringing about a change of government unlawfully and by force: *It is nearly eight years since a coup d'état brought the present Government into power* (London Times). [< French *coup d'état* (literally) stroke of state; see etym. under **coup**¹]

coup de thé|â|tre (kü' də tā ä'trə), *French.* **1** a sensational turn or trick in a play: *The text exhibits in a high degree Verdi's weaknesses in mistaking coups de théâtre for drama* (London Times). **2** any sudden action that produces a sensational effect. **3** (literally) stroke of theater.

coup d'oeil (kü dœ'yə), *French.* **1** a view taken in at a brief glance: *He prides himself on his penetrating coup d'oeil, which makes him a master at rapid chess and crossword puzzles, and at sizing up situations* (New Yorker). **2** (literally) stroke of eye.

***cou|pé** (kü pā'; *also* küp *for 1*), *n.* **1** a closed, two-door automobile seating two or five people. **2** a four-wheeled, closed carriage with a seat for two people inside and a seat for the driver outside. **3** an end compartment, with a seat on only one side, in a European railroad car, now not commonly seen. [< French *coupé* past participle of *couper* cut < Old French < *coup;* see etym. under **coup**¹]

automobile

***coupé** definitions 1,2

carriage

coupe (küp), *n.* = coupé.

couped (küpt), *adj. Heraldry.* having the extremities of a head or limb cut off evenly so as not to touch the edges of the shield. [< obsolete *coup* to cut (< Old French *coup;* see etym. under **coup**¹) + *-ed*²]

cou|ple (kup'əl), *n., v.,* **-pled, -pling.** —*n.* **1a** two things of the same kind that go together; pair: *a couple of dice. He bought a couple of tires for his bicycle.* **SYN**: mates, couplet. See syn. under **pair. b** *Informal.* a small number; a few, usually two: *She will arrive in a couple of hours. Give me a couple of those apples—about four of them.* **2** a man and a woman who are married, engaged, or partners in a dance: *It is observed in old couples ... who have been housemates for a course of years, that they grow alike* (Emerson). **3** *Mechanics.* a pair of equal, parallel forces acting in opposite directions, and tending to produce rotation. **4** *Electricity.* a voltaic couple; thermocouple. **5** that which unites two.
—*v.t.* **1** to join together; join together in pairs: *The brakeman coupled two freight cars.* **2** *Informal.* to marry. **3** *Electricity.* to connect by a coupling.
—*v.i.* **1** to join in a pair; pair. **2** to copulate: *Begin these wood birds but to couple now?* (Shakespeare).

couples, a leash for holding two hounds together: *Hounds yelled in their couples* (Scott).
[< Old French *cople* < Latin *cōpula* bond. See etym. of doublet **copula.**]

▶ **Couple** means strictly two persons or things associated in some way: *a married couple.* In everyday speech *couple* is equivalent to the numeral *two: He borrowed a couple of pencils.* Sometimes *couple* means several but not many; a few: *Lend me a couple of dollars—four, to be exact.*

cou|pled (kup'əld), *adj.* **1** tied, joined together: *coupled hounds.* **2** placed near to one another or side by side, especially in pairs: *coupled windows, coupled columns.*

cou|ple|ment (kup'əl mənt), *n.* **1** a connecting device; coupling. **2** *Obsolete.* the act of coupling or fact of being coupled.

cou|pler (kup'lər), *n.* **1** a person or thing that couples. **2** a device used to join two railroad cars; coupling. **3** a device in a pipe organ for coupling keys or keyboards so that they can be played together. **4** a device used to connect electric circuits, such as a transformer that joins parts of a radio apparatus together by means of induction.

cou|ples (kup'əlz), *n.pl.* See under **couple.**

cou|plet (kup'lit), *n.* **1** two successive lines of poetry, especially two that rhyme and have the same number of feet. *Example:*

"Whose woods these are I think I know.
His house is in the village though."
(Robert Frost)

2 a couple; pair. [< Middle French *couplet* (diminutive) < *couple* couple < Old French *cople;* see etym. under **couple**]

***coupling** definition 3

***cou|pling** (kup'ling), *n.* **1** the act or process of joining together: *The coupling and uncoupling of railroad cars usually requires an engine.* **2** a device for joining together parts of machinery, such as the ends of shafts, especially in order to transmit motion. **3** a device used to join two railroad cars; coupler. **4** *Electricity.* **a** a device or arrangement for transferring electrical energy from one circuit to another. **b** the relation between two circuits resulting from such a device or arrangement. **5** the part of the body of a dog or horse between the hips and the shoulders.

coupling pin, a pin used in joining railroad cars and parts of machines.

cou|pon (kü'pon, kyü'-), *n.* **1a** a part of a ticket, advertisement, or package, that gives the person who holds it certain rights: *She saved the coupons from boxes of soap to get a free set of cups and saucers.* **b** a form for name and address to order goods or obtain information. **2** a printed statement of interest due on a bond that can be cut from the bond and presented for payment. [< Old French *coupon* piece cut off < *couper* to cut < *coup;* see etym. under **coup**¹]

coup stick (kü), a stick carried into battle by some American Indians with which the warrior tried to touch an opponent without killing him, as a mark of bravery. [< *coup*¹]

cour|age (kėr'ij), *n.* **1** bravery; meeting danger without fear; fearlessness: *Although blinded by the explosion, he faced the future with courage.* **2** *Obsolete.* heart; mind; disposition.

have the courage of one's convictions, to act as one believes one should: *He believed in the efficacy of the birch, and had the courage of his convictions* (Hall Caine).

[< Old French *corage* < *cuer* heart, ultimately < Latin *cor* heart]

—*Syn.* **1 Courage, bravery** mean fearlessness. **Courage** applies to moral strength that makes a person face any danger, trouble, or pain steadily and without showing fear: *The pioneer women faced the hardships of the westward trek with courage.* **Bravery** applies to a kind of courage that is shown by bold, fearless, daring action in the presence of danger: *They owed their lives to the bravery of the firemen.*

cou|ra|geous (kə rā'jəs), *adj.* fearless; brave; full of courage. **SYN**: valiant, dauntless, intrepid, plucky, valorous, heroic, daring, bold, hardy. See syn. under **brave.** —**cou|ra'geous|ly,** *adv.* —**cou|ra'geous|ness,** *n.*

cou|rante or **cou|rant** (kü ränt'), *n.* **1** a former European dance in triple time, characterized by a running or gliding step. **2a** a piece of music for or suited to this dance. **b** (later) a composition in triple time, regularly following the allemande as a movement of the suite. Also, **coranto.** [< French *courante* (literally) running (dance) < *courir* run < Latin *currere*]

cour d'hon|neur (kür' dô nœr'), *pl.* **cours d'hon|neur** (kür' dô nœr'). *French.* **1** the forecourt of a large and formal building. **2** (literally) court of honor.

cou|reur de bois (kü rœr' də bwä'), *pl.* **cou|reurs de bois** (kü rœr' də bwä'). a wandering woodsman, hunter, and trader in the early French settlements in Canada and adjoining parts of North America. [< French *coureur de bois*]

cour|gette (kür zhet'), *n. British.* a variety of summer squash; zucchini. [< French *courgette* (diminutive) < *courge* gourd]

cour|i|er (kėr'ē ər, kůr'-), *n.* **1** a special messenger: *A courier was sent to carry news of the expedition's successful attempt to climb the mountain. Government dispatches to their embassies were sent by couriers.* **2** a secret agent who transfers information to and from other agents. **3** a person who goes with a group of travelers and takes care of hotel reservations, tickets, etc. [< Middle French *courrier* < Italian *corriere* < *correre* run < Latin *currere*]

cour|lan (kůr'lən), *n.* = limpkin. [< French *courlan* < a native word]

course (kôrs, kōrs), *n., v.,* **coursed, cours|ing.** —*n.* **1** onward movement; forward progress; advance: (*Figurative.*) *the course of events. They slackened their course* (Samuel Johnson). (*Figurative.*) *Our history book traces the course of man's development from the cave to modern city living.* **2** the direction taken, especially by a ship or aircraft, often expressed in degrees: *Our course was straight to the north. The Hispaniola ... sailed a course that would just clear the island on the east* (Robert Louis Stevenson). **3** *Figurative.* a line of action; way of doing; procedure: *The only sensible course was to go home. You must take the course that leads to success.* **SYN**: process, method, mode. **4** a way, path, track, or channel: *the winding course of a stream.* **SYN**: road, passage. **5** a number of like things arranged in some regular order: *a course of lectures on first aid.* **SYN**: succession, sequence. **6** *Figurative.* regular order: *The course of nature decrees that spring follows winter. Mother gets little rest in the course of her daily work.* **7a** a series of studies in a school, college, or university.

A student must complete a certain course in order to graduate. **b** one of the studies in such a series: *Each course in geography lasts one term.* **8** a part of a meal served at one time: *The first course was chicken soup.* **9** a place for races or games: *a golf course, a race course.* **10** a row of brick or stone in a wall. SYN: row, layer. **11** the pursuit of game with hounds. **12** *Historical.* a charge of two combatants, as in a tournament: *We ran our course, my charger fell* (Scott). **13** *Archaic.* a race.
—*v.i.* **1** to race; run; flow swiftly: *The blood courses through the arteries. Tears coursing down her cheeks.* **2** to run in hunting with hounds or in a tournament. **3** to follow a course; direct one's course.
—*v.t.* **1** to run through or over; traverse: *Tears coursed his burning cheek* (Robert Southey). **2** to run after; chase; pursue. **3** to hunt (game) with dogs, especially by sight and not by scent. **4** to cause (dogs) to hunt for game.
a course of sprouts, *Informal.* severe discipline or training: *He put ... [the dogs] through a course of sprouts which ultimately developed brilliant though erratic working qualities* (Outing).
courses, a the points of the compass: *Lay her two courses to the wind.* **b** the menstrual discharge; menses.
in due course, at the proper or usual time; after a while: *I'll attend to you in due course.*
in the course of, during; in the process of: *He mentioned you a few times in the course of our discussion.*
lay a course, *Nautical.* to lie or sail in a certain direction without being obliged to tack: *A ship "lays her course" when, being close-hauled, the wind permits the desired course to be steered* (Lewis R. Hamersly).
of course, a surely; certainly: *Of course you can go! It would be easy, of course, to exaggerate this truth of the continuity of history into a falsehood* (Mark Pattison). **b** naturally; as should be expected: *She gave me a gift, and, of course, I accepted it. She made some very particular inquiries about my people which, of course, I was unable to answer* (John Hunter).
run one's course, a to be completed: *Once a fight starts, it must run its course unless it is stopped by outside interference* (Listener). **b** to come to an end: *This is gratifying assurance that the Camp fad ... has finally run its course* (Saturday Night).
[< Old French *cours* or *curs* < Latin *cursus, -ūs* < *currere* run; and < French *course* < Italian *corsa* a running, ultimately < Latin *currere*]

cours|er[1] (kôr′sər, kōr′-), *n.* **1** a person who practices the sport of coursing. **2** a dog for coursing. **3** *Archaic.* **a** a swift horse: *Nor any coursers like a page of prancing poetry* (Emily Dickinson). **b** a large powerful horse ridden in battle or in a tournament; charger. **c** any similar swift animal ridden or driven: *More rapid than eagles his coursers they flew, With a sleighful of toys and St. Nicholas, too!* (Clement Clarke Moore). [< Old French *coursier* < *cours* a running; see etym. under **course**]

cours|er[2] (kôr′sər, kōr′-), *n.* any one of certain birds related to and resembling the plovers and noted for swift running, native to Africa and Asia, but occasionally found in Europe. [< New Latin *Cursorius* the genus name < Latin *cursōrius* (literally) adapted to running, ultimately < *currere* run]

cours|es (kôr′siz, kōr′-), *n.pl.* See under **course.**

course|ware (kôrs′wãr′, kōrs′-), *n.* instructional materials designed for or stored in computers: *More than 2,000 users were preparing new courseware to use with or add to the PLATO-course catalogue* (Science News). [< *course* + (soft)*ware*]

cours|ing (kôr′sing, kōr′-), *n.* **1** the act of a person or thing that courses. **2** the sport of pursuing game, with greyhounds following by sight.

court (kôrt, kōrt), *n., v., adj.* —*n.* **1a** a place where justice is administered: *The prisoner was brought to court for trial.* **b** the persons who administer justice; judge or judges: *The court found him guilty.* **c** an assembly of such persons to administer justice: *Several cases await trial at the next court. Court is now in session.* **d** a session of a judicial body: *Superior Court will convene at ten o'clock. Abbr:* Ct. **2a** the place where a king, emperor, or other sovereign lives; royal palace. **b** the family, household, or followers of a king, emperor, or other sovereign: *The court of King Solomon was noted for its splendor.* **3a** a sovereign and his advisers as a ruling body or power: *"By order of the Court of St. James" is by order of the British government.* **b** an assembly held by a king, emperor, or other sovereign: *The queen held court to hear from her advisers.* **4** *Sports.* **a** a place marked off for a game: *a tennis court, a basketball court.* **b** one of the divisions of such a place: *the service court.* **5a** a short street, built around with houses. **b** *Obsolete.* a building or group of buildings in a courtyard; manorial house (now only in place names). **6a** a space without a roof, partly or wholly enclosed by walls or buildings: *The four apartment houses were built around a court of grass.* SYN: yard, courtyard. **b** a section or subdivision of the area of an exhibition building, a museum, or the like, open above (to the general roof). SYN: yard, courtyard. **7** the body of qualified members of a corporation or its managing board, or the meeting of such a body. **8** attention paid to get favor; effort to please.
—*v.t.* **1** to seek the favor of; try to please: *The nobles courted the king to get positions of power.* **2** to pay loving attention to; woo: *The young man courted the girl by bringing her flowers every day.* **3** *Figurative.* to try to get; seek: *to court applause. It is foolish to court danger.* SYN: invite. **4** to hold out inducements to: *Their representative courted the committee in charge of franchises with free trips and other gifts.* SYN: solicit, allure, attract.
—*v.i.* to pay loving attention; woo: *Long ago I have forgot to court* (Shakespeare).
—*adj.* of or belonging to a royal court; designed for use in a court: *a court beauty, court dress, court manners.*
out of court, a without the aid or sponsorship of a law court: *The lawsuit was settled privately by the two parties out of court.* **b** beyond or without claim to consideration: *The men who broke up the meeting put themselves out of court with public opinion.*
pay court to, a to pay attention to (a person) to get his favor; try to please: *He went to pay his court to the king.* **b** to pay loving attention to in order to marry; woo: *Many young men came to pay court to his daughter.*
[< Old French *cort* < Latin *cohors, -hortis* enclosure; cohort; retinue. See etym. of doublet **cohort.**]

court-bar|on (kôrt′bar′ən, kōrt′-), *n.* an English manorial court, now nearly extinct, presided over by the lord, or his steward, and having jurisdiction over disputes between tenants, local misdemeanors, and the like.

court bouillon, 1 a rich soup containing wine. **2** a stock for boiling fish, made from water and herbs.

court card, the king, queen, or jack of any suit of playing cards; a coat card; face card.

court cupboard, a kind of cabinet or sideboard with shelves, formerly used for the display of china.

court dance, 1 a formal and elaborate dance, as those performed at royal courts **2** music for it.

court dress, the costume at court and on other state occasions.

cour|te|ous (kėr′tē əs), *adj.* thoughtful of others; polite: *It was courteous of him to help the old lady with her bundles.* SYN: civil, urbane, deferential, obliging, gracious, affable. See syn. under **polite.** [Middle English *courteis* < Old French *corteis* < *cort;* see etym. under **court**] —**cour′te|ous|ly,** *adv.* —**cour′te|ous|ness,** *n.*

cour|te|san (kôr′tə zən, kōr′-, kėr′-), *n.* a prostitute at a court or among the nobility or wealthy classes. Also, **courtezan.** [< Middle French *courtisane* < Italian *cortigiana* (literally) woman of the court < *corte,* ultimately < Latin *cohors;* see etym. under **court**]

cour|te|sy (kėr′tə sē), *n., pl.* **-sies. 1** polite behavior; thoughtfulness for others: *Giving one's seat to a lady in a crowded bus is a sign of courtesy. There is always time enough for courtesy* (Emerson). *As surely as courage was Igaya's hallmark on skis, courtesy was his salient quality at all other times* (Newsweek). SYN: politeness, civility, courteousness, urbanity, complaisance. **2** a kindness; courteous act or expression; polite act: *Thanks for all your courtesies.* SYN: indulgence. **3** = curtsy.
by (or **of**) **courtesy,** as a favor or compliment, rather than as something rightfully owing: *The furniture for the play was supplied by courtesy of Blank Brothers. The title of Lord is only given of courtesy to the younger son of a duke.*
[< Old French *cortesie* < *corteis;* see etym. under **courteous**]

courtesy book, a manual of courtly manners and duties, such as one used by young noblemen in the Middle Ages and the Renaissance.

courtesy call, a short, formal visit paid by one government official or dignitary on another as an act of courtesy or etiquette: *Less than twelve hours after the mission's arrival here from Jeddah, [the] British High Commissioner ... threw normal colonial protocol to the winds and paid a courtesy call upon the mission* (Sunday Times).

courtesy car, an automobile, often chauffeured, which is made available by a hotel, business firm, or other organization to guests, customers, or visitors: *Bass River Marina ... provides six courtesy cars for local sightseeing or jaunts into Atlantic City* (Wall Street Journal).

courtesy card, a card issued by a hotel, store, bank, or other business establishment, entitling the bearer to certain privileges, such as reduced prices or rates.

courtesy flag, the national flag of the country a merchant ship visits, hoisted as the ship enters port.

courtesy light, a light inside an automobile which goes on when a door is opened.

courtesy title, *British.* a title given by social custom but having no legal validity, as to younger children of dukes and earls.

cour|te|zan (kôr′tə zən, kōr′-, kėr′-), *n.* = courtesan.

court hand, a style of handwriting formerly used in law courts and public records in England.

court|house (kôrt′hous′, kōrt′-), *n.* **1** a building where law courts are held. **2** a building used for the government of a county. It usually houses a court. **3** *U.S., especially Southern.* a county seat.

cour|ti|er (kôr′tē ər, kōr′-), *n.* **1** a person often present at the court of a king, prince, emperor, or other ruler; court attendant. **2** a person who tries to win the favor of another by flattering and pleasing him: *He played the courtier to the social arbiters of the city.* —**cour′ti|er|ship,** *n.*

cour|ti|er|ly (kôr′tē ər lē, kōr′-), *adj.* like a courtier; courtly.

court-leet (kôrt′lēt′, kōrt′-), *n.* an English court, now nearly extinct, held before a lord or his steward, and having jurisdiction over petty offenses and the civil affairs of its district. [< *court* + Anglo-French *lete* (origin uncertain)]

court|ly (kôrt′lē, kōrt′-), *adj.,* **-li|er, -li|est,** *adv.* —*adj.* **1** having manners fit for a king's court; polite, elegant, or polished: *The courtly gentleman was a favorite with the ladies.* SYN: refined, dignified, ceremonious. **2** trying hard to please one's superior; flattering. **3** disposed to favor or be subservient to a royal court.
—*adv.* in the manner or style of a royal court; in courtly fashion. —**court′li|ness,** *n.*

court-mar|tial (kôrt′mär′shəl, kōrt′-), *n., pl.* **courts-mar|tial** or **court-mar|tials,** *v.,* **-tialed, -tial|ing** or (*especially British*) **-tialled, -tial|ling.**
—*n.* **1** a military court for trying offenders against the laws of the armed forces: *The court-martial was made up of six officers.* **2** a trial by a military court: *The soldier's court-martial for disobedience was placed on his record.*
—*v.t.* to try by a military court: *... a remark which got him court-martialed for insubordination* (Newsweek).

court of appeals, = appellate court.

Court of Cassation, the highest court of appeal in France.

Court of Claims, *U.S.* **1** = United States Claims Court. **2** (in some states) a county court charged with the financial business of the county.

Court of Common Pleas, 1 (formerly, in England) a court for the trial of civil actions, one of the three superior courts of common law. **2** (in some states of the United States) an intermediate court with civil and criminal jurisdiction.

court of domestic relations, a court that may decide legal issues between members of a family; domestic relations court.

Court of Honor, 1 the planning or governing body of a group of boy scouts, girl scouts, or girl guides, consisting of patrol leaders, elected officers, and adult leaders. **2** a session of this court, especially held for awarding honors.

court of inquiry, a military court which investigates any accusation or imputation against an officer or soldier of the army.

court of law, a place where justice is administered; law court.

court of record, a court whose judgments are kept on permanent record and represent the law until revised by special writs.

Court of Session, the supreme civil tribunal of Scotland, established in 1532.

Court of St. James or **Court of St. James's,** the court of the British sovereign. It gets its name from St. James's Palace in London, where royal receptions were formerly held.

court order, an order issued by a court of law, enjoining someone to do or refrain from doing something; injunction: *Briggs seeks a court order to halt Crane's purchases of its stock* (Wall Street Journal).

court plaster, thin cloth with a sticky substance (usually isinglass and glycerin) on one side, used for covering slight cuts. [because formerly used as face patches by ladies at court]

Pronunciation Key: hat, āge, cãre, fär; let, ēqual, tėrm; it, īce; hot, ōpen, ôrder; oil, out; cup, pu̇t, rüle; child; long; thin; ᴛʜen; zh, measure; ə represents **a** in about, **e** in taken, **i** in pencil, **o** in lemon, **u** in circus.

court reporter, a stenographer who records the testimony given at a trial or other legal proceeding. He records every word spoken except proceedings the judge indicates should be omitted from the record.

court|room (kôrt′rüm′, kōrt′-; -rům′), *n.* a room where a law court is held.

court|ship (kôrt′ship, kōrt′-), *n.* **1a** the condition or time of courting in order to marry; wooing: *The brief courtship was a very happy one.* **b** the courting or wooing of a female animal. **2** solicitation, as of favors. **3** *Obsolete.* **a** courtly manners or behavior. **b** flattery. **4** *Obsolete.* the paying of court, as to a dignitary.

court tennis, an indoor game in which a ball is hit back and forth over a low net and may be bounced off the walls during play. It is played on an enclosed court, as distinguished from lawn tennis.

court|yard (kôrt′yärd′, kōrt′-), *n.* a space enclosed by walls in or near a large building.

cous|cous (küs′küs′), *n.* a North African dish consisting of steamed coarse ground wheat served with meat and broth. [< French *couscous* < Arabic *kuskus*]

cous|in (kuz′ən), *n.* **1** the son or daughter of one's uncle or aunt. First cousins have the same grandparents; second cousins have the same great-grandparents; and so on for third and fourth cousins. The children of brothers and sisters are called *cousins, cousins-german, first cousins,* or *full cousins;* children of first cousins are called *second cousins.* **2a** a distant relative. **b** (formerly, frequently) a nephew or niece. **c** *Law.* (formerly) the next of kin, including ancestors and descendants more remote than parent or child. **3** a citizen of a related nation: *The British, Canadians, and Americans might be called cousins.* **4** *Figurative.* a person or thing having affinity of nature to another: *That renegade is first cousin to a rattlesnake.* **5** a term used by one sovereign in speaking to another sovereign or to a great nobleman. [< Old French *cousin, cosin* < Latin *cōnsōbrīnus* mother's sister's child < *com-* together + *soror* sister]

cous|in|age (kuz′ə nij), *n.* **1** the condition of being cousins; kinship: *A mixed group of photographs ... reveal affinities and cousinages previously unsuspected* (Sunday Times). **2** cousins collectively; family; kinfolk: *On one page we are back in* [*his*] *New York boyhood, a welter of cousinage* (New York Times).

cous|in-ger|man (kuz′ən jėr′mən), *n., pl.* **cous|ins-ger|man.** a son or daughter of one's uncle or aunt; first cousin. [< Old French *cousin-germain.* Compare etym. under **cousin, german**[1].]

cous|in|hood (kuz′ən hu̇d), *n.* **1** the relation of a cousin or cousins. **2** cousins or kinsfolk collectively.

cous|in-in-law (kuz′ən in lô′), *n., pl.* **cous|ins-in-law. 1** the cousin of one's husband or wife. **2** the husband or wife of one's cousin.

Cousin Jack, a nickname for a Cornishman. [because of the common use of *cousin* as a familiar form of address in *Cornwall*]

cous|in|ly (kuz′ən lē), *adj., adv.* **—*adj.* 1** like a cousin; like a cousin's. **2** suitable for a cousin. **—*adv.*** in the manner of a cousin.

cous|in|ry (kuz′ən rē), *n.* cousins collectively; kinsfolk.

cous|in|ship (kuz′ən ship), *n.* the relationship of a cousin or cousins.

cou|teau (kü tō′), *n., pl.* **-teaux** (-tōz′). a knife, especially a large knife with two edges, used as a weapon. [< French *couteau*]

coûte que coûte (küt′kəküt′), *French.* cost what it may.

couth[1] (küth), *adj.* refined; sophisticated; graceful: *He has a couth and cultured wife* (Time). [back formation < *uncouth*] **—couth′ness,** *n.*

couth[2] (küth), *v., adj.* **—*v.*** *Obsolete.* a past tense and past participle of **can.**
—*adj.* 1 *Obsolete.* known; well-known; familiar. **2** *Scottish.* couthie.
[Old English *cūth,* past participle of *cunnan* can]

couth|ie (kü′thē), *adj. Scottish.* friendly or sociable; kind or pleasant. Also, **couthy.** [Middle English *couth* pleasant (Old English *cūth* known, familiar) + *-ie*]

couth|y (kü′thē), *adj. Scottish.* couthie.

cou|ture (kü tůr′; *French* kü tγr′), *n.* **1** dressmaking and fashion designing. **2** dressmakers and fashion designers. [< French *couture* < Old French; see etym. under **couturier**]

cou|tu|ri|er (kü tůr′ē ər; *French* kü tγ ryā′), *n.* a man dressmaker or designer of dresses. [< French *couturier,* Old French, a tailor < *couture* a sewing, seam, ultimately < Latin *cōnsuere* sew < *com-* together + *suere* sew]

cou|tu|rière (kü tγ ryer′), *n.* a woman dressmaker or designer of dresses: *Elsa Schiaparelli, Paris couturière and mainstay of international fashions* (Newsweek). [< French *couturière,* feminine of *couturier;* see etym. under **couturier**]

cou|vade (kü väd′), *n.* a practice among some primitive peoples by which, at the birth of a child, the father takes to bed and performs other acts natural to the mother rather than to the father: *When a man in a primitive culture like the Carib is asked why he practices couvade ... he replies that it has always been done* (Ogburn and Nimkoff). [< obsolete French *couvade* (literally) a hatching, brood < *couver,* Old French *cover* to brood; see etym. under **covey**]

co|va|lence (kō vā′ləns), *n. Chemistry.* **1** the total of the pairs of electrons which one atom can share with surrounding atoms. **2** the ability to form a bond in which two atoms share a pair of electrons. **3** the bond thus formed.

co|va|len|cy (kō vā′lən sē), *n., pl.* **-cies.** = covalence.

co|va|lent (kō vā′lənt), *adj.* of or having to do with covalence. **—co|va′lent|ly,** *adv.*

co|var|i|ance (kō vãr′ē əns), *n. Statistics.* the average value of the product of the deviations of two variables from their respective average values.

co|var|i|ant (kō vãr′ē ənt), *adj. Mathematics, Statistics.* varying with another quantity in such a way that the relationship between the two quantities remain proportionally the same.

cove[1] (kōv), *n., v.,* **coved, cov|ing. —*n.* 1** a small bay; mouth of a creek; inlet on the shore. See picture under **bay**[1]. **2** a sheltered place; nook. **3a** a sheltered place among hills or woods: *The bandits hid in a cove deep in the hills.* **b** *U.S. Dialect.* a gap or pass. **4** *Architecture.* any concave molding or member, often of large dimensions, such as the surface of a vault or a hollow curve between a wall and ceiling; a concavity.
—*v.t., v.i.* to arch or vault, especially to arch (a ceiling) at its junction with the wall.
[Old English *cofa* chamber]

cove[2] (kōv), *n. British Slang.* a person; fellow. [< Romany *kova* that man]

coved (kōvd), *adj.* forming an arch; arched; curving; concave: *The mosques and other buildings of the Arabians are rounded into domes and coved roofs* (Henry Swinburne).

co|vel|line (kō vel′in, -īn), *n.* a mineral, a native sulfide of copper, usually occurring in masses of an indigo-blue color. *Formula:* CuS [< Niccolò *Covelli,* 1790-1829, an Italian mineralogist + *-ine*[1]]

co|vel|lite (kō vel′īt), *n.* = covelline.

cov|en (kuv′ən), *n.* **1** a gathering of witches, especially of a group of thirteen witches: *It* [*book*] *treats of sorcery and midnight covens in a jolly matter-of-fact manner* (Punch). **2** any gathering or assembly. [variant of obsolete *covent* convent; see etym. under **convent**[1]]

cov|e|nant (kuv′ə nənt), *n., v.* **—*n.* 1** a solemn agreement between two or more persons or groups; compact: *The rival nations signed a covenant to reduce their armaments.* SYN: contract. **2** *Law.* **a** a formal agreement that is legal, especially one under seal; legal contract. **b** a particular clause of agreement forming part of the same sealed instrument. **c** (in common law) the action taken for recovery of damages when a sealed agreement or contract is broken. **3** a solemn agreement between a church's members, such as one for maintaining its faith. **4** (in the Bible) the solemn promises of God to man as set forth in the Old and New Testament; compact between God and man: *He hath remembered his covenant for ever* (Psalms 105:8).
—*v.t.* to agree solemnly (to do certain things). SYN: stipulate.
—*v.i.* to enter into a covenant or formal agreement.
[< Old French *covenant,* present participle of *covenir* < Latin *convenīre* < *com-* together + *venīre* come]

Cov|e|nant (kuv′ə nənt), *n.* any of certain bonds of agreement signed by the Scottish Presbyterians for the defense and furtherance of their religion.

cov|e|nant|ed (kuv′ə nən tid), *adj.* holding a position, situation, or condition, under a covenant or contract.

cov|e|nan|tee (kuv′ə nən tē′), *n.* the person to whom a promise by covenant is made.

cov|e|nant|er (kuv′ə nən tər), *n.* a person who makes a solemn agreement: [*The*] *grandson of the original covenanter ... believed a court should rule on the validity of the covenant* (New York Times).

Cov|e|nan|ter (kuv′ə nən tər, kuv′ə nan′-), *n.* a person who signed and supported either of the Covenants of the Scottish Presbyterians in the 1600's.

cov|e|nan|tor (kuv′ə nən tər), *n.* a person by whom a promise by covenant is made.

Cov|ent Garden (kuv′ənt, kov′-), **1** a famous flower and vegetable market district in London, formerly the garden of a convent. **2** a famous theater in this district, originally built in 1731, now the Royal Opera House.

Cov|en|try (kuv′ən trē, kov′-), *n.*
be in Coventry, to be ostracized or ignored: *I'm in social Coventry through leaving the receiver off* (Punch).
send to Coventry, to refuse to associate with: *When ... his neighbours learnt what he had been doing, he and his family were threatened and sent to Coventry by many of them* (Manchester Guardian Weekly).
[< *Coventry,* a city in central England, where Royalists were imprisoned during the Civil War]

cov|er (kuv′ər), *v., n.* **—*v.t.* 1** to put something over: *Pull the shade to cover the window. Cover this sleeping child with your coat. Cover this box with a wide board.* **2** to be over; occupy the surface of; spread over: *She covered the cake with icing. Snow covered the ground.* **3a** to clothe; wrap up: *People in the Arctic cover themselves with furs.* SYN: envelop. **b** *Figurative.* to invest (oneself or one's reputation): *He covered himself with glory.* **4** to be thick over: *Dust covered his clothes.* **5** *Figurative.* to hide; conceal: *Do not try to cover a mistake. He laughed to cover his anxiety.* SYN: screen, cloak, shroud. **6** to protect; shelter: *Our insurance covers our belongings against loss by fire. The cave covered him from the snow.* **7** to go over; travel: *The travelers covered 400 miles a day by car.* **8** *Figurative.* to include; take in: *The review covered everything we learned before Christmas.* **9** to be enough; provide for: *My allowance covers my lunch at school.* **10** *Sports.* **a** to stand behind; support: *The shortstop covered the second baseman in case he missed the ball.* **b** to guard (an opponent); defend (a position): *to cover the goal in soccer.* **11** to aim straight at: *He covered the animal with a rifle.* **12** *Military.* **a** to have within range: *The guns of the fort on the hill covered the territory around it.* **b** to protect (a soldier, policeman, position, etc.) from attack while maneuvering by watching for and being ready to fire at any enemy or attacker who appears. **c** to form or align in a straight file behind (men in front); align or order (troops) to align in straight files (off). **13a** to have as one's territory or sphere of work: *a salesman covering Ohio.* **b** to extend over; occupy: *a ranch covering a thousand acres.* **14** to put one's hat or cap on: *Cover your head when you are in the sun.* **15** to report or photograph (events, meetings, or the like): *The reporter covered the fire for his newspaper.* **16a** to deposit the equivalent of (money deposited in betting); accept the conditions of (a bet): *If you bet a dollar, I'll cover it.* **b** (in card games) to play a higher card than (the highest card previously played). **17** to buy (commodities or securities) for future delivery as protection against loss when the market rises. **18** (of a bird) to brood or sit on (eggs or chicks). **19** (of a male animal) to copulate with (the female).
—*v.i.* 1 to act as a substitute: *Please cover for me at the counter for a few minutes.* **2** to make excuses; protect by making excuses (for): *The drug addict's family kept covering for him.* **3** *Military.* to form or be in a straight file behind those in front.
—*n.* 1 something that covers: *the cover of a book. A box, can, or jar usually has a cover.* SYN: lid, top, case, wrapping. **2a** protection; shelter; something that hides, conceals, or screens: *We took cover in an old shed during the storm. A thicket makes good cover for animals to hide in.* (*Figurative.*) *The burglar escaped under the cover of darkness.* (*Figurative.*) *The spy's cover was to act as a bartender.* SYN: refuge, retreat. **b** vegetation considered as providing protection for smaller plants from the sun, severe weather, or other extremes. **c** a hiding place for game; covert. **3** funds adequate to cover or meet a liability or secure against possible loss. **4** a place for one person at a table, set with a plate, knife, fork, spoon, napkin, and glass. **5** in philately: **a** an envelope or wrapper with stamp and any postal markings affixed. **b** a letter addressed on the reverse side after folding to form an envelope. **6** the part of a shingle, slate, or tile, on a roof that is hidden by the lapping of the one above, the exposed part being called the *margin.* **7** a substitute; understudy: *The "cover" of the house had already been onstage, playing a different role* (Harper's). **8** = cover charge. **9** coverage: *a 25 per cent gold cover of paper money.* **10** *Cricket.* cover-point.

break cover, to come out in the open: *To reach the farmhouse the soldiers had to break cover and run across a field.*

cover up, a to cover completely: *Often ... feeling cold after having kicked off the bedclothes, he would say in his sleep: "Tom, cover me up"* (W. M. Thayer). **b** *Figurative.* to hide; conceal: *Göring and Hitler agreed to cover up the facts and used the incident to help "justify" the ruth-*

less Nazi invasion of the Low Countries (Newsweek).

from cover to cover, from the first page to the last; from beginning to end: *I read the book from cover to cover.*

under cover, a hidden; secret; disguised: *He kept his activities under cover.* **b** secretly: *The spies met their contacts under cover.*

[< Old French *covrir* < Latin *cooperīre* < *co-* (intensive) + *operīre* cover] —**cov′er|er,** *n.* —**cov′er|less,** *adj.*

cov|er|age (kuv′ər ij, -ə rij), *n.* **1** the risks covered by an insurance policy: *He has fire and theft coverage on his store.* **2** the amount of funds held to meet liabilities: *a 60 per cent gold coverage of paper money.* **3a** the scope and manner of presenting information by a reporter, newspaper, or the like: *The President's inauguration got broad coverage from all the radio and television stations. His coverage of the African situation was unbiased and complete.* **b** the section of the buying public presumably reached by a given advertising campaign, medium, or other exposure: *The network will "have the coverage to become extremely competitive" by late this fall* (Wall Street Journal).

***cov|er|all** (kuv′ər ôl′), *n.* **1** Often, **coveralls.** a work garment that includes shirt and trousers in a single piece of clothing. It resembles overalls but with sleeves. **2** an apron which covers all of a dress, front and back.

***coverall**
definition 1

cover charge, a charge made in some restaurants for service and entertainment in addition to the charge for food.

cover crop, a crop sown in a field or orchard to protect the soil from erosion, especially in winter, and provide humus when the crop is plowed under.

cov|ered (kuv′ərd), *adj.* **1** having a cover or covering: *a covered walk.* **2** wearing one's hat or cap.

***covered bridge,** a bridge protected from the weather by a shed or cover, usually of wood.

***covered bridge**

covered smut, a fungous disease of barley and other grains, in which spores enclosed in the glumes develop smut balls.

***covered wagon, 1** a wagon having an arched canvas cover that can be taken off, especially a prairie schooner. **2** *British.* a boxcar.

Conestoga wagon

***covered wagon**
definition 1
prairie schooner

covered way, an open corridor running along the top of the counterscarp around the outworks, covered from the enemy's fire by a parapet or embankment.

cover girl, an attractive girl or woman whose picture is used on the cover of a magazine.

cover glass, a piece of thin glass used to cover a microscopic preparation on a slide; coverslip.

cov|er|ing (kuv′ər ing), *n.* **1** anything that covers, such as a cloth to spread over something, clothing, or an outer coating: *A blanket is a bed covering.* **2** the buying of commodities or securities previously sold short, as a protection against loss when the market rises: *Brokers reported that some of the buying resulted from covering by speculators who had previously sold short* (Wall Street Journal).

covering letter or **note,** a letter or note accompanying or following a package or another letter, explaining or confirming its contents.

cov|er|let (kuv′ər lit), *n.* **1** an outer covering for a bed; bedspread. **2** any covering. [Middle English *coverlite,* apparently < Old French *covrir* (see etym. under **cover**) + *lit* bed < Latin *lectus*]

Cov|er|ley (kuv′ər lē), *n.* **Sir Roger de, 1** an amiable country squire belonging to the imaginary club in Joseph Addison's *Spectator.* **2** an English country-dance.

cov|er|lid (kuv′ər lid), *n.* = coverlet.

cov|er-point (kuv′ər point′), *n.* in cricket and lacrosse: **1** a position near point. **2** the player stationed at this position.

covers (no period), coversed sine.

co|versed sine (kō′vėrst), *Trigonometry.* the versed sine of the complement of a given angle or arc. *Abbr:* covers (no period).

cov|er|slip (kuv′ər slip′), *n.* = cover glass.

cover story, a story in a magazine associated with the illustration on its front cover.

co|vert (*adj. 1, n. 3* kō′vərt, kuv′ərt; *adj. 2,3; n. 1, 2* kuv′ərt, kō′vərt), *adj., n.* —*adj.* **1** kept from sight; secret; hidden; disguised: *The children cast covert glances at the box of candy they were told not to touch.* **SYN:** concealed. See syn. under **secret. 2** *Law.* married and under the authority or protection of her husband. **3** *Rare.* covered; sheltered.

—*n.* **1a** a hiding place; shelter. **b** a thicket in which wild animals or birds hide. **2** a covering. **3** = covert cloth.

coverts, the smaller and weaker feathers of a bird that cover the bases of the larger feathers of the wing and tail; tectrices: *The coverts of the wings are of a deep blackish green* (Goldsmith).

[< Old French *covert,* past participle of *covrir;* see etym. under **cover**] —**co′vert|ly,** *adv.* —**co′vert|ness,** *n.*

covert action or **operation,** a secret undertaking, especially to gather information, conducted by a police force or intelligence branch of government: *Veteran agency operatives often say that without covert action the C.I.A. would be nothing but a collection of sophisticated professors with mounds of intelligence* (New York Times).

cov|ert-bar|on (kuv′ərt bar′ən), *adj. Law.* covert.

co|vert cloth (kō′vərt, kuv′ərt), a cloth of wool, silk and wool, cotton, or rayon, used for coats, suits, and other clothing.

covert coat, *British.* a short, light overcoat of covert cloth, worn for sports.

cov|erts (kuv′ərts), *n. pl.* See under **covert.**

cov|er|ture (kuv′ər chůr, -chər), *n.* **1** a cover; covering. **2** a hiding place; shelter; refuge. **3** *Law.* the status of a woman during her married life, when she is legally under the authority or protection of her husband. **4** *Figurative.* a concealing covering; disguise.

cov|er-up (kuv′ər up′), *n.* **1** something that conceals or disguises, especially that conceals or disguises a defect or crime: *The SEC's use of the term [self-regulation] is nothing more than a cover-up for greater and greater Government control of our nation's capital markets* (Wall Street Journal). **2** a garment that covers up another garment: *A bikini cover-up, an evening dress with a matching sleeveless cover-up.*

cov|et (kuv′it), *v.t.* **1** to desire eagerly (something that belongs to another): *The other boys coveted his new bat.* **SYN:** See syn. under **envy. 2** to wish for, especially eagerly; long for. [< Old French *coveitier* < Gallo-Romance *cupidietāre* < Latin *cupiditās, -ātis* cupidity < *cupidus* desiring < *cupere* desire] —**cov′et|a|ble,** *adj.* —**cov′et|er,** *n.*

cov|et|ous (kuv′ə təs), *adj.* **1** desiring things that belong to others: *Russia long has cast covetous eyes southward toward the Persian Gulf* (Newsweek). **2** eagerly desirous, especially of money: *Covetous beyond all sense of humanity, he foreclosed mortgages right and left.* **SYN:** greedy, avaricious, grasping, rapacious. —**cov′et|ous|ly,** *adv.* —**cov′et|ous|ness,** *n.*

cov|ey (kuv′ē), *n., pl.* **-eys. 1** a small flock of partridges, quail, or similar birds: *He walked up to a covey of grouse, and getting off but one shot, picked up no less than five ... birds* (Atlantic). **2** *Figurative.* a small group; company: *the father of a covey of girls* (New Yorker). [< Old French *covee* < *cover* incubate, brood < Latin *cubāre* lie, sleep]

cov|in (kuv′ən), *n. Law.* a collusion between two or more persons harmful to a third. [< Old French *covin, convine* < Late Latin *convenium,* ultimately < Latin *com-* together + *venīre* come]

cov|ing (kō′ving), *n.* **1** an arched or coved part of a building projecting beyond the parts below. **2** a cove or series of coves. **3** coved work.

covings, the curved sides of a fireplace that narrow toward the back: *The covings ... of a fireplace are now commonly placed in an oblique position* (John Holland).

cov|in|ous (kuv′ə nəs), *adj. Law.* involving covin; collusive; fraudulent.

cow¹ (kou), *n., pl.* **cows** or (*Archaic or Dialect*) **kine. 1** the full-grown female of domestic cattle, especially the common dairy animal that furnishes milk. **2** the female of the buffalo, moose, and other large mammals, the male of which is called a bull: *A bull elephant followed by two young cows emerged from the trees.* **3** *Australian Slang.* a disagreeable person or thing.

till (or **until**) **the cows come home,** for a very long time; on and on: *You could be standing next to somebody suffering from typhoid until the cows come home and you would not get it so long as your food was not affected* (London Times).

[Old English *cū*] —**cow′like′,** *adj.*

cow² (kou), *v.t.* to make afraid; frighten: *The bully cowed many of the younger children with his threats.* **SYN:** intimidate, scare. [probably < Scandinavian (compare Old Icelandic *kūga*)]

cow³ (kou), *v.t. Scottish.* to poll (the head); cut short; top; prune. Also, **cowe.** [alteration of earlier *coll* < Scandinavian (compare Old Icelandic *kollr* head, poll)]

cow|a|bun|ga (kou′ə bung′gə), *interj.* a surfer's cry as he rides the crest of a wave. [origin unknown]

cow|age (kou′ij), *n.* = cowhage.

co-walk|er (kō wô′kər), *n.* an apparitional double of a living person.

cow|an (kō′ən), *n.* **1** *Scottish.* a person who builds stone walls without mortar (used contemptuously of one who works as a mason without having served the regular apprenticeship). **2** a person who is not a Freemason. [origin unknown]

cow|ard (kou′ərd), *n., adj.* —*n.* a person who lacks courage or is easily made afraid; one who runs from danger, trouble, or other difficulties: *Cowards die many times before their deaths* (Shakespeare). —*adj.* lacking courage; cowardly. [< Old French *coart* < *coe* tail < Latin *cōda,* dialectal variant of *cauda* (referring to an animal with its tail between its legs)]

cow|ard|ice (kou′ər dis), *n.* lack of courage; being easily made afraid: *The deserter was guilty of cowardice.* **SYN:** faintheartedness, pusillanimity.

cow|ard|ly (kou′ərd lē), *adj., adv.* —*adj.* **1** without courage: *I was too cowardly to do what was right* (Dickens). **SYN:** timorous, craven, pusillanimous, fainthearted. See syn. under **timid. 2** of a coward; like a coward: *He made his threats at a cowardly distance.* —*adv.* in a cowardly manner. —**cow′ard|li|ness,** *n.*

cow|bane (kou′bān′), *n.* any one of various plants of the parsley family, reputedly poisonous to cattle, such as the spotted cowbane, a North American plant with poisonous roots.

cow|bell (kou′bel′), *n.* **1** a bell hung around a cow's neck to indicate her whereabouts. **2** *U.S.* the bladder campion.

cow|ber|ry (kou′ber′ē, -bər-), *n., pl.* **-ries. 1** the berry or fruit of any one of several plants growing in pastures, such as the red huckleberry. **2** any of these plants. **3** a marsh plant of the rose family. **4** *U.S.* the partridgeberry (plant).

cow|bind (kou′bīnd′), *n.* either of two species of bryony.

cow|bird (kou′bėrd′), *n.* a small North American blackbird, often found with cattle. Most cowbirds lay their eggs in the nests of other birds.

cow blackbird, = cowbird.

cow|boy (kou′boi′), *n.* **1** a man whose work is looking after cattle on a ranch; cowhand. He rides horseback to do most of his work. **2** a man who rides horses in a rodeo. **3** *Slang.* a wild or irresponsible young man, especially a reckless driver: *The number of "cowboys" on the road is probably small ... but their behaviour is getting them all a bad name* (London Times). **4** *Historical.* a Tory partisan in the American Revolution in the vicinity of New York, especially a member of various lawless bands that made raids on the farms of the region.

cowboy boot, a high-heeled riding boot, often with fancy trimming on top, worn by cowboys and ranchers.

cowboy hat, a broad-brimmed hat worn by cowboys and ranchers; ten-gallon hat.

cowboys and Indians, a children's game in which players enact a battle between Indians and cowboys. It is played sometimes in the form of tag, in which those that are "it" are the cowboys chasing the Indians to tag them.

cow bunting, = cowbird.

***cow|catch|er** (kou′kach′ər), *n.* a metal frame on the front of a locomotive, streetcar, or the like, to clear the tracks of anything in the way.

***cowcatcher**

cow college, *U.S. Slang.* **1** an agricultural college. **2** any small, rural college.

cowe (kou), *v.t. Scottish.* cow[3].

cow|er (kou′ər), *v.i.* **1** to crouch or draw back in fear or shame: *The dog cowered under the table after being whipped by its master.* **SYN:** cringe, quail. **2** to draw back tremblingly from another's threats or blows. **SYN:** cringe, quail. [apparently < Scandinavian (compare Old Icelandic *kūra* doze, lie quiet)] **—cow′er|ing|ly,** *adv.*

cow-eyed (kou′īd′), *adj.* having bovine eyes; ox-eyed: *cow-eyed Junos* (Atlantic).

cow|fish (kou′fish′), *n., pl.* **-fish|es** or (*collectively*) **-fish. 1** a fish with hornlike projections above its eyes. **2** any one of certain small animals related to the whales, such as the dolphin or porpoise. **3** a sea cow such as a dugong or manatee.

cow|girl (kou′gėrl′), *n.* a woman or girl who works on a ranch, at rodeos, etc.

cow|hage (kou′ij), *n.* **1** the short, stiff hairs covering the pods of a tropical plant of the pea family, that cause intense itching. **2** the pods. **3** the plant. Also, **cowage, cowitch.** [< Hindustani *kawāch,* contraction of *kiwānch* < Sanskrit *kapikacchu* a tropical stinging plant < *kapi* monkey + *kacchu* itch]

cow|hand (kou′hand′), *n.* a person who works on a cattle ranch; cowboy: *Whitey, that intrepid young cowhand, and his cousin Josie found a wild horse caught in a washout* (Saturday Review).

cow|herd (kou′hėrd′), *n.* a person whose work is looking after cattle at pasture.

cow|hide (kou′hīd′), *n., v.,* **-hid|ed, -hid|ing.** **—*n.* 1** the hide of a cow: *Cowhide was checked for ticks and sores.* **2** leather made from it: *The cowboy's chaps were of cowhide.* **3** a strong, heavy whip made of rawhide or of braided leather: *The driver cracked his cowhide over the mule team's head.*
—*v.t.* to whip with a cowhide; flog.

cow hitch, = lark's-head.

cow|ish (kou′ish), *n.* **1** a plant of the parsley family, having edible tuberous roots used as food by the Indians in Oregon. **2** the root of this plant. [compare Nez Percé *kowish*]

cow|itch (kou′ich), *n.* = cowhage.

cow killer, a wingless wasp of the southeastern United States similar to an ant in appearance.

***cowl[1]** (koul), *n., v.* **—*n.* 1** a monk's cloak with a hood: *The wandering monk's cowl was mud-stained from head to foot.* **2** the hood itself: *Throwing back his cowl, he exposed his face.* **3** *Figurative.* anything shaped like a cowl: *Bateau neckline dips low in the back like a swimsuit, turns into a narrow cowl in front* (New York Times). **4** the part of an automobile body that supports the windshield, the dashboard, and the rear part of the hood. **5** the cowling of an airplane. **6** a covering for the top of a chimney to increase the draft. **7** a wire cage for the top of the funnel of a locomotive.
—*v.t.* 1 to put a monk's cowl on; make a monk of. **2** to cover with a cowl or something resembling a cowl.
[Old English *cūle, cugele* < Late Latin *cuculla,* variant of Latin *cucullus* hood]

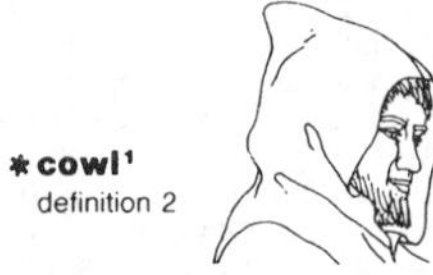

***cowl[1]**
definition 2

cowl[2] (koul), *n.* a large tub or the like for water or other liquid, especially one with two ears through which a cowlstaff can be passed. [Middle English *covelle,* apparently < Old French *cuvele* < Latin *cūpella* vat, cask (diminutive) < *cūpa*]

cowled (kould), *adj.* **1** wearing a cowl. **2** *Botany, Zoology.* shaped like a cowl; cucullate.

cow|lick (kou′lik′), *n.* a small tuft of hair that will not lie flat.

cow lily, the nuphar or spatterdock.

cowl|ing (kou′ling), *n.* **1** a metal covering over the engine of an aircraft; cowl. The cowling may be removed. **2** a similar part forming a continuous surface with the fuselage or the wing.

cowl|staff (koul′staf′, -stäf′), *n. Archaic or Dialect.* a staff or pole on which a cowl or other vessel or weight is carried between two persons.

cow|man (kou′mən), *n., pl.* **-men.** *U.S.* **1** an owner of cattle; ranchman. **2** a man who takes care of cattle.

co-work|er (kō wėr′kər), *n.* a person who works with another.

cow parsley, a European plant of the parsley family that was introduced as a weed in North America; wild chervil.

cow parsnip, any of a group of tall perennial plants of the parsley family.

cow|pea (kou′pē′), *n.* **1** a bushy annual plant of the pea family, that has very long pods and is grown in the southern United States for use as feed for cattle or fertilizer. **2** = black-eyed pea.

Cow|per's glands (kou′pərz, kü′-), a pair of small glands that empty into the male urethra; bulbourethral glands. [< William *Cowper,* 1666-1709, a British anatomist, who discovered them]

cow pilot, = pintano (fish).

cow plant, a woody, climbing plant of the milkweed family, found in Sri Lanka, the milky juice of which is used for food by the Singhalese.

cow poison, a native larkspur of California.

cow|poke (kou′pōk′), *n. U.S. Slang.* a cowboy.

cow pony, a pony used in herding cattle in the western United States.

cow|pox (kou′poks′), *n.* a contagious disease of cows causing small pustules on cows' udders and teats; vaccinia. Cowpox is a virus disease. Vaccine for smallpox is obtained from cows that have cowpox.

cow|punch|er (kou′pun′chər), *n. U.S. Informal.* a cowboy. [American English < *cow* + *puncher* < *punch* drive cattle (as if by prodding)]

***cow|rie** or **cow|ry** (kou′rē), *n., pl.* **-ries. 1** the brightly colored, smooth shell of a tropical mollusk, used as money in some parts of Africa and Asia: *The cowry, aristocrat among shells, is noted for its high natural polish* (Science News Letter). **2** the animal itself. [< Hindi *kaurī*]

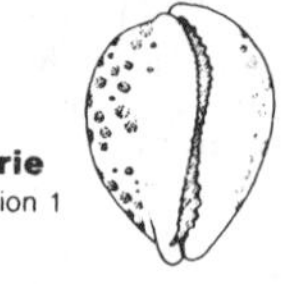

***cowrie**
definition 1

cow shark, a large shark with six pairs of gill slits, found in European and West Indian waters.

cow|skin (kou′skin′), *n.* = cowhide.

cow|slip (kou′slip), *n.* **1a** a wild plant with bright, yellow flowers that bloom in early spring; English primrose. **b** any one of various plants resembling this, such as the shooting star or the Virginia cowslip. **2** = marsh marigold. [Old English *cūslyppe* < *cū* cow + *slyppe* slime]

cow town, *U.S. and Canada.* a small town in a cattle-raising region: *Uranium turned this from a sleepy little cow town to a booming city* (Time).

cow tree, 1 a South American tree of the mulberry family, whose trunk yields a nutritious, milky juice. **2** any tree yielding a similar juice.

cow|wheat (kou′hwēt′), *n.* any one of a group of plants of the figwort family, especially a weed found in the wheat fields of Europe.

cox (koks), *n., pl.* **cox|es,** *v. Informal.* **—*n.*** a coxswain. **—*v.t., v.i.*** to act as cox or coxswain to (a boat). **—cox′less,** *adj.*

cox|a (kok′sə), *n., pl.* **cox|ae** (kok′sē). **1** *Anatomy.* **a** the hipbone. **b** the hip joint. **2** *Zoology.* the joint by which the leg is articulated to the body in arthropods. [< Latin *coxa* hip]

cox|al (kok′səl), *adj.* having to do with the hip or hip joint.

cox|al|gi|a (kok sal′jē ə), *n.* **1** pain in the hip. **2** disease of the hip joint. [New Latin *coxalgia* < *coxa* + Greek *álgos* pain]

cox|al|gic (kok sal′jik), *adj.* having to do with or affected with coxalgia.

cox|al|gy (kok′sal′jē), *n.* = coxalgia.

cox|comb (koks′kōm′), *n.* **1a** a vain, empty-headed man; conceited dandy. **SYN:** fop, popinjay. **b** *Obsolete.* a fool; simpleton. **2** = cockscomb (plant). **3** *Obsolete.* **a** a strip of red cloth, jagged like the comb of a cock, formerly worn in a jester's cap. **b** a cap with this strip of cloth. **4** *Obsolete.* the head. [variant of *cock's comb* (which it resembled in shape and color)]

cox|comb|i|cal or **cox|com|i|cal** (koks kom′ə-kəl, -kō′mə-), *adj.* of the nature of or resembling a coxcomb; conceited; foppish.

cox|comb|ry (koks′kōm′rē), *n., pl.* **-ries. 1** silly vanity; foolish conceit. **2** an example of this.

Cox|cox (kôs kôs′), *n. Mexican Mythology.* the counterpart of Noah and ancestor of the Toltecs and Aztecs.

cox|i|tis (kok sī′tis), *n.* inflammation of the hip joint. [< *cox*(a) + *-itis*]

Cox|sack|ie virus (kok sak′ē), one of a group of intestinal viruses associated with various diseases in man, especially respiratory diseases. [< *Coxsackie,* a city in New York where the virus was first found]

cox|swain (kok′sən, -swān′), *n., v.* **—*n.* 1** a person who steers a rowboat, racing shell, or other small boat. He often gives certain directions to the crew. **2** a person who usually steers and is in charge of a small boat and its crew.
—*v.t.* = cox. Also, **cockswain.**
[< *cock* cockboat + *swain*]

coy (koi), *adj., v.* **—*adj.* 1** shy or modest; bashful. **2** acting more shy than one really is; coquettishly reserved: *I am not trying to hide anything ... and I'm certainly not being coy* (Newsweek).
—*v.t.* 1 to render quiet; calm; appease. **2** to stroke or touch soothingly; pat; caress.
—*v.i.* *Archaic.* **1** to act or behave coyly; affect shyness or reserve. **2** to be slow or reluctant; make difficulty.
[< Old French *coi,* earlier *quei* < Vulgar Latin *quētus,* for Latin *quiētus* at rest. See etym. of doublets **quiet**[1] and **quit,** adjective.] **—coy′ly,** *adv.* **—coy′ness,** *n.*

coy|ote (kī′ōt, kī ō′tē), *n., pl.* **-otes** or (*collectively*) **-ote. 1** a small wolf living especially on the prairies and in the hills of western North America; prairie wolf. It is noted for loud howling at night. See picture under **dog. 2** a cunning, malicious figure, human or animal, in the myths of many North American Indian tribes. **3** *Slang.* a smuggler or exploiter of illegal immigrants to the United States, especially from Latin America: *He could not support his wife and ten children ... in El Salvador, he explained, so he had saved eight hundred dollars to pay a "coyote" ... who arranged his passage to Washington* (New Yorker). [American English < Mexican Spanish < Nahuatl *coyotl*]

Coyote State, a nickname for South Dakota.

co|yo|til|lo (kō′yō tēl′yō, kī′ō-; *Spanish* kō′yō-tē′yō), *n., pl.* **-los.** any plant of a group of poisonous shrubs of the buckthorn family found in the southwestern United States and in Mexico. [< Mexican Spanish *coyotillo* (diminutive) < *coyote;* see etym. under **coyote**]

coy|pu (koi′pü), *n., pl.* **-pus** or (*collectively*) **-pu.** a large water rodent of South America with webbed hind feet that has become established in parts of the southern and western United States; nutria. Its fur resembles beaver. [< Spanish *coipu* < Araucanian (Chile) *koypu*]

coz (kuz), *n. Informal.* cousin.

coze (kōz), *v.,* **cozed, coz|ing,** *n.* **—*v.i.*** to converse in a friendly way; chat. **—*n.*** a friendly talk; chat. [apparently < French *causer,* learned borrowing from Latin *causārī* to plead]

coz|en (kuz′ən), *v.t., v.i.* to deceive or trick; cheat; beguile. [origin uncertain] **—coz′en|er,** *n.*

coz|en|age (kuz′ə nij), *n.* the practice of cozening; deception or trick; fraud.

co|zy (kō′zē), *adj.,* **-zi|er, -zi|est,** *n., pl.* **-zies,** *v.i.,* **-zied, -zy|ing.** **—*adj.*** warm and comfortable; snug: *She likes to read in a cozy corner near the fireplace.* **SYN:** See syn. under **snug.**
—*n.* a padded cloth cover to keep a teapot warm: *knitted tea cozies for our precious teapot* (Atlantic).
—*v.i.* cozy up to, *Informal.* to attempt to gain favor with. Also, **cosey, cosie, cosy.**
[apparently < Scandinavian (compare Norwegian *koselig*)] **—co′zi|ly,** *adv.* **—co′zi|ness,** *n.*

co|zy|mase (kō zī′mās), *n.* = diphosphopyridine nucleotide: *Cozymase is a coenzyme containing the B vitamin nicotinamide* (Scientific American).

cp., 1 compare. **2** coupon.

c.p., 1 candle power. **2** chemically pure.

C.P., 1 chemically pure. **2** Command Post. **3** common pleas. **4** Communist Party. **5** Court of Probate.

CPA (no periods) or **C.P.A., 1** certified public accountant. **2** critical path analysis.

cpd., compound.

CPI (no periods), consumer price index.

Cpl. or **cpl.,** corporal.

cpm (no periods) or **c.p.m.,** cycles per minute.

C.P.M. or **CPM** (no periods), critical path method.

c.p.o. or **C.P.O.,** chief petty officer.

CPR (no periods), an emergency procedure performed on the victim of a cardiac arrest; cardiopulmonary resuscitation: *The revolutionary heart-starting technique known as CPR ... consists of hard pressure on the lower ... breastbone 60 to 70 times a minute (to force blood out of the heart) alternating with mouth-to-mouth ventilation* (Time).

cps (no periods), cycles per second.

CPU (no periods), central processing unit.

CQ (sē′kū′), *n.* the call used at the start of radiograms as of general information and warnings.
CQ (no periods), charge of quarters.
CQD (sē′kū′dē′), *n.* the radio code signal formerly used to summon assistance, as by ships in distress.
c quark, = charmed quark.
cr. or **Cr.,** **1** credit. **2** creditor.
Cr (no period), **1** chromium (chemical element). **2** cruzeiro.
C.R., **1** Costa Rica. **2** Keeper of the Rolls (Latin, *Custos Rotutorum*).
craal (kräl), *n.* = kraal.
***crab**[1] (krab), *n., v.,* **crabbed, crab·bing.** —*n.* **1** a broad, flat crustacean with eight legs and two claws. The small abdomen or the tail of a crab is folded under. Many kinds of crabs are good to eat. **2** any one of various similar animals, such as the hermit crab, coconut crab, and king crab. **3** a machine for raising heavy weights, originally one with claws. **4** *Figurative.* a cross, sour person. **5** = crab louse. **6a** the act or maneuver of crabbing an airplane. **b** the sideward movement of an airplane turning into a cross wind.
—*v.i.* **1** to catch crabs for eating. **2** *Informal.* to find fault; criticize; complain: *Don't crab so much. The man who ran the luncheonette where I ate did nothing but . . . crab about the noise we made* (New Yorker). **3** to turn an airplane slightly slantwise into a cross wind, to compensate for drift. **4** to move crabwise; go or climb sideways: *Children on skis crabbed up [the hill] and shot down constantly* (Atlantic). **5** (of hawks) to seize or claw each other.
—*v.t.* **1** to turn (an airplane) slightly slantwise into a cross wind, to compensate for drift. **2** (of hawks) to seize or claw (each other). **3** *Informal.* **a** to interfere with; spoil: *to crab someone's act, crab a deal.* **b** to find fault with; criticize.
catch a crab, to make a faulty stroke in rowing: *A boat upset . . . because one of the rowers caught a crab* (London Times).
crabs, a losing throw, such as two aces, in the game of hazard: *My . . . neighbor . . . called for fresh dice, and selected two of them with the utmost care only to throw crabs* (Whyte Melville).
[Old English *crabba*]

***crab**[1]
definitions 1, 2

stone crab

king crab

crab[2] (krab), *n.* = crab apple (applied to either the fruit or the tree). [Middle English *crabbe*]
Crab (krab), *n.* Cancer, a constellation of the zodiac. The Crab is the 4th sign of the zodiac. [see etym. under **crab**[1]]
crab apple, **1** a small, sour apple, used for making jelly. **2** a small, sour wild apple. **3** a tree on which crab apples grow. **4** *Informal, Figurative.* a crabby person: *Mr. Donaldson, a dry-tongued crab apple of a man, launched into the ironic verses* (Christopher Driver).
crab·bed (krab′id), *adj.* **1** hard to read or decipher because irregular: *The teacher refused to accept papers with crabbed handwriting.* **2** hard to understand; perplexing: *This writer has a crabbed style.* **3** peevish; ill-natured; cross. SYN: surly, testy, irascible, petulant. [< *crab*[1] + *-ed*[2] (because of its crooked motion and cross temper)] —**crab′bed·ly,** *adv.* —**crab′bed·ness,** *n.*
crab·ber[1] (krab′ər), *n.* **1** a person who fishes for crabs. **2** a boat used in crab fishing. [< *crab*[1], noun + *-er*[1]]
crab·ber[2] (krab′ər), *n. Informal.* a person who finds fault or criticizes severely. [< *crab*[1], verb + *-er*[1]]
crab·bing (krab′ing), *n.* the act of catching crabs; crab fishing.
crab·by (krab′ē), *adj.,* **-bi·er, -bi·est.** *Informal.* cross, peevish, or ill-natured; crabbed: *He is brought up under the . . . Puritan maxims of a crabby maiden aunt* (Time). —**crab′bi·ly,** *adv.* —**crab′bi·ness,** *n.*
crab cactus, = Christmas cactus.
crab·eat·er (krab′ē′tər), *n.,* or **crabeater seal,** any one of a group of very common seals of West Antarctica, that live among the ice packs and feed on shrimplike crustaceans of the region. They are about 8 feet long.
crab grass, or **crab·grass** (krab′gras′, -gräs′), *n.* a coarse grass that spreads rapidly and spoils lawns: *Letting good lawn grass grow taller is one simple way of combating crab grass* (New York Times). See picture under **grass family.**
crab·hole (krab′hōl′), *n.* **1** a hole made by a land crab or a crawfish. **2** the hollow formed from one of these burrows by rain or by a cave-in.
crab·like (krab′līk′), *adj., adv.* —*adj.* **1** like a crab. **2** suggesting the sideways movements of a crab in walking: *The crablike course of the graph indicates a decline in business.*
—*adv.* sideways: *They rowed crablike upstream.*
crab louse, a louse which infests parts of the human body, resembling a crab in appearance and having recurved feet, like claws, with which it hooks itself to its host.
Crab Nebula, a white, expanding gaseous cloud in the constellation Taurus, that is a powerful source of radio waves.
crabs (krabz), *n.pl.* See under **crab**[1].
crab's-eye (krabz′ī′), *n.* = jequirity.
crab spider, any one of a group of short, wide spiders that live on trees and flowers and sometimes walk sideways like crabs.
crab·stick (krab′stik′), *n.* **1** a stick or cudgel made of crab tree wood. **2** a cross, ill-natured person; crab.
crab tree, = crab apple (def. 3).
crab·wise (krab′wīz′), *adv., adj.* sideways or backwards, like a crab: *the crabwise movements of wrestlers grappling on the floor* (*adj.*). *The author approaches the horrendous social themes crabwise* (Saturday Review) (*adv.*).
crack (krak), *n., v., adj., adv.* —*n.* **1a** a split or opening made by breaking without separating into parts: *There is a crack in this cup.* **b** *Figurative.* a flaw or defect; weakness: *There were no cracks in her character. We tried to paper over the cracks in the script's dialogue.* **2** a narrow opening: *I can see between the cracks in the floorboards.* SYN: cleft, fissure, crevice, chink. **3** a sudden, sharp noise: *the crack of a whip or a rifle, a crack of thunder.* SYN: clap, report. **4** *Informal, Figurative.* a hard, sharp blow: *The falling branch gave me a crack on the head.* **5** *Informal.* an instant; moment: *We got up at the crack of dawn. I'll be with you in a crack.* **6** *Informal.* a try; effort; attempt: *to take a crack at dancing. I took a crack at the job and succeeded.* **7** *Slang, Figurative.* a funny or clever remark; joke. **8** *Informal, Figurative.* a cutting remark; gibe: *If he makes another crack about my singing, he'll be sorry.* **9** unsoundness of mind. **10** *Informal.* a superior person or thing: *She is a crack at skiing.* **11** a cracking of the voice. **12** *Slang.* **a** a burglary. **b** a burglar. **13** *U.S.* an extremely potent, free-based form of cocaine with a short-term effect: *Crack, a highly addictive form of cocaine, is available from most of the 50 drug dealers doing business in Washington Square Park and on Greenwich Village streets 24 hours a day* (New York Times). **14** *Archaic.* a boast. **15** *Scottish.* a chat; gossip.
[Middle English *crak.* Related to **crack,** verb.]
—*v.i.* **1** to break without separating into parts: *The glass cracked when I poured boiling water into it.* **2** to make a sudden, sharp noise; snap: *The whip cracked.* **3** to break with a sudden, sharp noise: *The tree cracked and fell when lightning struck it.* **4** to become harsh, broken, or shrill: *His voice cracked with emotion.* **5** *Informal.* to give way; break down: *His mind cracked under the strain of working for three days without sleep.* SYN: fail, collapse. **6** *Dialect.* to boast; brag. **7** *Scottish.* to chat; gossip.
—*v.t.* **1** to break without separating into parts: *You have cracked the window.* SYN: split, fracture. **2** to cause to make a sudden, sharp noise: *The stagecoach driver cracked the whip.* SYN: snap. **3** to break with a sudden, sharp noise: *We cracked the nuts.* **4** to hit with a hard, sharp blow: *The falling branch cracked me on the head. The boxer cracked his opponent on the jaw.* SYN: smack. **5** to make (the voice) harsh or shrill. **6** *Figurative.* to break into: *The burglar cracked the safe.* **7** *Informal, Figurative.* to break through: *to crack the sound barrier.* **8** *Informal.* to tell or say (something funny or clever): *She cracked a joke.* **9** *Figurative.* to figure out the meaning of (a code); decipher: *In wartime, each enemy tries to crack the other's code. She once cracked a Chinese code without knowing Chinese* (George S. Kaufman). **10** to separate (as petroleum or coal tar) into various substances: *The refinery cracks petroleum to make gasoline.* **11** to ruin; damage: *to crack someone's reputation or credit.* **12** to break with pain or grief: *The death of his dog cracked the boy's heart.* **13** *U.S. Informal, Figurative.* to open and use: *He did not crack a book until the final examination.* **14** *Obsolete.* to boast.
—*adj. Informal.* very good; excellent; first-rate: *a crack train. Buffalo Bill was a crack shot.*
—*adv.* with a crack; with a cracking sound.
crack down, *Informal.* to take stern measures: *The police cracked down and hauled away cars that were double-parked.*
cracked up, *Informal.* praised or claimed: *This book is not what it is cracked up to be.*
crack on, *British Informal.* to go on; carry on: *Big John with his immense experience had things under his personal control ("Crack on, lads!" was a favorite Big John order)* (Sunday Times).
crack up, a to crash or smash: *When the driver skidded off the road he cracked up his car against a tree. The airplane cracked up as it landed.* **b** to suffer a mental or physical collapse: *She was in danger of cracking up under the strain of overworking.* **c** *U.S. Slang.* to laugh or cause to laugh uncontrollably; convulse with laughter: *And then Fred shouts: "I am the great pumpkin!" The whole room cracks up* (Harper's).
[Old English *cracian*] —**crack′a·ble,** *adj.*
crack·a·jack (krak′ə jak′), *n., adj.* = crackerjack.
crack baby, a baby born with various disabilities or deformities caused by the mother's use of crack-cocaine while pregnant: *The most widely cited estimate—[of] fetally exposed babies (or "crack babies") born per year—is much too high* (Washington Post).
crack·brain (krak′brān′), *n.* a crazy or insane person.
crack·brained (krak′brānd′), *adj.* crazy; insane: *I cannot summarize here nine hundred pages of allegations that are usually crackbrained when they are not dishonest* (Harper's).
crack-co·caine (krak′ kō kān′, -kō′kān), *n.* = crack (def. 13).
crack·down (krak′doun′), *n. Informal.* the act of taking, or bringing to bear, stern measures or swift disciplinary action.
cracked (krakt), *adj.* **1** broken without separating into parts; broken coarsely: *cracked ice, cracked wheat, a cracked cup.* SYN: fractured. **2** having harsh notes; lacking evenness; broken: *The crying boy spoke in a cracked voice.* SYN: raucous. **3** *Informal.* crazy; insane. SYN: deranged.
crack·er (krak′ər), *n.* **1** a thin, crisp biscuit or wafer: *a soda cracker.* **2** a person or instrument that cracks. **3** a firecracker: *This rowdy element later entered the grounds of Union Buildings . . . climbed to the top of the adjoining General Botha statue and threw crackers* (London Times). **4** a small paper roll which explodes when it is pulled at both ends; cosaque. It is used as a party favor and sometimes contains a motto, candy, or other surprise. **5** something put at the end of a whiplash to make a cracking sound. **6** *U.S. Dialect.* a poor white person living in the hills or backwoods of Georgia, Florida, or other Southern state (often used in an unfriendly way). **7** the apparatus used for cracking petroleum, in a refinery. **8** *Obsolete.* **a** a boaster; braggart. **b** a liar.
cracker barrel, an open barrel of salted crackers, formerly often found in American country stores.
crack·er-bar·rel (krak′ər bar′əl), *adj.* having the plainness, robust humor, and informality of country people; unsophisticated; down-to-earth: *He has the cracker-barrel wit of a Will Rogers.*
cracker beak, a type of strong beak such as that of sparrows, grosbeaks, and other finches, used for cracking the hard shells of seeds which they eat.
crack·er·jack (krak′ər jak′), *n., adj. Slang.* —*n.* **1** a person or thing of superior ability or grade: *He is a crackerjack at dominoes.* **2** a kind of candied popcorn.
—*adj.* of superior ability or grade: *a crackerjack motorboat. He had his bartenders—five crackerjack men—try to find out what you could put with ginger beer to make it more attractive* (New Yorker).
[American English; (earlier) *crackajack*]
crack·ers (krak′ərz), *adj. British Slang.* crazy; mad: *Leatherjacket got it eventually we know that . . . and then went crackers* (Maurice Proctor).
crack·head (krak′hed′), *n. U.S. Slang.* a person addicted to crack (free-based cocaine).
crack·ing (krak′ing), *n., adj., adv.* —*n.* the process of changing certain hydrocarbons in petroleum and other oils into lighter hydrocarbons by heat and pressure and a catalyst. Cracking is used in producing ordinary gasoline.
—*adj. Informal.* **1** vigorous; brisk: *a cracking pace.* **2** thorough; complete: *a cracking bore.*
—*adv. Informal.* thoroughly: *a cracking good race.*
get cracking, *Informal.* to make a vigorous start; get going: *The five-minute rest period was up; time to stop speculating and get cracking* (Atlantic).

Pronunciation Key: hat, āge, cãre, fär; let, ēqual, tėrm; it, īce; hot, ōpen, ôrder; **oi**l, **ou**t; cup, pu̇t, rüle; **ch**ild; lo**ng**; **th**in; **ŦH**en; **zh**, measure; **ə** represents **a** in about, **e** in taken, **i** in pencil, **o** in lemon, **u** in circus.

crack|le (krak′əl), *v.*, **-led, -ling,** *n.* — ***v.i.*** **1** to make slight, sharp sounds: *A fire crackled in the fireplace. Twigs crackled beneath their feet.* **2** to become minutely cracked, as the surface of some kinds of china or glass does; craze. **3** *Figurative.* to be brilliant or lively; sparkle: *Its [the play's] succession of scenes crackles with good, colloquial dialogue* (Orville Prescott).
— ***v.t.*** **1** to cause to crackle; break with a crackling noise: *He crackled the letter viciously in his hand.* **2** to cover with a network of minute cracks; craze (china or glass).
— ***n.*** **1** a crackling; a slight, sharp sound, such as paper makes when it is crushed. **2** very small cracks on the surface of some kinds of china or glass. **3** china or glass made with such a surface; crackleware. **4** *Figurative.* brilliance; liveliness; sparkle: *The crackle and glow of H. L. Mencken lives on in these pages* (Charles Poore).
[< *crack,* verb + *-le* (frequentative)]

crack|led (krak′əld), *adj.* **1** covered with a network of minute cracks: *crackled porcelain, crackled glass.* **2** covered with crackling.

crack|le|ware (krak′əl wãr′), *n.* crackled china or glass; crackle.

crack|ling (krak′ling), *n., adj.* — ***n.*** **1** the making of slight, sharp sounds. **2** the crisp, browned skin of roasted pork.
— ***adj.*** **1** that crackles. **2** *Figurative.* brilliant; lively; sparkling: *crackling wit, crackling prose.*
cracklings, *Dialect.* **a** the crisp part left after lard has been fried out of hog's fat. **b** corn bread made with this: *Some cracklings were set before us, and we began eating* (American Pioneer).
— **crack′ling|ly,** *adv.*

crack|ly (krak′lē), *adj.* apt to crackle; crisp and brittle.

crack|nel (krak′nəl), *n.* a hard, brittle cake or biscuit: *Take with thee ten loaves, and cracknels, and a cruse of honey* (I Kings 14:3).
cracknels, small pieces of crisply fried fat pork.
[apparently alteration of Middle French *craquelin* < Middle Dutch *crakelinc* < *kraken* crack, crackle]

crack of doom, **1** the signal for the Last Judgment. **2** the Last Judgment; the day the world ends. **3** the signal for the end of everything.

crack|owe (krä′kou), *n.* a boot or shoe with a very long poulaine, in fashion at the end of the 1300's: *The crackowe had a pointed toe so long that a chain had to be used to hold it up* (Lynn Farnol). Also, **cracow.** [< *Cracow,* Poland, where it was used originally]

crack|pot (krak′pot′), *n., adj. Slang.* — ***n.*** a very eccentric or crazy person: *The detective ... discovers that Parker is not just another crackpot but perhaps the only sane individual present* (New York Times).
— ***adj.*** eccentric or impractical: *a crackpot inventor, crackpot ideas.* **SYN**: crackbrained.

crack|pot|ism (krak′pot′iz əm), *n. Informal.* eccentricity; lunacy: *The space program is the precise opposite of economic crackpotism. It is sensible conservatism's greatest future weapon against just such crackpotism* (William S. White).

cracks|man (kraks′mən), *n., pl.* **-men.** *Slang.* a burglar.

crack-the-whip (krak′ᴛʜə hwip′), *n.* a game in which the players run together in a line, hanging on to each other to avoid being thrown off balance as the leader suddenly turns and causes the line to swing around.

crack-up or **crack|up** (krak′up′), *n.* **1** a crash; smash: *The fast driver has been in more than one automobile crack-up.* **SYN**: smash-up. **2** *Informal.* a mental or physical collapse; breakdown.

crack willow, a variety of willow whose brittle twigs break off easily; brittle willow.

crack|y[1] (krak′ē), *adj.,* **crack|i|er, crack|i|est.** **1** having cracks or fractures: *cracky walls.* **2** *Dialect.* cracked; crazy.

crack|y[2] (krak′ē), *interj.* an exclamation or mild oath: *And, by cracky ..., it's not hard to understand why* (New York Times). [alteration of *crikey*]

cra|cow (krä′kou), *n.* = crackowe.

cra|dle** (krā′dəl), *n., v.,* **-dled, -dling.** — ***n. **1** a small bed for a baby, usually mounted on rockers. **SYN**: crib. **2** *Figurative.* **a** the place where a thing begins its growth: *the cradle of civilization, the cradle of literature and art. The sea is thought to have been the cradle of life. Churches whose origin goes back to the cradle of Christianity* (D. Hunter). **b** the first stage of life; infancy: *customs taught from the cradle, medical care provided by the state from the cradle to the grave.* **c** a place of rest or repose: *to sleep in the cradle of false security.* **3** any kind of framework looking like or used as a cradle. **4** a frame to support a ship, aircraft, or other large object while it is being built or repaired. **5** the part of a telephone that supports the receiver. **6** a box on rockers to wash earth from gold or other metals. **7a** a frame fastened to a scythe for laying grain evenly as it is cut. **b** = cradle scythe. **8** a low, wheeled frame on which a mechanic lies to work underneath an automobile. **9** the part of a gun mounting for supporting or raising the gun. **10** a frame or case for protecting a broken limb. **11** an engraver's tool for laying mezzotint grounds. **12** a framework used in the tanning process; rocker.
— ***v.t.*** **1** to put or rock in a cradle; hold as if in a cradle: *She cradled the baby in her arms.* **2** *Figurative.* to shelter or train in early youth: *The mother bear cradled her cub until he could take care of himself. He was cradled in the house of his uncle.* **SYN**: nurture. **3** to support (a ship, etc.) in a cradle. **4** to wash (gold or other metals) from earth in a cradle. **5** to cut with a cradle scythe: *to cradle oats.*
— ***v.i.*** **1** to lie in or as if in a cradle. **2** to cut grain with a cradle scythe.
rob the cradle, *Slang.* to choose a companion, or marry a person, much younger than oneself: *His friends teased him about robbing the cradle when he proposed, at 40, to a girl of 20.*
[Old English *cradol*] — **cra′dle|like′,** *adj.* — **cra′dler,** *n.*

***cradle**
definition 1

***cra|dle|board** (krā′dəl bôrd′, -bōrd′), *n.* a small wooden frame to which an infant is strapped, usually carried on the back of the women of most North American Indian tribes.

***cradleboard**

cradle cap, a yellowish, glossy crust often formed on the scalp of infants, caused by a glandular secretion of the skin.

cra|dle|land (krā′dəl land′), *n.* = cradle (def. 2).

***cradle scythe,** a scythe with a frame attached to it for laying grain evenly as it is cut.

***cradle scythe**

cra|dle|song (krā′dəl sông′, -song′), *n.* = lullaby.

cra|dle-to-grave (krā′dəl tə grāv′), *adj.* of or for a lifetime: *A fair degree of cradle-to-grave supervision has been achieved* (New York Times).

craft (kraft, kräft), *n., v.* — ***n.*** **1** special skill: *The carpenter shaped and fitted the wood into a cabinet with great craft.* **SYN**: skillfulness, dexterity, art. **2** a trade or art requiring special skill: *Carpentry is a craft. No two actors are more devoted to their craft or more relentlessly determined on perfection in every detail* (New Yorker). **3** the members of a trade requiring special skill: *He belongs to the craft of electricians.* **SYN**: guild. **4** skill in deceiving others; slyness; trickiness: *By craft the gambler tricked them out of all their money.* **SYN**: guile, wile, deceit, fraud. See syn. under **cunning. 5a** boats, ships, or aircraft: *Craft of all kinds come into New York harbor every day.* **b** a boat, ship, or aircraft: *A strange craft sailed into the harbor.*
— ***v.t.*** to work, make, or finish with skill or art: *Skillfully cured ... the woods are crafted by experts in the cabinetmaker's art* (Maclean's).
[Old English *cræft* skill, a craft; (originally) strength]

craft guild, = guild (def. 2).

crafts|man (krafts′mən, kräfts′-), *n., pl.* **-men.** **1** a skilled workman; artisan: *The master carpenter was a real craftsman.* **2** an artist or professional whose work shows technical skill but not necessarily of aesthetic merit. — **crafts′man|like′,** *adj.*

crafts|man|ship (krafts′mən ship, kräfts′-), *n.* the work or skill of a craftsman: *This skill, craftsmanship, and experience can only be acquired over years of sustained and patient activity* (London Times). **SYN**: craft.

craft union, a labor union made up of persons in the same craft. Unions of carpenters, plumbers, or bricklayers are craft unions.

craft|work (kraft′wėrk′, kräft′-), *n.* **1** work requiring or showing special skill: *an expert in ceramic craftwork.* **2** a thing or things made by such work: *an exhibition of American Indian craftwork.*

craft|y (kraf′tē, kräf′-), *adj.,* **craft|i|er, craft|i|est.** **1** skillful in deceiving others; sly; tricky: *a crafty villain. The crafty fox lured the rabbit from its hole.* **SYN**: cunning, wily. **2** *Dialect.* skillful; dexterous; clever; ingenious. — **craft′i|ly,** *adv.* — **craft′i|ness,** *n.*

crag[1] (krag), *n.* a steep, rugged rock or cliff rising above others; a projecting rock. [< Celtic (compare Gaelic *creag*)]

crag[2] (krag), *n. Scottish and Dialect.* the neck; throat. [Middle English *crage.* Compare Middle High German *krage.*]

crag|fast (krag′fast′, -fäst′), *adj.* caught between two crags and unable to go up or down, as a sheep on a craggy hillside.

crag|ged (krag′id), *adj.* = craggy. — **crag′ged|ness,** *n.*

crag|gy (krag′ē), *adj.,* **-gi|er, -gi|est.** **1** having many crags; steep and rugged; rough: *The craggy hill was difficult to climb.* **2** rough; uneven: *The old fisherman had a craggy, weathered face.*
— **crag′gi|ly,** *adv.* — **crag′gi|ness,** *n.*

crags|man (kragz′mən), *n., pl.* **-men.** a person used to or skilled in climbing crags.

crake (krāk), *n.* any one of various birds of the same family as the rail, with short bills, such as the corn crake and spotted crake. [Middle English *crak,* perhaps < Scandinavian (compare Old Icelandic *krāka* crow)]

cram (kram), *v.,* **crammed, cram|ming,** *n.* — ***v.t.*** **1** to force into; force down; stuff: *He crammed as many candy bars into his pockets as they would hold. I crammed all my clothes quickly into the bag.* **SYN**: ram. **2** to fill too full; crowd: *The hall was crammed, with many people standing.* **SYN**: pack. **3a** to eat too fast or too much of: *He felt ill after he had crammed down his lunch.* **SYN**: stuff. **b** to fill with too much food: *the little garden where I was crammed with gooseberries* (Scott). **SYN**: gorge. **c** to fatten (poultry or other domestic animals) by overfeeding. **4** *Informal, Figurative.* to stuff with knowledge or information. **5** *Informal, Figurative.* to learn hurriedly: *He is cramming facts and dates for his history examination.* **6** *Slang, Figurative.* to tell lies or exaggerated stories to.
— ***v.i.*** **1** to eat too fast or too much. **2** *Informal, Figurative.* to try to learn too much in a short time: *As he hasn't studied very hard during the year, he has to cram for his final tests.*
— ***n.*** *Informal.* **1** a crammed or crowded condition; crush: *It was a prodigious cram, and we turned away no end of people* (Dickens). **2** *Figurative.* the act of cramming a subject, especially in preparation for an examination. **3** *Figurative.* information acquired by cramming.
[Old English *crammian* < *crimman* to insert]
— **cram′mer,** *n.*

cram|be (kram′bē), *n.* **1** a broad-leaved plant of the mustard family grown in northern Africa, having small, white flowers, and pods whose seeds yield an oil used especially in synthetic rubber manufacture, plastics, and lubrication. **2** = sea kale. [< New Latin *Crambe* the genus name < Latin *crambē* cabbage < Greek *krambē*]

cram|bo (kram′bō), *n.* **1** a game in which a player must think up a rhyme for a word or line given by another. **2** a rhyme or rhyming (in contemptuous use). [earlier *crambe* < Latin *crambē repetīta* (literally) cabbage repeated; any repeated thing]

cram|oi|sy or **cram|oi|sie** (kram′oi zē, -ə-), *adj., n. Archaic.* — ***adj.*** crimson.
— ***n.*** crimson cloth.
[< Old French *crameisi* or Italian *chermesi* < Arabic *qirmāzī* < *qirmiz* the kermes insect. Compare etym. under **carmine, crimson, kermes.**]

cramp[1] (kramp), *v., n., adj.* — ***v.t.*** **1** to shut into a small space: *The two of us were cramped in the telephone booth.* **2** *Figurative.* to limit; restrict; restrain; hamper: *His work was cramped by the very short time he had left to spend on it. In the Middle Ages, science was cramped by ignorance and superstition.* **3** to turn sharply to one side or the other; steer: *He had to cramp his front wheels in order to get out of the tight parking space.* **4** to fasten together with a metal cramp; clamp.
— ***n.*** **1** a metal bar bent at both ends; cramp iron.

It is used for holding together things such as blocks of stone and timbers. **2** = clamp¹. **3** *Figurative.* something that confines or hinders; limitation; restriction. SYN: constraint. **4** *Figurative.* a confined state or part.
— ***adj.*** = cramped.
cramp one's style. See under **style**.
[< Middle Dutch *crampe,* or Middle Low German *krampe*]

cramp² (kramp), *n., v.* — ***n.*** **1** a sudden, painful contracting or pulling together of muscles, often from chill or strain: *The swimmer was seized with a cramp in his leg and had to be helped from the pool.* **2** a paralysis of particular muscles as a result of using them too much.
— ***v.t.*** to cause to have a contraction or paralysis of muscles: *The green apples he ate cramped his stomach.*
cramps, very sharp pains in the abdomen: *A light feeling of ... "cramps" during the first day or so can be relieved by a heating pad or hot-water bag placed on the abdomen* (Sidonie M. Gruenberg).
[< Old French *crampe* < Middle Dutch. Compare etym. under **cramp¹**.]

cramped (krampt), *adj.* **1** confined; limited; restricted: *The poor family lived in very cramped quarters.* **2** *Figurative.* unnaturally compressed; hard to make out; crabbed: *cramped handwriting, a cramped style.* **3** seized with cramp: *cramped fingers.*

cramp|fish (kramp′fish′), *n., pl.* **-fish|es** or (*collectively*) **-fish.** = electric ray (fish).

cramp iron, = cramp¹ (def. 1).

cram|pon (kram′pən), *n.* **1** a strong iron bar with one or more hooks at one end, used to grip heavy things, for lifting; grapnel; grappling iron. **2** a spiked iron plate on a shoe to prevent slipping, used in logging or mountain climbing. [< French *crampon* < unrecorded Frankish *krampo* iron hook]

cram|poon (kram pün′), *n.* = crampon.

cramps (kramps), *n.pl.* See under **cramp²**.

cran (kran), *n., pl.* **crans** or (*collectively*) **cran.** *British.* a capacity measure for fresh herring fixed at 37½ imperial gallons or about 750 fish: *Fishermen threw 200 cran of herring back into the sea rather than accept the price offered* (Manchester Guardian). [origin uncertain]

cran|ber|ry (kran′ber′ē, -bər-), *n., pl.* **-ries.** **1** a firm, sour, dark-red berry, used in making sauce and jelly. **2** a small shrub or trailing vine that these berries grow on. It grows in marshes or bogs and belongs to the heath family. **3** any one of various plants having fruit like the cranberry. [American English, perhaps < Low German *kraanbere*]

cranberry bog, a marsh where cranberries grow.

cranberry tree or **bush, 1** a North American shrub or small tree of the honeysuckle family, with large clusters of white flowers and a red fruit. **2** a closely related European shrub, also having white flowers and a red fruit; marsh elder; European cranberry bush. Its cultivated forms are known as *snowball* or *guelder-rose.*

cran|dall (kran′dəl), *n.* a hammerlike tool used by masons for dressing soft stone. [< *Crandall,* a proper name]

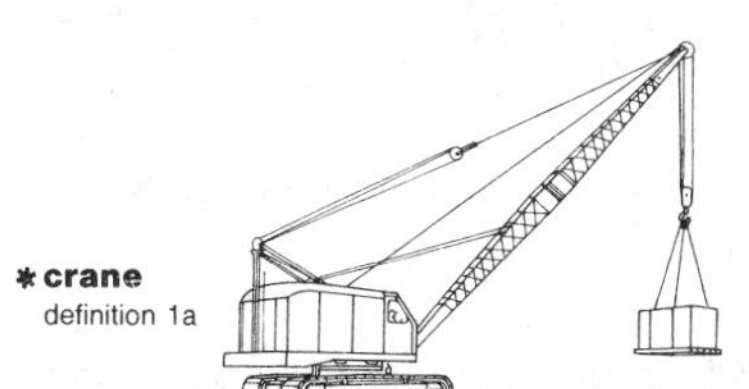
***crane**
definition 1a

crane** (krān), *n., v.* **craned, cran|ing.** — ***n. **1a** a machine with a long, swinging arm, for lifting and moving heavy weights. SYN: derrick. **b** any one of various other kinds of machines that lift, such as a traveling crane. **2** a swinging metal arm in a fireplace, used to hold a kettle or pot over the fire. **3** a large wading bird with long legs, neck, and bill, such as the whooping crane and the sandhill crane of North America. **4** any one of various herons, especially the great blue heron.
— ***v.t.*** **1** to move by, or as if by, a crane. **2** to stretch (the neck) as a crane does, in order to see better: *The little man craned his neck, trying to get a glimpse of the parade over the heads of the crowd.*
— ***v.i.*** **1** to stretch the neck as a crane does, in order to see better: *He was delighted to show them how fast it could go while they craned forward and chanted the rising figures* (London Times). **2** *Informal, Figurative.* to hesitate at danger or difficulty. **3** to stop and look before a dangerous leap in hunting.
[Old English *cran*] — **crane′like′,** *adj.*

crane|bill (krān′bil′), *n.* = crane's-bill.

crane fly, any one of a group of long-legged flies often confused with a large mosquito.

crane helicopter, a helicopter equipped with a crane for heavy lifting.

crane|man (krān′mən), *n., pl.* **-men.** a person who operates a crane.

crane's-bill or **cranes|bill** (krānz′bil′), *n.* **1** any wild geranium, so called from the long, slender beak of the fruit; heron's-bill. **2** any variety of geranium.

crani-, *combining form.* the form of **cranio-** before vowels, as in *cranial.*

cra|ni|a (krā′nē ə), *n.* a plural of **cranium.**

cra|ni|al (krā′nē əl), *adj.* of or having to do with the skull; from the skull: *cranial bones, the cranial capacity of a chimpanzee.* — **cra′ni|al|ly,** *adv.*

cranial index, = cephalic index.

cranial nerve, any one of 12 pairs of nerves that leave the brain directly through openings in the skull.

cra|ni|ate (krā′nē it, -āt), *adj., n.* — ***adj.*** **1** having a skull. **2** having to do with or belonging to a group of vertebrates comprising those which possess a skull and brain. The mammals, birds, reptiles, amphibians, and fishes are craniate animals.
— ***n.*** a craniate animal.

cranio-, *combining form.* cranium; skull: *Craniology = the science of skulls.* Also, **crani-** before vowels. [< Greek *krānion* skull]

cra|ni|o|fa|cial (krā′nē ō fā′shəl), *adj.* belonging to both the skull and the face.

cra|ni|og|no|my (krā′nē og′nə mē), *n.* the art of judging mental or personal qualities from the form and other characteristics of the skull. [< *cranio-* + Greek *gnṓmē* knowledge]

cra|ni|o|graph (krā′nē ə graf, -gräf), *n.* an instrument for making outline drawings of the skull.

cra|ni|og|ra|phy (krā′nē og′rə fē), *n.* the description of skulls.

craniol., craniology.

cra|ni|o|log|i|cal (krā′nē ə loj′ə kəl), *adj.* of or having to do with craniology. — **cra′ni|o|log′i|cal|ly,** *adv.*

cra|ni|ol|o|gist (krā′nē ol′ə jist), *n.* a person who studies craniology.

cra|ni|ol|o|gy (krā′nē ol′ə jē), *n.* the science that deals with the size, shape, and other characteristics of skulls.

craniom., craniometry.

cra|ni|om|e|ter (krā′nē om′ə tər), *n.* an instrument for measuring skulls.

cra|ni|o|met|ric (krā′nē ə met′rik), *adj.* having to do with craniometry. — **cra′ni|o|met′ri|cal|ly,** *adv.*

cra|ni|o|met|ri|cal (krā′nē ə met′rə kəl), *adj.* = craniometric.

cra|ni|om|e|trist (krā′nē om′ə trist), *n.* an expert in or student of craniometry.

cra|ni|om|e|try (krā′nē om′ə trē), *n.* the science of measuring skulls; measurement of skulls.

cra|ni|op|a|gus (krā′nē op′ ə gəs), *n., adj.* — ***n.*** a condition in which Siamese twins are born with their heads joined.
— ***adj.*** joined at the skull: *craniopagus twins.* [< *cranio-* + Greek *págos* that which is fixed]

cra|ni|o|plas|ty (krā′nē ə plas′tē), *n., pl.* **-ties.** plastic surgery on or near the cranium. [< *cranio-* + Greek *plastós* molded]

cra|ni|o|sa|cral (krā′nē ō sā′krəl), *adj.* of or having to do with the region of the autonomic nervous system centered in the brain and in the lower end of the spinal cord.

cra|ni|os|co|pist (krā′nē os′kə pist), *n.* an expert in or student of cranioscopy.

cra|ni|os|co|py (krā′nē os′kə pē), *n.* **1** the observation of the shape and other characteristics of the skull. **2** = phrenology. [< *cranio-* + *-scopy*]

cra|ni|ot|o|my (krā′nē ot′ə mē), *n., pl.* **-mies.** an operation in which the head of the fetus is opened and broken down when it presents an obstacle to delivery. [< *cranio-* + *-tomy*]

cra|ni|um (krā′nē əm), *n., pl.* **-ni|ums** or **-ni|a.** **1** the skull of a vertebrate: *The elephant has a huge cranium but a small brain.* **2** the part of the skull enclosing the brain: *The cranium is composed of eight bones, the face of fourteen* (Beals and Hoijer). [< Medieval Latin *cranium* < Greek *krānion*]

crank¹ (krangk), *n., v., adj.* — ***n.*** **1** a mechanical device for turning a shaft, or for converting one kind of motion to another: **a** a part or handle of a machine connected at right angles to another part to set it in motion. Some cranks have a handle so that they may be turned by hand. *I turned the crank of the sharpener to sharpen my pencil. This French window is opened or closed by a crank.* **b** a U-shaped offset in a rotating shaft connected by a bearing to a reciprocating shaft. **2** *Figurative.* a queer notion or act; whim; caprice. SYN: whimsy, fancy. **3** *Figurative.* a turn of speech or thought; conceit: *Quips and Cranks and wanton Wiles* (Milton). **4** *Informal, Figurative.* **a** an odd person; person with queer ideas or habits; person possessed, as by some idea or hobby. SYN: eccentric, monomaniac. **b** a cross or ill-tempered person. SYN: crab. **5** *Obsolete.* a bend; winding course.
— ***v.t.*** **1** to work or start by means of a crank: *The engines of automobiles do not have to be cranked by hand any more.* **2** to speed; accelerate; boost: *The Air Force probably would get orders to crank up production very soon* (Newsweek). **3** to bend into the shape of a crank. **4** to attach, fasten, or furnish with a crank.
— ***v.i.*** **1** to turn a crank. **2** to twist; wind.
— ***adj.*** **1** loose; shaky; unsteady: *crank machinery.* **2** *Figurative.* of or by a queer or eccentric person: *a crank telephone call, crank letters.* **3** *British Dialect.* weak; infirm; sickly.
crank out, *Informal.* to produce rapidly and steadily: *Congressmen cranked out a steady stream of updated press releases* (Wall Street Journal).
crank up, *U.S. Informal.* to get ready; get started: *Bayh instructed his staff to crank up for an all-out fight against the nomination* (New Yorker).
[Old English *cranc*]

crank² (krangk), *adj.* liable to lurch or capsize; unstable: *a crank boat.* [earlier *cranksided,* perhaps < Dutch *krengen* push over, careen]

crank³ (krangk), *adj. Dialect.* **1** in high spirits; lusty; sprightly; merry. **2** aggressively high-spirited; cocky. [origin uncertain]

crank|case (krangk′kās′), *n.* a heavy, metal case forming the bottom part of an internal-combustion engine. The crankcase of a gasoline engine contains lubricating oil and encloses the crankshaft, connecting rods, and other parts. See picture under **internal-combustion engine.**

crank|er|y (krang′kər ē), *n., pl.* **-er|ies.** the characteristics of a crank; eccentricity; monomania: *Crankery ranges all the way from dangerous approach to insanity to the one-idea fanatics in pseudoscientific research* (London Times).

crank|ish (krang′kish), *adj.* somewhat cranky.

cran|kle (krang′kəl), *n., v.,* **-kled, -kling.** — ***n.*** a bend or turn; crinkle. — ***v.t.*** to bend sinuously; crinkle. — ***v.i.*** to bend in and out; wind. [perhaps < *crank¹*, verb + *-le* (frequentative)]

crank|ous (krang′kəs), *adj. Scottish.* irritable; cranky: *This while she's been in crankous mood* (Robert Burns).

crank|pin (krangk′pin′), *n.* a pin or cylinder at the outer end or part of a crank, such as one for holding a connecting rod.

crank|shaft (krangk′shaft′, -shäft′), *n.* a shaft turning or turned by a crank. The crankshaft of an automobile engine is attached to the connecting rods and transfers power from the pistons to the clutch and transmission.

crank|y (krang′kē), *adj.,* **crank|i|er, crank|i|est.** **1** cross, irritable, or ill-natured. SYN: crotchety. **2** odd; queer; eccentric. SYN: touched. **3** liable to capsize; unstable. SYN: loose, shaky, rickety. **4** full of twists or windings; crooked. — **crank′i|ly,** *adv.* — **crank′i|ness,** *n.*

cran|nied (kran′ēd), *adj.* full of crannies: *Flower in the crannied wall, I pluck you out of the crannies* (Tennyson).

cran|nog (kran′əg), *n.* (in Ireland or Scotland) an ancient lake dwelling or artificial island in a lake. [< Irish Gaelic *crannog* (literally) structure of timbers < *crann* beam, tree]

cran|ny (kran′ē), *n., pl.* **-nies.** a small, narrow opening; crack; crevice; chink: *I looked in all the nooks and crannies of our house for the misplaced letter.* SYN: fissure. [Middle English *crani,* alteration of Old French *cran* notch, fissure]

cran|reuch (kran′rəʜ), *n. Scottish.* hoarfrost. [apparently < Scottish Gaelic *crann* tree + *reodhadh* freezing]

crants (krants), *n. Obsolete.* a garland; wreath. [< German *Kranz*]

crap¹ (krap), *n., v.,* **crapped, crap|ping.** *Slang.* — ***n.*** **1** stupid, foolish talk; nonsense. **2** rubbish; trash; junk.
— ***v.t.*** **1** to talk nonsense to. **2** to make a mess of; spoil.
crap around, *U.S. Slang.* to behave foolishly; waste time; mess around.
[Middle English *crappe* chaff, greaves]
► **Crap** is generally considered vulgar and is avoided by careful speakers and writers.

crap² (krap), *n. U.S.* **1** a losing, first throw of 2, 3, or 12 in craps. **2** = craps. [see etym. under **craps**]

Pronunciation Key: hat, āge, cãre, fär; let, ēqual, tėrm; it, īce; hot, ōpen, ôrder; oil, out; cup, pu̇t, rüle; child; long; thin; ᴛʜen; zh, measure; ə represents **a** in about, **e** in taken, **i** in pencil, **o** in lemon, **u** in circus.

crap|au|dine (krap′ə dēn′), *n.* an ulcer on the coronet of a horse's hoof. [< French *crapaudine* < *crapaud* toad]

crape (krāp), *n., v.* **craped, crap|ing.** —*n.* **1** = crepe (def. 1). **2** a piece of black crepe used as a sign of mourning: *According to all the rules, she should have been in the crape and I should have been offering the consolations of philosophy* (Harper's).
—*v.t.* **1** to cover, clothe, or drape with crape. **2** *Obsolete.* to crimp (the hair).
[variant of **crepe**]

crape|hang|er (krāp′hang′ər), *n. Slang.* a person who dampens enthusiasm with a gloomy outlook; pessimist. Also, **crepehanger.**

crape myrtle, a shrub of the loosestrife family having bright, rose-colored, purple, or sometimes white, crumpled petals, native to China but often grown in the southern United States. The shrub also grows wild in tropical Asia and Australia. Also, **crepe myrtle.**

crap game, = craps.

crap|pie (krap′ē), *n.* either of two species of small, freshwater fish of North America, used for food; calico bass or white crappie. Also, **croppie.** [American English, apparently < a dialectal Canadian French word]

crap|py (krap′ē), *adj.,* **-pi|er, -pi|est.** *Slang, usually considered vulgar.* worthless; inferior; junky; trashy.

craps (kraps), *n. U.S.* a gambling game played with two dice. [American English < Louisiana French *craps* the game of hazard < English *crabs* the lowest throw in hazard]

crap|shoot|er (krap′shü′tər), *n. U.S.* a person who plays craps.

crap|u|lence (krap′yə ləns), *n.* **1** sickness from drinking or eating too much. **2** gross intemperance; debauchery.

crap|u|lent (krap′yə lənt), *adj.* **1** sick from drinking or eating too much; crapulous. **2** given to such intemperance. [< Latin *crāpulentus* very intoxicated < *crāpula* excessive drinking < Greek *kraipálē* nausea]

crap|u|los|i|ty (krap′yə los′ə tē), *n.* inclination to drunkenness.

crap|u|lous (krap′yə ləs), *adj.* **1** given to or characterized by drinking or eating too much. **2** = crapulent.

crash[1] (krash), *n., v., adj.* —*n.* **1** a noise like many dishes falling and breaking, or like sudden, loud band music: *The bottles fell on the floor with a crash. The lightning was followed by a crash of thunder.* **2** a falling, hitting, or breaking with force and a loud noise: *the crash of dishes on the floor, the crash of a falling tree, the crash of stones hurled at the windows.* SYN: smash. **3a** a fall to the earth or a bad landing of an aircraft: *Only four passengers escaped injury in the crash of the plane.* **b** the violent striking of one solid thing against another; collision: *There was a crash of two cars at the corner.* **4** *Figurative.* sudden ruin; severe failure in business: *He lost all his money in the stock market crash.* SYN: bankruptcy.
—*v.i.* **1** to make a sudden, loud noise: *The cymbals crashed. The thunder is rumbling And crashing and crumbling* (James Russell Lowell). **2** to fall, hit, or break with force and a loud noise: *The table was upset and all the dishes crashed on the floor.* SYN: smash. **3** to strike violently and shatter; move or go with force and a loud noise: *The baseball crashed through the window.* **4a** to fall to the earth in such a way as to be damaged or wrecked: *The airplane went out of control and crashed in landing, but no one was hurt.* **b** to collide: *The two cars crashed into each other at an intersection. One of the drivers crashed in the first lap.* **5** *Figurative.* to be suddenly ruined; fail in business: *In bad times some companies crash.* **6a** *Informal.* to gate-crash a party, dance, or other social gathering: *Half the people at the inaugural ball had crashed in.* **b** *Slang.* to sleep over or lodge at a place without paying: *The man . . . said they could crash for the night at Love Inn* (New York Times). **7** (of a computer) to become inoperative because of a malfunction in the hardware or software: *Viruses . . . can modify a program's operation, causing computers to malfunction or crash* (Yonkers Herald Statesman).
—*v.t.* **1** to hit or break with force and a loud noise: *With a wide sweep of his arm, he crashed the dishes to the floor.* SYN: smash. **2** to force or drive in a noisy manner: *The hunters crashed their horses through the brushwood in pursuit of the fox.* **3a** *Informal.* to get into (a party or dance) without being invited; gate-crash: *So many crashed the dance that there was no room for the invited guests.* **b** *Slang.* to sleep over or lodge at (a place) without paying: *"When a transient arrives looking for a place to crash," says one communard, "we send him to a motel"* (Time). **4** to cause (an aircraft) to crash.
—*adj.* to be carried out with all possible speed, at whatever cost: *a crash program or project, a crash course in bookkeeping, a crash diet.*
[probably imitative derivative of *crack*]

crash[2] (krash), *n.* a coarse linen cloth, used for towels, curtains, upholstering, and clothing. [compare Russian *krashenyj* colored, dyed]

crash barrier, *British.* a guardrail on a highway or airport runway.

crash|boat (krash′bōt′), *n.* a small craft used in rescue and recovery work.

crash cymbal, a cymbal with a shallow cup and turned-up edge that produces a loud crash when struck with a drumstick.

crash dive, a sudden, very rapid dive by a submarine.

crash-dive (krash′dīv′), *v.,* **-dived, -div|ing.** —*v.i.* to make a crash dive.
—*v.t.* to dive suddenly and rapidly into: *to crash-dive an enemy boat.*

crash|er (krash′ər), *n.* **1** something that crashes or makes a crash; a loud, hard blow or percussion. **2** *Informal.* gate crasher. **3** *U.S. Slang.* burglar.

***crash helmet,** a heavily padded head covering worn by automobile racers, motorcyclists, roller skaters, and the like.

***crash helmet**

crash|ing (krash′ing), *adj. Informal.* **1** thorough, complete: *They and their cause are a crashing bore* (Saturday Night). **2** shocking; appalling: *a crashing lack of taste, a crashing error.* [< *crash*[1] + *-ing*[2]] —**crash′ing|ly,** *adv.*

crash-land (krash′land′), *v.t.* to land (an aircraft) in an emergency so that a crash results, especially to land with landing gear retracted. —*v.i.* to make a crash landing.

crash landing, an emergency landing of an aircraft so that a crash results.

crash pad, **1** = crash padding. **2** a pad or cushion around the edge of a cockpit or other part of an aircraft as a guard against head injury. **3** *Slang.* a place where one may sleep over or lodge free.

crash padding, a protective pad made of foam rubber or other synthetic foams for automobile dashboards.

crash|proof (krash′prüf′), *adj.* safe in the event of a crash: *a crashproof car. Airplanes are required to carry crashproof tape recorders.*

crash truck, a truck equipped to provide emergency help at the scene of an airplane crash.

crash|wor|thy (krash′wėr′ᴛʜē), *adj.* able to withstand a crash; safe in the event of a crash; crashproof. —**crash′wor′thi|ness,** *n.*

cra|sis (krā′sis), *n.* **1** the combination of the vowels of two syllables, especially at the end of one word and beginning of the next, into one long vowel or diphthong. **2** *Obsolete.* temperament. [< Greek *krâsis* combination < *kerannúnai* to mix]

crass (kras), *adj.* **1** gross or stupid; dense: *crass ignorance, a crass person.* SYN: obtuse, oafish. **2** thick; coarse. [< Latin *crassus* thick, fat, gross] —**crass′ly,** *adv.* —**crass′ness,** *n.*

cras|sa|men|tum (kras′ə men′təm), *n., pl.* **-tums, -ta** (-tə). the thick, jellylike part of coagulated blood; clot. [< Latin *crassāmentum* < *crassāre* to thicken < *crassus* solid, thick]

cras|sier (krä syā′), *n. French.* a hill of rubbish; dump.

cras|si|tude (kras′ə tüd, -tyüd), *n.* **1** the quality or state of being crass; gross ignorance. **2** thickness; coarseness.

cras|su|la (kras′yə lə), *n.* any one of a genus of crassulaceous plants native to South Africa. [< New Latin *Crassula* genus name (diminutive) < Latin *crassa* (*herba*) thick (plant)]

cras|su|la|ceous (kras′yə lā′shəs), *adj.* belonging to the orpine family of plants, a family of fleshy or succulent plants typified by the orpine, houseleek, and stonecrop. [< New Latin *Crassulaceae* the order name (< *Crassula* the genus; see etym. under **crassula**) + English *-ous*]

cratch (krach), *n.* **1** *British Dialect.* a crib to hold fodder for horses, etc.; manger. **2** *Archaic.* the manger in which the infant Jesus lay at Bethlehem. [Middle English *crecche* < Old French *creche;* see etym. under **crèche**]

crate (krāt), *n., v.,* **crat|ed, crat|ing.** —*n.* **1** a large frame, box, or basket made of strips of wood, for shipping or storing glass, china, fruit, household goods, or furniture. **2** *Slang.* an old, cheap, or inferior automobile or airplane.
—*v.t.* to pack in a crate: *to crate a mirror for moving.* [< Latin *crātis* wickerwork, lattice. See etym. of doublet **grate**[1].]

crate|ful (krāt′fu̇l), *n., pl.* **-fuls.** as many or as much as a crate holds.

cra|ter[1] (krā′tər), *n., v.* —*n.* **1** an opening at the top of a volcano, shaped like a bowl. See picture under **volcano. 2** a hole in the ground shaped like a bowl: *The battlefield was full of craters made by exploding shells. The meteor crashed to earth, forming a huge crater.* **3** a round, ringlike elevation on the surface of the moon, resembling the crater of a volcano. **4** a large bowl or jar used by the ancient Greeks and Romans, especially for mixing water with wine; krater.
—*v.t.* to cover (a highway or other flat area) with craterlike holes, as by heavy bombing: *The runways were effectively cratered and planes were destroyed on the ground* (Dwight D. Eisenhower).
—*v.i.* to form a crater or hollow.
[< Latin *crātēr* < Greek *krātēr* bowl for mixing wine with water < *kerannúnai* to mix]

crat|er[2] (krā′tər), *n.* a person or thing that packs or stores goods in a crate.

Cra|ter (krā′tər), *n., genitive* **Cra|ter|is.** a southern constellation between Hydra and Leo, supposed to represent a vase with two handles and a base; Cup. [< Latin *Crātēr, -ēris*]

cra|ter|al (krā′tər əl), *adj.* of, belonging to, or of the nature of a crater.

crater basin, 1 a depressed area in which volcanic craters occur. **2** a caldera.

cra|tered (krā′tərd), *adj.* having a crater or craters: *the cratered surface of the moon.*

cra|ter|i|form (krə ter′ə fôrm, krā′tər-), *adj.* having the form of a crater.

Cra|ter|is (krā′tər is), *n.* genitive of **Crater.**

crater lake, a deep lake occupying the crater or caldera of a volcano.

cra|ter|let (krā′tər lit), *n.* a small lunar crater.

C ration, a daily ration of packaged food provided by the U.S. Army for combat troops.

craunch (krônch, kränch), *v.t., v.i., n.* = crunch.

cra|vat (krə vat′), *n., v.,* **-vat|ted, -vat|ting.** —*n.* **1** a necktie, especially a wide one. **2** a neckcloth; scarf: *"Perhaps, Louisa," said Mr. Dombey, slightly turning his head in his cravat, as if it were a socket, "you would have preferred a fire?"* (Dickens).
—*v.t.* to furnish with or as if with a cravat: *. . . black dress cravatted in white organdie* (Sunday Times).
—*v.i.* to put on a cravat: *I redoubled my attention to my dress; I . . . cravatted* (Edward G. Bulwer-Lytton).
[< French *cravate,* apparently < special use of *Cravate* Croat < German *Kravatte* < Serbo-Croatian *Hrvat* (perhaps from the Croat soldiers' scarves)]

crave (krāv), *v.,* **craved, crav|ing.** —*v.t.* **1** to long for; desire very much: *The thirsty man craved water. The lonely orphan craved affection.* SYN: want, wish, covet. **2** to ask earnestly for; beg: *He craved a favor of the king.* SYN: beseech, entreat. **3** to need greatly; require: *My brain craves rest.*
—*v.i.* to beg or plead; long: *Some have too much, yet still do crave* (Edward Dyer). SYN: hanker, hunger, thirst.
[Old English *crafian* demand] —**crav′er,** *n.* —**crav′ing|ly,** *adv.*

cra|ven (krā′vən), *adj., n., v.,* —*adj.* **1** cowardly; weakhearted: *the craven nature of a traitor.* SYN: pusillanimous, timorous. **2** *Obsolete.* vanquished; defeated.
—*n.* = coward.
—*v.t.* to make craven: *a prohibition . . . that cravens my weak hand* (Shakespeare).
cry craven, to surrender; admit defeat: *I . . . will make that slanderous wretch cry craven in the dust* (Robert Southey).
[Middle English *cravant;* origin uncertain] —**cra′ven|ly,** *adv.* —**cra′ven|ness,** *n.*

Cra|ven|ette (krav′ə net′, krā′və-), *n. Trademark.* a waterproofed cloth used especially for raincoats, topcoats, and other outerwear. [< *Craven* Street, London, England]

cra|ven|ette (krav′ə net′, krā′və-), *v.t.,* **-et|ted, -et|ting.** to make (a fabric) waterproof by the process used in Cravenette or a similar process.

cra|ving (krā′ving), *n.* strong desire; longing; yearning: *The hungry man had a craving for food.* SYN: See syn. under **desire.**

craw (krô), *n.* **1** the crop of a bird or insect. **2** the stomach of any animal.
stick in one's craw, *U.S. Informal.* to be unpalatable, or impossible to accept: *To adore Winston Churchill or to demolish him might equally stick in our craws* (New Yorker).
[Middle English *crawe;* origin uncertain]

craw|craw (krô′krô′), *n.* a skin disease, probably parasitic, that affects chiefly the inner side of the thighs. It occurs among the inhabitants of the west coast of Africa. [apparently ultimately < Dutch *kraauw* scratch]

craw|dad (krô′dad′), *n. U.S. Dialect.* crawfish:

The lobster and his relatives the crab, shrimp and inland "crawdads" really are cousins of the insects (Science News Letter).

craw|fish (krô′fish′), *n., pl.* **-fish|es** or (*collectively*) **-fish**, *v.* **—*n.*** = crayfish.

—*v.i.* *U.S. Informal.* to back out of something; retreat: *We took down everything he said, but he crawfished. He didn't name a name* (Harper's). [American English; variant of *crayfish*]

crawk (krôk), *v.i.* to utter a hoarse sound; squawk. [imitative]

crawl[1] (krôl), *v., n.* **—*v.i.*** **1** to move slowly by pulling the body along the ground: *Worms and snakes crawl.* **2** to creep on hands and knees: *A baby crawls before it walks. The boys crawled through a hole in the wall.* **3** *Figurative.* to move very slowly: *The heavy traffic crawled through the narrow tunnel.* **4** to swarm with crawling things: *The ground under the garbage can was crawling with ants.* **5** to feel creepy: *My flesh crawled at the thought of the huge black snakes.* **6** *Figurative.* to move stealthily or slavishly: *The leopard crawled toward its prey. The dog crawled to its master's feet.* **7** to creep; trail: *A green ... vine that crawls along the side of yon small hill* (Milton). **8** to swim with alternate overarm strokes and a fast flutter kick. **—*v.t.*** to crawl upon: *The veriest wretch that crawls the earth* (Eliza Parsons).

—*n.* **1** a crawling; slow movement: *The crawl of traffic annoyed the impatient driver.* (*Figurative.*) *His progress seemed a mere crawl.* **2** a fast way of swimming by alternate overarm strokes combined with a fast flutter kick. **3** *British Slang.* a round made through the pubs or bars; pub-crawl. [apparently < Scandinavian (compare Old Icelandic *krafla*)] **—crawl′er,** *n.*

—*Syn.* *v.i.* **1, 3, 6. Crawl, creep,** used literally and figuratively, mean to move slowly. **Crawl** emphasizes the slow, dragging movement of a worm pulling its body along the ground, and is used of a thing or person that moves in this way or seems to grovel in the dirt like a worm: *He tried to crawl back into favor.* **Creep** emphasizes the slow movement of a person going on hands and knees or the stealthy manner of a cat: *The days creep by. Danger creeps nearer.*

crawl[2] (krôl), *n.* an enclosure of stakes in shallow water, used to hold turtles, fish, and the like. [< Dutch *kraal* < Spanish *corral.* See etym. of doublet **corral.**]

crawler tractor, a tractor that can travel over very rough ground on its two endless tracks; caterpillar tractor.

crawl|er|way (krô′lər wā′), *n.* a road built at a launching site to move large loads, such as rockets: *An eight-lane "crawlerway" ... led to the launch pad* (Time).

crawl|ing peg (krô′ling), *Economics.* a system in which a country's exchange rate is regulated by frequent but small adjustments to reflect trading values on the exchange markets: *The so-called crawling peg would be a lesser evil than freely floating exchange rates* (Manchester Guardian Weekly).

crawl space, a small open space above the ceiling or below the floor in a building that provides or facilitates access to the plumbing, heating units, wiring, and other parts of the building structure.

crawl|way (krôl′wā′), *n.* **1** = crawl space. **2** = crawlerway.

crawl|y (krô′lē), *adj.,* **crawl|i|er, crawl|i|est.** *Informal.* feeling as if things are crawling over one's skin; creepy.

***cray|fish** (krā′fish′), *n., pl.* **-fish|es** or (*collectively*) **-fish. 1** any one of numerous freshwater crustaceans that look much like small lobsters, to which they are closely related. **2** a similar but larger saltwater crustacean. Also, **crawfish.** [earlier *crevysshe,* variant of Middle English *creves* any crustacean < Old French *crevice* < Germanic (compare Old High German *crebis* crab)]

***crayfish** definition 1

cray|on (krā′ən, -on), *n., v.,* **-oned, -on|ing. —*n.*** **1** a stick or pencil of chalk, charcoal, or a waxlike, colored substance, used for drawing or writing: *The sick child spent hours using crayons to color pictures in a coloring book.* **2** a drawing made with a crayon or crayons: *The beautiful crayon of the mountains hung in a frame.*

—*v.t., v.i.* to draw with a crayon or crayons: *a contest to crayon posters.*

[< French *crayon* < Old French *croion* chalky earth < *craie* chalk < Latin *crēta*]

crayon board, a cardboard for crayon or pastel, usually with a roughened surface.

cray|on|ist (krā′ə nist), *n.* a person who draws with crayons.

craze (krāz), *n., v.,* **crazed, craz|ing. —*n.*** **1** a short-lived, eager interest in doing some one thing; fad: *One year the boys had a craze for collecting beetles; the next year they had a craze for making models of ships.* SYN: mania, rage. **2** an insane condition; insanity. **3** a tiny crack in the glaze of pottery or glass. **4** *Dialect.* a crack; defect; flaw. [< verb]

—*v.t.* **1** to make crazy; drive mad: *The broken leg nearly crazed the horse with pain. ... crazed with care, or crossed in hopeless love* (Thomas Gray). **2** to make tiny cracks all over the surface or glaze of (a dish, vase, or the like); crackle. **3** *Dialect.* to weaken in health; make infirm: *till length of years and sedentary numbness craze my limbs* (Milton). **4** *Dialect.* to crack. **5** *Obsolete.* to break; shatter.

—*v.i.* **1** to become crazy; go mad: *My tortured brain begins to craze* (Keats). **2** to become minutely cracked, as the glaze of some kinds of pottery does. **3** *Obsolete.* to break; crack.

[Middle English *crase* break, apparently < Scandinavian (compare Swedish *krasa* crack)]

crazed (krāzd), *adj.* **1** made crazy; insane; demented. **2** having the glaze covered with tiny cracks: *crazed pottery.*

cra|zy (krā′zē), *adj.,* **-zi|er, -zi|est,** *n., pl.* **-zies.**

—*adj.* **1** having a diseased or injured mind; insane; mad. A person who is crazy is not responsible for his actions and is often kept in an institution for the mentally ill. *A crazy person set fire to the house.* **2** greatly distressed or shaken by strong emotion, such as fear, rage, or grief; frantic: *The mother of the kidnaped child was crazy with worry.* **3** foolish, absurd, ridiculous, or fantastic: *That was a crazy idea—to jump off the barn.* SYN: unwise, senseless. **4** *Informal.* very eager or enthusiastic: *She is so crazy about cats that she brings home every stray she finds.* **5** not strong or sound; shaky; frail: *The crazy light blinks on and off whenever anyone jiggles the table.* **6** *U.S. Slang.* wonderful. **7** *Archaic.* ailing; sickly; infirm: *an indulgence conceded to his little crazy body* (Leigh Hunt).

—*n.* *Informal.* a crazy or eccentric person: *there are so many crazies around now* (New Yorker).

like crazy, *Slang.* like mad; without let-up: *When we saw the dog running toward us, we ran like crazy. Once the Canadian Broadcasting Corporation really got going people would be buying TV sets like crazy* (Maclean's).

—cra′zi|ly, *adv.* **—cra′zi|ness,** *n.*

—*Syn.* *adj.* **1 Crazy, mad, insane** mean showing characteristics of someone mentally ill. **Crazy** is the general word, applied commonly to any person who is mentally disturbed: *His absurd, incoherent statements made me wonder whether he was crazy.* **Mad** suggests being completely out of control or beyond reason, wildly foolish or reckless: *Such uncontrolled violence and wild ravings are to be expected of someone who is mad.* **Insane** suggests being utterly irrational or senseless: *He planned an insane revenge.* It is the legal term for a person who is adjudged not responsible for his actions because of mental disturbance: *The prisoner was found not guilty because she was insane.*

crazy bone, = funny bone.

crazy paving, *British.* paving consisting of irregularly shaped flagstones or tiles.

crazy quilt, 1 a quilt made of pieces of cloth of various shapes, colors, and sizes sewed together with no definite pattern. **2** a patchwork; something suggesting a crazy quilt.

cra|zy|weed (krā′zē wēd′), *n.* = locoweed.

C-re|ac|tive protein (sē′rē ak′tiv), an abnormal protein that appears in the bloodstream in response to injury or inflammation. *Abbr:* CRP (no periods).

creagh (kreH, kraH), *n.* in Ireland and the Scottish Highlands: **1** an incursion for plunder; raid; foray. **2** booty; prey.

creak (krēk), *v., n.* **—*v.i.*** to squeak loudly: *The hinges on the door creaked because they needed oiling.* **—*v.t.*** to cause to creak.

—*n.* a creaking noise; squeak: *The creak in the stairs of the old house was spooky.*

[Middle English *creken;* apparently imitative] **—creak′ing|ly,** *adv.*

creak|y (krē′kē), *adj.,* **creak|i|er, creak|i|est.** likely to creak; creaking: *creaky floors, creaky hinges. A creaky ride in a venerable elevator brings one to the fourth-floor laboratory* (Harper's). **—creak′i|ly,** *adv.* **—creak′i|ness,** *n.*

cream (krēm), *n., v., adj.* **—*n.*** **1** the oily, yellowish part of milk. Cream rises to the top when milk that is not homogenized is allowed to stand. Butter is made from cream. **2a** a fancy sweet dessert or candy made of cream; food like cream: *ice cream, chocolate creams, banana cream pie.* **b** a soup or purée made with milk or cream: *cream of tomato soup.* **3** an oily preparation put on the skin to make it smooth and soft: *vanishing cream.* SYN: ointment, salve. **4** a yellowish white. **5** a cream-colored animal, especially a horse or rabbit: *a pair of creams.* **6** *Figurative.* the best or choicest part of anything: *the cream of the crop. The cream of the class is made up of the best students.* SYN: élite. **7** a thick, sweet liqueur; crème.

—*v.t.* **1** to take the cream from; skim the cream from (milk). **2** to cook (food) with cream, milk, or a sauce made of cream or milk with butter and flour: *creamed peas, creamed asparagus.* **3** to make into a smooth mixture like cream: *She creamed the butter and sugar together for a cake.* **4** to put cream in: *to cream and sugar tea.* **5** to allow (milk) to form cream. **6** *Figurative.* to select the cream or best part of: *At the age of 15, a tough competitive exam creams off the country's most promising mathematical brains* (New Scientist). **7** *U.S. Slang.* to beat soundly; injure or defeat severely.

—*v.i.* **1** to form cream. **2** to form a thick layer like cream on the top; foam; froth.

—*adj.* **1** of or for cream: *a cream pitcher.* **2** containing cream or milk; resembling cream: *cream soup.* **3** yellowish-white; cream-colored: *cream lace.*

[< Old French *cresme* < Vulgar Latin *crāma* < Latin *chrisma* ointment < Greek *chrîsma* < *chríein* anoint. See etym. of doublet **chrism.**]

cream|cake (krēm′kāk′), *n. Especially British.* a cake with a filling of cream custard.

cream cheese, a soft, white cheese made from cream, or milk and cream.

cream-col|ored (krēm′kul′ərd), *adj.* of the color of cream; yellowish-white.

cream|cups (krēm′kups′), *n. sing. or pl.* a California plant of the poppy family, having small, yellowish or cream-colored flowers.

creamed (krēmd), *adj.* **1** having the cream formed or separated. **2** made, flavored, or mixed with cream.

cream|er (krē′mər), *n.* **1** a small pitcher for holding cream; cream pitcher. **2** a machine for separating cream from milk; separator. **3** a refrigerator in which milk is placed while the cream is rising. **4** a powdery creaming agent similar to dried milk but made of corn syrup solids and other ingredients, used especially in coffee: *a nondairy creamer.*

cream|er|y (krē′mər ē), *n., pl.* **-er|ies. 1** a place where butter and cheese are made. **2** a place where cream, milk, and butter are bought or sold. **3** a place where milk is set for the cream to rise.

cream nut, = Brazil nut. [< its color]

cream of tartar, a very sour, white powder used in medicine and in cooking, especially to make baking powder; potassium bitartrate. Cream of tartar is obtained from the deposit in wine casks. *Formula:* $KHC_4H_4O_6$

cream|om|e|ter (krē mom′ə tər), *n.* an instrument for determining the percentage of cream in a sample of milk.

cream puff, 1 a light pastry usually filled with whipped cream or custard. **2** *Slang.* a used car on the market that has been treated with care by its previous owner or owners and is still in excellent condition. **3** *Slang.* a sissy; weakling.

cream sauce, a sauce made of cream or milk with flour and butter.

cream soda, a vanilla-flavored carbonated soft drink.

cream|ware (krēm′wãr′), *n.* cream-colored china pottery, especially the Wedgwood ware known by that name.

cream-white (krēm′hwīt′), *adj.* yellowish-white; cream-colored.

cream|y (krē′mē), *adj.,* **cream|i|er, cream|i|est. 1** like cream; smooth and soft. **2** having much cream in it: *pie with a rich, creamy filling.* **3** yellowish-white. **—cream′i|ly,** *adv.* **—cream′i|ness,** *n.*

crease[1] (krēs), *n., v.,* **creased, creas|ing. —*n.*** **1** a line or mark made by folding cloth, paper, or the like; fold; ridge; furrow: *He likes a sharp crease in his trousers.* **2** a wrinkle: *The creases on his face showed that he was very old.* **3a** *Ice Hockey.* a rectangular area defined by lines in front of each goal cage, which attacking players may not enter except in certain specified circumstances. **b** *Lacrosse.* a circle with an 18-foot di-

Pronunciation Key: hat, āge, cãre, fär; let, ēqual, tėrm; it, īce; hot, ōpen, ôrder; oil, out; cup, pu̇t, rüle; child; long; thin; ᴛʜen; zh, measure; ə represents **a** in about, **e** in taken, **i** in pencil, **o** in lemon, **u** in circus.

ameter surrounding each goal. **4** *Cricket.* **a** one of the lines marked on the ground parallel to each of the wickets to define the positions of bowler and batsman. **b** the space defined by these lines: *A batsman leaving his crease is liable to be put out.*
—***v.t.*** **1** to make a crease or creases in: *Mother creased the pleats in her skirt with an iron. Some dress materials are easily creased. When the teacher is thinking he creases his forehead.* SYN: wrinkle. **2** to graze with a bullet. **3** *U.S.* to wound or stun (an animal) with a shot in the crest or surface of the neck. —***v.i.*** to become creased or wrinkled: *a tie that does not crease. Some cloth is too thick to crease well.*
[origin unknown] —**crease'less,** *adj.* —**creas'er,** *n.*

crease[2] (krēs), *n.* = creese. [< Malay *kĕris* dagger]

crease-re|sist|ance (krēs'ri zis'təns), *n.* the property of being able to resist wrinkling, as of fabrics: *Crease-resistance that permits cotton wearing apparel to be worn without ironing can be imparted to the fabric by resin treatment* (Science News Letter).

crease-re|sist|ant (krēs'ri zis'tənt), *adj.* **1** less likely to wrinkle than most fabrics. **2** chemically treated and pressed so as to resist wrinkling.

creas|y (krē'sē), *adj.,* **creas|i|er, creas|i|est.** full of creases.

cre|ate (krē āt'), *v.,* **-at|ed, -at|ing,** *adj.* —***v.t.*** **1** to make a thing which has not been made before; bring into being: *She created a garden in the desert. Composers create music. We men of the twentieth century, surrounded by hats "created" by Lili Daché...* (Erwin Panofsky). SYN: originate, produce, invent. **2** to give rise to; be the cause of: *The noise created a disturbance.* SYN: cause, occasion. **3** to make by giving a new character, function, or status to: *The queen created the man a knight.* SYN: appoint, constitute. **4** to be the first to represent (a part or role): *Maude Adams created the part of Barrie's Peter Pan.*
—***adj.*** *Archaic.* created.
[< Latin *creāre* (with English *-ate*[1])] —**cre|at'a|ble,** *adj.*

cre|a|tin (krē'ə tin), *n.* = creatine.

cre|a|tine (krē'ə tin, -tēn), *n.* a colorless, crystalline compound found chiefly in the muscles of vertebrate animals, which is involved with supplying energy for voluntary muscle contraction. *Formula:* $C_4H_9N_3O_2$ [< French *créatin* < unrecorded Greek *kreāt-,* a false stem of *kréas, -ōs* meat]

creatine phosphate, = phosphocreatine.

cre|at|i|nine (krē at'ə nin, -nēn), *n.* a constituent of urine produced by the breakdown of creatine, also found in blood, muscle, plants, soil, etc. *Formula:* $C_4H_7N_3O$

cre|a|tion (krē ā'shən), *n.* **1** the act of making a thing which has not been made before: *The gasoline motor led to the creation of the modern automobile.* SYN: origination, genesis. **2** a being created: *As when a new Particle of Matter doth begin to exist... which had before no Being; and this we call Creation* (John Locke). **3** all things that have been created; the world; the universe: *Let all creation praise the Lord.* SYN: cosmos. **4** a thing produced by intelligence or skill, usually an important or original one: *Poems, paintings, and symphonies are creations of the imagination.* SYN: invention, production. **5** a new article or style of clothing by a fashion designer: *The strapless dress was a Coco Chanel creation.*
the Creation, the creating of the universe by God: *The Bible says the Creation took six days. ... as if all India was theirs, by title, from the Creation* (Thomas Herbert).

cre|a|tion|al (krē ā'shə nəl), *adj.* of or having to do with creation.

cre|a|tion|ism (krē ā'shə niz əm), *n.* **1** the doctrine that all things were created by God substantially as they are now, and did not gradually evolve or develop. **2** the doctrine that God immediately creates a soul for every human infant born. —**cre|a'tion|ist,** *n.*

creation science, the teachings of creationism: *The creationists are flooding state Legislatures with bills and pressuring school boards to give "creation science"... equal time with evolution in the nation's science classrooms* (Tuscaloosa News).

cre|a|tive (krē ā'tiv), *adj., n.* —***adj.*** **1** having the power to create; inventive; productive: *Sculptors are creative artists.* **2a** approaching the realm of art; imaginative: *creative engineering.* **b** artistic; literary (limited to fiction and poetry): *the creative people of the theater. The writing of poems, stories, or plays is often called creative writing.* **3** constructive; purposeful; involving something useful or worthwhile: *The real secret of living with children... lies in knowing how to be creative in taking away* (Time).
—***n.*** *U.S. Informal.* a creative person: *Maybe all this recent talk about creativity is pushing the creatives to the top* (New York Times). —**cre|a'tive|ly,** *adv.* —**cre|a'tive|ness,** *n.*

creative evolution, *Philosophy.* (in Bergsonism) evolution seen as a process of constant creation under the impulse of the élan vital.

cre|a|tiv|i|ty (krē'ā tiv'ə tē), *n.* the quality of being creative; ability to create: *the creativity of contemporary architects.*

cre|a|tor (krē ā'tər), *n.* a person or thing that creates: *Leonardo da Vinci was the creator of many ideas for inventions.* SYN: originator, engenderer, maker, producer, inventor, author, designer.
the Creator, God: *Remember now thy Creator in the days of thy youth* (Ecclesiastes 12:1).
[< Latin *creātor*]

cre|a|tor|ship (krē ā'tər ship), *n.* the condition or function of a creator.

cre|a|tress (krē ā'tris), *n.* a woman who creates, produces, or constitutes.

cre|a|trix (krē ā'triks), *n., pl.* **cre|a|trix|es, cre|a|tri|ces** (krē'ə trī'sēz). = creatress. [< Latin *creātrix,* feminine of *creātor* creator]

crea|tur|al (krē'chər əl), *adj.* having to do with or of the nature of a creature or creatures; creaturely.

crea|ture (krē'chər), *n.* **1** any living person or animal; a person or beast: *Mother let us keep the lost dog, as the poor creature was starving.* **2** anything created; creation: *Ghosts are creatures of our imagination.* SYN: invention, production. **3** a farm animal (especially in the United States). **4** a person who is strongly influenced or controlled by another person or thing; person who is ready to do anything that another asks. SYN: dependent, tool. **5** *Figurative.* something produced by or developing from something else; result; product. **6** material comfort, especially food, drink, and the like: *Good wine is a good familiar creature* (Shakespeare). **7** intoxicating liquor, especially whiskey (humorous, from the passage I Timothy 4:4, "Every creature of God is good," used in defense of the use of wine). [< Old French *creature,* learned borrowing from Latin *creātūra* < *creāre* produce]

creature comforts, things that give bodily comfort. Food, clothing, and shelter are creature comforts.

crea|ture|hood (krē'chər hůd), *n.* the condition of being a creature.

crea|ture|ly (krē'chər lē), *adj.* of or having to do with a creature or creatures; creatural. —**crea'ture|li|ness,** *n.*

crea|ture|ship (krē'chər ship), *n.* creaturehood.

***crèche** (kresh, krāsh), *n.* **1** a model of the Christ child in the manger, with attending figures, often displayed at Christmas. **2** = day nursery. **3** an asylum or hospital for abandoned infants. [< French *crèche* < Old French *creche* < Old High German *chrippia* crib]

***crèche** definition 1

cre|dal (krē'dəl), *adj.* of or characterized by a creed; creedal. [< Latin *crēdō* I believe + *-al*[1]]

cre|dence (krē'dəns), *n.* **1** belief or credit: *The kind-hearted old lady seldom gave credence to gossip about her nieghbors.* SYN: faith, trust. **2** an introduction or recommendation in confidence; credential: *a letter of credence.* SYN: testimonial. **3** a small side table or shelf for holding elements and articles used in the Eucharistic service; credence table. **4** *Obsolete.* a serving table or sideboard. [< Medieval Latin *credentia* < Latin *crēdere* believe]

credence table, = credence.

cre|den|dum (kri den'dəm), *n., pl.* **-da** (-də). **1** a thing to be believed. **2** an article of faith. [< Latin *crēdendum,* neuter of *crēdendus,* gerundive of *crēdere* believe]

cre|dent (krē'dənt), *adj.* **1** believing; trustful; confiding. **2** *Obsolete.* having credit or repute; credible.

cre|den|tial (kri den'shəl), *n., adj.* —***n.*** something that gives or recommends credit or confidence: (*Figurative.*) *His open countenance was his best credential.* —***adj.*** giving or recommending credit or confidence.
credentials, letters of introduction; references: *The new ambassador from England presented his credentials to the President.*

cre|den|tialed (kri den'shəld), *adj.* furnished with credentials; accredited.

***cre|den|za** (kri den'zə), *n.* a sideboard or side table; buffet: [< Italian *credenza* < Medieval Latin *credentia;* see etym. under **credence**]

***credenza**

cre|de ut in|tel|li|gas (kred'ē ůt in tel'i gas), *Latin.* believe in order that you may understand.

cred|i|bil|i|ty (kred'ə bil'ə tē), *n.* the quality of being believable: *Once a physician's credibility is questioned, his status as an expert disappears* (Atlantic). SYN: trustworthiness, dependability.

credibility gap, **1** a discrepancy between the official statements and the actions of a government, resulting in the loss or weakening of the government's credibility. **2** *Figurative: Zurich bankers tend to see a credibility gap between professed aims and actual achievements* (London Times). *The central failure of the play is a credibility gap between the audience and the characters* (Time).

cred|i|ble (kred'ə bəl), *adj.* worthy of belief; believable; reliable; trustworthy: *That boy's excuse for being absent was hardly credible. It hardly seems credible that your son has grown so tall in one year.* [< Latin *crēdibilis* < *crēdere* believe] —**cred'i|ble|ness,** *n.* —**cred'i|bly,** *adv.*
►**Credible, creditable,** and **credulous** are sometimes confused. *Credible* means believable: *His story is hardly credible; how could all that happen to one person? Creditable* means bringing honor or praise: *He turned in a creditable performance, though his heart was no longer in his acting. Credulous* means too ready to believe: *Credulous people are easily fooled.*

cred|it (kred'it), *n., v.* —***n.*** **1a** belief in the truth of something; faith; trust: *I know he is sure of his facts and put credit in what he says.* **b** personal influence or authority based on the confidence of others or on one's own reputation: *Buckingham ... resolved to employ all his credit to prevent the marriage* (David Hume). **c** credibility; trustworthiness: *His revelations destroy their credit by running into detail* (Emerson). **2a** trust in a person's ability and intention to pay: *This store will extend credit to you by opening a charge account in your name.* **b** one's reputation in money matters: *If you pay your bills on time, your credit will be good.* **3a** money in a person's bank account: *When I deposit this check, I will have a credit of fifty dollars in my savings account.* **b** the balance in a person's favor in an account: *His bookseller's statement shows a credit of $5.* **4** *Bookkeeping.* **a** the entry of money paid on account. **b** the right-hand side of an account where such entries are made. **c** the sum entered, or the total shown, on this side. **5** delayed payment; time allowed for delayed payment: *The store allowed us six months' credit on our purchase.* **6** favorable reputation; good name: *The mayor was a man of credit in the community.* SYN: repute, standing, honor. **7** praise, honor, recognition: *The person who does the work should get the credit. He claims no credit for the scheme.* SYN: commendation, esteem, appreciation. **8** a person or thing that brings honor or praise: *Benjamin Franklin's great scientific achievements were a credit to his young country. You are a credit to the school* (Dickens). **9a** an entry on a student's record showing that he has passed a course of study: *You must pass the examination to get credit for the course.* **b** a unit of work entered in this way: *He needs three credits to graduate.* **c** *British.* a mark between a mere pass and distinction, awarded in examinations. **10** Usually, **credits. a** an acknowledgment of the authorship or source of material used in a publication, work done on a dramatic show, radio or television program, or other artistic production: *The credits are often listed at the beginning of a motion picture.* **b** a listing of the producers, directors, actors, technicians, and others who have given their skills to a motion picture, radio or television show, or a play. *Abbr:* cr.
—***v.t.*** **1** to have faith in; believe; trust: *I can credit all that you are telling me because I had a similar experience. I... am content to credit my senses* (Samuel Johnson). **2a** to enter on the credit side of an account: *The bank credited fifty dollars to his savings account.* **b** to assign to as a credit: *The grocer was credited with the value of two hundred deposit bottles.* **3** to give credit in a bank account or other statement of account. **4** to put an entry on the record of (a student) showing that he has passed a course of study. **5** *Archaic.* to bring honor to. **6** *Obsolete.* to supply with goods on credit.

credit to, to ascribe to; attribute to: *The shortage of wheat was credited to lack of rain. Some excellent remarks were ... borrowed from and credited to Plato* (Oliver Wendell Holmes).
credit with, to think that one has; give recognition to: *You will have to credit him with some sense for not panicking during the fire.*
do credit to, to bring honor or praise to: *The winning team did credit to the school's reputation.*
give credit for, a to think that one has: *Give me credit for some brains.* **b** to give recognition to: *Give him credit for the idea. [They] give her credit for sincerity* (J. Wilson).
give credit to, to have faith in; believe; trust: *He gives no credit to kings or emperors* (James Mozley).
on credit, on a promise to pay later. When you buy anything and promise to pay for it later, you are getting it on credit. *He bought a new car on credit since he could not afford to make such a large purchase in cash.*
to one's credit, to bring honor to; be to the honor or praise of; worthy of approval: *It is to the students' credit that they hate war and social injustice* (Fred M. Hechinger).
[< Middle French *crédit* < Italian *credito,* learned borrowing from Latin *creditum* a loan < *crēdere* trust, entrust, lend (money)] —**cred′it|less,** *adj.*
▶ **Credit with, accredit with** mean to believe someone or something responsible for saying, doing, feeling, or causing something. **Credit** emphasizes the idea of believing, not always with enough reason or evidence: *You credit me with doing things I never thought of.* **Accredit** emphasizes the idea of accepting because of some proof: *We accredit Peary with having discovered the North Pole.*

cred|it|a|bil|i|ty (kred′ə tə bil′ə tē), *n., pl.* **-ties. 1** the quality of being creditable. **2** a creditable thing. **3** something that ought to be believed although not an article of faith.

cred|it|a|ble (kred′ə tə bəl), *adj.* **1** bringing praise or honor: *Her record of perfect attendance is very creditable to her.* **SYN:** praiseworthy, meritorious, commendable. **2** respectable; reputable: *His performance, though not inspiring, was a creditable one.* **SYN:** satisfactory. **3** worthy of receiving credit, especially financial or academic credit: *a creditable bank, a creditable student.* **4** that can be ascribed or attributed (to): *an invention creditable to Edison.* —**cred′it|a|ble|ness,** *n.*
▶ See **credible** for usage note.

cred|it|a|bly (kred′ə tə blē), *adv.* in a creditable manner; with credit to oneself: *He had come to America at the very start of the war and had served creditably in the southern theater* (Atlantic).

credit agency or **bureau,** an organization which collects information about the credit standing of individuals and business concerns, and makes this information available to subscribers to the agency's services.

credit card, a wallet-size identification card that enables its holder to buy products and obtain services on credit from one or a variety of business firms: *Credit card spenders who shun cash transactions may help ease the increasing demand for coins* (Wall Street Journal).

credit insurance, 1 insurance to protect creditors against heavy losses from non-payment of accounts. **2** = credit life insurance.

credit letter, = letter of credit.

credit life insurance, life insurance covering payment of loans in case of the borrower's death; credit insurance.

credit line, a line appearing with a story, picture, dramatic production, or the like, acknowledging its source or a participant in its composition or production.

credit man, an employee in a business establishment who fixes the amount of credit to be allowed to customers.

credit memorandum, a written authorization of an allowance or deduction granted to a customer; credit slip.

cré|dit mo|bi|lier (krā dē′ mô bē lyā′), *French.* credit based on security consisting of movable or personal property.

cred|i|tor (kred′ə tər), *n.* **1a** a person to whom money or goods are due; one to whom a debt is owed. **b** a person who gives credit for money or goods in business transactions. **2** *Bookkeeping.* the credit side, or an entry on the credit side, of an account. *Abbr:* cr.

cred|i|tor|ship (kred′ə tər ship), *n.* the state of being a creditor.

credit rating, the reputation and financial standing of a business concern or individual, which establishes the extent to which money may be borrowed or credit obtained.

credits (kred′its), *n.pl.* See under **credit,** *n.*

credit slip, = credit memorandum.

credit squeeze, a restraint put on bank loans by the government to fight inflation.

credit standing, a reputation for good or bad credit.

credit union, a cooperative association that makes loans to its members at low rates of interest: *A credit union is simply a group of people who run their own borrowing and saving system under government supervision.*

cred|it|wor|thy (kred′it wėr′ᴛʜē), *adj.* worthy of financial credit: *asserting that many creditworthy small enterprises are denied reasonable credit accommodation by the commercial banks* (Wall Street Journal). —**cred′it|wor′thi|ness,** *n.*

cre|do (krē′dō, krā′-), *n., pl.* **-dos. 1** a statement of belief; creed: *Because the President has adopted it, the credo is of importance in American political history* (Atlantic). **2** Also, **Credo.** the Apostles' Creed or the Nicene Creed. [< Latin *crēdō* I believe < *crēdere.* See etym. of doublet **creed.**]

Cre|do (krē′dō, krā′-), *n.* **1** the music for the Apostles' Creed or the Nicene Creed. **2** = credo (def. 2).

cre|du|li|ty (krə dü′lə tē, -dyü′-), *n.* a too great readiness to believe.

cred|u|lous (krej′ə ləs), *adj.* **1** too ready to believe; easily deceived: *She was so credulous that the other children could fool her easily.* **SYN:** gullible. **2** characterized by or arising from credulity. [< Latin *crēdulus* (with English *-ous*) < *crēdere* believe] —**cred′u|lous|ly,** *adv.* —**cred′u|lous|ness,** *n.*
▶ See **credible** for usage note.

Cree (krē), *n., pl.* **Cree** or **Crees. 1** a member of a tribe of American Indians living in Montana and in central and southern Canada. **2** the Algonkian language of this tribe.

creed (krēd), *n.* **1** a brief statement of the essential points of religious belief as approved by some church. **2** any statement of faith, belief, or opinion: *"Honesty is the best policy" was his creed in all his business dealings.* **SYN:** credo, tenet, doctrine.
the Creed, the Apostles' Creed or the Nicene Creed: *They should learn the Christian faith as it is contained in the Creed* (John Gau).
[Old English *crēda* < Latin *crēdō* I believe. See etym. of doublet **credo.**] —**creed′less,** *adj.*

creed|al (krē′dəl), *adj.* of or having to do with a creed or creeds; based on religious faith: *This broadening horizon makes the job more difficult for the church that has built a strong creedal fence about itself* (Harper's).

creek (krēk, krik), *n.* **1** a small stream; brook. **2** a narrow bay running inland for some distance. **3** *Dialect.* a narrow or winding passage; nook; turn.
up the creek, *U.S. Slang.* in trouble: *The trucks stop delivering to this store and where am I? Up the creek* (Edwin A. Roberts).
[earlier *creke* inlet, Middle English *crike,* perhaps < Scandinavian (compare dialectal Swedish *krik*)]
▶ The pronunciation (krik) is common in many sections of the United States and is by no means rare in educated use.

Creek (krēk), *n., pl.* **Creek** or **Creeks. 1** a member of a group of Indian tribes formerly living in Alabama, Georgia, and northern Florida, now living mostly in Oklahoma. **2** the Muskhogean language of these tribes.

creek bottom, *U.S.* level ground beside a stream or brook: *plains of sagebrush, with no trees except a few aspens and cottonwoods in the creek bottoms* (New Yorker).

creek chub, a freshwater fish commonly found in small rivers and lakes of the middle and eastern United States and Canada; horned dace.

creek gum, a gum tree of Australia.

***creel** (krēl), *n.* **1** a basket for holding fish that have been caught. **2** a basketlike trap to catch fish and lobsters. **3** a framework with skewers on which bobbins are held in a spinning machine. [perhaps < Old French *creil,* ultimately < Latin *crātis* wickerwork. Compare **crate, grill.**]

***creel** definition 1

creep (krēp), *v.,* **crept, creep|ing,** *n.* —*v.i.* **1** to move slowly with the body close to the ground or floor; crawl: *The cat was creeping toward the mouse. A baby creeps on its hands and knees before it begins to walk.* **SYN:** See syn. under **crawl. 2** *Figurative.* to move slowly or little by little: *The fog crept in while we were asleep. The traffic is creeping over the narrow bridge. Despondency began to creep over their hearts* (Washington Irving). *The cedar's shadow ... creeps o'er its dial of gray moss* (James Russell Lowell). **SYN:** See syn. under **crawl. 3** *Figurative.* to move in a timid or stealthy way: *The robbers crept toward their victims. The beaten dog crept into the room on his belly.* **4** to grow along the ground or over a wall by means of clinging stems: *a creeping plant. Ivy had crept up the wall of the old house.* **5** *Figurative.* to feel as if things were creeping over the skin; shiver; shudder: *It made my flesh creep to hear the wolves howl.* **6** to slip slightly out of place. The spreading of a metal under tension or strain is due to its ability to creep. *The hall rug creeps until we pull it back. Railroad tracks moving under the weight of traffic are said to creep.* —**v.t.** *Poetic.* to creep along or over: *the meanest worm that creeps the earth* (Charles Wesley).
—*n.* **1** the act of creeping; slow movement: *Until a gentle creep, A careful moving caught my waking ears* (Keats). **2** the slow continuous deformation of a metal under stress below the yield point determined by a tensile test. **3** Physics. the process of softening, flexing, or melting of material with accompanying changes in shape and dimension that result from stress or increased temperature: *The creep properties of ice itself are still largely unexplored. Below a certain stress, creep will not take place at all* (Science News Letter). **4** *Geology.* slow movement of soil or disintegrated rock down a slope, due to gravity, frost, or ground water: *tangential creep, continental creep.* **5** an enclosure with a small entrance in which young animals can feed undisturbed: *A temporary creep was provided ... for the young calves* (London Times). **6** *Slang.* **a** an undesirable, unpleasant, or worthless person. **b** a petty thief; sneak thief. **c** petty thievery.
the creeps, *Informal.* a feeling of horror, as if things were creeping over one's skin: *The very thought of snakes gives her the creeps. For some reason she couldn't define he gave her the creeps* (John S. Strange).
[Old English *crēopan.* See related etym. at **cripple.**]

CREEP (no periods), Committee for the Reelection of the President. Also, **CRP** (no periods).

creep|age (krē′pij), *n.* a gradual movement.

***creep|er** (krē′pər), *n.* **1** a person or thing that creeps. **2** any plant that grows along a surface, sending out rootlets from the stem, such as the Virginia creeper and ivy. **3** a small bird that creeps around on trees and bushes looking for food, such as the brown creeper of North America. **4** a domestic fowl having very short legs. **5** a grapnel for dragging the bottom of the sea or a river, or other body of water. **6** a piece of canvas attached to a ski for better gripping in climbing uphill. **7** any one of various mechanical devices for conveying or feeding material slowly. **8** a low, wheeled frame used by automobile mechanics to lie on; cradle. **9** *Cricket.* a pitched ball which stays low.
creepers, a a garment combining shirt and pants, worn by babies: *... outerwear for infants, including creepers, sunsuits and nylon dresses* (Wall Street Journal). **b** spiked iron plates worn on shoes to prevent slipping: *Ice creepers are now on sale in certain shops of Newcastle* (Newcastle Weekly Chronicle).

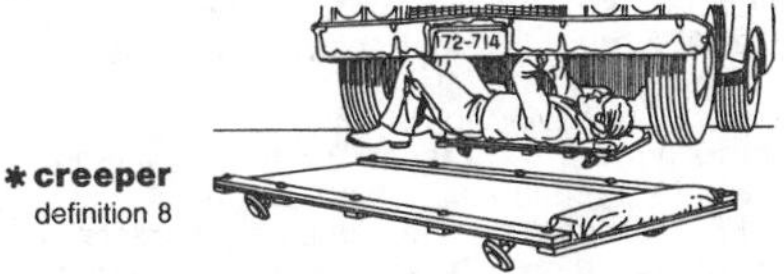

***creeper** definition 8

creep|hole (krēp′hōl′), *n.* **1** a hole by which to creep in or out. **2** a hole into which an animal creeps to escape notice or danger. **3** a trick; excuse.

creep|ie (krē′pē), *n.,* or **creepie stool,** *Scottish.* a low stool: *On the creepie stool, chubby Isaac absorbed the wonder of half-comprehended words* (New Yorker).

creep|ie-peep|ie (krē′pē pē′pē), *n.* a small, portable, battery-powered television camera: *Creepie-peepies and walkie-talkies manned by hard-running TV reporters* (Time). [< *creep* + *peep*[1],

Pronunciation Key: hat, āge, cãre, fär; let, ēqual, tėrm; it, īce; hot, ōpen, ôrder; oil, out; cup, pu̇t, rüle; child; long; thin; ᴛʜen; zh, measure; ə represents **a** in about, **e** in taken, **i** in pencil, **o** in lemon, **u** in circus.

perhaps patterned on *walkie-talkie*]

creep|ing (krē′ping), *adj.* **1** moving or developing in a gradual or imperceptible manner: (*Figurative.*) *creeping socialism, creeping aggression. Creeping inflation, we are told, is inevitable—all we can do is to accept it and learn to live with it* (Atlantic). **2** *Botany.* growing along or just beneath the surface of the ground, or on any other surface, and usually sending out rootlets at intervals.
— **creep′ing|ly**, *adv.*

creeping bent, a common type of lawn grass of temperate North America that spreads by sending out runners, grown especially to cover large areas, such as golf courses and playgrounds.

creeping buttercup, a buttercup with stolons that run along the ground and send out roots.

creeping Charlie, = moneywort.

creeping eruption, an eruption of itchy, red patches on the skin, caused by the burrowing of insect and worm larvae, such as those of the hookworm, into the surface of the skin.

creeping Jennie, = moneywort.

creeping Jesus, *British Slang.* a person who acts in an abject or slavish manner.

creeping paralysis, = locomotor ataxia.

creeping thyme, = wild thyme.

creep|y (krē′pē), *adj.*, **creep|i|er, creep|i|est.** **1** having a feeling of horror, as if things were creeping over one's skin; frightened: *Ghost stories make some children creepy.* **2** causing such a feeling: *The wind howling through the old house was creepy. The stillness was awful creepy and uncomfortable* (Mark Twain). **3** moving slowly; creeping. — **creep′i|ly**, *adv.* — **creep′i|ness**, *n.*

creep|y-crawl|y (krē′pē krô′lē), *adj., n., pl.* **-crawl|ies.** — *adj.* **1** that creeps and crawls. **2** sneaking; servile. **3** *Figurative.* full of eerie or uncanny suggestions: *a creepy-crawly feeling.*
— *n. British Informal.* an insect, spider, rodent, or other small crawling animal: *And all this gentle safari in perfect safety—there are no poisonous snakes, no deadly creepy-crawlies* (Sunday Times).

creese (krēs), *n.* a type of dagger having a wavy blade, used by the Malays. Also, **crease, kris.** [< Malay *kĕris*]

creesh (krēsh), *n., v.t. Scottish.* grease. [< Old French *craisse, cresse* < Latin *crassa,* feminine of *crassus* thick, fat]

cre|mains (krē′mānz′), *n.pl.* a cremated corpse: *He suggests a rather thorough overhauling of the language: ... flower car, not flower truck; cremains ... not ashes* (Jessica Mitford).

cre|mas|ter (krə mas′tər, krē-), *n.* a pointed or rounded part with many hooklike claws at the rear of a pupa's body. [< New Latin *cremaster* < Greek *kremastḗr* < *kremannynai* hang]

cre|mate (krē′māt), *v.t.,* **-mat|ed, -mat|ing.** **1** to burn (a dead body) to ashes instead of burying it. **2** to burn. [< Latin *cremāre* (with English *-ate*[1])]

cre|ma|tion (krē mā′shən), *n.* the burning of a dead body to ashes instead of burying it.

cre|ma|tion|ist (krē mā′shə nist), *n.* a person who advocates cremation instead of burial of the bodies of the dead.

cre|ma|tor (krē′mā tər, krē mā′-), *n.* **1** a person who cremates corpses. **2** a furnace for cremating dead bodies. **3** an incinerator for burning garbage, rubbish, or the like.

cre|ma|to|ri|um (krē′mə tôr′ē əm, -tōr′-; krem′ə-), *n., pl.* **-to|ri|ums, -to|ri|a** (-tôr′ē ə, -tōr′-). = crematory.

cre|ma|to|ry (krē′mə tôr′ē, -tōr′-; krem′ə-), *n., pl.* **-ries,** *adj.* — *n.* **1** a furnace for cremating dead bodies. **2** a building that has a furnace for cremating.
— *adj.* of or having to do with cremating.

crème (krem), *n.* **1** cream. **2** a thick, sweet liqueur. [< French *crème* type of liqueur, cream < Old French *cresme;* see etym. under **cream**]

crème de ca|ca|o (krem′ də kä kä ō′; *Anglicized* krēm′ də kō′kō), *French.* a brown liqueur with a chocolate flavor.

crème de la crème (krem′ də lä krem′), *French.* **1** the choicest. **2** (literally) cream of the cream.

crème de menthe (krem′ də mäɴt′; *Anglicized* krēm′ də mint′), *French.* a liqueur flavored with mint.

crem|o|carp (krem′ə kärp, krē′mə-), *n.* the characteristic dry fruit of plants of the parsley family, consisting of two one-seeded carpels which separate from each other at maturity and remain closed while hanging at the end of the axis. [< Greek *krema-* to hang + *karpós* fruit]

Cre|mo|na (kri mō′nə), *n.* any one of the violins of outstanding quality made by the Amati, Stradivari, and Guarneri families, and others, during the 1500's, 1600's, and 1700's in Cremona, a city in northern Italy.

cre|mone bolt (kri mōn′), one of a pair of vertical rods that operate the bolts of casement windows and French doors by being raised or lowered with a knob or handle. [< French *crémone,* apparently < *Crémone* Cremona (Italy)]

Cre|mo|nese (kri′mō nēz′, -nēs′), *adj., n., pl.* **-nese.** — *adj.* of or having to do with Cremona, Italy, or the violins of the same name made there.
— *n.* a native of Cremona.

cre|na (krē′nə), *n., pl.* **-nae** (-nē). **1** a notch or indentation. **2** a tooth or scallop. [< New Latin *crena;* origin uncertain]

cre|nate (krē′nāt), *adj.* with a scalloped edge: *Many leaves are crenate.* **SYN:** notched. [< New Latin *crenatus* < *crena* crena] — **cre′nate|ly,** *adv.*

cre|nat|ed (krē′nā tid), *adj.* = crenate.

cre|na|tion (kri nā′shən), *n.* a crenate formation; a series of scallops, for example on the margin of a leaf or shell or on the edges of a red blood cell as a result of shrinkage.

cren|a|ture (kren′ə chər, krē′nə-), *n.* **1** a crenate formation, for example on the margin of a leaf or shell. **2** a notch between teeth.

cren|el (kren′əl), *n., v.,* **-eled, -el|ing** or (*especially British*) **-elled, -el|ling.** — *n.* **1** an open space between merlons on a battlement; embrasure. See picture under **battlement. 2** a crenation or crenature. — *v.t.* = crenelate.
[< Old French *crenel* (diminutive) < *cren,* earlier *cran;* see etym. under **cranny**]

cren|el|ate (kren′ə lāt), *v.t.,* **-at|ed, -at|ing.** **1** to furnish with battlements. **2** to form with square indentations with a pattern resembling crenels: *Moldings are often crenelated.* Also, **crenel, crenelle.** [< Old French *creneler* (with English *-ate*[1]) < *crenel* notch; see etym. under **crenel**]

cren|el|at|ed (kren′ə lā′tid), *adj.* **1** embattled: *With its ... delicate cupolas and crenelated battlements* (Atlantic). **2** furnished with crenels: *the tall red brick crenelated walls of the Kremlin* (Time).

cren|el|a|tion (kren′ə lā′shən), *n.* **1a** the act of crenelating. **b** the state of being crenelated. **2** a battlement having crenels: *There is the bishop's residence bristling with the same crenelations as the fortress—those fierce crenelations which are cleft down the center like snakes' tongues* (Atlantic). **3** a notch or indentation, or a series of these.

cren|el|late (kren′ə lāt), *v.t.,* **-lat|ed, -lat|ing.** *Especially British.* crenelate.

cre|nelle (kri nel′), *v.t.,* **-nelled, -nel|ling.** = crenelate.

cren|u|late (kren′yə lit, -lāt), *adj.* minutely crenate, as a leaf or shell. [< New Latin *crenulatus* < *crenula* notch (diminutive) < *crena*]

cren|u|lat|ed (kren′yə lā′tid), *adj.* = crenulate.

cren|u|la|tion (kren′yə lā′shən), *n.* **1** crenulate state. **2** a minute crenation.

cre|o|dont (krē′ə dont), *n.* any animal of an extinct suborder of primitive, carnivorous mammals with small brains, regarded as the ancestors of the modern carnivores: *Early flesh-eating mammals called creodonts had long bodies and short legs* (S. P. Welles). [< New Latin *Creodonta* < Greek *kréas, kréōs* flesh + *odoús, odóntos* tooth]

Cre|ole or **cre|ole** (krē′ōl), *n., adj.* — *n.* **1** a descendant of early French or Spanish settlers in Louisiana: *"I am a Creole of Louisiana." ... I then explained ... that creole means native, and has no reference to color or race* (Harper's). **2a** the French language as spoken in Louisiana. **b** any French patois: *Haitian Creole.* **3** a French or Spanish person born in Latin America or the West Indies. **4** a person who is part Negro and part Creole. **5** a Canadian of French descent: *It was the neighboring Creoles and small Acadian planters* (Longfellow).
— *adj.* **1** of or having to do with the Creoles: *Compere Martin ... could ... play on the fiddle, an invaluable accomplishment in an old French creole village* (Washington Irving). **2** cooked in a sauce of stewed tomatoes, peppers, onion, and other spicy foods served over rice: *shrimp creole.*
[< French *créole* < Spanish *criollo* < Portuguese *crioulo* (originally) bred in one's house < *criar* bring up < Latin *creāre* create]

cre|o|li|za|tion (krē′ə lə zā′shən), *n.* the process by which a mixture of several languages becomes the standard native language: *The creolization of a pidgin language can happen voluntarily* (*as in certain modern villages in New Guinea*), *or involuntarily* (*as when Caribbean plantation owners deliberately separated slaves of the same language, in order to minimize the danger of conspiracy and revolt*) (Scientific American).

cre|o|lized language (krē′ə līzd), a language formed by a mixture of two languages and learned by later generations as their native tongue.

Cre|on (krē′on), *n. Greek Legend.* **1** a king of Thebes, contemporary with Oedipus. **2** a king of Corinth, the father-in-law of Jason.

cre|oph|a|gous (krē of′ə gəs), *adj.* flesh-eating; carnivorous.

cre|oph|a|gy (krē of′ə jē), *n.* the eating of flesh. [< Greek *kreophagiā* < *kréas, kréōs* flesh + *phagein* eat]

cre|o|sol (krē′ə sōl, -sol), *n.* a colorless to yellowish, oily liquid obtained from beechwood tar and the resin of the guaiacum tree, used as an antiseptic. Creosol is one of the active constituents of creosote. *Formula:* $C_8H_{10}O_2$ [< *creos*(ote) + *-ol*[1]]

cre|o|sote (krē′ə sōt), *n., v.,* **-sot|ed, -sot|ing.** — *n.* **1** an oily liquid with a penetrating odor, obtained by distilling wood tar. It is used to preserve wood and in cough medicine. *Creosote may be hydrogenated to make motor spirit and is widely used as a timber preservative* (London Times). **2** a similar substance obtained from coal tar.
— *v.t.* to treat with creosote.
[(originally) a meat preservative < Greek *kreo-,* for *kréas, kréōs* flesh + *sōtḗr* savior, preserver < *sôzein* save]

creosote bush, an evergreen shrub with resinous leaves and a strong odor of creosote, growing in the southwestern United States and northern Mexico.

crepe or **crêpe** (krāp), *n., adj.* — *n.* **1** a thin, light cloth with a finely crinkled surface; crape. Crepe may be silk, cotton, rayon, or wool. *She was stiff as starched crepe* (Winston Churchill). **2** = crepe paper. **3** a light, thin pancake. **4** = crepe rubber. **5** = crape (def. 2).
— *adj.* = creped: *crepe soles.*
[< French *crêpe* < Old French *crespe* < Latin *crispa,* feminine of *crispus* curled]

creped (krāpt), *adj.* having the texture of crepe; crinkled, so as to give a better grip: *creped paper tissues.*

crepe de Chine (krāp′ də shēn′), a soft, thin, medium-weight silk crepe. [< French *crêpe de Chine* China crepe]

crepe hair, plaited wool or vegetable fiber used as hair for false beards, wigs, and the like, especially on the stage.

crepe|hang|er (krāp′hang′ər), *n.* = crapehanger.

crêpe lisse (krāp′ lēs′), *French.* a very thin, fine crepe in which the crinkled surface is almost imperceptible, used especially for making ruching.

crepe or **crêpe myrtle**, = crape myrtle.

crepe paper, thin, crinkled paper that looks like crepe, used for making decorations.

crêpe|rie (krā prē′), *n. French.* a place where crêpes suzette and other pancakes are sold.

crepe rubber, crude rubber with a crinkled surface, used for the soles of shoes.

crêpe su|zette (krāp′ sü zet′), *pl.* **crêpes suzette** (krāps′ sü zet′), **crêpe su|zettes** (krāp′ sü-zets′). a thin pancake served for dessert, usually rolled, with a hot sauce of butter, sugar, citrus juice, and a liqueur or brandy, and often set ablaze when served. [< French *crêpe suzette* (literally) Suzette pancake]

crep|ey (krā′pē), *adj.,* **crep|i|er, crep|i|est.** = crepy.

crep|i|ness (krā′pē nis), *n.* crepy texture or quality.

cré|pi|nette (krā pē net′), *n. French.* minced meat with sauce or stuffing, wrapped in pieces of pork caul.

crep|i|tant (krep′ə tənt), *adj.* crackling; rattling; crepitating.

crep|i|tate (krep′ə tāt), *v.i.,* **-tat|ed, -tat|ing.** to crackle; rattle. [< Latin *crepitāre* (with English *-ate*[1]) crackle, rattle (frequentative) < *crepāre* rattle]

crep|i|ta|tion (krep′ə tā′shən), *n.* a crepitating: *the tiny crepitation of insect or field mouse close to my ear* (Geoffrey Household).

crep|i|tus (krep′ə təs), *n.* a harsh grating sound caused when broken ends of bone rub together. [< Latin *crepitus* crackled, past participle of *crepāre* rattle]

cré|pon (krā′pon; *French* krā pôɴ′), *n.* a dress material of wool, silk, or cotton, crinkled like crepe but heavier. [< French *crépon*]

crept (krept), *v.* the past tense and past participle of **creep**: *The baby crept across the floor. We had crept up on the enemy without their seeing us.*

cre|pus|cle (kri pus′əl), *n.* twilight; dusk. [< Latin *crepusculum* (diminutive) < *creper* dark; obscure]

cre|pus|cu|lar (kri pus′kyə lər) *adj.* **1** of twilight; resembling twilight; dim; indistinct. **2** appearing or flying at twilight, as certain birds and insects do.

cre|pus|cule (kri pus′kyül), *n.* = crepuscle.

cre|pus|cu|line (kri pus′kyə lin, -līn), *adj.* **1** having to do with twilight. **2** dusky; dim.

cre|pus|cu|lous (kri pus′kyə ləs), *adj.* = crepuscular.

cre|pus|cu|lum (kri pus′kyə ləm), *n.* twilight; dusk; crepuscle.

crep|y (krā′pē), *adj.,* **crep|i|er, crep|i|est.** of or like crepe; crinkled: *crepy fabrics.* Also, **crepey.**

cres. or **cresc.,** crescendo.

cre|scen|do** (krə shen′dō), *adj., adv., n., pl.* **-dos,** *v.,* **-doed, -do|ing.** **—*adj.*, *adv. *Music.* with a gradual increase in force or loudness: *a crescendo passage* (adj.). *Lullabies are not sung crescendo* (adv.). **—*n.*** **1** a gradual increase in force or loudness, especially in music. **2** *Music.* a crescendo passage. **—*v.i.*** to increase gradually in loudness or intensity. [< Italian *crescendo,* present participle of *crescere* increase < Latin *crēscere;* see etym. under **crescent**]

***crescendo**
definition 2

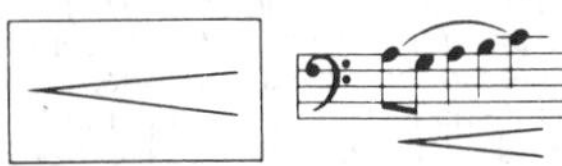

cres|cent** (kres′ənt), *n., adj.* **—*n. **1** the shape of the moon when it is small and thin. The moon is a crescent in its first and last quarter. **2** anything that curves in a similar way. A curved street or a curved row of houses is sometimes called a crescent. **3** the emblem of the former Turkish Empire and of the present republic of Turkey. **4** the Turkish or Moslem power. **5** a light roll, made of yeast dough, shaped like a crescent moon. **6** *Heraldry.* a bearing in the form of a new moon, usually borne horizontally with the horns uppermost as a mark of the second son. **7** a small butterfly with spotted brown wings with black margins on the upper side and a pale crescent spot on the under side of the wings.
—*adj.* **1** shaped like the moon when it is small and thin: *a crescent pin.* **2** growing; increasing; developing: *the crescent darkness.*
[< Latin *crēscēns, -entis* growing, present participle of *crēscere* arise, begin to grow < *creāre* produce, create] **—cres′cent|like′,** *adj.*

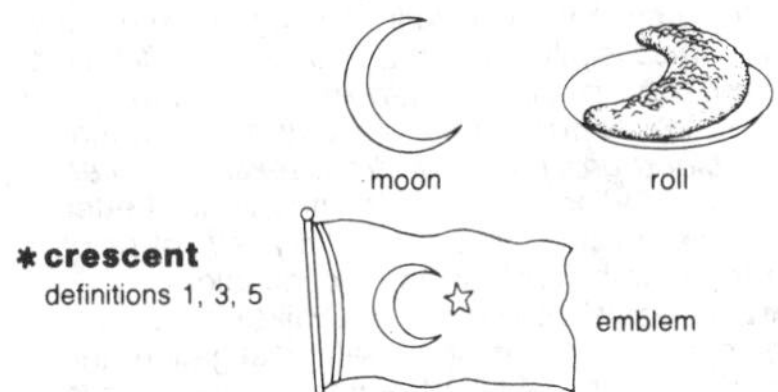

***crescent**
definitions 1, 3, 5

cres|cent|ed (kres′ən tid), *adj.* **1** formed as a crescent. **2** decorated with crescents.

cres|cen|tic (kre sen′tik), *adj.* crescent-shaped; crescentlike: *crescentic slopes.*

crescent of crisis, = arc of crisis: *Afghanistan . . . lies along the eastern tier of the "crescent of crisis," which in an oil-short world has become strategically vital to both the West and the Soviet Union* (Time).

cres|cent-shaped (kres′ənt shāpt′), *adj.* having the shape of a crescent or new moon.

cre|scit e|un|do (kres′it ē un′dō; krā′skit e ůn′dō), *Latin.* it grows as it goes (motto of New Mexico).

cres|cive (kres′iv), *adj.* growing; increasing; crescent.

cres|co|graph (kres′kə graf, -gräf), *n.* a device for observing and recording small movements of growth in plants, by greatly magnifying the actual movements. [< Latin *crēscere* to grow + *-graph*]

cres|co|graph|ic (kres′kə graf′ik), *adj.* of or having to do with the crescograph.

cre|sol (krē′sōl, -sol), *n.* **1** any one of three isomeric oily compounds obtained from coal tar, used as a disinfectant and in resins; hydroxytoluene. Creosote oil contains cresols. *Formula:* C_7H_8O **2** a mixture of these compounds. [alteration of *creosol*]

cress (kres), *n.* any one of various plants whose leaves have a peppery taste and are used as a garnish or in salad. Cress belongs to the mustard family. [Old English *cresse*]

cres|set (kres′it), *n.* a metal container for burning oil, wood, or other burnable material, to give light. Cressets are mounted on poles or hung from above. [< Old French *cresset,* earlier *craisset* < *craisse* grease < Latin *crassus* fat, thick]

Cres|si|da (kres′ə də), *n. Medieval Legend.* a Trojan woman who was faithless to her lover, Troilus.

cress|y (kres′ē), *adj.* abounding in cresses.

crest (krest), *n., v.* **—*n.*** **1** a tuft or comb on the head of a bird or animal. **2a** a decoration of plumes or feathers on the top of a helmet. **b** the apex or cone of a helmet. **c** = helmet. **3** a decoration at the top of a coat of arms. A family crest is sometimes put on silverware, dishes, or letter paper. **4** the top part; peak; summit: *The crest of a hill. The instrument is designed to count a sample of 300 waves, and to measure the height of each from trough to succeeding crest* (Science News Letter). SYN: ridge. **5a** the ridge of the neck of a horse, dog, or other animal with fur. **b** the mane of a horse, lion, or other animal with fur. **c** *Anatomy.* a ridge running along the surface of a bone: *the frontal crest of the skull.* **6** *Architecture.* = cresting.
—*v.t.* **1** to furnish with a crest or cresting. **2** to serve as a crest to; top; crown: *The stately mansion crested the hill.* **3** to reach the crest or summit of (a hill, wave, or other inclined surface).
—*v.i.* **1** to form or rise into a crest: *Wave upon wave crested during the storm.* **2** to reach its crest or highest point: *At LaCrosse, Wis., the river crested at 17.7 feet, 5.7 feet above flood stage* (New York Times). **3** *Dialect.* to hold oneself (up) proudly: *The old minister was standing with his back to the fire, cresting up erect* (James Boswell).
[< Old French *creste* < Latin *crista* tuft, crest] **—crest′like′,** *adj.*

crest|ed (kres′tid), *adj.* having a crest: *a crested bird, a crested shield.*

crested auklet, a small auk of the North Pacific and Bering Sea areas.

crested flycatcher, a large flycatcher, with a crest of eastern North America.

crested myna, a variety of myna with long feathers on its forehead and a bushy crest. It is native to India and Burma but is also found in Japan, the Philippines, and British Columbia.

crest|fall|en (krest′fô′lən), *adj.* with bowed head; dejected; discouraged: *She came home crestfallen because she had failed the examination.* SYN: depressed, dispirited, abject. **—crest′fall′en|ly,** *adv.* **—crest′fall′en|ness,** *n.*

crest|ing (kres′ting), *n. Architecture.* an ornamental finish of stone, metal, or other building material at the top of a structure, along the ridge of a roof, the top of a wall or parapet, or the like.

crest|less (krest′lis), *adj.* without a crest.

cres|yl (kres′əl, krē′səl), *n. Chemistry.* the univalent radical tolyl, of which cresol is the hydroxide.

cre|syl|ic (kri sil′ik), *adj.* of or obtained from cresol or creosote.

cre|ta|ceous (kri tā′shəs), *adj.* like chalk; containing chalk; chalky. [< Latin *crētāceus* (with English *-ous)* < *crēta* chalk]

Cre|ta|ceous (kri tā′shəs), *n., adj.* **—*n.*** **1** the last geological period of the Mesozoic era, after the Jurassic and before the Paleocene, characterized by the formation of chalk deposits. During this period flowering plants began to appear and dinosaurs became extinct. **2** the rocks formed during this period.
—*adj.* of or having to do with this period or its rocks.

Cre|tan (krē′tən), *adj., n.* **—*adj.*** of or having to do with Crete, its inhabitants, or their language.
—*n.* a person born or living in Crete.

cre|tic (krē′tik), *adj., n. Prosody.* **—*adj.*** denoting a foot of three syllables, the first and third being long, the second being short.
—*n.* a cretic foot or verse; amphimacer.
[< Latin *Crēticus* of Crete < *Crēta* Crete < Greek *Krētē*]

cre|tin (krē′tən; *especially British* kret′ən), *n.* **1** a person suffering from cretinism: *A cretin is a person born with a congenital absence of functioning thyroid gland* (Sunday Times). **2** a very stupid person; fool: *The cretin with the transistor radio has finally invaded the last remaining corners of silence* (Atlantic). [< French *crétin* < an Alpine dialect < Latin *Christiānus* Christian (the development of meaning was "man," then "fellow," then "poor fellow")]

cre|tin|ism (krē′tə niz əm; *especially British* kret′ə niz əm), *n.* a condition of severe mental and physical retardation caused by a deficiency in the thyroid gland. The deficiency may be inborn or it may develop in infancy.

cre|tin|oid (krē′tə noid; *especially British* kret′ə noid), *adj.* resembling a cretin or cretinism.

cre|tin|ous (krē′tə nəs; *especially British* kret′ə nəs), *adj.* **1** of or having to do with a cretin. **2** of the nature of cretinism.

Cre|to-My|ce|nae|an (krē′tō mī′sə nē′ən), *adj.* of or having to do with the civilization and culture of ancient Crete and Mycenae.

cre|tonne (kri ton′, krē′ton), *n.* a strong cotton or linen cloth with designs printed in colors on one or both sides. Cretonne is used especially for curtains, furniture covers, and other interior decoration. [< French *cretonne,* probably < *Creton,* a village in Normandy, where such stout linen cloth was made]

Cre|ü|sa or **Cre|u|sa** (krē ü′sə), *n.* **1** *Greek and Roman Legend.* a daughter of Priam and the wife of Aeneas, lost or killed on the night Troy fell. **2** *Greek Legend.* the wife of Jason, killed by Medea, whom Jason had deserted.

Creutz|feldt-Ja|kob disease (kroits′felt yä′kob, -kop), a degenerative brain disease of middle and late life, caused by infection with a prion: *The scientists had noted that Creutzfeldt-Jakob disease causes changes in brain tissue similar to those caused by kuru* (Richard R. Johnson). [< Hans G. *Creutzfeldt* (born 1883) and Alfons M. *Jakob* (1884–1931), German psychiatrists who first described the disease]

cre|val|le (krə val′ē), *n.* = cavalla (def. 1). [variant of *cavalla*]

cre|vasse (krə vas′), *n., v.,* **-vassed, -vass|ing.** **—*n.*** **1** a deep crack or split in the ice of a glacier, or in the ground after an earthquake: *Glaciologists investigate crevasses near the junction between grounded ice and floating ice shelf* (Science News Letter). **2** *U.S.* a break in the levee of a river, dike, or dam.
—*v.t.* to make crevasses in.
[< French *crevasse* < Old French *crevace.* See etym. of doublet **crevice.**]

cre|vette (krə vet′), *n., pl.* **-vettes.** = shrimp. [< French *crevette*]

crev|ice (krev′is), *n.* a narrow split or crack; cleft; rift; fissure: *Tiny ferns grew in crevices in the stone wall.* SYN: chink, slit. [< Old French *crevace* < Vulgar Latin *crepacia* < Latin *crepāre* crack, creak. See etym. of doublet **crevasse.**]

crev|iced (krev′ist), *adj.* having crevices; cracked; fissured.

crew[1] (krü), *n., v.* **—*n.*** **1** the men needed to work a ship, especially: **a** the common sailors of a ship's company. **b** a work section of a ship's company: *a boiler crew.* **2** a group of persons manning an aircraft. **3** a group of people working or acting together: *a crew of loggers, a maintenance crew. A train crew runs a railroad train.* SYN: team. **4** a band or company; gang; crowd: *The boys on that street are a rough crew.* SYN: group, mob. **5a** the members of a rowing team. **b** the sport of rowing as a crew: *He went out for crew in his sophomore year at college.* **6** *Obsolete.* a reinforcement of soldiers.
—*v.t.* **1** to staff (a ship) with a crew: *Arrangements had been made for the crewing of the ship to ensure this* (London Times). **2** to operate (a ship) as if with a crew: *The schooner was crewed by a retired sailor.*
—*v.i.* to act as a crewman; work with a crew.
[< Old French *creüe* increase; recruit < *creistre* grow < Latin *crēscere;* see etym. under **crescent**] **—crew′less,** *adj.*

crew[2] (krü), *v.* crowed; a past tense of **crow[1]**.

crew chief, 1 (in the U.S. Air Force) a noncommissioned officer who supervises a ground crew. **2** any person in charge of a ground crew, as at an airport or launch complex: *the countdown crew chief.*

crew cut, 1 a kind of very short haircut for men or boys. **2** a person wearing a crew cut.

crew-cut (krü′kut′), *adj.* wearing or displaying a crew cut: *a crew-cut freshman.*

crew|el (krü′əl), *n.* **1** a loosely twisted, woolen yarn, used for embroidery. **2** embroidery done with this yarn. [origin uncertain]

crew|el|work (krü′əl wėrk′), *n.* work done with crewels or worsted yarns, applied to a species of embroidery which became fashionable about 1860.

crew haircut, = crew cut.

crew|man (krü′mən), *n., pl.* **-men.** a member of a crew: *a crewman on a jet airliner.*

crew|mate (krü′māt′), *n.* a member of the same crew: *A crewmate accepted his medal for him* (Newsweek).

***crew neck** or **neckline,** a round, close-fitting neckline at the base of the throat, as on sweaters worn by boat crews.

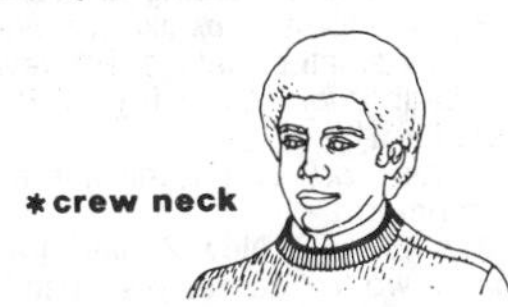

***crew neck**

cri|ant (krē äɴ′), *adj. French.* loud; garish.

crib (krib), *n., v.,* **cribbed, crib|bing.** **—*n.*** **1** a small bed with high barred sides to keep a baby from falling out. **2** a rack or manger for horses and cows to eat from. **3** a building, box, or bin for storing grain, salt, and the like: *Rats damaged much of the corn in the crib.* **4** a framework of logs or timbers used in building. The wooden lining inside a mine shaft is a crib. **5** a stall or

Pronunciation Key: hat, āge, cãre, fär; let, ēqual, tėrm; it, īce; hot, ōpen, ôrder; oil, out; cup, pu̇t, rüle; child; long; thin; ᴛʜen; zh, measure; ə represents **a** in about, **e** in taken, **i** in pencil, **o** in lemon, **u** in circus.

pen for cattle: *Where no oxen are, the crib is clean* (Proverbs 14:4). **6** *Informal.* the use of another's words or ideas as one's own; plagiarism. **7** *Informal.* notes or helps that are unfair to use in doing schoolwork or in examinations: *A translation of a work in a foreign language, used dishonestly, is a crib.* **8a** a small room or house. **b** *Figurative.* a confined space. **9** a water reservoir. **10** a set of cards in cribbage, made up of discards from each hand and scored by the dealer after the deal has been played. **11** (especially in Australia and New Zealand) a light meal or lunch, especially one carried by a worker to be eaten at his place of work. **12** (New Zealand) a small house at a seaside or vacation resort. **13** *Slang.* a safe. **14** *Obsolete.* a wicker basket; crate.

— ***v.t.*** **1** to provide with a crib or cribs in building. **2** to shut up in a small space, as if in a crib: *His restraint did not crib nor confine either the vast size of the drama or the rhythm of its unfolding* (London Times). **3** *Informal.* to use (another's words or ideas) as one's own; plagiarize.

— ***v.i.*** **1** *Informal.* **a** to use somebody's words or ideas in an unfair way: *He cribbed from the encyclopedia to write his report.* **b** to steal; pilfer. **2** = crib-bite.

crack a crib, *Slang.* to break into a house: *The burglars tried to crack a crib but were caught in the act.*

[Old English *cribb*]

***crib|bage** (krib′ij), *n.* a card game for two, three, or four people. The players keep score with a narrow board into which movable pegs fit. [< *crib,* noun + *-age*]

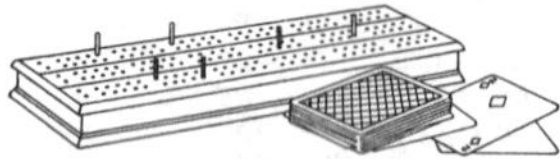

***cribbage**

crib|ber (krib′ər), *n.* **1** a person that cribs. **2** a horse that crib-bites.

crib|bing (krib′ing), *n.* **1** = crib-biting. **2** a mining crib. **3** the pieces of timber forming the lining of a shaft. **4** *Informal.* cheating; plagiarism: *Cribbing is of two distinctly different kinds: Copying the work of another student, and copying from a self-prepared pony* (Newsweek).

crib-bite (krib′bīt′), *v.i.,* **-bit, -bit|ten** or **-bit, -bit-ing.** (of horses) to engage in crib-biting. — **crib′-bit′er**, *n.*

crib-bit|ing (krib′bī′ting), *n.* a harmful habit of horses in which the sides of the stall, manger, or other objects are gnawed. It is accompanied by noisy breathing.

crib death, *U.S.* the sudden death of an infant in his sleep without any recognized warning symptoms or known cause: *"Crib deaths" happen in the best-doctored countries and to the best-cared-for babies* (Time). Also, *British.* **cot death.**

cri|bel|lum (krə bel′əm), *n., pl.* **-bel|la** (-bel′ə). a platelike organ by which some spiders spin additional silk. [< Late Latin *crībellum* small sieve (diminutive) < Latin *crībrum* sieve]

cri|blé (krē blā′), *adj.* **1** engraved by a method in which light and shade are indicated by numerous small round holes sunk in a wooden block. **2** decorated with minute punctures or depressions, as a surface of metal or wood. [< French *criblé,* past participle of *cribler* riddle with holes, ultimately < Latin *crībrum* sieve]

crib note or **sheet**, **1** a small piece of paper containing information from which students illicitly copy during a test. **2** any cribbing device.

crib|ri|form (krib′rə fôrm), *adj.* like a sieve; perforated with many small openings. [< New Latin *cribriformis* < Latin *cribrāre* to sift (< *crībrum* sieve) + *forma* form]

crib|rose (krib′rōs), *adj.* perforated with many small holes; cribriform.

crib tin, (in Australia and New Zealand) a container in which a worker carries his lunch to work.

crib|work (krib′wėrk′), *n.* work consisting of logs, beams, or the like, arranged in layers at right angles.

cri|cet|id (krī set′id, -sē′tid), *n., adj.* — ***n.*** any one of a large family of mouselike rodents that includes the hamsters, gerbils, lemmings, and voles.

— ***adj.*** of or belonging to this family.

[< New Latin *Cricetidae* the family name < *Cricetus* the genus name of hamsters < Slavic (compare Czech *křeček* hamster]

crick¹ (krik), *n., v.* — ***n.*** a muscular cramp; painful stiffness of muscles: *I got a crick in the neck from sleeping in the chair.*

— ***v.t.*** to give a crick to (the neck or back).

[origin uncertain]

crick² (krik), *n. U.S. Dialect.* creek (def. 1).

***crick|et¹** (krik′it), *n.* **1** a small, black leaping insect related to the grasshopper. Male crickets make a chirping noise by rubbing their front wings together. **2** a metal toy that fits in the hand and when pressed makes a sound like that of the cricket. [< Old French *criquet* < *criquer* creak, rattle]

***cricket¹**
definition 1

crick|et²** (krik′it), *n., adj., v.* — ***n. **1** an outdoor game played by two teams of eleven players each, with a ball, a flattened bat, and a pair of wickets. Cricket is very popular in England. *The sport of cricket and its curiously languid vocabulary ... "Well-played, sir," for "Great catch," and "How-zat?" for "Is he out?" are as British as a crumpet* (Newsweek). **2** *Informal.* fair play; good sportsmanship: *It's not cricket to bully little children. Many Englishmen think ill of some present policies of the government of South Africa. But Lord's is the last place to mention it. That would not be cricket* (New York Times).

— ***adj.*** *Informal.* according to good sportsmanship; fair; honest.

— ***v.i.*** to play the game of cricket.

[< Old French *criquet* goal post in game of bowls, stick, perhaps < Middle Dutch *cricke* stick, staff] — **crick′et|er**, *n.*

***cricket²**
definition 1

crick|et³ (krik′it), *n.* a small, low, wooden stool. [earlier *cracket;* origin uncertain]

cricket frog, any one of several small tree frogs that make a chirping noise resembling that of a cricket.

cri|coid (krī′koid), *adj., n.* — ***adj.*** **1** ring-shaped. **2** of or denoting the ring-shaped cartilage at the lower part of the larynx.

— ***n.*** the cricoid cartilage.

[< New Latin *cricoides* < Greek *krikoeidês* < *krikos* ring + *eîdos* form]

cri de coeur (krē də kœr′), *French.* **1** a heartfelt plea: *His words are a cri de coeur for peace.* **2** an appeal to sympathy: *The poor man's cri de coeur was impossible to resist.* **3** (literally) cry of the heart.

cried (krīd), *v.* the past tense and past participle of **cry**: *The baby cried for its mother. The baby has cried all day.*

cri|er (krī′ər), *n.* **1** an officer in a law court who makes the public announcements. **2** = town crier. **3** a person who shouts out announcements of goods for sale; hawker. **4** a person who cries or shouts.

cries (krīz), *n., v.* — ***n.*** plural of **cry**: *the cries of birds.*

— ***v.*** third person, present tense of **cry**: *The baby cries when he sees a stranger.*

cri|key (krī′kē), *interj.* an exclamation or mild oath. [altered pronunciation of *Christ*]

crim. con., *Law.* criminal conversation; adultery.

crime (krīm), *n.* **1** an act that is against the law. Any felony or misdemeanor is a crime. Murder, kidnaping, and treason are high crimes often punishable by death. *Murder is a vile and loathsome crime.* **2** the activity of criminals; violation of law: *Crime is increasing in the cities.* **3a** an evil or wrong act; sin: *It is a crime to let people live without food and clothing. War is a crime against humanity.* **b** *Figurative:* *It's a crime to neglect such a lovely garden.* [< Old French *crime* < Latin *crīmen, -inis* accusation, offense; of uncertain origin] — **crime′less,** *adj.*

— ***Syn.*** **1 Crime, offense** mean an act that breaks a law. **Crime** applies particularly to an act that breaks a law that has been made for the public good, and is punishable by public law: *Arson and swindling are crimes.* But what constitutes a crime varies to some extent with place and period. It is no longer a crime in Great Britain for a man to marry his deceased wife's sister. Certain conduct on the Sabbath may be a crime in one country and be entirely overlooked by the law in another country. **Offense** is more general, and applies to any act, not always serious, that breaks any moral, public, or social law: *Lying and cruelty are offenses.*

crime against nature, *Law.* unnatural sexual intercourse; sodomy.

Cri|me|an (krī mē′ən), *adj., n.* — ***adj.*** of or having to do with the Crimea, a large peninsula extending into the Black Sea from the north.

— ***n.*** a native or inhabitant of the Crimea.

crime|ful (krīm′fəl), *adj.* full of crime; criminal.

cri|men (krī′mən), *n. Latin.* a crime.

crime pas|si|on|nel (krēm′ pä syô nel′), *n., pl.* **crimes pas|si|on|nels** (krēm′ pä syô nel′). *French.* a crime of passion, especially a murder prompted by a wife's or husband's unfaithfulness.

crime-rid|den (krīm′rid′ən), *adj.* dominated by crime.

crime wave, a sudden surge of criminal activity; a noticeable increase in the number of crimes committed in an area at a given time: *They pointed with alarm to increasing unrest ... and new crime waves in the cities* (Newsweek).

crim|i|nal (krim′ə nəl), *n., adj.* — ***n.*** a person who has committed a crime: *The criminal was sentenced to prison for theft.* **SYN**: offender, lawbreaker, malefactor, felon, culprit.

— ***adj.*** **1** guilty of wrongdoing: *a criminal person.* **SYN**: culpable. **2** that is a crime: *Murder and stealing are criminal acts.* **SYN**: unlawful, illegal, felonious. **3** of or having to do with crime or its punishment: *a criminal court, criminal law.* **4a** like crime; wrong; sinful: *criminal behavior. It is criminal to let a pet die of neglect.* **b** *Figurative:* *As long as magnetic-tape recordings have certain built-in possibilities, it would be criminal to ignore them* (Harper's).

[< Old French *criminel,* learned borrowing from Latin *crīminālis* < *crīmen, -inis;* see etym. under **crime**]

criminal contempt, contempt of court due to evasion of a court order: *The Senate bill permits jury trials not only in cases involving voting—it permits jury trials in all criminal contempt cases* (Newsweek).

criminal conversation, *Law.* unlawful intercourse with a married person; adultery.

crim|i|nal|ist (krim′ə nə list), *n.* a person who studies criminal law or criminology: *A criminalist is a specialist, but not in any one scientific field. He must be qualified as an expert to identify any of a large number of different kinds of evidence from blood groups to ink, from textiles to metals, from vegetation to soils* (Science News Letter).

crim|i|nal|is|tic (krim′ə nə lis′tik), *adj.* of or having to do with criminalists or criminology.

crim|i|nal|is|tics (krim′ə nə lis′tiks), *n.* criminology; the method of crime investigation and detection that employs the latest scientific techniques (as comparison of blood types, or tape-recording analysis) to collect incriminating evidence.

crim|i|nal|i|ty (krim′ə nal′ə tē), *n., pl.* **-ties. 1** the fact or quality of being criminal; guilt: *A higher ratio of criminality is found among the unmarried and divorced than among those living a normal family life* (Emory S. Bogardus). **2** a criminal act.

crim|i|nal|ize (krim′ə nə līz), *v.t.,* **-ized, -iz|ing.** to declare (a person or activity) criminal; make liable for punishment as a crime: *to criminalize the use of addictive drugs.* — **crim′i|nal|i|za′tion**, *n.*

criminal law, the law of a community or state that deals with crimes and their punishment: *Criminal law is frankly a separate specialty and one which does not interest the corporate lawyers, though they will very occasionally undertake a defense in an unpopular cause célèbre* (Harper's).

criminal lawyer, a lawyer who deals with cases involving crime, as distinguished from civil cases or tort.

crim|i|nal|ly (krim′ə nə lē), *adv.* **1** in a criminal manner. **2** according to criminal law.

crim|i|nal|oid (krim′ə nə loid), *n.* a person of a type believed to be predisposed to criminal acts.

crim|i|nate (krim′ə nāt), *v.t.,* **-nat|ed, -nat|ing.** **1** to accuse of a crime. **2** to furnish evidence of the guilt of; incriminate. **3** to censure as criminal; condemn. [< Latin *crīminārī* (with English *-ate¹*) < *crīmen, -inis;* see etym. under **crime**] — **crim′i-na′tion**, *n.* — **crim′i|na|tor**, *n.*

crim|i|na|tive (krim′ə nā′tiv), *adj.* tending to or involving crimination; accusatory.

crim|i|na|to|ry (krim′ə nə tôr′ē, -tōr′-), *adj.* criminating.

crim|i|no|gen|ic (krim′ə nō jen′ik), *adj.* causing criminal behavior; predisposing to criminality: *criminogenic traits.* [< Latin *crīmen, -inis* crime + English *-gen* + *-ic*]

crim|i|no|log|ic (krim′ə nə loj′ik), *adj.* = criminological.

crim|i|no|log|i|cal (krim′ə nə loj′ə kəl), *adj.* of or having to do with criminology. — **crim′i|no|log′i-cal|ly**, *adv.*

crim|i|nol|o|gist (krim′ə nol′ə jist), *n.* a person who studies criminology.

crim|i|nol|o|gy (krim′ə nol′ə jē), *n.* the scientific study of crime and its prevention and of criminals and their treatment. [< Latin *crīmen, -inis* crime + English *-logy*]

crim|i|no-tech|ni|cian (krim′ə nō tek nish′ən), *n.* = criminalist.

crim|i|nous (krim′ə nəs), *adj.* **1** dealing with crime: *a criminous melodrama, a criminous plot.* **2** guilty of crime; criminal: *One may well think that Henry II was just in demanding that criminous clerks be tried in the King's courts* (W. H. Auden).

crim|mer (krim′ər), *n.* a gray fur resembling Persian lamb. Also, **krimmer**. [< German *Krimmer* < *Krim* the Crimea, where the lambs are raised]

crimp[1] (krimp), *v., n.* —*v.t.* **1** to press into small, regular, narrow folds; make wavy; frill: *The children crimped tissue paper to make paper flowers.* **2** to hinder; cramp: *Low prices earlier crimped both domestic output and foreign imports* (Wall Street Journal). **3** to fold the edges of (a cartridge case) inward so as to secure the wad and the charge. **4** to cause (the flesh of fish) to become firm by gashing it before cooking. **5** to bend or mold (leather) into shape.

—*n.* **1** something crimped; fold or wave. **2** the act of crimping. **3** a waved or curled lock of hair. **4** a wavy or curly condition, especially in wood that has dried too rapidly. **5** the natural curl or wave in wool fiber: *Although ordinary hair and wool are very similar, true hair lacks the crimp, or curl, that gives wool its resilience* (Charles P. Macaluso). **6** a crease put in sheet or plate metal to make it less flexible. **7** a device or tool for crimping leather.

put a crimp in, *U.S. Informal.* to interfere with; hinder; thwart (any scheme or agreement): *Hence . . . to scrimp on the Government's spending is to put a crimp in the economy* (Wall Street Journal).

[Old English *gecrympan* to crimp, curl] —**crimp′er**, *n.*

crimp[2] (krimp), *n., v.* —*n.* a person who makes a business of forcing or tricking men into becoming sailors or soldiers.

—*v.t.* to force or trick (men) into becoming sailors or soldiers.

[origin uncertain]

crimped (krimpt), *adj.* made with crimps; ripply: *Crimped fibers give a yarn a bulky appearance without increasing its weight* (Wall Street Journal).

crim|ple (krim′pəl), *v.t., v.i.*, **-pled, -pling**. to wrinkle; crumple; curl. **SYN:** crinkle. [< *crimp*[1] + *-le* (frequentative)]

crimp|y (krim′pē), *adj.*, **crimp|i|er, crimp|i|est**. having small, narrow folds; wavy; frizzy.

crim|son (krim′zən), *adj., n., v.* —*adj.* **1** deep-red: *In her embarrassment she turned crimson.* **2** sanguinary.

—*n.* **1** a deep red. **2** a crimson pigment or dye.

—*v.t., v.i.* to make or become deep red in color: *His face crimsoned with shame.*

[< Italian *cremesino* < *cremisi*, variant of *chermisi* the color < Arabic *qirmizī* < *qirmiz* the kermes insect (from which a red dye was derived) < Sanskrit *krmis* worm. Compare etym. under **carmine, cramoisy, kermes**.]

crimson clover, an annual clover with red, and sometimes white or yellow, flowers, grown especially in the southern United States for soil improvement and livestock feed; Italian clover.

crimson rambler, a climbing rose with clusters of bright-red flowers.

cringe (krinj), *v.*, **cringed, cring|ing**, *n.* —*v.i.* **1** to shrink from danger or pain; crouch in fear: *The dog cringed at the sight of the whip.* **SYN:** cower. **2** to try to get favor by slavish attention or behavior: *The courtiers cringed before the king.* **SYN:** fawn.

—*n.* the act of cringing.

[Middle English *crengen*, Old English *cringan* give way, fall in battle, perish] —**cring′er**, *n.* —**cring′ing|ly**, *adv.*

crin|gle (krin′gəl), *n.* a small loop or ring of rope on the edge of a sail. The sail can be fastened by putting a rope through the cringle. [apparently < Low German *kringel* (diminutive) < *kring* ring]

cri|nite[1] (krī′nīt), *adj.* **1** = hairy. **2** *Botany, Zoology.* having tufts of hairy growth on the surface. [< Latin *crīnītus* hairy < *crīnis* hair]

cri|nite[2] (krī′nīt, krin′īt), *n.* = encrinite. [< Greek *krínon* lily + English *-ite*[1]]

crin|kle (kring′kəl), *v.*, **-kled, -kling**, *n.* —*v.t., v.i.* **1** to wrinkle or ripple: *Crepe paper is crinkled.* **2** to rustle: *Paper crinkles when it is crushed.* **3** to bend without breaking off: *The piece of aluminum foil crinkled as she tried to tear it off.*

—*n.* **1** a wrinkle or ripple: *There is a crinkle in the tablecloth.* **2** a rustle: *The crinkle of starched petticoats accompanied the child as she ran.*

[Middle English *crenklen* (frequentative), Old English *crincan* to bend]

crin|kle|root (kring′kəl rüt′, -rut′), *n.* any one of various North American plants of the mustard family, having a fleshy, pungent rootstock; toothwort.

crin|kly (kring′klē), *adj.*, **-kli|er, -kli|est**. full of crinkles: *crinkly eyes.*

crin|kum-cran|kum (kring′kəm krang′kəm), *n.* *Archaic.* something full of twists and turns.

***cri|noid** (krī′noid, krin′oid), *n., adj.* —*n.* any one of a group of flower-shaped sea animals having a small, cup-shaped body with five branched, feathery arms, usually attached by a stalk; sea lily. The crinoids comprise a class of echinoderms.

—*adj.* **1** of or belonging to this class. **2** shaped like a lily.

[< Greek *krinoeidês* lilylike]

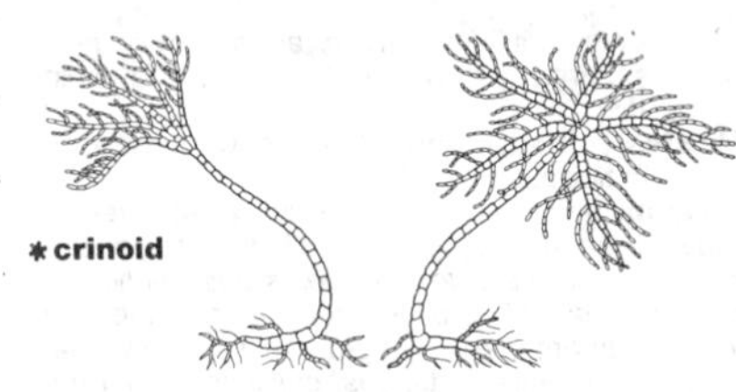

***crinoid**

cri|noi|dal (krī noi′dəl, kri-), *adj.* of or having to do with the crinoids.

crin|o|line (krin′ə lin, -lēn), *n.* **1** a stiff cloth used especially as a lining to hold a skirt out or make a coat collar stand up. Crinoline is sometimes used in bookbinding. **2** a petticoat of crinoline to hold a skirt out: *A great gathered skirt that's kept in full sail by an attached crinoline* (New Yorker). **3** = hoop skirt: *the before-the-War southern belles in their widespread crinolines.* [< French *crinoline* < Italian *crinolino* < *crino* horsehair (< Latin *crīnis* hair) + *lino* flax, thread < Latin *līnum* (from the original mixture of these fibers)]

cri|num (krī′nəm), *n.* any one of a genus of tall, bulbous, tropical and subtropical plants of the amaryllis family, having clusters of large, showy flowers. [< New Latin *Crinum* < Greek *krínon* lily]

crin vé|gé|tal (kraN′ vā zhā tȧl′), the fiber of any one of several fan palms of Europe and North Africa, especially the hemp palm, used widely as a substitute for horsehair. [< French *crin végétal* (literally) vegetable hair]

cri|ol|lo (krē ō′lō, -ōl′yō; *Spanish* krē ô′yô), *n., pl.* **-los**, *adj.* —*n.* **1** a Spanish-American native of European, especially Spanish, parentage; Creole. **2** an animal belonging to any of several breeds of cattle, sheep, or other domestic animals, raised in Latin America.

—*adj.* of or having to do with the criollos: *a Venezuelan criollo writer, criollo milk cows.*

[< Spanish *criollo;* see etym. under **Creole**]

cri|o|sphinx (krī′ə sfingks), *n.* a sphinx with the head of a ram. [< Greek *kriós* ram + *sphínx* sphinx]

cripes (krīps), *interj.* an exclamation or mild oath. [altered pronunciation of *Christ*]

crip|ple (krip′əl), *n., adj., v.*, **-pled, -pling**. —*n.* **1** a person or animal that cannot use his legs, arms, or body properly because of injury, deformity, or lack; lame person or animal: *Long John Silver was a cripple who limped on a wooden leg.* **2** (in building) any part of a frame that is shorter than full size. **3** *U.S.* a dense thicket in swampy or lowland. **4** a railroad car or locomotive that needs repair. **5** a temporary staging or support, as in washing windows.

—*adj.* disabled; lame.

—*v.t.* **1** to make a cripple of; lame. **2** *Figurative.* to damage; weaken: *The ship was crippled by the storm. Business was crippled by a series of strikes.* **SYN:** impair, disable.

[Old English *crypel*. See related etym. at **creep**.] —**crip′pler**, *n.*

—*Syn. v.t.* **1 Cripple, disable** mean to deprive of the ability or power to carry on normal activities. **Cripple** means to deprive a person or animal of the use of a leg, foot, or arm: *He has been crippled since he broke his hip.* **Disable** means to deprive of the ability to work or act normally: *The man is disabled by a heart condition.*

crise (krēz), *n. French.* crisis: (*Figurative.*) *Just as we were embarking, [she] was overtaken by a crise; all her notes . . . had disappeared* (New Yorker).

crise de con|fiance (krēz′ də kôN fyäNs′), *French.* crisis of confidence; a political crisis resulting from a lack of confidence in government policies.

crise de con|science (krēz′ də kôN syäNs′), *French.* crisis of conscience; severe moral doubts or scruples.

crise de nerfs (krēz′ də ner′), *French.* crisis of nerves; a nervous breakdown.

cri|sis (krī′sis), *n., pl.* **-ses** (-sēz). **1** the turning point in a disease, toward life or death: *The doctor said that when the patient's fever broke, the crisis would be passed.* **2** *Figurative.* **a** a point at which a change must come, either for the better or the worse; deciding event: *The Battle of Waterloo was a crisis in Napoleon's career.* **b** a time of difficulty and of anxious waiting: *The United States faced a crisis following the Japanese attack on Pearl Harbor.* **SYN:** See syn. under **emergency**.

[< Latin *crisis* < Greek *krísis* < *krínein* decide, judge, separate]

crisis center, a headquarters from which a disaster is monitored, emergency relief is controlled, psychological counseling is available, or other assistance is given during a time of difficulty: *[She] describes Poe as a kind of crisis center where pregnant teen-agers can count on support* (Tuscaloosa News).

crisis management, the expert handling of a crisis or emergency so as to reduce or eliminate danger, damage, or the like, especially in government and industry. —**crisis manager**.

crisp (krisp), *adj., v., n.* —*adj.* **1** hard and thin; breaking easily with a snap: *Dry toast and fresh celery are crisp.* **SYN:** brittle. **2** *Figurative.* sharp and clear: **a** fresh; bracing: *The air was cool and crisp.* **b** short and decided; clear-cut: *"Don't talk; fight," was his crisp answer. Hemingway wrote stories in a crisp style.* **SYN:** decisive. **3** *Figurative.* **a** brisk; animated: *a crisp manner.* **b** lively or sparkling: *crisp conversation.* **4** neat; clean-cut: *crisp clothes.* **5** curly and wiry: *crisp hair.* **6** rippled; wrinkled; undulating: *crisp waves.*

—*v.t., v.i.* to make or become crisp: *Crisp the lettuce in cold water.*

—*n.* **1** something crisp. **2** *British.* a thin slice of potato fried until crisp; potato chip. **3** *Dialect.* crackling (def. 2).

[Old English *crisp* curly < Latin *crispus* curled] —**crisp′ly**, *adv.* —**crisp′ness**, *n.*

cris|pate (kris′pāt), *adj.* crisped or curled.

cris|pat|ed (kris′pā tid), *adj.* = crispate.

cris|pa|tion (kris pā′shən), *n.* **1** a curling or being curled. **2** a slight contraction of a part, as of skin.

crisp|er (kris′pər), *n.* a person or thing that crisps: **a** a drawer in a refrigerator in which fruits and vegetables are stored to keep crisp. **b** = curling iron.

Cris|pin (kris′pən), *n.* = shoemaker. [< Saint *Crispin*, patron of shoemakers]

crisp|y (kris′pē), *adj.*, **crisp|i|er, crisp|i|est**. crisp: *We might have whitebait fried in deep fat, crispy and . . . hot* (Atlantic). —**crisp′i|ness**, *n.*

cris|sal (kris′əl), *adj.* of or having to do with the crissum.

criss|cross (kris′krôs′, -kros′), *v., adj., adv., n.* —*v.t.* **1** to mark or cover with crossed lines: *Little cracks crisscrossed the wall.* **2** to come and go across; move or pass back and forth: *Buses and cars crisscross the city.*

—*v.i.* to come and go; move back and forth.

—*adj.* made or marked with crossed lines; crossing: *Plaids have a crisscross pattern.*

—*adv.* **1** = crosswise. **2** *Figurative.* awry; askew.

—*n.* **1** a mark or pattern made of crossed lines: *His messy paper was a crisscross of lines.* **2** the game of tick-tack-toe. **3** = christcross.

[alteration of *christcross*]

criss|cross-row (kris′krôs′rō′, -kros′-), *n.* = christcross-row.

cris|sum (kris′əm), *n.* **1** the area surrounding the cloacal opening of a bird. **2** the feathers of this area. [< New Latin *crissum* < Latin *crissāre* move the haunches]

cris|ta (kris′tə), *n., pl.* **-tae**. a ridge or other crestlike process, such as the elevated sensory area in the wall of the ampulla of a semicircular canal. [< Latin *crista* crest]

cris|tae (kris′tē), *n.pl.* **1** plural of **crista**. **2** lamellar folds of the inner membrane of mitochondria, on which most of the respiratory enzymes are situated.

cris|tate (kris′tāt), *adj.* **1** having a crest; crested. **2** forming a crest. [< Latin *cristātus* < *crista* crest]

cris|tat|ed (kris′tā tid), *adj.* = cristate.

cris|to|bal|ite (kris tō′bə līt), *n.* silica occurring in small octahedral crystals as a high-temperature modification of quartz. [< Cerro San *Cristóbal*, near Pachuca, Mexico + *-ite*[1]]

crit., **1** critical. **2** criticism. **3** criticized.

cri|te|ri|a (krī tir′ē ə), *n.* a plural of **criterion**.

cri|te|ri|ol|o|gy (krī tir′ē ol′ə jē), *n.* the doctrine of criteria or standards of judgment.

cri|te|ri|on (krī tir′ē ən), *n., pl.* **-ri|a** or **-ri|ons**. a rule or standard for making a judgment; test: *The ultimate criterion of a good education is what the student gets out of it* (Newsweek). **SYN:** measure, touchstone, yardstick. See syn. under **standard**. [< Greek *kritḗrion* < *krínein* to judge]

crith (krith), *n. Physics.* the weight of one liter of

Pronunciation Key: hat, āge, cãre, fär; let, ēqual, tėrm; it, īce; hot, ōpen, ôrder; oil, out; cup, pu̇t, rüle; child; long; thin; ᴛʜen; zh, measure; ə represents **a** in about, **e** in taken, **i** in pencil, **o** in lemon, **u** in circus.

hydrogen at standard pressure and temperature, used as a unit of weight for gases. [< Greek *krithē* barleycorn, the smallest weight]

crit|ic (krit′ik), *n.* **1a** a person who makes judgments of the merits and faults of books, music, pictures, plays, acting, or other works of literature or art. Many critics write upon their subject as a profession. *We read what the critics in the newspapers had to say about the new play to find out if it was worth seeing.* **b** a person who judges the suitability or quality of anything. **2** a person who disapproves or finds fault; faultfinder: *She was such a constant critic that the other girls did not like her.* SYN: caviler, censurer, carper. **3** *Obsolete.* criticism. **4** *Obsolete.* a critical notice or review; critique. [< Latin *criticus* < Greek *kritikós* critical, able to judge < *krínein* to judge]

crit|i|cal (krit′ə kəl), *adj.* **1** inclined to find fault or disapprove: *a critical disposition. Do not be so critical.* SYN: faultfinding, censorious, carping, captious. **2** skilled as a critic. **3** coming from one who is skilled as a critic; involving criticism: *a critical judgment, a critical reading.* **4** belonging to the work of a critic: *critical essays.* **5** of a crisis; important at a time of danger and difficulty: *His delay in getting a doctor was critical. This is the critical moment.* SYN: crucial. **6** full of danger or difficulty: *The patient was in critical condition.* SYN: hazardous. **7** having to do with the crisis of a disease: *a critical period in an illness.* **8** necessary for some work or project but existing in inadequate supply: *Food supplies for the flood victims had become critical.* **9** *Physics, Chemistry.* having to do with or constituting a point at which some action, property, or condition undergoes a decisive change: *Critical phenomena are dramatic manifestations of fundamental properties of matter* (Science News). **10** *Nuclear Physics.* **a** having to do with, or capable of producing, a chain reaction. See also **critical mass.** **b** of or involving the operation of an atomic reactor: *a critical experiment.* **11** *Zoology, Botany.* distinguished by slight or questionable differences that are uncertain or difficult to determine: *a critical species.*

go critical, (of an atomic reactor) to begin a sustained chain reaction: *The reactor is to "go critical," or start nuclear fission reaction, next spring* (New York Times).

—**crit′i|cal|ly,** *adv.* —**crit′i|cal|ness,** *n.*

critical angle, 1 *Optics.* the smallest possible angle of incidence that gives total reflection: *The angle of incidence for which the refracted ray emerges tangent to the surface is called the critical angle* (Sears and Zemansky). **2** *Aeronautics.* the angle of attack of a wing at which maximum lift is momentarily reached and above which turbulence occurs, drag is greatly increased, lift is destroyed, and the airfoil tends to stall.

critical constants, *Physics.* the critical temperature, pressure, and density of a substance.

crit|i|cal|i|ty (krit′ə kal′ə tē), *n.* the point at which a nuclear reactor achieves a self-sustaining chain reaction: *This state, which seems to the layman pretty close to perpetual motion, is known to engineers as "criticality"* (Newsweek).

critical mass, 1 the minimum amount of fissionable material capable of producing a self-sustaining chain reaction. **2** *Figurative.* the point where conditions or opinions combine to produce change (of focus, direction, policy, or the like): *. . . that critical mass of public pressure necessary for effective, vigorous public policies* (Thomas B. Edsall).

critical path analysis or **method,** a method of planning and controlling a complex operation by making a chart or diagram of the sequence of steps and time for each step required to complete the operation, often by means of a computer: *Critical path methods can be employed to establish priorities while minimising the time and cost of development* (New Scientist).

critical point, *Physics.* the point at which two phases, especially the gaseous and liquid, of a substance merge: *The end of the vaporization curve is called the critical point* (Shortley and Williams).

critical pressure, *Physics.* the absolute pressure of a gaseous substance when at the critical temperature: *At any pressure over 3,206 pounds—the "critical pressure barrier"—water turns instantaneously to steam without passing through an intermediate stage of bubbling* (Wall Street Journal).

critical size, the size of a nuclear system undergoing fission, upon which a chain reaction depends.

critical speed, 1 *Aeronautics.* any speed at which the performance of an aircraft will change or come to an end. **2** any speed at which a craft or vehicle shows signs of disorder (as vibration or unsteadiness): *We . . . find that in any flexible ship there is a critical speed of towing above which flexing and shaking will occur* (New Scientist).

critical state, *Physics.* the state of a substance when it reaches the critical point.

critical temperature, *Physics.* that temperature of a substance above which it remains in the gaseous state and cannot be liquefied by pressure alone.

critical velocity, *Physics.* the velocity at which the flow of a fluid changes from laminar to turbulent.

crit|ic|as|ter (krit′ik as′tər), *n.* an inferior or incompetent critic. [< *critic* + Latin *-aster,* a diminutive suffix]

crit|i|cise (krit′ə sīz), *v.i., v.t.,* **-cised, -cis|ing.** *British.* criticize.

crit|i|cism (krit′ə siz əm), *n.* **1** unfavorable remarks or judgments; finding fault: *Mother could not let my rudeness to her guests pass without criticism.* SYN: disapproval, fault-finding. **2** the making of judgments; approving or disapproving; analysis of merits and faults: *Just criticism should be welcomed. Criticism is simply the method by which existing ideas and institutions are submitted to the test of principles, ideas, ideals, and possibilities* (Adlai Stevenson). **3** the art or principles of making careful judgments on the merits and faults of books, music, plays, acting, or other literary or artistic works: *literary criticism, drama criticism. Criticism should reveal the character, the spirit of writing, rather than attempt a tape measure estimate of the writer's status* (New York Times). **4** a critical comment, essay, or review; critique: *Before I finish this theme, I would appreciate your criticisms of what I have written.* SYN: See syn. under **review. 5** the critical science dealing with the text, character, composition, and origin of literary documents, especially of the Bible.

crit|i|cize (krit′ə sīz), *v.,* **-cized, -ciz|ing.** —*v.t.* **1** to blame; find fault with; disapprove: *Do not criticize him until you know all the circumstances.* SYN: reprove, censure, fault. **2** to judge or speak as a critic; discuss the merits and faults of: *The editor criticized the author's new novel, comparing it with his last one.* SYN: appraise, evaluate.

—*v.i.* **1** to find fault; disapprove. **2** to act or speak as a critic; pass judgment as to merits and faults.

—**crit′i|ciz′a|ble,** *adj.* —**crit′i|ciz′er,** *n.*

crit|i|cule (krit′ə kyül), *n.* a petty or minor critic: *Its [a novel's] flaws . . . any criticule could tabulate with jocose ease* (Vladimir Nabokov). [< *critic* + *-ule*]

cri|tique (kri tēk′), *n., v.* **-tiqued, -tiqu|ing.** —*n.* **1** a critical essay or review: *Some newspapers have critiques of new books. This provocative essay of close to three hundred pages is a critique of France today and yesterday—an angry inquiry into what happened to the fibre of the nation and that of its Frenchmen* (New Yorker). **2** the act or art of criticizing; criticism.

—*v.t.* to write a critique on; criticize; review: *He rules lightly, exercising his control largely by critiquing the editors monthly reports* (Time).

[< French *critique* < Greek *kritikḗ* (*téchnē*) the critical (art), feminine of *kritikós;* see etym. under **critic**]

crit|ter (krit′ər), *n.* **1** *U.S. Dialect.* a creature; animal. **2** an animal (such as a cow or pig) raised as livestock: *Marketings of top-quality critters have dwindled most* (Wall Street Journal). **3** *Informal.* any unusual animal, especially if it is fictional, mythical, microscopic, or prehistoric: *cartoon critters.*

croak (krōk), *n., v.* —*n.* the deep, hoarse sound made by a frog, crow, or raven.

[< verb]

—*v.i.* **1** to make a deep, hoarse sound. **2** *Figurative.* to be always prophesying misfortune; be dissatisfied; grumble. **3** *Slang.* to die.

—*v.t.* **1** to utter in a deep, hoarse voice: *He croaked a reply.* **2** *Slang.* to kill.

[Middle English *crok,* unrecorded Old English *crācian* to croak, related to *crācettan*]

croak|er (krō′kər), *n.* **1** a person, animal, or thing that croaks. **2** any one of various fishes that make a croaking or grunting noise: *Two types of fish—pan-sized gulf croakers and large, gamey corbinas—seem to be adapting to the desert sea's tepid waters* (Science News Letter). **3** a person who is always prophesying misfortune. **4** *Especially U.S. Slang.* a doctor.

croak|ing (krō′king), *n.* the act of making a deep, hoarse sound.

croak|y (krō′kē), *adj.* **croak|i|er, croak|i|est.** **1** making a croaking sound. **2** given to croaking. —**croak′i|ly,** *adv.*

Cro|at (krō′at), *n., adj.* —*n.* **1** a person born or living in Croatia; a Croatian. **2** the Croatian language.

—*adj.* = Croatian.

Cro|a|tian (krō ā′shən), *adj., n.* —*adj.* of or having to do with Croatia or the Croats.

—*n.* **1** = Croat. **2** the Slavic language of Croatia. Croatian and Serbian are virtually the same language written in different alphabets.

croc (krok), *n. Slang.* a crocodile.

cro|ce|in (krō′sē in), *n.* any one of several synthetic red and orange dyes, especially an azo dye. [< Latin *croceus* saffron-colored (< *crocus* saffron) + English *-in*]

***cro|chet** (krō shā′), *v.,* **-cheted** (-shād′), **-chet|ing** (-shā′ing), *n.* —*v.t., v.i.* to make wool or cotton thread into sweaters, shawls, and other things in a way somewhat like knitting, but using only one needle, with a hooked end, called a crochet hook.

[< noun]

—*n.* **1** the act of working in this way. **2** the work or fabric made by crocheting.

[< Old French *crochet* (diminutive) < *croc* hook < Germanic (compare Old Icelandic *krōkr*). See etym. of doublet **crocket, croquet, crotchet.**]

—**cro|chet′er,** *n.*

***crochet**

crochet hook, a needle that ends in a barblike hook, used in crocheting.

cro|chet|ing (krō shā′ing), *n.* **1** the making of crochet work. **2** = crochet work.

crochet work, work done with a crochet hook.

cro|ci (krō′sī), *n.* a plural of **crocus.**

cro|cid|o|lite (krō sid′ə līt), *n.* a mineral consisting chiefly of a silicate of iron and sodium, occurring in long blue fibers or in a golden-brown, hard form. The fibrous form is used as asbestos.

[< Greek *krokís,* variant of *krokýs, -ýdos* nap of woolen cloth + English *-lite*]

crock[1] (krok), *n.* a pot or jar made of baked clay. [Old English *crocca*]

crock[2] (krok), *n., v.* —*n.* **1** *Dialect.* an old ewe. **2** an old, worn-out horse. **3** *Slang.* a worthless, old, or decrepit person or thing.

—*v.t., v.i. Informal.* to disable or become disabled; injure or break down: *Summerby crocked from a . . . gratuitous body check from Storey* (Sunday Times).

[earlier *crok.* Compare Danish *krak* sickly beast.]

crock[3] (krok), *n., v.* —*n.* **1** dye that rubs off from cloth. **2** *Dialect.* smut; soot; dirt.

—*v.t., v.i.* to soil; stain; lose dye and color: *Fabric makers complained that they could not get much more than a pastel, and this tended to fade or "crock"* (Wall Street Journal).

[perhaps < *crock*[1] (from the soot clinging to pot bottoms)]

crocked (krokt), *adj. Slang.* drunk. [perhaps < past participle of *crock*[2]]

crock|er|y (krok′ər ē, krok′rē), *n.* dishes, jars, and similar things made of baked clay; earthenware.

crock|et (krok′it), *n.* **1** a carved ornament, usually made to resemble foliage, along the edges of a spire, pinnacle, gable, or other sloping part of a building. **2** a snag at the end of a stag's horn. [< Anglo-French *croket,* Old French *crochet.* See etym. of doublet **crochet, croquet, crotchet.**]

crock|et|ed (krok′ə tid), *adj.* **1** decorated with architectural crockets: *playfully crocketed pinnacles, ripe as corn on the cob* (Louis MacNeice). **2** (of a stag's horn) having crockets.

crock|y (krok′ē), *adj.,* **crock|i|er, crock|i|est.** smutty; sooty.

croc|o|dile (krok′ə dīl), *n.* **1a** a large reptile with a long body like a lizard, four short legs, a thick skin, a long narrow head, a long tail, and webbed hind feet. Crocodiles live in the rivers and marshes of the warm parts of Africa, Asia, Australia, and America. Some kinds are fourteen or more feet long when fully grown. See picture under **alligator. b** leather prepared from the skin of a crocodile. **2** any crocodilian. **3** *British.* a slowly moving procession of people: *A neat crocodile of earnest dark-suited men . . . struggled to overtake him* (London Times). [< Old French *cocodrille* < Medieval Latin *cocodrillus,* for Latin *crocodīlus* < Greek krokódīlos (earlier) lizard, (literally) pebbleworm < *krokē* pebble + *drîlos* worm]

crocodile bird, an African bird of the same family as the plover, that often sits on a basking crocodile and feeds on its insect parasites; trochilus.

crocodile tears, 1 pretended or insincere grief. It is so called because of the story that crocodiles shed tears to lure a man within reach or while devouring him. **2** a condition, caused by severe damage to the principal motor nerve of the face, in which involuntary tears are shed.

croc|o|dil|i|an (krok′ə dil′ē ən), *n., adj.* —*n.* any animal of an order of reptiles that includes crocodiles, alligators, and gavials.

—adj. **1** of or like a crocodile. **2** of or belonging to the crocodilians.

cro|co|i|site (krō kō′ə sīt), *n.* = crocoite.

cro|co|ite (krō′kō īt), *n.* a reddish native chromate of lead occurring in monoclinic crystals. *Formula:* $PbCrO_4$ [< French *crocoise* (< Greek *krokóeis* saffron-colored) + English *-ite*[1]]

cro|cus[1] (krō′kəs), *n., pl.* **cro|cus|es** or **cro|ci.** **1** a small plant that blooms in the early spring or fall and has white, yellow, or purple flowers. Crocuses grow from a bulblike corm and belong to the iris family. See picture under **iris family.** **2** the flower. **3** a deep-yellow color; saffron. **4** a polishing powder consisting of iron oxide: *Today's enlightened polishing is done judiciously, by hand, with jeweler's crocus, the finest abrasive known* (Emory Cook). **5** any one of various yellow or red powders formerly obtained from metals by calcination; colcothar. [< Latin *crocus* < Greek *krókos,* perhaps < Semitic (compare Hebrew *karkōm*)]

cro|cus[2] (krō′kəs), *n.* **1** coarse fabric, such as burlap, used especially for making sacks. **2** *pl.* **-cus|es.** a sack made of this fabric. [origin unknown]

crocus cloth, 1 a layer of jeweler's rouge on thick cloth backing, used for polishing metals and jewels. **2** = crocus[2]

crocus sack or **bag,** a sack or bag made of crocus. [origin unknown]

Croe|sus (krē′səs), *n.* any very rich person. [< *Croesus,* king of Lydia, Asia Minor, from 560 to 546 B.C., famous for his great wealth]

croft (krôft, kroft), *n. British.* **1** a small, enclosed field. **2** a very small rented farm. [Old English *croft*]

croft|er (krôf′tər, krof′-), *n. British.* a person who cultivates a very small farm.

croft|ing (krôf′ting, krof′-), *n.* **1** the tenancy of crofts. **2** the land and property of a crofter. **3** bleaching by sunlight by spreading cloth on the ground.

***crois|sant** (krwä säɴ′), *n.* a rich roll shaped like a crescent: *I take a light breakfast of café au lait with a brioche or croissant* (New Yorker). [< French *croissant* (literally) crescent < present participle of *croître* < Latin *crēscere;* see etym. under **crescent**]

***croissant**

croix de guerre (krwä′ də ger′), a French medal given to soldiers for bravery under fire. [< French *croix de guerre* (literally) war cross]

cro|ker sack (krō′kər), *Southern U.S.* a sack made of coarse fabric, such as burlap. [*croker,* alteration of *crocus*[2]]

cro|ki|nole (krō′kə nōl), *n.* **1** a game played by shooting disks with a snap of the finger so that they land in scoring circles or spots on a circular or hexagonal board. **2 Crokinole.** a trademark for this game.

Cro-Mag|non (krō mag′non), *adj., n.* *—adj.* of or belonging to a group of prehistoric people who lived about 25,000 years ago. They were characterized by large, long heads and tall stature. Considered of the same species as modern man, they used stone and bone implements, and some of them were skilled artists.

—n. a person of this group.

[< the *Cro-Magnon* cave, near Dordogne, France, where the first remains were found]

crom|lech (krom′lek), *n.* **1** a circle of upright stones built in prehistoric times. **2** upright stones with a large, flat stone laid horizontally on them; dolmen. [< Welsh *cromlech* < *crom* bent, curved + *llech* (flat) stone]

cro|mor|na (krə môr′nə), *n.* an organ stop which gives a tone like that of a clarinet. [< French *cromorne* < German *Krummhorn* crooked horn]

Crom|well|i|an (krom wel′ē ən), *adj., n.* *—adj.* having to do with or characteristic of the English general and Puritan leader Oliver Cromwell, or his age; stern; puritanical: *Cromwellian austerity.*

—n. **1** an adherent of Oliver Cromwell. **2** a soldier who fought under Cromwell.

crone (krōn), *n.* a withered old woman. [< Old North French *carogne* cross-grained woman, or Middle Dutch *croonje* old ewe < Old French *carogne* carcass. See etym. of doublet **carrion.**]

cronk[1] (krongk, krôngk), *n., v.* *—n.* a croaking or honking sound, such as made by a raven or wild goose.

—v.i. to make this sound: *There will still be plenty of competition with the networks still cronking . . . at one another in 16-in. cannon tones* (Time).

cronk[2] (krongk, krôngk), *adj. Australian Slang.* **1** liable to collapse; weak; sick. **2** unfit to run in a race: *a cronk horse.* **3** done or obtained by fraud. [probably < Yiddish or German *krank* sick]

Cro|nos (krō′nos), *n.* = Cronus.

Cro|nus (krō′nəs), *n. Greek Mythology.* a Titan, son of Uranus, and ruler of the universe until overthrown by his son Zeus. He was identified by the Romans with the god Saturn. Also, **Kronos.**

cro|ny (krō′nē), *n., pl.* **-nies.** a very close friend; chum: *The spirit of cronyism was not to his liking; he was not one of the cronies* (Newsweek). SYN: comrade, companion, pal. [perhaps < Greek *chrónios* lasting < *chrónos* time]

cro|ny|ism (krō′nē iz əm), *n.* the practice of appointing close friends to governmental posts regardless of their merit or experience; political favoritism.

crood (krüd), *v.i. Scottish.* to make a soft, murmuring sound, as a dove; coo. Also, **croud.** [imitative]

crook[1] (krůk), *v., n.* *—v.t.* **1** to make a curve or hook in; bend: *The hunter crooked his finger around the trigger of his gun. I crooked my leg around the branch to keep from falling.* **2** *U.S. Slang.* **a** to tamper with dishonestly: *to crook the books.* **b** to steal: *to crook equipment.*

—v.i. to bend or be bent; be turned from a right line.

—n. **1** a hook; bend; curve: *a crook in a stream.* SYN: turn. **2** a hooked, curved, or bent part: *the crook of the elbow, the crook of a cane.* **3a** a shepherd's staff. Its upper end is curved or bent into a hook. **b** the crosier of a bishop or abbot. **4** an implement or instrument having a bent or curved part, such as a hook or a pothook. **5** a curved piece of tubing added to a horn or cornet to lower the pitch. **6** *Informal.* a person who is not honest in his dealings; thief or swindler: *The crook stole all of my money.* SYN: sharper, cheat, scoundrel. **7** the act of crooking or bending. [Middle English *crōk* apparently < Scandinavian (compare Old Icelandic *krōkr*)]

crook[2] (krůk), *adj. Australian.* **1** sick or ailing: *to feel crook.* **2** bad; unpleasant; unsatisfactory: *crook weather.* **3** bad-tempered; angry. [perhaps alteration of *cronk*[2]]

crook|back (krůk′bak′), *n.* **1** = hunchback. **2** *Obsolete.* a crooked back.

crook|backed (krůk′bakt′), *adj.* having a crooked back; hunchbacked.

crook|ed (krůk′id), *adj.* **1** not straight; bent, curved, or twisted. **2** *Figurative.* not honest; fraudulent; wrong: *a crooked scheme.* **—crook′ed|ly,** *adv.* **—crook′ed|ness,** *n.*

crook|er|y (krůk′ər ē), *n.* dishonesty; crookedness.

Crookes space or **Crookes dark space** (krůks), the nonluminous portion of an electric discharge between the cathode and the negative glow, present when the discharge takes place in a tube containing a gas at very low pressure. [< Sir William *Crookes,* 1832-1919, an English physicist, who invented the Crookes tube]

Crookes tube, a form of vacuum tube which has been highly exhausted so as to permit free molecular motion. [< Sir William *Crookes*]

crook|neck (krůk′nek′), *n.* a kind of squash with a long, curved neck.

crook|necked (krůk′nekt′), *adj.* having a hooked or curved neck.

crool (krül), *v.i.* to make a sound more liquid and prolonged than a croak: *Baby is lying in mother's lap, crooling and gurgling* (Sunday Magazine). [imitative]

croon (krün), *v., n.* *—v.i., v.t.* **1** to hum, sing, or murmur in a low tone: *The mother was crooning to her baby.* **2** to sing in a low voice with exaggerated emotion. **3** *Scottish.* to utter a loud, deep, continuing sound; bellow; roar.

—n. a low humming, singing, or murmuring.

[apparently < Middle Low German (compare Middle Dutch *krōnen* murmur)]

croon|er (krü′nər), *n.* **1** a person who croons. **2** a man who sings popular songs in a low, sentimental voice.

crop (krop), *n., v.,* **cropped, crop|ping.** *—n.* **1** plants grown or gathered by people for use, especially as food: *Wheat, corn, and cotton are three main crops of the United States.* **2a** the whole amount (of wheat, corn, or the produce of any plant or tree) that is borne in one season: *The drought made the potato crop very small this year.* **b** the yield of some other product in a season: *the ice crop.* **3** *Figurative:* *a crop of lies, the annual crop of freshmen, a crop of new candidates.* SYN: series. **4** the act or result of cropping. A short haircut is a crop. **5** a mark produced by clipping the ears, especially of a domestic animal; earmark. **6a** a baglike swelling of the esophagus of many birds, where food is stored and prepared for digestion; craw: *Fuel consumption is so great that most birds have a kind of carburetor called a crop for straining and preparing their food before it is injected into the combustion cylinders of the stomach and intestines* (Atlantic). **b** a similar organ in other animals or in insects: *The honey sac of a bee is called a crop. The earthworm empties the food into the crop, which is a storage chamber from which the food is released in small portions to the gizzard* (A. M. Winchester). **7a** a short whip with a loop instead of a lash: *a riding crop.* **b** the handle or stock of a whip. **8** an entire tanned hide of an animal. **9** *Mining.* an outcrop of a vein or seam.

—v.t. **1** to cut or bite off the top of: *Sheep had cropped the grass very short.* **2** to clip or cut short; cut off a part of: *a cropped page or picture, a dog with a cropped tail. His hair was cropped in a crew cut.* **3** to cause to bear a crop or crops.

—v.i. **1** to plant, cultivate, or yield a crop or crops. **2** *Mining.* to come to the surface of the ground, as a vein of ore.

crop out, to appear or come to the surface: *Ridges of white rock crop out all over that hillside. Any wild trait unexpectedly cropping out in any of the domestic animals pleased* [*Thoreau*] *immensely* (John Burroughs).

crop up, to turn up unexpectedly: *Unless you plan carefully, all sorts of difficulties may crop up.*

[Old English *cropp* sprout, craw] **—crop′less,** *adj.*

— Syn. n. **1, 2a Crop, yield, harvest** mean a product of the land, grown or gathered for use. **Crop** is the general word, applying to the product while growing or when gathered: *The tomato crop was damaged by frost.* **Yield** applies to the quantity of a crop produced: *The yield from those apple trees was poor this year.* **Harvest** applies to the gathering of a crop, more specifically to the process or time of gathering or to the amount gathered in one season: *The winter wheat is ready for spring harvest.*

crop-dust (krop′dust′), *v.t.* to sprinkle (cotton, tobacco, or other crop or vegetation) with insecticide or fungicide, especially from an aircraft.

— v.i. to engage in crop-dusting: *A year later he went to Peru to crop-dust there* (Newsweek).

crop duster, an aircraft used in crop-dusting.

crop-eared (krop′ird′), *adj.* **1** having the ears cropped. **2** having the hair cropped short, so that the ears are conspicuous.

crop-full (krop′fůl′), *adj.* having the crop or stomach filled; filled to repletion: *Let poets be crop-full of jealousy* (Walter Savage Landor).

crop-haired (krop′hãrd′), *adj.* having the hair cut short.

crop insurance, insurance that provides partial protection for a farmer's income in case of bad weather or loss of crops.

crop|land (krop′land′), *n.* land used for the growing and harvesting of crops: *The typical farmer had a thousand acres of cropland* (Atlantic).

crop milk, a liquid secreted by the lining of a pigeon's or dove's crop during the brooding period: *In about 14 days the eggs hatch and the parents begin to feed their young "crop milk"* (Scientific American).

crop|per (krop′ər), *n.* **1** a person or thing that crops. **2** a machine for shearing cloth. **3** a person who raises a crop or crops, especially on land owned by another, receiving a share of the produce; sharecropper. **4** a plant that furnishes a crop: *The soybean is a hardy cropper.* **5** *Informal, Figurative.* a heavy fall; failure or collapse.

come a cropper, *Informal.* to meet with misfortune; come to grief; fail or collapse: *Proxy hunters for both sides occasionally come a cropper during the heat of the campaign* (Wall Street Journal).

crop|pie (krop′ē), *n.* = crappie.

crop rotation, a system of growing in one field a succession of crops with different food requirements to prevent the soil from exhausting its food supply on the unvarying needs of a single crop.

***croquet** definition 1

***cro|quet** (krō kā′; *especially British* krō′kā, -kē), *n., v.,* **-queted** (-kād′), **-quet|ing** (-kā′ing). *—n.*

Pronunciation Key: hat, āge, cãre, fär; let, ēqual, tėrm; it, īce; hot, ōpen, ôrder; oil, out; cup, půt, rüle; child; long; thin; ᴛʜen; zh, measure; ə represents **a** in about, **e** in taken, **i** in pencil, **o** in lemon, **u** in circus.

1 an outdoor game played by using mallets to knock wooden balls through small wire arches, called wickets, set in the ground. A croquet course is usually the shape of two diamonds set end to end. **2** a driving away of an opponent's ball by striking one's own when the two are in contact.
— v.t., v.i. to drive away (a ball) by a croquet. [< French *croquet* shepherd's crook, (perhaps) hockey stick, dialectal variant of Old French *crochet.* See etym. of doublet **crochet, crocket, crotchet.**]

cro|quette (krō ket′), *n.* a small mass of cooked meat, fish, or vegetables chopped and coated with crumbs and fried. [< French *croquette* < *croquer* crunch]

cro|quis (krô kē′), *n., pl.* **-quis** (-kē′). *French.* **1** a preliminary drawing or design prepared by an artist, designer, or the like: *From croquis to caption-writing, fashion is a major industry* (Punch).
2 (literally) a sketch.

crore (krôr, krōr), *n., pl.* **crores** or **crore.** a unit of 10 million (especially rupees) in India; 100 lakhs. [< Hindustani *karōr*]

***cro|sier** (krō′zhər), *n.* **1** an ornamental staff, ending in a hook like a shepherd's crook, carried by or before bishops or certain abbots; crook. It symbolizes their pastoral office and duties. **2** *Botany.* the curled top of a young fern. Also, **crozier.** [< Old French *crosier, crocier* crook bearer < *crosse, croce* hook < Vulgar Latin *croccia* < Germanic (compare Old High German *chruckjā* crook)]

***crosier** definition 1

***cross** (krôs, kros), *n., v., adj., adv.* *— n.* **1** a stick or post with another across it like a T or an X.
2 anything shaped like this. A cross is a symbol of the Christian religion, such as when mounted on a pole and carried in a religious procession, or as a sign made with the right hand as an act of devotion. A person who cannot write his name makes a cross instead. A soldier is sometimes given a cross for bravery in war. **3** any monument or memorial formed like this or with a cross on it. **4** a crossing or a place of crossing; lying or going across. **5** *Figurative.* **a** a burden of duty or suffering; trouble: *A patient person bears his cross without complaining.* SYN: trial, affliction. **b** anything that thwarts or obstructs. **6a** a mixing of kinds, breeds, or races. **b** the result of such mixing; crossbreed: *A mule is a cross between a horse and a donkey.* SYN: hybrid. **c** *Figurative.* a mixture or combination of qualities or features: *Cyrano de Bergerac was a cross between a soldier and a poet.* **7** a countering blow in boxing, crossing over the opponent's lead. **8** a pipe connection having four arms at right angles. **9** the accidental contact of two electrical conductors; short circuit. **10** *Slang.* something that is not fair, such as a game in which the winner is decided in advance.
— v.t. **1** to draw a line across: *In writing you cross the letter "t".* **2a** to cancel by drawing a line or lines across: *to cross off a name on a list. He crossed out the wrong word.* **b** to mark with an X. **3** to put or lay across: *He crossed his arms.* **4** to lie across; intersect: *Main Street crosses Market Street.* **5a** to move from one side to the other of; go across: *Cross the street at the corner. He crossed the ocean in a tramp steamer. The bridge crosses the river.* **b** to carry or transport across: *The ship crossed the soldiers to a new theater of battle.* **6** to meet and pass: *He crossed her on the stairs.* **7** to make the sign of the cross on or over: *The priest crossed himself before the altar. They cross'd themselves for fear* (Tennyson). **8** *Figurative.* to hinder; oppose: *If anyone crosses him, he gets very angry.* **9** to mix kinds, breeds, or races of: *A new plant is sometimes made by crossing two others.* **10** to cause a faulty or accidental connection between: *The telephone lines were crossed.* (*Figurative.*) *She and I must have got our wires crossed, since we never met as we had planned.* **11** *Slang.* to deceive or betray; double-cross.
— v.i. **1** to lie across; intersect: *the place where the two roads cross. Parallel lines cannot cross.* **2** to meet and pass: *My letter to her and her letter to me crossed in the mail.* **3** to move from one side or place to another. **4** to interbreed.
— adj. **1** lying or going across; crossing: *He stood at the intersection of the cross streets.* **2** in a bad temper; peevish: *She is cross because her cake burned. I have never had a cross word from him in my life* (Jane Austen). SYN: ill-tempered. **3** mixed in kind, breed, or race; crossbred; hybrid. **4** *Figurative.* contrary; opposite: *to confuse matters by bringing up a cross issue.* **5** unfavorable; adverse: *A very cross accident indeed!* (Richard Brinsley Sheridan). **6** involving interchange; reciprocal. **7** *Slang.* dishonest.
— adv. crosswise; across.
cross over, a *Biology.* to go from one homologous chromosome to another during meiosis: *The farther apart the genes are on the same chromosome, the greater is the opportunity for crossing over* (Harbaugh and Goodrich). **b** *Informal.* to die: *The old prospector kept digging till the day he crossed over.*
cross up, *Slang.* **a** to betray; double-cross: *The accused ... seemed to have been crossed up only by the one event of July 13 that the killer had overlooked* (Time). **b** to confuse: *Consumers crossed up the sales experts* (Wall Street Journal).
take the cross, to join a crusade: *Baldwin ... exhorted men to take the cross* (Richard Grafton).
the Cross, a the cross on which Christ died. It is a symbol of Christianity. *Those blessed feet ... nailed on the bitter Cross* (Shakespeare).
b Christ's sufferings and death; the Atonement: *the doctrine of the Cross, as the one great rule and hope of the world* (G. A. Poole). **c** the Christian religion: *Let us now take leave of the countries of the Half Moon ... and return ... into those of the Cross* (Bartholomew Harris). **d** the Southern Cross; Crux: *We saw again the Northern Star to our great joy; till then we had only the ... Cross in sight* (Christopher Fryke).
[Old English *cros* < Old Irish *cross* < Latin *crux, crucis.* See etym. of doublet **crux.**] *—* **cross′a|ble,** *adj.* *—* **cross′er,** *n.* *—* **cross′ly,** *adv.* *—* **cross′ness,** *n.*

cross-, *combining form.* **1** cross-shaped: *Cross-stitch = a stitch crossed over another.*
2 moving across: *Crossfire = lines of fire that cross.*
3 counter: *Cross-purpose = a purpose counter to another.*
4 across regular lines of affinity: *Cross-fertilization = the fertilization of one plant by the pollen from another.* [< *cross*]

cross action, legal action brought by a defendant against the plaintiff in the same case or suit.

cross|arm (krôs′ärm′, kros′-), *n.* the horizontal beam of a telephone pole or a similar pole, used for electricity distribution and transmission lines.

cross|band (krôs′band′, kros′-), *n. Zoology.* a stripe situated crosswise on the body of an animal.

cross|bar (krôs′bär′, kros′-), *n., v.,* **-barred, -barring.** *— n.* a bar, line, or stripe going crosswise.
— v.t. to mark with crossbars.

cross|beam (krôs′bēm′, kros′-), *n.* a beam that crosses another or extends from wall to wall.

cross|bed|ded (krôs′bed′id, kros′-), *adj. Geology.* having an original lamination oblique to the main stratification.

cross|bed|ding (krôs′bed′ing, kros′-), *n. Geology.* apparent lines of stratification crossing the real ones; false bedding.

cross|belt (krôs′belt′, kros′-), *n.* **1** a belt passing obliquely across the breast. **2** a belt worn over both shoulders, and crossing in front of the breast.

cross|bench (krôs′bench′, kros′-), *n. British.* a bench situated at right angles to other benches in the House of Lords on which independent or neutral members sometimes sit.

cross|bench|er (krôs′ben′chər, kros′-), *n. British.* an independent or neutral member of the

***cross** definition 2

House of Lords: *Lord Boothby, speaking with the freedom of a crossbencher, described the Treasury's policy as 'furtive, disastrous, and dishonest'* (Annual Register).

cross|bill (krôs′bil′, kros′-), *n.* a small finch whose powerful bill has points that cross each other when the bill is closed.

cross birth, a birth in which the child is presented in a position transverse to the uterus.

cross|bones (krôs′bōnz′, kros′-), *n.pl.* two large bones placed crosswise, usually below a skull, to mean death: *Poisonous medicines are sometimes marked with a skull and crossbones.*

***cross|bow** (krôs′bō′, kros′-), *n.* a medieval weapon for shooting arrows (called bolts) or stones, consisting of a bow fixed across a wooden stock, with a groove in the middle to direct the arrows or stones.

***crossbow**

cross|bow|man (krôs′bō′mən, kros′-), *n., pl.* **-men.** a soldier who used a crossbow.

cross|bred (krôs′bred′, kros′-), *adj., n., v.* —*adj.* produced by crossbreeding. SYN: hybrid, mongrel. —*n.* an animal or plant produced by crossbreeding: *Comebacks and crossbreds met very keen competition* (London Times). SYN: hybrid, mongrel. —*v.* the past tense and past participle of **crossbreed.**

crossbred wool, wool from a sheep that is a cross of two breeds of sheep, such as the Corriedale. Crossbred wool is brighter and coarser than Merino and is used especially in the making of hosiery and worsted serge.

cross|breed (krôs′brēd′, kros′-), *v.,* **-bred, -breed|ing,** *n.* —*v.t., v.i.* to breed by mixing kinds, breeds, or races: *You can crossbreed a horse and a donkey to get a mule.* SYN: cross, hybridize.
—*n.* an individual or breed produced by crossbreeding: *A loganberry is a crossbreed of a blackberry and a raspberry.* SYN: hybrid.

cross|breed|ing (krôs′brē′ding, kros′-), *n.* breeding by mixing kinds, breeds, or races: *It's a boon to biologists, who hope crossbreeding will do for trees what it's already achieved for corn and livestock* (Wall Street Journal).

cross|buck (krôs′buk′), *n.* a highway traffic sign consisting of two crosspieces forming an X to warn motorists that a railroad crossing is ahead.

cross buck, *Football.* a play in which two backs cross paths as they head into the line of scrimmage, one to fake receiving the ball and the other to receive it.

cross bun, a bun marked with a cross on top. Hot cross buns are often eaten on Good Friday or during Lent.

cross|bus|ing (krôs′bus′ing, kros′-), *n. U.S.* the busing of children from two different districts to each other's schools: *the hardening of racial attitudes caused by crossbusing to achieve racial balance* (New York Times).

cross-chan|nel (krôs′chan′əl, kros′-), *adj.* passing or situated across a channel, as the English Channel: *a cross-channel steamer.*

cross-check (krôs′chek′, kros′-), *v., n.* —*v.t.* **1** to check a second time; recheck: *The biographer must . . . check and cross-check every document* (New York Times). **2** to check more than twice: *rechecked later for accuracy . . . and cross-checked in over three times as many cases* (Harper's). **3a** *Anthropology.* to compare (a person's behavior) at different times. **b** to compare (two people's behavior) under the same conditions.
—*n.* a second or further check.

cross-chest carry (krôs′chest′, kros′-), a method of carrying someone in the water to rescue him from drowning by clamping an arm across his chest while swimming a sidestroke.

cross circulation, a technique similar to blood transfusion in which the arteries and veins of two individuals are linked so that the heart and lungs of the donor are used to circulate and oxygenate the patient's blood during a heart operation.

cross-con|nect (krôs′kə nekt′, kros′-), *v.t.* to interchange the connections of (electric wires).

cross-coun|try (krôs′kun′trē, kros′-), *adj., adv., n.* —*adj., adv.* **1** across fields or open country instead of by road: *a cross-country race.* **2** across an entire country, not merely a part: *a cross-country flight from New York to Seattle* (adj.). *The mission . . . had brought him cross-country to Los Angeles* (Time) (adv.).
—*n.* a sports event or events held across fields or open country, as cross-country skiing and long-distance running.

cross cousins, *Anthropology, Sociology.* cousins one of whom has a father who is the brother of the other's mother.

cross-cul|tur|al (krôs′kul′chər əl, kros′-), *adj.* crossing the boundaries of a culture; involving more than one culture: *The social sciences should study cross-cultural problems as well as those of our own culture.* —**cross′-cul′tur|al|ly,** *adv.*

cross|cur|rent or **cross-cur|rent** (krôs′kėr′ənt, kros′-), *n.* **1** a current of air blowing across another. **2** *Figurative.* an opposing tendency or trend: *the crosscurrents of political thought.*

cross|cut (krôs′kut′, kros′-), *n., adj., v.,* **-cut, -cut|ting.** —*n.* **1** a cut, course, or path going across. **2** a short cut: *The quickest way is to take the crosscut through the fields.* **3** *Mining.* a passageway cut across the course of a vein. **4** = crosscut saw.
—*adj.* **1** used or made for cutting across: *a crosscut chisel.* **2** cut across.
—*v.t.* to cut across: *Crosscut the field to take a short cut.*

crosscut saw, a saw made for cutting across the grain of wood.

cross-date (krôs′dāt′, kros′-), *v.,* **-dat|ed, -dat|ing.** —*v.t.* to establish the date or age of (trees, archaeological artifacts, or other specimens) by comparing systematically their characteristics with those of others whose age has been previously determined.
—*v.i.* to make such a comparison so as to establish a date or age: *With trees of known felling date the outer ring, and hence the rest, can be dated, and so by cross-dating can the outer rings of older trees or stumps which overlap the inner rings of the dated ones* (New Scientist).

cross-dress (krôs′dres′; kros′-), *v.i.* to dress in the clothing of the opposite sex: *Transvestites [range] from those who occasionally wear the clothes of the other sex in private to those who are only comfortable when cross-dressing in public* (Harper's). —**cross′-dress′er,** *n.*

cross-dress|ing (krôs′dres′ing, kros′-), *n.* = transvestism.

crosse (krôs, kros), *n.* the racket used in playing lacrosse.
[< French *crosse* < Old French *croce;* see etym. under **crosier**]

cross-ex|am|i|na|tion (krôs′ig zam′ə nā′shən, kros′-), *n.* **1** an examination to check a previous examination: *A lawyer questions witnesses for the opposing side by cross-examination to test the truth of their evidence.* **2** a close or severe questioning.

cross-ex|am|ine (krôs′ig zam′in, kros′-), *v.t., v.i.,* **-ined, -in|ing.** **1** to question closely (a witness for the opposing side) to check the truth of his testimony. SYN: interrogate. **2** to question closely or severely; cross-question. —**cross′-ex|am′in|er,** *n.*

cross-eye (krôs′ī′, kros′-), *n.* strabismus, especially the form in which both eyes are turned toward the nose and cannot focus on the same point.

cross-eyed (krôs′īd′, kros′-), *adj.* having both eyes turned toward the nose and unable to focus on the same point.

cross-fer|til|i|za|tion (krôs′fėr′tə lə zā′shən, kros′-), *n.* **1** *Botany.* the fertilization of one flower by pollen from another; allogamy. **2** *Biology.* **a** the fertilization of the ovum of one individual by the sperm of another. **b** the mating of a male of one variety with the female of another. **3** *Figurative.* a mingling or exchange (of ideas, techniques, or other findings) between different industries, cultures, or other groups that would result in mutual gain: *But documents often fail to reveal motives; they fail to show the genesis of ideas or the cross-fertilization and intellectual pin-pricking that takes place when two or more scientists are gathered together* (Bulletin of Atomic Scientists).

cross-fer|til|ize (krôs′fėr′tə līz, kros′-), *v.,* **-lized, -liz|ing.** —*v.t.* to cause the cross-fertilization of.
—*v.i.* to be subjected to cross-fertilization.

cross-file (krôs′fīl′, kros′-), *v.i.,* **-filed, -fil|ing.** *U.S.* to file for nomination on more than one party's ticket during Congressional or other primaries: *In the state of California, the candidates can cross-file and appear on several ballots.* —**cross′-fil′er,** *n.*

cross fire, or **cross|fire** (krôs′fīr′, kros′-), *n.* **1** *Military.* **a** gunfire coming from two or more opposite directions so as to cross; simultaneous fire along these lines: *A truck was overturned and the occupants were caught in the cross fire of Israeli sharpshooters* (Harper's). **b** one of these lines. **2** *Figurative.* a verbal attack or indictment from two or more sources or directions: *The cross fire between committee members and Pentagon representatives, called in to explain procurement methods, was sharp* (Newsweek).

cross-fire (krôs′fīr′, kros′-), *v.i.,* **-fired, -fir|ing.** **1** to make or take part in a cross fire. **2** to strike a hind foot against a front foot: *Pacers are more likely to cross-fire than trotters.* **3** to direct X rays from several points so that they cross or converge at one given point.

cross|foot (krôs′fu̇t′, kros′-), *adj., adv.* with the feet crossed; with one foot over the other: *a crossfoot spin* (adj.); *to dance or skate crossfoot* (adv.).

cross fox, a color phase of the red fox having dark fur in the shape of a cross along the back and across the shoulders.

cross-grained (krôs′grānd′, kros′-), *adj.* **1** having the grain arranged in crossing directions, or irregularly, instead of running straight: *cross-grained wood.* **2** *Figurative.* hard to get along with; contrary: *a cross-grained old miser.* SYN: intractable, perverse.

cross guard, a type of guard on a sword, made in the form of a bar at right angles with the blade.

cross hair, one of the fine strands of spider web, quartz fiber, or other material stretched across the focal plane of an optical instrument for defining accurately the line of sight; cross wire: *His face glued to the radarscope and its tireless, swinging line of light [he] made manual adjustments to keep the cross hairs on the pip that marked his target* (Time).

cross|hatch (krôs′hach′, kros′-), *v., n.* —*v.t., v.i.* to mark or shade (an engraving, drawing, or the like) with two sets of parallel lines crossing each other.
—*n.* one of these lines.

cross|hatch|ing (krôs′hach′ing, kros′-), *n.* **1** the making of crosshatches. **2** the marking or shading made.

cross|head (krôs′hed′, kros′-), *n.* **1** *Printing.* a heading printed across the page or column in the body of the text. **2** the bar or piece at the end of a piston rod connecting it with the connecting rod of a steam engine.

cross-im|mu|ni|ty (krôs′i myü′nə tē, kros′-), *n., pl.* **-ties.** immunity produced against a disease organism by inoculation with a different but related organism.

cross-im|mu|ni|za|tion (krôs′im′yù nə zā′shən, kros′-), *n.* the state or condition of having cross-immunity: *A cross-immunization test is one which seeks to find out whether antibodies to one virus will neutralize a different virus* (Scientific American).

cross index, an index of cross-references.

cross-in|dex (krôs′in′deks, kros′-), *v.t.* **1** to index (a reference) under another heading as a cross-reference. **2** to provide (a book, periodical, or index) with cross-references. —*v.i.* to be cross-indexed; contain a cross index.

cross-in|fec|tion (krôs′in fek′shən, kros′-), *n.* an infection transmitted between hospital patients having different infectious diseases.

cross|ing (krôs′ing, kros′-), *n.* **1** the place where lines or tracks cross; intersection: *"Railroad crossing! Stop! Look! Listen!"* **2** the place at which a street or river may be crossed: *White lines mark the crossing.* **3** the act of going across, especially a voyage across water: *The ocean liner makes the crossing from New York to England every two weeks.* **4** the part of a cruciform church where the transept crosses the nave. **5** an opposing; a thwarting. **6** = crossbreeding.

crossing guard, a person, usually uniformed, who, for pay or as a public service, directs traffic and helps school children cross the street at busy intersections.

crossing over, or **cross|ing-over** (krôs′ing ō′vər, kros′-), *n. Biology.* the mutual exchange of genes between homologous chromosomes during meiosis.

cross|jack (krôs′jak′, kros′-; *Nautical* krô′jik, kroj′ik), *n.* a square sail on the lower yard of a mizzenmast.

cross-kick (krôs′kik′, kros′-), *n., v. Rugby.* —*n.* a kick toward the side; sideways kick.
—*v.t.* to give (the ball) a cross-kick.
—*v.i.* to make a cross-kick.

cross-leg|ged (krôs′leg′id, kros′-; -legd′), *adj., adv.* **1** with one leg over the other and the knees together. **2** with the ankles crossed and the knees apart.

cross|let (krôs′lit, kros′-), *n.* a small cross, used as a bearing in heraldry. See diagram under **cross.**

cross-li|cense (krôs′lī′səns, kros′-), *n., v.,* **-censed, -cens|ing.** —*n.* an exchange of licenses to use each other's patents for a specified period: *The two companies arranged a royalty-free cross-license.*

Pronunciation Key: hat, āge, cãre, fär; let, ēqual, tėrm; it, īce; hot, ōpen, ôrder; **oi**l, **ou**t; cup, pu̇t, rüle; **ch**ild; lo**ng**; **th**in; **ᵺ**en; **zh**, measure; **ə** represents **a** in about, **e** in taken, **i** in pencil, **o** in lemon, **u** in circus.

—*v.i.* to exchange such licenses of patent.

cross|light (krôs′līt′, kros′-), *n.* a light that crosses the direction of another light and illuminates parts which the other leaves in shade. **crosslights, a** lights whose rays cross each other: *The windows on the other sides were darkened to avoid crosslights.* **b** enlightenment from various unrelated or conflicting sources: *The fluctuations and crosslights of Lawrence's criticism ... result in a view of literature of considerable subtlety and complexity* (Listener).

cross-link (krôs′lingk′, kros′-), *n., v.* —*n.* **1** a crosswise connection: *Links and cross-links make a pattern of overlapping spiders' webs* (Manchester Guardian). **2** *Chemistry.* a long molecular chain joined to another chain at intervals between atomic cores for the purpose of strengthening a material, as rubber in the process of vulcanization.
—*v.t.* to join (a molecular chain) to: *If the two threads of a chromosome were cross-linked before a cell divided, the two could not separate properly during division and abnormalities would result* (Scientific American).
—*v.i.* to establish cross-links: *Cross-linking increases strength and toughness in plastic film which has been irradiated* (Science News Letter).

cross-link|age (krôs′ling′kij, kros′-), *n.* **1** the process of establishing chemical bonds between atomic cores of different molecular chains: *Certain kinds of ... cross-linkages ... make the protein molecules incapable of taking further part in body processes* (Science News Letter). **2** = cross-link.

cross lode, *Mining.* a lode or vein which does not follow the regular and ordinary course of the productive lodes of the district, but intersects them at an angle.

cross-match (krôs′mach′, kros′-), *v.i.* to determine the compatibility of a donor's and a recipient's blood before transfusion. It is done by placing red cells of the donor and the recipient into the other's serum. If no agglutination occurs after cross-matching, the blood specimens are compatible. —*v.t.* to subject (blood) to cross-matching.

cross-mate (krôs′māt′, kros′-), *v.t., v.i.,* **-mat|ed, -mat|ing.** to mate or breed different varieties or species; cross; crossbreed.

cross-mo|dal (krôs′mō′dəl, kros′-), *adj. Psychology.* of or having to do with cross-modality.

cross-mo|dal|i|ty (krôs′mō dal′ə tē, kros′-), *n. Psychology.* the ability to match or associate things perceived through different senses, such as spoken words with written words.

cross-mod|u|la|tion (krôs′moj′ù lā′shən, kros′-), *n. Electronics.* a distortion or interference occurring when the carrier of a desired signal is modulated by an unwanted signal, as in radio transmission: *Watch for "cross-modulation," the undesirable presence of a strong, local station on two or three points around the dial* (Saturday Review).

cros|sop|te|ryg|i|an (kro sop′tə rij′ē ən), *adj., n.* —*adj.* of or having to do with a group of fish which, except for a species found off South Africa, is now believed to be extinct: *The crossopterygian fishes gave rise to the amphibians and vanished almost totally* (Scientific American).
—*n.* a crossopterygian fish.
[< New Latin *Crossopterygii* the group name (< Greek *krossós* tassel + *ptéryx, -ygos* fin) + English *-an*]

cross|o|ver (krôs′ō′vər, kros′-), *n.* **1** anything that crosses over or connects: **a** a small bridge over a highway or parkway. **b** a process of coordinating low and high frequencies over high-fidelity speakers by feeding the low frequencies to a bass speaker and the high frequencies to a treble speaker. **2** *Biology.* **a** = crossing over. **b** the characteristic inherited by crossing over. **3** a blend of the jazz form with other types of popular music or an adaptation of the jazz form to various styles and formats; fusion: *Although the crossover trend was the most conspicuous aspect of jazz, some artists gained respect through pure jazz performances that reached a small but loyal audience* (Leonard Feather).

cross|patch (krôs′pach′, kros′-), *n. Informal.* a cross, bad-tempered person.

cross peen, a machinists' hammer having a peen with a rounded edge running across or perpendicular to the direction of the handle.

cross|piece (krôs′pēs′, kros′-), *n.* a piece of wood, metal, or other material, that is placed across something: [*He*] *reflexively put his hand on a crosspiece between panes of glass, as if he had a mind to raise the window* (New Yorker).

cross-ply (krôs′plī′, kros′-), *adj. British.* of or having to do with a kind of tire in which the plies of cord fabric are laid to cross each other diagonally.

cross-pol|li|nate (krôs′pol′ə nāt, kros′-), *v.,* **-nat|ed, -nat|ing.** —*v.t.* to cause cross-pollination in.
—*v.i.* to be subjected to cross-pollination.

cross-pol|li|na|tion (krôs′pol′ə nā′shən, kros′-), *n.* **1** the transfer of pollen from the anther of one flower to the stigma of another, on the same plant or on another plant of the same species. Insects and wind are agents of cross-pollination. **2** = cross-fertilization: (*Figurative.*) *cultural cross-pollination.*

cross product, *Mathematics.* a vector quantity whose length is the product of the lengths of two vectors and the sine of the angle between them; vector product; outer product. It is denoted by a cross placed between the two vectors, as in *A* x *B.*

cross-pur|pose (krôs′pėr′pəs, kros′-), *n.* an opposing or contrary purpose.
at cross-purposes, a misunderstanding each other's purpose: *Let's set things right; we've been at cross-purposes.* **b** acting under such a misunderstanding: *For ten years the sisters continued at cross-purposes, though a single meeting would have cleared up their quarrel.*
cross-purposes, a game of questioning and answering in which words having different meanings are used: *I won't pay you the kisses you won from me last night at cross-purposes* (George Farquhar).

cross-ques|tion (krôs′kwes′chən, kros′-), *v., n.* —*v.t.* to question closely; cross-examine.
—*n.* a question asked in cross-examining.

cross|rail (krôs′rāl′, kros′-), *n.* a piece of wood, metal, or other material, that lies across something.

cross-re|fer (krôs′ri fėr′, kros′-), *v.t., v.i.,* **-ferred, -fer|ring. 1** to refer from one part to another. **2** to make a cross-reference.

cross-ref|er|ence (krôs′ref′ər əns, kros′-; -ref′rəns), *n., v.,* **-enced, -enc|ing.** —*n.* a reference from one part of a book, index, or table, to another. "See picture under **bit**³," at **brace**, is a cross-reference.
—*v.t.* **1** to provide with cross-references: *Well thought out, clearly printed, skillfully cross-referenced* (Scientific American). **2** = cross-refer.

cross relation, *Music.* a contradiction in chromatic relationship between notes in different voices sounded successively or simultaneously, as a C natural in one part and a C sharp in the other; false relation.

cross-re|sist|ance (krôs′ri zis′təns, kros′-), *n.* resistance to a new antibiotic that a germ transfers or develops from its resistance to another drug.

cross-re|sist|ant (krôs′ri zis′tənt, kros′-), *adj.* having or showing cross-resistance to a drug.

cross-rhythm (krôs′riтн′əm, kros′-), *n. Music.* the simultaneous use of strikingly different rhythms in different parts or voices.

cross|road (krôs′rōd′, kros′-), *n.* **1** a road that crosses another: *The hikers stopped at the crossroad puzzled at which way to go.* **2** a road that connects main roads: *We took the crossroad from the inland highway to the one along the coast.*

cross|roads (krôs′rōdz′, kros′-), *n.pl.* **1** the place where roads cross: *Near the crossroads we stopped and read the signs.* **2** *Figurative.* **a** a critical turning point: *The troubles of collective bargaining have brought labor to a serious crossroads* (Wall Street Journal). **b** a point at which two or more courses of action diverge: *He and Lucy had passed the crossroads of life now, their paths had cut away from each other* (James T. Farrell).
at the crossroads, in a situation where a choice must be made: *He found himself at the crossroads of his career when he had to decide between staying in business and entering politics.*

cross|ruff (krôs′ruf′, kros′-), *n., v.* —*n.* a series of plays in card games, in which each of two partners in turn leads a card that the other trumps.
—*v.i.* to trump cards in this way.
—*v.t.* **1** to trick or maneuver into. **2** to surpass; cap: *The orderly sequence of events was about to be crossruffed by exploding violence* (New Yorker).
[< *cross* + *ruff*² card game]

cross seat, a seat extending across a carriage or other conveyance.

***cross section, 1** the act of cutting anything across: *She sliced tomatoes for a salad by making a series of cross sections.* **2** a piece cut in this way: *A cross section of muscular tissue was observed under a microscope.* **3a** a drawing or diagram showing such a piece or the surface of such a cut. **b** a drawing showing levels and profiles, for example in surveying. **4** *Figurative.* a sample; small selection of people, animals, or things with the same qualities as the entire group: *If our neighborhood can be taken as a cross section of the town, then the mayor hasn't much chance of being reelected. He made a study of a cross section of middle-income families.* **5** *Physics.* that portion of a nucleus subjected to bombardment by neutrons or other particles, in which a particular reaction will occur.

***cross section**
definition 3a

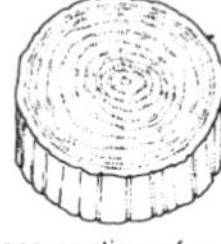

cross section of wood

cross-sec|tion (krôs′sek′shən, kros′-), *v.t.* **1** to cut into cross sections. **2** to make a cross section of: (*Figurative.*) *As the American samples opposite and overleaf show, the collection neatly cross-sections contemporary painting* (Time).

cross-sec|tion|al (krôs′sek′shə nəl, kros′-), *adj.* of, having to do with, or covering a cross section: *Basketball is native in origin and cross-sectional in appeal.*

cross-shaped (krôs′shāpt′, kros′-), *adj.* in the form or shape of a cross; cruciform.

cross-staff (krôs′staf′, kros′-; -stäf′), *n.* a surveying instrument for setting out right angles to a main line, no longer used in the United States.

***cross-stitch** (krôs′stich′, kros′-), *n., v.* —*n.* **1** one stitch crossed over another, forming an X. **2** embroidery made with this stitch.
—*v.t., v.i.* to embroider or sew with one stitch crossed over another.

***cross-stitch**

cross street, 1 a street that crosses another. **2** a street connecting main streets.

cross talk, 1 noises heard in a telephone or radio channel when currents from one channel interfere with those of another: *Cross talk happens when pairs of wire are positioned parallel to each other in a cable* (Scientific American). **2** *British.* an exchange of remarks between members of different parties in Parliament: *There was a good deal of cross talk on the origin of recent rumours about sterling* (London Times).

cross|tie (krôs′tī′, kros′-), *n.* a heavy piece of timber or iron placed crosswise to form a foundation or support. The rails of a railroad track are fastened to crossties about 21 inches apart.

cross-town (krôs′toun′, kros′-), *adj., adv.* —*adj.* that runs across the town: *a cross-town bus.*
—*adv.* across the town: *We took the bus cross-town to Lincoln Center.*

cross traffic, traffic moving crosswise at intersecting points: *a motorway, with no cross traffic and with all vehicles travelling in one direction should be the safest form of road in a fog* (Manchester Guardian).

cross-trans|fu|sion (krôs′trans fyü′zhən, kros′-), *n.* cross circulation in which two blood systems are connected by mechanical devices, such as pumps or tubes.

cross|trees (krôs′trēz′, kros′-), *n.pl.* two horizontal bars of wood or metal near the top of a ship's mast to support the top and spread the upper shrouds.

cross-ven|ti|la|tion (krôs′ven′tə lā′shən, kros′-), *n.* ventilation from two sources, as opposite windows in a room.

cross vine, a vine of the southern United States, so called because of the cross-shaped arrangement of inner tissue, as shown in a transverse section of the older stems.

cross|walk (krôs′wôk′, kros′-), *n.* an area marked with lines, used by pedestrians in crossing a street.

cross|way (krôs′wā′, kros′-), *n.* = crossroad.

cross|ways (krôs′wāz′, kros′-), *adv.* = crosswise.

cross wind, a wind that blows across the direction of movement of an aircraft, boat, or automobile.

cross wire, 1 a wire that crosses. **2** = cross hair.

cross|wise (krôs′wīz′, kros′-), *adv.* **1** so as to cross; across: *The tree fell crosswise over the stream.* SYN: athwart. **2** in the form of a cross: *The streets come together crosswise at the intersection.* **3** *Figurative.* opposite to what is required; wrongly: *You have assembled these pieces of your bookcase crosswise.*

cross|word (krôs′wėrd′, kros′-), *n.* = crossword

Pronunciation Key: hat, āge, cãre, fär; let, ēqual, tėrm; it, īce; hot, ōpen, ôrder; oil, out; cup, pu̇t, rüle; child; long; thin; тнen; zh, measure; ə represents **a** in about, **e** in taken, **i** in pencil, **o** in lemon, **u** in circus.

puzzle.
cross|word puzzle (krôs′wėrd′, kros′-), a puzzle with sets of numbered squares to be filled in with words, one letter to each square, so that the words may be read both across and down. Synonyms, definitions of the words, or other clues are given with numbers corresponding to numbers in the squares.
cross|yard (krôs′yärd′, kros′-), *n. Nautical.* a pole or spar fastened crosswise.
crot|a|line (krot′ə lin, krō′tə-; -līn), *adj.* of or resembling the rattlesnakes. [< New Latin *Crotalus* the rattlesnake genus (< Greek *krótalon* rattle, castanet) + English *-ine*[1]]
crot|a|lum (krot′ə ləm, krō′tə-), *n., pl.* **-la** (-lə). a rattle or clapper made of wood and bone, used in ancient Egypt and Greece. [< Latin *crotalum* < Greek *krótalon*]
crotch (kroch), *n.* **1** the place where a tree or bough divides into two limbs or branches: *The nest was in a crotch of the tree.* **2** the place where the human body divides into the two legs. **3** a forked piece or part, such as a forked stake or pole, used as a support. [< French *croche* crook < Old North French variant of *croc;* see etym. under **crotchet**; influenced by English *crutch*]
crotched (krocht), *adj.* having a crotch; forked.
crotch|et (kroch′it), *n.* **1** an odd notion; unreasonable whim: *The old man had many crotchets.* SYN: caprice, whimsy, vagary. **2** a small hook or hooklike part, organ, or instrument. **3** *Especially British.* a quarter note or its symbol in music. **4** *Obsolete.* a brooch. [< Old French *crochet* (diminutive) < *croc* hook. See etym. of doublet **crochet, crocket, croquet.**]
crotch|et|eer (kroch′ə tir′), *n.* a person having odd notions or unreasonable whims.
crotch|et|y (kroch′ə tē), *adj.* full of odd notions or unreasonable whims. —**crotch′et|i|ly**, *adv.* —**crotch′et|i|ness**, *n.*
cro|ton (krō′tən), *n.* **1** any one of a genus of tropical shrubs or trees of the spurge family, having a strong odor. The seeds of an Asian species yield croton oil. Cascarilla bark is obtained from certain species grown in the Bahamas. **2** any one of various related plants, often grown in gardens for their beautiful foliage. [< New Latin *Croton* the genus name < Greek *krotṓn* castor-oil plant; tick[2] (from the shape of its seed)]
Croton bug, a small, pale yellowish-brown cockroach, commonly found in houses near damp places; water bug; German cockroach. [American English < *Croton (water) bugs,* which were numerous in New York City after the *Croton* river became a source of the city's water through the *Croton* aqueduct into the city]
cro|ton|ic acid (krō ton′ik, -tō′nik), *Chemistry.* a colorless, crystalline substance used in organic synthesis. *Formula:* $C_4H_6O_2$
croton oil, a thick, bitter oil obtained from croton seeds, used in medicine as a cathartic and as a counterirritant.
crouch (krouch), *v., n.* —*v.i.* **1** to stoop low with bent legs like an animal ready to spring, or a person hiding: *The cat crouched in the corner waiting for the mouse to come out of its hole. The boys crouched under a bush when we played hide-and-seek.* **2** to shrink down in fear: *The frightened girl crouched in the bushes to hide from the dog.* SYN: cower. **3** to bow down in a timid or slavish manner; cringe. SYN: grovel, crawl, fawn.
—*v.t.* to bend low.
—*n.* **1** the act or state of crouching. **2** a crouching position.
[< Old French *crochir* become bent, crooked < *croc* hook < Germanic (compare Old Icelandic *krōkr*)] —**crouch′er**, *n.* —**crouch′ing|ly**, *adv.*
croud (krüd), *v.i. Scottish.* crood.
croup[1] (krüp), *n.* an inflammation or diseased condition of the throat and windpipe, especially in children, characterized by a hoarse cough and difficult breathing. [< obsolete *croup* to cry hoarsely, croak; imitative]
croup[2] (krüp), *n.* the rump of a horse or other quadruped; crupper. [< Old French *croupe* < unrecorded Frankish *kruppa*]
croup[3] (krüp), *v.t. U.S. Informal.* to take charge of as a croupier. [apparently back formation < *croupier*]
crou|pi|er (krü′pē ər), *n.* **1** an attendant at a gambling table who spins the wheel or throws the dice, rakes in the money, and pays the winners. **2** a person who sits at the lower end of the table at a public dinner and acts as assistant chairman. [< French *croupier* < *croupe* (originally) one who rides behind on the croup[2]]
croup|ous (krü′pəs), *adj.* = croupy.
croup|y (krü′pē), *adj.,* **croup|i|er, croup|i|est.** **1** sick with croup. **2** hoarse and having difficulty in breathing: *the wheeze of a croupy baby.* **3** of croup; resembling croup.
crouse (krüs), *adj. Scottish.* bold; brisk; lively; cheerful. [probably < Middle Low German *krūs* crisp] —**crouse′ly**, *adv.*
crous|tade (krü städ′), *n. French.* a cuplike form of bread, rice, hominy, or the like, usually fried crisp, and filled with meat, fish, oysters, or other seafood.
crou|ton (krü′ton), *n.* a small piece of toasted or fried bread, often served in soup. [< French *croûton* < *croûte,* earlier *crouste* crust < Latin *crusta*]
crow[1] (krō), *n.* **1** a large, glossy, black bird that has a harsh cry or caw. **2** any similar and related bird, such as a raven, magpie, or jay. **3** = crowbar.
as the crow flies, in a straight line; in or by the shortest way: *He lives exactly one mile from school as the crow flies.*
eat crow, to be forced to do something very disagreeable and humiliating: *I suppose Norris has explained our mistake and eaten crow for all of us* (W. M. Raine).
have a crow to pick with, *Informal.* to have a complaint or criticism against; have something unpleasant to talk over with: *The tenants in this building have a crow to pick with the landlord because he fails to provide the services required by law.*
[Old English *crāwe*]
crow[2] (krō), *n., v.,* **crowed** (*or* **crew** *for 1*), **crowed, crow|ing.** —*n.* **1** the loud cry of a rooster: *The fox started at the crow of the rooster.* **2** a happy sound made by a baby. **3** *Figurative.* an expression of happiness and pride: *a crow of triumph.* [< verb]
—*v.i.* **1** to make the cry of a rooster: *The cock crowed as the sun rose.* **2** to make the happy sound of a baby: *The baby crowed with laughter.* **3** *Figurative.* to show one's happiness and pride; boast: *The winning team crowed over its victory.*
[Old English *crāwan;* imitative]
Crow[1] (krō), *n., pl.* **Crow** or **Crows. 1** a member of a tribe of American Indians formerly living in Montana and Wyoming and now living in Montana. **2** the Siouan language of the Crow. [American English; partial translation of Hidatsa *absaroke,* literally, children of the (large-beaked) bird]
Crow[2] (krō), *n.* the southern constellation Corvus. [translation of Latin *corvus* crow]
***crow|bar** (krō′bär′), *n.* a strong bar of iron or steel used to lift things or pry them apart. It often has a curved or forked end, flattened into a wedge. [American English < *crow*[1] in sense of "crowbar" (from its resemblance to the beak of the bird) + *bar*[1]]

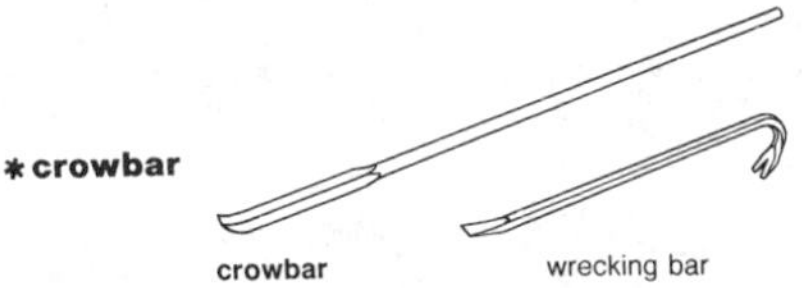

***crowbar**

crow|ber|ry (krō′ber′ē), *n., pl.* **-ries. 1** a tasteless black berry, the fruit of a small, evergreen, heathlike shrub of northern Europe and America. **2** the shrub itself; heathberry: *Flying northward in an airplane, you see occasional green patches where crowberry grows in the tundra* (Scientific American). **3** the American or large cranberry.
crow blackbird, any one of a group of North American birds noted for their dark plumage, such as the grackles.
crowd[1] (kroud), *n., v.* —*n.* **1** a large number of people together: *A crowd gathered at the scene of the fire. It was difficult to get through the crowd of shoppers.* **2** people in general; the masses: *Advertisements seek to appeal to the crowd.* **3** *Figurative.* a large number of things together; multitude: *all at once I saw a crowd, a host of golden daffodils* (Wordsworth). **4** *Informal.* a set; group; company: *The boy and his crowd went to the playground to play basketball.* [< verb]
—*v.i.* **1** to collect in large numbers: *The children crowded around the edge of the swimming pool to hear the instructor.* (*Figurative.*) *Suspicions and alarms crowded upon him* (Benjamin Jowett). SYN: throng, swarm. **2** to press forward; force one's way: *The people on the platform crowded into the subway car.* **3** to hasten; press on.
—*v.t.* **1** to press closely together; compress: (*Figurative.*) *In revolutions men live fast; the experience of years is crowded into hours* (Macaulay). **2** to fill; fill too full: *Christmas shoppers crowded the store.* SYN: cram, pack. **3** to push; shove: *The big man crowded the child out of his way.* **4** *U.S. Informal, Figurative.* to press with demands; urge; dun: *He was being crowded by his creditors.* **5** *U.S. Informal.* to come close to; approach: *Abel and Valerie are both single, both crowding 40* (Charles Poore).
crowd sail. See under **sail.**
[Old English *crūdan* to press]
—*Syn. n.* **1 Crowd, throng, swarm** mean a large number of people together. **Crowd** implies that people are pressed together rather closely and without much order: *A crowd was waiting in the lobby.* **Throng** implies greater numbers and more pressing together and pushing forward: *Just before Christmas there are throngs in the streets.* **Swarm** suggests a large, confused, moving mass: *A swarm of bees flew around the hive.*
crowd[2] (kroud), *n.* **1** an ancient Celtic musical instrument similar to a viol; crwth. **2** *Dialect.* a fiddle or a fiddler. [< Welsh *crwth* fiddle, bulging body]
crowd|ed (krou′did), *adj.* **1** filled with a crowd. **2** filled; filled too full; packed: (*Figurative.*) *One crowded hour of glorious life is worth an age without a name* (Scott). **3** close together; too close together. —**crowd′ed|ly**, *adv.* —**crowd′ed-ness**, *n.*
crowd|er (krou′dər), *n.* **1** a player on a crowd. **2** *Dialect.* a fiddler.
crow|die or **crow|dy** (krou′dē), *n. Scottish.* a thick mixture of oatmeal and water; gruel; porridge. [origin uncertain]
crowd puller, *Informal.* a person, thing, or event that attracts crowds; attraction: *The biggest crowd pullers among Christie's sales are their model train sales* (London Times).
crow|er (krō′ər), *n.* **1** a cock that crows. **2** a person that crows.
crow flight, 1 a flight of crows. **2** a direct journey or course; beeline.
crow|flow|er (krō′flou′ər), *n.* a crowfoot or any one of various similar plants, such as the ragged robin and the marsh marigold.
crow|foot (krō′fu̇t′), *n., pl.* **-foots** *for 1;* **-feet** *for 2, 3, and 4.* **1** a buttercup or other plant with deeply divided leaves shaped something like a crow's foot. **2** *Nautical.* an arrangement of small ropes of different lengths, used to suspend awnings or other canvas. **3** a sharp-pointed device thrown on the ground to hinder cavalry; crow's-foot; caltrop. **4** *U.S.* a piece of zinc shaped like a crow's foot, used as one of the poles or electrodes in some kinds of batteries.
***crowfoot family**, a large group of dicotyledonous herbs and shrubs having simple or compound leaves and one or many separate carpels. The family includes the buttercup, aconite, anemone, columbine, clematis, and peony. See picture below.
crow|hop (krō′hop′), *n., v.,* **-hopped, -hop|ping.** —*n.* **1** *Western U.S.* a hopping movement, like that of a crow, made by a bucking horse. **2** a short distance: *His ranch is just a crowhop from here.*
—*v.i.* to move in short jerky hops.
Crow Jim, *U.S. Slang.* discrimination against

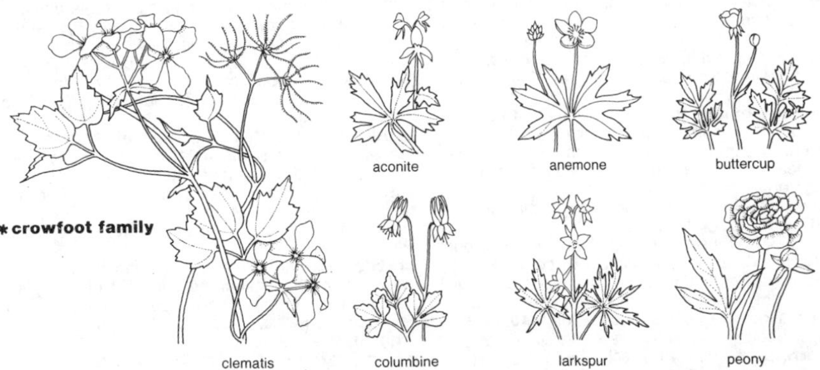

***crowfoot family**

whites; reverse racism: *Whites complain of "Crow Jim" when what they mean is that work is scarcer than ever—even for them* (Time). [reversed < *Jim Crow*]

Crow Jim|ism (jim′iz əm), *U.S. Slang.* the practice of discriminating against whites.

crow|keep|er (krō′kē′pər), *n.* **1** a person employed to keep the crows away from crops. **2** *Dialect.* a scarecrow.

crown (kroun), *n., v., adj.* **—*n.*** **1** a head covering, usually of precious metal and jewels, worn by a king or queen; diadem: *Uneasy lies the head that wears a crown* (Shakespeare). **2** *Figurative.* the power and authority of a king or queen; royal power: *Crowns and thrones may perish* (Sabine Baring-Gould). *One man with a dream . . . Shall go forth and conquer a crown* (A.W.E. O'Shaughnessy). **3** *Figurative.* a king or queen: *Always address the crown respectfully.* **4** a design or thing shaped like a crown. **5** a wreath for the head; garland: *The winner of the race received a crown.* **6** *Figurative.* an honor; reward: *He won the amateur boxing crown in his last bout.* **7** the head: *Jack fell down and broke his crown* (Nursery Rhyme). **8** the highest part; top: *the crown of the head, the crown of a hat, the crown of a mountain.* **SYN:** See syn. under **top. 9** *Figurative.* the highest state or quality of anything; perfection; consummation: *This Olympic victory was the crown of her athletic career.* **SYN:** See syn. under **top. 10a** the part of a tooth which appears beyond the gum, covered with enamel; corona. **b** the chewing surface of a tooth. **c** an artificial substitute for either of these. **11a** a former British silver coin, worth 5 shillings. **b** = krona or krone. **12** *Nautical.* the end of an anchor between the arms. **13** *Botany.* **a** the part of a plant at which the root and the stem join. The crown looks like the top of the root. **b** the corona of a flower or seed. **c** the leaves and branches of a tree or shrub. **14a** the crest of a bird. **b** the tip of a deer's horn. **15** = crown glass. **16** = crown lens. **17** the part of a cut gem above the girdle. **18** a size of printing paper, 15 × 19 inches (in England 15 × 20 inches).
—*v.t.* **1** to make king or queen: *The prince was crowned in London.* **2** *Figurative.* to honor; reward: *His hard work was crowned with success.* **3** to be on top of; cover the highest part of: *A fort crowns the hill.* **4** *Figurative.* to make perfect or complete; add the finishing touch to: *Exotic fruits and delicate pastries crowned the feast.* **5** to put a crown on (a tooth). **6** to make a king of (a checker that has been moved across a checkerboard). **7** *Informal.* to hit on the head.
—*adj.* of a crown or the Crown; having to do with a crown; or the Crown.
the Crown, a royal power; the supreme governing power in a monarchy: *The Crown granted lands in colonial America to William Penn. The assertion of passive obedience to the Crown grew obnoxious to the Crown itself* (Henry Hallam). **b** (in Great Britain and Canada) the government in its legal capacity: *by order of the Crown.*
[< Anglo-French *coroune* < Latin *corōna* crown, garland, wreath. See etym. of doublet **corona.**]

Crown Agent, 1 (in England) an agent for the Crown, especially in dealings with one of the colonies. **2** (in Scotland) a solicitor who, under the chief law officer of the Crown, takes charge of criminal proceedings.

crown|al (krou′nəl), *n. Archaic.* a coronet; garland. [variant of *coronal*]

crown antler, a topmost branch or antler of a stag's horn; sur-royal antler.

crown cap, = crown cork.

Crown colony, a colony under the control and authority of the British Crown, administered by a governor. Hong Kong is a Crown colony.

crown cork, the fluted, cork-lined metal cap of a bottle of carbonated soft drink or beer.

Crown corporation or **company,** (in Canada) a legal agency or company through which the federal government or the government of a province carries out certain regulatory and other functions.

crowned (kround), *adj.* having a crown: *lips of poets crowned and dead* (Algernon Charles Swinburne).

crowned eagle, an eagle of Africa that lives in the rain forests and feeds on monkeys.

crowned pigeon, a large pigeon native to New Guinea, with tufts of thin, lacy feathers forming a crest on its head.

crown|er¹ (krou′nər), *n.* one who or that which crowns or completes.

crown|er² (krou′nər), *n. British Dialect.* a coroner.

crown|et (krou′net), *n. Archaic.* = coronet.

crown gall, a tumorous growth caused by a bacillus that occurs in all parts of the world and attacks a variety of crops, such as orchard trees, sugar beets, and raspberries.

crown gear, = crown wheel.

crown glass, 1 a very clear glass used in optical instruments. **2** an old kind of window glass that is in round sheets with a thick place in the middle: *In the early 1800's . . . window glass was called crown glass . . . made by blowing a bubble of glass, then spinning it until it was flat* (C. J. Phillips).

crown imperial, a plant of the lily family, bearing hanging flowers under a whorl of leaves.

crown|ing (krou′ning), *adj.* that forms the crown or acme; consummating; highest; most perfect: *Fulton's last and crowning achievement was the building of the steamboat Clermont.*

crown jewel, 1 any one of the jewels which are the hereditary regalia of the crown or royal family of any country. **2** *Figurative.* the most valuable asset of a country, company, or the like: *The archipelago had been the crown jewel of the Dutch Empire for almost 350 years* (Arnold C. Brackman). *The Hughes Tool Co., crown jewel of the Howard Hughes financial empire* (Time).

crown land, 1 land belonging to a crown. The reigning king or queen or certain members of their family are entitled to receive the revenue from it. *Before the surrender of the crown lands the Monarchy used to pay for certain services that are now part of the budget* (Sunday Times). **2** one of the major administrative provinces of the former Austro-Hungarian Empire.

crown lens, the convex part of an achromatic lens, made of crown glass.

***crown of thorns, 1** a climbing species of spurge, having long stems covered with cactus-like spines. **2** = crown-of-thorns starfish.

***crown of thorns**
definition 1

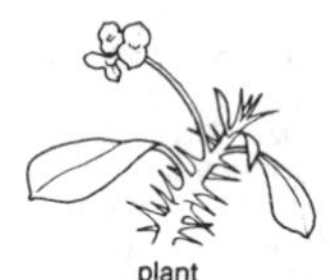
plant

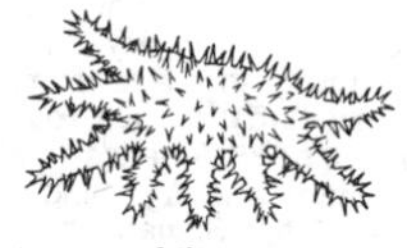
***crown-of-thorns starfish**

***crown-of-thorns starfish** (kroun′əv thôrnz′), a large starfish that feeds on coral polyps and is the main predator of coral reefs in the Pacific.

crown|piece (kroun′pēs′), *n.* **1** a piece that forms the crown or top of anything. **2** a piece of money; crown.

crown post, = king post.

crown prince, the oldest living son of a king or queen; male heir to the throne.

crown princess, 1 the wife of a crown prince. **2** the girl or woman who is heir to the throne.

***crown roast,** the ribs of lamb or pork arranged as a fancy roast, with the upper part of the bones trimmed and the roast so fastened that the center is hollow.

***crown roast**

crown rot, a common fungous disease of plants, causing decay at the crown of the root and blackening of the leaves.

crown rust, 1 a fungous disease of oats and other grasses, causing rust-colored spots to appear on the leaves. **2** the fungus causing it.

crown saw, a rotary saw with teeth on the end or edge of a hollow cylinder.

crown vetch, = axseed.

crown wheel, a wheel, especially in a clock or watch, with cogs set at right angles to its plane.

crown|work (kroun′wėrk′), *n.* **1** *Dentistry.* **a** the making or setting of artificial crowns. **b** an artificial crown. **2** *Historical.* a defensive outwork consisting of a central bastion with a wall and demibastion on each side, usually connected by a ditch to the main fortress.

crow's-foot (krōz′fu̇t′), *n., pl.* **-feet. 1** Often, **crow's-feet.** a tiny wrinkle at the outer corner of the eye. **2** a three-pointed embroidered design used to finish the ends of seams, openings, or the like, in tailored clothes. **3** = crowfoot; caltrop. **4** a group of short ropes arranged to divide the pull of some single rope.

crow's-nest (krōz′nest′), *n.* **1** a small, enclosed platform for the lookout, near the top of a ship's mast. **2** any similar platform ashore. **3** a cupola on a caboose in which the conductor or brakeman can observe the train.

croze (krōz), *n.* a cooper's tool for cutting the grooves at the ends of the staves of a barrel or cask. [perhaps < Old French *croz* hollow, groove < *croser* hollow out]

cro|zier (krō′zhər), *n.* = crosier.

CRP (no periods), C-reactive protein.

crs., 1 creditors. **2** credits.

CRT or **C.R.T.,** cathode-ray tube.

cru¹ (krü; *French* krʏ), *n., pl.* **crus** (krüz; *French* krʏ). a vintage of wine produced in one of the French vineyards: *Many clay sealings giving vineyards of origin were found there, and the years of the different crus were also recorded* (New Yorker). [< French *cru* < *crû,* past participle of *croître* to grow < Latin *crēscere;* see etym. under **crescent**]

cru² (krü), *n.* a proposed international currency or unit of money for use with other currencies in the reserves of the world's central banks. [< *c*(ollective) *r*(eserve) *u*(nit)]

cru|ces (krü′sēz), *n.* cruxes; a plural of **crux.**

cru|cial (krü′shəl), *adj.* **1** very important; decisive; critical: *It was crucial to perform an immediate operation on the injured man. The great crucial books of human thought outside what are called the exact sciences . . . always render articulate the results of fundamental new experiences to which human beings have to adjust themselves* (Edmund Wilson). **2** very trying; severe. **3** having the form of a cross; cross-shaped. [< New Latin *crucialis* < Latin *crux, crucis* cross (referring to a cross signpost at a fork in a road)] **—cru′cial|ly,** *adv.*

cru|ci|ate (krü′shē it, -āt), *adj.* **1** of the form of a cross; cross-shaped. **2** *Botany.* having petals arranged in the form of a cross: *a cruciate flower.* **3** *Zoology.* crossing each other diagonally: *an insect's cruciate wings.* [< New Latin *cruciatus* < Latin *crux, crucis* cross]

***cru|ci|ble** (krü′sə bəl), *n.* **1** a pot to melt metals in: *Crucibles in a school chemistry laboratory are usually made of clay, porcelain, or iron.* **2** the hollow part at the bottom of a metallurgical furnace in which molten metal collects. **3** *Figurative.* a severe test or trial. [< Medieval Latin *crucibulum* (originally) night lamp]

***crucible**
definition 1

crucible steel, a high grade of steel formerly prepared by melting crude or blister steel, later by melting selected cemented bars of steel or by melting together wrought iron, carbon, and flux in crucibles.

cru|ci|fer (krü′sə fər), *n.* **1** a person carrying a cross, especially in a religious procession. **2** a plant of the mustard family; a cruciferous plant. [< Late Latin *crucifer* < Latin *crux, crucis* cross + *ferre* to bear]

cru|cif|er|ous (krü sif′ər əs), *adj.* **1** bearing or wearing a cross. **2** of or belonging to plants of the mustard family whose flowers have a cross-like corolla bearing four petals.

cru|ci|fix (krü′sə fiks), *n.* **1** a cross with the figure of Christ crucified on it. **2** any cross. [< Late Latin *crucifixus,* alteration of Latin *cruci fixus* fixed to a cross < *crux, crucis* cross and *figere* fasten]

cru|ci|fix|ion (krü′sə fik′shən), *n.* **1** the act of crucifying: *Crucifixion is a cruel and unusual punishment.* **2** the fact or state of being crucified: (*Figurative.*) *He endeavored to persuade her that for each of the crucifixions of life there is a solace* (New Yorker). **3** *Obsolete.* torture; severe pain; anguish.

Cru|ci|fix|ion (krü′sə fik′shən), *n.* **1** the putting to death of Christ on the cross. **2** a picture or statue of this.

cru|ci|form (krü′sə fôrm), *adj.* shaped like a cross. [< Latin *crux, crucis* cross + English *-form*] **—cru′ci|form′ly,** *adv.*

cru|ci|fy (krü′sə fī), *v.t.,* **-fied, -fy|ing. 1** to put to death by nailing or binding the hands and feet to a cross: *The Romans, Greeks, and some Oriental peoples crucified criminals.* **2** *Figurative.* to treat severely; torture or persecute: *The other lawyers crucified him for defending a traitor.* **3** (in religious use) to mortify or subdue (as passion or sin). [< Old French *crucifier* < Late Latin *crucifigere,* alteration of Latin *cruci figere* (see etym. under **crucifix**); influenced by Old French verbs ending in *-fier* (< Latin *-ficāre*)] **—cru′ci|fi′er,** *n.*

Cru|cis (krü′sis), *n.* the genitive of **Crux.**

cru|ci|ver|bal|ist (krü′sə vėr′bə list), *n.* a person who makes up crossword puzzles: *The development of the cruciverbalist's art . . . is not subject to the same sorts of random whimsy that determine new trends in haute couture or pop culture* (Listener). [probably patterned on French *cruciverbiste* a crossword puzzle enthusiast]

crud (krud), *n., v.,* **crud·ded, crud·ding.** *—n.* 1 *Dialect.* curd. 2 *Slang.* **a** anything inferior, worthless, or disgusting; muck; filth. **b** a dirty or disgusting individual.
—v.t., v.i. Dialect. curd
[Middle English *crudde*]

crud·dle (krud′əl), *v.t., v.i.,* **-dled, -dling.** *Obsolete or Dialect.* to curdle.

crud·dy (krud′ē), *adj.,* **-di·er, -di·est.** *Slang.* 1 of or filled with muck; filthy: *cruddy slums.* 2 worthless; trashy: *a cruddy potboiler.*

crude (krüd), *adj.,* **crud·er, crud·est,** *n. —adj.* 1 in a natural or raw state; unrefined: *Oil, ore, and sugar are crude before being refined and prepared for use.* **SYN:** unfinished, unprocessed. See syn. under **raw.** 2 not mature; unripe: *crude fruit.* **SYN:** green. 3 rough; coarse: *a crude log cabin, a crude chair made out of a box.* 4 *Sociology.* roughly estimated or based on a yearly number (of births, deaths, or other vital statistics) per 1,000 people in a given area: *the crude marriage rate.* 5 lacking finish, grace, taste, or refinement: *the crude manners of a rude person, a crude remark.* **SYN:** rude.
—n. = crude oil.
[< Latin *crūdus* raw] —**crude′ly,** *adv.* —**crude′ness,** *n.*

crude oil, petroleum in its natural state, as obtained from the ground before refining.

cru·di·tés (krʏ dē tā′), *n.pl. French.* raw vegetables, usually with salad dressing, served as an appetizer.

cru·di·ty (krü′də tē), *n.* 1 *no pl.* crude quality or condition; lack of finish; roughness: *The crudity of the house contrasted with the shiny newness of the car parked in front.* 2 *pl.* **-ties.** a crude action or thing.

cruel (krü′əl), *adj.* 1 fond of causing pain to others and delighting in their suffering; not caring about the pain and suffering of others; hardhearted: *The cruel man whipped his horse.* 2 showing a cruel nature: *cruel acts.* 3 causing pain and suffering: *a cruel war. Arthritis is a cruel disease of the joints.* [< Old French *cruel* < Latin *crūdēlis* rough, related to *crūdus* crude] —**cru′el·ly,** *adv.* —**cru′el·ness,** *n.*
— Syn. 1 **Cruel, brutal, pitiless** mean unfeeling in treatment of people and animals. **Cruel** implies indifference to the physical or mental suffering of others and willingness to cause or add to it: *The cruel master mistreated his slaves. The cruel remark was difficult to forget.* **Brutal** suggests the cruelty of a wild animal, shown in acts of physical violence: *Brutal captors beat their prisoners.* **Pitiless** implies cold unwillingness to show mercy to those who are suffering: *The pitiless ruler refused to help the poor.*

cru·el·ty (krü′əl tē), *n.* 1 *no pl.* readiness to give pain to others or lack of concern for their suffering; having a cruel nature: *To hit a weaker person is a sign of cruelty. Physical or mental cruelty is often grounds for divorce.* 2 *pl.* **-ties.** a cruel act or acts: *I will never forget his cruelty to my little dog.*

cruelty man, *British Informal.* an official of the Royal Society for the Prevention of Cruelty to Animals.

cru·et (krü′it), *n.* a small glass bottle with a stopper, to hold vinegar, oil, or other liquids for the table. [Middle English *cruet* a church vessel < Old French (diminutive) < *cruie* pot < Germanic (compare Old Saxon *krūka*)]

cruise (krüz), *v.,* **cruised, cruis·ing,** *n. —v.i.* 1 to sail or travel about from place to place on pleasure or business: *We cruised to Bermuda on our vacation. The coastguard cutter cruised along the coast looking for smugglers.* 2 to travel or journey from place to place without a set destination: *Taxis cruise, looking for fares.* 3 to travel in an automobile, airplane, or boat, at the speed at which it operates best.
—v.t. 1 to sail over or about: *Freighters and oil tankers cruise the oceans of the world.* 2 to travel or journey over or about: *The taxicab cruised the city streets in search of passengers.* 3 to survey (a forest) to estimate the amount and value of the timber.
—n. 1 the act of sailing about from place to place on pleasure or business: *a cruise in search of buried treasure.* 2 a voyage made by cruising: *We went for a cruise on the Great Lakes last summer. The doctor prescribed an ocean cruise for the sick woman.*
[< Dutch *kruisen* < *kruis* cross < Latin *crux, crucis* cross]

cruise control, a computer controlled mechanism that regulates the speed of an automobile after it is set by the driver.

cruise missile, a guided missile that depends on air for support and cannot leave the earth's atmosphere.

cruis·er (krü′zər), *n.* 1 a warship with less armor and more speed than a battleship. 2 an airplane or taxi that cruises. 3 a motorboat having a cabin and equipped with facilities for living on board; cabin cruiser. 4 a police car for patrolling streets and highways, connected with headquarters by radio; patrol car; squad car: *A police cruiser had stopped him for a safety check a block earlier* (Maclean's). 5 a person who estimates the amount and value of the timber in a forest. 6 a person who sails about, travels, or vacations on a pleasure boat: *Cruisers, who take their leisure on the water, are almost fanatically independent people* (Newsweek).

cruis·er·weight (krü′zər wāt′), *n.* in boxing: 1 *British.* a light heavyweight. 2 *U.S.* an amateur designation for the lowest portion of the heavyweight class, from 177 to 186 pounds.

cruise·wear (krüz′wãr′), *n.* clothes for wearing on an ocean cruise.

cruis·ing (krü′zing), *adj. Aeronautics.* of or having to do with flight at a speed of maximum fuel economy: *cruising speed, cruising range.*

crul·ler (krul′ər), *n.* a piece of rich, sweet dough fried brown in deep fat. The dough is usually shaped in twists and cut in short pieces. Also, **kruller.** [American English < Dutch *kruller* < *krullen* curl]

crum (krum), *n., v.t., v.i. Archaic.* crumb.

crumb (krum), *n., v. —n.* 1 a very small piece of bread or cake broken from a larger piece: *He fed crumbs to the birds.* 2 a little bit: *a crumb of comfort.* 3 the soft, inside part of bread. 4 *Slang.* a worthless or contemptible person; crumb-bum.
—v.t. 1 to break into crumbs; crumble: *He nervously crumbed his roll into small pellets.* 2 to cover with crumbs for frying or baking: *Crumb the fritters before you fry them.* 3 *Informal.* to brush or wipe crumbs from (a tablecloth or table).
—v.i. to break into crumbs; crumble.
[Old English *cruma*]

crumb brush, a brush for sweeping crumbs off the table.

crumb-bum or **crum·bum** (krum′bum′), *n. Slang.* a person regarded as inferior or insignificant.

crumb·cloth (krum′klôth′, -kloth′), *n.* a cloth spread under a dining-room table to protect the carpet from falling crumbs or food.

crum·ble (krum′bəl), *v.,* **-bled, -bling,** *n. —v.t.* 1 to break into very small pieces or crumbs: *to crumble dirt between your hands. Do not crumble your bread on the table.* 2 to destroy; break down. **SYN:** disintegrate, decompose.
—v.i. 1 to break into very small pieces: *This cake crumbles too easily.* 2 to fall to pieces; decay: *The old wall was crumbling away at the edges.* (*Figurative.*) *If the Franco-German accord does crumble, other countries will be swallowed up in the gap thus opened* (Manchester Guardian Weekly). **SYN:** disintegrate, decompose.
—n. 1 something crumbling or crumbled. 2 *Dialect.* a tiny crumb; fragment.
[variant of Middle English *crimble* < unrecorded Old English *crymelen* (frequentative) < *gecryman* < *cruma* crumb]

crum·bly (krum′blē), *adj.,* **-bli·er, -bli·est.** tending to crumble; easily crumbled. —**crum′bli·ness,** *n.*

crumb·y (krum′ē), *adj.,* **crumb·i·er, crumb·i·est.** 1 full of crumbs. 2 soft like the inside part of bread. 3 *Informal.* inferior; bad.

crum·horn (krùm′hôrn′), *n.* = krumhorn.

crum·mie or **crum·my**[1] (krum′ē), *n., pl.* **-mies.** *Scottish.* a cow with crumpled or crooked horns. [< obsolete *crum* crooked + *-ie, -y*[2] (diminutive)]

crum·my[2] (krum′ē), *adj.,* **-mi·er, -mi·est,** *adv. Slang. —adj.* 1 disgusting; repulsive; dirty: *It* [*the city*] *not only has the most spectacular skyline, but also some of the crummiest slums* (Newsweek). 2 of no worth; unsatisfactory: *I had a crummy time at the party. It was a crummy deal.*
—adv. badly: *He pitched crummy at today's game.* [originally a variant of *crumby*]

crump (krump), *v., n., adj. —v.t., v.i.* to crunch.
—n. 1 a crunch: *the crump of a crashing airplane* (Time). 2 *British Military Slang.* a large explosive shell.
—adj. Scottish. brittle.
[probably imitative]

crum·pet (krum′pit), *n. Especially British.* a round, flat cake, thicker than a pancake, baked on a griddle. It is usually toasted and eaten while hot. [perhaps Old English *crompeht* a cake; perhaps Middle English *crompid* curled, past participle of obsolete *crump* to bend, curl up]

crum·ple (krum′pəl), *v.,* **-pled, -pling,** *n. —v.t.* to crush together; wrinkle: *He crumpled the paper into a ball.*
—v.i. 1 to become crumpled or crushed together. 2 to fall down; collapse: *She crumpled to the floor in a faint.* (*Figurative.*) *The haughty witness crumpled under the lawyer's severe questioning.*
—n. a wrinkle made by crushing something together.
[perhaps frequentative form < Old English *crump* bent]

crum·pled (krum′pəld), *adj.* crushed together; crushed out of shape; made untidy: *a crumpled tablecloth, a crumpled hat.*

crum·pler (krum′plər), *n.* 1 a person who crumples. 2 *Informal.* a cravat: *The fit of his crumpler and the crease of his breeches* (Richard D. Blackmore).

crum·ply (krum′plē), *adj.,* **-pli·er, -pli·est.** full of wrinkles.

crunch (krunch), *v., n. —v.t.* 1 to crush noisily with the teeth: *Someone sitting behind us was crunching peanut brittle.* 2 to crush or grind noisily.
—v.i. 1 to chew with a crunching sound. 2 to make, or move with, a crunching noise: *The hard snow crunched under our feet. The children crunched through the snow.*
—n. 1 the act or sound of crunching. 2 *Informal, Figurative.* **a** a critical or decisive point; crisis: *matters coming to the crunch. The next crunch could well come in Guinea* (Manchester Guardian Weekly). **b** crux: *I do—but she doesn't. That's the crunch of the trouble* (Encounter). Also, **craunch.**
[originally imitative; perhaps influenced by *crush, munch*]

crunch·y (krun′chē), *adj.,* **crunch·i·er, crunch·i·est.** *Informal.* brittle and crackling: *crunchy peanut brittle.*

cru·node (krü′nōd), *n. Geometry.* a point at which a curve crosses itself. [< Latin *crux* cross + English *node*]

cru·or (krü′ôr), *n.* 1 coagulated blood. 2 the part of the blood that forms the clot. [< Latin *cruor, -ōris* blood (flowing from the body)]

crup·per (krup′ər), *n.* 1 a strap attached to the back of a harness or saddle and passed under a horse's tail to prevent the harness or saddle from slipping forward. See picture under **harness.** 2 = croup[2]. 3 the buttocks. [< Old French *cropiere* < *crope;* see etym. under **croup**[2]]

cru·ra (krür′ə), *n.* plural of **crus.**

cru·ral (krür′əl), *adj.* 1 of or having to do with the leg. 2 = femoral. 3 of or having to do with any parts occurring in pairs or sets, resembling a pair of legs. [< Latin *crūrālis* < *crūs, crūris* leg]

crus (krus), *n., pl.* **cru·ra** (krür′ə). *Anatomy.* 1 the leg or hind limb, especially the part between the knee and ankle; shank. 2 any one of various parts, occurring in pairs or sets, resembling a leg. [< Latin *crūs, crūris* leg, especially the shank]

cru·sade (krü sād′), *n., v.,* **-sad·ed, -sad·ing.** *—n.* 1 Often, **Crusade.** any one of the Christian military expeditions between the years 1096 and 1291 to recover the Holy Land from the Moslems. 2a a war having a religious purpose and approved by the church; holy war. **b** an evangelistic campaign; a revival. 3 *Figurative.* a vigorous campaign against a public evil or in favor of some new idea: *Everyone was asked to join the crusade against cancer.*
—v.i. to take part in a crusade: (*Figurative.*) *We crusaded against littering.*
[Anglicized form of earlier *croisade* < French, and *crusada* < Spanish *cruzada,* ultimately < Latin *crux, crucis* cross]

cru·sad·er (krü sā′dər), *n.* a person who takes part in a crusade: *The crusaders of the Middle Ages tried to recover the Holy Land from the Moslems.* (*Figurative.*) *The crusaders for women's rights had a protest march.*

cru·sa·do (krü sā′dō), *n., pl.* **-does** or **-dos.** an old Portuguese gold or silver coin bearing the figure of a cross. Also, **cruzado.** [< Portuguese *cruzado* (literally) crossed < *cruz* cross < Latin *crux, crucis*]

cruse (krüz, krüs), *n.* a small jug, pot, or bottle made of earthenware or metal: *a cruse of oil, a cruse of vinegar.* [< Middle Dutch *croes*]

crush (krush), *v., n. —v.t.* 1 to squeeze together violently so as to break or bruise: *The bear's squeeze crushed two of the hunter's ribs.* 2 to wrinkle or crease by wear or rough handling: *His hat was crushed when the girl sat on it. My suitcase was so full that my clothes were crushed.* 3 to break into fine pieces by grinding, pounding, or pressing: *The ore is crushed between steel rollers. Sugar cane is first crushed in the mill.* 4 to flatten by heavy pressure: *The steam roller crushed the soft dirt.* 5 *Figurative.* **a** to subdue; put down; conquer: *The revolt was crushed and the leaders were imprisoned.* **SYN:** suppress. **b** to oppress: *Woe to him who crushes the soul with chain and rod* (John Greenleaf Whittier). 6 to force out by pressing or squeezing; extract: *Bacchus, that first from out the purple grape crushed*

---

the sweet poison of misused wine (Milton). **7** to drink (wine or ale); quaff: *You shall crush a cup of wine* (Scott). **—*v.i.*** **1** to become crushed. **2** to advance by crushing; press or crowd forcibly.
—*n.* **1a** the act of crushing. **b** the state of being crushed: *Unhurt amidst . . . the crush of worlds* (Joseph Addison). **2** a violent pressure like grinding or pounding: *He pushed his way through the crush of the crowd.* **3** a mass of people or things crowded close together: *There was a crush in the narrow exits after the football game. . . . a crush of carts and chairs and coaches* (Dickens). **4a** the pressing (of grapes or cottonseed) in the production of wine and oil: *The soybean crush during November totaled 733,200 tons.* **b** = crushings. **5** *Informal.* **a** a sudden, strong liking for a person: *None of her crushes last very long. Every schoolgirl at some time has a crush on an older man.* **b** the object of a sudden, strong liking. [< Old French *croissir* or *cruissir* < Germanic (compare Gothic *kriustan* gnash)] **—crush′a|ble,** *adj.*

crush|a|bil|i|ty (krush′ə bil′ə tē), *n.* the quality of being crushable.

crush|er (krush′ər), *n.* **1** a person or thing that crushes: **a** a person whose trade is to crush some article for economic purposes. **b** a machine for crushing or pulverizing raw material, such as seed, ore, or quartz. **2** *Informal.* something which overwhelms or overpowers: *It's Destiny, and mine's a crusher!* (Dickens). **3** *Informal.* a crushing blow.

crush hat, 1 a hat which can be crushed or folded without damage. **2** a soft felt hat. **3** an opera hat.

crush|ing (krush′ing), *adj., n.* **—*adj.*** that crushes; bruising; overwhelming: *dealt a crushing blow.*
—*n.* the act or process of pressing (grapes or seeds) in the production of wine and oil.
crushings, crushed grapes or seeds: *Soybean crushings . . . were up slightly from a year earlier* (Wall Street Journal). **—crush′ing|ly,** *adv.*

crush|mark (krush′märk′), *n.* a dent or mark made on an automobile window, especially the windshield, by flying bits of gravel or other hard objects.

crush|proof (krush′prüf′), *adj.* that will not crush: *a crushproof package.*

Cru|soe (krü′sō), *n.* = Robinson Crusoe.

crust (krust), *n., v.* **—*n.*** **1** the hard, outside part of bread: *Baking makes the crust hard and dry to protect the crumb inside.* **2a** a piece of this: *The boy was told to eat the crusts of his sandwich.* **b** any hard, dry piece of bread. **3** the rich dough rolled out thin and baked for pies: *A rich, flaky crust covered the top of the apple pie.* **4a** any hard outside covering: *The frozen crust on the snow was thick enough for us to walk on.* **b** the hard outer shell of an animal or plant: *the crust of a lobster.* **c** *Informal, Figurative.* impudence; effrontery; gall: *He had a lot of crust shooting his bazoo off when it wasn't any skin off his teeth* (James T. Farrell). **5** the solid outer layer of the earth: *When the earth's crust is subjected to a local stress, it appears to behave like a brittle material* (Scientific American). See picture under **core**[1]. **6** a scab. **7** a solid deposit on the inner surface of wine bottles; beeswing.
—*v.t.* **1** to cover with or as if with a crust; encrust: *The rocks were crusted with lichen.* **2** to form into a crust; harden: *the dirt of half a century, crusted on the glass* (Wilkie Collins). **3** to hunt (deer or other game) on the crust of snow.
—*v.i.* to form or become covered with a crust: *By the next day the snow had crusted over.*
[probably < Old French *crouste* < Latin *crusta* rind] **—crust′less,** *adj.* **—crust′like′,** *adj.*

Crus|ta|cea (krus tā′shə), *n.pl.* a class of arthropods composed of the crustaceans. [< New Latin *Crustacea* (coined by Lamarck) < Latin *crusta* shell, rind]

crus|ta|cean (krus tā′shən), *n., adj.* **—*n.*** any one of a group of animals with a hard shell, jointed body and appendages, and gills, that live mostly in water. Crabs, lobsters, and shrimps are crustaceans. **—*adj.*** of or belonging to this group.

crus|ta|ce|ol|o|gy (krus tā′shē ol′ə jē), *n.* the science or study of crustaceans. [< New Latin *Crustacea* (see etym. under **Crustacea**) + *-logy*]

crus|ta|ceous (krus tā′shəs), *adj.* **1** = crustacean. **2** having a shell or crust. **3** of or like a crust.

crus|tal (krus′təl), *adj.* of or having to do with a crust, especially of the earth or moon: *crustal rocks.*

crust-hunt (krust′hunt′), *v.i.* to hunt deer or other game on the crust of snow when it is strong enough to support the hunter but not the game. **—crust′-hunt′er,** *n.*

crus|tose (krus′tōs), *adj.* (of lichen and algae) growing in the form of crusts; sticking fast to soil, rock, or bark so as not to be detachable except in small fragments.

crust|y (krus′tē), *adj.,* **crust|i|er, crust|i|est. 1** of or like a crust; having a crust; hard: *crusty bread.* **2** *Figurative.* harsh in manner or speech; crabbed; surly: *a crusty old bachelor. The crusty sea captain had a quick temper.* **—crust′i|ly,** *adv.* **—crust′i|ness,** *n.*

crutch (kruch), *n., v.* **—*n.*** **1** a support to help a lame person walk. It is a stick with a padded crosspiece at the top to fit under a lame person's arm and support part of his weight in walking, or a shorter one that fits on the forearm and hand. **2** *Figurative.* anything like a crutch in shape or use; support; prop: *He used his father's help as a crutch to get through his homework.* **3** a forked rest for the leg in a sidesaddle. **4** *Nautical.* a forked prop placed under a boom or spar when the sails are not set. **5** a stick with a perforated piece of wood or iron at the end, used to stir ingredients in making soap. **6** = crotch (defs. 2, 3).
—*v.t.* to support with or as if with a crutch; prop; sustain. [Old English *crycc*]

crutched (krucht), *adj.* having or bearing a cross: *The crutched friars were an order of friars that carried or wore crosses.*

crutch|ing (kruch′ing), *n.* the shearing of sheep wool from around the breech to protect the flock from blowflies (which are not attracted by the breech of newly shorn sheep).

crux (kruks), *n., pl.* **crux|es** or **cru|ces. 1** the essential part; the most important point: *the crux of an argument. We had now reached the crux of our negotiations.* **2** a puzzling or perplexing question; difficult point to explain. **3** *Heraldry.* a cross. [< Latin *crux, crucis* cross]

Crux (kruks), *n., genitive* **Cru|cis.** *Astronomy.* the Southern Cross.

crux an|sa|ta (kruks′an sā′tə), = ankh. [< Latin *crux ansāta* ansate cross]

cru|za|do (krü zā′dō), *n., pl.* **-does** or **-dos.** **1** the monetary unit of Brazil, equal to 100 centavos. It replaced the cruzeiro in 1986. **2** = crusado.

cru|zei|ro (krü zăr′ō; *Portuguese* krü zā′rō, -rü), *n., pl.* **-ros.** the former monetary unit of Brazil, replaced by the cruzado. [< Portuguese *cruzeiro* < *cruz* cross < Latin *crux, crucis*]

crwth (krüth), *n.* = crowd[2].

cry (krī), *v.,* **cried, cry|ing,** *n., pl.* **cries. —*v.i.*** **1** to shed tears; weep: *The girl cried when her favorite doll broke.* **2** to make a noise from grief or pain or other strong feeling: *She cried with small whimpering sounds.* **3** to make an animal's usual noise or call: *The hounds cried in the moonlight.* **4** to call loudly; shout: *Call to each other and whoop and cry All night, merrily* (Tennyson).
—*v.t.* **1** to call out; call loudly; shout: *The drowning man cried "Help!" He cried her name in vain.* **2** to sell by calling on the streets: *Peddlers cry their wares in the street.* **3** to beg for; entreat in a loud voice: *to cry mercy, cry pardon, cry vengeance.* **4** to cause (oneself) to be by crying: *to cry oneself sick, to cry oneself to sleep.*
—*n.* **1** a loud call; shout: *the drowning man's cry for help.* **2** a fit of shedding tears: *She had a long cry when her favorite doll broke.* **3** a noise of grief or pain or other strong feeling: *a cry of rage.* **4** the noise or call of an animal: *the hungry cry of the wolf. The crows cried to one another from the treetops.* **5** a call to action; slogan: *"Forward" was the army's cry as it attacked.* **6** a call for help; appeal; entreaty: *"Won't anyone help me?" was her cry.* **7** a call that means things are for sale: *a peddler's cry.* **8** an opinion generally expressed; public voice: *The cry was that the city needed brighter street lights.* **9a** the yelping of hounds in the chase. **b** a pack of hounds. **10** *Obsolete.* clamor; tumult; outcry.
a far cry. See under **far cry.**
cry down, to make little of; speak of as unimportant or of little value; disparage; deprecate: *The critic cried down the book.*
cry for, a to ask earnestly for; beg for: *The child cried for the ice cream. The beggar cried for alms.* **b** *Figurative.* to need very much: *The rundown old house cried for a coat of paint. The city government cries for reform.*
cry havoc. See under **havoc.**
cry off, to break an agreement; refuse to do something: *Would she be the first to cry off from such a bargain?* (Anthony Trollope).
cry one's eyes out. See under **eye.**
cry one's heart out. See under **heart.**
cry out, a to call loudly; shout: *He cried out a goodnight.* **b** to scream; yell: *They will not cry out before they're hurt* (Byron). **c** *Figurative.* to protest: *Every living movement of human thought . . . cries out against it* (R. H. Hutton).
cry over spilt milk. See under **milk.**
cry up, to praise; speak of as important or valuable: *While kingmakers and idealists seek to cry up the incipient statesmanship and the high moral tone of their favorite senators, the professional politicians consult the statistics in the Governors' contest of the off-year election* (Alistair Cooke).
cry wolf. See under **wolf.**
in full cry, in close pursuit: *The pack of hounds was in full cry after the fox.*
within cry of, within calling distance of: *Villages and houses . . . each one was within cry of another* (William Lithgow).
[< Old French *crier* < Latin *quirītāre* (originally) implore the aid of the *Quirītes* Roman citizens]
—*Syn.* *v.i.* **4,** *v.t.* **1 Cry, shout, bellow** mean to call loudly. **Cry** applies whether meaningless sounds or distinct words are used: *He cried "Help!" She cried out in sudden pain.* **Shout** applies when words are used and are called out at the top of one's voice: *I shouted upstairs.* **Bellow** applies when a cry is uttered in a loud, angry, bull-like voice: *He bellowed when he hit his thumb.*

cry|ba|by (krī′bā′bē), *n., pl.* **-bies.** a person who cries easily or pretends to be hurt.

cry|ing (krī′ing), *adj.* **1** that cries. **2** demanding attention; very bad: *a crying evil. The slums in that city are a crying shame.*
for crying out loud, an exclamation of annoyance, protest, or surprise: *Well, for crying out loud: who got us into this mess in the first place?* (Jules Feiffer).
—cry′ing|ly, *adv.*

cry|mo|ther|a|py (krī′mō ther′ə pē), *n.* the treatment of disease by means of cold. [< Greek *krýmos* cold + English *therapy*]

cryo-, *combining form.* low temperature; cold; freezing, as in cryobiology, cryoscope. [< Greek *krýos* frost, cold]

cry|o|bank (krī′ō bangk′), *n., v.* **—*n.*** a place for storage of any of the various products or organs of the body at extremely low temperature. **—*v.t.*** to preserve in a cryobank: *The methodology for cryobanking human semen has undergone continuous refinement* (Patient Care).

cry|o|bi|o|log|i|cal (krī′ō bī′ə loj′ə kəl), *adj.* of or having to do with cryobiology. **—cry′o|bi′o|log′i|cal|ly,** *adv.*

cry|o|bi|ol|o|gist (krī′ō bī ol′ə jist), *n.* a person who studies cryobiology.

cry|o|bi|ol|o|gy (krī′ō bī ol′ə jē), *n.* the study of the effects of very low temperatures on living things.

cry|o|chem|i|cal (krī′ō kem′ə kəl), *adj.* of or having to do with cryochemistry.

cry|o|chem|is|try (krī′ō kem′ə strē), *n.* the study of the effects of very low temperatures on chemical actions and processes.

cry|o|e|lec|tron|ics (krī′ō i lek′tron′iks, -ē′lek-), *n.* the use of very low temperatures, especially of temperatures near absolute zero, in electronic processes and devices.

cry|o|gen (krī′ə jən), *n.* a substance for producing very low temperatures; freezing mixture.

cry|o|gen|ic (krī′ə jen′ik), *adj.* **1** of or having to do with cryogens or the production of very low temperatures. **2** of or having to do with cryogenics. **3** using very low temperatures: *cryogenic surgery.* **—cry′o gen′i|cal|ly,** *adv.*

cry|o|gen|i|cist (krī′ə jen′ə sist), *n.* an engineer or physicist specializing in cryogenics.

cry|o|gen|ics (krī′ə jen′iks), *n.* the branch of physics dealing with the behavior of matter at very low temperatures: *The new science of cryogenics is expanding into industry at an ever more rapid rate* (Christian Science Monitor).

cry|o|gen|ist (krī oj′ə nist), *n.* = cryogenicist.

cry|o|hy|drate (krī′ō hī′drāt), *n. Chemistry.* a mixture of ice and a crystallized salt, obtained by freezing a saturated water solution of the salt.

cry|o|lite (krī′ə līt), *n.* a mineral, a fluoride of sodium and aluminum, found in Greenland. It is used in making glass and ceramics and as a solvent for aluminum oxide in the preparation of aluminum metal. *Formula:* Na_3AlF_6 [< *cryo-* cold + *-lite* (for its icelike form)]

cry|om|e|ter (krī om′ə tər), *n.* a thermometer for the measurement of very low temperatures, such as one containing alcohol instead of mercury.

cry|on|ics (krī on′iks), *n.* the preservation of dead bodies from decay by a freezing process, especially with the idea of reviving them at such a time in the future when science will be able to restore life to bodies that have not undergone decay. [< *cryo-* + *-nics,* as in *bionics*]

cry|oph|o|rus (krī of′ər əs), *n.* an instrument for showing the freezing of water by evaporation. [< New Latin *cryophorus* < Greek *krýos* cold + *-phóros* bearing < *phérein* to bear]

cry|o|phys|ics (krī′ō fiz′iks), *n.* = cryogenics.

cry|o|pre|cip|i|tate (krī′ō pri sip′ə tāt, -tit), *n.* **1** a substance precipitated by chilling or freezing. **2** a concentrate of antihemophilic globulin prepared by cryoprecipitation.

cry|o|pre|cip|i|ta|tion (krī′ō pri sip′ə tā′shən), *n.* **1** the act or process of precipitating a substance by chilling or freezing. **2** the preparation of a concentrate of antihemophilic globulin by this process: *Cryoprecipitation . . . enables the anti-hemophilic factor from a pint of blood to be concentrated in a volume of only 10 ml.* (Martin C. G. Israëls).

cry|o|probe (krī′ō prōb′), *n.* an instrument for freezing tissues, usually with liquid nitrogen, in order to destroy or remove them.

cry|o|pro|tec|tive (krī′ō prə tek′tiv), *adj., n.* **—*adj.*** providing protection against supercooling: **—*n.*** a cryoprotective agent.

cry|o|scope (krī′ə skōp), *n.* an instrument for determining the freezing points of liquids.

cry|o|scop|ic (krī′ə skop′ik), *adj.* of or having to do with cryoscopy.

cry|os|co|py (krī os′kə pē), *n.* **1** the science or study of the freezing points of liquids and how they are determined. **2** *Medicine.* the examination of blood, urine, and other body fluids as a diagnostic technique by determination of their normal freezing points.

cry|o|stat (krī′ə stat), *n.* a refrigerating unit generating very low temperatures, that is capable of liquefying a gas, such as helium, by chilling it more than 450 degrees below zero Fahrenheit.

cry|o|sur|geon (krī′ō sėr′jən), *n.* a doctor who performs cryosurgery.

cry|o|sur|ger|y (krī′ō sėr′jər ē), *n.* surgery that uses very low temperatures to destroy or remove diseased tissue; cryogenic surgery: *Cryosurgery has been used in such eye operations as retinal detachments* (Science News Letter).

cry|o|sur|gi|cal (krī′ō sėr′jə kəl), *adj.* of or having to do with cryosurgery.

cry|o|ther|a|py (krī′ō ther′ə pē), *n.* = crymotherapy.

cry|o|tron (krī′ə tron), *n.* a very small device used in an electronic computer instead of a vacuum tube or transistor to conduct electric current. It is made of tantalum and niobium and is capable of losing practically all electrical resistance at temperatures below −420° Fahrenheit.

crypt (kript), *n.* **1** an underground room or vault. The crypt beneath the main floor of a church was formerly often used as a burial place. **2** *Anatomy.* a small tubular gland, cavity, or follicle. **3** *Informal.* a cryptogram. [< Latin *crypta* < Greek *krýptē* vault < *kryptós* hidden. See etym. of doublet **grotto**.]

crypt-, *combining form.* a variant of **crypto-** before some vowels, as in *cryptanalytic, cryptic.*

cryp|tal (krip′təl), *adj.* of or of the nature of a crypt.

crypt|a|nal|y|sis (krip′tə nal′ə sis), *n., pl.* **-ses** (-sēz). the breakdown and deciphering of coded messages, or the process of discovering the cryptographic system used in them: *He notes that cryptanalysis requires, among other things, concentration, perseverance, and a vivid imagination* (E. B. White). [< Greek *kryptós* hidden + English *analysis*]

crypt|an|a|lyst (krip tan′ə list), *n.* a person who does cryptanalysis.

crypt|an|a|lyt|ic (krip′tan ə lit′ik), *adj.* engaged in or responsible for the breakdown of codes, especially in wartime.

cryp|tic (krip′tik), *adj.* **1** having a hidden meaning; secret; mysterious: *a cryptic message. We could not fully understand his cryptic remark.* **2** *Zoology.* serving to hide or camouflage. [< Late Latin *crypticus* < Greek *kryptikós* < *kryptós* hidden] **—cryp′ti|cal|ly,** *adv.*

cryp|ti|cal (krip′tə kəl), *adj.* = cryptic.

crypto-, *combining form.* **1** hidden; secret: *Cryptogram = something written in secret code.* **2** secretly; disguised; not open or avowed: *Crypto-fascist = secretly fascist.* Also, **crypt-** before some vowels. [< Greek *kryptós* hidden]

cryp|to|a|nal|y|sis (krip′tō ə nal′ə sis), *n., pl.* **-ses** (-sēz). = cryptanalysis.

cryp|to|bi|o|sis (krip′tō bī ō′sis), *n.* **1** the ability of an organism, such as various lower invertebrates, to survive in a state of metabolic inactivity, as at certain very low temperatures. **2** the state of suspended animation in which such organisms are able to live. [< New Latin *cryptobiosis* < *crypto-* hidden + *biosis* mode of life]

cryp|to|bi|ote (krip′tō bī′ōt), *n.* a cryptobiotic organism.

cryp|to|bi|ot|ic (krip′tō bī ot′ik), *adj.* characterized by cryptobiosis; able to survive in a state of metabolic inactivity: *a cryptobiotic organism.*

cryp|to|clas|tic (krip′tō klas′tik), *adj.* composed of particles too small to be seen by the unaided eye: *cryptoclastic rocks.* [< Greek *kryptós* hidden + *klastós* broken off + English *-ic*]

cryp|to|coc|cal (krip′tə kok′əl), *adj.* caused by any one of a group of yeastlike, often pathogenic, fungi: *cryptococcal meningitis.*

cryp|to|coc|co|sis (krip′tə kok′ə sis), *n.* a highly fatal systemic infection, especially of the brain and its covering membranes, caused by a microscopic fungus. [< New Latin *Cryptococcus* genus name of the fungus (< Greek *kryptós* hidden + *kókkos* grain) + English *-osis*]

cryp|to-Com|mu|nist or **cryp|to-com|mu|nist** (krip′tō kom′yə nist), *n., adj.* **—*n.*** a person who is secretly a Communist or Communist sympathizer. **—*adj.*** secretly Communist or sympathizing with Communism.

cryp|to|crys|tal|line (krip′tō kris′tə lin, -līn), *adj. Mineralogy.* minutely crystalline; having crystals too small to be seen even with a microscope.

cryp|to-fas|cist (krip′tō fash′ist), *n., adj.* **—*n.*** a person who is secretly a fascist or fascist sympathizer. **—*adj.*** secretly fascist or sympathizing with fascism: *a crypto-fascist regime.*

cryp|to|gam (krip′tə gam), *n. Botany.* an old term for plants having no seeds, such as ferns and mosses. [< New Latin *Cryptogamia* < Greek *kryptós* hidden + *gámos* marriage, wedlock]

cryp|to|gam|ic (krip′tə gam′ik), *adj.* of cryptogams; resembling cryptogams.

cryp|tog|a|mous (krip tog′ə məs), *adj.* = cryptogamic.

cryp|to|gen|ic (krip′tə jen′ik), *adj.* (of a disease) of unknown origin; obscure. [< Greek *kryptós* hidden + English *-gen* + *-ic*]

cryp|tog|e|nous (krip toj′ə nəs), *adj.* = cryptogenic.

cryp|to|gram (krip′tə gram), *n.* something written in secret code or cipher: *I completed today's cryptogram in the morning newspaper, which I had never had enough patience to even begin in the past, in about one-half hour* (New Yorker). [< Greek *kryptós* hidden + English *-gram*]

cryp|to|gram|mat|ic (krip′tə grə mat′ik), *adj.* = cryptogrammic.

cryp|to|gram|mic (krip′tə gram′ik), *adj.* of, having to do with, or of the nature of a cryptogram.

cryp|to|graph (krip′tə graf, -gräf), *n.* = cryptogram.

cryp|tog|ra|pher (krip tog′rə fər), *n.* **1** an expert in cryptography. **2** a person who writes in cipher.

cryp|to|graph|ic (krip′tə graf′ik), *adj.* of or the nature of cryptography: *A branch of the movement bases its claims on cryptographic proofs . . . on evidence derived from ciphers or other cryptographic systems allegedly incorporated in the plays themselves* (Scientific American). **—cryp′-tograph′i|cal|ly,** *adv.*

cryp|to|graph|i|cal (krip′tə graf′ə kəl), *adj.* having to do with cryptography.

cryp|tog|ra|phist (krip tog′rə fist), *n.* = cryptographer.

cryp|tog|ra|phy (krip tog′rə fē), *n.* **1** the art or process of using or deciphering secret codes or ciphers. **2** anything written in secret codes or ciphers. [< New Latin *cryptographia* < Greek *kryptós* hidden + *-graphiā* writing]

cryp|to|log|ic (krip′tə loj′ik), *adj.* = cryptological.

cryp|to|log|i|cal (krip′tə loj′ə kəl), *adj.* of or having to do with cryptology: *a meticulous study of Elizabethan printing methods, combined with a whole series of highly technical cryptological checks* (Time).

cryp|tol|o|gist (krip tol′ə jist), *n.* a person who studies cryptology.

cryp|tol|o|gy (krip tol′ə jē), *n.* **1** the study of cryptograms; cryptography. **2** = cryptanalysis. [< Greek *kryptós* hidden + English *-logy*]

cryp|to|me|ri|a (krip′tə mir′ē ə), *n.* an evergreen tree of the taxodium family, native to China and Japan, often grown for ornament. [< New Latin *Cryptomeria* the genus name < Greek *kryptós* hidden + *méros* part (because the seeds are enclosed by scales)]

cryp|to|nym (krip′tə nim), *n.* a secret name. [< Greek *kryptós* hidden + dialectal *ónyma* name]

cryp|ton|y|mous (krip ton′ə məs), *adj.* having the name concealed; anonymous.

cryp|to|phyte (krip′tə fīt), *n.* = cryptogam. [< *crypto-* + Greek *phytón* plant]

cryp|tor|chid (krip tôr′kid), *n.* a male animal having one or two testicles that have not descended into the scrotum. [< Greek *kryptós* hidden + New Latin *orchid-*, false stem of Greek *órchis* testicle]

cryp|tor|chid|ism (krip tôr′ki diz′əm), *n.* failure of one or two testicles to descend into the scrotum.

cryp|tor|chism (krip tôr′kiz əm), *n.* = cryptorchidism.

cryp|to|vol|can|ic (krip′tō vol kan′ik), *adj.* of or relating to a cryptovolcano.

cryp|to|vol|ca|no (krip′tō vol kā′nō), *n., pl.* **-noes** or **-nos.** a volcanic eruption occurring at such great depth that it does not reach or deform the earth's surface, usually only producing a circular depression several miles wide with a central body of uplifted rocks. [< Greek *kryptós* hidden + English *volcano*]

cryp|to|zo|o|log|i|cal (krip′tō zō′ə loj′ə kəl), *adj.* **1** of legendary animals. **2** of or having to do with cryptozoology.

cryp|to|zo|ol|o|gist (krip′tō zō ol′ə jist), *n.* an expert in cryptozoology.

cryp|to|zo|ol|o|gy (krip′tō zō ol′ə jē), *n.* the study of and search for legendary animals: *The formation . . . of the International Society of Cryptozoology (the study of "hidden" animals) confers a new respectability on scientists who study the likes of . . . Sasquatch, the Himalayan Yeti, and the Loch Ness Monster* (Pat Ohlendorf). [< *crypto-* + *zoology*] **—cryp′to|zo|ol′o|gist,** *n.*

cryst., **1** crystalline. **2** crystallized. **3** crystallography.

crys|tal** (kris′təl), *n., adj.* **—*n. **1** a clear, transparent mineral that looks like ice, especially the transparent or nearly transparent form of pure quartz. **2** a piece of crystal cut into form for use or ornament. Crystals are used as beads, and hung around lights. **3a** a very transparent glass of great brilliance, used especially in making drinking glasses, serving dishes, pitchers, and vases: *goblets of crystal.* **b** glasses, dishes, or other articles made of crystal: *eyeing the plate and crystal* (Thackeray). **4** any clear, transparent substance, especially pure, clear water: *the liquid crystal.* **5** the transparent glass or plastic cover over a watch dial. **6** one of the regularly shaped pieces with angles and flat surfaces into which many substances solidify. In the physical sciences, a crystal is a solid particle in which the atoms, ions, or molecules are arranged in a regularly repeating, characteristic pattern or network of fixed points in space, with measurable distances between them. Crystals are classified into systems according to their shape, such as cubic or hexagonal, and all corresponding crystal faces in any system have the same angle between them. Crystals can grow in solution by accretion. *Crystals of sugar can be distinguished from crystals of snow by their difference in form.* **7** a group of such pieces or particles in a three-dimensional pattern: *Emeralds and most other gems are crystals.* **8** a crystalline material with special electrical properties, used in radio and other electronic devices, especially: **a** a piece of galena, Carborundum, or other crystalline material used as the rectifier in a crystal detector. **b** = crystal detector. **c** a crystal of a substance such as Rochelle salt possessing piezoelectric properties which cause it to develop electrostatic voltages when stretched or compressed, and conversely, to contract or expand in certain directions when an electrostatic field is applied. It is used in electromechanical transducers such as phonograph pickups and loudspeakers. **d** a crystal of quartz so cut that it vibrates at a single frequency when electric voltages of the same frequency are put across opposite sides, used to control the frequency of a radio-frequency oscillator or filter; quartz plate.
—*adj.* **1** clear and transparent like crystal: *crystal spring water.* **2** made of crystal: *crystal beads. Tap the rim with your fingernail and the clear ring reveals the exquisite perfection of this crystal glassware* (Newsweek). **3** having to do with or using a crystal or crystal detector in radio. [< Old French *cristal*, learned borrowing from Latin *crystallum* < Greek *krýstallos* clear ice, ultimately < *krýos* frost] **—crys′tal|like′,** *adj.*

***crystal**
definition 6

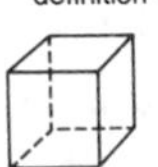
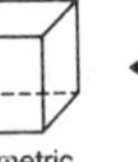

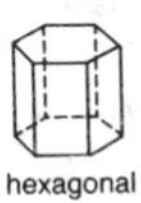

crystal ball, a ball of rock crystal or glass typically used by fortune tellers to gaze into and predict the future.

crys|tal-ball (kris′təl bol′), *Slang.* **—*v.t.*** to predict.
—*v.i.* to make predictions.

crystal-ball gazer, *Informal.* a person who speculates about the future or predicts the outcome of some future event: *The crystal-ball gazers who try to chart the course of the U.S. economy usually hedge any predictions with plenty of ifs and buts* (Time).

crys|tal-clear (kris′təl klir′), *adj.* **1** as clear as crystal: *crystal-clear diamonds.* **2** *Figurative:* *Being crystal-clear in his own mind, he speaks directly and vividly to the minds of the theatre-goer* (New York Times).

crystal detector, a device for rectifying the al-

Pronunciation Key: hat, āge, cãre, fär; let, ēqual, tėrm; it, īce; hot, ōpen, ôrder; oil, out; cup, pu̇t, rüle; child; long; thin; ᴛʜen; zh, measure; ə represents **a** in about, **e** in taken, **i** in pencil, **o** in lemon, **u** in circus.

ternating currents in a radio receiving apparatus, consisting of a crystal embedded in a soft metal.

crystal diode, a silicon or germanium crystal used as a diode.

crys·tal-gaz·er (kris′təl gā′zər), *n.* a person who stares steadily into a crystal ball in order to obtain a view of distant happenings or future events.

crystal gazing, **1** a steady staring into a crystal ball in order to obtain a view of distant happenings or future events. **2** speculation about the future: *We engaged in a bit of crystal gazing as to what life will be like in the year 2000.*

crystall., crystallography.

crystal laser, a laser that uses a ruby or other crystal usually of a cylindrical shape.

crystal lattice, the regular geometrical arrangement of atoms, ions, or molecules of a crystal.

crys·tal·lif·er·ous (kris′tə lif′ər əs), *adj.* bearing, containing, or yielding crystals.

crys·tal·lig·er·ous (kris′tə lij′ər əs), *adj.* = crystalliferous.

crys·tal·line (kris′tə lin, -līn), *adj., n.* **—*adj.*** **1** made of crystals; solidified in the form of crystals: *Sugar, salt, snowflakes, and diamonds are crystalline. Some rocks are crystalline.* **2** made of crystal: *crystalline pendants hanging from the chandelier.* **3** clear and transparent like crystal: *A crystalline sheet of ice covered the pond.* (*Figurative.*) *Simple, crystalline, and concise, her prose flows along swiftly, creating scene and character with striking immediacy and assurance* (Atlantic). **4** of or having to do with crystals and their formation.
—*n.* a light, soft dress material, similar to mousseline de soie.

crystalline heaven or **sphere**, *Astronomy.* a sphere in the Ptolemaic system, supposed to exist between the primum mobile outside and the firmament of the fixed stars inside, and to communicate motion to all within.

crystalline lens, the lens of the eye: *Immediately behind the iris is the crystalline lens, a somewhat plastic lens, the curvatures of whose surfaces can be changed by muscles around the edge in order to vary the focal length* (Shortley and Williams).

crys·tal·lin·i·ty (kris′tə lin′ə tē), *n.* crystalline quality or character: *Varieties of color, clarity and crystallinity found in natural diamonds have been observed in the man-made diamonds* (New York Times).

crys·tal·lise (kris′tə līz), *v.i., v.t.,* **-lised, -lis·ing.** *British.* crystallize.

crys·tal·lite (kris′tə līt), *n.* **1** a tiny globule or prism in glassy, igneous rock that is the beginning of a crystal. **2** *Physics.* a submicroscopic geometrical arrangement of atoms that is the center of growth of a crystal. [< *crystal* + *-ite*[1]]

crys·tal·li·tis (kris′tə lī′təs), *n.* an inflammation of the crystalline lens of the eye.

crys·tal·liz·a·bil·i·ty (kris′tə lī′zə bil′ə tē), *n.* the quality of being crystallized; capability of forming crystals: *Crystallizability is essential for a fiber-forming polymer* (Michaela Leitner).

crys·tal·li·za·tion (kris′tə lə zā′shən), *n.* **1** the act or process of crystallizing or quality or condition of being crystallized: *the crystallization of water by freezing.* **2** a crystallized substance or formation. **3** *Figurative.* the taking on of a real, concrete, or permanent form; realization: *The meeting resulted in the crystallization of our plans.*

crys·tal·lize (kris′tə līz), *v.,* **-lized, -liz·ing.** **—*v.i.*** **1** to form into crystals; solidify into crystals: *Water crystallizes to form snow.* **2** *Figurative.* to form into definite shape: *After much thought his vague ideas crystallized into a clear plan.*
—*v.t.* **1** to form into crystals; solidify into crystals. **2** *Figurative.* to give a definite form or shape to; realize: *Someday our hopes will become crystallized. When the controversy was over, the thought of the church, crystallized by the mind of St. Augustine, was clearer than it had ever been before* (Atlantic). **3** to coat with sugar. **—crys′tal·liz′a·ble,** *adj.* **—crys′tal·liz′er,** *n.*

crys·tal·lized (kris′tə līzd), *adj.* formed into crystals.

crys·tal·lo·gen·e·sis (kris′tə lə jen′ə sis), *n.* the science or study of the origin or formation of crystals. [< *crystal* + *genesis*]

crys·tal·lo·gen·ic (kris′tə lə jen′ik), *adj.* forming crystals; producing crystallization.

crys·tal·log·e·ny (kris′tə loj′ə nē), *n.* = crystallogenesis. [< *crystal* + *-gen* + *-y*[3]]

crys·tal·log·ra·pher (kris′tə log′rə fər), *n.* a person who studies crystallography.

crys·tal·lo·graph·ic (kris′tə lə graf′ik), *adj.* of or having to do with crystallography or crystals: *The final assault saw a concerted British attack . . . from the crystallographic department at Oxford* (London Times). **—crys′tal·lo·graph′i·cal·ly,** *adv.*

crys·tal·lo·graph·i·cal (kris′tə lə graf′ə kəl), *adj.* = crystallographic.

crys·tal·log·ra·phy (kris′tə log′rə fē), *n.* the science that deals with the form, structure, and properties of crystals: *Classical crystallography could suggest no explanation other than the possibility of some unknown long-range force between molecules* (Scientific American). [< *crystal* + *-graphy*]

crys·tal·loid (kris′tə loid), *adj., n.* **—*adj.*** like crystal.
—*n.* *Chemistry.* a substance (usually capable of crystallization) that, when dissolved in a liquid, forms a true solution and will diffuse readily through vegetable or animal membranes.
[< Greek *krystalloeidḗs* < *krýstallos* crystal + *eîdos* form]

crys·tal·loi·dal (kris′tə loi′dəl), *adj.* having to do with or of the nature of a crystalloid.

crys·tal·lo·lu·mi·nes·cence (kris′tə lō lü′mə nes′əns), *n.* the production of light, without a rise in temperature, occurring when a solution crystallizes.

crys·tal·lo·man·cy (kris′tə lə man′sē), *n.* divination by means of a crystal ball or other transparent body; crystal gazing. [< *crystal* + Greek *manteíā* divination]

crys·tal·lom·e·try (kris′tə lom′ə trē), *n.* the measuring of the angles of crystals.

crystal set, a radio receiver that uses a crystal detector instead of vacuum tubes to separate the signal from the carrier wave.

crystal system, each of the six different general methods in which various minerals crystallize, constituting the six classes of crystalline forms.

crystal violet, = gentian violet.

crystal vision, **1** visual perception, as of distant happenings or of the future, supposed to be aroused by crystal gazing. **2** the image or images which seem to be perceived.

cs., case or cases.

c.s., **1** capital stock. **2** civil service.

Cs (no period), **1** cesium (chemical element). **2** cirro-stratus.

CS (no periods), a potent tear gas that causes temporary blindness, used especially in riot control: *CS caused some severe irritation, and the average period of incapacity was from five to 15 minutes* (London Times). [< Ben B. *C*(orson), born 1896, and Roger W. *S*(toughton), 1906-1957, American chemists who discovered it]

C.S., an abbreviation for the following:
1 capital stock.
2 chemical society.
3a Christian Science. **b** Christian Scientist.
4 civil service.
5 Keeper of the Seal (Latin, *Custos Sigilli*).

C/S, cases.

C.S.A., **1** Confederate States Army. **2** Confederate States of America.

csar·das (chär′däsh), *n.* = czardas.

csc (no periods), cosecant.

CSC (no periods), Civil Service Commission.

C.S.C., *British.* Conspicuous Service Cross.

csch (no periods), hyperbolic cosecant.

CSE (no periods) or **C.S.E.**, *British.* Certificate of Secondary Education (awarded to secondary-school graduates, of lower value than the GCE or General Certificate of Education).

csk., cask.

CSM (no periods), **1** command and service module: *"I would like to make sure that the LM [lunar module] is okay before we power down the CSM"* (London Times). **2** corn, soya, milk: *The U.S. Department of Agriculture has developed a food made of corn, soybeans and milk, called CSM* (Science News).

CSO (no periods) or **C.S.O.**, Chief Signal Officer.

CST (no periods), **C.S.T.**, or **c.s.t.**, Central Standard Time.

ct., **1** cent or cents. **2** certificate.

Ct., an abbreviation for the following:
1 Connecticut. Official abbr: Conn.
2 count.
3 county.
4 court.

CT (no periods), **1** cell therapy. **2** Central Time. **3** Connecticut (in postal Zip Code).

C.T., Central Time.

CTC (no periods), Centralized Traffic Control.

cten·o·cyst (ten′ə sist, tē′nə-), *n.* the vesicle, containing clear fluid and otoliths, that constitutes the organ of sense in the ctenophores. [< Greek *kteís, ktenós* comb + English *cyst*]

cten·o·dac·tyl (ten ə dak′təl), *n.* a hystricomorphic rodent of northern Africa, with small ears, a stumpy tail, and hind limbs that have a fringe of bristles on the inner toes; comb rat; gundi. [< New Latin *Ctenodactylus* the genus name < Greek *kteís, ktenós* comb + *dáktylos* toe, finger]

cte·noid (tē′noid, ten′oid), *adj. Zoology.* having marginal projections resembling the teeth of a comb, as the teeth or scales of certain fishes do. [< New Latin *Ctenoidei* ctenoid fish < Greek *ktenoeidês* comb-shaped < *kteís, ktenós* comb + *eîdos* form]

cte·noi·de·an (ti noi′dē ən), *adj., n. Obsolete.* **—*adj.*** belonging to a large group of fishes, including those with ctenoid scales.
—*n.* a ctenoid fish.

Cte·noph·o·ra (ti nof′ər ə), *n.pl.* the phylum of animals comprising the ctenophores.

cte·noph·o·ran (ti nof′ər ən), *adj., n.* **—*adj.*** of or having to do with the ctenophores.
—*n.* a ctenophoran animal.

cten·o·phore (ten′ə fôr, -fōr; tē′nə-), *n.* **1** any one of a phylum of marine invertebrate animals resembling jellyfishes, having biradial symmetry, and swimming by means of eight rows of meridional ciliated plates; comb jelly: *There were the ctenophores, looking like beautiful luminescent Japanese lanterns* (New Yorker). **2** one of the rows of comb plates of a ctenophore. [< New Latin *Ctenophora* the class name < Greek *kteís, ktenós* comb + *phoreîn* to bear]

ctf., certificate.

ctge., cartage.

ctn (no period), **1** cotangent. **2** carton.

c to c (no periods), center to center.

CTOL (no periods), conventional take-off and landing.

ctr., center.

cts., **1** centimes. **2** cents. **3** certificates.

cu. or **cu** (no period), cubic.

Cu (no period), **1** *Chemistry.* copper (chemical element; Latin, *cuprum*). **2** cumulus.

cua·dri·lla (kwä drēl′yä, -drē′yä), *n., pl.* **-las.** *Spanish.* the group of persons who assist the bullfighter in the arena: *But he couldn't stay away from the bulls, . . . so he joined Pacote's cuadrilla as a banderillero* (Barnaby Conrad).

cuar·ta (kwär′tə), *n. Southwestern U.S.* a long rawhide whip. [American English < American Spanish *cuarta*]

cuat·ro (kwät′rō), *n., pl.* **-ros.** a four-stringed guitar used in Central America and the West Indies: *Finding a few diamonds, he would load his canoe with rum and float downriver, happily strumming the cuatro* (Time). [< American Spanish *cuatro* (literally) four < Spanish < Latin *quattuor*]

cub[1] (kub), *n., v.* **cubbed, cub·bing.** **—*n.*** **1** a young bear, fox, lion, tiger, or other wild animal: *With the fury of a bear which had been robbed of her cubs* (Scott). **2** *Figurative.* an inexperienced or awkward boy. **3** = cub scout. **4** = cub reporter.
—*v.i.* **1** to give birth to a cub or cubs. **2** to hunt fox cubs. **3** *British.* to train hounds to hunt by means of fox cubs.
[origin uncertain]

cub[2] (kub), *n.* **1** a stall or pen for cattle. **2** = coop[1]. **3** a crib for fodder. **4** a bin or chest. [origin uncertain; compare Low German *kübje* cattle shed]

cub., cubic.

cu·bage (kyü′bij), *n.* **1** the determination of cubic contents of a thing. **2** the cubic contents determined: *The volume of water it can displace is its cubage.*

Cu·ba li·bre (kyü′bə lē′brə), an alcoholic drink consisting of rum, a cola beverage, and lemon or lime juice. [< Spanish *Cuba libre* (literally) free Cuba]

Cu·ban (kyü′bən), *adj., n.* **—*adj.*** of or having to do with Cuba or its people.
—*n.* a person born or living in Cuba.

cu·bane (kyü′bān), *n.* a hydrocarbon whose carbon atoms are joined in the shape of a cube: *The first successful synthesis of cubane . . . paved the way to an extensive study of the chemistry of boxlike molecular structures* (London Times). [< *cub*(e) + *-ane*]

cub·an·gle (kyüb′ang′gəl), *n.* the solid angle formed by three lines meeting at right angles to one another, as in a corner of a cube.

Cuban heel, a medium-high heel for women's shoes, somewhat narrow at the base and slightly curved at the back.

Cu·ban·ize (kyü′bə nīz), *v.t.,* **-ized, -iz·ing.** to make Cuban in character, appearance, or other form: *Hoping to disguise Moscow's controlling arm, Roca set out to Cubanize the party* (Time).

Cu·ba·nol·o·gist (kyü′bə nol′ə jist), *n.* a student of Cuba and Cuban politics: *. . . Cubanologists, who sit in Florida and observe Havana via the microfilms in a university library* (Manchester Guardian Weekly).

Cuban Spanish, the dialect spoken by Spanish speakers in Cuba.

cu·ba·ture (kyü′bə chər), *n.* **1** the determination of the cubic contents of something. **2** cubic contents. [< *cube;* patterned on *quadrature*]

cub·bish (kub′ish), *adj.* like a cub; inexperienced or awkward. **—cub′bish·ness,** *n.*

cub·by (kub′ē), *n., pl.* **-bies.** **1** a snug, confined place. **2** a cubbyhole: *Up garret was a little cubby, with a pallet in it* (Mark Twain). [< *cub*[2] + *-y*[2]]

cub·by·hole (kub′ē hōl′), *n.* **1** a small enclosed

space: [*She*] *works in a tiny cubbyhole above Seventh Avenue, surrounded by button boxes, swatches of material, scrapbooks and half-finished dresses* (Time). **2** *Figurative.* category: *T. S. Eliot was a poet who could not be placed into an easily marked cubbyhole* (New York Times).

cube**[1] (kyüb), *n., v.,* **cubed, cub|ing.** **—*n. **1** a solid with six square faces or sides, all equal. **2a** anything shaped like a cube: *ice cubes, a cube of sugar.* **b** = flashcube. **3** the product obtained when a number is used three times as a factor: *125 is the cube of 5, because 5 X 5 X 5 = 125.*
—*v.t.* **1** to make or form into the shape of a cube: *The beets we had for supper were cubed instead of sliced.* **2** to tenderize (meat) by pounding a pattern of small cubes on the surface with a tenderizing mallet. **3** to use (a number) three times as a factor: *4 cubed is 64.* **4** to measure the cubic contents of.
[< Latin *cubus* < Greek *kýbos* cube; (originally) a die] **—cube′like′,** *adj.*

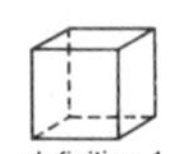

*cube[1] definitions 1, 3 — definition 1 — $5^3 = 5 \times 5 \times 5 = 125$ definition 3

cu|be[2] (kyü′bā), *n.* any one of various tropical American plants which yield rotenone. [< Spanish *quibey,* probably < the Carib name]

cu|beb (kyü′beb), *n.* **1** the dried, unripe berry of a tropical shrub or climbing vine of the pepper family. Cubebs were formerly crushed and smoked in pipes or cigarettes for the treatment of catarrh. They are also used as a spice and still used as a medicine in Asia. **2** a cigarette containing the crushed berries. [< Old French *cubebe,* learned borrowing from Medieval Latin *cubeba* < Arabic *kabāba*]

cube|let (kyü′blit), *n.* a small cube.

cube root, the number that produces a given number when used as a factor three times: *The cube root of 125 is 5.*

cu|bic (kyü′bik), *adj.* **1** shaped like a cube: *the cubic form of a block of ice.* **2** having length, breadth, and thickness. A cubic inch is the volume of a cube whose edges are one inch long. The cubic content of a room is the number of cubic feet it contains. *Abbr:* cu. **3** having to do with or involving the cubes of numbers; of the third degree. **4** *Crystallography.* = isometric.

cu|bi|cal (kyü′bə kəl), *adj.* shaped like a cube; cubic. **—cu′bi|cal|ly,** *adv.* **—cu′bi|cal|ness,** *n.*

cubic centimeter, a unit of cubic measure equal to an area 1 centimeter long, 1 centimeter wide, and 1 centimeter high, or .061 cubic inch. *Abbr:* cc.

cubic equation, an equation in which the highest power of the unknown quantity is a cube.

cubic foot, a unit of cubic measure, equal to an area 1 foot long, 1 foot wide, and 1 foot high, or .0283 cubic meter. *Abbr:* cu.ft.

cubic inch, a unit of cubic measure, equal to an area 1 inch long, 1 inch wide, and 1 inch high, or 16.387 cubic centimeters. *Abbr:* cu.in.

cu|bi|cle (kyü′bə kəl), *n.* **1** a very small room or compartment. **2** a small space for sleeping, especially a small division of a dormitory. [< Latin *cubiculum* bedroom (diminutive) < *cubāre* to lie down]

cubic measure, a system of measurement of volume in cubic units:
1728 cubic inches = 1 cubic foot
27 cubic feet = 1 cubic yard
1000 cubic millimeters = 1 cubic centimeter
1000 cubic centimeters = 1 cubic decimeter
1000 cubic decimeters = 1 cubic meter

cu|bi|cule (kyü′bə kyül), *n.* = cubicle.

cu|bic|u|lum (kyü bik′yə ləm), *n., pl.* **-la** (-lə). **1** = cubicle. **2** *Archaeology.* a burial chamber, as in catacombs. [< Latin *cubiculum*]

cubic yard, a unit of cubic measure, equal to an area 1 yard long, 1 yard wide, and 1 yard high, or .7646 cubic meter. *Abbr:* cu.yd.

cu|bi|form (kyü′bə fôrm), *adj.* having the form of a cube.

cub|ism (kyü′biz əm), *n.* a style of painting, drawing, and sculpture, developed in the early 1900's, in which objects are represented by cubes and other geometrical forms rather than by realistic details: *Picasso ... said that ... "Cubism is no different from any other school of painting ... it is an art dealing primarily with forms"* (New Yorker).

cub|ist (kyü′bist), *n., adj.* **—*n.*** an artist or sculptor whose art is based on cubism.
—*adj.* of or having to do with cubism or cubists: *Even in his great cubist period with its somber austere canvases ... the trivia of everyday life ... are recognizable* (Newsweek).

cu|bis|tic (kyü bis′tik), *adj.* = cubist. **—cu|bis′ti-cal|ly,** *adv.*

cu|bit (kyü′bit), *n.* an ancient measure of length, about 18 to 22 inches: *The cubit was based on the length of the forearm from the elbow to the tip of the middle finger.* [< Latin *cubitum, cubitus* elbow, cubit, related to *cubāre* lie down]

cu|bi|tal (kyü′bə təl), *adj.* **1a** of or having to do with the forearm: *a cubital vein.* **b** of or having to do with ulna. **2** of the length of a cubit.

cu|bi|tus (kyü′bə təs), *n., pl.* **-ti** (-tī). *Anatomy.* **1** = forearm. **2** = ulna. [< Latin *cubitus* cubit, elbow; see etym. under **cubit**]

cub|mas|ter (kub′mas′tər, -mäs′-), *n.* a man in charge of a pack of cub scouts.

cu|boid (kyü′boid), *adj., n.* **—*adj.*** **1** shaped like a cube; cubical. **2** *Anatomy.* of or denoting a cube-shaped bone, the outermost of the distal row of tarsal bones.
—*n.* **1** something shaped like a cube. **2** *Anatomy.* the cuboid bone. **3** *Mathematics.* a rectangular parallelepiped.

cu|boi|dal (kyü boi′dəl), *adj.* **1** = cuboid. **2** of or belonging to the cuboid bone.

cub reporter, *Informal.* a young, inexperienced newspaper reporter; cub.

cub scout or **Cub Scout,** a member of the junior division of the Boy Scouts. Cub scouts are 8 to 10 years of age.

cub shark, = ground shark.

cu|ca|ra|cha (kü′kə rä′chə; *Spanish* kü′kä rä′chä), *n., pl.* **-chas.** **1** a very fast popular dance of Mexico. **2** = cockroach. [< Spanish *cucaracha*]

cu|chi|fri|to (kü′chē frē′tō), *n., pl.* **-tos.** *Spanish.* a cube of pork dipped in batter and fried in deep fat.

Cu|chul|ainn or **Cu|chul|lain** (kü ʜul′in, -kul′-), *n.* a legendary Irish hero who defended the kingdom of Ulster single-handedly against invaders.

cuck|ing stool (kuk′ing), a chair into which common scolds, dishonest tradesmen, or others to be punished were strapped, left to be mocked and pelted by the crowd, or to be ducked [(literally) a toilet seat < Middle English *coken* to defecate]

cuck|old (kuk′əld), *n., v.* **—*n.*** the husband of an unfaithful wife.
—*v.t.* to make a cuckold of.
[< Old French *cucuault* < *coucou,* earlier, *cocu;* see etym. under **cuckoo** (because the female cuckoo changes mates)]

cuck|old|ry (kuk′əl drē), *n.* **1** making a cuckold of a husband. **2** *Obsolete.* cuckolds collectively.

cuck|oo (kü′kü; *especially for n.* ku̇k′ü), *n., pl.* **-oos,** *v.,* **-ooed, -oo|ing,** *adj.* **—*n.*** **1** a bird whose call sounds much like its name. The common European cuckoo lays its eggs in the nests of other birds instead of hatching them itself. The American cuckoo builds its own nest and has a call less like the name. Other members of this family in the Americas are the black-billed cuckoo, the yellow-billed cuckoo, the ani, and the road runner. **2a** the call of the cuckoo. **b** a bird call that sounds like the word *cuckoo.* **3** *Slang.* a silly or crazy person; fool.
—*v.i.* to make the sound of the cuckoo, or an imitation of it.
—*adj.* *U.S. Slang.* crazy; silly.
[Middle English *cuccu* < Old French *cocu;* imitative]

cuckoo bee, a solitary bee that lays its eggs in the nests of other solitary bees or takes the place of the queen in a bumblebee nest.

***cuckoo clock,** a clock with a little toy bird that makes a sound like that of the European cuckoo to mark intervals of time.

*cuckoo clock

cuck|oo|flow|er (kü′kü flou′ər, ku̇k′ü-), *n.* **1** a slender, erect plant of the mustard family, a variety of bitter cress, native to North America and Europe, having white or purple flowers; lady's-smock. **2** = ragged robin. **3** any one of certain related plants.

cuck|oo|pint (kü′kü pīnt, ku̇k′ü-), *n.* a common European arum; wake-robin.

cuckoo spit or **spittle,** **1** a frothy secretion exuded by certain homopterous insects as a protective covering for their larvae, found on the leaves, axils, and other parts of plants; toad spit or spittle; frog spit or spittle. **2** an insect that secretes this, such as the froghopper.

cuckoo wasp, any one of a family of wasps that has a hard integument of metallic colors, curls its abdomen under the body when attacked, and lays its eggs in the nests of other species of wasps and bees.

cu. cm. or **cu cm** (no periods), cubic centimeter or cubic centimeters.

cu|cu|li|form (kyü kyü′lə fôrm), *adj.* of or having to do with a large group of birds that includes the cuckoos, road runners, and anis. [< New Latin *Cuculiformes* the order < Latin *cucūlus* cuckoo + *forma* form]

cu|cul|late (kyü′kə lāt, kyü kul′āt), *adj. Botany, Zoology.* having a hood; shaped like a hood, as a leaf or nectary. [< Late Latin *cucullātus* < Latin *cucullus* cap, hood] **—cu′cul|late′ly,** *adv.*

cu|cul|lat|ed (kyü′kə lā′ tid, kyü kul′ā-), *adj.* = cucullate.

cu|cul|li|form (kyü kul′ə fôrm), *adj.* hood-shaped.

cu|cul|lus (kyü kul′əs), *n., pl.* **-li** (-lī). **1** a cowl or monk's hood. **2** *Zoology, Anatomy.* a hoodlike formation or coloration of the head. [< Latin *cucullus* cap, hood]

cu|cum|ber (kyü′kum bər), *n.* **1** a long, green vegetable with firm flesh and many seeds inside, eaten usually in thin slices in a salad, or used to make pickles. It belongs to the gourd family. See picture under **gourd family.** **2** the vine that it grows on. **3** any one of various similar plants or their fruit.
cool as a cucumber, a very cool: *It's cool as a cucumber outdoors.* **b** calm and unruffled; not excited: *Thucydides ... is ... cool as a cucumber upon every act of atrocity* (Thomas De Quincey).
[< Old French *cocombre, coucombre* < Latin *cucumis* cucumber; a sea plant of similar color and odor]

cucumber root, a plant of the lily family, having a fleshy rootstock which tastes like a cucumber; Indian cucumber.

cucumber tree, 1 any one of several American magnolias whose fruit resembles a small cucumber. **2** an East Indian tree with an acid fruit resembling a small cucumber and used for pickling; bilimbi.

cu|cu|mi|form (kyü kyü′mə fôrm), *adj.* shaped like a cucumber. [< Latin *cucumis* cucumber + English *-form*]

cu|cur|bit (kyü kėr′bit), *n.* **1** a gourd or any plant of the gourd family: *Scientists have discovered the "Adam" of the cucurbits, the family of plants that includes the squashes, pumpkins and ornamental gourds* (Science News Letter). **2** Also, **cucurbite.** a round, gourd-shaped dish formerly used as the lower part of a distilling apparatus. [< Middle French *cucurbite,* learned borrowing from Latin *cucurbita* gourd, gourd-shaped glass]

cu|cur|bi|ta|ceous (kyü kėr′bə tā′shəs), *adj.* belonging to the gourd family of plants, which includes the pumpkin, squash, cucumber, and watermelon.

cu|cur|bi|tal (kyü kėr′bə təl), *adj.* = cucurbitaceous.

cu|cur|bite (kyü kėr′bit), *n.* = cucurbit (def. 2).

cu|cu|yo (kü kü′yō), *n., pl.* **-yos.** = fire beetle. [< Spanish *cocuyo* cucuyo]

cud (kud), *n.* **1** a mouthful of food brought back from the first stomach of cattle or similar animals for a slow, second chewing in the mouth. **2** *Dialect.* a quid of tobacco.
chew the cud, a to chew the food that has been brought back from the first stomach: *Cows, sheep, and camels chew the cud.* **b** *Figurative.* to ponder or meditate; ruminate: [*I*] *left her a little while to chew the cud* (Henry Fielding).
[Old English *cudu,* variant of *cwidu*]

cu|da (kü′də), *n., pl.* **-da** or **-das.** *U.S. Dialect or Informal.* barracuda.

cud|bear (kud′bãr′), *n.* **1** a violet coloring matter obtained from various lichens, used for dyeing. **2** any lichen that yields it. [coined from his first name by Dr. *Cuthbert* Gordon, a Scottish physician, who patented it]

cud|ding (kud′ing), *n.* rumination (of animals).

cud|dle (kud′əl), *v.,* **-dled, -dling,** *n.* **—*v.t.*** to hold close and lovingly in one's arms or lap; hug tenderly: *She was cuddling the little kittens.* SYN: fondle.
—*v.i.* to lie close and comfortably; curl up: *The two puppies cuddled together in front of the fire.* SYN: nestle.
—*n.* a hug; embrace.
[perhaps related to **couth**]

cud|dle|some (kud′əl səm), *adj.* pleasing to cuddle.

Pronunciation Key: hat, āge, cãre, fär; let, ēqual, tėrm; it, īce; hot, ōpen, ôrder; oil, out; cup, pu̇t, rüle; child; long; thin; ᴛʜen; zh, measure; ə represents a in about, e in taken, i in pencil, o in lemon, u in circus.

cud|dly (kud′lē), *adj.*, **-dli|er, -dli|est.** **1** given to cuddling. **2** pleasing to cuddle; cuddlesome. —**cud′dli|ness,** *n.*

cud|dy¹ (kud′ē), *n., pl.* **-dies. 1a** a small cabin on a boat: *a log jam of moored living-sampans, whose residents poked their heads out from below the mat-thatched cuddies to watch* (Atlantic). **b** the small galley or pantry on a boat. **2** a small room or cupboard. [origin uncertain]

cud|dy² (kud′ē), *n., pl.* **-dies.** *Scottish.* **1** a donkey. **2** *Figurative.* a stupid person. [< *Cuddy,* probably short for *Cuthbert*]

cud|dy³ (kud′ē), *n., pl.* **-dies.** a coalfish, especially a young coalfish. [compare Gaelic *cudaig*]

cudg|el (kuj′əl), *n., v.,* **-eled, -el|ing** or (*especially British*) **-elled, -el|ling.** —*n.* a short, thick stick used as a weapon; club. —*v.t.* to beat with or as if with a cudgel: *If he were here, I would cudgel him like a dog* (Shakespeare).
cudgel one's brains. See under **brain.**
take up the cudgels for, to defend strongly: *His wife had taken up the cudgels for her friend* (Anthony Trollope).
[Old English *cycgel*] —**cudg′el|er,** *n.*

cud|weed (kud′wēd′), *n.* **1** any plant of a group of woolly herbs of the composite family, given to animals that have lost their cud; cottonweed. **2** any one of various related plants.

cue¹ (kyü), *n., v.t.,* **cued, cue|ing** or **cu|ing.** —*n.* **1a** an action or speech by an actor which serves as the signal for another actor to come on the stage or begin speaking. **b** a signal for some other person or persons in a stage production to do his part: *For a recent … meeting, the stage crew had to worry about 176 light cues, 124 sound cues, and 80 prop changes* (Newsweek). **2** a signal like this to a singer or musician. **3** *Figurative.* a hint as to what should be done: *Take your cue from me at the party about when it is time to leave. Being a stranger, he took his cue from the actions of the natives.* **4** the part one is to play; course of action. **5** a frame of mind; mood: *Nobody was in the cue to dance* (Hawthorne). **SYN:** disposition humor.
—*v.t.* to provide (a person) with a cue or hint: *During the rehearsal the director cued the actors.*
cue in, to insert or add (a camera shot, scene, passage of dialogue, or stage device) to a script: *Screens labeled Preset showed the picture on the camera that would be cued in next* (Harper's).
[perhaps < French *queue,* Old French *coue* tail, end < Latin *coda,* dialectal variant of *cauda* (from the "end" of a preceding actor's speech)]

cue² (kyü), *n., v.,* **cued, cue|ing** or **cu|ing.** —*n.* **1** a long, tapering stick used for striking the balls in billiards, pool, or the like. It has a pad at the tip. **2** = queue (pigtail).
—*v.t.* to twist (the hair) into a queue or cue.
[variant of *queue* < French < Old French *coue;* see etym. under **cue¹**]

cue ball, the ball, usually white, struck by the cue in billiards or pool.

cue|ca (kwā′kə; *Spanish* kwe′kä), *n., pl.* **-cas. 1** a light, gay dance of Chile and Bolivia, performed by couples. **2** the music to this dance. [< American Spanish *cueca*]

cue card, a card with key words and phrases used to prompt a speaker, chiefly during a telecast: *The tablet was a kind of cue card consisting of catchwords which gave the singer only the gist of his verses* (Scientific American).

cued speech (kyüd), a method of communication for the deaf which combines lip reading with manual signs by associating particular sounds with certain hand positions: *a method known as "cued speech" … consist[ing] of 12 hand signals that, when used with lip reading, allow a deaf person to see clearly any word that is spoken* (W.J. Cromie).

cue|ist (kyü′ist), *n.* **1** a person who uses a cue, as in billiards. **2** an expert in the use of the cue.

cue rack, a rack for holding billiard cues.

cue sheet, a list of cues, such as for lighting and music, used by a stage manager.

cues|ta (kwes′tə), *n. U.S.* a ridge with a gentle slope on one side and a steep slope on the other. See picture under **plain.** [< Spanish *cuesta* hill, slope]

cuff¹ (kuf), *n.* **1** a band around the wrist, either attached to a sleeve or separate: *His shirt cuffs got wet when he didn't pull his sleeves up to wash.* **2** a turned-up fold around the bottom of a trouser leg. **3** the part of a long glove that covers the wrist or part of the arm. **4** = handcuff.
off the cuff, without preparation; impromptu; offhand: *Only … where he spoke completely off the cuff did he seem to be establishing any great rapport with his audience* (Wall Street Journal).
on the cuff, on credit: *Epidemic living on the cuff is costing Americans more than a penny or two* (Wall Street Journal).
[Middle English *cuffe* glove; origin uncertain]

cuff² (kuf), *v., n.* —*v.t.* to hit with the hand; slap: *The older boy ducked in surprise as the little boy tried to cuff him on the ear.*
—*n.* a hit with the hand. [origin uncertain]

cuff button, a button for the cuff of a shirt, blouse, or coat.

cuffed (kuft), *adj.* having a cuff or cuffs: *cuffed sleeves and trousers.*

cuff|less (kuf′lis), *adj.* without cuff or cuffs.

cuff link, a link for the cuff of a shirt.

Cu|fic (kyü′fik), *adj.* of or denoting a kind of Arabic writing used by the copyists of Cufa in transcribing the Koran. Also, **Cuphic, Kufic.** [< *Cufa,* an ancient city near Babylon, a center of Moslem learning + English *-ic*]

cu. ft. or **cu ft** (no periods), cubic foot or cubic feet.

cui bo|no (kwē′ bō′nō, kī′), *Latin.* **1** for whose benefit? who profits by it? **2** (popularly but erroneously) to what use or good purpose?

cu. in. or **cu in** (no periods), cubic inch or cubic inches.

***cui|rass** (kwi ras′), *n., v.* —*n.* **1** a piece of armor for the body, made of a breastplate and a plate for the back fastened together. **2** the breastplate alone: *The troopers armed with cuirass and backplate …* (Scott). **3** the armor plate of a warship. **4** *Zoology.* a hard, bony protective covering of certain animals.
—*v.t.* to cover or protect with a cuirass.
[< Old French *cuirasse* < Italian *corazza* < Late Latin *coriācea* (*vestis*) (garment) of leather < Latin *corium* leather; form influenced by Old French *cuir* leather < Latin *corium*]

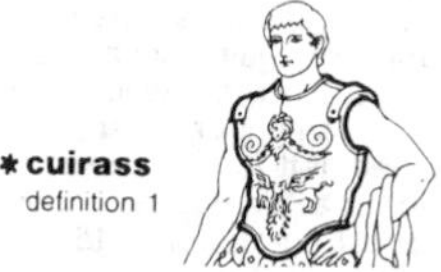

***cuirass**
definition 1

cui|rassed (kwi rast′), *adj.* furnished with a cuirass or other protective covering.

cui|ras|sier (kwir′ə sir′), *n.* a cavalry soldier wearing a cuirass.

cuir-bouil|li (kwēr′bü yē′), *n. French.* leather boiled or soaked in hot water and pressed into any required shape, which it is capable of retaining. Owing to its extreme hardness, it offers considerable resistance to cuts and blows.

***Cui|se|naire rod** (kwiz′ə nãr′), one of a set of ten rods of different related sizes and colors, used in teaching arithmetic. [< Georges *Cuisenaire,* a Belgian schoolteacher who developed a method of teaching with these rods]

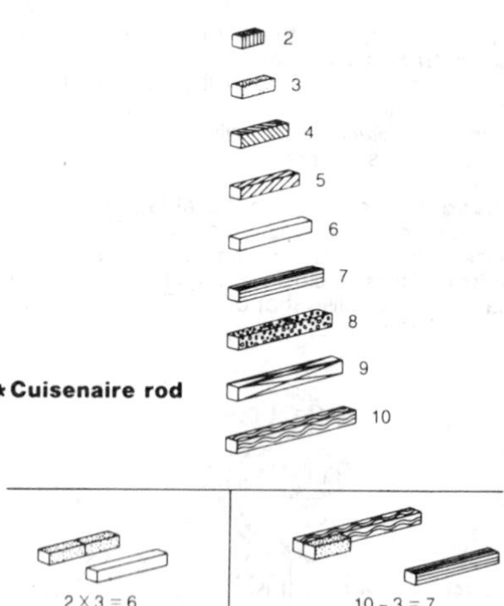

***Cuisenaire rod**

cuish (kwish), *n.* = cuisse.

cui|sine (kwi zēn′), *n.* **1** a style of cooking or preparing food; cooking; cookery: *Italian cuisine.* **2** food: *The cuisine is excellent at that restaurant.* **3** the kitchen. [< Old French *cuisine* < Latin *coquīna* kitchen < *coquere* to cook]

cuisine min|ceur (maɴ sœr′), a style of French cooking that restricts the use of ingredients having a high calorie content. [< French *cuisine minceur* cuisine of slimness]

cuisse (kwis), *n.* a piece of armor to protect the thigh. See picture under **armor.** [< Old French *cuisse* thigh < Latin *coxa* hip]

cuit|tle or **cui|tle** (kʏ′təl), *v.t.,* **-tled, -tling.** *Scottish.* **1** to wheedle; cajole; coax. **2** to tickle.

cuke (kyük), *n. Informal.* cucumber.

cul|bas|ti|ja (tsül bäs′ti yä), *n.* a Yugoslav dish of grilled pork or beef. [< Serbo-Croatian *culbastyá*]

culch (kulch), *n.* = cultch.

Cul|dee (kul′dē), *n.* a person belonging to a class of anchorites or hermits existing in Ireland, Scotland, and Wales from the 700's to the 1700's. [< New Latin *Culdei,* earlier *Keldei* < Old Irish *céle dé* anchorite < *céle* associate, servant + *dé* of God]

cul-de-four (kul′də fůr′, kůl′-), *n., pl.* **culs-de-four.** *Architecture.* a vault in the form of a quarter sphere, often used to cover a semidome, especially in Roman, Byzantine, and Romanesque architecture. [< French *cul-de-four* bottom of an oven]

cul-de-lampe (kul′də lamp′, kůl′-), *n., pl.* **culs-de-lampe. 1** *Architecture.* **a** an ornamental support of inverted conical form. **b** a pendant having this form. **2** an ornament used to fill up a blank space in a page, as at the end of a chapter when the lines stop short of the bottom. [< French *cul-de-lampe* bottom of a lamp]

cul-de-sac (kul′də sak′, kůl′-; *French* kʏd′ sák′), *n., pl.* **culs-de-sac** (kulz′də sak′, kůlz′-; *French* kʏd′sák′), **cul-de-sacs. 1** a street or passage open at only one end; blind alley: *The rare, clear sunshine of an English spring flooded the narrow cul-de-sac of Downing Street* (Newsweek). **2** *Figurative.* an impasse: *The author has reached a cul-de-sac in the writing of his novel.* **3** *Anatomy.* a vessel, tube, or sac open only at one end, such as the cecum. **4** a situation in which a military force is hemmed in on all sides except behind. [< Old French *cul-de-sac* bottom of the sack; *cul* < Latin *cūlus*]

cul|do|scope (kul′də skōp), *n.* a small, lighted, telescopic instrument used in culdoscopic examination.

cul|do|scop|ic (kul′də skop′ik), *adj.* of or having to do with culdoscopy.

cul|dos|co|py (kul dos′kə pē), *n.* gynecological examination of the female pelvic organs by means of a culdoscope placed in the posterior cul-de-sac of the cervix. [< *cul-d*(e-sac) + *-scopy*]

cu|let (kyü′lit), *n.* **1** the flat face forming the bottom of a diamond or other gem cut as a brilliant. **2** the part of a suit of armor protecting the back of the body below the waist. [< Old French *culet* (diminutive) < *cul* bottom < Latin *cūlus*]

cu|lex (kyü′leks), *n., pl.* **cu|li|ces** (kyü′lə sēz). any one of a large genus of mosquitoes that includes the most common mosquito of North America and Europe: *The fact that culex mosquitoes feed on birds raises a question as to a possible avian role in the spread of certain of the viruses* (Scientific American). [< Latin *culex, culicis* gnat]

cu|lic|id (kyü lis′id), *adj., n.* —*adj.* of or having to do with a family of insects comprising the mosquitoes.
—*n.* a culicid insect.
[< New Latin *Culicidae* the family name < Latin *culex, culicis* gnat]

cu|li|nar|y (kyü′lə ner′ē, kul′ə-), *adj.* **1** of or having to do with cooking or the kitchen: *After one of her meals, Mother is often praised for her skill in the culinary arts.* **2** used in cooking. [< Latin *culīnārius* < *culīna* kitchen] —**cu′li|nar′i|ly,** *adv.*

cull¹ (kul), *v., n.* —*v.t.* **1a** to pick out; select: *The lawyer culled important facts from the mass of evidence.* **b** to pick over; make selections from: *She culled the peaches, picking only the choicest ones.* **c** to discard: *She culled the spoiled berries from each box.* **2** to pick out (calves, cows, or other animals) according to their quality: *These increases in production per cow have been achieved through culling out poor milk givers* (Wall Street Journal).
—*n.* something inferior picked out. Poor fruit, stale vegetables, and animals not up to standard are called culls.
[< Old French *coillir* < Latin *colligere* < *com-* together + *legere* gather] —**cull′er,** *n.*

cull² (kul), *n. Dialect.* **1** a silly person; simpleton; fool. **2** a man; chap. [perhaps short for *cully* or for obsolete *cullings,* as if "inferior stock"]

cul|len|der (kul′ən dər), *n.* = colander.

cul|let (kul′it), *n.* fragments of broken or trimmed glass, remelted in making a new mixture of glass or something used as an ingredient of pottery glazes: *Upstairs, on top of a chest full of cullet (stained glass fragments)* (Punch). [variant of *collet* (as being originally the broken "necks" from blown glass)]

cull|ing (kul′ing), *n.* **1** the act of a person that culls. **2** something culled.
cullings, parts or pieces of inferior quality or size, selected and separated from a larger mass: *He picked the best grapes for himself, and left the cullings for us.*

cul|lion (kul′yən), *n. Obsolete.* a base, despicable, or vile person; rascal. [< Old French *couillon* rascal; (originally) testicle < Late Latin *culiō, -ōnis,* for Latin *cōleus* testicle; (originally) bag < Greek *koleós* sheath, scabbard]

cul|lis[1] (kul′is), *n.* a strong broth prepared like beef tea, but with any kind of meat. [< Middle French *coleïs,* ultimately < Latin *cōlāre* to strain, flow through]

cul|lis[2] (kul′is), *n. Architecture.* a gutter, as in a roof. [< French *coulisse* furrow, groove < *coulis,* ultimately < Latin *cōlāre* to strain, flow through]

cul|ly (kul′ē), *n., pl.* **-lies,** *v.,* **-lied, -ly|ing.** —*n. Informal.* **1** a person who is easily cheated or imposed upon; dupe; gull. **2** man; fellow; mate: *What's your hurry, cully?*
—*v.t. Rare.* to take in; deceive; cheat.
[perhaps short for *cullion*]

culm[1] (kulm), *n.* **1** small or refuse hard coal; slack. **2** hard coal of poor quality. [Middle English *culm,* perhaps related to *col* coal]

culm[2] (kulm), *n., v.* —*n. Botany.* the jointed stem characteristic of grasses, usually hollow.
—*v.i.* to form a culm. [< Latin *culmus* stalk]

Culm (kulm), *n. Geology.* a European formation of Lower Carboniferous strata, as of shales or sandstones, containing thin beds of inferior coal. [< *culm*[1]]

cul|mif|er|ous (kul mif′ər əs), *adj. Botany.* containing or producing culms. [< *culm*[1] + *-ferous*]

cul|mi|nant (kul′mə nənt), *adj.* culminating; reaching the greatest altitude; topmost.

cul|mi|nate (kul′mə nāt), *v.,* **-nat|ed, -nat|ing.**
—*v.i.* **1** to reach its highest point; reach a climax; result (in): *The science fair culminated in the awarding of prizes.* **2** to reach the highest altitude a heavenly body will; be on the meridian.
—*v.t.* to bring to its highest point or climax: *Their marriage culminated their long friendship.*
[< Late Latin *culmināre* (with English *-ate*[1]) to crown < Latin *culmen, -inis* top]

cul|mi|na|tion (kul′mə nā′shən), *n.* **1** the highest point; climax: *The culmination of the Christmas party was the appearance of Santa Claus.* **SYN:** acme, zenith, peak. **2** a reaching of the highest point. **3** a reaching of the meridian by a heavenly body; position of greatest altitude.

Culm measures or **series,** = Culm.

***cu|lottes** (kyü lots′; *French* kʏ lôt′), *n.pl.* a woman's skirt divided and sewed like trousers, but cut so full as to appear much like an ordinary skirt; divided skirt. [< French *culottes* trousers < Middle French < *cul* bottom < Latin *cūlus*]

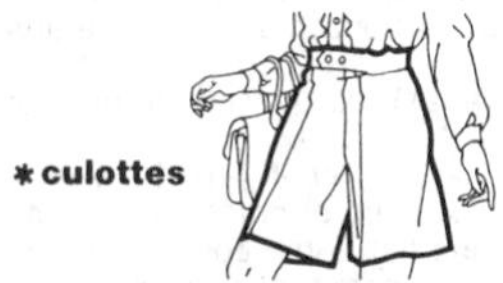
***culottes**

cul|pa|bil|i|ty (kul′pə bil′ə tē), *n.* the fact or condition of being culpable.

cul|pa|ble (kul′pə bəl), *adj.* deserving blame; blameworthy: *The policeman was dismissed for culpable neglect of duty.* [< Old French *coulpable* < Latin *culpābilis* < *culpa* fault, crime, blame]
—**cul′pa|ble|ness,** *n.*

cul|pa|bly (kul′pə blē), *adv.* in a culpable manner; blamably; reprehensibly.

cul|prit (kul′prit), *n.* **1** a person guilty of a fault or crime; offender: *The person who broke the window is the culprit; he should pay for it.* **2** a prisoner in court accused of a crime. [apparently < Anglo-French *cul. prit,* earlier *cul. prist; cul.,* short for *culpable* deserving punishment, and *prist,* variant of Old French *prest* ready (for trial), ultimately < Latin *praestō* I am on hand, or ready]

cult (kult), *n.* **1** a system of religious worship, especially with reference to its rites and ceremonies: *Buddhism includes many cults.* **2** great admiration for a person, thing, or idea; worship: *A cult of [Napoleon] grew up after his death* (H. G. Wells). **SYN:** devotion, homage. **3** a group showing such admiration; worshipers. **4** the object of such admiration: *The films of Charlie Chaplin have become a cult among many moviegoers.* **5a** a group or sect whose practices or beliefs are separated from generally accepted values and creeds. **b** the practices or beliefs of such a group or sect. [< Latin *cultus, -ūs* worship < *colere* cultivate, cherish]

cultch (kulch), *n.* **1** the stones, old shells, or other material laid down in an oyster bed, to which the young oysters attach themselves. **2** the spawn or young of oysters. Also, **culch.** [perhaps < Old French *culche* bed, layer, couch]

cul|te|ra|nis|mo (kül′tā rä nēs′mō, -nēz′-), *n.* a highly elaborate and affected style of writing cultivated in Spain during the 1500's and 1600's. [< Spanish *culteranismo* < *cultero* a person who affects great culture < *cultura* culture]

cult-fig|ure (kult′fig′yər, -ər), *n.* a person or figure that is the object of a cult or popular adulation: *We have not, so far, come up with a cult-figure to equal Father Christmas* (Punch).

cult|ic (kul′tik), *adj.* of or having to do with a cult or cults: *the numerous cultic sayings and ritualistic practices by which the believers in Naturism can be distinguished* (Time).

cul|ti|gen (kul′tə jən), *n.* **1** a cultivated plant of unknown or obscure origin, such as the cabbage. **2** any cultivated variety; cultivar: *Gardeners . . . have developed many cultigens, or garden varieties, of such common flowers as irises, orchids, roses, and tulips* (Harold N. Moldenke). [< *culti*(vate) + *-gen*]

cul|ti|pack (kul′tə pak′), *v.t., v.i.* to prepare (a seedbed) using a cultipacker. [back formation < *cultipacker*]

cul|ti|pack|er (kul′tə pak′ər), *n.* an agricultural tool used in the preparation of a seedbed, consisting of ridged rollers drawn by a tractor. [< *culti*(vation) + *packer*]

cult|ish (kul′tish), *adj.* **1** of or having to do with a cult. **2** suggestive or characteristic of a cult or cultists: *the cultish zeal of nature lovers.*

cult|ism (kul′tiz əm), *n.* adherence or devotion to a cult: *Though American intellectual history is rich in cultism, faddism, and large-scale self-deception, it offers no precedent for this tragic situation* (New Yorker). —**cult′ist,** *n., adj.*

cul|ti|va|bil|i|ty (kul′tə və bil′ə tē), *n.* the quality or condition of being cultivable.

cul|ti|va|ble (kul′tə və bəl), *adj.* that can be cultivated.

cul|ti|var (kul′tə vär, -vər), *n. Biology.* a variety produced by selective breeding; cultigen. [< *culti*(vate) + *var*(iant)]

cul|ti|vat|a|ble (kul′tə vā′tə bəl), *adj.* = cultivable.

cul|ti|vate (kul′tə vāt), *v.t.,* **-vat|ed, -vat|ing. 1** to prepare and use (land) to raise crops by plowing it, planting seeds, and taking care of the growing plants; till: *He cultivates a farm of 500 acres.* **2** to help (plants) grow by labor and care: *She cultivates most of her flowers from seed.* **3a** to loosen the ground around (growing plants) to kill weeds and help growth: *It took all afternoon to cultivate the corn.* **b** to loosen or break up (the ground) with a cultivator: *The farmer cultivated his fields just before planting time.* **4** *Figurative.* to improve or develop by education or training: *It takes time, thought, and effort to cultivate your mind.* **SYN:** train, refine. **5** *Figurative.* to give time, thought, and effort to; practice: *An artist cultivates his craft.* **SYN:** cherish. **6** *Figurative.* to promote the growth or development of (an art, science, or other undertaking or study). **SYN:** foster. **7** *Figurative.* to establish or strengthen: *Friendships cultivated in school often last a lifetime.* **8** *Figurative.* to seek the friendship of; seek better acquaintance with: *She cultivated people who could help her.* [< Medieval Latin *cultivare* (with English *-ate*[1]) < *cultivus* under cultivation < Latin *colere* till, cherish]

cul|ti|vat|ed (kul′tə vā′tid), *adj.* **1** prepared and used to raise crops: *A field of wheat is cultivated land; a pasture is not.* **2** produced by cultivation; not wild: *The American Beauty rose is a cultivated flower.* **3** *Figurative.* improved or developed: *a cultivated understanding.* **4** *Figurative.* cultured; refined: *cultivated tastes. France . . . still considers itself the most cultivated country in Europe* (New Yorker).

cul|ti|va|tion (kul′tə vā′shən), *n.* **1** the act of preparing land and growing crops by plowing, planting, and necessary care: *Better cultivation of soil will result in better crops.* **SYN:** husbandry. **2** the condition of being prepared by plowing, planting, and necessary care: *Only half the farm was under cultivation.* **3** *Figurative.* improvement or development. **4** *Figurative.* the act of giving time and thought to improving and developing (the body, mind, or manners): *Some adults stress the cultivation of good manners.* **5** *Figurative.* culture; result of improvement or growth through education and experience; refinement.

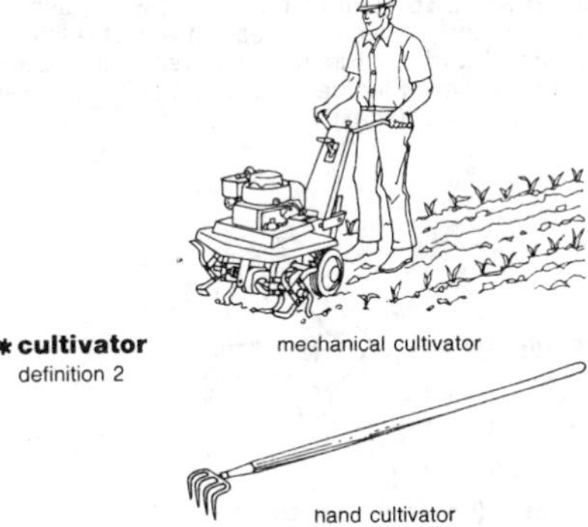

***cultivator**
definition 2

***cul|ti|va|tor** (kul′tə vā′tər), *n.* **1** a person or thing that cultivates: *Only the easygoing Malay, with no inherited business experience, has been left behind, following in most cases his traditional life as cultivator and fisherman* (Atlantic). **2** a tool or machine used to loosen the ground and destroy weeds. A cultivator is pulled or pushed between rows of growing plants.

cult of personality, a cult centering on the figure of a national leader or hero, especially one who encourages or enforces such a cultism, regarded in some Communist states as a negation of Marxist-Leninist doctrine.

cul|trate (kul′trāt), *adj.* sharp-edged and pointed, as a leaf or the beak of a bird. [< Latin *cultrātus* < *culter* knife]

cul|trat|ed (kul′trā tid), *adj.* = cultrate.

cult society, *Anthropology.* a society or social group held together by a religious motive.

cul|tur|a|ble (kul′chər ə bəl), *adj.* = cultivable.

cul|tur|al (kul′chər əl), *adj.* **1** having to do with culture; of development and training of the mind: *Literature, art, and music are cultural studies.* **2** at or in which cultural studies or pursuits are fostered: *[In the 1920's] Harlem became a black cultural center and attracted writers, musicians, artists, and entertainers* (Edgar Allan Toppin). **3** *Anthropology.* of or belonging to a culture: *cultural artifacts, cultural traits.* **4** of or having to do with the physical or mental developments of a culture: *cultural geography, cultural history.* **5** of or having to do with agriculture or horticulture: *The most widely used cultural controls are crop rotation, . . . raising insect-resistant breeds, and clearing the land of breeding grounds* (Albert A. LaPlante, Jr.). **6** of or having to do with biological cultures: *cultural methods for growing bacteria.* —**cul′tur|al|ly,** *adv.*

cultural anthropology, the branch of anthropology that deals with the origins, development, and functioning of human cultures: *In contrast to physical anthropology which . . . is concerned mainly with man's bodily structure, cultural anthropology deals with man's behavior and specifically with the ways in which human beings carry out the activities involved in daily living* (Beals and Hoijer). —**cultural anthropologist.**

cultural evolution, *Anthropology.* the gradual development of a culture through successive stages, usually of increasing complexity, as from savagery to barbarism and from barbarism to civilization.

cultural exchange, an exchange between two countries of visiting teachers, students, artists, athletes, or other groups, to promote mutual understanding by familiarizing the two peoples with one another's culture.

cul|tur|al|ize (kul′chər ə līz), *v.t.,* **-ized, -iz|ing.** to subject to the influence of civilization or culture: *to culturalize a primitive tribe.* —**cul′tur|al|i|za′tion,** *n.*

cultural lag, *Sociology.* the interval of time between technological change and social adaptation; culture lag.

cultural revolution, 1 a complete transformation of the institutions of a culture or society: *We need an alternative program, an alternative both to development and to merely political revolution. Let me call this alternative program either institutional or cultural revolution, because its aim is the transformation of both public and personal reality* (Ivan Illich). **2** Usually, **Cultural Revolution.** a major drive by Chinese Communists led by Mao Tse-tung, begun in 1966 and lasting several years, to enforce Maoist ideology and purge China of revisionist leaders and influences.

cultural revolutionary, an advocate or supporter of cultural revolution.

cul|tu|ra|ti (kul′chə rä′tē, -rā′tī), *n.pl.* the cultured class; cultured people. [< *culture,* patterned after *literati*]

cul|ture (kul′chər), *n., v.,* **-tured, -tur|ing.** —*n.* **1** fineness of feelings, thoughts, tastes, or manners; refinement: *He is a man of culture who appreciates the great art and fine sculpture in the museum.* **SYN:** breeding. See syn. under **education. 2** *Anthropology.* **a** the civilization of a given people or nation at a given time or over all time; its customs, its arts, and its conveniences: *The series of lectures included the culture of the Plains Indians, of the Pygmies, of the ancient Incas, and of modern Japan.* **b** socially inherited artifacts. **3** the development of the mind or body by education or training: *physical culture courses.* **4** the preparation of land to raise crops by plowing, planting, and necessary care; cultivation. **SYN:** tillage. **5a** the raising by proper or special care of

bees, fish, silkworms, oysters, or other plants or animals, for their natural products, especially as a source of food or profit: *the culture of the vine, the culture of silk.* **b** the rearing of plants or animals with the aim of improving them. **6** the growth of germs or bacteria in a special solution for scientific study or medicinal use. **b** the resulting colony or growth: *When cultures of this bacterium are kept for some time . . . their virulence becomes diminished* (Edward E. Klein).
—*v.t.* **1** = cultivate. **2** *Biology.* **a** to grow or propagate (bacteria, tissues, or other living matter) in a specially prepared artificial medium: *The organism has been successfully cultured.* **b** to use (a substance) as a source of or medium for culture: *to culture milk.*
[< Middle French *culture*, learned borrowing from Latin *cultūra* a tending < *colere* to till, cherish; see etym. under **cultivate**] —**cul'ture|less**, *adj.*

culture area, *Anthropology, Sociology.* the geographic area in which a culture complex is located.

culture center, *Anthropology, Sociology.* the place from which a culture trait or culture complex has emanated or where it is found in its most representative form; the center of a culture area.

culture complex, *Anthropology, Sociology.* a pattern of interrelated culture traits.

cul|tured (kul'chərd), *adj.* **1** having or showing culture; refined: *a cultured man of science.* SYN: polished, well-bred. **2** produced or raised by culture: *cultured oysters.* SYN: propagated.

culture diffusion, *Anthropology, Sociology.* the process by which a trait or pattern of culture spreads outward from the point of origin: *When missionaries are sent from one country to a "heathen" country, culture diffusion may take place by direction* (Emory S. Bogardus).

cultured pearl, a natural pearl produced by planting a tiny foreign body in an oyster to irritate its internal membranes and cause it to secrete a protective substance, that eventually hardens, around the irritating foreign body.

culture hero, *Anthropology.* any mythical hero of folklore and legend who is believed to be responsible for man's condition, advancement, and culture.

culture lag, = cultural lag.

culture medium, *Biology.* a solution or material in which microorganisms find nourishment and can reproduce: *The white, and even the yolk, of an egg provide a marvelous culture medium for microbes* (New York Times).

culture pearl, = cultured pearl.

culture shock, the disorientation a person experiences when thrust into a foreign culture or a new way of life: *The Chipewyans, apparently sunk in culture shock, have already made a shambles of the houses recently built for them* (Canadian Saturday Night).

culture trait, **1** *Anthropology, Sociology.* the basic unit or simplest element in a culture, as a particular artifact, a mode of dwelling, a type of worship, or a form of social organization. **2** any trait characteristic of or peculiar to a culture or society.

cul|ture-vul|ture (kul'chər vul'chər), *n. Slang.* a person who shows excessive interest in literature, art, or other intellectual pursuits; a cultural devotee or enthusiast: *I was a young library assistant . . . and an earnest culture-vulture* (London Times).

cul|tur|ist (kul'chər ist), *n.* **1** a person who cultivates. **2** a devotee of culture.

cul|tur|o|log|i|cal (kul'chər ə loj'ə kəl), *adj.* of or having to do with culturology. —**cul'tur|o|log'i|cal|ly**, *adv.*

cul|tur|ol|o|gist (kul'chə rol'ə jist), *n.* a person who studies culturology.

cul|tur|ol|o|gy (kul'chə rol'ə jē), *n.* the branch of anthropology that studies cultural institutions apart from or independently of the individuals who develop or are influenced by them.

cul|tus[1] (kul'təs), *n.* a religious cult. [< Latin *cultus;* see etym. under **cult**]

cul|tus[2] (kul'təs), *n.,* or **cultus cod**, a food fish of the North American Pacific coast; the ling cod. [< Chinook jargon *cultus* worthless]

cultus image or **statue**, any image or statue used in the cult of a deity.

cul|ver (kul'vər), *n.* a dove; pigeon. [Old English *culfre*]

cul|ver|in (kul'vər in), *n.* **1** a musket used in medieval times. **2** a long, heavy cannon used in the 1500's and 1600's. [< Middle French *coulevrine* < *coulevre* serpent < Latin *colubra* (names of reptiles were often given to early cannon)]

cul|ver|in|eer (kul'vər ə nir'), *n.* a soldier armed with or in charge of a culverin.

Cul|ver's root (kul'vərz), **1** the root of a plant of eastern North America belonging to the figwort family, used in medicines as a cathartic and emetic. **2** the plant itself. [< a Doctor *Culver,* who lived before the 1700's and used it in his practice]

cul|vert (kul'vərt), *n.* a drain or small channel for water crossing under a road, railroad, or canal. SYN: conduit. [origin uncertain]

cum (kum, kům), *prep.* with; together with; including: *a transfer of stocks cum dividend.* [< Latin *cum*]
▶**Cum** is often used in facetious or humorous combinations or hyphenated phrases: *a miniature ballet-cum-harmonica troupe* (New Yorker); *a perfect country-cum-sea holiday* (Observer).

Cu|mae|an sibyl (kyü mē'ən), a legendary woman seer of ancient times whose authority in matters of divination was acknowledged by the Romans and whose prophecies formed the Sibylline Books. [< *Cumae,* an ancient city in southwestern Italy + English *-an*]

Cu|ma|na (kü'mä nä'), *n., pl.* **-na** or **-nas**. **1** a member of a South American Indian tribe, prominent in the earlier history of Venezuela for its resistance to the efforts of missionaries and slave hunters. **2** the language of this tribe.

Cu|ma|na|go|to (kü'mä nä gō'tō), *n., pl.* **-to** or **-tos**. = Cumana.

cum|ber (kum'bər), *v., n.* —*v.t.* **1** = encumber. **2** *Obsolete.* to overwhelm, harass, or confound.
—*n.* **1** = encumbrance. **2** *Obsolete.* trouble, distress, or embarrassment.
[probably < Old French *combrer* impede < *combre* barrier, especially in a river; probably of Germanic origin] —**cum'ber|er**, *n.*

cum|ber|some (kum'bər səm), *adj.* **1** hard to manage; clumsy, unwieldy, or burdensome: *The armor worn by knights was often so cumbersome they had to be helped onto their horses.* SYN: ponderous, weighty. **2** inconvenient; embarrassing: *a cumbersome obligation.* SYN: onerous, troublesome. —**cum'ber|some|ly**, *adv.* —**cum'ber|some|ness**, *n.*

cum|bly (kum'blē), *n., pl.* **-blies**. a coarse woolen wrap or blanket worn in India as a cloak. [< Hindi *kamlī* < Sanskrit *kambala*]

cum|brance (kum'brəns), *n.* = encumbrance.

Cum|bri|an (kum'brē ən), *adj., n.* —*adj.* of or having to do with the county of Cumberland, in northwestern England.
—*n.* a native or inhabitant of Cumberland.
[< *Cumbria,* the ancient British kingdom which included Cumberland + *-an*]

cum|brous (kum'brəs), *adj.* = cumbersome. —**cum'brous|ly**, *adv.* —**cum'brous|ness**, *n.*

cum cp., with coupon.

cum div. or **cum d.**, with dividend.

cu|mene (kyü'mēn), *n.* a colorless liquid found in petroleum, soluble in alcohol and various organic solvents but not in water, used as an additive in aviation gasoline, in lacquers, and as a sterilizing agent for catgut; cumol. *Formula:* C_9H_{12} [< *cum*(in) + *-ene*]

cum|in (kum'ən), *n.* **1** a small plant native to the Mediterranean region, grown for its aromatic, seedlike fruits which are used in cookery and medicine. Cumin belongs to the parsley family. **2** its seedlike fruit. Also, **cummin**. [Old English *cymen* < Latin *cumīnum* < Greek *kýmīnon*]

cum int., with interest.

cum lau|de (kům lou'dē; kum lô'dē), **1** with distinction (added to the diploma of a person who has done especially good academic work): *to graduate cum laude.* **2** *Informal.* a graduate who has earned special praise or honor: *The place is crawling with Ph.D.'s and cum laudes* (New York Times). [< Latin *cum laude* with praise]

cum|mer (kum'ər), *n. Scottish.* **1** a godmother. **2** a woman companion. **3** a woman; girl or lass. **4** a witch. Also, **kimmer**. [< Old French *commere* < Late Latin *commāter* < Latin *com-* along with + *māter* mother]

***cum|mer|bund** (kum'ər bund), *n.* a wide sash worn around the waist, instead of a vest. Also, **kummerbund**. [< Hindustani, Persian *kamarband* < Arabic *kamar* leather belt (with pockets) + Persian *band* band(age)]

***cummerbund**

cum|min (kum'ən), *n.* = cumin.

cum|ol (kum'ōl), *n.* = cumene.

cum pri|vi|le|gi|o (kum priv'ə lē'jē ō), *Latin.* with privilege; authorized.

cum|quat (kum'kwot), *n.* = kumquat.

cum|shaw (kum'shô), *n.* (formerly, in Chinese ports) a present or tip. [< Chinese (Amoy) *kam siā,* pronunciation of *kan hsieh* grateful thanks]

cu|mu|late (*v.* kyü'myə lāt; *adj.* kyü'myə lit, -lāt), *v.,* **-lat|ed, -lat|ing**, *adj.* —*v.t., v.i.* to heap up; accumulate.
—*adj.* heaped up.
[< Latin *cumulāre* (with English *-ate*[1]) < *cumulus* a heap] —**cu'mu|la'tion**, *n.*

cu|mu|la|tive (kyü'myə lā'tiv, -lə-), *adj.* **1** heaped up; increasing or growing by additions; accumulated: *The cumulative effects of many illnesses made him a weak man.* **2** *Law.* imposed successively upon the same defendant for the same or for an additional offense: *cumulative penalties, a cumulative sentence.* —**cu'mu|la'tive|ly**, *adv.* —**cu'mu|la'tive|ness**, *n.*

cumulative dividend, a dividend that must be added to future dividends if it is not paid when due.

cumulative evidence, evidence that reinforces or supports previous evidence.

cumulative preferred stock, preferred stock on which the dividends, if not paid, accumulate.

cumulative stock, stock bearing cumulative dividends that increase or grow by successive additions.

cumulative voting, a system of voting where each voter has as many votes as there are persons to be elected. The voter may cast all his votes for one candidate or may divide them between several candidates.

cu|mu|li|form (kyü'myə lə fôrm), *adj.* having the form of cumulus clouds.

cu|mu|lo-cir|rus (kyü'myə lō sir'əs), *n., pl.* **-cir|ri** (-sir'ī). a cloud that is partly cumulus and partly cirrus.

cu|mu|lo-nim|bus or **cu|mu|lo|nim|bus** (kyü'myə lō nim'bəs), *n., pl.* **-bus|es, -bi** (-bī). a massive, vertical, cloud formation with peaks that sometimes resemble high mountains and sometimes spread out to resemble anvils, occurring at heights of between 1600 and over 20,000 feet; thundercloud.

cu|mu|lose (kyü'myə lōs), *adj.* **1** having a high content of humus: *cumulose soils.* **2** full of cumuli.

cu|mu|lo-stra|tus or **cu|mu|lo|stra|tus** (kyü'myə lō strā'təs), *n., pl.* **-ti** (-tī). a cumulus cloud with its base spread out horizontally like a stratus cloud.

cu|mu|lous (kyü'myə ləs), *adj.* having the form of a cumulus cloud.

cu|mu|lus (kyü'myə ləs), *n., pl.* **-li** (-lī). **1** a vertical cloud formation made up of detached clouds, rounded at the top and flat at the bottom. Cumuli are usually seen in fair weather and occur at heights of between 1600 and 20,000 feet. See picture under **cloud**. **2** a heap; pile. [< Latin *cumulus* heap]

Cu|na (kü'nə), *n., pl.* **-na** or **-nas**. **1** a member of a Caribbean Indian tribe inhabiting parts of Panama and nearby islands. The Cuna have an unusual number of albinos among them. **2** the Chibchan language of this tribe.

cu|nab|u|la (kyü nab'yə lə), *n.* **1** = cradle. **2** *Figurative.* the earliest abode: *the cunabula of the human race.* [< Latin *cūnābula* < *cunae*]

Cu|nard|er (kyü när'dər), *n.* any steamship of a line founded by Sir Samuel Cunard in 1839, originally to carry mail between Liverpool and New York.

cunc|ta|tion (kungk tā'shən), *n.* tardy action; delay. [< Latin *cūnctātiō, -ōnis* < *cūnctārī* delay]

cunc|ta|tive (kungk'tə tiv), *adj.* delaying.

cunc|ta|tor (kungk tā'tər), *n.* delayer.

cunc|ta|to|ry (kungk'tə tôr'ē, -tōr'-), *adj.* delaying.

cunc|tip|o|tent (kungk tip'ə tənt), *adj. Archaic.* all-powerful; omnipotent. [< Late Latin *cunctipotens, -entis* < Latin *cunctus* all + *potens, -entis* potent]

cu|ne|al (kyü'nē əl), *adj.* wedgelike; wedge-shaped. [< Latin *cuneus* wedge + English *-al*[1]]

cu|ne|ate (kyü'nē it, -āt), *adj.* tapering to a point at the base; wedge-shaped: *a cuneate leaf.* [< Latin *cuneātus* wedge-shaped < *cuneus* wedge] —**cu'ne|ate|ly**, *adv.*

cu|ne|at|ed (kyü'nē ā'tid), *adj.* = cuneate.

cu|ne|at|ic (kyü'nē at'ik), *adj.* = wedge-shaped.

***cuneiform**
n., definition 1
P A R SA I YA
translation: "Persia"

***cu|ne|i|form** (kyü nē'ə fôrm, kyü'nē-), *adj., n.* —*adj.* **1** wedge-shaped. **2** composed of cuneiform inscriptions: *cuneiform tablets.* **3** *Anatomy.* of or denoting any wedge-shaped bone.
—*n.* **1** the wedge-shaped characters used in the writing of ancient Babylonia, Assyria, Persia, and some other areas of the Near East: *The decipherment of cuneiform was not accepted by all*

informed students of antiquity until well after the end of the nineteenth century (New Yorker).
2 *Anatomy.* a wedge-shaped bone, especially one of three bones of the human ankle.
[< Latin *cuneus* wedge + English *-form*]

cu|ne|i|form|ist (kyü nē′ə fôr′mist, kyü′nē-), *n.* a student of or an expert in cuneiform writing.

cu|nic|u|lus (kyü nik′yə ləs), *n., pl.* **-li** (-lī). an underground passage, such as a burrow or a drain. [< Latin *cunīculus*]

cun|ner (kun′ər), *n.* either of two small Atlantic fishes allied to the wrasses, used for food. [origin uncertain]

cun|ni|lin|gus (kun′ə ling′gəs), *n.* oral stimulation of the female genital organs. [< New Latin *cunnilingus* < Latin *cunnus* vulva + *lingere* lick]

cun|ning (kun′ing), *adj., n.* — *adj.* **1** clever in deceiving; sly: *a cunning fox. The cunning thief outwitted the police and got away.* **SYN**: crafty, artful, guileful. See syn. under **sly**. **2** made, showing, or done with skill, knowledge, or cleverness: *The old watch was a fine example of cunning workmanship.* **SYN**: ingenious. **3** skillful; clever in doing: *With cunning hand the sculptor shaped the little statue. Esau was a cunning hunter* (Genesis 25:27). **SYN**: expert. **4** *Informal.* pretty and dear; cute: *Kittens and babies are cunning.* **SYN**: attractive.
— *n.* **1** skillful or sly ways of getting what one needs or wants, or of escaping one's enemies: *A fox has a great deal of cunning.* **2** skill; cleverness: *The old sculptor's hand never lost its cunning.*
[Old English *cunnung* < *cunnan* know (how). See related etym. at **can**[1].] — **cun′ning|ly**, *adv.*
— **cun′ning|ness**, *n.*
— *Syn. n.* **1 Cunning, craft** mean skill in getting what one wants. **Cunning** suggests slyness and the use of clever tricks or false appearances to hide one's real purpose and get the better of others: *He has the cunning of a cat with a mouse.* **Craft** suggests skill in deceiving others by making clever and artful plans and using underhand methods: *His swindle was planned with deliberate craft.*

cup (kup), *n., v.,* **cupped, cup|ping.** — *n.* **1** a hollow, rounded dish to drink from. Most cups have handles. **2** as much as a cup holds; cupful. In cooking directions, a cup equals a half pint. *She drank a cup of milk.* **3** a cup together with its contents. **4** anything shaped like a cup. The petals of some flowers form a cup. **5** an ornamental cup, vase, or other trophy, given to the winner of a contest: *the Davis Cup.* **6** the bowllike part of a goblet or wineglass that holds the contents. **7** *Figurative.* a drink or food served in a cup; mixture: *a claret cup, a cider cup, a fruit cup.* **SYN**: cocktail. **8a** the cup used in Communion. **SYN**: chalice. **b** the wine used in Communion. **SYN**: chalice. **9** *Figurative.* something to endure or experience; fate: *the bitter cup of defeat. ... to drink the bitterest cup of humiliation* (James Anthony Froude). **10** = cupping glass. **11** in golf: **a** = hole. **b** the metal lining of the hole. **12** either of two pouchlike supports for the breasts in a brassiere.
— *v.t.* **1** to shape like a cup: *She cupped her hands to catch the ball. The old man cupped a hand behind one ear.* **2** to take or put in a cup: *She cupped the flour from a bag and poured it into a mixing bowl.* **3** to take blood from (a person) by the process of cupping.
— *v.i.* **1** to become cup-shaped. **2** to use a cupping glass.
cup of tea, *Informal.* **a** just what one likes; something suited to one's taste, interest, or pleasure: *Human nature being what it is, [some] people are simply not other people's cup of tea* (Time). **b** a sort of thing; matter: *What actually did happen was another cup of tea altogether.*
cups, the drinking of intoxicating beverages: *the jolly Prince ... loving his cups and his ease* (Thackeray).
in one's cups, drunk: *She used to come home in her cups, and break the china* (John Arbuthnot).
[Old English *cuppe* < Late Latin *cuppa* < Latin *cūpa* tub] — **cup′like′**, *adj.*

Cup (kup), *n. Astronomy.* the southern constellation Crater.

cup and ball, **1** a toy consisting of a cup at the end of a stem to which a ball is attached by a string, the object being to toss the ball and catch it in the cup. **2** the game played with this.

cup-and-ring (kup′ən ring′), *adj.* of or having to do with prehistoric stone monuments marked with cuplike depressions surrounded by concentric rings.

cup anemometer, an anemometer consisting of three or four hemispherical cups for measuring wind velocity and pressure.

cup|bear|er (kup′bãr′ər), *n.* **1** (formerly) a person who filled and served cups of wine at banquets. **2** (formerly) a noble who tasted the wine before handing it to his master: *Nehemiah ... held the highly honored position of cupbearer to King Artaxerxes I in Persia* (Walter G. Williams).

cup|board (kub′ərd), *n.* **1** a closet or cabinet with shelves, especially for dishes and food supplies. **2** *British.* any small closet.

cupboard love, a love inspired by considerations of what one can get with it; interested affection.

cup|cake (kup′kāk′), *n.* a small cake baked in a pan shaped like a cup.

cup coral, any one of various cup-shaped forms of coral formed by the development of a single polyp.

cu|pel (kyü′pəl, kyü pel′), *n., v.,* **-peled, -pel|ing** or (*especially British*) **-pelled, -pel|ling.** — *n.* **1** a small, cuplike, porous dish used in assaying usually made of bone ash. **2** a receptacle in which silver is refined.
— *v.t.* to heat or refine in a cupel.
[< a Latinized spelling of Middle French *coupelle* (diminutive) < Old French *coupe* < Late Latin *cuppa* cup < Latin *cūpa* tub] — **cu′pel|er** or (*especially British*) **cu|pel′ler**, *n.*

cu|pel|la|tion (kyü′pə lā′shən), *n.* the use of a cupel in assaying or refining metals.

cup|fer|ron (kyüp′fer′ən), *n.* a crystalline compound soluble in water, alcohol, and ether, used especially as a reagent in separation of copper and iron from other metals. *Formula:* $C_6H_9N_3O_2$
[< Latin *cuprum* copper + *ferrum* iron]

cup|ful (kup′fůl), *n., pl.* **-fuls.** as much as a cup can hold. In cooking, a cupful equals a half pint or 8 oz.

cup fungus, any one of various fleshy ascomycetes found especially on decayed logs and leaves, having cup-shaped fruiting bodies.

Cu|phic (kyü′fik), *adj.* = Cufic.

cup|hold|er (kup′hōl′dər), *n.* the winner of a cup in a sports contest; champion.

***Cu|pid** (kyü′pid), *n.* the Roman god of love, son of Venus and either Mercury or Mars. The Greeks called him Eros. Cupid is usually represented as a winged boy with bow and arrows. [< Latin *Cupīdo* (literally) desire < *cupere* desire]

***Cupid**

cu|pid (kyü′pid), *n.* a figure of a winged child used as a symbol of love: *a valentine covered with little cupids.* [< *Cupid*] — **cu′pid|like′**, *adj.*

cu|pid|i|ty (kyü pid′ə tē), *n.* eager desire to possess something; greed: *They gazed with envy and cupidity at the noble mansions* (Cardinal Newman). **SYN**: avarice. [< Latin *cupiditās* < *cupidus* desirous < *cupere* desire]

Cu|pid's bow (kyü′pidz), **1** lips shaped like the double-curved bow of Cupid. **2** the double-curved bow shown in classical art.

***cu|po|la** (kyü′pə lə), *n., v.,* **-laed, la|ing.** — *n.* **1** a rounded roof; dome: *The Capitol at Washington, D.C. has a cupola.* **2** a small dome or tower on a roof, especially a small, often squarish tower on the roof of a barn with louvered sides to let in air. **3** a domelike thing or part. **4** *Geology.* a domelike rock formation projecting from the upper part of a batholith. **5** a small furnace used mainly for melting iron. **6** = headhouse.
— *v.t.* to construct or furnish with or as if with a cupola or cupolas: *cupolaed band shell.*
[< Italian *cupola* < Late Latin *cūpula* (diminutive) < Latin *cūpa* tub, cask. See etym. of doublet **cupule.**]

***cupola**
definition 2

cup|pa (kup′ə), *n. British Slang.* a cup of tea: *After the game there is never more than a quick cuppa before the visitors bundle back into the bus* (Sunday Times).

cupped (kupt), *adj.* = cup-shaped.

cup|per (kup′ər), *n.* a person who performs the operation of cupping.

cup|ping (kup′ing), *n.* the application of glass cups to the skin to create a partial vacuum, usually through heat, in order to draw blood to the surface of the skin.

cupping glass, a glass vessel in which a partial vacuum is created, used in cupping.

cup plant, a tall, yellow-flowered plant of the composite family, found in the United States, having large, opposite leaves, the upper pairs of which form a cuplike cavity.

cup|py (kup′ē), *adj.* **1** = cup-shaped. **2** full of cuplike cavities. **3** (of trees or timber) having cracks or fissures between the annual rings.

cu|pram|mo|ni|um (kyü′prə mō′nē əm), *n.,* or **cuprammonium rayon**, a rayon made by treating cellulose in a solution of ammonia and copper hydroxide: *Cuprammonium ... is widely used in suit and coat linings and in very sheer dress and blouse fabrics* (Wall Street Journal). [< Latin *cuprum* copper[1] + New Latin *ammonium*]

cuprammonium solution, **1** a solution of copper and ammonia. **2** = Schweitzer's reagent.

cu|pre|a bark (kyü′prē ə), the coppery-red bark of a South American tree and certain related trees, one of the sources of quinine. [< Latin *cuprea*, feminine of *cupreus;* see etym. under **cupreous**]

cu|pre|ous (kyü′prē əs), *adj.* **1** of or containing copper. **2** copper-colored. [< Latin *cupreus* (with English *-ous*) < *cuprum* copper[1]]

cu|pres|sin|e|ous (kyü′pre sin′ē əs), *adj.* of or having to do with the cypress family of trees and shrubs. [< New Latin *Cupressineae* the cypress tribe. (< Latin *cupressus* cypress) + English *-ous*]

cu|pric (kyü′prik), *adj. Chemistry.* of or containing copper, especially with a valence of two. [< Latin *cuprum* copper + English *-ic*]

cupric chloride, a green, crystalline compound used as a mordant in dyeing, in the manufacture of indelible inks, and as a wood preservative. *Formula:* $CuCl_2 \cdot 2H_2O$

cupric oxide, a black, powdery or granular compound used to desulfurize petroleum oils, as a coloring agent in ceramic glazes, and in artificial gems. *Formula:* CuO

cupric sulfate, = blue vitriol.

cu|prif|er|ous (kyü prif′ər əs), *adj.* yielding copper.

cu|prite (kyü′prīt), *n.* a mineral consisting of native cuprous oxide, occurring in crystals and granular masses, and forming an important ore of copper. *Formula:* Cu_2O

cu|proid (kyü′proid), *n.* a solid contained under twelve equal triangles, formed by erecting a pyramid on each of the triangular faces of a tetrahedron. [< Latin *cuprum* copper + English *-oid* (because the form occurs in the mineral tetrahedrite, a sulfide of copper)]

cu|pro|mag|ne|site (kyü′prō mag′nə sīt), *n.* a hydrous sulfate of copper and magnesium.

cu|pro|man|ga|nese (kyü′prō mang′gə nēs, -nēz), *n.* an alloy of copper and manganese.

cu|pro|nick|el (kyü′prō nik′əl), *n.* an alloy of copper and nickel.

cu|prous (kyü′prəs), *adj. Chemistry.* of or containing copper, especially with a valence of one. [< Latin *cuprum* copper + English *-ous*]

cuprous chloride, a white to grayish-white, crystalline compound used as a condensing agent for soaps, fats, and oils, in purifying acetylene, and as an insectide. *Formula:* CuCl

cuprous oxide, a dark-red, crystalline compound used in paints for ship bottoms, in making red glazes on pottery and glassware, and in treating the seeds of various vegetables to prevent damping-off. *Formula:* Cu_2O

cu|prum (kyü′prəm), *n. Latin.* copper. *Abbr:* Cu (no period).

cups (kups), *n.pl.* See under **cup**.

cup sculpture, a type of prehistoric sculpture in which cuplike depressions surrounded by concentric rings were carved into stone or rock; cup-and-ring sculpture.

cup|seed (kup′sēd′), *n.* a tall, climbing vine of the southern United States, bearing a large drupe which contains a bony seed hollowed out like a cup on one side.

cup shake, a crack or fissure sometimes occurring between the annual rings of a tree or timber.

cup-shaped (kup′shāpt), *adj.* shaped like a cup; cuplike.

cup tie, *British.* the deciding game or match played in competition for a cup.

cup-tied (kup′tīd′), *adj. British.* participating in a cup tie.

cu|pu|la (kyü′pyə lə), *n., pl.* **-lae** (-lē). **1** = cupule. **2** a jellylike substance on the crista of the semicircular canals. [< Latin *cūpula* cupule]

cu|pu|lar (kyü′pyə lər), *adj.* = cupulate.

Pronunciation Key: hat, āge, cãre, fär; let, ēqual, tėrm; it, īce; hot, ōpen, ôrder; oil, out; cup, pùt, rüle; child; long; thin; ᴛʜen; zh, measure; ə represents **a** in about, **e** in taken, **i** in pencil, **o** in lemon, **u** in circus.

cu|pu|late (kyü′pyə lāt), *adj.* shaped like a cupule; having a cupule.
cu|pule (kyü′pyül), *n.* **1** a cup-shaped involucre, such as that of the acorn. **2** the cup-shaped receptacle of certain fungi. **3** a cup-shaped sucker or similar part in an animal. [< Latin *cūpula.* See etym. of doublet **cupola.**]
cur (kėr), *n.* **1** a worthless dog of mixed breed; mongrel: *That snappish, ill-tempered cur bit the postman.* **2** *Figurative.* an ill-bred, contemptible person. [Middle English *curre,* earlier *kurdogge,* perhaps < Scandinavian (compare dialectal Swedish *kurre* house dog)]
cur., 1 currency. 2 current (this month).
cur|a|bil|i|ty (kyůr′ə bil′ə tē), *n.* the fact of admitting cure; curable character.
cur|a|ble (kyůr′ə bəl), *adj.* that can be cured: *With proper care and medicine tuberculosis is a curable disease.* —**cur′a|bly,** *adv.* —**cur′a|ble-ness,** *n.*
cu|ra|çao (kyůr′ə sō′), *n.* a liqueur or cordial made from the dried peel of a bitter kind of orange. [< *Curaçao,* an island in the West Indies (perhaps where first made)]
cu|ra|çoa (kyůr′ə sō′), *n.* = curaçao.
cu|ra|cy (kyůr′ə sē), *n., pl.* **-cies.** the position, rank, or work of a curate: *He was ordained ... to a curacy of St. Mary's, Leicester* (London Times).
cur|agh (kėr′əH, -ə), *n. Scottish and Irish.* currach.
cu|ra|ra (kyů rä′rə), *n.* = curare.
cu|ra|re or **cu|ra|ri** (kyů rä′rē), *n.* **1** a poisonous, blackish, resinlike substance obtained from certain tropical plants, used by certain South American Indians to poison arrows. It is employed in medicine to relax muscles during operations, and in electric-shock therapy. **2** a plant yielding this substance. [< Spanish *curaré* or Portuguese *curare* < the Tupi name]
cu|ra|rine (kyůr′ə rēn, -ər in), *n.* a bitter poisonous alkaloid obtained from curare. *Formula:* $C_{19}H_{26}N_2O$ [< *curar*(e) + *-ine*[2]]
cu|ra|rize (kyůr′ə rīz, kyů rä′-), *v.t.,* **-rized, -rizing.** to drug with curare. —**cu′ra|ri|za′tion,** *n.*
cu|ras|sow (kyůr′ə sō, kyů ras′ō), *n.* any one of several large, turkeylike, arboreal birds found in tropical South and Central America. [< *Curaçao,* an island in the West Indies]
cu|rat|age (kyůr′ət ij), *n.* the house or residence provided for a curate.
cu|rate (kyůr′it), *n.* **1** a clergyman who assists a pastor, rector, or vicar. **2** *Archaic.* a clergyman with pastoral duties.
the curate's egg, *British Informal.* something or someone of mixed quality (good and bad in parts): *Wintle was rather like the curate's egg, but Wilkinson played a quietly intelligent game* (London Times).
[< Medieval Latin *curatus* (one) having the cure of souls < *cura* cure (of souls) < Latin *cūra* care, charge. See etym. of doublet **curé.**]
cu|rat|ic (kyů rat′ik), *adj.* of or having to do with a curate.
cur|a|tive (kyůr′ə tiv), *adj., n.* —*adj.* having the power to cure; tending to cure; curing; remedial: *We do not seek a peace other than one which will be curative and creative* (Time).
—*n.* a means of curing; remedy. —**cur′a|tive|ly,** *adv.* —**cur′a|tive|ness,** *n.*
cu|ra|tor (kyů rā′tər; *for 3 also* kyůr′ə tər), *n.* **1** a person in charge of all or part of a museum, library, art gallery, zoo, or other establishment or collection; custodian. **2** a manager; overseer; steward. **3** *Law.* a guardian of a minor or of a person declared legally unfit. [< Anglo-French *curatour,* Old French *curateur,* learned borrowing from Latin *cūrātor* < *cūrāre* care for < *cūra* care]
cu|ra|to|ri|al (kyůr′ə tôr′ē əl, -tōr′-), *adj.* of or having to do with a curator.
cu|ra|tor|ship (kyů rā′tər ship, kyůr′ə-), *n.* the office or position of a curator: *a Museum of Natural History curatorship of invertebrate fossils* (New Yorker).
cu|ra|to|ry (kyůr′ə tôr′ē, -tōr′-), *n., pl.* **-ries. 1** the office of a curator. **2** a group of curators.
curb[1] (kėrb), *n., v.* —*n.* **1** Also, *especially British,* **kerb.** a raised border, especially one of concrete or stone, along the edge of a pavement or sidewalk, or around the top of a well; coaming: *He parked his car close to the curb.* **2** an enclosing framework or border supporting the base or outer edge of a dome, shaft, or the like. **3** *Figurative.* a check; restraint: *to put a curb on one's spending. Put a curb on your temper.* SYN: control. **4** a chain or strap fastened to a horse's bit and passing under its lower jaw. When the reins are pulled tight, the curb checks the horse. **5** a hard swelling below the hock of a horse's leg, often causing lameness. **6** = curb market.
—*v.t.* **1** to hold in check; restrain: *You must curb your laughter when you are in church. My hunger was curbed by the snack. So is the will of a living daughter curbed by the will of a dead father* (Shakespeare). SYN: See syn. under **check. 2** to put a curb on (a horse). **3** to provide with a curb. [< Old French *courbe,* ultimately < Latin *curvus* bent, crooked, curved] —**curb′a|ble,** *adj.* —**curb′-less,** *adj.*
curb[2] (kėrb), *v.t., v.i. Obsolete.* to curve; bend; bow. [earlier *courbe* < French *courber* to bend; influenced by *curve*]
curb bit, a horse's bit having a curb.
curb chain, a chain attached to a horse's bit; curb.
curb|er (kėr′bər), *n.* **1** a person or thing that curbs. **2** stones or other material forming a curb (of a street).
curb exchange, = curb market.
curb|ing (kėr′bing), *n.* **1** material for making a curb (for a street). **2** a raised border of concrete; curb.
curb key, a telegraphic key used in operating submarine cables, designed to prevent confusion of signals; curb sender.
curb market, a market for the sale of securities not dealt in on the regular stock exchange. The original curb markets were formed on city sidewalks and streets.
curb plate, 1 *Architecture.* **a** the wall plate of a circular or elliptical dome or roof. **b** the plate which receives the feet of the upper rafters of a curb roof. **2** the cylindrical frame of a well.
curb roof, a roof having two slopes on each side, with the lower one being the steeper. The gambrel roof and mansard roof are two types.
curb sender, = curb key.
curb service, service provided by an establishment to patrons seated in parked cars; drive-in service.
curb|side (kėrb′sīd′), *n., adj.* —*n.* the area of sidewalk at or near a curb: *a car hugging the curbside.*
—*adj.* **1** at or near a curb: *We went to a restaurant with curbside service.* **2** of the street; earthy: *Argentina has its Italianate curbside slang, Mexico has its Indian* (Time).
curb|stone (kėrb′stōn′), *n., adj.* —*n.* a stone or stones forming a curb; raised border of concrete or stone along the edge of a pavement or sidewalk. Also, *especially British,* **kerbstone.**
—*adj.* **1** at or near the curb; curbside. **2** *Informal.* homespun: *curbstone philosophy.*
curch (kėrch), *n. Scottish.* a kerchief for the head. [back formation < *curches,* plural < Old French *couvrechies,* plural of *couvrechief;* see etym. under **kerchief**]
cur|cu|li|o (kėr kyü′lē ō), *n., pl.* **-li|os.** any one of various snout beetles, especially a kind that destroys fruit. [< Latin *curculiō* corn worm, weevil]
cur|cu|ma (kėr′kyů mə), *n.* any one of various tropical plants of the ginger family, with perennial tuberous roots from which turmeric and zedoary are obtained. [< Medieval Latin *curcuma* < Arabic *kurkum* saffron, turmeric]
cur|cu|min (kėr′kyů min), *n.* **1** a yellow, crystalline substance, the coloring matter of turmeric. **2** an artificial yellow dye. [< *curcum*(a) + *-in*]
curd (kėrd), *n., v.* —*n.* **1** Often, **curds.** the thick part of milk that separates from the watery part when milk sours. Cheese is made from curds. **2** any similar food obtained by fermentation: *soybean curds.*
—*v.t., v.i.* to form into curds; curdle.
[earlier *crud,* Middle English *crudde*]
cur|dle (kėr′dəl), *v.t., v.i.,* **-dled, -dling. 1** to form into curds; coagulate: *Milk curdles when kept too long in a warm place.* **2** to thicken.
curdle the blood. See under **blood.**
[< *curd,* verb + *-le* (frequentative)]
curd|y (kėr′dē), *adj.* **1** full of curds. **2** like curdled milk.
cure (kyůr), *v.,* **cured, cur|ing,** *n.* —*v.t.* **1** to bring back to health; make well: *The doctor used strong medicine to cure the sick child of pneumonia.* (*Figurative.*) *Time cured him of his grief* (Washington Irving). **2** to get rid of: *Rest in bed will often cure a cold.* (*Figurative.*) *Only great determination can cure a bad habit like smoking.* (*Figurative.*) *What can't be cured must be endured* (Robert Burton). **3** to preserve (meat, fish, hide, lumber, or other material or food), especially by drying, salting, smoking, or pickling: *Tobacco leaves are hung in bunches to be cured before being prepared for smoking.* **4** to treat (concrete) by watering or chemical means in order to develop hardness and imperviousness. **5** to vulcanize (rubber): *The curing of rubber products by radiation has been known for a good many years* (New York Herald Tribune).
—*v.i.* **1** to be or become cured: *Tobacco leaves are often hung in barns to cure.* **2** to bring about a cure.
—*n.* **1** the act or fact of curing. **2** a means of curing; treatment intended to relieve or remove disease or any bad condition: *a rest cure, a cure for sore eyes,* (*Figurative.*) *a cure for laziness.* **3** a medicine that is a means of curing or relieving; remedy: *Quinine is a cure for malaria.* **4** a successful medical treatment; restoration to health. **5a** spiritual charge; religious care. **b** the office or district of a curate; curacy: *A small cure was offered me* (Oliver Goldsmith). **6a** a method or process of curing meat, fish, hide, lumber, or other material or food. **b** a quantity of meat, fish, hide, lumber, or other material or food, cured at one time or in one place.
[< Old French *curer* < Latin *cūrāre* care for < *cūra* care] —**cur′er,** *n.*
—*Syn. v.t.* **1, 2 Cure, heal, remedy** mean to make well or right. **Cure** applies particularly to bringing back to health after sickness or disease: *The new treatment cured his asthma; it cured him of asthma.* **Heal** means to make whole, and is used particularly of wounds, burns, or sickness: *This medicine will heal that cut.* **Remedy** means to put right, and applies to curing or relieving any unhealthy physical or mental condition: *The operation remedied his twisted foot.*
cu|ré (kyů rā′; *French* ky rā′), *n.* a parish priest. [< Old French *cure* < Medieval Latin *curatus* (one) having the cure of souls < *cura* cure (of souls) < Latin *cūra* care, charge. See etym. of doublet **curate.**]
cure-all (kyůr′ôl′), *n.* a remedy supposed to cure all diseases or evils; panacea: (*Figurative.*) *The toll road is only suitable through a densely populated area, is not a cure-all to the nationwide need for better roads* (Time).
cure|less (kyůr′lis), *adj.* without cure; incurable. —**cure′less|ly,** *adv.*
cu|ret|tage (kyů ret′ij, kyůr′ə täzh′), *n.* a scraping or cleaning with a curette; the process of curetting. [< French *curetage* < *curette;* see etym. under **curette**]
***cu|rette** or **cu|ret** (kyů ret′), *n., v.,* **-ret|ted, -ret-ting.** —*n.* a small, scoop-shaped surgical instrument used to scrape the walls of a body cavity.
—*v.t.* to scrape with a curette: *to curette a sinus.* [< Middle French *curette* < *curer* cleanse]

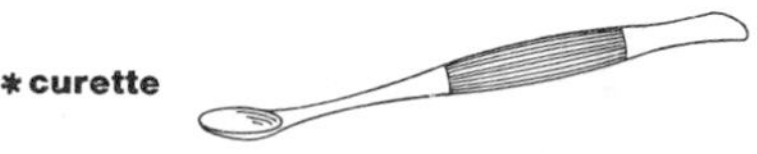
***curette**

cu|rette|ment (kyů ret′mənt), *n.* = curettage.
cur|few (kėr′fyü), *n.* **1a** a period of time, usually starting in the evening, during which the inhabitants of a city or other area are restricted to their homes or not permitted to appear in certain public places, especially in wartime: *Using a Jordanian law, a 21-hour curfew has been imposed in all the towns* (London Times). **b** a rule requiring certain persons to be off the streets or at home before a fixed time: *The mayor has established a 10 P.M. curfew for children in our city.* **2a** the ringing of a bell at a fixed time in the evening as a signal. In the Middle Ages, it was a signal to put out lights and cover fires in the camp or in the town. **b** a bell ringing such a signal: *Every night at nine the curfew rang. The curfew tolls the knell of parting day* (Thomas Gray). **c** the time when a curfew begins or is rung: *Everyone has to be in by curfew.* [< Anglo-French *coeverfu,* Old French *covrefeu* < *couvrir* cover (< Latin *cooperīre*) + *feu* fire < Latin *focus* hearth]
cur|fewed (kėr′fyüd), *adj.* regulated by a curfew: *a curfewed city.*
cu|ri|a (kyůr′ē ə), *n., pl.* **cu|ri|ae** (kyůr′ē ē). **1** a medieval council or law court. **2** the meeting place of the ancient Roman senate. **3** one of the ten divisions of each of the three ancient Roman tribes. **4** the meeting place of one of these divisions. **5** the senate of ancient Italian towns. [< Latin *cūria* < unrecorded *co-viria* gathering of male inhabitants < *co-* together + *vir* man]
Cu|ri|a (kyůr′ē ə), *n.* a group of high officials who assist the Pope in the government and administration of the Roman Catholic Church; the papal court of the Roman Catholic Church; Curia Romana.
cu|ri|al (kyůr′ē əl), *adj., n.* —*adj.* of or having to do with a curia.
—*n.* a member of an ancient Roman or an Italian curia.
cu|ri|al|ism (kyůr′ē ə liz′əm), *n.* a curial system, especially the policy or system of the papal Curia.
cu|ri|al|ist (kyůr′ē ə list), *n.* **1** a member of the papal Curia. **2** a supporter of the policy or authority of the papal Curia.
cu|ri|al|is|tic (kyůr′ē ə lis′tik), *adj.* of or having to do with curialists or curialism.
curia re|gis (rē′jis), the king's court or central administration in early Norman and Angevin England and Capetian France. [< Medieval Latin *curia regis* < Latin *cūria* (see etym. under **curia**), *rēx, rēgis* king]

Curia Ro|ma|na (rō mā′nə), the Curia.
cu|ri|ate (kyůr′ē āt, -it), *adj.* of or relating to the ancient Roman curiae.
cu|rie (kyůr′ē, kyů rē′), *n.* the unit for measuring the intensity of radioactivity. It is the quantity of a radioactive isotope which decays at the rate of 3.7×10^{10} disintegrations per second. Originally, it was the amount of radioactivity given off by one gram of radium. *The most powerful modern atomic bomb should release no more than 10 billion curies* (Scientific American). *Abbr:* c. [< Pierre *Curie,* 1859-1906, a French chemist and physicist and codiscoverer of radium]
Curie constant, *Physics.* the result of multiplying the magnetic susceptibility per unit mass of a paramagnetic substance by the absolute temperature. [see etym. under **curie**]
Curie point, *Physics.* the temperature above which a ferromagnetic substance, such as iron, loses its magnetization or becomes paramagnetic. [see etym. under **curie**]
Curie's law, *Physics.* the law that the magnetic susceptibility of gases is inversely proportional to the absolute temperature. [see etym. under **curie**]
Curie temperature, = Curie point.
cu|ri|o (kyůr′ē ō), *n., pl.* **-ri|os**. an object valued as a curiosity; a strange, rare, or novel object: *Marco Polo brought back many curios from China.* [short for *curiosity*]
cu|ri|o|log|ic (kyůr′ē ə loj′ik), *adj.* = cyriologic.
cu|ri|o|sa (kyůr′ē ō′sə), *n.pl.* books, manuscripts, or novel objects dealing with unusual, and often pornographic, subjects. [< Latin *cūriōsa* (literally) curious objects]
cu|ri|os|i|ty (kyůr′ē os′ə tē), *n., pl.* **-ties**. **1** an eager desire to know: *He satisfied his curiosity about animals by visiting the zoo every week.* **2** the condition of being too eager to know; inquisitiveness: *Curiosity got the better of her, and she opened her sister's mail. Curiosity killed the cat.* **3** a strange, rare, or novel object; something arousing curiosity; novelty: *One of his curiosities was a basket made from an armadillo shell. His unexpectedly erratic behavior is a curiosity.* **SYN:** curio, rarity, wonder. **4** an odd, unusual, or interesting quality: *The president's childish behavior is of some curiosity. He was intrigued with the curiosity of the place.* **5** *Obsolete.* carefulness; accuracy; skill.
cu|ri|ous (kyůr′ē əs), *adj.* **1** eager to know: *a curious student. Small children are very curious, and ask many questions. Girls have curious minds And fain would know the end of everything* (Elizabeth Barrett Browning). **2** too eager to know; prying: *Some people are always curious about their neighbors' business.* **3a** strange; odd; unusual: *I found a curious old box in the attic.* **b** (in booksellers' jargon) pornographic. **4** very odd; peculiar; eccentric: *curious notions. He is a very curious character.* **5** very careful; exact: *the curious inquiries of science.* **6** *Archaic.* made with skill. **7** *Obsolete.* accurate; expert; fastidious. [< Old North French *curius* (with English *-ous*), learned borrowing from Latin *cūriōsus* inquisitive, full of care, ultimately < *cūra* care] —**cu′ri|ous|ly**, *adv.* —**cu′ri|ous|ness**, *n.*
—*Syn.* **1, 2 Curious, inquisitive, prying** mean eager to find out about things. **Curious** means eager to learn things, but sometimes suggests being too eager to know about other people's business: *A normal child is curious about how things work. I was curious to know who was visiting our neighbors.* **Inquisitive** suggests constantly asking questions to find out what one wants to know, especially about personal matters: *She is too inquisitive about my dates.* **Prying** adds to *inquisitive* the idea of peeping and of busying oneself about other people's business: *I had prying neighbors.*
***cu|ri|um** (kyůr′ē əm), *n.* a radioactive, metallic chemical element produced artificially from plutonium and americium. [< Pierre *Curie,* 1859-1906, and Marie *Curie,* 1867-1934, codiscoverers of radium, + New Latin *-ium*]

★curium

symbol	atomic number	mass number	oxidation state
Cm	96	247	3

curl (kėrl), *v., n.* —*v.t.* **1** to twist into rings; roll into coils: *Mother curls her hair.* **2** to twist out of shape; bend into a spiral or curve: *She kept curling her handkerchief nervously around one finger. He curled his lips into a forced smile.* **3** *Obsolete.* to adorn with curls or ringlets.
—*v.i.* **1** to twist into rings; roll into coils: *Her sister's hair curls naturally.* **2** to twist out of shape; bend into a curve: *Paper curls as it burns.* **3** to rise in rings: *Smoke curled slowly from the campfire.* **4** to play at curling.
—*n.* **1** a curled lock of hair; ringlet: *A wet curl hung out from under her rain hat.* **2** anything curled or bent into a curve: *A carpenter's shavings form curls. The Indians' signal fire gave off curls of smoke.* **SYN:** convolution. **3** a curling or being curled. **SYN:** undulation. **4** any of several diseases of plants, especially peaches, in which the leaves are curled up. **5** *Surfing.* a hollow space formed between the spilling crest and the main body of a wave.
curl one's lip. See under **lip**.
curl up, a to draw up one's legs: *She curled up on the sofa.* **b** to roll up: *The snake curled up and died. He curls up as the mimosa leaf is said to do when the breeze turns from warm to cool* (Sunday Times). **c** *Informal.* to break down; give up: *At the half-distance Le Nord looked like winning easily; but he curled up in the last few strides* (London Daily News).
in curl, curled: *She had her hair in curl.*
[earlier *curlen* or *crullen* < Middle English *crul* curly] —**curl′a|ble**, *adj.*
curl|er (kėr′lər), *n.* **1** a person or thing that curls. **2** a device on which hair is twisted or wound to make it curl. **3** a person who plays at curling.
cur|lew (kėr′lü), *n., pl.* **-lews** or (*collectively*) **-lew**. a wading bird with a long, thin, curved bill. Curlews belong to the same family as the sandpipers. [< Old French *courlis,* earlier *courlieus;* perhaps imitative]
curl|i|cue or **curl|y|cue** (kėr′lē kyü), *n.* a fancy twist, curl, or flourish: *Curlicues in handwriting make it hard to read.* [< *curly* + *cue*² queue]
curl|i|cued or **curl|y|cued** (kėr′lē kyüd), *adj.* having curlicues.
***curl|ing** (kėr′ling), *n.* a game in which large, smooth, rounded stones with handles are slid over ice at a target: *The ancient sport of curling grows in winter popularity at Chicago golf clubs* (Wall Street Journal). [apparently < the curling motion given to the stones]

★curling

curling iron or **irons**, an instrument for curling or waving hair.
curling stone, one of the large, smooth, rounded stones used in curling.
curling tongs, = curling irons.
curl|pa|per (kėrl′pā′pər), *n.* a piece of soft, folded paper over which a lock of hair is rolled up tightly to curl it.
curl|y (kėr′lē), *adj.*, **curl|i|er, curl|i|est**. **1** curling; wavy: *curly hair.* **2** having curls or curly hair: *a curly head.* **3a** having a grain which forms a wavy pattern: *curly birch.* **b** forming a wavy pattern: *birch with a curly grain.* —**curl′i|ly**, *adv.* —**curl′i-ness**, *n.*
curl|y-coat|ed retriever (kėr′lē kō′tid), any one of a breed of hunting dogs having a black or liver-colored coat of thick, tight curls, and weighing from 60 to 70 pounds.
curly top, a highly infectious and destructive plant virus carried and transmitted by various leaf hoppers, affecting beets, tomatoes, beans, and squash. The leaves roll and become brittle around the edges and the plant shrivels up.
cur|mudg|eon (kər muj′ən), *n.* a cantankerous, stingy, bad-tempered person; miser: *Only a curmudgeon would argue that the country ought not to build more schools or hospitals* (Wall Street Journal). [origin unknown]
cur|mudg|eon|ly (kər muj′ən lē), *adj.* cantankerous; bad-tempered; miserly: *It will only be the most curmudgeonly of critical readers who will fail to learn a great deal at Mr. Spender's pleasantly informal school* (London Times).
curn (kėrn), *n. Scottish.* **1** a grain. **2** a small quantity or number; a few. [Middle English *curn,* related to *corn*]
curr (kėr), *v.i.* to make a low murmuring sound: *Doves and cats curr.* [imitative, perhaps < Scandinavian (compare Old Icelandic *kurra* murmur)]

★currach

***cur|rach** or **cur|ragh** (kėr′əʜ, -ə), *n. Scottish and Irish.* an open boat made of skin or canvas stretched over a frame of withes, larger than a coracle and boat-shaped. Also, **curagh**. [< Scottish Gaelic and Old Irish *curach* currach, carcass]
cur|ra|jong (kėr′ə jong), *n.* any one of various Australian trees or shrubs of the mallow and sterculia families whose strong, fibrous bark is used especially to make cordage and matting. Also, **cŭrrijong, kurrajong**. [< the native Australian name]
cur|rant (kėr′ənt), *n.* **1** a small raisin without seeds, made from certain sorts of small, sweet grapes. Currants are used in puddings, cakes, and buns. They are produced chiefly in the countries on the eastern Mediterranean Sea and in California; Corinthian raisin. **2a** a small, sour, red, black, or white berry, which is used in jelly, jam, wine, and pies. Currants grow in bunches on any one of various bushes that belong to the saxifrage family. **b** a bushy shrub that currants grow on. **3** any one of various similar fruits or shrubs. [< Anglo-French (*raisins de*) *Corauntz* raisins of Corinth]
currant borer or **clearwing**, a clearwing (moth), the larva of which bores in stems of currant shrubs.
currant gall, a small round gall, like an unripe currant, formed by a hymenopterous insect in the male flowers and upon the leaves of the oak.
cur|ren|cy (kėr′ən sē), *n., pl.* **-cies**. **1** money in actual use in a country: *Coins and paper money are currency in the United States.* **2** a passing from person to person; circulation: *People who spread a rumor give it currency.* **3** general use or acceptance; common occurrence: *Words such as "couldst" and "thou" have little currency now.* **SYN:** prevalence, vogue. **4** *Australian.* Australian-born whites as a group.
cur|rent (kėr′ənt), *n., adj.* —*n.* **1** a flow; stream. Running water or moving air makes a current. *The current swept the stick down the river. The draft created a current of cold air over my feet.* **SYN:** See syn. under **stream**. **2a** a flow of electricity through a wire. Metals are good conductors of electric current. *The current went off when lightning hit the power lines.* **b** the rate or amount of such a flow, usually expressed in amperes: *Heating requires much more current than lighting does. Abbr:* c. **3** *Figurative.* course or movement (of events or of opinions); general direction: *Newspapers influence the current of public opinion.*
—*adj.* **1** of the present time. The current issue of a magazine is the latest one issued. *We discuss current events in class whenever somebody reports on the news.* **2** *Figurative.* in general use; commonly occurring: *Long ago it was a current belief that the earth was flat.* **3** going around: passing from person to person: *A rumor is current that school will close tomorrow.* **SYN:** prevalent. **4** *Archaic.* running; flowing.
[alteration of Middle English *courant* < Old French *corant,* present participle of *corre* to run < Latin *currere*] —**cur′rent|ness**, *n.*
—*Syn. adj.* **2, 3 Current, present, prevailing** mean generally used or occurring at a certain time. **Current** emphasizes the idea of going on or going around from person to person, and means commonly known, used, accepted, or occurring now unless another time is stated: *We read the daily newspaper to keep up with the current situation and developments in different parts of the world.* **Present** emphasizes the idea of being in this place at this time: *This dictionary records present English usage.* **Prevailing** emphasizes the idea of being strongest or most common at a given time and place: *"Foolish" is now the prevailing meaning of "silly." In one period the prevailing sense of "silly" was "helpless."*
current account, **1** an account kept by a customer at a bank to meet his current expenses. **2** an account kept by two firms doing business with one another, to show their transactions.
current algebra, a form of algebra used in the study of charged elementary particles: *Current algebra involves a set of mathematical relations* [*in which*] *the term "current" refers to a current of some property of a particle in analogy with electric current* (Scientific American).
current assets, assets that can be converted into cash within a relatively short time: *The operating assets are divided by accountants into "current assets" and "fixed assets"* (Schmidt and Bergstrom).
current balance, an instrument for measuring electric currents precisely by using a system of fixed and moving coils of certain (specified) di-

mensions, used to determine the absolute value of the ampere.

current density, the amount of electric current flowing per unit of cross section of a conductor, usually expressed in amperes per square centimeter.

current dollar, a dollar the value of which is determined by its relative purchasing power at any given time.

cur|ren|te ca|la|mo (kə ren′tē kal′ə mō; kü ren′te kä′lä mō), *Latin.* **1** fluently; offhand. **2** (literally) with a running pen.

current events, news or a discussion of news of the present time.

current expenses, expenses necessary to the continuous carrying on of a business.

current liabilities, liabilities which will mature within a relatively short time.

current limiter, an electrical device for limiting the flow of current if the voltage applied exceeds a certain limit.

cur|rent|ly (kėr′ənt lē), *adv.* **1** at the present time; now: *The flu is currently going around the office and many people are absent from work.* **2** *Figurative.* generally; commonly: *a currently held belief among the world's scientists.*

current meter, an instrument for measuring the rate of flow of a body of running water, consisting of a wheel which rotates under the impact of the water, the rate of the wheel's revolutions determining the velocity of the running water.

current ratio, the ratio of current assets to current liabilities.

cur|ri|cle (kėr′ə kəl), *n.* a lightweight, two-wheeled carriage drawn by two horses abreast. [< Latin *curriculum.* See etym. of doublet **curriculum.**]

cur|ric|u|lar (kə rik′yə lər), *adj.* of or having to do with a curriculum: *Educators continued to develop their curricular practices around these concepts until psychological research proved these early ideas to be fallacious* (Atlantic).

cur|ric|u|lum (kə rik′yə ləm), *n., pl.* **-lums, -la** (-lə). **1** a course of study: *The curriculum in Grade 4 includes arithmetic, geography, reading, and spelling.* **2** a program of studies leading to a particular degree or certificate: *the curriculum of the Law School.* [< Latin *curriculum* course, chariot (diminutive) < *currus, -ūs* chariot < *currere* run. See etym. of doublet **curricle.**]

curriculum vi|tae (vī′tē), *pl.* **curricula vi|tae**. *Latin.* **1** a biographical summary; short account of a person's background, education, and professional career. SYN: résumé. **2** the course of a person's life: *As everyone knows, there is, in Le Corbusier's curriculum vitae, a superabundance of projects which, for one reason or another, were never acted upon* (Sunday Times).

cur|ried (kėr′ēd), *adj.* prepared with curry or curry powder: *curried shrimp.*

cur|ri|er (kėr′ē ər), *n.* **1** a person who curries tanned leather. **2** a person who curries horses. [< Old French *corier* < Latin *coriārius* tanner < *corium* hide, leather]

cur|ri|er|y (kėr′ē ər ē), *n., pl.* **-er|ies. 1** the occupation of a currier. **2** the place where a currier carries on his business.

cur|ri|jong (kėr′ə jong), *n.* = currajong.

cur|rish (kėr′ish), *adj.* of or like a cur; surly; contemptible; snarling. SYN: ill-bred, worthless, base, ignoble, quarrelsome. **—cur′rish|ly**, *adv.* **—cur′rish|ness**, *n.*

cur|ry¹ (kėr′ē), *v.t.,* **-ried, -ry|ing. 1** to rub and clean (a horse) with a brush or currycomb. **2** to prepare (tanned leather) for use by soaking, scraping, beating, or coloring. **3** to beat; thrash.
curry favor. See under **favor.**
[< Old French *correier* put in order < *con-* (< Latin *com-*) + *reier* arrange < Germanic (compare Gothic *garēdan* provide)]

cur|ry² (kėr′ē), *n., pl.* **-ries**, *v.,* **-ried, -ry|ing.** *—n.* **1** a peppery sauce made from a mixture of spices, seeds, and turmeric. Curry is a popular seasoning in India. **2** = curry powder. **3** a food flavored with curry.
—v.t. to prepare or flavor (food) with curry.
[< Tamil *kari* sauce]

cur|ry|comb (kėr′ē kōm′), *n., v. —n.* a comb or brush with metal teeth for rubbing and cleaning a horse.
—v.t. to use a currycomb on; brush with a currycomb.

curry powder, a powdered mixture of spices, seeds, and turmeric used in making curry.

curse (kėrs), *v.,* **cursed** or **curst, curs|ing**, *n.* *—v.t.* **1** to ask God to bring evil or harm on: *She lay in bed, crying and cursing them: "O God, Master of the Universe, may their hands and feet wither ..."* (James T. Farrell). *Thou shalt not ... curse the ruler of thy people* (Exodus 22:28). **2** to bring evil or harm on; torment: *Sure some fell fiend has cursed our line, that coward should e'er be son of mine* (Scott). **3** to swear at. **4** to excommunicate: *About this time ... a Bull was sent from the Pope, which cursed both the King and the Realm* (Sir Richard Baker). **5** to speak profanely against (holy things); blaspheme.
—v.i. to swear; say bad words; blaspheme: *I drink not, I curse not, I cheat not; they are unnecessary vices* (John Dryden).
—n. **1** the words that a person says when he wishes evil or harm on someone or something: *The witch's curse was uttered against her enemies.* **2** something that is cursed. **3** the trouble or harm that comes as if in answer to a curse. **4** a cause of evil or harm: *His quick temper has been a curse to him all his life.* **5** the words used in swearing: *His talk was full of vile curses.* SYN: oath. **6** excommunication: *The waiting crowd ... stood to hear the priest rehearse, in God's name, the Church's curse* (John Greenleaf Whittier).
be cursed with, to have and suffer from: *He is cursed with a bad temper.*
the curse, *Informal.* menstruation.
[Old English *cursian* < *curs*, a curse] **—curs′er**, *n.*

—Syn. v.t. 3, *v.i.* **Curse, swear** mean to use profane language. **Curse** emphasizes anger or hatred, and implies a heartfelt wish to bring harm upon someone: *He cursed the poor waitress who had spilled soup on him. He cursed when a car almost hit him.* **Swear** suggests using holy names to punctuate one's speech or to express strong feelings: *He thinks it manly to swear. She swore when she stubbed her toe.*

curs|ed (kėr′sid, kėrst), *adj.* **1** under a curse: *Let us fly this cursed place* (Milton). SYN: anathematized. **2** deserving a curse; evil; hateful: *In that country there is a cursed custom: for they eat more gladly man's flesh, than any other flesh* (Sir John Mandeville). SYN: damnable, execrable, detestable. **3** wretched; execrable: *'Tis a cursed thing to be in debt* (Laurence Sterne). **—curs′ed|ly**, *adv.* **—curs′ed|ness**, *n.*

Cur|sil|lis|ta (kür′sēl yēs′tä), *n.* a person taking part in a Cursillo.

Cur|sil|lo (kür sēl′yō), *n.* **1** a method of revitalizing the interest and involvement of Roman Catholics in their faith through regular weekly or monthly meetings in small groups for study, prayer, and discussion. **2** *pl.* **-los.** such a weekly or monthly meeting. [< Spanish *cursillo* little course]

curs|ing (kėr′sing), *n.* **1** a curse; malediction; imprecation. **2** an anathema; excommunication. **3** blasphemy.

cur|sive (kėr′siv), *adj., n. —adj.* written with the letters joined together and with flowing strokes. Ordinary handwriting is cursive. *—n.* **1** a letter made to join other letters. **2** a style of printing type imitating handwriting. **3** cursive script. [< Medieval Latin *cursivus* < Latin *cursus, -ūs* a running < *currere* to run] **—cur′sive|ly**, *adv.*

cur|sor (kėr′sər), *n.* **1** the sliding glass of a slide rule or optical instrument, having a fine hairline on it, used to facilitate computing or sighting. **2** a flashing movable pointer on a computer display screen, indicating the position where a deletion, insertion, or other operation takes place. [< Latin *cursor* runner < *currere* run]

cur|so|ri|al (kėr sôr′ē əl, -sōr′-), *adj. Zoology.* **1** adapted or fitted for running: *cursorial limbs.* **2** having legs fitted for running: *The ostrich is a cursorial bird.*

cur|so|ry (kėr′sər ē), *adj.* without attention to details; hasty and superficial: *He gave the lesson a cursory glance, expecting to study it later. Even a cursory reading of the letter showed many errors.* SYN: rapid, hurried. [< Latin *cursōrius* of a race < *currere* run] **—cur′so|ri|ly**, *adv.* **—cur′so|ri|ness**, *n.*

curst (kėrst), *adj., v. —adj.* **1** = cursed. **2** *Archaic.* perversely disagreeable; ill-tempered; cantankerous. *—v.* cursed; a past tense and past participle of **curse.**

cur|sus (kėr′səs), *n., pl.* **-sus. 1** a stated order of daily prayer; ritual. **2** an academic course; curriculum. [< Latin *cursus* course; see etym. under **course**]

cur|sus ho|no|rum (kėr′səs ho nôr′əm), *Latin.* course of honors; sequence of offices (originally referring to the series of offices leading up to the Roman consulate): *Indeed, some might find it remarkable that such a cursus honorum—Dean of King's College London, Dean of Exeter, Dean of St. Paul's—should have fallen to so liberal a thinker* (Joseph McCulloch).

curt (kėrt), *adj.* **1** short; short and rude; abrupt: *a curt remark. His curt way of speaking makes him seem rude. A curt nod was the only notice he gave that he knew she was there.* SYN: brusque. See syn. under **blunt. 2** brief; terse: *a curt style of writing.* SYN: succinct. [< Latin *curtus* (cut) short] **—curt′ly**, *adv.* **—curt′ness**, *n.*

cur|tail (kėr tāl′), *v.t.* to cut short; cut off part of; reduce; lessen: *The boy's father curtailed his allowance from $1 to 50 cents.* SYN: abbreviate, abridge, diminish. See syn. under **shorten.** [variant of *curtal;* probably influenced by *tail*] **—cur|tail′er**, *n.* **—cur|tail′ment**, *n.*

cur|tail step (kėr′tāl), the lowest step of a stair, finished in a curve at its outer end.

cur|tain (kėr′tən), *n., v. —n.* **1** a cloth hung at windows or anywhere indoors for protection or ornament: *ruffled curtains.* SYN: hanging, drapery. **2a** the drapery or hanging screen separating the stage of a theater from the part where the audience sits. **b** the fall or closing of the curtain at the end of an act or scene. **c** the raising or opening of the curtain at the beginning of a play. **d** the action or speech in a play immediately before the curtain falls or closes; curtain line. **e** = curtain call. **3** *Figurative.* **a** anything that covers or hides: *a curtain of artillery fire. A curtain of fog fell over the harbor.* **b** a barrier of secrecy erected for defensive reasons: *a security curtain.* **4a** a flat stretch of wall connecting two bastions, towers, pavilions, or gates. **b** a low wall which supports no roof and serves only as a screen or enclosure.
—v.t. **1** to provide with a curtain or curtains; shut off with a curtain; decorate with a curtain: *A canopy which love had spread to curtain her sleeping world* (Shelley). **2** *Figurative.* to cover; hide: *Darkness curtained the burglar's movements. Night could not curtain his guilt.*
bring down the curtain on, to terminate; end: *The merger brought down the curtain on the independent company.*
curtain off, to separate or divide by means of a curtain or curtains: *The boys took two sheets and curtained off a space in the corner.*
curtains, *Slang.* **a** the end: *"It's curtains for us, I'm afraid," said the signalman, months before the closure of the Somerset and Dorset [railways]* (London Times). **b** death: *"... the primary reason was smoke inhalation. If my father-in-law had one good whiff, that would have been curtains, because he had this difficulty with his lungs"* (New Yorker).
draw the curtain over (or **on**), to conceal: *The committee chose to draw the curtain over the more controversial aspects of the investigation.*
raise the curtain on, to disclose; reveal: *The police investigation raised the curtain on a new gang of criminals operating in the city's underworld.*
ring down the curtain, a to lower a theater curtain: *"I'll ring down the curtain and give everybody their money back"* (Time). **b** *Figurative.* to draw a close or finish (on): *His retirement rings down the curtain on a distinguished career.*
ring up the curtain, a to raise a theater curtain: *The director gave a signal to ring up the curtain and the play began.* **b** *Figurative.* to set out (on); start; embark: *The British Isles Rugby Football team rings up the curtain on their Antipodean tour* (London Times).
the Curtain, the Iron Curtain: *Private scientific societies are wasting no time preparing to follow up ... proposals for freer movement of ideas across the Curtain* (Newsweek).
[< Old French *curtine* < Late Latin *cortīna* (diminutive) < Latin *cors, cortis* enclosure, courtyard] **—cur′tain|less**, *adj.*

curtain call, the return to the stage of a performer after a performance to acknowledge the applause of the audience: *Almost no one left before the end. Indeed, the people remained in their seats for all the curtain calls* (New York Times).

curtain lecture, a scolding given in private, especially one given by a wife to her husband, as behind the curtains with which beds were once enclosed.

curtain line, the last line spoken by a performer before the curtain falls: *This has all the marks of a stage curtain line—though its message could have been conveyed quite differently* (Punch).

curtain raiser, 1 a short play given before the main play in a theater. **2** *Figurative.* something small used to introduce something bigger: *He called the inquiry a "curtain raiser" for a "thorough re-examination" of monetary policies next year* (Wall Street Journal).

curtain speech, 1 an acknowledgment of applause by an author, producer, or leading actor at the end of a performance. **2** the last speech of a scene, act, or play: *In an overexplicit curtain speech, [James] Stewart says contritely that he has learned the bitter lesson of power* (Time).

curtain time, the time at which a play, concert, or other performance is scheduled to begin.

cur|tain-up (kėr′tən up′), *n. British.* the start of a play, concert, or the like.

curtain wall, a wall between columns or piers of a frame or skeleton of a building which supports no load other than its own weight, and is not supported by girders or beams: *The term "curtain wall" is used nowadays to describe the* *sheath, or "skin," of a modern building* (Scientific American).

curtain walling, the material or materials used in constructing a curtain wall.

cur|tal (kėr′təl), *adj., n. Obsolete or Archaic.* —*adj.* **1** short; brief; curt. **2** having the tail docked: *a curtal horse.* **3** wearing a short frock: *a curtal friar.*
—*n.* **1** any animal that has had its tail docked. **2** anything cut short. **3** a short cannon used in the 1500's and 1600's. **4** Also, **curtall.** a kind of bassoon used in the 1500's.
[< Middle French *courtauld* < Old French *curtald* cut off short < *court* short < Latin *curtus*]

curtal ax, *Archaic.* a cutlass.

cur|tall (kėr′təl), *n.* = curtal (def. 4).

cur|tate (kėr′tāt), *adj.* shortened; reduced. [< Latin *curtātus* < *curtāre* to cut short < *curtus* shortened]

cur|te|sy (kėr′tə sē), *n., pl.* **-sies.** *Law.* the right a husband has in certain inherited property of his wife, especially real estate, after her death. [variant of *courtesy*]

cur|ti|lage (kėr′tə lij), *n. Law.* the area of land occupied by a dwelling and its yard and outbuildings, actually enclosed or considered as enclosed. [< Anglo-French *curtilage* courtyard < Old French *courtil* court, ultimately < Latin *cohortālis* of a (barn)yard < *cohors;* see etym. under **court**]

curt|sey (kėrt′sē), *n., pl.* **-seys,** *v.i., v.t.,* **-seyed, -sey|ing.** = curtsy.

***curt|sy** (kėrt′sē), *n., pl.* **-sies,** *v.,* **-sied, -sy|ing.** —*n.* a bow of respect or greeting by women and girls, made by bending the knees and lowering the body slightly or almost to the floor: *Her low curtsy to the queen was a gesture of respect.*
—*v.i., v.t.* to make a curtsy: *The actress curtsied when the audience applauded.* [variant of *courtesy*]

***curtsy**

cu|rule (kyůr′ül), *adj.* **1** denoting the curule chair or the privilege of occupying it. **2** of the highest rank. [< Latin *curūlis* < *currus, -ūs* (triumphal) chariot < *currere* run]

***curule chair**, a special seat, inlaid with ivory and shaped like a campstool with curved legs, reserved for certain of the highest magistrates or officials of ancient Rome; chair of state.

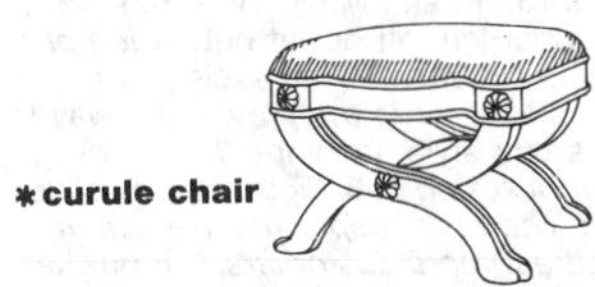

***curule chair**

cur|va|ceous (kėr vā′shəs), *adj. Informal.* having a curving or well-shaped female figure; attractively or well proportioned. [< *curv*(e) + *-aceous*] —**cur|va′ceous|ly,** *adv.*

cur|vant (kėr′vənt), *adj. Heraldry.* curved or bowed.

cur|vate (kėr′vit, -vāt), *adj.* bent in a regular form; curved.

cur|vat|ed (kėr′vā tid), *adj.* = curvate.

cur|va|tion (kėr vā′shən), *n.* a curving or being curved.

cur|va|ture (kėr′və chůr, -chər), *n.* **1** the act of curving or condition of being curved, especially an abnormal condition: *a curvature of the spine.* **2** a curved piece or part; curve: *The carved table has many delicate curvatures.* **3** the degree of curving; curve: *the curvature of the earth's surface.* [< Latin *curvātūra* a bending; vault < *curvāre* to curve]

***curve** (kėrv), *n., v.,* **curved, curv|ing,** *adj.* —*n.* **1** a line that has no straight part; a continuously bending line without angles. A circle is a closed curve. **SYN:** arc. **2** something having the shape of a curve; bend: *The automobile had to slow down to go around the curves in the road.* **SYN:** turn. **3a** a baseball pitched to swerve just before it reaches the batter. **b** the spin or swerve of the ball. **4** *Mathematics.* **a** a line or lines on which every point can be defined by an equation or equations. **b** the path of a moving point. **c** the line where two surfaces intersect. **5** *Statistics.* a line or set of lines showing the values which a function of a variable passes through as the value of the variable changes. **6** a curved ruler used by draftsmen.
—*v.t.* **1** to bend so as to form a line that has no straight part; cause to take a curved form: *The strong man curved the iron bar. The cabinetmaker curved the back of the sofa in a graceful arc.* **2** to pitch (a curve) in baseball.
—*v.i.* **1** to bend in a line that has no straight part; move in the course of a curve: *The highway curved to the right in a sharp turn.* **2** to pitch a curve in baseball.
—*adj.* = curved.
throw a curve, to play a trick; do mischief; deal unfairly with: *I notice that every time I'm riding high and start to congratulate myself Fate throws me a curve* (S. J. Perelman).
[< Latin *curvus* curved, bent] —**curve′less,** *adj.*

$y = x^2$
x-axis
y-axis

***curve**
definition 4a

curve ball, **1** a baseball curve: *Curve balls are classified as high and low and fast and slow curves. These balls curve, or "break" into or away from a batter, depending on the side thrown from and the side that the batter is on* (New York Times). **2** *Figurative.* a trick or ruse: *Numbers of people will argue heatedly that Government half-truths, cover-ups, obfuscations, sophistries, euphemisms and curve balls are permissible tools of the trade so long as a "real lie" (meaning outright and provable) is not employed to gull the people* (Tom Wicker).

curved (kėrvd), *adj.* bent so as to form a curve. —**curv′ed|ness,** *n.*

curve|some (kėrv′səm), *adj.* = curvaceous.

cur|vet (*n.* kėr′vit; *v.* kėr vet′, kėr′vit), *n., v.,* **-vet|ted, -vet|ting** or **-vet|ed, -vet|ing.** —*n.* a leap in the air made by a horse. The forelegs are raised first and then the hind legs, so that all four legs are off the ground for a second.
—*v.i.* **1** to leap in this way. **2** to cause one's horse to do this. **3** to leap about; frisk: *porpoises keeping a rendezvous in the Gulf of Aden and curvetting by the hundred, high in the air, in a kind of courtship ballet* (New Yorker).
—*v.t.* to cause (a horse) to make a curvet.
[< Italian *corvetta* (diminutive) < *corvo* curve < Latin *curvus* curved, bent]

curvi-, *combining form.* curved, as in *curvifoliate.* [< Latin *curvus*]

cur|vi|fo|li|ate (kėr′və fō′lē it, -āt), *adj. Botany.* having curved leaves.

cur|vi|form (kėr′və fôrm), *adj.* having a curved form.

cur|vi|lin|e|al (kėr′və lin′ē əl), *adj.* = curvilinear.

cur|vi|lin|e|ar (kėr′və lin′ē ər), *adj.* **1** consisting of a curved line or lines: *The Einsteinian universe is curvilinear, with four dimensions* (New York Times). **2** enclosed by curved lines. —**cur′vi|lin′e|ar|ly,** *adv.*

cur|vo|graph (kėr′və graf, -gräf), *n.* = cyclograph.

cur|vous (kėr′vəs), *adj.* bent; crooked; curved.

cur|vu|late (kėr′vyə lit, -lāt), *adj.* slightly curved.

curv|y (kėr′vē), *adj.* **1** *Informal.* curvaceous. **2** having a curve or curves.

cus|cus[1] (kus′kəs), *n.* a small mammal of New Guinea and the northern tip of Australia, with woolly fur, large eyes, and short ears. It lives in trees and hunts mostly at night. The female carries her young in a pouch. [< a native name in New Guinea]

cus|cus[2] (kus′kəs), *n.* the long, fibrous root of an aromatic grass of India, used for making screens and ornamental baskets. [< Hindi *khas khas*]

cu|sec (kyü′sek), *n.* one cubic foot a second, used as a unit to measure the volume of flow, especially in engineering. [< *cu*(bic) + *sec*(ond)]

Cush (kush), *n.* **1** the eldest son of Ham and father of Nimrod (in the Bible, Genesis 10:6-8). **2** the country of his supposed descendants in northeastern Africa. Ancient Cush was a kingdom along the Nile River in what is now northeastern Sudan from about 2000 B.C. to about 350 A.D., and was an important trading center. Also, **Kush.**

cush|at (kush′ət), *n.* = ringdove. [Old English *cūscute*]

cu|shaw (kə shô′), *n.* any one of various long-necked squashes, especially a crookneck. Also, *U.S.,* **cashaw.** [American English < Algonkian (perhaps Powhatan) *escushaw* it is raw or green]

cush-cush (kůsh′kůsh′), *n.* a yam grown principally in tropical America, noted for its delicious flavor. [origin unknown]

Cush|ing's disease or **syndrome** (kůsh′ingz), a disease caused by an abnormal cellular growth associated with adenoma of the pituitary gland. [< Harvey W. *Cushing,* 1869-1939, an American surgeon, who described it]

cush|ion (kůsh′ən), *n., v.* —*n.* **1** a soft pillow or pad used to sit, lie, or kneel on: *I rested my head by laying it on a cushion. … sit on a cushion and sew a fine seam* (Nursery Rhyme). **2** anything that makes a soft place: *a cushion of moss under a tree.* **3** a thing shaped or used like a cushion: **a** a small pillow used in making lace. **b** a pad worn by women under the hair. **c** = pincushion. **4a** anything that softens, lessens, or protects from a shock, jar, or jolt. Air or steam forms a protective cushion in some machines. *The bush acted as a cushion to my fall.* **b** *Figurative.* anything that lessens the effects of distress or adversity, relieves a burden, or makes for greater comfort or ease: *During her years of working she created a cushion of savings against sickness or retirement.* **c** *Figurative.* a special benefit, especially a reduction or relief: *a tax cushion.* **5** the elastic padding on the sides of a billiard table. **6** the layer of soft rubber in the casing of a pneumatic tire.
—*v.t.* **1** to put or seat on a cushion; support with cushions: *The nurse cushioned the patient's head.* **2** to supply with a cushion or cushions: *to cushion a chair.* **3** to protect (a machine or machine part) from sudden shocks or jars with a cushion of steam or air. **4** *Figurative.* to soften or ease the effects of; protect: *His family's wealth had always cushioned him against failure. Nothing could cushion the shock of his father's death.* **5** *Figurative.* to suppress quietly; ignore: *There my courage failed: I preferred to cushion the matter* (Charlotte Brontë). **6** *Figurative.* to soften: *Please cushion your voice.*
[< Old French *coissin, coussin* seat cushion, probably < Vulgar Latin *coxīnum* < Latin *coxa* hip] —**cush′ion|like′,** *adj.*

cush|ion|craft (kůsh′ən kraft′, -kräft′), *n., pl.* **-craft.** a vehicle that travels on a cushion of air; an air cushion vehicle or hovercraft.

cush|ion|ing (kůsh′ə ning), *n.* material or materials for making cushions.

cushion rafter, a rafter placed beneath a principal one, to relieve an unusual strain.

cushion scale, a very common scale insect, injurious to oranges and other trees, having a large waxy, fluted ovisac resembling a cushion attached to the bodies of the females.

cush|ion|y (kůsh′ə nē), *adj.* cushionlike; soft and elastic: *a cushiony carpet.*

Cush|ite (kush′īt), *n.* a native or inhabitant of ancient Cush. Also, **Kushite.**

Cush|it|ic (kə shit′ik), *n., adj.* —*n.* a group of Hamitic languages of Ethiopia and eastern Africa.
—*adj.* of or having to do with this group of languages. Also, **Kushitic.** [< *Cush*]

cush|y (kůsh′ē), *adj.,* **cush|i|er, cush|i|est.** *Informal.* soft; comfortable; easy: *a cushy job. Queen Alexandra … recounts her cushy Odyssean upbringing as the only child of a deposed Greek princess* (New Yorker). [< Hindustani *khush* pleasant + English *-y*[1]] —**cush′i|ly,** *adv.* —**cush′i|ness,** *n.*

cusk (kusk), *n.* **1** an edible fish of the same family as the cod; torsk. **2** = burbot. [American English; perhaps < a Scandinavian word]

cusp (kusp), *n.* **1a** a point or pointed end. A crescent has two cusps. **b** *Geometry.* spinode. **2** a blunt or pointed end on the crown of a tooth or a valve of the heart. **3** *Architecture.* a point or projecting figure formed by the meeting of two arcs, such as one of the pointed projections that sometimes decorate the internal curve of an arch. **4** *Astronomy.* either of the pointed ends of a crescent moon or of an inferior planet, such as Venus, in the crescent phase. **5** *Astrology.* **a** the beginning or entrance of a house, or of a sign of the zodiac. **b** a person born on the day of such a beginning or entrance. [< Latin *cuspis, -pidis* a point, pointed end of anything]

cus|pate (kus′pit, -pāt), *adj.* = cusped.

cus|pat|ed (kus′pā tid), *adj.* = cusped.

cusped (kuspt), *adj.* **1** having a cusp or cusps. **2** shaped like a cusp.

cus|pid (kus′pid), *n.* a tooth having one cusp; canine tooth. [< Latin *cuspis, -pidis;* see etym. under **cusp**]

cus|pi|dal (kus′pə dəl), *adj.* **1** of or having to do with a cusp. **2** having a pointed end.

cus|pi|date (kus′pə dāt), *adj.* having a sharp, pointed end: *cuspidate leaves.*

cus|pi|dat|ed (kus′pə dā′tid), *adj.* = cuspidate.

cus|pi|da|tion (kus′pə dā′shən), *n.* decoration

Pronunciation Key: hat, āge, cãre, fär; let, ēqual, tėrm; it, īce; hot, ōpen, ôrder; oil, out; cup, pu̇t, rüle; child; long; thin; ᴛʜen; zh, measure; ə represents **a** in about, **e** in taken, **i** in pencil, **o** in lemon, **u** in circus.

with cusps, as in architecture.

cus|pi|dor (kus′pə dôr), *n.* a container to spit into; spittoon. [American English < Portuguese *cuspideira* < *cuspir* to spit < Latin *conspuere* spit on < *com-* (intensive) + *spuere* spit]

cus|poid (kus′poid), *adj.* of or like a geometric cusp; like that of a geometric cusp.

cuss (kus), *n., v. Informal.* —*n.* **1** a curse. **2** an odd or troublesome person or animal: *Independent, religious, a ruthless old cuss, restless—the prototype of the wandering American* (V. S. Pritchett). —*v.t., v.i.* to curse. [variant of *curse*]

cuss|ed (kus′id), *adj. U.S. Informal.* **1** cursed. **2** stubborn; perverse; cantankerous. —**cuss′ed|ly,** *adv.* —**cuss′ed|ness,** *n.*

cus|so (ku̇s′ō, kus′-), *n.* the dried flower clusters of an Abyssinian tree of the rose family, used especially as a drug to expel the tapeworm. [< a native word]

cuss|word (kus′wėrd′), *n. Informal.* a word used to express a curse or oath: *The epithet should not ... be taken as a political cussword* (Economist).

cus|tard (kus′tərd), *n.* a baked, boiled, or frozen pudding made of eggs, sugar, and milk. Custard is used as a dessert or as a food for sick people. [variant of earlier *crustade* < Old French *croustade* < Old Provençal *croustado* pasty[2] < Latin *crustāre* cover with crust < *crusta* crust, rind]

custard apple, **1** a heart-shaped tropical fruit with sweet, yellowish flesh. **2** the tree that it grows on, raised chiefly in the West Indies. **3** any one of various trees and shrubs of the same genus, such as the papaw.

cus|tard-ap|ple family (kus′tərd ap′əl), a group of largely tropical dicotyledonous shrubs and trees, some widely cultivated in South America for their fruit. The family includes the sweetsop, papaw, ylang-ylang and custard apple.

custard cup, a cup in which a custard is baked, made of heat-resistant material.

cus|tard-pie (kus′tərd pī′), *adj.* having to do with or resembling slapstick comedy, such as that of the early silent motion pictures in which one comic routine was to throw a pie filled with custard at the face of another actor.

cus|to|des (kus tō′dēz), *n.* the plural of **custos.**

cus|to|di|al (kus tō′dē əl), *adj., n.* —*adj.* having to do with custody or custodians: *custodial workers.* —*n.* a vessel for preserving sacred objects, such as relics.

cus|to|di|an (kus tō′dē ən), *n.* **1** a person in charge; guardian; keeper: *When his father died his uncle became his legal custodian.* **2** a person who takes care of a building or offices; janitor; caretaker: *A school custodian* (*a modern euphemism for "janitor"*) *often receives a higher salary than the teacher* (Saturday Review). —**cus|to′di|an|ship,** *n.*

cus|to|dy (kus′tə dē), *n., pl.* **-dies. 1** watchful keeping; charge; care: *Parents have the custody of their young children. All the important papers are in the lawyer's custody.* **SYN:** guardianship. **2** a being confined or detained; imprisonment: *He maintained that his custody had been unduly prolonged.*

in custody, in prison or under arrest; in the care of the police: *The newspaper reports that the hit-and-run driver has been apprehended and is now in custody.*

take into custody, to arrest: *The suspect was taken into custody by the police.*

[< Latin *custōdia* < *custos, -ōdis* guard]

cus|tom (kus′təm), *n., adj.* —*n.* **1** any usual action or practice; habit: *It was his custom to rise early every morning.* **2** the accepted way of acting in a community or other group; convention; tradition: *Custom required our dressing for dinner.* **SYN:** propriety, etiquette. **3** a long-established habit that has almost the force of law: *Common law is based on custom. The social customs of many countries differ from ours.* **4a** the regular business given by a customer: *The new gas station would like to have your custom.* **SYN:** patronage. **b** customers of a store or shop, as a group. **SYN:** clientele. **5** a tax, rent, or service regularly due from feudal tenants to their lord. **6** an import duty. See also **customs.**

—*adj.* **1** made for a special order: *custom work. Custom clothes are made specially according to the order of one individual.* **2** making things to order; not selling ready-made goods: *He had that suit made by a custom tailor.*

[< Old French *costume, custume* < Vulgar Latin *cōstūmen,* for *cōnsuētūmen* < Latin *cōnsuēscere* < *com-* (intensive) + *suēscere* accustom. See etym. of doublet **costume.**]

—*Syn. n.* **1 Custom, habit, practice** mean a usual action or way of acting. **Custom** applies to an action or way of doing things that has become established by a person or a group as the result of being repeated over a period of time: *It was his custom to go to the movies every Saturday. Eating hot dogs is an American custom.* **Habit** applies to an action that a person has repeated so often that he does it naturally and without thinking: *She had the habit of winding her watch before going to bed. He had a bad habit of interrupting people.* **Practice** applies to a usual or customary procedure that a person has established by deliberate choice: *He had made a practice of getting up early.*

cus|tom|a|ble (kus′tə mə bəl), *adj.* = dutiable.

cus|tom|ar|y (kus′tə mer′ē), *adj., n., pl.* **-ar|ies.** —*adj.* **1** according to custom; as a habit; usual: *a customary celebration, his customary friendliness. It is customary to exchange gifts at Christmas.* **SYN:** habitual. See syn. under **usual. 2** holding or held by custom; having to do with or established by custom, as distinguished from law: *customary rent.* **3** subject to feudal dues.

—*n. Law.* **1** Also, **customaries.** a collection of legal customs, or customary laws, as of a manor, city, or province. **2** a book or document containing them. —**cus′tom|ar′i|ly,** *adv.* —**cus′tom|ar′i|ness,** *n.*

customary law, law which is derived by immemorial custom from ancient times: *The application of customary law is today practically limited to civil law, and mainly to land tenure, succession, tort, contract, marriage and divorce, family, and other personal relations* (London Times).

cus|tom-built (kus′təm bilt′), *adj.* made or built to order; not ready-made: *custom-built homes. The tests are custom-built to fit the demands of the particular situation* (Scientific American).

cus|tom|er (kus′tə mər), *n.* **1** a person who buys, especially a regular shopper at a particular store; buyer; purchaser: *This openhanded buying approach reflected a free-spending public, but everyone was also agreed that the customer was getting more finicky* (Newsweek). **SYN:** client. **2** *Informal.* a person one has to deal with; fellow; chap: *He can be a rough customer when he gets angry.* **SYN:** body. —**cus′tom|er|less,** *adj.*

cus|tom|er's man (kus′tə mərz), an employee of a brokerage house who is registered with the stock exchange as authorized to advise clients on investments in stocks and other securities.

custom house, a government building or office, usually at a seaport, airport, or border-crossing point, where taxes on things brought into a country are collected.

cus|tom|ize (kus′tə mīz), *v.t.,* **-ized, -iz|ing.** to make specially for a customer; make to order: *executive interiors customized to fit your own firm's requirements* (Wall Street Journal).

cus|tom|iz|er (kus′tə mī′zər), *n.* **1** a person who makes something specially for a customer. **2** a person who rebuilds or otherwise alters an automobile, especially by using parts from different models.

cus|tom-made (kus′təm mād′), *adj.* made to order or measure; made especially for an individual; not ready-made: *a custom-made suit.*

cus|toms (kus′təmz), *n.pl.* **1** duties or taxes paid to the government on things brought in from a foreign country: *I paid $4 in customs on the $100 Swiss watch.* **2** the department of the government that collects these taxes.

customs broker, a person who, for a fee, specializes in clearing goods for importers through customs.

customs duties, = customs (def. 1).

custom smelter, a plant in which ore is smelted for small companies which do not have their own smelting facilities.

customs union, an agreement between two or more countries to create a single area among them for customs purposes: *Europe would then form a customs union, and such unions are preferential by definition* (New York Times).

cus|tom-tai|lor (kus′təm tā′lər), *v.t.* = tailor-make.

cus|tos (kus′tos), *n., pl.* **cus|to|des.** *Latin.* a custodian; guardian.

custos mo|rum (môr′əm, mōr′-), *Latin.* a guardian of morals; censor.

cus|trel (kus′trəl), *n.* the bearer of a knight's armor; squire. [Middle English *custrell*]

cus|tu|mal (kus′chu̇ məl), *n.* a written collection of the legal customs of a province, city, or other area; customary. [< Medieval Latin *custumalis* < Vulgar Latin *cōstūmen;* see etym. under **custom**]

cut[1] (kut), *v.,* **cut, cut|ting,** *adj., n.* —*v.t.* **1** to divide, separate, open, or remove with a knife or any tool that has a sharp edge; sever: *to cut a string, to cut wheat, to cut timber into logs. The butcher cut the meat with a knife. We cut a branch from the tree.* **2** to pierce or wound with something sharp: *She cut her finger on the broken glass.* **SYN:** gash, slash. **3** to make by cutting: *to cut a statue, to cut a suit. He cut a hole through the wall with an ax.* **4a** to make a recording on: *to cut a record or tape.* **b** to prepare (a stencil) for mimeographing or the like: *to cut a stencil.* **5** to have (a tooth) grow through the gums. **6** *Figurative.* **a** to reduce; decrease: *We must cut our expenses to save money.* **SYN:** lessen; lower. **b** to weaken by mixing; dilute: *to cut a drink.* **7** to shorten by removing a part or parts; trim: *to cut one's hair or nails, to cut the hedge,* (*Figurative.*) *to cut a speech.* **SYN:** pare, prune, clip. **8** to divide by crossing; go across; pass through: *A brook cuts that field.* **SYN:** intersect. **9** to hit or strike sharply: *to cut a horse with a whip. The cold wind cut me to the bone.* **10** to hit (a ball) with a slicing stroke in tennis, baseball, or other games played with a racket or club: *She cut the ball so that it bounded almost backward.* **11** *Figurative.* to hurt the feelings of: *The mean remark cut me.* **12** to switch off; stop: *to cut an engine.* **13** *Informal.* to refuse to recognize (a person) socially: *No one in the class cut the new boy although he was very unfriendly.* **14** *Informal.* to be absent from (a class, lecture, or other meeting): *We wanted to cut history when we heard there was going to be a test.* **15** to make less sticky or stiff; dissolve: *Gasoline cuts grease and tar.* **16a** to draw (a card) at random from a pack. **b** to divide (a pack of playing cards) at random. **17** *Informal, Figurative.* to do; perform; make: *to cut a poor figure.* **SYN:** execute. **18** *U.S.* to separate (cattle) from a herd.

—*v.i.* **1a** to make a cut, opening, or channel with or as if with a sharp instrument: *You did not cut deep enough. After laying out the pattern, she was ready to cut.* **b** to perform the functions of, or be like, a sharp instrument: *The razor cuts well. The wind cuts like a knife.* (*Figurative.*) *Her remark cut.* **2** to be cut; admit of being cut: *Stale bread cuts better than fresh bread. Cheese cuts easily.* **3** to go by a short, direct way; go: *Let's cut through the woods and get ahead of them.* **4** to divide by crossing; cross: *A brook cuts through that field.* **5** to stop photographing a motion picture or television scene: *The cameraman said "Cut!" This epic stint ended without so much as a bang or a whimper ...* [*the*] *director of photography quietly said "Cut," ... and that was that* (New York Times). **6** to hit a tennis or other ball with a slicing stroke. **7** (of the teeth) to grow through the gums. **8** *Slang.* to leave a place; make off: *Let's cut.*

—*adj.* **1** that has been cut: *a cut pie, cut cloth, a cut finger.* **2** shaped, formed, or ornamented by cutting. **3** *Figurative.* reduced; lessened: *cut prices.* **4** *Figurative.* abridged; edited: *a cut version of a long novel.* **5** *Sports.* that has been made to bounce irregularly or curve: *a cut ball or shot.* **6** *Botany.* having the edges indented or divided: *cut leaves.*

—*n.* **1** an opening made by cutting, especially a wound; gash: *He put a bandage on his leg to cover the cut.* **2** a passage or channel made by cutting or digging: *a cut for a road. The biggest job* [*in building the Panama Canal*] *was digging the Gaillard Cut* (John and Mavis Biesanz). **3a** a piece that has been cut off or cut out: *A leg of lamb is a tasty cut of meat.* **b** an excision or omission of a part: *a cut in the play.* **4** the way in which a thing is cut; style; fashion: *the narrow, close-fitting cut of his coat.* **5** *Figurative.* a reduction; decrease: *The shopkeeper made a cut in his prices to attract more customers.* **6** a quicker way; short cut. **7** a sharp blow or stroke with a whip, sword, or cane: *After they were found guilty ... one was sentenced to eight cuts with the cane and the other to three cuts* (London Times). **8** in tennis, baseball, and other games played with a racket or club: **a** a slicing stroke: *He took a cut at the ball with his bat.* **b** the spin given to the ball by such a stroke. **9** *Figurative.* an action or speech that hurts the feelings: *This was the most unkindest cut of all* (Shakespeare). **SYN:** slight. **10** *Informal.* a refusal to recognize socially: *She gave him the cut direct.* **11** *Informal.* absence from a class, lecture, or the like: *The old-style rebel griped about compulsory chapel and got into trouble with the dean's office by taking frequent cuts* (Wall Street Journal). **12a** a block or plate with a picture engraved on it, used in printing. **b** a picture made from such a block or plate. **13** *Informal.* a share: *Each partner has a cut of the profits.* **14a** a random division of a pack of playing cards. **b** the random selection of one card.

a cut above, *Informal.* superior to (another or others): *Wade ... saw himself a cut above the others in toughness and cunning* (London Times).

cut a caper. See under **caper.**

cut across, a to go straight across or through: *He cut across the field to save time.* **b** to disregard: *When he voted, he cut across party lines.*

cut and dried. See **cut-and-dried.**

cut and run, a *Informal.* to make off quickly; hurry off: *I'd give a shilling if they had cut and run* (Dickens). **b** *Nautical.* to cut the anchor cable and make sail instantly: *Greek and Turkish craft*

... *were obliged to 'cut and run' before the wind* (Byron).

cut back, a to reduce or curtail: *The companies had to cut back production because orders fell off.* **b** to go in a different direction suddenly (in football, hockey, and other field games): *On signal, the right guard cuts back to protect the passer.* **c** to shorten by cutting off the end or ends of (a plant): *Early in March cut back all the shoots* (Shirley Hibberd). **d** to return to an earlier point in the sequence of a plot, as in a motion picture or novel: *If you can not use a crowd perhaps you can cut back to some single person who overlooks the crime and later tells the story* (E. W. Sargent).

cut down, a to cause to fall by cutting: *to cut down a tree.* **b** *Figurative.* to reduce; decrease: *to cut down one's allowance. Did the author correct the proofs? And, if so, did he in the process cut down ... the obviously long sentences, and so upset the original and natural order?* (C. B. Williams). **c** to kill in battle: *to cut down the enemy. Hunters cut down most of the buffalo of our plains.* **d** to injure or disable: *Shipp ... was cut down by a vicious block by Calgary's Don Luzzi during the exhibition season* (Maclean's).

cut down on, to lessen or slow down; reduce: *This is no time to cut down on the drive against crime* (Manchester Guardian Weekly).

cut down to size. See under **size**[1].

cut ice. See under **ice**.

cut in, a to break in; interrupt: *She cut in with a remark while I was talking.* **b** to interrupt a dancing couple to take the place of one of them: *Nobody else has got a right to cut in and dance with you more than the one you go with* (Booth Tarkington). **c** to move a vehicle suddenly into a line of moving traffic: *When the cabdriver cut in he collided with another car.* **d** to introduce or admit into a group or activity: *to cut in debaters as they signal to speak.* **e** to connect or join, especially to a machine or working part: *to cut in an automatic pilot.*

cut it fine. See under **fine**[1].

cut it out, *Slang.* stop it; don't do that: *I began to cry ... "Hey, cut it out, honey," he said, embarrassed* (Atlantic).

cut loose, a to separate from anything; break a connection or relation: *At a congress in ... 1912, the Bolsheviks finally cut loose from the Mensheviks and became ... an independent party* (Edmund Wilson). **b** to run away; free oneself: *I will cut loose from every entanglement* (A. E. Barr). **c** *Figurative.* to act without restraint: *improvisation that gives each of the musicians a chance to cut loose on his own* (New Yorker).

cut no ice. See under **ice**.

cut off, a to remove by cutting: *Cut off that branch.* **b** to shut off: *to cut off the water.* **c** to stop suddenly: *to cut off all hope of success.* **d** to break; interrupt: *to cut off a retreat.* **e** to disinherit: *The will cut off his daughter without a dollar.* **f** to intercept: *to cut off the mails.* **g** to isolate: *Rural homes were cut off by the storm.*

cut of one's jib, *Informal.* one's outward appearance: *Elizabeth likes the cut of Raleigh's jib—and his beard too* (Time).

cut one's teeth. See under **teeth**.

cut out, a to remove by cutting: *to cut out a cyst. He cut out the picture from a newspaper.* **b** to take out; leave out: *Why did you cut out this part of the play?* **c** to take the place of; get the better of: *to cut out a rival.* **d** to make or shape by cutting: *to cut out a dress.* **e** *Figurative.* to plan; map out: *She has her work cut out for her.* **f** to stop doing or using (something): *to cut out candy. Please cut out the noise.* **g** *Informal.* to leave suddenly or abruptly: *We cut out of the party and went home.* **h** *Figurative.* to suit as if by nature: *She was cut out to be a teacher.* **i** to move a vehicle out of a line of moving traffic, especially without warning: *She forgot I was there and cut out like a race driver, cornering without touching the brake and gunning it coming out of the turn* (Atlantic). **j** to separate from a herd: *to cut out a steer.*

cut short, to end suddenly; interrupt: *Sickness threatened to cut short his vacation. An exclamation ... cut the lawyer short* (Dickens).

cut up, a to cut to pieces: *Every lady ... was instructed how to cut up a turkey* (Illustrated London News). (*Figurative.*) *They will very soon cut up and destroy all we have in this country* (John H. Burton). (*Figurative.*) *Wilson's tongue cut up both men in one clean, neat stroke* (Maclean's). **b** *Informal.* to hurt: *I believe he was dreadfully cut up at my going away* (F. E. Trollope). **c** *Slang.* to show off; play tricks: *The old 'Squire got pretty riley when he heard how the rebels was cutting up* (C. F. Browne).

[Middle English *cutten;* origin uncertain. Compare Old Icelandic *kuti* knife.]

—***Syn.*** *v.t.* **1 Cut, chop, hack** mean to separate or remove with something sharp. **Cut** is the general word: *He cut some branches for kindling.* **Chop** means to cut by hitting: *He chopped the wood.* **Hack** means to cut or chop roughly and unevenly, and often suggests that the implement should be sharper or its user more skilled: *You certainly hacked that roast when you carved it.*

cut[2] (kut), *n.* one of several pieces of straw, wood, or paper, used in drawing lots: *He drew the shortest cut.* [origin uncertain]

cut-and-cov|er (kut'ən kuv'ər), *n., adj.* —*n.* a method of tunnel construction in which the surface is excavated and after construction filled with the excavated material.
—*adj.* of or designating this method.

cut-and-dried (kut'ən drīd'), *adj.,* or **cut and dried, 1** ready for use; arranged in advance: *It is clear that in these circumstances the man who would turn this report into a cut-and-dried prescription for politicians had better tread carefully* (Manchester Guardian). **2** *Figurative.* dull; uninteresting: *His speech was cut and dried because he had nothing new to say.*

cut and fill, a method employed in building roads and canals or in mining, in which excavated material from the worked areas is used to form adjacent embankments.

cut and thrust, 1 the action, especially in swordplay, of cutting and thrusting. **2** active interplay between opposing interests: *a master at cut and thrust in debate* (Wall Street Journal).

cut-and-try (kut'ən trī'), *adj.* based on trial and error; characterized by or involving repeated experimentation: *All of these mechanisms have been fashioned largely by cut-and-try methods rather than on scientific principles* (Scientific American).

cu|ta|ne|ous (kyü tā'nē əs), *adj.* of the skin; having to do with or on the skin: *cutaneous nerves.* [< New Latin *cutaneus* (with English *-ous*) < Latin *cutis* skin]

cu|ta|ne|ous|ly (kyü tā'nē əs lē), *adv.* by or through the skin.

***cut|a|way** (kut'ə wā'), *n., adj.* —*n.* **1** a coat having the lower part cut back in a curve or slope from the waist in front to the tails in back. Cutaways are used by men for formal wear in the daytime. **2** an object, or a model or drawing of an object, having part of its covering removed to show a section of its working parts for examination.
—*adj.* showing or representing an object with part of its covering removed: *a cutaway model. The cutaway view shows a small portion of the machinery that powers and operates this world's most modern ship* (Time).

***cutaway**
definition 1

cutaway dive, a dive in which the diver stands with his back to the water but turns and enters it in a forward position.

cut|back (kut'bak'), *n.* **1** a reduction in quantity, number, or rate; curtailment: *a cutback in expenditures. The factory made a cutback in production when many of its orders were canceled. In spite of talk of cutbacks, defense spending still is headed upward* (Wall Street Journal). **2** a plant that has been pruned by cutting off shoots close to the main stem. **3** a scene that returns the action to an earlier time in a play, motion picture, television play, novel, or other literary piece: *The cutbacks to his youth are many ..., for he keeps probing himself on why he ever left Old Pompey and whether Manhattan is worth the price* (Atlantic). **4** *Surfing.* a swinging back into the wave while riding the surfboard.

cut|bank (kut'bangk'), *n.* the steep, overhanging, concave wall of a stream having a meandering course.

cutch[1] (kuch), *n.* = catechu. [< Malay *kachu*]

cutch[2] (kuch), *n.* a pile of leaves of a very thin, tough paper between which sheets of gold are laid to be beaten into gold leaf. [< French *caucher* < *caucher* to press down, ultimately < Latin *calcāre* to tread on < *calx, calcis* heel]

cut|cher|ry (kə cher'ē), *n., pl.* **-ries.** in India: **1** a courthouse. **2** an administrative office. [Anglo-Indian < Hindustani *kachahrī* audience chamber]

cutch|er|y (kuch'ər ē), *n., pl.* **-er|ies.** = cutcherry.

cut|down (kut'doun'), *adj., n.* —*adj.* **1** reduced in size; shortened: *a cutdown automobile.* **2** abridged; condensed: *a cutdown version of a novel.*
—*n.* **1** that which is cut down. **2** the act or process of cutting down; curtailment: *a cutdown in spending.*

cute (kyüt), *adj.,* **cut|er, cut|est.** *Informal.* **1** pretty and dear; pleasing or attractive; winsome; dainty: *a cute baby.* **SYN:** charming. **2** *U.S.* consciously or intentionally stylish or mannered: *cute dialogue. A good deal of [the plot] is painfully cute and contrived* (Newsweek). **SYN:** affected. **3** clever; shrewd; cunning; keenwitted; sharp: *a cute trick.* **SYN:** astute. [< *acute*] —**cute'ly,** *adv.* —**cute'ness,** *n.*

cute|sy (kyüt'sē), *adj.,* **-si|er, -si|est.** *U.S. Informal.* consciously or affectedly cute.

cut|ey (kyü'tē), *n., pl.* **-eys.** *U.S. Informal.* cutie.

cut glass, glass shaped or decorated by grinding and polishing.

cut-grass (kut'gras'), *n.* any grass having rough-edged blades which can cut the skin.

cu|ti|cle (kyü'tə kəl), *n.* **1a** the outer skin of vertebrates; epidermis. **b** any superficial skin or integument, such as the transparent membrane which envelopes annelids. **2** the hard skin around the outside of a fingernail or toenail. **3** *Botany.* a very thin film covering the surface of a plant. [< Latin *cutīcula* (diminutive) < *cutis* skin]

cu|tic|u|la (kyü tik'yə lə), *n., pl.* **-lae** (-lē). the outer layer of the skin of certain lower organisms, especially insects. [< Latin *cutīcula* (diminutive) < *cutis* skin]

cu|tic|u|lar (kyü tik'yə lər), *adj.* **1** of or having to do with a cuticle. **2** like cuticle.

cu|tic|u|lar|ize (kyü tik'yə lə rīz), *v.t.,* **-ized, -iz|ing. 1** to make a cuticle of. **2** *Botany.* to cutinize.

cut|ie (kyü'tē), *n.* **1** *Informal.* an attractive, personable, vivacious girl or young woman: *The nurses in the outfit are cuties one and all* (New Yorker). **2** *U.S. Slang.* **a** a person clever at maneuvering or outsmarting opponents: *The Assembly's old cuties had calculated that Faure was ... leftist enough to cut the ground from under Mendès with the voters* (Time). **b** a clever or shrewd maneuver: *Although [Archie] Moore had taken control of the fight one minute from the end of the first round, the finish was startlingly sudden. That is an old cutie of Moore* (New York Times).

cutie pie, 1 *Informal.* **a** a cute girl or young woman; cutie. **b** a sweetheart; darling. **2** *Slang.* a scintillation counter.

cu|ti|fi|ca|tion (kyü'tə fə kā'shən), *n.* formation or grafting of skin.

cu|ti|fy (kyü'tə fī), *v.i.,* **-fied, -fy|ing.** to form or graft skin.

cu|tin (kyü'tin), *n. Botany.* a waxy substance that is the chief ingredient of the outer skin of many plants. [< Latin *cutis* skin + English *-in*]

cut-in (kut'in'), *n., adj.* —*n.* **1** the act or an instance of cutting in. **2** a motion-picture shot inserted into a sequence so that it breaks continuity.
—*adj.* inserted into a film sequence: *a cut-in close-up, a cut-in flashback.*

cu|tin|i|za|tion (kyü'tə nə zā'shən), *n. Botany.* a modification of cell walls by which they become impermeable to water through the presence of cutin.

cu|tin|ize (kyü'tə nīz), *v.t., v.i.,* **-ized, -iz|ing.** to change into cutin: *Epidermal cells are usually cutinized, while cork cells tend to become suberized* (Heber W. Youngken).

cu|tis (kyü'tis), *n.* the skin beneath the epidermis; dermis; corium. [< Latin *cutis*]

***cut|lass** or **cut|las** (kut'ləs), *n.* **1** a short, heavy, slightly curved sword, used in former times especially by sailors. **2** a large, heavy knife; machete. [< French *coutelas* < *couteau, coutel* < Latin *cultellus* (diminutive) < *culter* knife]

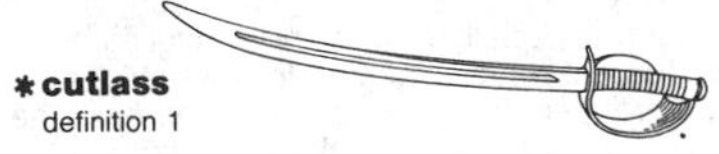

***cutlass**
definition 1

cutlass fish, a long, slender saltwater fish with long, doglike teeth and a dorsal fin that extends the length of its body. It lives in the waters of the West Indies, the western Pacific Ocean, and the southern United States.

cut|ler (kut'lər), *n.* a person who makes, sells, or repairs knives, scissors, and other cutting instruments. [< Old French *coutelier* < *coutel* small knife; see etym. under **cutlass**]

cut|ler|y (kut'lər ē), *n.* **1** cutting instruments, such as knives and scissors. **2** knives, forks, spoons,

Pronunciation Key: hat, āge, cãre, fär; let, ēqual, tėrm; it, īce; hot, ōpen, ôrder; oil, out; cup, pu̇t, rüle; child; long; thin; ᴛʜen; zh, measure;
ə represents **a** in about, **e** in taken, **i** in pencil, **o** in lemon, **u** in circus.

and other implements for table use. **3** the work or business of a cutler.

cut|let (kut′lit), *n.* **1** a slice of meat cut from the leg or ribs for broiling or frying: *a veal cutlet.* **2** a flat, fried cake of chopped food, such as meat, chicken, or fish; croquette. [< Old French *côtelette* (diminutive) < *coste* < Latin *costa* rib, side]

cut|line (kut′līn′), *n.* information printed below a cut or illustration in a newspaper, magazine, or other publication; caption or legend.

cut|off (kut′ôf′, -of′), *n., adj.* —*n.* **1** a short way across or through; short cut: *We'll save time if we take the cutoff across the park.* **2a** a new and shorter passage cut by a river through a bend. **b** the water in the old channel, thus cut off. **3a** a stopping of the passage of steam or working fluid to the cylinder of an engine. **b** the valve or other device that stops the passage of liquid or gas through a pipe or opening. **c** the point in the stroke at which the admission of fluid is stopped. **4** the act or an instance of cutting off; cessation; end. **5** the point in an electrical circuit at which a mechanism prevents the flow of current of certain frequencies to or from the circuit. **6** the interception of a baseball thrown to a base from the outfield.
—*adj.* at or in which anything is cut off: *a cutoff period. A cutoff date ends this agreement.*

cutoff valve, a valve that stops the passage of a fluid to the cylinder of an engine.

cut|out (kut′out′), *n., adj.* —*n.* **1** a shape or design to be cut out of paper, cloth, cardboard, wood, or plastic: *Some books for children have cutouts to be removed and pasted together. The shoes had cutouts and little heels* (New York Times). **2** a device for disconnecting an internal-combustion engine from its muffler: *Automobiles have cutouts to let the exhaust from the engine out into the air.* **3** a device for breaking or closing an electric circuit. **4** *Slang.* a person who acts as a contact or middleman between espionage agents. **5** the act or an instance of cutting out.
—*adj.* made or designed with a cutout or cutouts: *a gown with a cutout back. Rudi Gernreich . . . made dresses that were both cutout and transparent* (Angela Taylor).

cut|over (kut′ō′vər), *adj., n.* —*adj.* from which the trees have been cut: *They replanted the cutover land.*
—*n.* a tract of land from which the trees have been cut; land cleared of timber.

cut-price (kut′prīs′), *adj.* = cut-rate.

cut|purse (kut′pėrs′), *n.* = pickpocket. [< the practice of stealing purses by cutting them from belts to which they were attached]

cut-rate (kut′rāt′), *adj., n.* —*adj.* **1** reduced in price; at reduced rates: *cut-rate merchandise, selling at cut-rate prices no one else can match.* **2** offering goods or services at reduced rates or prices: *a cut-rate store, a cut-rate dealer.*
—*n.* a reduced rate or price: *The normal British foreign holiday is now a "package tour" at cut-rates* (Sunday Times).

cut stone, stone cut or chiseled to a particular shape, for use as keystone, skewback, or other purpose.

cut|ta|ble (kut′ə bəl), *adj.* that can be cut.

cut|tage (kut′ij), *n.* the propagating of plants by means of cuttings.

cut|ter (kut′ər), *n.* **1** a person who cuts: *A garment cutter cuts out pieces of fabric to be made into clothes.* **2** a tool or machine for cutting: *The blade of a meat cutter is very sharp.* **3** a small, light sleigh, usually pulled by one horse. **4** a small sailboat with one mast, rigged like a sloop. **5a** a small, armed ship used by the coast guard, especially for patrolling and for clearing and maintaining waterways. **b** a small, armed ship used by the coast guard, especially to prevent smuggling; revenue cutter. **6** a boat belonging to a warship, used to carry people and supplies to and from the ship. **7** *U.S.* **a** an old cow or steer. **b** a grade of beef for such animals.

cutter bar, 1 the bar in a mowing or reaping machine that bears the knife or blade. **2** the bar bearing the cutter in a lathe.

cut|ter|head (kut′ər hed′), *n.* the revolving head of a tool with cutters or sharpened edges.

cut|throat (kut′thrōt′), *n., adj.* —*n.* **1** a person who kills; murderer. SYN: assassin. **2** cutthroat bridge. **3** = cutthroat trout. **4** *Especially British.* an open razor: *I started shaving with a cutthroat and still do so in spite of my 74 years* (Cape Times).
—*adj.* **1** murderous: *a cutthroat band of pirates.* **2** *Figurative.* without mercy; relentless or severe: *cutthroat competition.* SYN: merciless. **3** played by three card players, each of whom scores for himself: *cutthroat bridge.*

cutthroat trout, a trout found in rivers and lakes of northwestern North America.

cut time, = alla breve.

cut|ting (kut′ing), *n., adj.* —*n.* **1** a thing cut off or out. **2** a small shoot cut from a plant to grow a new plant; scion; slip: *Mother started the new flower pots with cuttings from the older plants.* **3** *Especially British.* a newspaper or magazine clipping. **4** *Especially British.* a way cut through high ground for a road or track: *One sees children . . . perched like a swarm of bees on the railings overlooking a railway cutting* (London Times). **5** a phonograph recording. **6** the act or an instance of cutting or cutting out.
—*adj.* **1** that cuts; sharp: *Shears and scissors are cutting tools. A cutting wind whistled over the frozen lake.* SYN: keen, acute, trenchant. **2** *Figurative.* hurting the feelings; sarcastic: *He was offended by her cutting remark.* SYN: biting, caustic. **3** on or in which cutting is done: *a cutting table, a cutting room.* —**cut′ting|ly,** *adv.*

cutting board, a board used on a bench or on the lap for cutting leather or cloth.

cutting edge, *Figurative.* the foremost or leading position; vanguard: *Ever since it outlawed public school segregation . . . the U.S. Supreme Court has been on the cutting edge of civil rights advances* (Time).

cutting horse, a horse on a cattle ranch specially trained for the job of separating or cutting out calves, steers, or cows picked for market.

cutting oil, a specially prepared, usually emulsified oil used as a lubricant for tools which cut metals.

cut|tle (kut′əl), *n.* = cuttlefish.

***cut|tle|bone** (kut′əl bōn′), *n.* the hard internal shell of cuttlefish. It is used for making polishing powder and as food for cage birds.

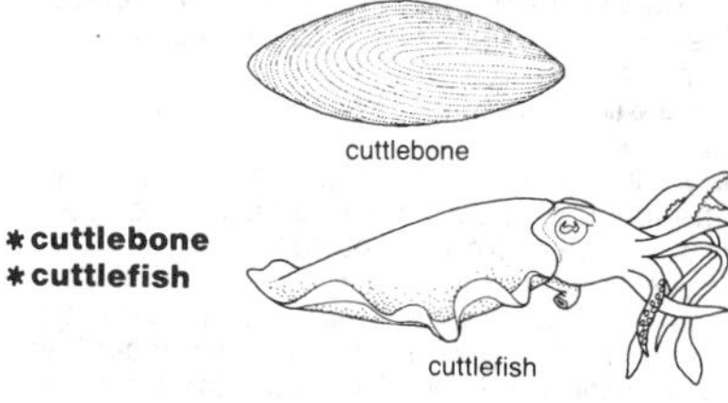

***cuttlebone**
***cuttlefish**

***cut|tle|fish** (kut′əl fish′), *n., pl.* **-fish|es** or (*collectively*) **-fish.** a saltwater mollusk having ten arms with suckers, two of which are especially long, and a hard internal shell. The cuttlefish is related to the squid. When frightened, one kind of cuttlefish squirts out an inky fluid, which is the source of sepia. [earlier *cotul,* Old English *cudele* cuttlefish + *fish*]

cut|ty (kut′ē), *n., pl.* **-ties,** *adj. Scottish.* —*n.* **1** a short spoon. **2** a tobacco pipe with a short stem. **3** a hussy. —*adj.* short; cut short. [< *cut*[1], verb + *-y*[1]]

cutty stool, *Scottish.* **1** a low stool. **2** a seat in churches where offenders against chastity, or other delinquents, had to sit.

cut|up (kut′up′), *n.* **1** *Slang.* a person who shows off or plays tricks. **2** the act or an instance of cutting up.

cut velvet, velvet in which the loops of the warp are cut.

cut|wa|ter (kut′wôt′ər, -wot′-), *n.* **1** the front part of a ship's prow or stem. **2** the wedge-shaped end of a pier of a bridge for dividing the current, breaking up ice, or deflecting debris.

cut|work (kut′wėrk′), *n.* **1** embroidery in which part of the material is cut away. **2** appliqué work.

cut|worm (kut′wėrm′), *n.* a caterpillar that cuts off the stalks of young plants near or below the ground when feeding on them at night. It is the larva of a moth.

cu|vée (ky vā′), *n. French.* **1** the contents of a vat or cask of wine. **2** the vintage of this wine.

cu|vette (kyü vet′), *n.* **1** a transparent tube or container used in laboratory work: *The procedure consists of placing [the] reaction mixture in the cuvette of a light measuring instrument* (New Scientist). *Naturally lit enclosures called cuvettes were used to surround small ecological systems* (L. G. Morris and G. A. Carpenter). **2** an ornamental basin of pottery, porcelain, or the like. [< French *cuvette* (diminutive) < *cuve* vat < Latin *cūpa* tub]

Cu|vi|er|i|an (kyü′vē ãr′ē ən, -vir′ē-), *adj.* of or having to do with the French naturalist Georges Cuvier or his system of animal classification.

cv. or **cv't.,** convertible.

CVA (no periods) or **C.V.A.** or **c.v.a.,** cerebrovascular accident.

CW (no periods), **1** chemical warfare. **2** continuous wave.

cwm (küm), *n., pl.* **cwms.** *Geology.* a natural amphitheater; cirque. [< Welsh *cwm,* Old English *cumb*]

c.w.o. or **C.W.O.,** cash with order.

CWO (no periods), chief warrant officer.

cwt., hundred weight; 100 lbs. in the United States; 112 lbs. in Great Britain (Latin *centum* + English *weight*).

-cy, *suffix added to nouns or adjectives to form nouns.* **1** office, position, or rank of ______: *Captaincy = rank of a captain.* **2** quality, condition, or fact of being ______: *Bankruptcy = condition of being bankrupt.* [< French *-cie, -tie,* learned borrowings) or directly < Latin *-cia, -tia,* or Greek *-kiā, -keia, -tiā, -teia*]

cy|an (sī′an), *n.* a color between green and blue. It is one of the three used in the subtractive color process in color photography. [< Greek *kýanos* blue]

cyan-, *combining form.* the form of **cyano-** before vowels, as in *cyanic, cyanhydrin.*

cy|an|a|mid (sī an′ə mīd, sī′ə nam′id), *n.* = cyanamide.

cy|an|a|mide (sī an′ə mīd, -mid; sī′ə nam′īd, -id), *n.* **1a** a white, crystalline compound prepared by the action of ammonia on cyanogen chloride and in other ways. *Formula:* CH_2N_2 **b** a salt of this compound. **2** = calcium cyanamide. [< *cyan-* + *amide*]

cy|a|nate (sī′ə nāt), *n.* a salt or ester of cyanic acid.

cyan blue, = cyan.

cy|an|hy|drin (sī′ən hī′drin), *n.* = cyanohydrin.

cy|an|ic (sī an′ik), *adj.* **1** of cyanogen; containing cyanogen. **2** blue. Flower colors in all shades of blue, and passing through violet and purple to red, are called cyanic.

cyanic acid, a colorless, poisonous liquid. *Formula:* HOCN

cy|a|nid (sī′ə nid), *n.* = cyanide.

cy|a|ni|da|tion (sī′ə nə dā′shən), *n.* = cyanide process.

cy|a|nide (sī′ə nīd, -nid), *n., v.,* **-nid|ed, -nid|ing.** —*n.* any one of various metallic salts containing carbon and nitrogen. Cyanide is used in making plastics and insecticides, in extracting gold and silver from ores, and in treating metals. Potassium cyanide is extremely poisonous.
—*v.t.* to treat with a cyanide.

cyanide process, a method of extracting gold and silver from ores by treatment with a dilute solution of potassium or sodium cyanide.

cy|a|nine (sī′ə nēn, -nin), *n.* a blue or bluish dye used in photography as a sensitizer. It is the blue coloring matter of certain flowers. *Formula:* $C_{29}H_{35}IN_2$

cy|a|nite (sī′ə nīt), *n.* a silicate of aluminum, usually occurring in blue, blade-shaped crystals. *Formula:* Al_2SiO_5 Also, **kyanite.**

cy|a|nize (sī′ə nīz), *v.t.,* **-nized, -niz|ing.** to convert into cyanide.

cyano-, *combining form.* **1** blue or dark-blue, as in *cyanometer, cyanotype.* **2** of cyanogen; containing cyanogen, as in *cyanohydrin cyanoacetylene.* Also, **cyan-** before vowels. [< Greek *kýanos* dark-blue color or substance.]

cy|a|no|a|cet|y|lene (sī′ə nō ə set′ə lēn, -lin), *n.* a large organic molecule discovered in cosmic gas clouds: *Cyanoacetylene* (HC_3N), *the most complex organic molecule found in space so far, has now come to light in the radio source at the galactic centre* (New Scientist).

cy|a|no|co|bal|a|min (sī′ə nō kō bal′ə min), *n.* a dark-red, crystalline compound, one of the three forms of vitamin B_{12}. *Formula:* $C_{63}H_{90}N_{14}PCo$ [< *cyano-* + *cobal*(t) + (vit)*amin*]

cy|a|no|eth|yl|ate (sī′ə nō eth′ə lāt), *v.t.,* **-at|ed, -at|ing.** to treat with cyanoethylene (acrylonitrile): *cyanoethylated cotton products.*

cy|a|no|eth|yl|a|tion (sī′ə nō eth′ə lā′shən), *n.* the process of treating with acrylonitrile: *cyanoethylation of cotton.*

cy|a|no|eth|yl|ene (sī′ə nō eth′ə lēn), *n.* = acrylonitrile.

cy|an|o|gen (sī an′ə jən), *n. Chemistry.* **1** a colorless, poisonous, inflammable gas with the odor of bitter almonds. *Formula:* C_2N_2 **2** a univalent radical (—CN) consisting of one atom of carbon and one of nitrogen, found in the cyanides, the cyanates, and hydrocyanic acid. [< French *cyanogène* < Greek *kýanos* dark-blue substance + French *-gène* -gen (from its being a constituent of Prussian blue)]

cy|a|no|ge|net|ic (sī′ə nō jə net′ik), *adj.* tendng to yield or produce hydrocyanic or prussic acid, as certain gases.

cy|a|no|hy|drin (sī′ə nō hī′drin), *n.* any one of a group of organic compounds which contain both the CN and the OH radicals. Also, **cyanhydrin.**

cy|a|nom|e|ter (sī′ə nom′ə tər), *n.* an instrument for measuring degrees of blueness, as of the sky.

cy|a|nom|e|try (sī′ə nom′ə trē), *n.* the measurement of the intensity of the blueness of the sky.

cy|a|no|sis (sī′ə nō′sis), *n.* blueness or lividness of the skin and mucous membranes caused by lack of oxygen in the blood, and associated with high altitudes, suffocation, shock, and certain forms of heart disease. [< New Latin *cyanosis* <

Greek *kýanōsis* dark-blue color < *kýanos* dark-blue + *-ōsis* condition]

cy|a|not|ic (sī′ə not′ik), *adj.* having to do with or affected with cyanosis: *a heart operation to provide a blood supply to the lungs of cyanotic children.*

cy|an|o|type (sī an′ə tīp), *n.* **1** = blueprint. **2** a process of making blueprints.

cy|a|nu|rate (sī′ə nůr′āt, -nyůr′-), *n.* a salt or ester of cyanuric acid.

cy|a|nu|ric acid (sī′ə nůr′ik, -nyůr′-), a white or colorless crystalline acid, used in organic synthesis. *Formula:* $C_3H_3N_3O_3$

Cyb|e|le (sib′ə lē), *n.* a nature goddess of ancient peoples in Asia Minor, identified with the Greek goddess Rhea.

cy|ber|cul|tur|al (sī′bər kul′chər əl), *adj.* of or having to do with the effects of cybernation on culture or society.

cy|ber|cul|ture (sī′bər kul′chər), *n.* a culture or society dominated by cybernation.

cy|ber|nate (sī′bər nāt), *v.t.*, **-nat|ed, -nat|ing.** to automate through the use of computers: *The ... bakery in Chicago is cybernated; there are practically no workmen at all* (New Yorker). [back formation < *cybernation*]

cy|ber|na|tion (sī′bər nā′shən), *n.* automation through the use of computers: *Cybernation continues to cut into the supply of unskilled and semiskilled jobs* (New York Times). [coined in 1962 by Donald N. Michael, an American communications expert < *cybern*(etics) + *-ation*]

cy|ber|net|ic (sī′bər net′ik), *adj.* of or having to do with cybernetics.

cy|ber|ne|ti|cian (sī′bər nə tish′ən), *n.* = cybernetist.

cy|ber|net|i|cist (sī′ber net′ə sist), *n.* = cybernetist.

cy|ber|net|ics (sī′bər net′iks), *n.* the comparative study of the human and animal nervous system and certain mechanical systems in order to better understand communication and control of impulses and responses in both types of systems. [coined in 1948 by Norbert Wiener, 1894-1964, an American mathematician < Greek *kybernētikós* of a pilot < *kybernētēs* pilot < *kybernân* to steer]

cy|ber|net|ist (sī′bər net′ist), *n.* a person who studies cybernetics.

cy|ber|pho|bi|a (sī′bər fō′bē ə), *n.* an excessive fear of computers: *Our surveys indicate a strong relationship between creativity and cyberphobia: people scoring on the very top and very bottom of a creativity scale seem most anxious about computers* (Discover). **—cy′ber|pho′bic,** *adj.*

cy|borg (sī′bôrg), *n.* a human body or other organism whose functions are taken over in part by various electronic or electromechanical devices: *The futuristic cyborg, or combination man and machine, will consist of a stationary, computerlike human brain, served by machines to fill its limited physical needs and act upon its commands* (Time). [< *cyb*(ernetic) *org*(anism)]

cyc., **1** cyclopedia. **2** cyclopedic. **3** cyclorama.

***cy|cad** (sī′kad), *n.* any one of a family of large, subtropical and tropical, palmlike plants with a cluster of long, fernlike leaves either rising from an underground stem or borne at the top of a thick, usually unbranched, columnlike trunk. Cycads bear cones. [< New Latin *Cycas, -adis* genus name < assumed Greek *kýkas,* a scribe's error for *kóïkas,* plural of *kóïx* a kind of palm]

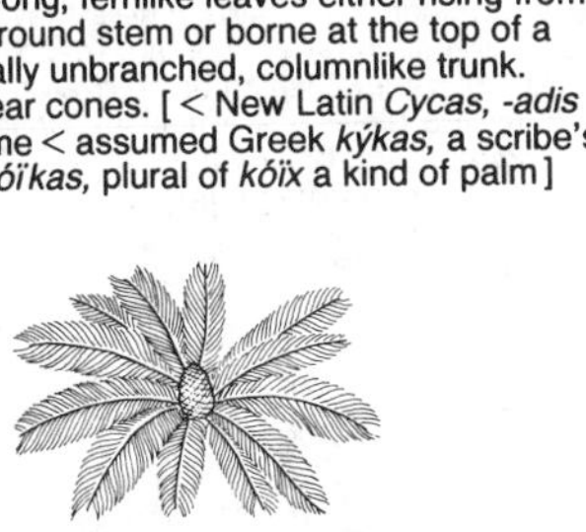

***cycad**

cyc|a|da|ceous (sik′ə dā′shəs), *adj.* of or belonging to the cycads.

cyc|a|do|phyte (sik′ə də fīt), *n.* a cycadlike plant of the Mesozoic era. [< *cycad* + Greek *phytón* plant]

cy|cas (sī′kas), *n.* any one of a group of cycads that resemble both the ferns and the palms. [< New Latin *Cycas;* see etym. under **cycad**]

cycl-, *combining form.* the form of **cyclo-** before a vowel, as in *cyclic.*

Cy|clad|ic (si klad′ik, sī-), *adj.* of or having to do with the Cyclades, a group of Greek islands in the Aegean Sea, and the prehistoric civilization that flourished there: *Cycladic statues.*

cy|clage (sī′klij), *n.* electrical power expressed in full periods of alternating electric current: *The well-known accuracy of the electric clock [is] due to the precise regulation of the cyclage of the electric current by the central station* (Science News Letter).

cyc|la|mate (sik′lə māt, sī′klə-), *n.* a white, crystalline powder with a very sweet taste, formerly much used as a sweetening agent. It is a calcium or sodium salt of an organic acid. [< *cycl-* + (sulf)*amate* the salt of sulfamic acid]

cyclamate calcium or **sodium,** = Sucaryl.

cyc|la|men (sik′lə men), *n.* any one of a group of plants with heart-shaped leaves and showy white, purple, pink, or crimson flowers, whose five petals bend backward. It belongs to the primrose family. [< New Latin *Cyclamen* < Latin *cyclamīnos* < Greek *kyklámīnos* a species of cyclamen]

cyc|la|min (sik′lə min, sī′klə-), *n.* a vegetable principle found in the root of various kinds of cyclamen. It is white, amorphous or in minute crystals, and has a bitter, acrid taste. [< *cyclam*(en) + *-in*]

cy|claz|o|cine (sī klaz′ə sēn, -sin), *n.* an analgesic drug used in the treatment of heroin addiction. Its action precipitates the symptoms of withdrawal. *Formula:* $C_{18}H_{25}NO$ [< *cycl-* + *azo-* + *-cine* (perhaps as in *medicine*)]

cy|cle (sī′kəl), *n., v.,* **cy|cled, cy|cling.** ***—n.*** **1** any period of time or complete process of growth or action that repeats itself in the same order. The seasons of the year—spring, summer, autumn, and winter—make a cycle. **SYN:** round. **2** a complete set, course, or series: *a cycle of events, a cycle of songs.* **SYN:** collection. **3a** all the stories, poems, legends, or ballads told about a certain hero or event: *There is a cycle of stories about the adventures of King Arthur and his knights.* **b** a series of miracle or mystery plays: *the Coventry cycle.* **4** a very long period of time; age: *Better fifty years of Europe than a cycle of Cathay* (Tennyson). **SYN:** epoch. **5** a complete or double alternation or reversal of an alternating electric current. The number of cycles per second is the measure of frequency. **6** a bicycle, tricycle, or motorcycle. **7** *Biology.* a recurring series of changes. **8** *Botany.* a closed circle or whorl of leaves. **9** *Astronomy.* an orbit or circle in the heavens: *the cycle of a planet.* **10** *Physics.* a series of operations by which a substance or operation is finally brought back to the initial state. **11** the series of strokes of a piston in the cylinder of an engine.
—v.i. **1** to pass through a cycle or cycles; occur over and over again in the same order. **2** to ride a bicycle, tricycle, or motorcycle.
[< Late Latin *cyclus* < Greek *kýklos* wheel, circle, ring]

cy|cle|car (sī′kəl kär′), *n.* a small, light motor vehicle having an open driving compartment and either three or four wheels.

cy|cler (sī′klər), *n.* the rider of a bicycle, tricycle, or motorcycle.

cycle rickshaw, = pedicab.

cy|cle|way (sī′kəl wā′), *n. British.* a road reserved for cyclists; bikeway: *There are 14 miles of cycleway separate from the roads, and they have been designed to be a joy to use* (London Times).

cy|clic (sī′klik, sik′lik), *adj.* **1** of a cycle: *the cyclic motion of a steam-engine piston.* **2** moving in cycles; coming in cycles: *the cyclic nature of the seasons. These cyclic operations will be controlled remotely and automatically from a control room* (Times Supplement). **3** *Chemistry.* **a** containing a ring of atoms. **b** of or having to do with an arrangement of atoms in a ring or closed chain. **4** *Botany.* arranged in whorls. **—cy′cli|cal|ly,** *adv.*

cy|cli|cal (sī′klə kəl, sik′lə-), *adj.* = cyclic.

cyclic AMP, a chemical compound that acts as an intercellular messenger in carrying out the action of hormones, especially the hormones of the pituitary gland; adenosine monophosphate.

cyclic pitch control, control of the forward, backward, and sideways movements of a helicopter by a cyclic pitch stick.

cyclic pitch stick, a control stick used in a helicopter to change the pitch of each main rotor blade so that it takes the smallest bite of air in the direction in which the pilot wishes to fly.

cyclic poets, the Greek poets following Homer who wrote epics about the Trojan War.

cy|clist (sī′klist), *n.* the rider of a bicycle, tricycle, or motorcycle.

cy|clize (sī′klīz, sik′līz), *v.t., v.i.,* **-clized, -cliz|ing.** *Chemistry.* to establish a closed chain or ring formation in. **—cy′cli|za′tion,** *n.*

cy|cli|zine (sī′klə zēn), *n.* an antihistaminic drug used to control motion sickness; Marezine. *Formula:* $C_{18}H_{22}N_2$ [< *cycli*(c) + (a)*zine*]

cy|clo (sē′klō), *n., pl.* **-clos.** = cyclo-pousse: *the bow-backed driver of a Laotian cyclo* (Maclean's).

cyclo-, *combining form.* **1** circle; of a circle: *Cycloid = shaped somewhat like a circle.*
2 cycle; alternation: *Cyclothymia = alternation of mental attitude.*
3 *Chemistry.* cyclic: *Cyclohexane = cyclic hexane.* Also, **cycl-** before vowels.
[< Greek *kýklos* ring, wheel]

cy|clo|al|kane (sī′klō al′kān, sik′lō-), *n.* an alicyclic compound.

cy|clo|al|kene (sī′klō al′kēn, sik′lō-), *n.* = cycloolefin.

cy|clo-cross (sī′klō krôs′, -kros′), *n.* a cross-country bicycle race.

cy|clo|gen|e|sis (sī′klə jen′ə sis), *n.* the formation or development of a storm, especially of a cyclone.

cy|clo|gi|ro (sī′klō jī′rō), *n., pl.* **-ros.** an aircraft similar to the autogiro but with airfoils feathered to rotate parallel to the ground on each cycle of rotation.

cy|clo|graph (sī′klə graf, -gräf; sik′lə-), *n.* a camera that takes a panoramic picture of the periphery of an object; curvograph.

cy|clo|hex|ane (sī′klō hek′sān, sik′lō-), *n.* C_6H_{12}, considered as a ring of six bivalent radicals (CH_2): *Textile companies make synthetic fibers from cyclohexane* (Richard C. McCurdy).

cy|clo|hex|a|nol (sī′klō hek′sə nōl, -nol; sik′lō-), *n.* an alcohol derived from cyclohexane. *Formula:* $C_6H_{11}OH$

cy|clo|hex|a|none (sī′klō hek′sə nōn, sik′lō-), *n.* a ketone prepared by oxidizing cyclohexanol. *Formula:* $C_6H_{10}O$

cy|clo|hex|i|mide (sī′klō hek′sə mīd, sik′lō-), *n.* a crystalline compound derived from a moldlike soil microorganism, used especially as a fungicide for the control of leaf spot and turf diseases; Actidione. *Formula:* $C_{15}H_{23}NO_4$

cy|cloid** (sī′kloid), *adj., n.* ***—adj. **1** like a circle; somewhat circular. **2a** somewhat circular, with smooth edges and concentric striations. Certain fishes have cycloid scales. **b** having cycloid scales: *a cycloid fish.* **3** of or having cyclothymia. ***—n.*** **1** *Geometry.* a curve traced by a point on the circumference or on a radius or a prolonged radius of a circle when the circle is rolled along a straight line and kept in the same plane. **2** a cycloid fish. **3** a cyclothymic person.
[< Greek *kykloeidês* circular < *kýklos* circle + *eîdos* form]

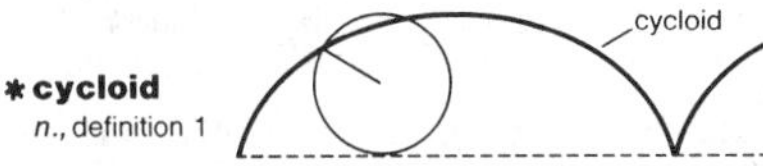

***cycloid**
n., definition 1

cy|cloi|dal (sī kloi′dəl), *adj.* = cycloid. **—cy|cloi′dal|ly,** *adv.*

cy|clom|e|ter (sī klom′ə tər), *n.* **1** an instrument that measures the distance that a wheel travels by recording the revolutions that it makes. **2** an instrument for measuring arcs of circles.

cy|clo|met|ric (sī′klə met′rik), *adj.* of or having to do with cyclometry.

cy|clom|e|try (sī klom′ə trē), *n.* the science of measuring circles.

cy|clo|nal (sī klō′nəl), *adj.* = cyclonic.

cy|clone (sī′klōn), *n.* **1** a storm or winds moving around and spiraling in toward a calm center of low pressure, which also moves. The winds of a cyclone move counterclockwise in the Northern Hemisphere and clockwise in the Southern Hemisphere. *Many errors in forecasting are caused by overattention to comparatively local conditions, without proper regard to the grand movement upon which the cyclones—the parents of rain and sunshine—are borne* (London Times). **SYN:** typhoon, hurricane. **2** any very violent windstorm, such as a tornado. **SYN:** whirlwind. [ultimately < Greek *kýklos* circle; probably influenced by Greek *kyklôn,* present participle of *kykloyn* move around in a circle]

cyclone cellar, an underground shelter from cyclones or tornadoes.

cyclone fence, **1** = chain link fence. **2 Cyclone Fence.** a trademark for such a fence.

cyclone furnace or **boiler,** a furnace for burning crushed and very moist subbituminous coal by using a liquid fuel and preheated air that produce a whirling column of flames in which the combustible material is burned and the slag is melted.

cy|clon|ic (sī klon′ik), *adj.* **1** of a cyclone: *a cyclonic wind.* **2** like a cyclone: *cyclonic circulations.* **—cy|clon′i|cal|ly,** *adv.*

cy|clon|i|cal (sī klon′ə kəl), *adj.* = cyclonic.

cy|clo|nite (sī′klə nīt, sik′lə-), *n.* RDX; a powerful explosive of high sensitivity, combined with other explosives for use in certain bombs; hexogen.

cy|clo|nol|o|gy (sī′klō nol′ə jē), *n.* the scientific study of cyclones.

Pronunciation Key: hat, āge, cãre, fär; let, ēqual, tėrm; it, īce; hot, ōpen, ôrder; oil, out; cup, pu̇t, rüle; child; long; thin; ᴛʜen; zh, measure; ə represents a in about, e in taken, i in pencil, o in lemon, u in circus.

cy|clo|no|scope (sī klō′nə skōp), *n.* a device for determining the center of a cyclone.

cy|clo|o|le|fin (sī′klō ō′lə fin, sik′lō-), *n.* any one of a group of alicyclic hydrocarbons with an unsaturated ring, having the general formula C_nH_{2n-2}; cycloalkene.

cy|clo|par|af|fin (sī′klō par′ə fin, sik′lō-), *n.* any one of a group of alicyclic hydrocarbons with a saturated ring, having the general formula C_nH_{2n}; naphthene.

Cy|clo|pe|an (sī′klə pē′ən), *adj.* **1** of or resembling the Cyclopes: *a searchlight went on like a Cyclopean eye and swiveled its beam toward me* (Guy Endore). **2** Also, **cyclopean.** huge; gigantic; massive. **3** *Architecture.* in or resembling a very early style of masonry using huge stones more or less irregular in shape.

cy|clo|pe|di|a or **cy|clo|pae|di|a** (sī′klə pē′dē ə), *n.* **1** a book or set of books giving information on all branches of one subject. It is made up of articles which are usually arranged alphabetically. **2** a book or set of books giving information on many branches of knowledge; encyclopedia.

cy|clo|pe|dic or **cy|clo|pae|dic** (sī′klə pē′dik), *adj.* **1** wide and varied. **2** having to do with a cyclopedia. **—cy′clo|pe′di|cal|ly, cy′clo|pae′di|cal|ly,** *adv.*

cy|clo|pe|dist or **cy|clo|pae|dist** (sī′klə pē′dist), *n.* a person who makes a cyclopedia or writes articles for one.

cy|clo|pen|tane (sī′klə pen′tān, sik′lə-), *n.* a colorless, saturated hydrocarbon present in certain petroleums. *Formula:* C_5H_{10}

Cy|clo|pes (sī klō′pēz), *n.* plural of **Cyclops.**

cy|clo|pho|ri|a (sī′klə fôr′ē ə, -fōr′-; sik′lə-), *n.* involuntary rotation of the eyeball, tilting the vertical axis to the side, due to weakness of the oblique muscles. [< *cyclo-* + Greek *-phoriā* < *phérein* to bear]

cy|clo|phos|pha|mide (sī′klə fos′fə mīd, sik′lə-; -mid), *n.* a drug related to nitrogen mustard, used in the treatment of various cancers and to suppress the rejection of transplanted tissue.

cy|clo|pi|a (sī klō′pē ə), *n.* a massive abnormality in which the eyes are partly or wholly fused. [< New Latin *cyclopia* < Greek *kýklos* circle + *ōps* eye]

Cy|clop|ic (sī klop′ik), *adj.* belonging to or like a Cyclops; monstrous; Cyclopean: *poking television's Cyclopic eye into every nook and cranny of the amphitheatre* (Time).

cy|clo|ple|gi|a (sī′klə plē′jē ə, sik′lə-), *n.* paralysis of the ciliary muscle of the eye. [< New Latin *cycloplegia* < Greek *kýklos* circle + *plēgē* a stroke]

cy|clo|ple|gic (sī′klə plē′jik, sik′lə-), *n., adj.* **—*n.*** a remedy or agent for treating cycloplegia.
—*adj.* of or producing cycloplegia.

cy|clo|pro|pane (sī′klə prō′pān, sik′lə-), *n.* a colorless, saturated, gaseous hydrocarbon considered as a closed ring of three methylene radicals (CH_2), used as an anesthetic. *Formula:* C_3H_6

Cy|clops (sī′klops), *n., pl.* **Cy|clo|pes.** *Greek Legend.* one of a group of giants with one eye in the middle of the forehead.
[< Latin *Cyclops* < Greek *Kýklōps* < *kýklos* circle + *ōps* the eye]

cy|clops (sī′klops), *n., pl.* **-clops.** any one of a group of tiny free-swimming crustaceans having a single eye in the middle of the head region; water flea. [< *Cyclops*]

cy|clo|ram|a (sī′klə ram′ə, -rä′mə), *n.* **1** a large picture of a landscape, battle, or other scene, on the wall of a circular room. **2** a curved curtain or backdrop on a stage, used to give the illusion of distance or unlimited space in the background.
[< *cyclo-* + Greek *hórāma* spectacle]

cy|clo|ram|ic (sī′klə ram′ik), *adj.* having to do with or like a cyclorama.

cy|close (sī′klōs), *n. Chemistry.* a sugar containing a closed carbon chain in the molecule.

cy|clo|ser|ine (sī′klə ser′ēn), *n.* an antibiotic formed in cultures of various species of streptomyces, used in the treatment of tuberculosis and certain other bacterial infections; Seromycin. *Formula:* $C_3H_6N_2O_2$ [< *cyclo-* + *ser*(um) + *-ine*]

cy|clo|sis (sī klō′sis), *n. Biology.* the rotary streaming movement of protoplasm in a cell, especially of the endoplasm. [< New Latin *cyclosis* < Greek *kýklōsis* < *kykloyn* move in a circle]

cy|clo|spor|ine (sī′klə spôr′ēn, -spōr′-), or **cy|clo|spor|in** (sī′klə spôr′in, -spōr′-), *n.* an immunosuppressive drug derived from certain brown algae, effective in stopping the rejection of transplanted tissue without destroying the body's immune system. [< New Latin *Cyclosporinae* the class of brown algae]

Cy|clo|sto|ma|ta (sī′klə stō′mə tə), *n.pl.* the class of vertebrates comprising the cyclostomes.

cy|clos|to|mate (sī klos′tə mit, -māt), *adj.* = cyclostomatous.

cy|clo|stom|a|tous (sī′klə stom′ə təs, -stō′mə-; sik′lə-), *adj.* **1** having a circular mouth. **2** belonging to the cyclostomes.

cy|clo|stome (sī′klə stōm, sik′lə-), *n., adj.* **—*n.*** any animal of a class of slender, snakelike fishes, having a round, sucking mouth and no jaws. Lampreys and hagfishes belong to this class.
—*adj.* of or belonging to this class.
[< *cyclo-* + Greek *stóma* mouth]

cy|clos|to|mous (sī klos′tə məs), *adj.* = cyclostomatous.

cy|clo|stroph|ic (sī′klə strof′ik, sik′lə-), *adj.* denoting winds strongly affected by centrifugal force. [< *cyclo-* + Greek *strophē* a turning + *-ic*]

cy|clo|style (sī′klə stīl, sik′lə-), *n., v.,* **-styled, -styl|ing. —*n.*** an apparatus for printing copies of writing by means of a stencil.
—*v.t.* to copy by means of a cyclostyle: *to cyclostyle a letter.*

Cy|clo-teach|er (sī′klō tē′chər), *n. Trademark.* a teaching machine using printed disks for programmed instruction.

cy|clo|them (sī′klə them, sik′lə-), *n. Geology.* a series of beds deposited in one sedimentary cycle. [< *cyclo-* + Greek *théma* something set down]

cy|clo|thyme (sī′klə thīm, sik′lə-), *n.* **1** a person who alternates between liveliness and depression. **2** = manic-depressive.

cy|clo|thy|mi|a (sī′klə thī′mē ə, sik′lə-), *n.* alternation of liveliness and depression. [< *cyclo-* + Greek *-thymiā* < *thymós* mind]

cy|clo|thy|mic (sī′klə thī′mik, sik′lə-), *adj., n.* **—*adj.*** **1** alternating between liveliness and depression. **2** = manic-depressive.
—*n.* = cyclothyme.

cy|clot|o|my (sī klot′ə mē), *n.* **1** *Surgery.* an operation for division of the ciliary muscle, practiced to relieve tension in glaucoma. **2** *Mathematics.* the theory of the partition of the circle.

cy|clo|tron (sī′klə tron, sik′lə-), *n.* **1** a particle accelerator that greatly increases the speed and energy of protons and other atomic particles; atom smasher. An alternating electric field in a constant magnetic field accelerates the particles in a spiral path away from their sources and causes the particles to collide with nuclei at very high velocities, and break up atoms and cause radioactivity. **2** an apparatus for developing large beam currents by passing positive ions through repeated accelerating potentials. [< *cyclo-* + *-tron,* as in *electron*]

cy|der (sī′dər), *n. British.* cider.

cyg|net (sig′nit), *n.* **1** a young swan. **2** a highly energetic and penetrating form of radiation believed to come from the constellation Cygnus and certain other celestial sources: *These cygnets have become the ugly ducklings of underground astronomy* (Science News). [perhaps diminutive of Old French *cygne* < Latin *cygnus* < Greek *kýknos*]

Cyg|ni (sig′nī), *n.,* genitive of **Cygnus.**

Cyg|nus (sig′nəs), *n., genitive* (def. 2) **Cyg|ni.** **1** *Greek Mythology.* the swan into which Zeus changed himself when he visited Leda to court her. **2** a northern constellation in the Milky Way, seen by ancient astronomers as having the rough outline of a swan in flight; Swan. [< Latin *Cygnus* (literally) swan]

cyl., **1** cylinder. **2** cylindrical.

cyl|i|ces (sil′ə sēz), *n.* the plural of **cylix.**

***cylinder**
definition 1a

right circular cylinder

oblique cylinder

cyl|in|der** (sil′ən dər), *n., v.* **—*n. **1a** a solid bounded by two equal, parallel circles and by a curved surface, formed by moving a straight line of fixed length so that its ends always lie on the two parallel circles. In a right circular cylinder the circles are perpendicular to the line; in an oblique circular cylinder they are not. **b** a solid bounded by two parallel planes and a curved surface formed by moving a straight line so that it constantly describes a given curve and remains parallel to its original position. **c** a curved surface formed by either of these motions. **d** the volume of any such solid. **2** any long, round object, solid or hollow, with flat ends: *Tin cans and rollers are cylinders.* **3** the rotating part of a revolver that contains chambers for cartridges. **4a** the piston chamber of an internal-combustion engine. **b** the barrel of a pump. **5** *Printing.* **a** a revolving drum, forming part of a flat-bed press, which produces the impression. **b** one of two or more revolving drums on a rotary press which carry the printing plate or the blanket or receive the impression. **6** *Archaeology.* **a** a cylindrical stone seal used by the Babylonians and Assyrians. **b** a hollow, barrel-shaped object of baked clay bearing cuneiform inscriptions. **7a** a vessel or container having the form of a cylinder. **b** its contents.
—*v.t.* **1** to furnish with a cylinder or cylinders. **2** to subject to the action of a cylinder or cylinders.
[< Latin *cylindrus* < Greek *kýlindros* < *kylíndein* to roll]

cylinder block, = engine block.

cylinder gate, a cylindrical gate or valve used to regulate the amount of water flowing to a turbine.

cylinder head, a detachable plate closing the end of the cylinder or engine block of an internal-combustion engine and sometimes carrying the valves.

cylinder oil, a heavy, viscous grade of oil for lubricating the cylinder of a steam engine.

cylinder press, a printing press in which one revolving cylinder forces the paper against the form, which is moved back and forth on a flat bed.

cyl|in|dra|ceous (sil′ən drā′shəs), *adj.* like a cylinder; shaped like a cylinder.

cy|lin|dric (sə lin′drik), *adj.* = cylindrical.

cy|lin|dri|cal (sə lin′drə kəl), *adj.* **1** shaped like a cylinder; having the form of a cylinder. Cans of fruit, candles, and water pipes are usually cylindrical. **2** of or having to do with a cylinder. **—cy|lin′dri|cal|ly,** *adv.*

cy|lin|dri|cal|i|ty (sə lin′drə kal′ə tē), *n.* cylindrical quality or form.

cyl|in|drite (sil′ən drīt), *n.* a sulfide of lead, antimony, and tin, occurring in massive forms with concentric cylindrical structure, found in Bolivia.

cyl|in|droid (sil′ən droid), *n., adj.* **—*n.*** a solid having the form of a cylinder with equal and parallel elliptical bases.
—*adj.* **1** like a cylinder. **2** like a cylindroid.
[< Greek *kylindroeidḗs* < *kýlindros* (see etym. under **cylinder**) + *eîdos* form]

cy|lix (sī′liks, sil′iks), *n., pl.* **cyl|i|ces.** a shallow drinking cup with a tall stem and two handles, used in ancient Greece. Also, **kylix.** [< Greek *kýlix*]

Cyl|le|ni|an (si lē′nē ən), *adj.* of or having to do with Hermes (Mercury), said to have been born on Mount Cyllene in Greece.

Cym., Cymric.

cy|ma (sī′mə), *n., pl.* **-mae** (-mē). **1** a molding whose outline is concave and convex. **2** *Botany.* a cyme. [< New Latin *cyma* < Greek *kyma* (originally) anything swollen; young sprout of a plant]

cy|ma|graph (sī′mə graf, -gräf), *n.* an instrument for tracing an outline or contour, especially of moldings or profiles. [< New Latin *cyma* (< Greek *kyma* anything swollen; a wave, a waved molding) + English *-graph*]

cy|mar (si mär′), *n.* a simar, a loose garment formerly worn by women. [< French *cimarre, simarre* < Italian *zimarra* long robe, probably < Spanish *zamarra* shepherd's garment < Arabic *sammūr* sable. See etym. of doublet **chimere, simar.**]

cy|ma|ti|um (si mā′shē əm), *n., pl.* **-ti|a** (-shē ə). *Architecture.* a cyma. [< Latin *cȳmatium* an ogee, volute of an Ionic column < Greek *kymátion* (diminutive) < *kyma;* see etym. under **cyma**]

***cym|bal** (sim′bəl), *n.* one of a pair of brass plates used as a musical instrument. When cymbals are struck together or hit with beaters they make a loud ringing sound. Cymbals are made from long coils of spun metal which are brazed together in the form of a plate. [Old English *cimbal* < Latin *cymbalum* < Greek *kýmbalon* < *kýmbē* hollow of a vessel, bowl, drinking cup]

***cymbal**

suspended cymbals

hand cymbals

cym|baled (sim′bəld), *adj.* furnished with cymbals.

cym|bal|ist (sim′bə list), *n.* a player on the cymbals or the cymbalom.

cym|ba|lom (sim′bə lom), *n.* an ancient stringed musical instrument.

cym|bate (sim′bāt), *adj.* boat-shaped. [< Latin *cymba* boat + English *-ate*[1]]

Cym|be|line (sim′bə lēn), *n.* a drama by Shakespeare, first produced around 1609-10, based on a tale by Boccaccio.

cym|bid|i|um (sim bid′ē əm), *n., pl.* **-bid|i|ums, -bid|i|a** (-bid′ē ə). any flower of a genus of tropical, terrestrial orchids, grown in greenhouses for their spikes of showy, boatshaped flowers. See picture under **orchid**. [< New Latin *Cymbidium* the genus name < Latin *cymba* boat]

cym|bi|form (sim′bə fôrm), *adj.* boat-shaped; longer than broad; convex, and keeled like the bottom of a boat: *cymbiform insects, cymbiform spores.* [< Latin *cymba* boat + English *-form*]

***cyme** (sīm), *n.* a flower cluster in which there is a flower at the top of the main stem and of each branch of the cluster. The flowers in the center open first. The sweet william has cymes. [< Latin *cȳma;* see etym. under **cyma**]

***cyme**

cy|mene (sī′mēn), *n.* a colorless, liquid hydrocarbon with a lemonlike odor, that occurs in the oil of cumin and other plants in three isometric forms (orthocymene, metacymene, and paracymene). *Formula:* $C_{10}H_{14}$ [< Latin *cumīnum* (see etym. under **cumin**) + English *-ene*]

cy|mif|er|ous (sī mif′ər əs), *adj.* producing cymes.

cy|mo|gene (sī′mə jēn), *n.* an inflammable, gaseous mixture of hydrocarbons, obtained in distilling petroleum, and used to produce low temperatures. [< *cym*(ene) + *-gen*]

cy|mo|graph (sī′mə graf, -gräf), *n.* **1** = kymograph. **2** = cymagraph. [< Greek *kýma* wave + English *-graph*]

cy|moid (sī′moid), *adj.* having the form of a cyme.

cy|mom|e|ter (sī mom′ə tər), *n.* an instrument for measuring wave frequency of electric waves. [< Greek *kýma* wave + English *-meter*]

cy|mo|phane (sī′mə fān), *n.* = chrysoberyl. [< Greek *kýma* wave + *phaínein* appear]

cy|mo|scope (sī′mə skōp), *n.* a device for detecting the presence of electric or electromagnetic waves. [< Greek *kýma* wave + English *-scope*]

cy|mose (sī′mōs, sī mōs′), *adj. Botany.* **1** having a cyme or cymes. **2** like a cyme. **3** = determinate: *a cymose flower cluster.* [< Latin *cȳmōsus* < *cȳma;* see etym. under **cyma**] —**cy′mose|ly,** *adv.*

Cym|ric (kim′rik, sim′-), *adj., n.* —*adj.* **1** of or having to do with the Welsh people or their language. **2** of or having to do with the group of Celts that includes the Welsh, Cornish, and Bretons, or their languages; Brythonic.
—*n.* **1** = Welsh. **2** the Brythonic division of the Celtic languages. Also, **Kymric.**

Cym|ru (kim′rü), *n.* Wales.

Cym|ry (kim′rē), *n.* **1** the Welsh people. **2** the branch of the Celts that includes the Welsh, Cornish, and Bretons. Also, **Kymry.** [< Welsh *Cymry* the Welsh]

cy|mule (sī′myül), *n. Botany.* a simple or diminutive cyme, either by itself or forming part of a compound cyme.

cyn|e|get|ic (sin′ə jet′ik), *adj.* of or having to do with hunting or the chase. [< Greek *kynēgetikós* < *kynēgétēs* huntsman < *kýōn, kynós* dog + *ēgétēs* leader]

cyn|e|get|ics (sin′ə jet′iks), *n.* hunting; the chase.

cyn|ic (sin′ik), *n., adj.* —*n.* **1** a person inclined to doubt the sincerity and goodness of human motives and to show this doubt by sneers and sarcasm: *He cast a cynic's doubting eye on every good deed in a naughty world.* **2** a sneering, sarcastic person.
—*adj.* = cynical.
[< Latin *Cynicus* Cynic philosopher < Greek *Kynikós* (literally) doglike < *kýōn, kynós* dog]

Cyn|ic (sin′ik), *n., adj.* —*n.* a member of a group of ancient Greek philosophers who taught that virtue constitutes happiness, and that self-control is the essential part of virtue. They despised pleasure, money, and personal comfort.
—*adj.* of or having to do with the Cynics or their doctrines.

cyn|i|cal (sin′ə kəl), *adj.* **1** doubting the sincerity and goodness of others: *There are many other people ... who are just as cynical as these youngsters about local politicians* (Harper's). **2** sneering; sarcastic: *The boys made several cynical remarks to cover up their disappointment at being left out of the play.* —**cyn′i|cal|ly,** *adv.* —**cyn′i|cal|ness,** *n.*
—*Syn.* **1 Cynical, pessimistic** mean doubting and mistrustful. **Cynical** emphasizes a tendency to doubt the honesty and sincerity of people and their motives for doing things: *It is difficult to make friends with a person who is cynical about friendship.* **Pessimistic** emphasizes a disposition to look on the dark side of things and to expect the unpleasant or worst to happen: *He has a very pessimistic attitude toward the value of this work.*

cyn|i|cism (sin′ə siz əm), *n.* **1** cynical quality or disposition: *The smugness has gone out of cynicism and the skeptics are asking the questions which will lead at length to affirmation of some kind* (Atlantic). **2** a cynical remark.

Cyn|i|cism (sin′ə siz əm), *n.* the doctrines of the Cynics.

cyn|i|pid (sin′ə pid), *n.* any one of a family of small insects that deposit larvae on the leaves of plants and trees and produce galls; gallfly. [< New Latin *Cynipidae* the family name < *Cynips* the typical genus < Greek *kýōn, kynós* dog + *íps* wood worm]

cyn|o|ceph|a|lous (sin′ə sef′ə ləs, sī′nə-), *adj.* having a head like that of a dog. [< Greek *kýōn, kynós* dog + *kephalḗ* head + English *-ous*]

cyn|o|dont (sin′ə dont, sī′nə-), *n.* any one of a class of upright reptiles of the Triassic period. [< New Latin *Cynodontia* < Greek *kýōn, kynós* dog + *odoús, odóntos* tooth]

cyn|o|gnath|us (sin′ə nath′əs), *n.* a prehistoric reptile with differentiated teeth and skull and legs much like those of a mammal. [< New Latin *Cynognathus* the genus name < Greek *kýōn, kynós* dog + *gnáthos* jaw]

Cyn|o|su|ra (sin′ə shůr′ə, sī′nə-), *n.* **1** *Greek Mythology.* a nymph of Mount Ida, and nurse of Zeus, metamorphosed into the constellation Ursa Minor. **2** = Cynosure.

cy|no|su|ral (sī′nə shůr′əl, sin′ə-), *adj.* attracting attention.

cy|no|sure (sī′nə shůr, sin′ə-), *n.* **1** a center of attraction, interest, or attention. **2** *Figurative.* something used for guidance or direction: *Every eye watched every motion of the Englishman, a cynosure, to store him for future nourishment* (Atlantic). [< *Cynosure*]

Cy|no|sure (sī′nə shůr, sin′ə-), *n.* **1** the northern constellation Ursa Minor, which contains the North Star and which was formerly used by sailors as a guide. **2** the North Star (Polaris). [< Latin *Cynosūra* Ursa Minor < Greek *kynósoura* (literally) dog's tail < *kýōn, kynós* dog + *ourā́* tail]

Cyn|thi|a (sin′thē ə), *n.* **1** *Greek and Roman Mythology.* Artemis or Diana, regarded as the goddess of the moon. **2** the moon.

Cynthia moth, a large, brown moth with white markings that feeds on the ailanthus, one of the few insects known to do this.

C.Y.O. or **CYO** (no periods), Catholic Youth Organization.

cy|per|a|ceous (sī′pə rā′shəs), *adj.* belonging to the sedge family of plants. [< New Latin *Cyperus* the typical genus (< Latin *cypērus* rush, sedge < Greek *kýpeiros*) + English *-aceous*]

cy|pher (sī′fər), *n., v.i., v.t.* = cipher.

cy pres (sē′ prā′), *Law.* as nearly as possible (to the intent of a person who leaves a will or trust that cannot be executed literally). [< Anglo-French *cy pres,* Old French *si pres* as near(ly) (as possible)]

cy|press[1] (sī′prəs), *n.* **1** any one of a group of evergreen trees with hard wood and dark-green, overlapping leaves like scales. It belongs to the cypress family. Cypress is cultivated in western Asia, southern Europe, and the southern and western United States. **2** any one of various cone-bearing trees, related to the true cypress, such as the bald or swamp cypress. **3** the wood of any cypress tree. Cypress is much used for boards and shingles and for doors. **4** the branches of the cypress, used as a symbol of mourning, from their ancient use at funerals. **5** any one of various plants in some way resembling the true cypress. [< Old French *cipres,* learned borrowing from Late Latin *cypressus* < Greek *kypárissos*]

cy|press[2] (sī′prəs), *n. Obsolete.* **1** a fine, thin, black fabric formerly much used for mourning: *wearing mourning scarfs of cypress* (London Gazette). **2** an expensive satin. [probably < Old French *Cypre* Cyprus, from which many fabrics were imported in the Middle Ages]

cy|pressed (sī′prəst), *adj.* planted with cypress trees.

cypress family, a widely distributed group of gymnospermous trees and shrubs having scalelike or needlelike leaves and widely used for lumber and for ornamental purposes. The family includes the cypress, arbor vitae, juniper, and red cedar.

cypress knee, a large, hollow, conical excrescence which rises from the roots of the bald cypress. The presumed cause of its growth is to provide air for the roots.

cypress vine, a garden plant of the morning-glory family, having finely divided leaves and bright-red or white, tubular flowers.

Cyp|ri|an (sip′rē ən), *adj., n.* —*adj.* **1** of or having to do with Cyprus, an island in the eastern Mediterranean, famous for its worship of Aphrodite (Venus). **2** lewd; licentious.
—*n.* **1** a native or inhabitant of Cyprus. **2** a lewd or licentious person.
[< Latin *Cyprius* Cyprian (< *Cyprus* Cyprus, an ancient center for the worship of Venus) + English *-an*]

cy|prid (sī′prid), *n., pl.* **-prids, -pri|des** (-prə dēz′). **1** any one of a genus of minute, freshwater crustaceans with delicate bivalve shells. **2** = cypris. [< New Latin *Cyprididae* the genus name < Greek *Kýpris* Aphrodite]

cy|pri|nid (si prī′nid, sip′rə-), *n., adj.* = cyprinoid.

cy|prin|i|form (si prin′ə fôrm, -prī′nə-), *adj.* carplike in form or structure. [< Latin *cyprīnus* carp (< Greek *kyprînos*) + English *-form*]

cy|prin|o|dont (si prin′ə dont, -prī′nə-), *n.* any one of a group of small, soft-finned fishes, mostly inhabiting fresh or brackish water, and including the killifishes and certain minnows. [< New Latin *Cyprinodon* the typical genus < Greek *kyprînos* carp + *odoús, odóntos* tooth]

cyp|ri|noid (sip′rə noid, si prī′-), *n., adj.* —*n.* any one of a large group of freshwater fishes, including the carps, suckers, goldfishes, breams, and most freshwater minnows.
—*adj.* of or belonging to this group of freshwater fishes.
[< Latin *cyprīnus* carp (< Greek *kyprînos*) + English *-oid*]

Cyp|ri|ot (sip′rē ət), *n., adj.* —*n.* **1** a person born or living in Cyprus. **2** the Greek dialect of Cyprus.
—*adj.* of or having to do with Cyprus; Cyprian.
[< Greek *Kypriṓtes* < *Kýpros* Cyprus]

Cyp|ri|ote (sip′rē ōt), *n., adj.* = Cypriot.

cyp|ri|pe|di|um (sip′rə pē′dē əm), *n., pl.* **-di|a** (-dē ə). any one of a group of orchids that have drooping flowers with a protruding, saclike lip, including lady's-slippers and moccasin flowers. [< New Latin *Cypripedium* the genus name < Greek *Kýpris* Aphrodite + *pódion* (diminutive) < *poús, podós* foot]

cy|pris (sī′pris), *n.* the stage after the nauplius in the development of a barnacle; a larval form with a bivalve shell and a pair of anterior antennae; cyprid. [< Greek *Kýpris* Aphrodite]

cy|pro|hep|ta|dine (sī′prō hep′tə dēn), *n.* a drug that opposes the effects of histamine and serotonin, used especially against pruritus and asthma. *Formula:* $C_{21}H_{21}N$ [< *cy*(clo-) + *pro-*[1] + *hepta-* + (piperi)*dine*]

cyp|se|la (sip′sə lə), *n., pl.* **-lae** (-lē). *Botany.* an achene having an adherent calyx. [< New Latin *cypsela* < Greek *kypsélē* hollow vessel, box]

cyp|se|line (sip′sə līn, -lin), *adj.* **1** having to do with or resembling a swift. **2** belonging to the same family of birds as the swift. [< Latin *cypselus* the swift (< Greek *kýpselos*) + *-ine*[1]]

Cy|ra|no de Ber|ge|rac (sir′ə nō də bėr′zhə rak; *French* sē rȧ nō′ də ber zhə rȧk′), the hero of a play by Edmond Rostand. Cyrano is famous for his large nose.

Cyr|e|na|ic (sir′ə nā′ik, sī′rə-), *adj., n.* —*adj.* **1** of Cyrenaica, an ancient country in northern Africa, or Cyrene, its chief city. **2** of or having to do with a school of ancient Greek philosophers that taught that pleasure is the only rational aim in life.
—*n.* **1** a native or inhabitant of Cyrenaica. **2** a disciple of the Cyrenaic philosophy.

Cy|re|ne (sī rē′nē), *n. Greek Mythology.* a water nymph beloved by Apollo, by whom she bore Aristaeus.

***Cy|ril|lic** (si ril′ik), *adj.* of or having to do with an ancient Slavic alphabet from which the Russian, Bulgarian, and Serbian alphabets have developed. [< *Cyril,* an apostle to the Slavs in the 800's, who developed an earlier Slavic alphabet from which the Cyrillic alphabet was derived]

***Cyrillic**

Аэрофлот

cyr|i|o|log|ic (sir′ē ə loj′ik, sī′rē-), *adj.* denoting or having to do with a form of hieroglyphic writing in which objects are represented by pictures, not by symbols. Also, **curiologic.** [< Greek *kȳriologikós* speaking literally < *kȳ́rios* proper + *lógos* speech]

Pronunciation Key: hat, āge, cãre, fär; let, ēqual, tėrm; it, īce; hot, ōpen, ôrder; oil, out; cup, pu̇t, rüle; child; long; thin; ᴛʜen; zh, measure; ə represents a in about, e in taken, i in pencil, o in lemon, u in circus.

cyr|to|lite (sėr′tə līt), *n.* a mineral related to zircon in form or composition, but hydrous, and perhaps resulting from its alteration. The faces of the crystals are commonly convex. [< Greek *kyrtós* curved + English *-lite*]

cyr|tom|e|ter (sėr tom′ə tər), *n.* an instrument for measuring and recording the curved surface of the chest and other parts of the body. [< Greek *kyrtós* curved + English *-meter*]

cyr|to|sis (sėr tō′sis), *n.* curvature of the spine. [< New Latin *cyrtosis* < Greek *kýrtōsis* < *kyrtós* curved]

cyr|to|style (sėr′tə stīl), *adj., n.* —***adj.*** having columns arranged in a projecting curve, as a portico. —***n.*** a portico with columns arranged in a projecting curve. [< Greek *kyrtós* curved + English *style*]

cyst (sist), *n.* **1** a small sac in animals or plants, usually containing liquid and diseased matter produced by inflammation. Cysts are often caused by the blocking of some passage, for example in a gland. **2** a thin-walled, hollow organ or cavity in an animal body or plant; a bladder, sac, or vesicle, for example in rockweeds. **3** a spore in green algae during a period of dormancy, after which it germinates to produce a new plant; resting spore. **4** a cell or cavity containing reproductive bodies, embryos, or bacteria in a resting stage. **5** a small, round sac, such as that enclosing an embryonic tapeworm or a pair of certain parasitic protozoans before sporulation. **6** any similar protective capsule. [< New Latin *cystis* < Greek *kýstis* pouch, bladder]

cys|ta|thi|o|nine (sis′tə thī′ə nēn, -nin), *n.* an amino acid that is an intermediate in the conversion of methionine to cysteine. *Formula:* $C_7H_{14}N_2O_4S$ [< *cyst*(eine) + (me)*thionine*]

cys|tec|to|my (sis tek′tə mē), *n., pl.* **-mies.** the surgical removal of a cyst or bladder.

cyst|ed (sis′tid), *adj.* having a cyst.

cys|te|ine (sis′tē ēn, -in), *n.* a crystalline amino acid present in proteins and derived from cystine. *Formula:* $C_3H_7O_2NS$

cys|ten|chy|ma (sis teng′kə mə), *n.* a kind of fluid-filled tissue in certain sponges, similar to the parenchyma of plants.

cyst|ic (sis′tik), *adj.* **1** of or like a cyst. **2** having a cyst or cysts. **3** enclosed in a cyst; encysted. **4** of the bladder. **5** of the gall bladder.

cys|ti|cer|coid (sis′tə sėr′koid), *n.* the larva of certain tapeworms, somewhat similar to the cysticercus but having a very small, or rudimentary, bladder.

cys|ti|cer|cus (sis′tə sėr′kəs), *n., pl.* **-cer|ci** (-sėr′sī). the encysted larva of certain tapeworms. [< New Latin *cysticercus* < Greek *kýstis* bladder + *kérkos* tail]

cystic fibrosis, a hereditary disease of the pancreas, primarily beginning in childhood, characterized by excessive secretion from internal organs, malnutrition, and accompanying respiratory infection.

cys|ti|form (sis′tə fôrm), *adj.* having the form of a cyst or bladder. [< *cyst* + *-form*]

cys|tin (sis′tin), *n.* = cystine.

cys|tine (sis′tēn, -tin), *n.* a crystalline amino acid found in many proteins, especially keratin: *To speed the healing of a wound, whether in battle or in an operating room, the human body needs one particular chemical, a protein building block called cystine* (Science News Letter). *Formula:* $C_6H_{12}N_2O_4S_2$ [< Greek *kýstis* bladder + *-ine* (from its discovery in a urinary calculus)]

cys|ti|nu|ri|a (sis′tə nůr′ē ə, -nyůr′-), *n.* the presence of cystine in the urine.

cys|ti|tis (sis tī′tis), *n.* inflammation of the urinary bladder.

cysto-, *combining form.* bladder; sac; cyst, as in *cystocyte, cystoscope.* [< Greek *kýstis* bladder]

cys|to|carp (sis′tə kärp), *n. Botany.* the multicellular body, consisting of a mass of asexual spores (carpospores), that develops after fertilization in the red algae, sometimes contained in a special cellular envelope (pericarp). [< *cysto-* + Greek *karpós* fruit]

cys|to|cele (sis′tə sēl), *n.* a hernia in which the bladder protrudes. [< *cysto-* + Greek *kḗlē* tumor]

cyst|oid (sis′toid), *adj., n.* —***adj.*** resembling a cyst; like a bladder. —***n.*** a cystoid formation.

cys|to|lith (sis′tə lith), *n. Botany.* an outgrowth of the walls of some cells, containing tiny crystals of calcium carbonate. [< *cysto-* + Greek *líthos* stone]

cys|to|ma (sis tō′mə), *n., pl.* **-ma|ta** (-mə tə). a tumor containing cysts.

cys|to|scope (sis′tə skōp), *n.* an instrument for examining the interior of the urinary bladder.

cys|to|scop|ic (sis′tə skop′ik), *adj.* **1** having to do with a cystoscope. **2** performed with a cystoscope.

cys|tos|co|py (sis tos′kə pē), *n.* an examination of the urinary bladder with a cystoscope.

cys|tot|o|my (sis tot′ə mē), *n., pl.* **-mies.** the surgical operation of cutting into the urinary bladder, especially to remove stones.

cyt-, *combining form.* the form of **cyto-** before vowels, as in *cytase.*

cy|tase (sī′tās), *n.* an enzyme found especially in the cells of dates, Brazil nuts, and barley, useful in the hydrolysis of cellulose.

cy|tas|ter (sī tas′tər, sī′tas′-), *n.* a star-shaped figure appearing in a cell during mitosis, consisting of a centrosphere and threads radiating from it; aster. [< *cyt-* + Greek *astḗr* star]

-cyte, *combining form.* a cell: *Leucocyte = a white* (*blood*) *cell.* [< Greek *kýtos* anything hollow]

Cyth|er|e|a (sith′ə rē′ə), *n.* Aphrodite (Venus), the goddess of love and beauty. [< the island *Cytherea,* near which Aphrodite was fabled to have risen from the waves]

Cyth|er|e|an (sith′ə rē′ən), *adj.* **1** having to do with Aphrodite (Venus). **2** having to do with the planet Venus.

cyt|i|dine (sī′tə din, sit′ə-; -dēn), *n.* a white, crystalline nucleoside of ribose and cytosine, prepared from yeast ribonucleic acid. *Formula:* $C_9H_{13}N_3O_5$

cyt|i|dyl|ic acid (sī′tə dil′ik, sit′ə), a nucleotide of ribonucleic acid which on hydrolysis yields cytosine, ribose, and phosphoric acid. *Formula:* $C_9H_{14}N_3O_8P$

cyto-, *combining form.* cell or cells: *Cytoplasm = protoplasm of a cell.* Also, **cyt-** before vowels. [< Greek *kýtos* anything hollow]

cy|to|an|a|lyz|er (sī′tō an′ə lī′zər), *n.* an electronic device for use in pathology by means of which specimens of suspicious tissue may be automatically analyzed to detect the presence of cancer, based on the fact that cancerous cells have larger and denser nuclei than those of normal cells.

cy|to|ar|chi|tec|ture (sī′tō är′kə tek′chər), *n.* the cellular arrangement of a tissue, organ, or other part of the body.

cy|to|cha|las|in (sī′tō kə las′in), *n.* any one of a group of substances isolated from mold cultures, that cause cells to expel their nuclei and that induce cessation of cell movement and of cytoplasmic activity: *My associate ... has used cytochalasin to study the movement of nerve cells and migratory cells* (Norman K. Wessells). [< *cyto-* + Greek *chálasis* loosening, slackening + English *-in*]

cy|to|chem|i|cal (sī′tō kem′ə kəl), *adj.* of, having to do with, or based on the principles or methods of cytochemistry.

cy|to|chem|is|try (sī′tō kem′ə strē), *n.* the science of the chemistry of cells.

cy|to|chrome (sī′tə krōm), *n.* any one of various pigments concerned with cellular respiration, important as catalysts in the oxidation process.

cytochrome oxidase, an oxidizing enzyme containing iron and porphyrin, found in mitochondria and responsible for the formation of a large part of adenosine triphosphate.

cy|tog|a|my (sī tog′ə mē), *n.* the union or conjugation of cells.

cy|to|gene (sī′tə jēn), *n.* a particle of cytoplasm able to reproduce itself.

cy|to|gen|e|sis (sī′tə jen′ə sis), *n.* the formation of cells.

cy|to|ge|net|ic (sī′tō jə net′ik), *adj.* having to do with cytogenesis.

cy|to|ge|net|i|cist (sī′tō jə net′ə sist), *n.* a specialist in cytogenetics.

cy|to|ge|net|ics (sī′tō jə net′iks), *n.* the branch of biology dealing with the relation of cells to the phenomena of heredity and variation.

cy|to|gen|ic (sī′tə jen′ik), *adj.* **1** producing cells. **2** characterized by the formation of cells.

cy|to|ki|ne|sis (sī′tō ki nē′sis, -kī-), *n.* the changes occurring in the cytoplasm of a cell during mitosis, meiosis, and fertilization.

cy|to|ki|net|ic (sī′tō ki net′ik, -kī-), *adj.* of or having to do with cytokinesis.

cy|to|ki|nin (sī′tō kī′nən), *n.* a plant hormone that directs the differentiation of cells into the roots and shoots of young plants: *The cytokinins are closely related to adenine, one of the bases found in nucleic acids, and compounds with strong cytokinin activity occur in transfer RNA* (New Scientist).

cy|to|list (sī′tə list), *n.* an enzyme which dissolves the cell wall. [< *cytol*(ysis) + *-ist*]

cy|to|log|ic (sī′tə loj′ik), *adj.* = cytological.

cy|to|log|i|cal (sī′tə loj′ə kəl), *adj.* of or having to do with cytology. —**cy′to|log′i|cal|ly**, *adv.*

cy|tol|o|gist (sī tol′ə jist), *n.* a person who studies cytology.

cy|tol|o|gy (sī tol′ə jē), *n.* **1** the branch of biology that deals with the formation, structure, and function of cells. **2** cellular structure and functions.

cy|tol|y|sin (sī tol′ə sin), *n.* a substance able to cause cytolysis.

cy|tol|y|sis (sī tol′ə sis), *n.* the dissolution or destruction of cells.

cy|to|lyt|ic (sī′tə lit′ik), *adj.* of or having to do with cytolysis.

cy|to|me|gal|ic inclusion disease (sī′tō mə gal′ik), a serious disease of newborn babies that affects the brain, liver, kidneys, and lungs, characterized by a great enlargement of epithelial cells, with nuclei containing large inclusion bodies. It is caused by a cytomegalovirus. [< *cyto-* + Greek *mégas, megálou* great + English *-ic*]

cy|to|meg|a|lo|vi|rus (sī′tō meg′ə lō vī′rəs), *n.* any one of a group of DNA-containing viruses, related to the herpesvirus, that cause the cellular enlargement characteristic of cytomegalic inclusion disease.

cy|to|path|ic (sī′tə path′ik), *adj.* of or having to do with cytopathy.

cy|to|path|o|gen|ic (sī′tō path′ə jen′ik), *adj.* attacking living cells.

cy|to|path|o|log|ic (sī′tō path′ə loj′ik), *adj.* of cytopathology; involving diseases of cells. —**cy′to|path′o|log′i|cal|ly**, *adv.*

cy|to|path|o|log|i|cal (sī′tō path′ə loj′ə kəl), *adj.* = cytopathologic.

cy|to|pa|thol|o|gy (sī′tō pə thol′ə jē), *n.* **1** the study of cellular diseases; cell pathology. **2** the conditions or characteristics of a diseased cell or cells.

cy|top|a|thy (sī top′ə thē), *n.* degeneration or disease in a living cell. [< *cyto-* + *-pathy*]

cy|toph|a|gy (sī tof′ə jē), *n. Biology.* = phagocytosis. [< *cyto-* + Greek *phageîn* eat]

cy|to|phar|ynx (sī′tə far′ingks), *n.* a gullet or tube in certain protozoans leading from the cytoplasm into the endoplasm.

cy|to|plasm (sī′tə plaz əm), *n.* the living substance or protoplasm of a cell outside of the nucleus: *The main body of the cell, its cytoplasm, corresponds to the factory area where workers are manufacturing the specified product from incoming raw materials* (Scientific American). See picture under **cell.**

cy|to|plas|mic (sī′tə plaz′mik), *adj.* having to do with cytoplasm.

cy|to|plast (sī′tə plast), *n.* = cytoplasm.

cy|to|plas|tic (sī′tə plas′tik), *adj.* of or like the cytoplasm of a cell.

cy|to|sine (sī′tə sin, -sēn), *n.* a substance present in nucleic acid in cells. It is one of the pyrimidine bases of both DNA and RNA. *The genetic code of* [*the*] *DNA molecule are the four bases, or chemical subunits, adenine, guanine, cytosine, and thymine* (Scientific American). *Formula:* $C_4H_5N_3O$ *Abbr:* C (no period). [< *cyto-* + *-ose*[2] + *-ine*[2]]

cy|to|skel|e|ton (sī′tə skel′ə tən), *n.* the essential framework in cell structure.

cy|to|some (sī′tə sōm), *n.* the body of protoplasm in a cell, exclusive of the nucleus.

cy|to|stat|ic (sī′tə stat′ik), *adj.* stopping or inhibiting the growth of cells: *Another approach to cancer-cell inhibition is the use of cytostatic drugs* (Morris Fishbein).

cy|to|stome (sī′tə stōm), *n.* the mouth of a cell, leading into the cytopharynx in protozoans.

cy|to|tax|is (sī′tə tak′sis), *n.* the movement of cells, or of cell masses, in relation to one another.

cy|to|tax|o|nom|ic (sī′tə tak′sə nom′ik), *adj.* of or having to do with cytotaxonomy.

cy|to|tax|on|o|my (sī′tə tak son′ə mē), *n.* taxonomic classification based on the study of cellular structures, especially the chromosomes.

cy|to|tech|nol|o|gist (sī′tə tek nol′ə jist), *n.* a person who studies specimens of cells to detect changes in cell structure, especially in the diagnosis of cancer.

cy|to|tox|ic (sī′tə tok′sik), *adj.* of or produced by a cytotoxin.

cy|to|tox|in (sī′tə tok′sin), *n.* a toxin or antibody having a specific harmful effect on certain cells.

cy|to|trop|ic (sī′tə trop′ik), *adj. Biology.* **1** characterized by cytotropism. **2** that has an affinity for or is attracted by cells.

cy|tot|ro|pism (sī tot′rə piz əm), *n. Biology.* the growing or bending of cell masses, or of cells, toward or away from one another.

C.Z. or **CZ** (no periods), Canal Zone (Panama).

Cza|pek's medium (chä′peks), a culture medium on which to grow molds to be tested for the production of antibiotics. [< Friedrich *Czapek,* a Czech scientist of the 1900's]

czar (zär), *n.* **1** an emperor. When Russia had an emperor, his title was czar. **2** *Figurative.* a person with absolute or dictatorial power; autocrat: *the czar of baseball, the czar of the underworld.* **SYN:** monarch, dictator. Also, **tsar, tzar.** [< Russian *car′,* ultimately < Latin *Caesar* Caesar. See etym. of doublets **Caesar, Kaiser.**]

czar|das (chär′däsh), *n.* a Hungarian national dance in double time, consisting of a slow and a fast movement, and including a great variety of

steps and figures. Also, **csardas**. [< Hungarian *csárdás*]
czar|dom (zär′dəm), *n.* the office, power, or territory of a czar.
czar|e|vitch (zär′ə vich), *n.* **1** the eldest son of a Russian czar; cesarevitch. **2** a son of a Russian czar. Also, **tsarevitch**, **tzarevitch**. [< Russian *carevich* < *car′*; see etym. under **czar**]
cza|rev|na (zä rev′nə), *n.* **1** a daughter of a Russian czar. **2** the wife of a czarevitch. Also, **tsarevna**, **tzarevna**. [< Russian *carevna* < *car′*; see etym. under **czar**]
cza|ri|na (zä rē′nə), *n.* the wife of a czar; a Russian empress. Also, **tsarina**, **tzarina**. [< German *Zarin* (earlier *Czarin*), feminine of *Zar* < Russian *car′*; see etym. under **czar**]
czar|ism (zär′iz əm), *n.* autocratic government; absolutism; despotism. Also, **tsarism**, **tzarism**.
czar|ist (zär′ist), *adj., n.* —***adj.*** **1** of or having to do with a czar or czarism: *a czarist regime, policies, or powers.* **2** of, or as of, the time of a czar or czars: *czarist days, a czarist restaurant.*
—***n.*** a follower of a czar or czars; a supporter of czarism. Also, **tsarist**, **tzarist**.
czar|ist|ic (zä ris′tik), *adj.* = czarist.
cza|rit|za (zä rit′sə), *n.* = czarina. Also, **tsaritza**, **tzaritza**. [< Russian *carica*, feminine of *car′*; see etym. under **czar**]
Czech (chek), *n., adj.* —***n.*** **1** a member of a branch of the Slavs. Bohemians, Moravians, and Silesians are Czechs. **2** their Slavic language.
—***adj.*** of or having to do with Czechoslovakia, its people, or their languages.
Czech., Czechoslovakia.
Czech|ic (chek′ik), *adj.* = Czech.
Czech|ish (chek′ish), *adj.* = Czech.
Czech|ize (chek′īz), *v.t.*, **-ized**, **-iz|ing**. to make Czech, especially in language or character.
Czech|o|slo|vak (chek′ə slō′vak, -väk), *adj., n.* —***adj.*** of or having to do with Czechoslovakia, its people, or their language.
—***n.*** **1** a person born or living in Czechoslovakia. **2** either of the languages, Czech or Slovak, of Czechoslovakia.
Czech|o|slo|va|ki|an (chek′ə slō vä′kē ən, -vak′ē-), *adj., n.* = Czechoslovak.

✱D[1] or **d** (dē), *n., pl.* **D's** or **Ds**, **d's** or **ds**. **1** the fourth letter of the English alphabet. There are two *d's* in *Dad.* **2** any sound represented by this letter. **3** (as a symbol) the fourth (of an actual or possible series): *row D in the balcony.* **4** the lowest passing grade in schools and colleges: *to get a D in physics.* **5** *Music.* **a** the second tone in the scale of C major. **b** a symbol representing this tone. **c** a key, string, etc., that produces this tone. **d** the scale or key that has D as its keynote: *a concerto in D.* **6** the Roman numeral for 500.

✱D[1]
definition 5b

D[2] (dē), *n., pl.* **D's**. anything shaped like the letter D.

-'d[1] , a spelling representing the informal pronunciation of: **a** had. *Examples:* We'd come too early. What'd happened? **b** did. *Example:* Where'd they disappear? **c** would. *Examples:* They'd never go there. It'd be awful if they did.

-'d[2], *suffix.* a form of **-ed**[2], used with words ending in a vowel, as in *henna'd hair, mascara'd eyes.*

D- or **d-**, *combining form.* dextro- (right handed) in configuration: *d-glyceraldehyde = dextro-glyceraldehyde.* [< *d*(extro-)]

d (no period), an abbreviation or symbol for the following:
1 deci-.
2 *Physics.* density.
3 diameter.
4 dyne.
5 *British.* penny (Latin, *denarius*) or pence (Latin, *denarii*), used before decimalization in 1971.

d., an abbreviation for the following:
1 dam (mother).
2 date.
3 daughter.
4 day or days.
5 dead.
6 degree.
7 deputy.
8 died.
9 dime.
10 dividend.
11 dollar.
12 dose.

D (no period), an abbreviation or symbol for the following:
1 Department: *DOT = Department of Transportation.*
2 deuterium (chemical isotope).
3 *Chemistry.* didymium.
4 dinar.
5 *Physics.* displacement.
6 Dutch.

D., an abbreviation for the following:
1 deacon.
2 December.
3a Democrat. **b** Democratic.
4 Department.
5 Doctor: *M.D. = Doctor of Medicine. Ph.D. = Doctor of Philosophy.*
6 dowager.
7 Duchess.
8 Duke.
9 duodecimo.
10 Dutch.
11 God (Latin, *Deus*).
12 Lord (Latin, *Dominus*).

da[1] (dä), *n. Dialect or Informal.* father: *Your da gave you advice and you resented it* (Sean O'Faolain). [apparently < children's speech]

da[2] (dä), *adv., n. Russian.* yes: *They made concessions where the conceding did them no hurt: a da instead of a nyet in the U.N. Security Council* (Time).

da (no period), deca-.

da., **1** daughter. **2** day or days.

Da., Danish.

DA (no periods), an abbreviation for the following:
1 delayed action.
2 deposit account.
3a documents against acceptance. **b** documents for acceptance.
4 don't answer.

D.A., district attorney.

dab[1] (dab), *v.,* **dabbed, dab|bing,** *n.* **—*v.t.*** **1** to touch lightly; pat with something soft or moist; tap: *The nurse dabbed my cut with a piece of cotton.* **2** to put on with light strokes: *I dabbed ointment on my sunburn.* **3** to strike sharply; pick holes in. **4** *Slang.* to fingerprint: *Wall Street firms are required to "dab" ... every employee from messenger boy to president* (London Times).
—*v.i.* **1** to pat with something soft or moist. **2** to strike lightly; peck. **3** to use a dabber.
—*n.* **1** a quick, light touch or blow; pat or tap; peck: *The cat made a dab at the butterfly with its paw.* **2** a small, soft or moist mass: *I put little dabs of butter on the bread.* **3** a little bit: *Put a dab of paint on this spot you missed.* **4** *Slang.* a fingerprint.
[Middle English *dabben;* probably imitative]

dab[2] (dab), *n.* **1** any one of various flatfishes related to the flounder, such as the sand dab of the North Atlantic. **2** = flatfish. [origin uncertain]

dab[3] (dab), *n. Informal.* an expert: ... *'something of a dab' ... at the shoemaking business* (Hawthorne). [origin uncertain]

dab|ber (dab'ər), *n.* **1a** a person or thing that dabs. **b** a person who takes part in something or works at something without serious intent; dabbler. **2** a pad or ball used by printers and engravers to apply ink.

dab|ble (dab'əl), *v.,* **-bled, -bling.** **—*v.t.*** to dip (hands, feet, shoes, or the like) in and out of water; splash: *We sat and dabbled our feet in the pool.*
—*v.i.* **1** to play in water with the hands; splash. **SYN:** sprinkle, spatter. **2** *Figurative.* to do anything in a slight or superficial manner; work a little: *He dabbled at painting but soon gave it up. The businessman dabbled in the stock market.*
[earlier *dabbel.* Compare Flemish *dabbelen.*]

dab|bler (dab'lər), *n.* a person who dabbles; dilettante.

dab|chick (dab'chik'), *n.* **1** the little grebe, a small European water bird. **2** the pied-billed grebe of North America. **3** a small yacht of five tons or under. [earlier *dapchick;* origin uncertain]

dab hand, *British Informal.* a skillful or expert person: *He was ... full of good will, a dab hand at any chore* (Punch).

dab|ster (dab'stər), *n.* **1** *Informal.* an amateur or superficial worker; dabbler. **2** *Dialect.* an expert.

da ca|po (dä kä'pō), *Italian.* **1** *Music.* from the beginning (a direction to repeat a passage). **2** the passage to be thus repeated. **3** (literally) from the head.

d'ac|cord (dȧ kôr'), *French.* **1** in accord; agreed. **2** *Music.* in tune.

dace (dās), *n., pl.* **dac|es** or (*collectively*) **dace.** **1** a small, European freshwater fish, related to the carp. **2** any one of various similar or related fishes of the United States. [Middle English *darse* < Old French *dars*]

da|cha (dä'chə), *n. Russian.* a house in the suburbs or country: *His office is in the Kremlin, but he lives in a spacious dacha outside Moscow* (Time).

dachs|hund (däks'hůnd', daks'-, dash'-; *German* däks'hůnt'), *n.* a small dog with a long body, very short legs, and large, drooping ears. It has a smooth, short-haired or long-haired coat, or a wire-haired coat. The dachshund is of a German breed that originally came from France and was widely used for hunting. *The dachshund is a strong, hardy dog with a good sense of smell* (Henry P. Davis).
[< German *Dachshund* < *Dachs* badger + *Hund* dog]

Dach|stein (däk'stīn), *n. Geology.* a division of the Triassic formation in the northern and southern Alps. [< German *Dachstein,* mountains in the Austrian Alps]

Da|cian (dā'shən), *adj., n.* **—*adj.*** of or having to do with Dacia, an ancient Roman province in southern Europe, or with its people.
—*n.* a native or inhabitant of Dacia.

da|cite (dā'sīt), *n.* an igneous rock in which the crystals are scattered through a mass of fine-grained minerals: *Dacites occur in dikes and intrusions as well as in lava flows* (Fenton and Fenton). [< *Dacia,* a Roman province, where it is found, + *-ite*[1]]

da|cit|ic (də sit'ik), *adj.* having to do with or having the characteristics of dacite.

dack|er (dak'ər), *v.i. Scottish.* **1** to totter or saunter. **2** to vacillate; equivocate. [apparently < Middle Flemish *daeckeren*]

da|coit (də koit'), *n., v.* **—*n.*** a member of a gang of robbers in India or Burma, who plunder in armed bands. **—*v.i.*** to plunder or rob in an armed band.
[< Hindustani *ḍakāit* < *ḍakā* gang robbery]

da|coit|y (də koi'tē), *n., pl.* **-coit|ies.** **1** the system of robbery as practiced by dacoits: *Acharya Bhave said that the problem of dacoity could be solved if the people were fearless and philanthropic* (Times of India). **2** a robbery of this kind.
[< Hindustani *ḍakāitī* < *ḍakāit* dacoit]

Da|cron (dā'kron, dak'ron), *n. Trademark.* an artificial fiber or fabric that does not wrinkle or fade easily. It is used for shirts, dresses, suits, and other cloth articles. *Dacron dresses were ordered for summer selling* (New York Times).

dac|ry|o|lin (dak'rē ə lin), *n.* an albuminous component of tears. [< Greek *dákry* tear + English *-ol*[1] + *-in*]

dac|tyl (dak'təl), *n.* **1** a foot in modern English verse having one accented syllable followed by two unaccented syllables. *Example:* "This'is the/ for'est pri/ me'val. The/ mur'mur ing/ pines' and the/ hem'locks." **2** a foot in classical verse having three syllables consisting of one long syllable followed by two short syllables. *Example:* "Ārmăvĭr/ūmqŭe că/nō." **3** *Zoology.* a finger or toe. [< Latin *dactylus* < Greek *dáktylos* finger, dactyl. See etym. of doublet **date**[2].]

dac|tyl|ate (dak'tə lit), *adj.* having fingerlike processes; fingered.

dac|tyl|ic (dak til'ik), *adj., n.* **—*adj.*** **1** consisting of dactyls: *Longfellow's attempt to transport classic dactylic hexameter into English* (New Yorker). **2** of dactyls. **—*n.*** dactylic verse.

dac|tyl|i|cal|ly (dak til'ə klē), *adv.* with a dactylic rhythm: *"Ulutanua the isle of the sea," read that verse dactylically and you get the beat* (Robert Louis Stevenson).

dac|tyl|i|og|ly|phy (dak til'ē og'lə fē), *n.* the art of engraving gems for rings and the like. [< Greek *daktylioglyphiā* < *dáktylios* finger ring + *glýphein* carve]

dac|tyl|i|og|ra|phy (dak til'ē og'rə fē), *n.* the description or study of finger rings. [< Greek *dáktylios* finger ring]

dac|tyl|i|o|man|cy (dak til'ē ə man'sē), *n.* divination by means of a finger ring. [< Greek *dáktylios* finger ring + *manteíā* divination]

dac|ty|li|tis (dak'tə lī'tis), *n.* inflammation of a finger or toe.

dac|tyl|o|gram (dak til'ə gram), *n.* = fingerprint.

dac|ty|log|ra|phy (dak'tə log'rə fē), *n.* **1** the science of fingerprinting, especially as a method of criminal identification: *Dactylography is a fascinating chapter in forensic science* (Keith Simpson). **2** = dactylology.

dac|ty|lol|o|gy (dak'tə lol'ə jē), *n.* communication by signs made with the fingers, especially as practiced by people who are deaf and dumb.

dac|ty|los|co|py (dak'tə los'kə pē), *n.* the identification of criminals or other persons by means of fingerprints.

dad (dad), *n. Informal.* father. [apparently < children's speech]

Da|da or **da|da** (dä'də, -dä), *n.* a movement in modern art and literature rejecting the standards and values of society by proposing unrestrained expression in behavior and artistic form; Dadaism: *Dada got its start in Zurich, Switzerland, during World War I with a group of rebellious young artists who thought the world was going nowhere* (Time). [< French *Dada* (originally) a child's word meaning "hobbyhorse"]

Da|da|esque (dä'də esk'), *adj.* like Dada; characteristic of Dada.

✱D[1]
definition 1

Dd — Script letters look like examples of fine penmanship. They appear in many formal uses, such as invitations to social functions.

Dd Dd — Handwritten letters, both manuscript or printed (left) and cursive (right), are easy for children to read and to write.

Dd *Dd* — Roman letters have *serifs* (finishing strokes) adapted from the way Roman stonecutters carved their letters. This is *Times Roman* type.

Dd ***Dd*** — Sans-serif letters are often called *gothic.* They have lines of even width and no serifs. This type face is called *Helvetica.*

Dd *Dd* — Between roman and gothic, some letters have thick and thin lines with slight flares that suggest serifs. This type face is *Optima.*

D — Computer letters can be sensed by machines either from their shapes or from the magnetic ink with which they are printed.

Da|da|ism or **da|da|ism** (dä′də iz əm), *n.* = Dada.

Da|da|ist or **da|da|ist** (dä′də ist), *n., adj.* **—*n.*** a follower or adherent of Dada: *The Dadaists reacted to what they believed were outworn traditions in art, and the evils they saw in society. They tried to shock and provoke the public with outrageous pieces of writing, cabaret skits, poetry recitals, and art exhibitions* (Marcel Franciscono). **—*adj.*** having to do with or belonging to Dada: *It was a large and very rusty collection of wheels, gears, and cams, all brought together in the shape of some fantastic Dadaist engine* (New Yorker).

Da|da|is|tic or **da|da|is|tic** (dä′də is′tik), *adj.* having to do with Dada; Dadaist: *In the Dadaistic gag paintings in which Picasso has stuck odd bits of newspaper, there is the wonderful color* (Wall Street Journal).

dad|dy (dad′ē), *n., pl.* **-dies. 1a** *Informal.* father: *I suppose every boy looks forward to the day when he can have the opportunity of bestowing an honor upon his daddy* (New York Times). **b** *Figurative: To say that all news is local is to utter the daddy of journalistic clichés* (Saturday Review). **2** *U.S. Slang.* = sugar daddy.

daddy bug, = daddy longlegs.

daddy longlegs, or **dad|dy-long|legs** (dad′ē-lông′legz′, -long′-), *n., pl.* **-legs. 1** an animal that looks much like a spider, but does not bite; harvestman. It has a small body and long, thin legs. **2** *British.* a crane fly.

Dad|dy-o or **dad|dy-o** (dad′ē ō), *n. Slang.* a familiar form of address for any man: *He called the English teacher 'Daddy-o'* (New Yorker).

da|do (dā′dō), *n., pl.* **-does** or **-dos,** *v.,* **-doed, -do|ing. —*n.* 1** the part of a pedestal between the base and the cap or cornice. **2** a broad finish of wood, or sometimes wallpaper or fabric, on the lower part of an inside wall of a room. **3a** a rectangular groove made in woodworking to form a joint. **b** the joint made with this groove. **c** a tool used to cut such a groove.
—*v.t.* 1 to provide with a dado. **2** to cut or insert a dado in.
[< Italian *dado* cube, die < Latin *datum* thing given, (originally) neuter past participle of *dare* give. See etym. of doublets **datum, die[2].**]

DAE (no periods), Dictionary of American English.

dae|dal (dē′dəl), *adj. Poetic.* **1** ingenious; skillful: *the sculptor's daedal hand.* **2** variously adorned; diversified. **3** intricate; mazelike. [< Latin *daedalus* < Greek *daídalos* skillful; skillfully wrought < *daidállein* work cunningly]

Dae|da|li|an or **Dae|da|le|an** (di dā′lē ən, -dāl′yən), *adj.* **1** skillful; ingenious. **2** intricate; mazelike.

Daed|a|lus (ded′ə ləs), *n. Greek Legend.* a skillful architect and sculptor who built the Labyrinth in Crete; with his son Icarus he escaped from imprisonment in it by using wings he contrived of feathers fastened by wax. *The envy of birds is very old in human history; the fable of Daedalus and Icarus has come down to us from classical antiquity* (Atlantic).
[< Latin *Daedalus* < *daedalus* skillful; see etym. under **daedal**]

Daem|mer|schlaf (dem′ər shläf′), *n. German.* Dämmerschlaf.

dae|mon (dē′mən), *n.* = demon.

dae|mon|ic (di mon′ik), *adj.* = demonic.

dae|mon|i|cal|ly (di mon′ə klē), *adv.* = demonically.

daff[1] (daf, däf), *v., n. Scottish.* **—*v.i.*** to act the fool; play; jest.
—*n.* 1 a simpleton; fool. **2** a coward.
[Middle English *daffe* a fool, perhaps related to *dafte* daft]

daff[2] (daf, däf), *v.t.* **1** *Archaic.* to put or turn aside: *The nimble-footed madcap Prince of Wales, And his comrades, that daff'd the world aside . . .* (Shakespeare). **2** *Obsolete.* to doff. [variant of *doff*]

daf|fa|dil|ly (daf′ə dil′ē), *n., pl.* **-lies.** *Dialect.* a daffodil.

daf|fa|down|dil|ly (daf′ə doun dil′ē), *n., pl.* **-lies.** *Dialect.* a daffodil.

daf|fi|ness (daf′ē nis), *n. Informal.* silliness.

daf|fo|dil (daf′ə dil), *n.* **1** a plant with long, slender leaves and yellow or white flowers that bloom in the spring. It is one kind of narcissus and grows from a bulb. The daffodil belongs to the amaryllis family. See picture under **amaryllis family. 2** its flower. It has a long, trumpet-shaped corona growing out from the center of the petals. **3** bright yellow, the color of the common daffodil. [variant of earlier *affodill* < Vulgar Latin *affodillus* < Latin *asphodelus* < Greek *asphódelos* asphodel. See etym. of doublet **asphodel.**]

daf|fo|dil|ly (daf′ə dil′ē), *n., pl.* **-lies.** *Dialect.* a daffodil.

daf|fo|down|dil|ly (daf′ə doun dil′ē), *n., pl.* **-lies.** *Dialect.* a daffodil.

daff|y (daf′ē), *adj.,* **daff|i|er, daff|i|est.** *Informal.* **1** foolish; silly. **2** crazy; insane. [perhaps < *daft,* or *daff[1],* noun]

daf|fy|down|dil|ly (daf′ə doun dil′ē), *n., pl.* **-lies.** *Dialect.* a daffodil.

daft (daft, däft), *adj.* **1** without sense or reason; silly; foolish; stupid: *Go out in this rain? You must be daft.* **2** crazy; insane; mad: *to go daft.* **3** *Scottish.* madly gay: *in a frolic daft* (Robert Burns). [Middle English *dafte,* Old English *gedæfte* gentle. See related etym. at **deft.**] **—daft′ly,** *adv.* **—daft′ness,** *n.*

dag[1] (dag), *n., v.,* **dagged, dag|ging. —*n.* 1** *British.* a daglock. **2a** an end hanging loose. **b** a decorative edging on garments; dagging.
—*v.t.* *British.* to cut off the daglocks from (sheep). [< earlier *dag* to slash]

dag[2] (dag), *n.* a heavy pistol, no longer used. [origin unknown]

Da|gan (dä′gän), *n.* the Babylonian god of the earth.

dag|ga (dag′ə), *n.* Indian hemp, smoked as a narcotic: *Dagga belongs to the same drug family as hashish, kief, and marijuana* (New Yorker). [< Afrikaans *dagga* < Khoikhoi *daxa-b* species of shrub yielding it]

***dag|ger** (dag′ər), *n., v.* **—*n.* 1** a small weapon with a short, pointed blade, used for stabbing: *He wrote of himself: "Each line shall stab, shall blast, like daggers and like fire"* (Time). **2** a sign like a cross, used in printing to refer the reader to a footnote or other reference; obelisk: *The dagger after a man's name means posthumous publication* (Science News Letter).
—*v.t.* 1 to stab with a dagger. **2** to mark with a dagger sign.
at daggers drawn, ready or disposed to fight; hostile: *The U.S. gas industry, long at daggers drawn with the electric utility industry which has been snatching away every gas user it can grab . . .* (Wall Street Journal).
look daggers (at), to look (at) with hatred or anger; look fiercely or savagely: *She looked daggers at me. And she's never spoken to me since* (Maclean's).
[probably < earlier *dag* to stab + *-er[1]*]

***dagger**
definition 2

† . . . preliminary figures are given in the report†.

†Report of the Committee . . .

dag|gered (dag′ərd), *adj.* equipped with a dagger or daggers: *Feisal, majestically robed and daggered, represented his country* (Time).

dag|ger|like (dag′ər līk′), *adj.* like a dagger: *A daggerlike pain shot up his arm.*

dagger of lath, 1 a counterfeit dagger made of wood, carried by the actor personifying Vice in the old morality plays. **2** a weak means of attack or defense.

dag|ging (dag′ing), *n.* **1** a decorative edging on garments in medieval times. **2** = daglock. [< *dag[1]* + *-ing[1]*]

dag|gle (dag′əl), *v.t., v.i.,* **-gled, -gling.** to drag or trail through mud or water. [< earlier *dag,* in sense of "hang down" + *-le*]

Da|ghe|stan (dä′gə stän′), *n.* a Caucasian rug made usually with gray wool and having geometric designs. [< *Daghestan,* an autonomous Soviet republic in the eastern Caucasus, where the rug is made]

dag|lock (dag′lok′), *n.* a dirty lock of wool near a sheep's tail.

da|go or **Da|go** (dā′gō), *n., pl.* **-gos** or **-goes.** *Slang.* a person of Spanish, Portuguese, or Italian origin (now used only in an unfriendly way). [American English; supposedly < *Diego* James, a common Spanish name]

da|go|ba (dä′gə bə), *n.* a dome-shaped monument containing relics of Buddha or of a Buddhist saint. [< Singhalese *dāgaba*]

Da|gom|ba (də gom′bə), *n., pl.* **-ba** or **-bas. 1** a member of a people of West Africa, living in northeastern Ghana and in Togo. **2** the Gur language of this people.

Da|gon (dā′gon), *n.* the chief god of the Philistines and later of the Phoenicians, half man and half fish (in the Bible, Judges 16:23).

da|guerre|o|type (də ger′ə tīp, -ē ə-), *n., v.,* **-typed, -typ|ing. —*n.* 1** an early method of photography. The pictures were made on silvered metal plates made sensitive to light. **2** a picture made in this way: *He presented the first successful daguerreotype, as still life, to the curator of the Louvre* (Scientific American).
—*v.t., v.i.* to photograph by this method.
[< French *daguerréotype* < Louis *Daguerre,* 1787-1851, who invented it]

da|guerre|o|typ|ing (də ger′ə tī′ping, -ē ə-), *n.* the making of a daguerreotype: *A number of leading scientists interested themselves in daguerreotyping* (Scientific American).

da|guerre|o|typ|ist (də ger′ə tī′pist, -ē ə-), *n.* a photographer who used the daguerreotype process.

da|guerre|o|typ|y (də ger′ə tī′pē, -ē ə-), *n.* the daguerreotype process.

dah[1] (dä), *n.* a dash in the Morse code: *Whenever I listened in on very high frequencies . . . I heard a series of high-pitched dits and dahs* (John Ciardi). [imitative]

dah[2] (dä), *n.* a short sword with a heavy back, used also as a knife, especially in Burma. Also, **dha, dao.** [< Burmese *dah*]

***da|ha|be|ah** or **da|ha|bee|yah** (dä′hə bē′ə), *n.* a kind of houseboat or passenger boat, used on the Nile. It originally had one or more lateen sails, and now has sails or engines, or both. *On the trip she dined with Lord Kitchener in a dahabeah on the Nile* (Time). Also, **diabeah.** [< Arabic *dhahabīyah* golden state barge of the Egyptian Moslem rulers < *dhahab* gold]

***dahabeah**

da|ha|bi|ya or **da|ha|bi|yeh** (dä′hə bē′ə), *n.* = dahabeah.

dahl|ia (dal′yə, däl′-; *especially British* dāl′yə), *n.* **1** a tall plant with large, showy flowers of many colors and varieties that bloom in late summer and autumn. It belongs to the composite family; the roots are tuberous. Dahlias are native to Mexico and Central America. **2** its flower. **3** a violet color used in dyeing, derived from rosaniline. [< New Latin *Dahlia* the genus name < Anders *Dahl,* 1751-1789, a Swedish botanist]

Da|ho|man (də hō′mən), *adj., n.* **—*adj.*** of or having to do with Dahomey, former name of Benin, a country in western Africa.
—*n.* a native of Dahomey.

Da|ho|me|an or **Da|ho|mey|an** (də hō′mē ən), *adj., n.* = Dahoman.

da|hoon (də hün′), *n.,* or **dahoon holly,** a type of holly with pointed leaves, native to the southern United States.

dai|ker (dā′kər), *v.i. Scottish.* to dacker.

dai|kon (dī′kən), *n.* a Japanese radish with a large, sweet, white root, also grown in the western United States. [< Japanese *daikon* (literally) great root]

Dail (dôl, doil), *n.* = Dail Eireann.

Dail Eir|eann (dôl ãr′ən, doil), the lower house of parliament of the Republic of Ireland. [< Irish *dáil* assembly + *Éireann,* genitive of *Éire* Ireland]

dai|ly (dā′lē), *adj., adv., n., pl.* **-lies. —*adj.* 1** done, happening, or appearing every day, or every day but Sunday: *a daily paper, a daily visit.* **SYN:** diurnal, quotidian. **2** lasting a day: *the daily rotation of the earth on its axis.* **3** of or for a day: *to receive daily wages.*
—*adv.* every day; day by day: *to deliver daily. The bus runs daily.*
—*n.* 1 a newspaper printed every day, or every day but Sunday: *An undetermined number of other morning dailies throughout France were unable to publish tonight because of a Communist-led nuisance strike* (New York Times). **2** *British.* a domestic servant, especially a maid, who lives outside the household.

daily double, in horse or dog racing: **1** a combination bet to pick the winners in two specified races, usually the first two, in the course of a day. **2** these two races.

daily dozen, *Informal.* a set of physical exercises performed daily.

dai|men (dā′min), *adj. Scottish.* occasional.

dai|mio (dī′myō), *n., pl.* **-mio** or **-mios.** = daimyo.

dai|mon (dī′mōn), *n.* an attendant or guiding spirit; demon: *A painter . . . allows his daimon to be choked by the constant pressure of domestic and social life* (Listener). [< Greek *daímōn.* Compare etym. under **demon.**]

dai|mon|e|lix (dī mon′ə liks), *n.* a gigantic, spiral fossil, probably of vegetable origin, found in parts of Nebraska, Wyoming, and South Dakota; devil's

Pronunciation Key: hat, āge, cãre, fär; let, ēqual, tėrm; it, īce; hot, ōpen, ôrder; oil, out; cup, pu̇t, rüle; child; long; thin; ᴛʜen; zh, measure; ə represents **a** in about, **e** in taken, **i** in pencil, **o** in lemon, **u** in circus.

corkscrew. [< Greek *daímōn* divinity, demon + *hélix* a spiral]
dai|mon|ic (dī mon′ik), *adj.* influenced by a guiding spirit; demonic.
dai|myo (dī′myō), *n., pl.* **-myo** or **-myos.** one of the great feudal nobles of Japan who were vassals of the emperor. Also, **daimio.** [< Japanese *daimyō* (literally) great name]
Dai Nip|pon (dī′ni pon′, nip′on, nēp′pôn′), a former Japanese name of Japan. [< Japanese *Dai Nihon* < *dai* great + *Nihon* Nippon]
dain|ti|ly (dān′tə lē), *adv.* in a dainty manner; elegantly; fastidiously; delicately.
dain|ti|ness (dān′tē nis), *n.* **1** dainty quality or character; a being dainty. **2** fineness of taste.
dain|ty (dān′tē), *adj.,* **-ti|er, -ti|est,** *n., pl.* **-ties.**
—*adj.* **1** having delicate beauty; fresh and pretty: *The violet is a dainty spring flower.* **SYN:** exquisite. See syn. under **delicate. 2a** delicate in tastes and feeling; particular: *She is dainty about her eating, never spilling or taking big bites.* **SYN:** fastidious, neat, trim. **b** too particular; overnice: *When men were starving, they could not afford to be dainty* (John L. Motley). **3** good to eat; delicious: *Wasn't that a dainty dish to set before the king?* (Nursery Rhyme). [< noun]
—*n.* **1** something very good to eat; a delicious bit of food: *Candy and nuts are dainties.* **SYN:** delicacy. **2** *Obsolete.* thing esteemed or choice.
[< Old French *deinte* < Latin *dignitās* worthiness. See etym. of doublet **dignity.**]
dai|qui|ri (dī′kər ē, dak′ər-), *n.* a cocktail consisting of rum, lime juice, and sugar, shaken vigorously with ice. [< *Daiquirí,* a locality in Cuba]
dair|y (dãr′ē), *n., pl.* **dair|ies,** *adj.* —*n.* **1** a store or company that sells milk, cream, butter, and cheese. **2** = dairy farm. **3** a room or building where milk and cream are kept and made into butter and cheese. **4** business of producing milk, cream, butter and cheese. **5** = dairy cattle.
—*adj.* of or made with milk, cream, butter, or cheese: *dairy products, dairy foods.*
[Middle English *deierie* < *deie* maid, Old English *dǣge* breadmaker + *-erie* -ery]
Dairy Belt, a region in the northern United States, extending from New England to Minnesota, where dairy farming is practiced.
dairy cattle, cows of certain breeds kept for the milk they give.
dairy farm, a farm where milk, cream, butter, and cheese are made.
dairy farmer, farmer who works a dairy farm.
dairy farming, the business of raising cows to produce milk and cream.
dair|y|ing (dãr′ē ing), *n.* **1** the business of processing milk and cream, or of making butter and cheese to sell: *But not only have scientists affected dairying, dairy research has furthered academic science* (J. A. Barnett). **2** = dairy farming.
dair|y|land (dãr′ē land′), *n.* any area especially suitable for dairying: *Four counties, covering 90 miles of prosperous dairyland, were hit by the funnels of boiling wind* (Newsweek).
dair|y|maid (dãr′ē mād′), *n.* a girl or woman who works in a dairy.
dair|y|man (dãr′ē mən), *n., pl.* **-men. 1** a man who works in a dairy. **2** a man who owns or manages a dairy.
dairy ranch, *Western U.S.* a ranch that produces milk and milk products commercially.
dairy shorthorn, = Milking Shorthorn.
dair|y|wom|an (dãr′ē wu̇m′ən), *n., pl.* **-wom|en.** a woman who owns or manages a dairy.
da|is (dā′is, dās, dī′is), *n.* a raised platform at one end of a hall or large room. A throne, seats of honor, or a desk may be set on a dais. [< Old French *deis* < Latin *discus* quoit, dish < Greek *dískos.* See etym. of doublets **desk, discus, dish, disk.**]
dai|sied (dā′zid), *adj. Poetic.* full of daisies; adorned with daisies: *daisied lawns* (John Gay).
dai|sy (dā′zē), *n., pl.* **-sies,** *adj.* —*n.* **1** a plant, originally of Europe, whose flowers or petals are usually white or pink around a yellow center. It belongs to the composite family. See picture under **composite family. 2** a tall plant of the same genus as the chrysanthemum, whose flower heads have a yellow disk and white rays; the common "white daisy" or oxeye daisy of North America. **3** the flower of either of these plants.
4 *Slang.* something fine or first-rate. **5** *U.S.* a cut of pork from the shoulder, salted, smoked, and boned; daisy ham. **6** a long, iced drink, made with alcoholic liquor flavored with grenadine, lemon juice, or the like.
—*adj. U.S. Slang.* first-rate; outstanding.
push up (the) daisies, *Slang.* to be dead; be in the grave: *I'm not like Dylan Thomas. After all, he's been pushing up daisies some time now* (Tim Heald).
[Old English *dæges ēage* day's eye] —**dai′sy-like′,** *adj.*
daisy chain, 1 a chain of daisies formed by joining their stems. **2** *Figurative.* a loosely connected series: *A daisy chain of anecdotes introduces the reminiscences* (Punch).
daisy cutter, *Slang.* **1** a ball batted in baseball or cricket so that it skims or bounds close to the ground. **2** a horse that lifts its feet only a little way from the ground in trotting.
daisy ham, = daisy (def. 5).
daisy printer or **wheel,** a wheel in a typewriter or word-processing machine that prints from letters mounted on the ends of spokes radiating from a spindle: *The 401 comes equipped with . . . a daisy printer that can print out an average business letter in less than 30 seconds* (Time).
dak (däk), *n.* in India: **1** transportation of travelers or letters by relays of men or horses. **2** the post or mail: *I recognized it, from descriptions in books, as a spear carried by dak (mail) runners* (Atlantic). Also, **dawk.** [Anglo-Indian < Hindustani *ḍāk*]
dak bungalow, (in India) an inn or other lodging for travelers: *In the smaller towns one stays in places variously described as dak bungalows, circuit houses, rest houses* (Santha Rama Rau).
da|ker hen (dā′kər), the corn crake or land rail. [origin unknown]
Da|kin's solution (dā′kənz), a neutral antiseptic solution containing about 0.5 per cent of sodium hypochlorite, developed during World War I for treating infected wounds. [< Henry D. *Dakin,* 1880-1952, an English chemist in the United States, who developed it]
da|koit (də koit′), *n., v.i.* = *dacoit.*
da|koit|y (də koi′tē), *n., pl.* **-koit|ies.** = dacoity.
Da|ko|ta (də kō′tə), *n., pl.* **-ta** or **-tas. 1** a member of an American Indian tribe living on the plains of the northern United States and southern Canada; Sioux: *The competitive Kwakiutl and the co-operative Dakota are hunters* (Ogburn and Nimkoff). **2** the Siouan language of this tribe. [American English < Siouan (Dakota) tribal name *dakoʹta,* also an adjective meaning "friendly, feeling affection for"]
Da|ko|tan (də kō′tən), *adj., n.* —*adj.* **1** of North Dakota and South Dakota, or either of them. **2** of or having to do with the Dakota Indians.
—*n.* **1** a native or inhabitant of North Dakota or South Dakota. **2** a Dakota Indian.
Dak|sha (däk′shə), *n. Hindu Mythology.* a son of Brahma, of whom grotesque legends were told. [< Sanskrit *Daksha* power]
dal (däl), *n.* in the East Indies: **1** a split pea used for porridge. **2** a plant yielding this pea. **3** a cooked dish made with lentils and spices. [< Hindi *dāl*]
Da|lai La|ma (dä lī′ lä′mə), the chief priest of the religion of the Buddhist priests in Tibet and Mongolia, now living in India; Grand Lama: *Before Communist China's soldiers entered Tibet in 1950, the Dalai Lama was both spiritual and temporal leader* (New York Times). [< Mongol *dalai* (literally) ocean; vast + Tibetan *blama* priest, lama]
dal|a|pon (dal′ə pon), *n.* a herbicide used especially against couch grass. [probably < *d*(i-[1]) + *al*(ph)*a* + *p*(ropi)*on*(ic acid)]
Da|lar|ni|an (də lär′nē ən), *adj.* of or having to do with a series of Pre-Cambrian rocks in Sweden. [< *Dalarne,* a former Swedish province]
da|la|si (də lä′sē), *n., pl.* **-si** or **-sis.** the unit of money of Gambia, equal to 100 butut. [< the native name in Gambia]
dale (dāl), *n.* a valley; vale. [Old English *dæl*]
Da|lek or **da|lek** (dä′lek), *n. British.* a robot that talks with a rasping, monotonous voice: *Like programmed daleks, the French military planners proceed to their "second generation" . . . of 18 intermediate range ballistic missiles* (London Times). [< the name of a robot on "Dr. Who," a BBC science-fiction television series]
dales|man (dālz′mən), *n., pl.* **-men.** a person who lives in a dale or valley, especially in the northern counties of England.
da|leth (dä′leth, -let), *n.* the fourth letter of the Hebrew alphabet. [< Hebrew *dāleth* (literally) door]
Da|li|esque (dä′lē esk′), *adj.* in the style of the Spanish painter Salvador Dali (born 1904) or his art: *You can't say it [the painting] was really totally abstract—more of a Daliesque surrealist collage* (Punch).
Dal|las (dal′əs), *n.* = Dallis.
Dal|las|ite (dal′ə sīt), *n.* a native or inhabitant of Dallas, Texas.
dalles (dalz), *n.pl.* **1** rapids flowing over a flat rock bottom in a narrowed portion of a river.
2 the steep, almost vertical cliffs on the sides of a canyon or ravine. [American English < Canadian French *dalles* < Middle French *dalle* flagstone < Middle Dutch *dal* board]
dal|li|ance (dal′ē əns), *n.* **1** a dallying; trifling: *Like a . . . reckless libertine, Himself the primrose path of dalliance treads* (Shakespeare). **2** a flirtation.
dal|li|er (dal′ē ər), *n.* a person who dallies.
Dal|lis (dal′əs), *n.,* or **Dallis grass,** a tall perennial water or marsh grass of South America. It is grown in the southern United States for pasture and forage. Also, **Dallas.**
Dall sheep (dôl), a wild sheep of Alaska and northwestern Canada, pure white or with brownish upper parts; white sheep; bighorn. [< William Healey *Dall,* 1845-1927, an American naturalist]
Dall's sheep (dôlz), = Dall sheep.
dal|ly (dal′ē), *v.,* **-lied, -ly|ing.** —*v.i.* **1** to act in a playful manner: *The spring breeze dallies with the flowers.* **2** to flirt (with danger, temptation, etc., or with a person); trifle: *He dallied with the offer for days, but finally refused it.* **SYN:** See syn. under **trifle. 3** to linger idly; loiter: *He was late for school because he dallied along the way.* **SYN:** dawdle.
—*v.t.* to waste (time); idle: *He dallied the afternoon away daydreaming.*
[< Old French *dalier* to chat]
dal|ly|ing|ly (dal′ē ing lē), *adv.* in a trifling or dallying manner.
Dal|ma|ni|tes (dal′mə nī′tēz), *n.pl.* a group of trilobites in which the test is distinctly divided into three subequal areas both longitudinally and horizontally. [< New Latin *Dalmanites* the genus name < Johan *Dalman,* a Swedish naturalist of the 1800's + *-ites*]
Dal|ma|tian (dal mā′shən), *n., adj.* —*n.* **1** a large, short-haired dog, usually white with black or brown spots; coach dog. **2** a native or inhabitant of Dalmatia, a region in western Yugoslavia, especially one who speaks the native Slavic language. **3** an extinct Romance language of Dalmatia.
—*adj.* of or having to do with Dalmatia, its people, or their language.
dal|mat|ic (dal mat′ik), *n.* **1** a loose-fitting outer vestment worn by deacons and bishops of the Roman Catholic Church on certain occasions.
2 a similar robe worn by kings and emperors at coronation and other formal occasions. **3** a garment formerly worn by noblemen and gentlemen. [< Latin *Dalmatica* (*vestis*) Dalmatian (garment) < *Dalmaticus* of Dalmatia < Greek *Dalmatiā*]
dal se|gno (däl sā′nyō), *Music.* repeat the section starting at the sign. *Abbr:* D.S. [< Italian *dal segno* from the sign]
dal|ton (dôl′tən), *n.* a unit of mass in biochemistry, equal to the mass of a single hydrogen atom. [< John *Dalton,* 1766-1844, an English chemist and physicist]
Dal|to|ni|an (dôl tō′nē ən), *adj., n.* —*adj.* **1** relating to or discovered by John Dalton: *the Daltonian atomic theory of the union of different atoms in definite quantitative proportions to form compounds.* **2** of or relating to color blindness.
—*n.* a color-blind person.
Dal|ton|ism or **dal|ton|ism** (dôl′tə niz əm), *n.* color blindness, especially the inability to distinguish red from green. [< French *daltonisme* < John *Dalton,* 1766-1844, an English chemist and physicist, who first described color blindness]
Dal|ton|ist (dôl′tə nist), *n.* a color-blind person.
Dal|ton Plan (dôl′tən), a method of individual instruction in public schools in which students work at their own rate. [< *Dalton,* Massachusetts, High School, where it was first used]
Dal|ton's law (dôl′tənz), the law that in a mixture of gases which do not enter into chemical reaction but are in equilibrium, the total pressure is the same as the sum of the pressures which would be exerted by each individually if the others were not present. [< John *Dalton;* see etym. under **dalton**]
***dam**[1] (dam), *n., v.,* **dammed, dam|ming.** —*n.*
1 a wall built to hold back the water of a stream, creek, or river: *There was a flood when the dam burst. The sleepy pool above the dam, The pool beneath it never still* (Tennyson). **SYN:** dike. **2** a body of water held back by a dam. **3** anything resembling a dam, such as an underground wall in a mine to hold back air or gas.
—*v.t.* **1** to provide with a dam; hold back (water) by means of a dam: *The beavers had dammed a brook and formed a pond* (Francis Parkman).
2 *Figurative.* to hold back; block up.
[Middle English *dame.* Compare Old English *demman* to dam.] —**dam′like′,** *adj.*

***dam**[1]
definition 1

dam[2] (dam), *n.* **1** the female parent of sheep, cattle, horses, and other four-footed animals: *I laid* *down the dam, and took the kid in my arms* (Daniel Defoe). **2** a mother: *What! All my pretty chickens and their dam At one fell swoop?* (Shakespeare). [Middle English *damme,* variant of *dame* female superior, dame]

dam|age (dam′ij), *n., v.,* **-aged, -ag|ing.** **—*n.*** **1** harm or injury that lessens value or usefulness: *The accident did very little damage to either car. No human being can arbitrarily dominate over another without grievous damage to his own nature* (Thomas Huxley). **SYN:** detriment, impairment. **2** *Informal.* cost; expense: *Many thanks, but I must pay the damage* (Byron). **SYN:** price.
—*v.t.* to harm or injure so as to lessen value or usefulness; harm; hurt: *I damaged my sweater playing football. I damaged the canoe when I paddled it against a rock.* **SYN:** impair, disfigure, spoil, mar. See syn. under **harm.**
—*v.i.* to receive damage or injury: *Wool usually damages if washed in hot water.*
damages, money claimed or paid by law to make up for some harm done to a person or his property: *The man who was injured by the car asked for $50,000 in damages.*
[< Old French *damage* < *dam* loss < Latin *damnum* loss, hurt, damage] **—dam′ag|ing|ly,** *adv.*

dam|age|a|ble (dam′ə jə bəl), *adj.* that can be damaged; susceptible to injury.

damage control, any means used to minimize or reduce the damage caused by an accident, crime, financial loss, adverse publicity, or other calamity: (*Figurative.*) *It's a stunning scene where old grudges and suspicions are suddenly dredged up and flung in a fit of emotion, devoid of damage control* (Washington Times).

damage suit, a lawsuit in which the claimant seeks damages: *Unhappy side effects of the steady stream of new drugs are minimized or ignored until the doctor discovers them in his own patients, by which time it is too late for anything but a damage suit* (New Scientist).

dam|an (dam′ən), *n.* **1** a small, rabbitlike, hoofed mammal native to Asia Minor. The daman is called a cony in the Bible. **2** = hyrax. [< Arabic *damān* (*'Isrā'īl*) sheep (of Israel)]

dam|ar (dam′ər), *n.* = dammar.

Da|ma|ra (dä mä′rä), *n., pl.* **-ras.** a member of a Bantu tribe living in Damaraland, the central part of South West Africa.

dam|a|scene (dam′ə sēn, dam′ə sēn′), *v.,* **-scened, -scen|ing,** *n., adj.* **—*v.t.*** Also, **damaskeen.** to ornament (metal) with inlaid gold or silver or with a wavy design: . . . *helmet designs and devices that were etched, gilded, embossed and damascened on the steel plate* (Time).
[< adjective]
—*n.* the ornament itself.
—*adj.* of or like such ornament.
[< *Damascene*] **—dam′a|scen′er,** *n.*

Dam|a|scene (dam′ə sēn, dam′ə sēn′), *adj., n.* **—*adj.*** of or having to do with the city of Damascus or its people.
—*n.* a native or inhabitant of Damascus.
[< Latin *Damascēnus* < Greek *Damaskēnós*]

dam|a|scen|ing (dam′ə sē′ning, dam′ə sē′-), *n.* **1** the making of damascened metal or articles. **2** a damascened design, pattern, etc.

Da|mas|cus blade (də mas′kəs), a sword blade made of Damascus steel; damask blade.

Damascus steel, 1 a kind of ornamented steel with fine, wavy, white, silver, or black lines, originally made at Damascus, used for sword blades. **2** any similarly ornamented steel. Also, **damask, damask steel.**

Damascus sword, a sword made of Damascus steel.

dam|ask (dam′əsk), *n., adj., v.* **—*n.*** **1** a firm, shiny, reversible linen, silk, or cotton fabric with woven designs: *hangings of damask.* **2** a linen material of this type used especially for tablecloths and napkins: *Spotless damask covered the table.* **3a** a rose color; pink. **b** = damask rose. **4a** = Damascus steel. **b** any damascened metal.
—*adj.* **1** made of damask: *damask tablecloths.* **2** rose-colored; pink: *damask cheeks.* **3** of or named after the city of Damascus: *the damask plum, damask rose.*
—*v.t.* **1** = damascene. **2** to weave with the design of damask fabric. **3** to deface or destroy by stamping or marking: *to damask seditious books.*
[< Latin *Damascus* < Greek *Damaskós*]

damask blade, = Damascus blade.

dam|a|skeen (dam′ə skēn′), *v.t.* = damascene.

damask rose, a large, fragrant, pink rose originally of Asia Minor, from which attar of roses is made.

damask steel, = Damascus steel.

da|mas|sé (dȧ mȧ sā′), *adj. French.* having a woven pattern, as silk.

dam|bon|ite (dam′bə nīt), *n. Chemistry.* a crystalline derivative of inositol, occurring in a certain kind of caoutchouc from western Africa. [< a native name + English *-ite*[1]]

dame (dām), *n.* **1** lady; madam (now used only figuratively, in personifications): *Dame Fortune. Our secrets have been betrayed—not by men, but by Dame Nature, that fickle dispenser of truth* (Bulletin of Atomic Scientists). **2** an elderly woman. **3** *Slang.* a woman. **4** *Archaic.* the mistress of a household or of a school. [< Old French *dame* Latin *domina* lady, mistress of the house < *domus* house. See etym. of doublets **dona, doña, donna, duenna.**]

Dame (dām), *n.* in Great Britain: **a** a title of honor given to a woman, corresponding to the rank of a knight: *Miss Fonteyn, premiere danseuse of the Sadler's Wells Ballet, was made a Dame of the British Empire* (Newsweek). **b** the legal title of the wife or widow of a knight or baronet. **c** the wife or daughter of a lord.

dame d'hon|neur (dȧm′ dô nœr′), *French.* a maid of honor; lady in waiting.

dame school, *Obsolete.* an elementary school for children, kept by a woman (dame).

dame's violet or **rocket,** a tall fragrant rocket of Europe and Asia, with light purple flowers.

dam|fool (dam′fül′), *n., adj. Informal.* **—*n.*** a very stupid person.
—*adj.* very stupid.

dam|i|an|a (dam′ē an′ə, -ā′nə), *n.* a drug consisting of the leaves of certain Mexican plants, used as a tonic, stimulant, and aphrodisiac. [American English < Mexican Spanish *damiana,* probably < a native name]

Da|mi|an|ist (dā′mē ə nist), *n.* a follower of Damian, patriarch of Alexandria in the 500's, who denied the separate godhead of the three persons of the Trinity.

dam|mar or **dam|mer** (dam′ər), *n.* **1** a resin obtained from various Australian and East Indian evergreens, used to make colorless varnish. **2** any one of various resins obtained from East Indian trees of different families. Also, **damar.** [< Malay *damar* resin]

Däm|mer|schlaf (dem′ər shläf′), *n. German.* twilight sleep. Also, **Daemmerschlaf.**

damn (dam), *v., n., adj., adv., interj.* **—*v.t.*** **1** to declare (something) to be bad or inferior; condemn: *The critics damned the new book.* **SYN:** denounce, proscribe, execrate. **2** to cause to fail; ruin: *Lack of funds damned the project from its beginning. Hence, vile instrument! Thou shalt not damn my hand* (Shakespeare). **3** to doom to hell. **4** to swear or swear at by saying "damn"; curse. **SYN:** imprecate. **5** *Obsolete.* to pronounce guilty; sentence; doom.
—*v.i.* to say "damn"; curse.
—*n.* **1** a saying of "damn"; curse. **2** *Informal.* a trifle; the merest bit; hoot; straw: *not care or give a damn, not worth a damn.*
—*adj., adv.* = damned.
—*interj.* an exclamation of anger or annoyance.
damn with faint praise. See under **praise.**
[< Old French *damner,* learned borrowing from Latin *damnāre* condemn < *damnum* damage, loss, hurt] **—damn′er,** *n.*
►See **darn**[2] for usage note.

dam|na|ble (dam′nə bəl), *adj.* **1** abominable or outrageous; detestable. **2** deserving condemnation; execrable, heinous. **—dam′na|ble|ness,** *n.*

dam|na|bly (dam′nə blē), *adv.* **1** odiously; detestably; abominably. **2** in a manner to incur severe censure, condemnation, or damnation.

dam|nant quod non in|tel|li|gunt (dam′nant kwod non in tel′ə gunt), *Latin.* they condemn what they do not comprehend.

dam|na|tion (dam nā′shən), *n., interj.* **—*n.*** **1** a damning or a being damned; condemnation. **2** condemnation to eternal punishment; perdition. **3** a sin bringing or deserving eternal punishment. **4** a curse.
—*interj.* an exclamation of anger or annoyance.

dam|na|to|ry (dam′nə tôr′ē, -tōr′-), *adj.* damning; assigning to damnation; condemnatory.

damned (damd), *adj., n., adv.* **—*adj.*** **1** cursed; abominable. **SYN:** detestable. **2** outrageous; damnable. **3** doomed to eternal punishment.
—*n.* Usually, **the damned,** the souls in hell: *In dreadful apparition, saw before his vision pass the shadows of the damned* (Robert Pollok).
—*adv.* *Slang.* very. **SYN:** extremely.
►See **darn**[2] for usage note.

damned|est (dam′dist), *adj., n.* **—*adj.*** most damned.
—*n.* *Informal.* the greatest possible effort; utmost: *to do one's damnedest to win.*

dam|ni|fi|ca|tion (dam′nə fə kā′shən), *n. Law.* a damnifying; damage; injury; loss.

dam|ni|fy (dam′nə fī), *v.t.,* **-fied, -fy|ing.** *Law.* to cause loss or damage to; hurt in person, estate, or interest; injure.

damn|ing (dam′ing), *adj.* that damns or condemns; that brings damnation. **—damn′ing|ly,** *adv.*

dam|no|sa he|re|di|tas (dam nō′sə hə red′ə tas), *Latin.* a hurtful or disadvantageous inheritance.

dam|nous (dam′nəs), *adj. Law.* of or having to do with damage; causing loss or damage. [< Latin *damnosus* < *damnum* hurt]

dam|num fa|ta|le (dam′nəm fə tā′lē), *Law.* damages caused by chance, that is, by the happening of an event which could not be foreseen or guarded against by the highest degree of prudence or care. [< New Latin *damnum fatale*]

Dam|o|cle|an (dam′ə klē′ən), *adj.* of or having to do with Damocles.

Dam|o|cles (dam′ə klēz), *n. Greek and Roman Legend.* a flatterer and courtier of Dionysius, king of Syracuse, who glorified the happiness and riches of kings. The king made Damocles aware of the constant dangers surrounding kings by seating him at a banquet under a sword suspended by a single hair.

Dam|o|cle|tian (dam′ə klē′shən), *adj.* of or like Damocles; having to do with Damocles: *No sense of Damocletian doom hangs over its* [*Thailand's parliament*] *discussions, and a gift for easygoing scepticism greases the cogs of its political life* (James Morris).

Da|moe|tas (də mē′təs), *n.* **1** (in Theocritus and Virgil) a herdsman. **2** (in pastoral poetry) a rustic. **3** (in Sidney's *Arcadia*) a foolish country clown.

dam|oi|selle (dam′ə zel′), *n. Archaic.* damsel.

Da|mon (dā′mən), *n. Roman Legend.* a man who pledged his life for his friend Pythias, who had been sentenced to death. Because of their devotion, the lives of both were spared.

dam|o|sel or **dam|o|zel** (dam′ə zel), *n. Archaic.* damsel: *The blessed damozel leaned out From the gold bar of Heaven* (Dante Gabriel Rossetti).

damp (damp), *adj., n., v.* **—*adj.*** **1** slightly wet; moist: *My feet were damp from walking home in the rain. Use a damp mop for the floor.* **2** *Archaic.* depressed; dejected: *With looks downcast and damp* (Milton). [< noun]
—*n.* **1** moisture: *When it's foggy you can feel the damp in the air.* **2** *Figurative.* a thing that checks or deadens; check; discouragement: *Your illness cast a damp over the party.* **SYN:** damper, dejection. **3** any harmful gas that collects in mines, such as chokedamp or firedamp: *The mine disaster was caused by exploding damp.* **4** *Archaic.* dejection.
—*v.t.* **1** to make moist or slightly wet; dampen; moisten: *Mother damped the clothes before she ironed them.* **2** *Figurative.* to check or deaden: **a** to depress; discourage: *Weariness damped the traveler's enthusiasm.* **b** to stifle; choke; extinguish: *to damp a fire.* **c** *Music.* to stop the vibrations of (a string, etc.). **3** *Physics.* to reduce or lessen the amplitude of (oscillations or waves).
[< noun]
damp down, to check or stifle; discourage; suppress: *Taxation damps down demand, and so does borrowing outside the banking system* (Sunday Times). *This technique not only inhibits genuine thinking but also damps down curiosity* (Listener).
damp off, a to rot, as the stems and leaves of plants when the soil and atmosphere are too wet or cold. **b** *Figurative.* to decline in power, strength, wealth, beauty, or other attribute; decay; deteriorate: *"We Churchills always damp off after 40," he* [*Sir Winston*] *is supposed to have said* (Manchester Guardian Weekly).
[< Middle Dutch, or Middle Low German *damp* vapor] **—damp′ly,** *adv.* **—damp′ness,** *n.*
—*Syn.* *adj.* **1 Damp, moist, humid** mean somewhat wet. **Damp** implies a slight degree of wetness and usually suggests that it is unpleasant or unwanted: *This house is damp in rainy weather.* **Moist** implies less wetness than *damp,* with no suggestion of unpleasantness: *The moist air was scented with violets.* **Humid** is commonly used to describe a high degree of moisture in the air: *In the East, the air is humid in summer.*

damped (dampt), *adj.* **1** dampened. **2** deadened. **3** retarded in action. **4** *Physics.* reduced gradually in amplitude: *The new analysis breaks sound into a new kind of element called a damped curve, described as "dying away like the vibration of a plucked guitar string"* (Science News Letter).

damped waves, *Physics.* waves of a group or series that are gradually lessened in amplitude.

damped wave train, *Telegraphy.* **1** a wave train composed of electric waves which are large in amplitude at or near the beginning of the group or series, and gradually decrease in amplitude as the end is approached. **2** a form of wave train characteristic of certain telegraph systems, each wave train separated from the one ahead and the one behind by an interval of time.

Pronunciation Key: hat, āge, cãre, fär; let, ēqual, tėrm; it, īce; hot, ōpen, ôrder; oil, out; cup, pu̇t, rüle; child; long; thin; ᴛʜen; zh, measure; ə represents **a** in about, **e** in taken, **i** in pencil, **o** in lemon, **u** in circus.

damp|en (dam′pən), *v.t.* **1** to make damp; moisten: *Mother sprinkles water over the clothes to dampen them before ironing.* SYN: wet. **2** *Figurative.* to cast a chill over; depress; discourage: *The sad news dampened our spirits.* SYN: lessen, dull, deaden. —*v.i.* to become damp: *The camp supplies dampened and molded during the long rains.* —**damp′en|er**, *n.*

***damp|er** (dam′pər), *n.* **1** a person or thing that discourages or checks: *The results are likely to clamp a damper on hopes for tax cuts any time soon* (Wall Street Journal). **2** a movable plate to control the draft in a stove or furnace: *In the pipe leading to the chimney we find a circular piece of metal, called a damper* (Beauchamp, Mayfield, and West). **3** *Music.* **a** a device for checking vibration and reducing the volume of sound, especially of piano strings. **b** a mute for muffling the sound of a horn, or other brass or woodwind instrument. **4** *Electricity.* **a** a device for checking the vibration of a magnetic needle. **b** a piece of copper in or near the poles of a synchronous machine to decrease hunting. **5** *Australian.* a kind of unleavened bread made of flour and water and baked in hot ashes: *to feed you on damper, or some other nameless abomination* (Charles Kingsley).

put a damper on, to suppress; curb; curtail; squelch: *The chairman put a damper on every suggestion the committee made.*

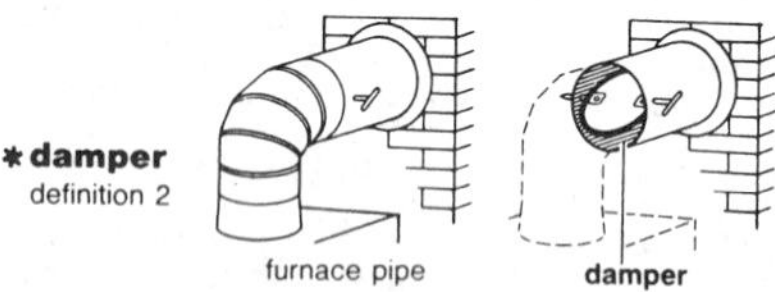

***damper** definition 2

damp|ing (dam′ping), *n. Physics.* the act or process of lessening the amplitude (of waves or oscillations).

damp|ing-off (dam′ping ôf′), *n.* a disease that causes the decay of young plants, especially seedlings and cuttings, at the surface of the ground, caused by various fungi that live near the surface of the soil.

damp|ish (dam′pish), *adj.* somewhat damp. —**damp′ish|ness**, *n.*

damp-proof (damp′prüf′), *adj., v.* —*adj.* that will not let dampness through or cause damage: *a damp-proof floor, damp-proof shoes.* —*v.t.* to make damp-proof: *to damp-proof a building.*

dam|sel (dam′zəl), *n. Archaic.* **1** a young girl; maiden. **2** a young unmarried lady. [< Old French *dameisele,* ultimately < Latin *domina* lady, mistress of the house; see etym. under **dame**. See related etym. at **demoiselle**.]

damsel bug, a small, brown or black, soft-bodied insect that eats aphids, leaf hoppers, and some other plant pests.

dam|sel|fish (dam′zəl fish′), *n., pl.* **-fish|es** or (*collectively*) **-fish**. any one of various brightly colored fishes which live around coral reefs.

damsel fly, or **dam|sel|fly** (dam′zəl flī′), *n.* an insect that holds its four wings vertically together when resting; devil's-darning-needle. It is similar to a dragonfly, but is smaller and more delicate. Damsel flies comprise a suborder.

dam|site (dam′sīt′), *n.* a site of or for a dam.

dam|son (dam′zən), *n.* **1** a small, dark-purple plum. **2** the tree that it grows on: *The damson blossom is out in the Lyth valley, several weeks late* (Manchester Guardian). [< Old French *damascene,* learned borrowing from Latin (*prunum*) *damascēnum* (plum) of Damascus < Greek *Damaskēnón* Damascus plum, damson]

damson plum, **1** = damson. **2** (in England) a plum like the damson but sweeter.

dam|yan|kee (dam′yang′kē) *n. U.S. Informal.* a Northerner: *He can hardly be called a damyankee since he was born in Texas* (Wall Street Journal). [< *damn* + *Yankee*]

dan¹ (dan), *n.* a small buoy with a pole displaying a flag by day and a lantern by night, used to indicate the position of deep-sea fish lines or a center about which a trawler is worked. [origin unknown]

dan² or **Dan¹** (dän, dan), *n.* any one of several grades or ranks of proficiency in Japanese sports and games: *Iyeda . . . now ranks as a fifth Dan professional (ninth Dan is highest) in his native Japan* (Time). [< Japanese *dan*]

Dan² (dan), *n.* **1** the fifth son of Jacob. Bilhah was his mother (in the Bible, Genesis 30:6). **2** the Hebrew tribe descended from him, that migrated to northern Palestine.

Dan³ (dan), *n. Archaic.* an honorable title equivalent to *Master* or *Sir: Dan Chaucer, Dan Cupid.* [< Old French *dan* < Latin *dominus* master < *domus, -ūs* home. See etym. of doublets **Dom**, **don**.]

Dan., **1** Daniel. **2** Danish.

Dan|a|e or **Dan|a|ë** (dan′ē ē), *n. Greek Legend.* the mother of Perseus. After she was visited by Zeus in the form of a shower of gold she bore him a son, Perseus.

Da|na|id or **Da|na|ïd** (dan′ē id), *n.* one of the Danaides.

Dan|a|id|e|an (dan′ē id′ē ən, -ē ə dē′-), *adj.* **1** having to do with or suggestive of the Danaides. **2** *Figurative.* laborious, useless, and endless; futile: *a Danaidean task.*

Da|na|i|des or **Da|na|ï|des** (də nā′ə dēz), *n.pl. Greek Legend.* the fifty daughters of Danaus. All but one, Hypermnestra, killed their husbands on their wedding night and were condemned to draw water with a sieve forever in Hades.

Dan|a|kil (dan′ə kil), *n., pl.* **-kils** or **-kil**. = Afar (a Hamitic people).

Dan|a|us or **Dan|a|üs** (dan′ē əs), *n. Greek Legend.* a king of Argos. See also **Danaides**.

dan|bur|ite (dan′bėr īt), *n.* a mineral, a borosilicate of calcium, of a white to yellowish color, often occurring in fine crystals resembling topaz. [< *Danbury,* Connecticut, where it occurs + *-ite¹*]

dance (dans, däns), *v.,* **danced, danc|ing**, *n., adj.* —*v.i.* **1** to move in rhythm, usually in time with music: *The ballerina can dance very gracefully.* **2** to jump up and down; move in a lively way: *The little boy danced with delight.* **3** *Figurative.* to bob up and down: *a boat dancing on the water.* —*v.t.* **1** to do, perform, or take part in (a dance): *They danced a waltz.* **2** to cause to dance: *He danced me around the room.* **3** to bring about by dancing: *She danced holes in her shoes.* —*n.* **1** movement in rhythm, usually in time with music: *The dances of primitive peoples were usually mass dances* (Emory S. Bogardus). **2** some special group of steps: *The waltz is a well-known dance.* **3** a party where people dance; dancing party: *My older sister is going to the high-school dance.* **4** one round of dancing: *May I have the next dance?* **5** a piece or type of music for dancing. **6** the art of dancing. **7** *Figurative.* movement up and down; lively movement: *the dance of shadows on the wall.* —*adj.* **1** of or having to do with dancing. **2** for dancing: *dance music.*

dance attendance on. See under **attendance**.

dance to one's tune. See under **tune**.

[< Old French *danser,* perhaps < Germanic (compare Old High German *dansōn* draw along)]

dance|a|ble (dan′sə bəl, dän′-), *adj.* that can be danced to: *The Moiseyev performers showed their ready assimilation of any danceable pattern* (Saturday Review).

dance drama, a drama in which the story is told by elaborate dance movements, formalized gestures, and chanting or dialogue. Japanese no plays are dance dramas.

dance|hall (dans′hôl′, däns′-) *n.* dance music that is an electronic mixture of various popular music styles accompanied by talking or rapping to the rhythm of the music: *Historically, [Jamaican] dancehall can be viewed as the antecedent to American rap* (Rolling Stone). —**dance′-hall′**, *adj.*

dance hall, a public hall or room in which dances are held.

dance of death, a representation in which a skeleton, Death, dances with people to suggest the everpresent danger of death.

danc|er (dan′sər, dän′-), *n.* **1** a person who dances: *The dancers sat down and began to talk after the music was over.* **2** a person whose occupation is dancing: *Bright polished brass like the cymbals of King David's dancers* (Langston Hughes).

danc|er|cise (dan′sər sīz), *n.* the practice of dancing, especially in a group, as a type of physical exercise. [blend of *dance* and (ex)*ercise*]

dan|cette (dan set′), *n.* **1** *Architecture.* a molding with a pattern of zigzags or chevrons. **2** *Heraldry.* a fess dancetté. [alteration of *dancetté*]

dan|cet|té (dan se tā′, -set′ē), *adj. Heraldry.* having large and deeply marked indentations or zigzags, usually three in number: *a fess dancetté.* [apparently alteration of French *danché,* ultimately < Latin *dēns, dentis* tooth]

danc|ing (dan′sing, dän′-), *n., adj.* —*n.* **1** the performance of a dance: *The ballerina's dancing was superb.* **2** the art of performing dances; dance. —*adj.* that dances: *dancing flames.*

dancing card, a card on which to write the names of the persons with whom one has agreed to dance in a single evening.

dancing dervish, a monk or friar of a Mohammedan religious order that has a ceremony in which they dance and spin about violently; whirling dervish.

dancing girl, a professional woman dancer, especially of the Middle East and the Orient; nautch dancer.

dancing mania, = tarantism.

dancing master, an instructor of dancing, especially in a dancing school: *A dancing master . . . came by on a bus with his dancing class on an outing* (John Ciardi).

dancing school, a school in which social and ballroom dancing are taught, especially to children.

danc|y (dan′sē, dän′-), *adj.,* **danc|i|er, danc|i|est**. dancing; lively and spry: . . . *[the] slightly dancy step of an old athlete* (John Cheever). [< *dance* + *-y¹*]

D and C or **D & C** (no periods), dilation and curettage (the operation of dilating the cervix and scraping the uterus to remove a cyst, perform an abortion, or the like).

D. & D. or **D and D** (no periods), *U.S. Slang.* **1** deaf and dumb: *Playing D. & D. with cops was a lesson taught in the quiet back rooms of precinct houses* (Time). **2** drunk and disorderly: *The red-faced man whispered, "I'm in on a D and D, son, I don't want any trouble, I'm getting out tomorrow"* (Harper's).

dan|de|li|on (dan′də lī′ən), *n.* **1** a weed with deeply notched leaves and bright-yellow flowers on a hollow stalk. Dandelions bloom in the spring. They belong to the composite family. See picture under **composite family**. **2** any one of various related plants. [< Middle French *dent de lion* lion's tooth, translation of Medieval Latin *dens leonis* < Latin *dens* tooth, *leō, leōnis* lion (because of its toothed leaves)]

dandelion greens, the tender leaves of young dandelions, used as potherbs.

dan|der¹ (dan′dər), *n. Informal.* temper; anger. [origin uncertain]

get one's dander up, to get angry; lose one's temper: *He 'pears to know just how long he can torment me before I get my dander up* (Mark Twain).

dan|der² (dan′dər), *n.* **1** = dandruff. **2** particles like dandruff that fall from skin, feathers, or hair: *They were told the mist contained allergens, such as pollen, dust, or animal dander* (Science News). [related to **dandruff**]

dan|der³ (dan′dər), *v.i. Scottish.* **1** to stroll; saunter. **2** to talk incoherently. [origin uncertain]

dan|di (dan′dē), *n.* = dandy³.

dan|di|a|cal (dan dī′ə kəl), *adj.* like that of a dandy: *dandiacal clothes.*

Dan|die Din|mont (dan′dē din′mont), or **Dandie Dinmont terrier**, a small terrier with a long body, long ears, short legs, and a rough coat, that originated in the Cheviot Hills between England and Scotland. [< *Dandie Dinmont,* a character in Sir Walter Scott's *Guy Mannering,* who owned such terriers]

dan|di|fi|ca|tion (dan′də fə kā′shən), *n.* **1** a dandifying or being dandified. **2** something that dandifies.

dan|di|fy (dan′də fī), *v.t.,* **-fied, -fy|ing**. to make trim or smart like a dandy; make foppish: *Roy was conscious of his hands. They were square and smooth, with dandified nails* (New Yorker).

dan|di|prat (dan′dē prat), *n.* **1** a small English coin worth three halfpence, used in the 1500's. **2** a child; urchin. **3** an insignificant person; whipper-snapper. **4** *Obsolete or Archaic.* a dwarf; pygmy. Also, **dandyprat**. [origin unknown]

dan|dle (dan′dəl), *v.t.,* **-dled, -dling**. **1** to move (a child) up and down on one's knees or in one's arms. **2** *Figurative.* to pet; pamper: *Pianist Ellis Larkins . . . has a sophisticated beat all his own and a sweet, gentle way of dandling a tune* (Time). [earlier *dandyll.* Compare Italian *dandolare,* and *dondolare* to toss, swing.]

dan|dler (dan′dlər), *n.* a person who dandles or fondles.

dan|druff (dan′drəf), *n.* small, whitish scales of dead skin that flake off the scalp; scurf: . . . *dandruff in children is most frequently associated with the glandular changes of adolescence* (Sidonie M. Gruenberg). [origin uncertain]

dan|druff|y (dan′drəf ē), *adj.* having dandruff; scurfy.

dan|dy¹ (dan′dē), *n., pl.* **-dies**, *adj.,* **-di|er, -di|est**. —*n.* **1** a man who is too careful of his dress and appearance: . . . *a silver-haired dandy who showed up at London first nights in a swirling black cape* (Time). SYN: fop. **2** *Informal.* an excellent or first-rate thing: *That new bike is a dandy.* **3** *Nautical.* **a** a type of British yawl having a leg-of-mutton sail on the mast at the stern. **b** the tall, narrow after sail or mizzen on such a yawl. **4** an openwork basket or vessel, used either to carry fuel, or to confine fuel in a larger grate, or to hold pig iron in a furnace hearth for preliminary heating. —*adj.* **1** of a dandy; too carefully dressed. SYN: foppish. **2** *Informal.* excellent; first-rate: *He got a dandy new bike.* [originally Scottish, perhaps < slang *Dandy* (diminutive) < Saint *Andrew*]

dan|dy[2] (dan′dē), *n.* an infectious fever; dengue; dandy fever. [apparently < *dengue* + *-y*[3]]

dan|dy[3] (dan′dē), *n., pl.* **-dies.** in India: **1** a boatman of the Ganges. **2** an ascetic, especially one who carries a staff. **3** a kind of litter consisting of a strong cloth strung like a hammock to a bamboo staff. Also, **dandi.** [< Hindi *ḍanḍī*]

dandy fever, = dandy[2].

dan|dy|funk (dan′dē fungk), *n.* a kind of pudding formerly well known among seafaring men.

dandy horse, = velocipede (def. 2a): *Bicycles ... introduced into England in 1818 ... were called hobbyhorses* [*or*] *dandy horses* (Franklin M. Reck).

dan|dy|ish (dan′dē ish), *adj.* like a dandy; foppish.

dan|dy|ism (dan′dē iz əm), *n.* the style or manners of a dandy; foppishness.

dan|dy|prat (dan′dē prat), *n.* = dandiprat.

dandy roll or **roller,** a roller used in papermaking for solidifying the web of paper and for putting on the watermark. [origin uncertain]

Dane (dān), *n.* **1** a person born or living in Denmark. **2** a person of Danish descent. **3** = Great Dane.

the Dane, Hamlet.

Dane|geld or **dane|geld** (dān′geld′), *n.* (in English history) a tax collected regularly to buy off the Danish invaders, and later continued as a land tax: *If once you have paid him the Danegeld, You never get rid of the Dane* (Rudyard Kipling). [Middle English *Danegeld* < *Dane* Dane + Old English *gield* payment]

Dane|gelt or **dane|gelt** (dān′gelt′), *n.* = Danegeld.

Da|ne|la|ga (dä′nə lä′gə), *n.* = Danelaw.

Dane|law or **Dane|lagh** (dān′lô′), *n.* **1** the set of laws enforced by the Danes when they held northeast England in the 800's and 900's A.D. **2** the part of England under these laws. [Old English *Dena lagu*]

Danes'-blood (dānz′blud′), *n.* any one of several plants supposed to have sprung originally from the blood of Danes slain in battle, such as the pasqueflower or the bellflower.

dang (dang), *adj., adv., v.t., v.i., n. Informal.* damn; darn: *Dang my bones* (Dickens). [euphemism for *damn*]

danged (dangd), *adj., adv. Informal.* = darned.

dan|ger (dān′jər), *n.* **1** a chance of harm; nearness to harm; risk; peril: *A soldier's life is full of danger. There is some danger in mountain climbing.* **2** a thing that may cause harm: *Hidden rocks are a danger to ships.* SYN: menace, threat. **3** *Archaic.* **a** power; jurisdiction. **b** power to reach or harm. **4** *Obsolete.* harm; injury: *We put a sting in him, That at his will he may do danger with* (Shakespeare). [< Old French *dangier,* ultimately < Latin *dominium* sovereignty < *dominus* master]

—*Syn.* **1 Danger, peril** mean threat of harm. **Danger,** the more general word, always suggests a definite chance of harm even though it may not be near or certain: *Miners at work are always in danger.* **Peril** implies that great harm is near at hand and probable: *When a mine caves in, the miners are in peril.*

dan|ger|less (dān′jər lis), *adj.* without danger; free from danger.

danger line, a line marking the boundary between apparent safety and danger: *If the figures above have given the impression that the rim states have escaped the desert or conquered it, and are now safe beyond the danger line, that impression must be corrected* (Harper's).

danger money, *Especially British.* extra pay for undertaking a dangerous assignment or special risk: *This is paid to him ... as a rock 'n' roll singer—and perhaps also as danger money, since his young admirers have on two occasions rushed him ... and pulled out handfuls of his hair as souvenirs* (Manchester Guardian Weekly).

dan|ger|ous (dān′jər əs), *adj.* likely to cause harm; not safe; risky: *Shooting off firecrackers can be dangerous.* SYN: perilous, hazardous, precarious, unsafe. —**dan′ger|ous|ly,** *adv.* —**dan′ger|ous|ness,** *n.*

danger signal, a sign, object, light, sound, or the like giving notice of danger: *Late in the afternoon, scientists at Britain's Windscale plant ... saw danger signals on a temperature control instrument* (Time).

dan|ger|some (dān′jər səm), *adj.* full of danger; very dangerous.

danger zone, a definite area or region within which some danger exists.

dan|gle (dang′gəl), *v.,* **-gled, -gling,** *n.* —*v.i.* **1** to hang and swing loosely: *The curtain cord dangles.* (*Figurative.*) *Some choppy editing abruptly disposes of whole characters, leaving several plot lines dangling* (Eugene Archer). SYN: flap, oscillate. **2** *Figurative.* to wait around; hang about; follow: *The pretty girl had several boys dangling after her.*

—*v.t.* **1** to hold or carry (a thing) so that it swings loosely: *The cat played with the string I dangled in front of it. The nurse dangled the toys in front of the baby.* **2** to cause to dangle. **3** *Figurative.* to keep (a hope or anticipation) hanging uncertainly before one: *He* [*the President*] *dangled before the country the prospect of budget cuts* (New York Times).

—*n.* **1** the act of dangling. **2** something that dangles.

[probably < Scandinavian (compare Danish *dangla*)] —**dan′gler,** *n.*

dan|gle|ber|ry (dang′gəl ber′ē), *n., pl.* **-ries.** = tangleberry.

dan|gle-doll|y (dang′gəl dol′ē), *n., pl.* **-doll|ies.** *British.* a small doll hung in a car window as a charm or decoration.

dan|gling participle (dang′gling), a participle not clearly connected with the word it modifies. In "Sitting on the porch, a beautiful moon can be seen," *sitting* is a dangling participle.

►**A dangling participle** is objectionable because of its ludicrous effect (*Walking down the street, the church steeple came into view*) or its lack of immediate clarity: *Toddling down the walk, I saw the neighbor's child. Working at his desk, the sudden noise proved startling.* Clarity is achieved by placing the participle next to the word it modifies (*... the child toddling down the walk*) and by stating the word it modifies (*Working at his desk, he was startled by ...*). A participle which technically dangles but is neither ludicrous nor at all unclear is called an absolute participle, and it is generally regarded as acceptable: *Strictly speaking, a tomato is a fruit. Barring accidents, we shall be at home by six. Talking of flower shows, did you see the one of 1975?*

dan|gly (dang′glē), *adj.,* **-gli|er, -gli|est.** that dangles; dangling: *a dangly earring, necklace, or bracelet.*

Da|ni|an (dā′nē ən), *n. Geology.* the uppermost division of the Cretaceous system in France and Belgium, not in the English series. [< Latin *Dānia* Denmark (< *Dāni* Danes) + English *-an*]

Dan|iel (dan′yəl), *n.* **1** a Hebrew prophet who lived in Babylon during the Captivity and whose great faith in God kept him unharmed in a den of lions (in the Bible, Daniel 6:16-27). **2** a book of the Old Testament that tells about him. *Abbr:* Dan., Danl.

Dan|iell cell (dan′yəl), a galvanic cell, having a copper cathode and a zinc anode. [< John Frederic *Daniell,* 1790-1845, an English physicist]

da|ni|o (dā′nē ō), *n., pl.* **-ni|os.** any one of several brightly colored tropical fishes of India and Ceylon (Sri Lanka), related to the goldfish. Danios are often kept in aquariums. [< New Latin *Danio,* the genus name]

Dan|ish (dā′nish), *adj., n.* —*adj.* of or having to do with Denmark, its people, or their language.

—*n.* **1** *pl. in use.* the people of Denmark; the Danes. **2** the Scandinavian language of Denmark. **3** = Danish pastry.

Danish pastry, 1 a rich, flaky pastry made with yeast, in which the process of rolling the dough, dotting it with shortening, and folding it is repeated several times before it is pulled into small pieces and baked: *Fragile, fruity Danish pastry in cunning shapes* (Maclean's). **2** a piece of this pastry.

Dan|ite (dan′īt), *n.* **1** a descendant of Dan (in the Bible, Judges 13:2). **2** a member of an alleged secret order of Mormons, supposed to have been formed about 1837 and to have been guilty of various atrocious crimes.

dank (dangk), *adj.* unpleasantly damp; moist; wet: *The cave was dark, dank, and chilly.* [Middle English *danke,* perhaps < Scandinavian (compare Swedish *dank* marshy spot)] —**dank′ly,** *adv.* —**dank′ness,** *n.*

dan|ke schön (däng′kə shœn′), *German.* thank you.

dank|ish (dang′kish), *adj.* somewhat dank; damp.

Dan|ne|brog (dan′ə brog), *n.* **1** the Danish national flag. **2** a Danish order of merit awarded to Danes and citizens of other countries for deeds of civilian or military distinction. [< Danish *Dannebrog* < *Dane* Danish + Old Danish *brog* cloth]

Da|no-Nor|we|gian (dā′nō nôr wē′jən), *n.* = Riksmål.

danse du ven|tre (däɴs′ dʏ väɴ′trə), *French.* belly dance.

danse ma|ca|bre (däɴs′ mȧ kȧ′brə), *French.* the dance of death: *Much of the imaginative art and literature of our time is preoccupied by the theme of the danse macabre* (Bulletin of Atomic Scientists).

dan|seur (däɴ sœr′), *n.* a male dancer, especially in a ballet. [< French *danseur* < Old French *danser,* noun use of infinitive; see etym. under **dance**]

dan|seur no|ble (däɴ sœr′ nô′blə), *pl.* **dan|seurs no|bles** (däɴ sœr′ nô′blə). a male ballet dancer of noble appearance and manners: *There are male performers who have the dash and elevation of danseurs nobles* (New York Times). [< French *danseur noble* noble dancer]

dan|seuse (däɴ sœz′), *n., pl.* **-seuses** (-sœz′). a female dancer, especially in a ballet: *The assemblage ... incorporates some of the handsomest danseuses of the season* (New Yorker). [< French *danseuse,* feminine of *danseur* < Old French *danser;* see etym. under **dance**]

Dan|te|an (dan′tē ən, dan tē′-), *adj., n.* —*adj.* **1** of or having to do with Dante or his writings. **2** = Dantesque.

—*n.* a student or admirer of Dante.

Dan|tesque (dan tesk′), *adj.* like Dante or his style; elevated; solemn; somber: *... a Dantesque catalogue of the psychological and physical tortures of a company of men and women trapped in Warsaw's sewers during the abortive 1944 uprising against the Nazis* (Time). [< *Dante* Alighieri, 1265-1321, Italian poet and author of the *Divine Comedy* + *-esque*]

Dan|ton|esque (dan′tə nesk′), *adj.* of, like, or in the manner of Danton; bold and audacious: *In addition to his Dantonesque boldness in meeting the foe, he had the constructive mind which is rare in a man of action* (Atlantic). [< Georges Jacques *Danton,* 1759-1794, one of the chief figures in the French Revolution + *-esque*]

Dan|ton|ist (dan′tə nist), *n.* a follower of Danton.

Dan|u|bi|an (dan yü′bē ən), *adj.* of or having to do with the Danube or the people living near the Danube.

dan|za (dän′sä, -zä), *n.* a formal dance of the Middle Ages, danced in couples or singly. [< Spanish *danza* dance]

da|o (dä′ü), *n., pl.* **da|os.** = dah[2].

dap (dap), *v.,* **dapped, dap|ping.** —*v.i.* **1** to fish by letting the bait dip and bob lightly on the water. **2** to dip lightly or suddenly into water. **3** to rebound; bounce. —*v.t.* **1** to bounce; skip. **2** to cut a notch in for joining: *to dap timber.* [perhaps variant of *dab*[1]]

daph|ne (daf′nē), *n.* **1** any one of a group of small, ornamental, European and Asiatic shrubs with very fragrant, pink or purplish flowers, such as the mezereum. **2** the laurel. [< Latin *daphne* < Greek *dáphnē* laurel]

Daph|ne (daf′nē), *n. Greek Legend.* a nymph pursued by Apollo, from whom she was saved by being changed into a laurel tree. [< Greek *Dáphnē* (originally) laurel]

Daph|ne|pho|ri|a (daf′nē fôr′ē ə, -fōr′-), *n.* an ancient Greek festival, a kind of Maypole ceremony, held in Thebes. [< Greek *daphnēphoriā,* ultimately < *dáphnē* laurel + *phérein* to bear]

daph|ni|a (daf′nē ə), *n.* a tiny freshwater crustacean often having a bivalve shell covering its transparent body except for the head and two sets of antennae, and moving by jerking the second set of large antennae; water flea. [< New Latin *Daphnia* the genus name < Latin *daphne* daphne]

Daph|nis (daf′nis), *n. Greek Mythology.* a minor Greek pastoral god, regarded as the inventor of bucolic poetry.

Daphnis and Chlo|ë (klō′ē), two lovers in a Greek pastoral romance of about the 300's or 400's A.D. They are regarded as the model of typical, unsophisticated lovers.

dap|per (dap′ər), *adj.* **1** neat; trim; spruce: *The dandy is very dapper about his fine clothes.* SYN: smart, natty. **2** small and active: *Trip the pert faeries and the dapper elves* (Milton). SYN: brisk, nimble. [Middle English *dapyr.* Compare Middle Dutch *dapper* agile, strong, sturdy.] —**dap′per|ly,** *adv.* —**dap′per|ness,** *n.*

dap|per|ling (dap′ər ling), *n.* a little, dapper fellow.

dap|ping (dap′ing), *n.* a method of fishing in which the bait dips and bobs lightly on the water.

dap|ple (dap′əl), *adj., v.,* **-pled, -pling,** *n.* —*adj.* marked with spots; spotted: *a dapple horse.* SYN: pied, variegated.

—*v.t., v.i.* to mark or become marked with spots: *The bleach dappled the dark cloth* (v.t.). *The dark cloth dappled in the bleach solution* (v.i.).

—*n.* **1** a spotted appearance or condition. **2** an animal with a spotted or mottled skin or coat, especially a horse. SYN: piebald.

[Middle English *dappel.* Compare Old Icelandic *depill* spot.]

dap|pled (dap′əld), *adj.* spotted; mottled.

dap|ple-gray (dap′əl grā′), *adj.* gray with spots of darker gray.

dapple gray, a dapple-gray horse or other animal.

Pronunciation Key: hat, āge, cãre, fär; let, ēqual, tėrm; it, īce; hot, ōpen, ôrder; oil, out; cup, pu̇t, rüle; child; long; thin; ᴛʜen; zh, measure; ə represents **a** in about, **e** in taken, **i** in pencil, **o** in lemon, **u** in circus.

D.A.R. or **DAR** (no periods), Daughters of the American Revolution, a society of women who are descended from Americans who fought in the Revolutionary War.

darb (därb), *n. U.S. Slang.* an excellent or admirable person or thing: *The children . . . are three little darbs* (Time). [origin uncertain]

dar|by (där′bē), *n., pl.* **-bies. 1** a plasterer's tool for leveling a surface of plaster. **2** *Slang.* a handcuff. [< *Darby, Derby*, an English town and shire]

Dar|by and Joan (där′bē ənd jōn′), the typical old married couple, contented and devoted to each other. [< *Darby and Joan*, characters in an old song]

dar|cy (där′sē), *n., pl.* **-cys.** a measure of the permeability of a porous medium: *Permeability is commonly measured in darcys and millidarcys (thousandth of a darcy) . Even the tavern loafers of an oil town now speak enthusiastically of a permeability of 500 millidarcys* (Gilluly, Waters, and Woodford). [< Henri *Darcy*, 1803-1858, a French hydrologist]

Dard (därd), *n.* **1** any one of an Indo-Aryan people living in the northwestern part of the Indian subcontinent. **2** a group of related Indic languages spoken by this people, including Kashmiri; Dardic.

Dar|dan (där′dən), *adj., n.* = Trojan. See also **Dardanus.** [< Latin *Dardanus* < Greek *Dárdanos*, or *Dardánios* Trojan < *Dárdanos* Dardanus]

Dar|da|ni|a (där dā′nē ə), *n.* legendary Troy.

Dar|da|ni|an (där dā′nē ən), *adj., n.* = Trojan.

Dar|da|nus (där′də nəs), *n. Greek Legend.* a son of Zeus, the mythical ancestor of the Trojans.

Dar|dic (där′dik), *n.* the Indic languages of the Dards.

dare[1] (dãr), *v.,* **dared** or (*Archaic*) **durst, dared, dar|ing,** *n.* —*v.i.* to have courage; be bold; be bold enough: *You wouldn't dare! The will to do, the soul to dare* (Scott).
—*v.t.* **1** to have courage to try; be bold enough for; not be afraid of: *The explorer dared the dangers of the icy north. She dared contradict the teacher.* **2** to meet and resist; face and defy: *to dare the power of a dictator. I saw and felt London at last . . . I dared the perils of the crossings* (Charlotte Brontë). SYN: brave. **3** to challenge: *I dare you to jump the puddle.*
—*n.* **1** a challenge: *I took his dare to jump.* **2** *Obsolete.* daring; boldness.
[Old English *dearr*, first person singular, indicative of *durran* to dare] —**dar′er,** *n.*
—*Syn. v.i.* **Dare, venture** mean to be courageous or bold enough to do something. **Dare** emphasizes the idea of meeting fearlessly any danger or trouble, especially in doing something that is or seems important: *Only the fireman dared to enter the burning building.* **Venture** emphasizes the idea of being willing to take chances: *He ventured to cross the rickety bridge when none of the rest of us would even set foot on it.*
▶**dare, dares.** Either *dare* or *dares* is used with the third person singular: *He dare not. He dares to do many reckless things.*

dare[2] (dãr), *v.t.,* **dared, dar|ing. 1** *Dialect.* to terrify; daunt. **2** *Obsolete.* to daze; fascinate. [Old English *darian* to lurk, lie hid]

dare|dev|il (dãr′dev′əl), *n., adj.* —*n.* a reckless person.
—*adj.* recklessly daring: *The speeder's daredevil driving caused an accident. This was not the first time he had shown daredevil tendencies* (Harper's).

dare|dev|il|ry (dãr′dev′əl rē), *n., pl.* **-ries.** = daredeviltry.

dare|dev|il|try (dãr′dev′əl trē), *n., pl.* **-tries.** reckless daring: *There was the usual thrilling, high-altitude daredeviltry, including an act on a weird upside-down unicycle* (Wall Street Journal).

dare|ful (dãr′fəl), *adj.* full of daring.

dare|say (dãr′sā′), *v.t., v.i.,* or dare say, to venture to say; assume as probable; presume: *I daresay his success was due to his hard work. I, daresay you have thought me very neglectful* (Jane Carlyle). SYN: believe.
▶**Daresay** or **dare say** is always used in the first person singular, present tense: *I daresay you are right. You and I, I dare say, agree.*

darg or **dargue** (därg), *n. Scottish.* **1** a day's work. **2** a set task. [reduction of Middle English *dawerk* < *day* day + *werk* work]

dar|ic (dar′ik), *n.* an ancient Persian gold coin. [< Greek *Dāreikós (statēr)* (a coin) of Darius]

dar|ing (dãr′ing), *n., adj.* —*n.* boldness; courage to take risks: *The old soldier proudly recalled the daring of his youth.*
—*adj.* bold; fearless; courageous: *Saving the dog from the burning building was a daring act.* SYN: audacious, intrepid, rash, venturesome. —**dar′ing|ly,** *adv.* —**dar′ing|ness,** *n.*

Dar|jee|ling (där jē′ling), *n.* a kind of fine India tea having a delicate flavor, grown chiefly in the Himalayan mountains. [< *Darjeeling*, a district in northern India]

dark (därk), *adj., n., v.* —*adj.* **1** without light or with very little light: *A night without a moon is dark.* **2** reflecting or radiating little light; nearly black in color: *dark clouds. She has dark-brown eyes.* **3** not light-colored: *a dark complexion, dark meat.* **4** *Figurative.* gloomy; dull; dismal: *to look on the dark side of things. Rain and clouds make a dark day.* SYN: dreary, morose. **5** *Figurative.* hidden; secret: *The spy had a dark plan.* **6** *Figurative.* hard to understand or explain: *a dark chapter in a book. God's ways seem dark* (John Greenleaf Whittier). SYN: obscure, abstruse, enigmatical, inscrutable. **7** *Figurative.* without knowledge or culture; ignorant; unenlightened: *a dark period in history.* **8** *Figurative.* evil; wicked: *The treacherous murder was a dark deed.* SYN: sinister. **9** *Figurative.* sad, sullen, or frowning: *a dark look.* **10** *Figurative.* silent; reticent: *Be dark as the hush'd silence of the grave* (Thomas Otway). **11** *Phonetics.* (of *-l* sounds) having the quality of a back vowel. *Example: -l* in *wool* is darker than in *lean.* SYN: mute. **12** not broadcasting: *During the power failure all the local radio and television stations were dark.*
—*n.* **1** the absence of light; darkness: *Do not be afraid of the dark.* **2** night; nightfall: *The dark comes early in winter.* **3** a dark color. **4** *Figurative.* obscurity. **5** *Figurative.* secrecy. **6** *Figurative.* ignorance.
—*v.t.* , *v.i. Obsolete.* to darken.
after dark, after night has fallen: *Before we got to the foot of the mountain, which was not till after dark* (Lady M. W. Montague).
in the dark, without knowledge or information; in ignorance: *He said nothing, leaving me in the dark about his plans.*
keep dark, to keep silent about; not tell about: *Of course, I'll keep as dark about it as possible* (Century Magazine).
whistle in the dark, to try to be courageous or hopeful in a fearful or trying situation: *[He] said he was not whistling in the dark or crying alarms, but declared he had tremendous confidence that business is basically strong* (Wall Street Journal).
[Middle English *derke*, Old English *deorc*]
—*Syn. adj.* **1 Dark, dim** mean without light. **Dark** means without any light or with very little light: *The house is dark; not a light is on.* **Dim** means without enough light to see clearly or distinctly: *With only the fire burning, the room was dim.*

dark-a|dapt (därk′ə dapt′), *v.t.* to adjust (the pupils of the eyes) to darkness.

dark adaptation, the adjustment of the pupils of the eyes to darkness or dim light: *Some night-blind people can improve their dark adaptation by taking large doses of vitamin A* (Scientific American).

Dark Ages or **dark ages, 1** the early part of the Middle Ages, from about 400 A.D. to about 1000 A.D., when learning and culture in western Europe were at a low ebb. **2** the period between ancient and modern times, from about the 400's A.D. to about A.D. 1450; the Middle Ages.
▶Definition 1. represents the dominant view of contemporary historians. Definition 2. is that of an earlier generation who contrasted the Middle Ages with the Renaissance to the disadvantage of the former.

Dark and Bloody Ground, 1 a supposed translation of the word *Kentucky.* **2** a name given to Kentucky in reference to its early Indian warfare.

dark brown star, a source of infrared radiation but little visible light discovered in the Milky Way.

dark comedy, 1 = black humor. **2** = black comedy.

Dark Continent, the continent of Africa (because formerly little was known about it): *That part of the Dark Continent . . . has a well-defined belt of virulent ailments caused by heavy rains and dense jungle growths* (Newsweek).

dark|en (där′kən), *v.t., v.i.* **1** to make or become dark or darker; dim: *We darkened the room by drawing the shades. As the storm approached, the sky darkened.* **2** to make or become blind. —**dark′en|er,** *n.*

dark|ey (där′kē), *n., pl.* **-eys.** = darky.

dark-field illumination (därk′fēld′), a system of illumination, used especially in an ultramicroscope, lighting the field from the side, making a light object on a dark background.

dark-field microscope, a microscope equipped with dark-field illumination.

dark-fired (därk′fīrd′), *adj.* fire-cured (used especially of tobacco): *Farms in the north-central section produce dark-fired tobacco, which is cured with heat and smoke rather than with air like most tobaccos* (Isabel Howell).

dark horse, 1 an unexpected winner about whom little is known. **2** a person who is unexpectedly nominated for a political office: *Dark horses in both parties were bobbing up everywhere* (Newsweek). [< the practice of altering a horse's color in order to mask its identity]

dark|ie (där′kē), *n., pl.* **-ies.** = darky.

dark|ish (där′kish), *adj.* somewhat dark. —**dark′ish|ness,** *n.*

dark lantern, a lantern whose light can be hidden by a cover or dark glass.

dar|kle (där′kəl), *v.,* **-kled, -kling.** —*v.i.* **1** to appear dark or indistinct. **2** to grow or become dark. **3** to become dark with anger. —*v.t.* to make dark or obscure. [back formation < *darkling*]

dark-line spectrum (därk′līn′), a spectrum of dark lines on a bright background: *Sunlight produces a dark-line spectrum* (Robert H. Baker).

dark|ling (där′kling) *adv., adj.* —*adv.* in the dark.
—*adj.* **1** dark: *It is late, and I am tired of darkling colors* (New Yorker). **2** *Figurative.* dim; obscure; darksome. [< *dark* + Old English *-ling*, an adverbial suffix indicating state or manner]

darkling beetle, a large beetle with a hard, black, brown, or gray body, that cannot fly and prefers dry places in which it feeds as a scavenger on decaying vegetable matter.

dark|ly (där′klē), *adv., adj.* —*adv.* in a dark manner. —*adj.* dark-looking; somewhat dark.

dark matter, *Astronomy.* a hypothetical form of matter that does not emit or absorb electromagnetic radiation: *This missing matter is unlike ordinary matter that gives off or absorbs light, hence the name—dark matter* (Stephen S. Murray).

dark nebula, a large, dark or nearly dark, starless region in the sky occupied by clouds of dust and gas which hide or dim the view of stars behind them. Some dark nebulae are easily visible because they reflect the light of the stars around them. *A succession of dark nebulae produces the great rift in the Milky Way* (Robert H. Baker).

dark|ness (därk′nis) *n.* **1** the quality or state of being dark: *A voice in the darkness, a knock at the door* (Longfellow). SYN: dimness, duskiness. **2** *Figurative.* gloom; sorrow or trouble. **3** *Figurative.* wickedness; evil: *Oftentimes, to win us to our harm, The instruments of darkness tell us truths* (Shakespeare). **4** *Figurative.* obscurity; concealment; secrecy. **5** *Figurative.* blindness; ignorance.

dark|room (därk′rüm′, -rům′), *n.* a room cut off from all outside light and arranged for developing photographs. It usually has a very dim, colored light.

dark|some (därk′səm), *adj.* **1** dark. **2** *Figurative.* gloomy; somber: *a darksome wood.* **3** *Figurative.* obscure. **4** *Figurative.* fearsome: *a darksome fiend.* —**dark′some|ness,** *n.*

dark star, a star that cannot be seen: **1** one that is so cool that all or most of its light waves are in the infrared portion of the spectrum. **2** one that no longer gives off any light; dead star.

dark|y (där′kē), *n., pl.* **dark|ies.** *Informal.* a Negro (often used in an unfriendly way). Also, **darkey, darkie.**

Dar|lan (där′lan), *n. Trademark.* a synthetic fiber made from a chemical related to adiponitrile.

Dar|ley Arabian (där′lē), one of the three stallions from which all English thoroughbred race horses are descended. [< Richard *Darley*, an Englishman, who acquired the horse in 1704]

dar|ling (där′ling), *n., adj.* —*n.* **1** a person or animal very dear to another; person or animal much loved: *The baby is the family darling.* **2** a favorite: *My sister is my mother's darling.* (*Figurative.*) *Trade, that pride and darling of our Ocean* (Emerson). SYN: pet. **3** *Informal.* a charming, pleasing, or attractive person or thing: *Isn't that baby a darling?*
—*adj.* **1** very dear; much loved: *"My darling daughter," her letter began. We are all ready for a glowing story about this darling girl* (George S. Kaufman). SYN: beloved. **2** favorite: *the darling member of the family.* **3** *Informal.* pleasing or attractive: *Oh, isn't that just the classiest, darlingest coat you ever saw!* (Theodore Dreiser).
[Old English *dēorling* < *dēore* dear + *-ling* -ling]
—**dar′ling|ly,** *adv.* —**dar′ling|ness,** *n.*

darn[1] (därn), *v., n.* —*v.t.* , *v.i.* to mend by making rows of stitches back and forth across a hole or torn place. —*n.* **1** a place mended by darning. **2** the act of darning.
[< dialectal Middle French *darner* mend < *darne* a piece < Breton *darn*]

darn[2] (därn), *adj., adv., v., n. Informal.* —*adj.* troublesome; exasperating; detestable (an expression of irritation): *The darn thing doesn't work right.*
—*adv.* very; extremely: *She was a darn attractive girl, very vivacious* (Time).
—*v.t.* , *v.i.* to swear or swear at mildly; say "darn": *Darn it! I'll be late!*
—*n.* **1** a saying of "darn." **2** a contemptible amount: *not worth a darn.*
[< *damn*; probably influenced by *tarnal*, informal for *eternal*]
▶**Darn** and **darned** are used as expressions of annoyance or the like (*a darn* or *darned nuisance*)

or as intensives (*darn* or *darned attractive*) of a milder nature than **damn** or **damned**, often by those who avoid the latter words as possibly offensive because of their religious connotations.

darned (därnd), *adj., adv. Informal.* = darn².

dar|nel (där′nəl), *n.* a weed with poisonous seeds that looks somewhat like rye. It often grows in grainfields. The darnel is an annual grass. [probably < Old North French *darnelle* < a Germanic word]

darn|er (där′nər), *n.* **1** a person who darns. **2** = darning needle. **3** = darning egg.

darn|ing (där′ning), *n.* **1** the act of mending with stitches. **2** articles darned or to be darned: *Her work box was piled high with darning.*

darning cotton, cotton thread used in darning.

darning egg, an egg-shaped piece of wood, plastic, or, sometimes, glass over which an article to be darned is drawn smooth.

darning needle, **1** a long needle with a large eye for heavy thread, used in darning. **2** = dragonfly.

dar|o|bok|ka (dar′ə bok′ə), *n.* a drum struck with two hands, used in Egypt and North Africa. [< Arabic *darābukkah* tambourine]

da|ro|ga (də rō′gə), *n.* a title applied in India to various executive officers; overseer; governor. [< Hindustani *dārōghah*]

dar|rein (dar′ān, də rān′), *adj.* (in old law) last; dernier. [< Old French *darrain,* ultimately < Latin *dē retrō* behind]

darrein presentment, (in old law) the last or previous presentation to an ecclesiastical benefice regarded as proof of the right to make presentation.

dar|shan (där′shən), *n. Hinduism.* a spiritual experience or blessing conferred by the sight of an important teacher or leader: *They have not come to hear Nehru but for darshan, the spiritual impact of being in the presence of a great personality* (Time).

D'Ar|son|val galvanometer (där′sən vôl, -val), a galvanometer with a coil that pivots on an iron core between the poles of a permanent magnet: *The D'Arsonval galvanometer is one of the most commonly used galvanometers* (D. D. Ewing). [< Jacques Arsene *d'Arsonval,* 1851-1940, a French physicist]

***dart** (därt), *n., v.* —*n.* **1** a slender, pointed weapon or short stick tipped with a sharp metal point. It may be thrown by the hand or shot from a blowgun. **2** anything like a dart, such as an arrow or javelin. **3** a sudden, swift movement. SYN: dash. **4** the stinger of an insect. **5** a short seam to make a garment fit better. **6** *Figurative.* a sharp look, word, or retort. **7** *Australian Informal.* a scheme; plan.
—*v.t.* **1** to throw or shoot suddenly and swiftly: *The Eskimos darted spears at the seal.* SYN: hurl, launch. **2** to send suddenly: (*Figurative.*) *The girl darted an angry glance at her younger sister.* **3** to fit with a dart or darts: *to dart the waistline of a dress.*
—*v.i.* **1** to move suddenly and swiftly: *The deer saw us and darted away.* SYN: dash, bolt, spring. **2** to throw a dart or other weapon.
darts, a game in which darts are thrown at a target: *There are many games and contests which require skill in aiming or throwing, such as darts* (Bernard S. Mason).
[< Old French *dart* < Germanic (compare Old English *daroth*)] —**dart′like′**, *adj.*

***dart** definition 1

***dartboard**

***dart|board** (därt′bôrd′, -bōrd′), *n.* the target in the game of darts.

dart|er (där′tər), *n.* **1** an animal or person that moves suddenly and swiftly. **2** a small freshwater fish, of the same family as the perch. **3** = snakebird.

dart|ing (där′ting), *adj.* moving or shooting suddenly and swiftly: *His darting touch gives a piano almost the crispness of a harpsichord* (Atlantic). —**dart′ing|ly**, *adv.*

dart|ist (där′tist), *n.* a person who plays the game of darts.

dar|tle (där′təl), *v.t., v.i.,* **-tled, -tling.** to dart or shoot forth repeatedly. [< *dart,* verb + *-le*]

Dart|moor pony (därt′mu̇r, -môr, -mōr), any one of a breed of English ponies raised in Devonshire, noted for their ability as work horses: *Dartmoor ponies are a hardy, sure-footed breed with small heads and ears* (Margaret C. Self). [< *Dartmoor,* a region in Devonshire, England]

dar|tre (där′tər), *n.* any one of various skin diseases, such as herpes. [< French *dartre* < Late Latin (Gaul) *derbita* < Celtic (compare Breton *dervoed*)]

dar|trous (där′trəs), *adj.* having to do with or like dartre.

darts (därts), *n.pl.* (*singular in use*). See under **dart**.

darts-board (därts′bôrd′, -bōrd′), *n. Especially British.* dartboard: . . . *loud-voiced patronizing young men and women who inexpertly monopolize the darts-board* (Punch).

dart snake, any one of a group of serpentlike lizards that dart on their prey.

Dar|von (där′von), *n. Trademark.* a drug used to relieve pain: *He has often dispatched a nurse for codeine or Darvon* (Harper's). *Formula:* $C_{22}H_{29}NO_2$

Dar|win|i|an (där win′ē ən), *adj., n.* —*adj.* of Charles Darwin, English scientist (1809-1882) or his theory of evolution, as stated and defended in his works *The Origin of Species* (1859) and *The Descent of Man* (1871).
—*n.* a person who believes in Darwinism.

Darwinian theory, = Darwinism.

Dar|win|ism (där′wə niz əm), *n.* the theory of evolution through natural selection, developed by Charles Darwin, according to which natural selection results in the survival of some plant and animal forms but not others. Among a number of slight variations those best adapted to the environment survive, ultimately resulting in new, usually more complex species.

Dar|win|ist (där′wə nist), *adj., n.* = Darwinian.

Dar|win|is|tic (där′wə nis′tik), *adj.* = Darwinian: *W. C. Wells formulated what was practically a Darwinistic statement on natural selection in . . . 1813* (Science News Letter).

Dar|win tulip (där′wən), any one of a variety of tall-growing, late-blooming tulips having a wide range of uniformly colored single flowers.

***dash¹** (dash), *v., n.* —*v.t.* **1** to throw, drive, or strike: *In a fit of anger he dashed his ruler against the door. We dashed water over him.* **2** to splash: *She dashed some paint on the paper and called it a tree.* **3** to strike violently or throw so as to break; smash: *He dashed the bowl to bits on a rock. The waves dashed the boat to pieces.* SYN: shatter, crush. **4** *Figurative.* to ruin or destroy: *Our hopes were dashed by the bad news.* **5** to depress; discourage. SYN: deject. **6** to mix with a small amount of something else. **7** to abash; confound: *He was dashed by the sudden questioning of the teacher.* **8** *British Informal.* to damn: *Dashed if I know* (Dickens).
—*v.i.* **1** to strike violently: *The waves dashed against the rocks.* **2** to rush: *They dashed by in a hurry.* SYN: dart.
—*n.* **1a** a splash: *the dash of waves against the rocks. He was sprayed by a dash of mud.* **b** the sound of splashing. **2** a rush: *He made a dash for safety.* **3** a violent blow or stroke; smash: *the dash of the oar against the water.* **4** a thing that depresses or discourages; check: *The accident was a dash to our hopes.* **5** a small amount: *Put in just a dash of pepper.* SYN: touch, tinge, smack. **6** a short race: *the hundred-yard dash.* **7** energy; spirit; liveliness: *The winning team played with dash against the losers.* **8** *Figurative.* showy appearance or behavior: *The well-dressed couple cut a dash at the party. The instructors, who were mostly technicians, or pilots grounded by injury, cared nothing for soldierly dash* (New Yorker). **9** a mark used in writing or printing to show a break in sense, explanatory material, omitted letters or words, or the like. **10** a hasty stroke: *He crossed out the sentence with a dash of the pen.* **11** a long sound used in sending messages by telegraph or radiotelegraph: *The difference between a dot and a dash is the difference in time between two clicks* (Beauchamp, Mayfield, and West). **12** = dashboard. **13** *Especially British.* a mild curse; damn: *He didn't care a dash.*
dash off, a to do or write quickly: *He dashed off a letter to his friend. You can sometimes dash off a favorable review in twenty minutes, it's panning that is difficult* (Saturday Review). **b** to go in a hurry; run: *She dashed off to catch the 8 o'clock express.*
[Middle English *daschen.* Compare Danish *daske* slap.]

***dash¹**

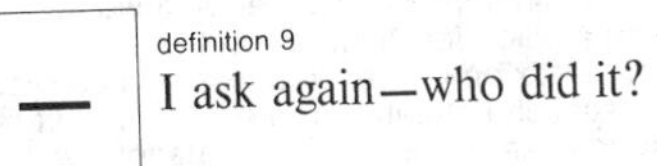

definition 9

dash² (dash), *n., v.* —*n.* (in Africa) a gift or gratuity; tip.
—*v.t.* (in Africa) to bestow a dash on; tip: *Until recently, one of the worst torments of African travel for a white man arose out of this necessity of dashing every chief he visited* (New Yorker). [shortening of earlier *dashee,* a native word on the Guinea coast]

Dash|a|ha|ra (dash′ə hə rä′), *n.* (in India) an annual festival in commemoration of a form of the goddess Devi. [< Hindi *dasahrā* < Sanskrit *dasaharā* (literally) one that removes ten sins]

dash|board (dash′bôrd′, -bōrd′), *n.* **1** the panel with instruments, gauges, and certain controls in front of the driver in an automobile, truck, aircraft, or boat. **2** protection on the front of a wagon, carriage, or boat, that prevents mud or water from being splashed into it; dasher.

da|sheen (da shēn′), *n.* a kind of taro grown in Hawaii, the southern United States, and various tropical areas for its edible sprouts and tubers, which are used like potatoes. [apparently < French *de Chine* of China]

dash|er (dash′ər), *n.* **1** a person or thing that dashes. **2** a device for stirring the cream in a churn or ice-cream freezer. **3** = dashboard (def. 2). **4** *Informal.* a dashing person.

***da|shi|ki** (də shē′kē), *n., pl.* **-kis.** a loose shirtlike garment, often colorfully printed or embroidered, put on by pulling it over the head. [< a West African word]

***dashiki**

dash|ing (dash′ing), *adj.* **1** full of energy and spirit; lively: *a dashing young man. Feuer's favorite cold-weather sport is skiing, to which he has a dashing approach* (New Yorker). **2** *Figurative.* showy or stylish: *The men in the band wore bright, dashing uniforms. . . . young men with dashing mustaches, heavy fringes of beard, and foils* (Edmund Wilson). —**dash′ing|ly**, *adv.*

dash-plate (dash′plāt′), *n.* a plate sometimes fixed in a marine boiler, over the fire box, to prevent the crown sheet from being left bare when the ship rolls heavily.

dash|pot (dash′pot′), *n.* a device for checking motion in a machine, consisting of a cylinder or chamber in which the movement of a piston is retarded by a cushion of air or liquid.

dash|y (dash′ē), *adj.,* **dash|i|er, dash|i|est.** dashing; showy; stylish.

das|n't or **dass|n't** (das′ənt), *U.S. Dialect.* dare not.

das|sie (das′ē), *n.* a South African cony; the hyrax: *These stony kloofs afforded shelter to innumerable "dassies," singular little creatures between a rat and a rabbit* (T. J. Lucas). [< Afrikaans *dasje* (diminutive) < Dutch *das* badger]

das|tard (das′tərd), *n., adj.* —*n.* a mean coward; sneak; poltroon.
—*adj.* mean and cowardly; sneaking; dastardly. [Middle English *dastard* (originally) a dullard, apparently < *dased,* past participle of *dasen* to daze]

das|tard|li|ness (das′tərd lē nis), *n.* cowardliness.

das|tard|ly (das′tərd lē), *adj.* mean and cowardly; like a dastard; sneaking: *The traitor was caught in the dastardly act of betraying his country.*

da|sym|e|ter (da sim′ə tər), *n.* an instrument for measuring the density of gases. [< Greek *dasýs* dense + English *-meter*]

das|y|ure (das′ē yu̇r), *n.* any animal of a group of small, carnivorous marsupials of Tasmania and Australia, such as the Tasmanian devil. [< New Latin *Dasyurus* the genus name < Greek *dasýs* dense, shaggy + *ourá* tail]

dat., dative.

DAT (no periods), digital audiotape: *Unlike CDs, which cannot be used to copy live music or other recorded tapes, the DAT is . . . able to rerecord and play back sounds* (B.A. Leerburger).

da|ta (dā′tə, dat′ə, dä′tə), *n.pl.* of **da|tum.** things known or granted; information; facts: *Names, ages, and other data about the class are written in the teacher's notebook.*
►**Data** is the plural of the seldom-used singular *datum.* Since its meaning is often collective, referring to a group of facts as a unit, *data* is often

Pronunciation Key: hat, āge, cãre, fär; let, ēqual, tėrm; it, īce; hot, ōpen, ôrder; oil, out; cup, pu̇t, rüle; child; long; thin; ᴛʜen; zh, measure; ə represents **a** in about, **e** in taken, **i** in pencil, **o** in lemon, **u** in circus.

used with a singular verb in informal English: *The data we have collected is not enough to be convincing.* Formal English continues to regard *data* as a plural rather than as a collective noun: *Our task is to analyze the data that have been secured.*

da|ta|bank (dā′tə bangk′, dat′ə-, dä′tə-), *n., v.,* or **data bank.** —*n.* **1** a large collection of records stored on a computer system from which specialized data may be extracted or organized as desired: *In defence of databanks, one can point to major benefits in medicine, in research, in industry and in commerce which stem directly from the centralization of information* (London Times). **2** such a computer system with its data. **3** the place where such a computer system is located. **4** any data storage system.
—*v.t.* to put or store in a databank.

da|ta|base (dā′tə bās′, dat′ə-, dä′tə-), *n.* **1** a collection of related records or information, stored on a computer and organized to make any part of it easily accessible. **2** = databank.

dat|a|ble (dā′tə bəl), *adj.* that can be dated: *Though none of the coins is precisely datable, analysis of the whole group makes it possible to say with certainty that the ship was buried between 650 and 670* A.D. (Scientific American). Also, **dateable.**

da|ta et ac|cep|ta (dā′tə et ak sep′tə, dat′ə, dä′tə), *Latin.* **1** things given and received. **2** expenditures and receipts.

da|ta|flow (dā′tə flō′, dat′ə-, dä′tə-), *n.* the flow or transfer of data between computers or within a network of computers: *In . . . the dataflow approach, the individual processors automatically carry out instructions when the data becomes available* (Economist).

data link, a communications link for direct transmission of data from one or more distant points to a central computer or data processing unit: *Data links now direct central operation of wholly automated and widely separated factory and distribution centres* (L.V. Berkner).

da|ta|ma|tion (dā′tə mā′shən, dat′ə-, dä′tə-), *n.* the automatic processing of data by computers, especially as a branch of commerce and industry.

da|ta|phone (dā′tə fōn′, dat′ə-, dä′tə-), *n.* an apparatus for sending information from one computer to another over telephone lines.

data processing, the handling and sorting of complex data by means of electronic computers.

data processor, a computer or person who codes information for use by a computer.

data reduction, the conversion of information into meaningful and useful form, such as graphs or tables, usually by an electronic computer.

da|ta|ry (dā′tər ē), *n., pl.* **-ries. 1** an officer, in recent years a cardinal, of the papal court in charge of matters relating to papal benefices. **2** his office or function.
[< Medieval Latin *datarius* the officer, or *datario* the office < Latin *datārius* about to be given away < *datus, -ūs* gift < *dare* give]

date¹ (dāt), *n., v.,* **dat|ed, dat|ing.** —*n.* **1** the time when something happens or happened: *Give the date of your birth. July 4, 1776, is the date of the signing of the Declaration of Independence.* **2** a statement of time: *There is a date stamped on every piece of U.S. money.* **3** a period of time: *At that date there were no airplanes.* SYN: day, age. **4** *Informal.* **a** an appointment for a certain time: *Don't forget to keep your Monday morning date with the dentist.* SYN: rendezvous. **b** an engagement of an entertainer; booking: *[He] does only four or five dates a month because he doesn't want to take all that money to the graveyard* (Time). **5** *Informal.* a person of the opposite sex with whom a social appointment is made: *He asked her to be his date for the school dance.* **6** the time that anything lasts; duration: *Ages of endless date founded in righteousness* (Milton).
—*v.t.* **1** to mark the time of; put a date on: *Please date your papers before handing them in.* **2** to find out the date of; give a date to: *The scientist was unable to date the fossil. Some of Shakespeare's plays cannot be dated exactly.* **3** to make old-fashioned or out of date: *Wearing a stiff collar dates Grandpa. Her old-fashioned hats date her.* **4** *Informal.* to make a social appointment with (a person of the opposite sex): *My brother has been dating his girl friend regularly.*
—*v.i.* **1** to be dated; have a date on it: *This letter dates from Paris.* **2** to belong to a certain period of time; have its origin: *The oldest house in town dates from the 1780's. The Christian Era dates from the birth of Christ.* **3** to be or become old fashioned or out of date: *Some of the material has inevitably dated, and some of it is overfamiliar, but these are my only quibbles with an entertainment that endows nostalgia with more charm* (Kenneth Tynan). **4** to have social engagements with members of the opposite sex: *She doesn't date often.*
down to date, to the present time: *Should the language of the King James Bible be brought down to date?* (Mario Pei).
of even date, of the same date: *I telephoned your office last Monday morning, and sent my letter of even date that afternoon.*
out of date, old-fashioned; not in present use: *That old, long dress even looks out of date. No flower girls in the market, for flowers are out of date* (R. H. Stoddard).
to date, till now; yet: *To date, very little has been done, nationwide, to translate medical knowledge . . . into classroom practice* (Saturday Review).
up to date, a *Figurative.* in fashion; modern: *Her clothes are always up to date. Why, then, should Lord Salisbury sharpen his faculties and keep them . . . up to date?* (London Daily News). **b** up to the present time: *Can you bring me up to date on the developments?*
[< French *date,* learned borrowing from Medieval Latin *data,* noun use of feminine past participle of Latin *dare* give, chiefly in the phrase *data* (*epistola Romae*) (letter) given (at Rome)]
▶**dates.** In using figures to write dates, American usage is to place the month before the day: 7/14/76. British usage commonly places the day of the month first: 14/7/76.

date² (dāt), *n.* **1** the sweet fruit of a kind of palm tree. Dates are oblong and fleshy with a single hard seed and grow in large clusters. **2** the tree that bears it; date palm. [< Old French *date,* ultimately < Latin *dactylus* < Greek *dáktylos* date; finger. See etym. of doublet **dactyl.**]

date|a|ble (dā′tə bəl), *adj.* = datable.

date|book (dāt′bůk′), *n.* a book used for noting important days, events, appointments, expenditures, and the like.

dat|ed (dā′tid), *adj.* **1** marked with a date; showing a date on it. **2** out-of-date: *Jazzy and theatrically insistent, they [torch songs by Kurt Weill] have a lot of fascination, even if they are as dated as an Emil Jannings movie* (New Yorker). SYN: passé. —**dat′ed|ly,** *adv.* —**dat′ed|ness,** *n.*

date|less (dāt′lis), *adj.* **1** without a date; not dated. **2** endless; unlimited. **3** so old that it cannot be given a date: *from dateless usage* (Wordsworth). **4** old but enduring; ageless. **5** *Informal.* without social appointments.

date line, an imaginary line agreed upon as the place where each calendar day first begins; International Date Line. It runs north and south through the Pacific, mostly along the 180th meridian. When it is Sunday just east of the date line, it is Monday just west of it. *The date line . . . was set up by agreement between commercial steamship lines* (Bernhard, Bennett, and Rice).

date|line (dāt′līn′), *n., v.,* **-lined, -lin|ing.** —*n.* a line, especially in a letter or newspaper article, giving the date and often the place of writing.
—*v.t.* to give a dateline to; inscribe with a dateline: *to dateline a newspaper story.*

date|mark (dāt′märk′), *n., v.* —*n.* a mark noting the time of manufacture, shipping, etc.
—*v.t.* to provide with a datemark.

date palm, a tree on which dates grow, having a crown of large, feathershaped leaves. It belongs to the palm family. Most date palms are from 40 to 100 feet high.

date plum, 1 the fruit of any of various trees, such as the persimmon. **2** any of these trees.

dat|er (dā′tər), *n.* **1** a person who dates. **2** a machine for stamping dates.

date rape, the act of having forced sexual intercourse with a female while on a social date: *The popular term is the narrower "date rape" which suggests an ugly ending to a raucous night on the town* (Time).

date sugar, sugar made from the sap or fruit of the date palm.

da|til (dä′til), *n.* any one of several South American palms whose leaves yield a fiber that is braided into hats and baskets. [< Spanish *dátil* date]

dat|ing (dā′ting), *n.* **1** the practice or an instance of having social engagements with a person or persons of the opposite sex. **2** a term of sale meaning that the time (usually 30, 60, or 90 days) allowed for the payment of the merchandise does not begin to run until a specified date in the future.

dating bar, *U.S.* a barroom that seeks the patronage of unmarried young men and women by providing a place for them to meet.

Da|tism (dā′tiz əm), *n.* brokenness or incorrectness of speech natural to a foreigner; a fault or mistake in speaking a foreign language: *We can understand that a small Athenian boy should commit a Datism in Latin* (Saturday Review). [< Greek *Dātismós* speaking like *Datis,* the Medean commander at Marathon]

da|tive (dā′tiv), *adj., n.* —*adj.* **1** showing the indirect object of a verb or the object of a preposition. Latin and some other languages have a dative case. In English, the dative function is expressed by word order or a prepositional phrase: *Give* him *the book. Give the book* to him. In the Latin, *Puero librum dedit,* "He gave the boy a book," *puero* (indirect object) is in the dative case. In *Puero est liber* ("a book is to the boy"), the dative case shows possession. **2** *Law.* **a** that can be given or disposed of at one's pleasure. **b** (of an officer) that can be removed.
—*n.* **1** the dative case. **2** a word or form in this case.
[< Latin *datīvus* (*cāsus*) (case) of giving < *datus, -ūs* a giving < *dare* give] —**da′tive|ly,** *adv.*
▶**dative case.** Older grammars of English stated that nouns or pronouns used as indirect objects of a verb are in the dative case. Noun: *The old woman gave the boy a nod as she walked by.* Pronoun: *I bought her a fountain pen.* Most English grammars now include the dative and the accusative cases under the general term *objective case.*

da|to or **dat|to** (dä′tō), *n., pl.* **-tos. 1** the chief of a Moro tribe in the Philippines. **2** the headman of a barrio (village) or tribe in Malay countries.
[< Malay *dato'*]

dat|o|lite (dat′ə līt), *n.* a complex silicate containing boron and calcium, found as glassy crystals in various colors. [< Greek *dateîsthai* divide + English *-lite*]

da|tum (dā′təm, dat′əm, dä′təm), *n., pl.* **-ta. 1** a fact from which conclusions can be drawn. **2** something known or assumed as fact: *The head as well as the heart declines to accept any single datum as final* (Saturday Review). [< Latin *datum* (thing) given, neuter past participle of *dare* give. See etym. of doublets **dado, die².**]
▶See **data** for usage note.

datum level, line, plane, or **point,** a level, line, plane, or point, from which heights and depths are measured in engineering and surveying.

da|tu|ra (də tyůr′ə, -tůr′-), *n.* **1** any one of a group of coarse, bad-smelling plants of the nightshade family, having funnel-shaped flowers, prickly pods, and narcotic properties, such as the jimson weed; thorn apple. **2** the flower of one of these plants. [< Hindustani *dhatūrā*]

dat|u|rism (dat′yə riz əm), *n.* poisoning by datura or stramonium.

dau., daughter.

daub (dôb), *v., n.* —*v.t.* **1** to cover with plaster, clay, mud, or any soft material that will stick: *The mason filled the cracks in the wall by daubing them with cement.* **2** to apply (greasy or sticky stuff) to a surface. SYN: smear. **3** to make dirty; soil; stain: *Your skirt is daubed with mud.* SYN: sully, defile. **4a** to paint (something) unskillfully. **b** to lay on (colors) unskillfully: *The Prime Minister himself daubed in some glaring new patches of color* (Time).
—*v.i.* **1** to daub something. **2** to paint unskillfully: *She is no artist; she just daubs.* **3** *Archaic.* to put on a false show.
—*n.* **1** anything daubed on: *Just a few daubs of glue will mend the plate.* **2** a picture that shows a lack of skill in the painting. **3** an act of daubing. **4** material for daubing, such as rough plaster or mortar.
[< Old French *dauber* (originally) to whitewash, plaster < Latin *dealbāre* < *dē-* from + *albus* white]

daube (dōb), *n. French.* a dish of braised meat and vegetables.

daub|er (dô′bər), *n.* **1** a person or thing that daubs. **2** something to daub with, such as a brush to spread shoe polish. **3** an unskillful painter. **4** = mud dauber.

daub|er|y (dô′bər ē), *n., pl.* **-er|ies. 1** a daubing. **2** the work of a dauber.

daub|ry (dô′brē), *n., pl.* **-ries.** = daubery.

daub|y (dô′bē), *adj.,* **daub|i|er, daub|i|est. 1** of or like a daub. **2** that daubs.

daud (dôd), *v.t. Scottish.* **1** to throw. **2** to throw things at. [imitative]

daugh|ter (dô′tər), *n., adj.* —*n.* **1a** a female child. A girl is the daughter of her father and mother. *Abbr:* dau. **b** a daughter-in-law. **c** a kindly term of address to a girl as from an older person, priest, or the like. **2a** a female descendant. Women are sometimes figuratively called daughters of Eve. **b** *Figurative.* a girl or woman attached to a country, cause, organization, project, or other undertaking, as a child is to its parents: *a daughter of France, daughters of liberty. A daughter of our meadows* (Tennyson). **c** anything thought of as a daughter in relation to its origin: *The Romance tongues are the daughters of the Latin language.*
—*adj.* **1** like a daughter. **2** of a daughter. **3** *Biology.* having the relationship of offspring of the first generation, or resulting from a primary division or segmentation. See also **daughter chromosome.**

[Old English *dohtor*]
daughter atom, an atom of a daughter element.
daughter cell, one of two new cells formed when an old cell of an organism divides: *In my view, cancer is brought about through a random mutation or change in the character of body cells and this change is propagated through succeeding generations of daughter cells* (Observer).
daughter chromosome, one of the two chromosomes which arise by the equal division of a single chromosome in a mother cell: *Each chromosome divides lengthwise, giving rise to two daughter chromosomes* (Beals and Hoijer).
daughter element, an element produced by the decay of a radioactive element.
daugh|ter-in-law (dô′tər in lô′), *n., pl.* **daugh-ters-in-law.** the wife of one's son.
daugh|ter|li|ness (dô′tər lē nis), *n.* conduct or feeling proper for a daughter: *cared for her with a tender daughterliness.*
daugh|ter|ly (dô′tər lē), *adj.* **1** of a daughter: *daughterly love toward her mother.* **2** like that of a daughter: *The girl's daughterly behavior endeared her to the teacher.* **3** proper for a daughter: *daughterly duties.*
daughter nucleus, one of two cell nuclei derived by division from a single mother nucleus.
Daugh|ters of the American Revolution (dô′tərz). See **D.A.R.**
daunt (dônt, dänt), *v.t.* **1** to frighten; overcome with fear: *Danger did not daunt the hero.* SYN: intimidate, cow. **2** to discourage; lessen the courage of: *Not daunted by his first failure, he tried again.* SYN: dismay, dishearten. [< Old French *danter* < Latin *domitāre* (frequentative) < *domāre* to tame] —**daunt′er,** *n.*
daunt|ing|ly (dôn′ting lē, dän′-), *adv.* in a terrifying manner.
daunt|less (dônt′lis, dänt′-), *adj.* not to be frightened or discouraged; brave: *He is a dauntless pilot; he will fly anywhere.* SYN: daring, courageous, fearless, bold. —**daunt′less|ly,** *adv.* —**daunt′-less|ness,** *n.*
daun|ton (dôn′tən, dän′-), *v.t. Scottish.* to daunt.
dau|phin (dô′fən; *French* dō fan′), *n.* the title of the oldest son of the king of France, used as a title from 1349 to 1830. [< Middle French *dauphin,* Old French *daufin* (originally) a family name < Medieval Latin *Dalphinus,* for Latin *delphīnus* (literally) dolphin < Greek *delphîs, -înos.* See etym. of doublet **dolphin.**]
dau|phine (dô′fēn), *n.* the wife of a dauphin. [< French *dauphine,* feminine of Middle French *dauphin;* see etym. under **dauphin**]
dau|phin|ess (dô′fə nis), *n.* = dauphine.
daut (dôt, dät), *v.t. Scottish.* to pet; fondle; caress. Also, **dawt.** [origin unknown]
dauw (dou), *n.* the common zebra of southern and eastern Africa, with broad stripes across its body; Burchell's zebra. [< Afrikaans *dauw* < a native name]
D.A.V., Disabled American Veterans.
Dav., David.
dav|en|port (dav′ən pôrt, -pōrt), *n.* **1** a long couch with a back and arms. Some davenports can be made into beds. *... not a davenport, not a settee, but simply a battered old leather couch* (Robert Traver). **2** *Especially British.* a writing desk with drawers and a hinged shelf to write on. [probably < the maker's name]
Da|vid (dā′vid), *n.* a Hebrew warrior, poet, and second king of Israel, about 1000 B.C. He succeeded Saul and organized the Jewish tribes into a national state. According to tradition, he wrote many Psalms of the Bible (in the Bible, II Samuel, 1-24).
David Cop|per|field (kop′ər fēld), a novel by Charles Dickens, published in 1849-50.
Da|vid|ic (də vid′ik), *adj.* of or having to do with David as king of Israel, or as the reputed author of the Psalms: *the glories of the ancient Davidic monarchy* (E. Grubb).
David's harp, = double harp.
Da|vis Cup (dā′vis), a tennis trophy held for a year by the winning country in an international tournament. [< Dwight *Davis,* 1879-1945, an American statesman and sportsman, who donated the cup in 1900]
dav|it (dav′it; *Nautical* dā′vit), *n.* **1** one of a pair of curved, metal or wooden arms at the side of a ship, used to hold or lower a small boat: *Suspended from davits on the Simon Lake is a small, two-man plastic and steel submarine* (Wall Street Journal). **2** a crane formerly used for shifting the anchor of a ship from the cathead to stowage on the forecastle deck. [< Anglo-French *daviot,* Old French *daviet* (originally, diminutive) < *Davi* David]
Da|vus (dā′vəs), *n.* (in Latin comedies) a conventional name for a slave. [< Latin *Dāvus*]
Da|vy Jones (dā′vē jōnz′), the spirit of the sea; the sailor's devil. [origin uncertain]
Davy Jones's locker or **Davy Jones' locker,** **1** the grave of those who die at sea; bottom of the ocean: *one boat's crew of 'em is gone to Davy Jones' locker* (Herman Melville). **2** the ocean.
***Davy lamp,** a miner's safety lamp in which the flame is enclosed by a fine wire screen, used to prevent gas explosions. [< Sir Humphry *Davy,* 1778-1829, an English chemist, who invented it]

***Davy lamp**

daw¹ (dô), *n.* **1** = jackdaw. **2** *Archaic, Figurative.* a silly person; simpleton. [Middle English *dawe.* Compare Old High German *taha.*]
daw² (dô), *n., v.i. Scottish.* dawn. [Old English *dagian*]
daw|dle (dô′dəl), *v.,* **-dled, -dling,** *n.* —*v.i.* to waste time; be idle; loiter; dally: *Don't dawdle over your work.* SYN: trifle, lag, idle.
—*v.t.* to waste by trifling: *He dawdled a whole afternoon away.* SYN: fritter.
—*n.* **1** a person who dawdles. **2** the act of dawdling.
[origin uncertain]
daw|dler (dô′dlər), *n.* a person who dawdles; trifler; idler.
daw|dling (dô′dling), *adj.* sauntering; idling. —**daw′dling|ly,** *adv.*
Dawes Plan (dôz), a plan for reorganizing the finance and stabilizing the currency of Germany, drawn up in 1924 by an international committee under the chairmanship of Charles G. Dawes.
dawk¹ (dôk), *n.* = dak.
dawk² (dôk), *n. U.S.* a person who disapproves of war but is unwilling to oppose it actively; one who is neither a hawk nor a dove in politics: *The Republican dawks could not convincingly square their criticism of U.S. war policy with their insistence that they still support the war* (Time). [blend of *dove* and *hawk*]
dawn (dôn), *n., v.* —*n.* **1** the beginning of day; the first light in the east: *Each dawn heralds a new day.* SYN: aurora, daybreak, sunrise. **2** *Figurative.* the beginning: *Dinosaurs roamed the earth before the dawn of man. This man, born at the dawn of the Age of Reason, was to turn into a madman* (Time). SYN: appearance.
—*v.i.* **1** to grow bright or clear in the morning: *It was dawning when I woke.* **2** to grow clear to the eye or mind: *The ocean dawned on our view.* (*Figurative.*) *After the hint she gave, it dawned on me that she was expecting a present.* **3** *Figurative.* to begin; appear: *Day dawns in the east. A new era of progress is dawning in Africa.*
[short for Middle English *dawning,* probably < Scandinavian (compare Danish *dagning*)]
dawn chorus, **1** radio interference associated with the aurora or atmospheric storms. It is usually received in the early morning: *Only the best equipment ... will enable you to hear the so-called "dawn chorus," the mysterious "tweeks," "bonks" and "swishes"* (Scientific American). **2** the twittering made by awakening birds at dawn.
dawn horse, = eohippus.
dawn|light (dôn′līt′), *n.* the grayish light appearing at dawn: *Booted soldiers, their blue coats black in the dawnlight, scuffed across the porch* (Atlantic).
Dawn man, = Piltdown man.
dawn patrol, **1** an early-morning military flight to patrol enemy positions. **2** the personnel working on radio or television programs in the early morning.
dawn redwood, a deciduous tree related to the sequoias, that bears its cones on long, naked stalks rather than on needle-bearing branches, found in several areas of China.
dawn stone, = eolith.
dawt (dôt, dät), *v.t. Scottish.* daut.
day (dā), *n.* **1** the time of light between sunrise and sunset: *Days are longer in summer than in winter. Even the fall of leaves in autumn may be postponed by an artificial increase in the length of day* (Eric Ashby). **2** the light of day; daylight: *a cloudy day, a sunny day.* **3a** the 24 hours of day and night; time it takes for the earth to make one rotation on its axis: *The day is increasing in length by about one- or two-thousandths of a second per century* (Scientific American). **b** the time in which any heavenly body rotates once upon its axis. **4** a day as a point or unit of time or on which something happens: *The third day he shall rise again* (Matthew 20:19). **5** a day or date set aside for a particular purpose or celebration: *a school day, a fast day, Christmas Day, New Year's Day.* SYN: festival, holiday. **6** hours for work; workday: *An eight-hour day is common. Our company has a seven-hour day.* **7** a time; period: *the present day. In days of old, people used candles instead of electric lights.* SYN: age. **8** *Figurative.* a period of life, activity, power, or influence: *He has seen better days. Great Britain has had its day as a great colonial power.* **9** a game, battle, or contest: *The debate was over; our side won the day. The argument of the prosecution had carried the day, and the prosecutor leaned back in his chair with a sigh of satisfaction* (Atlantic). SYN: conflict. **10** a victory: *The trumpets sound retreat, the day is ours* (Shakespeare).
any day, *Informal.* **a** in every instance; every time; always: *"You can have a pastoral garden," she said ... "I'll take a formal garden any day"* (New Yorker). **b** in every way: *He is better looking than Gil, any day, I think* (Theodore Dreiser).
call it a day, *Informal.* to stop work or any other activity: *After rehearsing the play for three hours, the director called it a day. Some who lost their boats, or had them damaged beyond repair, have called it a day, so far as boating is concerned* (New York Times).
day after day, each day: *Day after day the birds came back for crumbs.*
day by day, each day; daily: *I cannot give you, day by day, an account of this ... journey* (Elizabeth Griffith). *We live with him and his troubles ... day by day* (Alistair Cooke).
day in, day out, every day; continuously: *The major day in, day out business of society has been acquiring the necessities of life* (Bulletin of Atomic Scientists).
from day to day, each day: *Tomorrow, and tomorrow, and tomorrow, Creeps in this petty pace from day to day* (Shakespeare). *Over 300 reporters ... are sending back information on the situation from day to day* (Listener).
in this day and age, in the age we live in; at the present time: *To do "El Capitan" in this day and age, the director and cast must bring to the operetta a tongue-in-cheek quality* (Harold C. Schonberg).
that'll be the day, *Informal.* it will never happen: *"Everything here is on a cash basis from now on." "That'll be the day," he said* (New Yorker).
[Old English *dæg*]
Day|ak (dī′ak), *n.* = Dyak.
da|yal (dä yäl′), *n.* any one of various songbirds of the East Indies. [< Hindi *dahiyāl*]
day bed, or **day|bed** (dā′bed′), *n. Especially U.S.* a bed, usually narrow, that has a low headboard and footboard of equal height. A day bed can be used as a couch by day.
day blindness, = hemeralopia.
day book, **1** *Bookkeeping.* a book in which a record is kept of each day's business. **2** a diary; journal.
day boy, a nonresident student who attends a boarding school: *He had been a happy day boy at his preparatory school and won a scholarship to a public school, where he was also happy as a boarder* (Sunday Times).
day|break (dā′brāk′), *n.* **1** dawn; time when it first begins to get light in the morning: *The world rolls into light; It is daybreak everywhere* (Longfellow). **2** a very early hour.
day-by-day (dā′bī dā′), *adj.* daily: *day-by-day charts of a comet's position. Mothers and fathers can see the day-by-day progress of these attempts* (Sidonie M. Gruenberg).
day camp, a summer camp for children who return home each night: *The second of three permanent day camp sites that will provide facilities for 5,000 New York children will be opened in June at Orangeburg, N.Y.* (New York Times).
day-care (dā′kãr′), *adj.* of or for the daytime care of preschool children: *Day-care centers are clearly needed for those mothers who want to work* (Harper's).
day coach, an ordinary railroad passenger car, with seats only: *Often he travels from Toronto to Lindsay on Friday evenings in a day coach and spends the whole time moving down the seats chatting with passengers* (Maclean's).
day|dream (dā′drēm′), *n., v.,* **-dreamed** or **-dreamt, -dream|ing.** —*n.* **1** a dreamy thinking about pleasant things; reverie. **2** something imagined but not likely to come true: *Now these daydreams are literally wish-fulfillments, fulfillments of ambitious or erotic wishes* (Sigmund Freud).
—*v.i.* to think about pleasant things in a dreamy way: *I would pace up and down, half listening,*

Pronunciation Key: hat, āge, cãre, fär; let, ēqual, tėrm; it, īce; hot, ōpen, ôrder; oil, out; cup, pu̇t, rüle; child; long; thin; ᴛʜen; zh, measure; ə represents **a** in about, **e** in taken, **i** in pencil, **o** in lemon, **u** in circus.

half daydreaming, wishing my name would appear on Preston's list of people who had elements of greatness (New Yorker). —**day′-dream′er**, *n.*

day|dream|y (dā′drē′mē), *adj.* of or like a daydream: *The kids fell into daydreamy boredom ... because they missed the main event* (Time).

day fighter, a fighter plane designed for daytime operations.

day|flow|er (dā′flou′ər), *n.* any one of a group of plants of the spiderwort family, most of which bear racemes of small, blue flowers that live for about a day.

day|fly (dā′flī′), *n., pl.* **-flies**. a May fly; ephemerid: *May flies are often called dayflies because ... adult May flies live only a few hours or a few days* (E. G. Linsley).

Day-Glo (dā′glō′), *n. Trademark.* a fluorescent paint that gives off a variety of brilliant colors when exposed to light.

day|glow (dā′glō′), *n.* airglow occurring in the daytime: *Successful measurements of dayglow were obtained by using ultraviolet spectrometers carried on sounding rockets* (Science News Letter).

day hospital, a hospital for outpatients only: *As the name implies, the day hospital is for patients who need many of the therapeutic activities available in the hospital but who do not need the 24-hour protection inherent in living in the hospital* (Science News Letter).

day in court, **1** a day or part of a day during which a person appears in court. **2** an opportunity to explain one's ideas or defend one's point of view: *The company was not going to forfeit its day in court ... not when its good name had been impugned up and down the land* (New Yorker).

day labor, labor done or hired by the day.

day laborer, an unskilled or manual worker who is paid by the day.

day|length (dā′lengkth′, -length′), *n.* = photoperiod: *... the onset of winter with its low temperature and shorter daylength* (New Scientist).

day letter or **lettergram**, *U.S.* a telegram with a low charge for fifty words, sent during the day. It is slower than a regular telegram.

day|light (dā′līt′), *n., v.* —*n.* **1** the light of day: *It is easier to read by daylight than by lamplight. From a strictly scientific standpoint, it is preferable to define daylight as the radiation falling on the earth from the entire sky* (Hardy and Perrin). **2** = daytime. **3** dawn; daybreak: *He was up at daylight in order to get an early start.* **4** *Figurative.* publicity; openness: *The newspapers brought the mayor's graft into daylight and forced him to resign.* **5** an open space; gap.

—*v.t., v.i.* to expose to daylight, especially by building to allow the maximum amount of daylight to enter.

daylights, *Slang.* vital parts; insides: *to knock the daylights out of a boxer, to scare the daylights out of someone.*

see daylight, *Informal.* **a** to get the meaning; understand: *No matter how much we tried to explain it to her, she just could not see daylight.* **b** to approach the end of a hard or tiresome job: *I didn't think I could finish painting the garage today, but now I'm beginning to see daylight.*

daylight saving, = daylight-saving time.

day|light-sav|ing time (dā′līt′sā′ving), time that is one hour ahead of standard time. It gives more daylight after working hours. Clocks are set ahead one hour in the spring and back one hour in the fall.

day lily, **1** any one of a genus of plants of the lily family, bearing clusters of large, yellow, orange, or sometimes red flowers that last about a day. **2** = plantain lily. **3** the flower of any one of these plants.

day|long (dā′lông′, -long′), *adj., adv.* through the whole day: *Castro kept on the move constantly, toughening his men by daylong forced marches* (Time).

day|mare (dā′mãr′), *n.* an experience that is like a bad dream; a very distressing experience: *A peaceful drive through farmland suddenly turns into a daymare* (Time). [< *day* + (night)*mare*]

day-neu|tral plant (dā′nü′trəl, -nyü′-), a plant growing and blooming independent of the amount of light: *Day-neutral plants, such as dandelions, apparently are insensitive to the length of day as they will bloom in any season if they receive enough heat and moisture* (Harbaugh and Goodrich).

day nursery, a nursery for the care of small children during the day; crèche.

Day of Atonement, Yom Kippur, the most sacred fast observed by the Jews.

day of doom, = Day of Judgment.

Day of Judgment, the day of God's final judgment of mankind at the end of the world; the end of the world; Judgment Day.

day owl, **1** = hawk owl. **2** any one of various owls which fly by day and look somewhat like hawks.

day release, (in Great Britain) a part-time release from employment to allow a worker to attend courses at a technical school.

day-re|turn (dā′ri tėrn′), *n. Especially British.* a railroad ticket for going and returning only on the same day, usually sold at cheaper rates: *a day-return to London.*

day|room (dā′rüm′, -ru̇m′), *n.* a room in a military barracks with reading and recreational facilities: *Nights are taken up with movies, bull sessions in dayrooms, or sentry duty* (Newsweek).

days (dāz), *adv.* during the day; in the daytime: *What does he do days now that he works nights?*

day school, **1** a school held in the daytime (contrasted with *night school*). **2** a private school for students who live at home. **3** an elementary school held on weekdays.

day shift, **1** a group of workers working through the day: *As the day shift filed from the plant, Knowland stuck out a warm and brawny hand and said, "I'm Senator Bill Knowland"* (Newsweek). **2** the period of time during which they work.

days|man (dāz′mən), *n., pl.* **-men**. **1** a day laborer. **2** *Archaic.* an arbitrator; mediator.

days of grace, extra days allowed for payment after a bill or note falls due.

days of obligation, days on which everyone is required to abstain from work and to attend religious services, holy days of obligation.

day|spring (dā′spring′), *n. Poetic.* dawn; daybreak.

day|star (dā′stär′), *n.* **1** the morning star. **2** the sun.

day student, a nonresident student who comes to a school or college during the day for classes or study.

day tank, a furnace for melting a large quantity of glass over a period of about 24 hours: *Day tanks hold one to four tons of glass* (C. J. Phillips).

day|time (dā′tīm′), *n., adj.* —*n.* the time when it is day and not night: *My baby brother sleeps even in the daytime. Daytime is the period naturally associated with work, as nighttime is with recreation* (Matthew Luckiesh).

—*adj.* of the daytime; occurring during the day: *the daytime hours, daytime activities, daytime TV programs.*

day-to-day (dā′tə dā′), *adj.* daily; day by day: *We go about the day-to-day routine of our lives with a feeling of security and comfort* (Time).

day-trad|er (dā′trā′dər), *n.* a person who engages in day-trading: *... to play the market like professional day-traders* (London Times).

day-trad|ing (dā′trā′ding), *n.* the buying and selling of the same listed stocks on the stock exchange in the course of a single day: *Requirements are tightened on day-trading, the technique by which speculators move in and out of stock on the same day and count on rising prices to pay off their purchase and provide a profit as well* (Time).

day-trip|per (dā′trip′ər), *n.* a person who goes on a short trip or excursion and returns the same day: *Busloads of day-trippers ... overrun the châteaus* (Atlantic).

day|work (dā′wėrk′), *n.* **1** work done in the daytime. **2** work paid for by the day or hour.

day|work|er (dā′wėr′kər), *n.* a person who works by the day or the hour.

daze (dāz), *v.,* **dazed, daz|ing**, *n.* —*v.t.* **1** to make unable to think clearly; confuse; bewilder; stun: *A blow on the head dazed him so that he could not find his way home.* (*Figurative.*) *The winner was dazed by his good luck.* SYN: benumb, stupefy, confound. **2** to hurt (one's eyes) with light; dazzle: *The child was dazed by the bright lights.* —*n.* a dazed condition; bewilderment: *He was in a daze from the accident and could not understand what was happening.* SYN: stupefaction. [Middle English *dasen*, probably < Scandinavian (compare Old Icelandic *dasa-sk* become exhausted)]

daz|ed|ly (dā′zid lē), *adv.* in a dazed, bewildered, or stupid manner: *In the final set he did little more than go through the motions of a tennis player, smiling dazedly as the ball whizzed by, often yards out of reach* (New Yorker).

daz|ing|ly (dā′zing lē), *adv.* in a dazing, benumbing, or stupefying manner: *Visually, "The Nun's Story" is almost dazingly beautiful* (Time).

daz|zle (daz′əl), *v.,* **-zled, -zling**, *n.* —*v.t.* **1** to hurt (the eyes) with too bright light or with quick-moving lights: *To look straight at headlights dazzles the eyes.* SYN: blind, daze. **2** to overcome the sight or the mind of with anything very bright or splendid: (*Figurative.*) *The children were dazzled by the richness of the king's palace.*

—*v.i.* **1** to be confused or overpowered by light. **2** *Figurative.* to excite admiration by brilliance.

—*n.* a dazzling; bewildering brightness: *the dazzle of powerful electric lights;* (*Figurative.*) *the dazzle of high society.*

[< *daze* + *-le*]

daz|zle|ment (daz′əl mənt), *n.* **1** the act of dazzling or condition of being dazzled. **2** something that dazzles.

dazzle painting, the painting of ships in dazzling patterns during World War I to make it difficult for attacking submarines to estimate the course.

daz|zler (daz′lər), *n.* a person or thing that dazzles.

daz|zling (daz′ling), *adj.* brilliant or splendid: *the magician's dazzling display of skill.* (*Figurative.*) *Give me the splendid silent sun, with all his beams full-dazzling* (Walt Whitman). —**daz′-zling|ly**, *adv.*

db (no period), **db.**, or **dB** (no periods), decibel or decibels.

d.b., **1** daybook. **2** double-breasted.

dBA (no periods), decibel A (a unit for measuring noise in which A represents a weighing scale for loudness): *... Central London rush-hour street noise is 63 dBA* (Sunday Times).

DBA or **dba** (no periods), doing business as.

D.B.A., Doctor of Business Administration.

D.B.E., Dame Commander of the British Empire.

dbh (no periods), diameter breast-high.

DBI (no periods), *Trademark.* a drug used orally in the treatment of diabetes: *An antidiabetic pill, DBI, or phenformin, was developed especially for children* (Science News Letter). *Formula:* $C_{10}H_{15}N_5$

D. Bib., Douay Bible.

dbl. or **dble.**, double.

DBS (no periods), Dominion Bureau of Statistics (of Canada).

dbt., debit.

d.c. or **d-c** (no periods), direct current (of electricity).

► These abbreviations are now widely used as modifiers: *d-c power.*

DC (no periods), **1** direct current. **2** District of Columbia (with postal Zip Code).

D.C., an abbreviation for the following:
1 da capo.
2 direct current.
3 district commissioner.
4 District of Columbia.
5 Doctor of Chiropractic.

D.C.L., Doctor of Civil Law (an honorary degree).

D.C.M., *British.* Distinguished Conduct Medal.

dd., delivered.

d.d., **1** days after date. **2** delayed delivery. **3** demand draft.

DD (no periods), dishonorable discharge.

D.D., Doctor of Divinity (Latin, *Divinitatis Doctor*).

D-day (dē′dā′), *n.* **1** June 6, 1944, the day of Allied assault on the beaches of Normandy against the Germans in World War II. **2** the day on which a previously planned military attack is to be made, or on which an operation is to be started. [probably on analogy of *H-hour*]

DDD (no periods), **1** dichlorodiphenyldichloroethane (a less toxic insecticide than DDT). **2** Direct Distance Dialing.

DDE (no periods), dichlorodiphenyldichloroethylene (a less toxic insecticide than DDT).

D.D.R., Deutsche Demokratische Republik (German Democratic Republic; East Germany).

D.D.S., Doctor of Dental Surgery.

D.D.Sc., Doctor of Dental Science.

DDT (no periods) or **D.D.T.**, a very powerful, odorless insecticide. *Formula:* $C_{14}H_9Cl_5$ [< *d*(ichloro)*d*(iphenyl)-*t*(richloroethane), the chemical name of the substance]

DDVP (no periods), dimethyl dichlorovinyl phosphate, the chemical name of the insecticide dichlorvos.

de or **De** (də, dē), *prep.* of; from (an element in many names of places or persons, chiefly of French origin): *Honoré de Balzac.* [< French *de*]

de-, *prefix.* **1** to do the opposite of: *Decentralize = to do the opposite of centralize.*
2 down; lower: *Depress = to press down.*
3 away; off: *Derail = (to run) off the rails.*
4 to remove or take away: *Defrost = to remove the frost.*
5 entirely; completely: *Despoil = to spoil entirely.*
[< Latin *dē-* < *dē* away from, or < Old French *de-* < Latin *dē-*]

DE (no periods), Delaware (with postal Zip Code).

Dea., deacon.

DEA (no periods) or **D.E.A.**, Department of Economic Affairs (of Great Britain).

de|ac|ces|sion (dē′ak sesh′ən), *v.t. U.S.* to sell or auction off (a museum piece, coin collection, or other collection or part of one) in order to raise funds for new acquisitions: *He intended to deaccession some 235 paintings of all periods, 38 tapestries, and an unspecified quantity of medieval items* (New York Times Magazine).

de|a|cet|y|late (dē'ə set'ə lāt), *v.t.,* **-lat|ed, -lat|ing.** to remove one or more radicals of acetic acid from (an organic compound).

de|a|cet|y|la|tion (dē'ə set ə lā'shən), *n.* a deacetylating.

dea|con (dē'kən), *n., v.* **—*n.*** **1** an officer of a church who helps the minister in church duties not connected with the preaching: *A board of deacons governs church business affairs.* **2** a member of the clergy next below priest in rank: *The deacon read the lesson from the Bible.*
—*v.t.* **1** *U.S. Informal.* to read (a hymn) aloud one or two lines at a time, the congregation singing the lines as soon as read. **2** *U.S. Slang.* **a** to pack (fruit or other produce) with the best on top. **b** to falsify; adulterate.
[Old English *diacon* < Latin *diāconus* < Greek *diākonos* religious official; (originally) servant]

dea|con|ate (dē'kə nit, -nāt), *n.* = diaconate.

dea|con|esque (dē'kə nesk'), *adj.* of or like a deacon: *a tall, slender, deaconesque man* (New Yorker).

dea|con|ess (dē'kə nis), *n.* a woman who is an official assistant in church work, especially in caring for the sick and the poor.

dea|con|like (dē'kən līk'), *adj. Informal.* sanctimonious.

dea|con|ry (dē'kən rē), *n., pl.* **-ries. 1** the position of deacon. **2** deacons collectively or as a group.

dea|con|ship (dē'kən ship), *n.* the position or status of a deacon.

de|ac|ti|vate (dē ak'tə vāt), *v.t.,* **-vat|ed, -vat|ing. 1** to remove (a group of soldiers) from active service; demobilize: *They said they also intend to mothball 375 naval vessels, deactivate three air divisions, cut armaments and military budgets* (Time). **2** to make inactive: *to deactivate a nerve or a solution. Sleep comes when this waking center is deactivated, probably by enzymes* (Time). **3** to stop the use of: *to deactivate a factory.*

de|ac|ti|va|tion (dē ak'tə vā'shən), *n.* a deactivating.

de|ac|ti|va|tor (dē ak'tə vā'tər), *n.* a person or thing that deactivates.

dead (ded), *adj., n., adv.* **—*adj.*** **1** with life gone from it; no longer living; that has died: *a dead flower, dead leaves.* **2** without life; inanimate: *Stone and water are dead matter.* **3** like death: *She fell over in a dead faint.* **4a** not active; dull or quiet: *a dead volcano, dead coals, a dead market. Summer is never a dead season at camp. At midnight this neighborhood of houses is dead.* **b** not productive; yielding nothing: *dead capital, dead soil.* **SYN:** unprofitable, unproductive, barren. **c** not moving: *a dead pulley. The dead ball was out of play.* **SYN:** motionless. **5** having no power: **a** without force, spirit, or feeling; lifeless; flat: *dead colors,* (*Figurative.*) *a dead rule. The dead tennis ball would hardly bounce. There are few dead spots in Mr. Killmayer's explosive texture, and he is undoubtedly a composer to watch* (New York Times). **SYN:** ineffectual. **b** carrying no electric current: *a dead circuit. The car won't start because the battery is dead. The telephone line is dead.* **c** not radioactive: *dead rocks.* **6** *Figurative.* no longer in use: **a** obsolete: *a dead issue. The language of the ancient Romans is a dead language.* **SYN:** extinct. **b** past its usefulness: *That old war slogan is dead. The printing type for yesterday's newspaper is all dead type.* **7** *Informal.* very tired; worn-out: *I'm so dead from shopping, I must sit down and take off my shoes. [He] was so dead with fatigue that he did not even try to make an escape* (Edmund Wilson). **8** sure; certain: *Tomorrow's sunrise is a dead certainty. Buffalo Bill was a dead shot with a rifle.* **9** complete; absolute: *The sunken ship was a dead loss. There was dead silence in the library.* **10a** without stopping: *The boy ran home at a dead trot.* **b** to the limit of one's endurance: *to collapse after a dead sprint.* **11** having no sound; not receiving sound: *a dead spot in the auditorium.* **12** *Law.* deprived of civil rights.
—*n.* Usually, **the dead. 1** the time when there is the least life stirring: *the dead of winter. The plane landed in the dead of night.* **2** a dead person or persons: *enough noise to wake the dead. We honor the dead of our wars on Memorial Day.*
—*adv.* **1** completely; absolutely; utterly: *You are dead right. He was dead tired. He stopped dead* (Dickens). **2** directly; straight: *The bridge is dead ahead of us. Don't take any side streets but walk dead ahead two miles.*
be caught dead, *Informal.* to be seen or found having anything to do with (something unpleasant or embarrassing): *The whole thing looked a little like an invalid's wheelchair, and a boy wouldn't have been caught dead on one unless he was clowning* (New Yorker).
[Old English *dēad*] **—dead'ness,** *n.*
—*Syn.* *adj.* **1,2 Dead, deceased, lifeless** mean without life. **Dead** emphasizes the idea of dying, and applies particularly to someone or something that was living or alive, but no longer is: *The flowers in the garden are dead.* **Deceased,** a technical word, applies only to a dead person: *The deceased parent left no will.* **Lifeless** emphasizes the idea of being without life, and is used both of what now is or seems to be without life of any kind and of things that never had life: *a lifeless body, lifeless stones.*

dead air, 1 air that is prevented from circulating for purposes of insulation. Double-walled houses are insulated by dead air between the two walls. **2** a period of time when nothing is being broadcast on radio or television.

dead-air (ded'ãr'), *adj.* having to do with or using dead air: *The weather protection is maintained in either sub-zero or blistering tropical temperatures by dead-air space insulation in the boat's canopy and floor liner* (Science News Letter).

dead angle, an angle or space outside a fortification which cannot be reached by the fire of its defenders; dead space.

dead-ball line (ded'bôl'), *Rugby.* a line parallel to and behind the goal line, beyond which the ball is considered out of play.

dead|beat (ded'bēt'), *adj., n.* **—*adj.*** **1** making successive beats with intervals of rest and no recoil, as the mechanism of a watch. **2** *Physics.* stopping with little or no oscillation, as the needle of certain compasses; free from oscillation.
—*n.* *Slang.* a dead beat: *a sort of transit camp for artist bums and odd deadbeats* (Punch).

dead-beat (ded'bēt'), *adj. Informal.* all tired out.

dead beat, *Slang.* **1** *U.S.* a person who avoids paying for what he gets: *... a robustious clown, a seam-splitting glutton, and a lovable dead beat* (Time). **2** a lazy person; loafer: *The battalion Personnel Selection Officer was usually a dead beat, unfit for anything better* (New Statesman).

dead|born (ded'bôrn'), *adj.* = stillborn.

dead-burned (ded'bėrnd'), *adj.* heated at extremely high temperatures until freed of carbon dioxide: *dead-burned minerals.*

dead center, 1 the position of the crank and connecting rod in an engine, at which the connecting rod has no power to turn the crank; dead point. Dead center occurs at each end of a stroke, when the crank and the connecting rod are in the same straight line. **2** a center in a lathe, etc., which does not rotate. **3** the exact center.

dead drop, a telephone booth, public lavatory, or similar site used in espionage to deposit and pick up messages and other material according to a prearranged schedule: *In a dead drop ... the sender and receiver avoid the risk entailed in making a transfer during a personal encounter* (New Yorker).

dead duck, *Slang.* a person or thing that has become utterly played out or worthless. *Most Chicagoans regarded the reform movement as a dead duck* (Newsweek).

dead|ee (de dē'), *n. U.S.* a portrait of a person who has died, painted from a photograph.

dead|en (ded'ən), *v.t.* **1** to make dull or weak; lessen the force of: *Some medicines are given to deaden pain. Thick walls deaden the noises from the street. The force of the blow was deadened by his heavy clothing.* **SYN:** blunt, impair, benumb. **2** to make soundproof: *The curtains, carpets, and thick walls deadened the room.* **3a** to kill (trees) by girdling. **b** to clear (land) by killing the trees in this manner. **—*v.i.*** to become dead. **—dead'en|er,** *n.*

dead end, 1 a street or passage closed at one end: *The Fifty-eighth Street dead end has a name of its own—Sutton Place* (New York Times). **2** *Figurative.* a point beyond which progress, advancement, or achievement is impossible: *The discussion reached a dead end.*

dead-end (ded'end'), *adj., n., v.* **—*adj.*** **1** closed at one end: *Her humor comes from walking into dead-end streets rather than into custard pies* (New York Times). **2** *Figurative.* having no opportunity for progress, advancement, or achievement; fruitless: *a dead-end conference, a dead-end job.* **3** of the slums; tough: *a dead-end gang. G.I.'s chipped in to help him build a church for Seoul's dead-end kids* (Time).
—*n.* = dead end.
—*v.t.* **1** to make a dead end of: *The new highway dead-ended our street.* **2** to bring to a dead end: (*Figurative.*) *to dead-end an unpopular proposal.*
—*v.i.* to reach a dead end: (*Figurative.*) *When an executive dead-ends, he may give a different name to his predicament* (Wall Street Journal).

dead|en|ing (ded'ə ning), *n.* **1** the act of a person or thing that deadens. **2** something that deadens, especially sound or color. **3** *U.S.* a clearing made by deadening trees.

dead|er (ded'ər), *n. Slang.* a dead person; corpse.

dead|eye (ded'ī'), *n., adj.* **—*n.*** *Nautical.* a round, flat, wooden block that is used to fasten the shrouds of a ship.
—*adj.* *Informal.* absolutely accurate: *deadeye aim.*

dead|fall (ded'fôl'), *n.* **1** a trap for animals made so that a heavy weight falls upon and holds or kills the animal. **2** a mass of fallen trees and underbrush: *The deadfalls of centuries make the forests impassable in summer* (Atlantic).

dead freight, very heavy or bulky, nonperishable freight, as lumber, bricks, or machinery.

dead furrow, the furrow that remains open in the center of a field in plowing.

dead giveaway, *Informal.* a complete betrayal.

dead hand, *Law.* mortmain; inalienable possession.

Dead Hand, = Raynaud's phenomenon.

dead|head (ded'hed'), *n., v., adv.* **—*n.*** **1** *Informal.* a person who rides on a vehicle, train, or airplane, or sees a game or other entertainment, without paying: *The passengers, all specially invited guests, were Cabinet members, senators, ambassadors, and other distinguished deadheads* (New Yorker). **2a** a locomotive, empty railroad car, or train of empty cars being hauled from one place to another: *Putting trailers on flat cars ... makes use of cars that would otherwise be idle or "deadheads"* (Wall Street Journal). **b** a vehicle, train, or airplane traveling without passengers or freight. **3** a person who does not participate in or contribute to something, such as a social party, a business meeting, or some undertaking, but who is present.
—*v.t.* to give (a person) permission to ride, etc., as a deadhead. **—*v.i.*** **1** to be a deadhead. **2** to make a trip without passengers or freight.
—*adv.* without passengers or freight: *In times of growing crisis, we would gradually deposit a few divisions in Europe and fly our planes back deadhead* (Wall Street Journal). **—dead'head'er,** *n.*

dead-head (ded'hed'), *v.i., v.t. British.* to remove or cut off the dead flowers of a plant: *Lilacs, camellias, rhododendrons and azaleas should be dead-headed* (Sunday Times).

dead heat, a race that ends in a tie: *The dead heat in the first race, naturally, made for two daily doubles* (New York Times).

dead-heat (ded'hēt'), *v.i.* to end a race in a tie: *After a lapse of about 10 minutes the judge announced that the pair had dead-heated* (London Times). **—dead'-heat'er,** *n.*

dead horse, *Slang.* **1** something that has ceased to be of use; dead duck. **2** (in printing) bogus: *The printer looks up sullenly. "Give me some live copy, not that ... dead horse"* (Harper's).
beat (or **flog) a dead horse,** to try to revive a feeling or interest that has died out; engage in fruitless effort: *The talk turned to the city budget, whereupon Gray said, "I think you're both beating a dead horse"* (New Yorker). *In parliament he again pressed the necessity of reducing expenditure. Friends warned him that he was flogging a dead horse* (John Morley).

dead|house (ded'hous'), *n.* a building or place where dead bodies are kept for a time; morgue.

dead|ish (ded'ish), *adj.* somewhat dead; lifeless; not lively: *Stockholm, I felt, was a deadish city* (Manchester Guardian Weekly).

dead latch, a door latch with a spring bolt opened by a key or by turning a knob: *The automatic dead latch is specially designed for glass panelled doors* (Punch).

dead letter, 1 an unclaimed letter; letter that cannot be delivered or returned because of a wrong address. **2** *Figurative.* **a** a law or rule that is no longer observed: *Conservation laws are dead letters there* (New York Times). **b** that which has lost its original power or significance: *The treaty is now a dead letter.*

dead letter box or **drop,** a place for depositing secret messages and other material without having to come in direct contact with the recipient: *Ever since coming to West Germany Guillaume had been collecting intelligence material and dispatching it to his masters—either by radio, by courier or through 'dead letter' boxes* (Annual Register).

dead-let|ter office (ded'let'ər), the department of a post office where dead letters are sent to be opened and returned to the writer or destroyed.

dead-lift (ded'lift'), *v.t.* to lift (a weight) in the dead lift: *Ladd can dead-lift 700 lbs.* (Time).

dead lift, 1 a direct lifting of a dead weight. **2** an exercise in weight lifting in which a barbell is raised in one motion from the floor to the upper

---

Pronunciation Key: hat, āge, cãre, fär; let, ēqual, tėrm; it, īce; hot, ōpen, ôrder; oil, out; cup, pu̇t, rüle; child; long; thin; ᴛʜen; zh, measure; ə represents **a** in about, **e** in taken, **i** in pencil, **o** in lemon, **u** in circus.

thighs. 3 *Archaic, Figurative.* a situation in which one can do no more; an extremity: *to help someone who is at a dead lift.*

dead|light (ded′līt′), *n.* 1 *Nautical.* **a** a strong shutter of wood or metal fitted over a cabin window or porthole to keep out water. **b** a heavy glass window fixed in the deck or side of a ship, framed with metal. 2 a skylight that will not open.

dead|li|ly (ded′lə lē), *adv.* in a deadly manner.

dead|line (ded′līn′), *n.* 1 a time limit; the latest possible time to do something: *The teacher made Friday afternoon the deadline for handing in all book reports. April 15 is the deadline for filing individual income-tax returns.* 2 the time when all copy for a newspaper or the like must be in: *The reporter's deadline was 8 P.M. for the morning edition.* 3 a line around a prison which no prisoner can cross without being shot. 4 a line or boundary that must not be crossed.

dead|li|ness (ded′lē nis), *n.* deadly quality or character.

dead load, a permanent and fixed load, such as the weight of a bridge or building; dead weight.

dead|lock (ded′lok′), *n., v.* —*n.* 1 a condition or situation in which activity between two opposing sides stops because they are equally strong and neither one will give in; complete standstill: *Employers and strikers had reached a deadlock in their dispute over higher wages.* 2 *U.S.* a tied score in a game: *Pennsylvania produced the first of the game's two deadlocks at 5:26 of the second quarter* (New York Times). 3 a very strong, springless lock with a bolt opened by a key or by turning a knob: *Lock him out with a Yale ... deadlock* (Punch).
—*v.t., v.i.* 1 to bring or come to a complete standstill: *The employer and strikers have been deadlocked for almost a week. Both disputants denied any part in deadlocking the collective bargaining process* (Wall Street Journal). *Yale and Harvard had deadlocked for the team title* (New York Times). 2 to lock with a deadlock: *Both handle and bolt are automatically deadlocked against turning* (Punch).

dead|ly (ded′lē), *adj.,* **-li|er, -li|est,** *adv.* —*adj.* 1 causing death; likely to cause death; fatal: *a deadly wound, a deadly disease, the deadly berries of a poisonous bush.* SYN: mortal, lethal. See syn. under **fatal.** 2 like that of death: *deadly paleness, deadly stillness.* SYN: deathly. 3 until death: *The deadly enemies had a fierce hatred for each other.* SYN: implacable. 4 causing death of the soul: *Envy and pride are deadly sins.* 5 dull; boring: *a deadly lecture by a tiresome speaker.* 6 *Informal.* extreme; intense: *Why such deadly haste to make money?* (Thomas Carlyle). SYN: excessive. 7 absolutely accurate: *Daniel Boone was a deadly shot.* 8 penetrating; incisive: *Its smiling but deadly analysis of the upper strata of French society is the product of the Dreyfus period* (Edmund Wilson).
—*adv.* 1 like death: *deadly pale. So coldly sweet, so deadly fair* (Byron). SYN: deathly. 2 extremely; intensely: *deadly cold weather. "Washing dishes is deadly dull," she said.* 3 as if dead. 4 *Obsolete.* mortally; fatally.

deadly agaric, any of various poisonous mushrooms, as the fly agaric and the death cup.

deadly nightshade, = belladonna (def. 1a).

deadly sins, = seven deadly sins.

dead-mail office (ded′māl′), = dead-letter office.

dead-man's control (ded′manz′), a control of a locomotive, heavy machinery, or other dangerous equipment that automatically engages a brake when the operator's hand or foot is removed from the control.

dead-man's float, floating motionless on the surface of the water with the head down.

dead-man's handle, pedal, or **throttle,** = dead-man's control.

dead march, a solemn funeral march, especially at a military funeral.

dead-mouthed (ded′mouᴛʜd′, -moutht′), *adj.* (of a horse) having a mouth no longer sensitive to the bit: *... provided also that if I have deadmouthed horses I am allowed proper bits in which to drive them* (New Yorker).

dead-on-ar|riv|al (ded′on ə rī′vəl, -ôn-), *n. U.S.* an electronic circuit which fails to operate when first used in equipment.

dead|pan (ded′pan′), *n., adj., adv., v.,* **-panned, -pan|ning.** *Slang.* —*n.* an expressionless face, person, or manner.
—*adj.* showing no expression or feeling: *a deadpan comedian, deadpan language, a deadpan news story.* SYN: expressionless, poker-faced.
—*adv.* in a deadpan manner: *The lines were read deadpan. The official Yugoslav newspaper, Borba, reprinted—deadpan—a Pravda article* (Newsweek).
—*v.t., v.i.* to act or perform in a deadpan manner: *to deadpan a joke, to deadpan through a party.*

dead point, 1 = dead center (def. 1). 2 any point of no mechanical action.

dead reckoner, an instrument for dead reckoning: *an automatic dead reckoner that continuously plots a ship's position.*

dead reckoning, 1 the calculation of the position of a ship or aircraft without observations of the sun, stars, or other heavenly bodies, by using a compass and studying the record of the navigator: *Dead reckoning, although it serves to indicate roughly the location of boat or aircraft, does not do so accurately* (Bernhard, Bennett, and Rice). 2 the location determined in this manner. 3 the calculation of one's location by natural landmarks: *Daniel Boone made his way back to the settlement by dead reckoning.*

dead ringer, *Slang.* a person or thing exactly like someone or something else: *The synthetic article is a dead ringer for the imported glass* (Wall Street Journal).

Dead Sea Scrolls, a collection of ancient papyrus and leather scrolls discovered in several caves in the Qumran Valley near the Dead Sea. They contain the oldest known copies of most of the books of the Bible. Many scrolls have been added since the first ones were found in 1947, most written in Hebrew and Aramaic about 2,000 years ago. They contain comments and explanations on Biblical writing and the monastic rules of the Qumran Community.

dead-set (ded′set′), *adj.* firmly fixed; very determined or resolute: *... dead-set against any compromise* (Newsweek).

dead set, 1 an abrupt stop or stand made by a hunting dog in pointing game. 2 *Figurative.* **a** a determined stand: *The disaffected sections of the Irish population made a dead set against him from the first* (Manchester Evening News). **b** a determined attempt to gain someone's affections: *There was a girl at Dumdum ... who made a dead set at me* (Thackeray).

dead soldier, *U.S. Slang.* 1 an empty wine or whiskey bottle. 2 an empty beer can or bottle.

dead space, = dead angle.

dead-stick landing (ded′stik′), a landing of an aircraft with the engine off: *Gravity slows him and beckons him back to earth and a dead-stick landing* (Time).

dead storage, the storage of property in a warehouse for a long period of time.

dead stroke, a stroke in power hammers in which the hammer is not instantly withdrawn after striking and the blow is inelastic in effect.

dead water, *Nautical.* the water that eddies about the stern of a ship as it moves along.

dead weight, 1 the weight of anything lifeless, rigid, and unyielding. 2 *Figurative.* a very great or oppressive burden: *It will take some time before the spiritual dead weight of 10 years of occupation is finally thrown off* (London Times). 3 the weight of a railroad car or other vehicle without cargo or load. 4 = dead load.

dead weight ton, or **dead|weight ton** (ded′wāt′) a long ton (2,240 pounds) used in calculating dead weight tonnage.

dead weight tonnage, or **deadweight tonnage,** the capacity in long tons of the cargo, crew, passengers, fuel, supplies, and spare parts of a merchant ship: *Dead weight tonnage in cargo ships almost always exceeds gross tonnage* (New York Times).

dead|wood (ded′wu̇d′), *n.* 1 dead branches or trees. 2 *Figurative.* useless people or things: *The new manager got rid of the deadwood by firing half of the staff.* 3 *Figurative.* a conventional word or phrase that adds nothing to the meaning of a sentence. 4 the solid timber structure set near the keel of a wooden ship at the bow or stern. 5 a pin or pins knocked down in bowling and lying in the alley or gutters.

De|ae Ma|tres (dē′ē mā′trēz), the three Teutonic goddesses of plenty. [< New Latin *Deae Matres* < Latin *deae,* plural of *dea* goddess + *mātrēs,* plural of *māter, -tris* mother]

de|aer|ate (dē ār′āt), *v.t.,* **-at|ed, -at|ing.** to remove gas, especially in the form of bubbles, from: *to deaerate water.*

de|aer|a|tion (dē′ār ā′shən), *n.* a deaerating.

de|aer|a|tor (dē ār′ā tər), *n.* an apparatus for removing the gas, especially in the form of bubbles, from a liquid or, sometimes, a compartment: *Conventional types of deaerators are not suitable where cold deaerated water is required for process purposes* (New Scientist).

de-aes|thet|i|ci|za|tion (dē′es thet′ə sə zā′shən, *especially British* -ēs-), *n.* the removal of aesthetic qualities from art: *The movement toward de-aestheticization is both a reaction against and a continuation of the trend toward formalistic overrefinement in the art of the sixties* (Harold Rosenberg).

de-aes|thet|i|cize (dē′es thet′ə sīz, *especially British* -ēs-), *v.t.,* **-cized, -ciz|ing.** to rid (art or a work of art) of aesthetic qualities.

de|a ex ma|chi|na (dē′ə eks mak′ə nə), *Latin.* 1 a female deus ex machina: *But lo! in the wings is a dea ex machina, a glittering fairy godmother to bring the happy ending* (Manchester Guardian Weekly). 2 (literally) a goddess from a machine.

deaf (def; *see note below*), *adj., v.* —*adj.* 1 not able to hear: *The deaf man learned to read lips well.* 2 not able to hear well: *The deaf old man sat up front to hear the orchestra better.* 3 *Figurative.* not willing to hear; heedless: *The miser was deaf to all requests for money.*
—*v.t.* to deafen.
deaf and dumb, unable to hear and speak: *I couldn't follow their rapid conversation, so I just stood smiling vaguely, like a well-meaning deaf and dumb person* (New Yorker).
[Old English *dēaf*] —**deaf′ly,** *adv.* —**deaf′ness,** *n.*
▶**Deaf** is now generally pronounced (def). Formerly (dēf) was in good use but is now rare in the English of educated people.

deaf aid, *British.* hearing aid.

deaf ears, ear lobes of domesticated fowl.

deaf|en (def′ən), *v.t.* 1 to make deaf: *A hard blow on the ear deafened him for life.* 2 to stun with noise: *A sudden explosion deafened us for a moment.* 3 to drown out by a louder sound. 4 to make soundproof; deaden.

deaf|en|ing (def′ə ning), *adj.* that deafens or stuns with noise. —**deaf′en|ing|ly,** *adv.*

deaf-mute (def′myüt′), *n., adj.* —*n.* a person who is unable to hear and speak. Born deaf-mutes usually cannot speak because of their inability to hear others and learn speech from them.
—*adj.* being a deaf-mute; unable to hear and speak.

deaf-mut|ism (def′myü′tiz əm), *n.* 1 the condition of being a deaf-mute: *Hereditary deaf-mutism is usually caused by a recessive gene* (C. Auerbach). 2 a usage in speech or writing that is peculiar to deaf-mutes.

deal[1] (dēl), *v.,* **dealt, deal|ing,** *n.* —*v.i.* 1 to have to do (with): *Arithmetic deals with numbers. The first volume or two of Michelet's history, dealing with the early races of Gaul* (Edmund Wilson). 2 to act; behave: *Brothers do not always deal kindly with one another.* 3 to occupy oneself; take action: *The courts deal with those who break the laws.* 4 to carry on a business; buy and sell: *This garage deals in gasoline, oil, and tires. A butcher deals in meat.* 5 to distribute playing cards: *It's your turn to deal.*
—*v.t.* 1 to give or deliver: *One fighter dealt the other a hard blow.* SYN: inflict. 2 to give a share of to each; distribute: *The Red Cross dealt out food to the hungry soldiers.* SYN: apportion, divide. 3 to distribute (playing cards).
—*n.* 1 *Informal.* **a** a business arrangement; bargain: *If you buy this television set on sale you can get a good deal.* **b** anything that is agreed upon, such as an arrangement or a meeting: *It's a deal, I'll meet you after school.* 2 *Informal.* distribution; arrangement; plan: *He is proposing that we substitute a new deal for the old one.* 3 a secret or underhanded arrangement: *The corrupt mayor was caught in a deal to take public money.* 4 in cardplaying: **a** the distribution of cards. **b** a player's turn to deal. **c** the time during which one deal of cards is being played. **d** the cards held by a player; hand. 5 a quantity; amount: *I took a deal of trouble.* 6 a dealing; distributing. 7 *Informal.* a thing; item: *The whole deal is $35* (New Yorker).
a good (or **great**) **deal, a** a large part, portion, or amount: *A great deal of her money goes for rent.* **b** to a great extent or degree; much: *He is always going to the beach because he likes to swim a good deal.*
[Old English *dǣlan* < *dǣl,* noun]

deal[2] (dēl), *n., adj.* —*n.* 1 a stout board of pine or fir, usually between 7 and 9 inches wide and 6 feet long: *I lingered ... to smell the smell of piled up deals and feel the salt wind blowing* (Cecily Fox-Smith). 2 boards like this. 3 pine or fir wood.
—*adj.* made of deal: *The judge took his place behind a deal table while on his right, six jurors shifted ... uncomfortably* (Maclean's).
[< Middle Dutch or Middle Low German *dele*]

de|a|late (dē ā′lāt), *adj., n.* —*adj.* deprived of wings (said of the queens of ants or other insects whose wings are shed after the nuptial flight).
—*n.* a dealate insect. [< *de-* + *alate*]

de|a|lat|ed (dē ā′lā tid), *adj.* = dealate.

de|a|la|tion (dē′ā lā′shən), *n.* a being or becoming dealate; the shedding of wings after nuptial flight.

deal|er (dē′lər), *n.* 1 a person who makes his living by buying and selling: *Father bought a used car from a car dealer.* SYN: trader, merchant. 2 a person who distributes the cards in a card game. 3 a person who acts in some specified manner:

a treacherous dealer. **4** a person who has dealings (with another or in something): *a dealer with the Devil, a dealer in sorcery.*

dealer's choice, any game of cards in which the dealer decides which game or variation of a game will be played, depending on the number of players at the table.

deal|er|ship (dē′lər ship), *n.* the business, franchise, or territory of a dealer: *The mere fact that other dealers are eliminated doesn't make an exclusive dealership illegal* (Wall Street Journal).

deal|fish (dēl′fish′), *n., pl.* **-fish|es** or (*collectively*) **-fish**. any one of a group of deep-sea fishes having long, flat bodies; ribbonfish. [< *deal*[2] + *fish*]

deal|ing (dē′ling), *n.* **1** a way of doing business: *The grocer is respected for his honest dealing.* **2** a way of acting; behavior toward others; conduct: *The judge is known for his fair dealing.* **3** distribution, especially of playing cards.
dealings, a business relations: *That company has dealings with firms all over the world.* **b** friendly relations.

dealt (delt), *v.* the past tense and past participle of **deal**[1]: *The knight dealt his enemy a blow. The cards have been dealt.*

de|am|bu|la|to|ry (dē am′byə lə tôr′ē, -tōr′-), *adj., n., pl.* **-ries**. —*adj.* going from place to place; ambulatory: *The deambulatory hero moves along his uncharted course* (Saturday Review).
—*n.* ambulatory.
[< Late Latin *deambulātōrium* a gallery for walking < Latin *deambulāre* to walk away < *de-* away + *ambulāre* to walk]

de-A|mer|i|can|i|za|tion (dē′ə mer′ə kə nə zā′shən), *n.* the act or process of de-Americanizing: *The platform calls for a "progressive de-Americanization" of the war* (New York Times).

de-A|mer|i|can|ize (dē′ə mer′ə kə nīz), *v.t.,* **-ized, -iz|ing.** to rid or divest of American influence or control: *While Ford of Europe will continue to be largely American-run, national operations henceforth will be significantly de-Americanized* (Time).

de|am|i|nate (dē am′ə nāt), *v.t.,* **-nat|ed, -nat|ing.** *Chemistry.* to alter (a compound) by removing the amino radical —NH_2; deaminize. [< *de-* + *amin*(e) + *-ate*[1]]

de|am|i|na|tion (dē am′ə nā′shən), *n. Chemistry.* the process of removing the amino radical —NH_2 from a chemical compound.

de|am|i|ni|za|tion (dē am′ə nə zā′shən), *n.* = deamination.

de|am|i|nize (dē am′ə nīz), *v.t.,* **-nized, -niz|ing.** = deaminate.

dean[1] (dēn), *n.* **1** a member of the faculty of a school, college, or university who has charge of the behavior or studies of the students: *the dean of women.* **2** a head of a division or school in a college or university: *the dean of the Law School.* **3** a high official of a church. A dean is often in charge of a cathedral. **4** a person who has belonged to a group longest; senior member; doyen: *He [Bill Zorach] was the dean of carvers and one of America's leading artists* (New York Times). *William Byrd in 1600 ... was the dean of London musicians* (Harold C. Schonberg). **5** *British.* **a** the president of a faculty or the head of a college within a university. **b** a fellow of a college at Oxford or Cambridge charged with disciplinary functions. [< Old French *deien* < Late Latin *decānus* master of ten < Latin *decem* ten. See related etym. at **doyen**.]

dean[2] (dēn), *n. British.* dene.

dean|er|y (dē′nər ē), *n., pl.* **-er|ies**. **1** the position or authority of a dean. **2** the residence or district of a dean: *... those joint church magazines which are published by the rural deaneries* (J. W. Robertson Scott).

dean|ship (dēn′ship), *n.* the position, office, or rank of a dean: *He succeeds to the deanship vacated by the resignation* (Science).

dean's list, a list published by the dean of a college, containing the names of students who have achieved the highest grades during the school term or year; honor roll.

de|an|thro|po|mor|phize (dē an′thrə pə môr′fīz), *v.t.,* **-phized, -phiz|ing.** to deprive of anthropomorphic attributes or character.

dear[1] (dir), *adj., n., adv., interj.* —*adj.* **1** much loved; precious: *His sister was very dear to him. This is an old story but somehow each time more dear* (Atlantic). **SYN**: beloved. **2** much valued; highly esteemed. *Dear* is used as a form of polite address at the beginning of letters: *Dear Sir.* **3** *Figurative.* costing much; high in price: *Fresh strawberries are dear in winter.* **SYN**: costly, high-priced. See syn. under **expensive**. **4** charging high prices; high: *That grocer is very dear.* **5** *Obsolete.* heartfelt; earnest. **6** *Obsolete.* worthy; honorable.
—*n.* **1** a dear one; a darling: *"Come, my dear," said her mother.* **2** a very attractive or engaging person: *The distinguished actress ... is a dear and a doll in the leading role* (Bosley Crowther).
—*adv.* **1** with affection; fondly: *The old lady held dear the memories of her childhood.* **2** *Figurative.* at a high price; much; very much: *That mistake will cost you dear. "Buy cheap, sell dear" was his motto.*
—*interj.* an exclamation of surprise, trouble, regret, etc.: *Oh dear! I lost my pencil. Dear me, I'm late again!*
[Old English *dēore.* Compare etym. under **darling**.] —**dear′ness**, *n.*

dear[2] (dir), *adj. Archaic.* hard; severe; grievous; dire: *... in our dear peril* (Shakespeare). Also, **dere**. [Old English *dēor*]

dear|born (dir′bərn), *n. U.S.* a kind of four-wheeled country carriage. [American English, probably < Henry *Dearborn,* 1751-1829, an American general and Congressman]

Dear John letter, *U.S. Slang.* **1** a letter to a man from his wife or fiancée, informing him that she has found another man: *A Dear John letter ended their marriage* (Wall Street Journal). **2** any letter declaring the end of a relationship: *Dear John letters from Birch Society sympathizers told of their cooled ardor* (Harper's).

dear|ly (dir′lē), *adv.* **1** fondly: *Mother loves her baby dearly.* **2** *Figurative.* at a high price: *He bought his new car quite dearly.* **3** *Figurative.* very much: *You will regret your foolish behavior dearly in years to come.*

dearness allowance, in India: **1** an agreement to grant an increase in wages in case of a rise in the cost of living. **2** such a wage increase.

dearth (dėrth), *n.* **1** a scarcity; lack; too small a supply: *A dearth of food caused the prices to go up. The orphan suffered from a dearth of affection.* **SYN**: want. See syn. under **scarcity**. **2** a scarcity of food; famine: *Drought in China is often followed by dearth and disease.* **SYN**: poverty. [Middle English *derthe* (originally) costliness < Old English *dēore* dear, precious]

dear|y or **dear|ie** (dir′ē), *n., pl.* **dear|ies**. *Informal.* a dear one; darling.

death (deth), *n., adj.* —*n.* **1** the act or fact of dying; the ending of any form of life in people, animals, or plants: *The old man's death was calm and peaceful.* **SYN**: decease, demise, passing. **2** any ending that is like dying: *the death of a newspaper, the death of an empire,* (*Figurative.*) *the death of one's hopes. In every parting there is an image of death* (George Eliot). **3** a being dead: *eyes closed in death. In death his heart was still.* **4** any condition like being dead: *No longer being well-liked was death to the salesman.* **5** a cause of dying: *His high blood pressure was his death.* **6** bloodshed; murder. **7** extinction; destruction: *The wages of sin is death* (Romans 6:23). **8** *Figurative.* loss or absence of spiritual life: *His death occurred when he retired, though he still lived on for years.* **9** way of dying: *Let me die the death of the righteous* (Numbers 23:10). **10** *Obsolete.* a pestilence.
—*adj.* of or having to do with death: *the death agonies of the damned.* **SYN**: mortal.
at death's door, almost dead; dying: *Poor Mrs. Crawley had been at death's door* (Anthony Trollope).
be death on, *Informal.* to be well-equipped at handling; be able to deal with firmly: *Fanny ... was always death on you English chaps* (E. Fawcett).
catch one's death, *Informal.* to catch a bad cold: *What if it is snowing or raining and I catch my death?* (Earl Hines).
do to death, a to kill; murder: *Done to death by slanderous tongues was the hero that here lies* (Shakespeare). **b** to do, act, or say the same thing so often that it becomes boring: *The play was done to death over the years, so that it no longer attracts audiences.*
in at the death, a present when the game is killed by the hounds: *The hunter was close enough to the fox to be in at the death.* **b** *Figurative.* present at the end of something: *Reporters reached the scene late, and only one managed to be in at the death of the fire.*
put to death, a to kill or execute: *The farmer must put his herd of diseased beef cattle to death.* **b** killed: *By the ancient law of the forest, poachers were put to death.*
to death, beyond endurance; excessively: *She was bored to death.*
to the death, to the last resource or extremity: *to fight tyranny to the death.*
[Old English *dēath*]

Death (deth), *n.* the power that destroys life, often represented as a skeleton dressed in black and carrying a scythe or spade and mattock. [< *death*]

death adder, a common venomous snake of Australia, related to the cobra.

death angel, **1** (in Jewish and Moslem tradition) Azrael, the angel who takes the soul from the body at the moment of death. **2** = death cup.

death ash, radioactive fallout: *... thermonuclear explosion in the Pacific that sifted death ash on Japanese fishermen 71 miles away* (Time).

death|bed (deth′bed′), *n., adj.* —*n.* **1** the bed on which a person dies: *The sick old man lay on his deathbed.* **2** the last hours of life: *He spent his deathbed in futile recriminations.*
—*adj.* during the last hours of life: *The murderer made a deathbed confession.*

death bell, a bell tolled at the death of a person; passing bell.

death benefit, insurance money paid to beneficiaries.

death block, a block of death cells: *a story about a warden's wife who was in love with a condemned man in the death block* (Atlantic).

death|blow (deth′blō′), *n.* **1** a blow that kills: *The knight received a deathblow early in the battle.* **2** *Figurative.* a thing that puts an end (to something): *His illness was the deathblow to hopes for a trip to Europe.*

death camas or **camass**, **1** a perennial plant of the lily family common in the western United States, with grasslike leaves, cream-colored flowers, and a bulb poisonous to cattle, sheep, and other grazing animals. **2** its bulb.

death camp, = extermination camp: *... Auschwitz, the largest and most famous of the death camps* (Hannah Arendt).

death cell, one of a row of cells in a death house: *The first play is set in a death cell an hour or so before its occupant, a lawyer, is to be hanged* (New Yorker).

death certificate, a certificate by a doctor on which the facts relating to a person's death, such as the date, time, and cause, are recorded: *Investigators double-checked both the primary cause of death and other contributory diseases with the physician who signed the death certificate* (Time).

death chamber, **1** a room in which condemned prisoners are executed. **2** a room where someone lies dead or dying.

death control, the prolonging of human life by improved medical care.

death cup, **1** a very poisonous, white mushroom found in woodlands, that has a cuplike enlargement at the base of the stem: *Rabbits can digest the death cup* (New Scientist). **2** the cuplike enlargement.

death damp, the cold sweat that sometimes precedes death.

death-deal|ing (deth′dē′ling), *adj.* causing death; fatal.

death dust, = death sand.

death duty, *British.* an inheritance tax.

death|ful (deth′fəl), *adj.* **1** full of or fraught with death; deadly; fatal; destructive: *Oh! Deathful stabs were dealt apace, The battle deepened in its place* (Tennyson). **2** like death: *The deathful hue of his countenance* (Jane Porter). **3** *Archaic.* liable to death; mortal. —**death′ful|ly**, *adv.* —**death′ful|ness**, *n.*

death house, *U.S.* a place where condemned criminals are kept until put to death.

death instinct, (in Freudian psychology) an instinct that makes man wish to repress his desires for pleasure and, at its extreme, seek to annihilate himself, a drive associated with feelings of guilt. [translation of German *Todestrieb*]

death knell, **1** the sound of a bell tolled at the death of a person; knell. **2** *Figurative.* a signal of the death or passing away of anything: *The Civil War sounded the death knell of slavery.*

death|less (deth′lis), *adj.* living forever; immortal; eternal: *Shakespeare's deathless fame, deathless prose.* **SYN**: imperishable, perpetual. —**death′less|ly**, *adv.* —**death′less|ness**, *n.*

death|like (deth′līk′), *adj.* like that of death; deathly: *There was a deathlike silence before the storm.*

death|li|ness (deth′lē nis), *n.* deathly quality; resemblance to death.

death|ly (deth′lē), *adj., adv.* —*adj.* **1** like that of death; deathlike: *Long illness had brought a deathly pallor to his face.* **2** causing death; deadly: *The rats were killed with a deathly poison.* **SYN**: fatal. **3** *Poetic.* of death.
—*adv.* **1** as if dead: *The sick man grew deathly pale.* **2** extremely: *She is deathly afraid of deep water. Again the Great Hall was deathly silent* (Time).

death march, a long, forced march, usually of prisoners of war, under conditions exceeding the normal limits of human endurance: *The soldiers*

Pronunciation Key: hat, āge, cãre, fär; let, ēqual, tėrm; it, īce; hot, ōpen, ôrder; oil, out; cup, pu̇t, rüle; child; long; thin; ᴛʜen; zh, measure; ə represents **a** in about, **e** in taken, **i** in pencil, **o** in lemon, **u** in circus.

were survivors of a nightmarish 400-mile Communist death march that followed Dienbienphu's fall (Life).

death mask, a clay, wax, or plaster likeness of a person's face made from a cast taken after the person's death.

death penalty, punishment of a criminal by death; capital punishment: *With the death penalty for murderers apparently here for a while yet, things will likely go easier on lesser offenders* (Maclean's).

death|place (deth′plās′), *n.* the place where one dies: *The messages were pouring in today to Bertrand Russell's anchorage and deathplace, Phas Penrhyn* (London Times).

death rate, the proportion of the number of deaths per year to the total population, or to some other stated number: *The death rate did not exceed about 5 to 10 per cent of the population* (Fenner and Day).

death rattle, a rattling sound made in the throat of a dying person.

death ray, an invisible, high-energy electronic or radioactive beam, such as the beam from a laser, capable of destroying most objects.

death|roll (deth′rōl′), *n. Especially British.* a list of persons killed: *... the deathroll was the largest since the emergency began* (Economist).

death row, a block or row of cells in a death house: *Premiers are like men in death row ... wondering and worrying when the big knife will fall* (Time).

death sand, *Military.* radioactive dust.

death sentence, **1** a decree by a judge or court condemning a person to death. **2** *Figurative.* a condemning to collapse, ruin, or oblivion; deathblow; doom: *Whether this is good or bad policy, it is a death sentence for the company* (Wall Street Journal).

***death's-head** (deths′hed′), *n.* a human skull, used as a symbol of death: *The pleasant trappings ... were all whisked away and and you saw a death's-head leering into your face* (Harper's).

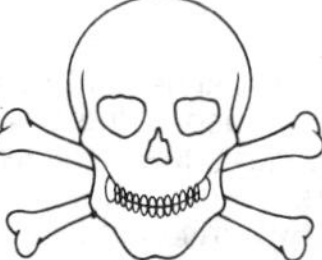

death's-head moth, a large hawk moth with markings on the back of the thorax that resemble the figure of a skull.

deaths|man (deths′mən), *n., pl.* **-men**. *Archaic.* an executioner.

death squad, an organized group of killers, especially ones hired by a government to assassinate suspected political enemies.

death star, = Nemesis: *The possible mechanism that has stirred the greatest interest and debate ... is the one involving the Sun's theorized companion star called Nemesis, or the "death star"* (John N. Wilford).

death|trap (deth′trap′), *n.* **1** a building or structure where the risk of fire or collapse is great. **2** a very dangerous situation.

death|ward (deth′wərd), *adv.* toward death.

death warrant, **1** an official order for a person's death. **2** *Figurative.* anything that dooms to death or to an end that is like death: *In his doctor's face the sick man read his death warrant.*

death|watch (deth′woch′, -wôch′), *n.* **1** a watch kept beside a dying or dead person. **2** a guard for a person about to be put to death. **3** a small, destructive beetle that lives in wood and makes a ticking sound which was once believed to foretell death.

deathwatch beetle, = deathwatch (def. 3).

death wish, (in Freudian psychology) a wish, either conscious or unconscious, for one's own or someone else's death: *His hero is a writer whose nature is destructive; at the beginning, we see him with a pronounced death wish which he seems to conquer as he becomes a successful playwright* (Malcolm Bradbury). [translation of German *Todeswunsch*]

death wound, a wound that causes death.

death|y (deth′ē), *adj., adv.* = deathly.

deave (dēv), *v.t.*, **deaved**, **deav|ing**. *Scottish.* to make deaf; deafen. [Old English *dēafian,* implied in *adēafian* become deaf < *dēaf* deaf]

deb (deb), *n. Informal.* a debutante: *The newest of the Maisonette's debs is being introduced to New York social life* (New Yorker).

deb., debenture.

de|ba|cle or **dé|bâ|cle** (dā bä′kəl, -bak′əl; di-), *n.* **1** a sudden downfall or collapse; overwhelming breakdown or failure; disaster: *The election was a great debacle for the party in power, since most of its candidates lost. After several verbal débâcles we realized we could no longer discuss the care and feeding of Anne in her presence* (Harper's). **2** the breaking up of ice in a river. **3** a violent rush of waters carrying debris. [< French *débâcle* < *débâcler* to free < *dé-* un- (< Latin *dis-*) + *bâcler* to bar]

de|bag (dē bag′), *v.t.*, **-bagged**, **-bag|ging**. *British Slang.* to remove the trousers from.

de|bar (di bär′), *v.t.*, **-barred**, **-bar|ring**. to bar out; shut out; prevent; prohibit: *School rules debarred him from playing on the school team until his grades improved. To debar one from leaving the country is a denial of a very material natural right* (New York Times). SYN: exclude, forbid, restrain.

de|bark[1] (di bärk′), *v.i., v.t.* to get off a ship, aircraft, or other vehicle: *passengers debarking from a bus. After the passengers debarked in port, the captain debarked his crew. Scientists and Seabees finally began debarking themselves and their gear* (Newsweek). SYN: land. [< French *débarquer* < *dé-* parting from (< Latin *dis-*) + *barque* bark, ship]

de|bark[2] (dē bärk′), *v.t.* to remove bark from: *Once debarked, the logs will be moved from Bow to the company's Lawrence papermaking plant* (Wall Street Journal). [< *de-* + *bark*[1]] —**de-bark′er**, *n.*

de|bar|ka|tion (dē′bär kā′shən), *n.* a debarking or being debarked; landing from a ship, aircraft, or other vehicle.

de|bar|ment (di bär′mənt), *n.* a debarring or being debarred.

de|bar|rass (di bar′əs), *v.t.* **1** = disembarrass. **2** to relieve (oneself) of; disencumber: *... debarrassing himself of his cup and saucer* (New Yorker). [< French *débarasser* < *dé-* un- (< Latin *dis-*) + (*em*) *barasser* embarrass]

de|base (di bās′), *v.t.*, **-based**, **-bas|ing**. to make low or lower; lessen the value of: *He debased himself and his character by evil actions. The country's paper money was debased when the government could no longer give the full amount of gold or silver for it.* SYN: corrupt, deteriorate.

de|based (di bāst′), *adj.* **1** lowered in quality or character. **2** *Heraldry.* (of a charge) borne upside down; reversed.

de|base|ment (di bās′mənt), *n.* **1** a debasing or a being debased: *the debasement of silver money by increasing the amount of alloy in it.* **2** anything that debases or is debased. **3** *Obsolete.* abasement.

de|bas|er (di bā′sər), *n.* a person or thing that debases or lowers in estimation or value.

de|bas|ing (di bā′sing), *adj.* that debases. —**de-bas′ing|ly**, *adv.*

de|bat|a|ble (di bā′tə bəl), *adj.* **1** capable of being debated; open to debate. To be debatable a topic must have at least two sides. SYN: moot, questionable. **2** not decided; in dispute: *Once the two countries agreed, the boundary line was no longer debatable.* SYN: uncertain.

debatable land, land between two countries that is claimed by both.

de|bat|a|bly (di bā′tə blē), *adv.* in a debatable manner: *One suave rationalist detained me en route to point out, somewhat debatably, that "there must be a scientific reason for everything that happens in the world"* (Punch).

de|bate (di bāt′), *v.*, **-bat|ed**, **-bat|ing**, *n.* —*v.t.* **1** to talk about reasons for and against (something); consider; discuss: *I am debating buying a camera.* SYN: deliberate. See syn. under **discuss**. **2** to argue about (a question or topic) in a public meeting: *The two candidates debated the right of government employees to go out on strike for higher wages. Will the Administration handling of foreign policy be debated and do you think it should be?* (Newsweek). **3** *Archaic.* to fight for; contend.

—*v.i.* **1** to argue about a question, topic, or other matter in a public meeting. **2** to consider; deliberate. **3** *Obsolete.* to fight, quarrel; contend: *debate with angry swords* (Shakespeare).

—*n.* **1** a discussion of reasons for and against; discussion: *There has been much debate about which boy to choose for captain.* SYN: argument. **2** a public argument for and against a question in a meeting. A formal debate is a contest between two sides to see which one has more skill in speaking and reasoning. *We heard a debate over the radio. After a lively debate, the congress endorsed the statement on foreign policy* (London Times). **3** *Archaic.* fighting; strife; contention.

[< Old French *debat* < *debatre* strive < Late Latin *dēbattere* < Latin *dēbattuere* < *dē-* down, completely + *battuere* to beat]

de|bat|er (di bā′tər), *n.* a person who debates; disputer; wrangler: *The booklets will go to, among others, the 100-or-so high school debaters who write in weekly for information on aid, which is a national debate topic for high-schoolers this year* (Wall Street Journal).

de|bat|ing|ly (di bā′ting lē), *adv.* in the manner of debate.

de|bat|ing society (di bā′ting), a club or group of persons (usually at a school or college) formed for the purpose of debating. *Lloyd developed his argumentative skill at Cambridge as president of the Union, the university debating society that serves as a training ground for many British politicians* (Newsweek).

de|bauch (di bôch′), *v., n.* —*v.t.* **1** to lead away from duty, virtue, or morality; corrupt or seduce; demoralize: *Bad companions had debauched the boy.* **2** to corrupt; pervert; deprave: (*Figurative.*) *to debauch humor.* SYN: vitiate.

—*v.i.* to indulge too much in sensual pleasures, eating, drinking, etc.

—*n.* **1** a period of excessive eating, drinking, etc.: *One drunken debauch after another ruined his health.* **2** = debauchery.

[< French *débaucher* entice from duty < Old French *desbaucher* < *de-* from + *balc*, or *bauch* beam < Germanic (compare Old High German *balko*)] —**de|bauch′er**, *n.*

de|bauched (di bôcht′), *adj.* morally corrupted; depraved; perverted.

de|bauch|ed|ly (di bô′chid lē), *adv.* in a debauched manner; pervertedly.

deb|au|chee (deb′ô chē′, -shē′), *n.* an intemperate, corrupt, dissipated, or depraved person. SYN: libertine, rake.

de|bauch|er|y (di bô′chər ē), *n., pl.* **-er|ies**. **1** excessive indulgence in sensual pleasures, eating, drinking, etc. SYN: sensuality, dissipation, licentiousness, intemperance, debauch. **2** a departure from duty, virtue, or morality. SYN: corruption. **3** an orgy.

de|bauch|ment (di bôch′mənt), *n.* **1** a debauching; a leading away from duty, virtue, or morality. **2** a debauched condition; debauchery. **3** = debauch (def. 1).

de|beak (dē bēk′), *v.t., v.i.* to remove the beak of (a bird): *Debeaking turkeys reduces losses from cannibalism* (Science News Letter).

de|ben|ture (di ben′chər), *n.* **1** a written acknowledgment of a debt. **2** = debenture bond. **3** a certificate of drawback, such as is given to a person or business that reexports imported goods. [< Latin *dēbentur* there are owing, third person plural, present passive of *dēbēre* to owe; see etym. under **debt**]

debenture bond, a bond issued by a company acknowledging indebtedness for a sum on which interest is due until the principal is repaid.

deb|ile (deb′əl), *adj. Archaic.* weak; feeble. [< French *débile*, learned borrowing from Latin *dēbilis* weak]

de|bil|i|tate (di bil′ə tāt), *v.t.*, **-tat|ed**, **-tat|ing**. to make weak or feeble; weaken: *A hot, wet, tropical climate debilitates those who are not used to it.* SYN: enervate, exhaust. See syn. under **weaken**. [< Latin *dēbilitāre* (with English *-ate*[1]) < *dēbilis* weak]

de|bil|i|tat|ed (di bil′ə tā′tid), *adj.* weakened; enfeebled: *The populations are far less debilitated than they were* (Atlantic).

de|bil|i|ta|tion (di bil′ə tā′shən), *n.* **1** the act of debilitating. **2** a debilitated condition; weakening.

de|bil|i|ta|tive (di bil′ə tā′tiv), *adj.* tending to debilitate; causing debilitation.

de|bil|i|ty (di bil′ə tē), *n., pl.* **-ties**. the condition of being weak; weakness; feebleness: *Long illness caused such debility in him that he found even walking difficult.* SYN: languor, exhaustion. [< Latin *dēbilitās* < *dēbilis* weak]

deb|it (deb′it), *n., v. Bookkeeping.* —*n.* **1** an entry of something owed in an account. **2** the left-hand side of an account, where such entries are made. **3** the sum or total shown on this side. *Abbr:* dr.

—*v.t.* **1** to charge with or as a debt: *The bank debited his account $500.* **2** to enter on the debit side of an account.

[alteration of earlier *debte;* spelling influenced by Latin *dēbitum.* Compare etym. under **debt**.]

debit card, a small plastic card with a code number enabling a bank customer to withdraw cash or make deposits by an automatic teller machine and to charge purchases directly to funds on deposit in the bank: *The debit card will be used to initiate a transaction at the bank itself, at a retail outlet, or at a remote unattended location where money can be deposited or withdrawn around the clock* (Rod N. Thorpe).

de|blat|er|ate (di blat′ə rāt), *v.i.*, **-rat|ed**, **-rat|ing**. **1** to babble; prate. **2** to complain bitterly against something. [< Latin *dēblaterāre* (with English *-ate*[1]) < *dē-* of + *blaterāre* to prate]

de|blat|er|a|tion (di blat′ə rā′shən), *n.* **1** the act or fact of babbling; prating. **2** the act or fact of complaining.

de|bloom (dē blüm′), *v.t.* to remove the bloom or bluish fluorescence from (an oil).

deb|o|nair or **deb|o|naire** (deb′ə nãr′), *adj.* **1** gay; cheerful. SYN: light-hearted. **2** pleasant;

courteous: *His debonair ways made the dashing young man a favorite among the ladies.* SYN: urbane, gracious. [< Old French *debonaire* < *de bon aire* of good disposition] —**deb′o|nair′ly,** *adv.* —**deb′o|nair′ness,** *n.*

de|bone (dē bōn′), *v.t.,* **-boned, -bon|ing.** to remove bone from: *deboned fish.*

de bon goût (də bôɴ gü′), *French.* in good taste.

de bonne grâce (də bôn gräs′), *French.* with good grace; willingly.

de|boost (dē büst′), *v., n.* —*v.i.* to reduce the thrust of a spacecraft or missile in flight, especially in order to lower the orbiting altitude of a spacecraft or to slow down a warhead before impact: *This combination would prevent anti-ballistic missile radar. . . . from ascertaining the point of impact until the rocket "deboosts"—about three minutes and 500 miles from target* (Time).
—*n.* the act of reducing the thrust of an orbiting spacecraft or missile: *The second "deboost" maneuver dropped Orbiter 2 from its taxiing orbit of 1,150 miles high and 130 miles low* (New York Times).

Deb|o|rah (deb′ər ə), *n.* a prophetess of Israel who was one of the judges (in the Bible, Judges 4 and 5).

de|boss (dē bôs′, -bos′), *v.t.* to press down or sink (a design or pattern) below the surface. [< *de-* + *boss²*, n.]

de|bouch (di büsh′), *v., n.* —*v.i.* **1** to come out from a narrow or confined place into open country: *The soldiers debouched from the valley into the plain.* **2** (of a ravine, river, pass, or other geographical feature) to issue into a wider place or space, such as a larger valley or plain. **3** to come out; emerge; issue: *From it [a station wagon] debouched my future parents-in-law, my future sister-in-law, my parents, and two guests* (Atlantic).
—*n.* = débouché.
[< French *déboucher* < *dé-* parting from (< Latin *dis-*) + *bouche* mouth < Latin *bucca* the cheek]

dé|bou|ché (dā bü shā′), *n. French.* **1** an opening in a fortress or other fortification, for troops to march out. **2** an exit. **3** an opening for trade; market; outlet.

de|bouch|ment (di büsh′mənt), *n.* **1** the act of debouching. **2** a mouth; outlet: *the debouchment of a river.* SYN: egress, exit.

de|bou|chure (dā′bü shür′), *n.* a mouth or outlet, as of a river or a pass; debouchment: *Some rivers, like the Mississippi, combine all three stages from source to debouchure* (White and Renner). [< French *débouchre* < *déboucher;* see etym. under **debouch**]

de|bride (dā brēd′), *v.t.,* **-brid|ed, -brid|ing.** to treat (a wound) by debridement. [back formation < *debridement*]

de|bride|ment (dā′brēd mäɴ′), *n.* the cleansing of a wound by cutting away dead or infected tissue, foreign matter, bone, or other debris. *Under conditions of shock and delayed debridement of wounds which occur in mass casualties, antibiotics may be less effective* (Science News Letter). [< French *débridement* < *débrider* to unbridle]

de|brief (dē brēf′), *v.t.* to question or obtain information from (someone, such as an emissary, pilot, or intelligence officer) on his return from a mission. —*v.i.* to be debriefed: *Other planes are still landing as I go below to debrief* (Saturday Evening Post).

de|bris or **dé|bris** (də brē′, dā′brē; *especially British* deb′rē), *n.* **1** scattered fragments; ruins; rubbish: *The street was covered with broken glass, stone, and other debris from the explosion.* **2** *Geology.* a mass of large fragments worn away from rock; detritus: *the debris left by a glacier.* [< French *débris* < Old French *debrisier* < *de-* away (< Latin *dē-*) + *brisier* to break]

de Bro|glie wave (də brô lyē′), a wave or group of waves thought to surround moving particles, as electrons, protons, or neutrons. [< Louis V. *de Broglie,* born 1892, a French physicist]

dé|brouil|lard (dā brü yär′), *adj., n. French.* —*adj.* talented and resourceful in shifting for oneself: *But abroad you are not clever enough, not flexible enough, not débrouillard enough to really get along in France* (Harper's).
—*n.* a person who is débrouillard: *Always virtuoso débrouillards, they [Hungarians] have had a lot of experience in adapting to strong regimes* (New Yorker).

debt (det), *n.* **1** something owed to another: *Having borrowed money a few times, he had debts to pay back to several people. My debt for her kindness can never be repaid.* SYN: duty. **2** the condition of owing; indebtedness: *to get out of debt. He is in debt to the automobile dealer for his car.* SYN: arrears. **3** *Figurative.* a sin; trespass: *Forgive us our debts.* [< Old French *dete,* or *debte* < Latin *dēbitum* (thing) owed, neuter past participle of *dēbēre* to owe; (originally) keep (something) from someone < *dē-* away + *habēre* have. Compare etym. under **debit.**]

debt limit, the limit, as established by law or constitution, beyond which a government may not incur indebtedness: *I have no alternative but to ask Congress to again increase the debt limit* (New York Times).

debt of honor, a betting or gambling debt.

debt|or (det′ər), *n.* **1** a person who owes something to another: *If I borrow a dollar from you, I am your debtor.* **2** *Bookkeeping.* the debit side of an account. *Abbr:* dr.

debt|or|ship (det′ər ship), *n.* the quality, state, or condition of being in debt.

debt service, the total yearly payment of interest and principle due on a debt.

de|bug (dē bug′), *v.t.,* **-bugged, -bug|ging. 1** to remove or correct the defects or difficulties of: *During this period, the new weapon is extensively tested and "debugged" by the Air Force* (Wall Street Journal). **2** to find and remove hidden microphones and other electronic spying devices from (a room, building, automobile, airplane, or telephone): *Top company executives will . . . be shown how to bug and debug a board room* (London Times).

de|bunk (dē bungk′), *v.t. Informal.* **1** to remove nonsense or sentimentality from association with: *Debunking Washington, however, has never been popular* (Sunday Times). **2** to prove incorrect or false; refute: *to debunk a theory, to debunk the claims of an advertiser.* [American English < *de-* take away + *bunk²*] —**de|bunk′er,** *n.*

de|burr (dē bėr′), *v.t.* to remove metal burrs from (a part, gear, or other machinery). —**de|burr′er,** *n.*

de|bus (dē bus′), *v.,* **-bussed, -bus|sing.** —*v.i.* to alight from a bus.
—*v.t.* to let (passengers) get off a bus.

De|bus|sy|an or **De|bus|si|an** (də bʏ′sē ən), *adj., n.* —*adj.* of or having to do with Claude Debussy (1862-1918), his music, theories, or style: *The work teeters uneasily between Debussian impressionism, Wagnerian brassiness, and artificial invention* (New Yorker).
—*n.* an admirer of Debussy's style or theory of music.

De|bus|sy|esque (də bʏ′sē esk′), *adj.* like Debussy or his music: *Duke Ellington's magnificent two-platoon band . . . is pulsing away, and so is the modernized Debussyesque music* (New Yorker).

De|bus|sy|ite (də bʏ′sē īt), *adj., n.* = Debussyan.

de|but or **dé|but** (dā′byü; di byü′, dā-), *n., v.* —*n.* **1** a first public appearance: *a young actor's debut on the stage.* **2** a first formal appearance of a young woman in society: *a girl's debut.* SYN: coming-out. **3** the first appearance of anything: *the debut of the latest model cars.*
—*v.i.* to make a debut: *Other new models will debut in coming weeks* (Wall Street Journal).
[< French *début* < *débuter* make the first stroke (in billiards) < *dé-* + *but* goal < Old French]

deb|u|tant or **dé|bu|tant** (deb′yə tänt, -tənt), *n.* a man making a debut, especially an actor or speaker.

deb|u|tante or **dé|bu|tante** (deb′yə tänt, -tant; deb′yə tänt′), *n.* **1** a young woman during her first season in society: *For five or six years he had been escorting debutantes to parties in St. Louis* (New Yorker). **2** a woman making a debut. [< French *débutante* (originally) feminine present participle of *débuter;* see etym. under **debut**]

dec-, *combining form.* the form of **deca-** before vowels, as in *decathlon.*

dec., an abbreviation for the following:
1 deceased.
2 decimeter.
3 declension.
4 declination.
5 decrease.
6 decrescendo.

Dec., December.

deca-, *combining form.* ten: *Decagram = ten grams.* Also, **dec-, dek-** (before vowels), **deka-.** [< Greek *déka* ten]

dec|a|bo|rane (dek′ə bôr′ān, -bōr′-), *n.* a crystalline compound of boron used especially in making high-energy fuels for rockets, missiles, etc. *Formula:* $B_{10}H_{14}$

de|cac|er|ous (di kas′ər əs), *adj.* having ten horns or hornlike arms, tentacles, or other appendages, as the squid. [< Greek *déka* ten + *kéras* horn + English *-ous*]

dec|ad (dek′ad), *n.* **1** the number ten. **2** a group of ten; decade. [< Greek *dekás, dekádos* group of ten. See etym. of doublet **decade.**]

dec|a|dal (dek′ə dəl), *adj.* of or having to do with a decad or decade.

dec|ade (dek′ād), *n.* **1** ten years. From 1900 to 1910 was a decade. Two decades ago means twenty years age. **2** a group, set, or series of ten: *A set of rosary beads is divided into five groups called decades, with ten beads per decade* (Time). [< Middle French *décade,* learned borrowing from Late Latin *decas, decadis* < Greek *dekás, dekádos* group of ten < *déka* ten. See etym. of doublet **decad.**]

de|ca|dence (di kā′dəns, dek′ə-), *n.* **1** a falling off; growing worse; decline; decay: *The appearance of poor books is a sign of a decadence in literature. The decadence of morals was one of the causes of the fall of Rome.* SYN: degeneration, deterioration. **2** a period of decline in art, literature, or other cultural activities. [< Middle French *décadence,* learned borrowing from Medieval Latin *decadentia,* ultimately < Latin *dē-* apart, down + *cadere* to fall]

de|ca|den|cy (di kā′dən sē, dek′ə-), *n., pl.* **-cies.** = decadence.

de|ca|dent (di kā′dənt, dek′ə-), *adj., n.* —*adj.* **1** falling off; growing worse; declining; decaying: *a decadent nation.* **2** of or like the French decadents.
—*n.* **1** a decadent person: *He who sees it only from a gondola gets little more than a glimpse of the lifeless Venice of the decadents* (Guido Piovene). **2** one of a group of French writers and artists, such as Baudelaire, Verlaine, and Mallarmé, of the late 1800's, whose work was characterized by great refinement of style and a tendency to glorify the abnormal and artificial qualities in life and literature. See also **symbolist.** —**de|ca′dent|ly,** *adv.*

de|ca|dent|ism (di kā′dən tiz əm, dek′ə dən tiz′əm), *n.* the literary movement or theories of the decadents.

decade ring, a ring used like a rosary in counting prayers, usually having on the circumference ten knobs or bosses of one form for aves, with an additional knob for the pater, and sometimes also a twelfth for the credo.

de|cad|ic (di kad′ik), *adj.* of or having to do with tens; based upon ten or tens; denary: *the decadic logarithm of two.* [< Greek *dekadikós* < *dekás, dekádos* group of ten]

dec|a|drachm or **dec|a|dram** (dek′ə dram), *n.* an ancient Greek silver coin worth ten drachmas.

de|caf|fe|in|ate (dē kaf′ē ə nāt), *v.t.,* **-at|ed, -at|ing.** to remove caffeine from: *A cup of regular "decaffeinated" coffee still contains about one-third as much caffeine as the straight Java, but instant coffee can be decaffeinated to one-eighth of normal* (Time).

de|caf|fe|in|ize (dē kaf′ē ə nīz), *v.t.,* **-ized, -iz|ing.** = decaffeinate.

*__dec|a|gon__ (dek′ə gon), *n.* a plane figure having ten angles and ten sides. [< Greek *dekágōnon* < *déka* ten + *gōniā* corner, angle]

*__decagon__

*__decahedron__

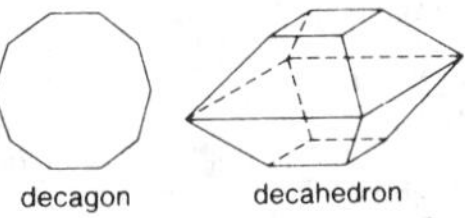

decagon decahedron

de|cag|o|nal (de kag′ə nəl), *adj.* **1** of or having to do with a decagon. **2** having the shape of a decagon; ten-sided.

dec|a|gram (dek′ə gram), *n.* a unit of mass in the metric system equal to 10 grams or 0.3527 ounce. *Abbr:* dkg. Also, **dekagram.** [< French *décagramme* < Greek *déka-* deca- + French *gramme* gram]

dec|a|gramme (dek′ə gram), *n. Especially British.* decagram.

dec|a|he|dral (dek′ə hē′drəl), *adj.* having the shape of a decahedron; ten-sided.

*__dec|a|he|dron__ (dek′ə hē′drən), *n., pl.* **-drons, -dra** (-drə). a solid figure having ten flat, sharp-angled surfaces. See picture above. [< Greek *déka* ten + *-hedron,* as in *dodecahedron*]

de|cal (dē′kal, di kal′), *n.* a design or picture to be transferred especially to glass, wood, or plastic, treated so that it will stick fast; decalcomania. [< *decal* (comania)]

de|cal|ci|fi|ca|tion (dē kal′sə fə kā′shən), *n.* **1** the act of decalcifying. **2** the state or condition of being decalcified.

de|cal|ci|fi|er (dē kal′sə fī′ər), *n.* a thing that decalcifies.

de|cal|ci|fy (dē kal′sə fī), *v.t.,* **-fied, -fy|ing.** to remove lime or calcium from: *to decalcify bone. Strontium-90 in milk, resulting from atomic fallout, can be removed by decalcifying the milk* (Science News Letter).

de|cal|co|ma|ni|a (di kal′kə mā′nē ə), *n.* **1** = decal. **2** the process of decorating glass, wood, or

Pronunciation Key: hat, āge, cãre, fär; let, ēqual, tėrm; it, īce; hot, ōpen, ôrder; oil, out; cup, pu̇t, rüle; child; long; thin; ᴛʜen; zh, measure; ə represents **a** in about, **e** in taken, **i** in pencil, **o** in lemon, **u** in circus.

plastic by applying decals. [< French *décalcomanie* < *décalquer* transfer a tracing + *manie* mania]

de|ca|les|cence (dē′kə les′əns), *n.* the sudden absorption of heat as a metal passes a certain temperature. [< *de-* + *calescence*]

de|ca|les|cent (dē′kə les′ənt), *adj.* (of a metal during heating) suddenly absorbing heat as it passes a certain temperature.

dec|a|li|ter (dek′ə lē′tər), *n.* a unit of measure of volume in the metric system, equal to 10 liters, 9.08 quarts U.S. dry measure, or 2.64 gallons U.S. liquid measure. *Abbr:* dkl. Also, **dekaliter**. [< French *décalitre* < *déca-* deca- + *litre* liter]

dec|a|li|tre (dek′ə lē′tər), *n. Especially British.* decaliter.

Dec|a|logue or **Dec|a|log** (dek′ə lôg, -log), *n.* the Ten Commandments (in the Bible, Exodus 20:2-17). [< Middle French *décalogue* < Late Latin *decalogus* < Greek *dekálogos* < *déka lógos* Ten Commandments]

dec|a|logue or **dec|a|log** (dek′ə lôg, -log), *n.* any set of ten commandments or rules. [< *Decalogue*]

De|cam|er|on (di kam′ər ən), *n.* a collection of 100 tales written by Boccaccio and published in Italy in 1353. [< Italian *Decamerone* < Greek *déka* ten + *hēméra* day (because ten tales were told on each day)]

de|cam|er|ous (di kam′ər əs), *adj. Botany.* having ten parts in each whorl (generally written *10-merous*): *decamerous flowers.* [< Greek *déka* ten + *méros* part + English *-ous*]

dec|a|me|ter (dek′ə mē′tər), *n.* a unit of measure of length in the metric system equal to 10 meters, or 32.8 feet. *Abbr:* dkm. Also, **dekameter**. [< French *décamètre* < *déca-* deca- + *mètre* meter]

dec|a|me|tre (dek′ə mē′tər), *n. Especially British.* decameter.

dec|a|met|ric (dek′ə met′rik), *adj.* **1** of or having to do with decameters; measured in decameters. **2** of or having to do with radio waves ranging from 10 to 100 meters in length, or a frequency of 3 to 30 megahertz: *Storms have been observed at decametric wavelengths (3 to 30 megahertz)* (Science News). Also, **dekametric**.

de|camp (di kamp′), *v.i.* **1** to leave quickly, secretly, or without ceremony; run away; flee: *The thieves had decamped by the time the police came.* **SYN:** abscond, escape. **2** to leave a camp or camping ground; break camp: *The army of the King of Portugal was at Elvas on the 22nd of the last month, and was to decamp on the 24th* (The Tatler). [< French *décamper* < *dé-* departing from (< Latin *dis-*) + *camp* camp]

de|camp|ment (di kamp′mənt), *n.* **1** the act of decamping. **2** a quick departure.

dec|a|nal (dek′ə nəl, di kā′-), *adj.* of a dean or deanery. [< Late Latin *decānus* dean + English *-al*[1]] —**dec′a|nal|ly**, *adv.*

dec|ane (dek′ān), *n.* a colorless, liquid hydrocarbon of the methane series, found in several isomeric forms. *Formula:* $C_{10}H_{22}$ [< *dec-* + *-ane*]

de|cant (di kant′), *v.t.* **1** to pour off (liquor or a solution) gently without disturbing the sediment: *The waiter decanted the wine.* **2** to pour from one container into another. **3** *Figurative.* to unload as if by pouring or spilling out: *The wagonette had decanted us at some ideal site for . . . picnicking* (New Yorker). [probably < Medieval Latin *decanthare* < Latin *dē-* down from + *canthus,* with unrecorded meaning "rim, lip" < Celtic (compare Welsh *cant* rim). Compare etym. under **cant**[2].]

de|can|ta|tion (dē′kan tā′shən), *n.* the act or process of decanting.

de|cant|er (di kan′tər), *n.* **1** a glass bottle with a stopper, used for serving wine or liquor. **2** a vessel for decanting or receiving decanted liquors.

de|ca|pac|i|tate (dē′kə pas′ə tāt), *v.t.,* **-tat|ed, -tat|ing.** to inhibit capacitation in (sperm).

de|ca|pac|i|ta|tion (dē′kə pas′ə tā′shən), *n.* the act or process of decapacitating; inhibition of the capacity of sperm to fertilize an egg.

de|cap|i|tal|i|za|tion (dē kap′ə tə lə zā′shən), *n.* a decapitalizing.

de|cap|i|tal|ize (dē kap′ə tə līz), *v.t.,* **-ized, -iz|ing. 1** to deprive of capital: *to decapitalize a firm. The Argentine landowner has been progressively decapitalized* (Atlantic). **2** to convert from upper to lower case: *to decapitalize a letter.*

de|cap|i|tate (di kap′ə tāt), *v.t.,* **-tat|ed, -tat|ing.** to cut off the head of; behead: *In Germanic nations, as is well known, culprits were decapitated by means of the heavy-bladed broad two-handed sword* (Notes and Queries). [< Late Latin *dēcapitāre* (with English *-ate*[1]) < Latin *dē-* un- + *caput, capitis* head]

de|cap|i|ta|tion (di kap′ə tā′shən), *n.* **1** the act of decapitating. **2** a being decapitated.

de|cap|i|ta|tor (di kap′ə tā′tər), *n.* a person who decapitates.

dec|a|pod (dek′ə pod), *n., adj.* —*n.* **1** any one of an order of crustaceans having ten legs or arms, such as a lobster, crab, or crayfish. **2** any one of a suborder of mollusks having ten arms or tentacles, such as a squid or cuttlefish.
—*adj.* having ten legs, arms, or tentacles.
[< New Latin *Decapoda* the order name < Greek *déka* ten + *poús, podós* foot]

de|cap|o|dal (di kap′ə dəl), *adj.* of or having to do with a decapod.

de|cap|o|dous (di kap′ə dəs), *adj.* having the form or shape of a decapod crustacean.

de|car|bon|ate (dē kär′bə nāt), *v.t.,* **-at|ed, -at|ing.** to remove carbon dioxide or carbonic acid from.

de|car|bon|a|tor (dē kär′bə nā′tər), *n.* a person or thing that decarbonates.

de|car|bon|i|za|tion (dē kär′bə nə zā′shən), *n.* the act or process of decarbonizing.

de|car|bon|ize (dē kär′bə nīz), *v.t., v.i.,* **-ized, -iz|ing.** to remove carbon (from); decarburize: *Iron is decarbonized in making steel.*

de|car|bon|iz|er (dē kär′bə nī′zər), *n.* a person or thing that decarbonizes.

de|car|box|yl|ate (dē′kär bok′sə lāt), *v.t.,* **-at|ed, -at|ing.** *Chemistry.* to free from the carboxyl group -COOH

de|car|box|yl|a|tion (dē′kär bok′sə lā′shən), *n. Chemistry.* the removal of one or more carboxyl groups, -COOH, as by removing carbon dioxide from an organic acid.

de|car|bu|ri|za|tion (dē kär′bər ə zā′shən, -byər-), *n.* = decarbonization.

de|car|bu|rize (dē kär′bə rīz, -byə-), *v.t.,* **-rized, -riz|ing.** = decarbonize.

dec|ar|chy (dek′är kē), *n., pl.* **-chies.** a board of ten that governed the Greek states which Sparta had freed from Athenian rule. [< Greek *dekarchiā* < *déka* ten + *archós* ruler]

dec|are (dek′ār, dek ār′), *n.* a unit of square measure in the metric system, equal to 10 ares, 1,000 square meters, or about 1,196 square yards. [< French *décare* < Greek *déka* ten + French *are* are < Latin *ārea* area]

de|car|tel|ise (dē kär′tə līz), *v.t.,* **-ised, -is|ing.** *Especially British.* decartelize.

de|car|tel|i|za|tion (dē kär′tə lə zā′shən), *n.* **1** the dissolving of a cartel or cartels. **2** an instance of this.

de|car|tel|ize (dē kär′tə līz), *v.t.,* **-ized, -iz|ing.** to dissolve a cartel or cartels in (a business or industry). —**de|car′tel|iz′er**, *n.*

dec|a|stere (dek′ə stir), *n.* a unit of measure of volume in the metric system equal to 10 steres, 10 cubic meters, or about 13.08 cubic yards. Also, **dekastere**. [< French *décastère* < *déca-* deca- + *stère* stere]

dec|a|stich (dek′ə stik), *n.* a poem consisting of ten lines. [< Greek *déka* ten + *stíchos* verse]

dec|a|style (dek′ə stīl), *adj.* having ten columns in front, as a temple or a portico. [< Latin *decastȳlus* < Greek *dekástylos* < *déka* ten + *stŷlos* column]

de|cas|u|al|i|za|tion (dē kazh′ů ə lə zā′shən), *n.* the abolition of casual labor.

de|cas|u|al|ize (dē kazh′ů ə līz), *v.t.,* **-ized, -iz|ing.** to make no longer casual; change from a casual or uncertain condition by giving a regular or permanent character: *to decasualize labor by providing steady employment.*

dec|a|syl|lab|ic (dek′ə sə lab′ik), *adj., n.* —*adj.* having ten syllables: *a decasyllabic line of poetry.* —*n.* = decasyllable.

dec|a|syl|la|ble (dek′ə sil′ə bəl), *n.* a line of poetry having ten syllables.

de|cath|lete (di kath′lēt), *n.* an athlete who competes in a decathlon: *Gerhard Auer, No. 3 in the West German boat, was once a decathlete, accumulating over 6,500 points* (London Times). [blend of *decathlon* and *athlete*]

de|cath|lon (di kath′lon), *n.* an athletic contest with ten different parts, such as running, jumping, and throwing the javelin. It is held during two days. The person who scores the most points for all ten parts is the winner: *The modern decathlon consists of the 100-meter dash, broad jump, shot put, high jump, 400-meter run, 110-meter hurdles, discus throw, pole vault, javelin throw, 1,500-meter run* (Time). [< *dec-* ten + Greek *âthlon* contest. Compare etym. under **athlete**.]

de|cay (di kā′), *v., n.* —*v.i.* **1** to become rotten; rot: *The old apples got soft and decayed. Her teeth decayed because she ate too many sweets. The beams of the old house had decayed and fallen in.* **2** to grow less in power, strength, wealth, or beauty: *Many nations have grown great and then decayed. The power of the Roman Empire was decaying at the time of Nero.* **SYN:** deteriorate, decline. **3** to decrease in number, volume, intensity, or power. **4** *Physics.* (of radioactive substances) to disintegrate by the emission of various types of rays: *This radioactivity "decays," or decreases, rapidly but the fission products can contaminate* (Hanson W. Baldwin). **5** *Aerospace.* (of an orbiting earth satellite) to slow down because of atmospheric friction.
—*v.t.* to cause to decay: *Too many sweets may decay the teeth.*
—*n.* **1** a rotting: *tooth decay. The decay of the tree trunk proceeded so rapidly the tree fell over in a year. If bacterial decay did not occur, the life activities of plants and animals would of necessity come to a standstill* (Fred W. Emerson). **SYN:** putrefaction. **2** a decayed condition: *Round the decay of that colossal wreck* (Shelley). **3** a loss of power, strength, wealth, or beauty: *The decay of the old lady's health and vigor was very gradual. Age is not all decay* (George MacDonald). **SYN:** deterioration, decline. **4** a decrease in number, volume, intensity, or power. **5** *Physics.* the loss in quantity of a radioactive substance through disintegration of its component nuclei, as by the emission of alpha particles or beta particles. **6** *Aerospace.* reduction in speed of an orbiting earth satellite, caused by atmospheric friction. **7** *Obsolete.* **a** destruction; ruin. **b** consumption; phthisis.
[< Old French *decair* < *de-* down (< Latin *dē-*) + *cair* < Latin *cadere* to fall] —**de|cay′er**, *n.*
—*Syn. v.i.* **1 Decay, rot, decompose** mean to change from a good or healthy condition to a bad one. **Decay** emphasizes the idea of changing little by little through natural processes: *Some diseases cause the bones to decay.* **Rot**, more emphatic, emphasizes the idea of spoiling and applies especially to plant and animal matter: *The fruit rotted on the vines.* **Decompose** emphasizes the idea of breaking down into original parts, by natural or chemical processes: *Bodies decompose after death.*

de|cay|a|ble (di kā′ə bəl), *adj.* liable to decay.

decay constant, the ratio of the rate of disintegration of a radioactive substance to the amount of the substance left unchanged: *The decay constants of potassium are somewhat uncertain* (Scientific American).

de|cayed (di kād′), *adj.* **1** having fallen away or declined from a former state of excellence or well-being. **2** reduced in fortune: *An ancient asylum for superannuated tradesmen and decayed householders* (Washington Irving). **3** affected with physical decay, as buildings, teeth, or fruit.

de|cay|less (di kā′lis), *adj.* without decay; not subject to decay.

decd., deceased.

de|cease (di sēs′), *n., v.,* **-ceased, -ceas|ing.**
—*n.* the act or fact of dying; death: *The general's unexpected decease left the army without a leader.* **SYN:** demise.
—*v.i.* to die: *deceasing without leaving an heir.* **SYN:** expire.
[< Old French *deces* < Latin *dēcessus, -ūs* death, departure < *dēcēdere* < *dē-* away + *cēdere* go]

de|ceased (di sēst′), *adj., n.* —*adj.* no longer living; dead: *The deceased man's belongings were sent to his widow.* **SYN:** See syn. under **dead**.
—*n.* Usually, **the deceased**, a dead person or persons: *The deceased had been a famous actor.*

de|ce|dent (di sē′dənt), *n. U.S. Law.* a dead person. [< Latin *dēcēdēns, -entis,* present participle of *dēcēdere;* see etym. under **decease**]

decedent estate, *U.S. Law.* the estate left by a person at death.

de|ceit (di sēt′), *n.* **1** the act of making a person believe as true something that is false; deceiving, lying, or cheating: *The swindler's open, frank face made him seem incapable of deceit.* **2** a dishonest trick; a lie spoken or acted: *A polite deceit sometimes backfires on the deceiver.* **SYN:** stratagem, wile. **3** the quality in a person that makes him tell lies or cheat; deceitfulness: *The dishonest trader was full of deceit.* **SYN:** cunning. [< Old French *deceite* < *deceveir;* see etym. under **deceive**]
—*Syn.* **1 Deceit, deception, guile** mean false or misleading representation. **Deceit** implies concealing or twisting the truth in order to mislead and gain advantage over others: *The trader was truthful and without deceit.* **Deception** applies to the act that gives a false or wrong idea, but does not always suggest a dishonest purpose: *A magician uses deception.* **Guile** suggests craftiness and slyness and deception by means of trickery: *He got what he wanted by guile, not work.*

de|ceit|ful (di sēt′fəl), *adj.* **1** ready or willing to deceive or lie: *A liar is a deceitful person.* **SYN:** insincere, disingenuous. **2** meant to deceive; deceiving; misleading: *She told a deceitful story to avoid punishment.* **SYN:** false, fraudulent. —**de|ceit′ful|ly**, *adv.* —**de|ceit′ful|ness**, *n.*

de|ceiv|a|ble (di sē′və bəl), *adj.* **1** that can be deceived. **2** *Archaic.* deceitful; deceptive. —**de|ceiv′a|ble|ness**, *n.*

de|ceiv|a|bly (di sē′və blē), *adv.* in a deceivable manner.

de|ceive (di sēv′), *v.*, **-ceived, -ceiv|ing.** — ***v.t.*** **1** to make (a person) believe as true something that is false; mislead: *The magician deceived his audience into thinking he had really sawed the woman in half. The boy tried to deceive his mother, but she knew what he had done.* **SYN:** delude, fool, trick, beguile, dupe. See syn. under **cheat. 2** *Obsolete.* to while away (time).
— ***v.i.*** to lie; use deceit; act deceitfully: *Ah, what a tangled web we weave, When first we practise to deceive!* (Scott).
[< Old French *deceveir* < Latin *dēcipere* ensnare, catch < *dē-* away + *capere* take]

de|ceiv|er (di sē′vər), *n.* a person who deceives; cheat; impostor.

de|ceiv|ing|ly (di sē′ving lē), *adv.* in a manner so as to deceive.

de|cel|er|ate (dē sel′ə rāt), *v.t., v.i.*, **-at|ed, -at|ing.** to decrease the velocity (of); slow down: *By firing small rockets the astronauts decelerated the spaceship. The wheel slowly decelerated.* [< *de-* + (ac) *celerate*]

de|cel|er|a|tion (dē sel′ə rā′shən), *n.* the act of decelerating; decrease in velocity; negative acceleration: *Highway surfaces become polished and slippery in places where traffic is heavy, where acceleration or deceleration is great, and at curves* (Science News Letter).

deceleration parachute, a parachute attached to an aircraft for slowing it down during landing.

de|cel|er|a|tor (dē sel′ə rā′tər), *n.* **1** a person or thing that decelerates. **2** a device for reducing the speed of an engine: *the decelerator which automatically throttles the engine whenever the clutch is disengaged* (Westminster Gazette).

de|cel|er|om|e|ter (dē sel′ə rom′ə tər), *n.* a device for measuring the rate of deceleration, especially of vehicles. [< *deceler*(ate) + *-meter*]

de|cel|er|on (dē sel′ə ron), *n.* an aileron on some jet aircraft for slowing it down in flight. [< *decel-er*(ate) + (ailer) *on*]

De|cem|ber (di sem′bər), *n.* the 12th and last month of the calendar year. It has 31 days. *December 25th is Christmas. Abbr:* Dec. [< Old French *decembre,* learned borrowing from Latin *December* < *decem* ten (in the early Roman calendar it was the tenth and last month)]

De|cem|brist (di sem′brist), *n., adj.* — ***n.*** (in Russian history) a person who took part in a military conspiracy in December, 1825, to limit the power of Czar Nicholas I.
— ***adj.*** of or having to do with this conspiracy: *This Decembrist uprising failed miserably, but it marked the first appearance of a revolutionary force in Russia* (Ballis, McLane, and Shabad).

de|cem|vir (di sem′vər), *n., pl.* **-virs, -vi|ri** (-və rī). **1** a member of a council of ten magistrates in ancient Rome. The decemvirs in 451 and 450 B.C. prepared the earliest Roman law code. **2** a member of a council of ten men, such as that of the Venetian Republic. [< Latin *decemvir,* singular of *decemvirī* < *decem* ten + *virī* men, plural of *vir* man]

de|cem|vi|ral (di sem′vər əl), *adj.* of or having to do with the decemvirs.

de|cem|vi|rate (di sem′vər it, -və rāt), *n.* **1** the office or government of decemvirs: *The decemvirate seems indeed to have exhibited the perfect model of an aristocratical royalty, vested not in one person but in several* (Thomas Arnold). **2** a group or council of ten men or decemvirs.

de|cen|a|ry (di sen′ər ē), *adj., n., pl.* **-ries.** — ***adj.*** of or having to do with a tithing.
— ***n.*** a tithing; ten freeholders and their families. Also, **decennary.** [< Medieval Latin *decenarius* < *decena* a tithing < Latin *decem* ten]

de|cen|cy (dē′sən sē), *n., pl.* **-cies. 1** the quality or state of being decent: *Common decency requires that you pay for the window you broke.* **2** proper behavior; a conforming to the standard of good taste: *Immodest words admit of no defence, For want of decency is want of sense* (Earl of Roscommon). **SYN:** decorum. **3** a proper regard for modesty or delicacy; respectability. **SYN:** seemliness.
decencies, a things decent or proper; suitable acts; proper observances: *Being courteous, tolerant, and kind are some of the decencies of life.* **b** the things required for a proper standard of living.

de|cen|na|ry¹ (di sen′ər ē), *n., pl.* **-ries,** *adj.* — ***n.*** a period of ten years.
— ***adj.*** of or having to do with a period of ten years.
[< Latin *decennis* of ten years (< *decem* ten + *annus* year) + English *-ary*]

de|cen|na|ry² (di sen′ər ē), *adj., n., pl.* **-ries.** = decenary.

de|cen|ni|ad (di sen′ē ad), *n.* = decennium.

de|cen|ni|al (di sen′ē əl), *adj., n.* — ***adj.*** **1** of or for ten years. **2** happening every ten years.
— ***n.*** a tenth anniversary or its celebration.
[< Latin *decennium* a decade (< *decennis* of ten years < *decem* ten + *annus* year) + English *-al*¹]

de|cen|ni|al|ly (di sen′ē ə lē), *adv.* every ten years.

de|cen|ni|um (di sen′ē əm), *n., pl.* **-ni|ums, -ni|a** (-nē ə). a period of ten years; decade; decenniad. [< Latin *decennium* < *decennis* of ten years < *decem* ten + *annus* year]

de|cent (dē′sənt), *adj.* **1** proper and right: *It is not decent to laugh at a crippled person.* **SYN:** suitable, appropriate. **2** modest; free from vulgarity; not obscene: *His study was simple and serious and showed a more decent taste* (Edmund Wilson). **3** having a good reputation; respectable: *decent people.* **SYN:** decorous, dignified. **4** good enough; fairly good: *He gets decent marks at school.* **SYN:** tolerable, passable. **5** suitable to one's position; adequate: *He is not rich but he earns a decent living.* **6** not severe; rather kind: *The teacher was very decent to excuse my absence when my mother was ill.* **7** *Informal.* dressed; not naked: *Mother's voice asked if I were decent. "Pyjamas," I replied* (Punch). **8** *Obsolete.* handsome; comely. [< Latin *decēns, -entis* becoming, fitting, present participle of *decēre* be fitting, proper, or suitable] — **de′cent-ness,** *n.*

de|cen|ter (dē sen′tər), *v.t.* to put out of center; make eccentric.

de|cent|ly (dē′sənt lē), *adv.* in a decent manner; properly; respectably; fairly.

de|cen|tral|ise (dē sen′trə līz), *v.t., v.i.*, **-ised, -is|ing.** *Especially British.* decentralize.

de|cen|tral|ist (dē sen′trə list), *n., adj.* — ***n.*** a person who advocates or supports decentralization.
— ***adj.*** of or having to do with decentralization or decentralists.

de|cen|tral|i|za|tion (dē sen′trə lə zā′shən), *n.* **1** the act of decentralizing: *He believed in decentralization, and preferred scattered farms* (Sunday Times). **2** the state of being decentralized.

de|cen|tral|ize (dē sen′trə līz), *v.*, **-ized, -iz|ing.** — ***v.t.*** **1** to spread or distribute (authority or power) among more groups or local governments: *He ... emphasized in a speech published here today that the Soviet Union's decentralized system of agricultural planning was to take effect immediately* (New York Times). *We* [*should*] *spend the money to return to the safety of decentralized power* (New York Times). **2** to reorganize (a large industry, business, school system, or other institution) into smaller units of management and operation: *The congregation has approved changes that will decentralize the* [*Jesuit*] *order to the extent of giving its individual provinces more discretionary powers* (Robert C. Doty).
— ***v.i.*** to become decentralized; undergo decentralization: *Failure of the ... regime to decentralize has resulted in continued high costs and low productivity* (Richard A. Pierce).

de|cep|tion (di sep′shən), *n.* **1** the act of deceiving: *The twins' deception in exchanging places fooled everybody except their mother.* **SYN:** imposture, subterfuge, trickery. See syn. under **deceit. 2** the state of being deceived: *The deception of the magician's audience was almost complete.* **3** a thing that deceives; illusion. **4** a trick meant to deceive; fraud; sham: *The scheme is all a deception.* **SYN:** hoax, ruse, artifice, stratagem. [< Late Latin *dēceptiō, -ōnis* < Latin *dēcipere;* see etym. under **deceive**]

de|cep|tious (di sep′shəs), *adj. Obsolete.* deceitful; deceptive.

de|cep|tive (di sep′tiv), *adj.* **1** deceiving or misleading: *Thirsty travelers on the desert are often fooled by the deceptive appearance of trees and water. He played the piano with deceptive ease.* **2** meant to deceive; *deceptive glances. The deceptive friendliness of the fox fooled the rabbit.* **SYN:** fraudulent, false, specious. — **de|cep′tive|ly,** *adv.* — **de|cep′tive|ness,** *n.*

de|cer|e|brate (dē ser′ə brāt), *v.*, **-brat|ed, -brat-ing,** *adj.* — ***v.t.*** to remove the cerebrum from: *to decerebrate a frog.*
— ***adj.*** **1** decerebrated. **2** lacking reason or intelligence: *the decerebrate acts of a mob.*

de|cern (di sern′), *v.t.* **1** = discern. **2** (in Scots law) to decree; adjudge. — ***v.i.*** to see distinctly; distinguish. [< Latin *dēcernere* decide, determine; see etym. under **decree**]

de|cer|ti|fi|ca|tion (dē sėr′tə fə kā′shən), *n.* a decertifying.

de|cer|ti|fy (dē sėr′tə fī), *v.t.*, **-fied, -fy|ing.** to remove or discontinue the certification or accreditation of; refuse certification to: *to decertify a labor union.*

de|chlo|rin|ate (dē klôr′ə nāt, -klōr′-), *v.t.*, **-at|ed, -at|ing.** to free (a substance) of chlorine; take away chlorine from.

de|chlo|rin|a|tion (dē klôr′ə nā′shən, -klōr′-), *n.* the act or process of dechlorinating: *dechlorination of water by means of a carbon filter.*

de|chris|tian|i|za|tion (dē kris′chə nə zā′shən), *n.* the process of divesting of Christian character.

de|chris|tian|ize (dē kris′chə nīz), *v.t.*, **-ized, -iz-ing.** to divest of Christian character.

deci-, *combining form.* one tenth of: *Decigram = one tenth of a gram.* [< Latin *decimus* tenth < *decem* ten]

dec|i|are (des′ē ãr), *n.* a unit of measure of area in the metric system equal to 1/10 of an are, 10 square meters, or 11.96 square yards. [< French *déciare* < *déci-* deci- + *are* are < Latin *ārea* area]

dec|i|bel (des′ə bel), *n.* **1** a unit for measuring the relative intensity of sounds, equal to 1/10 of a bel: *Most people speak in a range between 45 and 75 decibels* (Wall Street Journal). **2** a unit for expressing power ratios, equivalent to ten times the logarithm to the base ten of the ratio of any two power magnitudes. *Abbr:* db. [< *deci-* + *bel*]

de|cid|a|ble (di sī′də bəl), *adj.* that can be decided.

de|cide (di sīd′), *v.*, **-cid|ed, -cid|ing.** — ***v.t.*** **1** to settle (a question or dispute) by giving victory to one side; give a judgment or decision about: *Let us decide the question by tossing a penny. Fighting is a poor way to decide an argument.* **2** to cause (a person) to reach a decision: *What decided you to vote for him?*
— ***v.i.*** **1** to give a judgment or decision: *Her sister decided in favor of the blue dress instead of the yellow one. The court decided in favor of the defendant.* **2** to make up one's mind; resolve: *He decided to be a sailor.*
[< Latin *dēcīdere* decide; (literally) cut off < *dē-* away + *caedere* to cut]
— ***Syn.*** *v.i.* **2 Decide, determine, resolve** mean to make up one's mind regarding a course of action. **Decide** emphasizes the idea of coming to a conclusion after some question, talk, or thinking over: *I decided to take the position at the bank.* **Determine** suggests fixing one's mind so firmly on doing something that nothing could shake one loose from his decision or purpose: *I determined to make a success of it.* **Resolve** further implies that one has promised to oneself to do or not to do something: *I resolved to do good work.*

de|cid|ed (di sī′did), *adj.* **1** clear or definite; unquestionable: *There is a decided difference between black and white. His height gave the basketball player a decided advantage. I find much cause to reproach myself that I have lived so long, and have given no decided and public proof of my being a Christian* (Patrick Henry). **SYN:** undeniable, indisputable. **2** firm; determined; resolute: *He studied hard because he had a decided wish to go to college. Henry Smith spoke out boldly, and in a decided voice* (Scott). **SYN:** positive, emphatic. — **de|cid′ed|ness,** *n.*
▶ **Decided, decisive** mean clear and firm. *Decided* means definite or unquestionable: *His weight gave the boxer a decided advantage. Decisive* means having or producing a clear result: *The Battle of Saratoga was a decisive victory for the Americans.*

de|cid|ed|ly (di sī′did lē), *adv.* **1** clearly; definitely; without question: *Her work is decidedly better than his. It was a decidedly warm day.* **SYN:** certainly, surely, doubtless. **2** in a determined manner; firmly: *The candidate spoke decidedly and to the point.*

de|cid|er (di sī′dər), *n.* a person or thing that decides (a question or dispute): *The minority—the late deciders—may tip the scales and carry an election* (Science News Letter).

de|cid|u|a (di sij′ů ə), *n.* the part of the lining of the uterus in which a fertilized ovum is embedded and which is cast off at birth. [< New Latin (*membrana*) *decidua* deciduous (membrane)]

de|cid|u|al (di sij′ů əl), *adj.* of or having to do with the decidua.

de|cid|u|ate (di sij′ů it), *adj.* **1** characterized by or having a decidua: *a deciduate mammal.* **2** having to do with a decidua.

deciduate placenta, a placenta which is composed in part of a decidua.

***de|cid|u|ous** (di sij′ů əs), *adj.* **1a** shedding leaves each year. Maples, elms, and most oaks are deciduous trees. **b** having such trees or shrubs: *Deciduous forests are limited to regions where there is sufficient rainfall* (Fred W. Emerson). **2** falling off at a particular season or stage of growth: *Maples have deciduous leaves that fall in autumn. Antlers are deciduous horns.* **3** *Figurative.* not permanent; fleeting; transitory: *There is much that is deciduous in books* (James Russell Lowell). [< Latin *dēciduus* (with English *-ous*) <

Pronunciation Key: hat, āge, cãre, fär; let, ēqual, tėrm; it, īce; hot, ōpen, ôrder; oil, out; cup, pu̇t, rüle; child; long; thin; ᴛʜen; zh, measure; ə represents a in about, e in taken, i in pencil, o in lemon, u in circus.

dēcidere < *dē-* away, off + *cadere* to fall] —**de·cid′u|ous|ly**, *adv.* —**de|cid′u|ous|ness**, *n.*

***deciduous**
definition 1a

deciduous trees:

chokecherry

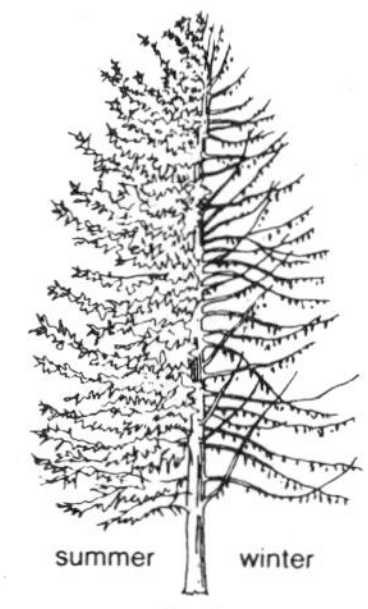

larch

evergreen trees:

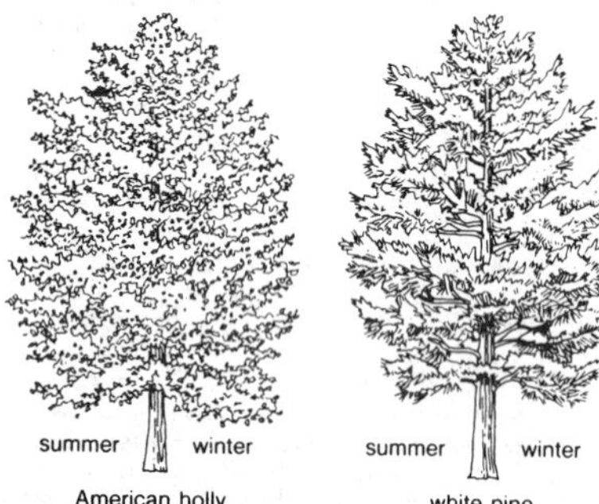

American holly white pine

deciduous holly, = black alder.
deciduous tooth, = milk tooth.
dec|i|gram (des′ə gram), *n.* a unit of measure of mass in the metric system equal to one tenth of a gram, about 1.5432 grains, or 0.003527 ounce. *Abbr:* dg. [< French *décigramme* < *déci-* deci- + *gramme* gram]
dec|i|gramme (des′ə gram), *n. Especially British.* decigram.
dec|ile (des′əl), *n., adj. Statistics.* —*n.* one of the points on a scale of the frequency distribution of data which divide the data into ten parts, each having the same frequency.
—*adj.* of or having to do with deciles; being a decile.
[< Latin *decem* ten; patterned on *quartile*]
dec|i|li|ter (des′ə lē′tər), *n.* a unit of measure of volume in the metric system equal to one tenth of a liter, 6.102 cubic inches U.S. dry measure, or about 3.38 fluid ounces U.S. liquid measure. *Abbr:* dl. [< French *décilitre* < *déci-* deci- + *litre* liter]
dec|i|li|tre (des′ə lē′tər), *n. Especially British.* deciliter.
de|cil|lion (di sil′yən), *n., adj.* **1** 1 with 33 zeros following it (in the U.S., Canada, and France). **2** 1 with 60 zeros following it (in Britain and Germany). [< *dec-* + (m)*illion*]
de|cil|lionth (di sil′yənth), *adj., n.* —*adj.* **1** having to do with a decillion. **2** having the magnitude or position of one of a decillion equal parts.
—*n.* **1** the quotient of unity divided by a decillion. **2** one of a decillion equal parts.
decim., decimeter.
dec|i|mal (des′ə məl), *n., adj.* —*n.* **1** a fraction like .04 or 4/100, .2 or 2/10; decimal fraction. **2** a number containing a decimal fraction. *Examples:* 75.24, 3.062, .7, .091.
—*adj.* of tens; proceeding by tens: *United States money has a decimal system. The metric system is a decimal system of measurement.* SYN: denary, decadic.
[< Medieval Latin *decimalis* of tithes or tenths < Latin *decima,* feminine of *decimus* tenth]
decimal classification, a system of library classification using numbers and decimals, such as the Dewey decimal system.
decimal fraction, a fraction whose denominator is ten or a multiple of ten, expressed by placing a decimal point to the left of the numerator. *Examples:* .04 = 4/100, .2 = 2/10.
dec|i|mal|ise (des′ə mə līz), *v.t.,* **-ised, -is|ing.** *Especially British.* decimalize.
dec|i|mal|ist (des′ə mə list), *n.* **1** an expert in the use of the decimal system. **2** an exponent of a decimal notation.
dec|i|mal|i|za|tion (des′ə mə lə zā′shən), *n.* a decimalizing; reduction to a decimal system: *A bill for the decimalization of the Union's coinage would also be introduced* (Cape Times).
dec|i|mal|ize (des′ə mə līz), *v.t., v.i.,* **-ized, -iz|ing.** to reduce to a decimal system: *The century-old battle for reform of Britain's currency seemed to be over ... The Government announced that it would drop pounds, shillings, and pence and decimalize* (Anthony Lewis).
dec|i|mal|ly (des′ə mə lē), *adv.* **1** by means of decimals. **2** by tens.
decimal point, a period placed before a fraction expressed in decimal figures, as in 2.03 or .623.
decimal system, **1** any system of numeration which is based on units of ten. **2** = decimal classification.
dec|i|mate (des′ə māt), *v.t.,* **-mat|ed, -mat|ing.** **1** to destroy much of; kill a large part of: *War had decimated the tribe, but the survivors kept on fighting.* **2** to select by lot and execute every tenth man of: *The mutineers were decimated by order of the captain.* **3** to take or destroy one tenth of. **4** *Obsolete.* to take a tenth or tithe from. [< Latin *decimāre* (with English *-ate*[1]) take a tenth < *decimus* tenth < *decem* ten]
dec|i|ma|tion (des′ə mā′shən), *n.* **1** a decimating or being decimated: *If full-scale nuclear war developed, their people and territories would share in the general decimation* (Bulletin of Atomic Scientists). **2** *Obsolete.* **a** the taking of tithes or tenths. **b** the tithe.
dec|i|ma|tor (des′ə mā′tər), *n.* **1** a person or thing that decimates. **2** *Obsolete.* a collector of tithes or tenths.
dé|cime (dā sēm′), *n. French.* a French copper coin equal to 10 centimes or formerly about two cents, no longer used.
dec|i|me|ter (des′ə mē′tər), *n.* a unit of measure of length in the metric system equal to one tenth of a meter, or about 3.937 inches. *Abbr:* dm. [< French *décimètre* < *déci-* deci- + *mètre* meter]
dec|i|me|tre (des′ə mē′tər), *n. Especially British.* decimeter.
dec|i|met|ric (des′ə met′rik), *adj.* **1** having to do with decimeters; measured in decimeters. **2** of or having to do with radio waves ranging from 0.1 to 1 meter in length, or a frequency of 300 to 3000 megahertz: *This magnetosphere is believed to be the source of the decimetric (not to be confused with the dekametric) radio emanations that come from the planet [Jupiter]* (Science News).
dec|i|nor|mal (des′ə nôr′məl), *adj. Chemistry.* in one tenth of its normal strength.
de|ci|pher (di sī′fər), *v.t.* **1** to make out the meaning of (something that is not clear): *I can't decipher this poor handwriting. We just couldn't decipher the mystery.* SYN: interpret, translate, unravel, explain. **2** to change (something in code) into ordinary language; interpret (secret writing) by using a key; decode: *The spy deciphered the secret message.* **3** *Archaic.* to describe; depict.
—**de|ci′pher|er**, *n.*
de|ci|pher|a|ble (di sī′fər ə bəl), *adj.* that can be deciphered: *The form which affairs in Europe may assume is not yet decipherable by those out of the cabinet* (Thomas Jefferson).
de|ci|pher|ment (di sī′fər mənt), *n.* **1** the act of deciphering. **2** something deciphered.
de|ci|sion (di sizh′ən), *n., v.* —*n.* **1** the act of making up one's mind; resolution: *Not knowing which color he would like, I have not come to a decision on what sweater to buy him.* **2a** the deciding or settling of a question or dispute by giving judgment to one side. **b** *Boxing.* the winning of a match on points or by the verdict of the referee and judges, rather than by a knockout: *Carter, appearing in his eleventh title fight ... gained a decision over Smith in Cincinnati in 1950* (New York Times). **3** the judgment reached or given: *The jury brought in a decision of not guilty. In this contest, the decision of the judges is final.* SYN: verdict, decree, order. **4** firmness and determination; being decided: *to act with decision. She is a woman of decision who makes up her mind what to do and then does it.*
—*v.t. Informal, Boxing.* to defeat (an opponent) by a decision: *In his 13th bout Machen decisioned Nino Valdes* (Saturday Evening Post).
[< Latin *dēcīsiō, -ōnis* < *dēcīdere;* see etym. under **decide**]
de|ci|sion|al (di sizh′ə nəl), *adj.* of or having to do with a decision: *The judges work from what is called decisional law—the body of legal theory built up over the years by the state courts deciding similar cases before them* (Harper's).
decision procedure, *Mathematics, Statistics.* a formal method by which any problem expressible in a given formula can be solved in a finite number of steps: *Decision procedures—sometimes called algorithms—are familiar in everyday mathematics. For example, the technique of long division represents a decision procedure for the predicate "x is divisible by y," where x and y can be any natural numbers* (Scientific American).
decision table, a table listing all the conditions of a problem and the possible actions to be taken, used to help make decisions or plans in any system.
decision tree, a diagram in the form of a branching tree representing alternate strategies or methods and the respective values assigned to them, used to help make decisions or plans in any system.
de|ci|sive (di sī′siv), *adj.* **1** having or giving a clear result; settling something beyond question or doubt: *The team won by 20 points, which was a decisive victory. The Battle of Saratoga was a decisive defeat for the British.* SYN: conclusive. **2a** having or showing decision: *When I asked for a decisive answer, he said flatly, "No."* SYN: resolute, determined. **b** calling for a decision or decisions: *a decisive moment.* —**de|ci′sive|ly**, *adv.* —**de|ci′sive|ness**, *n.*
▶See **decided** for usage note.
dec|i|stere (des′ə stir), *n.* a unit of measure of volume in the metric system equal to one tenth of a stere, 1/10 cubic meter, or .1308 cubic yard. [< French *décistère* < *déci-* deci- + *stère* stere]
de|civ|i|li|za|tion (dē siv′ə lə zā′shən), *n.* a decivilizing or being decivilized.
de|civ|i|lize (dē siv′ə līz), *v.t.,* **-lized, -liz|ing.** to reduce or degrade from a civilized condition.
deck (dek), *n., v.* —*n.* **1** one of the floors or platforms extending from side to side and often end to end of a ship. The upper, main, middle, and lower decks of a ship are somewhat like the stories of a house. Often the upper deck has no roof over it. **2** a part or floor resembling this: *the deck of an airplane, a parking deck. On the roof of the porch is a large sundeck.* **3** a pack of playing cards: *He shuffled the deck and dealt the cards.* **4** *Journalism.* a line or lines of a headline set in the same type; bank. **5** the basic mechanical part of a tape recorder, without amplifiers, speakers, or other attachments; tape deck. **6** *U.S. Slang.* a package of heroin, especially a package of three grains.
—*v.t.* **1** to cover, dress, or adorn: *The little girl was decked out in white linen. Deck the halls with boughs of holly* (Christmas carol). SYN: array, attire, clothe. **2** to provide with a deck. **3** *U.S. Slang.* to knock down; floor: *Bonavena struggled up at the count of eight and Ali decked him again* (Time).
clear the deck or **decks**, **a** to remove unnecessary objects from the decks of a warship, to prepare for action: *The sailors cleared the decks for a fight before the pirate ship closed in.* **b** *Figurative.* to make ready for any action: *... to clear the decks for an expected filibuster* (Wall Street Journal).
hit the deck, *U.S. Slang.* **a** to get up from bed: *"Hit the deck, boys!" said the old seaman who awoke us.* **b** to drop on the ground or floor: *When the shots rang out, everyone hit the deck. The contender hit the deck twice in the fifth round.*
on deck, **a** present and ready to do something; on hand: *The coach is sick and won't be on deck for practice for at least one week.* **b** *Baseball.* next at bat. A player on deck usually waits at an assigned spot away from the batter's box.
stack the deck, *Informal.* **a** to arrange a pack of cards dishonestly: *The gambler's deck was stacked with five aces.* **b** *Figurative.* to prepare circumstances in advance: *When [the company] pits a piece of its "New, Super-strength ... Wrap" against "ordinary wrap," it stacks the deck by seeing to it that the "ordinary wrap" is deliberately torn and severely wrinkled* (Time).
[perhaps < Middle Dutch *dec* a roof, cover < *decken* to cover]
deck boy, a person working on the deck of a ship; deck hand.
deck chair, a folding chair with a wooden or canvas seat and arm rests, and sometimes a footrest.
deck|el (dek′əl), *n.* = deckle.
deck|er (dek′ər), *n.* **1** anything with a deck or (a specified number of) decks: *a three-decker sandwich.* **2** a person or thing that decks.
deck hand, a sailor who works on deck, not rated as an able-bodied seaman; common sailor.
deck|head (dek′hed′), *n.* the underside of a deck: *... trapped between rising water and a steel deckhead* (Maclean's).
deck|house (dek′hous′), *n.* a house or room built on the deck of a ship: *The Third Mate emerged from the deckhouse and thumped down his seabag* (Atlantic).
deck|ing (dek′ing), *n.* material used in constructing a deck: *The decking is coated with skid-proof enamel abrasive tread* (Science News Letter).
deck|le (dek′əl), *n.* in papermaking: **1** a device for keeping the pulp from spreading beyond desired limits. A deckle is used to determine the size or width of the sheet. **2** = deckle edge. [< German *Deckel* (diminutive) < *Decke* cover]

deckle edge, 1 the rough edge of untrimmed paper: *The deckle edges are left at the side and bottom, the top edge alone being cut* (Bookseller). 2 an edge made to look like this; an imitation of it.
deck|le-edged (dek′əl ejd′), *adj.* having a deckle edge: *a book bound with deckle-edged paper.*
deck|load (dek′lōd′), *n.* the cargo or load stowed on the deck of a ship: *All I would have to do was step across from our deckload of timber* (Harper's).
deck|o (dek′ō), *n.* = dekko.
deck passage, traveling accommodations on the deck of a ship. It is the cheapest passage obtainable.
deck sport, any sport suitable for or played on the deck of a ship, such as deck tennis.
deck tennis, a game played on a small court, often on the deck of a ship, in which a ring of rope or the like is tossed, caught, and tossed back over the net.
decl., declension.
de|claim (di klām′), *v.i.* 1 to speak like an orator in a loud and emotional manner; speak or write for effect: *Everyone at the table listened as the old soldier declaimed against the lack of patriotism. His eyes and face were wild and he was declaiming, though one could not understand him* (Atlantic). **SYN**: rail, inveigh. 2 to recite in public; make a formal speech. **SYN**: orate. — ***v.t.*** to recite aloud, especially with artificial expression: *He then declaimed the following passage rather with too much than too little emphasis* (Scott). [< Latin *dēclāmāre* < *de-* forth + *clāmāre* to cry, call, shout] —**de|claim′er**, *n.*
dec|la|ma|tion (dek′lə mā′shən), *n.* 1 the act or art of reciting in public; making formal speeches: *That which gave most effect to his declamation was the air of sincerity, of vehement feeling, or moral elevation which belonged to all that he said* (Macaulay). 2 a formal speech or selection of poetry or prose for reciting: *He practiced his long declamation many times before giving it before an audience.* 3 the act of talking loudly and emotionally: *Declamation roar'd, while Passion slept* (Samuel Johnson). 4 loud and emotional talk; a noisy speech. **SYN**: harangue. 5 *Music.* the proper enunciation of words, especially in recitative.
de|clam|a|to|ry (di klam′ə tôr′ē, -tōr′-), *adj.* 1 having to do with declamation. 2 loud and emotional.
de|clar|a|ble (di klar′ə bəl), *adj.* that has to be declared, as for customs.
de|clar|ant (di klãr′ənt), *n. Law.* 1 a person who makes a statement that may thereafter be used as evidence: *The object of requiring the signature of the declarant is to fix liability for false declarations* (London Times). 2 *U.S.* an alien who has signed his first naturalization papers, thus declaring his intention to become a citizen.
dec|la|ra|tion (dek′lə rā′shən), *n.* 1 the act of declaring: *a declaration of love. The king's declaration of war was a signal for the army to begin fighting.* **SYN**: assertion, announcement, avowal. 2 the thing declared; open or public statement: *The royal declaration was announced in every city and town.* 3 the document containing a declaration: *The Declaration of Tehran stated, in part, that the three Allied nations "shall work together in the war and in the peace"* (Payson S. Wild, Jr.). 4 a statement of goods or other property for taxation or customs: *The importer gave the customs agent a declaration showing what merchandise he was bringing into the country.* 5 a very strong statement. 6a a bid in bridge, especially the winning bid. b an announcement of a player's score while playing bezique and other card games; meld. 7 *Cricket.* a tactical decision by one side to close its innings. 8 *Law.* a the formal statement in an action in which a plaintiff first presents his claim and requests judgment. b a simple statement made by a witness instead of an oath. A declaration is subject to the laws of perjury.
Declaration of Independence, the public statement declaring that the American colonies were independent of Great Britain. It was adopted by the Second Continental Congress on July 4, 1776.
declaration of intention, = first papers: *The law no longer requires a person to "take out first papers," or file a declaration of intention to become an American citizen* (Robert Rienow).
Declaration of Rights, = Bill of Rights.
Declaration of the Rights of Man, the preamble to the French constitution of 1789.
de|clar|a|tive (di klar′ə tiv), *adj., n.* —***adj.*** making a statement; explaining. "I am eating" and "The dog has four legs" are declarative sentences. —***n.*** that which declares: *American policy is seldom cast in the harsh declaratives and imperatives favored by the Russians* (Richard H. Rovere). —**de|clar′a|tive|ly**, *adv.*

▶ **Declarative sentences** make statements and total considerably more than nine-tenths of the sentences we write: *That was the most delicious breakfast we had ever tasted. Phaëthon drove the chariot of the sun for a day.*
de|clar|a|tor (di klar′ə tər), *n.* a legal declaration establishing a fact: *... a declarator that tweed hand-woven in the Outer Hebrides but otherwise processed on the Scottish mainland is Harris tweed* (Manchester Guardian Weekly).
de|clar|a|to|ry (di klar′ə tôr′ē, -tōr′-), *adj.* 1 that declares or explains the law or the legal rights of parties in a dispute: *a declaratory act, a declaratory judgment.* 2 = declarative.
de|clare (di klãr′), *v.*, **-clared, -clar|ing.** —***v.t.*** 1 to announce publicly or formally; make known; say; proclaim: *Congress has the power to declare war. The company has just declared a dividend on its stock. Peace was declared at last.* **SYN**: See syn. under **announce**. 2 to say openly or strongly; affirm: *The boy declared that he would never go back to school again. I declare the story to be false.* 3 to reveal; show: *The heavens declare the glory of God* (Psalms 19:1). 4 to make a statement of (goods or property) for taxation or customs: *Travelers returning to the United States must declare the things which they bought abroad.* 5a to announce (what suit will be played as trumps) in bridge. b to announce (the score) during play in bezique and other card games; meld. 6 *Cricket.* to call close of (an innings) before the usual number of wickets have fallen.
—***v.i.*** to make a declaration; proclaim oneself: *The students declared against cheating.*
declare oneself, to declare love to another person; propose: *He was told either to declare himself or to stop courting the girl.*
I declare! an exclamation of surprise or pleasure.
[< Latin *dēclārāre* make evident or clear < *dē-* (intensive) + *clārāre* make clear < *clārus* clear]
—***Syn.*** ***v.t.*** 2 **Declare, assert** mean to say positively. **Declare** means to state firmly and openly, sometimes in spite of possible contradictions: *The Continental Congress declared that the colonies were free and independent. The weather bureau declares that the rain will stop by morning.* **Assert** means to state vigorously, usually without proof and sometimes in spite of proof that one is wrong, but often because one believes he is right: *You assert that you were not there, but ten people saw you.*
de|clared (di klãrd′), *adj.* publicly or formally made known; avowed; professed.
de|clar|ed|ly (di klãr′id lē), *adv.* with formal declaration; professedly; avowedly.
de|clar|er (di klãr′ər), *n.* 1 a person or thing that exhibits, sets forth, or makes known. 2 a person who makes or signs a declaration. 3 a person who declares at bridge, bezique, and other card games: *The four quick tricks in dummy were a mixed consolation to Kaplan, the declarer* (Observer).
de|class (dē klas′, -kläs′), *v.t.* to remove or degrade from one's class; cause to lose standing: *The Beats have some collateral relationships to working-class life (they appropriate its décor in any event) but, fundamentally, they are declassed* (Saturday Review).
dé|clas|sé (dā klä sā′), *adj., n. French.* —***adj.*** degraded from one's class in society; declassed: *He was ... the déclassé son of a solid middle-class family* (Hannah Arendt).
—***n.*** a declassed person.
dé|clas|sée (dā klä sā′), *adj., n. French.* the feminine form of **déclassé**: *In no way are they déclassées. They move without prejudice in the highest circles* (Hamilton Basso).
de|clas|si|fi|a|ble (dē klas′ə fī′ə bəl), *adj.* that can be declassified; subject to declassification: *It is imperative that information not be just declassifiable but positively unclassified ...* (Wall Street Journal).
de|clas|si|fi|ca|tion (dē klas′ə fə kā′shən), *n.* 1 the act or process of declassifying: *The declassification of nuclear knowledge had, indeed, been continuous* (London Times). 2 the material declassified.
de|clas|si|fy (dē klas′ə fī), *v.t.*, **-fied, -fy|ing.** to remove (documents, codes, or other material or undertakings) from the list of restricted, confidential, or secret information: *Important sectors like thermonuclear research have not been declassified* (Bulletin of Atomic Scientists).
de|clen|sion (di klen′shən), *n.* 1 *Grammar.* a the giving of the different endings or forms to nouns, pronouns, and adjectives according to their case, number, and gender, or their relation to other words in the sentence. **SYN**: inflection. b the giving of variant forms of a word for case only. The declension of *who* is: nominative case, *who;* possessive case, *whose;* objective case, *whom.* c all such forms of a word written or recited in a given order. d a group of words whose endings for the different cases, number, or gender, are alike: *Latin nouns are usually grouped in five declensions.* 2 a downward movement, bend, or slope: *the declension of the sun toward the west.* **SYN**: incline, declination, declivity, dip. 3 *Figurative.* a sinking into a lower or inferior condition; decline. **SYN**: deterioration, decadence, degeneration. 4 *Figurative.* a turning away (from one's religion, faith, or other beliefs); deviation from a standard. **SYN**: defection. 5 a polite refusal. [perhaps < Old French *déclinaison,* learned borrowing from *dēclīnātiō, -ōnis* < *dēclīnāre;* see etym. under **decline**]
de|clen|sion|al (di klen′shə nəl), *adj.* of or belonging to declension.
de|clin|a|ble (di klī′nə bəl), *adj.* 1 *Grammar.* that can be given in different cases; that has different forms for its different cases. 2 that can be refused or declined.
dec|li|nate (dek′lə nit), *adj. Botany, Zoology.* bent or bending downward or aside.
***dec|li|na|tion** (dek′lə nā′shən), *n.* 1 a downward bend or slope. **SYN**: declension. 2 a polite refusal: *I mailed our declination for the tea.* 3a the deviation of the needle of a compass from true north or south. b the angular measure of this deviation; variation. 4 *Astronomy.* the angular distance of a star, planet, etc., from the celestial equator. The declination of a star is used to locate its north or south position in the heavens: *The declination of a star is similar to geographical latitude and is given in degrees* (Bernhard, Bennett, and Rice). *Symbol:* δ 5 a turning aside or a deviating from a standard. 6 *Obsolete.* decline; decay.

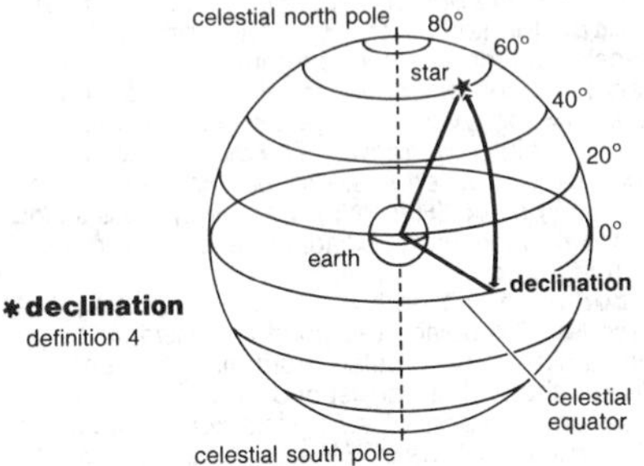

***declination** definition 4

de|clin|a|to|ry (di klī′nə tôr′ē, -tōr′-), *adj.* 1 expressing or suggesting declination. 2 expressing refusal.
de|clin|a|ture (di klī′nə chər), *n.* the act of declining; polite refusal.
de|cline (di klīn′), *v.*, **-clined, -clin|ing,** *n.* —***v.t.*** 1 to turn away from doing; refuse (to do something): *The boy declined to do what he was told.* **SYN**: reject. See syn. under **refuse**. 2 to refuse politely: *I have to decline your invitation because Mother expects me at home now. He declined my offer of help.* 3 to cause to bend or slope down. 4 *Grammar.* to give the different cases or case endings of (a noun, pronoun, or adjective); inflect. See also **declension**, def. 1.
—***v.i.*** 1 to refuse something politely. 2 *Figurative.* to grow less in power, strength, wealth, or beauty; grow worse; decay: *Great nations have risen and declined. A man's strength declines as he grows old.* **SYN**: deteriorate, degenerate. 3 to bend or slope down: *The hill declines to a fertile valley.* 4 *Figurative.* to draw toward the close: *The day declines early during the winter.* 5 to stoop, especially to something unworthy. 6 *Obsolete.* to turn aside; deviate.
—***n.*** 1 a falling to a lower level; sinking: *a decline in prices, the decline of the sun to the horizon.* 2 *Figurative.* a losing of power, strength, wealth, or beauty; growing worse: *the decline of the Roman Empire. The old man's decline was apparent in his halting walk. In the decline of the ancient world it was saints rather than sages who were needed* (Edmund Wilson). **SYN**: decay, deterioration, diminution. 3 the last part of anything: *He grew old and weak in the decline of his life.* 4 a wasting disease; consumption; tuberculosis of the lungs. 5 a downward incline or slope: *The wagon rolled down the decline.* **SYN**: declivity. [< Latin *dēclīnāre* < *dē-* from + *clīnāre* to bend]
de|clin|er (di klī′nər), *n.* a person who declines.
de|clin|ing balance (di klī′ning), a system of depreciating property at an accelerated rate, by applying an increased percentage of yearly de-

preciation to the unamortized balance rather than to the original cost.

dec|li|nom|e|ter (dek′lə nom′ə tər), *n.* an instrument for measuring magnetic declination. [< *declin*(ation) + *-meter*]

de|cliv|i|tous (di kliv′ə təs), *adj.* considerably steep: *There was a dangerous shower stall with a declivitous floor* (New Yorker).

de|cliv|i|ty (di kliv′ə tē), *n., pl.* **-ties.** a downward slope: *The declivity of the mountain pass was so steep that even the mules had difficulty.* SYN: descent, inclination, gradient. [< Latin *dēclīvitās* < *dēclīvis* sloping downward < *dē-* down + *clīvus* slope]

de|cli|vous (di klī′vəs), *adj.* sloping downward.

Dec|lo|my|cin (dek′lō mī′sin), *n. Trademark.* a drug used to check or kill bacteria and viruses. It is an antibiotic of the tetracycline group, related to Aureomycin. *Formula:* $C_{21}H_{21}ClN_2O_8$

de|clutch (dē kluch′), *v.t., v.i.* to disengage (a clutch): *There's a control lever that allows the machine's pulling power to be stepped up without the driver having to declutch, shift gears, or touch the throttle* (Wall Street Journal).

de|coct (di kokt′), *v.t.* **1** to extract desired substances from (something) by boiling. **2** *Obsolete.* to boil down; boil; cook. [< Latin *dēcoctus,* past participle of *dēcoquere* < *dē-* away + *coquere* to cook]

de|coc|tion (di kok′shən), *n.* **1** the act of boiling to extract some desired substance. **2** a preparation made by boiling a substance in water or other liquid; extract obtained by boiling: *They had drunk a decoction prescribed by a native doctor who claimed that those who drank it while the eclipse was on would become younger* (London Times).

de|code (dē kōd′), *v.t.,* **-cod|ed, -cod|ing. 1** to translate (secret or coded information) into ordinary language or understandable form; decipher: *Hittite hieroglyphics . . . are being decoded* (Newsweek). (*Figurative.*) *The plot needs to be decoded and when it is, not much seems . . . to be taking place* (Harper's). **2** to apply the spelling-sound relationship to (reading), especially in the learning process.

de|cod|er (dē kō′dər), *n.* **1** a person or thing that decodes. **2** a device designed to unscramble mixed signals or to select from many electronic signals those that correspond to the result of a situation: *The scrambled signals would produce a blur on the screens of TV sets not equipped with a decoder* (Science News Letter). *Transmitted signals will be picked up by a special decoder on each light that selects only the signals meant for its own intersection* (Wall Street Journal).

de|co|here (dē′kō hir′), *v.t., v.i.,* **-hered, -her|ing.** *Electricity.* to return to normal condition of sensitiveness; restore by means of a decoherer.

de|co|her|ence (dē′kō hir′əns), *n. Electricity.* decohering action.

de|co|her|er (dē′kō hir′ər), *n. Electricity.* a device for restoring a coherer to normal condition after it has been affected by an electric wave.

de|co|he|sion (dē′kō hē′zhən), *n. Electricity.* **1** the act of decohering. **2** the effect of decoherence.

de|col|late (di kol′āt), *v.t.,* **-lat|ed, -lat|ing.** to remove the head of; behead. [< Latin *dēcollāre* (with English *-ate*[1]) < *dē-* down from + *collum* neck]

de|col|la|tion (dē′kə lā′shən), *n.* **1** the act of decollating; beheading. **2** the fact of being beheaded.

de|col|la|tor (dē′kə lā′tər), *n.* a person who decollates; headsman.

de|col|lec|ti|vi|za|tion (dē′kə lek′tə və zā′shən), *n.* **1** the act or process of decollectivizing. **2** that which has been decollectivized, as a farm group.

de|col|lec|ti|vize (dē′kə lek′tə vīz), *v.t.,* **-ized, -iz|ing.** to remove from collective management: *Peasant families nibbled at the state farms, decollectivized an estimated six million acres* (Time).

dé|colle|tage (dā′kol täzh′, -ko lə-; dek′lə-), *n.* **1** the neck of a dress cut low so as to leave the neck and shoulders exposed: *Décolletage has probably caused less stir than almost any facet of women's clothing* (Newsweek). **2** a dress or blouse cut in this way. [< French *décolletage* < *décolleté;* see etym. under **décolleté**]

dé|colle|té (dā′kol tā′, -ko lə-; dek′lə), *adj.* **1** = low-necked. **2** wearing a low-necked dress or blouse. [< French *décolleté,* past participle of Old French *decolleter* bare the neck]

de|col|o|ni|za|tion (dē kol′ə nə zā′shən), *n.* **1** the act or process of decolonizing: *In much of Africa south of the Sahara, decolonization is now in full swing* (Newsweek). **2** that which has been decolonized.

de|col|o|nize (dē kol′ə nīz), *v.,* **-nized, -niz|ing.** —*v.t.* **1** to establish as a self-governing area; remove from colonial status: *Having achieved political freedom, most African states face the problem of decolonizing their economics* (Atlantic). **2** to deprive of a colony or colonies.

—*v.i.* to divest itself of a colony or colonies: *My country [Spain] is the only one in the world which, while it is decolonizing, is itself the victim of colonialism* (Fernando Castiella y Maiz). —**de-col′o|niz′er,** *n.*

de|col|or (dē kul′ər), *v.t.* to remove the color of; bleach; decolorize. Also, *British,* **decolour.**

de|col|or|ant (dē kul′ər ənt), *n., adj.* —*n.* a substance that bleaches or removes color.

—*adj.* that can remove color; bleaching.

de|col|or|a|tion (dē′kul ə rā′shən), *n.* **1** loss of color. **2** *Obsolete.* discoloration.

de|col|or|i|za|tion (dē kul′ər ə zā′shən), *n.* the act of depriving of color.

de|col|or|ize (dē kul′ə rīz), *v.t.,* **-ized, -iz|ing.** = decolor.

de|col|or|iz|er (dē kul′ə rī′zər), *n.* an agent that decolorizes, such as alcohol, acetic acid, and glycerine.

de|col|our (dē kul′ər), *v.t. Especially British.* decolor.

de|com|mer|cial|ise (dē′kə mėr′shə līz), *v.t.,* **-ised, -is|ing.** *Especially British.* decommercialize.

de|com|mer|cial|i|za|tion (dē′kə mėr′shə lə-zā′shən), *n.* the act or process of decommercializing: *. . . the decommercialization of pharmacies, whereby the pharmacist would be prohibited from selling nonpharmaceutical goods* (London Times).

de|com|mer|cial|ize (dē′kə mėr′shə līz), *v.t.,* **-ized, -iz|ing.** to stop the commercialization of; remove the methods and spirit of commerce from (an institution, industry, or activity): *a crusade to decommercialize Christmas* (New Yorker).

de|com|mis|sion (dē′kə mish′ən), *v.t.* **1** to take out of active service; retire: *A short simple ceremony today decommissioned a great fighting ship—the battleship Missouri* (New York Times). **2** to deprive of one's commission: *to decommission an officer.*

de|com|mu|ni|za|tion (dē kom′yə nə zā′shən), *n.* the act or process of decommunizing: *. . . a recent partial decommunization of agriculture [in China] to give peasants incentive to labor once again for good crops* (Wall Street Journal).

de|com|mu|nize (dē kom′yə nīz), *v.t.,* **-nized, -niz|ing.** to undo the communization of; remove the methods and practices of communism from (an industry, society, or institution): *The Red-directed General Federation of Labor called the strike to protest [against] a bill designed to decommunize the printing trades* (New York Times).

de|com|part|men|tal|i|za|tion (dē kom′pärt-men′tə lə zā′shən), *n.* the act or process of decompartmentalizing: *The Renaissance was a period of decompartmentalization: a period which broke down the barriers which had kept things in order* (Erwin Panofsky).

de|com|part|men|tal|ize (dē kom′pärt men′-təlīz), *v.t.,* **-ized, -iz|ing.** to undo the compartmentalization of; free of boundaries, divisions, categories, or the like: *To make Germany an operating concern . . . Germany had to be decompartmentalized and the zones abolished* (Theodore H. White).

de|com|pen|sate (dē kom′pən sāt), *v.i.,* **-sat|ed, -sat|ing.** to suffer from decompensation.

de|com|pen|sa|tion (dē kom′pən sā′shən), *n.* **1** *Medicine.* failure of the heart to maintain normal circulation because of a loss in its ability to compensate for a defect. **2** *Psychology.* loss of the ability or desire to compensate for some inadequacy; loss of compensation: *She had . . . symptoms of hysteria and a tendency to decompensation* (Manchester Guardian Weekly).

de|com|plex (dē′kəm pleks′), *adj.* **1** compounded of parts that are themselves complex. **2** repeatedly complex.

de|com|pos|a|bil|i|ty (dē′kəm pō′zə bil′ə tē), *n.* decomposable quality or property.

de|com|pos|a|ble (dē′kəm pō′zə bəl), *adj.* that can be decomposed: *The major energy sources comprising all forms of decomposable carbon compounds are present* (New Scientist).

de|com|pose (dē′kəm pōz′), *v.,* **-posed, -pos-ing.** —*v.i.* **1** (of a substance) to become separated into its parts. **2** to become rotten; decay: *The old fruits and vegetables decomposed quickly in the heat.* SYN: See syn. under **decay.**

—*v.t.* **1** to separate (a substance) into what it is made of: *A prism decomposes sunlight into its various colors. Most nonmetal chlorides are decomposed by water—some violently so* (J. Crowther). **2** to rot; decay.

de|com|pos|er (dē′kəm pō′zər), *n.* something that decomposes; decomposing agent.

de|com|pos|ite (dē′kəm poz′it, di kom′pə zit), *adj., n.* —*adj.* **1** compounded more than once. **2** compounded of things already composite; decompound: *a decomposite leaf.*

—*n.* anything compounded of composite things.

de|com|po|si|tion (dē′kom pə zish′ən), *n.* **1** the act or process of decomposing: *the decomposition of water into hydrogen and oxygen.* SYN: breakup, disintegration. **2** decay; rot: *fruit spoiled by decomposition.*

de|com|pound (dē′kəm pound′), *v., adj., n.* —*v.t.* **1** to compound a second time; compound further; compound (something already compounded). **2** = decompose.

—*adj.* composed of things already compounded: *A decompound leaf is one whose petiole has additional petioles, each one supporting a compound leaf.*

—*n.* something that is decompound.

de|com|press (dē′kəm pres′), *v.t.* **1** to remove pressure from. **2** to lessen the pressure of air on: *When the diver comes to the surface, however, he must be decompressed slowly* (Time).

de|com|pres|sion (dē′kəm presh′ən), *n.* the removal or lessening of pressure, especially of air pressure: *to undergo decompression in an airlock. Gradual decompression is necessary for deep-sea divers as they are brought to the surface.*

decompression chamber, an airtight compartment in which a person working under abnormal air pressure is gradually readjusted to normal atmospheric pressure. Decompression chambers are also used to accustom flyers to low pressures encountered in high-altitude flying.

decompression sickness, sickness that is a result of changing too suddenly from abnormal air pressure to ordinary air pressure; caisson disease. *High-altitude flights in jet planes may be dangerous for fat people, it appears from two fatal cases of decompression sickness in jet plane flights reported to the Aero Medical Association in Washington* (Science News Letter).

de|con|cen|trate (dē kon′sən trāt), *v.t.,* **-trat|ed, -trat|ing.** to break up the concentration of; decentralize: *to deconcentrate a compound in a solution. Under post-war Allied control, the great Ruhr coal and steel trusts were deconcentrated* (Wall Street Journal).

de|con|cen|tra|tion (dē kon′sən trā′shən), *n.* **1** a deconcentrating or being deconcentrated: *Some families . . . weathered the storm of deconcentration, and still control large business organizations* (Manchester Guardian). **2** that which is deconcentrated.

de|con|di|tion (dē′kən dish′ən), *v.t.* **1** to remove a conditioned response or responses from: *The best way to decondition his animals was to . . . remove them completely from the scene of conditioning* (Science News Letter). **2** to cause to deteriorate in physical condition: *. . . the deconditioning phenomena of bed rest* (Howard A. Rusk).

de|con|gest (dē′kən jest′), *v.t.* to free from congestion; eliminate congestion in: *To decongest London . . . , the administrative capital should be shifted bodily to a British Brasilia, somewhere between York and Harrogate* (Annual Register).

de|con|ges|tant (dē′kən jes′tənt), *n.* something used to eliminate or relieve congestion.

de|con|ges|tion (dē′kən jes′chən), *n.* the act or process of decongesting or the condition of being decongested: *These same cities are . . . faced with urban decongestion; people are moving out of town* (Wall Street Journal).

de|con|ges|tive (dē′kən jes′tiv), *adj.* lessening congestion: *The decongestive effect of a drug.*

de|con|se|crate (dē kon′sə krāt), *v.t.,* **-crat|ed, -crat|ing. 1** to undo the consecration of. **2** deprive of sacred character: *deconsecrated cathedrals.*

de|con|se|cra|tion (dē kon′sə krā′shən), *n.* **1** the act or ceremony of deconsecrating. **2** that which is deconsecrated.

de|con|sid|er (dē′kən sid′ər), *v.t.* to deprive of consideration; discredit.

de|con|sid|er|a|tion (dē′kən sid′ə rā′shən), *n.* the act or process of deconsidering.

de|con|struc|tion (dē′kən struk′shən), *n.* a method of literary criticism, applied especially to poetry, in which the text is reduced to its basic linguistic and semantic elements. *He [Harold Bloom] makes the refreshing suggestion that his exemplary American texts will prove resistant to deconstruction . . . because both criticism and poetry "in the American grain" affirm "the self over language"* (New York Times Book Review). —**de′-con|struc′tion|ist,** *n.*

de|con|struc|tiv|ism (dē′kən struk′tə viz əm), *n.* a movement in modern architecture that seeks to change conventional ways of perceiving form and space by producing buildings of sharp, clashing angles, skewed shapes, and incomplete forms.

de|con|tam|i|nant (dē′kən tam′ə nənt), *n.* anything used to eliminate or check contamination.

de|con|tam|i|nate (dē′kən tam′ə nāt), *v.t.,* **-nat-ed, -nat|ing. 1** to make free from poison gas or harmful radioactive agents: *The reactor had to be extensively decontaminated and reconstructed* (Science). **2** to free from any sort of contamination. **3** to remove the secret or sensitive parts of (a classified document) to make its publication harmless: *It was only when Secretary of Defense*

Laird refused to decontaminate and declassify the documents for the Foreign Relations Committee that men who had worked on the papers and reporters who had heard about them set out to expose the blunders and the cover-up (James Reston).

de·con·tam·i·na·tion (dē′kən tam′ə nā′shən), *n.* the act or process of decontaminating: *Prompt decontamination measures were important factors in reducing the incidence and severity of the external symptoms* (New York Times).

de·con·trol (dē′kən trōl′), *v.*, **-trolled, -trol·ling,** *n.* —***v.t.*** to remove controls from: *to decontrol rents.*
—***n.*** a removal of controls: . . . *a formula for automatic decontrol at certain price levels* (Newsweek).

de·con·trol·ler (dē′kən trō′lər), *n.* a person or thing that decontrols: *The government handed decontrollers orders to fix the prices of steel stock at levels that guarantee no dramatic loss for the nation's exchequer* (Wall Street Journal).

dé·cor or **de·cor** (dā kôr′), *n.* **1** = decoration. **2a** the arrangement of furnishings in a room, store, lobby, or other area, especially in a building. **b** the scenery on a stage: *Some of the costumes are attractive, but the décor . . . is uneven in style and invention* (London Times). [< Middle French *décor* < *décorer* to ornament, learned borrowing from Latin *decorāre;* see etym. under **decorate**]

dec·o·rate (dek′ə rāt), *v.t.*, **-rat·ed, -rat·ing. 1** to make beautiful; trim; adorn: *We decorated the Christmas tree with shining balls.* **2** to paint or paper (a room, house, or other area): *The old rooms looked like new after they had been decorated.* **3** to give a badge, ribbon, or medal to (a person) as an honor: *The general decorated the soldier for his brave act.* [< Latin *decorāre* (with English *-ate*[1]) < *decus, -oris* adornment < *decēre* be fitting, suitable. Compare etym. under **decent.**]
—***Syn.* 1 Decorate, ornament, adorn** mean to add something to give or increase beauty. **Decorate** means to trim with flowers, ornaments, or other trimmings to add color, variety, or a festive appearance: *We decorated the church with lilies for Easter.* **Ornament** suggests adding, often permanently, something which especially suits a thing and adds to its general effect and beauty: *Stained-glass windows ornament the church.* **Adorn** suggests adding something which is beautiful itself and therefore increases the beauty of a thing or person: *She adorned her hair with flowers.*

dec·o·rat·ed (dek′ə rā′tid), *adj.* **1** ornamented; adorned: *a brightly decorated birthday cake.* **2** *Architecture.* having to do with the decorated style.

decorated style, the Gothic style of architecture prevailing in England throughout most of the 1300's, characterized by more elaborate patterns in window tracery, moldings, and other features than in the preceding period.

dec·o·ra·tion (dek′ə rā′shən), *n.* **1** a thing used to decorate; ornament: *We put pictures and other decorations up in the classroom.* **SYN:** embellishment. **2** a badge, ribbon, or medal given as an honor: *The sailor's decorations showed that he had seen much active service.* **3** the act or process of decorating: *Decoration of the room took most of the day before the spring festival.* **SYN:** adornment.

Decoration Day, = Memorial Day.

dec·o·ra·tive (dek′ə rā′tiv, dek′rə-), *adj.* decorating; ornamental; helping to make beautiful: *The colored paper chains gave a decorative effect to the room. The ballet . . . offers great scope to the writer of decorative music* (New Yorker). **—dec′o·ra′tive·ly,** *adv.* **—dec′o·ra′tive·ness,** *n.*

decorative arts, the art of decorating with ornamental objects or the skill of decorating objects with ornamental designs. The decorative arts include carving, ceramics, and interior decoration.

dec·o·ra·tor (dek′ə rā′tər), *n.* **1** a person who decorates. **2** a person who plans and arranges the furnishings and color schemes of homes, offices, clubs, and other rooms and buildings; interior decorator. **3** a person whose work is painting or papering rooms.

decorator color or **shade,** any unconventional or radically new color or shade, especially one used in experimental or futuristic interior decoration.

dec·o·rous (dek′ər əs; di kôr′-, -kōr′-), *adj.* acting properly; in good taste; well-behaved; dignified: *Quiet, decorous behavior is requested in the library.* **SYN:** proper, appropriate, fit. [< Latin *decōrus* (with English *-ous*) < *decor, -ōris* seemliness, comeliness < *decēre* be seemly, fitting, suitable] **—dec′o·rous·ly,** *adv.* **—dec′o·rous·ness,** *n.*

de·cor·ti·cate (dē kôr′tə kāt), *v.*, **-cat·ed, -cat·ing,** *adj.* —***v.t.* 1a** to remove the bark, husk, or outer covering from; peel. **b** to remove the cortex from. **2** *Figurative.* to expose; criticize severely.
—***adj.* 1** without an outer covering; stripped, peeled, or husked. **2** having the cortex removed; decorticated.
[< Latin *decorticāre* (with English *-ate*[1]) < *dē-* from + *cortex, -icis* bark]

de·cor·ti·ca·tion (dē kôr′tə kā′shən), *n.* the act or process of decorticating.

de·cor·ti·ca·tor (dē kôr′tə kā′tər), *n.* **1** a person or thing that decorticates. **2** a machine or instrument for decorticating.

de·co·rum (di kôr′əm, -kōr′-), *n.* **1** *no pl.* proper behavior; good taste in conduct, speech, or dress: *You behave with decorum when you act politely.* **SYN:** respectability. **2** *often pl.* an observance or requirement of polite society: *The girl's mother had taught her to observe all the little decorums that mark a lady.* [< Latin *decōrum* (that which is) seemly < *decor, -ōris* seemliness < *decēre* be seemly]

de·cou·page or **dé·cou·page** (dā′kü päzh′), *n., v.*, **-paged, -pag·ing.** —***n.* 1** a picture made by pasting paper cutouts together. **2** the art of making such pictures.
—***v.t.*** to decorate with decoupages.
[< French *découpage* < *decouper* cut out]

de·cou·ple (di kup′əl), *v.*, **-pled, -pling.** —***v.t.* 1** to separate or split up: . . . America was *"decoupling" its own defense from that of NATO* (New York Times). **2** to reduce the shock waves of (a nuclear explosion) by detonating underground.
—***v.i.* 1** to become separated; split up. **2** to eliminate the dependence of one country upon another, especially of a developing country upon an industrialized one.

de·coy (*v.* di koi′; *n.* dē′koi, di koi′), *v., n.* —***v.t.* 1** to lead (wild birds or animals) into a trap or near a hunter: *The farmer decoyed the rats with cheese.* **2** *Figurative.* to lead or tempt (a person) into danger by trickery; entice: *You cannot decoy us into the prison camp* (New York Times). **SYN:** allure, inveigle. —***v.i.*** to be decoyed.
[< noun]
—***n.* 1** an artificial bird used to lure birds into a trap or near a hunter: *The duck hunter floated decoys on the water.* **2** a bird or other animal trained to lure others of its kind into a trap. **3** *Figurative.* any person or thing used to lead or tempt into danger; lure. **SYN:** bait. **4** a place into which wild birds or animals are lured.
[earlier *coy,* perhaps < Dutch (*de*) *koye* (the) cage < Latin *cavea* cave] **—de·coy′er,** *n.*

decoy duck, 1 a duck, or an imitation of one, used as a decoy. **2** *Figurative.* a person who entices another into a trap or danger.

de·crease (*v.* di krēs′; *n.* dē′krēs, di krēs′), *v.*, **-creased, -creas·ing,** *n.* —***v.i.*** to grow or become less; lessen: *Hunger decreases as one eats.*
—***v.t.*** to make less; lessen: *to decrease prices. Decrease the dose of medicine as you feel better.*
—***n.* 1** a growing or becoming less: *Toward night there was a decrease in heat.* **SYN:** lessening, abatement. **2** the amount by which a thing becomes or is made less: *The decrease in heat was ten degrees.* **SYN:** reduction, loss.
on the decrease, decreasing: *Travel by railroad has been on the decrease since World War II largely because of the speed of air travel.*
[< Old French *descreiss-,* stem of *descreistre* < Latin *dēcrēscere* < *dē-* down + *crēscere* grow < *creāre* make, beget]
—***Syn.* *v.i., v.t.* Decrease, diminish, dwindle** mean to become or make less. **Decrease** suggests steadily going down little by little: *The rainfall is decreasing.* **Diminish** suggests becoming smaller in size, amount, or importance because someone or something keeps taking away a part: *The medical bills during my long sickness have diminished my savings.* **Dwindle** emphasizes the idea of wasting away, of becoming smaller until nothing is left: *Our supplies dwindled.*

de·creas·ing (di krē′sing), *adj.* becoming less; diminishing; lessening. **—de·creas′ing·ly,** *adv.*

de·cree (di krē′), *n., v.*, **-creed, -cree·ing.** —***n.* 1** something ordered or settled by authority; official decision: *The condemned man was pardoned by a decree of the Governor.* **SYN:** proclamation, fiat, ordinance. **2** *Law.* a decision or order of a court or judge. **SYN:** mandate. **3** *Ecclesiastical.* a law of a church council, especially one settling a disputed point of doctrine or discipline. **SYN:** decretal. **4** *Theology.* one of the eternal purposes of God whereby events are foreordained.
—***v.t.*** to order or settle by authority: *The city government decreed that all dogs must be licensed. Fate decreed that Ulysses should travel long and far.* **SYN:** decide, determine, enact, ordain.
—***v.i.*** to decide; determine: *God decrees; man agrees.*
[< Old French *decre,* variant of *decret,* ultimately < Latin *dēcernere* to decide < *dē-* from + *cernere* decide]

de·cree·a·ble (di krē′ə bəl), *adj.* that can be decreed.

de·cree-law (di krē′lô′), *n.* a decree which has or is given the force of a law. *A decree-law, which went into effect at midnight, forbade the export of all capital from France* (New York Times).

decree ni·si (nī′sī), *Law.* a conditional decree of divorce, which becomes final later.

de·cre·er (di krē′ər), *n.* a person who decrees.

dec·re·ment (dek′rə mənt), *n., v.* —***n.* 1** a growing gradually less; slow loss; decrease. **SYN:** diminution. **2** the amount lost by growing gradually less. **3** *Mathematics.* the amount by which the value of a variable decreases.
—***v.t.*** to show a decrease in or on: *Apart from becoming one of the main instruments to identify us electronically to the banking system, they* [*bank cards*] *may also be used as a sort of portable bank account. In this case it will be the card itself, not the account held at the bank's computer centre, which is decremented as we make our payments* (New Scientist).
[< Latin *dēcrēmentum* < *dēcrēscere;* see etym. at **decrease.** Compare etym. at **increment.**]

de·crep·id (di krep′id), *adj.* an obsolete spelling of **decrepit.**

de·crep·it (di krep′it), *adj.* **1** broken down or weakened by old age; old and feeble: *He was too decrepit to climb the stairs.* **SYN:** infirm, wasted. See syn. under **weak. 2** *Figurative.* worn or broken down from use. **SYN:** infirm, wasted. See syn. under **weak.** [< Latin *dēcrepitus* broken down < *dē-* down + *crepāre* rattle, creak, crack] **—de·crep′it·ly,** *adv.*

de·crep·i·tate (di krep′ə tāt), *v.*, **-tat·ed, -tat·ing.**
—***v.t.*** to roast or calcine (a salt or mineral) so as to cause crackling or until crackling stops.
—***v.i.*** (of salts and minerals) to make a crackling noise when roasting.

de·crep·i·ta·tion (di krep′ə tā′shən), *n.* **1** the calcining of a salt or mineral until it ceases to crackle with the heat. **2** the crackling and disintegration of a salt or mineral when exposed to sudden heat.

de·crep·i·tude (di krep′ə tüd, -tyüd), *n.* feebleness, usually from old age; decrepit condition; weakness.

decresc. or **decres.,** decrescendo.

de·cres·cence (di kres′əns), *n.* a waning state or condition.

de·cre·scen·do (dē′krə shen′dō, dā′-), *n., pl.* **-dos,** *adj., adv.* —***n.* 1** a gradual decrease in force or loudness; diminuendo. **2** a passage to be played or sung in this way.
—***adj., adv.*** with a gradual decrease in force or loudness; diminuendo.
[< Italian *decrescendo,* gerund of *decrescere* < Latin *dēcrēscere;* see etym. under **decrease**]

de·cres·cent (di kres′ənt), *adj.* decreasing; growing gradually less; waning: *a decrescent moon.*

de·cre·tal (di krē′təl), *n., adj.* —***n.* 1** a decree or reply by the pope settling some question of doctrine or ecclesiastical law: *Justice was administered in the name and according to the decretals of Rome* (Lew Wallace). **2** any decree.
—***adj.*** of or containing a decree or decrees.
[< Medieval Latin *decretale* < Latin *dēcrētālis* of or having a decree < *dēcernere;* see etym. under **decree**]

de·cre·tal·ist (di krē′tə list), *n.* an expert in the Decretals.

De·cre·tals (di krē′təlz), *n.pl.* a collection of decrees by the pope forming a part of canon law.

de·cre·tist (di krē′tist), *n.* an expert in canon law.

de·cre·tive (di krē′tiv), *adj.* = decretory. **—de·cre′tive·ly,** *adv.*

dec·re·to·ry (dek′rə tôr′ē, -tōr′-; *especially British* di krē′tər ē), *adj.* having to do with or like a decree; definitive; decisive.

de·cri·al (di krī′əl), *n.* the act of decrying.

de·cri·er (di krī′ər), *n.* a person who decries.

de·crim·i·nal·i·za·tion (dē krim′ə nə lə zā′shən), *n.* the act or process of decriminalizing: *The Swedish report . . . recommending decriminalization of pornography was followed by legislation implementing the proposal* (William D. Hawkland).

de·crim·i·nal·ize (dē krim′ə nə līz), *v.t.*, **-ized, -iz·ing.** to declare not criminal; legalize (something previously treated as a crime or offense): *to decriminalize gambling.*

de·cruit (dē krüt′), *v.t. U.S.* to place (an older or unneeded employee) in a lower-level position.
[< *de-* + (re)*cruit*]

de·cry (di krī′), *v.t.*, **-cried, -cry·ing. 1** to express strong disapproval of; condemn; cry out against: *From his pulpit the minister decried all forms of gambling.* **SYN:** denounce. **2** to make little of; try to lower the value of by slighting statements: *The librarian decried television as the only*

Pronunciation Key: hat, āge, cāre, fär; let, ēqual, tėrm; it, īce; hot, ōpen, ôrder; oil, out; cup, pu̇t, rüle; child; long; thin; ᴛʜen; zh, measure; ə represents **a** in about, **e** in taken, **i** in pencil, **o** in lemon, **u** in circus.

source of entertainment. The lumber dealer decried the use of concrete for houses. SYN: disparage. [< French *decrier* < *de-* out (< Latin *dis-*) + *crier* to cry < Latin *quirītāre*]

de|crypt (dē kript′, di-), *v.t.* to decode (a cryptogram).

de|cu|bi|tus (di kyü′bə təs), *n.* **1** the position assumed by the body when lying down. **2** = bedsore. [< New Latin *decubitus* < Latin *dēcumbere* lie down; see etym. under **decumbent**]

decubitus ulcer, = bedsore.

dec|u|man (dek′yu̇ mən), *adj.* **1** very large; immense: *decuman waves.* **2** (in Roman history) having to do with the tenth cohort of a legion (used especially of the main gate of a fortified camp, the primary defense of which was the responsibility of the tenth cohort). [< Latin *decumānus*, variant of *decimānus* of a tenth < *decimus* tenth < *decem* ten (because of the belief that every tenth wave was larger)]

de|cum|bence (di kum′bəns), *n.* a decumbent condition or position.

de|cum|ben|cy (di kum′bən sē), *n.* = decumbence.

de|cum|bent (di kum′bənt), *adj.* **1** *Botany.* lying or trailing on the ground with the end tending to climb: *decumbent stems or branches.* **2** lying down; reclining. [< Latin *dēcumbēns, -entis*, present participle of *dēcumbere* lie down < *dē-* down + *cumbere* lie down]

dec|u|ple (dek′yu̇ pəl), *adj., n., v.,* **-pled, -pling.** —*adj.* ten times as great; tenfold.
—*n.* a number or quantity ten times another; tenfold amount.
—*v.t.* to make ten times as great.
[< Middle French *decuple*, learned borrowing from Late Latin *decuplus* < Latin *decem* ten + *-plus* -fold]

de|cu|ri|on (di kyu̇r′ē ən), *n.* in Roman history: **1** an officer commanding a group of ten horsemen. **2** the head of a decury. **3** any commander of ten. **4** a member of a colonial or municipal senate. [< Latin *decuriō, -ōnis* leader of a *decuria;* see etym. under **decury**]

***de|cur|rent** (di kėr′ənt), *adj. Botany.* extending down the stem: *decurrent leaves.* [< Latin *dēcurrēns, -entis*, present participle of *dēcurrere* < *dē-* down + *currere* run] —**de|cur′rent|ly**, *adv.*

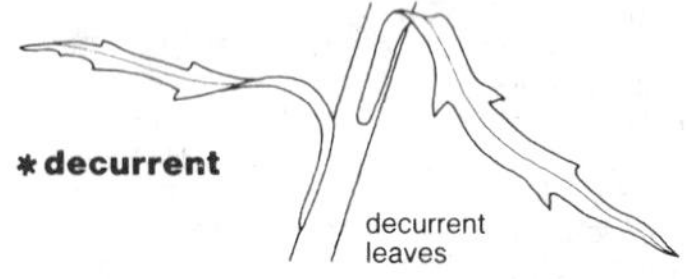

***decurrent**

de|cur|va|tion (dē′kėr vā′shən), *n.* **1** the act or process of decurving. **2** the condition of being curved downward.

de|curve (dē kėrv′), *v.t., v.i.,* **-curved, -curv|ing.** to curve downward.

dec|u|ry (dek′yər ē), *n., pl.* **-ries.** in Roman history: **1** a group of ten, as of judges or scribes. **2** a group, division, or class of any size. [< Latin *decuria* < *decem* ten]

***de|cus|sate** (di kus′āt), *adj., v.,* **-sat|ed, -sat|ing.** —*adj.* **1** in the form of the letter X; crossed; intersecting. **2** *Botany.* arranged along the stem in pairs, each pair at right angles to the pair next above or below: *decussate leaves.*
—*v.t., v.i.* to cross in the form of the letter X; intersect.
[< Latin *decussāre* (with English *-ate*[1]) to form an X intersection < *decussis* the number ten (X), a coin worth ten asses < *decem* ten + *as* as, Roman coin] —**de|cus′sate|ly**, *adv.*

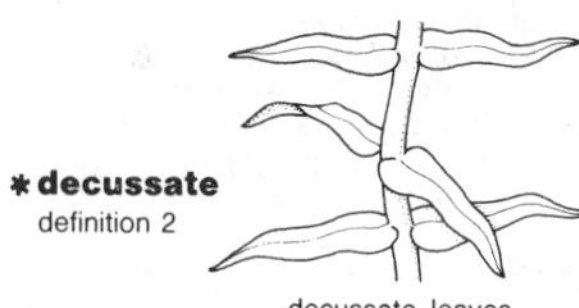

***decussate**
definition 2

de|cus|sa|tion (dē′kə sā′shən), *n.* **1** the crossing of lines, rays, fibers, or the like so as to form a figure like the letter X; intersection. **2** *Anatomy.* a band of nerve fibers crossing the central nervous system and connecting unlike centers on the two sides.

Pronunciation Key: hat, āge, cãre, fär; let, ēqual, tėrm; it, īce; hot, ōpen, ôrder; oil, out; cup, pu̇t, rüle; child; long; thin; ᴛʜen; zh, measure; ə represents **a** in about, **e** in taken, **i** in pencil, **o** in lemon, **u** in circus.

ded., **1** dedicated. **2** dedication. **3** dedicatory.

D. Ed., Doctor of Education. Also, **Ed.D.**

de|dal (dē′dəl), *adj.* = daedal.

de|dans (də däN′), *n.* in court tennis: **1** an open gallery for spectators at the service end of the court. **2** the spectators. [< French *dedans*]

ded|i|cant (ded′ə kənt), *n.* a person who dedicates.

ded|i|cate (ded′ə kāt), *v.,* **-cat|ed, -cat|ing,** *adj.* —*v.t.* **1** to set apart for a purpose: *The land on which the battle of Gettysburg was fought was dedicated to the memory of the soldiers who had died there. The new altar was dedicated at a special service.* SYN: consecrate. **2** to celebrate the opening of (a bridge, institution, meeting, or other function or structure) with an official ceremony. **3** *Figurative.* to give up wholly or earnestly to some person or purpose: *A minister or priest is dedicated to the service of God. The doctor dedicated his life to improving hospital care in his community. Marlowe's play is . . . unrelievedly dedicated to blood and thunder* (Newsweek). SYN: See syn. under **devote.** **4** to address (a book, poem, or other literary or artistic work) to a friend or patron as a mark of affection, respect, or gratitude: *The author dedicated his book to his teacher.*
—*adj. Archaic.* dedicated.
[< Latin *dēdicāre* (with English *-ate*[1]) proclaim, affirm < *dē-* + *dicāre* proclaim < *dīcere* speak]

ded|i|cat|ed (ded′ə kā′tid), *adj.* designed or used for a particular task or purpose: *Other dedicated machines include statistical and financial calculators and metric converters* (New Scientist).

ded|i|ca|tee (ded′ə kə tē′), *n.* a person to whom anything, especially a book, is dedicated.

ded|i|ca|tion (ded′ə kā′shən), *n.* **1** the act of setting apart or state of being set apart for a purpose: *the dedication of a church.* SYN: consecration. **2** a ceremony attending the official opening of something, such as a building, institution, or convention: *the dedication of a new library wing.* **3** *Figurative.* the act or state of giving up wholly or earnestly to some person or purpose: *The old man regretted his complete dedication to making money.* SYN: devotion. **4** the words dedicating a book, poem, or the like, to a friend or patron. SYN: inscription.

ded|i|ca|tive (ded′ə kā′tiv), *adj.* = dedicatory.

ded|i|ca|tor (ded′ə kā′tər), *n.* a person who dedicates.

ded|i|ca|to|ry (ded′ə kə tôr′ē, -tōr′-), *adj.* of dedication; as a dedication: *Ten eminent physicists have contributed to a dedicatory volume on the development of physics* (Bulletin of Atomic Scientists).

de di|e in di|em (dē dī′ē in dī′əm), *Latin.* from day to day.

de|dif|fer|en|ti|ate (dē dif′ə ren′shē āt), *v.i.,* **-at|ed, -at|ing.** *Biology.* to undergo dedifferentiation; lose special form or function: *When the tadpole metamorphoses into the frog, some of its tissues start to dedifferentiate* (Haldane and Huxley).

de|dif|fer|en|ti|a|tion (dē dif′ə ren′shē ā′shən), *n. Biology.* a process in which a cell, tissue, organ, or organism loses its special form or function; loss of specialization.

de do|lo ma|lo (dē dō′lō mā′lō), *Latin.* from evil intent; from fraud.

de|duce (di düs′, -dyüs′), *v.t.,* **-duced, -duc|ing.** **1** to reach (a conclusion) by reasoning; infer: *Her instructions are so complicated I cannot deduce from them what she wants.* See also **induce.** SYN: See syn. under **conclude.** **2** to trace the course, descent, or origin of: *to deduce the development of a culture from archeological remains.* [< Latin *dēdūcere* lead (down), derive < *dē-* down + *dūcere* to lead]

de|duc|i|ble (di dü′sə bəl, -dyü′-), *adj.* that can be deduced or inferred: *The opinions of an expert are, where rational, deducible* (Manchester Guardian Weekly).

de|duct (di dukt′), *v.t.* **1** to take away; subtract: *The father deducted the costs of the broken window from his son's allowance.* SYN: See syn. under **subtract.** **2** *Obsolete.* to deduce. [< Latin *dēductus*, past participle of *dēdūcere;* see etym. under **deduce**]

de|duct|i|bil|i|ty (di duk′tə bil′ə tē), *n.* the quality of being deductible: *The actions of the Internal Revenue Service concerning tax deductibility for organizations have been nothing short of high-handed* (Harper's).

de|duct|i|ble (di duk′tə bəl), *adj.* that can be deducted.

de|duc|tion (di duk′shən), *n.* **1** the act of taking away; subtraction: *No deduction from one's pay is made for absence due to illness.* SYN: reduction. **2** an amount deducted: *There was a deduction of $50 from the bill for damage caused by the movers.* SYN: rebate, discount. **3** a reaching of conclusions by reasoning; inference. A person using deduction reasons from general laws to particular cases. *Example:* All animals die; this cat is an animal; therefore, this cat will die. **4** a thing deduced; conclusion: *Sherlock Holmes reached his clever deductions by careful study of the facts.*
▶**Deduction, induction** are names of opposite processes of reasoning, the two ways in which we think. *Deduction* applies to the process by which one starts with a general principle that is accepted as true, applies it to a particular case, and arrives at a conclusion that is true if the starting principle was true, as in *All female mammals secrete milk; this is a female mammal; therefore, this will secrete milk. Induction* applies to the process by which one collects many particular cases, finds out by experiment what is common to all of them, and forms a general rule or principle which is probably true, as in *Every female mammal I have tested secreted milk; probably all female mammals secrete milk.*

de|duc|tive (di duk′tiv), *adj.* of or using deduction; reasoning by deduction: *In mathematics plausible reasoning . . . is only the prelude to deductive proof* (Scientific American). SYN: inferential. —**de|duc′tive|ly**, *adv.*

de|du|pli|ca|tion (dē′dü plə kā′shən, -dyü-), *n. Botany.* the congenital separation of one organ into two or more.

dee (dē), *n., adj.* —*n.* **1** the letter D or d. **2** either of the two D-shaped, semicircular, hollow cylinders of a cyclotron. When electrons are accelerated in the dees to a speed of 28,000 miles per second they are released to create a beam in the cyclotron. —*adj.* shaped like a D.

deed (dēd), *n., v.* —*n.* **1** something done; an act or action: *To feed the hungry is a good deed.* **2** a brave, skillful, or unusual act: *The song that nerves a nation's heart Is in itself a deed* (Tennyson). SYN: feat, exploit. **3** doing; performance: *Deeds, not words, are needed.* SYN: action. **4** a written or printed document, sealed and signed, containing some contract: *The buyer of real estate receives a deed legally transferring the ownership to him.*
—*v.t.* to transfer by deed: *He deeded his house to his oldest son.*
in deed, in fact; actually: *The chiefs became the chiefs in deed as well as in name* (Arthur P. Stanley). See **indeed.**
[Old English *dǣd*, and *dēd.* See related etym. at **do**[1].]

deed|ful (dēd′fəl), *adj.* active; effective.

deed|less (dēd′lis), *adj.* without deeds or action; inactive.

deed of defeasance, *Law.* a collateral deed made at the same time as another and containing conditions that must be met for the first deed to remain in effect.

deed poll, *British.* a deed executed by one party only.

dee|jay (dē′jā′), *n. U.S. Slang.* disk jockey. [< *d*(isk) *j*(ockey)]

deek (dēk), *n. U.S. Slang.* a policeman: *The regulars long since recognized them as "deeks"—street slang for cop—but not because they had seen the policemen's snapshots or because they were white* (New Yorker). [probably alteration or variant of *dick*]

deem (dēm), *v., n.* —*v.t., v.i.* to think, believe, or consider; form or have an opinion: *The police deemed it necessary for the town's safety to arrest most speeders.* SYN: judge, regard, suppose.
—*n. Obsolete.* a judgment; opinion.
[Old English *dēman* < *dōm* judgment, doom]
—**deem′er**, *n.*

de-em|pha|sis (dē em′fə sis), *n.* the act of de-emphasizing or condition of being de-emphasized.

de-em|pha|size (dē em′fə sīz), *v.t.,* **-sized, -siz|ing.** to remove emphasis from; modify emphasis on: *The trend is to de-emphasize varsity sports* (Newsweek).

deem|ster (dēm′stər), *n.* either of the two judges of the Isle of Man. Also, **dempster.** [Middle English *demestre* < *demere* one who deems, judge]

deem|ster|ship (dēm′stər ship), *n.* the office of deemster in the Isle of Man.

de-en|er|gize (dē en′ər jīz), *v.t.,* **-gized, -giz|ing.** to deprive (a piece of machinery, an electrical circuit, etc.) of its source of power: *. . . allowing the solenoid to de-energize and release the brakes* (Toboldt and Purvis).

deep (dēp), *adj., adv., n., v.* —*adj.* **1** going a long way down from the top or surface: *The ocean is deep here. The men dug a deep well to get pure water.* **2a** going a long way back from the front: *a deep forest.* **b** in depth; having a depth of: *The lot on which the house stands is 100 feet deep.* **3** from far down or back: *Take a deep breath.* **4** far down or back: *a deep cut.* **5** *Figurative.* far on: *to be deep in the study of physics.* **6** *Figurative.* low in pitch: *She heard the low tones of her father's deep voice.* **7** *Figurative.* making one go a long way or take much time in thinking; hard to understand: *a deep subject, a deep book.* SYN:

abstruse, obscure. **8** *Figurative.* **a** heartfelt; earnest: *deep sorrow. Deep feeling is hard to put into words.* SYN: profound. **b** strong; great; intense; extreme: *deep silence. A deep sleep is one that is hard to be awakened from.* **9** *Figurative.* strong and dark in color; rich: *a deep red.* **10** *Figurative.* with the mind fully taken up; absorbed: *deep in thought. There he is at it, deep in Greek* (Robert Browning). SYN: engrossed. **11** *Figurative.* going below the surface: *a speech of deep importance. A deeper knowledge of man's present psychology will lead to a more vital advance than the splitting of the atom* (New Yorker). **12** *Figurative.* learned; wise; shrewd: *a deep scholar.* SYN: astute. **13** *Figurative.* sly; crafty: *You're a deep one, Mr. Pip* (Dickens). SYN: artful, cunning. **14** *Figurative.* grave; serious: *in deep disgrace.* **15** *Figurative.* much involved: *deep in debt.*

—adv. **1** far down or back: *The men dug deep before they found water. They went deep into the forest.* **2** *Figurative.* well along in time; far on in time: *She studied deep into the night.* **3** *Figurative.* intensely; profoundly; deeply: *We went deep into the problem.*

—n. **1** a deep place. **2** *Figurative.* the most intense part: *the deep of winter.* **3** *Nautical.* one of the unmarked points at intervals of one fathom from one another or from any of the 9 marks on a sounding line. On a 200-fathom line the deeps are at 1, 4, 6, 8, 9, 11, 12, 14, 16, 18, and 19 fathoms, the remaining depths being marks. **4** any ocean area more than 18,000 feet deep: *Dr. Trask came on the trench while collecting samples of the ocean floor from what are known as deeps* (New York Times).

—v.t., v.i. to deepen.

in deep water. See under **water**.

jump (or **go**) **off the deep end.** See under **end**[1].

the deep, the sea; the ocean: *Frightened sailors thought they saw monsters from the deep.*

[Old English *dēop*] **—deep′ly,** *adv.* **—deep′ness,** *n.*

deep-chest|ed (dēp′ches′tid), *adj.* having a thick chest.

deep-dish (dēp′dish′), *adj.* baked in a deep dish with a crust on top only: *a deep-dish pie.*

deep-draft (dēp′draft′, -dräft′), *adj.* (of a ship) that draws or displaces deep water: *deep-draft ocean vessels.*

deep-draw (dēp′drô′), *v.t.,* **-drew, -drawn, -draw|ing.** to cold-work (sheet metal) into cup-shaped or other extended forms by forcing it into or through a die.

deep-dyed (dēp′dīd′), *adj.* thoroughgoing; absolute; complete: *deep-dyed skepticism.*

deep|en (dē′pən), *v.t.* to make deep or deeper: *We deepened the hole.* *—v.i.* to become deep or deeper: *The water deepened as the tide came in.* (*Figurative.*) *The evening deepened into dark.* **—deep′en|er,** *n.*

deep fat, enough fat or oil in a pan to cover completely the food to be cooked.

deep freeze, a state of postponement, inactivity, or delay: *The Government would put in the deep freeze its program for authorizing a new subsidized fleet* (New York Times).

deep-freeze (dēp′frēz′), *v.,* **-froze** or **-freezed, -fro|zen** or **-freezed, -freez|ing,** *n.* *—v.t.* to freeze and store for later use: *It had been caught, filleted, skinned, and deep-frozen in a factory trawler some 2,000 miles away* (Listener). *—n.* a box or container for freezing and storing food; freezer.

deep-freez|er (dēp′frē′zər), *n.* **1** = deep-freeze. **2** a person or thing that deep-freezes.

deep-fry (dēp′frī′), *v.t.,* **-fried, -fry|ing.** to fry in deep fat. **—deep′-fry′er,** *n.*

deep|ie (dē′pē), *n. British Slang.* a three-dimensional motion picture; 3-D film.

deep|ish (dē′pish), *adj.* somewhat deep: *He took a deepish breath and waited* (J. D. Salinger).

deep-laid (dēp′lād′), *adj.* planned secretly and carefully: *deep-laid schemes.*

deep|most (dēp′mōst), *adj.* deepest.

deep-mouthed (dēp′mouᴛʜd′, -moutht′), *adj.* **1** having a deep, sonorous voice: *The deep-mouth'd bloodhound's heavy bay* (Scott). **2** deep and sonorous, as the baying of a hound: *deep-mouth'd welcome* (Byron).

deep pocket, *Informal.* **1** a person or company with strong financial resources: *A "deep pocket" is an entity that is perceived to have large assets and insurance* (Christian Science Monitor). **2** Usually, **deep pockets.** a large amount of capital; strong financial resources: *By bringing in a partner with deep pockets, ... the company was in a position to offer a more attractive deal* (New York Times).

deep-root|ed (dēp′rü′tid, -rut′id), *adj.* **1** deeply rooted: *a tall and deep-rooted tree.* **2** *Figurative.* firmly fixed: *deep-rooted traditions. Many people have a deep-rooted fear of snakes.* SYN: established, ingrained, confirmed.

deep scattering layer, microscopic marine organisms that form a layer deep in the ocean, causing a reflection of sonar impulses similar to those detected from reflections off the ocean floor and often confused with them.

deep-sea (dēp′sē′), *adj.* of or in the deeper parts of the sea: *a deep-sea diver, deep-sea biological research.*

deep-sea angler, an angler fish having a large head and mouth, sharp teeth, and a luminous gland at the tip of a stalk that rises from the end of the snout.

deep-seat|ed (dēp′sē′tid), *adj.* **1** far below the surface; set deeply: *For treatment of deep-seated cancers, both neutrons and gamma rays will be provided by the reactor* (Science News Letter). **2** *Figurative.* firmly fixed: *He has a deep-seated love of nature. All three countries are welfare states but have a deep-seated respect for what free enterprise can do* (Newsweek).

deep-set (dēp′set′), *adj.* **1** set deeply: *She has deep-set eyes.* **2** *Figurative.* firmly fixed: *a deep-set dread of debt, deep-set opposition.*

deep six, *U.S. Slang.* **1** burial, especially at sea. **2** a place for trash or discarded material or ideas: *In the Navy Department, ... the wastebasket is referred to as the Deep Six* (Clarence Stratton).

to give one the deep six, to throw overboard; reject; discard: *The last Japanese plane [in the story] crashes ..., giving most of the characters the deep six* (Newsweek).

deep-six (dēp′siks′), *v.t. U.S. Slang.* to throw overboard; give one the deep six.

deep South or **Deep South,** *U.S.* the Southern states regarded as most typical of the South, generally including Georgia, Alabama, Mississippi, Louisiana, and South Carolina: *In the states of the Deep South ... generations of traditions are being challenged* (Wall Street Journal).

deep space, space beyond the earth and the moon (as distinguished from *outer space* in the sense of the space immediately beyond the earth's atmosphere): *Laws will have to be drawn up to regulate travel by human beings ... in so-called deep space* (New Yorker).

deep structure, *Linguistics.* the basic or underlying structure of a sentence from which its surface or phonetic expression is generated: *Transformational-generative grammar assigns to each sentence a "deep structure" in an attempt to generalize about language—and reproduce, from all constituent parts, all the possible sentences of a language* (New York Times).

deep therapy, the use of X rays or other devices capable of producing a deeply penetrating beam of radiation, especially as in the treatment of cancer: *Deep therapy with million-volt radiation was possible before the war; it depended on the use of gamma rays from radium* (New Scientist).

deep|wa|ter (dēp′wôt′ər, -wot′-), *adj.* **1** of or in deep water: *deepwater shrimp, a deepwater channel, deepwater swimming.* **2** for use in deepwater: *a deepwater sailboat.* **3** at or near an ocean: *For the first three centuries of our history, our biggest cities were deepwater ports* (Harper's).

***deer** (dir), *n., pl.* **deer** or (*rarely*) **deers. 1** a swift, graceful mammal that has hoofs and chews the cud. Most male deer and some female deer have antlers, which are shed and grow again every year. Deer are herbivorous. The smaller species of these mammals include the white-tailed (or Virginia) deer and the mule deer of America, the red deer of Europe and Asia, and the fallow deer of Europe. Elk, moose, and caribou belong to the same family. See picture below. **2** *Obsolete.* any beast, especially a wild beast. [Old English *dēor* animal. Compare etym. under **dear**[2].] **—deer′like′,** *adj.*

deer|ber|ry (dir′ber′ē), *n., pl.* **-ries. 1** a shrub of the heath family growing in the eastern United States and bearing tart, inedible berries. **2** = partridgeberry. **3** = wintergreen.

deer fly, 1 any one of a group of horseflies that suck blood: *We were constantly annoyed by mosquitoes, black flies and deer flies which appeared in swarms and bit us unmercifully* (Scientific American). **2** = snipe fly.

deer-fly fever (dir′flī′), = tularemia.

deer grass, any one of various grasses, especially the common meadow beauty.

deer|hound (dir′hound′), *n.* a dog of a Scottish breed, resembling a greyhound but larger and with a shaggy coat; Scottish deerhound.

deer|let (dir′lit), *n.* **1** a little deer. **2** = chevrotain.

deer lick, a salt lick to which deer come to lick the earth.

deer mouse, 1 any one of a group of North American mice with white underparts and feet and large ears; white-footed mouse. **2** a yellowish-brown jumping mouse of America.

deer|skin (dir′skin′), *n., adj.* *—n.* **1** the skin of a deer. **2** leather made from it. **3** clothing made of this leather.

—adj. made of deerskin: *a deerskin flying suit.*

deer|slay|er (dir′slā′ər), *n.* a hunter who kills deer, especially in excess of what is considered sportsmanlike: *Rural roads and rural lodges are filled by an army of wool-shirted deerslayers* (Newsweek).

***deer|stalk|er** (dir′stô′kər), *n.* **1** a close-fitting cap with earflaps, originally worn by hunters in stalking deer. It is the kind that Sherlock Holmes wore. **2** a person who stalks deer.

***deerstalker**
definition 1

deer|stalk|ing (dir′stô′king), *n.* the hunting of deer by stalking, especially by stealing within shooting range.

deer tiger, = cougar.

deer|weed (dir′wēd′), *n.* a California plant of the pea family with yellow flowers and trifoliate leaves.

de-es|ca|late (dē es′kə lāt), *v.t., v.i.,* **-lat|ed, -lat|ing.** to reduce in scale or size: *The debate followed the adoption of a resolution charging the Administration with failing to de-escalate the war* (New York Times). *Those who might be expecting in these excerpts some of the qualities imparted to this [musical] work by Elisabeth Schwarzkopf, Nicolai Gedda, and Erich Kunz in their famous Angel production are warned to de-escalate their expectations* (Saturday Review).

de-es|ca|la|tion (dē es′kə lā′shən), *n.* the reverse of escalation; reduction in scale or size: *A de-escalation of the war is needed, rather than the escalation that we now see imminent* (New York Times).

de-es|ca|la|to|ry (dē es′kə lə tôr′ē, -tōr′-), *adj.* of or having to do with de-escalation: *de-escalatory measures to reduce tension.*

deet (dēt), *n. U.S.* = diethyl toluamide. [< pronunciation of *d.t.*, abbreviation of *diethyl toluamide*]

def., an abbreviation for the following:
1 defective.
2 defendant.
3 deferred.
4a defined. **b** definite. **c** definition.

de|face (di fās′), *v.t.,* **-faced, -fac|ing. 1** to spoil the appearance of; mar: *Thoughtless boys have defaced the desks by marking on them. Scribbled pictures and notes defaced the pages of the book.* **2** *Figurative.* to blot out; obliterate: *to deface the record.* [< Old French *defacer* < *de-* away from (< Latin *dis-*) + *face* face] **—de|face′a|ble,** *adj.*

—Syn. **1 Deface, disfigure** mean to spoil the appearance of someone or something. **Deface** means to spoil the surface of something by blotting out an important detail, by scratching something in, or by wearing down, as by the result of

***deer**
definition 1

white-tailed deer

elk

moose

caribou

weather or age: *The walls of the subway were defaced with crude drawings and jokes. The inscription is too badly defaced to be read.* **Disfigure** suggests spoiling the beauty of a person or thing by permanent injury too deep or serious to repair: *The accident left her face disfigured.*

de|face|ment (di fās′mənt), *n.* **1** the act of defacing. **2** the state of being defaced. **3** a thing that defaces.

de|fac|er (di fā′sər), *n.* a person or thing that defaces.

de fac|to (dē fak′tō), **1** in fact; in reality: *We must look at it as a matter de facto, not imaginary.* **2** actually existing, whether lawful or not: *the dictator's de facto government, de facto racial segregation.* [< Latin *dēfactō* from the fact < *dē* from, *factō*, ablative of *factum*, neuter past participle of *facere* do, act]

def|ae|cate (def′ə kāt), *v.*, **-cat|ed, -cat|ing.** = defecate.

def|ae|ca|tion (def′ə kā′shən), *n.* = defecation.

de|fal|cate (di fal′kāt, -fôl′-), *v.i.*, **-cat|ed, -cat|ing.** to steal or misuse money entrusted to one's care: *The collector defalcated with the rents.* [< Medieval Latin *defalcare* (with English *-ate*[1]) (literally) to cut off with a sickle < Latin *dē-* down, away + *falx, falcis* sickle, pruning knife] **—de|fal′ca|tor,** *n.*

de|fal|ca|tion (dē′fal kā′shən, -fôl-), *n.* **1** the theft or misuse of money entrusted to one's care: *The cashier's defalcation was discovered.* SYN: embezzlement, misappropriation. **2** the amount stolen or misused.

def|a|ma|tion (def′ə mā′shən, dē′fə-), *n.* the act of defaming or condition of being defamed; slander or libel: *It contrives to mention accusingly or suspiciously a far larger number of scholars and public figures than any earlier exercise in defamation* (Harper's).

de|fam|a|to|ry (di fam′ə tôr′ē, -tōr′-), *adj.* defaming; slanderous or libelous.

de|fame (di fām′), *v.t.*, **-famed, -fam|ing.** **1** to attack the good name of; harm the reputation of; speak evil of; slander or libel: *Men in public life are sometimes defamed by opponents. Other ventures have tried to defame respectable people by use of the . . . principle of guilt by association* (Harper's). SYN: calumniate, vilify, malign. **2** *Archaic.* to disgrace. **3** *Obsolete.* to accuse. [< Old French *diffamer*, and Medieval Latin *defamare*, both < Latin *diffāmāre* damage by rumor, spread rumor < *dis-* abroad + *fāma* rumor]

de|fam|er (di fā′mər), *n.* a slanderer or libeler; detractor; calumniator.

de|fang (dē fang′), *v.t.* **1** to remove the fangs of. **2** to disarm: *The U.S. has defanged and debunked the class struggle* (Time).

de|fas|sa (di fas′ə), *n., pl.* **-sa.** the more widespread of the two kinds of waterbucks or African antelopes. The defassa makes a good pet when caught young. [< New Latin *defassa* the species name]

de|fat (dē fat′), *v.t.*, **-fat|ted, -fat|ting.** **1** to remove fat from: *the defatting and drying effects of soap.* **2** to deprive of fat.

de|fault (di fôlt′), *n., v.* **—*n.*** **1** failure to do something or to appear somewhere when due; neglect. If, in any contest, one side does not appear, it loses by default. SYN: negligence, omission. **2** failure to pay when due: *a default on an installment payment.* **3** *Law.* failure to appear in court at the time assigned to plead or defend a case. **4** *Obsolete.* a want; lack; absence. **5** *Obsolete.* a fault; mistake; misdeed.

—*v.i.* **1** to fail to do something or appear somewhere when due: *They defaulted in the tennis tournament.* **2** to fail to pay ones debts when due. **3** *Law.* **a** to fail to appear in court at the proper time. **b** to lose a case because of failure to appear. **—*v.t.*** **1** to fail to perform or pay when due. **2** *Law.* to declare (a person) in default. **3** to lose by default.

in default of, in the absence of; having no; lacking: *In default of evidence, the case was dismissed.*

[< Old French *defaute*, earlier *defaulte* < *defaillir* < *de-* de- (< Latin *dē-*) + *faillir*, ultimately < Latin *fallere* deceive]

de|fault|er (di fôl′tər), *n.* **1** a person who defaults: *Under exchange rules a defaulter must pay a buyer a fair market price for the undelivered potatoes* (New York Times). **2** a person who steals or uses money entrusted to his care. **3** *British.* a soldier convicted of a military offense.

de|fea|sance (di fē′zəns), *n.* **1** a making null and void. **2** *Law.* **a** a condition stated in a contract or deed which, if carried out, makes the contract or deed null and void. **b** a contract or deed expressing such a condition. [< Old French *defesance* < *desfaire*; see etym. under **defeat**]

de|fea|si|bil|i|ty (di fē′zə bil′ə tē), *n.* the quality of being defeasible.

de|fea|si|ble (di fē′zə bəl), *adj.* that can be or is liable to be made null and void. **—de|fea′si|ble|ness,** *n.*

de|feat (di fēt′), *v., n.* **—*v.t.*** **1** to win a victory over; overcome: *to defeat an army, to defeat an opponent in an election. Washington defeated Cornwallis at Yorktown.* **2** *Figurative.* to make useless; cause to fail: *to defeat someone's plans. His effort to toughen himself by going without an overcoat defeated itself, for he caught a bad cold.* SYN: frustrate, thwart. **3** *Figurative.* to do out of; deprive: *His bad temper defeated him of ultimate success.* SYN: defraud. **4** *Law.* to make null and void; annul. **5** *Obsolete.* to undo; destroy; ruin: *His unkindness may defeat my life* (Shakespeare).

—*n.* **1** a defeating: *Washington's defeat of Cornwallis ended the Revolutionary War.* SYN: conquest. **2** a being defeated: *Cornwallis's defeat at Yorktown marked the end of British power in the United States.* SYN: loss, overthrow. **3** *Figurative.* a making useless. **4** *Obsolete.* undoing; destruction; ruin.

[< Old French *desfeit*, past participle of *desfaire* < Vulgar Latin *diffacere* < Latin *dis-* un-, not + *facere* do]

—*Syn.* *v.t.* **1 Defeat, conquer, vanquish, overcome** mean to win a victory over someone or something. **Defeat** means to win a victory, at least for the moment: *We defeated Lincoln High School in baseball yesterday.* **Conquer** emphasizes final achievement after a long effort in winning control over people, things, or feelings: *Some countries may be defeated but never conquered. Doctors are seeking ways to conquer disease. Try to conquer your fears.* **Vanquish** emphasizes completely overpowering another, usually in a single encounter: *The champion vanquished the challengers one by one.* **Overcome** implies getting the better of someone or something, especially a habit or feeling: *He could not overcome his dislike for that man.*

de|feat|er (di fē′tər), *n.* a person or thing that defeats.

de|feat|ism (di fē′tiz əm), *n.* the attitude or behavior of a defeatist; conduct tending to bring about acceptance of defeat.

de|feat|ist (di fē′tist) , *n., adj.* **—*n.*** a person who expects, wishes for, or admits defeat.

—*adj.* having to do with or characterized by defeatism: *This defeatist attitude is induced by early training* (Harper's).

de|fea|ture (di fē′chər), *n.* **1** *Archaic.* disfigurement; defacement. **2** *Obsolete.* defeat; ruin; overthrow.

def|e|cate (def′ə kāt), *v.* **-cat|ed, -cat|ing.** **—*v.i.*** **1** to discharge waste matter from the intestines; have a movement of the bowels. **2** to become clear of impurities.

—*v.t.* to clear of impurities; purify; refine.

[< Latin *dēfaecāre* (with English *-ate*[1]) cleanse, purify < *dē-* from + *faecēs* dregs]

def|e|ca|tion (def′ə kā′shən), *n.* **1** the act of defecating; purification. **2** that which has been defecated.

def|e|ca|tor (def′ə kā′tər), *n.* a person or thing that defecates or purifies.

de|fect (*n.* dē′fekt; *v.* di fekt′), *n., v.* **—*n.*** **1** a fault; blemish; imperfection: *The hole was a defect in the material. A bad temper was the defect in his nature.* **2** lack of something needed for completeness; a falling short: *A defect in his sense of right and wrong made him steal.* SYN: want, deficiency.

—*v.i.* to forsake one's own country, group, party, or religion, for another, especially another that is opposed to or different from it: *After he lost the nomination, he defected to the other party. A top Polish officer has defected to the West and is now hiding in the U.S.* (Wall Street Journal).

[< Latin *dēfectus, -ūs* revolt, failure < *dēficere*; see etym. under **deficient**]

—*Syn.* *n.* **1 Defect, flaw, blemish** mean an imperfection or fault. **Defect,** the general word, applies to any imperfection on the surface or in the makeup of a person or thing: *A hearing aid helps to overcome defects in hearing. No person is without defects.* **Flaw** applies to a defect in structure, suggesting a crack or break when used literally, a fault in character when used figuratively: *That bubble is a flaw in the glass. Jealousy is the great flaw in his character.* **Blemish** applies to an external defect, such as a stain on the surface of some object or a pimple on the skin, and when used figuratively suggests a slight defect: *His reputation is without blemish.*

defect., defective.

de|fec|ti|bil|i|ty (di fek′tə bil′ə tē), *n.* liability of falling short; a being defective.

de|fec|ti|ble (di fek′tə bəl), *adj. Obsolete or Rare.* liable to fall short; subject to defect.

de|fec|tion (di fek′shən), *n.* **1** a falling away from loyalty, duty, or belief; desertion: *The candidate was blamed for defection from his political party.* SYN: apostasy, renunciation. **2** a falling short; failure: *I underwent . . . miserable defections of hope* (Charlotte Brontë).

de|fec|tive (di fek′tiv), *adj., n.* **—*adj.*** **1** having a flaw or blemish; not complete; not perfect; faulty: *A watch with defective parts will not keep time. . . . leaning his head sideways as though he was trying to hear something through a defective telephone* (Graham Greene). SYN: imperfect. **2** lacking one or more of the usual forms of grammatical inflection. "Ought" is a defective verb. **3** *Psychology.* below normal in behavior or intelligence.

—*n.* **1** a defective person or thing. **2** a person who has some defect of body or mind. **3** *Grammar.* a defective word. **—de|fec′tive|ly,** *adv.* **—de|fec′tive|ness,** *n.*

defective virus, any one of a class of viruses that contain only a small amount of genetic material and can therefore replicate only in the presence of a normal virus: *The delta agent [is] a defective virus that exists only in conjunction with the hepatitis B virus* (Science News).

defective year, the shortest of the three common years of the Jewish calendar, having 353 days.

de|fec|tol|o|gy (dē′fek tol′ə jē, di fek′-), *n.* the study of the causes and remedies of defects in human development or mechanical composition.

de|fec|tor (di fek′tər), *n.* a person who defects: *I have just returned from . . . Western Germany, where I have been talking to the Soviet defectors* (Time).

de|fed|er|al|ize (dē fed′ər ə līz, -fed′rə-), *v.t.*, **-ized, -iz|ing.** **1** to break up or dissolve (a federal union). **2** to withdraw from the control of the federal government.

de|fem|i|nize (dē fem′ə nīz), *v.t.*, **-nized, -niz|ing.** to deprive of feminine qualities or characteristics: *This physiological revolution . . . has defeminized Eve and demoralized Adam* (Atlantic).

de|fence (di fens′), *n. Especially British.* defense.

de|fend (di fend′), *v.t.* **1** to keep safe; guard from attack or harm; protect: *As the wolves closed in the dog stood rigid, ready to defend his master. In sports, the defense is in charge of defending the goal.* SYN: See syn. under **guard. 2** to act, speak, or write in favor of: *The newspapers defended the governor's action. A district attorney defends the rights and privileges of the citizens.* SYN: uphold, maintain. **3** *Law.* **a** to fight or contest (a claim or lawsuit). **b** to act or speak on behalf of (a person accused): *The lawyer defended the man charged with theft before a judge. A State Supreme Court order . . . demands that public funds be used to defend indigents* (New York Times). **4** *Obsolete.* to prohibit; forbid: *No interdict Defends the touching of these viands pure* (Milton).

—*v. i.* to make or enter a defense. [< Old French *defendre* < Latin *dēfendere* ward off < *dē-* from, away + *fendere* to strike, push]

de|fend|a|ble (di fen′də bəl), *adj.* that can be defended.

de|fend|ant (di fen′dənt), *n.,* adj. **—*n.*** a person accused or sued in a law court: *This defendant is charged with theft.* **—*adj.*** **1** defending; being a defendant. **2** *Obsolete.* defensive.

►See **accused** for usage note.

de|fend|er (di fen′dər), *n.* **1** a protector; guardian. **2** *Sports.* a person or team that stands ready to defend its championship.

Defender of the Faith, a title held by the sovereigns of England. Pope Leo X conferred it on Henry VIII in 1521.

de|fend|ress (di fen′dris), *n.* a woman defender.

de|fen|es|trate (di fen′ə strāt), *v.*., **-trat|ed, -trat|ing.** to throw (a person or thing) out of a window. [back formation < *defenestration*]

de|fen|es|tra|tion (di fen′ə strā′shən), *n.* the act of throwing a person or thing out of a window. [< Latin *dē-* from + *fenestra* window + English *-ation* (coined for the Defenestration of Prague in 1618, a famous instance of this)]

de|fense (di fens′), *n., v.*, **-fensed, -fens|ing.** **—*n.*** **1** any thing, act, or word that defends, guards, or protects; thing used to guard against attack or harm: *A wall around a city was a defense against enemies. A well-built house or a warm coat is a defense against cold weather.* SYN: protection. **2** the act of defending or protecting; a guarding against attack or harm: *The armed forces are responsible for the defense of the country.* Millions for defense, but not one cent for tribute (Robert G. Harper). **3** an action, speech, or writing in favor of something: *The poet Shelley wrote a defense of poetry.* SYN: support, justification. **4** a defending team or force, especially the players defending a goal in a game: *Our football team has a good defense.* **5a** the act or skill of defending oneself in boxing or fencing. **b** the method of such defense. **6a** a defendant and his lawyers. **b** the answer of a defendant to an accusation or lawsuit against him. **c** the methods adopted by the defendant's lawyers in conducting his case.

— ***v.t.*** *U.S. Football.* to put up a defense against (an opposing team, player, or tactic): *A team is not "defended against" but "defensed"* (Time). Also, *especially British,* **defence.**
[< Old French *defens* < Latin *dēfensa* prohibition, defense < *dēfendere;* see etym. under **defend**]
▶ When **defense** and **offense** are frequently used together, as in the description of football games, the first syllable is often stressed to emphasize the contrast. In a similar way, the adjectives *defensive* and *offensive* are often pronounced (dē′fen siv) and (of′en siv).

defense in depth, a system of military defense providing, behind the most forward position, a series of lines or installations spaced at intervals, or a large area into which units may withdraw and regroup.

de|fense|less (di fens′lis), *adj.* having no defense; helpless against attack or harm; unprotected: *A baby is defenseless; he cannot prevent what is done to him.* —**de|fense′less|ly,** *adv.* —**de|fense′less|ness,** *n.*

de|fense|man (di fens′mən), *n., pl.* **-men.** either one of two hockey players assigned to defend the area in front of a goal: *If a defenseman can't stop the puck, he falls on it* (Maclean's).

defense mechanism or **reaction, 1** any self-protective reaction by an organism, such as the development of resistance to infection. **2** *Psychology.* any psychological device by which a person limits or prevents his own awareness of unpleasant feelings such as guilt or anxiety, by rationalizing or denying a situation, concealing or repressing an unacceptable drive, or transferring emotion to a new object or activity.

de|fen|si|bil|i|ty (di fen′sə bil′ə tē), *n.* the quality of being defensible.

de|fen|si|ble (di fen′sə bəl), *adj.* **1** that can be defended. **2** *Figurative.* justifiable; proper. —**de-fen′si|ble|ness,** *n.*

de|fen|si|bly (di fen′sə blē), *adv.* justifiably; properly.

de|fen|sive (di fen′siv), *adj., n.* —***adj.*** **1** ready to defend; intended to defend; defending: *a defensive war, a defensive end in football.* **2** used for defense: *a defensive weapon.* **SYN:** protective. **3** of defense: *a defensive attitude.*
—***n.*** **1** a position or attitude of defense. **2** a thing that defends.
on the defensive, ready to defend, apologize, or explain: *Casual comments about her new hairdo put her on the defensive.*
—**de|fen′sive|ly,** *adv.* —**de|fen′sive|ness,** *n.*
▶ See **defense** for usage note.

de|fer[1] (di fėr′), *v.t., v.i.,* **-ferred, -fer|ring.** to put off; delay: *Examinations were deferred because so many students were sick.* **SYN:** postpone. See syn. under **delay.** [spelling for earlier alternate pronunciation of *differ*]

de|fer[2] (di fėr′), *v.i.,* **-ferred, -fer|ring.** to yield in judgment or opinion; submit courteously: *Children should defer to their parents' wishes.* [< Middle French *déférer,* learned borrowing from Latin *dēferre* < *dē-* down, away + *ferre* carry]

def|er|ence (def′ər əns), *n.* **1** a yielding to the judgment, opinion, or wishes of another; courteous submission. **2** great respect: *Boys and girls should show deference to persons who are much older and wiser.* **SYN:** See syn. under **honor.**
in deference to, out of respect for the wishes or authority of: *... the resignation of a Prime Minister in deference to the will of the House of Commons* (Homersham Cox).
pay (or **show**) **deference to,** to submit to the superior claims, skill, judgment, or other qualities of another: *Now, Sir, you shall stay and see what a deference they pay to my skill and authority* (Richard Estcourt).

def|er|ent[1] (def′ər ənt), *adj.* = deferential. [< *defer*[2] + *-ent*]

def|er|ent[2] (def′ər ənt), *adj., n.* —***adj.*** carrying down or away; efferent.
—***n.*** **1** something that carries or conveys; conductor: *All of them are dull and inapt deferents except air* (Francis Bacon). **2** (in Ptolemaic astronomy) a circle around the earth, along the circumference of which the orbits of the other planets were supposed to rotate. See diagram under **epicycle.**
[< Latin *dēferēns, -entis,* present participle of *dēferre;* see etym. under **defer**[2]]

def|er|en|tial (def′ə ren′shəl), *adj.* showing deference; respectful. —**def′er|en′tial|ly,** *adv.*

de|fer|ment (di fėr′mənt), *n.* a putting off; delay; postponement: *a deferment from military service, a deferment in paying a loan.*

de|fer|ra|ble (di fėr′ə bəl), *adj., n.* —***adj.*** that can be deferred.
—***n.*** a person or thing that can be deferred.

de|fer|ral (di fėr′əl), *n.* = deferment.

de|ferred (di fėrd′), *adj.* **1** postponed; delayed. **2** withheld for a certain period: *Such an account is a deferred expense and is shown in the balance sheet as an asset* (Schmidt and Bergstrom).

deferred annuity, a annuity which does not begin until after a period or number of years, or until the death of some person, or until some future event.

deferred charge, *Accounting.* a current expenditure incurred for a future operation, and written off in the future.

deferred income, *Accounting.* income received or placed on record before earned or due, such as rent payments received in advance.

deferred pay, *British.* a part of the pay of a soldier or other member of the armed forces which is held over to be paid at his discharge, or at death.

deferred shares, stock shares not entitling the holder to a full share of profits, or to any at all, until a future date or some future occurrence.

de|fer|rer (di fėr′ər), *n.* a person who defers.

de|fer|ves|cence (dē′fər ves′əns, def′ər-), *n.* the abatement of fever; decrease in body temperature in recovering from fever. [< German *Defervеszenz* < Latin *dēfervēscens,* present participle of *dēfervēscere* to cool down < *dē-* down + *fervēscere* begin to boil < *fervere* be hot]

de|feu|dal|ize (dē fyü′də līz), *v.t.,* **-ized, -iz|ing.** to deprive of feudal character.

de|fi (di fī′), *n. Informal.* a defiance; challenge.

de|fi|ance (di fī′əns), *n.* **1** the act of defying; standing up against authority and refusing to recognize or obey it; open resistance to power: *He shouted defiance at the policeman and was promptly arrested.* **2** a challenge to meet in a contest, to do something, or to prove something: *A defiance, once made, must be sustained.*
bid defiance to, to defy: *See how scornfully they look down upon you, and bid defiance to the elements* (Richard J. Sullivan).
in defiance of, without regard for; in spite of: *in defiance of authority. He goes without a hat all winter in defiance of the cold weather.*
[< Old French *defiance* < *defier;* see etym. under **defy**]

de|fi|ant (di fī′ənt), *adj.* showing defiance; openly resisting; disobedient; challenging: *The boy said, "I won't," in a defiant manner. ... the man's heart that dare rise defiant against Hell itself* (Thomas Carlyle). **SYN:** rebellious, recalcitrant.
—**de|fi′ant|ly,** *adv.* —**de|fi′ant|ness,** *n.*

de|fi|brate (dē fī′brāt), *v.t., v.i.,* **-brat|ed, -brat-ing.** to reduce (wood or paper) to fibers; break down to fibrous form.

de|fi|bril|late (dē fī′brə lāt), *v.,* **-lat|ed, -lat|ing.**
—***v.t.*** to cause defibrillation in: *It has been possible in a hospital to defibrillate the heart by electric shock and then to start it beating again within a relatively few minutes after "death"* (Paul Dudley White).
—***v.i.*** to undergo defibrillation.

de|fi|bril|la|tion (dē fī′brə lā′shən), *n.* **1** the act of relaxing fibrillating muscle fibers of the heart, especially by electric shock. **2** the condition so produced.

de|fi|bril|la|tor (dē fī′brə lā′tər), *n.* an electrical device for overcoming the effects of fibrillation of the muscle fibers of the heart: *Every operating theater should have emergency equipment: oxygen, an electric "defibrillator" to shock the heart back into action* (Time).

de|fi|bri|nate (dē fī′brə nāt), *v.t.,* **-nat|ed, -nat-ing.** to deprive (blood) of fibrin; remove fibrin from (blood).

de|fi|bri|na|tion (dē fī′brə nā′shən), *n.* the act of defibrinating.

de|fi|cience (di fish′əns), *n.* = deficiency.

de|fi|cien|cy (di fish′ən sē), *n., pl.* **-cies. 1** a lack or absence of something needed; incompleteness: *a deficiency of judgment, deficiency of moral fiber. A deficiency of calcium in your diet can cause weak teeth.* **2** the amount by which a thing falls short or is too small: *If a bill to be paid is $10 and you have only $6, the deficiency is $4.* **SYN:** deficit, shortage. **3** *Genetics.* the loss of a gene or group of genes from a chromosome: *Under the microscope a deficiency can be detected most easily in the giant chromosomes of the salivary glands* (Theodosius Dobzhanky).

deficiency disease, any disease caused by a lack of essential substances in the diet, especially of certain vitamins and minerals, as in pellagra or rickets.

deficiency judgment, *U.S. Law.* a judgment for the balance due on a debt, part of which has been paid or met by the forfeiture of the security.

de|fi|cient (di fish′ənt), *adj., n.* —***adj.*** **1** not complete; defective: *The child's knowledge of arithmetic is deficient.* **SYN:** imperfect, incomplete. **2** not enough; lacking; not sufficient in amount, force, or quality: *This bread is deficient in protein and the milk is deficient in fat.* **SYN:** short, scant, inadequate.
—***n.*** a deficient person or thing.
[< Latin *dēficiēns, -entis* failing, present participle of *dēficere* < *dē-* down, away + *facere* do, make]
—**de|fi′cient|ly,** *adv.*

deficient number, a positive number whose divisors have a sum less than twice that number. *Example:* 8 is a deficient number because 1 + 2 + 4 = 7.

def|i|cit (def′ə sit), *n.* **1a** the amount by which a sum of money falls short; shortage: *Since the club owed $15, and had only $10 in the treasury, there was a deficit of $5 to be made up by the members.* **b** an excess of expenditure or liabilities over income or assets: *The City Housing Authority since 1952 has raised rents over 70 per cent and is still operating with a deficit* (New York Times). **2** *Figurative.* any deficiency or shortage: *The total housing deficit [in Latin America] is about 15 million units* (Rómulo Betancourt). *Such a concentration has left the country with an enormous deficit of unmet social needs* (Manchester Guardian Weekly). [< Latin *dēficit* it is wanting < *dēficere;* see etym. under **deficient**]

deficit financing, the management and provision of money for deficit spending: *The Planning Commission is also now convinced that deficit financing must be kept to a minimum* (Times of India).

deficit spending, spending more money than is received, using accumulated funds or credit. A government employs deficit spending in emergency, to carry out long-term projects quickly, or to increase business and employment during economic depression: *We cannot switch from years of deficit spending to a balanced budget in too short a time* (New York Times).

de fi|de (dē fī′dē), *Latin.* **1** of the faith. **2** *Roman Catholic Church.* authoritative; held by the Church as true, and to be revealed as truth.

de|fi|er (di fī′ər), *n.* a person who defies.

def|i|lade (def′ə lād′), *v.,* **-lad|ed, -lad|ing,** *n.*
—***v.t., v.i.*** to arrange the position of (troops, a fortification, tanks, or artillery) against enemy fire, especially to secure shelter through protective terrain against fire from the side (enfilading fire) and against plunging fire from nearby heights.
—***n.*** the act or operation of defilading.
[< French *défiler;* see etym. under **defile**[2]. Compare etym. under **enfilade.**]

de|file[1] (di fīl′), *v.t.,* **-filed, -fil|ing. 1** to make dirty, bad-smelling, or in any way disgusting: *The children's muddy shoes defiled all the rugs in the house.* **SYN:** pollute, contaminate, befoul. **2** to destroy the pureness or cleanness of (anything sacred); desecrate; corrupt: *The barbarians defiled the church by using it as a stable.* **SYN:** debase, profane. **3** to make ceremonially unclean: *The heathen are come into thine inheritance; thy holy temple have they defiled* (Psalms 79:1). **4** to stain; dishonor; sully: *The pretty girl's reputation was defiled by malicious gossips.* **5** *Archaic.* to ravish. [alteration of Middle English *defoulen* (< Old French *defouler* trample down, violate); influenced by Middle English *filen* befoul, Old English *fȳlan* < *fūl* foul] —**de|fil′ing|ly,** *adv.*

de|file[2] (di fīl′, dē′fīl), *v.,* **-filed, -fil|ing,** *n.* —***v.i.*** to march in single file or a narrow column: *The troops defiled through the pass.*
—***n.*** a narrow place through which troops can march only in narrow columns; a steep and narrow valley: *a narrow pass or defile, between ... closely hanging hills* (John Motley).
[< French *défilé,* noun use of past participle of *défiler* march by files < *dé-* off + *file* file]

de|file|ment (di fīl′mənt), *n.* **1** the act of defiling; pollution: *The defilement of the air and water by industrial wastes is a growing problem.* **2** the state of being defiled. **3** a thing that defiles. [< *defile*[1] + *-ment*]

de|fil|er (di fī′lər), *n.* a person or thing that defiles; corrupter.

de|fin|a|bil|i|ty (di fī′nə bil′ə tē), *n.* the quality of being definable.

de|fin|a|ble (di fī′nə bəl), *adj.* that can be defined.

de|fin|a|bly (di fī′nə blē), *adv.* in a definable manner.

de|fine (di fīn′), *v.t.,* **-fined, -fin|ing. 1** to make clear the meaning of; explain: *A dictionary defines words.* **SYN:** interpret. **2** to make clear; make distinct: *The shadow defined the shape of the building.* **3** to fix; settle: *The powers of the courts are defined by law. The laws define what are the rights to use and to enjoy and to dispose of property* (Atlantic). **SYN:** establish, specify. **4** to settle the limits of: *The boundary between the*

United States and Canada is defined by treaty. The surveyor defined the boundaries of the property. SYN: circumscribe. **5** to be a distinguishing feature of; characterize: *Perseverance usually defines success.* [< Middle French *définir* < Latin *dēfīnīre* to limit < *dē-* completely + *fīnīre* to bound < *fīnis* a bound, limit]

de|fine|ment (di fīn′mənt), *n.* the act of defining; description; definition.

de|fin|er (di fī′nər), *n.* a person or thing that defines.

de|fin|i|en|dum (di fin′ē en′dəm), *n., pl.* **-da** (-də). the subject of a definition; something defined or to be defined. [< Latin *dēfīnīendum,* neuter gerundive of *dēfīnīre* to limit]

de|fin|i|ens (di fin′ē enz), *n., pl.* **de|fin|i|en|tia** (di-fin′ē en′chə, -en′chē ə). the phrase, words, or terms that constitute a definition; something that defines. [< Latin *dēfīnīens,* present participle of *dēfīnīre* to limit]

def|i|nite (def′ə nit), *adj.* **1** clear or exact; precise; not vague: *definite proof. Say "Yes" or "No," or give me some definite answer.* SYN: explicit, positive. **2** having settled limits; limited; restricted. **3** limiting; restricting: *The contract's definite articles are very precise.* SYN: specific. **4** *Botany.* (of an inflorescence) determinate. [< Latin *dēfīnītus,* past participle of *dēfīnīre;* see etym. under **define**] —**def′i|nite|ness,** *n.*

▶ **Definite** and **definitive,** although overlapping in meaning, are not synonyms. *Definite,* meaning perfectly clear and exact, is a synonym of *distinct: I expect a definite answer, either yes or no. Definitive,* meaning final and complete, is a synonym of *decisive: We have appealed to the Supreme Court for a definitive answer.*

definite article, 1 the English article *the.* It is used to limit or restrict the sense of a noun (*The king died last night*) or to generalize its sense (*The dog is a domesticated animal*). **2** its equivalent in other languages.

definite inflections, *Grammar.* those inflections of the adjective in German and early English which are used when preceded by the definite article or its equivalent.

def|i|nite|ly (def′ə nit lē), *adv.* **1** in a definite manner: *Say definitely what you have in mind.* SYN: clearly. **2** certainly: *Will you go? Definitely.* SYN: surely, unquestionably, assuredly.

▶ **Definitely** is one of the most frequently misspelled words. Remember there is no *a* in it and associate def i *ni* tion with def i *ni*te and def i *ni*tely. In current English, *definitely* is often used as a counter word in the sense of "certainly" or "quite" instead of in its exact sense of "in a definite manner": *She definitely is unpopular. I definitely don't want ice cream.*

def|i|ni|tion (def′ə nish′ən), *n.* **1** the act of explaining the nature of a thing; act of making clear the meaning of a word: *Definition tries to account for the characteristics and nature of a thing and so explain or identify what a thing is.* SYN: elucidation, exposition, interpretation. **2** a statement that makes clear the meaning of a word; explanation. One definition of "home" is "the place where a person or family lives." *Coleridge's definition of prose was "words in their best order," and of poetry, "the best words in their best order."* **3** a formal or precise statement in which the nature of a thing is made clear: *It has been found hard to describe man by an adequate definition* (Samuel Johnson). **4** the power of making clear and distinct. The capacity of a lens to give a clear, distinct image of an object is called its definition. *With the small camera, covering a field 20 degrees wide with good definition, we can photograph these galaxies* (Scientific American). **5** clearness; distinctness: *Good photographs have definition. A person with a well-developed body has muscular definition.* **6** the accuracy with which sound or images are reproduced by a radio or television receiver.

def|i|ni|tion|al (def′ə nish′ə nəl), *adj.* of a definition; having to do with or of the nature of a definition: *Attention should be called to another matter which is partly a definitional problem and partly a methodological one* (Stone and Taylor).

de|fin|i|tive (di fin′ə tiv), *adj., n.* —*adj.* **1a** that decides or settles a question; conclusive; final: *Mother gave a definitive answer: we could not go unless we finished our homework first. A jury had pronounced: the verdict was definitive* (Macaulay). SYN: decisive, unconditional. **b** completely reliable; authoritative: *a definitive edition. Lotte Lenya is Kurt Weill's widow, and the definitive interpreter of the songs he wrote* (New Yorker). **2a** limiting; defining: *a definitive word.* **b** established; limited: *... the universe has no definitive size* (Time). **3** *Biology.* completely formed: *a definitive organ.*

—*n.* **1** *Grammar.* a word that limits or defines a noun, such as *the, this, all,* or *none.* **2** an issue of a postage stamp, or a series of them, assigned for regular use.

▶ See **definite** for usage note.

definitive host, the host of an adult parasite, in which it may reproduce sexually: *Some [insects] ... are intermediate hosts for parasitic protozoans or other organisms that they transmit to other or definitive hosts* (Tracy I. Storer).

de|fin|i|tive|ly (di fin′ə tiv lē), *adv.* **1** so as to decide or settle the matter; decisively; conclusively; finally; definitely: *Definitively thus I answer you* (Shakespeare). **2** *Metaphysics.* so as to have a definite position, but not take up space.

de|fin|i|tive|ness (di fin′ə tiv nis), *n.* the quality of being definitive; decisiveness.

de|fin|i|ti|za|tion (di fin′ə tə zā′shən), *n.* the act of making definite.

de|fin|i|tize (di fin′ə tīz), *v.t.,* **-tized, -tiz|ing.** to make definite: *The new contract "definitizes" previous Air Force letters authorizing Convair to proceed with the project* (Wall Street Journal).

de|fin|i|tor (di fin′ə tər), *n.* an officer in certain religious orders whose duty is to decide points of discipline.

de|fin|i|tude (di fin′ə tüd, -tyüd), *n.* the quality of being definite; definiteness.

def|la|grate (def′lə grāt, dē′flə-), *v.t., v.i.,* **-grat|ed, -grat|ing.** to burn suddenly and violently. [< Latin *dēflagrāre* (with English *-ate*[1]) burn away < *dē-* away + *flagrāre* to burn]

def|la|gra|tion (def′lə grā′shən, dē′flə-), *n.* the act of deflagrating; sudden, violent burning.

def|la|gra|tor (def′lə grā′tər, dē′flə-), *n.* a device for producing deflagration.

de|flat|a|ble (di flā′tə bəl), *adj.* that can be deflated.

de|flate (di flāt′), *v.,* **-flat|ed, -flat|ing.** —*v.t.* **1** to let air or gas out of (a balloon, tire, football, or other inflated thing); collapse: *We found that a nail had deflated the tire.* **2** *Figurative.* to reduce the amount, size, or importance of; reduce: *to deflate currency, deflate prices. The cities were to be deflated and the population distributed in villages* (Edmund Wilson). *After the initial flurry of excitement, he sought to deflate the story* (New York Times). **3** to injure or destroy the conceit or confidence of: *Our laughter soon deflated him.*
—*v.i.* **1** to become deflated: *A punctured tire quickly deflates.* **2** to reduce the amount of available money in circulaton; cause deflation: *The Chancellor ... wanted to deflate—to take spending money out of the economy* (Manchester Guardian Weekly).
[probably < *de-* do the opposite of + (in)*flate*]

de|fla|tion (di flā′shən), *n.* **1** the act of letting the air or gas out: *the deflation of a tire.* **2** a being deflated. **3** a reduction of the amount of available money in circulation so that the value of money increases and prices go down. **4** *Geology.* the removal of solid particles by the wind, leaving the rocks exposed to the weather.

de|fla|tion|ar|y (di flā′shə ner′ē), *adj.* of or having to do with deflation: *My present pocket money, at six shillings a week, is dangerously deflationary* (Punch).

de|fla|tion|ist (di flā′shə nist), *n.* a person who supports monetary deflation.

de|fla|tor (di flā′tər), *n.* a person or thing that deflates.

de|flect (di flekt′), *v.t., v.i.* to bend or turn aside; change the direction of: *The wind deflected the arrow's path. The ball deflected from its straight course. The V2 rockets were steered by deflecting the hot exhaust gases of the jet* (J. M. Stephenson). (*Figurative.*) *His thoughts were deflected by her constant chatter.* SYN: swerve, deviate. [< Latin *dēflectere* < *dē-* away + *flectere* to bend]

de|flec|ta|ble (di flek′tə bəl), *adj.* that can be deflected.

de|flect|ed (di flek′tid), *adj.* **1** turned aside or from a direct course. **2** *Botany and Zoology.* bent abruptly downward.

de|flec|tion (di flek′shən), *n.* **1** a bending or turning aside: *Strong winds caused some deflection from the arrow's expected flight. The deflection of electrons by an electric field is used to control the direction of an electron stream in many electronic devices* (Sears and Zemansky). **2** the amount of bending or turning. **3** a bending downward. **4** *Physics.* the movement of the needle or indicator of a scientific instrument from its zero or normal position. **5** *Mechanics.* the amount of bending or twisting in a structure under load. **6** *Optics.* the bending of rays of light from a straight line. Also, *especially British,* **deflexion.**

de|flec|tive (di flek′tiv), *adj.* **1** causing deflection. **2** tending to deflect.

de|flec|tor (di flek′tər), *n.* a thing that deflects, especially a device for deflecting a current of air, gas, or the like: *Then part of the air strikes deflectors that look a little like a Venetian blind* (Time).

de|flex (di fleks′), *v.t.* to deflect downward: *to deflex wings.* [< Latin *dēflexus,* past participle of *dēflectere;* see etym. under **deflect**]

de|flex|i|bil|i|ty (di flek′sə bil′ə tē), *n.* the capability of being deflected.

de|flex|ion (di flek′shən), *n. Especially British.* deflection.

de|floc|cu|late (di flok′yə lāt), *v.,* **-lat|ed, -lat|ing.** —*v.t.* to change from a flocculated state; separate into finely divided particles.
—*v.i.* to become deflocculated.

de|floc|cu|la|tion (di flok′yə lā′shən), *n.* separation into finely divided particles.

de|floc|cu|la|tor (di flok′yə lā′tər), *n.* a dispersing or suspending agent.

de|floc|cu|lent (di flok′yə lənt), *n.* = deflocculator.

def|lo|rate (def′lə rāt, dē′flə-), *adj., v.,* **-rat|ed, -rat|ing.** —*adj.* having lost its flowers or shed its pollen.
—*v.t.* to deflower.

def|lo|ra|tion (def′lə rā′shən, dē′flə-), *n.* the action of deflowering or condition of being deflowered. [< Old French *defloracion,* learned borrowing from Latin *dēflōrātiō, -ōnis* < *dēflōrāre;* see etym. under **deflower**]

de|flow|er (dē flou′ər), *v.t.* **1** to strip flowers from: *Garlands ... from vales deflower'd* (Keats). **2** to deprive (a woman) of her virginity. **3** *Figurative.* to rob of beauty, excellence, or purity; spoil; ruin; ravish. SYN: ravage, desecrate, violate. [< Old French *desflourer,* learned borrowing from Latin *dēflōrāre* < *dē-* from + *flōs, flōris* flower]

de|flow|er|er (dē flou′ər ər), *n.* a person or thing that deflowers.

def|lu|ent (def′lü ənt), *adj.* flowing or running downward; decurrent.

de|fluor|i|date (dē flür′ə dāt, -flü′ər ə-), *v.t.,* **-dat|ed, -dat|ing.** to check, diminish, or end the fluoridating of (drinking water): *The Bartlett water was defluoridated to a level of 1 ppm* (Joan Banus).

de|fluor|i|nate (dē flür′ə nāt, -flü′ər ə-), *v.t.,* **-nat|ed, -nat|ing.** to take fluorine from; free or deprive of fluorine.

de|flux|ion (di fluk′shən), *n. Medicine, Obsolete.* a flow or discharge, such as of mucus during a cold. [< Late Latin *dēfluxiō, -ōnis* < Latin *dēfluere* flow down < *dē-* down + *fluere* to flow]

de|foam (dē fōm′), *v.t.* to remove foam or bubbles from: *This mixture is then defoamed and the freshly oxygenated blood is sent to the pump for return to the body* (Science News Letter). —**de-foam′er,** *n.*

de|fo|cus (dē fō′kəs), *v.,* **-cused, -cus|ing** or (*especially British*) **-cussed, -cus|sing.** —*v.t.* to cause to deviate from a focused position or point. —*v.i.* to be defocused; go out of focus.

de|fog (dē fog′, -fôg′), *v.t.,* **-fogged, -fog|ging.** to remove haze or mist from, especially by means of a defogger.

de|fog|ger (dē fog′ər), *n.* a device that mechanically removes haze or mist formed by condensation on the windshield or rear window of a motor vehicle.

de|fo|li|ant (di fō′lē ənt), *n.* a chemical agent used to strip plants or trees of their leaves: *A new tool in cancer research may be a chemical now used as a weedkiller and cotton defoliant* (Science News Letter).

de|fo|li|ate (di fō′lē āt), *v.,* **-at|ed, -at|ing.** —*v.t.* to strip (a tree or plant) of leaves.
—*v.i.* to be stripped of leaves.
[< Late Latin *dēfoliāre* (with English *-ate*[1]) < Latin *dē-* away from + *folium* leaf]

de|fo|li|a|tion (di fō′lē ā′shən), *n.* a loss or shedding of leaves: *Defoliation helps keep mechanically picked cotton clean and free from leaves* (Burt Johnson).

de|fo|li|a|tor (di fō′lē ā′tər), *n.* **1** a chemical that defoliates. **2** an insect that strips trees of their leaves.

de|force (di fôrs′, -fōrs′), *v.t.,* **-forced, -forc|ing.** *Law.* **1** to deprive (a person) of property by force; keep (a person) from his property by force. **2** to withhold (something) by force from the rightful owner. [< Anglo-French *deforcer,* Old French *desforcier* < *des-* dis- (< Latin *dis-*) + *forcier* to force]

de|force|ment (di fôrs′mənt, -fōrs′-), *n. Law.* the act or process of deforcing or state of being deforced.

de|for|ciant (di fôr′shənt, -fōr′-), *n. Law.* a person who deforces. [< Anglo-French *deforceant,* (originally) present participle of *deforcer;* see etym. under **deforce**]

de|for|est (dē fôr′ist, -for′-), *v.t.* to remove the trees from; clear of trees or forests: *The land had to be deforested before the settlers could farm it.*

de|for|est|a|tion (dē fôr′ə stā′shən, -for′-), *n.* the act of deforesting or condition of being deforested: *By excessive deforestation and by the destruction of other vegetational cover, flood control is becoming increasingly difficult* (Fred W. Emerson).

de|for|est|er (dē fôr′ə stər, -for′-), *n.* a person or thing that clears land of trees or forests.

de|form[1] (di fôrm′), *v.t.* **1** to spoil the form or shape of: *Shoes that are too tight deform the feet.* **SYN:** disfigure, misshape. **2** to make ugly: *Hate and anger deformed the witch's face.* **3** to change the form of; transform. **4** *Physics.* to change the shape of by stress: *A metal crystal can be plastically deformed without fracture* (J. Crowther). **—*v.i.*** to become deformed. [< Old French *desformer* < Latin *dēfōrmāre* < *dē-* from + *forma* shape]

de|form[2] (di fôrm′), *adj. Archaic.* deformed; ugly. [< Latin *dēfōrmis* < *dē-* from + *forma* shape]

de|form|a|ble (di fôr′mə bəl), *adj.* that can be deformed.

de|for|mal|i|za|tion (dē fôr′mə lə zā′shən), *n.* the act or process of deformalizing or state of being deformalized: *... the deformalization of social life and the clothes to wear for it* (London Times).

de|for|mal|ize (dē fôr′mə līz), *v.t.,* **-ized, -iz|ing.** to reduce the formal aspects of; make less formal: *to deformalize the structure of an organization.*

de|for|ma|tion (dē′fôr mā′shən, def′ər-), *n.* **1** the act of deforming: (*Figurative.*) *His modest deformation of his subject matter over the years has come to seem ... merely the masterly signature of his individualism* (New Yorker). **2** a deformed condition; disfigurement: *A crippling disease caused deformation of his body. The twisted branches of that tree are deformations caused by the snow.* **3** a change of form. **4** a changed form. **5** *Physics.* a change in the shape or dimensions of a body, resulting from stress; strain: *The application of similar heat cycles produced no deformation of cubic metals like lead and aluminium* (F. A. Fox). **6** *Geology.* **a** any change in the original state or size of rock masses, especially as produced by faulting. **b** an instance of this.

de|formed (di fôrmd′), *adj.* **1** not properly formed: *A hunchback is deformed.* **SYN:** misshapen, disfigured. **2** ugly. **—de|form′ed|ly,** *adv.*

de|form|er (di fôr′mər), *n.* **1** a person or thing that deforms. **2** (in controversial use) the opposite of reformer.

de|form|i|ty (di fôr′mə tē), *n., pl.* **-ties. 1** something in the shape of a body that is not as it should be, such as hump on the back: *a deformity of the hand.* **SYN:** malformation. **2** the condition of being improperly formed: *Doctors can now cure many deformities.* **SYN:** disfigurement. **3** an improperly formed person or thing. **4** *Figurative.* moral disfigurement or ugliness: *the deformity of evil living, the criminal's deformity of conduct.*

de|fraud (di frôd′), *v.t.* to take money, rights, or other interests away from by fraud; cheat: *to defraud citizens of their rights. The company defrauded the government of millions of dollars in taxes.* **SYN:** swindle, cozen. [< Latin *dēfraudāre* < *dē-* (intensive) + *fraus, fraudis* fraud] **—de|fraud′er,** *n.*

de|frau|da|tion (dē′frô dā′shən), *n.* the act of defrauding or state of being defrauded.

de|fray (di frā′), *v.t.* **1** to pay (costs or expenses): *The expenses of national parks are defrayed by the taxpayers.* **2** *Archaic.* to meet the expense of; pay for. [< Middle French *desfraier* < *de-* out (< Latin *dē-*) + Old French *frais* costs < Frankish (compare Old High German *fridu* peace)] **—de|fray′a|ble,** *adj.* **—de|fray′er,** *n.*

de|fray|al (di frā′əl), *n.* payment of costs or expenses.

de|fray|ment (di frā′mənt), *n.* = defrayal.

de|frock (dē frok′), *v.t.* to deprive of priestly dress and position; unfrock: *Adolf Lanz was a defrocked Roman Catholic priest who left the Church ... in 1899* (Atlantic).

de|frost (dē frôst′, -frost′), *v.t.* **1a** to remove frost or ice from: *to defrost the refrigerator.* **b** = defog. **2** to thaw out (frozen foods): *The fish was defrosted, cut into portions, well battered, and then fried* (Listener). **—*v.i.*** to thaw out; become defrosted: *The weather was hot. The dinners defrosted* (Wall Street Journal).

de|frost|er (dē frôs′tər, -fros′-), *n.* **1** a device that removes frost or ice, either through heat or mechanically. Defrosters are used on the wings of planes and in refrigerators. **2** = defogger.

deft (deft), *adj.* quick and skillful in action; nimble; clever: *The fingers of a violinist or surgeon must be deft. ... one of the deftest juggling performances since the late W. C. Fields laid aside his Indian clubs* (Time). **SYN:** See syn. under **dexterous.** [Old English *gedæfte* gentle. See related etym. at **daft.**] **—deft′ly,** *adv.* **—deft′ness,** *n.*

deft., defendant.

de|fu|el (di fyü′əl), *v.t.,* **-eled, -el|ing** or (*especially British*) **-elled, -el|ling.** to remove the fuel rods of a nuclear reactor: *Removal of the sump water, expected to be among the most difficult tasks of the clean-up operation, must be accomplished before full scale decontamination and defuelling of the reactor can begin* (New Scientist).

de|funct (di fungkt′), *adj., n.* **—*adj.*** no longer in existence; dead; extinct; deceased: *A business that fails is defunct.* **—*n.*** Usually, **the defunct.** a dead person or persons: *Accosting a servant ... he demanded the name of the defunct* (Washington Irving). [< Latin *dēfūnctus,* past participle of *dēfungī* finish < *dē-* off, completely + *fungī* perform (a duty)]

de|func|tive (di fungk′tiv), *adj. Rare.* of or having to do with dying: *The cold Brussels sprout rolled off the page of the book I was reading and lay inert and defunctive in my lap* (Newsweek).

de|funct|ness (di fungkt′nis), *n.* the quality or condition of being defunct.

de|fuse (dē fyüz′), *v.t.,* **-fused, -fus|ing. 1** to remove the fuze from (a bomb, mine, or other explosive device): *The bomb was expertly defused and trucked off to a bomb graveyard where the explosive filling could be steamed out in safety* (Time). **2** *Figurative:* [*The President*] *has defused chronic student protest by releasing jailed students* (Time). *Miss Bacall defuses and obliterates every other talent on stage* (Alistair Cooke).

de|fus|er (dē fyü′zər), *n.* a person or thing that defuses.

de|fy (*v.* di fī′; *n.* di fī′, dē′fī), *v.,* **-fied, -fy|ing,** *n., pl.* **-fies. —*v.t.*** **1** to set oneself openly against (authority); resist boldly: *As soon as the boy was earning his own living he defied his father's strict rules. The thief defied the law and was arrested.* **SYN:** brave. **2** to be beyond the power of; withstand; resist: *This strong fort defies capture. Granite defies weathering more than sandstone.* **3** to challenge (a person) to do or prove something: *We defy you to show that our game is not fair. Betty ... defied me to deny it* (Richard D. Blackmore). **SYN:** dare. **4** *Archaic.* to challenge to a combat or contest.
—*n.* *Informal.* a challenge to a combat or contest: *So keyed-up during a race that he must shout a glad defy* (New York Times).
[< Old French *defier* < Vulgar Latin *disfīdāre* < Latin *dis-* away + *fīdus* faithful]

de|fy|ing|ly (di fī′ing lē), *adv.* with defiance; defiantly.

deg., degree or degrees: *Even in "cool" north Iraq the temperature for several weeks has been well over 100 deg. F. in the shade* (London Times).

dé|ga|gé (dā gȧ zhā′), *adj.* **1** easy in manner; not embarrassed; unconstrained: *We drift out, dégagé, a little blasé, to find the Harvard men with whom we came* (New Yorker). **2** *Ballet.* having the working foot disengaged in readiness for a step. [< French *dégagé* disengaged, put at ease]

de|gas (dē gas′), *v.t.,* **-gassed, -gas|sing. 1** to remove a gas from. **2** to remove poison gas from. **—de|gas′ser,** *n.*

de|gas|i|fi|ca|tion (dē gas′ə fə kā′shən), *n.* the act of degassing.

de|gas|i|fi|er (dē gas′ə fī′ər), *n.* an agent that degasses: *The water is passed through a degasifier where the carbon dioxide is removed* (Scientific American).

de|gas|i|fy (dē gas′ə fī), *v.t.,* **-fied, -fy|ing.** = degas.

de Gaull|ism (də gô′liz əm, -gō′-), = Gaullism.

de Gaull|ist (də gô′list, -gō′-), = Gaullist.

de|gauss (dē gous′, -gôs′), *v.t.* **1** to neutralize the magnetic field of (a steel ship) so that explosive magnetic mines will not be attracted to its hull. A coil of electric cable is put around the ship's hull. **2** to demagnetize: *Before making any colour adjustments the engineer will have to degauss the face of the screen which contains the metal shadow-mask ... as well as the metal screen* (New Scientist). [< *de-* + *gauss*]

de|gen|er|a|cy (di jen′ər ə sē), *n.* **1** degenerate condition or character. **2** the act or process of degenerating.

de|gen|er|ate (*v.* di jen′ə rāt; *adj., n.* di jen′ər it), *v.,* **-at|ed, -at|ing,** *adj., n.* **—*v.i.*** **1** to grow worse; decline in physical, mental, or moral qualities: *His health degenerated with disease and old age. How the son degenerates from the sire!* (Alexander Pope). **SYN:** deteriorate. **2** *Biology.* to sink to a lower type; lose the normal or more highly developed characteristics of one's race or kind: *The eyes of the electric eel are cloudy, degenerated, and useless in adult life* (A. W. Haslett). **SYN:** deteriorate.
—*adj.* **1** that has degenerated; showing a decline in physical, mental, or moral qualities: *The thief was a degenerate member of a fine family.* **2** *Biology.* that has lost the normal or more highly developed characteristics of its race or kind. **3** *Quantum Mechanics.* having the low quantum states composed of atoms with very dense electrons and nuclei: *degenerate matter.* **4** *Genetics.* that codes redundantly for a particular or the same amino acid: *a degenerate codon. Is the* [*genetic*] *code degenerate, that is, does more than one kind of triplet correspond to a particular amino acid?* (J. M. Thoday and J. A. Pateman).
—*n.* a degenerate person; person having an evil or unwholesome character: *Only a degenerate could have committed such a horrible crime.* **SYN:** deviate.
[< Latin *dēgenerāre* (with English *-ate*[1]) depart from one's race or kind, ultimately < *dē-* from + *genus, generis* race, kind] **—de|gen′er|ate|ly,** *adv.* **—de|gen′er|ate|ness,** *n.*

degenerate gas, a gas in which the electronic particles and nuclei are densely distributed, and thus can liberate energy, as in white dwarf stars.

de|gen|er|a|tion (di jen′ə rā′shən), *n.* **1** the process of degenerating. **SYN:** deterioration. **2** a degenerate condition. **SYN:** degeneracy. **3** *Medicine.* a deterioration in tissues or organs of the body, caused by disease, injury, etc.: *The gangrenous degeneration rapidly extended* (E. A. Parkes). **4** *Biology.* a gradual change to a less highly developed or lower type. **SYN:** devolution.

de|gen|er|a|tive (di jen′ə rā′tiv, -ər ə-), *adj.* **1** tending to degenerate. **2** characterized by degeneration; showing degeneration: *degenerative changes of the tissues. Many diseases which are not caused by organisms, notably those connected with the degenerative changes of old age, are ever-present and ever-increasing problems* (A. J. Birch).

degenerative disease, a disease associated with old age and the breakdown or failure of an organ or system, such as arteriosclerosis.

de|germ (dē jėrm′), *v.t.* **1** to eliminate disease germs from. **2** to remove the seeds or kernels from (a grain): *to degerm wheat.*

de|gla|ci|a|tion (dē glā′shē ā′shən), *n.* the disappearance of glacial ice from an area: *... changes in the climate of Britain associated with the last glacial maximum and the following deglaciation* (G. H. Dury).

de|glam|or|ize (dē glam′ə rīz), *v.t.,* **-ized, -iz|ing.** to divest of glamour or of a glamorous appearance or reputation: *It was the Dreyfus affair that deglamorized high society for Proust* (Time).

de|glu|ti|nate (di glü′tə nāt), *v.t.,* **-nat|ed, -nat|ing. 1** to remove gluten from. **2** *Obsolete.* to unglue. [< Latin *dēglūtināre* (with English *-ate*[1]) < *dē-* away, un- + *glūtināre* to glue < *glūten, -inis* glue]

de|glu|ti|na|tion (di glü′tə nā′shən), *n.* the act or process of removing gluten from; deglutinating.

de|glu|ti|tion (dē′glü tish′ən, deg′lü-), *n.* the act or power of swallowing: *Judgment untempered by feeling is too bitter and husky a morsel for human deglutition* (Charlotte Brontë). [< French *déglutition* < Latin *dēglūtīre* swallow down < *dē-* down + *glūtīrī* to swallow. Compare etym. under **glut, glutton.**]

de|glu|ti|to|ry (di glü′tə tôr′ē, -tōr′-), *adj.* of or having to do with deglutition.

de|grad|a|bil|i|ty (di grā′də bil′ə tē), *n., pl.* **-ties.** susceptibility to decomposition, especially chemical decomposition.

de|grad|a|ble (di grā′də bəl), *adj.* susceptible to decomposition, especially chemical decomposition: *There has been a reduction of the residual amounts of synthetic detergent material in the ... river sources of supply after the complete substitution in packets of washing powder retailed in Britain of anionic detergents which are biologically degradable* (Nature).

deg|ra|dand (deg′rə dand), *n.* a person who is to be degraded or reduced in rank.

deg|ra|da|tion (deg′rə dā′shən), *n.* **1** a degrading: *A poor diet may cause a gradual degradation of health.* **SYN:** deterioration. **2** a being degraded: *Failure to obey orders caused the sergeant's degradation to the rank of private. For, in the absence of debate, unrestricted utterance leads to the degradation of opinion* (Atlantic). **SYN:** debasement, degeneracy. **3** a degraded condition: *The drunkard, filthy and half-starved, lived in degradation.* **4** *Geology.* the wearing down of land, rocks, or other land formations, by erosion: *The processes of gradation are of two types: ... called degradation and aggradation* (Finch and Trewartha). **5** the degrading of complex chemical compounds.

deg|ra|da|tion|al (deg′rə dā′shə nəl), *adj.* of or having to do with degradation.

deg|ra|da|tive (deg′rə dā′tiv), *adj.* of or tending to degradation: *The principle ... is that molecules containing radioactive atoms can be traced* *through the courses of their synthetic or degradative metabolisms* (F. Fowden).

de|grade (di grād′), *v.*, **-grad|ed, -grad|ing.** — ***v.t.*** **1** to reduce to a lower rank, often as a punishment; take away a position or an honor from: *The sergeant was degraded to private for disobeying orders.* **SYN**: demote. **2** to make worse; lower; debase: *You degrade yourself when you steal.* **SYN**: defile, dishonor. **3** *Chemistry.* to reduce systematically the molecule of (a compound) into others of less complex structure; decompose: *This treatment "degraded" some of the virus, separating the rods into nucleic acid and protein molecules* (Time). **4** to reduce in price, strength, purity, or other quality: *to degrade food or drugs. In coordinated bomber-missile attacks, ballistic missiles can precede the bomber strikes and "degrade" the enemy's defenses* (United States Air Force Report on the Ballistic Missile). **5** *Geology.* to wear down (land, rocks, or other land formations) by erosion. **6** to tone down in color. **7** *Biology.* to reduce to a lower classification.
— ***v.i.*** to become reduced or degraded: *This polymerized herbicide degrades in moist soil at a controlled rate* (Science News).
[< Old French *degrader,* learned borrowing from Late Latin *dēgradāre* reduce the rank of < Latin *dē-* down + *gradus, -ūs* step, grade]

de|grad|ed (di grā′did), *adj.* reduced to lower rank, position, etc.; debased. — **de|grad′ed|ly,** *adv.* — **de|grad′ed|ness,** *n.*

de|grad|er (di grā′dər), *n.* a person or thing that degrades; debaser.

de|grad|ing (di grā′ding), *adj.* that degrades or debases: *The poor man believed that accepting charity was degrading.* — **de|grad′ing|ly,** *adv.*

dé|gras (dā grä′), *n. French.* the fat or grease recovered after treating certain skins with fish oil, and used as a dressing for hides: *In composition, dégras is nothing more or less than emulsified fat ... of buttery or salvelike consistency* (C. Salter).

de gra|ti|a (dē grā′shē ə), *Latin.* from or by favor.

de|grease (dē grēs′), *v.t.*, **-greased, -greas|ing.** to remove grease from, especially by using chemicals: *Remember the trouble the Home Guard had in 1940 degreasing those lend-lease American rifles!* (Punch).

de|greas|er (dē grē′sər), *n.* a person or thing that degreases.

de|greas|ing (dē grē′sing), *n.* **1** the act or process of removing grease from a greasy object. **2** the removal of fatty matter from raw sheep's wool by the solvent action of petroleum naphtha.

***de|gree** (di grē′), *n.* **1a** a unit for measuring temperature. A degree on the centigrade (Celsius) scale is 1.8 times a degree on the Fahrenheit scale. *The freezing point of water is 32 degrees* (*32°*) *Fahrenheit or 0 degrees* (*0°*) *centigrade* (*Celsius*). **b** one of the marks on a thermometer or other device, representing a degree. **2a** a unit for measuring the opening of an angle or an arc of a circle; 1/90 of a right angle or 1/360 of the circumference of a circle. Forty-five degrees is half a right angle or one eighth of the line bounding a circle. **b** a position on the earth's surface or the celestial sphere as measured by degrees of latitude or longitude. **3** amount; extent: *To what degree are you interested in reading?* **SYN**: measure, range. **4** a step in a scale; a stage in a process: *He has advanced only one degree in promotion.* **SYN**: gradation. **5** rank; social station; grade: *A princess is a lady of high degree. Here lies a lady of beauty and high degree* (John Crowe Ransom). **SYN**: standing. **6** a rank or title given by a college or university to a student whose work fulfills certain requirements, or to a noted person as an honor: *a bachelor's degree, a master's degree. Applicant should have an Honours Degree, and also practical experience* (Sunday Times). **7** *Law.* the relative measure of the seriousness of a crime: *murder in the first degree.* **8** *Grammar.* one of the three stages in the comparison of adjectives or adverbs. The positive degree of *fast* is *fast;* the comparative degree is *faster;* the superlative degree is *fastest.* **9** *Algebra.* rank as determined by an exponent or sum of exponents: *A^3 and a^2b are terms of the third degree; $x^2y^2z^3$ is a term of the seventh degree.* **10** a relative condition, manner, way, or respect: *A bond and a stock may both be wise investments, each in its degree.* **11** any one of various grades conferred by a fraternal society, or the like, upon its members. **12** a step in direct line of descent: *a cousin two degrees removed.* **13** *Music.* **a** an interval between any note of the scale and the next note. **b** a line or space on the staff showing the position of the notes. **c** an interval between two of these lines or spaces. **14** *Obsolete.* a step, as of a stair; row; tier.
by degrees, gradually: *By degrees the lake gets warm enough to swim in. What wound did ever heal but by degrees?* (Shakespeare).
to a degree, a to a large amount; to a great extent: *A Czarina obstinate to a degree;* [*she*] *would not consent* (Thomas Carlyle). **b** a little; somewhat; slightly: *He was stubborn to a degree, but we finally persuaded him to go along with our plans.*
to the nth degree. See under **nth.**
[< Old French *degre* < Vulgar Latin *dēgradus* < Late Latin *dēgradāre* divide into steps; see etym. under **degrade**]

***degree**
definitions 1b, 2a

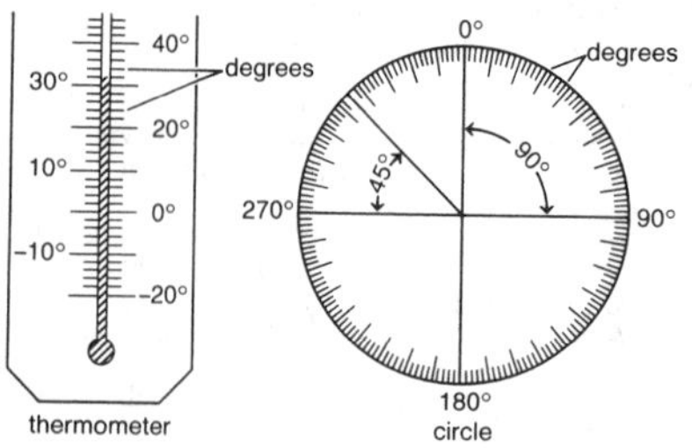

40° 30° 20° 10° 0° -10° -20° degrees
thermometer

0° 90° 180° 270° 45° 90° degrees
circle

de|greed (di grēd′), *adj.* having one or more academic degrees: *This degreed man must be able to boast a minimum of 3 to 5 years of successful engineering-sales activity* (New York Times).

de|gree-day (di grē′dā′), *n., pl.* **-days.** a unit representing one degree of deviation below a standard (usually 65 degrees) in the mean temperature out of doors for one day. It is used in statistics to determine fuel requirements.

de|gree|less (di grē′lis), *adj.* **1** lacking an academic degree. **2** not providing academic degrees: *a degreeless university.*

degree mill, *Informal.* an educational institution that confers academic degrees without proper authorization or adequate academic standards.

degree of freedom, 1 *Physics.* any one of the ways in which a body may be displaced or a system changed without loss of equilibrium. **2** *Statistics.* any one of the number of unrestricted and independent values that may be assigned arbitrarily to a distribution.

degrees of frost, degrees below the freezing point of water.

de|gres|sion (di gresh′ən), *n.* **1** the decrease in rate for sums below a certain amount, especially in degressive taxation. **2** a going down; descent. [< Latin *dēgressiō, -ōnis* < *dēgredī* to descend < *dē-* from + *gradī* go]

de|gres|sive (di gres′iv), *adj.* of or having to do with a system of taxation in which the rate is constant on sums of and above a certain fixed amount, but diminishes gradually on sums below it.

dé|grin|go|lade (dā graN gô lȧd′), *n. French.* a swift, involuntary descent; steep, downward course: *... The day the white rabble of Algiers rioted and frightened Premier Guy Mollet, will be chosen to mark the beginning of the second dégringolade* (A. J. Liebling).

deg|u (deg′ü), *n.* **1** a brownish, ratlike rodent of Peru with large ears and a bushy-tipped tail. **2** any one of various South American rodents of the same family, such as the coypu. [< Spanish *degu* < a native name]

de|gum (dē gum′), *v.t.*, **-gummed, -gum|ming.** to free from gum.

de|gust (di gust′), *v.t., v.i.* to taste attentively, so as to appreciate the flavor. [< Latin *dēgustāre* < *dē-* (intensive) + *gustāre* to taste < *gustus, -ūs* a tasting]

de|gus|tate (di gus′tāt), *v.t., v.i.*, **-tat|ed, -tat|ing.** = degust. [< Latin *dēgustāre* (with English *-ate*[1]); see etym. under **degust**]

de|gus|ta|tion (dē′gus tā′shən), *n.* the act of tasting: *As Waythorn sat despatching his hurried luncheon he looked across half enviously at the other's leisurely degustation of his meal* (Edith Wharton).

de gus|ti|bus non est dis|pu|tan|dum (dē gus′tə bəs non est dis′pyü tan′dəm), *Latin.* there is no accounting for tastes; it is useless to argue about matters of taste.

de|gut (dē gut′), *v.t.*, **-gut|ted, -gut|ting.** *British.* to remove the guts or innards of; eviscerate: *to degut fish.* (*Figurative.*) *Mr. Stone has attempted to degut the musical of its more absurd moments* (Derek Malcolm).

de|hair (dē hãr′), *v.t.* to remove the hair from (an animal or its hide or skin): *They sent the qiviut through the special machinery they have designed for dehairing Cashmere* [*goats*], *and found that it works perfectly* (Atlantic).

de haut en bas (də ō′ tän bä′), *French.* **1a** from top to bottom. **b** from head to foot. **2** superciliously; disdainfully: *The patterns and values of this prescientific agricultural society ... have always been seen de haut en bas* (Sunday Times).

de|hire (dē hīr′), *v.t.*, **-hired, -hir|ing.** *U.S.* to discharge from hired employment; fire: *In a depression, the boss is sacked and jumps from a window. In the "recedence," he is "dehired"* (Manchester Guardian Weekly).

de|hisce (di his′), *v.i.*, **-hisced, -hisc|ing.** *Biology.* (of an organ, seed pod, or other enclosed process) to burst open along a definite line, providing for discharge of the seeds or other contents. [< Latin *dehīscere* < *dē-* away from + *hīscere* < *hiāre* be open, gape]

de|his|cence (di his′əns), *n. Biology.* the bursting open of an organ, pod, anther, or other enclosed process, in order to discharge seeds, pollen, or other contents.

de|his|cent (di his′ənt), *adj.* (of dry fruits such as legumes and capsules) bursting open to scatter seeds.

de|horn (dē hôrn′), *v.t.* to remove the horns from: *Dehorned cattle have had their horns removed by cutting them out with a knife or burning them out with a hot iron* (Hilton M. Briggs).

de|horn|er (dē hôr′nər), *n.* an instrument for cutting off the horns of cattle.

de|hors (də ôr′), *prep. Law.* **1** outside. **2** outside of: *a fact dehors the contract.* **3** foreign to. [< French *dehors,* adverb < Late Latin *dēforīs* < Latin *dē-* from + *forīs* out of doors]

de|hort (di hôrt′), *v.t.* to seek to dissuade: *Croker dehorts me from visiting Ireland* (Robert Southey). [< Latin *dehortārī* < *dē-* from + *hortārī* exhort] — **de|hort′er,** *n.*

de|hor|ta|tion (dē′hôr tā′shən), *n.* the act of dehorting; earnest dissuasion.

de|hor|ta|tive (di hôr′tə tiv), *adj., n.* — ***adj.*** **1** having the quality or purpose of dehorting. **2** = dehortatory.
— ***n.*** a dehortative address or argument.

de|hor|ta|to|ry (di hôr′tə tôr′ē, -tōr′-), *adj., n., pl.* **-ries.** — ***adj.*** characterized by dehortation.
— ***n.*** *Obsolete.* a dehortatory address.

de|hu|man|i|za|tion (dē hyü′mə nə zā′shən), *n.* a dehumanizing or being dehumanized.

de|hu|man|ize (dē hyü′mə nīz), *v.t.*, **-ized, -iz|ing.** to deprive of human qualities, such as interest or sympathy: *The knowledge, for which Buchenwald is a compact symbol, that men can be dehumanized, ... is not a reason for casting out the knowledge of good and evil* (New Yorker). **SYN**: brutalize.

de|hu|mid|i|fi|er (dē′hyü mid′ə fī′ər), *n.* a device for treating air in a building, room, or other enclosed area, to regulate and, usually, decrease the amount of moisture in the air: *Torrential rains in many areas of the country are bringing a sales flood for dehumidifiers* (Wall Street Journal).

de|hu|mid|i|fy (dē′hyü mid′ə fī), *v.t.*, **-fied, -fy|ing.** to remove moisture from (the air).

de|hy|drase (dē hī′drās), *n.* **1** = dehydrogenase. **2** = dehydratase.

de|hy|dra|tase (dē hī′drə tās), *n.* an enzyme that causes the removal of water from a compound.

de|hy|drate (dē hī′drāt), *v.*, **-drat|ed, -drat|ing.** — ***v.t.*** **1** to take water or moisture from; dry: *to dehydrate vegetables. High fever dehydrates the body.* **2** to deprive (a chemical compound) of water or the elements of water.
— ***v.i.*** to lose water or moisture.

de|hy|dra|tion (dē′hī drā′shən), *n.* the removal of water from the body, or from vegetables, fruits, or other foods, or from chemical compounds.

de|hy|dra|tor (dē hī′drā tər), *n.* a device that dehydrates: *Dehydrators take less time than the other means of drying to process the same amount of food. Some dehydrators use a partial vacuum to make water evaporate at a low temperature* (John T. R. Nickerson).

de|hy|dro|chlo|rin|ase (dē hī′drə klôr′ə nās, -klōr′-), *n.* an enzyme that causes dehydrochlorination.

de|hy|dro|chlo|rin|ate (dē hī′drə klôr′ə nāt, -klōr′-), *v.t.*, **-at|ed, -at|ing.** to remove hydrogen and chlorine from (a compound).

de|hy|dro|chlo|rin|a|tion (dē hī′drə klôr′ə nā′shən, -klōr′-), *n.* the removal of hydrogen and chlorine from a compound: *Mosquitoes immune to DDT by having mastered the art of inactivating it by dehydrochlorination ...* (New Scientist).

de|hy|dro|freez|ing (dē hī′drō frē′zing), *n.* a process for preserving fruits and vegetables by partial dehydration and quick-freezing.

de|hy|dro|fro|zen (dē hī′drō frō′zən), *adj.* preserved by dehydrofreezing: *It includes everything from dehydrofrozen soup to irradiated nuts* (Science News Letter).

de|hy|dro|gen|ase (dē hī′drə jə nās), *n.* an enzyme that activates hydrogen and causes its removal, as from body tissue: *In bacterial respiration the most important enzymes are the dehydrogenases* (Dible, MacLennan, and Barber). [< *de-* + *hydrogen* + *-ase*]

de|hy|dro|gen|ate (dē hī′drə jə nāt), *v.t.*, **-at|ed**, **-at|ing.** to remove hydrogen from (a compound).
de|hy|dro|gen|a|tion (dē hī′drə jə nā′shən), *n.* the removal of hydrogen from a compound.
de|hy|dro|gen|i|za|tion (dē hī′drə jə nə zā′shən), *n.* dehydrogenation.
de|hy|dro|gen|ize (dē hī′drə jə nīz), *v.t.*, **-ized**, **-iz|ing.** = dehydrogenate.
de|hyp|no|tize (dē hip′nə tīz), *v.t.*, **-tized**, **-tiz|ing.** to bring out of the hypnotic state.
De|ia|ni|ra (dē′ə nī′rə), *n. Greek Legend.* the wife of Hercules, who unknowingly killed him by giving him a poisoned shirt.
de|ice (dē īs′), *v.t.*, **-iced**, **-ic|ing.** to prevent ice from forming on; remove ice from (an aircraft or other surface): *There was a brief delay while the wings were deiced, and then the plane taxied out onto the field* (New Yorker).
***de|ic|er** (dē ī′sər), *n.* a device or substance for removing or preventing the formation of ice on airplane wings, the windshield of a car, or other surface.

***deicer**

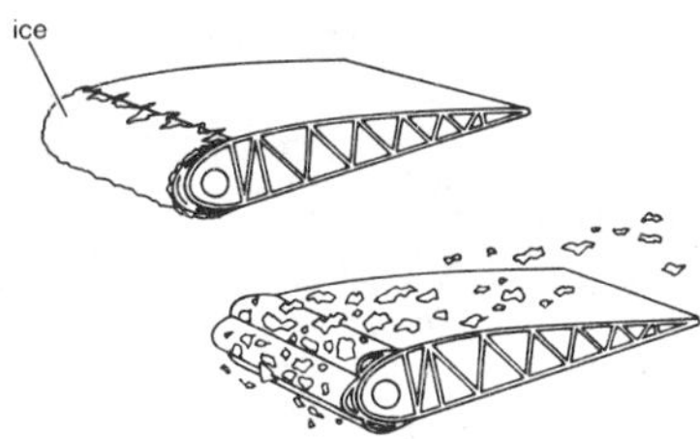

de|i|cid|al (dē′ə sī′dəl), *adj.* of or having to do with deicide; god-killing.
de|i|cide¹ (dē′ə sīd), *n.* a person who kills a god, as in some primitive rituals. [< Late Latin *deicīda* < Latin *deus* god + *-cīda* -cide¹]
de|i|cide² (dē′ə sīd), *n.* the killing of a god: *The deicide principle in Marx rebelled against the Absolute Idea* (Edmund Wilson). [< New Latin *deicidium* < Latin *deus* god + *-cīdium* -cide²]
deic|tic (dīk′tik), *adj.* **1** *Logic.* that proves directly. **2** *Grammar.* pointing out; demonstrative. Also, **deiktic.** [< Greek *deiktikós* showing, able to show < *deiknýnai* to show] **—deic′ti|cal|ly,** *adv.*
de|i|de|ol|o|gize (dē ī′dē ol′ə jīz), *v.t.*, **-gized**, **-giz|ing.** to remove ideology or doctrine from: *The time has come ... to get down to the task of demythologizing and deideologizing the teaching office in the church* (Hans Kung).
de|if|ic (dē if′ik), *adj.* **1** deifying; making divine. **2** divine; godlike. [< Latin *deificus* (one) deifying; consecrated < *deus* god + *facere* make]
de|i|fi|ca|tion (dē′ə fə kā′shən), *n.* **1** a deifying: *The deification of the emperor was customary in ancient Rome. I would suggest that deification of the state ... is surely not in the American tradition* (Atlantic). **2** a being deified: *After his deification, altars were erected to him throughout the empire.* **3** *Theology.* the absorption of anything into the divine nature or deity.
de|i|fi|er (dē′ə fī′ər), *n.* a person or thing that deifies.
de|i|form (dē′ə fôrm), *adj.* having the form of a god; godlike. [< Medieval Latin *deiformis* < Latin *deus* god + *forma* form, shape]
de|i|form|i|ty (dē′ə fôr′mə tē), *n.* the quality or condition of being deiform.
de|i|fy (dē′ə fī), *v.t.*, **-fied**, **-fy|ing.** **1** to make a god of: *Many American Indians deified and worshiped streams, trees, animals, and other objects of nature.* **2** to worship or regard as a god: *Some deify wealth, others, power.* SYN: adore, idolize. [< Old French *deifier* < Late Latin *deificāre* < Latin *deificus;* see etym. under **deific**]
deign (dān), *v.i.* to think fit; condescend: *So great a man would never deign to quarrel with such trifling critics.* SYN: stoop. **—*v.t.*** **1** to condescend to give (an answer, a reply, or other acknowledgment): *She did not deign even a nod to show that she had heard.* SYN: vouchsafe. **2** *Obsolete.* to condescend to accept: *I fear my Julia would not deign my lines* (Shakespeare). [< Old French *deignier* < Latin *dignārī* < *dignus* worthy, ultimately < *decēre* be of worth]
De|i gra|ti|a (dē′ī grā′shē ə; de′ē grä′tē ä), *Latin.* by the grace of God.
deik|tic (dīk′tik), *adj.* = deictic.
deil (dēl), *n. Scottish.* a devil.
De Im|i|ta|ti|o|ne Chris|ti (dē im′ə tā′shē ō′nē kris′tī), *Latin.* a famous medieval religious treatise, of disputed authorship, but commonly ascribed to Thomas à Kempis.
Dei|mos (dī′mos), *n.* the smaller and slower satellite of Mars, discovered in 1877. [< New Latin *Deimos* < Greek *Deimós* a son of Mars < *deimós* fear, terror]
de|in|dex (dē in′deks), *v.t.* **1** to remove or separate (income, interest rates, and the like) from cost-of-living or inflation rates: *The proposals to tax certain short-term benefits, deindex others, and reduce and tax strike benefits will produce an outcry from the unions* (Manchester Guardian Weekly). **2** to remove from an index: *If there is no possibility to deindex recipients, then it's only fair that we protect taxpayers through an indexation of taxes* (Time). **—de|in′dex|a′tion,** *n.*
de|in|di|vid|u|al|ize (dē in′də vij′ù ə līz), *v.t.*, **-ized**, **-iz|ing.** = depersonalize.
de|in|dus|tri|al|ize (dē′in dus′trē ə līz), *v.t.*, **-ized**, **-iz|ing.** to reduce or break up the industry or industrial capacity of (a defeated or occupied country): *The policy of deindustrializing Germany was abandoned in 1948* (London Times).
de|ink (dē ingk′), *v.t.* to remove the ink from (paper, especially newsprint or wastepaper).
de|in|sti|tu|tion|al|ize (dē in′stə tü′shə nə līz, -tyü′-), *v.t.*, **-ized**, **-iz|ing.** **1** to remove the institutional quality or character from: *Even the 8-by-10-foot bathrooms have been deinstitutionalized* (New York Times). **2** to remove from an institution or institutional environment: *It is a really visionary little organization, anxious to deinstitutionalize the disabled* (London Times). **—de|in′sti|tu′tion|al|i|za′tion,** *n.*
de in|te|gro (dē in′tə grō), *Latin.* anew; afresh.
de|in|ter|mix|ture (dē′in tər miks′chər), *n.* the geographical separation of very-high-frequency stations from ultrahigh-frequency stations so that only one type will broadcast in a given area.
de|i|on|ise (dē ī′ə nīz), *v.t.*, **-ised**, **-is|ing.** *Especially British.* deionize.
de|i|on|i|za|tion (dē ī′ə nə zā′shən), *n.* the act of deionizing.
de|i|on|ize (dē ī′ə nīz), *v.t.*, **-ized**, **-iz|ing.** to purify (water) by converting ionic salts into acids and removing them by means of an absorbing agent. **—de|i′on|iz′er,** *n.*
De|ïph|o|bus or **De|iph|o|bus** (dē if′ə bəs), *n. Greek Legend.* a Trojan warrior, son of Priam and Hecuba. He married Helen after the death of Paris and when Troy fell was killed by Menelaus.
deip|nos|o|phist (dīp nos′ə fist), *n.* a person who converses learnedly at dinner. [< Greek *deipnosophistēs* one wise in kitchen matters < *deîpnon* the main meal + *sophistēs* a master, a Sophist]
Deir|dre (dir′drē; *Irish* dār′drā), *n. Celtic Legend.* the princess whom Conchobar, king of Ulster, reared and intended to make his wife, but who ran away with a lover. When Conchobar killed her lover and his brothers, Deirdre died of grief.
de|ism (dē′iz əm), *n.* **1** belief in God on the evidence of reason and nature, and without accepting any particular religion. **2** the belief that God exists entirely apart from our world and does not influence the lives of human beings (contrasted with *atheism, pantheism,* and *theism*). [< Latin *deus* god + English *-ism;* probably patterned on French *déisme*]
de|i|so|late (dē ī′sə lāt, -is′ə-), *v.t.*, **-lat|ed**, **-lat|ing.** to remove from isolation; bring into the company of others: *Now we are being urged to take the initiative to "deisolate" Red China by entering into "scientific and technical cooperation" with Peking* (Bruno Shaw).
de|i|so|la|tion (dē ī′sə lā′shən, -is′ə-), *n.* removal from isolation: *At stake, in the process of China's deisolation, are questions of ... peace in a quadripolar East Asia* (*U.S., U.S.S.R., Japan and China*) (New York Times).
de|ist (dē′ist), *n.* a person who believes in deism: *A deist without a church, he was a free-thinking Freemason with a handsome wit and an easy mastery of prose ... in short, the multilateral Eighteenth Century Man* (Newsweek).
de|is|tic (dē is′tik), *adj.* of or having to do with deists or deism: *reason is the common ground on which men can meet intellectually, and all religions, be they scientistic or deistic, must come before its bar initially* (A. T. Macqueen). **—de|is′ti|cal|ly,** *adv.*
de|is|ti|cal (dē is′tə kəl), *adj.* **1** = deistic. **2** inclined or tending to deism.
de|i|ty (dē′ə tē), *n., pl.* **-ties.** **1** a god or goddess; one of the gods worshiped by a people or a tribe; divine being: *Jupiter was the ruler of the ancient Roman deities. Neptune was a deity of the sea.* **2** divine nature; being a god; godhood; divinity: *Christians believe in the deity of Christ.* **the Deity,** God: *We see the wisdom and the greatness of the Deity in all seeming worlds that surround us* (Oliver Goldsmith). [< Old French *deite,* learned borrowing from Late Latin *deitās* < Latin *deus* god]
dé|jà vu (dā′zhä vü′; *French* dā zhä vY′), *n.* **1** the illusion of having already experienced the situation one is in for the first time; paramnesia. **2** recognition of something already seen or known; tiresome familiarity: *Unfortunately, the book as a whole gives us a sense of déjà vu* (Saturday Review). [< French *déjà vu* already seen]
de|ject (di jekt′), *v., adj.* **—*v.t.*** **1** to depress the spirits of; dishearten: *His troubles did not long deject him.* **2** *Archaic.* to throw or cast down. **—*adj.*** *Archaic.* dejected; downcast. [< Latin *dējectus,* past participle of Latin *dējicere* < *dē-* down + *jacere* to throw]
de|jec|ta (di jek′tə), *n.pl.* excrements. [< Latin *dējecta,* neuter plural of *dējectus;* see etym. under **deject**]
de|ject|ed (di jek′tid), *adj.* **1** in low spirits; sad; discouraged: *She was feeling dejected and unhappy until the good news cheered her up. Today glad—tomorrow dejected* (Edward Bulwer-Lytton). SYN: downcast, disheartened. See syn. under **sad.** **2** *Archaic.* **a** thrown or cast down. **b** downcast: *dejected eyes.* **3** *Obsolete.* abased; humbled. **—de|ject′ed|ly,** *adv.* **—de|ject′ed|ness,** *n.*
de|jec|tile (di jek′təl), *n. Military.* a missile hurled down on an enemy. [< Latin *dējectus* (see etym. at **deject**); on analogy of English *projectile*]
de|jec|tion (di jek′shən), *n.* **1** lowness of spirits; sadness; discouragement: *Her face showed her dejection at missing the party.* SYN: depression, melancholy, despondency. **2** *Medicine.* **a** defecation. **b** excrement; feces.
de|jeune (di jün′), *n. Obsolete.* déjeuner. [< Old French *desjeun* breakfast]
dé|jeu|né (dā zhœ nā′), *n. French, Obsolete.* déjeuner.
dé|jeu|ner (dā zhœ nā′), *n. French.* **1** breakfast. **2** luncheon.
de ju|re (dē jùr′ē), *Latin.* by right; according to law; legal (contrasted with *de facto*): *Will de jure sovereignty and membership in the Western alliance add to West Germany's security?* (New York Times).
deka- or **dek-,** *combining form.* variant spellings of **deca-** or **dec-,** as in *dekagram.*
Dek|a|brist (dek′ə brist), *n.* = Decembrist.
dek|a|gram (dek′ə gram), *n.* = decagram.
deke (dēk), *n., v.,* **deked, dek|ing.** *Canadian Slang.* **—*n.*** a sham maneuver in hockey; feint. **—*v.t.*** to maneuver (a shot, movement, or player) in hockey by feinting. [< *decoy*]
dek|ko (dek′ō), *n. British Slang.* a look: *But once I'd grabbed hold of the script and taken a good dekko at it, my worst fears were confirmed* (Kenneth Tynan). Also, **decko.** [< Hindustani *dekho,* imperative of *dekhnā* to look]
de|knight (dē nīt′), *v.t.* to deprive of knighthood; degrade from the rank of knight.
del., 1a delegate. **b** delegation. **2** delete. **3** delivery.
Del., Delaware.
de|laine (di lān′), *n.* a thin woolen material, often having a printed pattern; mousseline de laine. [< French (*mousseline*) *de laine* (muslin) of wool; *laine* < Latin *lāna* wool]
De|laine sheep (di lān′), one of a strain of merino raised in the United States. It is a source of delaine.
de|lam|i|nate (dē lam′ə nāt), *v.t., v.i.,* **-nat|ed**, **-nat|ing.** to split into separate layers.
de|lam|i|na|tion (dē lam′ə nā′shən), *n.* **1** a splitting apart into layers. **2** *Embryology.* the separation of certain groups of cells from others to form distinct cellular masses during morphogenesis.
De|la|ney clause or **amendment,** a clause in the U.S. Food, Drug and Cosmetic Act forbidding the use of any food additive shown to cause cancer in animals or people. [< J.J. *Delaney,* born 1901, New York Congressman]
de|late (di lāt′), *v.t.,* **-lat|ed**, **-lat|ing.** **1** to accuse; inform against; denounce: *If a minister be thus left at liberty to delate sinners from the pulpit ... he may often blast the innocent* (Samuel Johnson). **2** *Archaic.* to relate; report. [< Latin *dēlatus,* past participle of *dēferre* bear down, accuse, defer]
de|la|tion (di lā′shən), *n.* **1** denouncement; accusation. **2** the act of delating.
de|la|tor (di lā′tər), *n.* **1** an informer; accuser. **2** a secret or professional informer.
Del|a|ware (del′ə wãr), *n.* **1a** a member of a tribe of American Indians, most of whom formerly lived in the valley of the Delaware River. **b** the Algonkian language of this tribe. **2** an American variety of grape, having small, sweet, light-red fruits. **3** any one of an American breed of chickens having white feathers, black-barred hackles and tails, and raised chiefly for production of meat.
Del|a|war|e|an (del ə wãr′ē ən), *adj., n.* **—*adj.*** of or having to do with the state of Delaware.

Pronunciation Key: hat, āge, cãre, fär; let, ēqual, tėrm; it, īce; hot, ōpen, ôrder; oil, out; cup, pu̇t, rüle; child; long; thin; ᴛʜen; zh, measure; ə represents a in about, e in taken, i in pencil, o in lemon, u in circus.

—*n.* a native or inhabitant of Delaware.

de|law|yer (dē lô′yər), *v.t.* to remove the need for legal action or the use of lawyers in (some settlement or legal process): *In other areas, procedural reforms such as no-fault insurance offer ways to "delawyer" particular problems* (Thomas Ehrlich). *Several states have enthusiastically embraced "delawyering" proposals* (David C. Beckwith).

de|lay (di lā′), *v., n.* —*v.t.* **1** to put off till a later time: *We will delay the party for a week and hold it next Saturday.* **2** to make late; keep waiting; hinder the progress of: *The accident delayed the train for two hours. Ignorance delays progress.* SYN: retard. —*v.i.* to be late; go slowly; stop along the way; wait: *Do not delay on this errand.* SYN: linger, loiter.

—*n.* **1** the act of delaying; a stopping along the way: *We were so late that we could afford no further delay.* **2** the fact of being delayed; a being put off till a later time: *The delay upset our plans.*

[< Old French *delaier* < *de-* + *laier* leave, let]

—**de|lay′er**, *n.*

—*Syn. v.t.* **1 Delay, defer, postpone** mean to put off doing something. **Delay** often suggests either holding off for some reason but planning to act at some later time or putting off indefinitely: *I delayed seeing the dentist.* **Defer** usually suggests deciding to put off until a better time, with the intention of acting then: *I deferred going until I had more time.* **Postpone** suggests deferring until a definite time, after something has been done, learned, etc.: *I postponed going until next week.*

de|layed-ac|tion (di lād′ak′shən), *adj.* **1** not acting immediately: *Using a camera with a delayed-action shutter makes it possible for you to snap your own picture.* **2** (of a bomb) having a time fuze; not exploding immediately upon hitting the target.

de|layed neutron (di lād′), a neutron emitted after the initial radioactive decay of a nuclear explosion.

de|lay|ing action (di lā′ing), **1** a defensive military maneuver designed to slow up the enemy's advance without engaging in a decisive battle. **2** defensive play in sports to keep the ball or puck away from the opposing team until a period of play or the game is over, usually to maintain a scoring advantage.

de|lay|ing|ly (di lā′ing lē), *adv.* in a manner so as to delay or detain.

delay line, **1** an electronic transmission line or circuit in which a signal or wave is purposely delayed for a set length of time. **2** a device in an electronic computer which stores information by delaying signals between input and output so as to circulate them in the computer for as long as necessary.

del cred|er|e (del kred′ər ē, krē′dər ē), **1** *Law.* denoting the obligation of a factor or agent to guarantee the solvency of the third parties with whom he contracts for his principal. **2** (literally) of belief or trust. [< Italian *del credere* < *del* of the + *credere* to believe; a belief]

del credere agent, a factor or agent who guarantees his principal against loss due to insolvency on contracts which he has made with third parties.

de|le (dē′lē), *v.,* **-led, -le|ing,** *n.* —*v.t., v.i. Printing.* to cross out; delete. This instruction is indicated on copy or proofs by a stylized form of delta or *d* (originally, δ, ∂).

—*n.* the mark indicating the instruction to dele.

[< Latin *dēlē*, imperative of *dēlēre* delete; or perhaps short for *dēleātur* let it be deleted. Compare **stet**.]

de|lec|ta|bil|i|ty (di lek′tə bil′ə tē), *n.* the quality of being delectable.

de|lec|ta|ble (di lek′tə bəl), *adj.* very pleasing; delightful: *a delectable meal, the delectable taste of freshly baked bread. Trees of God, Delectable both to behold and taste* (Milton). [< Middle French *délectable*, learned borrowing from Latin *dēlectābilis* < *dēlectāre;* see etym. under **delight**] —**de|lec′ta|ble|ness**, *n.*

de|lec|ta|bly (di lek′tə blē), *adv.* in a delectable manner; delightfully; charmingly.

de|lec|tate (di lek′tāt), *v.t.,* **-tat|ed, -tat|ing.** = delight. [< Latin *dēlectāre* (with English *-ate*[1]); see etym. under **delight**]

de|lec|ta|tion (dē′lek tā′shən), *n.* great pleasure; delight; entertainment: *The magician did many tricks for our delectation.* SYN: enjoyment.

de|lec|tus (di lek′təs), *n., pl.* **-tus|es** or (*Latin*) **-tus.** a selection of passages for translation, especially from Latin or Greek authors. [< Latin *dēlectus, -ūs* < *dēligere* select < *dē-* from + *legere* to gather]

del|e|ga|ble (del′ə gə bəl), *adj.* that can be delegated: *delegable authority.*

del|e|ga|cy (del′ə gə sē), *n., pl.* **-cies. 1** a group of delegates; delegation. **2** the sending or appointing of a delegate. **3** the position or authority of a delegate: *hope for a delegacy to a convention* (James Bryce).

de|le|gal|ize (dē lē′gə līz), *v.t.,* **-ized, -iz|ing.** to end the legal authority for.

del|e|gant (del′ə gənt), *n. Law.* a debtor who, to discharge his debt, assigns to his creditor a debt of a third party due to himself.

del|e|gate (*n.* del′ə git, -gāt; *v.* del′ə gāt), *n., v.,* **-gat|ed, -gat|ing.** —*n.* **1** a person given power or authority to act for others; representative: *Our club sent two delegates to the state meeting. The three Moroccan delegates to the former sultan of Morocco ... returned to Paris by air this morning* (London Times). SYN: deputy. **2** a representative of a territory in the U.S. House of Representatives who has a seat and the right to speak but no vote. **3** a member of the lower branch of the legislature (House of Delegates) in Maryland, Virginia, and West Virginia.

—*v.t.* **1** to appoint or send (a person) as a representative: *Each club delegated one member to attend the state meeting. The children delegated her to buy the flowers.* SYN: depute. **2** to give over (one's power or authority) to another so that he may act for one: *The teacher delegated the task of keeping order to the biggest boy in class. The states delegated the control of foreign affairs to the federal government.* **3** *Law.* to assign (one's own debtor) to a creditor to replace oneself as a debtor.

—*v.i.* to give over power or authority: *A terrorist ... must delegate to a rather sanguinary and unscrupulous class of subordinate* (John Kenneth Galbraith).

[< Latin *dēlēgātus, past participle of dēlēgāre* < *dē-* + *lēgāre* send (with a commission) < *lēx, lēgis* law]

del|e|ga|tee (del′ə gə tē′), *n. Law.* a person to whom a debtor is assigned in satisfaction of another's debt; assignee of a delegant.

del|e|gate|ship (del′ə git ship, - gāt-), *n.* the office or position of a delegate.

del|e|ga|tion (del′ə gā′shən) *n.* **1** the act or process of delegating or fact of being delegated: *The Senator's delegation of power to an aide did not cover any important rights.* **2** a group of delegates: *Each club sent a delegation to the state meeting.* **3** the position or authority of a delegate or group of delegates.

del|e|ga|tor (del′ə gā′tər), *n.* a person who delegates: *Roncalli, on the other hand, is a great delegator of work* (Maclean's).

de|len|da (di len′də), *n.pl.* things to be deleted, erased, or blotted out. [< Latin *dēlēnda,* gerundive of *dēlērē* destroy]

de|len|da est Car|tha|go (di len′də est kär thā′gō; dā len′dä est kär tä′gō), *Latin.* Carthage must be destroyed (a course urged by Cato the Elder when speaking publicly on any subject whatever).

de|lete (di lēt′), *v.t., v.i.,* **-let|ed, -let|ing. 1** to strike out or take out (anything written or printed); cross out; remove; omit: *In order to decrease the number of pages, many long passages were deleted from the book before printing.* **2** *Figurative.* to wipe out; erase; expunge: *The patient's high fever deleted most of his memories.* **3** *Genetics.* to cause the loss of (a section) of a chromosome. **4** *Linguistics.* to remove (part of a phrase or sentence) in performing a transformation or derivation.

[< Latin *dēlētus,* past participle of *dēlēre* destroy]

del|e|te|ri|ous (del′ə tir′ē əs), *adj.* causing harm; injurious: *'Tis pity wine should be so deleterious* (Byron). *The deleterious genetic effects* [*of radiation*] *would persist for hundreds of generations* (Bulletin of Atomic Scientists). SYN: harmful, noxious, pernicious. [< New Latin *deleterius* (with English *-ous*) < Greek *dēlētērios* < *dēlētēr* destroyer < *dēléesthai* hurt, injure] —**del′e|te′ri|ous|ly,** *adv.* —**del′e|te′ri|ous|ness,** *n.*

de|le|thal|ize (dē lē′thə līz), *v.t.,* **-ized, -iz|ing.** to modify the design of (a dashboard, seat, or other fixture) in a vehicle so that it will not cause death or lethal injury in a collision or crash.

de|le|tion (di lē′shən), *n.* **1** the act of deleting. **2** the fact of being deleted. **3** a deleted part. **4** *Genetics.* the loss of a section of a chromosome: *Characteristic malformations have been related to deletion of parts of specific chromosomes* (Victor A. McKusick). **5** *Linguistics.* the removal of any part of a phrase or sentence to perform a transformation or derivation. *Example:* In the sentence "She is napping in the bedroom" the sentence "She is napping" can be derived by deletion of the phrase "in the bedroom."

delf (delf), *n.* = delft.

delft (delft), *n.* **1** a kind of glazed earthenware made in the Netherlands, usually decorated in blue on a white background. **2** any pottery like this. [< *Delft,* a city in the Netherlands, where it is made]

delft|ware (delft′wãr′), *n.* = delft.

del|i (del′ē), *n., pl.* **del|is.** *U.S. Informal.* delicatessen: *And it's time for lunch. He goes out and buys a pastrami sandwich at the deli* (New Yorker). [< *deli*(catessen)]

De|li|an (dē′lē ən), *adj., n.* —*adj.* of or belonging to Delos.

—*n.* a native or inhabitant of Delos.

de|lib|er|ate (*adj.* di lib′ər it, -lib′rit; *v.* di lib′ə rāt), *adj., v.,* **-at|ed, -at|ing.** —*adj.* **1** done on purpose; intended; thought over beforehand: *His rude answer was a deliberate attempt to provoke her. They were the first great social thinkers of their century to try to make themselves, by deliberate discipline, both classless and international* (Edmund Wilson). **2** slow and careful in deciding what to do: *A deliberate person takes enough time to make up his mind.* SYN: thoughtful, cautious, circumspect. **3** slow; not hurried: *The old man walked with deliberate steps.* SYN: See syn. under **slow**.

—*v.i., v.t.* **1** to think over carefully; consider: *He was slow to answer, deliberating over each question. I am deliberating where to put up my new picture. The woman who deliberates is lost* (Joseph Addison). **2** to talk over reasons for and against something; discuss; debate: *Congress deliberated the question of raising taxes.*

[< Latin *dēlīberātus,* past participle of *dēlīberāre* to deliberate < *dē-* + *lībrāre* weigh < *lībra* a pound, scale. Compare etym. under **deliver**.]

—**de|lib′er|ate|ness**, *n.*

—*Syn. adj.* **1 Deliberate, intentional** mean done on purpose. **Deliberate** suggests that what it describes was thought over in advance and done with a clear idea of what one is doing: *His attempt to deceive the customs authorities was deliberate. The actor delivered his lines with deliberate emphasis. The lawyer made a deliberate attempt to confuse the jury.* **Intentional** emphasizes the idea of a purpose, and means done with a definite end in mind: *His unkind remark was intentional; he wanted to make you angry.*

de|lib|er|ate|ly (di lib′ər it lē, -lib′rit-), *adv.* **1** on purpose. **2** slowly.

de|lib|er|a|tion (di lib′ə rā′shən), *n.* **1** careful thought: *After long deliberation, I decided not to go.* SYN: reflection, study, consideration. **2** a talking about reasons for and against an action; discussion; debate: *the deliberations of Congress over raising taxes. This sentence, after a lengthened deliberation between the Home Secretary and the Judges, was commuted for one of transportation for life* (Lytton Strachey). **3** slowness and care: *The hunter aimed his gun with great deliberation.* **4** slowness: *His everlasting deliberation used to infuriate his wife.*

de|lib|er|a|tive (di lib′ə rā′tiv), *adj.* **1** for deliberation; having to do with deliberation; discussing reasons for and against something: *Congress is a deliberative body.* **2** characterized by deliberation; coming as a result of deliberation: *The judge made a just and deliberative decision.* —**de|lib′er|a′tive|ly**, *adv.* —**de|lib′er|a′tive|ness**, *n.*

de|lib|er|a|tor (di lib′ə rā′tər), *n.* a person who deliberates.

del|i|ble (del′ə bəl), *adj.* that can be erased or removed. [< Latin *dēlēbilis* < *dēlēre* destroy]

del|i|ca|cy (del′ə kə sē), *n., pl.* **-cies. 1** fineness of weave, quality, or make; slightness and grace: *the delicacy of lace, the delicacy of a flower, the delicacy of a baby's skin.* **2** fineness of feeling for small differences; sensitiveness: *The pianist had a great delicacy of touch.* **3** a need of care, skill, or tact: (*Figurative.*) *His refusal required delicacy; he did not wish to hurt his friend's feelings.* **4** *Figurative.* thought for the feelings of others; consideration: *The minister had an inborn feeling of delicacy.* **5** a shrinking from what is offensive or not modest: *A false delicacy is affectation, not politeness* (Sir Richard Steele). **6** a being easily hurt or made ill; weakness; frailty: *The child's delicacy was a constant worry to his mother.* **7** a choice kind of food; dainty. Nuts and candy are delicacies. Caviar is considered a delicacy. **8** exquisite fineness or skill: *the delicacy of some of Shakespeare's sonnets.* **9** *Obsolete.* gratification; pleasure.

del|i|cate (del′ə kit), *adj., n.* —*adj.* **1** pleasing to the senses; light, mild, or soft: *delicate foods, delicate colors. Roses have a delicate fragrance. A baby's skin is delicate.* SYN: tender, subdued. **2** of fine weave, quality, or make; thin, easily torn: *A spider's web is delicate.* **3** requiring care, skill, or tact: *a delicate situation, a delicate question.* SYN: ticklish. **4** easily damaged; fragile: *delicate china, delicate flowers.* **5** very quickly responding to slight changes of condition; finely sensitive: *delicate instruments, a delicate sense of touch.* **6** easily hurt or made ill: *a weak and delicate child.* SYN: frail, weakly. **7** *Figurative.* hard to appreciate; subtle: *a delicate point in reasoning.* **8** *Figurative.* careful of the feelings of others; considerate. SYN: tactful. **9** avoiding anything that is offensive or immodest; fastidious. **10** *Obsolete.*

self-indulgent; loving ease or luxury.
—*n.* **1** *Archaic.* a delicacy: *These delicates he heap'd with glowing hand* (Keats). **2** *Obsolete.* a luxury. **3** *Obsolete.* a person who loves luxury. [< Latin *dēlicātus* soft, tender, pampered] —**del′i|cate|ly**, *adv.* —**del′i|cate|ness**, *n.*
—*Syn. adj.* **1 Delicate, dainty, exquisite** mean pleasing to the senses. **Delicate** suggests fineness or softness of texture, lightness in quality, or exactness and fineness in the making which especially please any of the five senses or the mind: *Roses have a delicate fragrance. He does delicate work with water colors.* **Dainty** suggests smallness, perfection in the making, and fragile beauty which especially please the sense of sight or taste: *The baby wore a dainty dress.* **Exquisite** suggests such great perfection of quality and workmanship as would satisfy the most refined taste: *an exquisite jewel.*

del|i|ca|tes|sen (del′ə kə tes′ən), *n.* **1** *sing. in use.* a store that sells prepared foods, such as cooked meats, smoked fish, cheese, salads, pickles, and sandwiches: *The delicatessen closes at nine o'clock.* **2** *pl. in use.* the foods sold at such a store: *Delicatessen usually require little preparation for serving.* [American English < German *Delikatessen,* plural of *Delikatesse* a delicacy < Middle French *délicatesse* < *délicate* delicate, learned borrowing from Latin *dēlicātus*]

de|li|cious (di lish′əs), *adj.* **1** very pleasing to taste or smell: *delicious fruit, a delicious cake.* **2** very pleasing; delightful: *a delicious color combination.* [< Old French *delicieus* (with English *-ous*) < Late Latin *dēliciōsus* < *dēliciae* a delight < *dēlicere* entice; see etym. under **delight**] —**de|li′cious|ly**, *adv.* —**de|li′cious|ness**, *n.*
—*Syn.* **1 Delicious, luscious** mean delighting the senses. **Delicious** is used chiefly to mean delightfully pleasing in flavor, less often in fragrance or aroma: *This dessert is delicious. The coffee smells delicious.* **Luscious** adds to *delicious* the suggestion of richness or sweetness, and when applied to fruit, ripeness or juiciness: *a luscious apple pie.*

De|li|cious (di lish′əs), *n.* a kind of red or yellow apple with a fine flavor. [< *delicious*]

de|lict (di likt′), *n. Law.* a misdemeanor; transgression; offense. [< Latin *dēlictum* offense, neuter past participle of *dēlinquere* fail, offend; see etym. under **delinquent**]

del|i|gate (del′ə gāt) *v.t.,* **-gat|ed, -gat|ing.** to tie off; apply a ligature to.

de|light (di līt′), *n., v.* —*n.* **1** great pleasure; joy: *The little girl took great delight in her dolls. Teach us Delight in simple things, And Mirth that has no bitter springs* (Rudyard Kipling). **SYN**: ecstasy, rapture. See syn. under **pleasure**. **2** a thing that gives great pleasure: *Dancing is her delight.* **3** delightfulness: *Sweets grown common lose their dear delight* (Shakespeare).
—*v.t.* to please greatly: *The circus delighted the children. The little girl was delighted with her birthday presents. Who can predict what will delight the public next week?* **SYN**: gladden.
—*v.i.* **1** to have great pleasure: *Children delight in surprises.* **2** to give great pleasure: *The old actress had delighted for years.*
[< Old French *delit* < *delitier* < Latin *dēlectāre* to charm (frequentative) < *dēlicere* entice < *dē-* (intensive) + *lacere* entice] —**de|light′er**, *n.*

de|light|ed (di lī′tid), *adj.* **1** greatly pleased; very glad; joyful: *I am delighted to be home again.* **2** *Obsolete.* delightful. —**de|light′ed|ly**, *adv.* —**de|light′ed|ness**, *n.*

de|light|ful (di līt′fəl), *adj.* very pleasing; giving joy: *a delightful visit from an old friend, a delightful person.* **SYN**: enjoyable, pleasurable. —**de|light′ful|ly**, *adv.* —**de|light′ful|ness**, *n.*

de|light|less (di līt′lis), *adj.* having or giving no delight; cheerless.

de|light|some (di līt′səm), *adj.* = delightful. —**de|light′some|ly**, *adv.* —**de|light′some|ness**, *n.*

De|li|lah (di lī′lə), *n.* **1** a woman who betrayed Samson, her lover, to the Philistines (in the Bible, Judges 16). **2** a false, treacherous woman; temptress.

de|lime (dē līm′), *v.t.,* **-limed, -lim|ing,** to remove lime from, as skins.

de|lim|it (di lim′it), *v.t.* to fix limits of; mark the boundaries of; define: *The border between Sikkim and Tibet has been formally delimited* (Manchester Guardian).

de|lim|i|tate (di lim′ə tāt), *v.t.,* **-tat|ed, -tat|ing.** = delimit.

de|lim|i|ta|tion (di lim′ə tā′shən), *n.* **1** a delimiting or being delimited. **2** the determination of a limit or boundary: *Recent developments in aeronautics have set statesmen and international lawyers new problems in frontier delimitation* (Bulletin of Atomic Scientists).

de|lim|i|ta|tive (di lim′ə tā′tiv), *adj.* having the function of delimitation.

de|lin|e|ate (di lin′ē āt), *v.t.,* **-at|ed, -at|ing. 1** to trace the outline of: *The map delineated clearly the boundary between Mexico and Texas.* **2** to draw; sketch. **3** *Figurative.* to describe in words; portray: *He delineated his plan in a thorough report.* **SYN**: depict, picture. [< Latin *dēlīneāre* (with English *-ate*[1]) < *dē-* + *līnea* line]

de|lin|e|a|tion (di lin′ē ā′shən), *n.* **1** the act of delineating. **2** the thing delineated; diagram, sketch, portrait, or description: (*Figurative.*) *The author's character delineations are forceful and realistic.*

de|lin|e|a|tive (di lin′ē ā′tiv), *adj.* serving to delineate or depict.

de|lin|e|a|tor (di lin′ē ā′tər), *n.* **1** a person or thing that delineates. **2** a tailors' pattern that can be adjusted for cutting garments of different sizes.

de|lin|quen|cy (di ling′kwən sē), *n., pl.* **-cies. 1** failure in a duty; neglect of an obligation. **SYN**: guilt. **2a** failure to meet payments when due: *Many an American has pushed his credit close to the limit, so that any drop in income might bring a flood of delinquencies and repossessions* (Wall Street Journal). **b** overdue bills, taxes, or notes. **3** the condition or habit of behaving unlawfully: *We can curb juvenile delinquency by education.* **4** a fault; offense; misdeed; shortcoming.

de|lin|quent (di ling′kwənt), *adj., n.* —*adj.* **1** failing in a duty; neglecting an obligation: *He was delinquent in paying his overdue taxes.* **2** guilty of a fault or an offense: *The delinquent boys had been breaking windows in the neighborhood.* **3** due and unpaid; overdue: *The owner lost his house when it was sold for delinquent taxes.* **4** having to do with delinquents.
—*n.* a delinquent person; offender; criminal: *He had been a delinquent since early childhood.*
[< Latin *dēlinquēns, -entis,* present participle of *dēlinquere* fail < *dē-* off + *linquere* leave] —**de|lin′quent|ly**, *adv.*

de|lint (dē lint′), *v.t.* to remove the fiber, or lint, from cotton or similar seeds.

de|lint|er (dē lin′tər), *n.* a kind of cotton gin for removing the short fibers, or lint, that remain on the cotton seed after the first ginning; linter.

del|i|quesce (del′ə kwes′), *v.i.,* **-quesced, -quesc|ing. 1** *Chemistry.* to melt or become liquid by absorbing moisture from the air: *Certain salts, such as calcium chloride and zinc chloride, deliquesce readily.* **SYN**: liquefy, dissolve. **2** *Botany.* **a** to divide into small branches or veins. **b** to melt away: *Certain parts of some fungi deliquesce in the process of growth.* (*Figurative.*) *His articles ... too often deliquesce into a maudlin fine writing* (Punch). [< Latin *dēliquescere* < *dē-* (intensive) + *liquēscere* become fluid < *liquere* be liquid]

del|i|ques|cence (del′ə kwes′əns), *n.* **1** the act or process of deliquescing or melting away. **2** the liquid or solution produced when something deliquesces.

***del|i|ques|cent** (del′ə kwes′ənt), *adj.* **1** becoming liquid by absorbing moisture from the air: *deliquescent crystals.* **2** *Botany.* branching in such a way that the main stem or axis is lost in the branches: *Trees like the elm, cottonwood, oak, hickory, and many others are deliquescent.*

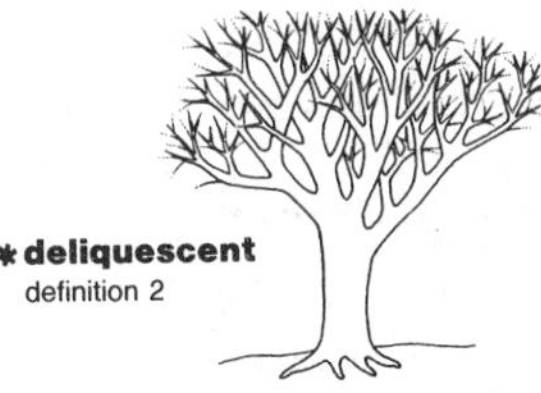

***deliquescent**
definition 2

de|liq|ui|um[1] (di lik′wē əm), *n.* **1** a failure of vital force; mental failing or weakness. **2** a fainting caused by cerebral anemia; syncope. [< Latin *dēliquium* < *dēlinquere* fail; see etym. under **delinquent**]

de|liq|ui|um[2] (di lik′wē əm), *n. Obsolete.* deliquescence. [< Latin *dēliquium* flowing down < *dēliquāre* clear off < *dē-* (intensive) + *liquāre* liquefy, dissolve]

del|i|ra|tion (del′ə rā′shən), *n.* mental disorder; delirium; madness: *in this universal dotage and deliration* (Thomas Carlyle). [< Latin *dēlīrātiō, -ōnis* < *dēlīrāre;* see etym. under **delirium**]

de|lir|i|ant (di lir′ē ənt), *adj., n.* —*adj.* causing delirium: *a deliriant drug.*
—*n.* a deliriant agent or drug: *Hashish is a deliriant.*

de|lir|i|fa|cient (di lir′ə fā′shənt), *adj., n.* —*adj.* causing or producing delirium.
—*n.* a substance that produces delirium.

de|lir|i|ous (di lir′ē əs), *adj.* **1** out of one's senses for a short time; wandering in mind; raving; lightheaded: *The patient's high fever made him delirious.* **2** *Figurative.* wildly excited: *The students were delirious with joy when their team won the tournament.* **3** caused by or characteristic of delirium: *delirious ravings.* —**de|lir′i|ous|ly**, *adv.* —**de|lir′i|ous|ness**, *n.*

de|lir|i|um (di lir′ē əm), *n., pl.* **-lir|i|ums, -lir|i|a** (-lir′ē ə). **1** a temporary disorder of the mind that occurs during fevers, insanity, drunkenness, or a drugged state. Delirium is characterized by restlessness, excitement, strange ideas, and wild talk. *He died in a sanitarium, wracked by delusions and delirium* (Newsweek). **2** *Figurative.* wild excitement: *He jumped up, shouted, clapped his hands, and danced in a delirium of joy* (Washington Irving). **SYN**: hysteria, frenzy. [< Latin *dēlīrium* < *dēlīrāre* rave, be crazy; (literally) go out of the furrow (in plowing) < *dē-* out of + *līra* furrow]

delirium tre|mens (trē′mənz), a mental and nervous disorder accompanied by violent tremblings and terrifying hallucinations, usually caused by prolonged and excessive drinking of alcoholic liquor, with associated malnutrition. [< New Latin *delirium tremens* trembling delirium]

de|list (dē list′), *v.t.* to remove officially (a stock or security) from the list of a stock exchange: *The board may at any time suspend or delist a security, on the basis of certain set standards* (Wall Street Journal).

del|i|tes|cence (del′ə tes′əns), *n.* **1** the condition of lying hid; concealment; seclusion. **2** *Medicine.* **a** the sudden disappearance of inflammation. **b** the subsidence of a tumor. **c** incubation (of a disease).

del|i|tes|cent (del′ə tes′ənt), *adj.* lying hid; concealed. [< Latin *dēlitescēns, -entis,* present participle of *dēlitēscere* hide away < *dē-* away + *latēscere* lie hid < *latēre*]

de|liv|er (di liv′ər), *v., adj.* —*v.t.* **1** to carry and give out; distribute: *The postman delivers letters.* **2** to give up; hand over: *Dick delivered his mother's message to Mrs. Brown. The traitor delivered the fort to the enemy.* **SYN**: surrender, yield. **3** to give forth in words: *The traveler delivered a series of talks on his travels. The jury delivered its verdict.* **SYN**: utter, enunciate. **4** to strike; throw: *The pitcher delivered a curve. The boxer delivered a blow.* **SYN**: cast, discharge. **5** to set free; rescue; save: *to deliver an animal from a trap. A passing ship delivered the shipwrecked passengers from a certain death at sea. "Deliver us from evil."* **SYN**: liberate, release. See syn. under **rescue**. **6** to help (a woman) give birth to a child: *She was delivered of twins.* **7** to help in the birth of: *to deliver a baby.* **8** *Obsolete.* to make known; assert; impart.
—*v.i.* **1** to make a delivery or deliveries: *Our store delivers every afternoon.* **2** *U.S., Figurative.* to carry out or fulfill an expectation; make good: *This autumn the President has a major opportunity to deliver on his pledge* (New York Times).
—*adj. Archaic.* active; nimble; agile.
deliver oneself of, to speak; give out: *The witness delivered himself of all his pent-up hatred.*
[< Old French *delivrer* < Late Latin *dēlīberāre* to set free < Latin *dē-* away + *līberāre* to free < *līber* free]

de|liv|er|a|bil|i|ty (di liv′ər ə bil′ə tē), *n.* the quality of being deliverable: *Additional facilities at the firm's underground storage reservoir near Herscher, Ill., ... would increase peak deliverability of gas from 430 million to 500 million cubic feet daily* (Wall Street Journal).

de|liv|er|a|ble (di liv′ər ə bəl), *adj.* that can be or is to be delivered.

de|liv|er|ance (di liv′ər əns), *n.* **1** the act of setting free or the state of being set free; rescue; release: *The soldiers rejoiced in their deliverance from prison.* **SYN**: freedom, liberation. **2** a formal opinion or judgment: *Approval is asked for a deliverance which urges once again on the Government the need for an amendment of the law* (Observer). **SYN**: verdict.

de|liv|er|er (di liv′ər ər), *n.* **1** a person who sets free or releases; liberator; rescuer: *He stood forth as the deliverer of his country* (Edward Gibbon). **2** a person who delivers by transferring or handing over: *The postman is a deliverer of the mail.*

de|liv|er|ly (di liv′ər lē), *adv. Archaic.* lightly; nimbly; deftly.

de|liv|er|y (di liv′ər ē, -liv′rē), *n., pl.* **-er|ies. 1** the act of carrying and giving out letters, goods, or other items; act of distributing: *There is one delivery of mail a day in our city.* **2** a giving up; handing over; surrender: *the delivery of a town to the enemy. The captive was released upon the delivery of his ransom.* **3** manner of speaking;

Pronunciation Key: hat, āge, cãre, fär; let, ēqual, tėrm; it, īce; hot, ōpen, ôrder; oil, out; cup, pu̇t, rüle; child; long; thin; ᴛʜen; zh, measure; ə represents **a** in about, **e** in taken, **i** in pencil, **o** in lemon, **u** in circus.

way of giving a speech or lecture: *Our minister has an excellent delivery. I was charmed with the gracefulness of his . . . delivery* (Joseph Addison). **SYN:** enunciation, locution. **4** the act or way of striking or throwing: *That pitcher has a fast delivery.* **5** a rescue; release. **SYN:** liberation, deliverance. **6** a giving birth to a child; childbirth. **SYN:** confinement. **7** anything that is delivered; goods to be delivered. **8** *Law.* the formal handing over of property to another.

delivery boy, **1** a boy or man employed to deliver parcels to customers. **2** a boy who delivers papers; paperboy.

de|liv|er|y|man (di liv′ər ē man′, -mən; -liv′rē-), *n., pl.* **-men.** a man who delivers packages or goods, especially with a truck: *The strike of 4,400 deliverymen had laid a high cost on the nine newspapers and on the city* (Time).

delivery room, **1** a room in a hospital given over to the delivery of babies: *As an R.N. assisting in the delivery room, I am always profoundly impressed at the miracle of life* (Time). **2** a room or area in a library in which books are delivered to borrowers and returned by them.

dell (dell), *n.* a small, sheltered glen or valley, usually with trees in it: *That break [in the forest] is a dell; a deep hollow cup lined with turf* (Charlotte Brontë). **SYN:** vale, dale, dingle. [Old English *dell.* Related to **dale.**]

Del|la Crus|can (del′ə krus′kən), **1** having to do with or in the style of the Accademia della Crusca, an academy established at Florence in 1582, mainly to sift and purify the Italian language. **2** having to do with a school of English poetry affecting an artificial style, started by certain Englishmen at Florence toward the end of the 1700's.

Del|la Rob|bi|a (del′ə rob′ē ə), **1** the enameled terra cotta ware made by Luca Della Robbia and his successors. **2** any similar ware. **3** *Printing.* a kind of type.

de|lo|cal|i|za|tion (dē lō′kə lə zā′shən), *n.* **1** the act or process of delocalizing. **2** the state of being delocalized.

de|lo|cal|ize (dē lō′kə līz), *v.,* **-ized, -iz|ing.** **—*v.t.*** **1** to detach or remove from the proper or usual locality; free from local limitations: *We can have no St. Simons or Pepyses till we have a Paris or London to delocalize our gossip and give it historic breadth* (James Russell Lowell). **2** *Chemistry.* to move (electrons) from one point on a molecule to another: *Analysis of its electronic spectrum suggests that the unpaired election is delocalized* (Sheldon G. Shore).
—*v.i. Chemistry.* to move from one point on a molecule to another: *To understand the nature of the reaction, it is important to know if the ionic charge really does "delocalize"* (Ralph C. Dougherty).

de|lo|mor|phic (dē′lə môr′fik), *adj.* **1** of appreciable size. **2** denoting those cells of the stomach glands that supposedly secrete the hydrochloric acid. [< Greek *dêlos* visible + *morphê* form + English *-ic*]

de|lo|mor|phous (dē′lə môr′fəs), *adj.* = delomorphic.

de|loul (də lül′), *n.* = dromedary.

de|louse (dē lous′, -louz′), *v.t.,* **-loused, -lous|ing.** to remove lice from.

de|lous|er (dē lou′sər, -zər), *n.* an agent that delouses.

Del|phi|an (del′fē ən), *adj.* = Delphic.

Del|phic (del′fik), *adj.* **1** having to do with the oracle of Apollo at Delphi. **2** having a double meaning; obscure; oracular: *His landlady was wont to deliver Delphic utterances in foreboding tones.*

del|phic|al|ly or **Del|phic|al|ly** (del′fik lē), *adv.* in an obscure, enigmatic, or ambiguous manner: *"You may go on that assumption," he answered Delphically* (Nigel Nicolson). **SYN:** cryptically.

Delphic oracle, the oracle of Apollo at Delphi. The oracle often gave ambiguous answers to questions.

Del|phin (del′fin), *adj.* of or having to do with the dauphin of France. [< Latin (*ad ūsum*) *Delphīnī* (for the use) of the *dauphin*]

Del|phi|ni (del fī′nī), *n.* genitive of **Delphinus.**

del|phi|nin (del′fə nin), *n.* a pigment derived from a variety of larkspur. Its chloride is solunble in water. *Formula:* $C_{41}H_{39}ClO_{21}{\cdot}2H_2O$ [< *delphin*(ium) + *-in*]

del|phi|nine (del′fə nēn, -nin), *n.* a bitter, poisonous, crystalline alkaloid obtained from various species of larkspur. *Formula:* $C_{33}H_{45}NO_9$[< *delphin*(ium) + *-ine*[2]]

del|phin|i|um (del fin′ē əm), *n.* = larkspur. [< New Latin *Delphinium* the genus name < Greek *delphīnion* larkspur, dolphin flower < *delphīn, -înos* dolphin (because of the shape of the nectar gland)]

Del|phi|nus (del fī′nəs), *n., genitive* **Del|phi|ni.** a northern constellation near Pegasus; the Dolphin. [< Latin *delphīnus* (literally) dolphin < Greek *delphîn, -înos*]

Del|rin (del′rin), *n. Trademark.* a strong, resilient plastic, produced by the polymerization of formaldehyde. *Formula:* $(\text{-OCH}_2\text{-})_n$

Del|sar|ti|an (del sär′tē ən), *adj.* of or having to do with François Delsarte (1811-1871) or his theories of music and drama.

***del|ta** (del′tə), *n.* **1** a deposit of earth and sand that collects at the mouths of some rivers and is usually three sided: *the delta of the Nile, the Mississippi delta.* **2** the fourth letter of the Greek alphabet. It is equivalent to English *D, d.* **3** anything shaped like a triangle; triangular space or figure. The delta of a fingerprint is the point around which the skin ridges form a triangle. **4** one of several possible positions of atoms or groups of atoms which are substituted in a chemical compound. **5** = delta wing. [< Greek **Δ** *délta* the letter or *d* (because of the shape of the capital)]

***delta**
definitions 1, 2

river delta

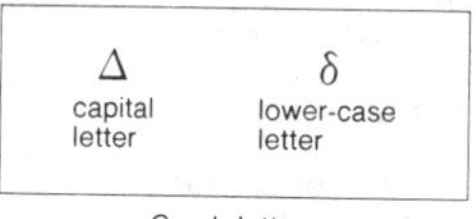

Greek letter

Del|ta (del′tə), *n. U.S.* a code name for the letter *d,* used in transmitting radio messages.

delta agent or **virus**, a defective virus that can exist only in combination with the virus which causes serum hepatitis: *The delta agent . . . believed to be on the rise world-wide, can make chronic hepatitis B infection lethal* (J. Silberner).

Delta Cephei, a large variable star in the constellation Cepheus, characterized by pulsation from bright to dim in its interval of about five days and nine hours.

del|ta|ic (del tā′ik), *adj.* **1** of or having to do with a delta: *the deltaic population of the Lower Ganges* (London Standard). **2** forming a delta; like a delta.

delta iron, an allotrope of iron having a crystal structure similar to that of alpha iron, produced by heating gamma iron above 1400 degrees centigrade (Celsius).

del|tal (del′təl), *adj.* of or having to do with a delta: *the rich land of the deltal formations in the lower Mississippi River.*

delta plain, the nearly level lowland portion of a delta above water.

delta plateau, **1** = sand plain. **2** a delta formed at the front of a regional glacier.

delta ray, an electron emitted when a fast-moving charged particle, such as an alpha particle, penetrates matter.

delta wave, a large, slow brain wave marking the deepest level of sleep: *High-amplitude delta waves in sleep are almost typical of youth. With increasing age, however, the EEG [electroencephalogram] of the delta waves becomes smaller and flatter* (Segal and Luce).

***delta wing**, a triangular, swept-back aircraft wing designed to give high speed and great lift.

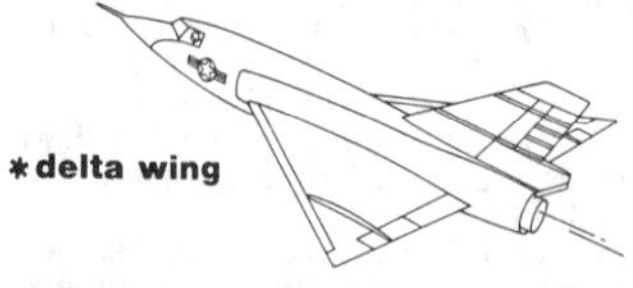

***delta wing**

del|ta-wing (del′tə wing′), *adj.* having a delta wing.

del|ta-winged (del′tə wingd′), *adj.* = delta-wing.

del|tic (del′tik), *adj.* deltaic.

del|ti|ol|o|gist (del′tē ol′ə jist), *n.* a person who collects post cards as a hobby.

del|ti|ol|o|gy (del′tē ol′ə jē), *n.* the hobby of collecting post cards. [< Greek *deltion* (diminutive < *déltos* writing tablet) + English *-logy*]

del|toid (del′toid), *adj., n.* **—*adj.*** **1** shaped like the Greek delta; triangular: *a deltoid leaf.* **2** of or having to do with the deltoid muscle.
—*n.* = deltoid muscle.
[< New Latin *deltoides* < Greek *deltoeidês* < *délta* delta + *eîdos* form]

deltoid muscle, a large, triangular muscle of the shoulder. It lifts the arm away from the side of the body. See picture under **arm**[1].

de|lud|a|ble (di lü′də bəl), *adj.* that can be deluded.

de|lude (di lüd′), *v.t.,* **-lud|ed, -lud|ing.** **1** to mislead the mind or judgment of; trick or deceive: *The spy deluded me into thinking he was on my side. She deluded herself into thinking she was still the slender, pretty girl of her youth.* **SYN:** dupe, trick, beguile, gull, hoodwink. **2** *Obsolete.* to trifle with. **3** *Obsolete.* to elude; evade. [< Latin *dēlūdere* < *dē-* (pejorative) + *lūdere* to play]

de|lud|er (di lü′dər), *n.* a person who deludes.

de|lud|ing|ly (di lü′ding lē), *adv.* in a way so as to delude.

del|uge (del′yüj), *n., v.,* **-uged, -ug|ing.** **—*n.*** **1** a great flood: *After the dam broke, the deluge washed away the bridge. The Johnstown flood was a deluge that has gone down in history.* **SYN:** inundation. See syn. under **flood.** **2** a heavy fall of rain; downpour: *We were caught in a deluge on the way home.* **3** *Figurative.* any overwhelming rush: *Most stores have a deluge of orders just before Christmas.*
—*v.t.* **1** to flood or overflow: *Water deluged our cellar when the big pipe broke.* **SYN:** inundate. **2** *Figurative.* to overwhelm: *The movie star was deluged with requests for his autograph. At length corruption, like a general flood . . . Shall deluge all* (Alexander Pope).
the Deluge, the great flood in the days of Noah; the Flood (in the Bible, Genesis 7): *Her hat looked as if it had been worn at the Deluge, it was so shabby and out of style.*
[< Old French *deluge* < Latin *dīluvium* < *dīluere* < *dis-* away + *luere* wash. See etym. of doublet **diluvium.**]

de|lun|dung (del′ən dung), *n.* a small, striped and spotted, carnivorous mammal of the cat family, found in Java. It resembles a civet cat but has shorter legs and a longer tail. [< a native name]

de|lu|sion (di lü′zhən), *n.* **1** a false belief or opinion: *She was under the delusion that she could pass any test without studying for it. The belief that a pleasant personality alone will make a man successful is a delusion.* **SYN:** See syn. under **illusion.** **2** the act of deluding. **SYN:** deception. **3** the state of being deluded: *The disappointment of manhood succeeds to the delusion of youth* (Benjamin Disraeli). **4** a fixed belief maintained in spite of unquestionable evidence to the contrary. People with mental disorders, especially schizophrenics, often have delusions. *The insane man had a delusion that he was George Washington.* [< Latin *dēlūsiō, -ōnis* < *dēlūdere;* see etym. under **delude**]

de|lu|sion|al (di lü′zhə nəl), *adj.* having to do with or characterized by delusions: *delusional insanity. The text goes on to speak of "delusional beliefs which become the uppermost and guiding theme of the patient's life"* (Harper's).

de|lu|sion|ar|y (di lü′zhə ner′ē), *adj.* delusive; delusional: *Each . . . nurses a delusionary hope* (Time).

de|lu|sive (di lü′siv), *adj.* misleading the mind or judgment; deceptive; false: *All the delusive seduction of martial music* (Fanny Burney). *. . . the desperate and delusive belief that this is the only alternative to recession and unemployment* (Newsweek). **SYN:** fallacious. **—de|lu′sive|ly,** *adv.* **—de|lu′sive|ness,** *n.*

de|lu|so|ry (di lü′sər ē), *adj.* delusive; deceptive.

de|lus|tered (dēlus′tərd), *adj.* reduced in luster; treated with a delustrant during manufacture: *delustered satin.*

de|lus|trant (dēlus′trənt), *n.* a chemical used to reduce the luster of yarns and fabrics: *Titanium dioxide . . . acts as a delustrant, removing excessive sheen from the fibre* (New Scientist). [< *de-* + *luster* + *-ant*]

de|luxe (də lůks′, -luks′), *adj.,* or **de luxe,** of exceptionally good quality; elegant: *a de luxe model, deluxe accommodations. Two typically fine books have just been brought out by Tériade and his Verve publishing house in deluxe editions* (New Yorker). [< French *de luxe* (literally) of luxury]

delve (delv), *v.,* **delved, delv|ing,** *n.* **—*v.i.*** **1** to search carefully for information: *The scholar delved in many libraries for facts to support his theories.* **SYN:** explore, ferret. **2** *Archaic.* to dig: *When Adam delved and Eve span* (Richard Hampole).
—*v.t. Dialect.* to dig; make or obtain by digging.
—*n.* **1** an act of digging. **2** a hollow. **3** *Archaic.* an excavation; pit; cave.
[Old English *delfan*]

delv|er (del′vər), *n.* **1** a patient and laborious investigator. **2** *Archaic.* a person who digs with or as if with a spade.

Dem., 1 Democrat. 2 Democratic.

de|mag|net|i|za|tion (dē mag′nə tə zā′shən), *n.* the act or process of demagnetizing.

de|mag|net|ize (dē mag′nə tīz), *v.,* **-ized, -iz|ing.** —*v.t.* to deprive of magnetism or magnetic properties: *A sample may be demagnetized by reversing the magnetizing current a number of times, decreasing its magnitude with each reversal* (Sears and Zemansky).
—*v.i.* to be demagnetized: *Unwanted recordings may simply be erased by demagnetizing and the tape reused almost indefinitely* (New Yorker).
—**de|mag′net|iz′er,** *n.*

dem|a|gog (dem′ə gôg, -gog), *n.* = demagogue.

dem|a|gog|ic (dem′ə goj′ik, -gog′-), *adj.* **1** of a demagogue. **2** like a demagogue: *Demagogic leaders stirred up the people.* —**dem′a|gog′i|cal|ly,** *adv.*

dem|a|gog|i|cal (dem′ə goj′ə kəl, -gog′-), *adj.* = demagogic.

dem|a|gog|ism (dem′ə gôg′iz əm, -gog′-), *n.* = demagoguery.

dem|a|gogue (dem′ə gôg, -gog), *n.* **1** a popular leader who stirs up the people by appealing to their emotions and prejudices. The chief aim of most demagogues is to get power and money for themselves alone: . . . *the mean arts and unreasonable clamours of demagogues* (Macaulay). **2** a leader of the people (in ancient history). [< Greek *dēmagōgós* a popular leader < *dêmos* people + *agōgós* leader, a leading < *ágein* to lead]

dem|a|gogu|er|y (dem′ə gôg′ər ē, -gog′-), *n.* *Especially U.S.* the methods or principles of a demagogue; demagogism.

dem|a|gogu|ism (dem′ə gôg′iz əm, -gog′-), *n.* = demagoguery.

dem|a|go|gy (dem′ə gō′jē, -gôg′ē, -gog′-), *n.* = demagoguery.

de mal en pis (də mȧl′äɴ pē′), *French.* from bad to worse.

de|mand (di mand′, -mänd′), *v., n.* —*v.t.* **1** to ask for as a right: *The prisoner demanded a trial. Teachers demand attention.* **2** to ask for with authority: *The policeman demanded the boys' names.* **3** to ask to know or to be told: *to demand an answer. "Where is my mother?" the little boy demanded.* **4** *Figurative.* to call for; require; need: *Training a puppy demands patience. Karl Marx's great book "Das Kapital" is a unique and complex work, which demands a different kind of analysis from that which it usually gets* (Edmund Wilson). **5** to require to appear; summon: *He demanded his servant.*
—*v.i.* to make a demand; ask.
—*n.* **1** the act of demanding: *a demand for a bigger allowance.* **2** a thing demanded. **3** a claim; requirement: *A mother has many demands on her time.* **4a** the desire and ability to buy: *Because of the large crop, the supply of apples is greater than the demand.* **b** the quantity of a commodity wanted at a particular price. **5** a legal claim. **6** *Archaic.* a request; question; query.
in demand, wanted: *Taxicabs are in great demand on rainy days.*
on demand, upon request; on being claimed: *a note payable on demand.*
[< Old French *demander* to request < Latin *dēmandāre* entrust < *dē-* (intensive) + *mandāre* to order] —**de|mand′er,** *n.*
—***Syn.*** *v.t.* **1, 2 Demand, claim, require** mean to ask or call for something as a right or need. **Demand** emphasizes insisting on getting something a person has the right to call for: *I demand a fair hearing.* **Claim** emphasizes having, or stating that one has, the right to get what is demanded: *Three different heirs claimed the inheritance.* **Require** emphasizes authority to make a demand: *The bank requires evidence of financial stability before a loan is granted.*

de|mand|a|ble (di man′də bəl, -män′-), *adj.* that can be demanded.

de|mand|ant (di man′dənt, -män′-), *n.* **1** a person who demands. **2** *Law.* **a** the plaintiff in a real action. **b** any plaintiff or claimant.

demand bill, a bill of exchange payable on demand.

demand deposit, a bank deposit which may be withdrawn at any time the depositor wishes.

demand draft, a draft payable on demand.

de|mand-driv|en (di mand′driv′ən, -mänd′-), *adj.* caused by increased demand for a product or service: *Rubber has had a demand-driven price rise. The price of rubber depends on the demand for tyres, and thus on the state of the car industry* (Economist).

de|man|deur (də mäɴ dœr′), *n. French.* applicant; petitioner.

demand inflation, = demand-pull.

de|mand|ing (di man′ding, -män′-), *adj.* that demands; making severe demands; making many or excessive demands: *a demanding job, a demanding husband.* —**de|mand′ing|ly,** *adv.*

demand loan, = call loan.

demand note, 1 a note payable on demand. **2** one of the notes comprising the first issue of United States paper money, authorized by Congress in July of 1861.

de|mand-pull (di mand′pu̇l′), *n.* inflation caused by excessive demand for goods and services forcing the cost of production higher and therefore raising market prices.

de|mand-side (di mand′sīd′, -mänd′-), *adj.* of or having to do with economic policy theoretically designed to stimulate demand in a nation's economy by such methods as increasing government spending to create a demand for goods and services that will be met by increased employment.

de|man|toid (di man′toid), *n.* a brilliant green garnet. [< Swedish, or Dutch *demant* diamond + English *-oid*]

de-Mao|i|za|tion (dē mou′ə zā′shən), *n.* the repudiation or reversal of the policies of the Chinese Communist leader Mao Tse-tung (Mao Zedong), 1893-1976: *Just as the de-Stalinisation debate in Russia was part of the struggle for power between Stalin's successors, so the de-Maoisation debate is a sign of a similar struggle . . . in Peking* (Manchester Guardian Weekly).

de|mar|cate (dē′mär kāt, di mär′-), *v.t.,* **-cat|ed, -cat|ing. 1** to set and mark the limits of: *Night after night, groups of infiltrators crossed a ditch which demarcates the armistice lines* (Harper's). **2** *Figurative.* to separate; distinguish. [back formation < *demarcation*]

de|mar|ca|tion (dē′mär kā′shən), *n.* **1** the act of setting and marking the limits: (*Figurative.*) *the demarcation of a country's authority.* **2** *Figurative.* separation; distinction: *the demarcation of infancy from childhood. The speculative line of demarcation, where obedience ought to end and resistance must begin* (Edmund Burke). Also, **demarkation.** [< Spanish *demarcación* < *demarcar* to delimit < *de-* off + *marcar* to mark]

de|mar|ca|tor (di mär′kā tər, dē′mär kā′-), *n.* a person or thing that marks out boundaries.

de|march (dē′märk), *n.* the chief magistrate of a deme. [< Latin *dēmarchus* < Greek *dêmarchos* < *dêmos* district + *árchein* to rule]

dé|marche (dā mȧrsh′), *n. French.* **1** a plan of action: *The diplomat had cordially rejected Hacking's démarche in my favor* (A. J. Liebling). **2** a change of plans. **3** a walk; step; proceeding: *In his opinion British démarches against Athens radio broadcasts were unjustified* (London Times).

de|mar|ga|rin|at|ed (dē mär′jər ə nā′tid, -gər-), *adj.* (of an oil) having the stearin or solid part removed.

de|mark (dē märk′, di-), *v.t.* = demarcate.

de|mar|ka|tion (dē′mär kā′shən), *n.* = demarcation.

de|ma|te|ri|al|i|za|tion (dē′mə tir′ē ə lə zā′shən), *n.* a depriving or loss of material character or form.

de|ma|te|ri|al|ize (dē′mə tir′ē ə līz), *v.,* **-ized, -iz|ing.** —*v.t.* to deprive of material character or form: *For me light is not décor, but a means to dematerialize the stage until only the personality of the singing actor remains* (Newsweek).
—*v.i.* to lose material character or form.

de mau|vais goût (də mō ve′ gü′), *French.* in bad taste.

deme (dēm), *n.* **1** *Biology.* a small group or population of organisms that interbreed, such as an anthill, or all the frogs in a pond. **2** an administrative division or township in ancient Attica and, formerly, modern Greece; commune. [< Greek *dêmos* country district; its people]

de|mean[1] (di mēn′), *v.t.* to lower in dignity or standing; humble: *to demean oneself by insulting a friend. The duke's son would not demean himself by working.* SYN: debase, degrade. [< *de-* down + *mean*[2]; patterned on *debase*]

de|mean[2] (di mēn′), *v.t.* **1** to behave or conduct (oneself): *He demeans himself well.* **2** *Obsolete.* to carry on; manage. [< Old French *demener* < *de-* de- (< Latin *dē-*) + *mener* lead, direct < Latin *mināre* drive]

de|mean|ing (di mē′ning), *adj.* that demeans; debasing: *a demeaning work environment.*

de|mean|or (di mē′nər), *n.* the way a person acts and looks; behavior; manner; conduct: *She has a quiet, modest demeanor.* SYN: bearing, deportment. [Middle English *demenure* < *demenen* behave < Old French *demener;* see etym. under **demean**[2]]

de|mean|our (di mē′nər), *n. British.* demeanor.

de|ment (di ment′), *v., adj., n.* —*v.t.* to make mad or insane. —***adj.*** *Archaic.* out of one's mind; mad; insane. —***n.*** *Rare.* a demented person. [< Late Latin *dēmentāre* < Latin *dēmēns, -mentis* mad < *dē-* out of + *mēns, mentis* mind]

de|men|ta|tion (dē′men tā′shən), *n.* the act of making demented or the condition of being demented; madness.

de|ment|ed (di men′tid), *adj.* mentally ill; insane; crazy: *an act of demented folly.* SYN: mad, crazed. —**de|ment′ed|ly,** *adv.* —**de|ment′ed|ness,** *n.*

dé|men|ti (dā mäɴ tē′), *n. French.* **1** the act of lying. **2** a formal or official denial, as of a report.

de|men|tia (di men′shə), *n.* a partial or complete deterioration of mind: (*Figurative.*) *Tied up in costly appeal proceedings, . . . Bruce became a mad, abject figure, a classic instance of litigant's dementia* (New York Times). SYN: insanity, lunacy. [< Latin *dēmentia* < *dēmēns, -mentis* mad; see etym. under **dement**]

de|men|tial (di men′shəl), *adj.* mad; insane.

dementia par|a|lyt|i|ca (par′ə lit′ə kə), paresis, a disorder resulting from chronic syphilitic infection of the brain, characterized by progressive moral and intellectual deterioration, and often by delusions of grandeur. [< New Latin *dementia paralytica* paralytic dementia]

dementia prae|cox or **pre|cox** (prē′koks), = schizophrenia: *Among the psychoses are schizophrenia, first called dementia praecox (adolescent insanity) by Emil Kraepelin in 1896, and changed by Eugen Bleuler in 1911 to the now more generally accepted term schizophrenia* (Marguerite Clark). [< New Latin *dementia praecox* precocious insanity]

de|men|to (di men′tō), *n., pl.* **-tos,** *U.S. Slang.* a demented person; lunatic: *All the electronic gear in Miami could not replicate the effect of 60,000 live dementos in Little Rock's War Memorial Stadium* (New York Times Magazine). *Can she have been peering through her curtains at some other lone demento?* (Harper's)

dem|e|rar|a (dem′ə rãr′ə, -rä′rə), *n.* a crystalline, yellowish-brown, raw cane sugar. [< *Demerara,* in Guyana]

de|mer|it (dē mer′it), *n.* **1** a fault or defect. **2** a mark against a person's record for bad behavior or poor work: *The prisoner had so many demerits on his record that he was not eligible for parole.* **3** *Obsolete.* merit; desert: *Envy not the demerits of those who are most conspicuously distinguished* (John Gay). [< Medieval Latin *demeritum* fault (with *de-* taken pejoratively) < Latin *dēmerērī* deserve < *dē-* (intensive) + *merērī* to merit]

de|mer|i|to|ri|ous (di mer′ə tôr′ē əs, -tōr′-), *adj.* = blameworthy.

Dem|er|ol (dem′ə rōl, -rol), *n. Trademark.* meperidine hydrochloride, a sedative.

de|mer|sal (di mėr′səl), *adj.* **1** on, near, or sinking to the bottom: *demersal eggs.* **2** living on or near the bottom, as a fish: *shallow waters teeming with cod, haddock, and demersal, or bottom-loving fish* (Wall Street Journal). [< Latin *dēmersus,* past participle of *dēmergere* to plunge down into (< *dē-* down + *mergere* to plunge) + English *-al*[1]]

de|mes|mer|ize (dē mes′mə rīz, -mez′-), *v.t.,* **-ized, -iz|ing.** to bring out of hypnotic influence.

de|mesne (di mān′, -mēn′), *n.* **1** a house and land belonging to a lord and used by him. **2** a domain; realm. **3** *Figurative.* a district; region. **4** *Law.* the possession of land as one's own. **5** land, or land and buildings, possessed as one's own; real estate. [< Anglo-French *demesne,* Old French *demeine* domain. See etym. of doublet **domain.**]

De|me|ter (di mē′tər), *n. Greek Mythology.* the goddess of agriculture, fruitfulness, and marriage. The Romans called her Ceres.

dem|e|ton (dem′ə ton), *n.* a highly toxic organic phosphate used in agriculture as a systemic insecticide; Systox. *Formula:* $C_8H_{19}O_3PS_2$

de|mi (dē′mī), *n.* plural of **demos.**

demi-, *prefix.* **1** half; partial: *Demigod = a half god.* **2** smaller than ordinary: *Demitasse = a small cup of coffee, or the cup itself.*
[< Old French *demi-* half < Latin *dīmidius* < *dis-* apart + *medius* middle]

dem|i|bas|tion (dem′ē bas′chən), *n.* a projecting part of a fortification consisting of one face and one flank; half of a bastion.

dem|i|god (dem′ē god′), *n.* **1** one who is partly divine and partly human. Hercules was a demigod. **2** a minor or lesser god. **3** *Figurative.* a person who is held in high esteem; hero: *actors, athletes, and other modern demigods.*

dem|i|god|dess (dem′ē god′is), *n.* a woman demigod.

dem|i|john (dem′ē jon), *n.* a large bottle of glass or earthenware enclosed in wicker. Demijohns have a small neck and one or two handles. [< French *dame-jeanne* Lady Jane, a popular name of the bottle]

dem|i|lance (dem′ē lans′, -läns′), *n.* **1** a short, light lance. **2** a horseman who carried such a lance. [< French *demie lance*]

Pronunciation Key: hat, āge, cãre, fär; let, ēqual, tėrm; it, īce; hot, ōpen, ôrder; oil, out; cup, pu̇t, rüle; child; long; thin; ᴛʜen; zh, measure; **ə** represents **a** in about, **e** in taken, **i** in pencil, **o** in lemon, **u** in circus.

de|mil|i|ta|rise (dē mil′ə tə rīz), *v.t.*, **-rised, -ris|ing.** *Especially British.* demilitarize.

de|mil|i|ta|ri|za|tion (dē mil′ə tər ə zā′shən), *n.* the act or process of demilitarizing or the state of being demilitarized: *... a decade's retrogression from demilitarization with its uncertain consequences* (Economist).

de|mil|i|ta|rize (dē mil′ə tə rīz), *v.t.*, **-rized, -riz|ing. 1** to free from military control; deprive of military character: *to demilitarize a zone or boundary between enemy countries. ... deliberate attempt to de-Prussianize and demilitarize its 48 million inhabitants* (Atlantic). **2** to place under civil instead of military control.

dem|i|lune (dem′ē lün), *n.* **1** a half moon; crescent. **2** a triangular-shaped structure set at the entrance to a fortification or between two bastions; ravelin. [< French *demilune*]

dem|i-min|i (dem′ē min′ē), *adj., n., pl.* **-min|is.** *—adj.* shorter than mini.
—n. a skirt or dress shorter than mini.

dem|i|mon|daine (dem′ē mon dān′), *n.* a woman of the demimonde. [< French *demimondaine* < *demimonde;* see etym. under **demimonde**]

dem|i|monde (dem′ē mond, dem′ē mond′), *n.* **1** a class of women whose reputation and morals are doubtful. **2** a woman of this class; demimondaine. **3** prostitutes generally. **4** = demiworld: *... a familiar figure in the demimonde of European government gatherings* (London Times). [< French *demimonde* < *demi-* half, demi- + *monde,* learned borrowing < Latin *mundus* world]

de|min|er|al|ise (dē min′ər ə līz), *v.t.*, **-ised, -is|ing.** *Especially British.* demineralize.

de|min|er|al|i|za|tion (dē min′ər ə lə zā′shən), *n.* the act or process of demineralizing or condition of being demineralized: *Realistic accomplishment in demineralization of saline water anywhere rests wholly on permissible cost* (Science News Letter).

de|min|er|al|ize (dē min′ər ə līz), *v.t.*, **-ized, -iz|ing.** to remove or greatly reduce the mineral content of: *A major drawback in the past to demineralizing water by freezing has been the cost* (Time).

de|min|er|al|iz|er (dē min′ər ə lī′zər), *n.* something that demineralizes.

de mi|ni|mis non cu|rat lex (dē min′ə məs non kyůr′at leks′), *Latin.* the law does not concern itself with trifles.

de|mi-pen|sion (də mē päɴ syôɴ′), *n. French.* **1** an arrangement in a boarding house, hotel, or dormitory to eat only some meals, usually the noon meal. **2** (literally) half-board.

dem|i|pique (dem′ē pēk′), *adj., n. —adj.* (of a saddle) half-peaked; having a peak of about half the height of that of the older war saddle.
—n. a demipique saddle.
[< *demi-* + *peak*[1]; spelling influenced by French *pique* pike, spear]

de|mi-pli|é (də mē plē ā′), *n. French.* **1** (in ballet) a position with the knees bent about halfway to a full plié. **2** (literally) half bent.

de|mi-pointe (də mē pwaɴt′), *n. French.* **1** (in ballet) a position with the foot raised about halfway to the erect position and the weight borne upon the ball of the foot. **2** (literally) half toe.

dem|i|qua|ver (dem′ē kwā′vər), *n. Music.* a semiquaver; sixteenth note.

dem|i|re|lief (dem′ē ri lēf′), *n.* **1** = mezzo-relievo. **2** the appearance of standing halfway out, given by shading, color, or line. [< *demi-* + *relief*]

dem|i|re|lie|vo or **dem|i|ri|lie|vo** (dem′ē ri-lē′vō), *n., pl.* **-vos.** = demirelief. [< *demi-* + Italian (*alto*)*rilievo* alto-relievo]

dem|i|rep (dem′ē rep′), *n.* a woman of doubtful or compromised reputation; demimondaine. [< *demi-* + *rep*[2], short for *reputation*]

de|mis|a|ble (di mī′zə bəl), *adj.* that can be demised or transferred.

de|mise (di mīz′), *n., v.,* **-mised, -mis|ing.** *—n.* **1** death; decease: *The Odyssey does not bring us to the demise of Odysseus* (William Gladstone). *The continued growth of television as a medium for mass advertising was responsible for the demise ... of the Saturday Evening Post and the This Week Sunday newspaper supplement* (Walter Joyce). **2** *Law.* **a** the transfer of an estate by a will or lease. SYN: conveyance. **b** a death which causes the transfer of an estate. **3** a transfer of royal power by death or abdication.
—v.t. **1** *Law.* to transfer (an estate) by a will or lease. SYN: convey. **2** to transfer (royal power) by death or abdication. **3** *Obsolete.* to convey; transmit.
—v.i. **1** *Law.* to pass by bequest or inheritance. **2** = die.
[< Old French *demise,* feminine past participle of *desmettre* to put away < *des-* away (< Latin *dis-*) + *mettre* to put < Latin *mittere* send]

dem|i|sea|son (dem′ē sē′zən), *adj.* intermediate between two seasons, as in style.

dem|i|sem|i (dem′ē sem′ē), *adj.* half of a half.

dem|i|sem|i|qua|ver (dem′ē sem′ē kwā′vər), *n. Music.* a thirty-second note, or the symbol for it.

de|mis|sion (di mish′ən), *n.* **1** a putting away or letting go; giving up; resignation; abdication. **2** *Archaic.* a sending away; dismissal. [< Old French *demission* < *desmettre;* see etym. under **demise**]

de|mist (dē mist′), *v.t. Especially British.* to defrost: *A device to demist the back window and enable the motorist to see out of it is still considered optional* (New Scientist).

de|mist|er (dē mis′tər), *n. Especially British.* a defroster: *One buys a car and discovers one needs windscreen washers and foglamps and demisters* (Punch).

de|mit (di mit′), *v.,* **-mit|ted, -mit|ting,** *n. —v.t.* **1** to resign; abdicate. **2** *Archaic.* to let go; send away; dismiss.
—v.i. to resign; abdicate.
—n. **1** an act of demission or transfer of membership, as from one masonic lodge to another. **2** the letter which officially certifies to such a transfer.
[< French *démettre* < Old French *desmettre;* see etym. under **demise**]

dem|i|tasse (dem′ē tas′, -täs′), *n.* **1** a very small cup of black coffee. **2** a small cup for serving black coffee. [< French *demitasse* half cup < *demi-* half + *tasse* cup]

dem|i|tint (dem′ē tint′), *n.* = half-tint.

dem|i|toi|let (dem′ē toi′lit), *n.* a way of dressing, intermediate between ordinary and full dress.

dem|i|urge (dem′ē ėrj), *n.* **1** a magistrate in certain ancient Greek states; demiurgos; demiurgus. **2** *Figurative.* a person who is likened to the Demiurge; a prime mover; creative force: *... a war of giants in which he, the demiurge of the new age, would by sheer human will power reverse the seeming inevitability of history* (Atlantic). [< Greek *dēmiourgós* skilled public craftsman < *dḗmios* public (< *dêmos* people) + *érgon* work]

Dem|i|urge (dem′ē ėrj), *n.* **1** (in Platonic philosophy) the Creator of the world; Maker. **2** (in Gnostic philosophy) a supernatural being believed to be subordinate to the Supreme Being, and sometimes regarded as the creator of evil.

dem|i|ur|geous (dem′ē ėr′jəs), *adj.* of or like a demiurge.

dem|i|ur|gic (dem′ē ėr′jik), *adj.* of or having to do with a demiurge. —**dem′i|ur′gi|cal|ly,** *adv.*

dem|i|ur|gi|cal (dem′ē ėr′jə kəl), *adj.* = demiurgic.

dem|i|ur|gos (dem′ē ėr′gos), *n.* = demiurge.

dem|i|ur|gus (dem′ē ėr′gəs), *n., pl.* **-gi** (-jī). = demiurge.

de|mi-vierge (də mē vyerzh′), *n. French.* **1** a girl or woman of low morals but still a virgin. **2** (literally) half-virgin.

dem|i|volt or **dem|i|volte** (dem′ē vōlt), *n.* a half turn with the forelegs raised, made by a horse. [< French *demivolte* < *demi-* half, demi- + *volte* vault. Compare etym. under **volta.**]

dem|i-wolf (dem′ē wůlf′), *n., pl.* **-wolves. 1** a cross between a wolf and a dog. **2** a wolflike dog.

dem|i|world (dem′ē wėrld′), *n.* a world or sphere on the fringes of conventional, wealthy, or reputable society; demimonde: *His impressive set of academic credentials opened the doors of literary society, a demiworld about which Podhoretz writes entertainingly and knowledgeably* (Time). [partial translation of French *demimonde*]

dem|o (dem′ō), *n., pl.* **dem|os.** *Informal.* **1** a recording for distribution to disk jockeys, agents, etc., to advertise a new song or performing group. **2** = demonstration: *The nuclear-disarmament marchers were making their demo* (Punch). **3** = demonstrator: *Not a single demonstrator ... was armed with* [*the*] *standard "demo" equipment* (London Times).

Dem|o (dem′ō), *n., pl.* **Dem|os.** *U.S. Informal.* a Democrat: *The most powerful Demo in the State, Pat Brown* (San Francisco Chronicle).

de|mob (dē mob′), *v.,* **-mobbed, -mob|bing,** *n. Informal. —v.t.* to demobilize: *In 1945, aged 29, he was demobbed from the British army with the rank of major* (Time).
—n. Especially British. demobilization: *After the war, and before my demob, I found myself behind a desk in Belgium* (Lord Mancroft).

de|mo|bi|lise (dē mō′bə līz), *v.t.*, **-lised, -lis|ing.** *Especially British.* demobilize.

de|mo|bi|li|za|tion (dē mō′bə lə zā′shən), *n.* the act or process of demobilizing or the condition of being demobilized.

de|mo|bi|lize (dē mō′bə līz), *v.t.*, **-lized, -liz|ing.** to remove from military service, status, or control: *When a war is over, the soldiers are demobilized and sent home. Demobilized in 1920, he was appointed secretary of the ... missions in Palestine* (London Times).

Dem|o-Chris|tian (dem′ō kris′chən), *n., adj.* Christian Democrat.

de|moc|ra|cy (di mok′rə sē), *n., pl.* **-cies. 1** a government that is run by the people who live under it. In a democracy, the people rule either directly through meetings that all may attend, such as the town meetings in New England, or indirectly through the election of certain representatives to attend to the business of running government: *Democracy means the community's governing through its representatives for its own benefit* (Thomas P. Thompson). *Puritanism ... laid, without knowing it, the egg of democracy* (James Russell Lowell). **2** a country, state, or community in which the government is a democracy: *The United States is a democracy.* **3** the common people, distinguished from the privileged class, or their political power. **4** the treating of other people as one's equals: *The teacher's democracy made her popular among her pupils.* [< Middle French *démocratie,* learned borrowing from Medieval Latin *democratia* < Greek *dēmokratíā* < *dêmos* people + *krátos* rule, power]

De|moc|ra|cy (di mok′rə sē), *n.* **1** the Democratic Party in the United States. **2** its principles and policies. [< *democracy*]

dem|o|crat (dem′ə krat), *n.* **1** a person who believes that a government should be run by the people who live under it. **2** a person who treats other people as his equals. **3** = democrat wagon.

Dem|o|crat (dem′ə krat), *n.* a member of the Democratic Party. *Abbr:* Dem.

dem|o|crat|ic (dem′ə krat′ik), *adj.* **1** of a democracy; like a democracy. **2** of or having to do with the common people. **3** treating other people as one's equals: *The queen's democratic ways made her dear to her people.*

Dem|o|crat|ic (dem′ə krat′ik), *adj.* of or having to do with the Democratic Party. [< *democratic*]

dem|o|crat|i|cal (dem′ə krat′ə kəl), *adj.* = democratic.

dem|o|crat|i|cal|ly (dem′ə krat′ə klē), *adv.* in a democratic manner; according to the principles of democracy: *Puerto Rico's ... democratically elected government supplies aid and incentives* (Time).

Democratic Party, one of the two main political parties in the United States. It was derived from the Democratic-Republican Party. The other is the Republican Party.

Dem|o|crat|ic-Re|pub|li|can (dem′ə krat′ik ri-pub′lə kən), *adj., n. —adj.* of or having to do with the Democratic-Republican Party.
—n. a member of this party.

Democratic-Republican Party, an American political party of the early 1800's, derived from the Antifederal Party, which opposed a strong central government.

de|moc|ra|tise (di mok′rə tīz), *v.t., v.i.,* **-tised, -tis|ing.** *Especially British.* democratize.

de|moc|ra|tism (di mok′rə tiz əm), *n.* the theory or system of democracy.

de|moc|ra|tist (di mok′rə tist), *n.* a person who favors or supports democracy.

de|moc|ra|ti|za|tion (di mok′rə tə zā′shən), *n.* a democratizing or being democratized: *It is a period of the democratization of all institutions* (James Bryce).

de|moc|ra|tize (di mok′rə tīz), *v.t., v.i.,* **-tized, -tiz|ing.** to make or become democratic: *... today's new era of democratized monarchy* (Time).

democrat wagon, a two-seated, open wagon; democrat.

De|moc|ri|te|an (di mok′rə tē′ən), *adj.* of or having to do with Democritus or with the atomic theory associated with his name.

dé|mo|dé (dā mô dā′), *adj. French.* outmoded: *France's démodéindustry and old-fashioned agricultural system can run only another three or four years* (New Yorker).

dem|o|dec|tic mange (dem′ə dek′tik), *Veterinary Medicine.* a skin disease (mange) caused by a parasitic mite. [< New Latin *Demodex* the genus name (< Greek *dēmós* tallow + *dêx* wood worm) + English *-ic*]

de|mod|ed (dē mō′did), *adj.* out of fashion; outmoded: *His cult of aristocratic individualism would secretly have been disdained as demoded* (New York Times).

De|mod|o|cus (di mod′ə kəs), *n.* (in Homer's *Odyssey*) a famous bard at the court at Phaeacia.

de|mod|u|late (dē moj′ə lāt), *v.t.,* **-lat|ed, -lat|ing.** *Electronics.* to obtain from a modulated wave or current a signal which reproduces the original signal wave or current; detect.

de|mod|u|la|tion (dē moj′ə lā′shən), *n.* the act or process of demodulating; detection.

de|mod|u|la|tor (dē moj′ə lā′tər), *n.* a device, such as a rectifier, used in demodulating; detector.

De|mo|gor|gon (dē′mə gôr′gən, dem′ə-), *n.* (in medieval mythology) a mysterious and dreadful god or demon. [< Late Latin *Dēmogorgōn,* apparently ultimately < Greek *daímōn* demon + *gorgós* grim, terrible. Compare **Gorgon.**]

de|mog|ra|pher (di mog′rə fər), *n.* a person who

studies demography: *As projected by some demographers, the explosion point—i.e., the time when the earth's known resources no longer can feed all human life—could be reached in 1987* (Newsweek).

dem|o|graph|ic (dem′ə graf′ik), *adj.* of or having to do with demography: *Migration offers little by way of a solution of the world's demographic problem* (Wall Street Journal). —**dem′o|graph′i|cal|ly**, *adv.*

dem|o|graph|i|cal (dem′ə graf′ə kəl), *adj.* = demographic: *demographical studies of population changes.*

dem|o|graph|ics (dem′ə graf′iks), *n.pl.* demographic data.

de|mog|ra|phist (di mog′rə fist), *n.* = demographer.

de|mog|ra|phy (di mog′rə fē), *n.* the science dealing with statistics of human populations, including size, distribution, diseases, births and deaths: *The analysis of fluctuations of animal populations has importance for human demography* (F. S. Bodenheimer). [< Greek *dêmos* people + English *-graphy*]

de|moid (dē′moid), *adj.* characteristic of a region or period or of a particular geological formation (used of fossils that are so common as to be typical). [< Greek *dēmoeidês* common < *dêmos* people]

dem|oi|selle (dem′wä zel′), *n.* **1** a young girl; damsel. **2** a crane of Asia, Europe, and Africa, having long, white plumes behind the eyes; Numidian crane. **3** a dragonfly with a slender body that holds its wings vertically when at rest. **4** = damselfish. **5** = tiger shark. [< Middle French *demoiselle* < Old French *dameisele.* See related etym. at **damsel**.]

de|mol|ish (di mol′ish), *v.t.* **1** to pull or tear down; reduce to ruin: *Shells and bombs demolished the fortress. The slums were demolished before the town was extended.* SYN: ruin, raze. See syn. under **destroy**. **2** *Figurative: Princeton demolished . . . one of the best Dartmouth teams* (New Yorker). *Professor Lattimore . . . demolishes several of the accepted legends about early Mongolian history* (Manchester Guardian Weekly). [< Middle French *démoliss-*, stem of *démolir,* learned borrowing from Latin *dēmōlīrī* tear down < *dē-* down + *mōlēs, mōlis* mass, might] —**de|mol′ish|er**, *n.*

de|mol|ish|ment (di mol′ish mənt), *n.* = demolition.

dem|o|li|tion (dem′ə lish′ən, dē′mə-), *n.* a demolishing or being demolished; destruction; ruin: *The demolition of several buildings with explosives cleared the land for a new highway.*

demolition bomb, a bomb with a relatively large explosive charge, used especially for destroying buildings and other important objects.

demolition derby, *U.S.* a contest in which old cars are driven against each other until all are wrecked except the winner's.

dem|o|li|tion|ist (dem′ə lish′ə nist, dē′mə-), *n.* a person who seeks to demolish existing social and political institutions.

de|mol|o|gy (di mol′ə jē), *n.* = demography.

de|mon (dē′mən), *n., adj.* —*n.* **1** an evil spirit; devil; fiend: *In his dream the boy was chased by seven green demons. . . . haunted by woman wailing for her demon-lover!* (Samuel Taylor Coleridge). **2a** a very wicked or cruel person: *The hero was a demon in disguise.* **b** a person or thing viewed by another as an evil, harmful, or disruptive influence. **3** *Figurative.* an evil influence: *The demon of greed ruined the miser's happiness.* **4** a person who has great energy or vigor: *My music teacher is a demon for practicing.* **5** an attendant or guiding spirit. **6** *Greek Mythology.* an inferior or minor god.
—*adj.* = demoniac: *the demon Senate Majority leader who could swing almost anything, the big wheeler-dealer* (New York Times). Also **daemon**. [< Latin *daemonium* < Greek *daimónion* divine (thing), demigod; (in Christian writings) evil spirit < Greek *daímōn* divinity, spirit] —**de′mon|like′**, *adj.*

de|mon|ess (dē′mə nis), *n.* a woman demon.

de|mon|e|ti|za|tion (dē mon′ə tə zā′shən, -mun′-), *n.* a demonetizing or being demonetized.

de|mon|e|tize (dē mon′ə tīz, -mun′-), *v.t.,* **-tized, -tiz|ing.** **1** to deprive of its standard value as money: *Demonetizing gold and printing money to suit national policy would produce chaos since other nations would do the same thing* (Wall Street Journal). **2** to withdraw from use as money.

de|mo|ni|ac (di mō′nē ak), *adj., n.* —*adj.* **1** of or like demons. **2** devilish; fiendish: *Burning people at the stake was a demoniac custom.* SYN: diabolic, satanic. **3** *Figurative.* raging; frantic: *In a demoniac fit the cat clawed the leg of the woman who kicked it.* **4** possessed by an evil spirit.
—*n.* a person supposed to be possessed by an evil spirit.

de|mo|ni|a|cal (dē′mə nī′ə kəl), *adj.* = demoniac. —**de′mo|ni′a|cal|ly**, *adv.*

de|mo|ni|an (di mō′nē ən), *adj.* having to do with or like a demon or demons.

de|mon|ic (di mon′ik), *adj.* **1** of or caused by evil spirits; demoniac; devilish. **2** influenced by a guiding spirit; inspired. Also, **daemonic, daimonic.** —**de|mon′i|cal|ly**, *adv.*

de|mon|i|cal (di mon′ə kəl), *adj.* = demonic.

de|mon|ism (dē′mə niz əm), *n.* **1** belief in demons. **2** the worship of demons.

de|mon|ist (dē′mə nist), *n.* **1** a believer in demons. **2** worshiper of demons.

de|mon|ize (dē′mə nīz), *v.t.,* **-ized, -iz|ing.** **1** to make into or like a demon. **2** to subject to the influence of demons.

de|mon|oc|ra|cy (dē′mə nok′rə sē), *n., pl.* **-cies.** **1** the rule of demons. **2** a ruling body of demons.

de|mon|og|ra|pher (dē′mə nog′rə fər), *n.* a person who studies demonography.

de|mon|og|ra|phy (dē′mə nog′rə fē), *n.* the description of demons; descriptive study or treatise of demons.

de|mon|ol|a|ter (dē′mə nol′ə tər), *n.* a worshiper of demons.

de|mon|ol|a|try (dē′mə nol′ə trē), *n.* the worship of demons. [< *demon* + Greek *latreíā* worship]

de|mon|o|log|i|cal (dē′mə nə loj′ə kəl), *adj.* of or having to do with demonology: *The two wizards cross wands in a demonological duel to the death* (Time). —**de′mon|o|log′i|cal|ly**, *adv.*

de|mon|ol|o|gist (dē′mə nol′ə jist), *n.* a person who studies demonology.

de|mon|ol|o|gy (dē′mə nol′ə jē), *n., pl.* **-gies.** **1** the study of demons or of beliefs about demons. **2** a treatise on demons. **3** a grouping of persons or things viewed by their opponents as evil, harmful, or disruptive influences: *Like his patron, the President,* [*Murray*] *Chotiner is one of the fixtures of liberal demonology, and one, as it happens, who can never be counted out* (Atlantic).

de|mon|o|man|cy (dē′mə nə man′sē), *n. Obsolete.* divination by the help of demons. [< *demon* + Greek *manteíā* divination]

de|mon|o|pho|bi|a (dē′mə nə fō′bē ə), *n.* an unhealthy fear of demons.

demon star, = Algol.

de|mon|stra|bil|i|ty (di mon′strə bil′ə tē, dem′ən-), *n.* demonstrable quality or condition.

de|mon|stra|ble (di mon′strə bəl, dem′ən-), *adj.* **1** that can be shown or proved: *a demonstrable proposition.* **2** evident; apparent. —**de|mon′stra|ble|ness**, *n.*

de|mon|stra|bly (di mon′strə blē, dem′ən-), *adv.* **1** in a manner that can be proved; clearly: *This kind of program is a luxury this country demonstrably cannot afford* (Wall Street Journal). **2** by demonstration.

de|mon|strant (di mon′strənt), *n.* **1** a person who demonstrates. **2** a person who takes part in a public demonstration.

dem|on|strate (dem′ən strāt), *v.,* **-strat|ed, -strat|ing.** —*v.t.* **1** to establish the truth of, for example by argument or deduction; show clearly; prove; attest: *Can you demonstrate that the earth is round?* **2** to explain by carrying out experiments, or by showing and explaining samples or specimens; show how (a thing) is done: *The science teacher demonstrated the use of the magnet and the balance in class.* **3** to show, advertise, or make known by carrying out a process in public; show the merits of (a thing for sale): *The salesman washed some clothes to demonstrate his washing machine to us.* SYN: exhibit. **4** to show (feeling) openly: *She demonstrated her love for the baby by giving it a big hug when she arrived home.* SYN: evince, reveal, evidence. **5** *Obsolete.* to point out; indicate.
—*v.i.* **1** to take part in a parade or meeting to protest or to make demands: *An angry crowd demonstrated in front of the mayor's office for more police protection.* SYN: manifest. **2** to display military strength to frighten or deceive an enemy. **3** to teach by demonstrating.
[< Latin *dēmōnstrāre* (with English *-ate*[1]) < *dē-* (intensive) + *mōnstrāre* to show < *mōnstrum* (originally) divine omen; wonder]

dem|on|stra|tion (dem′ən strā′shən), *n.* **1** clear proof: *a demonstration that the earth is round. The ease with which he solved the hard problem was a demonstration of his ability in arithmetic.* **2** teaching by carrying out experiments or by showing and explaining samples or specimens: *A compass was used in a demonstration of the earth's magnetism.* **3** a showing of some new product or process in a public place; a showing of the merits of a thing for sale: *the demonstration of a washing machine.* SYN: exhibition, display. **4** an open show or expression of feeling: *The mother greeted her long-lost son with every demonstration of joy.* SYN: manifestation. **5** a parade or meeting to protest or make demands: *The tenants held a demonstration against the raise in rent.* **6** a display of military strength to frighten or deceive an enemy. **7a** *Logic.* an argument or series of propositions that proves a conclusion. **b** *Mathematics.* the process of proving that certain assumptions necessarily produce a certain result.

dem|on|stra|tion|al (dem′ən strā′shə nəl), *adj.* of or having to do with demonstration.

demonstration city, a city used to demonstrate the techniques and advantages of urban renewal: *Congress, however, did approve measures . . . in attacking urban decay through a "demonstration cities" program* (Richard Worsnop).

dem|on|stra|tion|ist (dem′ən strā′shə nist), *n.* a person who takes part in a demonstration; demonstrator.

de|mon|stra|tive (di mon′strə tiv), *adj., n.* —*adj.* **1** expressing one's affections freely and openly: *The girl's demonstrative greetings embarrassed her shy brother.* **2** *Grammar.* pointing out. "This" and "that" are demonstrative pronouns and also demonstrative adjectives. **3** showing clearly; explanatory. **4** giving proof; conclusive.
—*n. Grammar.* a pronoun or adjective that points out. —**de|mon′stra|tive|ly**, *adv.* —**de|mon′stra|tive|ness**, *n.*
► *This, these, that, those* are called **demonstrative adjectives** or **pronouns**, according to their use in sentences. Adjective: *This car was bought in May.* Pronoun: *This costs considerably more than that.*

dem|on|stra|tor (dem′ən strā′tər), *n.* **1** a person or thing that demonstrates. **2** a vehicle, appliance, or other merchandise used by a dealer to demonstrate the product to customers: *The dealer uses this car as a demonstrator.* **3** a person who takes part in a demonstration. **4** an instructor who teaches by practical demonstrations, for example in a medical or dental school.

dem|on|stra|tor|ship (dem′ən strā′tər ship), *n. Especially British.* a college or university teaching assistantship, especially in science.

dem|o-pack (dem′ō pak′), *n.* a package of high explosives used by members of an underwater demolition team.

dem|o|phil (dem′ə fil), *n.* = demophile.

dem|o|phile (dem′ə fīl, -fil), *n.* a friend of the people. [< Greek *dêmos* people + English *-phile*]

de|mor|al|ise (di môr′ə līz, -mor′-), *v.t.,* **-ised, -is|ing.** *Especially British.* demoralize.

de|mor|al|i|za|tion (di môr′ə lə zā′shən, -mor′-), *n.* **1** the action of demoralizing. **2** the state of being demoralized.

de|mor|al|ize (di môr′ə līz, -mor′-), *v.t.,* **-ized, -iz|ing.** **1** to lower the morals or principles of; corrupt; deprave: *The drug habit demoralizes its victims.* **2** to lower the morale of; weaken the spirit, courage, or discipline of; dishearten: *Lack of food and ammunition demoralized the besieged soldiers.* **3** to throw into confusion or disorder: *Threats of war demoralized the stock market.* [American English (coined by Noah Webster) < *de-* + *moralize,* or *moral* + *-ize*]

de|mor|al|iz|er (di môr′ə lī′zər, -mor′-), *n.* a person or thing that demoralizes.

de|mor|al|iz|ing|ly (di môr′ə lī′zing lē, -mor′-), *adv.* in a demoralizing manner; so as to demoralize: *A British officer had infiltrated into Ludendorff's staff and played demoralizingly on his mind* (London Times).

de|mor|phism (di môr′fiz əm), *n. Geology.* the decomposition, disintegration, or weathering of rocks, as contrasted with their metamorphism or transformation into other rocks.

de mor|tu|is nil ni|si bo|num (dē môr′chù is nil nī′sī bō′nəm), *Latin.* of the dead (say) nothing except good.

de|mos (dē′mos), *n., pl.* **-mi.** **1** the common people of an ancient Greek state. **2** the populace; common people. **3** a township in ancient Attica. [< Greek *dêmos* district, its people]

De|mos|then|ic (dem′əs then′ik, dē′məs-), *adj.* having to do with or characteristic of Demosthenes, the great Athenian orator, 384?-322 B.C.

de|mote (di mōt′), *v.t.,* **-mot|ed, -mot|ing.** to put back to a lower grade; reduce in rank; degrade: *The new girl was demoted from fourth grade to third when the teacher found she could not do the work. He was demoted from corporal to private.* [American English < *de-* + (pro)*mote*]

de|moth|ball (dē môth′bôl′, -moth′-), *v.t.* to return (military or naval equipment) to use by removing the preservative coating in which it has been stored.

de|mot|ic (di mot′ik), *adj., n.* —*adj.* **1** of the com-

mon people; popular: *demotic customs, the demotic mind. There will never be a successful working-class English novel until someone invents or discovers a method of writing demotic speech* (Observer). **2** having to do with or denoting the ancient Egyptian form of simplified writing, derived from the hieratic character. **3** having to do with or denoting the standard spoken and written form of modern Greek.
—*n.* **1** a simplified form of ancient Egyptian writing. **2** the standard spoken and written form of modern Greek, especially as contrasted with katharevousa, the literary language of the 1800's.
[< Greek *dēmotikós* of or for the people < *dêmos* the people]

de|mot|ics (di mot′iks), *n.* the study of people and society; sociology.

de|mot|i|ki (di mot′ē kē), *n.* = demotic (*n.* def. 2). [< New Greek *dēmotikē* < Greek *dēmotikós* of the people < *dêmos* the people]

de|mo|tion (di mō′shən), *n.* **1** the act of demoting. **2** the fact of being demoted.

de|mot|ist (di mot′ist), *n.* a person who studies demotic script.

de|mount (dē mount′), *v.t.* **1** to remove from a mounting. **2** to take apart. —*v.i.* = dismount.

de|mount|a|bil|i|ty (dē moun′tə bil′ə tē), *n.* demountable quality.

de|mount|a|ble (dē moun′tə bəl), *adj.* that can be removed: *a demountable wheel rim.*

demp|ster (demp′stər), *n.* = deemster.

de|mul|cent (di mul′sənt), *adj., n.* —*adj.* soothing.
—*n.* a soothing ointment or medicine.
[< Latin *dēmulcēns, -entis,* present participle of *dēmulcēre* < *dē-* down + *mulcēre* soothe]

de|mul|si|fi|er (di mul′sə fī′ər), *n.* a chemical agent that breaks down or prevents the formation of an emulsion.

de|mur (di mėr′), *v.,* **-murred, -mur|ring,** *n.* —*v.i.* **1** to show disapproval or dislike; object; take exception: *The clerk demurred at working overtime without extra pay.* **2** *Law.* to put in a demurrer. **3** *Obsolete.* to hesitate; pause; delay.
—*n.* **1** the act of demurring; objection; exception: *The clerk's demur was ignored by his boss. Her gentle demur went unnoticed in the fury of the argument.* **2** *Law. Obsolete.* a demurrer.
[< Old French *demurer* < Latin *dēmorārī* < *dē-* + *morārī* to delay < *mora* a pause, delay]

de|mure (di myůr′), *adj.,* **-mur|er, -mur|est.** **1** seeming more modest and proper than one really is; coy: *the demure smile of a flirt.* **SYN:** prim. See syn. under **modest. 2** serious; thoughtful; sober: *The modest maiden was demure.* **SYN:** grave, sedate. [< *de-* (perhaps intensive) + obsolete *mure* demure < Old French *meür* discreet, mature < Latin *mātūrus*] —**de|mure′ly,** *adv.* —**de|mure′ness,** *n.*

de|mur|ra|ble (di mėr′ə bəl), *adj.* that may be demurred to.

de|mur|rage (di mėr′ij), *n.* **1** failure to load or unload a ship, railroad car, or truck within the time specified. **2** the payment made for this. [< Old French *demorage* < *demurer;* see etym. under **demur**]

de|mur|ral (di mėr′əl), *n.* a demurring; demur.

de|mur|rant (di mėr′ənt), *n. Law.* a party to an action who puts in a demurrer.

de|mur|rer (di mėr′ər), *n.* **1** a person who objects. **2** an objection; exception: *This reply is met by the demurrer that it is beside the question* (Herbert Spencer). **3** *Law.* a plea by a defendant that a lawsuit or part of a lawsuit be dismissed because the facts, even if true, do not sustain the plaintiff's claim or because there is some legal defect in his claim.

de|my (di mī′), *n., pl.* **-mies. 1** a size of writing paper (in the United States 16 x 21, in Great Britain 15½ x 20, inches) or of printing paper (17½ x 22½ inches). **2** a holder of a scholarship at Magdalen College, Oxford. [variant of *demi-* half]

de|my|e|li|nate (dē mī′ə lə nāt), *v.t.,* **-nat|ed, -nat|ing.** to remove or destroy myelin or the myelin sheath of (nerves).

de|my|e|li|na|tion (dē mī′ə lə nā′shən), *n.* **1** the act of demyelinating. **2** the result of demyelinating.

de|my|ship (di mī′ship), *n.* a scholarship at Magdalen College, Oxford.

de|mys|ti|fi|ca|tion (dē mis′tə fə kā′shən), *n.* the act or process of demystifying; enlightenment: *In an age of unfolding rationality and demystification of the world, the numerical growth of scientists, technologists and technicians has been accompanied by the development of a new faith and a new priesthood* (New Scientist and Science Journal).

de|mys|ti|fy (dē mis′tə fī), *v.t.,* **-fied, -fy|ing.** to make understandable; clarify by explanation or study: *The French government in the past fortnight at least "successfully demystified the obscure science of gold and brought it into the forefront of politics"* (New Yorker).

de|myth|i|ci|za|tion (dē mith′ə sə zā′shən), *n.* the act or process of demythicizing: *Demythicization began with the demythicizing of God and the Holy Trinity . . . to end with the demythicization of the priesthood* (London Times).

de|myth|i|cize (dē mith′ə sīz), *v.t., v.i.,* **-cized, -ciz|ing.** to strip or rid of myths; demythologize.

de|my|thol|o|gise (dē′mi thol′ə jīz), *v.t.,* **-gised, -gis|ing.** *British.* demythologize.

de|my|thol|o|gi|za|tion (dē′mi thol′ə jə zā′shən), *n.* the act or process of demythologizing.

de|my|thol|o|gize (dē′mi thol′ə jīz), *v.t.,* **-gized, -giz|ing.** to remove myths or mythological elements from (a religion, doctrine, cult, and the like): *German Biblical Critic Rudolf Bultmann . . . argues that the essential Gospel message must be "demythologized" by liberating it from antiquated supernatural language* (Time). *A religion that was completely demythologized would . . . be a very dull religion* (London Times). *Mr. Blake goes very slightly too far in the attempt to demythologize Disraeli* (John Grigg). —**de′my|thol′o|giz′er,** *n.*

den (den), *n., v.,* **denned, den|ning.** —*n.* **1** a wild animal's home; lair: *The bear's den was in a cave.* **2** a cavern, cave, or other place in which to take shelter or hide. **3** *Figurative.* a place where thieves or the like have their headquarters. **4** *Figurative.* a small, dirty or neglected room or dwelling. **5** *Figurative.* one's private room for reading and work, usually small and cozy. **6** a group of two to eight cub scouts.
—*v.i.* **1** to live in or as if in a den. **2** to escape into or hide in a den.
den up, *U.S.* **a** to retire into a den for the winter, as a hibernating animal does. **b** to retire to one's den or private room.
[Old English *denn*] —**den′like′,** *adj.*

Den., Denmark.

de|nar|i|us (di nãr′ē əs), *n., pl.* **-nar|i|i** (-nãr′ē ī). **1** an ancient Roman silver coin. **2** an ancient Roman gold coin. **3** *British.* a penny. *Abbr:* d (no period). [< Latin *dēnārius* containing ten; a coin worth ten asses[2] < *dēnī* ten at a time, ultimately < *decem* ten. See related etym. at **denary.** See etym. of doublets **denier**[2], **dinar.**]

den|a|ry (den′ər ē, dē′nər-), *adj.* of or having to do with the number ten; having ten as the basis of reckoning; decimal. [< Latin *dēnārius.* See related etym. at **denarius.**]

de|na|sal|ize (dē nā′zə līz), *v.t.,* **-ized, -iz|ing.** to make (speech sounds) less nasal; remove the nasal quality from (the voice).

de|na|tant (dē nā′tənt), *adj.* swimming or migrating with the current, not against it: *denatant fishes.*

de|na|tion|al|i|za|tion (dē nash′ə nə lə zā′shən, -nash′nə-), *n.* the process of denationalizing or state of being denationalized.

de|na|tion|al|ize (dē nash′ə nə līz, -nash′nə-), *v.t.,* **-ized, -iz|ing. 1** to deprive of national rights, scope, or character. **2** to turn over, or return, to private ownership or operation, as an industry or undertaking previously owned or operated by a government or an agency of the government.

de|na|tion|al|iz|er (dē nash′ə nə lī′zər, -nash′nə-), *n.* a person or thing that denationalizes.

de|nat|u|ral|i|za|tion (dē nach′ər ə lə zā′shən, -nach′rə-), *n.* a denaturalizing or being denaturalized.

de|nat|u|ral|ize (dē nach′ər ə līz, -nach′rə-), *v.t.,* **-ized, -iz|ing. 1** to make unnatural: *The lyrical ballad . . . is almost always denaturalized by culture* (Francis T. Palgrave). **2** to withdraw citizenship from (a naturalized citizen): *Gambler Frank Costello, 72 . . . was denaturalized in 1959* (Newsweek).

de|na|tur|ant (dē nā′chər ənt), *n.* a denaturing substance or agent.

de|na|tur|a|tion (dē nā′chə rā′shən), *n.* the act or process of denaturing or condition of being denatured.

de|na|ture (dē nā′chər), *v.t.,* **-tured, -tur|ing. 1** to change the nature of. **2** to make unfit for eating or drinking without destroying its usefulness for other purposes: *denatured alcohol.* **3** *Biochemistry.* to change the properties of (a protein) by changing its structure, for example by heat or the addition of chemicals.

de|na|tur|ize (dē nā′chə rīz), *v.t.,* **-ized, -iz|ing.** to denature.

de|na|tur|iz|er (dē nā′chə rī′zər), *n.* something that denatures.

de|na|zi|fi|ca|tion (dē nät′sə fə kā′shən, -nat′-), *n.* the act or process of denazifying or state of being denazified.

de|na|zi|fy (dē nät′sə fī, -nat′-), *v.t.,* **-fied, -fy|ing.** to rid of Nazi doctrines or Nazi influences: *Among the new arrests were people of great prominence under the Nazis, most of whom had already been denazified by the German courts* (Hannah Arendt).

dendr-, *combining form.* a form of **dendro-** before vowels, as in *dendriform.*

den|dri|form (den′drə fôrm), *adj.* like a tree in form.

den|drite (den′drīt), *n.* **1** the branching part at the receiving end of a nerve cell; dendron. **2** *Geology.* **a** a stone or mineral with branching, treelike markings, caused by crystallization of foreign minerals. **b** such a treelike marking. **3** a crystalline growth of branching form. [< Greek *dendrîtēs* of a tree < *déndron* tree]

den|drit|ic (den drit′ik), *adj.* formed or marked like a dendrite; treelike.

den|drit|i|cal (den drit′ə kəl), *adj.* = dendritic.

den|drit|i|cal|ly (den drit′ə klē), *adv.* in a dendritic manner; as a tree.

dendro-, *combining form.* of a tree; of trees: *Dendrology = study of trees.* [< Greek *déndron* tree]

den|dro|chron|o|log|i|cal (den′drō kron′ə loj′ə-kəl), *adj.* of or having to do with dendrochronology: *Dendrochronological techniques . . . can be confidently employed in the Southwest because the dry climate has preserved wood more than fifteen hundred years* (Melville J. Herskovits). —**den′dro|chron′o|log′i|cal|ly,** *adv.*

den|dro|chro|nol|o|gist (den′drō krə nol′ə jist), *n.* a person who studies dendrochronology.

den|dro|chro|nol|o|gy (den′drō krə nol′ə jē), *n.* the study of tree rings as a means of establishing dates and environmental conditions in the past.

den|dro|graph (den′drə graf, -gräf), *n.* a device for recording the growth of a tree by measuring the trunk's changes in volume. [< Greek *déndron* tree + English *-graph*]

den|droid (den′droid), *adj.* like a tree in form; dendriform; arborescent. [< Greek *dendroeidēs* < *déndron* tree + *eîdos* form]

den|droi|dal (den droi′dəl), *adj.* = dendroid.

den|drol|a|try (den drol′ə trē), *n.* the worship of trees.

den|dro|lite (den′drə līt), *n.* a petrified or fossil tree or part of a tree.

den|dro|log|ic (den′drə loj′ik), *adj.* = dendrological.

den|dro|log|i|cal (den′drə loj′ə kəl), *adj.* of or having to do with dendrology.

den|drol|o|gist (den drol′ə jist), *n.* a person who studies dendrology.

den|drol|o|gous (den drol′ə gəs), *adj.* having to do with dendrology.

den|drol|o|gy (den drol′ə jē), *n.* the branch of botany dealing with the study of trees.

den|drom|e|ter (den drom′ə tər), *n.* an instrument for measuring trees.

den|dron (den′dron), *n.* = dendrite (def. 1).

den|dro|phile (den′drə fīl), *n.* a lover of trees.

den|droph|i|lism (den drof′ə liz əm), *n.* love of trees.

den|droph|i|lous (den drof′ə ləs), *adj.* **1** tree-loving: *The Pembroke Arbor Society* [*is*] *a dendrophilous organization that had long been urging Bermudians to spare their cedars and not wastefully chop them down for Christmas trees* (New Yorker). **2** growing on or twining about trees: *Many dendrophilous vines are harmful to trees.* [< Greek *déndron* tree + *phílos* fond (with English *-ous*)]

dene (dēn), *n. British.* a bare, sandy tract by the sea; a low sand hill. Also, **dean.** [Middle English *den;* origin uncertain]

Den|eb (den′eb), *n.* a star of the first magnitude in the northern constellation Cygnus, used by navigators as a guide. Deneb is 60,000 times as bright as the sun. [< Arabic *dhanab* tail[1]]

De|neb|o|la (də neb′ō lə), *n.* a star in the tail of the constellation Leo. [< Arabic *dhanab-al-asad* tail of the lion]

den|e|ga|tion (den′ə gā′shən), *n.* denial; contradiction. [< Latin *dēnegātiō, -ōnis* < *dēnegāre;* see etym. under **deny**]

de|ne|go|ti|ate (dē′ni gō′shē āt), *v.t.,* **-at|ed, -at|ing.** to negotiate the breaking of (an agreement): *The French took pains to denegotiate the accord* (New York Times).

dene|hole (dēn′hōl′), *n.* one of the many ancient artificial excavations or pits found chiefly in the chalk formations in Essex and Kent in England and in the valley of the Somme in France. [apparently < dialectal *Dene* Dane + *hole* (because the Danes supposedly hid plunder in them)]

de|ner|vate (dē nėr′vāt), *v.t.,* **-vat|ed, -vat|ing. 1** to remove a nerve or nerves from. **2** to cut off the nerves to.

de|ner|va|tion (dē′nėr vā′shən), *n.* the process of denervating or condition of being denervated: *Permanent denervation, to stop the pain, is best done by an operation in which the nerve is cut* (Science News Letter).

de|neu|tral|i|za|tion (dē nü′trə lə zā′shən, -nyü′-), *n.* the act or process of deneutralizing or state of being deneutralized: *The deneutralization of Formosa marks an important change in the* *conduct of the cold war* (Newsweek).

de|neu|tral|ize (dē nü′trə līz, -nyü′-), *v.t.,* **-ized, -iz|ing.** to abolish the neutral status of (a country, territory, etc.).

den|gue (deng′gā, -gē), *n.* an infectious, epidemic or sporadic fever with severe pain in the head, joints, and muscles and usually skin rash, caused by a virus transmitted by an aëdes mosquito; breakbone fever. [American English < Spanish (West Indies) *dengue* < Swahili (Zanzibar) (*ki*)*dinga* (*popo*) a kind of sudden cramp (of the evil spirit)]

de|ni|a|bil|i|ty (di nī′ə bil′ə tē), *n. U.S.* the ability to deny having any knowledge or connection with an illegal or improper activity: *The use of middlemen, of trusted aides-de-camp, of cash instead of checks are all techniques that give the political figure who gets the money "deniability" —he can say he knows nothing about the matter* (Nicholas M. Horrock).

de|ni|a|ble (di nī′ə bəl), *adj.* that can be denied.

de|ni|al (di nī′əl), *n.* **1** the act of saying that something is not true: *a denial of the existence of ghosts. Your denial is fruitless; we have proof.* SYN: contradiction. **2** the act of saying that one does not hold to or accept (a belief): *Galileo was forced to make a public denial of his belief that the earth went around the sun.* **3** a refusing: *His denial of our request seemed very rude.* SYN: noncompliance. **4** a refusing to acknowledge; disowning: *Peter's denial of Christ.* SYN: disavowal. **5** a doing without things that one wants; self-denial. **6** *Law.* the opposing by the defendant of a plea, claim, or charge made against him.

de|nic|o|tin|ize (dē nik′ə tə nīz), *v.t.,* **-ized, -iz|ing.** to remove all or part of the nicotine from (tobacco).

de|ni|er[1] (di nī′ər), *n.* a person who denies.

den|ier[2] (den′yər, də nir′ *for 1;* də nir′ *for 2 and 3*), *n.* **1** a unit of weight used to express the fineness of silk or synthetic yarn, such as rayon or nylon, or other fiber, based on the number of .05 grams (of weight) in 450 meters of length: *A 15-denier nylon stocking is finer than a 30-denier stocking.* **2** an old French coin, originally silver, about 1/12 of a sou, later having little value. **3** a very small sum. [< Old French *denier* < Latin *dēnārius.* See etym. of doublets **denarius, dinar.**]

den|i|grate (den′ə grāt), *v.t.,* **-grat|ed, -grat|ing.** **1** to blacken the character or reputation of (a person, group, or organization); defame: *To say that integration has failed is to ignore and denigrate the thousands of Southern citizens who ... have faithfully tried to obey what they believed was the law of the land* (Tom Wicker). SYN: sully, stain. **2** *Rare.* to blacken with dirt, smoke, or the like. [< Latin *dēnigrāre* (with English *-ate*[1]) blacken thoroughly < *dē-* (intensive) + *nigrāre* blacken < *niger, nigrī* black] —**den′i|gra′tor,** *n.*

den|i|gra|tion (den′ə grā′shən), *n.* the act of blackening a reputation; defamation: *They regard the denigration of the craft of journalism as ... lamentable* (Columbia Journalism Review).

den|i|gra|to|ry (den′ə grə tôr′ē, -tōr′-), *adj.* denigrating; slanderous: *Some of them were dropping mildly denigratory digs about the Russians* (Harper's).

den|im (den′əm), *n.* a heavy, coarse cotton cloth with a diagonal weave, used especially for overalls and for upholstery and sports clothes. **denims,** overalls or trousers made of denim: *The anarchists are tousle-haired young people, dressed in denims and winter pullovers* (London Times).
[< French (*serge*) *de Nîmes* (serge) from *Nîmes,* a town in France]

de|ni|trate (dē nī′trāt), *v.t.,* **-trat|ed, -trat|ing.** to free from nitric acid, nitrates, oxides of nitrogen, or the nitro group.

de|ni|tra|tion (dē′nī trā′shən), *n.* the process of denitrating.

de|ni|tra|tor (dē nī′trā tər), *n.* an apparatus for denitration.

de|ni|tri|fi|ca|tion (dē nī′trə fə kā′shən), *n.* a denitrifying or being denitrified.

de|ni|tri|fi|er (dē nī′trə fī′ər), *n.* an agent that denitrifies.

de|ni|tri|fy (dē nī′trə fī), *v.t.,* **-fied, -fy|ing.** **1** to remove nitrogen or its compounds from. **2** to change (nitrates) by reduction into nitrites, nitrogen, or ammonia.

den|i|za|tion (den′ə zā′shən), *n.* **1** the act of making one a denizen. **2** the fact of being made a denizen.

den|i|zen (den′ə zən), *n., v.* —*n.* **1** a person or animal that lives in a place; inhabitant; occupant: *Fish are denizens of the sea.* **2** a foreign word, plant, or animal that has been naturalized: *The common English sparrow is a denizen of America; it was first brought from Europe to America about 1850.* **3** a foreigner who is given certain rights.
—*v.t.* to make a denizen; naturalize.
[< Anglo-French *deinzein* < *deinz* within (< Late Latin *deintus* < Latin *dē* from + *intus* within) + *-ein* one that is < Latin *-āneus*]

den|i|zen|ship (den′ə zən ship), *n.* the state of being a denizen.

den mother, 1 a woman who is in charge of a den of cub scouts. **2** *Figurative: She's spending her life as den mother to Toronto's ... dope addicts* (Maclean's).

den|ner (den′ər), *n.* the leader of a den of cub scouts.

den|net (den′it), *n.* a light, open two-wheeled carriage similar to a gig and fashionable in England in the early 1800's. [origin unknown]

de|nom|i|na|ble (di nom′ə nə bəl), *adj.* that can be denominated or named.

de|nom|i|nate (di nom′ə nāt), *v.t.,* **-nat|ed, -nat|ing.** to give a name to; name. [< Latin *dēnōmināre* (with English *-ate*[1]) < *dē-* (intensive) + *nōmen, -inis* name]

de|nom|i|nate number (di nom′ə nit, -nāt), a number used with the name of the kind of unit: *4 oz., 10 in., and 9 lb. are denominate numbers.*

de|nom|i|na|tion (di nom′ə nā′shən), *n.* **1** a name for a group or class of things; name. SYN: appellation, designation, title. **2** a religious group or sect: *Methodists and Baptists are two large Protestant denominations. The presence of many different denominations and sects in a society means that the culture is differentiated into many parts, with differing group interests and viewpoints* (Ogburn and Nimkoff). **3** a class or kind of units: *Reducing 5/12, 1/3, and 1/6 to the same denomination gives 5/12, 4/12, and 2/12. Reducing 5 ft. and 10 in. to the same denomination gives 70 in. The United States coin of lowest denomination is a cent.* **4** a class; sort; kind. **5** the act of naming.

de|nom|i|na|tion|al (di nom′ə nā′shə nəl, -nāsh′nəl), *adj.* having to do with or controlled by some religious denomination; sectarian: *a denominational school.*

de|nom|i|na|tion|al|ism (di nom′ə nā′shə nəliz′əm, -nāsh′nə liz-), *n.* **1** denominational principles. **2** division into denominations. **3** adherence to or advocacy of denominational principles or a denominational system.

de|nom|i|na|tion|al|ist (di nom′ə nā′shə nə list, -nāsh′nə-), *n.* **1** a member of a denomination. **2** a person who favors or supports denominationalism.

de|nom|i|na|tion|al|ize (di nom′ə nā′shə nə līz, -nāsh′nə-), *v.t.,* **-ized, -iz|ing.** to make denominational.

de|nom|i|na|tion|al|ly (di nom′ə nā′shə nə lē, -nāsh′nə-), *adv.* according to a denominational method; in a sectarian manner.

de|nom|i|na|tive (di nom′ə nā′tiv, -ə nə-), *adj., n.* —*adj.* **1** giving a distinctive name; naming. **2** *Grammar.* derived from a noun or an adjective. "To center" and "to whiten" are denominative verbs. —*n. Grammar.* a word derived from a noun or an adjective. —**de|nom′i|na′tive|ly,** *adv.*

de|nom|i|na|tor (di nom′ə nā′tər), *n.* **1** the number below the line in a fraction, which states the size of the parts in their relation to the whole: *In ¾, 4 is the denominator, and 3 is the numerator.* **2** *Figurative.* **a** a quality or characteristic shared by all; common denominator. **b** a yardstick or criterion; standard: *The individual is the denominator that counts* (Terry Sanford). **3** *Rare.* a person or thing that names.

de nos jours (də nō zhür′), *French.* **1** of our time; of the present age: *This monster ... is in a way the Gargantua de nos jours* (Punch). **2** (literally) of our days.

de|not|a|ble (di nō′tə bəl), *adj.* that can be denoted.

de|no|ta|tion (dē′nō tā′shən), *n.* **1** the meaning, especially the exact, literal meaning: *The denotation of "home" is "place where one lives," but it has many connotations.* **2** a denoting or marking out; indication. **3** a mark; sign; symbol. **4** *Logic.* **a** the class, type, or number of things included in a given term; extension. **b** a value, quantity, or other attribute, represented by a symbol.
▶The **denotation** of a word is the exact, literal meaning of that word as contrasted with its **connotation,** the added meaning the word suggests or implies. The denotation of *slender* and *skinny* is thin, but *slender* connotes approval and *skinny,* disapproval.

de|no|ta|tive (dē′nō tā′tiv, di nō′tə tiv), *adj.* **1** having the quality of denoting; designative; indicative. Proper names are denotative. **2** of or having to do with denotation. —**de|no′ta|tive|ly,** *adv.*

de|note (di nōt′), *v.t.,* **-not|ed, -not|ing.** **1** to be the sign of; indicate: *A fever usually denotes sickness. If the teacher writes an "A" on your paper, it denotes very good work.* **2** to be a name for; mean: *The word "stool" denotes a small chair without a back.* **3** to stand for as a symbol: *The character "X" denotes multiplication.* [< Middle French *dénoter,* learned borrowing from Latin *dēnotāre* denote, mark out < *dē-* from, out + *notāre* to mark < *nota* mark]
▶See **denotation** for usage note.

de|note|ment (di nōt′mənt), *n.* a sign; indication.

de|no|tive (di nō′tiv), *adj.* serving to denote; indicative; denotative.

de|noue|ment or **dé|noue|ment** (dā′nü mäɴ′), *n.* **1a** the solution of a plot in a story, play, situation, or the like: *The particulars of the dénouement you shall know in due season* (Tobias Smollett). *It's all fairly conventional and unsubtle, with an anticlimactic dénouement; but the Cornish setting is attractive* (New York Times). **b** the passage in the story, play, or other literary work, in which this takes place. **2** outcome; end: *He also, no doubt, wanted to go himself as a fitting denouement to his career* (Atlantic). [< French *dénouement* < *dénouer* untie < *dé-* (< Latin *dis-*) out + *nouer* < Latin *nōdāre* to tie < *nōdus* knot]

de|nounce (di nouns′), *v.t.,* **-nounced, -nounc|ing.** **1** to speak against; express strong disapproval of; condemn; censure: *The preacher denounced war, calling it immoral.* **2** to give information against; accuse: *The chief denounced one of his own police officers as a thief. The scientists denounced most cancer cures as frauds.* **3** to give formal notice of the termination of (a treaty or other agreement). **4** *Archaic.* to proclaim or announce (a calamitous event). **5** *Obsolete.* to portend. [< Old French *denoncer* < Latin *dēnūntiāre* < *dē-* down + *nūntiāre* proclaim < *nūntius* messenger] —**de|nounc′er,** *n.*

de|nounce|ment (di nouns′mənt), *n.* the act of denouncing; denunication.

de nou|veau (də nü vō′), *French.* anew; afresh; again.

de no|vo (dē nō′vō), *Latin.* anew; starting again: *It is naive to imagine that leaders initiate plans de novo, especially in a country like the United States where so many pressure groups exist* (Ogburn and Nimkoff).

dense (dens), *adj.,* **dens|er, dens|est.** **1** closely packed together; thick: *a dense forest, a dense fog. Dense patches of briers are difficult to walk through.* SYN: compact, close. **2** *Figurative.* very great; intense; impenetrable: *dense ignorance.* SYN: profound. **3** *Figurative.* thick-headed; stupid: *His dense look showed he did not understand the problem.* **4** relatively opaque, with strong contrasts of light and shade: *a dense photographic negative.* [< Latin *dēnsus*] —**dense′ly,** *adv.* —**dense′ness,** *n.*

den|si|fi|ca|tion (den′sə fə kā′shən), *n.* a densifying or being densified.

den|si|fy (den′sə fī), *v.t.,* **-fied, -fy|ing.** to make dense: *Densified wood, with characteristics of the original board changed by compression, will be another popular item* (Wall Street Journal).

den|sim|e|ter (den sim′ə tər), *n.* an apparatus for measuring the density or specific gravity of a solid or liquid. [< Latin *dēnsus* dense]

den|si|met|ric (den′sə met′rik), *adj.* of or by a densimeter: *a densimetric analysis.* —**den′si|met′ri|cal|ly,** *adv.*

den|sim|e|try (den sim′ə trē), *n.* the use of the densimeter, especially in determining the density of samples of gunpowder.

den|si|tom|e|ter (den′sə tom′ə tər), *n.* **1** an instrument for measuring the density of a photographic negative. **2** = densimeter. [< *density*]

den|si|tom|e|try (den′sə tom′ə trē), *n.* the study of the density of photographic negatives.

den|si|ty (den′sə tē), *n., pl.* **-ties.** **1** the condition or quality of being dense; having parts very close together; compactness; thickness: *The density of the forest prevented us from seeing more than a little way ahead.* **2** the amount of matter to a unit of bulk; the ratio of the mass of a given volume of a substance to that of an equal volume of a standard substance. Water is the standard for solids and liquids, and hydrogen or air for gases. *The density of lead is greater than the density of wood. Abbr:* D. or d. **3** the quantity of anything per unit area: *population density.* **4** *Figurative.* stupidity. **5** *Photography.* the relative opaqueness of a developed negative. **6** *Electricity.* **a** the quantity of electricity per unit of area on a charged surface. **b** = current density.

density current, 1 *Physics.* the passage by gravity of a liquid or gas through or around a fluid of slightly different density. **2** = turbidity current.

dent[1] (dent), *n., v.* —*n.* **1** a hollow made by a blow or pressure: *The boys threw rocks that made dents in the steel doors. The fall put a dent in my bicycle fender.* **2** a weak spot; the

---

Pronunciation Key: hat, āge, cãre, fär; let, ēqual, tėrm; it, īce; hot, ōpen, ôrder; oil, out; cup, pu̇t, rüle; child; long; thin; ᴛʜen; zh, measure; ə represents **a** in about, **e** in taken, **i** in pencil, **o** in lemon, **u** in circus.

start of a break, hole, or cut: (*Figurative.*) *The purchase of a new car made a dent in our savings.* (*Figurative*). *The rebuke left a dent in the boy's stubborn attitude.*
—***v.t.*** to make a dent in: *The movers dented the top of the table when they banged it against the doorknob. 125 workers labored 48 hours a week most of the past year trying to dent their backlog* (Wall Street Journal).
—***v.i.*** to become dented: *Soft wood dents easily. The teakettle dented when it was dropped on the floor.*
[Middle English *dente* stroke; striking, variant of *dint*]

dent[2] (dent), *n.* **1** a toothlike part in a gearwheel, lock, or mechanical device. **2** a notch or indentation: *High was his comb . . . In dents embattled like a castle wall* (John Dryden). [< Old French *dent* tooth < Latin *dēns, dentis*]

dent., **1** dental. **2** dentist. **3** dentistry.

den|tal (den′təl), *adj., n.* —***adj.*** **1** of or for the teeth: *dental cream. Proper dental care can prevent tooth decay.* **2** of or for a dentist's work: *a dental drill.* **3** *Phonetics.* (of speech sounds) produced by placing the tip of the tongue against or near the back of the upper front teeth.
—***n.*** *Phonetics.* a dental sound. "T" and "d" are dentals.
[< Late Latin *dentālis* < Latin *dēns, dentis* tooth] —**den′tal|ly**, *adv.*

dental floss, a strong, waxed thread for cleaning between the teeth.

dental formula, a formula or tabular statement of the number and kinds of teeth a mammal may have.

dental hygiene, that part of dentistry related to keeping the teeth, gums, and mouth healthy.

dental hygienist, an assistant to a dentist who cleans the teeth and performs routine examinations.

den|ta|li|um (den tā′lē əm), *n., pl.* **-li|ums, -li|a** (-lē ə). a tooth shell; scaphopod: *Dentalium . . . shells kept on strings were the money of the Indians on the Pacific coast* (Tracy I. Storer). [< New Latin *Dentalium* the genus name < Late Latin *dentālis* < Latin *dēns, dentis* tooth]

den|tal|i|za|tion (den′tə lə zā′shən), *n.* **1** the act of making into a dental sound. **2** a dental sound.

den|tal|ize (den′tə līz), *v.t.*, **-ized, -iz|ing.** *Phonetics.* to make into a dental sound.

dental pulp, the soft, sensitive substance containing the nerves and blood vessels that fills the cavity of a mature tooth.

dental technician, a person who makes bridges, dentures, crowns, and other restorative devices, to dentists' specifications.

den|ta|ry (den′tər ē), *adj.* **1** of or having to do with the teeth; dental. **2** bearing teeth. [< Late Latin *dentārius* < Latin *dēns, dentis* tooth]

dentary splenial, the fused dentary and splenial bones, or a bone which takes the place of those two in forming the jaw.

***den|tate** (den′tāt), *adj.* having toothlike projections; toothed; notched: *a dentate leaf.* [< Latin *dentātus* < *dēns, dentis* tooth] —**den′tate|ly**, *adv.*

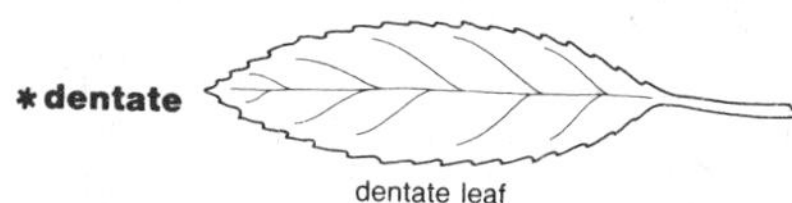

dentate leaf

den|tat|ed (den′tā tid), *adj.* = dentate.

den|ta|tion (den tā′shən), *n.* **1** dentate condition or form. **2** *Zoology.* one or more toothlike parts or projections: *the dentation on the wings of a butterfly or moth.*

dent corn, a variety of Indian corn in which the kernels indent on maturing: *He selected some of the varieties of . . . dent corn then commonly grown and planted them together in a field isolated from other corn* (Scientific American). See picture under **corn**[1].

den|tel (den′təl), *n.* = dentil.

den|te|lat|ed (den′tə lā′tid), *adj.* having small toothlike markings; finely notched. [< French *dentelé* toothed + English *-ate*[1] + *-ed*[2]]

denti-, *combining form.* of a tooth or teeth; dental: *Dentiform = of the form of a tooth.* Also, **dento-**. [< Latin *dēns, dentis* tooth]

den|ti|care (den′tə kãr′), *n.* (in Canada) a government-sponsored program of free dental care for children. [patterned on *Medicare*]

den|ti|cle (den′tə kəl), *n.* **1** a small tooth or toothlike part. **2** = dentil. [< Latin *denticulus* agricultural fork (diminutive) < *dēns, dentis* tooth]

den|tic|u|lar (den tik′yə lər), *adj.* **1** having the form of a small tooth: *. . . converted into a gizzard by the development of denticular processes* (Francis J. Bell). **2** *Architecture.* having dentils.

den|tic|u|late (den tik′yə lit, -lāt), *adj.* **1** finely toothed or notched: *a denticulate leaf.* **2** *Architecture.* having or decorated with dentils. —**den|tic′u|late|ly**, *adv.*

den|tic|u|lat|ed (den tik′yə lā′tid), *adj.* = denticulate.

den|tic|u|la|tion (den tik′yə lā′shən), *n.* **1** denticulate condition or form. **2** a denticle or denticles.

den|ti|cule (den′tə kyül), *n.* = dentil.

den|ti|form (den′tə fôrm), *adj.* of the form of a tooth; tooth-shaped.

den|ti|frice (den′tə fris), *n.* a paste, powder, or liquid for cleaning the teeth. [< Middle French *dentifrice* < Latin *dentifricium* < *dēns, dentis* tooth + *fricāre* to rub]

den|tig|er|ous (den tij′ər əs), *adj.* bearing teeth; supplied with teeth.

***den|til** (den′təl), *n. Architecture.* one of a series of small, rectangular blocks, arranged like a row of teeth, used as an ornament, as on the molding of a cornice; denticle; denticule. Also, **dentel**. [< Middle French *dentille* (diminutive) < *dent* tooth < Latin *dēns, dentis*]

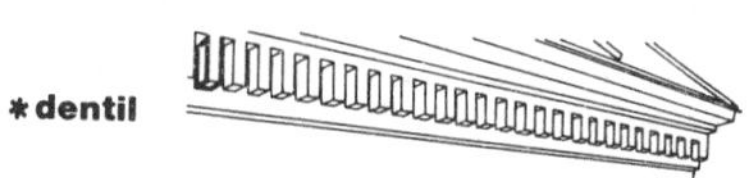

den|ti|la|bi|al (den′tə lā′bē əl), *adj., n.* = labiodental.

den|ti|lin|gual (den′tə ling′gwəl), *adj., n. Phonetics.* —***adj.*** (of speech sounds) produced with the tongue against or near the teeth: *"Th" in "think" and "then" are dentilingual sounds.*
—***n.*** a dentilingual sound. Also, **dentolingual**.

den|tin (den′tin), *n.* the hard, bony material beneath the enamel of a tooth. It forms the main part of a tooth.

den|ti|nal (den′tə nəl), *adj.* of or having to do with the dentin: *Sting rays . . . inflict their injuries by means of a dentinal sting that is located on the back surface of the animal's tail* (Science News Letter).

den|ti|na|sal (den′tə nā′zəl), *adj., n.* —***adj.*** (of certain sounds) dental and nasal, as the consonant *n.*
—***n.*** a dentinasal sound.

den|tine (den′tēn, -tin), *n.* = dentin.

den|ti|phone (den′tə fōn), *n.* an instrument held against the teeth to assist hearing by transmitting sound vibrations to the auditory nerve; audiphone.

den|ti|ros|tral (den′tə ros′trəl), *adj.* **1** having a toothed or notched bill. **2** (in old classifications) belonging to or having to do with a group of passerine birds including the shrikes, which have a tooth or notch on each side of the upper mandible near the tip.

den|tist (den′tist), *n.* a doctor whose work is the care of teeth. A dentist fills cavities in teeth, cleans, straightens, or extracts them, supplies artificial teeth, and treats diseases of the mouth and gums. [< French *dentiste* < *dent* tooth < Latin *dēns, dentis*]

den|tis|tic (den tis′tik), *adj.* having to do with dentistry or dentists.

den|tis|ti|cal (den tis′tə kəl), *adj.* = dentistic.

den|tist|ry (den′tə strē), *n.* the work, art, or profession of a dentist: *The discovery of anesthesia was one of the most important steps in the history of dentistry* (Robert G. Kesel).

den|ti|tion (den tish′ən), *n.* **1** the growth of teeth; teething. **2** the kind, number, and arrangement of the teeth: *Dogs and wolves have the same dentition.* [< Latin *dentītiō, -ōnis* < *dentīre* to get or cut teeth < *dēns, dentis* tooth]

dento-, *combining form.* a form of **denti-**, as in *dentolingual.*

den|toid (den′toid), *adj.* shaped like a tooth; toothlike.

den|to|lin|gual (den′tə ling′gwəl), *adj., n.* = dentilingual.

den|to|sur|gi|cal (den′tō sėr′jə kəl), *adj.* of or having to do with dentistry and surgery.

den|ture (den′chər), *n.* **1** a set of artificial teeth. **2** a set of teeth. [< French *denture* < *dent* tooth < Latin *dēns, dentis*]

den|tur|ist (den′chər ist), *n.* (in Canada) a person who sells and fits false teeth, and is legally authorized to do so in some provinces, although not a dentist. [< *denture* + *-ist;* patterned on *optometrist*]

de|nu|cle|ar|i|za|tion (dē nü′klē ər ə zā′shən, -nyü′-), *n.* the action of denuclearizing or state of being denuclearized: *Restoration of Japanese sovereignty and denuclearization of the island* [*Okinawa*] (C. L. Sulzberger).

de|nu|cle|ar|ize (dē nü′klē ə rīz, -nyü′-), *v.t.*, **-ized, -iz|ing.** **1** to stop the production or testing of nuclear weapons in: *to denuclearize a zone.* **2** to deprive of nuclear weapons: *to denuclearize a nation.*

de|nu|cle|ate (dē nü′klē āt, -nyü′-), *v.t.*, **-at|ed, -at|ing.** to remove the nucleus or nuclei from: *to denucleate an egg cell. How trees manage to denucleate the water in their sap ducts before subjecting it to negative pressure remains a fascinating problem for botanists to solve* (New Scientist).

de|nu|cle|a|tion (dē nü′klē ā′shən, -nyü′-), *n.* the act or process of denucleating; removal of a nucleus or nuclei.

de|nu|dant (di nü′dənt, -nyü′-; den′yu̇-), *n. Geology.* any agent or agency that causes denudation.

de|nu|date (den′yu̇ dāt; di nü′-, -nyü′-), *v.*, **-dat|ed, -dat|ing,** *adj.* —***v.t.*** = denude.
—***adj.*** denuded; bare.

de|nu|da|tion (dē′nü dā′shən, -nyü-; den′yu̇-), *n.* **1** the action of denuding. **2** a denuded condition. **3** *Geology.* the laying bare of rock by erosion: *Denudation of the rocks of the Alps has laid bare massive sections whose slopes can be measured as they disappear down below other rock layers* (New Scientist).

de|nu|da|tive (di nü′də tiv, -nyü′-), *adj.* of or having to do with denudation.

de|nude (di nüd′, -nyüd′), *v.t.*, **-nud|ed, -nud|ing.** **1** to make bare; strip (something) of its clothing or covering: *Most trees are denuded of their leaves in winter.* (*Figurative.*) *to denude the sea of valuable fish.* (*Figurative.*) *Medical and space research is denuding the world of its monkeys* (New Scientist). **2** *Geology.* to lay (a rock or land) bare by removing what lies above, especially by erosion: *. . . rapidly denuded by rain and rivers* (Alfred R. Wallace).
[< Latin *dēnūdāre* < *dē-* away + *nūdāre* to strip < *nūdus* bare] —**de|nud′er**, *n.*

de|nu|mer|a|bil|i|ty (di nü′mər ə bil′ə tē, -nyü′-), *n.* the quality or condition of being denumerable.

de|nu|mer|a|ble (di nü′mər ə bəl, -nyü′-), *adj. Mathematics.* that can be counted or numbered successively, even though infinite, as if having the power of finite cardinal numbers.

de|nu|mer|a|bly (di nü′mər ə blē, -nyü′-), *adv.* in a denumerable manner, by or with denumerable elements.

de|nu|mer|ant (di nü′mər ənt, -nyü′-), *n.* the numbers expressing how many solutions exist for a given system of equations.

de|nun|ci|ate (di nun′sē āt, -shē-), *v.t.*, **-at|ed, -at|ing.** = denounce.

de|nun|ci|a|tion (di nun′sē ā′shən, -shē-), *n.* **1** an expression of strong disapproval; condemnation; denouncing: *the mayor's denunciation of crime, the teacher's denunciation of cheating.* **2** the act of informing against; accusation: *His denunciation of his neighbor as a thief shocked everyone.* **3** a formal notice of the intention to end a treaty or other agreement. **4** a declaration of a curse, revenge, or other retribution; warning; threat: *. . . full of malignity and denunciations against a man whose name they had never heard* (Samuel Johnson). **5** *Obsolete.* a public announcement; proclamation.
[< Latin *dēnūntiātiō, -ōnis* < *dēnūntiāre;* see etym. under **denounce**]

de|nun|ci|a|tive (di nun′sē ā′tiv, -shē-), *adj.* = denunciatory. —**de|nun′ci|a′tive|ly**, *adv.*

de|nun|ci|a|tor (di nun′sē ā′tər, -shē-), *n.* a person who denounces.

de|nun|ci|a|to|ry (di nun′sē ə tôr′ē, -tōr′-; -shē-), *adj.* condemning; accusing; threatening: *The mayor received a denunciatory letter from the protesting citizens.*

de|nu|tri|tion (dē′nü trish′ən, -nyü-), *n.* lack of nutrition.

Den|ver|ite (den′və rīt), *n.* a native or inhabitant of Denver.

Den|ver sandwich (den′vər), = Western sandwich. [< *Denver,* Colorado]

de|ny (di nī′), *v.t.*, **-nied, -ny|ing.** **1** to say (something) is not true: *The prisoner denies the charges against him. The mayor denied the existence of slums in the city.* **2** to say that one does not hold to or accept (a belief): *Though frightened of the dark, she denied a belief in ghosts and witches.* **3** to refuse to give or grant: *I could not deny the stray cat some milk. I could not deny her so small a favor.* **4** to refuse to acknowledge; disown: *He denied his signature. . . . Verily I say unto thee, That this night, before the cock crow, thou shalt deny me thrice* (Matthew 26:34). **SYN:** repudiate, disclaim. **5** to refuse to accept. **6** *Obsolete.* to forbid.

deny oneself, to do without the things one wants: *A person who diets to lose weight has to deny himself candy, cake, and other rich foods. Mothers frequently deny themselves so that their children may have more.*

deny oneself to, to refuse to see: *Illness forced Mrs. Smith to deny herself to all callers.*
[< Old French *denier* < Latin *dēnegāre* < *dē-* (intensive) + *negāre* say no] —**de|ny′ing|ly**, *adv.*
—***Syn.*** **1 Deny, contradict** mean to declare something not true. **Deny** means to state defi-

nitely or emphatically that something is untrue or cannot be true: *She denied that she planned to leave town.* **Contradict** means to assert strongly that the truth is the opposite of what has been said: *He contradicted the testimony of the preceding witness.*

de|ob|stru|ent (dē ob′strü ənt), *adj., n.* —*adj.* **1** removing obstructions: *a deobstruent drug.* **2** = laxative.
—*n.* a deobstruent drug or medicine.
[< *de-* + *obstruent*]

de|o|dand (dē′ə dand), *n.* **1** a thing to be forfeited or given to God. **2** (in early English law) a personal chattel which had been the immediate cause of a person's death. It was then forfeited to the crown to be put to a pious use. [< Anglo-French *deodande* < Medieval Latin *deodandum* < *Deo dandum* (literally) thing to be given to God; *Deo,* dative of Latin *deus* god, *dandum,* neuter gerundive of Latin *dare* give]

de|o|dar (dē′ə där), *n.* a cedar tree of the Himalayas, cultivated as a shade tree and for its very durable wood. [< Hindustani *deodār* < Sanskrit *devadāru* wood of the gods]

de|o|dor|ant (dē ō′dər ənt), *n., adj.* —*n.* a preparation that neutralizes odors, especially bad odors.
—*adj.* that neutralizes odors.

de|o|dor|ise (dē ō′də rīz), *v.t.,* **-ised, -is|ing.** *Especially British.* deodorize.

de|o|dor|i|za|tion (dē ō′dər ə zā′shən), *n.* the act of deodorizing or state of being deodorized.

de|o|dor|ize (dē ō′də rīz), *v.t.,* **-ized, -iz|ing. 1** to destroy or neutralize the odor of. **2** *Figurative: The Italian socialists ... may share the desire to deodorize some Italian films* (New York Times).
—**de|o′dor|iz′er,** *n.*

De|o fa|ven|te (dē′ō fə ven′tē), *Latin.* God favoring; with God's help.

De|o gra|ti|as (dē′ō grā′shē as; de′ō grä′tē äs), *Latin.* thanks to God.

De|o ju|van|te (dē′ō jü van′tē), *Latin.* God helping.

de|on|to|log|i|cal (di on′tə loj′ə kəl), *adj.* having to do with deontology.

de|on|tol|o|gist (dē′on tol′ə jist), *n.* a person who studies deontology.

de|on|tol|o|gy (dē′on tol′ə jē), *n.* the science of duty or moral obligation. [< Greek *déon, -ontos* duty + English *-logy*]

de-or|bit (dē ôr′bit), *v., n.* —*v.t.* to take out of orbit: *First of all, warheads de-orbited from satellites could reach their targets so quickly that a defending nation would lose the previous minutes of warning for which the United States has purchased such costly facilities as the Ballistic Missile Early Warning System* (Atlantic).
—*n.* the act of taking or coming out of orbit: *The critical factor will be to determine the moment of de-orbit* (New Scientist).

De|o vo|len|te (dē′ō vō len′tē), *Latin.* if God is willing. *Abbr:* D.V.

de|ox|i|dant (dē ok′sə dənt), *n.* a deoxidizing agent.

de|ox|i|date (dē ok′sə dāt), *v.t.,* **-dat|ed, -dat|ing.** = deoxidize.

de|ox|i|da|tion (dē ok′sə dā′shən), *n.* = deoxidization.

de|ox|i|dise (dē ok′sə dīz), *v.t.,* **-dised, -dis|ing.** *Especially British.* deoxidize.

de|ox|i|di|za|tion (dē ok′sə də zā′shən), *n.* the act or process of deoxidizing.

de|ox|i|dize (dē ok′sə dīz), *v.t.,* **-dized, -diz|ing.** to remove oxygen from; reduce from the oxide state. —**de|ox′i|diz′er,** *n.*

deoxy-, *combining form.* containing fewer atoms of oxygen in the molecule than (the specified compound), as in *deoxycholic* (*acid*). [< *de-* from, away + *oxy*(gen)]

de|ox|y|cho|lic acid (dē ok′sə kō′lik, -kol′ik), a crystalline acid occurring in the bile of certain mammals including man and containing one less hydroxyl group than cholic acid. *Formula:* $C_{24}H_{40}O_4$ Also, **desoxycholic acid.**

de|ox|y|cor|ti|cos|ter|one (dē ok′sə kôr′tə kos′tə rōn), *n.* a crystalline compound obtained from the cortex of the adrenal gland or produced synthetically, used especially in its acetate form in the treatment of adrenal deficiency, epilepsy, and certain conditions of hypotension: *Deoxycorticosterone and the other natural adrenal hormones control electrolyte and water balance* (New Scientist). *Formula:* $C_{21}H_{30}O_3$

de|ox|y|gen|ate (dē ok′sə jə nāt), *v.t.,* **-at|ed, -at|ing.** to remove oxygen, especially free oxygen, from (a compound or mixture, such as water); deoxygenize.

de|ox|y|gen|a|tion (dē ok′sə jə nā′shən), *n.* the act or process of removing oxygen: *A ... wholesale extermination of fish through deoxygenation of water takes place sometimes in summer, when fish that have been landlocked in a pond or lagoon find the water getting too warm* (Science News Letter).

de|ox|y|gen|i|za|tion (dē ok′sə jə nə zā′shən), *n.* = deoxygenation.

de|ox|y|gen|ize (dē ok′sə jə nīz), *v.t.,* **-ized, -iz|ing.** = deoxygenate.

de|ox|y|ri|bo|nu|cle|ase (dē ok′sə rī′bō nü′klē ās, -nyü′-), *n.* an enzyme that promotes the hydrolysis of deoxyribonucleic acid. Also, **desoxyribonuclease.**

* **de|ox|y|ri|bo|nu|cle|ic acid** (dē ok′sə rī′bō nü klē′ik, -nyü-), an acid found in the nucleus of all living cells. It is the substance of which most genes are made and is chiefly responsible for the transmission of inherited characteristics; thymus nucleic acid. A single molecule consists of two parallel twisted chains of alternating units of phosphoric acid and deoxyribose, linked by crosspieces of the purine bases, adenine and guanine, and the pyrimidine bases, cytosine and thymine. *In the case of higher animals, the cell's instructions are carried by long, coiled-up molecules of DNA* (*deoxyribonucleic acid*) (Time). *Abbr:* DNA (no periods). Also, **desoxyribonucleic acid.** [< *deoxyribo*(se) + *nucleic acid*]

***deoxyribonucleic acid**

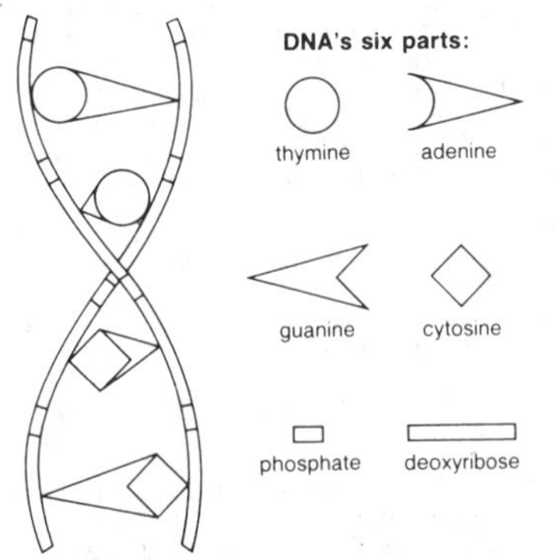

de|ox|y|ri|bo|nu|cle|o|pro|tein (dē ok′sə rī′bō nü′klē ō prō′tēn, -tē in; -nyü′-), *n.* a nucleoprotein containing deoxyribose.

de|ox|y|ri|bo|nu|cle|o|side (dē ok′sə rī′bō nü′klē ə sīd, -sid; -nyü′-), *n.* a nucleoside containing deoxyribose: *In our first attempt to achieve DNA synthesis in a cell-free system we used the deoxyribonucleoside called deoxythimidine* (Arthur Kornberg).

de|ox|y|ri|bo|nu|cle|o|tide (dē ok′sə rī′bō nü′klē ə tīd, -tid; -nyü′-), *n.* a nucleotide containing deoxyribose.

de|ox|y|ri|bose (dē ok′sə rī′bōs), *n.* the sugar constituent of deoxyribonucleic acid. *Formula:* $C_5H_{10}O_4$ [< *deoxy-* + *ribose*]

deoxyribose nucleic acid, = deoxyribonucleic acid.

dep., **1** depart. **2** department. **3** departure. **4** deponent. **5** deposed. **6** deposit. **7** depot. **8** deputy.

de|paint (di pānt′), *v.t. Archaic.* to paint; depict.

de|pal|a|tal|i|za|tion (dē pal′ə tə lə zā′shən), *n.* the removal or lessening of palatal quality: *He had enormous difficulty with depalatalization, never managing to remove the extra Russian moisture from t's and d's before the vowels he so quaintly softened* (New Yorker).

de|pan|cre|a|tize (dē pan′krē ə tīz), *v.t.,* **-tized, -tiz|ing.** to remove the pancreas from: *The maximal positive effect reported was a temporary disappearance of glycosuria in depancreatized dogs* (Science).

de|part (di pärt′), *v., n.* —*v.i.* **1** to go away; leave: *The flight departs at 6:15. We arrived in the village in the morning, and departed that night.* **2** *Figurative.* to turn away; change (from): *He became very untidy, departing from his usual neat ways. Depart from evil, and do good* (Psalms 34:14). **SYN:** diverge, deviate. **3** to pass away; die.
—*v.t.* to go away from: *He departed this life at the age of seventy.*
—*n. Obsolete.* **1** a departing; departure. **2** death.
[< Old French *departir* < Late Latin *departīre* divide < Latin *dē-* (intensive) + *partīre* divide < *pars, partis* part] —**de|part′er,** *n.*
—*Syn. v.i.* **1 Depart, withdraw, retire** mean to go away or leave. **Depart** suggests going away from some definite place or person: *He departed from his home.* **Withdraw** suggests departing for a certain reason: *I withdrew while they discussed my qualifications for the job.* **Retire** suggests prolonged or permanent change of condition: *to retire from business. The author retired to a mountain cabin to write his book.*

de|part|ed (di pär′tid), *n., adj.* —*n.* Usually, **the departed.** a dead person or persons: *the dear departed.*
—*adj.* **1** dead. **2** gone; past: *departed joys.*

dé|par|te|ment (dā pär tə mäN′), *n. French.* an administrative district under French rule; department: *In government ... the two islands have been integrated into highly centralized metropolitan France as départements* (New York Times).

de|part|ment (di pärt′mənt), *n.* **1** a separate part of some whole; special branch; division: *Our city government has a fire department and a police department.* **2** a main division of governmental administration: *the Department of Justice.* **3** a special division within a company, store, or other organization: *the toy department, the legal department, the furniture department, the complaint department.* **4** a section within a university, college, or school, giving instruction in a certain field: *the history department.* **5** one of the administrative districts into which a country, such as France or Paraguay, is divided. **6** one of the large geographical divisions of the United States as divided for military purposes. **7** a part; portion; section. *Abbr:* dept.

de|part|men|tal (dē′pärt men′təl, di pärt′-), *adj.* **1** having to do with a department: *departmental policies.* **2** divided into departments: *The business is so large that it must be handled on a departmental basis.* —**de′part|men′tal|ly,** *adv.*

de|part|men|tal|ism (dē′pärt men′tə liz əm, di-pärt′-), *n.* a tendency towards or advocacy of departmentalizing: *... the complexity and departmentalism of ... the special sciences* (Harper's).

de|part|men|tal|ist (dē′pärt men′tə list, di pärt′-), *n.* a person who follows or advocates departmental methods and policies.

de|part|men|tal|i|za|tion (dē′pärt men′tə lə zā′shən), *n.* the action of departmentalizing or condition of being departmentalized.

de|part|men|tal|ize (dē′pärt men′tə līz), *v.t.,* **-ized, -iz|ing. 1** to make or arrange into departments; form departments of: *The faculty, departmentalized though it be, will form a defensive circle and moan to high heaven at any aggressive initiative by an administrative wolf* (Atlantic). **2** to classify or restrict as if in departments: *to departmentalize learning. He decided to departmentalize his life* (New Yorker).

departmental store, *Especially British.* a department store.

department store, a store that sells many different kinds of articles in separate departments under one management.

de|par|ture (di pär′chər), *n.* **1** the act of going away; act of leaving: *His departure was very sudden.* **2** *Figurative.* a turning away; change: *a departure from our old custom.* **SYN:** divergence, deviation. **3** *Figurative.* a starting on a new course of action or thought: *Attending this dancing class will be a new departure for me, for I have never done anything like it. The present law makes a fresh departure in commercial legislation.* **4** *Nautical.* **a** the distance eastward or westward covered by a ship on any course, measured according to the number of meridians traveled. **b** the bearing of an object on the coast, taken at the commencement of a voyage, from which the dead reckoning begins. **5** *Archaic.* death.

de|pas|tur|age (di pas′chər ij, -päs′-), *n.* **1** the eating of growing grass, plants, etc., by grazing animals. **2** the right of pasture.

de|pas|ture (di pas′chər, -päs′-), *v.,* **-tured, -tur|ing.** —*v.t.* **1** to eat the growing grass or plants of (land) by grazing. **2** to pasture or feed (cattle).
—*v.i.* = graze.

de|pau|per|ate (di pô′pə rāt), *v.,* **-at|ed, -at|ing,** *adj.* —*v.t.* **1** to make poor; impoverish. **2** to reduce in quality, vigor, or capacity.
—*adj.* impoverished; reduced in quality, vigor, or capacity.
[< Medieval Latin *depauperare* (with English *-ate*[1]) < Latin *dē-* (intensive) + *pauperāre* impoverish < *pauper* poor man]

de|pau|per|a|tion (di pô′pə rā′shən), *n.* = impoverishment.

de|pau|per|i|za|tion (di pô′pər ə zā′shən), *n.* a freeing or being freed from poverty.

de|pau|per|ize (di pô′pə rīz), *v.t.,* **-ized, -iz|ing.** to free from poverty.

dé|pêche (dā pesh′), *n. French.* a dispatch; telegram; message.

de|pe|nal|ize (di pē′nə līz, -pen′ə-), *v.t.,* **-ized, -iz|ing.** to reduce the penalties or disadvantages of: *My vote is going to the Party—if any—that depenalizes the self-employed* (London Times).

de|pend (di pend′), *v.i.* **1** to be a result of; be controlled or influenced by something else: *The success of our picnic will depend partly upon the*

Pronunciation Key: hat, āge, cãre, fär; let, ēqual, tėrm; it, īce; hot, ōpen, ôrder; oil, out; cup, pu̇t, rüle; child; long; thin; ᴛʜen; zh, measure; ə represents **a** in about, **e** in taken, **i** in pencil, **o** in lemon, **u** in circus.

weather. **2** to have as a support; get help from; rely (on or upon) for help: *Children depend on their parents for food and clothing. Over the next ten years the [party] continued to depend on a coalition, but the unity of the party was increasingly strained* (Observer). **SYN**: See syn. under **rely**. **3** to rely (on or upon); trust: *You can depend on the timetable to tell you when the airplanes leave.* **SYN**: See syn. under **rely**. **4** to hang down; be suspended: *The chandelier depends from the ceiling.* **5** *Obsolete.* to wait in suspense. [< Old French *dependre,* learned borrowing from Latin *dēpendēre* < *dē-* from + *pendēre* hang] —**de|pend′er**, *n.*

de|pend|a|bil|i|ty (di pen′də bil′ə tē), *n.* reliability; trustworthiness: *Close, discriminating judgment of human character ... has not kept pace in its growth, refinement, and dependability with the steadily increasing job market* (Harper's).

de|pend|a|ble (di pen′də bəl), *adj.* that can be depended on; reliable; trustworthy: *Almanacs have fairly dependable information.* —**de|pend′a|ble|ness**, *n.*

de|pend|a|bly (di pen′də blē), *adv.* in a dependable manner.

de|pend|ance (di pen′dəns), *n.* = dependence.

de|pend|an|cy (di pen′dən sē), *n., pl.* **-cies**. = dependency.

de|pend|ant (di pen′dənt), *adj., n.* = dependent.

de|pend|ence (di pen′dəns), *n.* **1** the fact or condition of being dependent: *the dependence of crops on good weather. The former addict's medical dependence on methadone is a parallel to the diabetic's dependence on insulin* (New York Times). **2** the relation of trusting or relying on another for support, help, or existence: *The boy wished to go to work so that he could end his dependence on his uncle.* **3** trust; reliance: *You can put your dependence in the delivery boy, for he is always on time.* **4** a person or thing relied on: *The old man's small income from rents was his only dependence. Also,* **dependance**.

de|pend|en|cy (di pen′dən sē), *n., pl.* **-cies**. **1** a country or territory controlled by another country: *Puerto Rico and the Virgin Islands are dependencies of the United States.* **2** the condition of trusting or relying on another for support or existence; dependence: *The dependency of his mother irritated the older boy very much.* **3** a thing that depends on another for existence, support, or help. **4** an annex to a building. Also, **dependancy**.

***de|pend|ent** (di pen′dənt), *adj., n.* —*adj.* **1** trusting or relying on another person or thing for support or help: *A child is dependent on its parents.* **2** depending; possible if something else takes place: *A farmer's success is dependent on having the right kind of weather for his crops. Promotion in that company is dependent on consistent hard work.* **SYN**: contingent, conditional. **3** under the control or rule of another; subject. **4** hanging down; pendent: *dependent clusters of cherries.* **5** *Mathematics and Statistics.* **a** (of a variable) relying on the values assumed by one or more independent variables. **b** (of an equation) that can be derived from another equation. x + y = 3 and 2x + 2y = 6 are dependent equations.

—*n.* **1** a person who is supported or helped by another. **SYN**: subordinate, retainer. **2** *Obsolete.* a subordinate thing or part. Also, **dependant**.
—**de|pend′ent|ly**, *adv.*

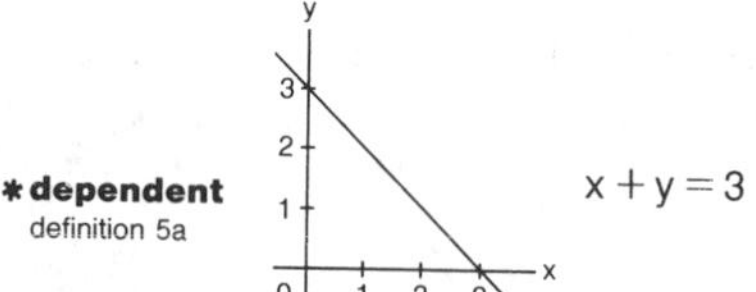

***dependent**
definition 5a

dependent clause, = subordinate clause.

dependent variable, See **dependent** (*adj.* def. 5a.).

de|peo|ple (dē pē′pəl), *v.t.,* **-pled, -pling**. to deprive of people; depopulate.

de|perm (dē pėrm′), *v.t.* to demagnetize (a ship) by placing electric coils vertically around the hull. [< *de-* + *perm*(anent magnetism)]

de|per|son|al|ise (dē pėr′sə nə līz), *v.t.,* **-ised, -is|ing**. *Especially British.* depersonalize.

de|per|son|al|i|za|tion (dē pėr′sə nə lə zā′shən), *n.* **1** the process of depersonalizing or condition of being depersonalized. **2** *Psychology.* a loss of the sense of personal identity, occurring especially in some forms of mental illness: *Their [mental patients'] desire for correction of a minor or nonexistent disfigurement is actually an early feeling of depersonalization and withdrawal from reality* (Newsweek).

de|per|son|al|ize (dē pėr′sə nə līz), *v.t.,* **-ized, -iz|ing**. to remove the personal quality or character of; make impersonal: *In the ... rural communes that were to convert 500 million peasants into depersonalized, multipurpose labor units, there is apathy and despair* (Time).

de|phase (dē fāz′), *v.t.,* **-phased, -phas|ing**. *Physics.* to put out of phase.

de|phlo|gis|ti|cate (dē′flə jis′tə kāt), *v.t.,* **-cat|ed, -cat|ing**. **1** *Medicine.* to reduce inflammation in. **2** *Obsolete.* to deprive of phlogiston.

de|phlo|gis|ti|cat|ed (dē′flə jis′tə kā′tid), *adj. Obsolete.* deprived of phlogiston.

de|phlo|gis|ti|ca|tion (dē′flə jis′tə kā′shən), *n.* the act or process of reducing inflammation.

de|phos|pho|ri|za|tion (dē fos′fər ə zā′shən), *n.* the act or process of removing phosphorus.

de|phos|pho|rize (dē fos′fə rīz), *v.t.,* **-rized, -riz|ing**. to remove phosphorus from.

de|pict (di pikt′), *v.t.* to represent by drawing, painting, or describing; show; picture; portray: *The artist and the poet both tried to depict the splendor of the sunset.* [< Latin *dēpictus,* past participle of *dēpingere* < *dē-* down + *pingere* to paint] —**de|pict′er**, *n.*

de|pic|tion (di pik′shən), *n.* **1** the act of drawing or painting. **2** a thing that represents; picture; description: *The artist's depiction of the English countryside shows him at his best. The real meat of the book is in the depiction of the moral conflicts keenly felt by these men, and their inner struggles to resolve the problems* (Bulletin of Atomic Scientists).

de|pic|tive (di pik′tiv), *adj.* having the function or quality of depicting: *a depictive essay on American artists.*

de|pic|ture[1] (di pik′chər), *n.* = depiction. [< Latin *dēpictus* (see etym. under **depict**) + *-ūrā* process of]

de|pic|ture[2] (di pik′chər), *v.t.,* **-tured, -tur|ing**. **1** = depict. **2** = imagine.

de|pig|ment (dē pig′mənt), *v.t.* to deprive of pigment: *A dark-skinned animal kept in a dark room for several years would tend to become depigmented, etiolated, and its skin would appear white, but as soon as it was exposed to the sun the pigment would begin to return* (Newsweek).

de|pig|men|ta|tion (dē pig′mən tā′shən), *n.* the condition of being deprived of pigment: *Blond hair is doubtless a side effect of the general depigmentation of men that has occurred in northern Europe* (Scientific American).

de|pig|ment|ize (dē pig′mən tīz), *v.t.,* **-ized, -iz|ing**. = depigment.

dep|i|late (dep′ə lāt), *v.t.,* **-lat|ed, -lat|ing**. to remove hair from. [< Latin *dēpilāre* (with English *-ate*[1]) < *dē-* from + *pilus* hair]

dep|i|la|tion (dep′ə lā′shən), *n.* a depilating or being depilated.

dep|i|la|tor (dep′ə lā′tər), *n.* a person or thing that removes hair.

de|pil|a|to|ry (di pil′ə tôr′ē, -tōr′-), *n., pl.* **-ries**, *adj.* —*n.* a paste, liquid, or other preparation for removing hair.
—*adj.* that can remove hair.

de|pil|i|tant (di pil′ə tənt), *n.* a depilatory agent or preparation.

de|plane (dē plān′), *v.i.,* **-planed, -plan|ing**. to get off an airplane after landing: *At last his Royal Highness deplaned, impeccably frozen yet smiling* (Manchester Guardian).

de pla|no (dē plā′nō), *Latin.* **1** without argument. **2** by self-evident right; plainly.

de|plen|ish (di plen′ish), *v.t.* to empty; deplete.

de|ple|ta|ble (di plē′tə bəl), *adj.* that is being or becoming depleted; nearing depletion: *depletable natural resources.*

de|plete (di plēt′), *v.t.,* **-plet|ed, -plet|ing**. **1** to reduce the fullness of; empty or exhaust by using up resources, strength, vitality, or the like: *Because the traveler's funds were depleted, he went home. In many countries, years of mining have depleted the coal deposits.* **2** *Medicine.* to empty or relieve (the system, overcharged vessels, etc.) by bloodletting or purgatives. [< Latin *dēplētus,* past participle of *dēplēre* to empty < *dē-* un- + *plēre* fill]

de|ple|tion (di plē′shən), *n.* **1** the act or process of emptying; exhausting: *Years of mining have caused a depletion of coal deposits in the mines.* **SYN**: exhaustion. **2** the condition of being depleted; exhaustion: *At the present rate of depletion, the Canadian forest can remain commercially productive for only a very few decades* (J. J. De Gryse). **SYN**: exhaustion. **3** *Accounting.* the reduction or consumption of capital assets.

depletion allowance, a tax deduction for companies that extract natural resources such as minerals, oil, or timber, granted on the grounds that such production represents a reduction in capital assets as well as income.

de|ple|tive (di plē′tiv), *adj.* tending to deplete; depleting.

de|ple|to|ry (di plē′tər ē), *adj.* = depletive.

de|plor|a|bil|i|ty (di plôr′ə bil′ə tē, -plōr′-), *n.* deplorable quality; deplorableness.

de|plor|a|ble (di plôr′ə bəl, -plōr′-), *adj.* **1** that is to be deplored; regrettable; lamentable: *a deplorable accident, a deplorable misuse of money.* **2** wretched; miserable: *Deplorable living conditions existed in the slums.* **SYN**: grievous, sad.
—**de|plor′a|ble|ness**, *n.*

de|plor|a|bly (di plôr′ə blē, -plōr′-), *adv.* in a deplorable manner; lamentably.

dep|lo|ra|tion (dep′lə rā′shən), *n.* a deplorable state or condition; wretchedness.

de|plore (di plôr′, -plōr′), *v.t.,* **-plored, -plor|ing**. **1** to be very sorry about; express great sorrow for; regret deeply; lament: *We deplore the accident.* **SYN**: bewail, bemoan. **2** to find fault with; regard as grievous or to be regretted: *The report deplored the almost universal lack of direct radio communications between ambulance services* (New York Times). *We strongly deplore the large-scale retaliatory raid ... on Jordanian territory* (Arthur J. Goldberg). [< Latin *dēplōrāre* < *dē-* (intensive) + *plōrāre* weep] —**de|plor′er**, *n.* —**de|plor′ing|ly**, *adv.*

de|ploy (di ploi′), *v., n.* —*v.t.* **1** to spread out (troops, military units, or other forces) from a column into a long battle line. **2** to distribute (forces) in convenient positions for future use: *A fleet of ships were deployed over the area in which the astronauts were expected to land.* **3** *Figurative: ... an English poet deploying all the forces of his genius* (Matthew Arnold).
—*v.i.* **1** (of troops or other forces) to spread out into a long battle line from a column. **2** *Figurative: The seat was even equipped with an inflatable dinghy which deploys automatically if the astronaut lands in the water* (Science News Letter).
—*n.* the action of deploying; deployment.
[< French *déployer* < Old French *desployer* < *des-* un- (< Latin *dis-*) + *ployer* fold < Latin *plicāre.* See related etym. at **display**.]

de|ploy|ment (di ploi′mənt), *n.* the act of deploying or condition of being deployed: *... a conventional war that would allow time for the mobilization and deployment of the reserves* (London Times).

de|plu|mate (dē plü′māt), *adj.* stripped of feathers.

de|plu|ma|tion (dē′plü mā′shən), *n.* **1** the process of depluming or state of being deplumed. **2** molting.

de|plume (dē plüm′), *v.t.,* **-plumed, -plum|ing**. **1** to deprive of plumage or feathers. **2** *Figurative.* to strip of honor, wealth, or the like. [< Old French *deplumer* < *de-* de- + *plume* feather < Latin *plūma*]

de|po|lar|i|za|tion (dē pō′lər ə zā′shən), *n.* the act or process of depolarizing or state of being depolarized: *Even when a frog muscle is cooled to the freezing point of water, the depolarization of the muscle membrane throws the whole fiber into action within 40 thousandths of a second* (Scientific American).

de|po|lar|ize (dē pō′lə rīz), *v.t.,* **-ized, -iz|ing**. to destroy or neutralize the polarity or polarization of.

de|po|lar|iz|er (dē pō′lə rī′zər), *n.* a substance that unites chemically with the hydrogen bubbles attached to the carbon plate of a primary cell and removes them from the carbon so that the cell can deliver a steady current.

de|po|lit|i|cize (dē′pə lit′ə sīz), *v.t.,* **-cized, -ciz|ing**. to diminish the influence of politics or political parties in or on (a government, industry, controversy, or legal issue): *... the question whether and to what extent judges should be depoliticized* (London Times).

de|pol|lute (dē′pə lüt′), *v.t.,* **-lut|ed, -lut|ing**. to free from pollution: *There is no question that just as technology has polluted the country, it can also depollute it* (Time).

de|pol|lu|tion (dē′pə lü′shən), *n.* the act or process of depolluting: *The Trent River Authority at least is on the side of depollution* (New Scientist and Science Journal).

de|pol|y|mer|i|za|tion (dē pol′ē mər ə zā′shən), *n.* the action of depolymerizing or condition of being depolymerized: *This enzyme acts to change another chemical, hyaluronic acid, by a process called depolymerization* (Science News Letter).

de|pol|y|mer|ize (dē pol′ē mə rīz), *v.t.,* **-ized, -iz|ing**. to remove the polymeric properties of (a compound) to the original state before polymerization: *Under extremely small doses of radiation the nucleoprotein is depolymerized and loses its gel-like quality* (Scientific American).

de|pone (di pōn′), *v.t., v.i.,* **-poned, -pon|ing**. to testify in writing under oath. [< Latin *dēpōnere* put down (in Medieval Latin, testify) < *dē-* down + *pōnere* put]

de|po|nent (di pō′nənt), *n., adj.* —*n.* **1** a person who testifies, especially in writing, under oath.

2 (in Greek and Latin grammar) a verb passive in form but active in meaning.
— *adj.* having passive form but active meaning.
[< Latin *dēpōnēns, -entis,* present participle of *dēpōnere;* see etym. under **depone**]

de|pop|u|lar|ize (dē pop′yə lə rīz), *v.t.,* **-ized, -iz|ing.** to deprive of popularity.

de|pop|u|late (dē pop′yə lāt), *v.,* **-lat|ed, -lat|ing,** *adj.* — *v.t.* **1** to deprive of inhabitants, wholly or in part; reduce the population of: *The conquerors depopulated the enemy's capital by driving the inhabitants away.* **2** *Obsolete.* to plunder; lay waste.
— *adj. Archaic.* deprived of inhabitants; depopulated.

de|pop|u|la|tion (dē pop′yə lā′shən, dē′pop-), *n.* **1** the act of depopulating. **2** the condition of being depopulated.

de|pop|u|la|tor (dē pop′yə lā′tər), *n.* a person or thing that depopulates.

de|port (di pôrt′, -pōrt′), *v., n.* — *v.t.* **1** to force to leave a country; banish; expel; remove. When an alien is deported, because his presence is undesirable or illegal, he is sent out of the country, usually back to his native land. **SYN:** exile. See syn. under **banish.** **2** to behave or conduct (oneself) in a particular manner: *The boys were trained to deport themselves like gentlemen.*
— *n. Obsolete.* deportment.
[< Old French *deporter* < Latin *dēportāre* < *dē-* away + *portāre* carry] — **de|port′er,** *n.*

de|port|a|ble (di pôr′tə bəl, -pōr′-), *adj.* that can be or should be deported: *The best the FBI could do was ask the Immigration and Naturalization Service to arrest [him] as a deportable alien* (Time).

de|por|ta|tion (dē′pôr tā′shən, -pōr-), *n.* the removal from a country by banishment or expulsion: *Deportation of criminals from England to Australia was once common. Of 79 underworld personalities exposed by the committee as possible candidates for deportation, only seven have left the country* (Newsweek).

de|por|tee (dē′pôr tē′, -pōr-), *n.* a person who is or has been deported: *Many of the deportees were newcomers to Shanghai who had flocked there from food-short villages* (Newsweek).

de|port|ment (di pôrt′mənt, -pōrt′-), *n.* the way a person acts; behavior; conduct: *A gentleman is known by his deportment. Many schools are doing away with the system of reporting on children's schoolwork only with respect to subject matter and that vague term, "deportment"* (Sidonie M. Gruenberg). **SYN:** demeanor, bearing. See syn. under **conduct.**

de|pos|al (di pō′zəl), *n.* a deposing; deposition.

de|pose (di pōz′), *v.,* **-posed, -pos|ing.** — *v.t.* **1** to put out of office or a position of authority, especially a high one like that of king: *The king was deposed by the revolution. You may my glories and my state depose* (Shakespeare). **2** to declare under oath, especially in writing; testify: *The witness deposed that she had seen the accused on the day of the murder.*
— *v.i.* to testify under oath, especially in writing.
[< Old French *deposer* < *de-* down, de- (< Latin *dē-*) + *poser* put, pose[1]] — **de|pos′a|ble,** *adj.* — **de|pos′er,** *n.*

de|pos|it (di poz′it), *v., n.* — *v.t.* **1** to put down; lay down; leave lying: *He deposited his bundles on the table.* **2** to leave lying as sediment: *The flood deposited a layer of mud in the streets.* **3** to put in a place to be kept safe: *Deposit your money in the bank.* **4** to pay as a pledge for carrying out a promise to do something or to pay more later: *If you will deposit $5, the store will reserve the coat for you until you pay the rest.* **5** *U.S.* to leave (a certain amount of farm land) uncultivated under the provisions of a farm parity program: *They generally deposited their scrubby highland acres and planted their more fertile bottom-land acreage* (Wall Street Journal). — *v.i.* **1** to settle or be precipitated. **2** to make or pay a deposit.
— *n.* **1** something laid down or left lying by natural means: *There is often a deposit of sand and mud at the mouth of a river.* **2** something put in a certain place to be kept safe: *Money put in a bank is a deposit.* **3** money paid as a pledge to do something or to pay more later: *He put down a $50 deposit on the coat, planning to pay the balance of $100 by Christmas.* **4** a mass of some mineral in rock or in the ground: *deposits of coal.* **5** a depositing. **6** = depository.
on deposit, a in a bank: *to have $100 on deposit in a savings account.* **b** in a place for safekeeping: *jewelry on deposit in a safe.*
[< Latin *dēpositus, past participle of dēpōnere;* see etym. under **depone**]

de|pos|i|tar|y (di poz′ə ter′ē), *n., pl.* **-tar|ies,** *adj.* — *n.* **1** a person or company that receives something for safekeeping; trustee. **2** = depository (def. 1).
— *adj.* **1** of or having to do with deposits: *a depositary bank.* **2** serving as a deposit or depository: *a depositary library.*

dep|o|si|tion (dep′ə zish′ən, dē′pə-), *n.* **1** the act of putting out of office or a position of authority; removal from power. **2a** the giving of testimony under oath. **b** the testimony so given, especially a sworn statement in writing: *The prisoner made a deposition to use in appealing his case. A deposition made before the witness left town was used as evidence in the trial.* **3** the act or process of depositing: *the deposition of silt from the floodwaters, the deposition of funds in a bank.* **4** a thing deposited; deposit.

dep|o|si|tion|al (dep′ə zish′ə nəl, dē′pə-), *adj.* of or having to do with a deposition: *... depositional areas such as flood plains, old sea floor, or lake beds* (White and Renner).

Deposition from the Cross, 1 the taking down of Christ's body from the cross. **2** the representation of this in a work of art.

de|pos|i|tor (di poz′ə tər), *n.* **1** a person who deposits. **2** a person who deposits money in a bank: *Depositors in savings banks may receive interest on the money deposited.*

de|pos|i|to|ry (di poz′ə tôr′ē, -tōr′-), *n., pl.* **-ries.** **1** a place where anything is stored for safekeeping; storehouse. **2** = depositary (def. 1).

deposit slip, a printed slip on which a bank depositor lists the amount of checks, bills, or coins to be credited to his account.

de|pot (*n.* dē′pō *for 1; also* dep′ō *for 2-4; British also* dep′ō *for 1; v.* dē′pō), *n., v.* — *n.* **1** a railroad or bus station. **2** a storehouse; warehouse: *It predicts in advance what the depots will need and has parts shipped before they are requisitioned* (Newsweek). **3** a place where military supplies are stored. **4** a place where recruits are brought together and trained.
— *v.t.* to place in a depot: *When near the summit, Captain Scott told ... the party to depot their surplus and return* (H. G. Ponting).
[< French *dépôt* < Old French *depost,* ultimately < Latin *dēpōnere;* see etym. under **depone**]

dep|ra|va|tion (dep′rə vā′shən, dē′prə-), *n.* the action of depraving or fact of being depraved; deterioration; corruption: *It is to these ... [circumstances] that the depravation of ancient polite learning is principally to be ascribed* (Oliver Goldsmith).

de|prave (di prāv′), *v.t.,* **-praved, -prav|ing.** **1** to make bad; injure morally; corrupt; pervert: *Drinking too much alcoholic liquor often depraves a person's character.* **2** *Obsolete.* to defame. [< Latin *dēprāvāre* < *dē-* (intensive) + *prāvus* crooked, wrong] — **de|prav′er,** *n.*

de|praved (di prāvd′), *adj.* having very bad morals; corrupt; perverted: *A murderer is so depraved that he has no regard for human life.* **SYN:** vicious. See syn. under **corrupt.**

de|prav|ed|ly (di prā′vid lē), *adv.* in a depraved manner; corruptly; perversely.

de|prav|ed|ness (di prā′vid nis), *n.* depraved quality or condition; depravity.

de|prave|ment (di prāv′mənt), *n.* = depravity.

de|prav|i|ty (di prav′ə tē), *n., pl.* **-ties.** **1** the quality or condition of being depraved; wickedness; viciousness; corruption: *a monster of depravity* (T. S. Eliot). **2** a corrupt act; bad practice.

dep|re|cate (dep′rə kāt), *v.t.,* **-cat|ed, -cat|ing.** **1** to express strong disapproval of; plead against; protest against: *Lovers of peace deprecate war.* **2** to belittle; disparage: *It must take an unusual amount of moxie to deprecate Richard Rodgers' music* (Dorothy Kilgallen). *Without deprecating the value of what currently is being done on the air, it would seem sensible to explore further [what] the best means* (New York Times). **3** *Archaic.* to seek to avert by prayer. [< Latin *dēprecārī* (with English *-ate*[1]) plead in excuse; avert by prayer < *dē-* away + *precārī* pray < *prex, precis* prayer]
▶ **Deprecate, depreciate,** although overlapping in meaning, were not synonymous. *Deprecate* meant to protest against; *depreciate* meant to belittle: *Many deprecate the commercialism of intercollegiate football. Few depreciate the benefits of exercise.* Now even the best writers have melded the two to become one.

dep|re|cat|ing|ly (dep′rə kā′ting lē), *adv.* in a manner that expresses deprecation; deprecatorily.

dep|re|ca|tion (dep′rə kā′shən), *n.* **1** a strong expression of disapproval; pleading or protesting against something: *a look of deprecation* (George Eliot). **2** belittling; disparagement: *Granted all the evils of colonialism, there has been too much deprecation of the European contribution to Asia* (Sydney Hook).

dep|re|ca|tive (dep′rə kā′tiv), *adj.* = deprecatory. — **dep′re|ca′tive|ly,** *adv.*

dep|re|ca|tor (dep′rə kā′tər), *n.* a person who deprecates.

dep|re|ca|to|ri|ly (dep′rə kə tôr′ə lē, -tōr′-), *adv.* in a deprecatory manner.

dep|re|ca|to|ri|ness (dep′rə kə tôr′ē nis, -tōr′-), *n.* deprecatory quality or condition.

dep|re|ca|to|ry (dep′rə kə tôr′ē, -tōr′-), *adj.* **1** deprecating. **2** = apologetic.

de|pre|ci|a|ble (di prē′shē ə bəl, -shə bəl), *adj.* that can be depreciated.

de|pre|ci|ate (di prē′shē āt), *v.,* **-at|ed, -at|ing.** — *v.t.* **1** to lessen the value or price of: *The government has the power to depreciate currency.* **2** *Figurative.* to speak slightingly of; belittle: *That lazy boy is always depreciating the value of exercise.* **SYN:** underrate, disparage.
— *v.i.* to lessen in value: *The longer an automobile is driven the more it depreciates.*
[< Latin *dēpretiāre* (with English *-ate*[1]) < *dē-* down + *pretium* price] — **de|pre′ci|at′ing|ly,** *adv.*
▶ See **deprecate** for usage note.

de|pre|ci|a|tion (di prē′shē ā′shən), *n.* **1a** a lessening or lowering in price, value, or estimation: *The depreciation of a car is greatest during its first year.* **b** such a loss figured as part of the cost of doing business: *Depreciation, of course, is a bookkeeping charge which reduces reported earnings but does not involve the expenditure of cash* (Wall Street Journal). **2** a reduction in the value of money: *Foreign currency depreciation is a result of economic depression in the country concerned.* **3** *Figurative.* a speaking slightingly (of); belittling; disparagement.

depreciation reserve, *Accounting.* a reserve account to offset the cost of equipment that is depreciating and will ultimately have to be replaced or renewed.

de|pre|ci|a|tive (di prē′shē ā′tiv), *adj.* = depreciatory. — **de|pre′ci|a′tive|ly,** *adv.*

de|pre|ci|a|tor (di prē′shē ā′tər), *n.* a person or thing that depreciates: *Counterfeiters and inflation are depreciators of money.*

de|pre|ci|a|to|ry (di prē′shē ə tôr′ē, -tōr′-), *adj.* tending to depreciate, disparage, or undervalue.

dep|re|date (dep′rə dāt), *v.t., v.i.,* **-dat|ed, -dat|ing.** to ravage; plunder: *... those hasty improvements of the past century which had been allowed to depredate the city* (Columbia University Forum).

dep|re|da|tion (dep′rə dā′shən), *n.* the act of plundering; robbery; a ravaging: *Intertribal depredations were frequent among savages. Today deer, protected and multiplying, are committing serious depredations on farmlands and gardens* (Atlantic). [< Late Latin *dēpraedātiō, -ōnis* < *dēpraedārī* to pillage, thieve < Latin *dē-* away + *praeda* booty]

dep|re|da|tor (dep′rə dā′tər), *n.* a person or thing that depredates.

dep|re|da|to|ry (dep′rə dā′tər ē; di pred′ə tôr′-, -tōr′-), *adj.* depredating; plundering; ravaging.

de|press (di pres′), *v.t.* **1** to make sad or gloomy; cause to have low spirits: *Rainy weather always depresses me. "This house depresses and chills one," said Kate* (Dickens). *She was depressed by the bad news from home.* **SYN:** deject, sadden, dispirit. **2** to press down; push down; lower: *When you play the piano, you depress the keys.* **3** *Figurative.* to make less active; weaken: *Some medicines depress the action of the heart.* **4** to lower in amount or value: *The price of potatoes has been depressed by the tremendous size of the harvest this year. Liquidation again depressed the market* (Wall Street Journal). **5** *Music.* to lower (the voice or tone) in pitch; flat. **6** *Obsolete.* to suppress; overcome. [< Old French *depresser,* ultimately < Latin *dēprimere* press down < *dē-* down + *premere* press]

de|pres|sant (di pres′ənt), *n., adj.* — *n.* a drug or other substance that reduces the body's reactions and relaxes muscles; depressor: *an appetite depressant.* **SYN:** sedative.
— *adj.* decreasing the rate of vital activities; quieting.

de|pressed (di prest′), *adj.* **1** gloomy; low-spirited; sad: *depressed vacationers during a spell of rainy weather.* **SYN:** dejected, downcast. See syn. under **sad.** **2** pressed down; lowered. **3** *Figurative.* lowered in force, amount, quality, or value: *depressed electric power caused by wet wires during a storm.* **4a** affected or hurt by a business depression: *... personnel cuts in depressed industries* (Wall Street Journal). **b** economically deprived: *depressed classes of society, a depressed region.* **5** *Botany, Zoology.* flattened down; broader than high.

depressed area, a region characterized by poverty, unemployment, and their accompanying ills: *Its [the federal government's] criterion for defin-*

Pronunciation Key: hat, āge, cãre, fär; let, ēqual, tėrm; it, īce; hot, ōpen, ôrder; oil, out; cup, pu̇t, rüle; child; long; thin; ᴛʜen; zh, measure; ə represents **a** in about, **e** in taken, **i** in pencil, **o** in lemon, **u** in circus.

ing a depressed area is based on unemployment figures from the Labor Department (New Yorker).

de|press|i|ble (di pres′ə bəl), *adj.* that can be depressed.

de|press|ing (di pres′ing), *adj.* **1** that depresses. **2** causing depression or lowness of spirits. —**de|press′ing|ly**, *adv.*

de|pres|sion (di presh′ən), *n.* **1** the act of pressing down; lowering or sinking: *A rapid depression of the mercury in a barometer usually indicates the approach of a storm.* **2** a depressed condition: *The barometer showed a depression. The heavy weight of snow caused a depression of the shed's roof.* **3** a low place; hollow: *Rain formed puddles in the depressions in the ground.* **4a** low spirits; sadness or gloominess: *Failure usually brings on a feeling of depression. These warm and sunny days completely cured the boy's depression.* SYN: dejection, melancholy. **b** *Psychology.* a mental disorder characterized by prolonged feelings of despair and dejection, often accompanied by fatigue, headaches, and other physical symptoms: *Depression is the most widespread of all psychiatric disorders.* **5** a lowering of business activity, usually for an extensive period of time, generally affecting national income and much of industrial and agricultural production; dullness of trade: *Many men lost their jobs during the depression of the 1930's. Here were cycles of industrial prosperity which always collapsed into industrial depressions* (Edmund Wilson). **6** *Medicine.* a lowering of the vital functions or powers, as by relaxing muscle tissue or depressing activity. **7** *Astronomy.* the angular distance of a star, planet, or other heavenly body below the horizon. **8** *Surveying.* the angular distance of an object below the horizontal plane through the point of observation. **9** *Meteorology.* an area of low barometric pressure; low.

de|pres|sive (di pres′iv), *adj., n.* —***adj.*** **1** tending to produce or characterized by depression; depressing. **2** having to do with or characterized by psychological depression: *Two or three persons out of every 100 in the world live in the shadow of depressive illness. The causes of this most widespread of mental disorders are not known* (Science News).
—***n.*** a person suffering from psychological depression: *With what are generally termed psychotics—schizophrenics, paranoids, depressives—the most valid approach seems to lie not in psychotherapy at all but in somatic medicine* (Renata Adler).
—**de|pres′sive|ly**, *adv.* —**de|pres′sive|ness**, *n.*

de|pres|so|mo|tor (di pres′ō mō′tər), *adj., n. Physiology.* —***adj.*** retarding motor activity: *depressomotor nerves.*
—***n.*** a depressomotor agent or drug.
[< *depresso*(r) + *motor*]

de|pres|sor (di pres′ər), *n.* **1** a person or thing that depresses. **2** *Anatomy.* a muscle that depresses or draws down a part. **3a** a medical or surgical instrument for pressing down some part or organ: *A doctor uses a tongue depressor when looking into the throat.* **b** a drug or medicine that reduces vital functions, relaxes muscles, or has other effects of lowering activity; depressant.

depressor nerve, a nerve that acts to lower the blood pressure when stimulated.

de|pres|sur|i|za|tion (dē presh′ər ə zā′shən), *n.* the removal or release of air pressure from a pressurized interior.

de|pres|sur|ize (dē presh′ə rīz), *v.t.,* **-ized, -iz|ing.** to remove or release air pressure from (a pressurized interior): *In their suits at last, the astronauts depressurized their cabin . . . and opened the hatch* (von Braun and Ordway).

de|print (dē′print′), *v., n.* —***v.t.*** to reprint (a separate article) from the original type.
—***n.*** a reprinted article.
[< *de-* + *print*]

de|priv|a|ble (di prī′və bəl), *adj.* that can be deprived; liable to be deprived.

de|priv|al (di prī′vəl), *n.* = deprivation.

dep|ri|va|tion (dep′rə vā′shən), *n.* **1** the act of depriving: *a deprivation of civil rights.* **2** the condition of being deprived; loss; privation: *The cobbler's family suffered great deprivation during his long illness.*

de|priv|a|tive (di priv′ə tiv), *adj.* tending to deprive; characterized by deprivation.

de|prive (di prīv′), *v.t.,* **-prived, -priv|ing. 1** to take away from by force: *The people deprived the cruel king of his power.* SYN: dispossess, divest, strip. **2** to keep from having or doing: *The children were deprived of supper. Worrying deprived him of sleep. Cold weather and heavy snow deprives animals of pasturage* (Wall Street Journal). **3** to remove from or divest of ecclesiastical office. **4** *Obsolete.* to take away.
[< Old French *depriver* < *de-* (intensive) (< Latin *dē-*) + *priver* deprive < Latin *prīvāre* (originally) exempt < *prīvus* deprived of, without] —**de|priv′er**, *n.*

de|prived (di prīvd′), *adj.* lacking advantages available to others; underprivileged: *A culturally deprived child who has not attended kindergarten may need as many as four or five* [*extra*] *sessions . . . It is important to keep the deprived child from developing a sense of failure or defeat at the start of his schooling* (Scientific American).

de pro|fun|dis (dē prō fun′dis), *Latin.* from the depths (of sorrow, misery, or despair).

De Pro|fun|dis (dē prō fun′dis), **1** the 130th Psalm. **2** the first words of the 130th Psalm in Latin.

de|pro|gram (dē prō′gram, -grəm), *v.i., v.t.* **-grammed, -gram|ming** or **-gramed, -gram|ing.** to try to dissuade (a person) from a set of wayward ideas or beliefs, often by forceful means: *Other accounts of deprogramming indicate that the process, which can last from two days to two weeks, is something between a brainwashing and an inquisition* (Time). —**de|pro′gram|mer**, *n.*

de pro|pri|o mo|tu (dē prō′prē ō mō′tü), *Latin.* of one's or its own motion; spontaneously.

de|pro|tein|ize (dē prō′tē nīz, -tē ə nīz), *v.t.,* **-ized, -iz|ing.** to deprive of protein; take protein from: *The amount of sugar in blood is shown by the color that a concentrated, deproteinized blood filtrate turns when treated with certain chemicals, then boiled and shaken* (Science News Letter).

dep|sid (dep′sid), *n.* = depside.

dep|side (dep′sīd, -sid), *n.* any one of a group of esters formed from phenolic carboxylic acids.
[< Greek *dépsein* to tan (< *dépsa* skin, hide) + English *-ide*]

dept., **1** department. **2** deputy.

depth (depth), *n.* **1** the distance from top to bottom: *the depth of a hole. The depth of the lake was so great we could not see the bottom.* **2** the distance from front to back: *The depth of our playground is 250 feet.* **3** a deep place: (*Figurative.*) *From a depth of unrecorded time* (Shelley). **4** the deepest part: *in the depths of the earth,* (*Figurative.*) *the depths of one's heart.* **5** the most central part; middle: (*Figurative.*) *in the depth of winter. He was lost in the depth of the forest.* **6** the quality or condition of being deep; deepness: *The other students admired his depth of understanding.* **7** *Figurative.* intensity (of feelings, interest, or the like): *The boy's depth of interest in trains was so great he spent all his time reading about them.* **8** *Figurative.* deep understanding; profoundness; profundity: *A philosopher should have depth of mind. The story has a good plot but it has no depth at all.* **9** lowness of pitch. **10** *Figurative.* intensity, as of color, silence, or darkness.
beyond (or **out of**) **one's depth, a** in water too deep for safety: *He remained three hours in the water, afraid to move, lest he should get out of his depth* (Pall Mall Gazette). **b** beyond one's ability to understand or do: *Launch not beyond your depth, but be discreet* (Alexander Pope).
in depth, going below the surface; penetrating; extensive; deep: *analysis in depth. During the extra time he hopes to do more stories in depth and features related to the news* (New York Times).
[Middle English *depthe* < *dep* deep, Old English *dēop*]

depth bomb, = depth charge.

depth-bomb (depth′bom′), *v.t.* to bomb with a depth charge or charges: *to depth-bomb a submarine.*

depth charge, an explosive charge dropped from a ship or airplane and set to explode at a certain depth under water. It is used especially against submarines.

depth-charge (depth′chärj′), *v.t.,* **-charged, -charg|ing.** = depth-bomb.

depth finder, an instrument for measuring the depth of water, especially by means of sonar: *Commercial fishermen are using acoustic finders patterned after the Navy depth finders to locate schools of fish* (Scientific American).

depth gauge, an apparatus for the precise measurement of the depth of a hole or recess, or of the height of a projection above a plane surface.

depth indicator, = fathometer.

depth interview, an interview that seeks fuller explanations and more personal responses than those obtained by means of questionnaires: *Depth interviews uncovered the motivational and emotional reasons why doctors use some publications more than others* (Drug Trade News).

depth|less (depth′lis), *adj.* **1** without depth; shallow: *Even when the clouds of gauze parted, it was to reveal the frustrating depthless world seen with one eye* (New Yorker). **2** of immeasurable depth; fathomless: *the depthless ocean.* **3** superficial: *the banal chatter of a trivial, depthless character.*

depth of field, *Photography.* the distance between the nearest and farthest objects clearly focused by a lens at a given opening: *If extremely sharp definition of the image is not essential, there is evidently a certain range of object distances, called the depth of field, such that all objects within this range are simultaneously "in focus"* (Sears and Zemansky).

depth perception, the ability to judge the distance and relation of distant things to each other and to the observer: *The old yardsticks, such as reaction time, depth perception, coordination and general intelligence, have little value in differentiating the safe from the unsafe driver* (Science News Letter).

depth psychology, the study or analysis of unconscious mental processes; psychoanalysis: *Within the field of psychology, the special branch that concerns itself with the relation between mental illness and the creative development of personality is depth psychology* (Ira Progoff).

depth sounder, = depth finder.

dep|u|rate (dep′yə rāt, di pyůr′āt), *v.,* **-rat|ed, -rat|ing.** —***v.t.*** to purify; cleanse.
—***v.i.*** to become purified.
[< Medieval Latin *depurare* (with English *-ate*[1]) < Latin *dē-* from + *pūrāre* purify < *pūrus* clean, pure]

dep|u|ra|tion (dep′yə rā′shən), *n.* the act of purifying or cleansing: *the depuration of a wound.*

dep|u|ra|tive (dep′yə rā′tiv, di pyůr′ə-), *adj., n.* —***adj.*** purifying; cleansing.
—***n.*** a purifying agent or medicine.

dep|u|ra|tor (dep′yə rā′tər), *n.* a person or thing that cleanses.

de|purge (dē pėrj′), *v.t.,* **-purged, -purg|ing.** to restore to favor, especially by official pardon: *to depurge a war criminal.*

dep|u|ta|ble (dep′yə tə bəl), *adj.* that can be deputed.

dep|u|ta|tion (dep′yə tā′shən), *n.* **1** a group of persons sent to represent others; delegation: *The factory workers appointed a deputation of their fellows to bargain for higher pay.* **2** the act of deputing: *The deputation of committee functions was the duty of the chairman.* **3** *Obsolete.* appointment or assignment to an office or function.

de|pute (di pyüt′), *v.t.,* **-put|ed, -put|ing. 1** to appoint to do one's work or to act in one's place; delegate: *The teacher deputed a pupil to take charge of the room while she was gone.* **2** to give (one's work, authority, responsibility, or obligation) to another; transfer: *The owner deputed the repair of the building to his partner.* [< Old French *deputer,* learned borrowing from Late Latin *dēputāre* assign < Latin, consider as < *dē-* away, apart + *putāre* think, count]

dep|u|tise (dep′yə tīz), *v.t., v.i.,* **-tised, -tis|ing.** *Especially British.* deputize: *He will assist generally in the running of the factory and deputise for him in his absence* (Sunday Times).

dep|u|tize (dep′yə tīz), *v.,* **-tized, -tiz|ing.** —***v.t.*** to appoint as deputy: *He was deputized as sheriff for three months.*
—***v.i.*** to act as deputy.

dep|u|ty (dep′yə tē), *n., pl.* **-ties,** *adj.* —***n.*** **1** a person appointed to do the work of or to take the place of another: *The sheriff appointed special deputies to help him enforce the law.* SYN: proxy, delegate, agent. **2** an assistant to certain public officials: *the deputy mayor of New York.* **3** a representative in certain lawmaking assemblies: *In France, the citizens elect deputies to the lower house of the national legislative body, formerly called the Chamber of Deputies.* **4** *British.* an inspector of safety in a coal mine: *The deputies . . . test the beams and other protective appliances* (Daily News).
—***adj.*** acting as a deputy.
[< Middle French *député,* noun use of past participle of Old French *deputer;* see etym. under **depute**]

dep|u|ty|ship (dep′yə tē ship), *n.* the office or position of a deputy.

der., **1** derivation. **2** derivative. **3** derived.

de|ra|cial|i|za|tion (dē rā′shə lə zā′shən), *n.* the elimination of racial characteristics or features.

de|ra|cial|ize (dē rā′shə līz), *v.t.,* **-ized, -iz|ing.** to remove racial characteristics, qualities, or attitudes from: *to deracialize a group, a segregated school, etc.*

de|rac|i|nate (di ras′ə nāt), *v.t.,* **-nat|ed, -nat|ing.** to tear up by the roots; uproot; eradicate; exterminate: (*Figurative.*) *Neither arms, nor victories* [*were*] *able to deracinate or root out this doctrine* (B. Harris). [< Old French *desraciner* (with English *-ate*[1]) < *des-* out (< Latin *dis-*) + *racine* root < Late Latin *rādīcīna* < Latin *rādīx, -īcis*]

de|rac|i|na|tion (di ras′ə nā′shən), *n.* eradication.

dé|ra|ci|né (dā rá sē nā′), *adj., n. French.* —***adj.*** uprooted from one's native or other natural environment; displaced: *For if ever there was a nation that is déraciné, uprooted from its traditional ties and anchorages, it is post-war Germany* (Atlantic).

—*n.* an uprooted or displaced individual: *A déraciné, a man who has been torn up by the roots, cannot be replanted* (Listener).

de|ra|di|cal|ize (dē rad′ə kə līz), *v.t.*, **-ized, -iz|ing.** to cause to abandon or retreat from radicalism: *Today Obst's cigars are longer than his hair, and he admits that hobnobbing with publishing fat cats has tended to deradicalize him* (Newsweek). —**de|rad′i|cal|i|za′tion,** *n.*

de|raign (di rān′), *v.t. Obsolete.* **1** *Law.* **a** to dispute or contest (a claim), especially by wager of battle. **b** to prove or vindicate (a right), especially by wager of battle. **2a** to arrange (an army) for battle. **b** to set (troops) in battle array. [< Anglo-French *desreiner,* Old French *desraisnier* explain, defend < *des-* away (< Latin *dis-*) + *raisnier* speak, account for < Vulgar Latin *ratiōnāre* < Latin *ratiō, -ōnis* reason]

de|raign|ment (di rān′mənt), *n. Obsolete.* a deraigning or being deraigned.

de|rail (dē rāl′), *v.t.* **1** to cause (a train, car, or other device that moves on rails) to run off the rails: *Already ten major fires of unknown origin had caused heavy losses, and several trains were derailed* (Newsweek). **2** *Figurative: Bitter fights among . . . major political groups have derailed attempts to form a stable government* (Wall Street Journal). —*v.i.* to run off the rails. [perhaps back formation < *derailment*]

de|rail|er (dē rā′lər), *n.* a person or thing that derails.

de|rail|leur (di rā′lər; *French* dā rä yœr′), *n.* **1** a device on a bicycle which moves the chain from one gearwheel to another; bicycle gearshift. See picture under **bicycle.** **2** a bicycle equipped with a derailleur. [< French *dérailleur* < *dérailler* derail; see etym. under **derailment**]

de|rail|ment (dē rāl′mənt), *n.* the act of derailing or condition of being derailed: *The train's speed at derailment was at least 57 m.p.h.* (London Times). [< French *déraillement* < *dérailler* derail < *dé-* from + *rail* rail]

de|range (di rānj′), *v.t.*, **-ranged, -rang|ing. 1** to disturb the order or arrangement of; throw into confusion: *Sudden illness in the family deranged plans for the trip. She had run for the nearest doctor in the middle of the night, but he was not a man to derange himself* (New Yorker). SYN: disorder, disarrange. **2** to make insane: *The mother of the kidnaped baby was temporarily deranged by grief.* [< French *déranger* < Old French *desrengier* < *des-* (< Latin *dis-*) + *ranger* to range]

de|ranged (di rānjd′), *adj.* **1** disarranged; disordered. **2** = insane.

de|range|ment (di rānj′mənt), *n.* **1** a disturbance of order or arrangement: *Any derangement of the furniture upset her. Where mass opinion dominates the government, there is a morbid derangement of the true functions of power* (Atlantic). SYN: disarrangement, disorder, disorganization. **2** = insanity. **3** *Mathematics.* inversion.

de|rate (dē rāt′), *v.t.*, **-rat|ed, -rat|ing. 1** *Especially British.* to reduce the assessed valuation of (industrial property or the like) as a benefit to business: *The derating of industry was introduced to assist manufacturers in certain heavy industries during the prewar depression* (Sunday Times). **2** to operate (an engine) at reduced power.

de|ra|tion (dē rā′shən), *v.t.* to free from rationing; remove from rationing: *to deration meat.*

de|rat|i|za|tion (dē rat′ə zā′shən), *n.* the getting rid of rats: *deratization of ships.*

de|ray (di rā′), *n. Archaic or Dialect.* disorder; uproar; disorderly merrymaking. [< Old French *desrai* < *desreër* to act disorderly < *des-* out (< Latin *dis-*) + *rei* order, rank < a Germanic word]

Der|by (dėr′bē; *British* där′bē), *n., pl.* **-bies. 1** a famous horse race in England founded by the Earl of Derby in 1780 and run every year at Epsom Downs, near London. **2** a horse race of similar importance: *the Kentucky Derby.* **3** a variety of porcelain made at Derby. [< 12th Earl of *Derby,* died 1834]

***der|by** (dėr′bē; *British* där′bē), *n., pl.* **-bies. 1** an important race or competition: *a soapbox derby.* **2** a stiff hat with a rounded crown and narrow brim; a bowler. [< *Derby,* the horse race]

***derby**
definition 2

Derby cheese, a hard, pressed cheese made from partly skimmed milk, produced chiefly in the Derbyshire district of England.

Der|by|shire cheese (dėr′bē shir, -shər; *British* där′bē shir, -shər), = Derby cheese.

dere (dir), *n., adj. Obsolete.* —*n.* **1** dear. **2** deer. —*adj.* dear.

de|rec|og|ni|tion (dē rek′əg nish′ən), *n.* withdrawal of recognition, as from a country or government: *Because of Britain's derecognition of the Chinese Republic of Taiwan, there were difficulties over the granting of visas to the Taiwan delegation* (Manchester Guardian Weekly).

de|rec|og|nize (dē rek′əg nīz), *v.t.*, **-nized, -niz|ing.** to withdraw recognition or formal acknowledgment of: *to derecognize a country or government. One advanced M.Sc. course within London University has been "derecognized"* (New Scientist).

de|reg|is|ter (dē rej′ə stər), *v.t. British.* to remove from a register; take away the registration of: *Party policy is to compel the unions to . . . register with a new registrar (who would have power to deregister them)* (London Times).

de rè|gle (də re′glə), *French.* according to rule; in order: *Since this was a championship bout, hostilities were de règle as soon as the fallen man got to his feet* (New Yorker).

de|reg|u|late (dē reg′yə lāt), *v.t.*, **-lat|ed, -lat|ing. 1** to remove regulations or restrictions from: *. . . a plan to liberalize all broadcast regulation and virtually deregulate radio* (June B. Csida). **2** to remove price or rate controls from: *A parallel Administration bill to deregulate natural gas has been shelved* (London Sunday Times.) —**de|reg′u|la′tion,** *n.* —**de|reg′u|la′tor,** *n.*

der|e|lict (der′ə likt), *adj., n.* —*adj.* **1** that has been abandoned; forsaken; deserted: *a derelict ship.* **2** failing in one's duty; negligent: *The guard was found derelict in letting the prisoner escape.* SYN: delinquent, unfaithful.
—*n.* **1** a ship abandoned and afloat at sea. **2** a poor, homeless person who is unwilling or unable to care for himself: *The ragged old derelict begged for money to buy a meal.* **3** any useless, discarded, or forsaken thing. **4** *Law.* land left dry by the gradual receding of water.
[< Latin *dērelictus,* past participle of *dērelinquere* abandon < *dē-* (intensive) + *re-* behind + *linquere* leave]

der|e|lic|tion (der′ə lik′shən), *n.* **1** a failure in one's duty; negligence: *Because of the watchman's dereliction, thieves managed to enter the bank.* **2** abandonment; a forsaking; desertion. **3** *Law.* **a** a leaving of dry land by the gradual receding of water: *Land gained by the dereliction of water* (Henry T. Colebrooke). **b** the land left dry.

de|re|press (dē′ri pres′), *v.t. Genetics.* to induce (a gene) to operate by disengaging the repressor: *The group . . . now hopes to find out how genes are repressed and derepressed—turned off and on—so that genes can be made to operate when required* (Charles S. Marwick).

de|re|pres|sor (dē′ri pres′ər), *n. Genetics.* a biochemical mechanism that activates a gene by disengaging the repressing mechanism, or repressor; inducer.

de|req|ui|si|tion (dē rek′wə zish′ən), *n., v. British.* —*n.* the return of property to civilian control after requisition by military authority.
—*v.t.* to return (property) to civilian control.

de re|rum na|tu|ra (dē rir′əm nə tůr′ə, -tyůr′-), *Latin.* on the nature of things.

de|res|in|a|tion (dē rez′ə nā′shən), *n.* the act or process of removing resin.

de|re|strict (dē′ri strikt′), *v.t.* to remove restrictions from: *The average number of fatalities per 100 million miles on derestricted rural roads in Britain varies between twelve and sixty-nine* (Sunday Times).

de|re|stric|tion (dē′ri strik′shən), *n.* a derestricting or being derestricted.

Dergue or **Dirgue** (dėrg, dirg), *n.* the ruling military council of Ethiopia, established after the deposition of Emperor Haile Selassie. [< Amharic *dergue, dirgue* (literally) committee]

de|ride (di rīd′), *v.t.*, **-rid|ed, -rid|ing.** to make fun of; laugh at in scorn; ridicule with contempt; mock: *The boys derided him for his fear of the dark.* SYN: See syn. under **ridicule.** [< Latin *dērīdēre* < *dē-* down + *rīdēre* laugh] —**de|rid′er,** *n.* —**de|rid′ing|ly,** *adv.*

de ri|gueur (də rē gœr′), *French.* required by etiquette; according to custom; proper: *Rome grows more Americanized every day. Blue jeans and cowboy suits are currently de rigueur among teen-agers* (New Yorker).

de|ris|i|ble (di riz′ə bəl), *adj.* subject to derision; worthy of derision.

de|ri|sion (di rizh′ən), *n.* **1** scornful laughter; ridicule; contempt: *Children dread the derision of their playmates.* **2** an object of ridicule: *I was a derision to all my people* (Lamentations 3:14). [< Latin *dērīsiō, -ōnis* < *dērīdēre;* see etym. under **deride**]

de|ri|sive (di rī′siv), *adj.* mocking; ridiculing: *derisive laughter.* —**de|ri′sive|ly,** *adv.* —**de|ri′sive|ness,** *n.*

de|ri|so|ry (di rī′sər ē), *adj.* **1** mocking; derisive: *Derisory laughter greeted his stale jokes.* **2** laughable; ridiculous: *Their pay is derisory by comparison with that of politicians in other countries* (Manchester Guardian Weekly).

deriv., 1 derivation. **2** derivative.

de|riv|a|ble (di rī′və bəl), *adj.* that can be derived: *It says that the formula in question is not derivable from the axioms of arithmetic* (Scientific American).

de|riv|al (di rī′vəl), *n.* = derivation.

der|i|vate (der′ə vit), *n., adj.* —*n.* **1** something derived. **2** a derivative, such as a word or a chemical product. —*adj. Archaic.* derived.

der|i|va|tion (der′ə vā′shən), *n.* **1** the act or fact of deriving: *The derivation of many of our laws from Roman law is unmistakable.* **2** the state of being derived. **3** origin; source: *The celebration of Halloween is of Scottish derivation.* **4** the system in a language for making new words from old by using prefixes and suffixes and by other methods. *Example: Quickness* = *quick* + suffix *-ness.* **5** a statement of how a word was formed; etymology. **6** *Mathematics.* the operation of deducing from one function another function considered or treated as its derivative, such as the operation of finding a differential coefficient in differential calculus. **7** = evolution.

der|i|va|tion|al (der′ə vā′shə nəl), *adj.* having to do with derivation.

der|i|va|tion|ist (der′ə vā′shə nist), *n.* a person who holds the theory of derivation or evolution of organic types; evolutionist.

de|riv|a|tive (di riv′ə tiv), *adj., n.* —*adj.* **1** not original; derived: *derivative poetry.* **2** of derivation; derivational.
—*n.* **1** something derived: *Many medicines are derivatives of roots and herbs. They spoke a derivative of the Malay language* (Harper's). **2** a word formed by adding a prefix or suffix to another word. *Quickness* and *quickly* are derivatives of *quick.* **3** a chemical substance obtained from another by modification or by partial substitution of components: *Acetic acid is a derivative of alcohol.* **4** *Mathematics.* **a** the instantaneous rate of change of a function with respect to its variable. **b** a function derived from another in differential calculus; differential coefficient. —**de|riv′a|tive|ly,** *adv.* —**de|riv′a|tive|ness,** *n.*

de|rive (di rīv′), *v.*, **-rived, -riv|ing.** —*v.t.* **1** to obtain from a source or origin; get; receive: *He derives much pleasure from reading adventure stories.* **2** to trace (a word, custom, or title) from or to a source or origin: *The word "December" is derived from the Latin word "decem," which means "ten."* **3** to obtain by reasoning; deduce. **4** to obtain (a chemical substance) from another by substituting a different element. **5** *Obsolete.* to lead; bring; direct.
—*v.i.* to come from a source or origin; originate: *This story derives from an old legend.*
[< Old French *deriver,* learned borrowing from Latin *dērīvāre* lead off, draw off (water) < *dē-* off + *rīvus* stream] —**de|riv′er,** *n.*

de|rived (di rīvd′), *adj.* drawn, obtained, or originating from a source; not original or native: *On the other hand, many of the derived races may not genetically be the result of mixture, but rather the product of special types of genetic adaptation* (Beals and Hoijer). *Abbr:* der.

derived protein, = proteose.

derived unit, *Physics.* any unit which is a derivative of one or more primary units, such as of mass, length, or time.

derm (dėrm), *n.* = dermis.

der|ma[1] (dėr′mə), *n.* = dermis. [< Greek *dérma, -atos* skin]

der|ma[2] (dėr′mə), *n.* a casing of beef stuffed with a spicy flour mixture and roasted; kishke. [< Yiddish *derme,* plural of *darm* intestine < Middle High German]

derm|a|bra|sion (dėr′mə brā′zhən), *n.* the removal of epidermis by freezing and applying a high-speed, motor-driven wire brush, used especially on scars.

der|mal (dėr′məl), *adj.* of the skin; dermic.

der|map|ter|an (dər map′tər ən), *adj., n.* —*adj.* of or belonging to the order of insects comprising the earwigs. —*n.* = earwig.
[< New Latin *Dermaptera* the order name < Greek *dérma* skin + *pterón* wing]

dermat- or **dermato-,** *combining form.* of the skin: *Dermatotherapy* = *treatment of the skin.* [< Greek *dérma, -atos* skin]

der|mat|ic (dėr mat′ik), *adj.* of or having to do with the skin; dermal.

der|ma|ti|tis (dėr′mə tī′tis), *n.* inflammation of the skin.

Pronunciation Key: hat, āge, cãre, fär; let, ēqual, tėrm; it, īce; hot, ōpen, ôrder; oil, out; cup, pu̇t, rüle; child; long; thin; ᴛʜen; zh, measure; ə represents **a** in about, **e** in taken, **i** in pencil, **o** in lemon, **u** in circus.

der|mat|o|gen (dər mat′ə jən, dėr′mə tə-), *n. Botany.* a thin layer of growing tissue from which the epidermis is developed.

der|ma|to|glyph|ics (dėr′mə tə glif′iks), *n.* **1** the pattern of lines in the palm of the hand, or the sole of the foot. **2** the study of these patterns, especially in infants, to detect disease or abnormality. [< *dermato-* + Greek *glýphein* to carve]

der|ma|tog|ra|phy (dėr′mə tog′rə fē), *n.* the anatomical description of the skin.

der|ma|toid (dėr′mə toid), *adj.* resembling skin; skinlike.

der|ma|to|log|ic (dėr′mə tə loj′ik), *adj.* = dermatological.

der|ma|to|log|i|cal (dėr′mə tə loj′ə kəl), *adj.* of or having to do with dermatology. **—der′ma|to|log′i|cal|ly**, *adv.*

der|ma|tol|o|gist (dėr′mə tol′ə jist), *n.* a person who studies dermatology and usually practices medicine treating the skin and its diseases.

der|ma|tol|o|gy (dėr′mə tol′ə jē), *n.* the branch of medicine that deals with the skin, its structure, and its diseases.

der|ma|tome (dėr′mə tōm), *n.* **1** an instrument for cutting skin grafts. **2** *Embryology.* the part of the mesoderm from which the dermis develops. [< *derma* + Greek *-tomíā* a cutting]

der|ma|to|my|co|sis (dėr′mə tō mī kō′sis), *n., pl.* **-ses** (-sēz). any fungous disease of the skin, such as ringworm. [< *dermato-* + *mycosis*]

der|ma|to|my|o|si|tis (dėr′mə tō mī′ə sī′tis), *n.* a disease marked by inflammation of the muscular tissues and the skin. [< *dermato-* + Greek *mŷs, myós* muscle + English *-itis*]

der|ma|to|phyte (dėr′mə tə fīt), *n.* any fungus parasitic on the skin, causing diseases such as athlete's foot or ringworm.

der|ma|to|phyt|ic (dėr′mə tə fit′ik), *adj.* of dermatophytes; having to do with or caused by dermatophytes.

der|ma|to|phy|to|sis (dėr′mə tō fī tō′sis), *n.* a fungous disease of the skin, caused by dermatophytes.

der|ma|to|plas|ty (dėr′mə tə plas′tē), *n.* plastic surgery of the skin. [< *dermato-* + Greek *plastós* something formed]

der|ma|to|sis (dėr′mə tō′sis), *n., pl.* **-ses** (-sēz). any disease of the skin.

der|mat|o|some (dėr mat′ə sōm), *n. Botany.* one of the granular bodies which are thought to form the cell wall of a plant. Dermatosomes occur in rows and are united and surrounded by protoplasm.

der|ma|to|ther|a|py (dėr′mə tō ther′ə pē), *n.* treatment of the skin and its diseases.

der|mes|tid (dėr mes′tid), *n.* any one of a group of small beetles whose larvae are especially injurious to dried meats, wool, fur, and other animal matter. [< New Latin *Dermestidae* the family name < Greek *dérmēstēs* a worm < *dérma* skin + *esthíein* to eat]

der|mic (dėr′mik), *adj.* = dermal.

der|mis (dėr′mis), *n.* **1** the sensitive layer of skin beneath the epidermis; cutis; corium. See diagram under **skin.** **2** = skin. Also, **derm, derma.** [< New Latin *dermis,* reduction of Greek *epidermis* epidermis]

der|mo|graph|i|a (dėr′mə graf′ē ə), *n.* an extremely sensitive or irritable condition of the skin in which lines drawn on it leave a reddish, elevated mark. [< New Latin *dermographia* < Greek *dérma* skin + *gráphein* write]

der|mog|ra|phism (dər mog′rə fiz əm), *n.* = dermographia.

der|moid (dėr′moid), *adj.* skinlike; dermatoid.

der|mop|ter|an (dər mop′tər ən), *adj., n.* **—*adj.*** of or belonging to the order of mammals comprising the flying lemurs. **—*n.*** = flying lemur. [< New Latin *Dermoptera* the order name < Greek *dérma* skin + *pterón* wing]

der|mo|skel|e|ton (dėr′mō skel′ə tən), *n.* the exoskeleton. [< Greek *dérma* skin + English *skeleton*]

dern[1] (dėrn), *adj. Scottish.* **1** hidden or secret: *There's not a dern nook, or cove . . . that he's not acquainted with* (Scott). **2** dark; somber; dreary. [Old English *derne*]

dern[2] (dėrn), *interj., adv. U.S. Slang.* darn: *Dern it!* (interj.). *I dern nigh broke my leg climbing the fence* (adv.).

der|ni|er (dėr′nē ər; *French* der nyā′), *adj.* last; ultimate; final. [< French *dernier* < Old French *derrenier* < *dererain* (the) back, ultimately < Latin *dē-* from + *retrō* back(wards)]

der|nier cri (der nyā′ krē′), *French.* **1** the latest word. **2** the latest style.

der|nier res|sort (der nyā′ rə sôr′), *French.* the last resort or resource.

der|o|gate (der′ə gāt; *adj. also* der′ə git), *v.,* **-gat|ed, gat|ing,** *adj.* **—*v.i.*** **1** to take away a part of something so as to impair it; detract: *The king felt that summoning a parliament would derogate from his authority.* **2** to become worse; degenerate. **—*v.t.*** **1** to take away (something) from a thing so as to impair it. **2** *Obsolete.* to detract from; depreciate.
—*adj.* *Rare.* deteriorated; debased.
[< Latin *dērogāre* (with English *-ate*[1]) < *dē-* away from + *rogāre* ask] **—der′o|gate|ly,** *adv.*

der|o|ga|tion (der′ə gā′shən), *n.* **1** a lessening or impairment (of power, law, position, or other status): *To him, marriage meant only the derogation of his independence.* **2** the state of becoming worse; deterioration; debasement. **3** disparagement; detraction.

de|rog|a|tive (di rog′ə tiv), *adj.* = derogatory. **—de|rog′a|tive|ly,** *adv.*

der|o|ga|tor (der′ə gā′tər), *n.* a person who derogates.

de|rog|a|to|ri|ly (di rog′ə tôr′ə lē, -tōr′-), *adv.* in a derogatory manner.

de|rog|a|to|ri|ness (di rog′ə tôr′ē nis, -tōr′-), *n.* the quality of being derogatory.

de|rog|a|to|ry (di rog′ə tôr′ē, -tōr′-), *adj.* **1** showing an unfavorable opinion of some person or thing; disparaging; belittling: *The stranger's derogatory remarks about the town and its people made him unpopular.* **2** lessening the value; detracting.

der|rick** (der′ik), *n., v.* **—*n. **1** a machine for lifting and moving heavy objects. A derrick has a long arm that swings at an angle from the base of an upright post or frame. **2** a towerlike framework over an oil well that holds the drilling and hoisting machinery.
—*v.t.* **1** to lift or move by or as if by derrick. **2** *U.S. Slang.* to remove (a pitcher) from a ball game.
[earlier, gallows; hangman < *Derrick,* a hangman at Tyburn, London, around 1600]

***derrick**
definitions 1, 2

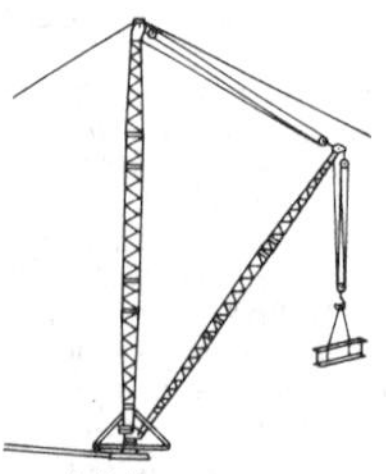
definition 1

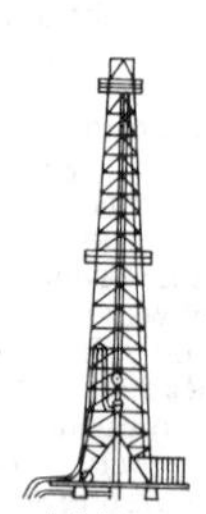
definition 2

der|ri|ère or **der|ri|ere** (de′rē ãr′), *n.* the rump; buttocks. [< French *derrière* < adjective, back < Old French *deriere* < Latin *de retrō* from behind]

der|ring-do (der′ing dü′), *n.,* or **derring do,** daring deeds; heroic daring: *But where in the older picaresque tradition the adventures are feats of physical derring-do, here they are adventures of the spirit* (Wall Street Journal). [Middle English (Chaucer) *dorryng don* daring to do; subsequently misunderstood by Spenser to be a compound noun, and popularized by Sir Walter Scott]

***der|rin|ger** (der′ən jər), *n. U.S.* a short pistol that has a large caliber. [American English < Henry *Deringer,* 1786-1868, an American inventor]

***derringer**

der|ris (der′is), *n.* **1** any one of a group of mostly climbing, East Indian and African plants of the pea family. The roots of various East Indian species yield the insecticide and fish poison rotenone. **2** an extract of these roots. [< New Latin *Derris* the genus name < Greek *dérris* leather cover]

der|ry (der′ē), *n., pl.* **-ries. 1** a meaningless word in the refrains of songs and ballads. **2** a song or ballad.

der|ry-down (der′ē doun′), *n.* = derry.

der Tag (dər täk′), *German.* **1** the day (a phrase used by the Nazis to signify the day on which Germany would begin her conquests). **2** the day of any important event.

derv (dėrv), *n. British.* diesel fuel. [< *d*(iesel) *e*(ngine) *r*(oad) *v*(ehicle)]

der|vish (dėr′vish), *n.* **1** a member of a Moslem religious order that practices unusual self-denial and devotion. Some dance and spin about violently. **2** a member of any one of the tribes of upper Egypt and the Sudan who followed the Mahdi and revolted against the British and Egyptians in the period 1880-1885. [< Turkish *derviş* < Persian *darvīsh*]

DES (no periods), diethylstilbestrol.

de|sa|cral|i|za|tion (dē sā′krə lə zā′shən, -sak′rə-), *n.* the act or process of desacralizing: *Artists . . . demand the "desacralization" of art and condemn the worship of the art object by museums, collectors, dealers, and art lovers* (New Yorker).

de|sa|cral|ize (dē sā′krə līz, -sak′rə-), *v.t.,* **-ized, -iz|ing.** to divest (an idea or institution) of its sacredness; make less sacred: *We must desacralize the nuclear deity, . . . relegating it to the destructive material entity that it is* (Atlantic).

de|sal|i|nate (dē sal′ə nāt), *v.t.,* **-nat|ed, -nat|ing.** = desalt.

de|sal|i|na|tion (dē sal′ə nā′shən), *n.* the removal of salt or saline content, especially from seawater.

de|sal|i|nize (dē sal′ə nīz), *v.t.,* **-nized, -niz|ing.** = desalt. **—de|sal′i|ni|za′tion,** *n.*

de|sal|i|vate (dē sal′ə vit), *adj.* having the salivary glands removed: *In a second series of experiments, the researchers applied vaseline to the lips of desalivate pups every two hours during the daytime* (New Scientist and Science Journal).

de|salt (dē sôlt′), *v.t.* to remove salt from; deprive of saline content: *to desalt seawater.* **—de|salt′er,** *n.*

de|sat|u|rate (dē sach′ə rāt), *v.t.,* **-rat|ed, -rat|ing.** to decrease the saturation of (a color).

de|scale (dē skāl′), *v.t.,* **-scaled, -scal|ing.** to remove the crust or hard coating from, especially that produced by the minerals in water: *Polishing is done after fabrication and the best results are obtained from ordinary descaled . . . stainless steel* (New Scientist).

des|ca|mi|sa|do (des′kä mē sä′dō; *Spanish* des′kä mē sä′ŦHō), *n., pl.* **-dos. 1** an ultra-liberal revolutionist of the Spanish revolution of 1820-23. **2** an Argentine worker of the poorest class: *He rode back to power on the shoulders of his descamisados* (Newsweek). [< Spanish *descamisado* (literally) shirtless]

des|cant (*v.* des kant′, dis-; *n.* des′kant), *v., n.* **—*v.i.*** **1** to talk at great length; discourse; make comments: *She descanted upon the wonders of her trip to Europe.* **2** *Music.* to sing or play a melody in harmony with another melody. **3** to sing.
—*n.* **1** *Music.* **a** part music. **b** a melody to be played or sung with another melody. It is the earliest form of counterpoint. **c** the art of singing or composing music in parts. **d** the upper part or voice in part music, especially the soprano. **2** any song or melody. **3** extended comment; discourse.
[< Old French *deschanter* < Medieval Latin *discantāre* < Latin *dis-* apart + *cantus -ūs* song] **—des|cant′er,** *n.*

de|scend (di send′), *v.i.* **1** to go or come down from a higher place to a lower place: *The river descends from the mountains to the sea. He descended in a parachute.* (*Figurative.*) *The shades of evening began to descend* (William Forbes). SYN: fall, sink. **2** to go or come down from an earlier to a later time: *a superstition descended from the Middle Ages.* **3** to go from greater to fewer numbers; go from higher to lower on any scale: *The numbers 75-50-25 form a series that descends.* **4** to slope downward: *The path descended from the cliff to the beach.* **5a** to make a sudden attack: *The wolves descended on the sheep and killed them.* **b** *Figurative: Hordes of relatives began to descend on the rich man.* **6** to be handed down from parent to child; pass by inheritance: *This land has been in our family for 150 years, descending from father to son.* **7** to come down or spring from; have as ancestors: *He is descended from pioneers.* **8** *Figurative.* to lower oneself; stoop: *In order to eat she descended to stealing.* **9** to proceed from general things to particular things in speaking or writing. **10** *Astronomy.* to move toward the horizon or toward the south. **—*v.t.*** to go or come down; move downward upon or along: *to descend the stairs to the basement. The winding trail descends the mountain.* [< Old French *descendre* < Latin *dēscendere* < *dē-* down + *scandere* climb]

de|scend|a|ble (di sen′də bəl), *adj.* = descendible.

de|scend|ant (di sen′dənt), *n., adj.* **—*n.*** **1** a person born of a certain family or group: *a descendant of the Pilgrims.* **2** an offspring; child, great-grandchild, and so on. You are a direct descendant of your parents, grandparents, great-grandparents, and earlier ancestors.
—*adj.* descending; going or coming down.

de|scend|ent (di sen′dənt), *n., adj.* = descendant.

de|scend|er (di sen′dər), *n.* **1** a person or thing that descends. **2a** *Printing.* the lower part or tail of such lower-case letters as *g, p, q, j,* and *y.* **b** any such letter.

de|scend|i|ble (di sen′də bəl), *adj.* **1** that can be descended. **2** *Law.* that can descend; inheritable: *a descendible estate.*

de|scend|ing (di sen′ding), *adj.* **1** that descends:

the descending sun, a descending scale. **2** *Botany.* (of an inflorescence) determinate.

descending colon, the part of the large intestine that descends on the left side of the abdomen, between the transverse colon and the sigmoid flexure. See diagram under **intestine**.

descending letter, *Printing.* a letter with a long stem which descends below the line.

descending node, = node (def. 6).

de|scen|sion (di sen′shən), *n. Rare.* descent.

de|scen|sion|al (di sen′shə nəl), *adj.* of or having to do with descension or descent.

de|scen|sive (di sen′siv), *adj.* tending to descend; descending.

de|scent¹ (di sent′), *n.* **1** a coming or going down from a higher to a lower place: *The descent of the balloon was more rapid than its rise had been.* **2** a downward slope: *We climbed down a steep descent.* **3** a way or passage down; means of descending: *There was only one descent into the old mine.* **4** a handing down from parent to child; a descending or coming down in a family line: *We can trace the descent of blond hair in this family through five generations.* **5** a family line; ancestors: *We can trace our descent back to a family in England.* SYN: ancestry. **6** *Figurative.* **a** a sinking to a lower condition; decline; fall. **b** a lowering of oneself. **7** a sudden attack: *The descent of the bandits on the village was totally unexpected.* **8** *Law.* a handing down of an estate by inheritance. **9** *Obsolete.* a single stage in the line of descent from an ancestor; generation. [< Old French *descente* < *descendre;* see etym. under **descend**]

de|scent² (dē sent′), *v.t.* to deprive of scent; remove the scent gland of: *Pablo is a striped skunk who ... has been "descented"* (London Times). [< *de-* + *scent*]

de|school (dē skül′), *v.t.* to abolish traditional schools in: *The radical deschooling of society begins, therefore, with the unmasking by cultural revolutionaries of the myth of schooling* (Ivan Illich).

de|scram|bler (dē skram′blər), *n.* a device for unscrambling scrambled telephone, radio, or television signals: *Video-scramblers are used in subscription television to make the telecast unintelligible to viewers whose sets are not equipped with a descrambler* (Scientific American).

de|scrib|a|ble (di skrī′bə bəl), *adj.* that can be described.

de|scribe (di skrīb′), *v.t.,* **-scribed, -scrib|ing.** **1** to tell in words how a person looks, feels, or acts, or how a place, a thing, or an event looks or happened; tell or write about: *The reporter described the accident in detail. He described his sufferings as a prisoner of war. There are no books which I more delight in than in ... those that describe remote countries* (Joseph Addison). SYN: depict. **2** to trace or form; draw the outline of: *The spinning top described a figure 8.* SYN: trace. **3** *Obsolete.* to descry. [< Latin *dēscrībere* copy off, write down < *dē-* down, out + *scrībere* write] **—de|scrib′er,** *n.*

— *Syn.* 1 Describe, narrate mean to tell or to write about something. **Describe** means to tell what a person, place, or thing looks like or is like, by giving details of appearance, character, and other features, and arranging them so that the hearer or reader will get a clear picture: *He described the people he saw from the window.* **Narrate** means to tell a story, by arranging details of events so the hearer or reader will understand what happened: *He narrated the history of the Forty-Niners.*

de|scri|er (di skrī′ər), *n.* a person who descries.

de|scrip|tion (di skrip′shən), *n.* **1** the act of describing; telling in words how a person, place, thing, or event looks, behaves, or happened. **2** a composition or account that gives a picture in words: *The vivid description of the hotel fire made me feel as if I had seen it.* **3** kind; sort; type: *I have seen no dog of any description today. In the crowd there were people of every description.* **4** the act of tracing; act of drawing in outline; delineation. [< Latin *dēscrīptiō, -ōnis* < *dēscrībere;* see etym. under **describe**]

de|scrip|tive (di skrip′tiv), *adj.* **1** describing; using description: *A descriptive booklet tells about the places to be seen on the trip. Write a descriptive paragraph about a flower garden.* **2** *Grammar.* **a** serving to describe. "Big" in "big house" is a descriptive adjective. **b** = nonrestrictive. **3** (of a branch of science) having to do with objective description; based upon observed or empirical facts exclusive of historical, theoretical, or other considerations: *descriptive linguistics, descriptive botany.* **—de|scrip′tive|ly,** *adv.* **—de|scrip′tive|ness,** *n.*

descriptive geometry, 1 the branch of geometry that solves three-dimensional problems by making projections of figures on two planes that are perpendicular to each other. **2** geometry in which projections are used in solving problems.

de|scrip|tor (di skrip′tər, -tôr), *n.* **1** a word, phrase, or symbol that identifies a particular subject in the storage unit of a computer: *When a research worker wants to extract from the microfilm all the material bearing on a certain item of information, he punches the descriptors defining this item on a card and inserts the card in the machine* (Scientific American). **2** a subject heading or key word.

de|scry (di skrī′), *v.,* **-scried, -scry|ing,** *n.* **—*v.t.*** **1** to catch sight of; be able to see; make out; see at a distance; see with difficulty: *to descry an island on the horizon. We descried the little boat two miles away.* **2** to discover by observation; see; detect; perceive: *He thought he could descry a way out of his troubles.* **3** *Obsolete.* to disclose; reveal.

—n. Obsolete. a sight or discovery of something distant or obscure.

[< Old French *descrier* proclaim < *des-* dis- (< Latin *dis-*) + *crier* cry < Latin *quirītāre.* See related etym. at **decry**.]

Des|de|mo|na (dez′də mō′nə), *n.* the young wife of Othello in Shakespeare's tragedy *Othello.* Her husband smothered her when Iago tricked him into believing her unfaithful.

de|seam (dē sēm′), *v.t. Metallurgy.* to remove surface blemishes, such as seams, from (ingots); scarf.

des|e|crate (des′ə krāt), *v.t.,* **-crat|ed, -crat|ing.** to treat or use without respect; disregard the sacredness of; profane: *The enemy desecrated the church by using it as a stable.* [< *de-* + (con)*secrate;* perhaps influenced by Old French *dessacrer* < *des-* dis- (< Latin *dis-*) + *sacrer* consecrate < Latin *sacrāre* < *sacer* sacred]

des|e|crat|er (des′ə krā′tər), *n.* a person who desecrates.

des|e|cra|tion (des′ə krā′shən), *n.* **1** the act of desecrating; profanation: *The Puritans felt that work or amusement on Sunday was a desecration of the Sabbath.* **2** the fact or condition of being desecrated.

des|e|cra|tor (des′ə krā′tər), *n.* = desecrater.

de|sec|tion|al|ize (dē sek′shə nə līz), *v.t.,* **-ized, -iz|ing.** to free from sectionalism; widen in scope by the removal of whatever limits or divides.

de|seg|men|ta|tion (dē′seg mən tā′shən), *n.* **1** the state or quality of not being segmented; change from a segmented condition. **2** the reduction of the number of segments by the coalescence of two or more, as in the carapace of a lobster.

de|seg|ment|ed (dē seg′mən tid), *adj.* showing or characterized by desegmentation.

de|seg|re|gate (dē seg′rə gāt), *v.,* **-gat|ed, -gat|ing.** **—*v.t.*** to abolish racial segregation in: *to desegregate a public school.*

—*v.i.* to become desegregated; bring about desegregation: *The national guard desegregated, putting Negroes and whites in the same units.*

de|seg|re|ga|tion (dē seg′rə gā′shən), *n.* the doing away with the practice of providing separate schools and other public facilities for racial groups, especially blacks and whites: *The device of closing public schools as a defense against desegregation is taking a heavy toll in terms of education, economics—and human emotions* (Wall Street Journal).

de|seg|re|ga|tion|ist (dē seg′rə gā′shə nist), *n.* a person who supports or actively works for desegregation: *Democrats faced a critical problem ... how to keep the Northern desegregationists and the Southern segregationists from ripping the party apart* (Newsweek).

de|se|lect (dē′si lekt′), *v.t. U.S.* to discharge (a trainee) during training: *The road from application to trainee to overseas volunteer is a hard one. Many individuals do not follow through. Many are "deselected"* (New York Times).

de|sen|si|ti|za|tion (dē sen′sə tə zā′shən), *n.* the act or process of desensitizing or state of being desensitized: *They treated a small number of patients by desensitization with a series of injections of weak solutions of ... antigen* (Science News Letter).

de|sen|si|tize (dē sen′sə tīz), *v.t.,* **-tized, -tiz|ing.** **1** to make less sensitive. **2** *Photography.* to make less sensitive to light. **3** *Medicine.* to reduce or eliminate the sensitivity of (a person, organism, organ, or tissue): *Meanwhile, for the hay fever sufferer this season, shots to desensitize, or immunize, him against the pollens are the best that can be offered* (Science News Letter). **4** *Psychiatry.* to relieve (a person) of an emotional disturbance. **—de|sen′si|tiz′er,** *n.*

de|se|ques|trate (dē′si kwes′trāt), *v.t.,* **-trat|ed, -trat|ing.** *Especially British.* to free from sequestration; release (something confiscated): *This property ... has now been desequestrated and in most cases returned to its owners or their agents* (Manchester Guardian Weekly).

De|se|ret (dez′ə ret), *n.* a region in the Western United States comprising Utah, Arizona, Nevada, and parts of New Mexico, Colorado, Wyoming, and California, organized into a state by the Mormons in 1849 but refused admission to the Union by Congress: *The Mormon pioneers ... called the region Deseret. This name ... stands for industry and hard work* (A. Russell Mortensen). [< *deseret,* a word meaning "honeybee" in the Book of Mormon]

des|ert¹ (dez′ərt), *n., adj.* **—*n.*** **1a** a barren region with little or no rainfall, usually sandy and without trees. The Sahara is a great desert in the northern part of Africa. **b** a barren region with little or no vegetation because of cold, perpetual snow, or ice: *Physiologically the Antarctic is a desert, the air is extremely dry and the surface frozen* (Gabriele Rabel). **2** a region that is not inhabited or cultivated; wilderness. **3** *Figurative.* a place or environment lacking intellectual or spiritual stimulation: *a cultural desert.*

—*adj.* **1** dry and barren: *Arabia is largely desert land. The board would build dams to harness electrical power and irrigate desert wastelands* (Newsweek). **2** not inhabited or cultivated; wild: *Robinson Crusoe was shipwrecked on a desert island.* **3** *Archaic.* deserted; abandoned.

[< Latin *dēsertum* (thing) abandoned, neuter past participle of Latin *dēserere;* see etym. at **desert²**]

— *Syn.* *n.* 1a, 2 Desert, wilderness mean an uninhabited or uncultivated region. **Desert** emphasizes dryness and barrenness and applies to a region that is usually sandy and without water, trees, or inhabitants: *Great sections of desert in Arizona and California have been made into farmland by irrigation.* A *desert island,* however, might be a verdant place which is merely deserted. **Wilderness** emphasizes lack of trails and roads and applies particularly to a region where few men have ever been and which is covered with dense vegetation: *Daniel Boone lived in Kentucky when it was still a wilderness.*

de|sert² (di zėrt′), *v.t.* **1** to go away and leave (a person or a place, especially one that should not be left); forsake: *A husband should not desert his wife and children. After the family deserted the farm, its buildings fell into ruin.* SYN: abandon. **2** to run away from (duty); leave without permission and without intending to return: *The young boy deserted the army because he was afraid.* **3** to fail (one) when needed; leave: *His self-confidence deserted him.* **—*v.i.*** **1** to run away from duty. **2** to leave military service without permission and without intending to return: *A soldier who deserts is punished.* [< Old French *deserter* < Late Latin *dēsertāre* (frequentative) < Latin *dēserere* abandon < *dē-* away + *serere* join]

— *Syn.* *v.t.* 1 Desert, forsake, abandon mean to leave someone or something completely. **Desert** suggests breaking a vow or running away from a duty and without intending to return, therefore almost always implying blame: *He deserted his country and helped the enemy.* **Forsake** suggests breaking away from someone or something once regarded with affection, but does not necessarily imply blame: *He forsook his family to study medicine.* **Abandon** emphasizes that the action is final and complete: *They abandoned the wrecked plane.*

de|sert³ (di zėrt′), *n.* **1** Usually, **deserts.** what one deserves; suitable reward or punishment: *The reckless driver got his just deserts when he was fined and his driver's license was suspended. The characters of great men ... sooner or later receive the wages of fame or infamy according to their true deserts* (William Cowper). **2** meritoriousness; excellence; worth: *The greatest desert cannot be pleaded in answer to a charge of ... transgression* (Macaulay). **3** the act or fact of deserving. [< Old French *deserte,* past participle of *deservir* < Latin *dēservīre;* see etym. under **deserve**]

***desert boot**

***des|ert boot** (dez′ərt), **1** a loose-fitting suede shoe reaching just above the ankle and now usually loosely laced, originally worn by soldiers in North Africa. **2 Desert boot,** a trademark for this or a similar type of casual shoe.

Pronunciation Key: hat, āge, cãre, fär; let, ēqual, tėrm; it, īce; hot, ōpen, ôrder; oil, out; cup, pu̇t, rüle; child; long; thin; ᴛʜen; zh, measure; ə represents **a** in about, **e** in taken, **i** in pencil, **o** in lemon, **u** in circus.

de|sert|ed (di zėr′tid), *adj.* abandoned; forsaken: *The deserted house fell into ruins.*

de|sert|er (di zėr′tər), *n.* **1** a person who deserts. **2** a soldier or sailor who runs away from duty or leaves military service without permission and without intending to return.

desert fox, = kit fox.

desert holly, a small, dense shrub of the goosefoot family, found in the deserts of southwestern North America and in Mexico. The spiny foliage is used for decoration at Christmastime.

de|ser|tic (di zėr′tik), *adj.* of or having to do with a desert or deserts.

des|er|ti|fi|ca|tion (dez′ər tə fə kā′shən), *n.* the process of turning into arid or desert land: *An ugly word, desertification, has been coined to describe the relentless creep of the desert into the semiarid regions* (London Times). *Desertification is thought to result more from land mismanagement than from uncontrollable climatic changes* (New York Times).

de|ser|tion (di zėr′shən), *n.* **1** the act of deserting. **2** the condition of being deserted; desolation: *Desertion caused the old house to fall into ruin. Desertion hurt her pride more than her heart.* **3** a running away from duty. **4** a leaving military service without permission and without intending to return. **5** *Law.* intentional abandonment of one's wife or husband in violation of legal or moral obligation.

des|ert lark (dez′ərt), any of various larks native to Asian and African deserts.

de|sert|less (di zėrt′lis), *adj.* **1** without reward or merit. **2** undeserving: *O miserable and desertless that I am* (Algernon Charles Swinburne).

des|ert lily (dez′ərt), a lily with long, narrow leaves and showy flowers, found in flat, dry areas of the southwestern United States.

desert locust, a very destructive migratory locust found in northern Africa and in Asia Minor.

desert rat, **1** any rat adapted to life in the desert, such as a kangaroo rat. **2** *U.S. Slang.* a prospector in the deserts of the western United States: *Huge industrial plants are the modern successors to the itinerant "desert rat"* (New York Times). **3** *Slang.* a soldier who fought in northern Africa during World War II: *In sad pubs and clubs one often finds them, those once dashing desert rats and fighter pilots* (Manchester Guardian Weekly).

desert varnish, a glossy coating of iron oxide and other chemicals found on rocks and pebbles after long exposure in desert regions.

de|serve (di zėrv′), *v.,* **-served, -serv|ing.** **—*v.t.*** to have a right to; have a claim to; be worthy of; merit: *A hard worker deserves good pay. One good turn deserves another.* **—*v.i.*** to be worthy: *That he, who best deserves, alone may reign* (John Dryden). [< Old French *deservir* < Latin *dēservīre* serve well < *dē-* (intensive) + *servīre* serve < *servus* a slave] **—de|serv′er,** *n.*

de|served (di zėrvd′), *adj.* rightfully earned; merited.

de|serv|ed|ly (di zėr′vid lē), *adv.* according to what is deserved; justly; rightly: *The criminal was deservedly punished.*

de|serv|ed|ness (di zėr′vid nis), *n.* the quality of having deserved; worthiness.

de|serv|ing (di zėr′ving), *adj., n.* **—*adj.*** **1** that deserves; worthy (of something): *Those thieves are deserving of punishment.* **2** worth helping: *The deserving student received a scholarship.*
—*n.* what is deserved; deserts; merit. **—de|serv′ing|ly,** *adv.* **—de|serv′ing|ness,** *n.*

de|sex (dē seks′), *v.t.* **1** to deprive of sexual characteristics. **2** to remove the reproductive organs of. **3** *U.S.* to remove sexual or sexist references from.

de|sex|u|al|i|za|tion (dē sek′shu̇ ə lə zā′shən), *n.* the act or process of desexing.

de|sex|u|al|ize (dē sek′shu̇ ə līz), *v.t.,* **-ized, -iz|ing.** to desex.

des|ha|bille (dez′ə bēl′), *n.* = dishabille.

des|ic|cant (des′ə kənt), *n., adj.* **—*n.*** an agent or drug that dries or desiccates. **—*adj.*** drying; desiccating.

des|ic|cate (des′ə kāt), *v.,* **-cat|ed, -cat|ing.** **—*v.t.*** **1a** to deprive of moisture or water; dry thoroughly; dry: *The soil in a desert is desiccated by the dry air and sun.* **b** *Figurative.* to make intellectually or spiritually dry: *that desiccated and discouraged brain* (Lytton Strachey). **2** to preserve by drying thoroughly; dehydrate: *desiccated fruit.* **—*v.i.*** to become dry.
[< Latin *dēsiccāre* (with English *-ate*[1]) < *dē-* down, out + *siccus* dry]

des|ic|ca|tion (des′ə kā′shən), *n.* the action of desiccating or a desiccated condition: *Thus the powder kills through desiccation, literally drying the insect to death* (Science News Letter).

des|ic|ca|tive (des′ə kā′tiv), *adj.* tending to desiccate or dry; desiccant.

des|ic|ca|tor (des′ə kā′tər), *n.* **1** a person or thing that desiccates. **2** an apparatus for drying fruit, milk, or other foodstuffs, or for absorbing moisture in a chemical.

des|ic|ca|to|ry (des′ə kə tôr′ē, -tōr′-), *adj.* = desiccative.

de|sid|er|a|ta (di sid′ə rā′tə, -rä′-; -zid′-), *n.* plural of **desideratum.**

de|sid|er|ate (di sid′ə rāt, -zid′-), *v.t.,* **-at|ed, -at|ing.** to feel a desire for; long for; feel the want of; want: *... he desiderated something more on a level with himself* (Cardinal Newman). [< Latin *dēsīderāre* (with English *-ate*[1]) long for. See etym. of doublet **desire.**]

de|sid|er|a|tion (di sid′ə rā′shən, -zid′-), *n.* **1** longing; desire. **2** a thing desired.

de|sid|er|a|tive (di sid′ə rā′tiv, -zid′-), *adj., n.* **—*adj.*** **1** having or expressing desire; having to do with desire. **2** *Grammar.* (of a verb) formed from and expressing desire to do the action implied in another verb.
—*n.* *Grammar.* a desiderative verb.

de|sid|er|a|tum (di sid′ə rā′təm, -rä′-; -zid′-), *n., pl.* **-ta.** something desired or needed: *Health, security, and affection are desiderata. The only desideratum was a harpsichord to give vitality and bite to the strings* (London Times). [< Latin *dēsīderātum,* neuter past participle of *dēsīderāre* long for; see etym. under **desire**]

des|i|de|ri|um (des′ə dir′ē əm), *n., pl.* **-de|ri|a** (-dir′ē ə). a longing or ardent desire, as for something once possessed and now missed; a painful sense of loss. [< Latin *dēsīderium* < *dēsīderāre* to long for; see etym. under **desire**]

de|sight (dē sīt′), *n.* a thing unpleasant to look at; eyesore.

de|sign (di zīn′), *n., v.* **—*n.*** **1** a drawing, plan, or sketch made to serve as a pattern from which to work: *The design showed how to build the machine.* **2** the arrangement of details, form, and color in painting, weaving, building, or other artistic, architectural, or mechanical form: *a wallpaper design in tan and brown.* **3** the art of making designs, patterns, or sketches: *a school of design. Architects study and become skilled in design.* **4** a piece of artistic work. **5** a plan in mind to be carried out: *The design was to establish an unusual summer theater. I shall soon have gone too far in my design of deception ever to go back* (Graham Greene). **SYN:** See syn. under **plan.** **6** a scheme of attack; evil or crafty plan: *The thief had designs upon the safe.* **7** purpose; aim; intention: *Whether by accident or design, he overturned the lamp.* **SYN:** See syn. under **intention.** **8** adaptation of means to a planned end; underlying plan or conception: *the evidence of design in a communications satellite.* **9** *Archaic.* crafty scheming.
—*v.t.* **1** to make a first sketch of; plan out; arrange form and color of; draw in outline: *to design a dress, to design a bridge.* **2** to plan out; form in the mind; contrive: *The author of this detective story has designed an exciting plot.* **3** to have in mind to do; purpose; mean: *Did you design this, or did it just happen?* **4** to set apart; intend: *The nursery was designed for the baby's use. His parents designed him for the ministry.* **5** *Obsolete.* to point out; indicate. **6** *Obsolete.* to appoint; nominate. **—*v.i.*** **1** to make drawings, sketches, or plans: *He designs for our dress department.* **2** to form or fashion a work of art.
[< Middle French *desseign* < Italian *disegno* < *disegnare* < Latin *dēsignāre* < *dē-* from + *sīgnāre* to mark < *sīgnum* a mark]

des|ig|nate (*v.* dez′ig nāt; *adj.* dez′ig nit, -nāt), *v.,* **-nat|ed, -nat|ing,** *adj.* **—*v.t.*** **1** to mark out; point out; show: *Red lines designate main roads on this map. His uniform designates his rank.* **SYN:** indicate. **2** to name; entitle: *The ruler of Iran is designated Shah.* **3** to select for duty, office, or other position; appoint: *That man has been designated by the President as the next Secretary of State.*
—*adj.* appointed or nominated for office but not yet installed: *a premier designate.*
[< Latin *dēsīgnāre* (with English *-ate*[1]); see etym. under **design**]

des|ig|nat|ed hitter (dez′ig nā′tid), a baseball player designated by a team to bat in place of the pitcher throughout the game. The designated hitter for each game can appear anywhere in the batting order. *Abbr:* DH (no periods).

des|ig|na|tion (dez′ig nā′shən), *n.* **1** the act of marking out; pointing out; definite indication: *The designation of places on a map should be clear.* **2** a descriptive title; name: *"Your Honor" is a designation given to a judge.* **3** appointment to an office or position; selection for a duty: *The designation of Cabinet officers is one of the powers of the President.*

des|ig|na|tive (dez′ig nā′tiv), *adj.* serving to designate.

des|ig|na|tor (dez′ig nā′tər), *n.* a person or thing that designates.

des|ig|na|to|ry (dez′ig nə tôr′ē, -tōr′-), *adj.* = designative.

de|signed (di zīnd′), *adj.* planned; intended: *The route designed for us was closed to traffic.*

de|sign|ed|ly (di zī′nid lē), *adv.* by design; on purpose; intentionally. **SYN:** purposely.

des|ig|nee (dez′ig nē′), *n.* a person who is designated: *Such rules shall define the powers of the president or his designee with respect to disciplinary action* (New York Times).

design engineer, an engineer who plans each part of a device or structure and shows how the parts fit together and the materials to be used.

de|sign|er (di zī′nər), *n. adj.* **—*n.*** **1** a person who designs: *The dress designer made sketches and patterns for the new fall fashions of women's clothes.* **2** a plotter; schemer.
—*adj.* designed by and bearing the name of a fashion designer: *designer jeans.*

designer drug, *U.S.* a narcotic made so that it is not a chemically controlled substance: *"Designer drugs"—designed ... by underground chemists who tinker with the molecular structure of illegal narcotics to produce variants that are not explicitly banned by federal law* (Time).

de|sign|ing (di zī′ning), *adj., n.* **—*adj.*** **1** scheming; plotting: *The designing widow soon had the handsome bachelor in her net.* **2** showing plan or forethought. **—*n.*** the art of making designs, patterns, or sketches. **—de|sign′ing|ly,** *adv.*

de|sign|less (di zīn′lis), *adj.* without design, plan, or purpose; aimless; heedless.

de|sign|ment (di zīn′mənt), *n. Obsolete.* designation; design.

de|silt (dē silt′), *v.t.* to free (water) of silt: [*In*] *desilting basins ... sediment is removed* (Time).

de|sil|ver|i|za|tion (dē sil′vər ə zā′shən), *n.* the act or process of desilverizing.

de|sil|ver|ize (dē sil′və rīz), *v.t.,* **-ized, -iz|ing.** to remove the silver from.

des|i|nence (des′ə nəns), *n.* **1** termination; ending. **2** *Grammar.* a termination, suffix, or ending of a word. [< French *désinence,* ultimately < Latin *dēsinere* to close < *dē-* off + *sinere* to leave]

de|sip|i|ence (di sip′ē əns), *n.* silliness; trifling; nonsense. [< Latin *dēsipientia* < *dēsipere* lack understanding < *dē-* un- + *sapere* to know]

de|sip|i|ent (di sip′ē ənt), *adj.* trifling; foolish; playful.

de|sip|ra|mine (də zip′rə mēn), *n.* a drug used as an antidepressant or psychic energizer. *Formula:* $C_{18}H_{22}N_2$ [short for *des*(methyl)*i*(mi)*pramine,* its chemical name]

de|sir|a|bil|i|ty (di zīr′ə bil′ə tē), *n.* **1** *no pl.* the state or quality of being desirable: *Nobody doubts the desirability of good health.* **2** *pl.* **-ties.** a desirable condition or thing: *various desirabilities to choose from.*

de|sir|a|ble (di zīr′ə bəl), *adj., n.* **—*adj.*** worth wishing for; worth having; pleasing; good: *a quiet, desirable neighborhood. Main Street is a very desirable location for a large department store.* **SYN:** excellent. **—*n.*** a desirable person or thing. **—de|sir′a|ble|ness,** *n.*

de|sir|a|bly (di zīr′ə blē), *adv.* in a desirable manner.

de|sire (di zīr′), *n., v.,* **-sired, -sir|ing.** **—*n.*** **1** a wanting or longing; strong wish: *His desire is to travel. His predominant passion was desire of money* (Samuel Johnson). **2** a wish expressed in words; request: *I sent you, at your desire, the articles you wanted.* **3** a thing wished for: *His greatest desire was a bicycle. The desire of all nations is peace.* **4** sensual appetite; lust.
—*v.t.* **1** to wish earnestly for; long for: *The orphan desired love and approval.* **SYN:** long, yearn, crave. See syn. under **wish.** **2** to express a wish for; ask for: *The principal desires your presence in his office. I desired a room for the night.* **3** *Archaic.* to miss; regret the loss of. **4** *Obsolete.* to invite. **—*v.i.*** to have or feel a desire. **SYN:** long, yearn, crave. See syn. under **wish.**
[< Old French *desirer* < Latin *dēsīderāre* long for; (originally) to await the fate which the stars bring < *dē-* from + *sīdus, -eris* constellation. See etym. of doublet **desiderate.**] **—de|sir′er,** *n.*
—*Syn. n.* **1 Desire, longing, craving** mean a strong wish. **Desire** applies to any strong wish, good or bad, for something a person thinks or hopes he can get: *She felt a great desire to see her birthplace again.* **Longing** applies to an earnest or enduring desire, sometimes for something a person thinks he can get if he tries or wishes hard enough, but often for something that seems beyond reach: *the longing for the return of spring. His longing for a bicycle is pathetic.* **Craving** applies to a desire so strong that it amounts to a need or hunger: *a craving for excitement, a craving for candy.*

de|sir|ous (di zī′rəs), *adj.* **1** desiring; wishing; eager: *She is desirous of going to France on her vacation.* **2** *Obsolete.* desirable. **—de|sir′ous|ly,** *adv.* **—de|sir′ous|ness,** *n.*

de|sist (di zist′), *v.i.* to stop doing something; cease: *Desist at once! Men should therefore desist from this enormous crime* (Henry Fielding). [< Old French *desister*, learned borrowing from Latin *dēsistere* < *dē-* (intensive) + *sistere* stop, cause to stand < *stāre* stand]

de|sist|ance or **de|sist|ence** (di zis′tәns), *n.* a ceasing to act or proceed; stopping.

de|si|tion (di sish′әn), *n.* an ending; end; conclusion. [< Latin *dēsitus*, past participle of *dēsinere* (see etym. under **desinence**) + English *-ion*]

de|siz|ing (dē sī′zing), *n.* the process of removing size from cloth. [< *de-* + *size*² + *-ing*]

desk (desk), *n., adj., v.* **—*n.*** **1** a piece of furniture with a flat or sloping top on which to write or rest books for reading. A desk often has drawers. **2** any similar piece of furniture, such as a lectern or pulpit. **3** a stand for holding sheet music; musician's stand. **4** a department of work at a certain location or at a desk: *the information desk of a library, the copy desk of a newspaper.*
—*adj.* **1** for use on or at a desk: *a desk blotter, a desk calendar, a desk calculator.* **2** stationed at a desk in a certain capacity: *a desk sergeant. After husky . . . bellhops took possession of the baggage, the desk clerk directed us to the Intourist office, off the lobby* (Maclean's).
—*v.t.* to station at or assign to work at a desk, especially as compared to more vigorous activity: *to desk a pilot.*
[< Medieval Latin *desca* < Italian *desco* < Latin *discus* quoit, platter < Greek *dískos.* See etym. of doublets **dais, discus, dish, disk.**]

desk|bound (desk′bound′), *adj.* **1** confined to work at a desk: *a deskbound clerk, deskbound functionaries.* **2** more inclined to sit down than to be active: *a deskbound executive.*

de|skill (dē skil′), *v.t.* to reduce (a job or operation) to simple parts requiring no skill, especially through automation and specialization: *Many crafts have in fact become deskilled* (New Scientist).

desk|less (desk′lis), *adj.* without a desk: *a deskless room.*

desk|man (desk′man′), *n., pl.* **-men.** **1** an editor assigned to the copy desk in a newspaper office. **2** a person who does deskwork.

desk|mate (desk′māt′), *n.* a student who shares a desk with another in a classroom.

desk study, *British.* a study made without extensive field and laboratory investigation.

desk|top (desk′top′), *adj.* designed to be used or placed on top of a desk; tabletop: *a desktop computer.*

desktop publisher, person who uses a small computer to produce typeset copy for printing and distribution.

desktop publishing, electronic typesetting and the design and creation of charts, tables, and other graphics, prepared on small computers for printing: *Desktop publishing moved to the forefront of new and efficient ways to use personal computers . . . for easy and inexpensive preparation of school newspapers, corporate reports, and virtually any other publication that combines text and graphics on the same page* (J. Schefter). *Abbr:* DTP

desk|work (desk′wėrk′), *n.* work done or to be done at a desk: *. . . deskwork galore, throwing bits of vaguely worded papers from tray to tray* (Atlantic).

D. ès L., Doctor of Letters (French, *Docteur ès Lettres*).

des|ma (des′mә), *n., pl.* **-ma|ta** (-mә tә). an irregular spicule of a sponge. [< New Latin *desma* < Greek *désma* band < *deîn* to bind]

des|man (des′mәn), *n., pl.* **-mans.** either of two molelike, aquatic, insect-eating mammals of the Soviet Union and of the Pyrenees. They secrete musk. [< Swedish *desman-*(råtta) musk(rat)]

Des|mas (des′mas), *n.* = Dismas.

des|mid (des′mid), *n.* any one of a large group of microscopic, single-celled, freshwater, green algae of widely varying form. The cell is typically divided into distinct halves by a constriction. [< New Latin *Desmidium* the genus name (diminutive) < Greek *desmós* chain, band, bond]

des|mid|i|an (des mid′ē әn), *adj., n.* **—*adj.*** of or having to do with the desmids.
—*n.* = desmid.

des|mo|gen (des′mә jәn), *n.* the embryonic tissue of plants. [< Greek *desmós* chain, bond + English *-gen*]

des|moid (des′moid), *adj., n.* **—*adj.*** **1** *Anatomy.* resembling a ligament. **2** *Medicine.* interwoven in bundles; fibrous: *a desmoid tumor.*
—*n.* *Medicine.* a desmoid tumor.
[< Greek *desmós* chain, band, and *desmê* bundle + English *-oid*]

des|mo|sine (des′mә sīn), *n.* an amino acid that serves as a cross-link for molecules of elastin: *Desmosine [is] probably largely responsible for the elasticity and stability of elastin, the main protein of the aortic wall* (Scientific American). [< Greek *desmós* chain, bond + English *-ine*²]

des|mo|some (des′mә sōm), *n.* an adhesive part of an epithelial cell by which it adheres to adjoining cells: *The epithelial cells . . . are attached to one another at sites called desmosomes, each of which is somewhat like a spot weld* (Scientific American). [< Greek *desmós* chain, bond + English *-some*³]

de|so|cial|i|za|tion (dē sō′shә lә zā′shәn), *n.* **1** removal from society or from a social environment: *Worse even than locked doors was the intimate desocialization and dehumanization of the patients* (Time). **2** the removal of the principles or practice of socialism from an industry, government, etc.: *If desocialization of steel isn't finished by then, a victorious Labor Party could more easily carry out its . . . threat to reimpose state ownership on steel* (Wall Street Journal).

de|so|cial|ize (dē sō′shә līz), *v.t.,* **-ized, -iz|ing.** to subject to desocialization: *Darkness isolates and desocializes the citizen* (Harper's). **—de|so′cial|iz′er,** *n.*

dés|oeu|vre|ment (dā zœ vrә mäɴ′), *n. French.* idleness; lack of occupation: *I have nothing to write you, and write . . . from mere désoeuvrement* (Longfellow).

des|o|late (*adj.* des′ә lit; *v.* des′ә lāt), *adj., v.,* **-lat|ed, -lat|ing.** **—*adj.*** **1** not producing anything; laid waste; devastated; barren: *desolate land.* **SYN:** ravaged. **2** not lived in; deserted: *a desolate house.* **SYN:** uninhabited. **3** unhappy; forlorn; wretched: *The hungry child looked desolate. The unemployed, by and large, are not the desolate-looking or acting lot of the 1930's* (Wall Street Journal). **4** left alone; solitary; lonely: *No one so utterly desolate, But some heart, though unknown, Responds unto his own* (Longfellow). **SYN:** forsaken. **5** dreary; dismal: *a desolate life.*
—*v.t.* **1** to make unfit to live in; lay waste: *The Vikings desolated the lands they attacked.* **SYN:** devastate. **2** to make unhappy or forlorn: *We are desolated to hear that you are going away.* **3** to deprive of inhabitants. **SYN:** depopulate.
[< Latin *dēsōlātus*, past participle of *dēsōlāre* < *dē-* (intensive) + *sōlus* alone] **—des′o|late|ly,** *adv.* **—des′o|late|ness,** *n.*
—*Syn.* *adj.* **3 Desolate, disconsolate** mean unhappy and forlorn. **Desolate** implies feeling left alone, deserted by everyone, or, especially, separated from someone dear: *I was desolate when my mother died.* **Disconsolate** implies absence of hope, consolation, and comfort: *I was disconsolate when I lost my job and was unable to get another for several months.*

des|o|lat|er (des′ә lā′tәr), *n.* = desolator.

des|o|la|tion (des′ә lā′shәn), *n.* **1** the act of making desolate: *the desolation of the country by an invading army.* **SYN:** devastation. **2** a ruined, lonely, or deserted condition: *After the fire the forest land was in complete desolation. He described the utter desolation of the American Indians. Yon dreary plain . . . the seat of desolation* (Milton). **SYN:** ruin, barrenness. **3** a desolate place: *The old prospector lived in the desolation of the California hills.* **4** sadness; lonely sorrow: *desolation at the loss of loved ones.* **SYN:** grief.

des|o|la|tor (des′ә lā′tәr), *n.* a person or thing that desolates.

de|sorb (dē sôrb′, -zôrb′), *v.t.* to release (a gas or other substance) from a condition of being adsorbed or absorbed: *The gas removed from a leak-tight vessel at low pressures is that desorbed from the walls of the apparatus and the materials held in the vacuum* (New Scientist).
—*v.i.* to be or become desorbed.

dés|o|ri|en|té (dā zô ryäɴ tā′), *adj. French.* having lost one's bearings; disoriented.

de|sorp|tion (dē sôrp′shәn, -zôrp′-), *n.* the process of desorbing: *Even after the most careful preparation, desorption from the walls of the system constitutes a major source of the residual gas that keeps dribbling into an ultra-high-vacuum system* (Scientific American).

des|oxy|y|cho|lic acid (des ok′sә kō′lik, -kol′ik), = deoxycholic acid.

des|ox|y|cor|ti|cos|ter|one (des ok′sә kôr′tәkos′tә rōn), *n.* = deoxycorticosterone.

des|ox|y|ri|bo|nu|cle|ase (des ok′sә rī′bō nü′klē ās, -nyü′-), *n.* = deoxyribonuclease.

des|ox|y|ri|bo|nu|cle|ic acid (des ok′sә rī′bō-nü klē′ik, -nyü-), = deoxyribonucleic acid.

des|ox|y|ri|bose nucleic acid (des ok′sә rī′-bōs), = deoxyribonucleic acid.

de|spair (di spãr′), *n., v.* **—*n.*** **1** the loss of hope; state of being without hope; a dreadful feeling that nothing good can happen: *Despair seized us as we felt the boat sinking under us.* **SYN:** hopelessness. **2** a person or thing that causes despair: *Her temper tantrums were the despair of her parents.*
—*v.i.* to lose hope; be without hope: *The doctors despaired of saving the sick man's life.*
—*v.t.* *Archaic.* to give up hope of.
[< Old French *despoir* < *desperer* to despair < Latin *dēspērāre* < *dē-* without, out of + *spērāre* to hope] **—de|spair′er,** *n.*
—*Syn.* *n.* **1 Despair, desperation** mean hopelessness. **Despair** emphasizes loss of hope and usually suggests sinking into a state of discouragement: *In his despair over losing his job he fell in with bad companions.* **Desperation** suggests a recklessness that is caused by despair and is expressed in rash or frantic action as a last resort: *He had no job and no money, and in desperation robbed a bank.*

de|spair|ful (di spãr′fәl), *adj.* full of despair; despairing. **—de|spair′ful|ly,** *adv.*

de|spair|ing (di spãr′ing), *adj.* feeling, showing, or expressing despair; hopeless: *a despairing cry.* **SYN:** See syn. under **hopeless.** **—de|spair′ing|ly,** *adv.* **—de|spair′ing|ness,** *n.*

des|patch (dis pach′), *v.t., v.i., n.* = dispatch. **—des|patch′er,** *n.*

des|per|a|do (des′pә rā′dō, -rā′-), *n., pl.* **-does** or **-dos.** a bold, reckless criminal; dangerous outlaw: *Billy the Kid and Jesse James were two famous desperadoes of the Wild West.* [< Old Spanish *desperado* (literally) past participle of *desperar* to despair < Latin *dēspērāre*; see etym. under **despair.** See related etym. at **desperate.**]

des|per|ate (des′pәr it, des′prit), *adj.* **1** not caring what happens because hope is gone; reckless because of despair; violent: *Suicide is a desperate act.* **2** ready to run any risk: *a desperate robber.* **3** having little chance for hope or cure; very dangerous or serious: *a desperate illness.* **4** extremely bad; extreme; excessive: *The poor farmer lived in desperate circumstances.* **5** hopeless: *Lying is the last desperate resort of fools.* **SYN:** See syn. under **hopeless.** [< Latin *dēspērātus*, past participle of *dēspērāre*; see etym. under **despair.** See related etym. at **desperado.**] **—des′per|ate|ly,** *adv.* **—des′per|ate-ness,** *n.*

des|per|a|tion (des′pә rā′shәn), *n.* **1** a hopeless or reckless feeling; readiness to run any risk: *They jumped out of the window in desperation when they saw that the stairs were on fire.* **SYN:** See syn. under **despair.** **2** the act or fact of despairing.

des|pi|ca|bil|i|ty (des′pi kә bil′ә tē, des pik′ә-bil′-), *n.* a being despicable.

des|pi|ca|ble (des′pi kә bәl, des pik′ә-), *adj.* to be despised; contemptible: *Cowards and liars are despicable. It is despicable to go away and leave a cat behind to starve.* **SYN:** vile, base. [< Late Latin *dēspicābilis* < Latin *dēspicārī* despise < *dē-* down + *specere* look] **—des′pi|ca|ble|ness,** *n.*

des|pi|ca|bly (des′pi kә blē, des pik′ә-), *adv.* in a despicable manner; contemptibly.

de|spight (di spīt′), *n. Obsolete.* despite.

de|spin (dē spin′), *v.t., v.i.,* **-spun, -spin|ning.** to neutralize the effect of revolving motion by revolving an attached object in the opposite direction at the same speed: *To maintain permanent radio illumination of the Earth the horn aerial mounted at one axis is mechanically despun in the opposite direction to spin stabilization* (Science Journal).

de|spir|i|tu|al|ize (dē spir′ә chü ә līz), *v.t.,* **-ized, -iz|ing.** to deprive of spiritual character; affect with worldliness or materialism: *to despiritualize religion.*

de|spis|a|ble (di spī′zә bәl), *adj.* deserving to be despised; despicable.

de|spise (di spīz′), *v.t.,* **-spised, -spis|ing.** to look down upon; scorn; think of as beneath one's notice, or as too mean or low for one to do: *I despise baseball but I love basketball. Fools despise wisdom and instruction* (Proverbs 1:7). **SYN:** disdain, contemn. [< Old French *despis-*, stem of *despire* < Latin *dēspicere* < *dē-* down + *specere* look at. Compare etym. under **despicable.**] **—de-spis′er,** *n.*

de|spite (di spīt′), *prep., n., v.,* **-spit|ed, -spit|ing.**
—*prep.* in spite of: *The boys went for a walk despite the rain. Despite various drawbacks, India is determined to raise her standard of living* (Atlantic). [< noun]
—*n.* **1** insult or injury: *The hero avenged the despite done to his brother.* **2** malice; spite. **3** contempt; scorn: *The Globe developed a despite for the entire leadership of the Conservative Party* (Canada Month).
—*v.t.* *Archaic.* **1** to regard or treat with contempt. **2** to offend; vex.
in despite of, in spite of: *[They] seized my hand in despite of my efforts to the contrary* (Washington Irving).

Pronunciation Key: hat, āge, cãre, fär; let, ēqual, tėrm; it, īce; hot, ōpen, ôrder; oil, out; cup, pu̇t, rüle; child; long; thin; ᴛʜen; zh, measure; ә represents **a** in about, **e** in taken, **i** in pencil, **o** in lemon, **u** in circus.

[< Old French *despit* < Latin *dēspectus, -ūs* a looking down upon < *dēspicere;* see etym. under **despise**]

de|spite|ful (di spīt′fəl), *adj.* spiteful; malicious. —**de|spite′ful|ly,** *adv.* —**de|spite′ful|ness,** *n.*

des|pit|e|ous (des pit′ē əs), *adj. Archaic.* **1** contemptuous. **2** malicious; spiteful. [variant of Middle English *despitous* < Anglo-French < Old French *despit;* see etym. under **despite**] —**des·pit′e|ous|ly,** *adv.*

de|spoil (di spoil′), *v.t.* to strip of possessions; rob; plunder: *The cities of Greece and Asia were despoiled of their most valuable ornaments* (Edward Gibbon). [< Old French *despoillier* < Latin *dēspoliāre* < *dē-* (intensive) + *spoliāre* to spoil < *spolium* armor, booty] —**de|spoil′er,** *n.*

de|spoil|ment (di spoil′mənt), *n.* = despoliation.

de|spo|li|a|tion (di spō′lē ā′shən), *n.* robbery; plundering; pillage.

de|spond (di spond′), *v., n.* —*v.i.* to lose heart, courage, or hope: *Though very ill, he did not despond.*

—*n. Archaic.* despondency.

[< Latin *dēspondēre* lose courage, despair, give up < *dē-* down + *spondēre* to promise] —**de·spond′er,** *n.*

de|spond|ence (di spon′dəns), *n.* = despondency.

de|spond|en|cy (di spon′dən sē), *n.* a loss of heart, courage, or hope; discouragement; dejection: *Many disappointments caused his despondency and the old man retired to his farm to lead a hermit's life.*

de|spond|ent (di spon′dənt), *adj., n.* —*adj.* having lost heart, courage, or hope; discouraged; dejected: *Long lines of despondent-looking people lined up before the counter leading to Information Department* (New Yorker).

—*n.* a person who desponds. —**de|spond′ent|ly,** *adv.*

de|spond|ing (di spon′ding), *adj.* = despondent. —**de|spond′ing|ly,** *adv.*

des|pot (des′pət, -pot), *n.* **1** a monarch having unlimited power; absolute ruler: *In ancient times many rulers were despots.* **2** a person who does just as he likes; one who exercises tyrannical power; tyrant or oppressor. **3** a title meaning "master" or "lord," used in Byzantine times to refer to an emperor, or a ruler of one of certain local Byzantine states. **4a** a bishop or patriarch in the Greek Church. **b** a noble, prince, or military leader in Italian cities in the 1300's and 1400's. [< Middle French *despot,* learned borrowing from Medieval Greek *despótēs* absolute ruler, master < Greek, master (of the household)]

des|pot|ic (des pot′ik), *adj.* of a despot; having unlimited power; tyrannical.

des|pot|i|cal (des pot′ə kəl), *adj. Obsolete.* despotic.

des|pot|i|cal|ly (des pot′ə klē), *adv.* in a despotic manner; with absolute power: *In those days the father of the house ruled despotically.*

des|pot|ism (des′pə tiz əm), *n.* **1** government by a monarch having unlimited power. **2** tyranny or oppression. **3** *Figurative.* absolute power or control: *Such is the despotism of the imagination over uncultivated minds* (Macaulay).

de|spu|mate (di spyü′māt, des′pyü-), *v.,* **-mat|ed, -mat|ing.** —*v.t.* to skim; free (a liquid) of impurities; clarify.

—*v.i.* to become free of impurities.

[< Latin *dēspūmāre* (with English *-ate*[1]) < *dē-* from + *spūma* foam, scum]

des|pu|ma|tion (des′pyü mā′shən), *n.* a skimming or being skimmed.

de|spun (dē spun′), *v.* the past tense and past participle of **despin.**

des|qua|mate (des′kwə māt), *v.i.,* **-mat|ed, -mat·ing.** to come off in scales, as the epidermis in certain diseases; peel off. [< Latin *dēsquāmāre* (with English *-ate*[1]) < *dē-* off + *squāma* scale (of a fish, etc.)]

des|qua|ma|tion (des′kwə mā′shən), *n.* **1** a coming off in scales; peeling: *the desquamation following a bad sunburn.* **2** a thing that comes off in scales.

des|qua|ma|tive (di skwam′ə tiv), *adj.* having to do with desquamation.

des|qua|ma|to|ry (di skwam′ə tôr′ē, -tōr′-), *adj.* = desquamative.

D. ès S., Doctor of Sciences (French, *Docteur ès Sciences*).

des|sert (di zėrt′), *n., adj.* —*n.* a course of sweets or fruit at the end of a meal. In the United States, pie, cake, ice cream, fruit, and pudding are desserts. In Great Britain, "dessert" often means fruit, candy, or nuts.

—*adj.* of or used for the dessert: *dessert forks, dessert plates.*

[< Middle French *dessert* removal of main course < *desservir* clear the table < *des-* un- (< Latin *dis-*) + Old French *servir* to serve]

des|sert|spoon (di zėrt′spün′), *n.* a spoon larger than a teaspoon and smaller than a tablespoon, used in eating desserts.

des|sert|spoon|ful (di zėrt′spün′fu̇l), *n., pl.* **-fuls.** as much as a dessertspoon can hold; approximately 2½ fluid drams.

dessert wine, any one of various sweet wines often served with or after dessert, such as port, sherry, and Tokay.

des|sia|tine (des′yə tēn), *n.* a Russian unit of land measure, about 2.7 acres. [< Russian *desjatina*]

des|sous des cartes (də sü′dā kärt′), *French.* **1** the inside facts of a case; something not generally revealed. **2** (literally) the underside of the cards.

de|sta|bi|li|za|tion (dē stā′bə lə zā′shən), *n.* the act or process of destabilizing.

de|sta|bi|lize (dē stā′bə līz), *v.t.,* **-lized, -liz|ing.** to deprive of stability; make unsteady: *to destabilize a government.*

de|stain (dē stān′), *v.t., v.i.* to remove stain from (a microscopic specimen): *The alcohol tends to bleach the dye. The slide must be watched carefully ... to prevent total destaining* (Scientific American).

de|sta|lin|i|za|tion (dē stä′lə nə zā′shən), *n.* the systematic effort by the leaders of the Communist Party in the Soviet Union to discredit the reputation and dissociate themselves from the political principles and methods of Joseph Stalin: *Her stay in Russia coincided with the thaw that followed destalinization* (Time).

de|sta|lin|ize (dē stä′lə nīz), *v.t.,* **-ized, -iz|ing.** to subject to destalinization: *The Russians and their satellites were busy destalinizing their cities, changing Stalingrad's name to Volgograd and Stalino to Donetsk* (John R. Kerstetter).

de|ster|i|lize (dē ster′ə līz), *v.t.,* **-lized, -liz|ing.** to return to productive use (gold previously idle) in order to back a new issue of currency, support credit expansion, or the like.

***De Stijl** (də stīl′), a movement in modern art, originating in Holland in 1917, emphasizing abstract and geometric forms, especially rectangles, and the use of black and white and the primary colors; neoplasticism. [< Dutch *De Stijl* (literally) The Style, a magazine devoted to this movement, published from 1917 to 1928]

***De Stijl**

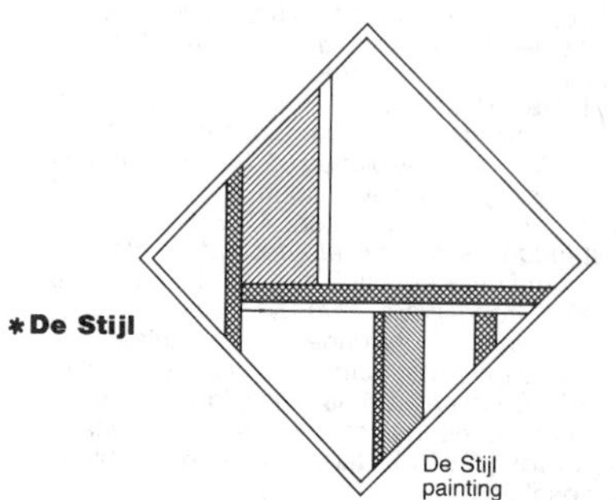

De Stijl painting

des|ti|na|tion (des′tə nā′shən), *n.* **1** the place to which a person or thing is going or is being sent: *the destination of a ship, letter, or package.* **2** a setting apart for a particular purpose or use; intention: *The destination of his study is the law.*

des|tine (des′tən), *v.t.,* **-tined, -tin|ing. 1** to set apart for a purpose or use; intend: *The prince was destined from his birth to be a king.* **2** to cause by fate: *My letter was destined never to reach him. We are decreed, Reserved, and destined to eternal woe* (Milton).

destined for, a intended to go to; bound for: *ships destined for England.* **b** intended for: *destined for the ministry.*

[< Old French *destiner* < Latin *dēstināre* determine, make fast, ultimately < *dē-* (intensive) + *stāre* to stand]

des|ti|ny (des′tə nē), *n., pl.* **-nies. 1** what becomes of a person or thing in the end; one's lot or fortune: *It was young Washington's destiny to become the first President of the United States. Within limits man now controls his destiny* (Atlantic). **SYN:** See syn. under **fate. 2** what will happen, believed to be determined beforehand in spite of all later efforts to change or prevent it: *He struggled in vain against his destiny. Marriage and hanging go by destiny* (Robert Burton). **3** the power that is believed to determine the course of events; overruling necessity; fate: *She felt that destiny had been unkind to her in making her poor.*

Des|ti|ny (des′tə nē), *n., pl.* **-nies.** *Greek and Roman Mythology.* the goddess of destiny.

the Destinies, the Fates; the powers supposed to preside over human life: *I shall not allow the Destinies to have had an hand in the deaths of the several thousands who have been slain in the late war* (Joseph Addison).

[< *destiny*]

des|ti|tute (des′tə tüt, -tyüt), *adj., n.* —*adj.* **1** lacking necessary things, such as food, clothing, and shelter: *A destitute family needs help from charity.* **2** *Obsolete.* abandoned; forsaken; deserted.

—*n.* Usually, **the destitute,** a destitute person or persons: *The destitute filled the streets after the earthquake.*

destitute of, having no; empty of; without: *A bald head is destitute of hair.*

[< Latin *dēstitutus,* past participle of *dēstituere* forsake < *dē-* away + *statuere* put, place] —**des′·ti|tute|ness,** *n.*

des|ti|tu|tion (des′tə tü′shən, -tyü′-), *n.* **1** a lack of the means of living; extreme poverty: *Destitution is the mark of the slums.* **SYN:** See syn. under **poverty. 2** the state of being without; lack: *Destitution and destruction are the results of war.*

de|stock (dē stok′), *v.t. Especially British.* to deplete the stock or livestock of: *The drought and floods have destocked the Masai* (Manchester Guardian Weekly).

de|stool (dē stül′), *v.t.* (in western Africa) to depose (a chief): *Every Ashanti chief has a stool, generally a low, slightly concave bench ... , and when a ruler is deposed, he is said to be destooled* (New Yorker).

de|stool|ment (dē stül′mənt), *n.* a destooling: *Failure to accept such guidance and advice was a legitimate cause for destoolment* (Robert S. Rattray).

de|stress (dē stres′), *v.t.* to eliminate excess strain on: *Immediate measures to guarantee the track's safety and eventual destressing* (*a heating process*) *of the entire existing mileage should prevent further serious trouble on these lines* (London Times).

des|tri|er (des′trē ər, des trir′), *n. Archaic.* a war horse; charger. [< Anglo-French *destrer,* Old French *destrier* < *destre* right hand < Latin *dextera* (*manus*) right (hand) (because it was led by the right hand of the squire)]

de|stroy (di stroi′), *v.t.* **1** to break to pieces; make useless; spoil; ruin: *Careless children destroy all their toys. Drought destroyed the corn crop.* **2** to put an end to; do away with: *A heavy rain destroyed all hope of a picnic.* **SYN:** abolish, extinguish. **3** to deprive of life; kill: *Fire destroys many trees every year.* **4** to counteract the effect of; make void: *A child's confidence can be destroyed by correcting his every move. The exceptions do not destroy the authority of the rule* (Macaulay). —*v.i.* to be destructive; destroy things. [< Old French *destruire* < Vulgar Latin *dēstrūgere* < Latin *dēstruere* < *dē-* un-, down + *struere* pile, build] —**de|stroy′ing|ly,** *adv.*

—*Syn. v.t.* **1 Destroy, demolish** mean to pull down or wreck the structure of something. **Destroy** means to make useless by breaking to pieces, taking apart, killing, or in any other of many ways: *The paintings were completely destroyed in the fire.* **Demolish** means to ruin by tearing down or smashing to pieces and applies only to things thought of as having been built up, such as buildings or, figuratively, arguments and theories: *The city demolished many buildings to make room for the speedway.*

de|stroy|a|ble (di stroi′ə bəl), *adj.* that can be destroyed.

***de|stroy|er** (di stroi′ər), *n.* **1** a person or thing that destroys. **2** a small, fast warship with guns, torpedoes, and other weapons. A destroyer is used to attack submarines and as an escort vessel with merchant convoys or larger warships. *Destroyers are the cavalry of the sea, fast, fierce scouts who rode herd on our convoys and flattops and drove the U-boat to bay* (Atlantic).

***destroyer** definition 2

***destroyer escort**

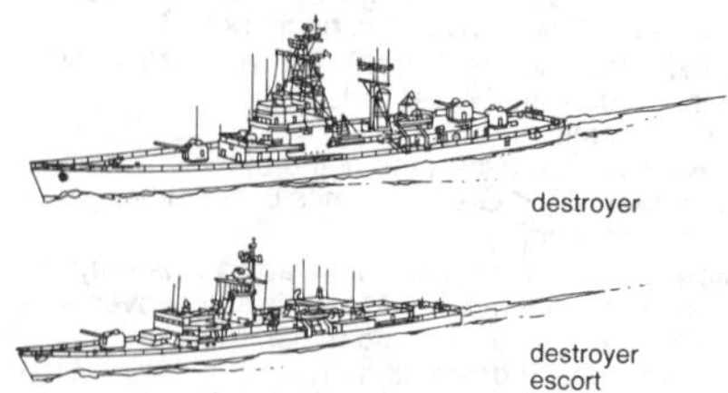

destroyer

destroyer escort

De|stroy|er (di stroi′ər), *n.* = Siva.

***destroyer escort,** a warship similar to a destroyer but somewhat smaller: *He got the Legion of Merit for a brilliant training job commanding the Atlantic Fleet's Bermuda-based shakedown group for new destroyers and destroyer escorts* (Time).

de|stroy|ing angel (di stroi′ing), a very poisonous mushroom; amanita.
Destroying Angel, a member of an alleged secret order of Mormons; Danite.
de|struct (di strukt′), *v., n. U.S. Aerospace.* —***v.t., v.i.*** to blow up a rocket or other missile that fails to function properly: *The Air Force ... must "destruct," as they put it, some 10 per cent of their test missiles to forestall their running berserk* (Newsweek).
—***n.*** the destructing of a rocket or missile. [back formation < *destruction*]
de|struct|i|bil|i|ty (di struk′tə bil′ə tē), *n.* the quality of being destructible.
de|struct|i|ble (di struk′tə bəl), *adj.* that can be destroyed. —**de|struct′i|ble|ness,** *n.*
de|struc|tion (di struk′shən), *n.* **1** the act of destroying: *A bulldozer was used in the destruction of the old barn.* **2** the state of being destroyed; ruin: *The storm left destruction behind it. The great fire caused the city's destruction.* **SYN:** See syn. under **ruin. 3** a thing that destroys; cause or means of destroying: *The destruction of the poor is their poverty* (Proverbs 10:15). [< Latin *dēstrūctiō, -ōnis* < *dēstruere;* see etym. under **destroy**]
de|struc|tion|al (di struk′shə nəl), *adj.* of, having to do with, or produced by destruction or destructive forces.
de|struc|tion|ist (di struk′shə nist), *n.* a person who believes in the policy of destroying existing political institutions.
de|struc|tive (di struk′tiv), *adj.* **1** tending to destroy; liable to cause destruction: *Termites are destructive insects.* **2** destroying; causing destruction: *Fires and earthquakes are destructive.* **3** tearing down; not helpful; not constructive: *Destructive criticism shows things to be wrong, but does not show how to correct them.* —**de|struc′tive|ly,** *adv.* —**de|struc′tive|ness,** *n.*
destructive distillation, *Chemistry.* the decomposition of a substance, such as wood or coal, by strong heat in a closed container, and the collection of the volatile matters evolved; dry distillation.
de|struc|tiv|i|ty (dē′struk tiv′ə tē, di struk′-), *n.* = destructiveness.
de|struc|tor (di struk′tər), *n.* **1** a furnace or incinerator for the burning of refuse. **2** something that destructs, especially an explosive for blowing up a missile or rocket under testing.
de|struc|tur|al|ize (dē struk′chər ə līz), *v.t.,* **-ized, -iz|ing.** to undo or take apart; disorganize.
de|sub|stan|ti|ate (dē′səb stan′shē āt), *v.t.,* **-at|ed, -at|ing.** to deprive of substance.
des|u|da|tion (des′yü dā′shən), *n. Medicine.* heavy or abnormal sweating. [< Latin *dēsūdātiō, -ōnis* < *dēsūdāre* sweat heavily < *dē-* (intensive) + *sūdāre* to sweat]
de|suete (di swēt′), *adj.* outdated; outmoded: ... *our artistic history and heritage we learn backwards, astonished to find what were once hailed as strokes of trenchant originality emerging from earlier now neglected and desuete masters* (Philip Hope-Wallace). [< French *désuète* < Latin *dēsuētus,* past participle of *dēsuēscere* put out of use; see etym. under **desuetude**]
des|ue|tude (des′wə tüd, -tyüd), *n.* disuse: *Many words once commonly used have fallen into desuetude.* [< French *désuétude,* learned borrowing from Latin *dēsuētūdō, -inis* < *dēsuēscere* put out of use < *dē-* away, from + *suēscere* to become used to]
de|sul|fur or **de|sul|phur** (dē sul′fər), *v.t.* to free from sulfur; desulfurize.
de|sul|fu|rate or **de|sul|phu|rate** (dē sul′fyə rāt, -fə-), *v.t.,* **-rat|ed, -rat|ing.** = desulfurize.
de|sul|fu|ri|za|tion or **de|sul|phu|ri|za|tion** (dē sul′fər ə zā′shən, -fyər-), *n.* the act or process of desulfurizing: *The melting and refining process is to be done in an electric furnace, said to offer the best metallurgical condition for desulphurization* (London Times).
de|sul|fu|rize or **de|sul|phu|rize** (dē sul′fə rīz, -fyə-), *v.t.,* **-rized, -riz|ing.** to free from sulfur; desulfur. —**de|sul′fu|riz′er, de|sul′phu|riz′er,** *n.*
de|sul|tor (di sul′tər), *n., pl.* **de|sul|tors, de|sul|to|res** (des′əl tôr′ēz, -tōr′-). a bareback rider in the Roman circus who rode two or more horses at once, leaping from one to another. [< Latin *dēsultor,* ultimately < *dē-* down + *salīre* to leap]
des|ul|to|ri|ly (des′əl tôr′ə lē, -tōr′-), *adv.* in a desultory or random manner; unmethodically: *Two boys from the school were playing desultorily at the other end of the yard, passing a football back and forth* (Harper's).
des|ul|to|ri|ness (des′əl tôr′ē nis, -tōr′-), *n.* the quality of being desultory; lack of method.
des|ul|to|ry (des′əl tôr′ē, -tōr′-), *adj.* **1** jumping from one thing to another; without aim or method; unconnected: *He read the book in a desultory manner, skipping chapters as he pleased. We talked in a desultory fashion* (Atlantic). **SYN:** aimless, fitful. **2** coming suddenly; random: *a desultory thought.* [< Latin *dēsultōrius* having to do with a leaper, ultimately < *dē-* down + *salīre* to jump, leap]
de|syn|on|y|mi|za|tion (dē′si non′ə mə zā′shən), *n.* the act or process of differentiating words.
de|syn|on|y|mize (dē′si non′ə mīz), *v.t.,* **-mized, -miz|ing.** to differentiate in meaning (words that appear to be synonyms).
DET (no periods), diethyltryptamine, a hallucinogenic drug.
Det., detective.
de|tach (di tach′), *v.t.* **1** to loosen and remove; unfasten; separate: *to detach a locomotive from a train. He detached his watch from the chain.* **2** to send away on special duty: *One squad of soldiers was detached to guard the road.* [< French *détacher* < *dé-* apart, un- (< Latin *dis-*) + *-tacher,* as in *attacher* attach] —**de|tach′er,** *n.*
de|tach|a|bil|i|ty (di tach′ə bil′ə tē), *n.* detachable quality or condition.
de|tach|a|ble (di tach′ə bəl), *adj.* that can be detached: *a notebook with detachable leaves.*
de|tached (di tacht′), *adj.* **1** separate from others; isolated; unattached: *A detached house is separated by land from neighboring houses.* **2** not influenced by others or by one's own interests and prejudices; impartial: *The judge listened to the claims of both sides with a detached air.* **3** reserved; aloof.
de|tach|ed|ly (di tach′id lē), *adv.* in a detached manner; disconnectedly; impartially: *Describe him as detachedly and clinically as possible* (Newsweek).
de|tach|ed|ness (di tach′id nis), *n.* the quality of being detached or of standing apart; separation; isolation.
de|tach|ment (di tach′mənt), *n.* **1** a taking apart; separation. **2** a lack of interest; standing apart; aloofness: *He watched the motion picture with detachment.* **3** freedom from prejudice or bias; impartial attitude: *Students were surprised at the professor's air of detachment in talking about his own books.* **4** a group of soldiers or ships sent away on some special duty: *The detonation tore the gun from its carriage, killed one member of the gun detachment, and seriously injured the other* (London Times). **5** the state of being on special duty: *a squad of soldiers on detachment.*
de|tail (di tāl′, dē′tāl; *see note below*), *n., v.* —***n.*** **1** a small or unimportant part; item; particular: *the details of a report. All the details of her costume carried out the brown color scheme. She does not enjoy the details of housekeeping.* **SYN:** See syn. under **item. 2** a dealing with small things one by one: *An engineer must have a grasp of detail. I will give you the broad outlines of the situation in Africa; there is not space to go into detail.* **3** a minute account; report of particulars: *We spend the first five minutes in a detail of symptoms* (Elisha K. Kane). **4a** a minor decoration or subordinate part in a building, picture, machine, etc. **b** such parts taken together: *The detail of the façade is more interesting than that of the interior.* **c** = detail drawing. **5a** the act of selecting a small group for some special duty. **b** a small group sent on some special duty: *The captain sent a detail of six soldiers to guard the bridge.* **SYN:** squad, detachment, party. **c** the special duty assigned to such a group.
—***v.t.*** **1** to tell fully; tell even the small and unimportant parts: *to detail a plan. The new boy detailed to us all the wonders he had seen in his travels.* **2** to select for or send on special duty: *Policemen were detailed to hold back the crowd watching the parade.*
in detail, with all the details; part by part: *Without concert ... without a leader, they would be destroyed in detail* (James A. Froude).
[< French *détail* < *détailler* cut in pieces, to relate in detail < *dé-* (intensive) (< Latin *dē-*) + *tailler* to cut] —**de|tail′er,** *n.*
▶ **detail.** Pronunciation of the noun is divided: di|tāl′ or dē′tāl. The first is older; the second especially common in situations where the word is used a great deal (army life, architecture, and other specialized uses). The pronunciation dē′tāl is also frequently used for def. 2 of the verb.

***detail drawing**

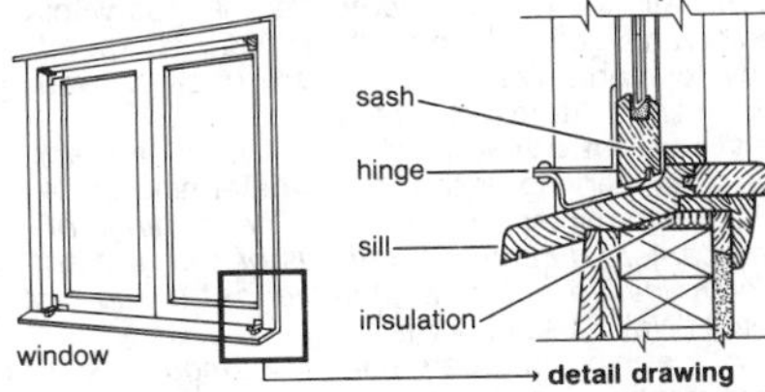

***detail drawing,** a drawing of a part of a building, machine, or apparatus, usually on a larger scale than the drawing of the whole, to show more clearly the relationship of parts, method of construction, or the like.
de|tailed (di tāld′, dē′tāld), *adj.* **1** full of details and particulars: *The witness gave a detailed account of the accident.* **2** exact; minute; particular: *With a microscope a scientist can make a detailed examination of bacteria.*
de|tail|ed|ly (di tā′lid lē), *adv.* in a detailed manner: *The president must know it as detailedly as he would a battle map* (Birmingham News).
de|tail|ed|ness (di tā′lid nis), *n.* detailed state or quality.
detail man, a person employed by a drug manufacturer to present his products to druggists, doctors, and hospitals: *A poll ... showed that 68% of doctors get their first information about a new drug from the detail man* (Wall Street Journal).
de|tain (di tān′), *v.t.* **1** to keep from going; hold back; delay; retard: *The heavy traffic detained us for almost an hour. I was detained ... partly by the rain, and partly by company that I liked very much* (William Cobbett). **2** to keep from going away; hold as a prisoner: *The police detained the suspected thief for questioning.* **SYN:** confine. **3** *Archaic.* to withhold. [< Old French *detenir* < Latin *dētinēre* < *dē-* from, away + *tenēre* hold] —**de|tain′ing|ly,** *adv.*
de|tain|ee (di tā′nē′), *n.* a person held in custody or confinement; prisoner: *Forty-one more Greek Cypriot political detainees held without trial were released yesterday* (Cape Times).
de|tain|er (di tā′nər), *n.* **1** a person or thing that detains. **2** *Law.* **a** a keeping possession of what belongs to another. **b** the detaining of a person in custody. **c** a writ for the further detention of a person already in custody.
de|tain|ment (di tān′mənt), *n.* = detention.
de|tas|sel (dē tas′əl), *v.t.* to remove the tassel of (a corn plant), especially to pollinate hybrid corn.
de|tect (di tekt′), *v.t.* **1** to find out; discover; catch: *The boy was detected stealing cookies in the pantry.* **2** to make out; discover the presence, existence, or fact of: *to detect an error in the account. Could you detect any odor in the room?* **3** *Radio, Television.* to separate the sound wave, or other signal being sent, from the carrier wave by a detector; demodulate. [< Latin *dētēctus,* past participle of *dētegere* < *dē-* un-, off + *tegere* to cover]
de|tect|a|bil|i|ty (di tek′tə bil′ə tē), *n.* the quality of being detectable: *the detectability of underground atomic explosions.*
de|tect|a|ble (di tek′tə bəl), *adj.* that can be detected: *Their shrill, brassy notes swept across the scrub of the airfield on the cold night air, so as to be just detectable to the crews above the purr of their engines* (Sunday Express).
de|tect|a|bly (di tek′tə blē), *adv.* in a detectable manner or way.
de|tec|ta|phone (di tek′tə fōn), *n.* a telephonic device able to pick up and transmit conversation from one room or place to another.
de|tect|er (di tek′tər), *n.* = detector.
de|tect|i|ble (di tek′tə bəl), *adj.* = detectable.
de|tec|tion (di tek′shən), *n.* **1** a finding out; discovery: *the detection of crimes or criminals.* **2** a being found out or discovered: *His detection will be a matter of only a few hours.* **3** *Radio, Television.* the separation in a receiving set of the sound wave, or other signal being sent, from the carrier wave; demodulation.
de|tec|tive (di tek′tiv), *n., adj.* —***n.*** **1** a policeman or other person whose business is to get information secretly, discovering who committed a crime or an act against another person: *In come the neighbors, the police ... arrive, along with a reporter and a photographer, the body is removed, and then appears the detective* (New Yorker). **2** a person who detects.
—***adj.*** **1** having to do with detectives and their work: *He liked reading detective stories.* **2** used in discovering or finding out: *Scientific detective methods are more accurate than guessing.*
de|tec|tiv|ism (di tek′tə viz əm), *n.* the work or activities of a detective: *a suspenseful piece of detectivism, literary detectivism.*
de|tec|tor (di tek′tər), *n.* **1** a person or thing that detects; detecter. **2** *Radio, Television.* a vacuum tube or other device in a receiving set that helps in the change of radio waves into sound waves by removing the carrier waves from the signal sent out by the microphone; demodulator. **3a** a simple, portable galvanometer for indicating the flow of a current of electricity, but not its strength. **b** any device used to determine the

Pronunciation Key: hat, āge, cãre, fär; let, ēqual, tėrm; it, īce; hot, ōpen, ôrder; **oil, out;** cup, pu̇t, rüle; **ch**ild; lo**ng**; **th**in; **ᴛʜ**en; **zh,** measure; **ə** represents **a** in about, **e** in taken, **i** in pencil, **o** in lemon, **u** in circus.

presence of electric waves, such as a coherer in a radio receiving set. **4** a device for causing the diaphragm of a telephone receiver to vibrate when a high-frequency current passes through. **5** a low-water indicator for a boiler. **6** *Obsolete.* an informer; accuser.

***detector car**, a car that travels over the rails of a railroad and discovers flaws with an electric detecting device.

***detector car**

det|en|ee (det′ə nē′), *n.* a person confined in a detention camp. [perhaps Anglicized form of French *détenu*]

de|tent (di tent′), *n.* any part of a mechanism that checks or releases motion, such as the catch in a lock, the catch that regulates a clock's striking, or a pawl. [< French *détente* < Old French *destente* < *destendre* slacken < *des-* from (< Latin *dis-*) + *tendre* stretch < Latin *tendere*]

dé|tente (dā tänt′), *n.* the easing of strained relations, especially between nations or political groups: *The huge and hoary obstacles in the way of a real détente remain* (Economist). [< French *détente;* see etym. under **detent**]

de|ten|tion (di ten′shən), *n.* **1** the act of detaining; act of holding back. **2** the condition of being detained; delay: *Detention after hours is a common punishment in school.* **3** the act of keeping in custody; confinement: *A jail is used for detention of persons who have been arrested.* **4** the act of keeping back; a withholding. Also, **detainment**. [< Late Latin *dētentiō, -ōnis* < Latin *dētinēre;* see etym. under **detain**]

detention camp, = concentration camp.

detention center, **1** *Especially British.* a reformatory. **2** a concentration camp.

detention home, a special building for the temporary housing of children who are called before a juvenile court to answer charges of delinquency.

dé|te|nu (dā tə ny′), *n. French.* a person detained in custody; prisoner.

dé|te|nue (dā tə ny′), *n. French.* feminine of **détenu**.

de|ter (di tėr′), *v.t.*, **-terred, -ter|ring.** to keep back; discourage or hinder; stop or prevent from acting or proceeding by fear or consideration of danger or trouble: *The extreme heat deterred us from going downtown. The barking dog deterred me from crossing the neighbor's yard. Lack of housing deters the ... location here of company headquarters* (New York Times). *Drugged with love as I was, why, nothing could deter me from marriage* (Saul Bellow). **SYN**: dissuade, restrain, prevent. [< Latin *dēterrēre* < *dē-* away + *terrēre* frighten]

de|terge (di tėrj′), *v.t.*, **-terged, -terg|ing.** **1** to wipe away; cleanse. **2** *Medicine.* to cleanse (a wound, an ulcer, or infection) by removing foul or morbid matter. [< Latin *dētergēre* < *dē-* off, away + *tergēre* wipe]

de|ter|gence (di tėr′jəns), *n.* = detergency.

de|ter|gen|cy (di tėr′jən sē), *n.* detergent quality; cleansing power.

de|ter|gent (di tėr′jənt), *n., adj.* —*n.* **1** a substance that acts like soap, used for cleansing. Detergents are chemical compounds made by combining bleaches and other ingredients into mixtures of granules, liquids, or tablets. Detergents, unlike soaps, clean effectively in hard water. **2** any substance used for cleansing. Soap is a detergent.
—*adj.* cleansing; purging; detersive.
[< Latin *dētergēns, -entis,* present participle of *dētergēre;* see etym. under **deterge**]

de|te|ri|o|rate (di tir′ē ə rāt), *v.*, **-rat|ed, -rat|ing.**
—*v.i.* to become worse; lessen in character, quality, or value; depreciate: *Machinery deteriorates rapidly if it is not taken care of. As the morning progressed the weather deteriorated more and more* (London Times). **SYN**: degenerate, decline, retrograde.
—*v.t.* to make worse: *A hot, damp climate deteriorates leather.* **SYN**: impair, corrupt.
[< Late Latin *dēteriōrāre* (with English *-ate*[1]) < Latin *dēterior* worse]

de|te|ri|o|ra|tion (di tir′ē ə rā′shən), *n.* **1** the action or process of deteriorating: *The old couch is beginning to show signs of deterioration.* **2** the condition of having deteriorated: *We had the book rebound because of the deterioration of the cover. Meaningful Federal assistance is essential to rescue metropolitan areas from deterioration and decay* (New York Times).

de|te|ri|o|ra|tive (di tir′ē ə rā′tiv), *adj.* tending to deteriorate.

de|te|ri|o|ra|tor (di tir′ē ə rā′tər), *n.* a person or thing that deteriorates.

de|te|ri|o|rism (di tir′ē ə riz′əm), *n.* the doctrine that the general tendency of all things is to grow worse. [< Latin *dēterior* worse + English *-ism*]

de|ter|ma (di tėr′mə), *n.* **1** a sturdy native wood of Guiana. **2** the tree that produces this wood. [< a native name]

de|ter|ment (di tėr′mənt), *n.* **1** a deterring. **2** a thing that deters; deterrent.

de|ter|mi|na|ble (di tėr′mə nə bəl), *adj.* **1** that can be settled or decided. **2** that can be found out exactly. **3** *Especially Law.* liable to be terminated.

de|ter|mi|na|cy (di tėr′mə nə sē), *n.* the state or quality of being determinate.

de|ter|mi|nant (di tėr′mə nənt), *adj., n.* —*adj.* determining; deciding: *The higher pay offered was the determinant factor in his changing jobs.*
—*n.* **1** a thing that determines; determining factor or agent: *Money and its rate of use are not the sole determinants of price* (Newsweek). **2** *Mathematics.* **a** a certain number of quantities arranged in a square block whose value is the sum of all the products that can be formed according to certain rules. **b** the square block itself. **3** *Biology.* = determiner.

de|ter|mi|nan|tal (di tėr′mə nan′təl), *adj.* having to do with or expressed in mathematical determinants.

***de|ter|mi|nate** (di tėr′mə nit), *adj.* **1** with exact limits; fixed; definite: *a determinate number of feet* (John Dryden). **SYN**: specific. **2** settled; positive: *a determinate rule or order.* **SYN**: decided. **3** determined; resolute. **4** having flowers which arise from terminal buds and thus terminate a stem or branch. A forget-me-not has determinate inflorescence. A determinate inflorescence is also called *cymose, definite,* or *descending.* [< Latin *dēterminātus,* past participle of *dētermināre;* see etym. under **determine**] —**de|ter′mi|nate|ly**, *adv.* —**de|ter′mi|nate|ness**, *n.*

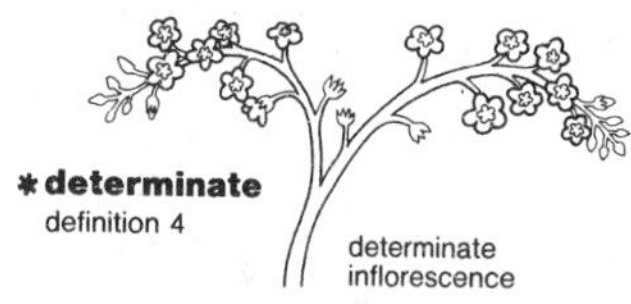

***determinate** definition 4

de|ter|mi|na|tion (di tėr′mə nā′shən), *n.* **1** great firmness in carrying out a purpose; fixed purpose: *My determination was not weakened by the difficulties I met.* **SYN**: resolve, resolution. **2** a finding out the exact amount or kind, by weighing, measuring, or calculating: *determination of the gold in a sample of rock.* **3** the act of deciding; act of settling beforehand: *The determination of the list of things to prepare for that important trip took a long time. The determination of the best name for the product called for considerable discussion. Determination of the U.S. price, which is the keystone of the world-wide structure of crude oil prices, is divorced from normal commercial forces* (Wall Street Journal). **4** the state of being determined; settlement; decision: *The doctor's determination was to operate at once.* **5** the result of finding out exactly; conclusion: *The doctor's determination was made after he received a report on the tests.* **6** fixed direction or tendency, as that of the blood toward a particular part of the body, or, *figuratively,* of the intellect or will toward some object or end. **7** a determining of bounds or limits; fixing the extent, position, or identity (of anything); delimitation: *The determination of the property lines was required before the sale.* **8** *Logic.* **a** the making of an idea, concept, etc., more precise in its outline by the addition of restrictive attributes or other qualifying features. **b** the defining of a concept by specifying its parts. **9a** a judicial or authoritative decision or settlement of a matter at issue, such as a controversy or suit. **b** the decision arrived at; authoritative or final ruling. **10** *Law.* a conclusion or termination. **11** *Embryology.* the changes within embryonic cells which fix their future course of development: *The gene is a unit of determination* (Bulletin of Atomic Scientists).

de|ter|mi|na|tive (di tėr′mə nā′tiv, -nə tiv), *adj., n.* —*adj.* serving or tending to determine or decide; determining; conclusive: *The earnings of the carriers during brief periods of time are not determinative of the reasonableness of the fare level* (Wall Street Journal).
—*n.* **1** a thing that determines. **2** *Linguistics.* **a** an ideographic sign in hieroglyphic writing, annexed to a word phonetically represented, to define its meaning. **b** in certain languages: (1) a spoken syllable having an analogous function. (2) a determinative or demonstrative word. —**de|ter′mi|na′tive|ly**, *adv.* —**de|ter′mi|na′tive|ness**, *n.*

de|ter|mi|na|tor (di tėr′mə nā′tər), *n.* a person or thing that determines; determiner.

de|ter|mine (di tėr′mən), *v.*, **-mined, -min|ing.**
—*v.i.* **1** to make up one's mind very firmly; come to a decision; resolve: *He determined to become the best scout in the troop. Narcissa determined to go at once* (Thomas Love Peacock). **SYN**: See syn. under **decide**. **2** to come to an end; expire. **3** *Archaic.* to take a course to a definite point or end.
—*v.t.* **1** to find out exactly (something previously unknown or uncertain) by observation, calculation, or surmise; fix: *to determine the height of a mountain. The captain determined the latitude and longitude of his ship's position.* **SYN**: ascertain, establish. **2** to be the deciding fact in reaching (a certain result); settle; regulate: *The number of answers you get right determines your mark on this test. Tomorrow's weather will determine whether we go to the beach or stay home. As in other things ... not the seller, but the buyer determines the price* (Thomas Hobbes). **3** to fix or settle beforehand; decide: *Can you now determine the date for our party? The boys determined which players should be on each team by lot.* **4** to put an end or limit to: **a** to limit in space, extent, quality, amount, or force; bound: *That hill determines our view.* **b** to clarify or define (an idea, concept, or argument) by determination: *The meaning of a word is partly determined by its use in a particular sentence.* **5** to settle as a judge or arbiter; decide: *to determine a dispute. The laws will ... determine the punishment of the criminal* (David Hume). **6** to fix the geometrical position of. **7** *Especially Law.* to bring to an end; put an end to; conclude; terminate. **8** to direct to some conclusion: **a** to give direction, tendency, or definite bias to; decide the course of; impel to (some destination): *Accidental impulses determine us to different paths* (Samuel Johnson). **b** *Figurative.* to decide the course of (a person); give an aim to; influence the choice of (to do something): *This circumstance determined him to the study of law.*
[< Old French *determiner,* learned borrowing from Latin *dētermināre* set limits to < *dē-* from + *terminus* end, limit]

de|ter|mined (di tėr′mənd), *adj.* **1** with one's mind firmly made up; resolved: *The determined explorer kept on his way in spite of the storm.* **SYN**: inflexible, staunch, decided. **2** firm; resolute: *a determined effort. His determined look showed that he had made up his mind. She is a lady of very determined character* (George Bernard Shaw). —**de|ter′mined|ly**, *adv.* —**de|ter′mined|ness**, *n.*

de|ter|min|er (di tėr′mə nər), *n.* **1** a person or thing that determines; determinant. **2** *Linguistics.* a limiting adjective or modifier which always accompanies and usually precedes a noun or noun phrase. *A* in *a hat, the* in *the big house,* and *every* in *every little thing* are determiners. *That, one, some, his,* in *that boy, one piece, some people,* and *his book* are English determiners. **3** *Biology.* **a** a secondary unit of germ plasm supposed to determine the character of a cell or group of cells in the organism. **b** a hereditary factor; gene.

de|ter|min|ism (di tėr′mə niz əm), *n.* **1** the doctrine that human actions are the necessary results of antecedent causes. **2** the doctrine that all events are determined by antecedent causes: *Determinism presumes that the initial state is given with absolute precision* (Bulletin of Atomic Scientists).

de|ter|min|ist (di tėr′mə nist), *n., adj.* —*n.* a person who believes in determinism: *While I don't want to sound like an economic determinist, things can't really get better until all of us here in the South settle some of our pressing economic problems* (Wall Street Journal).
—*adj.* relating to the doctrine of determinism: *... the determinist view of the forces that mold men's destinies* (New Yorker).

de|ter|min|is|tic (di tėr′mə nis′tik), *adj.* of or having to do with determinism or determinists: *It further appears that the deterministic description of psychological phenomena and the description in terms of "free will" are not at all contradictory but complementary, adapted to different, mutually exclusive conditions* (New Scientist). —**de|ter′min|is′ti|cal|ly**, *adv.*

de|ter|rence (di tėr′əns, -ter′-), *n.* **1** the act or process of deterring: *The main objects of imprisonment should be ... deterrence from crime and the reformation of offenders* (Contemporary Review). **2** a deterrent: *It seems likely that deterrence carried by bombers will be as effective as deterrence carried by ballistic missiles* (Bulletin of Atomic Scientists). **3** the use of a deterrent: *The strategy of deterrence consists essentially of maintaining the capability of striking a devastating nuclear retaliatory blow against any enemy* *who attacks us or our vital interests* (Hanson W. Baldwin).

de|ter|rent (di tėr′ənt, -ter′-), *adj., n.* —*adj.* discouraging or hindering; deterring; restraining: *A dog in the house is a deterrent influence on burglars. Atomic strength has been shifted back into a primarily deterrent role* (Atlantic).
—*n.* **1** something that deters: *Fear of sharks is a deterrent to swimming in those waters. The installed nuclear missile arsenal is not intended for use against an enemy, but to act as a deterrent against his use of nuclear missiles* (H. W. Katz). **2** a military weapon powerful enough to deter an enemy from aggression: *a nuclear deterrent. America's allies are dependent on the American deterrent for their security—but have had almost no control over strategic nuclear weapons* (Maclean's). —**de|ter′rent|ly**, *adv.*

de|ter|rer (di tėr′ər, -ter′-), *n.* a person or thing that deters: *Professor Kaufmann ... foresaw the possibility that the deterrer of war might be deterred, instead of the enemy* (New York Times).

de|ter|sion (di tėr′shən), *n.* **1** a detergent action. **2** a cleansing, as of a sore. [< Latin *dētersiō, -ōnis* < *dētergēre;* see etym. under **deterge**]

de|ter|sive (di tėr′siv), *n., adj.* = detergent.

de|test (di test′), *v.t.* **1** to dislike very much; hate: *Girls usually detest snakes. I have lived in such dishonour, that the gods Detest my baseness* (Shakespeare). *I don't like being subjected to propaganda—and I detest soapboxes* (Harold Pinter). **SYN:** abhor, loathe, abominate, despise, execrate. See syn. under **hate**. **2** *Obsolete.* to curse. [< Middle French *détester* express abhorrence, curse, learned borrowing from Latin *dētestārī* curse, calling the gods to witness < *dē-* from, down + *testis* witness] —**de|test′er**, *n.*

de|test|a|bil|i|ty (di tes′tə bil′ə tē), *n.* = detestableness.

de|test|a|ble (di tes′tə bəl), *adj.* deserving to be detested; hateful: *Murder is a detestable crime.* **SYN:** abhorrent, loathsome, abominable, execrable, odious, vile. —**de|test′a|ble|ness**, *n.*

de|test|a|bly (di tes′tə blē), *adv.* in a detestable manner; abominably.

de|tes|ta|tion (dē′tes tā′shən), *n.* **1** a very strong dislike; hatred: *My cat has a detestation of water.* **2** a detested person or thing: *Snakes are her detestation.*

de|throne (di thrōn′), *v.t.,* **-throned, -thron|ing.** **1** to remove from a throne; remove from ruling power; depose: *The rebels dethroned the weak king.* **2** *Figurative.* to remove from any dominant position: *Love, by dethroning Reason ... doth kill the Man* (Robert Boyle). —**de|thron′er**, *n.*

de|throne|ment (di thrōn′mənt), *n.* **1** the act of dethroning; removal from a throne or a high position. **2** the fact of being dethroned.

de|tin (dē tin′), *v.t.,* **-tinned, -tin|ning.** to remove the tin from. —**de|tin′ner**, *n.*

det|i|nue (det′ə nü, -nyü), *n. Law.* **1** the unlawful detention of personal property. **2** a common-law action, now rarely used, to recover the property so detained, or its value. **3** a writ used in such an action. [< Old French *detenue,* feminine past participle of *detenir* detain]

det|o|na|bil|i|ty (det′ə nə bil′ə tē, dē′tə-), *n.* the property or condition of being detonable: *the detonability of an explosive.*

det|o|na|ble (det′ə nə bəl, dē′tə-), *adj.* that can be detonated.

det|o|nat|a|ble (det′ə nā′tə bəl, dē′tə-), *adj.* detonable; detonative: *The explosive remains detonatable for up to four days in the open, even during pouring rain* (New Scientist).

det|o|nate (det′ə nāt, dē′tə-), *v.,* **-nat|ed, -nat|ing.** —*v.t.* to cause to explode with a loud noise: *The workmen detonated the dynamite.*
—*v.i.* to explode with a loud noise: *Suddenly the bomb detonated.*
[< Latin *dētonāre* (with English *-ate*[1]) < *dē-* down + *tonāre* thunder]

det|o|na|tion (det′ə nā′shən, dē′tə-), *n.* **1** the act of detonating. **2** an explosion with a loud noise. **3** a loud noise: *The detonation of the dynamite was heard for blocks.* **4** an improper burning of fuel in an internal-combustion engine or the sound it causes; knock: *Detonation ... is attributed to irregular and too rapid expansion or explosion of the gasoline and air mixture* (Toboldt and Purvis).

det|o|na|tive (det′ə nā′tiv, dē′tə-), *adj.* **1** tending to detonate; explosive. **2** of the nature of a detonation.

det|o|na|tor (det′ə nā′tər, dē′tə-), *n.* **1** a fuze, percussion cap, or similar device used to set off an explosive. **2** any explosive.

de|tor|sion (di tôr′shən), *n.* **1** *Biology.* the straightening or straight condition of an organism whose ancestors were twisted. **2** *Medicine.* the straightening of a twisted organ or part of the body. [< *de-* + *torsion*]

de|tour (dē′tůr, di tůr′), *n., v.* —*n.* **1** a road that is used when the main or direct road cannot be traveled: *The route you suggest is full of detours.* **2** *Figurative.* a roundabout way: *He took several detours before getting the right answer. A detour in reading often reveals unexpected pleasure.*
—*v.i.* to use a detour: *We detoured around the bridge that had been washed out. The car had to detour six times.*
—*v.t.* to cause to use a detour: *The police detoured all traffic on Broadway to keep it open for the parade. Road repairs were constantly detouring them.*
[< French *détour* < Old French *destourner* turn aside < *des-* away (< Latin *dis-*) + *tourner* to turn < Latin *tornāre*]

de|tox|i|cant (dē tok′sə kənt), *n.* a substance used to detoxicate someone; detoxicator: *... giving them [the birds] salt water to drink and milk as a detoxicant against the oil they have swallowed* (New Yorker).

de|tox|i|cate (dē tok′sə kāt), *v.t.,* **-cat|ed, -cat|ing.** to remove poison from; detoxify: *The explanation may lie in the tendency of the organism to detoxicate itself and distribute the alcohol evenly throughout the body* (New Scientist).

de|tox|i|ca|tion (dē tok′sə kā′shən), *n.* detoxification.

de|tox|i|ca|tor (dē tok′sə kā′tər), *n.* a drug or agent that detoxicates.

de|tox|i|fi|ca|tion (dē tok′sə fə kā′shən), *n.* **1** the act or process of detoxifying: *It is therefore necessary to collect the gaseous waste in suitable containers, pending chemical detoxification* (Scientific American). **2** the condition of being detoxified.

de|tox|i|fy (dē tok′sə fī), *v.,* **-fied, -fy|ing.** —*v.t.* to remove toxic or poisonous qualities from; remove a poison or its effects from: *Mosquitoes use the same enzyme as do flies to detoxify DDT* (Science News Letter).
—*v.i.* to be or become detoxified: *Methadone, an inexpensive synthetic material similar to heroin, is used to help addicts detoxify* (Science News).

de|tract (di trakt′), *v.i.* **1** to take away a part; remove some of the quality or worth: *The ugly frame detracts from the beauty of the picture. Modernizing the building's facade would ... enhance, rather than detract from the character of the neighborhood* (New York Times). **SYN:** depreciate, derogate. **2** to speak disparagingly: *That critic is always detracting in his remarks.* **SYN:** decry. —*v.t.* **1** to take away (a part) from a whole; remove (some of the quality or worth); withdraw; subtract; abate: *The ugly frame detracts something from the beauty of the picture. The defect detracts little from the intrinsic value.* **2** *Archaic.* to disparage; belittle; defame. **3** *Obsolete.* to draw away. [< Latin *dētractus,* past participle of *dētrahere* < *dē-* away + *trahere* draw] —**de|tract′ing|ly**, *adv.*

de|trac|tion (di trak′shən), *n.* **1** a taking away of some quality or worth; detracting: *Of course her squinting eyes are a slight detraction.* **2** an act of speaking evil; belittling: *Happy are they that hear detractions, and can put them to mending* (Shakespeare). **SYN:** defamation, calumny, slander, disparagement, traducement.

de|trac|tive (di trak′tiv), *adj.* **1** tending to detract. **2** speaking evil; belittling. —**de|trac′tive|ly**, *adv.*

de|trac|tor (di trak′tər), *n.* a person who speaks evil of or belittles another: *Detractors have branded the movement with [a] disapproving name* (London Times).

de|trac|to|ry (di trak′tər ē), *adj.* = detractive.

de|trac|tress (di trak′tris), *n.* a woman detractor.

de|train (dē trān′), *v.i.* to get off a railroad train: *The travelers had to detrain for customs at the border.* —*v.t.* to put off from a railroad train.

de|train|ment (dē trān′mənt), *n.* the act of getting off a railroad train.

de|trib|al|ise (dē trī′bə līz), *v.t.,* **-ised, -is|ing.** *Especially British.* detribalize.

de|trib|al|i|za|tion (dē trī′bə lə zā′shən), *n.* **1** the act of detribalizing. **2** the condition of being detribalized.

de|trib|al|ize (dē trī′bə līz), *v.t.,* **-ized, -iz|ing.** to deprive of tribal character or organization: *It is not only the intelligentsia who are detribalized, but thousands of men ... have left their reserves to seek employment in Nairobi and elsewhere* (London Times).

det|ri|ment (det′rə mənt), *n.* **1** loss, damage, or injury; harm; hurt: *No one can miss a month of school without detriment to his studies.* **SYN:** impairment, deterioration. **2** something that causes loss, damage, or injury: *His dishonesty was a detriment to his character. His lack of education was a serious detriment to his career.* [< Latin *dētrīmentum* < *dēterere* < *dē-* away + *terere* wear]

det|ri|men|tal (det′rə men′təl), *adj., n.* —*adj.* causing loss or damage; harmful; injurious: *Lack of sleep is detrimental to one's health.* **SYN:** hurtful, disadvantageous.
—*n.* a detriment; hindrance; handicap: *The sisters of the wife being considered detrimentals, are placed in Buddhist convents* (C. F. Gordon-Cumming). —**det′ri|men′tal|ly**, *adv.*

de|tri|tal (di trī′təl), *adj.* having to do with or composed of detritus.

de|trit|ed (di trī′tid), *adj.* reduced to detritus.

de|tri|tion (di trish′ən), *n.* the act of wearing away by rubbing.

de|tri|tus (di trī′təs), *n.* **1** *Geology.* an accumulation of small fragments, such as sand or silt worn away from rock. **2** any disintegrated material; debris: *The detritus left by the flood covered the highway. Its corners and closets were cluttered with the detritus of ages* (Time). [< Latin *dētrītus, -ūs* a rubbing away < *dēterere* < *dē-* away + *terere* rub]

De|troit|er (di troi′tər), *n.* a native or resident of Detroit.

de trop (də trō′), *French.* **1** too much or too many; superfluous: *Mentioning the weather is de trop, rather like bringing up the hopeless Parisian traffic situation* (Saturday Review). **2** unwelcome; in the way: *He assures me I won't be de trop* (New Yorker).

de|trude (di trüd′), *v.t.,* **-trud|ed, -trud|ing.** **1** to thrust out or away; expel. **2** to thrust or force down. [< Latin *dētrūdere* < *dē-* down, away + *trūdere* thrust]

de|trun|cate (di trung′kāt), *v.t.,* **-cat|ed, -cat|ing.** to reduce by cutting off a part. [< Latin *dētruncāre* (with English *-ate*[1]) < *dē-* off + *truncāre* to cut off, maim]

de|trun|ca|tion (dē′trung kā′shən), *n.* the act of reducing by cutting off a part: *detruncation of our syllables* (Samuel Johnson).

de|tru|sion (di trü′zhən), *n.* the act of detruding.

de|tu|mes|cence (dē′tü mes′əns, -tyü-), *n.* cessation or reduction of swelling.

de|tu|mes|cent (dē′tü mes′ənt, -tyü-), *adj.* characterized by detumescence; reduced in swelling.

de|tune (dē tün′, -tyün′), *v.t.,* **-tuned, -tun|ing.** to reduce in tune; change from a tuned condition: *to detune an engine, detune a piano string.* —**de|tun′er**, *n.*

de|tur (dē′tər), *n.* a prize awarded annually to undergraduates who have attained superior work. It is a specially bound book on some subject in the winner's field of study. [< Latin *dētur* let there be given]

Deu|ca|li|on (dü kā′lē ən, dyü-), *n. Greek Mythology.* a son of Prometheus. He and his wife Pyrrha survived a flood sent by Zeus and became ancestors of the succeeding human race by casting stones behind them from which men and women sprang.

deuce[1] (düs, dyüs), *n., v.,* **deuced, deuc|ing.**
—*n.* **1** a playing card marked with a *2.* **2** the side of a die having two spots. **3** a dice throw of two aces (in craps, a losing point on first cast). **4** (in a game of cards or dice) two. **5** *Tennis.* **a** a tie score at 40 each, or any subsequent tie score in a game. **b** a tie score of five or more games each in a set. **6** *U.S. Slang.* two dollars (originally, a two-dollar bill): *[He] slipped the judge a deuce to button up to the press* (S. J. Perelman).
—*v.t. Tennis.* to even the score of (a game or set) at deuce.
[< Old French *deus* two < Latin *duos,* accusative of *duo* two]

deuce[2] (düs, dyüs), *interj., n. Informal.* a mild oath or exclamation of annoyance; the dickens, the devil: *Who the deuce is he?*
deuce of a, *Informal.* **a** exceptional; extraordinary: *It was a deuce of a game.* **b** exceptionally: *We had a deuce of a good time.*
[< *deuce*[1]; possibly influenced by Low German *duus* the devil!; also, an unlucky throw at dice]

deuce-ace (düs′ās′, dyüs′-), *n.* **1** a low throw with dice, of deuce and ace. **2** *Figurative.* bad luck.

deuc|ed (dü′sid, dyü′-; düst, dyüst), *adj., adv. Informal.* —*adj.* devilish; excessive.
—*adv.* devilishly; excessively.

deuc|ed|ly (dü′sid lē, dyü′-), *adv.* devilishly; excessively.

deuces wild, a card game in which a deuce represents any card in the deck. Deuces wild is played in some forms of poker and in canasta.

de|ur|ban|ize (dē ėr′bə nīz), *v.t.,* **-ized, -iz|ing.** to deprive (a district or city) of its urban character.

de|us ex ma|chi|na (dē′əs eks mak′ə nə), *Latin.* **1** a person, god, or event that comes just in time to solve a difficulty in a story, play, or other literary or dramatic work, especially when

Pronunciation Key: hat, āge, cãre, fär; let, ēqual, tėrm; it, īce; hot, ōpen, ôrder; oil, out; cup, pu̇t, rüle; child; long; thin; ᴛʜen; zh, measure; ə represents **a** in about, **e** in taken, **i** in pencil, **o** in lemon, **u** in circus.

the coming is contrived or artificial: *There is ... Ferral, a French representative of big business, whom Malraux uses as the novel's deus ex machina* (New Yorker). (*Figurative.*) *Mr. Galbraith rejects the notion that somewhere in Wall Street there was a deus ex machina who somehow engineered the boom and bust* (New York Times). **2** (literally) a god from a machine (referring to a mechanical device used in the ancient Greek and Roman theater by which actors who played the parts of gods were lowered from above the stage to end or resolve the dramatic action).

De|us Mi|se|re|a|tur (de′ůs mē′se re ä′tůr; dē′əs miz′ər ē ā′tər), *Latin.* (may) God have mercy (the first words of, and a title for, Psalm 67).

De|us vo|bis|cum (dē′əs vō bis′kəm), *Latin.* God be with you.

De|us vult (dē′əs vult′; de′ůs vůlt′), *Latin.* God wills (it), the battle cry of the Crusades.

Deut., Deuteronomy (book of the Old Testament).

deu|ter|ag|o|nist (dü′tə rag′ə nist, dyü′-), *n.* **1** the character of second importance in the ancient Greek drama (after the protagonist). **2** *Figurative.* any secondary or minor character: *Like the philosopher McIndoe, the deuteragonist in Mr. Lister's poem, I have had thoughts in mid-air* (Eli Waldron). [< Greek *deúteros* second + *agōnistēs* combatant, actor]

deu|ter|a|nope (dü′tər ə nōp, dyü′-), *n.* a person suffering from deuteranopia.

deu|ter|a|no|pi|a (dü′tər ə nō′pē ə, dyü′-), *n.* lack of ability to see the color green. [< New Latin *deuteranopia* < Greek *deúteros* second + *a-* not + *ôps, ōpós* eye]

deu|ter|a|no|pic (dü′tər ə nō′pik, dyü′-), *adj.* of or having to do with deuteranopia.

deu|ter|at|ed (dü′tə rā′tid, dyü′-), *adj.* containing deuterium: *deuterated cells.*

deu|ter|a|tion (dü′tə rā′shən, dyü′-), *n.* the condition of becoming or being deuterated.

deu|ter|ide (dü′tə rīd, dyü′-), *n.* a compound of deuterium containing some other element or radical, as of lithium.

deu|te|ri|um (dü tir′ē əm, dyü-), *n.* an isotope of hydrogen; heavy hydrogen. Its atoms have about twice the mass of ordinary hydrogen. Deuterium occurs in heavy water. *Deuterium or double-weight hydrogen if "fused" into heavier elements would constitute a source of energy virtually without limit since it occurs in great abundance in sea water* (Science News Letter). [< New Latin *deuterium* < Greek *deutérion,* neuter, having second place < *deúteros* second]

deuterium oxide, *Chemistry.* = heavy water.

deu|ter|o|ca|non|i|cal (dü′tər ō kə non′ə kəl, dyü′-), *adj.* of or having to do with a second canon; forming a second canon. [< Greek *deúteros* second + English *canonical*]

deuterocanonical books, those books or sections of books of the Biblical canon as defined by the Council of Trent that include most of the Old Testament Apocrypha of the King James Version and are regarded by the Roman Catholic Church as constituting a second canon, accepted later than the first, but of equal authority.

deu|ter|o|cone (dü′tər ə kōn, dyü′-), *n.* the inner and anterior cusp of an upper premolar of mammals. [< Greek *deúteros* second + English *cone*]

deu|ter|og|a|mist (dü′tə rog′ə mist, dyü′-), *n.* a person who marries a second time.

deu|ter|og|a|my (dü′tə rog′ə mē, dyü′-), *n.* **1** a second marriage, after the death or divorce of a first husband or wife; digamy. **2** the custom of contracting such marriages. [< Greek *deuterogamiā* < *deúteros* second + *gámos* marrying]

deu|ter|on (dü′tə ron, dyü′-), *n.* the nucleus of an atom of deuterium, consisting of one proton and one neutron which have parallel spins: *His method ... is to direct a high energy beam of nuclear particles* (*deuterons*) *on to the gland* (London Times).

Deu|ter|o|nom|ic (dü′tər ə nom′ik, dyü′-), *adj.* **1** of or having to do with the book of Deuteronomy: *Deuteronomic law.* **2** having the literary or theological character of the book of Deuteronomy: *Deuteronomic phraseology.*

Deu|ter|on|o|mist (dü′tə ron′ə mist, dyü′-), *n.* the author, or one of the authors, of the book of Deuteronomy, or of any Deuteronomic part of the Old Testament.

Deu|ter|on|o|mis|tic (dü′tə ron′ə mis′tik, dyü′-), *adj.* of the nature or style of the writer of Deuteronomy.

Deu|ter|on|o|my (dü′tə ron′ə mē, dyü′-), *n.* the fifth book of the Old Testament. It contains a second statement of the Mosaic law. *Abbr:* Deut. [< Latin *Deuteronomium* < Greek *Deuteronómion* < *deúteros* second + *nómos* law]

deu|ter|op|a|thy (dü′tə rop′ə thē, dyü′-), *n. Medicine.* a secondary affection, sympathetic with or resulting from another. [< Greek *deúteros* second + English *-pathy*]

deu|ter|o|plasm (dü′tər ə plaz′əm, dyü′-), *n.* = deutoplasm.

deu|ter|ot|o|ky (dü′tə rot′ə kē, dyü′-), *n.* the form of parthenogenesis in which offspring of both sexes are produced.

deu|ton (dü′ton, dyü′-), *n.* = deuteron.

deu|to|plasm (dü′tə plaz′əm, dyü′-), *n. Biology.* the yolk or other material in an egg or cell that furnishes food for the nourishment of the embryo. [< Greek *deúteros* second + *plásma* something formed]

deu|to|plas|mic (dü′tə plaz′mik, dyü′-), *adj.* of or having to do with deutoplasm.

deu|tron (dü′tron, dyü′-), *n.* = deuteron.

Deut|sche mark (doi′chə), the unit of money in Germany, a coin equal to 100 pfennigs. *Abbr:* DM (no periods). [< German *Deutsche Mark* German mark]

Deut|sches Reich (doi′chəs rīн′), *German.* German realm (the former official name of Germany).

Deutsch|land (doich′länt′), *n. German.* Germany.

deut|zi|a (düt′sē ə, dyüt′-, doit′-), *n.* any one of a number of shrubs of the saxifrage family, native to China and Japan, several of which are grown for their showy, usually white, bell-shaped flowers. [< New Latin *Deutzia* the genus name < Johann van der *Deutz,* 1743–1784, a Dutch botanist]

deux-che|vaux (dœ′shə vō′), *n. French.* **1** an automobile with a badly worn-out engine with only as much power as one would suppose a two-horsepower engine to have. **2** (literally) two-horses.

deu|xième (dœ zyem′), *n. French.* a second performance (especially of a play) following the premiere: *Anyhow, "Pulses" is something truly new, even though this was the world deuxième* (London Times).

dev (dāv), *n.* = div.

de|va (dā′və), *n. Hinduism.* a god or divinity; one of the order of good spirits. [< Sanskrit *deva* god]

de|va|da|si (dā′və dä′sē), *n.* (in India) a girl or woman serving as a dancer and courtesan in a Hindu temple. [< Sanskrit *devadāsī*]

de|val|or|ize (dē val′ə rīz), *v.t.,* **-ized, -iz|ing.** to lower the value of; devaluate.

de|val|u|ate (dē val′yů āt), *v.,* **-at|ed, -at|ing.** — ***v.t.*** **1** to reduce the value of; deprive of value. **2** to fix a lower legal value on (a currency that has depreciated): *In 1967 Great Britain devaluated the pound from $2.80 to $2.40.* — ***v.i.*** **1** to lose value; diminish in value: *Diamonds are still a girl's best friend. They won't devaluate, and ... they're fun too* (Wendy Michener). **2** to introduce or effect a devaluation of currency.

de|val|u|a|tion (dē val′yů ā′shən), *n.* **1** the act or process of devaluating. **2** the state of being devaluated.

de|val|u|a|tion|ist (dē val′yů ā′shə nist), *n.* a supporter or advocate of the devaluation of a currency.

de|val|ue (dē val′yü), *v.,* **-ued, -u|ing.** — ***v.t.*** to devaluate: *Students at high-standard colleges were ... likely to feel that the war "devalued" their education* (Time). — ***v.i.*** to introduce or effect devaluation of currency.

De|va|na|ga|ri (dā′və nä′gə rē), *n.* the alphabet generally used in writing Sanskrit and many modern languages of India. [< Sanskrit *devanāgarī* < *deva* god + *nāgarī* writing; (literally) of the city < *nāgara* city]

De|var|shis (dā vär′shiz), *n.pl. Hinduism.* sages who have attained perfection on earth and have been exalted as demigods to heaven. [< Sanskrit *devarṣi,* singular < *deva* god]

dev|as|tate (dev′ə stāt), *v.t.,* **-tat|ed, -tat|ing.** to lay waste; destroy; ravage; make unfit to live in: *A long war devastated the country. The storms and floods that have devastated much of central and northern Italy have no precedent in recorded history* (New York Times). **SYN:** harry, pillage, plunder, sack, despoil. [< Latin *dēvāstāre* (with English *-ate*[1]) < *dē-* (intensive) + *vāstus* waste; empty; ravaged]

dev|as|tat|ing (dev′ə stā′ting), *adj.* **1** causing widespread destruction: *The first blow will be so devastating as to be decisive* (Bulletin of Atomic Scientists). **2** *Figurative.* effectively sarcastic, trenchant, or deflating: *The devastating analysis of the English scene ... will have widespread repercussions* (Canadian Saturday Night). **3** *Figurative.* very effective; powerful: [*He*] *can be devastating in a slow blues* (New Yorker). — **dev′as|tat′ing|ly,** *adv.*

dev|as|ta|tion (dev′ə stā′shən), *n.* the act of devastating, or condition of being devastated; destruction; desolation: *Every year fires cause the devastation of valuable forests.* **SYN:** ravage, havoc, ruin.

dev|as|ta|tive (dev′ə stā′tiv), *adj.* devastating; ravaging.

dev|as|ta|tor (dev′ə stā′tər), *n.* a person or thing that devastates or lays waste.

de|vein (dē vān′), *v.t.* to remove the vein of (a shrimp) after shelling it.

dev|el (dev′əl), *n., v. Scottish.* — ***n.*** a severe or stunning blow.
— ***v.t.*** to strike or knock down with a stunning blow. [origin uncertain]

de|vel|op (di vel′əp), *v.i.* **1** to come into being or activity; grow: *The seeds develop into plants. Plants develop from seeds.* **2** to change in character through successive periods; evolve: *Land animals are believed to have developed from sea animals.* **3** to become bigger, better, more useful, or improved: *His business developed very slowly.* **4** *Photography.* **a** to be treated with chemicals to bring out the latent image; undergo development: *This type of film develops in twenty minutes.* **b** to become visible, as an image does under the process of development. **5** to become known; become apparent: *His scheme developed at length.* — ***v.t.*** **1** to bring into being or activity; grow: *Scientists have developed many new drugs to fight disease. By experimentation botanists have developed many new plants.* **SYN:** generate, unfold. **2** to cause to change in character through successive periods; evolve: *Only six decades developed the Wrights' primitive plane into the modern jet.* **3** to come to have; display; show: *He developed an interest in collecting stamps.* **4** to make bigger, better, more useful, or improve: *Swimming will develop many different muscles.* **5a** to work out in greater and greater detail: *Gradually we developed our plans for the boys' club.* **b** *Music.* to elaborate (a theme or motive) by variation of rhythm, melody, harmony, or texture. **6** *Photography.* **a** to treat (a photographic film or plate) with chemicals to bring out the picture: *We shall print all the films we developed.* **b** to make (the latent image) visible on an exposed film or plate. **7** to bring to light; make known; reveal: *The detective's inquiry did not develop any new facts.* **8a** to bring forth; make more available: *to develop the water power of an area.* **b** to build on (open land) or rebuild (an old and often run-down area): *to develop an old farm into a new suburb.* **9** *Mathematics.* to expand, especially in the form of a series. **10** *Chess.* to move (a piece or pieces) to effective positions for use in a future play: *to develop one's bishops early in the game.* [< French *développer* unwrap. Compare etym. under **envelop.**]

de|vel|op|a|ble (di vel′ə pə bəl), *adj.* that can be developed.

de|vel|ope (di vel′əp), *v.i., v.t.,* **-oped, -op|ing.** *Rare.* develop.

de|vel|oped (di vel′əpt), *adj.* highly advanced economically; industrialized; wealthy: *Other countries also protected their producers, including developed countries like the U.S.* (Vivian Raven).

de|vel|ope|ment (di vel′əp mənt), *n. Rare.* development.

de|vel|op|er (di vel′ə pər), *n.* **1** a person or thing that develops. **2** a chemical used to bring out the picture on a photographic film or plate. **3** a person or company that develops land.

de|vel|op|ing (di vel′ə ping), *adj.* not yet developed; underdeveloped: *Representatives from developing nations complained that their concerns did not have much in common with those of industrialized nations* (Darlene R. Stille).

de|vel|op|ment (di vel′əp mənt), *n.* **1** the process of developing; growth: *The doctor followed the child's development closely.* **2** an outcome; result; new event: *The newspaper gives news about the latest developments in the elections.* **3** a working out in greater and greater detail: *The development of the plans for rocket flight to the moon took many years. The rubella vaccine* [*was*] *in an earlier stage of development than the mumps vaccine* (Harold J. Schmeck, Jr.). *The leaders of the political opposition had tried to prevent the development of an independent nuclear weapons programme by China* (Manchester Guardian Weekly). **4** a group of similar houses or apartment buildings built on open land or in place of old buildings: *Many developments in New York City are replacing the slums. The development contains 135 apartments and sixty-five garages* (New York Times). **5** the developing of a photograph. **6** a more elaborate form. **7** stage of advancement: *The tribe's development was more primitive than that of their neighbors.* **8** *Music.* the second movement of a sonata developing the principal and secondary subjects introduced in the exposition. **9** *Chess.* the move of a piece or pieces to effective positions for use in a future play.

de|vel|op|men|tal (di vel′əp men′təl), *adj.* of or having to do with development: *A slow development of certain functions of the nervous system ... is called a developmental lag* (Science News Letter). — **de|vel′op|men′tal|ly,** *adv.*

developmental biology, the study of the development of organisms: *The question developmental biology seeks to answer concerns the way in which a single fertilized cell can grow into an organized mass of millions of cells, of many different types, all functioning together as a whole* (New Scientist and Science Journal).

developmental psychology, the study of changes in human behavior from infancy to old age, especially the period between birth and the early 20's.

development area, *British.* an area of high unemployment in which the government undertakes to stimulate new industrial development.

development engineer, an engineer who improves products, builds and tests models of a new product, or makes products based upon the results and discoveries of research.

development section, *Music.* the section of a movement or composition in which the unfolding of the capacities of a musical theme or themes takes place, usually the middle section of a sonata form between exposition and recapitulation.

dé|ve|lop|pé (dā və lô pā'), *n., pl.* **-pés** (-pā'). *French.* a ballet movement in which the free leg is raised and the toe extended.

de|verb|a|tive (di vėr'bə tiv), *n., adj.* **—*n.*** a word formed on or derived from a verb. The nouns *engraver* and *engraving* are deverbatives.
—*adj.* derived from or formed on a verb: *a deverbative word, a deverbative ending.*

de|vest (di vest'), *v.t.* **1** *Law.* to divest. **2** *Obsolete.* to undress (a person or oneself). [< Old French *devester*, variant of *desvestir* undress < *des-* dis- (< Latin *dis-*) + *vestir* clothe < Latin *vestīre*]

De|vi (dā'vē), *n. Hinduism.* **1** a goddess of motherhood and fertility, the consort of Siva. **2** any goddess. [< Sanskrit *devī* goddess]

de|vi|a|ble (dē'vē ə bəl), *adj.* that can be caused to deviate; capable of being deflected.

de|vi|ance (dē'vē əns), *n.* **1** the quality or state of being deviant. **2** a deviation.

de|vi|an|cy (dē'vē ən sē), *n.* the quality or state of being deviant.

de|vi|ant (dē'vē ənt), *n., adj.* **—*n.* 1** = deviate. **2** anything that deviates from the norm: *[He] sees no reason why chemists cannot produce deviants from other medically important alkaloids such as quinine* (New Scientist).
—*adj.* that deviates; deviating: *... the persecution of deviant shades of opinion* (Time).

de|vi|ate (*v.* dē'vē āt; *n., adj. also* dē'vē it), *v.,* **-at|ed, -at|ing,** *n., adj.* **—*v.i.*** to turn aside (from a way, course, rule, truth, standard, or the like): *The principal deviated from her custom and did not attend the school's annual pet show. His statements sometimes deviated slightly from the truth.* **SYN:** See syn. under **diverge**.
—*v.t.* to cause to turn aside; deflect: *Light rays entering the earth's atmosphere from the sun or the stars are continuously deviated so as to follow a curved path* (Sears and Zemansky).
—*n.* 1 an individual who shows a marked deviation from the norm: *He wasn't a recluse or a deviate, but for some reason there was no family, no responsibility* (Atlantic). **2** *Statistics.* the value of a variable measured from some standard point, usually the mean.
—*adj.* 1 characterized by a marked deviation from the standard or norm. **2** that deviates; deviant.
[< Late Latin *dēviāre* (with English *-ate*[1]) < *dēvius* devious < *dē-* aside + *via* way]

de|vi|a|tion (dē'vē ā'shən), *n.* **1** an act or instance of turning aside from a way, course, rule, truth, standard, or the like; divergence; swerving; deflection: *The iron in the ship caused a deviation of the magnetic needle of the compass.* (*Figurative.*) *Running in the halls is a deviation from school rules and will not not be allowed.* **2** *Statistics.* **a** the difference between one value of a set of values and the arithmetic mean of the set. **b** the amount of this difference. **3** the action or conduct of a deviationist or a deviate. **4** any departure or divergence from a course of action.

de|vi|a|tion|ism (dē'vē ā'shə niz əm), *n.* a turning aside from party policies, especially from official Communist policies.

de|vi|a|tion|ist (dē'vē ā'shə nist), *n.* a person who turns aside from party policies, especially from official Communist policies: *In all his posts he has been the watchdog of the party line, the purger of deviationists* (Economist).

de|vi|a|tive (dē'vē ā'tiv), *adj.* of deviation; having to do with or causing deviation.

de|vi|a|tor (dē'vē ā'tər), *n.* a person or thing that deviates.

de|vice (di vīs'), *n.* **1** something invented, devised, or fitted for a particular use or special purpose; a mechanism or apparatus. A can opener and an electric razor are devices. *Our gas stove has a device for lighting it automatically. It was an improvement in the timing device, however, and not in the method of heartbeat detection* (New Scientist). **SYN:** contrivance. **2** a plan, scheme, or trick: *The thief used the device of acting as a repairman to get the boy to let him into the house.* **SYN:** expedient, artifice, stratagem, wile, ruse. **3** a drawing or figure used in a pattern or as an ornament: *A star and circle are used as a device in the border.* **SYN:** design. **4** a picture or design on a coat of arms, often accompanied by a motto. **5** = motto: *A banner with the strange device, Excelsior!* (Longfellow). **6** *Archaic.* the act or faculty of devising, contriving, or planning; inventiveness: *... full of noble device* (Shakespeare). **7** *Obsolete.* will; pleasure; fancy; desire.
leave to one's own devices, to leave to do as one thinks best: *The teacher left us to our own devices in choosing the books for our reports.*
[fusion of Middle English *devis* disposition (of work), talk, and of *devise* design, emblem, plan; both < Old French *devis* and *devise* < Latin *dīvidere* divide]
▶**Device** is the noun form, **devise** the verb: *He tried to perfect a device for removing clinkers. By various devices he was able to amass a huge fortune. Mary Ann devised a new plan for the organization.*

dev|il (dev'əl), *n., v.,* **-iled, -il|ing** or (*especially British*), **-illed, -il|ling.** **—*n.* 1** any evil spirit; fiend; demon: *Devils plucked my sleeve* (Tennyson). **2** a wicked or cruel person: *A devil, born a devil, on whose nature Nurture can never stick* (Shakespeare). **3** a very able, clever, energetic, or reckless person: *a mischievous devil, a lucky devil.* **SYN:** knave, rogue. **4** an unfortunate or wretched person: *The migrant workers, poor devils, are given miserable living quarters.* **5** the errand boy or youngest apprentice in a printing office; printer's devil. **6** a person who does literary work or legal research for another, for which the latter gets the credit or pay. **7** *Figurative.* something very bad; an evil influence or power: *A devil rises in my heart, Far worse than any death to me* (Tennyson). **8** a machine that has sharp teeth or spikes for tearing, cleaning, or picking. **9** (in India, South Africa, and other desert places) a dust storm or sandstorm.
—*v.t.* 1 *Informal.* to bother or tease; torment: *Her older brother deviled her all during the meal.* **SYN:** chaff, annoy. **2** to treat harshly. **3** to prepare (food) by grinding or mashing, and adding hot or savory seasoning: *to devil ham.* **4** to subject to the operation of a devil (machine), especially such as tearing (rags) to pieces. **SYN:** hack. **5a** to act as a legal or literary devil for. **b** to write or produce (a paper, thesis, or brief) as a legal or literary devil: *Everything you've written, he has deviled for you* (Atlantic).
—*v.i.* to act as a literary devil.
between the devil and the deep (blue) sea, caught in a dilemma; forced to decide between two unpleasant choices: *He could either go to Europe and displease his mother, or he could stay home and miss a fine opportunity; he was between the devil and the deep blue sea.*
devil of a, very bad; devilish; confounded: *We had the devil of a time getting out of ... uniform* (New Yorker).
give the devil his due, to be scrupulously fair even to a bad or disliked person: *He was never yet a breaker of proverbs: He will give the devil his due* (Shakespeare).
go to the devil, to go to ruin or perdition: *When a man's country's going to the devil* (Byron).
have the devil's own time, to experience great difficulty: *Sugar Merchant Henry Tate had the devil's own time getting the nation to accept his costly gift* (Time).
like the devil, with great force, cunning, etc.; extremely: *We're pushing like the devil to get as much as we can done now* (Wall Street Journal).
play the devil with, *Informal.* to do damage to; make havoc or ruin of: *Salt water plays the devil with a uniform* (Frederick Marryat).
raise the devil, *Informal.* to make a great disturbance: *When he finds out you broke his pipe, he will raise the devil. They have readers who raise the devil when they make a mistake* (Time).
talk (or **speak**) **of the devil**, mention someone and he will appear: *Talk of the devil!—Here comes Thiselton!* (G. Allen).
the Devil or **the devil, a** (in Jewish and Christian theology) the evil spirit; the enemy of goodness; Satan: *... till the door was broke, and the Devil came in* (Robert Southey). **b** (after an interrogative) an expletive expressing surprise, annoyance, impatience, etc.: *Why, who the devil are you?* (Henry Fielding). *What the devil makes him cry?* (Thomas Hood). **c** (as an interjection) an exclamation used to express disgust, anger, surprise, etc.: *"That is W," said the teacher. "The Devil!" exclaimed the boy, "is that W?"* (Emerson).
(the) devil take the hindmost, a do not worry about what happens to the slowest or last one; let each shift for himself: *The soldiers fled before the advancing enemy and let the devil take the hindmost.* **b** unconcerned, especially with the consequences: *Wilson now adopted a devil-take-the-hindmost attitude; he didn't seem to care much about the consequences* (Newsweek).
the devil to pay, much trouble ahead; awkward or unpleasant consequences: *Had he been laid up at present, there would have been the very devil to pay* (Jane Carlyle).
[Old English *dēofol*, ultimately < Greek *diábolos* slanderer < *diabállein* slander < *dia-* across, against + *bállein* throw]

devil dance, a frenzied dance performed among shamanists or the like, usually to frighten away disease demons or other evil spirits.

devil dancer, a person who performs a devil dance: *Devil dancers in Ceylon often use ugly masks ... in their ancient ceremonies* (Fred Eggan).

devil dog, *Informal.* a nickname for a member of the U.S. Marine Corps.

dev|il|dom (dev'əl dəm), *n.* **1** the rule of a devil. **2** the realm of devils. **3** devils collectively.

dev|iled (dev'əld), *adj.* ground up or mashed and highly seasoned: *deviled ham.* Also, *especially British,* **devilled**.

deviled eggs, hard-boiled eggs cut in halves lengthwise, their yolks made into a paste with mayonnaise and various seasonings, and heaped back into the halved whites.

dev|il|fish (dev'əl fish'), *n., pl.* **-fish|es** or (*collectively*) **-fish. 1** a large ray of warm seas that moves by a flapping motion of its broad fins; manta; manta ray. It is related to the shark and reaches a weight of over 3,000 pounds. **2** a large cephalopod, especially an octopus.

devil grass, any troublesome, fast-growing grass, such as couch grass.

dev|il|hood (dev'əl hu̇d), *n.* the condition or character of a devil.

devil horse, = mantis.

devil hound, **1** a nickname for a member of the U.S. Marine Corps. **2** a rendering of German *Teufelshund*, a name said to have been applied by the Germans to the marines during World War I, because of their fierceness in attack.

dev|il-in-the-bush (dev'əl in thə bu̇sh'), *n.* = love-in-a-mist.

dev|il|ish (dev'ə lish, dev'lish), *adj., adv.* **—*adj.* 1** like a devil; worthy of the Devil; very cruel; wicked: *a devilish temper.* **SYN:** diabolical, execrable, fiendish, satanic. **2** mischievous or daring: *The boys played devilish pranks on Halloween.* **3** *Informal.* very great; extreme: *He's got me into devilish trouble.*
—*adv.* *Informal.* excessively; very; extremely: *He's tough, ma'am, ... tough and devilish sly* (Dickens). **SYN:** exceedingly. **—dev'il|ish|ly,** *adv.* **—dev'il|ish|ness,** *n.*

dev|il|kin (dev'əl kin), *n.* a little devil; imp.

dev|illed (dev'əld), *adj. Especially British.* deviled.

dev|il-may-care (dev'əl mā kãr'), *adj.* very careless and reckless: *... a lively, devil-may-care cheerfulness that is infectious* (New Yorker).

dev|il|ment (dev'əl mənt), *n.* devilish actions or behavior; deviltry; mischief: *What devilment are the boys up to now?*

devil on two sticks, **1** the piece of wood used in the game of diabolo. **2** the game itself.

dev|il|ry (dev'əl rē), *n., pl.* **-ries.** *Especially British.* deviltry.
▶See **deviltry** for usage note.

dev|il's advocate (dev'əlz), **1** *Roman Catholic Church.* a person appointed to examine the evidence and present arguments that must be satisfactorily answered, against the beatification or canonization of a person; advocatus diaboli. **2** a critic who argues either against a popular cause or for an unpopular cause. [translation of Medieval or New Latin *advocatus diaboli*]

devil's apron, a tough, brown seaweed with very large leaves that have a wavy margin like an apron.

devil's bit, **1** any plant of a group of erect or spreading herbs native to Europe, having a fleshy root and heads of blue flowers. **2** any plant of a group of North American herbs of the lily family having showy clusters of flowers; blazing star.

devil's bite, = American hellebore.

devil's bones, = dice.

devil's claw, **1** a low American shrub with large, showy flowers and pods having a slender, curved thorn that hooks easily into the coat of any ani-

---

Pronunciation Key: hat, āge, cãre, fär; let, ēqual, tėrm; it, īce; hot, ōpen, ôrder; oil, out; cup, pu̇t, rüle; child; long; thin; ᴛʜen; zh, measure; ə represents **a** in about, **e** in taken, **i** in pencil, **o** in lemon, **u** in circus.

mal that brushes the plant. **2** a scorpion shell found in the Indian Ocean. **3** a very strong hook and chain used as a stopper for a chain cable.

devil's corkscrew, = daimonelix.

dev|il's-darn|ing-nee|dle (dev′əlz där′ning nē′-dəl), *n.* a dragonfly or damsel fly.

devil's food cake, a rich, dark chocolate cake.

devil's grip or **grippe**, = pleurodynia.

dev|il|ship (dev′əl ship), *n.* the condition of being a devil; character of a devil.

devil's paintbrush, = orange hawkweed.

devil's snuffbox, = puffball.

devil's tattoo, a drumming idly with the fingers on some object, as a sign of vexation or impatience, or in an irritating manner.

Devil's Triangle, = Bermuda Triangle.

devil's walking stick, = Hercules'-club (def. 2).

devil theorist, a person who believes in or favors a devil theory.

devil theory, any theory that attributes historical and other calamities to the actions of selfish individuals in power rather than to impersonal forces or causes: *Nothing so inexorably kills the liberty of the mind as a devil theory of history, inspiring as it must a search for the devil and proscription of his views* (Tom Wicker).

devil tree, a large tropical evergreen tree with soft white wood, a bitter bark, and a milky juice.

dev|il|try (dev′əl trē), *n., pl.* **-tries**. **1** evil action; wicked mischief. **2** mischievous or daring behavior: *The boys were full of deviltry on Halloween.* **3** great cruelty or wickedness. **4** diabolical magic or art. [alteration of *devilry*]

▶**Deviltry**, though of dubious formation, is firmly established in American use; in Great Britain it is dialectal, chiefly in the sense of "mischief." **Devilry**, which is better justified etymologically, is the more common form in British English but is rare in the United States.

dev|il|wood (dev′əl wu̇d′), *n.* a small evergreen tree of the olive family, having hard, close-grained wood, of the southern United States.

de|vi|ous (dē′vē əs), *adj.* **1** out of the direct way; winding; twisting; roundabout: *We took a devious route through side streets and alleys to avoid the crowded main streets.* **SYN:** circuitous, tortuous, rambling. **2** *Figurative.* straying from the right course; not straightforward; going astray: *His devious nature was shown in half lies and small dishonesties.* **SYN:** erring, sinful. [< Latin *dēvius* (with English *-ous*) < *dē-* out of + *via* the way]
—**de′vi|ous|ly**, *adv.* —**de′vi|ous|ness**, *n.*

de|vir|gin|ate (dē vėr′jə nāt), *v.t.*, **-at|ed**, **-at|ing**. to deprive of virginity or virginal character: *Last century, virgin land typified the American myth; devirginated America is today's symbol* (J. Wreford Watson).

de|vir|gin|ize (dē vėr′jə nīz), *v.t.*, **-ized**, **-iz|ing**. = devirginate.

de|vir|il|ize (dē vir′ə līz), *v.t.*, **-ized**, **-iz|ing**. **1** to deprive of virility or vitality; devitalize. **2** to deprive of masculine qualities.

de|vis|a|ble (di vī′zə bəl), *adj.* **1** that can be devised or contrived. **2** *Law.* that can be devised or bequeathed, as real property.

de|vis|al (di vī′zəl), *n.* the act of devising; contrivance; invention.

de|vise (di vīz′), *v.*, **-vised**, **-vis|ing**, *n.* —***v.t.*** **1** to think out; plan or contrive; invent: *The boys are trying to devise a scheme for earning money during the summer vacation. He devised a way of raising boards up to the roof by using a pulley.* **SYN:** concoct, concert, excogitate. **2** to give or leave (land, buildings, or other property) by a will. **3** *Obsolete.* to divide; separate; distribute. **4** *Obsolete.* to conceive; imagine; guess.
—***v.i.*** **1** to contrive; plan: *The captain was always devising how to get the mate into trouble.* **2** *Obsolete.* to imagine; guess: *I ... love thee better than thou canst devise* (Shakespeare).
—***n.*** *Law.* **1** a giving or leaving land, buildings, or other property, by a will. **2** a will or part of a will doing this. **3** property, especially real property, given or left in this way.
[< Old French *deviser* dispose in portions, arrange, ultimately < Latin *dīvidere* divide]
▶See **device** for usage note.

de|vis|ee (di vī′zē′, dev′ə zē′), *n. Law.* a person to whom land, buildings, or other property, are given or left by a will.

de|vis|er (di vī′zər), *n.* a person who devises; inventor; contriver.

de|vi|sor (di vī′zər, -zôr), *n. Law.* a person who gives or leaves land, buildings, or other property, by a will.

de vi|su (dē vī′sü), *Latin.* from or by sight.

de|vi|tal|i|za|tion (dē vī′tə lə zā′shən), *n.* **1** the act or process of devitalizing. **2** the state of being devitalized: *This devitalization of the governing power is the malady of democratic states* (Atlantic).

de|vi|tal|ize (dē vī′tə līz), *v.t.*, **-ized**, **-iz|ing**. **1** to take the life of; kill. **2** to make less vital; weaken; exhaust: *The times demand a renaissance in freedom of thought and freedom of expression, a renaissance that will end the orthodoxy that is threatening to devitalize us* (William O. Douglas). **SYN:** debilitate.

de|vi|ta|min|ize (dē vī′tə mə nīz), *v.t.*, **-ized**, **-iz|ing**. to remove the vitamins from.

de|vit|ri|fi|a|ble (dē vit′rə fī′ə bəl), *adj.* capable of being devitrified.

de|vit|ri|fi|ca|tion (dē vit′rə fə kā′shən), *n.* the action or process of depriving of vitreous character, especially the molecular change (of rocks) from a glassy to a crystalline condition.

de|vit|ri|fy (dē vit′rə fī), *v.t.*, **-fied**, **-fy|ing**. **1** to deprive of vitreous character or properties. **2** to cause (glass or a vitreous substance) to become opaque, hard, and crystalline in structure.

de|vize (di vīz′), *v.t., v.i.*, **-vized**, **-viz|ing**. *Especially British.* devise.

de|vo|cal|ize (dē vō′kə līz), *v.t.*, **-ized**, **-iz|ing**. *Phonetics.* to deprive of vocal or sonant qualities; unvoice. —**de|vo′cal|i|za′tion**, *n.*

de|voice (dē vois′), *v.t.*, **-voiced**, **-voic|ing**. *Phonetics.* to devocalize; unvoice: *Some speakers now devoice sounds which are historically "d" sounds* (W. P. Lehman).

de|void (di void′), *adj.* entirely without or wanting; empty; lacking; destitute (of): *A well devoid of water is useless. He is the total amateur, totally lacking in imagination, totally devoid of any technical skill* (John Canaday). **SYN:** vacant, void. [alteration of Middle English *devoided*, past participle of *devoiden* cast out, vacate < Old French *desvoidier* < *des-* away (< Latin *dis-*) + *voidier* to empty < *voide* empty, void]

de|voir (də vwär′, dev′wär), *n.* **1** Usually, **devoirs**. an act of civility or respect: *We paid our devoirs to our host.* **2** *Archaic.* duty; appointed task. [< Old French *deveir*, noun use of infinitive < Latin *dēbēre* owe]

dev|o|lu|tion (dev′ə lü′shən), *n.* **1** progression from stage to stage. **2** the transmitting or passing of property from person to person. **3** the passing on to a successor of any unexercised right. **4a** the delegating (of duty, responsibility, or authority) to another. **b** (in British politics) the granting of self-government to a division of the United Kingdom, especially to Scotland or Wales, and formerly in the 1800's to Ireland: *Their [Labour Government in London] answer, to be offered in detailed legislation soon is "devolution"—the granting of selected powers to a new and locally elected Scottish Assembly* (New York Times). **5** *Biology.* reversed evolution; degeneration: *Regression or devolution and extinction are quite as much a part of the total record as is progression* (Beals and Hoijer). [< Medieval Latin *devolutio, -onis* < Latin *dēvolvere;* see etym. under **devolve**]

dev|o|lu|tion|ar|y (dev′ə lü′shə ner′ē), *adj.* of or having to do with devolution.

dev|o|lu|tion|ist (dev′ə lü′shə nist), *n.* a person who supports the transfer of governmental authority from a higher to a lower level.

de|volve (di volv′), *v.*, **-volved**, **-volv|ing**. —***v.i.*** **1** to be handed down to someone else; be transferred: *If the president is unable to handle his duties, they devolve upon the vice-president. Her functions had now devolved upon the Prince, and in 1844, he boldly attacked the problem* (Lytton Strachey). **2** *Archaic.* to roll or flow down.
—***v.t.*** **1** to transfer (duty, work, or responsibility) to someone else: *... those who, because they are too busy or too ignorant to discharge the higher duties of self-government, have been glad to devolve them upon their representatives* (Charles H. Pearson). **2** *Archaic.* to roll down; cause to descend with a rolling motion.
[< Latin *dēvolvere* < *dē-* down + *volvere* roll]

de|volve|ment (di volv′mənt), *n.* the act of devolving.

Dev|on (dev′ən), *n.* any one of a breed of small, robust cattle originally from Devon, England.

De|vo|ni|an (də vō′nē ən), *n., adj.* —***n.*** **1** a native or inhabitant of Devon, England. **2** *Geology.* **a** the period of the Paleozoic era, after the Silurian and before the Carboniferous; Age of Fishes. It was characterized by the appearance of amphibians, wingless insects, and by an abundance of primitive fish, great expansion in the numbers and kinds of corals, and the presence of primitive trees. **b** the rocks formed during this period.
—***adj.*** **1** of or having to do with Devon, England. **2** *Geology.* of or having to do with the Devonian or its rocks: *During Devonian times ... mountains arose and much more of the land moved upward out of the water* (Fred W. Emerson).

De|von|ic (də von′ik), *adj.* = Devonian.

Dev|on|shire cream (dev′ən shir, -shər), a very thick, rich cream; clotted cream. [< *Devonshire*, a county in England]

dé|vot (dā vō′), *n. French.* a male devotee.

de|vote (di vōt′), *v.*, **-vot|ed**, **-vot|ing**, *adj.* —***v.t.*** **1** to give up (oneself, or one's money, time, or efforts) to some person, purpose, or service: *The mother devoted herself to her children. He devoted his efforts to the improvement of the parks in his city. Is the nation as yet devoting enough time and thought and energy and money and ingenuity to the ... often ignored problem of the ghetto school in the big city?* (Tom Wicker). **2** to set apart and consecrate to God or to a sacred purpose. **3** to set apart for any other particular purpose: *That museum devotes two floors to animal exhibits. The program was devoted to music by Casals, and there were speeches* (Harold C. Schonberg). **SYN:** appropriate, assign, apply. **4** *Archaic.* to consign to evil, as by a curse; doom; curse. —***adj.*** *Archaic.* devoted.
[< Latin *dēvōtus*, past participle of *dēvovēre* < *dē-* away + *vovēre* to vow. See etym. of doublet **devout**.]
—***Syn.*** *v.t.* **1, 2 Devote, dedicate, consecrate** mean to give something or someone up to a purpose. **Devote** emphasizes giving up seriously to a single purpose, shutting out everything else: *He devoted his time to study.* **Dedicate** emphasizes giving up or setting apart earnestly or solemnly for a serious or sacred use: *She dedicated her life to science. They dedicated the hospital.* **Consecrate** emphasizes setting the person or thing apart as sacred or glorified, by a solemn vow or ceremony: *A bishop consecrated the burial ground.*

de|vot|ed (di vō′tid), *adj.* **1** very loyal, affectionate, or faithful: *a devoted son. His dog is a devoted companion.* **SYN:** ardent, zealous, assiduous, attached. **2** dedicated; consecrated: *devoted churchgoers, a devoted shrine.* **3** *Archaic.* doomed; cursed: *He ... vowed revenge on her devoted head* (John Dryden). —**de|vot′ed|ly**, *adv.* —**de|vot′ed|ness**, *n.*

dev|o|tee (dev′ə tē′), *n.* **1** a person who is strongly devoted to something: *Many Americans and Japanese are devotees of baseball.* **SYN:** votary, enthusiast. **2** a person who is earnestly devoted to religion, especially to observances of an extreme kind. **SYN:** zealot.

de|vote|ment (di vōt′mənt), *n.* devotion; dedication: *His own personal devotement to the missionary cause* (Francis Wayland).

de|vo|tion (di vō′shən), *n.* **1** deep, steady affection; loyalty; faithfulness: *the devotion of a dog to its master, the devotion of a mother to her child. To a visiting Englishman there is not much to suggest a dogged devotion to the ... Empire in Canada today* (Geoffrey Moorhouse). **SYN:** love, attachment, fidelity, constancy, devotedness. **2** the act of giving up or condition of being given up to some person, purpose, or service: *the devotion of a lifetime to research. Her devotion to the Girl Scouts made her attend every meeting.* **3** the act of devoting or setting apart to a sacred use or purpose; solemn dedication; consecration: *The devotion of half his income to charity was a great example of human kindness.* **4** earnestness in religion; devoutness. **SYN:** reverence. **5a** religious worship or observance; divine worship. **SYN:** adoration. **b** (in the Roman Catholic Church) worship directed to a special religious relic. **c** a form of prayer or worship, intended for private or family use.
devotions, religious worship, prayers, or praying: *We saw several persons kneeling at their devotions* (Hawthorne).

de|vo|tion|al (di vō′shə nəl), *adj., n.* —***adj.*** having to do with religious devotion; used in worship: *devotional hymns, devotional services.* —***n.*** a devotional prayer or service. —**de|vo′tion|al|ly**, *adv.*

de|vo|tion|al|ism (di vō′shə nə liz′əm), *n.* devotional spirit or character.

de|vo|tion|al|ist (di vō′shə nə list), *n.* a person given to devotion; religious devotee.

de|vo|tions (di vō′shənz), *n.pl.* See under **devotion**.

de|vour (di vour′), *v.t.* **1** to eat (usually said of animals): *The lion devoured the sheep.* **2** to eat like an animal; eat very hungrily: *The hungry boy devoured his dinner.* **SYN:** gulp. **3** *Figurative.* to consume, waste, or destroy: *devoured by disease. The raging fire devoured the forest. Inflation devours wages and the worker must run faster and faster just to stand still* (Anthony B. Akers). **4** to swallow up; engulf: *The jaws of darkness do devour it up* (Shakespeare). **5** *Figurative.* to take in with eyes or ears in a hungry, greedy way: *He devoured the new book about airplanes.* **6** to absorb wholly: *devoured by curiosity. She was devoured by anxiety about her lost child. ... in sorrow all devour'd* (Shakespeare). [< Old French *devorer*, learned borrowing from Latin *dēvorāre* < *dē-* down + *vorāre* gulp] —**de|vour′er**, *n.* —**de|vour′ing|ly**, *adv.*

de|vour|ment (di vour′mənt), *n.* the act of devouring or consuming.

de|vout (di vout′), *adj.* **1** active in worship and prayer; religious: *The minister was a very devout*

man. SYN: godly. See syn. under **pious**. **2** showing or expressing devotion; reverential; devotional: *a devout prayer. With uplifted hands, and eyes devout, grateful to Heaven* (Milton). **3** earnest; sincere; hearty: *devout thanks. You have my devout wishes for your safety.* SYN: heartfelt. [< Old French *devot,* learned borrowing from Latin *dēvōtus.* See etym. of doublet **devote**.]
—**de|vout'ly**, *adv.* —**de|vout'ness**, *n.*

de|vul|can|ize (dē vul'kə nīz), *v.t.,* **-ized, -iz|ing.** to treat (vulcanized rubber) so as to restore or partially restore the condition of the original material.

dew (dü, dyü), *n., v.* —*n.* **1** moisture that condenses from the air and collects in small drops on cool surfaces during the night: *In the morning there are drops of dew on the grass and flowers.* **2** any moisture in small drops on a surface, such as tears or perspiration. **3** *Figurative.* something fresh or refreshing like dew: *the dew of sleep.* **4** *Figurative.* anything suggestive of morning and hence of youth: *in the morn and liquid dew of youth* (Shakespeare). **5** *U.S. Slang.* whiskey: *They still make a lively dew* (Time).
—*v.t.* to wet with or as if with dew; moisten: *It was enough to dew the eyes* (Time). *Give me thy hand, that I may dew it with my mournful tears* (Shakespeare).
[Old English *dēaw*]

De|wa|lee (di wä'lē), *n.* = Divali.

de|wan (di wän', -wôn'), *n.* in India: **1a** a prime minister of a state. **b** (formerly) a minister of finance of a state. **2** any high official. [< Arabic *dīwān* < Persian, earlier *dēvān* register (of accounts). See etym. of doublet **divan**.]

Dew|ar flask, vessel, bulb, or **tube** (dü'ər, dyü'-), a glass vessel with double, silvered walls, from between which the air has been removed, used especially as a container for liquefied gases. [< Sir James *Dewar,* 1842-1923, a Scottish chemist, who invented it]

de|wa|ter (dē wôt'ər, -wot'-), *v.t.* to remove water from, especially by draining or pumping: *to dewater coal, to dewater a pipeline.*

de|wax (dē waks'), *v.t.* to remove wax from: *Producing oils for use in cold climates is done by dewaxing the oil at a very low temperature* (Science News Letter). —**de|wax'er**, *n.*

dew|ber|ry (dü'ber'ē, dyü'-), *n., pl.* **-ries. 1a** (in North America) the fruit, a sweet, black berry, of various blackberry vines that grow along the ground. **b** (in England) the black, edible fruit of a bramble. **2** any of these plants; ground blackberry; running blackberry.

dew|bill (dü'bil', dyü'-), *n.* a fleshy growth at the base of a turkey's bill; snood.

dew|bow (dü'bō', dyü'-), *n.* an arc of colored light resembling a rainbow, occurring on a dew-covered surface. [< *dew* + (rain)*bow*]

dew cap, a short tube extending beyond the objective of a telescope to keep rain or spray from hitting the objective or to block off extraneous light.

***dew|claw** (dü'klô', dyü'-), *n.* **1** a small, useless inner claw or toe in some dogs and other animals; not reaching the ground in walking. **2** the false hoof of deer, hogs, and other hoofed mammals, consisting of two rudimentary toes.

***dewclaw** definition 1

dew|drop (dü'drop', dyü'-), *n.* a drop of dew: *In each dewdrop of the morning lies the promise of a day* (Thoreau).

De|wey|an (dü'ē ən, dyü'-), *adj.* of or having to do with the American philosopher and educator John Dewey (1859-1952) or his philosophy.

Dew|ey decimal system (dü'ē, dyü'-), a widely used system of library classification for books according to subject matter, in which specific three-digit numbers and decimals represent the various fields and their subdivisions. [< Melvil *Dewey,* 1851-1931, an American librarian, who devised it]

De|wey|ite (dü'ē īt, dyü'-), *n., adj.* —*n.* a student or follower of John Dewey.
—*adj.* = Deweyan.

dew|fall (dü'fôl', dyü'-), *n.* **1** the formation or deposition of dew: *Hear the dewfall sliding on the leaves* (Harper's). **2** the time in the evening when this begins.

dew|i|ly (dü'ə lē, dyü'-), *adv.* in a dewy manner; like dew.

dew|i|ness (dü'ē nis, dyü'-), *n.* the state of being covered or damp with dew.

***dew|lap** (dü'lap', dyü'-), *n.* **1** the loose fold of skin under the throat of cattle, certain dogs, and some other animals. **2** a pendulous fold of skin under the throat of certain birds. **3** *Humorous.* a pendulous fold of flesh on the throat of a human being. [Middle English *dewlappe* < *dew,* origin and meaning uncertain + *lap,* Old English *læppa* lobe, pendulous piece]

***dewlap** definition 1

dew|lapped (dü'lapt', dyü'-), *adj.* having a dewlap.

DEW line or **D.E.W. line**, Distant Early Warning line, a chain of radar stations across northern Canada, north of the Arctic Circle, designed to give the earliest possible warning of an attack on the United States or Canada by missiles or planes routed over the north polar region.

de|worm (dē wėrm'), *v.t.* to remove worms from: *In the deworming of dogs it is desirable to administer toluene or a chlorinated hydrocarbon* (Science Journal).

dew plant, a low, spreading plant of the carpetweed family, having thin, almost fleshless stems and rose-colored flowers, and commonly cultivated, as in window boxes; ice plant.

dew point, the temperature of the air at which dew begins to form: *Measuring the temperature of the dew point is the most accurate method of determining relative humidity* (Sears and Zemansky).

dew pond, a small and shallow pond, usually artificial, chiefly located on a hill, and supplied by mist or dew.

dew-ret (dü'ret', dyü'-), *v.t.,* **-ret|ted, -ret|ting.** to ret (flax or hemp) by exposing it to natural moisture in the open air: *It takes perhaps six weeks to dew-ret hemp* (Journal of the Royal Agricultural Society).

dew worm, = earthworm.

dew|y (dü'ē, dyü'-), *adj.,* **dew|i|er, dew|i|est.** **1** wet with dew: *from morn to dewy eve* (Milton). **2** *Figurative.* **a** fresh or refreshing like dew; sparkling. **b** coming gently; vanishing quickly. **3** of dew.

dew|y-eyed (dü'ē īd', dyü'-), *adj.* **1** sentimental; romantic. **2** artless; innocent: *They looked like debutantes, all dewy-eyed in filmy white* (Newsweek).

dex (deks), *n. U.S. Informal.* Dexedrine: *Amphetamine is the general name for a class of drugs, including Benzedrine (bennies), Dexedrine (dex), and Methedrine (meth or "speed"), which act as body stimulants* (New York Times).

dex|a|meth|a|sone (dek'sə meth'ə zōn), *n.* a synthetic steroid hormone used to treat arthritis. *Formula:* $C_{22}H_{29}FO_5$

dex|am|phet|a|mine (dek'sam fet'ə mēn, -min), *n.* = dextroamphetamine.

Dex|e|drine (dek'sə drin, -drēn), *n. Trademark.* = dextroamphetamine.

dex|ie (dek'sē), *n. U.S. Informal.* a Dexedrine pill: *... it is something else again for "bennies," "dexies" and other assorted pep pills to pile up on the locker-room shelf* (Time).

dex|i|o|car|di|a (dek'sē ə kär'dē ə), *n. Anatomy.* an abnormal condition in which the heart is on the right side; dextrocardia. [< Greek *dexiós* on the right side + *kardiā* heart]

dex|i|o|trop|ic (dek'sē ə trop'ik), *adj.* turning or rising from left to right; dextral. [< Greek *dexiós* to the right + *tropē* a turning + English *-ic*]

dex|ter (deks'tər), *adj.* **1** of or on the right-hand side. **2** *Heraldry.* situated on that part of an escutcheon to the right of the bearer, and hence to the left of the spectator. **3** *Obsolete.* auspicious; favorable; propitious. [< Latin *dexter* right]

Dex|ter (deks'tər), *n.* an Irish breed of cattle slightly larger than big dogs, noted for their hardiness and ability to thrive on any kind of pasturage: *There are only about a hundred and fifty head of Dexters in the whole country* (New Yorker). [probably < a proper name]

dex|ter|i|ty (dek ster'ə tē), *n.* **1** skill in using the hands: *A good surgeon works with dexterity.* **2** skill in using the body generally: *The champions had great dexterity and skill in swimming.* **3** skill in using the mind; cleverness: *Dexterity in questioning witnesses helped the lawyer win many cases. By his incomparable dexterity, he [Francesco Sforza] raised himself from the precarious and dependent situation of a military adventurer to the first throne of Italy* (Macaulay). **4** right-handedness.

dex|ter|ous (deks'tər əs, -trəs), *adj.* **1** having skill with the hands: *A typist needs to be dexterous.* **2** quick and skillful in bodily movements: *a dexterous acrobat.* **3** having or showing skill in using the mind; clever: *A successful manager must be dexterous in handling people.* **4** right-handed. Also, **dextrous.** —**dex'ter|ous|ly**, *adv.* —**dex'ter|ous|ness**, *n.*
—*Syn.* **1, 2, 3 Dexterous, deft, adroit** mean skillful in using the hands and body, or the mind. **Dexterous** suggests easy, quick, smooth movements and lightness and sureness of touch coming from practice: *Mary is a dexterous pianist.* **Deft** adds to *dexterous* the idea of neatness and exceptional lightness and swiftness: *A surgeon has to be deft.* **Adroit** adds to *dexterous* the idea of being quick-witted, and is used less often of physical skill than of mental quickness, resourcefulness, and cleverness in handling situations: *The adroit stewardess kept the passengers on the plane cheerful during the storm.*

dex|trad (deks'trad), *adv.* to the right. [< Latin *dextra,* feminine of *dexter* right hand + *ad* toward]

dex|tral (deks'trəl), *adj.* **1** of the right hand; right-hand; right. **2** right-handed. **3** having the spire or whorl rising from left to right when viewed from above, as most snail shells do. **4** *Obsolete.* auspicious; favorable. —**dex'tral|ly**, *adv.*

dex|tral|i|ty (dek stral'ə tē), *n.* **1** the state of being on the right side rather than the left. **2** right-handedness.

dex|tran (deks'tran), *n. Chemistry.* a white, slimy carbohydrate, produced in sugar solutions such as molasses or fermenting sugar beets, by the action of certain bacteria. It is used as a substitute for blood plasma in cases of shock. *Unlike blood plasma, scientists note, dextran can be stockpiled without refrigeration and it does not transmit certain types of virus* (Wall Street Journal). *Formula:* $(C_6H_{10}O_5)_n$ [< Latin *dexter* right hand (because of its dextrorotatory properties)]

dex|tra|nase (deks'trə nās), *n.* an enzyme produced by a fungus of the penicillium family, effective in preventing formation of dental plaque. [< *dextran* (which promotes formation of plaque) + *-ase*]

Dex|tri-Mal|tose (deks'trē môl'tōs), *n. Trademark.* a soluble powder of maltose and dextrins, used as a nutritive agent in infants' formulas.

dex|trin (deks'trin), *n.* a soluble, gummy substance formed from starch by the action of heat, dilute acids or alkalis, or enzymes (amylase). It is used as an adhesive and for sizing paper. [< French *dextrine* < Latin *dexter* right hand (because of its dextrorotatory properties)]

dex|trine (deks'trin, -trēn), *n.* = dextrin.

dex|trin|ize (deks'trə nīz), *v.t.,* **-ized, -iz|ing.** to convert partly or wholly into dextrin: *dextrinized starch.*

dex|trin|ous (deks'trə nəs), *adj.* having to do with or resembling dextrin.

dex|tro (deks'trō), *adj. Chemistry.* turning or turned to the right. [< Latin *dexter* right hand]

dextro-, *combining form.* **1** toward the right: *Dextrorotatory = rotatory toward the right.* **2** dextrorotatory: *Dextroglucose = dextrorotatory glucose.*
[< Latin *dexter* right hand]

dex|tro|am|phet|a|mine (deks'trō am fet'ə mēn, -min), *n.* a drug used as a stimulant and for controlling the appetite; Dexedrine. It is the dextrorotatory form of amphetamine. Also, **dexamphetamine.**

dex|tro|car|di|a (deks'trə kär'dē ə), *n.* = dexiocardia.

dex|tro|glu|cose (deks'trə glü'kōs), *n.* common dextrorotatory glucose; dextrose.

dex|tro|gy|rate (deks'trə jī'rāt), *adj.* = dextrorotatory.

dex|tro|gy|rous (deks'trə jī'rəs), *adj.* = dextrorotatory.

dex|tro|ro|ta|ry (deks'trə rō'tər ē), *adj.* = dextrorotatory.

dex|tro|ro|ta|tion (deks'trə rō tā'shən), *n.* **1** rotation toward the right hand. **2** *Physics, Chemistry.* rotation of the plane of polarization of light to the right.

dex|tro|ro|ta|to|ry (deks'trə rō'tə tôr'ē, -tōr'-), *adj.* **1** turning or causing to turn toward the right or in a clockwise direction. **2** *Physics, Chemistry.* characterized by turning the plane of polarization of light to the right, as a crystal, lens, or compound in solution.

dex|tror|sal (deks trôr'səl), *adj.* = dextrorse.

dex|trorse (deks'trôrs, deks trôrs'), *adj. Botany.* rising spirally from left to right, or in a clockwise direction when viewed from directly underneath or from the base: *the dextrorse stem of a vine.* [< Latin *dextrōrsum,* variant of *dextrovorsum* < *dexter* to the right + *versum* turned] —**dex'trorse|ly**, *adv.*

dex|trose (deks'trōs), *n.* a crystalline sugar less

Pronunciation Key: hat, āge, cãre, fär; let, ēqual, tėrm; it, īce; hot, ōpen, ôrder; oil, out; cup, pu̇t, rüle; child; long; thin; ᴛʜen; zh, measure; ə represents **a** in about, **e** in taken, **i** in pencil, **o** in lemon, **u** in circus.

sweet than cane sugar, occurring in many plant and animal tissues and fluids; grape sugar. It is a form of glucose. It is dextrorotatory to polarized light. *To keep going, he would salvage the so-called dextrose tablets from the K rations that the rest of us would throw away* (Harper's). *Formula:* $C_6H_{12}O_6$ [< *dextr*(o)- + *-ose*[2]]

dex|tro|thy|rox|ine (deks′trə thī rok′sēn, -sin), *n.* a drug that accelerates the breakdown of cholesterol in the blood. It is the dextrorotatory form of thyroxine.

dex|trous (deks′trəs), *adj.* = dexterous. **—dex′trous|ly,** *adv.* **—dex′trous|ness,** *n.*

dex|tro|ver|sion (deks′trə vėr′zhən, -shən), *n.* a turning or deviation from the left to the right side: *In "wrong-sided heart," known as dextroversion, the heart is placed as if it had been rotated . . . from its normal position* (Seattle Times).

dey (dā), *n., pl.* **deys.** **1** the former title of the ruler of Algiers, before the French conquest in 1830. **2** former title of the rulers of Tunis and Tripoli. [< Turkish *dayi* (originally) maternal uncle]

dey|ship (dā′ship), *n.* the position or dignity of a dey.

de|zinc|i|fi|ca|tion (dē zing′kə fə kā′shən), *n. Metallurgy.* **1** the separation of zinc from an alloy or composition in which it is present, especially from a metal in a liquid state. **2** loss of zinc by corrosion, as from brass.

de|zinc|i|fy (dē zing′kə fī), *v.t.,* **-fied, -fy|ing.** to subject to dezincification.

de|zy|mo|tize (dē zī′mə tīz), *v.t.,* **-tized, -tiz|ing.** to free from disease germs. [< *de-* + *zymot*(ic) + *-ize*]

DF (no periods), direction finder.

D.F., **1** Defender of the Faith (Latin, *Defensor Fidei*). **2** Federal District (Spanish, *Distrito Federal*).

D.F.A., Doctor of Fine Arts.

DFC (no periods), Distinguished Flying Cross.

DFL (no periods) or **D.F.L.,** Democratic-Farmer-Labor (party), a political party of Minnesota formed in 1944 by the merger of the Farmer-Labor Party and the Democratic Party.

DFM (no periods), Distinguished Flying Medal.

DFP (no periods), diisopropyl fluorophosphate.

dg., decigram or decigrams.

DG (no periods), director-general.

dghai|sa (dī′sə), *n.* a small Maltese boat that resembles a gondola. [< Maltese *dghaisa*]

d-glu|cose (dē′glü′kōs), *n.* = dextrose.

DH (no periods), designated hitter: *One manager . . . was thinking of using Don Buford as a leadoff DH* (National Review).

D.H., Doctor of Humanities.

dha (dä), *n.* = dah.

dha|i (dä′ē), *n.* (in India) a midwife. [< Hindustani *dhāī*]

dhak (däk, dôk), *n.* an East Indian tree of the pea family, noted for its brilliant orange-red flowers. It yields a form of the gum kino. [< Hindi *ḍhāk*]

dhal (däl), *n.* = dal.

dham|noo (däm′nü), *n.* **1** an East Indian tree of the same family as the linden. **2** the strong lumber from this tree. [< Hindi *dhamnoo*]

dhar|ma (där′mə, dėr′-), *n.* **1** *Hinduism and Buddhism.* the law, especially natural and moral law. **2** *Hinduism.* right behavior; virtue; righteousness: *In India, one was expected to follow the "dharma"—or the "style of life"—of one's caste* (Wall Street Journal). [< Sanskrit *dharma*]

***Dhar|ma Chak|ra** (där′mə chuk′rə; dėr′-), *Hinduism.* the wheel of law, an ancient symbol in the form of a many-spoked wheel, represented on the flag of India. [< Sanskrit *dharma* dharma + *cakrā* wheel, disk]

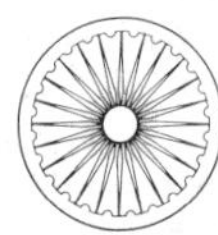

***Dharma Chakra**

Dhar|ma|shas|tra (där′mə shäs′trə, dėr′-), *n.* the whole body of Hindu law, especially the laws ascribed to Manu, Yajnavalkya, and other inspired sages. [< Sanskrit *dharma-śāstra* < *dharma* dharma + *śāstra* sastra]

dhar|na (där′nä, dėr′-), *n.* (in India) a way of extorting payment or compliance with a demand, in which the creditor sits fasting at the debtor's door until his demand is met. Also, **dhurna.** [< Hindi *dharnā*]

Dhe|gi|ha (dā′gē hä), *n.* a division of the Siouan stock of North American Indians.

D.H.L., Doctor of Hebrew Letters (or Literature).

dho|bi (dō′bē), *n.* (in India) a native washerman: *In cities like Cochin and Trivandrum, some college graduates work as . . . dhobis (laundrymen) for 20¢ a day* (Time). [< Hindi *dhōbī*]

dhole (dōl), *n., pl.* **dholes** or (*especially collectively*) **dhole.** a fierce, wild dog of Asia and Indonesia, that usually hunts in packs. [perhaps < Santali (a language of India) *dahal* wild dog]

dholl (dol), *n.* = dal.

dhoo|ti (dü′tē), *n.* = dhoti.

***dho|ti** (dō′tē), *n.* **1** a long, narrow loincloth worn by men in India: *He was . . . a magnificent man with grey moustaches and beard, and always dressed in a clean white dhoti and shirt* (London Times). **2** fabric for this garment. [< Hindi *dhōtī*]

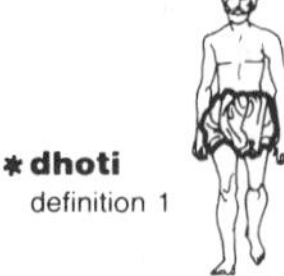

***dhoti**
definition 1

***dhow** (dou), *n.* a ship with lateen sails, used along the coasts of Arabia, India, and eastern Africa: *Out by the reef that made the harbor, the Frenchman's dhow lay at anchor* (New Yorker). [< Arabic *dāw;* origin uncertain]

***dhow**

dhur|na (dėr′nä), *n.* = dharna.

dhur|rie (dėr′ē), *n.* a kind of coarse, durable cotton carpeting made in India, usually in fringed squares. [< Hindustani *darī*]

di (dē), *n.* a tone of the musical scale between do and re. [variant of *do*[2]]

di., diameter.

di-[1], *prefix.* **1a** twice; double; twofold, as in *dicotyledon.* **b** two; having two, as in *digraph.* **2** containing two atoms, radicals, or the like, of the substance specified, as in *dioxide.* Also, **dis-** before *s.* [< Greek *dís* twice]

di-[2], *prefix.* the form of **dis-**[2] before *b, d, l, m, n, r, s, v,* and sometimes before *g* and *j,* as in *direct, digress.*

di-[3], *prefix.* the form of **dia-** before vowels, as in *diorama.*

Di (no period), *Chemistry.* didymium.

DI (no periods) or **D.I.,** **1** disability insurance. **2** discomfort index. **3** drill instructor (in the U.S. Marine Corps).

dia., diameter.

dia-, *prefix.* through; across; thoroughly, as in *diaphragm, diameter.* Also, **di-** before vowels. [< Greek *diá* through, throughout, apart]

di|a|base (dī′ə bās), *n.* **1** *Especially U.S.* a fine-grained, dark-colored, crystalline, granular igneous rock consisting essentially of augite and feldspar. **2** *Especially British.* an altered form of basalt or dolerite. **3** *Obsolete.* diorite. [< French *diabase,* perhaps < Greek *diábasis* a going over < *diá* through, over + *baínein* to walk, step, go]

di|a|ba|sic (dī′ə bā′sik), *adj.* of or having to do with diabase.

di|a|bat|ic (dī′ə bat′ik), *adj.* of or with transmission of heat; not adiabatic. [< Greek *diábatos* passable + English *-ic*]

di|a|be|ah (dē′ə bē′ə), *n.* = dahabeah.

di|a|be|tes (dī′ə bē′tis, -tēz), *n.* **1** a disease in which a person's system cannot properly absorb normal amounts of sugar and starch because the pancreas fails to secrete enough insulin; diabetes mellitus. It is characterized by excessive production of urine and abnormal thirst. *There exists a strong hereditary predisposition in both types of diabetes, although a greater one in the maturity-onset type* (George F. Cahill, Jr.). **2** = diabetes insipidus. [< New Latin *diabetes* < Greek *diabḗtēs* (literally) a passer-through; siphon < *diabaínein* go through < *dia-* through + *baínein* go]

diabetes in|sip|i|dus (in sip′ə dəs), a disorder marked by profuse secretion of urine (containing no sugar) and intense thirst, caused by a malfunction of the pituitary gland. [< New Latin *diabetes insipidus* (literally) insipid diabetes]

diabetes mel|li|tus (mel′ə təs), a disorder of carbohydrate metabolism generally due to failure of the pancreas to secrete enough insulin, characterized by the presence of sugar in the urine, abnormally high sugar content in the blood, loss of weight, extreme thirst and hunger, excessive secretion of urine, and, in severe cases, coma; sugar diabetes. Treatment includes the administration of insulin and rigid control of the diet. [< New Latin *diabetes mellitus* (literally) honey diabetes]

di|a|bet|ic (dī′ə bet′ik, -bē′tik), *adj., n.* **—*adj.*** **1** of or having to do with diabetes or its treatment. **2** having diabetes.
—*n.* a person having diabetes: *In the diabetic, the pancreas may not produce enough insulin* (Time).

di|a|be|to|gen|ic (dī′ə bē′tə jen′ik), *adj.* that produces diabetes: *The diabetogenic hormone seems to decrease sugar metabolism and, thus, is directly antagonistic to insulin* (A. M. Winchester).

di|a|be|tol|o|gist (dī′ə bə tol′ə jist), *n.* a doctor who specializes in diabetes or diabetic disorders.

di|a|ble|rie or **di|a|ble|ry** (di ä′blər ē), *n., pl.* **-ries.** **1** diabolic magic or art; sorcery; witchcraft: *His use of a Biblical phrase gave her a touch of shivers, of diablerie—the devil at his old game of quoting scripture* (Harper's). **2** reckless mischief; deviltry: *Miss Eva . . . appeared to be fascinated by her wild diablerie* (Harriet Beecher Stowe). **3** the domain or realm of devils. **4** the lore of devils; demonology. [< French *diablerie*]

di|a|blo|tin (dē ab′lə tin; *French* dyä blô taɴ′), *n.* **1** a little devil; imp. **2** the guacharo. [< French *diablotin,* diminutive of *diable* devil]

di|a|bol|a|try (dī′ə bol′ə trē), *n.* worship of the Devil.

di|a|bol|ic (dī′ə bol′ik), *adj.* **1** like the Devil; very cruel or wicked; devilish; fiendish: *The police discovered a diabolic plot to poison the city's drinking water.* SYN: satanic. **2** of or having to do with the Devil or devils. SYN: infernal. [< Late Latin *diabolicus* < Greek *diabolikós* < *diábolos;* see etym. under **devil**] **—di′a|bol′i|cal|ly,** *adv.* **—di′a|bol′i|cal|ness,** *n.*

di|a|bol|i|cal (dī′ə bol′ə kəl), *adj.* = diabolic.

di|ab|o|lism (dī ab′ə liz əm), *n.* **1** action aided by the Devil; sorcery; witchcraft. **2** diabolical or devilish action; deviltry: *Even the most vicious acts of his characters are felt as the deeds of black misunderstanding rather than diabolism* (Newsweek). **3** belief in or worship of a devil or devils. **4** the character or condition of a devil.

di|ab|o|list (dī ab′ə list), *n.* a person who believes in or writes on diabolism.

di|ab|o|lize (dī ab′ə līz), *v.t.,* **-lized, -liz|ing.** **1** to make diabolic or devilish. **2** to represent as diabolic. **3** to subject to diabolic influence.

***di|ab|o|lo** (dē ab′ə lō), *n., pl.* **-los.** **1** a game in which a piece of wood shaped like an hourglass is spun, tossed, and caught by means of two sticks with a cord stretched between them held in the hands. **2** the piece of wood. [< Italian *diabolo*]

***diabolo**
definition 1

di|a|bol|o|gy (dī′ə bol′ə jē), *n.* = diabolology.

di|a|bo|lol|o|gy (dī′ə bə lol′ə jē), *n.* doctrine concerning the Devil or devils; diabolic lore. [< Greek *diábolos* devil + English *-logy*]

di|ab|o|lus ex ma|chi|na (dī ab′ə ləs eks mak′ə nə), *Latin.* devil from a machine; an evil person or thing introduced into a story or account to provide an explanation or resolve a problem: *His analysis leaves him with no basis for rational optimism. His diabolus ex machina—technique—is greater than man* (Scientific American).
[patterned on *deus ex machina*]

di|a|caus|tic (dī′ə kôs′tik), *adj., n. Optics.* **—*adj.*** (of a surface or curve) formed by the intersection of refracted rays of light.
—*n.* a diacaustic curve or surface.
[< *dia-* across + *caustic*]

di|a|ce|tic acid (dī′ə sē′tik, -set′ik), a derivative of acetic acid, found in the urine in certain abnormal conditions, especially when diabetes is present. *Formula:* $C_4H_6O_3$

di|a|ce|to|nu|ri|a (dī′ə sē′tə nůr′ē ə, -nyůr′-), *n.* the presence of diacetic acid in the urine.

di|ac|e|tu|ri|a (dī as′ə tůr′ē ə, -tyůr′-), *n.* = diacetonuria.

di|ac|e|tyl|mor|phine (dī as′ə təl môr′fēn), *n.* = heroin.

di|a|chron|ic (dī′ə kron′ik), *adj.* **1** through the course of time or history; historical. **2** treating a subject or event from a historical perspective; not synchronic or descriptive: *Historical (diachronic) linguistics is an honorable field of study; so is structural (synchronic) linguistics* (George P. Faust).

di|a|chron|i|cal|ly (dī′ə kron′ə klē), *adv.* in a diachronic manner; historically.

di|ach|ro|ny (dī ak′rə nē), *n.* **1** diachronic or historical treatment or arrangement. **2** historical change or development.

di|ach|y|lon (dī ak′ə lon), *n.* an adhesive plaster consisting essentially of lead oxide and oil, much used as the basis for other plasters. Also, **di-achylum**, **diaculum**. [< Medieval Latin *diachylon* < Greek *diàchȳlôn* composed of juices]

di|ach|y|lum (dī ak′ə ləm), *n.* = diachylon.

di|ac|id (dī as′id), *adj. Chemistry.* (of a base or alcohol) able to form a salt or ester by combining with two molecules of a monobasic acid or with one of a dibasic acid.

di|ac|o|nal (dī ak′ə nəl), *adj.* of or having to do with a deacon: *diaconal office, diaconal ministrations.* [< Late Latin *diāconālis* < Latin *diāconus;* see etym. under **deacon**]

di|ac|o|nate (dī ak′ə nit, -nāt), *n.* **1** the rank or position of a deacon. **2** a group of deacons: *Our diaconate meets to discuss church affairs.* [< Late Latin *diāconātus* < Latin *diāconus;* see etym. under **deacon**]

di|a|con|i|con (dī′ə kon′ə kon), *n., pl.* **-ca** (-kə). (in the Eastern Church) a building or room adjoining the church, where vestments, ornaments, and other equipment and supplies are kept; sacristy; vestry. [< Greek *diākonikón*]

di|a|cous|tic (dī′ə küs′tik, -kous′-), *adj.* of or having to do with diacoustics.

di|a|cous|tics (dī′ə küs′tiks, -kous′-), *n.* the consideration of the properties of sound refracted by passing through media of different density.

di|a|crit|ic (dī′ə krit′ik), *adj., n.* —*adj.* **1** = diacritical. **2** *Medicine.* = diagnostic.
—*n.* a diacritical mark.
[< Greek *diakritikós* < *diakrínein* < *dia-* apart + *krínein* distinguish, separate]

di|a|crit|i|cal (dī′ə krit′ə kəl), *adj.* **1a** used or meant to distinguish; distinctive: *No attempt, of course, is made at exhaustive analysis; the aim, rather, is diacritical, which is all one may fairly demand of an encyclopedia* (Punch). **b** *Phonetics.* used to distinguish sounds or values of letters. See also **diacritical mark. 2** capable of distinguishing or discerning: *diacritical intellect or power.* —**di′a|crit′i|cal|ly**, *adv.*

***diacritical mark**, **point**, or **sign**, a mark placed over, under, or attached to a letter to indicate pronunciation, stress, accent, or other value.

***diacritical mark**

cañón, élève, façade

di|ac|tine (dī ak′tin), *adj., n.* —*adj.* (of a sponge spicule) pointed at both ends; having two rays.
—*n.* a straight or curved spicule with two rays.
[< *di-*[1] two + Greek *aktís, -înos* ray]

di|ac|tin|ic (dī′ak tin′ik), *adj. Physics.* capable of transmitting the actinic rays of light, as a lens filter.

di|ac|tin|ism (dī ak′tə niz əm), *n. Physics.* the condition of transmitting actinic rays.

di|ac|u|lum (dī ak′yə ləm), *n.* diachylon.

di|a|del|phous (dī′ə del′fəs), *adj. Botany.* **1** (of stamens) united so as to form two bundles or sets. **2** (of plants) having the stamens so united. [< New Latin *Diadelphia* the former class name (coined by Linnaeus) < Greek *di-* double + *adelphós* brother + English *-ous*]

di|a|dem (dī′ə dem), *n., v.* —*n.* **1** a crown: *Christ wore a diadem of thorns.* **2** an ornamental band of cloth formerly worn as a crown. **3** *Figurative.* royal power, authority, or dignity; sovereignty.
—*v.t.* to adorn with a diadem; crown: (*Figurative.*) *diadem'd with rays divine* (Alexander Pope).
[< Latin *diadēma* < Greek *diádēma* < *diadeîn* bind around < *dia-* across + *deîn* bind]

Di|ad|o|chi (dī ad′ə kī), *n.pl.* the six Macedonian generals of Alexander the Great, among whom his empire was divided after his death in 323 B.C.

di|ad|ro|mous (dī ad′rə məs), *adj.* that migrate between salt waters and fresh waters: *diadromous fish.* [< *dia-* + *-dromous* (as in *anadromous, catadromous*)]

di|aer|e|sis (dī er′ə sis; *especially British* dī ir′ə-sis), *n., pl.* **-ses** (-sēz). = dieresis.

di|ae|ret|ic (dī′ə ret′ik), *adj.* = dieretic.

di|a|gen|e|sis (dī′ə jen′ə sis), *n.* **1** *Geology.* the modification taking place in a sediment from the time of its deposition to the time when it undergoes metamorphism. **2** any chemical dissolution or recombination of elements. [< *dia-* + *genesis*]

di|a|ge|net|ic (dī′ə jə net′ik), *adj.* **1** of or having to do with diagenesis. **2** altered by diagenesis: *Pyrite and siderite grains are diagenetic* (Lawrence Ogden). —**di′a|ge|net′i|cal|ly**, *adv.*

di|a|ge|o|trop|ic (dī′ə jē′ə trop′ik), *adj.* tending to grow horizontally to the earth's surface, such as branches and roots. [< *dia-* + Greek *gê, geôn* the earth + *tropikós* having to do with turning]

di|a|ge|ot|ro|pism (dī′ə jē ot′rə piz′əm), *n.* the tendency of parts of plants to grow horizontally to the earth's surface.

di|ag|nos|a|ble (dī′əg nō′sə bəl), *adj.* that can be diagnosed: *Despite their professed aches and pains ... [they] have no diagnosable physical ailments* (Newsweek).

di|ag|nose (dī′əg nōs′, -nōz′), *v.t., v.i.,* **-nosed, -nos|ing.** to find out the nature of by an examination and careful study; make a diagnosis of (a disease or any other condition); diagnosticate: *The doctor diagnosed her illness as measles.* [back formation < *diagnosis*] —**di′ag|nos′er**, *n.*

di|ag|no|sis (dī′əg nō′sis), *n., pl.* **-ses** (-sēz). **1a** the act or process of finding out what disease a person or animal has by examination and careful study of the symptoms: *The doctor used X rays and blood samples in his diagnosis.* **b** the opinion resulting from such investigation: *To most people, a tuberculosis diagnosis comes as an enormous emotional shock* (Newsweek).
2 *Figurative.* **a** a careful study of the facts about something to find out its essential features, faults, or other characteristics: *The engineers made a complete diagnosis of the plane crash by examining the parts for defective workmanship.* **b** a decision reached after a careful study of symptoms or facts: *The diagnosis blamed the collapse of the bridge on faulty construction.*
3 *Biology.* a statement of the determining characteristics, as of a genus or species. [< Greek *diágnōsis* a discerning, distinguishing < *diá-* apart, through + *gnôsis* inquiry, investigation < *gignṓskein* (learn to) know]

di|ag|nos|tic (dī′əg nos′tik), *adj., n.* —*adj.* **1** of or having to do with diagnosis: *a diagnostic approach to the problems of education.* **2** helping in diagnosis; serving to indicate the nature or character of anything, as of a disease: *diagnostic tests.*
—*n.* **1** Also, **diagnostics.** diagnosis, especially as an art or science. **2** a symptom or characteristic of value in diagnosis: *Her pallor was a diagnostic.*

di|ag|nos|ti|cal|ly (dī′əg nos′tə klē), *adv.* **1** by means of diagnosis. **2** with reference to diagnosis.

di|ag|nos|ti|cate (dī′əg nos′tə kāt), *v.t., v.i.,* **-cat|ed, -cat|ing.** = diagnose.

di|ag|nos|ti|cian (dī′əg nos tish′ən), *n.* a person who is expert in making diagnoses: *This instrument makes it possible for diagnosticians to listen to the heart* (Scientific American).

***di|ag|o|nal** (dī ag′ə nəl), *n., adj., v.,* **-naled, -nal|ing** or (*especially British*) **-nalled, -nal|ling.** —*n.* **1a** a straight line or plane that cuts across in a slanting direction, often from corner to corner. **b** *Geometry.* a line connecting two nonadjacent corners of a plane figure having four or more sides. **2a** any slanting line, row, or arrangement of things. **b** = virgule. **3** a part of any structure, such as a beam or plank, placed diagonally.
—*adj.* **1** taking the direction of a diagonal; slanting; oblique: *a diagonal stripe in cloth. The ship sailed on a diagonal course across the Atlantic from New York to Cape Town.* SYN: bias. **2** having slanting lines, ridges, or parts, or having some part placed diagonally or obliquely: *a diagonal weave.* **3a** connecting two corners that are not next to each other in a four-sided or many-sided figure: *a diagonal line.* **b** (of a plane) extending from one edge of a polyhedron to another nonadjacent edge.
—*v.i.* to move in a diagonal; diagonalize: *Red tubes arch over a horizontal wall band of rainbow colors, then diagonal down to the floor* (New York Times).
[< Latin *diagōnālis* < Greek *diagônios* from angle to angle < *diá-* across + *goniā́* angle] —**di|ag′o-nal|ly**, *adv.*

***diagonal**
definitions 1b, 3b

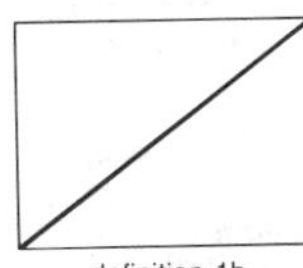
definition 1b

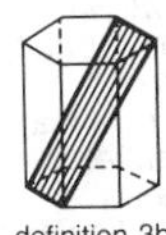
definition 3b

diagonal cloth, a twilled fabric having prominent diagonal ridges.

di|ag|o|nal|ize (dī ag′ə nə līz), *v.,* **-ized, -iz|ing.**
—*v.i.* to move in a diagonal.
—*v.t.* to make diagonal; align diagonally with.

di|a|gram (dī′ə gram), *n., v.,* **-gramed, -gram|ing** or (*especially British*) **-grammed, -gram|ming.**
—*n.* **1** a drawing or sketch showing important parts of a thing. A diagram may be an outline, a plan, a drawing, a figure, a chart, or a combination of any of these, made to show clearly what a thing is or how it works. *He drew a diagram to show us how to get to his house. The engineer drew a diagram of the bridge.* **2** a figure composed of lines, used to help in the proof of a geometrical proposition or to illustrate a definition or statement.
—*v.t.* to put on paper, a blackboard, or other writing surface, in the form of a drawing or sketch; make a diagram of: *to diagram the digestive system, to diagram a sentence. The architect diagramed the floor plan to show how he would divide the office space.*
[< Latin *diagramma* < Greek *diágramma* < *diá-* apart, out + *grámma* lines (of a picture, drawing) < *gráphein* write, mark]

di|a|gram|mat|ic (dī′ə grə mat′ik), *adj.* **1** in the form of a diagram. **2** in outline form only; sketchy: *The plot of my story was in a diagrammatic form, with details to be filled in later.*
—**di′a|gram|mat′i|cal|ly**, *adv.*

di|a|gram|mat|i|cal (dī′ə grə mat′ə kəl), *adj.* = diagrammatic.

di|a|gram|ma|tize (dī′ə gram′ə tīz), *v.t.,* **-tized, -tiz|ing.** to make a diagram of; diagram.

di|a|graph (dī′ə graf, -gräf), *n.* **1** an instrument used for drawing mechanically, on any desired scale, projections of objects, enlargements of maps, or the like. **2** a combined protractor and scale used in plotting. [< French *diagraphe* < Greek *diagráphein* mark out with lines < *diá-* across, through + *gráphein* draw, mark]

di|a|grid (dī′ə grid′), *n.* a framework of diagonally intersecting bars of metal or concrete, used as a supporting structure in a building, reactor, or the like. [< *dia*(gonal) *grid*]

di|a|ki|ne|sis (dī′ə ki nē′sis, -kī-), *n. Biology.* the last stage of the prophase of meiosis, in which the chromatids contract, making the chiasmata seem to move toward their ends. This is the stage in which the chromosomes in many organisms are most easily counted. [< *dia-* across + Greek *kī́nēsis* motion]

di|al (dī′əl), *n., v.,* **-aled, -al|ing** or (*especially British*) **-alled, -al|ling.** —*n.* **1** a marked surface on which a moving pointer shows time, degree, direction, or how much there is of something. The face of a clock or of a compass is a dial. A dial may show the amount of water in a tank or the amount of steam pressure in a boiler. **2** the plate or disk of a radio or television set, with numbers or letters on it for tuning in to a radio or television station. **3** the part of an automatic telephone consisting of a revolving disk with holes to indicate how far to turn it in order to encode the letters and numbers, used in making telephone calls. **4** a plate, disk, or wheel on a lock, with numbers or letters on it, used for opening the lock. **5** = sundial. **6** a miner's compass for underground surveying. **7** an instrument for holding a gem while it is being cut. **8** *Obsolete.* any timepiece or chronometer.
—*v.t.* **1** to tune in by using a radio or television dial: *He dials his favorite station every morning.* **2** to call by means of a telephone dial: *She dialed her father's office. You have dialed the wrong number.* **3** to turn a dial to (a combination) in order to open a lock: *He dialed the combination to open his locker.* **4** *Figurative.* to measure or record with or as if with a dial. **5** to survey or lay out with a miner's compass.
—*v.i.* to operate a dial.
match dials, *Railroading.* to compare time on watches: *The engineer and the conductor matched dials.*
[perhaps < unrecorded Medieval Latin (*rota*) *dialis* daily (wheel of a clock); *dialis* < Latin *diēs* day] —**di′al|er**, *especially British* **di′al|ler**, *n.*

dial., **1** dialect. **2** dialectal.

di|al|bird (dī′əl bėrd′), *n.* = dayal.

di|al|de|hyde (dī al′də hīd), *n. Chemistry.* a compound made up of two aldehydes.

dialdehyde starch, a strong, gluelike substance produced by the oxidation of the anhydroglucose in starch, used as a thickening, binding, and tanning agent.

di|a|lect (dī′ə lekt), *n., adj.* —*n.* **1** a form of speech spoken in a certain district or by a certain group of people: *The Scottish dialect of English has many words and pronunciations that are not used in Standard English. A dialect of French is spoken in southern Louisiana by descendants of French Canadians.* SYN: See syn. under **language.** **2** one of a group of closely related languages: *Some of the dialects descended from the Latin language are French, Italian, Spanish, and Portuguese.* **3** a distinct form or variety of a language: *the Sicilian dialect of Italian.* **4** words and pronunciations used by certain professions, classes of people, or other groups. **5** manner of speaking; phraseology; idiom.
—*adj.* = dialectal: *dialect speech, dialect poems.*

Pronunciation Key: hat, **ā**ge, c**ã**re, f**ä**r; let, **ē**qual, t**ė**rm; it, **ī**ce; hot, **ō**pen, **ô**rder; **oi**l, **ou**t; cup, p**ů**t, r**ü**le; **ch**ild; lo**ng**; **th**in; **ᴛʜ**en; **zh**, measure; **ə** represents **a** in about, **e** in taken, **i** in pencil, **o** in lemon, **u** in circus.

[< French *dialecte* < Latin *dialectus* < Greek *diálektos* discourse, conversation, ultimately < *diá-* between + *légein* speak]

▶ **Dialects** exist because of the separation of groups of speakers and are not peculiar to backward regions, for the "Oxford accent" forms a minor dialect, and the people of Boston and of New York speak differently from their neighbors. Nor do dialects depend upon education or social standing. An educated, as well as an uneducated, Westerner will speak somewhat differently from a Southerner or New Englander of a similar degree and quality of education.

di|a|lec|tal (dī′ə lek′təl), *adj.* of a dialect; like that of a dialect. —**di′a|lec′tal|ly**, *adv.*

dialect atlas, = linguistic atlas.

dialect geography, = linguistic geography.

di|a|lec|tic (dī′ə lek′tik), *n., adj.* —*n.* **1** Often, **dialectics.** the art or practice of logical discussion as a means of examining critically the truth of a theory or opinion: *Freedom of speech has become a central concern of the western society because of the discovery among the Greeks that dialectic, as demonstrated in the Socratic dialogues, is a principal method of attaining moral and political truth* (Atlantic). **2** discussion or debate, on the basis of logic, of the truth of a theory or opinion; logical argumentation. **3** a branch of logic that consists of formal rhetorical reasoning. **4** Often, **dialectics. a** a method of logic based on the resolution of contradictory opposites, thesis and antithesis, leading to synthesis. It was used by Hegel and later adapted by Marx. **b** a social, economic, or other change believed to result from the resolution of contradictory opposites.
—*adj.* **1** having to do with dialectics; dialectical: *a dialectic theory of history.* **2** = dialectal.
[< Old French *dialectique* < Latin *dialectica* < Greek *dialektikē* (*téchnē*) dialectic art, art of reasoning < *diálektikos* < *diálektos;* see etym. under **dialect**] —**di′a|lec′ti|cal|ly**, *adv.*

di|a|lec|ti|cal (dī′ə lek′tə kəl), *adj.* = dialectic.

dialectical materialism, a social and economic theory, elaborated by Karl Marx and Friedrich Engels from Georg Hegel's dialectic theory and held by Communists, which maintains that social and economic evolution must inevitably proceed through stages of conflict between economic classes, the dictatorship of the proletariat, and the gradual atrophy of the state to the eventual emergence of a classless society.

dialectical materialist, a person who supports dialectical materialism.

di|a|lec|ti|cian (dī′ə lek tish′ən), *n.* **1** a person skilled in dialectic; logician: *Skilled dialecticians drew them into arguments* (Newsweek). **2** a student of dialects.

di|a|lec|ti|cism (dī′ə lek′tə siz əm), *n.* **1** the characteristic tendency or influence of dialect. **2** dialectal speech or usage. **3** the practice of dialectic.

di|a|lec|tics (dī′ə lek′tiks), *n.* = dialectic (defs. 1, 4): *Dialectics explains change as the result of conflict between opposites which then ... fuse into a new kind of thing that embraces both opposites* (Louis O. Kattsoff).

di|a|lec|to|log|i|cal (dī′ə lek′tə loj′ə kəl), *adj.* of or having to do with dialectology. —**di′a|lec′to|log′i|cal|ly**, *adv.*

di|a|lec|tol|o|gist (dī′ə lek tol′ə jist), *n.* a person who studies dialectology; dialectician: *Dialectologists of the last century ... toiled diligently to gather in the rich harvest of words before the winter of standardization* (Simeon Potter).

di|a|lec|tol|o|gy (dī′ə lek tol′ə jē), *n.* the study of dialects. [< *dialect* + *-logy*]

di|al|ing (dī′ə ling), *n.* **1** the art of constructing dials. **2** *Mining.* surveying with a dial.

di|al|lage (dī′ə lij), *n.* a laminated or foliated variety of pyroxene, usually of a green color, found in basic igneous rocks. [< French *diallage* < Greek *diallagē* interchange, ultimately < *diá-* through + *allássein* to alter < *állos* other (because it cleaves in different planes)]

di|al|ling tone (dī′ə ling), *Especially British.* dial tone.

di|a|log (dī′ə lôg, -log), *n., v.,* **-loged, -log|ing.** = dialogue.

di|a|log|ic (dī′ə loj′ik), *adj.* **1** of or like a dialogue. **2** taking part in a dialogue. —**di′a|log′i|cal|ly**, *adv.*

di|a|log|i|cal (dī′ə loj′ə kəl), *adj.* = dialogic.

di|al|o|gism (dī al′ə jiz əm), *n.* the discussion of a subject by a speaker or writer under the form of an imaginary dialogue.

di|al|o|gist (dī al′ə jist), *n.* **1** a speaker in dialogue. **2** a writer of dialogue.

di|a|lo|gis|tic (dī′ə lə jis′tik), *adj.* in the form of a dialogue; consisting of dialogue.

di|al|o|gite (dī al′ə jīt), *n.* = rhodochrosite. [< Greek *dialogē* an accounting + English *-ite*[1]]

di|al|o|gize (dī al′ə jīz), *v.i.,* **-gized, -giz|ing.** to carry on a dialogue.

di|a|logue (dī′ə lôg, -log), *n., v.,* **-logued, -logu|ing.** —*n.* **1** a conversation: *Two actors had a dialogue in the middle of the stage.* **2** conversation in a play, story, novel, or other literary or dramatic work; conversation written out: *That book has a good plot and much clever dialogue. What is remarkable about the play is that the dialogue flows smoothly and momentously ... but never once ceases to pique our eager curiosity* (London Times). **3** a literary work in the form of a conversation. **4** an airing of views; discussion: *The debate in the* [*Senate*] *chamber itself has been what it should be, a probing public dialogue* (Wall Street Journal). **5** *Music.* a composition for two instruments or voices, or two groups of instruments or voices, each responding to the other or joining the other in a duet: *... four separate "dialogues," in each of which the quartet and orchestra treat a set of melodic and harmonic ideas* (Time).
—*v.t.* to put into the form of a dialogue; furnish with dialogue.
—*v.i.* to hold a dialogue or conversation: *Dost dialogue with thy shadow?* (Shakespeare). Also, **dialog.**
[< Latin *dialogus* < Greek *diálogos* < *diá-* between + *lógos* speech < *légein* to speak] —**di′a|logu′er**, *n.*

Dialogue Mass, a Low Mass in which the server's parts are recited in unison by the congregation.

dialogue of the deaf, a discussion or negotiation in which each side completely ignores the needs or arguments of the other: *Better communication is no panacea for every industrial dispute ... But English reserve does seem to lead, all too often, to a muted dialogue of the deaf* (London Times). [translation of French *dialogue des sourds*]

dial telephone or **phone**, a telephone equipped with a movable dial by which the user activates electronic devices at a central exchange to secure the connection desired.

dial tone, the humming sound that is heard on a dial telephone when the receiver is lifted. It indicates that a number may be dialed. Also, *especially British,* **dialling tone.**

di|al|y|sate (dī al′ə sāt, -zāt), *n.* **1** the product of dialysis; the dialyzed part of a substance. **2** the purifying liquid through which substances from the blood pass in hemodialysis. Also, **dialyzate.**

di|a|lyse (dī′ə līz), *v.t.,* **-lysed, -lys|ing.** *Especially British.* dialyze. —**di′a|lys′er**, *n.*

di|al|y|sis (dī al′ə sis), *n., pl.* **-ses** (-sēz). **1** *Chemistry.* the separation of colloids or large molecules from dissolved substances or small molecules by application of the principle that small molecules diffuse readily through a membrane and colloids or large molecules not at all or very slightly. **2** *Medicine.* separation of waste matter from the blood through a hemodialyzer; hemodialysis: *Some persons receive dialysis ... one to three times per week. They are leading active lives four to seven years after their kidneys have ceased to function* (Alton L. Blakeslee). [< Greek *diálysis* dissolution, separation < *dia-* apart + *lýsis* a loosening]

di|a|lyt|ic (dī′ə lit′ik), *adj.* having to do with or like dialysis; characterized by separation. —**di′a|lyt′i|cal|ly**, *adv.*

di|a|lyz|a|ble (dī′ə lī′zə bəl), *adj.* that can be dialyzed.

di|al|y|zate (dī al′ə zāt), *n.* = dialysate.

di|a|lyze (dī′ə līz), *v.t.,* **-lyzed, -lyz|ing. 1** to separate or obtain by dialysis. **2** to subject to dialysis: *Plastic tubes in a patient's arm conduct blood from an artery to an artificial kidney, where the blood is dialyzed, and then back to a vein* (John Bergan). —**di′a|lyz′er**, *n.*

diam., diameter.

di|a|mag|net (dī′ə mag′nit), *n.* a diamagnetic body or substance; diamagnetic: *A superconductor ... behaves as a perfect diamagnet—that is, it excludes magnetic fields from its interior* (Science).

di|a|mag|net|ic (dī′ə mag net′ik), *adj., n. Physics.* —*adj.* repelled by a magnet; taking a position at right angles to the lines of force of a magnet: *So that the electrons in the atoms shall interfere as little as possible, diamagnetic compounds are chosen, in which the electrons are distributed very symmetrically around the nuclei* (Science News).
—*n.* a diamagnetic body or substance, such as bismuth or silver.
[< *dia-* + *magnetic*] —**di′a|mag|net′i|cal|ly**, *adv.*

di|a|mag|net|ism (dī′ə mag′nə tiz əm), *n.* **1** diamagnetic quality. **2** diamagnetic phenomena. **3** the force to which these phenomena are attributed. **4** the science dealing with diamagnetic phenomena.

di|a|man|tane (dī′ə mən tān), *n.* a hydrocarbon having the same spatial arrangement of carbon atoms as the diamond.

dia|man|té (dyȧ mäɴ tā′), *adj., n. French.* —*adj.* set with diamonds or diamond chips: *a watch with diamanté numerals.*
—*n.* a material or fabric to which a sparkling effect is given by the use of rhinestones, paste, etc.: *Resplendent in white net and diamanté, the imperial crown gleaming on her head ... the young Queen read the Speech from the Throne* (Time).

di|a|man|tif|er|ous (dī′ə mən tif′ər əs), *adj.* yielding or producing diamonds. Also, **diamondiferous.** [< French *diamantifère* (< *diamant* diamond) + English *-ous*]

di|a|man|tine (dī′ə man′tin, -tēn, -tīn), *adj.* **1** consisting of a diamond. **2** like or suggesting a diamond in shape, brilliance, or hardness: *This aristocratic Danish author ... has fashioned a nonfictional still life, elegiac in mood, diamantine in craft* (Time).

di|a|mat (dī′ə mat′), *n.* = dialectical materialism. [< *dia*(lectical) *mat*(erialism)]

***di|am|e|ter** (dī am′ə tər), *n.* **1** a straight line passing from one side to the other through the center of a circle, sphere, cylinder, or other rounded form. **2** the length of such a line; measurement from one side to the other through the center of a figure or object; width; thickness: *the diameter of a pipe, rock, or crater. The diameter of the earth is about 8,000 miles. The tree trunk was almost 2 feet in diameter.* **3** a measure of the degree of magnification of a microscope or telescope lens. A microscope that makes an object appear 10 times larger has magnified the object 10 diameters, usually written 10X. *Abbr:* d., dia., diam. [< Old French *diametre,* learned borrowing from Latin *diametros* < Greek *diámetros* diagonal of a circle or parallelogram < *dia-* across + *métron* a measure]

***diameter**
definition 1

circle

sphere

di|am|e|tral (dī am′ə trəl) *adj.* of a diameter; having to do with or forming a diameter. —**di|am′e|tral|ly**, *adv.*

diametral pitch, the number of teeth per inch of diameter of a gear.

di|a|met|ric (dī′ə met′rik), *adj.* **1** of or along a diameter. **2** *Figurative.* exactly opposite: *The two candidates had diametric opinions on that issue. The speaker took a diametric view of the question.*

di|a|met|ri|cal (dī′ə met′rə kəl), *adj.* = diametric.

di|a|met|ri|cal|ly (dī′ə met′rə klē), *adv.* **1** as a diameter. **2** *Figurative.* directly; exactly; entirely: *The two men argued, their views diametrically opposed.*

di|a|mine (dī′ə mēn, -min; dī am′ēn, -in), *n. Chemistry.* any one of various compounds having two amino ($-NH_2$) radicals.

di|am|mo|ni|um phosphate, (dī ə mō′nē əm), a white crystalline or powdery substance used as a fertilizer, for flameproofing wood, paper, and textiles, and in making yeast, vinegar, and bread. *Formula:* $(NH_4)_2HPO_4$

***dia|mond** (dī′mənd, dī′ə-), *n., adj., v.* —*n.* **1a** a colorless or tinted precious stone, formed of pure carbon in crystals. Diamond is the hardest natural substance known. **b** an inferior specimen of this substance, or one artificially made, used chiefly in industry. Industrial diamonds are used to cut glass and metals and in drill bits. **2** a tool having a diamond tip for cutting glass. **3** a plane figure with four equal sides whose angles are not right angles; rhombus; lozenge. **4** a type of intersection, often between a primary and a secondary road, whose ramps form the shape of a diamond. **5** a playing card with one or more red designs like a diamond on it. **6** *Baseball.* **a** the space inside the lines that connect the bases; infield. **b** the whole field. **7** a very small size of printing type; 4½ point.
—*adj.* **1** made of diamond: *a diamond lens.* **2** set or furnished with a diamond or diamonds: *a diamond clasp.* **3** shaped like a diamond: *Its windows were old diamond-pane lattices* (Dickens).
—*v.t.* to adorn with or as if with diamonds.

diamond cut diamond, a dispute or struggle between two well-matched opponents: *It was a case of diamond cut diamond as the men fought to a draw.*

diamond in the rough, a person who has good qualities but lacks polish: *The nation's rural youth can be described as "underdeveloped human resources, diamonds in the rough, possessors of many ... talents"* (New York Times).

diamonds, the suit of playing cards with red designs like a diamond on them: *Clubs, Diamonds, Hearts, in wild disorder seen* (Alexander Pope).

[< Old French *diamant,* learned borrowing from Medieval Latin *diamas, -antis,* alteration of Latin *adamās* diamond, loadstone. See etym. of doublet **adamant.**] — **dia′mond|like′**, *adj.*

***diamond**
definitions *adj.*3, *n.*6a

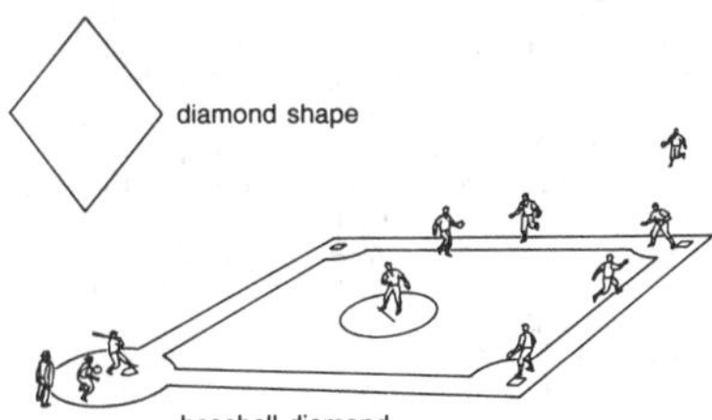

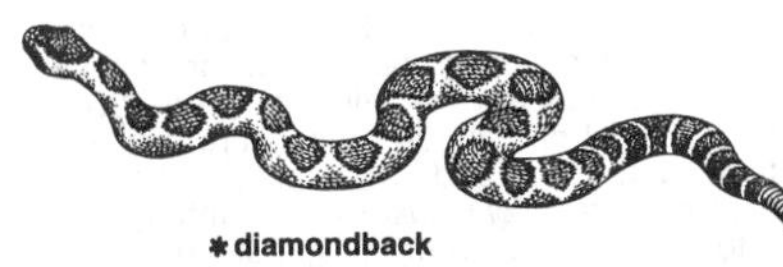

***diamondback**
definition 1

dia|mond|back** (dī′mənd bak′, dī′ə-), *n., adj.* — ***n. **1** any one of several large rattlesnakes having diamond-shaped markings on the back, found in the southern and western United States, such as the western diamondback rattlesnake. **2** = diamondback terrapin.
— ***adj.*** = diamond-backed.

dia|mond-backed (dī′mənd bakt′, dī′ə-), *adj.* having the back marked with diamond-shaped figures.

diamondback moth, a small, destructive European and American moth, having gray or brownish wings which exhibit white diamond-shaped markings when closed. It feeds on cabbage leaves, cauliflower, and similar plants.

diamondback terrapin, an edible turtle that has diamond-shaped markings on its shell. It lives in salt marshes along the North American coast of the Atlantic and Gulf of Mexico.

diamond beetle, a large, black, South American beetle studded with points of brilliant golden green.

diamond drill, a drill or borer which cuts by means of diamonds set like teeth in an annular bit.

diamond dust, a powder of crushed or ground diamonds, used as an abrasive.

dia|mond|ed (dī′mən did, dī′ə-), *adj.* **1** set with or as if with diamonds: (*Figurative.*) ... *the diamonded night* (Tennyson). **2** having parts shaped like diamonds or lozenges: *A casement ... diamonded with panes of quaint device* (Keats).

diamond hitch, a hitch used in fastening a pack on an animal, in which a diamond-shaped arrangement of rope is formed on the top of the pack.

diamond horseshoe, *U.S.* the dress circle in a theater, opera house, or other auditorium or grandstand.

dia|mon|dif|er|ous (dī′mən dif′ər əs, dī′ə-), *adj.* = diamantiferous.

diamond jubilee, the 75th anniversary, or sometimes the 60th or 70th, of the founding of an organization or the happening of some event: *Anatomists from all parts of the world attended the diamond jubilee ... of the American Association of Anatomists* (Science News Letter).

dia|mon|doid (dī′mən doid, dī′ə-), *adj.* having the form of a diamond: *However, the large diamondoid hydrocarbon diamantane, although known, was extremely difficult to prepare and has thus remained a chemical curiosity* (New Scientist and Science Journal).

dia|mond-point (dī′mənd point′, dī′ə-), *adj.* **1** having a point or tip made of diamond: *a diamond-point phonograph needle, a diamond-point chisel.* **2** made with diamond-point instruments: *a diamond-point engraving.*

diamond powder, = diamond dust.

dia|monds (dī′məndz, dī′ə-), *n.pl.* See under **diamond.**

diamond saw, a circular saw, edged with diamond dust, for cutting stone: *Diamond saws ... are used to saw diamond crystals in half* (Frederick H. Pough).

dia|mond-shaped (dī′mənd shāpt′, dī′ə-), *adj.* having the shape of a diamond or lozenge.

dia|mond-skin disease (dī′mənd skin′, dī′ə-), a form of erysipelas in swine, marked by the appearance of red, diamond-shaped patches on the skin.

Diamond State, Delaware.

diamond wedding, the 75th anniversary of a wedding, or sometimes the 60th or 70th.

di|a|mor|phine (dī′ə môr′fēn, -mōr′-; -fin), *n.* = heroin.

Di|a|mox (dī′ə moks), *n. Trademark.* acetazoleamide.

Di|an (dī′an), *n. Poetic.* Diana: *Dian, goddess of the golden bow* (William Cowper).

Di|an|a (dī an′ə), *n.* **1** *Roman Mythology.* the goddess of the hunt and of the moon. She was worshiped especially as the protectress and helper of women. The Greeks called her Artemis. **2** *Poetic.* the moon. **3** a young woman of fine physique and easy, graceful carriage.

Diana monkey, a monkey with a black back, white belly, and striking, long white beard, found near the coast of western Africa.

di|an|drous (dī an′drəs), *adj. Botany.* **1** having two stamens: *diandrous flowers.* **2** having flowers with two stamens: *diandrous plants.* [< New Latin *diandrus* (with English *-ous*) < Greek *di-* twice + *anḗr, andrós* man]

di|a|no|et|ic (dī′ə nō et′ik), *adj., n.* — ***adj.*** of or having to do with thought or reasoning, especially discursive reasoning. — ***n.*** the part of logic that deals with discursive reasoning. [< Greek *dianoētikós* < *dianoêsthai* to think, reason < *diá-* through + *noeîn* think < *nóos* mind]

di|an|thus (dī an′thəs), *n.* any one of various plants of the pink family, as the carnations and sweet williams; pink. [< New Latin *Dianthus* the genus name < Greek *Diós,* genitive of *Zeús* Zeus + *ánthos* flower]

di|a|pa|son (dī′ə pā′zən, -sən), *n.* **1** a swelling musical sound: *a glorious diapason of heavenly voices.* **2** the whole range of a voice or instrument. **3** a fixed standard of musical pitch. **4** a tuning fork or its pitch. **5** either of two principal stops in an organ. Open diapason is a stop that gives full, majestic tones. Stopped diapason is a stop that gives powerful, flutelike tones. **6** harmony of tones or parts: *Through all the compass of the Notes it ran, The diapason closing full in man* (John Dryden). **7** a melody; strain. **8** *Obsolete.* harmony; agreement. **9** *Obsolete.* the interval of an octave. [< Latin *diapāsōn* < Greek *diapāsôn* octave < *dià pasôn* (*chordôn*) across all (the notes of the scale)]

di|a|pa|son|al (dī′ə pā′zə nəl, -sə-), *adj.* = diapasonic.

di|a|pa|son|ic (dī′ə pə zon′ik, -son′-), *adj.* of or having to do with the diapason or melody.

di|a|pause (dī′ə pôz′), *n.* a period in the life cycle of insects and certain other animals during which their physiological activity is very low and they are highly resistant to unfavorable external conditions: *Many species survive unfavourable conditions by going into a state of diapause in which they roll themselves up into a tight ball in spherical earthen cells which are lined with mucus* (Betty I. Roots).

di|a|paus|ing (dī′ə pô′zing), *adj.* in diapause: *A diapausing silkworm pupa ... withstands 100 times as much X-ray radiation as a human being* (Science News Letter).

di|a|pe|de|sis (dī′ə pə dē′sis), *n.* the movement or passage of blood cells, especially phagocytes, through the unruptured walls of the capillary blood vessels into the tissues. [< New Latin *diapedesis* < Greek *diapḗdēsis* an oozing through < *diapēdan* to ooze through < *diá-* through + *pēdan* to leap, throb]

di|a|pen|te (dī′ə pen′tē), *n.* the interval of the fifth in ancient and medieval music. [< Latin *diapente* < Greek *dià pénte* (*chordôn*) through five (notes)]

di|a|per (dī′ə pər, dī′pər), *n., v.* — ***n.*** **1** a piece of cloth or other soft, absorbent material folded and used as underpants for a baby. **2** a pattern of small, constantly repeated, geometric figures. **3** a white cotton or linen woven with such a pattern. **4** a towel, napkin, or cloth of this material.
— ***v.t.*** **1** to put a diaper on: *to diaper the baby after his bath.* **2** to ornament with a diaper pattern: ... *many a floating fold ... diaper'd with inwrought flowers, or cloth of gold* (Tennyson).
[< Old French *diapre,* variant of *diaspre* ornamental cloth < Medieval Latin *diasprus* < Medieval Greek *díaspros* < Greek *diá-* (intensive) + *áspros* white]

diaper rash, an irritation in the form of a rash in the diaper area: *The booklet is part of a nationwide campaign to eliminate diaper rash, a skin ailment few infants escape* (Science News Letter).

di|a|phane (dī′ə fān), *n.* **1** a transparent resin solution used to cover microscopic slides. **2** the transparent membrane that covers an organ or cell. [< Middle French *diaphane* diaphanous < Medieval Latin *diaphanus*]

di|a|pha|ne|i|ty (dī′ə fə nē′ə tē), *n.* the power of transmitting light; transparency. [apparently < Greek *diaphấneia* transparency (< *diaphanḗs;* see etym. under **diaphanous**) + English *-ity*]

di|aph|a|nous (dī af′ə nəs), *adj.* **1** transparent; translucent: *Gauze is a diaphanous fabric. ... new leaves, delicate as butterflies' wings, and diaphanous as amber* (Thomas Hardy). **SYN:** pellucid. **2** *Figurative.* light; delicate; airy: *A diaphanous Juliet appeared on her balcony* (Newsweek). **SYN:** ethereal. [< Medieval Latin *diaphanus* (with English *-ous*) < Greek *diaphanḗs* < *diá-* through + *phaínein* show] — **di|aph′a|nous|ly**, *adv.* — **di|aph′a|nous|ness**, *n.*

di|a|phone (dī′ə fōn), *n.* **1** *Phonetics.* any variation of the same allophone, as of the *e* in *merry.* **2** a fog signal with a two-tone blast used as an aid in navigation. [< *dia-* + *-phone*]

di|aph|o|rase (dī af′ə rās), *n.* a flavoprotein active in the transfer of electrons from the reduced form of diphosphopyridine nucleotide to molecular oxygen. [< Greek *diáphoros* different + English *-ase*]

di|a|pho|re|sis (dī′ə fə rē′sis), *n. Medicine.* perspiration, especially when artificially produced. [< Late Latin *diaphorēsis* < Greek *diaphórēsis* evaporation, perspiration < *diá-* through + *phoreîn* carry (frequentative) < *phérein*]

di|a|pho|ret|ic (dī′ə fə ret′ik), *adj., n. Medicine.* — ***adj.*** producing perspiration.
— ***n.*** a diaphoretic medicine.

di|a|phragm** (dī′ə fram), *n., v.* — ***n. **1** a partition of muscles and tendons separating the cavity of the chest from the cavity of the abdomen; midriff. Contraction of the diaphragm causes the lungs to expand. **2** a thin, dividing partition, such as that in a galvanic cell or in some shellfish. **3** a thin disk or cone that moves rapidly to and fro when sounds are directed at it, used in telephone receivers, loudspeakers, earphones, microphones, and other instruments. **4** a disk with a hole in the center for controlling the amount of light entering a camera, microscope, etc. **5** a contraceptive pessary. **6** a connecting stiffener between the webs of a girder in a bridge or other construction.
— ***v.t.*** **1** to furnish with a diaphragm. **2** to act upon with a diaphragm.
diaphragm down, to reduce the aperture of (a lens or objective) by means of a diaphragm: ... *both lenses are diaphragmed down to the same aperture* (British Journal of Photography).
[< Latin *diaphragma* < Greek *diáphragma* < *diá-* across + *phrágma* fence < *phrássein* to fence, or hedge in]

***diaphragm**
definitions 1, 3, 4

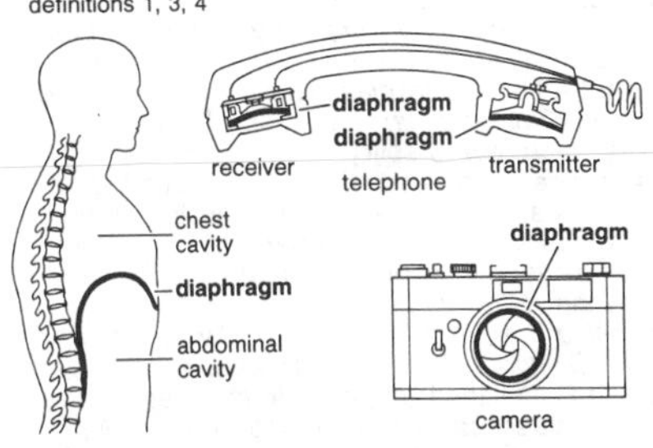

di|a|phrag|mat|ic (dī′ə frag mat′ik), *adj.* **1** having to do with a diaphragm. **2** like a diaphragm. — **di′a|phrag|mat′i|cal|ly**, *adv.*

di|a|phys|i|al or **di|a|phys|e|al** (dī′ə fiz′ē əl), *adj.* **1** having to do with a diaphysis. **2** extending continuously between two ends, as the shaft of a bone.

di|aph|y|sis (dī af′ə sis), *n., pl.* **-ses** (-sēz). **1** *Anatomy.* the shaft of a long bone. **2** *Botany.* abnormal proliferation of a flower or of a flower cluster. [< Greek *diáphysis* < *diá-* through + *phýsis* growth < *phýein* grow, wax, spring up]

di|a|pir (dī′ə pir), *n. Geology.* an anticlinal fold in which a mobile core, such as salt, has pierced through the more brittle overlying rock: *Both young mountain ranges and mid-ocean ridges are differentiation products of the mantle and are breaking through the crust as diapirs* (Science Journal). [< Greek *diapeirein* to pierce through]

di|a|pir|ic (dī′ə pir′ik), *adj.* of or by diapirs: *diapiric structures, diapiric intrusion.*

di|ap|o|phys|i|al (dī′ap ə fiz′ē əl), *adj.* of or having to do with a diapophysis.

di|a|poph|y|sis (dī′ə pof′ə sis), *n., pl.* **-ses** (-sēz). *Anatomy, Zoology.* the transverse part of a vertebra. [< *di-* + *apophysis*]

di|a|pos|i|tive (dī′ə poz′ə tiv), *n. Photography.* a positive transparency produced from a negative,

Pronunciation Key: hat, āge, cãre, fär; let, ēqual, tėrm; it, īce; hot, ōpen, ôrder; oil, out; cup, pu̇t, rüle; child; long; thin; ᴛʜen; zh, measure; ə represents a in about, e in taken, i in pencil, o in lemon, u in circus.

such as a lantern slide.

di|ap|sid (dī ap′sid), *adj.* having two pairs of temporal arches, as certain reptiles: *a diapsid skull.* [< *di-* + Latin *apsīs, -īdis* apse]

di|ar|chal (dī är′kəl), *adj.* of or having to do with a diarchy.

di|ar|chi|al (dī är′kē əl), *adj.* = diarchal.

di|ar|chic (dī är′kik), *adj.* = diarchal.

di|ar|chy (dī′är kē), *n., pl.* **-chies.** government in which the executive power is vested in two rulers or ruling authorities. Also, **dyarchy.** [< Greek *di-* twice + *archós* ruler (< *árchein* to rule) + English *-y*[3]]

di|ar|i|al (dī är′ē əl), *adj.* of or having to do with a diary.

di|a|rist (dī′ər ist), *n.* a person who keeps a diary.

di|a|ris|tic (dī′ə ris′tik), *adj.* **1** of or having to do with a diary. **2** like that of a diary: *a story in diaristic form.*

di|a|rize (dī′ə rīz), *v.i.,* **-rized, -riz|ing.** to write in a diary.

di|ar|rhe|a or **di|ar|rhoe|a** (dī′ə rē′ə), *n.* the condition of having too many and too loose movements of the bowels. [< Latin *diarrhoea* < Greek *diárrhoia* < *diá-* through + *rheîn* flow]

di|ar|rhe|al or **di|ar|rhoe|al** (dī′ə rē′əl), *adj.* of or having to do with diarrhea.

di|ar|rhe|ic or **di|ar|rhoe|ic** (dī′ə rē′ik), *adj.* = diarrheal.

di|ar|rhet|ic or **di|ar|rhoet|ic** (dī′ə ret′ik), *adj.* = diarrheal.

di|ar|thro|di|al (dī′är thrō′dē əl), *adj.* of or like diarthrosis.

di|ar|thro|sis (dī′är thrō′sis), *n., pl.* **-ses** (-sēz). *Anatomy.* a kind of articulation that permits considerable motion, as in the hip or shoulder. [< Greek *diarthrōsis* < *diá* through + *arthrōsis* a jointing < *arthroûn* to be jointed < *árthron* a joint]

di|a|ry (dī′ər ē), *n., pl.* **-ries. 1** an account, written down each day, of what has happened to one, or what one has done or thought, during the day: *The entries in many a famous man's private diary have revealed interesting facts of history.* **2** a blank book with a space for each day, in which to keep a daily record: *She received a beautiful leather-bound diary each year.* **3** a printed book or calendar giving general information about each day of the year. [< Latin *diārium* daily allowance; journal < *diēs* day]

di|as|chi|sis (dī as′kə sis), *n.* inability of a part of the nervous system to function, due to damage in another part: *... a temporary reduction in autonomic reactivity due to diaschisis* (Morris Fishbein). [< New Latin *diaschisis* < Greek *diáschisis* division < *diaschízein* to split apart < *dia-* apart + *schízein* to split]

Di|as|po|ra (dī as′pər ə), *n.* **1** the scattering of the Jews after their captivity in Babylon. **2** the Jews thus scattered. **3** the parts of the world in which Jews live outside of Israel or, formerly, Palestine: *Other Israeli leaders joined them in stressing the need for a strong Zionist movement in the Diaspora* (New York Times). **4** the early Jewish Christians living outside of Palestine. **5** Also, **diaspora.** the scattering of any group; dispersion: *During the last years of the Republic, there had begun the great Diaspora of Florentine artists. Michelangelo went to Rome. Pietro Torrigiano and the Rovezzano sculptors went to England. Jacopo Sansovino went to Venice* (Mary McCarthy). [< Greek *diasporá* a scattering < *diá-* through, apart + *sporá* a sowing < *speírein* to sow. See etym. of doublet **diaspore.**]

di|a|spore (dī′ə spôr, -spōr), *n.* a native hydroxide of aluminum varying in color from white to violet, occurring in scaly, crystalline masses. *Formula:* $Al_2O_3 \cdot H_2O$ [< French *diaspore* < Greek *diasporá* (because of its dispersion when heated). See etym. of doublet **diaspora.**]

Di|as|po|ric (dī as′pər ik), *adj.* of or having to do with the Diaspora.

di|a|stase (dī′ə stās), *n.* amylase, especially certain extracts from molds or germinating seeds: *malt diastase.* [< French *diastase* < Greek *diástasis* separation < *diá-* apart + *stásis* a standing < *histánai* to stand]

di|a|sta|sic (dī′ə stā′sik), *adj.* = diastatic.

di|as|ta|sis (dī as′tə sis), *n., pl.* **-ses** (-sēz). **1** separation of bones without fracture; dislocation. **2** the rest period of the cardiac cycle, occurring between the diastole and the systole. [< Greek *diástasis* separation; see etym. under **diastase**]

di|a|stat|ic (dī′ə stat′ik), *adj.* **1** of or having to do with diastase. **2** having the properties of amylase; capable of breaking down starch into dextrins and of reducing sugar.

di|a|stem (dī′ə stem), *n. Geology.* a minor break in sedimentary rocks, accompanied by little or no erosion. [< Greek *diástēma* interval. See etym. of doublet **diastema.**]

di|a|ste|ma (dī′ə stē′mə), *n., pl.* **-ma|ta** (-mə tə). a gap or space between teeth in a jaw of an animal. [< Latin *diastēma* < Greek *diástēma* interval. See etym. of doublet **diastem.**]

di|a|ste|mat|ic (dī′ə sti mat′ik), *adj.* having to do with or of the nature of a diastema.

di|as|ter (dī as′tər), *n. Biology.* a stage in mitosis when the chromosomes, after splitting and separating, have formed two star-shaped groups near the ends of the spindle. [< *di-*[1] + Greek *astḗr* star]

di|a|ster|e|o|i|so|mer (dī′ə ster′ē ō ī′sə mər, -stir′-), *n.* one of two or more stereoisomers that are not mirror images of each other.

di|a|ster|e|o|i|so|mer|ic (dī′ə ster′ē ō ī′sə-mer′ik, -stir′-), *adj.* having the nature or characteristic of a diastereoisomer.

di|as|to|le (dī as′tə lē), *n.* **1** the regular expansion of the heart each time its cavities fill with blood. It alternates with the contraction (systole), the two making up the cardiac cycle that includes brief intervening periods of inactivity (diastases). **2** (in ancient prosody) the lengthening of a short syllable when metrically accented or before a pause. [< Late Latin *diastolē* < Greek *diastolḗ* prolongation, expansion, ultimately < *diá-* apart + *stéllein* send]

di|as|tol|ic (dī′ə stol′ik), *adj.* having to do with diastole: *The diastolic pressure is that in the arteries when the heart is relaxed* (Science News Letter).

di|as|tral (dī as′trəl), *adj.* of or having to do with the diaster stage in mitosis.

di|a|stroph|ic (dī′ə strof′ik), *adj.* of or like diastrophism.

di|as|tro|phism (dī as′trə fiz əm), *n. Geology.* the action of the forces that have caused the deformation of the earth's crust, producing mountains, continents, and other geological features: *Diastrophism includes earthquakes, the rising and sinking of land, and the slow heaving up of mountains* (T. Walter Wallbank). [< Greek *diastrophḗ* distortion (< *diá-* through + *stréphein* to turn) + English *-ism*]

di|a|style (dī′ə stīl), *adj., n. Architecture.* **—*adj.*** of or having to do with an arrangement of columns in which the space between two columns measures three diameters. **—*n.*** a diastyle colonnade. [< Latin *diastȳlos* < Greek *diástȳlos* < *diá-* through + *stȳ̂los* pillar]

di|a|tes|sa|ron (dī′ə tes′ə ron), *n.* **1** a consecutive narrative based on the four Gospels; a harmony of the four Gospels. **2** (in Greek and medieval music) the interval of a fourth. [< Late Latin *diatessarōn* < Greek *dià tessárōn* composed of four]

di|a|ther|mal (dī′ə thėr′məl), *adj.* = diathermic (def. 1).

di|a|ther|mance (dī′ə thėr′məns), *n.* = diathermancy.

di|a|ther|man|cy (dī′ə thėr′mən sē), *n. Physics.* diathermanous quality; property of transmitting radiant heat. [< French *diathermansie* < Greek *diá-* through + *thérmansis* a heating < *thermaínein* to heat]

di|a|ther|ma|nous (dī′ə thėr′mə nəs), *adj. Physics.* freely permeable by radiant heat; that can freely transmit radiant heat.

di|a|ther|mi|a (dī′ə thėr′mē ə), *n.* = diathermy.

di|a|ther|mic (dī′ə thėr′mik), *adj.* **1** of or having to do with diathermy. **2** *Physics.* diathermanous. [< French *diathermique* < Greek *diá-* through + *thérmē heat*]

di|a|ther|mist (dī′ə thėr′mist), *n.* a person who treats disease by diathermy: *Diathermists who treat thread veins will usually remove these* (London Times).

di|a|ther|mi|za|tion (dī′ə thėr′mə zā′shən), *n.* the administering of diathermy.

di|a|ther|mize (dī′ə thėr′mīz), *v.t.,* **-mized, -miz|ing.** to treat by means of diathermy.

di|a|ther|my (dī′ə thėr′mē), *n., pl.* **-mies. 1** a method of treating disease by heating the tissues under the skin with high-frequency electric currents. **2** the machine used for this. [< New Latin *diathermia* < Greek *diá-* through + *thérmē* heat]

di|ath|e|sis (dī ath′ə sis), *n.* a constitutional tendency to some particular disease. [< New Latin *diathesis* < Greek *diáthesis* condition, arrangement < *diatithénai* arrange, < *diá-* through + *tithénai* to place]

di|a|thet|ic (dī′ə thet′ik), *adj.* of or having to do with diathesis; constitutional.

***diatom**

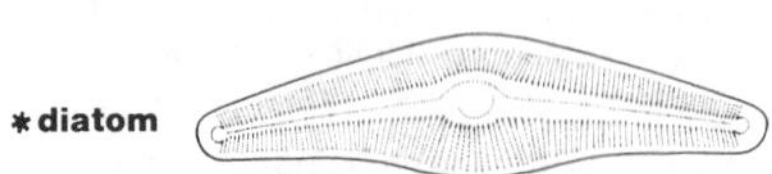

***di|a|tom** (dī′ə tom, -təm), *n.* any one of numerous microscopic, one-celled, aquatic algae that have hard shells composed mostly of silica: *Diatoms float free in the water and, upon death, settle to the bottom, contributing to the rich organic mud that supports a great population of annelid worms* (Science News Letter). [< New Latin *Diatoma* the typical genus < Greek *diátomos* cut in half < *diá-* through + *témnein* to cut]

di|a|to|ma|ceous (dī′ə tə mā′shəs), *adj.* **1** of or having to do with diatoms. **2** consisting of or containing diatoms or their fossil remains: *Many of the diatomaceous earths are useful as absorbent and polishing powders* (Heber W. Youngken).

di|a|tom|ic (dī′ə tom′ik), *adj. Chemistry.* **1** having two atoms in each molecule: *The oxygen molecule is diatomic.* **2** containing two replaceable atoms or groups. **3** = bivalent.

di|at|o|min (dī at′ə min), *n.* a brown pigment found in certain diatoms, associated with the photosynthetic process.

di|at|o|mite (dī at′ə mīt), *n.* earth consisting of the fossil remains of diatoms; diatomaceous earth; kieselguhr. It is used as an abrasive, insulator, and filter.

di|a|ton|ic (dī′ə ton′ik), *adj. Music.* **1** of or using only the eight tones of a standard major or minor musical scale without chromatic alteration. **2** (in Greek music) of or using the tetrachord divided into two whole tones and a half tone. [< Latin *diatonicus* < Greek *diatonikós* < *diá-* through + *tónos* tone < *teínein* stretch (a gut string)]

di|a|ton|i|cal|ly (dī′ə ton′ə klē), *adv.* in a diatonic manner.

di|a|ton|i|cism (dī′ə ton′ə siz əm), *n.* the use of tones belonging to a standard major or minor musical scale.

***diatonic scale,** a standard major or minor scale of eight musical tones in the octave, with no chromatic intervals.

***diatonic scale**

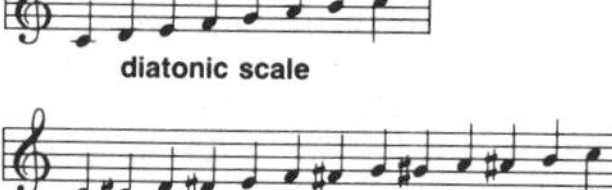

di|a|treme (dī′ə trēm), *n.* a volcanic vent produced through solid rock by exploding gases. [< *dia-* + Greek *trêma* perforation]

di|a|tribe (dī′ə trīb), *n.* **1** a speech or discussion bitterly and violently directed against some person or thing: *Even the candidate's friends were shocked by his violent diatribes during the campaign.* SYN: denunciation, invective, tirade. **2** *Archaic.* a discourse; critical dissertation. [< Latin *diatriba* discussion < Greek *diatribḗ* discourse, study, pastime < *diá-* away + *tríbein* to wear]

di|a|trib|ist (dī′ə trī′bist), *n.* **1** a person who writes or makes a diatribe. **2** *Archaic.* the writer of a critical dissertation.

di|a|trop|ic (dī′ə trop′ik), *adj.* (of plant organs) exhibiting diatropism.

di|at|ro|pism (dī at′rə piz əm), *n. Botany.* a tendency of certain organs in various plants to take a position transverse to the direction of the stimulus.

di|az|e|pam (dī az′ə pam), *n.* a chemical substance widely used as a tranquilizer: *Finally, hostile tendencies can often be remarkably controlled by drugs, like Librium and diazepam, which are not sedatives, and which do not depress the general level of cerebral activity, but which act specifically and selectively on the aggressive circuits* (New Scientist). *Formula:* $C_{16}H_{13}ClN_2O$ [< *di-* two + *az-* nitrogen + *ep-* besides, distinctive + *-am* ammonia]

di|a|zin (dī′ə zin, dī az′in), *n.* = diazine.

di|a|zine (dī′ə zēn, -zin; dī az′ēn, -in), *n. Chemistry.* one of three isomeric hydrocarbons, each having a ring of four carbon and two nitrogen atoms. *Formula:* $C_4H_4N_2$ [< *di-*[1] + *azo* + *-ine*[2]]

di|az|i|non (dī az′ə non), *n.* a colorless, highly toxic liquid, used as an insecticide, especially against houseflies. *Formula:* $C_{12}H_{21}N_2O_3PS$

di|az|o (dī az′ō, -ā′zō), *adj., n.* **—*adj.* 1** *Chemistry.* of or containing a group of two nitrogen atoms, N_2, united with one hydrocarbon radical or with one hydrocarbon radical and another atom or group of atoms. **2** of or having to do with the diazo process: *Diazo copy paper is coated with a solution that is sensitive to ultraviolet light* (Wall Street Journal).
—*n.* a diazo compound, especially a diazo dye. [< *di-*[1] + *azo*]

diazo compound, *Chemistry.* any one of a group of organic compounds having a group of two nitrogen atoms, N_2, combined with a hydrocarbon radical.

di|a|zole (dī′ə zōl, dī ā′-), *n. Chemistry.* any one of a group of hydrocarbons having a ring of three carbon and two nitrogen atoms.

di|a|zo|ma (dī′ə zō′mə), *n., pl.* **-ma|ta** (-mə tə). a walkway through the middle of an ancient Greek

theater. [< Greek *diázōma* < *diá-* through + *zōma* zone]
di|az|o|meth|ane (dī az′ō meth′ān, -ā′zō-), *n. Chemistry.* a poisonous, yellow, gaseous compound used in organic synthesis. *Formula:* CH_2N_2
di|a|zo|ni|um compound (dī′ə zō′nē əm), *Chemistry.* any one of a group of compounds containing the radical ArN:N—. [< *di-*[1] + *azo* + (ammo)*nium*]
diazonium salts, *Chemistry.* a group of compounds having the general formula (ArN:N)x, the *x* representing an acid radical.
diazo process, a method for producing prints or copies on paper treated with a diazo compound: *Only one method will make copies for one cent apiece. That's the diazo process* (Wall Street Journal).
di|az|o|ti|za|tion (dī az′ə tə zā′shən), *n. Chemistry.* the act or process of forming a diazonium salt.
di|az|o|tize (dī az′ə tīz), *v.t.*, **-tized, -tiz|ing.** *Chemistry.* to treat so as to form a diazonium compound.
dib (dib), *v.i.*, **dibbed, dib|bing.** to fish by letting the bait (usually a natural insect) dip and bob lightly on the water; dab; dibble. [apparently variant of *dab*[1]]
di|ba|sic (dī bā′sik), *adj. Chemistry.* **1** having two hydrogen atoms that can be replaced by two atoms or radicals of a base in forming salts: *a dibasic acid.* **2** having two basic atoms, each with a valence of 1.
dib|a|tag (dib′ə tag), *n.* a rare, cinnamon-colored antelope of desert areas of northeastern Africa, having a long neck, legs, and tail. [< a Somali word]
dib|ber (dib′ər), *n.* = dibble[1].
dib|ble[1] (dib′əl), *n., v.,* **-bled, -bling.** —*n.* a pointed tool for making holes in the ground for seeds, bulbs, or young plants.
—*v.t.* **1** to make a hole in (the soil) with or as if with a dibble. **2** to sow or plant (seeds or seedlings) in this way. —*v.i.* to use a dibble.
[origin uncertain]
dib|ble[2] (dib′əl), *v.i.*, **-bled, -bling. 1** to dabble; move or paddle in water. **2** = dib. [perhaps variant of *dabble*]
dib|bler (di′blər), *n.* **1** a person or thing that dibbles. **2** an Australian mammal, a brown, ratlike marsupial, regarded as extinct since the 1800's and rediscovered in 1967: *The animal is the rat-like marsupial, Antechinus apicalis, popularly known (to those who have even heard of it) as the Dibbler. Mouse-brown in colour with a long snout and a short tail it had apparently been dibbling away on the outskirts of a big city, undisturbed because nobody even suspected it was there* (New Scientist).
dib|buk (dib′u̇k), *n.* = dybbuk.
di|bo|rane (dī bôr′ān, -bōr′-), *n.* a gaseous compound of boron and hydrogen used in making rocket fuels. *Formula:* B_2H_6
di|bran|chi|ate (dī brang′kē it, -āt), *adj., n.* —*adj.* belonging to a group of cephalopods, having two gills, eight or ten arms with suckers, and an ink sac containing a fluid useful for protection and escape.
—*n.* a dibranchiate cephalopod, such as the squid, octopus, or cuttlefish.
di|bro|mide (dī brō′mīd, -mid), *n.* a compound containing two atoms of bromine with another element or radical.
dibs[1] (dibz), *n.pl.* **1** a game somewhat like jacks but played with small pieces of bone or the like. **2** the pieces used in this game. **3** *Slang.* money: *Bad as wages were ... they did bring in the ... dibs* (New Yorker).
dibs on, *Slang.* **a** a demand on; claim on: *The automobile business gets first dibs on steel* (Harper's). **b** a claim to be the first to do, to be, to choose, etc.: *Dibs on the cookies.*
[earlier *dibstones;* origin uncertain]
dibs[2] (dibz), *n.* a thick, sweet syrup made in countries of the East, especially the Middle East, from grape juice or dates. [< Arabic *debs*]
di|car|box|yl|ic acid (dī kär′bok sil′ik), any organic compound containing two carboxyl groups, -COOH.
di|cast (dī′kast, dik′ast), *n.* any one of the 6,000 citizens chosen in ancient Athens annually to try cases in the courts of law in a capacity that combined the function of the modern judge and juryman. [< Greek *dikastḗs* < *dikázein* give judgment < *díkē* legal rights]
di|cas|ter|y (dī kas′tər ē), *n., pl.* **-ter|ies. 1** one of the courts in which the dicasts sat. **2** a group of dicasts.
di|cas|tic (dī kas′tik), *adj.* of or having to do with the dicasts.
***dice** (dīs), *n., pl. of* **die**[2], *v.,* **diced, dic|ing.** —*n.* **1a** small cubes with a different number of spots (one to six) on each side. Dice are used in pairs and shaken and thrown from the hand or a box in playing some games and in gambling. **b** any small cubes or square blocks. **2a** a game played with dice. **b** the throwing or use of dice.
—*v.i.* **1a** to play games or gamble with dice, tossing them to see how many spots there will be on the sides that turn up. **b** *Figurative: to dice with death. Liverpool, too, will not wish to dice unduly with the conditions and the fates* (London Times). **2** to split into small fragments when broken: *We make the glass so that it will dice when it implodes, disintegrating to pieces small enough to pass through valves and pumps without damaging them* (Scientific American). **3** (in automobile racing) to jockey at close quarters for the lead.
—*v.t.* **1** to cut into small cubes: *Carrots are sometimes diced before being cooked. Most of the celery is diced right at the farm before it is sent to Duluth* (Wall Street Journal). **2** to mark or ornament with a pattern of cubes or squares; checker. **3** to lose or throw away by gambling with dice: *He diced his fortune away.*
load the dice, *Informal.* to decide beforehand the chances for success or failure; insure the outcome of anything in advance: *The producer loads the dice against a company ... by introducing so much background noise* (Manchester Guardian Weekly).
no dice, *Informal.* **a** a refusal; no: *A friend of mine wanted to interview me. I said no dice* (Jon Ruddy). *It was payment in full or no dice* (New Yorker). **b** to no avail; in vain: *Enticed them to talk about other London clubs, hoping for a little Old Boy backlash, but no dice* (Punch).
[< Old French *dez,* plural of *de* die[2]]

***dice**
definition 1a

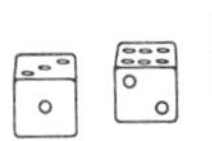
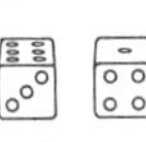

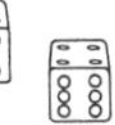

Di|ce (dī′sē), *n. Greek Mythology.* the daughter of Zeus and Themis. She represented justice. Also, **Dike.** [< Greek *Díkē* (originally) judgment; legal rights]
dice|box (dīs′boks′), *n.* a box for throwing dice in games and gambling.
di|cen|tra (dī sen′trə), *n.* any plant of a group of perennial herbs of the fumitory family, having drooping, heart-shaped flowers, such as the bleeding heart, Dutchman's-breeches, and squirrel corn. [< New Latin *Dicentra* the genus name < Greek *díkentros* having two spurs < *di-* two + *kéntron* spur, (sharp) point]
di|cen|tric (dī sen′trik), *adj.* having two centromeres: *Variegation was studied in a hybrid ... and found to be due to dicentric chromosomes* (Harold W. Rickett).
di|ceph|a|lous (dī sef′ə ləs), *adj.* having two heads. [< Greek *diképhalos* (with English *-ous*) < *di-* two + *kephalḗ* head]
dic|er (dī′sər), *n.* **1** a person who plays at dice. **2** a device for cutting into small cubes. **3** *Slang.* a hat, especially a stiff hat: *Enveloped in a billowing vicuña coat, a green velours dicer cocked on his head ...* (New Yorker).
dic|ey (dī′sē), *adj. British Slang.* **1** chancy; risky: *... when a patient goes into an operating theatre, which can be just as dicey as an emergency landing* (Punch). **2** doubtful; uncertain: *At a guess I'd say we're in for a dicey transitional period on the boards* (Alan Coren).
di|cha|si|al (dī kā′zhē əl, -zē-), *adj. Botany.* having to do with or like a dichasium.
di|cha|si|um (dī kā′zhē əm, -zē-), *n., pl.* **-si|a** (-zhē ə, -zē ə). *Botany.* a cymose inflorescence in which the main axis produces a pair of lateral axes below the terminal flower, each of which similarly produces a pair, and so on. [< New Latin *dichasium* < Greek *díchasis* division < *dicházein* divide < *dícha* in two]
di|chla|myd|e|ous (dī′klə mid′ē əs), *adj. Botany.* having both a calyx and a corolla. [< Greek *di-* two + *chlamýs, -ydos* cloak + English *-ous*]
di|chlo|rid (dī klôr′id, -klōr′-), *n.* = dichloride.
di|chlo|ride (dī klôr′īd, -id; -klōr′-), *n.* a chloride whose molecules contain two atoms of chlorine; bichloride: *They tested the ... dichlorides of manganese, iron and cobalt* (Science News Letter).
di|chlo|ro|ben|zene (dī klôr′ō ben′zēn, -klōr′-; -ben zēn′), *n.* = paradichlorobenzene.
di|chlo|ro|di|phen|yl-tri|chlo|ro|eth|ane (dī-klôr′ō dī fen′əl trī klôr′ō eth′ān, -klōr′-), *n. Chemistry.* DDT.
di|chlor|vos (dī klôr′vəs, -klōr′-), *n.* an organic phosphate used as an insecticide in aerosol form or by impregnating a resin strip with it. *Formula:* $C_4H_7Cl_2O_4P$ *Abbr:* DDVP (no periods). [< *di-chlor*(o)*v*(inyl)(ph)*os*(phate)]
di|cho|gam|ic (dī′kə gam′ik), *adj.* = dichogamous.
di|chog|a|mous (dī kog′ə məs), *adj. Botany.* hermaphroditic, with the stamens and pistils maturing at different times, thus preventing self-fertilization.
di|chog|a|my (dī kog′ə mē), *n. Botany.* dichogamous condition. [< Greek *dícho-* separately + English *-gamy*]
di|chon|dra (dī kon′drə), *n.* any one of a genus of tropical creeping vines of the morning-glory family, used for ground cover and on lawns. [< New Latin *Dichondra* the genus name < *di-* twice + Greek *chóndros* grain]
di|chop|tic (dī kop′tik), *adj.* having the eyes widely separated: *a dichoptic insect.*
di|cho|tom|ic (dī′kə tom′ik), *adj.* = dichotomous.
di|chot|o|mist (dī kot′ə mist), *n.* a person who dichotomizes.
di|chot|o|mi|za|tion (dī kot′ə mə zā′shən), *n.* **1** division into two parts or into pairs. **2** separation or classification by dual or binary subdivision.
di|chot|o|mize (dī kot′ə mīz), *v.,* **-mized, -miz|ing.** —*v.t.* to divide into two parts; divide into pairs: *A correct answer can not be dichotomized into the two categories, yes or no* (Ogburn and Nimkoff).
—*v.i. Botany.* to separate into two parts, as a root, stem, or leaf vein; become dichotomous.
di|chot|o|mous (dī kot′ə məs), *adj.* **1** divided or dividing into two parts. **2** *Botany.* branching by repeated divisions into two. —**di|chot′o|mous|ly,** *adv.*
***di|chot|o|my** (dī kot′ə mē), *n., pl.* **-mies. 1** division into two parts: *the arts-science dichotomy. Between the blueprints in the ivory tower and the working models on the ground there is a slight dichotomy* (Punch). **2a** *Botany.* a branching by repeated division into two parts. **b** *Zoology.* a form of branching in which each successive axis divides into two; repeated bifurcation, such as that of the veins. **3** *Logic.* classification by division, or by successive subdivision, into two mutually exclusive groups or sections: *the dichotomy in the universe of the living and the nonliving.* **4** *Astronomy.* the phase of the moon, or of an inferior planet, when half of its face is visible. [< Greek *dichotomíā* a cutting in half < *dícha* in two + *témnein* to cut]

***dichotomy**
definitions 2a, 2b

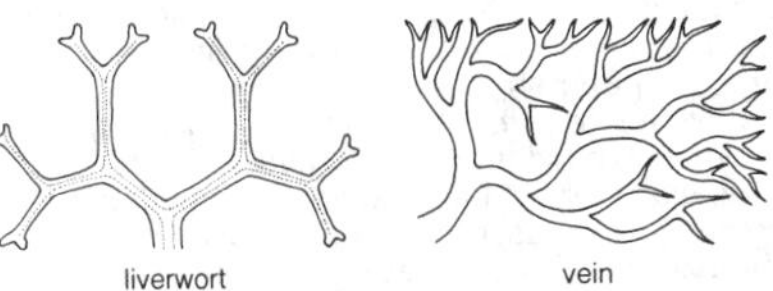

di|chro|ic (dī krō′ik), *adj.* **1** having or showing two colors. **2** *Mineralogy.* (of a crystal) showing two different colors according to the direction of transmitted light, due to difference in the amount of absorption of the rays. **3** *Chemistry.* (of a solution) showing different colors for different concentrations, as a solution of chlorophyll.
di|chro|ism (dī′krō iz əm), *n.* **1** the quality of being dichroic; dichromaticism. **2** = dichromatism (def. 1). [< French *dichroïsme* < Greek *díchroos* < *di-* two + *chrṓs, chrōtós* color (of the skin)]
di|chro|ite (dī′krō īt), *n.* iolite, a mineral whose crystals are often dichroic.
di|chro|it|ic (dī′krō it′ik), *adj.* = dichroic.
di|chro|mat (dī′krō mat), *n.* a person suffering from dichromatism: *There are three types of dichromats, known as protanopes, deuteranopes and tritanopes respectively* (New Scientist).
di|chro|mate (dī krō′māt), *n.* a compound whose molecules have two chromium atoms; bichromate.
di|chro|mat|ic (dī′krō mat′ik), *adj.* **1** having two colors; dichroic; dichromic. **2** *Zoology.* showing two color phases independent of phases correlated with age, sex, or season: *Various birds and insects are dichromatic.* **3** of or affected with dichromatism (def. 2).
di|chro|mat|i|cism (dī′krō mat′ə siz əm), *n.* = dichroism (def. 1).
dichromatic vision, = dichromatism.
di|chro|ma|tism (dī krō′mə tiz əm), *n.* **1** the quality or condition of being dichromatic. **2** *Medicine, Psychology.* color blindness in which only two of the primary colors can be seen; dichromatic vision.
di|chro|mic[1] (dī krō′mik), *adj.* having to do with or including two colors only. [< Greek *díchrōmos* two-colored (< *di-* two + *chrôma* color) + English *-ic*]

Pronunciation Key: hat, āge, cãre, fär; let, ēqual, tėrm; it, īce; hot, ōpen, ôrder; oil, out; cup, pu̇t, rüle; child; long; thin; ᴛʜen; zh, measure; ə represents a in about, e in taken, i in pencil, o in lemon, u in circus.

di|chro|mic[2] (dī krō′mik), *adj. Chemistry.* containing two chromium atoms (or their equivalents). [< *di-*[1] two + *chromic*]

dichromic acid, a hypothetical acid from which a series of salts, the dichromates or bichromates, are formed. *Formula:* $H_2Cr_2O_7$

dichromic vision, = dichromatism.

di|chro|o|scope (dī krō′ə skōp), *n.* = dichroscope.

di|chro|scope (dī′krə skōp), *n.* an instrument for testing the dichroism of crystals. [< *dichro*(ism) + *-scope*]

di|chro|scop|ic (dī′krə skop′ik), *adj.* having to do with the dichroscope.

dic|ing (dī′sing), *n.* **1** playing at dice. **2** a decoration with cubelike figures.

dick (dik), *n. Slang.* a detective: *The bloke slides out of the bathroom window, the only one in the house which hadn't got a dick sitting under the sill, and leaps into the fog* (Margery Allingham). [American English, perhaps a reduction of *detective*]

dick|cis|sel (dik sis′əl), *n.* a finch common in the grasslands of central United States, the male of which has a yellow breast and black crescent on the throat. [American English; supposedly imitative]

dick|ens (dik′ənz), *n., interj.* Usually, **the dickens**, a mild oath or exclamation of surprise or annoyance; the deuce; the devil: *I cannot tell what the dickens his name is* (Shakespeare). *The dickens! Has the Rogue of a Count play'd us another trick then?* (Vanbrugh and Cibber). [perhaps < *Dickon* (diminutive) < *Dick*, for *Richard*, a man's name]

Dick|en|si|an (di ken′zē ən), *adj., n.* **—*adj.*** having to do with or like the style of Charles Dickens or his writings: *Another officer awaited, writing at a high Dickensian dais* (Punch).
—*n.* an admirer or student of the works of Dickens: *He may regard himself as an inveterate Dickensian* (New York Times).

dick|er[1] (dik′ər), *v., n.* **—*v.i., v.t.*** to trade by barter or by petty bargaining; haggle: *She dickered with the butcher over the price of steaks.*
—*n.* **1** a petty bargain: *I made a dicker with him to take care of my hens during my absence in return for the eggs the hens laid.* **2** the act or practice of dickering; barter; petty bargaining. [American English; perhaps < *dicker*[2]]

dick|er[2] (dik′ər), *n.* **1** the number or quantity ten. **2** a lot of ten hides or skins. [Middle English *diker*, ultimately < Latin *decuria* ten (perhaps referring to hides used in barter) < *decem* ten]

dick|ey[1] (dik′ē), *n., pl.* **-eys. 1** a shirt front that can be detached. **2** an insert worn at the neck opening of a blouse, jacket, etc.: *Buttoned-in dickeys can also make cocktail necklines prim* (New Yorker). **3** = vestee. **4** a high collar on a shirt. **5** a child's bib or pinafore. **6** Also, **dickey box.** the driver's seat on the outside of a carriage. **7** a seat at the back of a carriage, for servants. **8** *British.* an automobile rumble seat. **9** a small bird. **10** a donkey. Also, **dickie, dicky.** [perhaps partly < *Dick*, for *Richard*, a man's name]

dick|ey[2] (dik′ē), *adj. Informal.* poor in quality or condition: unsound; shaky. Also, **dicky.** [origin uncertain]

dick|ey|bird (dik′ē bėrd′), *n.* = dickybird.

dickey box, = dickey[1] (def. 6).

dick|ie (dik′ē), *n., pl.* **dick|ies.** = dickey[1].

dick|ite (dik′īt), *n.* a crystalline silicate of aluminum identical in chemical composition to kaolinite, found in hydrothermal veins. [< Allan B. *Dick*, 1833–1926, an English mineralogist]

Dick test (dik), *Medicine.* a test for susceptibility to scarlet fever, in which a reaction to the injection into the skin of the scarlet fever toxin indicates a lack of immunity. [< George F. and Gladys *Dick*, American bacteriologists, who developed it in 1923]

dick|ty (dik′tē), *adj.,* **-ti|er, -ti|est.** = dicty.

dick|y[1] (dik′ē), *n., pl.* **dick|ies.** = dickey[1].

dick|y[2] (dik′ē), *adj.,* **dick|i|er, dick|i|est.** *Informal.* dickey; shaky: *Things were rather dicky in the markets just then* (New Yorker).

dick|y|bird (dik′ē bėrd′), *n.* a small bird: *Dickybird, dickybird fly away home . . .* (nursery rhyme).

di|cli|nism (dī′klə niz əm), *n. Botany.* the condition of being diclinous.

di|cli|nous (dī′klə nəs, dī klī′-), *adj. Botany.* **1** having the stamens and pistils in separate flowers either on the same plant (monoecious), or on separate plants of the same species (dioecious). **2** (of a flower) having only stamens or only pistils; unisexual. [< New Latin *Diclines* earlier class name (< Greek *di-* double + *klīnē* bed < *klīnein* to lie) + English *-ous*]

di|cot (dī′kot), *n.* = dicotyledon.

di|cot|yl (dī kot′əl), *n.* = dicotyledon.

di|cot|y|le|don (dī kot′ə lē′dən), *n. Botany.* a flowering plant that has two cotyledons or seed leaves in the embryo. The dicotyledons, which include many trees and most cultivated plants, are angiosperms, one of the two large subclasses of plants that have the seeds enclosed in an ovary. Dicotyledons have leaves with a network of veins and flower parts in fours or fives. See picture under **cotyledon**. See also **monocotyledon**.

di|cot|y|le|don|ous (dī kot′ə lē′də nəs), *adj.* having two cotyledons or seed leaves; belonging to the dicotyledons.

di|cou|ma|rin (dī kü′mər in), *n.* a white, crystalline compound obtained from spoiled clover or made synthetically, used to prevent blood coagulation. *Formula:* $C_{19}H_{12}O_6$ [< *di-*[1] + *coumarin*]

di|cou|ma|rol (dī kü′mə rōl, -rol), *n.* = dicoumarin.

di|crot|ic (dī krot′ik), *adj. Medicine.* **1** (of the pulse) having two arterial beats for each beat of the heart. **2** of or having to do with such a pulse. [< Greek *díkrotos* (< *di-* double + *krótos* noise of beating) + English *-ic*]

di|cro|tism (dī′krə tiz əm, dik′rə-), *n.* dicrotic condition.

dict., **1** dictator. **2** dictionary.

dic|ta (dik′tə), *n.* dictums; a plural of **dictum:** *He did not expect his dicta to be taken with such seriousness by so many* (Atlantic).

dic|ta|belt (dik′tə belt′), *n.* a plastic belt on which dictation is recorded in a dictating machine: *My secretaries in New York, Los Angeles, Washington, and San Francisco . . . get dictabelts from me every day* (New Statesman). [< *dicta*(tion) + *belt*]

dic|ta|graph (dik′tə graf, -gräf), *n.* = Dictograph.

Dic|ta|phone (dik′tə fōn), *n. Trademark.* an instrument that records and subsequently reproduces for transcription words that are spoken into it. [< *dicta*(te) + *-phone*]

dic|tate (*v.* dik′tāt, dik tāt′; *n.* dik′tāt), *v.,* **-tat|ed, -tat|ing,** *n.* **—*v.t.*** **1** to say or read (something) aloud for another person or persons to write down: *The teacher dictated a spelling list. A businessman often dictates letters to his secretary.* **2** to command with authority; order in clear and definite terms: *The country that won the war dictated the terms of peace to the country that lost.* SYN: decree.
—*v.i.* **1** to say or read something to be written down: *The businessman dictated to his secretary.* **2** to speak with authority; make others do what one says; lay down the law; give orders: *Big nations sometimes dictate to little ones.*
—*n.* a direction or order that is to be carried out or obeyed: *the dictates of a ruler, the dictates of common sense. An honest man follows the dictates of his conscience.* SYN: command.
[< Latin *dictāre* (with English *-ate*[1]) say often (frequentative) < *dīcere* say, tell. See etym. of doublet **dight.**]

dic|tat|ing machine (dik′tā ting, dik tā′-), a machine for taking dictation.

dic|ta|tion (dik tā′shən), *n.* **1** the act of saying or reading (something) aloud for another person or persons who writes them down: *The pupils wrote down the spelling words at the teacher's dictation. The ransom note was scribbled at the kidnaper's dictation.* **2** words said or read aloud to be written down: *The secretary took the dictation in shorthand and typed it out later. We have dictation during the first five minutes of our French class.* **3** the act of giving orders that must be obeyed; making rules: *The boy was tired of his sister's constant dictation and refused to obey her.*

dic|ta|tion|al (dik tā′shə nəl), *adj.* of or belonging to dictation.

dic|ta|tor (dik′tā tər, dik tā′-), *n.* **1** a person who uses absolute authority, especially a person who, without having any claim through inheritance or free popular election, seizes control of a government: *Dictators, almost by definition, distrust their people and are afraid to allow a free play of public opinion* (New York Times). (*Figurative.*) *French dress designers have long been the dictators in the world of fashion.* SYN: autocrat, despot. **2** (in Roman history) an official given absolute authority over the state in times of emergency. *Abbr:* dict. **3** a person who says or reads words aloud to another who writes them down: *Who was the dictator of this letter?*

dic|ta|to|ri|al (dik′tə tôr′ē əl, -tōr′-), *adj.* **1** of or like that of a dictator; absolute: *That country has a dictatorial government.* SYN: autocratic. **2** fond of commanding and giving orders; domineering; overbearing: *The younger children disliked the dictatorial manner of their older brother.* SYN: arbitrary, imperious. **—dic′ta|to′ri|al|ly,** *adv.* **—dic′ta|to′ri|al|ness,** *n.*

dic|ta|tor|ship (dik tā′tər ship, dik′tā-), *n.* **1** the position or rank of a dictator: *The dictatorship of almost every country that has one is filled by a military tyrant.* **2** the period of time a dictator rules: *The dictatorship of the tyrant was an unhappy time for teachers, students, and writers.* **3** power to give orders that must be obeyed: *The majority were the more radical, and took charge, establishing a dictatorship of the proletariat* (Emory S. Bogardus). **4** a country under the rule of a dictator: *The little dictatorship was rocked by a revolution.*

dic|ta|to|ry (dik′tə tôr′ē, -tōr′-), *adj.* = dictatorial.

dic|ta|tress (dik tā′tris), *n.* a woman dictator.

dic|ta|ture (dik tā′chər), *n.* = dictatorship.

dic|tion (dik′shən), *n.* **1** the manner of expressing ideas in words; style of speaking or writing. Good diction implies a skillful choice of words accurately used to express clearly the speaker's or writer's ideas. *He has a clearly understood diction that challenges, moves, and convinces.* **2** the manner of pronouncing words; enunciation; articulation: *The radio announcer is very easy to understand because he has very clear diction.* [< Latin *dictiō, -ōnis* a saying < *dīcere* say]
— *Syn.* **1 Diction, phraseology, wording** mean the way of using words. **Diction** emphasizes the care and skill with which words are chosen: *The diction acceptable in speech is usually less formal than that required in writing.* **Phraseology** applies to the words, used by a particular group, profession, or individual: *I don't understand legal phraseology.* **Wording** applies to both words and grouping, emphasizing their special suitability for a given purpose: *He changed the wording of the telegram to make it clearer.*

dic|tion|ar|y (dik′shə ner′ē), *n., pl.* **-ar|ies. 1** a book that explains the words of a language, or some special kind of words. It is usually arranged alphabetically. One can use a dictionary to find out the meaning, pronunciation, or spelling of a word. A medical dictionary explains words used in medicine. A German-English dictionary translates German words into English. A dictionary of biography has accounts of people's lives arranged in alphabetical order of their names. *From the time of* [*Samuel*] *Johnson on, the dictionary has been a conservative and standardizing agency for the spelling of the language as well as for its other aspects* (Stuart Robertson). SYN: lexicon. **2** a book of information or reference on any subject or branch of knowledge, the items of which are arranged in some stated order, often alphabetical: *a dictionary of folklore, a Dictionary of the Bible.* **3** *Figurative.* any repository of knowledge or information: *Life is our dictionary* (Emerson). *Burnet was eminently qualified to be of use as a living dictionary of British affairs* (Macaulay). *Abbr:* dict. [< Medieval Latin *dictionarium* < Latin *dictiō, -ōnis;* see etym. under **diction**]

Dic|to|graph (dik′tə graf, -gräf), *n. Trademark.* a machine with a transmitter so sensitive that no mouthpiece is needed, capable of recording in one room sounds or conversation made in another. Also, **dictagraph.** [American English < Latin *dictum* thing said + English *-graph*]

dic|tum (dik′təm), *n., pl.* **-tums** or **-ta. 1** a formal comment; authoritative opinion: *The dictum of the critics was that the play was excellent.* SYN: pronouncement. **2** a maxim; saying: *The old dictum says that love is blind. A dictum of George Bernard Shaw, often quoted, is "If parents would only realize how they bore their children!"* SYN: adage. **3** *Law.* an opinion by a judge on a point not directly involved in the case at trial: *It did no injustice but the dictum in it is wrong* (London Times). [< Latin *dictum* thing said, neuter past participle of *dīcere* say]

dic|ty (dik′tē), *adj.,* **-ti|er, -ti|est.** *U.S. Slang.* **1** high-class; high-style. **2** excellent: *. . . a dicty cure for spasms* (New Yorker). Also, **dickty.** [origin unknown]

dic|ty|o|some (dik′tē ə sōm), *n.* the basic unit of the Golgi apparatus; Golgi body: *The dictyosomes consist of stacks of lamellar vesicles and associated vesicles* (J. Cronshaw). [< Greek *díktyon* net + English *-some*[3]]

dic|ty|o|ste|le (dik′tē ə stē′lē), *n. Botany.* a siphonostele whose vascular mass is broken up into a number of longitudinal strands or vascular bundles: *A dictyostele . . . is common to most monocotyl stems* (Heber W. Youngken). [< Greek *díktyon* net + English *stele*]

Di|cu|ma|rol (dī kü′mə rōl, -rol), *n. Trademark.* dicoumarin; dicoumarol.

di|cy|an|di|am|ide (dī sī′ən dī am′īd, -id), *n.* a crystalline compound obtained by the polymerization of cyanamide, used in making resins, plastics, etc., and in fertilizers. *Formula:* $C_2H_4N_4$ [< *di-*[1] two + *cyan*(ide) + *di-* two + *amide*]

di|cyn|o|dont (dī sin′ə dont), *n.* any animal of a genus of extinct herbivorous reptiles, having heavy limbs and two tusks. [< *di-*[1] two + Greek *kýōn, kynós* dog + *odoús, odóntos* tooth]

did (did), *v.* past tense of **do**[1]: *I did my work.*

Did|a|che (did′ə kē), *n.* a Christian treatise, probably of the 100's A.D. (full title, *The Teaching of the Twelve Apostles*).
[< Greek *Didachē* (*tôn dōdeka apostólōn*)

Teaching (of the Twelve Apostles)]

Did|a|chist (did'ə kist), *n.* the writer or compiler of the Didache.

Did|a|chog|ra|pher (did'ə kog'rə fər), *n.* = Didachist.

di|dact (dī'dakt), *n.* a person who is inclined to teach others; pedagogue or pedant.

di|dac|tic (dī dak'tik, di-), *adj.* **1** meant to instruct: *Aesop's "Fables" are didactic stories; each one has a moral.* **SYN:** educative. **2** inclined to instruct others; teacherlike: *The older brother was called "Professor" because of his didactic manner. This didactic tendency . . . has been a common feature in our modern writing* (Atlantic). **SYN:** preceptorial. [< Greek *didaktikós* apt at teaching < *didáskein* teach] —**di|dac'ti|cal|ly,** *adv.*

di|dac|ti|cal (dī dak'tə kəl, di-), *adj.* = didactic.

di|dac|ti|cism (dī dak'tə siz əm, di-), *n.* didactic quality, character, or manner: *His didacticism was directed as much at posterity as at ourselves* (Wall Street Journal).

di|dac|ti|cist (dī dak'tə sist, di-), *n.* a person whose aim is to teach others; a didactic writer or speaker: *Godard remains a poet, although he truly means now to be only a didacticist and an inquirer* (Penelope Gilliatt).

di|dac|tics (dī dak'tiks, di-), *n.* the science or art of giving instruction or teaching.

di|dac|tyl (dī dak'təl), *adj. Zoology.* having only two fingers, claws, or toes to each limb. [< *di-*[1] two + Greek *dáktylos* finger, toe]

di|dac|ty|lous (dī dak'tə ləs), *adj.* = didactyl.

di|dap|per (dī'dap'ər), *n.* a dabchick, especially the pied-billed grebe. [contraction of *divedapper.* See related etym. at **dive, dip.**]

did|da|koi (did'ə koi), *n.* = didicoi.

did|der (did'ər), *v.i. British Dialect.* to tremble; shiver; quiver. [origin uncertain]

did|dle[1] (did'əl), *v.t.,* **-dled, -dling.** *Informal.* **1** to cheat; swindle: *He diddled his landlady out of two weeks' rent. Do it yourself, and you won't be diddled* (New Yorker). **2** to waste (time). **3** to ruin; undo.

diddle away, to trifle away; waste in a trifling manner: *A day diddled away, and nothing to show for it!* (Scott).

[origin uncertain] —**did'dler,** *n.*

did|dle[2] (did'əl), *v.i.,* **-dled, -dling.** *Informal or Dialect.* to move from side to side by jerks; shake; quiver. [perhaps related to **didder**]

***did|ger|i|doo, did|jer|i|doo,** or **did|jer|i|du** (dij'ər ə dü'), *n.* (in Australia) a native musical wind instrument consisting of a long hollow sapling or bamboo stem that makes a droning or wailing sound.

***didgeridoo**

did|i|coi (did'ə koi), *n., pl.* **-cois.** *British.* a Gypsy half-caste: *The didicois . . . are those with less than half Romany blood* (Listener). [< Romany *didekai*]

did|n't (did'ənt), did not.

di|do (dī'dō), *n., pl.* **-dos** or **-does.** *U.S. Informal.* a mischievous or disorderly action; prank; trick.

cut (up) a dido (or **didos**), to make mischief; cut a caper: *Three sailors on leave in San Francisco . . . cut up a lot of old-fashioned didos and shenanigans* (Newsweek).

[origin uncertain]

Di|do (dī'dō), *n. Roman Legend.* the founder and queen of Carthage. In Virgil's *Aeneid* she receives Aeneas hospitably, falls in love with him, and kills herself on a funeral pyre when he goes away.

didst (didst), *v. Archaic.* did (used only with *thou*). "Thou didst" means "You did."

di|dy (dī'dē), *n., pl.* **-dies.** *U.S. Informal.* a baby's diaper. [< children's pronunciation of *diaper*]

di|dym (dī'dəm), *n.* = didymium.

di|dym|i|um (dī dim'ē əm), *n. Chemistry.* a mixture of the elements neodymium and praseodymium. It is a rare-earth metal, formerly believed to be an element, usually found in association with lanthanum. *Taking cerium out of the rare earth mixture leaves a collection of rare earths we call "didymium"* (Scientific American). [< New Latin *didymium* < Greek *dídymos* twin]

did|y|mous (did'ə məs), *adj. Botany, Zoology.* growing in pairs; paired; twin. [< French *didyme* (< Greek *dídymos* twin) + English *-ous*]

Did|y|mus (did'ə məs), *n.* the surname of the Apostle Thomas (in the Bible, John 11:16).

di|dyn|a|mous (dī din'ə məs), *adj. Botany.* having four stamens arranged in two pairs of unequal length. [< *di-*[1] twice + Greek *dýnamis* power]

die[1] (dī), *v.i.,* **died, dy|ing. 1** to stop living; become dead: *The flowers in the garden died from frost. It matters not how a man dies, but how he lives* (Samuel Johnson). **2** *Figurative.* to lose force, strength, or active qualities: *My sudden anger died. . . . and so dies my revenge* (Shakespeare). **3** *Figurative.* to come to an end; stop: *My secret must die with me* (George Du Maurier). **4** to stop running or functioning: *The motor sputtered and died.* **5** *Informal, Figurative.* to want very much: *I'm dying to go to Alaska. The little boy was dying for an ice-cream cone.* **6** *Figurative.* to pass gradually away; fade away: *A wave died along the shore. I hear soft music die along the grove* (Alexander Pope). **7** *Figurative.* to pass gradually (into): *The twilight died into the dark* (Tennyson). **8** *Figurative.* to become suddenly faint: *It might be seen . . . how her heart died within her* (Robert Southey). **9** *Figurative.* to suffer as if dying: *Cowards die many times before their deaths* (Shakespeare). **10** *Theology.* to suffer spiritual death: *The soul that sinneth, it shall die* (Ezekiel 18:4).

die away (or **down**), to stop or end little by little; lose force or strength gradually: *The music died away. He thought the criticism . . . that had followed his announcement would die down* (New York Times).

die hard, a to struggle until death; resist to the very end; refuse to give in: *The old politician died hard, refusing to concede victory of the election to his young opponent until all of the votes had been counted.* **b** to go on without loss of force; persist indefinitely: *Old customs die hard.*

die off, to die one after another until all are dead: *The whole herd of cattle died off in the epidemic of hoof-and-mouth disease.*

die out, a to stop or end little by little: *The old ways are dying out.* **b** to cease or end completely: *He is the last of the family; after his death the name will die out.*

[Middle English *dien,* earlier *deghen,* perhaps < Scandinavian (compare Old Icelandic *deyja*)]

—***Syn.* 1, 3 Die, perish** mean to stop living or existing. **Die,** the general word, meaning to stop living, is also used figuratively of things that have been active in any way: *The noisy conversation of the class died suddenly when the teacher came into the room.* **Perish,** more formal or literary than *die,* implies dying through violence or hardship, and used figuratively means to go out of existence permanently: *She feared that the unleashing of atomic power would cause civilization to perish.*

▶**Die** is generally used with *of* before an illness: *He died of* (not *from* or *with*) *cancer.* However, *from* is sometimes used to express "from the effects of": *He died from a wound.*

***die**[2] (dī), *n., pl.* **dies** *for 1, 3, 4,* **dice** *for 2, v.,* **died, die|ing.** —*n.* **1** any tool or apparatus for shaping, cutting, punching, or stamping things. It is usually a metal block or plate cut in a way to fit its purpose. Different kinds of dies are used for coining money, for raising letters up from the surface of paper, and for giving a certain shape to articles made by forging and cutting. *A few feet away a begrimed hammer operator thrusts another hot piece of steel into his die* (Wall Street Journal). **2** one of a set of dice. **3** any small cube or square block. **4** *Architecture.* a cubical dado of a pedestal.

—*v.t.* to mold, shape, or cut with a die.

the die is cast, the decision is made and cannot be changed: *The die is cast—I cannot go back* (George Meredith).

[< Old French *de* < Latin *datum* thing given (that is, by fortune), neuter past participle of *dare* give. See etym. of doublet **datum.**]

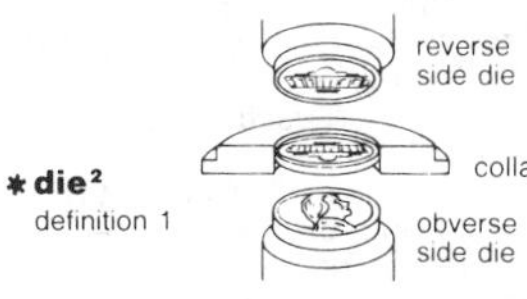

***die**[2]
definition 1

die-a|way (dī'ə wā'), *adj.* languishing; languid.

die|back (dī'bak'), *n.* a condition of trees and bushes, especially of orange and other citrus trees and of the coffee plant, in which the tree or bush dies from the outer parts inward or from the top downward: *Foresters call it a "dieback," a term they use for a variety of diseases in which the tree "dies back" slowly from the outer twigs and leaves inward* (Maclean's).

die-cast (dī'kast', -käst'), *adj., v.,* **-cast, -cast|ing.** —*adj.* made by the process of die casting: *a die-cast engine block.*

—*v.t.* to subject to or make by die casting: *Manufacturers do not die-cast steel and iron because these metals do not melt at low temperatures* (Allison Butts).

die caster, a person who makes die castings: *Special high grade zinc is used by die casters for the automobile and appliance industries* (Wall Street Journal).

die casting, 1 a process for making castings by pressing molten metal into metallic molds under pressure. **2** a casting made this way.

di|e|cious (dī ē'shəs), *adj.* = dioecious.

di|ec|ta|sis (dī ek'tə sis), *n. Prosody.* lengthening by the insertion of a syllable. [< Greek *diéktasis* < *diekteínein* to lengthen < *diá-* apart + *ekteínein* to stretch]

die-cut (dī'kut'), *v.t.,* **-cut, -cut|ting.** to cut out with a die or dies. —**die'-cut'ter,** *n.*

dief|fen|bach|i|a (dē'fən bak'ē ə), *n.* any one of several ornamental plants of parti-colored foliage native to tropical America, including the dumb cane: *Dieffenbachias are tropical cousins of the jack-in-the-pulpit* (New York Times). [< New Latin *Dieffenbachia* the genus name < J. F. *Dieffenbach,* 1794-1847, a German botanist]

die-hard or **die|hard** (dī'härd'), *adj., n.* —***adj.*** resisting to the very end; refusing to give in: *The Senator was a die-hard opponent of any changes in the Constitution. His book is an . . . account of the struggle for public housing against the owners of slums and die-hard politicians* (New Yorker).

—***n.*** a person who refuses to give in: *Grandfather was a die-hard; he refused to use modern machinery on his farm. The waitresses were shooing out the last die-hards, turning off the lights in earnest* (New Yorker).

die-hard|ism (dī'här'diz əm), *n.* the principles or spirit of a die-hard: *In the case of Ezra Pound, American die-hardism and nonconformity were pushed to tragic limits* (London Times Literary Supplement).

di|el (dī'əl, dē'əl), *adj., n. Ecology.* —***adj.*** occurring with a periodicity of 24 hours; daily: *the diel cycle of lizards.*

—***n.*** the 24-hour period; day. [< Latin *dies* day]

di|el|drin (dī el'drin), *n.* a very poisonous insecticide obtained by the oxidation of aldrin with certain acids, used especially against soil-infesting insects, such as locusts and grasshoppers. *Formula:* $C_{12}H_8OCl_6$ [< *Diel*(s-Alder reaction, an important organic reaction) + *-drin,* as in *aldrin*]

di|e|lec|tric (dī'i lek'trik), *adj., n. Electricity.* —***adj.* 1** nonconducting. **2** having to do with a nonconducting medium or with the transmission of electricity without conduction.

—***n.*** a dielectric substance or medium, such as glass, rubber, or wood.

[< *di-*[3] across + *electric* (because induction takes place "across" it)] —**di'e|lec'tri|cal|ly,** *adv.*

di|e|lec|tri|cal (dī'i lek'trə kəl), *adj.* = dielectric.

dielectric constant or **coefficient,** *Electricity.* a measure of the degree to which a nonconductor increases the capacitance of a condenser when placed around or between its plates: *The dielectric constant is a number denoting the ability of a material to resist the flow of electric current through it* (Science News Letter).

dielectric heating, heating of a nonconductor in a varying electric field, due to dielectric loss: *Dielectric heating can now be used for drying and setting textile materials* (New Scientist).

dielectric loss, loss of energy in a dielectric subjected to a varying electric field. This energy is converted to heat.

dielectric strength, the maximum electrical intensity against which a given dielectric can provide effective insulation: *Dielectric strength determines how much voltage [a] condenser will stand without breaking down* (Shortley and Williams).

die|mak|ing (dī'mā'king), *n.* the process of molding dies used to shape metals.

di|en|ce|phal|ic (dī'en sə fal'ik), *adj.* of or having to do with the diencephalon.

di|en|ceph|a|lon (dī'en sef'ə lon), *n. Anatomy.* the posterior part of the forebrain, connecting the cerebrum to the midbrain and including the optic vesicles and pineal body; interbrain. See picture under **brain.** [< New Latin *diencephalon* < Greek *diá-* through + *enképhalon* brain]

di|ene (dī'ēn, dī ēn'), *n. Chemistry.* an aliphatic hydrocarbon having two double bonds; diolefin. [< *di-*[1] + *-ene*]

die-off (dī'ôf', -of'), *n.* the dying off of a population of animals or plants in a particular locality: *Scientists have investigated a number of less spectacular alewife "die-offs" in recent years, but they still have conflicting theories about the*

Pronunciation Key: hat, āge, cãre, fär; let, ēqual, tėrm; it, īce; hot, ōpen, ôrder; oil, out; cup, pu̇t, rüle; child; long; thin; ᴛʜen; zh, measure; ə represents a in about, e in taken, i in pencil, o in lemon, u in circus.

cause of the phenomenon (Time). *Stage-4 degeneration is characterized by shrub die-offs* (*as a result of overbrowsing and a low water table*) (New Scientist).

di|er (dī′ər), *n.* a person who dies.

★**di|er|e|sis** (dī er′ə sis; *especially British* dī ir′ə-sis), *n., pl.* **-ses** (-sēz). **1** two dots placed over the second of two consecutive vowels to indicate that the second vowel is to be pronounced in a separate syllable. *Examples: Noël, naïve, diploë.* **2** the division of one syllable into two, especially by the separation of a diphthong into two simple vowels. **3** *Prosody.* the break which occurs when the end of a foot coincides with the end of a word. **4** (in the pronunciations in this book) a mark over *a* to show that it is pronounced as in *far* (fär), and over *u* to show that it is pronounced as in *rule* (rül). Also **diaeresis**. [< Late Latin *diaeresis* < Greek *diairesis* separation, division < *diaireîn* divide < *diá-* apart + *haireîn* take]

▶**dieresis**. With prefixes, a hyphen is still often used instead of a dieresis, especially in words with *re-* (*re-enlist*). In words of common occurrence, the tendency is to drop both dieresis and hyphen (*cooperation, zoology, reentry*). In the body of a word, however, the dieresis is still sometimes used (*Chloë, Phaëthon*).

★**dieresis**

definition 1
• • naïve
definition 4
fär, rüle

di|e|ret|ic (dī′ə ret′ik), *adj.* of or having to do with dieresis. Also, **diaeretic**.

di|es (dī′ēz, dē′ās), *n., pl.* **di|es**. *Latin.* day.

die|sel or **Die|sel** (dē′zəl, -səl), *n., adj., v.* —*n.* **1** = diesel engine. **2** a truck, locomotive, train, tractor, or construction equipment, run by a diesel engine. **3** = diesel oil.
—*adj.* **1** equipped with or run by a diesel engine: *a diesel locomotive. Its truck fleets include 250 diesel tractors* (Wall Street Journal). **2** of or for a diesel engine: *diesel fuel.*
—*v.i.* (of an internal combustion engine) to continue firing after the ignition has been shut off: *When hot, the engine would diesel ... after the ignition was switched off* (Popular Science).
[< Rudolf *Diesel,* 1858-1913, a German engineer, who invented the diesel engine in the 1890's]

diesel or **Diesel cycle**, a thermodynamic cycle of operations, performed in four strokes or two strokes by a diesel engine. It consists of intake of air, compression of air, injection and ignition of fuel accompanied by expansion of burned mixture, and exhaustion of combustion products.

die|sel-e|lec|tric or **Die|sel-e|lec|tric** (dē′zəl i-lek′trik, -səl-), *adj.* having an electric motor supplied with electricity from a generator run by a diesel engine: *a diesel-electric locomotive.*

diesel or **Diesel engine**, an internal-combustion engine in which fuel oil is ignited by heat from compression of air in the cylinder heads.

die|sel|ing or **Die|sel|ing** (dē′zə ling), *n.* a brief continued idling of an automobile after the ignition is turned off. Dieseling may occur in standard automobiles that use lean fuel mixtures for idling in order to reduce the emission of exhaust pollutants.

die|sel|ise or **Die|sel|ise** (dē′zə līz, -sə-), *v.t.,* **-ised, -is|ing.** *Especially British.* dieselize.

die|sel|i|za|tion or **Die|sel|i|za|tion** (dē′zə lə-zā′shən, -sə-), *n.* the process of dieselizing or state of being dieselized.

die|sel|ize or **Die|sel|ize** (dē′zə līz, -sə-), *v.t.,* **-ized, -iz|ing.** to equip with, or convert to use of, a diesel engine or engines: *It pinched the French railway system, almost completely dieselized* (Newsweek).

diesel or **Diesel motor**, = diesel engine.

diesel oil or **fuel**, a light fuel oil burned by diesel engines and obtained after the distillation of gasoline and kerosene from crude oil.

di|es faus|tus (dī′ēz fôs′təs; dē′ās fous′tùs), *Latin.* a lucky or auspicious day.

di|es in|faus|tus (dī′ēz in fôs′təs; dē′ās in fous′-tùs), *Latin.* an unlucky or inauspicious day.

die|sink|er (dī′sing′kər), *n.* a person who makes dies for shaping or stamping.

die|sink|ing (dī′sing′king), *n.* the making of dies for shaping or stamping.

Di|es I|rae (dī′ēz ī′rē; dē′ās ē′rā), **1** a medieval liturgical poem which describes the Day of Judgment and usually forms the second section of the Requiem Mass. **2** a musical setting of it, either the traditional plain song or an original composition [< Medieval Latin *Dies Irae* Day of Wrath, first line of the poem]

di|e|sis (dī′ə sis), *n., pl.* **-ses** (-sēz). *Printing.* the double dagger. [< Latin *diesis* < Greek *diesis* quarter tone (for which the sign was used); (literally) a sending through, ultimately < *diá-* through + *hiênai* pass, send]

di|es non (dī′ēz non′), *Law.* a day on which law courts are not open; day when courts do not transact business. [< Latin *diēs nōn* (*jūridicus*) not a (court) day]

die|so|hol (dē′zə hôl, -hol), *n.* a mixture of diesel oil and ethyl alcohol, used as a fuel in diesel engine: *As prices for petroleum products rise the economics should become favorable for gasohol and for the diesel fuel-ethanol combination, called diesohol* (John Patrick Jordan). [< *dies*(el) + (alc)*ohol*]

die|stock (dī′stok′), *n.* the stock or handle for holding the dies used in cutting screws.

di|es|trum (dī es′trəm), *n. Zoology.* an inactive period in the estrous cycle; anestrum.

di|et[1] (dī′ət), *n., v.* —*n.* **1** the usual kind of food and drink for a person or animal: *My diet is made up of meat, fish, vegetables, fruits, water, and milk. Grass is a large part of a cow's diet.* SYN: fare, victuals. **2** any special selection of food eaten in sickness, or to make oneself fatter or thinner: *The doctor ordered a liquid diet for the sick child. The doctor put my uncle on a diet because he was too fat.* SYN: regimen. **3** *Figurative.* a habitual or repeated exposure to something: *She served him a steady diet of complaints.*
—*v.i.* **1** to eat special food as a part of a doctor's treatment, or in order to gain or lose weight: *Don't give me any cake; I'm dieting to lose weight.* **2** to eat food; feed. —*v.t.* **1** to cause to eat special or limited amounts of food and drink. **2** to feed with a particular kind of food. [< Old French *diete,* learned borrowing from Latin *diaeta* < Greek *díaita* way of life] —**di′et|er**, *n.*

di|et[2] (dī′ət), *n.* **1** a formal assembly for discussion. SYN: congress, convention, council. **2** the national lawmaking body in certain countries. Switzerland and Japan are governed by diets. SYN: parliament. **3** *Scottish.* **a** a day set for a particular meeting or assembly. **b** a session or sitting, as of a court. **4** a formal assembly in the Holy Roman Empire to discuss or act upon public or state affairs. [< Medieval Latin *dieta* day's work, session of councilors < Latin *diaeta;* see etym. under **diet**[1]; influenced by Latin *diēs* day]

di|e|tar|i|an (dī′ə tãr′ē ən), *n.* a person who follows a dietary or diet.

di|e|tar|y (dī′ə ter′ē), *adj., n., pl.* **-tar|ies**. —*adj.* having to do with diet: *Dietary rules tell what foods to eat for healthy living.*
—*n.* **1** an allowance of food, in a prison, hospital, etc. SYN: ration. **2** a system or course of diet.

dietary fiber, roughage in food, such as bran and fruit skins.

dietary laws, a code of laws, observed chiefly by Orthodox Jews, dealing with the foods that one is permitted or not permitted to eat, the slaughtering of animals, the foods that may or may not be eaten together, and dishes and utensils to be used at various times.

di|e|tet|ic (dī′ə tet′ik), *adj.* of or having to do with diet or dietetics: *Many dietetic foods are without sugar, salt, or fats.* —**di′e|tet′i|cal|ly**, *adv.*

di|e|tet|i|cal (dī′ə tet′ə kəl), *adj.* = dietetic.

di|e|tet|ics (dī′ə tet′iks), *n.* the science that deals with the amount and kinds of food needed by the body.

di|e|tet|ist (dī′ə tet′ist), *n.* a person who studies dietetics.

di|eth|yl|car|ba|ma|zine (dī eth′əl kär′bə mə-zēn), *n.* a white, crystalline, odorless powder, used in medicine, especially as a drug destructive of filariae. *Formula:* $C_{10}H_{21}N_3O$

di|eth|yl ether (dī eth′əl), = ether (def. 1).

di|eth|yl|stil|bes|trol or **di|eth|yl|stil|boes|trol** (dī eth′əl stil bes′trōl, -trol), *n. Biochemistry.* a colorless, synthetic substance used like estrone but not itself an estrogen; stilbestrol.

diethyl toluamide, a colorless liquid insect repellent with a mild odor and low toxicity, used also as a solvent for resins; deet.

di|e|ti|cian (dī′ə tish′ən), *n.* = dietitian.

di|e|ti|tian (dī′ə tish′ən), *n.* a person trained to plan meals that have the right amounts of various kinds of food. Many hospitals and schools employ dietitians.

diet kitchen, a kitchen, usually connected with a hospital, where special diets for invalids and other patients are prepared.

di|et|less (dī′ət lis), *adj.* without a diet; not following a diet.

Diet of Worms, the meeting of the German lawmaking assembly, in 1521, at which Martin Luther defended his doctrines.

di|e|to|ther|a|py (dī′ə tə ther′ə pē), *n.* the treatment of disease by the regulation of diet.

diet pill, *U.S.* any of various hormones, diuretics, or other drugs in tablet form, prescribed to reduce weight, usually by speeding up metabolism.

dietz|e|ite (dēt′zə īt), *n.* a mineral consisting of the iodate and chromate of calcium, occurring in yellow prismatic crystals and fibrous masses. [< August *Dietze,* a German chemist of the 1800's + English *-ite*[1]]

Dieu a|vec nous (dyœ′ ȧ vek nü′), *French.* God with us.

Dieu et mon droit (dyœ′ ā môɴ drwȧ′), *French.* God and my right (the motto on the royal arms of Great Britain and Northern Ireland).

Dieu vous garde (dyœ′ vü gȧrd′), *French.* God keep you (a form of salutation).

dif-, *prefix.* the form of **dis-**[2] before *f,* as in *diffuse.*

diff., **1** difference. **2** different.

dif|fer (dif′ər), *v.i.* **1** to be not the same; be unlike; be different (from): *My answer to the arithmetic problem differed from hers. The twins differ from each other in their interests.* **2** to hold or express a different opinion; disagree: *The two of us differ as to how we should spend the money. I differed from him in the solution he offered. I never differ with your plans.* SYN: dissent. **3** *Obsolete.* to dispute; quarrel. [< Old French *differer,* learned borrowing from Latin *differre* to set apart; differ < *dis-* apart + *ferre* carry. Compare etym. under **defer**[1].]

dif|fer|ence (dif′ər əns, dif′rəns), *n., v.,* **-enced, -enc|ing.** —*n.* **1** the condition of being different: *the difference of night and day.* **2** a way in which people or things are different: *The only difference between the twins is that Katy weighs five pounds more than Rebecca.* **3** what is left after subtracting one number from another; the amount by which one quantity is different from another: *The difference between 6 and 15 is 9.* **4** the condition of having a different opinion; disagreement: *The clerk's difference with the manager cost him his job.* **5** a quarrel; dispute: *The children had a difference over a name for the new puppy.* **6** *Heraldry.* an alteration made to differentiate the coats of arms of two persons, which would otherwise be identical. *Abbr:* diff.
—*v.t.* **1** to cause or constitute a difference in or between; make different. **2** to see the difference in or between; discriminate. **3** *Heraldry.* to add a difference to: *The third son differences his paternal coat with a mullet* (John E. Cussana).

make a difference, **a** to give or show different treatment: *The mother never made a difference between her two sons.* **b** to be important; have an effect or influence; matter: *A person's appearance makes a difference in how others judge him. It makes no difference what you say after you are found guilty.*

split the difference, **a** to divide what is left in half: *You offer five, I ask ten; we'll split the difference at seven-fifty.* **b** to meet halfway; compromise: *My adviser was always ready to split the difference.*

[< Old French *difference,* learned borrowing from Latin *differentia* < *differre;* see etym. under **differ**. See etym. of doublet **differentia**.]

—*Syn. n.* **1 Difference, discrepancy, disparity** mean unlikeness between two things. **Difference** applies to a lack of sameness or any likeness, large or small, in a detail, quality, etc.: *The difference between red and green is not apparent to some color-blind people.* **Discrepancy** applies to a lack of agreement between things that should be alike or balanced: *There was a discrepancy between the two newspaper reports of the trial.* **Disparity** applies to a difference in equality, suggesting that one thing is noticeably lower, smaller, etc., than the other: *There is always a disparity between my expenses and my income.*

difference tone, *Physics.* a tone formed by the sounding of two tones simultaneously, the frequency of which is the difference between that of the two tones.

dif|fer|ent (dif′ər ənt, dif′rənt), *adj., adv.* —*adj.* **1** not alike; not like: *People have different names. An automobile is different from a boat. We saw different kinds of animals at the zoo.* SYN: dissimilar, unlike. **2** not the same; separate; distinct: *We called three different times but never found her at home. Different people have told us the same thing about her. That is a different matter altogether.* **3** not like others or most others; unusual: *Our teacher is quite different; she never gives us homework.*
—*adv. Informal.* differently: *With her in the house, everyone acted different* (Jetta Carleton).
—**dif′fer|ent|ly**, *adv.* —**dif′fer|ent|ness**, *n.*

▶**different**. The standard American usage with *different* is *from: His second book was entirely different from his first.* Informal usage is divided, using *from* occasionally, sometimes *to* (which is a common British usage), and more often *than: She was different than any other girl I had ever known. Different than* is becoming more common when the object is a clause: *The house was a good deal different than he remembered it.*

dif|fer|en|ti|a (dif′ə ren′shē ə), *n., pl.* **-ti|ae**

(-shē ē). *Logic.* the quality or condition that distinguishes one species from all the others of the same genus or class. [< Latin *differentia.* See etym. of doublet **difference**.]

dif|fer|en|ti|a|bil|i|ty (dif′ə ren′shē ə bil′ə tē), *n.* the quality or condition of being differentiable.

dif|fer|en|ti|a|ble (dif′ə ren′shē ə bəl), *adj.* that can be differentiated.

dif|fer|en|tial (dif′ə ren′shəl), *adj., n.* —*adj.* **1** of a difference; showing a difference; depending on a difference: *The differential rates in freight charges are for carrying heavier packages longer distances.* SYN: diverse. **2** distinguishing; distinctive: *a differential feature peculiar to itself.* **3** having to do with distinguishing characteristics or specific differences: *A differential diagnosis attempts to distinguish between two similar diseases.* **4** *Mathematics.* having to do with or involving differentials. **5** *Physics, Mechanics.* concerning the difference of two or more motions, pressures, temperatures, or other measurable quantities. **6** *Geology.* producing different or selective effects on formations or constituents of rocks, soils, or other land material: *differential erosion, differential weathering.*
—*n.* **1a** a differential duty, rate, or charge: *The decline in the differentials has not been evenly paced and has been interrupted by one recovery* (London News Chronicle). **b** the difference involved: *Despite the price differential, consumers will buy canned soft drinks if they are made available* (Sales Management). **2** = differential gear. **3** *Mathematics.* the product of the derivative of a function containing one variable multiplied by the increment of the independent variable. **4** *Electricity.* a coil or wire so related to another coil as to produce polar action contrary to that of the other coil. —**dif′fer|en′tial|ly**, *adv.*

differential analyzer, an analog computer used to solve differential equations: [*The*] *differential analyzer ... can solve advanced mathematical problems of physics, electrical engineering, and other sciences* (Louis N. Ridenour).

differential calculus, the branch of higher mathematics that investigates differentials, derivatives, and their relations.

differential coefficient, *Mathematics.* the limit of the ratio of change of a function to the corresponding change of a variable in it, as the change of the variable approaches zero.

differential equation, *Mathematics.* an equation containing or involving differential coefficients and differentials.

***differential gear**, an arrangement of gears to permit differences in speed in different parts of a mechanism, especially one in an automobile axle that allows one of the rear wheels to turn faster than the other in going around a corner or curve; compensating gear; differential.

***differential gear**

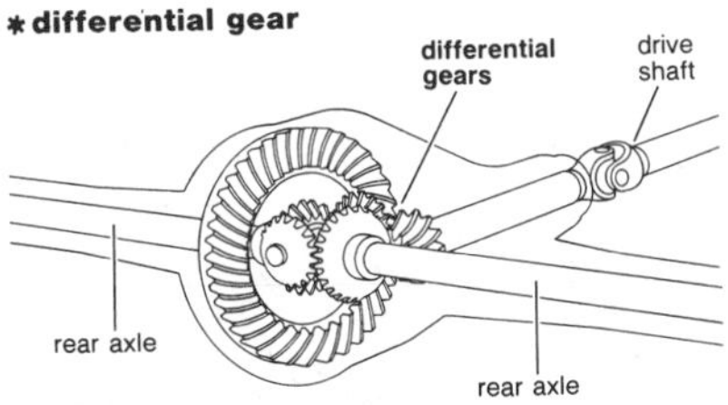

differential quotient, = differential coefficient.

differential rate, the lower or lowest of two or more rates arrived at by railroads, or other common carriers, competing for traffic.

differential windlass, a windlass in which the drum consists of two parts of different diameters, the hoisting rope unwinding from one part while it is being wound on the other; Chinese windlass.

dif|fer|en|ti|ate (dif′ə ren′shē āt), *v.,* **-at|ed, -at|ing,** *n.* —*v.t.* **1** to make different; cause to have differences: *Consideration for others differentiates a thoughtful person from a bad-mannered one. It is the accumulated knowledge of centuries which differentiates modern Man from his ancestor in the dawn of civilization* (Bulletin of Atomic Scientists). **2** to find or tell the difference in or between; find or show to be different: *Almost anyone can differentiate a cow from a horse. The botanist differentiated varieties of plants.* SYN: See syn. under **distinguish**. **3** *Biology.* to make different in the process of growth or development; make unlike by modification. **4** *Mathematics.* to obtain the differential or differential coefficient of: *to differentiate an equation.*
—*v.i.* **1** to become different: *This genus of plants differentiates into many species.* **2** to tell the difference; find or show what is different: *A doctor must differentiate between diseases to give the right treatment.* SYN: See syn. under **distinguish**. **3** *Biology.* to become differentiated or specialized: *The cells of an embryo differentiate into organs and parts as it grows.*
—*n.* **1** *Geology.* any of a group of rocks derived from a parent mass and differentiated into constituents either more acidic or more basic than the original mass. **2** *Mathematics.* = differential coefficient.

dif|fer|en|ti|a|tion (dif′ə ren′shē ā′shən), *n.* the act, process, or result of differentiating; alteration; modification; distinction: *Science is an intellectual endeavor, but there are differentiations in the levels of mental demand that it makes* (John E. Owen).

dif|fer|en|ti|a|tor (dif′ə ren′shē ā′tər), *n.* a person or thing that differentiates.

dif|fi|cile (dif′ə sēl′, di fis′əl; *French* dē fē sēl′), *adj. Obsolete, except as French.* (of persons) hard to deal with; hard to please or satisfy; troublesome: [*He*] *fought back and acquired the reputation of being difficile, as the French would say* (New York Times). [< Middle French *difficile,* learned borrowing from Latin *difficilis;* see etym. under **difficulty**]

dif|fi|cult (dif′ə kult, -kəlt), *adj.* **1** hard to do or understand: *Arithmetic is difficult for some pupils. Cutting down the tree was difficult. Poetry became, if anything, more "difficult" and esoteric* (Saturday Review). SYN: arduous. See syn. under **hard**. **2** hard to manage; hard to please: *That difficult member of the team always wants his own way. I found my new employer difficult.* SYN: trying. **3** presenting obstacles or trouble: *a thing difficult to imagine, a place difficult of access.* **4** hard to persuade; unwilling. [perhaps back formation < *difficulty*] —**dif′fi|cult|ly**, *adv.* —**dif′fi|cult|ness**, *n.*

dif|fi|cul|ty (dif′ə kul′tē, -kəl tē), *n., pl.* **-ties. 1** the fact or condition of being difficult; degree to which something is difficult: *The difficulty of the job kept us from finishing it on time.* **2** hard work; much effort: *The lame man walked with difficulty.* **3** something which stands in the way of getting things done; thing that is hard to do or understand; obstacle: *He tried to overcome the difficulties presented by his lack of people to help him. My quick temper is my chief difficulty.* SYN: hindrance. **4** trouble: *in difficulty with the police. What is your difficulty? Some children have great difficulty in learning how to spell.* SYN: hardship, dilemma, predicament. **5** financial trouble: *He has been in difficulties ever since he started to gamble.* **6** a disagreement; quarrel. **7** reluctance; unwillingness; objection: *Men should consider that raising difficulties concerning the mysteries in religion cannot make them more wise, learned, or virtuous* (Jonathan Swift).
make a difficulty, to be unwilling; object: *My mother made no difficulty when I bought a car.*
[< Latin *difficultās* < *difficilis* hard < *dis-* not, away from + *facilis* easy, facile]

dif|fi|da|tion (dif′ə dā′shən), *n.* **1** a formal renouncing of faith, allegiance, or friendship. **2** a solemn defiance of an enemy. [< Medieval Latin *diffidatio, -onis,* ultimately < Latin *dis-* away + *fīdere* trust]

dif|fi|dence (dif′ə dəns), *n.* lack of self-confidence; shyness: *He began to speak with a diffidence that disappeared as soon as he felt sure of himself.* SYN: bashfulness.

dif|fi|dent (dif′ə dənt), *adj.* **1** lacking in self-confidence; shy; bashful: *... a serious young man, diffident and withdrawn* (Time). SYN: modest. **2** = distrustful. [< Latin *diffidēns, -entis,* present participle of *diffīdere* < *dis-* away + *fīdere* trust] —**dif′fi|dent|ly**, *adv.*

dif|flu|ence (dif′lü əns), *n.* the quality or condition of being diffluent: *... the diffluence of channels in a river delta* (Science News).

dif|flu|ent (dif′lü ənt), *adj.* tending to flow apart; readily dissolving. [< Latin *diffluēns, -entis,* present participle of *diffluere* flow away < *dis-* away + *fluere* to flow]

dif|form (di fôrm′), *adj.* **1** differing in form; unlike; dissimilar. **2** irregular in form; not uniform. [< Medieval Latin *difformis* < Latin *dis-* un- + *forma* shape]

dif|form|i|ty (di fôr′mə tē), *n., pl.* **-ties. 1** difference or diversity in form. **2** lack of uniformity.

dif|fract (di frakt′), *v.t.* **1** *Physics.* to break up by diffraction: *The neutrons are scattered or diffracted by the atoms just as X rays are* (Science News Letter). **2** to break in pieces; break up. [< Latin *diffractus,* past participle of *diffringere* < *dis-* apart + *frangere* break]

dif|frac|tion (di frak′shən), *n. Physics.* **1** a spreading of light around an obstacle into a series of light and dark bands or into colored bands of the spectrum: *Newton had attempted to infer from ... diffraction phenomena the size of the corpuscles of matter* (Scientific American). **2** a similar spreading of other waves, such as sound waves, as when a wave front changes from a straight line to a curved line. **3** a change in the direction of an electron beam, such as occurs when the beam comes in contact with a crystal of nickel.

diffraction grating, *Physics.* a plate of glass or polished metal with very fine and close parallel lines, used to produce spectra by diffraction: *The light is then dispersed by a diffraction grating* (Scientific American).

dif|frac|tive (di frak′tiv), *adj.* having to do with diffraction; tending to diffract. —**dif|frac′tive|ly**, *adv.* —**dif|frac′tive|ness**, *n.*

dif|frac|tom|e|ter (dif′rak tom′ə tər), *n.* an instrument for measuring diffraction: *A diffractometer which can determine the orientation of crystals in any plane without resetting is on offer now* (New Scientist).

dif|frac|to|met|ric (di frak′tə met′rik), *adj.* of or having to do with a diffractometer.

dif|fran|gi|bil|i|ty (di fran′jə bil′ə tē), *n.* **1** quality of being diffrangible. **2** the degree of diffraction.

dif|fran|gi|ble (di fran′jə bəl), *adj.* that can be diffracted. [< *dif-* + *frangible*]

dif|fuse (*v.* di fyüz′; *adj.* di fyüs′), *v.,* **-fused, -fus|ing,** *adj.* —*v.t.* **1** to spread out so as to cover a large space or surface; scatter widely: *The sun diffuses light and heat. Schools and libraries and many television programs diffuse knowledge.* SYN: disseminate, disperse. **2** *Physics.* to spread by diffusion.
—*v.i.* **1** to scatter widely; spread. **2** *Physics.* to mix together by spreading into one another: *Alcohol and water will diffuse; oil and water will not. Oxygen diffuses through air about 10,000 times faster than through water* (Albert R. Grable).
—*adj.* **1** not drawn together at a single point; spread out: *diffuse light.* SYN: widespread, scattered, dispersed. **2** using many words where a few would do: *a diffuse writer. A diffuse book is very tiresome to read. Too strong and concise, not diffuse enough for a woman* (Jane Austen). SYN: wordy.
[< Latin *diffusus,* past participle of *diffundere* < *dis-* apart (in every direction) + *fundere* pour]
—**dif|fuse′ly**, *adv.* —**dif|fuse′ness**, *n.*

dif|fus|ed|ly (di fyü′zid lē), *adv.* in a diffused manner.

diffuse nebula, a dark or slightly luminous galactic nebula. The lack of a regular and distinct shape distinguishes the diffuse nebulae from the planetary nebulae.

dif|fuse-po|rous (di fyüs′pôr′əs, -pōr′-), *adj.* having pores uniform in size and distribution, unchanging in spring and summer, and unable to be seen by the naked eye, such as the wood of the maple, birch, and cherry.

dif|fus|er (di fyü′zər), *n.* **1** a person or thing that diffuses. **2** *Aeronautics.* a chamber used to reduce the velocity and increase the static pressure of air or other fluid in relative motion.

dif|fus|i|bil|i|ty (di fyü′zə bil′ə tē), *n.* the quality of being diffusible.

dif|fus|i|ble (di fyü′zə bəl), *adj.* that can be diffused.

dif|fu|sion (di fyü′zhən), *n.* **1** the act or fact of diffusing; a spreading or scattering widely: *The invention of printing greatly increased the diffusion of knowledge. The spreading of patterns and traits from one group or area to another is known as cultural diffusion.* **2** a being widely spread or scattered; diffused condition. **3a** a mixing together of the atoms or molecules of substances by spreading into one another: *the diffusion of gases, liquids, or solids. An example of a new relation is found in the combination of diffusion and heat flow* (R. O. Davies). **b** the scattering of light resulting from its being reflected from a rough surface. See **scatter**. **4** the use of too many words; wordiness.

dif|fu|sion|al (di fyü′zhə nəl), *adj.* of diffusion; having to do with or produced by diffusion.

diffusion board, a porous, chemically treated board, similar in appearance to fiberboard, having the ability to filter out such contaminants as gases and noxious or radioactive particles while allowing oxygen and carbon dioxide to pass through freely.

dif|fu|sion|ism (di fyü′zhə niz əm), *n.* any theory that emphasizes diffusion, especially the theory that different cultures arise by diffusion from a single source: *Most archaeologists were schooled in ... diffusionism. This notion holds that civilization and advanced technology arose in Egypt and the Middle East and then, starting about 2500 B.C., diffused, or flowed, northward into Europe* (Robert C. Cowen).

Pronunciation Key: hat, āge, cãre, fär; let, ēqual, tėrm; it, īce; hot, ōpen, ôrder; **oil**, **out**; cup, pu̇t, rüle; **ch**ild; lo**ng**; **th**in; **ᴛʜ**en; **zh**, measure; ə represents **a** in about, **e** in taken, **i** in pencil, **o** in lemon, **u** in circus.

dif|fu|sion|ist (di fyü′zhə nist), *n., adj.* **—*n.*** a person who believes in some theory of diffusion, such as the theory of culture diffusion.
—*adj.* of or in the manner of a diffusionist; favoring a theory of diffusion: *"The Rise of the West" by William H. McNeill . . . This diffusionist history of how the world was Europeanized won a National Book Award* (Saturday Review).

diffusion pump, a pump for producing a vacuum in an X-ray tube, radio tube, lamp bulb, or the like, usually by means of a column of mercury which pushes out air molecules: *The final pressure at which the tube works is achieved by means of a diffusion pump* (Scientific American).

dif|fu|sive (di fyü′siv), *adj.* **1** tending to diffuse. **2** showing diffusion. **3** using too many words; wordy: *He is less diffusive and more pointed than usual* (Sir Leslie Stephen). **SYN:** verbose. **—dif|fu′sive|ly,** *adv.* **—dif|fu′sive|ness,** *n.*

dif|fu|siv|i|ty (dif′yü siv′ə tē), *n. Physics.* capacity of diffusion (as a measurable quality of liquids, gases, heat, or other physical phenomena).

dif|fu|sor (di fyü′zər), *n.* = diffuser.

dig (dig), *v.,* **dug** or (*Archaic*) **digged, dig|ging,** *n.* **—*v.i.*** **1** to use a machine, shovel, spade, hands, claws, or snout to make a hole or to turn over the ground: *Dogs bury bones and dig for them later.* **SYN:** delve, spade, grub. **2** to make a way by digging: *to dig through a hill. They dug through a mountain to build a tunnel.* **3** *Figurative.* to make a careful search or inquiry (for information or into the works of some author): *The writer dug into the family records for the story of his pioneer ancestors.* **4** *Informal, Figurative.* to work or study hard. **5** *Slang.* **a** to understand: *Adults may not dig, but how could 20 million teen-agers be wrong?* (Time). **b** to look; keep an eye (on): *OK, that's me posted at the corner digging on all the frozen chickies rushing it home from work* (Al Young).
—*v.t.* **1** to break up and turn over (ground) with a spade, or other tool or machinery. **2** to make by digging and removing material: *to dig a well. The workmen dug a cellar. Under the wide and starry sky Dig the grave and let me lie* (Robert Louis Stevenson). **SYN:** excavate. **3** to get by digging: *to dig potatoes. We dug clams at the beach yesterday.* **SYN:** unearth. **4** to make a thrust or stab; prod: *The cat dug her claws into my hand. I dug my horse with my spurs to make him run faster.* **5** *Slang.* **a** to understand; appreciate: *to dig the mellower things in life* (Time). **b** to notice; observe: *Dig that new style.* **c** to like; admire: *to dig a baseball player.*
—*n.* **1** a thrust or poke: *The boy gave his friend a playful dig in the ribs.* **2** *Figurative.* a sarcastic remark: *The candidate made a dig at his opponent.* **3** *Informal.* an archaeological excavation: *I don't think I can remember a single dig in which something at least was not found* (London Times). **4** the act of digging: *A careful dig with a trowel loosened the roots.* **5** *U.S. Informal.* a diligent, hard-working student.
dig in, *Informal.* **a** to dig trenches for protection: *. . . evidence of Syrian military units digging in on the frontier* (London Times). **b** to work or study hard: *The scholar dug in as the subject became more and more confused.* **c** to establish oneself in a position: *South Africans are anything but pessimistic about their future on this continent. Not only are they digging in for a long stay; they look for it to be a prosperous one, too* (Wall Street Journal).
dig into, *Informal.* **a** to work hard at: *He seemed to dig into his subject* (The Examiner). **b** to give up from; hand over, especially upon a second demand: *So long as the need for education facilities and for municipal services continues to grow, state and local taxpayers will have to keep digging deeper into their pockets* (Wall Street Journal).
digs, *Especially British Informal.* a place to live; diggings: *Jim also, unquestionably, lives in the smartest of digs* (New Yorker).
dig up (or **out**), **a** to unearth: *to dig up potatoes.* **b** to excavate: *The contractor's men began to dig up the lot next door for a basement.* **c** *Figurative.* to find out; discover; obtain as if by digging: *Ogden digs up a deck of cards* (O. Henry).
[Middle English *dyggen,* perhaps < Old French *diguer* < *digue* dike, perhaps < Middle Dutch *dijc.* Compare etym. under **dike, ditch.**]

dig., digest.

di|ga|met|ic (dī′gə met′ik), *adj. Biology.* producing two kinds of gametes or germ cells, such as one containing an X chromosome and another a Y chromosome.

di|gam|ma (dī gam′ə), *n.* a letter in the early Greek alphabet (F). It represented a sound similar to that of the English *w.* [< Latin *digamma* < Greek *digamma* < *di-* twice + *gámma* gamma]

di|gam|mat|ed (dī gam′ā tid), *adj.* spelled with or having the digamma.

dig|a|mous (dig′ə məs), *adj.* **1** married a second time; practicing digamy. **2** of or having to do with digamy.

dig|a|my (dig′ə mē), *n.* second marriage; marrying again after the death of the first husband or wife. [< Latin *digamia* < Greek *digamíā* < *di-* twice + *gámos* marrying]

di|gas|tric (dī gas′trik), *adj., n. Anatomy.* **—*adj.*** designating or having to do with a muscle having two fleshy parts connected by a tendon: *a digastric or two-bellied muscle.*
—*n.* a muscle of the lower jaw, thick at its extremities and thin and tendinous in the middle, by which the hyoid bone is raised in swallowing.
[< New Latin *digastricus* < Greek *di-* two + *gastḗr, gastrós* stomach (because of the shape)]

Dig|by (dig′bē), *n., pl.* **-bies,** or **Digby chicken,** a variety of small herring caught and cured at Digby, Nova Scotia.

di|gen|e|sis (dī jen′ə sis), *n., pl.* **-ses** (-sēz). *Biology.* alternation of sexual and asexual reproduction in successive generations.

di|ge|net|ic (dī′jə net′ik), *adj. Biology.* having to do with or like digenesis.

di|gest (*v.* də jest′, dī-; *n.* dī′jest), *v., n.* **—*v.t.*** **1** to change (food) in the mouth, stomach and intestines so that the body can absorb it: *We digest our food slowly. I like milk, but I can't digest it* (Newsweek). **2** to promote the digestion of (food): *Cheese is believed to digest everything except itself.* **3** *Figurative.* to think over (something) until one understands it clearly, or until it becomes a part of one's thoughts: *It often takes a long time to digest new ideas. Some books are to be tasted, others to be swallowed, and some few to be chewed and digested* (Sir Francis Bacon). **SYN:** consider, assimilate. **4** to make a brief statement of; summarize: *The author refused to allow the publisher to digest his book.* **5** *Figurative.* to bear; endure; tolerate: *Such ill-mannered behavior is more than I can digest.* **SYN:** brook, stomach. **6** *Chemistry.* to soften by combinations of heat, moisture, pressure, or chemical action; dissolve or decompose.
—*v.i.* **1** to be digested; undergo digestion: *Our food digests slowly.* **2** to digest food. [< Latin *dīgestus,* past participle of *dīgerere* separate, dissolve < *dis-* apart + *gerere* carry]
—*n.* **1** a brief statement of what is in a longer book, article, or statement; summary: *a digest of law.* **SYN:** See syn. under **summary.** **2** a collection of summaries or condensations: *a digest of great novels.* **SYN:** compendium. **3** the product of the action of enzymes on food.
[< *Digest*]

Di|gest (dī′jest), *n.* a collection of Roman law compiled in the 500's by order of Emperor Justinian. [< Late Latin *Dīgesta* (originally) neuter plural of Latin *dīgestus;* see etym. under **digest,** verb]

di|gest|ant (də jes′tənt), *adj., n.* = digestive.

di|gest|er (də jes′tər, dī-), *n.* **1** a person who makes a digest. **2** an apparatus for softening or dissolving a substance by heat, pressure, moisture, and the like. **3** a thing, especially an organ or agent, that digests or promotes digestion.

di|gest|i|bil|i|ty (də jes′tə bil′ə tē, dī-), *n.* the quality of being digestible.

di|gest|i|ble (də jes′tə bəl, dī-), *adj.* that can be digested; easily digested. **—di|gest′i|ble|ness,** *n.*

di|gest|i|bly (də jes′tə blē, dī-), *adv.* in a digestible form or condition.

***di|ges|tion** (də jes′chən, dī-), *n.* **1** the digesting of food: *Proper digestion is necessary for good health.* **2** the ability to digest food: *A person's digestion can be affected by illness.* **3** *Figurative.* the act of digesting (books or the like): *the easy digestion of simple ideas.* **4** *Chemistry.* decomposition, as of sewage. **5** *Obsolete.* a digest.

di|ges|tive (də jes′tiv, dī-), *adj., n.* **—*adj.*** **1** of or for digestion: *Saliva is one of the digestive juices. The stomach is an important digestive organ.* **2** helping digestion: *digestive tablets.*
—*n.* **1** something, especially a medicine, that aids digestion. **2** *British.* a kind of whole-meal biscuit. **—di|ges′tive|ly,** *adv.*

dig|ger (dig′ər), *n.* **1** a person or thing that digs. **2** the part of a machine that turns up the ground. **3** any tool for digging. **4** *Informal.* an Australian or New Zealander (a nickname used especially in World War I).

Dig|ger[1] (dig′ər), *n.* a member of a tribe or group of North American Indians who lived on roots dug from the ground or on the nuts of the Digger pine.

Dig|ger[2] (dig′ər), *n.* any one of a group of hippies devoted to helping others, especially other hippies, as by giving them free food and clothing. [< *Diggers,* a group of English idealists of the 1600's who applied communist principles to agriculture, digging and planting publicly held lands]

Digger pine, a pine native to California and Nevada, whose nuts provided one of the chief sources of food for the Digger Indians.

digger wasp, any one of various solitary wasps that dig their nests in the ground.

dig|ging (dig′ing), *n.* **1** the act of a person or thing that digs. **2** something dug out. **3** a place where digging is carried on; excavation.
diggings, a a mine, archaeological site, or other place where digging is being done: *she sometimes pans a little gold out of the old diggings* (Harper's). **b** the material that is dug out. **c** *Informal.* a place to live: *Once they were the temporary diggings of Lord Byron, Shelley, Heine . . .* (Newsweek).

digging stick, a pointed stick or bone used among the American Indians and other primitive people for simple cultivation.

dight (dīt), *v.t.,* **dight** or **dight|ed, dight|ing.** *Archaic or Dialect.* **1** to dress; adorn: *Slowly, in all his splendors dight, The great sun rises* (Longfellow). **2** to equip; prepare; make ready. **3** to repair; put in order. [Old English *dihtan* compose, arrange < Latin *dictāre.* See doublet **dictate.**]

dig|it (dij′it), *n.* **1** any one of the figures 0, 1, 2, 3, 4, 5, 6, 7, 8, 9. Sometimes 0 is not called a digit. **2** a finger or toe. **3** the breadth of a finger used in ancient times as a measure of length, usually about ¾ inch. **4** *Astronomy.* 1/12 the apparent diameter of the sun or moon. [< Latin *digitus* finger] **—dig′it|like,** *adj.*

dig|it|al (dij′ə təl), *adj., n.* **—*adj.*** **1** of, having to do with, or using a digit or digits: *Digital telephone numbers, such as 941-2898, are replacing the old letter and number combinations, such as WI 1-2898.* **2** having digits. **3** like a digit or digits. **4** of, having to do with, or based on the principle of a digital computer: *a digital code.* **5** or or having to do with the recording of sound by means of electrical signals coded into binary digits: *digital recording, digital sound.*
—*n.* **1** a finger. **2** a key of an organ, piano, etc., played with the fingers. **—dig′it|al|ly,** *adv.*

***digestion**
definition 1

the digestive system:

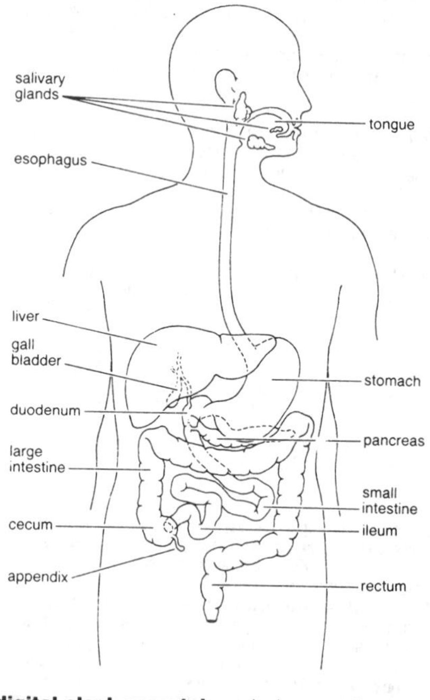

salivary glands
tongue
esophagus
liver
gall bladder
stomach
duodenum
pancreas
large intestine
small intestine
cecum
ileum
appendix
rectum

digital clock or **watch,** a clock or watch, often electronically operated, which shows the time by displaying it in digits, such as 5:30, instead of by hands moving around a dial.

digital computer, a type of electronic calculating machine using numbers expressed as digits of some numerical system to solve problems which can be expressed mathematically: *Increasing use is being made of analogue and digital computers for analysis of data* (Science News).

digital disk or **disc,** a sound recording whose quality is enhanced by processing with a digital computer: *The first fully digital discs, compact and metallic, gleaming with rainbow colors, their music free of all interference . . . tracked by a laser beam* (Manchester Guardian Weekly).

dig|i|tal|in (dij′ə tal′in, -tā′lin), *n.* **1** a poisonous, crystalline glycoside obtained from the seeds of a common European fox glove. *Formula:* $C_{36}H_{56}O_{14}$ **2** a mixture of glycosides obtained from the seeds of this foxglove.

dig|i|tal|is (dij′ə tal′is, -tā′lis), *n.* **1** a medicine used for stimulating the heart, obtained from the leaves and seeds of some varieties of foxglove: *Digitalis, used to treat heart conditions, is an example of a steroid in plants* (Science News Letter). **2** any of a group of tall, European and Asiatic herbs of the figwort family; foxglove. [< New Latin *digitalis* < Latin *digitālis* having to do with the finger < *digitus* finger (because of the shape of its corolla)]

dig|i|tal|ism (dij′ə tə liz′əm), *n.* a disorder of the body produced by the excessive use of digitalis.

dig|i|tal|i|za|tion (dij′ə tə lə zā′shən), *n.* treatment with digitalis.

dig|i|tal|ize (dij′ə tə līz), *v.t.,* **-ized, -iz|ing. 1** to treat with digitalis. **2** to make (data) suitable for handling by digital computer; digitize.

dig|i|tate (dij′ə tāt), *adj.* **1** having separate or divided fingers or toes. **2** having radiating divisions or leaflets like fingers: *a digitate leaf.* — **dig′i-tate′ly,** *adv.*

dig|i|tat|ed (dij′ə tā′tid), *adj.* = digitate.

dig|i|ta|tion (dij′ə tā′shən), *n.* **1** digitate condition or formation. **2** a digitlike process or division in an animal or plant.

dig|i|ti|form (dij′ə tə fôrm), *adj.* fingerlike; digitate.

dig|i|ti|grade (dij′ə tə grād), *adj., n.* — ***adj.*** having feet shaped so that the toes, but not the heels, are on the ground: *Dogs, cats, and horses are digitigrade animals.* — ***n.*** a digitigrade animal. [< New Latin *digitigrada* < Latin *digitus* finger, toe + *gradus, -ūs* step, grade, < *gradī* to walk]

dig|i|ti|za|tion (dij′ə tə zā′shən), *n.* conversion into a digit or digits; representation in digital form: *There is an extra processing stage between the digitization of the character and its recognition* (New Scientist).

dig|i|tize (dij′ə tīz), *v.t.,* **-tized, -tiz|ing. 1** to convert (data), as from an analog computer, into a number or numbers expressed in digits in a scale of notation. **2** to count, manipulate, or treat (something) with the fingers. — **dig′i|tiz′er,** *n.*

dig|i|to|nin (dij′ə tō′nən), *n.* a saponin derived from the seeds of digitalis, used in determining the level of cholesterol in blood plasma and tissue. *Formula:* $C_{56}H_{92}O_{29}$ [< *digit*(alis) + (sap)*onin*]

dig|i|to|plan|tar (dij′ə tō plan′tər), *adj.* of or having to do with the sole of the foot and the toes.

dig|i|to|ri|um (dij′ə tôr′ē əm, -tōr′-), *n., pl.* **-to-ri|a** (-tôr′ē ə, -tōr′-). a small portable keyboard used for exercising and strengthening the fingers in piano playing; a dumb piano.

dig|i|tox|in (dij′ə tok′sin), *n.* a highly toxic white or buff, crystalline glycoside found in digitalis, used in cardiac treatment. *Formula:* $C_{41}H_{64}O_{13}$ [< *digi*(talis) + *toxin*]

di|glad|i|a|tion (dī glad′ē ā′shən), *n. Archaic.* **1** a combat with swords. **2** *Figurative.* a contest; quarrel; dispute. [< Latin *dīgladiārī* contend fiercely (< *dis-* asunder + *gladius* sword) + English *-ation*]

di|glos|si|a (dī glos′ē ə), *n.* **1** the condition of having the tongue divided into two parts by a cleft. **2** *Linguistics.* the use of different forms of the same language or, sometimes, of different languages in the same speech area, one of which is often considered superior to the other: *The diglossia problem of the lower-class black is unusual because he does not speak a colloquial or "incorrect" form of Standard English* (Peter Farb).

di|glot (dī′glot), *adj., n.* — ***adj.*** using or in two languages; bilingual. — ***n.*** a diglot book or edition. [< Greek *diglōttos* interpreter, (one) speaking two languages < *di-* double + *glôtta,* variant of *glôssa* tongue]

di|glot|tic (dī glot′ik), *adj.* = diglot.

di|glyc|er|ide (dī glis′ə rīd, -ər id), *n.* any one of a group of fatty compounds formed when two acid radicals replace two of the hydrogen atoms of the -OH (hydroxyl) groups in glycerol: *Because a molecule of glycerol has three reactive sites, it is possible to have monoglycerides, diglycerides, and triglycerides, depending on how many molecules of fatty acid react with each molecule of glycerol* (Scientific American).

dig|ni|fi|ca|tion (dig′nə fə kā′shən), *n.* the act of dignifying or the state of being dignified.

dig|ni|fied (dig′nə fīd), *adj.* having dignity; noble; stately: *The President has a dignified manner.* — **dig′ni|fied′ly,** *adv.*

dig|ni|fy (dig′nə fī), *v.t.,* **-fied, -fy|ing. 1** to give dignity to; make noble, worthwhile, or worthy: *The low farmhouse was dignified by the great elms around it.* **2** to give a high-sounding name or title to: *The boys dignified their old sailboat with the title of Ocean Queen.* [< Old French *dignifier,* learned borrowing from Latin *dīgnificāre* < *dīgnus* worthy + *facere* make]

dig|ni|tar|i|al (dig′nə tãr′ē əl), *adj.* of or belonging to a dignitary.

dig|ni|tar|y (dig′nə ter′ē), *n., pl.* **-tar|ies,** *adj.* — ***n.*** a person who has a position of honor. A bishop is a church dignitary.
— ***adj.*** of or having to do with a dignity or high position, especially in a church.

dig|ni|ty (dig′nə tē), *n., pl.* **-ties. 1** proud and self-respecting character or manner or stately appearance: *the dignity of a cathedral. Milton's poetry has dignity.* **2** the quality of character or ability that wins respect and high opinion of others: *A judge should maintain the dignity of his position.* **3** a high office, rank, or title; position of honor: *He may attain the dignity of the presidency.* **SYN:** eminence. **4** worth; nobleness: *Honest work has dignity; idleness has none. A peace above all earthly dignities* (Shakespeare). **5** *Archaic.* a person of high office, rank, or title; dignitary. **6** *Astrology.* a situation of a planet in which its influence is heightened. [< Old French *dignete,* learned borrowing from Latin *dīgnitās* worthiness < *dīgnus* worthy. See etym. of doublet **dainty.**]

dig|ox|in (dij ok′sən), *n.* a highly toxic, odorless, colorless to white crystalline glycoside derived from digitalis leaves, used to restore or increase cardiac contraction. *Formula:* $C_{41}H_{64}O_{14}$ [< *dig*(italis) + (t)*oxin*]

di|gram (dī′gram), *n.* = digraph.

di|graph (dī′graf, -gräf), *n.* **1** two letters used together to spell a single sound. *Examples: ea* in *each, th* in *with, sh* in *shop.* **2** any combination of two letters: *The cryptographer treats digraphs, or pairs of the letters of his plain text, as the elements for encipherment* (L. D. Callimahos).

di|graph|ic (dī graf′ik), *adj.* **1** of, having to do with, or like a digraph. **2** written in two different characters or alphabets. — **di|graph′i|cal|ly,** *adv.*

di|gress (də gres′, dī-), *v.i.* **1** to turn aside from the main subject in talking or writing: *A speaker should not digress too far or too often if he wishes to hold the full attention of his audience.* **SYN:** See syn. under **diverge. 2** = swerve. [< Latin *dīgressus,* past participle of *dīgredī* deviate < *dis-* apart, aside + *gradī* to step, go] — **di-gress′er,** *n.*

di|gres|sion (də gresh′ən, dī-), *n.* a digressing; turning aside from the main subject in talking or writing: *The speaker's many digressions made the lecture longer than usual. Digressions ... are the sunshine ... the life and soul of reading* (Laurence Sterne).

di|gres|sion|al (də gresh′ə nəl, dī-), *adj.* = digressive.

di|gres|sion|ar|y (də gresh′ə ner′ē, dī-), *adj.* of the nature of a digression; digressive.

di|gres|sive (də gres′iv, dī-), *adj.* characterized by digression; tending to digress; digressing. **SYN:** rambling. — **di|gres′sive|ly,** *adv.* — **di|gres′sive-ness,** *n.*

digs (digz), *n.pl.* See under **dig.**

***di|he|dral** (dī hē′drəl), *adj., n.* — ***adj.* 1** *Mathematics.* having or formed by two plane surfaces which meet along an edge: *a dihedral angle.* **2** *Aeronautics.* (of wings) set at a dihedral angle to each other, each rising from the horizontal.
— ***n.* 1** the figure formed by two intersecting plane surfaces. **2** an angle between two planes; dihedral angle. **3** the angle at which the wings of an aircraft are inclined to each other.
[< *di-*[1] two + Greek *hédrā* seat, base + *-al*[1]]

***dihedral**
definitions 1, 2

definition 1 definition 2

di|hy|brid (dī hī′brid), *adj., n. Biology.* — ***adj.*** having parents whose genetic make-up differs in two pairs of inheritable characters.
— ***n.*** a dihybrid organism.

di|hy|dric (dī hī′drik), *adj. Chemistry.* containing two hydroxyl groups: *dihydric alcohols.*

di|hy|dro|strep|to|my|cin (dī hī′drō strep′tə mī′-sin), *n.* a compound derived from streptomycin, similar in use but less toxic in effect. *Formula:* $C_{21}H_{41}N_7O_{12}$

di|hy|dro|ta|chys|ter|ol (dī hī′drō tə kis′tə rōl, -rol), *n. Biochemistry.* a sterol yielded by an ergosterol derivative and possessing vitamin D activity. *Formula:* $C_{28}H_{43}O$

di|hy|drox|y|ac|e|tone (dī hī drok′sē as′ə tōn), *n.* a colorless, crystalline powder, used in solution for spreading on the skin to produce an artificial suntan: *Overnight tanners are based on dihydroxyacetone and they mix with the amino acids in the skin to produce a surface brownness which varies in intensity according to the number of applications* (London Times). *Formula:* $C_3H_6O_3$

di|i|so|pro|pyl fluo|ro|phos|phate (dī ī′sə prō′-pəl flür′ə fos′fāt, flü′ər ə-), an extremely toxic oily liquid used in the treatment of glaucoma; DFP (no periods). *Formula:* $C_6H_{14}FPO_3$

di|kar|y|on (dī kar′ē ôn), *n. Biology.* **1** a cell containing two haploid nuclei which divide simultaneously. **2** a mycelium or a hypha containing such cells. [< *di-*[1] + Greek *káryon* kernel]

dik-dik (dik′dik′), *n.* a tiny, harelike African antelope, usually about 14 or 15 inches high at the shoulder. [< the native name in East Africa]

***dike**[1] (dīk), *n., v.,* **diked, dik|ing.** — ***n.* 1** a bank of earth or a dam built as a defense against flooding by a river or the sea: *More than 5,000 years ago the Chinese were controlling the Yellow River floods with dikes* (New York Times). **SYN:** embankment. **2** a ditch or channel for water. **3** a bank of earth thrown up in digging. **SYN:** earthwork. **4** a low wall of earth or stone used to enclose or divide a field; causeway. **5** *Figurative.* a barrier; obstacle: *A vital ... dike against inflation will be swept away* (Arthur Krock). **6** *Geology.* a long, usually narrow mass of igneous rock which was thrust, while molten, into a fissure in older rock: *There is no sharp distinction between veins and dikes, but in general, the material of veins was deposited gradually* (George B. Clark).
— ***v.t.* 1** to provide with a dike or dikes. **2** to drain with a ditch or channel for water. **3** *Scottish.* to enclose or divide (land) with dikes.
— ***v.i.*** to dig or build dikes. Also, **dyke.**
[Old English *dīc.* See related etym. at **ditch.**]
— **dik′er,** *n.*

***dike**[1]
definition 1

dike[2] (dīk), *n. Slang.* = dyke[2].

Di|ke (dī′kē), *n.* = Dice.

di|ke|tone (dī kē′tōn), *n. Chemistry.* a compound having two carbonyl (—CO) radicals.

dik|tat or **Dik|tat** (dik tät′), *n.* an imposed mandate, decree, or the like, the terms of which are regarded as excessively strict or taxing: *He is ... a fully fledged Dictator, who having abolished Parliamentary Government at home, now seeks to impose his rule in Europe by diktat* (London Times). [< German *Diktat* dictate]

di|lac|er|ate (də las′ə rāt, dī-), *v.t.,* **-at|ed, -at|ing.** to tear in pieces; tear apart. [< Latin *dīlacerāre* (with English *-ate*[1]) < *dis-* apart + *lacerāre* lacerate]

di|lac|er|a|tion (də las′ə rā′shən, dī-), *n.* a tearing apart or in pieces.

Di|lan|tin (dī lan′tin), *n. Trademark.* a white, powdery drug used in treating epilepsy; diphenylhydantoin. *Formula:* $C_{15}H_{11}N_2O_2Na$ [< *di* (pheny)*l*-(hyd)*ant*(o)*in*]

di|lap|i|date (də lap′ə dāt), *v.,* **-dat|ed, -dat|ing.**
— ***v.t.* 1** to cause or allow to fall into ruin or decay: *Time had dilapidated the old mansion.* **2** *Figurative.* to squander; waste: *to dilapidate an estate.* — ***v.i.*** to fall into ruin or decay.
[< Latin *dīlapidāre* (with English *-ate*[1]) destroy with stones < *dis-* (intensive) + *lapidāre* to stone < *lapis, -idis* stone]

di|lap|i|dat|ed (də lap′ə dā′tid), *adj.* falling to pieces; partly ruined or decayed through neglect: *The ghost town was full of dilapidated houses.*

di|lap|i|da|tion (də lap′ə dā′shən), *n.* a partial ruin; a falling to pieces; tumble-down condition: (*Figurative.*) *the dilapidation of the national resources* (Thomas Matthews). **SYN:** disrepair.

di|lap|i|da|tor (də lap′ə dā′tər), *n.* a person who causes or allows dilapidation.

di|lat|a|bil|i|ty (dī lā′tə bil′ə tē, də-), *n.* the quality of being dilatable.

di|lat|a|ble (dī lā′tə bəl, də-), *adj.* that can be dilated.

di|lat|an|cy (dī lā′tən sē, də-), *n.* **1** *Physics.* the property of granular masses of expanding in bulk with change of shape, due to the increase of space between the rigid particles as they change positions. **2** the quality or property of dilating.

dilatancy theory, a theory that the measurable change in volume of rocks under pressure can be used to predict earthquake: *The dilatancy theory arose after seismologists noticed that in the months before several earthquakes, compressional waves in the vicinity of the quake site slowed down, then speeded up again* (Science News).

di|lat|ant (dī lā′tənt, də-), *adj., n.* — ***adj.* 1** *Phys-*

Pronunciation Key: hat, āge, cãre, fär; let, ēqual, tėrm; it, īce; hot, ōpen, ôrder; oil, out; cup, pu̇t, rüle; child; long; thin; ᴛʜen; zh, measure; ə represents a in about, e in taken, i in pencil, o in lemon, u in circus.

ics. exhibiting or characterized by dilatancy. **2** dilating; expanding.
—***n.*** **1** = dilator. **2** a substance that can dilate.

di·la·tate (dī lā′tāt, dī′lə-), *adj.* = dilated.

dil·a·ta·tion (dil′ə tā′shən, dī′lə-), *n.* **1** the act or process of dilating; enlargement; expansion; widening: *dilatation of the blood vessels.* **2** a dilated condition: *an arterial dilatation.* SYN: distention. **3** a dilated part. **4** amplification; expatiation: *I have spoken of Spenser's fondness for dilatation as respects thoughts and images* (James Russell Lowell).

dil·a·ta·tion·al (dil′ə tā′shə nəl, dī′lə-), *adj.* of or having to do with dilatation.

dil·a·ta·tor (dil′ə tā′tər, dī′lə-), *n.* = dilator.

di·late (dī lāt′, də-), *v.*, **-lat·ed, -lat·ing.** —***v.t.*** **1** to make larger or wider; expand; enlarge: *When you take a deep breath you dilate your nostrils.* SYN: See syn. under **expand**. **2** *Obsolete.* to describe at great length.
—***v.i.*** **1** to become larger or wider; expand; enlarge: *The pupil of the eye dilates when the light gets dim. His nostrils dilated with anger.* **2** *Figurative.* to speak or write at length: *That mother never gets tired of dilating on her children's successes.* SYN: expatiate.
[< Middle French *dilater,* learned borrowing from Latin *dīlātāre* < *dis-* apart + *lātus* wide]

di·lat·ed (dī lā′tid, də-), *adj.* widened; expanded.

di·lat·er (dī lā′tər, də-), *n.* = dilator.

di·la·tion (dī lā′shən, də-), *n.* **1** the act of dilating; enlargement; widening: *dilation of the thorax. The dilation of the patient's pupils took twenty minutes.* **2** the condition of being dilated: *Dilation of her pupils was the result of applying drops in her eyes.* SYN: distention. **3** a dilated part.

di·la·tive (dī lā′tiv, də-), *adj.* serving to dilate; dilating.

dil·a·tom·e·ter (dil′ə tom′ə tər), *n.* an instrument for determining the dilation of liquids or other substances.

dil·a·to·met·ric (dil′ə tə met′rik), *adj.* having to do with or determined by the dilatometer.

di·la·tor (dī lā′tər, də-), *n.* **1** a person or thing that dilates. **2** a muscle that dilates some part of the body. **3** a surgical instrument for dilating wounds or canals of the body; dilatant.

dil·a·to·ri·ly (dil′ə tôr′ə lē, -tōr′-), *adv.* in a dilatory manner: *He was dilatorily throwing up a piece of wood into the fire every now and then* (Thomas Hardy).

dil·a·to·ri·ness (dil′ə tôr′ē nis, -tōr′-), *n.* the quality of being dilatory; tendency to delay; tardiness: *Dilatoriness and reluctance to look at the Middle East as it is impose the severest possible strain on Western unity* (Spectator).

dil·a·to·ry (dil′ə tôr′ē, -tōr′-), *adj.* **1** tending to delay; not prompt: *People who are dilatory in paying their bills are poor customers.* SYN: tardy. **2** causing delay: *The carpenter's dilatory work habits held up completion of the building for weeks. The congressman's dilatory tactics kept the bill tied up for weeks.* [< Latin *dīlātōrius* < *dīlātōr* a delayer < *differre* defer, delay]

Di·lau·did (dī lô′did), *n. Trademark.* a powerful narcotic derived from morphine. *Formula:* $C_{17}H_{19}NO_3$

dil·do (dil′dō), *n., pl.* **-dos** or **-does. 1** *Slang.* an object made to substitute for a penis; artificial penis. **2** *Obsolete.* a word used in the refrains of old songs. [origin unknown]

di·lem·ma (də lem′ə), *n.* **1** a situation requiring a choice between two evils; any embarrassing or perplexing situation; a difficult choice: *Her dilemma was whether to go to the party in her old dress or stay at home. They may manage to find a way out of their dilemma, for there are some very canny politicians among them* (Newsweek). SYN: See syn. under **predicament**. **2** an argument forcing an opponent to choose one of two alternatives equally unfavorable to him: *Swear, fool, or starve; for the dilemma's even; A tradesman thou! and hope to go to heaven?* (John Dryden).
[< Late Latin *dilemma* < Greek *dilēmma* < *di-* two + *lēmma* premise, anything taken < *lambánein* take]

dil·em·mat·ic (dil′ə mat′ik), *adj.* having to do with or like a dilemma.

dil·et·tant (dil′ə tant, dil′ə tant′), *n., adj., v.i.* = dilettante.

dil·et·tan·te (dil′ə tänt′, -tan′tē), *n., pl.* **-tes, -ti** (-tē), *adj., v.,* **-ted, -te·ing.** —***n.*** **1** a person who follows some art or science without learning much about it; dabbler: *He was a dilettante in a dozen fields, an expert in none.* SYN: amateur. **2** a lover of the fine arts. **3** a trifler.
—***adj.*** of or like a dilettante: *The hero of The Spider's House is a dilettante culture vulture named John Stenham* (Time).
—***v.i.*** to play the dilettante.
[< Italian *dilettante* < *dilettare* to charm, delight < Latin *dēlectāre*]

dil·et·tan·te·ish (dil′ə tan′tē ish, -tän′-), *adj.* = dilettantish.

dil·et·tan·te·ism (dil′ə tan′tē iz əm, -tän′-), *n.* = dilettantism.

dil·et·tan·ti (dil′ə tan′tē, -tän′-), *n.* dilettantes; a plural of **dilettante**.

dil·et·tan·tish (dil′ə tän′tish, -tan′-), *adj.* like a dilettante; characterized by dilettantism.

dil·et·tant·ism (dil′ə tän′tiz əm, -tan′-), *n.* the quality or practice of a dilettante.

dil·et·tant·ist (dil′ə tan′tist, -tän′-), *adj.* = dilettantish.

dil·i·gence[1] (dil′ə jəns), *n.* **1** a working hard; careful effort; being diligent; ability to work steadily: *The student's diligence was rewarded with high marks. He will respond to his most challenging assignment with diligence and resourcefulness* (Newsweek). SYN: industry, perseverance. **2** *Law.* the attention and care due from a person, especially from a party to a contract. **3** *Obsolete.* speed; haste. [< Old French *diligence,* learned borrowing from Latin *dīligentia* < *dīligere;* see etym. under **diligent**]

dil·i·gence[2] (dil′ə jəns), *n.* a public stagecoach, formerly used in France and other parts of Europe. [special use of *diligence*[1] < French (*carrosse de*) *diligence* fast (coach)]

dil·i·gent (dil′ə jənt), *adj.* **1** hard-working; industrious: *The diligent student kept on working until he had finished his homework.* SYN: assiduous. See syn. under **busy**. **2** careful and steady: *The detective made a diligent search for clues.* [< Latin *dīligēns, -entis,* present participle of *dīligere* value highly, love < *dis-* apart + *legere* choose] —**dil′·i·gent·ly,** *adv.*

dill[1] (dil), *n.* **1** an annual herb whose spicy seeds or leaves are used to flavor pickles, in cookery and perfumes, and in medicine as a carminative. It belongs to the parsley family. **2** its seeds or leaves. [Old English *dile*]

dill[2] (dil), *n. Australian Slang.* a simpleton; gull; a gullible person.

dill pickle, a cucumber pickle flavored with dill.

dill water, an aromatic carminative prepared from the volatile oil of dill and water.

dil·ly[1] (dil′ē), *n., pl.* **-lies.** a small tree of the sapodilla family found in southern Florida and the West Indies, having a heavy, hard, dark-brown wood and bearing a small, globular fruit. [short for *sapodilla*]

dil·ly[2] (dil′ē), *n., pl.* **-lies.** *U.S. Slang.* a person or thing regarded as unique, outstanding, odd, eccentric, etc.; corker: *a dilly of an actor. The game was a dilly. I've heard some dillies in my day, but that's the payoff* (New Yorker). [apparently < *del*(ightful) + *-y*[2]]

dil·ly-dal·ly or **dil·ly·dal·ly** (dil′ē dal′ē), *v.i.,* **-lied, -ly·ing.** to waste time; loiter; trifle: *There is no time to dilly-dally in our work* (Robert Louis Stevenson). [varied reduplication of *dally*]

dil·u·ent (dil′yü ənt), *adj., n.* —***adj.*** **1** that dilutes; diluting. **2** dissolving.
—***n.*** a diluting or dissolving agent, especially one that dilutes the blood.
[< Latin *dīluēns, -entis,* present participle of *dīluere;* see etym. under **dilute**]

di·lute (də lüt′, dī-), *v.,* **-lut·ed, -lut·ing,** *adj.* —***v.t.*** **1** to make weaker or thinner by adding water or some other liquid: *Mother diluted the concentrated orange juice with several cups of water. When the vaccine is diluted to one part in four, it still prevents paralysis in every case* (Scientific American). **2** *Figurative.* to take away the strength or force of; weaken; lessen: *The judge diluted the boy's punishment because he was so young. The high price of a new car diluted our enthusiasm for buying one.* SYN: reduce. **3** *British.* to lower the proportion of skilled workers in (a labor force) by hiring unskilled workers.
—***v.i.*** to become diluted: *The harsh colors diluted in the strong sunlight.*
—***adj.*** weakened or thinned by the adding of water or some other liquid: *a dilute acid. A dilute solution is one which contains a relatively small amount of a dissolved substance per unit volume of solution* (Parks and Steinbach).
[< Latin *dīlutus,* past participle of *dīluere* < *dis-* apart + *luere* wash] —**di·lute′ness,** *n.* —**di·lut′·er,** *n.*

di·lut·ed (də lü′tid, dī-), *adj.* weakened; thinned.

di·lu·tee (də lü′tē′, dī-), *n. British.* an unskilled or semiskilled person working at a skilled trade: *The dilutees should be stood off when "skilled" labour becomes available* (New Scientist).

di·lu·tion (də lü′shən, dī-), *n.* **1** the act of diluting. **2** the fact or state of being diluted: *Dilution . . . with some solvent, such as alcohol, results in extremely high yields of the radioactive element* (D. G. Tuck). **3** something diluted. **4** *British.* the substitution of unskilled for skilled workers.

di·lu·vi·al (də lü′vē əl, dī-), *adj.* **1** of or having to do with a flood. **2** made up of debris left by a flood or glacier. [< Latin *dīluviālis* < *dīluvium* flood; see etym. under **diluvium**]

di·lu·vi·an (də lü′vē ən, dī-), *adj.* = diluvial.

di·lu·vi·an·ism (də lü′vē ə niz′əm, dī-), *n.* the theory that attributes certain geological phenomena to a deluge that once occurred.

di·lu·vi·um (də lü′vē əm, dī-), *n., pl.* **-vi·a** (-vē ə). *Geology.* a coarse, superficial deposit formed by glacial action, once thought to be due to floods. [< Latin *dīluvium* < *dīluere* < *dis-* apart + *luere* wash. See etym of doublet **deluge**.]

dim (dim), *adj.,* **dim·mer, dim·mest,** *v.,* **dimmed, dim·ming,** *n.* —***adj.*** **1** not bright; not clear; not distinct: *the dim light of dusk. With the shades drawn, the room was dim.* SYN: faint. See syn. under **dark**. **2** not clearly seen, heard, or understood: *We could see only the dim outline of the mountain in the distance. We could barely understand the dim voice.* **3** *Figurative.* not clear to the mind; vague: *Grandfather has a somewhat dim recollection of his childhood days.* **4** without luster; dull: *dim colors.* **5** not seeing, hearing, or understanding clearly: *Grandfather's eyesight is getting dimmer.* **6** *Informal, Figurative.* adverse; unfavorable: *The outlook for spring sales is dim. She takes a dim view of our chances to win.*
—***v.t.*** to make dim: *We dimmed our lights when we reached the city streets. The writer of essays . . . seldom . . . dims his eyes with the perusal of antiquated volumes* (Samuel Johnson).
—***v.i.*** to become dim: *The lights in the house dimmed several times during the storm. The old man's eyes dimmed with tears.*
—***n.*** **1** dimness; dusk: *to sit in the dim.* **2** the low beam of a headlight or a parking light: *It was snowin' real hard, and I guess he couldn't see where he was . . . "He should've used his dims," the old man commented* (New Yorker). **3** = dimout: *A power "dim" affected three areas at breakfast time* (London Times).
dim out, to make nearly but not absolutely dark, by allowing light to appear only through slits, by use of blue lights, etc.: *to dim out the stage for the final scene.*
[Old English *dimm*] —**dim′ly,** *adv.* —**dim′ness,** *n.*

dim., **1** dimension. **2** diminuendo. **3** diminutive.

dime (dīm), *n.* **1** a coin of the United States, worth 10 cents, made of copper and nickel and formerly of silver. Ten dimes make one dollar. **2** a silver coin of Canada, worth 10 cents. **3** *U.S. Slang.* ten dollars' worth of a narcotic drug: *There I was repeatedly accosted by dealers chanting, "Jumbos, dimes, crack"* (Dennis Watlington).
a dime a dozen, *Informal.* plentiful and easily available; so common as to be little valued: *Sunday night at the cocktail party and buffet supper, choice fishing stories were a dime a dozen* (Galveston News).
[American English, earlier English *disme* a tenth, tithe < Old French < Latin *decima* (*pars*) tenth (part) < *decem* ten]

di·men·hy·dri·nate (dī′mən hī′drə nāt), *n.* a drug used against motion sickness and similar disorders; Dramamine. *Formula:* $C_{24}H_{28}ClN_5O_3$

dime novel, a sensational story with little or no literary merit.

***dimension**
definition 1

one dimension (length)

two dimensions (length, breadth)

three dimensions (length, breadth, thickness)

di·men·sion** (də men′shən), *n., adj., v.* —n.*** **1** a measurement of length, breadth, or thickness: *He ordered wallpaper for a room of the following dimensions: 16 ft. long, 12 ft. wide, and 8 ft. high.* **2** Also, **dimensions.** size or extent; scope: *a hall enormous in dimension.* (*Figurative.*) *Building a park in the slum area was a project of large dimensions. Our forum had no idea of the full dimensions of the postwar auto market* (Newsweek). **3** *Figurative.* a characteristic; quality; part: *There is another dimension to the story which is hardly hinted at* (Saturday Review). **4** *Geometry.* a mode of linear measurement, magnitude, or extension in a particular direction, usually as coexisting with similar measurements or extensions in other directions. **5** *Algebra.* a literal factor as counted in describing a term: *A^3, a^2b, and abc are all terms of three dimensions.*
—***adj.*** cut into particular sizes, especially for building: *dimension lumber.*
—***v.t.*** to measure or mark the dimensions of: *Electronic engineers can realize substantial improvements in dimensioning tolerances . . . by using a new line of high-stability, precision grid patterns* (Science News).
[< Middle French *dimension,* learned borrowing from Latin *dīmēnsiō, -ōnis* < *dīmētīrī* measure out < *dis-* out + *mētīrī* to measure]
►The three **dimensions** of a body, or of ordi-

nary space (compare **fourth dimension**), are length, breadth, and thickness (or depth); a surface has only two dimensions (length and breadth); a line has only one (length). Here the notion of measurement or magnitude is commonly lost, and the word denotes merely a particular mode of spatial extension.

di|men|sion|al (də men′shə nəl), *adj.* having to do with dimension or dimensions. —**di|men′sion|al|ly**, *adv.*

di|men|sion|al|i|ty (də men′shə nal′ə tē), *n.* the quality or condition of having or being within certain dimensions: *There is no depth and no dimensionality, and the figures, uprooted like the corpses in the graveyard, stare out as though they were apparitions* (Mary McCarthy).

dimensional sound, sound, as music, resulting from a multiplicity of reproducers, each supplied from a pickup by an independent channel and arranged to produce certain effects, as stereophonic illusion or artistic enhancement.

di|men|sioned (də men′shənd), *adj.* having or marked with a certain dimension or dimensions: *dimensioned drawings.*

di|men|sion|less (də men′shən lis), *adj.* **1** without dimension or physical extension. **2** of a size, importance, or degree too small to be measured; minute. **3** measureless; boundless; vast.

dimension stone, stone in natural blocks or slabs cut in definite shapes and sizes. Dimension stone includes granite, limestone, sandstone, marble, and slate.

di|mer (dī′mər), *n. Chemistry.* a compound formed by the joining together of two molecules of the same substance, especially as produced by polymerization. [< *di-* two + Greek *méros* part]

di|mer|cap|rol (dī′mər kap′rōl, -rol), *n.* = BAL. [reduced form of *dimercapto-propanol*]

di|mer|ic (dī mer′ik), *adj.* **1** *Chemistry.* of or having to do with a dimer. **2** = dimerous.

dim|er|ism (dim′ə riz əm), *n.* dimerous quality or nature.

di|mer|i|za|tion (dī′mə rə zā′shən), *n. Chemistry.* the act or process of forming a dimer: *A second ... reaction, which could be lethal, is dimerization, in which two identical adjacent units in the DNA chain join together* (New Scientist).

di|mer|ize (dī′mə rīz), *v.t., v.i.,* **-ized, -iz|ing.** *Chemistry.* to form a dimer; join together to form a single molecule: *The process is an electrolytic one, in which acrylonitrile dimerizes ... to form adiponitrile* (New Scientist).

dim|er|ous (dim′ər əs), *adj.* **1** consisting of two parts or divisions. **2** (of a flower) having two members in each whorl (generally written *2-merous*). **3** *Entomology.* having two-jointed tarsi. [< New Latin *dimerus* (with English *-ous*) < Greek *dimerḗs* having two parts < *di-* two + *méros* part]

dime store, *U.S.* a store selling a large variety of low-priced articles; variety store: *In late August the dime store windows were full of notebooks and yellow pencils* (Harper's).

dim|e|ter (dim′ə tər), *n.* a line of poetry having two feet. *Example: The hood′ed bat′ Twirls soft′ly by′* (Walter de la Mare). [< Latin *dimetrus* < Greek *dímetros* < *di-* two + *métron* meter]

di|meth|yl (dī meth′əl), *adj.* (of a compound) having two methyl radicals (C_2H_6).

di|meth|yl|a|mine (dī meth′ə lə mēn′, -lam′in), *n.* a highly flammable gas or liquid obtained from methanol and ammonia, used especially as a solvent, in missile fuels and soaps. *Formula:* CaH_7N

di|meth|yl|hy|dra|zine (dī meth′əl hī′drə zin, -zēn), *n.* a flammable liquid, prepared from dimethylamine and ammonia in the presence of a catalyst, used in fuels for jet planes and rockets. *Formula:* $C_2H_8N_2$

dimethyl phthalate, an oily, colorless, slightly aromatic liquid, used especially as an insect repellent, and in making plastics and synthetic fibers. *Formula:* $C_{10}H_{10}O_4$ *Abbr:* DMP (no periods).

dimethyl sulfoxide, a by-product of wood pulp manufacture, long used as a solvent and now in experimental medicine to relieve pain and prevent ice crystallization in body cells. *Formula:* C_2H_6OS *Abbr:* DMSO (no periods).

di|meth|yl|tryp|ta|mine (dī meth′əl trip′tə mēn), *n.* a hallucinogenic drug derived from various South American plants. It is similar to LSD but not as potent. *Formula:* $C_{12}H_{16}N_2$ *Abbr:* DMT (no periods) [< *dimethyl* + *tryptamine*]

di|met|ric (dī met′rik), *adj.* = tetragonal.

di|met|ro|don (dī′met rə don), *n.* a prehistoric, carnivorous reptile having long spines on the back that supported a web of skin resembling a sail. [< New Latin *Dimetrodon* the genus name < *di-*[1] double + Greek *métron* measure + *odoús, odóntos* tooth]

di|mid|i|ate (də mid′ē āt, dī-), *v.,* **-at|ed, -at|ing,** *adj.* —*v.t.* to divide into halves; reduce to half. —*adj.* **1** divided into halves; halved. **2** *Biology.* (of an organ) lacking or appearing to lack one half. [< Latin *dīmidiāre* (with English *-ate*[1]) < *dis-* apart + *medium* the middle]

di|mid|i|a|tion (də mid′ē ā′shən, dī-), *n.* **1** the act of halving. **2** the state of being halved.

dimin., **1** diminuendo. **2** diminutive.

di|min|ish (də min′ish), *v.t.* **1** to make smaller in size or amount; lessen; reduce: *Poor crops so diminished the food supply that people were starving. The long walk diminished his energy.* **SYN:** See syn. under **decrease**. **2** to lessen the importance, power, or reputation of; degrade. **3** *Architecture.* to cause to taper. **4** *Music.* to decrease (a minor or perfect interval) by a half step. **5** *Archaic.* to disparage; belittle. —*v.i.* **1** to become smaller in size or amount; lessen; decrease: *The heat diminished as the sun went down. A sound diminishes as you get farther away from its source.* **SYN:** See syn. under **decrease**. **2** to become less in importance, power, or reputation. **3** *Architecture.* to taper. [blend of Middle English *diminuen* (< Latin *dīminuere,* variant of *dēminuere* < *dē-* (intensive) + *minuere* lessen), and *menusen* to become less < Old French *menuisier* make small, ultimately < Latin *minūtus* small. Compare etym. under **minish**.] —**di|min′ish|er**, *n.* —**di|min′ish|ing|ly**, *adv.*

di|min|ish|a|ble (də min′i shə bəl), *adj.* that can be diminished.

***di|min|ished** (də min′isht), *adj.* **1** made smaller; lessened. **2** degraded; belittled: *The hero had a diminished reputation when people found out he was mean.* **3** *Music.* (of an interval) smaller by a half step than the corresponding perfect or minor interval: *a diminished fifth.* **4** tapered: *a diminished column.*

***diminished**
definition 3

perfect fifth

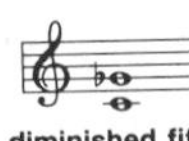

diminished fifth

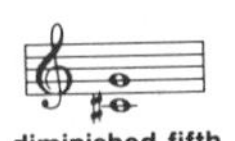

diminished fifth

di|min|ish|ing returns (də min′i shing), *Economics.* the fact that above a certain level increasing the amount of labor, capital, advertising, or other expenditures, used to produce a commodity does not cause a proportionate increase in the amount produced.

di|min|ish|ment (də min′ish mənt), *n.* = diminution.

***di|min|u|en|do** (də min′yù en′dō), *n., pl.* **-dos,** *adj., adv., v.* **-doed, -do|ing.** —*n.* **1** a gradual lessening of loudness. In music the sign for a diminuendo is dim., dimin., or >. **SYN:** decrescendo. **2** a passage to be played or sung with a diminuendo.
—*adj., adv.* with a diminuendo: (*Figurative.*) *All he could hear for a while was the buzzing and chirring and clicking of metallic insects, diminuendo, receding through a lead tube, far away* (Punch). **SYN:** decrescendo.
—*v.i.* to decrease gradually in loudness; become fainter: (*Figurative.*) *"Don't say that," he began to howl and diminuendoed down to a mutter* (Manchester Guardian Weekly).
[< Italian *diminuendo,* present participle of *diminuire* diminish]

***diminuendo**
definition 1

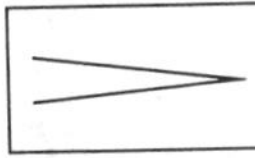

dim|i|nu|tion (dim′ə nü′shən, -nyü′-), *n.* **1** a diminishing; lessening; reduction; decrease: *The colonists fought to prevent any diminution of their rights by the king. Age brought a gradual diminution of his strength and energy. The diminution of true freedom of the intellect through a deadening but voluntary conformity ...* (Time). **2** *Music.* a theme or subject repeated or imitated in notes of shorter length than those originally used. [< Old French *diminution,* learned borrowing from Latin *dīminūtiō, -ōnis* < *dīminuere;* see etym. under **diminish**]

dim|i|nu|tion|al (dim′ə nü′shə nəl, -nyü′-), *adj.* tending toward diminution; reductive: *His is a diminutional talent: he can make things clear by making them small* (Atlantic).

di|min|u|ti|val (də min′yə tī′vəl), *adj.* of, having to do with, or like a diminutive.

di|min|u|tive (də min′yə tiv), *adj., n.* —*adj.* **1** small; little; tiny: *diminutive china figures. The doll's house contained diminutive furniture.* **SYN:** minute. See syn. under **little**. **2** *Grammar.* expressing smallness: *"Droplet" and "lambkin" have diminutive endings. In most languages the objects of love are spoken of under diminutive epithets* (Edmund Burke).
—*n.* **1** a small person or thing; a miniature. **2** *Grammar.* a word or part of a word expressing smallness. The suffixes *-ling, -let,* and *-kin* are called diminutives. *Example: Droplet = a small drop.*
[< Medieval Latin *diminutivus* < Latin *dīminuere;* see etym. under **diminish**] —**di|min′u|tive|ly**, *adv.* —**di|min′u|tive|ness**, *n.*

dim|is|so|ri|al (dim′ə sôr′ē əl, -sōr′-), *adj.* = dimissory.

dim|is|so|ry (dim′ə sôr′ē, -sōr′-), *adj.* granting leave to depart; dismissing. [< Late Latin *dīmissōrius* < *dīmittere* dismiss]

dimissory letter, **1** a letter dismissing a clergyman from one diocese and recommending him to another. **2** a letter from a pope, bishop, abbot, or other official, authorizing the bearer as a candidate for ordination.

dim|i|ty (dim′ə tē), *n., pl.* **-ties.** **1** a thin cotton cloth woven with heavy threads in striped or checked arrangement, used for dresses, curtains, etc.: *Corded cotton fabrics include dimity, pajama checks ... and other novelties* (Bernice G. Chambers). **2** a strong cotton cloth woven with raised patterns, used for draperies, coverings for furniture, etc. [< Italian *dimiti,* plural of *dimito* < Greek *dímitos* of double thread < *di-* double + *mítos* warp thread]

dim|ma|ble (dim′ə bəl), *adj.* that can be dimmed: *dimmable headlight bulbs.*

dim|mer (dim′ər), *n.* **1** a person or thing that dims. **2** a device that dims an electric light, especially automobile headlights.

dim|mish (dim′ish), *adj.* somewhat dim.

di|morph (dī′môrf), *n.* one of the two forms in which a dimorphic thing or substance exists.

di|mor|phic (dī môr′fik), *adj.* existing or occurring in two distinct forms; exhibiting dimorphism; dimorphous.

***di|mor|phism** (dī môr′fiz əm), *n.* **1** the occurrence of two different forms of the same plant, animal, organ, or substance: **a** *Botany.* the occurrence of two different forms of flowers, leaves, or other parts on the same plant or in the same species, as in the disk and ray florets of the daisy, or the young and adult foliage of eucalyptus. **b** *Zoology.* the occurrence of two forms different in structure, coloration, etc., among animals of the same species. **c** *Chemistry, Mineralogy.* the property of some substances of crystallizing in two different forms. **2** *Linguistics.* the occurrence in a language of two or more words, such as *dent* and *dint* or *church* and *kirk,* that come from the same source. [< Greek *dímorphos* (< *di-* two + *morphḗ* form) + English *-ism*]

***dimorphism**
definition 1a

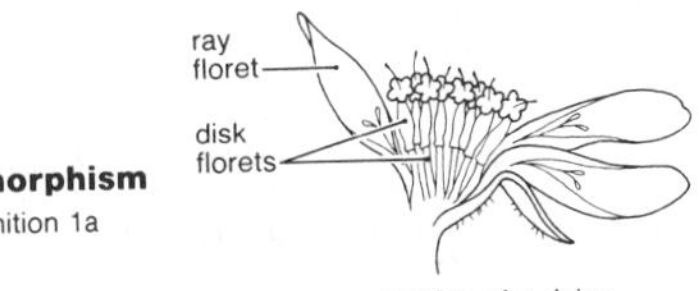

section of a daisy

di|mor|phous (dī môr′fəs), *adj.* = dimorphic.

dim|out (dim′out′), *n.* a lessening or concealing of light at night: *Newfoundland ... was already on a war footing, complete with ration laws and dimouts* (Maclean's).

dim|ple (dim′pəl), *n., v.,* **-pled, -pling.** —*n.* **1** a small, hollow place in the skin, usually in the cheek or chin: *She has dimples in her cheeks when she smiles. There's a boil on his ear and a corn on his chin—He calls it a dimple but dimples stick in* (James Whitcomb Riley). **2** any small, hollow place, such as a dip in the surface of land or a ripple on the water.
—*v.t.* to make or show dimples in: *The shower dimpled the surface of the pond.*
—*v.i.* to form dimples: *She dimples whenever she smiles.*
[Middle English *dympull;* origin uncertain]

dim|ply (dim′plē), *adj.* having dimples.

dim sum (dim′ sum′), a Chinese appetizer of steamed, meat-filled dumplings. [< Cantonese *dim sum*]

dim|wit (dim′wit′), *n. Informal.* a stupid person; simpleton; fool: *... a slothful, inconsistent dimwit which gets along solely on a few inherited habits* (Time).

dim|wit|ted (dim′wit′id), *adj. Informal.* stupid; foolish. —**dim′wit′ted|ly**, *adv.* —**dim′wit′ted|ness**, *n.*

din (din), *n., v.,* **dinned, din|ning.** —*n.* a loud,

Pronunciation Key: hat, āge, cãre, fär; let, ēqual, tėrm; it, īce; hot, ōpen, ôrder; oil, out; cup, pu̇t, rüle; child; long; thin; ᴛʜen; zh, measure; ə represents **a** in about, **e** in taken, **i** in pencil, **o** in lemon, **u** in circus.

confused noise that lasts: *The din of the cheering crowd watching the game was deafening.* SYN: See syn. under **noise**.
—*v.i.* to make a din.
—*v.t.* **1** to strike with a din. **2** to say (one thing) over and over again; repeat in a tiresome way: *He was always dinning into our ears the importance of hard work.*
[Old English *dynn*]

di·nan·de·rie (di nan′də rē, dē′nan drē′), *n.* fine antique metallic vessels and utensils. [< *Dinand,* former name of *Dinant,* Belgium, noted for its brass kitchen utensils]

di·nar (di när′), *n.* **1a** the unit of money of Yugoslavia, equal to 100 paras. **b** the unit of money in several countries of the Mediterranean area, especially Algeria, Iraq, Jordan, Kuwait, Tunisia, and Yemen (Aden). The Algerian dinar is equal to 100 centimes, the Tunisian to 1,000 millimes, and the others to 1,000 fils. **2** a coin worth one dinar. **3** any one of various gold coins used in ancient Arab countries. [< Arabic or Persian *dīnār* < Late Greek *dēnárion* < Latin *dēnārius.* See etym. of doublets **denarius, denier², dinero.**]

Di·nar·ic (di nar′ik), *adj.* **1** of or having to do with the mountain range which extends along the eastern side of the Adriatic. **2** of or having to do with a hypothetical racial group inhabiting the northern Adriatic coast, characterized by tallness, a very short head, dark wavy hair, and straight or aquiline nose. [< *Dinara,* a mountain in Yugoslavia + English *-ic*]

din·dle (din′dəl, din′əl), *v.,* **-dled, -dling,** *n. Scottish.* —*v.i., v.t.* to tingle; ring; vibrate.
—*n.* a thrill; tingle. Also, **dinnle.**
[origin uncertain. Probably related to **din.**]

dine (dīn), *v.,* **dined, din·ing,** *n.* —*v.i.* to eat dinner: *We usually dine at six o'clock.*
—*v.t.* to give a dinner to; give a dinner for: *The Chamber of Commerce dined the famous traveler.*
—*n. Obsolete except Dialect.* dinner.
dine out, to eat dinner away from home: *We dined out last night to celebrate my birthday.*
[< Old French *disner* (originally) take the first meal of the day < Vulgar Latin *disjējūnāre* to breakfast < *dis-* un- + *jējūnium* a fasting. See related etym. at **disjune.**]

din·er (dī′nər), *n.* **1** a person who is eating dinner. **2** a railroad car in which meals are served; dining car: *We sat in the same coach but in different seats, and we did not go into the diner together for lunch* (New Yorker). **3** a small eating place that often looks like a railroad car.

di·ner·ic (dī ner′ik), *adj. Physics.* having to do with or constituting the boundary between two liquids that cannot mix. [< *di-¹* two + Greek *nēros* liquid + English *-ic*]

di·ne·ro (dē nā′rō, *for 1;* də när′ō *for 2*), *n., pl.* **-ros. 1** a silver coin of Peru, no longer used. **2** *U.S. Slang.* money: *He insisted he had no dinero.* [< Spanish *dinero* < Latin *dēnārius.* See etym. of doublets **denarius, denier², dinar.**]

din·er-out (dī′nər out′), *n., pl.* **din·ers-out.** a person who dines at a restaurant, night club, or place other than at home: *Men who daily play host to New York's diners-out dine out themselves* (New York Times).

di·nette (dī net′), *n.* **1a** a small dining room or dining space. **b** the table and chairs used in a dinette. **2** *British.* a luncheon; small meal. [American English < *dine* + *-ette* (definition 2) < French *dinette* (diminutive of *dîner* dinner)]

ding (ding), *v., n.* —*v.i., v.t.* **1** to make the sound of a bell; ring continuously. **2** *Informal.* to say over and over; din.
—*n.* **1** the sound made by a bell. **2** *Surfing.* a dent, scratch, or hole on a surfboard.
[probably imitative]

Din·gaan's Day (din gänz′), a holiday in South Africa, December 16, commemorating the victory of a small force of Boers over the Zulus under their king, Dingaan, in 1838.

ding-a-ling (ding′ə ling′), *n. U.S. Slang.* a crazy person. [probably so called from the idea of hearing imaginary bells]

Ding an sich (ding′än ziH′), *German. Philosophy.* thing-in-itself: *He distinguishes between appearance and substance (the latter being probably what Kant called "Ding an sich")* (Max Born).

ding·bat (ding′bat), *n.* **1** *U.S. Slang.* a gadget; invention: *The drawings . . . contain an exploded view of the parts, above the assembled dingbat* (Scientific American). **2** *U.S. Slang.* **a** a strange, silly, or stupid person. **b** a beggar; hobo. **3** *Printing.* a distinctive type face or ornament, used in headings, at the beginning of a paragraph, between columns, etc. [< earlier *ding* to thump + *bat* club]

ding-dong (ding′dông′, -dong′), *n., adj., v.* —*n.* **1** the sound made by the continuous ringing of a bell. **2** a jingle; rhyme in verse or song.
—*adj.* **1** continuously ringing or striking. **2** *Informal.* very vigorous; closely contested: *a ding-dong contest, a ding-dong race. A ding-dong labor war is about to break into the news* (Newsweek).
—*v.i.* to sound with the regularity of the ding-dong of a bell.
—*v.t. Informal.* to annoy with repetitious complaints, requests, taunts, etc.
[imitative]

dinge (dinj), *v.t.,* **dinged, dinge·ing,** *n.* = dent. [origin uncertain]

din·gey (ding′ē), *n., pl.* **-geys.** = dinghy.

***din·ghy** (ding′ē), *n., pl.* **-ghies. 1** a small rowboat. **2** a small boat used as a tender by a large boat, such as a yacht or warship. **3** a small racing boat with no deck and a single mast rigged with a mainsail and often a jib. **4** a rowboat or sailboat used in India and the East Indies. Also, **dingey, dingy.** [< Hindi *ḍingī,* variant of *ḍengī* small boat]

***dinghy**
definitions 1, 3

definition 1 definition 3

din·gi·ly (din′jə lē), *adv.* in a dingy manner.

din·gi·ness (din′jē nis), *n.* dingy quality or condition; lack of cleanness and freshness.

din·gle¹ (ding′gəl), *n.* a small, deep, shady valley: *Searched each thicket, dingle, hollow* (Longfellow). SYN: dell. [origin uncertain]

din·gle² (ding′gəl), *v.i.,* **-gled, -gling. 1** to tinkle; jingle. **2** to tingle, as from cold. **3** to vibrate. [apparently diminutive of *ding*]

din·go (ding′gō), *n., pl.* **-goes.** a wolflike wild dog of Australia that feeds chiefly on wallabies and sheep. Dingoes hunt alone or in packs. See picture under **dog.** [< a native name]

ding·us (ding′əs), *n. Slang.* **1** something which is unknown, unfamiliar, or forgotten. **2** a gadget; invention: *The various slides and clips that replaced the tiepin of yesteryear are in turn being replaced, we're told, by a new sort of dingus adapted from Army insignia* (New Yorker). [< Dutch *dinges* < *ding* thing, object]

din·gy¹ (din′jē), *adj.,* **-gi·er, -gi·est,** dirty-looking; lacking brightness or freshness; dull: *Dingy curtains covered the windows of the dusty old room. The dingy tenements stood row on row.*

din·gy² (ding′ē), *n., pl.* **-gies.** = dinghy.

din·ing car (dī′ning), diner; a railroad car in which meals are served.

dining hall, a large, public dining room, as in a college or school dormitory or a military base.

dining room, a room in which dinner and other meals are served.

di·ni·tro·ben·zene (dī nī′trō ben′zēn), *n. Chemistry.* one of three white or yellowish isomeric compounds produced by the action of boiling nitric acid on either benzene or nitrobenzene, and used in making dyes. *Formula:* $C_6H_4N_2O_4$

di·ni·tro·phe·nol (dī nī′trō fē′nōl, -nol), *n.* a yellow crystalline compound, used in the manufacture of dyes, as a preservative for timber, and in explosives. *Formula:* $C_6H_4N_2O_5$ *Abbr:* DNP (no periods).

dink¹ (dingk), *adj., v. Scottish.* —*adj.* neatly dressed; fine; trim: *The mechanic, in his leather apron, elbowed the dink and dainty dame* (Scott).
—*v.t.* to dress neatly or finely: . . . *too old to dink myself as a gallant* (Scott).
[origin uncertain]

dink² (dingk), *n. U.S.* a skullcap worn by freshmen in certain colleges and universities: *A dink was on the back of my head, a textbook lay open in my lap* (Harper's). [American English, apparently back formation < *dinky*]

dink³ (dingk), *n., v.* —*n.* a drop shot in tennis: *His service returns were good, notably his backhand "dinks"* (London Times).
—*v.t.* to hit with a drop shot: *She has a strong serve and the finesse to . . . dink her returns of service, to throw off her opponent's timing* (New Yorker).
[imitative]

dink⁴ (dingk), *n. U.S. Slang.* a derogatory name in the army for a Vietnamese. [origin unknown]

Din·ka (ding′kä), *n., pl.* **-ka** or **-kas. 1** a member of a Negro people living in areas around the upper Nile. The Dinka work principally at raising livestock. *This is the territory of the Dinka tribe, and here almost immediately, you emerge from the influence and sophistication of the Arab Moslems* (New Yorker). **2** their Nilotic language.

dink·ey (ding′kē), *n., pl.* **-eys. 1** *U.S.* a small locomotive, used for pulling freight cars around in a railroad yard, for hauling logs, or for work in industrial plants, foundries, and the like. **2** a donkey engine, used for doing work which requires small horsepower. **3** a pair of wheels on an axle used to carry the weight of a beam or pole in erecting structures, telephone lines, etc. [American English spelling variant of *dinky*]

dinks or **DINKS** *n.pl. U.S. Slang.* a childless couple with a double income: *They have wooed the busy yuppie couples known to market researchers as dinks . . .* (Economist). [< d(ouble) i(ncome), n(o) k(ids)]

din·kum (ding′kəm), *adj., adv. British and Australian Slang.* —*adj.* honest; genuine; very good: *a dinkum welcome.* —*adv.* honestly; genuinely: *What he did was fair dinkum.*

dink·y (ding′kē), *adj.,* **dink·i·er, dink·i·est,** *n., pl.* **dink·ies.** *Informal.* —*adj.* **1** small and insignificant: *Do you expect me to live in this dinky town?* **2** neat; trim; dainty. —*n.* = dinkey. [< *dink¹* + *-y¹*]

din·ner (din′ər), *n.* **1** the main meal of the day. On weekdays, dinner is usually eaten in the evening. A Sunday dinner is usually eaten in the afternoon. *In the city we have dinner at night, but in the country we have dinner at noon.* **2** a formal meal in honor of some person or occasion: *The city officials gave the mayor a dinner to celebrate his reelection.* SYN: banquet. **3** a meal served at a fixed time or price; table d'hôte: *A four-course dinner this week for three . . . came to the yen equivalent of $50 on the menu* (New York Times). [< Old French *disner,* noun use of infinitive; see etym. under **dine**]

dinner bell, a bell, gong, iron pipe, or the like, rung to announce dinner, especially as used on a farm to summon field hands.

dinner bucket, = dinner pail.

dinner coat or **jacket,** a semiformal coat without tails, usually black with satin lapels, worn by men in the evening; the jacket of a tuxedo.

dinner dance, a dinner followed by dancing: *I was wearing my dinner jacket, and someone was going to pick me up and take me to a dinner dance at the club* (New Yorker).

dinner hour, any particular time when people usually eat dinner: *The dinner hour in Chicago is between 5:30 and 6:30.*

dinner music, music played during dinner or the dinner hour, especially light music.

dinner pail, a pail, bucket, or lunch box in which a workman carries his dinner with him.

dinner party, a party of guests invited to dinner.

dinner plate, a large plate on which the main course of a dinner is served to one person.

dinner ring, a showy ring, often with a large ornamental stone or a number of small stones, worn at ceremonies.

dinner theater, a restaurant where theatrical productions, especially plays, are presented following dinner.

din·ner·time (din′ər tīm′), *n.* **1** the time at which dinner is served. **2** = dinner hour.

din·ner·ware (din′ər wãr′), *n.* the plates, platter, and other dishes for serving dinner.

din·nle (din′əl), *v.i., v.t.,* **-nled, -nling,** *n. Scottish.* dindle.

di·noc·er·as (dī nos′ər əs), *n.* a huge mammal with hoofs and three pairs of horns which lived during the Eocene epoch in North America. [< New Latin *Dinoceras* the genus name < Greek *deinós* terrible + *kéras, -atos* horn]

di·no·cer·a·tan (dī′nə ser′ə tən), *adj.* of or having to do with a dinoceras.

di·no·flag·el·late (dī′nə flaj′ə lāt), *n.* any one of an order of tiny marine flagellates, some species of which produce a red, toxic substance poisonous to fish. [< New Latin *Dinoflagellata* the order name < Greek *dînos* rotation, whirling + Latin *flagellum;* see etym. under **flagellate**]

di·nor·nis (dī nôr′nis), *n.* any of a group of huge, flightless birds, including the typical moas. [< New Latin *Dinornis* the genus name < Greek *deinós* terrible + *órnis* bird]

di·no·saur (dī′nə sôr), *n.* **1** any one of two orders of extinct reptiles that dominated the earth many millions of years ago. Some dinosaurs were bigger than elephants; others were smaller than cats. *The Mesozoic Era frequently is called the Age of Dinosaurs, because these creatures were the most striking animals of the time and were world-wide in distribution.* **2** *Figurative:* . . . *this mindless dinosaur of a musical* (New Yorker). *Rear-engine cars . . . have made the Offenhauser roadster a dinosaur* (New York Times). [< New Latin *Dinosaurus* the typical genus < Greek *deinós* terrible + *saûros* lizard]

di·no·sau·ri·an (dī′nə sôr′ē ən), *adj., n.* —*adj.* of or like a dinosaur.
—*n.* = dinosaur.

di·no·sau·ric (dī′nə sôr′ik), *adj.* like a dinosaur: (*Figurative.*) . . . *the dinosauric bigness of modern science* (Scientific American).

di·no·there (dī′nə thir), *n.* any one of a group of elephantlike mammals of the Tertiary period in

Europe and Asia, having a pair of tusks curving downward from the lower jaw. [< New Latin *dinotherium* < Greek *deinós* terrible + *thēr* beast]

di|no|the|ri|um (dī′nə thir′ē əm), *n., pl.* **-the|ri|a** (-thir′ē ə). = dinothere.

dint (dint), *n., v.* **—*n.*** **1** = dent. SYN: indentation. **2** *Obsolete.* a blow; stroke.
—*v.t.* = dent.
by dint of, by the force or effective action of: *By dint of hard work the job was completed on schedule.*
[Old English *dynt*]

dint|less (dint′lis), *adj.* without dints (dents); making no dints.

di|nu|cle|o|tide (dī nü′klē ə tīd, -nyü′-; -tid), *n.* a substance formed by the union of two nucleotides.

di|oc|e|san (dī os′ə sən, dī′ə sē′-), *adj., n.* **—*adj.*** of or having to do with a diocese: *Bishop Welles told his diocesan convention that he would not proceed with canonization unless they wished it, although he felt that he had the power to canonize the two bishops* (Newsweek).
—*n.* **1** the bishop of a diocese. **2** a clergyman or person belonging to a diocese.

di|o|cese (dī′ə sis, -sēs), *n.* the church district over which a bishop has authority; bishopric; see. [< Old French *diocise*, learned borrowing from Late Latin *diocēsis* < Greek *dioikēsis* diocese, province; (originally) economy, housekeeping < *diá-* through + *oîkos* house]

di|ode (dī′ōd), *n. Electronics.* a vacuum tube or semiconducting device having two electrodes, especially a rectifier which permits the flow of electrons in only one direction. [< *di-*[1] two + Greek *hodós* way]

di|oe|cious (dī ē′shəs), *adj. Botany.* having male and female flowers in separate plants of the same species. The asparagus and willows are dioecious. Also, **diecious, dioicous.** [< New Latin *Dioecia* a typical genus (< Greek *di-* double + *oîkos* house) + English *-ous*] **—di|oe′cious|ly,** *adv.*

di|oe|cism (dī ē′siz əm), *n.* the quality or condition of being dioecious.

di|oes|trum (dī es′trəm, -ēs′-), *n.* the interval between rutting periods. See **rut**[2]. [< *di-*[1] + *oestrum*]

di|oi|cous (dī oi′kəs), *adj.* = dioecious.

di|ol (dī′ōl), *n.* a dihydric alcohol, such as glycol. [< *di-*[1] + *-ol*[1]]

Di|o|la (dē ō′lə), *n., pl.* **-la** or **-las.** a member of one of the six major tribes of Senegal, the leading rice growers. Most of the Diola practice their tribal religions, but a few are Moslems.

di|o|le|fin (dī ō′lə fin), *n.* = diene.

Di|o|med (dī′ə med), *n.* = Diomedes.

Di|o|mede (dī′ə mēd), *n.* = Diomedes.

Di|o|me|des (dī′ə mē′dēz), *n. Greek Legend.* a Greek hero in the Trojan War who helped Odysseus steal the statue of Athena from Troy.

di|o|nae|a (dī′ə nē′ə), *n.* = Venus's-flytrap. [< New Latin *Dionaea* the genus name < Greek *Diōnē* Dione]

Di|o|ne (dī ō′nē), *n.* **1** *Greek Mythology.* a woman Titan, daughter of Oceanus and Tethys, and mother by Zeus of Aphrodite. **2** *Astronomy.* a satellite of Saturn, discovered in 1684.

Di|o|ny|si|a (dī′ə nish′ē ə, -nis′-), *n.pl.* any set of festivals in honor of the Greek god Dionysus (Bacchus).

Di|o|nys|i|ac (dī′ə nis′ē ak), *adj.* = Dionysian.

Di|o|ny|sian (dī′ə nish′ən, -nis′ē ən), *adj.* **1** of or having to do with Dionysus (Bacchus) or the Dionysia. **2** highly individualistic; romantic; exuberant: *In this concert he was at his Dionysian best* (New Yorker).

Di|o|ny|sus or **Di|o|ny|sos** (dī′ə nī′səs), *n.* the Greek god of wine; Bacchus.

Di|o|phan|tine analysis (dī′ə fan′tīn, -tēn, -tin), analysis of Diophantine equations to determine the presence and nature of integral solutions. [< *Diophantus* of Alexandria, Greek mathematician of the 200's A.D.]

Diophantine equation, an equation whose coefficients are integers, studied to determine the possibility or range of integral solutions: *This reduces to 98y − 199x = 5, a Diophantine equation with an infinite number of integral solutions* (Scientific American).

di|op|side (dī op′sīd, -sid), *n. Mineralogy.* a transparent variety of pyroxene. *Formula:* $CaMgSi_2O_6$ [< French *diopside* < Greek *di-* twice + *ópsis* aspect]

di|op|tase (dī op′tās), *n. Mineralogy.* a translucent silicate of copper, found in green, six-sided crystals. [< French *dioptase* < Greek *diá-* through + *optasiā* appearance < *optós* visible]

di|op|ter or **di|op|tre** (dī op′tər), *n. Optics.* a unit of refractive power, equal to that of a lens whose focal length is one meter; dioptrie: *In the empty, cloudless sky, the eye involuntarily exerts about one dioptre of accommodation* (Science News Letter). [< French *dioptre* < Latin *dioptra* an ancient optical measuring instrument < Greek *dióptra* < *diá-* through + *optós* visible]

di|op|tom|e|ter (dī′op tom′ə tər), *n.* an optical instrument used to measure the refraction of the eye. [< *di-*[1] + *optometer*]

di|op|tom|e|try (dī′op tom′ə trē), *n.* the measurement of the accommodation and refraction of the eye.

di|op|tral (dī op′trəl), *adj.* = dioptric.

di|op|tric (dī op′trik), *adj.* **1** of or having to do with a diopter. **2** of or having to do with dioptrics. **3** having to do with the refraction of light; refractive; refracting. **4** assisting vision; giving a medium for the sight: *a dioptric lens.* **—di|op′tri|cal|ly,** *adv.*

di|op|tri|cal (dī op′trə kəl), *adj.* = dioptric.

di|op|trics (dī op′triks), *n.* the branch of optics dealing with the refraction of light, especially by lenses.

di|op|trie or **di|op|try** (dī op′trē), *n., pl.* **-tries.** = diopter.

di|o|ram|a (dī′ə ram′ə, -rä′mə), *n.* **1** a scene or exhibit showing a group of lifelike sculptured figures of men, animals, and surrounding objects against a painted or modeled background. A diorama is viewed through a windowlike opening. **2** a picture that is usually looked at through a small opening and is lighted from above, the light being diminished or increased to represent changes in the weather, etc. **3** a place where such pictures or scenes are exhibited. [< French *diorama* < Greek *diá-* through + *hórāma* sight < *horân* see, look]

di|o|ram|ic (dī′ə ram′ik), *adj.* having to do with or like a diorama.

di|o|rite (dī′ə rīt), *n.* a coarse-grained igneous rock consisting essentially of hornblende and feldspar. [< French *diorite* < Greek *diorízein* distinguish (< *diá-* through + *orízein* mark a boundary) + French *-ite*]

di|o|rit|ic (dī′ə rit′ik), *adj.* having to do with or like diorite.

di|os|co|re|a (dī′os kôr′ē ə, -kōr′-), *n.* any one of a group of tropical or temperate vines, many of which bear an edible tuber; yam. They also yield synthetic hormones, such as diosgenin. [< New Latin *Dioscorea* the genus name < *Dioscorides*, a Greek physician and naturalist]

di|os|co|re|a|ceous (dī′os kôr′ē ā′shəs, -kōr′-), *adj.* belonging to the family of plants typified by the yam.

Di|os|cu|ri (dī′ə skyůr′ī), *n.pl. Greek and Roman Mythology.* the twin brothers Castor and Pollux, sons of Zeus; Castor was said to be mortal, while Pollux was immortal. After death they were placed in heaven as the constellation Gemini. [< Greek *Dióskouroi* < *Diós*, genitive of *Zeús* Zeus + *koûros* boy, son]

Di|os|cu|ric (dī′ə skyůr′ik), *adj.* of, having to do with, or resembling the legend of the twins Castor and Pollux.

di|os|ge|nin (dī os′jə nin), *n.* a synthetic female hormone derived from Mexican yams. [< *dios*(corea) + *-gen* + *-in*]

di|os|mose (dī oz′mōs, -os′-), *v.,* **-mosed, -mosing,** *n.* **—*v.t.*** = osmose. **—*n.*** = osmosis.

di|os|mo|sis (dī′oz mō′sis, -os-), *n.* = osmosis.

di|os|mot|ic (dī′oz mot′ik, -os-), *adj.* = osmotic.

di|os|py|ra|ceous (dī os′pə rā′shəs), *adj.* = ebenaceous. [< Latin *diospyros* a kind of plant (< Greek *dióspyros* < *Diós*, genitive of *Zeús* Zeus + *pȳrós* wheat) + *-aceous*]

di|o|vu|lar (dī ō′vyə lər), *adj.* having two ovules.

di|ox|ane (dī ok′sān), *n. Chemistry.* a colorless liquid used as a solvent, in making varnishes and lacquers, and in the textile industry. *Formula:* $C_4H_8O_2$ [< (diethylene) *diox*(ide) + *-ane*]

di|ox|id (dī ok′sid), *n.* = dioxide.

di|ox|ide (dī ok′sīd, -sid), *n. Chemistry.* an oxide having two atoms of oxygen for each molecule.

di|ox|in (dī ok′sən), *n.* a very poisonous and persistent substance, formed in the manufacture of certain herbicides and other chemicals. It has been found to cause deformities in fetuses.

dip (dip), *v.,* **dipped** or **dipt, dip|ping,** *n.* **—*v.t.*** **1** to put under water or any liquid and lift quickly out again: *She dipped her hand into the pool to see how cold the water was.* **2** to put (one's hand, a spoon, or fork) into to take out something: *He dipped his hand into the jar and snatched a handful of cookies.* **3** to take up in the hollow of the hand or with a pail, pan, or other container: *to dip water from a bucket, dip up a sample of wheat.* **4** to lower and raise again quickly: *The ship's flag was dipped as a salute.* **5** to make (a candle) by putting a wick over and over into hot tallow or wax. **6** to dye by dipping in a liquid: *to dip a dress.* **7** to wash or clean by dipping in a liquid. **8** to immerse in a solution for plating or galvanizing. **9** to immerse (a sheep or other animal) in a disinfectant solution. **10** to baptize by immersion. **11** *British.* to dim (automobile headlights). **12** *Archaic.* to wet as if by immersion; chill: *A cold shuddering dew dips me all o'er* (Milton). **13** *U.S.* to use (snuff) by dipping it from the container and rubbing it on the teeth and gums.
—*v.i.* **1** to go under water and come quickly out again: *He dipped a few times in the ocean to cool himself off.* **2** to sink or drop down: *The bird dipped low over the water in its flight. The price of eggs dipped below a dollar last week.* **3** to slope downward: *The road dips into the valley.* **4** to put one's hand, a spoon, fork, or other implement into something to take out some of its contents: *to dip from a kettle of soup.* **5** = curtsy. **6** *Aeronautics.* to make a short, sudden dive to gain momentum for a climb.
—*n.* **1** a dipping of any kind, especially a quick plunge into and out of a tub of water, the sea, or a pool: *He felt cool after a dip in the ocean.* **2** a liquid in which to dip something, especially a mixture in which to dip something for washing or cleaning: *The sheep were driven through a dip to disinfect their coats.* **3** a creamy mixture of foods eaten by dipping into with a cracker, piece of bread, or the like: *a cheese dip, a lobster dip.* **4** a sudden drop or downward slope: *a dip in prices. The dip in the road made the car bounce.* **5** a candle made by dipping: *Tom ... was surveying his drenched garments by the light of a tallow dip* (Mark Twain). **6** that which is taken out or up by dipping. **7** the amount of slope down: *The dip increased as we went on.* **8** a sinking down and out of sight; setting: *the dip of the sun.* **9** *Mining and Geology.* the downward slope of a stratum or vein. **10** *Surveying and Astronomy.* the angular distance of the visible horizon below the horizontal plane through the observer's eye. **11** the downward inclination of the magnetic needle at any particular place; the angle which the direction of the needle makes with the horizontal. **12** *Gymnastics.* an exercise on the parallel bars, the body being lowered until the chin is even with the bars, and then raised until the arms are straight. **13** *U.S. Slang.* a pickpocket: *... the deftness of the dip, the skill of the safecracker* (Time).
dip into, a to take something out of: *to dip into a box of candy, dip into one's savings.* **b** to read or look at for a short time; glance at: *He dipped into a book on astronomy. A blasphemy so like these Molinists', I must suspect you dip into their books* (Robert Browning). **c** to engage in superficially: *to dip into astronomy.*
[Old English *dyppan*] **—dip′pa|ble,** *adj.*
—*Syn.* ***v.t.*** **1 Dip, plunge, immerse** mean to put into a liquid. **Dip** emphasizes taking right out again after putting or lowering partly in or wholly under: *I dipped my handkerchief in the cool water.* **Plunge** emphasizes throwing or putting completely under, suddenly or with force: *I plunged the vegetables into boiling water.* **Immerse** emphasizes keeping completely under long enough to get thoroughly soaked: *I immersed my clothes in the soapy water.*

di|pep|ti|dase (dī pep′tə dās), *n.* an enzyme that hydrolyzes dipeptides into its constituent amino acids.

di|pep|tide (dī pep′tīd, -tid), *n.* a peptide that, upon hydrolysis, releases two amino-acid molecules. [< *di-*[1] + *peptide*]

di|pet|al|ous (dī pet′ə ləs), *adj.* having two petals; bipetalous.

di|phase (dī′fāz′), *adj. Electricity.* having two phases; denoting or having to do with a system combining two alternating currents that differ from each other in phase by one quarter of a cycle (90 degrees).

di|phas|ic (dī fā′zik), *adj.* = diphase.

di|phen|yl (dī fen′əl, -fē′nəl), *n.* = biphenyl.

di|phen|yl|am|in (dī fen′ə lam′in, -fē′nə-), *n.* = diphenylamine.

di|phen|yl|am|ine (dī fen′ə lə mēn′, -lam′in; -fē′nə-), *n. Chemistry.* a colorless, crystalline compound produced by heating aniline with the hydrochloride of aniline, used in making dyes, explosives, etc. *Formula:* $C_{12}H_{11}N$

di|phen|yl|hy|dan|to|in (dī fen′əl hī dan′tō in, -fē′nəl-), *n.* = Dilantin. [< *diphenyl* + *hyd*(rogen) + (all)*antoin*]

di|phos|gene (dī foz′jēn), *n.* a substance used as a poison gas in World War I. *Formula:* $C_2Cl_4O_2$

di|phos|pho|gly|cer|ic acid (dī fos′fō gli ser′ik, -glis′ər-), a substance present in blood and tissues that regulates the release of oxygen by hemoglobin: *Diphosphoglyceric acid ... is manufactured in the red blood cells from glucose*

Pronunciation Key: hat, āge, cãre, fär; let, ēqual, tėrm; it, īce; hot, ōpen, ôrder; oil, out; cup, pu̇t, rüle; child; long; thin; ᴛʜen; zh, measure; ə represents **a** in about, **e** in taken, **i** in pencil, **o** in lemon, **u** in circus.

and phosphate (New York Times). *Abbr:* DPG (no periods). [< *di-*[1] + *phosph*(ate) + *glyceric acid*]

di|phos|pho|pyr|i|dine nucleotide (dī fos′fō-pir′ə dēn, -din), a coenzyme first isolated from yeast, necessary for the fermentation of glucose and the dehydrogenation of substances in cellular metabolism; cozymase. *Formula:* $C_{21}H_{27}N_7O_{14}P_2$ *Abbr:* DPN (no periods).

diph|ros (dif′ros), *n., pl.* **-roi** (-roi). a portable folding chair used by the ancient Greeks. [< Greek *diphrós*]

diph|the|ri|a (dif thir′ē ə, dip-; *see note below*), *n.* a dangerous, infectious disease of the throat. It is accompanied by high fever and the formation of a membranous substance that hinders breathing, and is caused by a bacillus. [< French *diphthérie* < Greek *diphthérā* hide, leather (because of the tough membrane developed on the affected parts)]

▶While *diphtheria* is probably changing to the pronunciation (dip thir′ē ə) for most laymen, its derived forms such as *diphtherial* are of isolated enough use in medical circles to preserve the pronunciation (dif thir′ē əl) for a time.

diph|the|ri|al (dif thir′ē əl, dip-), *adj.* having to do with diphtheria; diphtheritic.

diph|ther|ic (dif ther′ik, dip-), *adj.* = diphtheritic.

diph|the|rit|ic (dif′thə rit′ik, dip′-), *adj.* **1** of or like diphtheria. **2** suffering from diphtheria or the diphtheria bacillus.

diph|the|roid (dif′thə roid, dip′-), *adj., n.* —*adj.* of or like diphtheria.

—*n.* a bacterium that resembles the diphtheria bacillus: *Research has been concentrated on seeking methods to eliminate* [*dental*] *plaque formed by diphtheroids* (Lou Joseph).

diph|thong (dip′thông, dif′-; -thong), *n.* **1** a vowel sound made up of two vowel sounds pronounced in one syllable, such as *ou* in *house, oi* in *noise.* **2** two vowel letters joined together in printing, such as *æ* and *œ;* a ligature. **3** two vowel letters representing a single sound, such as *ea* in *eat;* a digraph. [earlier *diptonge* < Old French *diptongue* < Late Latin *diphthongus* < Greek *díphthongos* < *di-* double + *phthóngos* sound, voice]

▶A **diphthong** is often represented by only one letter, as *i* in *ice* or *u* in *abuse.*

diph|thon|gal (dip thông′gəl, dif-; -thong′-), *adj.* of or like a diphthong.

diph|thong|ic (dip thông′gik, dif-; -thong′-), *adj.* = diphthongal.

diph|thong|ise (dip′thông īz, -gīz; dif′-; -thong-), *v.t., v.i.* **-ised, -is|ing.** *Especially British.* diphthongize: *Because the vowels are jumbled up they tend to change character and diphthongise* (Manchester Guardian).

diph|thong|i|za|tion (dip′thông ə zā′shən, -gə-; dif′-; -thong-), *n.* the changing of a vowel into a diphthong.

diph|thong|ize (dip′thông īz, -gīz; dif′-; -thong-), *v.,* **-ized, -iz|ing.** —*v.t.* to change (a vowel or vowels) into a diphthong.

—*v.i.* to become a diphthong.

diph|y|cer|cal (dif′ə sėr′kəl, dif′i-), *adj.* **1** (of fishes) having a tail in which the upper and lower lobes are symmetrical and are equally divided by the end of the spine. **2** of or having to do with this kind of tail: *The tail is usually altered from the heterocercal type . . . to the homocercal and diphycercal forms* (Tracy I. Storer). [< Greek *diphuēs* double + *kérkos* tail + English *-al*[1]]

di|phy|let|ic (dif′ə let′ik), *adj.* **1** having two lines of descent; derived from two distinct sets of ancestors. **2** of or having to do with a classification of groups of animals on the theory that they have a diphyletic origin.

di|phyl|lous (dī fil′əs), *adj. Botany.* having two leaves. [< *di-*[1] two + Greek *phýllon* leaf + English *-ous*]

diph|y|o|dont (dif′ē ə dont), *adj., n.* —*adj.* having two successive sets of teeth, as most mammals.

—*n.* a diphyodont mammal.

[< Greek *diphuēs* double + *odoús, odóntos* tooth]

dipl., diplomat.

dip|la|cu|sis (dip′lə kyü′sis), *n.* an abnormal condition of hearing in which one tone is heard as if it were two tones of different pitch. [< New Latin *diplacusis* < Greek *diplóos* double + *ákousis* hearing < *akoúein* to hear]

di|ple|gi|a (dī plē′jē ə), *n.* a paralysis affecting similar parts on both sides of the body, such as the hands, legs, or arms. [< New Latin *diplegia* < Greek *di-* twice + *plēgē* stroke]

dip|lei|do|scope (dip lī′də skōp), *n.* an instrument consisting of a pair of mirrors tilted toward each other at an angle slightly more than 90 degrees, and covered by a sheet of glass, which indicates the passage of the sun, a star, or satellite over the meridian, by the coincidence of two images of the object, one formed by single and the other by double reflection. [< Greek *diplóos* double + *eîdos* form + English *-scope*]

di|pleu|ro|gen|e|sis (dī plür′ə jen′ə sis), *n.* **1** the symmetry of the right and left halves of the body in higher members of the animal kingdom. **2** evolution through the development of this kind of symmetry.

di|plex (dī′pleks), *adj.* of or denoting a telegraph or radio broadcast system for sending two messages in the same direction at the same time. [< *di-*[1] two + (du)*plex*]

dip|lo|blas|tic (dip′lə blas′tik), *adj.* having two germ layers, the ectoderm and endoderm, as coelenterates do. [< Greek *diplóos* double + *blastós* germ, sprout + English *-ic*]

dip|lo|car|di|ac (dip′lə kär′dē ak), *adj. Zoology.* having the right and left sides of the heart completely separate, as birds and mammals do. [< Greek *diplóos* twofold + English *cardiac*]

dip|lo|caul|us (dip′lə kôl′əs), *n.* a prehistoric amphibian with a crescent-shaped head, eyes near the front, and a skull equal to the whole length of the animal, adapted for living on the lake bottom. [< New Latin *diplocaulus* < Greek *diplóos* double + *kaulós* stalk]

dip|lo|coc|cal (dip′lə kok′əl), *adj.* of or like a diplococcus.

dip|lo|coc|cic (dip′lə kok′sik), *adj.* = diplococcal.

dip|lo|coc|cus (dip′lə kok′əs), *n., pl.* **-coc|ci** (-kok′sī). *Bacteriology.* any one of a group of elongated, parasitic bacteria, occurring typically as paired cells enclosed in a capsule, especially the species that causes lobar pneumonia. See also **streptococcus.** [< New Latin *Diplococcus* the genus name < Greek *diplóos* double + New Latin *coccus* coccus]

***di|plod|o|cus** (də plod′ə kəs), *n.* any one of an extinct genus of gigantic, plant-eating dinosaurs of the Upper Jurassic period of western North America: *Diplodocus was one of the largest land animals on record; skeletons more than 60 feet long have been found* (Robert M. Garrelo). [< New Latin *Diplodocus* the genus name < Greek *diplóos* double + *dokós* wooden beam]

***diplodocus**

dip|lo|ë (dip′lō ē), *n. Anatomy.* the spongy, porous bony tissue between the hard inner and outer walls of the bones of the skull. [< Greek *diplóē* a fold < *diplóos* double]

di|plo|ic (də plō′ik), *adj.* of or having to do with the diploë: *diploic tissue.*

dip|loid (dip′loid), *adj., n.* —*adj. Biology.* having double the number of chromosomes characteristic of germ cells of the species: *The body cells of a normal salamander are diploid: they have two sets of chromosomes* (Scientific American). See also **haploid.**

—*n.* **1** *Biology.* a diploid organism or cell. **2** *Crystallography.* a solid belonging to the isometric system, having 24 similar trapezoidal planes. [< Greek *diplóos* double + English *-oid*]

di|plo|ma (də plō′mə), *n., pl.* **-mas, -ma|ta** (-mə tə), *v.,* **-maed, -ma|ing.** —*n.* **1** a written or printed paper given by a school, college, or university which says that a person has completed a certain course of study, or has been graduated after a certain amount of work. **2** any certificate that bestows certain rights, privileges, honors, or titles. **3** an official document; charter.

—*v.t.* to furnish with a diploma: *It would delight a newly diplomaed psychologist, this spectacle of antisocial withdrawal* (Saturday Evening Post). [< Latin *diplōma* < Greek *diplōma* chart; (literally) paper folded double < *diploûn* to double < *diplóos* double]

▶The classical plural **diplomata** is now rare and is never used in the ordinary sense of *diploma.*

di|plo|ma|cy (də plō′mə sē), *n., pl.* **-cies. 1** the management of relations between nations. The making of treaties, international agreements, and the like, is an important part of diplomacy. *But diplomacy is negotiation, and the legitimate purpose of negotiation is to make agreements* (New York Times). **2** skill in managing such relations: *The statesman's great diplomacy prevented an outbreak of war between the two countries.* **3** skill in dealing with people; tact: *My older brother used diplomacy in being helpful at home the day before he asked to use the car.* [< French *diplomatie* < *diplomate* diplomat]

di|plo|ma|ism (də plō′mə iz əm), *n.* undue emphasis on the acquisition of an academic degree, especially as a qualification for hiring personnel: *The obvious question is whether a degreeless society would produce enough skilled people to bring technology under control. It is one thing to lambaste the tyranny of diplomaism, but quite another to expect nations to function without high standards of excellence* (Time).

diploma mill, *Informal.* = degree mill.

dip|lo|mat (dip′lə mat), *n.* **1** a person whose work is to handle the relations of his country with other nations. Ambassadors, envoys, and chargés d'affaires are diplomats. *Abbr:* dipl. or DPL. **2** a person who is skillful in dealing with people; a tactful person: *How do you know I am a diplomat? By the skillful way you hide your claws* (Edmond Rostand).

dip|lo|mate (dip′lə māt), *n.* a physician who has been certified in a field of specialization by any of various medical boards: *He received his medical degree from Emory University, . . . and is a diplomate of the American Board of Pediatrics* (New York Times). [< *diplom*(a) + *-ate,* as in *curate*]

dip|lo|mat|ic (dip′lə mat′ik), *adj.* **1** of or having to do with the management of relations between nations: *Ministers and consuls to foreign countries are in the diplomatic service. Ambassadors are the highest-ranking members of the diplomatic service.* **2** skillful in dealing with people; tactful: *a diplomatic policeman. He gave a diplomatic answer to avoid hurting his friend's feelings.* SYN: politic. [< New Latin *diplomaticus* having to do with original documents (usually legal ones) < Greek *diplōma;* see etym. under **diploma**]

dip|lo|mat|i|cal|ly (dip′lə mat′ə klē), *adv.* in a diplomatic manner; with diplomacy: *Remind him diplomatically that he hasn't paid his subscription yet. Diplomatically, Smith said he doubted that the goings-on at the investigation had anything to do with the falling market* (Time).

diplomatic corps, all of the ambassadors, ministers, and other official representatives of foreign nations at the capital of a country.

diplomatic immunity, special privileges accorded to diplomats and their families and staffs by international agreement, including freedom from arrest, search, and taxation.

dip|lo|mat|ics (dip′lə mat′iks), *n.* **1** = diplomacy. **2** the science of deciphering ancient documents and determining their age, authenticity, and certain other characteristics.

di|plo|ma|tism (də plō′mə tiz əm), *n.* = diplomacy.

di|plo|ma|tist (də plō′mə tist), *n. Especially British.* a diplomat.

di|plo|ma|tize (də plō′mə tīz), *v.i.,* **-tized, -tiz|ing.** to use diplomacy or tact.

dip|lont (dip′lont), *n.* an organism whose cells, except for the gametes, are diploid throughout life.

dip|lo|phase (dip′lō fāz′), *n.* the diploid phase of an organism: *. . . the alternation of haplophases and diplophases in the life cycle of different organisms* (Scientific American).

dip|lo|phon|ic (dip′lə fon′ik), *adj.* (of hearing) in which a single sound seems to come from two directions. [< Greek *diplóos* double + *phōnē* sound + English *-ic*]

di|plo|pi|a (də plō′pē ə), *n.* a disorder of the eyes in which objects are seen double. [< New Latin *diplopia* < Greek *diplóos* double + *ôps* eye]

di|plop|ic (də plop′ik), *adj.* seeing double.

dip|lo|pod (dip′lə pod), *n., adj.* —*n.* = millipede.

—*adj.* of or having to do with diplopods.

[< New Latin *Diplopoda* class name < Greek *diplóos* double + *poús, podós* foot]

di|plo|sis (də plō′sis), *n. Biology.* a doubling of the number of chromosomes, occurring when two haploid sets fuse during the union of germ cells. [< Greek *díplōsis* a doubling]

dip|lo|ste|mo|nous (dip′lə stē′mə nəs, -stem′ə-), *adj. Botany.* having two series of stamens, or twice as many stamens as petals. [< Greek *diplóos* double + *stēmōn* warp, thread (taken as *stêma* stamen) + English *-ous*]

dip|lo|tene (dip′lə tēn), *n.* a stage of the prophase of meiosis in which chiasmata begin to appear. [< Greek *diplóos* double + *tainiā* band]

di|plu|ran (də plür′ən), *n.* any one of an order of insects that have slender, whitish bodies but no eyes and no wings. They live in rotten wood or under leaves or stones. [< New Latin *Diplura* the order name (< Greek *diplóos* double + *ourā* tail) + English *-an*]

dip needle, = dipping needle.

dip|net (dip′net′), *n., v.,* **-net|ted, -net|ting.** —*n.* a net with a long handle for scooping up fish.

—*v.t., v.i.* to catch (fish) with a dipnet: *Dipnetting of Chinook salmon by Indians at the Celilo Falls . . .* (New Scientist).

dip|no|an (dip′nō ən), *adj., n.* —*adj.* of or belonging to a group of fishes having both gills and lungs.

—*n.* a dipnoan fish; lungfish.

[< New Latin *Dipnoi* the subclass name < Greek *dípnoos* having two breathing apertures < *di-*

two + *pneîn* to breathe]
dip|no|ous (dip′nō əs), *adj.* **1** having both gills and lungs, as the dipnoans. **2** like a dipnoan.
di|pode (dī′pōd), *adj., n.* **—*adj.*** biped; having two feet.
—*n.* a lizard with rudimentary pectoral limbs, so that it appears to have only two feet.
dip|o|dy (dip′ə dē), *n., pl.* **-dies**. *Prosody.* **1** a group of two feet. **2** a verse having two feet; dimeter. [< Late Latin *dipodia* < Greek *dipodiā* < *dipous, -podos* two-footed < *di-* two + *poús, podós* foot]
di|po|lar (dī pō′lər), *adj.* having two poles; having to do with two poles: *A dipolar quantity reversed remains the same.*
di|pole (dī′pōl′), *n. Physics, Chemistry.* **1** two equal electric charges or magnetic poles of opposite sign which are separated by a specified distance, as in a molecule. **2a** a molecule or other object that can be thought of as having two such charges or poles: *Each water molecule is a small dipole, that is, its positive and negative charges do not coincide* (Sears and Zemansky). **b** a small copper wire having such properties, especially one of a number placed in orbit about the earth to reflect radio signals. **3** = dipole antenna.
dipole antenna, a radio or television antenna having two separated conducting rods one-half wave in length.
dip|per (dip′ər), *n.* **1** a person or thing that dips. **2** a long-handled cup or larger container for dipping water or other liquids. **3** a large scoop or shovel attached to a derrick by a chain. It is shaped like a box with a door on the bottom which can be pulled open with a long cord to dump dirt or mud. **4** = dipper dredge. **5** any one of various diving birds, such as the water ouzel, the kingfisher, and the grebe.
Dip|per (dip′ər), *n.* either of two groups of stars in the northern sky each somewhat like the shape of a dipper; Big Dipper or Little Dipper.
dipper dredge, a floating dredge that has a large scoop shovel or dipper that hangs on a chain from a derrick. Both the dipper and the derrick can be raised and lowered.
dip|per|ful (dip′ər fu̇l), *n., pl.* **-fuls**. as much as a dipper can hold.
dip|pi|ly (dip′ə lē), *adv. U.S. Slang.* in a dippy manner.
dip|pi|ness (dip′ē nis), *n. U.S. Slang.* being dippy; foolishness.
dipping needle, a magnetic needle mounted so as to be capable of moving freely in a vertical plane about its center of gravity, and indicating by its dip the direction of the earth's magnetism; dip needle. See also **inclinometer**.
dip|py (dip′ē), *adj.,* **-pi|er, -pi|est**. *U.S. Slang.* **1** crazy; foolish; dimwitted: *A fisherman has to be a little dippy, like the left-handed baseball players, to stay with it* (Newsweek). **2** intoxicated; light-headed; dizzy: *One minute somebody is dippy on ether fumes ...* (Time).
di|pro|to|don (dī prō′tə don), *n.* an extinct marsupial of Australia, resembling the wombat, and about the size of a rhinoceros. [< Greek *di-* two + *prôtos* first; front + *odoús, odóntos* tooth]
dip|sa|ca|ceous (dip′sə kā′shəs), *adj.* of or belonging to a family of Old World herbs typified by the teasel. [< New Latin *Dipsacaceae* the family name (< Greek *dipsakos* teasel < *dípsa* thirst) + English *-ous* (because the plant retains water)]
dip|sas (dip′səs), *n., pl.* **-sa|des** (-sə dēz). a serpent whose bite was believed to produce a deadly thirst: *It thirsted as one bit by a dipsas* (Shelley). [< Latin *dipsas* < Greek *dípsas* (originally) causing thirst < *dípsa* thirst]
dip|sey or **dip|sy** (dip′sē), *adj. Nautical.* deep-sea.
dip|so (dip′sō), *n., pl.* **-sos**. *Slang.* dipsomaniac.
dip|so|ma|ni|a (dip′sə mā′nē ə), *n.* an abnormal, uncontrollable craving for alcoholic liquors. [< New Latin *dipsomania* < Greek *dípsa* thirst + *maniā* mania]
dip|so|ma|ni|ac (dip′sə mā′nē ak), *n., adj.* **—*n.*** a person who has dipsomania.
—*adj.* of or having to do with dipsomania or a dipsomaniac.
dip|so|ma|ni|a|cal (dip′sə mə nī′ə kəl), *adj.* = dipsomaniac.

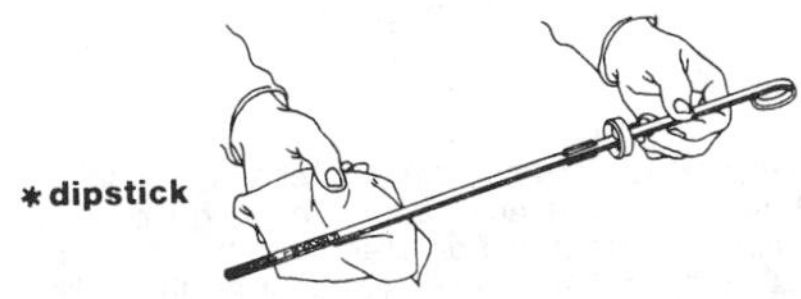

***dipstick**

***dip|stick** (dip′stik′), *n.* a graduated rod for measuring the level of a liquid in a container, such as the oil in the crankcase of an internal-combustion engine: *A dashboard gauge shows the level of oil in the engine, obviating the messy dipstick and rag* (New Yorker).
dip|switch (dip′swich′), *n. British.* a switch for dimming the headlights of an automobile: *Switches for the screenwasher and wipers ... come immediately to hand, and there is a floor button dipswitch* (London Times).
dip|sy-do or **dip|sy-doo** (dip′sē dü′), *n. U.S. Slang.* **1** *Baseball.* a slow or fast curve that is very difficult to hit. **2** tricky maneuvering: *the dipsy-do of a magician.*
dip|sy-doo|dle (dip′sē dü′dəl), *n., v.,* **-dled, -dling**. *U.S. Slang.* **—*n.*** **1** *Baseball.* **a** a dipsy-do. **b** a pitcher adept at throwing a dipsy-do. **2** a deceptive person; tricky thing.
—*v.t., v.i.* to deceive; trick.
dipt (dipt), *v.* dipped; a past tense and a past participle of **dip:** *He dipt water from the well.*
Dip. Tech., *British.* Diploma in Technology.
dip|ter (dip′tər), *n.* a dipterous insect.
Dip|ter|a (dip′tər ə), *n.pl.* the order of insects comprising the dipterans. [< New Latin *Diptera* the order name < Greek *dípteros;* see etym. under **dipterous**]
dip|ter|al (dip′tər əl), *adj.* **1** *Architecture.* having two rows of columns on all sides. **2** dipterous.
dip|ter|an (dip′tər ən), *adj., n.* **—*adj.*** = dipterous.
—*n.* any one of a large order of insects that, except for some wingless parasitic forms, have one pair of membranous wings, the usual second pair of wings being replaced by small club-shaped organs. Mosquitoes, gnats, and houseflies belong to this order.
dip|ter|ist (dip′tər ist), *n.* a person who studies dipterology: *Competition ... between the dipterists and the lepidopterists* (Oliver Wendell Holmes).
dip|ter|o|carp (dip′tər ō kärp′), *n., adj.* **—*n.*** a dipterocarpaceous tree.
—*adj.* of or containing such trees: *a dipterocarp forest.*
dip|ter|o|car|pa|ceous (dip′tər ō kär pā′shəs), *adj.* belonging to a large family of tropical Asiatic trees, having a two-winged fruit from which fragrant oils and resins are obtained, such as the gurjun. [< New Latin *Dipterocarpus* the genus name (< Greek *dípteros* two-winged + *karpós* fruit) + English *-aceous*]
dip|ter|ol|o|gy (dip′tə rol′ə jē), *n.* the study of dipterous insects.
dip|ter|on (dip′tə ron), *n.* a dipterous insect.
***dip|ter|ous** (dip′tər əs), *adj.* **1** (of insects) having one pair of wings. **2** of or belonging to the dipterans. **3** *Botany.* having two winglike appendages, as certain fruits and seeds do. [< New Latin *dipterus* (with English *-ous*) two-winged < Greek *dípteros* < *di-* two + *pterón* wing]

***dipterous**
definition 3

***dip|tych** (dip′tik), *n.* **1** an ancient writing tablet consisting of two pieces of wood or ivory hinged together, with the inner sides waxed for writing on with a stylus. **2** a pair of paintings or carvings on two panels hinged together. **3** anything folded so as to have two leaves. [< Late Latin *diptycha*, neuter plural < Greek *díptychos* folded double < *di-* twice + *ptychḗ* a fold]

***diptych**
definition 2

di|quat (dī′kwät), *n.* a herbicide activated by photosynthesis upon contact with weeds: *Diquat ... is now widely used throughout the world to control weeds in such diverse crops as cotton, rubber, potatoes, sugar beet and tea* (New Scientist). *Formula:* $C_{12}H_{12}Br_2N_2$ [< *di-*[1] + *quat*(ernary), part of the formula]
dir., director.
Dir|cae|an (dėr sē′ən), *adj.* **1** of or having to do with the fountain Dirce, near Thebes, in Boeotia. Pindar, who lived in Thebes, was called "the Dircaean Swan" by Horace. **2** Pindaric; poetic.
dir|dum (dir′dəm, dėr′-), *n. Scottish.* **1** a scolding; outcry; blame. **2** uproar; noise; din. [origin uncertain. Compare Gaelic *diardan* anger.]
dire (dīr), *adj.,* **dir|er, dir|est**. causing great fear or suffering; dreadful: *the dire consequences of a nuclear war, dire necessity. Dire was the noise of conflict* (Shakespeare). [< Latin *dīrus*] **—dire′ly**, *adv.* **—dire′ness**, *n.*
di|rect (də rekt′, dī-), *v., adj., adv.* **—*v.t.*** **1** to manage or guide; control: *to direct a play, direct a business. A teacher directs the work of the pupils. A mounted policeman used to direct the traffic here, but now it's all signals.* SYN: See syn. under **manage**. **2** to instruct to do something; order; command: *The policeman directed the traffic to stop.* SYN: See syn. under **command**. **3** to tell or show the way; give information about where to go or what to do: *Can you direct me to the airport? Signposts direct travelers.* **4** to turn (something) straight to or at; point (to) or aim (at): *The fireman directed his hose at the flames. We should direct our efforts to a useful end.* **5** to address (a letter or package) to a person or place. **6** to address (words, facial expressions, or gestures) to a person: *He directed his request to the king.*
—*v.i.* to give directions; order: *I am not directing here any longer; I have resigned.*
—*adj.* **1** without a stop or turn; straight: *a direct route. Our house is in direct line with the school. A bee makes a direct flight to the hive.* **2** in an unbroken line; lineal: *a direct heir. The man is a direct descendant of John Adams.* **3** *Figurative.* without anyone or anything in between; not through others; immediate: *direct influence. The new teacher took direct charge of the library. Selling door to door is direct selling.* **4** *Figurative.* straightforward; frank; truthful; plain: *The boy gave a direct answer. He made a direct denial of the charge of cheating.* **5** exact; absolute: *the direct opposite.* **6** of or produced by the action of the people as voters, without intermediaries or representatives: *direct elections.* **7** that uses a speaker's exact words. In the sentence *He said, "You're right"* the words "You're right" are a direct quotation. **8** *Mathematics.* following the natural order. **9** not requiring a mordant to fix the color: *a direct dye.* **10** *Astronomy.* (of a heavenly body or its motion) proceeding in the order of the signs of the zodiac; proceeding from west to east.
—*adv.* directly; without deviation: *The airplane goes to Los Angeles direct, without stopping between here and there. They are able to buy direct with obvious advantages* (Advertising Age).
[< Latin *dīrēctus* straight, past participle of *dīrigere* set straight < *dis-* apart + *regere* guide]
—di|rect′ing|ly, *adv.* **—di|rect′ness**, *n.*
—*Syn.* *adj.* **1, 3 Direct, immediate** mean proceeding from one to another without a break. **Direct** implies that the line is unbroken, though there may be many steps between: *Overwork and too great strain were the direct causes of his death.* **Immediate** implies that there is nothing between: *A heart attack was the immediate cause of his death.*
▶**Direct address** is the name or descriptive term used in addressing someone. It is set off from the rest of the sentence by comma(s): *Examples:* My friends, I wish you would forget this night. It's all right, Mrs. Williams, for you to come into the room now.
di|rect|a|ble (də rek′tə bəl, dī-), *adj.* that can be directed; dirigible.
direct action, an act or acts intended to gain an end immediately, such as strikes, boycotts, or sabotage, used by workers to wrest concessions from employers, rather than through political representatives.
direct actionist, a person who advocates a policy of direct action.
direct cost, *Accounting.* a cost which can be assigned to a definite process or operation or to the manufacture of a particular product, as distinguished from overhead.
direct current, a steady electric current that flows in one direction only. The current from all batteries is direct current. *Abbr:* D.C., d.c.
direct discourse, a quoting of what a person says in his exact words. *Example:* He said, "Let's go now."
Direct Distance Dialing, telephone dialing from one region to another by using an area code. *Abbr:* DDD (no periods).
direct drive, a drive in which the driving and driven parts are mounted on a common shaft: *Direct drive provides top efficiency at cruising speeds* (Newsweek).
direct dye, a dye that does not require fixing with a mordant. It is used chiefly on cellulose fibers.
di|rect|ed (də rek′tid, dī-), *adj.* **1a** guided; organized; supervised: *directed sports activities.* **b** aiming at some practical objective; applied: *directed research.* **2** *Mathematics.* **a** having a positive or negative direction: *a directed line segment.*

Pronunciation Key: hat, āge, cãre, fär; let, ēqual, tėrm; it, īce; hot, ōpen, ôrder; **oil**, **out**; cup, pu̇t, rüle; **ch**ild; lo**ng**; **th**in; ᴛʜen; **zh**, measure; ə represents **a** in about, **e** in taken, **i** in pencil, **o** in lemon, **u** in circus.

b preceded by a plus or a minus sign: *a directed number.*

di|rect|ed-en|er|gy weapon (də rek′tid en′ər jē, dī-), a weapon that fires particle beams or laser beams, especially against nuclear missiles; beam weapon: *There are a couple of hundred ... blue-eyed boys in Los Alamos, New Mexico, working on hunter-killer satellites and directed-energy weapons like satellite-launched high-energy lasers* (Rolling Stone).

di|rect|ed|ness (də rek′tid nis, dī-), *n.* the quality of being directed or under guidance.

directed verdict, a verdict specifically demanded of the jury by the court: *When the facts are so clearly in favor of one party that the jury could not reasonably decide any other way, the judge may direct the jury to return a directed verdict* (Arthur E. Sutherland).

di|rec|tee (də rek′tē′, dī′rek-), *n.* a person who is directed or is under direction.

di|rect|er (də rek′tər, dī-), *n.* = director.

direct evidence, the evidence of a witness who testifies that a fact to be proved is true of his own knowledge.

direct examination, the first examination of a witness by the party who has called him to testify.

direct grant school, (in Great Britain) a private school that receives a grant directly from the Ministry of Education.

di|rec|tion (də rek′shən, dī-), *n.* **1** guidance; managing; control: *the direction of a play or motion picture. The school is under the direction of a good teacher.* **SYN:** management. **2** an order; command: *It was his direction that I prepare a report.* **3** Also, **directions.** a knowing or telling what to do, how to do, where to go, or other instruction: *He needs directions to the lake. Can you give me directions for driving to Chicago?* **4** the address on a letter or package. **5** the course taken by a moving body, such as a ball or a bullet. **6** any way in which one may face or point. North, south, east, and west are directions. *Our school is in one direction and the post office is in another.* **7** *Figurative.* a course along which something moves; way of moving; tendency: *This town shows improvement in many directions.* **8** *Music.* a word, phrase, or sign for the tempo or style in which a score or part of a score should be played. **9** a body of directors; directorate: *I will ask some of the direction* (Thackeray).

—*Syn.* **7 Direction, trend, tendency** mean line or course of action. **Direction** applies when the course of action is set and steady: *The investigation has taken a new direction.* **Trend** applies when the course is more general and involves some twistings and turnings: *The trend is toward higher wages and prices.* **Tendency** applies when the course is definite but the progress, though inclined in this direction, is uncertain: *The tendency is toward higher taxes.*

di|rec|tion|al (də rek′shə nəl, dī-), *adj.* **1** of or having to do with direction in space: *If the main weight is behind the centre of the car directional control is not so good* (London News Chronicle). **2a** *Radio.* fitted for determining the direction from which signals come, or for sending signals in a particular direction. **b** receiving signals from a particular direction; that can be turned in a particular direction: *a directional antenna, a directional reflector.* **3** indicating direction: *Hand-signaling remains an important safety factor for drivers although most cars are equipped with flashing directional indicators* (New York Times). —**di|rec′tion|al|ly**, *adv.*

di|rec|tion|al|i|ty (də rek′shə nal′ə tē, dī-), *n.* **1** the condition of having direction. **2** the degree or extent to which anything has direction.

directional wireless, **1** wireless employed to discover position through the direction of messages received or intercepted, as by the navigator of an aircraft or of a ship at sea. **2** wireless in which the waves are sent out in only one direction, as from one station to another.

direction finder, a device for finding the direction of incoming radio waves. It is usually a loop aerial which rotates freely on a vertical axis.

direction indicator, a device used in navigating an aircraft, consisting of a needle set for the desired course and a compass which shows the actual course.

di|rec|tion|less (də rek′shən lis, dī-), *adj.* having no direction: *He writes with the meandering, seemingly directionless flow of much of life itself* (Newsweek). —**di|rec′tion|less|ly**, *adv.*

di|rec|tive (də rek′tiv, dī-), *n., adj.* —*n.* an order or instruction telling what to do, how to do, or where to go: *The captain gave a directive to his lieutenants. This advisory ... had the force of a directive because of the willing, not to say anxious, compliance of newspaper editors and publishers* (Bulletin of Atomic Scientists).

—*adj.* directing; serving to direct. —**di|rec′tive|ly**, *adv.* —**di|rec′tive|ness**, *n.*

di|rec|tiv|i|ty (də rek′tiv′ə tē, dī′rek-), *n.* directional condition or quality; directionality: *The real advantage ... of such an antenna in long-distance reception is its directivity* (L. F. B. Carini).

direct labor, *Accounting.* the cost of labor expended directly upon production, exclusive of maintenance, clerical costs, and other overhead charges.

direct liability, a definite obligation, such as a loan or a purchase of goods or services on credit, which can be paid as specified, as distinguished from a contingent liability.

di|rect|ly (də rekt′lē, dī-), *adv., conj.* —*adv.* **1** in a direct line or manner; straight: *This road runs directly into the center of town.* **2** *Figurative.* straightforwardly; frankly; plainly; truthfully. **3** exactly; absolutely: *directly opposite.* **4** immediately; at once: *Come home directly. I shall be with you directly.*

—*conj.* *Especially British.* as soon as: *I left directly he called.* See also **immediately**.

direct mail, **1** mail sent by business firms, nonprofit organizations, or other groups, directly to potential customers or contributors, advertising something or requesting their patronage, membership, help, or the like. **2** this method or form of advertising: *Direct mail costs more to reach the customer than other forms of advertising* (Marion Harper, Jr.).

direct material, the raw material of a manufactured product whose cost can be identified and measured.

direct object, *Grammar.* a word or words showing the person or thing undergoing the action expressed by the verb. In "The boat struck a rock," *rock* is the direct object of the verb *struck.*

***Di|rec|toire** (dē rek twär′), *n., adj.* —*n.* the Directory. —*adj.* of or in the style of the period of the French Directory; extravagant; ornate: *Some of her daytime dresses are "Directoire," with gathered skirts falling loosely from high-belted bodices* (New York Times). [< French *Directoire* < Latin *dīrēctus;* see etym. under **direct**]

***Directoire**

di|rec|tor (də rek′tər, dī-), *n.* **1** a manager; person who directs; leader. A person who plans and directs the performance of a play, a motion picture, or a show on television or radio is called a director. **2** one of a group of persons chosen to direct the affairs of a company or institution: *The owners of a company elect the directors. Company directors have certain functions which really come down to giving advice out of their experience in the business world generally* (Newsweek). *Abbr:* dir. **3** a gunsight that coordinates the firing of a number of guns. Also, **directer.**

di|rec|tor|ate (də rek′tər it, dī-), *n.* **1** the position of director. **2** a group of directors: *Interlocking directorates should be prohibited* (Wall Street Journal).

di|rec|tor-gen|er|al (də rek′tər jen′ər əl, dī-), *n.* a person appointed as the overall director: *Sir Julian Huxley, the distinguished biologist and writer, was the first director-general of Unesco* (Bulletin of Atomic Scientists).

di|rec|to|ri|al (də rek′tôr′ē əl, -tōr′-; dī′rek-), *adj.* having to do with a director or directorate. —**di|rec′to′ri|al|ly**, *adv.*

director's chair, a type of light folding chair used by motion-picture directors: *Jungle version of director's chair, with zebra-striped canvas seat and back, bamboo-patterned frame* (Good Housekeeping).

di|rec|tor|ship (də rek′tər ship, dī-), *n.* the position or term of office of a director: *He resigned his directorships with several other large corporations* (Wall Street Journal).

di|rec|to|ry (də rek′tər ē, dī-; -trē), *n., pl.* **-ries,** *adj.* —*n.* **1** a list of names and addresses, usually in alphabetical order. A telephone book is a directory of people who have telephones. **2** a group of directors; directorate. **3** a book of rules or instructions. **4** a book containing directions for the order of worship.

—*adj.* serving to direct; directing; advisory.

Di|rec|to|ry (də rek′tər ē, dī-; -trē), *n.* the group of five men who governed France from 1795 to 1799. [translation of French *Directoire;* see etym. under **Directoire**]

direct primary, *U.S.* a primary in which the voters of a political party choose the candidates of their party for office by direct vote rather than at a convention.

direct question, a question in a person's exact words. *Example:* He asked, "Shall we go now?"

di|rec|tress (də rek′tris, dī-), *n.* a woman director.

di|rec|trice (də rek′trēs′), *n.* = directress. [< French *directrice* < New Latin *directric-, directrix* directrix]

di|rec|trix (də rek′triks, dī-), *n., pl.* **di|rec|trix|es, di|rec|tri|ces** (dī′rek trī′sēz). **1** *Geometry.* a fixed line used in determining a conic section. **2** = directress. [< New Latin *directrix,* feminine of Latin *dīrēctor* < *dīrēctus;* see etym. under **direct**]

direct tax, a tax that cannot be passed on to another, for example in the form of higher prices, but must be paid directly by the taxed person. Income taxes, property taxes, and inheritance taxes are direct taxes.

dire|ful (dīr′fəl), *adj.* dire; dreadful; terrible: *direful news. One has no great hopes from Birmingham; I always say there is something direful in the sound* (Jane Austen). —**dire′ful|ly**, *adv.* —**dire′ful|ness**, *n.*

dir|et|tis|si|ma (dir′ə tis′ə mə), *n. Mountaineering.* a direct ascent:... *a school in Switzerland specializing in direttissima, an innovation that ignores the traditional zigging and zagging around danger spots for a damn-the-obstacles, straight-up climb to the top* (Time). [< Italian *direttissima* most direct]

dire wolf, a large wolflike mammal whose remains were found among North American Pleistocene deposits.

dirge (dėrj), *n.* **1** a funeral song or tune: *A dirge for her, the doubly dead in that she died so young* (Edgar Allan Poe). **2** in the Roman Catholic Church: **a** the choral funeral service. **b** a funeral hymn or Requiem. [contraction of Latin *dīrige* direct !, imperative of *dīrigere;* see etym. under **direct** (because of its use as first word in Office of the Dead] —**dirge′like′**, *adj.*

dirge|ful (dėrj′fəl), *adj.* = mournful.

dir|ham (dir ham′), *n.* **1** a unit of money in Morocco, a coin or note equal to 100 francs. **2** a measure of weight in Egypt, equal to about 3.12 grams. Also, **dirhem.** [< Arabic *dirham* < Latin *drachma* drachma]

dir|i|gi|bil|i|ty (dir′ə jə bil′ə tē, də rij′ə-), *n.* the fact or quality of being dirigible.

dir|i|gi|ble (dir′ə jə bəl, də rij′ə-), *n., adj.* —*n.* a kind of balloon that can be steered; airship. A dirigible is filled with gas that is lighter than air. [< adjective]

—*adj.* that can be directed.

[< Latin *dīrigere* to direct + English *-ible*]

dir|i|gism (dir′ə jiz əm), *n.* = dirigisme.

di|ri|gisme (dē rē zhēsm′), *n. French.* **1** government intervention or control in the nation's economy. **2** (literally) planning; direction.

di|ri|giste (dē rē zhēst′), *adj. French.* of or characterized by dirigisme.

di|ri|go (dir′ə gō), *Latin.* I direct; I guide (the motto of Maine).

dir|i|ment (dir′ə mənt), *adj.* that makes absolutely void; nullifying. [< Latin *dirimēns, -entis,* present participle of *dirimere* separate, break off < *dis-* apart + *emere* take]

diriment impediment, a condition, such as consanguinity or the fact that one of the partners is already married, that makes a marriage null and void from the beginning.

dirk (dėrk), *n., v.* —*n.* = dagger.

—*v.t.* to stab with a dirk.

[origin uncertain]

dirl (dirl, dėrl), *Scottish.* —*v.i.* to vibrate; tingle.

—*v.t.* to cause to vibrate or tingle.

[probably related to **thirl**]

***dirn|dl** (dėrn′dəl), *n.* **1** an Alpine peasant girl's costume consisting of a blouse, a tight bodice, and a full, brightly colored skirt, gathered at the waist. **2** a dress imitating it. **3** a skirt of this type. [< dialectal German *Dirndl* girl (diminutive) < *Dirne* maid]

***dirndl**
definition 1

dirn|dled (dėrn′dəld), *adj.* **1** of or like a dirndl. **2** dressed in a dirndl: *You see buzzing factories, garlanded cattle and dirndled girls* (New Yorker).

dirt (dėrt), *n.* **1** mud, dust, earth, or anything like them. Dirt soils whatever it touches. *She treats me as if I were the dirt under her feet.* **2** loose earth or soil. **3** *Figurative.* an unclean thing, action, or speech. **4** uncleanness; meanness. **5** *Informal, Figurative.* scandal; gossip: *Do you know*

the latest dirt? **6** *Informal, Figurative.* anything worthless: *We were only singing seamen from the dirt of London town* (Alfred Noyes). **7** *Mining.* the earth, gravel, or other material from which gold is separated by washing.
do (someone) **dirt,** *Informal.* to do (a person, his family or associates, or his reputation) intentional and malicious harm: *He was somehow doing these people dirt, defiling their clean, hopeful lives* (Saturday Evening Post).
eat dirt, *Informal.* to submit to degrading treatment; make a humiliating apology or retraction: *In times of revolution a good many pecks of dirt have to be eaten* (Saturday Review).
[Middle English *drit,* perhaps < Scandinavian (compare Old Icelandic *drit* excrement from birds)]

dirt bike, *U.S.* a lightweight motorcycle for racing on a dirt track.

dirt-cheap (dėrt′chēp′), *adj., adv.* **—*adj.*** very cheap: *By American standards, tuition in Germany is dirt cheap* (Holiday).
—*adv.* = cheaply.

dirt farmer, *Informal.* a farmer who has practical experience in doing his own work.

dirt·i·ly (dėr′tə lē), *adv.* in a dirty manner.

dirt·i·ness (dėr′tē nis), *n.* a dirty condition.

dirt·less (dėrt′lis), *adj.* void of dirt.

dirt-poor (dėrt′pu̇r′), *adj.* very poor: *For all its glamor and greatness, ancient Greece was dirt-poor* (Life).

dirt road, a road with dirt or gravel surface.

dirt track, an outdoor track of dirt, cinders, or the like for racing.

dirt·y (dėr′tē), *adj.,* **dirt·i·er, dirt·i·est,** *v.,* **dirt·ied, dirt·y·ing,** *adv.* **—*adj.* 1** soiled by dirt; unclean: *dirty hands.* **2** that makes dirty; soiling: *a dirty job.* **3** *Figurative.* not clean or pure in action, thought, or speech: *a dirty joke.* **4** *Figurative.* low; mean; vile: *a dirty, low-down rascal. Politics is neither "sweetness and light" nor "too dirty to get into"* (New York Times). SYN: base. **5** not clear or pure in color; clouded: *a dirty red.* **6** stormy or windy; rough: *The hurricane was the dirtiest weather I ever saw. It begins to look very dirty to windward* (Frederick Marryat). **7** being on drugs; using drugs: *Two weeks ago four new men came into the group meeting and each admitted he was then "strung-out." Each was given 10 days to appear on the list as "clean." At the meeting 10 days later each was "dirty"* (London Times). **8** causing a great amount of radioactive fallout: *dirty bombs.*
—*v.t.* to make dirty; soil; pollute: *Don't dirty your new dress by playing outside in this wet weather.*
—*v.i.* to become dirty or soiled: *A white shirt will dirty faster than a dark one.*
—*adv.* *Informal.* dirtily: *to fight dirty.*
—*Syn.* *adj.* **1 Dirty, filthy, foul** mean unclean. **Dirty** means soiled in any way: *dirty shoes. Children playing in mud get dirty.* **Filthy,** often implying an attitude of disgust, suggests being extremely dirty, covered or stained with greasy or sticky dirt or littered with trash: *a filthy kitchen. In some cities and towns the streets are filthy.* **Foul** implies still greater disgust and suggests being filled or covered with filth or with something unhealthy, impure, or rotten: *The water in the swamp is foul.*

dirty pool, *U.S. Slang.* unfair or dishonest conduct; foul play: *samples of dirty pool in the business world* (New York Times).

dirty tricks, *U.S.* underhanded activities and practices to achieve political gain: *economic and psychological subversion of the . . . government, including such dirty tricks as introducing counterfeit money* (Time).

dirty war, the use of terrorism, death squads, or other unorthodox means of waging war: *. . . more than 5,100 missing persons, victims of . . . a "dirty war" against leftist guerrillas* (Richard Boudreaux).

dirty word, 1 a coarse or obscene word. **2** anything vile or contemptible; an evil: *The steel industry is still under the threat of nationalization and . . . profits are considered a dirty word by many* (London Times).

dirty work, *U.S. Slang.* dishonest, corrupt, or unethical activity; foul play.

Dis (dis), *n.* **1** the Roman god of the lower world, identified with the Greek god Pluto. **2** the lower world; Hades.

dis (dis), *v.t.,* **dissed, dis·sing.** *Slang.* to show disrespect; scorn: *We hope that you guys don't dis us for it* (New York Magazine).

dis-[1], *prefix.* the form of **di**[1] before *s,* as in *dissyllable.*

dis-[2], *prefix.* **1** opposite of; lack of; not: *Dishonest = opposite of honest. Discomfort = lack of comfort.* **2** do the opposite of: *Disentangle = do the opposite of entangle. Disallow = do the opposite of allow.* **3** apart; away, as in *dismiss, dispel.*
Also: **di-** before *b, d, l, m, n, r, s, v,* and sometimes before *g* and *j;* **dif-** before *f.* [< Old French *des-* < Latin *dis-* apart, or directly < Latin]

di·sa (dī′sə), *n.* any one of a large genus of distinctively formed and colorful South African orchids. [< New Latin *Disa* the genus name; origin unknown]

dis·a·bil·i·ty (dis′ə bil′ə tē), *n., pl.* **-ties. 1** lack of ability or power: *The player's disability was caused by illness.* **2** something that disables: *Deafness is a disability for a musician.* **3** something that disqualifies: *Relationship to an accused man is a disability which disqualifies a person for service on the jury at his trial.*

disability clause, a provision in life-insurance contracts freeing the insured from further payments if he becomes totally disabled, and, in certain policies, giving him an income.

dis·a·ble (dis ā′bəl), *v.t.,* **-bled, -bling. 1** to make unable; make unfit for use or action; cripple: *A sprained ankle disabled the football player for three weeks. She was disabled by polio.* SYN: See syn. under **cripple. 2** to disqualify legally.

dis·a·bled (dis ā′bəld), *adj.* deprived of ability or power; crippled: *He suggested that Congress, with the help of the executive branch of the government, resolve the constitutional doubt about when and by whom a President might be declared disabled so that his duties could be taken over by another official* (Newsweek).

dis·a·ble·ment (dis ā′bəl mənt), *n.* the condition of being deprived of ability or power; deprivation: *Where there had been permanent and substantial worsening of the war disablement higher pensions were awarded* (John Moss).

dis·a·bus·al (dis′ə byü′zəl), *n.* the act of disabusing.

dis·a·buse (dis′ə byüz′), *v.t.,* **-bused, -bus·ing.** to free from deception or error: *Education should disabuse people of foolish prejudices.*

di·sac·cha·rid (dī sak′ər id), *n.* = disaccharide.

di·sac·cha·ri·dase (dī sak′ə rə dās), *n.* any enzyme, such as invertase (sucrase), that hydrolyzes disaccharides.

di·sac·cha·ride (dī sak′ə rīd, -ər id), *n.* any one of a group of carbohydrates, such as lactose, maltose, sucrose, and various other sugars, which hydrolysis changes into two simple sugars (monosaccharides): *Ordinary table sugar and milk sugar belong to the disaccharide class of sugars* (Science News Letter). [< *di-*[1] + *saccharide*]

di·sac·cha·rose (dī sak′ə rōs), *n.* = disaccharide.

dis·ac·cord (dis′ə kôrd′), *v., n.* **—*v.i.*** to disagree; be out of harmony: *His arguments disaccord with the facts.*
—*n.* disagreement; lack of harmony; variance.

dis·ac·cord·ant (dis′ə kôr′dənt), *adj.* disagreeing; not in accord.

dis·ac·cred·i·ta·tion (dis′ə kred′ə tā′shən), *n.* withdrawal of accreditation: *Delegates arguing for the disaccreditation of the Nationalist Chinese included representatives of Byelorussia . . . and Burma* (New York Times).

dis·ac·cus·tom (dis′ə kus′təm), *v.t.* **1** to cause (a person) to lose a habit. **2** *Archaic.* to make (something) no longer customary.

dis·a·dapt (dis′ə dapt′), *v.t.* to make difficult or unable to adapt: *The two cosmonauts remained 'disadapted' to normal gravity much longer than would have been predicted on a basis of the previous (American) longest duration flight* (Science Journal).

dis·ad·van·tage (dis′əd van′tij, -vän′-), *n., v.,* **-taged, -tag·ing. —*n.* 1** lack of advantage; unfavorable condition: *Her shyness was a disadvantage in company. The deaf child was at a disadvantage in school.* **2** a loss or injury: *The candidate's enemies spread rumors that were to his disadvantage.*
—*v.t.* to subject to disadvantage; place in an unfavorable position.

dis·ad·van·taged (dis′əd van′tijd, -vän′-), *adj., n.* **—*adj.*** lacking advantages; being in an unfavorable condition; underprivileged: *Many disadvantaged children live in the slums. . . . the achievement of equal participation and opportunity for members of minority and disadvantaged groups* (New York Times).
—*n.* the disadvantaged, persons who are disadvantaged or underprivileged: *The program is forcing responsible teachers of the disadvantaged to re-examine some of their cherished clichés* (Harper's).

dis·ad·van·ta·geous (dis ad′vən tā′jəs, dis′ad-), *adj.* causing disadvantage; unfavorable. **—dis·ad′·van·ta′geous·ly,** *adv.* **—dis·ad′van·ta′geous·ness,** *n.*

dis·ad·vise (dis′əd vīz′), *v.t.,* **-vised, -vis·ing. 1** to advise against (a course, etc.). **2** to advise (a person) against a course, etc.

dis·af·fect (dis′ə fekt′), *v.t.,* to make unfriendly, disloyal, or discontented.

dis·af·fect·ed (dis′ə fek′tid), *adj.* unfriendly, disloyal, or discontented: *The disaffected crew decided to mutiny. A spokesman said the disaffected workers reported on the job yesterday morning* (Wall Street Journal).

dis·af·fec·tion (dis′ə fek′shən), *n.* unfriendliness, disloyalty, or discontent: *Lack of food and supplies caused disaffection among the soldiers.*

dis·af·fil·i·ate (dis′ə fil′ē āt), *v.t., v.i.,* **-at·ed, -at·ing.** to withdraw from affiliation with: *I wish to disaffiliate myself from any association with this enterprise* (New Yorker).

dis·af·fil·i·a·tion (dis′ə fil′ē ā′shən), *n.* **1** the act of withdrawing from affiliation with a society, an organization, or other group. **2** the state of being disaffiliated.

dis·af·firm (dis′ə fėrm′), *v.t.* **1** to contradict; deny. **2** *Law.* to reverse; repudiate; annul: *The witness disaffirmed his previous testimony.*

dis·af·firm·ance (dis′ə fėr′məns), *n.* **1** contradiction; denial. **2** *Law.* repudiation; annulment.

dis·af·fir·ma·tion (dis′af ər mā′shən), *n.* = disaffirmance.

dis·af·for·est (dis′ə fôr′ist, -for′-), *v.t.* **1** (in English law) to return to the legal status of ordinary land from that of a forest. **2** to strip or clear of forests or trees.

dis·af·for·est·a·tion (dis′ə fôr′ə stā′shən, -for′-), *n.* the act or process of disafforesting.

dis·af·for·est·ment (dis′ə fôr′ist mənt, -for′-), *n.* **1** the act of disafforesting. **2** the state of being disafforested.

dis·ag·gre·gate (*v.* dis ag′rə gāt; *adj.* dis ag′rəgit, -gāt), *v.,* **-gat·ed, -gat·ing,** *adj.* **—*v.t.*** to separate or break up into component parts.
—*adj.* disassembled; disjointed; disorganized: *Modern education is often a mélange of disaggregate studies.*

dis·ag·gre·ga·tion (dis ag′rə gā′shən), *n.* **1** the act or process of separating or breaking up into component parts. **2** the state of being disaggregated.

dis·ag·i·o (dis aj′ē ō), *n., pl.* **-i·os.** a charge levied for the exchange of a depreciated foreign currency.
[< *dis-*[2] + *agio*]

dis·a·gree (dis′ə grē′), *v.i.,* **-greed, -gree·ing. 1** to fail to agree; be different: *Your account of the incident disagrees with his.* **2** to have unlike opinions; differ: *Doctors sometimes disagree about the proper way to treat a patient.* **3** to quarrel; dispute: *The two neighbors never spoke to each other again after they disagreed about their boundary line.* **4** to have a bad effect; be harmful: *He can't eat strawberries because they disagree with him.*

dis·a·gree·a·ble (dis′ə grē′ə bəl), *adj., n.* **—*adj.* 1** not to one's liking; unpleasant: *to speak a disagreeable truth. A headache is disagreeable.* SYN: offensive. **2** not friendly; unkind; bad-tempered; cross: *She is sometimes disagreeable before breakfast.*
—*n.* a disagreeable thing: *. . . always . . . seeing difficulties and disagreeables in everything* (Elizabeth Gaskell). **—dis′a·gree′a·ble·ness,** *n.*

dis·a·gree·a·bly (dis′ə grē′ə blē), *adv.* in a disagreeable manner; unpleasantly: *Swedenborg is disagreeably wise . . . and repels* (Emerson).

dis·a·gree·ment (dis′ə grē′mənt), *n.* **1** a failure to agree; difference of opinion; dissent: *The disagreement that existed between members of the jury led to a new trial.* **2** a quarrel; dispute: *Their disagreement led to blows.* **3** difference; unlikeness: *There is a disagreement between his account of the incident and mine.* **4** unwholesome effect; unsuitableness.

dis·al·low (dis′ə lou′), *v.t.* to refuse to allow; deny the truth or value of; reject: *The court disallowed the man's claim to the property.*

dis·al·low·a·ble (dis′ə lou′ə bəl), *adj.* that may be or is subject to being disallowed.

dis·al·low·ance (dis′ə lou′əns), *n.* the act of disallowing; rejection: *He subsequently claimed the expenditure as a deductible business expense. This was disallowed by the tax collector and the disallowance was upheld in the courts* (Wall Street Journal).

dis·am·big·u·ate (dis′am big′yu̇ āt), *v.t.,* **-at·ed, -at·ing.** to rid (a sentence, statement, or the like) of ambiguity: *Given a syntactically ambiguous grammar, it is possible to use semantic information to disambiguate its syntax and construct a similar unambiguous grammar* (New Yorker).

dis·am·big·u·a·tion (dis′am big′yu̇ ā′shən), *n.* the act or process of disambiguating: *Harris has neglected an important problem, the disambiguation of homonymous structures* (Language).

dis·a·men·i·ty (dis′ə men′ə tē, -mē′nə-), *n. British.* **1** *no pl.* a lack or loss of amenity; inconvenience; trouble: *Two other rapidly growing sources of disamenity . . . are air travel and tourism* (New

Pronunciation Key: **hat, āge, cãre, fär; let, ēqual, tėrm; it, īce; hot, ōpen, ôrder; oil, out; cup, pu̇t, rüle; child; long; thin; ᴛʜen; zh,** measure;
ə represents **a** in about, **e** in taken, **i** in pencil, **o** in lemon, **u** in circus.

Scientist). **2** *pl.* **-ties**. a disagreeable feature or condition: *[He] regards much of modern building as ugly, and dreams of an enlightened committee with powers to deal with these disamenites* (Sunday Times).

dis|an|i|mate (dis an′ə māt), *v.t.*, **-mat|ed, -mat|ing. 1** to deprive of life; make lifeless. **2** to discourage; dishearten.

dis|an|i|ma|tion (dis an′ə mā′shən), *n.* **1** the act of depriving of life. **2** discouragement; a disheartening.

dis|an|nex (dis′ə neks′), *v.t.* to separate; disjoin; detach.

dis|an|nex|a|tion (dis an′ek sā′shən), *n.* the process of disannexing; separation.

dis|an|nul (dis′ə nul′), *v.t.*, **-nulled, -nul|ling.** to annul completely; make void.

dis|an|nul|ment (dis′ə nul′mənt), *n.* = annulment.

dis|a|noint (dis′ə noint′), *v.t.* to undo the anointing or consecration of.

dis|ap|pear (dis′ə pir′), *v.i.* **1** to pass from sight; stop being seen: *The little boy disappeared around the corner.* **2** to pass from existence; stop being; be lost: *When spring comes, the snow disappears.* **—dis′ap|pear′er,** *n.*

—*Syn.* 1 Disappear, vanish, fade mean to pass from sight. **Disappear,** the general term, means to pass out of sight slowly or quickly, gradually or suddenly: *He disappeared into the night.* **Vanish** means to disappear without a trace, usually suddenly, often in some strange or mysterious way: *The stranger suddenly vanished from town. When hungry boys sit down to eat, the food quickly vanishes.* **Fade** means to disappear little by little: *The ship faded into the fog.*

dis|ap|pear|ance (dis′ə pir′əns), *n.* the act of disappearing; vanishing: *The disappearance of the airplane brought about a search of the area. Not likely to be remembered a moment after their disappearance* (Joseph Addison).

dis|ap|pear|ing gun (dis′ə pir′ing), a gun which after being fired descends to the loading position behind the protection of a parapet.

dis|ap|point (dis′ə point′), *v.t.* **1** to fail to satisfy one's desire, wish, or hope; leave wanting something: *The circus disappointed him, for there was no elephant.* **2** to fail to keep a promise to: *You said you would help; do not disappoint me.* **3** to keep from happening; oppose and defeat: *He disappointeth the devices of the crafty, so that their hands cannot perform their enterprise* (Job 5:12). **—*v.i.*** to cause disappointment: *Sometimes, too, a character will disappoint by failing to emerge as I had hoped* (Saturday Review). **—dis′ap|point′er,** *n.*

dis|ap|point|ed (dis′ə poin′tid), *adj.* **1** made dissatisfied; not having one's hopes or desires realized; frustrated; thwarted: *a disappointed loser. And on the other side I heard recede the disappointed tide* (Emily Dickinson). **2** *Obsolete.* improperly equipped or prepared.

dis|ap|point|ed|ly (dis′ə poin′tid lē), *adv.* in a disappointed manner: *A large number of us old mossbacks disappointedly read the papers describing and detailing the trend toward a government to "do all for all" in Washington* (Wall Street Journal).

dis|ap|point|ing|ly (dis′ə poin′ting lē), *adv.* in a disappointing manner: *Although he seems to feel that American policy toward China has missed important opportunities, he is disappointingly vague on the specifics* (New York Times).

dis|ap|point|ment (dis′ə point′mənt), *n.* **1** the state of being or feeling disappointed; the feeling one has when one does not get what was expected or hoped for: *When she did not get a new bicycle, the disappointment seemed too great to bear. I have been too familiar with disappointments to be very much chagrined* (Abraham Lincoln). **2** a person or thing that causes disappointment: *Her lazy son was a disappointment to her.* **3** the act or fact of disappointing: *His disappointment of our wishes showed we could not rely on him.*

dis|ap|pro|ba|tion (dis′ap rə bā′shən), *n.* = disapproval.

dis|ap|pro|ba|tive (dis ap′rə bā′tiv), *adj.* expressing disapprobation; disapproving.

dis|ap|pro|ba|to|ry (dis ap′rə bə tôr′ē, -tōr′-), *adj.* = disapprobative.

dis|ap|prov|al (dis′ə prü′vəl), *n.* **1** opinion or feeling against; expression of an opinion against; dislike: *Hisses from the audience showed its disapproval of the speaker's remarks.* **2** the refusal to consent; rejection.

dis|ap|prove (dis′ə prüv′), *v.*, **-proved, -prov|ing. —*v.t.* 1** to consider not good or not suitable; have or express an opinion against: *Mother disapproves of rough games in the house. We disapprove rash behavior. Doctor Johnson condemns whatever he disapproves* (Fanny Burney). **2** to refuse consent to; reject: *The judge disapproved the verdict.* **—*v.i.*** to show dislike (of): *Most children disapprove of going to school in the summer.* **—dis′ap|prov′ing|ly,** *adv.*

dis|arm (dis ärm′), *v.t.* **1** to take weapons away from: *The police captured the robbers and disarmed them.* **2** to deprive of munitions of war or means of defense, often by tearing down or dismantling. **3** *Figurative.* to remove anger, dislike, or suspicion from; make friendly; calm the anger of: *The little boy's smile could always disarm those who were about to scold or punish him.* **4** to make harmless: *The soldiers disarmed the bomb by removing its fangs.* **—*v.i.* 1** to put down weapons. **2** to stop having an army and navy; reduce or limit armed forces or weapons: *The nations agreed to disarm.*

dis|ar|ma|ment (dis är′mə mənt), *n.* **1** the act of disarming. **2** the reduction of armies, navies, and their equipment: *Only controlled disarmament can make a viable world in the nuclear age* (Stuart Chase).

dis|arm|er (dis är′mər), *n.* **1** a person that disarms. **2** a proponent of disarmament: *Where would that early, wrathful disarmer [the prophet Isaiah] see any swords being beaten into plowshares?* (New Yorker).

dis|arm|ing (dis är′ming), *adj.* that disarms opponents; winning; agreeable: *He confessed his ignorance of farm problems in a most disarming way* (Maclean's). *With disarming open-mindedness, Brecht accepted . . . criticisms* (New York Times).

dis|arm|ing|ly (dis är′ming lē), *adv.* in a disarming manner.

dis|ar|range (dis′ə rānj′), *v.t.*, **-ranged, -rang|ing.** to disturb the arrangement of; put out of order: *The wind disarranged her hair.* **—dis′ar|rang′er,** *n.*

dis|ar|range|ment (dis′ə rānj′mənt), *n.* a disarranging or being disarranged.

dis|ar|ray (dis′ə rā′), *n.*, *v.* **—*n.* 1** lack of order; disorder; confusion: *There was disarray on the busy street after the bank robbers were chased and caught.* **2** disorder of clothing: *A wicked Hag . . . In ragged robes and filthy disarray* (Edmund Spenser).

—*v.t.* 1 to put into disorder or confusion. **2** to undress; strip.

dis|ar|tic|u|late (dis′är tik′yə lāt), *v.t., v.i.*, **-lat|ed, -lat|ing.** to separate at the joints: *One of the party, . . . found a large part of the disarticulated skeleton of a mammoth, an extinct elephant* (Science News Letter).

dis|ar|tic|u|la|tion (dis′är tik′yə lā′shən), *n.* the act or process of separating or condition of being separated at the joints.

dis|ar|tic|u|la|tor (dis′är tik′yə lā′tər), *n.* a person or thing that disarticulates.

dis|as|sem|ble (dis′ə sem′bəl), *v.t.*, **-bled, -bling.** to take apart: *The mechanic disassembled the motor to repair it. The 65 crystal chandeliers in the U.S. Capitol had been taken down, disassembled, washed prism by prism, reassembled and rehung* (Time).

dis|as|sem|bly (dis′ə sem′blē), *n.*, *pl.* **-blies. 1** the act or process of disassembling. **2** the state of being disassembled.

dis|as|sim|i|late (dis′ə sim′ə lāt), *v.t.*, **-lat|ed, -lat|ing.** to transform (assimilated substances) into less complex or waste substances; transform by catabolism.

dis|as|sim|i|la|tion (dis′ə sim′ə lā′shən), *n.* the act or process of disassimilating; catabolism.

dis|as|so|ci|ate (dis′ə sō′shē āt), *v.t.*, **-at|ed, -at|ing.** = dissociate.

dis|as|so|ci|a|tion (dis′ə sō′sē ā′shən, -shē-), *n.* = dissociation.

dis|as|ter (də zas′tər, -zäs′-), *n.* **1** an event that causes much suffering or loss; great misfortune. A destructive fire, flood, earthquake, or shipwreck, or great loss of money is a disaster. *Some unhappy master whom unmerciful disaster followed fast and followed faster* (Edgar Allan Poe). **2** *Obsolete.* an unfavorable aspect of a star or planet. [< Middle French *désastre* < Italian *disastro* < Latin *dis-* away, without + *astrum* star < Greek *ástron*]

—*Syn.* 1 Disaster, calamity, catastrophe mean a great misfortune. **Disaster** applies to an event which happens suddenly or unexpectedly, through human fault, mechanical or structural failure, or the forces of nature, and causes much loss and suffering: *The failure of the bank was a disaster for the farmers.* **Calamity** applies especially to a disaster which causes intense suffering and grief to a great number: *The attack on Pearl Harbor was a calamity.* **Catastrophe** suggests a disaster which is final and complete, causing loss that can never be made up: *A modern war is a catastrophe.*

disaster area, 1 any area which has suffered a disaster. **2** any area in the United States so severely stricken by disaster, such as a hurricane, earthquake, or business depression, that the people living in it are unable to maintain normal economic activity. By decree of the President such an area may become entitled to federal assistance.

dis|as|trous (də zas′trəs, -zäs′-), *adj.* **1** bringing disaster; causing much suffering, loss, pain, or sorrow; calamitous: *A disastrous hurricane struck the city, leaving thousands of people without food or homes.* **2** *Archaic.* foreboding disaster; or evil omen: *As when the sun . . . In dim eclipse, disastrous twilight sheds* (Milton). **—dis|as′trous|ly,** *adv.* **—dis|as′trous|ness,** *n.*

dis|a|vow (dis′ə vou′), *v.t.* to deny that one knows about, approves of, or is responsible for; disclaim; repudiate: *The prisoner disavowed any share in the plot to escape.* **—dis′a|vow′er,** *n.*

dis|a|vow|al (dis′ə vou′əl), *n.* a disavowing; denial; repudiation: *An official disavowal followed* (Edward Edwards).

dis|bal|ance (dis bal′əns), *n.* the state of being unbalanced; disproportion: *Undeveloped countries have a disbalance between population growth and economic resources.*

dis|band (dis band′), *v.t.* **1** to break up (a band or company); dismiss from service: *When peace is declared, armies are disbanded.* **2** *Obsolete.* to dissolve; disintegrate. **—*v.i.*** to break ranks; become scattered: *The class disbanded for the summer vacation.*

dis|band|ment (dis band′mənt), *n.* the act or process of disbanding or state of being disbanded: *There are those whose attachment to the traditions of our conventional forces prevents their accepting the disbandment of famous regiments or the closing of historic dockyards* (Sunday Times).

dis|bar (dis bär′), *v.t.*, **-barred, -bar|ring.** to take away from (a lawyer) the right to practice law.

dis|bar|ment (dis bär′mənt), *n.* the act or process of disbarring or state of being disbarred.

dis|be|lief (dis′bi lēf′), *n.* lack of belief; refusal to believe: *When he heard the shocking rumor, he immediately expressed disbelief. His father showed disbelief in Michael's fantastic story of lions and tigers.* **SYN:** See syn. under **unbelief.**

dis|be|lieve (dis′bi lēv′), *v.*, **-lieved, -liev|ing. —*v.t.* 1** to have no belief in; refuse to believe: *His father disbelieved the boy's story that a lion had come into his room in the middle of the night.* **2** to reject as false or undocumented: *The extermination camps of the Nazi terror are in danger of being forgotten or disbelieved by some people* (Manchester Guardian).

—*v.i.* to have no faith or belief (in).

dis|be|liev|er (dis′bi lē′vər), *n.* a person who disbelieves.

dis|be|liev|ing (dis′bi lē′ving), *adj.* of or showing disbelief: *He broke off, realizing that . . . he was getting no more than a polite and disbelieving attention* (Harper's). **—dis′be|liev′ing|ly,** *adv.*

dis|bench (dis bench′), *v.t.* **1** to remove from or deprive of a bench or seat. **2** (in English law) to deprive of the status of a bencher.

dis|bench|ment (dis bench′mənt), *n.* the act or process of disbenching or state of being disbenched.

dis|ben|e|fit (dis ben′ə fit), *n.* a lack or absence of benefit: *The disbenefits are difficult to establish and easy to underestimate: how much is a clean river worth to the citizens along its banks?* (New Scientist and Science Journal).

dis|bod|y (dis bod′ē), *v.t.*, **-bod|ied, -bod|y|ing.** = disembody.

dis|bos|om (dis bu̇z′əm, -bü′zəm), *v.t.* = unbosom.

dis|bound (dis bound′), *adj.* having a torn, loose, or poor binding; having come unbound: *Disbound copies of books should be repaired.*

dis|bow|el (dis bou′əl), *v.t.*, **-eled, -el|ing.** or (*especially British*) **-elled, -el|ling.** = disembowel.

dis|brain (dis brān′), *v.t.* to deprive of the brain; remove the brain from.

dis|branch (dis branch′, -bränch′), *v.t.* **1** to cut or break off the branches of. **2** to cut or break off (a branch).

dis|bud (dis bud′), *v.t.*, **-bud|ded, -bud|ding. 1** to deprive of buds or shoots. **2** to remove unnecessary buds from: *Many plants, if they are disbudded, will produce larger, though fewer, flowers.*

dis|bur|den (dis bėr′dən), *v.t.* **1** to relieve of a burden: (*Figurative.*) *The boy disburdened his mind to his mother by confessing that he had broken the expensive lamp accidentally.* **2** to get rid of (a burden); unload. **—*v.i.*** to unload; discharge a load.

dis|bur|den|ment (dis bėr′dən mənt), *n.* the act of disburdening or state of being disburdened.

dis|burs|a|ble (dis bėr′sə bəl), *adj.* that can be disbursed.

dis|bur|sal (dis bėr′səl), *n.* the act of disbursing; disbursement.

dis|burse (dis bėrs′), *v.t.*, **-bursed, -burs|ing.** to pay out; expend: *The treasurer is in charge of disbursing money to pay the club's bills. Our city treasurer disburses thousands of dollars each week.* SYN: See syn. under **spend**. [< Old French *desbourser* < *des-* away (< Latin *dis-*) + *bourse* purse < Late Latin *bursa* < Greek *býrsa* leather. Compare etym. under **bursa**.]

dis|burse|ment (dis bėrs′mənt), *n.* **1** the act of paying out: *Our treasurer attends to the disbursement of funds.* **2** money paid out; expenditure: *Disbursements must stay within the budget.*

dis|burs|er (dis bėr′sər), *n.* a person or thing that disburses.

dis|bur|then (dis bėr′ᴛʜən), *v.t., v.i. Archaic.* disburden.

dis|bur|then|ment (dis bėr′ᴛʜən mənt), *n. Archaic.* disburdenment.

disc[1] (disk), *n., v.t.* = disk.

disc[2] (disk), *n. Informal.* discothèque: *After that, how about a night on the town at one of the local discs* (New Yorker).

disc., **1** discount. **2a** discovered. **b** discoverer.

dis|cage (dis kāj′), *v.t.,* **-caged, -cag|ing.** to release from or as if from a cage.

dis|caire (dis kãr′), *n.* a person who selects the records to be played at a discothèque. [< French *disquaire*]

dis|cal (dis′kəl), *adj.* of a disk; having to do with or like a disk.

dis|cal|ce|ate (dis kal′sē it, -āt), *adj.* barefooted; unshod. [< Late Latin *discalceātus,* past participle of *discalceāre;* see etym. under **discalced**]

dis|calced (dis kalst′), *adj.* barefooted; unshod: *The members of certain orders of friars and nuns are discalced.* [< Late Latin *discalceāre* pull off one's shoes (< *dis-* off + *calceāre* to shoe < *calceus* shoe < *calx, calcis*) + English *-ed*[2]]

dis|cant (*v.* dis kant′; *n.* dis′kant), *v.i., n.* = descant.

dis|card (*v.* dis kärd′; *n.* dis′kärd), *v., n.* — ***v.t.*** **1** to give up as useless or worn out; throw aside: *You can discard clothes, ways of doing things, or beliefs. Father repaired the toy that I had discarded.* SYN: reject. **2a** to get rid of (playing cards not wanted) by throwing them aside or playing them. **b** to play (a card that is not a trump and not of the suit led).
— ***v.i.*** to throw out an unwanted card.
— ***n.*** **1** the act of throwing aside as useless or not wanted: *the deliberate discard of superstition comes with learning.* SYN: rejection. **2** a thing or things thrown aside as useless or not wanted: *Although she needed clothes, she was too proud to take my discards.* **3** the cards thrown aside or played as not wanted.
[< *dis-*[2] + *card*[1]] — **dis|card′er**, *n.*

dis|card|a|ble (dis kär′də bəl), *adj.* **1** that can be discarded; worthless: *... a yard of discardable verbiage* (Sunday Times). **2** that can be thrown away after being used once; disposable: *discardable containers. Discardable clothing made of miracle fibres ... are also future possibilities* (Maclean's).

dis|card|ment (dis kärd′mənt), *n.* the act of discarding; rejection.

dis|car|nate (dis kär′nit, -nāt), *adj.* divested of the flesh or the body; disembodied.

dis|car|na|tion (dis′kär nā′shən), *n.* = disembodiment.

dis|case (dis kās′), *v.t.,* **-cased, -cas|ing.** to uncase; strip.

disc brake, = disk brake.

dis|cept (di sept′), *v.i.* to dispute; debate; differ. [< Latin *disceptāre* debate, determine < *dis-* separately + *captāre* strive after (frequentative) < *capere* to catch]

dis|cep|ta|tion (dis′ep tā′shən), *n.* a dispute; controversy.

dis|cern (də zėrn′, -sėrn′), *v.t.* to perceive; see clearly; distinguish or recognize: *Through the fog I could just discern a car coming toward me. When there are many conflicting opinions, it is hard to discern the truth. Not till the hours of light return, All we have built do we discern* (Matthew Arnold). — ***v.i.*** to distinguish; make a distinction; discriminate: *The Philosopher whose discoveries now dazzle us could not once discern between his right hand and his left* (William Ellery Channing). [< Old French *discerner* distinguish, separate, learned borrowing from Latin *discernere* < *dis-* off, away + *cernere* distinguish, separate] — **dis|cern′er**, *n.*

dis|cern|i|ble (də zėr′nə bəl, -sėr′-), *adj.* that can be discerned; perceptible: *The island was barely discernible through the mist.* — **dis|cern′i|ble|ness**, *n.*

dis|cern|i|bly (də zėr′nə blē, -sėr′-), *adv.* in a manner so as to be discerned; perceptibly.

dis|cern|ing (də zėr′ning, -sėr′-), *adj.* keen in seeing and understanding; with good judgment; shrewd; acute; discriminating: *A more discerning mind, a shrewder tongue, I have never met.* — **dis|cern′ing|ly**, *adv.*

dis|cern|ment (də zėrn′mənt, -sėrn′-), *n.* **1** keenness in seeing and understanding; good judgment; shrewdness: *The eye of the soul acquires a discernment whereby some can instantly read the character of others* (Cardinal Manning). SYN: See syn. under **insight**. **2** the act of discerning: *It is in the discernment of place, of time, and of person that the inferior artists fail* (Macaulay).

dis|cerp (də sėrp′), *v.t. Archaic.* **1** to tear into pieces; divide into parts. **2** to tear off; separate. [< Latin *discerpere* < *dis-* apart + *carpere* to pluck]

dis|cerp|ti|bil|i|ty (də sėrp′tə bil′ə tē), *n.* = divisibility.

dis|cerp|ti|ble (də sėrp′tə bəl), *adj.* that can be torn into pieces or divided into parts; divisible; separable. [< Latin *discerptus,* past participle of Latin *discerpere* (< *dis-* apart + *carpere* to pluck) + English *-ible*]

dis|cerp|tion (də sėrp′shən), *n.* the act of tearing apart into pieces; division into parts.

dis|charge (*v.* dis chärj′; *n.* dis chärj′, dis′chärj), *v.,* **-charged, -charg|ing,** *n.* — ***v.t.*** **1** to release; let go; dismiss: *to discharge a patient from a hospital, discharge a committee, discharge a lazy employee, discharge a prisoner.* SYN: See syn. under **dismiss**. **2** to fire off; shoot: *The policeman discharged his gun at the fleeing robbers.* **3** to give off; let out: *The infection discharged pus.* **4a** to unload (cargo or passengers) from a ship, train, bus, automobile, or airplane: *The taxi discharged its passengers at the hotel.* **b** to unload (a ship). **5** to rid of an electric charge; withdraw electricity from. **6** *Figurative.* to perform (a duty or function): *to discharge the duties of postman. He discharged all the errands he had been given.* SYN: See syn. under **perform**. **7** to pay (a debt or other obligation): *You discharge a loan when you return the money.* **8** *Figurative.* to release from an obligation; exempt: *to discharge a debtor from his debts.* **9** *Law.* to cancel or set aside (a court order). **10** *Architecture.* **a** to transfer and distribute (a load). **b** to relieve (a part) of weight or pressure by distributing over adjacent parts. **11** to remove or bleach (a dye or color) from a textile, cloth, etc.
— ***v.i.*** **1** (of a gun) to go off: *The pistol discharged accidentally.* **2** to come or pour forth: *The river discharges into a bay.* **3** to lose an electric charge. **4** to unload cargo or passengers from a ship, train, bus, automobile, or airplane. **5** (of ink, dye, or other coloring matter) to run.
— ***n.*** **1a** a release; a letting go; a dismissing: *an honorable discharge from the army. The prisoner expects his discharge from jail next week.* **b** a writing that shows a person's release or dismissal; certificate of release: *Many members of the armed forces got discharges when the war ended.* **2** a firing off of a gun or a blast: *The discharge of dynamite could be heard for three miles.* **3** a giving off; a letting out: *Lightning is a discharge of electricity in the atmosphere.* **4** a thing given off or let out: *a watery discharge from the eye.* **5** the rate of flow: *The discharge from the pipe is ten gallons a second.* **6** an unloading: *The discharge of this cargo will not take long.* **7** *Figurative.* the performing of a duty: *A public servant should be honest in the discharge of his duties.* **8** *Figurative.* payment (of a debt or other obligation): *Money was set aside for the discharge of the debt.* **9** *Electricity.* **a** the transference of electricity between two charged bodies when placed in contact with or near each other. **b** the equalization of electric potential difference between terminals. **10** *Law.* **a** exoneration; acquittal. **b** the dismissal or reversal of a court order.
[< Old French *descharger* < Vulgar Latin *discarricāre* < Latin *dis-* away, un- + *carricāre* to charge]

dis|charge|a|ble (dis chär′jə bəl), *adj.* that can be or is to be discharged: *The notes are dischargeable in three years.*

dis|charg|er (dis chär′jər), *n.* **1** a person or thing that discharges. **2** *Electricity.* an instrument or device for discharging the electricity from a charged body.

discharge tube, a vacuum tube containing a low-pressure gas or vapor which conducts an electric current when sufficient voltage is applied.

dis|ci (dis′ī), *n.* discuses; a plural of **discus**.

dis|cif|er|ous (də sif′ər əs), *adj. Botany.* bearing disks; having a disk. [< Latin *discus* disk + English *-ferous*]

***discifloral**

discifloral flower

***dis|ci|flo|ral** (dis′ə flôr′əl, -flōr′-), *adj. Botany.* having flowers in which the receptacle is enlarged into a conspicuous disk surrounding the ovary, and usually distinct from the calyx. [< Latin *discus* disk + English *floral*]

dis|ci|form (dis′ə fôrm), *adj.* disk-shaped; discoid. [< Latin *discus* disk + English *-form*]

dis|cig|er|ous (də sij′ər əs), *adj.* bearing disks. [< Latin *discus* disk + *gerere* to bear + English *-ous*]

dis|ci|ple (də sī′pəl), *n., v.,* **-pled, -pling.** — ***n.*** **1** a believer in the thought and teaching of a leader; follower: *The famous doctor had many disciples among his young medical students.* SYN: See syn. under **follower**. **2** one of the followers of Jesus, especially one of the twelve Apostles: *The disciples of Jesus spread Christianity throughout much of the area around the Mediterranean.*
— ***v.t.*** **1** *Archaic.* to make a disciple or disciples of. **2** *Obsolete.* to teach; train; educate.
[Old English *discipul* < Latin *discipulus* pupil < unrecorded *discipere* to grasp, apprehend < *dis-* apart, away + *capere* seize]

dis|ci|ple|ship (də sī′pəl ship), *n.* **1** the state of being a disciple. **2** the time of being a disciple.

Dis|ci|ples of Christ (də sī′pəlz), a Protestant religious sect founded in the United States in 1809 that rejects all forms and creeds and seeks to unite Christians on the basis of the New Testament only; Christian Church.

dis|ci|plin|a|ble (dis′ə plin′ə bəl), *adj.* **1** that can be disciplined or instructed. **2** deserving discipline.

dis|ci|pli|nal (dis′ə plī′nəl, dis′ə plə nəl), *adj.* of or having to do with discipline.

Dis|ci|plin|ant (dis′ə plə nənt), *n.* a member of a former religious order in Spain whose followers whipped and punished themselves publicly. [< Spanish *disciplinantes,* plural < Medieval Latin *disciplinare* chastise, beat with rods < Latin *disciplīna* discipline]

dis|ci|plin|ant (dis′ə plə nənt), *n.* a person who subjects himself to discipline.

dis|ci|pli|nar|i|an (dis′ə plə nãr′ē ən), *n., adj.* — ***n.*** a person who enforces discipline or who believes in strict discipline.
— ***adj.*** = disciplinary.

dis|ci|pli|nar|i|an|ism (dis′ə plə nãr′ē ə niz′əm), *n.* the principles and practice of a disciplinarian.

dis|ci|pli|nar|y (dis′ə plə ner′ē), *adj.* **1** having to do with discipline: *Our teacher has no disciplinary problems, since the children in the class are well behaved.* **2** for discipline; intended to improve discipline: *After the prisoners rioted, the warden took disciplinary measures.*

dis|ci|pli|na|to|ry (dis′ə plə nā′tər ē), *adj.* disciplinary.

dis|ci|pline (dis′ə plin), *n., v.,* **-plined, -plin|ing.** — ***n.*** **1** training, especially training of the mind or character: *Children who have had no discipline are often hard to teach.* **2** the training effect of experience, misfortune, or other happenings: *The discipline of his early hardships contributed to his success.* **3** a trained condition of order and obedience: *Learning a language imposes a discipline on the mind.* **4** order kept among school pupils, soldiers, or members of any group: *When the fire broke out, the students showed good discipline.* **5** a particular system of rules for conduct: *The discipline of a military school is usually strict.* **6** punishment; chastisement: *A little discipline would do him good.* **7** a branch of instruction or education: *Both Latin and mathematics are disciplines that require an analytical approach.* **8** methods or rules for regulating the conduct of members of a church. **9** control exercised over members of a church.
— ***v.t.*** **1** to train; bring to a condition of order and obedience; bring under control: *An officer must know how to discipline the untrained recruits.* **2** to punish; chastise: *You ought to discipline that rude boy for bad behavior.*
[< Latin *disciplīna* < *discipulus;* see etym. under **disciple**]

dis|ci|plin|ed|ly (dis′ə plind lē, -plin′id lē), *adv.* in a disciplined or controlled manner; with discipline: *The ... performers all work disciplinedly at their jobs in the best tradition of ensemble acting* (Saturday Review).

dis|ci|plin|er (dis′ə plə nər), *n.* a person who disciplines.

dis|cip|u|lar (də sip′yə lər), *adj.* of or befitting a disciple; being a disciple.

disc jockey, = disk jockey.

dis|claim (dis klām′), *v.t.* **1** to refuse to recognize as one's own; deny connection with: *The motorist disclaimed responsibility for the accident.* **2** to give up all claim to: *She disclaimed any share in the inheritance.* **3** *Obsolete.* to renounce; disa-

Pronunciation Key: hat, āge, cãre, fär; let, ēqual, tėrm, it, īce; hot, ōpen, ôrder; oil, out; cup, pu̇t, rüle; child; long; thin; ᴛʜen; zh, measure; ə represents **a** in about, **e** in taken, **i** in pencil, **o** in lemon, **u** in circus.

vow. —*v.i.* to give up all legal claim or right.

dis|claim|er (dis klā′mər), *n.* **1** the act of disclaiming; denial; rejection. **2** a person who disclaims. **3a** a statement denying responsibility for some act or condition. **b** a clause in an agreement relieving one party of responsibility for carrying out certain provisions under certain circumstances.

dis|cla|ma|tion (dis′klə mā′shən), *n.* the act of disclaiming; renunciation; disavowal.

dis|clam|a|to|ry (dis klam′ə tôr′ē, -tōr′-), *adj.* disclaiming; like a disclamation.

disc|less (disk′lis), *adj.* = diskless.

dis|close (dis klōz′), *v.*, **-closed, -clos|ing,** *n.* —*v.t.* **1** to open to view; uncover: *The lifting of the curtain disclosed a beautiful painting.* **2** to make known; reveal: *This letter discloses a secret.* **SYN:** See syn. under **reveal. 3** *Obsolete.* to unfold; unfasten. —*n. Obsolete.* disclosure.

dis|clos|er (dis klō′zər), *n.* a person who discloses or reveals.

dis|clo|sure (dis klō′zhər), *n.* **1** the act of disclosing: *disclosure of a secret. His reluctant disclosure of his whereabouts led to many misunderstandings.* **2** a thing disclosed; revelation: *The newspaper's disclosures shocked the public.*

dis|co (dis′kō), *n., pl.* **-cos,** *v.,* **-coed, -co|ing.** —*n.* **1** *Informal.* discothèque. **2** *U.S.* music played in discothèques, especially rhythm and blues characterized by a strong, rhythmic bass: *WPIX-FM recently switched several hours of its nightly programming over to "disco"* (New York Times).
—*v.i. U.S.* to dance to disco music: *You can disco to your heart's content at Clark Center* (New York Post).

dis|cob|o|lus (dis kob′ə ləs), *n., pl.* **-li** (-lī). a thrower of the discus in ancient Greece or Rome. [< Latin *discobolus* < Greek *diskobólos* < *dískos* discus + *bólos* a throwing (of a fishing net) < *bál-lein* to throw]

Dis|cob|o|lus (dis kob′ə ləs), *n.* a statue of a man about to throw the discus, made by the Greek sculptor Myron in the 400's B.C.

dis|cog|ra|pher (dis kog′rə fər), *n.* the compiler of a discography.

dis|co|graph|ic (dis′kə graf′ik), *adj.* = discographical.

dis|co|graph|i|cal (dis′kə graf′ə kəl), *adj.* of or having to do with discography.

dis|cog|ra|phy (dis kog′rə fē), *n., pl.* **-phies. 1** a list of phonograph disks or of writings about them: *The 120-page discography is exhaustive* (Manchester Guardian). **2** the history of recorded music, records, and recording performers.

dis|coid (dis′koid), *adj., n.* —*adj.* **1** having the form of a disk; disk-shaped. **2** *Botany.* (of composite plants) having a flower head containing only tubular flowers in the central disk, with no ray flowers. The tansy is a discoid plant. —*n.* a disk-shaped thing. [< Late Latin *discoīdes* < Greek *diskoeidês* < *diskos* discus + *eîdos* form]

dis|coi|dal (dis koi′dəl), *adj.* = discoid.

dis|col|or (dis kul′ər), *v.t.* to change or spoil the color of; stain: *Smoke had discolored the building.* —*v.i.* to become changed in color: *Many materials fade and discolor if exposed to sunshine.* [< Old French *descoulourer* < Late Latin *discolōrārī* < *dis-* away + *colōr* color]

dis|col|or|a|tion (dis kul′ə rā′shən), *n.* **1** the act of discoloring. **2** the state of being discolored. **3** a stain.

dis|col|or|ment (dis kul′ər mənt), *n.* = discoloration.

dis|col|our (dis kul′ər), *v.t., v.i. Especially British.* discolor.

dis|co|ma|ni|a (dis′kə mā′nē ə), *n.* love of phonograph records: *The most disturbing feature of the current discomania is that many quite sincere music lovers are losing the taste for live music* (Punch).

dis|com|bob|u|late (dis′kəm bob′yə lāt), *v.t.,* **-lat|ed, -lat|ing.** *Slang.* to confuse; disconcert; perplex: *... a platoon of press agents and photographers, who had instructions to discombobulate opponents* (New Yorker). [probably alteration of *discompose* and *discomfit*]

dis|com|bob|u|la|tion (dis′kəm bob′yə lā′shən), *n. Slang.* a discombobulated state or condition.

dis|com|fit (dis kum′fit), *v., n.* —*v.t.* **1** to defeat completely; rout: *The enemy was discomfited by our sudden attack from ambush. Joshua discomfited Amalek and his people with the edge of the sword* (Exodus 17:13). **SYN:** overthrow, vanquish. **2** to defeat the plans or hopes of; frustrate: *Our dreams are often discomfited by reality.* **SYN:** foil. **3** to embarrass greatly; confuse; disconcert: *Those who did not do the reading were discomfited by the teacher's question.* **SYN:** abash.
—*n. Obsolete.* discomfiture.
[< Old French *desconfit,* past participle of *desconfire* undo, destroy < *des-* completely (< Latin *dis-*) + *confire* make, accomplish < Latin *conficere* finish up, destroy < *com-* with, together + *facere* make, do] —**dis|com′fit|er,** *n.*

dis|com|fit|ing|ly (dis kum′fit ing lē), *adv.* in a discomfiting manner; embarrassingly: *By discomfitingly small margins, the measure squeaked through Congress* (Time).

dis|com|fi|ture (dis kum′fi chůr, -chər), *n.* **1** a complete defeat; rout. **SYN:** overthrow. **2** a defeat of plans or hopes; frustration: *After five days' exertion, this man of indomitable will and invincible fortune resigns the task in discomfiture and despair* (Benjamin Disraeli). **3** great embarrassment; confusion: *The crowd laughed at the discomfiture of the fireman who had to ask where the fire was.*

dis|com|fort (dis kum′fərt), *n., v.* —*n.* **1** lack of comfort; uneasiness: *Embarrassing questions cause discomfort.* **2** a thing that causes discomfort: *Mud and cold were the discomforts the campers minded most.* **SYN:** inconvenience.
—*v.t.* to make uncomfortable or uneasy: *The hiker was discomforted by a pair of tight boots.*

dis|com|fort|a|ble (dis kum′fər tə bəl), *adj.* making uncomfortable or uneasy; lacking comfort or convenience: *Pacing to and fro in his discomfortable house* (Robert Louis Stevenson).

discomfort index, = temperature-humidity index. *Abbr:* DI (no periods), D.I.

dis|com|mend (dis′kə mend′), *v.t.* **1** to find fault with; express disapproval of: *Who else shall discommend her choice* (Coventry Patmore). **2** to bring into disfavor. —**dis′com|mend′er,** *n.*

dis|com|mend|a|ble (dis′kə men′də bəl), *adj.* to be discommended; worthy of censure.

dis|com|men|da|tion (dis′kom ən dā′shən), *n.* the act of discommending; dispraise: *Following the guidebook line, 'Nothing need detain the tourist here,' some discommendations for persons planning a trip to Europe* (Joseph Wechsberg).

dis|com|mode (dis′kə mōd′), *v.t.,* **-mod|ed, -mod|ing.** to put to inconvenience; disturb; trouble: *His late arrival discommoded us.*

dis|com|mo|di|ous (dis′kə mō′dē əs), *adj.* causing trouble or inconvenience; disadvantageous; troublesome. —**dis′com|mo′di|ous|ly,** *adv.* —**dis′com|mo′di|ous|ness,** *n.*

dis|com|mod|i|ty (dis′kə mod′ə tē), *n., pl.* **-ties. 1** inconvenience: *You go about, in rain or fine, at all hours, without discommodity* (Charles Lamb). **2** a disadvantage; source of inconvenience or trouble. **3** *Economics.* a thing that should be gotten rid of.

dis|com|mon (dis kom′ən), *v.t. Law.* **1** to deprive of the right to use a common. **2** to change (land) from a common to private land. **3** *Especially British.* to deprive (a tradesman) of the privilege of selling to students, especially at Oxford and Cambridge universities.

dis|com|pose (dis′kəm pōz′), *v.t.,* **-posed, -pos|ing. 1** to disturb the self-possession of; make uneasy; ruffle: *The grins of his friends discomposed him when he tried to make his report before the class.* **SYN:** agitate, disquiet, confuse. **2** to bring into disorder; disarrange; unsettle: *Better for Us ... That never passion discompos'd the mind* (Alexander Pope). **SYN:** disorder.

dis|com|pos|ed|ly (dis′kəm pō′zid lē), *adv.* in a discomposed manner; uneasily.

dis|com|pos|ing|ly (dis′kəm pō′zing lē), *adv.* in a way that discomposes or disturbs.

dis|com|po|sure (dis′kəm pō′zhər), *n.* the state of being discomposed; confusion; uneasiness; embarrassment. **SYN:** agitation, perturbation.

dis|con|cert (dis′kən sėrt′), *v.t.* **1** to disturb the self-possession of; embarrass greatly; confuse: *He was disconcerted to find that he had come to school wearing one brown sock and one black sock. I was disconcerted by this unexpected opposition.* **SYN:** See syn. under **confuse. 2** to upset or frustrate (plans or measures); disorder: *The chairman's plans were disconcerted when the speaker of the evening did not show up.*

dis|con|cert|ed (dis′kən sėr′tid), *adj.* disturbed from self-possession; confused; embarrassed. —**dis′con|cert′ed|ly,** *adv.* —**dis′con|cert′ed|ness,** *n.*

dis|con|cert|ing|ly (dis′kən sėr′ting lē), *adv.* in a disconcerting manner.

dis|con|cer|tion (dis′kən sėr′shən), *n.* = disconcertment.

dis|con|cert|ment (dis′kən sėrt′mənt), *n.* **1** the act of disconcerting. **2** the state of being disconcerted.

dis|con|firm (dis′kən fėrm′), *v.t.* to refuse to confirm; reject; invalidate; disprove: *to disconfirm an order, a theory, etc.*

dis|con|fir|ma|tion (dis kon′fər mā′shən), *n.* the act of disconfirming; invalidation; disproval: *Criteria of valid deduction can be and have been supplied providing general criteria of confirmation and disconfirmation* [*of hypotheses*] (Scientific American).

dis|con|form (dis′kən fôrm′), *v.i.* to not conform; be dissimilar: *The buyers had failed to prove that the cloth disconformed to contract* (London Times).

dis|con|form|a|ble (dis′kən fôr′mə bəl), *adj.* not conformable.

dis|con|for|ma|tion (dis kon′fôr mā′shən), *n.* a disconforming; failure or refusal to conform.

dis|con|form|i|ty (dis′kən fôr′mə tē), *n., pl.* **-ties. 1** the refusal or failure to conform; nonconformity. **2** *Geology.* an unconformity in which the strata above and below the contact are parallel.

dis|con|nect (dis′kə nekt′), *v., n.* —*v.t.* to undo or break the connection of; separate; unfasten; detach: *He disconnected the electric fan by pulling out the plug.*
—*n.* **1** something that disconnects: *The ... combination starter is equipped with a circuit breaker as the disconnect* (Scientific American). **2** a disconnection: *He got a busy signal, two no-answers, and a disconnect* (New York Times).

dis|con|nect|ed (dis′kə nek′tid), *adj.* **1** not connected; separate: *Our house and the garage are entirely disconnected.* **2** without order or connection; incoherent; broken: *The injured man could give only a disconnected account of the accident.* —**dis′con|nect′ed|ly,** *adv.* —**dis′con|nect′ed|ness,** *n.*

dis|con|nec|tion (dis′kə nek′shən), *n.* **1** the act of disconnecting. **2** the state of being disconnected; separation.

dis|con|nex|ion (dis′kə nek′shən), *n. Especially British.* disconnection.

dis|con|sid|er (dis′kən sid′ər), *v.t.* to discredit; bring into disrepute: *The man was now disconsidered and as good as deposed* (Robert Louis Stevenson).

dis|con|sid|er|a|tion (dis′kən sid′ə rā′shən), *n.* **1** the act of disconsidering. **2** the fact of being disconsidered; disrepute.

dis|con|so|la|cy (dis kon′sə lə sē), *n.* a being disconsolate; disconsolateness; unhappiness: *The false face may be used to conceal age, ill-health, tiredness, or disconsolacy* (New Yorker).

dis|con|so|late (dis kon′sə lit), *adj.* **1** without hope; forlorn; unhappy: *The cat was disconsolate because her kitten died.* **SYN:** dejected, sad. **2** causing discomfort; cheerless; gloomy; dismal: *a long and disconsolate day.* **SYN:** See syn. under **desolate.** [< Medieval Latin *disconsolatus* < Latin *dis-* away, un- + *cōnsōlārī* < *com-* (intensive) + *sōlārī* soothe] —**dis|con′so|late|ly,** *adv.* —**dis|con′so|late|ness,** *n.*

dis|con|so|la|tion (dis kon′sə lā′shən), *n.* disconsolate state or feeling; disconsolateness.

dis|con|tent (dis′kən tent′), *n., v., adj.* —*n.* **1** a dislike of what one has and a desire for something different; uneasy feeling; dissatisfaction; restlessness: *Low pay and long hours of work caused discontent among the factory workers. Lose not in sullen discontent your peace* (John Gay). **SYN:** uneasiness. **2** a discontented person; malcontent: *It should not be assumed, however, that all the Tory discontents approach the defence problem from the same point of view* (Manchester Guardian).
—*v.t.* to displease; dissatisfy: *So fearful I am of discontenting my wife* (Samuel Pepys). *... attempts to discontent the public mind* (George Washington).
—*adj.* discontented; dissatisfied.

dis|con|tent|ed (dis′kən ten′tid), *adj.* not contented; not satisfied; displeased and restless: *She was discontented with the lonely life in the country. The unhappy woman habitually wore a discontented expression. The discontented workers went on strike. The troops, discontented with his treatment of them ... refused to obey* (Robert Watson). **SYN:** dissatisfied. —**dis′con|tent′ed|ly,** *adv.* —**dis′con|tent′ed|ness,** *n.*

dis|con|tent|ment (dis′kən tent′mənt), *n.* discontented state or feeling; discontent.

dis|con|tin|u|ance (dis′kən tin′yů əns), *n.* **1** the act of stopping or breaking off; cessation: *a discontinuance of electric service. Losses from the manufacture of low-priced electric blankets ... have led to the discontinuance of those products* (Wall Street Journal). **2** *Law.* the termination of an action at the plaintiff's request or by his failure to take the proper steps to keep it pending.

dis|con|tin|u|a|tion (dis′kən tin′yů ā′shən), *n.* **1** the act of breaking off; a stopping; a ceasing. **SYN:** cessation. **2** a break; interruption.

dis|con|tin|ue (dis′kən tin′yü), *v.,* **-tin|ued, -tin|u|ing.** —*v.t.* **1** to give up; stop; put an end or stop to; break off: *That train has been discontinued. After the patient got well, the doctor discontinued his visits.* **2** to cease from; cease to take, use, receive, give, or pay: *They decided to discontinue the evening newspaper.* **SYN:** quit. **3** *Law.* to terminate (a suit) by request of the plaintiff or by his failing to continue it.
—*v.i.* to come to an end or stop; cease: *When the strike began railroad service discontinued abruptly.*

dis|con|tin|u|er (dis′kən tin′yü ər), *n.* a person who discontinues a rule or practice.

dis|con|ti|nu|i|ty (dis′kon tə nü′ə tē, -nyü′-), *n., pl.* **-ties.** **1** lack of connection: *The story's plot was ruined by its discontinuity.* **2** a break or gap in something: *Colour distortions caused by sharp discontinuities in spectral radiation are generally unacceptable for interior lighting where the visual environment is of any consequence* (J. B. Collins). **3** *Geology.* the boundary of a layer or formation at which marked changes in earthquake waves occur, such as the Mohorovicic discontinuity or the surface of the earth itself.

discontinuity layer, 1 the layer between the earth's crust and mantle; Mohorovicic discontinuity. **2** a layer of water between parts that differ markedly in temperature; thermocline.

dis|con|tin|u|ous (dis′kən tin′yü əs), *adj.* not continuous; having gaps or breaks; interrupted; intermittent: *Wide spread the discontinuous ruins lie* (Nicholas Rowe). SYN: broken. **—dis′con|tin′u|ous|ly,** *adv.* **—dis′con|tin′u|ous|ness,** *n.*

discontinuous spectrum, = bright-line spectrum.

discontinuous variation, *Biology.* a sudden change in the form or structure of an organism virtually without intermediate forms; mutation: *When we study physiology as well as morphology, discontinuous variation turns out to be very common* (J. B. S. Haldane).

dis|co|or|di|na|tion (dis′kō ôr′də nā′shən), *n.* lack of coordination: *... production of discoordination and stupor by overdosage* (New Scientist).

dis|co|phil (dis′kə fil), *n.* = discophile.

dis|co|phile (dis′kə fīl, -fil), *n.* a person who loves phonograph records and discography: *The discophile can hear his favourite performance whenever he wishes; there is no denying the almost fatal convenience of the gramophone* (London Times). [< Latin *discus* disk + English *-phile*]

dis|cord (*n.* dis′kôrd; *v.* dis kôrd′), *n., v.* **—n.** **1** difference of opinion; disputing; disagreement: *Constant argument caused angry discord that spoiled the meeting.* SYN: dissension, strife. **2** *Music.* **a** a lack of harmony in notes sounded at the same time; dissonance. **b** a combination of notes not in harmony with each other. **3** harsh, clashing sounds: *Arms on armour clashing bray'd horrible discord* (Milton). **4** a harsh or unpleasing sound.
—*v.i.* to disagree.
[< Old French *discord* < *discorder* to be at variance, learned borrowing from Latin *discordāre* < *discors, -cordis* discordant < *dis-* apart + *cor, cordis* heart]

dis|cord|ance (dis kôr′dəns), *n.* **1** a discord of sounds. SYN: dissonance. **2** disagreement: *There was an ironical discordance between the inner history of the man and his apparent fortunes* (Lytton Strachey). SYN: conflict.

dis|cord|an|cy (dis kôr′dən sē), *n.* = discordance.

dis|cord|ant (dis kôr′dənt), *adj.* **1** not in agreement; not fitting together; differing; disagreeing: *A quarrel started after several discordant opinions had been expressed.* **2** not in harmony: *a discordant note in music.* **3** harsh; clashing: *Many automobile horns sounding at once are discordant.* **—dis|cord′ant|ly,** *adv.*

Dis|cor|di|a (dis kôr′dē ə), *n. Roman Mythology.* the goddess of dissension (the counterpart of the Greek goddess Eris).

dis|co|thèque or **dis|co|theque** (dis′kə tek, dis′kə tek′; *French* dēs kō tek′), *n., v.,* **-thèqued, -thèqu|ing** or **-thequed, -thequ|ing.** **—*n.*** a night club or other place of entertainment where customers or performers dance or sing to recorded music: *The young generation loves the noisy nightclubs and the discothèques* (New York Times).
—*v.i.* to dance to recorded music at a discothèque: *Most older men will only react by trying doubly hard to prove how young they are, sweating it out on the tennis court or discothequing it way past their bedtime* (Time).
[< French *discothèque* (literally) record library < *disque* disk, record + *-thèque* (as in *bibliothèque* library); originally applied to a record shop, then to a café or bar where customers chose records to be played from a selection]

discothèque dress, a short, low-necked dress, often black and with frills at the hemline, originally worn by go-go girls at discothèques.

dis|count (*v.* dis′kount, dis kount′; *n.* dis′kount), *v., n.* **—*v.t.*** **1** to take off a certain amount from (a price): *The store discounts 3 per cent on all bills paid when due.* SYN: rebate. **2** *Figurative.* to believe only part of; allow for exaggeration in (a statement): *You must discount what he tells you, for he is too fond of a good story.* **3** *Figurative.* to leave out of account; disregard: *In his plans he discounted the expense.* **4** *Figurative.* to take (an expected event, opinion, policy) into account beforehand, and so lessen its effect or interest when it occurs: *The price of the stock fell before its dividend was reduced, for the reduction had already been discounted.* **5** to buy, sell, or lend money on (a note, bill of exchange, or other obligation), deducting a certain percentage to allow for unpaid interest.
—*v.i.* **1** to sell goods at a discount: *Many stores do not discount at all.* **2** to lend money, deducting the interest in advance.
—*n.* **1** the amount taken off from a price: *During the sale the dealer allowed a 10 per cent discount on all cash purchases.* SYN: reduction. **2** a percentage charged for buying, selling, or lending money on a note, bill of exchange, or other obligation. **3** interest deducted in advance. **4** the act of discounting.
at a discount, a at less than the regular price; below par: *Though one system of coinage were adopted for all countries, claims on foreign countries would nevertheless vary in price, and would still be either at a premium or at a discount* (George J. Goschen). **b** *Figurative.* in low esteem; reduced in estimation or regard. *Originality, vigour, courage, straightforwardness are excellent things, but they are at a discount in the market* (H. N. Oxenham).
[< Old French *desconter* count out < *des-* away (< Latin *dis-*) + *conter* to count < Latin *computāre*]

dis|count|a|ble (dis′koun tə bəl), *adj.* that can be discounted.

dis|coun|te|nance (dis koun′tə nəns), *v.,* **-nanced, -nanc|ing,** *n.* **—*v.t.*** **1** to refuse to approve; discourage: *This high school discountenances secret societies.* **2** to make ashamed; embarrass greatly; abash; disconcert: *She was discountenanced by her mother's angry look.*
—*n.* *Archaic.* a show of disapproval.

dis|coun|te|nanc|er (dis koun′tə nən sər), *n.* a person who discountenances; one who refuses to countenance, encourage, or support.

dis|count|er (dis′koun tər), *n.* **1** a merchant who sells goods at a discount: *The discounters claim to offer cut-rate prices through low markups and high volume* (Wall Street Journal). **2** = discount house.

discount house, 1 a large retail store or distributor that regularly sells merchandise for less than the manufacturers' list prices, making its profits from a large sales volume with low overhead: *The discount houses are a growing and virtually indispensable outlet for goods* (Newsweek). **2** *British.* a financial establishment which trades in discounted notes, loans, or securities.

discount rate, 1 the rate of interest charged for discounting notes. **2** = rediscount rate.

discount store, = discount house (def. 1).

dis|cour|age (dis kėr′ij), *v.t.,* **-aged, -ag|ing.** **1** to take away the courage or confidence of; destroy the hopes of; dishearten: *Failing again and again discourages anyone.* SYN: depress, daunt. **2** to try to prevent by disapproving; frown upon; dissuade: *All her friends discouraged her from such a dangerous swim.* **3** to make seem not worth while; prevent or hinder: *The chill of winter soon discouraged our picnics. Most lines have been deliberately discouraging passenger traffic through poor service ... and the steadily declining frequency and availability of trains* (New York Times).
[< Old French *descoragier* < *des-* away (< Latin *dis-*) + *corage* courage]

dis|cour|age|a|ble (dis kėr′ij ə bəl), *adj.* capable of being discouraged: *Too intelligent to be vain, he is evidently discourageable—should anything happen, that is to say, to discourage him* (Manchester Guardian Weekly).

dis|cour|aged worker (dis kėr′ijd), *U.S.* an unemployed person of working age who is not actively looking for a job: *The number of discouraged workers goes up as unemployment rises....For each 1 percent rise in the unemployment rate, the number of discouraged workers increases by 100,000* (New York Times).

dis|cour|age|ment (dis kėr′ij mənt), *n.* **1** the condition of being or feeling discouraged; lack of spirit or confidence: *Discouragement showed in every line of her drooping figure.* **2** something that discourages; a disheartening influence: *The out-of-town tryout of the play was a discouragement to its producer.* **3** the act of discouraging: *Her father's discouragement of her ambitions led her to leave home.*

dis|cour|ag|er (dis kėr′ə jər), *n.* a person or thing that discourages or disheartens.

dis|cour|ag|ing (dis kėr′ə jing), *adj.* that discourages; disheartening: *It is discouraging to lose faith in the human race.* **—dis|cour′ag|ing|ly,** *adv.*

dis|course (*n.* dis′kôrs, -kōrs, dis kôrs′, -kōrs′; *v.* dis kôrs′, -kōrs′), *n., v.,* **-coursed, -cours|ing.** **—*n.*** **1** a long written or spoken discussion of some subject: *Lectures and sermons are discourses.* SYN: oration, treatise, essay. **2** talk; conversation: *I ... laid hold of that opportunity of entering into discourse with him* (Jonathan Swift). **3** *Archaic.* the process or the faculty of reasoning. **4** *Obsolete.* the faculty of conversing.
—*v.i.* **1** to speak or write formally or at length on some subject: *The scholar discoursed at great length on the poetic style of John Keats.* **2** to talk; converse: *Rather than he will not discourse he will hire men to hear him* (Ben Jonson). SYN: confer. **—*v.t.*** *Archaic.* **1** to utter (sounds or music): *Give it breath with your mouth and it will discourse most eloquent music* (Shakespeare). **2** to discuss; tell; narrate: *Or by what means got'st thou to be released? Discourse, I prithee, on this turret's top* (Shakespeare).
[< Latin *discursus, -ūs* a running about (in Late Latin, discourse) < *discurrere* < *dis-* apart (in different directions) + *currere* to run]

dis|cours|er (dis kôr′sər, -kōr′-), *n.* a person who discourses; speaker.

dis|cour|te|ous (dis kėr′tē əs), *adj.* not courteous; not polite; rude: *discourteous waiters.* SYN: impolite, disrespectful. **—dis|cour′te|ous|ly,** *adv.* **—dis|cour′te|ous|ness,** *n.*

dis|cour|te|sy (dis kėr′tə sē), *n., pl.* **-sies.** **1** lack of courtesy; impoliteness; rudeness: *I think one of the greatest destroyers of domestic peace is discourtesy* (Harriet Beecher Stowe). **2** a rude or impolite act: *It is a discourtesy to interrupt another person's remarks.* SYN: incivility.

dis|cov|er (dis kuv′ər), *v.t.* **1** to see or learn of for the first time; find out: *Until Balboa discovered the Pacific Ocean most Europeans did not know it existed. No one has discovered a way to turn copper into gold.* **2** to make known to the public; hail as a discovery: *Stutterin' Sam, who was 6 feet 3 inches tall, was "discovered" by Billy Rose, the showman* (New York Times). *One by one the famous old fishing villages of Cornwall have been noisily "discovered"—by a prominent painter, perhaps, or a best-selling novelist* (John Malcolm Brinnin). **3** *Archaic.* to make known; reveal: *The knight would not discover his name to the prince.* **4** *Archaic.* to exhibit; display: *to discover his gold lace and scarlet.* **5** *Obsolete.* to uncover. [< Old French *descovrir* < Late Latin *discooperīre* < Latin *dis-* un- + *cooperīre* to cover] **—dis|cov′er|er,** *n.*
—*Syn.* **1 Discover, invent** mean to find something not known before. **Discover** means to find or find out something that already existed, but was not known about or had not been seen: *Pierre and Marie Curie discovered radium.* **Invent** means to make or work out something that did not exist before: *Thomas Edison invented the electric light bulb.*

dis|cov|er|a|ble (dis kuv′ər ə bəl), *adj.* that can be discovered.

dis|cov|ert (dis kuv′ərt), *adj. Law.* not under the protection or authority of a husband: *A widow is said to be discovert.* [< Old French *descouvert,* past participle of *descovrir;* see etym. under **discover**]

dis|cov|er|ture (dis kuv′ər chür, -chər), *n. Law.* the state of a woman not under the protection or authority of a husband.

dis|cov|er|y (dis kuv′ər ē, -kuv′rē), *n., pl.* **-er|ies.** **1** the act of discovering; a seeing or learning of something for the first time: *Dr. Fleming's discovery of penicillin occurred in 1928.* **2a** a thing found out: *One of Benjamin Franklin's discoveries was that lightning is electricity.* **b** a person whose particular talent has recently been discovered, such as an actor, entertainer, or athlete: *That young pianist was the discovery of a famous conductor.* **3** *Law.* the compulsory disclosure of facts, documents, etc.

Dis|cov|er|y (dis kuv′ər ē, -kuv′rē), *n.* the small English ship which made five important voyages of exploration to North America between 1602 and 1616.

Discovery Day, = Columbus Day.

disc parking, *British.* a system for parking vehicles in which disks showing the time of parking are given to motorists for display on their cars.

disc plough, *Especially British.* = disk plow.

disc plow, = disk plow.

dis|cre|ate (dis′krē āt′), *v.t.,* **-at|ed, -at|ing.** to undo (anything created); reduce to nothing; annihilate: *Thou hast set thine hand to unmake and discreate* (Algernon Charles Swinburne).

dis|cre|a|tion (dis′krē ā′shən), *n.* the undoing of creation or of anything created.

dis|cred|it (dis kred′it), *v., n.* **—*v.t.*** **1** to cast doubt on; destroy belief, faith, or trust in: *The lawyer discredited the witness by proving that he had been bribed.* SYN: dishonor. **2** to refuse to be-

---

Pronunciation Key: hat, āge, cãre, fär; let, ēqual, tėrm; it, īce; hot, ōpen, ôrder; oil, out; cup, pu̇t, rüle; child; long; thin; ᴛʜen; zh, measure; ə represents a in about, e in taken, i in pencil, o in lemon, u in circus.

lieve; decline to trust or have faith in: *We discredit her because she has lied so often.* **SYN**: disbelieve. **3** to do harm to the good name or standing of; give a bad reputation to: *Being caught cheating discredited the boy among his classmates. Losing five battles discredited the general.*
—*n.* **1** loss of belief, faith, or trust; doubt: *These photographs throw discredit on your account of the accident. Columbus's voyage cast discredit on the theory that the earth is flat.* **SYN**: disrepute. **2** loss of good name or standing: *The young thief brought discredit to his family.* **SYN**: disrepute. **3** a person or thing that causes loss of good name or standing; disgrace: *The young thief is a discredit to his family.*

dis|cred|it|a|ble (dis kred′ə tə bəl), *adj.* bringing discredit; disgraceful: *My own conduct in making no effort to prevent or stop this treatment of the horse has grown more and more discreditable to me* (Atlantic). **SYN**: dishonorable.

dis|cred|it|a|bly (dis kred′ə tə blē), *adv.* in a discreditable manner.

dis|cred|i|ta|tion (dis kred′ə tā′shən), *n.* **1** the act of discrediting. **2** the state or condition of being discredited.

dis|creet (dis krēt′), *adj.* very careful in speech and action; showing good judgment; wisely cautious: *A discreet person does not spread gossip. "Perhaps" is a discreet answer. You are a discreet man, and I make no doubt can keep a secret* (Washington Irving). **SYN**: prudent, wary. [< Old French *discret,* learned borrowing from Latin *discrētus* separated (in Medieval Latin, discerning), past participle of *discernere;* see etym. under **discern**. See etym. of doublet **discrete**.] —**dis|creet′ly**, *adv.* —**dis|creet′ness**, *n.*
► **Discreet** and **discrete** no longer have the same meaning. *Discreet* is a synonym of *prudent; discrete* is a synonym of *distinct* or *separate.*

dis|crep|ance (dis krep′əns), *n.* = discrepancy.

dis|crep|an|cy (dis krep′ən sē), *n., pl.* **-cies**. **1** lack of consistency; difference; disagreement: *There was a discrepancy in the two reports of the accident.* **SYN**: See syn. under **difference**. **2** an example of inconsistency: *The lawsuit was lost because of discrepancies in the statements of the witnesses.*

dis|crep|ant (dis krep′ənt), *adj.* showing lack of harmony; disagreeing; different; inconsistent. **SYN**: discordant, inharmonious. [< Latin *discrepāns, -antis,* present participle of *discrepāre* sound differently < *dis-* apart, off + *crepāre* to sound] —**dis|crep′ant|ly**, *adv.*

dis|crete (dis krēt′), *adj., n.* —*adj.* **1** distinct from others; separate; individual: *An apple and a stone are discrete objects.* **2** consisting of distinct or individual parts; discontinuous: *Wages paid to employees, the population of a community, the birth rate, and the like, furnish discrete series of data* (Emory S. Bogardus).
—*n.* a separate part or piece of equipment, often a component part of a large system, such as a high-fidelity system: *Most manufacturers of discretes are—to quote an industry marketing manager—"up to our ears in transistors"* (New Scientist and Science Journal).
[< Latin *discrētus* separated, past participle of *discernere;* see etym. under **discern**. See etym. of doublet **discreet**.] —**dis|crete′ly**, *adv.* —**discrete′ness**, *n.*
► See **discreet** for usage note.

dis|cre|tion (dis kresh′ən), *n.* **1** the quality of being discreet; good judgment; care in speech or action; wise caution: *My brother rushed in front of the car, but I showed more discretion. It requires discretion to criticize someone without hurting his feelings.* **SYN**: prudence, sagacity. **2** freedom to judge or choose: *It is within the principal's discretion to punish a pupil.* **SYN**: choice. **3** *Obsolete.* judgment; decision. **4** *Obsolete.* separation; distinction.
at the discretion of, according to the way one pleases, chooses, or thinks fit: *This fund will be used at the discretion of the chairman.*

dis|cre|tion|al (dis kresh′ə nəl), *adj.* = discretionary. —**dis|cre′tion|al|ly**, *adv.*

dis|cre|tion|ar|i|ly (dis kresh′ə ner′ə lē; *especially British* dis kresh′ə nər ə lē), *adv.* in a discretionary way.

dis|cre|tion|ar|y (dis kresh′ə ner′ē; *especially British* dis kresh′ə nər ē), *adj.* with freedom to decide or choose; left to one's own judgment: *The law gave the mayor certain discretionary powers. A discretionary account arises when an investor in effect says to his broker: "I trust you and I think your judgment is great. I don't have time to worry over my stocks. You buy and sell whenever you think best"* (New York Times).

discretionary income, disposable income in excess of the amount needed for necessities such as clothing, housing, and food: *Since 1940, U.S. discretionary income ... has increased sixfold* (Time).

dis|cre|tive (dis krē′tiv), *adj.* **1** serving to separate or divide. **2** = disjunctive. —**dis|cre′tive|ly**, *adv.*

dis|crim|in|a|bil|i|ty (dis krim′ə nə bil′ə tē), *n.* capability of being distinguished.

dis|crim|in|a|ble (dis krim′ə nə bəl), *adj.* that can be discriminated or distinguished: *It is estimated that there are ten million discriminable colors.*

dis|crim|i|nance (dis krim′ə nəns), *n.* something that helps to discriminate or distinguish; discriminant: *Existing seismic capabilities for the identification of underground nuclear explosions can identify, in the northern hemisphere, 50 kiloton events in hard rock. By the inclusion of other types of discriminance this identification could, in principle, be reduced by a factor of about five* (New Scientist and Science Journal).

dis|crim|i|nant (dis krim′ə nənt), *n.* **1** anything which serves as a discriminating or distinguishing quality or characteristic: *Length of flower stalk is another useful discriminant* (R. H. Richens). **2** *Mathematics.* an algebraic expression used to distinguish or separate other expressions in a quantity or equation.

dis|crim|i|nate (*v.* dis krim′ə nāt; *adj.* dis krim′ə-nit), *v.,* **-nat|ed, -nat|ing**, *adj.* —*v.i.* **1** to see or note a difference; make a distinction: *It is often difficult to discriminate between a mere exaggeration and a deliberate falsehood.* **SYN**: See syn. under **distinguish**. **2** to show a difference in treatment: *It is wrong to discriminate against people because of their race, religion, or nationality.*
—*v.t.* **1** to make or see a difference between: *Some boys cannot discriminate red from green easily. Can you discriminate a good book from a poor one?* **SYN**: See syn. under **distinguish**. **2** to constitute a difference between; differentiate: *Communicating knowledge discriminates human beings from animals.*
—*adj.* **1** having discrimination; making careful distinctions: *Bright students and slow students should have discriminate treatment.* **2** *Archaic.* distinguished; distinct.
[< Latin *discrīmināre* (with English *-ate*[1]) < *discrīmen, -inis* separation < root of *discernere;* see etym. under **discern**] —**dis|crim′i|nate|ly**, *adv.*

dis|crim|i|nat|ing (dis krim′ə nā′ting), *adj.* **1** able to discriminate well; discerning: *The art collector has discriminating taste.* **2** that discriminates: *She is discriminating in her choice of friends.* **3** differential: *Makers wanted a discriminating duty on imports.* Also, **discriminative**. —**dis|crim′i|nat′ing|ly**, *adv.*

dis|crim|i|na|tion (dis krim′ə nā′shən), *n.* **1** the act of making or recognizing differences and distinctions: *Do not buy clothes without discrimination. Discrimination between fact and theory is sometimes difficult to make.* **SYN**: discernment, insight, acumen. **2** the ability to discriminate accurately between things that are very much alike; good judgment: *He lacked discrimination in his choice of friends. It does ... credit to your discrimination that you should have found such a very excellent young woman* (Dickens). **3** a making a difference in favor of or against: *Racial or religious discrimination in hiring workers is against the law.* **4** *Obsolete.* something that serves to differentiate.

dis|crim|i|na|tion|al (dis krim′ə nā′shə nəl), *adj.* of or having to do with discrimination, especially racial discrimination.

discrimination reaction, *Psychology.* a reaction in which the movement of response is delayed until the mind of the subject has identified the stimulus.

discrimination time, *Psychology.* the total duration of the time of a discrimination reaction, or the time necessary for the identification of the stimuli.

dis|crim|i|na|tive (dis krim′ə nā′tiv), *adj.* **1** discriminating. **2** showing discrimination: *discriminative trade laws.* —**dis|crim′i|na′tive|ly**, *adv.*

dis|crim|i|na|tor (dis krim′ə nā′tər), *n.* **1** a person or thing that discriminates. **2** *Electronics.* a circuit that converts one type of signal to another: *The original picture or composite telephone signals are obtained at the output of the discriminator, the FM counterpart of the detector in popular radio practice* (New Scientist).

dis|crim|i|na|to|ri|ly (dis krim′ə nə tôr′ə lē, -tōr′-), *adv.* so as to discriminate; discriminatively: *... punishing discriminatorily any person exercising or seeking to exercise his right to vote* (New York Times).

dis|crim|i|na|to|ry (dis krim′ə nə tôr′ē, -tōr′-), *adj.* discriminative; showing partiality or prejudice: *Proponents of the bill argued that Federal regulation of natural-gas production ... was discriminatory, since the government did not attempt to fix prices on coal, iron, copper* (Newsweek).

dis|crown (dis kroun′), *v.t.* to deprive of royal power; depose. **SYN**: uncrown.

dis|cul|pate (dis kul′pāt), *v.t.,* **-pat|ed, -pat|ing**. to free from blame or fault; exculpate. [< Medieval Latin *disculpare* (with English *-ate*[1]) < Latin *dis-* not + *culpāre* to blame < *culpa* fault]

dis|cul|pa|tion (dis′kul pā′shən), *n.* freedom from blame or fault; exculpation.

dis|cum|ber (dis kum′bər), *v.t.* = disencumber. [< *dis-*[2] + *cumber*]

dis|cur|sion (dis kėr′shən, -zhən), *n.* a digression: *The discussion of ghost stories turned into a discursion on personal experiences.*

dis|cur|sive (dis kėr′siv), *adj.* **1** wandering from one subject to another; rambling: *His carefully planned speech was not discursive but stayed right on the subject. ... a slow-paced, leisurely, ... and discursive novel* (New York Times). **SYN**: digressive. **2** proceeding by reasoning or argument: *Johnson ... is always a man of intuitions rather than of discursive intellect* (Leslie Stephen). [< Latin *discursus, -ūs* (see etym. under **discourse**) + English *-ive*] —**dis|cur′sive|ly**, *adv.* —**dis|cur′sive|ness**, *n.*

***dis|cus** (dis′kəs), *n., pl.* **-cus|es** or **-ci**. **1** a heavy, circular plate of rubber, plastic, or wood with a metal rim. It is used in athletic games as a test of skill and strength in throwing. Discuses were formerly made of stone or metal. **2** the throwing of the discus as a test of skill or as a contest. [< Latin *discus* < Greek *dískos* platter. See etym. of doublets **dais, desk, dish, disk**.]

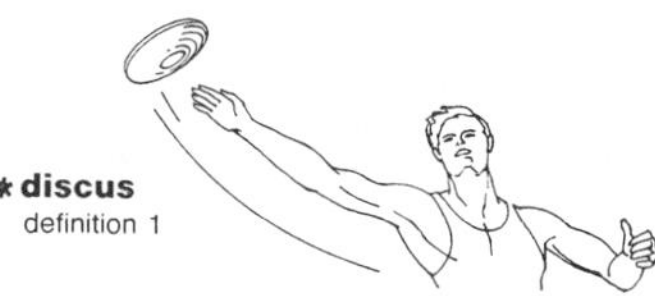

***discus**
definition 1

dis|cuss (dis kus′), *v.t.* **1** to consider from various points of view; talk over: *His mother and father always discuss the news. Congress is discussing tax rates. Senior public education officials ... gathered here to discuss how to improve the big-city school systems* (New York Times). **2** *Archaic.* to try the qualities of (food or drink) by eating or drinking; consume: *They allowed him to discuss the question, while they discussed his port wine* (Frederick Marryat). **3** (in civil law) to take all possible steps to recover a debt from (the person primarily liable) before proceeding against the person secondarily liable. **4** *Archaic.* to dispel; disperse: *a pomade ... of virtue to discuss pimples* (Samuel Johnson). **5** *Obsolete.* to make known; reveal: *Art thou a gentleman? What is thy name? discuss* (Shakespeare). [< Latin *discussus,* past participle of *discutere* strike asunder (in Late Latin, discuss) < *dis-* apart + *quatere* to shake] —**dis|cuss′er**, *n.*
—*Syn.* **1 Discuss, argue, debate** mean to talk something over with others in order to arrive at a conclusion. **Discuss** suggests considering all sides of a question: *We discussed the best road to take.* **Argue** suggests taking one side and bringing forward facts and reasons for it and against the other side: *I argued for taking the new highway.* **Debate** suggests more formal arguing, often publicly, between clearly drawn-up sides: *The question of federal aid to schools was hotly debated in the Senate.*

dis|cuss|a|ble (dis kus′ə bəl), *adj.* = discussible.

dis|cus|sant (dis kus′ənt), *n.* a person participating in a discussion: *Let one of the discussants so much as intimate a fresh idea or engage another of the panelists in controversy, and there is Mr. Smith, quick on the switch, shunting the discussion into more neutral territory* (Time).

dis|cuss|i|ble (dis kus′ə bəl), *adj.* that can be discussed: *This kind of protection has recently come into the realm of the imaginable and discussible, as Peter F. Drucker demonstrates in "The Medical Insurance We Need Most"* (Harper's).

dis|cus|sion (dis kush′ən), *n.* **1** a talk about the reasons for and against: *After two hours' discussion, the members of the club seemed near a decision.* **2** the act of discussing things; talk: *a classroom discussion on modern art. His arrival caused much discussion in the village.* **3** the second section of a fugue in which the subject and answer of the exposition are informally repeated.

dis|cus|sion|al (dis kush′ə nəl), *adj.* **1** of or having to do with discussion. **2** subject to discussion: *The plan is still in its discussional stage.*

discus throw, a sports event in which the discus is thrown for distance.

dis|cu|tient (dis kyü′shənt), *adj., n.* —*adj.* serving to disperse diseased matter: *a discutient medicine.*
—*n.* a discutient medicine or agent.
[< Latin *discutiēns, -entis,* present participle of

discutere; see etym. under **discuss**]

dis|dain (dis dān′), *v., n.* — ***v.t.*** to look down on; consider beneath oneself or one's notice; scorn: *The honest official disdained the offer of a bribe. Now that she is rich, she disdains to speak to her old friends.* **SYN**: despise, spurn.
— ***n.*** the act of looking down on a person or an action as beneath one; scorn: *The conceited boy treated his brothers and sisters with disdain.* **SYN**: contempt. See syn. under **scorn**.
[< Old French *desdeignier* < *des-* down (< Latin *dis-*) + *deignier* to deign < Latin *dignārī*] — **dis-dain′er**, *n.*

dis|dain|ful (dis dān′fəl), *adj.* proud and scornful; feeling or showing disdain: *a disdainful toss of the head.* **SYN**: contemptuous, scornful. — **dis-dain′ful|ly**, *adv.* — **dis|dain′ful|ness**, *n.*

dis|ease (də zēz′), *n., v.,* **-eased, -eas|ing.** — ***n.*** **1** sickness; illness; a condition in which an organ, system, or part does not function properly: *Cleanliness helps prevent disease. People, animals, and plants are all liable to suffer from disease. Great strides are also being made in ... immunology—the study of the body's natural defenses against disease* (James E. Brody). **SYN**: ailment. **2** any particular illness: *Measles and chicken pox are two diseases of childhood.* **3** an unhealthy condition of a plant or a product: *the diseases of grains.* **4** *Figurative.* a disordered or bad condition, such as that of mind, morals, or public affairs: *It is the disease of not listening, the malady of not marking, that I am troubled withall* (Shakespeare). *The disease with which the human mind now labors is want of faith* (Emerson). **5** *Obsolete.* dis-ease; uneasiness.
— ***v.t.*** to cause sickness or illness in; infect.
[< Old French *desaise* < *des-* without, away (< Latin *dis-*) + *aise* ease, opportunity]

dis-ease (dis′ēz′), *n.* uneasiness; discomfort; disturbance.

dis|eased (də zēzd′), *adj.* **1** having a disease; showing signs of sickness or illness: *a diseased heart. A diseased lung may be removed by an operation.* **2** *Figurative.* disordered: *An insane person has a diseased mind.*

dis|ease|ful (də zēz′fəl), *adj.* **1** = diseased. **2** producing disease; unwholesome.

dis|e|con|o|my (dis′i kon′ə mē), *n., pl.* **-mies.** something that is economically harmful, inefficient, or unprofitable; misuse of the economy: *The old stock example of a diseconomy ... was the factory pouring out smoke and grime to the detriment of the family washing on the line* (Sunday Times). *The analogy is supported by the many similar diseconomies that are fostered under the two systems of financing, all dissipating some of the potential benefits of the public and private money spent for medical care* (Scientific American).

dis|edge (dis ej′), *v.t.,* **-edged, -edg|ing.** to take the edge off; blunt; dull: *served a little to disedge the sharpness of that pain* (Tennyson).

dis|ed|i|fi|ca|tion (dis ed′ə fə kā′shən), *n.* the act of disedifying; a scandal.

dis|ed|i|fy (dis ed′ə fī), *v.t.,* **-fied, -fy|ing.** to scandalize.

dis|e|lec|tri|fi|ca|tion (dis′i lek′trə fə kā′shən), *n.* the act or process of diselectrifying.

dis|e|lec|tri|fy (dis′i lek′trə fī), *v.t.,* **-fied, -fy|ing.** to free from electricity; make nonelectric.

dis|em|bark (dis′em bärk′), *v.t., v.i.* to get off or land from a ship, aircraft, or other vehicle; debark: *... disembarking at the Wall Street heliport* (New York Times). *The cabin stopped, and the skiers began to disembark* (Irwin Shaw).

dis|em|bar|ka|tion (dis′em bär kā′shən), *n.* the act of disembarking.

dis|em|bar|rass (dis′em bar′əs), *v.t.* **1** to free from something that holds back or entangles; disengage; disentangle: *... disembarrassing himself of contact with any faction within the State* (London Times). **2** to relieve; rid: *He appeared to have disembarrassed himself of all traces of the good manners in which he had been trained.* **3** to free from embarrassment or uneasiness.

dis|em|bar|rass|ment (dis′em bar′əs mənt), *n.* **1** the act of disembarrassing. **2** the state of being disembarrassed.

dis|em|bed (dis′em bed′), *v.t.,* **-bed|ded, -bed-ding.** to free or remove (something embedded).

dis|em|bel|lish (dis′em bel′ish), *v.t.* to deprive of embellishment.

dis|em|bod|ied (dis′em bod′ēd), *adj.* separated from the body: *Ghosts are usually thought of as disembodied spirits.*

dis|em|bod|i|ment (dis′em bod′ē mənt), *n.* **1** the act of disembodying. **2** the state of being disembodied.

dis|em|bod|y (dis′em bod′ē), *v.t.,* **-bod|ied, -bod-y|ing.** to separate (a soul, spirit, etc.) from the body.

dis|em|bogue (dis′em bōg′), *v.t., v.i.,* **-bogued, -bo|guing.** **1** (of a river, lake, strait, or the like) to pour forth (its waters) at the mouth. **2** *Figurative.* to emerge or discharge. [< Spanish *desembocar* < *des-* in reverse (< Latin *dis-*) + *embocar* run (as the tide) up into a river < *em-* in + *boca* mouth < Latin *bucca* cheek]

dis|em|bogue|ment (dis′em bōg′mənt), *n.* **1** a pouring forth of water. **2** the place where water pours forth.

dis|em|bos|om (dis′em bu̇z′əm, -bü′zəm), *v.t.* to disclose; reveal. — ***v.i.*** to unburden oneself.

dis|em|bow|el (dis′em bou′əl), *v.t.,* **-eled, -el|ing** or (*especially British*) **-elled, -el|ling.** **1** to take or rip out the bowels or entrails of; eviscerate: *The sharp horns of the antelope disemboweled the lion.* **2** *Figurative: to disembowel an engine.* Also, **disentrail.**

dis|em|bow|el|ment (dis′em bou′əl mənt), *n.* the act or process of disemboweling; evisceration.

dis|em|broil (dis′em broil′), *v.t.* to free from embroilment, entanglement, or confusion.

dis|em|plane (dis′em plān′), *v.i.,* **-planed, -plan-ing.** to get off an airplane; deplane: *One of his wives was promptly told to disemplane ... and the Nawab took off for Pakistan* (London Times).

dis|em|ploy (dis′em ploi′), *v.t.* to dismiss or release from employment; put out of work: *Would industry stop dead when it disemployed the last man ...?* (New Yorker).

dis|em|ploy|ment (dis′em ploi′mənt), *n.* lack of employment; a being unemployed: *Instead of saying that a lot of people might lose their jobs and become unemployed, the economists talked about increasing "disemployment"* (Tuscaloosa News).

dis|en|a|ble (dis′en ā′bəl), *v.t.,* **-bled, -bling.** to make unable; disable: *He thought ... that the absurdly strong colouring of the picture would disenable the work from doing either good or harm* (Anthony Trollope). — **dis′en|a′ble|ment**, *n.*

dis|en|chant (dis′en chant′, -chänt′), *v.t.* to free from enchantment or illusion; disillusion: *I thought that he would be charming, but I was disenchanted when I met him. The most deeply entrenched tyrant can be destroyed by aroused public opinion and disenchanted military leaders* (Time). — **dis′en|chant′ed|ly**, *adv.* — **dis′en-chant′er**, *n.* — **dis′en|chant′ing|ly**, *adv.*

dis|en|chant|ment (dis′en chant′mənt, -chänt′-), *n.* a freeing or being freed from enchantment or illusion: *If the new election is delayed, the disenchantment with* [*the candidate*] *might grow enough to defeat him* (Wall Street Journal). *This general disenchantment with the world ... only intensified her sense of forlornness* (George Eliot).

dis|en|cum|ber (dis′en kum′bər), *v.t.* to free from a burden, annoyance, or trouble: *She disencumbered herself of her pile of Christmas parcels.* **SYN**: disembarrass, release.

dis|en|cum|ber|ment (dis′en kum′bər mənt), *n.* **1** the act of disencumbering. **2** the fact of being disencumbered.

dis|en|dow (dis′en dou′), *v.t.* to deprive (a church or other institution) of endowments. — **dis′en-dow′er**, *n.*

dis|en|dow|ment (dis′en dou′mənt), *n.* the act or fact of disendowing.

dis|en|fran|chise (dis′en fran′chīz), *v.t.,* **-chised, -chis|ing.** **1** to take any right or privilege away from: *to disenfranchise rowdy children. The philosophy is, if you can't lick 'em, disenfranchise 'em* (Wall Street Journal). **2** = disfranchise (def. 1).

dis|en|fran|chise|ment (dis′en fran′chīz mənt), *n.* **1** the act or process of disenfranchising. **2** the state of being disenfranchised.

dis|en|gage (dis′en gāj′), *v.,* **-gaged, -gag|ing.**
— ***v.t.*** **1** to free or release from anything that holds; detach; loosen: *The mother gently disengaged her hand from that of the sleeping child. Disengage the clutch.* **SYN**: free. **2** to free from an engagement, pledge, or obligation. **SYN**: release. **3** *Military.* to withdraw from combat or contact with (an enemy).
— ***v.i.*** **1** to free oneself; get loose. **2** *Military.* to withdraw from an engagement; retreat: *The French disengaged quite rapidly after Dien Bien Phu, and indeed they performed an extraordinary evacuation* (Listener).

dis|en|gaged (dis′en gājd′), *adj.* **1** released; detached: *Though her manner seemed disengaged, she was aware of all they said.* **2** not busy; free from appointments: *Will you be disengaged on Tuesday?*

dis|en|gag|ed|ness (dis′en gā′jid nis), *n.* the quality of being disengaged.

dis|en|gage|ment (dis′en gāj′mənt), *n.* **1** the act of disengaging. **2** the state of being disengaged: *He has never believed in European disengagement from the East-West conflict* (New York Times). **3** freedom from obligation or occupation; ease of manner.

dis|en|gag|er (dis′ən gā′jər), *n.* a person or thing that disengages.

dis|en|no|ble (dis′en nō′bəl), *v.t.,* **-bled, -bling.** to deprive of nobility; make ignoble; degrade: *unworthy behaviour ... disennobles a man* (Joseph Addison).

dis|en|tail (dis′en tāl′), *v.t. Law.* to free (an estate) from entail.

dis|en|tail|ment (dis′en tāl′mənt), *n. Law.* the act of disentailing; breaking an entail.

dis|en|tan|gle (dis′en tang′gəl), *v.,* **-gled, -gling.**
— ***v.t.*** to free (anything) from tangles or complications; untangle: *to disentangle rope,* (*Figurative.*) *to disentangle fact from fancy. The police tried to disentangle the confused victim's story.* **SYN**: disengage, extricate.
— ***v.i.*** to become disentangled: *Nylon rope often disentangles more easily than hemp.*

dis|en|tan|gle|ment (dis′en tang′gəl mənt), *n.* **1** the act of disentangling. **2** the state of being disentangled.

dis|en|tan|gler (dis′en tang′glər), *n.* a person who disentangles.

dis|en|thrall or **dis|en|thral** (dis′en thrôl′), *v.t.* to set free from enthrallment or bondage; liberate: *In straits and in distress Thou didst me disenthrall* (Milton).

dis|en|thrall|ment or **dis|en|thral|ment** (dis′-en thrôl′mənt), *n.* a freeing or a being freed from enthrallment or bondage; liberation.

dis|en|throne (dis′en thrōn′), *v.t.,* **-throned, -thron|ing.** = dethrone.

dis|en|throne|ment (dis′en thrōn′mənt), *n.* dethronement.

dis|en|ti|tle (dis′en tī′təl), *v.t.,* **-tled, -tling.** to deprive of title or right.

dis|en|tomb (dis′en tüm′), *v.t.* to disinter or unearth.

dis|en|tomb|ment (dis′en tüm′mənt), *n.* the act of disentombing; disinterment.

dis|en|trail (dis′en trāl′), *v.t.* = disembowel.

dis|en|train (dis′en trān′), *v.t., v.i.* = detrain.

dis|en|trance (dis′en trans′, -träns′), *v.t.,* **-tranced, -tranc|ing.** to arouse from a trance.

dis|en|trance|ment (dis′en trans′mənt, -träns′-), *n.* recovery from a trance.

dis|en|twine (dis′en twīn′), *v.,* **-twined, -twin|ing.**
— ***v.t.*** to disentangle; untwine; untwist.
— ***v.i.*** to become disentwined.

di|sep|a|lous (dī sep′ə ləs), *adj. Botany.* having two sepals. [< *di-*[1] two + *sepalous*]

dis|e|qui|li|brate (dis ē′kwə lī′brāt, -i kwil′ə-), *v.t.,* **-brat|ed, -brat|ing.** to throw out of balance: *Too much light can disequilibrate you—just like the strobe lights at the Electric Circus do* (New York Times).

dis|e|qui|li|bra|tion (dis ē′kwə lī brā′shən, -i kwil′ə-), *n.* a throwing out of balance; disequilibrium.

dis|e|qui|lib|ri|um (dis ē′kwə lib′rē əm), *n., pl.* **-ri-ums, -ri|a** (rē ə). **1** loss of equilibrium or stability; the condition of being out of balance: *Overflowing granaries may make for economic disequilibrium but hardly for spiritual frustration* (Wall Street Journal). **2** an amount by which something is out of balance: *Britain wants the monetary system to be operated in such a way that temporary disequilibria in payments can be financed without upsetting ... the adjustment process* (London Times).

dis|es|tab|lish (dis′es tab′lish), *v.t.* **1** to deprive of the character of being established. **2** to withdraw special state recognition or support from (a church): *She* [*Queen Victoria*] *feared that if the Liberals insisted upon disestablishing the Irish Church, her Coronation Oath might stand in the way* (Lytton Strachey).

dis|es|tab|lish|ment (dis′es tab′lish mənt), *n.* **1** the act of disestablishing. **2** disestablished condition: *Disestablishment would mean loss of state protection, possibly some lands, and the privilege of crowning England's monarchs* (Time).

dis|es|tab|lish|men|tar|i|an (dis′es tab′lish mən-tãr′ē ən), *n.* a person who favors or supports disestablishmentarianism.

dis|es|tab|lish|men|tar|i|an|ism (dis′es tab′lish-mən tãr′ē ə niz′əm), *n.* the doctrine of withdrawing state recognition or support from a church.

dis|es|teem (dis′es tēm′), *v., n.* — ***v.t.*** to scorn or dislike. **SYN**: slight, despise.
— ***n.*** low esteem or regard; scorn; disfavor: *How I should like to distil my disesteem of my contemporaries into prose so perfect that all of them would have to read it!* (Logan Pearsall Smith). **SYN**: dislike.

di|seur (dē zœr′), *n.* a male entertainer who specializes in monologue: *Another, an accomplished diseur, related a ghost story* (New Yorker). [< French *diseur* (literally) speaker]

Pronunciation Key: hat, āge, cãre, fär; let, ēqual, tėrm, it, īce; hot, ōpen, ôrder; **oil, out**; cup, pu̇t, rüle; **ch**ild; lo**ng**; **th**in; **ᴛʜ**en; **zh**, measure; **ə** represents **a** in about, **e** in taken, **i** in pencil, **o** in lemon, **u** in circus.

di|seuse (dē zœz′), *n.* a woman entertainer who specializes in monologue: *no mere monologist or diseuse; she describes herself as a character actress* (Time). [< French *diseuse* (literally) female speaker]

dis|fa|vor (dis fā′vər), *n., v.* —*n.* **1** unfavorable regard; dislike or disapproval: *The workers looked with disfavor on any attempt to lower their wages.* **2** the condition of having lost favor or trust: *The defeated general was in disfavor with the government. The poor young Prince ... had fallen into open disfavour* (Thomas Carlyle).
—*v.t.* to dislike or disapprove: *The legislator disfavored every bill that would increase taxes.*

dis|fa|vour (dis fā′vər), *n., v.t. Especially British.* disfavor.

dis|fea|ture (dis fē′chər), *v.t.,* **-tured, -tur|ing.** to mar the features of; disfigure.

dis|fea|ture|ment (dis fē′chər mənt), *n.* disfeatured condition; disfigurement; defacement.

dis|fig|u|ra|tion (dis fig′yə rā′shən), *n.* = disfigurement.

dis|fig|ure (dis fig′yər), *v.t.,* **-ured, -ur|ing.** to spoil the appearance of; hurt the beauty of: *A scar disfigured his face. Large billboards disfigured the countryside.* SYN: deform.

dis|fig|ure|ment (dis fig′yər mənt), *n.* **1** the act of disfiguring: *the disfigurement of walls by scribblers.* **2** a disfigured condition: *The disfigurement of his face was caused by an explosion.* SYN: defacement, deformity. **3** something that disfigures; defect: *The scar tissue on his face was a small disfigurement.* SYN: blemish.

dis|fig|ur|er (dis fig′yər ər), *n.* a person who disfigures.

dis|fig|ur|ing|ly (dis fig′yər ing lē), *adv.* in a disfiguring manner; so as to disfigure.

dis|flu|en|cy (dis flü′ən sē), *n.* **1** a stutter. **2** *pl.* **-cies.** an instance of stuttering.

dis|for|est (dis fôr′ist, -for′-), *v.t.* **1** to disafforest. **2** to clear of forests or trees.

dis|for|est|a|tion (dis fôr′ə stā′shən, -for′-), *n.* **1** the act of disforesting. **2** disforested condition.

dis|fran|chise (dis fran′chīz), *v.t.,* **-chised, -chis|ing.** **1** to take the rights of citizenship away from: *A disfranchised person cannot vote or hold office.* **2** = disenfranchise (def. 1). Also, **disenfranchise.**

dis|fran|chise|ment (dis fran′chīz mənt), *n.* **1** the act or process of disfranchising. **2** the state of being disfranchised. Also, **disenfranchisement.**

dis|frock (dis frok′), *v.t.* = unfrock.

dis|func|tion (dis fungk′shən), *v.i., n.* = dysfunction.

dis|fur|nish (dis fėr′nish), *v.t.* to deprive of furniture or belongings; strip (of).

dis|fur|nish|ment (dis fėr′nish mənt), *n.* **1** the act of disfurnishing. **2** the state of being disfurnished.

dis|gav|el (dis gav′əl), *v.t.,* **-elled, -el|ling.** (in English law) to relieve (land) from the tenure of gavelkind. [< *dis-*[2] + *gavel* (kind)]

dis|gorge (dis gôrj′), *v.,* **-gorged, -gorg|ing.**
—*v.t.* **1** to throw up (what has been swallowed); vomit forth. SYN: spew. **2** to pour forth; discharge: *Swollen streams disgorged their waters into the river.* **3** *Figurative.* to give up unwillingly: *The robbers were forced to disgorge their plunder.*
—*v.i.* to throw up; empty; discharge. [< Old French *desgorger* < *des-* out (< Latin *dis-*) + *gorge* gorge, throat]

dis|gorge|ment (dis gôrj′mənt), *n.* the act of disgorging.

dis|gorg|er (dis gôr′jər), *n.* **1** a person or thing that disgorges. **2** a device for extracting a gorged hook from the throat of a fish.

dis|grace (dis grās′), *n., v.,* **-graced, -grac|ing.**
—*n.* **1** loss of honor or respect; shame: *The disgrace of being sent to prison was too much for him to bear.* **2** loss of favor or trust: *The king's former adviser is now in disgrace.* **3** a person or thing that causes dishonor or shame: *The rude boy was a disgrace to his parents.*
—*v.t.* **1** to cause disgrace to; bring shame upon: *The traitor disgraced his family and friends.* **2** to dismiss in disgrace: *The cowardly officer was disgraced for failing to do his duty.*
[< French *disgrâce* misfortune; deformity < Italian *disgrazia* < *dis-* out of (< Latin *dis-*) + *grazia* grace < Latin *grātia* esteem]
—*Syn. n.* **1 Disgrace, dishonor, ignominy** mean loss of good name or respect. **Disgrace** suggests losing the respect and approval of others: *He was in disgrace after his ungentlemanly behavior.* **Dishonor** suggests losing one's self-respect and honor: *For neglect of duty, he was stripped of his rank with dishonor.* **Ignominy** suggests being put to public shame and held in contempt: *He brought on himself the ignominy of being caught cheating in the game.*

dis|grace|ful (dis grās′fəl), *adj.* causing dishonor or loss of respect; shameful: *a disgraceful scene. The rude girl's behavior was disgraceful.* SYN: dishonorable, disreputable. —**dis|grace′ful|ly,** *adv.* —**dis|grace′ful|ness,** *n.*

dis|grac|er (dis grā′sər), *n.* a person or thing that disgraces or exposes to disgrace; a person or thing that brings disgrace, shame, or contempt upon others, or upon a cause.

dis|grun|tle (dis grun′təl), *v.t.,* **-tled, -tling.** to put in a bad humor; disgust; displease: *A poor breakfast disgruntles him for the rest of the day.* [< *dis-*[2] + *gruntle*]

dis|grun|tled (dis grun′təld), *adj.* in a bad humor; discontented; disgusted; displeased: *Nothing would please him in his disgruntled mood.* —**dis|grun′tled|ly,** *adv.*

dis|grun|tle|ment (dis grun′təl mənt), *n.* moody discontent: *These will create disgruntlement and opposition in every school district in the country* (Newsweek).

dis|guise (dis gīz′), *v.,* **-guised, -guis|ing,** *n.*
—*v.t.* **1** to hide who one really is by looking like someone else: *Uncle disguised himself as Santa Claus. The spy disguised himself as an old woman.* **2** to hide what (a thing) really is; make (a thing) seem like something else; misrepresent: *The pirates disguised their ship as a trading vessel. She disguised her handwriting by writing with her left hand. He disguised his hate by a false show of friendliness.*
—*n.* **1** the use of a changed or unusual dress and appearance in order not to be known: *Detectives sometimes depend on disguise.*
2 clothes, actions, or other artificial means used to hide or deceive: *Woman's clothes and a wig formed the spy's disguise.* **3** *Figurative.* a false or misleading appearance; deception; concealment: *Her outward friendliness was only a disguise for her hate.* **4** a disguised condition or form: (*Figurative.*) *a blessing in disguise. A weed is no more than a flower in disguise* (James Russell Lowell).
[< Old French *desguisier* < *des-* away (< Latin *dis-*) + *guise* guise < Germanic (compare Old High German *wīsa* manner)]

dis|guised (dis gīzd′), *adj.* **1** having the appearance altered by a disguise. **2** *Archaic.* intoxicated.

dis|guis|ed|ly (dis gī′zid lē), *adv.* with or in disguise.

dis|guise|ment (dis gīz′mənt), *n.* **1** a disguising or being disguised. **2** something that disguises; disguise.

dis|guis|er (dis gī′zər), *n.* a person or thing that changes appearances and makes things appear other than they are.

dis|gust (dis gust′), *n., v.* —*n.* a strong dislike; sickening dislike: *We feel disgust for bad odors or tastes.* SYN: distaste, loathing, repugnance. See syn. under **dislike.**
—*v.t.* to cause to feel disgust: *The smell of a pigpen disgusts many people.*
[< Middle French *desgoust* distaste < *desgouster* to loathe < *des-* away (< Latin *dis-*) + *goust* taste < Latin *gustus, -ūs*]

dis|gust|ed (dis gus′tid), *adj.* filled with disgust: *He was disgusted with the behavior of the selfish child.* —**dis|gust′ed|ly,** *adv.* —**dis|gust′ed|ness,** *n.*

dis|gust|ful (dis gust′fəl), *adj.* disgusting: *... the tragical and too often disgustful history of witchcraft ...* (James Russell Lowell). —**dis|gust′ful|ly,** *adv.* —**dis|gust′ful|ness,** *n.*

dis|gust|ing (dis gus′ting), *adj.* that disgusts; unpleasant; distasteful: *Garbage often has a disgusting smell.* SYN: sickening, repulsive. —**dis|gust′ing|ly,** *adv.*

***dish** (dish), *n., v.* —*n.* **1** anything to serve food in, such as a plate, bowl, cup, or saucer. Dishes can be made of glass, pottery, or plastic, but paper plates are usually not called dishes. *She brought forth butter in a lordly dish* (Judges 5:25). **2** the amount of food served in a dish; as much as a dish can hold: *I ate two dishes of ice cream.* **3** food served: *Sliced peaches and cream is the dish I like best.* **4** a thing shaped like a dish. **5** a concavity in the shape of a dish. **6** concave state or the degree of concavity, for example of a wheel. **7** a large antenna usually having the shape of a paraboloid, especially the antenna of a radio telescope. **8** *Slang.* anything that is in accord with one's tastes or desires: *Rough, exhausting games are not my dish.* **9** *Slang.* a pretty girl: *Here was the best looking girl aboard the train, a dish* (New Yorker).
—*v.t.* **1a** to serve (food) by putting it in a dish: *You may dish the dinner now.* **b** *Figurative: This story has been dished around in a hundred different ways.* **2** to shape like a dish; make concave: *The pie crust needs to be dished a little more.* **3** *Slang.* to defeat; ruin: *My competitors have dished me.* SYN: frustrate, circumvent.
—*v.i.* to be or become concave.

dish it out, *Slang.* to abuse or punish someone physically or verbally: *If you dish it out, you must learn to take it as well.*

dish out (or **up**), **a** to serve (food): *The chef dished out the salad.* **b** *Informal.* to give out; dispense: *Exclusive excerpts of [his] confession were dished up* (Manchester Guardian Weekly). **c** *Informal.* to inflict; administer; give: *to dish out a series of knockout blows. ... the roach's record of taking and surviving the worst that man can dish up* (New York Times).
[Old English *disc* < Latin *discus* < Greek *dískos* discus, platter. See etym. of doublets **dais, desk, discus,** and **disk.**]

***dish**
definition 7

dis|ha|bille (dis′ə bēl′), *n.* **1** informal, careless dress: *At eight in the morning we go in dishabille to the pump room* (Tobias Smollett). **2** a garment or costume worn in dishabille. **3** the condition of being partly undressed. Also, **deshabille.** [< French *déshabillé,* past participle of Middle French *déshabiller* < *dés-* away (< Latin *dis-*) + *habiller* to dress]

dis|ha|bit|u|ate (dis′hə bich′ů āt), *v.t.,* **-at|ed, -at|ing.** to cause to lose or give up a habitual action; disaccustom.

dis|hal|low (dis hal′ō), *v.t.* to destroy the sacredness of; profane: *Ye that so dishallow the holy sleep, Your sleep is death* (Tennyson).

dis|har|mon|ic (dis′här mon′ik), *adj.* **1** characterized by physical features that lack symmetry: *Disharmonic faces, it may be noted, are ... characteristic of the Eskimos* (Beals and Hoijer). **2** = disharmonious.

dis|har|mo|ni|ous (dis′här mō′nē əs), *adj.* unharmonious; discordant; dissonant.

dis|har|mo|nize (dis här′mə nīz), *v.,* **-nized, -niz|ing.** —*v.t.* to make inharmonious.
—*v.i.* to be inharmonious.

dis|har|mo|ny (dis här′mə nē), *n., pl.* **-nies.** **1** lack of harmony; discord; dissonance: *disharmony of mind and tongue* (Thomas Carlyle). **2** something discordant.

dish|cloth (dish′klôth′, -kloth′), *n.* a cloth to wash dishes with; dishrag.

dishcloth gourd, **1** any of a group of plants of the gourd family, having gourds whose spongy inner portion may be used as a cloth. **2** the gourd itself.

dish|clout (dish′klout′), *n. Archaic or Dialect.* dishcloth.

dish cross, a metal stand to support a hot dish, shaped like a cross: *Dish rings ... were quickly superseded by the more elaborate dish cross which had adjustable arms, and often a spirit lamp in the centre* (London Times).

dis|heart|en (dis här′tən), *v.t.* to cause to lose hope; discourage; depress; dispirit: *Long illness is disheartening. The long drought disheartened the farmer.* SYN: deject.

dis|heart|en|ing|ly (dis här′tə ning lē), *adv.* in a disheartening manner; so as to discourage.

dis|heart|en|ment (dis här′tən mənt), *n.* = discouragement.

dished (disht), *adj.* **1** shaped like a dish; made slightly concave: *a dished mirror, a dished steering wheel. The land was dished so that water collected in the pond.* **2** having a curved surface: *a dished-in steering wheel to protect the driver, the dished-out surface of a watch crystal.* **3** set at a camber; tilted so as to be closer together at the bottom than at the top: *a dished pair of automobile wheels.* **4** *Slang.* ruined; defeated; frustrated.

dis|helm (dis helm′), *Archaic.* —*v.t.* to deprive of a helmet.
—*v.i.* to take off one's helmet.
[< *dis-*[2] + *helm*[2]]

dis|her|i|son (dis her′ə sən), *n.* the act of disinheriting; disinheritance. [earlier *disheriteson* < Old French *desheriteisun,* ultimately < Latin *dis-* not + *hērēditās* inheritance]

dis|her|it (dis her′it), *v.t. Obsolete.* to disinherit. [Middle English *diseriter* < Old French *desheriter,* ultimately < Latin *dis-* not + *hērēditās* inheritance]

dis|her|it|ment (dis her′it mənt), *n. Obsolete.* disinheritance.

di|shev|el (də shev′əl), *v.t.,* **-eled, -el|ing** or (*especially British*) **-elled, -el|ling.** to disarrange or rumple (hair, clothing, bedding, feathers, or other arranged things). [back formation from *disheveled*]

di|shev|eled (də shev′əld), *adj.* **1** not neat; rumpled; mussed; untidy: *His disheveled appearance showed that he had slept with his clothes on.* SYN: disordered. **2** hanging loosely or in disorder;

unkempt: *disheveled hair.* SYN: tousled. **3** poorly organized; disjointed: *A disheveled comedy about Organization Men at a Convention* (New Yorker). [< Old French *descheveler* (< *des-* apart + *chevel* hair < Latin *capillus*) + English *-ed*²]

di|shev|elled (də shev′əld), *adj. Especially British.* disheveled.

di|shev|el|ment (də shev′əl mənt), *n.* **1** the act of disheveling. **2** disheveled condition: *He apologized for his dishevelment and offered to repair it* (Harper's).

dish-faced (dish′fāst′), *adj.* having a flattened or somewhat hollow face: ... *a short, shrivelled little fellow, dish-faced and battered* (New Yorker).

dish|ful (dish′fu̇l), *n., pl.* **-fuls.** as much as a dish can hold.

dish gravy, meat juice in the platter after carving meat.

dish|ing (dish′ing), *adj.* **1** that dishes. **2** taking or having the form of a dish; concave.

dis|hoard (dis hôrd′, -hōrd′), *v.t., v.i.* to release (that which was hoarded): *Such dishoarding was a major influence in curtailing the earlier recessions* (E. C. Harwood).

dis|hon|est (dis on′ist), *adj.* **1** not fair play; showing lack of honesty: *Lying, cheating, and stealing are dishonest.* SYN: corrupt, underhand. **2** not honest; ready to cheat; not upright: *A person who lies or steals is dishonest.* SYN: thievish. **3** arranged to work in an unfair way: *dishonest scales weighted to cheat the customer.* SYN: fraudulent.

dis|hon|es|ty (dis on′ə stē), *n., pl.* **-ties. 1** lack of honesty: *A liar, cheater, or thief can't be trusted because of his dishonesty. The dishonesty of the city officials was exposed by the newspapers.* **2** a dishonest act.

dis|hon|or (dis on′ər), *n., v.* **—*n.*** **1** loss of reputation or standing; shame; disgrace: *The robber brought dishonor to his family.* SYN: See syn. under **disgrace. 2** a person or thing that causes dishonor: *The team's poor sportsmanship in the tournament was a dishonor to the school.* **3** the refusal or failure to pay a check, bill, or other obligation.
—*v.t.* **1** to bring reproach or shame upon: *The player who cheated dishonored the entire team.* **2a** to refuse or fail to pay (a check, bill, or other obligation): *A bank will dishonor your checks if you do not have money in the bank to pay them.* **b** to fail to keep (a promise or the like): *On a few rare occasions an individual elector has dishonored his commitment* (New Yorker). **—dis|hon′or|er,** *n.*

dis|hon|or|a|ble (dis on′ər ə bəl), *adj.* **1** causing loss of honor; shameful; disgraceful: *a dishonorable career.* SYN: base, ignominious. **2** without honor; unprincipled: *A dishonorable student has no scruples about cheating.* SYN: despicable. **—dis|hon′or|a|ble|ness,** *n.*

dishonorable discharge, a military discharge given for such reasons as theft, desertion, and destruction of government property. It deprives the holder of all veteran benefits and some citizenship rights.

dis|hon|or|a|bly (dis on′ər ə blē), *adv.* in a dishonorable manner; with dishonor.

dis|hon|our (dis on′ər), *n., v.t. Especially British.* dishonor.

dis|horn (dis hôrn′), *v.t.* to remove the horns from; dehorn.

dis|house (dis houz′), *v.t.,* **-housed, -hous|ing. 1** to evict from a house. **2** to clear (ground) of houses.

dish|pan (dish′pan′), *n.* a pan in which to wash dishes.

dishpan hands, chapped hands, especially as caused by frequent immersion in water containing detergent compounds, soap flakes, and the like.

dish|rag (dish′rag′), *n. U.S.* **1** a cloth to wash dishes with; dishcloth. **2** anything wet and limp. **3** = dishcloth gourd.

dish-shaped (dish′shāpt′), *adj.* shaped like a dish: *With this 140-foot, dish-shaped antenna to catch radio radiation from vast regions of space* ... (Science News Letter).

dish|tow|el (dish′tou′əl), *n.* a towel to dry dishes with.

dish|ware (dish′wãr′), *n.* dishes used for meals: chinaware: *The quake jarred dishware off the shelves but no severe damage was reported* (San Francisco Chronicle).

dish|wash|er (dish′wosh′ər, -wôsh′-), *n.* **1** a machine for washing dishes, pots, glasses, and silverware: *These modern heaters can deliver ... superhot water for laundry and dishwasher* (Harper's). **2** a person who washes dishes in a restaurant kitchen or the like: *I've been a dishwasher all my life and I'm sick of it* (Maclean's).

dish|wash|ing (dish′wosh′ing, -wôsh′-), *n., adj.* **—*n.*** the washing of dishes.
—*adj.* for washing dishes: *a dishwashing machine, a dishwashing compound.*

dish|wa|ter (dish′wôt′ər, -wot′-), *n.* **1** water to wash dishes with. **2** water in which dishes have been washed: (*Figurative.*) *You don't win campaigns with a diet of dishwater and milk toast* (Newsweek).

dish|wa|ter|y (dish′wôt′ər ē, -wot′-), *adj.* resembling dishwater.

dish|y (dish′ē), *adj.,* **dish|i|er, dish|i|est.** *Especially British. Slang.* attractive; pretty: ... *two dishy chicks with plenty talent* (Observer). *Charbol's "Les Bonnes Femmes" defined very exactly what it is to be a dishy girl bored stiff with selling electrical equipment* (New Yorker). [< *dish* (def. 9) + *-y*¹]

dis|il|lu|sion (dis′i lü′zhən), *v., n.* **—*v.t.*** to free from illusion; deprive of one's belief or hope; disappoint; disenchant: *The boys became disillusioned about the romance of camping once the heavy rains collapsed their tent and soaked their bedding. ... a chic forty-year-old who is disillusioned but not embittered* (New Yorker).
—*n.* freedom from illusion; disenchantment: *a painful disillusion.*

dis|il|lu|sion|er (dis′i lü′zhə nər), *n.* a person or thing that disillusions.

dis|il|lu|sion|ist (dis′i lü′zhə nist), *n.* = disillusioner.

dis|il|lu|sion|ize (dis′i lü′zhə nīz), *v.t.,* **-ized, -iz|ing.** = disillusion.

dis|il|lu|sion|ment (dis′i lü′zhen mənt), *n.* **1** the process of disillusioning. **2** the state of being disillusioned: *Ravel's great orchestral suite, La Valse, is a brilliant study of the composer's own disillusionment* (New Yorker).

dis|il|lu|sive (dis′i lü′siv), *adj.* tending to disillusion.

dis|im|mure (dis′i myu̇r′), *v.t.,* **-mured, -mur|ing.** to free from confinement; liberate.

dis|im|pas|sioned (dis′im pash′ənd), *adj.* dispassionate; calm.

dis|im|pris|on (dis′im priz′ən), *v.t.* to release from imprisonment. **—dis′im|pris′on|ment,** *n.*

dis|im|prove (dis′im prüv′), *v.t., v.i.,* **-proved, -prov|ing.** to make or become worse.

dis|im|prove|ment (dis′im prüv′mənt), *n.* a worsening: ... *an utter neglect and disimprovement of the earth* (John Norris).

dis|in|cen|tive (dis′in sen′tiv), *n.* a thing that discourages effort or incentive: *High taxation is one of the causes of inflation, and a disincentive to hard work* (Economist).

dis|in|cli|na|tion (dis in′klə nā′shən), *n.* slight dislike; unwillingness; averseness: *His most noticeable quality was a marked disinclination for work.* SYN: reluctance.

dis|in|cline (dis′in klīn′), *v.,* **-clined, -clin|ing.** **—*v.t.*** to make unwilling; turn away; alienate: *to disincline one's affections. The hard rain disinclined him to go.* **—*v.i.*** to be unwilling: *Many hobos disincline to work.*

dis|in|clined (dis′in klīnd′), *adj.* unwilling; averse: *The lazy boy was disinclined to clean up his room.* SYN: loath.

dis|in|cor|po|rate (dis′in kôr′pə rāt), *v.t.,* **-rat|ed, -rat|ing.** to remove from the state of incorporation; deprive of the privileges of incorporation: *to disincorporate a village.*

dis|in|cor|po|ra|tion (dis′in kôr′pə rā′shən), *n.* **1** the act of disincorporating. **2** the state of being disincorporated.

dis|in|fect (dis′in fekt′), *v.t.* to destroy the disease germs in or on: *to disinfect dental instruments. Garbage chutes lead into a ... device that compresses the refuse, disinfects it, and even sprays it with perfume* (New York Times). SYN: sterilize. **—*v.i.*** to destroy disease germs; act as a disinfectant: *"Don't wipe the edge [of the cup]," said Michael. "The brandy disinfects"* (Joanna Ostrow).

dis|in|fect|ant (dis′in fek′tənt), *n., adj.* **—*n.*** a substance or means used to destroy disease germs. Alcohol, iodine, and carbolic acid are disinfectants. Heat is a disinfectant.
—*adj.* used to destroy disease germs: *a disinfectant soap.*

dis|in|fec|tion (dis′in fek′shən), *n.* the destruction of disease germs.

dis|in|fec|tor (dis′in fek′tər), *n.* a person or thing that disinfects.

dis|in|fest (dis′in fest′), *v.t.* to destroy infesting insects, rodents, or pests in: *to disinfest a cellar.*

dis|in|fes|ta|tion (dis in′fes tā′shən), *n.* the destruction of infesting insects, rodents, or other pests.

dis|in|flate (dis′in flāt′), *v.t.,* **-flat|ed, -flat|ing.** to reduce (prices) without bringing about deflation; reverse from a state of inflation.

dis|in|fla|tion (dis′in flā′shən), *n.* reversal of an economy from a state of continuous inflation, especially by reducing prices to increase the purchasing power of consumers without bringing about deflation.

dis|in|fla|tion|ar|y (dis′in flā′shə ner′ē), *adj.* **1** of or having to do with disinflation. **2** producing or tending to produce disinflation: ... *a very real incentive to make some sacrifice in order to save, thus producing a disinflationary trend* (London Times).

dis|in|form (dis′in fôrm′), *v.t.* to give distorted or false information to: *to disinform the public.* [back formation from *disinformation*]

dis|in|for|ma|tion (dis in′fər mā′shən), *n.* distorted or false information designed to mislead: *Lonsdale is working for the KGB's "Department of Disinformation"— an outfit dedicated to sowing dissent and confusion among Western intelligence networks* (Time). [translation of Russian *dezinformatsiya*]

dis|in|ge|nu|i|ty (dis in′jə nü′ə tē, -nyü′-), *n.* disingenuous quality; disingenuousness: *Mr. Butler, with an air of disingenuity, pretended that he was only anxious that as many Labour voters should get to the poll as possible* (Punch).

dis|in|gen|u|ous (dis′in jen′yu̇ əs), *adj.* lacking in frankness; insincere; covertly guileful; crafty: *a disingenuous apology. Persons entirely disingenuous, who really do not believe the opinion they defend* (David Hume). SYN: artful. **—dis′in|gen′u|ous|ly,** *adv.* **—dis′in|gen′u|ous|ness,** *n.*

dis|in|her|i|son (dis′in her′ə zən), *n.* disherison; disinheritance.

dis|in|her|it (dis′in her′it), *v.t.* to prevent from inheriting; take away an inheritance from: *A father disinherits his son if he leaves none of his property to his son.*

dis|in|her|it|ance (dis′in her′ə təns), *n.* **1** the act of disinheriting. **2** the state of being disinherited.

dis|in|hi|bi|tion (dis′in ə bish′ən, dis in′hi-), *n. Psychology.* the failure of an inhibition to operate, caused by an extraneous stimulus, a distraction, drug, or other factor that impedes inhibition.

dis|in|hume (dis′in hyüm′), *v.t.,* **-humed, -hum|ing.** to unearth; exhume.

dis|in|sec|tion (dis′ən sek′shən), *n.* = disinsectization.

dis|in|sect|i|za|tion (dis′ən sek′tə zā′shən), *n.* the act or process of ridding an aircraft, ship, truck, or other enclosed area of insects.

dis|in|te|gra|ble (dis in′tə grə bəl), *adj.* that can be disintegrated.

dis|in|te|grant (dis in′tə grənt), *n.* a substance causing disintegration of a medicinal tablet: *A mixture of sodium bicarbonate plus tartaric acid also acts as a disintegrant by generating carbon dioxide when the tablet is placed in water* (New Scientist and Science Journal).

dis|in|te|grate (dis in′tə grāt), *v.,* **-grat|ed, -grat|ing. —*v.t.*** **1** to break up; separate into small parts or bits: *The bomb disintegrated the building.* (*Figurative.*) *We cannot modify our class distinctions without risk of disintegrating the social structure* (George Meredith). **2** to change the structure of an atomic nucleus, especially by bombarding it with charged particles: *The target nucleus is of course also disintegrated* (E. P. George). **—*v.i.*** **1** to become disintegrated; break up: *The old papers had disintegrated into a pile of fragments and dust.* SYN: decompose, crumble. **2** (of atomic nuclei) to undergo disintegration.

***dis|in|te|gra|tion** (dis in′tə grā′shən), *n.* **1** a breaking up; separation into small parts or bits: *Rain and frost had caused the gradual disintegration of the rock.* (*Figurative.*) *The decay of moral principles which hastened the disintegration of Roman society* (Charles Merivale). **2** a change in the structure of an atomic nucleus by its emission of particles or rays; decay. Disintegration occurs naturally in the nuclei of radioactive substances or can be induced in other substances by bombarding their nuclei with fast-moving particles or rays.

***disintegration**
definition 2

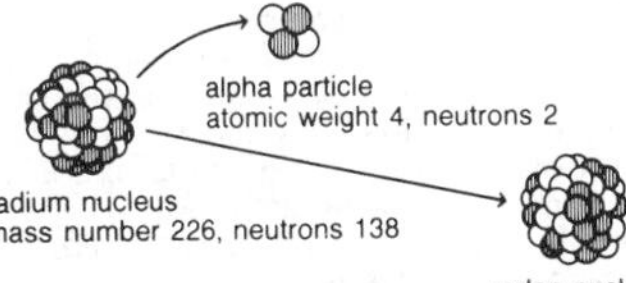

disintegration product, *Physics, Chemistry.* **1** a substance formed by the disintegration of another substance. **2** a substance produced by the breaking down of a radioactive substance.

Pronunciation Key: hat, āge, cãre, fär; let, ēqual, tėrm; it, īce; hot, ōpen, ôrder; oil, out; cup, pu̇t, rüle; child; long; thin; ᴛʜen; zh, measure; ə represents **a** in about, **e** in taken, **i** in pencil, **o** in lemon, **u** in circus.

dis|in|te|gra|tive (dis in′tə grā′tiv), *adj.* tending to disintegrate or produce disintegration; disintegrating: . . . *the integrative and disintegrative processes within the social system of the nation* (Bulletin of Atomic Scientists). —**dis|in′te|gra′tive|ly**, *adv.*

dis|in|te|gra|tor (dis in′tə grā′tər), *n.* **1** a person or thing that causes disintegration. **2** a machine for disintegrating a substance: *Some big-volume wineries, by contrast, use disintegrators advertised to "grind whole clusters* [*of grapes*], *including stems!"* (Newsweek).

dis|in|ter (dis′in tėr′), *v.t.*, **-terred, -ter|ring.** **1** to take out of a grave or tomb; dig up. SYN: exhume. **2** *Figurative.* to bring to light; discover and reveal: *It may be a very good idea not to disinter the entire range of activities of the giants whose names today grace the foundations* (Atlantic). SYN: unearth.

dis|in|ter|est (dis in′tər ist, -trist), *n., v.* —*n.* **1** lack of interest; indifference; unconcern: *Her disinterest in music was due to a boring teacher. What Kafka typifies, of course, is a disinterest in character as such* (American Scholar). **2** disinterestedness; impartiality: *He forever stayed serene and firm in his disinterest toward his opposition* (Emmet John Hughes).
—*v.t.* to rid of interest or concern: *Wodehouse's true offense was to have disinterested himself in the war* (New Statesman).

dis|in|ter|est|ed (dis in′tər əs tid, -tris-; -tə res′-), *adj.* **1** free from selfish motives; impartial; fair: *An umpire makes disinterested decisions. Never have statesmen needed so much the disinterested wisdom which a philosophic temper alone can give* (Manchester Guardian). SYN: unbiased, unprejudiced. **2** not interested; unconcerned; uninterested: *A disinterested pupil can spoil a class. He was tired, preoccupied, disinterested* (Dayton Rommel). —**dis|in′ter|est′ed|ly**, *adv.* —**dis|in′ter|est′ed|ness**, *n.*
▶**Disinterested** and **uninterested** can be used to make a useful distinction of meaning. *Uninterested* means having no concern about the matter and paying no attention: *I find it difficult to entertain anyone so uninterested in everything I suggest doing.* In careful usage, *disinterested* means having no reason or desire to be anything but strictly impartial and fair: *A judge should be disinterested.* Increasingly, however, *disinterested* is being used with the meaning of *uninterested.* Because of this, it is wise to make sure that context makes the intended meaning of *disinterested* unmistakable.

dis|in|ter|me|di|a|tion (dis′in tər mē′dē ā′shən), *n. U.S. Finance.* heavy withdrawals from intermediate institutions, such as savings and commercial banks, for direct investment in the securities market.

dis|in|ter|ment (dis′in tėr′mənt), *n.* **1** the act of disinterring. **2** the state of being disinterred. **3** something disinterred.

dis|in|tox|i|cate (dis′in tok′sə kāt), *v.t.*, **-cat|ed, -cat|ing.** to free from the effects of intoxication or an intoxicating drug: *to disintoxicate addicts.*

dis|in|tox|i|ca|tion (dis′in tok′sə kā′shən), *n.* **1** the act or process of disintoxicating: *disintoxication from alcohol.* **2** treatment for drug addiction or alcoholism: *a disintoxication clinic.*

dis|in|vest (dis′in vest′), *v.t., v.i.* to withdraw stock, savings, capital, or the like, from investment: . . . *the tendency of British shareholders and companies to disinvest* (London Times).

dis|in|vest|ment (dis′in vest′mənt), *n.* a disinvesting or being disinvested.

dis|in|vi|ta|tion (dis′in və tā′shən), *n.* **1** the act of disinviting. **2** the state of being disinvited.

dis|in|vite (dis′in vīt′), *v.t.*, **-vit|ed, -vit|ing.** to cancel an invitation to.

dis|jas|ked, dis|jas|ket, or **dis|jas|kit** (dis jas′kit), *adj. Scottish.* broken down; dilapidated; decayed. [apparently alteration of *dejected*]

dis|ject (dis jekt′), *v.t.* to cast or break apart; scatter; disperse. [< Latin *disjectus,* past participle of *disjicere* < *dis-* apart + *jacere* to throw]

dis|jec|ta mem|bra (dis jek′tə mem′brə), *Latin.* scattered members; disjointed fragments: *A light rain fell on the old newspapers, ice-cream cartons, orange-peel, and the rest of the disjecta membra of a thousand separate retreats into illusion* (Punch).

dis|jec|tion (dis jek′shən), *n.* **1** the act of disjecting. **2** the fact or condition of being disjected.

dis|join (dis join′), *v.t.* to keep from joining; prevent from being joined; separate. SYN: disunite, part, sever. —*v.i.* to become separated.

dis|joint (dis joint′), *v., adj.* —*v.t.* **1** to take apart at the joints: *The butcher disjointed the chicken for Mother.* SYN: dismember. **2** *Figurative.* to break up; put out of order; disconnect: *War disjoints a nation's affairs.* **3** to put out of joint; dislocate: *He disjointed his wrist when he fell.*
—*v.i.* to come apart; be put out of joint: *Let the frame of things disjoint* (Shakespeare).
—*adj.* **1** *Mathematics.* having no members in common. The set of even numbers and the set of odd numbers are disjoint. The sets (1,2,3) and (3,4,5) are not disjoint because they have 3 in common. **2** *Obsolete.* disjointed; out of joint.

dis|joint|ed (dis join′tid), *adj.* **1** taken apart at the joints: *a disjointed chicken.* SYN: disjoined. **2** *Figurative.* broken up; disconnected; incoherent: *disjointed speech. The nervous boy gave a rambling and disjointed account of the book he had read.* **3** out of joint: *a disjointed wrist.* —**dis|joint′ed|ly**, *adv.* —**dis|joint′ed|ness**, *n.*

dis|junct (dis jungkt′), *adj., n.* —*adj.* **1** disjoined; separated: *The Petrassi piece is in a disjunct chromatic idiom not usually associated with the . . . Italian composer* (New York Times). **2** having the head, thorax, and abdomen separated by deep constrictions. Ants are disjunct insects.
—*n. Logic.* any one of the alternatives of a disjunctive proposition.
[< Latin *disjūnctus,* past participle of *disjungere* < *dis-* away + *jungere* join]

dis|junc|tion (dis jungk′shən), *n.* **1** the act of disjoining. **2** the state of being disjoined; separation. **3** *Logic.* **a** the relation between the terms of a disjunctive proposition. **b** a disjunctive proposition.

dis|junc|tive (dis jungk′tiv), *adj., n.* —*adj.* **1** causing separation; separating. **2** *Grammar.* showing a choice or contrast between two ideas, words, clauses, etc. *But, yet,* and *either . . . or* are disjunctive conjunctions. *Otherwise* and *else* are disjunctive adverbs. **3** *Logic.* involving alternatives. A disjunctive proposition asserts that one or the other of two things is true but both cannot be true. Also, **discretive.**
—*n.* **1** *Grammar.* a disjunctive conjunction. **2** *Logic.* a statement involving alternatives. —**dis|junc′tive|ly**, *adv.*

dis|junc|ture (dis jungk′chər), *n.* = disjunction.

dis|june (dis jün′), *n. Scottish.* breakfast. [< Old French *desjun* < *desjuner* to break a fast < Vulgar Latin *disjunāre,* variant of *disjējūnāre.* See related etym. at **dine.**]

***disk** (disk), *n., v.* —*n.* **1** a thin, round, flat object shaped like a coin. **2** a round, flat surface, or a surface that seems so: *the sun's disk.* **3** a round, flat part in a plant or animal: *The yellow center of a daisy is a disk.* **4** *Anatomy, Zoology.* any one of various round, flat structures, especially the mass of fibrous cartilage lying between the bodies of adjacent vertebrae. **5** anything resembling a disk. **6** = phonograph record. **7** a floppy disk, hard disk, or similar magnetic disk for storing data: *Disks contain more recorded information now than ever before* (New York Times). **8** the puck used in ice hockey. **9** *Obsolete.* a discus.
—*v.t.* to work (the soil) with a disk harrow. Also, **disc.**
[< Latin *discus* < Greek *dískos* discus. See etym. of doublets **dais, desk, discus, dish.**]
—**disk′like′**, *adj.*

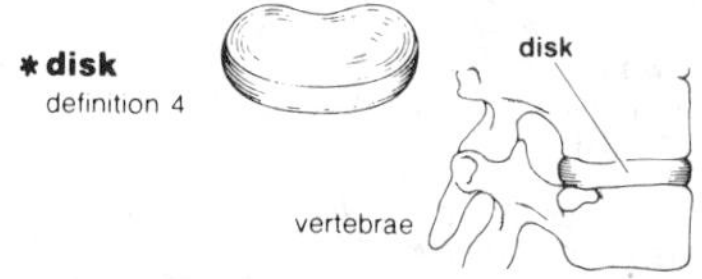

***disk** definition 4

disk brake, an automobile brake in which flat plates are pressed against both sides of a revolving disk attached to the wheel. See picture under **brake**[1]. Also, **disc brake.**

disk drive, the machinery of a computer that turns a disk to retrieve information stored on the disk: *In addition to floppy disk drives, there are hard disk drives, which rapidly spin hard, metal disks that store vastly greater amounts of information than do floppy disks* (New York Times).

disk|ette (dis′ket, dis ket′), *n.* = floppy disk.

disk flower or **floret**, one of the florets with tubular corollas in the central portion or disk of a daisy, aster, or other composite flower head. See picture under **dimorphism.**

***disk harrow**, a harrow with a row of sharp, revolving disks, used in preparing ground for planting or sowing, or in cultivating certain plants.

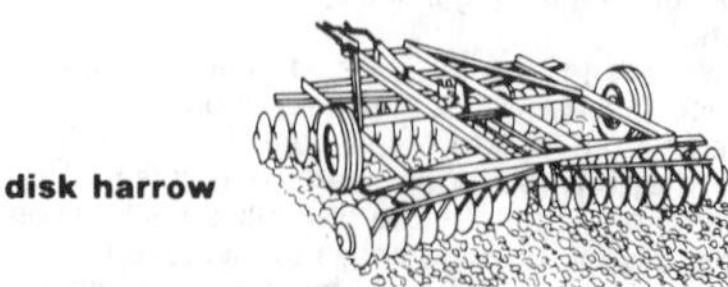
***disk harrow**

disk jockey, *Informal.* an announcer for a radio program that consists chiefly of recorded popular music: *Brad Phillips, disk jockey, will conduct the program from the stage of the Rivoli Theatre* (New York Times). Also, **disc jockey.**

disk|less (disk′lis), *adj.* without a disk; not showing a disk.

dis|kog|ra|phy (dis kog′rə fē), *n.* a method of taking X-ray pictures of an intervertebral disk after injecting a radiopaque substance: *Diskography has proved of value in the demonstration of damaged intervertebral disks in instances when routine myelography has been ineffective* (Morris Fishbein).

disk pile, an iron pile, having a disk or flange as a foot, used for foundations in sand.

disk plow, a plow with revolving disks, in place of plow shares. It is used especially in plowing hard, sticky, or stony land. Also, **disc plow.**

disk-shaped (disk′shāpt′), *adj.* having the shape of a disk.

disk wheel, a wheel with a solid surface instead of spokes.

disk winding, a winding on an armature in which the convolutions are flat.

dis|leaf (dis lēf′), *v.t.* = disleave.

dis|leave (dis lēv′), *v.t.*, **-leaved, -leav|ing.** to deprive of leaves: *bare trunk and disleaved bough* (James Russell Lowell).

dis|lik|a|ble (dis lī′kə bəl), *adj.* worthy of being disliked; displeasing; distasteful.

dis|like (dis līk′), *v.*, **-liked, -lik|ing,** *n.* —*v.t.* **1** to not like; object to; have a feeling against: *He dislikes studying and would rather play football. Cats dislike being wet.* **2** *Obsolete.* **a** to displease; offend. **b** to show dislike for.
—*n.* **1** a feeling of not liking; a feeling against: aversion; repugnance: *I have a dislike of rain and fog.* **2** *Obsolete.* disagreement; discord. —**dis|lik′er**, *n.*
—*Syn. n.* **1 Dislike, distaste, disgust** mean a feeling of not liking someone or something. **Dislike,** the general word, applies to any degree of this feeling: *I have a dislike for studying and would rather play baseball.* **Distaste** applies to a fixed dislike for something one finds unpleasant or disagreeable: *He has a distaste for chocolate.* **Disgust** applies to a strong dislike for something that is offensive, sickening, or loathsome: *We feel disgust for dirty streets, bad odors, or polluted water.*

dis|like|a|ble (dis lī′kə bəl), *adj.* = dislikable: *The three victims of this hair-raising novel . . . are each in their own way wholly dislikeable* (London Times).

dis|lik|en (dis lī′kən), *v.t. Obsolete.* to make unlike; disguise: *Muffle your face . . . and, as you can, disliken the truth of your own seeming* (Shakespeare).

dis|limn (dis lim′), *Archaic.* —*v.t.* to obliterate (a picture); efface; blot out.
—*v.i.* to become dislimned.

dis|link (dis lingk′), *v.t.* = unlink.

dis|lo|cate (dis′lō kāt), *v.t.*, **-cat|ed, -cat|ing.** **1** to put out of joint: *The football player dislocated his shoulder when he fell.* **2** *Figurative.* to put out of order; disturb; upset: *Our plans for the picnic were dislocated by the rain.* SYN: disarrange, disconcert. **3** to put out of place; displace.

dis|lo|ca|tion (dis′lō kā′shən), *n.* **1** the act of dislocating: (*Figurative.*) *His dislocation of the family's plans did not upset the children.* **2** the state of being dislocated. **3** *Physics.* an imperfection in the crystal structure of a metal or other solid resulting from the absence of an atom or atoms in one or more layers of a crystal.

dis|lo|ca|tive (dis′lō kā′tiv), *adj.* dislocating; producing dislocation: . . . *the dislocative shifts caused by new technology and by the mass movement of people from farms to cities* (New York Times).

dis|lo|ca|tor (dis′lō kā′tər), *n.* a person or thing that dislocates: (*Figurative.*) *The war, though, was the great dislocator* (New Yorker).

dis|lo|ca|to|ry (dis′lō kā′tər ē), *adj.* dislocating; dislocative.

dis|lodge (dis loj′), *v.*, **-lodged, -lodg|ing.** —*v.t.* to drive or force out, as of a place or position: *The workman used a crowbar to dislodge a heavy stone from the wall. Heavy gunfire dislodged the enemy from the fort.*
—*v.i.* to go away from a lodging place.

dis|lodge|a|ble (dis loj′ə bəl), *adj.* that can be dislodged.

dis|lodge|ment (dis loj′mənt), *n. Especially British.* dislodgment.

dis|lodg|ment (dis loj′mənt), *n.* **1** the act of dislodging. **2** the state of being dislodged.

dis|loy|al (dis loi′əl), *adj.* not loyal; unfaithful: *A disloyal servant let robbers into the house.* SYN: false, traitorous. —**dis|loy′al|ly**, *adv.*

dis|loy|al|ist (dis loi′ə list), *n.* a person who is disloyal.

dis|loy|al|ty (dis loi′əl tē), *n., pl.* **-ties.** **1** lack of loyalty; unfaithfulness: *The traitor was imprisoned for disloyalty to his country.* **2** a disloyal act: *Re-*

vealing secrets to the enemy in wartime is a disloyalty.

—*Syn.* **1 Disloyalty, treachery, treason** mean faithlessness. **Disloyalty** means unfaithfulness to the allegiance owed to persons, friends, one's country, or the like: *They reproached me with disloyalty to my school.* **Treachery** suggests some definite act of betraying trust while pretending to be loyal: *Secretly working to hurt a friend is treachery.* **Treason** applies to treachery to one's country, shown by doing something openly to help the enemy: *As an American citizen, he was guilty of treason for broadcasting enemy propaganda.*

dis|mal (diz′məl), *adj., n.* —*adj.* **1** dark and gloomy; dreary: *A damp cave or a rainy day is dismal.* SYN: somber. **2** depressed; miserable: *Sickness or bad luck often makes a person feel dismal.* SYN: sad. **3** cheerless; depressing: *Oliver Twist was born in a dismal workhouse.* **4** *Archaic.* disastrous; calamitous. **5** *Obsolete.* evil; unlucky.
—*n.* **1** something dismal. **2** *Obsolete.* a dismal person.
the dismals, *Dialect.* low spirits; the dumps: *I was simply trying to joke away the dismals* (George Washington Cable).
[Middle English *dismall,* perhaps < Old French *dis mal* evil (unlucky) days (in astrology) < Latin *diēs malī*] —**dis′mal|ly,** *adv.* —**dis′mal|ness,** *n.*

dismal science, political economy; economics (a term coined by Thomas Carlyle): *Whatever became of the dismal science? It went to the United States ... and became a gay, laughing, happy child again, a brainchild indeed of Keynes* (Sunday Times). —**dismal scientist.**

dis|man|tle (dis man′təl), *v.t.,* **-tled, -tling. 1** to remove furniture or equipment from; unfurnish: *to dismantle a house. The warship was dismantled before the hull was sold for scrap metal.* **2** to pull down; take apart: *We had to dismantle the bookcases in order to fit them through the doorway. It is almost impossible to dismantle an ... expeditionary force of over 300,000 men, with all their equipment, within six months* (James Reston). [< Old French *desmanteler* < *des-* off, away (< Latin *dis-*) + *mantel* mantle]

dis|man|tle|ment (dis man′təl mənt), *n.* the act or process of dismantling.

dis|man|tler (dis man′tlər), *n.* a person who dismantles or strips.

Dis|mas (diz′məs), *n.* the legendary name of the penitent thief crucified with Christ. Also, **Desmas.**

dis|mask (dis mask′, -mäsk′), *v.t. Obsolete.* to unmask.

dis|mast (dis mast′, -mäst′), *v.t.* to take the mast or masts from; break down the mast or masts of.

dis|mast|ment (dis mast′mənt, -mäst′-), *n.* **1** the act of dismasting. **2** the state of being dismasted.

dis|may (dis mā′), *n., v.* —*n.* loss of courage because of dislike or fear of what is about to happen or what has happened: *And each In other's countenance read his own dismay* (Milton). [< verb]
—*v.t.* to trouble greatly; make afraid; paralyze with fear or hopelessness: *The thought that she might fail the arithmetic test dismayed her.*
[Middle English *desmayen,* perhaps < unrecorded Anglo-French *desmaier* < Vulgar Latin *dismagāre* deprive of strength, for *exmagāre* < *ex-* away, out + Germanic (compare Old High German *magan* have strength)]
—*Syn. n.* **Dismay, consternation** mean a feeling of being unnerved or overwhelmed by the thought of what is going to happen next. **Dismay** suggests loss of ability to face or handle something frightening, baffling, or upsetting: *The mother was filled with dismay when her son confessed he had robbed a store.* **Dismay** is often used in a weakened sense: *To my dismay, my son gave up literature for mathematics.* **Consternation** suggests dismay and dread so sudden or great that a person cannot think clearly or, sometimes, move: *To our consternation the child darted out in front of the speeding car.*

dis|may|ing|ly (dis mā′ing lē), *adv.* in a dismaying manner; so as to trouble or make afraid.

dis|mem|ber (dis mem′bər), *v.t.* **1** to cut or tear the limbs from; divide limb from limb: *The wolves dismembered the deer's carcass.* **2** *Figurative.* to pull apart; cut to pieces; separate or divide into parts: *After the war the defeated country was dismembered and could no longer be called a nation. Three physicists ... dismembered one of the most intractable problems of the atom* (Walter Sullivan). —**dis|mem′ber|er,** *n.*

dis|mem|ber|ment (dis mem′bər mənt), *n.* **1** the act of dismembering: (*Figurative.*) *The Russians were also pressing for the complete dismemberment of Germany* (Newsweek). **2** the state of being dismembered.

dis|miss (dis mis′), *v.t.* **1** to send away; allow to go: *At noon the teacher dismissed the class for lunch.* **2** to remove from office or service; not allow to keep a job: *We dismissed the painter because his work was so poor.* **3** to put out of mind; stop thinking about: *Dismiss your troubles and be happy with what you have.* **4** to refuse to consider (a complaint, plea, etc.) in a court: *The judge dismissed the case because of lack of evidence.* **5** to deal with briefly or quickly: *The teacher dismissed all irrelevant questions in order to finish the lesson in one period.* [< Old French *desmis,* past participle of *desmettre* send away, learned borrowing from Vulgar Latin *dismittere,* for Latin *dīmittere* < *dī-* away + *mittere* send]
—*Syn.* **1, 2 Dismiss, discharge, release** mean to let someone go from his job, duty, etc. **Dismiss** applies whether he is forced to go or permitted to do so: *The students are not dismissed before 3:15. The principal dismissed the truant boy from school.* **Discharge** is often used when a person is forced to go but is also used especially of hospital patients when released: *The manager discharged the bookkeeper. After five days in the hospital, the patient was discharged.* **Release** applies when he is freed of his obligation to stay: *The soldier was released from duty for two days.*

dis|miss|al (dis mis′əl), *n.* **1** the act of dismissing: *The dismissal of five workmen caused a strike.* **2** the state or fact of being dismissed: *The company refused to announce the reason for the workers' dismissal. The teacher's dismissal under fire put him on the blacklist.* **3** a written or spoken order dismissing someone: *The workers received their dismissal last Friday.*

dis|miss|i|ble (dis mis′ə bəl), *adj.* that can be dismissed.

dis|mis|sion (dis mish′ən), *n.* = dismissal.

dis|mis|sive (dis mis′iv), *adj.* **1** characterized by dismissal; tending to dismiss. **2** that deals with summarily: *a dismissive gesture.* —**dis|mis′sive|ly,** *adv.* —**dis|mis′sive|ness,** *n.*

dis|mis|so|ry (dis mis′ər ē), *adj.* **1** sending away; dismissing to another jurisdiction. **2** giving permission to leave.

dis|mount (dis mount′), *v., n.* —*v.i.* **1** to get off a horse or other animal or get off a vehicle such as a bicycle: *The cavalry dismounted and led their horses across the stream.* SYN: alight. **2** *Obsolete.* to come down from a height; descend.
—*v.t.* **1** to throw or bring down from a horse; unhorse: *The first knight dismounted the second.* **2** to deprive (troops) of horses or mounts: *The Indians dismounted the troops by stealing their horses.* **3** to take (a thing) from its setting, framework, or support: *The cannons were dismounted for shipping to another fort.* **4** to take apart; take to pieces: *The mechanic dismounted the typewriter in order to fix the keys.*
—*n.* the act or manner of dismounting.

dis|mount|a|ble (dis moun′tə bəl), *adj.* that can be dismounted.

dis|mu|ta|tion (dis′myü tā′shən), *n. Chemistry.* a process in which a substance is simultaneously oxidized and reduced, producing two substances.

dis|na|ture (dis nā′chər), *v.t.,* **-tured, -tur|ing.** to make unnatural.

Dis|ney|esque (diz′nē esk′), *adj.* resembling or characteristic of the fanciful creations of Walt Disney, 1901-1966, American producer of animated cartoons and motion pictures; fanciful; fantastic; unreal: *I lay ... in a house haunted to the shadowy corners by Disneyesque menaces with clutching fingernails* (John Updike). *We were billeted in a Disneyesque castle outside Malines* (Lord Mancroft).

Dis|ney|ish (diz′nē ish), *adj.* = Disneyesque.

dis|o|be|di|ence (dis′ə bē′dē əns), *n.* refusal to obey; failure to obey: *Disobedience cannot be allowed in the army.* SYN: insubordination, recalcitrance.

dis|o|be|di|ent (dis′ə bē′dē ənt), *adj.* failing to follow orders or rules; refusing to obey; rebellious: *The disobedient child would not do his homework.* —**dis′o|be′di|ent|ly,** *adv.*

dis|o|bey (dis′ə bā′), *v.t.* to refuse to obey; fail to obey; defy: *The soldier who disobeyed orders was punished harshly.* —*v.i.* to be disobedient: *The law finally punishes those who disobey.* —**dis′o|bey′er,** *n.*

dis|o|bey|al (dis′ə bā′əl), *n.* a disobeying.

dis|o|blige (dis′ə blīj′), *v.t.,* **-bliged, -blig|ing. 1** to neglect to oblige; refuse to oblige; refuse to do a favor for: *I'm sorry to disoblige you, but I haven't enough money to lend any.* **2** to give offense to: *My plan has given offence to some gentlemen whom it would not be very safe to disoblige* (Joseph Addison). SYN: offend, affront. **3** to inconvenience: *The weather seemed determined to disoblige us.* SYN: incommode.

dis|o|blig|er (dis′ə blī′jər), *n.* a person who disobliges.

dis|o|blig|ing (dis′ə blī′jing), *adj.* not obliging; unwilling to accommodate others: *a disobliging driver, disobliging neighbors.* —**dis′o|blig′ing|ly,** *adv.* —**dis′o|blig′ing|ness,** *n.*

di|so|di|um cro|mo|gly|cate (dī sō′dē əm krō′mə glī′kāt), a drug used to prevent allergic bronchial asthma: *Disodium cromoglycate ... prevents the development of asthma by interfering with the antigen-antibody reaction* (Irwin J. Polk). *Formula:* $C_{23}H_{14}Na_2O_{11}$ [*disodium* containing two sodium atoms < *di-*[1] + *sodium; cromoglycate* < *c*(h)*romo-* + *glyc*(ine) + *-ate*[2]]

dis|op|er|a|tion (dis op′ə rā′shən), *n. Biology.* that behavior of organisms inhabiting the same place which results in harm or disadvantage to the organisms themselves.

dis|orb (dis ôrb′), *v.t. Archaic.* **1** to throw out of orbit. **2** to deprive of the orb of sovereignty.

dis|or|der (dis ôr′dər), *n., v.* —*n.* **1** a lack of order; confusion: *The room was in disorder after the birthday party.* SYN: jumble. **2** a public disturbance; tumult; riot; unruly conduct: *Mounted troops were called out to put an end to the disorder in the streets.* SYN: commotion. **3** a sickness; disease: *Eating the wrong food can cause a stomach disorder.* SYN: ailment.
—*v.t.* **1** to destroy the regular order or working of; throw into confusion: *A series of accidents disordered the shop.* SYN: upset. **2** to cause sickness in: *Anxiety may disorder the heart or stomach.* —**dis|or′der|er,** *n.*

dis|or|dered (dis ôr′dərd), *adj.* **1** not in order; confused: *The boy failed for his disordered lesson.* **2** sick; disturbed: *a disordered mind.* —**dis|or′dered|ly,** *adv.* —**dis|or′dered|ness,** *n.*

dis|or|der|li|ness (dis ôr′dər lē nis), *n.* a disorderly condition: *She was scolded for the disorderliness of her room.*

dis|or|der|ly (dis ôr′dər lē), *adj., adv., n.* —*adj.* **1** not orderly; untidy; confused: *The troops fled in a disorderly retreat. An untidy, messy room is disorderly.* SYN: irregular. **2** causing disorder; making a disturbance; breaking rules; unruly: *A disorderly mob ran through the streets, shouting and breaking windows.* SYN: lawless, riotous. **3** *Law.* against the law; contrary to good morals or decency. See also **disorderly conduct.**
—*adv.* in a disorderly manner.
—*n.* = disorderly person.

disorderly conduct, *Law.* any action contrary to good morals or decency: *The drunkard was charged with disorderly conduct.*

disorderly house, *Law.* a gambling house, house of prostitution, or other building and its occupants engaged in illegal pursuits.

disorderly person, *Law.* a person guilty of disorderly conduct.

dis|or|gan|ise (dis ôr′gə nīz), *v.t.,* **-ised, -is|ing.** *Especially British.* disorganize.

dis|or|gan|i|za|tion (dis ôr′gə nə zā′shən), *n.* **1** the act of disorganizing; breaking up of order or system: *the disorganization of a government or an army.* **2** absence of organization or orderly arrangement; the condition of being disorganized; disorganized state: *Disorganization results from the impact of forces producing social change* (Ogburn and Nimkoff).

dis|or|gan|ize (dis ôr′gə nīz), *v.t.,* **-ized, -iz|ing.** to throw into confusion or disorder; upset the order and arrangement of: *Heavy snowstorms delayed all flights and disorganized the airline schedule.*

dis|or|gan|ized (dis ôr′gə nīzd), *adj.* not properly organized; lacking organization: *He describes our theatre's method of recruiting directors as, in general, "disorganized, arbitrary, and basically amateur"* (Michael Billington).

dis|or|gan|iz|er (dis ôr′gə nī′zər), *n.* a person who disorganizes; one who destroys regular order or system.

dis|o|ri|ent (dis ôr′ē ent, -ōr′-), *v.t.* **1** to cause to lose one's bearings. **2** *Figurative.* to cause to lose one's reckoning with respect to truth; disconcert; embarrass: *His sudden rise to fame and fortune disoriented him at first.* **3** *Psychiatry.* to cause disorientation in. **4** *Obsolete.* to turn from the east.

dis|o|ri|en|tate (dis ôr′ē en tāt, -ōr′-; -ôr′ē en′-, -ōr′-), *v.t.,* **-tat|ed, -tat|ing.** = disorient.

dis|o|ri|en|ta|tion (dis ôr′ē en tā′shən, -ōr′-), *n.* **1** the condition of having lost one's bearings; uncertainty as to direction: *In weightless space, scientists believe men may experience a disorientation* (Wall Street Journal). **2** *Psychiatry.* a mental disorder in which a person is unaware of or unable to respond, especially to other people or his surroundings, and is completely without a sense of time.

dis|own (dis ōn′), *v.t.* to refuse to recognize as one's own; cast off: *He disowned his wayward*

Pronunciation Key: hat, **ā**ge, c**ã**re, f**ä**r; let, **ē**qual, t**ė**rm, it, **ī**ce; hot, **ō**pen, **ô**rder; **oi**l, **ou**t; cup, p**u̇**t, r**ü**le; **ch**ild; lo**ng**; **th**in; **ŦH**en; **zh,** measure; **ə** represents **a** in about, **e** in taken, **i** in pencil, **o** in lemon, **u** in circus.

son. *They disown their principles out of fear* (Jonathan Swift). **SYN**: renounce, repudiate.

dis|own|ment (dis ōn′mənt), *n.* the act of disowning; repudiation.

dis|par|age (dis par′ij), *v.t.*, **-aged, -ag|ing. 1** to speak slightingly of; say (something) is of less value or importance than it actually is; belittle: *The coward disparaged the hero's brave attempt to rescue the drowning child.* **SYN**: depreciate. **2** to lower the reputation of; discredit. **SYN**: dishonor. [< Old French *desparagier* to marry beneath one's station < *des-* away (< Latin *dis-*) + *parage* rank, lineage < Latin *pār, paris* equal]

dis|par|age|ment (dis par′ij mənt), *n.* **1** the act of disparaging; detraction: *The disparagement of his mother made him bristle.* **2** something that lowers a thing or person in worth or importance. **SYN**: aspersion. **3** a lessening in esteem or standing; discredit: *Say nothing that will be to his disparagement with his new employer.*

dis|par|ag|er (dis par′ə jər), *n.* a person who disparages or dishonors; one who belittles, vilifies, or disgraces.

dis|par|ag|ing (dis par′ə jing), *adj.* that disparages; slighting: *The drama critic made disparaging comments on the new play.*

dis|par|ag|ing|ly (dis par′ə jing lē), *adv.* so as to disparage; slightingly.

dis|pa|rate (dis′pər it), *adj.* distinct in kind; essentially different; unlike: *A dog and a snake are disparate animals. Capitalism and communism have disparate political values. English chess players seem to accommodate their play to two disparate styles* (Al Horowitz). **SYN**: dissimilar. [< Latin *disparātus,* past participle of *disparāre* divide, separate < *dis-* apart + *parāre* get ready, prepare, arrange] — **dis′pa|rate|ly,** *adv.* — **dis′pa|rate|ness,** *n.*

dis|par|i|ty (dis par′ə tē), *n., pl.* **-ties. 1** lack of equality: *disparity in numbers. The old man ignored the disparity in their ages as he enjoyed the company of the young man. The continuing economic disparity between the "haves" and the "have nots" is a growing concern in world capitals* (New York Times). **SYN**: See syn. under **difference. 2** the quality of being unlike; difference: *The disparity in the accounts of the two witnesses puzzled the policeman.*

dis|park (dis pärk′), *v.t. Archaic.* **1** to divest of the character of a park. **2** to throw open (a private park) to common use.

dis|par|lure (dis′pär lu̇r′), *n.* a synthetic form of the sex attractant of the female gypsy moth, more potent than gyplure: *Availability of the synthetic pheromone disparlure has . . . greatly increased the efficiency of the trapping program, and led to the possibility of direct control of the moth* (Mortin Beroza). [< (Porthetria) *dispar,* species name of the gypsy moth + English *lure*]

dis|part (dis pärt′), *v., n.* — *v.t.* to separate; divide into parts: *Till death disparts the union.* — *v.i.* to separate; break up.
— *n.* **1** the difference between the radius of the bore at the breech of a gun and that at the swell of the muzzle. **2** Also, **dispart sight.** a sight which allows for this difference.
[probably < Italian *dispartire* divide, learned borrowing from Latin *dispartīre* distribute < *dis-* apart + *partīre* to part, share]

dis|part|ment (dis pärt′mənt), *n.* **1** separation; division into parts. **2** an opening caused by separation.

dis|pas|sion (dis pash′ən), *n.* freedom from emotion or prejudice; calmness; impartiality.

dis|pas|sion|ate (dis pash′ə nit), *adj.* free from emotion or prejudice; calm and impartial: *To a dispassionate observer, the drivers of both cars seemed equally to blame for the accident.* **SYN**: composed, cool. — **dis|pas′sion|ate|ly,** *adv.* — **dis|pas′sion|ate|ness,** *n.*

dis|patch (dis pach′), *v., n.* — *v.t.* **1** to send off to some place or for some purpose: *to dispatch a telegram. The captain dispatched a boat to bring a doctor on board ship.* **2** to get (something) done promptly or speedily: *The teacher dispatched the roll call and began the lesson.* **SYN**: settle, conclude. **3** to give the death blow to; kill: *He dispatched the deer with his first shot.* **4** *Informal.* to finish off; eat up: *The hungry boy quickly dispatched the meal.* **5** to dispose of; get rid of: *The housewife dispatched the salesman. He started predicting the round in which he would dispatch each opponent* (New Yorker).
— *v.i.* **1** *Archaic.* to hasten away; make haste: *Butler Gilbert, dispatch, thou knave* (Scott). **2** *Obsolete.* to conclude an affair or business.
— *n.* **1** a sending off (of a letter or messenger) to some place or for some purpose: *Please hurry up the dispatch of this telegram. There are periods best suited to the dispatch of a probe to Mars* (Walter Sullivan). **2** a written message, such as special news or government business: *This dispatch has been two days on the way. The correspondent rushed dispatches to his newspaper in New York about the fire in Paris.* **3** promptness in doing something; speed: *The boys worked with neatness and dispatch.* **SYN**: haste, expedition. **4** a putting to death; a killing: *The Japanese are … taught … the science … or accomplishment of "Happy Dispatch"* (London Times). **5** an agency for conveying goods: *The package was sent by dispatch.* **6** *Obsolete.* dismissal; discharge. Also, **despatch.**
[< Italian *dispacciare* hasten, or Spanish *despachar* < *dis-* not (< Latin *dis-*) + *empachar* impede, perhaps < Late Latin *impedicāre* hinder < *in-* (intensive) + *pedica* snare < *pēs, pedis* foot]

dispatch boat, a fast boat for carrying messages.

dispatch box, 1 = dispatch case. **2** *British.* either of two boxes placed on a table before the House of Commons, one on the Government side, the other on the Opposition side, from behind which a member of the Government or a leader of the Opposition may address the House.

dispatch case, a briefcase for carrying papers, such as dispatches or documents.

dis|patch|er (dis pach′ər), *n.* a person who dispatches. A train dispatcher is in charge of sending off the trains on schedule.

dis|pau|per (dis pô′pər), *v.t. Law.* **1** to decide (a person) to be no longer a pauper. **2** to disqualify from suing as a pauper (without payment of fees).

dis|pau|per|i|za|tion (dis pô′pər ə zā′shən), *n.* **1** the act of dispauperizing. **2** the state of being dispaupered.

dis|pau|per|ize (dis pô′pə rīz), *v.t.*, **-ized, -iz|ing. 1** to free from the state of pauperism. **2** to free from paupers.

dis|peace (dis pēs′), *n.* want of peace or quiet; uneasiness; dissension. [< *dis-*[2] + *peace*]

dis|pel (dis pel′), *v.t.*, **-pelled, -pel|ling.** to drive away and scatter; disperse: *to dispel darkness or gloom. The captain's cheerful laugh dispelled our fears.* **SYN**: See syn. under **scatter.** [< Latin *dispellere* < *dis-* away + *pellere* to drive]

dis|pel|ler (dis pel′ər), *n.* a person or thing that dispels: *The sun is the dispeller of darkness.*

dis|pend (dis pend′), *v.t. Obsolete.* to pay out; expend; spend. [< Old French *despendre* expend < Latin *dispendere* pay out < *dis-* out + *pendere* pay, weigh]

dis|pen|sa|bil|i|ty (dis pen′sə bil′ə tē), *n.* the quality of being dispensable.

dis|pen|sa|ble (dis pen′sə bəl), *adj.* **1** that can be done without; unimportant: *Television will never make books dispensable.* **SYN**: unessential, omissible. **2** that can be dispensed or administered: *The amount of dispensable funds was greatly reduced by Congress.* **3** *Ecclesiastical.* **a** that can be condoned: *a dispensable offense or sin.* **b** that can be declared not binding: *a dispensable law or rule.* — **dis|pen′sa|ble|ness,** *n.*

dis|pen|sa|ry (dis pen′sər ē), *n., pl.* **-ries.** a place where medicines, medical care, and medical advice are given free or for a small charge.

dis|pen|sa|tion (dis′pən sā′shən), *n.* **1** the act of giving out; act of distributing: *the dispensation of food and clothing to the flood victims.* **2** a thing given out or distributed: *They gave thanks for the dispensations of Providence.* **3** rule; management: *From 1558 to 1603 England was under the dispensation of Elizabeth I.* **4** the management or ordering of events by divine Providence or Nature: *The dispensations … of Providence continued to be strange* (Lytton Strachey). **5** a religious system: *the Christian dispensation, the Jewish dispensation.* **6** in the Roman Catholic Church: **a** official permission to disregard a rule, law, obligation, or the like, without penalty. **b** the writing giving such permission. **7** a doing away with or a doing without something: *The dispensation with reading the minutes saved time at club meetings.*

dis|pen|sa|tion|al (dis′pən sā′shə nəl), *adj.* of or having to do with dispensation or a dispensation.

dis|pen|sa|tor (dis′pən sā′tər), *n.* a person who dispenses; distributor; administrator.

dis|pen|sa|to|ry (dis pen′sə tôr′ē, -tōr′-), *n., pl.* **-ries. 1** a book that tells how to prepare and use medicines; an unofficial pharmacopoeia. **2** *Obsolete.* a dispensary.

dis|pense (dis pens′), *v.*, **-pensed, -pens|ing,** *n.* — *v.t.* **1** to give out; distribute: *The Red Cross dispensed food and clothing to the flood victims.* **SYN**: allot, apportion. See syn. under **distribute. 2** to carry out; put in force; apply: *Judges and law courts dispense justice.* **3** to prepare and give out: *Druggists must dispense medicines with the greatest care.* **4** to release; excuse: *He appeared to think himself … dispensed from all necessity of providing for himself* (Samuel Johnson). — *v.i.* to grant dispensation.
— *n. Obsolete.* a dispensation.

dispense with, a to do away with; make unnecessary: *The electric light has dispensed with the task of cleaning and filling oil lamps.* **b** to do without; get along without: *I shall dispense with these crutches as soon as my leg heals.*
[< Old French *dispenser,* learned borrowing from Latin *dispēnsāre* distribute (frequentative) < *dispendere;* see etym. under **dispend**]

dis|pens|er (dis pen′sər), *n.* a person or thing that dispenses or administers: *a paper-cup dispenser, a dispenser of patronage.*

dis|peo|ple (dis pē′pəl), *v.t.*, **-pled, -pling.** to deprive of all or many people or inhabitants; depopulate: *They thought it but compliance with the Divine command to dispeople the land of the Philistines* (Henry Hart Milman).

dis|peo|ple|ment (dis pē′pəl mənt), *n.* the process of dispeopling; depopulation.

di|sper|mous (dī spėr′məs), *adj. Botany.* (of fruits and their cells) containing two seeds.

di|sper|my (dī′spėr′mē), *n. Biology.* the entrance of two spermatozoa into a single egg.

dis|pers|a|ble (dis pėr′sə bəl), *adj.* = dispersible.

dis|per|sal (dis pėr′səl), *n.* the act of scattering or state of being scattered; dispersing: *Soldiers forced the dispersal of a mob. … the dispersal of industry from bomb-vulnerable cities* (Newsweek). **SYN**: dispersion.

Dis|per|sal (dis pėr′səl), *n.* = Diaspora.

dis|per|sant (dis pėr′sənt), *n.* an agent, especially a chemical compound, that aids in the dispersion of a substance.

dis|perse (dis pėrs′), *v.*, **-persed, -pers|ing,** *adj.* — *v.t.* **1** to send or drive off in different directions; scatter: *The police dispersed the rioters.* **SYN**: See syn. under **scatter. 2** to distribute; circulate: *Children went through the crowd dispersing handbills.* **SYN**: disseminate. **3** to cause to disappear; dispel; dissipate: *The swelling on his arm was dispersed by cold compresses.* **4** *Optics.* to divide (white light) into rays of different colors. **5** *Chemistry.* to scatter (the particles of a colloid) throughout another substance or a mixture.
— *v.i.* **1** to spread in different directions; scatter: *The crowd dispersed when it began raining.* **SYN**: See syn. under **scatter. 2** to disappear; be dispelled: *The chill night air dispersed with the dawn.*
— *adj.* dispersed. [< Middle French *disperser* < Latin *dispergere* < *dis-* apart + *spargere* scatter]

dis|pers|ed|ly (dis pėr′sid lē), *adv.* in a dispersed manner: *It is obviously much easier to write dispersedly than to construct the well-made play* (London Times).

dis|pers|ed|ness (dis pėr′sid nis), *n.* the quality or condition of being dispersed: *the dispersedness of our pioneer population.*

dis|persed phase (dis pėrst′), = disperse phase.

disperse phase, *Chemistry.* the particles in a colloidal system which are dispersed throughout a medium.

dis|pers|er (dis pėr′sər), *n.* a person or thing that disperses.

dis|pers|i|bil|i|ty (dis pėr′sə bil′ə tē), *n.* the quality or condition (of a substance) of being dispersible: *Separation is also affected by the dispersibility of the clays and shales in water* (Israel Berkovitch).

dis|pers|i|ble (dis pėr′sə bəl), *adj.* that can be dispersed.

***dis|per|sion** (dis pėr′zhən, -shən), *n.* **1** a dispersing: *Dispersion is the only real answer to atomic attack* (New York Times). **2** a being dispersed. **3** *Physics.* **a** the separation of light into its different colors. **b** a similar separation of electromagnetic waves, etc. **c** the difference between the deviations of any two wave lengths passing through and refracted by a prism, because of the different amounts of refraction for rays of different wave length. **4** *Chemistry.* **a** a substance that has been dispersed. **b** the system consisting of the dispersed colloidal particles and the medium in which they are dispersed. **5** *Military.* the scattered fall of missiles fired from a gun or guns set at the same range or of bombs dropped under identical conditions. **6** *Statistics.* the difference in size in the values of a variable or variables.

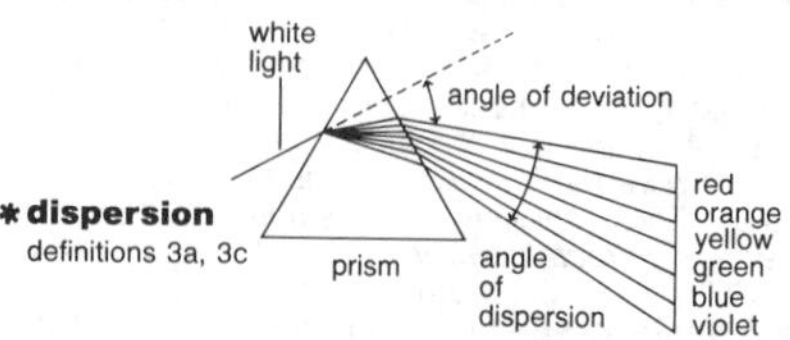

***dispersion**
definitions 3a, 3c

Dis|per|sion (dis pėr′zhən, -shən), *n.* = Diaspora.

dispersion error, *Military.* **1** variation in the fall of a series of shots. **2** the distance of one of these shots from the center of the group.

dispersion medium, *Chemistry.* the medium in which the particles in a colloidal system are dispersed; continuous phase.

dis|per|sive (dis pėr′siv), *adj.* dispersing; tending to disperse: *The material of an ordinary lens is dispersive* (John B. Walsh). —**dis|per′sive|ly,** *adv.* —**dis|per′sive|ness,** *n.*

dispersive power, *Physics.* the power of a substance to separate light rays by diffraction. It is measured by the ratio of the dispersion of the red and blue wave lengths to the deviation of the yellow produced by a prism of small angle.

dis|per|soid (dis pėr′soid), *n. Chemistry.* **1** a colloidal system having a relatively high degree of dispersion. **2** a colloid.

dis|pir|it (dis pir′it), *v.t.* to lower the spirits of; depress; discourage; dishearten: *Three defeats in a row dispirited the team. A week of rain dispirited us all.* SYN: deject.

dis|pir|it|ed (dis pir′ə tid), *adj.* depressed; discouraged; disheartened; dejected: *He returned wet, hungry, and dispirited.* —**dis|pir′it|ed|ly,** *adv.* —**dis|pir′it|ed|ness,** *n.*

dis|pir|it|ing (dis pir′ə ting), *adj.* that dispirits; depressing; disheartening. —**dis|pir′it|ing|ly,** *adv.*

dis|pir|it|ment (dis pir′it mənt), *n.* **1** the act of dispiriting. **2** the state of being dispirited; discouragement.

dis|pit|e|ous (dis pit′ē əs), *adj. Archaic.* pitiless; cruel. [variant of *despiteous*]

dis|place (dis plās′), *v.t.,* **-placed, -plac|ing.** **1** to take the place of; put something else in the place of: *The automobile has displaced the horse and buggy.* SYN: replace, supplant. **2** to remove from a position of authority: *The mayor displaced the police chief.* **3** to put out of place; move from its usual place or position: *Please do not displace any of my tools. A floating object displaces its own weight of liquid.* **4** to force out; remove; banish.

dis|place|a|ble (dis plā′sə bəl), *adj.* that can be displaced; liable to be displaced.

displaced homemaker, *U.S.* a married woman who has lost her means of support by divorce, separation, or the death or disability of her husband: *The term displaced homemaker was invented by another Californian . . . who was divorced at 57 and . . . not eligible for unemployment insurance because homemaking is not considered work* (Time).

dis|placed person (dis plāst′) a person forced out of his own country by war, famine, political disturbance, or because of his political convictions: *The displaced person has become a world-wide phenomenon* (Emory S. Bogardus).

dis|place|ment (dis plās′mənt), *n.* **1** the act of displacing. **2** a being displaced: *His laziness caused his displacement from office.* **3a** the weight of the volume of liquid or gas displaced by a body floating in it. This weight is equal to that of the floating object. **b** the difference between the initial position of a body and its position at a later instant, measured from some chosen point. **4** the volume in a pump or engine cylinder displaced by the stroke of the piston. **5** the distance of movement of rocks or strata in a geological fault. **6** *Psychiatry.* a form of defense mechanism in which an emotion that is repressed when first experienced is later expressed in connection with something unrelated; transference.

displacement ton, a unit of weight in terms of volume, equal to 35 cubic feet, or 0.9905 cubic meter, approximately the volume of salt water displaced by one long ton.

displacement tonnage, the weight of a ship in terms of the number of long tons displaced by it.

dis|plac|er (dis plā′sər), *n.* **1** a person or thing that displaces. **2** *Pharmacy.* an apparatus for obtaining an extract by displacement; percolator.

dis|plant (dis plant′, -plänt′), *v.t.* **1** to uproot (a plant). **2** *Obsolete.* to dislodge (people) from their settlements or country.

dis|play (dis plā′), *v., n., adj.* —*v.t.* **1** to put on view; show: *The American flag is displayed on the 4th of July.* **2** to show in a special way so as to attract attention: *The stores are displaying the new spring clothes in their windows.* **3** to let appear unintentionally or incidentally; reveal: *He displayed his good nature by answering all our questions.* **4** to spread out; unfold: *to display a banner.* **5** *Printing.* to make (certain words) prominent or conspicuous by the use of large, heavy, or distinctive type.
—*v.i.* to engage in display.
—*n.* **1** a showing; exhibition: *He did not like the boy's display of bad temper.* SYN: See syn. under **show.** **2** a showing off; ostentation: *Her fondness for display led her to buy showy clothes.* **3** a planned showing of a thing, for some special purpose; exhibit: *The local school had two displays of children's drawings in store windows.* **4** *Printing.* **a** the choice and arrangement of type so as to make certain words, etc., prominent. **b** printed matter so chosen and arranged. **5a** a visual presentation of radar signals or computer data on a screen. **b** a device for this: *The basic hardware for graphical output is the cathode-ray-tube display, known around computer installations as the CRT display* (Scientific American). **6** a presentation of colors and plumage by birds in certain patterns: *a courtship display, intimidation display. Many of the color patches used in display no doubt serve as signaling devices* (Leonard W. Wing).
—*adj.* **1** for display, especially as samples: *display goods.* **2** on, at, or in which samples of articles to be sold are on display: *a display counter.*
[< Old French *despleier* < Latin *displicāre* scatter < *dis-* un-, apart + *plicāre* to fold] —**dis|play′er,** *n.*
—*Syn. v.t.* **1, 2, 3 Display, exhibit, evince** mean to show. **Display** implies showing something so that others may see it clearly and examine it: *The saleswoman displayed her new cosmetics on the table.* **Exhibit** implies showing something especially worth looking at and in a way that draws attention: *The museum is exhibiting a rare collection of coins.* **Evince** applies only to something that cannot be seen with the eyes, such as feeling or quality: *He evinced obvious displeasure when he learned he would have to stay after school.*

display advertisement, an advertisement using striking typographical arrangement, color, illustrations, and the like.

dis|played (dis plād′), *adj. Heraldry.* turned full face with wings, talons, and tail feathers outstretched and the head looking over the right shoulder: *an eagle displayed.*

dis|please (dis plēz′), *v.,* **-pleased, -pleas|ing.** —*v.t.* to not please; be disagreeable to; offend; annoy: *You displease your father when you don't obey him. Glaring colors displease the eye.* SYN: anger, vex, chafe, provoke, pique.
—*v.i.* to be disagreeable or offensive.

dis|pleas|ed|ly (dis plē′zid lē), *adv.* in a displeased or disapproving manner; with displeasure.

dis|pleas|ing|ly (dis plē′zing lē), *adv.* in a displeasing, annoying, or offensive manner; disagreeably.

dis|pleas|ure (dis plezh′ər), *n., v.,* **-ured, -ur|ing.** —*n.* **1** the feeling of being displeased; slight anger; annoyance; dislike; dissatisfaction: *When Queen Victoria said, "We are not amused," she was expressing displeasure. We feel displeasure at something we dislike.* **2** *Archaic.* discomfort; uneasiness. **3** *Archaic.* offense; injury.
—*v.t. Archaic.* to displease.

dis|pleas|ure|ment (dis plezh′ər mənt), *n. Archaic.* displeasure.

dis|plen|ish (dis plen′ish), *v.t. Scottish.* deplenish.

dis|plen|ish|ing sale (dis plen′ə shing), *Scottish.* a sale of household furniture or of farm stock and utensils, as at the expiration of a lease.

dis|plode (dis plōd′), *v.t., v.i.,* **-plod|ed, -plod|ing.** *Obsolete.* to explode. [< Latin *displōdere* < *dis-* apart + *plaudere* clap]

dis|plo|sion (dis plō′zhən), *n. Obsolete.* explosion.

dis|plume (dis plüm′), *v.t.,* **-plumed, -plum|ing.** = deplume.

dis|pone (dis pōn′), *v.,* **-poned, -pon|ing.** —*v.t.* **1** (in Scottish law) to assign or convey legally. **2** *Obsolete.* to arrange; dispose. —*v.i. Obsolete.* to arrange. [< Latin *dispōnere* < *dis-* apart + *pōnere* to place]

dis|pon|er (dis pō′nər), *n.* (in Scottish law) a person who legally transfers property from himself to another.

dis|ponge (dis punj′), *v.t.,* **-ponged, -pong|ing.** to let drip as if from a sponge. [variant of *dispunge*]

dis|pope (dis pōp′), *v.t.,* **-poped, -pop|ing.** to deprive of the dignity of pope.

dis|port (dis pôrt′, -pōrt′), *v., n.* —*v.t.* to amuse (oneself); sport: *People laughed at the clumsy bears disporting themselves in the water.*
—*v.i.* to entertain oneself; play: *The baby disported with the new toy in great glee.* SYN: frolic, gambol.
[< Anglo-French *disporter,* Old French *desporter* < *des-* away (< Latin *dis-*) + *porter* carry, bear < Latin *portāre*]
—*n. Archaic.* a pastime; amusement. SYN: recreation, entertainment, sport.
[< Anglo-French *disport,* Old French *desport* < *disporter;* see the verb]

dis|port|ment (dis pôrt′ment, -pōrt′-), *n. Archaic.* the act of disporting; amusement; sport; play.

dis|pos|a|bil|i|ty (dis pō′zə bil′ə tē), *n.* the quality or condition of being disposable.

dis|pos|a|ble (dis pō′zə bəl), *adj., n.* —*adj.* **1** that can be disposed of after use; that can be thrown away: *disposable containers of foil, disposable paper napkins.* **2** at one's disposal; available: *Disposable income is money for spending or saving after taxes are paid.*
—*n.* a disposable article: *Hosts of "disposables" —items thrown away after a single use—are entering the hospital field* (Wall Street Journal).

dis|pos|al (dis pō′zəl), *n., adj.* —*n.* **1** the act of getting rid (of something): *the disposal of radioactive waste. The city takes care of the disposal of garbage.* **2** the act of giving away: *His will provided for the disposal of his property after his death.* **3** a selling; sale: *The disposal of government surplus items is arranged for Monday.* **4** the power or authority to dispose of or use something; control: *The trustees had the disposal of the estate.* SYN: command. **5** a dealing with; a settling of affairs: *His disposal of the difficulty pleased everybody.* **6** the act of putting in a certain order or position; arrangement: *a very tasteful disposal of flowers. The disposal of the chairs along the sides of the hall left plenty of space for dancing in the middle.* SYN: disposition. **7** a means of or a device for disposing. One kind of garbage disposal is an electric grinder installed in a kitchen sink to reduce garbage to liquid form or finely chopped particles so that it goes down into the sewage system. **8** *Obsolete.* regulation; dispensation; administration.
—*adj.* in which waste material is disposed of: *a disposal plant, a disposal drum.*
at (or **in**) **one's disposal,** ready for one's use or service at any time; under one's control or management: *I will put my room at your disposal.*

dis|pose (dis pōz′), *v.,* **-posed, -pos|ing,** *n.* —*v.t.* **1** to put in a certain order or position; arrange: *The flags were disposed in a straight line for the parade.* SYN: distribute, disperse. **2** to arrange (matters); settle (affairs); determine. **3** to make ready or willing; influence; incline: *More pay and shorter hours disposed him to take the new job.* **4** to make liable or subject: *Getting your feet wet disposes you to catching cold.* **5** to make fit; prepare: *Hardship disposes man to meet adversity.* **6** *Obsolete.* to regulate; order: *. . . he who is now sovereign can dispose and bid what shall be right* (Milton). **7** *Obsolete.* to bestow; distribute.
—*v.i.* **1** to control the course of events; settle affairs; determine: *Man proposes, but God disposes* (Thomas à Kempis). **2** *Obsolete.* to make terms.
—*n.* **1** *Archaic.* disposition; habit. **2** *Obsolete.* arrangement; regulation; disposal.
dispose of, a to get rid of: *Dispose of that rubbish.* **b** to give away: *I shall dispose of this clothing to the Salvation Army.* **c** to sell: *The owner disposed of his house for $35,000.* **d** to eat or drink: *The boys soon disposed of the picnic lunch.* **e** to arrange; settle: *The committee disposed of all its business in an hour.*
[< Old French *disposer* arrange < *dis-* apart, on various sides (< Latin) + *poser* to place, pose]

dis|posed (dis pōzd′), *adj.* willing; inclined: *Most young boys are more disposed to play than to study. The manager of this store is well disposed toward young people.*

dis|pos|ed|ness (dis pō′zid nis), *n.* the quality or state of being disposed; disposition; inclination.

dis|pos|er (dis pō′zər), *n.* a person or thing that disposes; a distributor, bestower, or director: *food waste disposers.*

dis|po|si|tion (dis′pə zish′ən), *n.* **1** one's natural way of acting toward others or of thinking about things; nature: *a cheerful disposition, a selfish disposition, a changeable disposition.* **2** tendency; inclination; natural bent: *a disposition to argue. A quarrelsome person has a disposition to start trouble.* **3** the act of putting in order or position; arrangement: *The general planned the disposition of his soldiers for the battle. The disposition of the papers on my desk had been changed.* **4** a disposing; settlement: *the satisfactory disposition of a difficult problem. What disposition did the court make of his case?* SYN: management. **5** disposal: *He had a large sum of money at his disposition. Safe disposition of radioactive waste requires the greatest care.* **6** *Obsolete.* physical constitution or state.
—*Syn.* **1 Disposition, temperament, temper** mean the qualities that characterize a person as an individual. **Disposition** applies to the controlling mental or emotional quality that determines a person's natural or usual way of thinking and acting: *He has a quarrelsome disposition.* **Temperament** applies to the combined physical, emotional, and mental qualities that determine a person's whole nature: *He has an artistic temperament.* **Temper** applies to the combined natural and acquired qualities that determine the state of mind in which a person meets problems and troubles: *He is calm in temper. Temper* may also be applied to a more temporary state: *I found*

Pronunciation Key: hat, āge, cãre, fär; let, ēqual, tėrm; it, īce; hot, ōpen, ôrder; oil, out; cup, pu̇t, rüle; child; long; thin; ᴛʜen; zh, measure; ə represents **a** in about, **e** in taken, **i** in pencil, **o** in lemon, **u** in circus.

him in a good temper.

dis|po|si|tion|al (dis′pə zish′ə nəl), *adj.* of or having to do with disposition.

dis|po|si|tioned (dis′pə zish′ənd), *adj.* having a (certain kind of) disposition: *a well-dispositioned boy.*

dis|pos|i|tive (dis poz′ə tiv), *adj.* disposing; regulating; controlling: *the dispositive clause of a contract.*

dis|pos|sess (dis′pə zes′), *v.t.* **1** to force to give up the possession of a house, land, or other real estate; oust: *The tenant was dispossessed for not paying his rent.* **SYN:** evict, remove, dislodge. **2** to take away from; deprive: *Fear dispossessed him of his senses.*

dis|pos|ses|sion (dis′pə zesh′ən), *n.* **1** the act of dispossessing: *The long process of dispossession . . . has all but stripped the Indians of their resources* (Harper's). **2** the state of being dispossessed.

dis|pos|ses|sor (dis′pə zes′ər), *n.* a person who dispossesses.

dis|pos|ses|so|ry (dis′pə zes′ərē), *adj.* having to do with dispossession.

dis|po|sure (dis pō′zhər), *n. Archaic.* disposal; disposition.

dis|praise (dis prāz′), *v.* **-praised, -prais|ing.** *n.* **—*v.t.*** to express disapproval of; speak against; blame. **SYN:** censure.
—*n.* the expression of disapproval; blame: *In praise and in dispraise the same, A man of well-attemper'd frame* (Tennyson). **SYN:** censure. **—dis-prais′er,** *n.* **—dis|prais′ing|ly,** *adv.*

dis|pread (dis pred′), *v.t., v.i.* to spread out; extend. Also, **disspread.**

dis|priv|i|lege (dis priv′ə lij), *v.t.,* **-leged, -leg|ing.** to deprive of privileges; make underprivileged.

dis|prize (dis prīz′), *v.t.,* **-prized, priz|ing.** *Archaic.* to disdain.

dis|prod|uct (dis prod′əkt, -ukt), *n.* a harmful product, especially one that is the result of negligence on the part of the producer: *The National Bureau of Economic Research . . . is trying to revise the system of economic accounting so that it will gauge the cost of noxious factories, landscape wreckers, noise and other "disproducts"* (Time).

dis|prof|it (dis prof′it), *v., n. Archaic.* **—*v.t.*** to bring disadvantage to; damage; inconvenience.
—*n.* a disadvantage; damage; loss.

dis|proof (dis prüf′), *n.* **1** a disproving; refutation. **SYN:** confutation. **2** a fact or reason that disproves something.

dis|pro|por|tion (dis′prə pôr′shən, -pōr′-), *n., v.* **—*n.*** **1** the lack of proper proportion; lack of symmetry: *This personal approach breathes life into the account but also leads to disproportion in treatment* (Scientific America). **2** something out of proportion.
—*v.t.* to make disproportionate: *Statutes that disproportion punishment to crime* (Edward G. Bulwer-Lytton).

dis|pro|por|tion|a|ble (dis′prə pôr′shə nə bəl, -pōr′-), *adj.* = disproportionate. **—dis′pro|por′-tion|a|ble|ness,** *n.*

dis|pro|por|tion|a|bly (dis′prə pôr′shə nə blē, -pōr′), *adv.* = disproportionally.

dis|pro|por|tion|al (dis′prə pôr′shə nəl, -pōr′-), *adj.* not in proportion; disproportionate.

dis|pro|por|tion|al|ly (dis′prə pôr′shə nə lē, -pōr′-), *adv.* without proportion; unequally.

dis|pro|por|tion|ate (*adj.* dis′prə pôr′shə nit, -pōr′-; *v.* dis′prə pôr′shə nāt, -pōr′-), *adj. v.,* **-at-ed, -at|ing. —*adj.*** out of relation in size, number, or other factor (to something else); not in proper proportion: *A penny would be disproportionate pay for a day's work.* **SYN:** disproportionable.
—*v.i. Chemistry.* to undergo disproportionation. **—dis′pro|por′tion|ate|ness,** *n.*

dis|pro|por|tion|ate|ly (dis′prə pôr′shə nit lē, -pōr′-), *adv.* in a disproportionate degree; inadequately or excessively: *Our public authorities and public-minded citizens, whenever they embark upon a civic project, surround it with open spaces that are frightfully and disproportionately expensive* (New Yorker).

dis|pro|por|tion|a|tion (dis′prə pôr′shə nā′shən, -pōr′-), *n. Chemistry.* the formation of two dissimilar molecules or substances from a single parent molecule or substance.

dis|prov|a|ble (dis prü′və bəl), *adj.* that can be disproved; refutable.

dis|prov|al (dis prü′vəl), *n.* the act of disproving; disproof.

dis|prove (dis prüv′), *v.t.,* **-proved, -prov|ing.** to prove false or incorrect; refute: *Experiment has disproved the old idea that heavy objects fall faster than lighter objects. A witness disproved the defendant's statements.* **SYN:** rebut, invalidate.

dis|punge (dis punj′), *v.t.,* **-punged, -pung|ing.** *Archaic.* dispone. [< *di-*[2] + obsolete *spunge* sponge]

dis|put|a|bil|i|ty (dis pyü′tə bil′ə tē, dis′pyů-), *n.* the quality of being disputable or controvertible.

dis|put|a|ble (dis pyü′tə bəl, dis′pyů-), *adj.* liable to be disputed, questioned, or discussed; uncertain; questionable: *The existence of flying saucers is disputable.*

dis|put|a|bly (dis pyü′tə blē, dis′pyů-), *adv.* in a disputable manner or degree; questionably.

dis|pu|tant (dis′pyů tənt, dis pyü′-), *n., adj.* **—*n.*** a person who takes part in a dispute or debate: *Behind the debates were fundamentals of supreme importance to the disputants* (Newsweek).
—*adj.* disputing.

dis|pu|ta|tion (dis′pyů tā′shən), *n.* **1** debate; discussion; controversy: *[Marx] was nearly arrested and only escaped by entangling the policeman in one of his irresistible disputations* (Edmund Wilson). **2** a dispute. **3** an exercise in which parties attack and defend a thesis, as was the practice in medieval universities. **4** *Obsolete.* a discourse; conversation: *a philosophical disputation.*

dis|pu|ta|tious (dis′pyů tā′shəs), *adj.* fond of disputing; inclined to argue: *The Copernicus-Galileo theory might have prevailed if disgruntled scholars and disputatious monks had not begun a muttering campaign against Galileo* (Time). **SYN:** quarrelsome, contentious. **—dis′pu|ta′tious|ly,** *adv.* **—dis′pu|ta′tious|ness,** *n.*

dis|put|a|tive (dis pyü′tə tiv), *adj.* = disputatious.

dis|pute (dis pyüt′), *v.,* **-put|ed, -put|ing,** *n.* **—*v.i.*** **1** to give reasons or facts for or against something; discuss; argue; debate: *The lawmakers disputed over the need for new taxes.* **2** to quarrel: *The robbers disputed violently over the stolen gold.* **SYN:** wrangle.
—*v.t.* **1** to argue about; discuss; debate: *The lawyers disputed the case before the judge.* **2** to disagree with (a statement); say (something) is false or doubtful; call in question: *The insurance company disputed his claim for damages to his car. My right there is none to dispute* (William Cowper). **SYN:** contest, deny. **3** to fight against; oppose; resist: *The rebels disputed the troops behind street barricades.* **4** to fight for; fight over: *The soldiers disputed every inch of ground when the enemy attacked.* **SYN:** contest. **5** to try to win; compete for: *The losing team disputed the victory up to the last minute of play.*
—*n.* **1** argument; debate: *There is a dispute over where to build the new school.* **SYN:** contention, controversy. See syn. under **argument. 2** a quarrel: *The boys' dispute ended in a fight.* **3** *Obsolete.* a struggle; contest; fight.
beyond dispute, a not to be disputed or questioned: *The bank teller's honesty is beyond dispute.* **b** final; settled. **c** in a settled condition; finally: *The boundary has been fixed beyond dispute.*
in dispute, being disputed: *The reliability of the evidence is in dispute.*
[< Old French *desputer,* or disputer, learned borrowing from Latin *disputāre* examine, discuss, argue < *dis-* apart, separately + *putāre* calculate]

dis|put|er (dis pyü′tər), *n.* a person who disputes, or who is given to disputation or controversy: *Where is the disputer of this world?* (I Corinthians 1:20).

dis|qual|i|fi|ca|tion (dis kwol′ə fə kā′shən), *n.* **1** the act or process of disqualifying. **2** the state of being disqualified. **3** something that disqualifies: *I hope you don't think good looks a disqualification for the business* (Dickens).

dis|qual|i|fy (dis kwol′ə fī), *v.t.,* **-fied, -fy|ing.** **1** to make unable to do something: *His lame foot disqualified him for most sports.* **2** to declare unfit or unable to do something; deprive of a right or privilege: *The judge disqualified himself because he was a friend of the person on trial.* **3** *Sports.* to refuse permission to take part in a contest or declare unqualified during a contest because of failure to meet certain requirements or an infraction of rules: *Failure to follow the coach's training rules disqualified him from the football team.*

dis|quan|ti|ty (dis kwon′tə tē), *v.t.,* **-tied, -ty|ing.** **1** to deprive (syllables) of metrical quantity. **2** *Obsolete.* to lessen in quantity.

dis|qui|et (dis kwī′ət), *v., n., adj.* **—*v.t.*** to make uneasy or anxious; disturb; worry: *The strange actions of the feverish boy disquieted his mother. Rumors of a revolution disquieted the king.* **SYN:** trouble, alarm.
—*n.* uneasy feelings; anxiety: *Her disquiet made the rest of us uneasy, too.* **SYN:** worry, restlessness, uneasiness, unrest.
—*adj. Archaic.* restless; uneasy; disturbed. **—dis-qui′et|ness,** *n.*

dis|qui|et|en (dis kwī′ə tən), *v.t.* = disquiet.

dis|qui|et|ing (dis kwī′ə ting), *adj.* disturbing: *A very disquieting rumor spread.* **—dis|qui′et|ing|ly,** *adv.*

dis|qui|et|ly (dis kwī′ə lē), *adv.* in an uneasy manner; anxiously.

dis|qui|e|tude (dis kwī′ə tüd, -tyüd), *n.* uneasiness; anxiety: *A profound disquietude devoured him* (Lytton Strachey). **SYN:** restlessness, disturbance, disquietness.

dis|qui|si|tion (dis′kwə zish′ən), *n.* a long or formal speech or writing about a subject; dissertation: *scholastic craggy disquisitions* (John Trapp). **SYN:** treatise. [< Latin *disquīsītiō, -ōnis* < *disquīrere* inquire < *dis-* apart + *quaerere* seek]

dis|qui|si|tion|al (dis′kwə zish′ə nəl), *adj.* of the nature of a disquisition: *. . . the tyrannous flow of Henry Worthington's disquisitional lava* (John Updike).

dis|quis|i|tive (dis kwiz′ə tiv), *adj.* **1** having to do with or given to disquisition. **2** inquiring.

dis|quis|i|tor (dis kwiz′ə tər), *n.* the author of a disquisition.

dis|quis|i|to|ry (dis kwiz′ə tôr′ē, -tōr′-), *adj.* investigating; inquiring; disquisitive: *"Getting Married" (1908) is the first of what Shaw called his "disquisitory plays"* (London Times).

Dis|rae|li|an (diz rā′lē ən), *adj.* having to do with or characteristic of Benjamin Disraeli (1804-1881), English statesman and novelist, or his writings: *. . . a vision akin to Disraelian romanticism* (Listener). *He austerely declines . . . to quote all the celebrated Disraelian epigrams* (Harper's).

dis|rate (dis rāt′), *v.t.,* **-rat|ed, -rat|ing.** to reduce to a lower rank.

dis|re|gard (dis′ri gärd′), *v., n.* **—*v.t.*** **1** to pay no attention to; take no notice of: *Disregarding the child's screams, the doctor cleaned and bandaged the cut.* **SYN:** neglect. **2** to treat without proper regard or respect; slight: *The gang disregards all authority.*
—*n.* **1** lack of attention; neglect: *Continued disregard to his studies led to the boy's failure. The reckless driver was arrested for his complete disregard of the traffic laws.* **2** lack of proper regard or respect: *a deliberate disregard for tradition.* **SYN:** irreverence. **—dis′re|gard′er,** *n.*

dis|re|gard|ful (dis′ri gärd′fəl), *adj.* lacking in regard; neglectful; careless: *The state . . . is by its nature disregardful or ill-informed* (Bulletin of Atomic Scientists).

dis|rel|ish (dis rel′ish), *n., v.t.* dislike: *Taking his punishment with characteristic disrelish* (Amelia B. Edwards). **SYN:** *n.* distaste.

dis|re|mem|ber (dis′ri mem′bər), *v.t. Informal.* to fail to remember; forget: *I disremember her name* (Mark Twain).

dis|re|pair (dis′ri pār′), *n.* bad condition; need of repairs: *The old, vacant house was in disrepair. Many of the physical facilities of various Treasury Department bureaus are in such states of disrepair* (Wall Street Journal).

dis|rep|u|ta|bil|i|ty (dis rep′yə tə bil′ə tē), *n.* disreputable quality or state.

dis|rep|u|ta|ble (dis rep′yə tə bəl), *adj.* **1** having a bad reputation: *a disreputable old rascal, a disreputable dance hall.* **SYN:** base, infamous. **2** not respectable; not fit to be used or seen; in poor condition: *The boy was well dressed except for a disreputable old hat.* **3** discreditable; dishonorable: *a disreputable adventure.* **—dis|rep′u|ta|ble-ness,** *n.*

dis|rep|u|ta|bly (dis rep′yə tə blē), *adv.* in a disreputable manner; discreditably.

dis|rep|u|ta|tion (dis rep′yə tā′shən), *n. Archaic.* disrepute.

dis|re|pute (dis′ri pyüt′), *n.* loss or absence of reputation; discredit; disfavor: *Many old remedies for illness have fallen into disrepute among doctors.* **SYN:** disesteem, disgrace, dishonor.

dis|re|spect (dis′ri spekt′), *n., v.* **—*n.*** lack of respect; rudeness; impoliteness; discourtesy: *He meant no disrespect by his hasty remark. Older people criticized the boy's disrespect for his parents.*
—*v.t.* to regard or treat rudely or impolitely.

dis|re|spect|a|bil|i|ty (dis′ri spek′tə bil′ə tē), *n.* the quality of being disrespectable.

dis|re|spect|a|ble (dis′ri spek′tə bəl), *adj.* not respectable.

dis|re|spect|ful (dis′ri spekt′fəl), *adj.* showing no respect; lacking in courtesy to elders or superiors; impolite; rude: *The disrespectful boy made fun of his father.* **—dis′re|spect′ful|ly,** *adv.* **—dis′re|spect′ful|ness,** *n.*

dis|robe (dis rōb′), *v.t., v.i.,* **-robed, -rob|ing.** = undress. **—dis|robe′ment,** *n.*

dis|rob|er (dis rō′bər), *n.* a person or thing that strips off clothing or covering: *The trees swept bare by autumn's gale—that swift and merciless disrober* (Sir P. Felis).

dis|roof (dis rüf′, -růf′), *v.t.* = unroof.

dis|root (dis rüt′, -růt′), *v.t.* to uproot; dislodge.

dis|rupt (dis rupt′), *v., adj.* **—*v.t., v.i.*** to break up; burst apart; split: *The rioters tried to disrupt the assembly. Slavery seemed likely to disrupt the Union. The proposed routes would . . . slash through beautiful rural scenery and disrupt residential communities* (New York Times). *The old man said that smoking stunted a boy's growth, ruined his health, disrupted his moral sense* (James T. Farrell). **SYN:** shatter.

—*adj.* disrupted: *Their disrupt friendship was later renewed.*
[< Latin *disruptus,* past participle of *disrumpere* < *dis-* apart + *rumpere* to break] —**dis|rupt′ing|ly**, *adv.*

dis|rupt|er (dis rup′tər), *n.* a person or thing that disrupts: *Joe, the disrupter, is actively disliked* (New York Times).

dis|rup|tion (dis rup′shən), *n.* **1** the act or process of breaking up; a splitting; bursting apart; shattering: *Arguments led to the disruption of their partnership.* **2** the condition of being broken up; a being split: *There was a disruption of telephone service during the storm.*

dis|rup|tion|ist (dis rup′shə nist), *n.* a person who disrupts or favors disruption.

dis|rup|tive (dis rup′tiv), *adj.* causing disruption; tending to break up: *a disruptive influence.* —**disrup′tive|ly**, *adv.* —**dis|rup′tive|ness**, *n.*

disruptive discharge, a sudden increase in electric current through an insulating medium caused by the breakdown of the medium under stress.

dis|rup|tor (dis rup′tər), *n.* = disrupter.

dis|rup|ture (dis rup′chər), *v.t.,* **-tured, -tur|ing.** = disrupt.

dis|sat|is|fac|tion (dis′sat is fak′shən), *n.* the state of being dissatisfied; discontent; displeasure: *Poor food caused the dissatisfaction among the soldiers.*

dis|sat|is|fac|to|ry (dis′sat is fak′tər ē, -fak′trē), *adj.* causing discontent; unsatisfactory.

dis|sat|is|fied (dis sat′is fīd), *adj.* **1** discontented; displeased: *When we do not get what we want, we are dissatisfied.* **2** showing discontent or displeasure: *a dissatisfied expression.*

dis|sat|is|fi|ed|ly (dis sat′is fī′id lē, -fīd′ lē), *adv.* in a dissatisfied manner; with dissatisfaction: *She remains dissatisfiedly mute* (Rhoda Broughton).

dis|sat|is|fy (dis sat′is fī), *v.t.,* **-fied, -fy|ing.** to fail to satisfy; make discontented; displease: *The boy's poor grades dissatisfied his parents. Envy may dissatisfy us with our lot.*

dis|save (dis sāv′), *v.i.,* **-saved, -sav|ing.** to use up one's savings; spend more than one earns: *Rising prices are, it would seem, causing people to dissave—and pour the money into goods—for fear of further depreciation in the value of their savings* (Malcolm Crawford). —**dis|sav′er**, *n.*

dis|sav|ing (dis sā′ving), *n.* the using up of one's savings; a spending more than one earns: *The period immediately before Christmas has traditionally been one of dissaving* (Sunday Times).

dis|seat (dis sēt′), *v.t.* = unseat.

dis|sect (di sekt′, dī-), *v.t.* **1** to cut apart (an animal, plant, organ, or tissue) in order to examine or study the structure. **SYN**: anatomize. **2** *Figurative.* to examine carefully part by part; analyze: *Let us dissect that statement and find out just what it means. Biblical scrolls have been studied, dissected, and made available to scholars* (Harold J. Plenderleith). **SYN**: scrutinize. **3** to cut in pieces; divide into parts: *It appears that normal stream-erosion had already dissected large blocks* [*of rock*] (E. F. Roots). [< Latin *dissectus,* past participle of *dissecāre* < *dis-* apart + *secāre* to cut]

dis|sect|ed (di sek′tid, dī-), *adj.* **1** cut up; divided. **2** *Botany.* cut or divided into many lobes: *dissected leaves.* **3** *Geology.* cut up by irregular valleys: *a dissected plateau.*

dis|sect|i|ble (di sek′tə bəl, dī-), *adj.* that can be dissected.

dis|sec|tion (di sek′shən, dī-), *n.* **1** the act of cutting apart an animal or plant, or any part of an animal or plant, in order to examine or study the structure: *At Padua, the center of medical studies, the first public dissection* (*as opposed to occasional private autopsies which were performed whenever a person of consequence had died under mysterious circumstances*) *took place in 1341* (Erwin Panofsky). **2** an animal, plant, etc., that has been dissected. **3** *Figurative.* examination of something in detail or point by point; analysis: *A dissection of your argument shows several inconsistencies.*

dis|sec|tor (di sek′tər, dī-), *n.* **1** a person who dissects. **2** an instrument used in dissecting.

dis|seise (dis sēz′), *v.t.,* **-seised, -seis|ing.** = disseize.

dis|seize (dis sēz′), *v.t.,* **-seized, -seiz|ing.** *Law.* **1** to deprive (a person) of possession wrongfully or by force. **2** to dispossess; oust. [< Anglo-French *disseisir,* Old French *dessaisir* dispossess < *des-* away, un- (< Latin *dis-*) + *saisir* get possession of, seize]

dis|sei|zee (dis′sē zē′, dis sē′zē′), *n. Law.* a person who is disseized.

dis|sei|zin (dis sē′zin), *n. Law.* **1** the act of disseizing. **2** the state of being disseized. [< Anglo-French *disseisine,* Old French *dessaisine* < *des-* away, without (< Latin *dis-*) + *saisine* formal possession, related to *saisir* seize]

dis|sei|zor (dis sē′zər, -zôr), *n. Law.* a person who disseizes; dispossessor.

dis|sel|boom (dis′əl büm), *n.* (in South Africa) the pole of a wagon, by which it is hauled: *The last two oxen are yoked to the disselboom, to which is attached a long chain, or rope of hemp; to this the other yokes are attached* (Richard Cadbury). [< Afrikaans *disselboom* < Dutch < *dissel* shaft of a wagon + *boom* tree, pole]

dis|sem|blance (di sem′bləns), *n.* **1** the act of dissembling; dissimulation. **2** *Archaic.* lack of resemblance; unlikeness; dissimilarity.

dis|sem|ble (di sem′bəl), *v.,* **-bled, -bling.** —*v.t.* **1** to hide (one's real feelings, thoughts, plans, or motives); disguise: *She dissembled her anger with a smile.* **2** to put on the appearance of; pretend; feign: *The bored listener dissembled an interest he didn't feel.* **3** to pretend not to see or notice; disregard; ignore; neglect.
—*v.i.* to conceal one's real feelings, thoughts, plans, or motives; be a hypocrite; dissimulate: *Families that quarrel in the privacy of the home do well to dissemble when they go out to dinner* (Harper's).
[alteration of obsolete *dissimule* to dissimulate; patterned on *resemble*]

dis|sem|bler (di sem′blər), *n.* a person who dissembles; one who practices duplicity; a deceiver; hypocrite: *A deep dissembler, not of his affections only, but of religion* (Milton).

dis|sem|bling|ly (di sem′bling lē), *adv.* in a dissembling manner; deceptively.

dis|sem|i|nate (di sem′ə nāt), *v.t.,* **-nat|ed, -nat|ing.** to scatter widely; spread abroad: *News is disseminated by means of television and radio.* **SYN**: diffuse, promulgate. [< Latin *dissēmināre* (with English *-ate*[1]) < *dis-* in every direction + *sēmināre* to plant, propagate < *sēmen, -inis* seed]

dis|sem|i|nat|ed (di sem′ə nā tid), *adj. Medicine.* spread throughout a tissue, organ, or the entire body: *disseminated neurodermatitis.*

disseminated sclerosis, *British.* = multiple sclerosis.

dis|sem|i|na|tion (di sem′ə nā′shən), *n.* the act or process of scattering or state of being scattered widely; a spreading abroad; diffusion: *The chief function of a newspaper is the dissemination of information to the public.*

dis|sem|i|na|tive (di sem′ə nā′tiv), *adj.* disseminating.

dis|sem|i|na|tor (di sem′ə nā′tər), *n.* a person or thing that disseminates: *The disseminator spreads or distributes facts freely* (Emory S. Bogardus).

dis|sem|i|nule (di sem′ə nyül), *n. Botany.* a seed, spore, or other propagating part of a plant: *Many birds, including those that retain seeds for only a few hours, may play a significant role in the movement of disseminules from upland to aquatic sites* (Science). [< *dissemin*(ate) + *-ule*]

dis|sen|sion (di sen′shən), *n.* a disputing; a quarreling; hard feeling caused by a difference in opinion: *The club broke up because of dissension among its members.* **SYN**: discord, disagreement, contention. Also, **dissention.** [< Old French *dissension,* learned borrowing from Latin *dissensiō, -ōnis* < *dissentīre;* see etym. under **dissent**]

dis|sent (di sent′), *v., n.* —*v.i.* **1** to disagree; think differently; express a different opinion from others: *Most of the class wanted to have a picnic, but three boys dissented. Two of the judges dissented from the decision of the other three.* **2** to withhold consent. **3** to refuse to conform to the rules and beliefs of an established church: *The Puritans dissented from the doctrines of the established or state church of England.*
—*n.* **1** disagreement; difference of opinion: *Dissent among the members broke up the club. My dissent went unnoticed. Our long and proud tradition of dissent—persecuted only in moderation—has always challenged the established order* (Manchester Guardian Weekly). **2** a declaration of disagreement of opinion about something, especially as written by a judge dissenting from the majority opinion: *The members of the minority usually agree among themselves on who will write the dissent* (New Yorker). **3** refusal to conform to the rules and beliefs of an established church: *The Puritans' dissent caused their separation from the Church of England.*
[< Latin *dissentīre* < *dis-* apart, differently + *sentīre* think, feel]

dis|sent|er (di sen′tər), *n.* a person who dissents: *These dissenters readily admit they are in the minority* (Newsweek).

Dis|sent|er (di sen′tər), *n.* a Protestant in England or Scotland who belongs to some church other than the established church; Nonconformist. [< *dissenter*]

dis|sen|tience (di sen′shəns), *n.* dissentient condition; difference of opinion.

dis|sen|tient (dis sen′shənt), *adj., n.* —*adj.* dissenting, especially from the opinion of the majority: *There is some dissentient voice raised against every reform.* **SYN**: dissident.
—*n.* a person who dissents: *The motion was carried despite the dissentients.*

dis|sent|ing (di sen′ting), *adj.* **1** dissentient; differing or disagreeing: *a dissenting opinion.* **2** refusing to accept the rules and beliefs of a state church. —**dis|sent′ing|ly**, *adv.*

dis|sen|tion (di sen′shən), *n.* = dissension.

dis|sen|tious (di sen′shəs), *adj.* full of dissension; given to dissension; quarrelsome; contentious.

dis|sep|i|ment (di sep′ə mənt), *n. Botany, Zoology.* a partition in some part or organ; septum. [< Latin *dissaepīmentum* < *dissaepīre* to separate < *dis-* apart + *saepīre* set a boundary < *saepēs, -is* partition, hedge]

dis|sep|i|men|tal (di sep′ə men′təl), *adj.* of or like a dissepiment.

dis|sert (di sėrt′), *v.i.* to discourse on a subject: *It is not amiss ... to be able to dissert upon the growth and flavour of wines* (Lord Chesterfield). [< Latin *dissertus,* past participle of *disserere* discuss, examine < *dis-* apart + *serere* compose; join words]

dis|ser|tate (dis′ər tāt), *v.i.,* **-tat|ed, -tat|ing.** to make a dissertation; discourse.

dis|ser|ta|tion (dis′ər tā′shən), *n.* a formal discussion of a subject. A university student who is working for a doctor's degree is required to write a dissertation. *He talked at length ... giving a dissertation on his weight and dietetic virtues of tapioca pudding to the reporters* (New York Times). [< Latin *dissertātiō, -ōnis* < *dissertāre* (frequentative) < *disserere;* see etym. under **dissert**]

dis|ser|ta|tor (dis′ər tā′tər), *n.* a person who dissertates.

dis|serve (dis sėrv′), *v.t.,* **-served, -serv|ing.** to do an ill turn to; harm: *Bernstein persuaded himself that it was possible to omit a third of the total work and still not disserve the composer ... and not disserve the mood and style of the setting* (Saturday Review).

dis|serv|ice (dis sėr′vis), *n.* bad treatment; harm; injury; detriment: *You do a disservice to him when you fail to give him credit for his efforts. The bar association's position is a disservice to the bench, since it would disqualify an excellent judge; ... and it is a disservice to the bar association, since it reflects an unreasoned prejudice* (Francis W. H. Adams).

dis|serv|ice|a|ble (dis sėr′vi sə bəl), *adj.* harmful; injurious; detrimental.

dis|sev|er (di sev′ər), *v.t.* **1** to sever; separate: *Life dissevers many early friends.* **SYN**: disjoin, disunite. **2** to cut into parts.
—*v.i.* to separate; part.

dis|sev|er|ance (di sev′ər əns), *n.* the act or fact of dissevering; separation.

dis|sev|er|a|tion (di sev′ə rā′shən), *n.* = disseverance.

dis|sev|er|ment (di sev′ər mənt), *n.* = disseverance.

dis|si|dence (dis′ə dəns), *n.* disagreement in opinion, character, or motive; dissent: *There are now grounds for hope that the hounding of dissidence, innocent of treason, will come to a halt* (Bulletin of Atomic Scientists).

dis|si|dent (dis′ə dənt), *adj., n.* —*adj.* disagreeing in opinion, character, or motive; dissenting: *There were many dissident voices raised in objection.*
—*n.* a person who disagrees or dissents: *the dissidents from public opinion.*
[< Latin *dissidēns, -entis,* present participle of *dissidēre* < *dis-* apart + *sedēre* sit]

dis|sight (dis sīt′), *n.* an unsightly object; eyesore.

dis|sil|i|ence (di sil′ē əns), *n.* = dissiliency.

dis|sil|i|en|cy (di sil′ē ən sē), *n.* the quality of being dissilient.

dis|sil|i|ent (di sil′ē ənt), *adj.* **1** flying or springing apart. **2** *Botany.* bursting open with force, as the dry pod or capsule of some plants. [< Latin *dissiliēns, -entis,* present participle of *dissilīre* < *dis-* apart + *salīre* leap]

dis|sim|i|lar (di sim′ə lər), *adj.* not similar; unlike; different: *The brothers had markedly dissimilar characteristics.* —**dis|sim′i|lar|ly**, *adv.*

dis|sim|i|lar|i|ty (di sim′ə lar′ə tē), *n., pl.* **-ties.** **1** lack of similarity; unlikeness; difference: *dissimilarity of tastes.* **2** a point of difference.

dis|sim|i|late (di sim′ə lāt), *v.t., v.i.,* **-lat|ed, -lat|ing.** to make or become unlike. [< Latin *dissimilis* unlike, on the analogy of *assimilate*]

Pronunciation Key: hat, āge, cãre, fär; let, ēqual, tėrm, it, īce; hot, ōpen, ôrder; oil, out; cup, pu̇t, rüle; child; long; thin; ᴛʜen; zh, measure; ə represents **a** in about, **e** in taken, **i** in pencil, **o** in lemon, **u** in circus.

dis|sim|i|la|tion (di sim′ə lā′shən), *n.* **1** the act of making or becoming unlike. **2** *Biology.* the breakdown of organic compounds into simpler ones; catabolism. **3** *Phonetics.* the change in a speech sound making it less like a similar sound nearby, such as the change of the first *r* to *l* in Italian *pellegrino* from Latin *peregrinus,* both meaning "foreign."

dis|sim|i|la|tive (di sim′ə lā′tiv), *adj.* tending to dissimilate or causing dissimilation.

dis|si|mil|i|tude (dis′sə mil′ə tüd, -tyüd), *n.* **1** unlikeness; difference. **SYN**: dissimilarity, diversity. **2** a point of difference.

dis|sim|u|late (di sim′yə lāt), *v.,* **-lat|ed, -lat|ing.** —***v.t.*** to disguise or hide under a pretense; hide the truth about; dissemble: *He dissimulated his cowardice by bragging about how brave he was.* —***v.i.*** to hide the truth; dissemble: *He could neither simulate nor dissimulate* (Henry James). [< Latin *dissimulāre* (with English *-ate*[1]) < *dis-* away, not + *simul* together < *similis* similar, like]

dis|sim|u|la|tion (di sim′yə lā′shən), *n.* the act of dissimulating; pretense; deceit; hypocrisy: *Without some dissimulation no business can be carried on at all* (Lord Chesterfield). *Let love be without dissimulation* (Romans 12:9). **SYN**: duplicity.

dis|sim|u|la|tive (di sim′yə lā′tiv), *adj.* having to do with or characterized by dissimulation.

dis|sim|u|la|tor (di sim′yə lā′tər), *n.* a person who dissimulates; dissembler.

dis|si|pate (dis′ə pāt), *v.,* **-pat|ed, -pat|ing.** —***v.t.*** **1** to spread in different directions; scatter. *The sun dissipated the mist. After a brisk morning wind dissipated the clouds, the sky was clear all day.* **2** to cause to disappear; dispel: (*Figurative.*) *What little romantic glamour this Christmas homecoming had held for her was dissipated* (Theodore Dreiser). **3** to spend foolishly; waste on things of little value; squander: *The extravagant son soon dissipated his father's fortune.* —***v.i.*** **1** to scatter so as to disappear; disperse: *The morning haze had dissipated by ten o'clock.* **2** to disappear; vanish: (*Figurative.*) *His disappointment dissipated when he realized that he was an adventurer, journeying to fight for love* (James T. Farrell). **3** to indulge too much in sensual or foolish pleasures. [< Latin *dissipāre* (with English *-ate*[1]) < *dis-* apart + *supāre* throw]

dis|si|pat|ed (dis′ə pā′tid), *adj.* **1** indulging too much in sensual or foolish pleasures; dissolute: *A youth who spends his time in drinking and gambling is dissipated.* **2** wasted: *a dissipated life, a dissipated fortune.* **3** scattered; dispersed. —**dis′si|pat′ed|ly,** *adv.* —**dis′si|pat′ed|ness,** *n.*

dis|si|pat|er (dis′ə pā′tər), *n.* = dissipator.

dis|si|pa|tion (dis′ə pā′shən), *n.* **1** the process of dissipating or state of being dissipated; a scattering in different directions. **2** a wasting by misuse: *the dissipation of energy for worthless ends.* **3** too much indulgence in sensual or foolish pleasures; intemperance. **4** amusement; diversion, especially harmful amusements: *Crowds without company and dissipation without pleasure* (Edward Gibbon). **5** disintegration; dissolution.

dis|si|pa|tive (dis′ə pā′tiv), *adj.* tending to dissipate: *a dissipative force.*

dis|si|pa|tor (dis′ə pā′tər), *n.* a person or thing that dissipates; dissipater.

dis|so|ci|a|ble (di sō′shē ə bəl, -shə-), *adj.* **1** that can be dissociated; separable. **2** unsociable. **3** that tends to dissociate or separate.

dis|so|cial (dis sō′shəl), *adj.* = unsociable.

dis|so|ci|ate (di sō′shē āt), *v.,* **-at|ed, -at|ing.** —***v.t.*** **1** to break the connection or association with; separate: *When the honest man discovered that his companions were thieves, he dissociated himself from them. The new appointee to the Cabinet dissociated himself from his business in order to avoid a conflict of interest.* **SYN**: sever. **2** *Chemistry.* to separate or decompose by dissociation. —***v.i.*** **1** to withdraw from association. **2** *Chemistry.* to be subjected to dissociation. Also, **disassociate.** [< Latin *dissociāre* (with English -ate[1]) < *dis-* apart + *sociāre* to join < *socius* ally]

dis|so|ci|at|ed personality (di sō′shē ā′tid), *Psychology.* a pathological state of the mind in which two or more distinct personalities exist in the same person.

dis|so|ci|a|tion (di sō′sē ā′shən, -shē-), *n.* **1a** the act of dissociating. **SYN**: division, disunion. **b** the state of being dissociated. **SYN**: division, disunion. **2** *Chemistry.* **a** the usually reversible changing of a substance into two or more simpler substances, such as occurs when calcium carbonate is heated to a high temperature and gradually decomposes into calcium oxide and carbon dioxide in such a way that upon subsequent lowering of the temperature the freed substances recombine into calcium carbonate. **b** the separation of molecules of an electrolyte into constituent ions; ionization. Sodium and chlorine ions are formed by the dissociation of sodium chloride molecules in water. **3** *Psychology.* the separation of an idea or feeling from the main stream of consciousness. Also, **disassociation.**

dis|so|ci|a|tive (di sō′shē ā′tiv), *adj.* having to do with or causing dissociation.

dis|so|conch (dis′ə kongk), *n. Zoology.* **1** the shell of a mollusk in the veliger stage. **2** the shell of an adult bivalve. [< Greek *dissós* double + English *conch*]

dis|sog|e|ny (di soj′ə nē), *n. Biology.* a form of reproduction among the ctenophores, in which there are two periods of sexual maturity in the same individual, one in the larval and another in the adult form. [< Greek *dissós* double + English *-gen* + *-y*[3]]

dis|sog|o|ny (di sog′ə nē), *n.* = dissogeny.

dis|sol|u|bil|i|ty (di sol′yə bil′ə tē), *n.* the fact or quality of being dissoluble.

dis|sol|u|ble (di sol′yə bəl), *adj.* that can be dissolved. —**dis|sol′u|ble|ness,** *n.*

dis|so|lute (dis′ə lüt), *adj.* **1** living an immoral life; very wicked; immoral: *The dissolute young man had a very bad reputation. The nobles were lawless and dissolute* (John R. Green). **SYN**: dissipated, licentious, profligate, lewd. **2** *Obsolete.* lax; negligent; unrestrained. [< Latin *dissolūtus,* past participle of *dissolvere;* see etym. under **dissolve**] —**dis′so|lute′ly,** *adv.* —**dis′so|lute′ness,** *n.*

dis|so|lu|tion (dis′ə lü′shən), *n.* **1** a breaking up; an ending of an association of any kind: *the dissolution of the English monasteries under Henry VIII. The partners arranged for the dissolution of their partnership.* **2** the breaking up of an assembly by ending its session: *the dissolution of parliament.* **3** ruin; destruction: *the dissolution of an empire.* **4** separation of parts which compose a connected system or body: *the dissolution of nature or of government.* **5** the separation of soul and body; death: *He waits for the day of his dissolution with a resignation mixed with delight* (Sir Richard Steele). **6** disintegration; decomposition: *The dissolution of a compound into its elements.* **7a** the act or process of dissolving, or changing from a solid to a liquid state. **b** the condition of undergoing liquefaction; dissolving.

dis|so|lu|tive (dis′ə lü′tiv), *adj.* having to do with or involving dissolution.

dis|solv|a|ble (di zol′və bəl), *adj.* that can be dissolved; dissoluble.

dis|solve (di zolv′), *v.,* **-solved, -solv|ing,** *n.* —***v.t.*** **1** to make liquid, especially by putting into a liquid: *I dissolved two spoonfuls of sugar in my cup of coffee.* **SYN**: thaw. See syn. under **melt. 2** to change from a solid or gas to a liquid: *The warm air dissolved the ice.* **SYN**: thaw. See syn. under **melt. 3** to break up; end: *They dissolved the partnership because they could not agree on how to conduct the business. The cabinet was dissolved because the members could not agree with the prime minister.* **SYN**: disperse. **4** to separate into parts; decompose. **5** (in motion pictures and television) to cause (a picture or scene) to fade gradually from the screen while the succeeding picture or scene slowly appears. **6** to solve; explain; clear up: *The mystery was dissolved.* **7** *Law.* to annul: *to dissolve an injunction.* **8** *Archaic.* to destroy the binding power or effect of: *To ... dissolve these magic spells* (Milton). —***v.i.*** **1** to become liquid, especially by being put into a liquid; become dissolved: *The teacher explained that salt or sugar will dissolve in water.* **SYN**: thaw. See syn. under **melt. 2** to change from a solid or gas to a liquid: *The ice dissolved in the warm air.* **SYN**: thaw. See syn. under **melt. 3** to break up; end: *But though the Icarions did not dissolve until amost the end of the century, their moments of prosperity were modest and few* (Edmund Wilson). **4** to fade away: *The dream dissolved when she woke up.* **5** to separate into parts; decompose. **6** (in motion pictures and television) to fade gradually from the screen while the succeeding picture or scene slowly appears. **7** to lose its binding force or effect. —***n.*** (in motion pictures and television) the gradual disappearing of a picture or scene while the succeeding picture or scene slowly appears: *One technique used in taking one camera off the air and putting another in its place is called a dissolve* (Jack Gould).

dissolve in tears. See under **tear**[1].

[< Latin *dissolvere* < *dis-* apart + *solvere* to loose, loosen]

dis|sol|vent (di zol′vənt), *adj., n.* —***adj.*** dissolving; solvent. —***n.*** = solvent.

dis|solv|er (di zol′vər), *n.* **1** a person or thing that dissolves, or has the power of dissolving something. **2** (in motion pictures and television) an apparatus for dissolving a picture.

dis|solv|ing (di zol′ving), *adj.* that dissolves. —**dis|solv′ing|ly,** *adv.*

dissolving view, picture that fades into the next view when projected on a screen.

dis|so|nance (dis′ə nəns), *n.* **1** a harshness and unpleasantness of sound; discord: *The dissonance of many tooting taxi horns.* **2** *Music.* **a** the relationship or sound of two or more tones in a combination which is conventionally considered to be in a condition of unrest needing resolution or completion; discord. **b** a combination of tones out of harmonic relation in such a way as to cause pulsations due to interference. **3** *Figurative.* lack of harmony; disagreement: *Dissonance among the three partners doomed the project.* **SYN**: incongruity, discord.

dis|so|nan|cy (dis′ə nən sē), *n. Obsolete.* dissonance.

dis|so|nant (dis′ə nənt), *adj.* **1** harsh in tone or sound; clashing; not harmonious: *No sound is dissonant which tells of life* (Samuel Taylor Coleridge). **SYN**: incongruous, discordant. **2** *Music.* marked by dissonance; discordant: *This music is ... dissonant as dissonance can be* (Harper's). **3** *Figurative.* out of harmony with other conditions, persons, policies, or opinions; disagreeing: *The dirty, crowded houses of slums are dissonant with the richness of our country.* [< Latin *dissonāns, -antis,* present participle of *dissonāre* < *dis-* apart + *sonāre* to sound] —**dis′so|nant|ly,** *adv.*

dis|spread (dis pred′), *v.t., v.i. Archaic.* dispread.

dis|suade (di swād′), *v.t.,* **-suad|ed, -suad|ing.** **1** to persuade not to do something: *The father finally dissuaded his son from leaving school.* **2** to advise against. [< Latin *dissuādēre* < *dis-* from, away + *suādēre* to urge]

dis|suad|er (di swā′dər), *n.* a person who dissuades.

dis|sua|sion (di swā′zhən), *n.* the act of dissuading.

dis|sua|sive (di swā′siv), *adj.* attempting to dissuade; tending to dissuade. —**dis|sua′sive|ly,** *adv.* —**dis|sua′sive|ness,** *n.*

dis|syl|lab|ic (dis′sə lab′ik, dis′ə-), *adj.* having two syllables. Also, **disyllabic.** —**dis′syl|lab′i|cal|ly,** *adv.*

dis|syl|la|ble (di sil′ə bəl, dis′sil′-) *n.* a word having two syllables, such as *about, bandage,* or *candy.* Also, **disyllable.** [< French *dissyllable,* learned borrowing from Latin *disyllabus* < Greek *disýllabos* < *di-* two + *syllabē̂* syllable; spelling influenced by English *syllable*]

dis|sym|met|ric (dis′si met′rik), *adj.* = dissymmetrical.

dis|sym|met|ri|cal (dis′si met′rə kəl), *adj.* **1** not symmetrical. **2** symmetrical in reverse; having the same form but not superposable: *The right and left hands of a person are dissymmetrical.* —**dis′sym|met′ri|cal|ly,** *adv.*

dis|sym|me|try (dis sim′ə trē), *n., pl.* **-tries. 1** the lack or absence of symmetry. **2** dissymmetrical form or character.

dist., **1** distance. **2a** distinguish. **b** distinguished. **3** district.

dis|tad (dis′tad), *adv. Anatomy.* toward the end or distal part. [< *dist*(ant) + Latin *ad* toward]

dis|taff** (dis′taf, -täf), *n., adj.* —n.*** **1** a stick, split at the tip, to hold wool or flax for spinning by hand. **2** the staff on a spinning wheel for holding wool or flax. **3** woman's work or affairs. **4** the female sex; woman or women. **5** the female branch of a family. **6** a female heir. —***adj.*** of women; having to do with or suited to women or their affairs; female: *There are only two distaff members in the Senate* (Parade). *It's a very informal, distaff operation, and the women all love the feeling that they are close to the publishing world* (Saturday Review). [Old English *distæf* < *dis-* flax + *stæf* staff]

***distaff** definition 2

distaff

distaff side, the mother's side of a family, household, or hereditary line: *My cousin and I are related on the distaff side.*

dis|tain (dis tān′), *v.t. Archaic.* **1** to discolor; stain. **SYN**: dye, tinge. **2** *Figurative.* to dishonor; disgrace. **SYN**: defile, sully. [< Old French *desteindre* < *des-* apart (< Latin *dis-*) + *teindre* to dye < Latin *tingere*]

dis|tal (dis′təl), *adj. Anatomy.* away from the center or point of origin; terminal: *Fingernails are at the distal ends of fingers.* [< *dist*(ant) + *-al,* as in *dorsal*] —**dis′tal|ly,** *adv.*

dis|tance (dis′təns), *n., v.,* **-tanced, -tanc|ing.** —***n.*** **1** space in between: *The distance from the*

farm to town is 5 miles. **2** the condition of being far away: *Because of the lake's distance, we will have to stop overnight on the way.* **3** a place far away: *The sailors saw a light in the distance.* **4** the time in between; interval: *The increasing distance between thunderclaps meant the storm was moving away.* **5** *Music.* the interval or difference between two tones. **6** *Figurative.* lack of friendliness or familiarity; coldness of manner; reserve: *A certain distance in the old man's manner made the children respect him.* **7** *Figurative.* remoteness in relation or degree; amount of difference: *the distance between a descendant and his ancestor. The distance in color of the two fabrics is very noticeable.* **8** *Painting.* **a** the distant part of a landscape: *One sees cattle grazing in the distance.* **b** the part of a picture that represents this: *There is no distance in his paintings, which are all flat and two-dimensional.* **9** a space measured back from the winning post in horse racing. In order to qualify for further heats, a horse must be within this space when the winner finishes. **10** *Obsolete.* disagreement; dissension; dispute.
—*v.t.* **1** to leave far behind; do much better than: *He distanced all the other runners in the mile race.* **2** to beat by a distance: *The big black horse distanced the others.* **3** *Figurative.* to leave behind at a distance, as if in a race: *She distances her rivals in charm.* **4** to cause to appear distant or remote: *Mountains, which the ripe Italian air distances* (James Russell Lowell).
at a distance, a long way: *The farm is at a distance from the road.*
go the distance, *Sports.* **a** to play an entire game without substitution: *Jack Shanafelt and Jack Cannon also went the whole distance for Pennsylvania* (New York Times). **b** to fight or last an entire match without being knocked out: *Only two opponents have gone the distance against him* (New York Times).
keep at a distance, to refuse to be friendly or familiar with; treat coldly: *The captain kept his crew at a distance.*
keep one's distance, to be not too friendly or familiar: *The shy boy kept his distance and did not mingle with his new classmates. But for my children, I would have them keep their distance from the thickening center* (Robinson Jeffers).
[< Old French *distance,* learned borrowing from Latin *distāns;* see etym. under **distant**]

distance measuring equipment, a radar device in an aircraft for automatically computing the distance between the aircraft and a suitably equipped airport or ground station. *Abbr:* DME (no periods).

distance medley, a track relay race in which each runner of a team runs a different distance, usually in the order of a quarter mile, half mile, three-quarters of a mile, and one mile.

dis|tant (dis′tənt), *adj.* **1** far away in space: *The sun is distant from the earth.* **2** away: *The town is three miles distant.* **3** *Figurative.* far apart in time, relationship, or likeness; not close: *A third cousin is a distant relative. We may take a trip to Europe in the distant future.* **4** *Figurative.* not friendly: *She gave him only a distant nod.* **SYN**: aloof, reserved. **5** at a distance; from a distance; not near: *a distant vision, a distant journey. The old man had only a distant memory of the school he attended as a boy.* **6** *Obsolete.* different; diverse. [< Middle French *distant,* learned borrowing from Latin *distāns, -antis,* present participle of *distāre* stand apart < *dis-* apart + *stāre* to stand] —**dis′tant|ly**, *adv.* —**dis′tant|ness**, *n.*
—*Syn.* **1, 2 Distant, far, remote** mean not near. **Distant** suggests a considerable space unless the exact measure is stated: *He lives in a distant city. The city is 10 miles distant from Chicago.* **Far** suggests a long but somewhat indefinite distance away; **remote** suggests a long distance from the center of things: *Vietnam is a far country; to Americans it used to be remote.*

Distant Early Warning line, = DEW line.

dis|taste (dis tāst′), *n., v.,* **-tast|ed, -tast|ing.** —*n.* dislike: *a distaste for formality, a distaste of society. His distaste for carrots showed clearly on his face. He took a sip of the iced water with distaste as though it were medicine* (Graham Greene). **SYN**: See syn. under **dislike**.
—*v.t. Obsolete.* **1** to dislike. **2** to displease; offend. **3** to dislike the taste of.

dis|taste|ful (dis tāst′fəl), *adj.* unpleasant; disagreeable; offensive: *a distasteful medicine. Cleaning out the garbage cans is a distasteful task.* **SYN**: repugnant. —**dis|taste′ful|ly**, *adv.* —**dis|taste′ful|ness**, *n.*

Dist. Atty., district attorney.

***dis|tel|fink** (dis′təl fingk), *n. U.S.* a design or reproduction of a stylized, brightly colored bird, which figures prominently in the folklore of the Pennsylvania Dutch and is often painted on furniture or cloth and used in decoration. [< German *Distelfink* goldfinch]

***distelfink**

dis|tem|per¹ (dis tem′pər), *n., v.* —*n.* **1a** an infectious disease of dogs and other animals, accompanied by fever, a short, dry cough, and weakness. It is caused by a virus and affects chiefly young dogs. **b** a serious viral disease of cats; feline enteritis: *Kittens should get injections to protect them against distemper.* **c** a bacterial disease of horses; strangles. **2** a sickness of the mind or body; disorder; disease: *Of no distemper, of no blast he died* (Milton). **3** *Figurative.* disturbance. **SYN**: disorder, derangement. [partly < verb; partly on analogy of *temper*¹]
—*v.t.* to make unbalanced; disturb; disorder: ... *the plight of the decent man in a sorely distempered society* (Atlantic). **SYN**: trouble, vex, upset. [Middle English *destempren* mix badly, or derange (the bodily humors) < Old French *destemprer* < Late Latin *distemperāre* mix improperly < Latin *dis-* not + *temperāre* mix in proper proportion]

dis|tem|per² (dis tem′pər), *n., v.* —*n.* **1** paint made by mixing the colors with eggs or glue instead of oil; tempera. Distemper is often used for painting on plaster walls. **2** a method of painting with such a mixture. **3** a picture painted by this method. **4** *British.* calcimine. [< verb]
—*v.t.* **1** to paint in distemper. **2** to mix (colors) by the distemper method. **3** *British.* to calcimine. **4** *Obsolete.* to dilute; dissolve; soak.
[< Old French *destemprer* dissolve, soak < Late Latin *distemperāre* mix thoroughly; see etym. under **distemper¹**]

dis|tem|per|a|ture (dis tem′pər ə chər, -prə-), *n. Archaic.* **1** distempered or disordered condition; disturbance of health or mind. **2** excess; intemperateness.

dis|tend (dis tend′), *v.t.* to stretch out by pressure from within; swell out; expand: *The balloon was distended almost to the bursting point. Blowing a trumpet distends your cheeks.*
—*v.i.* to become distended; swell out; expand: *The stomachs of starving people often distend.* (*Figurative.*) *Now his heart Distends with pride* (Milton).
[< Latin *distendere* < *dis-* apart + *tendere* stretch] —**dis|tend′er**, *n.*

dis|ten|si|bil|i|ty (dis ten′sə bil′ə tē), *n.* the quality of being distensible; capacity for distention.

dis|ten|si|ble (dis ten′sə bəl), *adj.* that can be distended.

dis|ten|sile (dis ten′səl, -sīl), *adj.* capable of distending; causing distention.

dis|ten|sion (dis ten′shən), *n.* = distention.

dis|tent (dis tent′), *adj.* distended. [< Latin *distentus,* past participle of *distendere;* see etym. under **distend**]

dis|ten|tion (dis ten′shən), *n.* **1** the act of distending. **2** the state of being distended.

dis|tich (dis′tik), *n., pl.* **-tichs.** two lines of verse forming a stanza, and usually making complete sense; couplet. *Example:*
Those who in quarrels interpose
Must often wipe a bloody nose.
[< Latin *distichon* < Greek *dístichon* < *di-* two + *stíchos* line]

dis|tich|ous (dis′ti kəs), *adj. Botany.* arranged alternately in two vertical rows on opposite sides of an axis: *distichous leaves.* [< Latin *distichus* in two ranks (with English *-ous*) < Greek *dístichos* < *di-* two + *stíchos* line] —**dis′tich|ous|ly**, *adv.*

dis|til (dis til′), *v.t., v.i.,* **-tilled, -til|ling.** *Especially British.* distill.

dis|till (dis til′), *v.,* **-tilled, -till|ing.** —*v.t.* **1** to make (a liquid or other substance) pure by turning it into a vapor and then cooling it into a liquid form again: *to distill water for drinking.* **2** to obtain by distilling; refine: *Gasoline is distilled from crude oil. Alcoholic liquor is distilled from mash made from grain.* **3** *Figurative.* to get out the essential principle; extract: *A jury must distill the truth from the testimony of witnesses.* **4** to give off in drops: *These flowers distill a sweet nectar.* **SYN**: exude. **5** to let fall in drops: *The sky distills the dew.*
—*v.i.* **1** to fall in drops; drip; trickle: *Tears distilled slowly from her eyes.* **2** to undergo distillation.
[< Late Latin *distīllāre,* for *dēstillāre* < Latin *dē-* down + *stīlla* drop]

dis|till|a|ble (dis til′ə bəl), *adj.* that can be distilled; fit for distillation.

dis|til|late (dis′tə lit, -lāt), *n.* **1** a distilled liquid; something obtained by distilling; distillation: (*Figurative.*) *Riding aboard this train, with its distillate of everyone and everything associated with the Kennedys over the years, one often had an eerie sense ...* (Russell Baker). **2** any of various petroleum products.

distillate oil, oil specially processed for use as fuel.

***dis|til|la|tion** (dis′tə lā′shən), *n.* **1** the act of distilling: *the distillation of water to purify it.* (*Figurative.*) *Ordinarily, decisions which must be made when life and death are at stake require a profundity of reflection, a weighing of factors, and the eventual distillation of a choice* (Atlantic). **2** the process of distilling; heating a liquid or solid in a retort, still, etc., and condensing the vapor given off by cooling it in order to purify and condense the thing heated: *Distillation is important both in the laboratory and in industry* (William N. Jones). **3** something distilled; extract; the refined or concentrated essence: (*Figurative.*) *"Lover Man," written in 1941, [is] recorded by him for the first time on this disk with a simple, direct persuasiveness that can only be the distillation of 25 years of playing it in every conceivable fashion* (New York Times).

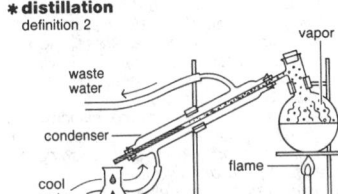

***distillation**
definition 2

vapor
waste water
condenser
flame
cool water
distillate

dis|til|la|to|ry (dis til′ə tôr′ē, -tōr′-), *adj., n., pl.* **-ries.** —*adj.* having to do with distillation.
—*n. Obsolete.* an apparatus for distillation.

dis|tilled (dis tild′), *adj.* obtained by distilling; purified: *distilled water.*

dis|till|er (dis til′ər), *n.* **1** a person or thing that distills. **2** a person or company that makes whiskey, rum, brandy, or other alcoholic beverages.

dis|till|er|y (dis til′ər ē, -til′rē), *n., pl.* **-er|ies.** **1** a place where distilling is done. **2** a place where whiskey, rum, brandy, or other alcoholic beverages are made; still.

dis|till|ment (dis til′mənt), *n.* = distillation.

dis|til|ment (dis til′mənt), *n. Especially British.* distillment.

dis|tinct (dis tingkt′), *adj.* **1** not the same; separate: *two distinct sounds. She asked me about it three distinct times.* **SYN**: different. **2** different in quality or kind: *Mice are distinct from rats. Reading is distinct from writing.* **SYN**: distinctive, dissimilar. **3** clear; easily seen, heard, or understood; plain: *Large distinct print is easy to read. Your speech and writing should be distinct.* **SYN**: obvious. **4** unmistakable; definite; decided: *A tall player has a distinct advantage in basketball.* **SYN**: positive, substantial. **5** distinguishing clearly: *The area of distinct vision in the eye is known as the yellow spot.* **6** decorated; adorned: *Dark blue the deep sphere overhead, Distinct with vivid stars inlaid* (Tennyson). **7** *Obsolete.* distinguished. [< Latin *distinctus,* past participle of *distinguere;* see etym. under **distinguish**] —**dis|tinct′ness**, *n.*

dis|tinc|tion (dis tingk′shən), *n.* **1** the act of distinguishing from others; making a difference: *She treated all her children alike without distinction.* **SYN**: discrimination. **2** difference: *The distinction between hot and cold is easily noticed. What is the distinction between ducks and geese?* **3** a special quality or feature; point of difference: *a dubious distinction. He has the distinction of being the tallest boy in the class.* **4** honor: *The soldier served with distinction.* **5** a mark or sign of honor: *He received many medals as distinctions for bravery.* **6** excellence; superiority: *The President should be a man of great distinction.* **SYN**: eminence.
distinction without a difference, a false distinction; artificial difference: *The distinction which is sometimes made between civil privileges and political power is a distinction without a difference* (Macaulay).

dis|tinc|tive (dis tingk′tiv), *adj.* **1** distinguishing from others; special; characteristic: *Policemen*

Pronunciation Key: hat, āge, cãre, fär; let, ēqual, tėrm, it, īce; hot, ōpen, ôrder; **oi**l, **ou**t; cup, pu̇t, rüle; **ch**ild; lo**ng**; **th**in; **ᴛʜ**en; **zh**, measure; **ə** represents **a** in about, **e** in taken, **i** in pencil, **o** in lemon, **u** in circus.

wear a distinctive uniform. **2** (of speech sounds) serving to distinguish significantly: *The difference between "p" and "b" is distinctive in English because it alone distinguishes the word "pat" from "bat."* — **dis|tinc′tive|ly,** *adv.* — **dis|tinc′tive-ness,** *n.*

dis|tinct|ly (dis tingkt′lē), *adv.* **1** clearly; plainly: *Speak distinctly.* **2** unmistakably; decidedly: *It is distinctly my turn to take you to dinner.* SYN: clearly, indubitably.

dis|tin|gué (dis′tang gā′, dis tang′gā), *adj.* looking important or superior; distinguished: *Sylvia came of a most distingué family* (New York Times). [< French *distingué,* past participle of *distinguer* to distinguish < Latin *distinguere;* see etym. under **distinguish**]

dis|tin|guish (dis ting′gwish), *v.t.* **1** to see or show the difference in; tell apart: *Can you distinguish cotton cloth from wool?* **2** to see or hear clearly; make out plainly: *On a clear, bright day you can distinguish things far away.* SYN: discern, perceive. **3** to make different; be a special quality or feature of: *A trunk distinguishes the elephant. Ability to talk distinguishes human beings from the lower animals.* SYN: differentiate, characterize. **4** to make famous or well-known; confer distinction on: *He distinguished himself by winning three prizes.* **5** to separate into different groups; classify: *Things are commonly distinguished into animal, vegetable, and mineral.* **6** *Archaic.* to single out for special attention; honor: *They who first distinguished you have the best claim to your attention* (Samuel Johnson).
— ***v.i.*** to see or show the difference; discriminate: *You learn to distinguish between right and wrong. The expert had a good eye for distinguishing between a fake and the genuine item.*
[< Latin *distinguere* < *dis-* between + *stinguere* to separate; patterned on verbs ending in *-ish,* as in *languish*] — **dis|tin′guish|er,** *n.*
— *Syn.* *v.t.* **1,** *v.i.* **Distinguish, differentiate, discriminate** mean to see or show the differences in or between things. **Distinguish** means to recognize the qualities and features of a thing that give it its special character and set it off from others: *He distinguished the violins from the cellos in the orchestra.* **Differentiate** means to point out the exact differences between one thing and others of the same class: *The teacher differentiated between Shakespeare's sonnets and Milton's.* **Discriminate** means to see the fine shades of difference between things: *Sometimes only experts can discriminate counterfeit bills from genuine money.*

dis|tin|guish|a|bil|i|ty (dis ting′gwi shə bil′ə tē), *n.* the quality or state of being distinguishable; distinguishableness.

dis|tin|guish|a|ble (dis ting′gwi shə bəl), *adj.* that can be distinguished; perceptible: *Whatever objects are different are distinguishable* (David Hume).

dis|tin|guish|a|ble|ness (dis ting′gwi shə bəl-nis), *n.* the quality or state of being distinguishable.

dis|tin|guish|a|bly (dis ting′gwi shə blē), *adv.* in a distinguishable manner; perceptibly.

dis|tin|guished (dis ting′gwisht), *adj.* **1** famous; well-known: *a distinguished artist.* SYN: celebrated. See syn. under **eminent. 2** looking important or superior: *Your new suit gives you a distinguished look.*

Distinguished Conduct Medal, *British.* a medal awarded to warrant officers, noncommissioned officers, and men for distinguished conduct in the field. *Abbr:* D.C.M.

Distinguished Flying Cross, 1 *U.S.* a bronze medal for heroism or exceptional service in an aerial flight. **2** *British.* a medal awarded to officers and warrant officers for heroism or exceptional service while flying in combat. *Abbr:* D.F.C. or DFC (no periods).

Distinguished Service Cross, 1 *U.S.* a bronze cross awarded for heroism or exceptional conduct in combat, next in rank to the Medal of Honor. **2** *British.* a similar award in the British Navy. *Abbr:* D.S.C.

Distinguished Service Medal, *U.S.* an award for exceptionally meritorious service to the government in the performance of a duty entailing great responsibility: *The National Aeronautics and Space Administration awards a Distinguished Service Medal to astronauts.* **2** *British.* a medal for distinguished conduct in war. *Abbr:* D.S.M.

Distinguished Service Order, *British.* an order awarded for exceptional services in combat. *Abbr:* D.S.O.

dis|tin|guish|ing (dis ting′gwi shing), *adj.* that distinguishes or makes distinguished: *a distinguishing characteristic.* — **dis|tin′guish|ing|ly,** *adv.*

dis|tin|guish|ment (dis ting′gwish mənt), *n.* **1** the act of distinguishing. **2** the state of being distinguished. **3** a thing that distinguishes.

dis|tort (dis tôrt′), *v.t.* **1** to pull or twist out of shape; make crooked or ugly; change the normal appearance of: *Rage distorted his face, making it very ugly.* SYN: contort. **2** *Figurative.* to change from the truth; give a twist or turn to (the mind, thoughts, views): *The driver distorted the facts of the accident to escape blame. The medium of television can strikingly if unintentionally distort events out of true focus* (C. L. Sulzberger). SYN: misrepresent, falsify. [< Latin *distortus,* past participle of *distorquēre* < *dis-* (intensive) + *torquēre* twist] — **dis|tort′er,** *n.* — **dis|tort′ing|ly,** *adv.*

dis|tort|ed (dis tôr′tid), *adj.* **1** pulled or twisted out of shape; made crooked: *The detective saw the distorted face of a victim of poison.* **2** *Figurative.* misrepresented; falsified: *He gave a distorted account of his experiences to make a better story.* — **dis|tort′ed|ly,** *adv.* — **dis|tort′ed-ness,** *n.*

dis|tor|tion (dis tôr′shən), *n.* **1** a distorting; twisting out of shape: (*Figurative*) *Exaggeration is a distortion of the truth.* **2** the fact or condition of being distorted: *The sick man's face was in complete distortion.* **3** anything distorted: *His story of the fishing trip was full of distortions.* **4** a distorted form or image. **5** *Electronics.* the inaccurate reproduction of a signal by modification of the wave form during amplification or transmission: *Distortion tends to run somewhat higher [on a cassette tape] than on other media, especially at high frequencies* (Charles Lincoln).

dis|tor|tion|al (dis tôr′shə nəl), *adj.* of or having to do with distortion.

dis|tor|tive (dis tôr′tiv), *adj.* tending to distort: (*Figurative.*) *We know now how distortive it was to talk of the [land] enclosure movement of the eighteenth century as the dispossession of the English peasantry* (Manchester Guardian Weekly).

distr., 1 distribute. **2** distribution. **3** distributor.

dis|tract (dis trakt′), *v., adj.* — ***v.t.*** **1** to draw away (the mind or attention): *Noise distracts my attention from studying.* SYN: divert. **2** to confuse; disturb; bewilder: *Several people talking at once distract a listener.* SYN: perplex. **3** to put out of one's mind; make insane: *The dog was distracted with fear.* SYN: craze, derange. **4** *Obsolete.* to draw apart; divide.
— ***adj.*** *Archaic.* distracted.
[< Latin *distractus,* past participle of *distrahere* < *dis-* away + *trahere* draw] — **dis|tract′er,** *n.*

dis|tract|ed (dis trak′tid), *adj.* **1** confused; disturbed; bewildered. **2** made insane; crazed. — **dis-tract′ed|ly,** *adv.* — **dis|tract′ed|ness,** *n.*

dis|tract|i|bil|i|ty (dis trak′tə bil′ə tē), *n.* the state or quality of being distractible: *We're developing a generation with a tremendous need for distractibility* (Wall Street Journal).

dis|tract|i|ble (dis trak′tə bəl), *adj.* that can be distracted.

dis|tract|ing (dis trak′ting), *adj.* that distracts: *Noises are distracting to a person trying to study.* — **dis|tract′ing|ly,** *adv.* — **dis|tract′ing|ness,** *n.*

dis|trac|tion (dis trak′shən), *n.* **1** the act of drawing away the mind or attention. **2** a thing that draws away the mind or attention: *Noise is a distraction when you are trying to study.* **3** a confusion of mind; disturbance of thought: *The mother of the lost children scarcely knew what she was doing in her distraction.* **4** relief from continued thought, grief, or effort; amusement: *Movies and television are popular distractions. She needed some mental distraction after the long strain.* SYN: relaxation, diversion. **5** insanity; madness. **6** confusion; perplexity; dissension.
to distraction, beyond endurance; to the point of madness: *Your constant whining is driving me to distraction.*

dis|trac|tive (dis trak′tiv), *adj.* distracting; tending to distract: *Noisy students have a distractive effect on those who want to study.*

dis|train (dis trān′), *Law.* — ***v.t.*** **1** to seize (goods) for unpaid rent or other debts: *The landlord distrained his tenants' trunks.* **2** to levy a distress upon (a person).
— ***v.i.*** to levy a distress: *Our goods were distrained upon in lieu of rent* (New Statesman).
[< Old French *destreindre* force, oppress < Latin *distringere* molest < *dis-* apart + *stringere* draw, contract]

dis|train|a|ble (dis trā′nə bəl), *adj. Law.* liable to be distrained.

dis|train|er or **dis|train|or** (dis trā′nər), *n. Law.* a person who distrains.

dis|train|ment (dis trān′mənt), *n. Law.* **1** the act of distraining. **2** the state of being distrained.

dis|traint (dis trānt′), *n. Law.* the act of distraining; distress.

dis|trait (dis trā′; *French* dēs tre′), *adj.* not paying attention; absent-minded: *She answered their questions in a distrait manner, her thoughts far away.* [< Middle French *distrait,* past participle of *distraire* to distract < Latin *distrahere*]

dis|traite (dēs tret′), *adj. French.* the feminine form of **distrait.**

dis|traught (dis trôt′), *adj.* **1** in a state of mental conflict and confusion; distracted; bewildered: *The lost child wandered about distraught with fear. The death of Jefferson's wife in September, 1782, left him stunned and distraught.* **2** crazed: *Distraught from grief, she flung herself overboard.* [spelling variant of *distract,* adjective < Latin *distractus;* see etym. under **distract**] — **dis-traught′ly,** *adv.* — **dis|traught′ness,** *n.*

dis|tress (dis tres′), *n., v.* — ***n.*** **1** great pain or sorrow; anxiety; trouble: *The boy's low grades caused his father distress.* SYN: grief, agony, anguish. See syn. under **sorrow. 2** something that causes distress; misfortune: *The high cost of living is a distress to most people.* SYN: calamity. **3** a dangerous condition; difficult situation: *A ship sinking or burning at sea is in distress.* **4** *Law.* **a** the legal seizure of the goods of another as payment for debt or as security; distraint. **b** goods seized in this way.
— ***v.t.*** **1** to cause great pain or sorrow to; make unhappy or troubled: *Your tears distress me.* SYN: afflict, vex. **2a** to subject to pressure, stress, or strain: *Several of the oarsmen were fearfully distressed* (London Times). **b** *Figurative.* to alter the appearance of by being subjected to wear, hard use, or blows: *The [furniture] faker strips such pieces with lye or paint remover ... and then "distresses" them with chains and mallets—that is, he gives them a good pounding to lend the battered allure of great age* (Time). **3** to constrain. **4** *Law.* to levy a distress upon; distrain.
[< Old French *distrece,* perhaps < Vulgar Latin *dīstrictia* < Latin *distringere* < *dis-* apart + *stringere* draw]

distress call, 1 a characteristic call, note, or other sound made by an animal in danger or distress: *American eastern crows ... will respond to the distress call of the French jackdaw, a relative they have never seen* (Scientific American). **2** = distress signal.

dis|tressed (dis trest′), *adj.* **1** suffering; distressful. **2** to be sold at less than the market price: *distressed goods.* **3** *Figurative.* altered in appearance by wear, hard use, or blows, especially deliberately to produce an antique appearance: *This modern furniture has been given a distressed finish, a process that is usually reserved for period reproduction furniture to make it look old* (New York Times).

distressed area, a region characterized by widespread unemployment, poverty, or other conditions of hardship: *Unemployment was so bad ... that the city just escaped being officially termed a distressed area* (New York Times).

dis|tress|ed|ly (dis tres′id lē), *adv.* in a distressed or troubled manner.

dis|tress|ful (dis tres′fəl), *adj.* **1** causing distress; painful. **2** feeling or showing distress; suffering. — **dis|tress′ful|ly,** *adv.* — **dis|tress′ful|ness,** *n.*

dis|tress|ing (dis tres′ing), *adj.* causing distress; painful: *It is distressing to see hungry children begging for food.* — **dis|tress′ing|ly,** *adv.*

distress merchandise, merchandise offered for cash sale at less than the market price.

distress selling, the selling of distress merchandise: *Few ranchers here saw any need for distress selling* (Wall Street Journal).

distress signal, 1 a signal used to call for help in an emergency, especially a code signal, such as an SOS: *A U.S. Navy search plane ... picked up a faint distress signal in the Atlantic* (Wall Street Journal). **2** any urgent call for help: *Amnesia patients seem to be flying a distress signal* (Science News Letter).

dis|trib|ut|a|ble (dis trib′yə tə bəl), *adj.* that can be distributed: *Light packages are distributable by letter carriers.*

dis|trib|u|tar|y (dis trib′yə ter′ē), *n., pl.* **-tar|ies.** a branch of a river that flows away from, rather than into, the main stream and never rejoins it: *Finally, the Mississippi ... divides into several arms (known as distributaries) which empty into the Gulf of Mexico* (Loyal Durand, Jr.).

dis|trib|ute (dis trib′yůt), *v.t.,* **-ut|ed, -ut|ing. 1** to give some of to each; divide and give out in shares; deal out: *Mother distributed candy among the children. The teacher distributed paper to each member of the class.* **2** to spread; scatter: *A painter should distribute the paint evenly over the wall.* SYN: disperse. **3** to divide into parts or groups: *The children were distributed into small groups for the trip to the museum. The Life Guards ... were then distributed into three troops* (Macaulay). **4** to put each in its place; sort out; arrange; classify: *A mail clerk distributes mail when he puts each letter into the proper bag. The flowering plants are distributed into over 20 well-marked classes.* SYN: sort. **5** to sell (goods) to a particular market. **6** *Logic.* to use (a term) so that it includes every member of a class. *Example: dogs* in the sentence "All dogs are animals." **7** *Printing.* to take apart and return (composed type) to the proper compartments in the case. **8** *Obsolete.* to administer (justice). [< Latin *distributus*, past participle of *distribuere* < *dis-* apart, individually + *tribuere* assign]

—*Syn.* **1 Distribute, dispense** mean to give something to each of several people. **Distribute** implies dividing it among them in definite though not necessarily equal shares: *The dividends were distributed to the stockholders.* **Dispense** implies measuring it out among them according to their needs or deserts: *The club dispensed new clothing to the children in the orphanage.*

dis|trib|u|tee (dis trib′yə tē′), *n. Law.* a person who receives a share in the distribution of the estate of an intestate: *The new deadline, of course, does not apply to returns of beneficiaries or other distributees* (Wall Street Journal).

dis|trib|ut|er (dis trib′yə tər), *n.* = distributor.

dis|tri|bu|tion (dis′trə byü′shən), *n.* **1** the act of distributing: *After the contest the distribution of prizes to the winners took place.* **2** the way of being distributed: *If some get more than others, there is an uneven distribution. Great changes ... in the distribution of land and water have undoubtedly caused great alterations in the climates of the world in the past million years* (Thomas A. Blair). **3** a thing distributed: *The food distribution fell short of the agency's expectations and had to be supplemented.* **4** the distributing to consumers of goods grown or made by producers. **5** the area over which a particular thing is spread: *the distribution of a species of animal.* **6** division and arrangement; classification. **7** *Statistics.* a systematic arrangement of numerical data.

dis|tri|bu|tion|al (dis′trə byü′shə nəl), *adj.* of or having to do with distribution.

distribution curve, *Statistics.* a curve representing a frequency distribution smoothed out to eliminate chance deviation due to inadequate sampling.

dis|trib|u|tist (dis trib′yə tist), *n.* a person who favors the equalization of private wealth; an advocate of land reform: *The distributist asks for a culture founded upon the land, the foundation of every great culture of the past; he asks that every one may have private property, and its correlative, private responsibility* (Times of India).

dis|trib|u|tive (dis trib′yə tiv), *adj., n.* —*adj.* **1** of or having to do with distribution; distributing. **2** *Grammar.* referring to each individual of a group considered separately. *Each, every, either,* and *neither* are distributive words. **3** *Mathematics.* of or having to do with the distributive law; giving the same product when performed on a set of numbers as when performed on the individual members of the set. *Example:* $6(7+3) = (6\times7)+(6\times3)$. *a distributive operation.* [*The*] *distributive rule of ordinary arithmetic states in symbols that* $a(b+c) = ab+ac$ (Scientific American). **4** *Logic.* (of a term) given its full extension.

—*n. Grammar.* a word that divides or distributes. *Each* and *every,* which represent the individuals of a collective number as separate, are distributives. —**dis|trib′u|tive|ness**, *n.*

distributive education, *U.S.* a special high-school program in which students hold part-time jobs and take courses related to their employment.

distributive fault, *Geology.* a fault in which the displacement is distributed among several parallel planes at short distances from one another instead of being confined to a single plane. See picture under **fault**.

distributive law, *Mathematics.* a law stating that the product of a number x and a sum $(y+z)$ is equal to the sum of the two products xy and xz. *Example:* $3(4+5) = (3\times4)+(3\times5)$.

dis|trib|u|tive|ly (dis trib′yə tiv lē), *adv.* **1** by distribution; not collectively. **2** in a distributive sense.

dis|trib|u|tiv|i|ty (dis trib′yə tiv′ə tē), *n. Mathematics.* the property of being distributive.

***dis|trib|u|tor** (dis trib′yə tər), *n.* **1** a person or thing that distributes. **2** a person or company that distributes goods to consumers, especially a wholesaler who buys from the manufacturer and sells to retailers. **3** a part of a gasoline engine that distributes electric current to the spark plugs.

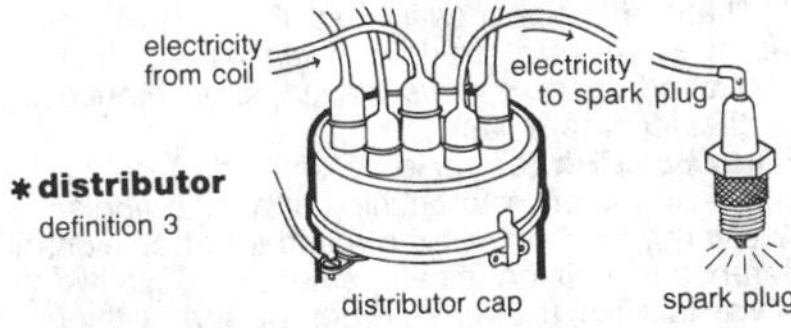

***distributor** definition 3

dis|trib|u|tor|ship (dis trib′yə tər ship), *n.* the business or territory of a distributor (def. 2): *an automobile parts distributorship.*

dis|trict (dis′trikt), *n., v.* —*n.* **1** a part of a larger area; region: *The leading farming district of the United States is in the Middle West. They lived in a fashionable district of the city.* **SYN**: locality, quarter. **2** a part of a country, state, or city marked off for a special purpose, such as providing schools or law courts, electing certain government officers, or supporting a church: *a school district. The Samoan village ... is usually associated with other villages in a larger political entity called a district* (Beals and Hoijer). *Abbr:* dist.

—*v.t.* to divide into districts: *Unlike many large cities which have rigid school districting, Baltimore allows its youngsters, from kindergarten through high school, to go to any school of their choice in the city* (New York Times).

[< Medieval Latin *districtus* territory under the jurisdiction of a feudal lord < Latin *distringere;* see etym. under **distress**]

district attorney, a lawyer who handles cases for the government within a certain district of a state or the country. *Abbr:* D.A.

district check, a plaid pattern or fabric based upon one worn in a particular district of Scotland: *He knows how to relax—does so in Van Heusen's sports shirt—district checks of ... polyester and cotton* (New Yorker).

district council, *British.* the local council of an urban or rural district.

district court, *U.S. Law.* **1** a state court with jurisdiction over a state judicial district. **2** a federal court with jurisdiction over a federal judicial district.

district curves, (in terrestrial magnetism) curves obtained by joining the successive points where isogonals, isoclinals, and the like intersect the lines of latitude.

dis|trict-heat|ed (dis′trikt hē′tid), *adj.* supplied by or using district heating: *In the City of Winnipeg, Canada ... the business area has been district-heated for nearly half a century* (New Scientist).

district heating, a system by which all heating and hot-water requirements of a district or community are supplied from a central source: *Like colour television, district heating—supplying several consumers from one central source—has been around for years without being exploited on any scale in this country* (Sunday Times).

district judge, the judge presiding over a district court.

district lines, (in terrestrial magnetism) district curves.

Di|stri|to Fe|de|ral (dēs trē′tō fā′ᴛʜä räl′), *Spanish.* Federal District. *Abbr:* D.F.

dis|trust (dis trust′), *v., n.* —*v.t.* to have no confidence in; not trust; be suspicious of; doubt: *A fat man learns to distrust wobbly chairs. They distrust strangers in that town.*

—*n.* lack of trust; lack of belief in the goodness of; suspicion: *She could not overcome her distrust of the stranger.* **SYN**: mistrust. See syn. under **suspicion**. —**dis|trust′er**, *n.*

dis|trust|ful (dis trust′fəl), *adj.* not trusting; suspicious: *They are distrustful of the ability of the new mayor to cope with the city's problems.* **SYN**: doubtful, diffident, incredulous. —**dis|trust′ful|ly**, *adv.* —**dis|trust′ful|ness**, *n.*

dis|truth (dis trüth′), *n.* lack of truth; falsity; untruth: *"At the moment, I am rather aggravated about the distruth of statements made by certain druids," he commented* (New Yorker).

dis|tune (dis tün′, -tyün′), *v.t.,* **-tuned, -tun|ing.** *Archaic.* to put out of tune: *What thought distempers and distunes thy woe?* (Algernon Charles Swinburne).

dis|turb (dis tėrb′), *v.t.* **1** to destroy the peace, quiet, or rest of: *Heavy truck traffic disturbed the neighborhood.* **SYN**: trouble, agitate, perturb. **2** to break in upon with noise or change: *Do not disturb the baby; he is asleep.* **3** to put out of order; interfere with: *Someone has disturbed my books; I can't find the one I want.* **4** to make uneasy; trouble: *He was disturbed to hear of his friend's illness.* **5** to move or put (oneself) out so as to oblige somone; inconvenience: *Don't disturb yourself; I can do it.* [< Old North French *disturber* < Latin *disturbāre* < *dis-* (intensive) + *turbāre* disturb < *turba* commotion] —**dis|turb′er** *n.*

dis|turb|ance (dis tėr′bəns), *n.* **1** the act of disturbing or fact of being disturbed. **2** a thing that disturbs. **3** confusion; disorder: *The police were called to quiet the disturbance at the street corner.* **SYN**: tumult. **4** uneasiness; trouble; worry. **SYN**: discomposure.

dis|turbed (dis tėrbd′), *adj.* **1** mentally or emotionally ill: *disturbed children, a disturbed patient.* **2** of or for disturbed people: *the disturbed ward of a hospital.*

dis|turb|ing (dis tėr′bing), *adj.* causing worry or anxiety; alarming; disquieting: *disturbing news, disturbing developments. The cold statistics of the ... poll will make disturbing reading for the Negro people* (Wall Street Journal). —**dis|turb′ing|ly**, *adv.*

di|style (dis′tīl, dī′stīl), *adj., n. Architecture.* —*adj.* having two columns, as a portico.

—*n.* a distyle portico.

[< *di-*[1] two + Greek *stŷlos* pillar]

di|sul|fate or **di|sul|phate** (dī sul′fāt), *n. Chemistry.* **1** a salt of pyrosulfuric (disulfuric) acid. **2** = bisulfate.

di|sul|fide or **di|sul|phide** (dī sul′fīd, -fid), *n. Chemistry.* a compound consisting of two atoms of sulfur combined with another element or radical.

di|sul|fi|ram (dī sul′fə ram), *n.* a crystalline compound widely used in the treatment of chronic alcoholism: *A dose of disulfiram causes a person who then drinks an alcoholic beverage to suffer extreme discomfort, including heavy breathing, nausea, and vomiting* (Sydney N. Fisher). *Formula:* $C_{10}H_{20}N_2S_4$ [< tetraethylthiu*ram disulfi*de, the chemical name]

di|sul|fu|ric acid (dī′sul fyür′ik), = pyrosulfuric acid.

dis|u|ni|fy (dis yü′nə fī), *v.t.,* **-fied, -fy|ing.** to cause disunion in; disunite: *Petty jealousies disunify an office.*

dis|un|ion (dis yün′yən), *n.* **1** separation; division: *Foreigners would believe that we are on the very verge of disunion; but the fact is otherwise* (George Washington). **SYN**: severance, disjunction. **2** lack of unity; disagreement; unfriendliness. **SYN**: dissension.

dis|un|ion|ism (dis yün′yə niz əm), *n.* the doctrine of disunionists.

dis|un|ion|ist (dis yün′yə nist), *n.* **1** a person who advocates or works for disunion. **2** a secessionist during the U.S. Civil War.

dis|u|nite (dis′yü nīt′), *v.,* **-nit|ed, -nit|ing.** —*v.t.* **1** to separate; divide. **2** to destroy the unity of; cause to disagree or to become unfriendly: *She tried to disunite the two friends by making each one jealous of the other. The country was disunited by the issue of slavery.*

—*v.i.* to become disunited; separate; part.

dis|u|ni|ty (dis yü′nə tē), *n.* lack of unity; disunion: *It was recognized that the allies must first concert policy among themselves; otherwise the Russians would be sure to exploit allied disunity* (New York Times). **SYN**: dissension, discord.

dis|use (*n.* dis yüs′; *v.* dis yüz′), *n., v.,* **-used, -us|ing.** —*n.* lack of use; not being used: *The old tools were rusted from disuse. Many words common in Shakespeare's time have fallen into disuse.*

—*v.t.* to stop using; discontinue the use or practice of.

dis|used (dis yüzd′), *adj.* no longer used: *The disused part of the cool beer cellar of this fifteenth-century hotel had to be whitewashed* (Manchester Guardian).

dis|u|til|i|ty (dis′yü til′ə tē), *n.* lack of utility; quality of causing inconvenience or harm.

dis|u|ti|lize (dis yü′tə līz), *v.t.,* **-lized, -liz|ing.** to divert from a useful purpose; make useless.

dis|val|ue (dis val′yü), *v.,* **-ued, -u|ing,** *n.* —*v.t.* to treat as of no value; depreciate.

—*n.* Usually, **disvalues.** *Sociology.* the reverse of values; things that the members of a society regard as undesirable, harmful, evil, etc.

dis|war|ren (dis wôr′ən, -wor′-), *v.t.* (in English law) to deprive (land) of the character of a warren; make common.

di|syl|lab|ic (dis′ə lab′ik), *adj.* = dissyllabic.

di|syl|la|ble (di sil′ə bəl), *n.* = dissyllable.

dis|yoke (dis yōk′), *v.t.,* **-yoked, -yok|ing.** to free from or as if from a yoke; unyoke.

dit[1] (dit), *n.* a dot in the Morse code: *The first two satellites ... transmitted the word "Hi" (four dits, pause, two dits)* (Gary L. Foskett). [imitative]

dit[2] (dit), *v.t.,* **dit|ted, dit|ting.** *Scottish.* to stop up; fill up; obstruct: *Dit your mouth with your meat* (Scottish Proverb). [Old English *dyttan*]

di|ta (dē′tə), *n.* **1** a tropical tree of the dogbane family, found in the Philippines and Asiatic countries, whose bark is used in medicines as a tonic and antiperiodic. **2** its bark. [< a native word]

di|tat De|us (dī′tat dē′əs), *Latin.* God enriches (the motto of Arizona).

ditch (dich), *n., v.* —*n.* **1** a long, narrow place dug in the earth. Ditches are usually used to irrigate fields and carry off water. **2** a natural channel or waterway. **3** a narrow channel in the ground around the playing area of a bowling green.

Pronunciation Key: hat, āge, cãre, fär; let, ēqual, tėrm, it, īce; hot, ōpen, ôrder; **oi**l, **ou**t; cup, pu̇t, rüle; **ch**ild; lo**ng**; **th**in; **ᴛʜ**en; **zh**, measure; **ə** represents **a** in about, **e** in taken, **i** in pencil, **o** in lemon, **u** in circus.

—*v.t.* **1** to dig a ditch in or around; provide with ditches: *With the skill of a Missouri farmer ditching a meadow* (New York Times). **2** to drive or throw into a ditch: *The careless driver ditched his car.* **3** to land (an airplane not equipped for the purpose) on water. **4** to cause (a train) to run off the rails; derail. **5** *Informal.* to get rid of: *The robber ditched his gun in a sewer. And it could even ditch . . . the whole grab-bag bid for the farmer's vote* (Wall Street Journal).
—*v.i.* **1** to dig a ditch or ditches. **2** to land an airplane on water in an emergency, with the expectation of abandoning it: *One Corsair pilot ditched at sea* (New York Times).
to the last ditch, to the last or utmost extremity; to the end: *It is a value eminently worth cherishing and preserving—and defending to the last ditch* (William Henry Chamberlain). *Britain would fight to the last ditch to maintain the level of the pound* (New York Times).
[Old English *dīc.* See related etym. at **dike.**]

ditch|a|ble (dich′ə bəl), *adj. Informal.* that can be ditched; discardable: *. . . a world full of expensive, ditchable commodities* (Penelope Gilliatt).

ditch|dig|ger (dich′dig′ər), *n.* a person who digs ditches or a machine for digging ditches: *An army of axmen and ditchdiggers fell to work digging trenches.*

ditch|dig|ging (dich′dig′ing), *n., adj.* —*n.* the work of digging ditches.
—*adj.* for digging ditches: *a ditchdigging machine.*

ditch|er (dich′ər), *n.* **1** a person who makes and repairs ditches. **2** a machine used to make ditches; ditching machine. **3** *Bowls.* a bowl which runs or is driven off the green.

ditch|ing machine (dich′ing), a ditcher.

ditch rider, *U.S.* a person who takes care of an irrigation system, keeping it in good repair, checking the water level, adjusting the gates, etc: *Of the four ditch riders . . . three are women* (Seattle Times).

ditch riding, taking care of an irrigation system, its ditches, and other equipment.

ditch|wa|ter (dich′wôt′ər, -wot′-), *n.* foul, stagnant water, such as is found in ditches.

di|the|ism (dī′thē iz əm), *n.* **1** belief in two supreme gods. **2** belief in two independent, antagonistic principles, one of good and the other of evil.

di|the|ist (dī′thē ist), *n.* a person who believes in ditheism.

di|the|is|tic (dī′thē is′tik), *adj.* having to do with or like ditheism.

dith|er (diтн′ər), *n., v.* —*n.* **1** a confused, excited condition: *He's in a dither about tomorrow's test. The children were all in a dither when they heard that the circus was coming to town.* **2** a tremble; shiver; quiver. **SYN:** vibration. [< verb]
—*v.i.* **1** to waver with uncertainty or fear: *to dither on making a decision.* **2** to tremble; shiver; quiver. **SYN:** thrill.
[apparently variant of Middle English *didderen;* origin uncertain] —**dith′er|er,** *n.*

dith|er|y (diтн′ər ē), *adj.* **1** confused and excited; flustered. **2** somewhat uncertain; trembling: *He . . . felt dithery and confused and old* (Graham Greene). **3** wavering; indecisive: *a dithery performance.*

di|thi|az|a|nine (dī′thī az′ə nēn, -nin), *n.* a crystalline compound used as a sensitizing agent for photographic emulsions, and as a drug in the treatment of hookworm and similar conditions. *Formula:* $C_{23}H_{23}IN_2S_2$ [< *di-*[1] + *thi-* + *az-* + (cy)-*anine*]

di|thi|on|ic acid (dī′thī on′ik), an acid occurring only in solution or in its salts. *Formula:* $H_2S_2O_6$ [< *di-*[1] + *thionic acid*]

di|thi|o|nite (dī thī′ə nīt), *n.* = hyposulfite. [< *di-*[1] + Greek *theîon* sulfur + English *-ite*[2]]

di|thi|o|nous (dī thī′ə nəs), *adj.* = hyposulfurous.

di|thi|zone (dī′thī zōn), *n.* a crystalline organic compound that forms colors with certain metals, such as silver and lead, used as a selective reagent: *Using a coloring agent, dithizone, the solution will turn from green to orange if there are barbiturate poisons in the blood* (Science News Letter). *Formula:* $C_{13}H_{12}N_4S$ [< *di*(phenyl)*thi*-(ocarba) *zone,* the full chemical name]

dith|y|ramb (dith′ə ram, -ramb), *n.* **1** a Greek choral song in honor of Dionysus. **2** a poem that is full of wild emotion or enthusiasm. **3** *Figurative.* any speech or writing like this. [< Latin *dīthyrambus* < Greek *dīthýrambos*]

dith|y|ram|bic (dith′ə ram′bik), *adj.* **1** of or like a dithyramb. **2** *Figurative.* wildly enthusiastic: *She expressed her boundless satisfaction in a dithyrambic letter to the Prime Minister* (Lytton Strachey).

dith|y|ram|bi|cal|ly (dith′ə ram′bə klē), *adv.* in or as in dithyrambs; with dithyrambic expression.

dits|y or **dits|ey** (dit′sē), *adj. U.S. Slang.* flighty, confused, or eccentric; dizzy: *He thinks women who want equality are ditsey* (New Yorker). Also, *ditzy.* [perhaps alteration of *dizzy*]

dit|ta|ny (dit′ə nē), *n., pl.* **-nies. 1** a perennial plant of the rue family cultivated for its showy white, pink, or purple flowers; fraxinella. **2** either of several plants of the mint family with clusters of purplish flowers. [alteration of Old French *ditan* < Latin *dictamnus* < Greek *diktamnon,* perhaps < *Diktē* the mountain Dicte on Crete, where the herb grew]

dit|tied (dit′id), *adj.* composed or sung as a ditty.

dit|to (dit′ō), *n., pl.* **-tos,** *v.,* **-toed, -to|ing,** *adv., adj.* —*n.* **1** the same; exactly the same as appeared or was said before. **2** the ditto mark or the abbreviation (do.) that stands for "ditto." **3** a copy; duplicate: *Rip's son and heir, who was the ditto of himself* (Washington Irving).
—*v.t.* to copy; duplicate; match: *The Navy and Marine Corps dittoes an average of 6,569 releases every working day* (Harper's).
—*adv. Informal.* as said before; likewise: *There is a research thesis waiting for somebody on the effects of dieting on conversation, ditto vegetarianism* (Atlantic). —*adj.* matching; similar: *a mixed-up film version of* [*his*] *offbeat romance between a frustrated American housewife and a ditto American working man* (Maclean's).
[< Italian *ditto* (literally) said < Latin *dictus,* past participle of *dīcere* say]

dit|to|graph (dit′ə graf, -gräf), *n.* a letter or series of letters repeated unintentionally in writing or copying.

dit|to|graph|ic (dit′ə graf′ik), *adj.* of or like a dittograph.

dit|tog|ra|phy (di tog′rə fē), *n., pl.* **-phies. 1** the unintentional repetition of a letter or word, or of a series of letters or words, in writing or copying. **2** a passage having such repetition. [< Greek *dittós* double + English *-graphy*]

***ditto mark**, a mark used to avoid repeating something written immediately above. Ditto marks are often used on long lists, bills, and tables. *Example:* 6 lb. butter at 75′ . . . \$4.50
4 ″ ″ ″ ″ . . . 3.00

***ditto mark**

” The Complete Plays of Shaw
” ” ” ” Synge

dit|ty (dit′ē), *n., pl.* **-ties.** a short, simple song or poem: *The series includes twenty-one lively ditties intended for 5- to 10-year-old boys and girls* (New York Times). [< Old French *dittie* < Latin *dictātum* (thing) dictated, neuter past participle of *dictāre* (frequentative) < *dīcere* say]

ditty bag, a small bag, used especially by sailors, to hold needles and thread, buttons, soap, laundry, and other items for household chores away from home.

ditty box, a small box used like a ditty bag.

ditz (dits), *n. U.S. Slang.* a flighty, confused, or eccentric person: *A nurse . . . inadvertently administers a fatal overdose to a patient—and catches all kinds of flak for being such a ditz* (Rolling Stone). [< *ditzy*]

ditz|y (dit′sē), *adj.* = ditsy.

di|u|re|sis (dī′yů rē′sis), *n.* excessive discharge of urine. [< New Latin *diuresis* < Greek *diá-* through + *oûresis* uresis]

di|u|ret|ic (dī′yů ret′ik), *adj., n.* —*adj.* causing an increase in the flow of urine.
—*n.* a drug or agent that causes an increase in the flow of urine: *These drugs include a diuretic for the elimination of excess water in the body* (Wall Street Journal).
[< Late Latin *diurēticus* < Greek *diourētikós,* ultimately < *diá-* through + *oureîn* urinate]

di|u|ret|i|cal (dī′yů ret′ə kəl), *adj., n. Obsolete.* diuretic.

Di|ur|il (dī yůr′əl), *n. Trademark.* chlorothiazide.

di|ur|nal (dī ėr′nəl), *adj., n.* —*adj.* **1** occurring every day; daily: *Sunrise is a diurnal event.* **SYN:** quotidian. **2** of or belonging to the daytime: *Diurnal temperatures are usually higher than those of the night.* **3** active only during the day, as certain animals and insects are: *Butterflies are diurnal.* **4** lasting a day; opening by day and closing by night, as certain flowers do.
—*n.* **1** *Ecclesiastical.* a service book containing the offices for the day hours of prayer. **2** *Archaic.* a diary; journal. **3** *Archaic.* a daily newspaper.
[< Late Latin *diurnālis* < Latin *diurnus* < *diēs* day. See etym. at doublet **journal.**] —**di|ur′nal|ly,** *adv.*

diurnal arc, the part of a circle which a heavenly body appears to pass through above the horizon.

diurnal circle, the apparent circle described by a heavenly body in its daily motion of rising and setting, resulting from the rotation of the earth. The diurnal circles of the stars are parallel and are described in the same period, but those of the sun, moon, and planets are not parallel and have different periods.

diurnal hibernation, hibernation that occurs at certain periods each day among some animals. Some bats spend the day in hibernation and become active at night. The diurnal hibernation of some hummingbirds takes place at night.

di|ur|nal|i|ty (dī′ėr nal′ə tē), *n.* the quality, condition, or habit of being diurnal: *Studies of the physiology of vertebrate eyes suggest that diurnality and nocturnality come and go as mutation and ecological expedience direct* (J. L. Cloudsley-Thompson).

diurnal libration, an apparent oscillation of the moon as perceived by an observer, produced by the effect of the earth's rotation.

diurnal motion, the apparent daily rotation of the heavenly bodies from east to west, an effect produced by the earth's rotation on its axis from west to east.

diurnal parallax, the parallax that a heavenly body would have if viewed from two points on the earth separated by an angle of 90° with the earth's center; geocentric parallax.

di|ur|na|tion (dī′ər nā′shən), *n.* the habit of sleeping or being inactive during the day, as contrasted with being active at night.

di|u|ron (dī′yə ron), *n.* a highly toxic, white, crystalline solid used as a weedkiller. *Formula:* $C_9H_{10}Cl_2N_2O$ [< *di*(chlorophenyl)*ur*(ea), part of the chemical name + *-on*]

di|u|tur|nal (dī′yů tėr′nəl), *adj.* of long duration.

di|u|tur|ni|ty (dī′yů tėr′nə tē), *n.* long duration; length of time: *I promise myself, if not immortality, yet diuturnity of being read* (Charles Lamb). [< Latin *diūturnitās* < *diūturnus* lasting < *diū* for a long time]

div (div), *n. Persian Mythology.* an evil spirit; demon; evil genius. Also, **dev.** [< Persian *dīv*]

div., **1** divided. **2** dividend. **3** division. **4** divorced.

di|va (dē′və), *n., pl.* **-vas.** a prima donna; famous woman opera singer.
[< Italian *diva* < Latin *dīva* goddess, feminine of *dīvus* divine (one)]

di|va|gate (dī′və gāt), *v.i.,* **-gat|ed, -gat|ing.** to wander; stray from one place or subject to another. [< Latin *dīvagārī* (with English *-ate*[1]) < *dis-* apart, in different directions + *vagārī* wander < *vagus* wandering]

di|va|ga|tion (dī′və gā′shən), *n.* the action of divagating; wandering or straying; deviation; digression: *The only divagation from the story that he enjoys is the "spot" in which small children from the audience join him in the fun on the stage* (London Times).

di|va|ga|to|ry (dī′və gə tôr′ē, -tōr′-), *adj.* characterized by divagating; digressive: *It all makes for a relaxed, divagatory mode of speech* (John Russell).

di|va|lence (dī vā′ləns, div′ə-), *n.* divalent quality or condition.

di|va|lent (dī vā′lənt, div′ə-), *adj. Chemistry.* having a valence of 2; bivalent.

Di|va|li (dē vä′lē), *n.* the Hindu festival of lights to commemorate the new year: *One of the prettiest of India's celebrations is Divali* (Santha Rama Rau). Also, **Dewalee, Diwali.** [< Hindustani *Dīvālī*]

di|van (dī′van, də van′), *n.* **1** a long, low, soft couch or sofa. **2a** a court or council in Turkey and other Oriental countries. **b** a council chamber or hall. **3** a smoking room: *She . . . directed him to the cigar divan on the other side of the street* (Anthony Trollope). **4** a collection of Persian or other Oriental poems, especially a series by a single author: *His chief work was a divan . . . of about 700 of his poems* (Walter J. Fischel).
[< Turkish *divān* < Arabic *dīwān* < Persian, earlier *dēvān* a council room with a raised cushioned section; (originally) register of documents. See etym. of doublet **dewan.**]

di|var|i|cate (*v.* dī var′ə kāt, də-; *adj.* dī var′ə kit, -kāt; də-), *v.,* **-cat|ed, -cat|ing,** *adj.* —*v.i.* **1** to spread apart; branch; diverge. **2** *Botany, Zoology.* to diverge at a wide angle, as certain plant branches or insect wings.
—*v.t.* to divide into branches.
—*adj.* **1** spreading apart at a wide angle; widely divergent. **2** *Botany, Zoology.* branching at a wide angle.
[< Latin *dīvāricāre* (with English *-ate*[1]) < *dis-* apart + *vāricāre* straddle < *vāricus* with legs stretched apart < *vārus* bowed, knock-kneed]
—**di|var′i|cate|ly,** *adv.*

di|var|i|ca|tion (dī var′ə kā′shən, də-), *n.* **1** a spreading apart or branching at a wide angle. **2** divergence from a fixed standard of opinion; difference of opinion; disagreement.

di|var|i|ca|tor (dī var′ə kā′tər, də-), *n.* a thing that divaricates.

dive (dīv), *v.,* **dived** or (*U.S. Informal and British Dialect*) **dove, dived, div|ing,** *n.* —*v.i.* **1** to plunge headfirst into water. **2** to go down or out of sight suddenly: *The thief dived into an alley to escape from the police.* **3** to plunge the hand suddenly into anything: *He dived into his pockets and brought out a dollar.* **4** *Figurative.* to plunge with the mind; begin with energy and zeal: *She dived into her work with enthusiasm. He has been diving into the history of the Incas.* **5a** to plunge downward at a steep angle: *The hawk dived straight at the field mouse.* **b** (of a submarine) to submerge. **—*v.t.*** to cause to dive; direct into a dive: *to dive an airplane or a submarine.* **—*n.*** **1** the act of diving: *We applauded the swimmer's graceful dive.* **2** a downward plunge at a steep angle: *The submarine made a dive toward the bottom.* **3** *Football.* a play in which the quarterback jumps head foremost and runs parallel to the line of scrimmage giving the ball to a back. **4** *Informal.* a low, cheap tavern or night club. [Old English *dȳfan* dip, submerge; meaning influenced by Old English *dūfan* to dive]

► See **dove**² for usage note.

dive-bomb (dīv′bom′), *v.t., v.i.* to bomb at low altitude with a dive bomber.

dive bomber, a bomber that releases its bomb load just before it pulls out of a dive toward the target: *Stuka dive bombers screamed down on roads clogged with refugees* (Newsweek).

dive brake, a speed brake attached to a wing or a fuselage for use in a dive.

div|er (dī′vər), *n.* **1** a person or thing that dives. **2** a person whose occupation is working or diving under water: *a pearl diver. The diver went down to examine the ship that had sunk.* **3** a diving bird. Loons, grebes, penguins, and auks are divers.

di|verge (də vėrj′, dī-), *v.*, **-verged, -verg|ing.** **—*v.i.*** **1** to move or lie in different directions from the same point; branch off: *Their paths diverged at the fork in the road; he turned left, and she turned right. Two roads diverged in a wood, and I—I took the one less traveled by* (Robert Frost). **2** *Figurative.* to differ; vary; deviate: *Contestants who diverge from the rules will be eliminated from the competition. Pronunciations which diverged too far from the prevailing usage of polite society were publicly discouraged* (Simeon Potter). **3** *Mathematics.* to increase indefinitely as more terms are added to a series. **—*v.t.*** to cause to diverge: *A lens thicker at the edges than in the center tends to diverge incident parallel rays* (Shortley and Williams). [< Late Latin *dīvergere* < *dis-* in different directions + *vergere* to slope]

—*Syn.* *v.i.* **1 Diverge, deviate, digress** mean to turn or move in a different direction. **Diverge** means to branch out in different directions like a Y from a main or former course: *Our paths diverged when we left school.* **Deviate** means to turn aside in one direction from a normal or regular path, way of thinking or acting, rule, or the like: *The teacher deviated from her custom and gave us no homework.* **Digress** applies chiefly to turning aside from the main subject while speaking or writing: *I lose interest if an author digresses too much.*

di|ver|gence (də vėr′jəns, dī-), *n.* **1** the act or state of diverging; a deviating or differing; difference: (*Figurative.*) *divergence from the rules. The committee couldn't come to an agreement because of the wide divergence of opinion among its members.* **2** *Mathematics.* the fact of diverging. **3** *Meteorology.* the flowing of air out of a particular region.

di|ver|gen|cy (də vėr′jən sē, dī-), *n., pl.* **-cies.** = divergence.

di|ver|gent (də vėr′jənt, dī-), *adj.* **1** diverging; different: (*Figurative.*) *a welter of divergent opinions.* **2** for use in different directions: *a divergent nozzle.* **—di|ver′gent|ly,** *adv.*

divergent squint or **strabismus**, a squint characterized by the turning of the eye outward.

di|verg|er (də vėr′jər), *n.* **1** a person or thing that diverges. **2** *Psychology.* a person who excels in far-ranging and imaginative thought: *Among the "trendy" biological subjects during the past few years have been both the psychological aspects of dreaming and the personality differences between convergers and divergers* (New Scientist and Science Journal).

***di|verg|ing lens** (də vėr′jing, dī-), a concave lens which causes a beam of light to diverge upon passing through it.

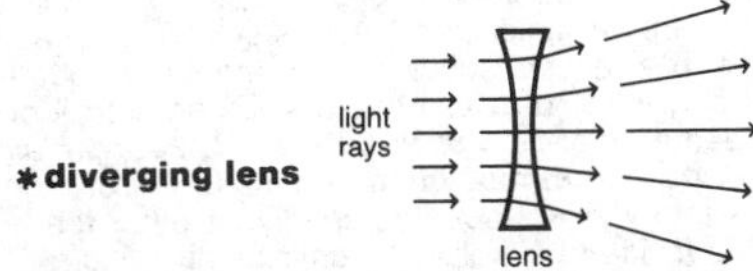

***diverging lens**

di|verg|ing|ly (də vėr′jing lē, dī-), *adv.* in a diverging manner.

di|vers (dī′vərz), *adj.* **1** more than one; several different; various: *A well-balanced diet is made up of divers foods. Divers queens who die with Antony But live a great while first with Julius* (James Branch Cabell). **SYN:** sundry. **2** *Obsolete.* diverse. [< Old French *divers,* ultimately < Latin *dīvertere;* see etym. under **divert**]

di|verse (də vėrs′, dī-), *adj.* **1** different; completely unlike: *A great many diverse opinions were expressed at the meeting. But O the truth, the truth! the many eyes That look on it! the diverse things they see* (George Meredith). **2** varied: *A person of diverse interests can talk on many subjects.* **SYN:** multiform, diversified. [variant of *divers;* the *-e* added on analogy of *converse, reverse*] **—di|verse′ly,** *adv.* **—di|verse′ness,** *n.*

di|ver|si|fi|a|ble (də vėr′sə fī′ə bəl, dī-), *adj.* that can be diversified; able to assume various forms: *Mr. Blunden always keeps close to the English tradition, which is still infinitely diversifiable* (Robert Graves).

di|ver|si|fi|ca|tion (də vėr′sə fə kā′shən, dī-), *n.* **1** the act or process of diversifying: *Earnings were not affected by the decline ... because of the firm's recent diversification into other lines* (Wall Street Journal). **2** the state of being diversified: *The state has high diversification in climate and a luxuriance in plant growth* (Atlantic).

di|ver|si|fied (də vėr′sə fīd, dī-), *adj.* in various forms; varied; diverse: *diversified producers, diversified investments.*

diversified farming, the growing of several different crops on a farm instead of depending on one, as cotton.

di|ver|si|fi|er (də vėr′sə fī′ər, dī-), *n.* a person or thing that diversifies.

di|ver|si|form (də vėr′sə fôrm, dī-), *adj.* of various forms; differing in form.

di|ver|si|fy (də vėr′sə fī, dī-), *v.*, **-fied, -fy|ing.** **—*v.t.*** **1** to make diverse; give variety to; vary: *Mountains, plains, trees, and lakes diversify the landscape. The hillocks ... diversified the contour of the vale* (Thomas Hardy). *Sometimes the solemnity of the evening was diversified by a concert, an opera, or even a play* (Lytton Strachey). **2** to spread or distribute (investments) among different companies or types of securities: [*An investment*] *club should attempt to diversify its holdings, for adequate diversification reduces investment risk* (Helen J. McLane and Patricia Hutar). **3** to enlarge (a company or business) by making diverse products. **—*v.i.*** to become diversified: *It is also diversifying into the lucrative stainless-steel market* (Time). [< Old French *diversifier,* learned borrowing from Medieval Latin *diversificare* < Latin *dīvertere* (see etym. under **divert**) + *facere* make]

di|ver|sion (də vėr′zhən, dī-), *n.* **1** the act or process of diverting; turning aside: *A magician's talk creates a diversion of attention so that people do not see how he does his tricks. High tariffs often cause a diversion of trade from one country to another.* **SYN:** deviation. **2** a relief from work or care; amusement; entertainment; pastime: *Watching television is a popular diversion. Golf is my father's favorite diversion.* **SYN:** sport, recreation. **3** an attack or feint intended to distract an opponent's attention from the point of main attack. **SYN:** distraction. [< Late Latin *dīversiō, -ōnis* < Latin *dīvertere;* see etym. under **divert**]

di|ver|sion|ar|y (də vėr′zhə ner′ē, dī-), *adj.* of or like a diversion or feint, especially in military tactics: *diversionary action.*

diversionary missile, a missile that distracts an enemy so that the main missile attack may hit its targets.

di|ver|sion|ist (də vėr′zhə nist, dī-), *n.* a person who diverges from the established principles and practices of his group, party, etc.; deviationist: *He pleaded guilty to political crimes and diversionist activity* (London Times).

di|ver|si|ty (də vėr′sə tē, dī-), *n., pl.* **-ties. 1** the quality or condition of being diverse; complete difference; unlikeness: *The quiet student and the active athlete were close friends in spite of the diversity of their dispositions. ... the curious diversity of human ambitions* (Lytton Strachey). **2** a point of unlikeness. **3** variety: *The diversity of food on the table made it hard for him to choose.* **SYN:** See syn. under **variety.**

diversity factor, *Electricity.* the ratio of the sum of the maximum power demands of the subdivisions of any system or parts of a system to the maximum demand of the whole system or of the part of the system under consideration, measured at the point of supply.

di|vers|ly (dī′vərz lē), *adv.* in divers or various ways.

divers' palsy, = the bends; caisson disease.

di|vert (də vėrt′, dī-), *v.t.* **1** to turn aside: *A ditch diverted water from the stream into the fields.* **2** to amuse; entertain: *We were diverted by the clown's tricks. Listening to music diverted him after a hard day's work. I diverted myself with talking to my parrot* (Daniel Defoe). **3** to distract: *A juggler or magician diverts attention from one hand by making feints with the other. The siren of the fire engine diverted the audience's attention from the play.* **4** *Figurative.* to embezzle; steal: *The dishonest treasurer diverted funds from the club's treasury.* **—*v.i.*** to turn aside from a course: *They ordered the pilot of the routine domestic flight to divert to North Korea* (Manchester Guardian Weekly). [< Old French *divertir,* learned borrowing from Latin *dīvertere* < *dis-* aside, apart + *vertere* turn]

di|vert|er (dī vėr′tər), *n.* **1** a person or thing that diverts: *Angling was ... a rest to his mind ... a diverter of sadness* (Izaak Walton). **2** = divertor.

di|vert|i|ble (də vėr′tə bəl, dī-), *adj.* that can be diverted.

di|ver|tic|u|lar (dī′vər tik′yə lər), *adj.* of or having to do with a diverticulum.

di|ver|tic|u|li|tis (dī′vər tik′yə lī′tis), *n.* inflammation of one or more diverticula, especially in the intestine.

di|ver|tic|u|lo|sis (dī′vər tik′yə lō′sis), *n.* a condition in which several diverticula are present in the intestines.

di|ver|tic|u|lum (dī′vər tik′yə ləm), *n., pl.* **-la** (-lə). *Anatomy, Medicine.* an abnormal, blind, tubular sac or process branching off from a canal or cavity. [< Latin *dīverticulum,* variant of *dēverticulum* by-path < *dēvertere* turn aside < *dē-* down, away + *vertere* turn]

di|ver|ti|men|to (dē ver′tē men′tō), *n., pl.* **-ti** (-tē), **-tos. 1** *Music.* an entertaining and light instrumental composition, usually in several movements: *Haydn ... is thought to have written ... well over two hundred divertimenti for chamber ensembles* (New Yorker). **2** a diversion; divertissement: *The spy thrillers that have been awesomely climbing the bestseller polls ... are divertimenti, if you will, on the abrasive themes of retail and wholesale slaughter* (Charles Poore). [< Italian *divertimento*]

di|vert|ing (də vėr′ting, dī-), *adj.* that diverts; entertaining; amusing. **—di|vert′ing|ly,** *adv.*

di|ver|tisse|ment (də vėr′tis mənt; *French* dē ver tēs mäɴ′), *n.* **1** a diversion; amusement; entertainment. **2** a short ballet performed between the acts of a play or between longer ballets. **3** *Music.* a divertimento. [< French *divertissement* < Old French *divertir;* see etym. under **divert**]

di|ver|tive (də vėr′tiv, dī-), *adj.* diverting; amusing; entertaining.

di|ver|tor (dī vėr′tər), *n.* a resistor connected in parallel with the winding of a machine to divert some of the current.

Di|ves (dī′vēz), *n.* **1** the rich man in the parable of the rich man and the beggar (in the Bible, Luke 16:19-31). **2** any rich man. [< Latin *dīves* rich (man)]

di|vest (də vest′, dī-), *v.t.* **1** to rid or free; strip: *The sailor divested himself of his clothes and dived into the water.* (*Figurative.*) *The company divested itself of its holdings in the losing factory.* **2** to force to give up; deprive: *A person in prison is divested of his right to vote.* **3** *Law.* to take away (property). [< Medieval Latin *divestire* remove privileges < Old French *desvestir* < *des-* away (< Latin *dis-*) + *vestir* to clothe < Latin *vestīre*]

di|vest|i|ble (də ves′tə bəl, dī-), *adj.* that can be divested.

di|vest|i|ture (də ves′tə chər, dī-), *n.* **1** the act of divesting. **2** the state or condition of being divested.

di|vest|ment (də vest′mənt, dī-), *n.* = divestiture.

di|ves|ture (də ves′chər, dī-), *n.* = divestiture.

di|vette (dē vet′), *n.* a lesser diva, especially a singer of musical comedy or the like. [< French *divette* (diminutive) < *diva* diva]

div|i (div′ē), *n. British Informal.* dividend, especially a dividend paid to members of a local cooperative society: *The Rochdale Pioneers did make their idealism work and now we have the Cooperative Wholesale Society, though some think today's divi isn't really worth it* (Sunday Times).

di|vid|a|ble (də vī′də bəl), *adj.* that can be divided; divisible.

di|vide (də vīd′), *v.*, **-vid|ed, -vid|ing,** *n.* **—*v.t.*** **1** to separate into parts: *A brook divides the field.* **SYN:** sever, split. See syn. under **separate. 2a** to separate into equal parts: *When you divide 8 by 2, you get 4.* **b** to be a divisor of without a remainder: *13 divides 65.* **3** to give some of to

Pronunciation Key: hat, āge, cãre, fär; let, ēqual, tėrm, it, īce; hot, ōpen, ôrder; oil, out; cup, pu̇t, rüle; child; long; thin; ᴛʜen; zh, measure; ə represents **a** in about, **e** in taken, **i** in pencil, **o** in lemon, **u** in circus.

each; share; apportion: *We divided the candy.* (*Figurative.*) *He divided his life between the country and the city.* **SYN:** dispense. **4** to cause to disagree; cause to differ in feeling, opinion, or interest: *Jealousy divided us.* **5** to separate (a legislature or other voting group) into two groups in voting. **6** to mark off in parts; graduate (a scale, instrument, or other measuring device). **7** to distinguish by kinds; sort out; classify.

—v.i. **1** to separate into parts; part: *The road divides and forms two roads.* **2** to do arithmetical or algebraic division: *He adds well, but has trouble dividing.* **3** to share; split: *The profits are counted; let's divide.* **4** to disagree; differ in feeling, opinion, or interest: *The school divided on the choice of a motto.* **5** to vote by separating into two groups.

—n. **1** a ridge of land so situated that the streams on one side flow in the opposite direction to the streams on the other side; ridge between two regions drained by different river systems; watershed: *The Rocky Mountains form part of the Continental Divide. The minor spurs ... of the upland serve merely as divides between small tributaries* (Finch and Trewartha). **2** the act of dividing; division.

[< Latin *dīvidere* < *dis-* apart + an unrecorded root *vid-* to separate, related to *vidua* widow]

Di|vide (də vīd′), *n.* = Great Divide.

di|vid|ed (də vī′did), *adj.* **1** separated. **2** disagreeing in feeling, opinion, etc.: *Divided and tumultuous assemblies* (Macaulay). *A divided court, and a discontented people* (Edward Gibbon). **3** having a partition or dividing strip between opposite lanes: *a divided expressway.* **4** *Botany.* cut to the base so as to form distinct portions: *a divided leaf.* **—di|vid′ed|ly,** *adv.* **—di|vid′ed|ness,** *n.*

▶divided usage. Usage is said to be divided when two or more forms exist and are equally reputable. *Divided usage* is not applied to localisms (like *poke* for *bag*) or to differences, like *ain't* and *isn't,* which belong to separate levels of the language. It applies to spellings, pronunciations, or constructions on which speakers and writers of similar education might differ. The two pronunciations of *either* (ē′ᴛʜər and ī′ᴛʜər), the two spellings of *catalog* (*catalog* and *catalogue*), and the two past tenses of *sing* (*sang* and *sung*) are examples of divided usage.

divided highway, a highway with a median strip between lanes of traffic going in opposite directions: *Divided highways engineered for high-speed driving are completed ... from Augusta, Me., to the Illinois line* (New York Times).

divided skirt, = culottes.

di|vi|de et im|pe|ra (div′ə dē et im′pər ə), *Latin.* divide and rule.

div|i|dend (div′ə dend), *n.* **1** a number or quantity to be divided by another: *In 8 ÷ 2, 8 is the dividend.* **2** money earned as profit by a company and divided among the owners or stockholders of the company. **3** a share of such money. **4** a refund of part of the premiums paid to an insurance company, given to a person holding a participating insurance policy out of the company's surplus earnings: *With our policy-holder dividends your total savings can be really surprising* (Newsweek). **5** *Law.* a sum of money divided among the creditors of a bankrupt estate. **6** *Especially British.* a bonus: *Soldiers are citizens of death's grey land, Drawing no dividend from time's tomorrows* (Siegfried Sassoon). [< Latin *dīvidendum* (thing) to be divided; neuter gerundive of *dīvidere;* see etym. under **divide**]

dividend warrant, an order to pay a dividend to a stockholder.

di|vid|er (də vī′dər), *n.* **1** a person or thing that divides: *There is a concrete divider in the center of the parkway.* **2** a partition, such as a screen or bookcase, for dividing a room into parts or areas. **3** a sheet of cardboard or the like for separating a notebook or a file of cards into parts: *a loose-leaf divider, a card file separated by alphabetical dividers.*

dividers, a compass for dividing lines, measuring distances, charting a course, or the like: *She was like a child with a pair of dividers* (Graham Greene).

di|vid|ing line (də vī′ding), a real or imaginary line regarded as separating two positions, points of view, ideas, periods of time, or conditions: *A sea-barrier forms a far more fundamental dividing line than any land frontier* (J. F. Pain). *The dividing line between sanity and insanity is often hard to establish.*

div|i-div|i (div′ē div′ē), *n.* **1a** a tropical American shrub or small tree of the pea family, whose astringent pods contain gallic and tannic acids that are used in tanning and dyeing. **b** its pods. **2a** a related tree whose pods are used for making ink. **b** its pods. [< American Spanish *dividivi,* probably < a Carib (French Guiana) name]

di|vid|u|al (də vij′ù əl), *adj.* **1** divisible; dividable. **2** separated; distinct. **3** distributed; shared: *The obligation is dividual* (Henry T. Colebrook). [< Latin *dīviduus* divisible, separated (< *dīvidere;* see etym. under **divide**) + English *-al*[1]] **—di|vid′u|al|ly,** *adv.*

di|vin|a|ble (də vī′nə bəl), *adj.* that can be divined.

Di|vi|na Com|me|dia (dē vē′nä kôm me′dyä), *Italian.* Dante's *Divine Comedy.*

div|i|na|tion (div′ə nā′shən), *n.* **1** the act of foreseeing the future or foretelling the unknown by inspiration, by magic, or by signs and omens: *It is quite legitimate for a scientist to investigate whether such phenomena as, for example, mind reading or divination of the future (clairvoyance) do exist* (Bulletin of Atomic Scientists). **SYN:** augury, prophecy. **2** a skillful guess or prediction.

div|i|na|tor (div′ə nā′tər), *n.* a person who practices divination.

di|vin|a|to|ry (də vin′ə tôr′ē, -tōr′-), *adj.* having to do with divination or a diviner.

di|vine (də vīn′), *adj., n., v.,* **-vined, -vin|ing.**

—adj. **1** of God or a god: *The Bible describes the creation of the world as a divine act. Accept the place the divine providence has found for you* (Emerson). *To err is human, to forgive divine* (Alexander Pope). **2** given by or coming from God: *The king believed that his power to rule was a divine right. Do you claim divine guidance for your system?* (Manchester Guardian). **3** to or for God; sacred; holy: *divine service, divine worship.* **4** like God or a god; heavenly. **5** *Informal, Figurative.* excellent or delightful; unusually good or great: *"What a divine hat!" she cried.* **6** having to do with divinity or theology.

—n. a clergyman who knows much about theology; minister; priest: *It is a good divine that follows his own instructions* (Shakespeare).

—v.t. **1** to foresee or foretell by inspiration, by magic, or by signs and omens; predict. **2** to find out without actually knowing; guess correctly: *She divined what had happened to the missing cake from the boys' guilty looks.* **3** to interpret; explain: *For reasons that are difficult to divine* (London Times). **4** *Obsolete.* to portend.

—v.i. to practice divination; prophesy.

[< Old French *divin,* learned borrowing from Latin *dīvīnus* of a deity < *dīvus* deity] **—di|vine′ness,** *n.*

Divine Comedy, a famous Italian poem, written by Dante (1300-1318), having three parts, *Inferno, Purgatorio,* and *Paradiso.*

divine healing, 1 the healing of physical ills by God's direct intervention: *Pentecostals and most revivalists believe in divine healing* (Maclean's). **2** the practice of seeking this healing through prayers and other expressions of faith; faith cure.

Divine Liturgy, the Communion service, especially in the Greek Orthodox Church.

di|vine|ly (də vīn′lē), *adv.* **1** in a divine or godlike manner. **2** by the agency or influence of God: *An angel is a divinely appointed messenger.* **3** *Informal.* supremely well: *She dances divinely.*

divine office, or **Divine Office,** the stated service of daily prayer; canonical hours.

di|vin|er (də vī′nər), *n.* **1** a person who foresees the future or perceives the unknown, or professes to do these things; prophet. **SYN:** soothsayer, magician, sorcerer. **2** a person who makes a skillful guess or prediction: *Most of Pennsylvania's unlicensed political diviners made their decisions weeks ago* (New York Times).

di|vin|er|ess (də vī′nər is), *n.* a woman diviner.

divine right, = divine right of kings: *The first blow at divine right was the execution of the English king, Charles I, in 1649* (J. S. Schapiro).

divine right of kings, the right to rule, thought to have been given to kings by God, not by the consent of the governed.

div|ing (dī′ving), *adj., n.* ***—adj.*** **1** that dives: *diving petrels.* **2** used in diving: *a diving helmet.*

—n. **1** the act of one that dives. **2** a water sport performed by plunging into water after performing various acrobatic falls.

diving beetle, any one of a group of large predacious aquatic beetles that swim freely in the water, and may often be seen diving rapidly to the bottom. See picture under **beetle**[1].

diving bell, a large, hollow container filled with air and open at the bottom. People can work in it under water.

diving board, a board projecting some distance over the water, from which a swimmer dives: *For a brief instant, a state of near zero gravity may be experienced when springing from a diving board* (Newsweek).

diving duck, any one of a group of ducks, including scoters and scaup ducks, which dive for their food: *Diving ducks live both in the sea and in inland waters. Most of them breed in grassy sloughs and lakes* (Joseph J. Hickey).

diving petrel, a variety of petrel that lives only in the Southern Hemisphere.

diving reflex, a bodily reflex of mammals that takes place when the head is submersed in cold water slowing the heartbeat and diverting blood to the brain, heart, and lungs, to delay suffocation: *The diving reflex ... is especially strong in younger persons* (Science News).

diving saucer, a type of deep-diving submarine for oceanographic study that has weights attached on the outside to make it sink.

diving suit, a waterproof suit with a helmet into which air can be pumped through a tube. Diving suits are worn by persons working under water.

***di|vin|ing rod, stick,** or **wand** (də vī′ning), a forked stick believed by some to be useful in locating water, oil, metal, and other things underground by dipping downward when held over a deposit of the substance sought.

***divining rod**

di|vin|i|ty (də vin′ə tē), *n., pl.* **-ties. 1** a divine being; a god or goddess. **2** divine nature or quality: *... such divinity doth hedge a king* (Shakespeare). **3** the study of God, religion, and divine things; theology. **4** a creamy, white fudge candy.

the Divinity, God: *'Tis the Divinity that stirs within us* (Joseph Addison).

divinity circuit, a flexible leather book-binding with projecting flaps which enclose the edges of the book, used for binding Bibles and other books of special edition.

divinity school, a school or college of theology.

div|i|ni|za|tion (div′ə nə zā′shən), *n.* the act of making divine; deification.

div|i|nize (div′ə nīz), *v.t.,* **-nized, -niz|ing.** to make divine; deify.

di|vi|si (dē vē′zē), *adj. Music.* separate (used as a direction for instruments playing from a single staff of music to separate, one playing the upper and the other the lower notes). [< Italian *divisi* < Latin *dīvīsus,* past participle of *dīvidere* divide; see etym. under **divide**]

di|vis|i|bil|i|ty (də viz′ə bil′ə tē), *n.* the quality of being divisible.

di|vis|i|ble (də viz′ə bəl), *adj.* **1** that can be divided. **SYN:** separable. **2** that can be divided without leaving a remainder: *12 is divisible by 1, 2, 3, 4, 6, and 12.*

di|vis|i|ble|ness (də viz′ə bəl nis), *n.* = divisibility.

di|vis|i|bly (də viz′ə blē), *adv.* in a divisible manner.

divisor 36 quotient
29 / 1048 dividend
87
178
174
4 remainder
long division

divisor 4 quotient
3 / 12 dividend
short division

***division** definition 3

***di|vi|sion** (də vizh′ən), *n.* **1** the act or process of dividing or state of being divided: *the division of time into hours, days, and weeks.* **SYN:** partition, severance. **2** the act of giving some to each; a sharing: *A fair division of the work among the children got the chores done quickly. Making large numbers of automobiles is possible only by a division of labor, in which each worker has a certain part of the work to do.* **SYN:** allotment, distribution, apportionment. **3** the process of dividing one number by another: *26 ÷ 2 = 13 is a simple division.* **4** a thing that divides. A boundary or a partition is a division. **5** one of the parts into which a thing is divided; group; section; department: *the research division of a drug company, the engineering division of a university. The cat family is a division of the carnivorous animals.* **6** *Botany.* a major group in the plant kingdom. The plants in a division are thought to be related by descent from a common ancestral group. **7a** a military unit made up of several brigades or regiments plus supporting troops, usually commanded by a major general. It is smaller than a corps. **b** a tactical subdivision of a fleet or squadron, consisting of two or more ships or aircraft of the same type: *How long will Canada keep an air division ... in Europe?* (Maclean's). **8** one of the parts into which a country, county, or other territory is divided for political, administrative, judicial, or military purposes: *a court in the seventh division.* **9** a difference of opinion, thought, or feeling; disagreement: *There was a division in school* *over whether to substitute soccer for football. There still are divisions among the American people* (Newsweek). **SYN:** dissension, disunion. **10a** the separation of a legislative body into two groups for voting. **b** the vote registered by such a separation. *Abbr:* div. [< Old French *division,* learned borrowing from Latin *dīvīsiō, -ōnis* < *dīvidere;* see etym. under **divide**]

di|vi|sion|al (də vizh′ə nəl), *adj.* of or having to do with a division; divisionary: *divisional management.*

di|vi|sion|al|i|za|tion (də vizh′ə nə lə zā′shən), *n.* the act or process of separating into divisions; decentralization.

di|vi|sion|al|ize (də vizh′ə nə līz), *v.t., v.i.,* **-ized, -iz|ing.** to separate into divisions; make divisions of; decentralize: *to divisionalize labor.*

di|vi|sion|ar|y (də vizh′ə ner′ē), *adj.* = divisional.

division bell, a bell in the British House of Commons, used to summon members to vote when there is a parliamentary division over a motion.

di|vi|sion|ism (də vizh′ə niz əm), *n.* = pointillism.

di|vi|sion|ist (də vizh′ə nist), *n.* a painter who practices divisionism.

division mark, = division sign.

division of labor, 1 the distribution of separate small parts of a process among many workers, for example on an assembly line, in order to facilitate mass production. **2** the condition under which the work of a society is divided among various trades and professions such as those of a priest, soldier, and shoemaker.

division sign, the symbol ÷ placed between two numbers to indicate that the first is to be divided by the second.

di|vi|sive (də vī′siv), *adj.* tending to cause division or disagreement: *divisive trade restrictions.* —**di|vi′sive|ly,** *adv.* —**di|vi′sive|ness,** *n.*

di|vi|sor (də vī′zər), *n.* **1** a number or quantity by which another is to be divided: *In 728 ÷ 16, 16 is the divisor.* **2** a number or quantity that divides another without a remainder.

di|vorce (də vôrs′, -vōrs′), *n., v.,* **-vorced, -vorc|ing.** —*n.* **1** the legal ending of a marriage. **2** *Figurative.* a separation: *In this country there is a complete divorce of government and religion.*
—*v.t.* **1** to end legally a marriage between: *The judge divorced Mr. and Mrs. Jones.* **2** to separate from by means of a divorce: *She divorced her husband.* **3** *Figurative.* to separate: *In sports, exercise and play are not divorced.*
—*v.i.* to separate by means of a divorce: *There are, of course, those who divorce, but I suspect that the high rate of divorce in America comes from the tremendous expectation placed on marriage* (Time).
[< Old French *divorce,* learned borrowing from Latin *dīvōrtium* < *dīvertere;* see etym. under **divert**]

di|vor|cé (də vôr′sā′, -vōr′-), *n.* a divorced man. [< French *divorcé,* past participle of *divorcer* to divorce < Old French *divorce* divorce]

di|vorce|a|ble (də vôr′sə bəl, -vōr′-), *adj.* that can be divorced.

di|vor|cee (də vôr′sē′, -vōr′-), *n.* a divorced person.

di|vor|cée (də vôr′sā′, -vōr′-), *n.* a divorced woman. [< French *divorcée,* feminine of *divorcé;* see etym. under **divorcé**]

di|vorce|ment (də vôrs′mənt, -vōrs′-), *n.* = divorce.

divorce mill, *Informal.* a court, city, or state in which divorces are granted on minimal legal grounds and requirements.

di|vorc|er (də vôr′sər, -vōr′-), *n.* a person or thing that brings about a divorce or separation.

div|ot (div′ət), *n.* **1** a small piece of turf or earth dug up by a golf club in making too low a stroke. **2** *Scottish.* a slice of earth with grass on it; turf; sod. **3** *U.S. Slang.* a toupee. [variant of Scottish *duvate;* origin uncertain]

di|vul|gate (də vul′gāt), *v.t.,* **-gat|ed, -gat|ing.** to make known publicly; divulge. [< Latin *dīvulgāre* (with English *-ate*[1]); see etym. under **divulge**]

di|vul|gat|er (də vul′gā tər), *n.* a person or thing that divulgates.

div|ul|ga|tion (div′ul gā′shən), *n.* **1** the act of divulging. **2** the state of being divulged.

di|vul|ga|tor (də vul′gā tər), *n.* = divulgater.

di|vul|ga|to|ry (də vul′gə tôr′ē, -tōr′-), *adj.* making known publicly; divulging.

di|vulge (də vulj′), *v.t.,* **-vulged, -vulg|ing. 1** to make known; make public; tell; reveal: *The traitor divulged secret plans to the enemy. I divulged the news of our misfortune* (Oliver Goldsmith). **SYN:** impart, communicate, disclose. **2** *Obsolete.* to publish. [< Latin *dīvulgāre* publish, make common < *dis-* apart + *vulgāre* make common (property) < *vulgus* common people]

di|vulge|ment (də vulj′mənt), *n.* the act of divulging.

di|vul|gence (də vul′jəns), *n.* the act of divulging.

di|vulg|er (də vul′jər), *n.* a person or thing that divulges.

di|vul|sion (də vul′shən), *n.* the act of tearing or pulling apart or in pieces. [< Latin *dīvulsiō, -ōnis* < *dīvellere* tear apart]

di|vul|sive (də vul′siv), *adj.* tending to tear or pull apart or in pieces.

Div|vers (div′ərz), *n. British, Students' Slang.* a public examination in the Scriptures, formerly given at Oxford University. [short for *div*(inity) (mod)*er*(ation)*s*]

div|vy (div′ē), *v.,* **-vied, -vy|ing,** *n., pl.* **-vies.** *Slang.* —*v.t., v.i.* to share or divide: *I divvied the plastering bill with her* (Life). *Both the dealer and the car buyer can, in effect, divvy up the factory bonus* (Wall Street Journal).
—*n.* **1** a share; part: *A memorandum of the divvy arrangement will be deposited in some safe as a check against memory* (Harper's). **2** division: *France grabbed Morocco . . . in that grand African divvy on the eve of World War II in which Britain got a free hand in Egypt* (Time).
[variant of *divide*]

Di|wa|li (dē wä′lē), *n.* = Divali.

di|wan (di wän′, -wôn′), *n.* **1** = dewan. **2** a chief steward. [see etym. under **dewan**]

dix (dēs), *n.* **1** the lowest trump in bezique and various other card games. **2** a score of ten points for this trump in pinochle.
[< French *dix* ten]

dix-hui|tième (dēzwē tyem′), *adj. French.* **1** of the eighteenth century; belonging to or characteristic of the 1700's: *It is in this self-consciously dix-huitième style that Russell prefers to recount his experiences of China in the early Twenties* (Listener). **2** (literally) eighteenth.

Dix|i|can (dik′sē kən), *n. U.S.* a Republican of the southern United States.
[American English < *Dixi*(e) + (Republi)*can;* patterned on *Dixiecrat*]

dix|ie (dik′sē), *n. British Slang.* a pot or pan for cooking, used especially in the field by a soldier: *Old Cookie just flung the tea-leaves and sugar together into the boiling water in a dixie* (Punch).
[< Hindustani *degchi* < Persian *degcha* (diminutive) < *deg* iron pot, kettle]

Dix|ie (dik′sē), *n., adj.* —*n.* **1** the Southern States of the United States, especially those which united to form the Confederacy in 1861; Dixie Land. **2** a lively song about the South, written in 1859 by Daniel D. Emmett (1815-1904). It was sung during the Civil War and is still popular.
—*adj.* of or having to do with the South of the United States; Southern.
[American English; origin uncertain]

Dix|ie|crat (dik′sē krat), *n.* **1** a Southern Democrat who opposed first the civil rights program of the Truman Administration and later the civil rights plank of the 1948 platform of the Democratic Party: *The Dixiecrats took four states from him [President Truman] in '48, but he was elected, nevertheless* (Newsweek). **2** a later follower of the Dixiecrats. [American English < *Dixie* + (demo)*crat*]

Dix|ie|crat|ic (dik′sē krat′ik), *adj.* of or having to do with the Dixiecrats: *I hope the new Republicans don't paint themselves into that old Dixiecratic corner* (Jack Spalding).

Dixiecrat Party, a political party formed by a group of Southern Democrats who voted against the Democratic Party in 1948 in opposition to the civil rights plank of the platform.

Dixie or **dixie cup,** *U.S.* **1** a paper cup or dish used for beverages, ice cream, soft cheeses, etc. **2 Dixie Cup,** a trademark for a paper cup of this kind.

Dix|ie|land (dik′sē land′), *n.* **1** a jazz style associated with New Orleans, marked by rapid tempo and lively improvisation. **2** a composition or music played in this style: *some of the merriest . . . most earsplitting Dixieland ever heard* (New Yorker).

Dixie Land, = Dixie (def. 1).

Dix|ie|land|er (dik′sē lan′dər), *n.* **1** a musician who specializes in Dixieland. **2** a devotee of Dixieland.

Dixieland jazz, = Dixieland.

DIY (no periods), *British.* do-it-yourself: *In six years he has captured about 70 per cent of the DIY ceramic tile market* (London Times).

diz|en (diz′ən, dī′zən), *v.t.* to dress with gaudy clothes or ornaments; bedizen. [earlier *disyn, disen.* Compare Middle Dutch *disen* wind up flax, Middle Low German *dise* bunch of flax on distaff]

diz|en|ment (diz′ən mənt, dī′zən-), *n.* dizened condition.

di|zo|ic (dī zō′ik), *adj. Zoology.* producing two young: *a dizoic spore.*

di|zy|got|ic (dī′zī got′ik), *adj.* developed from two zygotes; fraternal: *dizygotic twins.*

di|zy|gous (dī zī′gəs), *adj.* = dizygotic.

diz|zi|ly (diz′ə lē), *adv.* in a dizzy manner.

diz|zi|ness (diz′ē nis), *n.* a dizzy condition.

diz|zy (diz′ē), *adj.,* **-zi|er, -zi|est,** *v.,* **-zied, -zy|ing.** —*adj.* **1** likely to fall, stagger, or spin around; not steady; giddy: *When you spin round and round, and stop suddenly, you feel dizzy.* **2** having the sensation that things about one are whirling: *Riding on a merry-go-round makes some people dizzy.* **3** confused; bewildered: *The noise and crowds of the city streets made the little boy dizzy. Prospects of winning his first election made the candidate dizzy.* **4** likely to make dizzy; causing dizziness: *the dizzy height of the balcony.* **5** *Informal.* foolish; stupid.
—*v.t.* to make dizzy.
[Old English *dysig* foolish]

diz|zy|ing (diz′ē ing), *adj.* causing dizziness or confusion: *Japan's bankers and economists began warning . . . that a crisis was at hand unless Japan throttled down its dizzying rate of economic growth* (Time). —**diz′zy|ing|ly,** *adv.*

DJ (no periods), **1** disk jockey. **2** Also **D.J.** District Judge. **3** Dow-Jones (average, usually referring to the industrial average).

djeb|el (jeb′əl), *n.* a mountain or hill in Arab countries: *The lake . . . was Prussian blue against the naked, snow-tipped djebels on the other shore* (New Yorker). Also, **jebel, gebel.** [< Arabic *jebel*]

***djel|la|ba** or **djel|la|bah** (jə lä′bə), *n.* a loose-fitting outer robe worn especially in Arab countries: *Dressed in [an] immaculate white djellabah edged with brocaded silk* (Time). Also, **jellaba.** [< Arabic *jallabah*]

***djellaba**

Djer|ma (dyer′mə, dē er′-), *n., pl.* **-ma** or **-mas. 1** a member of a Negroid people living in the southwestern part of Niger. Most Djerma raise such crops as rice, cotton, millet, and peanuts on small farms near the Niger River. **2** the Sudanic language of this people, a dialect of Songhai.

Dji|bou|ti|an (jə bü′tē ən), *adj., n.* —*adj.* of or belonging to Djibouti, a country in eastern Africa (formerly the French Territory of Afars and Issas), independent since 1977.
—*n.* a native or inhabitant of Djibouti.

djin or **djinn** (jin), *n.* = jinn: *Her interests lie in djinns and prophets, cults and ceremonies* (Observer).

DJ-ing (dē jā′ing) *n.* talking over or with a recording, in time to the beat of the music: *The guys who spin the songs would rap on top of the rhythm, which we call DJ-ing* (Rolling Stone).

djin|nee or **djin|ni** (ji nē′), *n., pl.* **djinn.** = jinni.

Djin|nes|tan (jin′ə stan), *n.* the land of the jinn; Jinnestan.

D.J.S., Doctor of Juridical Science.

dk., 1 deck. **2** dock.

dkg., decagram or decagrams.

dkl., decaliter or decaliters.

dkm., decameter or decameters.

dl., deciliter or deciliters.

D layer, the lowest layer of ionized particles in the ionosphere, about 50 miles above the earth's surface; D region. The energy of short-wave radio waves reflected by other layers is absorbed on the D layer.

D. Lit. or **D. Litt., 1** Doctor of Letters (Latin, *Doctor Literarum* or *Litterarum*). **2** Doctor of Literature (Latin, *Doctor Literarum* or *Litterarum*).

D.L.P., Democratic Labour Party (of Australia).

D.L.S., *U.S.* Doctor of Library Science.

dm., decimeter or decimeters.

DM (no periods), **1** adamsite. **2** Deutsche mark.

D-Mark (dē′märk′), *n.* Deutsche mark.

D.M.D., Doctor of Dental Medicine (Latin, *Dentariae Medicinae Doctor*).

DMP (no periods), dimethyl phthalate.

DMSO (no periods), dimethyl sulfoxide.

DMT (no periods), dimethyltryptamine.

D. Mus., Doctor of Music.

DMZ (no periods), demilitarized zone (applied especially to the demilitarized zone between what was formerly South Vietnam and North Vietnam.

DNA (no periods), deoxyribonucleic acid, the substance of which most genes are made and that is chiefly responsible for the transmission of inherited characteristics: *Inside the nucleus of every cell are spiral molecules called DNA* (Life). *DNA . . . is the substance that conveys the genetic*

Pronunciation Key: hat, āge, cãre, fär; let, ēqual, tėrm; it, īce; hot, ōpen, ôrder; oil, out; cup, pu̇t, rüle; child; long; thin; ᴛʜen; zh, measure; ə represents **a** in about, **e** in taken, **i** in pencil, **o** in lemon, **u** in circus.

information which tells ourselves how to grow (C. P. Snow).

DNAase (dē′en′ā′ās′), *n.* = deoxyribonuclease.

DNA fingerprint, a distinctive pattern of bands formed by repeating sequences of base pairs of satellite DNA, used as a means of personal identification because of its unique quality to one individual; genetic fingerprint: *Except for identical twins, even close relatives can be distinguished by these DNA fingerprints* (J.A. Miller).

DNA fingerprinting, the technique of analyzing satellite DNA in a specimen of body tissue or fluid to reveal a person's DNA fingerprint; genetic fingerprinting: *It is envisaged that DNA fingerprinting will revolutionize forensic biology particularly with regard to the identification of rape suspects* (Science News).

DNA polymerase, an enzyme that promotes the formation of new nucleotides of DNA by a process of replication: *Besides its copying abilities, DNA polymerase can repair strands of DNA damaged by ultraviolet light* (London Times).

DNase (dē′en′ās′), *n.* = deoxyribonuclease.

DNB (no periods), a German news agency (Deutsches Nachrichtenbüro).

D.N.B., *British.* Dictionary of National Biography.

D notice, *British.* a formal government request to editors to withhold a certain item of news from publication in the interest of national security. [< *D*(efense) *notice*]

DNP (no periods), dinitrophenol.

do[1] (dü), *v., present singular* 1 **do**, 2 (*Archaic*) **doest** or **dost**, 3 **does** or (*Archaic*) **doeth** or **doth**; *plural* **do**; *past tense* **did**; *past participle* **done**; *present participle* **doing**; *n.* —*v.t.* **1** to carry through to an end any action or piece of work; carry out; perform: *She did her work well.* **2** to complete; finish; end: *That's done!* **3** to make; produce: *He did a book on his travels in Africa. Walt Disney did a movie about the seven dwarfs.* **4** to be the cause of; bring about: *Do good. Your work does you credit.* **5** to render: *to do homage, do justice.* **6** to deal with; take care of; put in order: *to do the dishes, do one's hair.* **7** to be satisfactory or enough for; serve: *It's a small house, but it will do us.* SYN: suffice, answer. **8** to work out; solve: *to do a puzzle, do a sum.* **9** to cook: *The roast will be done in an hour.* **10** to cover; traverse: *We did 50 miles in an hour.* **11** *Informal.* to cheat; trick.
—*v.i.* **1** to act; behave: *He did very well today. You have done wisely.* **2** to get along; manage; fare: *How do you do? My brother is doing well in his new job.* SYN: prosper. **3** to be satisfactory; be enough; serve: *This hat will do. That shovel will do.* **4** *Do* has special uses where it has no definite meaning: **a** in asking questions: *Do you like milk?* **b** in emphasizing a verb: *I do want to go. Do come and visit us.* **c** in standing for a verb already used: *My dog goes where I do. Her brother walks just as she does.* **d** in expressions that contain *not: People talk; animals do not.* **e** in inverted constructions, as after adverbs such as *rarely, hardly,* or *little: Rarely did she laugh.*
—*n.* **1** *British.* ado; commotion; stir. **2** *Informal.* entertainment; show: *At Christmas the office staff put on a great do.* **3** *Slang.* a swindle; fraud. **4** a command to do (something specified); rule; regulation: *the do's and don'ts of etiquette.*

do away with, a to put an end to; get rid of; abolish: *to do away with a rule.* **b** to kill: *The farmer did away with the sick chickens.*

do by, to act or behave toward; treat: *His father did well by him, sending him to the best schools.*

do down, *British Informal.* to get the better of; overcome; bring to grief: *Poor Fanny! She was such a lady, and so straight and magnificent. And yet everything seemed to do her down* (D. H. Lawrence).

do for, a to ruin or damage: *That fire means my business is done for.* **b** *Informal* to act as housekeeper for: *The young girl did for her widowed father.* **c** to provide for; manage: *to do for one's children.*

do in, a to ruin: *If you engage a second-rate man, who isn't used to this make of car, he'll do it in for you pretty quick* (W. J. Locke). **b** *Informal.* to kill: *. . . them that pinched it done her in* (George Bernard Shaw). **c** to exhaust: *I was done in by the long hike.* **d** to cheat: *It seems funny that the first blooming order I got in Enfield I should be done in* (London Daily Chronicle).

do one proud. See under **proud**.

do one's thing. See under **thing**[1].

do or die, *Informal.* to exert oneself to the utmost: *At 15 he entered the village amateur events, determined, as he recalls it, to do or die for his widowed mother* (Time).

do out of, to take away by fraud: *to do a man out of his savings.*

do over, a to do once again: *Do the problem over; your answer is all wrong.* **b** to redecorate: *to do over a living room.*

do up, a to wrap or tie up: *Please do up this package more securely.* **b** to arrange: *to do up one's hair.* **c** to clean and get ready for use: *Working together the children did up the kitchen quickly.* **d** to wear out; exhaust: *The children were done up from the long trip.* **e** *Slang.* to beat up: *The wogs just caught up with him and done him up proper* (Punch).

do with, to find useful or pleasant: *We could do with a nap after our long hike.*

do without, to get along though not having the thing mentioned or implied: *But there are some things which . . . all the real talent and resolution in England, will never enable us to do without* (John Ruskin).

have to do with, to relate to; deal with: *Abstract art has little to do with everyday experience.*

make do. See under **make**[1].

[Old English *dōn*]

—*Syn. v.t.* **1 Do, perform, accomplish** mean to carry on an activity to its end. **Do,** the most general term, applies to almost every kind of activity: *He did nothing today. I did my homework after school so I could go to the game.* **Perform,** a rather formal word in this meaning, usually implies that the activity is completed and often suggests that it is one regularly engaged in: *He performed none of his duties today. She performed wonders by making all arrangements for the field trip in two hours.* **Accomplish** implies that the activity is carried out successfully: *He worked but accomplished very little today.*

*****do**[2] (dō), *n. Music.* **1** the first and last tone of the diatonic scale. Do, re, mi, fa, sol, la, ti, do are the names of the tones of the scale. **2** the keynote of any natural scale. [< Italian *do,* arbitrary substitution of *ut;* see etym. under **gamut**]

key of C:

do	re	mi	fa	sol	la	ti	do
C	D	E	F	G	A	B	C

*****do**[2]
definition 1

do., ditto.

D.O., 1 defense order. 2 Doctor of Osteopathy.

DOA (no periods), dead on arrival.

doable (dü′ə bəl), *adj.* that can be done.

do-all (dü′ôl′), *n.* a person who does all kinds of work in a business or other enterprise; factotum.

doat (dōt), *v.i.* = dote.

doating (dō′ting), *adj.* = doting.

dobber (dob′ər), *n. U.S.* the float of a fishing line. [American English < Dutch *dobber* float, buoy]

dobbin (dob′ən), *n.* a slow, gentle, plodding horse, especially a farm horse. [(diminutive) < *Dob,* variant of *Bob,* nickname for *Robert.* Compare etym. under **robin**.]

dobby or **dobbie** (dob′ē), *n., pl.* **-bies. 1a** an attachment to a loom for the weaving of small, often geometric, figures. **b** Also, **dobby weave.** the pattern of figures woven with this attachment. **2** *Dialect.* a goblin; sprite; brownie. [perhaps < *Dobbie* (diminutive) < *Dob;* see etym. under **dobbin**]

dobe (dō′bē), *n., adj. U.S. Informal.* adobe.

Dobell's solution (dō belz′), an antiseptic solution containing sodium borate, phenol, sodium bicarbonate, glycerin, and water, used as a nose and throat spray. [< Henry B. *Dobell,* 1828-1917, a British physician]

Doberman pinscher (dō′bər mən), any one of a breed of medium-sized, slender, alert dogs, with short, dark, smooth hair, originally developed for police work. [< Ludwig *Dobermann,* a German dog breeder of the 1800's + German *Pinscher* pinscher]

dobie (dō′bē), *n., pl.* **-bies,** *adj. U.S. Informal.* adobe.

dobla (dō′blä), *n.* a former Spanish gold coin. [< Spanish *dobla* < Latin *duplus.* See etym. of doublets **dobra, double.**]

doblon (dō blōn′), *n., pl.* **-blones** (-blō′nās). = doubloon. [< Spanish *doblón*]

dobra (dō′brə), *n.* **1** the unit of money of São Tomé and Príncipe (island country off the west coast of Africa). **2** any one of several former Portuguese coins, especially a gold coin worth 2 johannes. [< Portuguese *dobra,* or *dobla* < Latin *duplus.* See etym. of doublets **dobla, double.**]

dobson (dob′sən), *n.* the large, black larva of the dobson fly; hellgrammite. [origin uncertain]

dobson fly, a large winged insect whose larva, hellgrammite, is often used as bait by anglers.

Dobu (dō bü′), *n., pl.* **-bus. 1** any one of a group of Melanesians of the Dobu Island in the Pacific, noted for their fierce and competitive individualism, treachery, and general paranoia. **2** the language of this people.

Dobuan (dō bü′ən), *adj., n.* —*adj.* of or having to do with the Dobus. —*n.* = Dobu.

doby (dō′bē), *n., pl.* **-bies,** *adj. U.S. Informal.* adobe.

doc (dok), *n. U.S. Informal.* doctor.

doc., document.

docent (dō′sənt), *n.* **1** a lecturer at a college or university. A docent is often a graduate student, not on the regular faculty. **2** a person trained as a guide and lecturer to conduct groups through a picture gallery, museum, etc. [< earlier German *Docent,* now *Dozent* < Latin *docēns, -entis,* present participle of *docēre* teach. Compare etym. under **doctor**.]

docentship (dō′sənt ship), *n.* **1** the position or function of a docent. **2** the time of being a docent.

Docetae (dō sē′tē), *n.pl.* a sect of heretics from the early Christian Church, who held that Christ's body was not human and that the sufferings of the earthly Christ were only apparent but not real. [< New Latin *Docetae* < Greek *Dokētai* < *dokéin* to seem, appear]

Docete (dō sēt′), *n.* a member or follower of the Docetae; Docetist.

Docetic or **docetic** (dō sē′tik, -set′ik), *adj.* of or having to do with the Docetae.

Docetism (dō sē′tiz əm, -set′iz-), *n.* the beliefs of the Docetae.

Docetist (dō sē′tist, -set′ist), *n.* a follower of Docetic teaching; Docete.

doch-an-dorris (doH′ən dor′is), *n.* a farewell drink; stirrup cup. [< Scottish Gaelic *deoch an doruis* drink at the door]

dochmiac (dok′mē ak), *adj.* of or having to do with a dochmius.

dochmius (dok′mē əs), *n., pl.* **-mii** (-mē ī). a foot of five syllables in ancient Greek and Latin verse usually with the first syllable and fourth short and the rest long. [< Latin *dochmius* < Greek *dóchmios*]

docile (dos′əl; *especially British* dō′sīl, dos′īl), *adj.* **1** easily managed; obedient: *Persons who are just starting to ride should use a docile horse.* SYN: tractable. See syn. under **obedient**. **2** easily taught; willing to learn: *The docile pupils in the class usually get the highest marks in conduct.* SYN: teachable. [< Middle French *docile,* learned borrowing from Latin *docilis* < *docēre* teach]
—**doc′ilely**, *adv.*

docility (dō sil′ə tē, do-), *n.* docile quality.

docimastic (dos′ə mas′tik), *adj.* of or having to do with a docimasy.

docimasy (dos′ə mə sē), *n., pl.* **-sies. 1** (in ancient Greece) a judicial inquiry into the fitness of candidates for public office or citizenship. **2** the process of determining something by test, such as the quality of metals or drugs, or whether a child was born alive. [< Greek *dokimasíā* scrutiny, examination < *dokimázein* to examine]

*****dock**[1] (dok), *n., v.* —*n.* **1** a platform built on the shore or out from the shore; wharf. Ships load and unload beside a dock. **2** the water between two piers, permitting the entrance of ships. **3** a place where a ship may be repaired, often built watertight so that the water may be kept high or pumped out. **4** a place for inspecting or repairing aircraft. **5** a room in a theater for the storage of scenery.
—*v.t.* **1** to bring (a ship) to dock; tie up at a dock: *The sailors docked the ship and began to unload it.* **2** = dry-dock. **3** to join (two spacecraft, such as a command module and a lunar module or a space station and a shuttle) while in space.
—*v.i.* **1** to come into a dock; moor at a dock: *The ship docked during the night.* **2** to be joined with another spacecraft while in space: *The manned orbital workshop was assembled yesterday when the three-man ferry craft Soyuz II docked with the Salyut, a big instrumented station that was sent aloft without a crew* (New York Times).
[< Middle Dutch, or Middle Low German *docke*]

*****dock**[1]
definitions 1, 2

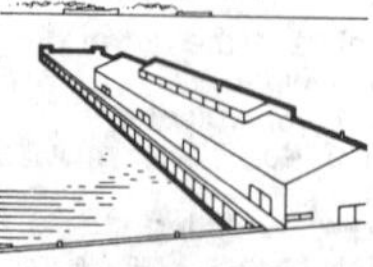
definition 1

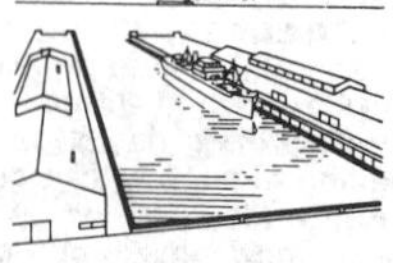
definition 2

dock[2] (dok), *v., n.* —*v.t.* **1** to cut down; cut some off of: *The company docked the men's wages if they came late to work.* SYN: curtail. **2** to cut short; cut off the end of. Horses' and dogs' tails are sometimes docked. SYN: truncate.
—*n.* **1** the solid, fleshy part of an animal's tail. **2** the part of a tail left after cutting or clipping. [Old English *-docca,* as in *finger-docca* finger muscle]

dock[3] (dok), *n.* the place where an accused person stands in a law court to be tried.
in (or **on**) **the dock, a** being tried: *18 members of the Ku Klux Klan . . . were in the dock in a trial that had drawn national attention* (New York Times). **b** *Figurative.* facing accusation or censure; being in a defensive position: *Liberalism is on the dock* (London Times). *The United States was obviously relieved to find the Russians in the dock once again* (Max Frankel).
[perhaps < Flemish *dok* pen]

dock[4] (dok), *n.* any one of various large, coarse weeds having sour or bitter leaves and clusters of greenish flowers; sorrel. It belongs to the buckwheat family. *Their cornland will remain choked with dock, thistle and couch* (J. W. Robertson Scott). [Old English *docce*]

dock|age[1] (dok′ij), *n.* **1** a place to dock ships: *Plans include 3,500 feet of deep-sea dockage in Lake Calumet* (Newsweek). **2** a charge for using a dock. **3** the docking of ships. [< *dock*[1] + *-age*]

dock|age[2] (dok′ij), *n.* the act of cutting down; act of cutting some off. [< *dock*[2] + *-age*]

dock|a|min|i|um (dok′ə min′ē əm), *n. U.S.* a berth for a boat or ship sold as a piece of real estate. [< *dock*[1] + (condo)*minium*]

dock|er[1] (dok′ər), *n.* **1** a person who works on a dock; dockworker; longshoreman: *11,000 dockers were able to work on vessels completing loading and unloading* (London Times). **2** a person who lives near docks. [< *dock*[1] + *-er*[2]]

dock|er[2] (dok′ər), *n.* a person or thing that docks, cuts short, or cuts off. [< *dock*[2] + *-er*[1]]

dock|et (dok′it), *n., v.,* **-et|ed, -et|ing.** **—*n.*** **1** a list of lawsuits to be tried by a court: *crowded Federal court dockets.* **2** a summary or list of law-court decisions. **3** any list of matters to be considered by some person or group. **4** a label or ticket giving the contents, such as those of a package or document.
—*v.t.* **1** to enter on a docket: *So far this year he has docketed 22 new cases* (Newsweek). **2** to make a summary or list of (law-court decisions). **3** to mark with a docket.
clear the docket, *U.S.* to dispose of, especially by bringing to trial or dismissing the cases pending before a court: *The court had cleared the docket by sitting to unseemly hours of the night* (Booth Tarkington).
[earlier *dogget;* origin uncertain]

dock|hand (dok′hand′), *n.* = dockworker.

dock|ing (dok′ing), *n.* the joining of orbiting or navigating spacecraft: *Rendezvous and docking in orbit is a difficult operation; even with men in charge. The first Gemini attempt nearly ended in disaster* (Science Journal).

dock|land (dok′land′), *n. British.* an area of piers and wharves in a port: *He gave a press conference in the rough-and-tumble slum area of London's dockland* (Maclean's).

dock|mack|ie (dok′mak ē), *n.* a shrub of the honeysuckle family, having small clusters of yellowish-white flowers and a red fruit which turns blue-black. [American English < Algonkian (Delaware) *dogekumak*]

dock|side (dok′sīd′), *n., adj.* **—*n.*** the area on or at the side of a dock: *A whole new fleet of fast and attractive little vessels is tethered at the dockside* (Atlantic).
—*adj.* **1** on or at the side of a dock: *a dockside terminal.* **2** of or having to do with a dock or docks, especially the general area around docks: *a dockside scene in a play.*

docks|man (doks′mən), *n., pl.* **-men.** a man employed at a dock or docks.

dock|wal|lop|er (dok′wol′ə pər), *n. U.S. Slang.* a longshoreman; docker.

dock|wal|lop|ing (dok′wol′ə ping), *n. U.S. Slang.* the work of a dockwalloper.

dock|work|er (dok′wėr′kər), *n.* a longshoreman; docker.

dock|yard (dok′yärd′), *n.* **1** a place where ships are built, equipped, and repaired. A dockyard contains docks, workshops, and warehouses for supplies. **2** *British.* a navy yard.

dock|yard|man (dok′yärd′mən), *n., pl.* **-men.** *British.* a man who works in a navy yard.

doc|tor (dok′tər), *n., v.* **—*n.*** **1** a person who knows how to treat diseases or physical or mental disorders; physician, dentist, or surgeon. A doctor must have a license to practice medicine. *Abbr:* Dr. **2** any person who treats diseases: *a witch doctor.* **3** a person who has the highest degree given by a university: *a Doctor of Philosophy, a Doctor of Laws.* **4** the academic degree held by such a person. *Abbr:* Dr. **5** any one of various mechanical devices for certain purposes, usually for curing defects, regulating, adjusting, or feeding, such as the doctor blade. **6** = donkey engine. **7** a gaudy artificial fly used in angling. **8** *Archaic.* a learned man; teacher: *Who shall decide, when doctors disagree?* (Alexander Pope). **9** *Archaic Slang.* a false or loaded die.
—*v.t.* *Informal.* **1** to treat disease in (a person, animal, or, sometimes, plants): *Mother doctors us for ordinary colds and stomachaches.* **2** *Figurative.* to tamper with: *The dishonest cashier doctored the accounts. Police documents have disappeared . . . have been burned, have been doctored* (New Yorker). **SYN:** falsify, adulterate. **3** to repair; mend: *The old man carefully doctored the split in the cane seat.* **—*v.i.*** *Informal.* **1** to be a doctor; practice medicine: *"They say there's no money in doctoring these days," said the man* (Punch). **2** to take medicine.
[< Old French *doctour,* learned borrowing from Latin *doctor* teacher < *docēre* teach]

doc|tor|al (dok′tər əl), *adj., n.* **—*adj.*** **1** having to do with a doctor or doctorate: *a doctoral dissertation.* **2** having a doctorate.
—*n.* *Informal.* a doctoral thesis or dissertation.

doc|to|rand (dok′tə rand), *n.* a candidate for a doctor's degree. [< German *Doktorand* < Medieval Latin *doctorandus,* ultimately < Latin *doctor;* see etym. under **doctor**]

doc|to|ran|dus (dok′tə ran′dəs), *n., pl.* **-di** (-dī). = doctorand. [< Medieval Latin *doctorandus*]

doc|tor|ate (dok′tər it), *n.* the degree of doctor given by a university.

doctor blade, a blade used to remove excess material, especially from a rotating surface: *As the cylinder* [*of a printing press*] *revolves, a steel blade called a "doctor blade" wipes the surface clean* (J. S. Mertle).

doc|tor|ess (dok′tər is), *n.* a woman doctor.

doc|tor|fish (dok′tər fish′), *n., pl.* **-fish|es** or (*collectively*) **-fish.** = surgeonfish.

doc|tor|less (dok′tər lis), *adj.* without a doctor or doctors: *Alaska is virtually doctorless* (Time).

Doc|tors' Commons (dok′tərz), **1** the buildings formerly occupied by the College of Doctors of Civil Law in London (originally, the dining hall of the college), where the courts dealing with wills, matrimonial cases, and admiralty matters sat. **2** the site on which these buildings formerly stood.

doctor's degree, = doctorate.

doc|tor|ship (dok′tər ship), *n.* the position, character, or function of a doctor.

doctor solution, a solution, usually consisting of sodium and lead oxide, used in petroleum refining to remove certain impurities and bad odors.

doc|tress (dok′tris), *n. Rare.* a woman doctor.

doc|tri|naire (dok′trə nãr′) *adj., n.* **—*adj.*** stubbornly trying to apply a theory without considering the actual circumstances; impractical; stubbornly theoretical: *We might . . . allow considerations of our own survival to take precedence over doctrinaire ideas* (Observer).
—*n.* a doctrinaire person; impractical theorist.
[< French *doctrinaire* < Old French *doctrine*]

doc|tri|nair|ism (dok′trə nãr′iz əm), *n.* the principles or practice of a doctrinaire: *I was suffering from doctrinairism on the part of some interior decorator* (New Yorker).

doc|tri|nal (dok′trə nəl), *adj.* of or having to do with doctrine: *We heard a doctrinal sermon on baptism.* **—doc′tri|nal|ly,** *adv.*

doc|tri|nar|i|an|ism (dok′trə nãr′ē ə niz′əm), *n.* = doctrinairism.

doc|tri|nar|i|ly (dok′trə nãr′ə lē), *adv.* in a doctrinary manner; doctrinally.

doc|tri|nar|y (dok′trə ner′ē), *adj.* = doctrinal.

doc|trine (dok′trən), *n.* **1** what is taught as the belief of a church, a nation, or a group of persons; belief; principle: *Christian doctrine. . . . the doctrine of the equality of all men* (Edmund Burke). **SYN:** dogma, tenet. **2** what is taught; teachings: *I wish to preach, not the doctrine of ignoble ease, but the doctrine of the strenuous life* (Theodore Roosevelt). **3** *Obsolete.* the act of teaching; lesson. [< Old French *doctrine,* learned borrowing from Latin *doctrīna* (literally) having to do with a teacher < *doctor;* see etym. under **doctor**]

docu-, *combining form.* a documentary: *a new kind of historical production—docuhistory* (Manchester Guardian).

doc|u|dra|ma (dok′yə drä′mə, -dram′ə), *n.* a television dramatization based on facts: *Popular novels play breezily with the lives of public and semipublic figures. Popular television has followed into the same area, calling the results "docudramas"* (New Yorker). [< *docu* (mentary) + *drama*]

doc|u|ment (*n.* dok′yə mənt; *v.* dok′yə ment), *n., v.* **—*n.*** **1** something written or printed that gives information and can be used as proof of some fact; any object used as evidence. Letters, maps, and pictures are documents. *A constitution is a precious document in a democracy, guaranteeing as it does the civil liberties of the people* (Andreas G. Papandreou). **2** old or historical fabric or design, of the kind found in museums, used or copied by fashion and interior designers: *He has fabrics created to suit him, frequently taking the pattern from a piece of antique cloth known as a "document"* (Maclean's). **3** *Obsolete.* evidence; proof. **4** *Obsolete.* a lesson; teaching.
—*v.t.* **1** to prove or support by means of documents or the like: *Can you document your theory with facts?* **2** to provide (a book, deed, or other document or account) with references as proof of the facts stated in it: *He documented all his quotations with copies of the original sources.* **3** to provide with official papers or documents. **4** *Obsolete.* to teach. [< Latin *documentum* example, proof < *docēre* show, teach]**—doc′u|ment′er,** *n.*

doc|u|men|ta|ble (dok′yů men′tə bəl), *adj.* that can be documented.

doc|u|men|tal (dok′yə men′təl), *adj.* = documentary.

doc|u|men|tal|ist (dok′yə men′tə list), *n.* a person, usually a librarian, who specializes in the gathering, classifying, and organization of documents, especially for research or use in archives.

doc|u|men|tar|i|an (dok′yə men tãr′ē ən), *n.* a writer, producer, or director of documentaries.

doc|u|men|ta|rist (dok′yə men′tə rist), *n.* = documentarian.

doc|u|men|ta|ry (dok′yə men′tər ē, -trē), *adj., n., pl.* **-ries.** **—*adj.*** **1** consisting of documents; in writing, print, or on film: *The man's own letters were documentary evidence of his guilt.* **2** presenting or recording factual information without fictionalizing but in an artistic fashion: *a documentary film about the history of Boston.* **—*n.*** a documentary book, motion picture, or radio or television program: *. . . something of the immediacy of a documentary* (New York Times).

doc|u|men|ta|tion (dok′yə men tā′shən), *n.* **1** the preparation and use of documentary evidence. **2** the documents used: *The noncritical air that pervades this book is somewhat compensated by the full documentation* (Edward D. Goldberger). **3** the collection, classification, processing, and transmission of information, especially through computers and other automatic equipment.

doc|u|tain|ment (dok′yə tān′mənt), *n. U.S.* television or other entertainment based on or including documentary material: *"I call it 'variety docutainment'," says the production's executive producer . . . "We'll be using documentary inserts combined on stage with drama, song, and dance"* (Washington Post). [< *docu-* + (enter)*tainment*]

DOD (no periods), Department of Defense.

do|dad (dü′dad), *n. Informal.* doodad.

dod|der[1] (dod′ər), *v.i.* to be unsteady; shake or tremble from frailty; totter: *The old man doddered from his chair to the door.* [origin uncertain. Compare etym. under **dither.**]**—dod′der|er,** *n.*

dod|der[2] (dod′ər), *n.* any one of a genus of slender, yellowish or reddish plants without chlorophyll, that live as parasites by twining their threadlike stems around flax, clover, thyme, and other plants and absorbing food from them by means of special roots called suckers or haustoria; goldthread; love vine. The dodder belongs to the morning-glory family. [Middle English *doder.* Compare German *Dotter* yolk.]

dod|dered (dod′ərd), *adj.* **1** that has lost its branches through age or decay: *a doddered oak.* **2** doddering; feeble; frail: *a doddered old man.*

dod|der|ing (dod′ər ing), *adj.* shaking; trembling; tottering.

dod|der|y (dod′ər ē), *adj.* = doddering.

dod|dle (dod′əl), *v.i.,* **-dled, -dling.** *Dialect.* dodder[1].

dod|dy (dod′ē), *n., pl.* **-dies.** **1** a cow or bull without horns. **2** Aberdeen Angus. [< dialectal *dod* to make hornless]

***do|dec|a|gon** (dō dek′ə gon), *n.* a plane figure having 12 angles and 12 sides. [< Greek *dōdekágōnon* < *dṓdeka* twelve + *gōníā* angle]

***dodecagon**
***dodecahedron**

dodecagon

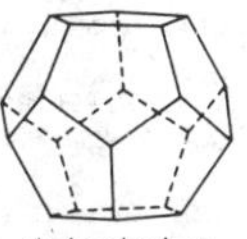
dodecahedron

do|de|cag|o|nal (dō′de kag′ə nəl), *adj.* having 12 angles and 12 sides.

do|dec|a|he|dral (dō′de kə hē′drəl), *adj.* like a dodecahedron; having 12 surfaces.

***do|dec|a|he|dron** (dō′de kə hē′drən), *n., pl.* **-drons, -dra** (-drə). a solid figure having 12 surfaces. [< Greek *dōdekáedron* twelve-sided < *dṓdeka* twelve + *hédrā* seat, base]

Pronunciation Key: **hat, āge, cãre, fär; let, ēqual, tėrm; it, īce; hot, ōpen, ôrder; oil, out; cup, pủt, rüle; child; long; thin; ᴛʜen; zh,** measure; **ə** represents **a** in about, **e** in taken, **i** in pencil, **o** in lemon, **u** in circus.

Do|dec|a|nese (dō'dek ə nēs', -nēz'), *adj.* of or having to do with the Dodecanese Islands (group of islands in the Aegean Sea near the coast of Turkey).

do|dec|a|phon|ic (dō'de kə fon'ik), *adj. Music.* twelve-tone; chromatic. **—do'dec|a|phon'i|cal|ly**, *adv.*

do|de|caph|o|nism (dō'de kaf'ə niz əm), *n.* = dodecaphony (def. 2).

do|de|caph|o|nist (dō'de kaf'ə nist), *n.* a musician who specializes in music written in a twelve-tone scale: *Like the majority of dodecaphonists, he presents music governed by strict logic and organization* (New York Times).

do|de|caph|o|ny (dō'de kaf'ə nē), *n.* **1** music employing a twelve-tone scale. **2** theory or use of the twelve-tone scale: *Twentieth-century chromaticism, [was] simplified about 1926 by Schönberg into a rule of thumb known as serial dodecaphony (or the twelve-tone row technique)* (Atlantic). [< Greek *dōdeka* twelve + *phōnē* sound]

do|dec|a|style (dō dek'ə stīl), *adj., n. Architecture.* **—*adj.*** having 12 columns in front, as a temple or portico. **—*n.*** a dodecastyle structure. [< Greek *dōdeka* twelve + *stylos* pillar]

do|dec|a|syl|lab|ic (dō'de kə sə lab'ik), *adj.* having 12 syllables.

do|dec|a|syl|la|ble (dō'de kə sil'ə bəl), *n.* a verse or a word of 12 syllables. [< Greek *dōdeka* twelve + English *syllable*]

do|de|cath|e|on (dō'de kath'ē on), *n.* = shooting star (def. 2). [< New Latin *Dodecatheon* the genus name < Latin *dōdecatheon* a kind of herb]

dod|gast|ed (dod gas'tid), *adj. Slang.* cursed; confounded.

dodge (doj), *v.,* **dodged, dodg|ing,** *n.* **—*v.i.*** **1** to move or jump quickly to one side: *As I looked around, the squirrel dodged behind a bush. The boy dodged just in time to avoid the speeding truck.* **2** to move quickly in order to get away from a person, a blow, or something thrown: *When he saw the other's raised fist, he dodged.* **3** to use evasive methods; use trickery; be deceitful. SYN: prevaricate. **4** *Photography.* to lighten a part of a print by shading it during enlarging. **—*v.t.*** **1** to move quickly in order to get away from (a person, a blow, or something thrown): *He dodged the snowball that came toward him. The pioneer dodged the Indian's arrow.* **2** to avoid by cleverness; get away from by some trick: *He dodged our questions by changing the subject.* SYN: elude. **3** *Photography.* to lighten (a part of a print) by shading while enlarging it.
—*n.* **1** a sudden movement to one side: *With a quick dodge into the brush the deer was hidden from the hunters.* **2** a trick to cheat: *a clever dodge. Some American film people have been accused of taking up Swiss residence as a tax dodge* (Esquire). SYN: contrivance. **3** *U.S. Slang.* a line of business: *The pictures sold so well that now Sears is in the art dodge big* (Time).
on the dodge, *Slang.* hiding from the police: *The bank robbers were on the dodge for a month, going from town to town, until they were finally caught.*
[origin uncertain]

dodge ball, a game in which several players form a ring and throw a large, inflated ball at one or more players inside the ring who try to catch or dodge the ball.

dodg|em (doj'əm), *n.,* or **dodgem car,** any one of various small cars ridden for entertainment in rinks at amusement parks or fairs: *It was as meaningless as watching a crowd of dodgem cars bumping and whirling at a fair* (Josephine Tey).

dodg|er (doj'ər), *n.* **1** a person who dodges. **2** a shifty or dishonest person: *the Artful Dodger* (Dickens). **3** *U.S.* a small handbill: *A number of printed dodgers were distributed in different parts of the city* (Philadelphia Times). **4** *U.S.* a kind of corn bread; corn dodger.

dodg|er|y (doj'ər ē), *n., pl.* **-er|ies.** the use of dodges; trickery: *What dodgery are you up to next?* (Dickens).

dodg|i|ly (doj'ə lē), *adv.* evasively; trickily.

dodg|y (doj'ē), *adj.,* **dodg|i|er, dodg|i|est.** full of or given to dodges; tricky; evasive: *In the intervals of dodging the Russian spaceships, our hero will signal down information for his earthbound colleagues to make dodgy deductions from* (Punch).

***do|do** (dō'dō), *n., pl.* **-dos** or **-does. 1** a large, clumsy bird not able to fly. Dodos lived on the island of Mauritius in the Indian Ocean and became extinct in the 1600's. **2** *Figurative.* **a** anyone or anything out-of-date: *The 1961 Constitution, though not officially revoked, is a political dodo* (Manchester Guardian Weekly). **b** a dull or stupid person: *an old dodo.*
dead as a (or **the**) **dodo,** out-of-date; outmoded; extinct: *I think this idea is as dead as a dodo* (U Thant). *Hand-done arithmetic, apart from keeping of household accounts, is as dead as the dodo* (Maclean's).
[< Portuguese *doudo* foolish, silly]

***dodo**
definition 1

dodo ball, a weighted bowling ball: *Balls that have been craftily hollowed out or packed with lead can be made to roll in tricky curves—"dodo balls," they are called* (New Yorker).

Do|do|nae|an or **Do|do|ne|an** (dō'də nē'ən), *adj.* of or having to do with Dodona, an ancient town of Epirus, famous for a sanctuary and oracle of Zeus located there in a grove of oaks.

doe (dō), *n., pl.* **does** or (*collectively*) **doe.** a female deer, goat, antelope, rabbit, or hare, or the female of most other animals whose male is called a *buck.* [Old English *dā*]

Doe (dō), *n.* See **John Doe, Jane Doe.**

DOE (no periods), **1** Department of Energy (formed in the United States in 1977): *DOE ... was built around three former agencies—the Federal Energy Administration, the Federal Power Commission, and the Energy Research and Development Administration* (Madelyn Krzak). **2** Department of the Environment (formed in Great Britain in 1971): *The DOE—as it has come to be called—swallowed ... three other independent and quite powerful ministries: Transport, Public Building and Works, and Housing* (London Times).

doe-eyed (dō'īd'), *adj.* having eyes that look as innocent and naive as those of a doe: *a doe-eyed beauty.*

doek (dük), *n.* a kerchief, usually of white cloth, worn round the head by native South African women. [< Afrikaans *doek* < Dutch]

do|er (dü'ər), *n.* a person who does something, especially with energy and drive: *He is a dreamer, but his brother is a doer.*

does (duz), *v.* the third person singular, present indicative of **do**[1]: *He does all the work.*

doe|skin (dō'skin'), *n.* **1** the skin of a doe. **2** leather made from it. **3** a very soft, supple leather with a fine suede finish made from the inner split of lamb or calfskin. **4** a smooth, soft woolen cloth, used for clothing.

does|n't (duz'ənt), does not.

do|est (dü'ist), *v. Archaic.* second person singular of **do**[1]. "Thou doest" means "you do."

do|eth (dü'ith), *v. Archaic.* does.

doff (dof, dôf), *v.t.* **1** to take off; remove: *He doffed his hat as the flag passed by.* **2** *Figurative.* to get rid of; throw aside. [contraction of *do off.* Compare etym. under **don**[2], **dup.**]

doff|er (dof'ər), *n.* **1** a person that doffs something. **2** a stationary machine used to remove cotton from the spindles of a mechanical picker.

dog** (dôg, dog), *n., v.,* **dogged, dog|ging,** *adv.* **—*n. **1** a four-legged, flesh-eating mammal used as a pet, for hunting, and for guarding property. Dogs are related to wolves, foxes, and jackals. They are bred in a great number of varieties. *My dog guards the house. His dog hunts rats.* **2** any animal of the same family as the dog, including wolves, foxes, and jackals. **3** a male of the same family as the dog, such as the fox or wolf. **4** any one of various animals somewhat like or suggesting a dog, such as the prairie dog or ferret. **5** *Informal.* a man; fellow: *He is a gay dog.* SYN: chap, blade. **6** *Figurative.* a low, contemptible man: *Die, like the dog you are!* **7** *Informal.* outward show. **8** a device similar to a dog's teeth, to hold or grip something. **9** = andiron. **10** a fogdog, sundog, or similar meteorological phenomenon. **11** *U.S. Slang, Figurative.* an unattractive, inferior, or unsuccessful person or thing: *That new singer is a dog. The used-car lots are full of dogs.* **12** *Slang.* = hot dog.
—*v.t.* **1** to hunt or follow like a dog: *The police dogged the suspected thief until they caught him. Spies dogged their footsteps.* SYN: track, pursue. **2** *Figurative.* to worry as if by a dog; beset; afflict: *Injuries dogged the baseball team all season.* **3** to drive or chase with a dog or dogs. **4** to fasten or secure by means of a mechanical dog: *When the log reached the carriage it was dogged ... by the simple movement of a lever* (G. W. Hotchkiss).
—*v.i.* to pursue or follow relentlessly.
—*adv.* thoroughly; extremely; utterly: *He had on a dog-worn coat.*
dog eat dog, competition characterized by ruthless practices: *If a man is hungry enough, he'll take what he can get and undercut the next fellow by a nickel an hour just to get the job. It's dog eat dog* (Time).
dog in the manger, *Informal.* a person who prevents others from using or enjoying something of no value to himself (in allusion to the fable of the dog that stationed himself in a manger and would not let the ox or horse eat the hay): *Why, what a dog in the manger you must be—you can't marry them both* (Frederick Marryat).
dog it, *Informal.* to avoid work; shirk responsibility: *Sometimes a boxer dogs it notoriously until the final minute* (New Yorker).
dogs, *Slang.* the feet: *My dogs are killing me!*
every dog has his day, everyone gets some attention or luck sometime in his life: *Young blood must have its course, lad, And every dog his day* (Charles Kingsley).
go to the dogs, to be ruined: *Rugby and the School-house are going to the dogs* (Thomas Hughes).
let sleeping dogs lie, to avoid arousing a source of possible trouble; refrain from disturbing the way things are: *It is arguable that the essence of conservatism is to let sleeping dogs lie* (Manchester Guardian Weekly).
put on (the) dog, *Informal.* to put on an outward show, as of wealth or refinement: *The Italians, by the way, are great dressers, and the more dog ... you can put on the better* (Manchester Guardian Weekly). *He won't let on he knows me when he's puttin' on dog* (A. H. Rice).
teach an old dog new tricks, to get an older person to accept new ideas or ways of doing things: *They used to say that you can't teach an old dog new tricks, but Grandma likes her new washing machine much better than her old washboard.*
throw to the dogs, to throw away as worthless: *He threw diplomacy to the dogs* (W. Irving).
[Old English *docga*]

Dog (dôg, dog), *n. Astronomy.* either of two constellations, Canis Major (Great Dog) or Canis Mi-

***dog**
definitions 1, 2

nor (Little Dog), near Orion.
do|ga|na (dō gä′nä), *n. Italian.* a custom house.
dog ape, a baboon or similar monkey.
do|gate (dō′gīt), *n.* the position or authority of a doge. [< *dog*(e) + *ate*³]
dog|bane (dôg′bān′, dog′-), *n.* any one of a genus of plants, many of them poisonous, with clusters of small, white or pink, bell-shaped flowers, including the Indian hemp. Its bitter root was used in medicines as a substitute for ipecac.
***dogbane family**, a group of dicotyledonous, mainly tropical herbs, shrubs, and trees, having a milky juice. The family includes many poisonous plants as well as others, such as the periwinkle and oleander, that are cultivated for ornament.

***dogbane family**
oleander periwinkle

dog|ber|ry (dôg′ber′ē, dog′-; -bər-), *n., pl.* **-ries.** **1** the berry or fruit of the European dogwood. **2** the plant. **3** any one of various other shrubs or trees, or their fruit, such as the chokeberry, the mountain ash, or one species of wild gooseberry of the United States, and the guelder-rose, the bearberry, and the dog rose of Europe.
Dog|ber|ry (dôg′ber′ē, dog′-; -bər-), *n., pl.* **-ries.** **1** a foolish, talkative constable in Shakespeare's "Much Ado About Nothing." **2** an ignorant, pompous official.
dog biscuit, **1** a hard, dry biscuit for dogs, made from ground food. **2** *U.S. Slang.* hardtack.
dog|cart (dôg′kärt′, dog′-), *n.* **1** a small cart pulled by dogs. **2** a small, open, horse-drawn carriage with two seats that are back to back.
dog|catch|er (dôg′kach′ər, dog′-), *n.* a person whose work is to catch and detain stray or unlicensed dogs.
dog-cheap (dôg′chēp′, dog′-), *adv., adj. Archaic.* at a very low price.
dog collar, **1** a collar for a dog. **2** a loose chain or cord worn around the neck to hold military identification tags. **3** a band or necklace of beads or jewels fitting closely around the neck. **4** *Slang.* the collar of a clergyman: *He's not a bit like a vicar. He doesn't even wear his dog collar except on Sundays* (New Yorker).
dog-day cicada (dôg′dā′, dog′-), any of various American cicadas heard especially during the hot days of late summer.
dog days, **1** a period of very hot and uncomfortable weather during July and August: *Come the crab-grass and the dog days, we'll have faint excuse to flee the trowel for the hammock* (Wall Street Journal). **2** *Figurative.* an evil time. [translation of Latin *diēs canīculārēs* days of the Dog Star; because this is the period when the rising of the Dog Star (Sirius) coincides with the rising of the sun]
dog|dom (dôg′dəm, dog′-), *n.* the world of dogs or of those interested in breeding or showing dogs: *the bluest blue ribbon in U.S. dogdom* (Time).
doge (dōj), *n.* the chief magistrate of Venice or Genoa when they were republics. [< dialectal Italian *doge* < Latin *dux* leader. See etym. of doublets **duce, duke.**]
dog-ear (dôg′ir′, dog′-), *n., v.* **—*n.*** a folded-down corner of a page in a book: *I made a dog-ear to mark the page where I stopped reading.*
—*v.t.* to fold down the corner of (a page or pages of a book).
dog-eared (dôg′ird′, dog′-), *adj.* having pages with corners folded down.
dog-eat-dog (dôg′ēt dôg′; dog′-, -dog′), *adj.* characterized by ruthless practices; fierce; cutthroat: *dog-eat-dog competition.*
doge|dom (dōj′dəm), *n.* **1** the authority or rule of a doge. **2** doges as a group.
dog-end (dôg′end′, dog′-), *n. British Slang.* a cigarette butt: *The familiar litter of used cups and dog-ends was much in evidence* (London Times).
doge|ship (dōj′ship), *n.* the rank, position, or authority of a doge.
dog|face (dôg′fās, dog′-), *n. U.S. Slang.* a common soldier; infantryman.
dog-faced (dôg′fāst′, dog′-), *adj.* having a face like that of a dog: *a dog-faced baboon.*
dog|fall (dôg′fôl′, dog′-), *n.* **1** a fall in which two wrestlers strike the ground at the same time. **2** a contest with no victor; draw: *A dogfall thus it ended—a dogfall it deserved to be* (Birmingham News). **3** an inadequate throw of a steer: *In a "dogfall," the steer collapses with its legs tucked under its body, then has to be raised and thrown again* (Time).
dog fennel, **1** = mayweed. **2** = heath aster. Also, **dog's fennel.**
dog|fight (dôg′fīt′, dog′-), *n., v.* **-fought, -fight|ing.** **—*n.*** **1** a combat between individual fighter planes at close quarters: *The long dogfights of the past are over . . . as far as the struggle between jet and jet is concerned* (Bulletin of Atomic Scientists). **2** a brawl; melee.
—*v.i.* to engage in a dogfight: *Chennault argued that the individual dogfighting of World War I was a throwback to the tactics of King Arthur* (Newsweek).
dog|fish (dôg′fish′, dog′-), *n., pl.* **-fish|es** or (*collectively*) **-fish.** **1** Also, **dogfish shark.** any one of several kinds of small shark, such as the smooth dogfish of the Atlantic and the spiny or piked dogfish of Atlantic and Pacific coasts. **2** any one of certain other fishes, such as the mudfish, the blackfish of Alaska and Siberia, and the wrasse.
dog fox, a male fox.
dog|ged (dôg′id, dog′-), *adj.* not giving up; stubborn; obstinate; persistent: *In spite of his weakness a dogged determination helped him to win the race.* SYN: headstrong, pertinacious. [< *dog* + *-ed*²] **—dog′ged|ly**, *adv.* **—dog′ged|ness**, *n.*
***dog|ger¹** (dôg′ər, dog′-), *n.* a boat with a broad bow and two masts, used by fishermen in the North Sea. [Middle English *doggere;* origin uncertain]

***dogger¹**

dog|ger² (dôg′ər, dog′-), *n.* **1** a person who dogs. **2** (in lumbering) a person who attaches dogs or hooks to a log when it is to be drawn by means of a cable. **3** *Australian.* a person who traps dingoes. [< *dog* + *-er*¹]
dog|ger|el (dôg′ər əl, dog′-), *n., adj.* **—*n.*** very poor poetry; poetry that is not artistic in form or meaning: *What the child wrote was doggerel; but what she felt and did was often a lyric* (Harper's).
—*adj.* **1** of or like doggerel; not artistic; crude; poor: *doggerel verses. A doggerel ballad . . . in which their wrongs were expressed with uncouth vigor* (John Motley). **2** (of verse) comic in style and irregular in form. Also, **doggrel.** [Middle English *doggerel,* adjective; origin uncertain]
dog|ger|el|ist (dôg′ər ə list, dog′-), *n.* a writer of doggerel: *English born doggerelist Robert W. Service . . . successfully mined a heap of gold with his pen* (Time).
dog|ger|el|ize (dôg′ər ə līz, dog′-), *v.i., v.t.,* **-ized, -iz|ing.** to write or turn into doggerel.
dog|ger|y (dôg′ər ē, dog′-), *n., pl.* **-ger|ies.** **1** mean or mischievous action or conduct. **2** dogs. **3** worthless people; rabble; riffraff. **4** *U.S. Slang.* a cheap saloon; bar.
dog|gie (dôg′ē, dog′-), *n.* **1** a little dog. **2** a pet name for a dog. Also, **doggy.**
doggie bag, = doggy bag.
dog|gish (dôg′ish, dog′-), *adj.* **1** of or like a dog; canine. **2** mean; surly; snarling; cynical. **3** *Informal.* stylish. **—dog′gish|ly**, *adv.* **—dog′gish|ness**, *n.*
dog|go (dôg′ō, dog′-), *adj., adv. Slang.* hidden; in hiding: *to lie doggo.*
dog|gone (dôg′gôn′, dog′gon′), *adj.,* **-gon|er, -gon|est,** *adv., v.,* **-goned, -gon|ing.** *U.S. Slang.*
—*adj.* damned; darned.
—*adv.* very: *The test was doggone hard.*
—*v.t.* to damn; darn: *Doggone it, man! Make haste then!* (Mayne Reid).
dog|goned (dôg′gônd′, dog′gond′), *adj., adv. U.S. Slang.* doggone: *Television might be a lot more exciting if the audience and the networks weren't so doggoned predictable* (TV Guide).
dog grass, = couch grass.
dog|grel (dôg′rəl, dog′-), *n., adj.* = doggerel.
dog|gy (dôg′ē, dog′-), *adj., adj.,* **-gi|er, -gi|est,** *n., pl.* **-gies.** **—*adj.*** **1** like a dog. **2** very fond of dogs: *the doggy set.* **3** *Informal.* outwardly showy or stylish.
—*n.* = doggie.
doggy bag, *U.S.* a bag given to a customer of a restaurant to carry home leftover food supposedly to feed a dog: [*His*] *wife couldn't finish her turkey sandwich. The elderly waitress put it in a doggy bag for her* (New Yorker).
dog-head|ed (dôg′hed′id, dog′-), *adj.* having a head like that of a dog; cynocephalous.
dog|hole (dôg′hōl′, dog′-), *n.* **1** a hole or a kennel for a dog. **2** a burrow of a prairie dog. **3** a place fit only for dogs; dirty place to live. **4** *U.S. Slang.* a small coal mine.
dog|house (dôg′hous′, dog′-), *n.* **1** a small house or shelter for a dog; kennel. **2** a place where the batch is fed into a furnace in glassmaking.
in the doghouse, *Slang.* out of favor: *He is in the doghouse with his mother for stealing cookies. Being in the doghouse, he had already been condemned to some menial task like checking the inventory of bales of carbon paper* (New Yorker).
do|gie (dō′gē), *n. Western U.S. and Canada.* **1** a calf without a mother, especially on the range or in a herd of cattle. **2** an undersized calf; runt. Also, **dogy.** [American English; origin uncertain]
dog Latin, **1** incorrect Latin. **2** an imitation of Latin; English with Latin endings.
dog|leg (dôg′leg′, dog′-), *adj., n., v.,* **-legged, -leg|ging.** **—*adj.*** bent like a dog's hind leg; having sharp angles; zigzagging: *a dogleg fence.*
—*n.* anything shaped like a dog's hind leg: **a** a fairway on a golf course of this shape: *Many of the long holes on the courses . . . are characterized by doglegs* (New York Times). **b** a route, passage, or course of this shape: *And they don't draw the streets quite straight; they give each a little dogleg* (Harper's).
—*v.i.* to take a dogleg turn; angle off: *He then proceeded to misplay the thirteenth, a 475-yard par 5 that doglegs sharply to the left* (New Yorker). **—*v.t.*** to turn aside from; avoid: *That particular office tends to be . . . doglegged by the City patronage* (Manchester Guardian Weekly).
dog|leg|ged (dôg′leg′id, -legd′; dog′-), *adj.* = dogleg.
dog|like (dôg′līk′, dog′-), *adj., adv.* in the manner of or like a dog: *His doglike faithfulness was touching* (adj.). *The workers curled up, doglike, under the shade* (adv.).
dog|ma (dôg′mə, dog′-), *n., pl.* **-mas, -ma|ta** (-mə tə). **1** a belief taught or held as true, especially by authority of a church; doctrine: *Gist of the charges against them: refusal to accept Biblical authority on essentials of Lutheran dogma, notably the virgin birth and Christ's physical resurrection and ascension* (Time). **2** any system of established principles and tenets. **3** *Figurative.* an opinion asserted in a positive manner as if it were of the highest authority. [< Latin *dogma* < Greek *dógma, -atos* opinion < *dokeîn* think]
dog|man (dôg′mən, dog′-), *n., pl.* **-men.** **1** a person who breeds or shows dogs; an authority on dogs: [*He*] *was my uncle's dogman, as well as butler and groom* (New Yorker). **2** *Australian.* a person who directs a crane driver during building operations.
dog|mat|ic (dôg mat′ik, dog-), *adj.* **1** of or having to do with dogma; doctrinal. **2** *Figurative.* positive and emphatic in asserting opinions; overbearing: *The audience disliked the speaker's dogmatic manner in stating his opinions as if they were facts. He is no longer interrogative but dogmatic* (Benjamin Jowett). **3** *Figurative.* asserted in a positive and emphatic manner: *He has no evidence to prove his dogmatic statement that the textbook was wrong. . . . dogmatic jargon learnt by heart* (John Gay). **—dog|mat′i|cal|ly**, *adv.*
dog|mat|i|cal (dôg mat′ə kəl, dog-), *adj.* = dogmatic.
dog|mat|i|cal|ness (dôg mat′ə kəl nis, dog-), *n.* the quality of being dogmatic; positiveness.
dog|ma|ti|cian (dôg′mə tish′ən, dog′-), *n.* **1** a student of dogmatics. **2** = dogmatist.
dog|mat|ics (dôg mat′iks, dog-), *n.* dogmatic or doctrinal theology.
dog|ma|tise (dôg′mə tīz, dog′-), *v.i., v.t.,* **-tised, -tis|ing.** *Especially British.* dogmatize.
dog|ma|tism (dôg′mə tiz əm, dog′-), *n.* positive and emphatic assertion of opinion. *Dogmatism is likely to arouse opposition. Where there is most doubt there is often the most dogmatism* (William H. Prescott).
dog|ma|tist (dôg′mə tist, dog′-), *n.* **1** a person who asserts opinions as if they were authoritative. **2** a person who states dogmas.
dog|ma|ti|za|tion (dôg′mə tə zā′shən, dog′-), *n.* the act of dogmatizing.
dog|ma|tize (dôg′mə tīz, dog′-), *v.,* **-tized, -tiz|ing.** **—*v.i.*** to assert opinions in a positive or authoritative manner; speak or write in a dogmatic way: *It is difficult, without intimate knowledge, to dogmatize too freely about the climate of opinion* (Wall Street Journal).
—*v.t.* to assert or deliver as a dogma.
dog|ma|tiz|er (dôg′mə tī′zər, dog′-), *n.* a person who dogmatizes; dogmatist.

Pronunciation Key: hat, āge, cãre, fär; let, ēqual, tėrm; it, īce; hot, ōpen, ôrder; oil, out; cup, pu̇t, rüle; child; long; thin; ᴛʜen; zh, measure; ə represents a in about, e in taken, i in pencil, o in lemon, u in circus.

dog|nap (dôg′nap, dog′-), *v.t., v.i.,* **-napped, -nap|ping** or **-naped, -nap|ing.** to steal (a dog or dogs) to collect ransom or to sell them. —**dog′-nap|per, dog′nap|er,** *n.*

Do|gon (dō′gon), *n., pl.* **-gons** or **-gon.** a member of a Sudanic-speaking people of Mali in western Africa. They live in rocky cliffs and are farmers.

do-good (dü′gůd′), *v., adj. Informal.* —*v.i.* to be or act like a do-gooder.
—*adj.* of or characteristic of do-gooders or do-goodery: . . . *the cultural vagaries of do-good endeavours that swing from Homes for Old Ladies to Junior League* (New Yorker).

do-good|er (dü′gůd′ər), *n. Informal.* a person who is too eager to correct or set things right: *an emotional, unthinking, compulsive and naïve do-gooder* (Ellis Magazine).

do-good|er|y (dü′gůd′ər ē), *n. Informal.* the beliefs or actions of a do-gooder or do-gooders: *Slogans . . . well-worn by international do-goodery* (New Scientist).

do-good|ism (dü′gůd′iz əm), *n. Informal.* do-goodery: *the phraseology of do-goodism* (Wall Street Journal).

dog paddle, a form of swimming similar to the paddling of a dog, in which quick, short strokes are used without bringing the arms out of the water: *After learning the float and kick, the beginner is ready for the dog paddle.*

dog-pad|dle (dôg′pad′əl, dog′-), *v.i.,* **-pad|dled, -pad|dling.** to swim with quick, short strokes without bringing the arms out of the water, as a dog does.

dog-poor (dôg′půr′, dog′-), *adj.* very poor.

dog pound, an enclosed place in which to keep stray dogs.

dog race, a race in which greyhounds or whip pets run around a track in pursuit of a mechanical rabbit, which runs ahead of them on a rail.

dog rose, a wild rose of Europe with pink or white flowers and hooked spines; wild brier: . . . *blossom like dog roses in the hedges* (Sunday Times).

dogs (dôgz, dogz), *n.pl. Slang.* See under **dog.**

dog's age, *U.S. Informal.* a long time: *We haven't seen you in a dog's age.*

dog salmon, = chum² (def. 2).

dog's-bane (dôgz′bān′, dogz′-), *n.* = dogbane.

dogs|bod|y (dôgz′bod′ē, dogz′-), *n.,* **-bod|ies.** *British Slang.* a hack; drudge: *She spent thirty-eight years as a kind of unpaid dogsbody, and then collected all her father's notes into this book after his death* (Rosemary Edisford). [originally *dog's body,* British nautical slang for a sea biscuit soaked in sugar water]

dog's chance, *Informal.* the slightest chance.

dog's-ear (dôgz′ir′, dogz′-), *n., v.t.* = dog-ear.

dog's-eared (dôgz′ird′, dogz′-), *adj.* = dog-eared.

dog's fennel, = dog fennel.

dog-sick (dôg′sik′, dog′-), *adj.* as sick as a dog; very sick.

dog|skin (dôg′skin′, dog′-), *n.* **1** the skin of a dog. **2** leather made from this skin or some substitute, such as sheepskin.

***dog sled** or **sledge,** a sled that is pulled by dogs: *Rev. Thomas Umaok . . . changes to a clerical collar and Eskimo furs to make calls by dog sled* (Newsweek).

***dog sled**

dog sledding, riding on a dog sled.

dog|sleep (dôg′slēp′, dog′-), *n.* a light, restless sleep.

dog's letter, the letter *r,* especially when pronounced with a trill.

dog's life, a miserable life.

dog's mercury, a perennial weedlike plant of the spurge family, with a slender rootstock, an unbranched stem, and small clusters of green leaves, common in England and western Europe.

dog's-tail (dôgz′tāl′, dogz′-), *n.,* or **dog's-tail grass, 1** any one of a group of grasses in which the flowers in each panicle all point one way, like the hairs of a dog's tail. **2** the yard grass.

Dog Star, 1 = Sirius. **2** = Procyon.

dog's-tongue (dôgz′tung′, dogz′-), *n.* = hound's-tongue.

dog's-tooth violet (dôgz′tüth′, dogz′-), = dogtooth violet.

dog tag, 1 *Informal.* a metal identification disk worn on a neck chain by a member of the armed forces. **2** a tag on the collar of a dog, such as a license tag or identification tag.

dog team, a team of dogs, especially for pulling a dog sled: *As he was sledging over the glacier, his dog team stopped dead and he moved forward on skis to investigate* (Walter Sullivan).

dog tent, *Slang.* a shelter tent.

dog-tired (dôg′tīrd′, dog′-), *adj.* very tired; worn-out; dog-weary.

dog|tooth (dôg′tüth′, dog′-), *n., pl.* **-teeth. 1** = canine tooth. **2** *Architecture.* a toothlike ornament, usually a pyramidal projection made up of radiating parts, or a series of these, as on a medieval molding.

dogtooth spar, a variety of calcite occurring in sharp crystals that resemble canine teeth.

dogtooth violet, a small plant of the lily family that has one yellow, white, purple, or pink flower and, in some species, mottled leaves; adder's-tongue; trout lily. See picture under **adder's-tongue.** Also, **dog's-tooth violet** .

dog|track (dôg′trak′, dog′-), *n.* a race track for dogs.

dog|trot (dôg′trot′, dog′-), *n., v.,* **-trot|ted, -trot-ting.** —*n.* a gentle, easy trot.
—*v.i.* to go or move at a dogtrot: *Reed dogtrotted and walked until the last 9 miles, which he ran* (Newsweek).

dog|vane (dôg′vān′, dog′-), *n.* a small vane of bunting, cork, or feathers on the weather gunwale of a ship to show the direction of the wind.

dog violet, a wild violet of northern Europe and the British Isles, bearing four to six blue flowers: *The dog violet is so called by the English because it lacks fragrance* (Theodor Just).

dog|watch (dôg′woch′, dog′-; -wôch′), *n. Nautical.* a two-hour period of work on a ship. There are two dogwatches a day, one from 4 to 6 P.M. and the other from 6 to 8 P.M.

dog-wea|ry (dôg′wir′ē, dog′-), *adj.* = dog-tired.

dog whelk, a small, marine mud snail.

dog whistle, a whistle for calling a dog, especially such a whistle with a high-frequency sound inaudible to people.

dog|wood (dôg′wůd′, dog′-), *n.* **1** any one of various trees or shrubs, especially: **a** a common North American tree bearing springtime blossoms that consist of tiny flowers surrounded by large white or pinkish leaves; cornel. It bears red berries in the fall. **b** a common European shrub with dark-red branches, greenish-white flowers, and dark-purple berries; cornel. **2** the hard wood of any of these trees. **3** any shrub or tree of the same family as the dogwood.

dogwood family, a group of dicotyledonous herbs, shrubs, and trees, found chiefly in north temperate regions. The family includes the flowering dogwood, bunchberry, aucuba, and cornel.

do|gy (dō′gē), *n., pl.* **-gies.** = dogie.

doiled (doild), *adj. Scottish.* stupid; foolish; crazed. [perhaps variant of Middle English *dold* made dull, variant past participle of *dullen* to dull. Compare etym. under **dolt.**]

doilt (doilt), *adj. Scottish.* = doiled.

doi|ly (doi′lē), *n., pl.* **-lies. 1** a small piece of linen, lace, paper, or plastic, used under plates, other dishes, or vases on a table. **2** a small, ornamental napkin used at dessert. **3** *U.S. Slang.* a toupee. [earlier *doiley-napkin* < *doiley* (originally) a woolen fabric, supposedly < a Mr. *Doiley,* a London dry-goods dealer]

do|ing (dü′ing), *n.* action; performance; execution: *Talking about the project was easier than the doing. To get him to give that large amount will take some doing.*
doings, a things done; actions; deeds: *The story is the story of Bart's doings and of the mark he leaves on those who love him* (Atlantic). **b** conduct; behavior. **c** *U.S. Dialect.* food or drink.

doit (doit), *n.* **1** a former Dutch copper coin worth about ¼ cent. **2** *Figurative.* a small sum; trifle; bit: *No one cares a doit what he thinks.* [< Dutch *duit*]

doit|ed (doi′tid, -tit), *adj. Scottish.* enfeebled, especially by age. [perhaps variant of *doted*]

do-it-your|self (dü′it yər self′), *adj.* designed for assembly or use by an amateur: *a do-it-yourself repair kit. Sometimes they buy do-it-yourself valentine boxes that contain all the materials needed to make valentines* (Elizabeth H. Sechrist).

do-it-your|self|er (dü′it yər sel′fər), *n. Informal.* a handy person; person who does himself work usually done by a handyman or professional.

do-it-your|self|er|y (dü′it yər sel′fər ē), *n.* the activities of a do-it-yourselfer.

do-it-your|self|ism (dü′it yər sel′fiz əm), *n.* the practice of being a do-it-yourselfer.

do|jo (dō′jō), *n., pl.* **-jos.** a place where judo, karate, and other Japanese arts of self-defense are taught. [< Japanese *dōjō*]

do|ku|san (dō′kə san), *n.* a formal private meeting between a Zen master and a disciple: *None of the following dialogues should be confused with what takes place in dokusan, the student's face-to-face encounter with the roshi in private* (Philip Kapleu). [< Japanese *dokusan*]

dol (dol), *n.* a unit of pain intensity, based on the application of heat from a lamp to the skin, and measured on a scale of 1-10, representing increasing degrees of intensity on a dolorimeter: *The pain in the second stage of childbirth registers ten and a half dols* (Science News Letter). [< Latin *dolor* pain]

dol., dollar or dollars.

do|lab|ri|form (dō lab′rə fôrm), *adj. Botany, Zoology.* shaped like an ax or a cleaver. [< Latin *dolābra* pickax + English *-form*]

Dolby (dôl′bē, dōl′-), *adj.* of or designating any of various electronic devices that reduce or eliminate noise from tape and other sound recordings: *Consumers . . . can record and replay their own material through the Dolby circuitry to keep tape hiss at bay* (New Scientist). [< *Dolby System,* a trademark]

Dol|by|ized (dôl′bē īzd, dōl′-), *adj.* recorded or provided with a Dolby device or equipment: *Dolbyized cassettes.*

dol|ce (dōl′chā), *adj., n.* —*adj.* **1** *Italian.* sweet. **2** *Music.* sweet and soft (a direction).
—*n.* a plate organ stop of soft tone.

dol|ce far nien|te (dōl′chā fär nyen′tā), *Italian.* **1** pleasant idleness: *the dolce far niente of the young scions of the new rich* (Harper's). **2** (literally) it is sweet doing nothing.

dol|ce vi|ta (dōl′chā vē′tä), *Italian.* **1** a way of life given over to pleasure and amusement; self-indulgent or dissolute living. **2** (literally) sweet life.

dol|drums (dol′drəmz, dōl′-), *n.pl.* **1** dullness; gloomy feeling; low spirits: *My brother has been in the doldrums since he failed to get on the swimming team.* **2** certain regions of the ocean near the equator where the wind is very light or constantly shifting. When a sailing ship gets in the doldrums, it makes hardly any headway. **3** the calm or windless weather characteristic of these regions.
[perhaps Middle English *dol* dull, on the analogy of English *tantrum*]

dole¹ (dōl), *n., v.,* **doled, dol|ing.** —*n.* **1** a portion of money or food given in charity: *a full measure of bread, wine and olives being his dole* (Cardinal Newman). SYN: alms. **2** a small portion. **3** relief money given by a government to unemployed workers. **4** a dealing out of money or food given in charity. **5** *Archaic.* lot; fate.
—*v.t.* **1** to deal out in portions to the poor; distribute in charity. **2** to give in small portions: *Mother doled out one piece of candy a day to each child.*
on (the) dole, in receipt of relief money from the government: *Of Perry County's 36,000 people, 14,000 exist on dole* (Time).
[Old English *dāl.* See related etym. at **deal¹.**]

dole² (dōl), *n. Archaic.* sorrow; grief: *She died. So that day there was dole in Astolat* (Tennyson). [< Old French *doel* < Late Latin *dolus* grief < Latin *dolēre* grieve]

dole|ful (dōl′fəl), *adj.* very sad or dreary; mournful; dismal: *a doleful expression. The hound gave a doleful howl.* SYN: sorrowful, woeful, plaintive. —**dole′ful|ly,** *adv.* —**dole′ful|ness,** *n.*

do|lent (dō′lənt), *adj. Archaic.* grieving; sorrowful; mournful.

do|len|te (dō len′tā, -tē), *adv., adj. Music.* plaintive; with sadness (used as a direction): *[a] wordless chorus wailing dolente* (Punch). [< Italian *dolente*]

dol|er|ite (dol′ə rīt), *n.* **1** a coarse-grained basalt. **2** *British.* diabase. **3** *U.S.* any dark igneous rock whose elements can be identified only with the microscope. [< French *dolérite* < Greek *dolerós* deceptive (< *dólos* trick) + French *-ite* -ite¹, because of the difficulty of identification)]

dol|er|it|ic (dol′ə rit′ik), *adj.* consisting of or like dolerite.

dole|some (dōl′səm), *adj. Archaic.* doleful.

dol|i|cho|ce|phal (dol′ə kō sē′fəl), *n.* a dolichocephalic person: . . . *the tall, fair, blue-eyed dolichocephals of north Europe* (Arthur C. Haddon).

dol|i|cho|ce|phal|ic (dol′ə kō sə fal′ik), *adj.* having a long, narrow head; having a breadth of skull less than four-fifths of the length from front to back. [< Greek *dolichós* long + English *cephalic*]

dol|i|cho|ceph|a|lism (dol′ə kō sef′ə liz əm), *n.* the quality or condition of being dolichocephalic.

dol|i|cho|ceph|a|lous (dol′ə kō sef′ə ləs), *adj.* = dolichocephalic.

dol|i|cho|ceph|a|ly (dol′ə kō sef′ə lē), *n.* = dolichocephalism.

dol|i|cho|mor|phic (dol′ə kō môr′fik) *adj.* having disproportionately long bodily members, as the head and neck.

dol|i|chos (dol′ə kos), *n.* any plant of a group of tropical vines having clusters of purple or white flowers and slightly curved, flat pods containing edible beans. [< New Latin *Dolichos* the genus name < Greek *dolichós* long (because of the size of the pods)]

do-lit|tle (dü′lit′əl), *n., adj. Informal.* —*n.* a per-

son who does or seeks to do as little as possible.
—*adj.* seeking to do or doing as little as possible: *a do-little legislature.*

doll (dol), *n., v.* —*n.* **1** a child's toy made to look like a baby, a child, or a grown person. **2** a pretty child, girl, or woman: *If the Russians or the Greeks lacked a word for her, one American did not. "There," a new admirer ... said last week, "goes a doll"* (Time). **3** a very likable person; a darling: *The distinguished actress, Sylvie, is a dear and a doll in the leading role* (Bosley Crowther). **4** a dandy; fop: *A sturdy lad ... is worth a hundred of these city dolls* (Emerson). **5** *U.S. Slang.* a stimulant, sedative, or tranquilizing drug in pill form; a sleeping pill, pep pill, or the like: *Patty is ... perpetually drunk on booze and zonked by "dolls"* (Time).
—*v.t., v.i. Slang.* to dress (up) in a stylish or showy way: *She was dolled up for the party.*
[< *Doll,* nickname for *Dorothy*] —**doll'-like'**, *adj.*

dol|lar (dol'ər), *n.* **1** a unit of money in the United States. One hundred cents make one dollar. $1.00 means one dollar. *Symbol:* $. *Abbr:* dol. **2** a similar unit of money equal to 100 cents, used in Australia, Canada, New Zealand, and various other countries, such as Bahamas, Belize, Ethiopia, Fiji, Guyana, Jamaica, Liberia, Malaysia, Trinidad and Tobago, and the British West Indies. **3** any of various units of money used mainly in trade, such as the Hong Kong dollar, the Taiwan dollar or yuan, the Levant dollar, and the Straits dollar. **4** a silver coin or piece of paper money worth one dollar. **5** a gold coin no longer used in the United States.
bet one's bottom dollar, *U.S. Slang.* **a** to bet the last dollar that one possesses: *He bet his bottom dollar at the races and now he is broke.* **b** to be completely sure: *I'll bet my bottom dollar the train will be late again.*
(it is) dollars to doughnuts, *U.S. Slang.* (it is) a sure thing; a certainty: *Dollars to doughnuts that Sullivan is right-handed!* (Time).
[earlier *daler* < Low German or Dutch *daler,* abstracted from German *Joachimsthaler* a silver coin from St. Joachim's valley in Bohemia. Compare etym. under **thaler**.]

dollar area, a group of countries in which foreign trade is transacted in currency freely convertible into dollars: *... the United Kingdom retains tariffs on imports from the dollar area* (Wall Street Journal).

dollar averaging, a system of buying securities in fixed amounts of money at regular intervals. By this system, more securities are bought when prices are low and fewer when prices are high, thus keeping the purchase price below average over a period of time.

dol|lar-a-year man (dol'ər əyir'), *U.S.* a person serving the federal government at the salary of one dollar a year.

dol|lar|bird (dol'ər bėrd'), *n.* a roller of Africa, India, and Australia that has a round, light-blue spot on its outspread wing.

dollar bloc, a group of countries that have adjusted their currencies and foreign exchange in accordance with the value of the U.S. dollar.

dollar crisis, the condition resulting when a country reduces its supply of dollars through failure to balance its trade with the United States.

dollar diplomacy, diplomacy associated with lending money to needy countries in order to advance the lending country's commercial interests there.

dol|lar|fish (dol'ər fish'), *n., pl.* **-fish|es** or (*collectively*) **-fish**. **1** a small, oval fish abundant along the eastern coast of the United States; butterfish. **2** either of several varieties of moonfish, especially a carangoid fish of the Atlantic with a compressed oblong body and silvery skin.

dollar gap, the shortage of dollars (for exchange) in a country suffering from a dollar crisis.

dollar imperialism, the extending of control and authority into foreign countries through the buying power of the dollar.

dol|lar|less (dol'ər lis), *adj.* having little or no money; worthless: *a dollarless adventurer seeking a rich heiress.*

dollar sale, *U.S.* a sale at which diverse articles of merchandise are sold for one dollar each.

∗**dollar sign** or **mark**, the symbol meaning dollar or dollars, placed regularly before a number. *Example:* $1 (one dollar); $5 (five dollars).

∗**dollar sign**

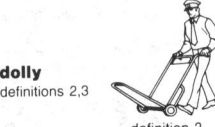

$ — $1 = one dollar; $2.10 = two dollars and ten cents

dollar spot, a fungous disease of lawns and golf greens, in which the grass develops brownish discolorations in areas about the size of a silver dollar.

dol|lar|wise (dol'ər wīz'), *adv.* with respect to dollars: *the highest sales dollarwise in the company's history.*

doll|house (dol'hous'), *n.* a toy house for children to use in playing with dolls; playhouse.

doll|ish (dol'ish), *adj.* somewhat like a doll; pretty but without much intelligence. —**doll'ish|ly**, *adv.* —**doll'ish|ness**, *n.*

dol|lop (dol'əp), *n., v. Informal.* —*n.* a portion or serving, large or small: *cake with a dollop of whipped cream.* SYN: quantity.
—*v.t.* to spread on; apply thickly or heavily: *to dollop butter on bread.*
[perhaps < Scandinavian (compare dialectal Norwegian *dolp* lump)]

∗**dol|ly** (dol'ē), *n., pl.* **dol|lies**, *v.,* **dol|lied**, **dol|ly|ing**. —*n.* **1** a child's name for a doll: *The little girl was crying, saying that a dog had taken her rag dolly.* **2** a small low frame on wheels, used to move heavy things: *The refrigerator was moved into the house on a dolly. He put the baggage on his dolly and wheeled it out to the taxi stand* (New Yorker). **3** a platform on wheels on which a motion-picture or television camera can be moved about. **4** *U.S.* a small locomotive run on narrow-gauge tracks, used in switching, construction jobs, etc. **5** *Mining.* a device for shaking and washing ore in a vessel. **6** *British Dialect.* a wooden pole for stirring or twisting clothes in washing. **7** a bar with a flat or cup-shaped piece set at an angle on one end, used to form or hold the head of a rivet. **8** a block placed on the top of a pile while it is being driven. **9** = dolly block. **10** *British Slang.* = dolly bird. **11** *Cricket.* = dolly catch.
—*v.t., v.i.* to move on a dolly: *The camera dollied in for the final scene.*
[< *doll* + *-y*^{2}]

∗**dolly**
definitions 2,3

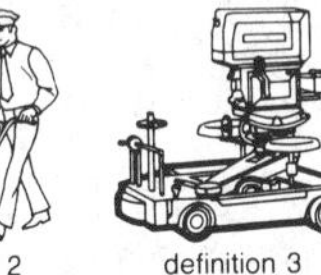

definition 2 — definition 3

dolly bag, *British Informal.* a Dorothy bag.

dolly bird, *British Slang.* an attractive or fashionable girl; a doll.

dolly block, a block placed behind sheet metal that is to be shaped with a hammer; dolly: *Select a dolly block with a face of the same general curvature as the panel* (Toboldt and Purvis).

dolly catch, *Cricket.* an easy catch.

dol|ly|man (dol'ē mən), *n., pl.* **-men**. a person who pushes or operates the dolly of a motion-picture or television camera: *It takes a fast dollyman on the camera to keep Douglas MacArthur in focus* (Time).

dol|ly|rock|er (dol'ē rok'ər), *n. British Slang.* **1** a young girl who is very up-to-date on the latest styles in clothes, music, and other items of interest to young people. **2** a style of clothing worn by such girls.

∗**Dolly Var|den** (vär'dən), **1** a dress printed with a large flower pattern, worn with the skirt gathered up in loops. **2** a large hat with one side bent downward and trimmed with flowers, formerly worn by women. **3** a trout of western North America with red spots on the sides, closely related to the brook trout. *The native char of the Pacific coastal waters is the Dolly Varden, a fish with a slender body and no wavy markings on the back* (Carl L. Hubbs). [< *Dolly Varden,* a character in Dickens's *Barnaby Rudge*]

∗**Dolly Varden**
definition 1

dol|ma (dōl'mə), *n.* a Turkish dish consisting of a vegetable stuffed with rice and meat, and boiled. [< Turkish *dolma*]

dol|ma|des (dōl mä'dēz), *n.pl.* = dolma. [< Greek *dolmádhes* < Turkish *dolma*]

∗**dol|man** (dol'mən, dōl'-), *n., pl.* **-mans**. **1** a woman's coat or cloak with capelike flaps instead of sleeves. **2** a long robe open in front, with narrow sleeves, worn by the Turks. **3** a short jacket in the uniform of the Hungarian hussars, worn loosely on the shoulders like a cape. [< French *dolman* < German *Dolman,* ultimately < Turkish *dolama* a coat with sleeves]

∗**dolman**
definition 2

∗**dolman sleeve**

dolman — dolman sleeve

∗**dolman sleeve**, a sleeve of a woman's dress or coat, close-fitting at the wrist and often to the elbow, full at the shoulder, and set deep into the garment's bodice.

dol|men (dol'mən), *n.* a prehistoric monument, generally regarded as a tomb, made by laying a large, flat stone across several upright stones. [< French *dolmen,* perhaps < Celtic (compare Breton *tol* table + *men* stone)]

dol|o|mite (dol'ə mīt), *n.* **1** a rock consisting mainly of calcium and magnesium carbonate. Much white marble is dolomite. *Dolomite is a granular ... limestone* (David Page). **2** the mineral, calcium and magnesium carbonate composing this rock. *Formula:* $CaCO_3 \cdot MgCO_3$ [< French *dolomite* < Déodat G. de *Dolomieu,* 1750-1801, a French geologist + *-ite* -ite^{1}]

dol|o|mit|ic (dol'ə mit'ik), *adj.* consisting of or containing dolomite: *dolomitic limestone.*

dol|o|mit|ize (dol'ə mə tīz), *v.t.,* **-ized**, **-iz|ing**. to convert into dolomite. —**dol'o|mit'i|za'tion**, *n.*

do|lor (dō'lər), *n.* sorrow; grief. [< Old French *dolour* < Latin *dolor* < *dolēre* suffer]

do|lor|e|site (də lôr'ə sīt), *n.* a black, anhydrous oxide of vanadium, associated with carbonaceous deposits in Colorado. *Formula:* $3V_2O_4 \cdot 4H_2O$ [< *Dolores,* a river in Colorado + *-ite*^{1}]

dol|o|rim|e|ter (dol'ə rim'ə tər), *n.* a device for measuring the intensity of pain in terms of dols. [< Latin *dolor* pain + English *-meter*]

dol|o|rol|o|gy (dol'ə rol'ə jē), *n.* the scientific study of pain: *Not until the specialty of dolorology began to emerge did the study of pain itself gain a new emphasis and respectability* (New York Times Magazine). [< Latin *dolor* pain + English *-logy*] —**dol'o|rol'o|gist**, *n.*

do|lo|ro|so (dō'lō rō'sō), *adj. Music.* soft and plaintive. [< Italian *doloroso*]

dol|or|ous (dol'ər əs, dō'lər-), *adj.* **1** full of or expressing sorrow; mournful: *a little dolorous cry.* SYN: sorrowful, doleful. **2** causing or giving rise to sorrow; grievous; painful. SYN: severe, acute. —**dol'or|ous|ly**, *adv.* —**dol'or|ous|ness**, *n.*

do|lour (dō'lər), *n. British.* dolor.

dol|phin (dol'fən), *n.* **1a** any one of a group of sea mammals related to the whale, but smaller. It has a snout like a beak and remarkable intelligence. Dolphins belong to the same order as whales and porpoises. **b** = porpoise. **2** either of two large, edible, saltwater fishes that are remarkable for their changes of color when taken from the water and for their ability to swim rapidly; dorado. **3** a post, especially several piles driven close together and capped or lashed together at the top, or a buoy used to moor a ship, raft of logs, etc. [< Old French *daulphin* < Latin *delphīnus* < Greek *delphīs, -înos.* See etym. of doublet **dauphin**.] —**dol'phin|like'**, *adj.*

Dol|phin (dol'fən), *n.* the northern constellation Delphinus.

dol|phin|ar|i|um (dol'fə nãr'ē əm), *n., pl.* **-i|ums**, **-i|a** (-ē ə). an aquarium for dolphins.

dol|phin|fish (dol'fən fish'), *n., pl.* **-fish|es** or (*collectively*) **-fish**. = dolphin (def. 2).

dolphin striker, a small spar under the bowsprit that helps support the jib boom; martingale.

dolt (dōlt), *n.* a dull, stupid person; blockhead; numskull: *Oh dolt, as ignorant as dirt* (Shakespeare). SYN: dunce. [apparently variant of Middle English *dold,* past participle of *dullen* to dull < Old English *dol* dull. Compare etym. under **doiled**.]

dolt|ish (dōl'tish), *adj.* like a dolt; dull and stupid: *a doltish clown.* SYN: foolish, thick-headed, senseless. —**dolt'ish|ly**, *adv.* —**dolt'ish|ness**, *n.*

dom (dōm), *n.* = doum palm.

Dom (dom; *Portuguese* dōN), *n.* **1** a title given to

Pronunciation Key: hat, āge, cãre, fär; let, ēqual, tėrm; it, īce; hot, ōpen, ôrder; oil, out; cup, pu̇t, rüle; child; long; thin; ᴛʜen; zh, measure; ə represents **a** in about, **e** in taken, **i** in pencil, **o** in lemon, **u** in circus.

Benedictine and Carthusian monks, and formerly to other Catholic dignitaries. **2** a title used in Portugal and Brazil before the Christian name by royalty, cardinals, bishops, and gentlemen on whom the sovereign conferred it. [< Portuguese *dom* < Latin *dominus* master, ruler. See etym. of doublets **Dan**[3], **don**[1].]

-dom, *suffix forming nouns.* **1** (*added to nouns*) the position, rank, or realm of a ___: *Earldom = the rank of an earl. Kingdom = the realm of a king.*
2 (*added to adjectives*) the condition or fact of being ___: *Freedom = the condition of being free.*
3 (*added to nouns*) all those who are ___: *Heathendom = all those who are heathen.*
[Old English *-dōm* state, rank, related to *dōm;* see etym. under **doom**]

dom., **1** domestic. **2** dominion.

DOM (no periods), dimethoxy-methylamphetamine (the chemical name of the hallucinogenic STP).

D.O.M., to God, the Best, the Greatest (Latin, *Deo Optimo Maximo*).

do|main (dō mān′), *n.* **1** the lands under the rule of one ruler or government: *Great Britain is a large island domain under the Crown of England.* **SYN**: realm, dominion. **2** land owned by one person; estate. **SYN**: manor. **3** *Law.* the absolute ownership of land. **4** *Figurative.* field of thought or action; sphere: *the domain of science, the domain of religion. Edison was a leader in the domain of invention.* **SYN**: province. **5** a region within a ferroelectric or ferromagnetic crystal, spontaneously polarized in a single direction. A crystal contains many domains polarized in a variety of directions, offsetting one another's energy. When domains are placed in a magnetic field, those favorably directed in respect to the field tend to grow at the expense of those unfavorably directed. **6** *Mathematics.* the set of all numbers which can be assigned to the algebraic variable *x* in an equation with two variables. Since the members of such a set may serve as replacements for the variable in a given relation, the set is sometimes called *replacement set.* [< French *domaine* < Old French *demaine,* earlier *demeine,* learned borrowing from Latin *dominium* < *dominus* lord, master < *domus* house. See etym. of doublet **demesne.**]

do|mal (dō′məl), *adj.* = domical: *domal mountains, resulting from the vertical uplift and doming of a circular or oval area* (White and Renner).

do|ma|ni|al (dō mā′nē əl), *adj.* having to do with domains or estates.

dome (dōm), *n., v.,* **domed, dom|ing.** —*n.* **1** a large, rounded roof or ceiling on a circular or many-sided base; cupola: *Nearly every state capitol has a dome.* **2** anything shaped like a dome; something high and rounded: *the dome of the sky, the rounded dome of a hill.* **3** *Archaic.* a house; mansion: *In Xanadu did Kubla Khan A stately pleasure-dome decree* (Samuel Taylor Coleridge). **4** *Crystallography.* a prism whose faces meet in a horizontal edge, like the roof of a house. **5** = dome car. **6** *Geology.* an anticlinal formation, circular or elliptical in structure, characteristic of oil and salt deposits, extrusions of volcanic lava, etc.: *Most of the world's sulfur today comes from deposits along the Gulf Coast of this country known as "domes"* (Wall Street Journal).
—*v.t.* **1** to cover with or as if with a dome. **2** to shape like a dome.
—*v.i.* to rise or swell like a dome.
[< Middle French *dôme* < Provençal *doma* < Late Latin *dōma* roof, house < Greek *dōma* house; (def. 3) < Latin *domus* house] —**dome′-like′**, *adj.*

dome car, a railroad car with a dome-shaped upper level that is enclosed with glass for sightseeing: *One thing is certain, the dome cars add much to sightseeing* (New York Times).

dome|lin|er (dōm′lī′nər), *n.* a railroad train having one or more dome cars.

dome mountain, a domical mountain, such as the Black Hills of South Dakota.

domes|day (dümz′dā′, dōmz′-), *n.* = doomsday.

Domesday Book, a record of a survey of the lands of England made by order of William the Conqueror in 1086, giving the ownership, value, assessment of taxes, and other facts, of all estates. Also, **Doomsday Book.** [Old English *dōmesdæg* (literally) day of judgment; *dōmes,* genitive of *dōm* law, judgment, doom (because it would be the book by which all men were judged)]

dome-shaped (dōm′shāpt′), *adj.* having the shape of a dome.

do|mes|tic (də mes′tik), *adj., n.* —*adj.* **1** of the home, household, or family affairs: *domestic problems, a domestic scene. Mother has many domestic duties.* **SYN**: household. **2** fond of home and family life: *The explorer was not a very domestic person.* **SYN**: domesticated. **3** not wild; tame; living with man or under the care of man. Cats, dogs, cows, horses, sheep, and pigs are domestic animals. *This herd of horses was domestic, but out on the plains they became wild.* **SYN**: domesticated. **4** of one's own country; not foreign: *Most newspapers publish both domestic and foreign news.* **SYN**: internal. **5** made in one's own country; native: *domestic woolens, domestic cheese.* **SYN**: home-grown, homemade, indigenous. **6** for home consumption: *domestic coal.*
—*n.* a servant in a household. A cook or a maid is a domestic.
domestics, a goods or products made in one's own country: *Competition is increasing between domestics and foreign imports.* **b** *U.S.* cloth articles used in the home, such as towels and bed linen: *That store sells fine handmade domestics and dress accessories.*
[< Middle French *domestique,* learned borrowing from Latin *domesticus* < *domus* house]

do|mes|ti|ca|ble (də mes′tə kə bəl), *adj.* that can be domesticated: *The potentially domesticable plants and animals were surely available to the bands of food-gatherers who lived in southwestern Asia and similar habitats in various parts of the globe* (Scientific American).

do|mes|ti|cal|ly (də mes′tə klē), *adv.* in a domestic manner; so far as concerns domestic affairs.

domestic art, = home economics.

do|mes|ti|cate (*v.* də mes′tə kāt; *n.* də mes′tə kit, -kāt), *v.,* **-cat|ed, -cat|ing,** *n.* —*v.t.* **1** to change (animals, savages, or plants) from a wild to a tame or cultivated state; tame. **2** *Figurative.* to make fond of home and family life: *A frontier widow ... makes an unsuccessful attempt to domesticate a hero* (Newsweek). **3** *Figurative.* to cause to be or feel at home; naturalize. —*v.i.* to live much at home; become domestic: *In spite of her efforts, Jessica had not quite domesticated* (Jetta Carleton).
—*n.* a plant or animal that has been domesticated: *In the ... phase ... dating from 7000 to 5000 B.C., there are traces of domesticated squash ... and of possible domesticates of peppers, gourds, and small beans* (Science). —**do-mes′ti|ca′tion**, *n.* —**do mes′ti|ca′tor**, *n.*

domestic fowl, any of various birds, especially chickens, which have been domesticated.

do|mes|tic|i|ty (dō′mes tis′ə tē), *n., pl.* **-ties.** **1** home and family life. **2** fondness for home and family life.
domesticities, domestic affairs.

do|mes|ti|cize (də mes′tə sīz), *v.t.,* **-cized, -ciz-ing.** to make domestic; domesticate.

domestic relations court, = court of domestic relations: *Domestic relations courts ... exist in some cities to deal with disputes within a family* (Sidonie M. Gruenberg).

do|mes|tics (də mes′tics), *n.pl.* See under **domestic.**

domestic science, = home economics.

domestic system, = cottage industry.

dom|ett (dom′it), *n.* outing flannel; a light cotton flannel. [origin uncertain]

dom|i|cal (dō′mə kəl, dom′ə-), *adj.* **1** having a dome or domes. **2** like a dome; domelike; domal: *The boundaries of the domical uplift constituting the Colorado Plateau—actually a series of plateaus—have never been rigidly defined* (Bulletin of Atomic Scientists). [< *dom*(e) + *-ic* + *-al*[1]] —**dom′i|cal|ly**, *adv.*

dom|i|cil (dom′ə səl), *n.* = domicile.

dom|i|cile (dom′ə səl, -sīl), *n., v.,* **-ciled, -cil|ing.** —*n.* **1** a dwelling place; house; home; residence. **SYN**: habitation, abode. **2** a place of permanent residence. One may have several residences, but only one legal domicile at a time.
—*v.t.* to settle in a domicile: *Domiciled at 26 Bay Street, ... the society maintained children in sixty-eight homes* (New York Times).
—*v.i.* to dwell; reside: *They domiciled in Italy part of the year.*
[< Middle French *domicile,* learned borrowing from Latin *domicilium* < *domus* house, probably + *colere* dwell]

dom|i|cil|i|ar (dom′ə sil′ē ər), *n. Obsolete.* a canon of a minor order, having no voice in a chapter.

dom|i|cil|i|ar|y (dom′ə sil′ē er′ē), *adj., n., pl.* **-ar-ies.** —*adj.* of or having to do with a domicile.
—*n. U.S.* a home for veterans who do not require hospital care, but are unable to earn a living and have no means of support. *All Veterans Administration hospitals and domiciliaries abolished racial segregation* (Dorothy B. Porter).

dom|i|cil|i|ate (dom′ə sil′ē āt), *v.,* **-at|ed, -at|ing.** —*v.t.* to settle in a domicile.
—*v.i.* to dwell; reside.

dom|i|cil|i|a|tion (dom′ə sil′ē ā′shən), *n.* **1** the act of settling in a domicile. **2** the state of being settled in a domicile.

dom|i|nance (dom′ə nəns), *n.* **1** a controlling influence; supreme authority; rule; control. **SYN**: ascendancy. **2** *Biology.* the quality or condition of being or having a dominant character.

dom|i|nan|cy (dom′ə nən sē), *n., pl.* **-cies.** = dominance.

***dom|i|nant** (dom′ə nənt), *adj., n.* —*adj.* **1** most powerful or influential; controlling; ruling; governing: *The British were formerly dominant in India. The President was the dominant figure at the cabinet meeting. Football is the dominant sport in the fall.* **2** rising high above its surroundings; occupying a commanding position: *A dominant cliff rose at the bend of the river.* **3** *Music.* based on or having to do with the fifth note of a scale. **4** *Biology.* of or designating a dominant character: *The character or trait of roundness is dominant over wrinkledness* (Beals and Hoijer).
—*n.* **1** *Music.* the fifth note of a scale. G is the dominant in the key of C. **2** *Biology.* **a** a dominant character or gene. **b** an individual possessing or transmitting a dominant character.
3 *Botany.* the most extensive and characteristic species in a plant community, determining the type and abundance of other species in the community.
[< Old French *dominant,* learned borrowing from Latin *dominā̆ns, -antis,* present participle of *dominārī.* See etym. under **dominate.**] —**dom′i|nant-ly**, *adv.*
—*Syn. adj.* **1 Dominant, predominant, paramount** mean uppermost. **Dominant** means ruling, and therefore having the most influence, power, or authority: *Efficiency is the dominant idea in many businesses.* **Predominant** means before others in influence, power, or authority, and therefore principal or superior: *Love of liberty is predominant in struggles for independence.* **Paramount** means first in importance, authority, or rank, and therefore supreme: *It is of paramount importance that we finish the work on time.*

***dominant**
definition 3

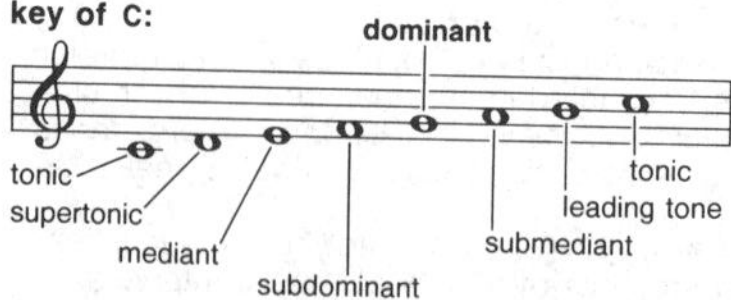

dominant character, the one of any pair of contrasting characters that prevails in an animal or plant when both are present in the germ plasm. *Example:* If a child inherits one gene for brown eyes from its mother, and one gene for blue eyes from its father, it will have brown eyes, as brown eyes are dominant and blue eyes are recessive.

dominant tenement or **estate**, *Law.* land in favor of which a servitude exists over another tenement.

dominant wavelength, the wavelength in a spectrum which matches, or most nearly corresponds to, a sample of color under analysis, used as an approximate determinant of the hue of the sample.

dom|i|nate (dom′ə nāt), *v.,* **-nat|ed, -nat|ing.** —*v.t.* **1** to control or rule by strength or power; prevail over: *The boy dominated his smaller brother. The chairman's strong will dominated the committee, which did what he wanted without arguing.* [*These writers*] *were attempting ... to dominate the confusion of history by imposing on it the harmony of art* (Edmund Wilson). **SYN**: master, sway. **2** to rise high above; hold a commanding position over: *The mountain dominates the city and its harbor.* **SYN**: command.
—*v.i.* **1** to exercise control; predominate; prevail: *Dandelions will dominate over grass if they are not kept out.* **2** to hold a commanding position: *How explain the charm with which he* [*Shakespeare*] *dominates* (James Russell Lowell).
[< Latin *dominārī* (with English *-ate*[1]) < *dominus* lord, master]

dom|i|na|tion (dom′ə nā′shən), *n.* the act of dominating; the exercise of ruling power; control; rule: *The tyrant's domination was challenged by the rebels.*
dominations, the fourth of the nine orders of angels in medieval theology; dominions: *Thrones, dominations, princedoms, virtues, powers; Hear my decree* (Milton).

dom|i|na|tive (dom′ə nā′tiv), *adj.* dominating; controlling.

dom|i|na|tor (dom′ə nā′tər), *n.* a ruler; ruling power.

dom|i|ne (dom′ə nē, dō′mə-), *n. Obsolete.* lord; master. [< Latin *dominē,* vocative of *dominus* master]

do|mi|ne di|ri|ge nos (dom′ə nē dir′ə jē nōs), *Latin.* Lord, guide us (the motto of London).

dom|i|neer (dom′ə nir′), *v.i.* to rule (over) at one's own will; assert one's authority or opinions in an arrogant way; tyrannize: *The oldest child in a family often domineers over his brothers and sisters.* **—*v.t.*** to tyrannize over; dominate: [< Dutch *domineren* < Old French *dominer,* learned borrowing from Latin *dominārī* to rule; see etym. under **dominate**] **—dom′i|neer′er,** *n.*

dom|i|neer|ing (dom′ə nir′ing), *adj.* inclined to dominate; arrogant; overbearing: *A bully has a domineering attitude.* **SYN:** tyrannical, despotic, authoritarian. **—dom′i|neer′ing|ly,** *adv.* **—dom′i-neer′ing|ness,** *n.*

do|min|i|cal (də min′ə kəl), *adj.* **1** of or having to do with Jesus Christ as Lord. **2** of or having to do with Sunday (the Lord's Day). [< Late Latin *dominicālis* < *dominica* (*diēs*) the Lord's day, Sunday, noun use of Latin *dominicus* of a lord; imperial < *dominus* lord, master]

dominical letter, one of the seven letters A to G used in calendars to mark Sundays throughout a particular year, and serving primarily in determining the date of Easter.

Do|min|i|can (də min′ə kən), *adj., n.* **—*adj.*** **1** of or having to do with Saint Dominic or the religious orders founded by him. **2** of or having to do with the Dominican Republic. **3** of or having to do with the island country of Dominica (a former British colony in the West Indies)
—*n.* **1** a friar or nun belonging to the Dominican order. **2** a person born or living in the Dominican Republic.

Dom|i|nick (dom′ə nik), *n.* = Dominique.

dom|i|nie (dom′ə nē; *for 3 also* dō′mə nē), *n.* **1** *Especially Scottish.* a schoolmaster: *Now, Dr. Wirt in early and middle life had been a dominie of note* (Atlantic). **2** *Informal.* a clergyman. **3** a pastor of the Dutch Reformed Church in the United States. [variant of *domine*]

do|min|ion (də min′yən), *n.* **1** the power or right of governing and controlling; rule; control: *The ancient Romans had dominion over a large part of the world.* (*Figurative.*) *Which shall have ultimate dominion, Dream, or dust?* (Don Marquis). **SYN:** sovereignty, influence, sway. **2** the lands under the control of one ruler or government. **3** a self-governing territory.
dominions, dominations: *Powers and Dominions, Deities of Heav'n* (Milton).
[< Middle French *dominion,* learned borrowing from Medieval Latin *dominio, -onis,* alteration of Latin *dominium* ownership. See etym. of doublet **dominium.**]

Do|min|ion (də min′yən), *n., adj.* **—*n.*** a name formerly used for a self-governing country within the British Commonwealth. Canada, Australia, and New Zealand were formerly Dominions. Canada is now a *Commonwealth nation,* a constitutional monarchy in form of government.
—*adj.* Also, **dominion.** *Canada.* relating to the country as a whole; national in scope.
[< *dominion*]

Dominion Day, the former name of *Canada Day,* honoring the establishment of the Dominion of Canada in 1867.

Dom|i|nique (dom′ə nēk′), *n.* any one of an American breed of chickens having yellow shanks, a rose comb, and grayish, barred plumage. Also, **Dominick.** [American English < French *Dominique* Dominica, an island in the West Indies, where they were bred]

do|min|i|um (də min′ē əm), *n. Law.* absolute or complete ownership; right of possession or use. [< Latin *dominium.* See etym. of doublet **dominion.**]

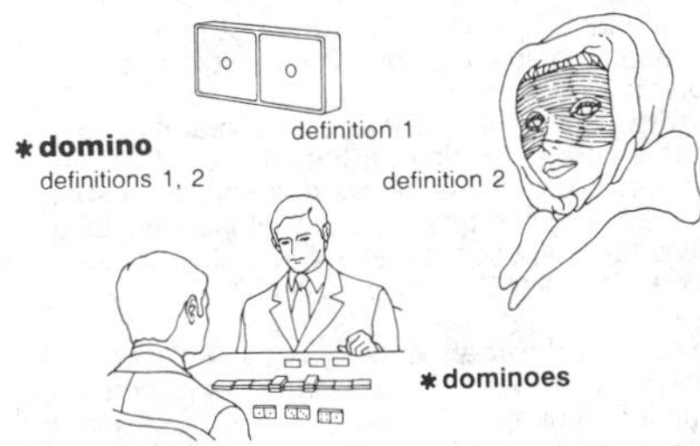

***dom|i|no** (dom′ə nō), *n., pl.* **-noes** or **-nos. 1** one of a set of small, oblong pieces of bone, wood, or ivory marked with spots and used in playing dominoes. **2** a loose cloak with a hood and a small mask covering the upper part of the face. It was formerly worn as a disguise, especially at masquerades. **3** the small mask. **4** a person wearing a domino. **5** any one of a group of things so positioned that if one of them should fall, all the others would fall in turn, like a row of dominoes. [< French *domino* < Medieval Latin, an ecclesiastical hooded garment, apparently < Latin *dominō,* dative of *dominus* master]

dom|i|noed (dom′ə nōd), *adj.* wearing a domino.

***dom|i|noes** (dom′ə nōz), *n.pl.* a game played with 28 flat, oblong pieces of bone, wood, or ivory that are either blank or marked with dots. Players try to match pieces having blanks or the same number of dots, usually one to six, in some sets one to nine. [< *domino* a half mask (because of the imagined resemblance of the pieces used to the mask)]
▶**Dominoes,** though plural in form, is usually singular in use: *Dominoes is played with 28 flat, oblong pieces of bone or wood.*

domino theory, 1 the political theory that if one country falls to an expansionist power, the next or neighboring countries will inevitably fall in turn: *The domino theory guided U.S. foreign policy . . . If Laos went, so, like a row of dominoes, would South Viet Nam, Thailand and the rest of Southeast Asia* (Time). **2** any similar theory or assumption: *If there is "action" on the book in the shops, the owners will order more. Which means people calling up and ordering or coming in and buying it. It's the domino theory: One book bought is another book sold* (Goodman Ace).

Do|mi|nus il|lu|mi|na|ti|o me|a (dom′ə nəs i lü′mi nā′shē ō mē′ə; dô′mi nu̇s i lü′mi nä′tē ō me′ä), *Latin.* the Lord is my light (the motto of Oxford University).

Do|mi|nus vo|bis|cum (dom′ə nəs vō bis′kəm; dô′mi nu̇s wō bis′ku̇m), *Latin.* the Lord be with you.

don[1] (don), *n.* **1** a Spanish gentleman; Spaniard. **2** a distinguished person: *the great dons of wit* (John Dryden). **3** *Informal.* a head, fellow, or tutor of a college at Oxford or Cambridge Universities in England. **4** *U.S. Slang.* the head of a secret criminal society or syndicate: *a Mafia don.* [< Spanish *don* < Latin *dominus* lord, master. See etym. of doublets **Dan[3], Dom.**]

don[2] (don), *v.t.,* **donned, don|ning.** to put on (clothing or anything worn): *The knight donned his armor. The soldiers donned their gas masks. She dons the airs of a princess.* [contraction of *do on.* Compare etym. under **doff, dup.**]

Don (don), *n.* a Spanish title meaning Mr. or Sir: *Don Felipe.*

do|na (dō′nə), *n.* a Portuguese or Brazilian lady. [< Portuguese *dona* < Latin *domina* mistress. See etym. of doublets **dame, doña, donna, duenna.**]

Do|na (dō′nə), *n.* a Portuguese title meaning Lady or Madam: *Dona Inés.*

do|ña (dō′nyä), *n.* a Spanish lady. [< Spanish *doña* < Latin *domina* mistress. See etym. of doublets **dame, dona, donna, duenna.**]

Do|ña (dō′nyä), *n.* a Spanish title meaning Lady or Madam: *Doña Maria.*

Do|nar (dō′när), *n. German Mythology.* the ancient god of thunder, associated with the Norse god Thor.

do|nate (dō′nāt), *v.t.,* **-nat|ed, -nat|ing.** to give; contribute, especially to a fund or institution: *He donated ten dollars to the Red Cross. Paul Mellon has donated to Yale University about $35-million worth of British paintings . . . and rare books* (New York Times). **SYN:** bestow, grant. [American English; back formation < *donation*]

do|na|tion (dō nā′shən), *n.* **1** a gift; contribution: *He makes the same donation to the church each year.* **2** the act of giving or contributing: *By his donation the church was able to build a new Sunday school.* **SYN:** bestowal, grant. [< Old French *donation,* learned borrowing from Latin *dōnātiō, -ōnis* < *dōnāre* to give < *dōnum* gift]

Don|a|tism (don′ə tiz əm), *n.* the doctrine or principles of the Donatists.

Don|a|tist (don′ə tist), *n.* a member of a schismatic and heretical sect of Christians that arose in North Africa in the year 311, out of a dispute about the election of Caecilian as bishop of Carthage. [< Medieval Latin *Donatista* < Bishop *Donatus* of Casae Nigrae, who led the opposition to Caecilian]

don|a|tive (don′ə tiv, dō′nə-), *n., adj.* **—*n.*** a gift or donation: *The Roman Emperor's custom was at certain solemn times to bestow on his soldiers a donative* (Richard Hooker).
—*adj.* characterized by being donated; of the nature of a donation: *a donative fund.*

do|na|tor (dō′nā tər, dō nā′-), *n.* a person who donates; donor.

don|cel|la (don sel′ə), *n.* any one of certain fishes, especially of the labroid group, found in waters around the West Indies and Florida. [< Spanish *doncella* (literally) damsel]

done (dun), *adj., v.* **—*adj.*** **1** finished; completed; through: *He is done with his homework.* **SYN:** performed, accomplished, settled. **2** ended; over: *The play is done. Then, the great drama done the pace accelerates and the scope opens out again* (Edmund Wilson). **3** Also, **done up.** *Informal.* worn out; exhausted: *She was completely done up after cleaning house.* **4** cooked enough: *The roast is almost done. I want my steak well done.* **5a** conforming to custom or convention; good manners or good taste: *Eating peas with a knife is not done.* **SYN:** proper, fitting. **b** *Slang.* fashionable: *It is "done" to go as a tourist to Russia* (Manchester Guardian Weekly). **c** past participle of **do[1]**: *Have you done your chores?*
done for, a ruined; damaged: *That fire means his business is done for.* **b** at an end; finished: *Hesitation meant his chance was done for.*
done in, *Informal.* exhausted: *Barker arrived absolutely done in,* [*and*] *he had to lie down* (New Yorker).
done with, *Informal.* finished; completed: *I'd like to get this done with.*

done deal, *U.S. Informal.* an accomplished fact; fait accompli: *The 50 percent raise [for members of Congress] is a done deal (barring miracles)* (Sarasota Herald-Tribune).

do|nee (dō nē′), *n.* **1** a person who has been given something as a gift. **2** *Law.* a person who has been given a power.

done|ness (dun′nis), *n.* the state of being cooked enough: *The cook tested the doneness of the roast.*

dong (dông, dong), *n.* the unit of money of Vietnam, equal to 100 sau. The unit of former South Vietnam was the piaster. [< Annamese *dong*]

don|ga (dong′gə), *n.* (in South Africa) a gully; ravine: *It was difficult and dangerous riding, for the ground was seamed with deep dongas* (B. Mitford). [< a Zulu word]

Don|go|la kid or **leather** (dong′gə lə), leather from goatskin or sheepskin tanned to resemble kid. [< *Dongola,* a province in the Sudan]

Dongola process, a process of tanning goatskin or sheepskin to resemble kid.

don|jon (dun′jən, don′-), *n.* a large, strongly fortified tower of a medieval castle; keep. [early form of *dungeon*]

Don Juan (don wän, hwän, jü′ən), **1** a nobleman in Spanish legends, who had many love affairs. He is the hero of many literary works, appearing in plays by Molière and George Bernard Shaw, an opera by Mozart, and a poem by Lord Byron. **2** a man leading an immoral life; libertine. **SYN:** rake, roué.
▶**Don Juan** is usually pronounced (don wän *or* don hwän), in imitation of the Spanish. When it applies to the title or hero of Byron's poem, it is traditionally pronounced (don jü′ən).

Don Juan|esque (don wä nesk′, hwä-, jü′ə-nesk′), of, having to do with, or resembling a Don Juan: *Byron's manner was tinged with a vein of Don Juanesque recklessness* (William Graham).

Don Juan|ism (don wä′niz əm, hwä′-, jü′ə-), an abnormal psychological condition in males, marked by a desire for sexual conquest, caused by insecurity or anxiety. *The same unconscious homosexual attraction is also usually found at the root of prostitution, nymphomania, and Don Juanism* (Saturday Review).

don|key (dong′kē, dung′-; dông′-), *n., pl.* **-keys. 1** an animal somewhat like a horse but smaller, with longer ears, a shorter mane, and a tuft of hair on the end of its tail; the domesticated ass or burro. See picture under **horse. 2** a stubborn person. **3** a silly or stupid person. **4** = donkey engine. [origin uncertain]

don|key|back (dong′kē bak′, dung′-; dông′-), *n., adv.* **—*n.*** the back of a donkey: *to cross a mountain on donkeyback.*
—*adv.* on donkeyback.

donkey boiler, a small, usually upright boiler for use on a ship when the main boilers are inactive.

donkey engine, a small steam engine, especially one which operates an anchor, heating system, or derrick.

donkey jacket, *British.* a thick jacket worn by workmen for protection against water, mud, or dirt.

don|key|man (dong′kē mən′, dung′-; dông′-), *n., pl.* **-men.** a man who operates a donkey engine.

donkey's years or **ears,** *Slang.* a very long time: *I've known old Nipper practically all my life. He's been here for donkey's years, you know* (Maurice Proctor).

donkey vote, (in Australia) a preferential vote in which the voter's order of choice is the same as the order in which the names are listed, probably indicating a lack of preference.

donkey work, *Informal.* monotonous and laborious work; drudgery: *Euclidean geometry has*

Pronunciation Key: hat, āge, cãre, fär; let, ēqual, tėrm; it, īce; hot, ōpen, ôrder; oil, out; cup, pu̇t, rüle; child; long; thin; ᴛʜen; zh, measure; ə represents **a** in about, **e** in taken, **i** in pencil, **o** in lemon, **u** in circus.

been cut to the bone partly because it is a dead-end subject and partly because of the donkey work involved in its study (New Scientist).

don|na (don′ə; *Italian* dôn′nä), *n.* an Italian lady. [< Italian *donna* < Latin *domina* lady, mistress. See etym. of doublets **dame**, **dona**, **doña**, **duenna**.]

Don|na (don′ə; *Italian* dôn′nä), *n.* an Italian title meaning Lady or Madam.

don|nard (don′ərd), *adj. Scottish.* donnered.

don|née (dô nā′), *n. French.* **1** a gift. **2** a datum. **3** the fundamental idea of a literary or dramatic work; basic premise: *The weakness of this enormously clever novel is very evident to the reader; it is, simply, that the donnée is vastly over-extended, as de Montherlant virtually confesses in his Preface* (Punch).

don|nered (don′ərd), *adj. Scottish.* stunned; stupefied; stupid. [past participle of Scottish *donner* or *dunner* stun with a blow or noise, perhaps (frequentative) < Middle English *donen* to din]

Don|ner|wet|ter (don′ər vet′ər), *interj. German.* **1** an exclamation of anger or annoyance. **2** (literally) thunder weather.

don|nish (don′ish), *adj.* like or characteristic of a university don; pedantic: *The question "Are Women Worth Educating?" trembles on every donnish lip* (Punch). **—don′nish|ly**, *adv.* **—don′nish|ness**, *n.*

Don|ny|brook or **don|ny|brook** (don′ē brük), *n.* a great commotion; riotous gathering; disorder; fighting: *Knocko ... returned to South Boston, where he ran a saloon that was the scene of many a celebrated Donnybrook* (Time). [< *Donnybrook*, a town in the Irish Republic, site of a fair suppressed in 1855 for its wild brawls]

do|nor (dō′nər), *n.* **1** a person who gives; giver; contributor. A person who gives his blood for transfusion is a blood donor; a person from whose body an organ or other part is removed for transplantation is also called a donor. **2** *Law.* a person who gives an estate or confers a power. **3** the atom that supplies the two electrons to form a semipolar bond with an acceptor. [< Anglo-French *donour*, Old French *doneur* < Latin *dōnātor* < *dōnāre;* see etym. under **donation**]

donor card, a card designating which organs may be used in transplant surgery upon the bearer's death: *If a person carries a donor card, ... that should overrule any objections by the coroner unless there is a reason, such as damage to the body, why the organ should not be used* (London Times).

do-noth|ing (dü′nuth′ing), *n., adj.* **—*n.*** **1** a person who lacks initiative or is reluctant to upset existing conditions by taking action. **2** a person who does nothing; idler. **—*adj.*** doing nothing; idle; reluctant to act: *Strangely enough, the strongman who had once bent 40 million Brazilians to his will turned out to be a do-nothing President* (Time). **—do′-noth′ing|ness**, *n.*

do-noth|ing|ism (dü′nuth′ing iz əm), *n.* do-nothing policy or practice.

Don Qui|xo|te (don ki hō′tē; kwik′sət, -sōt), **1** a story by Miguel de Cervantes that satirizes chivalric romances. It was published in two parts, in 1605 and 1615. **2** its hero, who is chivalrous and idealistic, but also foolish and impractical.

don|sie or **don|sy** (don′sē), *adj. Dialect.* **1** *U.S.* poor; in low spirits. **2** *Scottish.* unlucky; unfortunate. [origin uncertain]

don't (dōnt), do not. **—*n.*** a command not to do (someting specified): *a list of don'ts of etiquette.* ▶**Don't** is universally used in conversation and often in writing when *do not* would seem too emphatic or when rhythm seems more comfortable with the shorter form. In substandard usage *don't* = *doesn't: He don't look as well as he used to.*

don't-know (dōnt′nō′), *n.* a person or thing that is undecided, especially an undecided voter or vote: *Both Labour and Conservatives report up to 33⅓ per cent "don't-knows," even in some of the marginal seats, which looks as though a large protest vote could be garnered by the Liberals who are contesting every seat* (Sunday Times). [< one of the responses (*Yes/No/Don't know*) listed in the forms which are circulated among voters in the public opinion polls]

don|to|pe|dal|o|gy (don′tō pe dal′ə jē), *n.* a natural propensity or talent for putting one's foot in one's mouth (for saying something indiscreet, foolish, or embarrassing). [coined by Prince Philip, born 1921, the Duke of Edinburgh < *donto-* (< Greek *odoús, odóntos* tooth) + *pedal* (< Latin *pedālis* of the foot) + *-logy*]

do|num (də num′), *n.* a unit of land measurement in Turkey, Yugoslavia, and certain countries of the Near East. [< Turkish *dönüm*]

do|nut (dō′nut′), *n.* = doughnut.

don|zel (don′zəl), *n. Obsolete.* a young gentleman not yet knighted; squire; page. [< Italian *donzello* < Old Provençal *donsel* < Vulgar Latin *dominicellus* (diminutive) < Latin *dominus* lord]

doo|da or **doo|dah** (dü′dä), *n. Slang.* a state of excitement.

all of a dooda, *Slang.* in a state of excitement: *As her birthday approached, the little girl was all of a dooda.*

[< *dooda*(h), refrain of the plantation song "Camptown Races"]

doo|dad (dü′dad), *n. Informal.* **1** a fancy, trifling ornament: *In dozens of displays, such items as Danish bronze fruit bowls, Israel olive wood and Venetian glass liquor decanters have pushed Yankee whatnots and doodads from the choice eye-catching window space* (Wall Street Journal). **2** any contrivance or gadget: ... *electric can openers and other doodads* (New York Times). Also, **dodad**. [American English; origin uncertain]

doo|dle[1] (dü′dəl), *v.*, **-dled**, **-dling**, *n.* **—*v.i., v.t.*** to make drawings or marks absent-mindedly while talking or thinking: *He doodled his own face a lot* (New Yorker).

—*n.* a drawing or mark made absent-mindedly. [American English, apparently < dialectal English *doodle*, or *dudle* to trifle, fritter away time] **—doo′dler**, *n.*

doo|dle[2] (dü′dəl), *n. U.S.* = doodlebug[1].

doo|dle|bug[1] (dü′dəl bug′), *n. U.S.* the larva of the ant lion. The doodlebug digs a pit to catch other insects. [American English, perhaps < earlier English *doodle* simpleton + *bug*]

doo|dle|bug[2] (dü′dəl bug′), *n., v.*, **-bugged**, **-bugging**. *U.S. Informal.* **—*n.*** **1** any one of various devices with which it is claimed mineral and oil deposits can be located. **2** = buzz bomb.

—*v.i.* to use doodlebugs in prospecting. [apparently special use of *doodlebug*[1]] **—doo′dle|bug′ger**, *n.*

doo|hick|ey (dü′hik′ē), *n. Informal.* a thing; gadget; dingus: *The ingenious foreman thought up a doohickey to straighten out the 2,500 wire trash baskets crushed each year* (New York Times). [a coined word]

dool (dül), *n. Archaic.* dole; sorrow.

doo|lie[1] (dü′lē), *n.* = dooly.

doo|lie[2] (dü′lē), *n. Slang.* a plebe at the United States Air Force Academy: *As at the older service academies, first-year men—here called "doolies"—are subjected to special discipline* (New York Times). [origin unknown]

doo|ly (dü′lē), *n., pl.* **-lies**. a simple litter used in India. [< Hindi *ḍōlī* (diminutive) < *ḍōlā* swinging cradle < Sanskrit *dōlā* < *dul* to swing]

doom (düm), *n., v.* **—*n.*** **1** fate: *Doom stalked his footsteps.* SYN: destiny, lot, portion. See syn. under **fate**. **2** an unhappy or terrible fate; ruin or death: *The soldiers marched to their doom in battle. As the ship sank they faced their doom.* SYN: destruction. **3** a judgment; sentence: *The judge pronounced the guilty man's doom.* SYN: condemnation. **4** the end of the world; God's final judgment of mankind (in Christian belief). **5** *Obsolete.* a law; statute.

—*v.t.* **1** to condemn to some fate: *Poor health doomed him to an inactive life.* **2** to destine to an unhappy or terrible fate: *Keats was doomed to an early death.* **3** to condemn (to punishment) by a judgment or sentence: *The prisoner was doomed to death.* **4** to make a bad or unwelcome outcome certain: *The weather doomed our hopes of a picnic.* **5** *Obsolete.* to pronounce as a judgment or sentence; decree: *The Emperor in his rage will doom her death* (Shakespeare).

[Old English *dōm* law, judgment]

doom|er (dü′mər), *n. Archaic.* a doomster.

doom|ful (düm′fəl), *adj.* full of doom; fateful: *the doomful times of the 1930's.*

doom|like (düm′līk′), *adj.* like doom; fateful.

doom palm, = doum palm.

dooms (dümz), *adv. Scottish.* very; exceedingly. [origin uncertain]

doom|say|er (düm′sā′ər), *n.* a person who prophesies doom: *When Charles de Gaulle came to power in France ... doomsayers were quick to compose their epitaphs on European unity* (Time).

doom|say|ing (düm′sā′ing), *adj.* prophesying doom.

dooms|day or **Dooms|day** (dümz′dā′), *n.* the end of the world; the day of God's final judgment of mankind; Judgment Day.

Doomsday Book, = Domesday Book.

Doomsday Machine, a hypothetical machine designed to trigger automatic nuclear destruction under certain conditions without anyone being able to stop it: *the so-called Doomsday Machine that can destroy all human life, will become not only technologically feasible but inexpensive* (Herman Kahn and Anthony J. Wiener).

doom|ster (düm′stər), *n.* **1** a person who predicts calamity; doomsayer: *With the ... negotiations still in the early stages, the views of both the doomsters and the boosters are solidly founded* (Maclean's). **2** *Archaic.* a person who pronounces doom or sentence. **3** *Obsolete.* (in Scotland) the official, usually the executioner, who read or repeated the sentence. [alteration of *deemster;* influenced by *doom*]

door (dôr, dōr), *n.* **1** a movable part to close an opening in a wall. A door turns on hinges or about a post; some doors slide open and shut. A room usually has one door; a house or building may have many doors. **2** any movable part that suggests a door: *Some ground spiders make a door to their nests like a hinged lid.* **3** an opening where a door is; doorway: *He walked into the room through the door. The salesman had a foot in the door. I will not kill one grasshopper vain Though he eats a hole in my shirt like a door* (Vachel Lindsay). **4** the room, house, or building to which a door belongs: *His house is three doors down the street.* **5** *Figurative.* a way to go in or out; way to get something; access: *a door to opportunity. The door to knowledge is study. Always leave the door open to further negotiation* (New York Times).

darken one's door, to appear on one's threshold; come to see or visit one: *Rose did not want to turn away from Hubert and tell him never to darken her door again* (New Yorker).

in doors, in a house or building; inside: *You had better remain in doors* (Edward White). See **indoors**.

lay at the door of, to blame on; impute to: *The ... grievances he listed have long been laid principally at the door of Washington by other French officials* (New York Times).

lie (or **be**) **at one's door**, to be imputable or chargeable to one: *Lady Clara Vere de Vere, ... The guilt of blood is at your door* (Tennyson).

next door to, a in or at the house next to: *The preacher lives next door to the church.* **b** almost; very close to: *Cheating is an act next door to a crime. To be next door to starving* (Daniel Defoe).

out of doors, not in a house or building; outside: *They pawned everything at one time or another, including the children's shoes and Marx's coat—which prevented them from going out of doors* (Edmund Wilson).

show the door, to ask to leave: *Show that persistent salesman the door.*

slam (or **close**) **the door**, *Informal.* to reject, exclude, or shut off any opening: *The rejection ... slammed the door on any reapproachment between Peking and Moscow* (New York Times). *The N.U.R. executive did not completely close the door yesterday. They said they were ready to continue talks* (London Times).

[Old English *duru*] **—door′like′**, *adj.*

door|bell (dôr′bel′, dōr′-), *n.* a bell to be rung as a signal that someone wishes to have the door opened. A doorbell is usually inside a house and connected to a button or handle outside the door.

door chain, a chain for locking a door from the inside of a room.

do-or-die (dü′ər dī′), *adj.* that must be successfully done or met for survival: *[He] recognized the directive for what it was: a do-or-die order to solve a problem that had already become desperate* (Time).

doored (dôrd, dōrd), *adj.* having a door or doors.

door|frame (dôr′frām′, dōr′-), *n.* the frame in a doorway in which a door is set.

door|jamb (dôr′jam′, dōr′-), *n.* the upright piece forming the side of a doorway; doorpost.

door|keep|er (dôr′kē′pər, dōr′-), *n.* **1** a person who guards a door. **2** = doorman.

door|knob (dôr′nob′, dōr′-), *n.* a handle on a door, used for opening or closing the door.

door|less (dôr′lis, dōr′-), *adj.* having no door.

door|man (dôr′man′, dōr′-; -mən), *n., pl.* **-men**. **1** a man whose work is opening the door of a hotel, store, apartment house, or other building, for people going in or out. **2** a person who guards a door or an entrance; doorkeeper.

door|mat (dôr′mat′, dōr′-), *n.* **1** a mat placed near a door for wiping off the dirt from the bottoms of one's shoes before entering. **2** *Informal, Figurative.* a person or group that is easily taken advantage of, used, defeated, etc. **3** = knotgrass.

door|nail (dôr′nāl′, dōr′-), *n.* a nail with a large head.

dead as a doornail, entirely dead: *Without tourism the town would be as dead as a doornail* (London Times).

door-o|pen|er (dôr′ō′pə nər, dōr′-), *n. Informal.* a means of entrance, access, or admission: *One [course] is Government auto insurance, which the industry dreads as a door-opener to further Government intervention in the insurance business* (Time).

door|piece (dôr′pēs′, dōr′-), *n.* **1** a thing to be attached to or hung on a door: *I didn't like traveling on streetcars with large wreaths or floral doorpieces for funerals* (Saul Bellow). **2** = doorframe.

door|plate (dôr′plāt′, dōr′-), *n.* a metal plate on a

door with a name, number, or the like, on it.
door|post (dôr′pōst′, dōr′-), *n.* = doorjamb.
between you, me, and the doorpost, *Informal.* as a secret; confidentially: *Between you, me, and the doorpost, our friend is in trouble.*
door prize, a prize given to a person attending a motion-picture theater, party, or other gathering. Door prizes are usually awarded by drawing numbers that correspond to those on the tickets of the attending persons.
door|sill (dôr′sil′, dōr′-), *n.* = threshold.
door|step (dôr′step′, dōr′-), *n.* a step, or a set of steps, leading from a door to the ground.
at (or **on**) **one's doorstep,** close by; within one's sphere of interest, responsibility, or competence: *It is galling for the Americans to see a ruthless dictatorship established on their doorstep* (Manchester Guardian Weekly).
door|stop (dôr′stop′, dōr′-), *n.* a device for holding a door open or for stopping a door from opening beyond a certain point.
door-to-door (dôr′tə dôr′, dōr′tə dōr′), *adj., adv.* —*adj.* **1** going from one house, apartment, office, or other building, to the next and so on: *a door-to-door salesman.* **2** going from the starting point to the destination: *door-to-door delivery.*
—*adv.* **1** from one house, apartment, office, or other building, to the next: *to sell door-to-door.* **2** from the starting point to the destination.
door|trap (dôr′trap′, dōr′-), *n.* a trap with a door that swings shut upon the entry of an animal.
door|way (dôr′wā′, dōr′-), *n.* **1** an opening in a wall to be closed by a door; portal. **2** *Figurative.* a way to get something; access: *the doorway to success.*
door|weed (dôr′wēd′, dōr′-), *n.* = knotgrass.
door window, a window reaching to the floor and opening like a door.
door|yard (dôr′yärd′, dōr′-), *n.* a yard near the door of a house: *When lilacs last in the dooryard bloom'd* (Walt Whitman).
doo-wop (dü′wop), *n. Slang.* rock'n'roll group harmony music with a lead singer, especially popular in the 1950's and early 1960's. [imitative of the background harmony]
doo|zer (dü′zər), *n.* = doozy.
doo|zy (dü′zē), *n., pl.* **-zies.** *U.S. Slang.* a remarkable thing. [probably alteration of *deuce of*]
dop[1] (dop), *n.* a cup for holding a diamond while it is being cut. [< Dutch *dop* husk, shell, cover]
dop[2] (dop), *n.* a brandy made from the skins of grapes after the juice has been pressed out. [< Afrikaans *dop* < Dutch, husk, shell, cover]
do|pa (dō′pə), *n.* an amino acid found in various plants, isolated from a variety of bean or made synthetically. *Formula:* $C_9H_{11}NO_4$ [< *d*(ihydr)*o* (xy)*p*(henyl)*a*(lanine)]
do|pa|mine (dō′pə mēn), *n.* a hormone produced by the adrenal glands that is essential to the normal nerve activity of the brain: *These hormones, particularly dopamine, play an intimate role in the tremors experienced by patients with Parkinson's disease* (Science News). [< *dop*(a) + *amine*]
do|pant (dō′pənt), *n.* an impure substance added in very small amounts to a semiconductor to vary its conductive properties [< *dope* verb, to treat or coat one substance with another + *-ant*]
dope (dōp), *n., v.,* **doped, dop|ing.** —*n.* **1** *Slang.* a narcotic drug, such as opium or morphine. **2** *Slang.* information; forecast; prediction: *"Where did you get all that inside dope?" asked Darby* (James T. Farrell). **3** *Slang.* a very stupid person. **4** oil, grease, or fuel additive, used to make machinery run smoothly. **5** varnish or similar liquid applied to a fabric to strengthen or waterproof it. It was formerly put on the cloth parts of an airplane to make them stronger, waterproof, and airtight. **6** an absorbent material used in the manufacture of dynamite. **7** *Slang.* a drug used illegally to make a race horse run faster or an athlete perform better. **8** *U.S. Slang.* a drink containing a stimulant, especially a kola.
—*v.t.* **1** *Slang.* to give or apply dope to. **2** to treat or coat with another substance. **3** *Slang.* = dope out.
—*v.i. Slang.* to use dope: *The boys are too kempt; . . . they dope not, neither do they drink* (Observer).
dope off, *Slang.* to act as if drugged; be or become dopey: *I was so busy manipulating, inside me, all sorts of imaginary events that I would dope off into staring silences* (Harper's).
dope out, a to work out; figure out; discover: *All the same, I believe it was the hand of Fate that doped out the way for me to find her* (O. Henry). **b** to forecast; predict: *We would study the morning papers and . . . from them try to dope out the winners* (R. H. Davis).
[American English, sauce < Dutch *doop* dipping sauce < *dopen* dip] —**dop′er,** *n.*
dope addict, = drug addict.
dope fiend, *Slang.* = drug addict.
dope|head (dōp′hed′), *n. Slang.* = drug addict.
dope pusher or **peddler,** *Slang.* a person who sells or distributes dope.
dope sheet, *Slang.* a publication or part of a publication offering information on the condition and record of race horses.
dope|ster (dōp′stər), *n. U.S. Slang.* **1** a person who gathers information in order to predict the outcome of future events, such as horse races or elections. **2** an analyst.
dope|y (dō′pē), *adj.,* **dop|i|er, dop|i|est. 1** *Slang.* drugged; affected by or as if by dope; drowsy. **2** very stupid. Also, **dopy.**
dop|i|ness (dō′pē nis), *n. Slang.* state of being drugged or muddled; dopey quality or condition.
Dop|pel|gän|ger or **dop|pel|gän|ger** (dop′əl-geng′ər), *n.* the ghost or double of a living person; doubleganger: (*Figurative.*) *This was Boswell's role in life: Doppelgänger to men of genius* (John Wain). [< German *Doppelgänger* double goer]
Dop|per (dop′ər) *n.* a member of a strict Calvinistic sect in South Africa.
Dop|pler broadening (dop′lər), the broadening of a line or lines of a spectrum due to the Doppler effect, as a result of a relative difference in velocity of the radiating atoms or molecules.
Doppler effect, *Physics.* the apparent change in wave frequency when either the source of waves or the observer moves toward or away from the other. *Example:* the increase and decrease in the pitch or frequency of a train's whistle as the train passes an observer. [< Christian J. *Doppler,* 1803-1853, Austrian physicist, who described it]
Doppler radar, 1 a radar for determining the velocity of a moving object, such as an aircraft or a speeding car by the use of dovap. **2** = dovap.
Doppler shift, the apparent shift in the lines of a luminous body's spectrum as the body approaches or recedes from an observer.
dop|y (dō′pē), *adj.,* **dop|i|er, dop|i|est.** = dopey.
dor[1] (dôr), *n.,* or **dor bug, 1** a European dung beetle. **2** any one of various other beetles, such as the cockchafer. Also, **dorr.** [Old English *dora*]
dor[2] (dôr), *n. Obsolete.* mockery; (practical) joke. [perhaps < Scandinavian (compare Old Icelandic *dār* mockery)]
do|ra|do (də rä′dō), *n., pl.* **-dos.** = dolphin (def. 2). [< Spanish *dorado* dolphin; (literally) golden (because of their coloration)]
Do|ra|do (də rā′dō), *n. genitive* **Do|ra|dus.** a southern constellation between Carina and Phoenix, the site of the larger of the two Magellanic Clouds. [< *dorado* (because of its shape)]
Do|ra|dus (də rā′dəs), *n.* genitive of **Dorado.**
dor|bee|tle (dôr′bē′təl), *n.* = dor[1].
dor|cas (dôr′kəs), *n.,* or **dorcas gazelle,** a very small, light-brown gazelle; ariel. [< New Latin *Dorcas* the genus name < Greek *dorkás* deer, gazelle]
Dor|cas (dôr′kəs), *n.* a woman who made clothes for the poor (in the Bible, Acts 9:36-41).
do|ré (dô rā′), *adj., n.* —*adj.* **1** golden; gilded: *a steel-and-bronze doré inkstand.* **2** containing gold: *doré metal. Doré bullion is silver that contains small parts of gold.*
—*n.* an alloy of silver and gold. [< French]
do-re-mi (dō′rā′mē′), *n. U.S. Slang.* money; dough: *Corst doesn't have enough do-re-mi in his pocket to acquire a second-hand mousetrap* (Time). [< *do*[2] + *re*[1] + *mi* musical notes (because *do* is pronounced the same as slang *dough* money)]
dor|hawk (dôr′hôk′), *n.* the goatsucker or nightjar of Europe; nighthawk. [< *dor*[1] + *hawk*[1]]
Do|ri|an (dôr′ē ən, dōr′-), *n., adj.* —*n.* a member of a warlike Hellenic people who invaded the Peloponnesus, Crete, and Rhodes in the 1100's B.C. and put an end to Mycenaean culture.
—*adj.* of or having to do with the Dorians.
Dorian mode, 1 one of the modes in ancient Greek music, characterized by simplicity and solemnity. **2** a mode of medieval church music, beginning and ending on the note D.
***Dor|ic** (dôr′ik, dor′-), *adj., n.* —*adj.* **1** of or having to do with the oldest and simplest kind of Greek architecture. The capital of a Doric column has a rounded molding. **2** = Dorian. **3** not refined; rustic: *a Doric dialect.*
—*n.* **1** the Greek dialect spoken in Doris, a division of ancient Greece. **2** an unrefined or rustic dialect of English, such as Scottish.
Dor|i|cism (dôr′ə siz əm, dor′-), *n.* a Doric peculiarity of speech.
Dor|i|den (dôr′i dən), *n. Trademark.* glutethimide.
Do|ris (dôr′is, dōr′-), *n. Greek Mythology.* the mother of the Nereids.
dor|je (dôr′jə), *n.* a scepter in the form of a thunderbolt, held by Tibetan lamas as a symbol of the power of Buddha. [< Tibetan *dorje*]
dork (dôrk), *n. Slang.* a dull, stupid, or ineffectual person. [origin unknown]
Dor|king (dôr′king), *n.* any one of an English breed of chickens that have long, heavy bodies and five toes on each foot. [< *Dorking,* a town in Surrey, England]
dork|y (dôr′kē), *adj.,* **dork|i|er, dork|i|est.** *Slang.* dull, stupid, or ineffectual: *She asked Kate what she thought of Cle. "He's dorky," Kate responded. She didn't like his glasses* (Chicago Tribune).
dor|lach (dôr′ləн), *n. Scottish.* **1** a bundle; package. **2** a valise; portmanteau. **3** *Obsolete.* a quiver[2]. [< Gaelic *dorlach* handful, large quantity]
dorm (dôrm), *n. Informal.* a dormitory. [American English; short for *dormitory*]
dor|man|cy (dôr′mən sē), *n.* dormant condition: *Many seeds preserve their dormancy until they have been wet by a series of rains* (Scientific American).
dor|mant (dôr′mənt), *adj.* **1** sleeping or apparently sleeping; quiet as if asleep: *Bears and other animals that hibernate are dormant during the winter.* **2** inactive: *Many volcanoes are dormant.* (*Figurative.*) *The artist's talent for painting was dormant until his teacher discovered it.* SYN: quiescent. See syn. under **inactive. 3** with development suspended; not growing: *The plants, bulbs, and seeds were dormant during the cold of winter.* **4** used during the dormant period of plants: *a dormant spray.* **5** *Heraldry.* (of an animal) lying down with its head on its forepaws. [< Old French *dormant,* present participle of *dormir* to sleep < Latin *dormīre.* See etym. of doublet **dormient.**]
***dor|mer** (dôr′mər), *n.* **1** an upright window that projects from a sloping roof. **2** the projecting part of a roof that contains such a window: *Notice the splendid mansard roof, with its double tier of dormers and fancy iron crestings* (New Yorker). [originally, a sleeping room, its window < Old French *dormeor* < Latin *dormītōrium.* See etym. of doublet **dormitory.**]

***dormer**
definition 1

dor|mered (dôr′mərd), *adj.* having dormers: *There is a dormered . . . attic which can be finished into two additional bedrooms* (New York Times).
dormer window, a window built out from a sloping roof; dormer.
dor|mice (dôr′mīs′), *n.* plural of **dormouse.**
dor|mie (dôr′mē), *adj.* = dormy.
dor|mi|ent (dôr′mē ənt), *adj.* sleeping; dormant. [< Latin *dormiēns, -entis,* present participle of *dormīre* sleep. See etym. of doublet **dormant.**]
dor|min (dôr′min), *n.* = abscisic acid. [< *dorm*(ant) + *-in*]
dor|mi|tion (dôr mish′ən), *n.* **1** sleeping; a falling asleep. **2** dying; death. [< Middle French *dormition* < Latin *dormītiō, -ōnis* < *dormīre* to sleep]

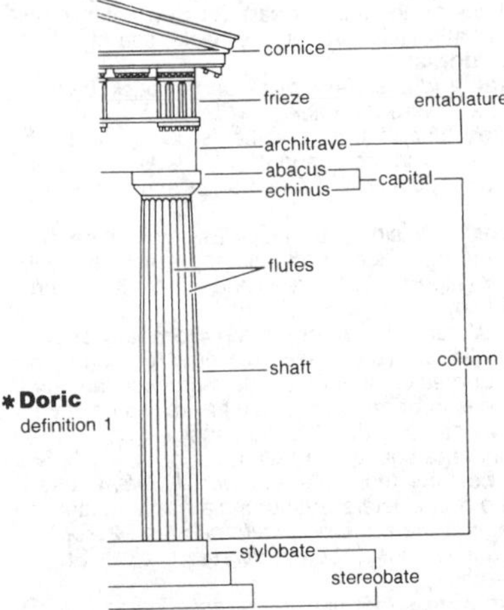

***Doric**
definition 1

dor|mi|to|ry (dôr′mə tor′ē, -tōr′-), *n., pl.* **-ries. 1** a building with many rooms for sleeping in. Many colleges have dormitories for students whose homes are far away. **2** a room for sleeping in containing several beds, for example in a boarding

Pronunciation Key: hat, āge, cãre, fär; let, ēqual, tėrm; it, īce; hot, ōpen, ôrder; oil, out; cup, pu̇t, rüle; child; long; thin; ᴛʜen; zh, measure; ə represents **a** in about, **e** in taken, **i** in pencil, **o** in lemon, **u** in circus.

school: *The queerest little dormitories which . . . had once been nun's cells* (Charlotte Brontë). 3 *Especially British.* a suburb in which commuters live. [< Latin *dormītōrium* < *dormīre* to sleep. See etym. of doublet **dormer**.]

dor·mo·bile (dôr′mə bēl), *n. British.* 1 a kind of small van or bus. *He was being prodded into the back of a dormobile in one of the connecting lanes* (Sunday Times). 2 **Dormobile**. a trademark for such a vehicle.

dor·mouse (dôr′mous′), *n., pl.* **-mice**. a small animal of the Old World that looks somewhat like a squirrel and somewhat like a mouse. It sleeps most of the winter. Dormice are rodents. [origin uncertain; perhaps < dialectal *dorm* to sleep, doze (< French *dormir* < Latin *dormīre*) + *mouse*]

dor·my (dôr′mē), *adj.* leading in golf by as many holes as remain to be played. [apparently < dialectal *dorm* to sleep (since further effort is of no value)]

dor·nick[1] (dôr′nik), *n.* a kind of linen cloth used in Scotland especially for tablecloths. [< *Doornik,* the Flemish name for *Tournay,* a city in Belgium, where it was first made]

dor·nick[2] (dôr′nik), *n. U.S.* a pebble, stone, or small boulder. [American English, probably < Irish *dornog* fist, small stone for throwing]

dor·nock (dôr′nək), *n.* = dornick.

do·ron·i·cum (də ron′ə kəm), *n.* any one of a group of European and Asiatic composite plants which are cultivated for their yellow flowers; leopard's-bane. [< New Latin *Doronicum* the genus name < New Greek *doroneikon* < Arabic *durūnaj*]

Dor·o·thy bag (dôr′ə thē, dor′-), *British.* a woman's handbag drawn together with purse strings and carried on the wrist. [< the name *Dorothy*]

dorp (dôrp), *n.* a village or town: *Swellendam is now a quietly thriving platteland dorp with . . . a total population of nearly 4,000 people* (Forbes Stuart). [< Dutch *dorp.* See related etym. at **thorp**.]

Dor·per (dôr′pər), *n.* any one of a breed of mutton sheep raised in South Africa. [< *Dor*(set)[2] + *Per*(sian)]

dorr (dôr), *n.* = dor[1].

dorr·bee·tle (dôr′bē′təl), *n.* = dor[1].

dor·sa (dôr′sə), *n.* plural of **dorsum**.

dor·sad (dôr′sad), *adv. Anatomy.* toward the back. [< Latin *dorsum* back + *ad* toward]

dor·sal[1] (dôr′səl), *adj., n.* —*adj.* 1 of the back; on or near the back: *a dorsal nerve. A shark has a dorsal fin.* 2 *Botany.* of or on the back of an organ or part: *the dorsal surface of a leaf.* 3 *Phonetics.* articulated with the back of the tongue.
—*n.* 1 *Biology.* a dorsal part, such as a dorsal fin or vertebra. 2 *Phonetics.* a dorsal sound.
[< Late Latin *dorsālis* < Latin *dorsum* the back]

dor·sal[2] (dôr′səl), *n.* = dossal.

dorsal fin, a fin or finlike part on the back of most aquatic vertebrates. See picture under **fin**[1].

dor·sa·lis (dôr sā′lis), *n.* an artery which supplies the back of an organ or part. [< New Latin *dorsalis* (in Latin, adjective, on the back); see etym. under **dorsal**[1]]

dor·sal·ly (dôr′sə lē), *adv.* 1 on the back; by the back. 2 toward the back.

d'or·say (dôr sā′), *n.* a woman's pump with each side cut low in the shape of a V. [< Count Alfred *d'Orsay,* 1801-1852, French artist and society figure]

Dor·set[1] (dôr′sit), *n.* an arctic Eskimo culture, believed to have flourished until approximately 1000 A.D. [< Cape *Dorset,* Greenland, where it was first identified]

Dor·set[2] (dôr′sit), *n.,* or **Dorset Horn**, any one of an English breed of sheep having large horns and wool of medium length. Dorsets produce lambs at any season of the year. They are raised chiefly for their meat along the Atlantic coast. [< *Dorset*(shire), a county in England]

dor·sif·er·ous (dôr sif′ər əs), *adj.* 1 *Botany.* bearing the fruit clusters of sporangia on the underside or back of the frond: *a dorsiferous fern.* 2 *Zoology.* dorsiparous. [< Latin *dorsum* back + English *-ferous*]

dor·sip·a·rous (dôr sip′ər əs), *adj. Zoology.* hatching the young on the back: *Certain toads are dorsiparous.* [< Latin *dorsum* back + *parere* to bear, give birth to + English *-ous*]

dor·si·spi·nal (dôr′sə spī′nəl), *adj.* having to do with the spinous processes of the vertebrae. [< Latin *dorsum* back + English *spinal*]

dor·si·ven·tral (dôr′sə ven′trəl), *adj.* 1 *Botany.* having distinct dorsal and ventral sides: *Most foliage leaves are dorsiventral.* 2 *Zoology.* dorsoventral. —**dor′si·ven′tral·ly**, *adv.*

dor·so·lat·er·al (dôr′sō lat′ər əl), *adj.* of or affecting both the back and the side. [< Latin *dorsum* back + English *lateral*]

dor·so·ven·tral (dôr′sō ven′trəl), *adj.* 1 *Zoology.* extending from the back to the abdominal side: *the dorsoventral axis.* 2 *Botany.* dorsiventral. [< Latin *dorsum* back + English *ventral*] —**dor′so·ven′tral·ly**, *adv.*

dor·sum (dôr′səm), *n., pl.* **-sa**. 1 the back; outer surface of an organ or part: *the dorsum of the hand.* 2 *Phonetics.* the back part of the tongue. [< Latin *dorsum*]

dort·y (dôr′tē), *adj. Scottish.* ill-humored; sulky.

***do·ry[1]** (dôr′ē, dōr′-), *n., pl.* **-ries**. a rowboat with a narrow, flat bottom and high sides. It was formerly much used by fishermen. [American English, perhaps < Miskito (a language of Nicaragua) *dóri*]

***dory[1]**

do·ry[2] (dôr′ē, dōr′-), *n., pl.* **-ries**. 1 = John Dory. 2 any one of various related fishes, such as the walleyed pike of North America. [< French *dorée* (literally) gilded. Compare etym. under **dorado**.]

do·ry·man (dôr′ē mən, dōr′-), *n., pl.* **-men**. a man who rows a dory.

DOS, disk operating system.

dos-à-dos (dō′zə dō′; *in dance calling, usually* dō′sē dō′), *n., pl.* **-dos** (-dōz′), *adv.* —*n.* 1 a figure in dancing in which two persons pass each other back to back and return to their places; do-si-do. 2 an open vehicle or piece of furniture made for people to sit back to back.
—*adv.* back to back.
[< French *dos à dos* (literally) back to back; *dos* < Old French; see etym. under **dosser**]

dos·age (dō′sij), *n.* 1a the amount of a medicine to be taken at one time: *The correct dosage is very important in the treatment of sickness.* b *Figurative.* a portion of anything; dose: *His mail brings him a daily dosage of opinion in which he is by turn vilified and glorified* (Time). 2 the giving of medicine in doses. 3 the intensity or length of application of X rays in certain methods of therapy. 4 the measured addition of ingredients to a substance to give it a certain strength or flavor: *A dosage of brandy or sugar is sometimes added to wine.*

dose (dōs), *n., v.,* **dosed, dos·ing**. —*n.* 1 the amount of a medicine to be given or taken at one time: *a dose of cough medicine.* SYN: dosage. 2 the intensity or length of exposure to heat, X rays, or other radiation: *The biological effects of radiation are measured by the dose received* (Bulletin of Atomic Scientists). 3 *Figurative.* the amount of anything given or taken at one time; portion: *a dose of flattery.* 4 a portion of an ingredient added to a substance to give it strength or flavor. 5 *Figurative.* anything unpleasant or disagreeable to take or endure: *Father always says that a good dose of work never hurt anyone.* 6 *Slang.* a venereal disease, especially gonorrhea.
—*v.t.* 1 to give medicine to in doses; treat with medicine: *The doctor dosed the boy with penicillin.* 2 to administer in doses; divide into doses. 3 to add a dose to; blend; adulterate: *to dose wine with sugar.*
—*v.i.* to take doses of medicine: *That sickly fellow is always dosing.*
[< Middle French *dose,* learned borrowing from Late Latin *dosis* < Greek *dósis* dose, a giving < *didónai* give] —**dos′er**, *n.*

dose·me·ter (dōs′mē′tər), *n.* = dosimeter.

dose rate, the intensity of radiation to which a person or thing is exposed.

dose-re·sponse (dōs′ri spons′), *adj.* showing the relationship of dosage (of a drug, gas, radiation, or other substance) to the physiological effect produced: *A dose-response chart would have a line going from zero to maximum dose, with the risk accelerating* (New York Times).

do-si-do (dō′sē dō′), *n., pl.* **-dos**, *v.,* **-doed, -doing**. —*n.* = dos-à-dos (def. 1).
—*v.i.* to execute a dos-à-dos.

do·sim·e·ter (dō sim′ə tər), *n.* a small device a person may wear for measuring the doses of atomic radiation received over a given period of time: *For safety's sake in the atom age, he may be equipped with a fountain-pen-sized "dosimeter"* (Wall Street Journal). [< Greek *dósis* dose + English *-meter*]

do·si·met·ric (dō′sə met′rik), *adj.* having to do with the measurement of doses or with a dosimeter.

do·sim·e·try (dō sim′ə trē), *n.* the measurement of doses.

dos·ing tank (dō′sing), a tank in a sewage treatment system for storing sewage before it is discharged into the next part of the system.

doss (dos), *n., v. Slang.* —*n.* 1 a bed, as in a cheap rooming house. 2 a doss house. 3 sleep.
—*v.i.* to sleep; bed down: *It was here that we dossed down for our first night in the desert* (Atlantic).
[probably < French, Old French *dos;* see etym. under **dosser**]

dos·sal or **dos·sel[1]** (dos′əl), *n.* an ornamental cloth hung at the back of an altar or throne or at the sides of the chancel. Also, **dorsal**. [< Medieval Latin *dossale,* and *dorsale,* neuter of Late Latin *dorsālis;* see etym. under **dorsal**[1]]

dos·sel[2] (dos′əl), *n.* = dossil; a plug of lint.

dos·ser (dos′ər), *n.* 1 an ornamental cloth covering the back of a seat, especially of a throne. 2 a basket for carrying things on the back; pannier. [< Old French *dossier* < *dos* the back < Vulgar Latin *dossum* < Latin *dorsum*]

doss house, a cheap rooming house: *We have to halt at . . . a village without eating-place and only a doss house* (Manchester Guardian).

dos·si·er (dos′ē ā, -ər), *n.* a collection of documents or papers about some subject or person. [< French, Old French *dossier* bundle of papers; see etym. under **dosser** (because the bundle of papers has a label on the back)]

dos·sil (dos′əl), *n.* 1 a plug of lint or cotton for stopping a wound; pledget. 2 *Printing.* a roll of cloth for wiping excess ink from the surface of a plate. [< Old French *dosil* spigot, plug < Late Latin *duciculus* (diminutive) < *dux, ducis* leader]

doss·y (dos′ē), *adj.,* **doss·i·er, doss·i·est**. *Informal.* stylish; smart. [apparently < Scottish *doss* neat, spruce]

dost (dust), *v. Archaic.* second person singular of **do**[1]. "Thou dost" means "you do."

Dos·to·ev·ski·an or **Dos·to·ev·sky·an** (dos′tə yef′skē ən), *adj.* 1 of Fyodor Dostoevsky, Russian novelist and short-story writer (1821-1881). 2 in the style of Dostoevsky.

do svi·da·nia (dô svē dä′nyə), *Russian.* goodbye. *They [the Russian delegation to Czechoslovakia] . . . bade their hosts do svidania, climbed aboard their own train and sped a bare mile across the border to dine and sleep in the security of their own country* (Time).

dot[1] (dot), *n., v.,* **dot·ted, dot·ting**. —*n.* 1 a tiny, round mark; very small spot; point. There is a dot over each *i* in this line. 2 a small spot; speck: *a blue necktie with white dots.* 3 a short sound used in sending messages by telegraph or radio. 4 *Music.* a a tiny, round mark after a note or rest that makes it half again as long. b a point placed under or over a note to indicate that it is to be played staccato. 5 *British Informal.* an unspecified time very long ago (usually in the phrase *the year dot*): *Investigative journalism has been the core of the trade since the newspaper year dot* (London Times).
—*v.t.* 1 to mark with a dot or dots: *Dot your i's and j's.* 2 to be here and there in; give variety to: *Trees and bushes dotted the broad lawn.*
—*v.i.* 1 to make a dot or dots. 2 *Archaic.* to limp: *to dot and go one means to hobble.*
dot the i's and cross the t's, to make something very clear: *[He] dotted our i's and crossed our t's with a vengeance about the lack of men in the Navy* (London Daily Chronicle).
on the dot, *Informal.* at exactly the right time; at the specified time: *Our train arrived on the dot. Though he was there every day on the dot for ten years, no patron ever appeared* (Edmund Wilson).
[Old English *dott* speck, head of a boil]

dot[2] (dot), *n.* = dowry. [< Old French *dot,* learned borrowing from Latin *dōs, dōtis* dowry]

DOT (no periods), Department of Transportation.

dot·age (dō′tij), *n.* 1 a weak-minded and childish condition that sometimes accompanies old age; senility: *The old man was in his dotage and spent much of his time mumbling to himself.* 2a excessive love or fondness; foolish affection: *Merlin fell in a dotage on the damsel* (Sir Thomas Malory). b the object of such a love or fondness: *those two main plagues and common dotages of human kind, wine and women* (Robert Burton). [< *dote* + *-age*]

do·tal (dō′təl), *adj.* of or having to do with a dot (dowry).

do·tard (dō′tərd), *n.* a person who is weak-minded and childish because of old age: *Thou were an old dotard and a fool* (William Caxton). [< *dote*]

do·ta·tion (dō tā′shən), *n.* the act of endowing; endowment. [< Latin *dōtātiō, -ōnis* < *dōtāre* endow < *dōs;* see etym. under **dot**[2]]

dote (dōt), *v.i.,* **dot·ed, dot·ing**. to be foolish and childish because of old age. Also, **doat**.
dote on (or **upon**), to be foolishly fond of; be too fond of; lavish too much affection on: *That mother dotes on her only son, spoiling him by granting his every wish. . . . now she could be romantic every evening, and dote upon Albert, without a single distraction, all day long* (Lytton Strachey).
[Middle English *doten,* perhaps < Middle Dutch, be childish] —**dot′er**, *n.*

dot·ed (dō′tid), *adj.* 1 decayed or unsound: *doted timber.* 2 *Obsolete.* foolish.

doth (duth), *v. Archaic.* does. "He doth" means "he does."

dot|ing (dō′ting), *adj.* **1** foolishly fond; too fond: *Doting parents see no fault in their children.* **2** weak-minded; childish; senile. **3** *Botany.* (of trees) decaying from age. Also, **doating.** **—dot′ing|ly,** *adv.*

dot map, a map on which statistical information is projected by means of dots, each representing a certain distributed quantity.

dot-ma|trix (dot′mā′triks, -mat′riks), *adj.* of or having to do with a printing process or device using a rectangular pattern of small dots to generate characters on a printer or computer display screen: *The dot-matrix impact printers . . . use dots arranged close together to make letters* (Computer Readout).

dot product, *Mathematics.* the scalar quantity which is the product of the lengths of two vectors and the cosine of the angle between them; scalar product; inner product. It is denoted by a dot placed between the vectors, as in A · B.

***dot|ted** (dot′id), *adj.* **1** marked with or as if with a dot or dots: *This butterfly has dotted orange and black wings.* **2** formed of dots: *Sign on the dotted line.* **3** *Music.* (of a note or rest) followed by a dot, thus making it half again as long: *a dotted eighth.*

***dotted**
definition 3

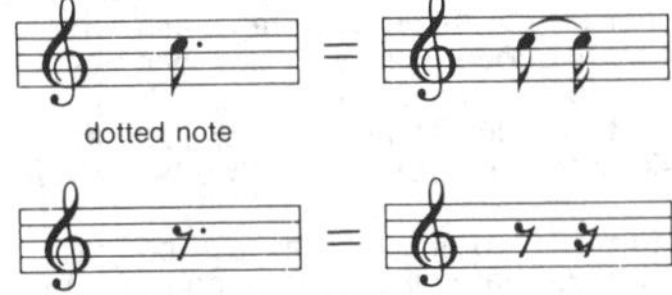

dotted note

dotted rest

dot|ted-line (dot′id līn′), *adj.* having to do with a direct relationship; lineal; close: *. . . Safety officer with dotted-line link to the Director of Research* (New Scientist).

dotted swiss, a sheer cotton material with a pattern of raised dots. [< *Swiss* (muslin)]

dot|tel (dot′əl), *n.* = dottle.

dot|ter (dot′ər), *n.* a person or thing that dots; instrument for making dots.

dot|ter|el (dot′ər əl), *n.* **1** a short-billed plover of Europe and Asia that is easily caught. **2** any related bird. **3** *Dialect.* a stupid person who is easily fooled or cheated. [< *dote* + *-rel,* as in *wastrel*]

dot|ti|ly (dot′ə lē), *adv.* in a dotty way; unsteadily: *The cold-weather birds, double their summer size, hopped dottily about the crisp, rimed grass* (New Yorker).

dot|ti|ness (dot′ē nis), *n.* dotty quality or condition: *When he said I was lovely he had a slightly dotty look, but I think the dottiness was no more than skin-deep* (Punch).

dot|tle (dot′əl), *n.* tobacco left in the bowl of a pipe after smoking. [earlier, plug, stopper, perhaps < *dot*[1] + *-le*]

dot|trel (dot′rəl), *n.* = dotterel.

dot|ty (dot′ē), *adj.,* **-ti|er, -ti|est. 1** *Informal.* feeble-minded; half-witted; partly insane: *The most striking is Miss Hare, a dotty old oddity who goes on alone in her crumbling family mansion and at intervals sees a vision of God riding past in his chariot* (Punch). **2** *Informal.* unsteady; shaky; feeble: *It is not really a good novel but it has a dotty brilliance that makes it linger in the memory* (Punch). **3** *Informal.* very enthusiastic: *I'm not dotty about people* (New York Times). **4** full of dots. [< *dot*[1] + *-y*[1]]

dot|y (dō′tē), *adj. Dialect.* decayed; decaying: *a doty tree.* [< *dot* (e) + *-y*[1]]

Dou|ai Bible (dü′ā), = Douay Bible.

Dou|a|la (dü ä′lə), *n.,* pl. **-la** or **-las.** a member of the principal tribe, of Bantu stock, of southern Cameroon in western Africa. Also, **Duala.**

douane (dwän), *n. French.* a custom house.

doua|nier (dwä nyā′), *n. French.* an official of a custom house: *The douaniers examined my passport and retained it* (London Times).

dou|ar (dü är′), *n.* an encampment of Arab tents grouped in a circle around a central enclosure for cattle: *among the Moslems who live in the medinas and douars of Algeria* (Saturday Review). [< Arabic *dūār*]

Dou|ay Bible or **Version** (dü′ā), an English translation of the Latin Vulgate Bible, made by a group of Roman Catholic scholars. The New Testament was published at Reims in 1582, the Old Testament at Douay (now Douai), France, in 1609. The Douay Bible is used by English-speaking Roman Catholics. *Abbr:* D.V.

dou|ble (dub′əl), *adj., adv., n., v.,* **-bled, -bling.** **—*adj.*** **1** twice as much, as many, as large, or as strong: *a double dip of ice cream. The man was given double pay for working on Sunday.* **SYN:** twofold. **2** for two: *a double room.* **3** made of two like parts; in a pair: *double doors.* **4** having two unlike parts; having two meanings or characters. The spelling *b-e-a-r* has a double meaning: *carry* and *a certain animal.* **5** *Figurative.* insincere; deceitful; false: *a double tongue, double-faced.* **SYN:** hypocritical. **6** having more than one set of petals: *Some roses are double, others are single.* **7** *Music.* **a** having two beats or a multiple of two beats to the measure. **b** producing a tone an octave lower than the ordinary instrument: *a double trumpet.*
—*adv.* **1** twice; doubly: *He was paid double by mistake. Be double careful when you cross the street.* **2** two (of everything) instead of one: *The blow on the head made him see double.* **3** two together: *. . . thy hand in mine With pulses that beat double* (Elizabeth B. Browning).
—*n.* **1** a number or amount that is twice as much: *Four is the double of two.* **2** a person or thing just like another: *Here is the double of your lost glove.* **SYN:** counterpart. **3** a substitute. In a motion picture an actor often has a double to do the dangerous scenes. **4** a fold; bend. **5** a sharp turn or backward bend; shift: *He made a sudden double and passed us again.* **6** *Baseball.* a hit by which a batter gets to second base. **7** *Bridge.* **a** the act of doubling a bid: *The double is at least a warning that North finds the prospect of game for his side very slim* (New York Times). **b** a hand strong enough to double on. **8** *U.S. Informal.* = daily double. **9** *Informal.* a double portion of an alcoholic drink. **10** *Printing.* a doublet. **11** *Archaic.* a variation in music.
—*v.t.* **1** to make twice as much or twice as many: *He doubled his money in ten years by investing it wisely.* **2** to fold; bend: *He doubled his slice of bread to make a sandwich.* **3** to close tightly together; clench: *He doubled his fists in anger.* **4** to sail or go around: *The ship doubled Cape Horn.* **5** to be the double of. **6** to be or have twice as much as: *The enemy's ships double our own.* **7** *Bridge.* to increase the points or penalties of (an opponent's bid). **8** *Music.* to add the upper or lower octave to (a note or notes).
—*v.i.* **1** to become twice as much or as many: *Money left in a savings bank will double in about twenty years.* **2** to take the place of another; substitute: *The principal is doubling for the teacher today. The understudy doubled for the leading actor when he got sick.* **3** to serve two purposes; play two parts: *The maid doubled as cook. He doubled on trumpet and drums in the school band.* **4a** to bend or turn sharply backward: *The fox doubled on his track and escaped the dogs.* **b** to bend over in pain, laughter, shock, or other emotion: *The runner doubled in pain with a cramp.* **5** *Baseball.* to hit a double: *He doubled but was put out trying for a triple.*
double back, a to fold over: *It ruins a book to double back the pages as a bookmark.* **b** to go back the same way that one came: *The fox doubled back to avoid capture.*
doubles, a game of tennis, etc., with two players on each side. *Pat Ward, Great Britain, and Christiane Mercelis, Belgium, won the women's doubles* (New York Times).
double up, a to fold up; curl up: *He spent the rainy day doubled up on the sofa, reading.* **b** to bend over: *He doubled up with laughter.* **c** to share room, bed, or quarters with another: *Since there was only one room left at the hotel, the two men doubled up for the night.*
on (or **at**) **the double, a** quickly: *The policeman answered the call for help on the double. Our Exeter hose goes happily into the washer, does not shrink, and dries on the double* (Wall Street Journal). *For two days he was all smiles and did everything at the double* (Harper's). **b** in double time: *Ellsworth detailed twenty men . . . and went 'at the double' down Pennsylvania Avenue* (Chambers's Journal).
[< Old French *duble* or *doble* < Latin *duplus.* See etym. of doublets **dobla, dobra, duple.**]
—dou′ble|ness, *n.*
▶**double letter.** In abbreviations, a double letter often indicates plurality: *pp.* = *pages; LLB.* = *Bachelor of Laws.*

dou|blé(dü blā′), *adj.* having or made with a doublure: *a doublébinding.* [< French *doublé,* past participle of *doubler* to double, put a lining in]

dou|ble-act|ing (dub′əl ak′ting), *adj.* = double-action (defs. 1, 2): [*A*] *double-acting pump . . . throws water at each stroke* (Edward Knight).

dou|ble-ac|tion (dub′əl ak′shən), *adj.* **1** that acts or applies power in two directions: *Perhaps his* [*James Watt's*] *most important improvement was the use of the double-action principle . . .* [*in which*] *the steam is used first on one side of the piston, then on the other side* (Otto A. Uyehara). **2** that has twice the usual effect: *Double-action baking powder contains both phosphate and sulfate powders.* **3** cocked and fired by a single pull of the trigger: *a double-action revolver.*

double agent, a secret agent who while working for one group is also an agent for an enemy or rival group: *Colonel Chang had been unmasked as a double agent passing secrets to the mainland* (Time).

double ax, an ax having a blade with two cutting edges, used as a decorative design in prehistoric remains of the Levant. A symbol associated with Zeus, it is found on Hittite, Cypriot, and Mycenaean objects.

dou|ble-bank (dub′əl bangk′), *v.t.* **1** to provide with two rowers: *The crewmen double-banked each of the oars.* **2** *British.* **a** to ride two on (a horse, bicycle, or other vehicle). **b** = double-park. **c** *Figurative.* to double: *Throughout the 1960s, under Conservative and Labour Prime Ministers, the practice has been to double-bank Treasury Ministers in the Cabinet* (London Times). [back formation < *double-banked*]

dou|ble-banked (dub′əl bangkt′), *adj.* **1** having two rowers on the same thwart, but rowing on opposite sides. **2** having two rowers at the same oar. **3** having two rows of oars, one above the other, as certain galleys.

double bar, *Music.* a double line on a staff that marks the end of a movement or of an entire piece of music.

dou|ble-bar|rel (dub′əl bar′əl), *adj.* = double-barreled.

dou|ble-bar|reled (dub′əl bar′əld), *adj.* **1** having two barrels: *a double-barreled shotgun.* **2** *Figurative.* having a twofold purpose: *Eliminating the repeated threats to the public interest from strikes in steel . . . calls for double-barreled action* (Wall Street Journal). **3** *Figurative.* having a double meaning: *a double-barreled compliment.* **4** having two parts: *Some of the biggest names in British exports are double-barreled: Rolls-Royce, Mini-Minor, Terry-Thomas* (Time).

double bass, a deep-toned, stringed musical instrument shaped like a cello but much larger; bass viol; contrabass. The player stands, or sits on a high stool, to play. See picture at **bass**[1].

dou|ble-bass (dub′əl bās′), *n., adj.* = contrabass.

dou|ble-bass|ist (dub′əl bā′sist), *n.* = contrabassist.

double bassoon, a large bassoon, an octave lower in pitch than the ordinary bassoon; contra bassoon.

double bed, a bed built to accommodate two persons. Most double beds have a standard size, usually 74 inches long and 54 inches wide.

dou|ble-bed|ded (dub′əl bed′id), *adj.* **1** having a double bed. **2** having two single beds.

double bill, two motion pictures, plays, or the like, on one program, for which a single admission is charged: *a double bill of opera and ballet* (Atlantic).

double bind, *Psychology.* an experience or situation in which a person receives contradictory cues or signals as to what he should do, so that whatever he does appears to be wrong.

dou|ble-bit|ted (dub′əl bit′əd), *adj.* having two cutting edges: *a double-bitted ax.*

dou|ble-blind (dub′əl blīnd′), *adj., n.* **—*adj.*** having to do with or designating a test or experiment in which neither the subjects nor the investigators know which of the subjects or substances are being tested and which are used as controls.
—*n.* a double-blind test or experiment: *Double-blind means that half the people in a test project are given real pills, and half are given dummies, with neither they nor the doctors knowing at the time which is which* (Good Housekeeping).

double boiler, a pair of pans, one of which fits part way down into the other. The food in the upper pan is cooked gently by the heat from the boiling water in the lower pan.

double bond, *Chemistry.* a compound in which two single valence bonds join two atoms, a characteristic of unsaturated compounds.

dou|ble-book (dub′əl bu̇k′), *v.t.* **1** to accept two reservations for (the same hotel room) so as to help insure its occupancy in the event of a cancellation. **2** to make two reservations for (a hotel room or the like) to be assured of obtaining it.

dou|ble-breast|ed (dub′əl bres′tid), *adj.* overlapping enough to make two thicknesses across the breast and having a double row of buttons: *a double-breasted jacket or coat.*

double bridle, a bridle having two reins, one controlling a curb bit, the other controlling a snaffle bit.

Pronunciation Key: hat, āge, cãre, fär; let, ēqual, tėrm; it, īce; hot, ōpen, ôrder; oil, out; cup, pu̇t, rüle; child; long; thin; ᴛʜen; zh, measure; ə represents **a** in about, **e** in taken, **i** in pencil, **o** in lemon, **u** in circus.

dou|ble-bub|ble (dub′əl bub′əl), *adj.* having a shape or structure the cross section of which is somewhat like that of one bubble on top of another: *a double-bubble fuselage.*

dou|ble-check (dub′əl chek′), *v., n.* —*v.t., v.i.* to check twice: *to double-check a report, to double-check for factual errors. Local police, who double-checked, decided he could go his way* (Time). —*n.* a check of something twice: *to make a double-check of safety apparatus.*

double chin, a soft fold of flesh under the chin.

dou|ble-chinned (dub′əl chind′), *adj.* having a double chin.

dou|ble-claw (dub′əl klô′), *n.* = unicorn plant.

dou|ble-clutch (dub′əl kluch′), *v.i.* to engage the clutch in neutral just prior to downshifting.

double coconut, a large, lobed coconut of the Seychelles, in the Indian Ocean; coco-de-mer.

dou|ble-con|cave lens (dub′əl kon′kāv, -kong′-), a lens with two concave surfaces, used in reducing glasses. See picture under **lens.**

dou|ble-con|vex lens (dub′əl kon veks′, -kən-), a lens with two convex surfaces, used in various magnifying glasses. See picture under **lens.**

double counterpoint, *Music.* a counterpoint with two parts that may be inverted, the lower part becoming the higher, or the higher part the lower.

dou|ble-cov|er (dub′əl kuv′ər), *v.t.* to cover (an opponent) with two players; double-team: *The other teams have to double-cover him all the time* (Time).

dou|ble-crest|ed cormorant (dub′əl kres′tid), the common cormorant of the coasts and inland waters of eastern North America, a large, greenish-black water bird with two crests on its head in summer.

dou|ble-crop|ping (dub′əl krop′ing), *n.* the raising of two or more crops on the same land in one season.

double cross, **1** *Informal.* an act of treachery: [*He*] *called the contract "a sell-out by the union and a double cross by the company"* (Wall Street Journal). **2** *Genetics.* the hybrid produced by two single crosses of inbred lines: *Jones' solution was simply to use seed from a double cross instead of a single cross* (Scientific American).

dou|ble-cross (dub′əl krôs′, -kros′), *v.t., v.i. Informal.* to promise to do one thing and then do another; be treacherous (to): *A wealthy uncle who double-crossed them by leaving his money to charities* (P. G. Wodehouse). —**dou′ble-cross′er,** *n.*

Dou|ble-Cros|tic (dub′əl krôs′tik, -kros′-), *n. Trademark.* a kind of crossword puzzle in which the words formed produce a quotation, which is then transcribed so that the initial letters of its words form an acrostic of the author of the quotation and the title of the work in which the quotation appears.

***double dagger,** a mark used to refer the reader to another section or to a note in a book; diesis.

***double dagger**

‡ …preliminary figures are given in the report‡.

‡Report of the Committee…

dou|ble-dare (dub′əl dãr′), *v.t.,* **-dared, -dar|ing.** to challenge or dare with double emphasis: *But the little boy said, "Who's scared of your grandma? I just double-dare her!"* (Guy Endore).

double date, a date in which two couples go out together.

dou|ble-date (dub′əl dāt′), *v.i.,* **-dat|ed, -dat|ing.** to go out with a person of the opposite sex and another couple.

dou|ble-deal (dub′əl dēl′), *v.i.,* **-dealt** (-delt′), **-deal|ing.** to practice deception; cheat; deceive: *It is Don Lope who is ill and she who double-deals pretending to call a doctor for him with her finger pressed firmly down on the telephone rest* (Penelope Gilliatt). [back formation < *double-dealing*] —**dou′ble-deal′er,** *n.*

dou|ble-deal|ing (dub′əl dē′ling), *n., adj.* —*n.* a pretending to do one thing and then doing another; deceitful action or behavior: *There were some who feared the U.S. could expect only grief and double-dealing in any … conferences with the Communists* (Newsweek).
—*adj.* ready to deceive; deceitful.

dou|ble-deck (dub′əl dek′), *adj., v.* —*adj.* having or consisting of two decks, levels, tiers, or layers: *a double-deck bus, a double-deck garage, a double-deck bed.*
—*v.t.* to make or arrange in two decks, levels, etc.: *to double-deck a bridge.*

dou|ble-decked (dub′əl dekt′), *adj.* = double-deck.

***dou|ble-deck|er** (dub′əl dek′ər), *n.* **1** something with two decks, floors, levels, tiers, or layers, such as a ship with two decks above the main deck, or a bus, railroad car, or aircraft having an upper floor with seats: *A bed with two levels, one above the other, is a double-decker.* **2** *U.S.* a sandwich made with three slices of bread and two layers of filling.

***double-decker** definition 1

double decomposition, *Chemistry.* metathesis (def. 2).

dou|ble-dig|it (dub′əl dij′it), *adj.* having to do with or marked by increases of 10 per cent or more, especially as shown in economic indicators, such as the consumer price index: *double-digit inflation, double-digit unemployment.*

double dipping, *U.S. Informal.* the system or policy of allowing a person who has retired from government service, especially military service, to continue receiving his pension after taking another government job: *Critics of the dual compensation …, including many Congressmen, consider "double dipping" typical of the ways in which the military pension system has become overly generous* (New York Times).

dou|ble|dome (dub′əl dōm′), *n. U.S. Slang.* a person of advanced intellect and refined taste; highbrow: *Miss Dunham has lectured at Yale University. She must have been the most popular visiting doubledome* (Wall Street Journal).

double dribble, *Basketball.* a violation in which a player dribbles the ball with both hands at the same time or stops dribbling and starts again.

double dummy, a game of bridge or whist for two players in which two hands are exposed, so that each of the players manages two hands.

double Dutch, a language or speech which is not understandable; gibberish.

dou|ble-du|ty (dub′əl dü′tē, -dyü′-), *adj.* that can be used in two ways; serving two functions: *a double-duty food mixer that can be used as both a mixer and a drink blender* (Wall Street Journal).

dou|ble-dye (dub′əl dī′), *v.t.,* **-dyed, -dye|ing.** **1** to dye twice. **2** *Figurative.* to imbue deeply.

dou|ble-dyed (dub′əl dīd′), *adj.* **1** twice dyed. **2** *Figurative.* deeply imbued; thorough; complete: *The speaker is a double-dyed fundamentalist.*

double eagle, a former gold coin of the United States, worth 20 dollars.

dou|ble-edged (dub′əl ejd′), *adj.* **1** having two cutting edges; two-edged. **2** cutting or acting both ways; as much against as for: *a double-edged compliment.*

dou|ble-end|ed (dub′əl en′did), *adj.* identical or very similar at both ends: *a double-ended walking stick. They grow a double-ended coconut* (Time).

dou|ble-end|er (dub′əl en′dər), *n.* **1** anything that is double-ended. **2** a ferryboat, trolley car, subway train, locomotive, etc., so designed and equipped as to be able to travel in either direction.

dou|ble-en|ten|dre (dü blän tän′drə), *n.* a word or expression with two meanings, one of which is often indelicate or improper: *He can make a double-entendre palatable to the worst prude* (Newsweek). [< obsolete French *double entendre* double meaning]

dou|ble en|tente (dü blän tänt′), *French.* double meaning; a vague or ambiguous sense.

double entry, a system of bookkeeping in which each transaction is written down twice, once on the credit side of the ledger and once on the debit side of the ledger.

dou|ble-en|try (dub′əl en′trē), *adj.* in or using the system of double entry.

double envelopment, a closing in and surrounding both flanks of an enemy at the same time.

double exposure, *Photography.* the exposure of the same surface or section of a roll of film twice: *In amateur photography the beginner's classic blunder is the double exposure* (Newsweek).

dou|ble-faced (dub′əl fāst′), *adj.* **1** having two faces or aspects: *double-faced cloth, a double-faced problem.* **2** *Figurative.* pretending to be what one is not; hypocritical; two-faced: *Fame, if not double-faced, is double-mouthed* (Milton).
SYN: insincere, deceitful.

double fault, *Tennis.* the making of two successive faults, causing the loss of a point.

dou|ble-fault (dub′əl fôlt′), *v.i. Tennis.* to make a double fault.

double feature, two motion pictures on one program for which a single admission is charged; double bill: *During the depression in the 1930's, movie theaters began to present double features* (Eric Johnston).

double fertilization, *Botany.* fertilization of the egg nucleus by one male nucleus and the polar nuclei by another male nucleus, especially characteristic of angiosperms.

double first, **1** the highest honors in two subjects at an English university. **2** a student who wins these honors.

dou|ble-flow|ered (dub′əl flou′ərd), *adj.* having double flowers; having flowers with an unusually large number of petals.

double fugue, *Music.* a fugue having two themes.

dou|ble|gang|er (dub′əl gang′ər), *n.* = Doppelgänger. [partial translation of German *Doppelgänger*]

double glazing, glazing consisting of two layers of glass separated by an air space: *A storm window provides the simplest kind of double glazing.*

double harp, a triangular shaped harp, with two separately tuned rows of catgut strings; David's harp.

dou|ble-head|ed (dub′əl hed′id), *adj.* **1** having two heads: *a double-headed ax.* **2** having good and bad qualities: *Atomic energy remains a double-headed creature* (Manchester Guardian). **3** double; twofold: *the double-headed threat to security—inflation and war.*

dou|ble-head|er (dub′əl hed′ər), *n.* **1** two baseball games between the same teams played one after the other on the same day. **2a** a railroad train pulled by two locomotives. **b** two locomotives attached to one train.

dou|ble-heart|ed (dub′əl här′tid), *adj.* false at heart; deceitful; treacherous. —**dou′ble-heart′ed-ness,** *n.*

dou|ble-hel|i|cal (dub′əl hel′ə kəl), *adj.* consisting of two strands that coil around each other to form a double spiral or helix: *Until the dramatic announcement of the double-helical structure of DNA, there was complete ignorance of how a chemical substance could carry out the multifold activities needed for a genetic substance* (James D. Watson).

double helix, **1** the structure of a molecule of DNA, made up of two helical strands of alternating phosphate and sugar units connected by bases of adenine, guanine, thymine, and cytosine: *The irony was that the physicists-turned-biologists and their immediate collaborators promptly … discovered the double helix, and opened up vistas of genetic engineering that were anything but "safe"* (Donald Fleming). **2** the DNA molecule itself.

dou|ble-hung (dub′əl hung′), *adj.* (of a window) having two sashes, one above the other, each counterbalanced by weights or friction devices.

double image, an image in a painting that represents two widely differing things at the same time, such as a chair that is also a human figure or a hill that is also a sleeping animal.

double indemnity, a provision or clause in a life insurance policy, whereby the company agrees to pay the beneficiary twice the face value of the policy in the event of the insured person's accidental death.

double jeopardy, *U.S. Law.* the trying of a person a second time for an offense he was acquitted of at a previous legal trial. Double jeopardy is prohibited by the fifth amendment of the Constitution.

dou|ble-job|ber (dub′əl job′ər), *n. British.* a person who works at a second job to supplement the wages of the regular job.

dou|ble-job|bing (dub′əl job′ing), *n. British.* the practice of working at a second job to supplement the wages of the regular job.

dou|ble-joint|ed (dub′əl join′tid), *adj.* having joints that let fingers, arms, legs, and other appendages, bend in unusual ways.

double knit, a specially stitched fabric having twice the usual thickness: *A double knit is any knit made with two sets of needles, creating a fabric of double thickness* (Duncan G. Steck).
—**dou′ble-knit′,** *adj.*

dou|ble|leaf (du′bəl lēf′), *n., pl.* **-leaves.** any one of several orchids having broad leaves; twayblade.

dou|ble-lock (dub′əl lok′), *v.t.* to lock by two turns of the key, as in some forms of lock.

dou|ble-mind|ed (dub′əl mīn′did), *adj.* undecided in mind; wavering: *A double-minded man is unstable in all his ways* (James 1:8). —**dou′ble-mind′ed|ness,** *n.*

double negative, a statement having two negative words and expressing a negative meaning. *Example:* "There wasn't no answer to my call" = "There was no answer to my call" or "There wasn't any answer to my call."

► **double negative.** In earlier English the use of two or more negative terms was quite permissible: *I can't see no wit in her* (Charles Lamb), but it is now considered as substandard. Currently, on the educated level, the double negative is likely to occur only in connection with *hardly, scarcely, but,* etc.: *There was hardly nothing to eat* (properly, *hardly anything*). *He can't help but think so* (properly, *can't help thinking* or *cannot but think*) .

dou|ble-nick|el (dub′əl nik′əl), *n. U.S. Slang.* 55 miles per hour (the nationwide highway speed limit established in 1973): *If you are driving at 55, you are doing the double-nickel* (Michael Harwood).

double obelisk, = double dagger.

double or nothing, the doubling of a bet or of the stakes in order to retrieve or cancel out previous losses.

dou|ble-park (dub′əl pärk′), *v.t., v.i.* to park (a car, truck, or bus) beside another vehicle which is occupying the parking space. —**dou′ble-park′er**, *n.*

double play, a defensive play in baseball in which two players are put out: *Dusty Rhodes, batting for Katt, grounded sharply to the mound and Newk had an easy double play by way of second* (New York Times).

dou|ble-play (dub′əl plā′), *adj. Baseball.* **1** adept at making double plays: *a double-play combination.* **2** having to do with or leading to a double play: *double-play position.*

double pneumonia, pneumonia affecting both lungs.

double possessive, a phrase indicating possession, both by the preposition *of* and by the possessive case. *Example:* a book of mine, a play of Shakespeare's.

double printing, the producing of two or more negatives on one print to give the appearance of a single composition.

dou|ble-quick (dub′əl kwik′), *n., adj., adv., v.* —***n.*** the next quickest step to a run in marching; double time.
—***adj.*** very quick.
—***adv.*** in double-quick time.
—***v.i.***, ***v.t.*** to march in double-quick step.

dou|bler (dub′lər), *n.* a person or thing that makes doubles, as by folding or copying.

dou|ble-reed (dub′əl rēd′), *adj.* having two reeds bound together in the mouthpiece that are made to vibrate against each other by the breath, thus producing the tone: *The oboe and bassoon are double-reed instruments.*

double refraction, *Physics.* the formation of two unequally refracted rays when a ray of light passes through certain types of crystals.

double rhyme, a rhyme of two syllables of which the second is unstressed, as in *cavern, tavern.*

dou|ble-ring (dub′əl ring′), *adj.* in which bride and groom give each other a wedding ring: *a double-ring ceremony.*

dou|ble-rip|per (dub′əl rip′ər), *n.* a double-runner.

dou|ble-rule (dub′əl rül′), *v.t.*, **-ruled, -rul|ing.** *Bookkeeping.* to draw two lines beneath (accounts that are balanced).

dou|ble-run|ner (dub′əl run′ər), *n.* two sleds connected by a board, for coasting.

dou|bles (dub′əlz), *n.pl.* See under **double.**

double salt, *Chemistry.* a salt that ionizes in solution as two separate salts, but forms a single substance on crystallization: *Alum is a double salt composed of aluminum and another salt, such as potassium.*

double scull, a light racing boat for two rowers.

dou|ble-scull (dub′əl skul′), *v.t., v.i.* to row (a double scull) with four oars.

∗**double sharp**, a sign that a note must be raised two half tones above the natural pitch.

∗**double sharp**

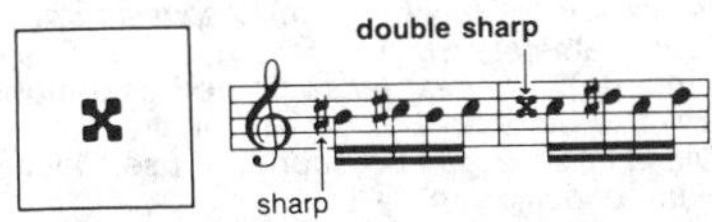

double shift, two groups or shifts of persons at work in a factory, school, or other institution or business, one following the other: *It is already overcrowded and must operate on a double shift . . . to accommodate all 1,280 children* (Atlantic).

dou|ble-shift (dub′əl shift′), *adj.* operating on a double shift: *double-shift classes at school.*

dou|ble-space (dub′əl spās′), *v.t., v.i.*, **-spaced, -spac|ing.** to leave a blank space between every line in typing: *to double-space a letter .*

dou|ble|speak (dub′əl spēk′), *n.* speaking falsely; speaking to deceive: *Before it had learned caution and the art of doublespeak, the American Communist Party advocated the violent overthrow of democratic institutions* (Saturday Review). [coined by George Orwell, 1903-1950, an English novelist]

double spread, an illustration or advertisement spread across two adjoining pages of a book, magazine, or newspaper: *These magnificent double spreads are scattered throughout all three volumes* (Harper's).

double standard, a standard applied more leniently to one group than to another, especially the stricter moral behavior demanded of women than of men: *He maintains a double standard throughout his diary, using one set of values for his side and another for the enemy* (New Yorker).

double star, **1** two stars so close together that they look like one to the naked eye: *Since double stars are so plentiful in the Galaxy, it is clear that they are no casual and trivial phenomenon* (W. H. Marshall). **2** = binary star.

double steal, *Baseball.* the stealing of or the attempt to steal two bases by two runners on the same play, usually with one runner starting out before the other.

double stem, a skiing movement in which the toes of the skis are brought together and the rear ends are pushed outward, thus slowing down the skier's speed.

dou|ble-stop (dub′əl stop′), *n., v.*, **-stopped, -stop|ping.** —***n.*** the stopping of two strings (of a violin, cello, or other bowed string instrument) at the same time. —***v.i.*** to stop two strings of an instrument at the same time.

double summer time, *British.* time that is two hours ahead of Greenwich Time, or one hour ahead of daylight-saving time.

∗**dou|blet** (dub′lit), *n.* **1** a man's close-fitting jacket, with or without sleeves. Men in Europe wore doublets from the 1400's to the 1600's. **2** a pair of two similar or equal things; couple. **3** one of a pair. **4** one of two or more different words in a language derived from the same original source but coming by different routes. *Example:* 1) *aptitude* and *attitude. Aptitude* came into English as a direct borrowing from Late Latin *aptitudo, aptitudinis.* However this Latin word was taken into Italian in the form *attitudine,* which was later further changed to *attitude* in French, from which it came into English. 2) *fragile* and *frail. Fragile* came into English as a direct borrowing from the Latin *fragilis.* However, the word *fragilis* changed to *frele* (or *fraile*) in French, from which it came into English in the form *frail.* **5** an imitation gem made of two pieces of glass or crystal with a layer of color between them. **6** *Printing, U.S.* a word or phrase set a second time by mistake.
doublets, two dice thrown that show the same number on each side facing up.
[< Old French *doublet* (originally) a "double" fabric < *doubler* to double + *-et* -et]

∗**doublet**
definition 1

double tackle, a system of ropes and blocks in which each block contains two grooved wheels.

dou|ble-take (dub′əl tāk′), *n.* an unthinking acceptance of a remark or situation followed by a second, delayed response displaying a surprised, sudden understanding, often used as a comic device by actors.

dou|ble|talk (dub′əl tôk′), *n., v.* —***n.*** **1** speech that is purposely meaningless, but seems meaningful because normal words and intonations are mixed in. **2** evasive, ambiguous, or deceitful talk: *political doubletalk.*
—***v.i.*** to speak in doubletalk: *Powerful newspapers still cower, leading churchmen still doubletalk* (Newsweek).
—***v.t.*** to use doubletalk on: *He'd go back in there day after day and doubletalk those people wonderfully* (Time). —**dou′ble|talk′er**, *n.*

dou|ble-team (dub′əl tēm′), *v.t. Sports.* **1** to assign two players to guard or block (an opponent). **2** to join together to guard or block (an opponent): *to double-team a tall center in basketball.*

dou|blet|ed (dub′lə tid), *adj.* wearing a doublet.

Double Ten, the national holiday of Taiwan (Nationalist China), celebrated on October 10, the anniversary of the founding of the Chinese republic in 1911. Its name refers to the date, which is the 10th day of the 10th month.

dou|ble|think or **dou|ble-think** (dub′əl thingk′), *n., v.* —***n.*** the ability to hold and accept two contradictory points of view at the same time: *By a strange exercise of doublethink, he seems to have felt simultaneously fulfilled and frustrated when his play became a hit* (New Yorker).
—***v.i.*** to engage in doublethink. —***v.t.*** to manage or maneuver by doublethink: *I suppose your Left-wing intellectuals will be able to double-think their way around that!* (Manchester Guardian Weekly). [coined by George Orwell, 1903-1950, an English novelist] —**dou′ble-think′er**, *n.*

double time, **1** a rate of marching in the United States Army in which 180 paces, each of 36 inches, are taken in a minute; double-quick. **2** double the usual rate of pay, for example for working overtime.

dou|ble-time (dub′əl tīm′), *v.*, **-timed, -tim|ing.**
—***v.i.*** to march at double time.
—***v.t.*** to order to march at double time.

dou|ble|ton (dub′əl tən), *n. Bridge.* an original holding of only two cards in a given suit. [< *double* + (single) *ton*]

dou|ble-tongue (dub′əl tung′), *v.i.*, **-tongued, -tongu|ing.** to vibrate the tongue very fast against the teeth and the hard palate in playing staccato passages on the trumpet, flute, or other wind instrument.

dou|ble-tongued (dub′əl tungd′), *adj.* speaking inconsistently; deceitful in speech.

dou|ble-tooth (dub′əl tüth′), *n.* a composite herb with prickly, seedlike fruit; bur marigold.

double touch, an adjustment of the keyboard action of an organ by which different effects are produced when the keys are depressed partially or wholly.

dou|ble|tree (dub′əl trē′), *n.* the crossbar on a carriage, wagon, plow, or other horse-drawn vehicle or machinery. When two horses are used, the singletrees of their harnesses are attached to this crossbar.

dou|blets (dub′lits), *n.pl.* See under **doublet.**

double vision, a disorder of the eyes in which objects are seen double; diplopia.

dou|ble|wide (dub′əl wīd′), *n.* a mobile home formed of two trailers fastened together side-by-side: *The industry expects doublewides to capture 50% of the market in three years* (Wall Street Journal).

double wing formation, an offensive formation in football with two wing backs.

dou|bling (dub′ling), *n.* **1** the act of a person or thing that doubles. **2** the second distillation of wine. **3** something that is doubled or folded over; fold. **4** an addition that makes double, such as the lining of a cloak.

dou|bloon (du blün′), *n.* a Spanish gold coin widely used in Spanish America until the 1800's, and equal to four pistoles. [< Spanish *doblón* < *doble* double < Latin *duplus*]

dou|blure (dü blʏr′), *n.* an ornamental lining, usually of leather or silk, on the inside of a book cover. [< French *doublure* < Old French *doubler;* see etym. under **double**]

dou|bly (dub′lē), *adv.* **1** in a double manner, amount, or degree; twice as; twice: *Doubly careful means twice as careful.* **2** two at a time. **3** *Archaic.* deceitfully.

doubt (dout), *v., n.* —***v.t.*** **1** to not believe or trust; not be sure of; feel uncertain about: *The captain doubted whether the leaking ship would reach land. I doubt that he wrote the letter.* SYN: mistrust, question. **2** *Archaic.* to be afraid of; fear.
—***v.i.*** to be uncertain or undecided: *O thou of little faith, wherefore didst thou doubt?* (Matthew 14:31).
—***n.*** **1** difficulty in believing; lack of trust or confidence; uncertainty: *Faith casts out doubt.* SYN: See syn. under **suspicion. 2** a feeling of uncertainty; uncertain state of mind: *We were in doubt as to the right road.* **3** an uncertain condition of affairs: *The ship's fate is still in doubt. In such a case, the defendant is entitled to the benefit of the doubt.* **4** *Obsolete.* fear; apprehension.
beyond doubt, surely; certainly: *He is beyond doubt the smartest boy in the class.*
no doubt, a certainly; surely: *No doubt we will win in the end.* **b** probably: *No doubt you're right, but others don't agree.*
without doubt, surely; certainly: *You can accept his decision without doubt.*
[< Old French *douter* < Latin *dubitāre* < *dubius* doubtful; spelling influenced by Latin]
—**doubt′er**, *n.*
▶**doubt.** The standard idiom in negative statements is *doubt that* (rather than *doubt but that* or *doubt but what*): *I do not doubt that he means well.* In positive statements it is *doubt whether* though now especially *doubt if* has taken its place: *I doubt whether he means well. I doubt if I can come.*

doubt|a|ble (dou′tə bəl), *adj.* that can be doubted.

doubt|ful (dout′fəl), *adj.* **1** full of doubt; not sure; undecided; uncertain: *We are doubtful about the*

Pronunciation Key: hat, āge, cãre, fär; let, ēqual, tėrm; it, īce; hot, ōpen, ôrder; oil, out; cup, pu̇t, rüle; child; long; thin; ᴛʜen; zh, measure; ə represents **a** in about, **e** in taken, **i** in pencil, **o** in lemon, **u** in circus.

weather for tomorrow. **2** causing doubt; open to question or suspicion: *Her sly questions made her sincerity doubtful. Any fact, any assumption, any theory, that has not been tested ... is at best a doubtful thing* (Atlantic). **3** of questionable character: *a person of doubtful reputation.* — **doubt′ful|ly**, *adv.* — **doubt′ful|ness**, *n.*

— *Syn.* **1 Doubtful, dubious** mean uncertain. **Doubtful** usually implies only lack of certainty: *I am doubtful about his ability to do that kind of work.* **Dubious** often implies suspicion: *I am dubious about his stories of early success.*

doubt|ing (dou′ting), *adj.* that doubts. — **doubt′ing|ly**, *adv.*

doubting Thomas, a person who doubts everything: *If there were any doubting Thomases, they thought it prudent to keep their doubts to themselves* (Punch). [< *Thomas,* the Apostle who doubted Christ's resurrection. John 20:24-29.]

doubt|less (dout′lis), *adv., adj.* — ***adv.*** **1** without doubt; surely; certainly. **SYN**: unquestionably, undoubtedly. **2** probably; no doubt: *Doubtless the United States Supreme Court eventually will find these cases on its docket* (Wall Street Journal).
— ***adj.*** having no doubts; sure; certain. **SYN**: undoubted, indubitable. — **doubt′less|ly**, *adv.*
— **doubt′less|ness**, *n.*

douce (düs), *adj.* **1** *Scottish.* quiet; steady; modest: *A douce woman she was, civil to the customers* (Scott). **2** *Obsolete.* sweet; pleasant. [< Old French *doux,* earlier *dous* and *dulz* sweet < Latin *dulcis*] — **douce′ly**, *adv.* — **douce′ness**, *n.*

dou|ce|peres (düs′pãrz′), *n.pl.* = douzepers.

dou|ceur (dü sœr′), *n.* **1** a fee or tip. **2** a bribe. **3** sweetness; agreeableness; amiability. [< French *douceur* < Old French *dousor,* earlier *dulçur* < *dous,* and *dulz* sweet; see etym. under **douce**]

dou|ceur de viv|re (dü sœr′ də vēv′rə), *French.* **1** the pleasures or good things of life; enjoyment of living: *We think of that* [*Edwardian*] *time as tinted by an even tone of elegance: clothes, panelled rooms, paintings, letters, manners, cooking, all contributory to an infinite douceur de vivre* (Sunday Times). **2** (literally) sweetness of living.

douche (düsh), *n., v.,* **douched, douch|ing.** — ***n.*** **1** a jet of water, antiseptic solution, or the like applied on or into any part of the body: *A douche of salt water up my nose helped relieve the cold in my head.* **2** the application of a douche. **3** a spray, syringe, or other device for applying a douche.
— ***v.t.*** to apply a douche to.
— ***v.i.*** to take a douche.
[< French *douche* < Italian *doccia* shower; conduit, ultimately < Latin *dūcere* to lead]

dough (dō), *n.* **1** a soft, thick mixture of flour, milk or water, fat, and other materials from which bread, biscuits, cake, and pie crust are made. **2** any soft, thick mass like this. **3** *Informal.* money: *Great, all right, to be earning your own dough* (James T. Farrell). **4** *U.S. Informal.* an infantryman; doughboy: *These, in our generation, have been known first as the Doughboys, and then the Doughs, and now the Dogfaces* (Harper's). [Old English *dāg*] — **dough′like′**, *adj.*

dough bird, = Eskimo curlew.

dough|boy (dō′boi′), *n.* **1** *U.S. Informal.* an infantryman in the United States Army during World War I. **2** a dumpling. [< *dough* + *boy* (supposedly because the soldiers in the Mexican War used dough to make hot meals, after fighting)]

dough|face (dō′fās′), *n.* **1** a face having the appearance of dough. **2** a person with such a face. **3** a person who is easily influenced; yielding person. **4** *U.S. History.* a Northern politician who was too eager to agree with the wishes of the South on slavery.

dough|foot (dō′fůt′), *n., pl.* **-feet.** *U.S. Informal.* doughboy.

dough|head (dō′hed′), *n. U.S. Slang.* a stupid person; dimwit.

dough|less (dō′lis), *adj.* **1** *U.S. Slang.* without money. **2** not made with dough.

dough|nut (dō′nut′), *n.* **1** a small cake of sweetened dough cooked in deep fat. A doughnut is usually cut in the shape of a ring. **2** a circular tube in a betatron or synchrotron that contains a vacuum in which electrons whirl and collide with the nuclei of the atoms in a small tungsten target to produce extremely powerful X rays and gamma rays. **3** any doughnut-shaped device: *Recent results reported by Soviet workers indicate that Tokamak 3's doughnut may well be leading the field* (New Scientist).
(it is) dollars to doughnuts. See under **dollar**.

dought (dout), *v.* past tense of **dow**[1].

dough|ti|ly (dou′tə lē), *adv.* in a doughty manner: *The old scheme has seldom been so doughtily exploited* (Time).

dough|ti|ness (dou′tē nis), *n.* doughty quality; bravery.

dough|ty (dou′tē), *adj.,* **-ti|er, -ti|est.** strong and bold; stout; brave; valiant: *doughty knights.* **SYN**: worthy, formidable. [Old English *dohtig* < *dugan* be good, worthy]

dough|y (dō′ē), *adj.,* **dough|i|er, dough|i|est.** of or like dough; soft and thick; pale and flabby.

Doug|las fir (dug′ləs), an evergreen tree of the pine family, often over 200 feet high, common in the western United States and in British Columbia, Canada. Its strong, durable wood is used for construction, railroad ties, etc. [American English < David *Douglas,* 1798-1834, a Scottish botanist and explorer]

Douglas spruce, pine, or **hemlock**, = Douglas fir.

Douglas squirrel, a squirrel of the Pacific coast forests, considered by some to be a subspecies of the red squirrel of North America; chickaree.

Dou|kho|bors (dü′kə bôrz), *n.pl.* a Russian Christian sect whose members migrated in large numbers to Canada in 1899 because they refused military service; spirit wrestlers. Also, **Dukhobors**. [< Russian *dukhobortsy* < *dukh* spirit + *bortsy* wrestlers]

doum (düm), *n.* = doum palm.

Dou|ma or **dou|ma** (dü′mə), *n.* = Duma.

doum palm, a large palm of northern and central Africa which bears an edible fruit about the size of an apple and tastes somewhat like gingerbread; gingerbread tree. [< Arabic *daum*]

doup|pi|o|ni (dü′pē ō′nē, dyü′-), *n.* = dupion.

dour (důr, dour), *adj.* **1** gloomy or sullen: *The boy was sulking in dour silence.* **2** stern; severe: *a dour look. His dour remarks frightened the child. The Prime Minister is immensely popular among the stolid and dour northerners* (New York Times). **SYN**: hard, fierce. **3** stubborn; obstinate. [< Latin *dūrus* hard, stern. See etym. of doublets **dure**[1], **duro.**] — **dour′ly**, *adv.* — **dour′ness**, *n.*

dou|ra or **dou|rah** (důr′ə), *n.* = durra.

dou|ri|cou|li (důr′i kü′lē), *n., pl.* **-lis.** a South American monkey about 12 inches long and with large eyes. It is active only at night. [< a native name]

dou|rine (dů rēn′), *n.* a venereal disease of horses, asses, and mules caused by a sporozoan parasite. [< French *dourine*]

dou|rou|cou|li (důr′ü kü′lē), *n., pl.* **-lis.** = douricouli.

Dou|sa|bel (dü′sə bel), *n.* a common name for a rustic sweetheart in old pastoral poems. Also, **Dowsabel.** [variant of *Dulcibella,* a proper name]

douse[1] (dous), *v.,* **doused, dous|ing,** *n.* — ***v.t.*** **1** to plunge into water or any other liquid: *to clean fruit by dousing it in cold water.* **SYN**: immerse. **2** to throw water over; drench: *The fireman doused the flames.*
— ***v.i.*** to plunge or be plunged into a liquid.
— ***n.*** a thorough dousing; drench: *I used to have to pick mint leaves for a last-minute macerating with vinegar and sugar—a horrid douse* (M. F. K. Fisher). Also, **dowse.**
[origin uncertain]

douse[2] (dous), *v.,* **doused, dous|ing,** *n.* — ***v.t.*** **1** *Informal.* to put out (a light); extinguish: *Douse the candles. He rose every morning before dawn to douse the same lights* (New York Times). **2** *Informal.* to take off; doff: *He doused his hat before entering the house.* **3** to lower or slacken (a sail) in haste. **4** to close (a porthole).
— ***n.*** a blow; stroke: *He gave the young man a douse in the chops* (Tobias Smollett). Also, **dowse.**
[perhaps < Middle Dutch *dossen* to beat, strike]

dous|er[1] (dou′sər), *n.* a person or thing that douses or drenches. [< *dous*(e)[1] + *-er*[1]]

dous|er[2] (dou′sər), *n.* **1** a person or thing that douses or extinguishes. **2** *Motion Pictures.* the shutter of a film projector which intercepts the light from reaching the film. Also, **dowser.** [< *dous*(e)[2] + *-er*[1]]

do ut des (dō′ ut dēz′), *Latin.* I give that you may give (used of a contract or its conditions).

dou|ze|pers (düz′pãrz′), *n.pl., sing.* **-per** (-pãr′). **1** the twelve peers or paladins represented in old romances as in attendance on Charlemagne. **2** a group of twelve great spiritual and temporal peers of medieval France. [< Old French *douze pers* twelve peers]

do|vap (dō′vap), *n.* a method for determining the velocity and position of a moving object, especially a missile, rocket, or aircraft, by means of radio signals which are sent out in a certain frequency, received and returned by the moving object, and then interpreted in accordance with the Doppler effect. [< *Do*(ppler) *v*(elocity) *a*(nd) *p*(osition)]

DoVAP (no periods), dovap; Doppler velocity and position.

dove[1] (duv), *n.* **1** a bird with a thick body, short legs, and a beak enlarged at the tip. It is a small kind of pigeon that is not domesticated. The dove is often a symbol of peace. **2** *Informal, Figurative.* a person who is opposed to war or to confrontation of force; person who seeks accommodation with an enemy instead of making war: *In our opinion, the general run of Americans—whether hawks or doves, or neither—are deeply preoccupied with the war* (New Yorker). *The President took partial account of views held by the two extreme poles of thinking, the war "hawks" ... and the peace "doves"* (New York Times). **3** *Figurative.* an innocent, gentle, or loving person.
(the) Dove, the Holy Ghost: *Return, O holy Dove, return* (William Cowper).
[perhaps Old English *dūfe-,* as in *dūfe-doppa* dabchick] — **dove′like′**, *adj.*

dove[2] (dōv), *v.* a past tense of **dive**: *The diver dove deep into the water after the sunken treasure.*
► **dove, dived.** Though *dived* is generally regarded as the proper form, *dove* is commonly used, especially in informal English.

dove color, a gray with a tinge of pink or purple.

dove-col|ored (duv′kul′ərd), *adj.* gray with a tinge of pink or purple.

dove|cot (duv′kot′), *n.* = dovecote.

dove|cote (duv′kōt′), *n.* a small house or shelter for doves or pigeons; columbary: *Like an eagle in a dovecot* (Shakespeare).

dove|house (duv′hous′), *n.* = dovecote.

dove|ish (duv′ish), *adj.* = dovish.

dove|kie or **dove|key** (duv′kē), *n.* **1** a small black and white auk with a short, stout bill, common in the north Atlantic and Arctic regions; rotche. **2** = black guillemot. [Scottish diminutive of *dove*[1]]

dove plant, an orchid of Central America. The central part of its flower looks somewhat like a white dove with expanded wings.

dove pox, an infectious disease which attacks doves; pigeon pox.

do|ver (dō′vər), *v., n. Scottish.* — ***v.i.*** to fall into a state between sleeping and waking; slumber.
— ***n.*** a state of slumber. [apparently frequentative of dialectal *dove* doze]

Do|ver's powder (dō′vərz), a medicine containing ipecac and opium, used especially to induce perspiration and reduce pain. [< Thomas *Dover,* 1660-1742, an English physician, who used it]

dove|tail** (duv′tāl′), *n., v.* — ***n. **1** a projection at the end of a piece of wood, metal, or plastic, that can be fitted into a corresponding opening at the end of another piece to form a joint. **2** the joint formed in this way.
— ***v.t.*** **1** to fasten, join, or fit together with dovetails. **2** *Figurative.* to join compactly or harmoniously: *The plan ... would dovetail limitations on nuclear weapons with cutbacks in conventional arms* (Wall Street Journal).
— ***v.i.*** **1** to fit together exactly: *The various pieces of evidence dovetailed so completely that the mystery was solved at once.* **2** *Figurative.* to fit compactly or harmoniously.

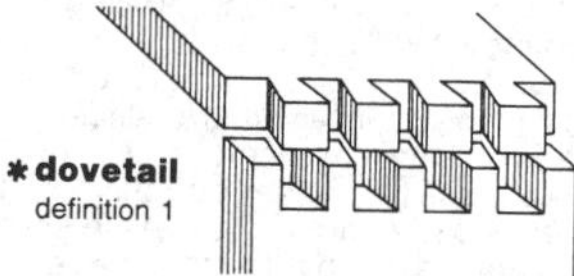

***dovetail**
definition 1

dove|tailed (duv′tāld′), *adj. Heraldry.* broken into dovetails, as a dividing line of a shield.

dove tree, a hardy, deciduous tree common to China, often attaining a height of 60 feet. It belongs to the dogwood family.

dov|ish (duv′ish), *adj.* **1** like a dove. **2** *Informal, Figurative.* opposed to war or to the use of force in a conflict; tending to seek accommodation with an enemy instead of making war: *New Hampshire is considered hawkish and Wisconsin dovish* (David Halberstam).

dow[1] (dou, dō), *v.i., past tense* **dowed** or **dought.** *Scottish.* **1** to be able. **2** to do well; thrive; prosper. [Old English *dugan* be strong, of use. Compare etym. under **doughty.**]

dow[2] (dou), *n.* = dhow.

Dow (dou), *n. U.S. Informal.* = Dow-Jones average (especially the Dow-Jones Industrial Average).

Dow., dowager.

dow|a|ble (dou′ə bəl), *adj. Law.* entitled to dower.

dow|a|ger (dou′ə jər), *n.* **1** a widow who holds some title or property from her dead husband: *The queen and her mother-in-law, the queen dowager, were both present.* **2** *Informal.* a dignified, elderly woman, usually of high social position. [< Old French *douagere* < *douage* dower < *douer* endow < Latin *dōtāre* < *dōs, dōtis* dowry, dot]

dow|di|ly (dou′də lē), *adv.* in a dowdy manner; shabbily.

dow|di|ness (dou′dē nis), *n.* dowdy quality or condition; shabbiness.

dow|dy (dou′dē), *adj.*, **-di|er, -di|est,** *n., pl.* **-dies.** —*adj.* poorly dressed; not neat; not stylish; shabby: *a dress ... dowdy with age* (Anthony Trollope).
—*n.* a woman whose clothes are shabby or not stylish: *The Duchess of Albemarle, who is ever a plain, homely dowdy* (Samuel Pepys).
[perhaps < earlier *dowd* a dowdy person; origin uncertain]

dow|dy|ish (dou′dē ish), *adj.* somewhat dowdy; like a dowdy.

***dow|el** (dou′əl), *n., v.,* **-eled, -el|ing** or (*especially British*) **-elled, -el|ling.** —*n.* **1** a peg on a piece of wood, metal, or plastic, made to fit into a corresponding hole in another piece, so as to form a joint fastening the two pieces together. **2** a piece of wood driven into a wall to receive nails or screws.
—*v.t.* to fasten with dowels; furnish with dowels. [Middle English *dowle,* perhaps related to Middle Low German *dovel* plug, tap (of a cask)]

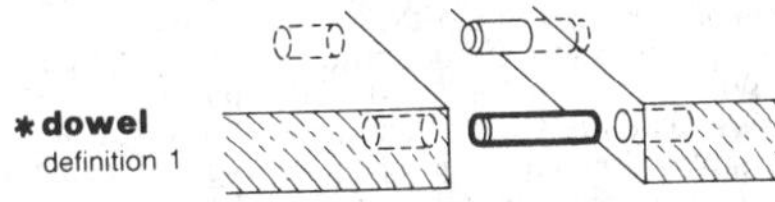
***dowel**
definition 1

dow|er (dou′ər), *n., v.* —*n.* **1** *Law.* a widow's share for life of her dead husband's property. **2** = dowry. **3** *Figurative.* a natural gift, talent, or quality; endowment.
—*v.t.* to provide with a dower; endow: *Nature has dowered her with both beauty and brains.*
[< Old French *douaire,* earlier *doaire* < Medieval Latin *dotarium* < Latin *dōtāre* endow; see etym. under **dowager**]

dower chest, a chest in which a bride stores items of her trousseau.

dow|er-house (dou′ər hous′), *n. Especially British.* a house provided for the residence of a widow as part of her dower.

dow|er|less (dou′ər lis), *adj.* without a dower or dowry.

dow|er|y (dou′ər ē), *n., pl.* **-er|ies.** = dowry.

dowf (douf, düf), *adj. Scottish.* **1** dull; flat. **2** lifeless; stupid. [Middle English *dolf,* and *doof,* perhaps < Scandinavian (compare Old Icelandic *daufr* deaf)]

Dow|gate (dou′gāt′; *especially British* dou′git), *n.* the original water gate of London.

dow|ie (dou′ē, dō′-), *adj. Scottish.* dull; melancholy; dismal. [apparently variant of earlier *dolly,* perhaps < Middle English *dol* dull]

dow|itch|er (dou′i chər), *n.* an American shore bird with a long bill, similar to a snipe. [American English, perhaps < Iroquoian (compare Onondaga *tawish*)]

Dow-Jones average or **index** (dou′jōnz′), *U.S.* an index or average of stock-market quotations for industrials, railroads, and utilities, issued daily to show the relative price of stocks. [< Charles H. *Dow,* 1851-1902, and Edward D. *Jones,* died 1920, American economists]

dowl (doul), *n.* one of the fine filaments branching off the shaft to form the vane of a feather. [origin uncertain. Compare Old French *douelle,* variant of *douille* soft; that which is soft.]

dow|las (dou′ləs), *n.* **1** a coarse linen cloth much used in the 1500's and 1600's. **2** a cotton cloth like this. [< *Daoulas,* a region near Brest, France]

Dow metal (dou), *Trademark.* any one of various alloys of magnesium containing at least 85 per cent of magnesium, that are light, easy to work, and have high tensile strength. [< the *Dow* Chemical Company]

down¹ (doun), *adv., prep., adj., v., n.* —*adv.* **1** from a higher to a lower place or condition: *They ran down from the top of the hill. The soldiers laid down their arms.* **2** in a lower place or condition: *Down in the valley the fog still lingers.* SYN: below. **3** to or in a place or condition thought of as lower: *She lives in New York, but goes down to Florida every winter.* **4** into or in a fallen or inferior position or condition: *to knock a man down. You can't keep a good man down.* **5** from an earlier to a later time or person: *The story has come down through many years. The house was handed down from father to son.* **6** from a larger to a smaller amount, degree, station, or condition: *everyone from the hotel manager down to the bellhop. The temperature has gone down. Prices have come down.* **7** actually; really: *Stop talking and get down to work.* **8** on paper; in writing: *Take down what I say.* **9** in cash when bought: *You can pay $10 down and the rest later.* **10** into a heavier or more concentrated form: *The maple sap was boiled down into syrup.*
—*prep.* down along, through, or into: *You can ride down a hill, walk down a street, or sail down a river.*
—*adj.* **1** in a lower place or condition: *The sun is down.* **2** going or pointed down: *the down train, a down escalator.* **3** sick; ill: *She is down with a cold.* **4** sad; discouraged: *He felt down about his failure.* SYN: downcast, dejected. **5** (of a football) no longer in play. **6** behind an opponent by a certain number of points. **7** *Baseball.* out: *One down and two to go.* **8** in cash when bought: *We made a down payment on a television set.*
—*v.t.* **1** to put, throw, knock, or get down: *He downed the medicine at one swallow. He was downed in a fight.* **2** to defeat: *Our baseball team downed Lincoln High School.*
—*v.i.* to get down; lie down: *Down, Fido!*
—*n.* **1** a piece of bad luck: *the ups and downs of life.* **2a** a chance to move a football forward. A team has four downs to make ten or more yards. **b** the declaring of the ball as down, or the play leading to this. **3** a downward movement; descent. **4** *Informal.* a grudge: *to have a down on someone.* **5** *U.S. Slang.* a downer (def. 1).
be down on, *Informal.* to be angry at; have a grudge against; show disapproval or dislike of: *The other players were down on him for quitting the game. In the next issue of the paper Mr. Henry Fairlie was down on Mr. Grimond "like a cartload of bricks," as Victorians used to say* (Annual Register).
down and out, completely without health, money, friends, or other resources; wretched; forsaken: *The old tramp was down and out without any place to turn for help.*
down with, a to put down; throw down: *Down with tyranny! Down with your guns!* **b** to get rid of: *Down with the lords of the forest* [*i.e. trees*] (Charles Mackay).
[Old English *dūne,* short for *adūne,* earlier *of dūne* from (the) hill. Compare etym. under **down³**.]

down² (doun), *n.* **1** soft feathers: *a pillow made of down, the down of a young bird.* **2** soft hair or fluff: *The down on a boy's chin develops into a beard.* **3** *Botany.* **a** a fine, soft hair on some plants and fruits: *peach down.* **b** the soft, feathery pappus of some seeds, as in the dandelion and thistle. [Middle English *doun* < Scandinavian (compare Old Icelandic *dūnn*)]

down³ (doun), *n.* a mound or ridge of sand heaped up by the wind; dune.
downs, rolling, grassy land.
[Old English *dūn* hill. See related etym. at **dune.**]

Down (doun), *n.* any one of certain breeds of sheep originally of the hills of Southern England (the Downs).

down-and-out (doun′ən out′), *adj., n.* —*adj.* **1** completely without health, money, friends, etc.; wretched; forsaken. SYN: impoverished, forlorn. **2** knocked out in boxing.
—*n.* = down-and-outer: *To children, down-and-outs, canaries, and stray dogs he is instinctive friend* (Manchester Guardian Weekly).

down-and-out|er (doun′ən ou′tər), *n.* a down-and-out person.

down-at-heel (doun′ət hēl′), *adj., adv.* = down-at-the-heel.

down-at-the-heel (doun′ət ᴛʜə hēl′), *adj., adv.* shabby; slovenly: *He had a ragged down-at-the-heel look.*

***down|beat** (doun′bēt′), *n., adj.* —*n. Music.* **1** the first beat in the bar. **2** the downward motion of a conductor's hand or baton to indicate this beat: *His downbeat was followed by a crashing fortissimo that made me jump* (New Yorker).
—*adj. Slang.* gloomy; pessimistic; unhappy: *a downbeat forecast, a downbeat movie.*

***downbeat**
definition 2
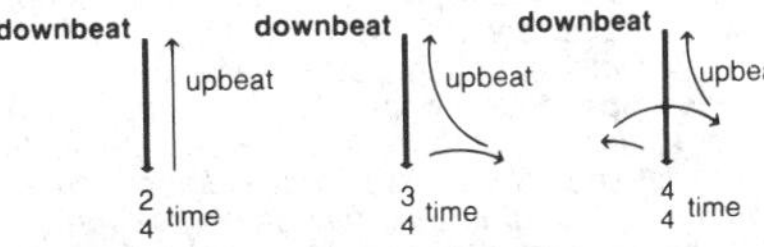

down|bound (doun′bound′), *adj., adv.* downward bound: *There were substantial increases in downbound traffic but decreases in upbound cargoes* (David M. L. Farr).

***down-bow**

***down-bow** (doun′bō′), *n.* a stroke across the strings of a violin, viola, or other bowed instrument, made by drawing the bow hand away from the instrument.

down|burst (doun′bėrst′), *n.* a strong downdraft creating a sudden destructive air current near the ground: *T. T. Fujita at the University of Chicago, who coined the word "downburst" ... showed that they were responsible for a number of commercial airplane accidents* (Louis J. Battan). *Downbursts often accompany tornadoes* (Science News).

down|cast (doun′kast′, -käst′), *adj., n.* —*adj.* **1** turned downward; directed downward: *Ashamed of his mistake, he stood before us with downcast eyes.* **2** *Figurative.* dejected; sad; discouraged: *One failure after another had made her downcast.* SYN: depressed.
—*n.* **1** a downcast look. **2** a casting down; overthrow. **3** a shaft in a mine for conveying fresh air downward.

down|come (doun′kum′), *n.* **1** downfall; descent. **2** = downcomer.

down|com|er (doun′kum′ər), *n.* a pipe or tube that carries a gas or liquid downward. It is used in a blast furnace and in certain steam boilers.

down|court (doun′kôrt′, -kōrt′), *adj., adv. Basketball.* in or toward the area of the offensive basket: *a downcourt pass* (adj.). *He dribbled downcourt and scored* (adv.).

down|draft (doun′draft′, -dräft′), *n.* **1** a downward current of air or wind: *The ventilation was bad, and what downdraft there was never seemed to reach our two rooms to clear the air* (New Yorker). **2** a downward movement or trend, especially in business activity: *The government's decision to tighten up on credit started a downdraft.*

down|draught (doun′draft′, -dräft′), *n. Especially British.* downdraft.

down|drift (doun′drift′), *n.* a drifting down; a slight or gradual downdraft.

down East, 1 New England. **2** the northeastern part of New England, especially Maine.

down-East (doun′ēst′), *adj., adv.* —*adj.* of or having to do with northeastern New England, especially Maine: *a down-East twang.*
—*adv.* in, to, or toward New England, especially Maine.

down-East|er (doun′ēs′tər), *n.* a person who lives in or comes from New England, especially Maine: *... a spare, porch-sitting down-Easter* (Time).

down-East|er|ner (doun′ēs′tər nər), *n.* = down-Easter.

down|er (dou′nər), *n. U.S. Slang.* **1** a sedative or depressant drug: *... Janis* [*Joplin, a rock singer*], *along with her famous Southern Comfort, harbored a sometime penchant for downers and hardstuff* (New York Times). **2** a dull, tiresome person or thing. **3** a decrease in force or intensity: *The movement has always been characterized by uppers and downers* (Time).

down|fall (doun′fôl′), *n.* **1** a bringing or coming to ruin; overthrow; ruin: *the downfall of an empire, the moral downfall of a person. Pride was his downfall.* **2** a heavy fall of rain or snow: *The downfall was too heavy to last long.* **3** a kind of trap in which a weight falls upon the prey.

down|fall|en (doun′fô′lən), *adj.* fallen; overthrown; ruined.

down-fault|ed (doun′fôl′tid), *adj. Geology.* having or characterized by a downward fault.

down-field (doun′fēld′), *adj., adv. Football.* in or toward a part of the field beyond the line of scrimmage; in the secondary: *downfield blocking* (adj.). *An ineligible receiver caught a pass downfield* (adv.).

down|flow (doun′flō′), *n.* **1** a flowing down. **2** something that flows down.

down|fold (doun′fōld′), *n. Geology.* a downward fold or depression; syncline: *The oil did not come from the arches or anticlines, but from the downfolds* (Glasgow Herald).

down|grade (doun′grād′), *n., v.,* **-grad|ed, -grad|ing,** *adj., adv.* —*n.* a downward slope, course, or tendency.
—*v.t.* **1** to move to a lower position with a smaller salary: *to downgrade a job, to downgrade an employee.* SYN: demote. **2** to lower, especially in status or reputation: *He downgrades people he does not like, in spite of their merits.*
—*adj.* , *adv.* = downward.
on the downgrade, growing less in strength, power, value, or interest; declining: *His health has been on the downgrade since he stopped exercising.*

down|haul (doun′hôl′), *n. Nautical.* a rope or tackle for hauling down a sail or yard.

down|heart|ed (doun′här′tid), *adj.* in low spirits; discouraged; dejected; depressed. —**down′heart′ed|ly,** *adv.* —**down′heart′ed|ness,** *n.*

Pronunciation Key: hat, āge, cãre, fär; let, ēqual, tėrm; it, īce; hot, ōpen, ôrder; oil, out; cup, pu̇t, rüle; child; long; thin; ᴛʜen; zh, measure; ə represents a in about, e in taken, i in pencil, o in lemon, u in circus.

down|hill (doun′hil′), *adv., adj., n.* **—*adv.*** **1** down the slope of a hill; downward. **2** *Figurative: His business has been going downhill lately.*
—*adj.* **1** going or sloping downward: *a downhill race.* **2** *Figurative: The house was in a downhill condition of repair.*
—*n.* **1** a downhill race in skiing: *The duke fell twice in the downhill, each time losing a ski* (Time). **2** the downward slope of a hill. **3** *Figurative: the downhill of life.*

down|hill|er (doun′hil′ər), *n.* a downhill racer in a ski competition.

down|hold (doun′hōld′), *n., v.,* **-held, -hold|ing.** **—*n.*** *U.S.* a strict limitation or curtailment: *a downhold on expenses.*
—*v.t.* to hold down or reduce.

down-home (doun′hōm′), *adj. Slang.* **1** *U.S.* having to do with or characteristic of the South of the United States; hillbilly; Dixie: *He is also a nonpareil down-home blues singer* (New Yorker). **2** of or from the country; rustic: *Despite his down-home appearance, Joe knows next to nothing about agriculture* (Maclean's).

down|i|ly (dou′nə lē), *adv.* in a downy manner; like down.

down|i|ness (dou′nē nis), *n.* downy quality.

Down|ing Street (dou′ning), **1** a street in London where several important offices of the British government are located. The official residence of the Prime Minister is at 10 Downing Street. **2** the British government.

down jacket, a quilted jacket, often sleeveless, filled with goose down.

down|land (doun′land′, -lənd), *n.* land forming downs or upland tracts: *Small fields of groundnuts, millet and maize rise gently to the open downland beyond* (Manchester Guardian Weekly).

down|less (doun′lis), *adj.* without down or downy growth.

down|light (doun′līt′), *n.* **1** a beam or beams of light directed downward: *Embedded in the ceiling were small stars that furnished downlight* (New Yorker). **2** the source of such light: *The ceiling [was] spotted with downlights* (Architectural Forum).

down|link (doun′lingk′), *n.* the communications connection for the transmission of signals from a spacecraft or satellite to a ground station.

down|load (doun′lōd′), *v.t., v.i.* to transmit information from a databank to a terminal.

down-mar|ket (doun′mär′kit), *adj., adv. Especially British.* **—*adj.*** of or for the lower-income consumer; of lower grade or quality: *They still make first-class cutlery in Sheffield. But down-market imports are threatening to flood the market* (Manchester Guardian Weekly). **—*adv.*** in or into the down-market field: *There is no reason to believe the paper will move 'down-market' in search of popularity* (Listener).

down|most (doun′mōst), *adv., adj.* (*superlative*) furthest down.

down payment, a payment in part or as a deposit for something bought or to be bought, especially in installment buying: *With their first pay check, they would make the down payment on a car* (Harper's).

down|pipe (doun′pīp′), *n. British.* a downspout.

down|play (doun′plā′), *v.t. U.S. Informal.* to understate; play down: *The Soviets might be ... downplaying the danger of small wars to allay the suspicion that they intend to start some* (Wall Street Journal).

down|pour (doun′pôr′, -pōr′), *n.* a heavy rain: *A heavy downpour ... and a thunderstorm interrupted play during the course of two of the semifinals* (London Times).

down quark, a quark having a downward spin and a charge of $-\frac{1}{3}$ and a spin of $+\frac{1}{2}$: *To explain the common, well-behaved particles such as neutrons or protons requires two quarks (and their corresponding antiquarks) designated "up quark" and "down quark"* (Science News).

down|range (doun′rānj′), *adj., adv.* along or on the line of a range in a direction away from a starting point, such as a launching pad.

down|rate (doun′rāt′), *v.t.,* **-rat|ed, -rat|ing.** to place lower or too low in rank, value, or regard: *... outcries that he is downrating military advice* (Fortune).

down|right (doun′rīt′), *adj., adv.* **—*adj.*** **1** thorough; complete: *a downright thief, a downright lie. This would be downright fraud* (Newsweek). SYN: absolute. **2** plain; positive: *Her downright answer left no doubt as to what she thought.* SYN: definite, straightforward. **3** plain and direct in speech or behavior: *a downright person.* **4** directed straight downward.
—*adv.* **1** thoroughly; completely: *They were downright rude to me.* SYN: absolutely, outright. **2** plainly; definitely. **3** straight down. **—down′right′ly,** *adv.* **—down′right′ness,** *n.*

down|riv|er (doun′riv′ər), *adv., adj.* = downstream: *No punts were out at this time of year, and swans generally stayed downriver* (New Yorker) (adv.). *St. Marc ... is the adjacent downriver village on the Richelieu* (Maclean's) (adj.).

down|rush (doun′rush′), *n.* a downward rush.

downs (dounz), *n.pl.* See under **down**[3].

down|scale (doun′skāl′), *adj. U.S.* below a certain scale, especially of income or wealth; not upscale: *The Ewings' ranch house is ... definitely downscale from "Giant." Large but not huge; white, serene, and grandly suburban* (New Yorker).

down|shift (doun′shift′), *v., n.* **—*v.t., v.i.*** to shift from a higher to a lower gear.
—*n.* a shifting from a higher to a lower gear.

down|side (doun′sīd′), *n., adj.* **—*n.*** **1** the under or lower side. **2** that part of a graph or chart which shows a decline or low level. **—*adj.*** of or on the downside: *a downside movement in trading.*
on the downside, lower; declining: *Stock averages for the day were on the downside.*

down|size (doun′sīz′), *v.t.,* **-sized, -siz|ing.** to reduce in size; scale down.

down|slope (doun′slōp′), *n., adj.* **—*n.*** a downward slope; downgrade: *They built their house on the downslope of the property.* **—*adj.*** in a downward slope: *downslope movement.*

downs|man (dounz′mən), *n., pl.* **-men.** a native or inhabitant of the downs, especially the downs of southern England.

down|spout (doun′spout′), *n.* a pipe that carries rain water from a roof to the ground or to a sewer or drain; drainspout.

Down's syndrome (dounz), a congenital disorder characterized by extreme mental deficiency and Mongoloid features; Mongolism: *Down's syndrome [is] a genetic disease that results from an extra No. 21 chromosome in the child's cells* (New York Times). [< John L. *Down,* 1828-1896, an English physician, who first described it]

down|stage (doun′stāj′), *adv., adj., n.* **—*adv.*** toward the footlights; in or to the front of the stage.
—*adj.* having to do with or at the front of the stage. **—*n.*** the front part of a stage.

down|stair (doun′stãr′), *adj.* = downstairs.

down|stairs (doun′stãrz′), *adv., adj., n.* **—*adv.*** **1** down the stairs: *He slipped and fell downstairs.* **2** on or to a lower floor: *Look downstairs for my glasses.* **—*adj.*** on a lower floor: *The downstairs rooms are dark.*
—*n.* the lower floor or floors: *The downstairs consisted of three large rooms.*

down|state (doun′stāt′), *n., adv., adj. U.S.* **—*n.*** the area of a state away from metropolitan or industrial centers, usually to the south.
—*adv., adj.* in, of, or toward downstate: *a downstate medical center* (adj.). *He practices medicine downstate* (adv.). **—down′stat′er,** *n.*

down|stream (doun′strēm′), *adv., adj.* **1** with the current of a stream; down a stream: *It is easy to swim or row downstream* (adv.). *The downstream current was swift after the flood* (adj.). **2** in, of, or toward the distribution and marketing end of any industry: *Fibre-makers who merged "downstream" would be working to the disadvantage of the ultimate consumer* (London Times). **3** *Molecular Biology.* in or toward the end point of a genetic segment or transcription: *other sequences which may lie ... downstream from the mRNA start point* (Science).

down|stream|er (doun′strē′mər), *n.* a person or thing that goes or lives downstream.

down|street (doun′strēt′), *adv.* further along or down a street.

down|stroke (doun′strōk′), *n.* **1** a downward stroke of a pen, pencil, etc. **2** a stroke delivered downwards: *the downstroke of a piston.*

down|sweep (doun′swēp′), *v.,* **-swept, -sweep|ing,** *n.* **—*v.t.*** to cause to be downswept.
—*v.i.* to be downswept: *Herefords ... with long, downsweeping horns* (New Yorker).
—*n.* a downswept thing, part, or arrangement.

down|swept (doun′swept′), *adj., v.* **—*adj.*** curving or slanting downward, especially in a smooth or regular line: *The Skylark sports downswept doors [and] long, flowing fenders* (Newsweek).
—*v.* the past tense and past participle of **downsweep.**

down|swing (doun′swing′), *n.* **1** a downward movement or trend: *a sharp downswing in sales.* **2** a swinging down, as of an arm or a lever.

down|take (doun′tāk′), *n.* a pipe or passage leading downward, as for conducting coal, ore, or gaseous products.

down-the-line (doun′ᴛʜə līn′), *adj.* thoroughgoing; complete: down-the-line bureaucrats.

down|throw (doun′thrō′), *n.* **1** a throwing down or a being thrown down; overthrow. **2** *Geology.* the downward displacement of rock on one side of a fault.

down|time (doun′tīm′), *n.* the time in which a machine, department, or the like is inactive or not working: *cut maintenance and downtime.*

down-to-earth (doun′tə ėrth′), *adj.* **1** not fanciful; matter of fact; practical; realistic: *a down-to-earth businessman. Conrad developed an appetite for adventure and daydreams which completely mystified his down-to-earth uncle* (Wall Street Journal). **2** not lofty or haughty: *His kind of down-to-earth campaigning goes well in the farm country* (Newsweek). **—down′-to-earth′ness,** *n.*

down|town (doun′toun′), *adv., adj., n.* **—*adv., adj.*** **1** to or in the main part or business part of a town or city: *Mother has gone downtown shopping* (adv.). *His office is in downtown Honolulu* (adj.). **2** to, toward, or in the lower part of a town or city: *We took a cab downtown to the docks* (adv.). *We crossed over to the other platform to take the downtown train* (adj.).
—*n.* the business section or main part of a town or city: *The center of Manchester is more like an American downtown than like an old English market place* (St. Louis Post-Dispatch).

down|trend (doun′trend′), *n.* a declining trend or tendency, especially in business activity: *Mortgage bankers and lenders look for the downtrend to continue* (Wall Street Journal).

down|trod (doun′trod′), *adj.* = downtrodden.

down|trod|den (doun′trod′ən), *adj.* **1** tyrannized over; oppressed. **2** trodden down; trampled upon.

down|turn (doun′tėrn′), *n.* = downtrend.

Down Under, **1** the region including Australia and New Zealand. **2** in or to the region including Australia and New Zealand. **3** of the region including Australia and New Zealand: *Britain relies on the Down Under area for meat and wool* (Newsweek).

down|ward (doun′wərd), *adv., adj.* **1** toward a lower place or condition: *The bird swooped downward on its prey* (adv.). *The downward trip on the elevator was very slow* (adj.). **2** toward a later time: *There has been great progress in science from the 1900's downward.* **—down′ward|ly,** *adv.* **—down′ward|ness,** *n.*

down|wards (doun′wərdz), *adv.* = downward.

down|warp (doun′wôrp′), *v., n. Geology.* **—*v.t., v.i.*** to fold or bend in a synclinal manner: *Successive downwarping and uplifting of the earth's crust ... have built up many layers of sedimentary rock* (Scientific American).
—*n.* a downwarped condition or area.

down|wash (doun′wosh′, -wôsh′), *n.* **1** *Aeronautics.* a deflection of air in a downward direction: *The downwash from a helicopter is about 30 mph* (Newsweek). **2** any downward movement or flow; downdraft; current: *a downwash of smoke.*

down|wind (doun′wind′), *adj., adv.* in the same direction as the wind, away from a certain point: *a downwind drift or current* (adj.). *The boat glided easily downwind* (adv.).

down|y (dou′nē), *adj.,* **down|i|er, down|i|est.** **1** made or consisting of soft feathers, hair, or fluff: *a downy pillow.* **2** covered with soft feathers or hair: *a downy chick.* **3** *Figurative.* like down; soft and fluffy: *A kitten's fur is downy. The only other sound's the sweep Of easy wind and downy flake* (Robert Frost).

downy hawthorn, a hawthorn with downy clusters of white and red flowers. The flower is the state flower of Missouri.

downy mildew, **1** any one of various fungi destructive to grape, potato, cantaloupe, and other plants, producing a downy white growth on the under surface of the leaves. **2** the disease produced by these fungi.

downy woodpecker, a small black and white woodpecker, the male of which has red on the back of the head.

DOW process, a method of extracting magnesium from seawater. [< the *Dow* Chemical Company]

dow|ry (dou′rē), *n., pl.* **-ries.** **1** the money or property that a woman brings to her husband when she marries him: *Dowry ... is not to be conceived as an inducement to marriage but as a device whereby the bride's family seek to aid their daughter's husband set up an economically stable household* (Beals and Hoijer). SYN: dot. **2** *Figurative.* a gift of nature; natural talent: *Good health and intelligence are a precious dowry.* **3** *Obsolete.* a present given by a man to his bride. **4** *Obsolete.* a widow's dower. Also, **dower, dowery.** [< Anglo-French *dowaire,* Old French *douaire;* see etym. under **dower**]

Dow|sa|bel (dou′sə bel), *n.* = Dousabel.

dow|sa|bel (dou′sə bel), *n. Obsolete.* a sweetheart. [< *Dowsabel;* see etym. under **Dousabel**]

dowse[1] (douz), *v.i.,* **dowsed, dows|ing.** to use a divining rod to locate water, minerals, or other natural resources. [origin unknown]

dowse[2] (dous), *v.t., v.i.,* **dowsed, dows|ing,** *n.* = douse[1].

dowse[3] (dous), *v.t.,* **dowsed, dows|ing,** *n.* = douse[2].

dows|er[1] (dou′zər), *n.* **1** a person who uses a divining rod. **2** = divining rod.

dows|er[2] (dou′sər), *n.* = douser[2].

dows|ing rod (dou′zing), = divining rod.

Dow theory, *U.S.* a theory for forecasting trends in the stock market by observing stock prices in the Dow-Jones averages, especially for industrials.

dox|ie (dok′sē), *n.* = doxy[2].

dox|og|ra|pher (dok sog′rə fər), *n.* a writer who collects and records the opinions of the Greek philosophers: *The Greek doxographers know of no astronomer before Thales* (Journal of Hellenic Studies).

dox|o|graph|i|cal (dok′sə graf′ə kəl), *adj.* of or having to do with doxography or doxographers: *doxographical evidence, doxographical testimony.*

dox|og|ra|phy (dok sog′rə fē), *n.* a collection of philosophical opinions. [< Greek *dóxa* opinion + English *-graphy*]

dox|o|log|i|cal (dok′sə loj′ə kəl), *adj.* having to do with or like a doxology; praising; glorifying.

dox|ol|o|gy (dok sol′ə jē), *n., pl.* **-gies.** a hymn or statement praising God. Three of the best-known doxologies begin: "Glory to God in the highest" (greater doxology), "Glory be to the Father and to the Son and to the Holy Ghost" (lesser doxology), and "Praise God from whom all blessings flow." [< Medieval Latin *doxologia* < Greek *doxologíā* < *doxologeîn* to praise < *dóxa* glory, praise + *légein* speak]

dox|y[1] (dok′sē), *n., pl.* **dox|ies.** *Informal.* an opinion or doctrine, especially in religion or theology: *Orthodoxy is my doxy,—heterodoxy is another man's doxy* (Bishop William Warburton). [abstracted from *orthodoxy, heterodoxy,* etc.]

dox|y[2] (dok′sē), *n., pl.* **dox|ies.** *Slang.* a mistress; prostitute. Also, **doxie.** [origin uncertain]

doy|en (doi′en, dwä′yen; *French* dwȧ yaN′), *n.* a dean; senior member of a group: *He had been the doyen of diamond men in Antwerp* (New Yorker). [< French *doyen* < Old French *deien;* see etym. under **dean**[1]]

doy|enne (doi′ən, dwä′yən; *French* dwȧ yen′), *n.* the feminine form of **doyen**: *The book is dedicated to Simone de Beauvoir, doyenne of French existentialists* (Time).

doy|ley (doi′lē), *n., pl.* **-leys.** = doily.

doy|ly (doi′lē), *n., pl.* **-lies.** = doily.

do|yo (dō′yō), *n. Japanese.* a children's poem; nursery rhyme.

doz., dozen or dozens.

doze[1] (dōz) , *v.,* **dozed, doz|ing,** *n.* —*v.i.* to sleep lightly; be half asleep: *After dinner my father dozes in his chair. Most of the time the sick man just dozed.* SYN: nod.

—*v.t.* **1** to pass or spend (time) in dozing: *The lazy boy dozed away his afternoons.* **2** to make drowsy.

—*n.* a light sleep; a nap.

doze off, to fall into a doze: *The cat dozed off by the fire. Before I dozed off, I was going to tell you what Mr. and Mrs. Tulliver were talking about* (George Eliot).

[perhaps < Scandinavian (compare Danish *döse* make dull)]

doze[2] (dōz) , *v.t.,* **dozed, doz|ing.** to grade with a bulldozer; bulldoze: *... our American earth ... dozed and paved into oblivion* (St. Louis Post-Dispatch).

doz|en[1] (duz′ən), *n., pl.* **-ens** or (*after a number*) **-en.** twelve; a group of twelve: *We had to have dozens of chairs for the party. Mother ordered three dozen eggs and a dozen rolls. Abbr:* doz.

the dozens, *U.S. Slang.* a children's contest of exchanging insults directed against each other's relatives: *Playin' the dozens in inner-city schools may cause more fights and disruptions than any other activity. The dozens or playin' the dozens has many names, but most youngsters probably refer to the game as "talkin' about moms"—making derogatory allegations about mothers* (Today's Education).

[< Old French *dozeine* < *douse* twelve < Latin *duodecim* < *duo* two + *decem* ten]

doz|en[2] (dō′zən), *v.t. Scottish.* to stun; daze. [Middle English *dosen.* See related etym. at **doze**[1].]

doz|enth (duz′ənth), *adj.* the 12th.

doz|er[1] (dō′zər), *n.* a person who dozes.

doz|er[2] (dō′zər), *n. Informal.* a bulldozer.

doz|i|ly (dō′zə lē), *adv.* in a dozy manner; drowsily; sleepily.

doz|i|ness (dō′zē nis), *n.* drowsiness; sleepiness.

doz|y (dō′zē), *adj.,* **doz|i|er, doz|i|est. 1** drowsy; sleepy: *The preacher preaches like a Sandhurst sergeant-major, with a violent enunciation of each syllable and a voice ferocious enough to reach the doziest cadet in the rear rank* (Manchester Guardian). **2** decaying: *dozy timber.*

DP (no periods), an abbreviation for the following:
1 data processing.
2 degree of polymerization.
3 displaced person.
4 durable press.

DPG (no periods), diphosphoglyceric acid.

D.P.H., Doctor of Public Health.

D. Phil., *British.* Doctor of Philosophy.

DPL (no periods), diplomat (as on automobile license plates).

dpm (no period), *Nuclear Physics.* disintegrations per minute.

DPN (no periods), diphosphopyridine nucleotide.

D.P.O., Distributing Post Office.

D.P.P., Director of Public Prosecutions (of Great Britain).

dps (no period), *Nuclear Physics.* disintegrations per second.

dpt., **1** department. **2** deponent.

DPT (no periods), Diphtheria, Pertussis (whooping cough), Tetanus. The serums for these three diseases are combined into one injection administered three times.

D.P.W., Department of Public Works.

d quark, = down quark.

dr., **1** debit. **2** debtor. **3** door. **4** drachma. **5** dram or drams. **6** drawer.

Dr (no period), doctor.

Dr., **1** debit. **2** debtor. **3** doctor. **4** door. **5** drive.

DR (no periods), dead reckoning.

drab[1] (drab), *adj.,* **drab|ber, drab|best,** *n., v.,* **drabbed, drab|bing.** —*adj.* **1** lacking brightness or color; not attractive; dull: *the drab houses of the smoky mining town.* (*Figurative.*) *The life of a person who never does anything is dull and drab.* SYN: monotonous, unattractive. **2** dull brownish- or yellowish-gray. SYN: dun.

—*n.* **1** a dull, brownish gray or yellowish gray. **2** a cloth of natural or undyed color.

—*v.t.* **1** to treat (hair, especially after bleaching) so as to remove excess color or glare. **2** to cause (a person) to look drab.

[earlier *drap* kind of cloth < Old French; see etym. under **drape**]—**drab′ly,** *adv.* —**drab′ness,** *n.*

drab[2] (drab), *n., v.,* **drabbed, drab|bing.** —*n.* **1** a dirty, untidy woman. SYN: slut, slattern. **2** = prostitute. SYN: harlot, strumpet.

—*v.i.* to associate with prostitutes.

[origin uncertain. Compare Irish *drabog,* Scottish Gaelic *dràbag* slattern.]

drab[3] (drab), *n.* a small amount, quantity, or sum.

in dribs and drabs. See under **drib.**

[origin uncertain]

dra|ba (drā′bə), *n., pl.* **-bas.** any one of a large group of low, usually perennial herbs of the mustard family, found in cold and mountainous regions of the Northern Hemisphere: *Edinburgh's scree ... provides splendid drainage for such rare alpines as lewisias ... and drabas* (New Yorker). [< New Latin *Draba* the genus name < Greek *drábē* a plant of the mustard family]

drab|bet (drab′it), *n.* a drab linen or cotton cloth used especially for men's working clothes.

drab|ble (drab′əl), *v.,* **-bled, -bling.** —*v.t.* to make wet and dirty by contact with muddy water or mud. —*v.i.* **1** to fish with a rod and long line by dragging the hook along the bottom. **2** to become wet and dirty.

[Middle English *drabelen.* Compare Low German *drabbeln* to splash, wade around in water.]

dra|bi (drä′bē), *n.* (in India) a muleteer. [alteration of English *driver*]

dra|cae|na (drə sē′nə), *n.,* or **dracaena palm,** any one of a group of tropical trees or shrubs of the agave family, such as the dragon tree. [< New Latin *Dracaena* the genus name < Greek *drákaina,* feminine of *drákōn;* see etym. under **dragon**]

drachm (dram), *n.* **1** *British.* a dram. **2** = drachma.

drach|ma (drak′mə), *n., pl.* **-mas, -mae** (-mē).
1 a unit of money of modern Greece, a coin equal to 100 lepta and worth about 3⅓ cents.
2 an ancient Greek silver coin, varying in value.
3 a small ancient Greek weight. **4** any one of various modern weights, especially a dram. *Abbr:* dr. [< Latin *drachma* < Greek *drachmē* (originally) handful < *drássesthai* to grasp < *dráx, drákos* handful. See etym. of doublet **dram.**]

Dra|co (drā′kō), *n., genitive* **Dra|co|nis.** a northern constellation part of which forms a semicircle around the Little Dipper; Dragon. [< Latin *Dracō, -ōnis* (literally) dragon]

Dra|co|ne (drə kō′nā), *n. Trademark.* a boat-sized, collapsible, and flexible container of rubber-coated nylon, used for the bulk transport of liquids and usually towed by a boat: *The purchase from Britain by Zambia of five Dracones ... raises the hope that these vessels will be used to carry Zambia's oil supply over lake Tanganyika* (New Scientist). [< Greek *drákōn* dragon; because of its appearance in the water]

dra|co|ni|an (drə kō′nē ən), *adj.* = draconic.

Dra|co|ni|an (drə kō′nē ən), *adj.* **1** of or having to do with Draco, a legislator of Athens in the 600's B.C., or his severe code of laws. **2** severe; cruel; harsh.

Dra|co|ni|an|ism (drə kō′nē ə niz′əm), *n.* Draconian principles or practices.

dra|con|ic (drə kon′ik), *adj.* having to do with or like a dragon. [< Latin *dracō, -ōnis* dragon + English *-ic*]

Dra|con|ic (drə kon′ik), *adj.* = Draconian: *In his Draconic drive to eliminate corruption from South Korea, austere Strongman General Park Chung Hee has cracked down hardest on the nation's smugglers* (Time).

Dra|con|i|cal|ly (drə kon′ə klē), *adv.* in a Draconic manner; vigorously; severely.

Drac|o|nid (drak′ə nid), *n.* any one of a shower of meteors seeming to radiate from the constellation Draco and frequently reappearing about October 9. [< New Latin *Draconides,* plural < *Draco* Draco]

Dra|co|nis (drə kō′nis), *n.* genitive of **Draco.**

drae|ger|man (drā′gər mən), *n., pl.* **-men.** a mine worker or volunteer who is specially trained in rescue and disaster operations. [< Alexander B. *Dräger,* 1870-1928, a German scientist, who devised the special equipment used by these men + *man*]

draff (draf, dräf), *n.* the remains of malt after brewing or distilling; dregs; lees. [probably < Scandinavian (compare Old Icelandic *draf*)]

draff|y (draf′ē, dräf′-), *adj.,* **draff|i|er, draff|i|est. 1** full of draff or dregs. **2** like draff; worthless.

draft (draft, dräft), *n., v., adj.* —*n.* **1** a current of air, especially in a room, chimney, stove, or any enclosed space: *I caught cold from sitting in a draft.* **2** a device for controlling a current of air in a fireplace, stove, or other place for holding a fire: *He opened the draft of the furnace to make the fire burn faster.* **3** a plan; sketch: *Before building, he had the architect make a draft of how the finished house should look.* SYN: outline, delineation. **4** a rough copy: *He made three different drafts of his book report before he handed it in in final form.* **5** the selection of persons for some special purpose. Men needed as soldiers are supplied to the army by draft. SYN: levy. **6** the persons selected for special service. **7** the act of pulling loads. **8** the quantity pulled: *That draft is too much for my team of horses to pull.* SYN: load. **9a** the pulling in of a net to catch fish. **b** all the fish caught in one drawing of a net. **10** a heavy demand or drain on anything: *Her long illness was a draft on her resources.* **11** a note to a bank, ordering that a certain sum of money be paid to the person named. SYN: bill of exchange. **12** the depth of water that a ship needs for floating or the depth to which a ship sinks into the water. A ship's draft is greater when it is loaded than when it is empty. **13a** a single act of drinking: *I emptied the glass at one draft.* **b** the amount taken in one drink. **c** the breathing in of air, smoke, and the like. **d** air, smoke, and the like, breathed in. **e** the drawing of beer, ale, or wine directly from a barrel when ordered. Beer is sold on draft and in cans or bottles. **14** *Masonry.* a line or border chiseled at the edge of a stone to serve as a guide in leveling the surface. **15** *Metallurgy.* the slight taper given to a pattern for a casting so that it may be removed from the sand without harming the mold. **16** the area of an opening for a flow of water, as in a sluice gate. **17** *Commerce.* a small allowance made for waste of certain goods sold by weight. **18** *U.S.* a gully; glen.

—*v.t.* **1** to make a plan or a sketch of: *It was well drafted to appeal to our Allies, neutrals, and the captive peoples* (Newsweek). **2** to write out a rough copy of: *Three members of the club drafted a set of rules to be discussed and voted on by the membership.* **3** to select for some special purpose, especially, to conscript (persons) for military service: *At eighteen he was drafted. The army drafted millions of young men. The convention drafted the President for a second term.* **4** to draw off or away. **5** *Masonry.* to cut a draft on (a stone).

—*adj.* **1** for pulling loads: *A big, strong horse or ox is a draft animal.* **2** drawn up in rough or sketchy form: *a draft letter.* **3** drawn from a barrel when ordered: *The customers ordered draft beer.*

[Middle English *draht,* verbal noun < Old English *dragan* to draw, drag]

▶See **draught** for usage note.

draft|a|ble (draf′tə bəl, dräf′-), *adj.* **1** that can be drafted. **2** eligible for a draft: *A steamship company wouldn't hire him because he's draftable* (Wall Street Journal).

draft board, a board of appointed officials for selecting and drafting men who are eligible for military service: *The ordinary life of a young man is turned quite about at the moment the mail brings him that well-known communication from the draft board in which are extended to him certain greetings from the President of the United*

Pronunciation Key: hat, āge, cãre, fär; let, ēqual, tėrm; it, īce; hot, ōpen, ôrder; oil, out; cup, pu̇t, rüle; child; long; thin; ᴛʜen; zh, measure; ə represents a in about, e in taken, i in pencil, o in lemon, u in circus.

States (Harper's).

draft card, *U.S.* a card identifying a man for the selection process of military service.

draft dodger, *U.S. Informal.* a man who seeks to avoid being drafted into military service.

draft|ee (draf tē′, dräf-), *n.* a person who is drafted for military service. [American English < *draft* + *-ee*]

draft|er (draf′tər, dräf′-), *n.* **1** a person who drafts: *the drafters of the Constitution of the United States.* **2** a draft horse.

draft horse, a horse for pulling heavy loads.

draft|i|ly (draf′tə lē, dräf′-), *adv.* in a drafty manner.

draft|i|ness (draf′tē nis, dräf′-), *n.* drafty quality or condition: *The house was not insulated and he noticed its draftiness.*

draft|ing (draf′ting, dräf′-), *n.* the work of a draftsman; mechanical drawing.

drafting board, = drawing board.

drafting paper, a hard grade of paper for use by draftsmen.

drafting room, a room or office in which drafting is done: *The decorative arts will eventually find their way back to the drafting room* (Harper's).

draft lottery, a system of drafting eligible men for military service by a chance drawing of their birth dates from a bowl to determine the order of induction. A draft lottery was adopted in the United States in 1969 and discontinued in 1975.

drafts (drafts, dräfts), *n.pl. U.S.* draughts.

drafts|man (drafts′mən, dräfts′-), *n., pl.* **-men**. **1a** a person who makes plans or sketches. A draftsman draws designs or diagrams from which buildings and machines are made. **b** an artist who draws especially well. **2** a person who writes out rough copies of documents, speeches, etc. **3** a person who draws up legal or official documents.

drafts|man|ship (drafts′mən ship, dräfts′-), *n.* the work of a draftsman.

draft|y (draf′tē, dräf′-), *adj.*, **draft|i|er**, **draft|i|est**. **1** in a current of air: *I had a drafty seat near the window.* **2** having many currents of air: *a drafty room.* **3** causing a current of air: *a drafty fireplace.*

drag (drag), *v.*, **dragged**, **drag|ging**, *n.* — *v.t.* **1** to pull along heavily or slowly; pull or draw along the ground: *A team of horses dragged the big log out of the forest.* **SYN**: haul, tug. See syn. under **draw**. **2** to pull a net or hook along for some purpose; search: *The fishermen dragged the bay for fish. The fire department dragged the lake for the drowned person's body.* **3** to break up (land) with a drag or harrow. **4** *Slang.* to bore: *I started lessons on drums six years ago, and on the side I played in rock groups. Both experiences dragged me* (Whitney Balliett).
— *v.i.* **1** to move along heavily or slowly: *The crippled old man dragged along slowly.* **SYN**: trail. **2** to go too slowly: *Time drags when you have nothing to do.* **3** to lag: *The baritone was dragging.* **4** *Slang.* to puff or inhale on a cigarette, pipe, or cigar, or suck on a straw: *Just then, an older man in brown walked up, dragging on a cigarette* (New Yorker). **5** to use a drag. **6** *U.S. Slang.* to take part in a drag race.
— *n.* **1** a net, hook, implement, or device used in dragging. **2** the act of dragging. **3** a thing dragged. **4** *Figurative.* anything that holds back; obstruction; hindrance: *That lazy, complaining boy is a drag on the team. Some old ideas and ways are a drag on progress.* **SYN**: impediment. **5** a low, strong sled for carrying heavy loads. **6** a heavy harrow or other implement drawn over land to level it and break up clods. **7** a device for slowing down the rotation of the wheels of a vehicle. **8** the force acting on a body in motion through a fluid in a direction opposite to the body's motion and produced by friction: *Airplanes flew faster as improved design reduced drag.* **9** *Slang.* a person or thing that is extremely boring: *I don't like public transportation, and driving back and forth every day is a drag. The traffic and the traveling create tension, and who needs more tension?* (Ernest Dunbar). **10** *Slang.* a street: *the main drag.* **11** *Slang.* a puff or inhalation on a cigarette, pipe, or cigar, or a suck on a straw: *He leaned back and took a deep drag from his cigarette* (Atlantic). **12** *U.S. Slang.* a girl taken out on a date: *One can see names of "drags" inscribed on desks in Mahan Hall* (*Barbara, Sharon, Prudence*) (Harper's). **13** *Slang.* influence: *The only thing that'll work now is drag. You need a really important figure to go to bat for you* (New Yorker). **14** *U.S.* = drag race. **15** *Slang.* **a** clothing appropriate to the opposite sex; transvestite clothing: *The cabaret dances are suitably twenty-ish and naughty, and, in one of them, one of the chorus "girls" turns out to be Mr. Grey in drag* (London Times). **b** clothing, especially that considered to be worn by a certain group, class, or type: *Perhaps it is timely to ... follow Bonnie and Clyde* (*a distinctive couple in 'thirties gangster drag*) (Punch). **16** *Nautical.* sea anchor (def. 1). **17a** a brake to prevent excessive spin in a fishing reel. **b** a pull on a fishing line caused by a water current. **18** in hunting: **a** an animal's trail or scent. **b** an artificial scent dragged on the ground to leave a trail for hounds. **c** = drag hunt. **19** a big coach with seats inside and on top, that used to be drawn by four or more horses: *Behind her came ... a drag, or private stage-coach with four horses* (Thackeray). **20** *Railroading.* a slow freight train. **21** *Metallurgy.* the bottom of a flask used in casting, that contains the gate and the cavity that is filled with molten metal.

drag in, to bring (something irrelevant) into a discussion: *Whatever we talk about, you drag in stamp collecting.*

drag on (or **out**), **a** to make or be too slow: *The events of the day drag themselves on tediously in such a country house* (Anthony Trollope). **b** to make or last too long: *The barking of the neighbor's dogs dragged on and jangled our nerves.*

drag one's feet (or **heels**). See under **feet** and **heel**[1].

[< Scandinavian (compare Old Icelandic *draga*), or, perhaps < dialectal variant of *draw*]

drag|bar (drag′bär′), *n.* = drawbar (iron rod).

drag|bolt (drag′bōlt′), *n.* = coupling pin.

drag bunt, *Baseball.* a bunt made by pulling back the bat as the ball is hit. It is usually used by a batter who wants to reach first base.

dra|gée (drȧ zhā′), *n. French.* **1** sugar-coated candy. **2** a sugar-coated tablet.

drag|ger (drag′ər), *n.* **1** a person or thing that drags. **2** a boat used in fishing with a dragnet; trawler.

drag|ging (drag′ing), *adj.* very slow; tedious: *a dragging pace.* — **drag′ging|ly**, *adv.*

drag|gle (drag′əl), *v.*, **-gled**, **-gling**. — *v.t.* to make wet or dirty by dragging through mud, water, dust, or wet snow.
— *v.i.* **1** to become wet or dirty by dragging through mud, water, dust, or wet snow. **2** to follow slowly; lag behind; straggle: *With heavy hearts they draggled at the heels of his troop* (Washington Irving). **3** to trail on the ground.

drag|gle|tail (drag′əl tāl′), *n.* a bedraggled or untidy woman; slut.

drag|gle|tailed (drag′əl tāld′), *adj.* bedraggled; untidy; sluttish.

drag|gly (drag′lē), *adj.*, **-gli|er**, **-gli|est**. = bedraggled.

drag|gy (drag′ē), *adj.*, **-gi|er**, **-gi|est**. dragging; slow-moving; boring: *a draggy plot, a draggy contest. The idea was to bring something of the Christmas spirit into the middle of a draggy summer* (New York Times).

drag|hound (drag′hound′), *n.* a hound trained to follow a drag or artificial scent.

drag hunt, a hunt with a drag or artificial scent.

drag|less (drag′lis), *adj.* having no drag.

***drag|line** (drag′līn′), *n.* **1** = dragrope (def. 2). **2** an excavating machine with a boom on a rotating platform and cables for controlling a bucket. Draglines are used for dredging, excavating, and earthwork: *Draglines began creating straight lines of canals and levees across the wastes* (Harper's). **3** a silk thread which a spider spins behind itself. It often uses it to escape from enemies.

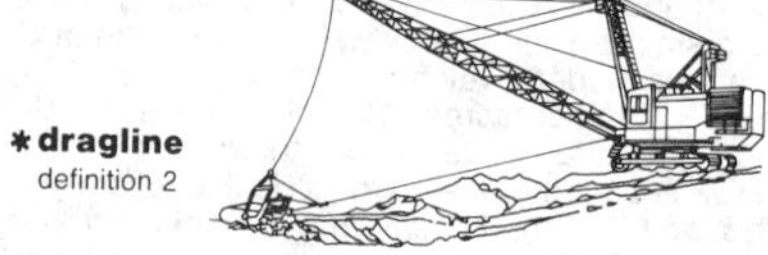

***dragline** definition 2

drag link, a link that connects the cranks of two shafts.

drag mill, = arrastra.

drag|net (drag′net′), *n.* **1** a net pulled over the bottom of a river, pond, or lake, or along the ground. Dragnets are used to catch fish and small birds. **2** *Figurative.* a means of catching or gathering in: *All kinds of criminals were caught in the police dragnet.*

drag|o|man (drag′ə mən), *n., pl.* **-mans** or **-men**. an interpreter in the Orient: *It was a little like traveling through the British Isles with a Gurkha dragoman who insisted on carrying on all intercourse with the natives* (New Yorker). [< Old French *drogman* < Medieval Latin *dragumannus* < Late Greek *dragoúmanos* < Old Arabic *targumān* < an Aramaic word]

***drag|on** (drag′ən), *n.* **1** a huge, fierce animal in old stories, supposed to look like a snake or lizard with wings, claws, and scales. Dragons often breathed out fire and smoke. **2** *Figurative.* a fierce, violent person. **3** *Figurative.* a very strict and watchful woman; stern chaperon. **4** *Figurative.* a tyrannical power; evil influence: *Harder still it has proved to resist and rule the dragon Money, with his paper wings* (Emerson). **5** *Zoology.* any one of various lizards with winglike membranes that can make long, flying leaps; flying dragon; flying lizard. **6** *Botany.* any one of various plants of the arum family, such as the jack-in-the-pulpit. **7** a large snake, whale, crocodile, or jackal in the Bible. **8** *Archaic.* a huge snake. **9** an armored tractor: *tanks, dragons, light and heavy guns.* **10** *Obsolete.* **a** a short musket used by mounted infantry. **b** a soldier armed with this musket; dragoon. [< Old French *dragon*, learned borrowing from Latin *dracō, -ōnis* < Greek *drákōn.* See etym. of doublet **drake**[2].]
— **drag′on|like′**, *adj.*

***dragon** definition 1

Drag|on (drag′ən), *n.* **1** *Astronomy.* the northern constellation Draco. **2** *Archaic.* Satan: *The Dragon, put to second rout, Came furious down to be revenged on man* (Milton). [< *dragon*]

dragon eel, an eel with eyeballs on the ends of long optic nerves. Its eyes grow into normal sockets as it gets older.

drag|on|esque (drag′ə nesk′), *adj.* like or like that of a dragon.

drag|on|ess (drag′ə nis), *n.* a female dragon.

drag|on|et (drag′ə nit), *n.* **1** a small or young dragon. **2** a small, often brightly colored marine fish. [< Old French *dragonet* (diminutive) < *dragon;* see etym. under **dragon**]

drag|on|fish (drag′ən fish′), *n., pl.* **-fish|es** or (*collectively*) **-fish**. = dragonet (def. 2).

***drag|on|fly** (drag′ən flī′), *n., pl.* **-flies**. a large, harmless insect with a long, slender body and two pairs of wings; darning needle; devil's-darning-needle. It flies about very rapidly to catch flies, mosquitoes, and other insects and is often found near water: *Deep in the sun-searched growths the dragonfly Hangs like a blue thread loosened from the sky* (Dante Gabriel Rossetti).

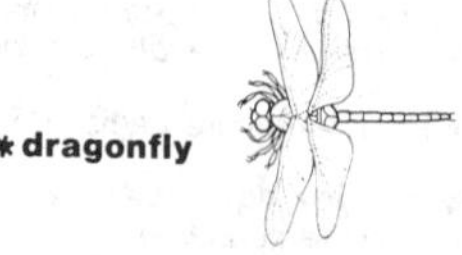

***dragonfly**

drag|on|head (drag′ən hed′), *n.* any plant of a group of herbs of the mint family with blue, purple, or white corollas.

drag|on|ish (drag′ə nish), *adj.* in the form of a dragon; like a dragon.

dragon lizard or **dragon of Komodo**, a very large lizard of Indonesia, sometimes 10 feet long and weighing up to 300 pounds. It is believed to be the largest lizard in the world. Also, **Komodo dragon**. [< *Komodo,* an island in Indonesia]

drag|on|nade (drag′ə nād′), *n.* **1** the persecution of the French Protestants by the troops of Louis XIV. **2** any persecution by soldiers. [< French *dragonnade* < Old French *dragon;* see etym. under **dragon**]

drag|on|root (drag′ən rüt′, -rủt′), *n.* **1** = jack-in-the-pulpit. **2** = green dragon.

drag|on's blood (drag′ənz), **1** a red resin obtained from the fruit of a palm of the Malay Archipelago, used in making varnishes, and in photoengraving. **2** any one of various similar resins from other trees, especially from varieties of dracaena.

***dragon's head**, **1** = dragonhead. **2** *Astronomy.* the point where the orbit of the moon or a planet intersects the ecliptic as the body moves northward.

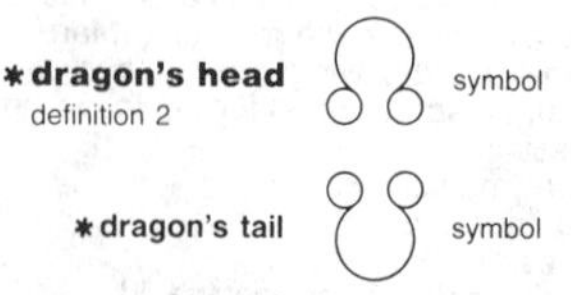

***dragon's head** definition 2 symbol

***dragon's tail** symbol

***dragon's tail**, *Astronomy.* the point where the orbit of the moon or a planet intersects the ecliptic as the body moves southward.

dragon's teeth, **1** the teeth of the dragon which were sown by Cadmus. **2** a row or rows of cone-shaped obstacles placed on a road: *The danger* *from heavy snow has been removed by ... earth mounds called "dragon's teeth," built on the principle of obstacles used against tanks, which brake avalanches* (London Times).

sow dragon's teeth, to sow seeds of destruction and dissension, injurious to oneself as well as to others: [*They*] *sowed the dragon's teeth which sprung up into the hydras of rebellion and apostasy* (John B. Marsden).

drag|on|tail (drag′ən tāl′), *n.* = green dragon.

dragon tree, a large tree of the agave family, from which a variety of dragon's blood is obtained. It grows in the Canary Islands.

dragon withe, a climbing plant bearing winged fruits like the paired ones of the maple. It grows in the West Indies.

dra|goon (drə gün′), *n., v.* — ***n.*** **1** a soldier who fights on horseback. Dragoons formerly rode horses to the battlefield, but fought on foot. **2** any one of a breed of domestic pigeons that produce large squabs, raised chiefly as food. **3** *Obsolete.* a short musket; dragon.
— ***v.t.*** **1** to compel by oppression or persecution: *Many prisoners were dragooned into working in labor camps.* **SYN:** pressure, coerce. **2** to oppress or persecute by dragoons.
[< French *dragon* pistol < Old French, (because it breathes fire like a dragon); see etym. under **dragon**]

dragoon bird, = umbrella bird.

drag-out (drag′out′), *n. Informal.* a dragging out; prolongation: *if the drag-out of the recession continues* (Christian Science Monitor).

***drag parachute,** a parachute used especially to slow down an aircraft on the runway in landing; brake parachute: *It will* [*land*] *at 250 m.p.h., and may use a drag parachute to check its speed on the ground* (Time).

***drag parachute**

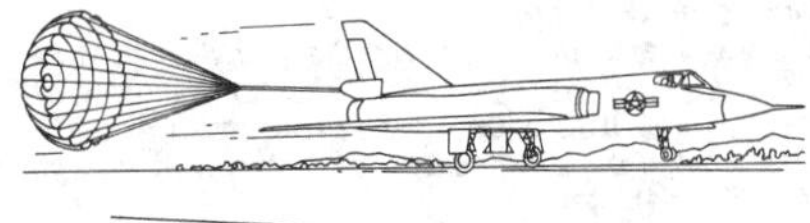

drag race, a race between cars, usually hot rods, to determine which can accelerate faster over a given distance, usually a quarter of a mile in the sport of drag racing.

drag racer, a person who takes part in a drag race.

drag racing, the racing of cars in a drag race, now especially as a recognized sport.

drag|rope (drag′rōp′), *n.* **1** a rope for pulling something, especially an artillery weapon. **2** a rope dragging from something, such as the guide rope sometimes hung downward from a balloon.

drag sail or **sheet,** a sea anchor equipped with a sail.

drag sein|ing, (sā′ning) = beach seining.

drags|man (dragz′mən), *n., pl.* **-men.** **1** the driver of a drag or coach. **2** a person hired to drag a river bed, etc.

***drag|ster** (drag′stər), *n. Slang.* **1** a car used in a drag race; hot rod: *The dragsters are usually concocted from a fantastic variety of car parts and bear little resemblance to any of the cars from which their parts were taken* (Wall Street Journal). **2** a person who takes part in a drag race; drag racer: *Glenn Leasher, a 26-year-old dragster from Burlingame, Calif., showed up with an improbable creation called Infinity* (Time).

***dragster**
definition 1

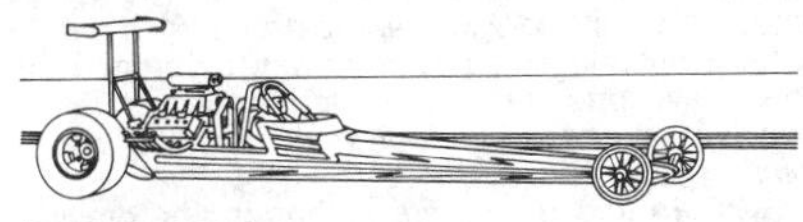

drag strip, a straight road, usually of concrete or asphalt, set aside by local police or municipal authorities, or specially laid, for drag races: *Your article about hot-rodding has sparked renewed interest in obtaining a drag strip in the Buffalo area* (Wall Street Journal).

drags|ville (dragz′vil), *n. Slang.* something boring: *University? That's just dragsville* (Mark Boxer). [< *drag* + *-ville*]

draht|haar (drät′här′), *n.* any one of a German breed of wire-haired pointers. [< German *Draht* wire + *Haar* hair]

drail (drāl), *n. U.S.* a fishhook with a weighted shank, for trolling: *A 2 to 4-ounce drail ... is used to carry the bait or lure to the bottom* (New York Times). [American English, apparently alteration of *trail*]

drain (drān), *v., n.* — ***v.t.*** **1** to draw off slowly: *That ditch drains water from the swamp.* **SYN:** remove. **2** to draw water or other liquid from; empty or dry by draining: *The farmers drained the swamps to get more land for crops.* **3** *Figurative.* to take away from slowly; use up little by little; exhaust: *The war drained the country of its people and money. His energy was drained by working too long in the hot sun.* **SYN:** deplete, deprive. **4** *Figurative.* to empty by drinking; drink dry: *In one drink he drained the cup.* **5** to strain (liquid) through a filter.
— ***v.i.*** **1** to flow off slowly: *The water drains into a river.* **2** to dry; lose moisture by dripping or flowing: *Set the dishes here to drain.* **3** to get rid of its surplus water; find an outlet for water: *Vast areas of the United States drain into the Gulf of Mexico.*
— ***n.*** **1** a channel, trench, or pipe for carrying off water or waste of any kind: *She carried the tray back to the kitchen* [*and*] *dumped the beer and coffee down the drain* (New Yorker). **2** anything that drains: *Strips of gauze are used as drains for pus from wounds.* **3** a slow taking away; a using up little by little: (*Figurative.*) *Working or playing too hard is a drain on your strength.*
drains, dregs: *I had ... emptied some dull opiate to the drains* (Keats).
go down the drain, a to become worthless: *His savings went down the drain on a bad investment.* **b** to be left out or forgotten: *Only about thirty new* [*television*] *programs are selected each year. The rest go down the drain* (Goodman Ace). *This isn't a play about a man going down the drain. It's about a man ... desperately fighting against doing so* (Saturday Review).
[Old English *drēahnian.* See related etym. at **dry.**]
— **drain|er,** *n.*

drain|a|ble (drā′nə bəl), *adj.* that can be drained.

drain|age (drā′nij), *n.* **1** the act or process of draining; a drawing off or flowing off of water: *The drainage of swamps improves a town.* **2** a system of channels or pipes for carrying off water or waste of any kind. **3** what is drained off. **4** an area that is drained.

drainage basin, the area that is drained by a river and its tributaries.

drainage cycle, *Geology.* the beginning, development, and maturity of a network of streams to the time of interruption introduced by new conditions.

drain|board (drān′bôrd′, -bōrd′), *n.* **1** a metal board, usually enamel-covered, on one side of a sink, set at a slight downward angle, for draining water from dishes, pots, and pans into the sink: *A plump old Irishwoman, who was mopping the drainboards, cooked him some supper* (New Yorker). **2** a matlike rubber tray on which dishes, pots, and pans are placed for drying after washing.

drain|less (drān′lis), *adj.* that cannot be drained or used up.

drain|pipe (drān′pīp′), *n.* a pipe for carrying off water or other liquid.

drainpipe trousers, = stovepipe trousers.

drains (drānz), *n.pl.* See under **drain.**

drain|spout (drān′spout′), *n.* = downspout.

drai|sine (drā zēn′), *n.* an early form of the velocipede, invented in 1816-17. [< German *Draisine* < Baron Karl von *Drais,* its inventor]

drake[1] (drāk), *n.* a male duck. [Middle English *drake.* Compare Low German *drake.*]

drake[2] (drāk), *n.* **1** = May fly. **2** *Obsolete.* a type of small cannon. **3** *Obsolete.* a dragon (def. 1). [Old English *draca* < Latin *dracō.* See etym. of doublet **dragon.**]

drake fly, a May fly, especially an artificial one, used for bait.

dram (dram), *n., v.,* **drammed, dram|ming.** — ***n.*** **1** a small weight. In apothecaries' weight, 8 drams make one ounce and each dram is 3.88 grams; in avoirdupois weight, 16 drams make one ounce and each dram is 1.77 grams. *Abbr:* dr. **2** = fluid dram. **3** a small drink of intoxicating liquor. **4** *Especially British, Figurative.* a small amount of anything. Also, *British,* **drachm.**
— ***v.i.*** to drink drams; tipple.
— ***v.t.*** to give a dram or drams to.
[< Old French *drame,* also *dragme* < Latin *drachma.* See etym. of doublet **drachma.**]

dra|ma (drä′mə, dram′ə), *n.* **1** a play such as one sees in a theater; story written to be acted out by actors on the stage: *The play "Hamlet" is a chilling drama about a king and queen of Denmark and their son.* **2** the art of writing, acting, or producing plays: *He is studying drama.* **3** a part of real life that seems to have been planned like a story or play: *The history of America is a great and thrilling drama.* **4** dramatic quality; action or excitement.
the drama, the branch of literature having to do with plays: *The Drama, which makes so great and so lucrative a part of Poetry* (Alexander Pope).
[< Late Latin *drāma* < Greek *drâma, -atos* play, deed < *drân* to do]

Dram|a|mine (dram′ə mēn), *n. Trademark.* dimenhydrinate.

dra|mat|ic (drə mat′ik), *adj.* **1** of drama; having to do with plays: *a dramatic actor, a dramatic success. The players are all accomplished ... but the total effect they give is that of performing a rather difficult exercise at an advanced school of dramatic art* (New Yorker). **2** seeming like a drama or play; full of action or feeling; exciting: *Abraham Lincoln's life was dramatic, from its beginnings to its end.* **3** striking; impressive: *a dramatic combination of colors.*
— *Syn.* **2 Dramatic, theatrical, melodramatic,** as applied to situations in real life, mean having qualities suitable to plays or the stage. **Dramatic** suggests exciting the imagination and deeply moving the feelings: *The reunion between the returning veterans and their wives was dramatic.* **Theatrical** suggests artificial or cheap effects, and calling directly on the feelings: *Her show of gratitude is theatrical.* **Melodramatic** emphasizes falseness and exaggeration, especially in trying to stir up the feelings: *The paper gave a melodramatic account of the child's rescue.*

dra|mat|i|cal (drə mat′ə kəl), *adj.* = dramatic.

dra|mat|i|cal|ly (drə mat′ik lē), *adv.* in a dramatic manner.

dramatic irony, a theatrical or literary device in which the audience is aware of some fact or action that acts upon one or all of the characters without their knowledge.

dra|mat|i|cism (drə mat′ə siz əm), *n.* dramatic character.

dramatic monologue, a poem in which only one character speaks.

dra|mat|ics (drə mat′iks), *n.* **1** the art of acting or producing plays. **2** plays given by amateurs. **3** tendency to show off; dramatic behavior: *Such dramatics as that child goes into, the minute you let her loose!*
► **Dramatics,** meaning the art of acting or producing plays, is singular in use: *Dramatics is taught in some colleges.* When *dramatics* means plays given by amateurs, it is plural in use: *Dramatics are presented in many theaters in the summer.*

dramatic tenor, **1** a rich, powerful tenor voice with a heavier and stronger lower range than the lyric tenor. **2** a man with such a voice, especially one who sings operatic parts written for this type of voice; heroic tenor.

dra|mat|i|cule (drə mat′ə kyül), *n.* a small or minor play: *The anniversary is celebrated by ... a volume of collected prose pieces and a short "dramaticule" or one-scene play, "Come and Go"* (Cyril Connolly). [diminutive form < Greek *drâma, -atos*]

dram|a|tise (dram′ə tīz, drä′mə-), *v.t., v.i.,* **-tised, -tis|ing.** *Especially British.* dramatize.

dram|a|tism (dram′ə tiz əm, drä′mə-), *n.* **1** dramatic quality; dramaticism. **2** a dramatization.

dram|a|tis per|so|nae (dram′ə tis pər sō′nē), **1** the characters or actors in a play: *To prove a point ... Mr. Hawley has first to put his extensive dramatis personae through a series of terrifying ordeals* (Wall Street Journal). **2** a list of them: *The dramatis personae calls for more than 100 Negro performers* (London Times). **3** the characters in a novel, poem, motion-picture, or anything dramatic: *The dramatis personae of his pictures are mostly glistening fish, their hue a glowing red or livid blue* (London Times). *Another gentleman got into the elevator with me, Mr. Norman Mack, one of the chief dramatis personae of the plot* (Esquire). *Abbr:* dram. pers.
[< Latin *dramatis personae* (literally) persons of a drama]

dram|a|tist (dram′ə tist, drä′mə-), *n.* a writer of plays; playwright: *The dramatist rewrote some of the scenes of his play to suit the story better.*

dram|a|tiz|a|ble (dram′ə tī′zə bəl, drä′mə-), *adj.* that can be dramatized; suitable for dramatization.

dram|a|ti|za|tion (dram′ə tə zā′shən, drä′mə-), *n.* **1** the act of dramatizing: *The children's dramatization of Rip Van Winkle was funny.* **2** what is dramatized: *That play is a dramatization of the life of Lincoln.*

dram|a|tize (dram′ə tīz, drä′mə-), *v.,* **-tized, -tiz|ing.** — ***v.t.*** **1** to arrange or present in the form of a play; make a drama of: *The children dramatized the story of Rip Van Winkle.* **2** to make seem exciting and thrilling; show or express in a

Pronunciation Key: hat, āge, cãre, fär; let, ēqual, tėrm; it, īce; hot, ōpen, ôrder; oil, out; cup, pu̇t, rüle; child; long; thin; ᴛʜen; zh, measure; ə represents **a** in about, **e** in taken, **i** in pencil, **o** in lemon, **u** in circus.

dramatic way: *The speaker dramatized his adventures with many actions and gestures.*
—*v.i.* **1** to behave dramatically; act in an exaggerated or emotional manner: *Stop dramatizing and describe exactly what happened.* **2** to adapt to dramatization: *The story would dramatize admirably* (New Monthly Magazine). **3** to write plays: *the language in which Shakespeare dramatized.*

dram|a|tiz|er (dram′ə tī′zər, drä′mə-), *n.* a person who dramatizes.

dram|a|turge (dram′ə tėrj, drä′mə-), *n.* = dramatist.

dram|a|tur|gic (dram′ə tėr′jik, drä′mə-), *adj.* having to do with dramaturgy. —**dram′a|tur′gi|cal|ly**, *adv.*

dram|a|tur|gi|cal (dram′ə tėr′jə kəl, drä′mə-), *adj.* = dramaturgic.

dram|a|tur|gist (dram′ə tėr′jist, drä′mə-), *n.* = dramaturge; dramatist.

dram|a|tur|gy (dram′ə tėr′jē, drä′mə-), *n.* the art of writing or producing dramas: *a triumph of motion picture dramaturgy* (Newsweek). [< Greek *drāmatourgiā* < *drâma, -atos* drama + *érgon* work]

drame à clef (drȧm′ ȧ klā′), *French.* **1** a play whose characters and situations represent real people and events. **2** (literally) drama with a key (to the actual people and events portrayed).

drame à thèse (drȧm′ ȧ tez′), *French.* a play with a thesis; play created for the purpose of expounding or illustrating an idea, doctrine, or theory.

dram|e|dy (dram′ə dē), *n., pl.* **-dies.** *U.S.* a situation comedy containing elements of realistic drama. [< *dram*(a) + (com)*edy*]

dram|mach (dram′əʜ), *n.* = drammock.

dram|ma gio|co|so (drȧm′mä jō kō′sō), *Italian.* jocose drama; comedy. *Paisiello's little opera is a delicious sample of the older dramma giocoso—not a Himalayan masterpiece, but a masterly comedy of the second rank* (Saturday Review).

dram|mock (dram′ək), *n. Scottish.* meal mixed with water, without cooking. Also, **drummock.** [origin uncertain. Compare Gaelic *dramag* foul mixture.]

dram. pers., dramatis personae.

dram|shop (dram′shop′), *n. Especially British.* a place where intoxicating liquor is sold; saloon; barroom.

Drang nach Os|ten (dräng′ näʜ ôs′tən), *German.* drive to the east; Germany's former imperialistic plan to dominate regions as far east as Asia: *For half a century Germany's diplomats and big industrialists, deep in Drang nach Osten . . . talked of a Berlin-to-Baghdad railway* (Time).

drank (drangk), *v.* past tense of **drink**: *She drank her milk an hour ago.*

drap|a|bil|i|ty (drā′pə bil′ə tē), *n.* the quality of being drapable: *. . . drapability, that is, hanging like cloth* (Listener).

drap|a|ble (drā′pə bəl), *adj.* that can be draped or made into a drape: *A highly drapable fabric for toques and turbans is satin* (New Yorker).

drape (drāp), *v.*, **draped, drap|ing,** *n.* —*v.t., v.i.* **1** to cover or hang with cloth falling loosely in folds, especially as a decoration: *The buildings were draped with red, white, and blue bunting.* **2** to arrange (clothes, hangings, or other cloth) to hang loosely in folds: *The servant draped the cape around his master's shoulders.*
—*n.* cloth hung in folds; hanging; drapery: *There are heavy drapes on the large windows in the living room.*
[earlier weave, make into cloth < Old French *draper* < *drap* cloth < Late Latin *drappus* piece of cloth]

drape|a|bil|i|ty (drā′pə bil′ə tē), *n.* = drapability.

drape|a|ble (drā′pə bəl), *adj.* = drapable.

drap|er (drā′pər), *n.* **1** *Especially British.* a dealer in cloth or dry goods. **2** a person who drapes: *Then the garment returns to the draper, who adjusts the skirt and waist on a dummy figure* (Bernice G. Chambers).

dra|per|ied (drā′pər ēd), *adj.* covered with or as if with drapery; draped.

dra|per|y (drā′pər ē, drāp′rē), *n., pl.* **-per|ies.** **1** hangings or clothing arranged in folds, especially such hangings hung as curtains: *The gay colors of the drapery made the living room bright and cheery.* **2** the graceful arrangement of hangings or clothing, especially in painting and sculpture. **3** cloths or fabrics; dry goods. **4** the business of a draper: *I've been working for him at the drapery . . . for nearly five years* (Punch).

dras|tic (dras′tik), *adj.* acting with force or violence; extreme; vigorous: *The police took drastic measures to put a stop to the wave of robberies. Drastic ills need drastic remedies.* [< Greek *drastikós* effective < *drâston* (thing) to be done < *drân* to do] —**dras′ti|cal|ly**, *adv.*

drat (drat), *v.t.,* **drat|ted, drat|ting.** *Dialect or Informal.* to damn; confound: *Drat it!* [short for expletive *'od rot,* for *God rot!*]

D ration, an emergency field ration issued to troops of the United States Army, consisting of three four-ounce bars of concentrated chocolate, each bar equal to a regular meal.

draught (draft, dräft), *n., v.t., adj.* = draft. —**draught′er**, *n.*

▶**draft, draught.** The pronunciation (draft) has caused the spelling *draught* to give way to *draft.* In current American usage, *draft* is always the spelling for a *bank draft,* the *military draft,* a *draft of a composition,* a *draft of air* and is the more usual spelling for a *ship's draft* (*draught*), a *draft* (*draught*) *of fish,* and especially for a *draft* (*draught*) *of ale* or *beer on draft* (*draught*). Usage, once divided, is now fairly well settled on *draftsman.* In Great Britain the usual spelling is *draught.*

draught|board (draft′bôrd′, dräft′-; -bōrd′), *n. British.* checkerboard.

draughts (drafts, dräfts), *n.pl. British.* the game of checkers.

draughts|man (drafts′mən, dräfts′-), *n., pl.* **-men.** **1** = draftsman. **2** *British.* a checker.

drave (drāv), *v. Archaic.* drove; a past tense of **drive.**

Dra|vid|i|an (drə vid′ē ən), *adj., n.* —*adj.* of or having to do with a group of intermixed races in southern India and in Ceylon (Sri Lanka) or their languages.
—*n.* **1** a member of any of these races: *In India the first farmers were the ancestors of the Dravidians, who still occupy the plains and coasts of the southern part of the peninsula* (Atlantic). **2** their languages. Dravidian constitutes a family that includes Tamil, Malayalam, Kanarese, and Telugu.

Dra|vid|ic (drə vid′ik), *adj.* = Dravidian.

draw (drô), *v.*, **drew, drawn, draw|ing,** *n.* —*v.t.* **1** to pull or drag; cause to move by the use of force or effort; haul: *The horses drew the wagon.* **2** to pull out, up, or back; cause to come out; get out: *to draw a pistol or a sword. He drew his hand from his pocket. Draw a pail of water from the well. She drew ten dollars from the bank. Draw five cards from the pack.* SYN: extract. **3a** to take the contents out of; empty: *to draw a chicken before cooking, to draw a lake. A hot poultice was used to draw the boil.* **b** to make by extracting the essence: *to draw tea.* **4** to take; get; receive: *Each partner draws $200 a week as salary.* **5** *Figurative.* to find out by reasoning; infer; derive: *to draw a conclusion.* **6** *Figurative.* to cause to come; attract; bring: *to draw a laugh from the audience. A parade always draws a crowd. Your actions draw praise or blame on yourself.* SYN: entice, allure. **7a** to make a picture or likeness of with pencil, pen, chalk, crayon, or charcoal: *Draw a circle.* SYN: trace, sketch. **b** *Figurative.* to describe; depict: *The characters in this novel are not fully drawn; they seem unreal.* **c** *Figurative.* to mark out; distinguish: *He cannot draw the line between a loan and a gift.* **d** *Figurative.* to form; formulate: *The judge drew a careful distinction between evidence and hearsay.* **8** to write out in proper form; frame; draft: *to draw a check, draw a will.* **9a** to breathe in; inhale: *Draw a deep breath.* **b** to utter: *He drew a sigh of relief.* **10** to make longer; stretch: *The men drew the rope taut.* (*Figurative.*) *His speech was drawn too long.* SYN: lengthen, prolong. **11** to make small or smaller; shrink: *She drew her mouth into a pucker.* **12** to sink to a depth of; need for floating: *A ship draws more water when it is loaded than when it is empty. The big ship draws 35 feet of water.* **13** to make the same score in (a game); finish with neither side winning. **14** to temper (steel) by gentle reheating. **15** to shape (glass) directly from a molten state by passing it through water-cooled rollers, hollow tubes, or other shaped holes. **16** to hit (the cue ball in billiards) so that it spins backward. **17** to hit (a cricket ball) with a slight turn of the bat so that it goes to the batsman's side of the wicket. **18** to slide (the stone) gently in curling. **19** to search (woods) for game.
—*v.i.* **1** to move; come; go: *The car drew near. We drew near the fire to get warm.* **2** to take out a pistol, sword, etc., for action. **3** to make a picture or likeness with pen, pencil, chalk, crayon, or charcoal; make drawings: *He draws very well for a six-year-old.* **4** to make a demand; be a drain: *The noisy students drew on the teacher's patience.* **5** to become long or longer; stretch. **6** to become small or smaller; shrink. **7** to make a current of air to carry off smoke: *The old, dirty chimney does not draw well.* **8** to make the same score in a game; finish with neither side winning. **9** to draw lots. **10** to attract; be an attraction: *That play is still drawing.* **11** *Hunting.* of a hound: **a** to move slowly toward the game after pointing. **b** to track game by scent. **12** to have the essence extracted; steep: *Let the tea draw for five minutes.*
—*n.* **1** the act of drawing: *The gunman was quick on the draw. A draw on the short end of the rope will release the knot.* **2** an amount drawn; something drawn. **3** a thing that attracts: *A good circus is a draw.* **4** a tie. A game is a draw when neither side wins. **5** a drawing of lots; lottery. **6** the lot drawn. **7** the part of a drawbridge that can be moved. **8** a small land basin into or through which water drains; a kind of valley: *The rancher found his stray cattle grazing in a draw.*

beat to the draw, *U.S.* **a** to draw a gun sooner than (one's opponent) is able to: *The marshal beat the gunman to the draw.* **b** *Figurative.* to do anything sooner than (one's opponent or opponents): *The unexpected sale beat the competition to the draw by two days.*

draw a bead on. See under **bead.**

draw a blank. See under **blank.**

draw away, to get ahead of others in a race: *Rather against the expectations of the crowd, it was the Spanish boy who drew away to win* (Listener).

draw back, to withdraw; recoil; retreat: *The crowd drew back as the fire truck approached.* (*Figurative.*) *The candidate was too deeply committed to draw back just before elections.*

draw down, to use up or be used up; consume: *Frost's fame is like that bottle: . . . it won't draw down however it is drunk* (Archibald MacLeish).

draw in, **a** to induce to come in or take part; entice; ensnare: *He was not the man to be drawn in to do what . . . he disliked* (H. Martineau). *The contemporary writer . . . has the problem of drawing in the reader with an insight and artistry that will hold him* (Gertrude Samuels). **b** to draw tight; contract; shrink: *The gown has to be drawn in to fit her.* **c** to draw to a close: *Hours passed and the day drew in.* **d** to become gradually shorter: *It was in the late summer and evenings were beginning to draw in already.*

draw off, **a** to move off; withdraw: *The tired soldiers drew off on both sides. The hunter drew off the hounds.* **b** to cause to flow off; drain away: *The Israelis began to draw off water from the Jordan River* (Listener).

draw on, **a** to come near; approach: *Evening drew on.* **b** *Figurative.* to use as a source; make use of: *As the fund grows, the money is there for you to draw on in case of emergency* (Harper's). *Mr. Mansour drew on his "progressive intellectuals" to form a Cabinet* (New York Times).

draw oneself up, to stand up straight: *He drew himself up to his full height.*

draw out, **a** to persuade to talk: *It is hard to draw out a shy person.* **b** to make or become longer; stretch; extend: *to draw out a rubber band. It was hard to draw out his meager income to cover a month's expenses for the entire family.*

draw the line. See under **line**[1].

draw up, **a** to arrange in order: *The marchers were drawn up in formation for the parade. The troops were drawn up in battle array.* **b** to write out or compose; frame; draft; formulate: *Mr. Steel's Bill has been drawn up with care* (Manchester Guardian Weekly). *A timetable for withdrawal has been drawn up* (Saturday Review). *The first good map of the Moon was drawn up by two German astronomers* (Listener). *The only workable answer lies in . . . a U.N. that can draw up the rules of the game for international behavior* (Norman Cousins). **c** to stop; pull up: *A car drew up in front of the house.*
[Old English *dragan.* Compare etym. under **draft, drag.**]
—*Syn. v.t.* **1 Draw, drag, haul** mean to pull. **Draw** suggests smoothness or ease of movement: *I drew a chair to the table.* **Drag** suggests resistance and means to pull with force, sometimes slowly: *We dragged the piano across the room.* **Haul** suggests pulling or moving something very heavy, often in or with a large vehicle: *Two engines are needed to haul trains over the mountains.*

draw|a|ble (drô′ə bəl), *adj.* **1** that can be drawn: *a drawable plan.* **2** that can be drawn on: *drawable funds.*

draw|back (drô′bak′), *n.* **1** anything that makes a situation or experience less complete or satisfying; unfavorable condition; disadvantage; hindrance: *Our trip was interesting, but the rainy weather was a drawback.* **2** money paid back from a charge made: *A drawback is made on customs duties on imported goods when they are later exported. Goods for which an export license is needed or which are being exported on drawback* (Birmingham Post). SYN: rebate. **3** a withdrawal: *Representative Ogden Reid . . . emphasized the need . . . to arrange a drawback of the missile installations* (New York Times).

draw|bar (drô′bär′), *n.* **1** a bar on the back of a tractor to which implements are attached. **2** a device on a trailer for attaching it to the towing vehicle. **3** an iron rod with a hole at each end, formerly used as a coupling for railroad cars.

draw|bore (drô′bôr′, -bōr′), *n. Carpentry.* a pinhole bored through a tenon so that the pin can draw the tenon and mortise tightly together.

*****draw|bridge** (drô′brij′), *n.* a bridge that can be entirely or partly lifted, lowered, or moved to one side. In old castles, drawbridges were lifted to keep enemies from crossing the moat and entering. A drawbridge over a river is lifted or turned to let tall boats pass. *The Earl Amurray seizes her, lifts her onto his horse and they ride over the drawbridge together and out into the world* (Harper's).

*** drawbridge**

draw|card (drô′kärd′), *n.* = drawing card.

draw|down (drô′doun′), *n.* **1** the lowering of a fluid level by pumping, as in a well. **2** the extent of such lowering. **3** *U.S.* a reduction; cutback: *In what may be the beginning of a worldwide drawdown, the President announced that 14,900 troops will be brought home from various stations abroad* (Time).

draw|ee (drô′ē′), *n.* a person for whom an order to pay money to a third person (the payee) is written.

drawer (drôr *for 1;* drô′ər *for 2 and 3*), *n.* **1** a box that slides in and out of a table, desk, or bureau: *He kept his shirts in the dresser drawer.* **2** a person or thing that draws: *A tapster, a draftsman, or a drawing instrument is a drawer.* **3** a person who writes an order to pay money.

drawer|ful (drôr′fu̇l), *n., pl.* **-fuls.** as much or as many as a drawer can hold; large quantity.

drawers (drôrz), *n.pl.* an undergarment fitting over the legs and around the waist. [< *draw* + *-er*[1] + *-s*[1] (probably because they are drawn onto the legs)]

draw|gate (drô′gāt′), *n.* a sluice gate, as in a lock in a canal, to hold back the water or to let part of it escape.

draw|gear (drô′gir′), *n.* **1** a harness for draft horses. **2** *British.* a coupling for railway carriages.

draw|ing (drô′ing), *n.* **1** a picture, sketch, plan, or design done with pencil, pen, chalk, crayon, or charcoal; lines representing a person or thing: *In the sketchbook were 35 exquisite drawings no bigger than his hand* (Time). **SYN:** delineation. **2** the act or process of making such a sketch, plan, or design; representing objects by lines. **3** a lottery. **4** a small amount of tea to be steeped.

drawing account, an account that shows withdrawals of money in a business for expenses. A drawing account shows how much money a salesman has drawn against his future salary, commissions, or expenses.

drawing board, a board on which paper can be fastened for drawing or drafting; drafting board.

on the drawing board, in a preliminary stage of development or design: *The Vanguard . . . is still only a set of plans on the drawing board* (Time).

drawing card, a person or thing that attracts people to a show or event; attraction.

drawing knife, = drawknife.

drawing pin, *British.* a thumbtack.

drawing room, **1** a room for receiving or entertaining guests; parlor. **2** the guests assembled in a drawing room. **3** *U.S.* a private compartment for two or more people in a railroad sleeping car. **4** a formal reception, such as one by a king or queen. [short for *withdrawing room*]

draw|ing-room (drô′ing rüm′, -ru̇m′), *adj.* of or having to do with a drawing room; suitable for a drawing room: *drawing-room furniture, drawing-room manners, a drawing-room comedy. The little drawing-room operas were shoved aside by 19th century grand opera* (Time).

drawing-room car, = parlor car.

drawing table, **1** = drawing board. **2** = extension table.

drawk (drôk), *v.t. Scottish.* to saturate with moisture, as flour or quicklime with water. [compare Old Icelandic *drekkja* drench]

draw|knife (drô′nīf′), *n., pl.* **-knives.** a woodworking tool having a blade with a handle at each end, used to shave off surfaces; drawshave; spokeshave. The workman pulls a drawknife toward him.

drawl (drôl), *v., n.* **—*v.t., v.i.*** to talk in a slow, lazy way, drawing out the vowels: *He drawled his words as if the effort of speech was too great for him.*

—*n.* a slow, lazy way of talking: *The captain strolls about in a relaxed manner, speaking in a calm, casual drawl* (Newsweek).

[apparently < Dutch *dralen* to linger, delay]

—drawl′er, *n.* **—drawl′ing|ly,** *adv.*

drawl|y (drô′lē), *adj.* of the nature of a drawl; characterized by drawling: *a drawly dialect.*

drawn (drôn), *v., adj.* **—*v.*** past participle of **draw:** *That old horse has drawn many loads.*

—*adj.* made tense; strained: *His face was drawn and stiff with pain.*

drawn butter, *U.S.* melted butter as sauce.

draw|net (drô′net′), *n.* = dragnet.

drawn glass, glass made by drawing, pulling, or rolling when heated, instead of by blowing or pressing: *Tubing is drawn glass.*

drawn-out (drôn′out′), *adj.* extended; prolonged; tedious: *a long and drawn-out story.*

drawn work, ornamental work done by drawing threads from a fabric, the remaining portions usually being formed into patterns by needlework.

draw|plate (drô′plāt′), *n.* a plate with tapering holes through which wire is drawn to regulate its size and shape.

draw poker, a form of poker in which the players may discard and draw cards to improve their hands.

draw|shave (drô′shāv′), *n.* = drawknife.

draw|sheet (drô′shēt′), *n.* a narrow sheet placed under a patient so that it can be withdrawn without having to make over the whole bed.

draw shot, *Billiards.* a shot in which the player strikes the cue ball so that it draws back after striking the object ball.

draw|span (drô′span′), *n.* the draw in a drawbridge.

draw|string (drô′string′), *n.* a string or cord run through the folded border of a bag or the waistline or hem of a garment, so that it can be tightened or loosened.

draw|tube (drô′tüb′, -tyüb′), *n.* a tube sliding within another tube, such as the tube carrying the eyepiece in a microscope.

draw water, = European goldfinch.

draw well, a well from which water is drawn with a rope or chain and a bucket: *In the end, as from the bottom of a deep draw well and by the aid of a heavy and rusty chain, he heaved up a recollection* (Atlantic).

draw works, equipment used to lower and raise the drill stem in an oil well, consisting of a hoisting drum and cable and two large blocks.

dray[1] (drā), *n., v.* **—*n.*** **1** a low, strong cart for carrying heavy loads: *A team of horses pulled the dray filled with barrels.* **2** a sledge or sled.

—*v.t.* to transport or carry on a dray.

[Middle English *dreye.* Compare Old English *dræge* dragnet < *dragan* to draw]

dray[2] (drā), *n.* = drey.

dray|age (drā′ij), *n.* **1** the act of hauling a load on a dray. **2** a charge for hauling a load on a dray.

dray horse, a horse that pulls a dray.

dray|man (drā′mən), *n., pl.* **-men.** a man who drives a dray.

dread (dred), *v., n., adj.* **—*v.t.*** **1** to look forward to with fear; dislike to experience; fear greatly: *He dreaded his visit to the dentist. Cats dread water.* **SYN:** apprehend. **2** *Archaic.* to regard with awe; venerate. **—*v.i.*** to feel great fear: *Dread not, nor be dismayed* (I Chronicles 22:13).

—*n.* **1** fear, especially fear of something that will happen, or may happen: *. . . thrice came on in fury And thrice turned back in dread* (Macaulay). **SYN:** See syn. under **fear. 2** a person or thing inspiring fear: *Sanctify the Lord of hosts . . . and let him be your dread* (Isaiah 8:13).

—*adj.* **1** dreaded; dreadful: *The dread day of his trial was approaching.* **SYN:** terrible, fearful. **2** held in awe; awe-inspiring: *the dread sight of the immense, glowing volcano.* **SYN:** awful.

[Old English *drǣdan*] **—dread′er,** *n.* **—dread′ing|ly,** *adv.* **—dread′ly,** *adv.* **—dread′ness,** *n.*

dread|ful (dred′fəl), *adj., n.* **—*adj.*** **1** causing dread; terrible; fearful; awe-inspiring: *The dragon was a dreadful creature. Death, be not proud, though some have called thee Mighty and dreadful* (John Donne). **SYN:** dire, awful. **2** very bad; very unpleasant: *a dreadful place to live in. I have a dreadful cold.*

—*n.* *British.* a cheap, sensational story or magazine. See **penny dreadful. —dread′ful|ness,** *n.*

dread|ful|ly (dred′fə lē), *adv.* **1** in a dreadful manner. **2** very; exceedingly.

dread|less (dred′lis), *adj.* having no fear; fearless; undaunted.

dread|locks (dred′loks′), *n.pl.* hair with long, entwined curls, worn especially by Rastafarians: *Knees pumping and braided "dreadlocks" swirling around his head in time to the music, he* [*Bob Marley*] *drove home the message* (Maclean's).

dread|naught or **dread|nought**[1] (dred′nôt′), *n.* **1** a large, powerful battleship with heavy armor and large guns. **2** *Figurative.* any large, powerful person or thing: *In choosing so many dreadnoughts—the heaviest, Muller, is 18 stone and square as a tank—the team may lack mobility* (Manchester Guardian Weekly). [< *Dreadnought,* a British battleship launched in 1906, first of its type]

dread|nought[2] (dred′nôt′), *n.* **1** a heavy coat or jacket of thick cloth with a long pile. **2** a thick cloth with a long pile. [< *dread* + *nought*]

dream (drēm), *n., v.,* **dreamed** (drēmd) or **dreamt** (dremt), **dream|ing,** *adj.* **—*n.*** **1** something thought, felt, seen, or heard during sleep: *I had a bad dream last night.* **2** *Figurative.* something as unreal as a dream: *Life is an empty dream* (Robert Browning). **SYN:** vision, fantasy. **3** the state in which a person has dreams: *In his dream he seemed to be flying.* **4** *Figurative.* something having great beauty or charm: *She was a dream of loveliness.* **5** *Figurative.* a daydream; reverie: *The boy had dreams of being a hero. The search after the great is the dream of youth* (Emerson). *It's the only dream you can have—to come out number-one man* (Arthur Miller).

—*v.t.* **1** to think, feel, see, or hear during sleep; see in a dream: *The little boy dreamed that he was flying. On that last night . . . I dreamed a vision of the dead* (Tennyson). **2** *Figurative.* to think of (something) as possible; suppose in a vague way; imagine: *The day seemed so bright that we never dreamed it would rain.* **3** *Figurative.* to spend in dreaming: *I dream away my life in others' speculations* (Charles Lamb). **—*v.i.*** **1** to have dreams: *During the night the little boy dreamed of having a dog.* **2** *Figurative.* to have daydreams: *She dreamed of being in the movies.* **3** *Figurative.* to think of something as possible; conceive: *I wouldn't dream of doing it.* **4** *Figurative.* to hover or hang without stirring, especially dreamily or drowsily: *Mist . . . dreamed along the hills* (Hawthorne).

—*adj.* *Informal.* realizing a perfection not expected except in a dream; desirable or ideal: *a dream vacation. The only trouble with a dream house is that the owner never dreams how much it's going to cost* (Wall Street Journal).

dream up, *Informal.* to create (an invention, plan, or the like) mentally: *In his spare time he was always dreaming up new gadgets. He is studying new scores, or worrying about an oncoming script, or dreaming up ideas for Philharmonic programs* (Harper's).

[Old English *drēam* joy, music; meaning influenced by Old Icelandic *draumr* dream]

—dream′ing|ly, *adv.*

dream allegory, = dream vision.

dream|boat (drēm′bōt′), *n. U.S. Slang.* **1** a very attractive person: *I was assured by the ladies of the Nawab's party that the delegation's leader, Sheik Mohamad Abdullah Ali Riza . . . was an absolute dreamboat* (New Yorker). **2** a very imaginative invention, idea, or plan: *Today's commonplaces are often yesterday's dreamboats.*

dream|er (drē′mər), *n.* **1** a person who dreams: *We are the music makers, We are the dreamers of dreams* (Arthur O'Shaughnessy). **2** *Figurative.* a person who does not fit his ideas to real conditions; an impractical person; visionary: *a dreamer, planning a perfect world for the future.*

dream|ful (drēm′fəl), *adj.* full of dreams; dreamy.

dream|i|ly (drē′mə lē), *adv.* in a dreamy manner; as in a dream: (*Figurative.*) *Humbert's obsession began in a dreamily distant beach resort where he met and desperately loved a girl* (Time).

dream|i|ness (drē′mē nis), *n.* dreamy state or condition.

dream|land (drēm′land′), *n.* **1** a place where a person seems to be when he is dreaming. **2** an ideal place existing only in the imagination; an unreal place. **3** sleep.

dream|less (drēm′lis), *adj.* free of dreams: *Above thy deep and dreamless sleep, the silent stars go by* (Phillips Brooks). **—dream′less|ly,** *adv.* **—dream′less|ness,** *n.*

dream|like (drēm′līk′), *adj.* like a dream; as vague, shadowy, or ideal as a dream: *A new world of dreamlike glory* (Emerson).

dream|scape (drēm′skāp), *n.* a dreamlike picture or view: *His attempts to jolt us with the horrific dreamscapes of Tueuse's final breakdown swell with merely literary passion* (Listener). [< *dream* + *-scape*]

dreamt (dremt), *v.* dreamed; a past tense and a past participle of **dream.**

dream vision, a type of medieval poem in which

Pronunciation Key: hat, āge, cãre, fär; let, ēqual, tėrm; it, īce; hot, ōpen, ôrder; oil, out; cup, pu̇t, rüle; child; long; thin; ᴛʜen; zh, measure; ə represents **a** in about, **e** in taken, **i** in pencil, **o** in lemon, **u** in circus.

the poet describes a dream whose content forms an allegory; dream allegory. *The Pilgrim's Progress* is an example of the dream vision.

dream world, a world that a person enters in dreams; world of dreams or illusions: *In the paper industry's dream world, women wear paper dresses and bake pies in disposable paper pans* (Wall Street Journal).

dream|y (drē′mē), *adj.*, **dream|i|er, dream|i|est.** **1** full of dreams: *a dreamy sleep.* **2** *Figurative.* like a dream; vague; dim: *a dreamy recollection.* **3** *Figurative.* fond of daydreaming; fanciful; not practical: *a dreamy person.* SYN: visionary. **4** causing dreams; soothing: *a dreamy lullaby, dreamy songs.* **5** *U.S. Slang, Figurative.* beyond comparison; exciting or attractive; wonderful: *a dreamy car, a dreamy dress.*

drear (drir), *adj.* = dreary: *They have waited for this time through the long drear months of winter* (Sports Illustrated).

drear|i|ly (drir′ə lē), *adv.* in a dreary manner; dismally: *She got up drearily, wondering if her troubles would ever end.*

drear|i|ness (drir′ē nis), *n.* dreary condition; cheerlessness.

drear|i|some (drir′ē səm), *adj.* = dreary: *Currently retail stores are gearing up for another profitable—and drearisome—Davy Crockett-type craze* (Saturday Evening Post).

drear|y (drir′ē), *adj.*, **drear|i|er, drear|i|est,** *v.*, **drear|ied, drear|y|ing.** —*adj.* **1** dull; without cheer; gloomy; depressing: *A cold, rainy day is dreary. Once upon a midnight dreary* (Edgar Allan Poe). SYN: cheerless, tedious, tiresome, dismal. **2** *Archaic.* sad; sorrowful.
—*v.t.* to make dreary: *... the high frequencies most people don't seem to notice are like to split my eardrums. Besides, it* [*television*] *drearies the ball game* (Jean Goldschmidt).
[Old English *drēorig* sad; (originally) bloodstained]

dreck (drek), *n. Slang.* worthless stuff; junk; trash: *My house was filling up with ... all sorts of dreck like radios, phonograph machines* (Jane Kramer). [< Yiddish *drek* dung, filth, rubbish < Middle High German *drec*]

***dredge**[1] (drej), *n., v.*, **dredged, dredg|ing.** —*n.* **1** a machine with a scoop, series of buckets, or suction pipe for cleaning out or deepening a harbor or channel, or for excavating: *Two enormous barn-red dredges, working round the clock, sucked an acre and a half of clay off the lake bottom each day* (Newsweek). **2** a machine with a net, used for gathering oysters or fish. It is dragged along the bottom of a river or the sea. **3** a boat equipped for dredging.
—*v.t.* **1** to clean out, deepen, or excavate with a dredge. **2** to bring up or gather with a dredge: *Samples of sandstone have been dredged from the seabed off the American shelf* (Gaskell and Hill). **3** *Figurative.* to dig up; collect: *The old gossip was perpetually dredging up long-forgotten scandals.* —*v.i.* to use a dredge: *In Dale Bay there is a sandy bottom, with opportunities for dredging ... from the Centre's boat* (A. W. Haslett).
[unrecorded Middle English *dregge*]

***dredge**[1]
definition 1

dredge[2] (drej), *v.t.*, **dredged, dredg|ing.** **1** to sprinkle: *The cook dredged the meat with flour.* **2** to sift: *to dredge flour.* [apparently Middle English *dredge* a grain mixture < Old French *dragie* sweetmeat < Latin *tragēmata* < Greek *tragēmata* spices]

dredge|a|ble (drej′ə bəl), *adj.* that can be dredged: *The material of the sea—or riverbed—is dredgeable* (New Scientist).

dredg|er[1] (drej′ər), *n.* **1** a person who dredges or uses a dredge. **2** a boat used in dredging. **3** = dredge[1] (def. 1). [< *dredg* (e)[1] + *-er*[1]]

dredg|er[2] (drej′ər), *n.* a box with holes on top for sprinkling flour, sugar, or seasoning. [< *dredg*(e)[2] + *-er*[1]]

dredg|ing (drej′ing), *n.* **1** the act of a person or thing that dredges. **2** the material dredged up.

dredging machine, = dredge[1] (def. 1).

Dred Scott Decision (dred′ skot′), a decision by the United States Supreme Court in 1857, upholding the right of a master in his slave as property and denying the constitutionality of the Missouri Compromise. [< *Dred Scott,* about 1795-1858, an American Negro slave, a principal in the case]

dree (drē), *v., adj. Scottish.* —*v.t.* to endure; suffer; bear: *The bold adventurer ... dree'd pain and dolour* (Scott).
—*adj.* **1** severe or tedious; wearisome. **2** dreary; dull.
[Old English *drēogan.* See related etym. at **drudge.**]

dreegh or **dreigh** (drēʜ), *adj.* = dree.

dreen (drēn), *v.t., v.i., n. Dialect.* drain.

dreep (drēp), *v.i., v.t., n. Dialect.* drip.

dreg|gy (dreg′ē), *adj.*, **-gi|er, -gi|est.** containing dregs; muddy.

D region, = D layer: *The D region ... is of great practical importance, since it contributes largely to the absorption of radio waves reflected from the ionosphere at any frequency, and determines the characteristics of waves on lower frequencies* (New Scientist).

dregs (dregz), *n. pl.* **1** solid bits of matter that settle to the bottom of a liquid; lees: *After pouring the tea, she rinsed the dregs out of the teapot.* SYN: sediment, grounds. **2** *Figurative.* the most worthless part; least desirable part: *Murderers are the dregs of humanity.* [< Scandinavian (compare Old Icelandic *dregg,* singular)]

***drei|del** (drā′dəl), *n.* **1** a top spun with the fingers that has four sides marked with Hebrew letters and is played with on the Jewish holiday of Hanukkah. **2** a game of chance played with the dreidel. [< Yiddish *dreydl* < *dreyen* to turn, spin]

***dreidel**
definition 1

drei|kan|ter (drī′kän′tər), *n.pl.* angular and prismatic pebbles whose faces have been cut by wind-blown sand. [< German *Dreikanter* (literally) three-cornered things < *drei* three + *Kante* corner]

drench (drench), *v., n.* —*v.t.* **1** to wet thoroughly; soak: *A heavy rain drenched the campers and they had to dry out their wet clothing.* SYN: See syn. under **wet.** **2** to cause to drink; compel (an animal) to swallow a medicine: *to drench a cow.*
—*n.* **1** a thorough wetting; soaking. **2** something that drenches; a solution for soaking. **3** a draft of medicine given to an animal.
[Old English *drencan* (causative) < *drincan* to drink] —**drench′er,** *n.* —**drench′ing|ly,** *adv.*

Dres|den china (drez′dən), **1** a kind of fine porcelain made in Meissen, Saxony, near Dresden; Meissen ware. It was the first true porcelain made in Europe. **2** something made of china that resembles Dresden ware. **3a** of Dresden china: *the ... Dresden china clock on the mantelpiece* (New Yorker). **b** resembling Dresden china: (*Figurative.*) *She had a delicate Dresden china beauty.* [< *Dresden,* a city in East Germany (probably because it was the best-known center for the ware)]

dress (dres), *n., adj., v.*, **dressed** or **drest, dress|ing.** —*n.* **1** an outer garment worn by women, girls, and babies. SYN: frock, gown. **2** an outer covering, such as the feathers of birds. **3** clothing, especially outer clothing: *neat dress. Boys think less about dress than girls do.* **4** formal clothes: *in full dress.* **5** *Figurative.* the outer form under which anything is presented. [< verb]
—*adj.* **1** of or for a dress: *a dress pattern, dress trimmings.* **2** of formal dress; characterized by formal dress: *a dress occasion.* **3** for semiformal or business wear: *A dress shirt and tie are required attire in most business offices.* [< verb]
—*v.t.* **1a** to put clothes on: *She dressed the baby quickly on cold mornings.* SYN: attire, garb. See syn. under **clothe. b** to provide clothes for; design clothes for: *Federico Forquet dresses some of the youngest society women in Rome* (New York Times). **2** to put formal clothes on. **3** to decorate; trim; adorn: *The store windows were dressed for Christmas.* **4** to make ready for use; prepare (food, skins, ore, timber, soil, etc.) by some particular process: *to dress a sheepskin. The butcher dressed the chickens by pulling out the feathers, cutting off the heads and feet, and taking out the insides.* **5** to comb, brush, and arrange (hair): *Mother has her hair dressed each week.* **6** to put medicine or a bandage on (a wound or sore): *The nurse dressed the wound every day.* **7** to form in a straight line: *The captain ordered the soldiers to dress their ranks.* **8** to smooth; finish: *to dress leather.* —*v.i.* **1** to put clothes on oneself: *He is dressing for dinner.* **2** to put on formal clothes. **3** to wear clothes properly and attractively: *Some people don't know how to dress.* **4** to form in a straight line.

dress down, a to scold; rebuke: *He retains an aversion to bureaucratic lingo and recently dressed down a couple of tax experts interviewing him on the radio for using the time-honored tax cliché "spouse"* (Newsweek). **b** *Informal.* to beat; thrash: *He was dressed down till he was black and blue.* **c** to dress casually or informally: *Canadian women, though hardly as staid as their men, have made a habit of dressing down* (Macleans).

dress ship. See under **ship.**

dress to kill, *Slang.* to dress very elegantly: *I had on my blue cotton dress, the one with the paisley print, and my white heels and white gloves. I was really dressed to kill* (Atlantic).

dress up, a to put on one's best clothes; dress with care or elegance: *You see very often a king of England or France dressed up like a Julius Caesar* (Joseph Addison). **b** to put on formal clothes: *Will this be an informal dinner or do we have to dress up?* **c** *Figurative: The Nagas want independence and no diplomatic formula can dress up a solution that falls short of this aim* (Manchester Guardian Weekly).
[< Old French *dresser* arrange < Vulgar Latin *dīrēctiāre* < Latin *dīrēctus* straight; see etym. under **direct**]
—*Syn. n.* **3 Dress, apparel, attire** mean clothing. **Dress,** the general word for outer clothing of all kinds, often suggests clothing suitable for some occasion or purpose: *I can't go camping without the proper dress.* **Apparel** applies particularly to outer clothing: *You can't buy underwear in that store; it carries only apparel.* **Attire** suggests rich or splendid clothing: *We need neat clothes, not fine attire.*

dres|sage (dres′ij; *French* dre sȧzh′), *n.* the guiding of a horse through various paces and postures without using reins or noticeable signals. [< French *dressage* < Old French *dresser;* see etym. under **dress**]

dress circle, a circle or section of seats in a theater, originally reserved for persons in formal dress.

dress coat, a formal coat with an open front and two long tails, worn by men for formal occasions.

dressed lumber (drest), lumber that comes in smooth, evenly cut boards.

dress|er[1] (dres′ər), *n.* **1** a person who dresses (himself, another person, a shop window, or a wound): *the dresser for an actress. He ... prided himself on being an immaculate dresser* (Newsweek). **2** a tool or machine to prepare things for use. [< *dress* + *-er*[1]]

dress|er[2] (dres′ər), *n.* **1** a piece of furniture with drawers for clothes and usually a mirror; bureau. **2** a piece of furniture with shelves for dishes: *The pewter plates on the dresser Caught and reflected the flame* (Longfellow). **3** *Obsolete.* a table on which to get food ready for serving. [< Old French *dresseur* < *dresser;* see etym. under **dress**]

dresser set, a set of toilet articles, such as a comb, hairbrush, and mirror.

dress form, a frame, sometimes of wire, in the form of a woman, used for fitting dresses. It is usually without arms and legs and is mounted on a stand.

dress goods, cloth for women's and children's dresses.

dress|i|ness (dres′ē nis), *n.* dressy quality; showiness; stylishness.

dress|ing (dres′ing), *n.* **1** a medicine or bandage put on a wound or sore. **2** a mixture of bread crumbs, seasoning, and sometimes meat and celery, used to stuff chicken, turkey, or other fowl. **3** a sauce for salads, fish, meat, and other foods: *French dressing.* **4** what is put on or in something to get it ready for use, such as: **a** fertilizer. **b** the glaze or sizing for a fabric. **5** the act of one that dresses. **6** = dressing-down.

dressing case, a case containing toilet articles, such as a comb, hairbrush, and mirror.

dress|ing-down (dres′ing doun′), *n. Informal.* **1** a scolding; rebuke: *She had given the bewildered desk clerk a ten-minute dressing-down for the hotel's ... lack of fire protection* (New Yorker). **2** a beating; thrashing.

dressing gown, a loose robe worn while dressing or resting: *It ... contained everything the painfully well-dressed man would require for the night—silk pyjamas, silk dressing gown* (Geoffrey Household).

dressing room, a room in which to dress, especially one in a theater in which actors put on makeup and costume.

dressing sack, a loose jacket worn while dressing or resting.

dressing station, a temporary building or place for the emergency treatment of wounded or injured persons.

dressing table, a table with a mirror; vanity. A woman sits at it to comb her hair and put on makeup.

dress|mak|er (dres′mā′kər), *n., adj.* **—*n.*** a person whose work is making or altering women's dresses and other clothing.
—*adj.* (of women's clothing) having delicate or flowing lines and decoration.

dressmaker form, = dress form.

dress|mak|ing (dres′mā′king), *n.* the act or work of making dresses and other women's clothing.

dress parade, a formal parade of soldiers or sailors in dress uniform.

dress rehearsal, a rehearsal of a play with costumes and scenery as for a regular performance.

dress shield, a pad worn by women under the arm to protect clothes from perspiration.

dress suit, a man's suit worn on special occasions, especially in the evening.

dress uniform, a special uniform worn for formal occasions. Dress uniforms are worn by members of the armed forces at social and state functions.

dress|y (dres′ē), *adj.*, **dress|i|er, dress|i|est.** *Informal.* **1** fond of wearing showy clothes: . . . *especially the gangsters, who were always the dressiest of the lot* (Atlantic). **2** stylish; fashionable: *The dressy dress with the warm sweater or jacket is universally beloved* (New Yorker).

drest (drest), *v.* dressed; a past tense and a past participle of **dress**.

drew (drü), *v.* past tense of **draw**: *He drew a picture of his mother.*

drey (drā), *n. Especially British.* a squirrel's nest. Also, **dray**.
[origin uncertain]

Drey|fu|sard (drā′fə särd, drī′-), *n.* a supporter or defender of or sympathizer with Alfred Dreyfus, a French army officer who was convicted of treason in 1894, but proved innocent in 1906.
[< French *Dreyfusard* < Alfred *Dreyfus,* 1859-1935]

drib (drib), *v.*, **dribbed, drib|bing,** *n. Obsolete or Dialect.* **—*v.i., v.t.*** to drip; dribble.
—*n.* a very small amount; drop.
in dribs and drabs, in very small quantities: *Contributions arrived in dribs and drabs.*
[variant of *drip*]

drib|ble (drib′əl), *v.*, **-bled, -bling,** *n.* **—*v.i.*** **1** to flow in drops or small amounts; trickle; drip: *That leaky faucet dribbles.* **2** to let saliva run from the mouth; drool: *The baby dribbles on his bib.* **SYN:** drivel. **3** to move a ball along by bouncing it or giving it short kicks so as to keep control of it.
—*v.t.* **1** to let flow in drops or small amounts; trickle: *That leaky faucet is constantly dribbling water.* **SYN:** drip. **2** to move (a ball) along by bouncing it or giving it short kicks: *to dribble a basketball, dribble a soccer ball.*
—*n.* **1** a dropping; dripping; trickle: *There's a dribble of milk running down your chin.* **2** a small amount: (*Figurative.*) *In the Funds a dearth of buyers and a dribble of sales were reflected in further losses* (London Times). **3** a very light rain; drizzle. **4** the act of dribbling a ball.
[< *drib* + *-le*] **—drib′bler,** *n.*

drib|let or **drib|blet** (drib′lit), *n.* a small amount: *He paid off his big debt in driblets, a dollar or two a week.* [< *drib* + *-let*]

driech or **driegh** (drēʜ), *adj.* = dree.

dried (drīd), *v.* past tense and past participle of **dry**: *I dried my hands. The dishes have already been dried.*

dried beef, beef cut into strips, salted, and cured by drying in the sun or by smoking.

dried milk, milk that is dehydrated and made into a powder; powdered milk: *Dried milk . . . is produced chiefly for human use, such as direct consumption in the home or for use by bakers and other processors* (Wall Street Journal).

dried-up (drīd′up′), *adj.* withered; shriveled; wizened: *dried-up bracken stalks,* (*Figurative.*) *a dried-up aristocrat.*

dri|er (drī′ər), *adj., n.* **—*adj.*** more dry; comparative of **dry**: *This towel is drier than that one.*
—*n.* **1** a person or thing that dries. **2** = dryer. (def. 1) **3** a substance put in paint, varnish, ink, or other liquid, to make it dry more quickly; dryer.

dries (drīz), *v., n.* **—*v.t., v.i.*** the third person, present tense of **dry**: *Dad dries the dishes.*
—*n.* a plural of **dry**.

dri|est (drī′ist), *adj.* most dry; superlative of **dry**: *Which is the driest towel?*

drift (drift), *v., n.* **—*v.t.*** **1** to carry along by currents of water or air: *The current was drifting our boat onto the rocks.* **2** to heap up; pile up: *The wind is so strong it's drifting the snow.* **3** to enlarge or shape (a hole) with a steel drift. **4** *Mining.* to excavate horizontally. **5** *Western U.S.* to drive (stock) slowly, letting them feed as they go: *to drift cattle. They would drift the horses along with two outfits instead of four* (John M. Hunter).
—*v.i.* **1** to be carried along by currents of water or air: *A raft drifts if it is not steered. When he was a young man, Lincoln drifted down the Mississippi in a flatboat.* **SYN:** float. **2a** to pass without special intention: *People drifted in and out of the meeting.* (*Figurative.*) *Decent and able men . . . drifted out of politics* (H. G. Wells). **b** *Figurative.* to go along without knowing or caring where one is going: *Some people have a purpose in life; others just drift.* **c** to move or appear one at a time or in small groups as drift does on a beach: *The students drifted into class.* **3** to be heaped up by the wind: *The snow drifted along the fence.*
[< noun]
—*n.* **1** a drifting: *the drift of an iceberg. As for Modern English, the drift of stress to the initial syllable is still a living issue* (Simeon Potter). **2** the direction of drifting: *The drift of this current is south.* **3** *Figurative.* tendency or trend: *Many politicians watch the drift of public opinion to see what to do next.* **4** *Figurative.* the direction of thought; meaning: *Please explain that again; I did not get the drift of your words.* **SYN:** intent. **5** *Geology.* sand, gravel, rocks, or dirt moved from one place and left in another by a river, glacier, or the wind. **6a** snow or sand heaped up by the wind: *After the heavy snow there were deep drifts in the yard.* **b** floating matter driven by currents of water, such as a log or a mass of wood: *Near the breakwater is a drift of old boards.* **7** a current of water or air caused by the wind. **8a** the sideways movement of an aircraft or ship off its projected course due to cross-currents of air or water. **b** the distance that an aircraft or ship is off course because of currents. It is usually expressed as an angle between the craft's heading and its actual path. **9** an almost horizontal passageway in a mine along a vein of ore, coal, or the like. **10** *Linguistics.* cumulative changes in a language in some special direction. **11** *Economics.* the tendency of earnings to rise somewhat faster than official wages: *The average rise in wages had been 6 per cent, to which must be added 2 per cent or so for drift* (London Times). **12** a round, tapering piece of steel for enlarging holes in metal or adjusting holes to receive rivets. **13** a tool used for ramming or driving piles or forcing other objects into something. **14** (in South Africa) a ford.
[Middle English *drift,* gerund, a driving < Old English *drīfan* to drive] **—drift′ing|ly,** *adv.*

drift|age (drif′tij), *n.* **1** the act or process of drifting. **2** the distance drifted. **3** what has drifted; material that drifts around in water or is washed up on the shore.

drift anchor, = sea anchor.

drift|bolt (drift′bōlt′), *n.* a bolt used for driving out other bolts.

drift bottle, a sealed bottle, carrying a message, set adrift at a specified point in the ocean. On its recovery, the known time and place of its entry and the time and place of its recovery indicate the speed and direction of ocean currents.

drift|er (drif′tər), *n.* **1** a person or thing that drifts. **2** *Slang.* a vagrant; tramp: *The speech of the two drifters is considered authentic rendition of low-pressure, Texas-drawl humor* (Newsweek). **3** a boat for fishing with drift nets: *Some drifters, unable to land their haul, left for fishing ports on the Continent* (London Times).

drift fence, *Western U.S.* a fence built to prevent cattle from drifting too far from their home range.

drift ice, masses of detached floating ice drifting with ocean currents or the wind.

drift indicator, = drift meter.

drift|less (drift′lis), *adj.* **1** having no drift, direction, or purpose; aimless. **2** *Geology.* free from drift. **—drift′less|ness,** *n.*

drift|less area (drift′lis), *Geology.* an area, including parts of the present states of Wisconsin, Minnesota, Iowa, and Illinois, which was presumably not covered by ice during the glacial epoch.

drift meter, an instrument for measuring the drift of aircraft; drift indicator.

drift-net (drift′net′), *v.i.*, **-net|ted, -net|ting.** to fish with a drift net: *Danish and Faroese fishermen drift-netting off western Greenland . . .* (London Times). **—drift′-net′ter,** *n.*

drift net, a large fishing net that is set out in a long line, usually supported at the top edge by floats or buoys, used especially for herring fishing.

drift pin, a smooth, tapered punch or guiding tool, used to draw adjacent pieces together to align holes for rivets or bolts.

drift sail, a sea anchor made from a sail or the like.

drift tube, *Electronics.* a hollow space or tube in a klystron or a linear accelerator, in which electrons move at a constant velocity.

drift|way (drift′wā′), *n.* **1** a road over which cattle, etc., are driven. **2** *Nautical.* leeway. **3** *Mining.* a drift (def. 9).

drift|weed (drift′wēd′), *n.* seaweed drifted on shore.

drift|wood (drift′wu̇d′), *n.* wood carried along by water; wood washed ashore from the water.

drift|y (drif′tē), *adj.*, **drift|i|er, drift|i|est.** characterized by drifts.

drill[1]** (dril), *n., v.* **—*n. **1** a tool or machine for boring holes: *The carpenter made a hole for the screw with his drill.* **2** teaching or training by having the learners do a thing over and over for practice: *The teacher gave the class plenty of drill in arithmetic.* **SYN:** See syn. under **exercise**. **3** group instruction and training in physical exercises or in marching, handling a gun, and other duties of soldiers. **4** any one of numerous marine snails that bore into and destroy oysters and other mollusks.
—*v.t.* **1** to bore a hole in; pierce with a drill: *A pit was dug in the ice shelf to a depth of 14 metres (46 ft.), and various bore holes drilled to depths of as much as 100 metres (325 ft.)* (E. F. Roots). **2** to teach by having the learner do a thing over and over again. **3** to cause to do military or physical exercises: *The sergeant drilled the new soldiers.* **4** *Slang.* to shoot at and hit: *The sheriff drilled the outlaw with his gun.*
—*v.i.* **1** to use a drill; pierce with a drill: *That dull bit will not drill through the wood.* **2** to be taught or trained by doing a thing over and over again. **3** to take part in military or physical exercises.
[< Dutch *dril* < *drillen* to bore (a hole). See related etym. at **thirl, thrill.**]

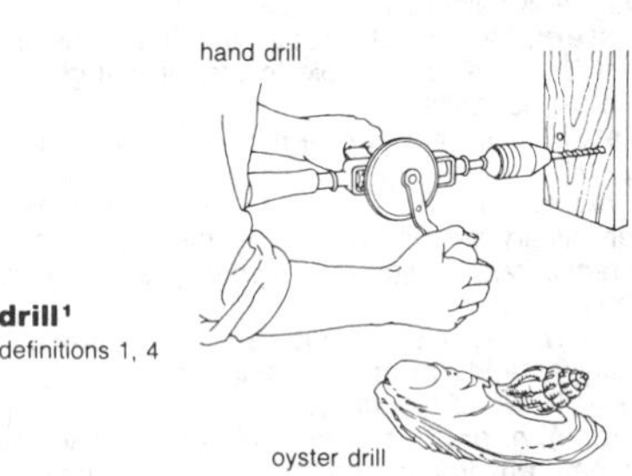

***drill[1]**
definitions 1, 4

drill[2]** (dril), *n., v.* **—*n. **1** a machine for planting seeds in rows. It makes a small hole or furrow, drops the seed, and then covers it. **2** a small furrow to plant seeds in. **3** a row of planted seeds.
—*v.t.* to plant in small furrows.
[origin uncertain]

***drill[2]**
definition 1

drill[3] (dril), *n.* a strong twilled cloth of cotton and formerly also of linen, used especially for overalls and linings; drilling: *Volume had increased enough to allow some mills to raise their prices for drill fabrics* (Wall Street Journal).
[short for *drilling* < German *Drillich,* half translation of Latin *trilix* of three threads < *ter* thrice + *līcium* thread]

drill[4] (dril), *n.* a baboon of western Africa, with a black face and stumpy tail, of the same genus as the mandrill but smaller. [apparently < a native West African name]

drill|a|ble (dril′ə bəl), *adj.* that can be drilled.

drill chuck, an adjustable device to hold a drill.

drill collar, a joint of hollow steel pipe fastening the drill pipe to the bit.

drill|er (dril′ər), *n.* a person or thing that drills.

drill hole, an exploratory hole made by a drill in probing for mineral, gas, or oil deposits: *The heavy trading was touched off by reports of a rich drill hole in a copper vein* (Time).

drill|ing[1] (dril′ing), *n., adj.* **—*n.*** **1** the act of a person or thing that drills. **2** the material removed by a drill. **3** training in military or physical exercises. **4** learning by doing a thing over and over again.
—*adj.* of, having to do with, or for drilling: *a drilling site, a drilling barge.*
[< *drill*[1] + *-ing*[1]]

drill|ing[2] (dril′ing), *n.* = drill[3]. [see etym. under **drill[3]**]

drilling mud, mud used to lubricate the drills, especially in drilling for oil, made of local clay or of prepared compounds, such as barite, bentonite, and fuller's earth.

drill instructor, an officer, usually noncommis-

Pronunciation Key: hat, āge, cãre, fär; let, ēqual, tėrm; it, īce; hot, ōpen, ôrder; oil, out; cup, pu̇t, rüle; child; long; thin; ᴛʜen; zh, measure;
ə represents **a** in about, **e** in taken, **i** in pencil, **o** in lemon, **u** in circus.

sioned, who drills soldiers in marching, handling guns, and other military maneuvers: . . . *the determined enthusiasm of a platoon of boots bent on appeasing an exacting drill instructor* (Time).

drill|lion (dril′yən), *adj., n. U.S. Slang.* an enormously large but indefinite number; zillion. . . . *a handful of bittersweet memories—plus about a drillion dollars from the dad who forgives him for marrying a Rhode Island Italian, now that she is dead* (Time). [probably alteration of *trillion*]

drill|mas|ter (dril′mas′tər, -mäs′-), *n.* **1** = drill instructor. **2** *Figurative.* a person who drills others in anything.

drill pipe, a pipe for driving a rotary drill, such as is used in well drilling.

drill press, a machine tool for drilling holes, especially in metal. It usually has a frame in which the drill turns and is lowered toward the work.

drill sergeant, a noncommissioned officer who serves as a drill instructor.

drill|ship (dril′ship′), *n.* a ship designed to drill for oil under water: *The well was drilled to a depth of 354 metres into the sea bed, by the drillship Discoverer Seven Seas, 64 km south-east of Tarragona* (New Scientist).

drill stem, the part of a rotary drill that transmits power from the rotary table to the bit that grinds and crushes rocks.

drill|stock (dril′stok′), *n.* a holder for the shank of a drill.

drill team, a team trained for exhibition in close-order military drill: *In unison, like the answer of a drill team, came a shouted, single-syllable: "Yes!"* (Atlantic).

drill yard, a special railroad yard for receiving, classifying, and forwarding freight cars.

dri|ly (drī′lē), *adv.* = dryly.

drin (drin), *n.* a group of toxic chemicals made of chlorinated hydrocarbons, used chiefly as insecticides: *Marcus Fox, Under Secretary of State for the Environment, told the House that the drins should indeed be controlled, but that they are not in wide use* (New Scientist). [abstracted from *aldrin, dieldrin,* etc.]

drin|am|yl (drin′ə məl), *n. British.* a narcotic drug combining a barbiturate and an amphetamine in the form of a tablet; purple heart. [< *d*(ext) *r*(oamphetam)*in*(e) + *amyl*]

Dr. Ing., Doctor of Engineering (German, *Doktor-Ingenieur*).

drink (dringk), *v.,* **drank** or (*formerly*) **drunk**; **drunk** or (*formerly or as predicate adjective*) **drunk|en**; **drink|ing**, *n.* —*v.t.* **1** to swallow (anything liquid): *A person must drink water to keep in good health.* **2** to suck up; absorb: *The dry ground drank up the rain.* **3** to swallow the contents of (a cup or other container): *Drink a cup of tea.* **4** to drink in honor of.
—*v.i.* **1** to swallow anything liquid such as water or milk: *We drank from paper cups.* **2** to drink alcoholic liquor: *He does not drink.* **3** to drink alcoholic liquor to excess: *He was fired because he drank and neglected his job.*
—*n.* **1** a liquid swallowed or to be swallowed: *Water is a good drink to quench one's thirst.* **2** a portion of a liquid: *Please give me a drink of milk. The drunkard wanted just one more drink.* **3** alcoholic liquor: *The problem is that she becomes extremely excited, overactive, aggressive and almost manic after she has had drink* (Parade). **4** too much drinking of alcoholic liquor. **5** *Slang.* a body of water; ocean, lake, pool, etc.: *Alongside is a . . . golf course—where a misplay lands you in the salty drink* (Saturday Review).
drink in, to take in through the senses with eagerness and pleasure: *Our ears drank in the music.*
drink to, to drink in honor of; drink with good wishes for: *The guests drank to the happiness of the bride and groom. Drink to me only with thine eyes* (Ben Jonson).
[Old English *drincan.* Compare etym. under **drench.**]
—*Syn. v.t.* **1 Drink, sip, imbibe** mean to swallow a liquid. **Drink** is the general word: *A person or animal must drink water in order to stay alive.* **Sip** means to drink little by little in very small quantities: *One should sip, not gulp, very cold or hot liquids.* **Imbibe**, a formal word, is now for the most part used humorously in the literal sense of drinking, but is used figuratively with the meaning "to absorb": *His one desire is to imbibe more knowledge.*
►See **drunk** for usage note.

drink|a|bil|i|ty (dring′kə bil′ə tē), *n.* drinkable condition or quality: *the drinkability of various wines.*

drink|a|ble (dring′kə bəl), *adj., n.* —*adj.* fit to drink: *Programs for bringing drinkable water to Egyptian and Iraqi villages are well under way* (Atlantic).
—*n.* something to drink: *I never have courage till I see the eatables and drinkables brought upon the table* (Oliver Goldsmith).

drink|er (dring′kər), *n.* **1** a person who drinks. **2** a person who drinks alcoholic liquor often or too much: *Citing controlled experiments with drinkers, Dr. Greenberg said that a person who drinks ten ounces of whiskey in two hours becomes drunk, scientifically* (Science News Letter).

drink|er|y (dring′kər ē), *n., pl.* **-er|ies.** *Informal.* a place where alcoholic liquor is sold and drunk.

drink|ing (dring′king), *n., adj.* —*n.* the consumption of liquids or alcoholic liquor.
—*adj.* **1** fit or safe to drink: *drinking water.* **2** at or from which to drink: *a drinking hole, a drinking fountain, a drinking cup.* **3** fond of alcoholic liquor: *a drinking man.*

drinking bout, a period of drinking, especially to excess.

drinking song, a song about drinking or to be sung while drinking.

drink|less (dringk′lis), *adj.* without anything to drink.

drink money, money given as a tip to be spent on drink or trifles.

drip (drip), *v.,* **dripped** or **dript**, **drip|ping**, *n.* —*v.i.* **1** to fall in drops: *Rain drips from an umbrella.* (*Figurative.*) *Jackets often dripped with fringe* (Patricia Peterson). **2** to be so wet that drops fall: *His forehead was dripping with perspiration.* **3** *Figurative.* to give out slowly; ooze: . . . *his voice dripping with sarcasm* (New York Times). *The spacious drawing rooms and dining room dripped with good will* (Henry Giniger).
—*v.t.* to let fall in drops: *The awning dripped water onto our heads.* (*Figurative.*) *The pages drip the names of notable acquaintances* (New Yorker). SYN: dribble.
—*n.* **1** the act of falling in drops: *The drip of the faucet kept me awake.* **2** a liquid that falls in drops. **3** *Architecture.* a part that projects, such as a coping or a cornice, to keep water off the parts below. **4** *Slang.* a person considered objectionable for any reason: *This commander of hers may be an absolute drip—she wouldn't know* (Emily Hahn). **5** *British.* drip-feed: *"I do not want to hear that the patient next door has had a Bad Turn and is on a drip"* (Catholic Herald).
drips, drippings: *An awning . . . to keep the drips off* (V. L. Cameron).
[Old English *dryppan* < *dropa* a drop]

drip cloth, *Aeronautics.* a strip of cloth around the equator of a balloon that keeps rain drippings away from the basket.

drip coffee, coffee made in a pot that allows boiling water to drip slowly down through finely ground coffee.

drip-dry (drip′drī′), *adj., v.,* **-dried**, **-dry|ing**, *n., pl.* **-dries.** —*adj.* that can be washed and hung to dry without wringing, requiring little or no ironing: *a drip-dry shirt.*
—*v.i., v.t.* to wash and hang to dry without wringing and with little or no ironing: *to drip-dry a shirt.*
—*n. U.S. Informal.* a drip-dry garment.

drip-feed (drip′fēd′), *adj., n. British.* —*adj.* of or for feeding a medicinal solution intravenously one drop at a time: *A baby was wheeled on a hospital trolley across a busy main road as a nurse held a drip-feed bottle because the men refused to turn out* (London Times).
—*n.* a course of intravenous feeding of a medicinal solution one drop at a time.

drip irrigation, a process of supplying water to the soil near the roots through a network of pipes: *Drip irrigation, feeding water directly to the roots, promotes faster growth with less water and fertilizer* (Marcella M. Memolo).

drip|less (drip′lis), *adj.* that does not drip: *The strands are said to be highly absorbent . . . dripless and durable* (Science News Letter).

drip painting, **1** a form of action painting executed by dripping or splattering paint instead of by using brushstrokes. *In addition, he* [*André Masson, an artist*] *squeezed color directly onto his canvases from a special tube, thereby antedating the drip paintings of Jackson Pollock by 20 years* (Time). **2** the style or technique of making such paintings.

drip|ping (drip′ing), *n., adj., adv.* —*n.* the act of anything that drips.
—*adj., adv.* sufficiently saturated to drip: *dripping wet.* —**drip′ping|ly**, *adv.*

dripping or **drip pan**, a pan put under roasting meat to catch and hold the drippings.

drip|pings (drip′ingz), *n.pl.* **1** the melted fat and juices that drip down from meat while it is roasting. **2** liquids that have dripped down.

drip pot, a pot used to make drip coffee.

drip|py (dri′pē), *adj.,* **drip|pi|er**, **drip|pi|est.** **1**characterized by dripping; wet; rainy. **2** *Slang.* silly; corny: *a drippy musical comedy.*

drips (drips), *n.pl.* See under **drip**.

drip|stone (drip′stōn′), *n.* **1** *Architecture.* a projecting stone molding or cornice for keeping water off the parts below. **2** calcium carbonate in the form of stalactites and stalagmites.

dript (dript), *v.* dripped; a past tense and a past participle of **drip**.

driv|a|ble (drī′və bəl), *adj.* **1** capable of being driven. **2** suitable for driving: *He came down a path that passes the highest drivable level of the ruins, and there was a busload of tourists* (Atlantic). Also, **driveable**.

drive (drīv), *v.,* **drove** or (*Archaic*) **drave**, **driv|en**, **driv|ing**, *n.* —*v.t.* **1** to make go: *Drive the dog away. Grief drove her insane.* **2** to manage or operate successfully; direct the movement of: *to drive a team of horses. Can you drive a car?* **3** to carry in an automobile or carriage: *He drove us to the station.* **4** *Figurative.* to force; urge on: *Hunger drove him to steal. Persecution drove them out of the country. To drive life into a corner, and reduce it to its lowest terms* (Thoreau). SYN: impel, push. **5** *Figurative.* to bring about or obtain by cleverness or force: *He drove a good bargain at the store.* SYN: effect. **6** *Figurative.* to compel to work hard: *The men said the boss drove them too hard.* SYN: overwork. **7** to force; direct by a blow or thrust: *to drive a nail into a board.* **8** to set in motion; supply power for: *The wind drives the windmill.* **9** *Sports.* to hit very hard and fast: *to drive a golf ball, to drive a double off the fence.* **10** to get or make by drilling, boring, or the like: *to drive a well.* **11** *Mining.* to excavate horizontally; make (a drift). **12** to go through an area and herd or direct (game) toward waiting hunters with guns.
—*v.i.* **1** to direct the movement of an automobile, carriage, or other vehicle or an animal: *Can you drive?* **2** to go in an automobile, carriage, or other vehicle: *We want to drive through the mountains on the way home.* **3** to work hard. **4** to dash or rush with force; dash violently: *The ship drove on the rocks. We drove against the enemy in a surprise attack.* **5** to aim; strike. **6** *Sports.* to hit a ball or puck.
—*n.* **1** a trip in an automobile, carriage, etc.: *On Sunday we took a drive in the country.* SYN: See syn. under **ride**. **2** a road to drive on: *He built a drive from the street to his house.* **3** *Figurative.* a driving force; pressure: *Hunger is a drive to action. The craving for approval is a strong drive in people.* **4** vigor; energy; initiative: *a young man with drive.* **5** *Figurative.* a special effort of a group for some purpose; campaign: *The town had a drive to get money for charity.* **6** *Sports.* **a** a very hard, fast hit: *The batter's drive went into deep left field.* **b** the way of hitting a ball or puck. **7** a military attack, often a large-scale, forceful attack: *The drive on the western front crushed the enemy.* **8** a driving, especially a rounding up or moving for some purpose or to some place: *a cattle drive.* **9** the thing or things driven: *a drive of cattle.* **10a** a part that drives machinery. **b** the means by which power is transmitted to the wheels in a motor vehicle: *fluid drive, four-wheel drive, front-wheel drive.* **11** *Mining.* drift (def. 9).
drive at, to mean; intend: *What are you driving at?*
let drive, to strike; aim: *The fighter let drive a left to the jaw.*
[Old English *drīfan.* Compare etym. under **drift.**]

Drive (drīv), *n.* a wide street or avenue, usually residential; boulevard: *Lake Shore Drive. Abbr:* Dr.

drive|a|ble (drī′və bəl), *adj.* = drivable.

drive-in (drīv′in′), *adj., n.* —*adj.* arranged and equipped so that customers may drive in and be served or entertained while remaining in their cars: *a drive-in movie theater, a drive-in bank.*
—*n.* a place so arranged and equipped.

driv|el (driv′əl), *v.,* **-eled**, **-el|ing** or (*especially British*) **-elled**, **-el|ling**, *n.* —*v.i.* **1** to let saliva run from the mouth. SYN: dribble, slaver. **2** to flow like saliva running from the mouth. **3** *Figurative.* to talk in a stupid, foolish manner; talk nonsense.
—*v.t.* **1** to say in a stupid, foolish manner: *driveling folly without end* (William Cowper). **2** to waste (time, energy, or other resources) in a stupid, foolish way.
—*n.* **1** saliva running from the mouth. **2** *Figurative.* silly talk; nonsense.
[Middle English *drivelen,* probably variant of *drevelen,* Old English *dreflian*]

driv|el|er (driv′ə lər), *n.* a person who drivels.

drive|line (drīv′līn′), *n.* the universal joint, drive shaft, and other parts connecting the transmission of an automobile with the driving axle.

driv|el|ler (driv′ə lər), *n. Especially British.* driveler.

driv|en (driv′ən), *v., adj.* **a** past participle of **drive**: *The milkman has just driven past our house.*
—*adj.* **1** urged onward; impelled: *The creative individual is a driven man. He has an inner compulsion to bring something new into the world*

(Atlantic). **2** carried along and gathered into heaps by the wind; drifted: *driven snow.* —**driv′en|ness**, *n.*

drive-on (drīv′on′, -ôn′), *adj.* **1** onto which an automobile or other vehicle can be driven: *a drive-on ferry.* **2** having to do with drive-on ferries or the vehicles using them: *drive-on traffic.*

driv|er (drī′vər), *n.* **1** a person who drives: *A cowboy who rounds up cattle is a driver.* **2** a person who drives an automobile, horses, or a carriage: *The driver of the truck admitted that the accident was his fault* (Time). **3** *British.* the engineer of a locomotive. **4** *Figurative.* a person who makes the people under him work very hard. **5** a golf club with a wooden head. It is used in hitting the ball off the tee. **6** a part of a machine, such as a gear or wheel, that transmits motion to another part or parts. **7** a tool for driving, such as a mallet or drift.
in the driver's seat, in full control; in a commanding position: *In that business, the owner is really in the driver's seat.*

driver ant, any one of a group of African, European, and Asian army ants, that travel in great swarms and eat other insects and animals.

driv|er|less (drī′vər lis), *adj.* without a driver: *a driverless car.*

***drive shaft**, a shaft that transmits power from an engine to the various working parts of a machine, especially such a device in an automobile connecting the transmission and the rear axle.

***drive shaft**

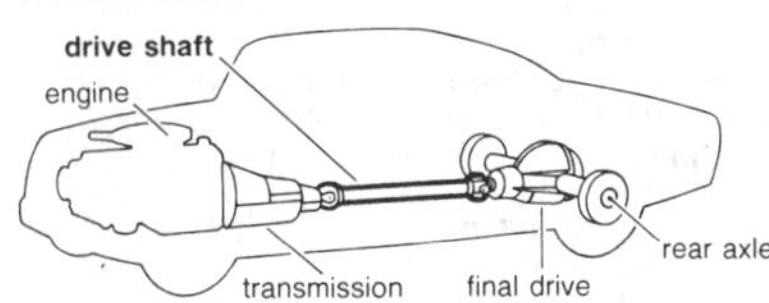

drive-up window (drīv′up′), *U.S.* a window through which patrons can be served while seated in their cars.

drive|way (drīv′wā′), *n.* **1** a road to drive on; drive. A driveway often leads from a house or other building to the public street or road. **2** a road or way along which vehicles or animals are driven.

driv|ing (drī′ving), *adj.* **1** setting in motion; moving: *The chief driving power in the rise of production has not been consumer spending but capital investment* (Manchester Guardian Weekly). **2** moving or falling rapidly; very hard; severe: *a driving wind, a driving rain.* **3** of or having to do with motor vehicle driving or drivers: *a driving examiner, a driving test.* —**driv′ing|ly**, *adv.*

driving clock, a clock used to drive an apparatus at a rate which is proportional to the passage of time. A driving clock attached to an equatorial telescope directs it continuously towards the same point in the sky.

driving iron, a golf club with a steel head, and a face with almost no pitch.

driving range, a field for practicing golf shots and drives, usually equipped with distance markers.

driving wheel, a main wheel which transmits motion to another or other wheels or which produces motion by friction against a stationary surface, such as the main wheel of a locomotive or bicycle.

driz|zle (driz′əl), *v.*, **-zled, -zling**, *n.* —*v.i.* **1** to rain very gently or in very small drops like mist. **2** to fall in fine drops: *As the farmer sprayed his orchard the insecticide drizzled over the plants.*
—*v.t.* **1** to shed or let fall in fine drops: *The air doth drizzle dew* (Shakespeare). **2** to sprinkle or wet with fine drops: *. . . drizzled by the ceaseless spray* (Scott).
—*n.* very small drops of rain like mist: *A steady drizzle made it hard to see across the field.*
[perhaps Middle English *dresen* to fall, Old English *drēosan* + *-le*]

driz|zly (driz′lē), *adj.*, **-zli|er, -zli|est.** having a light rain; drizzling: *a cold, drizzly afternoon.*

dro|gher (drō′gər), *n.* a slow, clumsy sailing boat of the West Indies. [< Middle French *drogueur* ship that fished and dried herring < Middle Dutch *drogher* drier]

drogue (drōg), *n.* **1** a parachute for decelerating or stabilizing an aircraft while in flight. **2** a device shaped like a large funnel at the end of the hose used to refuel planes in flight: *The pilot guided the nose of his plane up to the drogue.* **3** a type of small sea anchor. [perhaps variant of *drag*]

droid (droid), *n. Informal.* android: *The Nader droids are reading through the real-life Nader's Raiders files looking for "anything of social significance"* (Maclean's).

droit (droit; *French* drwȧ), *n.* **1** a legal right or claim. **2** something that a person has a legal right or claim to; a due. **droits**, dues; customs; duties: *The pilferings of the orchard and garden I confiscated as droits* (Frederick Marryat).
[< Old French *dreit*, later *droit* < Latin *dīrēctum*, neuter of *dīrēctus* straight, direct]

droit au tra|vail (drwȧ′ tō trȧ vȧ′yə), *French.* the right to labor or to employment.

droit d'au|baine (drwȧ′ dō ben′), *French.* **1** right of escheat. **2** the right formerly exercised by sovereigns of France to take over the property of a resident alien at his death.

droit des gens (drwȧ′ dā zhäN′), *French.* law of nations; international law.

droit du sei|gneur (drwȧ′ dY sā nyœr′), **1** the supposed right of a feudal lord to have sexual intercourse with a vassal's bride on her wedding night. **2** *Figurative.* any lordly or arrogant claim: *My stepfather seemed to think that he had a sort of droit du seigneur over all cheese in the house* (Oliver Woods). [< French *droit du seigneur* (literally) right of the lord]

droi|tu|ral (droi′chər əl), *adj. Law.* having to do with the right of property, as distinguished from the right of possession. [< French *droiture* rightness + English *-al*[1]]

drôle (drōl), *n. French.* a rogue; amusing rascal.

droll (drōl), *adj., n., v.* —*adj.* odd and amusing; quaint and laughable: *We smiled at the monkey's droll tricks.* SYN: comical.
—*n.* a funny person; jester; buffoon.
—*v.i.* to joke; jest.
[< French *drôle* (originally) noun, good fellow, probably < Dutch *drol* fat little fellow]—**droll′ness**, *n.*

droll|er|y (drō′lər ē, drōl′rē), *n., pl.* **-er|ies.**
1 something odd and amusing; a laughable trick.
2 quaint humor: *the rich drollery of "She Stoops to Conquer"* (Macaulay). **3** a jesting; joking.
4 *Obsolete.* a comic play, farce, or puppet show.

drol|ly (drōl′lē), *adv.* in a droll manner; amusingly.

-drome, *combining form.* **1** a large space or area, as in *airdrome, cosmodrome.*
2 a race course or track, as in *motordrome.*
[abstracted < (hippo)*drome*]

drom|e|dar|y (drom′ə der′ē), *n., pl.* **-dar|ies.** a swift camel with one hump and short hair, found in parts of India, Arabia, and northern Africa and used for riding; Arabian camel: *The troops included cavalry on Australian Walers and camel troops on big dun dromedaries* (New Yorker). See picture under **camel**. [< Late Latin *dromedārius* a certain kind of camel, for Latin *dromas, -adis* < Greek *dromás* (*kámēlos*) running (camel) < *drómos* a running]

dro|moi (drō′moi, drom′oi), *n.* a plural of **dromos**.

drom|o|ma|ni|a (drom′ə mā′nē ə, drō′mə-), *n.* an exaggerated urge to travel: *Partly it was a dromomania I have—I even have it when I drive a car* (Edward R. Murrow). [< Greek *drómos* a running + English *mania*]

drom|on (drom′ən, drum′-), *n.* = dromond.

drom|ond (drom′ənd, drum′-), *n.* a large, fast sailing ship of the Middle Ages. [< Anglo-French *dromund*, Old French *dromont* < Medieval Latin *dromo, -onis* < Late Greek *drómōn* a light vessel < Greek *drómos* a running]

dro|mos (drō′məs, drom′əs), *n., pl.* **-moi.** *Archaeology.* a passage, often between rows of columns or statues, leading to a temple, or to an underground tomb: *Each of the four chamber tombs was accessible through a long dromos which had burial niches hewn on both sides* (London Times). [< Greek *drómos* a running, race course, avenue]

drone[1] (drōn), *n., v.*, **droned, dron|ing.** —*n.* **1** a male bee, especially a male honeybee. Drones do not sting and do not work. *A typical beehive will contain a single queen, several hundred drones, and many thousand workers* (A. M. Winchester). See picture under **bee**[1]. **2** *Figurative.* a person not willing to work; idler; loafer. SYN: sluggard. **3** a pilotless aircraft or vessel directed by remote control.
—*v.t., v.i.* to spend (time) idly; loaf (away).
[Old English *drān*]

drone[2] (drōn), *v.*, **droned, dron|ing**, *n.* —*v.i.* **1** to make a deep, continuous humming sound: *Bees droned among the flowers.* **2a** to talk in a monotonous tone: *Several people in the audience fell asleep as the speaker droned on.* **b** *Figurative: The meeting droned on, but Don Hewitt had lost all interest* (Time).
—*v.t.* to say in a monotonous voice: *The weary beggar droned a prayer.*
—*n.* **1** a deep, continuous humming sound: *the drone of mosquitoes. The hikers heard the drone of a far-off motorcar.* **2** *Music.* **a** a bass pipe of a bagpipe. **b** the continuous tone produced by bass pipes. **c** a bagpipe or similar instrument. **3** a monotonous speaker.
[apparently special use of *drone*[1]]

dron|go (drong′gō), *n., pl.* **-gos** or **-goes.** **1** any one of various crowlike, insect-eating birds of Asia and Africa, with long, forked tails. **2** *Australian Slang.* a silly or stupid person. [< Malagasy *drongo*]

drongo shrike, = drongo (def. 1).

dron|ing (drō′ning), *adj.* **1** making a dull, monotonous sound. **2** in a monotonous tone: *a droning lecture on a dull subject.* —**dron′ing|ly**, *adv.*

dron|ish (drō′nish), *adj.* like a drone; lazy; inactive.

drool (drül), *v., n.* —*v.i.* **1** to let saliva run from the mouth as a teething baby does; drivel: *Although all infants usually do some drooling at one time or another, saliva running from a baby's mouth may often be an indication that he's hungry* (Sidonie M. Gruenberg). SYN: slaver.
2 *Slang, Figurative.* to talk foolishly.
—*n.* **1** saliva running from the mouth. **2** *Slang, Figurative.* foolish talk; drivel; nonsense: *The Guardian was one of the first papers to print weekly pieces commenting on trends in religion in preference to the pious drool often favoured elsewhere in Fleet Street* (Punch).
[apparently alteration of *drivel*]

droop (drüp), *v., n.* —*v.i.* **1** to hang down; bend down: *These flowers will soon droop if they are not put in water. His eyelids drooped as he tried to fight off sleep.* SYN: sag. **2** to become weak; lose strength and energy: *The hikers were drooping by the end of their walk in the hot sun. The old woman's body drooped with weariness.* SYN: sink, languish. **3** to become discouraged or depressed; be sad and gloomy: *In the summer, my sister drooped around the house because all her friends went to camp.* **4** to go down; sink: *As sunset approached the sun drooped in the western sky.* —*v.t.* **1** to hang down; let sink lower.
2 to turn (the eyes or face) toward the ground.
—*n.* **1** the act or fact of hanging down; a bending position: *The droop of the branches brought them within our reach.* **2** Also, **Droop.** a wide, loose, flowing dress similar to the tent dress: *On Fifth Avenue, the droops were out in droves, completely concealing even the shapeliest women's protrusions* (New York Times).
[< Scandinavian (compare Old Icelandic *drūpa*). See related etym. at **drop**.]

droop|ing (drü′ping), *adj.* **1** that droops; hanging or bending down: *Keep my drooping eyelids open wide* (Shakespeare). **2** losing strength and energy. **3** discouraged; depressed. —**droop′ing|ly**, *adv.*

droop nose or **snoot**, an aircraft nose or foremost point that can be deflected to permit better visibility in landing.

droop|y (drü′pē), *adj.*, **droop|i|er, droop|i|est.**
1 hanging down; drooping: *a droopy hat.* **2** discouraged; depressed.

drop (drop), *n., v.*, **dropped** or **dropt, drop|ping.**
—*n.* **1** a small amount of liquid in a somewhat round shape: *a drop of rain, a drop of blood.* SYN: globule. **2a** a very small amount of liquid: *Take a few drops of this medicine.* **b** = minim. **3** *Figurative.* a very small amount of anything: *Show her a drop of kindness.* **4** anything roundish like a drop: *She wore crystal drops on her ears. He offered me a lemon drop candy.* **5** a sudden fall: (*Figurative.*) *a drop in temperature, a drop in prices.* **6** the distance down; length of a fall: *From the top of the cliff to the water is a drop of 200 feet.* **7** a thing arranged to fall or let fall. A letter drop is a slot, usually with a hinged cover. A trap door and a backdrop on a stage are sometimes called drops. **8** the act of letting bombs, supplies, or other material or personnel fall from an airplane: *The plane made a mail and supply drop to the lonely weather station in Antarctica.* **9** *Slang.* a place used by spies to deposit secret messages or information: *"A Crime of One's Own" [by] Edward Grierson—Amusing beginning in a bookshop . . .; funny espionage, with some genuine thrills when Mitty-ish bookseller decides that his lending library is a drop and that laundry list bookmarks may conceal microdots* (Punch). **10** *Baseball.* a pitch that suddenly dips downward as it reaches the plate.
—*v.i.* **1** to fall in very small amounts. **2** to take a sudden fall; fall suddenly: *The acrobat dropped from the high rope into the net below. The price of sugar will drop soon. The patient's temperature dropped overnight.* **3** to fall: *It was so quiet you could hear a pin drop.* **4** to fall dead, wounded, or tired out: *After working all day I was ready to drop.* **5** to go lower; sink: *Her voice dropped to a whisper.* **6** *Figurative.* to pass into a less active or a worse condition: *The stock market dropped today.* **7** *Figurative.* to come to an

---

Pronunciation Key: hat, **ā**ge, c**ã**re, f**ä**r; let, **ē**qual, t**ė**rm; it, **ī**ce; hot, **ō**pen, **ô**rder; **oi**l, **ou**t; cup, p**u̇**t, r**ü**le; **ch**ild; lo**ng**; **th**in; **ᴛʜ**en; **zh**, measure; **ə** represents **a** in about, **e** in taken, **i** in pencil, **o** in lemon, **u** in circus.

end or stop: *The matter is not important; let it drop.* **8** *Figurative.* to come casually or unexpectedly: *Drop over and visit me some day.* **9** to go along with the current or tide: *The raft dropped down the river.* **10** (of animals) to give birth or be born.

—*v.t.* **1** to let fall in drops. SYN: drip. **2** to let fall suddenly: *He dropped his package.* **3** to cause to fall: *He dropped his opponent in the first round.* **4** to cause to fall dead; kill: *The hero always drops the villain at the first shot.* **5** to make lower: *Please drop your voice.* **6** *Figurative.* to let go; dismiss: *Members who do not pay their dues will be dropped from the club. He was dropped from college for poor grades.* **7** *Figurative.* to leave out; omit: *Drop the "e" in "drive" before adding "ing."* **8** *Figurative.* to stop; end: *The matter is not important; let's drop it.* **9** *Figurative.* to send (a letter or post card): *While you are away on your trip, drop me a card. I'll drop a line to you.* **10** *Figurative.* to give or express: *She dropped a hint that she would like to be invited to my party.* **11** to set down from a ship, automobile, carriage, etc.: *The taxi driver dropped his passengers at Main Street.* **12** (of animals) to give birth to: *The mare dropped a colt.* **13** *Slang.* to lose: *The team dropped four straight games.* **14** *Slang.* to swallow or ingest (a drug, especially a narcotic): *For every pain or problem we take a drink, smoke a cigarette of one type or another, or drop a pill* (New York Times Book Review). **15** *Cookery.* to poach (an egg). **16a** (in Rugby football) to make (a goal) by a drop kick. **b** (in American football) to drop-kick (a ball). **17** *Archaic.* to sprinkle with or as if with drops: *a coat dropped with gold.*

at the drop of a hat, a when a signal is given: *A well-trained dog responds at the drop of a hat.* **b** at once; willingly: [*He*] *will deliver homilies on the Street at the drop of a hat* (New Yorker).

drop a brick, See under **brick**.

drop back, to go toward the rear; retreat: *The troops dropped back in alarm when they saw the enemy tanks advancing toward them.*

drop behind, to lose ground; fall behind: *Two of the marchers dropped behind so far that the others had to stop and wait for them to catch up.*

drop by, to come in or call casually or unexpectedly; pay a casual visit: *We dropped by the Institute on Manhattan's 66th Street, a fine old town house* (Saturday Review).

drop in, to come in casually or unexpectedly; drop by: *My neighbor dropped in for a chat.*

drop in the bucket, a very small amount compared to the rest: *From the general impression of railway finances ... it looks more and more as if cash actually paid through the booking-office window is a mere drop in the bucket* (Punch).

drop off, a to go away; disappear: *She dropped off into the shadows.* **b** to go to sleep: *Whenever they saw me dropping off,* [*they*] *woke me up* (Dickens). **c** to become less; fall; sink: *The membership of the Society began dropping off* (Century Magazine).

drop out, a to leave school or college before completing a course or a term; become a dropout: *The first stage ...* [*is*] *catching the children still in school but likely to drop out* (Maclean's). **b** to withdraw from conventional society because of disillusionment with its standards and values: *Being a hippie, to them, means dropping out completely, and finding another way to live, to support oneself physically and spiritually* (Harper's).

drops, liquid medicine given in drops: *nose drops, eye drops. Here, Betty, let me take my drops* (Jonathan Swift).

get (or **have**) **the drop on,** *Slang.* **a** to point a gun at (a person) before he can point his gun at you: *Robles got the "drop" on his captors, and relieved three of them of their pistols* (Newsweek). **b** to get or have an advantage over: *The Philippine delegate had got the drop on Mr. Molotov in proposing that the meeting make some kind of declaration for world peace* (New York Times).

[Old English *dropa*] —**drop′like′,** *adj.*

drop biscuit, a biscuit formed by letting biscuit dough drop onto a pan or cookie sheet from a spoon instead of rolling and cutting it.

drop cake, 1 a small cake made by dropping thick batter from a spoon into boiling oil, or on a greased pan for baking in the oven. **2** a small cake baked in a muffin tin to be served individually, instead of in layers or a loaf to be cut.

drop|cloth (drop′klôth′, -kloth′), *n.* a cloth, canvas, or plastic sheet for protecting furniture, surfaces, machinery, or other articles and areas, during painting or repairing.

drop cookie or **cooky,** a cookie made by letting cookie dough drop onto a cookie sheet from a spoon and then baking it.

drop curtain, a curtain lowered between the acts of a play.

drop-forge (drop′fôrj′, -fōrj′), *v.t.,* **-forged, -forging.** to beat (hot metal) into shape with a very heavy hammer or weight. —**drop′-forg′er,** *n.*

drop forging, a drop-forged forging.

drop-front (drop′frunt′), *adj.* having a hinged front part that can be lowered to a horizontal position: *a drop-front desk or table.*

drop hammer, a very heavy weight used in forging or shaping metal. It is lifted by machinery and then dropped on the metal to be beaten into shape.

drop|head (drop′hed′), *n. British.* **1** an automobile with a top that can be folded down; convertible: *Production of the car, a two-seater drophead sports coupe, will begin in the spring* (London Times). **2** a part of a desk or cabinet that holds a typewriter or sewing machine and that may be lowered so as to leave a flat surface.

drop-in (drop′in′), *n., adj.* —*n.* **1** a person who drops in to a place; casual visitor: *The pilot was Captain Itchy Bourne ... He despised all generals, especially drop-ins from Washington* (John Fischer). **2** a place where people drop in or visit casually: *The rubbish came from Alice's Restaurant, a drop-in for dropouts built out of a deconsecrated church in Stockbridge, Mass.* (Derek Malcolm).

—*adj.* designed to be inserted: *Each window has a drop-in name plaque* (Time).

drop jaw, a form of rabies characterized by paralysis of the muscles in the jaw and neck.

drop keel, = centerboard.

drop kick, a kick given to a football as it touches the ground after being dropped from the hands.

drop-kick (drop′kik′), *v.t.* to give (a football) a drop kick. —*v.i.* to make a drop kick. —**drop′-kick′er,** *n.*

drop|lamp (drop′lamp′), *n.* a droplight.

drop leaf, a hinged table leaf that folds down when not in use.

drop-leaf (drop′lēf′), *adj.* having a drop leaf: *a drop-leaf table.*

drop|let (drop′lit), *n.* a tiny drop.

droplet infection, infection spread through the air by droplets of moisture expelled from the mouth in coughing, sneezing, or speaking: *In young children mononucleosis is believed to be spread by droplet infection* (New York Times).

drop letter, *U.S.* a letter to be delivered from or by the same post office in which it is posted.

drop|light (drop′līt′), *n.* a gas or electric lamp connected with a fixture by a tube or wire so that it may be lowered above a desk or table.

drop line, a fish line lowered by hand; handline.

drop-off (drop′ôf′, -of′), *n.* **1** a decline or lessening; curtailment: *a drop-off in production.* **2** a part that drops steeply; steep slope: *Mud ... builds up for years on the edge of the ocean's drop-off* (Science News Letter). **3** *Informal.* delivery: *The FBI had not bothered to notify the police of the ransom drop-off* (New York Times).

drop|out or **drop-out** (drop′out′), *n.* **1** a student who leaves a school or college before completing a course of study or before the end of a term: *California has the most college graduates ... Wisconsin the fewest dropouts* (Time). **2** a person who withdraws from any part of established or conventional society: *... the alienated societal dropouts of today* (New York Times). **3** the act of leaving or withdrawing in this way.

drop|out|ism (drop′out′iz əm), *n.* the practice of dropping out; tendency to become a dropout: *emotional problems proved to be the most ... predominant cause of both school difficulties and "dropoutism"* (Frances A. Mullen).

drop|pa|ble (drop′ə bəl), *adj.* **1** that can be dropped. **2** suitable for dropping: *a droppable nuclear bomb.*

dropped goal (dropt), a goal made by a drop kick in Rugby football.

drop|per (drop′ər), *n.* **1** a small glass tube with a hollow rubber cap at one end and a small opening at the other end from which a liquid can be made to fall in drops; pipette. **2** a person or thing that drops.

drop|per-in (drop′ər in′), *n., pl.* **drop|pers-in.** a casual visitor; drop-in: *I am not much inclined towards droppers-in; but sometimes one can't very well get out of providing a meal for the uninvited guest* (R. G. G. Price).

drop|ping (drop′ing), *n.* **1** the act of a person or thing that drops. **2** something that drops or falls in drops.

droppings, a the dung of animals and birds: *Officials claim that two fatal cases of brain infection in the past three months can be traced to a fungus ... which flourishes in pigeon droppings and pollutes the air* (Wall Street Journal). **b** what is dropped: *Like eager droppings into milk* (Shakespeare).

drop pipe, = airlift pump.

drop press, a machine used in stamping or embossing, similar in operation to a drop hammer.

drops (drops), *n.pl.* See under **drop**.

drop scene, 1 a scene that drops like a curtain. **2** a final scene on which a curtain drops.

drop seat, a hinged seat that folds down when not in use: *Some taxicabs and limousines have drop seats.*

drop shipment, merchandise shipped by a manufacturer, printer, or the like, directly to a retailer, the wholesaler receiving credit for having made the sale (distributional rights and profits being thus protected).

drop shot, 1 a kind of gunshot made by dropping melted metal into cold water. **2** (in tennis) a ball hit so as to fall just beyond the net and bounce very little: *The player sought to stay in the match with drop shots and tricky angle placements.*

drop|si|cal (drop′sə kəl), *adj.* **1** of or like dropsy: *She had congestive heart failure, a disorder marked by a dropsical condition* (Science News Letter). **2** having dropsy. —**drop′si|cal|ly,** *adv.* —**drop′si|cal|ness,** *n.*

drop|sonde (drop′sond), *n.* a radiosonde dropped by parachute from a high-flying aircraft to measure weather conditions. [< *drop* + (radio) *sonde*]

drop|sy (drop′sē), *n.* an abnormal condition in which a watery fluid collects in certain tissues or cavities of the body, often accompanied by swelling; edema. [short for earlier *hydropsy* < Old French *idropisie* < Latin *hydrōpisis* < Greek *hýdrōps, -ōpos* dropsy < *hýdōr* water]

dropt (dropt), *v.* dropped; a past tense and a past participle of **drop**.

drop test, a test of the strength of an object or piece of equipment by dropping it from a height or by dropping something weighty on it: *During the first drop test ... the vehicle failed to level out after the initial pitch-over* (Science News).

drop-test (drop′test′), *v.t.* to put to a drop test: *Small-scale models* [*of a boat dropped from a spacecraft*] *have been repeatedly drop-tested in laboratory experiments* (Time).

drop worm, a larva of a geometrid moth, or of certain other insects, that drops from trees by means of a thread.

drop|wort (drop′wėrt′), *n.* **1** a European and Asiatic herb of the rose family, having clusters of small white flowers. **2** a North American herb of the parsley family, growing in marshes and ditches.

drop zone, an area set aside for troops or supplies to be dropped from aircraft.

dros|er|a (dros′ər ə), *n., pl.* **-as.** = sundew. [< New Latin *Drosera* the genus name < Greek *droserós* dewy]

dros|er|a|ceous (dros′ə rā′shəs), *adj.* belonging to the family of plants typified by the sundew. [< New Latin *Droseraceae* the family name (< Greek *droserós* dewy) + English *-ous*]

***drosh|ky** (drosh′kē), *n., pl.* **-kies. 1** a low, four-wheeled, open carriage formerly used in Russia. It had a long, narrow bench on which the passengers sat astride or sideways, their feet resting on bars near the ground. **2** any of the various other horse-drawn vehicles used in Russia and other European countries. [< Russian *drozhki* (diminutive) < *drogi* wagon]

***droshky**
definition 2

dros|ky (dros′kē), *n., pl.* **-kies.** = droshky.

dro|som|e|ter (drə som′ə tər), *n.* an instrument for measuring the quantity of dew deposited. [< French *drosomètre* < Greek *drósos* dew + French *mètre* meter]

dro|soph|i|la (drə sof′ə lə), *n., pl.* **-lae** (-lē). = fruit fly. [< New Latin *Drosophila* the genus name < Greek *drósos* dew + *philos* loving]

dross (drôs, dros), *n.* **1** the waste or scum that comes to the surface of melting metals. **2** waste material; rubbish: *Thou puttest away all the wicked of the earth like dross* (Psalms 119:119). *When the author finds a treasure in a mass of dross, he insists on describing everything he found* (Scientific American). SYN: refuse. [Old English *drōs*]

dross|i|ness (drôs′ē nis, dros′-), *n.* drossy quality or condition.

dross|y (drôs′ē, dros′-), *adj.,* **dross|i|er, dross|i|est.** having or containing dross; like dross; impure.

drought (drout), *n.* **1** a long period of dry weather; continued lack of rain: *A drought of three months ruined the wheat.* **2** lack of water; dryness. SYN: aridity. **3** *Archaic.* thirst. Also, **drouth**.

[Old English *drūgath*. See related etym. at **dry**.]
▶**drought**, **drouth**. Both forms are in good use, though *drought* is more usual in formal English.
drought|y (drou′tē), *adj.*, **drought|i|er**, **drought|i|est**. **1** showing or suffering from drought: *a droughty, withered crop.* **2** lacking moisture; dry: *a droughty, desert region.* **3** *Archaic.* thirsty.
—**drought′i|ness**, *n.*
drouk (drük), *v.t.*, **drouked** (drükt), **drouk|it** or **drouk|et** (drü′kit), **drouk|ing**. *Scottish.* to drench (as with heavy rain). [perhaps < Scandinavian (compare Old Icelandic *drukna* be drowned)]
drouth (drouth), *n.* = drought.
▶See **drought** for usage note.
drouth|y (drou′thē), *adj.*, **drouth|i|er**, **drouth|i|est**. = droughty.
drove[1] (drōv), *v.* past tense of **drive**: *We drove two hundred miles today.*
drove[2] (drōv), *n., v.*, **droved**, **drov|ing**. —*n.* **1** a group of cattle, sheep, hogs, or other farm animals moving or driven along together; flock; herd: *The rancher sent a drove of cattle to market.* **2** many people moving along together; crowd: *Athletes and spectators began to drop in droves* (Time). **3a** a type of chisel with a wide head, used to finish the face of stone. **b** the finished face of a stone chiseled by a drove.
—*v.t., v.i.* **1** to drive or deal in (cattle) as a drover: *One Australian stockman passed lonely months droving in the Northern Territory* (Cape Times). **2** to chisel or finish the face of (stone) with a drove.
[Old English *drāf* act of driving, crowd]
drove chisel, = drove[2] (def. 3a).
dro|ver (drō′vər), *n.* **1** a person who drives cattle, sheep, hogs, or other farm animals to market. **2** a dealer in cattle.
drove work, = drove[2] (def. 3b).
drow (drü), *n. Scottish.* a cold mist; drizzle; shower. [origin uncertain]
drown (droun), *v.i.* to die under water or other liquid because of lack of air to breathe: *The fisherman almost drowned when his boat overturned.*
—*v.t.* **1** to kill by keeping under water or other liquid: *The flood drowned all the cattle in the lowlands.* **2** to cover with water; flood: *All the fields were drowned by the flood.* **3** *Figurative.* to be stronger or louder than; keep from being heard: *The boat's whistle drowned out what she was trying to tell us.* **4** to get rid of: *He tried to drown his sorrow in excitement.* [Middle English *drounen*. Compare Old English *druncnian*. See related etym. at **drink**.] —**drown′er**, *n.* —**drown′ing|ly**, *adv.*
drowned valley, a valley along a coastline that has been permanently flooded by the ocean so that it has become a bay or estuary. Chesapeake Bay and Delaware Bay are drowned valleys.
drown|proof|ing (droun′prü′fing), *n.* a method of staying alive in deep water for a long time by making use of controlled breathing and the body's natural buoyancy. *A new technique of water survival called "drownproofing" has been in official use as part of the* [*Marine Corps*] *training program here since April. It has virtually superseded conventional swimming instructions in water survival courses* (New York Times).
drowse (drouz), *v.*, **drowsed**, **drows|ing**, *n.* —*v.i.* **1** to be half asleep; be drowsy: *She drowsed, but did not quite fall asleep.* SYN: doze. **2** *Figurative.* to be dull or sluggish.
—*v.t.* **1** to make heavy, dull, or inactive, as if with sleep. **2** to pass (time) drowsily or in drowsing: *She drowsed the day away.*
—*n.* a being half asleep; sleepiness: *Aiken's is a massive, quiet, unending music, which if listened to long enough produces anodyne drowse* (New York Times Book Review).
[Old English *drūsian* sink, become slow]
drow|si|head or **drow|sy|head** (drou′zē hed), *n. Archaic.* drowsy condition; drowsiness.
drow|si|hood (drou′zē hůd), *n.* = drowsiness.
drow|si|ly (drou′zə lē), *adv.* in a drowsy manner; sluggishly; inactively.
drow|si|ness (drou′zē nis), *n.* **1** the state of being drowsy; sleepiness. **2** *Figurative.* intellectual or moral dullness; sloth: *His vivacity relieved the drowsiness of mere antiquarianism* (Benjamin Disraeli).
drow|sy (drou′zē), *adj.*, **-si|er**, **-si|est**. **1** half asleep; sleepy; dozing. SYN: See syn. under **sleepy**. **2** making one sleepy; lulling: *It was a warm, quiet, drowsy afternoon. Drowsy tinklings lull the distant folds* (Thomas Gray). **3** caused by sleepiness.
drub (drub), *v.*, **drubbed**, **drub|bing**, *n.* —*v.t.* **1** to beat with a stick; whip soundly; thrash; cudgel. SYN: flog. **2** to defeat by a large margin in a fight, game, contest, etc.: *The Cleveland Browns won their . . . football championship, drubbing the Los Angeles Rams, 38 to 14* (Newsweek). **3** *Figurative.* to inflict abuse upon. **4** to stamp (the feet).
—*v.i.* to beat; stamp: *The dog kept drubbing on the ground with its front paws.*
—*n.* a blow with a stick; thump; knock.
[perhaps < Arabic *ḍaraba* he beat] —**drub′ber**, *n.*
drub|bing (drub′ing), *n.* **1** a beating; thrashing. **2** a thorough defeat.
drudge (druj), *n., v.*, **drudged**, **drudg|ing**. —*n.* a person who does hard, tiresome, or disagreeable work: *I was not born to be the household drudge* (Tobias Smollett). *Diana has been the family drudge, keeping house for her father . . . and the four younger children* (New York Times). SYN: toiler, slave, hack.
—*v.i.* to do hard, tiresome, or disagreeable work: *College tutors do indeed work; they drudge* (M. Pattison).
—*v.t.* to put to hard, tiresome, or distasteful work: *A hardness of heart which cares not how his brother man is drudged . . .* (R. W. Hamilton).
[Middle English *druggen*. Compare Old English *drēogan* work, suffer. See related etym. at **dree**.]
drudg|er (druj′ər), *n.* a person who drudges; drudge.
drudg|er|y (druj′ər ē, druj′rē), *n., pl.* **-er|ies**. work that is hard, without interest, or disagreeable; dull or distasteful work: *My sister thinks that washing dishes every day is drudgery.* SYN: travail.
drudg|ing|ly (druj′ing lē), *adv.* in a hard, laborious manner; with drudgery.
drug (drug), *n., v.*, **drugged**, **drug|ging**. —*n.* **1** a substance (other than food) that, when taken into the body, produces a change in it. If the change helps the body, the drug is a medicine; if the change harms the body, the drug is a poison. Aspirin is a drug. Drugs are obtained from molds, parts of plants, parts of animals, and minerals or are prepared synthetically. *The West has discovered every major drug group: antibiotics, vitamins, sulfa drugs, . . . hormones, antihypertensives, and mental health drugs* (Science News Letter). **2** a drug that brings drowsiness or sleep, or lessens pain by dulling the nerves; narcotic. Opium is a habit-forming drug. **3** (formerly) any ingredient used in chemistry, pharmacy, dyeing, or the arts.
—*v.t.* **1** to give drugs to (a person), particularly drugs that are harmful or cause sleep: *The witch drugged the princess.* **2** to mix harmful drugs with (food or drink): *The spy drugged the soldier's wine.* **3** to affect or overcome (the body or the senses) in a way that is not natural: *drugged by exhaustion. The wine had drugged him.*
—*v.i. Informal.* to take drugs, especially as a habitual practice: *He drank, drugged, and in general lived with great violence* (Punch).
drugs, stocks, securities, or other financial holdings in companies that make or deal in drugs.
[< Middle French *drogue*, perhaps < Middle Dutch *droge* dry, or < Middle Low German *droge-fate* dry barrels, with *droge-* taken as name of the contents]
drug addict, a person who is addicted to narcotic drugs such as heroin or morphine.
drug|ger (drug′ər), *n.* a person who administers a drug.
drug|ger|y (drug′ər ē), *n., pl.* **-ger|ies**. **1** drugs collectively; medicine. **2** a place where drugs are kept for sale or use.
drug|get (drug′it), *n.* **1** a coarse, thick woolen fabric used for rugs. Sometimes the warp is cotton. **2** a rug or carpet made of drugget. **3** (formerly) a woolen or mixed fabric used for clothing. [< French *droguet*, perhaps < *drogue* (see etym. under **drug**) + *-et* -et]
drug|gist (drug′ist), *n.* **1** a person who sells drugs, medicines, toilet articles, and similar things. SYN: apothecary. **2** a person licensed to fill prescriptions; pharmacist.
drug|gy (drug′ē), *n., pl.* **-gies**, *adj.*, **-gi|er**, **-gi|est**. *U.S. Informal.* —*n.* a person who takes drugs: *The various student types . . . joiners and doers, druggies, and drunks* (James Reston).
—*adj.* having to do with taking drugs: *druggy sentiments.*
drug|less (drug′lis), *adj.* without a drug or drugs.
drug|mak|er (drug′mā′kər), *n.* a manufacturer of drugs.
drug|o|la (drə gō′lə), *n. U.S. Slang.* secret payment made to police or other authorities for permission to sell illegal narcotics without interference: *Federal investigators throughout the country are looking for friendly witnesses who will be granted immunity for telling what they know about payola and drugola* (Newsweek). [< *drug* + (pay)*ola*]
drug on the market, an article that is too abundant, is no longer in demand, or has too slow a sale.
drug|push|er (drug′půsh′ər), *n. Informal.* a pusher (of narcotics): *In a routine part, nightclub proprietress in league with drugpushers, she showed what real acting can do with the most unpromising, thin material* (Punch).
drugs (drugz), *n.pl.* See under **drug**.
drug|ster (drug′stər), *n.* a drug user or addict: *Injection of amphetamines has grown into an important procedure amongst drugsters* (Science Journal).
drug|store (drug′stôr′, -stōr′), *n.* a store that sells drugs and other medicines and often also soft drinks, cosmetics, magazines, and other merchandise.
drugstore beetle, a small destructive beetle, cylindrical in shape, that feeds on various drugs and cereals. It is related to the deathwatch.
drugstore cowboy, *U.S. Slang.* a man who hangs around a drugstore; loafer.
Dru|id or **dru|id**[1] (drü′id), *n.* a member of a religious order of priests, prophets, and poets among the ancient Celts of Britain, Ireland, and France. The Druids were very powerful leaders and judges until the Christian religion was accepted by the Celts. They appear in Welsh and Irish legend as sorcerers and soothsayers. *His great adversaries were the druids, who could divine the future by means of rods of yew and magic wheels* (New Yorker). [< Old French *druide*, learned borrowing from Latin *druidae*, plural < Gaulish (compare Old Irish *drui* sorcerer)]
dru|id[2] (drü′id), *n.* a person awarded the second degree of achievement in poetry and music at an eisteddfod. [< *Druid*]
Dru|id|ess or **dru|id|ess** (drü′ə dis), *n.* a female Druid; a Druidic prophetess.
Dru|id|ic or **dru|id|ic** (drů id′ik), *adj.* of or having to do with the Druids.
dru|id|i|cal or **Dru|id|i|cal** (drů id′ə kəl), *adj.* = druidic.
dru|id|ism or **Dru|id|ism** (drü′ə diz əm), *n.* the religion, ceremonies, or beliefs of the Druids.
*✱***drum**[1] (drum), *n., v.*, **drummed**, **drum|ming**. —*n.* **1** a musical percussion instrument that makes a sound when it is beaten. A drum is hollow with a covering usually parchment or leather, stretched tightly over the ends, and is played with one or a pair of beaters, sticks, brushes, or the hands. See picture on next page. **2a** the sound made by beating a drum: *Spring had come Like the silver needle-note of a fife . . . And a jubilant drum* (Joseph Auslander). **b** any sound like this: *the drum of rain on a roof.* **3** *Especially Military.* a person who plays the drum; drummer. **4** anything shaped somewhat like a drum, as the soundboard of a banjo or tambourine. **5** a drum-shaped container such as one to hold oil or food. See picture on next page. **6a** a thick bar or cylinder in a machine on which something is wound: *a drum of cable.* **b** a cylindrical tank on a machine or the like: *the steam drum of a boiler.* **7** *Architecture.* **a** a circular or polygonal structure upon which a dome is erected. **b** the block of stone making up one section of the shaft of a column. **8** *Anatomy.* the membrane between the middle ear and the outer ear; tympanum; eardrum. **9** the hollow part of the middle ear. **10** a natural organ by which an animal produces a loud or bass sound. **11** any one of various kinds of large, carnivorous, spiny-finned North American fishes that have an air bladder and can make a drumming sound; drumfish. **12** *Australian Slang.* a bundle or roll of clothes carried by a swagman; a swag. **13** *Obsolete.* a crowded assembly of fashionable people at a private house in the evening.
—*v.i.* **1** to beat or play a drum: *He drums in the school dance band.* **2** to beat, tap, or strike again and again, often with a rhythmical noise: *Stop drumming on the table with your fingers.* **3** to sound like a drum; resound: *The noise drummed in his ears.* **4** (of birds and insects) to make a hollow, reverberating sound, such as that made by quivering the wings: *The gnats drummed around him.*
—*v.t.* **1** to teach or drive into one's mind by repeating over and over: *His lessons had to be drummed into him because he did not learn quickly.* **2** to call or summon by or as if by beating a drum. **3** to beat rhythmically; perform (a tune) by drumming.
beat the drum (or **drums**), *Informal.* to give vigorous support; promote or advocate (something): *So far the response of the Government . . . and the call by the Minister of Science* [*Lord Hailsham*] *that we should "beat the drum" have done this country's reputation immense harm* (Jo Grimond).
drum out of, to send away from in disgrace: *The cowardly soldier was drummed out of the regiment.*
drum up, **a** to call together: *We could not drum up enough boys to make a football team.* **b** to

---

Pronunciation Key: hat, āge, cãre, fär; let, ēqual, tėrm; it, īce; hot, ōpen, ôrder; oil, out; cup, půt, rüle; child; long; thin; ᴛʜen; zh, measure; ə represents **a** in about, **e** in taken, **i** in pencil, **o** in lemon, **u** in circus.

get by asking again and again; solicit or obtain: *The company's advertising campaign drummed up more business. One bank official, however, called the move by the Justice Department "another ridiculous attempt to drum up more publicity"* (Wall Street Journal). **c** to concoct: *I would soon find the legislator in question drumming up some objection to the bill* (C. A. Eastman). **d** to rouse up: *The showman drummed up his grit* (Mark Twain). [perhaps short for earlier *drumslade* drum, drummer < Dutch, or Low German *trommelslag* drumbeat] —**drum′like′**, *adj.*

drum[2] (drum), *n.* **1** *Scottish and Irish.* a long, narrow hill or ridge. **2** *Geology.* a drumlin. [< Irish, or Scottish Gaelic *druim* ridge; (literally) back. See related etym. at **dorsum.**]

drum|beat (drum′bēt′), *n.* the sound made when a drum is beaten.

drum-beat|er (drum′bē′tər), *n. Informal.* **1** a publicity agent; advertising agent: *a drum-beater for a circus.* **2** *Figurative.* a person who proclaims his support of something in a loud manner or with a great deal of publicity: *a drum-beater for disarmament.*

drum|ble (drum′bəl, drům′əl), *v.i.*, **-bled, -bling.** *Dialect.* to move sluggishly. [< earlier *dumble* < *dumb* + *-le*]

drum brake, a brake, especially in an automobile, with brake bands that press outward against the inside rim of a brake drum.

drum corps, a group of drum players led or directed by a drum major.

drum|fire (drum′fīr′), *n.* **1** gunfire so heavy and continuous as to sound like the beating of drums. **2** *Figurative.* a continuous, unrelenting assault: *a drumfire of criticism.*

drum|fish (drum′fish′), *n., pl.* **-fish|es** or (*collectively*) **-fish.** = drum[1] (def. 11).

drum|head (drum′hed′), *n., adj.* —*n.* **1** the parchment or membrane stretched tightly over one or both ends of a drum. **2** = eardrum. **3** the top of a capstan. —*adj.* without delay and formality; brief and direct: *a drumhead meeting.*

drumhead court-martial, a court-martial on the battlefield or while troops are moving, held in order to try offenders without delay. [because originally the court used a large drum as a table]

drum|lin (drum′lən), *n.* a ridge or oval-shaped hill formed by glacial drift. See picture under **glacier.** [apparently short for unrecorded *drumling* < *drum*[2] + *-ling*]

drum|ly (drum′lē, drům′-), *adj.*, **-li|er, -li|est.** *Scottish.* **1** cloudy. **2** discolored; turbid. **3** troubled; gloomy. [variant of obsolete *drubly,* alteration of Middle English *trobly* troubled]

drum machine, an electronic instrument that stores and reproduces sounds of percussion instruments. It is most commonly used in popular music.

drum major, the leader or director of a marching band.

drum majorette, a girl or woman drum major, especially one who leads parades, twirling a baton; majorette.

drum|mer (drum′ər), *n.* **1** a person who plays a drum, especially in a band. **2** *U.S. Informal, Figurative.* a traveling salesman or commercial traveler.

drum|mock (drum′ək), *n. Scottish.* drammock.

Drum|mond light (drum′ənd), = limelight (defs. 2a, b.) [< Captain Thomas *Drummond,* 1797-1840, a Scottish engineer, who invented it]

Drummond phlox, a species of phlox with a wide range of colors that grows wild in Texas, and from which all annual varieties of phlox are derived. [< Thomas *Drummond,* a British botanist of the 1800's]

drum|roll (drum′rōl′), *n.* a roll of drums; the sound or beating of a drum or drums: *With the quietest of diplomatic drumrolls, he relinquished control of the 60 divisions in NATO's European defense mechanism* (Time).

drum|stick (drum′stik′), *n.* **1** a stick for beating a drum. **2** the lower half of the leg of a cooked chicken, turkey, or other fowl: *He fell asleep clutching a half-eaten turkey drumstick in his right fist* (Time).

drunk (drungk), *adj., n., v.* —*adj.* **1** overcome by alcoholic liquor; intoxicated; inebriated: *He was so drunk he could not stand up. The offender was arrested for being drunk and disorderly.* **2** *Figurative.* very much excited or affected: *The general was drunk with success. If, drunk with sight of power, we loose Wild tongues* (Rudyard Kipling). **3** *Archaic.* saturated; drenched: *a bee drunk with honey. I will make mine arrows drunk with blood* (Deuteronomy 32:42). —*n.* **1** a person who is drunk; intoxicated person: *The drunk was hustled off to jail.* **2** *Informal.* a spell of drinking alcoholic liquor; drinking bout: *Many alcoholics go on drunks that continue for days at a time.* **a 3** past participle of **drink**: *Has the baby drunk his milk?* **4** *Archaic.* drank; a past tense of **drink.**

▶**drunk, drunken.** The predicate adjective is regularly *drunk: The man was drunk* (not *drunken*). The attributive adjective is now either *drunk* or *drunken: The drunken* (or *drunk*) *man staggered in the door.*

drunk|ard (drung′kərd), *n.* a person who is often drunk; person who drinks too much alcoholic liquor.

drunk|en (drung′kən), *adj., v.* —*adj.* **1** overcome by alcoholic liquor; drunk: *The noisy, drunken man was arrested by the police.* SYN: intoxicated. **2** caused by being drunk: *a drunken act, drunken words.* **3** often drinking too much alcoholic liquor; habitually intemperate: *The soldier was a drunken brute.* **4** *Archaic.* saturated; drenched: *Let the earth be drunken with our blood* (Shakespeare). **5** (of a screw, bolt, or pipe) unevenly threaded. **a** *Archaic.* drunk; a past participle of **drink.** —**drunk′en|ly**, *adv.* —**drunk′en|ness**, *n.*

▶See **drunk** for usage note.

drunk|om|e|ter (drung kom′ə tər), *n.* a device for determining the alcoholic content of the blood by analysis of the breath, used on motorists who are suspected of being intoxicated while driving.

dru|pa|ceous (drü pā′shəs), *adj. Botany.* **1** resembling a drupe. **2** producing drupes: *drupaceous trees.*

drupe (drüp), *n. Botany.* a fruit whose seed is contained in a hard pit or stone surrounded by soft, pulpy flesh with a thin outer covering; a stone fruit. Plums, cherries, apricots, and peaches are drupes. See picture under **fruit.** [< New Latin *drupa* < Latin *drūpa,* for *druppa* very ripe olive < Greek *drýppa* olive]

dru|pel (drü′pəl), *n.* = drupe. [< New Latin *drupella* (diminutive) < *drupa;* see etym. under **drupe**]

drupe|let (drüp′lit), *n. Botany.* one of the small drupes of which certain fruits, such as the raspberry and blackberry, are made up.

dru|pe|ole (drü′pē ōl), *n.* = drupelet. [a diminutive of *drupe*]

druse (drüz), *n.* **1** a crust of small crystals lining the sides of a cavity in a rock. **2** the crystal-lined cavity. [< German *Druse*]

Druse or **Druze** (drüz), *n.* one of a people or sect in Syria, Lebanon, and Israel, whose basically Moslem religion contains some Christian elements. [< Arabic *Durūz*]

Dru|se|an or **Dru|si|an** (drü′zē ən), *adj.* of or having to do with the Druses.

dru|sy (drü′zē), *adj.* **1** covered or lined with small projecting crystals. **2** (of a rock) containing crystal-lined cavities, or druses.

druth|ers (druᴛʜ′ərz), *n. U.S. Dialect.* what one prefers; choice: *The mass of voters, if given their druthers, will vote for all spending projects and against all tax increases* (Wall Street Journal). [< (woul)*d rather*]

dru|zhin|nik (drü zhē′nik), *n., pl.* **-ni|ki** (-ni kē). a civilian auxiliary policeman in the Soviet Union: *The Druzhinniki . . . are also to be found guarding courtrooms during political trials* (London Times). [< Russian *druzhinnik* < (*Narodnaya*) *Druzhina* (People's) Patrol]

DRV (no periods) or **DRVN** (no periods), Democratic Republic of Vietnam (formerly North Vietnam).

dry (drī), *adj.*, **dri|er, dri|est,** *v.*, **dried, dry|ing,** *n., pl.* **drys** or **dries.** —*adj.* **1** not wet; not moist: *dry clothes. Dust is dry.* **2** having little or no rain: *a dry season. Arizona has a dry climate. Here I am, an old man in a dry month, Being read to by a boy, waiting for rain* (T. S. Eliot). SYN: droughty. **3** having little or no natural or ordinary moisture: *a dry tongue.* **4** not giving milk: *That cow has been dry for a month.* **5** empty of water or other liquid; evaporated: *I can't write with a dry fountain pen. The kettle has boiled dry.* **6a** wanting a drink; thirsty: *I'm dry after that hike.* **b** causing thirst: *Cutting lawns is dry work.* **7** not under, in, or on water: *He was glad to be on dry land and away from the swamp.* **8a** not liquid; solid: *dry wares, dry cargo.* **b** of or having to do with nonliquid substances or commodities: *dry measure.* **9** not shedding or accompanied by tears: *dry sobs. After the sad play there wasn't a dry eye in the theater.* **10** not fresh: *dry bread.* **11** *Figurative.* showing no feeling; stiff; cold or restrained: *a dry answer.* **12** *Figurative.* quiet and intelligent; humorous in an unemotional or somewhat sarcastic way: *His dry humor was said without a smile.* **13** *Figurative.* not interesting; dull: *a dry subject. A book full of facts and figures is dry.* **14** *Figurative.* inactive; slow; barren: *a dry business season. A dry period in politics . . . left him without much to do* (New Yorker). **15** free from sweetness or fruity flavor; low in sugar content: *dry wine.* **16** without mucus: *a dry cough.* **17a** *Informal.* having or favoring laws against making and selling alcoholic drinks: *Oklahoma used to be a dry state.* **b** in abstention from drinking alcoholic beverages: *Alcoholics must remain dry to cure themselves.* **18** without butter: *dry toast.* **19** bald; plain; unadorned: *a list of dry facts.* **20** *Figurative.* having stiff and formal outlines, as a work of art: *That painter's work is dry and without feeling.* **21** *Military.* practiced or rehearsed without live ammunition. **22** *Botany.* (of a simple fruit) characterized by the absence of moisture in the pericarp at maturity. **23** (of money) paid in cash. **24** *Obsolete.* without bloodshed: *a dry blow, a dry fight.*
—*v.t.* **1** to make dry: *to dry one's eyes.* **2** to wipe away: *to dry one's tears.* **3** to evaporate.
—*v.i.* **1** to become dry: *Clothes dry in the sun.* **2** to evaporate: *A shallow puddle dries rapidly.*
—*n.* **1** *Informal.* a person who favors laws against making and selling alcoholic drinks; prohibitionist: *Mr. Sinclair concludes that if only the drys had accepted the limited notion of a ban on hard spirits, prohibition might have survived* (Punch). **2** dryness; drought: *Dead water during the dries, and a lake with two outlets after the annual rains* (R. F. Burton).

dry out, to treat or be treated for alcoholic or drug addiction: *If he agrees to try to give up drinking he will be dried out in the clinic* (London Times). *They are not only making firmer contacts with the addicts in the streets but also giving some of those they have "dried out" a purpose which helps them, too, to come off the drug* (Manchester Guardian Weekly).

dry up, a to make or become completely dry: *The wells all dried up during the drought.* **b** *Slang.* to stop talking: *When first-rate directors talk like third-rate intellectuals, it's time for someone to tell them to dry up* (New Statesman). **c** to stop; run out; go out of existence: *It is highly probable that without profit the illicit channels would close and the supply of narcotics would dry up* (Wall Street Journal). **d** (of an actor) to

bass drum · bongo drums · conga drum · snare drum

★**drum**[1] definitions 1, 5

tenor drum · kettledrums · oil drum

forget one's words: *No matter how well you knew your words, you'd dry up when you got before the footlights* (George Moore). [Old English *drȳge*]
—***Syn.*** *adj.* **1 Dry, arid** mean without moisture. **Dry** does not necessarily imply being completely without moisture: *This bread is dry.* **Arid** implies being completely dry or dried out and adds the idea of barrenness, particularly when applied to land: *No crops will grow in arid soil.*

dry|ad or **Dry|ad** (drī′əd, -ad), *n., pl.* **-ads, -a|des** (-ə dēz). *Greek Mythology.* a nymph that lives in a tree; wood nymph; hamadryad: *Knock at the rough rind of this ilex-tree, and summon forth the Dryad!* (Hawthorne). [<Latin *Dryas, -adis* <Greek *Dryás, -ádos* <*drys* tree]

dry|ad|ic (drī ad′ik), *adj.* of or having to do with dryads.

dry|as|dust (drī′əz dust′), *n.* = pedant. [<the fictitious Dr. *Dryasdust,* of the prefatory matter of some of Sir Walter Scott's novels]

dry-as-dust (drī′əz dust′), *adj.* very dry or uninteresting; overly pedantic; spiritless; prosaic: *a dry-as-dust lecture, a dry-as-dust teacher.*

dry battery, **1** a set of dry cells connected to produce electric current. **2** a dry cell.

dry bean, a fully ripe navy bean.

dry bob, *British Slang.* a person, especially a schoolboy, who engages in such sports as cricket and Rugby.

dry bone ore, = smithsonite.

dry-brush (drī′brush′), *adj.* of or having to do with a technique of water-color painting done with concentrated paint on a brush that is almost dry.

dry-bulb thermometer (drī′bulb′), the one of the two thermometers of a psychrometer whose bulb is kept dry when humidity determinations are being made.

dry camp, *U.S.* a camp or halt where there is no water: *We must make a dry camp tonight* (J. H. Beadle).

***dry cell,** an electric cell in which the chemical producing the current is made into a paste with gelatin, sawdust, or the like, so that its contents cannot spill.

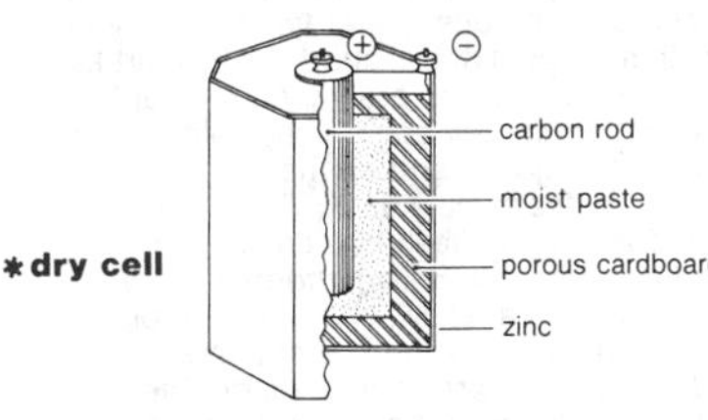

***dry cell**

dry cereal, any one of various types of breakfast cereal eaten without further cooking or preparation, usually with milk or cream.

dry-clean (drī′klēn′), *v.t.* to clean (clothes or other cloth articles) with naphtha, benzine, or the like, and little or no water. —***v.i.*** to undergo dry cleaning: *It dry-cleans beautifully and wrinkles hang out* (New York Times).

dry-clean|a|ble (drī′klē′nə bəl), *adj.* that can be dry-cleaned: *a dry-cleanable sheepskin coat.*

dry cleaner, 1 a person or business that does dry cleaning. **2** naphtha, benzine, or the like, used in dry cleaning.

dry cleaning, 1 the cleaning of cloth with little or no water, using liquids such as naphtha or benzine. **2** clothes or other articles that have been dry-cleaned: *to pick up some dry cleaning.*

dry-cleanse (drī′klenz′), *v.t.,* **-cleansed, -cleansing.** = dry-clean.

dry-cure (drī′kyůr′), *v.t.,* **-cured, -cur|ing.** to cure (meat) by salting and drying.

dry distillation, *Chemistry.* destructive distillation as applied to the decomposition of wood, coal, or other substance, by heat to yield liquid products; pyrolysis. Dry distillation is not a true distillation, since the original substances are changed in the process.

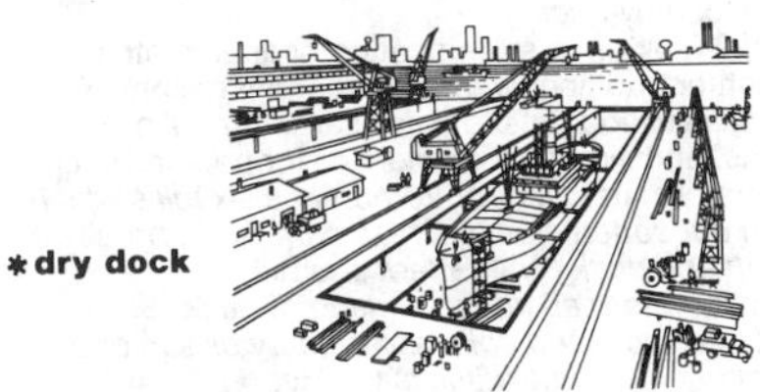
***dry dock**

***dry dock,** a dock built watertight so that the water may be pumped out or kept high. Dry docks are used for repairing or building ships. *The dry dock, which will form an essential part of Pakistan's shipbuilding programme, will accommodate vessels of up to 12,000 tons* (London Times).

dry-dock (drī′dok′), *v.t.* **1** to place (a ship) in a dry dock. **2** *Figurative.* to suspend the duties of (a person). —***v.i.*** **1** to go into dry dock. **2** *Figurative.* to be relieved of one's duties.

dry|er (drī′ər), *n.* **1** a device or machine that removes water, especially by heat or air: *a clothes dryer.* **2** = drier (def. 3).

dry-eyed (drī′īd′), *adj.* unable to weep; tearless: *The next day I packed my bag and took dry-eyed leave of the Morpions* (Punch).

dry-farm (drī′färm′), *v.t., v.i.* to farm (land) where there is little rain and no irrigation; practice dry farming: *In the dry-farmed fields the wheat that was still in the ground had taken on a dying pallor* (New York Times).

dry farmer, a person who does dry farming.

dry farming, farming in regions having little rainfall and no irrigation, by using methods which conserve the soil moisture and by raising crops which survive drought: *Dry farming, which is a direct response to aridity, was inaugurated on this continent in Utah* (White and Renner).

dry fly, a fishing lure made to imitate a May fly or other insect and designed to float on the water's surface.

dry-fly fishing (drī′flī′), fishing by casting a dry fly.

dry fog, *Meteorology.* a haze caused chiefly by smoke or dust (not a true fog).

dry|foot (drī′fůt′), *adv.* **1** with dry feet: *He was able to make his way over the stream dryfoot by leaping from rock to rock.* **2** *Obsolete.* (in hunting) by the scent of the foot.

dry gangrene, gangrene in which the affected tissue becomes shriveled and discolored or black, losing all feeling, due to occlusion of an artery which cuts off circulation.

dry gas, natural gas free from liquid hydrocarbons, often usable without refining.

dry goods, *Especially U.S.* cloth, ribbons, laces, and similar textile fabrics.

dry-gulch (drī′gulch′), *v.t. U.S.* **1a** to ambush treacherously and kill in a quiet place: *In the West's 20th century uranium rush, only one prospector thus far has been dry-gulched in 19th century fashion* (Time). **b** to kill by stampeding into a dry gulch, ravine, or other enclosed area. **2** *Informal, Figurative.* to ambush; beat up severely.

dry hole, a well which after drilling yields little or no oil or gas.

dry ice, 1 a very cold, white solid formed when carbon dioxide is greatly compressed and then cooled. It is used for cooling because it changes from a solid back to a gas without becoming liquid. **2 Dry Ice.** a trademark for this substance.

dry|ing (drī′ing), *adj.* **1** that dries: *a drying wind.* **2** having the quality of drying quickly: *Drying oils are used in paints and varnishes.*

dry|ish (drī′ish), *adj.* somewhat dry: *dryish ground, a dryish aftertaste, dryish humor.*

dry kiln, an enclosure in which lumber is dried and seasoned under controlled heat.

dry lake, a dried-up salt lake that may be covered with water after a rainstorm; playa; salt pan.

dry-land farmer (drī′land′), = dry farmer.

dry-land farming, = dry farming.

dry law, a law prohibiting the making and selling of alcoholic liquor.

dry|lot (drī′lot′), *adj.* of or having to do with an enclosed area in which cattle are fed without grazing, often by mechanized delivery of feed: *drylot dairying. Combined drylot feeding and grain-pasture grazing proved better for fattening steers in the South than drylot feeding alone* (E. G. Moore).

dry|ly (drī′lē), *adv.* in a dry manner or state: *He spoke little and dryly. Mr. Thompson said dryly that he was not offended, but what about the Premier* (New York Times Magazine). Also, **drily.**

dry measure, a system for measuring the volume of such things as grain, vegetables, or fruit. In the United States:
2 pints = 1 quart (67.2 cu. in. or 1.10 liters)
8 quarts = 1 peck (537.6 cu. in. or 8.81 liters)
4 pecks = 1 bushel (2150.42 cu. in).
In Great Britain a bushel equals 2219.360 cu. in., a gallon equals 4 quarts, and a quarter (one fourth of a hundredweight) equals 8 bushels.

dry milk, = dried milk.

dry mop, = dust mop.

dry|ness (drī′nis), *n.* dry quality or condition: (*Figurative.*) *Powell's dryness proceeds, first, from his view of life and, second, from his verbal felicity* (Newsweek).

dry nurse, 1 a nurse who takes care of a baby, but does not suckle it. **2** *Figurative.* a person who instructs someone in his duties.

dry-nurse (drī′nėrs′), *v.t.,* **-nursed, -nurs|ing.** to act as dry nurse to.

Dry|o|pe (drī′ə pē), *n. Greek Mythology.* a Thessalian princess beloved by Apollo and changed into a poplar by the hamadryads.

dry|o|pith|e|cine (drī′ō pith′ə sēn, -sīn), *adj., n.* —***adj.*** of, related to, or resembling Dryopithecus: *. . . the transition from the dryopithecine apes of the Miocene-Pliocene epoch (25 million to two million years ago) to the first true hominids* (Scientific American).
—***n.*** a dryopithecine ape: *Some proposed dryopithecines do not belong in this subfamily having proved instead to be monkeys* (Ian Tattersall).

Dry|o|pith|e|cus (drī′ō pith′ə kəs), *n.* an extinct anthropoid ape of the late Miocene and Pliocene of Europe, Africa, and Asia, from which man and certain other primates may have developed. [<New Latin *Dryopithecus* <Greek *drys* tree + *pithēkos* ape]

dry pack, a dry blanket put on the body for medical purposes.

dry painting, = sand painting.

dry pan, a rotating pan with heavy rollers in which crushed clay is thoroughly ground, to be used in making bricks.

dry plate, an early, gelatin-coated glass photographic plate, no longer used.

dry pleurisy, a painful form of pleurisy in which the surfaces of the pleura become dry and rough, and rub together.

dry point, 1 an engraving made from a copper plate that has been engraved with a hard needle without using acid: *Her dry points seemed to have come from another hand, strong and straight, no nonsense about it* (New Yorker). **2** the needle used. **3** this method of engraving.

dry rot, 1 a decay of seasoned wood, causing it to crumble to a dry powder, caused by various fungi. **2** a disease of vegetables and fruits, caused by a fungus which dries and kills the tissues. **3** any one of these fungi. **4** *Figurative.* hidden or unsuspected moral or social decay: *Lack of new people and new ideas often causes dry rot in an organization.*

dry-rot (drī′rot′), *v.i., v.t.,* **-rot|ted, -rot|ting.** to decay or cause to decay with dry rot: (*Figurative.*) *He was left to dry-rot in the vast paleface reservation* (Atlantic).

dry run, 1 any practice test or session; drill in, or practice of, a series of operations, using simulated equipment or a simulated situation; rehearsal: *The alert was a dry run of the dispersal of high officials intended in the event of actual nuclear attack. Before allowing the show to go on the air, [he] put it through 17 dry runs to smooth out the kings* (Time). **2** a practice, drill, or test in attacking or bombing without use of live ammunition.

dry-salt (drī′sôlt′), *v.t.* = dry-cure.

dry|salt|er (drī′sôl′tər), *n. British.* a dealer in salted and dried meats, pickles, or fish, or in drugs, dyestuffs, and gum.

dry|salt|er|y (drī′sôl′tər ē), *n., pl.* **-er|ies.** *British.* **1** a drysalter's store or business. **2** the articles dealt in by a drysalter.

dry sand, sand containing a special binder, the surface of which is dried with an open flame, used in casting metals.

dry shaver, *British.* an electric razor.

dry-shod (drī′shod′), *adj., adv.* having dry shoes; without getting the feet wet.

dry sink, a cabinet with a hollow part or basin for a dishpan, much used in the 1800's, especially in rural areas: *. . . old Canadian rocking chairs, cradles, and dry sinks* (Maclean's).

dry-ski (drī′skē′), *adj.* of or for practice or instruction in skiing that takes place indoors or on rollers or other artificial, dry surfaces: *a dry-ski school, dry-ski classes.*

dry steam, steam containing no moisture or not more than one half of one per cent moisture.

dry-stone (drī′stōn′), *adj.* built of stone without the use of mortar: *. . . some of the best examples of dry-stone walling I have seen for a long time* (Manchester Guardian).

dry sump, a type of engine lubrication in which the oil supply is contained in a separate oil tank and pumped to the moving parts.

dry wall, a wall built without mortar, now usually a prefabricated wall.

dry wash, *U.S.* clothes or linens that have been washed and dried but not ironed; rough-dry wash.

dry well, = dry hole.

ds (no period), decistere; decisteres.

d.s., 1 *Music.* dal segno (from the sign). **2** *Com-*

Pronunciation Key: hat, āge, cãre, fär; let, ēqual, tėrm; it, īce; hot, ōpen, ôrder; oil, out; cup, pu̇t, rüle; child; long; thin; ᴛʜen; zh, measure; ə represents **a** in about, **e** in taken, **i** in pencil, **o** in lemon, **u** in circus.

merce. days after sight.
Ds (no period), dysprosium (chemical element).
D.S., 1 *Music.* dal segno (from the sign). 2 dental surgeon. 3 Doctor of Science.
D.Sc., Doctor of Science.
D.S.C., 1 Distinguished Service Cross. 2 Doctor of Surgical Chiropody.
D.S.I.R. or **DSIR** (no periods) , *British.* Department of Scientific and Industrial Research.
DSL (no periods) or **D.S.L.**, deep scattering layer.
D.S.M., Distinguished Service Medal.
D.S.O., *British.* (Companion of the) Distinguished Service Order.
DSRV (no periods), Deep Submergence Rescue Vehicle.
DST (no periods) or **D.S.T.**, daylight-saving time.
d.t., delirium tremens.
D.T., **D.Th.**, or **D.Theol.**, Doctor of Theology.
DTP (no periods), desktop publishing.
d.t.'s, *Informal.* delirium tremens.
Du., 1 duke. 2 Dutch.
du|ad (dü′ad, dyü′-), *n.* a group or combination of two; couple; pair. [< Greek *dyás, - ádos*; spelling influenced by Latin *duo* two. See etym. of doublet **dyad.**]
du|al (dü′əl, dyü′-), *adj., n.* —*adj.* 1 composed or consisting of two parts; double; twofold: *The automobile had dual controls, one set for the learner and one for the teacher. The third and fourth boys . . . quickly became inseparable and were the dual delight of their father* (Newsweek). 2 of two; showing two: *the dual law which accounts for negative and positive electricity.* 3 *Grammar.* (in certain languages including Old English) designating a number category signifying two persons or things: *the dual number in Greek, a dual verb form.*
—*n. Grammar.* 1 the dual number: *Many languages have three numbers: singular, dual, and plural. Dual refers to two of a kind. In such a system, plural applies to three or more* (Henry A. Gleason). 2 a word in the dual number.
[< Latin *duālis* < *duo* two] —**du′al|ly**, *adv.*
Du|a|la (dü ä′lə), *n., pl.* **-la** or **-las.** = Douala.
dual citizen, a person who is a citizen of two countries, with allegiance to both; person having two nationalities: *Many states, such as Greece, Switzerland . . . still cling to the view that citizenship at birth continues despite naturalization in other states and such dual citizens may obtain passports in both countries* (New York Times).
dual citizenship, the condition of being a dual citizen. Also, **dual nationality**.
dual fund, a closed-end trust whose stock is divided between shares of income and shares of capital stock. Also, **dual-purpose fund.**
du|al|in (dü′ə lin, dyü′-), *n.* an explosive consisting of a mixture of nitroglycerin with sawdust and saltpeter. [< *dual* + *-in*]
du|al|ine (dü′ə lin, -lēn; dyü′-), *n.* = dualin.
du|al|ism (dü′ə liz əm, dyü′-), *n.* 1 dual condition; twofold division; duality: *a dualism between knowing and being* (Edward Caird). 2 *Philosophy.* the doctrine that all the phenomena of the universe can be explained by two separate and distinct substances or principles, such as mind and matter. 3 a doctrine of two principles in conflict, one good and one evil. 4 *Theology.* **a** the doctrine that Christ consisted of two personalities. **b** the doctrine that two distinct elements are constituted in man, such as body and spirit.
du|al|ist (dü′ə list, dyü′-), *n.* a believer in a doctrine of dualism: *Moravia is a dualist deeply conscious of a conflict between "civilization" and "nature," intellect and instinct* (Atlantic).
du|al|is|tic (dü′ə lis′tik, dyü′-), *adj.* 1 of or having to do with dualism. 2 based on dualism: *. . . a dualistic philosophy of the individual and the state* (Newsweek). 3 = dual. —**du′al|is′ti|cal|ly**, *adv.*
du|al|i|ty (dü al′ə tē, dyü-), *n., pl.* **-ties.** dual condition or quality: *There are many other dualities which the architect must respect: Color and texture, form and space, the building and the landscape* (Newsweek).
du|al|i|za|tion (dü′ə lə zā′shən, dyü′-), *n.* 1 the act of dualizing. 2 the condition of being dualized.
du|al|ize (dü′ə līz, dyü′-), *v.t.*, **-ized, -iz|ing.** 1 to make dual: *We say in projective geometry that we have dualized the original statement* (Scientific American). 2 to represent or regard as dual.
dual nationality, = dual citizenship.
du|a|logue (dü′ə lôg, dyü′-; -log), *n.* = dialogue (def. 1).
dual personality, a psychological condition in which a person exhibits the characteristics or behavior of two dissimilar personalities.
du|al-pur|pose (dü′əl pėr′pəs, dyü′-), *adj.* 1 for two purposes: *A few years ago he made a dual-purpose pilgrimage to Scotland: to visit old Cumnock, the home of his ancestors, and to play at St. Andrews* (Time). **2a** raised for both meat and milk: *dual-purpose cattle.* **b** raised for both meat and eggs: *dual-purpose chickens.*
dual-purpose fund, = dual fund.
Du|ar|te plum (dyü är′tē), a variety of Japanese plum grown on the Pacific coast of the United States.
dub[1] (dub), *v.t.*, **dubbed, dub|bing.** 1 to give a title to: *A man of wealth is dubbed a man of worth* (Alexander Pope). SYN: style. 2 to name or call: *Because of his light hair, the boys dubbed him "Whitey."* SYN: nickname. 3 to make (a man) a knight by striking his shoulder lightly with a sword. 4 to make smooth by cutting, rubbing, or scraping: *The lumberman hewed the log flat and then dubbed it with an adz.* 5 to dress, trim, or crop. 6 to dress (an artificial fly). [Old English *dubbian*]
dub[2] (dub), *n., v.*, **dubbed, dub|bing.** *U.S. Slang.* —*n.* 1 a poor hand at anything. 2 an awkward, clumsy player.
—*v.t., v.i.* to do or play awkwardly; bungle.
[American English, perhaps < *dub*[3]]
dub[3] (dub), *v.*, **dubbed, dub|bing,** *n.* —*v.t.* 1 to thrust; poke. 2 to beat (a drum). —*v.i.* 1 to make a thrust or dab; poke (at). 2 to make the sound of a drum: *trumpets braying and drums dubbing.*
—*n.* **1a** a beat of a drum. **b** the sound of a drum when beaten. 2 a thrust or blow.
[origin uncertain. Compare East Frisian *dubben* to beat, strike.]
dub[4] (dub), *v.*, **dubbed, dub|bing,** *n.* —*v.t.* 1 to add music, voices, or sound effects to (a motion-picture film, a radio or television broadcast, or a recording) by making a new sound track: *The dialogue spoken by the German and French is dubbed in heavily accented English* (Bosley Crowther). 2 to add (sounds) to. 3 to make a record of (a previously made recording).
—*v.i.* to make a new sound track, especially by adding one's own voice to a film, broadcast, or recording: *A star dubber can earn $50. One American dubbed for a year* (New York Times).
—*n.* 1 the act or process of dubbing: *The Instant Voice, as her husband calls her . . . makes about $10,000 for a major film dub* (Time). 2 the sounds added in dubbing.
[short for *double*] —**dub′ber**, *n.*
dub[5] (dub, dủb), *n. Scottish.* 1 a muddy or stagnant pool. 2 a puddle. 3 a deep, still pool in a river. [origin uncertain]
dub|bin (dub′ən), *n.* = dubbing (def. 2).
dub|bing (dub′ing), *n.* 1 the act of dubbing; the conferring of knighthood. 2 a grease used for softening and waterproofing leather: *to apply dubbing to new hiking boots.* 3 a flour paste used by weavers. 4 (in fishing) the materials used for the body of an artificial fly.
Dub|he (dủb′he), *n.* one of two stars (the other being Merak) situated at the bowl of the Big Dipper, and pointing in the direction of Polaris, the polestar. [< Arabic *dubb* bear]
du|bi|e|ty (dü bī′ə tē, dyü-), *n., pl.* **-ties.** 1 doubtfulness; dubiousness; uncertainty: *The twilight of dubiety never falls on him* (Charles Lamb). SYN: doubt. 2 something which is doubtful. [< Late Latin *dubietās* < Latin *dubius* doubtful]
du|bi|os|i|ty (dü′bē os′ə tē, dyü′-), *n., pl.* **-ties.** dubiety; dubiousness: *Men swallow dubiosities for certainties* (Sir Thomas Browne).
du|bi|ous (dü′bē əs, dyü′-), *adj.* 1 doubtful; uncertain; ambiguous: *a dubious compliment, a dubious friend. Many books in the Bible are of dubious authorship.* SYN: undetermined, indistinct, vague. See syn. under **doubtful.** 2 of uncertain issue or result: *in dubious battle* (Milton). 3 feeling doubt; wavering or hesitating in opinion; inclined to doubt: *She looked this way and that in a dubious manner.* 4 of questionable character; probably bad: *The police are investigating the swindler's dubious scheme for making money.* [< Latin *dubiōsus* < *dubium*, noun, doubt, neuter of *dubius*, adjective, doubtful] —**du′bi|ous|ly**, *adv.* —**du′bi|ous|ness**, *n.*
du|bi|ta|ble (dü′bə tə bəl, dyü′-), *adj.* that can be doubted; liable to doubt or question.
du|bi|tant (dü′bə tənt, dyü′-), *adj., n.* —*adj.* = doubting. —*n.* = doubter.
du|bi|tate (dü′bə tāt, dyü′-), *v.i.*, **-tat|ed, -tat|ing.** = doubt.
du|bi|ta|tion (dü′bə tā′shən, dyü′-), *n.* 1 the act of doubting. 2 the condition of being doubtful; uncertainty; hesitation. [< Latin *dubitātiō, -ōnis* < *dubitāre* to doubt < *dubius* doubtful]
du|bi|ta|tive (dü′bə tā′tiv, dyü′-), *adj.* inclined or given to doubt; expressing doubt or hesitancy: *turning his head . . . in a dubitative manner* (George Eliot). —**du′bi|ta′tive|ly**, *adv.*
Dub|lin|er (dub′lə nər), *n.* a native or resident of Dublin: *. . . . chapters of reminiscence by Dubliners who knew [James] Joyce both as a fierce young student and a world celebrity* (Punch).
Du|bon|net (dü′bə nā′, dyü′-), *n. Trademark.* a sweet French wine to which aromatic herbs and spices have been added, used as an apéritif.
duc (dʏk), *n. French.* duke.
du|cal (dü′kəl, dyü′-), *adj.* of or having to do with a duke or dukedom: *His lengthy, fragile fingers were ducal* (Atlantic). [< Late Latin *duc ālis* < Latin *dux, ducis* leader] —**du′cal|ly**, *adv.*
duc|at (duk′ət), *n.* 1 any one of various gold or silver coins once used in Europe, with varying value, especially a former Italian silver coin. 2 any piece of money. 3 *Slang.* a ticket. [< Middle French *ducat* < Italian *ducato* < Medieval Latin *ducatus* < *dux, ducis* duke (because it bears the title of the ducal power issuing it)]
duc|a|toon (duk′ə tün′), *n.* a former European silver coin of varying value. [< French *ducaton*, ultimately < Italian *ducato*; see etym. under **ducat**]
du|ce (dü′chā), *n.* a leader.
Il Duce, a title given to Benito Mussolini as head of Fascist Italy: *Il Duce was dictator of Italy until he was killed in 1945.*
[< Italian *duce* < Latin *dux, ducis* leader. See etym. of doublets **doge, duke.**]
Du|chenne dystrophy (dü shen′), a form of muscular dystrophy: *Muscular dystrophy is in fact a group of diseases. In the best known, Duchenne dystrophy, which is inherited and affects only boys, the muscles start to waste away from an early age* (London Times). [< Guillaume Armand *Duchenne,* 1806-1875, a French neurologist, who described it]
duch|ess (duch′is), *n.* 1 the wife or widow of a duke. 2 a lady with a rank equal to a duke's. [< Old French *duchesse*, feminine of *duc*; see etym. under **duke**]
Duch|ess (duch′is), *n.* a red-striped, oval-shaped apple. It is a favorite cooking-apple.
du|chesse (dü shes′; *French* dʏ shes′), *n.* = duchess.
duchesse lace, a type of lace consisting of individually woven floral designs which are corded together: *The gown was of heavy corded silk, with a fichu of duchesse lace* (New York Times).
[< French *duchesse* duchess]
duch|y (duch′ē), *n., pl.* **duch|ies.** the lands ruled by a duke or duchess; dukedom. [< Old French *duchee*, later *duche* < *duc*; see etym. under **duke**]
duck[1] (duk), *n., pl.* **ducks** or (*collectively*) **duck.** 1 any one of numerous wild or tame swimming birds with a broad, flat bill, short neck, short legs, and webbed feet. Ducks are very often kept to use as food or for their eggs. They belong to the same family as geese and swans. See picture under **goose.** 2 a female duck. The male is called a drake. 3 the flesh of a duck used as food. 4 Often, **ducks.** *British Informal.* a darling; pet. 5 *U.S. Slang.* a fellow; chap. 6 a marble, especially one used as the object of a shot. 7 *Cricket Slang.* no score; zero; naught: *The best batsmen sometimes make ducks* (London Times).
like water off a duck's back. See under **water**.
[Old English *dūce*. See related etym. at **duck**[2].]
—**duck′like′**, *adj.*
duck[2] (duk), *v., n.* —*v.i.* 1 to plunge or dip the head or the whole body under water and come up quickly, as a duck does. 2 to lower the head or bend the body quickly to keep from being hit or seen: *She ducked to avoid a low branch.* 3 *Figurative.* to cringe; yield. 4 *Slang.* to get away; withdraw; make off: *He ducked out of town to avoid paying his bills.* SYN: abscond. 5 (in bridge) to hold back a covering card and play low.
—*v.t.* 1 to plunge or dip in water momentarily: *We . . . always "ducked" the boy that told* (James Whitcomb Riley). 2 to lower (the head) or bend (the body) suddenly and momentarily; jerk down. 3 *Informal.* to get or keep away from; avoid; dodge: *to duck a blow. He ducked my question. He ducks many of the parties which many other officials think they must attend* (Newsweek).
—*n.* 1 a sudden plunge or dip under water and out again. 2 a sudden lowering of the head or bending of the body to keep from being hit or seen; a rapid, jerky bow or dodging motion: *The ducks and nods which weak minds pay to rank* (Charles Lamb).
[Middle English *duken, douken*; spelling influenced by *duck*[1]]
duck[3] (duk), *n.* a strong cotton or linen cloth with a lighter and finer weave than ordinary canvas. Duck is used to make small sails, tarpaulins, tents, and clothes for sailors or for people living in hot climates. *Mount Vernon has six mills which turn out cotton cloth such as print cloth, broadcloth and duck* (Wall Street Journal).
ducks, *Informal.* trousers made of duck: *Solly puts six thousand dollars in century bills in one pocket of his brown ducks* (O. Henry).
[< Dutch *doek* cloth]
***duck[4]** (duk), *n.* an amphibious truck with a watertight body so that it may move through the water like a boat: *Swarms of helicopters and Army amphibious "ducks" were pressed into action*

(Time). [spelling for pronunciation of *DUKW,* its code name]

*duck⁴

duck and drake, = ducks and drakes.
duck ant, = termite.
duck|bill (duk′bil′), *n.* a small water mammal of Australia and Tasmania that lays eggs; platypus. It has webbed feet and a bill like a duck's.
duck|billed (duk′bild′), *adj.* **1** having a bill like that of a duck: *a duckbilled fish.* **2** shaped like a duck's bill: *a duckbilled plate, duckbilled lips.*
duckbilled dinosaur, a dinosaur with a broad bill, many small teeth, and webbed feet, that lived mostly near water; hadrosaur.
duckbilled platypus, = duckbill.
duck|board (duk′bôrd′, -bōrd′), *n.* a low structure of boards used in wet or muddy places, as for a temporary sidewalk, or to provide traction for vehicles.
duck call, an instrument used by hunters to imitate a duck's quacking.
duck|er¹ (duk′ər), *n.* **1** a person who raises ducks. **2** a person who hunts ducks.
duck|er² (duk′ər), *n.* a person or thing that ducks or dives.
duck|er|y (duk′ər ē), *n., pl.* **-er|ies.** a place for breeding ducks.
duck-foot|ed (duk′fu̇t′id), *adj.* (of poultry) having the fourth or hind toe inclined to the front.
duck hawk, 1 a falcon of North America, 15 to 20 inches in length, that is dark bluish-gray on top and whitish with black bars below. It is the American variety of the peregrine falcon. **2** (in England) a species of harrier.
duck|ie (duk′ē), *n.* = ducky.
duck|ing¹ (duk′ing), *n.* **1** the act of plunging or being plunged into water. **2** immersion in water: *In colonial times, gossips were punished by ducking.* **3** a sudden lowering of the head or body. [< *duck²* + *-ing¹*]
duck|ing² (duk′ing), *n.* the catching or shooting of wild ducks. [< *duck¹* + *-ing¹*]
***ducking stool,** a stool at the end of a plank on which a person was tied and ducked into water as a punishment for minor offenses. It was used in early Colonial America.

*ducking stool

duck-leg|ged (duk′leg′id, -legd′), *adj.* having noticeably short legs.
duck|ling (duk′ling), *n.* a young duck.
duck|mole (duk′mōl′), *n.* = duckbill.
duck on drake, a game in which one of the players places his duck (small stone) upon a drake (large stone). The other players then try to knock it off with their ducks, and to regain these and run home before the first player can replace his duck and tag them.
duck on the rock, = duck on drake.
duck|pin (duk′pin′), *n.* a short bowling pin, used in the game of duckpins.
duck|pins (duk′pinz′), *n.pl.* a game somewhat like bowling, but played with smaller balls and pins: *Other forms of bowling include duckpins, popular in New England and some Southern states* (Wall Street Journal).
ducks (duks), *n.pl.* See under **duck³**.
ducks and drakes, the game of tossing flat stones or shells along the surface of water so they bounce several times before sinking. Also, **duck and drake.**
make ducks and drakes of, to play ducks and drakes with; squander: *A miser has it in his power to make ducks and drakes of his guineas* (Abraham Tucker).
play ducks and drakes with, to throw away idly or carelessly; handle or use recklessly: *Peter Sellers, Cecil Parker, Isabel Jeans, and Ian Carmichael play disrespectful but not at all dangerous ducks and drakes with the Church of England* (New Yorker).
duck snipe, = willet.
duck soup, *U.S. Slang.* anything that is easily done; a cinch: *This is duck soup for O'Brien compared to some of the occasions when he has been called upon* (New Yorker).
duck stamp, *U.S.* a Federal stamp required on the licenses of hunters of wild fowl. The funds resulting from its sale are used to acquire wetlands to assure the perpetuation of the flights of migratory birds.
duck|stone (duk′stōn′), *n.* one of the small stones used in the game of duck on drake; duck.
duck|tail (duk′tāl), *n.* a style of boys' or men's haircut in which the hair is left long on the sides and swept back, somewhat like a duck's tail.
duck-walk (duk′wôk′), *n., v.* —*n.* **1** = duckboard. **2** *Informal.* a waddling walk. —*v.i.* to walk like a duck; waddle: *He lifts weights, he duck-walks for miles . . .* (Time).
duck|weed (duk′wēd′), *n.* any one of a group of very small plants having no stem, that grow in water and often form dense green scum on the surface. Duckweed has a tiny disklike thallus beneath which are short, hairlike roots and is commonly grown in aquariums.
duck|y (duk′ē), *adj.,* **duck|i|er, duck|i|est,** *n., pl.* **duck|ies.** *Informal.* —*adj.* **1** darling; charming: *You can wear one of those ducky little lace caps* (Punch). **2** excellent; wonderful: *. . . a simply ducky dinner way up in the super swanky Rainbow Room* (New Yorker).
—*n.* darling; pet: *"My ducky, we mustn't be late!" she exclaimed* (Time). Also, **duckie.**
duct (dukt), *n., v.* —*n.* **1** a tube, pipe, or channel for carrying liquid, air, sand, grain, or other granular solid: *The hot air from our furnace reaches the bedrooms by metal heat ducts.* SYN: conduit. **2** a single pipe for electric or telephone cables. **3** a tube or canal in the body for carrying a bodily fluid, especially one for a fluid secreted by a gland: *tear ducts.* **4** *Botany.* one of the tracheae or vessels of the xylem of plants, serving to conduct water and dissolved minerals.
—*v.t.* to transmit (a substance) through a duct: *[He] favors . . . ducting the air downwards for take-off and channelling it through the normal tailpipe for forward flight* (New Scientist).
[< Latin *ductus, -ūs* a leading, command < *dūcere* to lead] —**duct′like′,** *adj.*
duct|ed fan or **propeller** (duk′tid), a fan or propeller that turns within a cylinderlike duct which captures air normally thrown aside by the propeller. Ducted fans are used in some aircraft engines and on air cushion vehicles.
duc|tile (duk′təl), *adj.* **1** that can be hammered out thin or drawn out into a wire; malleable: *The chief ductile metals are copper, iron, brass, platinum, gold, silver, and aluminum* (Walter R. Williams, Jr.). **2** easily molded or shaped; flexible: *Wax is ductile when it is warm.* SYN: pliant, plastic. **3** *Figurative.* easily managed or influenced; docile: *The man was in truth childishly soft and ductile* (Mrs. Humphry Ward). SYN: tractable, pliable, pliant. [< Latin *ductilis* < *dūcere* to lead] —**duc′tile|ly,** *adv.* —**duc′tile|ness,** *n.*
duc|til|i|ty (duk til′ə tē), *n., pl.* **-ties.** ductile quality: *Most polymers lose their ductility when given even moderate exposures* (Scientific American). (*Figurative.*) *Greater ductility and energy of language* (Macaulay). SYN: flexibility, pliableness, malleability, docility, tractableness.
duct|ing (duk′ting), *n.* **1** = ductwork. **2** the act of furnishing with a duct or ducts.
duct|less (dukt′lis), *adj.* having no duct.
ductless gland, a gland without a duct whose secretion passes directly into the blood or lymph circulating through it; endocrine gland. The thyroid, the pituitary, and the thymus are ductless glands.
duct|ule (duk′tyül), *n.* a small duct. [< *duct* + *-ule*]
duc|tus ar|te|ri|o|sus (duk′təs är tir′ē ō′səs), a blood vessel that connects the pulmonary artery with the aorta before birth and closes up following birth, after the supply of oxygen from the placenta has been cut off and the newborn has to use its own lungs. [< New Latin *ductus arteriosus* arterial duct]
duct|work (dukt′wėrk′), *n.* the arrangement of a duct or system of ducts: *The entire ductwork for the heating system for a seven-room house . . .* (Wall Street Journal).
dud¹ (dud), *n. Obsolete.* an article of clothing.
duds, *Informal.* **a** clothes: *I bought some new duds.* **b** possessions; belongings: *He had few duds and traveled light.* **c** old, ragged clothes: *Away I went to sea, with my duds tied in a handkerchief* (Harriet Beecher Stowe).
[Middle English *dudde* cloth, coarse cloth; origin uncertain]
dud² (dud), *n., adj.* —*n.* **1** a shell or bomb that fails to explode. **2** *Slang.* a failure: *The rocket test was a dud.* **3** any useless or inefficient person or thing: *He certainly turned out to be a dud at bowling.*
—*adj.* **1** ineffective; useless; good-for-nothing: *There isn't a dud number in the bunch, or a dud performance, either* (New Yorker). **2** out of order. **3** adverse, as weather.
[probably related to **dub²**]
dud|dy or **dud|die** (dud′ē), *adj. Scottish.* ragged.
dude (düd, dyüd), *n., v.,* **dud|ed, dud|ing.** —*n.* **1** *Especially U.S.* a man who pays too much attention to his clothes; a man of affected or excessive refinement in manners, speech, or dress; dandy. SYN: swell. **2** *Western U.S. and Canada.* a person raised in the city, especially an Easterner who vacations on a ranch. **3** *Slang.* any man; fellow; guy: *I'd already scored 22 points and was helping out this 6′9″ dude* (Sports Illustrated).
—*v.t. Informal.* Usually, **dude up.** to dress or make up like a dandy; decorate: *. . . getting duded up with makeup and hair spray so he can sing before a bank of lights* (Maclean's). (*Figurative.*) *All sorts of ranches had sprung up around Banders, many of them duded up with swimming pools* (Saturday Review).
[American English; origin unknown]
du|deen (dü dēn′), *n.* an Irish tobacco pipe made of clay, with a short stem. [< Irish *dūidīn* short smoking pipe (diminutive) < *dūd* pipe; horn; ear]
dude ranch, a ranch run as a tourist resort.
dudg|eon¹ (duj′ən), *n.* a feeling of anger, resentment, or offense; ill humor: *He recorded his impressions with some dudgeon and may I suggest, some relief* (Maclean's). SYN: ire, indignation.
in high dudgeon, very angry; resentful: *He was in high dudgeon when he found out that we had left without him.*
[origin unknown]
dudg|eon² (duj′ən), *n. Obsolete.* **1** a kind of wood used by turners, especially for handles of knives, daggers, and other tools. **2** the hilt of a dagger, made of this wood. **3** a dagger having a hilt of such wood: *It was a serviceable dudgeon, Either for fighting or for drudging* (Samuel Butler).
[< Anglo-French *digeon;* origin unknown]
du|dheen (dü dēn′), *n.* = dudeen.
dud|ish (dü′dish, dyü′-), *adj.* characteristic of a dude; foppish: *He ran for a touchdown every time he carried the ball against the dudish Harvard palefaces* (A. J. Liebling). —**dud′ish|ly,** *adv.*
duds (dudz), *n.pl.* See under **dud¹**.
due (dü, dyü), *adj., n., adv.* —*adj.* **1** owed as a debt; to be paid as a right: *The money due him for his work was paid today.* SYN: unpaid, owing, payable. **2** proper; rightful; fitting: *Respect is due to older people. We receive the due reward of our deeds* (Luke 23:41). SYN: appropriate, suitable. **3** as much as needed; enough: *He was driving without due care.* SYN: sufficient, requisite, adequate. **4** looked for; expected; set by agreement; promised to come: *The next train is due in ten minutes. Your report is due tomorrow.* **5** (of notes, bills, or other obligations) becoming payable; having reached maturity; mature. SYN: maturing. **6** (of dates) on which notes, bills, or other obligations become mature.
—*n.* a person's right; what is owed to a person: *Courtesy is his due while he is your guest. I am asking no more than my due.*
—*adv.* **1** straight; exactly; directly: *The ship sailed due west.* **2** *Archaic.* duly.
become (or **fall**) **due,** to become immediately payable, as a note does on reaching maturity; be required to be paid: *Income which has become due and has not yet been paid over* (Law Times).
dues, a the amount of money owed or to be paid to a club or other organization by a member: *Members who do not pay dues will be suspended from the club.* **b** a legal charge, tax, fee, or other payment: *He charges them with having defrauded the masters under whom he studied of their dues* (Connop Thirlwall).
due to, a caused by: *The accident was due to his careless use of the gun.* **b** because of; on account of: *The game was called off due to rain. It is solely due to Lord Denning's own high standing and repute that the public believed him* (Manchester Guardian Weekly).
give a person his due, to be fair to a person; do full justice to him: *And yet, give him his due, he always pays his share. Being of that honest few, who give the Fiend himself his due* (Tennyson).
[< Old French *deü,* past participle of *devoir* owe < Latin *dēbēre*]
▶**Due** was originally used only as an adjective, and in formal English it is still restricted by many

Pronunciation Key: hat, āge, cãre, fär; let, ēqual, tėrm; it, īce; hot, ōpen, ôrder; oil, out; cup, pu̇t, rüle; child; long; thin; ᴛʜen; zh, measure; ə represents a in about, e in taken, i in pencil, o in lemon, u in circus.

writers to this use: *Economic depressions are due to uncontrolled inflation* (modifies *depressions*). *Due to* as a preposition (*Due to his bad temper most people avoid him*) is in general use and appears in the writing of many American and British authors, although some users of formal English do not approve of the construction. One can easily avoid using *due to* as a preposition by substituting *because of* or *on account of* or by recasting the sentence: General: *Due to the storm he postponed his canoe trip.* Formal: *Because of the storm he postponed his canoe trip. The postponement of his canoe trip was due to the storm.*

due bill, a brief written acknowledgment of a debt, not payable to order or transferable by mere endorsement.

due date, the date on which a bill or other obligation falls due.

du|el (dü′əl, dyü′-), *n., v.,* **-eled, -el|ing** or **-elled, -el|ling.** *—n.* **1** a formal fight to settle a quarrel or avenge an insult. Duels are fought with guns, swords, or other weapons between two persons in the presence of witnesses called seconds. *A duel was fought ... between two colonels* (Jonathan Swift). **2** any fight or contest between two opposing parties, whether persons, animals, or political parties: *The two opposing lawyers fought a duel of wits in the law court.*
—v.i. to fight a duel; engage in single combat.
—v.t. Obsolete. to overcome or kill in a duel.
[< Middle French *duel* < Medieval Latin *duellum* a combat between two < Latin *duellum,* early form of *bellum* war. See etym. of doublet **duello.**]
—du′el|er, du′el|ler, *n.*

du|el|ing or **du|el|ling** (dü′ə ling, dyü′-), *n.* **1** the act of fighting a duel. **2** the practice of fighting duels.

dueling pistol, a pistol with a long barrel, to insure accuracy, used in dueling.

du|el|ist or **du|el|list** (dü′ə list, dyü′-), *n.* a person who fights a duel or duels: *His wife balanced upon the balustrade with an expression of infinite disdain and juggled languidly with her jewels as the routed duellists made hastily off* (Punch).

du|el|is|tic or **du|el|lis|tic** (dü′ə lis′tik, dyü′-), *adj.* of or having to do with a duel or duelist.

du|el|lo (dü el′ō), *n., pl.* **-los. 1** dueling, especially according to rigid laws and rules. **2** the established code of duelists; code duello. **3** *Obsolete.* a duel. [< Italian *duello* < Latin *duellum.* See etym. of doublet **duel.**]

duen|de (dwen′dā), *n. Spanish.* **1** a magic or mysterious spell; enchantment: *As a Latin, Busoni approaches the idea of death through a feeling for what Lorca called duende—that Spanish apprehension of the dark magic of death which lurks behind life and behind all great works of art* (Listener). **2** (literally) demon; ghost; fairy.

du|en|na (dü en′ə, dyü-), *n.* **1** an elderly woman who is the governess and chaperon of young girls in a Spanish or Portuguese family. **2** a governess or chaperon. [< Spanish *dueña* < Latin *domina* mistress, lady. See etym. of doublets **dame, dona, doña, donna.**]

due process or **due process of law**, the legal steps and measures to which a person is entitled to protect himself and his interests.

dues (düz, dyüz), *n.pl.* See under **due.**

du|et (dü et′, dyü-), *n., v.,* **-et|ted, -et|ting.** *—n.* **1** a piece of music for two voices or instruments. See also **duo. 2** two singers or players performing together.
—v.i. to sing or play a duet: *She was most thrilling when duetting with Marilyn Horne* (London Times).
—v.t. to sing or play together as a duet: *to duet a song.*
[< Italian *duetto* (diminutive) < *duo;* see etym. under **duo**]

du|et|tist (dü et′ist, dyü-), *n.* a person who takes part in a duet: *... immaculate timing, in the course of which the duettists emerge as a joint personality* (New Yorker).

duff[1] (duf), *n.* a flour pudding boiled in a cloth bag. [dialectal variant of *dough*]

duff[2] (duf), *n. Scottish and U.S.* **1** the decaying vegetable matter, such as fallen leaves, covering the ground in a forest. **2** fine coal. [perhaps imitative of the sound made by striking a soft substance]

duff[3] (duf), *v., adj.* *—v.t. Dialect* or *Slang.* **1** to manipulate (a thing) so as to make it pass for new or for something different. **2** in Australia: **a** to alter the brand on (stolen cattle). **b** to steal (cattle) by doing this. **3** to cheat.
—adj. British Slang. worthless; defective: *a duff product.*
[origin unknown]

duff[4] (duf), *n. U.S. Slang.* the rump; buttocks: *"The market is there," says he, "if we get off our duffs"* (Time). [origin uncertain]

duff[5] (duf), *v.t. British Slang.* to beat up: *Perhaps he will leap out from behind a lamp post and duff me up next time I go shopping* (Sunday Times). [origin uncertain]

duf|fel (duf′əl), *n., adj.* *—n.* **1** a coarse woolen cloth with a thick nap. **2** camping equipment. **3** = duffel coat: *Coats that are so typically British—reversible car coats, leather-trimmed duffels* (Wall Street Journal).
—adj. **1** made or consisting of duffel. **2** used for carrying duffel. Also, **duffle.**
[< Dutch *duffel* < *Duffel,* name of a town near Antwerp, Belgium]

duffel or **duffle bag**, **1** a large canvas sack used by soldiers, campers, and the like, for carrying clothing and other belongings. **2** a bag of stout material.

***duffel** or **duffle coat**, a knee-length coat of duffel, usually with an attached hood.

***duffel coat**

duff|er[1] (duf′ər), *n. Informal.* a clumsy, stupid, or incompetent person: *He was clever at mathematics but a duffer at English. The helicopter is still too tricky for the average road duffer to fly* (Scientific American). [origin uncertain]

duff|er[2] (duf′ər), *n. Slang.* **1** a peddler or hawker. **2** a person who sells trashy goods. **3** *Australian.* a cattle thief. [< *duff*[3] + *-er*[1]]

duff|er[3] (duf′ər), *n.* = duffel coat. [origin uncertain]

duf|fle (duf′əl), *n.* = duffel.

dug[1] (dug), *v.* past tense and past participle of **dig**: *The dog dug a hole in the ground. The potatoes have all been dug.*

dug[2] (dug), *n.* a nipple; teat, especially of a female animal. [origin uncertain. Compare Danish *daegge* to suckle.]

***du|gong** (dü′gong), *n.* a large, fish-shaped, herbivorous sea mammal of south Asia and Australian coastal waters with flipperlike forelimbs and a forked tail; sea cow. It is of the same order as the manatee. [< Malay *duyong*]

***dugong**

dug|out (dug′out′), *n.* **1** a rough shelter or cave formed by digging into the side of a hill, trench, or the like, and often reinforced with logs: *During war, soldiers use dugouts for protection against bullets, bombs, and shells.* **2** a small shelter at the side of a baseball field, partly below the surface of the ground. It is used by players who are not at bat or on the field. **3** a boat made by hollowing out a large log.

du haut en bas (dy ō′ tän bä′), *French.* **1** in a patronizing manner. **2** (literally) from on high down.

du|i (dü′ē), *n.* Italian plural of **duo.**

dui|ker (dī′kər), *n.* any one of various small South African antelopes: *Duikers are generally seen in pairs and are partial to bush country* (C. S. Stokes). Also, **duyker, duykerbok.** [< Afrikaans *duiker* (*bok*) diver (buck)]

dui|ker|bok (dī′kər bok′), *n.* = duiker.

dui|ker|buck (dī′kər buk′), *n.* = duiker.

du|ka or **duk|ka** (dü′kə), *n.* a retail shop in Kenya and some other parts of eastern Africa: *... the shops and garages were Indian-owned and the open-fronted bars, the dukkas selling every conceivable item from comic books to bicycles, the tea-rooms and the food stores were all Indian* (Manchester Guardian Weekly). [probably < Hindustani *dukān*]

du|ka|wal|lah (dü′kə wol′ə), *n.* a shopkeeper in Kenya and some other parts of eastern Africa: *The first Asians went to East Africa well ahead of the British ... They became the colony's "dukawallahs" (or shopkeepers), running every kind of establishment from the smart shops in the capital to tiny stores in dusty African villages* (Listener). [< *duka* + *wallah*]

duke (dük, dyük), *n.* **1** a nobleman of the highest title in Great Britain and other European countries, ranking next below a prince and above a marquis: *The peerage now includes the following titles in descending order of rank: duke, marquis, earl, viscount, and baron* (Marion F. Lansing). **2** a prince in some parts of Europe who rules a small state or country called a *duchy.* **3** a hybrid cherry that is a cross between the sweet cherry and the sour cherry.
dukes, *Slang.* the hands or fists: *Put up your dukes.*
[< Old French *duc* < Latin *dux, ducis* leader. See etym. of doublets **doge, duce.**]

duke|dom (dük′dəm, dyük′-), *n.* **1** the lands ruled by a duke; duchy. **2** the title or rank of a duke.

duke|ling (dük′ling, dyük′-), *n.* a little or petty duke.

dukes (düks, dyüks), *n.pl.* See under **duke.**

duke|ship (dük′ship, dyük′-), *n.* the state or dignity of a duke.

Du|kho|bors (dü′kə bôrz), *n.pl.* = Doukhobors.

DUKW or **Dukw** (no periods), duck[4].

dul|cet (dul′sit), *adj., n.* *—adj.* **1** soothing, especially to the ear; sweet or pleasing: *The singer was famous for her dulcet voice. Dulcet symphonies and voices sweet* (Milton). **SYN:** agreeable, gentle. **2** *Archaic.* sweet to the taste or smell.
—n. an organ stop resembling the dulciana, but an octave higher than the dulciana in pitch.
[Middle English *doucet* < Old French, (diminutive) < *doux,* earlier *dulz* sweet < Latin *dulcis*]
—dul′cet|ly, *adv.*

dul|ci|an|a (dul′sē an′ə), *n.* a type of organ stop having metal pipes and giving clear, singing, somewhat stringlike tones. [< New Latin *dulciana,* apparently < Medieval Latin, an ancient instrument; kind of song < Latin *dulcis* sweet]

dul|ci|fi|ca|tion (dul′sə fə kā′shən), *n.* the act of sweetening.

dul|ci|fy (dul′sə fī), *v.t.,* **-fied, -fy|ing.** to sweeten; render more agreeable; mollify; appease: *Time had not dulcified the tempers of the three elder* (Blackwood's Magazine).

***dul|ci|mer** (dul′sə mər), *n.* **1** a musical instrument with metal strings, played by striking the strings with two light hammers: *It was an Abyssinian maid And on her dulcimer she played* (Samuel Taylor Coleridge). **2** a wind instrument, especially a kind of bagpipe (in the Bible, Daniel 3:5). [< Old French *doulcemer,* or *doulcemele* < Latin *dulcis* sweet + *melos* song < Greek *mélos*]

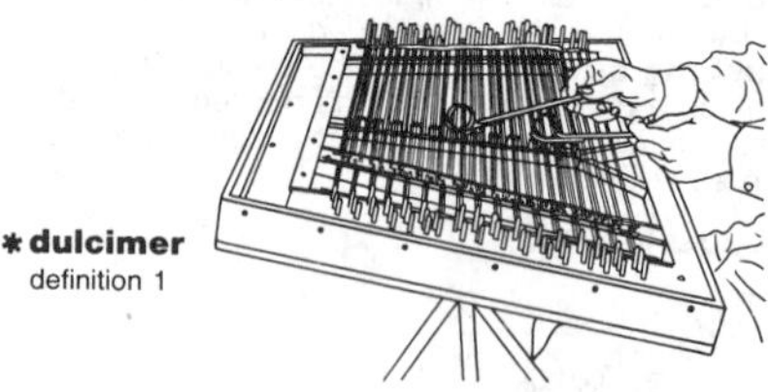
***dulcimer**
definition 1

Dul|cin|e|a (dul sin′ē ə, dul′sə nē′-), *n.* **1** the name given by Don Quixote to the coarse peasant girl he supposed to be a beautiful lady and chose for his sweetheart. **2** any sweetheart thought of as ideal.

du|li|a (dü lī′ə, dyü-), *n.* the veneration due saints and angels in the Roman Catholic Church. See also **hyperdulia, latria.** [< Medieval Latin *dulia* worship, service < Greek *douleiā* service < *doûlos* servant]

dull (dul), *adj., v.* *—adj.* **1** not sharp or pointed; blunt: *It is hard to cut with a dull knife.* **2** not bright or clear; lacking in vividness, brightness, or intensity: *a dull sound, a dull green, a dull day of rain.* **SYN:** obscure, dim, indistinct, cloudy, gloomy, overcast. **3** slow to understand; stupid: *The child had a dull mind.* **SYN:** obtuse, doltish. See syn. under **stupid. 4** having little feeling; insensitive: *You never would hear it; your ears are so dull* (Tennyson). **SYN:** insensible, unfeeling. **5** not felt sharply; vague; indistinct: *The dull pain of a bruise.* **6** not interesting; tiresome; boring: *a dull joke. History no longer shall be a dull book* (Emerson). **SYN:** uninteresting, colorless, tedious. **7** having little life, energy, or spirit; not active; sluggish: *a dull fire. The fur coat business is usually dull in the summer. This is the dull season for automobiles.* **SYN:** inert, stagnant, lifeless, slow, inactive. **8** not much in demand; not easily salable: *Flour is dull at $7.30* (Thomas Jefferson). **9** lacking zest; depressed; sad: *You are dull tonight; prithee be merry* (Sir Richard Steele). **SYN:** listless, downcast.
—v.t. to make dull: *Chopping wood dulled the ax.* (*Figurative.*) *Men have dulled their eyes with sin* (Henry Van Dyke).
—v.i. to become dull: *This cheap knife dulls very easily.*
[Middle English *dul,* related to Old English *dol* dull-witted] **—dull′ness, dul′ness,** *n.*
—Syn. adj. **1 Dull, blunt** mean without a sharp edge or point. **Dull** suggests that the object described has lost the sharpness it had or is not as

sharp as it should be: *This knife is dull.* **Blunt** suggests that the edge or point is not intended to be sharp or keen: *The blunt side of a knife will not cut meat. The weapon was a blunt instrument, possibly a poker.*

dull|ard (dul′ərd), *n.* a person who is stupid and learns very slowly; dolt; dunce. SYN: blockhead.

dull-brained (dul′brānd′), *adj.* having a dull brain; slow to understand or comprehend: *This arm of mine hath chastised the petty rebel, dull-brain'd Buckingham* (Shakespeare).

dull coal, = durain.

dull|head (dul′hed′), *n.* a person of dull understanding; a blockhead.

dull|ish (dul′ish), *adj.* somewhat dull: *A dullish French villa of the bourgeois class with the usual fountain of terra cotta and glazed tiles* (Harper's).

Dulls|ville or **dulls|ville** (dulz′vil), *n., adj. U.S. Slang.* —*n.* a condition of utter boredom; something very dull.
—*adj.* very dull: [*He*] *is square, folksy and dullsville, sounding just like dozens of boring politicians from the past* (Time).
[< *dull* + *-ville*]

dull-wit|ted (dul′wit′id), *adj.* stupid: *The trick at this point is to create just enough confusion to get the dull-witted to sharpen up their minds* (New Yorker). —**dull′-wit′ted|ness**, *n.*

dul|ly (dul′ē), *adv.* in a dull manner.

du|lo|sis (dü lō′sis, dyü-), *n.* the practice by some groups of ants of enslaving individuals or colonies of other ants.
[< Greek *doúlōsis* slavery < *douloûn* to enslave < *doûlos* servant, slave]

du|lot|ic (dü lot′ik, dyü-), *adj.* exhibiting dulosis; practicing the enslavement of other insects: *dulotic army ants.*

dulse (duls), *n.* any one of several coarse edible seaweeds having bright-red, deeply divided fronds: *Here we find growths of dulse, its . . . deeply indented red fronds somewhat suggesting the shape of a hand* (New Yorker). [< Irish, or Scottish Gaelic *duileasg*]

du|ly (dü′lē, dyü′-), *adv.* **1** according to what is due; rightly; suitably: *The documents were duly signed before a lawyer.* SYN: properly, fitly. **2** as much as is needed; enough. **3** when due; at the proper time: *I shall duly pay you back. The debt will be duly paid.*

Du|ma (dü′mə), *n.* in Russia: **1** the national legislature established in 1906 by Nicholas II and abolished in 1917. **2** Usually, **duma.** an elective council. Also, **Douma, douma.** [< Russian *duma* thought; counsel, ultimately < Germanic (compare Gothic *dōms* judgment). See related etym. at **deem, doom.**]

dumb (dum), *adj., v.* —*adj.* **1** not able to speak: *dumb animals. Helen Keller learned to speak; she was blind and deaf but not dumb.* **2** silenced for the moment by fear, surprise, shyness, or other emotion: *She was struck dumb with astonishment.* **3** unwilling to speak; silent; not speaking: *Yet should you bid me name him, I am dumb* (Edna St. Vincent Millay). SYN: taciturn, reticent. **4** *Informal.* slow in understanding; stupid; dull. SYN: foolish. **5** not characterized by or accompanied by speech, words, or sound: *dumb gestures. A land where newspapers were dumb From scandal and from scare* (Andrew Lang). **6** lacking some property, quality, or accompaniment normally belonging to others of the same type: *A dumb barge or craft is one without sails or propelling power.*
—*v.t.* **dumb down,** *U.S. Informal.* to make less intelligent; lower the intellectual level of: *They are generally blamed . . . as having been a major force in dumbing down textbooks nationwide* (Atlanta Constitution).
[Old English *dumb;* (definition 4) influenced by German *dumm* stupid] —**dumb′ly**, *adv.* —**dumb′ness**, *n.*
—*Syn.* **1, 2 Dumb, mute, speechless** mean without speech. **Dumb** means without the power of speech, and although often used interchangeably with *mute* and *speechless,* it is the term applied particularly to animals: *Even intelligent animals are dumb.* **Mute** emphasizes being silent for some strong reason, and applies particularly to people who have never been able to speak because they were born deaf or became deaf in very early life and have never or practically never heard sounds: *Many mute children now are taught to speak.* **Speechless** applies particularly to someone who is temporarily unable to talk because of emotion, surprise, or the like: *His remark left me speechless with rage.*

dumb ague, a malaria without the characteristic chills.

Dum|bar|ton Oaks (dum bär′tən), a place in the District of Columbia where conferences were held, August—October, 1944, to discuss tentative proposals for the United Nations Organization.

***dumb|bell** (dum′bel′), *n.* **1** a short bar of wood or iron with large, heavy balls or disks at the ends. Dumbbells are generally used in pairs and are lifted or swung around to exercise the muscles of the arms, back, etc. **2** *Slang.* a very stupid person; blockhead.

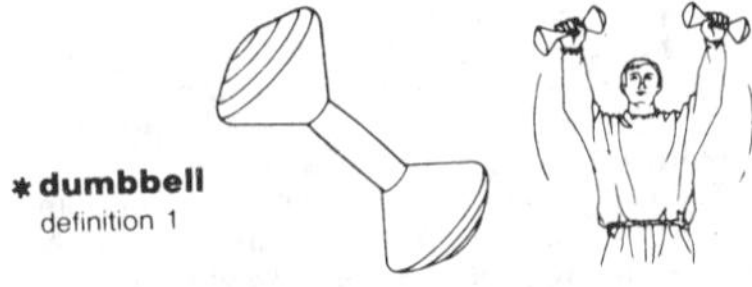

***dumbbell**
definition 1

Dumbbell Nebula, a nebula of the planetary type in the constellation Vulpecula, having the shape of a dumbbell.

dumb cane, a tropical American herb of the arum family, the stem of which when chewed causes the tongue to swell.

dum|bek (dum′bek), *n.* a kind of small drum of the Middle East, played with flattened hands.
[< Arabic *dumbeka*]

dumb|found (dum′found′), *v.t.* = dumfound. —**dumb′found′ing|ly**, *adv.*

dumb|found|er (dum′foun′dər), *v.t.* = dumfound.

dumb piano, a contrivance having a set of keys like a piano and used for exercising the fingers.

dumb rabies, a form of rabies characterized by paralysis of the jaw and throat muscles.

dumb show, **1** gestures without words; pantomime: *He indicated by dumb show that he wanted to speak to me privately.* **2** (in Elizabethan drama) a part of a play represented in pantomime.

dumb-show (dum′shō′), *adj.* done in dumb show; that uses dumb show.

dumb-struck (dum′struk′), *adj.* unable to speak; confused; dumfounded.

dumb|wait|er (dum′wā′tər), *n.* **1** a small box with shelves that can be pulled up and down a shaft. A dumbwaiter is used to send dishes, food, cooking utensils, or small parcels from one floor of a building to another. *His flat is on the floor above hers; when she wants him, she bangs on the ceiling with a broom, and he sneaks down through the dumbwaiter* (Time). **2** a small stand placed near a dining table to hold food, dishes, cooking utensils, or silverware.

dum|dum[1] (dum′dum′), *n.,* or **dumdum bullet**, a bullet having a soft or hollow nose that spreads out when it strikes, causing a serious wound.
[< *Dum Dum,* a town near Calcutta, India, where they were first produced]

dum|dum[2] (dum′dum′), *n. U.S. Slang.* a dumb person; dummy. [alteration and reduplication of *dumb*]

dumdum fever, = kala-azar. [< *Dum Dum,* India]

dum|found (dum′found′), *v.t.* to amaze and make unable to speak; bewilder; confuse; nonplus. SYN: confound. Also, **dumbfound.**
[< *dumb* + (con)*found*] —**dum′found′ing|ly**, *adv.*

dum|found|er (dum′foun′dər), *v.t.* = dumfound.

dum|ka (dům′kə), *n., pl.* **-ky** (-kē), **-kas.** a type of Slavic folk song or music, usually sad and merry in turn: *. . . Czech folk music, or dumka ("little thought"), the unpretentious but satisfying Slavic themes that delighted Dvorak* (Time). [< Czech *dumka*]

dumm|kopf or **dum|kopf** (dům′kôpf′), *n. Slang.* a stupid person; blockhead; dummy: *What a crippling burden. What a dummkopf he was to take it on* (Punch).
[< German *Dummkopf* < *dumm* stupid + *Kopf* head]

dum|my (dum′ē), *n., pl.* **-mies,** *adj., v.,* **-mied, -my|ing.** —*n.* **1** a figure of a person, used to display clothing in store windows, to shoot at in rifle practice, to tackle in football, or in other ways: *a tailor's dummy, a ventriloquist's dummy.* **2** an empty or imitation package or article used for display or advertisement: *All the articles in the window are dummies.* **3** *Printing.* **a** a sample volume, bound or unbound, and usually either blank or only partly printed, to show size and general appearance (in Great Britain called a *size copy*). **b** a format for parts or the whole of a magazine, book, or other publication, made up of printer's proofs pasted down upon empty pages to show the general arrangement of the material; layout. **4** anything made to resemble a real thing; imitation; counterfeit. **5** *Informal.* a stupid person; blockhead; dolt: *Werner and I went to the same high school, like all the boys in the neighborhood except the dummies who had to go to trade school* (Hortense Calisher). **6** a person who has nothing to say or who takes no active part in affairs: *That man is just a dummy, though he's a director on the board.* **7** a person who seems to be acting for himself, but is really acting for another. **8** *Slang.* a dumb person; mute. **9** in card games: **a** a player whose cards are laid face up on the table and played by his partner. **b** the hand played in this way. **c** a game in which there is such a hand. **d** an imaginary player represented by an exposed hand which is played by and serves as partner to one of the players. **10** a former type of steam locomotive with a silent exhaust.
—*adj.* **1** made to resemble the real thing; counterfeit; imitation: *dummy ammunition. The boys played soldier with dummy swords made of wood.* **2** acting for another while supposedly acting for oneself. SYN: vicarious. **3** (of card games) played with an exposed hand, or with three players instead of the usual four: *dummy whist.*
—*v.t. U.S.* to make a dummy of: *to dummy a newspaper, book, or page.*
—*v.i.* (in Australia) to occupy land for a person who will later assume ownership.
[< *dumb* + *-y*[1]]

dum|my-head torpedo (dum′ē hed′), a torpedo with the explosive removed, used for practice.

du|mor|ti|er|ite (dü môr′tē ə rīt, dyü-), *n. Mineralogy.* an aluminum silicate often occurring in gneiss: *. . . dumortierite, a rare mineral used in spark plugs and other refractory products* (Wall Street Journal).
[< Eugène *Dumortier,* a French paleontologist of the 1800's + *-ite*[1]]

dump[1] (dump), *v., n.* —*v.t.* **1** to empty out; throw down (anything) in a heap; unload in a mass: *The truck backed up to the hole and dumped the dirt in it.* **2** *Informal, Figurative.* to get rid of; abandon; reject: *The political party dumped the unpopular candidate. Finally, the movie was "dumped"—opened without the usual publicity and advance screenings* (New Yorker). **3** to sell in large quantities at a low price or below cost. **4** to put (surplus goods) for sale in this manner in a foreign country at a price below that in the home country. **5** to deposit as stores in a dump: *I dumped the oxygen apparatus* (E. F. Norton). **6** *U.S. Slang.* to throw (a game, race, etc.): *Without actually "dumping" or purposely losing a game, it is possible to "shave" or manipulate the point spread* (New York Times). **7** to print out all or part of (the contents of a computer memory).
—*v.i.* **1** to unload rubbish. **2** to unload materials in a mass. **3** to sell goods at very low prices, especially in selected foreign markets. **4** to drop down suddenly; flop down: *Down we dump in the dead rushes* (London Daily News).
—*n.* **1** a place for throwing rubbish: *Garbage is taken to the city dump.* **2** a heap of rubbish or refuse. **3** a reserve supply of ammunition, military stores, equipment, etc. **4** a place for storing military supplies: *an ammunition dump. Their projects range from a big bomber base . . . to a supply dump* (Wall Street Journal). **5** *Slang.* a dirty, shabby, untidy, or otherwise depressing place: *Life in this dump is unbearable.* **6** a printout of the contents of a computer memory: *When computers hit a snag they often print out dense reams of digits, which represent all the data that's been given to them. This is called a "dump." Searching out the error in a dump . . . occupies much of any programmer's time* (Atlantic).

dump on, *U.S. Slang.* to attack verbally; criticize severely: *Black leaders were angrily dumping on President Carter for his scaled-down urban program* (New York Times).
[perhaps < Scandinavian (compare Danish *dumpe* fall with a thud)]

dump[2] (dump), *n. Obsolete.* **1** a mournful melody or song. **2** a tune. **3** See **dumps.** [origin uncertain. Compare Low German *dump* dull, depressed.]

dump[3] (dump), *n.* **1** any object of dumpy shape. **2** a counter of lead used by children in games. [perhaps back formation < *dumpy*[1]]

dump|age (dum′pij), *n.* **1** the act of dumping. **2** a pile of dumped refuse or rubbish. **3** the privilege of dumping rubbish in a certain place. **4** the fee paid for this privilege.

dump cart, a cart that opens at the bottom or tips to discharge its contents.

dump|er (dum′pər), *n.* **1** a person or thing that dumps. **2** (in surfing) a large breaking wave; fall.

dump|i|ly (dum′pə lē), *adv.* in a dumpy manner.

dump|i|ness (dum′pē nis), *n.* dumpy condition.

dump|ing (dum′ping), *n.* the selling of surplus goods, securities, or other commodities in large quantities and at low prices, especially in foreign markets: *A dumping duty has been applied by the Canadian government on fresh strawberry imports . . . which have been entering Canada at unusually low prices* (Wall Street Journal).

dump|ish (dum′pish), *adj.* **1** sad; melancholy; moping. **2** dull; stupid. —**dump′ish|ly**, *adv.* —**dump′ish|ness**, *n.*

Pronunciation Key: hat, āge, cãre, fär; let, ēqual, tėrm; it, īce; hot, ōpen, ôrder; oil, out; cup, pu̇t, rüle; child; long; thin; ᴛʜen; zh, measure; ə represents a in about, e in taken, i in pencil, o in lemon, u in circus.

dump|ling (dump′ling), *n.* **1** a rounded piece of dough, boiled or steamed, and usually served with meat. **2** a small pudding made by enclosing fruit in a piece of dough and baking or steaming it. **3** a dumpy animal or person, short and of rounded outlines. [< earlier *dump* a badly shaped piece + *-ling*]

dump rake, a hayrake consisting of curved steel teeth mounted on an axle between two wheels. When the rake is full, the operator dumps the hay by pulling a lever that lifts the teeth from the ground.

dumps (dumps), *n.pl. Informal.* low spirits; gloomy feelings: *. . . needs must I wail, As one in doleful dumps* (Sir Richard Steele). **SYN:** depression, melancholy.

in the dumps, feeling gloomy or sad: *After she crumpled the car fender she was really in the dumps.*

dump|ster (dump′stər), *n. U.S.* a large receptacle for refuse which is emptied into a garbage truck or can be loaded on a flat-bed truck to carry to a garbage dump.

***dump truck**, a truck that can be unloaded by tipping the bed or by opening downward.

***dump truck**

dump|y¹ (dum′pē), *adj.,* **dump|i|er, dump|i|est.** short and fat; squat: *Her stature tall—I hate a dumpy woman* (Byron). [origin uncertain]

dump|y² (dum′pē), *adj.,* **dump|i|er, dump|i|est.** melancholy; dejected; sulky. [< *dump²* + *-y¹*]

dumpy level, a spirit level used in surveying and construction, having a short telescope with a large aperture.

dum spi|ro spe|ro (dum spī′rō spir′ō), *Latin.* while I breathe, I hope (one of the two mottoes of South Carolina, the other being *animis opibusque parati*).

dum vi|vi|mus, vi|va|mus (dum viv′i məs, vi vā′məs), *Latin.* let us live while we live; let us enjoy life.

dun¹ (dun), *v.,* **dunned, dun|ning,** *n.* **—*v.t.*** to demand payment of a debt from (someone) again and again: *The store dunned him until his overdue bills were finally paid.*
—*v.i.* to pester or plague constantly: *If you keep on dunning, I'll never pay.*
—*n.* **1** a demand for payment of a debt. **2** a person who keeps demanding payment of a debt.
[earlier, make a din < Scandinavian (compare Old Icelandic *duna* to thunder)]

dun² (dun), *adj., n.* **—*adj.*** dull grayish-brown.
—*n.* **1** a dull grayish brown. **2** a horse of a dun color. **3** a grayish-brown natural or artificial May fly used in angling. [Old English *dunn,* perhaps < Celtic (compare Old Irish *donn,* Welsh *dwn*)]

dun³ (dun), *n.* a hill; fortified eminence. [< Irish or Scottish Gaelic *dun*]

du|nam (də nam′), *n.* = donum.

Dun and Brad|street (dun′ ən brad′strēt), a commercial agency that publishes financial directories, and prepares and distributes credit information to its subscribers.

***Dun|can Phyfe** (dung′kən fīf′), designating a style of gracefully proportioned and soundly constructed furniture designed by Duncan Phyfe, 1768-1854, an American cabinetmaker and furniture designer.

***Duncan Phyfe**

dunce (duns), *n.* **1** a child slow at learning his lessons in school. **2** a stupid person; blockhead; dullard: *Blockhead! dunce! ass!* (John Arbuthnot). **SYN:** dolt, ninny. **3** *Obsolete.* **a** a dull pedant: *a dunce, void of learning but full of books* (Thomas Fuller). **b** a sophist. [earlier *duns* < *Dunsman* or *dunceman,* a name applied by his attackers to any follower of John *Duns* Scotus, an English theologian of the 1200's]

dunce cap, a tall, cone-shaped cap formerly worn as a punishment by a child who was slow in learning his lessons in school.

dunc|er|y (dun′sər ē), *n.* intellectual dullness; stupidity.

dunce's cap, = dunce cap.

dunch (dunsh, du̇nsh), *n., v.t. Scottish.* push; jog; nudge. [origin unknown]

dun|der|head (dun′dər hed′), *n.* a stupid, foolish person; dunce; blockhead; numskull: *Myself, I have always been an absolute dunderhead at mathematics* (New Yorker). [< earlier *dunder* (origin uncertain) + *head*]

dun|der|head|ed (dun′dər hed′id), *adj.* stupid; thick-headed. **—dun′der|head′ed|ness,** *n.*

dun|der|pate (dun′dər pāt′), *n.* = dunderhead.

Dun|drear|y (dun drir′ē), *n., pl.* **-drear|ies,** or **Dundreary whiskers**, long whiskers on both sides of the face but not on the chin. [< *Dundreary,* a character in the play *Our American Cousin* (1858) by Tom Taylor]

dune (dün, dyün), *n.* a mound or ridge of loose sand heaped up by the wind: *Over the shoulders and slopes of the dune I saw the white daisies go down to the sea* (Bliss Carman). [< Old French *dune* < Middle Dutch *dūnen,* or Middle Low German *dūne.* See related etym. at **down³**.]

***dune buggy**, a motor vehicle with very large tires, used for driving on sand dunes and beaches; beach buggy.

***dune buggy**
definition 1

dune|land (dün′land′, dyün′-; -lənd), *n.* a barren region characterized by dunes and little or no vegetation.

dun|fish (dun′fish′), *n.* codfish salted and cured in a special way.

dun fly, = dun² (*n.* def. 3).

dung (dung), *n., v.* **—*n.*** waste matter from the intestines of animals, much used as a fertilizer; manure. **SYN:** droppings.
—*v.t.* to put dung on as fertilizer: *I decided to make an experiment and kept one field free from any artificial [fertilizer] and dunged it regularly* (Punch).
[Old English *dung*]

dun|ga|ree (dung′gə rē′, dung′gə rē), *n.* a coarse cotton cloth, used especially for work clothes and sails.
dungarees, trousers, work clothes, or overalls made of this cloth: *Seaman Stringer, clad in dungarees and holding an oilcan, told the President, wearing sports slacks, about a fish called a "hog snapper"* (Newsweek). [< Hindi *dungrī*]

dung beetle, any one of certain beetles that feed on or breed in dung, such as the tumblebug; scarab.

Dun|ge|ness crab (dun′jə nis, dunj′nis; -nes), an edible crab caught in shallow waters from California to Alaska, and canned in Oregon, Washington, and Alaska. [< *Dungeness,* a fishing village in Washington]

dun|geon (dun′jən), *n., v.* **—*n.*** **1** a dark underground room or cell to keep prisoners in: *Beneath the castle I could discern vast dungeons* (George M. Berkeley). (*Figurative.*) *My body, which my dungeon is* (Robert Louis Stevenson). **2** = donjon.
—*v.t.* to confine in a dungeon; imprison.
[< Old French *donjon,* perhaps < a Germanic word]

dung|hill (dung′hil′), *n.* **1** a heap of dung or refuse: *a dunghill in the farmyard.* **2** *Figurative.* a vile place or person.

dung|y (dung′ē), *adj.,* **dung|i|er, dung|i|est. 1** full of dung. **2** like dung; foul; filthy; vile.

dun|ie|was|sal (dü′nē wos′əl), *n.* **1** a Scottish Highland gentleman of secondary rank. **2** a cadet of a family of rank. [< Gaelic *duine uasal* person of gentle (literally, respected) birth]

dun|ite (dun′īt), *n.* an igneous rock of granitic structure, composed chiefly of olivine with small amounts of chromite and other minerals. [< *Dun* Mountain, in New Zealand, an area where it is found + *-ite¹*]

dunk (dungk), *v., n. Informal.* **—*v.t.*** **1** to dip (something, especially food) into a liquid: *to dunk doughnuts in coffee, to dunk one's head in water.* **2** to lower or drop (a basketball) into the basket from above; place (a dunk shot): *Manny Leaks, the 6-foot-7-inch Niagara star, dunked a shot, grabbing the rim with both hands on the way down* (New York Times). **—*v.i.*** to dip into water: *The kids are dunking in the pool.*
—*n.* **1** a dunking; dip; immersion: *A detergent dunk is all it needs to keep it clean* (McCall's). **2** = dunk shot.
[American English, apparently < German *tunken* to dip] **—dunk′er,** *n.*

Dunk|ard (dung′kərd), *n.* a member of the Church of the Brethren, a sect practicing adult baptism by triple immersion, opposing oaths and military service, and observing severe simplicity of dress and speech. [American English, variant of *Dunker* < Pennsylvania Dutch *Dunker* (in German, *Tunker*) < *dunken* to dip, baptize]

Dunk|er (dung′kər), *n.* = Dunkard.

Dun|kirk (dun′kėrk, dun kėrk′), *n.* **1** a hasty retreat in the face of disaster: *It was essential for General Eisenhower to know whether the Afrika Korps was going to stage a Dunkirk* (Reader's Digest). **2** any difficult or dangerous situation; crisis: *The pound "is going through a Dunkirk"* (London Times). [< *Dunkirk,* a seaport in northern France where British forces were hastily evacuated in 1940]

dunk shot, *Basketball.* a shot in which the player jumps high enough to drop the ball into the basket: *Even in the pre-game warm-ups Alcindor's dunk shots would draw gasps and applause. Alcindor was particularly adept at the backward dunk* (Bill Becker).

dun|lin (dun′lən), *n., pl.* **-lins** or (*collectively*) **-lin.** a small wading bird of northern regions that has a broad black patch across the abdomen during breeding season; red-backed sandpiper. [probably for unrecorded *dunling* < *dun²* + *-ling*]

Dun|lop (dun′lop), *n.,* or **Dunlop cheese,** a white cheese made from unskimmed milk. [< *Dunlop,* a parish in Scotland where it was made originally]

dun|nage (dun′ij), *n.* **1** loose packing of branches, mats, or soft refuse, such as wastepaper or plastic, beneath, wedged among, or placed around a cargo to prevent damage by water or chafing or to protect freight in a railroad car: *We covered the bottom of the hold . . . with dried brush, for dunnage* (Richard Henry Dana). **2** *Figurative.* miscellaneous baggage. **3** *Slang.* a sailor's or tramp's clothes: *The tramp carried his dunnage tied to a stick.* [origin uncertain]

dun|ner (dun′ər), *n.* a person who duns.

dunn|ite (dun′īt), *n.* an explosive consisting of ammonium picrate, used in the head of projectiles. [< Colonel B. W. *Dunn,* 1860-1936, of the United States Army, who invented it + *-ite¹*]

dun|nock (dun′ək), *n.* a small European warbler; hedge sparrow. [apparently < *dun²* + *-ock,* a diminutive suffix]

dunt (dunt, du̇nt), *n., v. Scottish.* **—*n.*** **1** a hard blow making a dull sound. **2** a wound produced by such a blow. **3** a beat of the heart.
—*v.t.* to knock with a dull sound, as with the fist in the back or ribs.
—*v.i.* **1** to strike with a dull sound. **2** (of the heart) to beat; throb.
[variant of *dint.* Compare Swedish *dunt* dint.]

du|o (dü′ō, dyü′-), *n., pl.* **du|os** or (*Italian*) **du|i.** **1** a duet (used especially of instrumental music): *The Don Shirley duo will start unravelling its bittersweet harmonics* (New Yorker). **2** *Informal, Figurative.* a pair. [< Italian *duo* < Latin *duo* two]

du|o|de|cil|lion (dü′ə di sil′yən, dyü′-), *n.* **1** (in the U.S., Canada, and France) 1 with 39 zeros after it. **2** (in Great Britain and Germany) 1 with 72 zeros after it. [< Latin *duodecim* twelve + English *-illion,* as in *million*]

du|o|dec|i|mal (dü′ə des′ə məl, dyü′-), *adj., n.* **—*adj.*** having to do with twelfths or twelve; expressed by twelves.
—*n.* **1** one of a system of numerals, the base of which is twelve instead of ten. **2** one twelfth.
duodecimals, a system of numerals based upon twelve instead of ten: *Duodecimals . . . is generally employed by painters, bricklayers, etc., in measuring work* (Barnard Smith).
[< Latin *duodecimus* twelfth (< *duodecim* twelve < *duo* two + *decem* ten) + English *-al¹*] **—du′o|dec′i|mal|ly,** *adv.*

du|o|dec|i|mo (dü′ə des′ə mō, dyü′-), *n., pl.* **-mos,** *adj.* **—*n.*** **1** the page size of a book in which each leaf is one-twelfth of a whole sheet of paper, or about 5 by 7½ inches; twelvemo. *Abbr:* 12mo or 12°. **2** a book having pages of this size.
—*adj.* **1** of this size. **2** having pages of this size.
[< Latin *in duodecimō* in a twelfth (of a sheet)]

du|o|de|na (dü′ə dē′nə, dyü′-; dů od′ə-, dyů-), *n.* a plural of **duodenum.**

du|o|de|nal (dü′ə dē′nəl, dyü′-; dů od′ə-, dyů-), *adj.* of or having to do with the duodenum: *a duodenal ulcer.*

duodenal ulcer, an ulcer in the wall of the duodenum, caused entirely or in part by the digestive action of gastric juice: *Studies have revealed that of 1000 adult patients with duodenal ulcer, 26 had symptoms traceable to as early as four years of age* (Science News Letter).

du|o|den|ar|y (dü′ə den′ər ē, dyü′-; -dē′nər-; dů-od′ə ner′ē, dyů-), *adj.* having to do with or based on the number twelve; proceeding by twelves. [< Latin *duodēnārius* of twelve < *duodēnī;* see etym. under **duodenum.**]

du|o|de|ni|tis (dü′ə də nī′tis, dyü′-), *n.* inflammation of the duodenum. [< *duoden*(um) + *-itis*]

du|o|de|nos|to|my (dü′ə də nos′tə mē, dyü′-), *n.,pl.* **-mies.** the making of a permanent opening into the duodenum by surgery. [< *duoden*(um) +

Greek *stóma* mouth; opening + English -*y*[3]]

du|o|de|not|o|my (dü′ə də not′ə mē, dyü′-), *n., pl.* **-mies.** surgical incision of the duodenum. [< *duoden*(um) + Greek *-tomiā* a cutting]

du|o|de|num (dü′ə dē′nəm, dyü′-; dů od′ə-, dyů-), *n., pl.* **-na** or **-nums.** the first part of the small intestine, just below the stomach, which ends at the jejunum. See picture under **digestion.** [< Medieval Latin *duodenum* < Latin *duodēnī* twelve each < *duodecim* twelve < *duo* two + *decem* ten (because of its length, about twelve fingerbreadths)]

du|o|dra|ma (dü′ə drä′mə, dyü′-; -dram′ə), *n.* a play for two players in which the dialogue is spoken against an instrumental background. [< Italian *duodramma* < *duo* two + *dramma* drama]

du|o|graph (dü′ə graf, dyü′-; -gräf), *n.* = duotone. [< Latin *duo* two + English *-graph*]

du|o|logue (dü′ə lôg, dyü′-; -log), *n.* **1** a conversation between two persons; dialogue. **2** a dramatic performance or piece in the form of a dialogue: *The new play is a duologue in which the male character listens to the female character* (New York Times). [< Latin *duo* two + English (mono)*logue*]

duo|mo (dwô′mō), *n., pl.* **-mi** (-mē). *Italian.* a cathedral.

du|o-pi|an|ist (dü′ō pē an′ist, -pē′ə nist), *n.* a member of a duet playing at separate pianos: *Buck Whittemore and Jack Lowe ... began their career as duo-pianists in 1936* (Newsweek).

du|op|o|list (dů op′ə list, dyů-), *n.* a person who has a duopoly or favors duopoly.

du|op|o|ly (dů op′ə lē, dyů-), *n., pl.* **-lies.** exclusive control of a product by two competing companies: *Businesses controlled by "duopolies" ... can dictate prices in much the same manner as a classical monopoly* (Wall Street Journal). [< Latin *duo* two + English (mono)*poly*]

du|op|so|ny (dů op′sə nē, dyů-), *n.* exclusive control of the demand for a product by two competing purchasers of that product. [< Latin *duo* two + Greek *opsōniā* purchase of food]

du|o|rail (dü′ə rāl′, dyü′-), *n.* the conventional railroad consisting of two rails, as distinguished from the monorail: *On grounds of cost, comfort, and convenience, the duorail was the most practical of all sytems studied* (Ernest Davies).

du|o|tone (dü′ə tōn, dyü′-), *adj., n.* —*adj.* printed or done in two tones or colors.
—*n.* a printing process by which a one-color original is reproduced in two tones or colors; duograph.
[< Latin *duo* two + English *tone*]

du|o|toned (dü′ə tōnd, dyü′-), *adj.* printed or done in two tones or colors.

dup (dup), *v.t.,* **dupped, dup|ping.** *Archaic.* to open: *And dupp'd the chamber door* (Shakespeare). [contraction of *do up.* Compare etym. under **don**[2], **doff.**]

dup., duplicate.

dup|a|bil|i|ty (dü′pə bil′ə tē, dyü′-), *n.* = gullibility.

dup|a|ble (dü′pə bəl, dyü′-), *adj.* gullible.

dupe[1] (düp, dyüp), *n., v.,* **duped, dup|ing.** —*n.* **1** a person easily deceived or tricked: *the ready dupe of astrologers and soothsayers* (Scott). **2** a person who is being deluded or tricked: *The young politician's inexperience is making him the dupe of some unscrupulous schemers.*
—*v.t.* to make a dupe of; deceive or trick; delude: *The dishonest peddler duped all of his customers.* **SYN:** gull, cheat.
[< French *dupe,* variant of *huppe* < Latin *upupa* hoopoe (supposedly because it is a stupid bird)]
—**dup′er,** *n.*

dupe[2] (düp, dyüp), *adj., n., v. Photography, Informal.* = duplicate. [short for *duplicate*]

dup|er|y (dü′pər ē, dyü′-), *n., pl.* **-er|ies. 1** deception; trickery. **2** the condition of one who is duped.

du|pi|on (dü′pē ōn, dyü′-), *n.* **1** a double cocoon formed by two silkworms spinning together. **2** the coarse silk furnished by such double cocoons: ... *the immensely popular slub-textured cloths of the shantung and dupion type* (London Times). Also, **dupioni, douppioni.** [< French *doupion* < Italian *doppione,* augmentative of *doppio* double < Latin *duplus;* see etym. under **duple**]

du|pi|o|ni (dü′pē ō′nē, dyü′-), *n.* = dupion.

du|pla|tion (dü plā′shən, dyü-), *n.* multiplication by doubling. [< Latin *duplātiō, -ōnis* < *duplāre* to double]

du|ple (dü′pəl, dyü′-), *adj.* **1** double; twofold. **2** *Music.* having two or a multiple of two beats to the measure. [< Latin *duplus* double < *du-* two + *-plus* -fold. See etym. of doublets **dobla, dobra, double.**]

duple measure, = duple time.

duple ratio, a ratio in which the antecedent is double the consequent, as 2 to 1, or 8 to 4.

du|plet (dü′plit, dyü′-), *n.* **1** *Chemistry.* a pair of electrons shared by two atoms, constituting a covalent bond. **2** any group of two: *an eighth-note duplet in music.* [< *dupl*(e) + *-et*]

duple time, two-part time; music with two beats to the measure.

du|plex (dü′pleks, dyü′-), *adj., n.* —*adj.* **1** having two parts; double; twofold. **2** (of a machine) having two similar or corresponding main parts.
—*n.* a duplex house or duplex apartment.
[< Latin *duplex* < *du-* two + *-plex, -plicis,* related to *plaga* flat(ness)]

duplex apartment, an apartment having rooms on two floors.

du|plex|er (dü′plek sər, dyü′-), *n.* a switch that makes it possible to use only one radar antenna by automatically switching the transmitter or the receiver onto the antenna line as each is needed.

duplex house, a house built to accommodate two families.

du|plex|i|ty (dü plek′sə tē, dyü-), *n.* = doubleness.

duplex pump, a two-cylinder pump.

duplex telegraphy, a system for sending two messages over the same wire at the same time, especially in opposite directions.

du|pli|cate (*adj., n.* dü′plə kit, dyü′-; *v.* dü′plə kāt, dyü′-), *adj., n., v.,* **-cat|ed, -cat|ing.** —*adj.* **1** exactly like something else; corresponding to something else: *We have duplicate keys for the front door.* **2** having two corresponding parts; double; twofold: *A person's lungs are duplicate, but he has only one heart.* **3** (in card games) having the same hands played by different players: *duplicate bridge.*
—*n.* **1** one of two or more things exactly alike; an exact copy: *He mailed the letter but kept a duplicate.* **SYN:** facsimile, replica. **2** a card game played at duplicate competition, such as bridge.
—*v.t.* **1** to make an exact copy of; repeat exactly: *to duplicate an action. Duplicate the picture so that we may both have copies of it. Once is enough; don't duplicate the mistake.* **SYN:** reproduce. **2** to make double or twofold; double.
—*v.i.* **1** to be duplicated; replicate. **2** *Obsolete.* to double or fold on itself.
in duplicate, in two copies exactly alike: *Using carbon paper, he typed the application in duplicate. Receipts for refunds are taken in duplicate* (Harper's).
[< Latin *duplicāre* (with English *-ate*[1]) to double < *du-* two + *plicāre* to fold]

duplicate whist, a form of whist in which the hands are played over again, when each side holds the cards formerly held by its opponents.

du|pli|ca|tion (dü′plə kā′shən, dyü′-), *n.* **1** the act of duplicating; making anything twice as many or as much; repetition of an action or thing: *Duplication of effort is a waste of time.* **2** the condition or fact of being duplicated. **3** a duplicate copy; counterpart: *Her answers were a duplication of her sister's. Reorganize ... eliminating personnel duplications and other waste* (Newsweek).

du|pli|ca|tive (dü′plə kā′tiv, dyü′-), *adj.* having the quality of doubling; producing two instead of one.

du|pli|ca|tor (dü′plə kā′tər, dyü′-), *n.* a machine for making many exact copies of anything written, typed, or drawn.

du|pli|ca|to|ry (dü′plə kə tôr′ē, -tōr′-; dyü′-), *adj.* duplicating; repeating something exactly: *So long as the space race continues, this kind of essentially duplicatory activity is unavoidable* (New York Times).

du|pli|ca|ture (dü′plə kā′chər, dyü′-), *n.* **1** = duplication. **2** a fold.

du|plic|i|tous (dü plis′ə təs, dyü-), *adj.* deceitful; treacherous: [*His*] *candid essay tears the mask off this duplicitous thinking in a way nothing else in recent literature has* (Commentary). —**du|plic′i-tous|ly,** *adv.*

du|plic|i|ty (dü plis′ə tē, dyü-), *n., pl.* **-ties. 1** the character or practice of secretly acting one way and openly acting in another in order to deceive; deceitfulness; double-dealing; treachery: *the duplicity of the king's conduct* (Isaac D'Israeli). *The duplicity of the spy was exposed when his collaborators confessed.* **SYN:** dissimulation. **2** the state of being double, especially as applied to stars. [< Old French *duplicite* < Late Latin *duplicitās* doubleness < Latin *duplex, -plicis;* see etym. under **duplex**]

du|ra[1] (důr′ə, dyůr′-), *n.* = dura mater.

du|ra[2] (důr′ə), *n.* = durra.

du|ra|bil|i|ty (důr′ə bil′ə tē, dyůr′-), *n.* lasting quality; ability to withstand decay or wear; permanence: *We think of rock as a symbol of durability, yet even the hardest rock shatters and wears away when attacked by rain, frost, or surf* (New Yorker).

du|ra|ble (důr′ə bəl, dyůr′-), *adj.* **1** able to withstand wear or decay: *Work clothes are made of durable fabric.* **SYN:** strong. **2** lasting or existing a long time; not soon injured or worn out; lasting: *a durable marriage. Another war destroyed all hopes of a durable peace between the two nations.* **SYN:** permanent, stable, enduring, persistent.

durables, durable goods: *"Durables" like household furnishings and appliances have become available in mass quantities for the first time in Mexico* (Harper's).
[< Old French *durable* < Latin *dūrābilis* < *dūrāre* to last, harden < *dūrus* hard] —**du′ra|ble|ness,** *n.*

durable goods, manufactured goods not consumed by the purchaser, such as machinery, appliances, furniture, or hardware: *Behind autos and homes, appliances rank as the third biggest ... durable goods item* (Wall Street Journal).

durable press, 1 a textile-manufacturing process in which creases, pleats, and seams are set into fabric by the use of chemicals: *Durable press ... permits clothes to be taken out of the dryer and worn without a touch of the iron* (Time). **2** the pressed condition of textiles treated by this process: *Fabrics containing a durable press ... have been widely used in men's and boys' apparel* (New York Times). Also, **permanent press.**

du|ra|bly (důr′ə blē, dyůr′-), *adv.* in a durable manner; so as to withstand wear or decay; lastingly.

du|rain (də rān′), *n.* a hard, dull layer of bituminous coal, composed chiefly of decayed plant matter and clay. [< Latin *dūrus* hard + English *-ain,* as in *fusain*]

du|ral (důr′əl, dyůr′-), *adj.* of or having to do with the dura mater.

Du|ral|u|min (dů ral′yə mən, dyů-), *n.* **1** *Trademark.* a light alloy of aluminum containing copper, manganese, magnesium, and sometimes silicon or iron, comparable in strength and hardness to soft steel. **2 duralumin.** any one of various alloys of this kind. [< *dur*(able) + *aluminum*(um)]

du|ra ma|ter (důr′ə mā′tər, dyůr′-), *Anatomy.* the tough, fibrous membrane forming the outermost of the three coverings of the brain and spinal cord. [< Medieval Latin *dura mater* (literally) hard mother (that is, hard source). Compare etym. under **pia mater.**]

du|ra|men (dů rā′mən, dyů-), *n. Botany.* the central wood or heartwood of an exogenous tree. [< Latin *dūrāmen* hardness; woody branch of a vine < *dūrāre* to harden < *dūrus* hard]

du|rance (důr′əns, dyůr′-), *n.* **1** forced confinement; imprisonment: *In durance vile here must I wake and weep* (Robert Burns). **2** *Archaic.* endurance: *the durance of a granite ledge* (Emerson). [< Old French *durance* duration < Latin *dūrāre;* see etym. under **durable**]

Du|ra|ni (dü rä′nē), *n., pl.* **-ni** or **-nis.** a member of a large Pathan tribe in Afghanistan.

du|ran|te vi|ta (dů ran′tē vī′tə, dyů-), *Latin.* during life.

du|ra|tion (dů rā′shən, dyů-), *n.* length of time; the time during which anything continues: *The storm was of short duration.* **SYN:** term, period.
for the duration, until the end, especially of a war: *He enlisted in the army for the duration of the war.*
[< Middle French *duration,* learned borrowing from Late Latin *dūrātiō, -ōnis* < Latin *dūrāre;* see etym. under **durable**]

du|ra|tive (důr′ə tiv, dyůr′-), *adj.* designating a verb aspect in Russian and other languages which marks action as going on.

dur|bar (dėr′bär), *n.* **1** an official audience or reception held by a native prince of India or, formerly, by a British governor or viceroy in India: *The festivities center on Mysore City, the capital of the state, where the maharaja holds a ten-day durbar with all the splendid panoply of his ancestors* (Santha Rama Rau). **2** the court of a native prince or ruler: *Then, one morning Gopal came to the durbar with the golden box* (Times of India). **3** a hall or place where a durbar is held. [< Hindustani *darbār* < Persian *darbār* court < *dar* door + *-bār* place]

dure[1] (důr, dyůr), *adj. Archaic.* hard; severe. [< Old French *dure* < Latin *dūrus* hard. See etym. of doublets **dour, duro.**]

dure[2] (důr, dyůr), *v.i., v.t.,* **dured, dur|ing.** *Archaic.* to endure; last. [< Old French *durer* < Latin *dūrāre;* see etym. under **durable**]

Dür|er|esque (dʏ′rər esk′), *adj.* in the manner or style of Albrecht Dürer, 1471-1528, the famous German painter, engraver, and designer.

du|ress (dů res′, dyů-; důr′is, dyůr′-), *n.* **1** the use of force; compulsion: *A person cannot be legally forced to fulfill a contract signed under duress.* **SYN:** constraint, coercion, force. **2** imprisonment; confinement. [< Old French *duresse* < Latin

---

Pronunciation Key: **hat, āge, cãre, fär; let, ēqual, tėrm, it, īce; hot, ōpen, ôrder; oil, out; cup, půt, rüle; child; long; thin; ᴛʜen; zh,** measure; **ə** represents **a** in about, **e** in taken, **i** in pencil, **o** in lemon, **u** in circus.

dūritia hardness < *dūrus* hard]

Dur|ga (dů r′gä), *n.* a Hindu goddess, a wife of Siva, embodying or representing an aspect of female energy, also called Kali and other names.

Dur|ham (dėr′əm), *n.* a breed of shorthorned cattle; shorthorn. [< *Durham,* the county in England where it originated]

Durham boat, a long, narrow kind of keelboat used on North American rivers in the 1700's and 1800's. [probably < Robert *Durham,* a Pennsylvania boat builder of the 1700's]

Durham Rule, *U.S.* the rule that an accused person is not criminally responsible if his crime was the product of a diseased or defective mental condition. [< U.S. vs. *Durham,* a case tried in 1954 < Monte *Durham,* the accused in this case]

du|ri|an (dů r′ē ən), *n.* **1** the bad-smelling but edible fruit of a tree of the bombax family of southeastern Asia, with a hard, prickly rind and cream-colored pulp: *Piles of fruit—mangosteens, smelly durians, big green pomelos—lay about partly sheltered by banana leaves* (New Yorker). **2** the tree itself. [< Malay *durian* < *duri* thorn]

dur|ing (dů r′ing, dyů r′-), *prep.* **1** throughout the whole time of; throughout: *The boys played inside during the storm.* **2** at some time in; in the course of: *Come to see me during my office hours. During the night the rain turned to snow.* [present participle of *dure*[2]]

Dur|i|ron (dů r′ī′ərn, dyů r′-), *n. Trademark.* an acid-resisting alloy of steel containing about 14 per cent silicon. It is cast into pipes, valves, fittings, etc., for use in industries handling acids.

dur|mast (dėr′mast, -mäst), *n.* a European oak with a dark, heavy, elastic wood, used in making furniture and in building. [< *dur,* meaning uncertain + *mast*[2] acorns]

durn (dėrn), *v.t., n., adv., adj. Dialect or Informal.* darn: *It may not win any Oscars, but durn if it don't take the blue ribbon for country corn* (Time).

durned (dėrnd), *adj., adv. Dialect or Informal.* darned: *Now, that's durned nice* (Holiday).

du|ro (dü′rō), *n., pl.* **-ros**. an old Spanish silver dollar, worth a peso. [< Spanish *duro* < (*peso*) *duro* hard (solid) peso < Latin *dūrus.* See etym. of doublets **dour, dure**[1].]

Du|roc (dů r′ok, dyů r′-), *n.* any one of an American breed of large, quick-maturing red hogs with drooping ears.

Du|roc-Jer|sey (dů r′ok jėr′zē, dyů r′-), *n.* = Duroc.

du|rom|e|ter (dü rom′ə tər, dyü-), *n.* an instrument for determining the hardness of substances. [< Latin *dūrus* hard + English *-meter*]

dur|ra (dů r′ə), *n.* a cereal grass, a species of sorghum, with slender stalks, widely cultivated in the Mediterranean region and the Orient for food and for fodder; Indian millet; Guinea corn. Also, **dura, doura, dourah**. [< Arabic *dhura*]

durst (dėrst), *v. Archaic.* dared; a past tense of **dare**.

du|rum (dů r′əm, dyů r′-), *n.,* or **durum wheat**, a species of wheat from whose hard grain or kernels the flour used in macaroni, spaghetti, and the like, is made. [< Latin *dūrum,* neuter of *dūrus* hard]

dusk (dusk), *n., adj., v.* **—*n.*** **1** the darker stage of twilight before it is quite dark at night; time just before dark: *We saw the evening star at dusk. In the dusk of the evening* (James Mabbe). **2** shade; gloom: *the dusk of a forest.*
—*adj.* dusky; dark-colored.
—*v.t.* to make dusky; darken; obscure; dim: *That shadow which dusketh the light of the moon* (Josiah G. Holland). **—*v.i.*** to grow dusky or dim.
[Middle English *dusk, dosk,* alteration of Old English *dox*]

dusk|en (dus′kən), *v.t., v.i.* to make or become dusk.

dusk|i|ly (dus′kə lē), *adv.* in a dusky manner; with partial darkness.

dusk|i|ness (dus′kē nis), *n.* dusky condition or state; partial darkness.

dusk|ish (dus′kish), *adj.* somewhat dusky.

dusk|y (dus′kē), *adj.,* **dusk|i|er, dusk|i|est.** **1** somewhat dark; dark-colored: *Dusky woman, who are you?* (Walt Whitman). **2** dim; obscure: *the dusky light of the late afternoon.* **3** sad; gloomy; melancholy.
—*Syn.* **1 Dusky, swarthy** mean somewhat dark. **Dusky** means either dark-colored or dim, and applies to almost anything: *It was a dusky old warehouse.* **Swarthy** means dark-colored, and applies only to complexion: *He has a swarthy skin.*

dusky shark, a medium-sized shark which is not dangerous to man, common on the Atlantic coast of North America.

Dus|se|rah (dus′ə rä), *n.* = Dashahara.

dust (dust), *n., v.* **—*n.*** **1** fine, dry earth: *Dust lay thick on the road.* **2** any fine powder, such as an insecticide or a pollen.: *The old papers had turned to dust. The bee is covered with yellow dust from the flowers.* **3** earth; ground. **4** a cloud of dust floating in the air: *The speeding car on the dirt road raised a great dust.* **5** *Figurative.* what is left of a dead body after decay: *The tomb contains the dust of kings.* SYN: remains. **6** *Figurative.* a low or humble condition: *to raise the poor from the dust.* **7** *Figurative.* a worthless thing or person: *to treat someone like dust. Others may sing of the wine and the wealth and the mirth ... Mine be the dirt and the dross, the dust and scum of the earth* (John Masefield). **8** *British.* ashes or refuse. **9** *Figurative.* confusion; disturbance; turmoil: *to raise a lot of dust about nothing.* **10** = gold dust. **11** *Slang.* money; cash. **12** a single particle; a grain.
—*v.t.* **1** to brush or wipe the dust from: *Mother always dusts the furniture after sweeping.* **2** to brush off as dust: *Dust the crumbs from your lap.* **3** to get dust on; soil with dust: *Please wipe your shoes or you will dust the carpet.* **4** to sprinkle with dust or powder: *to dust a cake with sugar, to dust vegetable plants. The nurse dusted powder over the baby.* **5** *Figurative.* to sprinkle as dust: *to dust pepper on meat.*
—*v.i.* **1** to wipe or brush off dust, as from a room: *I'll sweep, and later, you can dust.* **2** to become dusty.
bite the dust, *Slang.* **a** to fall dead or wounded: *He ... had made numerous lions bite the dust* (C. J. Andersson). **b** to be defeated, dismissed, or eliminated: *Thruway billboard bites the dust in state attack* (New York Times). **c** to be thoroughly humiliated: *He bit the dust after the principal scolded him in front of the class.*
dust off, to introduce again later; reintroduce: *to dust off an old scheme.*
dust out, *U.S.* to make homeless or destitute by the effects of a dust storm: *The farmer became a migratory worker after he and his family had been dusted out.*
gather dust, to be ignored or neglected: *The two-year old report ... was circulated to certain officials and then set aside to gather dust* (New Scientist). *Slang such as "skiddoo" lie gathering dust and forgotten* (Arthur Krock).
hit the dust, *Slang.* to fall down; be knocked down: *The dazed boxer hit the dust in the third round. Treasured old buildings have steadily hit the dust, and more of them probably will* (New York Times).
lick the dust, a to fall dead or wounded: *Another redskin licked the dust.* **b** to humble oneself slavishly; grovel: *He licked the dust in order to curry favor with the political boss.*
settle the dust, (of affairs or circumstances) to quiet down; return to normal: *Expressing hope that "after the initial dust has settled" some good might evolve from the decision* (New York Times). *The association's leaders said they had taken no stand until the present because they wanted "to let the dust settle"* (Wall Street Journal).
shake the dust off one's feet, to go away feeling angry or scornful: *He shook the dust of that place off his feet and vowed to get even.*
throw dust in one's eyes, to confuse, deceive, or mislead; defy: *It required a long discourse to throw dust in the eyes of common sense* (Benjamin Franklin).
[Old English *dūst*] **—dust′like′**, *adj.*

dust bag, a bag in the tank of a vacuum cleaner into which the dust is blown.

dust|bin (dust′bin′), *n. British.* a bin or receptacle for the dust, ashes, and other refuse of a house; garbage can.

dust bowl or **Dust Bowl**, an area, especially in the western plains of the United States and Canada, where dust storms are frequent and violent: *Choking dust storms were stirred up over the dust bowl* (Science News Letter).

dust bowler, *U.S. Informal.* a person living in or coming from a dust bowl: *By 1938, 221,000 dust bowlers had entered California* (Atlantic).

dust cart, *British.* a cart or truck for carrying dust, refuse, and rubbish from the streets.

dust|cloth (dust′klôth′, -kloth′), *n.* a cloth used for removing dust from furniture, books, or other things; duster.

dust|coat (dust′kōt′), *n. British.* a lightweight outer garment; duster.

dust counter, an instrument for counting the number of particles of dust in a unit volume of air.

dust cover, *British.* a dust jacket.

dust devil, a small whirlwind that picks up and carries a column of dust as it moves along, especially in the plains area of the western United States.

***dust|er** (dus′tər), *n.* **1** a person or thing that dusts. **2** a cloth, brush, or the like, used to get dust off things. **3** an apparatus for sifting or blowing dry poisons on plants to kill insects. **4** a contrivance for removing dust from sifting; sieve. **5a** a long, lightweight garment worn over the clothes to keep dust off them: *Riding along dusty country roads in open cars called for a special garment to protect the clothes, and so the duster, a long coat of linen completely covering the wearer's clothes, came into being* (Bernice G. Chambers). **b** a similar garment, without a belt, worn by women as a dress, especially indoors: *In budget-priced coats, faille and linen dusters, both lined and unlined, look like big spring sellers* (New York Times). **6** *U.S. Informal.* a dust storm: *What was described by some weathermen as the worst duster in 25 years hit parts of seven states* (Newsweek). **7** *U.S.* an unproductive oil well; dry hole: *He invested in 56 dusters in a row before striking it rich* (Wall Street Journal). **8** *Baseball Slang.* a pitch purposely thrown at or near a batter's head; beanball: *His penchant for throwing "dusters" prompted ... Hank Aaron to label him a "mean" pitcher* (Time). **9** *U.S. Military Slang.* a type of motorized vehicle on a caterpillar track, and equipped with 40-millimeter guns: *The duster, maneuvering from one side to the other, fired hundreds of exploding shells into the hamlet* (New York Times).

***duster**
definition 5a

dust|fall (dust′fôl′), *n.* **1** the settling of dust from the atmosphere. **2** the amount of dust settling within a given time and area: *In an average month there are about 69 tons per square mile of sootfall, dustfall, and fly ash* (New Yorker).

dust|heap (dust′hēp′), *n.* a pile of dirt or rubbish: *We found one of its* [*a doll's*] *legs on the dustheap, and stuck it on* (New Yorker). (*Figurative.*) *Already one former Gaullist minister ... who broke away, has been voted into the dustheap* (New York Times).

dust|i|ly (dus′tə lē), *adv.* **1** in a dusty manner. **2** with dust.

dust|i|ness (dus′tē nis), *n.* dusty condition.

dust|ing powder (dus′ting), **1** an antiseptic powder, for dusting over wounds or surgical incisions. **2** a scented powder applied to the body, especially after bathing.

dust jacket, an outer paper cover for protecting a book; jacket.

dust|less (dust′lis), *adj.* **1** without dust. **2** not causing dust.

dust|man (dust′man′, -mən), *n., pl.* **-men**. **1** *British.* a man who collects and carts away refuse from dustbins; garbage collector: *The service provided by the dustman is no less socially useful than that provided by the teacher* (New Statesman). **2** a popular personification of sleep or sleepiness (in allusion to the rubbing of the eyes as if there were dust in them); sandman.

dust mop, a long-handled mop for dusting floors, walls, or ceilings; dry mop.

dust|off (dust′ôf′, -of′), *n. U.S. Military Slang.* a helicopter for evacuating casualties from a combat zone; medevac: *Wounded are picked up and shuttled away from enemy fire, then quickly evacuated on "dustoff" helicopters to the nearest U.S. hospital* (Time).

dust|pan (dust′pan′), *n.* a flat, broad pan with a handle, onto which dust can be swept from the floor.

dust|proof (dust′prüf′), *adj.* **1** that will let no dust through; resistant to dust: *dustproof storage.* **2** free from dust.

dust sheet, a large sheet thrown over furniture to protect it from dust, when not in use.

dust storm, a strong wind carrying clouds of dust across or from a dry region.

dust|up (dust′up′), *n. Informal.* a disturbance; controversy; commotion: *His involvement in last week's dustup consisted mainly of his friendship with several of the plotters* (Time).

dust whirl, = dust devil.

dust wrapper, *British.* = dust jacket.

dust|y (dus′tē), *adj.,* **dust|i|er, dust|i|est.** **1** covered with dust; filled with dust: *He found some dusty old books in the attic.* **2** like dust; dry and powdery: *dusty chalk.* **3** having the color of dust; grayish: *a dusty brown.* **4** of or having to do with dust: (*Figurative.*) *And all our yesterdays have lighted fools The way to dusty death* (Shakespeare).

dusty answer, a cold, unfeeling, or empty reaction or response: *He recalled many western attempts to get a genuine settlement but everyone ... had been given a dusty answer* (London Times).

dusty miller, **1** any one of various plants covered with white, woolly hairs, such as the rose campion. 2 a variety of artificial fishing fly, especially a brightly colored streamer fly used for salmon.

dusty wing, a small, neuropteran insect whose wings are powdered with whitish scales. It is a natural enemy of citrus mites and scales.

Du|sun (dü′sən), *n., pl.* **-sun** or **-suns**. a member of a tribe of Dyaks which makes up the largest part of the population of Sabah, in Malaysia.

Dutch (duch), *adj., n.* **—*adj.*** **1** of the Netherlands, its people, or their language. **2** *Slang.* German; Teutonic.
—*n.* **1** *pl. in use.* the people of the Netherlands. **2** the Germanic language of the Netherlands. **3** *pl. in use.* the people of Germany. The ancestors of the Pennsylvania Dutch came from Germany, not the Netherlands. **4** *Slang.* the German language.
beat the Dutch, *Informal.* to be very strange or surprising; outdo anything seen or heard of before: *"Well, you women do beat the Dutch," said her brother* (Mary E. Wilkins-Freeman).
get one's Dutch up, to make or become angry: *Walker had warned his lawyer not to get "Frank's Dutch up," but Curtin did so when he patronized Roosevelt about his knowledge of the law* (Atlantic). *Some people get their Dutch up, others are as meek as Moses* (Time).
go Dutch, *Informal.* to have each person pay for himself: *Since neither one of us could afford to take the other to the movies we went Dutch. She certainly cannot, for example, ask a boy she likes for a date, nor can she pay the expenses when she goes out with him (although she may sometimes "go Dutch")* (Harper's).
in Dutch, *Slang.* in disgrace; in trouble: *He not only had missed the take-off but was in Dutch with his superior officers* (New Yorker). *He wished that he was back at St. Patrick's, instead of being in high school and in Dutch for bumming* (James T. Farrell).
[< Middle Dutch *dutsch* Dutch, German]
▶Especially in the United States in the 1800's people around the immigrants misinterpreted **Dutch** for *Deutsch* meaning German. In present standard English, *Dutch* is used only with reference to the Netherlands (Holland), its people, their language, and the like, but the use in the sense of "German" still survives in the name *Pennsylvania Dutch,* for a people whose ancestors came from Germany. Otherwise it is now found only in slang.
▶The various derogatory expressions compounded of *Dutch,* such as *Dutch courage* and *Dutch uncle,* are a legacy from the Dutch-English commercial rivalry of the 1600's and 1700's.

Dutch auction, a public sale in which articles are reduced in price until sold.

Dutch barn, a shelter for farm produce that resembles a barn but has open sides. Dutch barns are common in England.

Dutch Belted, any one of a breed of dairy cattle, originally of the Netherlands, black with a broad white belt.

***Dutch cap**, a woman's cap, pointed at the top, and flaring at the sides in two triangular pieces.

***Dutch cap**

Dutch cheese, **1** a small, round, firm cheese made from skim milk. **2** = cottage cheese.

Dutch colonial, of or in an American colonial style typified by brick or stone houses with sloping roofs, small windows, and wooden shutters: *Dutch colonial houses in the middle colonies showed the influence of Dutch, German, Swedish, and English architectural styles* (E. D. Stone).

Dutch courage, *Informal.* courage brought on by drinking alcoholic liquor.

***Dutch door**, a door divided in two horizontally, so that the top half may be open while the other is closed.

***Dutch door**

Dutch elm disease, a disease of elm trees in which the leaves turn yellow and fall off and the tree dies, caused by a fungus carried by a beetle; elm blight.

Dutch|er (duch′ər), *n.* **1** = Dutchman (def. 2). **2** one of the Pennsylvania Dutch.

Dutch foil, leaf, gold, or **metal**, an alloy of copper and zinc in the form of thin sheets, used as a cheap imitation of gold leaf.

Dutch hoe, a hoe which is pushed instead of pulled.

Dutch|man (duch′mən), *n., pl.* **-men. 1** a person born or living in the Netherlands; Hollander; Netherlander. **2** *Slang.* a German; Teuton. **3** a Dutch ship. **4** *Carpentry.* a piece driven into an opening to close it, especially in a badly made joint.

Dutch|man's-breech|es (duch′mənz brich′iz), *n. sing. and pl. U.S.* **1** a creamy-white, fragrant spring wild flower with two slender projections shaped somewhat like breeches. **2** the plant that bears it, belonging to the same family as the bleeding heart, the fumitory family. See picture under **fumitory family**.

Dutch|man's-pipe (duch′mənz pīp′), *n. U.S.* a climbing vine of the birthwort family with large leaves, and curved flowers resembling the bowl of a tobacco pipe.

Dutch oven, **1** a heavy iron kettle with a close-fitting cover. Some Dutch ovens are covered with hot coals and used for baking. **2** a metal box that opens in front, used especially for roasting meat before an open fire or on top of a stove. **3** a brick oven in which the walls are first heated, and food is put in to cook after the fire goes out or is removed.

Dutch pink, a yellow lake pigment prepared from the bark of the black oak.

Dutch treat, *Informal.* a meal or entertainment at which each person pays for himself.

Dutch uncle, *Informal.* a person who sternly criticizes or scolds another: *Koussevitzky spent three hours one evening telling him, Dutch-uncle fashion, what a shocking waste of talent it had been for him to fritter away six months on a Broadway musical* (New Yorker).

Dutch wife, an open frame of rattan or cane to support the limbs while in bed.

du|te|ous (dü′tē əs, dyü′-), *adj.* dutiful; obedient: *duteous service.* SYN: submissive, subservient. **—du′te|ous|ly,** *adv.* **—du′te|ous|ness,** *n.*

du|ti|a|ble (dü′tē ə bəl, dyü′-), *adj.* on which a duty or tax must be paid: *Perfumes imported into the United States are dutiable goods.*

du|ti|ful (dü′tə fəl, dyü′-), *adj.* **1** doing one's duty; obedient: *She is a dutiful daughter to her parents, always helping around the house.* SYN: submissive. **2** required by duty; proceeding from or expressing a sense of duty: *dutiful words. The Princess gave her mother her dutiful regards* (Lytton Strachey). **3** *Obsolete.* relating to duty or obligation. **—du′ti|ful|ly,** *adv.* **—du′ti|ful|ness,** *n.*

du|ty (dü′tē, dyü′-), *n., pl.* **-ties. 1** a thing that is right to do; what a person ought to do; obligation: *It is your duty to obey the laws. You will always find those who think they know what is your duty better than you know it* (Emerson). **2** the compelling or binding force of what is right: *A sense of duty makes a person do what he thinks is right even when he does not want to do it. He gives only the worthless gold Who gives from a sense of duty* (James Russell Lowell). **3** the thing that a person has to do in doing his work; function; business; office: *the duties of a bookkeeper. A policeman's duties include enforcing the laws and arresting people who break them. The mailman's duties were to sort and deliver the mail.* SYN: responsibility. **4a** the proper behavior owed to an older or superior person; obedience and respect: *Such duty as the subject owes the prince* (Shakespeare). SYN: deference, homage, reverence, submission. **b** an act of respect, or an expression of respectful consideration: *our duty to your Honour* (Shakespeare). SYN: deference, homage, reverence, submission. **5** a payment due and enforced by law or custom, especially: **a** a tax on taking articles out of, or bringing them into, a country, or on the sale of certain articles or commodities; customs charge; excise. **b** a tax on the performance of certain transactions or the execution of various deeds and documents. **6** a measure of the effectiveness of an engine; the amount of work done by an engine per unit amount of fuel consumed; utility. **7** the amount of irrigation water required for a particular crop in a given area.
do duty for, to serve in place of; act as substitute for: *The children marched with broomsticks doing duty for guns.*
off duty, not at one's work or occupation: *When off duty . . . Captain Dick often came to console his friends* (Thackeray).
on duty, at one's work or occupation: *The night watchman is on duty from 8 p.m. to 6 a.m.*
[< Anglo-French *dueté* < *du,* or *due,* Old French *deü;* see etym. under **due**]
—*Syn.* ***n.*** **1 Duty, obligation** mean what a person ought to do. **Duty** applies to what a person ought to do at all times because it is legally or morally right: *Every person has a duty to his country.* **Obligation** applies more to what is required at a particular time by custom or by an agreement or contract: *A good citizen has certain obligations to society.*

du|ty-bound (dü′tē bound′, dyü′-), *adj.* bound or obliged by one's sense of duty: *He was duty-bound to confess his part in the prank.*

du|ty-free (dü′tē frē′, dyü′-), *adj.* free from payment of duty; exempt from duty: *These imports are mainly raw materials that are duty-free* (Time).

du|um|vir (dü um′vər, dyü-), *n., pl.* **-virs, -vi|ri** (-və rī). either of two men in ancient Rome who shared the same governmental position between them. [< Latin *duumvir* (literally) a man of two]

du|um|vi|rate (dü um′vər it, dyü-), *n.* **1** a governmental position shared by two men: *The consulship of ancient Rome was a duumvirate. For the first few months of this Janus-faced duumvirate it was Faure, nominally the Prime Minister, who was running the country's foreign policy* (Atlantic). **2** a union or partnership of two men.

du|vet (dü vā′), *n.* **1** a quilt stuffed with down or feathers; down comforter. **2** a downy growth. [< French *duvet* swan's down]

du|ve|tine (dü′və tēn), *n.* = duvetyn.

du|ve|tyn or **du|ve|tyne** (dü′və tēn), *n.* a soft, closely woven fabric of wool, sometimes combined with silk, cotton, or rayon, having a velvety nap. [< French *duvet* swan's down, earlier *dumet* (< *dum* down) + English *-yn,* early variant of *-ine*[1] (because of its downy nap)]

Du|wa|mish (də wä′mish, dwä′-), *n.* a member of a small tribe of North American Indians formerly living near Seattle, Washington.

dux (duks, du̇ks), *n. British.* the head pupil in a class or division of a school. [< Latin *dux* leader]

duy|ker (dī′kər), *n.* = duiker.

duy|ker|bok (dī′kər bok′), *n.* = duiker.

D.V., **1** God willing (Latin, *Deo Volente*). **2** Douay Version.

D.V.M., Doctor of Veterinary Medicine.

DW or **dw** (no periods), dead weight.

dwale (dwāl), *n.* = belladonna (def. 1a). [probably < Scandinavian (compare Old Icelandic *dvali* delay, sleep)]

dwalm or **dwam** (dwäm), *n., v. Scottish.* **—*n.*** a swoon; fainting fit. **—*v.i.*** to faint; swoon. [earlier *dwawm.* Compare Old English *dwolma* confusion, chaos.]

dwarf (dwôrf), *n., pl.* **dwarfs, dwarves** (dwôrvz), *adj., v.* **—*n.*** **1** a person, animal, or plant much smaller than the usual size for its kind: *Mr. Bruce met a dwarf, dressed as a clown, who had entertained at parties in his own childhood* (New Yorker). **2** (in fairy tales) an ugly little man with magic power. **3** any one of a class of stars of small size and luminosity, including the sun, as distinguished from a giant star; dwarf star: *The Mount Wilson and Palomar workers conclude that the oldest dwarfs were formed while the galaxy was in its initial gravitational contraction from a larger protogalaxy* (Scientific American).
—*adj.* **1** below the usual size for its kind; stopped in growth: *dwarf furniture. The northern parts of these forests extend into the Arctic regions where the trees are smaller, and at their extreme northern limit, even dwarf* (Fred W. Emerson). SYN: dwarfish, pygmy. **2** belonging to a species much smaller than related species: *a dwarf marigold.*
—*v.t.* **1** to keep from growing large; check in growth; stunt: *The Pygmies of the deep forests . . . may be dwarfed descendants of some of the Olduvai . . . folk* (Harper's). **2** *Figurative.* to cause to look or seem small by contrast or by distance: *That tall building dwarfs all those around it.* **3** *Figurative.* to make small or insignificant in extent or character: *The incessant repetition of the same handiwork dwarfs the man* (Emerson).
—*v.i.* to become dwarfed or smaller.
[Middle English *dwerf,* Old English *dweorg*]
—dwarf′ness, *n.*
—*Syn.* ***n.*** **1 Dwarf, midget** mean a person very much smaller than normal. **Dwarf** applies particularly to a person whose growth has been stunted, usually by glandular deficiency, and who often has limbs that are very short compared with the head and body, which may be normal in size: *Walt Disney used dwarfs in a movie. Dwarf* may be applied to a stunted animal or plant. With plants, however, *dwarf* usually refers not to the individual but to a *kind* or *variety* smaller than

Pronunciation Key: hat, āge, cãre, fär; let, ēqual, tėrm; it, īce; hot, ōpen, ôrder; oil, out; cup, pu̇t, rüle; child; long; thin; ᴛʜen; zh, measure; ə represents **a** in about, **e** in taken, **i** in pencil, **o** in lemon, **u** in circus.

related varieties, either because of natural differentiation or because of breeding: *the dwarf birch.* **Midget** applies to a tiny person who is perfectly shaped and normal in every way except size: *We see midgets in vaudeville or the circus.*

dwarf alder, a small North American buckthorn whose leaves resemble those of the alder.

dwarf chestnut, = chinquapin (def. 1).

dwarf cornel, a low herb of the dogwood family, having red berries; the bunchberry.

dwarf|ish (dwôr′fish), *adj.* like a dwarf; much smaller than average; diminutive: *What is an Epigram? A dwarfish whole, Its body brevity, and wit its soul* (Samuel Taylor Coleridge). SYN: pygmy, puny. —**dwarf′ish|ly**, *adv.* —**dwarf′ish|ness**, *n.*

dwarf|ism (dwôr′fiz əm), *n.* the condition or character of being a dwarf; a generally underdeveloped condition of growth, especially in the bony tissue of the limbs: *Efforts to use the cattle hormone in humans to treat dwarfism have not been successful* (Science News Letter).

dwarf|like (dwôrf′līk′), *adj.* like a dwarf; dwarfish: *Maryan's "personages" are dwarflike figures in odd hats* (Time).

dwarf mallow, a native European herb of the mallow family, growing along the ground. It has roundish leaves and pale lilac or white flowers.

dwarf mistletoe, a small mistletoe which grows parasitically in clusters on the branches of spruce, pine, fir, and hemlock trees.

dwarf palmetto, a low palmetto that grows along the southeastern coast of the United States and in the West Indies.

dwarf star, = dwarf (def. 3): *Discovery of flare-ups on two red dwarf stars raised to five the number of stars known to have flares similar to those on the sun* (Science News Letter).

dwarf sumac, a low sumac of eastern North America whose leaves contain much tannin and are used in tanning leather; black sumac; mountain sumac.

dwarves (dwôrvz), *n.* a plural of **dwarf**.

dweeb (dwēb), *n. U.S. Slang.* a foolish or inept person. [origin uncertain]

dweeb|y (dwē′bē), *adj. U.S. Slang.* foolish or inept: . . . *the dweeby high-school principal played by Jeff Daniels in the puppyish new movie "Sweet Hearts Dance"* (Vanity Fair).

dwell (dwel), *v.i.*, **dwelt** or **dwelled, dwell|ing.** **1** to make one's home; live: *They dwell in the country but work in the city.* SYN: reside, abide. **2** *Obsolete.* to linger or pause; delay. SYN: tarry.
dwell on (or **upon**), **a** to think, speak, or write about for a long time; fix one's attention on: *His mind dwelt on his pleasant day in the country.* **b** to put stress on: *The speaker dwelt especially on the great need for teachers.* **c** to sustain (a note) in music: *She dwells on high C with ease.*
[< Old English *dwellan* delude; (later) delay]

dwell|er (dwel′ər), *n.* a person who lives in a place; resident: *A city dweller lives in the city.* SYN: inhabitant.

dwell|ing (dwel′ing), *n.* **1** the place in which one lives; house; residence. SYN: habitation. **2** continued or habitual residence; abode.

dwelling house, a house in which people live.

dwelling place, = dwelling (def. 1). *Oh! that the desert were my dwelling place* (Byron).

dwelt (dwelt), *v.* a past tense and past participle of **dwell**: *We dwelt there for a long time. We have dwelt in the country for years.*

dwin|dle (dwin′dəl), *v.*, **-dled, -dling.** —*v.i.* **1** to become smaller and smaller; shrink; diminish: *During the storm the trapper's supply of food dwindled day by day.* SYN: lessen, decline, wane. See syn. under **decrease**. **2** *Figurative.* to fall away, as in quality; degenerate: *The writers dwindled into mere analysts* (John Green).
—*v.t.* to make smaller and smaller; cause to shrink: *Drought has dwindled the crops.*
[< *dwine* + *-le*; the *-d-* is intrusive]

dwin|dle|ment (dwin′dəl mənt), *n.* a dwindled state or condition; decreased size, strength, etc. or other characteristic.

dwine (dwīn), *v.i.*, **dwined, dwin|ing.** *Scottish.* to waste or pine away; fade. SYN: languish, wither. [Old English *dwīnan*]

dwt., pennyweight or pennyweights.

DX (no periods), or **D.X.**, (in radio) distance or distant.

Dy (no period), dysprosium (chemical element).

dy|ad (dī′ad), *n., adj.* —*n.* **1** a group of two; couple; duad. **2** *Biology.* **a** one of the groups of chromosome pairs formed when a tetrad splits: *In the two divisions that follow, the tetrads are divided in two planes, first into double bodies called dyads, next into their single components* (A. Franklin Shull). **b** a secondary unit of organization consisting of an aggregate of monads or single-celled organisms. **3** *Chemistry.* an element, atom, or radical having a valence of 2. **4** a meaningful dialogue, encounter, or relationship between two people: *The T-group has a special lingo, a mixture of hippie talk and social science jargon. People are always "hung-up" or "uptight," trying to discover "where I'm at." They don't talk; they "have a dyad"* (Ted J. Rakstis).
—*adj.* = dyadic. [< Latin *dyas, dyadis* < Greek *dyás, -ádos* two in number. See etym. at **duad**.]

dy|ad|ic (dī ad′ik), *adj.* of or having to do with a dyad or group of two.

Dy|ak (dī′ak), *n.* **1** a member of a group of Indonesian people living in Borneo and speaking a Malayan language. **2** the language of the Dyaks. Also, **Dayak**.

dy|ar|chic (dī är′kik), *adj.* = diarchal.

dy|ar|chi|cal (dī′är′kə kəl), *adj.* = diarchal.

dy|arch|y (dī′är kē), *n., pl.* **-arch|ies.** = diarchy.

dyb|buk (dib′ůk), *n.* a spirit in Jewish folklore, either an evil spirit, or the soul of a person who has died before his time, that enters and takes possession of a living person. Also, **dibbuk**. [< Hebrew *dibbug* (originally) cement, glue]

dye (dī), *n., v.*, **dyed, dye|ing.** —*n.* **1a** a coloring matter used to color cloth, hair, and other things. Some dyes are vegetable or animal, others chemical. **b** a liquid containing such coloring matter: *We bought a bottle of blue dye.* **2** a color produced by such coloring matter; tint; hue: *A good dye will not fade or run.*
—*v.t.* **1** to color (cloth, leather, or hair), by putting in a liquid containing coloring matter: *to have a dress dyed.* **2** to impart (color) with a dye: *A green may be made by dyeing a blue over a yellow.* **3** to color or stain; tinge: *The spilled grape juice dyed the tablecloth purple.* —*v.i.* **1** to become colored when treated with a dye: *This material dyes easily and quickly.* **2** (of dyes) to give or change color: *Black will dye over other colors.*
of deepest (or **blackest**) **dye**, of the lowest or vilest kind: *a mean and loathsome villain of the deepest dye.* [Old English *dēag*]

dye|a|bil|i|ty (dī′ə bil′ə tē), *n.* capability of being dyed: *Rayon has long been known for its fine dyeability* (Wall Street Journal).

dye|a|ble (dī′ə bəl), *adj.* that can be dyed: *New dyeable and printable surfaces are being grafted, through radiation, onto slick-finish, heat-resistant plastics* (Wall Street Journal).

dye|bath (dī′bath′, -bäth′), *n.* a solution of coloring matter in which substances to be colored are immersed.

dyed-in-the-wool (dīd′in ᴛʜə wůl′), *adj.* **1** thoroughgoing, complete: *a dyed-in-the-wool conservative in politics.* **2** dyed before being woven into cloth.

dye house, a building in which dyeing is done.

dye|ing (dī′ing), *n.* the coloring of fabrics with dye.

dye laser, a chemical laser using the fluorescence of certain organic dyes, such as rhodamine and fluorescein, to produce intense coherent light over a wide range of possible frequencies: *Ruby crystal lasers can produce pulses as short as five picoseconds; . . . dye lasers should be able to emit even shorter ones with durations in the 10^{-13} second range* (New Scientist).

dye marker, a dye, usually fluorescein, which, when dropped, colors ocean water enough to be seen from the air.

dy|er (dī′ər), *n.* a person whose work or business is dyeing cloth or leather.

dy|er's-broom (dī′ərz brüm′), *n.* = woadwaxen.

dy|er's-weed (dī′ərz wēd′), *n.* any one of several plants that yield a dye, as the weld, dyeweed, or woad.

dye|stuff (dī′stuf′), *n.* any one of various substances used as a dye or yielding a dye. Indigo and cochineal are dyestuffs.

dye|weed (dī′wēd′), *n.* **1** an Old World yellow-flowered shrub of the pea family, yielding a yellow dye; dyer's-weed. **2** a small North American composite herb with white flowers.

dye|wood (dī′wůd′), *n.* any wood, such as logwood, yielding a coloring matter used for dyeing.

dy|ing (dī′ing), *adj., v., n.* —*adj.* **1** at the point of death; about to die; ceasing to live: *a dying man.* SYN: moribund, mortal, expiring. **2** *Figurative.* coming to an end: *the dying year. Only the dying moans of the sirens continued for a moment or two to vibrate within the ear* (Graham Greene). **3** of death; at death: *dying words.* **a** the present participle of **die**[1]: *The storm is dying down.*
—*n.* = death. —**dy′ing|ly**, *adv.*

dyke[1] (dīk), *n., v.t., v.i.*, **dyked, dyk|ing.** = dike[1].

dyke[2] (dīk), *n. Slang.* (generally used in an unfriendly way) a homosexual woman; Lesbian. Also, **dike**. [origin unknown]

dyn. or **dynam.**, dynamics.

dy|na|graph (dī′nə graf, -gräf), *n.* an apparatus used on a railroad car to determine and record the condition of the track, speed of the train, resistance of the car, or other operating factor. [< Greek *dýnamis* power + English *-graph*]

dy|nam|e|ter (dī nam′ə tər), *n.* an instrument for determining the magnifying power of telescopes. [< Greek *dýnamis* power + English *-meter*]

dy|nam|ic (dī nam′ik), *adj., n.* —*adj.* **1** of or having to do with energy or force in motion. **2** of or having to do with force producing motion. **3** of or having to do with the science of dynamics. **4** *Figurative.* active; forceful; energetic: *a dynamic personality, dynamic plans.* SYN: potent, effective. **5** *Medicine.* functional; not organic: *a dynamic disease.* **6** (of a computer memory) requiring electrical recharging to retain data; not static: *In the "dynamic" version developed by Texas Instruments . . . the method of storage is not permanent, but must be refreshed regularly* (New Scientist).
—*n.* **1** the science of dynamics. **2** *Figurative.* active force: *It is regular worship which continually reconstitutes the Church and gives it its dynamic* (Maclean's). [< Greek *dynamikós* < *dýnamis* power < *dýnasthai* be powerful]

dy|nam|i|cal (dī nam′ə kəl), *adj.* = dynamic.

dy|nam|i|cal|ly (dī nam′ə klē), *adv.* in a dynamic manner.

dynamic electricity, an electric current; a stream of charges in motion.

dy|nam|i|cist (dī nam′ə sist), *n.* **1** a specialist in dynamics. **2** a person who believes in dynamism.

dy|nam|ics (dī nam′iks), *n.* **1** *sing. in use.* the branch of physics dealing with the motion of bodies and the action of forces on bodies either in motion or at rest. Dynamics includes kinematics, kinetics, and statics. **2** *sing. in use.* the science of force acting in any field. **3** *pl. in use.* the forces, physical or moral, at work in any field: *the dynamics of education.* **4** *pl. in use.* the variation and contrast of force or loudness in the production of musical sounds.

dy|na|mism (dī′nə miz əm), *n.* **1** any one of various doctrines or philosophical systems which seek to explain the phenomena of nature by the action of some force. **2** dynamic quality; energetic quality; forcefulness: *The visitor to Germany finds in the air a quick, nervous dynamism, which cannot be expressed in facts and figures but can only be sensed on the spot* (Wall Street Journal).

dy|na|mist (dī′nə mist), *n.* a person who believes in a doctrine of dynamism.

dy|na|mis|tic (dī′nə mis′tik), *adj.* **1** of dynamism; having to do with or of the nature of dynamism. **2** according to the doctrine of dynamists.

dy|na|mi|tard (dī′nə mə tärd′), *n.* = dynamiter.

dy|na|mite (dī′nə mīt), *n., v.*, **-mit|ed, -mit|ing,** *adj.* —*n.* **1a** a powerful explosive used in blasting, made mainly of nitroglycerin mixed with an absorbent material and pressed into round sticks. **b** any similar explosive containing ammonium nitrate or other substance instead of nitroglycerin. **2** *Figurative: The Three Flames . . . whose songs and music are dynamite* (New Yorker).
—*v.t.* **1** to blow up or destroy with dynamite: *The rebels dynamited a government fort.* **2** to mine or charge with dynamite: *The road builders dynamited the rocky hill they intended to blast and level.* **3** *Figurative.* to destroy; torpedo: *Opponents of the bill were determined to dynamite it in the legislature.*
—*adj. U.S. and Canadian Slang.* outstanding, impressive, or exciting; extraordinarily good; superlative: *A dynamite opening . . . at the Palladium* (New York Post). *The emphasis will be on development of a "dynamite" music and entertainment program for the park* (New Orleans States-Item).
[< Greek *dýnamis* power + English *-ite*[1]; coined by Alfred Nobel, who invented it]

dynamite gun, *Military.* a gun in which a shell containing dynamite or other high explosive is thrown by compressed air or gas.

dy|na|mit|er (dī′nə mī′tər), *n.* a person who uses dynamite and similar explosives, especially for unlawfully destructive or revolutionary purposes.

dy|na|mit|ic (dī′nə mit′ik), *adj.* of or having to do with dynamite or dynamiters. —**dy′na|mit′i|cal|ly**, *adv.*

dy|na|mit|i|cal (dī′nə mit′ə kəl), *adj.* = dynamitic.

dy|na|mit|ism (dī′nə mī tiz′əm), *n.* the use of dynamite and similar explosives for unlawful, especially anarchistic, purposes.

dy|na|mit|ist (dī′nə mī′tist), *n.* = dynamiter.

dy|na|mo (dī′nə mō), *n., pl.* **-mos.** **1** a machine that changes mechanical energy into electric energy; generator. It generally consists of an electromagnet, which furnishes a magnetic field, and an armature, usually made up of insulated copper wire wound around an iron core. The electric current is developed in the armature when it is rotated in the field or has the field rotated about it. *The welders made their own electricity with a small dynamo run by a gasoline engine.* **2** a motor which turns electrical energy into mechanical energy. **3** *Informal, Figurative.* a dynamic person, especially one who sparks some activity or enterprise: *Gascon is actor, director . . . agitator and dynamo of French-Canadian theater* (Maclean's). [short for *dynamo-electric machine; dynamo* < Greek *dýnamis* power]

dy|na|mo|e|lec|tric (dī′nə mō i lek′trik), *adj.* having to do with the transformation of mechanical energy into electric energy, or electric energy into mechanical energy.
dy|na|mo|e|lec|tri|cal (dī′nə mō i lek′trə kəl), *adj.* = dynamoelectric.
dy|na|mo|gen|e|sis (dī′nə mō jen′ə sis), *n.* production of increased nervous activity.
dy|nam|o|graph (dī nam′ə graf, -gräf), *n.* a dynamometer which automatically measures muscular power.
dy|na|mom|e|ter (dī′nə mom′ə tər), *n.* an apparatus for measuring force or power: *Most automakers measure horsepower by means of a dynamometer* (Time).
dy|na|mo|met|ric (dī′nə mō met′rik), *adj.* **1** having to do with a dynamometer or with dynamometry. **2** made with the aid of a dynamometer.
dy|na|mo|met|ri|cal (dī′nə mō met′rə kəl), *adj.* = dynamometric.
dy|na|mom|e|try (dī′nə mom′ə trē), *n.* the measurement of force or power.
dy|na|mo|tor (dī′nə mō′tər), *n.* a combined electric motor and dynamo for changing the voltage of an electric current.
dy|nast (dī′nast, -nəst; *especially British* din′ast, -əst), *n.* **1** a hereditary ruler; member or founder of a dynasty. **2** any ruler. [< Latin *dynastēs* < Greek *dynastês* < *dýnasthai* be powerful]
dy|nas|tic (dī nas′tik), *adj.* having to do with a dynasty or dynasties. **—dy|nas′ti|cal|ly,** *adv.*
dy|nas|ti|cal (dī nas′tə kəl), *adj.* = dynastic.
dy|nas|ti|cism (dī nas′tə siz əm), *n.* dynastic rule.
dy|nas|ty (dī′nə stē; *especially British* din′ə stē), *n., pl.* **-ties.** **1** a series of rulers who belong to the same family; a line of kings or princes: *The Bourbon dynasty ruled France for more than 200 years.* **2** the period of time during which a dynasty rules. **3** *Figurative.* a line or succession of individuals who attain fame or distinction related as a family or by other ties: *Henry Adams . . . left Somerset, England in 1638 . . . and founded an American dynasty* (Time).
dy|na|tron (dī′nə tron), *n.* **1** *Electronics.* a vacuum tube in which an increase in the plate voltage causes secondary emission of electrons from the plate and a decrease in plate current. Dynatrons were used in radio as oscillators. **2** *Physics.* meson. [< Greek *dýnamis* power (< *dýnasthai* be powerful) + (elec)*tron*]
dyne (dīn), *n.* the amount of force required to give a mass of one gram an acceleration of one centimeter per second for each second the force is applied. *Abbr:* d. [< French *dyne* < Greek *dýnamis* power < *dýnasthai* be powerful]
dyne-cen|ti|me|ter (dīn′sen′tə mē′tər), *n.* the unit of force in the centimeter-gram-second system equal to an erg.
Dy|nel (dī′nəl, dī nel′), *n. Trademark.* a modacrylic fiber used in making fabrics for clothing.
dy|node (dī′nōd), *n.* one of the supplementary electrodes providing the secondary emission of electrons in an electron multiplier, photomultiplier, etc. [< Greek *dýnamis* power + *hodós* way]
dy|on (dī′on), *n.* a hypothetical nuclear particle carrying both a magnetic charge and an electric charge: *Dyons effectively combined magnetic monopoles and quarks* (Science News). [(coined by Julian Schwinger, born 1918, an American physicist) < Greek *dy*(ás) two + English *-on*]
dys-, *prefix.* bad, abnormal, or defective, as in *dysfunction, dystrophy.* [< Greek *dys-*]
dys|aes|the|si|a (dis′es thē′zē ə, -zhə), *n. Medicine.* deranged or impaired sensation. [< Greek *dysaisthesiā* < *dys-* bad + *aisthēsis* sensation]
dys|ar|thri|a (dis är′thrē ə), *n.* inability to articulate words distinctly due to brain damage. [< New Latin *dysarthria* < Greek *dys-* bad + *árthron* joint]
dys|ar|thric (dis är′thrik), *adj.* **1** having to do with dysarthria. **2** having dysarthria.
dys|au|to|no|mi|a (dis ô′tə nō′mē ə), *n.* an inherited disorder of the nervous system, found chiefly among Jews of European descent, in which sensory perception and many autonomic functions are impaired. [< New Latin *dysautonomia* < Greek *dys-* bad + *autonomiā* autonomy]
dys|au|to|nom|ic (dis ô′tə nom′ik), *adj., n.*
—*adj.* of, having to do with, or affected by dysautonomia: *Mercifully, not every dysautonomic child has all the symptoms* (Newsweek).
—*n.* a person affected with dysautonomia: *Dysautonomics, compared with normal subjects, had a threefold increase in blood-serum levels of [the] substance* (Scientific American).
dys|bar|ism (dis′bə riz əm), *n.* = caisson disease. [< *dys-* + Greek *báros* weight + English *-ism*]
dys|che|zi|a or **dys|chi|zi|a** (dis kē′zē ə, -zhə), *n. Medicine.* painful or difficult excretion from the bowels. [< New Latin *dyschezia* < Greek *dys-* bad + *chézein* to defecate]
dys|chro|nous (dis′krə nəs), *adj.* not agreeing as to time; separate as to time. [< Greek *dys-* bad + *chrónos* time + English *-ous*]
dys|cra|si|a (dis krā′zē ə, -zhə), *n. Medicine.* an abnormal condition of the body, particularly of the blood. [< Greek *dyscrasiā* < *dys-* bad + *krâsis* a mixing]
dys|cras|ic (dis kraz′ik, -kras′-), *adj.* **1** of the nature of dyscrasia. **2** caused by dyscrasia. **3** having dyscrasia.
dys|cra|site (dis′krə sīt), *n.* a mineral consisting of antimony and silver. It occurs in crystals and also in massive and granular form.
dys|en|ter|ic (dis′ən ter′ik), *adj.* **1** of the nature of dysentery. **2** having dysentery.
dys|en|ter|y (dis′ən ter′ē), *n.* a disease of the intestines, producing diarrhea with blood and mucus. It is caused by any one of several microorganisms or by irritants. [< Old French *dissenterie,* learned borrowing from Latin *dysenteria* < Greek *dysenteriā* < *dys-* bad + *éntera* intestines]
dys|func|tion (dis fungk′shən), *n., v. Medicine.*
—*n.* a functional abnormality or impairment, for example of an organ.
—*v.i.* to cease to function properly or normally; to break down: *"I'm convinced that the next ruling generation is going to be all pillheads . . . If they haven't dysfunctioned completely to the point where they can't stand for office"* (Atlantic). Also, **disfunction.**
dys|func|tion|al (dis fungk′shə nəl), *adj.* **1** *Medicine.* having to do with dysfunction. **2** performing badly or improperly; malfunctioning: *Handsome though it is, the classic wood-and-paper architecture of Japan is wildly dysfunctional for a Northern climate* (John Fischer).
dys|gen|e|sis (dis jen′ə sis), *n.* difficulty in breeding; sterility; infecundity. [< New Latin *dysgenesis* < Greek *dys-* bad + *génesis* generation]
dys|gen|ic (dis jen′ik), *adj.* having to do with or causing degeneration in the type of offspring produced. Also, **disgenic.**
dys|gen|ics (dis jen′iks), *n.* the study of the causes of degeneration in offspring; cacogenics.
dys|graph|i|a (dis graf′ē ə), *n.* = agraphia.
dys|hi|dro|sis (dis′hi drō′sis), *n.* a disease of the sweat follicles, in which they become distended with the retained secretion.
dys|i|dro|sis (dis′i drō′sis), *n.* = dyshidrosis.
dys|la|li|a (dis lā′lē ə), *n.* inability to speak distinctly due to malformation of the organs of speech or to defects of the motor nerves. [< New Latin *dyslalia* < Greek *dys-* bad + *laliá* speech]
dys|lex|i|a (dis lek′sē ə), *n.* a form of aphasia marked by the inability to read properly: *Dyslexia is a neurological ailment which bears no more relation to intelligence than, say, color blindness* (Benjamin H. Pearse). [< New Latin *dyslexia* < Greek *dys-* bad + *léxis* word]
dys|lex|ic (dis lek′sik), *adj., n.* **—*adj.*** affected with dyslexia: *A dyslexic child's visual and auditory senses cannot perceive and record without distortion* (Saturday Review).
—*n.* a person affected with dyslexia: *To the parents of a dyslexic, the child's behavior may be profoundly perplexing. Often the child exhibits exceptional ingenuity and creativity, yet fails totally at school* (New York Times).
dys|lo|gis|tic (dis′lə jis′tik), *adj.* expressing disapproval or censure. **—dys′lo|gis′ti|cal|ly,** *adv.*
dys|lo|gy (dis′lə jē), *n. Rare.* dispraise; discommendation; censure.
dys|men|or|rhe|a or **dys|men|or|rhoe|a** (dis′men ə rē′ə), *n.* difficult or painful menstruation; cramps. [< New Latin *dysmenorrhea* < Greek *dys-* bad + *mên* month + *rheîn* flow]
dys|men|or|rhe|al or **dys|men|or|rhoe|al** (dis′men ə rē′əl), *adj.* of or having to do with dysmenorrhea.
dys|met|ri|a (dis met′rē ə), *n. Psychiatry.* loss of the sense of distance in relation to muscular actions, associated with certain brain lesions. [< New Latin *dysmetria* < Greek *dys-* bad + *métron* a measure]
dys|or|gan|i|za|tion (dis ôr′gə nə zā′shən), *n. Psychiatry.* impaired or inefficient mental organization.
dys|pa|thy (dis′pə thē), *n.* disagreement of feeling or sentiment; antipathy; aversion.
dys|pep|si|a (dis pep′sē ə, -shə), *n.* poor digestion; indigestion. [< Latin *dyspepsia* < Greek *dyspepsiā* < *dys-* bad + *péptein* ripen, digest]
dys|pep|sy (dis pep′sē), *n. Archaic.* dyspepsia.
dys|pep|tic (dis pep′tik), *adj., n.* **—*adj.*** **1** having to do with dyspepsia. **2** suffering from dyspepsia. **3** *Figurative.* gloomy; pessimistic: *a dyspeptic outlook on the world.* **SYN:** morbid.
—*n.* a person who has dyspepsia. **—dys|pep′ti|cal|ly,** *adv.*
dys|pep|ti|cal (dis pep′tə kəl), *adj.* = dyspeptic.
dys|pha|gi|a (dis fā′jē ə), *n. Medicine.* difficulty in swallowing. [< New Latin *dysphagia* < Greek *dys-* bad + *phageîn* eat]
dys|phag|ic (dis faj′ik), *adj.* **1** having to do with dysphagia. **2** having dysphagia.
dys|pha|si|a (dis fā′zē ə, -zhə), *n.* difficulty in understanding or using language, caused by brain damage. [< New Latin *dysphasia* < Greek *dys-* bad + *phásis* speech]
dys|pha|sic (dis fā′zik), *adj.* **1** having to do with dysphasia. **2** having dysphasia.
dys|phe|mism (dis′fə miz əm), *n.* **1** the use of a harsh or unpleasantly direct expression instead of one that is mild or neutral. **2** a harsh or unpleasantly direct expression used in this way: *"Kick the bucket" is a dysphemism for "die."* [< *dys-* + (eu)*phemism*]
dys|pho|ni|a (dis fō′nē ə), *n. Medicine.* difficulty in vocalizing sounds. [< Greek *dysphōniā* < *dys-* bad + *phōnē* sound, voice]
dys|phon|ic (dis fon′ik), *adj.* **1** having to do with dysphonia. **2** having dysphonia.
dys|pho|ri|a (dis fôr′ē ə, -fōr′-), *n. Medicine.* a condition characterized by restlessness, mental discomfort, and general unhappiness. [< Greek *dysphoriā* discomfort, ultimately < *dys-* bad + *phoreîn* to suffer]
dys|phor|ic (dis fôr′ik, -for′-), *adj.* **1** having to do with dysphoria. **2** having dysphoria. **3** characterized by dysphoria.
dys|pho|tic (dis fō′tik), *adj.* growing or occurring where there is little light, as at great depths of water: *dysphotic vegetation.*
dys|pla|sia (dis plā′zhə), *n.* abnormal development or growth of tissues, organs, or other structures. [< New Latin *dysplasia* < Greek *dys-* bad + *plásis* a molding]
dys|plas|tic (dis plas′tik), *adj.* **1** having to do with dysplasia. **2** having dysplasia.
dysp|ne|a or **dysp|noe|a** (disp nē′ə), *n. Medicine.* difficult or labored breathing. [< Latin *dyspnoea* < Greek *dýspnoia* < *dyspnoieîn* breathe with difficulty < *dys-* badly + *pneîn* breathe]
dysp|ne|al or **dysp|noe|al** (disp nē′əl), *adj.* of or belonging to dyspnea.
dysp|ne|ic or **dysp|noe|ic** (disp nē′ik), *adj.* **1** of the nature of dyspnea; characteristic of dyspnea. **2** having dyspnea. **3** accompanied by dyspnea.
dys|prax|i|a (dis prak′sē ə), *n.* = apraxia.
***dys|pro|si|um** (dis prō′sē əm, -shē-), *n.* a rare-earth metallic chemical element found in various minerals which forms highly magnetic compounds. [< New Latin *dysprosium* < Greek *dysprósiton,* neuter of *dysprósitos* hard to get at + New Latin *-ium,* a suffix meaning "element"]

***dysprosium**

symbol	atomic number	atomic weight	oxidation state
Dy	66	162.50	3

dys|rhyth|mi|a (dis riᴛʜ′mē ə, -rith′-), *n.* a disturbance in the rhythm of the brain waves, usually associated with a tendency toward convulsions or epilepsy. [< New Latin *dysrhythmia* < Greek *dys-* bad + *rhythmós* rhythm]
dys|rhyth|mic (dis riᴛʜ′mik, -rith′-), *adj.* of or having to do with dysrhythmia.
dys|tel|e|o|log|i|cal (dis′tel ē ə loj′ə kəl, -tē lē-), *adj.* **1** having to do with dysteleology. **2** showing absence of purpose or design.
dys|tel|e|ol|o|gy (dis′tel ē ol′ə jē, -tē lē-), *n.* **1** the doctrine of purposelessness in nature, as opposed to the doctrine of design (teleology). **2** the science of rudimentary or vestigial organs with reference to this doctrine. [< German *Dysteleologie* < *dys-* not + *Teleologie* teleology]
dys|thy|mi|a (dis thī′mē ə), *n.* mental depression; melancholy. [< New Latin *dysthymia* < Greek *dys-* bad + *-thymiā* < *thymós* mind]
dys|thy|mic (dis thī′mik), *adj.* **1** having to do with dysthymia. **2** having dysthymia. **3** characterized by dysthymia.
dys|to|ci|a (dis tō′shē ə), *n. Medicine.* difficult birth. [< New Latin *dystocia* < Greek *dystokiā* < *dys-* bad + *tókos* birth]
dys|to|ni|a (dis tō′nē ə), *n.* a disorder or disturbance of bodily tone. [< New Latin *dystonia* < Greek *dys-* bad + *tónos* tension]
dys|ton|ic (dis ton′ik), *adj.* **1** having to do with dystonia. **2** having dystonia.
dys|to|pi|a (dis tō′pē ə), *n.* the opposite of a utopia; place or condition that is bad or imperfect: *It may be that only a vision of Utopia can combat the dystopia of contemporary life* (Time). [< *dys-* bad + (u)*topia*]
dys|to|pi|an (dis tō′pē ən), *adj.* of or having to do with a dystopia: *Catherine, who takes after her mother, is also worried about life, and it seems*

Pronunciation Key: hat, āge, cãre, fär; let, ēqual, tėrm; it, īce; hot, ōpen, ôrder; oil, out; cup, pu̇t, rüle; child; long; thin; ᴛʜen; zh, measure; ə represents a in about, e in taken, i in pencil, o in lemon, u in circus.

that her friend Brigitte ... is encouraging her to take the dystopian view (Anthony Burgess).
dys|tro|phi|a (dis trō′fē ə), *n.* = dystrophy.
dys|troph|ic (dis trof′ik), *adj., n.* —*adj.* **1** having to do with or resembling dystrophy. **2** having dystrophy: *The research team reported it was able "to study the whole life history of a dystrophic muscle"* (Wall Street Journal). **3** depleted in nutrients and plant and animal life: *dystrophic lakes, the dystrophic wastes of the arctic.*
—*n.* a person affected with dystrophy.
dys|tro|phi|ca|tion (dis′trə fə kā′shən), *n.* the pollution of streams, lakes, and other bodies of water, by domestic and industrial wastes and runoff from fertilized agricultural areas: *The sea can probably tolerate the runoff indefinitely but along the way the nitrogen creates algal "blooms" that are hastening the dystrophication of lakes and estuaries* (Scientific American).
dys|tro|phy (dis′trə fē), *n. Medicine.* **1** defective nutrition. **2** defective development or degeneration: *muscular dystrophy.* [< Greek *dys-* bad + *trophḗ* nourishment]
dys|u|ri|a (dis yu̇r′ē ə), *n. Medicine.* difficult or painful urination. [< Late Latin *dysūria* < Greek *dysouriā* < *dys-* bad + *oûron* urine]
dys|u|ric (dis yu̇r′ik), *adj.* **1** having to do with dysuria. **2** having dysuria.
dz., dozen or dozens.
dzig|ge|tai (dzig′ə tī), *n.* a wild ass living in herds in central Asia. [< Mongolian *tchikhitei* long-eared < *tchikhi* ear]
dzo (dzō), *n.* a hybrid animal, the result of a cross between the water buffalo and the domesticated yak. [< Tibetan *dso*]
dzong (dzong), *n.* a fortified Buddhist monastery in Bhutan. [< Tibetan *dsong*]

E e

***E**[1] or **e** (ē), *n., pl.* **E's** or **Es**, **e's** or **es**. **1** the fifth letter of the English alphabet. There are two *e's* in *see.* **2** any sound represented by this letter. **3** *E* is used as a symbol for the fifth (of an actual or possible series): *bedroom E in a Pullman car.* **4a** a conditional failing grade in some American schools and colleges. **b** a mark or grade of excellence (in other American schools and colleges). **5** *Music.* **a** the third tone of the scale of C major. **b** a symbol representing this tone. **c** a key, string, etc., that produces this tone. **d** the scale or key which has E as its keynote: *a concerto in E.*

***E**[1]
definition 5b

E[2] (ē), *n., pl.* **E's**. anything shaped like the letter E.

e-, *prefix.* the form of **ex-**[1] before consonants (except *c, f, p, q, s,* and *t*), as in *evaporate, emerge, erase, evoke.*

e (no period), an abbreviation or symbol for the following:
1a east. **b** eastern.
2 *Astronomy.* eccentricity.
3 erg.
4 *Baseball.* error or errors.
5 *Mathematics.* the quantity 2.71828+, the base of natural logarithms.

e., an abbreviation for the following:
1a east. **b** eastern.
2 electron.
3a engineer. **b** engineering.
4 entrance (a direction in plays).
5 *Baseball.* error or errors.

E (no period), an abbreviation or symbol for the following:
1a east. **b** eastern.
2 Egyptian (formerly used with the symbol for *pound,* monetary unit): *£E215.*
3 einsteinium (chemical element).
4 *Electricity.* electromotive force (measured in volts).
5 *Astronomy.* elliptical system.
6 *Physics.* energy expressed in ergs: $E = mc^2$.
7 English.
8 (in the U.S. Navy) excellence.
9 excellent.

E., an abbreviation for the following:
1 earl.
2 earth.
3a east. **b** eastern.
4 English.

E|a (ā'ä), *n.* the god of the ocean and subterranean springs, and of wisdom, in the religion of ancient Babylonia and Assyria.

ea., each.

E.A. or **EA** (no periods), *Psychology.* educational age.

each (ēch), *adj., pron., adv.* —***adj.*** every one (of two or more persons, things, etc.) considered separately or one by one: *Each boy has a name.*
—***pron.*** each one; this one and that one and the other ones: *Each went his way. Each of the five girls has a doll.*
—***adv.*** for each; to each; apiece: *These pencils are five cents each.*
[Old English *ǣlc* < *ā* ever + *gelīc* alike]
—***Syn.*** *adj.* **Each, every** mean one and all (of a number or group). **Each** emphasizes that one and all of a number, or one and the other of two, are thought of singly, as individuals: *Each dog has a name* = any one of the dogs in the group has a name of its own. **Every**, relating to a group, means that one and all are included, with no exceptions: *Every dog has a name* = all the dogs in the group have names of their own. In a more inclusive sense, *every* means one and all everywhere: *Every dog has his day.*
▶ **each**. As a pronoun, *each* is singular: *Each of the three has a different instructor.*

each other, **1** each one the other one: *They struck each other,* that is, they struck, *each* striking *the other.* **2** one another: *They struck at each other.*
▶ **Each other, one another**. Though commonly used indiscriminately, *each other* applies particularly to two, and *one another* to more than two: *The two people were shouting at each other. The people were all shouting at one another.* General: *The men from farms on both sides of the river were shouting to each other.* Formal: *The men from farms on both sides of the river were shouting to one another.*

each-way (ēch'wā'), *adj. British.* **1** made in a horse race for both first and second place: *an each-way bet.* **2** that can go either way; even: *an each-way chance.*

EAE (no periods), experimental artificial encephalomyelitis (a disease artificially induced in animals to study the cause of multiple sclerosis).

ea|ger[1] (ē'gər), *adj.* **1** wanting very much; desiring very strongly; anxious to do or get something: *The child is eager to have the candy.* **2** characterized by or showing keenness of desire or strength of feeling: *eager looks, an eager contest.* **3** *Archaic.* biting; keen: *It is a nipping and an eager air* (Shakespeare). **4** *Obsolete.* fierce.
[< Old French *aigre* < Latin *ācer, ācris* keen]
—**ea'ger|ly**, *adv.* —**ea'ger|ness**, *n.*
—***Syn.* 1 Eager, keen, anxious** mean strongly moved by desire or interest. **Eager** suggests being excited or impatient about something one wants to do or have: *The boys were eager to start building the clubhouse.* **Keen** suggests being moved to energetic or enthusiastic action by great interest or sharp desire: *They were keen to get the work done.* **Anxious** sometimes suggests fear of being disappointed and not getting what is wanted: *She is anxious that we should all like her new friend.*

ea|ger[2] (ē'gər, ā'-), *n.* = eagre.

eager beaver, *U.S. Informal.* an overly hard-working, ambitious, or enthusiastic person: *An eager beaver with a fever to achieve can leave his rut and cut a wide swath by investing $5,000 and his talent in a distributorship* (Wall Street Journal).

ea|ger-bea|ver (ē'gər bē'vər), *adj. U.S. Informal.* anxious for priority or recognition to the point of rashness; too ambitious: *An eager-beaver underling, concluding that the boss frowns on all treks to the refreshment bar, bans coffee breaks for his 20 women clerks* (Wall Street Journal).

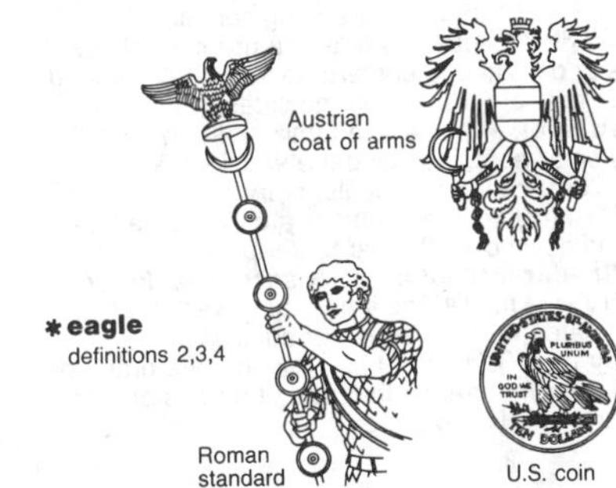

***eagle**
definitions 2,3,4

ea|gle** (ē'gəl), *n., adj., v.,* **-gled, -gling.** —n.*** **1** any one of a group of large birds of prey that have hooked beaks, keen sight, and powerful wings. The eagle is related to the hawk. The bald eagle is the national emblem of the United States. There are 48 different kinds of eagles in the world, but only the bald eagle and the golden eagle breed in the United States and Canada. **2** a design or picture shaped like an eagle, often used on a flag, coat of arms, coin, or stamp: *the white eagle of Poland.* **3** a standard bearing such a figure, especially the standard of the ancient Roman army. **4** a former gold coin of the United States with an eagle engraved on it, worth $10. **5** a score of two strokes less than par for a hole on a golf course: *An eagle on the fourth hole sent Burke on his way to the day's finest round* (New York Times).
—***adj.*** like that of an eagle: *The eagle eye of the guide saw every move the deer made.*
—***v.t.*** to score an eagle on (a hole) in golf: *He eagled the No. 2 hole and birdied No. 6* (New York Times).
eagles, the insignia of rank worn by a colonel in the United States Army: *Dressed in a coat and trousers of a captain of infantry, but recast as a colonel of cavalry by a pair of well-worn eagles that General Granger had kindly given me ...* (P. H. Sheridan).
[< Old French *egle,* learned borrowing from Latin *aquila*]

Ea|gle (ē'gəl), *n.* **1** the northern constellation Aquila. **2** a member of the Fraternal Order of Eagles, an organization founded in 1898 to promote health research, education, and social legislation.

eagle eye, a sharp eye or lookout: *As new convenience foods come under Institute scrutiny, we keep an eagle eye out for those that seem to us exceptional* (Good Housekeeping).

ea|gle-eyed (ē'gəl īd'), *adj.* sharp-sighted, like an eagle: *The injected dogs are watched with eagle-eyed care* (Time).

eagle owl, the largest owl inhabiting Europe, preying on other birds only at night.

eagle ray, any one of a group of sting rays whose large pectoral fins resemble eagle's wings.

ea|gles (ē'gəlz), *n.pl.* See under **eagle**.

eagle scout, *U.S.* a boy scout of the highest rank in scouting, having earned 21 merit badges.

ea|gle|stone (ē'gəl stōn'), *n.* a small, round lump of iron oxide mixed with clay. It was formerly supposed that eagles carried eaglestones to their nests to help in laying eggs.

ea|glet (ē'glit), *n.* a young eagle. [< Old French *aiglette* (diminutive) < *aigle,* earlier *egle;* see etym. under **eagle**]

eagle vulture, a large African bird that has certain characteristics of the hawk and the vulture.

ea|gre (ē'gər, ā'-), *n.* a high tidal wave rushing up a narrowing estuary; bore. Also, **eager**. [Middle English *higre*]

eal|dor|man or **eal|der|man** (ôl'dər mən), *n., pl.* **-men.** *Obsolete.* alderman.

EAM (no periods), National Liberation Front, a Greek underground movement in World War II against the Nazi occupation (Greek *Ethniko Apeleftherotiko Metopo*): *Thus, for instance, EAM, the left-wing force which Greek reaction, with Western support, tried to destroy, is represented in rather ideal terms* (Saturday Review).

Eames chair (ēmz), a molded plywood or plastic chair: *She threw away all her former possessions except one Eames chair* (Ernestine Carter). [< Charles *Eames,* born 1907, an American designer]

ean (ēn), *v.i. Obsolete.* to yean. [Old English *ēanian* to bring forth lambs]

-ean, *suffix.* a form of **-an**, as in *Mozartean.*

E. & O.E., errors and omissions excepted (added to statements and accounts).

ean|ling (ēn'ling), *n. Obsolete.* a young lamb; yeanling. [< *ean* + *-ling*]

***ear**[1] (ir), *n.* **1** the part of the body by which people and animals hear; organ of hearing. It consists of the external ear, the middle ear, and the inner ear. See picture on next page. **2** outer part of the ear; auricle: *The horse laid his ears back. One variety of ear is small and round with little or no lobe development and a deeply rolled helix or rim* (Beals and Hoijer). **3** a thing shaped somewhat like the outer part of an ear. The handle of a pitcher or the part of a bell by which it is hung is called an ear. **4** Also, **ears**. the sense of hearing; the power of distinguishing sounds: *There is no need to shout; we have good ears. A buzzing sound of bees his ears alarms* (John Dryden). **5** the ability to hear small differences in sounds: *a musician with a very good ear for pitch. She has a good ear for music.* **6** listening; attention: *Please give ear to my request. Give every man thine ear but few thy voice* (Shakespeare). **7** a projecting part of an animal that resembles an ear. The winglike projections where the ligament unites the two valves of a scallop are ears. **8** *Journalism.* either of the small boxes or

***E**[1]
definition 1

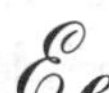

Script letters look like examples of fine penmanship. They appear in many formal uses, such as invitations to social functions.

Ee *Ee*

Handwritten letters, both manuscript or printed (left) and cursive (right), are easy for children to read and to write.

Ee *Ee*

Roman letters have *serifs* (finishing strokes) adapted from the way Roman stonecutters carved their letters. This is *Times Roman* type.

Ee *Ee*

Sans-serif letters are often called *gothic.* They have lines of even width and no serifs. This type face is called *Helvetica.*

Ee *Ee*

Between roman and gothic, some letters have thick and thin lines with slight flares that suggest serifs. This type face is *Optima.*

E

Computer letters can be sensed by machines either from their shapes or from the magnetic ink with which they are printed.

spaces in the upper corners of the front page of a newspaper, in which weather reports, slogans, etc., are printed.
be all ears, *Informal.* to listen eagerly; pay careful attention: *The children were all ears as the sailor described his adventures. Let me in on the secret; I'm all ears.*
believe one's ears, to credit what one hears: *He . . . blamed my partner, who could scarcely believe his ears* (Hugh Conway).
bend one's ear, *Slang.* to hold one stubbornly in a conversation: *Why, people have been bending our ears all day, and would gladly have continued into the night* (New Yorker).
by the ears, in a state of discord or contention: *In one place, we fight for a sword; in another for a horse; in short, we are all by the ears together* (Tobias Smollett).
chew one's ears off, *U.S. Slang.* to lecture or scold: *The clumsy player got his ears chewed off by the coach after the game.*
fall on deaf ears, to receive no attention; go unheeded: *His request for a raise in pay fell on deaf ears.*
go in one ear and out the other, to make no impression: *She listened to his explanation, but it just went in one ear and out the other.*
have (hold or **keep) one's ear to the ground,** *Informal.* to pay attention to what people are thinking and saying so that one can act accordingly: *If these associations are filled with the broad national principles of conservation, then the lawmakers will hold their ears to the ground* (National Conservation Congress).
incline one's ear, to listen favorably: *He inclined his ear to her tale of woe.*
lay back one's ears, *British Sports Slang.* to run at full speed; sprint: *His [the captain of a Rugby team's] try came from an interception in his own half, when, seeming to be considerably less surprised than his opponents, he laid back his ears and made it untouched to the posts* (U. A. Titley).
lend an ear, to listen; pay attention: *Friends, Romans, countrymen, lend me your ears* (Shakespeare).
over head and ears, deeply absorbed or involved; overwhelmed: *I am over head and ears in writings* (Thomas Gray).
play by ear, a to play (a piece of music or a musical instrument) without using written music: *She can't read notes but she can play any tune on the piano by ear.* **b** to handle (a matter) without adequate preparation or guidance: *The Administration has decided to play this by ear* (Newsweek).
prick (up) the ears, a to point the ears upward, especially to listen carefully: *The dog pricked up his ears when he heard his master's footsteps.* **b** *Figurative.* to give sudden attention: *I pricked up my ears when I heard my name mentioned.*
set by the ears, to cause to disagree or quarrel; stir up trouble between: *Does it [Turkey] fancy that it will obtain security for itself by setting Greek and Bulgarian by the ears?* (M. E. Grant Duff).
set on one's ear, to get very stirred up or excited: *"We set New York on its ear with the Picasso benefit . . ." Mrs. Smith said* (New Yorker). *They have . . . a chance to hoodwink local nabobs and set some unsuspecting prairie town on its ear* (Maclean's).
turn a deaf ear (or **ears**), to refuse to listen; pay no attention: *The President recently turned deaf ears on an S.O.S. plea from a group of G.O.P.ers* (Wall Street Journal).
up to the (or **one's**) **ears,** *Informal.* deeply taken up; thoroughly involved; almost overwhelmed: *I . . . was up to my ears in law* (Washington Irving).
wet behind the ears, too young to know very much; green; inexperienced: *[He] was wet behind the ears if he believed the charges thus far aired were unfounded* (New York Times).
[Old English *ēare*] **—ear′like′,** *adj.*

ear^2 (ir), *n., v.* **—*n.*** the part of certain plants that contains the grains. The grains of corn, wheat, oats, barley, and rye are formed on ears.
—*v.i.* to grow ears; form ears: *Soon the corn will ear.* [Old English *ēar*]

ear^3 (ir), *v.t. Archaic.* to plow. [Old English *erian*]

ear|ache (ir′āk′), *n.* pain in the ear; otalgia.

ear|bash|ing (ir′bash′ing), *n., adj. British Informal.* **—*n.*** a long or noisy speech; harangue; tirade: *Sometimes these occasions are used to give the audience a political earbashing* (London Times). **—*adj.*** earsplitting; deafening: *an earbashing . . . score, which sounds as if it is being played by a Marine Band . . .* (Manchester Guardian).

ear|bend|er (ir′ben′dər), *n. U.S. Informal.* a person or thing that compels one to listen.

ear|bob (ir′bob′), *n.* a dangling earring.

ear candy, *U.S. Slang.* smoothly arranged and pleasant-sounding popular music: *Synthesizers . . . fulfill pop music's never-ending quest for fresh ear candy* (Time).

ear-catch|er (ir′kach′ər), *n.* something that attracts attention by its sound, such as a catchy tune or lyric.

ear-catch|ing (ir′kach′ing), *adj.* having a sound that attracts attention: *Little clusters of grace notes intrigue Stockhausen, and his grouping of sound splashes are pleasant and ear-catching* (Oliver Daniel).

ear|clip (ir′klip′), *n.* an earring or other ornament fastened to the ear with a clip.

ear|cock|le (ir′kok′əl), *n.* a disease of wheat caused by a small nematode worm.

ear conch, the auricle of the ear; pinna.

ear cornet, a small ear trumpet formerly worn in the hollow of the ear.

ear crystal, a calcareous body formed in the internal ear of invertebrates; otolith.

ear|drop (ir′drop′), *n.* an earring with an ornament hanging from it.

ear|drum (ir′drum′), *n.* **1** a thin membrane across the middle ear that vibrates when sound waves strike it; tympanic membrane; tympanum: *Sound waves enter the outer ear, travel down the ear canal, and strike a thin membrane called the eardrum, which forms the boundary between the outer ear and the middle ear* (Shortley and Williams). See picture under **ear** ^{1}. **2** = middle ear.

eared^1 (ird), *adj.* **1** having ears or earlike parts. **2** having visible external ears. [< *ear*^{1} + *-ed*^{2}]

eared^2 (ird), *adj.* having ears: *eared barley.* [< *ear*^{2} + *-ed*^{2}]

eared grebe, a grebe of western North America with a tuft of long, golden feathers on each side of the head during the breeding season.

eared pheasant, any one of a group of pheasants of central and eastern Asia, marked by long white tufts of feathers on the sides of the head.

eared seal, any one of a family of seals with very small ears, including the sea lions and fur seals but not the hair seals; otary.

ear|flap (ir′flap′), *n.* a part of a cap that can be turned down over the ear to keep it warm.

ear|flow|er (ir′flou′ər), *n.* = sacred earflower.

ear fluid, a fluid in the inner ear of vertebrates, associated with the sense of equilibrium.

ear|fly (ir′flī′), *n., pl.* **-flies.** any one of a group of horseflies that attack the ears of horses and cattle, and also bite people.

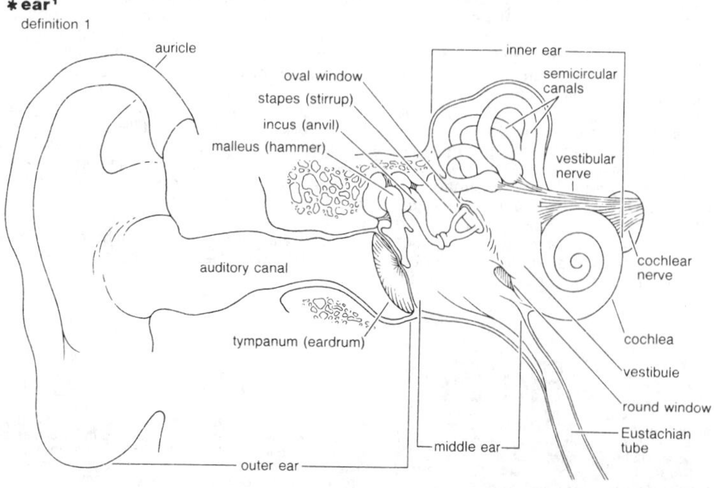

***ear**^{1}
definition 1

ear|ful (ir′fu̇l), *n., pl.* **-fuls.** *U.S. Informal.* **1** a startling or important disclosure: *If you want to get an earful, listen to this.* **2** more than enough: *I've had an earful of this radio program.* **3** a scolding: *They can expect an earful or two . . . on what the slump is doing economically* (Wall Street Journal).

ear guard, either of a pair of light cups of plastic or other material worn by jet pilots on the ears to exclude noise.

ear|hole (ir′hōl′), *n.* the opening of the ear.

ear|ing (ir′ing), *n.* a small rope attached to a cringle of a sail, used in reefing. [perhaps use of *earring,* or perhaps < *ear*^{1} + *-ing*^{1}]

earl (ėrl), *n.* **1** a British nobleman ranking below a marquis and above a viscount. The wife or widow of an earl is called a countess. **2** a noble in Anglo-Saxon England who was the governor of a county or shire. [Old English *eorl*]

ear|lap (ir′lap′), *n.* **1** = earflap. **2** = earlobe. **3** = external ear.

earl|dom (ėrl′dəm), *n.* **1** the lands ruled by an earl. **2** the title or rank of an earl.

earl|duck (ėrl′duk′), *n.* = red-breasted merganser.

ear|less (ir′lis), *adj.* **1** having no ears: *the American earless lizard.* **2** deaf.

earless seal, = hair seal.

ear|let (ir′lit), *n.* a small ear.

ear|li|ness (ėr′lē nis), *n.* the state of being early.

Earl Marshal, a high officer of state in Great Britain, who is head of the Heralds' College, appointing its officers, and who directs all ceremonies of state. The office is now hereditary in the line of the dukes of Norfolk.

ear|lobe (ir′lōb′), *n.* **1** the soft, loosely hanging lower part of the external ear. **2** the fleshy fold beside the ear of some fowls.

ear|lock (ir′lok′), *n.* **1** a lock of hair worn next to either ear by ultra-Orthodox Jews (in obedience to a Biblical commandment, Leviticus 19:27, prohibiting the rounding off of hair on the temples). **2** a lock of hair near the ear.

earl palatine, an English earl who formerly exercised royal prerogatives within his county.

earl|ship (ėrl′ship), *n.* the position, rank, or authority of an earl.

ear|ly (ėr′lē), *adv., adj.,* **-li|er, -li|est,** *n., pl.* **-lies.** **—*adv.*** **1** near the beginning; in the first part: *The sun is not hot early in the day.* SYN: betimes. **2** before the usual time: *Please come early.* SYN: beforehand. **3** long ago; far back in time; in ancient times: *Horses were very small early in their development.* **4** before very long; soon: *Spring may come early this year.* SYN: presently, shortly.
—*adj.* **1** of or occurring in the first part: *In his early years, he liked ships.* **2** occurring before the usual time: *We had an early dinner today.* **3** happening far back in time: *early history.* SYN: ancient. **4** occurring in the near future: *an early end to the strike, an answer at an early date.*
—*n.* a vegetable or fruit produced early in the season: *The glut of earlies has been caused by a slightly bigger acreage and an abnormal growing season* (London Times).
early on, at, from, or near the beginning; at an early time or stage: *Early on, young Mackie was keen at sports* (Newsweek).
[Old English *ǣrlīce* < *ǣr* ere + *-līce* -ly^1]

Early American, made or built in, or characterized by the styles of the American Colonial or post-Revolutionary periods, often displaying both Dutch and English influences.

early bird, *Informal.* a person who gets up, arrives, or does something early: *The company was an early bird in marketing computers.* [< the proverb "the *early bird* catches the worm"]

Early Bird, *Trademark.* an active communications satellite designed to relay microwave signals between North America and Europe.

early blight, a disease affecting the leaves of potato and tomato plants, caused by a fungus and similar to late blight.

Early English architecture, the pointed Gothic style of medieval architecture in England developed from the Norman style of the 1100's and the early 1200's.

early goldenrod, a goldenrod that blooms in eastern North America in August.

ear|ly|ish (ėr′lē ish), *adj.* rather early: *It is an earlyish work . . . and has long been unobtainable in this country* (Manchester Guardian).

ear|ly-warn|ing (ėr′lē wôr′ning), *adj.* designed to give warning well in advance of danger: *A group of four seismological monitoring stations is being installed in Chile, as part of an earthquake early-warning network to extend throughout South America* (Science News). [abstracted from *early-warning radar*]

early-warning radar, a radar set or system designed to detect aircraft at as great a distance as possible, and used near the periphery of a defended area to warn of approaching aircraft.

early wood, the lighter part of a tree's annual ring, which develops each spring; springwood.

ear|mark (ir′märk′), *n., v.* —*n.* **1** a mark made on the ear of an animal to show who owns it. **2** *Figurative.* a special mark, quality, or feature that gives information about a person or thing; sign: *Careful speech is an earmark of the educated man.*
—*v.t.* **1** to make an earmark on. **2** *Figurative.* to identify or give information about: *Careless work earmarks a poor student. A capital adorned with acanthus leaves earmarks the Corinthian column.* **3** *Figurative.* to set aside for some special purpose: *Money earmarked to buy books for the library cannot be spent for anything else.*

ear-mind|ed (ir′mīn′did), *adj.* having a marked tendency to carry on mental operations most readily by auditory images; thinking in sounds.

ear mite, a mite that infests the ears of mammals.

ear|muffs (ir′mufs′), *n.pl.* a pair of coverings to put over the ears to keep them warm or protect them from noise.

earn[1] (ėrn), *v.t.* **1** to get in return for work or service; be paid: *She earns 25 dollars a day.* **2** to do enough work for; do good enough work for; deserve; be worth: *He is paid more than he really earns.* SYN: merit. **3** to bring or get as deserved: *Her hard work earned her the respect of her teachers.* SYN: win. **4** to gain as a profit or return: *Money well invested earns good interest.* [Old English *earnian*] —**earn′er**, *n.*

earn[2] (ėrn), *v.i. Obsolete.* to desire strongly; long; yearn. [apparently variant of *yearn*]

earned run (ėrnd), a run in baseball which is not the result of an error by the defending team, scored against a pitcher.

earned run average, the average number of earned runs scored against a pitcher in a 9-inning game. *Abbr:* ERA (no periods), or E.R.A.

earned surplus, the net earnings of a corporation from the date of its incorporation; retained earnings.

ear|nest[1] (ėr′nist), *adj., n.* —*adj.* **1** strong and firm in purpose; eager and serious: *The earnest pupil tried very hard to do his best.* SYN: sincere, diligent, zealous. **2** important: *Life is real, life is earnest* (Longfellow).
—*n.* seriousness (of intention or purpose).
in earnest, determined or sincere; serious: *The young man is in earnest about becoming a famous painter.*
[Old English *eornost*] —**ear′nest|ly**, *adv.* —**ear′nest|ness**, *n.*

ear|nest[2] (ėr′nist), *n.* **1** a part given or done in advance as a pledge for the rest: *Take this money as an earnest of the amount I still owe you. Part of the price he paid to the seller was an earnest that the rest would be paid.* **2** *Figurative.* anything that shows what is to come; pledge; token: *The primrose flower Peeped forth to give an earnest of the Spring* (Wordsworth). *His eloquence and religious fervor had already given the earnest of high eminence in his profession* (Hawthorne). [Middle English *ernes*, apparently alteration (by association with *-ness*) of *erres* < Old French *erres*, plural < Latin *arrha* < Greek *arrhabôn* < Hebrew *'ērābon* pledge]

earnest money, money paid as a pledge: *The couple paid five thousand dollars earnest money on the house.*

earn|ing power (ėr′ning), **1** the capacity of a business or investment to yield profits. **2** a person's ability to earn a certain income.

earn|ings (ėr′ningz), *n.pl.* money earned; wages or profits. SYN: income.

* **ear|phone** (ir′fōn′), *n.* a receiver for a telephone, telegraph, radio, television, or hearing aid that is fastened in or placed over the ear; headphone.

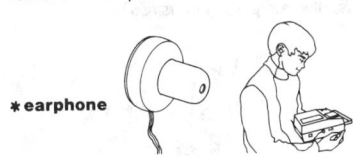

* **earphone**

ear|piece (ir′pēs′), *n.* **1** the part of any equipment that is connected to or held up by the ear. **2** = earflap. **3** one of the usually curved ends of the frame of eyeglasses that rests upon the ear.

ear piercer, a person who pierces the earlobe so that an earring may be worn in it.

ear-pierc|ing (ir′pir′sing), *adj.* piercing or irritating to the ear, as a shrill or sharp sound: *an ear-piercing scream.*

ear|plug (ir′plug′), *n.* **1** a small, rounded piece of wax, rubber, or plastic, used to insert into the ear to exclude noise. **2** a small, usually plastic, earphone connected to a portable, transistor, or other type of small radio, used for private listening.

ear|reach (ir′rēch′), *n.* = earshot.

ear|ring (ir′ring′), *n.* an ornament for the lobe of the ear.

ear shell, an abalone or other gastropod with an ear-shaped shell.

ear|shot (ir′shot′), *n.* the distance a sound can be heard; range of hearing: *We shouted, but he was out of earshot and could not hear our voices.*

ear|split|ting (ir′split′ing), *adj.* overpoweringly loud; deafening: *The bomb exploded with an earsplitting sound. An earsplitting musical about life among the contemporary Indians* (New Yorker).
—**ear′split′ting|ly**, *adv.*

ear|spool (ir′spül′), *n.* a cylindrical, ornamental plug worn in the earlobe by ancient peoples of North and South America.

ear stone, = otolith.

ear tag, an identification tag, usually of metal or leather, attached to the ear of an animal.

ear-tag (ir′tag′), *v.t.*, **-tagged, -tag|ging.** to attach an identification tag to the ear of (an animal).

* **earth** (ėrth), *n., v.* —*n.* **1** Also, **Earth.** the planet on which we live; the globe. The earth is the fifth largest planet in the solar system, and the third in distance from the sun. *China is on the other side of the earth. The earth is a large ball or sphere of mineral matter, some 8,000 miles in diameter, the depressions on which are filled with water* (White and Renner). See picture under **solar system.** **2** all the people who live on this planet: *The whole earth rejoiced in the feat of the astronauts who traveled to the moon. And the whole earth was of one language* (Genesis 11:1). **3** this world as the place where man lives (often in contrast to heaven and hell): *Earth's crammed with heaven, And every common bush afire with God* (Elizabeth Barrett Browning). **4** dry land; ground: *the earth, the sea, and the sky. God called the dry land earth* (Genesis 1:10). **5** soil; dirt: *The earth in the garden is good, soft soil.* **6** the hole of a fox or other burrowing animal. **7** worldly matters: . . . *all the fuming vanities of earth* (Wordsworth). **8** a metallic oxide from which it is hard to remove the oxygen, such as alumina: *the alkaline earths, the rare earths.* **9** *British.* the connection of an electrical conductor with the earth; ground. **10** *Obsolete.* a land or country: *this blessed plot, this earth, this realm, this England* (Shakespeare).
—*v.t.* **1** to connect (an electrical wire or other conductor) with the earth; ground. **2** to cover with soil: *to earth up a plant or its roots.* **3** *Dialect.* to hide in the earth; bury. **4** to drive (a fox or other quarry) to its burrow.
—*v.i.* to hide in the earth: *The fox earthed.*
back (or **down) to earth**, seeing things as they really are; practical; realistic: *Marx and Engels . . . had brought Hegel down to earth; and certainly nobody had ever labored more . . . to hold men's minds to their practical problems* (Edmund Wilson).
go to earth, a to go to its hole or burrow: *The river rises, and the master sends his groom to request Michael dig out a vixen and her cubs who have gone to earth on the bank* (Atlantic). **b** to go into hiding: *They've gone to earth, and we can't find them.*
on earth, ever; in the world: *My father kept saying: "What on earth are you doing?"* (Manchester Guardian). *"There is no way on earth" that operation of commuter railroads, such as the Long Island, "can be made profitable"* (New York Times).
run to earth, a to chase game, such as a fox, to its hole or burrow: *a vixen run to earth with her cub.* **b** to capture or find (something or someone) after a long search: *All the men who helped to run to earth the various members of the Ruthven family . . . were richly rewarded* (Spectator).
[Old English *eorthe*]
—*Syn. n.* **1, 3 Earth, world, globe** mean the planet on which we live. **Earth** applies to this planet covered by land and water, in contrast to the other planets and sun, stars, etc., or, sometimes, to heaven and hell: *the gravitational attraction of the earth.* **World** applies to the earth as the home of man, usually suggesting all mankind and human affairs: *all the nations of the world.* In the works of older writers, *world* sometimes means the visible universe, including the sun, moon, stars, etc.: *It is a Christian belief that the world will end on Judgment Day.* **Globe** emphasizes the roundness of the earth: *Today a traveler can fly around the globe in a few days.*

* **earth** definition 1

symbol

earth almond, = chufa.

earth apple, = Jerusalem artichoke.

earth art, art consisting of earthworks: *A lot of people have not yet made up their minds about earth art. . . . examples of it are so inaccessible that hardly anyone has actually seen an earthwork* (Calvin Tomkins).

earth ball, an edible fungus growing in the soil; truffle.

earth|board (ėrth′bôrd′, -bōrd′), *n.* the moldboard of a plow.

earth bob, a grub, the larva of a beetle.

earth|born (ėrth′bôrn′), *adj.* **1** born or sprung from the earth. **2** human; mortal.

earth|bound (ėrth′bound′), *adj.* **1** bound or limited to this earth: *Within a single generation man has ceased to be earthbound.* **2** *Figurative.* practical; down-to-earth: *Violaine . . . is the essence of sainthood and charity, Mara is fierce and earthbound* (New York Times).

earth-cir|cling (ėrth′sėr′kling), *adj.* going around the earth in an orbit: *It would start on its Martian journey from an earth-circling space platform* (Science News Letter).

earth current, an irregular electric current that flows through the ground, sometimes interfering with the flow in electric wires and telegraph cables.

Earth Day, a day in April set aside by environmentalists to dramatize the need for pollution control: *By the time Earth Day dawned on April 22, eco-activists of all ages were suffused with quasi-religious fervor* (Time).

earth|day (ėrth′dā′), *n.* the 24-hour day of the earth applied to measuring time on other celestial bodies or artificial satellites: *For just over 14 earthdays the sun will not shine on the barren surface of the [moon's] Sea of Rains, where the Lunokhod began its historic mission* (London Times).

earth|en (ėr′thən), *adj.* **1** made of baked clay: *an earthen jug.* **2** made of earth: *a low earthen dam.*

earth|en|ware (ėr′thən wãr′), *n., adj.* —*n.* **1** dishes or containers made of baked clay; crockery. Coarse pottery is earthenware. It is fired to a lower temperature than stoneware or porcelain. *Earthenware is made from purer, whiter clay than that used for tiles and, molded in various other forms, is manufactured the same as bricks* (Monroe M. Offner). **2** fired clay.
—*adj.* made of earthenware: *an earthenware pot.*

earth|fall (ėrth′fôl′), *n.* = landslide.

earth|fast (ėrth′fast′, -fäst′), *adj.* firm in the earth and hard to move.

earth-fill dam (ėrth′fil′), a dam constructed primarily of earth.

earth|flea (ėrth′flē′), *n.* = chigoe.

earth|fly (ėrth′flī′), *n., pl.* **-flies.** = chigoe.

earth|gall (ėrth′gôl′), *n.* a plant of the gentian family; centaury.

earth hog, = aardvark.

earth|i|an (ėr′thē ən), *n., adj.* —*n.* an earthman; earthling.
—*adj.* of the earth; earthly.

earth|i|ly (ėr′thə lē), *adv.* in a vigorous, earthy way: *Italy's expert actress Magnani [gave] one of her earthily explosive performances* (Time).

earth|i|ness (ėr′thē nis), *n.* **1** earthy nature or properties: *Mr. Munch and the orchestra gave the three symphonies balanced, vigorous readings in which were that blend of earthiness and sublimity that make Beethoven what he is* (New York Times). **2** = earthliness.

earth ivy, = ground ivy.

earth|light (ėrth′līt′), *n.* = earthshine.

earth|like (ėrth′līk′), *adj.* **1** like the earth: *Mars is more moonlike than earthlike* (Time). **2** like that of the earth: *an earthlike atmosphere.*

earth|li|ness (ėrth′lē nis), *n.* earthly quality or character; worldliness.

earth|ling (ėrth′ling), *n.* **1** an inhabitant of the earth; human being; mortal. SYN: man. **2** a worldly person. SYN: worldling.

earth lodge, a dwelling used by some North American Indian tribes, consisting of a pit in the ground with the structure above it roofed with sod.

earth|ly (ėrth′lē), *adj.,* **-li|er, -li|est.** **1** having to do with the earth, not with heaven: *man's earthly existence. The Duke's earthly possessions were of a negative character* (Lytton Strachey). **2** possible; conceivable: *That rubbish is of no earthly use to us; throw it away.* **3** *Archaic.* earthy.
—*Syn.* **1 Earthly, terrestrial, worldly** mean having to do with the earth. **Earthly** describes things connected with life in this world, in contrast to heavenly things: *to acquire money and other earthly possessions.* **Terrestrial** is used particularly to refer to the earth as a planet, or to the

land of the earth as opposed to water: *a terrestrial globe. People are terrestrial beings; fish are aquatic beings.* **Worldly** emphasizes the pleasures, success, vanity, and the like, of this life as contrasted with spiritual or religious values: *They enjoy parties, dances, and other worldly pleasures.*

earthly position, = substellar point.

earth|man (ėrth′man′, -mən), *n., pl.* **-men.** a human being; earthling: *A plasma engine some day may power earthmen to Mars* (Science News Letter).

earth mother, **1** (in mythology and folklore) a spirit or being taken as a symbol of the earth. **2** the earth regarded as the source of life. [translation of German *Erdmutter*]

earth mover, **1** a person or thing that moves earth, dirt, or rock, by pushing or scraping it from one place to another. **2** = bulldozer.

earth|mov|ing (ėrth′mü′ving), *adj.* having to do with the excavation and transportation of large quantities of earth: *earthmoving machinery; ... excavating and crane equipment for earthmoving and construction operations* (Wall Street Journal).

earth|nut (ėrth′nut′), *n.* **1** an underground part of certain plants, such as a root, tuber, or underground pod: *Peanuts, truffles, and pignuts are earthnuts.* **2** any plant that produces such a root or tuber.

earth|pea (ėrth′pē′), *n.* a vine of the pea family whose pods ripen underground like peanuts; hog peanut.

earth pig, = aardvark.

earth pillar, *Geology.* a column of loose, unconsolidated material usually covered with stone at the top, produced by erosion of surrounding land.

earth-plate (ėrth′plāt′), *n. Electricity.* = ground plate.

earth|quake (ėrth′kwāk′), *n.* a shaking or sliding of the ground. It is caused by the sudden movement of masses of rock along a fault or by changes in the size and shape of masses of rock far beneath the earth's surface. Earthquakes are often associated with the violent activity of volcanoes. *Earthquakes can destroy whole cities.*

earth|quak|ing (ėrth′kwā′king), *adj.* **1** causing the earth to shake: *an earthquaking rumble.* **2** = earthshaking. **3** = earthquaky.

earth|quak|y (ėrth′kwā′kē), *adj.,* **-quak|i|er, -quak|i|est. 1** subject to earthquakes: *an earthquaky country.* **2** like the effect of an earthquake; suggesting the motion of an earthquake: *an earthquaky feeling.*

earth resources satellite, an artificial satellite that gathers data on the earth's natural resources: *The use of Landsat and other earth resources satellites is booming, not only among research scientists but among farmers, explorers, and a growing number of businessmen as well* (Timothy Hackler).

earth|rise (ėrth′rīz′), *n.* a view of the earth from the moon or from a spacecraft, in which the earth seems to be rising above the moon's horizon. [patterned on *sunrise*]

earth satellite, a satellite of the earth made by man, especially a metal sphere or other structure, launched by rockets into an orbit outside the earth's atmosphere.

earth|scape (ėrth′skāp′), *n.* a view of the earth from outer space.

earth science, any one of the sciences dealing with the origin, composition, and physical features of the earth and its atmosphere. Geology, geography, meteorology, and oceanography are earth sciences.

earth scientist, a person trained or skilled in one or more of the earth sciences.

earth|shak|er (ėrth′shā′kər), *n.* **1** an earthshaking person, thing, or event. **2** Also, **Earthshaker.** a name applied to Poseidon and (less often) Zeus.

earth|shak|ing (ėrth′shā′king), *adj.* great or important to an unusual degree: *The race for state legislature seats, ordinarily not an earthshaking matter for non-Californians, this year has unusual significance* (Wall Street Journal). **—earth′shak′ing|ly**, *adv.*

earth-shat|ter|ing (ėrth′shat′ər ing), *adj.* = earthshaking.

earth|shine (ėrth′shīn′), *n.* the faint light visible on the part of the moon not directly illuminated by the sun; earthlight. It is due to light the earth reflects on the moon and is best seen about four days before or four days after the new moon.

earth|shock (ėrth′shok′), *n.* **1** = earthquake. **2** a movement of the ground caused by an underground explosion.

earth shoe, **1** a shoe whose sole is thicker in front than in back, designed to lower the heel below the rest of the foot for greater comfort: *She got rid of the demure blue patent pumps she had been wearing and substituted earth shoes, supremely comfortable but odd-looking* (Maclean's). **2 Earth Shoe**, a trademark for such a shoe.

earth|slide (ėrth′slīd′), *n.* = landslide (defs. 1, 2).

earth|star (ėrth′stär′), *n.* a fungus whose outer covering splits into the form of a star.

earth station, a station on earth equipped with electronic apparatus to receive and rebroadcast signals transmitted from outer space.

earth tide, the gravitational pull of the moon and sun on the earth, causing tidelike motions of the earth's crust several inches high. From the amount of distortion of the solid rocks by earth tides, the rigidity of the earth can be calculated.

earth|ward (ėrth′wərd), *adv., adj.* toward the earth: *The burning airplane hurtled earthward* (adv). *The spacecraft started its earthward descent* (adj.).

earth|wards (ėrth′wərdz), *adv.* = earthward.

earth wave, a seismic wave in the solid crust of the earth.

Earth Week, a week in April set aside for expression of public concern over the pollution of the earth's atmosphere.

earth|wom|an (ėrth′wům′ən), *n., pl.* **-wom|en.** a woman of the planet earth; a female earthling.

earth|work (ėrth′wėrk′), *n.* **1** a bank of earth piled up for a fortification: *Captain Pilkington ... asked the Minister of Works what action he was taking to preserve ancient barrows and earthworks* (London Times). **2** a moving of earth in engineering operations. **3** a work of art made by shaping or altering any natural feature of the environment, such as a piece of land or a sand dune, the finished work usually being exhibited in photographs.

earth|work|er (ėrth′wėr′kər), *n.* an artist who makes earthworks.

earth|worm (ėrth′wėrm′), *n.* **1** any one of various reddish-brown or grayish worms that live in the soil; angleworm. An earthworm is an annelid. It has minute bristles on each segment that aid in locomotion. Earthworms loosen the soil by burrowing and let air circulate through it. *Earthworms may be found almost everywhere that there is moist soil, and their tremendous value to agriculture can hardly be overestimated* (A. M. Winchester). **2** *Figurative.* a mean or groveling person.

earth|y (ėr′thē), *adj.,* **earth|i|er, earth|i|est. 1** of earth or soil: *Potatoes have an earthy smell.* **2** like earth or soil (in texture, color, or other feature): *The color of the field was a rich, earthy brown.* **3** not spiritual; worldly: *An earthy man is interested in material things. The first man is of the earth, earthy* (I Corinthians 15:47). **4** *Figurative.* natural; simple and frank; unsophisticated: *Miss Bettis ... has lost a great deal of her earlier earthy passion and has come to give a slightly false and fancy performance* (New York Times). **5** *Figurative.* not refined; coarse: *earthy humor.*

ear tick, a bloodsucking parasite which infests the ears of cattle, horses, sheep, dogs, and other animals. It is prevalent in the semiarid sections of the United States, where it causes heavy losses among livestock.

***ear trumpet**, a trumpet-shaped instrument held to the ear by a deaf person as an aid in hearing.

***ear trumpet**

ear|wax (ir′waks′), *n.* the sticky, yellowish substance secreted by glands along the canal of the outer ear; cerumen.

***ear|wig** (ir′wig′), *n., v.,* **-wigged, -wig|ging.** *—n.* **1** a slender insect somewhat like a beetle, found throughout the world. They have short, leathery forewings and forcepslike appendages at the end of the abdomen. Earwigs were once thought to crawl into people's ears; dermapteran. **2** a kind of long, narrow-bodied centipede.
—v.t. to try to influence with sly suggestions; whisper insinuations in the ear of, against another: *Each secretary of state is earwigged by a knot of sturdy beggars* (Blackwood's Magazine). [Old English *ēarwicga* < *ēare* ear[1] + *wicga* beetle, worm]

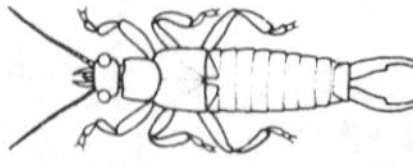
***earwig**
definition 1

ear|wit|ness (ir′wit′nis), *n.* a person who testifies, or can testify, to something he has heard: *The earwitness testimony ... is undependable in determining the source of any shots where there is a possibility of echoes* (New Yorker).

ear|worm (ir′wėrm′), *n.* = corn earworm.

ease (ēz), *n., v.,* **eased, eas|ing.** *—n.* **1** freedom from pain or trouble; comfort: *The rich young woman has a life of ease. I lean and loaf at my ease observing a spear of summer grass* (Walt Whitman). **2** freedom from trying hard; lack of effort; readiness: *You can do this lesson with ease. The reporter writes with great ease. Seeing how with great ease Nature can smile* (Tennyson). **3** freedom from embarrassment; natural or easy manner: *A certain graceful ease marks him as a man who knows the world* (Macaulay). **4** a lowering of the rate of interest on loans.
—v.t. **1** to make free from pain or trouble; give comfort to: *His kind words eased her worried mind.* **SYN:** relieve, soothe, calm. **2** to make less; lighten: *Some medicines ease pain. Aspirin eased my headache.* **SYN:** lessen. **3** to make easy; loosen: *The belt is too tight; ease it a little.* **4** to move slowly and carefully: *The movers eased the desk through the narrow door.* **5** to make (money, credit, etc.) available at low rates of interest. **6** *Nautical.* **a** to slacken or release the tension from (a rudder, sail, or rope). **b** to let (the helm or rudder) swing back slightly after turning far in one direction. **c** to turn the bow of (a ship) directly into a wave.
—v.i. **1** to become less rapid, stern, or otherwise intense: *Tension eased among the passengers as the fog lifted.* **2** to tend to decline in prices: *Coffee, rubber, burlap, wool, zinc, cottonseed oil and soybean oil rose; potatoes, hides and copper eased, and cocoa was mixed* (New York Times).
at ease, **a** free from pain or trouble; comfortable: *The doctor soon made the worried patient feel at ease. Louise was at ease, content* (Graham Greene). **b** with the body relaxed and the feet apart: *Soldiers standing at ease are permitted to talk.*
ease in, to break in with light work: *to ease in a new employee.*
ease off (or **up**), **a** to lessen; lighten: *It was an object with the king to ease off the taxation* (Stephen Dowell). **b** to loosen: *to ease off a rope.* **c** to slow down; relax: *Ease up; you are working too hard.*
ease out, to dismiss from or leave quietly (a job, an office, or other position or place): *The old player was about to ease himself out of the game. It is being suggested that the Russians are easing him out of office because of the resistance he is said to have shown towards some of their demands* (London Times).
ill at ease, uneasy; uncomfortable: *In such damp conditions everyone seemed ill at ease* (London Times).
take one's ease, to make oneself comfortable; rest: *Take your ease, for the journey ahead will be long and arduous.*
[< Old French *aise* comfort, opportunity < Vulgar Latin *adjacēns* neighborhood, noun use of Latin *adjacēns* adjacent]
*— **Syn.** n.* **1 Ease, comfort** mean freedom from strain. **Ease** suggests being relaxed or at rest: *When school is out, I am going to live a life of ease for a whole week.* **Comfort** suggests feeling well and contented and being well provided for: *Let others have wealth and fame; I want only comfort.*

ease|ful (ēz′fəl), *adj.* giving ease; comfortable; soothing: *easeful Death* (Keats). *The daughter sees all this as a dire threat to her happy, easeful life with her father* (Newsweek). **—ease′ful|ly**, *adv.* **—ease′ful|ness**, *n.*

***ea|sel** (ē′zəl), *n.* a stand for holding a picture, blackboard, or chart. [< Dutch *ezel* easel (literally) ass, ultimately < Latin *asinus*]

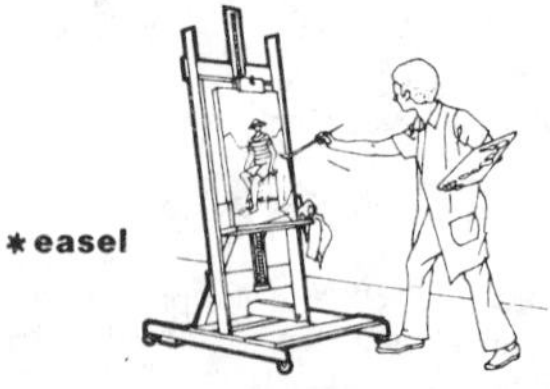
***easel**

ease|less (ēz′lis), *adj.* admitting of no relief; without ease: *Without Merman's 130 pounds of easeless energy, the fourth musical comedy of the season would never make it to the summer doldrums* (Newsweek).

ease|ment (ēz′mənt), *n.* **1** *Law.* a right held by one person to some limited use of land owned by another. **2** an easing; relief: *Perhaps ... the west had begun ... to perceive some signs of an easement of tension* (London Times). **3** a convenience.

eas|er (ē′zər), *n.* a person or thing that eases.

eas|i|ly (ē′zə lē), *adv.* **1** in an easy manner.

2 without trying hard; with little effort: *Her simple tasks were quickly and easily done.* **SYN**: readily. 3 without pain or trouble; comfortably: *A few hours after the operation, the patient was resting easily.* 4 smoothly; freely: *The cowboy rode his pony easily.* 5 by far; without question: *He is easily the best player on the field.* 6 very likely: *A war may easily happen if the two sides fail to reach an agreement.* **SYN**: probably.

eas|i|ness (ē′zē nis), *n.* **1** the quality or condition of being easy: *the easiness of a seat.* **2** carelessness or indifference.

east (ēst), *n., adj., adv.* —*n.* **1** the direction of the sunrise; direction just opposite west. On a compass, east is a point 90 degrees clockwise from north. *Abbr:* E. or E (no period). **2** Also, **East.** the part of any country toward the east.
—*adj.* **1** toward the east; farther toward the east: *Take the east road; it is the shortest way.* **2** coming from the east: *an east wind.* **3** in the east; facing the east: *the east wing of the house.* **4** toward the altar, as viewed from the nave.
—*adv.* **1** toward the east; farther toward the east; eastward: *Walk east to find the road.* **2** in the east: *The wind was blowing east.*
east of, further east than: *Ohio is east of Indiana.*
[Old English *ēast*]
▶ An **east** or **easterly** wind carries a ship *west* or on a *westerly* course.

East (ēst), *n.* **1a** the part of the United States to the east of the Allegheny Mountains, especially New England. **b** the part of the United States that lies to the east of the Mississippi River, especially the states north of Maryland and the Ohio River. **2** the countries in Asia as distinguished from those in Europe or America; the Orient. **3** the Soviet Union and its satellites in Eastern Europe: *It is normally taken for granted that the two main antagonists in the struggle between East and West are the United States and the Soviet Union* (Cape Times). **4** one of the four players or positions in bridge.

east|a|bout (ēst′ə bout′), *adv.* in an easterly direction.

east|bound (ēst′bound′), *adj.* going east; bound eastward.

east by north, 11°15′ to the north of east. *Abbr:* E b N, E by N

east by south, 11°15′ to the south of east. *Abbr:* E b S, E by S

East Coast fever, a serious disease of cattle in Africa caused by a sporozoan transmitted by ticks, characterized by high fever and swelling of the lymph glands.

East End, a crowded business and commercial section in east London, in which poorer people live.

East|er (ēs′tər), *n., adj.* —*n.* **1** the yearly celebration of the day on which Christ rose from the grave; Easter Sunday. Except in the Eastern Church, Easter comes between March 22 and April 25, usually on the first Sunday after the first full moon on or after March 21. **2** Eastertide, especially Easter week.
—*adj.* of or having to do with Easter; suitable for Easter: *Easter music.*
[Old English *ēastre* (originally) name of a goddess whose feast was celebrated in the spring < *ēast* east]

Easter bunny, a real or artificial rabbit used as a gift or decoration at Easter.

Easter egg, a colored egg, real or artificial, used as a gift or decoration at Easter.

Easter egg rolling or **roll,** a children's contest in which Easter eggs are rolled on a lawn with a spoon or mallet. The best-known Easter egg rolling is conducted each year on the lawn of the White House.

Easter Eve or **Even,** the day before Easter Sunday; Holy Saturday: *Part of special Holy Week rites that are steeped in traditions fifteen centuries old, the liturgy of Easter Even opened with the Blessing of the New Fire* (New York Times).

Easter Islander, a native or inhabitant of Easter Island in the South Pacific.

Easter lily, any one of several cultivated lilies with large, white, trumpet-shaped flowers. Easter lilies symbolize purity and are often used at Easter to decorate church altars.

east|er|ling (ēs′tər ling), *n.* **1** *Archaic.* a native or inhabitant of an eastern country or section. **2** (formerly, in England) a trader or native of one of the Hanse towns or of the Baltic shore in general. **3** an English silver penny of the 1100's to 1300's.

east|er|ly (ēs′tər lē), *adj., adv., n.* —*adj., adv.* **1** toward the east: *The house has an easterly outlook.* **2** from the east: *an easterly wind.*
—*n.* a wind that blows from the east.
easterlies, the prevailing easterly winds found in certain latitudes.
▶ See **east** for a usage note.

Easter Monday, the day after Easter.

east|ern (ēs′tərn), *adj., n.* —*adj.* **1** toward the east: *an eastern trip.* **2** from the east: *eastern tourists.* **3** of the east; in the east: *eastern schools.*
—*n.* a person living in an eastern region or country.
[Old English *ēasterne*]

East|ern (ēs′tərn), *adj., n.* —*adj.* **1** of, in, or from the eastern part of the United States: *an Eastern Congressman.* **2** of or in the countries of Asia; Oriental. **3** from or having to do with the Soviet Union and its east European satellites.
—*n.* a member of the Eastern Church.

Eastern Church, = Eastern Orthodox Churches.

eastern cottontail, the variety of cottontail (rabbit) common throughout the eastern United States and Mexico.

eastern diamondback rattlesnake, a rattlesnake with diamond-shaped markings, found from Louisiana to North Carolina.

Eastern Empire, = Eastern Roman Empire.

east|ern|er (ēs′tər nər), *n.* a person born or living in the east.

East|ern|er (ēs′tər nər), *n.* a person born or living in the eastern part of the United States.

Eastern Hemisphere, the half of the world that includes Europe, Asia, Africa, and Australia.

eastern hemlock, a medium to large hemlock of the eastern United States and Canada whose bark is an important source of tannin for the leather industry.

east|ern|ize or **East|ern|ize** (ēs′tər nīz), *v.t.,* **-ized, -iz|ing.** to make eastern or Eastern in character, ideas, ways, or the like: *Would the Japanese be easternized if an Eastern country were top dog?* (Maclean's).

eastern kingbird, a large North American flycatcher with slaty-black upper parts, white underparts, and an inconspicuous red patch on the crown; bee martin.

eastern larch, = tamarack.

eastern mole, a large, silvery or grayish mole with naked tail and broad front feet, found especially about lawns and gardens of the central and eastern United States.

east|ern|most (ēs′tərn mōst), *adj.* farthest east: *Far from neutral in the cold war, Austria is really the easternmost outpost of the Free World* (Wall Street Journal).

Eastern Orthodox, of or having to do with the Eastern Orthodox Churches.

Eastern Orthodox Churches, a group of Christian churches chiefly in eastern Europe, western Asia, and in Africa, most of which consider the patriarch of Constantinople as titular head of the church; Eastern Church; Orthodox Church.

eastern pip|is|trel (pip′ə strel′), a very small, brownish bat of the eastern United States and Mexico.

Eastern Question, the problems and complications in the international politics of Europe relating to the Near East.

Eastern Rite, **1** the church ceremonies and customs of the Eastern Orthodox Churches: *Churches in the Eastern Rite have always maintained a married priesthood* (Maclean's). **2** = Eastern Orthodox Churches.

eastern roll, a style of high jump in which the jumper clears the crossbar in a vertical position.

Eastern Roman Empire, the eastern part of the Roman Empire after its division in A.D. 395; Byzantine Empire. The Eastern Roman Empire ended with the capture of Constantinople by the Turks in 1453.

Eastern Standard Time or **Eastern Time,** the standard time in the eastern part of the United States and most of eastern Canada, a belt centered on the 75th meridian and extending 7 degrees 30 minutes, approximately, on each side of it. Eastern Standard Time is five hours behind Greenwich Time. *Abbr:* EST (no periods).

eastern tent caterpillar, a black tent caterpillar, with blue spots and a yellow stripe on the back, that lives in fruit and shade trees in eastern and central North America.

eastern willet, a willet that breeds along the Atlantic Coast between Virginia and the Bahama Islands, and migrates in winter as far south as Peru.

Easter Sunday, the Sunday on which Easter is celebrated.

East|er|tide (ēs′tər tīd′), *n.* **1** the week beginning with Easter Sunday; Easter week. **2** the fifty days from Easter to Whitsuntide, the forty days to Ascension Day, or the fifty-seven days to Trinity Sunday.

Easter time, = Eastertide.

Easter week, Easter Sunday and the week following.

East German, **1** of or having to do with East Germany. **2** a native or inhabitant of East Germany.

East Germanic, an extinct division of Germanic which included Gothic.

East India Company, The, **1** a British joint-stock company chartered in 1600 to trade with the East Indies. In the 1700's its conquests led to the organization of British India, and for a time it exercised sovereignty jointly with the crown. Its noncommercial functions were relinquished in 1858. **2** the name of similar companies chartered in Denmark, Sweden, France, and Holland.

East Indiaman, a strong, roomy, full-rigged ship used as a cargo carrier in the trade with the East Indies in the 1700's and 1800's.

East Indian, **1** of or having to do with the East Indies or its people. **2** a person born or living in the East Indies.

east|ing (ēs′ting), *n.* **1** the distance due east made by a ship. **2** distance eastward. **3** easterly departure. **4** a shifting eastward from a course. **5** easterly direction.

east-north|east (ēst′nôrth′ēst′), *n., adv., adj.*
—*n.* the point of the compass or the direction midway between east and northeast, two points or 22 degrees 30 minutes to the north of east.
—*adv., adj.* 22°30′ to the north of east. *Abbr:* ENE (no periods).

east-south|east (ēst′south′ēst′), *n., adv., adj.*
—*n.* the point of the compass or the direction midway between east and southeast, two points or 22 degrees 30 minutes to the south of east.
—*adv., adj.* 22°30′ to the south of east. *Abbr:* ESE (no periods).

east|ward (ēst′wərd), *adv., adj., n.* —*adv., adj.* toward the east; east: *He walked eastward* (adv.). *The orchard is on the eastward slope of the hill* (adj.).
—*n.* an eastward part, direction, or point.

east|ward|ly (ēst′wərd lē), *adj., adv.* **1** toward the east. **2** from the east: *an eastwardly wind.*

east|wards (ēst′wərdz), *adv.* = eastward.

East-West (ēst′west′), *adj.* between the East and the West: *East-West cooperation.*

eas|y (ē′zē), *adj.,* **eas|i|er, eas|i|est,** *adv.* —*adj.* **1** not hard to do or get; obtained with or requiring little effort: *an easy victory, easy work quickly done.* **2** free from pain, discomfort, trouble, or worry: *The rich young woman has an easy life.* **SYN**: tranquil, comfortable. **3** giving comfort or rest: *The old cot is an easy bed to lie on. 'Twas a green and easy world As she took it* (Elizabeth Barrett Browning). **4** fond of comfort or rest; lazy: *the easy man who sits at his own door,—and ... feeds in the sunshine* (Wordsworth). **SYN**: indolent. **5** not strict or harsh; not hard to get on with; not severe: *a teacher who is an easy marker. Father bought the new car on easy terms of payment.* **SYN**: lenient. **6a** not hard to influence; ready to agree with, believe in, or help anyone: *He was an easy victim for every get-rich-quick scheme.* **SYN**: compliant. **b** *Figurative:* *a woman of easy virtue.* **7** smooth and pleasant; not awkward: *She has easy manners. He has an easy way of speaking to everyone.* **SYN**: relaxed. **8** not steep; gradual: *an easy slope.* **9** not tight; loose: *an easy fit. Among her easy dresses is a sheath of black silk linen in a bud pattern of bright blue, light blue, and bright green* (New Yorker). **10** slow; not fast; not hurried: *The old horse moved at an easy pace.* **SYN**: gentle, moderate. **11** (of a commodity) not much in demand; not hard to get: *The supply situation for motorists in the metropolitan area remained generally easy, but Chicago was having increasing difficulty keeping its gasoline pumps going* (New York Times). **12** (of a money market) favorable to borrowers: *Federal Reserve Board authorities and the President's top advisers now plan to allow the money market to remain easy, but not "extra" easy* (Newsweek). **13** (of aces or honors in card games) divided evenly between the competing sides.
—*adv.* **1** *Informal.* without much trouble; at a leisurely pace; easily: *Everything was going on quite easy and comfortable* (Harriet Beecher Stowe). **2** without trying hard; with little effort.
easy come, easy go, *Informal.* something easily obtained may be spent or lost just as easily: *Once again a report ... will shock taxpayers with evidence or hints that Government departments spend money on the principle of easy come, easy go* (London Times).
easy does it, *Informal.* not so fast; take your time; be careful: *"Easy does it, sister," I said, stopping her. "Take your place in line"* (S. J. Perelman).
go easy on, a to be gentle or tactful with: *Go*

Pronunciation Key: hat, āge, cãre, fär; let, ēqual, tėrm; it, īce; hot, ōpen, ôrder; oil, out; cup, pu̇t, rüle; child; long; thin; ᴛʜen; zh, measure; ə represents **a** in about, **e** in taken, **i** in pencil, **o** in lemon, **u** in circus.

easy on the new neighbor when you complain about the dog. **b** to indulge in or use in moderation: *Most dentists recommend that children go easy on candy.*
take it (or **things**) **easy**, *Informal.* to refrain from exerting or disturbing oneself: *It was wisdom to take things easy and go along comfortably* (Mark Twain).
[< Old French *aisie,* past participle of *aisier* < *aäisier* set at east < *a-* at (< Latin *ad-*) + *aise;* see etym. under **ease**]
—*Syn. adj.* **1 Easy, simple, effortless** mean requiring little effort. **Easy** implies that little work is needed: *Dinner was easy to prepare.* **Simple** means easy to do, understand, use, etc., because not complicated in any way: *I can work out simple crossword puzzles.* **Effortless** means without effort, but suggests seeming to be easy or simple because a person or thing has developed control, power, or skill, usually through practice: *Watch the effortless movements of a cat.*
eas|y-care (ē′zē kãr′), *adj.* requiring little or no work after laundering, especially no ironing: *Now, polymers are the scientific basis for the innovation of products ranging from easy-care fabrics to artificial heart, kidney and artery supplements* (William O. Baker).
easy chair, a comfortable chair, usually having arms and cushions: *But sit down, Cluet. Take that easy chair* (Edgar Maass).
eas|y|go|ing (ē′zē gō′ing), *adj.* **1** taking matters easily; not worrying: *an easygoing way of life. The new teacher is pleasantly easygoing and relaxed with the class.* **2** having an easy gait or step: *an easygoing horse.* —**eas′y|go′ing|ness**, *n.*
easy mark, *Informal.* a person who is easily imposed upon: *Fat cats and fortune builders . . . are easy marks for agitators working among backcountry villagers who lack all sense of local identity and live in swamps of bitterness or apathy* (Harper's).
easy meat, *Especially British Slang.* **1** a person easily duped or imposed upon; easy mark. **2** an easy thing to do or get: *He himself says modestly, "It's easy meat, playing for England"* (Sunday Times).
easy money, **1** money borrowed or available for loan at a low rate of interest: *. . . policies to encourage business expansion—notably, stepped-up government spending and easy money* (Time). **2** money obtained by crime or deceit: *It may be this . . . spirit that inspires the midnight burglar . . ., not merely the desire for easy money* (Gertrude Atherton).
easy rider, *U.S. Slang.* **1** a guitar: *Old blues singers applied the term easy rider to the guitar, which, because of its shoulder strap, "rode easy"* (Time). **2** a male lover. **3** a man who lives off a woman's earnings.
easy street or **Easy Street**, *Informal.* the state of being financially secure or independent: *The only way East Street seems to have changed him is to have eliminated [his] need for . . . defiant extravagances* (Time).
on easy street or **Easy Street**, in comfortable circumstances; financially secure or independent: *As the heir to a fortune, he expects to be on easy street one day.*
eat (ēt), *v.*, **ate**, **eat|en**, **eat|ing** (see usage note below), *n.* —*v.t.* **1** to chew and swallow (food): *Cows eat grass and grain.* **2** to gnaw or devour: *Termites have eaten the posts and ruined the fence.* **3** *Figurative.* to destroy as if by eating; wear away; corrode: *This acid eats metal.* SYN: consume. **4** to make by eating: *Moths ate holes in my wool coat.* **5** *Informal, Figurative.* to bother; annoy: *I wonder what's eating him.*
—*v.i.* **1** to have a meal: *Where shall we eat?* **2** *Figurative.* to make a way, as if by gnawing or corrosion: *The sea has eaten into the north shore.*
—*n.* **eats**, *U.S. Slang.* food: *They smiled and smiled, they dandled babies, they staged fiestas with free eats* (Harper's).
eat crow. See under **crow**[1].
eat one's heart out. See under **heart**.
eat one's words. See under **word**.
eat out, to eat at a restaurant; eat away from home; dine out: *Let's eat out tonight instead of cooking a meal at home.*
eat out of one's hand. See under **hand**.
eat up, **a** to eat all of: *Eat up your spinach and then you may have dessert.* **b** *Figurative: Extravagant spending ate up his savings.* **c** *Informal.* to receive eagerly or greedily: *She is eating up the course in algebra. They offered him the most absurd flattery, and he ate it up.*
[Old English *etan*] —**eat′er**, *n.*
►**eat**. Formerly the past tense form (spelled either *eat* or *ate*) was pronounced (et). This pronunciation is still common in England and in some parts of the United States, especially the South, but it is now generally regarded as substandard in America.
eat|a|ble (ē′tə bəl), *adj., n.* —*adj.* fit to eat; edible: *It is inevitably eatable, usually tasty, always well-served, and priced moderately* (Time).
—*n.* **eatables**, things fit to eat; food items; edibles: *I set the stage for the making of these innocent little eatables* (Harper's).
eat|en (ē′tən), *v.* past participle of **eat**: *Have you eaten your dinner?*
eat|er|y (ē′tər ē), *n., pl.* **-er|ies**. *Informal.* a restaurant.
eath (ēᴛʜ, ēth), *adj., adv. Scottish.* —*adj.* easy. —*adv.* easily.
[Old English *ēathe* easily] —**eath′ly**, *adv.*
eat|ing (ē′ting), *n.* **1** the act of a person or thing that eats. **2** food with reference to its taste or quality when it is being eaten: *This fish is delicious eating.*
eating disorder, any one of various psychological conditions involving abnormal eating habits, such as anorexia nervosa and bulimia.
eating house, a restaurant, especially one of an inferior sort.
Eat|on agent (ē′tən), a microorganism, a variety of mycoplasma, that is the causative agent of primary atypical pneumonia.
[< Monroe D. *Eaton,* born 1904, American bacteriologist]
eau (ō), *n., pl.* **eaux**. *French.* water.
eau bé|nite (ō′ bā nēt′), *French.* holy water.
eau de co|logne or **Eau de Co|logne** (ō′ də kə lōn′), = cologne (def. 1). [< French *eau de Cologne* (literally) water of Cologne, where it was first made]
eau de nil (ō′ də nēl′), *French.* **1** Nile green. **2** (literally) water of the Nile.
eau de vie (ō′ də vē′, ōd vē′), *French.* **1** brandy. **2** (literally) water of life.
eau d'or (ō dôr′), *French.* **1** toilet water made from the flowers of the lily of the valley. **2** (literally) water of gold.
eau forte (ō fôrt′), *French.* **1** aqua fortis; nitric acid. **2** (literally) strong water.
eau su|crée (ō′ sʏ krā′), *French.* sugared or sweetened water: *Lemonade, eau sucrée—and drinkables mild* (Richard H. Barham).
eaux (ō), *n., French.* plural of **eau**.
***eaves** (ēvz), *n.pl.* the lower edge of a roof that stands out a little from the side of a building. [Old English *efes* (singular) edge, border]
►**Eaves**, originally singular, is now understood as plural, and a new singular, *eave,* is sometimes employed.

***eaves**

eaves|drop (ēvz′drop′), *v.*, **-dropped**, **-drop|ping**, *n.* —*v.i.* to listen to talk one is not supposed to hear; listen secretly to a private conversation: *Both travel widely and eavesdrop in trains and hotels for political intelligence* (Newsweek).
—*v.t. Archaic.* to listen to secretly.
—*n.* **1** water dripping from eaves. **2** the ground directly beneath the eaves of a building. **3** an act or instance of eavesdropping: *The statute places no termination date on the eavesdrop once the conversation sought is seized* (Time).
[< earlier sense of "standing under the eaves in order to listen," Old English *yfesdrype* the dripping of rainwater from eaves]
eaves|drop|per (ēvz′drop′ər), *n.* a person who listens to talk that he is not supposed to hear.
eaves swallow, a North American swallow that often builds its nest of mud under the eaves of buildings; cliff swallow.
eave trough or **spout**, a groove or gutter running along the eaves of a house to carry away rain water.
E.B., Encyclopaedia Britannica.
é|bauche (ā bōsh′), *n. French.* a first rough form, especially of a work of art; outline; sketch.
ebb (eb), *n., v.* —*n.* **1** a flowing of the tide away from the shore; fall of the tide: *The ebb uncovered the seaweed in the rocky pools.* **2** a flowing backward or away: (*Figurative.*) *I hate to learn the ebb of time From yon dull steeple's drowsy chime* (Scott). **3** *Figurative.* a growing less or weaker; decline; decay: *His faintness came not from despair, but nature's ebb* (Byron). **4** *Figurative.* a point of decline: *He realized that his fortunes were at an ebb.*
—*v.i.* **1** to flow out; fall: *We waded farther out as the tide ebbed.* **2** *Figurative.* to grow less or weaker; decline; decay: *His courage began to ebb as he neared the haunted house.* SYN: wane, decrease.
[Old English *ebba*]
ebb and flow, **1** the flowing of tidewater and its return to the sea. **2** *Figurative.* fluctuating circumstances: *the ebb and flow of life.*
ebb|less (eb′lis), *adj.* that does not ebb: *the salty ebbless waters of the Dead Sea.*
ebb tide, the flowing of the tide away from the shore. Ebb tide occurs twice every 24 hours in most parts of the world.
eb|e|na|ceous (eb′ə nā′shəs), *adj.* of or belonging to the family of trees and shrubs typified by the ebony; diospyraceous.
[< New Latin *Ebenaceae* the family name (< Greek *ébenos* ebony)]
e|be|ne|ous (i bē′nē əs), *adj.* of or having to do with ebony; like ebony.
Eb|e|ne|zer (eb′ə nē′zər), *n.* **1** (in the Bible) the name given by the prophet Samuel to the stone he erected in recognition of God's help in defeating the Philistines (in the Bible, I Samuel 7:12). **2** any memorial in recognition of God's help. **3** a place of worship of dissenters in England. [< Hebrew *eben ha-'ezer* (literally) stone of help]
é|bé|niste (ā bā nēst′), *n. French.* a cabinetmaker.
E|bi|o|nite (ē′bē ə nīt), *n.* one of a group of Christians formed before 100 A.D., who held that Jesus was a mere man and that the Mosaic law was binding upon Christians. In the 100's, they became a distinct sect. [< Latin *ebionita* < Hebrew *ebyōn* poor (in spirit)]
E|bi|o|nit|ic (ē′bē ə nit′ik), *adj.* of or having to do with the Ebionites or their doctrines.
E|bi|o|nit|ism (ē′bē ə nit iz′əm), *n.* the doctrines or system of the Ebionites.
Eb|la|ite (eb′lə īt, ē′blə-), *n.* an ancient Semitic language, used in the 2000's B.C., whose existence was discovered in 1976 through clay-tablet inscriptions found at Ebla, a ruined city near Aleppo, northern Syria: *Eblaite . . . is related to the Biblical Hebrew that was used about one thousand years later* (Science News).
Eb|lis (eb′lis), *n.* (in the Koran) the chief of the fallen angels; the Devil. Also, **Iblis**. [< Arabic *Iblīs* < Greek *diábolos* devil]
E b N (no periods) or **E by N** (no periods), east by north.
E-boat (ē′bōt′), *n. British.* a small, speedy type of surface torpedo boat. [< *e*(nemy) *boat*]
eb|on (eb′ən), *n., adj. Archaic.* —*n.* ebony.
—*adj.* **1** made of ebony. **2** black; dark: *Heaven's ebon vault, studded with stars unutterably bright* (Shelley).
eb|on|ist (eb′ə nist), *n.* a worker or dealer in ebony or other ornamental woods.
eb|on|ite (eb′ə nīt), *n.* a hard, black substance made by heating rubber with a large quantity of sulfur; vulcanite. Ebonite is used for combs and buttons, and for electric insulation. [< *ebon*(y)]
eb|on|ize (eb′ə nīz), *v.t.*, **-ized**, **-iz|ing**. to stain or finish in imitation of ebony.
eb|on|y (eb′ə nē), *n., pl.* **-on|ies**, *adj.* —*n.* **1** a hard, black wood, used especially for the black keys of a piano, for the backs and handles of brushes, and for ornamental woodwork. **2** a tropical tree that yields this wood. **3** any one of several similar woods or trees.
—*adj.* **1** made of ebony: *an ebony cane.* **2** like ebony; black; dark.
[< Late Latin *hebeninus* < Greek *ebéninos* of ebony < *ébenos* ebony < Egyptian *h-b-ny*]
Ebor., (Archbishop) of York (Latin, *Eboracensis*).
é|boule|ment (ā bül mäɴ′), *n. French.* **1** a falling down of walls, heavy masses, or other structures or formations. **2** a landslide.
e|brac|te|ate (ē brak′tē āt), *adj. Botany.* without bracts. [< New Latin *ebracteatus* < Latin *ex-* out of + *bractea* bract]
e|brac|te|at|ed (ē brak′tē ā′tid), *adj. Botany.* ebracteate; without bracts.
e|bri|e|ty (i brī′ə tē), *n.* drunkenness; inebriation. [< Latin *ēbrietās* < *ēbrius* drunk]
e|bri|ose (ē′brē ōs), *adj.* = drunk. [< Latin *ēbriōsus* < *ēbrius*]
E b S (no periods) or **E by S** (no periods), east by south.
EBS (no periods), Emergency Broadcast System (the civil-defense broadcasting system that replaced Conelrad in 1964).
e|bul|lience (i bul′yəns), *n.* **1** overflowing, lively enthusiasm: *the ebullience of youth.* SYN: effervescence. **2** a bubbling up like a boiling liquid. SYN: effervescence.
e|bul|lien|cy (i bul′yən sē), *n.* = ebullience.
e|bul|lient (i bul′yənt), *adj.* **1** overflowing with excitement or liveliness; very enthusiastic: *A small, dapper man with a waxed mustache and an ebullient air came upstairs and greeted the Count warmly* (New Yorker). **2** boiling up; bubbling.
[< Latin *ēbulliēns, -entis,* present participle of *ēbullīre* boil up < *ex-* out + *bullīre* to boil]
—**e|bul′lient|ly**, *adv.*

e|bul|li|om|e|ter (i bul′ē om′ə tər), *n.* = ebullioscope.
e|bul|li|o|scope (i bul′ē ə skōp), *n.* an instrument for determining the boiling points of liquids or solutions. [< French *ébullioscope* < Latin *ēbullīre* to boil + Greek *skopós* an observer]
e|bul|li|o|scop|ic (i bul′ē ə skop′ik), *adj.* of or having to do with the ebullioscope or ebullioscopy.
e|bul|li|os|co|py (i bul′ē os′kə pē), *n.* the study and use of the ebullioscope.
eb|ul|lism (eb′yə liz əm), *n.* the bubbling of body fluids resulting from a sudden reduction of air pressure: *The absence of an atmosphere on the Moon brings hazards of suffocation with a time of useful consciousness limited to a few seconds due to lack of oxygen and the ebullism—boiling of body fluids—due to lack of atmospheric pressure* (Science Journal). [< Latin *ēbullīre* boil up]
eb|ul|li|tion (eb′ə lish′ən), *n.* **1** an outburst (as of feeling): *This ebullition of feeling . . . came as a real shock to Lady and Lord Valleys* (John Galsworthy). **2** a boiling or bubbling up. [< Latin *ēbullītiō, -ōnis* < *ēbullīre* boil up < *ex-* out + *bullīre* boil]
e|bur|na|tion (ē′bər nā′shən, eb′ər-), *n. Medicine.* an abnormal hardening of bone or cartilage. [< Latin *eburnus* of ivory (< *ebur* ivory) + English *-ation*]
e|bur|ne|an (i bėr′nē ən), *adj.* of or like ivory. [< Latin *eburneus* made of ivory + English *-an*]
EBV (no periods) or **EB virus**, Epstein-Barr virus.
ec-, *prefix.* the form of **ex-**[2] before consonants, as in *eccentric, eclectic, ecstasy.*
EC (no periods), **1** Eastern Caribbean: *EC$3 million.* **2** European Community: *The EC expects to be one of the largest consumers of nuclear fuel by the year 2000* (Kenneth Brown).
E.C., East Central (a postal district in London).
ECA (no periods), Economic Cooperation Administration.
ECAFE (no periods), Economic Commission for Asia and the Far East.
e|car|i|nate (ē kar′ə nāt), *adj.* without a carina or keel; not carinate: *an ecarinate bird.*
é|car|té (ā′kär tā′), *n.* a card game for two people, played with 32 cards, in which discarding is a feature. [< French *écarté*, past participle of *écarter* to discard (a feature of the game) < *é-* out (< Latin *ex-*) + Middle French *carte* card[1]]
ec|bat|ic (ek bat′ik), *adj.* expressing result or consequence and not purpose or intention: *an ecbatic clause.* [< Greek *ekbatikós* < *ekbaínein* to result < *ékbasis* a consequence]
ec|cal|e|o|bi|on (e kal′ē ə bī′ən), *n.* an apparatus for hatching eggs by artificial heat; incubator. [coined < Greek *ekkaléo bíon* I call forth life]
ec|ce (ek′sē, ek′e), *interj. Latin.* lo! behold!
ec|ce ho|mo (ek′sē hō′mō, ek′e), **1** *Latin.* "Behold the man!"—the words with which Pilate presented Christ, crowned with thorns, to the Jews. John 19:5. **2** a picture or statue of Christ crowned with thorns.
***ec|cen|tric** (ek sen′trik), *adj., n.* —*adj.* **1** out of the ordinary; not usual; peculiar; odd: *People stared at the artist's eccentric clothes.* **SYN:** irregular, queer, whimsical. **2** not having the same center: *eccentric circles.* **3** not perfectly circular; not moving in a circle but in a related line. The orbit of an eccentric planet is elliptical. *The seventh satellite, which is much fainter, revolves in an eccentric orbit, at a mean distance of about six million miles, with a period of some 200 days* (Scientific American). **4** off center; having its axis set off center: *an eccentric wheel.*
—*n.* **1** a person who behaves in an unusual manner: *The behavior of an eccentric is hard to predict. Edgar Allan Poe was an eccentric.* **2** a disk or wheel set off center so that it can change circular motion into back-and-forth motion. **3** a circle not having the same center as another that is within it or that intersects it.
[< Medieval Latin *eccentricus* < Late Latin *eccentros* < Greek *ékkentros* < *ex-* out + *kéntron* center]

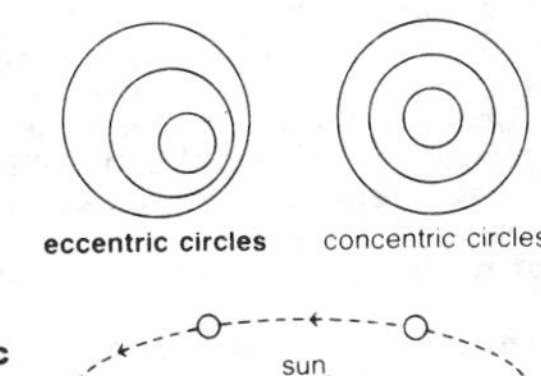
eccentric circles concentric circles

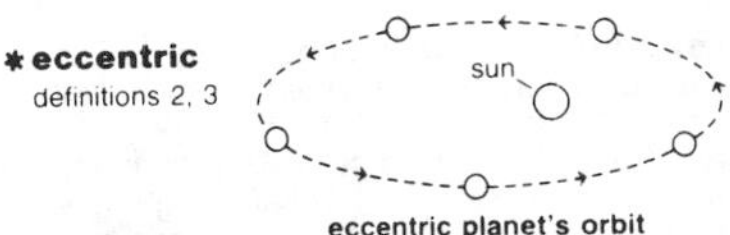

***eccentric** definitions 2, 3
eccentric planet's orbit

ec|cen|tri|cal (ek sen′trə kəl), *adj.* = eccentric.
ec|cen|tri|cal|ly (ek sen′trə klē), *adv.* in an eccentric manner or position; with eccentricity.
***ec|cen|tric|i|ty** (ek′sen tris′ə tē), *n., pl.* **-ties.** **1** something out of the ordinary; oddity; peculiarity: *One of his eccentricities was touching every lamppost he passed.* **SYN:** irregularity, whimsicality. **2** eccentric condition; being unusual or out of the ordinary: *The clock's eccentricity became noticeable when it struck three, whatever the hour.* **3** *Astronomy.* the amount of deviation of the orbit of a planet from a perfect circle: *Eccentricity is a numerical relation defining the shape of an ellipse* (Bernhard, Bennett and Rice). **4** the length of the back-and-forth stroke of an eccentric. **5** *Mathematics.* the ratio of the focal distance of any point in the curve of a conic section to the distance from the directrix.

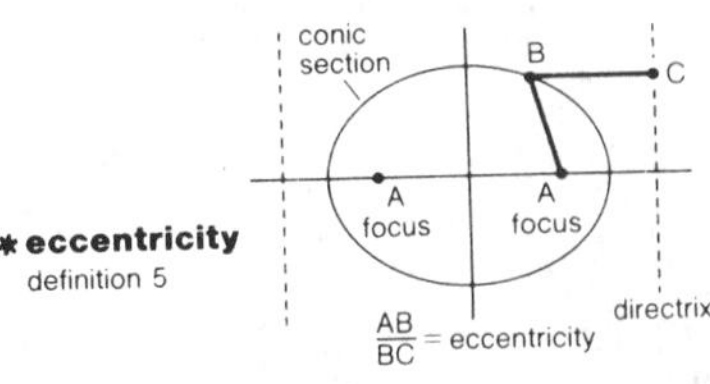

***eccentricity** definition 5

ec|ce sig|num (ek′sē sig′nəm, ek′e), *Latin.* see the proof; behold the sign.
ec|chon|dro|ma (ek′ən drō′mə), *n., pl.* **-mas, -ma|ta** (-mə tə). a tumor growing from a cartilage. [< New Latin *ecchondroma* < Greek *ex-* out + *chóndrōma* cartilage]
ec|chy|mo|ma (ek′ə mō′mə), *n., pl.* **-mas, -ma|ta** (-mə tə). a swelling caused by blood forced out of the blood vessels into the tissues under the skin, as by a bruise.
ec|chy|mosed (ek′ə mōzd), *adj.* having ecchymosis.
ec|chy|mo|sis (ek′ə mō′sis), *n.* a discoloration caused by the breaking of tiny blood vessels underneath the skin, as in a bruise. [< New Latin *ecchymosis* < Greek *ekchýmōsis* < *ekchymóesthai* pour out < *ex-* out + *chymós* juice]
eccl. or **eccles.**, ecclesiastical.
Eccl. or **Eccles.**, Ecclesiastes.
Ec|cles cake (ek′əlz), *British.* a fruit pastry similar to a Banbury tart but round. [< *Eccles*, a borough in Lancashire, England]
ec|cle|si|a (i klē′zhē ə, -zē-), *n., pl.* **-si|ae** (-zhē ē, -zē-). **1** a political assembly of the citizens of ancient Athens; ekklesia: *They met on the famous hill of the Pnyx, where the Ecclesia, the first of the great legislatures of a sovereign people, generally sat when the city was at the height of its glory* (London Times). **2** an assembly: *The exchange of letters with Stalin and Molotov in 1948 . . . led to his excommunication from the Communist ecclesia* (Time). **3** a congregation. **4** a church. [< Late Latin *ecclēsia* < Greek *ekklēsiā* church; (originally) an assembly < *ekkaleîn* call out < *ex-* out + *kaleîn* call]
ec|cle|si|al (i klē′zē əl), *adj.* of the church; ecclesiastical: *A united church with Roman Catholics and Anglicans coexisting in full ecclesial communion . . . is proposed* (London Times).
ec|cle|si|arch (i klē′zē ärk), *n.* **1** a ruler of the church. **2** a sacristan in the Greek Church. [< Greek *ekklēsiā* assembly + *-archos* ruler < *árchein* to rule]
ec|cle|si|ast (i klē′zē ast), *n.* a member of the ancient Athenian ecclesia.
the Ecclesiast, the Preacher (a title of the author of the book of Ecclesiastes).
[< Greek *ekklēsiastês;* see etym. under **Ecclesiastes**]
Ec|cle|si|as|tes (i klē′zē as′tēz), *n.* a book of the Old Testament, supposed to have been written by Solomon. *Abbr:* Eccl. or Eccles. [< Latin *Ecclēsiastes* < Greek *ekklēsiastês* preacher; member of the assembly < *ekklēsiā* church; see etym. under **ecclesia**]
ec|cle|si|as|tic (i klē′zē as′tik), *n., adj.* —*n.* a clergyman, or person in orders; a churchman as distinguished from a layman.
—*adj.* = ecclesiastical.
[< Late Latin *ecclēsiasticus* < Greek *ekklēsiastikós* < *ekklēsiastês;* see etym. under **Ecclesiastes**]
ec|cle|si|as|ti|cal (i klē′zē as′tə kəl), *adj.* of or having to do with the church or the clergy; churchly; clerical; not lay: *ecclesiastical courts.* —**ec|cle′si|as′ti|cal|ly**, *adv.*
ecclesiastical calendar, a calendar used by Christian churches to designate the days set apart for particular religious celebrations, as the days dedicated to canonized saints, feasts, vigils, and the like.
ecclesiastical law, **1** the law of the church as administered in the ecclesiastical courts. **2** the body of law relating to religion or religious institutions as administered in the civil courts.
ec|cle|si|as|ti|cism (i klē′zē as′tə siz əm), *n.* **1** ecclesiastical principles, practices, or spirit. **2** devotion to the principles or interests of the church; devotion to the extension of the influence of the church in its external relations.
Ec|cle|si|as|ti|cus (i klē′zē as′tə kəs), *n.* a book of proverbs included in the Douay Version of the Bible and in the Apocrypha. Also called "The Wisdom of Jesus, the Son of Sirach." *Abbr:* Ecclus.
ec|cle|si|ol|a|try (i klē′zē ol′ə trē), *n.* worship of the church; excessive reverence for churchly forms and traditions. [< Greek *ekklēsiā* church + English *-latry*]
ec|cle|si|o|log|i|cal (i klē′zē ə loj′ə kəl), *adj.* of or having to do with ecclesiology. —**ec|cle′si|o|log′i|cal|ly**, *adv.*
ec|cle|si|ol|o|gist (i klē′zē ol′ə jist), *n.* a student of or expert in ecclesiology.
ec|cle|si|ol|o|gy (i klē′zē ol′ə jē), *n.* **1** the study of the church as an organized society. **2** the science of church architecture and decoration. [< Greek *ekklēsiā* church + English *-logy*]
ec|cle|si|o|phile (i klē′zē ə fīl), *n.* a lover of church or religion: *For that reason, "Memories and Meanings" is a book of especial interest not merely to ecclesiophiles, but far more widely to all who find life's significance in the quest for truth* (Joseph McCulloch). [< Greek *ekklēsiā* church + English *-phile*]
Ecclus., Ecclesiasticus (a book of the Apocrypha).
ec|co (ek′kō), *interj. Italian.* behold! lo!
ec|crine (ek′rīn, -rin), *adj.* **1** of or having to do with certain sweat glands secreting a substance without a breakdown of its own cells: *The glands that actually produce sweat are of two general kinds: the apocrine glands, which are usually associated with hair follicles, and the eccrine glands, which are not* (Scientific American). **2** = exocrine. [< *ec-* + Greek *krīnein* to separate]
ec|cri|nol|o|gy (ek′rə nol′ə jē), *n.* the branch of physiology dealing with the bodily excretions and secretions.
ec|cri|sis (ek′rə sis), *n.* **1** the explulsion or excretion of any waste products or products of disease. **2** the excreted products themselves. [< New Latin *eccrisis* < Greek *ékkrisis* < *ekkrinein* secrete]
ec|crit|ic (e krit′ik), *adj., n.* —*adj.* that promotes excretion. —*n.* an eccritic medicine or drug.
ec|dem|ic (ek dem′ik), *adj.* occurring away from the place where it is endemic: *an ecdemic disease.* [< Greek *ex-* out + English *-demic;* patterned on *endemic*]
ec|dys|i|ast (ek diz′ē ast), *n.* a stripteaser. [American English (coined by H. L. Mencken) < Greek *ékdysis;* see etym. under **ecdysis**]
ec|dy|sis (ek′də sis), *n., pl.* **-ses** (-sēz). the shedding of the skin or shell by snakes, crustaceans, or insects or of feathers by a bird. [< New Latin *ecdysis* < Greek *ékdysis* a stripping, putting off < *ekdýein* < *ex-* off + *dýein* get into]
ec|dy|sone (ek′də sōn), *n.* a hormone produced in the prothoracic glands of insects that promotes growth and molting. [< *ecdys*(is) + (horm)*one*]
ECE (no periods) or **E.C.E.**, Economic Commission for Europe.
e|ce|sis (i sē′sis), *n.* the adaptation of a foreign plant to a new habitat. [< New Latin *ecesis* < Greek *oíkesis* a dwelling]
ECG (no periods), electrocardiogram.
é|chau|guette (ā shō get′), *n. French.* a small, overhanging turret on a wall; bartizan.
e|chelle (ā shel′), *n.* **1** *Physics.* a diffraction grating with relatively few lines or grooves, having a very high resolution over a narrow band of wavelengths. **2** a lacing of ribbons on the front of a stomacher. [< French *échelle* ladder; see etym. under **echelon**]
ech|e|lon (esh′ə lon), *n., adj., v.* —*n.* **1** the arrangement of troops, ships, planes, tanks, and other mechanized equipment, or artillery in a steplike formation. **2** *Figurative.* a level of command or authority. A unit of an army such as a company, battalion, division, or corps, is called an echelon. **3** a unit performing a special task or stationed in a certain position: *a maintenance echelon, a support echelon.*
—*adj.* **1** of or having to do with an echelon. **2** in the form of an echelon.
—*v.t., v.i.* to form into a steplike arrangement: *The army was echeloned along the road.*
[< French *échelon* round of a ladder < Old French *échelle* ladder < Late Latin *scāla* stair, slope]

Pronunciation Key: hat, āge, cãre, fär; let, ēqual, tėrm; it, īce; hot, ōpen, ôrder; oil, out; cup, pu̇t, rüle; child; long; thin; ᵺen; zh, measure; ə represents a in about, e in taken, i in pencil, o in lemon, u in circus.

echelon lens, a compound lens consisting of a series of concentric annular lenses arranged around a central lens.

ech|e|ve|ri|a (ek′ə vir′ē ə, ech′-), *n.* any one of a group of low-growing, tropical American plants of the orpine family. Some species are cultivated for use in bouquets and other decorations. [< New Latin *Echeveria* the genus name < Atanasio *Echeverria,* a Mexican botanical illustrator of the 1800's]

***e|chid|na** (i kid′nə), *n., pl.* **-nas, -nae** (-nē). a small, egg-laying, ant-eating mammal of Australia, Tasmania, and New Guinea, with a long, slender snout, no teeth, and a covering of spines; spiny anteater; porcupine anteater. [< Latin *echidna* < Greek *échidna* viper < *échis* viper]

***echidna**

E|chid|na (i kid′nə), *n. Greek Mythology.* a female monster, mother of Cerberus, the Chimera, and the Sphinx.

ech|i|nate (ek′ə nāt), *adj.* covered with spines; spiny; bristly. [< Latin *echinātus* < *echīnus* hedgehog < Greek *echînos*]

ech|i|nat|ed (ek′ə nā′tid), *adj.* = echinate.

e|chi|ni (i kī′nī), *n.* plural of **echinus**.

ech|i|nite (ek′ə nīt, i kī′-), *n.* a fossil sea urchin. [< Latin *echīnus* (see etym. under **echinus**) + English *-ite*[1]]

e|chi|no|coc|co|sis (i kī′nə kok′ə sis), *n.* a disease caused by the infestation of tissues and organs with the larvae of hydatid tapeworms. [< New Latin *Echinococcus* the genus name of the tapeworms + *-osis*]

***e|chi|no|derm** (i kī′nə dėrm, ek′ə-), *n.* any one of a group of small sea animals including starfish and sea urchins. An echinoderm has a spiny, stony shell and a body whose parts are arranged like the spokes of a wheel. [< New Latin *Echinodermata* the phylum name < Greek *echînos* sea urchin, (originally) hedgehog + *dérma, -atos* skin]

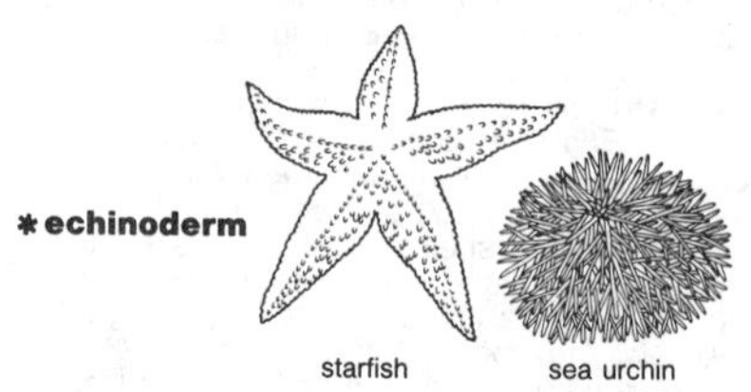

***echinoderm**

e|chi|no|der|mal (i kī′nə dėr′məl, ek′ə-), *adj.* = echinodermatous.

E|chi|no|der|ma|ta (i kī′nə dėr′mə tə), *n.pl.* the phylum of invertebrates comprising the echinoderms. [< New Latin]

e|chi|no|der|ma|tous (i kī′nə dėr′mə təs, ek′ə-), *adj.* **1** having a skin consisting of small, slender, bony, sharp-pointed pieces. **2** of or having to do with the echinoderms.

e|chi|noid (i kī′noid, ek′ə-), *adj., n.* **—adj. 1** like a sea urchin. **2** belonging to the class of sea urchins.
—n. = sea urchin.

e|chi|nu|late (i kī′nyə lit), *adj.* having or covered with small prickles; echinate: *echinulate spores.* **—e|chi′nu|late|ly,** *adv.*

e|chi|nus (i kī′nəs), *n., pl.* **-ni. 1** = sea urchin. **2** a rounded molding at the top of a Doric column. See picture under **Doric.** [< Latin *echīnus* < Greek *echînos* sea urchin]

ech|i|um (ek′ē əm), *n.* any plant of a group of herbs or shrubs of the borage family, cultivated for their showy, white, blue, or purple flowers; blueweed.
[< New Latin *Echium* the genus name < Greek *échion* name of a plant < *échis* viper]

ech|i|u|rid (ek′ē yůr′id), *adj., n.* = echiuroid.

ech|i|u|roid (ek′ē yůr′oid), *adj., n.* **—adj.** of or belonging to a group of marine worms related to the sipunculids.
—n. an echiuroid worm.
[< New Latin *Echiuroidea* the phylum name < Greek *échis* viper + *ourá* tail]

ech|o (ek′ō), *n., pl.* **ech|oes,** *v.,* **ech|oed, ech|o|ing. —n. 1** a sounding again; a repeating of a sound; sound heard after it is reflected from some object. You hear an echo if you shout and the sound is sent back by a cliff or hill or the walls of a large, empty room and heard again as if from a distance. *Blow, bugle, blow, set the wild echoes flying, And answer echoes, answer, dying, dying, dying* (Tennyson). **SYN:** reverberation. **2** *Figurative.* a person who repeats the words or imitates the feelings, acts, ideas, or style of another: *Better be a nettle in the side of your friend than his echo* (Emerson). **3** *Figurative.* a repeating the words or imitating the feelings, acts, ideas, or style of another: *His folly and his wisdom ... are all of his own growth, not the echo ... of other men* (Jonathan Swift). **4** *Figurative.* a sympathetic response: *Patriotic sentiments evoke an echo in every breast.* **5** a radio or sound wave which has been reflected. The detection of radio or sound wave reflections is the basis of radar and sonar: *... the familiar processes of radar to explore space around us by sending out powerful signals and looking carefully at the echoes when they come back* (A. J. Higgs). **6** *Music.* **a** a very soft repetition of a phrase. **b** a stop of an organ for producing soft or echolike tones. **7** a card-player's response to a signal from his partner or by a signal to his partner's lead.
—*v.i.* 1 to be heard again; sound again; be repeated in sound: *The gunshot echoed through the valley. Larks and nightingales make the sky echo with sound* (William Butler Yeats). **2** *Figurative.* to repeat or imitate the words, feelings, acts, ideas, or style of another: *I would repeat a stanza and he would softly echo.* **3** to give out a loud sound: *Drums and trumpets echo loudly* (Longfellow).
—*v.t.* 1 to sound again; repeat in sound: *The mountains echoed the yodeler's call.* **2** *Figurative.* to say or do always what another says or does: *That girl is always echoing what her mother says.*
[< Latin *ēchō* < Greek *ēchṓ*] **—ech′o|er,** *n.*

Ech|o (ek′ō), *n.* **1** *Greek Legend.* a nymph who pined away with love for Narcissus until only her voice was left. **2** echo personified. **3** *U.S.* a code name for the letter *e,* used in transmitting radio messages.

ech|o|car|di|og|ra|phy (ek′ō kär′dē og′rə fē), *n.* the use of ultrasonic apparatus for diagnosing cardiac tumors and diseased valves by analyzing the sound waves reflected from parts of the heart: *The principle underlying the technique is the graphic recording of high frequency sound waves as they bounce back to the recorder after striking an unusual structure within or outside the heart. This technique is also known as echocardiography* (Johnson McGuire and Arnold Iglauer).

echo chamber, a room designed to create echoes and other sound effects, especially for radio and phonograph records.

ech|o|en|ceph|a|log|ra|phy (ek′ō en sef′ə log′rə fē), *n.* the use of ultrasonic apparatus for diagnosing cerebral tumors and lesions by analyzing the sound waves reflected from parts of the brain: *Echoencephalography got its start in 1954 when Lars Leksell, a Swedish neurosurgeon, reported the use of pulsed ultrasound to reveal lateral shifts in certain structures which normally lie in the medial plane of the brain* (Science News).

ech|o|ey (ek′ō ē), *adj.* **1** of or like an echo; echoic: *The Brazilian pianist ... leads ... into a mad, echoey jumble such as that heard during the Schumann Toccata* (New York Times). **2** given to echoing: *It's very echoey, symmetrical, and penal looking* (Listener).

ech|o|gram (ek′ō gram), *n.* a chart or diagram drawn by an echograph: *Our echograms, drawn by an ultrasonic depth recorder, had delineated with unprecedented detail the profile of the bottom for 17,000 miles of our course* (Scientific American).

ech|o|graph (ek′ō graf, -gräf), *n.* a machine that emits sound waves and records them when they echo back after hitting an object. It is used to detect fish, chart ocean floors, and the like. [< *echo* + *-graph*]

e|cho|ic (e kō′ik), *adj.* **1** like an echo. **2** imitating a sound; onomatopoetic: *"Buzz," "caw," and "moo" are echoic words.*

ech|o|ing|ly (ek′ō ing lē), *adv.* so as to echo or reverberate sounds.

ech|o|ism (ek′ō iz əm), *n.* = onomatopoeia.

ech|o|la|li|a (ek′ə lā′lē ə), *n. Psychology.* the meaningless repetition of words. It is common in the speech of very young children and sometimes associated with mental disorder. [< *echo* + Greek *laliá* chatter]

ech|o|less (ek′ō lis), *adj.* **1** without any echo; acoustically good. **2** soundproof.

ech|o|lo|cate (ek′ō lō′kāt), *v.t.,* **-cat|ed, -cat|ing.** to locate distance and direction by means of echoes.

ech|o|lo|ca|tion (ek′ō lō kā′shən), *n.* **1** *Electronics.* a method of finding the range and direction of objects by measuring the time it takes sound or radio waves echoed from the objects to reflect back, used in radar and sonar. **2** a radarlike system or mechanism of orientation in the sensory organs of certain mammals, such as bats or whales, by which they translate their own echoes into directional signals that permit them to avoid all obstacles in their path: *However, another theory about moth behaviour, in which sound acts as an aid to navigation, suggests that they use a system of echolocation analogous with that of bats* (P. T. Haskell).

echo organ, a set of pipes in an organ, enclosed in a wooden box to give a distant sound effect.

ech|o|prax|i|a (ek′ə prak′sē ə), *n. Psychology.* the compulsive repetition of the actions of other people. [< *echo* + Greek *prâxis* a doing, acting]

echo ranging, a method of finding the range and direction of objects submerged under water by transmitting sound under water at supersonic frequencies, timing its speed, and measuring the direction of its echo.

echo sounder, an instrument that determines the depth of a body of water (notably the ocean's depth) by measuring the time it takes sound waves echoed from the water floor to reach the surface.

echo sounding, the technique of measuring the depth of a body of water by means of an echo sounder: *Echo sounding involves the use of sound waves emitted underwater from the hull of a vessel which travel to the bottom of the ocean and are reflected back* (Science News Letter).

ech|o|vi|rus (ek′ō vī′rəs), *n.,* or **ECHO virus**, a type of virus associated with various kinds of meningitis, intestinal diseases, and respiratory illnesses in human beings: *Polioviruses, reoviruses, echoviruses and infectious hepatitis virus still circulate widely* (New Scientist). [< *e*(nteric) *c*(ytopathogenic) *h*(uman) *o*(rphan) + *virus;* called "orphan" because when discovered it was not known to cause or be linked with specific diseases]

echt (eʜt), *adj., adv. German.* genuine: *To the echt Harvard man of yore, a gentleman should schedule no course before 11:00 A.M. or in a classroom above the second floor* (Harper's).

ECLA (no periods), Economic Commission for Latin America.

é|clair (ā klãr′), *n.* an oblong piece of pastry filled with whipped cream or custard and covered with icing. [< French *éclair* (literally) lightning < Old French *esclairer* to lighten < Latin *exclārāre* < *ex-* out + *clārus* clear]

é|clair|cisse|ment (ā kler sēs mäɴ′), *n. French.* a clearing up of something obscure; explanation.

ec|lamp|si|a (ek lamp′sē ə), *n.* a form of convulsions, usually recurrent, occurring especially during pregnancy or childbirth. [< New Latin *eclampsia* < Greek *éklampsis* a sudden development < *eklámpein* flash forth < *ex-* out + *lámpein* to shine]

ec|lamp|tic (ek lamp′tik), *adj.* having to do with or like eclampsia.

é|clat (ā klä′), *n.* **1** brilliant success: *That short potential stir that each can make but once, ... is the éclat of death* (Emily Dickinson). *We get on with great éclat* (Byron). **2** fame; glory; renown: *Yet the éclat it gave was enough to turn the head of a man less presumptuous* (W. H. Prescott). **3** a burst of applause or approval: *Her debut at the Metropolitan was hailed with great éclat.* [< Middle French *éclat* < *éclater,* Old French *esclater* < Latin *ex-* + a Frankish word]

ec|lec|tic (ek lek′tik), *adj., n.* **—adj. 1** selecting and using what seems best from various sources, systems, or schools of thought: *I shall be eclectic, going through the lists, since I cannot possibly evaluate more than a thousand recordings* (Atlantic). **2** made up of selections from various sources: *An anthology is an eclectic book.* **3** broad in acceptance of ideas or approval from other sources.
—n. a follower of an eclectic method.
[< Greek *eklektikós* < *eklégein* to select < *ex-* out + *légein* choose, pick] **—ec|lec′ti|cal|ly,** *adv.*

ec|lec|ti|cism (ek lek′tə siz əm), *n.* **1** the use or advocacy of an eclectic method: *He praises the romantic Gothic of the early nineteenth century and loves the showy grandeur of Stanford White's eclecticism at the end* (Harper's). **2** an eclectic system of philosophy, medicine, or other study.

eclectic medicine, a former medical system and practice in the United States that made much use of botanical remedies in the treatment of disease.

eclectic physician, a practitioner of eclectic medicine.

e|clip|sa|re|on (ē′klip sãr′ē on), *n.* a globe formerly used to illustrate the phenomena of solar and lunar eclipses.

***e|clipse** (i klips′), *n., v.,* **e|clipsed, e|clips|ing.**
—n. 1 a passing from sight because light is cut off. In an eclipse of the sun, the moon is between us and the sun, so that from any point within the moon's shadow the sun is not visible. An eclipse of the moon occurs when the moon enters the earth's shadow. **2** *Figurative.* a loss of

importance or reputation; a falling into obscurity: *The former champion has suffered an eclipse. The big upsurge of African nationalism has today stimulated deeper interest in the Africans . . . as the colonial era goes into eclipse* (Wall Street Journal). *Marxism is in relative eclipse. An era in its history has ended* (Edmund Wilson).
–*v.t.* **1** to cut off or dim the light from; darken: *As the moon eclipsed the sun the sky grew darker.* **2** *Figurative.* to cast into the shade; obscure the importance or reputation of; make less outstanding by comparison; surpass: *In sports he eclipsed his older brother. Napoleon eclipsed other generals of his time.* **SYN:** outshine, excel.
[< Old French *esclipse,* learned borrowing from Latin *eclīpsis* < Greek *ékleipsis* < *ex-* out + *leípein* to leave]

***eclipse**
definition 1

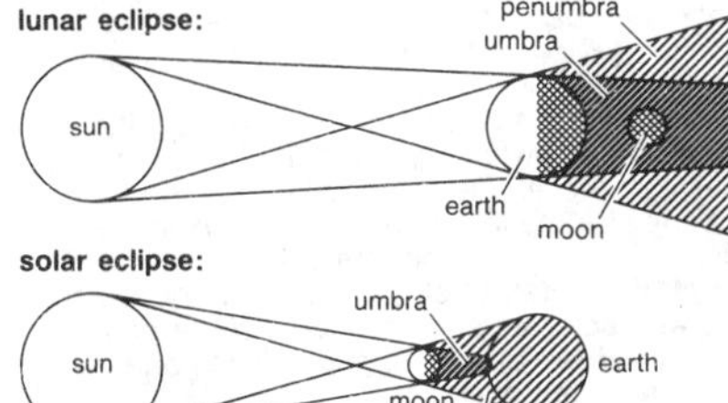

eclipse blindness, a form of temporary blindness from an injury of the retina by solar or nuclear radiation. Eclipse blindness most often happens to people who watch eclipses of the sun without protecting their eyes.
eclipse plumage, a dull or colorless plumage with which certain birds, such as male ducks, become covered at the close of the breeding season.
e|clips|er (ə klip′sər), *n.* **1** a person or thing that eclipses. **2** a mechanical device for automatically interrupting a beam of light, such as from a lighthouse or beacon.
e|clips|ing binary (i klip′sing), a variable star whose changes in brightness are due to apparent eclipse by its companion star in a binary system, which occurs when the plane of the orbit of the binary system almost coincides with the line of sight of the observer on earth.
e|clip|sis (i klip′sis), *n.* an omission of words or sounds needed to express something meaningfully. [< Greek *ékleipsis;* see etym. under **eclipse**]
e|clip|tic** (i klip′tik), *n., adj.* **–*n. **1** the path that the sun appears to travel in one year. It is that great circle of the celestial sphere which is cut by the plane containing the orbit of the earth. **2** the great circle on the terrestrial sphere which at any given moment lies in the plane of the celestial ecliptic.
–*adj.* **1** of the ecliptic. **2** having to do with an eclipse.
[< Latin *eclīpticus* < Greek *ekleiptikós* having to do with an *ékleipsis* eclipse]

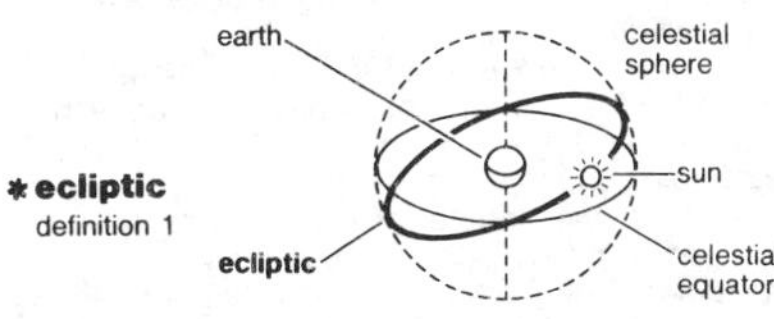

***ecliptic**
definition 1

e|clip|ti|cal (i klip′tə kəl), *adj.* = ecliptic.
ec|lo|gite (ek′lə jīt), *n.* a metamorphic rock consisting of green pyroxene, granular red garnet, and other minerals. [< Greek *eklogḗ* a selection + English *-ite*[1]]
ec|logue (ek′lôg, -log), *n.* a short poem about country life, often written as a dialogue between shepherds; idyllic poem: *For me, in those days, life was an eclogue interspersed with lyrics* (Harper's). **SYN:** pastoral, bucolic. [< Latin *ecloga* < Greek *eklogḗ* a selection < *eklégein;* see etym. under **eclectic**]
e|clo|sion (i klō′zhən), *n.* **1** emergence from concealment. **2** *Zoology.* the emerging of an insect from the pupa case. [< French *éclosion* < *éclore* hatch < *é-* from (< Latin *ex-*) + *clore* shut < Latin *claudere*]
ECM (no periods), **1** European Common Market. **2** electronic countermeasure.
ec|mne|sia (ek nē′zhə), *n.* a partial amnesia in which memory of recent events only is lost. [< New Latin *ecmnesia* < Greek *ex-* out + *mnē̂sis* memory]
eco-, *prefix.* of the environment or ecology; ecological, as in *ecosphere, ecosystem, ecocide.* [abstracted < *ecology*]

e|co-ac|tiv|ist (ē′kō ak′tə vist, ek′ō-), *n.* a person who is very active in matters dealing with the protection of the environment from pollution.
e|co-ac|tiv|i|ty (ē′kō ak tiv′ə tē, ek′ō-), *n., pl.* **-ties.** any project or undertaking to combat pollution or improve the quality of the environment.
e|co|ca|tas|tro|phe (ē′kə kə tas′trə fē, ek′ə-), *n.* a large-scale or world-wide disaster resulting from uncontrolled use of pollutants.
e|co|cid|al (ē′kə sī′dəl, ek′ə-), *adj.* having to do with or causing ecocide.
e|co|cide (ē′kə sīd, ek′ə-), *n.* the destruction of the earth's environment or ecology through the uncontrolled use of pollutants: *Ecocide—the murder of the environment—is everybody's business* (Herbert Kondo). [< *eco-* + *-cide* killing]
e|co|fact (ē′kō fakt′, ek′ō-), *n.* a natural object, such as a bone or grain, found together with artifacts at an archaeological site: *The evaluation of ecofacts reveals such information as what food people ate and whether they grew crops or gathered wild plants* (Barbara Voorhies). [< *eco-* + (arti)*fact*]
e|co|fal|low (ē′kə fal′ō, ek′ə-), *n.* a system that com-
bines crop rotation and reduced tillage to control the growth of weeds and conserve soil moisture.
e|co|freak (ē′kō frēk′, ek′ō-), *n. Slang.* an ardent conservationist or environmentalist (often used in an unfriendly way).
ecol., **1** ecological. **2** ecology.
é|cole (ā kôl′), *n. French.* school.
é|cole nor|male (ā kôl′ nôr mȧl′), *French.* a normal school.
é|cole po|ly|tech|nique (ā kôl′ pô lē tek nēk′), *French.* a technical school.
E. co|li (ē′ kō′lī), a common rod-shaped bacterium of the intestinal tract, strains of which have been grown in large amounts and used extensively in experiments dealing with protein synthesis, genetic transmission, immunity, and enzymology. [< *E*(scherichia) *coli,* the species name of the bacillus]
ec|o|log|ic (ek′ə loj′ik, ē′kə-), *adj.* = ecological.
ec|o|log|i|cal (ek′ə loj′ə kəl, ē′kə-), *adj.* of or having to do with ecology. **–ec′o|log′i|cal|ly,** *adv.*
ecological art, the art of making or sculpturing earthworks.
ecological succession, a change in the ecology that occurs very slowly when new types of systems in nature gradually replace old ones.
e|col|o|gist (ē kol′ə jist), *n.* a person who studies ecology.
e|col|o|gy (ē kol′ə jē), *n., pl.* **-gies. 1** the branch of biology that deals with the relation of living things to their environment and to each other; bionomics: *Ecology . . . is likewise a composite of the fundamental biological sciences* (A. Franklin Shull). **2** the branch of sociology that deals with the relations between human beings and their environment: *Ecology, or the patterns of culture whereby a people adjust to their environment, undoubtedly plays a large role in the initiation of political systems and in some aspects of their further development* (Beals and Hoijer). **3a** the balanced or harmonious relationship of living things to their environment: *Spurred by mounting public alarm over smog-choked cities and a generally threatened ecology. . .* (Time). **b** *Figurative: The introduction of a comprehensive computerized data base into a large company could well upset the 'ecology' of the firm to such an extent that it could take ages to reestablish a stable balance* (Science Journal). [< Greek *oîkos* dwelling, habitation, house + English *-logy*]
econ., **1** economic. **2** economics. **3** economy.
e|con|o|met|ric (i kon′ə met′rik, ek′ə nə-), *adj.* of or having to do with econometrics: *econometric analysis of the quantitative impact of fiscal policy* (Atlantic). **–e|con′o|met′ri|cal|ly,** *adv.*
e|con|o|me|tri|cian (i kon′ə mə trish′ən), *n.* a specialist in econometrics.
e|con|o|met|rics (i kon′ə met′riks, ek′ə nə-), *n.* a branch of economics that treats economic relationships mathematically by using statistical methods and measurements. [< *econom*(y) + *-metrics*]
e|co|nom|ic (ē′kə nom′ik, ek′ə-), *adj.* **1** of or having to do with economics. Economic problems have to do with the production, distribution, and consumption of goods and services. *Great economic and social forces flow with a tidal sweep* (John Morley). **2** having to do with the management of the income, supplies, and expenses of a household, community, government, or other group or organization: *The city treasurer deals with the economic problems of city government.* **3** having to do with the material welfare of a community or nation; practical or utilitarian in application or use: *economic botany, economic geology.* **4** economical; saving; thrifty. [< Latin *oeconomicus* < Greek *oikonomikós* < *oikonómos;* see etym. under **economy**]
e|co|nom|i|cal (ē′kə nom′ə kəl, ek′ə-), *adj.* **1** avoiding waste; thrifty; saving: *A good manager is economical in the use of his funds. The goal is to find economical ways of chemically treating water from the Columbia River so that it can be used to cool Hanford reactors operating at higher power than at present* (Science). **2** having to do with economics; economic. **3** *Archaic.* having to do with a household or its management.
–*Syn.* **1 Economical, frugal, thrifty** mean saving. **Economical** implies avoiding waste of money, time, work, or any other resources by careful planning and making the best and fullest possible use of what is spent: *He does more than others because he is economical of time and energy.* **Frugal** emphasizes saving by living simply and needing or using little: *The frugal widow bought and used food carefully.* **Thrifty** implies avoiding waste by planning well, spending carefully, and working hard: *Successful farmers are usually thrifty.*
e|co|nom|i|cal|ly (ē′kə nom′ə klē, ek′ə-), *adv.* **1** in an economical manner: *Try to live more economically.* **2** from the point of view of economics: *Economically, a large deficit does not always spell ruin.*
economic geography, a branch of geography that deals with the relation between physical and economic conditions and the development, production, and distribution of material goods.
economic good, *Economics.* any product or service that is relatively scarce and can be obtained only through money or effort.
economic rent, *Economics.* the theoretical difference between the yield from a good piece of land and the yield that could have been obtained with the same expenditure from the same amount of marginal land.
e|co|nom|ics (ē′kə nom′iks, ek′ə-), *n.* **1** *sing. in use.* the science of how people produce goods and services, how they distribute them among themselves, and how they use them; political economy. Economics deals with the material welfare of mankind and such problems as those of capital, labor, wages, prices, tariffs, and taxes. **2** *pl. in use.* the economic part; details of economy or management: *If the Concorde meets its promised performance specifications, the economics look quite good* (Wall Street Journal).
economic strike, a strike that results from disagreements over wages, hours, or working conditions.
economic zone, the area of coastal waters to whose fishing and mining resources a country claims exclusive rights: *The United Nations-sponsored confederation on the law of the sea . . . will favor 200 miles as the norm for "economic zones" controlled by coastal States* (Manchester Guardian Weekly).
e|con|o|mise (i kon′ə mīz), *v.t., v.i.,* **-mised, -mising.** *British.* economize. **–e|con′o|mis′er,** *n.*
e|con|o|mism (i kon′ə miz əm), *n.* great or undue emphasis on economics or economic theories: *It had subordinated every aspect of the national life to what [he] called economism . . . to the theory that man's chief end is merely to produce, distribute, consume, break records and grow rich* (Maclean's).
e|con|o|mist (i kon′ə mist), *n.* **1** an expert in economics: *In recent years, few groups have grown so fast or become so powerful as the professional economists* (Newsweek). **2** a person who is economical.
e|con|o|mi|za|tion (i kon′ə mə zā′shən), *n.* **1** the act or practice of economizing. **2** the result of economizing.
e|con|o|mize (i kon′ə mīz), *v.,* **-mized, -miz|ing.**
–*v.t.* to use little of; use to the best advantage: *If you can economize your time, you will get more done in less time.*
–*v.i.* to cut down expenses; avoid waste or extravagance: *We must economize or we will go into debt. The development they want in one direction is conditional on their economizing in another direction* (Maclean's).
e|con|o|miz|er (i kon′ə mī′zər), *n.* a person or thing that economizes.
e|con|o|my (i kon′ə mē), *n., pl.* **-mies,** *adj.* **–*n.*** **1** a making the most of what one has; avoiding waste in the use of anything; thrift: *By using economy in buying food and clothes, we were soon able to save enough money for the new car we needed.* **2** an instance of this: *The economy of going without a vacation bought new furniture for the house.* **3** a managing of affairs and resources so as to avoid waste; management: *Under President Franklin Roosevelt's administration,*

the country's economy improved greatly. SYN: husbandry. **4** the efficient arrangement of parts; organization; system. **5** a system of managing the production, distribution, and consumption of goods and services: *feudal economy. A creative economy is the fuel of magnificence* (Emerson). **6** *Theology.* the method of the divine administration of the world, especially as it affects a particular nation or time; dispensation: *The economy of Heaven is dark, and wisest clerks have missed the mark* (Charles Lamb). —*adj.* **1** less expensive than others of its kind; economical: *an economy car.* **2** of or having to do with economy class: *economy flights, economy fare.* **3** = economy-size. [< Latin *oeconomia* < Greek *oikonomiā* < *oikonómos* one who manages a house < *oîkos* house + *némein* manage, arrange]

economy class, a class of accommodations on airplanes and, sometimes, buses, trains, or ships, that is less expensive than first class and is usually the least expensive class; tourist class.

e|con|o|my-size (i kon′ə mē sīz′), *adj.* (of a packaged product) larger in size and offered as costing proportionately less than the standard-sized package: *You save when you buy a large, economy-size package* (Maclean's).

é|cor|ché (ā kôr shā′), *n. French.* **1** a subject so treated in painting or sculpture as to expose the muscular system. **2** (literally) skinned.

e|cor|ti|cate (ē kôr′tə kāt), *adj.* (of lichens, etc.) without a cortical layer.

e|co-safe (ē′kō sāf′), *adj.,* **-saf|er, -saf|est.** ecologically safe; not likely to damage the environment: *Eco-safe products for the home—biodegradable garbage bags, toilet paper and dishwashing soap, dioxin-free baby wipes and water-conservation kits* (Rolling Stone).

ECOSOC (no periods), (United Nations) Economic and Social Council.

e|co|spe|cies (ē′kə spē′shēz, ek′ə-), *n. sing. and pl. Biology.* a group of organisms only somewhat fertile with organisms of related groups, usually considered equivalent to a species.

e|co|spe|cif|ic (ē′kə spi sif′ik, ek′ə-), *adj.* of or having to do with an ecospecies. —**e′co|spe|cif′i|cal|ly,** *adv.*

e|co|sphere (ē′kə sfir, ek′ə-), *n.* any region suitable for life; biosphere. [< *eco-* + *sphere*]

e|cos|tate (ē kos′tāt), *adj. Biology.* not costate; without ribs.

e|co|sys|tem (ē′kə sis′təm, ek′ə-), *n.* a system made up of a group of living organisms and its physical environment, and the relationship between them. A pond, a lake, a forest, or an ocean may be an ecosystem. An ecosystem includes food supply, weather, and natural enemies.

e|co|te|lem|e|try (ē′kō tə lem′ə trē, ek′ō-), *n.* = biotelemetry.

e|co|ton|al (ē′kə tō′nəl, ek′ə-), *adj.* of or having to do with an ecotone.

e|co|tone (ē′kə tōn, ek′ə-), *n.* a region between two neighboring but unlike plant communities.

e|co|to|pi|an or **E|co|to|pi|an** (ē′kə tō′pē ən), *adj., n. Informal.* —*adj.* of or having to do with an ecologically ideal society. —*n.* a person who adopts an ecotopian way of life.

e|co|type (ē′kə tīp, ek′ə-), *n.* a group that is part of an ecospecies, usually considered as equivalent to a subspecies.

e|co|typ|ic (ē′kə tip′ik, ek′ə-), *adj.* of or having to do with an ecotype.

e|co|typ|i|cal|ly (ē′kə tip′ə klē, ek′ə-), *adv.* in an ecotypic way.

ec|phore (ek′fôr, -fōr), *v.t.,* **-phored, -phor|ing.** to evoke or revive (an emotion, a memory, or the like) by means of a stimulus. [< Greek *ekphoreîn* < *ékphoros* to be made known]

é|cra|seur (ā′krä zœr′), *n. French.* **1** a surgical instrument for removing tumors or other tissue by the gradual tightening of a chain or wire loop. **2** (literally) crusher.

é|cre|visse (ā krə vēs′), *n. French.* crayfish.

é|crou|le|ment (ā krül mäN′), *n. French.* a falling down or to pieces, such as a mass of rock or a building would; landslide.

ec|ru or **é|cru** (ek′rü, ā′krü), *adj., n.* —*adj.* pale-brown; light-tan. —*n.* **1** a pale brown; light tan. **2** light-tan or unbleached cloth. [< French *écru* raw, unbleached < Old French *escru* < *es-* (< Latin *ex-,* intensive) + Latin *crūdus* raw]

e|crus|ta|ceous (ē′krus tā′shəs), *adj. Botany.* (of lichens) having no thallus. [< *e-* not + *crustaceous*]

ECS (no periods), electroconvulsive shock.

ECSC (no periods), European Coal and Steel Community.

ec|sta|size (eks′tə sīz), *v.,* **-sized, -siz|ing.** —*v.t.* to throw into an ecstasy or transport of rapturous feeling; give pleasurable excitement to. —*v.i.* to go into ecstasies.

ec|sta|sy (eks′tə sē), *n., pl.* **-sies,** *v.,* **-sied, -sy|ing.** —*n.* **1** a condition of very great joy; strong feeling that delights or thrills the heart; rapture: *The little girl was in ecstasy over her new puppy. Crescendos of exalted ecstasy* (William Ellery Leonard). SYN: See syn. under **rapture. 2** any strong feeling that completely absorbs the mind; uncontrollable emotion: *A growing ecstasy of ordered, formal, passionate, increasing disregard for death* (Ernest Hemingway). **3** a trance: *Mystics, religious prophets, and poets have been known to go into ecstasy when meditating or seeking inspiration.* **4** Usually, **Ecstasy.** *U.S. Slang.* = MDMA: *Like all amphetamines, Ecstasy is probably bad for people with circulatory or heart disease* (Newsweek).
—*v.t.* to fill with great joy, delight, rapture, etc.: *The crowd was again ecstasied* (Thomas Hardy). [< Latin *extasis* < Greek *ékstasis* trance, distraction < *existánai* < *ex-* out + *histánai* to stand]

ec|stat|ic (ek stat′ik), *adj., n.* —*adj.* **1** very joyful and thrilled; full of ecstasy; showing ecstasy: *The young bride had an ecstatic look on her wedding day. For each ecstatic instant we must an anguish pay in keen and quivering ratio to the ecstasy* (Emily Dickinson). **2** caused by ecstasy: *He was in an ecstatic mood over the prize he had won.* **3** likely to show ecstasy.
—*n.* a person subject to fits of ecstasy.
ecstatics, fits of ecstasy; raptures: *She is in ecstatics over the newborn baby.*

ec|stat|i|cal (ek stat′ə kəl), *adj.* = ecstatic.

ec|stat|i|cal|ly (ek stat′ə klē), *adv.* in an ecstatic manner.

ECT (no periods), electroconvulsive therapy.

ec|tad (ek′tad), *adv. Anatomy.* on the outward side. [< *ect(o)-* + Latin *ad* to]

ec|tal (ek′təl), *adj. Anatomy.* external; superficial. —**ec′tal|ly,** *adv.*

Ec|the|sis (ek′thə sis), *n.* an edict of the Byzantine emperor Heraclius, promulgated in A.D. 638, maintaining the doctrine that Christ has only one will.

ecto-, *combining form.* to or on the outside: *Ectoderm = the outer cellular layer of an embryo.* [< Greek *ekto-* < *ektós* out of]

ec|to|blast (ek′tə blast), *n.* **1** *Biology.* the outermost membrane of a cell. **2** *Embryology.* the ectoderm. [< *ecto-* + Greek *blastós* sprout, germ]

ec|to|blas|tic (ek′tə blas′tik), *adj.* of or having to do with the ectoblast.

ec|to|cra|ni|al (ek′tə krā′nē əl), *adj.* of or having to do with the outer surface of the skull.

ec|to|derm (ek′tə dėrm), *n. Embryology.* the outer layer of cells formed during the development of the embryos of animals. Skin, hair, nails, the enamel of teeth, and the essential parts of the nervous system grow from the ectoderm: *There are now two distinct body layers, the cells forming the outside of the ball, the ectoderm, and the cells forming the tube within the ball, the endoderm* (A. M. Winchester). [< *ecto-* + Greek *dérma* skin]

ec|to|der|mal (ek′tə dėr′məl), *adj.* of or having to do with the ectoderm.

ec|to|der|mic (ek′tə dėr′mik), *adj.* = ectodermal.

ec|to|en|zym (ek′tō en′zim), *n.* = ectoenzyme.

ec|to|en|zyme (ek′tō en′zīm, -zim), *n.* an enzyme that acts or exists outside the cell.

ec|to|gen|e|sis (ek′tə jen′ə sis), *n. Biology.* the production of structures or bodies outside the organism.

ec|to|gen|ic (ek′tə jen′ik), *adj. Bacteriology.* originating or developed outside of the host, as certain disease-producing bacteria.

ec|tog|e|nous (ek toj′ə nəs), *adj.* = ectogenic.

ec|to|mere (ek′tə mir), *n. Embryology.* any of the blastomeres from which the ectoderm develops.

ec|to|mer|ic (ek′tə mer′ik), *adj.* of or having to do with an ectomere.

***ec|to|morph** (ek′tə môrf), *n.* one of three hypothetical body types used to explain certain aspects of personality, the other two being called *endomorph* and *mesomorph.* The ectomorph is characterized by a predominance of structures developed from the ectodermal layer (skin, nervous system) of the embryo, and is relatively thin and nervous. [< *ecto-* + Greek *morphē̂* form]

***ectomorph**

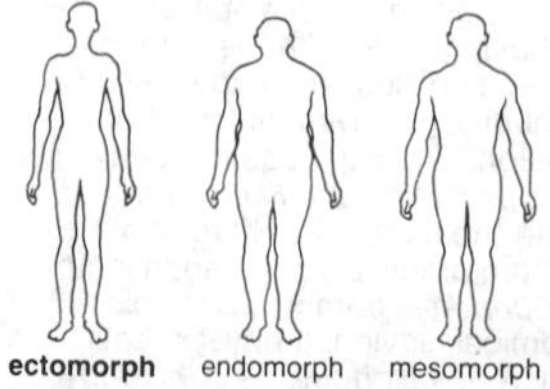

ectomorph endomorph mesomorph

ec|to|mor|phic (ek′tə môr′fik), *adj.* of or like an ectomorph; having to do with an ectomorph; designating the slender type of body build: *Ectomorphic persons are the linear, or beanpole type* (Science News). —**ec′to|mor′phi|cal|ly,** *adv.*

ec|to|mor|phy (ek′tə môr′fē), *n.* ectomorphic quality, character, or condition.

-ectomy, *combining form.* a surgical operation for removing a designated part of the body, as in *tonsillectomy.* [< Greek *ektomē̂* a cutting out]

ec|to|par|a|site (ek′tə par′ə sīt), *n.* a parasite living on the outside parts of the host. Lice and fleas are ectoparasites.

ec|to|par|a|sit|ic (ek′tə par′ə sit′ik), *adj.* having to do with, or of the nature of, external parasites.

ec|to|phyte (ek′tə fīt), *n.* a vegetable parasite living on the outside parts of the host. [< *ecto-* + Greek *phytón* plant]

ec|to|pi|a (ek tō′pē ə), *n.* a displacement of a part or parts of the body, usually congenital: *ectopia of the heart.*

ec|top|ic (ek top′ik), *adj.* away from its normal position: *Ectopic pregnancy is development of an embryo outside of the uterus.* [< Greek *éktopos* displaced (< *ex-* out + *tópos* place) + English *-ic*]

ec|to|plasm (ek′tə plaz əm), *n.* **1** *Biology.* the semiclear, somewhat rigid outer portion of the cytoplasm of a cell. **2** a supposed emanation from the body of a medium in a trance. [< *ecto-* + Greek *plásma* something formed]

ec|to|plas|mic (ek′tə plaz′mik), *adj.* of or having to do with ectoplasm. —**ec′to|plas′mi|cal|ly,** *adv.*

ec|to|rhi|nal (ek′tə rī′nəl), *adj.* situated on the outer side of the nose.

ec|to|sarc (ek′tə särk), *n.* the ectoplasm of a protozoan. [< *ecto-* + Greek *sárx, sarkós* flesh]

ec|to|skel|e|ton (ek′tə skel′ə tən), *n.* = exoskeleton.

ec|to|some (ek′tə sōm), *n.* the cortex, or outer part, of a sponge.

ec|tos|to|sis (ek′tos tō′sis), *n.* the growth of the bone around cartilage. It grows inward from without. [< *ecto-* + Greek *ostéon* bone + English *-osis*]

ec|to|ther|mic (ek′tə thėr′mik), *adj.* receiving heat from the outside; cold-blooded; poikilothermal.

ec|to|ther|mous (ek′tə thėr′məs), *adj.* = ectothermic.

ec|to|ther|my (ek′tə thėr′mē), *n.* the condition of being ectothermic; cold-bloodedness.

ec|to|troph|ic (ek′tə trof′ik), *adj.* deriving nourishment from the outside: *ectotrophic fungi.*

ec|to|zo|ic (ek′tə zō′ik), *adj.* having to do with ectozoons; being a parasite.

ec|to|zo|on (ek′tə zō′ən), *n.* an animal parasite that lives on an outside part of the host. [< *ecto-* + Greek *zôion* animal]

ec|tro|dac|ty|ly (ek′trə dak′tə lē), *n. Anatomy.* congenital absence of fingers or toes. [< New Latin *ectrodactylia* < Greek *ex-* from + *trō-* to damage + *dáktylos* finger]

ec|tro|me|li|a (ek′trə mē′lē ə), *n.* **1** the congenital absence of the whole or part of one or more limbs. **2** a virus disease of mice marked by the loss of feet and often other parts of the body; mouse pox. [< New Latin *ectromelia* < Greek *ex-* from + *trō-* to damage + *mélos* limb]

ec|tro|pi|on (ek trō′pē ən), *n.* an abnormal turning outward of the eyelid. [< Greek *ektrópion* < *ex-* out + *trépein* to turn]

ec|tro|pi|um (ek trō′pē əm), *n.* = ectropion.

ec|ty|pal (ek′tə pəl), *adj.* of or having to do with an ectype; like an ectype.

ec|type (ek′tīp), *n.* a copy; reproduction. [< Greek *éktypon,* neuter of *éktypos* worked in relief < *ex-* out + *týpos* figure, shape]

ecu or **ECU** (ā′kü; *sometimes* ē′sē′yü′), *n.* a money of account in the European Common Market, that is a standard in floating currencies within a narrow range. [< *E*(uropean) *C*(urrency) *U*(nit)]

é|cu (ā kʏ′), *n., pl.* **é|cus** (ā kʏ′). *French.* **1** the short, triangular shield carried by a mounted soldier in the Middle Ages. **2** any of several French gold or silver coins issued from the 1200's on, especially the silver five-franc piece.

E.C.U., English Church Union.

Ecua., Ecuador.

Ec|ua|do|re|an or **Ec|ua|do|ri|an** (ek′wə dôr′ē ən, -dōr′-), *adj., n.* —*adj.* of Ecuador or its people. —*n.* a native or inhabitant of Ecuador.

é|cuelle (ā kwel′), *n.* a low, two-handled bowl of wood, pewter, or silver, used for soup. [< French *écuelle,* ultimately < Latin *scutella* platter; see etym. under **scuttle**[1]]

ec|u|ma|ni|ac (ek′yů mā′nē ak), *n.* an extremely enthusiastic promoter of ecumenism.

ec|u|mene (ek′yů mēn, e kyü′mə nē), *n.* the habitable part of the world; the part of the world inhabited by man. [< Greek *oikouménē̂* (*gē̂*) the inhabited (world); see etym. under **ecumenical**]

ec|u|men|ic (ek′yů men′ik), *adj.* = ecumenical.

ec|u|men|i|cal (ek′yů men′ə kəl), *adj.* **1** general; universal. **2** of or representing the whole Christian Church: *How should he divide his responsibility to the local church and the ecumenical or* *world-wide church?* (Time). **3** promoting unity among all Christians or Christian, especially Protestant, denominations. Also, **oecumenical**. [< Latin *oecumenicus* < Greek *oikoumenikós* < *oikouménē* (*gê*) the inhabited (world), ultimately < *oîkos* dwelling + English *-al* [1]]

ecumenical council, a general church council supposed to represent the worldwide Christian Church. An ecumenical council of the Roman Catholic Church is one that is called by the Pope for a special purpose.

ec|u|men|i|cal|ism (ek′yů men′ə kə liz′əm), *n.* = ecumenicity.

ec|u|men|i|cal|ist (ek′yů men′ə kə list), *n.* = ecumenist.

ec|u|men|i|cal|ly (ek′yů men′ə klē), *adv.* in a general or ecumenical manner.

Ecumenical Patriarch, the title of the patriarch of Constantinople, who occupies the highest position of honor in the Eastern Orthodox Churches.

ec|u|men|i|cism (ek′yů men′ə siz əm), *n.* = ecumenicity.

ec|u|men|i|cist (ek′yů men′ə sist), *n.* = ecumenist.

ec|u|me|nic|i|ty (ek′yů me nis′ə tē), *n.* the championing of world-wide Christian harmony and unity, especially in the Protestant Church: *Other Protestants seek an authority in a revived church and a spate of books on ecumenicity shows eager and hopeful minds looking for union beyond denominational differences* (Harper's).

ec|u|men|ics (ek′yů men′iks), *n.* the study of the ecumenical character, history, and principles of the Christian Church.

ec|u|men|ism (ek′yů men′iz əm, ek′yů mə nizəm), *n.* **1** the principle of worldwide Christian harmony and unity. **2** = ecumenicity.

ec|u|men|ist (ek′yů men′ist), *n.* a supporter or champion of ecumenism.

ec|u|me|nop|o|lis (ek′yů me nop′ə lis), *n.* the world considered as one continuous city: *Are we going to succeed in making the inevitable ecumenopolis a tolerable habitat for human beings?* (Arnold Toynbee). [< Greek *oikouménē* the world + *pólis* city; coined by Constantinos A. Doxiadis, born 1913, a Greek architect and engineer]

ec|ze|ma (ek′sə mə, eg zē′-), *n.* an inflammation of the skin with itching and the formation of patches of scales and pimples. [< New Latin *eczema* < Greek *ékzema* < *ex-* out + *zeîn* to boil]

ec|zem|a|to|sis (eg zem′ə tō′sis), *n.* any eczematous inflammation.

ec|zem|a|tous (eg zem′ə təs), *adj.* **1** having to do with or caused by eczema. **2** having eczema.

-ed[1], a suffix that forms the past tense of many verbs, as in *wanted, edged, tried, dropped.* [Old English *-de, -ede, -ade, -ode*]

▶After *t* and *d*, **-ed** is pronounced as *id: wanted, faded;* after voiceless consonants (except *t*) it is pronounced as *t: dressed, washed;* after vowels and voiced consonants (except *d*) it is pronounced as *d: vowed, lagged.*

-ed[2], *suffix.* **1** forming the past participle of many verbs, as in *has echoed.*

2 forming adjectives from nouns with various meanings: **a** having ____ : *Long-legged = having long legs.* **b** having the characteristics of ____ : *Bigoted = having the characteristics of a bigot. Honeyed = having the characteristics of honey.*

[Old English *-d, -ed, -ad, -od*]

▶See **-ed**[1] for usage note.

ed., **1a** edited. **b** edition. **c** editor. **2** educated.

ED (no periods), **1** Education Department (the U.S. Department of Education): *Some 60 percent of ED's assistant secretaries and other top officials are women and minorities* (New York Times). **2** effective dose (of a drug or medicine).

e|da|cious (i dā′shəs), *adj.* **1** eating much; greedy in eating; voracious. SYN: ravenous. **2** *Figurative.: Concord Bridge has long since yielded to the edacious tooth of time* (James Russell Lowell). [< Latin *edāx, -ācis* (with English *-ous*) eating, tending to eat < *edere* eat]

e|dac|i|ty (i das′ə tē), *n.* edacious character; greediness; voracity.

E|dam (ē′dam, -dəm), *n.* = Edam cheese.

Edam cheese, a round, mild-flavored, yellow cheese, originally made in the Netherlands, usually having red wax on the outside. [< *Edam,* a village in the Netherlands]

e|daph|ic (i daf′ik), *adj.* having to do with or influenced by the soil, rather than by the climate: *A high ratio of potassium to magnesium in the area designated as edaphic desert may be one of the reasons for lower plant growth there* (Science News). [< Greek *édaphos* bottom, ground + English *-ic*]

edaphic climax, *Ecology.* a climax that is determined mainly by the conditions of the soil, for example whether it is moist, dry, or alkaline.

Ed.B., Bachelor of Education.

EDC (no periods), European Defense Community (France, Italy, West Germany, and the Benelux nations united for mutual defense).

Ed.D., Doctor of Education.

Ed|da (ed′ə), *n., pl.* **-das**. either of two Icelandic collections of the old Norse myths and legends, collected during the 1100's and 1200's. The Younger Edda is written in prose; the Elder Edda is written in poetry.

Ed|da|ic (e dā′ik), *adj.* = Eddic.

Ed|dic (ed′ik), *adj.* of or having to do with either Edda; in the style of either Edda.

Ed|ding|ton limit (ed′ing tən), *Astronomy.* the maximum brightness attainable by a celestial object of a given mass. [< Sir Arthur Stanley *Eddington,* 1882-1944, a British astronomer]

ed|dish (ed′ish), *n. British Dialect.* **1** grass or the like that grows after mowing; aftermath. **2** stubble. [origin uncertain; compare Old English *edisc* park, pasture]

ed|do (ed′ō), *n., pl.* **-does**. the edible root of the taro or of any of various related plants. [perhaps < Twi *ode* yam]

ed|dy (ed′ē), *n., pl.* **-dies**, *v.,* **-died**, **-dy|ing**. *—n.* **1** a small whirlpool or whirlwind; water, air, or smoke moving against the main current, especially when having a whirling motion: *The wind moved in an eddy near the sails. Cyclonic circulations can exist on widely varying scales, from eddies of minute size up to stable lows covering millions of square miles* (R. W. James). **2** any similar current of fog or dust. **3** *Figurative.* anything thought to resemble this: *Eddies of controversy grew around the new theory.*

—v.i., v.t. to whirl; move in circles: *The water eddied out of the sink.* (*Figurative.*) *Union stragglers crossing Rappahannock, . . . caught the mood of confusion that eddied in rear of countless battles* (Time). SYN: swirl.

[perhaps < Scandinavian (compare Old Icelandic *itha*)]

eddy current, an electric current induced in a conductor by a varying magnetic field. It causes loss of power in electrical equipment. *An all-metal construction was out because of eddy currents* (Scientific American).

eddy wind, the wind moving in an eddy near a sail, mountain, or other object.

E|del|fäu|le (ā′dəl foi′lə), *n. German.* **1** a mold that forms on the skins of ripening grapes, and through a biochemical process concentrates the sugar and the flavor within. **2** (literally) noble rot.

***e|del|weiss** (ā′dəl vīs), *n.* a small alpine plant of the composite family of Europe, Asia, and South America, with very small, white flowers in the center of star-shaped clusters of leaves that are covered with a white fuzz. [< German *Edelweiss* < *edel* noble + *weiss* white]

***edelweiss**

e|de|ma (i dē′mə), *n., pl.* **-mas**, **-ma|ta** (-mə tə). an abnormal accumulation of watery fluid in the tissues or cavities of the body, often causing visible swelling; dropsy. [< New Latin *edema* < Greek *oídēma* < *oídos* tumor, swelling]

e|dem|a|tose (i dem′ə tōs), *adj.* = edematous.

e|dem|a|tous (i dem′ə təs), *adj.* **1** having to do with or like edema. **2** having edema.

E|den (ē′dən), *n.* **1** the garden where Adam and Eve first lived (in the Bible, Genesis 2:8, 3:24). **2** *Figurative.* a delightful place; paradise: *Who loves a garden still his Eden keeps* (Bronson Alcott). **3** a state of perfect happiness. [< Hebrew *'eden*]

E|den|ic (i den′ik), *adj.* of or like Eden or an Eden.

e|den|ite (ē′də nīt), *n.* an aluminous variety of hornblende. [< German *Edenit* < *Eden*(ville), a town in Orange County, New York, where it is found + German *-ro -ite*[1]]

e|den|tal (ē den′təl), *adj.* = toothless.

e|den|tate (ē den′tāt), *n., adj.* *—n.* any one of an order of mammals that are toothless or have incomplete sets of teeth. Armadillos, sloths, and anteaters are edentates. *—adj.* **1** = toothless. **2** of or having to do with the edentates.

[< Latin *ēdentātus,* past participle of *ēdentāre* < *ex-* without + *dēns, dentis* tooth]

e|den|ta|tion (ē′den tā′shən), *n.* toothless condition.

e|den|tu|late (ē den′chə lāt), *adj.* without teeth or toothlike processes, as the mandibles of some insects.

e|den|tu|lous (ē den′chə ləs), *adj.* = toothless.[< Latin *ēdentulus* (with English *-ous*) toothless < *ex-* without + *dēns, dentis* tooth]

EDES (no periods), Hellenic National Democratic Party (Greek, *Ellinikos Dimokratikos Ethnikos Stratos*).

e|des|tin (i des′tin), *n.* a vegetable globulin found in the seed of the hemp and certain other plants, used to test for the presence of pepsin. [< Greek *edestós* eatable (< *édein* eat)]

Ed|gar (ed′gər), *n. U.S.* a bust of Edgar Allan Poe, awarded annually to a writer for the best current mystery fiction.

edge (ej), *n., v.,* **edged**, **edg|ing**. *—n.* **1** the line or place where something ends; part farthest from the middle; side: *flowers by the water's edge. This page has four edges.* **2** the extreme border or margin of anything; brink; verge: *The stag stood on the edge of the cliff.* (*Figurative.*) *The wretched spendthrift's business was on the edge of disaster.* **3** a thin, sharp side that cuts: *The blade of an ax or razor has an edge. The knife had a very sharp edge.* **4** the degree of sharpness of a blade. **5** *Figurative.* sharpness, keenness: *The remark had a biting edge to it. Archie Moore campaigned through most of the year as a heavyweight, trying to get back his fighting edge after he lost his bid for the heavyweight championship* (Paul Abramson). *Slander, Whose edge is sharper than the sword* (Shakespeare). **6** *Informal, Figurative.* advantage: *At the moment we appear to have an edge in aircraft quality and performance* (Bulletin of Atomic Scientists).

—v.t. **1** to put an edge on; form an edge on: *The gardener edged the path with white stones.* **2** to move sideways: *She edged her way through the crowd.* **3** to move little by little: *He edged his chair nearer the fire.* *—v.i.* **1** to move sideways: *She edged through the crowd.* **2** to move little by little: *The dog edged nearer the fire.* **3** to tilt a ski so that the edge cuts the snow.

edge in, to manage to get in: *He edged in some business while on vacation.*

edge out, to win by a narrow margin: *Kennedy edged out Nixon in the 1960 presidential election.*

on edge, **a** disturbed; irritated; tense: *His nerves were on edge from the constant noise. I'm all on edge over this landscape scheme* (R. W. Chambers). **b** eager; anxious; impatient: *The children were on edge as they awaited the start of the parade.*

on the edge of, at the point of (doing something): *He was now on the very edge of losing his office* (Richard W. Church).

set on edge, **a** to cause to feel excited or uncomfortable; disturb: *The constant noise set her nerves on edge.* **b** to make eager, anxious, or impatient: *He was set on edge by hours of waiting.*

take the edge off, to take away the force, strength, or enjoyment of: *The severe injury suffered by the winning pitcher took the edge off the team's victory.*

[Old English *ecg*]

—Syn. n. **1 Edge, border** mean the line or space that marks the end or side of something. **Edge** applies to a sharp line or very thin surface that marks the exact end of something: *We walked to the edge of the water.* **Border** applies to a line that marks the farthest limit of something or the space that runs along just inside the boundary or edge: *The handkerchief has a colored border.*

edge|bone (ej′bōn′), *n.* = aitchbone.

edged (ejd), *adj.* having an edge; sharp.

edge effect, *Ecology.* influence of neighboring plant communities on the types and numbers of animals in their adjoining fringes or borders.

edge-grain (ej′grān′), *adj.* (of lumber) sawed at right angles to the annual rings; quarter-sawed: *a roof laid with edge-grain shingles.*

edge|less (ej′lis), *adj.* having no edge: *an edgeless surface.* —**edge′less|ness**, *n.*

edge-on (ej′on′, -ôn′), *adv.* with the edge foremost: *The wall of the tube is so thin that even when it is viewed edge-on at a magnification of 1,000 diameters it is visible only as a line* (Scientific American).

edge plane, a carpenter's plane for trimming flat, round, or hollow edges on woodwork.

edg|er (ej′ər), *n.* **1** a person or thing that edges or puts an edge on anything. **2** a marble near the edge of the playing ring in the game of marbles. **3** a set of saws for trimming the rough edges of lumber. **4** a tool for trimming the edge of a lawn or the like.

edge roll, **1** a tool used in gilding and decorating the edges of book covers. **2** the ornament or

---

Pronunciation Key: hat, āge, cãre, fär; let, ēqual, tėrm; it, īce; hot, ōpen, ôrder; oil, out; cup, pu̇t, rüle; child; long; thin; ᴛʜen; zh, measure; ə represents a in about, e in taken, i in pencil, o in lemon, u in circus.

decoration so produced.
edge-rolled (ej′rōld′), *adj.* (of book covers) gilded or decorated with an edge roll.
edge·tool (ej′tül′), *n.* a tool with a sharp cutting edge, such as a chisel, plane, or ax.
edge·ways (ej′wāz′), *adv.* with the edge forward; in the direction of the edge.
edge·wise (ej′wīz′), *adv.* = edgeways.
get a word in edgewise, *Informal.* to manage to say something in conversation: *He talked so much that I couldn't get a word in edgewise.*
edge zone, a fold of tissue extending over the theca of various corals.
edg·i·ly (ej′ə lē), *adv.* sharply; impatiently.
edg·i·ness (ej′ē nis), *n.* sharpness; impatience: *He has acquired considerable confidence and know-how: gone is the edginess, the defensive rudeness* (Observer).
edg·ing (ej′ing), *n.* a thing forming an edge or put on along an edge; border or trimming for an edge: *an edging of pebbles for the rose garden, an edging of lace for a dress.*
edging lobelia, a low-growing, annual lobelia that is often cultivated in window boxes.
edg·y (ej′ē), *adj.,* **edg·i·er, edg·i·est. 1** impatient; irritable: *Father gets edgy when you ask him too many questions while he is reading the paper.* SYN: testy. **2** sharply defined: *edgy outlines.* **3** having an edge; sharp.
***edh** (eᴛʜ), *n.* **1** a letter of the Old English alphabet that represented either the voiced or voiceless dental fricative now spelled *th,* as in *then* and *thin.* **2** the symbol used in phonetic transcriptions to represent the voiced dental fricative as in *then.* Also, **eth.**

***edh**
definitions 1, 2

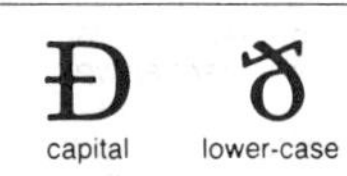

ðæt = that
Ðæt = That

ed·i·bil·i·ty (ed′ə bil′ə tē), *n.* fitness for eating.
ed·i·ble (ed′ə bəl), *adj., n.* —*adj.* fit to eat; eatable.
—*n.* **edibles,** things fit to eat; food: *The delightful hampers of edibles and drinkables* (George A. Sala). [< Late Latin *edibilis* < Latin *edere* eat]
—**ed′i·ble·ness,** *n.*
e·dict (ē′dikt), *n.* **1** a public order or command by some authority; decree: *The king issued an edict creating a new national holiday. In May, 1521, the emperor signed the Edict of Worms, which declared Luther to be an outlaw whom anyone could kill without punishment* (Lewis W. Spitz). SYN: See syn. under **proclamation. 2** *Figurative.* any similar order or command. [< Latin *ēdictum* < *ēdīcere* publish, proclaim < *ex-* out + *dīcere* say]
e·dic·tal (i dik′təl), *adj.* **1** having to do with or like an edict. **2** ordered or commanded by edict.
—**e·dic′tal·ly,** *adv.*
ed·i·fi·ca·tion (ed′ə fə kā′shən), *n.* moral improvement; spiritual benefit; instruction: *Good books provide edification of the mind. Never . . . was a sermon listened to with more impatience and less edification* (Scott). SYN: enlightenment.
ed·i·fi·ca·to·ry (ed′ə fə kā′tər ē; i dif′ə kə tôr′ē, -tōr′-), *adj.* that edifies or tends to edify.
ed·i·fice (ed′ə fis), *n.* a building, especially a large or impressive building, such as a cathedral, palace, or temple: *a spacious edifice of brick* (Hawthorne). SYN: See syn. under **building.** [< Old French *edifice,* learned borrowing from Latin *aedificium* < *aedificāre* build < *aedis* temple + *facere* make]
ed·i·fi·cial (ed′ə fish′əl), *adj.* having to do with a building; structural.
ed·i·fi·er (ed′ə fī′ər), *n.* a person who edifies.
ed·i·fy (ed′ə fī), *v.t.,* **-fied, -fy·ing. 1** to improve morally; benefit spiritually; instruct and uplift: *People go to church to be edified by the sermon and the religious lessons. Let us therefore follow after the things . . . wherewith one may edify another* (Romans 14:19). **2** *Archaic.* to build; construct. **3** *Obsolete.* to establish; organize. [< Old French *edifier* < Latin *aedificāre* build (up); see etym. under **edifice**] —**ed′i·fy′ing·ly,** *adv.*
e·dile (ē′dīl), *n.* = aedile.
Ed·i·son effect (ed′ə sən), the electric conduction from an incandescent filament to a cold positive electrode in the same lamp. [< Thomas Alva *Edison,* 1847-1931, an American inventor, who discovered it]
Ed·i·son-La·lande cell (ed′ə sən lə land′), an electric cell with a positive electrode of copper oxide, a negative electrode of amalgamated zinc, and an electrolyte of sodium hydroxide. [< Thomas Alva *Edison* and Felix *Lalande,* who invented it about 1880]
ed·it (ed′it), *v., n.* —*v.t.* **1** to prepare (another person's writings) for publication or presentation by correcting errors, checking facts, and the like; prepare an edition of: *The teacher is editing famous speeches for use in schoolbooks. Scholars often edit Shakespeare's plays.* **2** to have charge of (a newspaper, magazine, or other publication) and decide what shall be printed in it: *Two girls were chosen to edit the class bulletin.* **3** to revise or give final form to (motion-picture films, tape recordings, or other recorded material) by such means as cutting and splicing: *The performance you buy at the local record shop is . . . edited by a skilled technician so that the joins are imperceptible* (Punch). **4** to alter (a gene) by genetic engineering: *For large genes it is probably more practical to isolate the natural gene and then, when necessary, merely "edit" the gene with chemically synthesized DNA* (Science).
—*n. Informal.* **1** editing; editorial work: *Strick tosses in so many starts of parades and tourist views that at times the movie feels like a travelogue . . . luckily, the fast edit keeps the action from sagging* (New Yorker). **2** editorial: *As I read your edit in your issue of May 8, I felt like jumping up onto a soapbox and replying, "I'm glad you asked that question"* (Punch).
edit down, to shorten by or as if by editing: *The last 20 minutes [of a motion picture] could have been edited down* (Washington Times).
edit out, to delete while editing: *All references to the United States were . . . edited out of the tape* (Atlantic).
[< Latin *ēditus,* past participle of *ēdere* < *ex-* out + *dare* give; partly < English *editor*]
edit., **1** edited. **2** edition. **3** editor.
é·di·teur (ā dē tœr′), *n. French.* a publisher.
e·di·tion (i dish′ən), *n.* **1** all the copies of a book, newspaper, and other printed matter just alike and issued at or near the same time: *The first edition of "Robinson Crusoe" was printed in 1719. In the second edition of the book, many of the errors in the first edition had been corrected.* **2** the form in which a book is printed or published: *a one-volume edition of Shakespeare. The new edition of "Mother Goose" has better pictures than the older editions. Some books appear in paperback editions.* **3** an issue of the same newspaper, book, or other printed matter, published at different times with additions and changes: *the afternoon edition, a foreign edition.* [< Latin *ēditiō, -ōnis* < *ēdere;* see etym. at **edit**]
e·di·tion·al·ize (i dish′ə nə līz), *v.i.,* **-ized, -iz·ing.** to print several editions: *Indeed, where a national newspaper has no such connexion, it often tries to offset the handicap by editionalizing and by facsimile printing in more than one centre* (London Times).
é·di·tion de luxe (ā dē syôɴ′ də lʏks′), *French.* an especially elegant edition of a book or the like.
e·di·ti·o·nes ex·pur·ga·tae (i dish′ē ō′nēz eks′-pər gā′tē), *Latin.* expurgated editions.
e·di·ti·o prin·ceps (i dish′ē ō prin′seps), *Latin.* the first printed edition.
ed·i·tor (ed′ə tər), *n.* **1** a person who edits: *A large newspaper has many editors who are each responsible for a single department of news: a city editor, business editor, military editor, sports editor, etc. Abbr:* ed. **2** a person who writes editorials.
ed·i·to·ri·al (ed′ə tôr′ē əl, -tōr′-), *n., adj.* —*n.* **1** an article in a newspaper or magazine written by the editor or under his direction, giving the opinion or attitude of the paper upon some subject. **2** a radio or television broadcast expressing the editorial opinion or attitude of the program, station, or network.
—*adj.* of or having to do with an editor or an editorial: *editorial work, an editorial comment.*
ed·i·to·ri·al·ist (ed′ə tôr′ē ə list, -tōr′-), *n.* a writer of editorials.
ed·i·to·ri·al·ize (ed′ə tôr′ē ə līz, -tōr′-), *v.i.,* **-ized, -iz·ing. 1** to include comment or criticism in news articles. **2** to write an editorial: *Owing to the closeness of the Congressional elections in many parts of the country, the results were insufficiently clear to editorialize about* (New Yorker). —**ed′i·to′ri·al·i·za′tion,** *n.* —**ed′i·to′ri·al·iz′er,** *n.*
ed·i·to·ri·al·iz·ing (ed′ə tôr′ē ə lī′zing, -tōr′-), *n.* the making of (sometimes biased or distorted) assertions in the positive and authoritative manner of an editorial: *The modern style of predigested editorializing is apt to cause a vague uneasiness* (Atlantic).
ed·i·to·ri·al·ly (ed′ə tôr′ē ə lē, -tōr′-), *adv.* **1** in an editorial manner or capacity; as an editor: *She wrote editorially for a London paper* (Harper's). **2** in an editorial.
editor in chief, the editor in charge of a newspaper, magazine, dictionary, or other work compiled by a group of people.
ed·i·tor·ship (ed′ə tər ship), *n.* the position, duties, or authority of an editor.
ed·i·tress (ed′ə tris), *n.* a woman editor.
ed·i·trix (ed′ə triks), *n., pl.* **ed·i·trix·es, ed·i·tri·ces** (ed′ə trī′sēz). an editress.
E·di·ya (e dē′yə), *n.pl.* the tribes of black people that inhabit Fernando Póo in West Africa.
Ed.M., Master of Education.
E·do (ē′dō), *n., pl.* **E·do** or **E·dos. 1** a member of an agricultural people of West Africa, living chiefly in southern Nigeria. **2** their Kwa language.
Ed·o·hwe (ed′ə hwā), *n., pl.* **-hwe** or **-hwes.** a member of a tribe of North American Indians, formerly living in California.
E·dom (ē′dəm), *n.* Esau, Jacob's twin brother (in the Bible, Genesis 25:29, 30).
E·dom·ite (ē′də mīt), *n.* a native or inhabitant of Edom, a region in Palestine south of the Dead Sea (in the Bible, Numbers 20:14-21).
EDP (no periods) or **E.D.P.,** electronic data processing.
EDPM (no periods) or **E.D.P.M.,** electronic data processing machine.
eds., **1** editions. **2** editors.
E.D.S., English Dialect Society.
EDT (no periods), **E.D.T.,** or **e.d.t.,** Eastern Daylight Time.
EDTA (no periods), ethylenediamine tetra-acetic acid, a colorless, crystalline acid used as a metal chelating agent, as an anticoagulant, and in the treatment of chlorosis, calcinosis, lead poisoning, and other conditions. *Formula:* $C_{10}H_{16}N_2O_8$
educ., **1** educated. **2** education. **3** educational.
ed·u·ca·bil·i·ty (ej′u̇ kə bil′ə tē), *n.* **1** the ability to learn. **2** the opportunity to receive an education.
ed·u·ca·ble (ej′u̇ kə bəl), *adj., n.* —*adj.* that can be educated, taught, or trained.
—*n.* an educable person.
ed·u·cand (ej′u̇ kand), *n.* a person who is to be educated. [< Latin *ēducandus,* gerundive of *ēducāre* educate]
ed·u·cat·a·ble (ej′u̇ kā′tə bəl), *adj.* = educable.
ed·u·cate (ej′u̇ kāt), *v.,* **-cat·ed, -cat·ing.** —*v.t.* **1** to develop in knowledge, skill, ability, or character by training, study, or experience; teach; train: *The job of teachers is to educate the young.* SYN: instruct. **2** to send to school; provide schooling for: *My brother is being educated in the East and returns home only for vacations.* **3** to train for a particular calling or occupation.
—*v.i.* to give instruction; teach: *In my eyes the question is not what to teach, but how to educate* (Charles Kingsley).
[< Latin *ēducāre* (with English *-ate*[1]) bring up, raise, related to *ēdūcere;* see etym. under **educe**]
ed·u·cat·ed (ej′u̇ kā′tid), *adj.* **1** that has received an education; showing knowledge or training: *an intelligent and educated woman.* **2** refined: *an educated palate.* **3** based on expert interpretation of facts: *an educated opinion.* —**ed′u·cat′ed·ly,** *adv.* —**ed′u·cat′ed·ness,** *n.*
educated guess, an estimate, prediction, or opinion based on expert interpretation of incomplete, inadequate, or undigested data: *The educated guess by historians . . . is that the first two years of the Centennial saw between 250 and 300 books on the Civil War* (New York Times).
ed·u·ca·tee (ej′u̇ kə tē′), *n.* a person who is being educated; student: *It is not enough for the educator to pour fact after fact into the educatee* (Saturday Review).
ed·u·ca·tion (ej′u̇ kā′shən), *n.* **1** the development of knowledge, skill, ability, or character by teaching, training, study, or experience; teaching; training: *In the United States, public schools offer an education to all children. We cannot hope for significant advances in education without increased costs.* **2** the knowledge, skill, ability, or character gained through teaching, training, study, or experience: *A person with education knows how to speak, write, and read well. His education was limited to the three R's.* **3** the study of the methods, principles, and problems of teaching and learning: *The philosophy of education has been broadened by its association with anthropology.*
—*Syn.* **2 Education, enlightenment, culture** mean the qualities and knowledge a person gets from study, teaching, and experience. **Education** emphasizes the training, knowledge, and abilities a person gets through teaching or study: *A person with education knows how to speak and write well, and to read with understanding.* **Enlightenment** emphasizes the insight and understanding that make a person free from prejudice and ignorance: *A person with enlightenment can judge the intrinsic values in human relations.* **Culture** emphasizes the combination of enlightenment and taste that results from complete education: *A person of culture appreciates good music and art.*
ed·u·ca·tion·al (ej′u̇ kā′shə nəl), *adj.* **1** of or having to do with education: *The teachers in our school belong to the state educational associations.* **2** giving education; tending to educate: *Our science class saw an educational motion picture about wild animals.* SYN: instructive. —**ed′u·ca′tion·al·ly,** *adv.*

ed|u|ca|tion|al|ist (ej′ů kā′shə nə list), *n.* an authority on the methods and principles of education; educator: *These young people hardly need the vague group-games of the educationalists* (Richard D. Sullivan).

educational park, *U.S.* a group of elementary and secondary schools built on a large tract of land, with many facilities used in common: *The commission called educational parks, or clusters of schools, a "revolutionary" technique that might provide common experiences for children of different backgrounds* (New York Times).

educational psychology, the use of psychological knowledge and methods to study concepts and techniques of education and to solve educational problems: *We have concentrated on what are uniquely the concerns of educational psychology—what teachers are trying to do and why, how children's development affects what and how they learn, and how efficient learning can be fostered in the classroom* (William C. Morse and G. Max Wingo).

educational television, *U.S.* **1** noncommercial television broadcasting that features school and university-licensed instructional programs. **2** any television broadcasting that has educational or cultural appeal.

ed|u|ca|tion|ar|y (ej′ů kā′shə ner′ē), *n., pl.* **-ar|ies.** a person interested in education: *The educationaries, young and intent,* [*were*] *sitting before him in a large tiered classroom* (New York Times Magazine).

ed|u|ca|tion|ese (ej′ů kā′shə nēz′, -nēs′), *n.* the jargon of educators: *What kind of person is it who enjoys the aesthetics of a bell-shaped curve, the rhetoric of educationese, or the poetry of the primer?* (Saturday Review). [< *education* + *-ese*]

ed|u|ca|tion|ism (ej′ů kā′shə niz əm), *n.* undue emphasis on formal education and its institutions.

ed|u|ca|tion|ist (ej′ů kā′shə nist), *n.* = educationalist.

education park, = educational park.

ed|u|ca|tive (ej′ů kā′tiv), *adj.* **1** that educates; instructive: *the educative value of travel.* **2** of or having to do with education.

ed|u|ca|tor (ej′ů kā′tər), *n.* **1** a person whose profession is education; teacher: *The educator does not pour truths or untruths into the minds of others, but draws out of others their latent abilities and stimulates them to be original and creative* (Emory S. Bogardus). **2** an authority on methods and principles of education; leader in education.

ed|u|ca|to|ry (ej′ů kə tôr′ē, -tōr′-), *adj.* = educative.

e|duce (i düs′, -dyüs′), *v.t.*, **e|duced, e|duc|ing.** to bring out; draw forth; elicit; develop: *The science teacher's questions educed many facts about gardens and flowers.* **SYN**: extract. [< Latin *ēdūcere* < *ex-* out + *dūcere* lead]

e|duce|ment (i düs′mənt, -dyüs′-), *n.* **1** the act of educing. **2** the state of being educed.

e|duc|i|ble (i dü′sə bəl, -dyü′-), *adj.* that can be educed.

ed|u|crat (ej′ů krat), *n. U.S.* a representative or official of an educational system, agency, or institution. [< *edu*(cation) + (bureau)*crat*]

e|duct (ē′dukt), *n.* **1** something that is educed. **2** *Chemistry.* a substance extracted unchanged from another substance. [< Latin *ēductum,* neuter of *ēductus,* past participle of *ēdūcere;* see etym. under **educe**]

e|duc|tion (i duk′shən), *n.* **1** the act of educing. **2** something educed; educt. **3** an exhaust, such as that of steam after some device has completed its work.

e|duc|tive (i duk′tiv), *adj.* educing; tending to educe.

e|duc|tor (i duk′tər), *n.* a person or thing that educes.

e|dul|co|rate (i dul′kə rāt), *v.t.*, **-rat|ed, -rat|ing.** **1** *Chemistry.* to free from acids, salts, or impurities by washing. **2** *Obsolete.* to sweeten. [< Medieval Latin *ēdulcōrāre* (with English *-ate*[1]) < *ex-* out + Late Latin *dulcōrāre* sweeten < Latin *dulcor, -ōris* sweetness < *dulcis* sweet]

e|dul|co|ra|tion (i dul′kə rā′shən), *n.* **1** the act or process of edulcorating. **2** the state of being edulcorated.

∗Edwardian
definition 2

∗Ed|war|di|an (ed wär′dē ən), *adj., n.* —*adj.* **1** of or having to do with the reign of Edward VII, 1901-1910, of England. **2** having characteristics considered typical of Edwardians, especially in manners, elegance, and grandeur: *He was wearing a dark Edwardian suit with broad white stripes* (New Yorker).
—*n.* a person of the period of Edward VII.

Ed|war|di|a|na (ed wär′dē ä′nə, -an′ə, -ā′nə), *n.pl.* furniture, clothing, books, or other products of the Edwardian period: *These "junk shops" sell the antique dealers' cast-offs, late Victoriana, Edwardiana* (London Times).

Ed|war|di|an|ism (ed wär′dē ə niz′əm), *n.* **1** the ideas, beliefs, or way of living common during the reign of Edward VII: *The author, like so many of his generation, was obsessed with Edwardianism, its real opulence and unreal self-confidence* (Economist). **2** an object, manner of speech, style of dress, or the like, characteristic of the Edwardian period: *How like her aunt it was to use an out-of-date Edwardianism like "smitten"* (Josephine Tey).

Ed|war|dine (ed wär′dēn, -din), *adj.* = Edwardian.

ee (ē), *n. Scottish.* eye.

-ee, *suffix added to verbs to form nouns.* **1** a person who is ______: *Absentee = a person who is absent.*
2 a person who is ______ed: *Appointee = a person who is appointed.*
3 a person to whom something is ______ed: *Mortgagee = a person to whom something is mortgaged.*
4 a person who ______s: *Standee = a person who stands.*
[< Anglo-French *-e,* masculine past participle ending of verbs in *-er* < Latin *-ātus.* Compare etym. under **-ate**[1].]

e.e., errors excepted.

EE (no periods), **1** electrical engineer. **2** electrical engineering.

E.E., **1** Early English. **2a** electrical engineer. **b** electrical engineering. **3** errors excepted.

EEC (no periods), European Economic Community.

EEG (no periods), **1** electroencephalogram. **2** electroencephalograph. **3** electroencephalography.

∗eel (ēl), *n.* **1** a long, slippery fish shaped like a snake, with continuous dorsal, caudal, and anal fins and lacking ventral fins. Eels live in fresh water or salt water. **2** any one of various similar fishes, such as the electric eel and lamprey. **3** = eelworm. [Old English *ǣl*] —**eel′like′**, *adj.*

∗eel
definitions 1,2

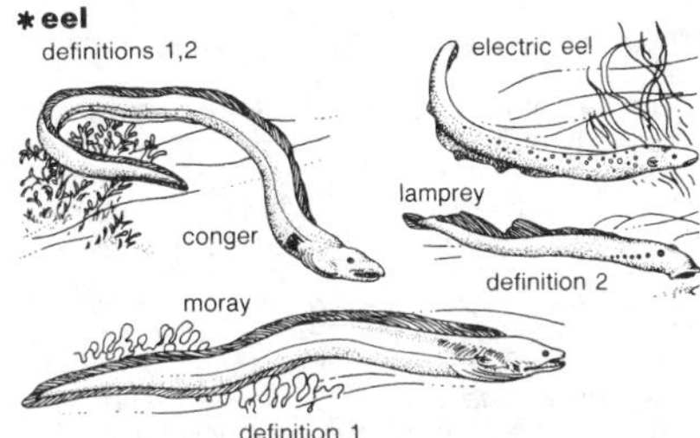

eel|er (ē′lər), *n.* a person who catches eels.

eel|fare (ēl′fãr′), *n.* **1** the passage of young eels up a river. **2** a brood of yound eels. [< *eel* + obsolete *fare* a journey]

eel|grass (ēl′gras′, -gräs′), *n. U.S.* **1** a sea plant with long, narrow leaves, growing under water along the Atlantic and Pacific coasts of North America. **2** a freshwater plant with ribbonlike leaves springing directly from the root, growing in shallow ponds; wild celery. It belongs to the frogbit family.

eel|ing (ē′ling), *n.* a fishing for eels.

eel|moth|er (ēl′muᴛʜ′ər), *n.* a European eelpout, a viviparous fish.

eel|pot (ēl′pot′), *n.* a basket or other container with a funnel-shaped entrance used for trapping eels: *In the late fall and early winter, when the eels in the river ... bring their highest prices, Mr. Ingold and Willy set eelpots* (New Yorker).

eel|pout (ēl′pout′), *n.* **1** a small, eellike saltwater fish. **2** = burbot. [Old English *ǣlepūte*]

eel|worm (ēl′wėrm′), *n.* any one of various small nematode worms, some injurious to plants, such as the vinegar eel.

eel|y (ē′lē), *adj.* of or like an eel; wriggling.

e'en (ēn), *adv.* even.

e'er (ãr), *adv.* ever.

-eer, *suffix added to nouns to form nouns and verbs.* **1** a person who directs or operates, as in *auctioneer, charioteer.*
2 a person who produces, as in *pamphleteer.*
3 to be concerned or deal with, as in *electioneer.*
[< Old French *-ier* < Latin *-ārius*]

ee|rie (ir′ē), *adj.*, **-ri|er, -ri|est.** **1** causing fear; strange; weird: *An eerie feeling crept upon us in the dark and eerie old house. At nightfall on the marshes, the thing was eerie and fantastic to behold* (R. L. Stevenson). **SYN**: See syn. under **weird**. **2** timid because of superstition. **SYN**: fearful. [Middle English *eri* timid, variant of *erg,* Old English *earg* cowardly, fearful]

ee|ri|ly (ir′ə lē), *adv.* in an eerie manner: *The wind whistled eerily in the chimney.*

ee|ri|ness (ir′ē nis), *n.* eerie quality or condition: *I won't say that it doesn't have the eeriness which is peculiar to all owls, but it seems more down to earth and nearer home* (Atlantic).

ee|ry (ir′ē), *adj.*, **-ri|er, -ri|est.** = eerie.

E.E.T.S., Early English Text Society.

EEZ (no periods), exclusive economic zone: *Our Government is talking about a British 200 mile EEZ* (London Times).

ef-, *prefix.* the form of **ex-**[1] before *f,* as in *effluent.*

ef|fa|ble (ef′ə bəl), *adj.* utterable; expressible. [< Latin *effābilis* < *effārī* utter < *ex-* out + *fārī* speak]

ef|face (ə fās′), *v.t.*, **-faced, -fac|ing.** **1** to rub out; blot out; do away with; destroy; wipe out: *The inscriptions on many ancient monuments have been effaced by time. It takes many years to efface the terrible memories of a war.* **SYN**: obliterate. See syn. under **erase. 2** *Figurative.* to keep (oneself) from being noticed; make inconspicuous: *The shy boy effaced himself by staying in the background.* [< Middle French *effacer* < Old French *esfacier* < *es-* away (< Latin *ex-*) + *face* face, appearance < Latin *faciēs* form]

ef|face|a|ble (ə fā′sə bəl), *adj.* that can be effaced.

ef|face|ment (ə fās′mənt), *n.* **1** the act of effacing. **2** the condition of being effaced.

ef|fac|er (ə fā′sər), *n.* a person or thing that effaces; destroyer.

ef|fect (ə fekt′), *n., v.* —*n.* **1** something made to happen by a person or thing; result: *The effect of the gale was to overturn several boats.* **2** the power to produce results; force; validity: *This contract is of no effect.* **3** influence: *The medicine had an immediate effect.* **4** an impression produced on the mind or senses, such as the combination of color and form in a picture: *Sunshine coming through leaves makes a lovely effect. The view gave the effect of a painting by Cézanne.* **5** something that produces such an impression: *The movie used many special effects with sounds and pictures to make the scenes appear real.* **6** purport; intent; meaning: *She did not openly say she opposed the measure but her speech was to that effect.*
—*v.t.* **1** to bring about; make happen; get done: *The war effected changes all over the world.* **SYN**: accomplish, achieve, realize, produce. **2** to make; construct.

effects, personal property; belongings; goods: *He lost all his personal effects in the fire. In ten minutes our effects were deposited in the guest's room of the Länsman's house* (Bayard Taylor).

for effect, for show in order to impress or influence others: *He said that only for effect; he really didn't mean it.*

give effect to, to put in operation; make active: *The teachers urged the principal to give effect to the proposal.*

in effect, a almost the same as; practically; virtually: *By constantly looking up at the clock he is saying, in effect, that he wants us to leave.* **b** in result or consequences: *The two methods are the same in effect.* **c** in force or operation; active: *The new rule has been in effect for a week.*

into effect, into operation; into action; into force: *When will the new rule go into effect?*

of no effect, with no results; useless: *Respectful message to his Majesty was of no effect* (Thomas Carlyle).

take effect, to begin to operate; become active: *The new regulations will take effect at once.*

to the effect, with the meaning or purpose: *He quotes ... a statement by Karl Kautsky to the effect that the proletariat, left to itself, can never arrive at socialism* (Edmund Wilson).

[< Latin *effectus, -ūs* < *efficere* work out, accomplish < *ex-* out + *facere* make] —**ef|fect′er,** *n.*

—*Syn. n.* **1 Effect, consequence, result** mean something produced by a cause. **Effect** applies to what happens directly and immediately: *The effect of raising the speed limit was an increase in the number of bad accidents.* **Consequence** applies to what follows, but not directly or immediately: *As a consequence, there was a state investigation of highway conditions.* **Result** ap-

Pronunciation Key: hat, āge, cãre, fär; let, ēqual, tėrm; it, īce; hot, ōpen, ôrder; **oi**l, **ou**t; cup, pu̇t, rüle; **ch**ild; lo**ng**; **th**in; **ᴛʜ**en; **zh**, measure; ə represents **a** in about, **e** in taken, **i** in pencil, **o** in lemon, **u** in circus.

plies to what happens as a final effect or consequence: *The result was a new set of traffic regulations.* See also **property** for synonym study including **effects**.

▶ See **affect**[2] for usage note.

ef|fect|i|ble (ə fek′tə bəl), *adj.* that can be effected.

ef|fec|tive (ə fek′tiv), *adj., n.* —*adj.* **1** able to cause something: *Light clothes are effective in keeping cool in warm weather.* **2** able to cause some desired result; getting results: *an effective medicine.* **3** in operation; active: *A bill passed by Congress becomes effective as soon as the President signs it.* **4** striking; impressive: *The artist made a very effective picture by using different shades of the same color.* **5** equipped and ready for fighting in the armed forces.
—*n.* **1** a member of the armed forces equipped and ready for fighting. **2** a military force equipped and ready for fighting. —**ef|fec′tive|ly**, *adv.* —**ef-fec′tive|ness**, *n.*
—*Syn. adj.* **1 Effective, effectual, efficient** mean producing an effect. **Effective** applies to anyone or anything that can or does produce an effect: *Several new drugs are effective in treating serious diseases.* **Effectual** implies that the effect produced is desirable or decisive: *The Christmas Seal campaign is an effectual means of teaching the public about tuberculosis.* **Efficient** implies that the effect is produced without waste of time or energy: *A skilled surgeon is efficient.*

effective horsepower, = brake horsepower.

effective resistance, the resistance of a conductor to an alternating current: *The actual resistance of a conductor at any frequency is called its effective resistance at that frequency* (Sears and Zemansky).

effective temperature, the temperature of a star as calculated by comparison of the star's radiation to optimum radiating conditions.

ef|fec|tiv|i|ty (ef′ek tiv′ə tē), *n.* effective quality; effectiveness: *Anaesthetics and related compounds that slow down respiration and all but prevent oxygen from reaching an area of effectivity are impractical to use but they do give some protection* (Alexander Hollaender).

ef|fect|less (ə fekt′lis), *adj.* without effect; ineffectual.

ef|fec|tor (ə fek′tər), *n.* a muscle or gland capable of responding to a nerve impulse: *Since the muscles and glands give the response they are termed effectors* (Harbaugh and Goodrich).

ef|fects (ə fekts′), *n.pl.* See under **effect**.

ef|fec|tu|al (ə fek′chu̇ əl), *adj.* **1** producing the desired effect; capable of producing the desired effect: *Quinine is an effectual remedy for malaria.* **SYN**: See syn. under **effective**. **2** valid. —**ef|fec′tu|al|ly**, *adv.* —**ef|fec′tu|al|ness**, *n.*

effectual calling, (in Calvinism) the special grace given to those elected to salvation.

ef|fec|tu|al|i|ty (ə fek′chu̇ al′ə tē), *n.* the quality of being effectual.

ef|fec|tu|ate (ə fek′chu̇ āt), *v.t.*, **-at|ed, -at|ing.** to make happen; bring about; carry into effect; cause. **SYN**: accomplish. [< Middle French *effectuer* (with English *-ate*[1]), learned borrowing from Latin *effectus;* see etym. under **effect**]

ef|fec|tu|a|tion (ə fek′chu̇ ā′shən), *n.* a causing; bringing about; accomplishment.

ef|fem|i|na|cy (ə fem′ə nə sē), *n.* lack of manly qualities; weakness or softness that is not manly: *It tempts him to exploit the effeminacy and vanity of Richard in the early scenes* (London Times).

ef|fem|i|nate (*adj., n.* ə fem′ə nit; *v.* ə fem′ə nāt), *adj., n., v.,* **-nat|ed, -nat|ing.** —*adj.* **1** lacking in manly qualities; showing weakness or softness that is not manly. **SYN**: womanish. **2** characterized by unmanly weakness or delicacy. **SYN**: womanish.
—*n.* an effeminate man or boy.
—*v.t.* to make effeminate.
—*v.i.* to become effeminate.
[< Latin *effēminātus,* past participle of *effēmināre* make a woman of < *ex-* + *fēmina* woman] —**ef-fem′i|nate|ly**, *adv.* —**ef|fem′i|nate|ness**, *n.*

ef|fem|i|na|tion (ə fem′ə nā′shən), *n.* the process of making or of becoming effeminate.

ef|fem|i|nize (ə fem′ə nīz), *v.t.*, **-nized, -niz|ing.** to make effeminate.

ef|fen|di (e fen′dē), *n., pl.* **-dis. 1** a former Turkish title of respect meaning about the same as "Sir" or "Master." **2** a person having this title in countries of the Near East, such as a Turkish doctor, official, or scholar. [< Turkish *efendi* < Greek *authéntēs* master, perpetrator, author, perhaps < *auto-* by oneself + unrecorded *héntēs* one who acts]

ef|fer|ent (ef′ər ənt), *adj., n.* —*adj.* carrying outward from a central organ or point. Efferent nerves carry impulses from the brain to the muscles.
—*n.* an efferent nerve. See picture under **afferent**.
[< Latin *efferēns, -entis,* present participle of *efferre* carry out < *ex-* out + *ferre* carry] —**ef′fer-ent|ly**, *adv.*

ef|fer|vesce (ef′ər ves′), *v.i.*, **-vesced, -vesc|ing. 1** to give off bubbles of gas; bubble: *Ginger ale effervesces.* **2** *Figurative.* to be lively and gay; be excited: *She effervesces at parties but is quiet and serious in private conversation.* **SYN**: sparkle. [< Latin *effervēscere* boil up < *ex-* out + *fervēscere* begin to boil < *fervēre* be hot]

ef|fer|ves|cence (ef′ər ves′əns), *n.* **1** the act or process of giving off bubbles of gas; bubbling. **2** *Figurative.* liveliness and gaiety: *Mr. Holbrook appeared at the door, rubbing his hands in very effervescence of hospitality* (Elizabeth Gaskell).

ef|fer|ves|cen|cy (ef′ər ves′ən sē), *n.* = effervescence.

ef|fer|ves|cent (ef′ər ves′ənt), *adj.* **1** giving off bubbles of gas; bubbling: *Ginger ale is effervescent. Effervescent waters contain large quantities of dissolved carbonic acid which, when exposed to the air, decomposes, liberating carbon dioxide* (Parks and Steinbach). **2** *Figurative.* lively and gay: *Our cheerleader has an effervescent personality.* —**ef′fer|ves′cent|ly**, *adv.*

ef|fer|vesc|i|ble (ef′ər ves′ə bəl), *adj.* that can effervesce.

ef|fer|ves|cive (ef′ər ves′iv), *adj.* tending to effervesce.

ef|fete (i fēt′), *adj., n.* —*adj.* **1** no longer able to produce; worn out; exhausted; decadent: *During the Middle Ages, Greek civilization declined and became effete. The critic takes the measure of our abundance ... and writes at white heat of our effete ways* (Saturday Review). **2** not manly; effeminate: *He is painfully effete and skittish as a girl* (New Yorker). *There is something ludicrous about superior, languid, effete Paters and Wildes identifying themselves with the ancient Greeks* (Stephen Spender).
—*n.* an effete person: *... a center for "effetes" and intellectuals* (Philip Roth).
[< Latin *effētus* worn out by bearing (of young) < *ex-* out + *fētus* having brought forth < a root *fē-* to bear] —**ef|fete′ly**, *adv.* —**ef|fete′ness**, *n.*

ef|fi|ca|cious (ef′ə kā′shəs), *adj.* producing the desired results; effective: *Vaccination is efficacious in preventing smallpox. When sickness develops, the average Japanese ... will not fail to visit a nearby Buddhist temple or Shinto shrine noted for its efficacious charms* (Atlantic). —**ef′fi-ca′cious|ly**, *adv.* —**ef′fi|ca′cious|ness**, *n.*

ef|fi|cac|i|ty (ef′ə kas′ə tē), *n., pl.* **-ties.** = efficacy.

ef|fi|ca|cy (ef′ə kə sē), *n., pl.* **-cies.** the power to produce the effect wanted; effectiveness: *The efficacy of aspirin in relieving headaches is well known.* [< Latin *efficācia* < *efficāx, -ācis* efficacious < *efficere* accomplish; see etym. under **efficient**]

ef|fi|cien|cy (ə fish′ən sē), *n., pl.* **-cies. 1** the ability to do things without waste of time or energy: *efficiency in household and business management. The skilled carpenter worked with great efficiency to finish the job quickly.* **SYN**: effectiveness, efficacy. **2a** efficient operation: *Friction lowers the efficiency of a machine.* **b** the ratio of the useful work performed or the energy generated by a motor, machine, or other device to the energy supplied. Efficiency is the amount of energy we get out of a machine divided by the amount of energy we put into the machine. **3** Also, **efficiency apartment.** an apartment usually consisting of one or two rooms designed for serviceable accommodation of single people or business couples: *One of the city's most popular motels, consisting of 33 efficiencies plus owner's apartment* (Wall Street Journal).

efficiency expert or **engineer**, a person whose profession is to devise more effective, economical methods of doing things: *Some businessmen are afraid that the appearance of an "efficiency expert" (a term most management consultants loathe) would hurt employe morale* (Newsweek).

ef|fi|cient (ə fish′ənt), *adj.* **1** able to produce the effect wanted without waste of time or energy; capable: *An efficient worker deserves good pay. And as the shift to the suburbs continues unabated, the need for efficient food distribution persists* (Wall Street Journal). **SYN**: competent. See syn. under **effective**. **2** actually producing an effect: *Heat is the efficient cause in changing water to steam.* [< Latin *efficiēns, -entis,* present participle of *efficere* < *ex-* out + *facere* do, make] —**ef|fi′cient|ly**, *adv.*

ef|fig|i|al (e fij′ē əl), *adj.* having to do with or like an effigy.

ef|fi|gi|es (e fij′ē ēz), *n. Latin.* an effigy.

ef|fig|ur|ate (e fig′yə rāt), *adj. Botany.* **1** having a definite form. **2** fully developed in its subordinate parts.

ef|fi|gy (ef′ə jē), *n., pl.* **-gies.** an image or statue, usually of a person: *The dead man's monument bore his effigy.*
burn (or **hang**) **in effigy**, to burn or hang an image of a person to show hatred or contempt: *As the revolution gained strength, the dictator was hanged in effigy.*
[< Middle French *effigie,* learned borrowing from Latin *effigiēs* < *effingere* to fashion < *ex-* out + *fingere* to form]

ef|fla|tion (e flā′shən), *n.* a blowing or breathing forth; emanation. [< Latin *efflātus,* past participle of *efflāre* to blow out (< *ex-* out + *flāre* to blow) + English *-ion*]

ef|fleu|rage (ef′lə räzh′), *n.* (in massaging) gentle, superficial rubbing with the palm of the hand. [< French *effleurage* < *effleurer* to graze or to touch]

ef|flo|resce (ef′lô res′, -lō-), *v.i.*, **-resced, -resc|ing. 1** to burst into bloom; blossom out. **SYN**: flower. **2** *Chemistry.* **a** to change either throughout or on the surface to a powder by loss of water of crystallization when exposed to air. **b** to become covered with a crusty deposit when water evaporates. [< Latin *efflōrēscere* < *ex-* out + *flōrēscere* begin to flower < *flōrēre* to flower < *flōs, flōris* flower]

ef|flo|res|cence (ef′lô res′əns, -lō-), *n.* **1** the act or process of bursting into bloom; a flowering. **2** the state or period of flowering: (*Figurative.*) *The efflorescence of romantic music occurred during the 1800's.* (*Figurative.*) *The development of sensational popular journalism coincided with the efflorescence of political and intellectual populism* (Bulletin of Atomic Scientists). **3** a mass of flowers. **4** *Figurative.* anything like a mass of flowers: *... a detestable human efflorescence upon what would otherwise have been good pasture* (H. G. Wells). **5** *Chemistry.* **a** a change that occurs when crystals lose their water of crystallization and become powder. **b** the powder formed in this way. **c** the deposit formed in this way. **d** the formation of a crusty deposit when water evaporates from a solution. **6** an eruption on the skin; rash.

ef|flo|res|cen|cy (ef′lô res′ən sē, -lō-), *n., pl.* **-cies.** = efflorescence.

ef|flo|res|cent (ef′lô res′ənt, -lō-), *adj.* **1** bursting into bloom; flowering. **2** that changes from crystals into powder by losing water of crystallization when exposed to air. **3** covered with a deposit formed by efflorescence.

ef|flu|ence (ef′lu̇ əns), *n.* **1** an outward flow, especially of water, light, electricity, magnetism, or anything resembling such a flow. **2** a thing that flows out; emanation; efflux: *The mist was an effluence from the swamp.* (*Figurative.*) *She alone had the right to enter where she could feel the effluence of a mysterious presence* (Lytton Strachey).

ef|flu|ent (ef′lu̇ ənt), *adj., n.* —*adj.* flowing out or forth.
—*n.* **1** a thing that flows out or forth; outflow: *A conservative limit has been set on this radioactivity so that the effluent will not damage aquatic life* (Science). **2** a stream flowing out of a larger stream, lake, or reservoir. **3** sewage, water used in industrial plants, or other liquid waste discharged into a river or lake: *Established procedure at sewage works has been adequate to deal with all ordinary effluents until recently* (Science News).
[< Latin *effluēns, -entis,* present participle of *effluere* to flow out < *ex-* out + *fluere* flow]

ef|flu|vi|a (i flü′vē ə), *n.* effluviums; a plural of **effluvium.**

ef|flu|vi|al (i flü′vē əl), *adj.* of or having to do with effluvium.

ef|flu|vi|um (i flü′vē əm), *n., pl.* **-vi|a** or **-vi|ums.** a vapor or odor, usually unpleasant: *The effluvium from the nearby marsh permeated the air.* [< Latin *effluvium* a flowing out < *effluere;* see etym. under **effluent**]

ef|flux (ef′luks), *n., pl.* **ef|flux|es. 1** an outward flow, as of water. **2** a thing that flows out; effluence. **3** an outflow of any kind: *the efflux of money from the treasury.* [< Latin *ex-* out + *flūxus, -ūs* a flux, flowing < *fluere* to flow]

ef|flux|ion (e fluk′shən), *n.* a flowing out; efflux: (*Figurative.*) *Due to the effluxion of time, the only remedy now available was an order of certiorari, which could be made only by the Divisional Court* (Manchester Guardian Weekly).

ef|fort (ef′ərt), *n.* **1** the use of energy and strength to do something; trying hard: *Climbing a steep hill takes effort. With much effort the little boy counted to 100.* **2** a hard try; strong attempt: *He did not win but at least he made the effort.* **3** the result of effort; thing done with effort; achievement: *Works of literature or art are literary or artistic efforts.* **4** *Mechanics.* a force upon a body due to a definite cause, such as the force which is applied in a simple machine. In a crowbar or lever, the effort is at one end, the load is

on the other, and the fulcrum is between them. [< Middle French *effort* < Old French *esfort* < *esforcier* to force, exert < *es-* out (< Latin *ex-*) + *forcier* < *force* force]
—*Syn.* **1 Effort, endeavor, application** mean active use of physical or mental power to do something. **Effort** implies trying hard, but not necessarily long or effectively: *I made an effort to finish my work today.* **Endeavor**, more formal, implies sincere and serious effort continued over some time: *By constant endeavor, the minister built up a large congregation.* **Application** emphasizes continued effort and close attention to what one is doing: *Strict application to his work has given success, though he has little talent.*

effort arm, the distance between the fulcrum of a lever and the applied force or effort.

ef|fort|ful (ef′ərt fəl), *adj.* exhibiting or full of effort; requiring effort. —**ef′fort|ful|ly**, *adv.* —**ef′fort|ful|ness**, *n.*

ef|fort|less (ef′ərt lis), *adj.* requiring or showing little or no effort; easy. **SYN**: See syn. under **easy**. —**ef′fort|less|ly**, *adv.* —**ef′fort|less|ness**, *n.*

ef|frac|tion (e frak′shən), *n.* the act of breaking open by force, as a door or safe.

ef|fron|ter|y (ə frun′tər ē, -trē), *n., pl.* **-ter|ies**. shameless boldness; impudence: *The politician had the effrontery to ask the people he had insulted to vote for him.* **SYN**: presumption, insolence, audacity. [< French *effronterie* < Old French *esfronte* shameless < Latin *effrōns* barefaced < *ex-* out + *frōns, frontis* brow]

ef|fulge (i fulj′), *v.t., v.i.,* **-fulged, -fulg|ing.** to shine or send forth brilliantly. [< Latin *effulgēre* < *ex-* out + *fulgēre* shine]

ef|ful|gence (i ful′jəns), *n.* brightness; radiance; splendor: *the effulgence of the full moon, the effulgence of the queen's jewels.* **SYN**: brilliance.

ef|ful|gent (i ful′jənt), *adj.* shining brightly; radiant: *Again I had the same little effulgent flash of intuition that she knew much more about him than, for some reason, she meant to indicate* (New Yorker). **SYN**: lustrous. [< Latin *effulgēns, -entis,* present participle of *effulgēre;* see etym. under **effulge**] —**ef|ful′gent|ly**, *adv.*

ef|fund (e fund′), *v.t.* to pour out.

ef|fuse (*v.* i fyüz′; *adj.* i fyüs′), *v.,* **-fused, -fus|ing,** *adj.* —*v.t.* to pour out; spill; shed: *Methodists wanted to increase literacy partly for the success of the religious tracts which their printing presses effused* (Harper's). —*v.i.* to exude.
—*adj.* **1** *Botany.* spread out loosely or without definite form: *effuse flowers.* **2** *Zoology.* (of certain shells) having the lips separated by a gap or groove.
[< Latin *effūsus,* past participle of *effundere* < *ex-* out + *fundere* pour]

ef|fu|sion (i fyü′zhən), *n.* **1** a pouring out, especially of a liquid: *There was an effusion of blood when he cut his finger. There was an effusion of lava from the erupting volcano.* **SYN**: gush. **2** *Figurative.* unrestrained expression of feeling in talking or writing: *Poets whose effusions entranced my soul* (Mary Shelley). **3** *Medicine.* **a** the escape of a fluid, such as blood or lymph, from its natural vessel into surrounding tissues or cavities. **b** the fluid that escapes. **4** *Physics.* the movement or flow of gas molecules through a small hole or holes.

ef|fu|sive (i fyü′siv), *adj., n.* —*adj.* **1** showing too much feeling; too demonstrative and emotional: *Peel ... was not effusive; he did not pour out his emotions* (Justin McCarthy). **2** *Geology.* formed by being poured out as lava on the surface of the earth. **3** *Archaic.* pouring out; overflowing.
—*n. Geology.* an effusive rock. —**ef|fu′sive|ly**, *adv.* —**ef|fu′sive|ness**, *n.*

Ef|ik (ef′ik), *n., pl.* **-ik** or **-iks. 1** a member of a tribe that lives around the estuary of the Cross and Old Kalabar rivers in southeastern Nigeria. **2** the Bantu language of this tribe.

eft[1] (eft), *n.* **1** a small newt. An eft lives on land until it matures. **2** (formerly) any small lizard. [Old English *efete.* Compare etym. under **newt.**]

eft[2] (eft), *adv. Archaic.* eftsoon; again; afterwards. [Old English *eft.* See related etym. at **after.**]

EFT or **EFTS**, electronic funds transfer (system): *EFTS (also referred to in some circles as the "checkless society") is a plan to eliminate paper by moving money among major financial institutions via computer* (New York Times).

EFTA (no periods), European Free Trade Association (an economic union of European countries not included in the Common Market, established in 1959).

eft|soon (eft sün′), *adv. Archaic.* **1** soon afterward. **2** again. [Old English *eftsōna* < *eft* again, eft[2] + *sōna* at once]

eft|soons (eft sünz′), *adv. Archaic.* eftsoon.

e.g., for example; for instance (Latin, *exempli gratia*).
► **E.g.** (not usually italicized) is regularly preceded by a comma or semicolon and followed by a comma or colon. In ordinary prose, formal or informal, it is now usually replaced by *for example.*

Eg., **1** Egypt. **2** Egyptian.

e|gad (i gad′), *interj.* a mild oath, like "by Jove." [probably alteration of *Oh God!*]

e|gal (ē′gəl), *adj. Obsolete.* equal. [< Old French *egal* < Latin *aequālis*]

e|gal|i|tar|i|an (i gal′ə tãr′ē ən), *n., adj.* —*n.* a person who believes that all people are equal; equalitarian: *I'm an egalitarian if you will translate the phrase to mean equality of opportunity and a casteless rather than classless society* (Newsweek).
—*adj.* believing that all people are equal: *Britain today is a comparatively egalitarian society* (Time).
[< French *égalitaire* (< *égalité;* see etym. under **equality**) + English *-ian*]

e|gal|i|tar|i|an|ism (i gal′ə tãr′ē ə niz′əm), *n.* belief in equality, especially in social equality.

é|ga|li|té (ā gȧ lē tā′), *n. French.* equality.

e|gal|i|ty (i gal′ə tē), *n., pl.* **-ties**. equality. [< French *égalité*]

e|gall (ē′gəl), *adj. Obsolete.* equal.

é|gare|ment (ā gȧr män′), *n. French.* **1** a going astray; wandering. **2** bewilderment; derangement.

Eg|bo (eg′bō), *n.* a Nigerian secret society, at one time existing as a political bond between various towns, especially in southeastern Nigeria.

EGD or **egd** (no periods), electrogasdynamic; electrogasdynamics.

E|ge|ri|a (i jir′ē ə), *n.* **1** *Roman Legend.* a nymph who gave prophetic advice to Numa Pompilius, the second king of Rome. **2** a guarding or protecting god.

e|gest (ē jest′), *v.t.* to discharge; excrete: *to egest waste matter. The skin egests sweat.* [< Latin *ēgestus,* past participle of *ēgerere* < *ex-* out + *gerere* carry, lead]

e|ges|ta (ē jes′tə), *n.pl.* matter discharged from the body; excrement. [< Latin *ēgesta,* neuter plural of *ēgestus;* see etym. under **egest**]

e|ges|tion (ē jes′chən), *n.* **1** the act or process of egesting. **2** something egested.

e|ges|tive (ē jes′tiv), *adj.* of or having to do with egestion.

***egg**[1]
definition 1

parts of an egg:

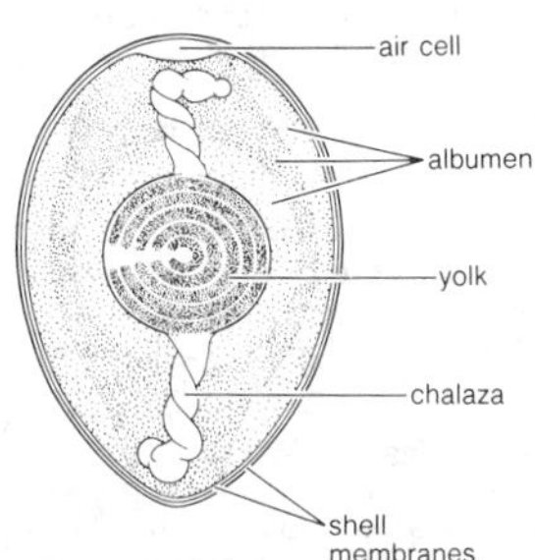

***egg**[1] (eg), *n., v.* —*n.* **1** a round or oval body that is laid by the female of birds, insects, many reptiles, amphibians, fishes, and other animals that do not bring forth living young. An egg is covered with a shell or membrane. Young animals hatch from these eggs. **2** the contents of an egg, especially a hen's egg, used as food: *Father likes two boiled eggs for breakfast. Prices of top-grade white eggs fell as much as six cents a dozen* (Wall Street Journal). **3** anything shaped like a hen's egg. **4** a female reproductive cell; egg cell; ovum. **5** *Informal.* a person: *a bad egg, a good egg.* **6** *Slang.* **a** an aerial bomb. **b** an underwater mine.
—*v.i.* **1** to prepare (food) with eggs. **2** to hit with (rotten) eggs.
egg on one's face, humiliation: *It is strange that these trends should coincide with the sudden splattering of egg on Uncle Sam's face in Madagascar* (C. L. Sulzberger).
have (or **put**) **all one's eggs in one basket**, to risk everything that one has on one chance: *[She] admonishes against putting "all our eggs in one basket—we don't want to lean too heavily upon the Eisenhower popularity"* (New York Times).
lay an egg, *Slang.* to fail utterly; flop: *What if "The Big Show" laid an egg? Worse yet, what if I laid an egg in "The Big Show"?* (Tallulah Bankhead).
walk on eggs, to act with extreme caution: *[They] are walking on eggs trying to avoid provoking Soviet indignation* (Canadian Saturday Night).
[< Scandinavian (compare Old Icelandic *egg*)]
—**egg′like′**, *adj.*

egg[2] (eg), *v.t.* to urge or encourage (on): *We egged the team on when it was behind.* **SYN**: incite. [< Scandinavian (compare Old Icelandic *eggja* < *egg* edge)]

egg albumin, the albumin which occurs in the white of eggs.

egg and anchor, = egg and dart.

egg and dart, a decorative pattern consisting of an egg-shaped ornament alternating with a dartlike, tonguelike, or anchorlike ornament. It is a characteristic decoration on the entablature of an Ionic column.

egg and spoon race, a race in which contestants must balance an egg in a spoon while running.

egg and tongue, = egg and dart.

egg apparatus, the group of cells at the micropylar end of the embryo sac in seed plants, only one of which is fertile.

egg apple, the fruit of the eggplant.

egg|beat|er (eg′bē′tər), *n.* **1** a device with revolving blades for beating eggs, cream, or batter. **2** *U.S. Slang.* a helicopter: *The egg beaters ... are a wonderfully reassuring sight to men who fly over water so cold that fifteen minutes' immersion could be fatal* (Saturday Evening Post).

egg bird, any one of various sea birds, such as the sooty tern, whose eggs are used for food.

egg-bound (eg′bound′), *adj.* (of hens) unable to discharge an egg from the oviduct.

egg carton, a paper container for holding a dozen or half-dozen eggs, especially a molded kind made of plastic or pasteboard.

egg case, **1** a membrane or covering around an egg. **2** = egg sac.

egg cell, the female reproductive cell produced by a plant or animal; ovum. A new animal or plant develops from a fertilized egg cell.

egg coal, coal from 5 to 3 inches in size.

egg cozy, *British.* a cover to keep a boiled egg warm.

egg cream, *U.S.* a drink made by mixing chocolate syrup and milk with soda water: *Wooden chairs at close-packed tables at which dedicated rock heads can sit sipping egg creams (oh, boy)* (New Yorker).

egg|cup (eg′kup′), *n.* an egg-shaped cup in which a boiled egg is served.

egg dance, a dance performed blindfolded among a number of eggs, a feat formerly popular in England.

egg|er (eg′ər), *n.* **1** a person who gathers eggs. **2** any one of various moths whose larvae eat foliage, such as the tent caterpillar.

egg flip, = eggnog.

egg foo yung (eg′ fü′ yung′), a fried omelet filled with bean sprouts, onions, and shrimp or pork, and seasoned with soy sauce. [< Chinese *fu yung*]

egg glass, **1** a glass for holding an egg. **2** a sandglass in which the running of the sand indicates the time during which an egg should be boiled.

egg|head (eg′hed′), *n. Informal,* an intellectual: *An intellectual is "one of the finest minds in the nation" when he agrees with us, and an impractical egghead when he doesn't* (Birmingham News).

egg|head|ed (eg′hed′id), *adj. Informal.* intellectual: *The concerns which give males dignity, integrity, authority, and true appeal ... are today regarded in the USA as eggheaded and silly* (Philip Wylie). —**egg′head′ed|ness**, *n.*

egg|head|ism (eg′hed′iz əm), *n. Informal.* intellectualism: *Los Alamos is replete with the apparatus of eggheadism—the little theater, the well-stocked library, the concert association* (Wall Street Journal).

egg|less (eg′lis), *adj.* having no egg or eggs; producing no eggs.

egg|nog (eg′nog′), *n.* a drink made of eggs beaten up with milk and sugar. It often has whiskey, brandy, or wine in it. [American English < *egg*[1] + *nog* strong ale]

egg|plant (eg′plant′, -plänt′), *n., adj.* —*n.* **1** a plant with a large, purple fruit shaped somewhat like an egg. It belongs to the nightshade family. Some ornamental varieties may be white, yellow, or striped. **2** the fruit, used as a vegetable; garden egg.
—*adj.* dark purple: *an eggplant organza.*

egg roll, a casing of egg dough containing a mixture of minced vegetables and roast pork, fried in deep fat.

egg rolling, **1** a race in which eggs are rolled

Pronunciation Key: hat, āge, cãre, fär; let, ēqual, tėrm; it, īce; hot, ōpen, ôrder; oil, out; cup, pu̇t, rüle; child; long; thin; ᴛʜen; zh, measure; ə represents **a** in about, **e** in taken, **i** in pencil, **o** in lemon, **u** in circus.

downhill. **2** Easter egg rolling.

egg sac, **1** the silken cocoon in which the eggs of most spiders are deposited and in which they hibernate. **2** one of the pair of egg-containing receptacles at the hinder end in crustaceans, such as some copepods.

eggs Benedict or **benedict**, a dish of poached eggs on a slice of broiled ham served on toast or English muffin and topped with hollandaise sauce. [< *Benedict*, a proper name]

egg|shell (eg′shel′), *n., adj.* **—*n.*** **1** the shell covering an egg. **2** a yellowish white.
—*adj.* **1** like an eggshell; very thin and delicate. **2** yellowish-white.

eggshell china or **porcelain**, porcelain ware of extreme thinness and delicacy.

egg timer, a small sandglass used for determining the time in boiling eggs.

egg tooth, a hard, toothlike projection developing in the jaws of embryo birds, chicks, snakes, and other oviparous animals, that serves to cut the egg membrane and shell at hatching and then drops off.

egg tray, = egg carton.

egg|walk (eg′wôk′), *v.i. Informal.* to move or advance with extreme care and tact: *... eggwalking through a series of compromises between the secular and sacred* (Time).

egg|whisk (eg′hwisk′), *n. British.* an eggbeater (def. 1).

egg white, the white of an egg; albumen.

egg|y (eg′ē), *adj.* **egg|i|er, egg|i|est.** of or like an egg; tasting of cooked eggs.

e|gi|lops (ē′jə lops, ej′ə-), *n.* an ulcer or fistula in the inner angle of the eye. Also, **aegilops.** [< Latin *aegilops* < Greek *aigílōps* < *aíx, aigós* goat + *ṓps* eye, face]

e|gis (ē′jis), *n.* = aegis.

Eg|la|more (eg′lə môr, -mōr), *n.* **Sir**, a brave knight and hero, one of King Arthur's Round Table.

Eg|la|mour (eg′lə mu̇r), *n.* **Sir**, = Eglamore.

eg|lan|tine (eg′lən tīn, -tēn), *n.* **1** a wild rose with a tall, prickly stem and single, pink flowers; sweetbrier. **2** any one of certain other plants, such as the woodbine and dog rose. [< Middle French *eglantine* (diminutive) < Old French *aiglent* < Vulgar Latin *aculentus* spiny < Latin *acus, -ūs* needle]

eg|la|tere (eg′lə tir), *n. Obsolete.* the eglantine. [< Old French *esglantier* < *aiglent;* see etym. under **eglantine**]

eg|le|ston|ite (eg′əl stə nīt), *n.* a native oxychloride of mercury, occurring in brownish isometric crystals. [< Thomas *Egleston*, 1832-1900, an American mining engineer + *-ite*[1]]

e|glo|mi|se or **é|glo|mi|sé** (ā′glə mi zā′), *adj.* painted on the back of a glass or glass panel so that the decoration may be seen on the front: *an eglomise mirror.* [< French *églomisé* < *Glomy*, a Parisian picture framer of the 1700's]

e|go (ē′gō, eg′ō), *n., pl.* **e|gos. 1** the individual as a whole in his capacity to think, feel, and act; self. **2** conceit; egotism: *The new boy's display of ego made the other students dislike him.* **3** *Psychoanalysis.* the part of the personality that is conscious of the environment and adapts to it. **4** *Philosophy.* the element of being that consciously and continuously enables an individual to think, feel, and act. [< Latin *ego* I]

e|go|cen|tric (ē′gō sen′trik, eg′ō-), *adj., n.* **—*adj.*** **1** self-centered; egoistic. **2** having or recognizing the self as the center of all things.
—*n.* an egocentric person.

e|go|cen|tri|cal|ly (ē′gō sen′trə klē, eg′ō-), *adv.* in an egocentric manner.

e|go|cen|tric|i|ty (ē′gō sen tris′ə tē, eg′ō-), *n.* egocentric quality or state; a being self-centered.

e|go|cen|trism (ē′gō sen′triz əm, eg′ō-), *n.* the condition of being egocentric; self-centeredness; egocentricity: *By the age of 7-8, egocentrism is lessening, and the child acquires skill in communicating and cooperating with others* (New Scientist).

e|go-de|fense (ē′gō di fens′, eg′ō-), *n. Psychology.* = defense mechanism.

e|go-dys|ton|ic (ē′gō dis ton′ik, eg′ō-), *adj. Psychology.* inacceptable to or inconsistent with the ego: *ego-dystonic processes.*

ego ideal, *Psychoanalysis.* a person's ideal of self-fulfillment, made up of certain characteristics of parents and others with whom he has identified himself.

e|go|ism (ē′gō iz əm, eg′ō-), *n.* **1** seeking the welfare of oneself only; selfishness. **2** talking too much about oneself; conceit; egotism. **3** the ethical doctrine that morality lies in the pursuit of individual self-interest, and that self-interest motivates all conduct. [< French *égoïsme* < New Latin *egoismus* < Latin *ego* I]
▶See **egotism** for usage note.

e|go|ist (ē′gō ist, eg′ō-), *n.* **1** a person who seeks the welfare of himself only; selfish person. **2** a person who talks too much about himself; conceited person. **3** a believer in egoism as a principle of human conduct.

e|go|is|tic (ē′gō is′tik, eg′ō-), *adj.* **1** seeking the welfare of oneself only; selfish. **2** talking too much about oneself; conceited. **—e′go|is′ti|cal|ly**, *adv.*

e|go|is|ti|cal (ē′gō is′tə kəl, eg′ō-), *adj.* = egoistic.

e|go|less (ē′gō lis, eg′ō-), *adj.* unhampered by the ego; unself-conscious: *There is a complete, egoless absorption, and no sensation of being used by or using circumstances and people* (Maclean's). **—e′go|less|ness**, *n.*

e|go|ma|ni|a (ē′gō mā′nē ə, eg′ō-), *n.* abnormal egotism.

e|go|ma|ni|ac (ē′gō mā′nē ak), *n.* an abnormally conceited person.

e|go|ma|ni|a|cal (ē′gō mə nī′ə kəl, eg′ō-), *adj.* characterized by egomania; abnormally conceited.

e|go-syn|ton|ic (ē′gō sin ton′ik, eg′ō-), *adj. Psychology.* acceptable to or consistent with the ego: *ego-syntonic impulses.*

e|go|tism (ē′gə tiz əm, eg′ə-), *n.* **1** a thinking, talking, or writing too much of oneself; excessive use of *I, my,* and *me;* conceit. **2** selfishness. [< Latin *ego* I + inserted *-t-* + English *-ism*]
▶**Egotism, egoism** mean a habit of thinking about oneself. Although some people use them interchangeably, the words retain different meanings in careful usage. *Egotism* emphasizes conceit, boasting, and selfishness in talking about oneself and one's own affairs: *His egotism keeps him from having friends. Egoism* emphasizes looking at everyone and everything only as it affects oneself and one's own welfare, but does not suggest boasting or annoying conceit, nor always selfishness: *We forget the natural egoism of a genius when he is charming.*

e|go|tist (ē′gə tist, eg′ə-), *n.* **1** a person who thinks, talks, or writes about himself too much; conceited person: *Perhaps the most eminent egotist that ever appeared in the world was Montaigne* (Joseph Addison). **2** a selfish person.

e|go|tis|tic (ē′gə tis′tik, eg′ə-), *adj.* **1** characterized by egotism; conceited. **2** selfish. **—e′go|tis′ti|cal|ly**, *adv.*

e|go|tis|ti|cal (ē′gə tis′tə kəl, eg′ə-), *adj.* = egotistic.

e|go|tize (ē′gə tīz, eg′ə-), *v.i.,* **-tized, -tiz|ing.** to talk or write too much about oneself; show egotism.

ego trip, *Informal.* something done mainly to show off or boost one's ego: *There is much more ... in this primary than those "ego trips" by diverse political personalities* (New York Times).

e|go-trip|per (ē′gō trip′ər, eg′ō-), *n. Informal.* a conceited or self-indulgent person.

e|gre|gious (i grē′jəs), *adj.* **1** very great; outrageous; flagrant: *He committed an egregious blunder in not stopping when the traffic light was red.* **2** remarkable; extraordinary: *She has an egregious need to be successful in everything she does.* [< Latin *ēgregius* (with English *-ous*) < *ex-* out + *grex, gregis* herd, flock] **—e|gre′gious|ly**, *adv.* **—e|gre′gious|ness**, *n.*

e|gress (ē′gres), *n., v.* **—*n.*** **1** going out: *The door was locked and no other egress was possible.* **2** a way out; exit: *The egress was plainly marked on the doors of the theater.* **SYN:** outlet. **3** the right to go out: *The deed reserved the right of egress from the neighboring property.* **4** *Astronomy.* the emergence of one heavenly body from behind or before the disk of another, for example at the end of an eclipse.
—*v.i.* to go out; go forth.
[< Latin *ēgressus, -ūs* < *ēgredī* go out < *ex-* out + *gradī* to step, go]

e|gres|sion (i gresh′ən), *n.* the action of going out; egress.

e|gret (ē′gret, eg′ret), *n.* **1** any one of various snow-white or grayish herons which in mating season grow tufts of beautiful, long plumes: *To ornithologists the true egret is "Egretta candidissima"—the whitest egret* (Science News Letter). **2** one of its plumes; aigrette. [< Middle French *aigrette* < Old French *egreste* heron < Old Provençal *aigron,* perhaps < a Germanic word]

e|gual|men|te (ā′gwäl men′tā), *adv. Italian. Music.* evenly.

e|gut|tu|late (i gut′yə lāt, -lit), *adj. Botany.* without spots.

Egypt., Egyptian.

E|gyp|ti|ac (i jip′tē ak), *adj.* of or having to do with ancient Egypt: *the Egyptiac civilization.*

E|gyp|tian (i jip′shən), *adj., n.* **—*adj.*** **1** of or having to do with Egypt or its people: *The Pyramids were built for ancient Egyptian monarchs.* **2** = Gypsy.
—*n.* **1** a person born or living in Egypt. **2** the Hamitic language of the ancient Egyptians. **3** = Gypsy.

spoil the Egyptians, to despoil the spoilers or oppressors, or those who are rich and powerful (in the Bible, Exodus 3:22 and 12:36): *Easing a world of such misproud priests ... of their jewels and their gimcracks, is a lawful spoiling of the Egyptians* (Scott).

Egyptian bean, the edible seed of the lablab.

Egyptian black, = basalt ware.

Egyptian blue, a blue pigment used by the ancient Egyptians, composed of the silicates of copper and lime.

Egyptian bondage, slavery like that of the Israelites in Egypt.

Egyptian clover, = berseem.

Egyptian cotton, a kind of cotton with lemon-colored flowers and long, silky, light-tan fibers, much grown in the United States.

Egyptian darkness, total darkness.

E|gyp|tian|ism (i jip′shə niz əm), *n.* an Egyptian characteristic or characteristics.

E|gyp|tian|i|za|tion (i jip′shə nə zā′shən), *n.* the act or process of Egyptianizing: *Tired of waiting politely for U.S. economic aid, Nasser suddenly decreed the Egyptianization of British and French banks, insurance companies, shipping and trading firms* (Newsweek).

E|gyp|tian|ize (i jip′shə nīz), *v.t.,* **-ized, -iz|ing.** to make Egyptian in appearance, customs, or character.

Egyptian jerboa, a species of North African jerboa living in communities maintained in underground galleries. Its body is from 6 to 8 inches long. Egyptian jerboas make good pets.

Egyptian pound, the basic Egyptian monetary unit worth about $2.30.

Egyptian vulture, = Pharaoh's hen.

Egyptol., Egyptology.

E|gyp|to|log|i|cal (i jip′tə loj′ə kəl), *adj.* of or having to do with Egyptology.

E|gyp|tol|o|gist (ē′jip tol′ə jist), *n.* an expert in Egyptology.

E|gyp|tol|o|gy (ē′jip tol′ə jē), *n.* the study of the monuments, history, language, and other aspects of the culture of ancient Egypt.

eh (ā), *interj.* **1** an exclamation expressing doubt, surprise, or failure to hear exactly: *Eh? What's that you said?* **2** an exclamation suggesting "Yes" for an answer: *That's a good joke, eh?*

e|heu, fu|ga|ces (la|bun|tur an|ni) (ā′hyü fü-gä′kās läbün′tu̇r än′ē), *Latin.* alas, (the years are) fleeting: *Old Paul is now dead and young Paul is fifty. Eheu, fugaces!* (New Yorker).

EHF or **ehf** (no periods), extremely high frequency (of or having to do with the electromagnetic spectrum between 30 and 300 gigahertz, especially with reference to radio transmission and reception).

EHT (no periods), extra high tension.

EHV (no periods), extra high voltage.

E.I., **1** East Indian. **2** East Indies.

ei|de (ī′dē, ā′dā), *n.* plural of **eidos**.

ei|dent (ī′dənt), *adj. Scottish.* diligent; busy. [Middle English *ithen* < Scandinavian (compare Old Icelandic *ithinn*)]

ei|der (ī′dər), *n.* **1** = eider duck. **2** = eider down (def. 1). [< Old Icelandic *æthar*, genitive of *æthr*]

eider down, or **ei|der|down** (ī′dər doun′), *n.* **1** the soft feathers from the breasts of eider ducks, used to stuff pillows and quilts, and as trimming; eider. **2** a quilt stuffed with these feathers. [ultimately < Scandinavian (compare Old Icelandic *æthar-dūn*)]

eider duck, any one of several large, northern sea ducks with very soft feathers on their breasts. The males are black with white heads and backs. The females line their nests with eider down plucked from their breasts.

eider yarn, a soft yarn made from merino wool.

ei|det|ic (ī det′ik), *adj.* of or having to do with extremely clear images of previous optical impressions: *eidetic imagery.* [< German *eidetisch* < Greek *eidētikós* < *eîdos* form] **—ei|det′i|cal|ly**, *adv.*

eidetic image, an image (experienced especially by children) which revives a previous optical impression with the clearness of hallucination.

ei|do|graph (ī′də graf, -gräf), *n.* an instrument for mechanical copying, especially of drawings or diagrams, upon the same or a reduced or enlarged scale. [< Greek *eîdos* form + English *-graph*]

ei|dol|ic (ī dol′ik), *adj.* of the nature of an eidolon; like an eidolon.

ei|do|lon (ī dō′lən), *n.* an image; specter; phantom. [< Greek *eídōlon* specter, image]

ei|dop|tom|e|try (ī′dop tom′ə trē), *n.* determination of the degree of acuteness of vision. [< Greek *eîdos* form + English *optometry*]

ei|dos (ī′dos, ā′-), *n., pl.* **ei|de.** the form or appearance of a culture, as distinguished from its spirit or ideals: *... a contrasting pair of aspects that have been called the ethos and the eidos of culture* (Alfred Kroeber). [< New Latin *eidos* < Greek *eîdos* form]

ei|gen|fre|quen|cy (ī′gən frē′kwən sē), *n., pl.* **-cies.** *Physics.* any one of the characteristic frequencies of the wave patterns of a vibrating system. [< German *Eigenfrequenz* < *eigen* own + *frequenz* frequency]

ei|gen|func|tion (ī′gən fungk′shən), *n.* **1** *Mathematics.* a solution in a differential or integral equation which satisfies given conditions for only certain values of a parameter. **2** *Physics.* one of the characteristic wave patterns of a vibrating system. [< German *Eigenfunktion* < *eigen* own + *Funktion* function]

ei|gen|val|ue (ī′gən val′yü), *n.* **1** *Mathematics.* one of the characteristic values of a parameter to which an eigenfunction belongs. **2** *Physics.* one of the values of the possible energy levels in a quantum-mechanical system. [partial translation of German *Eigenwert*]

eight (āt), *n., adj.* **—*n.*** **1** one more than seven; 8: *four and four make eight.* **2** a group of eight persons or things. **3** a crew of eight rowers. **4** a playing card, domino, billiard ball, or other part of a game with eight spots or an "8" on it.
—*adj.* being one more than seven.
[Middle English *eghte,* Old English *eahta*]

Eight (āt), *n.* **the Eight,** the Ashcan School of painters, so called because it was formed in 1907 by eight New York painters.

eight ball, 1 the black ball in the game of pool bearing an "8", which in certain varieties of the game the player is not allowed to shoot at until he has pocketed the other balls. If he accidentally pockets the eight ball, he loses the game.
2 *Radio,* a round microphone that can be used from any direction.
behind the eight ball, *U.S. Slang.* in a very bad position; in a jam: *The real forgotten man today is the high salaried executive who, without stock option and pensions, would be left behind the eight ball* (Wall Street Journal).

eight|een (ā′tēn′), *n., adj.* eight more than ten; 18: *In some states sixteen is the age at which one can first drive, in others it is two years later at eighteen.* [Old English *eahtatēne*]

eight|een|mo (ā tēn′mō), *n., adj.* = octodecimo.

eight|eenth (ā′tēnth′), *adj., n.* **1** next after the 17th; last in a series of 18. **2** one of 18 equal parts.

eight|fold (āt′fōld′), *adj., adv.* **—*adj.*** **1** having eight parts or members. **2** eight times as great or as much.
—*adv.* in eightfold measure.

eightfold way, *Nuclear Physics.* a theoretical classification of strongly interacting elementary particles into multiplets and supermultiplets, whose relationship is established by their having nearly the same mass, hypercharge, and isotopic spin; SU(3) symmetry. [< the Buddhist term for the eight paths to attain enlightenment; so called from the original suggestion that this classification would explain the relationship among a group of eight different elementary particles]

eighth (āth), *adj., n.* **—*adj.*** **1** next after the seventh; last in a series of 8: *August is the eighth month of the year.* **2** being one of 8 equal parts.
—*n.* **1** the next after the seventh; the last in a series of 8. **2** one of 8 equal parts. **3** *Music.* an octave. **—eighth′ly,** *adv.*

***eighth note,** a short note in music played for one eighth as long a time as a whole note; quaver.

***eighth note**
***eighth rest**

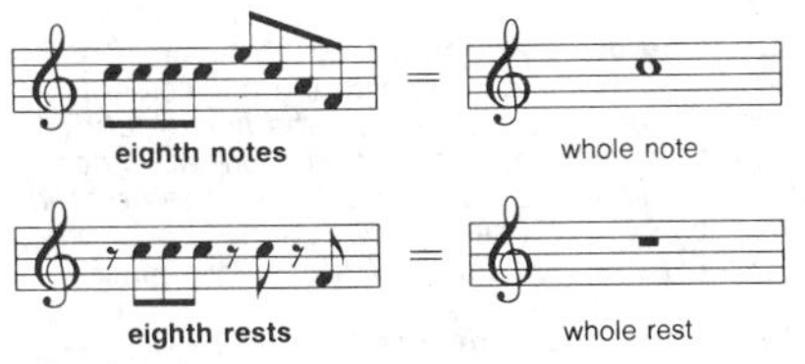

***eighth rest,** a rest, or sign for silence, in a musical notation equal in duration to an eighth note.

eight|i|eth (ā′tē ith), *adj., n.* **1** next after the 79th; last of a series of 80: *My grandfather is in his eightieth year.* **2** one of 80 equal parts: *The eightieth penny rolled under the radiator, leaving us seventy-nine cents.*

eight|ling (āt′ling), *n.* a compound or twin crystal consisting of eight individuals, such as are common with rutile.

eight|pen|ny (āt′pen′ē), *n., pl.* **-nies,** *adj.* **—*n.*** eight British pennies.
—*adj.* worth eight pence; costing eight pence: *An eightpenny nail is 2½ inches long, and it is so called because originally the nails cost eight pennies per hundred.*

eight-square (āt′skwãr′), *adj., n.* **—*adj.*** having eight corners; octagonal.
—*n.* an octagon or an octagonal solid.

eight|y (ā′tē), *n., pl.* **eight|ies,** *adj.* eight times ten; 80: *The eighty cows were milked in two groups, forty at a time.* [short for Old English *hundeahtatig*]

eight|y-nin|er (ā′tē nī′nər), *n.* a person who settled on a homestead in Oklahoma in 1889.

eight|y-six (ā′tē siks′), or **86,** *v.t.,* **-sixed, -six|ing** or **86′d, 86′ing.** *U.S. Slang.* to refuse to serve (a customer). [originally rhyming slang for *nix,* used in the jargon of cooks and waiters to indicate that there is nothing left of an item ordered from the menu]

ei|kon (ī′kon), *n., pl.* **ei|kons, ei|ko|nes** (ī′kə nēz). = icon. [< Greek *eikôn* image]

ei|kon|o|gen (ī kon′ə jen), *n.* an organic sodium salt used as a photographic developer. [< Greek *eikôn, -os* image + English *-gen*]

ei|le mit Wei|le (ī′ləmit vī′lə), *German.* make haste slowly.

Ein′ fes|te Burg ist un|ser Gott (īn fes′tə bu̇rk′ist u̇n′zər gôt′), *German.* "a mighty fortress is our God," the first line of a famous hymn by Martin Luther.

ein|korn (īn′kôrn′), *n.* a variety of wheat having a single grain, grown in central Europe. [< German *Einkorn* < *ein* one + *Korn* seed]

ein|mal ist kein|mal (īn′mäl ist kīn′mäl), *German.* once does not count.

ein|stein (īn′stīn), *n.* a unit of radiant energy, equivalent to the energy required to transform photochemically one mole of a photosensitive substance: *In the realm of chemistry the most useful unit for measuring the work that light can do is the einstein, the energy content of one mol of quanta* (Scientific American). [< Albert *Einstein,* 1879-1955, a German-born physicist]

Einstein equation, an equation expressing the relation of mass and energy; $E = mc^2$; mass-energy equation. E = the energy in ergs; m = the mass in grams; c = the velocity of light in centimeters per second.
[< Albert *Einstein*]

Ein|stein|i|an (īn stī′nē ən), *adj.* of or by Albert Einstein: *The Einsteinian universe is curvilinear, with four dimensions* (New York Times).

***ein|stein|i|um** (īn stī′nē əm), *n.* a rare radioactive, metallic chemical element, produced artificially from plutonium and uranium as a by-product of nuclear fission: *Five new twins, or isotopes, of the artificial element, einsteinium, have been created by scientists at the University of California* (Science News Letter). [American English < Albert *Einstein* + New Latin *-ium,* a suffix meaning "element"]

***einsteinium**

symbol	atomic number	mass number
Es	99	254

Einstein shift, a slight shift in the light spectrum of stars toward the red.

Einstein theory, the theory that there is no absolute motion, or motion with respect to absolute space filled with ether, but that all motion is relative, being that of one portion or manifestation of matter with respect to another portion of matter.

ei|ren|ic (ī ren′ik, -rē′nik), *adj.* = irenic.

ei|ren|i|con (ī ren′ə kon, -rē′nə-), *n.* = irenicon.

eis|bein (īs′bīn′), *n.* a German dish consisting of a stew of pork's knuckle, usually served with sauerkraut and mashed peas. [< German *Eisbein* (literally) ice bone]

eis|e|ge|sis (ī′sə jē′sis), *n., pl.* **-ses** (sēz). a reading of one's own ideas into a passage of the Bible; slanted or biased Biblical exegesis: *Says Preacher Cleland: "To translate débonnaire [meek] into debonair is a sign of eisegesis"* (Time).
[< Greek *eis* into + English (ex)*egesis*]

Ei|sen|bahn (ī′zən bän′), *n. German.* a railroad.

***Ei|sen|how|er jacket** (ī′zən hou′ər), a waist-length jacket originally part of a military uniform and now used for casual wear: *. . . one brown paper bag . . . jammed into the pocket of my Eisenhower jacket, where it didn't show too much* (Guy Endore). [< Dwight D. *Eisenhower,* 1890-1969 who wore such a jacket during World War II]

***Eisenhower jacket**

Ei|sen und Blut (ī′zən u̇nt blu̇t′), *German.* iron and blood.

eis|tedd|fod (ā steᴛʜ′vod, ī steᴛʜ′-), *n., pl.* **eis|tedd|fods, eis|tedd|fod|au** (ā′steᴛʜ vod′ī). a meeting of Welsh poets and musicians, especially as a modern festival at which prizes are awarded: *The eisteddfod . . . is a movable feast and held in a different city every year* (London Times).
[< Welsh *eisteddfod* session < *eistedd* sit]

eis|tedd|fod|ic (ā′steᴛʜ vod′ik, ī′steᴛʜ-), *adj.* of or having to do with an eisteddfod.

ei|ther (ē′ᴛʜər; *especially British* ī′ᴛʜər), *adj., pron., adv., conj.* **—*adj.*** **1** one or the other of two: *Either hat is becoming. You may read either book.* **2** each of two: *There are fields of corn on either side of the river.*
—*pron.* **1** one or other of the two: *You may wear either of the hats.* **2** each of two: *Either of the fields is suitable for growing corn.*
—*adv.* **1** any more than another: *If you do not go, I shall not go either.* **2** *Informal.* a word used to strengthen a negative in contradiction or retraction: *I've finished all my homework; no, I haven't either.*
—*conj.* one or the other of two: *Either come in or go out.*
[Old English *ǣgther,* reduction of *ǣghwæther* each of two < *ā* always + *gehwæther* each of two]

►either. a the pronunciation ī′ᴛʜər has not made so much progress in the United States as in England, and is sometimes heard in the same speech interchanged with ē′ᴛʜər by those who adopt the use of ī′ᴛʜər. **b** *Either* is usually construed as singular, though its use as a plural seems to be increasing: *Either is good enough for me. Either Grace or Phyllis is* (or *are*) *expected.*

ei|ther-or (ē′ᴛʜər ôr′; *especially British* ī′ᴛʜər ôr′), *adj., n.* **—*adj.*** limited to either one or the other; without alternative: *an either-or proposition. An either-or choice in such a conflict inevitably has far-reaching . . . consequences* (New York Times).
—*n.* an either-or choice or alternative: *[He] winces before the untender either-ors of history* (Time).

e|jac|u|late (i jak′yə lāt), *v.,* **-lat|ed, -lat|ing,** *n.* **—*v.t.*** **1** to say suddenly and briefly; exclaim. **2** to eject; discharge: *The violet seed pod burst open and ejaculated the seeds over a considerable distance.*
—*n.* *Physiology.* an ejection; discharge; ejaculation: *The speed with which sperms are formed in the adult is phenomenal: an ejaculate of human semen normally contains some 100-300 million sperms* (New Scientist).
[< Latin *ējaculārī* (with English *-ate*[1]) < *ex-* out + *jaculus* that which is thrown (diminutive) < *jacere* to throw]

e|jac|u|la|tion (i jak′yə lā′shən), *n.* **1** something said suddenly and briefly; an exclamation: *an impatient ejaculation of disgust.* **2** ejection; discharge: *the ejaculation of semen.*

e|jac|u|la|tive (i jak′yə lā′tiv), *adj.* of or like an ejaculation.

e|jac|u|la|tor (i jak′yə lā′tər), *n.* a person or thing that ejaculates.

e|jac|u|la|to|ry (i jak′yə lə tôr′ē, -tōr′-), *adj.* **1** said suddenly and briefly; containing exclamations. **2** ejecting; discharging. **3** *Physiology.* used for the ejaculation of sperm: *ejaculatory ducts.*

e|ject (i jekt′), *v., n.* **—*v.t.*** **1** to throw out from within: *The volcano ejected lava and ashes.* **2** to drive out; turn out; force out; expel: *The landlord ejected the tenant who did not pay his rent.*
—*n.* *Psychology.* something that is concluded to be real, but lies outside of one's ability to detect it consciously. *Example:* A person can conclude that he himself has a consciousness, but is unable to conclude this consciously in someone else.
[< Latin *ējectus,* past participle of *ējicere* < *ex-* out + *jacere* to throw]

e|jec|ta (i jek′tə), *n.pl.* matter ejected, as from a volcano: *Granitic rock fragments are never found in their [Pacific islands] volcanic ejecta* (Gilluly, Waters, and Woodford).
[< Latin *ējecta,* neuter plural of *ējectus;* see etym. under **eject**]

e|ject|a|ble (i jek′tə bəl), *adj.* that can be ejected: *The Navy recently unveiled an ejectable cockpit capsule.*

e|jec|ta|men|ta (i jek′tə men′tə), *n.pl.* = ejecta. [< Latin *ējectāmenta,* plural < *ējectāre* (frequentative) < *ējicere;* see etym. under **eject**]

e|jec|tion (i jek′shən), *n.* **1** the action of ejecting: *A landlord's ejection of a tenant always creates sympathy for the tenant.* **2** the state of being

Pronunciation Key: hat, āge, cãre, fär; let, ēqual, tėrm; it, īce; hot, ōpen, ôrder; oil, out; cup, pu̇t, rüle; child; long; thin; ᴛʜen; zh, measure; ə represents a in about, e in taken, i in pencil, o in lemon, u in circus.

ejected: *His ejection from the hall caused a riot.* **3** something ejected: *Lava is a volcanic ejection.*

ejection capsule, a detachable cockpit or cabin that can be ejected and parachuted from an airplane.

ejection seat, an airplane seat that in case of danger can be instantly ejected with its occupant into the air, where they are automatically separated and parachuted to earth.

e|jec|tive (i jek′tiv), *adj.* ejecting; serving to eject.

e|ject|ment (i jekt′mənt), *n.* **1** the action of ejecting; a dispossessing; an ousting. **2** *Law.* an action to recover a person's real property that has been wrongfully withheld.

e|jec|tor (i jek′tər), *n.* person or thing that ejects.

ejector seat, = ejection seat.

e|ji|dal (e hē′ᴛʜəl), *adj.* of or having to do with an ejido or ejidos: *The ejido in modern times is not economic and the ejidal system is faltering* (Canadian Forum).

e|ji|da|tar|i|o (e hē′ᴛʜä tär′ē ō), *n. Spanish.* a farmer belonging to an ejido.

e|ji|do (e hē′ᴛʜō), *n., pl.* **-dos** (-ᴛʜōs). (in Mexico) a cooperative or communal farm. [< Spanish *ejido*]

e|jus|dem ge|ne|ris (i jus′dem jen′ər is), *Latin.* of the same kind.

ek|a|haf|ni|um (ek′ə haf′nē əm), *n.* a tentative name given to element 104. [< *eka-* beyond, next in order (in the periodic table) (< Sanskrit *eka* one) + *hafnium*]

ek|a|lead (ek′ə led′), *n.* a hypothetical chemical element beyond the transactinide series: *Element 114, which we have mentioned so often, proves to be homologous with that very stable element lead; it can therefore be called "ekalead," using the terminology of Dmitri Mendeleev, the originator of the periodic table* (Glenn T. Seaborg and Justin L. Bloom). [< *eka-* beyond, next in order (in the periodic table) + *lead*]

eke[1] (ēk), *v.t.,* **eked, ek|ing.** *Archaic and Dialect.* to increase; enlarge; lengthen.

eke out, a to add to; increase; help; supplement: *The clerk eked out his regular wages by working in the evenings. . . . material in print eked out with scraps of hearsay* (New Statesman). **b** to barely manage to make (a living): *He eked out a living doing various odd jobs.* **c** to come by with difficulty of pains: *The champ, by the way, . . . eked out another shoddy win* (Esquire).

[variant of obsolete *echen* to augment, Old English *ēcan* < *ēaca* an addition]

eke[2] (ēk), *adv., conj. Archaic.* also; moreover; in addition. [Old English *ēac*]

EKG (no periods), electrocardiogram.

e|kis|tic (ē kis′tik), *adj.* of or having to do with ekistics.

e|kis|ti|cal (ē kis′tə kəl), *adj.* = ekistic.

e|kis|ti|cian (ē′kis tish′ən), *n.* a person who studies ekistics.

e|kis|tics (ē kis′tiks), *n.* the study of communities and settlements of people, especially with a view to improving them by extensive planning: *Although ekistics is a more compact term than "science of human settlements," it still derives from the "settling down" root, which to many of us seems all wrong now that the tendency is to move more and settle less* (Manchester Guardian Weekly). [< Greek *oikistikḗ* (< *oikistḗs* settler < *oîkos* house) + English *-ics;* coined by Constantinos A. Doxiadis, born 1913, a Greek architect]

ek|ka (ek′ä), *n.* a small, one-horse vehicle used in India. [Anglo-Indian < Hindustani *ekkā* < Sanskrit *eka* one]

ek|kle|si|a (i klē′zhē ə, -zē-), *n., pl.* **-si|as, -si|ae** (-zhē ē, -zē ē). **1** Also, **Ekklesia.** all those who have accepted the call to God's service. **2** = ecclesia (def. 1). [< Greek *ekklēsiā;* see etym. under **ecclesia**]

Ek|man layer (ek′mən), a layer of ocean water whose flow is at right angles to the wind's directions: *Thus the wind in the southern half of our square basin representing the North Atlantic transports water to the north in the thin Ekman layer* (Scientific American). [< V. Walfrid *Ekman,* a Swedish oceanographer, who first described it in the early 1900's]

ek|pwe|le (ek′pwə lā′), *n.* = ekuele.

ek|ue|le (ek′wə lā′), *n.* the unit of money of Equatorial Guinea, introduced in 1973, replacing the peseta. [< *ekpwele,* a native word in western Africa]

el (el), *n.* **1** *Informal.* an elevated railroad: *The crowded "el" train grinds to a halt at Friedrichstrasse station* (Alfred L. Malabre). **2** = ell[1]. **3** = ell[2].

El (el), *n.* a god of the Canaanites.

e|lab|o|rate (*adj.* i lab′ər it, -lab′rit; *v.* i lab′ə rāt), *adj., v.,* **-rat|ed, -rat|ing.** —*adj.* worked out with great care; having many details; complicated: *an elaborate banquet. The scientists made elaborate plans for landing a man on the moon. He read Shakespeare, and made an elaborate study of his method* (John Morley).

—*v.t.* **1** to work out with great care; add details to: *The inventor spent months in elaborating his plans for a new engine.* **2** to make with labor; produce.

—*v.i.* to talk, write, or plan in great detail; give added details: *The witness was asked to elaborate on one of his statements.*

[< Latin *ēlabōrātus,* past participle of *ēlabōrāre* < *ex-* out + *labor, -oris* work] —**e|lab′o|rate|ly,** *adv.* —**e|lab′o|rate|ness,** *n.*

—*Syn. adj.* **Elaborate, studied, labored** mean worked out in detail. **Elaborate** emphasizes the idea many details worked out with great care and exactness: *The elaborate decorations were perfect in every detail.* **Studied** emphasizes care in planning and working out details beforehand: *Studied politeness is insulting.* **Labored** emphasizes great and unnatural effort to work out details: *The boy gave a labored excuse for arriving late at school.*

e|lab|o|ra|tion (i lab′ə rā′shən), *n.* **1** the process of elaborating. **2** the condition of being elaborated. **3** something elaborated.

e|lab|o|ra|tive (i lab′ə rā′tiv), *adj.* elaborating; serving to elaborate.

e|lab|o|ra|tor (i lab′ə rā′tər), *n.* a person who elaborates.

e|la|brate (ē lā′brit), *adj. Zoology.* without a distinct labrum or upper lip. [< *e-* without + *labrum* + *-ate*[1]]

el|ae|op|ten (el′ē op′ten), *n.* = eleoptene.

el|ae|op|tene (el′ē op′tēn), *n.* = eleoptene.

E|laine (i lān′), *n. Arthurian Legend.* **1** a beautiful maiden who died for love of Sir Lancelot. **2** the mother of Sir Galahad.

E|lam|ite (ē′lə mīt), *n., adj.* —*n.* **1** a native or inhabitant of Elam, an ancient country and empire in what is now western Iran. **2** the language of the Elamites, used from about 2500 B.C. to A.D. 100, and believed to be unrelated to any other known language: *The trilingual inscription from Behistun in Persia . . . was in Old Persian, Elamite, and Babylonian* (Listener).

—*adj.* of Elam, its people, or their language.

é|lan (ā län′), *n.* enthusiasm or liveliness: spirit: *It was his revolutionary élan, his ruthless use of organized force, that made history* (New Yorker). SYN: verve. [< French *élan* < Old French *elancer* to dart < *e-* out (< Latin *ex-*) + *lancer* to throw (a lance) < Vulgar Latin *lanceāre* < Latin *lancea* a lance]

***e|land** (ē′lənd), *n.* a large, heavy, African antelope with twisted horns. It is the largest antelope found in Africa. *The eland is the biggest of antelopes. Its height is frequently six feet to the shoulder top, and occasionally more . . . Elands are harmless, and easily tamed* (C. S. Stokes). [< Dutch *eland* elk]

***eland**

el|a|net (el′ə net), *n.* any one of a group of small hawks or kites having weak bills and claws, short, square tails, and long, pointed wings, found in tropical and temperate climates. [< New Latin *Elanus* the genus name (origin uncertain) + English *-et*]

é|lan vi|tal (ā län′ vē tȧl′), *French.* the vital or creative force in life. According to the French philosopher Henri Bergson, it is responsible for the growth and evolution of all living things.

el|a|phine (el′ə fīn, -fin), *adj.* having to do with or resembling the red deer. [< Latin *elaphus* stag, deer (< Greek *élaphos*) + *-ine*[1]]

el|a|pid (el′ə pid), *adj., n.* —*adj.* belonging to a family of tropical snakes including many of the well-known poisonous varieties, such as the cobra, mamba, and coral snake.

—*n.* a snake of this family.

[< New Latin *Elapidae* the family name < Greek *élaps,* variant of *éllops* a kind of snake]

e|lapse (i laps′), *v.i.,* **e|lapsed, e|laps|ing.** to slip away; glide by; pass: *Many hours elapsed while he slept.* [< Latin *ēlapsus,* past participle of *ēlābī* < *ex-* away + *lābī* to slip, glide]

elapsed time, the time it takes a boat, automobile, or other racing vehicle to travel over a course without any adjustments, as for handicapping.

ELAS (no periods), Hellenic People's Army of Liberation of World War II (Greek, *Ellinikos Laikos Apeleftherotikos Stratos*).

e|las|mo|branch (i las′mə brangk, -laz′-), *n., adj.* —*n.* any one of a class of fishes whose skeletons are formed of cartilage and whose gills are thin and platelike; chondrichthian. Sharks and rays are elasmobranchs.

—*adj.* of or belonging to the elasmobranchs.

[< New Latin *Elasmobranchii* the class name < Greek *élasma, -atos* metal plate, beaten metal + *bránchia* gills]

e|las|mo|bran|chi|ate (i las′mə brang′kē āt, -it; -laz′-), *n., adj.* = elasmobranch.

e|las|mo|saur (i laz′mə sôr), *n.* any one of a group of large marine reptiles with very long necks, small heads, and paddlelike limbs and tail that lived during the Cretaceous period in North America.

e|las|tase (i las′tās), *n.* an enzyme occurring in the pancreatic juice that digests elastin. [< *elast*(in) + *-ase*]

e|las|tic (i las′tik), *adj., n.* —*adj.* **1** that can be stretched or pressed together and then return to its original shape, position, or size: *Toy balloons, sponges, and steel springs are elastic.* SYN: resilient. **2** springing back; springy: *an elastic step.* **3** *Figurative.* recovering easily and quickly; buoyant: *Her elastic spirits kept her from being discouraged for long.* **4** *Figurative.* easily changed to suit conditions; flexible; adaptable: *an elastic conscience. Mother has an elastic schedule.*

—*n.* **1** a tape, cloth, cord, or the like, woven partly of rubber. **2** = rubber band.

[< New Latin *elasticus* < Greek *elaúnein* to drive]

e|las|ti|cal|ly (i las′tə klē), *adv.* in an elastic manner; with elasticity.

e|las|ti|cat|ed (i las′tə kā′tid), *adj.* = elasticized: *The shoes have . . . elasticated gussets, making them easy to slip off and on* (Geoffrey Charles).

elastic clause, the final clause in Article I, Section 8 of the United States Constitution, which states that Congress may "make all laws which shall be necessary and proper," thereby allowing Congress to exercise many powers not granted to it specifically.

elastic collision, *Physics.* a collision between two particles in which their total kinetic energy after the collision is the same as before. The particles bounce off each other and no new particles are produced by the collision.

e|las|ti|cised (i las′tə sīzd), *adj. Especially British.* elasticized.

e|las|tic|i|ty (i las′tis′ə tē, ē′las-), *n.* elastic quality: *Rubber has great elasticity.* (*Figurative.*) *"Good" and "bad" are words having great elasticity of meaning.*

elasticity of volume, the tendency of liquids and gases to return to their original volume when the deforming force is released; resistance to change of volume. The slightest force can change their shape, but no force is great enough to change their volume permanently.

e|las|ti|cized (i las′tə sīzd), *adj.* woven or made with elastic: *The trousers have snaps on the elasticized waistbands to make them adjustable* (New Yorker).

elastic limit, the maximum stress that an elastic material can sustain and still return to its original form.

elastic scattering, *Physics.* the scattering of particles resulting from elastic collision.

e|las|tin (i las′tin), *n. Biochemistry.* a protein, similar to albumin, that is the basic substance of the elastic fiber of certain tissues. [< *elast*(ic) + *-in*]

e|las|to|hy|dro|dy|nam|ic (i las′tō hī′drō dī nam′ik, -di-), *adj.* dealing with the elasticity of fluids under force: *Sometimes the film of lubricant is so thin, and the fluid pressure acting on the bearing surfaces are so high, that the elastic deformation of these surfaces cannot be ignored; the regime is then called elastohydrodynamic* (Science Journal).

e|las|to|hy|dro|dy|nam|ics (i las′tō hī′drō dī nam′iks, -di-), *n.* the study of elastohydrodynamic effects.

e|las|to|mer (i las′tə mər), *n. Chemistry.* any elastic, rubberlike substance. [< *elastic* + Greek *méros* part]

e|las|to|mer|ic (i las′tə mer′ik), *adj.* having the properties of rubber.

e|las|to|plast (i las′tə plast′), *n. British.* **1** an elastic adhesive tape used especially as a bandage. **2 Elastoplast.** a trademark for this tape.

e|late (i lāt′), *v.,* **e|lat|ed, e|lat|ing,** *adj.* —*v.t.* to raise the spirits of; make joyful or proud: *His success in the contest elated him.* SYN: exhilarate.

—*adj.* inspired with joy or hope; exultant with success or victory.

[< Latin *ēlātus,* past participle of *efferre* < *ex-* out, away + *ferre* carry]

e|lat|ed (i lā′tid), *adj.* in high spirits; joyful or proud. SYN: exultant. —**e|lat′ed|ly,** *adv.* —**e|lat′ed|ness,** *n.*

e|la|ter[1] (el′ə tər), *n.* **1** *Botany.* an elastic, spiral filament for discharging and dispersing spores, such as that in the capsule of liverworts. **2** *Zoology.* = elaterid. **3** the forked, taillike appendage of a springtail, used in leaping. **4** *Obsolete.* elasticity. [< New Latin *elater* < Greek *elatêr* driver < *elaúnein* drive, set in motion]

e|lat|er[2] (i lā′tər), *n.* a person or thing that elates.

e|lat|er|id (i lat′ər id), *n.* any of a family of beetles that can spring into the air with a snap when turned on their backs; elater; click beetle; snapping beetle. [< New Latin *Elateridae* the family name < *elater;* see etym. under **elater**[1]]

e|lat|er|in (i lat′ər in), *n.* a white, crystalline substance that is the active principle of elaterium, used as a strong cathartic. *Formula:* $C_{20}H_{28}O_5$ [< *elater*(ium) + *-in*]

e|lat|er|ite (i lat′ə rīt), *n.* a brown mineral hydrocarbon, usually soft and elastic like rubber. [< *elater* elasticity + *-ite*[1]]

el|a|te|ri|um (el′ə tir′ē əm), *n.* the dried juice of the squirting cucumber, used as a cathartic. [< Latin *elatērium* < Greek *elatêrion* a purgative < *elaúnein* drive, set in motion]

e|la|tion (i lā′shən), *n.* high spirits; joy or pride; exultant gladness: *She was filled with elation at winning the prize.* **SYN**: jubilation.

E layer, a layer of the ionosphere about 50 to 90 miles above the earth's surface; Heaviside layer; Kennelly-Heaviside layer; E region. It reflects radio waves. *An Aerobee rocket experiment recently detected a sheet of current flowing in the E layer about 60 miles up* (Scientific American).

El|ba (el′bə), *n.* a place of exile or seclusion: ... *the comic figure waiting for the revolution to call him back in 1968 from his self-adopted Elba in the cafés of the Left Bank* (Sir Denis Brogan). [< *Elba,* the island to which Napoleon was exiled in 1814]

El|ber|ta (el bėr′tə), *n.* a variety of large, yellow, freestone peach, grown in the United States. [American English < *Elberta,* the wife of the originator of the variety]

el|bow (el′bō), *n., v.* **—*n.*** **1** the joint between the upper and lower arm; bend of the arm: *With elbows bent he sat, chin in his hands, fixedly staring at the TV.* **2** any bend or corner having the same shape as a bent arm. A sharp turn in a road or river may be called an elbow. **3** a bent joint for connecting pipes. **4** the raised arm of a chair or the end of a sofa, for supporting the elbow.

—*v.t.* **1** to push with the elbow; jostle: *Don't elbow me off the sidewalk. The shopper elbowed her competitors at the bargain counter.* (*Figurative.*) *The small farming class have been gradually elbowed out of their holdings* (Manchester Examiner). **2** to make (one's way) by pushing: *He elbowed his way through the crowd.*

—*v.i.* to make one's way by pushing: *Caught in the mob, he began to elbow right and left.*

at one's elbow, close to one: *I found at my elbow a pretty little girl* (Dickens). (*Figurative.*) *For one of history's momentous events, the outside world had only the carefully stage-managed story told by the handful of men at Stalin's elbow* (Time).

bend (lift, or **crook) an elbow**, *Informal.* to drink alcoholic beverages; drink to excess: *I am sure they will not waste time bending an elbow with a little old corn-pone Congressman and a lot of Wyoming hillbillies* (Harper's).

out at the elbow or **out at elbows**, worn out; ragged; shabby; poor: *He was himself just now so terribly out at elbows, that he could not command a hundred pounds* (Mary Martha Sherwood).

rub elbows with, to mingle with (people, especially of a different social level): *The lunatic, clad in a dapper pinstripe, was happily rubbing elbows with the window shoppers in the village* (Time).

up to one's elbow, a very busy: ... *up to our elbows making damson jam* (A. Robson). **b** deeply involved: *He's up to his elbow in new schemes.*

[Old English *elnboga* < *eln* length of lower arm + *boga* bow[2]]

el|bow-bend|ing (el′bō ben′ding), *adj. U.S. Informal.* given to drinking too much.

el|bow|board (el′bō bôrd′, -bōrd′), *n.* the board at the bottom of a window which forms the inner sill.

el|bow|bush (el′bō bủsh′), *n.* a shrub of the madder family, having sharply angled branches; buttonbush.

el|bow|chair (el′bō chãr′), *n.* a chair with elbows; armchair.

el|bowed (el′bōd), *adj.* **1** having elbows: *an elbowed sofa.* **2** shaped like an elbow; bent; curved: *elbowed grass.*

elbow grease, *Informal.* hard work; energy: *The trouble with economic equality is that it denies the cash value of that extra bit of efficiency, of education, of sharpness, skill, brains, or elbow grease* (Atlantic).

el|bow|room (el′bō rüm′, -rủm′), *n.,* or **elbow room**, plenty of room; enough room or space to move or work in: *Sufficient new dwelling units were added to the inventory to create ... elbow room* (Wall Street Journal).

elbow scissors, scissors having a bend in the blade for convenience in cutting.

el|bow|y (el′bō ē), *adj.* using elbows, as to push; elbowing: *elbowy arms.*

eld (eld), *n. Archaic.* **1** ancient times; former times; antiquity: *lands that contain the monuments of eld* (Byron). **2** old age: *Weak eld hath left thee nothing wise* (Edmund Spenser). [Old English *eldo* < *ald* old]

eld|er[1] (el′dər), *adj., n.* **—*adj.*** **1** older; senior: *my elder brother.* **2** of longer standing; prior in rank, validity, right, obligation, or service: *an elder title to an estate.* **3** earlier; former: *huge as the giant race of elder times* (Robert Southey).

—*n.* **1** Usually, **elders.** an older person; one's senior: *Children should respect their elders. But he took the advice of his elders and refrained from bringing out his book* (Edmund Wilson). **2** a person of advanced years. **3** an ancestor. **4** *Figurative.* one of the older and more influential men of a tribe or community; one to whom age and experience have brought wisdom and judgment: *Miss not the discourse of the elders* (Ecclesiasticus 8:9). **5** an officer in a church. **6** = presbyter. **7** a pastor or minister. **8** a member of a higher priesthood in the Mormon Church.

[Old English *eldra,* comparative of *ald* old]

▶ **elder, eldest.** These archaic forms of *old* survive in formal English and are used, when speaking of persons, chiefly for members of the same family: *the elder brother, our eldest daughter;* and in some set phrases: *the elder statesman.*

el|der[2] (el′dər), *n.* = elderberry. [Old English *ellærn*]

el|der|ber|ry (el′dər ber′ē), *n., pl.* **-ries. 1** any one of a group of shrubs or small trees with flat clusters of white flowers and black, purple, or red berries. It belongs to the honeysuckle family. **2** its berry. Elderberries are sometimes used in making wine or pies.

elder blow, = elderberry (def. 1).

Elder Edda, a collection of old Icelandic songs about gods and heroes collected during the 1100's and early 1200's.

elder hand, = eldest hand.

eld|er|ly (el′dər lē), *adj.* **1** somewhat old; beyond middle age; near old age: *He felt the need of companionship, to wander about the building, engaging in heartening snatches of acrimonious dispute with his elderly fellow residents* (Edwin O'Connor). **SYN**: See syn. under **old. 2** of or having to do with persons in later life.

eld|er|ship (el′dər ship), *n.* **1** the office or position of an elder in a church. **2** a group or court of elders; presbytery.

elder statesman, **1** an older statesman or politician, usually no longer in office, who is turned to for advice: *Next day the King desperately recalled one of the nation's elder statesmen ... to head a "caretaker" government* (Time). **2** a member of a group of advisers, having experience and high reputation in public affairs, who formerly advised the Japanese emperor; genro.

eld|est (el′dist), *adj.* = oldest (of brothers and sisters or of a group). [Old English *eldesta,* superlative of *ald* old]

▶ See **elder** for usage note.

eldest hand, the player on the dealer's left in card games.

el|ding (el′ding), *n. Dialect.* fuel. [< Scandinavian (compare Old Icelandic *eldīng* < *eldr* fire)]

ELDO (no periods), European Launcher Development Organization (a group of seven European countries engaged in a joint satellite development program).

El Do|ra|do, or **El|do|ra|do** (el′də rä′dō), *n., pl.* **-dos. 1** a legendary city supposed to be full of gold and treasure, sought by early Spanish explorers in America. **2** *Figurative.* any place said to be wealthy or where wealth is easily acquired. [< Spanish *El Dorado* (literally) the gilded; *dorado,* past participle of *dorar* to gild < Late Latin *dēaurāre* < Latin *dē-* of + *aurum* gold]

el|dritch (el′drich), *adj. Scottish.* weird; ghostly; unnatural; wild: *His [Whistler's] piercing, disturbing, eldritch "Ha- Ha" became a feature of his character* (Hesketh Pearson). [perhaps related to **elf**]

El|e|at|ic (el′ē at′ik), *adj., n.* **—*adj.*** **1** having to do with Elea, an ancient Greek town in southern Italy or Magna Graecia, or its inhabitants. **2** having to do with the philosophy of Xenophanes, who lived at Elea, and his followers Parmenides and Zeno. Its chief doctrine is that the only reality is an unchanging Being; the world that is perceptible to the senses is too unstable and perishable to be ultimate reality.

—*n.* **1** a native or inhabitant of Elea. **2** an adherent of Eleatic philosophy.

[< Latin *Eleāticus* of *Elea,* an ancient Greek colony in southwest Italy where Xenophanes lived]

El|e|at|i|cism (el′ē at′ə siz əm), *n.* the doctrine or system of the Eleatics.

El|e|a|zar (el′ē ā′zər), *n.* the third son of Aaron and his successor as high priest (in the Bible, Numbers 3:2-4, 32).

elec., **1** electric. **2** electrical. **3** electricity.

el|e|cam|pane (el′ē kam pān′), *n.* **1** a yellow-flowered plant of the composite family with bitter, aromatic leaves and root; horseheal. **2** a candy flavored with the root of this plant. [perhaps half translation of Medieval Latin *enula* (or *elena*) *campana* elecampane of the fields; *ele* < Middle French *alne,* ultimately < Latin *inula,* by influence of Greek *elénion*]

e|lect (i lekt′), *v., adj., n.* **—*v.t.*** **1** to choose by voting: *Americans elect a President every four years.* **2** to choose: *A student must take some subjects; he can elect others. The boys elected to play baseball, while the girls wanted to stay in and draw.* **SYN**: select, pick. **3** *Theology.* to select for salvation and eternal life.

—*v.i.* to choose.

—*adj.* **1** elected but not yet in office: *A President-elect of the United States becomes the President after his inauguration.* **2** specially chosen; selected: *the bride elect.* **3** chosen by God for salvation and eternal life.

—*n.* Usually, **the elect. a** the people selected or chosen by God for salvation and eternal life because He foresees their merit: *As God hath appointed the elect unto glory, so hath He, by the eternal and most free purpose of His will, foreordained all the means thereunto* (Westminster Confession of Faith). **b** people who belong to a group with special rights and privileges: *These reverend fathers, ... the elect of the land* (Shakespeare).

[< Latin *ēlectus,* past participle of *ēligere* < *ex-* out + *legere* choose]

elect., **1** electric. **2** electrical. **3** electricity.

e|lect|a|bil|i|ty (i lek′tə bil′ə tē), *n.* the condition of being electable.

e|lect|a|ble (i lek′tə bəl), *adj.* that can be elected: *In fact the primary made it more difficult rather than less so for the relatively unknown but potentially electable candidate to get the nomination* (Wall Street Journal).

e|lec|tion (i lek′shən), *n.* **1** a choosing by vote: *In our city we have an election for mayor every two years. It would be necessary to watch a Soviet 'election' to understand the working of the system and how different it is from the British parliamentary method* (J. V. Davidson-Houston). **2** the condition of being chosen for an office by vote: *The candidate's excellent campaign was the main reason for his election.* **3** choice; selection: *The election of winners in the art contest was announced after the board met.* **SYN**: preference. **4** selection by God for salvation. **5** *Obsolete.* persons chosen for salvation (in the Bible, Romans 11:7).

e|lec|tion|ar|y (i lek′shə ner′ē), *adj.* having to do with election.

election board, = board of elections.

Election Day, *U.S.* the day on which the election of public officials is held, the first Tuesday after the first Monday in November in most states; General Election Day.

e|lec|tion|eer (i lek′shə nir′), *v., n.* **—*v.i.*** to work for the success of a candidate or party in an election.

—*n.* a person who electioneers. **—e|lec′tion|eer′er,** *n.*

e|lec|tive (i lek′tiv), *adj., n.* **—*adj.*** **1** chosen by an election: *Senators are elective officials.* **2** filled by an election: *The office of President of the United States is an elective office.* **3** having the right to vote in an election. **4** based upon the principle of electing to office. **5** open to choice; not required: *Spanish is an elective subject in many high schools.* **SYN**: optional. **6** *Chemistry.* tending to combine with certain substances in preference to others.

—*n.* a subject or course of study that may be taken, but is not required. **—e|lec′tive|ly,** *adv.* **—e|lec′tive|ness,** *n.*

e|lec|tor (i lek′tər), *n.* **1** a person who has the right to vote in an election. **2** a member of the electoral college. **3** one of the princes who had the right to elect the emperor of the Holy Roman Empire.

e|lec|tor|al (i lek′tər əl), *adj.* **1** of electors: *electoral votes.* **2** of an election. **—e|lec′tor|al|ly,** *adv.*

Pronunciation Key: hat, āge, cãre, fär; let, ēqual, tėrm; it, īce; hot, ōpen, ôrder; **oil, out**; cup, pủt, rüle; **child**; long; **thin**; **ᴛʜen**; **zh**, measure; **ə** represents **a** in about, **e** in taken, **i** in pencil, **o** in lemon, **u** in circus.

electoral college, the group of people chosen by the voters to elect the President and Vice-President of the United States.

Electoral Commission, a board of commissioners created in 1877 by act of Congress to decide the validity of certain electoral votes following the election of 1876. Its decisions resulted in the election of Rutherford B. Hayes to the Presidency.

electoral vote, the votes cast by the electoral college.

e|lec|tor|ate (i lek′tər it), *n.* **1** the persons having the right to vote in an election. **2** the territory under the rule of an elector of the Holy Roman Empire. **3** the rank of an elector of the Holy Roman Empire.

e|lec|to|ri|al (i lek′tôr′ē əl, -tōr′-; ē′lek-), *adj.* = electoral.

e|lec|tor|ship (i lek′tər ship), *n.* the position or office of an elector.

electr-, *combining form.* the form of **electro-** before vowels.

E|lec|tra (i lek′trə), *n.* **1** *Greek Legend.* the daughter of Agamemnon and Clytemnestra. Electra urged her brother, Orestes, to kill their mother and her lover to avenge the murder of their father. **2** one of the Pleiades. **3** a style of modern printing type.

Electra complex, *Psychoanalysis.* a repressed, incestuous desire of a daughter for her father, the equivalent of an Oedipus complex in a son.

e|lec|tress (i lek′tris), *n.* **1** a woman elector. **2** the wife or widow of an elector of the Holy Roman Empire.

e|lec|tret (i lek′trit), *n.* a dielectric material that exhibits permanent polarity, as a magnet does: *Electrets are to electricity what permanent magnets are to magnetism—they exert a force on other electric bodies and don't lose their charge* (Science News). [< *electr*(icity) + (magn)*et*]

e|lec|tric (i lek′trik), *adj., n.* —*adj.* **1** of electricity; having to do with electricity: *an electric light, an electric current.* **2** charged with electricity: *an electric battery.* **3** run by electricity: *an electric stove.* **4** giving an electric shock: *an electric eel.* **5** played with electrically amplified guitars: *the transition from folk to electric rock.* **6** *Figurative.* exciting; thrilling: *an electric feeling.*

—*n.* **1** *Informal.* an automobile or railroad passenger car run by electricity. **2** a substance, such as amber or glass, that can exhibit electricity when rubbed.

[< New Latin *electricus* generated (by friction) from amber < Latin *ēlectrum* amber < Greek *ēlektron*]

e|lec|tri|cal (i lek′trə kəl), *adj.* **1** = electric. **2** producing or produced by electricity: *electrical impulses.* **3** having to do with or connected with electricity: *electrical experiments.*

electrical engineer, a person skilled in electrical engineering.

electrical engineering, the branch of engineering that deals with electricity, especially in industrial applications.

e|lec|tri|cal|ly (i lek′trə klē), *adv.* by electricity.

electrical storm, a storm accompanied by thunder and lightning; thunderstorm.

electrical transcription, **1** radiobroadcasting from a special phonograph record. **2** a special phonograph record so used.

electric arc, = arc (def. 3).

electric automobile, = electric car.

electric blanket, a blanket heated by an electric current that passes through a network of fine wires within it: *The 10,000-ohm relay is of the type used for controlling the heat of electric blankets* (Scientific American).

electric blue, a steely blue color, used especially in textile fabrics.

electric brain, = electronic brain.

electric cable, a protected bundle of wires to carry an electric current.

electric calamine, = calamine (def. 2a).

electric car, an automobile powered by a motor supplied with electric current from a storage battery or other device, such as a fuel cell; electromobile. Electric cars were popular between the late 1890's and 1910 and interest in them revives with new methods of generating electrical power.

electric catfish, a large African catfish that can give an electric shock.

electric chair, **1** a chair used in electrocuting criminals condemned to death. **2** a sentence of death in such a chair.

electric charge, an accumulation of electricity in a storage battery, condenser, fuel cell, or other device, which may again be discharged.

electric current, the flow of electricity through a conductor or transmitter.

electric drive, an automatic transmission in which a generator, connected with the engine, supplies power to a separate electric motor or motors, which drive the wheels. It is used in buses, trucks, and Diesel locomotives.

electric eel, a large South American fish resembling an eel, that can give strong electric shocks: *An electric eel of 3-4 ft. length can deliver a 600-volt shock through the discharge of some 6,000 batteries of plates, arranged in series down its length* (A. W. Haslett). See picture under **eel**.

electric eye, a photoelectric cell. An electric eye can operate a mechanism so as to open a door when its invisible beam is interrupted by the approach of a person. It is also used in motion pictures, television, and many other industries.

electric field, any space in which force due to an electric charge exists: *The action of the electric field on an electron is analogous to that of a gravitational field on a mass* (John R. Pierce).

electric fire, *British.* an electric heater.

electric fish, any one of about 250 species of fish having an electric organ and able to give shocks of varying intensity to their enemies or prey, including the electric catfish, electric eel, and various electric rays.

electric furnace, a furnace heated by electricity, usually to high temperatures, used for treating metals and alloys.

electric generator, a machine that produces electricity by changing mechanical energy into electrical energy; dynamo; generator.

electric guitar, a guitar connected by an electric cord to a combined speaker and amplifier and equipped with controls for increasing or modifying the sound. See picture under **bass**[1].

electric hare, an electrically driven, artificial hare, run on a track, which the dogs in a dog race chase.

electric heater, a portable device furnishing heat by small electric coils.

e|lec|tri|cian (i lek′trish′ən, ē′lek-), *n.* a person who repairs or installs electric wires, lights, motors, and the like.

electric induction, = electrostatic induction.

e|lec|tric|i|ty (i lek′tris′ə tē, ē′lek-), *n.* **1** a form of energy that can produce light, heat, magnetic force, and chemical changes. Electricity is produced in generators for people to buy and use, but can be produced by running a comb through your hair or by chemical change in a flashlight battery or fuel cell or by sunlight in a solar battery or cell. Electricity is regarded as consisting of oppositely charged particles, electrons and protons. Negative electricity is electricity in which the electron is the elementary unit; positive electricity has the proton as the elementary unit. Static electricity is electricity with the charges at rest; dynamic electricity has the charges in motion in a stream or current. *Lightning is caused by electricity.* **2** an electric current; flow of electrons: *Most refrigerators are run by electricity. Lightning cut off the town's electricity for about 10 minutes* (London Times). **3** the branch of physics that deals with electricity.

e|lec|tri|cize (i lek′trə sīz), *v.t.,* **-cized, -ciz|ing.** = electrify.

electric light, **1** a vacuum or gas lamp containing a filament of carbon or metal. When an electric current is passed through the filament, light is given off. **2** the light thus produced.

electric light bulb, = incandescent lamp.

electric meter, an instrument which measures the amount of electric current supplied and used.

electric organ, **1** a musical instrument whose tones, similar to those of a pipe organ, are produced by electrical rather than mechanical means. **2** a muscular tissue in various fish, controlled by the nervous system, modified to produce electricity. The power of the electricity and the morphology of the organ vary from one species of fish to another.

electric power, power produced by an electric generator, usually measured in kilowatt-hours.

electric ray, any one of a family of fishes with flat bodies, that have electric organs with which they can stun or kill their prey; torpedo: *The electric ray possesses organs in its body that actually generate electricity and when disturbed can give a powerful shock to any intruder on its privacy* (A. M. Winchester).

e|lec|trics (i lek′triks), *n.* the science of electricity.

electric shaver, an instrument powered by a small electric motor and used to shave the face or other parts of the body.

electric shock, a shock induced by electricity, especially in shock therapy: *Electric shock produces the same healing effects as the drug-induced fits, but the electric seizure is more accurately controlled and much less uncomfortable for the patient* (Marguerite Clark).

electric storm, = electrical storm.

electric thermometer, **1** = resistance thermometer. **2** = thermoelectric thermometer.

electric torch, *British.* a flashlight: *Jean took a turn at trying to stop lorries—using an electric torch* (Cape Times).

electric waves, **1** an electromagnetic disturbance or series of waves produced by oscillations of an electric discharge. **2** = electromagnetic wave.

e|lec|tric|weld (i lek′trik weld′), *adj.* having the seams joined or joints fixed by electric welding.

electric welding, = resistance welding.

e|lec|tride (i lek′trīd), *n.* any of a class of chemical compounds formed with atoms of metallic elements joined by unpaired electrons, analogous to sodium chloride. [< *electr*(on) + *-ide*]

e|lec|trif|er|ous (i lek′trif′ər əs, ē′lek-), *adj.* bearing or transmitting electricity.

e|lec|tri|fi|a|ble (i lek′trə fī′ə bəl), *adj.* that can be electrified.

e|lec|tri|fi|ca|tion (i lek′trə fə kā′shən), *n.* **1** the act or process of electrifying. **2** the state of being electrified.

e|lec|tri|fi|er (i lek′trə fī′ər), *n.* a person or thing that electrifies.

e|lec|tri|fy (i lek′trə fī), *v.t.,* **-fied, -fy|ing.** **1** to charge with electricity: *We electrified the main circuits to see if the fuses would blow.* **2** to equip for use with electric power: *Some railroads once run by steam are now electrified.* **3** to provide with electric power service: *Many rural areas will soon be electrified.* **4** to give an electric shock to. **5** *Figurative.* to excite; thrill: *The speaker electrified his audience. The spectators were electrified by the outfielder's diving catch.*

e|lec|tri|za|tion (i lek′trə zā′shən), *n.* = electrification.

e|lec|trize (i lek′trīz), *v.t.,* **-trized, -triz|ing.** = electrify (defs. 1, 2, 3, 4).

e|lec|triz|er (i lek′trī zər), *n.* a person or thing that electrifies.

e|lec|tro (i lek′trō), *n., pl.* **-tros.** an electrotype plate.

electro-, *combining form.* **1** electric or electrical: *Electromagnet = an electric magnet.* **2** electrically: *Electropositive = electrically positive.* **3** electricity: *Electromotive = producing a flow of electricity.* **4** electrolysis: *Electroplate = to cover with a thin coating of metal by electrolysis.* **5** electronic: *Electromusic = electronic music.* **6** electron: *Electrophile = a substance that attracts electrons.* [< Greek *elektro-* < *ēlektron* amber]

e|lec|tro|a|cous|tic (i lek′trō ə küs′tik, -kous′-), *adj.* = electroacoustical.

e|lec|tro|a|cous|ti|cal (i lek′trō ə küs′tə kəl, -kous′-), *adj.* of or having to do with electroacoustics.

e|lec|tro|a|cous|tics (i lek′trō ə küs′tiks, -kous′-), *n.* the science that deals with sound in its relationship to electricity.

e|lec|tro|a|nal|y|sis (i lek′trō ə nal′ə sis), *n.* *Chemistry.* analysis by means of electrolysis.

e|lec|tro|bath (i lek′trō bath′, -bäth′), *n.* the liquid used in electroplating, in which the metal to be deposited is held in solution.

e|lec|tro|bi|ol|o|gy (i lek′trō bī ol′ə jē), *n.* the branch of biology that deals with electrical phenomena in living organisms.

e|lec|tro|bi|os|co|py (i lek′trō bī os′kə pē), *n.* the examination of a body by means of an electric current, to discover muscular contractions as evidence of life.

e|lec|tro|cap|il|lar|i|ty (i lek′trō kap′ə lar′ə tē), *n.* a change in the capillary action of liquids when an electric current passes through them. It is used in measuring very small quantities of electricity.

e|lec|tro|cap|il|lar|y (i lek′trō kap′ə ler′ē), *adj.* having to do with changes in the capillarity of a liquid produced by electricity.

* **e|lec|tro|car|di|o|gram** (i lek′trō kär′dē ə gram), *n.* the tracing or record made by an electrocardiograph; cardiogram. *Abbr:* EKG (no periods).

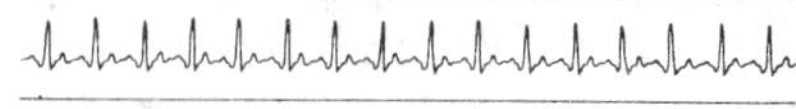

* **electrocardiograph**

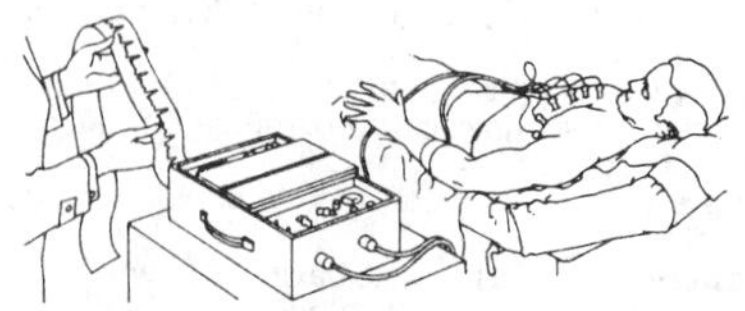

* **e|lec|tro|car|di|o|graph** (i lek′trō kär′dē ə graf, -gräf), *n.* an instrument that detects and records electrical impulses produced by the action of the heart with each beat; cardiograph. It is used in the diagnosis and treatment of diseases of the heart. *An electrocardiograph can be compared to*

instruments for testing the battery and spark plugs of an automobile (Science News Letter).

e|lec|tro|car|di|o|graph|ic (i lek′trō kär′dē ə graf′ik). *adj.* having to do with an electrocardiograph or electrocardiography: *an electrocardiographic tracing.* **–e|lec′tro|car′di|o|graph′i|cal|ly,** *adv.*

e|lec|tro|car|di|og|ra|phy (i lek′trō kär′dē og′rə fē), *n.* the science or technique of using an electrocardiograph.

e|lec|tro|cau|ter|i|za|tion (i lek′trō kô′tər ə zā′shən), *n* = electrocautery (def. 1).

e|lec|tro|cau|ter|y (i lek′trō kô′tər ē), *n., pl.* **-ter|ies. 1** the process of cauterizing with an electrically heated wire. **2** the instrument thus used: *More recently electrocauteries were devised by which small bleeding vessels could be coagulated without too much damage to surrounding tissues* (James Phinney Baxter).

e|lec|tro|chem|ic (i lek′trō kem′ik), *adj.* = electrochemical.

e|lec|tro|chem|i|cal (i lek′trō kem′ə kəl), *adj.* of or having to do with electrochemistry.

electrochemical equivalent, the weight of an element that can be liberated in electrolysis by one coulomb of electricity.

e|lec|tro|chem|i|cal|ly (i lek′trō kem′ə klē), *adv.* according to the laws of electrochemistry.

e|lec|tro|chem|ist (i lek′trō kem′ist), *n.* a person who studies electrochemistry.

e|lec|tro|chem|is|try (i lek′trō kem′ə strē), *n.* the branch of chemistry that deals with chemical changes produced by electricity, and the production of electricity by chemical changes.

e|lec|tro|chron|o|graph (i lek′trō kron′ə graf, gräf), *n.* an instrument for electrically recording exact instants of time.

e|lec|tro|co|ag|u|la|tion (i lek′trō kō ag′yə lā′shən), *n.* the sealing off of body tissue and small blood vessels through the use of high-frequency electric currents.

e|lec|tro|con|vul|sive (i lek′trō kən vul′siv), *adj.* administered with an electric current so as to produce muscular spasms: *electroconvulsive shock.*

electroconvulsive therapy or **treatment,** = electroshock therapy. *Abbr:* ECT (no periods).

e|lec|tro|cor|tin (i lek′trō kôr′tin), *n.* = aldosterone.

e|lec|tro|cul|ture (i lek′trō kul′chər), *n.* the use of electricity to stimulate the growth of plants.

e|lec|tro|cute (i lek′trə kyüt), *v.t.,* **-cut|ed, -cut|ing. 1** to kill in any way by electricity: *A live wire electrocuted the man when he touched it.* **2** to execute (a criminal) by an electric current. [American English < *electro-* + (exe)*cute*]

e|lec|tro|cu|tion (i lek′trə kyü′shən), *n.* execution or killing by the passage of a high voltage of electricity through the body.

e|lec|trode (i lek′trōd), *n.* either of the two terminals of a battery or any other source of electricity; a conductor by which a current is brought into a liquid or a gas. The anode and cathode of an electric cell are electrodes. *In the process of electrolytic conduction, electric current enters and leaves a solution at metallic plates called electrodes* (Shortley and Williams). [< *electro-* + Greek *hodós* way]

e|lec|trode|less (i lek′trōd lis), *adj.,* without electrodes.

e|lec|tro|del|ic (i lek′trō del′ik), *adj.* producing a psychedelic effect through the use of electric lights. [< *electro-* + (psyche)*delic*]

e|lec|tro|de|pos|it (i lek′trō di poz′it), *v., n.* **–*v.t.*** to deposit (a substance) by electrolysis. **–*n.*** a deposit produced by electrolysis.

e|lec|tro|dep|o|si|tion (i lek′trō dep′ə zish′ən), *n.* the depositing of a substance by electrolysis.

e|lec|tro|di|al|y|sis (i lek′trō dī al′ə sis), *n.* the process, carried on under the influence of an electric current, of separating compounds or substances by means of their different rates of diffusion through a semipermeable membrane. It is one method used to remove the salt from seawater.

e|lec|tro|di|a|lyt|ic (i lek′trō dī ə lit′ik), *adj.* of or having to do with electrodialysis.

e|lec|tro|dy|nam|ic (i lek′trō dī nam′ik, -di-), *adj.* **1** of or having to do with the force of electricity in motion. **2** of electrodynamics.

e|lec|tro|dy|nam|i|cal (i lek′trō dī nam′ə kəl, -di-), *adj.* = electrodynamic.

e|lec|tro|dy|nam|i|cal|ly (i lek′trō dī nam′ə klē), *adv.* according to the laws of electrodynamics.

e|lec|tro|dy|nam|ics (i lek′trō dī nam′iks, -di-), *n.* the branch of physics that deals with the mutual influence of electric currents, the interaction of currents and magnets, and the influence of an electric current on itself.

e|lec|tro|dy|na|mism (i lek′trō dī′nə miz əm), *n.* = electrodynamics.

e|lec|tro|dy|na|mom|e|ter (i lek′trō dī′nə mom′ə tər), *n.* an instrument for measuring the strength of an electric current by means of the attraction or repulsion mutually exerted between two coils of wire, one fixed and one movable. The current to be measured passes through one of these coils.

e|lec|tro|en|ceph|a|lo|gram (i lek′trō en sef′ə lə gram), *n.* a tracing made by an electroencephalograph, used in investigating the activity of the brain in health or disease.

e|lec|tro|en|ceph|a|lo|graph (i lek′trō en sef′ə lə graf, -gräf), *n.* a device for measuring the electrical activity of the brain, used in the diagnosis and treatment of brain disorders; encephalograph: *Ink tracings of brain waves made by an electroencephalograph almost always look the same whether they are taken from the right side or a corresponding point on the left* (Science News Letter).

e|lec|tro|en|ceph|a|log|ra|pher (i lek′trō en sef′ə log′rə fər), *n.* an expert in the use of the electroencephalograph.

e|lec|tro|en|ceph|a|lo|graph|ic (i lek′trō en sef′ə lə graf′ik), *adj.* of or having to do with an electroencephalograph or electroencephalography.

e|lec|tro|en|ceph|a|log|ra|phy (i lek′trō en sef′ə log′rə fē), *n.* the science or technique of using an electroencephalograph.

e|lec|tro|fish|ing (i lek′trō fish′ing), *n.* a method of fishing by using a positive electrical pole which attracts schools of fish into nets or traps.

e|lec|tro|form (i lek′trə fôrm′), *v.t.* to form (a substance) by electrodeposition on a mold.

e|lec|tro|form|ing (i lek′trō fôr′ming), *n.* the making of metal objects by electrodeposition.

e|lec|tro|gal|va|nize (i lek′trō gal′və nīz), *v.t.,* **-nized, -niz|ing.** to galvanize steel or iron articles by placing them in a solution in which zinc or zinc salts are dissolved. With the aid of electricity, the zinc is transferred onto the articles.

e|lec|tro|gas|dy|nam|ic (i lek′trō gas′dī nam′ik, -di-), *adj.* producing electric power by electrogasdynamics.

e|lec|tro|gas|dy|nam|ics (i lek′trō gas′dī nam′iks, -di-), *n.* the conversion of heat energy into electricity by sweeping charged particles through an electric field in a stream of gas: *Electrogasdynamics (egd for short) is a novel means of generating electricity. The principles involved are, however, quite simple. Small particles of dust (or smoke, fog, etc.) are charged in a low-voltage region and then transported by a gas stream to a high-voltage region, where the charges are removed. Work is done on the particles in moving them against the electric field and electricity generated* (New Scientist).

e|lec|tro|gen|e|sis (i lek′trə jen′ə sis), *n.* electrogenic activity; production of electricity: *The most important role of electrogenesis in animals is in . . . the propagation of nerve impulses* (Barry D. Lindley).

e|lec|tro|gen|ic (i lek′trə jen′ik), *adj.* producing electricity, especially in living organisms: *His research on electrogenic activity in different types of cells has included studies of the cells of protozoa* (Scientific American).

e|lec|tro|glow (i lek′trə glō′), *n. Astronomy.* a strong emission of ultraviolet light occurring on the sunlit side of various planets, especially Uranus: *Voyager 2 found that the glow was of yet another variety, which requires both UV sunlight and electrons, and Voyager scientists dubbed it "electroglow"* (Science News).

e|lec|tro|graph (i lek′trə graf, -gräf), *n.* **1** a record or tracing made automatically by an electrometer. **2** an electric apparatus used in transferring designs to plates or cylinders for printing. **3** an instrument for sending pictures or other written documents electrically. **4** a picture made by X rays. **5** a motion-picture projector that uses an arc light. **6** an instrument for registering electrical conditions.

e|lec|tro|graph|ic (i lek′trə graf′ik), *adj.* of or having to do with an electrograph.

e|lec|trog|ra|phy (i lek′trog′rə fē, ē′lek-), *n.* the science or technique of using an electrograph.

e|lec|tro|hor|ti|cul|ture (i lek′trō hôr′tə kul′chər), *n.* the growing of plants by means of electric light, the electric light either (and usually) supplementing the sunlight or affording the only illumination for the plants.

e|lec|tro|hy|drau|lic (i lek′trō hī drô′lik), *adj.* producing mechanical or chemical energy by electrohydraulics: *The eight nozzles [of a rocket engine] are swivelled by electrohydraulic jacks to control pitch, yaw and roll* (New Scientist).

e|lec|tro|hy|drau|lics (i lek′trō hī drô′liks), *n.* the conversion of electrical energy into mechanical or chemical energy by the controlled discharge of high-voltage electric arcs submerged in water or another liquid.

e|lec|tro|jet (i lek′trə jet), *n.* an electric current moving in an ionized layer in the upper atmosphere of the earth above the equator.

e|lec|tro|ki|ne|tic (i lek′trō ki net′ik), *adj.* of or having to do with electrokinetics.

e|lec|tro|ki|net|ics (i lek′trō ki net′iks), *n.* the branch of physics that deals with electric currents or electricity in motion.

e|lec|tro|ki|ne|to|graph (i lek′trō ki nē′tə graf, -gräf; -net′ə-), *n.* a device for determining the motion of ocean water by measuring its electric potentials as it moves through the earth's magnetic field.

e|lec|tro|less (i lek′trō lis), *adj.* not using or deposited by electrolysis: *electroless plating of metals, an electroless gold coating.*

e|lec|tro|lier (i lek′trə lir′), *n.* a chandelier or other support for electric lights. [< *electro-* + (chande)*lier*]

e|lec|trol|o|gist (i lek′trol′ə jist, ē′lek-), *n.* a person who removes excess hair, moles, or other blemishes by means of electrolysis.

e|lec|trol|o|gy (i lek′trol′ə jē, ē′lek-), *n.* the science of electricity.

e|lec|tro|lu|mi|nes|cence (i lek′trō lü′mə nes′əns), *n.* light produced without heat by passing an alternating current through a phosphorescent substance: *For example, electroluminescence . . . has already made possible decorative effects through lighted panels* (Harper's).

e|lec|tro|lu|mi|nes|cent (i lek′trō lü′mə nes′ənt), *adj.* having the properties of electroluminescence: *electroluminescent lighting.*

e|lec|tro|lyse (i lek′trə līz), *v.t.,* **-lysed, -lys|ing.** *Especially British.* electrolyze. **–e|lec′tro|lys′er,** *n.*

✱e|lec|trol|y|sis (i lek′trol′ə sis, ē′lek-), *n.* **1** the decomposition of a chemical compound into its ions by the passage of an electrical current through a solution of it (electrolyte). The electrolysis of metallic solutions is useful in putting metal coatings on objects. *One of the most important industrial applications of electrolysis is in the refining of metals* (Sears and Zemansky). **2** the subjection of a chemical compound to such a process. **3** the removal of excess hair, moles, or other blemishes by destruction with an electrified needle. [< *electro-* + Greek *lýsis* a loosening]

✱electrolysis
definition 1

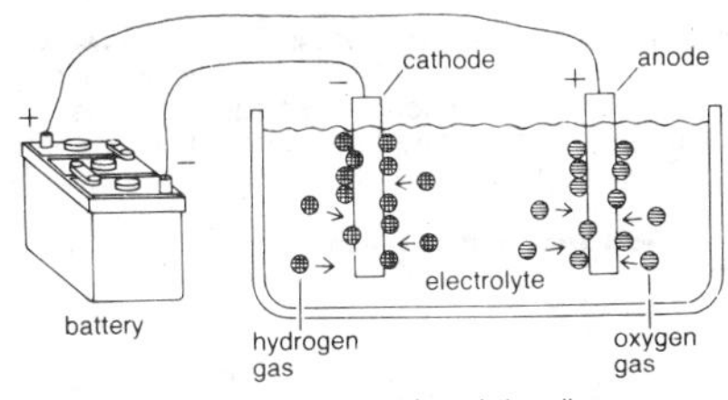

e|lec|tro|lyte (i lek′trə līt), *n.* **1** a chemical compound whose water solution will conduct an electric current; chemical compound that ionizes. Acids, bases, and salts are electrolytes. *Electrolytes . . . may be defined as compounds which when molten or when in solution conduct the electric current and are decomposed by it* (Monroe M. Offner). **2** a solution that will conduct an electric current. [< *electro-* + Greek *lytós* loosed]

e|lec|tro|lyt|ic (i lek′trə lik′ik), *adj.* of or having to do with electrolysis or with an electrolyte.

e|lec|tro|lyt|i|cal (i lek′trə lit′ə kəl), *adj.* = electrolytic.

e|lec|tro|lyt|i|cal|ly (i lek′trə lit′ə klē), *adv.* by means of electrolysis.

electrolytic cell, 1 the container which holds the electrolyte and the electrodes for use in electrolysis. **2** the electrolyte, its container, and the electrodes used in electrolysis.

electrolytic dissociation, the breaking down of the molecules of an electrolyte into ions.

e|lec|tro|ly|za|tion (i lek′trə lə zā′shən), *n.* decomposition by electrolysis.

e|lec|tro|lyze (i lek′trə līz), *v.t.,* **-lyzed, -lyz|ing.** to decompose by electrolysis.

e|lec|tro|lyz|er (i lek′trə lī′zər), *n.* an agent that electrolyzes.

✱e|lec|tro|mag|net (i lek′trō mag′nit), *n.* a piece of soft iron that becomes a strong magnet when an electric current is passed through wire coiled around it: *An electromagnet can be made by winding around a soft iron "core" a coil of in-*

sulated wire carrying electrical current (New York Herald Tribune).

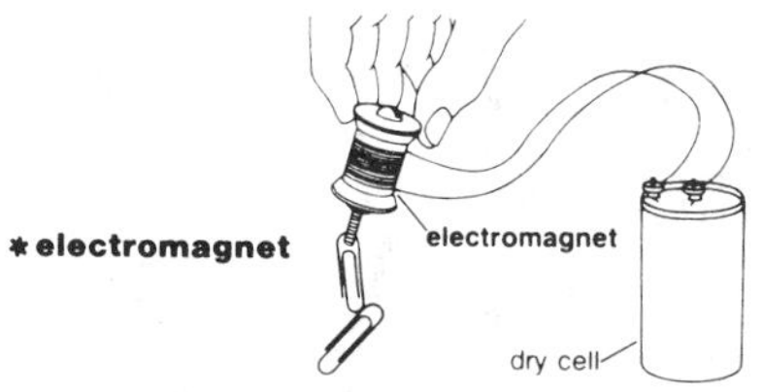

*** electromagnet**

e|lec|tro|mag|net|ic (i lek′trō mag net′ik), *adj.* **1** of or caused by an electromagnet. **2** of electromagnetism.

e|lec|tro|mag|net|i|cal (i lek′trō mag net′ə kəl), *adj.* = electromagnetic.

e|lec|tro|mag|net|i|cal|ly (i lek′trō mag net′ə klē), *adv.* **1** by means of an electromagnet. **2** by electromagnetism.

electromagnetic field, the field created by the interplay of an electric field and a magnetic field when an electric current passes through a wire: *An electromagnetic field consists of two kinds of energy: electrostatic, or potential energy, and electrodynamic, or kinetic energy* (Scientific American).

electromagnetic induction, the production of an electromotive force in a circuit by variation of the magnetic field with which the circuit is connected.

electromagnetic pulse, a powerful form of radiation released by a nuclear explosion, which has the effect of disrupting or disabling the electronically operated missile systems of a country: *The so-called "EMP" or electromagnetic pulse, induced by a major explosion, has widespread effects* (Hanson W. Baldwin).

electromagnetic radiation, the passage of energy through space or through material substances by electromagnetic waves: *Light, radio waves, and X rays are forms of electromagnetic radiation. Almost all our knowledge of extraterrestrial objects comes from emitted or reflected electromagnetic radiation—visible light or radio waves* (New Scientist).

***electromagnetic spectrum**, the entire range of the different types of electromagnetic waves. It goes from the very long, low-frequency radio waves, through infrared and light waves, to the very short, high-frequency cosmic rays and X rays.

*** electromagnetic spectrum**

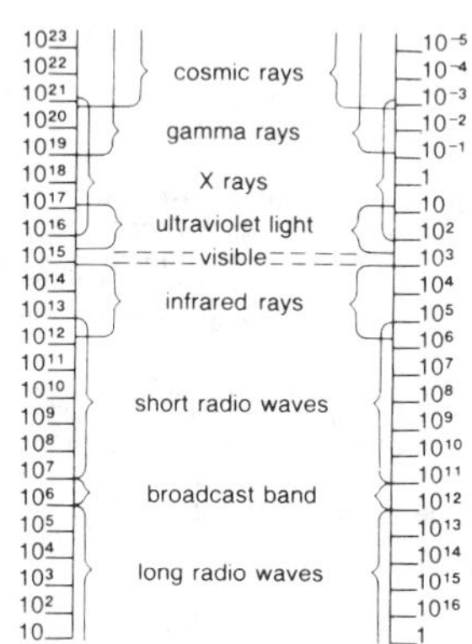

electromagnetic unit, any one of a group of units in the centimeter-gram-second system which are based on electromagnetism, such as the abampere, abcoulomb, abfarad, and abhenry. *Abbr:* e.m.u. or EMU (no periods).

electromagnetic wave, a wave of energy made up of an electric and a magnetic field, generated when an electric charge oscillates or is accelerated. Light waves and radio waves are electromagnetic waves, according to their frequencies and wavelengths. The chief kinds of electromagnetic waves, ranging from longest to shortest wave length, are long radio waves, short radio waves, infrared rays, visible light, ultraviolet light, X rays, and gamma rays. *In 1873, Maxwell showed that an oscillating electrical circuit should radiate electromagnetic waves* (Sears and Zemansky).

e|lec|tro|mag|net|ism (i lek′trō mag′nə tiz əm), *n.* **1** magnetism produced by a current of electricity. **2** the branch of physics that deals with electricity and magnetism.

e|lec|tro|mag|net|ist (i lek′trō mag′nə tist), *n.* a person who studies electromagnetism.

e|lec|tro|me|chan|i|cal (i lek′trō mə kan′ə kəl), *adj.* operated wholly or in part mechanically but powered or controlled by electricity. —**e|lec′tro|me|chan′i|cal|ly**, *adv.*

e|lec|tro|me|chan|ics (i lek′trō mə kan′iks), *n.* **1** the study of the mechanics in electricity or electric currents. **2** the study of electromechanical systems and processes.

e|lec|tro|met|al|lur|gi|cal (i lek′trō met′ə lėr′jə kəl), *adj.* of or having to do with electrometallurgy.

e|lec|tro|met|al|lur|gist (i lek′trō met′ə lėr′jist), *n.* a person who studies electrometallurgy.

e|lec|tro|met|al|lur|gy (i lek′trō met′ə lėr′jē), *n.* the branch of metallurgy that deals with the application of electricity to metallurgical processes, such as the use of electricity as a source of heat in refining metals.

e|lec|trom|e|ter (i lek′trom′ə tər, ē′lek-), *n.* an instrument for measuring differences in electrical charge or potential.

e|lec|tro|met|ric (i lek′trə met′rik), *adj.* having to do with electrometry.

e|lec|tro|met|ri|cal (i lek′trə met′rə kəl), *adj.* = electrometric.

e|lec|trom|e|try (i lek′trom′ə trē, ē′lek-), *n.* the measurement of electricity by an electrometer.

e|lec|tro|mo|bile (i lek′trə mə bēl), *n.* = electric car. [< *electro-* + (auto)*mobile*]

e|lec|tro|mo|tion (i lek′trə mō′shən), *n.* **1** electric motion; passage of an electric current. **2** mechanical motion produced by means of electricity.

e|lec|tro|mo|tive (i lek′trə mō′tiv), *adj.* **1** producing a flow of electricity. **2** of or having to do with electromotive force.

electromotive force, **1** the force due to differences of potential that causes an electric current. **2** the amount of energy derived from an electric source per unit of current passing through the source. Electromotive force is commonly measured in volts. *If two different metals are placed in contact, and the junction is warmed, an electromotive force is generated* (F. P. Bowden). *Abbr:* E.M.F., e.m.f., or emf (no periods).

electromotive series, *Chemistry.* a list of the metallic elements in the decreasing order of their tendencies to change to ions in solution, so that each metal displaces from solution those below it in the list, and is displaced by those above it; activity series.

e|lec|tro|mo|tiv|i|ty (i lek′trō mō tiv′ə tē), *n.* the production of a flow of electricity.

e|lec|tro|mo|to|graph (i lek′trō mō′tə graf, -gräf), *n.* an early form of a receiver for a telephone, invented by Edison.

e|lec|tro|mo|tor (i lek′trə mō′tər), *n.* **1** a machine producing electric current. **2** a motor run by electricity.

e|lec|tro|mu|sic (i lek′trō myü′zik), *n.* = electronic music.

e|lec|tro|my|o|gram (i lek′trō mī′ə gram), *n.* the record made by an electromyograph.

e|lec|tro|my|o|graph (i lek′trō mī′ə graf, -gräf), *n.* an instrument that records differences in the electric potential of muscles. It is used to diagnose muscular ailments. *Similar to the electrocardiograph, the electromyograph picks up clicks from sick muscles* (Marguerite Clark). [< *electro-* + Greek *mys, myós* muscle + English *-graph*]

e|lec|tro|my|o|graph|ic (i lek′trō mī′ə graf′ik), *adj.* having to do with or made by an electromyograph.

e|lec|tro|my|og|ra|phy (i lek′trō mī og′rə fē), *n.* the science or technique of using the electromyograph.

e|lec|tron (i lek′tron), *n.* a tiny particle carrying one unit of negative electricity; the unit charge of electricity found outside the nucleus of all atoms and having a mass about 1/1836 that of a proton. All atoms have electrons arranged about a nucleus. An electron may be positive (positron), but as the term is generally used, it refers to the negative form (negatron). *It is now recognized that the electrons do not always behave like tiny particles but sometimes manifest wave properties as well* (P. E. Hodgson). See picture under **atom**. Also, **elektron**. [< *electr*(ic) + *-on,* as in *ion*]

e|lec|tro|nar|co|sis (i lek′trō när kō′sis), *n.* unconsciousness produced by an electric current passing through the brain between electrodes placed on the temples.

electron beam, a stream of electrons moving in the same direction and with the same velocity: *The electron beam of the super-microscope has become a basic tool in research on disease* (Harper's).

electron cloud, (in a vacuum tube) the area between the electrodes which contains a great number of relatively stationary electrons.

electron diffraction, the diffraction of electrons when they pass through crystalline matter, useful in the study of the structure of materials.

e|lec|trone (i lek′trōn), *n.* = electronic organ.

e|lec|tro|neg|a|tive (i lek′trō neg′ə tiv), *adj., n.* —*adj.* **1** charged with negative electricity. **2** tending to pass to the positive pole (anode) in electrolysis. **3** tending to gain electrons; nonmetallic; acid.
—*n.* an electronegative substance. —**e|lec′tro|neg′a|tive|ly**, *adv.*

e|lec|tro|neg|a|tiv|i|ty (i lek′trō neg′ə tiv′ə tē), *n.* the condition of being electronegative.

e|lec|tro|neu|tral|i|ty (i lek′trō nü tral′ə tē, -nyü-), *n.* a condition in which the total charge of all the positive ions of a substance almost exactly equals the total charge of all the negative ions.

electron gas, any system of free electrons: *Each electron goes to form the communal "electron gas" which is responsible for the high electrical and thermal conductivity of the metallic state* (New Scientist).

electron gun, a device that produces and guides the flow of electrons and greatly increases their speed. In a television picture tube or an oscilloscope, the electron gun focuses a beam of electrons on the fluorescent screen at the end of the tube. Electron guns are also used in oil refining and various other industries.

e|lec|tron|ic (i lek′tron′ik, ē′lek-), *adj.* **1** of or having to do with electrons or electronics: *A skilled programmer must often spend days reducing the elements of a problem to numerical or electronic code before he can hold even a brief conversation with his machine* (Time). **2** computerized; stored in or controlled by a computer: *There were more than 2800 publicly available electronic databases of all types* (Science).

e|lec|tron|i|cal|ly (i lek′tron′ə klē, ē′lek-), *adv.* by electronic means; in an electronic manner: *to store data electronically.*

electronic art, a form of art that uses electronic materials, such as moving and flashing light displays, as the artistic medium: *Electronic music inspired him [Nam June Paik] to make electronic art, just as the Russian composer Scriabin made a motorized light display to accompany his Prometheus half a century ago* (Time).

electronic brain, a complex electronic computer, usually of the digital type, such as ENIAC; electric brain.

electronic church, *U.S.* religious television programs of a church or evangelistic service designed for mass audiences, usually conducted by preachers of great personal appeal.

electronic computer, = computer (def. 1).

electronic countermeasure, an electronic device that misdirects the guidance system of an enemy missile. *Abbr:* ECM (no periods).

electronic engineer, a person skilled in electronic engineering.

electronic engineering, the branch of electrical engineering that deals with electronics and the use of electronic devices in radio, television, automation, and computers.

electronic flash, = strobe light.

electronic funds transfer, a system for transferring funds from one account or location to another by computer: *Abbr:* EFT (no periods).

electronic intelligence, = elint.

electronic mail, **1** a system for sending messages by computer, Telex, facsimile telegraph, or other electronic means instead of by post; e-mail or E mail: *Electronic mail . . . is expected to capture a major portion of mail traffic* (Christian Science Monitor). **2** an international fax service operated by the U.S. Postal Service.

electronic music, music created by various electronic generators and filters and usually recorded on tape and edited to form musical compositions: *One form of electronic music is the conversion of familiar sounds into new sounds by varying frequency, intensity and other qualities* (New York Times).

electronic organ, an organ that uses electronic amplification to increase the volume of sound. An electronic organ has no pipes, but uses vacuum tubes to amplify the sound.

e|lec|tron|ics (i lek′tron′iks, ē′lek-), *n.* the branch of physics that deals with the production, activity, and effects of electrons in motion through vacuum tubes, gas-filled tubes, semiconductors, and other devices. Electronics has made possible the development of television, radio, radar, and computers.

electronic switching, an automatic system of switching electric circuits by means of electronic components, especially in telephone circuitry: *Electronic switching . . . allows a customer to transfer incoming calls automatically and to connect additional telephones to an existing call* (J. M. Freeman).

e|lec|tron|ize (i lek′trə nīz), *v.t.,* **-ized, -iz|ing.** to furnish with electronic equipment.

electron lens, the electrodes or conductors which set up electric or magnetic fields by which a beam of electrons can be focused, as light rays are by an optical lens.

electron micrograph, the photograph or image of an object under an electron microscope.

electron microscope, a microscope that uses beams of electrons instead of beams of light, and has much higher power than any ordinary microscope. An electron microscope is focused with an electron lens. Its enlarged images are not observable directly by the eye, but are projected upon a fluorescent surface or photographic plate. *A specimen for study under the electron microscope must be no "thicker" than .000003937 inch* (Science News Letter).

electron microscopist, a person skilled in the use of the electron microscope.

electron microscopy, the use of an electron microscope.

electron multiplier, a vacuum tube that amplifies a current by a series of accelerations and secondary emissions of electrons.

e|lec|tron|o|graph (i lek′tron′ə graf, -gräf), *n.* **1** a device using a vacuum tube to produce images on a fine-grain photographic emulsion exposed to an accelerated beam of electrons. **2** an image produced by such a device.

e|lec|tron|o|graph|ic (i lek′tron ə graf′ik, -gräf′-), *adj.* of or having to do with electronography: *The Spectracon electronographic image intensifier was developed for astronomers, who face the problem of recording two-dimensional pictures which contain a large amount of detail and have a very wide range of brightness* (Science Journal).

e|lec|tro|nog|ra|phy (i lek′tro nog′rə fē), *n.* the use of electronographs: *The cost of electronography to the user is high. Every time an exposed photographic plate is removed, the air destroys the highly reactive photosurface* (Scientific American).

e|lec|tron-op|ti|cal (i lek′tron op′tə kəl), *adj.* of or having to do with electron optics: *An electron-optical lens focuses the highly accelerated electrons into a tiny spot* (Paul H. Gleichauf).

electron optics, the branch of electronics that deals with the control of beams of electrons by an electric or magnetic field so that the rays act like rays of light in an optical instrument.

electron tube, **1** = vacuum tube. **2** a tube similar to a vacuum tube but filled with gas.

electron volt, a unit of electrical energy used in nuclear physics. It is equal to the energy gained by an electron when it moves from one point to a point higher in potential by one volt. It is equal to 1.6×10^{-12} ergs. In some particle accelerators, electrons having several billion electron volts of energy are produced. One Bev equals one billion electron volts. *Abbr:* e.v. or ev (no periods).

e|lec|tro|oc|u|lo|gram (i lek′trō ok′yə lə gram), *n.* a tracing made by an electrooculograph.

e|lec|tro|oc|u|lo|graph (i lek′trō ok′yə lə graf, -gräf), *n.* a device for measuring the speed and direction of eye movements by registering differences in electric potential.

e|lec|tro|oc|u|log|ra|phy (i lek′trō ok′yə log′rə fē), *n.* the technique of using the electrooculograph.

e|lec|tro|op|tic (i lek′trō op′tik), *adj.* = electrooptical. —**e|lec′tro|op′ti|cal|ly**, *adv.*

e|lec|tro|op|ti|cal (i lek′trō op′tə kəl), *adj.* of or having to do with electrooptics.

e|lec|tro|op|tics (i lek′trō op′tiks), *n.* the science of the relations between electricity and optics.

e|lec|tro|os|mo|sis (i lek′trō oz mō′sis, -os-), *n.* the flow of a liquid through a porous membrane as a result of an electric field created by electrodes placed on opposite sides of the membrane. It is utilized in drying and stabilizing soil.

e|lec|tro|os|mot|ic (i lek′trō oz mot′ik, -os-), *adj.* of or having to do with electroosmosis.

e|lec|tro|path|ic (i lek′trə path′ik), *adj.* of or having to do with electropathy.

e|lec|trop|a|thy (i lek′trop′ə thē, ē′lek-), *n.* = electrotherapy.

e|lec|tro|phile (i lek′trə fīl, -fil), *n.* a substance that is strongly attracted to electrons: *Then by dividing heterolytic* [*cell-destroying*] *reagents into nucleophiles and electrophiles, he* [*Sir Christopher Ingold*] *saw the basis of a scheme interrelating a great range of chemical reactions* (London Times).

e|lec|tro|phil|ic (i lek′trə fil′ik), *adj.* strongly attracted to electrons: *an electrophilic molecule or ion.*

e|lec|tro|phon|ic (i lek′trə fon′ik), *adj.* (of musical instruments) producing varied sounds by the varying of oscillations of an electric current.

e|lec|tro|pho|re|sis (i lek′trō fə rē′sis), *n.* **1** the movement of colloidal particles resulting from the influence of an electric field. **2** a technique based on this phenomenon, widely used to separate and analyze the molecular structure of substances such as blood plasma. [< *electro-* + Greek *phórēsis* a carrying < *phérein* carry]

e|lec|tro|pho|ret|ic (i lek′trō fə ret′ik), *adj.* having to do with or produced by electrophoresis: *electrophoretic analysis.* —**e|lec′tro|pho|ret′i|cal|ly**, *adv.*

e|lec|tro|pho|ret|o|gram (i lek′trō fə ret′ə gram), *n.* a record of the parts of a substance separated by electrophoresis.

e|lec|troph|o|rus (i lek′trof′ər əs, ē′lek-), *n., pl.* **-o|ri** (-ə rī). a simple device for producing charges of electricity by means of induction. [< *electro-* + Greek *phóros* bearing < *phérein* to bear]

e|lec|tro|pho|to|graph|ic (i lek′trō fō′tə graf′ik), *adj.* having to do with or using electrophotography: *an electrophotographic copier.*

e|lec|tro|pho|tog|ra|phy (i lek′trō fə tog′rə fē), *n.* photography that uses electric processes for producing images, as xerography.

e|lec|tro|phys|i|o|log|i|cal (i lek′trō fiz′ē ə loj′ə kəl), *adj.* having to do with or produced by electrophysiology: *From careful electrophysiological measurements it seems that a retina, even in total darkness, transmits a constant barrage of randomly scattered spontaneous responses to the brain* (Scientific American).

e|lec|tro|phys|i|ol|o|gist (i lek′trō fiz′ē ol′ə jist), *n.* a person who studies electrophysiology.

e|lec|tro|phys|i|ol|o|gy (i lek′trō fiz′ē ol′ə jē), *n.* **1** the science that studies the relationship between living organisms and electricity. **2** the electrical activity associated with any part of the body and its functions: *the electrophysiology of the retina.*

e|lec|tro|pism (i lek′trə piz əm), *n. Botany.* curvature of growth in plants due to slight electric currents. [< *elec*(tro-) + *tropism*]

e|lec|tro|plate (i lek′trə plāt′), *v.,* **-plat|ed, -plat|ing,** *n.* —*v.t.* to cover (silverware, printing plates, etc.) with a coating of metal by means of electrolysis.
—*n.* **1** silverware or other metal covered in this way. **2** a printing plate made by this process.
—**e|lec′tro|plat′er**, *n.*

e|lec|tro|plat|ing (i lek′trə plā′ting), *n.* the process of coating metal by means of electrolysis.

e|lec|tro|pneu|mat|ic (i lek′trō nü mat′ik, -nyü-), *adj.* moved by electric and pneumatic power: *The equipment ... works on an electropneumatic system* (New Scientist).

e|lec|tro|po|lar (i lek′trə pō′lər), *adj.* having one end or surface positive and the other negative, as an electrical conductor.

e|lec|tro|pol|ish (i lek′trō pol′ish), *v.t.* to polish (metal) by means of electrolysis: *As many as 900 components can be formed in an inch-diameter slice of electropolished silicon 0.01 in. thick* (New Scientist).

e|lec|tro|pol|ish|ing (i lek′trō pol′i shing), *n.* the polishing of metals by means of electrolysis, often used on curved parts which cannot be polished mechanically.

e|lec|tro|pos|i|tive (i lek′trō poz′ə tiv), *adj., n.* —*adj.* **1** charged with positive electricity. **2** tending to pass to the negative pole (cathode) in electrolysis. **3** tending to lose electrons; metallic; basic.
—*n.* an electropositive substance.

e|lec|tro|pos|i|tiv|i|ty (i lek′trō poz′ə tiv′ə tē), *n.* the condition of being electropositive.

e|lec|tro|pre|cip|i|ta|tor (i lek′trō pri sip′ə tā′tər), *n.* = electrostatic precipitator.

e|lec|tro|re|fine (i lek′trō ri fīn′), *v.t.,* **-fined, -fin|ing.** to refine (metal) by means of electrolysis: *The Interior Department reported progress in its search for commercially practical methods of electrorefining high-grade titanium from ... titanium scrap* (Wall Street Journal).

e|lec|tro|ret|i|no|gram (i lek′trō ret′ə nə gram), *n.* a chart of the electrical reaction of the retina to light, used to diagnose ailments of the eye. *Abbr:* ERG (no periods).

e|lec|tro|ret|i|nog|ra|phy (i lek′trō ret′ə nog′rə fē), *n.* the method of recording the electrical reaction of the retina to light.

***e|lec|tro|scope** (i lek′trə skōp), *n.* a device that indicates the presence of minute charges of electricity and shows whether they are positive or negative: *The electroscope is the oldest research tool of the nuclear physicist, indeed the oldest electrical measuring instrument* (Crammer and Peierls).

***electroscope**

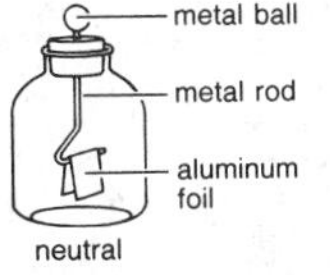

e|lec|tro|scop|ic (i lek′trə skop′ik), *adj.* of or having to do with an electroscope.

e|lec|tro|sen|si|tive (i lek′trō sen′sə tiv), *adj.* readily affected by electric current; sensitive to electricity: *electrosensitive paper.*

e|lec|tro|shock (i lek′trō shok′), *n.* **1** = electric shock. **2** = electroshock therapy.

electroshock therapy or **treatment**, shock therapy using an electric current passed through the brain: *He has received electroshock therapy to relieve his despondency* (New Scientist).

e|lec|tro|slag (i lek′trō slag′), *adj.* of or having to do with a method of welding or refining metals by passing an electric current through molten metal and a layer of slag in which impurities are dissolved.

e|lec|tro|sleep (i lek′trō slēp′), *n.* sleep induced by passing an electric current through the brain between electrodes placed on the temples: *Soviet physicians have indicated "good results" in using electrically induced relaxation and sleep—electrosleep—to treat various ailments* (New York Times).

e|lec|tro|stat|ic (i lek′trə stat′ik), *adj.* **1** of or having to do with static electricity: *The Van de Graaff electrostatic accelerator can produce ion beams having a very stable energy up to 5 Mev.* (Bulletin of Atomic Scientists). **2** of or having to do with electrostatics. —**e|lec′tro|stat′i|cal|ly**, *adv.*

electrostatic field, an electric field produced by electric charges which are stationary or at rest.

electrostatic generator, = Van de Graaff generator.

electrostatic induction, the production of an electric charge in a body by the influence of another body that is charged with electricity; electric induction.

electrostatic precipitator, a device for removing dust, pollen, or other particles from the air by subjecting them to an electrostatic charge so that they may be collected on a plate with an opposite charge: *Electrostatic precipitators are among the most important air cleaners because they run so efficiently and have so many different uses* (Frank H. Faust).

electrostatic printing, any process of printing or copying by the use of electrostatic charges instead of ink or pressure. The best known process of electrostatic printing is xerography.

e|lec|tro|stat|ics (i lek′trə stat′iks), *n.* the branch of physics that deals with static electricity and with objects charged with electricity.

electrostatic unit, *Electricity.* a unit based primarily upon the force exerted between two electric charges. The fundamental c.g.s. unit in this system is that unit charge which would repel with a force of one dyne a like and equal charge placed at a distance of one centimeter. *Abbr:* e.s.u. or esu (no periods).

e|lec|tro|steth|o|graph (i lek′trō steth′ə graf, -gräf), *n.* a very sensitive, electrically operated instrument used to record sounds of the heart: *The medical instrument is an electrostethograph, which gives doctors a high-fidelity record of heart sounds so faint they cannot be heard by the human ear even aided by a physician's stethoscope* (Science News Letter).

e|lec|tro|sur|ger|y (i lek′trō sėr′jər ē), *n.* the use of electric currents in surgery; surgical diathermy.

e|lec|tro|sur|gi|cal (i lek′trō sėr′jə kəl), *adj.* of or having to do with electrosurgery: *electrosurgical knives.*

e|lec|tro|tac|tic (i lek′trə tak′tik), *adj.* of or having to do with electrotaxis.

e|lec|tro|tax|is (i lek′trə tak′sis), *n.* the adjustment or movement of organisms or cells in relation to electric currents. [< *electro-* + Greek *táxis* arrangement]

e|lec|tro|tech|ni|cal (i lek′trō tek′nə kəl), *adj.* of or having to do with electrotechnology: *electrotechnical engineering.*

e|lec|tro|tech|ni|cian (i lek′trō tek nish′ən), *n.* a person who studies electrotechnology.

e|lec|tro|tech|nics (i lek′trō tek′niks), *n.* = electrotechnology.

e|lec|tro|tech|nol|o|gy (i lek′trō tek nol′ə jē), *n.* the science that deals with the practical applications of electricity: *This full sweep can already be discerned dimly in one recent episode in electrotechnology: the production of the transistor* (New Scientist).

e|lec|tro|ther|a|peu|tic (i lek′trō ther′ə pyü′tik), *adj.* of or having to do with electrotherapy.

e|lec|tro|ther|a|peu|ti|cal (i lek′trō ther′ə pyü′tə kəl), *adj.* = electrotherapeutic.

e|lec|tro|ther|a|peu|tics (i lek′trō ther′ə pyü′tiks), *n.* = electrotherapy.

e|lec|tro|ther|a|peu|tist (i lek′trō ther′ə pyü′tist),

Pronunciation Key: hat, āge, cãre, fär; let, ēqual, tėrm; it, īce; hot, ōpen, ôrder; oil, out; cup, pu̇t, rüle; child; long; thin; ᴛʜen; zh, measure; ə represents **a** in about, **e** in taken, **i** in pencil, **o** in lemon, **u** in circus.

n. = electrotherapist.

e|lec|tro|ther|a|pist (i lek′trō ther′ə pist), *n.* a person who studies electrotherapy.

e|lec|tro|ther|a|py (i lek′trō ther′ə pē), *n.* the treatment of disease by electricity, as in diathermy.

e|lec|tro|ther|mal (i lek′trō thėr′məl), *adj.* having to do with heat produced by electricity.

e|lec|tro|ther|mic (i lek′trō thėr′mik), *adj.* = electrothermal.

e|lec|tro|ton|ic (i lek′trə ton′ik), *adj.* of or having to do with electrotonus.

e|lec|tro|to|nic|i|ty (i lek′trō tə nis′ə tē), *n.* = electrotonus.

e|lec|trot|o|nus (i lek′trot′ə nəs, ē′lek-), *n.* the altered condition of a nerve or muscle during the passage of an electric current through it. [< *electro-* + *tonus*]

e|lec|tro|type (i lek′trə tīp), *n., v.,* **-typed, -typ-ing.** —*n.* **1** a metal or composition plate used in printing. It is a copy of a page of type, an engraving, or the like, made by electroplating a wax mold of the original. **2** a print made from such a plate. **3** = electrotyping.
—*v.t., v.i.* to make such a plate or plates (of).

e|lec|tro|typ|er (i lek′trə tī′pər), *n.* a person whose work is the making of electrotypes.

e|lec|tro-type|set|ter (i lek′trō tīp′set′ər), *n.* a machine that through electrically transmitted messages automatically sets type. Newspapers which use it can publish simultaneously in many cities.

e|lec|tro|typ|ic (i lek′trə tip′ik), *adj.* having to do with or made by means of electrotyping.

e|lec|tro|typ|ing (i lek′trə tī′ping), *n.* the process of making electrotypes; electrotypy.

e|lec|tro|typ|ist (i lek′trə tī′pist), *n.* a person skilled in electrotyping.

e|lec|tro|typ|y (i lek′trə tī′pē), *n.* the process of making electrotypes.

e|lec|tro|va|lence (i lek′trō vā′ləns), *n.* the number of electrons gained or lost by an atom when it becomes an ion in a compound; polar valence.

e|lec|tro|va|len|cy (i lek′trō vā′lən sē), *n., pl.* **-cies.** = electrovalence.

e|lec|tro|va|lent (i lek′trō vā′lənt), *adj.* of or producing electrovalence.

e|lec|tro|weak (i lek′trō wēk′), *adj. Physics.* uniting weak and electromagnetic interactions, as in the Weinberg-Salam theory: *Abdus Salam, one of the peole who started the work on the unified field theory, has been going around calling it "electroweak." This follows the historical precedent whereby the 19th century coined electromagnetism out of electricity and magnetism* (Science News).

e|lec|tro|win|ning (i lek′trō win′ing), *n.* the process of extracting metal from a solution by means of electrolysis. [< *electro-* + *winning*]

e|lec|trum (i lek′trəm), *n.* a pale-yellow, natural alloy of gold and silver, used by the ancients. [< Latin *ēlectrum* < Greek *ēlektron* (originally) amber]

e|lec|tu|ar|y (i lek′chů er′ē), *n., pl.* **-ar|ies.** a medicinal paste of powdered drugs and syrup or honey. [< Late Latin *ēlectuārium* < Greek *ekleiktón* a lozenge < *ekleíchein* lick out < *ex-* out + *leíchein* to lick]

el|e|doi|sin (el′ə doi′sən), *n.* a drug, originally obtained as an active polypeptide from the salivary glands of two species of octopuses, used to dilate blood vessels, reduce blood pressure, and stimulate smooth muscles. *Formula:* $C_{54}H_{85}N_{13}O_{15}S$ [< New Latin *Eledone* the octopus genus name]

el|ee|mos|y|nar|i|ly (el′ə mos′ə ner′ə lē, el′ē ə-), *adv.* by way of charity; charitably.

el|ee|mos|y|nar|y (el′ə mos′ə ner′ē, el′ē ə-), *adj.* **1** of or for charity; charitable: *But the monasteries still continue to train their monks and carry on education and eleemosynary work* (Atlantic). **2** provided by charity; free: *Eleemosynary relief never yet tranquilized the working classes—it never made them grateful* (Charlotte Brontë). **3** dependent on charity; supported by charity. [< Late Latin *eleēmosynārius* < Latin *eleēmosyna* < Greek *eleēmosýnē* compassion < *éleos* mercy. Compare etym. under **alms.**]

el|e|gance (el′ə gəns), *n.* **1** good taste; refined grace and richness; luxury free from coarseness: *We admired the elegance of the lady's clothes.* **SYN:** fineness, choiceness. **2** something elegant.

el|e|gan|cy (el′ə gən sē), *n., pl.* **-cies. 1** something elegant: *Clothes and their accessories, although elegancies, are also necessaries; cosmetics are vanities* (Punch). **2** good taste; elegance.

el|e|gant (el′ə gənt), *adj.* **1** showing good taste; refined; beautifully luxurious: *The palace had elegant furnishings.* **SYN:** superior. See syn. under **fine. 2** expressed with taste; correct and polished in expression or arrangement: *an elegant style of writing.* **3** *Informal.* nice; choice; fine. [< Old French *elegant*, learned borrowing from Latin *ēlegāns, -antis*, related to *ēligere* make a (proper) selection; see etym. under **elect**] —**el′e|gant|ly,** *adv.*

é|lé|gant (ā lā gäN′), *n. French.* a fashionable person.

é|lé|gante (ā lā gäNt′), *n. French.* a fashionable woman.

el|e|gi|ac (el′ə jī′ak, -ək; i lē′jē-), *adj., n.* —*adj.* **1** of or suitable for an elegy. **2** sad; mournful; melancholy: *elegiac grief.* **3** written in elegiacs.
—*n.* a dactylic hexameter couplet in Greek and Latin verse, the second line having no unaccented syllables in the third and sixth feet.
elegiacs, a poem written in such verses: *The Heroides and Tristia of Ovid are elegiacs.*

el|e|gi|a|cal (el′ə jī′ə kəl, i lē′jē-), *adj.* = elegiac.

el|e|gi|a|cal|ly (el′ə jī′ə klē, i lē′jē-), *adv.* in an elegiac way or manner: *Lully's heroic operas end elegiacally* (Listener).

el|e|gi|ast (e lē′jē ast), *n.* = elegist.

el|e|gist (el′ə jist), *n.* the writer of an elegy.

e|le|git (i lē′jit), *n. Law.* a writ of execution giving a creditor the property of a debtor until the debt is paid. [< Latin *ēlēgit* he has chosen < *ēligere* choose; see etym. under **elect**]

el|e|gize (el′ə jīz), *v.,* **-gized, -giz|ing.** —*v.t.* to write an elegy about.
—*v.i.* to write an elegy; lament.

el|e|gy (el′ə jē), *n., pl.* **-gies. 1** a mournful or melancholy poem, usually a lament for the dead. Milton's *Lycidas* and Shelley's *Adonais* are elegies. **2** a poem written in elegiac verses. **3** *Music.* a mournful piece to be played or sung. [< Middle French *élégie*, learned borrowing from Latin *elegīa* < Greek *elegeíā*, ultimately < *élegos* mournful poem, lament]

e|lek|tron (i lek′tron), *n.* = electron.

elem., 1 element or elements. 2 elementary.

el|e|me (el′ə mē), *n.* a variety of dried Smyrna figs from Turkey. [< Turkish *eleme* selected]

el|e|ment (el′ə mənt), *n.* **1** one of the simple substances, such as gold, iron, carbon, sulfur, oxygen, and hydrogen. An element cannot be separated into simpler parts by ordinary chemical means. There are over 100 elements, each composed of atoms that are chemically alike. *All material things in the universe known to our senses are composed of one or more chemical elements* (Science News Letter). **2** one of the parts of which anything is made up: *Honesty, industry, and kindness are elements of a good life.* **3** a simple or necessary part to be learned first; first principle; rudiment: *We learn the elements of arithmetic before the seventh grade.* **4** one of the four substances—earth, water, air, and fire—that were thought in ancient times to make up all other things. **5** *Figurative.* natural or suitable surroundings: *Every animal has his element assigned him, the birds have the air and man and beasts the earth* (Samuel Johnson). **6** the part that does the work in an electrical device. **7** *Military.* **a** any unit or part of a larger group, formation, or maneuver: *A column or squad is a military element.* **b** a unit of two or three planes flying in formation. **8** *Mathematics.* **a** a member of a set. **b** a very small part of a given magnitude similar in nature to the whole magnitude. **c** one of the lines, planes, or points that make up a geometrical figure. **9** *Electricity.* **a** one of the two unlike pieces that make up a voltaic couple. **b** the two electrodes of a voltaic couple when assembled. **10** *Radio, U.S.* an electrode in a vacuum tube. **11** *Astronomy.* one of the data required for the solution of a problem. **12** *Mechanics.* one of the parts making up a pair.
be in one's element, to be in the surroundings in which one feels at home: *A real bookworm, he is in his element in the library.*
be out of one's element, to be away from the surroundings in which one feels at home: *She was out of her element on the farm. When they came to make boards ... they were quite out of their element* (Daniel Defoe).
the elements, a the forces of the air, especially in bad weather: *The raging storm seemed a war of the elements.* **b** the bread and wine used in the Eucharist.
[< Latin *elementum* rudiment, first principle]
—*Syn.* **2 Element, component, constituent, ingredient** mean one of the parts of which something is made up. **Element,** the general word, applies to any essential or basic part of anything: *Kindness is an element of courtesy. The Latin element in English is surprisingly large.* **Component** means a part of something that is put together as a compound or mixture: *Quartz and feldspar are the chief components of granite.* **Constituent,** often used interchangeably with *component*, differs in suggesting active helping to form the whole instead of just being a part: *The colors of the rainbow are the constituents of white light.* **Ingredient** suggests that the helping parts lose individual identity in a mixture or combination: *Milk, eggs, and flour are basic ingredients in making a cake.*

element 104, an artificial, radioactive chemical element, the first of the transactinide series, produced in the form of various isotopes chiefly by bombarding californium with carbon ions; rutherfordium; kurchatovium.

element 105, an artificial, radioactive chemical element produced by bombarding californium with nitrogen nuclei or by bombarding americium with neon nuclei; hahnium.

element 106, an artificial, radioactive chemical element, the 14th of the transuranium elements and the third of the transactinides, produced by bombarding californium with oxygen ions or lead nuclei with chromium and molybdenum ions.

element 107, an artificial, radioactive chemical element produced by bombarding bismuth with nuclei of chromium.

el|e|men|tal (el′ə men′təl), *adj.* **1** of the forces of nature, especially the weather: *The storm showed elemental fury in its violence.* **2** as found in nature; simple but powerful: *Hunger is an elemental feeling.* **SYN:** natural. **3** = elementary. **SYN:** fundamental, basic. **4** of the four elements —earth, water, air, and fire. **5** *Figurative.* of the nature of an ultimate constituent; not compounded; simple. **6** being a necessary or basic part. —**el′e-men′tal|ly,** *adv.*

el|e|men|tal|ism (el′ə men′tə liz əm), *n.* **1** a method or theory that deifies the elemental powers of nature. **2** a system based upon elemental forces or characters.

el|e|men|tal|ist (el′ə men′tə list), *n.* an adherent of elementalism.

el|e|men|ta|ri|ly (el′ə men′tər ə lē, -trə-), *adv.* in an elementary manner.

el|e|men|ta|ri|ness (el′ə men′tər ē nis, -trē-), *n.* the quality or state of being elementary.

el|e|men|ta|ry (el′ə men′tər ē, -trē), *adj.* **1** dealing with the simple, necessary parts to be learned first; having to do with first principles; introductory: *a course in elementary botany.* **2** made up of only one chemical element; not a compound: *Silver is an elementary substance.* **3** having to do with a chemical element or elements. **4** elemental (def. 6). **5** of or having to do with basic or primary instruction: *elementary education.*
—*Syn.* **1 Elementary,** rudimentary, **primary** mean having to do with the beginnings of something. **Elementary** emphasizes the idea of being basic, and applies to the first steps or beginning facts and principles of anything: *I learned addition and subtraction in elementary arithmetic.* **Rudimentary** emphasizes the idea of being undeveloped, and applies to the first parts and principles of knowledge or a subject studied: *She has only a rudimentary knowledge of mathematics.* **Primary** emphasizes coming first in order or time: *Primary grades are the first three grades of elementary school.*

elementary particle, *Physics.* one of the fundamental units of which matter is composed; fundamental particle. The elementary particles include the electron, proton, and neutron, and the neutrino, neutretto, lambda, photon, and meson.

elementary school, 1 a school of six grades for pupils from about six to about twelve years of age, followed by junior high school. **2** a school of eight grades for pupils from about six to about fourteen, followed by a four-year high school.

el|e|men|toid (el′ə men′toid), *adj.* resembling an element; having the appearance of a simple substance: *an elementoid compound.*

el|e|ments (el′ə mənts), *n., pl.* See under **element.**

el|e|mi (el′ə mē), *n., pl.* **-mis.** a fragrant resin yielded by various tropical trees, used in ointments and plasters, in making varnish, etc. [< New Latin *gumi elimi* or Spanish *elemí* < Arabic *al-lāmī*]

e|len|chic (i leng′kik), *adj.* = elenctic.

e|len|chus (i leng′kəs), *n., pl.* **-chi** (-kī). *Logic.* **1** a refutation. **2** a false refutation. [< Latin *elenchus* < Greek *élenchos* cross-examination < *elénchein* refute]

e|lenc|tic (i lengk′tik), *adj.* **1** of or having to do with refutation. **2** of or having to do with cross-examination.

el|e|op|tene (el′ē op′tēn), *n. Chemistry.* the liquid part or hydrocarbon of an essential oil. [< Greek *élaion* olive oil + *ptēnós* winged]

***el|e|phant** (el′ə fənt), *n., pl.* **-phants** or (*collectively*) **-phant.** a huge, heavy mammal, the largest land animal now living. It has a long, muscular snout called a *trunk.* Ivory comes from its tusks, which develop from the upper incisor teeth. Elephants are practically hairless; they have five toes on each foot. Two species, the Asian and the African elephant, exist today. **African elephants** have large ears and both the males and females have tusks. **Indian** or **Asian elephants** have smaller ears than the African elephants and the females often have no tusks.

In some parts of India, travel by elephant is the only way a person can get through a dense jungle (A. M. Winchester). See picture below. [< Old French *olifant,* and *elefant,* learned borrowing from Latin *elephantus,* and *elephas* < Greek *eléphās, -antos* elephant, ivory]

***elephant beetle**, 1 any one of several lamellicorn beetles of enormous size, having a curved horn projecting at the front of the head, found especially in tropical America. See picture below. 2 any one of certain beetles or weevils having a long snout or proboscis.

***elephant bird**, a very large, extinct, flightless bird which formerly inhabited Madagascar; aepyornis. It stood about ten feet tall, weighed about 1,000 pounds, and laid eggs over thirteen inches long. See picture below.

elephant creeper, a woody climbing vine of the morning-glory family, growing in India, and reaching the tops of the tallest trees.

el|e|phant-ear (el′ə fənt ir′), *n.* or **elephant-ear sponge**, a large horny sponge found in the Mediterranean Sea, having a very fine texture and used commercially.

elephant grass, a tall perennial grass native to tropical Africa and Asia, grown in warm regions as a pasture grass.

el|e|phan|ti|as|ic (el′ə fan′tē as′ik), *n., adj.* —*n.* a person suffering from elephantiasis.
—*adj.* of or having to do with elephantiasis.

el|e|phan|ti|a|sis (el′ə fən tī′ə sis), *n.* **1** a disease in which parts of the body, usually the scrotum or legs, become greatly enlarged and the skin thickened and broken. It is caused by parasitic, filarial worms that block the flow of lymph. **2** *Figurative.* a disproportionate enlargement or exaggeration (of any object or quality): *It is a tremendous building, saved from elephantiasis by the skill of its architects* (Bulletin of Atomic Scientists).
[< Latin *elephantiasis* < Greek *elephantiāsis* < *eléphās, -antos* elephant]

el|e|phan|tine (el′ə fan′tin, -tīn, -tēn), *adj.* **1** like an elephant; huge, heavy, clumsy, and slow: *The Post Road . . . kept close to the base of the bluffs, which in this area were palisades of elephantine granite boulders* (New Yorker). **2** of elephants.

elephant man's disease or **elephant man disease**, = neurofibromatosis. [< *Elephant Man,* nickname of Joseph Merrick, an Englishman of the 1800's whose body was deformed by a disease identified with neurofibromatosis]

***elephant seal**, a very large, rare seal found along the Pacific Coast from the Antarctic to Southern California; sea elephant. The male has a long, overhanging proboscis and reaches a length of over twenty feet. *The sealing fleets concentrated on another variety, the so-called elephant seals, which although they provided no valuable fur turned out to be a source of oil* (New Scientist). See picture below.

el|e|phant's-ear (el′ə fənts ir′), *n.* **1** a plant with large leaves shaped like elephants' ears; caladium. **2a** the taro, especially when grown as an ornamental plant. **b** any one of various begonias with large, lopsided leaves.

el|e|phant's-foot (el′ə fənts fu̇t′), *n.* a South African plant having a large stem that is rough outside with a fleshy, edible interior.

***elephant shrew**, a small, leaping, insect-eating animal of Africa. It resembles a mouse and has a long snout like an elephant's trunk. See picture below.

el|e|phant's-tusk (el′ə fənts tusk′), *n.* a mollusk; one of the tooth shells.

El|eu|sin|i|a (el′yu̇ sin′ē ə), *n.pl.* the Eleusinian mysteries and the festival celebrated with them.

El|eu|sin|i|an (el′yu̇ sin′ē ən), *adj.* of or having to do with Eleusis, an ancient Greek city near Athens.

Eleusinian mysteries, the secret, religious ceremonies held yearly in ancient Greece at Eleusis in honor of the goddesses Demeter and Persephone.

El|eu|the|ri|a (el′yu̇ thir′ē ə), *n.pl.* the feast of liberty, an ancient Greek festival celebrated at Plataea in memory of the great victory won there by the Greeks over the Persians in 479 B.C.

e|leu|ther|o|dac|tyl (i lü′thər ə dak′təl), *adj.* = eleutherodactylous.

e|leu|ther|o|dac|tyl|ous (i lü′thər ə dak′tə ləs), *adj.* having the hind toe tendon free, as is the case with most passerine birds.

e|leu|ther|o|ma|ni|a (i lü′thər ə mā′nē ə), *n.* an abnormally great desire for freedom: *But most of these poems are marred by a false concept of poetry as a free excitement unattached to the hardness of things, an eleutheromania* (Atlantic).
[< Greek *eleútheros* free + English *mania*]

e|leu|ther|o|ma|ni|ac (i lü′thər ə mā′nē ak), *n.* a person who has an abnormally great desire for freedom.

elev., elevation.

el|e|vate (el′ə vāt), *v.,* **-vat|ed, -vat|ing,** *adj.* —*v.t.* **1** to lift up; raise: *He elevated the dumbwaiter to the second floor.* SYN: hoist. **2** *Figurative.* to raise in rank or station: *The soldier was elevated to a higher rank for bravery. When the president of the company retired, the vice-president was elevated to his position.* SYN: promote, advance, exalt. See syn. under **raise**. **3** *Figurative.* to raise in quality: *Reading good books elevates your mind.* SYN: promote, advance, exalt. See syn. under **raise**. **4** *Figurative.* to put in high spirits; make joyful or proud; elate. **5** to raise (the voice).
—***adj.*** *Poetic.* elevated.
[< Latin *ēlevāre* (with English *-ate*[1]) < *ex-* out + *levāre* lighten, raise < *levis* light]

el|e|vat|ed (el′ə vā′tid), *adj., n.* —***adj.*** **1** raised up; high: *an elevated train station, an elevated highway. He spoke from an elevated platform.* **2** *Figurative.* dignified; lofty; noble: *an elevated passage in the Bible.* SYN: exalted. **3** *Figurative.* in high spirits; joyful or proud: *an elevated mood.*
—*n. Informal.* an elevated railroad.

elevated pole, the visible celestial pole at any given place; the celestial pole which is above the horizon: *The south celestial pole . . . is the elevated pole for observers in the southern hemisphere* (Robert H. Baker).

elevated railroad, an electric railroad raised above the ground on a supporting frame; el. It is high enough for traffic to pass underneath.

el|e|va|tion (el′ə vā′shən), *n.* **1** a raised place; high place: *A hill is an elevation.* **2** height above the earth's surface: *The airplane flew at an elevation of 2,000 feet.* **3** height above sea level: *The elevation of Denver is 5,280 feet.* **4** *Figurative.* dignity; loftiness; nobility: *The doctor believed that the elevation of mankind is universal.* **5** a raising; lifting up: (*Figurative.*) *the elevation of Caesar from general to ruler of Rome.* **6** a being raised or lifted up. **7** *Architecture.* a flat scale drawing of the front, rear, or side of a building, as distinguished from a ground plan. **8** *Astronomy.* the angular distance of any heavenly body above the horizon. **9** *Surveying.* the angular distance of an object above the horizontal plane through the point of observation. **10** the ability to do an élévation in dancing. **11a** the raising of the Eucharistic elements during the Mass. **b** the part of the Mass at which this occurs.

é|lé|va|tion (ā lā vȧ syôɴ′), *n. French.* a leap of a ballet dancer.

el|e|va|tor (el′ə vā′tər), *n.* **1** something that raises or lifts up. **2** a moving platform or cage to carry people and things up and down in a building, mine, or the like; a lift: *Another interesting modern feature is the change-over from elevators to escalators* (London Times). **3** a building for storing grain: *Elevators are a familiar sight on the prairies.* **4** an adjustable flat piece, usually on the tail of an airplane, to cause it to go up or down: *The upward and downward course of the airplane is governed by the elevator* (Beauchamp, Mayfield, and West). See picture under **airplane**. [< Late Latin *ēlevātor* < *ēlevāre;* see etym. under **elevate**]

elevator shaft, a vertical passageway for an elevator.

elevator shoe, a shoe with raised heel and sole made for short men: *The champion didn't want his wife towering over him, and he refused to wear elevator shoes* (New Yorker).

el|e|va|to|ry (el′ə vā′tər ē), *adj.* serving to elevate.

é|lève (ā lev′), *n. French.* a pupil.

e|lev|en (i lev′ən), *n., adj.* —*n.* **1** one more than ten; 11: *We bought a dozen cookies but ate one and got home with only eleven.* **2** a team of eleven football or cricket players: *The Chicago eleven beat the team from Miami 14 to 7.*
—***adj.*** being one more than ten.
[Old English *endleofan* one left (over ten)]

e|lev|en-plus (i lev′ən plus′), *n.* a public-school examination administered in Great Britain to eleven-year-old children entering secondary school to determine if their future education should be technical or in the arts: *The years of preparation for the eleven-plus will continue to be the most aperient and depressing of all our social disciplines* (Punch).

e|lev|ens|es (i lev′ən ziz), *n.pl. British Informal.* a snack eaten before noon (originally at eleven o'clock) consisting of tea, coffee, or milk and biscuits: *several journalists in for elevenses this morning and several more for tea this afternoon* (Smith's London Journal).

e|lev|enth (i lev′ənth), *adj., n.* **1** next after the 10th; last in a series of 11. **2** one of 11 equal parts.

eleventh hour, the latest possible moment; time just before it is too late.

el|e|von (el′ə von), *n.* a movable control surface on an aircraft or missile that functions as both an elevator and an aileron.

elf[1] (elf), *n., pl.* **elves**. **1** a tiny being in the form of a human, that is full of mischief; fairy: *A sound as of some joyous elf Singing sweet songs to please himself* (Edna St. Vincent Millay). SYN: sprite, pixy. **2** a small, mischievous person. [Old English *ælf*]
—**elf′like′**, *adj.*

elf[2] (elf), *v.t. Obsolete.* to tangle (the hair) in elflocks. [< *elf*[1]]

elf[3] (elf), *n.* = elft.

ELF or **elf** (no periods), extremely low frequency (of or having to do with the electromagnetic spectrum between 30 and 300 hertz, especially in radio transmission and reception).

elf arrow, = elf bolt.

elf bolt, an arrowhead of flint or other stone found among paleolithic remains. [from the early belief that such stones were fairy arrowheads]

elf child, = changeling.

elf dart, = elf bolt.

elf|in (el′fən), *adj., n.* —***adj.*** **1** of or suitable for elves; like an elf's: *The child's elfin smile was very charming.* **2** diminutive.
—*n.* an elf.

elf|ish (el′fish), *adj.* like an elf; elfin; mischievous: *Thou strange and elfish child, whence didst thou come?* (Hawthorne). Also, **elvish**. —**elf′ish|ly**, *adv.* —**elf′ish|ness**, *n.*

elf|land (elf′land′), *n.* the land of the elves; fairyland: *the horns of elfland faintly blowing* (Tennyson).

elf|lock (elf′lok′), *n.* a tangled lock of hair caused by elves (according to superstition).

elf owl, a sparrow-sized, brown or grayish owl of the southwestern United States and Mexico. It is the smallest of American owls and commonly nests in an abandoned woodpecker's hole in the saguaro cactus.

elft (elft), *n.* a saltwater fish found around the coast of South Africa; elf: *The elft is three-quarters of a yard long or more, and is scaled much like a herring* (P. Kolben).

El|gar|i|an (el gär′ē ən), *adj., n.* —***adj.*** of or having to do with Sir Edward Elgar, 1857-1934, a

***elephant**

African elephant

Asian elephant

Pronunciation Key: hat, āge, cãre, fär; let, ēqual, tėrm; it, īce; hot, ōpen, ôrder; oil, out; cup, pu̇t, rüle; child; long; thin; ᴛʜen; zh, measure; ə represents **a** in about, **e** in taken, **i** in pencil, **o** in lemon, **u** in circus.

British composer, his work, or his style: *The music is a fine example of rich, glowing post-romanticism, with those Elgarian melodic leaps: so distinctive, so personal* (Harper's).
—*n.* a follower of Sir Edward Elgar's style of music.

El|gi|nism (el′gə niz əm), *n.* the practice of removing items of archaeological value, often illegally, from their original sites and transporting them to foreign countries for sale or exhibition: *A draft antiquities convention due to be considered by Unesco experts in Paris in April . . . uses the term "Elginism" as a synonym for archaeological plunder* (Peter Hopkirk). [< the *Elgin* Marbles, an ancient Greek frieze purchased and brought to England between 1803 and 1812 by the Earl of *Elgin.* Byron accused the Earl of vandalism for removing the sculptures from the Parthenon in Athens.]

E|li (ē′lī), *n.* a Hebrew high priest who trained Samuel to become the religious leader of his people (in the Bible, I Samuel 1-4).

E|li|as (i lī′əs), *n.* a name of Elijah (in the Bible, Matthew 16:14).

e|lic|it (i lis′it), *v.t.* to draw forth; bring out; draw out: *to elicit a reply, elicit applause, elicit the truth. The comedian's joke elicited laughter from the audience.* [< Latin *ēlicitus,* past participle of *ēlicere* < *ex-* out + *lacere* entice]
▶**Elicit, illicit** are not synonyms, but are sometimes confused because they sound alike. **Elicit** is a formal verb meaning to draw out in a skillful way or with difficulty something that is being hidden or held back: *I succeeded in eliciting from his secretary the information I needed.* **Illicit** is a formal adjective meaning unlawful or improper: *The police are trying to stop illicit sale of drugs.*

e|lic|it|a|ble (i lis′ə tə bəl), *adj.* that can be elicited.

e|lic|i|ta|tion (i lis′ə tā′shən), *n.* a drawing forth or being drawn forth.

e|lic|i|tor (i lis′ə tər), *n.* a person who elicits or draws forth.

e|lic|i|to|ry (i lis′ə tôr′ē, -tōr′-), *adj.* that elicits or tends to elicit: *an elicitory investigation.*

e|lide (i līd′), *v.t.,* **e|lid|ed, e|lid|ing. 1** to omit or slur over (a vowel or syllable) in pronunciation: *The "e" in "the" is elided in "th' inevitable hour."* **2** to strike out; suppress. **3** *Scottish Law.* to annul. [< Latin *ēlīdere* < *ex-* out + *laedere* dash, strike]

e|lid|i|ble (i lī′də bəl), *adj.* that can be elided.

el|i|gi|bil|i|ty (el′ə jə bil′ə tē), *n., pl.* **-ties.** fitness to be chosen; desirability; qualification.

el|i|gi|ble (el′ə jə bəl), *adj., n.* —*adj.* fit to be chosen; desirable; qualified: *an eligible bachelor. Pupils must pass in all subjects to be eligible for the school team.*
—*n.* an eligible person: *Beautiful, accomplished and an heiress, she had, of course, all the eligibles and non-eligibles of the other sex sighing at her feet* (Harriet Beecher Stowe).
[< Old French *eligible,* learned borrowing from Late Latin *eligibilis* < Latin *ēligere;* see etym. under **elect**]—**el′i|gi|ble|ness,** *n.*

eligible paper, bills, notes, or other financial paper acceptable for discount or rediscount by Federal Reserve Banks.

el|i|gi|bly (el′ə jə blē), *adv.* in an eligible manner.

E|li|hu (i lī′hyü, el′ə-), *n.* one of the friends of Job (in the Bible, Job 32-37).

E|li|jah (i lī′jə), *n.* a great Hebrew prophet who lived in the 800's B.C. (in the Bible, I Kings 17-19; II Kings 2:1-11).

e|lim|i|na|ble (i lim′ə nə bəl), *adj.* that can be eliminated: *Were other eliminable causes to turn up, such as malnutrition or the ingestion of some toxic substance, those, too, could be tackled* (Michael Abercrombie).

e|lim|i|nant (i lim′ə nənt), *n.* an agent that eliminates, as a chemical or drug.

e|lim|i|nate (i lim′ə nāt), *v.t.,* **-nat|ed, -nat|ing. 1** to get rid of; remove: *We had to eliminate the losing team from the competition. The new bridge over the railroad tracks eliminated danger in crossing.* SYN: See syn. under **exclude. 2** *Figurative.* to pay no attention to; leave out of consideration; omit: *The architect eliminated the cost of furniture, rugs, and other items, in figuring the cost of the house.* SYN: dismiss, rule out, ignore. **3** *Mathematics.* to get rid of (a symbol or unknown quantity) in two or more algebraic equations by combining them. **4** *Physiology.* to expel (waste) from the body; excrete: *In the kidneys these nitrogen wastes are taken out of the blood, sent to the bladder, and finally eliminated from the body in the urine* (Beauchamp, Mayfield, and West). [< Latin *ēlīmināre* (with English *-ate* [1]) < *ex-* off, out + *līmen, -inis* threshold]

e|lim|i|na|tion (i lim′ə nā′shən), *n.* **1** the act or process of eliminating: *the elimination of unsuitable candidates.* **2** the state of being eliminated.

e|lim|i|na|tive (i lim′ə nā′tiv), *adj.* tending or serving to eliminate.

e|lim|i|na|tor (i lim′ə nā′tər), *n.* a person or thing that eliminates.

e|lint or **ELINT** (i lint′), *n.* **1** a ship or aircraft equipped with electronic monitoring apparatus for gathering secret intelligence. **2** information obtained
by this means: *U.S. intelligence learned of the mishap through ELINT* (Time). [< *el*(ectronic) *int*(elligence)]

El|i|ot|i|an (el′ē ot′ē ən, -ō′tē ən), *adj.* = Eliotic.

El|i|ot|ic (el′ē ot′ik), *adj.* of or having to do with T. S. Eliot, 1888-1965, American-born British poet and critic.

E|LI|SA or **E|li|sa** (i lē′sə), *n.* a test for blood supplies to check for the presence of the virus that causes AIDS: *In an ELISA, broken-up pieces of the AIDS-related virus are stuck on a solid surface and washed with blood. If AIDS antibodies are in the blood, they'll stick to the virus* (J. Silberner). [< *e*(nzyme)-*l*(inked) *i*(mmuno)*s*(orbent) *a*(ssay)]

E|lis|a|beth (i liz′ə bəth), *n.* a cousin of the Virgin Mary and the mother of John the Baptist (in the Bible, Luke 1:5-45). Also, **Elizabeth.**

E|li|sha (i lī′shə), *n.* the Hebrew prophet of the 800's B.C. who was taught by Elijah (in the Bible, II Kings 2).

e|li|sion (i lizh′ən), *n.* **1** the suppression of a vowel or syllable in pronouncing. Elision is often used in poetry, and generally consists in cutting off a vowel at the end of one word when the next word begins with a vowel, as in *th' inevitable hour. As for elisions in the middle of a word, called syncope, even purists do not hesitate . . . to say Wenzday* (*Wednesday*) (Scientific American). **2** the omission of a word, sentence, or passage in a text for a specific purpose (such as the abridgment of a book). [< Latin *ēlīsiō, -ōnis* < *ēlīdere;* see etym. under **elide**]

e|li|sor (i lī′zər, el′ə-), *n. Law.* a person appointed in certain cases to return a panel of jurors or serve a writ. [< Old French *elisour* < *elis-,* stem of *elire* choose; see etym. under **elite**]

***e|lite** or **é|lite** (i lēt′, ā-), *n., adj.* —*n.* **1** the choice or distinguished part; those thought of as the best people: *Only the elite of society attended the reception for the new governor. Scholars are an important part of the intellectual elite of this country* (Saturday Review). **2** a size of typewriter type, smaller than pica, equivalent to 10-point printing type. There are 12 elite characters to the inch.
—*adj.* distinguished: *An elite group of scientists participated in the experiment.*
[< French *élite,* feminine past participle of *élire* choose < Old French *eslirero* < *Vulgar Latin exlegere,* for Latin *ēligere;* see etym. under **elect**]

***elite**
definition 2

The World Book Dictionary

É|lite (ā lēt′), *n.* the army of Switzerland.

Elite Guard, = SS Troops.

e|lit|ism or **é|lit|ism** (i lēt′iz əm, ā-), *n.* **1** rule or government by an elite: *He goes on to advocate a kind of tough-minded élitism* (Manchester Guardian). **2** the championing or support of such a rule.

e|lit|ist or **é|lit|ist** (i lē′tist, ā-), *adj., n.* —*adj.* **1** of, having to do with, or favoring elitism: . . . *the tendency of private institutions to be "restrictive, selective and elitist"* (Time). **2** of or having to do with the elite: *No doubt opera is all the things they say: an anachronism, an elitist pleasure* (New York Times).
—*n.* a person who favors or supports elitism.

e|lix|ir (i lik′sər), *n.* **1** a substance supposed to have the power of changing lead, iron, or other metal, into gold or of lengthening life indefinitely. The alchemists of the Middle Ages sought for it. **2** a universal remedy; cure-all: *He is a veritable necromancer, equipped with philters and elixirs of wondrous potency* (Harper's). **3** a medicine made of drugs or herbs mixed with alcohol and syrup. **4** *Figurative.* the quintessence of a thing; chief principle. [< Medieval Latin *elixir* < Arabic *al-iksīr* a form of the philosophers' stone, probably < Late Greek *xḗrion* powder for drying wounds < Greek *xērós* dry]

elixir of life, the elixir sought by the alchemists: *The energy spent by medieval alchemists in their search for the "elixir of life" might be compared to the efforts of modern chemists to find potent hormones, the elixirs that control life* (New York Herald Tribune).

e|lix|ir vi|tae (i lik′sər vī′tē), *Latin.* the elixir of life.

E|liz|a|beth (i liz′ə bəth), *n.* = Elisabeth.

E|liz|a|be|than (i liz′ə bē′thən, -beth′ən), *adj., n.* —*adj.* of the time when Elizabeth I ruled England (1558-1603).
—*n.* an Englishman, especially a writer, of the time of Elizabeth I: *Shakespeare is a famous Elizabethan.*

Elizabethan Age, the forty-five years of the reign of Queen Elizabeth I (1558-1603), usually regarded as the golden age of England.

Elizabethan architecture, the architecture of the times of Elizabeth I and James I, showing a marked Italian influence and characterized by large windows, long galleries, tall and highly decorated chimneys, and profuse ornamentation on parapets and the heads of windows.

E|liz|a|be|than|ism (i liz′ə bē′thə niz əm, -beth′ə-), *n.* a manner or style, or a particular feature of these, characteristic of the reign of Queen Elizabeth I of England (1558-1603).

Elizabethan sonnet, a type of sonnet having three stanzas of four lines each, followed by a couplet, written by Shakespeare and many other Elizabethans; Shakespearian sonnet; English sonnet. It has a rhyme scheme *abab, cdcd, efef, gg.*

elk (elk), *n., pl.* **elks** or (*especially collectively*) **elk. 1** a large deer of northern Europe and Asia. It has heavy, spreading antlers like those of a moose. The elk belongs to the same genus as the moose and closely resembles it. **2** a large, red deer of western North America; wapiti. See picture under **antler. 3** a soft leather made from elk hide or from calfskin or cowhide in imitation. [Middle English *elke,* Old English *eolh*]

Elk (elk), *n. U.S.* a member of the Benevolent and Protective Order of Elks, a fraternal organization founded in 1868.

elk|horn coral (elk′hôrn′), a very poisonous stony coral with a branched skeleton resembling somewhat the antlers of an elk.

elk|hound (elk′hound′), *n.* = Norwegian elkhound.

ell[1] (el), *n.* a measure of length, chiefly used in measuring cloth. In England, where it was formerly used, it was equal to 45 inches. (*Figurative.*) *Give him an inch and he'll take an ell.* Also, **el.** [Old English *eln* (originally) length of the lower arm]

ell[2] (el), *n.* **1** the letter *L, l.* **2** something shaped like a capital L, such as a pipe elbow. **3** *U.S.* an extension of a building at right angles to it; el.

el|la|chick (el′ə chik), *n.* a tortoise found on the Pacific coast of the United States in rivers or ponds, highly esteemed as food. [< Nisqually *ella-chick*]

el|lag|ic acid (i laj′ik), a crystalline substance found in the bark and galls of oak trees, formed by the hydrolysis of tannin. *Formula:* $C_{14}H_6O_8$[< French *ellagique* < *ellag,* anagram of *galle* gall (formed to prevent its confusion with *gallique* gallic acid)]

El|ling|to|ni|an (el′ing tō′nē ən), *adj., n.* —*adj.* having to do with or characteristic of the American jazz musician and composer Duke Ellington, his style, or his works. —*n.* an admirer or follower of Duke Ellington or his works.

***el|lipse** (i lips′), *n.* an oval having both ends alike. It is the plane curve formed by the path of a point that moves so that the sum of its distances from two fixed points (the foci) remains the same. Any conic section formed by a cutting plane inclined to the base but not passing through the base is an ellipse. [< Latin *ellīpsis* defect; see etym. under **ellipsis** (because the cutting plane makes a smaller angle with the base than does the side of the cone)]

***ellipse**

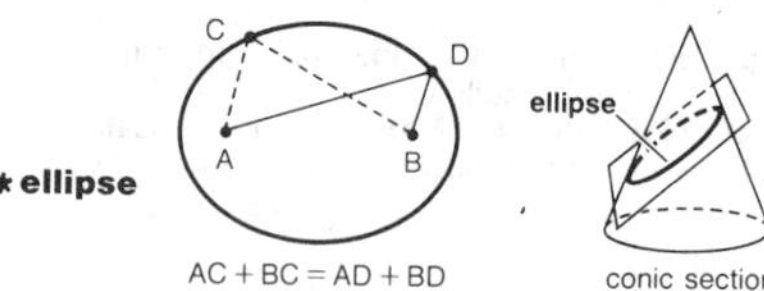

el|lip|ses (i lip′siz *for 1;* i lip′sēz *for 2*), *n.* **1** plural of **ellipse. 2** plural of **ellipsis.**

el|lip|sis (i lip′sis), *n., pl.* **-ses. 1** marks (. . . or * * *) used to show an omission in writing or printing. **2** the omission of a word or words needed to complete the grammatical construction, but not the meaning, of a sentence. *Example:* "She is as tall as her brother" instead of "She is as tall as her brother is tall." [< Latin *ellīpsis* < Greek *élleipsis* ellipse, ellipsis; defect < *elleípein* come short, leave out < *ek-* out + *leípein* to leave]

el|lip|so|graph (i lip′sə graf, -gräf), *n.* an instrument for drawing ellipses.

el|lip|soid (i lip′soid), *n., adj.* —*n.* **1** a solid figure of which all plane sections are ellipses or circles. **2** any surface of such a solid. —*adj.* having to do with or in the form of an ellipsoid.

el|lip|soi|dal (i lip′soi′dəl, el′ip-), *adj.* = ellipsoid.

el|lip|som|e|ter (i lip som′ə tər), *n.* an instrument for measuring ellipticity, used especially to determine the thicknesses of extremely thin films.

el|lip|som|e|try (i lip som′ə trē), *n.* the method or

technique of using an ellipsometer: *They followed film growth using the optical method of ellipsometry, which gives a direct, nonelectrical measure of film thickness* (Science News).

el|lip|tic (i lip′tik), *adj.* = elliptical. [< Greek *elleiptikós* defective < *elleípein* come short; see etym. under **ellipsis**]

el|lip|ti|cal (i lip′tə kəl), *adj., n.* —***adj.*** **1** shaped like an ellipse; of an ellipse. **2** of or showing ellipsis; having a word or words omitted: *If he is sometimes elliptical and obscure, it is because he has so much to tell us* (Edmund Wilson).
—***n.*** = elliptical galaxy.

elliptical galaxy, a galaxy that appears round or elliptical, without the spiral arms of a spiral galaxy: *The elliptical galaxies also form a sequence, ranging from almost spherical systems to flattened ellipsoids* (Scientific American).

el|lip|ti|cal|ly (i lip′tə klē), *adv.* **1** shaped like an ellipse. **2** with an ellipsis.

elliptic geometry, a system of geometry in which two or more lines passing through a point in a plane always intersect a given line in the plane (contrasted with *hyperbolic geometry*).

el|lip|tic|i|ty (i lip′tis′ə tē, el′ip-), *n.* **1** the quality of being elliptic. **2** the degree of deviation of an ellipse from a circle.

el|lip|toid (i lip′toid), *adj.* shaped somewhat like an ellipse; elliptical.

elm (elm), *n.* **1** a tall, graceful shade tree that often reaches a height of 75 to 100 feet. About 18 species of the elm tree are known. *The moan of doves in immemorial elms* (Tennyson). **2** its hard, heavy wood. [Old English *elm*]

elm bark beetle, any one of various beetles that harm elm trees, especially a beetle originally of Europe, the chief carrier of Dutch elm disease.

elm beetle, any one of various beetles that feed on the leaves of elm trees.

elm blight, = Dutch elm disease.

elm borer, any one of several coleopterous insects whose larvae bore into elm trees.

elm butterfly, any one of several nymphalid butterflies whose larvae feed on the leaves of the elm.

elm|en (el′mən), *adj. Archaic or Dialect.* of or belonging to the elm.

elm family, a group of deciduous shrubs and trees growing in temperate and tropical regions, having alternate, serrate, often asymmetrical leaves, and bearing a samara or drupe. The family includes the elms, hackberry, and planer tree.

elm leaf beetle, a beetle that feeds on elm trees in both the adult and larval stage, causing death by denudation of the leaves.

elm|wood (elm′wu̇d′), *n., adj.* —***n.*** the wood of the elm.
—***adj.*** made of elmwood: *elmwood armchairs, elmwood nursery furnishings.*

elm|y (el′mē), *adj.* having many elms; consisting of elms.

El Ni|ño (el nēn′yō), a periodic current of warm water flowing southward along the coast of Peru that kills the fish and causes the sea birds to migrate to find food: *Once in every ten years or so, a current of warm water called El Niño ... creeps stealthily down the coast* (Time). [< Spanish *El Niño* the Christ child (because the current usually appears near Christmas)]

e|loc|u|lar (ē lok′yə lər), *adj. Botany.* not partitioned; having no loculi.

el|o|cute (el′ə kyüt), *v.t., v.i.*, **-cut|ed, -cut|ing.** to say or speak in a declamatory manner; orate: [*He*] *elocutes lines that might better be spoken* (Time). *The amateur cast too would have more opportunity to show their acting ability whereas now they are obliged to richly elocute* (London Times). [back formation < *elocution*]

el|o|cu|tion (el′ə kyü′shən), *n.* **1** the art of speaking or reading clearly and effectively in public. Elocution includes the correct use of the voice, gestures, etc. **2** the manner of speaking or reading in public. **SYN:** delivery. [< Latin *ēlocūtiō, -ōnis* < *ēloquī* speak out < *ex-* out + *loquī* speak]

el|o|cu|tion|ar|y (el′ə kyü′shə ner′ē), *adj.* of or having to do with elocution.

el|o|cu|tion|ist (el′ə kyü′shə nist), *n.* **1** a person skilled in elocution. **2** a teacher of elocution.

e|lo|de|a (ə lō′dē ə), *n., pl.* **-de|as.** any one of a genus of American plants of the frogbit family, that grow submerged in water and have branching stems densely covered with leaves that grow even more crowded toward the tip; waterweed. Elodeas are commonly used in aquariums to keep the oxygen balance in the water. [< New Latin *Elodea* the genus name < Greek *helṓdēs* marshy < *helos* marsh]

é|loge (ā lôzh′), *n. French.* a eulogy; funeral oration.

E|lo|him (e lō′him), *n.* one of the names of God, of frequent occurrence in the Hebrew text of the Old Testament. [< Hebrew *ĕlohim,* plural of *ĕloăh*]

E|lo|hism (e lō′hiz əm), *n.* the worship of God as Elohim.

E|lo|hist (e lō′hist), *n.* the writer or writers of certain parts of the Hebrew text of the Hexateuch, in which God is referred to as *Elohim* instead of *Yahweh* (Jehovah).

El|o|his|tic (el′ō his′tik), *adj.* **1** characterized by the use of *Elohim* instead of *Yahweh* (Jehovah). **2** written by the Elohist.

e|loign or **e|loin** (i loin′), *v.t.* **1** to remove to a distance; carry off. **2** *Law.* to take out of legal jurisdiction or conceal (goods liable to distress). [< Old French *esloignier* < Late Latin *ēlongāre* remove; see etym. under **elongate**] —**e|loign′er** or **e|loin′er**, *n.*

e|loign|ment or **e|loin|ment** (i loin′mənt), *n. Obsolete.* **1** removal to a distance. **2** distance; remoteness.

E. long., east longitude.

e|lon|gate (i lông′gāt, -long′-), *v.,* **-gat|ed, -gat|ing,** *adj.* —***v.t., v.i.*** to make or become longer; lengthen; extend; stretch: *He elongated the rubber band to fit it around his papers.*
—***adj.*** **1** long and thin: *the elongate leaf of a willow. Earthworms have elongate bodies.* **2** lengthened. **SYN:** extended, prolonged.
[< Late Latin *ēlongāre* (with English *-ate*[1]) < *ex-* out + *longus* long]

e|lon|gat|ed (i lông′gā tid, -long′-), *adj.* long and thin; elongate: *an elongated snout.*

e|lon|ga|tion (ē′lông gā′shən, -long-), *n.* **1** a lengthening; extension. **2** a lengthened part; continuation. **3** the condition of being lengthened or extended. **4** *Astronomy.* the angular distance of a planet from the sun, or of a satellite from its primary.

e|lon|ga|tive (ē′lông gā′tiv, -long-), *adj.* that tends to elongate or lengthen out.

e|lope (i lōp′), *v.i.,* **e|loped, e|lop|ing.** **1** to run away with a lover, usually to get married. **2** to run away; escape. **SYN:** abscond. [apparently < Anglo-French *aloper* < Middle English *lopen* run; lope]

e|lope|ment (i lōp′mənt), *n.* the act of eloping; a running away: *While elopement is not as important a subject as newspaper reports and gossip would have people believe, yet it is socially significant* (Emory S. Bogardus).

e|lop|er (i lō′pər), *n.* a person who elopes.

el|o|quence (el′ə kwəns), *n.* **1** a flow of speech that has grace and force: *The eloquence of the President moved all hearts.* **2** the power to win by speaking; the art of speaking so as to stir the feelings: *Talking and eloquence are not the same: to speak, and to speak well, are two things* (Ben Jonson). **SYN:** elocution, oratory, rhetoric.

el|o|quent (el′ə kwənt), *adj.* **1** having the power of expressing one's feeling or thoughts with grace and force; having eloquence: *an eloquent speaker. The curse of this country is eloquent men* (Ralph Waldo Emerson). **SYN:** voluble, fluent, glib. **2** very expressive: (*Figurative.*) *eloquent eyes.* [< Latin *ēloquēns, -entis,* present participle of *ēloquī* < *ex-* out + *loquī* speak] —**el′o|quent|ly**, *adv.*

el|pas|o|lite (el pas′ə līt), *n.* a fluoride of aluminum, potassium, and sodium, first found in El Paso County, Colorado.

el|pi|dite (el′pə dīt), *n.* a silicate of zirconium and sodium occurring in masses, from white to brick-red, rarely in orthorhombic crystals, found in southern Greenland. [< Greek *elpís, -ídos* hope + English *-ite*[1]]

else (els), *adj., adv.* —***adj.*** **1** other; different; instead: *Will somebody else speak? What else could I say?* **2** in addition; more; besides: *The Browns are here; do you expect anyone else?*
—***adv.*** **1** differently: *How else can it be done?* **2** otherwise; if not: *Hurry, else you will be late.* **or else, a** or suffer the consequences: *From the sidelines comes a chorus of dark warnings that the networks had better shape up or else* (Commentary). **b** otherwise: *Speak fair words, or else be mute* (Shakespeare).
[Old English *elles*]
▶ When **else** is used with a preceding interrogative or indefinite pronoun, the possessive ending is now regularly added to *else: someone else's, who else's* (rather than *whose else*).

El|se|vier (el′zə vir, -vər), *adj., n.* = Elzevir.

else|where (els′hwãr), *adv.* somewhere else; in or to some other place: *Here as elsewhere, the Spanish Bourbons were no longer prepared to recognize opportunity in the New World* (Atlantic).

else|whith|er (els′hwiᴛʜ′ər), *adv. Archaic.* elsewhere.

else|wise (els′wīz), *adv.* = otherwise.

El Tor (el tôr′), a strain of the bacillus that causes cholera: *The epidemic is the latest flare-up of ... El Tor* (*named for the Egyptian quarantine station where it was first identified*) (Time).

el|u|ant (el′yü ənt), *n.* the solvent used in the process of elution.

el|u|ate (el′yü it), *n.* the solution obtained from the process of elution.

e|lu|ci|date (i lü′sə dāt), *v.t.,* **-dat|ed, -dat|ing.** to make clear; explain: *The scientist elucidated his theory by a few simple demonstrations.* **SYN:** clarify. [< Late Latin *ēlūcidāre* (with English *-ate*[1]) < Latin *ex-* out + *lūcidus* bright < *lūx, lūcis* a light]

e|lu|ci|da|tion (i lü′sə dā′shən), *n.* a making clear; explanation: *The elucidation of the tragedy is relayed to us by Edward's sister Isabel* (Atlantic).

e|lu|ci|da|tive (i lü′sə dā′tiv), *adj.* serving to elucidate; explanatory.

e|lu|ci|da|tor (i lü′sə dā′tər), *n.* a person who elucidates.

e|lu|ci|da|to|ry (i lü′sə də tôr′ē, -tōr′-; -dā′tər ē), *adj.* elucidative: *He cannot speak ... of "the world's opera houses" without adding an elucidatory "large, medium-sized, and small"* (New York Times).

e|lu|cu|bra|tion (i lü′kyə brā′shən), *n.* = lucubration.

e|lude (i lüd′), *v.t.,* **-lud|ed, -lud|ing.** **1** to avoid or escape by quickness or cleverness; slip away from: *The sly fox eluded the dogs.* **SYN:** evade, shun. See syn. under **escape. 2** to remain undiscovered or unexplained by; baffle: *The cause of cancer has eluded all research.* **SYN:** foil. [< Latin *ēlūdere* < *ex-* out, away + *lūdere* to play < *lūdus* game]

e|lud|er (i lü′dər), *n.* a person or thing that eludes.

e|lud|i|ble (i lü′də bəl), *adj.* that can be eluded.

el|u|ent (el′yü ənt), *n.* = eluant.

E|lul (e lül′, el′ül), *n.* the sixth month of the Hebrew ecclesiastical year or the twelfth of the civil year, corresponding to September and sometimes part of August. [< Hebrew *ĕlūl*]

e|lu|sion (i lü′zhən), *n.* an eluding; clever avoidance; evasion. [< Late Latin *ēlūsiō, -ōnis* < Latin *ēlūdere;* see etym. under **elude**]

e|lu|sive (i lü′siv), *adj.* **1** hard to describe or understand; baffling: *I had an idea that was too elusive to be put into words.* **2** tending to elude or escape: *The elusive enemy got away.* **SYN:** evasive. —**e|lu′sive|ly**, *adv.* —**e|lu′sive|ness**, *n.*

e|lu|so|ry (i lü′sər ē), *adj.* = elusive.

e|lute (i lüt′), *v.t.,* **-lut|ed, -lut|ing.** to separate or purify by elution: *The captured metal ions are then eluted and removed for final recovery by chemical precipitation* (New Scientist).

e|lu|tion (i lü′shən, -zhən), *n.* a process of extracting a substance from a mixture by treating it with a strongly active solvent and drawing off the solution. In combination with chromatography it is used especially to remove adsorbed material from an adsorbent. *By skilful choice of solutions for elution it proved possible to resolve mixtures of the rare earths into their components* (K. S. Spiegler). [< Latin *ēlūtiō, -ōnis* < *ēluere;* see etym. under **elutriate**]

e|lu|tri|ate (i lü′trē āt), *v.t.,* **-at|ed, -at|ing.** **1** to purify by washing or straining. **2** to separate the light and heavy particles of by straining. [< Latin *ēlūtriāre* (with English *-ate*[1]) < *ēluere* wash out < *ex-* out + *lavere* wash]

e|lu|tri|a|tion (i lü′trē ā′shən), *n.* purification by washing or straining.

e|lu|tri|a|tor (i lü′trē ā′tər), *n.* an apparatus for elutriating: *Current trends are towards long-period samplers* [*of air pollution*]*, ... incorporating elutriators to reject particles over 10 microns in size, which in the normal process of respiration do not enter the alveoli of the lungs* (Albert Roberts).

e|lu|vi|al (i lü′vē əl), *adj. Geology.* **1** having to do with or formed by eluviation. **2** having to do with or like eluvium.

e|lu|vi|ate (i lü′vē āt), *v.,* **-at|ed, -at|ing.** —***v.t.*** to remove by eluviation: *Some finely divided material has been carried out in suspension, or eluviated* (Finch and Trewartha).
—***v.i.*** to undergo eluviation.

e|lu|vi|a|tion (i lü′vē ā′shən), *n.* the downward removal of soil particles: *These processes include ... eluviation or the removal of materials from the upper levels of the soil ...* (White and Renner).

e|lu|vi|um (i lü′vē əm), *n., pl.* **-vi|a** (-vē ə). *Geology.* a deposit of soil, dust, etc., orginating in the place where found through decomposition of rock, or drifted there by winds (opposed to *alluvium*). [< New Latin *eluvium* < Latin *ex-* out + *luere* to wash; patterned on *alluvium*]

el|van (el′vən), *n.* = elvanite. [probably < Cornish *elven* spark]

Pronunciation Key: hat, āge, cãre, fär; let, ēqual, tėrm; it, īce; hot, ōpen, ôrder; oil, out; cup, pu̇t, rüle; child; long; thin; ᴛʜen; zh, measure; ə represents **a** in about, **e** in taken, **i** in pencil, **o** in lemon, **u** in circus.

el|van|ite (el′və nīt), *n.* a coarse porphyry composed of quartz and feldspar; granite porphyry.
el|van|it|ic (el′və nit′ik), *adj.* containing, resembling, or characterized by elvanite.
el|ver (el′vər), *n.* a young eel: *The young eels—elvers, they are called—find their way back home without guides, and re-stock the waters* (Science News Letter). [variant of *eelfare* the passing of young eels up a stream < *eel* + obsolete *fare* journey]
elves (elvz), *n.* plural of **elf**[1].
elv|ish (el′vish), *adj.* elfish. —**elv′ish|ly,** *adv.*
el|y|dor|ic (el′ə dôr′ik, -dor′-), *adj.* of or having to do with a method of painting, invented by Armand-Vincent de Montpetit in the 1700's, which uses both oil and water color. [< French *éludorique* < Greek *élaion* oil + *hýdōr* water]
É|ly|sée (ā lē zā′), *n.* **1** a palace in Paris, the official residence of the presidents of the republic, built in 1718. **2** the government of France.
E|ly|sian (i lizh′ən), *adj.* **1** of or having to do with Elysium. **2** *Figurative.* happy; delightful.
Elysian Fields, *Greek Mythology.* Elysium: (*Figurative.*) *The delegate . . . said that automation was "the key which would open the gates to the Elysian Fields of a new golden age"* (London Times).
E|ly|sium (i lizh′əm, -liz′ē əm), *n.* **1** *Greek Mythology.* a place where heroes and good people lived after death. **2** *Figurative.* any place or condition of perfect happiness; paradise: *Souls of Poets dead and gone, What Elysium have ye known . . . Choicer than the Mermaid Tavern?* (Keats). [< Latin *Ēlysium* < Greek *Ēlýsion* (*pedíon*) Elysian (field)]
el|y|tra (el′ə trə), *n.* plural of **elytron** or **elytrum.**
el|y|tral (el′ə trəl), *adj.* of or having to do with an elytron or elytra.
el|y|trif|er|ous (el′ə trif′ər əs), *adj.* elytrigerous.
el|y|tri|form (i lit′rə fôrm), *adj.* having the form of an elytron; elytroid.
el|y|trig|er|ous (el′ə trij′ər əs), *adj.* having elytra; bearing an elytron.
el|y|troid (el′ə troid), *adj.* similar to an elytron.
el|y|tron (el′ə tron), *n., pl.* **-tra.** either of a pair of thickened front wings that form a protective covering for the hind pair; wing case. Beetles and certain other insects have elytra. [< New Latin *elytron* < Greek *élytron* sheath < *eilýein* cover, wrap]
el|y|trous (el′ə trəs), *adj.* like the elytra of a beetle.
el|y|trum (el′ə trəm), *n., pl.* **-tra.** = elytron.
El|ze|vir (el′zə vir, -vər), *adj., n.* —*adj.* of or having to do with the Elzevir family or the style of type they developed.
—*n.* a book printed or a style of type developed by any of the Elzevir family. Also, **Elsevier.**
em[1] (em), *n., pl.* **ems,** *adj.* —*n.* **1** the letter *M, m.* **2** *Printing.* **a** the square of the body of any size of type; a unit for measuring the amount of print in a line, page, or other printed matter. It was originally the portion of a line occupied by the letter *m.* **b** a unit of pica type (equal to 1/6 inch) used to measure column width, etc.; a pica.
—*adj.* an em long or square: *an em dash, an em quad.* [a spelling for *M*]
'em or **em**[2] (əm), *pron. pl. Informal.* them: *Up and at 'em, boys!* [Middle English *'em,* unstressed form of *hem,* later replaced by *them*]
em-[1], *prefix.* the form of **en-**[1] before *b, p,* and sometimes *m,* as in *embark, employ, emmesh.*
em-[2], *prefix.* the form of **en-**[2] before *b, m, p, ph,* as in *emblem, emphasis.*
Em., *Chemistry.* emanation (of radioactive substance).
EM (no periods), an abbreviation for the following:
1 East Mark (the mark of East Germany, or ostmark, officially *DM East*) **2** electromagnetic.
3 electron microscope; electron microscopy. **4** enlisted man or men.
E.M., *U.S.* Engineer of Mines.
e|ma|ci|ate (i mā′shē āt), *v.t.,* **-at|ed, -at|ing.** to make unnaturally thin; cause to lose flesh or waste away: *A long illness had emaciated the patient.* [< Latin *ēmaciāre* (with English *-ate*[1]) < *ex-* out + *maciēs* leanness < *macer* lean, meager]
e|ma|ci|at|ed (i mā′shē ā′tid), *adj.* thin from losing flesh: *The invalid was pale and emaciated.*
e|ma|ci|a|tion (i mā′shē ā′shən, -sē-), *n.* an unnatural thinness from loss of flesh; wasting away: (*Figurative.*) *This is the steady emaciation, over the last 30 years or so, of the American patent system* (Wall Street Journal).
em|a|gram (em′ə gram), *n.* a meteorological chart showing temperature on a linear scale and pressure on a logarithmic scale. [< *em*[1] + (di)*agram*]
e-mail (ē′māl′), *n.,* or **E mail,** communications sent by computer; electronic mail.
em|a|lan|ge|ni (em′ə läng′gə nē), *n.* plural of **lilangeni.**
em|a|nant (em′ə nənt), *adj.* emanating; coming forth from a source.
em|a|nate (em′ə nāt), *v.,* **-nat|ed, -nat|ing.** —*v.i.* to come forth; spread out: *Fragrance emanated from the flowers. The rumor emanated from Chicago.*
—*v.t.* to send out; emit: (*Figurative.*) *"Ehrengard" emanates a sense of sophisticated simplicity* (New York Times Book Review). **SYN:** See syn. under **issue.**
[< Latin *ēmānāre* (with English *-ate*[1]) < *ex-* out + *mānāre* to flow]
em|a|na|tion (em′ə nā′shən), *n.* **1** the process of coming forth; spreading out. **SYN:** effluence. **2** anything that comes forth or spreads from a source: *Light and heat are emanations from the sun.* **3** *Chemistry.* a gas given off by a disintegrating, radioactive substance: *Thoron is an emanation of thorium.*
em|a|na|tion|ism (em′ə nā′shə niz əm), *n.* the theory or belief that all creation is the result of an emanation or series of emanations from the Divine Being.
em|a|na|tion|ist (em′ə nā′shə nist), *n.* a believer in emanationism.
em|a|na|tive (em′ə nā′tiv), *adj.* emanating; characterized by emanation.
em|a|na|tor (em′ə nā′tər), *n.* a person or thing that emanates.
em|a|na|to|ri|um (em′ə nə tôr′ē əm, -tōr′-), *n., pl.* **-to|ri|ums, -to|ri|a** (-tôr′ē ə, -tōr′-). a place for treating patients by means of radium emanation. [< *emana*(tion) + (sana)*torium*]
em|a|na|to|ry (em′ə nə tôr′ē, -tōr′-), *adj.* = emanative.
e|man|ci|pate (i man′sə pāt), *v.,* **-pat|ed, -pat|ing,** *adj.* —*v.t.* **1** to set free from slavery of any kind; release: *Lincoln emancipated the slaves on Jan. 1st, 1863. Women have been emancipated from many old restrictions.* (*Figurative.*) *Enlightened political leadership in the country could now succeed in emancipating science from military sponsorship* (Bulletin of Atomic Scientists). **SYN:** liberate. **2** *Roman Law.* to free (a child) from paternal control. —*adj.* emancipated.
[< Latin *ēmancipāre* (with English *-ate*[1]) < *ex-* away + *manceps, -cipis* purchaser < *manus* hand + *capere* take]
e|man|ci|pa|tion (i man′sə pā′shən), *n.* the act or process of setting free from slavery of any kind; release: *The emancipation of the slaves within any state in armed rebellion was proclaimed by President Lincoln in 1863.* (*Figurative.*) *The discoveries of science have led to man's emancipation from many old superstitions.* **SYN:** enfranchisement.
E|man|ci|pa|tion (i man′sə pā′shən), *n. British History.* the act of Parliament passed in 1829 that gave Roman Catholics equal civil rights (Catholic Emancipation Act).
e|man|ci|pa|tion|ist (i man′sə pā′shə nist), *n.* a person who favors or advocates emancipation from some legal, social, or other restraint. **SYN:** liberationist.
Emancipation Proclamation, *U.S. History.* the proclamation by President Lincoln on January 1, 1863, that declared free all persons held as slaves within any state or part of a state then in armed rebellion.
e|man|ci|pa|tive (i man′sə pā′tiv), *adj.* serving to emancipate.
e|man|ci|pa|tor (i man′sə pā′tər), *n.* a person who emancipates.
the Great Emancipator, Abraham Lincoln: *The Great Emancipator was also called "the railsplitter."*
e|man|ci|pa|to|ry (i man′sə pə tôr′ē, -tōr′-; *especially British* i man′sə pā′tər ē), *adj.* = emancipative.
e|man|ci|pist (i man′sə pist), *n.* an ex-convict in Australia.
e|man|dib|u|late (ē′man dib′yə lāt, -lit), *adj.* (of insects) having no mandibles, or having mandibles so modified that they cannot be used for grasping or biting.
e|mar|cid (i mär′sid), *adj. Botany.* flaccid; wilted. [< *e-* + Latin *marcidus* withered]
e|mar|gi|nate (i mär′jə nāt, -nit), *adj.* **1** notched at the margin. **2** *Botany.* having a shallow notch at the apex, as a leaf or petal. [< Latin *ēmargināttus,* past participle of *ēmargināre* take off the (straight) edge < *ex-* away + *margō, -inis* boundary, border]
e|mar|gi|nat|ed (i mär′jə nā′tid), *adj.* = emarginate.
e|mar|gi|na|tion (i mär′jə nā′shən), *n.* **1** emarginate condition. **2** a notch at the margin or tip of a petal or leaf.
e|mas|cu|late (*v.* i mas′kyə lāt; *adj.* i mas′kyə lit, -lāt), *v.,* **-lat|ed, -lat|ing,** *adj.* —*v.t.* **1** to remove the male reproductive glands of; castrate. **2** *Figurative.* to destroy the force of; weaken: *The editor emasculated the speech by cutting out its strongest passages. The Government appealed to the Supreme Court, claiming this decision "emasculates" the law* (Wall Street Journal).
—*adj.* deprived of force or vigor; weakened; effeminate: *. . . contemptuous of the fallacious notion that public service broadcasting need be square or emasculate* (New Statesman).
[< Latin *ēmasculāre* (with English *-ate*[1]) < *ex-* away + *masculus* male (diminutive) < *mās, maris* manly, male]
e|mas|cu|la|tion (i mas′kyə lā′shən), *n.* **1** the act or process of emasculating. **2** the condition of being emasculated.
e|mas|cu|la|tive (i mas′kyə lā′tiv), *adj.* tending to emasculate.
e|mas|cu|la|tor (e mas′kyə lā′tər), *n.* a person or thing that emasculates.
e|mas|cu|la|to|ry (i mas′kyə lə tôr′ē, -tōr′-), *adj.* = emasculative.
em|balm (em bäm′, -bälm′), *v.t.* **1** to treat (a dead body) with spices, chemicals, or drugs to keep it from decaying. **2** *Figurative.* to keep in memory; preserve: *Many fine sentiments are embalmed in poetry.* **3** to fill with sweet scent; perfume: *Roses embalmed the June air.* Also, **imbalm.** [< Middle French *embaumer* < *en-* in (< Latin *in*) + *baume* balm] —**em|balm′er,** *n.*
em|balm|ing fluid (em bä′ming, -bäl′-), a preserving fluid injected into the blood vessels of a corpse. It is composed of formaldehyde and various salts or alkaloids.
em|balm|ment (em bäm′mənt, -bälm′-), *n.* **1** the act or process of embalming. **2** the state of being embalmed. **3** preparation used for embalming.
em|bank (em bangk′), *v.t.* to protect, enclose, or confine with an embankment.
em|bank|ment (em bangk′mənt), *n.* **1** a raised bank of earth or stones used to hold back water or support a roadway. **SYN:** dike. **2** a protecting, enclosing, or confining with a bank of this kind.
em|bar (em bär′), *v.t.,* **-barred, -bar|ring. 1** to put within bars; enclose; imprison. **2** to stop; arrest.
em|bar|ca|der|o (em bär′kə der′ō), *n., pl.* **-der|os.** *Especially Western U.S.* a wharf, port, or landing place, frequently one serving an inland city or settlement. [< Spanish *embarcadero* < *embarcar* embark]
em|bar|ca|tion (em′bär kā′shən), *n.* = embarkation.
em|bar|go (em bär′gō), *n., pl.* **-goes,** *v.,* **-goed, -go|ing.** —*n.* **1** an order of a government forbidding merchant ships to enter or leave its ports: *During the War of 1812, Congress laid an embargo on commerce with Great Britain for 15 months.* **2** any restriction put on commerce by law: *Our Government would certainly place an embargo on gold sales of our stocks if they fell below $10 billion* (New York Times). **3** an order issued by a transportation company restricting the movement of certain freight over the company's lines because of traffic, strikes, bad weather, or similar conditions. **4** *Figurative.* restriction; restraint; hindrance: *There is a general embargo on appearances at functions promoting political or "controversial" organizations* (Manchester Guardian Weekly).
—*v.t.* to put under an embargo; forbid to enter or leave port: *The government embargoed all foreign ships. All vaccine not yet shipped from the manufacturers' plants was embargoed* (Time).
[< Spanish *embargo* < *embargar* restrain < *em-* in (< Latin *in-*) + *barra* bar[1]]
em|bark (em bärk′), *v.i.* **1** to go on board a ship, aircraft, or other vehicle: *Many people embark for Europe at New York harbor. Bus drivers have to climb down from the cab . . . to assist embarking or debarking passengers* (Manchester Guardian Weekly). **2** *Figurative.* to set out; start: *After leaving college, the young man embarked on a business career.* —*v.t.* **1** to put on board a ship, aircraft, or other vehicle: *The general embarked his troops.* **2** *Figurative.* to involve (a person) in an enterprise; invest (money) in an enterprise: *He foolishly embarked his fortune in the swindler's scheme and so lost it all.*
[< Middle French *embarquer* < *en-* in (< Latin *in-*) + *barque* bark < Late Latin *barca*]
em|bar|ka|tion (em′bär kā′shən), *n.* the act or process of embarking: *Mr. Kalatozov shows . . . the heroine's frantic search for her soldier boy among a mass of youths at an embarkation point for the front* (New Yorker).
em|bark|ment (em bärk′mənt), *n.* = embarkation.
em|bar|ras de ri|chesses (äɴ bȧ rä′də rē shes′), *French.* embarrassment of riches; embarrassing amount of wealth or good things: *Thus Ireland has an embarras de richesses in this type of experience* (Harper's).
►A common Anglicized form of the French idiom is *embarras de richesse,* as in the following quotation: *On page 2 of his book he starts to pile up examples . . . until at the end one finds oneself overwhelmed by a unique embarras de richesse* (Hannah Arendt).

em|bar|ras du choix (äɴ bä rä'dʏ shwä'), *French.* embarrassment of choice; too much to choose from: *The typical consumer is not often irresponsible, but in a free market of abundance he frequently suffers from "embarras du choix"* (G. C. F. Allen).

em|bar|rass (em bar'əs), *v.t.* **1** to make uneasy and ashamed; make self-conscious; fluster: *She embarrassed me by asking me if I really liked her.* **SYN:** discomfit, disconcert, abash. See syn. under **confuse. 2** to involve in difficulties; hamper; hinder: *Lack of trucks embarrassed the army's movements.* **SYN:** impede. **3** to complicate; mix up; make difficult: *He embarrasses discussion of the simplest subject by the use of a difficult technical vocabulary.* **4** to burden with debt; involve in financial difficulties: *I am embarrassed at the moment, but I will be able to pay you next month.* **—*v.i.*** to become disconcerted or confused: *The modern child embarrasses less easily than 50 years ago* (New Statesman). [< French *embarrasser* (literally) to block < *embarras* obstacle < Italian *imbarrazzo* < *imbarrare* to bar < *im-* in (< Latin *in-*) + Vulgar Latin *barra* bar¹]

em|bar|rassed|ly (em bar'əst lē), *adv.* in an embarrassed manner: *But while embarrassedly I stand, my handy neighbor takes a hand* (Wall Street Journal).

em|bar|rass|ing (em bar'ə sing), *adj.* that embarrasses: *an embarrassing situation.* **—em|bar'rass|ing|ly,** *adv.*

em|bar|rass|ment (em bar'əs mənt), *n.* **1** the act of embarrassing: *Embarrassment can be avoided by forgetting oneself.* **2** the condition of being embarrassed; uneasiness; shame: *She blushed in embarrassment at her son's rudeness to her friends.* **3** a thing that embarrasses: *He suffered the embarrassment of having forgotten her name.* **4** an excessive number or quantity from which it is difficult to select: *an embarrassment of riches, an embarrassment of friends.*

em|bas|sa|dor (em bas'ə dər, -dôr), *n.* = ambassador.

em|bas|sage (em'bə sij), *n. Archaic.* an embassy.

em|bas|sy (em'bə sē), *n., pl.* **-sies. 1** an ambassador and his staff of assistants. An embassy ranks next above a legation. **2** the residence and offices of an ambassador in a foreign country. **3** the position or duties of an ambassador. **4** a person or group officially sent to a foreign government with a special errand. **5** a special errand; important mission; official message. **6** the sending of ambassadors. [< Old French *embassee* < Italian *ambasciata* < Medieval Latin *ambactia* < Gaulish *ambactus* dependent, servant]

em|bathe (em bāᴛʜ'), *v.t.* **-bathed, -bath|ing.** to bathe; immerse; drench.

em|bat|tle¹ (em bat'əl), *v.t.,* **-tled, -tling. 1** to prepare for battle; form into battle order. **2** to fortify (a town or building). [< Old French *embatailler* < *en-* into (< Latin *in-*) + *bataille* battle¹]

em|bat|tle² (em bat'əl), *v.t.,* **-tled, -tling.** to provide a structure with battlements. [< *em-¹* + obsolete *battlen* battle², to furnish with battlements]

em|bat|tled¹ (em bat'əld), *adj.* **1a** drawn up ready for battle; prepared for battle. **b** engaged in a battle or struggle: *Another farm crisis may be riding down the already embattled Republicans* (Newsweek). **2** fortified.

em|bat|tled² (em bat'əld), *adj. Heraldry.* having an edge or outline shaped like a battlement; crenelated. See picture under **heraldry.**

em|bat|tle|ment (em bat'əl mənt), *n.* = battlement.

em|bay (em bā'), *v.t.* **1** to put or bring into a bay for shelter; force into a bay. **2** *Figurative.* to shut in; surround.

em|bay|ment (em bā'mənt), *n.* **1** the formation of a portion of water or coast into a bay. **2** a bay or baylike formation.

Emb|den goose (em'dən), a variety of domestic goose with pure-white plumage and orange beak and legs. [alteration of *Emden,* a city in Germany]

em|bed (em bed'), *v.t.,* **-bed|ded, -bed|ding. 1** to fix or enclose in a surrounding mass; fasten firmly: *Precious stones are often found embedded in rock. Even if the author writes badly in his own language, that is no reason to embed specifically English clichés in the text* (Observer). **2** to plant in a bed or something like a bed: *He embedded the bulbs in a box of sand.* **3** *Figurative.* to fix firmly in the mind: *Every detail of the accident is embedded in my memory.* Also, **imbed.**

em|bed|ded (em bed'id), *adj. Linguistics.* that is or may be inserted in a basic sentence by transformation: *an embedded adjective, phrase, or sentence.* In "The boy hitting the ball is left-handed," the clause "The boy hitting the ball" is an embedded clause in the basic sentence "The boy is left-handed." **—em|bed'ded|ness,** *n.*

em|bed|ment (em bed'mənt), *n.* the act of embedding or state of being embedded.

em|bel|lish (em bel'ish), *v.t.* **1** to add beauty to; decorate; adorn; ornament: *She embellished the simple dress with colorful embroidery. He embellished his letters with clever sketches.* **SYN:** beautify. **2** *Figurative.* to make more interesting by adding real or imaginary details; elaborate: *He embellished the old stories so that they sounded new. He embellished his account of the fight until it became a legend.* **—*v.i.*** to give embellishments; embroider. [< Old French *embelliss-,* stem of *embellir* < *en-* in (< Latin *in-*) + *bel* handsome < Latin *bellus*] **—em|bel'lish|er,** *n.*

em|bel|lish|ment (em bel'ish mənt), *n.* **1** decoration; adornment; ornament. **2** *Figurative.* detail, often imaginary, added to make a story or account more interesting. **3** the act or process of embellishing.

em|ber¹ (em'bər), *n.* a piece of wood or coal still glowing in the ashes of a fire.
embers, ashes in which there is still some fire: *He stirred the embers to make them blaze up again. The glowing embers in the fireplace threw shadows on the floor.* (*Figurative.*) *O joy! that in our embers Is something that doth live* (Wordsworth). (*Figurative.*) *The embers of American inflation . . . will again flame up* (Wall Street Journal).
[Middle English *eymbre,* Old English *ǣmerge*]

em|ber² (em'bər), *adj.* of or having to do with the Ember days. [Old English *ymbren,* or *ymbryne* course, (literally) a running around < *ymb* around + *ryne* a running. See etym. at **run.**]

Ember days, the four periods of three days each, set apart for fasting and prayer by the Roman Catholic, Anglican, and some other churches. They are the Wednesday, Friday, and Saturday following the first Sunday in Lent, Whitsunday, September 14, and December 13.

em|ber|goose (em'bər güs'), *n., pl.* **-geese.** the great northern diver, a loon that has a very loud call. [< Norwegian *emmergaas;* influenced by *goose*]

em|bers (em'bərz), *n.pl.* See under **ember¹.**

Ember week, one of the four weeks of the year in which the Ember days occur.

em|bez|zle (em bez'əl), *v.t.,* **-zled, -zling. 1** to steal (money entrusted to one's care): *The cashier embezzled $50,000 from the bank and left the country.* **SYN:** misappropriate. **2** *Obsolete.* to waste; squander; dissipate. [< Anglo-French *embesiler,* apparently < *en-* in (< Latin *in-*) + *beseler* destroy, perhaps < *bisel* a gouge; sloping edge < *biais* slant, bias]

em|bez|zle|ment (em bez'əl mənt), *n.* the theft of money entrusted to one's care. **SYN:** peculation.

em|bez|zler (em bez'lər), *n.* a person who embezzles.

em|bi|id (em'bē id, em bī'-), *n.pl.* any one of an order of small tropical or subtropical insects that resemble termites, live in colonies underground, and line their tunnels with silk spun by special organs on their forelegs; web spinner. [< New Latin *Embiidae* the family name < *Embia* the typical genus < Greek *émbios* having life]

em|bi|ot|o|cid (em'bē ot'ə sid), *n.* a North American viviparous fish with spiny fins, found chiefly in the shallow waters of the Pacific Coast. [< New Latin *Embiotocidae* the family name < Greek *émbios* having life + *tókos* offspring]

em|bi|ot|o|coid (em'bē ot'ə koid), *adj., n.* **—*adj.*** of or having to do with the embiotocids.
—*n.* an embiotocid.

em|bi|ra (em bē'rə), *n.* any one of a number of Brazilian trees that yield bast fiber. [< Portuguese *embira* < Tupi *embira* bark, bast]

em|bit|ter (em bit'ər), *v.t.* to make bitter; make more bitter: *The unhappy old man was embittered by the loss of all his money.* **SYN:** envenom.

em|bit|ter|ment (em bit'ər mənt), *n.* the action of embittering or condition of being embittered.

em|blaze¹ (em blāz'), *v.t.,* **-blazed, -blaz|ing. 1** to set ablaze; kindle. **2** to cause to light up, glow, or shine. **SYN:** illuminate. [< *em-¹* + *blaze,* noun]

em|blaze² (em blāz'), *v.t.,* **-blazed, -blaz|ing.** = emblazon. [< *em-¹* + *blaze,* verb]

em|blaz|er (em blā'zər), *n.* a person or thing that emblazes or illuminates.

em|bla|zon (em blā'zən), *v.t.* **1** to display conspicuously; picture in bright colors: *Posters were emblazoned on the walls of the room.* **2** to decorate; adorn: *The knight's shield was emblazoned with his coat of arms.* **3** *Figurative.* to praise highly; honor publicly; make known the fame of: *King Arthur's exploits were emblazoned in song and story.* [< *em-¹* + *blazon*] **—em|bla'zon|er,** *n.*

em|bla|zon|ment (em blā'zən mənt), *n.* **1** the act of emblazoning. **2** something emblazoned, such as a shield or escutcheon.

em|bla|zon|ry (em blā'zən rē), *n., pl.* **-ries. 1** brilliant decoration; adornment; conspicuous display. **2** a display of coats of arms; heraldic decoration.

✱em|blem (em'bləm), *n., v.* **—*n.*** **1** a symbol; sign of an idea; token: *The dove is an emblem of peace. The white flag is the emblem of surrender.* **2** a heraldic device. **3** any object used as a symbol: *Spades, the emblem of untimely graves* (William Cowper). **4** a picture suggesting a moral, often with an accompanying explanation, proverb, or the like. **5** *Obsolete.* an inlaid ornament; inlaid work.
—*v.t.* **1** to represent by an emblem; emblematize: *a medal struck to emblem a victory.* **2** to decorate with an emblem: *a uniform emblemed with stars and stripes.*
[< Latin *emblēma, -ātis* inlaid work < Greek *émblēma* insertion, embossed ornament < *en-* in + stem of *bállein* throw]
—*Syn.* *n.* **1 Emblem, symbol** mean something that stands for something else. **Emblem** applies to an object, or its likeness, that is especially suitable to suggest the nature of an idea, country, etc.: *The eagle is the emblem of the United States.* **Symbol,** often interchangeable with *emblem,* applies particularly to something chosen to stand for an idea or quality, without any thought of special fitness: *The skull and crossbones is a symbol of piracy. The swastika was the emblem of the Nazi party and a symbol of intolerance.*

✱emblem
definition 1

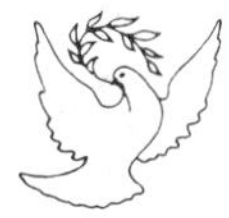
peace emblem

peace symbol

em|ble|ma (em blē'mə), *n., pl.* **-ma|ta** (-mə tə). an ornament in relief, either carved or mounted, on jewelry, vases, or other object. [< Latin *emblēma;* see etym. under **emblem**]

em|blem|at|ic (em'blə mat'ik), *adj.* of or used as an emblem; symbolic: *The lion is emblematic of courage. The cross is emblematic of Christianity. The lonely rider in the lonelier bush is still the emblematic figure of the Australian* (London Times). **—em'blem|at'i|cal|ly,** *adv.*

em|blem|at|i|cal (em'blə mat'ə kəl), *adj.* = emblematic.

em|blem|a|tist (em blem'ə tist), *n.* a designer, maker, or user of emblems.

em|blem|a|tize (em blem'ə tīz), *v.t.,* **-tized, -tiz|ing.** to serve as an emblem of; represent by an emblem; symbolize.

em|blem|a|tol|o|gy (em'blə mə tol'ə jē), *n.* the science of emblems; study of the origin and significance of emblems.

emblem book, a book of pictures that tell stories with a moral. Emblem books were very popular in England in the 1500's and 1600's.

em|ble|ments (em'blə mənts), *n.pl. Law.* the products or profits of land that has been sown or planted. [< Old French *emblaement* < *emblayer* sow with grain < *em-* in (< Latin *in-*) + *blef* field of grain < Medieval Latin *blada*]

em|bod|i|ment (em bod'ē mənt), *n.* **1** a person or thing symbolizing some idea or quality; that in which something is embodied: *Lincoln was an embodiment of democracy.* **SYN:** incarnation. **2** something embodied. **3** the act of embodying or the process or condition of being embodied.

em|bod|y (em bod'ē), *v.t.,* **-bod|ied, -bod|y|ing. 1** to put into a form that can be seen; express in definite form: *A building embodies the idea of the architect. Man can embody truth but he cannot know it* (Harper's). **SYN:** incarnate, materialize, externalize. **2** to bring together and include in a single book, law, or system; include; organize: *The Boy Scouts' "Scout Handbook" embodies the information needed to become a good scout.* **3** to make part of an organized book, law, system; incorporate: *The new engineer's suggestions were embodied in the revised plan.* **SYN:** embrace, assimilate. **4** to put into a body; provide with a body.

em|bog (em bog', -bôg'), *v.t.,* **-bogged, -bog|ging.** to cause to stick in a bog.

em|bold|en (em bōl'dən), *v.t.* to make bold; encourage; hearten: *Her success at playing the piano emboldened her to study other musical instruments.* **SYN:** nerve. **—em|bold'en|er,** *n.*

em|bo|le (em'bə lē), *n.* = emboly.

em|bo|lec|to|my (em'bə lek'tə mē), *n., pl.* **-mies.**

Pronunciation Key: hat, āge, cãre, fär; let, ēqual, tėrm; it, īce; hot, ōpen, ôrder; oil, out; cup, pu̇t, rüle; child; long; thin; ᴛʜen; zh, measure; ə represents **a** in about, **e** in taken, **i** in pencil, **o** in lemon, **u** in circus.

the surgical removal of an embolus. [< *embolus* + *-ectomy*]

em|bol|ic (em bol′ik), *adj.* **1** *Medicine.* having to do with an embolus or embolism. **2** *Embryology.* pushing or growing in during gastrulation.

em|bo|lism (em′bə liz əm), *n.* **1** a blocking of a blood vessel by a blood clot, a bit of fat, or other obstacle carried there by the blood. **2** the inserting of a day or days in a calendar to make it complete and accurate; intercalation. **3** a day or days so put in. [< Latin *embolismus* < Greek *embolê* insertion, or *émbolos* a plug, peg < *embállein* throw in < *en-* in + *bállein* throw]

em|bo|lis|mic (em′bə liz′mik), *adj.* **1** of or having to do with an embolism. **2** inserted in the calendar; intercalary: *The extra month of the Jewish calendar, Veadar, is an embolismic month.*

em|bo|lis|mi|cal (em′bə liz′mə kəl), *adj.* = embolismic.

embolismic year, a year consisting of thirteen lunar months: *Jewish leap years are embolismic years.*

em|bo|lite (em′bə līt), *n.* a mineral consisting chiefly of the chloride and bromide of silver, found in Chile and Mexico. [< Greek *embólion* insertion (< *émbolos* a plug) + English *-ite*[1]]

em|bo|li|um (em bō′lē əm), *n., pl.* **-li|a** (-lē ə). the margin of the corium in some hemipterous insects. [< New Latin *embolium* < Greek *embólion* insertion < *émbolos* a plug; see etym. under **embolism**]

em|bo|li|za|tion (em′bə lə zā′shən), *n. Medicine.* the appearance of an embolism; obstruction of a blood vessel by an embolus.

em|bo|lize (em′bə līz), *v.t., v.i.,* **-lized, -liz|ing.** *Medicine.* to cut off from the circulation by embolism.

em|bo|lon (em′bə lon), *n.* the beak of an ancient Greek or Roman warship, made of metal, and sharpened to pierce an enemy vessel below the water line.

em|bo|lum (em′bə ləm), *n.* = embolon.

em|bo|lus (em′bə ləs), *n., pl.* **-li** (-lī). *Medicine.* a clot, globule of fat, air bubble, or the like, carried in the bloodstream. It sometimes blocks up a blood vessel. [< Latin *embolus* < Greek *émbolos* peg; see etym. under **embolism**]

em|bo|ly (em′bə lē), *n., pl.* **-lies.** invagination; the process of forming the double-layered gastrula. [ultimately < Greek *embállein;* see etym. under **embolism**]

em|bon|point (äɴ bôɴ pwaɴ′), *n. French.* fatness; plumpness: *It was an impudence for any woman to carry on herself an embonpoint so flagrant* (New Yorker).

em|bor|der (em bôr′dər), *v.t. Archaic.* to furnish with or form into a border.

em|bos|om (em bůz′əm, -bü′zəm), *v.t.* **1** to surround; enclose; envelop: *the masses of noble wood embosoming the villages* (Charles Kingsley). **2** *Figurative.* to embrace or cherish.

em|boss[1] (em bôs′, -bos′), *v.t.* **1** to decorate with a design or pattern that stands out from the surface: *Our coins are embossed with letters and figures.* **2** to cause to stand out from the surface: *He ran his fingers over the letters to see if they had been embossed.* [< Old French *embocer* < *em-* (< Latin *in-*) + *boce* swelling, boss[2]] — **em|boss′er,** *n.*

em|boss[2] (em bôs′, -bos′), *v.t. Obsolete.* **1** to drive (a hunted animal) to exhaustion. **2** to cause to foam at the mouth. [Middle English *embosen,* perhaps < *en-*[1] + Old French *bos* wood]

em|boss|ment (em bôs′mənt, -bos′-), *n.* **1** a figure, carved or molded in relief. **2** a part that sticks out; bulge.

em|bouche|ment (äɴ büsh mäɴ′), *n. French.* the opening of one duct, channel, or vessel into another.

em|bou|chure (äm′bů shůr′), *n.* **1** the mouth of a river. **2** the widening of a river valley into a plain. **3** *Music.* **a** the mouthpiece of a wind instrument. **b** the shaping and use of the lips or tongue in playing such an instrument: *He picked up the trumpet without help, and the mellophone was no trouble at all after that, since it has the same fingering and a similar embouchure* (Time). [< Old French *embouchure* < *emboucher* put into, or discharge from, a mouth < *en-* in (< Latin *in-*) + *bouche* mouth < Latin *bucca*]

em|bour|geoise|ment (em′bůr zhwäz′mənt; *French* äɴ bür zhwáz mäɴ′), *n.* **1** the process of becoming bourgeois: *But China started from so far back that it will be long before embourgeoisement sets in there too* (Manchester Guardian). **2** the adoption of bourgeois ideas or practices: *The Soviet party, despite a new appearance of embourgeoisement, remained inherently Stalinist* (New York Times). [< French *embourgeoisement*]

em|bow (em bō′), *v.t. Archaic.* to bend or curve into a bow; arch; vault.

em|bow|el (em bou′əl), *v.t.,* **-eled, -el|ing** or (*especially British*) **-elled, -el|ling. 1** = disembowel. **2** *Obsolete.* to put into the bowels, or the innermost parts.

em|bow|er (em bou′ər), *v.t.* to enclose in a shelter of leafy branches: *A small Indian village, pleasantly embowered in a grove of spreading elms* (Washington Irving).

em|bow|er|ment (em bou′ər mənt), *n.* the act of embowering or of placing within a bower.

em|brace[1] (em brās′), *v.,* **-braced, -brac|ing,** *n.* — ***v.t.*** **1** to fold in the arms to show love or friendship; hold in the arms; hug: *The mother embraced her baby.* **2** *Figurative.* to take up; take for oneself; accept: *She eagerly embraced the offer of a trip to Europe. Some African tribes have embraced the Christian religion. American students have increasingly come to embrace a new value system which ... places human life over all other considerations* (Joseph Rhodes). **SYN:** adopt, espouse. **3** to include; take in; contain: *The cat family embraces cats, lions, tigers, and similar animals.* **SYN:** comprise. **4** to surround; enclose: *Vines embraced the hut. You'll see your Rome embraced with fire* (Shakespeare). **SYN:** encircle. **5** *Figurative.* to take in with the eye or mind. **6** *Obsolete.* to undertake.
— ***v.i.*** to hug one another: *The two girls embraced.*
— ***n.*** **1** a clasping in the arms; hug: *The little boy freed himself from his aunt's embrace.* (*Figurative.*) *Wrapt in the cold embraces of the tomb* (Alexander Pope). **2** a taking up or accepting: *the tribes' embrace of Christianity, their willing embrace of new values and ideas.*
[< Old French *embracer,* perhaps < Vulgar Latin *imbracchiāre* < Latin *in-* in + *bracchium* arm < Greek *brachīōn*]

em|brace[2] (em brās′), *v.t.,* **-braced, -brac|ing.** *Law.* to attempt to influence (a court or jury) illegally. [apparently back formation < *embraceor*]

em|brace|a|ble (em brā′sə bəl), *adj.* that can be embraced; inviting an embrace.

em|brace|ment (em brās′mənt), *n.* an embracing: (*Figurative.*) *... some of the foibles that attend mass embracement of art and culture* (Saturday Review).

em|brace|or (em brā′sər), *n. Law.* a person who tries to influence a court or jury illegally. [< Anglo-French *embraceor* < Old French *embraser* to set on fire; see etym. under **embrasure**]

em|brac|er[1] (em brā′sər), *n.* a person who embraces. [< *embrac*(e)[1] + *-er*[1]]

em|brac|er[2] (em brā′sər), *n. Law.* a person who practices embracery; embraceor. [< Anglo-French *embraceor;* see etym. under **embraceor**]

em|brac|er|y (em brā′sər ē), *n. Law.* the attempt to influence a court or jury illegally: *A summons alleging embracery, a charge which, it is believed, has not come before an English court since 1611, will be heard at Leeds Magistrates' Court on January 20* (London Times).

em|bra|cive (em brā′siv), *adj.* completely surrounding; encompassing: *The totalitarian state imposes embracive political and economic controls.*

em|branch|ment (em branch′mənt), *n.* **1** the act or state of branching off or out: *the embranchment of a river.* **SYN:** ramification. **2** a branch.

em|bran|gle (em brang′gəl), *v.t.,* **-gled, -gling.** to confuse; entangle; perplex.

em|bran|gle|ment (em brang′gəl mənt) *n.* confusion; entanglement: *The commissioner of parks is engaged in another jurisdictional embranglement.*

***em|bra|sure** (em brā′zhər), *n.* **1** an opening in a wall for a gun, with sides that spread outward to permit the gun to swing through a greater arc. **2** *Architecture.* a slanting off of the wall at an oblique angle on the inner sides of a window or door. [< French *embrasure* < Old French *embraser* set on fire < *en-* on (< Latin *in-*) + *braise,* earlier *breze* red-hot coal]

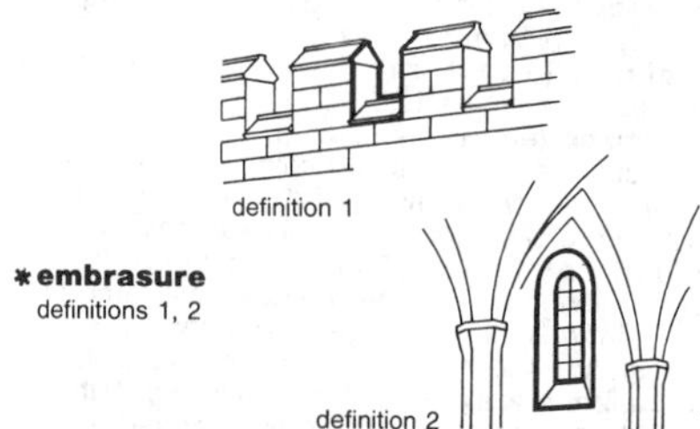

***embrasure**
definitions 1, 2

em|brit|tle (em brit′əl), *v.t.,* **-tled, -tling.** to cause (a metal) to become brittle: *Some—such as liquid oxygen—are so cold that they embrittle many constructional materials and evaporate continuously if not refrigerated* (New Scientist).

em|brit|tle|ment (em brit′əl mənt), *n.* the process of making or being made brittle: *Phosphorus in coking coals causes embrittlement of iron.*

em|bro|cate (em′brō kāt), *v.t.,* **-cat|ed, -cat|ing.** to bathe and rub with liniment or lotion. [< Late Latin *embrocāre* (with English *-ate*[1]) < *embrocha* lotion, infusion < Greek *embrochê* < *en-* in + *bréchein* to wet]

em|bro|ca|tion (em′brō kā′shən), *n.* **1** a liniment or lotion used for bathing and rubbing the body: *He went to Milan ... with a suspected touch of pleurisy. From then on his mother bought the embrocation wholesale* (Punch).

em|bro|glio (em brōl′yō), *n., pl.* **-glios.** = imbroglio.

em|broi|der (em broi′dər), *v.t.* **1** to ornament (cloth or leather) with a design or pattern of stitches: *She embroidered the handkerchief with his initials.* (*Figurative.*) *My sleep had been embroider'd with dim dreams* (Keats). **SYN:** decorate. **2** to make (an ornamental design or pattern) on cloth, leather, or other material, with stitches: *She embroidered silver stars on her blue dress.* **3** *Figurative.* to add imaginary details to; exaggerate: *The sailor didn't exactly tell lies, but he did embroider his stories.* **SYN:** embellish. — ***v.i.*** **1** to do embroidery. **2** *Figurative.* to give imaginary details; exaggerate or improvise: *to embroider on a story. In Bellini's day it was customary for the singer to embellish and embroider* (Harper's). [< *em-*[1] +Middle English *broideren* embroider < Old French *broder*] — **em|broi′der|er,** *n.*

em|broi|der|ess (em broi′dər is), *n.* a woman embroiderer: [*She*] *will be remembered by many for her skill as an embroideress who specialized in all kinds of needlework for Church furnishings* (London Times).

em|broi|der|y (em broi′dər ē, -drē), *n., pl.* **-der|ies. 1** the act or art of embroidering. **2** ornamental designs sewn in cloth or leather with a needle; embroidered work or material. **3** *Figurative.* imaginary details; exaggeration: *an embroidery of wishful thinking.*

embroidery frame, a frame on which material to be embroidered is fastened and stretched, so that it may not be drawn in the working.

em|broil (em broil′), *v.t.* **1** to involve (a person, country, or group) in a quarrel: *Even bystanders became embroiled in the riot. A wise person does not become embroiled in other people's disputes.* **2** to throw (affairs) into a state of confusion: *The accounts of the Crusades are embroiled with legends and myths.* **SYN:** disorder, confuse. [< French *embrouiller* < *en-* in + *brouiller* to disorder, mix; broil[2]] — **em|broil′er,** *n.*

em|broil|ment (em broil′mənt), *n.* **1** the act or process of embroiling. **2** the state of being embroiled.

em|brown (em broun′), *v.t.* to tan; darken.

em|brue (em brü′), *v.t.,* **-brued, -bru|ing.** = imbrue.

em|brute (em brüt′), *v.t.,* **-brut|ed, -brut|ing.** = imbrute.

em|bry|ec|to|my (em′brē ek′tə mē), *n., pl.* **-mies.** the surgical removal of an embryo. [< *embryo* + Greek *ektomê* a cutting out]

em|bry|o** (em′brē ō), *n., pl.* **-bry|os,** *adj.* — ***n. **1** an animal in the early stages of its development, before birth or hatching. A chicken within an egg is an embryo. A human embryo more than three months old is usually called a fetus. See picture on next page. **2** an undeveloped plant within a seed. See picture on next page. **3** *Figurative.* an undeveloped stage; the beginning or rudimentary stage of anything.
— ***adj.*** undeveloped; not mature; embryonic: (*Figurative.*) *an embryo idea.* **SYN:** rudimentary.
in embryo, in an undeveloped stage: *a plan in embryo.*
[< Medieval Latin *embryo* < Greek *émbryon* < *en-* in + *brýein* swell, be full]

em|bry|o|blast (em′brē ə blast), *n.* the inner cell mass of a blastula.

em|bry|o|car|di|a (em′brē ō kär′dē ə), *n.* a disorder of the heart in which its action resembles that of a fetal heart.

em|bry|oc|to|ny (em′brē ok′tə nē), *n.* the destruction of the embryo or fetus in the uterus.

em|bry|o|gen|e|sis (em′brē ō jen′ə sis), *n.* = embryogeny.

em|bry|o|ge|net|ic (em′brē ō jə net′ik), *adj.* = embryogenic.

em|bry|o|gen|ic (em′brē ō jen′ik), *adj.* of or having to do with embryogeny.

em|bry|og|e|ny (em′brē oj′ə nē), *n.* the formation and development of the embryo.

em|bry|oid (em′brē oid), *n.* a plant or animal form having the structure or function of an embryo: *Many of the embryoids developed into structures simulating globular or heart-shaped stages of dicotyledonous embryos* (A. C. Hildebrandt).

embryol., embryology.

em|bry|o|log|ic (em′brē ə loj′ik), *adj.* = embryological.

em|bry|o|log|i|cal (em′brē ə loj′ə kəl), *adj.* of or having to do with embryology. —**em′bry|o|log′i|cal|ly**, *adv.*
em|bry|ol|o|gist (em′brē ol′ə jist), *n.* an expert in embryology.
em|bry|ol|o|gy (em′brē ol′ə jē), *n.* the branch of biology that deals with the formation and development of embryos: *The object of the study of embryology ... is to discover how animals become what they are* (A. Franklin Shull).
em|bry|o|ma (em′brē ō′mə), *n., pl.* **-mas, -ma|ta** (-mə tə). a tumor composed of fetal tissues.
em|bry|on (em′brē on), *n.* = embryo. [< Greek *émbryon;* see etym. under **embryo**]
em|bry|o|nal (em′brē ə nəl), *adj.* = embryonic.
em|bry|o|nat|ed (em′brē ə nā′tid), *adj.* (of an egg) containing an embryo: *Dr. Harold Cox has succeeded in making at least one of the three polio viruses adapt itself to growth on embryonated hen's eggs* (Science News Letter).
em|bry|on|ic (em′brē on′ik), *adj.* **1** of the embryo: *an embryonic study. It now has human embryos from the earliest stage of development to the end of the embryonic period* (Science). **2** *Figurative.* not mature; undeveloped: *an embryonic leaf, an embryonic plan. It also means a new lease on life for the embryonic Spanish air force* (Harper's). SYN: immature.
em|bry|on|i|cal|ly (em′brē on′ə klē), *adv.* in an embryonic manner: (*Figurative.*) *This at a time when the internal combustion engine, aviation, synthetic chemistry, all brought to a high degree of development under capitalism, existed only embryonically or not at all* (Wall Street Journal).
embryonic disc, the part of the inner cell mass of the blastula from which the embryo develops. It is located between two cavities, the amniotic cavity and the yolk sac. It consists of three germ layers, the ectoderm, the mesoderm, and the endoderm.
embryonic plate, = embryonic disc.
em|bry|o|phyte (em′brē ə fīt), *n.* any one of a group of plants that develop embryos: *Mosses, ferns, and flowering plants are embryophytes.*
embryo sac, *Botany.* the large cell in the ovule that gives rise to the egg and the endosperm; megaspore (of seed plants). After fertilization, the egg becomes the embryo, which is contained within the embryo sac.
em|bu|ia (im bü′yə), *n.* = imbuia.
em|bus (em bus′), *v.,* **-bussed, -bus|sing.** *Especially British.* —*v.t.* to put on a bus.
—*v.i.* to get on a bus: *We embussed for Ridgewood the other afternoon, and soon found ourself in the waiting room of Dr. Weise's office* (New Yorker).
em|bus|qué (em′bə skā′; *French* äɴ bʏs kā′), *n.* a person who escaped war service by working in a government office or the like. [< French *embusqué,* (originally) past participle of *embusquer* to ambush]
em|buss|ment (em bus′mənt), *n. Especially British.* the act of embussing or state of being embussed: *As a respectful but distant admirer of Mac, I was invited to witness his embussment, en route to Liverpool* (London Times).
EMC (no periods), encephalomyocarditis.
em|cee (em′sē′), *n., v.,* **-ceed, -cee|ing.** *U.S. Informal.* —*n.* a master of ceremonies: *The Big Revue, a weekly hour-long musical show ... had an emcee, two featured singers, a six-member dance troupe, [and] a six-member vocal group* (Maclean's).
—*v.t., v.i.* to act as master of ceremonies (of): *Lord Harewood ... even emcees a TV show now and then* (Show).
[spelling for pronunciation of *M.C.*]
eme (ēm), *n. Dialect.* **1** an uncle. **2** a friend; gossip. [Old English *ēam*]
e|meer (ə mir′), *n.* = emir.
e|mend (i mend′), *v.t.* to free from faults or errors; correct; rectify: *The scholar emended the faulty text by suggesting changes so that it could be read more easily.* [< Latin *ēmendāre* < *ex-* out of + *mendum,* later *menda* fault. See etym. at doublet **amend.**] —**e|mend′er**, *n.*
e|mend|a|ble (i men′də bəl), *adj.* that can be emended.
e|men|date (ē′mən dāt), *v.t.,* **-dat|ed, -dat|ing.** = emend.
e|men|da|tion (ē′men dā′shən, em′en-), *n.* **1** the action of emending; correction; improvement. **2** a suggested change to free a faulty text, document, or the like, from error. **3** a change or correction.
e|men|da|tor (ē′mən dā′tər, em′ən-), *n.* a person who makes emendations.
e|men|da|to|ry (i men′də tôr′ē, -tōr′-), *adj.* **1** of or having to do with emendation. **2** serving to emend.
em|er|ald (em′ər əld, em′rəld), *n., adj.* —*n.* **1** a bright-green precious stone or jewel; transparent green beryl: *Beryl, colored green by traces of chromium, is the gem called emerald; colored blue-green it is called aquamarine* (Monroe M. Offner). **2** a bright-green variety of corundum or sapphire used as a precious stone. **3** a bright green. **4** *Printing.* a size of type (6½ point).
—*adj.* bright-green.
[< Old French *esmeralde* < Vulgar Latin *smaraldus* < Latin *smaragdus* < Greek *smáragdos*]
emerald copper, a translucent silicate of copper; dioptase.
emerald green, a bright green.
em|er|ald-green (em′ər əld grēn′, em′rəld-), *adj.* bright-green.
Emerald Isle, Ireland.
emerald moth, any one of a group of moths distinguished by their bright green color.
emerald nickel, a green, hydrous carbonate of nickel; zaratite.
emerald spodumene, an emerald-green variety of spodumene; hiddenite.
e|merge (i mėrj′), *v.i.,* **e|merged, e|merg|ing.** **1** to come out; come up; come into view: *The sun emerged from behind a cloud.* SYN: See syn. under **issue.** **2** to become known: *Many facts emerged as a result of the investigation.* **3** *Figurative.* to rise or come forth from obscurity, poverty, or other low condition: *Many distinguished men have emerged from slums.* [< Latin *ēmergere* < *ex-* out + *mergere* dip]
e|mer|gence (i mėr′jəns), *n.* **1** the act or fact of emerging; a coming into view: *the emergence of a chick from its egg.* **2** *Botany.* an outgrowth on the surface of an organ arising from tissue beneath the epidermis, such as a prickle.
e|mer|gen|cy (i mėr′jən sē), *n., pl.* **-cies,** *adj.* —*n.* **1** a sudden need for immediate action: *I keep a box of tools and a fire extinguisher in my car for use in an emergency.* **2** a situation in which such a need arises: *a national emergency.*
—*adj.* for a time of sudden need: *an emergency exit, an emergency fund. The surgeon performed an emergency operation. The Administration has invoked the emergency injunction of the Taft-Hartley Law only three times* (New York Times).
—*Syn. n.* **1, 2 Emergency, crisis** mean a trying or dangerous time or state of affairs. **Emergency** refers to a sudden or unexpected situation that calls for action without delay: *The failure of the city's electric power caused an emergency.* **Crisis** refers to a situation in which grave alternatives, sometimes life or death, hang in the balance and whose outcome will be decisive: *The floods brought on a crisis for the farmers.*
emergency brake, a second system of brakes on an automobile, usually operated by hand, and equipped with a ratchet or similar device which must be released in order to release the brake, used for holding an automobile in place while parked.
e|mer|gent (i mėr′jənt), *adj., n.* —*adj.* **1** emerging: *the emergent stars,* (*Figurative.*) *an emergent idea.* **2** rising from water or other liquid: *Today the continents happen to be largely emergent* (Scientific American). **3** *Figurative.* recently created; newly independent: *the emergent countries of Africa.* **4** *Figurative.* arising casually or unexpectedly: *emergent matters, emergent occasions.* **5** urgent: *a politically emergent issue.*
—*n.* **1** *Philosophy.* something that emerges or results from a combination of factors. **2** *Botany.* a plant growing in water whose upper parts grow above the water's surface. —**e|mer′gent|ly**, *adv.*
emergent evolution, a type of evolution which gives rise to unforeseen and unpredictable forms of life contrasted in philosophical theory with a type of evolution giving rise to predictable, expected forms.
emergent year, the epoch or date from which a people begin to compute time: *Our emergent year is the year of the birth of Christ.*
e|mer|gi|cen|ter (i mėr′jē sen′tər), *n. U.S.* a walk-in clinic for treating minor medical emergencies: *The emergicenter [is] a cross between a hospital emergency room and a family doctor's office ... generally located in shopping centers or along highways* (U.S. News & World Report).
e|mer|i|ta (i mer′ə tə), *adj., n., pl.* **-tae** (-tē).
—*adj.* (of a woman) honorably discharged; emeritus.
—*n.* a woman honorably discharged or retired from service.
[< Latin *ēmerita,* feminine of *ēmeritus;* see etym. under **emeritus**]
e|mer|i|tus (i mer′ə təs), *adj., n., pl.* **-ti** (-tī).
—*adj.* honorably discharged; retired from active service, but still holding one's rank and title: *At the age of seventy, Professor Arnold became professor emeritus.*
—*n.* a person, especially a man, honorably discharged or retired from service.
[< Latin *ēmeritus,* past participle of *ēmerēre* < *ex-* to the end + *merēre* serve]
em|e|rods (em′ə rodz), *n.pl. Archaic.* hemorrhoids.
e|mersed (i mėrst′), *adj.* **1** that has emerged; standing out. **2** *Botany.* standing out of water as part of an aquatic plant.
e|mer|sion (i mėr′zhən, -shən), *n.* **1** the action of emerging. **2** *Astronomy.* the reappearance of the sun, moon, or other heavenly body after an eclipse. [< Late Latin *ēmersiō, -ōnis* < Latin *ēmergere;* see etym. under **emerge**]
Em|er|so|ni|an (em′ər sō′nē ən), *adj., n.* —*adj.* of or having to do with Ralph Waldo Emerson, (1803–1882) American poet, essayist, and philosopher, his writings, or his views.
—*n.* **1** a supporter or imitator of Emerson. **2** an expert on Emerson.
em|er|y (em′ər ē, em′rē), *n.* a hard, dark rock which is used for grinding, smoothing, and polishing metals or stones: *Emery is essentially an intimate mixture of granular corundum and magnetite, and in powdered form has long been used as emery paper, emery cloth and emery wheels* (W. R. Jones). [< Middle French *émeri* < Old French *emmery* < Italian *smeriglio* < Vulgar Latin *smericulum* < Greek *smýris* abrasive powder]
emery bag, a small bag or case filled with emery, used for keeping needles bright and clean.
emery board, a very thin, flat piece of wood coated on both sides with powdered emery, used as a nail file.
emery cake, a compound of emery and beeswax used on the surfaces of wheels for buffing and glazing.
emery cloth, a sturdy cloth coated with powdered emery, used for smoothing or polishing.
emery paper, paper coated with powdered emery, used for smoothing or polishing.
emery wheel, a wheel for grinding or polishing, made of or coated with emery.
em|e|sis (em′ə sis), *n.* the action of vomiting. [< Greek *émesis* < *emeîn* to vomit]
em|e|ta|tro|phi|a (em′ə tə trō′fē ə), *n.* a wasting of the body resulting from the persistent vomiting of food. [< New Latin *emetatrophia* < Greek *émetos* vomiting + *tréphein* nourish]
e|met|ic (i met′ik), *adj., n.* —*adj.* causing vomiting. —*n.* a medicine that causes vomiting. [< Late Latin *ēmeticus* < Greek *emetikós* < *emeîn* to vomit]
emetic root, = flowering spurge.
em|e|tin (em′ə tin), *n.* = emetine.
em|e|tine (em′ə tēn, -tin), *n.* an alkaloid extracted from ipecac root, used as an emetic and in treat-

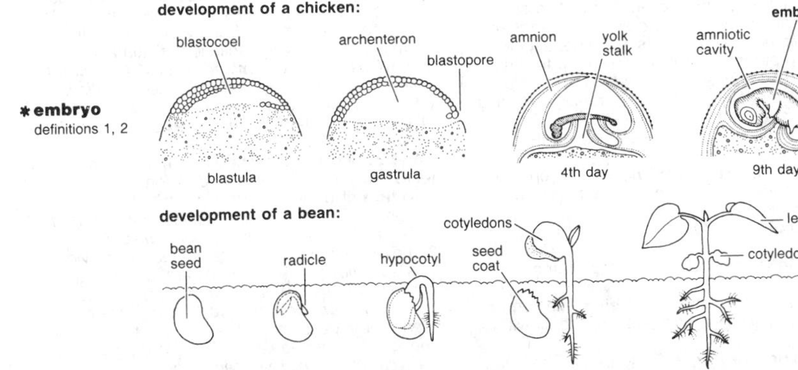

✱embryo
definitions 1, 2

Pronunciation Key: hat, āge, cãre, fär; let, ēqual, tėrm; it, īce; hot, ōpen, ôrder; oil, out; cup, pu̇t, rüle; child; long; thin; ᴛʜen; zh, measure; ə represents a in about, e in taken, i in pencil, o in lemon, u in circus.

ing amebic dysentery. *Formula:* $C_{29}H_{40}N_2O_4$ [< *emet*(ic) + *-ine*²]

e|meu (ē′myü), *n.* = emu.

é|meute (ā mœt′), *n. French.* an outbreak; a riot.

é|meu|tier (ā mœ tyā′), *n. French.* a rioter.

e.m.f., emf (no periods), or **E.M.F.**, electromotive force.

EMG (no periods), electromyogram.

-emia, *combining form.* condition of the blood: *Toxemia = a poisoned condition of the blood.* [< New Latin *-emia* < Greek *haîma* blood]

e|mic (ē′mik), *adj. Linguistics.* distinctive; contrastive; significant: *emic syllables, the transcription of emic sounds.* [abstracted < *phonemic, morphemic, graphemic,* etc.] —**e′mi|cal|ly**, *adv.*

e|mic|tion (i mik′shən), *n.* **1** the act of urinating. **2** = urine.

em|i|grant (em′ə grənt), *n., adj.* —*n.* a person who leaves his own country or region to settle in another: *My grandparents were emigrants from Ireland. It is expected that the total of emigrants from this country overseas will this year reach 220,000* (Manchester Guardian).
—*adj.* leaving one's own country or region to settle in another.
▶See **emigrate** for usage note.

em|i|grate (em′ə grāt), *v.i.*, **-grat|ed, -grat|ing.** to leave one's own country or region to settle in another: *My grandparents emigrated from Ireland to come to the United States.* [< Latin *ēmigrāre* (with English *-ate*¹) < *ex-* out + *migrāre* to move, migrate]
▶**emigrate, immigrate.** *Emigrate* means to move out of a country or region, *immigrate* to move into a country. One who *emigrates* from Norway might *immigrate* to the United States. An *emigrant* from Norway might be an *immigrant* to the United States.

em|i|gra|tion (em′ə grā′shən), *n.* **1** leaving one's own country or region to settle in another: *There has been much emigration from Italy to the United States. Emigration often removes the healthiest and most progressive element from an old country.* **2** a body of emigrants: *The largest emigration from Europe came to the United States in 1907.*

em|i|gra|tion|al (em′ə grā′shə nəl), *adj.* of or having to do with emigration.

em|i|gra|tor (em′ə grā′tər), *n.* = emigrant.

é|mi|gré or **e|mi|gré** (em′ə grā; *French* ā mē grā′), *n., pl.* **é|mi|grés** or **e|mi|grés** (em′ə grāz; *French* ā mē grā′). **1** = emigrant. **2** a royalist refugee from France during the French Revolution. **3** a refugee from Russia during and after the Russian Revolution: *He was 18 years old, an émigré from Pogar, a South Ukrainian village in Czarist Russia* (Newsweek). [< French *émigré,* (originally) past participle of *émigrer,* learned borrowing from Latin *ēmigrāre;* see etym. under **emigrate**]

E|mil|i|an (ē mil′ē ən), *adj.* of or belonging to Emilia, a fertile region of northern Italy between Lombardy and Tuscany: *the Emilian anatomist Malpighi, the farms of the Emilian plain.*

em|i|nence (em′ə nəns), *n.* **1** rank or position above all or most others; high standing; greatness; fame: *The surgeon's eminence was due to his superior skill in operating. His eminence in belles-lettres was unquestioned. Edison won eminence as an inventor.* SYN: distinction, prominence, renown. **2** a person of high rank or position; important person: *Winston Churchill was an eminence both in politics and literature.* **3** a high place; high point of land; lofty hill: *The lighthouse was built on an eminence rising many feet above the shore.*

Em|i|nence (em′ə nəns), *n.* a title of honor given to a cardinal in the Roman Catholic Church.

é|mi|nence grise (ā mē näns grēz′), *pl.* **é|mi|nences grises** (ā mē näns grēz′). *French.* **1** a person who wields power or exerts influence behind the scenes: *Krone sought the advice of the éminence grise of the chancellery, Globke* (Atlantic). **2** (literally) gray eminence. [originally used in French as the nickname of Père Joseph, a monk who was Cardinal Richelieu's confidential agent, after the gray habit which he wore, in contrast to the Cardinal's red habit]

em|i|nen|cy (em′ə nən sē), *n., pl.* **-cies.** *Obsolete.* eminence.

em|i|nent (em′ə nənt), *adj.* **1** above all or most others; outstanding; famous; distinguished; exalted: *Washington was eminent both as general and as President. Censure is the tax a man pays to the public for being eminent* (Jonathan Swift). **2** conspicuous; noteworthy: *The judge was a man of eminent fairness.* **3** high; lofty: *upon an high mountain and eminent* (Ezekiel 17:22). **4** standing out above other things; projecting; prominent. [< Latin *ēminēns, -entis,* present participle of *ēminēre* be prominent < *ex-* out + *minēre* to jut]
—*Syn.* **1 Eminent, prominent, distinguished** mean outstanding. **Eminent** implies standing high among or above all others of the same kind because of excellence in something: *Wordsworth and Coleridge were eminent English poets.* **Prominent** implies standing out from the crowd, and suggests being well known at least locally: *The president of the bank is a prominent man in his home town.* **Distinguished** implies being set off from others of the same kind because of outstanding qualities, and suggests being well known to the public: *President Eisenhower was also a distinguished general.*
▶**eminent, imminent.** *Eminent* means distinguished, exalted: *The new ambassador was eminent as both diplomat and scholar. Imminent* means likely to happen soon: *Convinced that bankruptcy was imminent, the company president called a meeting of the directors.*

eminent domain, *Law.* the right of the government to take private property for public use. The owner must be paid for the property taken.

em|i|nent|ly (em′ə nənt lē), *adv.* to an eminent degree; so as to be distinguished from others; specially: *Because of his long experience in the state legislature, he was eminently qualified to run for Congress.* SYN: notably, illustriously.

e|mir (ə mir′), *n.* **1** an Arabian chief, prince, or military leader. **2** a title of honor for the descendants of Mohammed. **3** the title of certain Turkish officials. Also, **amir, emeer.** [< Arabic *amīr* commander. Compare etym. under **admiral.**]

e|mir|ate (ə mir′it), *n.* **1** the rank or authority of an emir. **2** the territory governed by an emir. Also, **amirate.**

em|is|sar|y (em′ə ser′ē), *n., pl.* **-sar|ies,** *adj.* —*n.* **1** a person sent on a mission or errand: *I am your grandmother's emissary. She could not come herself* (Thomas Hardy). SYN: messenger. **2** a secret agent; spy.
—*adj.* sent forth on a mission.
[< Latin *ēmissārius* < *ēmittere;* see etym. under **emit**]

e|mis|sile (i mis′əl), *adj. Zoology.* that can be thrust out: *an emissile tubule.*

e|mis|sion (i mish′ən), *n.* **1** the act or fact of emitting: *the emission of light from the sun.* **2** a thing emitted; discharge: *It is from these bursts of emission that radio astronomers have obtained most of their new information about the sun's activities* (Scientific American). *Emissions in all categories—hydrocarbons, carbon monoxide, and oxides of nitrogen—were about 50% less than the standards set by the U.S. Environmental Protection Agency for gasoline engines* (Frank A. Smith). **3** circulation; issue. **4** *Electronics.* **a** the streaming out of electrons from the heated cathode of a vacuum tube. **b** the streaming out of electrons from an electrode subjected to irradiation or to the impact of electrons or ions. [< Latin *ēmissiō, -ōnis* < *ēmittere;* see etym. under **emit**]

emission control, regulation of the amount of pollutants released into the air, as from the exhaust of a motor vehicle, the smoke from manufacturing processes of a factory, or the heat from air-conditioning units of a building: *Emission control . . . will have to prevent significant deterioration of air quality in areas in which the quality equals or excels National Ambient Air Quality Standards* (Julian Josephson).

emission line, a line of radiation in spectrum analysis of stellar objects indicating the presence of a specific chemical element.

emission nebula, a very hot nebula that emits a luminous glow, having an emission spectrum, rather than an absorption spectrum.

emission spectrum, a spectrum produced by radiation of light from a luminous source: *The rainbow is an emission spectrum.*

e|mis|sive (i mis′iv), *adj.* emitting.

em|is|siv|i|ty (em′ə siv′ə tē), *n. Physics.* the relative ability of a surface to radiate energy, expressed in terms of a ratio to that of a black body with an equivalent temperature.

e|mit (i mit′), *v.t.*, **-mit|ted, -mit|ting.** **1** to send out; give off; discharge: *The sun emits light and heat. Volcanoes emit lava.* SYN: exude, expel, eject. **2** to put into circulation; issue. **3** to utter; express: *The trapped lion emitted roars of rage.* **4** to issue formally (as paper currency). [< Latin *ēmittere* < *ex-* out + *mittere* send]

e|mit|ter (i mit′ər), *n.* a person or thing that emits.

em|ma (em′ə), *n. British Slang.* a radio operator's code word for the letter *m,* as in *emma gee,* for MG (machine gun).

Em|man|u|el (i man′yü əl), *n.* = Immanuel (Christ).

em|mar|ble (e mär′bəl), *v.t.*, **-bled, -bling.** = enmarble.

em|mar|vel (e mär′vəl), *v.t.*, **-veled, -vel|ing** or (*especially British*) **-velled, -vel|ling.** to fill with wonder.

em|men|a|gogue (ə men′ə gog, -gôg; -mē′nə-), *n. Medicine.* a drug or agent that brings on the menstrual discharge. [< Greek *émmēna* the menses (< *en-* in + *mēn, mēnós* month) + *agōgós* leading < *ágein* lead]

em|me|nol|o|gy (em′ə nol′ə jē), *n.* the branch of medicine dealing with menstruation.

Em|men|ta|ler or **Em|men|tha|ler** (em′ən tä′lər), *n.* a firm, mild cheese with large holes; Swiss cheese as made in Switzerland. [< German *Emmentaler, Emmenthaler* < *Emmenthal,* a town in Switzerland]

Em|men|thal (em′ən täl), *n.* = Emmentaler.

em|mer (em′ər), *n.* a variety of wheat grown chiefly in European countries as food for livestock and to make flour for bread. Emmer has a brittle central spike. [< dialectal German *Emmer*]

em|mesh (e mesh′), *v.t.* = enmesh.

em|met (em′it), *n. Archaic or Dialect.* an ant. [Old English *ǣmete.* Compare etym. under **ant.**]

em|me|trope (em′ə trōp), *n.* a person having emmetropia.

em|me|tro|pi|a (em′ə trō′pē ə), *n.* the normal condition of the refraction of the eye, in which the rays of light are accurately focused on the retina and there is perfect vision. [< New Latin *emmetropia* < Greek *émmetros* in measure + *ôps* eye]

em|me|trop|ic (em′ə trop′ik), *adj.* having to do with or characterized by emmetropia.

***Em|my** (em′ē), *n., pl.* **-mies** or **-mys.** a statuette awarded annually by the Academy of Television Arts and Sciences for outstanding achievements in television programming, production, and acting. [apparently alteration of *immy,* nickname for an image orthicon camera tube]

***Emmy**

e|mol|lient (i mol′yənt), *adj., n.* —*adj.* softening or soothing: *She uses an emollient lotion on her hands after washing the dishes.*
—*n.* something that softens and soothes: *Cold cream is an emollient for the skin.*
[< Latin *ēmolliēns, -entis,* present participle of *ēmollīre* soften < *ex-* (intensive) + *mollis* soft]

e|mo|lo|a (ā′mō lō′ä), *n.* a grass of the Hawaiian Islands that grows in tufts from one to three feet high, and is distinguished from all other Hawaiian grasses by the roughness of its rachis and branches of the panicle. [< Hawaiian *emoloa*]

e|mol|u|ment (i mol′yə mənt), *n.* **1** profit from a job, office, or position; salary, fee, or wages: *These men were accustomed, in addition to the large regular emoluments of the office, to exact heavy fees from the prisoners* (James Lecky). SYN: remuneration, pay. **2** *Obsolete.* benefit; advantage. [< Latin *ēmolumentum* profit < *ēmolere* grind out < *ex-* out + *molere* grind]

e|mol|u|men|ta|ry (i mol′yə men′tər ē), *adj.* productive of emolument or profit; financially advantageous.

e|mote (i mōt′), *v.i.*, **-mot|ed, -mot|ing.** *Informal.* **1** to act, especially in an exaggerated manner: *Saturday's show . . . will keep Rooney on-screen for all but three minutes, singing, hoofing, and emoting* (Newsweek). **2** to show emotion: *You must "emote" in this music, unabashedly* (Harper's). [back formation < *emotion*]

e|mot|er (i mō′tər), *n.* a person who emotes.

e|mo|tion (i mō′shən), *n.* **1** a strong feeling of any kind. Hate, fear, excitement, anger, love, joy, and grief are emotions. *A ten-year old girl, totally blind and deaf from birth, showed emotions by facial expressions and gestures similar to those of children in full possession of their senses* (Ogburn and Nimkoff). SYN: See syn. under **feeling.** **2** *Obsolete.* a moving; agitation; disturbance: *The winds of Heaven mix for ever With a sweet emotion* (Shelley). [< Middle French *émotion* (after *motion*) < Old French *emouvoir* stir up, ultimately < Latin *ēmovēre* < *ex-* out + *movēre* move]

e|mo|tion|a|ble (i mō′shə nə bəl), *adj.* easily affected by emotion; liable to emotion.

e|mo|tion|al (i mō′shə nəl, -mōsh′nəl), *adj.* **1** of the emotions: *His constant fears show that he is suffering from a serious emotional disorder.* **2** showing emotion: *Her reaction to the movie was so emotional that she began to cry.* **3** appealing to the emotions: *The speaker made an emotional plea for money to help crippled children.* SYN: impassioned. **4** easily affected by emotion: *Emotional people are likely to cry if they hear sad music or read sad stories.*

e|mo|tion|al|ism (i mō′shə nə liz′əm, -mōsh′nə-liz-), *n.* **1** the tendency to show emotion too easily. **2** emotional quality or character. **3** appeal to the emotions.

e|mo|tion|al|ist (i mō′shə nə list, -mōsh′nə-), *n.* **1** a person who is easily affected by emotion. **2** a person who appeals to the emotions in attempting to persuade others. **3** a person who bases theories of conduct on the emotions.

e|mo|tion|al|i|ty (i mō′shə nal′ə tē), *n.* emotional quality or state: *Having examined the effects of a barren early upbringing on the dogs' activity, emotionality, and intelligence, we were curious to know how it would shape their social behavior* (Scientific American).

e|mo|tion|al|i|za|tion (i mō′shə nə lə zā′shən, -mōsh′nə-), *n.* the act of emotionalizing or state of being emotional: ... *the oversimplification and emotionalization of issues* (Arthur M. Schlesinger, Jr.).

e|mo|tion|al|ize (i mō′shə nə līz, -mōsh′nə-), *v.t.*, **-ized, -iz|ing.** to make emotional; deal with emotionally.

e|mo|tion|al|ly (i mō′shə nə lē, -mōsh′nə-), *adv.* **1** in an emotional manner. **2** with reference to the emotions: *emotionally mature.*

e|mo|tion|less (i mō′shən lis), *adj.* without emotion; devoid of feeling or passion: *a cold, emotionless attitude.* —**e|mo′tion|less|ness,** *n.*

e|mo|tive (i mō′tiv), *adj.* **1** showing or causing emotion: *She was in an emotive state.* **2** having to do with the emotions: *His cold nature forbade any emotive display.* —**e|mo′tive|ly,** *adv.* —**e|mo′tive|ness,** *n.*

e|mo|tiv|ism (i mō′tə viz əm), *n. Ethics.* the theory that moral statements express only our desires and emotions, and do not convey any knowledge or justify our preferences.

e|mo|tiv|ist (i mō′tə vist), *n.* an advocate of emotivism.

e|mo|tiv|i|ty (ē′mō tiv′ə tē), *n.* emotional quality, capacity, or state.

Emp., **1** emperor. **2** empress.

EMP (no periods), electromagnetic pulse.

em|pale (em pāl′), *v.t.*, **-paled, -pal|ing.** = impale.

em|pa|na|da (em′pə nä′də), *n.* a South American meat pie or turnover. [< American Spanish *empanada* (literally) breaded < Spanish *pan* bread < Latin *pānis*]

em|pan|el (em pan′əl), *v.t.*, **-eled, -el|ing** or (*especially British*) **-elled, -el|ling.** = impanel.

em|paque|tage (äɴ pȧk tȧzh′), *n.* a work of conceptual art consisting of an object wrapped tightly in canvas or other material and tied to form a distinctive bundle or package. [< French *empaquetage* packaging, package]

em|par|a|dise (em par′ə dīs), *v.t.*, **-dised, -dis|ing.** = imparadise.

em|pa|thet|ic (em pə thet′ik), *adj.* of, characterized by, or having empathy: *Alcoholics are ... empathetic to other alcoholics* (Harper's). —**em|pa|thet′i|cal|ly,** *adv.*

em|path|ic (em path′ik), *adj.* of or having to do with empathy.

em|pa|thist (em′pə thist), *n.* a person who maintains rapport with others through empathy.

em|pa|thize (em′pə thīz), *v.i.*, **-thized, -thiz|ing.** to engage in empathy; project into or identify with a person or object: *Kahn recognizes this psychological problem, but he is unable to empathize with his fellow Americans who evade it because they cannot cope with it* (Bulletin of Atomic Scientists).

em|pa|thy (em′pə thē), *n.* the quality or process of entering fully, through imagination, into another's feelings or motives, into the meaning of a work of art, or the like: *I had even carried empathy to the point of putting on weight and approaching the General's sort of pear-shaped silhouette* (New York Times). ... *an art with no conflict between image and perception, an art of complete empathy and at the same time of abstraction* (Atlantic). [< Greek *empátheia* < *en-* in + *páthos* feeling]

em|pen|nage (em pen′ij), *n.* the tail assembly of an aircraft. [< French *empennage* < Old French *empenner* to feather (an arrow) < *en-* on, in (< Latin *in-*) + *penne* feather < Latin *penna*]

em|per|or (em′pər ər), *n.* **1** a man who is the ruler of an empire: *Tiberius was the emperor of Rome during the life of Jesus Christ* (Mary F. Gyles). **SYN:** kaiser, czar. **2** a ruler who has the title of "emperor." Japan has an emperor. [< Old French *empereor* < Latin *imperātor* commander, emperor < *imperāre* command < *in-* in + *parāre* to order, prepare]

emperor fish, a large, oblong, edible fish with spiny fins and vivid coloring, found in the seas around southern Japan.

emperor goose, a bluish-gray goose with white head and tail that lives in coastal areas of Alaska and Siberia.

emperor of Japan, = emperor fish.

emperor penguin, a black-faced penguin of Antarctica, 3 feet tall and weighing about 60 pounds, the largest penguin known.

em|per|or|ship (em′pər ər ship), *n.* the rank, authority, or reign of an emperor.

em|per|y (em′pər ē), *n., pl.* **-per|ies. 1** absolute authority. **2** the territory of an empire. [< Old French *emperie* empire < *emperer* to rule]

em|pha|sis (em′fə sis), *n., pl.* **-ses** (-sēz). **1** special force; stress; importance: *My high school puts much emphasis on studies that prepare its students for college. For Tolman the emphasis is laid more on the organism's control of his environment, while for Hull the emphasis is on the environmental control of the organism* (F. H. George). **2** special force of voice put on particular syllables, words, or phrases: *In reading, our teacher puts emphasis on the most important words. A writer sometimes underlines important words for emphasis.* **SYN:** accent, accentuation. **3** intensity or force of expression or action: *A persuasive person speaks with emphasis.* [< Latin *emphasis* < Greek *émphasis* < *emphaínein* indicate < *en-* in + *phaínein* to show]

em|pha|sise (em′fə sīz), *v.t.*, **-sised, -sis|ing.** *Especially British.* emphasize.

em|pha|size (em′fə sīz), *v.t.*, **-sized, -siz|ing.** **1** to give special force to; make important; stress: *He emphasized her name by repeating it very loudly.* **SYN:** accentuate. **2** to call attention to: *The large number of automobile accidents emphasizes the need for careful driving.*

em|pha|siz|er (em′fə sī′zər), *n.* a person or thing that emphasizes.

em|phat|ic (em fat′ik), *adj.* **1** said or done with force or stress; strongly expressed: *Her answer was an emphatic "No!"* **SYN:** expressive, positive, energetic. **2** speaking with force or stress; expressing oneself strongly: *The emphatic speaker often pounded the table and shouted.* **SYN:** expressive, positive, energetic. **3** attracting attention; very noticeable; striking: *The club made an emphatic success of its party.* **4** *Grammar.* denoting a verbal construction that gives emphasis to the statement of the main verb. *Do come* and *did go* are emphatic forms of *come* and *go.* [< Greek *emphatikós* < *emphaínein;* see etym. under **emphasis**]

em|phat|i|cal|ly (em fat′ə klē), *adv.* in an emphatic manner; to an emphatic degree: *The President spoke emphatically.* **SYN:** unequivocally.

em|phrax|is (em frak′sis), *n.* an obstruction of a canal or duct, as the pores of the skin. [< Greek *émphraxis* obstruction < *emphrássein* to shut up < *en-* in + *phrássein* fence in]

em|phy|se|ma (em′fə sē′mə), *n.* **1** an abnormal enlargement of the air sacs in the lungs or body tissues caused by a loss of elasticity in the walls of the air sacs and a resulting inability to expel carbon dioxide: *Emphysema is a condition in which the lungs overexpand and breathing becomes difficult and less effective* (Science News Letter). **2** = heaves. [< New Latin *emphysema* < Greek *emphysēma* swelling < *emphysân* blow up]

em|phy|sem|a|tous (em′fə sem′ə təs, -sē′mə-), *adj.* **1** having to do with or like emphysema. **2** affected with emphysema.

em|piece|ment (em pēs′mənt), *n.* a piece of ornamental material inserted in a garment as a trimming.

em|pire (em′pīr), *n.* **1** a group of nations or states under one ruler or government, one country having some measure of control over the rest: *The Roman Empire consisted of many separate territories and different peoples.* **2** a country that has an emperor or empress: *the Japanese empire.* **SYN:** realm, domain. **3** absolute power; supreme authority; rule: *Westward the star of empire takes its way* (John Quincy Adams). **SYN:** sovereignty, dominion, sway. **4** *Figurative.* a large business or group of businesses under the control of a single person, family, or syndicate: *a real-estate empire. His empire included fertilizer sales, grain storage, cotton farming, a funeral home, and a newspaper* (Wall Street Journal). [< Old French *empire,* learned borrowing from Latin *imperium* rule, command < *imperāre;* see etym. under **emperor**]

***Empire**

Empire dress

Empire couch

***Em|pire** (em′pīr), *adj.* of or having to do with a style of dress, furniture, art, and decoration, in fashion during the first French Empire (1804-1815), characterized at its height by formal and complex design. An Empire dress or gown had a high waistline, loosely hanging skirt, and short, full sleeves. Empire furniture became large and heavy, with ornate carving, inlay, brass feet, and the like.

empire builder, a person who is committed to bring under his domination or control a group of countries, territories, industries, or other enterprises; a builder of a political or financial empire: *There were Russian empire builders who favored a "forward policy" in Mongolia, but on the whole the home Government was as reluctant to advance into Mongolia as the British were to advance into Tibet* (Manchester Guardian).

empire building, the practices and policies of an empire builder: *Under decentralization J. and J. found that it can spot ability quicker and, conversely, eliminate weak executives, cut down on buck passing,* [*and*] *stop empire building* (Wall Street Journal).

Empire Day, a British holiday in honor of Queen Victoria's birthday, May 24. The name was changed in 1947 to *Commonwealth Day.*

Empire State, a nickname for New York.

Empire State of the South, a nickname for Georgia.

em|pir|ic (em pir′ik), *n., adj.* —*n.* **1** a person who lacks theoretical or scientific knowledge and relies entirely on practical experience: *Like the ancient Egyptians, the Babylonians were often talented empirics* (Scientific American). **2** a person without regular or proper training; quack.
—*adj.* = empirical.
[< Latin *empīricus* < Greek *empeirikós* experienced < *en-* in + *peîra* experience; experiment]

em|pir|i|cal (em pir′ə kəl), *adj.* **1** based on experiment and observation: *Chemistry is largely an empirical science.* **2** based entirely on practical experience, without regard to science or theory: *an empirical knowledge of medicine.* —**em|pir′i|cal|ly,** *adv.*

empirical formula, a chemical formula used to indicate the simplest ratio of the number and kind of atoms in a chemical compound. It does not necessarily indicate the number of atoms in a molecule. *Example:* The empirical formula of acetylene is CH; the molecular formula is C_2H_2.

em|pir|i|cism (em pir′ə siz əm), *n.* **1** the use of methods based on experiment and observation: ... *the great influence exerted upon modern scientific thought by Newtonian physics, by the empiricism of Locke and Bacon, and by the optimistic rationalism of the eighteenth century* (John E. Owen). **2** undue reliance upon experience; unscientific practice; quackery. **3** the philosophical theory that all knowledge is based on experience.

em|pir|i|cist (em pir′ə sist), *n.* **1** a person who uses methods based on experiment and observation; experimenter. **2** a person who relies too much upon mere experience; quack. **3** a person who believes the philosophical doctrine of empiricism.

em|pir|i|cize (em pir′ə sīz), *v.t.*, **-cized, -ciz|ing.** to make empirical: *The measurement of social problems ... is crucial in what might be called the "empiricizing" process, that is, efforts to relate policy aims and actions to empirical conditions* (Richard Rose).

em|pi|rism (em′pə riz əm), *n.* = empiricism.

em|pi|ris|tic (em′pə ris′tik), *adj.* = empirical.

em|place (em plās′), *v.t.*, **-placed, -plac|ing.** to assign to a place or position; fix in or on an emplacement: *Already there are precise plans to erect in Europe some fourteen rocket positions in each of which will be emplaced perhaps fifteen missiles* (Bulletin of Atomic Scientists).

em|place|ment (em plās′mənt), *n.* **1** a space or platform for heavy weapons or equipment. **2** an assigning to a place; a locating.

em|plane (em plān′), *v.*, **-planed, -plan|ing.** —*v.i.* to get on an airplane: *He and a group of other travelers waiting to emplane looked out over the Paris airfield and saw a pillar of smoke* (Reporter).
—*v.t.* to put on an airplane. Also, **enplane.**

em|plas|tic (em plas′tik), *adj., n.* —*adj.* adhesive; fit to be applied as a plaster.
—*n.* an adhesive or glutinous substance.

em|plec|tite (em plek′tīt), *n.* a mineral consisting of sulfur, bismuth, and copper, occurring in thin

Pronunciation Key: hat, āge, cãre, fär; let, ēqual, tėrm; it, īce; hot, ōpen, ôrder; oil, out; cup, pu̇t, rüle; child; long; thin; ᴛʜen; zh, measure; ə represents **a** in about, **e** in taken, **i** in pencil, **o** in lemon, **u** in circus.

prismatic crystals of a grayish or white color and bright metallic luster. [< Greek *émplektos* woven + English *-ite*[1]]

em|ple|o|ma|ni|a (em plē′ə mā′nē ə), *n.* a mania for holding public office. [< Spanish *empleomanía* < *empleo* employ + *manía* mania]

em|ploy (em ploi′), *v., n.* —*v.t.* **1** to give work and pay to; use the services of: *That big factory employs many workers. The hotel employs two cooks.* **2** to use: *You employ a knife, fork, and spoon in eating. She employs her time wisely.* SYN: See syn. under **use**. **3** to keep busy; occupy: *She employed herself in reading. He employed himself in growing roses after he retired.*
—*n.* **1** the condition of being employed; service for pay; employment: *There are many workers in the employ of that big factory.* **2** *Archaic.* use: *to make full employ of a tool.* **3** *Archaic or Poetic.* work or occupation: *to find a good employ.*
[< Middle French *employer,* Old French *empleier* < Latin *implicāre* < *in-* in + *plicāre* fold. See etym. of doublets **implicate, imply.**]
—*Syn. v.t.* **1 Employ, hire** mean to give work and pay to someone. **Employ** suggests a certain regularity and dignity in the services: *The steel mill employs most of the men in town.* **Hire,** the more homely word, suggests temporary employment: *She hired a man to mow the lawn.*

em|ploy|a|bil|i|ty (em ploi′ə bil′ə tē), *n., pl.* **-ties.** fitness or availability for employment.

em|ploy|a|ble (em ploi′ə bəl), *adj., n.* —*adj.* that can be employed: *To produce "employable" graduates, Dunbar insists on promptness and tidiness* (Time).
—*n.* a person who is suitable or available for hiring.

em|ploy|e (em ploi′ē, em′ploi ē′), *n.* = employee.

em|ploy|é (äɴ plwȧ yā′), *n. French.* employee.

em|ploy|ee (em ploi′ē, em′ploi ē′), *n.* a person who works for some person or firm for pay: *This large factory has 800 employees who turn out cars for the public market.* [< French *employé,* (originally) past participle of *employer* to employ]

em|ploy|er (em ploi′ər), *n.* **1** a person or firm that employs one or more persons: *The automobile makers are about the largest employers in the country.* **2** a user.

em|ploy|less (em ploi′lis), *adj.* without employment or occupation: *the long, employless days of dead darkness* (Rudyard Kipling).

em|ploy|ment (em ploi′mənt), *n.* **1** what a person is doing; work; job: *He had no difficulty finding employment. His employment is sorting mail.* SYN: business, trade, profession. See syn. under **occupation**. **2** the act or process of employing: *A large office requires the employment of many people.* **3** the condition of being employed: *She enjoyed most her employment as baby sitter.* **4** use: *The painter was clever in his employment of brushes and colors.*

employment agency or **bureau,** an office or agency that helps a worker to find work or an employer to find a worker by bringing the two into contact.

em|pock|et (em pok′it), *v.t.* to put into one's pocket.

em|po|di|um (em pō′dē əm), *n., pl.* **-di|a** (-dē ə). a clawlike organ found between the true claws of many insects. [< New Latin *empodium* < Greek *en-* in + *poús, podós* foot]

em|poi|son (em poi′zən), *v.t. Archaic.* to poison; taint; embitter.

em|pol|der (em pōl′dər), *v.t.* to reclaim (a piece of land) from the sea or other body of water; bring under cultivation by building a dike, etc., for protection. [< *em-*[1] + *polder* a tract of low land]

em|po|ri|um (em pôr′ē əm, -pōr′-), *n., pl.* **-po|ri-ums, -po|ri|a** (-pôr′ē ə, -pōr′-). **1** a center of trade; market place. SYN: mart. **2** a large store selling many different things. **3** any large business: *a theatrical emporium, drive-in emporiums.* [< Latin *emporium* < Greek *empórion* < *émporos* merchant, traveler < *en-* on + *póros* voyage, ultimately < *peirein* to pass (through)]

em|pov|er|ish (em pov′ər ish, -pov′rish), *v.t.* = impoverish.

em|pow|er (em pou′ər), *v.t.* **1** to give power or authority to: *The secretary was empowered to sign certain contracts.* [*The Governor*] *said the incident might prompt him to sign a bill empowering him to close down schools where integration violence occurs* (Wall Street Journal). SYN: authorize, commission, license. **2** to enable; permit: *Man's erect position empowers him to use his hands freely.* Also, **impower.**

em|pow|er|ment (em pou′ər mənt), *n.* **1** the act of empowering or state of being empowered. **2** a taking or assuming of power, often political power; empowering: *As Housing Secretary, Jack Kemp is attempting to make "empowerment" of the poor more than a slogan by training public-housing tenants to manage and even own their projects* (Time).

em|pre|sa|ri|o (em′prə sä′rē ō), *n., pl.* **-ri|os.** one of a group of Americans who contracted with the Spanish or Mexican governments to found a colony in Texas before Texas became a republic. [< Spanish *empresario* manager, contractor < Italian *impresario;* see etym. under **impresario**]

em|press (em′pris), *n.* **1** the wife of an emperor: *Josephine was empress of France while her husband Napoleon was emperor.* **2** a woman who is the ruler of an empire: *Catherine the Great was empress of Russia in her own right and ruled with no emperor.* **3** a woman having supreme power. [< Old French *emperesse,* feminine of *emperere,* later *empereor;* see etym. under **emperor**]

empress cloth, a woolen fabric for women's dresses, having a finely repped or corded surface.

em|pres|sé (äɴ pre sā′), *adj. French.* eager; earnestly attentive or polite.

em|presse|ment (äɴ pres mäɴ′), *n. French.* cordiality; friendly eagerness.

em|prise or **em|prize** (em prīz′), *n. Archaic.* **1** an adventure; a daring undertaking. **2** knightly daring. [< Old French *emprise,* (originally) feminine past participle of *emprendre* undertake < *en-* in (< Latin *in-*) + *prendre* take < Latin *prehendere*]

Emp|so|ni|an (emp sō′nē ən), *adj.* of or having to do with the works, ideas, or style of William Empson, born 1906, an English poet and critic.

Emp|son|ic (emp son′ic), *adj.* = Empsonian.

emp|ti|er (emp′tē ər), *n., adj.* —*n.* a person or thing that empties.
—*adj.* comparative of **empty.**

emp|ti|ly (emp′tə lē), *adv.* in an empty manner.

emp|ti|ness (emp′tē nis), *n.* the condition of being empty; lack of contents.

emp|tor (emp′tôr), *n. Law.* a buyer. [< Latin *ēmptor* < *ĕmere* to buy]

emp|ty (emp′tē), *adj.,* **-ti|er, -ti|est,** *v.,* **-tied, -ty-ing,** *n., pl.* **-ties.** —*adj.* **1** with nothing or no one in it: *The birds had gone and their nest was left empty.* **2** vacant; unoccupied: *an empty room or house.* **3** having no cargo; unloaded: *an empty ship.* **4** *Figurative.* not real; without meaning: *An empty promise is one that you do not plan to keep. An empty threat has no force behind it.* SYN: hollow, unsubstantial, meaningless. **5** *Figurative.* lacking knowledge or sense; foolish; frivolous: *The empty coxcomb has no regard to anything . . . sacred* (Sir Richard Steele). **6** *Informal, Figurative.* hungry: *I found myself empty* (Daniel Defoe).
—*v.t.* to pour out or take out all that is in (a thing); make empty: *He emptied his glass quickly. He emptied the tobacco out of his pipe.* SYN: unload, unburden, evacuate. —*v.i.* **1** to become empty: *The hall emptied as soon as the concert was over.* **2** to flow out; discharge: *The Mississippi River empties into the Gulf of Mexico.*
—*n. Informal.* something that is empty, such as an empty container, freight car, or bottle: *The company makes its own cans and keeps 165,000 shiny empties in a 'jumble bin'* (New Yorker).
empty of, having no; devoid of: *Tired of wishes, Empty of dreams* (Carl Sandburg).
[Old English *ǣmettig* < *ǣmetta* leisure]
—*Syn. adj.* **1 Empty, vacant, blank** mean containing or occupied by nothing or no one. **Empty** means with nothing or with no one in it: *The house was empty when the fire broke out* (the occupants were out *or* nothing was in it). **Vacant** means unoccupied or not occupied by the proper person or thing: *The house was vacant* (nobody lived there). *The children play baseball on the vacant lot.* A position or office becomes *vacant,* not empty: *The position of school principal is vacant just now.* **Blank** applies to a surface with nothing on it or with empty or vacant spaces: *My window faces a blank wall.*

empty calorie, a calorie of food without any nutrient in it: *As a response to attacks on snack foods as "empty calories," the present trend is to enrich them with supplemental nutrients* (Scientific American).

empty field myopia, a temporary nearsightedness experienced by pilots flying at high altitudes, caused by absence of any well-defined distant object upon which the eye can focus.

emp|ty-hand|ed (emp′tē han′did), *adj.* having nothing in the hands; bringing or taking nothing, especially nothing of value, such as money or a present.

emp|ty-head|ed (emp′tē hed′id), *adj.* silly; stupid. SYN: witless.

emp|ty|ing (emp′tē ing), *n.* **1** the act of a person or thing that empties. **2** something emptied out.
emptyings, *U.S. Informal.* yeast prepared from the lees of beer, etc.

empty nester, a person whose children have grown up and left home.

empty nest syndrome, a form of depression supposedly common among women whose children have grown up and left home.

***empty set,** *Mathematics.* a set that has no members; null set. The set of natural numbers less than 0 is an empty set.

***empty set**

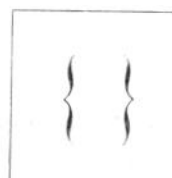

the set of all square triangles = ∅ or { }

emp|ty|sis (emp′tə sis), *n.* a spitting of blood from the lungs. [< Greek *émptysis* < *emptýein* to spit into]

em|pur|ple (em pėr′pəl), *v.t.,* **-pled, -pling.** to tinge or color with purple.

em|pur|pled (em pėr′pəld), *adj.* made purple; colored with purple.

Em|pu|sa (em pyü′sə, -zə), *n. Greek Legend.* a cannibal monster sent in various shapes by Hecate to frighten travelers.

em|py|e|ma (em′pē ē′mə, -pī-), *n., pl.* **-e|ma|ta** (-ē′mə tə, -em′ə-). *Medicine.* a collection of pus in a body cavity, especially in the lung cavity, resulting from infection of the lungs, as in pneumonia. [< New Latin *empyema* < Greek *empýēma* an abscess < *empyeîn* to suppurate < *en-* in, on + *pýon* pus]

em|py|e|mic (em′pē ē′mik, -pī-; -em′ik), *adj.* **1** having to do with or like empyema. **2** affected with empyema.

em|pyr|e|al (em pir′ē əl, em′pə rē′-), *adj., n.* —*adj.* **1** of the empyrean; celestial; heavenly; pure. **2** sublime; elevated. **3** formed of pure fire or light.
—*n.* the empyrean; region of celestial purity.
[< Late Latin *empyrius* (< Greek *empýrios* < *empýros* in or by fire < *en-* in + *pyr, pyrós* fire) + English *-al*[1]]

em|py|re|an (em′pə rē′ən), *n., adj.* —*n.* **1** the highest heaven, where the pure element of fire was once supposed to exist: . . . *this color is such an indescribably deep blue that one faintly grasps the medieval concept of the empyrean* (Hardy and Perrin). **2** the visible heavens; the sky; firmament; vault of the heavens: *the blue empyrean.* **3** the abode of God and the angels.
—*adj.* = empyreal.
[< Late Latin *empyrius* (see etym. under **empyreal**) + English *-an*]

em|py|reu|ma (em′pə rü′mə), *n.* the disagreeable smell or taste of organic substances burned in closed containers. [< Greek *empýreuma* a live coal covered with ashes < *empyreýein* ignite]

em|py|reu|mat|ic (em′pə rü mat′ik), *adj.* like empyreuma; smelling or tasting disagreeably.

EMS (no periods), European Monetary System.

e|mu (ē′myü), *n.* a large, three-toed Australian bird like an ostrich but smaller. Emus cannot fly, but they can run very fast. Also, **emeu.** [apparently < Portuguese *ema* crane, ostrich]

e.m.u. or **EMU** (no periods), electromagnetic unit or units.

emu apple, **1** an Australian tree of the mahogany family that has a sour, edible fruit. **2** the fruit.

emu bush, either of two Australian shrubs or small trees of the soapberry family, whose leaves are eaten by sheep for food when grass and other herbage are killed by drought and heat.

em|u|la|ble (em′yə lə bəl), *adj.* that can be emulated; worthy of emulation.

em|u|lant (em′yə lənt), *n.* a person who emulates; rival.

em|u|late (em′yə lāt), *v.,* **-lat|ed, -lat|ing,** *adj.* —*v.t.* **1** to try to equal or excell: *The ambitious young man emulated his father's ability to make friends easily. The proverb tells us to emulate the industry of the ant. After reading the life of Pitt, who became Prime Minister at 24, he* [*Randolph Churchill*] *frankly aspired to emulate him* (C. L. Sulzberger). **2** to rival with some success; vie with: *Thine eye would emulate the diamond* (Shakespeare).
—*adj. Obsolete.* ambitious; emulous.
[< Latin *aemulārī* (with English *-ate*[1]) < *aemulus* striving to equal]

em|u|la|tion (em′yə lā′shən), *n.* **1** imitation in order to equal or excel; desire to equal or excel: *Emulation of the lives of great men influences many ambitious young men.* **2** *Obsolete.* jealous rivalry; envy.

em|u|la|tive (em′yə lā′tiv), *adj.* **1** tending to emulate. **2** of or caused by emulation. —**em′u|la′-tive|ly,** *adv.*

em|u|la|tor (em′yə lā′tər), *n.* a person who emulates.

em|u|la|to|ry (em′yə lə tôr′ē, -tōr′-), *adj.* having to do with or like emulation.

e|mul|gent (i mul′jənt), *adj., n.* —*adj. Anatomy.* draining out, as a renal artery or vein.
—*n.* **1** *Anatomy.* an emulgent vessel. **2** *Phar-*

macy. a medicine or agent that stimulates the flow of bile.
[< Latin *ēmulgēns, -entis,* present participle of *ēmulgēre;* see etym. under **emulsion**]

em|u|lous (em′yə ləs), *adj.* **1** wishing to equal or excel: *Members of the team were emulous of the deeds of former athletes.* **2** *Obsolete.* jealous; envious. [< Latin *aemulus* (with English *-ous*)]
—em′u|lous|ly, *adv.* **—em′u|lous|ness,** *n.*

e|mul|si|fi|a|ble (i mul′sə fī′ə bəl), *adj.* that can be emulsified.

e|mul|si|fi|ca|tion (i mul′sə fə kā′shən), *n.* the act of emulsifying or process of being emulsified.

e|mul|si|fi|er (i mul′sə fī′ər), *n.* an agent or substance that emulsifies.

e|mul|si|fy (i mul′sə fī), *v.t.,* **-fied, -fy|ing.** to make or turn (an oil, fat, resin, or other substance) into an emulsion: *Juice from the pancreas emulsifies fat in the digestion of food.*

e|mul|sin (i mul′sin), *n.* an enzyme, found in the seeds of the almond and in the bark and leaves of certain plants of the rose family, capable of splitting glucosides.

e|mul|sion (i mul′shən), *n.* **1** a mixture of liquids that do not dissolve in each other; colloidal mixture. In an emulsion, one of the liquids contains minute drops of the other evenly distributed throughout. **2** *Pharmacy.* a milky liquid containing very fine drops of fat or oil. Cod-liver oil is made into an emulsion to improve its taste. **3** *Photography.* a coating on a camera film, plate, or photographic paper that is sensitive to light. [< New Latin *emulsio, -onis* < Latin *ēmulgēre* milk out < *ex-* out + *mulgēre* milk]

e|mul|sion|ize (i mul′shə nīz), *v.t.,* **-ized, -iz|ing.** = emulsify.

e|mul|sive (i mul′siv), *adj.* **1** like an emulsion. **2** yielding an emulsion.

e|mul|soid (i mul′soid), *n.* a colloid in which a solid exhibits strong affinity for the liquid in which it is dispersed. [< *emuls*(ion) + *-oid*]

e|munc|to|ry (i mungk′tər ē), *adj., n., pl.* **-ries.**
—*adj.* = excretory.
—*n.* a part or organ of the body, such as a kidney or the skin, that carries off waste products.
[< New Latin *emunctorius* cleansing, excretory < Latin *ēmungere* blow the nose, related to *mūcus* mucus]

emu wren, a small Australian bird whose tail feathers resemble those of the emu.

em|yd (em′id), *n.* any one of a group of chelonians consisting of the freshwater turtles, the freshwater tortoises, and the terrapins. [< Greek *emýs, -ýdos* freshwater tortoise]

e|myd|i|an (i mid′ē ən), *adj.* of or having to do with the emyds.

en (en), *n.* **1** the letter *N, n.* **2** *Printing.* half the width of an em.

en-[1], *prefix.* **1** to cause to be; make, as in *enable, enfeeble.*
2 to put in; put on, as in *encircle, enthrone.*
3 other meanings, as in *enact, encourage, entwine. En-* changes the meaning of a verb little or not at all except to make it more emphatic. Also, **em-** before *b, p,* and sometimes *m.*
[< Old French *en-* < Latin *in-* into, in, related to *in* in]
▶**en-, in-.** In several common words, usage is divided, though usually one form is more common. Americans at one time tended to use *in-* more, but emergence of *encrust, encase, enfold,* and others as preferred spellings in American publications shows a shift from this traditional usage.

en-[2], *prefix.* in; on, as in *energy.* Also, **em-** before *b, m, p, ph.* [< Greek *en-,* related to *en* in, into]

-en[1], *suffix forming verbs from adjectives and nouns.* **1** to cause to be; make, as in *blacken, sharpen.*
2 to cause to have, as in *heighten, strengthen.*
3 to become, as in *sicken, soften.*
4 to come to have; gain, as in *lengthen.*
[Old English *-nian*]

-en[2], *suffix added to nouns to form adjectives.* made of; having the look of, as in *woolen, silken, wooden, ashen.* [Old English *-en*]

-en[3], *suffix. -en* (or *-n*) is the ending of the past participles of many strong verbs, as in *fallen, shaken, written, sworn.* [Old English *-en*]

-en[4], a suffix used to form the plural of a few nouns, as in *children, oxen.* [Old English *-an*]

en|a|ble (en ā′bəl), *v.t.,* **-bled, -bling. 1** to make able; give ability, power, or means to: *Airplanes enable people to travel great distances rapidly.* SYN: empower, permit, authorize. **2** *Obsolete.* to make possible or easy.

en|a|bling act or **statute** (en ā′bling), **1** an act or statute enabling a person or corporation to do something that would otherwise be illegal: *The enabling act gives the Authority power to issue $30,000,000 of its own bonds to finance the sports center project* (New York Times). **2** an act of Congress authorizing the people of a territory to prepare a constitution and take the other steps leading to statehood.

en|act (en akt′), *v.t.* **1** to make into a law: *Congress enacted a bill to restrict the sale of guns.* **2** to decree; order. **3** to play the part of; act out; play: *He enacted the part of Long John Silver very well.*

en|act|a|ble (en ak′tə bəl), *adj.* that can be enacted.

en|ac|tion (en ak′shən), *n.* = enactment.

en|ac|tive (en ak′tiv), *adj.* of or having to do with the enactment of a law; enacting.

en|act|ment (en akt′mənt), *n.* **1** the action of enacting. **2** the state of being enacted: *The senator responsible for the enactment of the bill was asked to explain it.* **3** a law or a single provision of a law.

en|ac|tor (en ak′tər), *n.* a person who enacts.

en|ac|to|ry (en ak′tər ē), *adj.* = enactive.

en|al|la|ge (en al′ə jē), *n.* the substitution of one grammatical form for another, as the singular for the plural. [< Latin *enallagē* < Greek *enallagē* a change]

e|nam|el (i nam′əl), *n., v.,* **-eled, -el|ing** or (*especially British*) **-elled, -el|ling.** **—*n.*** **1** a glasslike substance melted and then cooled to make a smooth, hard surface. Different colors of enamel are used to cover or decorate different surfaces, such as metal or pottery. **2** a paint or varnish used to make a smooth, hard, glossy surface when dry: *We put a heavy coat of enamel on the baby's toys to prevent them from chipping.* **3** the smooth, hard, glossy outer layer that covers and protects the crown of a tooth: *The crown is covered with enamel, the hardest substance in the body, and the root is covered with cementum* (Harbaugh and Goodrich). **4** any smooth, hard, shiny coating or surface. **5** a thing or things covered or decorated with enamel; enamelware. **6** a cosmetic formerly applied to skin to make it smooth.
—*v.t.* **1** to cover or decorate with enamel: *We bought a bucket of paint and enameled the woodwork.* **2** to form a hard, glossy surface upon. **3** to adorn with various colors; decorate as if with enamel.
[< Anglo-French *enamayller* < *en-* on (< Latin *in-*) + *amayl,* Old French *esmail* enamel < Germanic (compare Old High German *smelzen* melt, to smelt)] **—e|nam′el|er** or *especially British* **e|nam′el|ler,** *n.* **—e|nam′el|like′,** *adj.*

e|nam|el|ing (i nam′ə ling), *n.* **1** the act or work of a person who enamels. **2** a decoration or coating of enamel. **3** the decorating of articles with enamel, as costume jewelry.

e|nam|el|ist (i nam′ə list), *n.* a person who enamels.

enamel kiln, a kiln in which pottery, glass, or other material are exposed to a low heat, suitable for fixing enamel colors, gold, and similar coatings.

e|nam|el|ling (i nam′ə ling), *n. Especially British.* enameling.

e|nam|el|list (i nam′ə list), *n. Especially British.* enamelist.

enamel organ, the enamel of an embryonic tooth after it has separated from the epithelium of the mouth and forms a cap over the dentin of the tooth.

e|nam|el|ware (i nam′əl wãr′), *n.* **1** pots, pans, serving dishes, and the like, that are made of metal coated with enamel: *Baked enamelware in gay colors and designs were ordered by nearly every visitor at his show booth* (Wall Street Journal). **2** bathroom fixtures, stoves, refrigerators, and other appliances made of metal coated with enamel.

en a|mi (äɴ nȧ mē′), *French.* as a friend.

en|am|or (en am′ər), *v.t.* **1** to arouse to love; cause to fall in love: *Her beauty enamored the prince.* SYN: captivate. **2** to charm; fascinate: *She was enamored by her own mirrored image.* SYN: captivate. [< Old French *enamourer* < *en-* in (< Latin *in-*) + *amour* love < Latin *amor* < *amāre* to love]

en|am|ored (en am′ərd), *adj.* very much in love; very fond; charmed: *The enamored prince gave up his throne to marry the beautiful peasant girl.*
enamored of, in love with; very fond of; charmed by: *He was enamored of the pretty girl. Where that lady lives of whom enamoured was my soul* (Robert Browning).

en|am|or|ment (en am′ər mənt), *n.* the state of being enamored.

en|am|our (en am′ər), *v.t. Especially British.* enamor.

en|an|ti|o|blas|tic (en an′tē ə blas′tik), *adj. Botany.* having the radicle turned away from the micropyle. [< Greek *enantíos* opposite + *blastós* sprout + English *-ic*]

en|an|ti|o|mer (en an′tē ə mər), *n.* = enantiomorph.

en|an|ti|o|mer|ic (en an′tē ō mer′ik), *adj.* = enantiomorphic.

en|an|ti|o|morph (en an′tē ə môrf), *n.* either of a pair of crystals, molecules, or compounds related to each other in the way that an object is related to its mirror image. [< Greek *enantíos* opposite + *morphḗ* form]

en|an|ti|o|mor|phic (en an′tē ə môr′fik), *adj.* having the nature or characteristic of an enantiomorph: *If we . . . imagine our enantiomorphic selves within our mirror image, then we realize that its definition of right and left would be reversed* (Scientific American).

en|an|ti|o|mor|phous (en an′tē ə môr′fəs), *adj.* = enantiomorphic.

en|an|ti|op|a|thy (en an′tē op′ə thē), *n.* allopathy; the treatment of disease by inducing an opposite condition.

en|an|ti|o|sis (en an′tē ō′sis), *n.* a figure of speech in which the opposite of what is meant is said; irony.

en|an|ti|o|trop|ic (en an′tē ə trop′ik), *adj.* (of different forms of the same substance) that can be transformed from one into the other in either direction. [< Greek *enantíos* opposite + *-tropos* a turning + English *-ic*]

en|arch (ā närk′), *n.* = enarchist.

en|ar|chist (ā när′kist), *n.* a high-ranking French civil service administrator selected from the top graduates of the National School of Administration. [< French *énarquiste* < *ENA,* École Nationale d'Administration + *-arque* leader + *-iste* -ist]

en|ar|gite (en är′jīt), *n.* a grayish-black copper ore, composed of sulfur, copper, arsenic, and sometimes antimony. [< Greek *enargḗs* clear + English *-ite*[1] (because its cleavage is apparent)]

en ar|rière (äɴ nȧ ryer′), *French.* in the rear; to the rear.

en|ar|thro|sis (en′är thrō′sis), *n. Anatomy.* a ball-and-socket joint. [< Greek *enárthrōsis* < *énarthros* jointed in < *en-* in + *árthron* a joint]

e|nate (ē′nāt), *adj., n.* **—*adj.*** related through the mother; maternally cognate.
—*n.* a relative on the mother's side.
[< Latin *ēnātus,* past participle of *ēnāscī* be born < *ex-* out + *nāscī* be born]

en at|ten|dant (äɴ nȧ täɴ däɴ′), *French.* **1** while waiting. **2** in the meantime.

en a|vant (äɴ nȧ väɴ′), *French.* forward.

en ba|di|nant (äɴ bȧ dē näɴ′), *French.* in jest; in sport.

en banc (äɴ bäɴk′), *French.* in full session with all the judges of the court on the bench; in banc.

en bloc (en blok′, än), all together; in one lump: *Music is at a great disadvantage when singing has to be taught en bloc* (Punch). *He would often sell off books in foreign languages acquired in en bloc purchases* (Atlantic).
[< French *en bloc*]

en bro|chette (äɴ brô shet′), *French.* cooked and served on a small spit or skewer.

en brosse (äɴ brôs′), *French.* cut short, so as to stand up like the bristles of a brush: *He had a handsome head of hair en brosse* (Atlantic).

enc., enclosure.

en ca|bo|chon (äɴ kȧ bô shôɴ′), *French.* **1** in the cabochon style: *a gem cut en cabochon.* **2** in rounded, convex form, without facets: *an emerald en cabochon.*

en ca|chette (äɴ kȧ shet′), *French.* in hiding; in secret; secretly.

en|cae|ni|a (en sē′nē ə), *n.pl.* ceremonies in honor of the founding of a city or the consecration of a church. [< Latin *encaenia* < Greek *enkaíniā* < *en-* in + *kainós* new]

En|cae|ni|a (en sē′nē ə), *n.pl.* ceremonies held each June at Oxford University in honor of its founders and benefactors. [< *encaenia*]

en|cage (en kāj′), *v.t.,* **-caged, -cag|ing.** to confine in or as if in a cage.

en|camp (en kamp′), *v.i.* **1** to make camp; settle in tents: *It took the soldiers only an hour to encamp.* SYN: camp. **2** to live in a camp for a time: *They encamped all night.* **—*v.t.*** to put in a camp: *They were encamped in tents.*

en|camp|ment (en kamp′mənt), *n.* **1** an encamping or a being encamped; forming a camp. **2** the place where a camp is; camp.

en|cap|si|date (en kap′sə dāt), *v.t.,* **-dat|ed, -dat|ing.** to enclose in the protein coat of a virus particle: *Once assembly begins the virion RNA will be sequestered . . . But since neither (-) strands nor coat protein mRNA are encapsidated . . . the production of virions can continue* (Nature). **—en|cap′si|da′tion,** *n.*

en|cap|su|lant (en kap′sə lənt), *n.* something

Pronunciation Key: hat, **ā**ge, c**ã**re, f**ä**r; let, **ē**qual, t**ė**rm; it, **ī**ce; hot, **ō**pen, **ô**rder; **oi**l, **ou**t; cup, p**u̇**t, r**ü**le; **ch**ild; lo**ng**; **th**in; **ŧh**en; **zh**, measure;
ə represents **a** in about, **e** in taken, **i** in pencil, **o** in lemon, **u** in circus.

that encapsulates, especially a substance used for encapsulating drugs: *a polymeric encapsulant.*

en|cap|su|late (en kap′sə lāt), *v.*, **-lat|ed, -lat|ing.** —*v.t.* **1** to enclose in a capsule: *The bacteria were encapsulated.* **2** to encase in a protective covering: *Unstable drugs can be encapsulated to protect them from air and moisture.*
—*v.i.* to become enclosed in a capsule: *Later these eggs will hatch; the larvae will burrow beneath the skin and then migrate to the back where they will encapsulate and grow to maturity* (Harper's).

en|cap|su|la|tion (en kap′sə lā′shən), *n.* the act or process of encapsulating: *By using silicon diodes, the latest insulating materials, and the technique of encapsulation in resin, an experimental cascade generator that provides 100 micro-amp. at 100 kv has been made* (New Scientist).

en|cap|sule (en kap′səl, -sül), *v.t., v.i.*, **-suled, -sul|ing.** = encapsulate.

en|car|nal|ize (en kär′nə līz), *v.t.*, **-ized, -iz|ing. 1** to give a fleshly form to. **2** to make carnal or sensual.

en|car|pi|um (en kär′pē əm), *n., pl.* **-pi|a** (-pē ə). = sporophore.

en|car|pus (en kär′pəs), *n., pl.* **-pi** (-pī). *Architecture.* a sculptured ornament in imitation of a festoon of fruits, leaves, flowers, or other objects, suspended between two points. [< Greek *énkarpos* containing fruit]

en|case (en kās′), *v.t.*, **-cased, -cas|ing. 1** to put into a case. **2** to cover completely; enclose: *Armor encased the knight's body.* Also, **incase.**

en|case|ment (en kās′mənt), *n.* **1** the act or process of encasing. **2** the state of being encased. **3** a thing that encases. **4** *Biology.* a former theory of reproduction according to which successive generations are produced by the successive development of innumerable germs encased one within another. Also, **incasement.**

en|cash (en kash′), *v.t. Especially British.* **1** to convert (checks, stocks, or other holdings) into cash: *Deposits can always be encashed at their full face value at agreed periods of notice of six months or less* (Economist). **2** to obtain (a sum) in the form of cash.

en|cash|a|ble (en kash′ə bəl), *adj. Especially British.* convertible into cash.

en|cash|ment (en kash′mənt), *n. Especially British.* conversion into cash: *Stick to banks rather than hotels ... for the best deal in encashment, they advised, and change larger rather than smaller amounts* (Spectator).

en casse|role (äɴ kȧs rôl′), *French.* cooked and served in a casserole.

en|cast|age (en kas′tij, -käs′-), *n.* the arrangement in a pottery or porcelain kiln of the pieces to be fired.

en|caus|tic (en kôs′tik), *n., adj.* —*n.* **1** the method or art of burning in colors, especially in painting and decorating, by mixing the colors with wax and then applying heat. **2** a painting or decorative object produced by this method.
—*adj.* prepared by heat; burnt in: *Encaustic tile is decorated with colored clays burnt in by firing.* [< Latin *encausticus* < Greek *enkaustikós* < *enkaíein* < *en-* in + *kaíein* to burn]

en|cave (en kāv′), *v.t.*, **-caved, -cav|ing.** to enclose or hide in or as if in a cave.

-ence, *suffix forming nouns chiefly from verbs.*
1 (*added to verbs*) the act or fact of ——ing: *Abhorrence = the act or fact of abhorring. Dependence = the act or fact of depending.*
2 (*added to adjectives ending in -ent*) the quality or condition of being ____ent: *Prudence = the quality of being prudent. Absence = the state of being absent.*
[< Old French *-ence* < Latin *-entia,* < *-ent-,* present participle stem + *-ia,* a noun suffix]
▶ **-ence** is the noun suffix often corresponding to the adjective suffix *-ent.* See also **-ency.**

en|ceinte[1] (en sānt′; *French* äɴ saɴt′), *adj.* being with child or young; pregnant. [< Old French *enceinte* < Late Latin *incincta* < Latin *in-* not + *cincta* girdled, feminine past participle of *cingere* gird, surround]

en|ceinte[2] (en sānt′; *French* äɴ saɴt′), *n.* **1** an enclosure; the wall around a fortified place. **2** the space enclosed by a wall. [< French *enceinte* < Old French *enceindre* to enclose < Latin *incingere* < *in-* in + *cingere* gird, surround]

En|cel|a|dus (en sel′ə dəs), *n. Greek Mythology.* a hundred-armed giant, son of Tartarus and Gaea. He was believed to lie beneath the volcano of Mt. Etna, in Sicily.

encephal-, *combining form.* the form of **encephalo-** before vowels, as in *encephalic.*

en|ce|phal|ic (en′sə fal′ik), *adj.* **1** of or having to do with the brain. **2** situated in the head or within the cranial cavity.

en|ceph|a|lit|ic (en sef′ə lit′ik), *adj.* **1** having to do with or like encephalitis: *encephalitic symptoms.* **2** having encephalitis.

en|ceph|a|li|ti|des (en sef′ə lī′tə dēz), *n.* plural of **encephalitis.**

en|ceph|a|li|tis (en sef′ə lī′tis), *n., pl.* **-ti|des.** inflammation of the brain caused by injury, infection, poison, or other agent. Sleeping sickness is one kind of encephalitis. [< Greek *enképhalos* the brain (see etym. under **encephalon**) + *-itis* disease]

encephalitis le|thar|gi|ca (lə thär′jə kə), = lethargic encephalitis. [< New Latin *encephalitis lethargica*]

en|ceph|a|li|to|gen (en sef′ə lī′tə jən), *n.* a virus or other agent that causes or tends to cause encephalitis.

en|ceph|a|li|to|gen|ic (en sef′ə lī′tə jen′ik), *adj.* that causes or tends to cause encephalitis: *an encephalitogenic protein, encephalitogenic activity.*

encephalo-, *combining form.* the brain: *Encephalomalacia = a softening of the brain.* Also, **encephal-** before vowels. [< Greek *enképhalos* brain]

en|ceph|a|lo|cele (en sef′ə lə sēl), *n.* protrusion of a portion of the brain through the cranium; a hernia of the brain. [< *encephalo-* + Greek *kḗlē* tumor]

en|ceph|a|lo|gram (en sef′ə lə gram), *n.* an X-ray photograph of the brain, after the cerebrospinal fluid has been drained off and replaced especially by air.

en|ceph|a|lo|graph (en sef′ə lə graf, -gräf), *n.* **1** = encephalogram. **2** = electroencephalograph.

en|ceph|a|lo|graph|ic (en sef′ə lə graf′ik), *adj.* of or having to do with encephalography.

en|ceph|a|log|ra|phy (en sef′ə log′rə fē), *n.* the science or technique of making encephalograms.

en|ceph|a|loid (en sef′ə loid), *adj.* resembling brain matter: *Encephaloid cancer is a soft, rapidly growing, malignant form of cancer, in which the diseased tissues resemble the cells of the brain.* [< *encephal-* + *-oid*]

en|ceph|a|lo|lith (en sef′ə lə lith), *n.* a concretion in the brain. [< *encephalo-* + Greek *líthos* stone]

en|ceph|a|lol|o|gy (en sef′ə lol′ə jē), *n.* **1** a description of the brain. **2** the science of the brain. [< *encephalo-* + *-logy*]

en|ceph|a|lo|ma (en sef′ə lō′mə), *n., pl.* **-ma|ta** (-mə tə), **-mas. 1** a brain tumor. **2** a hernia of the brain.

en|ceph|a|lo|ma|la|ci|a (en sef′ə lō mə lā′shē ə), *n.* **1** a condition characterized by softening of the brain. **2** a disease causing lesions of the brain in young poultry, caused by a deficiency of vitamin E in the diet. [< *encephalo-* + Greek *malakía* softness]

en|ceph|a|lo|me|nin|go|cele (en sef′ə lō mə ning′gə sēl), *n.* a protrusion through a fissure in the skull of brain substance with the attached membranes. [< *encephalo-* + *mening*(es) + Greek *kḗlē* tumor]

en|ceph|a|lo|mere (en sef′ə lə mir), *n.* an encephalic segment; one of the series of parts into which the embryonic brain is naturally divisible. [< *encephalo-* + *-mere*]

en|ceph|a|lo|my|e|li|tis (en sef′ə lō mī′ə lī′təs), *n.* inflammation of the tissues of the central nervous system, a disease of people, horses, other domestic animals, and birds: *Epidemiologists object even to a killed vaccine of this kind because it may bring on allergic encephalomyelitis, which is an inflammation of the brain and spinal cord* (New York Times). [< *encephalo-* + Greek *myelós* marrow + English *-itis* inflammation]

en|ceph|a|lo|my|o|car|di|tis (en sef′ə lō mī′ō kär dī′tis), *n.* inflammation of the brain and the heart muscle, a disease of children caused by any one of several viruses related to poliovirus. [< *encephalo-* + *myocard*(ium) + *-itis*] *Abbr:* EMC (no periods).

en|ceph|a|lon (en sef′ə lon), *n., pl.* **-la** (-lə). the brain of a vertebrate. [< New Latin *encephalon* < Greek *enképhalos* < *en-* (with)in + *kephalḗ* head]

en|ceph|a|lop|a|thy (en sef′ə lop′ə thē), *n., pl.* **-thies.** any disease of the brain: *Encephalopathy is commonest in children between 15 and 30 months of age* (Scientific American).

en|ceph|a|lous (en sef′ə ləs), *adj.* having a distinct head, as mollusks do.

en|chafe (en chāf′), *v.t.*, **-chafed, -chaf|ing.** *Archaic.* to heat; irritate; chafe.

en|chain (en chān′), *v.t.* **1** to fasten with a chain; put in chains; fetter; restrain. SYN: shackle. **2** *Figurative.* to attract and fix firmly; hold fast (attention or emotions): *The speaker's earnestness enchained the attention of his audience.* [< Old French *enchainer* < *en-* in (< Latin *in-*) + *chaine* chain]

en|chaîne|ment (äɴ shen mäɴ′), *n. French.* a sequence of ballet steps that form a complete movement.

en|chain|ment (en chān′mənt), *n.* the action of enchaining or state of being enchained.

en|chan|nel (en chan′əl), *v.t.*, **-neled, -nel|ing** or (*especially British*) **-nelled, -nel|ling.** to confine within its proper channel.

en|chant (en chant′, -chänt′), *v.t.* **1** to use magic on; put under a spell; bewitch: *The witch had enchanted the princess so that she slept for a month.* **2** *Figurative.* to delight greatly; charm: *The music enchanted us all. Bid me discourse, I will enchant thine ear* (Shakespeare). SYN: fascinate, captivate, enrapture. **3** to give a magical quality or effect to: *The sorceress enchanted the potion she gave him, so that he fell asleep.* **4** *Obsolete.* to delude; fool. [< Old French *enchanter* < Latin *incantāre* < *in-* against + *cantāre* to chant. See etym. of doublet **incant.**]

en|chant|er (en chan′tər, -chän′-), *n.* a person who enchants; magician.

enchanter's nightshade, any one of a group of low, white-flowered herbs of the evening primrose family, found in shady woods.

en|chant|ing (en chan′ting, -chän′-), *adj.* **1** that puts under a spell; bewitching: *The enchanting words were ended; the spell was complete.* **2** *Figurative.* very delightful; charming: *an enchanting child.* —**en|chant′ing|ly,** *adv.*

en|chant|ment (en chant′mənt, -chänt′-), *n.* **1** the use of magic spells: *In "The Wizard of Oz," Dorothy finds herself at home again by the enchantment of the Good Witch.* **2** the condition of being put under a magic spell. **3** a magic spell or charm: *In the Greek story, Circe turned men into pigs by her enchantments.* **4** *Figurative.* delight; rapture. **5** *Figurative.* something that delights or charms; great delight; charm: *We felt the enchantment of the moonlight on the lake.*

en|chant|ress (en chan′tris, -chän′-), *n.* **1** a woman who practices magic; witch: *Circe was an enchantress who changed Ulysses' men into swine.* SYN: sorceress. **2** *Figurative.* a very delightful, charming woman.

en|chase (en chās′), *v.t.*, **-chased, -chas|ing. 1** to place in a setting; mount; frame. **2** to ornament with engraved or embossed designs; decorate with gems or inlay: *The shield was enchased with gold and silver.* **3** to engrave (figures) on a surface: *His initials were enchased on the back of the watch.* [< Old French *enchasser* < *en-* in (< Latin *in-*) + *chasse* frame, case < Latin *capsa* box]

en|chi|la|da (en′chi lä′də), *n. Southwestern U.S.* a tortilla rolled around a filling of meat, cheese, peppers, etc., served with a peppery sauce: *Some Northerners never learn to like hush-puppies, grits and gravy, or chili and enchiladas* (New York Times). [American English < Mexican Spanish *enchilada,* ultimately < Spanish *en-* in (< Latin *in-*) + Nahuatl *chilli* chili]

en|chi|rid|i|on (en′kī rid′ē ən, -kə-), *n.* handbook or manual. [< Greek *encheirídion* handbook (diminutive) < *en-* in + *cheír* hand]

en|chon|dro|ma (en′kon drō′mə), *n., pl.* **-ma|ta** (-mə tə), **-mas.** a tumor that consists chiefly of cartilage. [< Greek *énchondros* cartilaginous (< *en-* in + *chóndros* cartilage) + English *-oma*]

en|chon|drom|a|tous (en′kon drom′ə təs, -drō′mə-), *adj.* of or having to do with enchondroma.

en|chon|dro|sis (en′kon drō′sis), *n.* an enchondroma rising from cartilage.

en|cho|ri|al (en kôr′ē əl, -kōr′-), *adj.* **1** belonging to or used in a particular country; native; domestic. **2** of or having to do with the demotic writing of the ancient Egyptians. [< Greek *enchṓrios* native (< *en-* in + *chṓrā* country) + English *-al*[1]]

en|chy|le|ma (en′kī lē′mə, -kə-), *n. Biology.* hyaloplasm. [< New Latin *enchylema* < Greek *en-* in + *chȳlós* juice, chyle]

en|chym|a|tous (en kim′ə təs), *adj.* (of glandular epithelial cells) infused; distended by infusion. [< Greek *énchyma* infusion]

en|ci|na (en sē′nə), *n.* the California live oak that has a hard, heavy wood: *They were taken with the live oak—the encinas—which abounds over the California hills, and named a place Encinas* (Alistair Cooke). [< Spanish *encina* < Vulgar Latin *īlicīna* the holm oak < Latin *īlex, īlicis*]

en|ci|nal (en sē′nəl), *adj.* of or having to do with the encina.

en|cinc|ture (en singk′chər), *v.*, **-tured, -tur|ing,** *n.* —*v.t.* to surround with or as if with a belt; encircle; girdle. —*n.* an encircling; enclosure.

en|ci|pher (en sī′fər), *v.t.* to put (a message) into cipher.

en|ci|pher|ment (en sī′fər mənt), *n.* **1** the act of enciphering. **2** the state of being enciphered: *We do not, in fact, know ... when the manuscript was written, or where, or what language lies at the basis of the encipherment* (Richard D. Altick).

en|cir|cle (en sėr′kəl), *v.t.*, **-cled, -cling. 1** to form a circle around; surround: *Trees encircled the pond.* SYN: encompass, gird. **2** to go in a circle around: *The moon encircles the earth.*

en|cir|cle|ment (en sėr′kəl mənt), *n.* **1** an encircling. **2** a being encircled.

En|cke's comet (eng′kəz), a comet of the Jupiter group, visible every 3.3 years. [< Johann *Encke,* 1791-1865, a German astronomer]

encl., enclosure.

en clair (äɴ kler′), *French.* in plaintext; not in code or cipher.

en|clasp (en klasp′, -kläsp′), *v.t.* to hold in or as if in a clasp; clasp tightly; embrace.

en|clave (en′klāv), *n., v.,* **-claved, -clav|ing.** *—n.* **1** a country or district surrounded entirely or in part by territory of another country, or a territory separated from its country by the territory of another country: *West Berlin is an enclave in East Germany.* **2** *Figurative.* **a** any small group existing apart from a larger group surrounding it: *They move in with relatives or friends in the little Italys and other ethnic enclaves in the poorer suburbs* (Arthur Koestler). **b** any small, isolated area: *[He] ... looked out into a spacious studio with a tall thicket of microphones to the left and, directly in front, an enclave containing a music stand, two microphones, and an upright piano* (Nat Hentoff).
— v.t. to enclose (foreign territory) within the territory of a country: *East Germany enclaves West Berlin.*
[< French *enclave* < Old French *enclaver* enclose < Vulgar Latin *inclavāre* < Latin *in-* in + *clavis* key]

en|clave|ment (en klāv′mənt), *n.* **1** the act of enclaving. **2** the condition of being an enclave.

en|cli|sis (eng′klə sis), *n.* pronunciation as an enclitic; attachment of an unstressed word to the previous word.

en|clit|ic (en klit′ik), *n., adj.* *—n.* a word or contraction which, having no stress, is pronounced as part of the preceding word. *Examples:* s in *Bert's here* (=*Bert is here*), *not* in *I cannot tell.*
— adj. pronounced as part of the preceding word.
[< Late Latin *encliticus* < Greek *enklitikós* < *enklínein* lean on < *en-* in, on + *klínein* lean, incline]

en|clit|i|cal|ly (en klit′ə klē), *adv.* in an enclitic manner.

en|clois|ter (en klois′tər), *v.t. Obsolete.* **1** to confine in a cloister. **2** to shut in; confine; immure.

en|close (en klōz′), *v.t.,* **-closed, -clos|ing.** **1** to shut in on all sides; surround: *The little park was enclosed on all sides by tall apartment buildings.* **SYN:** encompass. **2** to put a wall or fence around: *We are going to enclose our back yard to keep dogs out.* **3** to put in an envelope or package along with something else: *He enclosed a check when he mailed his order. Please enclose my card in the box of flowers.* **4** to contain: *a letter enclosing a dollar's worth of stamps.* Also, **inclose.** [< *en-*[1] in + *close,* verb, after Old French *enclos,* past participle of *enclore* to enclose]
▶ See **inclose** for usage note.

en|closed convent (en klōzd′), a convent of nuns who are fully isolated from the outside world, devoting themselves to worship, prayer, and contemplation as a means of attaining salvation for themselves and others.

en|clos|er (en klō′zər), *n.* a person or thing that encloses.

en|clo|sure (en klō′zhər), *n.* **1** an enclosed place: *Those cages are enclosures for the monkeys. A corral is an enclosure for horses.* **2** a thing that encloses. A wall or fence is an enclosure. **3** a thing enclosed: *The envelope contained a letter and $5 as an enclosure.* **4** the act of enclosing: *The enclosure of his resignation in his letter to the president gave him great satisfaction.* Also, **inclosure.**

en|cloud (en kloud′), *v.t.* to envelop in a cloud; becloud.

en|code (en kōd′), *v.t.,* **-cod|ed, -cod|ing.** to put into code: *The spy encoded his message and gave it to a courier for delivery. They encode the information and store it electronically for release on command* (Atlantic).

en|code|ment (en kōd′mənt), *n.* translation into code: *The ordinary way of breaking a cipher is to find an example of the use of this cipher sufficiently long so that the pattern of encodement becomes obvious to the skilled investigator* (Norbert Wiener).

en|cod|er (en kō′dər), *n.* **1** a person or thing that encodes. **2** a device which converts electronically one kind of signal into another. In computers, an encoder is used to convert one of several input signals into several coded outputs.

en coeur (äɴ kœr′), *French.* in the shape of a heart.

en|cof|fin (en kôf′ən, -kof′-), *v.t.* to put or enclose in a coffin.

en|coi|gnure (än′kwä nyůr′), *n.* a piece of furniture, especially of ornamental design, made with an angle to fit into a corner. [< French *encoignure* < *en-* in + *coin* corner]

en|col|pi|on (en kol′pē on), *n., pl.* **-pi|a** (-pē ə). (in the early and medieval church) a small reliquary or a casket containing a miniature copy of the Gospels, worn hanging in front of the breast.

en|col|pi|um (en kol′pē əm), *n., pl.* **-pi|a** (-pē ə). = encolpion.

en|co|mi|ast (en kō′mē ast), *n.* a writer or speaker of encomiums; eulogist. [< Greek *enkomiastês* < *enkômion;* see etym. under **encomium**]

en|co|mi|as|tic (en kō′mē as′tik), *adj.* giving high praise; eulogistic.

en|co|mi|as|ti|cal (en kō′mē as′tə kəl), *adj.* = encomiastic.

en|co|mi|as|ti|cal|ly (en kō′mē as′tə klē), *adv.* in an encomiastic manner.

en|co|mi|um (en kō′mē əm), *n., pl.* **-mi|ums, -mi|a** (-mē ə). an elaborate expression of praise; high praise; eulogy: *Give appreciation to the living rather than encomiums to the dead.* **SYN:** panegyric. [< Latin *encōmium* < Greek *enkômion,* neuter, laudatory < *en-* in + *kômos* revelry]

en|com|pass (en kum′pəs), *v.t.* **1** to go or reach all the way around; encircle: *The atmosphere encompasses the earth. Look how my ring encompasseth thy finger* (Shakespeare). **2** to include; contain: *Our history book encompasses all the important events in American history since 1607. The prince offered a jeweled casket, fit to encompass the rarer jewel it held.* **SYN:** enclose. **3** *Obsolete.* to outwit.

en|com|pass|ment (en kum′pəs mənt), *n.* the act of encompassing. **2** the condition of being encompassed.

en|coop (en küp′), *v.t.* to coop up.

en|core (äng′kôr, -kōr; än′-), *interj., n., v.,* **-cored, -cor|ing.** *— interj.* once more; again: *The audience liked the song so much they shouted, "Encore! Encore!"*
— n. **1** a demand by the audience for the repetition of a song or other performance, or for another appearance of the performer or performers: *There were only two encores in the whole show.* **2** the repetition by the performer in response to such a demand. **3** an extra song or appearance by the performer. **4** another appearance, match, bout, or the like involving the same people, in sports, the arts, or other performance.
— v.t. to call for a repetition of (a song or other performance) or the reappearance of (a performer): *The audience encored the singer.*
[< French *encore* yet; origin uncertain]

en|coun|ter (en koun′tər), *v., n.* *— v.t.* **1** to meet unexpectedly: *What if we should encounter a bear? I encountered an old friend on the train.* **2** to be faced with (difficulties, opposition, etc.): *He encountered many difficulties before the job was done. In "Pilgrim's Progress," the hero, Christian, encounters many hardships in his journey to the Celestial City.* **3** to meet as an enemy; meet in a fight or battle: *He encountered the strange knight in hand-to-hand conflict.* **SYN:** engage.
— v.i. to meet; meet unexpectedly; have an encounter: *We never met before, and never ... may again encounter* (Byron).
— n. **1** an unexpected meeting: *A fortunate encounter brought the two friends together after a long separation. Their first encounter was brief.* **2** a meeting face to face. **3** a meeting of enemies; fight; battle: *The two armies had a desperate encounter.* (*Figurative.*) *Who ever knew Truth put to the worse in a free and open encounter?* (Milton). (*Figurative.*) *This keen encounter of our wits* (Shakespeare). **SYN:** conflict, combat, skirmish. **4** *U.S.* a meeting or session of an encounter group. **5** *Obsolete.* behavior.
[< Old French *encontrer* < Vulgar Latin *incontrāre* < Latin *in-* in + *contrā* against]

encounter group, a group of people, especially people with different backgrounds, who get together to increase their self-awareness, sensitivity to others, and common interests or mutual objectives; T-group: *The encounter group, as it evolved at Esalen, is first of all a vehicle to provide an intense emotional experience* (Time).

en|cour|age (en kėr′ij), *v.t.,* **-aged, -ag|ing.** **1** to give hope, courage, or confidence to; urge on: *The cheers of their schoolmates encouraged the players to try to win the game for the school.* **SYN:** hearten, inspirit. **2** to give help to; be favorable to; support: *High prices for farm products encourage farming.* **SYN:** promote, advance, help. **3** to promote the development of; foster: *Sunlight encourages the growth of green plants.* [< Old French *encoragier* < *en-* in (< Latin *in-*) + *corage* courage]

en|cour|age|ment (en kėr′ij mənt), *n.* **1** the condition of being or feeling encouraged: *The singer drew his encouragement from the audience.* **2** something that gives hope, courage, or confidence: *The faith of his first teacher in his voice was his only encouragement.* **3** an urging on toward success; the act of encouraging: *Such encouragement as she gave was grudging.*

en|cour|ag|er (en kėr′ə jər), *n.* a person or thing that encourages.

en|cour|ag|ing (en kėr′ə jing), *adj.* that encourages; that increases hope or confidence: *an encouraging report.* **— en|cour′ag|ing|ly,** *adv.*

en|crim|son (en krim′zən), *v.t.* to make crimson; redden.

en|cri|nite (en′krə nīt), *n.* a fossil crinoid. Much of the world's marble is composed chiefly of fragments of encrinites. [< New Latin *encrinus* (< Greek *en-* in + *krínon* lily) + English *-ite*[1]]

en|croach (en krōch′), *v.i.* **1** to go beyond proper or usual limits; make gradual inroads on: *The sea encroached upon the shore and covered the beach.* **2** to trespass upon the property or rights of another; intrude: *The invading country encroached upon the territory of its neighbor. A good salesman does not encroach upon his customer's time.* **SYN:** See syn. under **intrude.** [< Old French *encrochier* to seize, fasten upon < *en-* in (< Latin *in-*) + *croc* hook. Compare etym. under **crochet.**] — **en|croach′er,** *n.*

en|croach|ing|ly (en krō′ching lē), *adv.* by encroachment.

en|croach|ment (en krōch′mənt), *n.* **1** an encroaching: *The cliff was being worn away by the encroachments of the sea. The way the utility businesses can prevent any future "encroachment" is by giving good service at low cost themselves* (Estes Kefauver). **SYN:** infringement, trespass. **2** a thing taken by encroaching.

en|crust (en krust′), *v.t.* **1** to cover with a crust or hard coating: *The inside of the kettle is encrusted with lime.* **SYN:** overspread. **2** to form a crust on; form into a crust: *The extremely cold weather during the night had encrusted the snow so that next morning it would bear our weight.* **3** to decorate with a layer of costly material: *The gold crown was encrusted with precious gems.*
— v.i. to form a crust: *The snow iced up and encrusted on the ground.* Also, **incrust.** [variant of *incrust*]

en|crus|ta|tion (en′krus tā′shən), *n.* **1** an encrusting. **2** a being encrusted. **3** a crust or hard coating. **SYN:** scale. **4** a decorative layer of costly material. Also, **incrustation.**

en|crust|ed (en krus′tid), *adj.* **1** forming a crust: *encrusted ice, encrusted enamel.* **2** *Figurative.* **a** hardened; inflexible: *encrusted prejudices. Outmoded restrictions and encrusted rules hobble the organization* (New York Times). **b** crabbed; crusty: *an encrusted old bachelor.* **— en|crust′ed|ly,** *adv.*

en|crypt (en kript′), *v.t.* to put into cipher or code: *to encrypt a secret message.*

en|cryp|tion (en krip′shən), *n.* an encrypting; a putting signals or messages into cipher or code.

en cuer|po (en kwer′pō), *Spanish.* **1** in the body. **2** without cloak, outer garment, or covering.

en|cui|rassed (en′kwi rast′), *adj. Zoology.* furnished with a structure or outer coat like a cuirass, such as is developed by certain infusorians; loricate.

en|cul|tu|rate (en kul′chə rāt), *v.t.,* **-rat|ed, -rat|ing.** to subject to enculturation.

en|cul|tu|ra|tion (en kul′chə rā′shən), *n.* the process by which a person becomes a part of his native culture: *The family is a sounder, more efficient instrument in the enculturation of the young than all our nursery schools, radio and TV, movies and comics rolled into one* (New York Times).

en|cul|tu|ra|tive (en kul′chər ə tiv), *adj.* of or having to do with enculturation: *Yet the enculturative experience is not terminated at the close of infancy* (Melville J. Herskovits).

en|cum|ber (en kum′bər), *v.t.* **1** to hold back (from running, doing, or being); hinder; hamper: *Heavy shoes encumber a runner in a race.* **2** to make difficult to use; fill; block up; obstruct: *Rubbish and old boxes encumbered the fire escape.* **3** to weigh down; burden with weight, difficulties, cares, or debt: *Mother is encumbered with household cares. The farm was encumbered with a heavy mortgage.* **4** *Figurative.* to make complicated; complicate. Also, **incumber.** [< Old French *encombrer* < *en-* in (< Latin *in-*) + *combre* barrier. Compare etym. under **cumber.**]

en|cum|ber|ment (en kum′bər mənt), *n.* the act of encumbering; obstruction; interference.

en|cum|brance (en kum′brəns), *n.* **1** something useless or in the way; hindrance; obstruction; burden: *Shoes would be an encumbrance to a swimmer. She refused to think of her handicap as an encumbrance.* **SYN:** impediment. **2** a dependent person: *The many encumbrances of a large family all living off of his small income, made it difficult to save any money.* **3** *Law.* a claim, mortgage, or other limitation on property:

Pronunciation Key: hat, āge, cãre, fär; let, ēqual, tėrm; it, īce; hot, ōpen, ôrder; oil, out; cup, půt, rüle; child; long; thin; ᴛʜen; zh, measure; ə represents **a** in about, **e** in taken, **i** in pencil, **o** in lemon, **u** in circus.

An encumbrance can limit an owner's use of his property ... [and] require that a piece of land be used only for a church (William Tucker Dean). Also, **incumbrance**.

en|cum|branc|er (en kum′brən sər), *n. Law.* a person who holds an encumbrance.

en|cur|tain (en kėr′tən), *v.t.* to curtain; enclose with curtains.

-ency, *suffix.* **1** (*added to verbs*) the act or fact of ___ing: *Dependency = the act or fact of depending.*
2 (*added to adjectives ending in -ent*) the quality or condition of being ___ent: *Frequency = the condition of being frequent.*
3 other meanings, as in *agency, currency.*
[< Latin *-entia;* see etym. under **-ence**]
▶ See **-ance** for usage note.

ency., encyc., or **encycl.**, encyclopedia.

en|cyc|lic (en sik′lik, -sī′klik), *n., adj.* = encyclical.

en|cyc|li|cal (en sik′lə kəl, -sī′klə-), *n., adj.* —***n.*** a letter from the Pope to his bishops, stating the position of the church on important questions.
—***adj.*** intended for wide circulation; general.
[< Late Latin *encyclicus* (< Greek *enkýklios* encircling < *en-* in + *kýklos* circle) + English *-al*[1]]

en|cy|clo|pe|di|a or **en|cy|clo|pae|di|a** (en sī′klə pē′dē ə), *n.* **1** a book or set of books giving information on all branches of knowledge, or on certain wide fields, with articles arranged alphabetically. **2** a book treating one subject very thoroughly, with its articles arranged alphabetically: *an encyclopedia of art. Abbr:* ency., encyc., or encycl. Also, **cyclopedia**, **cyclopaedia**. [< Late Latin *encyclopaedia* < Greek *enkýklios paideíā* well-rounded education; *enkýklios* (see etym. under **encyclical**); *paideíā* < *paideúein* educate < *país, paidós* child]

en|cy|clo|pe|dic or **en|cy|clo|pae|dic** (en sī′klə pē′dik), *adj.* **1** covering a wide range of subjects; possessing wide and varied information: *an expert with encyclopedic knowledge.* **SYN**: comprehensive. **2** of or having to do with an encyclopedia. Also, **cyclopedic**, **cyclopaedic**.

en|cy|clo|pe|di|cal or **en|cy|clo|pae|di|cal** (en sī′klə pē′də kəl), *adj.* = encyclopedic.

en|cy|clo|pe|di|cal|ly or **en|cy|clo|pae|di|cal|ly** (en sī′klə pē′də klē), *adv.* in an encyclopedic manner; comprehensively.

en|cy|clo|pe|dism or **en|cy|clo|pae|dism** (en sī′klə pē′diz əm), *n.* encyclopedic learning; knowledge presented in an encyclopedic way.

En|cy|clo|pe|dism (en sī′klə pē′diz əm), *n.* the doctrines of the French Encyclopedists.

en|cy|clo|pe|dist or **en|cy|clo|pae|dist** (en sī′klə pē′dist), *n.* a person who makes or compiles an encyclopedia.

En|cy|clo|pe|dist (en sī′klə pē′dist), *n.* one of the writers of the French *Encyclopedia* edited by Denis Diderot and Jean de Roland d'Alembert and published between 1751 and 1780, expressing many radical ideas.

en|cy|clo|pe|dize or **en|cy|clo|pae|dize** (en sī′klə pē′dīz), *v.t.*, **-dized, -diz|ing.** to treat, describe, or arrange as in an encyclopedia, or with encyclopedic fullness, accuracy, and system: *to encyclopedize knowledge.*

en|cyst (en sist′), *v.t., v.i.* to enclose or become enclosed in a cyst or sac.

en|cys|ta|tion (en′sis tā′shən), *n.* = encystment.

en|cyst|ed tumor (en sis′tid), a tumor enclosed in a well-defined membrane.

en|cyst|ment (en sist′mənt), *n.* **1** an enclosing or becoming enclosed in a cyst or sac. **2** the state of being encysted.

end[1] (end), *n., v., adj.* —***n.*** **1** the last part; conclusion: *the end of the year. He read to the end of the book.* **SYN**: termination, close, finish, expiration. **2** the part where a thing begins or where it stops: *Every stick has two ends. Drive to the end of this road. This is the end of the line; everyone must get off. The ends of this rope are frayed.* **3** purpose; what is aimed at in doing a piece of work; object: *He had gained his end. He had this end in mind—to do his work without a mistake. I have considered the happiness of the people as the end of government* (Edward Gibbon). **SYN**: intention, design, goal, aim. **4** result; outcome: *It is hard to tell what the end will be.* **SYN**: issue, consequence. **5** a part left over; fragment; remnant: *The store had a sale on fabric ends. On his table were some ends of verse and of candles* (Jonathan Swift). **SYN**: remainder. **6** death; destruction: *He met his end in the accident. ... a swan-like end, Fading in music* (Shakespeare). **SYN**: extermination, annihilation. **7** a cause of death or destruction. **8a** the player at either end of the line in football. **b** the position of this player. **9** a unit or division in the game of bowls and in curling; inning. **10** the furthest or most distant part of any region; extreme point: *She swore that she would go to the ends of the earth to find her lost child.* **11** a limit; boundary: *There was no end to her patience.*
—***v.t.*** **1** to bring to its last part; finish; stop: *Let us end this fight.* **2** to form the end of; be the end of: *This scene ends the play.* **3** to destroy; kill.
—***v.i.*** **1** to come to an end; finish: *The fight ended in a draw.* **2** to die.
—***adj.*** **1** coming at the end; final; last: *the end result of negotiations. The amateur's end impression is one of mixed astonishment and dismay* (Canadian Forum). **2** *U.S. Slang.* best; finest; most wonderful: *"My head's still in the clouds. I just had the absolutely, most fabulous, end birthday!"* (New Yorker).
at loose ends, a not settled or established: *"Fifteen years ago," she noted, "I was at loose ends—a widow with an ailing and aging mother"* (New York Times). **b** in confusion or disorder: *Things are getting worse and worse every day. We are all at loose ends* (Sylvester Judd).
end up, to wind up; come out: *Wasteful people usually end up in debt. So at retirement age you may end up with little more than Social Security* (Harper's).
get the short end of the stick, *Informal.* to fail to receive a full share; be slighted or overlooked: *Again the Czechs ... get the short end of the stick, simply because the terms of trade are against them* (Atlantic).
go off the deep end, *Slang.* to act suddenly and rashly without deliberation: *Don't go off the deep end and blame an innocent person for the accident just because you're upset.*
in the end, finally; ultimately: *He had some talent but in the end he had to give it [art] up* (Maclean's). *There is some reluctance to shoulder the whole burden of what, in the end, will simply be a useful addition to ... lines of communication* (Manchester Guardian Weekly).
keep (hold) up one's end, to sustain one's part or bear one's share fully in an undertaking or performance: *Our own impression was that the American doctors had held up their end rather better than fairly well* (New York Times).
make an end of, to stop; do no more: *Make an end of your quarreling.*
make (both) ends meet, to spend no more than one has; live within one's income: *The poor man had a hard time making ends meet. Worldly wealth he cared not for, desiring only to make both ends meet* (Thomas Fuller). *The other impecunious person contrived to make both ends meet by shifting his lodgings from time to time* (William Black).
no end, *Informal.* very much; very many: *I enjoyed myself no end at the concert.*
on end, a upright: *Place the log on end. His hair stood on end.* **b** one after another: *It snowed for days on end. Gallery enthusiasts announced that they would establish a world's record by queuing up for days on end in order to get one of the 539 standing-room admissions* (New Yorker).
put an end to, to do away with; stop, destroy, or kill: *In his desperation he threatened to put an end to himself.*
the (very, living) end, *U.S. Slang.* the best or finest; the most: *The very end in femininity is a one-piece bathing suit ... called the Beach Bunny* (Lois Long).
[Old English *ende*]
—***Syn.*** *v.t.* **1** *v.i.* **1 End, conclude, finish** mean to bring or come to a close. **End** merely suggests stopping, whether at an appropriate place or not: *My vacation ended when school started.* **Conclude** suggests a formal closing of a speech, essay, action, piece of business, etc.: *Singing the national anthem will conclude the meeting.* **Finish** suggests ending only after getting everything done that should be done: *He has finished writing the report. ... let us strive on to finish the work we are in* (Abraham Lincoln).

end[2] (end), *v.t. British Dialect.* to put (corn, hay, or other farm produce) into a barn, stack, or silo. [perhaps variant of *inn* to lodge, influenced by *end*[1], verb]

end-all (end′ôl′), *n.* the ultimate end; final touch: *Atomic energy is not the end-all of contemporary science.*

en|dam|age (en dam′ij), *v.t.*, **-aged, -ag|ing.** to damage; harm; injure.

en|dam|asked (en dam′əskt), *adj.* colored with or as with damask.

end|a|me|ba or **end|a|moe|ba** (en′də mē′bə), *n., pl.* **-bas, -bae** (-bē). any one of a genus of amebas or amebalike organisms that are parasitic on other forms of animal life, including the species that causes amebic dysentery. Also, **entameba.** [< New Latin *Endamoeba* the genus name < *endo-* + *amoeba*]

end-and-end (end′ən end′), *adj., n.* —***adj.*** having the warp laid out with alternating white and colored yarns or with any two alternating colors.
—***n.*** an end-and-end fabric: *The opening price of regular weight solids, end-and-ends, and colored woven stripes have been raised to $4.50* (Wall Street Journal).

en|dan|ger (en dān′jər), *v.t.* to cause danger to; expose to loss or injury: *Fire endangered the hotel's guests, but no lives were lost.* **SYN**: imperil.

en|dan|gered (en dān′jərd), *adj.* threatened with extinction: *The black rhino ... is recognized as an endangered mammal and has been placed on the official list of threatened species* (Science Journal).

en|dan|ger|ment (en dān′jər mənt), *n.* **1** the act of endangering. **2** the state of being endangered.

end|a|or|ti|tis (en′dā ôr tī′tis), *n.* inflammation of the lining of the aorta. [< *endo-* + *aorta* + *-itis*]

en|darch (en′därk), *adj. Botany.* having a single protoxylem, or several protoxylems surrounding a central parenchyma. [< Greek *éndon* within + *archē* origin]

end-a|round (end′ə round′), *n. Football.* a running play in which an end takes a hand-off from a back and runs around the opposite end of the line.

end|ar|ter|ec|to|my (en′där tə rek′tə mē), *n., pl.* **-mies.** the surgical removal of a thickened or diseased lining of an artery. [< *endarter*(ium) + *-ectomy*]

end|ar|ter|i|al (en′där tir′ē əl), *adj.* of or having to do with the endarterium.

end|ar|ter|i|tis (en′där tə rī′tis), *n.* inflammation of the lining of an artery. [< *endarterium* + *-itis*]

end|ar|ter|i|um (en′där tir′ē əm), *n., pl.* **-i|a** (-ē ə). *Anatomy.* the lining of an artery. [< New Latin *endarterium* < *endo-* + *arterium* artery]

end-blown (end′blōn′), *adj.* played by blowing through a mouthpiece at one end of a flute.

end body, = alexin.

end|brain (end′brān′), *n.* = telencephalon.

end bulb or **end bud,** a roundish body forming the enlarged ending of a nerve fiber. End bulbs range from simple terminations to very complex sensory organs and are dispersed in the skin, mucous membranes, muscles, etc.

end-con|sum|er (end′kən sü′mər), *n.* the ultimate consumer of a manufactured product. Also, **end-user.**

en|dear (en dir′), *v.t.* **1** to make dear; inspire or create affection for: *Her kindness endeared her to all of us.* **2** *Obsolete.* to win the affection of; attract: *to endear, and hold thee to me firmest* (Milton). **3** *Obsolete.* to make dear or costly.

en|dear|ing|ly (en dir′ing lē), *adv.* in an endearing manner; so as to endear.

en|dear|ment (en dir′mənt), *n.* **1** the fact of endearing or state of being endeared. **2** a thing that endears. **3** an act or word showing love or affection; caress.

en|deav|or (en dev′ər), *v., n.* —***v.i.*** to try hard; make an effort; strive. **SYN**: struggle, labor, essay. See syn. under **try**.
—***v.t.*** to try hard and earnestly; attempt: *A runner endeavors to win a race.*
—***n.*** an earnest attempt; hard try; effort: *With each endeavor she did better.* **SYN**: exertion, struggle. See syn. under **effort**.
[< *en-*[1] + *dever* (< Anglo-French *deveir,* Old French *devoir* duty) < phrase *se mettre en dever* to make it (one's) duty] —**en|deav′or|er,** *n.*

en|deav|our (en dev′ər), *v.i., v.t., n. Especially British.* endeavor.

en|dem|ic (en dem′ik), *adj., n.* —***adj.*** **1** regularly found among a particular people or in a particular locality: *Cholera is endemic in India.* **2** (of plants or animals) indigenous in a certain locality, especially those not found elsewhere: *Each scientist has noted some new species in the rich variety of flora and fauna that are endemic to the Seychelles* (Sunday Times).
—***n.*** **1** an endemic disease: (*Figurative.*) *Snobbishness is an insidious endemic* (Saturday Review). **2** an endemic plant or animal: *... species living in small, unique habitats as relicts or isolated endemics* (Science).
[< Greek *éndēmos* native (< *en-* in + *dêmos* people, district) + English *-ic*]

en|dem|i|cal (en dem′ə kəl), *adj.* = endemic.

en|dem|i|cal|ly (en dem′ə klē), *adv.* in an endemic manner.

en|de|mic|i|ty (en′də mis′ə tē), *n.* endemic character.

en|de|mism (en′də miz əm), *n.* the character or quality of being endemic.

end|er (en′dər), *n.* a person or thing that ends.

en|der|mic (en dėr′mik), *adj.* acting on or through the skin: *an endermic medicine.*

en dés|ha|bil|lé (äN dā zȧ bē yā′), *French.* partly or carelessly dressed: *For such a mythical figure to appear, and, moreover, en déshabillé, was a sensation* (New Yorker).

end-for-end (end′fər end′), *adj., adv.* with the ends reversed: *The spacecraft, turned end-for-end, passed behind the moon* (William J. Cromie).

end|game (end′gām′), *n.* **1a** the last stage of a game. **b** *Figurative:* *The Viet Cong struck at Tet*

. . . and from that point on, the Vietnam War was an endgame (Atlantic). **2** the third and final stage in a chess game, after the forces on both sides have been diminished during the opening and middle stages of the game.

end|gate (end′gāt′), *n. U.S.* the broad, movable board, usually hinged at the bottom, which closes in the rear of a truck or wagon; tailboard.

end-grain (end′grān′), *adj.* (of wood) with the end of the grain turned outward: *a cheeseboard of end-grain teak.*

en Dieu est ma fi|ance (äɴ dyœ′ e mȧ fē-äɴs′), *French.* in God is my trust.

end|ing (en′ding), *n.* **1** the last part; end: *The story has a sad ending.* **SYN:** conclusion, completion, termination. **2** death. **3** a letter or letters added at the end of a word or stem to change its meaning or to indicate its grammatical relationship to other words, such as *ly* in *kingly* or *s* in *kings;* suffix: *The common plural ending is "s" or "es." In Navaho, when it is necessary to indicate plurality, this is expressed by a separate word, not by an ending or* (*as in English mice*) *by a special form of the noun* (Beals and Hoijer).

en|disked (en diskt′), *adj.* recorded on a phonograph disk: *an endisked speech.*

en|dis|tance (en dis′təns), *v.t.,* **-tanced, -tanc|ing.** to make (an audience) feel distant from the action or characters of a play or motion picture, as by having the actors wear masks or continually shift roles: *. . . a deliberate attempt to "endistance" the audience from the subject matter of the film, in a manner to which we may apply . . . the now overused term "Brechtian"* (London Times).

en|dis|tance|ment (en dis′təns mənt), *n.* **1** the act or process of endistancing. **2** the effect produced by endistancing.

en|dite (en′dīt), *n. Zoology.* an appendage on the inner side of the limbs of a branchiopod crustacean. [< Greek *éndon* within + English *-ite*[1]]

end item, a finished item complete in itself, whether a simple piece or made up of many pieces, and ready for its intended use: *The measure* [*would*] *authorize the stockpiling of critical machine tools . . . —tools which need more time to make, in some cases, than the end items they are used to produce* (Wall Street Journal).

en|dive (en′dīv, än′dēv), *n.* **1** a kind of chicory, with broad, smooth leaves, used for salads; escarole. **2** a kind of chicory that has finely divided, curly leaves, used for salads; French endive. **3** a kind of chicory whose leaves are blanched to look like very smooth white celery, cooked or used for salads; witloof. [< Old French *endive,* learned borrowing from Late Latin *endivia,* ultimately < Greek *éntybon*]

end|less (end′lis), *adj.* **1** having no end; never stopping; lasting or going on forever: *the endless rotation of the earth around the sun. Depart upon thy endless cruise, old Sailor* (Walt Whitman). **SYN:** boundless, limitless, measureless, interminable, incessant, unceasing, continual, perpetual, everlasting. **2** seeming to have no end: *an endless scolding. Doing housework is an endless task.* **3** joined in a circle without ends; with the ends joined for continuous action: *The chain that turns the rear wheel of a bicycle is an endless chain.* **SYN:** continuous. **—end′less|ly,** *adv.* **—end′less|ness,** *n.*

endless screw, a screw whose threads engage the teeth of a gear and turn it.

end line, 1 *Basketball.* a line at each end of the court, at right angles to the sidelines. **2** *Football.* the boundary at each end of the playing field, ten yards behind the goal line. **3** *Tennis.* = base line.

end|long (end′lông′, -long′), *adv.* from end to end; lengthwise; on end. [perhaps re-formation of Old English *andlong;* or perhaps < Scandinavian (compare Old Icelandic *endelangr* from end to end)]

end man, 1 the man at either end of the line in a minstrel show who carries on a comic conversation with the interlocutor. **2** the man at an end of a line or row.

end moraine, = terminal moraine.

end|most (end′mōst), *adj.* most distant; last; farthest.

endo-, *combining form.* **1** inner: *Endoderm = the inner layer of embryo cells.*
2 within: *Endogamy = marrying within* (*one's tribe*).
3 inside: *Endophyte = a plant growing inside* (*another plant*).
[< Greek *endo-* < *éndon* within]

en|do|bi|ot|ic (en′dō bī ot′ik), *adj.* living as a parasite within the tissue of the host.

en|do|blast (en′dō blast), *n.* any of the blastomeres from which the endoderm develops. [< *endo-* + Greek *blastós* sprout, germ]

en|do|blas|tic (en′dō blas′tik), *adj.* having to do with or consisting of endoblast.

en|do|can|ni|bal|ism (en′dō kan′ə bə liz′əm), *n.* the practice of eating the flesh of persons belonging to the same tribe.

en|do|car|di|ac (en′dō kär′dē ak), *adj.* = endocardial.

en|do|car|di|al (en′dō kär′dē əl), *adj.* **1** in the heart. **2** of or having to do with the endocardium.

en|do|car|dit|ic (en′dō kär dit′ik), *adj.* having to do with endocarditis.

en|do|car|di|tis (en′dō kär dī′tis), *n.* inflammation of the endocardium.

en|do|car|di|um (en′dō kär′dē əm), *n., pl.* **-di|a** (-dē ə). the smooth membrane that lines the cavities of the heart. [< New Latin *endocardium* < Greek *éndon* within + *kardiā* heart]

en|do|carp (en′dō kärp), *n. Botany.* the inner layer of the pericarp of a fruit or ripened ovary of a plant. A peach stone is a hollow endocarp surrounding the seed. See picture under **fruit.** [< *endo-* + Greek *karpós* fruit]

en|do|cen|tric (en′dō sen′trik), *adj. Linguistics.* belonging to the same form class of grammatical construction as one of its immediate constituents. *Example:* The phrase *very fresh milk* is an endocentric construction, since it belongs to the same form class (noun) as the immediate constituent *milk.*

en|do|cor|pus|cu|lar (en′dō kôr pus′kyə lər), *adj.* within a corpuscle.

en|do|cra|ni|al (en′dō krā′nē əl), *adj.* of or belonging to the endocranium.

en|do|cra|ni|um (en′dō krā′nē əm), *n., pl.* **-ni|ums, -ni|a** (-nē ə). the inner surface of the skull, covering the brain; dura mater. [< *endo-* + *cranium*]

en|do|cri|nal (en′dō krī′nəl), *adj.* having to do with or like the endocrine glands.

en|do|crine (en′dō krin, -krīn), *adj., n.* **—*adj.*** of or having to do with the endocrine glands or the hormones they secrete: *In spring, the lengthening hours of light or rising temperature cause endocrine changes in many birds and fishes* (S. A. Barnett).
—*n.* **1** = endocrine gland. **2** its secretion. [< *endo-* + Greek *krínein* to separate]

***endocrine gland,** any one of various glands that produce secretions that pass directly into the bloodstream or lymph instead of into a duct; ductless gland; gland of internal secretion. The thyroid, the thymus, and the pituitary are endocrine glands. They secrete hormones that influence or regulate other organs in the body.

***endocrine gland**

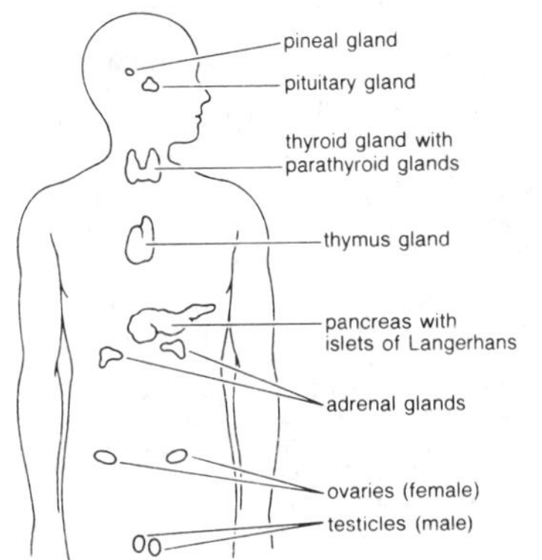

en|do|crin|ic (en′dō krin′ik), *adj.* = endocrinal.

en|do|cri|no|log|ic (en′dō kri′nə loj′ik), *adj.* = endocrinological.

en|do|cri|no|log|i|cal (en′dō kri′nə loj′ə kəl), *adj.* of or having to do with endocrinology.

en|do|cri|nol|o|gist (en′dō kri nol′ə jist, -krī-), *n.* a person who studies endocrinology.

en|do|cri|nol|o|gy (en′dō kri nol′ə jē, -krī-), *n.* the science dealing with the endocrine glands, especially in their relation to bodily changes and disease.

en|do|cri|no|path|ic (en′dō kri′nə path′ik), *adj.* of or having to do with endocrinopathy.

en|do|cri|nop|a|thy (en′dō kri nop′ə thē, -krī-), *n., pl.* **-thies.** *Medicine.* disease, or a diseased condition, due to improper functioning of one or more endocrine glands or organs. [< *endocrine* + *-pathy*]

en|doc|ri|nous (en dok′rə nəs), *adj.* = endocrinal.

en|do|cy|to|sis (en′dō sī tō′sis), *n.* the process by which cells take in or absorb substances: *Foreign particles such as bacteria are ingested by the process now known as endocytosis . . . The cell membrane folds inward to form a pocket, the edges of which fuse to enclose the particles* (Scientific American). [< *endo-* + (phago)*cytosis* or (pino)*cytosis*]

en|do|derm (en′dō dėrm), *n. Embryology.* the inner layer of cells formed during development of animal embryos. The lining of the organs of the digestive system develops from endoderm. [< *endo-* + Greek *dérma* skin]

en|do|der|mal (en′dō dėr′məl), *adj.* **1** *Zoology.* of or having to do with the endoderm. **2** *Botany.* of or having to do with the endodermis.

en|do|der|mic (en′dō dėr′mik), *adj.* = endodermal.

en|do|der|mis (en′dō dėr′mis), *n. Botany.* a layer of modified parenchyma cells which are united to form the inner boundary of the cortex and the sheath surrounding the vascular bundles of certain plants. [< *endo-* + (epi)*dermis*]

en|do|don|tia (en′dō don′shə, -shē ə), *n.* the branch of dentistry that deals with diseases of the dental pulp. [< New Latin *endodontia* < *endo-* + Greek *odoús, odóntos* tooth]

en|do|don|tic (en′dō don′tik), *adj.* of or having to do with endodontia.

en|do|don|tics (en′dō don′tiks), *n.* the science or practice of endodontia.

en|do|don|tist (en′dō don′tist), *n.* a dentist who specializes in endodontia.

en|do|en|zyme (en′dō en′zīm, -zim), *n.* an enzyme which acts or exists within a cell.

en|do|gam|ic (en′dō gam′ik), *adj.* = endogamous.

en|dog|a|mous (en dog′ə məs), *adj.* of or having to do with endogamy.

en|dog|a|my (en dog′ə mē), *n.* **1** the custom of marrying only within one's own tribe: *. . . marriage within a particular group, or endogamy, may exist along with exogamy* (Ogburn and Nimkoff). **2** *Botany.* pollination of a flower by another flower of the same plant. [< *endo-* + *-gamy*]

en|do|gas|tric (en′dō gas′trik), *adj.* situated within the abdomen.

en|do|gen (en′də jən), *n. Botany.* a former term for a plant in which new tissue is developed in the interior of the stem, which is not differentiated into wood and bark: *Monocotyledons are endogens.* [< *endo-* + *-gen*]

en|do|gen|e|sis (en′dō jen′ə sis), *n.* growth from within; endogeny.

en|do|ge|net|ic (en′dō jə net′ik), *adj.* having an origin from internal causes: *endogenetic diseases.*

en|do|gen|ic (en′dō jen′ik), *adj. Geology.* formed within the earth; proceeding from inside the earth: *a crater of endogenic origin.*

en|dog|e|nous (en doj′ə nəs), *adj.* **1** *Biology.* growing or proceeding from within; originating within. Cells or spores developing within a cell are endogenous. *In contrast, the causation of the chronic and progressive disorders of later years arises from within; they are endogenous rather than exogenous* (Edward J. Stieglitz). **2** *Physiology.* of or having to do with the metabolism of substances within cells or tissues without added nutrients. **3** *Anatomy.* produced within the body; autogenous. **4** *Geology.* = endogenic. **—en|dog′e|nous|ly,** *adv.*

en|dog|e|ny (en doj′ə nē), *n. Biology.* growth from within; endogenous cell formation.

en|do|glob|u|lar (en′dō glob′yə lər), *adj.* occurring within a blood globule, especially an erythrocyte.

en|dog|nath (en′dog nath), *n. Zoology.* the inner branch of the oral appendage of a crustacean. [< *endo-* + Greek *gnáthos* jaw]

en|do|lith|ic (en′dō lith′ik), *adj.* that lives under the surface of a rock or exists in a substance like stone. [< *endo-* + *lithic*[1]]

en|do|lymph (en′dō limf), *n.* the fluid of the inner ear.

en|do|lym|phan|gi|al (en′dō lim fan′jē əl), *adj.* situated or contained in a lymphatic vessel: *endolymphangial nodules.*

en|do|lym|phat|ic (en′dō lim fat′ik), *adj.* of or having to do with the endolymph: *the endolymphatic duct.*

en|do|me|tri|al (en′dō mē′trē əl), *adj.* of or having to do with the endometrium.

en|do|me|tri|o|sis (en′dō mē′trē ō′sis), *n.* a noncancerous disease of women in which tissue lining the uterus invades nearby areas. [< *endometri*(um) + *-osis*]

en|do|me|tri|um (en′dō mē′trē əm), *n.* the mucous lining of the uterus. [< New Latin *endometrium* < Greek *éndon* within + *mētra* womb]

en|do|mi|to|sis (en′dō mī tō′sis), *n.* a type of mitosis that occurs in certain plant and animal cells in which the chromosomes multiply but the nucleus does not divide.

en|do|mix|is (en′dō mik′sis), *n.* a process of nuclear reorganization similar to conjugation that takes place in certain solitary protozoans and ap-

Pronunciation Key: hat, āge, cãre, fär; let, ēqual, tėrm; it, īce; hot, ōpen, ôrder; oil, out; cup, pu̇t, rüle; child; long; thin; ᴛʜen; zh, measure; ə represents a in about, e in taken, i in pencil, o in lemon, u in circus.

pears to rejuvenate the organism. [< *endo-* + Greek *mixis* a mingling]

***en|do|morph** (en′dō môrf), *n.* **1** one of three hypothetical body types used to explain certain aspects of personality, the other two being called *ectomorph* and *mesomorph.* The endomorph is characterized by a predominance of structures developed from the endodermal layer of the embryo, and is inclined to be soft-skinned and fat, easy-going, and good natured. **2** a mineral enclosed within another mineral. [< *endo-* + Greek *morphê* form]

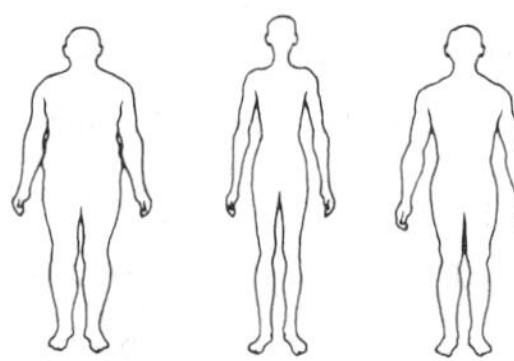

en|do|mor|phic (en′dō môr′fik), *adj.* **1** of or like an endomorph; having to do with an endomorph, especially as designating the fat type of body build. **2** *Mineralogy.* **a** enclosed by another mineral. **b** of or having to do with an endomorph or endomorphism. **c** taking place inside a mineral or rock. **—en′do|mor′phi|cal|ly,** *adv.*

en|do|mor|phism (en′dō môr′fiz əm), *n.* change in an endomorph due to reaction with the enclosing mineral.

en|do|mor|phy (en′dō môr′fē), *n.* endomorphic quality, character, or condition.

en|do|my|o|car|di|tis (en′dō mī′ō kär dī′tis), *n.* inflammation of the lining and muscular substance of the heart.

end on, 1 with the end pointing directly toward an object: *The ships collided end on.* **2** *Mining.* (of a mode of working a mass of coal) at right angles to the cleat.

end-on (end′on′, -ôn′), *adj.* of or on the end: *an end-on view, an end-on collision.*

en|do|nu|cle|ase (en′dō nü′klē ās, -nyü′-), *n.* an enzyme that breaks up strands of DNA into discontinuous segments: *The enzyme is an endonuclease, able to clip—in the test tube at least—the newly formed DNA helix into fragments shorter than the original RNA template* (New Scientist). [< *endo-* + *nuclease*]

en|do|par|a|site (en′dō par′ə sīt), *n.* an internal parasite, such as the tapeworm.

en|do|pep|ti|dase (en′dō pep′tə dās), *n. Biochemistry.* any one of various proteolytic enzymes, such as trypsin, that break down peptide bonds inside polypeptide chains.

en|do|pe|rid|i|um (en′dō pə rid′ē əm), *n., pl.* **-i|a** (-ē ə). *Botany.* the inner peridium of a fungus, when two are present.

en|do|per|ox|ide (en′dō pə rok′sīd), *n.* any one of a group of highly oxygenated compounds that are precursors of prostaglandins: *The endoperoxides are metabolized both to prostaglandins and to nonprostaglandin structures, and have unique biological actions on a number of different tissues* (Kenneth T. Kirton).

en|do|phyl|lous (en′dō fil′əs), *adj. Botany.* being or formed within a sheath. [< *endo-* + Greek *phýllon* leaf + English *-ous*]

en|do|phyte (en′dō fīt), *n. Botany.* a plant growing inside another plant. Certain algae are endophytes. [< *endo-* + *-phyte*]

en|do|phy|tic (en′dō fī′tik), *adj.* of or having to do with endophytes.

en|do|plasm (en′dō plaz əm), *n. Biology.* the inner portion of the cytoplasm of a cell.

en|do|plas|mic (en′dō plaz′mik), *adj.* of or having to do with endoplasm.

endoplasmic reticulum, a finely reticulated structure of the cytoplasm, visible in the electron microscope, especially in young cells, which stains with basic dyes, is covered with ribosomes, and is thought to provide surface for the activity of intracellular enzymes.

en|do|plast (en′dō plast), *n. Biology.* the nucleus of a protozoan. [< *endo-* + Greek *plastós* something formed]

en|do|pleu|ra (en′dō plůr′ə), *n. Botany.* the inner covering of a seed; tegmen. [< *endo-* + Greek *pleurá* side]

en|dop|o|dite (en dop′ə dīt), *n.* (in crustaceans) the inner branch of a biramous appendage. [< *endo-* + Greek *poús, podós* foot + English *-ite*[1]]

en|do|psy|chic (en′dō sī′kik), *adj.* that is within the soul.

en|do|ra|di|o|sonde (en′dō rā′dē ō sond), *n.* = radio pill.

end organ, *Physiology.* a specialized structure at the distal end of a sensory or motor nerve. The retina is the end organ for vision.

en|dor|phin (en dôr′fin), *n.* any one of a group of protein substances in the brain that suppress pain and control various physiological responses: *Endorphin . . . is 200 times more potent than morphine* (Science News). *Injected into animals, in laboratory tests, the endorphins (a chain of up to 31 amino acids) acted as pain killers* (Maclean's). [< *endo-* within + (m)*orphin*(e)]

en|dors|a|ble (en dôr′sə bəl), *adj.* that can be endorsed.

en|dor|sa|tion (en′dôr sā′shən), *n. Canadian.* approval; support; endorsement: *a newspaper's endorsation of a candidate.*

en|dorse (en dôrs′), *v.t.,* **-dorsed, -dors|ing.** **1a** to write one's name on the back of (a check, note, or other document): *He had to endorse the check before the bank would cash it.* **b** to make (a check, bill, note, or other document) payable to another person by signing one's name on the back of the instrument. **c** *British.* to make an entry of an offense on the back of (a license): *He was found guilty and fined £10 and his driving licence was endorsed* (London Times). **2** to sign one's name anywhere on (a bill, document, or the like): *The storekeeper endorsed my bill when I paid the full amount.* **3** *Figurative.* to approve; support: *Parents heartily endorsed the plan for a school playground.* SYN: sanction, uphold.

endorse out, (in South Africa) to send away from an urban to a rural area as part of a system of controlling the influx of black Africans into the cities: *Eyewitness reports from Johannesburg Station suggest that about 70 people a day were being "endorsed" out of that city alone* (Manchester Guardian Weekly).

[alteration of Middle English *endossen* approve by signing on the back < Old French *endosser* < *en-* on (< Latin *in-*) + *dos* back < Latin *dorsum*]

en|dor|see (en dôr′sē′, en′dôr-), *n.* a person to whom a check, note, or other document is assigned by endorsement.

en|dorse|ment (en dôrs′mənt), *n.* **1** a person's name on the back of a check, note, bill, or other document, in evidence of its transfer or assuring its payment. **2** the act of writing on the back of a check or other document. **3** *Figurative.* approval; support: *His idea received endorsement by the entire club.* **4** an additional provision or clause in an insurance contract by which the coverage described in the contract may be increased or diminished.

en|dors|er (en dôr′sər), *n.* a person who endorses.

en|do|sarc (en′dō särk), *n. Biology.* the endoplasm of a protozoan. [< *endo-* + Greek *sárx, sarkós* flesh]

en|do|scope (en′də skōp), *n. Medicine.* an instrument used to examine the interior of a hollow organ, such as the urethra or rectum.

en|do|scop|ic (en′də skop′ik), *adj.* of or having to do with endoscopy or an endoscope.

en|dos|co|pist (en dos′kə pist), *n.* a person skilled in endoscopy.

en|dos|co|py (en dos′kə pē), *n.* examination of a hollow organ by means of an endoscope.

en|do|skel|e|tal (en′dō skel′ə təl), *adj.* of or having to do with the endoskeleton.

***en|do|skel|e|ton** (en′dō skel′ə tən), *n.* the internal skeleton characteristic of vertebrates and allied forms.

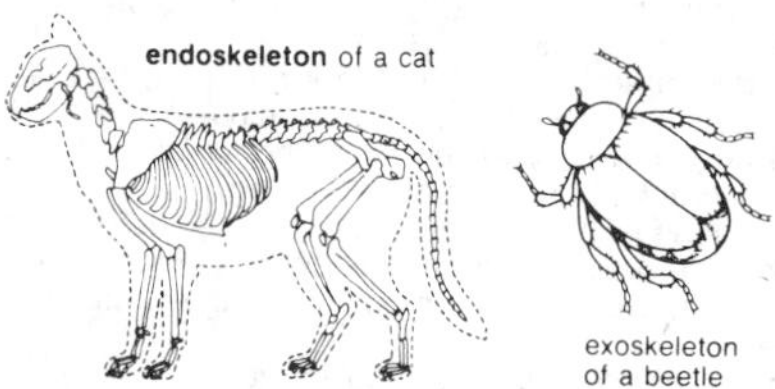

en|dos|mose (en′dos mōs, -doz-), *n.* = endosmosis.

en|dos|mo|sic (en′dos mō′sik, -doz-), *adj.* = endosmotic.

en|dos|mo|sis (en′dos mō′sis, -doz-), *n.* osmosis predominantly from an outer to an inner vessel or toward the solution of greater concentration. [alteration of French *endosmose* < Greek *éndon* within + *ōsmós* a thrusting, attack. Compare etym. under **osmosis.**]

en|dos|mot|ic (en′dos mot′ik, -doz-), *adj.* of or having to do with endosmosis.

en|do|sperm (en′dō spėrm), *n.* nourishment for the embryo of a plant, stored in the seed or ovule.

en|do|spore (en′dō spôr, -spōr), *n.* **1** *Botany.* the inner coat or wall of a spore of certain plants; endosporium. **2** *Bacteriology.* a spore formed within a cell of certain bacteria.

en|do|spo|ri|um (en′dō spôr′ē əm, -spōr′-), *n., pl.* **-spo|ri|a** (-spôr′ē ə, -spōr′-). *Botany.* an endospore. [< New Latin *endosporium* < Greek *éndon* within + *sporá* a sowing]

en|dos|po|rous (en dos′pər əs; en′dō spôr′əs, -spōr′-), *adj. Bacteriology.* forming spores within a cell.

en|dos|te|al (en dos′tē əl), *adj.* situated or occurring in the interior of a bone.

en|dos|te|um (en dos′tē əm), *n., pl.* **-te|a** (-tē ə). the membranous connective tissue lining the walls of the marrow space of a bone. [< New Latin *endosteum* < Greek *éndon* within + *ostéon* bone]

en|do|stome (en′də stōm), *n. Botany.* **1** the opening at the apex of the inner coat of the ovule. **2** the inner peristome of mosses.

en|dos|to|sis (en′dos tō′sis), *n.* the growth of bone within cartilage. [< *endo-* + Greek *ostéon* bone + *-ōsis* condition]

en|dos|tra|cum (en dos′trə kəm), *n., pl.* **-tra|ca** (-trə kə). the inner layer of the shell of a crustacean. [< New Latin *endostracum* < Greek *éndon* within + *óstrakon* shell]

en|do|style (en′dō stīl), *n.* a ventral groove in the pharynx of certain primitive chordates, such as the tunicates and amphioxus, that secretes a mucus which traps food particles. [< *endo-* + Greek *stylos* column]

en|do|sul|fan (en′dō sul′fan), *n.* a powerful insecticide containing chlorinated sulfate, used for protection of vegetable crops. *Formula:* $C_9H_6Cl_6O_3S$

en|do|sym|bi|ont (en′dō sim′bī ont, -bē-), *n.* a microorganism that has adapted itself to existence within the cell or cells of other organisms: *One attractive hypothesis is that the mitochondria and chloroplasts present today in plant and animal cells once were free-living organisms, distantly related to present-day bacteria, that were incorporated into larger cells and became endosymbionts during the subsequent course of evolution* (Scientific American).

en|do|sym|bi|o|sis (en′dō sim′bī ō′sis, -bē-), *n.* adaptation of a microorganism to living within a cell or cells of another organism: *There is an increasing amount of evidence, however, which suggests that a process of "endosymbiosis" of small procaryotic cells with larger procaryotic cells may have been involved* (New Scientist).

en|do|sym|bi|ot|ic (en′dō sim′bī ot′ik, -bē-), *adj.* having to do with endosymbiosis; living within a cell or cells of another organism: *endosymbiotic aerobic bacteria.* **—en′do|sym′bi|ot′i|cal|ly,** *adv.*

en|do|the|ci|um (en′dō thē′shē əm, -sē-), *n., pl.* **-ci|a** (-shē ə, -sē-). *Botany.* **1** the inner lining of the walls of the cells of an anther. **2** (in mosses) the central mass of cells in the spore case from which the archespore is usually developed. [< New Latin *endothecium* < Greek *éndon* within + *thêkē* a chest, box]

en|do|the|li|al (en′dō thē′lē əl), *adj.* having to do with endothelium: *The artery and the vein each put out a tendril of endothelial cells, and the two tendrils grow toward each other* (New Yorker).

en|do|the|li|oid (en′dō thē′lē oid), *adj.* like endothelium.

en|do|the|li|o|ly|sin (en′dō thē′lē ə lī′sin), *n.* a lysin that causes the destruction of vascular endothelial cells.

en|do|the|li|o|lyt|ic (en′dō thē′lē ə lit′ik), *adj.* of or having to do with endotheliolysin.

en|do|the|li|o|ma (en′dō thē′lē ō′mə), *n., pl.* **-mas, -ma|ta** (-mə tə). *Medicine.* a tumor originating from the endothelium.

en|do|the|li|um (en′dō thē′lē əm), *n., pl.* **-li|a** (-lē ə). the tissue that lines blood vessels, lymphatic vessels, the heart, etc. It is a form of epithelium. [< New Latin *endothelium* < Greek *éndon* within + *thēlē* nipple]

en|doth|e|loid (en doth′ə loid), *adj.* = endothelioid.

en|do|ther|mal (en′dō thėr′məl), *adj.* = endothermic.

en|do|ther|mic (en′dō thėr′mik), *adj.* **1** *Chemistry.* of or having to do with a chemical change in which heat is absorbed: *Reactions which must absorb energy in order to proceed are called endothermic reactions* (Monroe M. Offner). **2** *Biology.* maintaining a constant internal temperature; homeothermal: *Warm-blooded animals are endothermic.*

en|do|tho|rax (en′dō thôr′aks, -thōr′-), *n.* the internal processes of the thorax or cephalothorax of arthropods.

en|do|tox|ic (en′dō tok′sik), *adj.* of or having to do with endotoxin.

en|do|tox|in (en′dō tok′sin), *n.* a toxic substance, that remains inside the organism that produces it.

en|do|tra|che|al (en′dō trā′kē əl), *adj.* having to do with the inside of the trachea, or windpipe: *A thin tube, known as an endotracheal catheter,* *has been put down her windpipe to assure her a clear and controllable airway throughout the operation* (Harper's).

en|do|troph|ic (en′dō trof′ik), *adj.* deriving nourishment from within, as certain fungi living within the roots of plants and deriving nourishment from their inner cells. [< *endo-* + Greek *trophê* nourishment + English *-ic*]

en|dow (en dou′), *v.t.* **1** to give money or property to provide an income for: *The rich man endowed the college he had attended.* **2** *Figurative.* to give from birth; provide with some ability, quality, or talent: *Nature endowed her with both a good mind and good looks.* SYN: equip, invest. **3** *Obsolete.* to provide with a dowry. [< Old French *endouer* < *en-* on (< Latin *in-*) + *douer* endow < Latin *dotāre* bestow] —**en|dow′er**, *n.*

en|dow|ment (en dou′mənt), *n.* **1** money or property given to a person or institution to provide an income: *This college has a large endowment.* SYN: grant, donation. **2** *Figurative.* a gift from birth; ability; talent: *A good sense of rhythm is a natural endowment.* **3** the act of endowing.

endowment insurance, a form of life insurance providing for the payment of a fixed sum to the insured person at a specified time, or to his designated beneficiaries should he die before the time named.

en|do|zo|ic (en′dō zō′ik), *adj.* present within or living inside an animal: *endozoic algae.*

end paper, a sheet of paper folded in two leaves, one of which is pasted to the inside of the front or back cover of a book, the other serving as an extra flyleaf: *The illustrations of Furlinetta and the other animals are in color and the zoo as a whole is shown on the attractive end papers* (Saturday Review).

end pin, the button of a violin or other string instrument.

end plate, the expanded ending of a motor nerve in a muscular fiber.

end|play (end′plā′), *n., v. Contract Bridge.* —*n.* a play in which an opponent is forced into the lead so that he loses a trick. It usually occurs near the end of a contract.
—*v.t.* to force into the lead in an endplay: *South ... could see that he would be endplayed if he retained that card* (Alan Truscott).

end play, the longitudinal back-and-forth play of an axle, shaft, or the like: *Excessive end play in the crankshaft will produce an intermittent rap* (Toboldt and Purvis).

end point, **1** the conclusion of a chemical process or reaction. **2** a point in space where a line or segment stops or abruptly changes direction. **3** an object or goal.

end product, **1** the product resulting from any process at its conclusion: *Education is a process, not an end product* (New York Times). **2** *Nuclear Physics.* the last stable member of a series of isotopes, each produced by the radioactive decay of the preceding isotope.

en|drin (en′drin), *n.* a powerful insecticide, used especially in agriculture, an isomer of dieldrin, related to chlordane. It is also effective against rodents. *Formula:* $C_{12}H_{40}OCl_6$

end run, **1** *Football.* a play in which the ball carrier tries to advance the ball by circling one end of the defensive line. **2** *U.S.* anything that resembles an end run in football, such as the shape of a graph or an indirect military strategy.

end-run (end′run′), *v.t., v.i.,* **-ran**, **-run**, **-run|ning.** *U.S. Informal.* to evade an obstacle or barrier, by trickery or indirection; circumvent: *He is not the sort of officer who writes personal letters to old Army friends in order to end-run around official channels* (Newsweek).

end-stopped (end′stopt′), *adj.* (of blank verse) stopping or pausing at the end of the line, or of each line.

end stopping, a form of blank verse in which each line ends with a stop or pause, instead of freely running on into the next line.

Ends|ville (endz′vil), *adj. U.S. Slang.* wonderful; out of this world: *At the windup of his two-week tour, Soviet Cosmonaut Georgy Beregovoy announced that New York was strictly Endsville* (Time). [< *end* + *-ville*]

end table, a small table suitable for placing at either end of a couch or beside a chair.

end-to-end (end′tü end′), *adj., adv.* with the ends touching: *We laid the piece of string out end-to-end to see if by tying we would have a long enough piece.*

en|due (en dü′, -dyü′), *v.t.,* **-dued**, **-du|ing.** **1** to provide with a quality or power; furnish; supply: *The wisest man is not endued with perfect wisdom. The jungle ... answered, as if endued with life, by waving its boughs* (Frederick Marryat). **2** = clothe. **3** to put on. Also, **indue.** [< Old French *enduire* < Latin *indūcere* lead into < *in-* in + *dūcere* lead; later confused with Latin *induere* put on, invest with]

en|dur|a|ble (en dùr′ə bəl, -dyùr′-), *adj.* **1** that can be endured; bearable: *His pain was so severe that it was barely endurable.* **2** likely to endure or last.

en|dur|a|bly (en dùr′ə blē, -dyùr′-), *adv.* in an endurable manner; so as to be endurable.

en|dur|ance (en dùr′əns, -dyùr′-), *n.* **1** the power to last and to withstand hard wear: *A runner must have great endurance to run 30 miles in a day. Cheap, shoddy cloth has little endurance.* **2** the power to stand something without giving out; holding out; bearing up: *The wounded man's endurance of pain was remarkable.* SYN: fortitude, patience, forbearance, tolerance. **3** the act or an instance of enduring pain, hardship, etc.: *Patient endurance Attaineth to all things* (Longfellow). **4** continued existence in time; duration.

en|dur|ant (en dùr′ənt, -dyùr′-), *adj.* ready to endure; that endures or is capable of endurance: *a hardy, endurant variety of wheat.*

en|dure (en dùr′, -dyùr′), *v.,* **-dured**, **-dur|ing.**
—*v.i.* **1** to keep on; last; continue in existence: *Metal and stone endure for a long time. The Lord shall endure for ever* (Psalms 9:7). SYN: See syn. under **last**[2]. **2** to hold out; suffer patiently: *"I can't endure much longer," he whispered.*
—*v.t.* to put up with; bear; stand: *The wounded man endured much pain. How small of all that human hearts endure, That part which laws or kings can cause or cure!* (Samuel Johnson). SYN: suffer, tolerate, experience. See syn. under **bear**[2].
[< Old French *endurer* < Latin *indūrāre* make hard < *in-* in + *dūrus* hard]

en|dur|er (en dùr′ər, -dyùr′-), *n.* a person or thing that endures.

en|dur|ing (en dùr′ing, -dyùr′-), *adj.* lasting; permanent: *Mankind longs for an enduring peace. The works of great writers have enduring value.* SYN: abiding, unchanging. See syn. under **lasting.**
—**en|dur′ing|ly**, *adv.* —**en|dur′ing|ness**, *n.*

en|dur|o (en dùr′ō, -dyùr′-), *n., pl.* **-dur|os.** *U.S.* a race to test a runner's or driver's endurance. [probably < American Spanish *enduro* < *endurar* to endure]

end use, the particular function which a manufactured product serves or to which it is limited.

end-us|er (end′yü′zər), *n.* = end-consumer.

end|ways (end′wāz′), *adv., adj.* **1** on end; upright. **2** with the end forward; in the direction of the end. **3** = lengthwise. **4** with the ends placed so that they touch; end-to-end.

end|wise (end′wīz′), *adv., adj.* = endways.

En|dym|i|on (en dim′ē ən), *n. Greek Legend.* a beautiful youth loved by the moon goddess Selene.

end zone, the area beyond either goal line which is in bounds on a football field.

-ene, a suffix used in forming the names of many hydrocarbons, especially the olefin series, as in *benzene, naphthalene.* [< Latin *-ēnus,* an adjective suffix]

E.N.E., ENE (no periods), or **e.n.e.**, east-northeast.

en é|che|lon (äɴ nāsh lôɴ′), *French.* in echelon; like a flight of steps.

en ef|fet (äɴ ne fe′), *French.* in effect.

en|e|ma (en′ə mə), *n., pl.* **en|e|mas, e|nem|a|ta** (e nem′ə tə). **1** an injection of liquid into the rectum to flush the bowels; clyster. **2** the device used. [< Greek *enema* injection < *enīénai* send in < *en-* in + *hīénai* send]

en|e|my (en′ə mē), *n., pl.* **-mies**, *adj.* —*n.* **1** a person or group that hates and tries to harm another; opponent; adversary: *... while men slept, his enemy came and sowed tares among the wheat* (Matthew 13:25). *For every ten jokes thou hast got an hundred enemies* (Laurence Sterne). **2** a force, nation, army, fleet, or air force that opposes another; person, ship, or other agent of a hostile nation. Two countries at war with each other are enemies. **3** *Figurative.* anything that will harm: *Frost is an enemy of flowers. Every animal that consumes another animal is called an enemy, or predator, and the animal eaten is its prey* (Tracy I. Storer).
—*adj.* **1** of an enemy. **2** *Obsolete.* adverse; hostile.
the Enemy, the Devil; Satan: *Defend him from the danger of the Enemy* (Book of Common Prayer).
[< Old French *enemi,* earlier *inimi,* learned borrowing from Latin *inimīcus* < *in-* not + *amīcus* friendly, related to *amāre* to love]
— *Syn. n.* **1, 2 Enemy, foe** mean a hostile person, group, country, army, or other agent. **Enemy**, the common and general word, applies to any adversary and to any form of hostility shown: *His unscrupulous methods have made many enemies for that businessman.* **Foe**, now a somewhat literary word, suggests a dangerous adversary, actively or furtively demonstrating hostility: *The foes of the plan to move the city dump started a lawsuit against its supporters.*

enemy alien, an alien living in a country which is at war with his own country.

en|ep|i|der|mic (en ep′ə dėr′mik), *adj.* of or having to do with medical applications, such as plasters, to the skin.

en|er|ge|sis (en′ər jē′sis), *n. Botany.* catabolic change, making energy available within a plant cell. [< New Latin *energesis* < Greek *energeîn;* see etym. under **energetic**]

en|er|get|ic (en′ər jet′ik), *adj.* **1** full of energy; eager to work: *Cool autumn days make us feel energetic. The new office boy seemed energetic when he reported for work.* SYN: vigorous, strenuous. **2** full of force; active: *energetic reform measures. An energetic effort on the part of all members will ensure the success of our plan.* SYN: vigorous, strenuous. [< Greek *energētikós* active < *energeîn* be in action, operate < *en-* in + *érgon* work, deed]

en|er|get|i|cal|ly (en′ər jet′ə klē), *adv.* with energy; vigorously: *Astrid Varnay sang the part of Isolde very energetically and with some beauty of tone* (New Yorker).

en|er|get|ics (en′ər jet′iks), *n.* **1** the science of the laws of energy. **2** the amount and nature of the energy output or changes in any activity or system: *We worked out a theory of the energetics of grinding* (Canada Month). *We wished to investigate the energetics of flapping flight* (Scientific American). **3** use or output of energy: *It is interesting ... to dream about a possible, perhaps more practical, use of the moon for earth's energetics* (Bulletin of Atomic Scientists).

en|er|gic (en ėr′jik), *adj.* characterized by energy; energetic.

e|ner|gi|co (e nėr′jē kō), *adj. Italian, Music.* energetic; to be rendered with strong articulation and accentuation.

en|er|gid (en ėr′jid), *n. Biology.* the nucleus of a cell together with its active cytoplasm regarded as a vital unit. [< German *Energid* < *Energie* energy]

en|er|gism (en′ər jiz əm), *n.* the theory that the supreme good does not lie in pleasure but in a contented activity of mind. [< German *Energismus* < Late Latin *energīa;* see etym. under **energy**]

en|er|gize (en′ər jīz), *v.,* **-gized**, **-giz|ing.** —*v.t.* to give energy to; make active: *Ambition energizes people. Faith will energize us for any sort of work* (Walter McClaren).
—*v.i.* to put forth energy; act with vigor.

en|er|giz|er (en′ər jī′zər), *n.* **1** any one of several drugs used to relieve abnormal mental depression and to increase energy and alertness. **2** a small device that stores chemical energy, such as a dry cell, used to operate small mechanisms: *Entirely powered by an energizer of shirt-button size, the ... electric watch ... is considered to be the most accurate portable timepiece yet devised* (Wall Street Journal).

en|er|gu|men (en′ər gyü′mən), *n.* **1** a person who is possessed by an evil spirit; demoniac. **2** a fanatic; enthusiast. [< Late Latin *energūmenus* < Greek *energoúmenos,* present passive participle of *energeîn;* see etym. under **energetic**]

en|er|gy (en′ər jē), *n., pl.* **-gies.** **1** will to work; vigor: *That boy is so full of energy that he cannot keep still.* **2** the power to do work or act; force: *All our energies were used to keep the fire from spreading. Beware of rashness, but with energy and sleepless vigilance go forward* (Abraham Lincoln). **3** capacity for doing work, such as lifting or moving an object. Light, heat, and electricity are different forms of energy. Energy exists as potential or kinetic and is measured in various units, such as ergs, joules, or foot-pounds. *A steam engine changes heat into mechanical energy. According to the established principles of conservation in physics, energy is never created or destroyed, but is only transferred or transformed* (Atlantic). **4** ability to produce action or effect. [< Late Latin *energīa* < Greek *enérgeia* < *énergos* active < *en-* in + *érgon* work]

energy audit, a systematic check of the use of energy within a building, especially to determine where savings can be achieved: *If you have never had one, an energy audit is ... a survey of your home to see where the energy goes—and the money for it* (Christian Science Monitor).

energy crisis, a critical shortage in the supply of energy-producing fuels, such as gas, oil, and coal, usually attributed to increased consumption, depletion of natural resources, a decline in ex-

Pronunciation Key: hat, āge, cãre, fär; let, ēqual, tėrm; it, īce; hot, ōpen, ôrder; **oil**, **out**; cup, pu̇t, rüle; **ch**ild; lo**ng**; **th**in; **ᴛʜ**en; **zh**, measure; ə represents **a** in about, **e** in taken, **i** in pencil, **o** in lemon, **u** in circus.

ploration, and environmental protective legislation.

en|er|gy-drive (en′ər jē drīv′), *n.* underground pressure from gas or water that forces oil to the surface after drilling a well.

energy level or **state**, *Physics.* (in quantum theory) one of the usually stable states of energy of a physical system. In the atom, electrons cluster about the nucleus in various energy levels. *Each nucleus has discrete energy states, and in passing from one to another it sends out gamma rays of sharply defined energy* (Scientific American).

energy paper, a dry sheet of paper fiber impregnated with potassium persulfate and powdered carbon, that serves as the active material of a dry-cell battery and is easily replaceable when the battery runs out of power.

energy structure, a type of kinetic art structure having motorized, mechanical, or electronic parts.

en|er|vate (*v.* en′ər vāt; *adj.* i nėr′vit), *v.,* **-vat|ed, -vat|ing,** *adj.* — ***v.t.*** **1** to lessen the vigor or strength of; weaken: *A hot, damp climate enervates people who are not used to it.* **SYN**: debilitate. **2** to weaken mentally or morally: *Many civilizations were enervated by too much luxury.*
— ***adj.*** lacking vigor or strength; enervated: *I observed ... the enervate slightness of his frail form* (Edward Bulwer-Lytton).
[< Latin *ēnervāre* (with English *-ate*[1]) < *ex-* away + *nervus* sinew, nerve]

en|er|va|tion (en′ər vā′shən), *n.* **1** the act of enervating. **2** the condition of being enervated.

en|er|va|tive (en′ər vā′tiv), *adj.* tending to enervate; enervating.

en|er|va|tor (en′ər vā′tər), *n.* a thing that enervates.

en é|vi|dence (äɴ nā vē däɴs′), *French.* in evidence; in plain sight.

en|face (en fās′), *v.t.,* **-faced, -fac|ing. 1** to write, print, or stamp on the face of (a note, bill, or draft). **2** to write, print, or stamp (a mark or a form of words) on the face of a note, bill, or draft.

en face (äɴ fȧs′), *French.* **1** in the face; to one's face. **2** openly; boldly. **3** in front; opposite.

en|face|ment (en fās′mənt), *n.* what is written or printed on the face of a note, bill, check, etc.

en fa|mille (äɴ fȧ mē′yə), *French.* with one's family; at home; informally: *I think it must have been in the spring of 1929 that I received the invitation to dine en famille in St. John's Wood to meet Max Beerbohm* (Evelyn Waugh).

en|fant (äɴ fäɴ′), *n. French.* a child.

en|fant ché|ri (äɴ fäɴ′ shā rē′), *French.* **1** a pampered child (used chiefly figuratively in English): *Ivory Coast ... is the enfant chéri of France, showered with loans and French capital* (Atlantic). **2** (literally) cherished child.

en|fant gâ|té (äɴ fäɴ′ gä tā′), *French.* a spoiled child.

en|fants per|dus (äɴ fäɴ′ per dʏ′), *French.* **1** a squad of soldiers sent on a very dangerous mission. **2** (literally) lost children.

en|fant ter|ri|ble (äɴ fäɴ′ te rē′blə), *French.* **1** a child whose behavior or words embarrass older people. **2** a person or organization that is indiscreet, lacks a sense of responsibility, or is extremely unconventional: *By the year 1919, when he [John Maynard Keynes] was in his middle thirties, he had achieved international fame or notoriety as the enfant terrible of economics* (Punch). *"L'Express" has become the enfant terrible of postwar French journalism* (Newsweek). **3** (literally) terrible child.

en|fant trou|vé (äɴ fäɴ′ trü vā′), *French.* **1** a foundling. **2** (literally) found child.

en|fee|ble (en fē′bəl), *v.t.,* **-bled, -bling.** to make feeble; weaken.

en|fee|ble|ment (en fē′bəl mənt), *n.* **1** the act of enfeebling. **2** the condition of being enfeebled.

en|fee|bler (en fē′blər), *n.* a person or thing that enfeebles.

en|feoff (en fef′, -fēf′), *v.t. Law.* **1** to invest with a fee or fief. **2** to hand over as a fief: (*Figurative.*) *The skipping king ... Enfeoffed himself to popularity* (Shakespeare). [< Anglo-French *enfeoffer,* Old French *enfieffer* < *en-* into (< Latin *in-*) + *fief* fief]

en|feoff|ment (en fef′mənt, -fēf′-), *n.* **1** the act of giving a fee or fief. **2** the deed that gives a person the fee of an estate. **3** the estate obtained in this way.

en fête (äɴ fet′), *French.* in a festive manner; in holiday dress.

en|fet|ter (en fet′ər), *v.t.* to bind with or as if with fetters.

en|fe|ver (en fē′vər), *v.t.* **1** to throw into a fever. **2** *Figurative.* to incense.

En|field rifle (en′fēld), **1** a muzzleloading British musket, caliber .577, having a rifled bore, used in the United States in the Civil War. **2** a British bolt-action, breechloading rifle, caliber .303. **3** a similar rifle, caliber .30, used by American troops in World War I. [< *Enfield,* a village in Middlesex, England, near the site of an arms works]

en|fi|lade (en′fə lād′), *n., v.,* **-lad|ed, -lad|ing.** — ***n.*** gunfire that sweeps from the side at a line of troops or a position held by them.
— ***v.t.*** to fire guns at (a line of troops or the position held by them) from the side.
[< French *enfilade* < Old French *enfiler* to thread, pierce < *en-* on (< Latin *in-*) + *fil* thread < Latin *fīlum*]

en|fin (äɴ faɴ′), *adv. French.* **1** after all; at last. **2** in brief.

en|flame (en flām′), *v.t., v.i.,* **-flamed, -flam|ing.** = inflame.

en|flesh (en flesh′), *v.t.* **1** to clothe with flesh. **2** to give a fleshy form to; incarnate.

en|fleu|rage (äɴ flœ räzh′), *n.* a process of extracting perfumes by exposing odorless oils or fats to the exhalations of particular flowers. [< French *enfleurage* < *enfleurer* imbue with scent < *en-* in (< Latin *in-*) + *fleur* flower]

en|flow|er (en flou′ər), *v.t.* to adorn or deck with flowers: *Spring enflowers the fields.*

en|fold (en fōld′), *v.t.* **1** to fold in; wrap up: *The lady was enfolded in a shawl.* **SYN**: enclose, encompass. **2** *Figurative.* to embrace; clasp: *The mother enfolded her baby in her arms.* **3** to shape into a fold or folds. Also, **infold.** — **en|fold′er,** *n.*

en|fold|ment (en fōld′mənt), *n.* **1** a wrapping up; enclosure. **2** *Figurative.* an embrace.

en|force (en fôrs′, -fōrs′), *v.t.,* **-forced, -forc|ing. 1** to force obedience to; cause to be carried out; put into force: *The teacher will enforce the rules of the school. Policemen and judges will enforce the laws of the city.* **SYN**: execute, administer. **2** to force; compel: *The robbers enforced obedience to their demand by threats of violence. Illness enforced me to remain idle.* **3** to urge with force; emphasize: *The teacher enforced the principle of honesty by examples. Graphic illustrations of crippling from arthritis enforced the seriousness of the disease.* [< Old French *enforcier* < *en-* on (< Latin *in-*) + *force* force, noun]

en|force|a|bil|i|ty (en fôr′sə bil′ə tē, -fōr′-), *n.* the quality or state of being enforceable.

en|force|a|ble (en fôr′sə bəl, -fōr′-), *adj.* that can be enforced: *In Italy, the income-tax law is about as popular, and as enforceable, as Prohibition used to be in the U.S.* (Time).

en|for|ced|ly (en fôr′sid lē, -fōr′-), *adv.* by force or compulsion, not by choice.

en|force|ment (en fôrs′mənt, -fōrs′-), *n.* the act or process of enforcing; putting into force: *Strict enforcement of the laws against speeding will reduce automobile accidents.*

en|forc|er (en fôr′sər, -fōr′-), *n.* a person or thing that enforces.

en|for|ci|ble (en fôr′sə bəl, -fōr′-), *adj.* = enforceable.

en foule (äɴ fül′), *French.* in a crowd.

en|frame (en frām′), *v.t.,* **-framed, -fram|ing.** to enclose in or as if in a frame.

en|fran|chise (en fran′chīz), *v.t.,* **-chised, -chis|ing. 1** to give the right to vote to: *The 19th amendment to the Constitution enfranchised American women.* **2** to set free; release from slavery or restraint. [< Old French *enfranchiss-,* stem of *enfranchir* < *en-* in + *franc* free]

en|fran|chise|ment (en fran′chiz mənt), *n.* **1** the act or process of enfranchising. **2** the state of being enfranchised.

en|fran|chis|er (en fran′chī zər), *n.* a person or thing that enfranchises.

eng., 1a engine. **b** engineer. **c** engineering. **2a** engraved. **b** engraver. **c** engraving.

Eng., 1 England. **2** English.

en|gage (en gāj′), *v.,* **-gaged, -gag|ing.** — ***v.t.*** **1** to keep busy; occupy: *Work engages much of my time. He engaged me in conversation.* **2** to hire; employ; take for use or work; reserve (as seats, rooms, or a cab): *We engaged two rooms at the hotel. She engaged a carpenter to repair the porch.* **3** to promise or pledge to marry; betroth: *He was engaged to my sister. My sister and he are engaged.* **4** to catch and hold; attract: *Bright colors engage a baby's attention. This humanity and good nature engages everybody to him* (Joseph Addison). **5** to bind by a promise or contract; promise; commit; pledge: *He engaged himself as an apprentice to a printer.* **6** to fit into; lock together: *The teeth of geared wheels engage each other.* **7** to start a battle against; attack: *Our soldiers engaged the enemy.* **8** *Obsolete.* to pawn; mortgage.
— ***v.i.*** **1** to keep oneself busy; be occupied; be active; take part: *The two friends engaged in conversation. He engages in politics.* **2** to bind oneself; promise; pledge: *I will engage to be there on time.* **3** to fit; lock together; mesh: *The teeth of one gear engage with the teeth of the other.* **4** to join battle with an enemy: *The mob ... did not venture to engage against musketry and cannon with their knives* (Robert Southey).
[< Old French *engagier* < *en gage* under pledge]

en|ga|gé (äɴ gȧ zhā′), *adj. French.* committed or involved; not aloof or indifferent: *Reporting offers the sense of being engagé in the political process of one's own time* (Joseph and Stewart Alsop).

en|gaged (en gājd′), *adj.* **1** promised or pledged to marry: *The engaged girl wore a diamond ring.* **SYN**: betrothed, affianced. **2** busy; occupied: *Engaged in conversation, they did not see me.* **3** taken for use or work; hired. **4** fitted together; interlocked. **5** involved in a fight or battle. **6** *Architecture.* attached to or partly sunk into something else or looking as if it is built in this way: *a wall with engaged columns.*

en|gage|ment (en gāj′mənt), *n.* **1** the act of engaging. **2** the fact or condition of being engaged. **3** a promise; pledge: *An honest person fulfills all his engagements.* **SYN**: agreement. **4** a promise to marry: *Their parents announced the young couple's engagement.* **SYN**: betrothal. **5** a meeting with someone at a certain time; appointment: *He made a point of being punctual in all his engagements.* **6** a period of being hired; time of use or work: *The actor had an engagement of three weeks in a play.* **7** a battle; fight: *The greatest engagement of the Civil War was at Gettysburg.* **SYN**: encounter, combat, conflict. See syn. under **battle.**
engagements, financial obligations: *They were consequently unable to meet their own engagements* (Macaulay).

engagement ring, a ring, usually set with a diamond or diamonds, given by a man to his fiancée in token of their betrothal.

en|gag|er (en gā′jər), *n.* **1** a person who engages or secures. **2** a person who enters into an engagement or agreement; surety. **3** a person who engages the services of another; employer.

en|gag|ing (en gā′jing), *adj.* very attractive; pleasing; charming; winning: *She has an engaging smile.* — **en|gag′ing|ly,** *adv.* — **en|gag′ing|ness,** *n.*

en|garb (en gärb′), *v.t.* to dress; attire; garb.

en gar|çon (äɴ gȧr sôɴ′), *French.* as a bachelor; like a bachelor.

en garde (äɴ gȧrd′), *French.* **1** on guard: *To be perfectly ravishing this spring, a woman must wear a hat so avant-garde that the onlooker would do well to be en garde* (New Yorker). **2** *Fencing.* the starting position.

en|gar|land (en gär′lənd), *v.t.* to encircle with a garland.

Eng.D., Doctor of Engineering.

En|gel|mann spruce (eng′gəl mən), a tall evergreen tree of the pine family, found in western North America, whose wood is valued as lumber. [< George *Engelmann,* 1809-1884, a German-American botanist]

Engelmann spruce beetle, a very destructive beetle that attacks the bark of certain evergreen trees, especially the Engelmann spruce.

En|gel's law (eng′gəlz), *Economics.* the principle that as a family's income rises, a smaller share is spent for food and a larger share for education and recreation. [< Ernst *Engel,* 1821-1896, a German statistician, who originated the law]

en|gen|der (en jen′dər), *v.t.* **1** to bring into existence; produce; cause: *Filth engenders disease.* **2** to beget; procreate: *Violence naturally engenders violence* (Macaulay). — ***v.i.*** to be produced; come into existence. [< Old French *engendrer* < Latin *ingenerāre* < *in-* in + *generāre* beget, create < *genus, generis* race, kind]

en|gen|der|er (en jen′dər ər), *n.* a person or thing that engenders; begetter.

en|gen|der|ment (en jen′dər mənt), *n.* the act of engendering, procreating, or reproducing.

En|gi|du (en′gə dü), *n.* = Enkidu.

en|gild (en gild′), *v.t.* to gild; brighten.

engin., engineering.

en|gine[1] (en′jən), *n.* **1** a machine for applying power to some work, especially a machine that can start others moving. **2** a machine that pulls a railroad train; locomotive. **3** anything used to bring about a result; instrument or device: *Cannons are engines of war.* **4** = fire engine. **5** *Obsolete.* an artifice; device; plot; means: *Nor did he 'scape By all his engines* (Milton). [< Old French *engin* skill, cleverness < Latin *ingenium* inborn qualities, talent < *in-* in + *gen-,* root of *gignere* to beget, produce. Compare etym. under **genius, ingenious.**] — **en′gine|less,** *adj.*

en|gine[2] (en′jən), *v.t.,* **-gined, -gin|ing. 1** to furnish with an engine or engines. **2** *Obsolete.* to contrive or plan. [< Old French *enginier* < Medieval Latin *ingeniare* < Latin *ingenium;* see etym. under **engine**[1]]

★engine block, the main part of an engine, containing the cylinders, cast as a unit, without accessory parts and usually without the cylinder head.

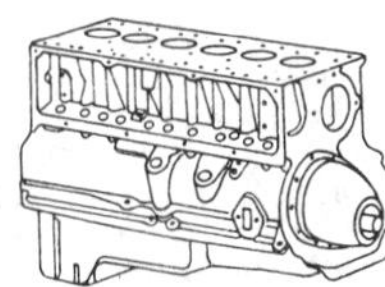
*engine block

engine driver, *Especially British.* the engineer of a locomotive.

en·gi·neer (en′jə nir′), *n., v.* —*n.* **1** a person who plans and builds engines, machines, roads, bridges, canals, forts, or the like; expert in engineering. **2** a person who takes care of or runs an engine. The man who runs a locomotive is an engineer. **3** a member of a military unit trained, equipped, and used for engineering work. *Abbr:* engr. **4** *Obsolete.* a person who contrives, designs, or invents.
—*v.t.* **1** to plan, build, direct, or work at as an engineer: *to engineer a road, bridge, or building.* **2** *Figurative.* to guide; manage: *She engineered the whole job from start to finish.*

en·gi·neered food (en′jə nird′), vegetable or synthetic substances to supplement or replace traditional foods that are too expensive, scarce, or not sufficiently nutritious; fabricated food: *The development of distinctly new types of foods, often designated as engineered or fabricated foods, was stimulated by the school lunch program* (Howard P. Milleville).

en·gi·neer·ing (en′jə nir′ing), *n.* **1** the science, work, or profession of an engineer. Engineering is needed in the planning, design, and supervision of construction of such things as railroads, bridges, dams, canals, buildings, machines, and electrical systems. *The Golden Gate Bridge is a triumph of engineering. Abbr:* engin. **2** *Figurative.* maneuvering; skillful contrivance: *Party engineering and the trickery of elections* (St. James's Gazette).

engineering drawing, *British.* = mechanical drawing.

engineer's chain, a measuring instrument consisting of 100 interlinked metal rods, 100 feet long.

en·gi·neer·ship (en′jə nir′ship), *n.* the position, work, or business of an engineer.

engine house, a station for a fire engine.

en·gine·man (en′jən mən), *n., pl.* **-men. 1** a man who operates an engine, as in a factory. **2** a petty officer in the United States Navy, in charge of diesel and gasoline engines.

en·gin·er (en′jə nər), *n. Obsolete.* an engineer.

engine room, the room, as of a ship or building, in which the engines are situated.

en·gine·ry (en′jən rē), *n.* **1** engines; machines. **2** skillful contrivance. **3** *Obsolete.* the making of engines or machines.

engine shaft, a shaft in a mine used exclusively for the pumping machinery.

en·gine-turned (en′jən tėrnd′), *adj.* ornamented with designs produced by engine turning.

engine turning, a kind of ornamental decoration, as on a watchcase, made by a lathe attachment. The most complicated is a rose engine turning.

en·gi·nous (en′jə nəs, en jē′-), *adj. Obsolete.* clever; cunning; deceitful.

en·gird (en gėrd′), *v.t.* = encircle.

en·gir·dle (en gėr′dəl), *v.t.,* **-dled, -dling.** = encircle.

en·gla·cial (en glā′shəl), *adj. Geology.* being within a glacier: *an englacial boulder.* —**en·gla′cial·ly**, *adv.*

Eng·land·er (ing′glən dər), *n.* an English person.

Eng·lish (ing′glish), *adj., n., v.* —*adj.* **1** of or having to do with England, its people, or their language. **2** belonging to the English language; written or spoken in the English language.
—*n.* **1** *pl. in use.* the people of England. **2** the language of England, including Old English or Anglo-Saxon (before 1100), Middle English (about 1100-1500), and Modern English (from about 1500). English is also spoken in the United States, Canada, the Republic of South Africa, Australia, New Zealand, and many other places. *Abbr:* Eng. **3** the English spoken in a certain place or by a certain group: *pidgin English.* **4** an English translation or equivalent. **5** Sometimes, **english.** a spinning motion given to a ball by hitting, throwing, or kicking on one side of its center: . . . *twisting it to give the ball the desired "english" or spin* (Harper's). **6** a large size of type; 14 point.
—*v.t.* **1** to translate into English; express in plain English. **2** to adopt (a foreign word) into English: *"Liqueur" is not yet Englished* (Walter S. Landor). **3** Sometimes, **english.** to give a spinning motion to (a ball).
[Old English *Englisc* <*Engle,* plural, the English people] —**Eng·lish·ness**, *n.*

English bond, a bond used in bricklaying, consisting of alternate courses of headers and stretchers in which the joints in alternate courses line up vertically.

English breakfast, a large breakfast, usually including eggs, sausages, toast, and tea, as distinguished from a Continental breakfast.

English Canadian, a Canadian of English, rather than of French, descent.

Eng·lish-Ca·na·di·an (ing′glish kə nā′dē ən), *adj.* of or having to do with English Canadians, their attitudes, customs, speech, or other attributes.

English class, any one of several breeds of chicken raised mostly for their meat, including the Australorp, Orpington, and Dorking breeds. The English class developed largely from poultry brought to England by the Romans about A.D. 43.

English cocker spaniel, any one of a breed of hunting dogs differing from the cocker spaniel chiefly in its larger size. It weighs from 26 to 34 pounds.

English daisy, the common European daisy.

English disease, **1** bronchitis (because bronchitis is common in England). **2** *Informal.* any one of various economic or labor problems originally associated with Great Britain, such as excessive attention to work rules, apparent control of management policy by shop stewards, and absenteeism: *At the same time, rapidly rising costs of factory production—first noticeable in Britain and nicknamed "the English disease"—have become manifest in other countries of west Europe and in North America* (London Times).

English elm, a European elm, with a broad spread of branches, common in England, and planted elsewhere.

English English, English as spoken in England; British English: *It is not universal kernel sentences and transformational rules but a manifold context of specific political history and social sensibility that makes a man "stand" for office in English English and "run" for it in American* (George Steiner).

English foxhound, any one of a breed of hunting dogs with a smooth, white, black, and tan coat and weighing from 60 to 75 pounds, used primarily for hunting foxes.

English hawthorn, a variety of hawthorn growing up to 15 feet high, with clusters of white flowers, native to Europe and northern Africa.

English horn, a wooden musical instrument resembling an oboe, but larger and having a lower tone. See picture under **oboe**. [a mistranslation of French *cor anglé* angled, cornered horn; *anglé* confused with *anglais* English]

Eng·lish·ism (ing′gli shiz əm), *n.* **1** devotion or loyalty to England or to its customs and traditions. **2** a word, phrase, or meaning originating in England. **3** a custom or trait peculiar to England.

English ivy, an ivy of the ginseng family having dark-green, shining leaves, and clusters of inconspicuous greenish-yellow flowers that are succeeded by dark berries. See picture under **ivy**.

Eng·lish·ize (ing′gli shīz), *v.t.,* **-ized, -iz·ing.** to make English in habits, customs, or character.

English laurel, = cherry laurel.

Eng·lish·man (ing′glish mən), *n., pl.* **-men. 1** a person born or living in England. **2** a person whose ancestry is English, such as some Canadians and Australians. **3** an English ship.

Englishman's tie, a type of knot used in joining two ends of rope.

Eng·lish·ment (ing′glish mənt), *n.* an English translation or version of a foreign work.

English muffin, a flat muffin made with yeast and baked on a griddle.

English pheasant, the common pheasant, naturalized in Great Britain prior to 1059.

English primrose, = cowslip.

English Revolution, the expulsion in 1688 of James II and the transfer of sovereignty to William and Mary.

English Round Hand, = copperplate.

Eng·lish·ry (ing′glish rē), *n.* **1** the fact or state of being English. **2** English people; people of English descent, as in Ireland. **3** friendship for or kinship with England.

English saddle, an almost flat saddle with only a slight pommel and a wide back.

English setter, a long-haired, black, white, and tan hunting dog, sometimes in mixtures of white, black, lemon, orange, and chestnut. It is trained to hunt with its nose pointed toward game.

English sickness, = English disease.

English sonnet, = Elizabethan sonnet.

English sparrow, a small, brownish-gray bird, a European finch now very common in America; house sparrow. It belongs to the same family as the weaverbird.

English springer spaniel, a large field spaniel that springs at game to drive it from its hiding place.

English system, the system of measurement that includes such units as the foot, pound, and gallon. The English system was replaced in Great Britain by the metric system.

English toy spaniel, a small spaniel with a round head and a short turned-up nose, weighing from about nine to twelve pounds. The English toy spaniel came from China or Japan and was a favorite with English noblemen in the 1600's.

English walnut, **1** a walnut tree from Asia, cultivated in Europe and North America and having a gray bark and a mild-flavored nut; Persian walnut. **2** its edible nut, used in candy, cakes, and as a condiment or hors d'oeuvre. **3** its soft wood.

English wheat, the poulard wheat in the forms grown in England.

Eng·lish·wom·an (ing′glish wu̇m′ən), *n., pl.* **-wom·en. 1** a woman born or living in England. **2** a woman whose ancestry is English.

Eng·lish·y (ing′glish ē), *adj.* typically English; suggesting English or England: *Uncle Hugh had lots of brothers and cousins who lived on ancestral acres in exotic, Englishy-sounding places like Beverly Farms and Bedford Village* (Michael J. Arlen).

English yew, a type of yew common to Europe and Asia, having heavy, elastic wood and dense, dark-green foliage.

en·globe (en glōb′), *v.t.,* **-globed, -glob·ing. 1** to enclose in a globe. **2** to form into a globe.

en·globe·ment (en glōb′mənt), *n.* the condition of being englobed.

en·glut (en glut′), *v.t.,* **-glut·ted, -glut·ting.** *Archaic.* **1** to swallow. **2** to gorge.

en·gobe (äɴ gōb′, en-), *n. Ceramics.* white or colored slip: *Painting on the clay with colored slip (engobe) either before or after firing it the first time is one of the best ways to decorate your work* (Helen Young). [<French *engobe* <*engober* to coat]

en·gorge (en gôrj′), *v.t., v.i.,* **-gorged, -gorg·ing. 1** to swallow greedily. **2** to glut; gorge. **3** to feed greedily. **4** *Medicine.* to congest with blood.
[<Old French *engorger* <*en-* in (<Latin *in-*) + *gorge* gorge, noun]

en·gorge·ment (en gôrj′mənt), *n.* **1** the act of engorging or condition of being engorged. **2** *Medicine.* congestion with blood.

en·gou·é (äɴ gü ā′), *adj. French.* infatuated.

en·goue·ment (äɴ gü mäɴ′), *n. French.* infatuation.

engr., **1** engineer. **2a** engraved. **b** engraver. **c** engraving.

en·graft (en graft′, -gräft′), *v.t.* **1** to graft (a shoot) from one tree or plant into or on another: *Peach trees can be engrafted on plum trees.* **2** *Figurative.* to fix in; implant: *Honesty and thrift are engrafted in his character.* Also, **ingraft.**

en·grail (en grāl′), *v.t.* to ornament with curved indentations: *hills with peaky tops engrail'd* (Tennyson).
[<Middle French *engreler* <Old French *engresler* <*en-* in (<Latin *in-*) + *gresle* hail (as if pitted by hail, or shaped like hailstones)]

en·grailed (en grāld′), *adj.* **1** having a ring of raised dots around the edges: *an engrailed coin or medal.* **2** *Heraldry.* cut into concave, semicircular notches: *a bordure engrailed.*

en·grail·ment (en grāl′mənt), *n.* **1** indentation in curved lines. **2** an engrailed circle or a ring or dots around the edge of a coin, medal, etc.

en·grain (en grān′), *v.t.* = ingrain. [Middle English *en grain* <Old French *en graine* in cochineal dye; later associated in French and English with *grain* fiber, used as "(to dye) in the fiber"]

en·gram (en′gram), *n.* **1** an enduring change, believed to occur in the protoplasm of nerve tissues in response to stimuli, which may account for the acquisition of skills and lasting memories. **2** *Psychology.* a permanent impression left on an individual by an experience.

en grand (äɴ gräɴ′), *French.* **1** on a large or grand scale. **2** as a whole.

en grande te·nue (äɴ gräɴd tə ny′), *French.* in full dress.

en grande toi·lette (äɴ gräɴd twä let′), *French.* in full dress.

en grand sei·gneur (äɴ gräɴ se nyœr′), *French.* as a great lord; in lordly style.

en·graph·i·a (en graf′ē ə), *n.* = engraphy. [<New Latin *engraphia* <Greek *en-* in + *-graphía* -graphy]

en·graph·ic (en graf′ik), *adj.* of or having to do with engraphy: *an engraphic stimulus.* —**en·graph′i·cal·ly**, *adv.*

Pronunciation Key: hat, āge, cãre, fär; let, ēqual, tėrm; it, īce; hot, ōpen, ôrder; oil, out; cup, pu̇t, rüle; child; long; thin; ᴛʜen; zh, measure; ə represents **a** in about, **e** in taken, **i** in pencil, **o** in lemon, **u** in circus.

en|gra|phy (en′grə fē), *n.* the making or receiving of an engram or engrams.

en|grav|a|ble (en grāv′ə bəl), *adj.* that can be engraved: *In Frost's case the reputation has . . . engraved Frost's very engravable face as in a kind of Mount Rushmore of the nation's consciousness* (James Dickey).

en|grave (en grāv′), *v.t.,* **-graved, -grav|ing.** **1a** to cut deeply in; carve in an artistic way: *The jeweler engraved the boy's initials on the back of the watch.* SYN: chisel. **b** to decorate by engraving: *to engrave silverware with crests.* **2** to cut (a picture, design, or map) in lines on a wood, stone, metal, glass, or plastic plate for printing. **3** *U.S.* to print from such a plate or block. **4** *Figurative.* to impress deeply; fix firmly: *His mother's face was engraved on his memory.* [< *en-*[1] + *grave*[3], probably patterned on obsolete French *engraver*]

en|grav|er (en grā′vər), *n.* a person who engraves plates or blocks for printing.

engraver beetle, = bark beetle.

en|grav|ing (en grā′ving), *n.* **1** the art or act of a person who engraves. **2** copy of a picture made from an engraved plate; print. **3** an engraved plate or block; engraved design or pattern.

en|gross (en grōs′), *v.t.* **1** to occupy wholly; fill the mind of; take up all the attention of: *The artist was so engrossed in his painting that he didn't notice the people watching him. She was engrossed by the interesting story.* SYN: absorb. **2** to copy or write in large, clear letters; write a beautiful copy of: *His name was engrossed on the diploma.* **3** to write out in formal manner; express in legal form. **4** to buy all or much of (the supply of some commodity) so as to control prices: *to engross the market for wheat.* **5** *Figurative.* to keep in one's own possession; monopolize. [(definitions 1,4,5) < *in gross* < Old French *en gros* wholesale, in a lump; (definitions 2,3) < Anglo-French *engrosser* < *en-* in (< Latin *in-*) + *grosse* large writing < Latin *grossus* thick, gross] **—en|gross′er,** *n.*

en|grossed (en grōst′), *adj.* wholly occupied in; absorbed.

en|gross|ing (en grō′sing), *adj.* fully occupying the attention; absorbing: *engrossing tales.* **—en-gross′ing|ly,** *adv.*

en|gross|ment (en grōs′mənt), *n.* **1** the act of engrossing: *the engrossment of a charter.* **2** the state of being engrossed: *complete engrossment in his studies.* **3** something that is copied out or expressed in legal form. **4** something that is bought up to control prices.

en|gulf (en gulf′), *v.t.* to swallow up; overwhelm; submerge: *A wave engulfed the small boat.* (*Figurative.*) *Civil war had engulfed the country.*

en|gulf|ment (en gulf′mənt), *n.* **1** the act of engulfing. **2** the state of being engulfed.

en|ha|lo (en hā′lō), *v.t.,* **-loed, -lo|ing.** to surround with or as with a halo: *that suavity which may rightly be looked for in a man enhaloed by the glory of God* (Marcel Aymé).

en|hance (en hans′, -häns′), *v.t.,* **-hanced, -hanc|ing.** to add to; make greater; heighten: *The gardens enhanced the beauty of the house. The growth of a city often enhances the value of land close to it.* SYN: increase, augment. [< Anglo-French *enhauncer,* Old French *enhaucier* < *en-* on, up (< Latin *in-*) + *haucier,* earlier *halcier* raise < Vulgar Latin *altiāre* < Latin *altus* high. See related etym. at **hawser.**]

en|hanced music (en hanst′, -hänst′), reproduced music in which certain modifications have been made to create artistic effects, as by varying the relative amplification in different stereophonic channels, or by increasing relatively the intensity of upper harmonics.

enhanced radiation weapon, a nuclear weapon designed to release large amounts of high-energy neutron radiation with lesser blast effects; neutron bomb: *Regular tactical nuclear weapons create more thermal and blast damage, and leave greater amounts of residual radiation, and thus such weapons are claimed to be inferior by proponents of enhanced radiation weapons . . . . Some of those in opposition to the enhanced radiation weapons suggested that it is immoral to design a weapon to kill persons but to spare property* (Robert M. Lawrence).

en|hance|ment (en hans′mənt, -häns′-), *n.* **1** the act of enhancing. **2** the state of being enhanced.

en|hanc|er (en han′sər), -hän′-), *n.* a person or thing that enhances.

en|han|cive (en han′siv, -hän′-), *adj.* that tends to enhance: *an enhancive landmark.*

en|har|mon|ic (en′här mon′ik), *adj., n. Music.* **—*adj.*** **1** having to do with notes on the scale with different names that have the same tone or sound on an instrument. *Example:* C sharp and D flat. **2** having to do with or designating a scale, a style of music, or an instrument employing intervals smaller than a semitone, especially quarter tones. **3** (in ancient Greek music) having to do with intervals smaller than a semitone. **—*n.*** enharmonic note, scale, or piece of music. [< Late Latin *enharmonicus* < Greek *enarmónios* < *en-* in + *harmónios* harmony; perhaps patterned on Greek *harmonikós* harmonic] **—en′-har|mon′i|cal|ly,** *adv.*

en haut (äɴ ō′), *French.* on high; above; aloft; upstairs.

en|heart|en (en här′tən), *v.t.* = hearten.

en|hy|drite (en hī′drīt), *n.* a mineral containing water closed up inside its cavities. [< Greek *énydros* (see etym. under **enhydrous**)]

en|hy|drous (en hī′drəs), *adj.* having water within; containing drops of water or other fluid: *enhydrous quartz.* [< Greek *énydros* (with English *-ous*) in water, containing water, living in water < *en-* in + *hýdōr* water]

E|nid (ē′nid), *n. Arthurian Legend.* the wife of Geraint.

e|nig|ma (i nig′mə), *n.* **1** a baffling or puzzling problem, situation, or person. *The mysteries of the universe are an enigma to man.* **2** a puzzling statement; riddle: *The riddle of the Sphinx was a famous enigma that was solved by Oedipus.* [< Latin *aenigma* < Greek *aínigma* < *aînos* fable, riddle]

en|ig|mat|ic (en′ig mat′ik, ē′nig-), *adj.* like an enigma or riddle; baffling; puzzling; mysterious: *She hides her real opinion behind an enigmatic smile.* **—en′ig|mat′i|cal|ly,** *adv.*

en|ig|mat|i|cal (en′ig mat′ə kəl, ē′nig-), *adj.* = enigmatic.

e|nig|ma|tize (i nig′mə tīz), *v.t.,* **-tized, -tiz|ing.** to make enigmatic.

en|isle (en īl′), *v.t.,* **-isled, -isl|ing.** *Poetic.* **1** to make an island of. **2** to place on an island; isolate. Also, **inisle.**

en|jail (en jāl′), *v.t.* to put in jail; imprison.

en|jamb|ment or **en|jambe|ment** (en jam′-mənt, -jamb′-; *French* äɴ zhäɴb mäɴ′), *n. Prosody.* the continuation of a sentence from one line or couplet into the next. [< French *enjambment* < Middle French *enjamber* encroach, stride < *en-* on (< Latin *in-*) + Old French *jambe* leg < Late Latin *gamba*]

en|jew|el (en jü′əl), *v.t.,* **-eled, -el|ing** or (*especially British*) **-elled, -el|ling.** = bejewel.

en|join (en join′), *v.t.* **1** to order, direct, or urge: *The father enjoined his son to be honest at all times.* SYN: prescribe, command, charge, bid. **2** to require or forbid by an authoritative command; issue an authoritative command to. **3** *Law.* to forbid; prohibit: *The judge enjoined the contractor from building a factory in an area set aside for homes.* [< Old French *enjoindre,* learned borrowing from Latin *injungere* to attack, charge < *in-* on + *jungere* join] **—en|join′er,** *n.*

en|join|a|ble (en joi′nə bəl), *adj.* that can be enjoined.

en|join|ment (en join′mənt), *n.* **1** the act of enjoining. **2** the state of being enjoined.

en|joy (en joi′), *v.t.* **1** to have or use with joy; be happy with; take pleasure in: *The children enjoyed their visit to the museum.* **2** to have as an advantage or benefit: *He enjoys good health.*
enjoy oneself, to be happy; have a good time: *Enjoy yourself at the party.*
[< Old French *enjoir* < *en-* in (< Latin *in-*) + *joir* enjoy < Latin *gaudēre* < *gaudium* joy] **—en|joy′er,** *n.*

en|joy|a|ble (en joi′ə bəl), *adj.* that can be enjoyed; giving joy; pleasant. **—en|joy′a|ble|ness,** *n.*

en|joy|a|bly (en joi′ə blē), *adv.* in an enjoyable manner.

en|joy|ment (en joi′mənt), *n.* **1** the act or state of enjoying: *Enjoyment anticipated is twice enjoyment fulfilled.* **2** a thing enjoyed: *His child's happiness was his chief enjoyment.* **3** pleasure; joy; delight: *Harsh criticism takes the enjoyment out of life.* SYN: happiness, felicity. See syn. under **pleasure.** **4** a having as an advantage or benefit; possession or use: *The son now has the enjoyment of his father's car. Laws protect the enjoyment of our rights.*

en|keph|a|lin (en kef′ə lin), *n.* any one of several protein substances in the brain that suppresses pain: *Enkephalins resemble morphine and other opiates because they all are able to interact with specific molecular receptors . . . , the enkephalins providing in-built pain killers* (New Scientist). [< Greek *enképhalon* brain + English *-in*]

en|ki|an|thus (en′kē an′thəs), *n.* a deciduous shrub of the heath family, native to the Far East. It is planted for its white, red, or yellow flowers and its scarlet foliage in autumn. [< New Latin *Enkianthus* genus name < Greek *énkyos* pregnant + *ánthos* flower (because of appearance)]

En|ki|du (en′kə dü), *n.* (in the Gilgamesh Epic) a wild man of the desert, created to combat Gilgamesh, whose friend he becomes instead. After his death, Gilgamesh tries and fails to rescue him from the underworld. Also, **Engidu.**

en|kin|dle (en kin′dəl), *v.t.,* **-dled, -dling. 1** to arouse; excite; stir up. **2** to light up; brighten. **3** = kindle.

en|kin|dler (en kin′dlər), *n.* a person or thing that enkindles.

enl., **1** enlarged. **2** enlisted.

en|lace (en lās′), *v.t.,* **-laced, -lac|ing. 1** to wind or lace about; encircle; enfold. **2** to twine together; interlace. SYN: interweave. [< Old French *enlacier* < *en-* in (< Latin *in-*) + *lacier* < Latin *laqueāre* < *laqueus* noose]

en|lace|ment (en lās′mənt), *n.* the act of enlacing or the state of being enlaced.

en l'air (äɴ ler′), *French.* **1** in the air; in a state of disorder or commotion. **2** without firm basis. **3** unsupported or unduly exposed, as the flank of an army.

en|large (en lärj′), *v.,* **-larged, -larg|ing.** **—*v.t.*** **1** to make larger; increase in size: *The factory was enlarged to make room for more machinery.* (*Figurative.*) *Good reading enlarges the mind.* SYN: augment, broaden, extend, expand. See syn. under **increase.** **2** *Photography.* to make (a print) larger than the original negative.
—*v.i.* to become or grow larger; increase in size: *The balloon enlarged as we pumped air into it.* SYN: augment, broaden, extend, expand. See syn. under **increase.**
enlarge on, to talk or write about in more detail: *He enlarged once more on the avarice and cowardice of the banks* (Harriet Martineau).
[< Old French *enlarger* < *en-* (< Latin *in-*) + *large* broad expansive < Latin *largus* copious]

en|large|a|ble (en lär′jə bəl), *adj.* that can be enlarged.

en|large|ment (en lärj′mənt), *n.* **1** the act of enlarging or state of being enlarged: *an enlargement of the chapel.* **2** an amount that is added; thing that enlarges something else; addition: *After we finished painting the enlargement, nobody could tell just where it was added to the garage.* **3** anything that is an enlarged form of something else. **4** *Photography.* a print that is made larger than the negative.

en|larg|er (en lär′jər), *n.* **1** a person or thing that enlarges. **2** *Photography.* an instrument for making enlargements.

en|lau|rel (en lôr′əl, lor′-), *v.t.* **-reled, -rel|ing** or (*especially British*) **-relled, -rel|ling.** *Poetic.* to crown with laurels.

en|leve|ment (en lēv′mənt), *n.* a kidnaping; abduction. [< French *enlèvement* < *enlever* to carry off < *en-* (< Latin *inde* away) + *lever* to lift]

en|light|en (en lī′tən), *v.t.* **1** to give the light of truth and knowledge to; free from prejudice, ignorance, or the like: *He found the lesson very enlightening.* **2** to inform; instruct. **3** *Archaic.* to give light to. **—en|light′en|er,** *n.*

en|light|ened (en lī′tənd), *adj.* **1** informed: *an enlightened populace.* **2** free from prejudice, ignorance, or the like: *enlightened views.*

en|light|en|ment (en lī′tən mənt), *n.* **1** the act or process of enlightening or state of being enlightened; information; instruction. SYN: See syn. under **education.** **2** *Buddhism.* the state of heightened perception in which the individual transcends the mind and body and attains nirvana.

En|light|en|ment (en lī′tən mənt), *n.* a philosophical movement in France and other European countries during the 1700's that emphasized rationalism, intellectual freedom, and freedom from prejudice and superstition in social and political activity. [translation of German *Aufklärung*]

en|list (en list′), *v.i.* **1** to join the army, navy, or some other branch of the armed forces, especially voluntarily: *He enlisted in the navy.* SYN: enroll. **2** *Figurative.* to join in some cause or undertaking; give help or support: *Many members of our class enlist in the Red Cross drive each year.* **—*v.t.*** **1** to get to join some branch of the armed forces; induct: *Many men were enlisted during the war.* **2** *Figurative.* to get to join in some cause or undertaking; secure the help or support of: *The students were enlisted in the school's cleanup program.* **3** to enter on a list; enroll. **—en|list′er,** *n.*

en|list|ed man (en lis′tid), a man in the armed forces who is not a commissioned officer, warrant officer, or cadet.

en|list|ee (en lis′tē, -lis′tē′), *n.* a person who enlists for military service.

en|list|ment (en list′mənt), *n.* **1** the act of enlisting: *Enlistment of help in an election takes long hours of persuasion.* **2** the condition of being enlisted. **3** the time for which a person enlists: *The old soldier's fifteen-year enlistment will be over in two years.*

en|liv|en (en lī′vən), *v.t.* **1** to make lively, active, gay, or cheerful: *Spring enlivens all nature. Bright curtains enliven a room.* SYN: exhilarate, brighten. **2** *Obsolete.* to give life to. **—en|liv′en|er,** *n.* **—en-liv′en|ing|ly,** *adv.*

en|liv|en|ment (en lī′vən mənt), *n.* **1** the act of

enlivening: *The enlivenment of trade is the constant care of businessmen.* **2** the state of being enlivened: *We rejoice in the recent enlivenment of trade.* **3** something that enlivens: *Full employment is an enlivenment to trade.*

en|lock (en lok′), *v.t.* to lock up; shut in; enclose.

en|mar|ble (en mär′bəl), *v.t.*, **-bled, -bling. 1** to sculpture in marble. **2** adorn or inlay with marble: *a richly enmarbled altar.* Also, **emmarble.**

en masse (en mas′; *French* äɴ màs′), in a group; all together: *Cockroaches migrate en masse* (Science News Letter). [< French *en masse* in mass]

en|mesh (en mesh′), *v.t.* to catch in a net; enclose in meshes; entangle: *The big gear at the extreme left ... enmeshes with a smaller gear on the starting motor when you use the "starter"* (Beauchamp, Mayfield, and West). Also, **emmesh, immesh, inmesh.**

en|mesh|ment (en mesh′mənt), *n.* the state of being enmeshed.

en|mi|ty (en′mə tē), *n., pl.* **-ties.** the feeling that enemies have for each other; hostility or hatred: *For enmity and hate are contrary to friendship and concord* (William Caxton). **SYN:** animosity, antipathy. [Middle English *enemitie* < Old French *ennemistie* < *ennemi* enemy < Latin *inimīcus*]

en|ne|ad (en′ē ad), *n.* a group of nine persons or things. [< Greek *enneás, -ádos* < *ennéa* nine]

en|ne|ad|ic (en′ē ad′ik), *adj.* having to do with an ennead or the number nine.

en|ne|a|gon (en′ē ə gon), *n. Geometry.* a plane figure having nine angles and nine sides. [< Greek *ennéa* nine + *gōníā* angle]

en|ne|ag|o|nal (en′ē ag′ə nəl), *adj. Geometry.* having nine angles and nine sides.

en|ne|a|he|dral (en′ē ə hē′drəl), *adj. Geometry.* having nine faces. [< Greek *ennéa* nine + *hédra* base + English *-al*[1]]

en|ne|a|he|dron (en′ē ə hē′drən), *n. Geometry.* a solid figure having nine faces. [< Greek *ennéa* nine + *hédra* base]

en|ne|a|style (en′ē ə stīl), *adj. Architecture.* having nine columns. [< Greek *ennéa* nine + *stŷlos* column]

en|no|ble (en nō′bəl), *v.t.*, **-bled, -bling. 1** to raise in the respect of others; make noble; dignify; exalt: *A good deed ennobles the person who does it.* **2** to raise to a noble rank; give a title of nobility to: *The king ennobled his general for winning the war.* **3** to make finer or more noble in nature; elevate: *His character had been ennobled through suffering.*

en|no|ble|ment (en nō′bəl mənt), *n.* **1** the act of ennobling. **2** the state of being ennobled: *His ennoblement did not change his character or his way of life.*

en|no|bler (en nō′blər), *n.* a person or thing that ennobles.

en|nui (än′wē), *n., v.*, **-nuied** or **-nuyed, -nuy|ing.** —*n.* a feeling of weariness and discontent that comes from having no occupation or interest; boredom: *Gilded halls upon gilded halls can add up to ennui* (A. H. Weiler).
—*v.t.* to affect with ennui; bore: *Evenings ... sacred to reading on his part, and mortally ennuying to myself* (Jane Welsh Carlyle).
[< French *ennui* < Old French *ennuyer* to chagrin. See related etym. at **annoy.**]

en|nuy|é (äɴ nwē yā′), *adj., n. French.* —*adj.* affected with ennui; bored: ... *the constrained effort of the ennuyé man of the world* (Edgar Allan Poe).
—*n.* a man who is bored.

en|nuy|ée (äɴ nwē yā′), *adj., n. French.* the feminine form of **ennuyé.**

E|noch (ē′nək), *n.* **1** the father of Methuselah (in the Bible, Genesis 5:18-24). **2** the eldest son of Cain (in the Bible, Genesis 4:17, 18).

Enoch Arden, 1 the hero of the narrative poem *Enoch Arden* (1864) by Tennyson. He is a shipwrecked sailor who returns home after some years to find that his wife had thought him dead and married his friend. **2** any missing person presumed to be dead but later discovered alive: *This deliberate Enoch Arden first wanted to know how they had found him* (Maclean's).

e|nod|al (ē nō′dəl), *adj. Botany.* without nodes; jointless. —**e|nod′al|ly,** *adv.*

e|nol (ē′nol, -nōl), *n. Chemistry.* the tautomeric form of a ketone, containing a hydroxyl group attached to a carbon atom with a double bond. [< Greek *hen-*, stem of *eîs* one + English *-ol*[1]]

e|nol|ase (ē′nə lās), *n.* an enzyme active in glycolysis, found in the muscles and in yeast. [< *enol* + *-ase*]

e|nol|ic (ē nō′lik, -nol′ik), *adj.* **1** of the nature of enol. **2** belonging to enol.

e|no|log|i|cal (ē′nə loj′ə kəl), *adj.* of or having to do with enology. Also, **oenological.**

e|nol|o|gist (ē nol′ə jist), *n.* a student of enology; person who knows much about wines. Also, **oenologist.**

e|nol|o|gy (ē nol′ə jē), *n.* the art of making wine or knowledge or study of wines. Also, **oenology.** [< Greek *oînos* wine + English *-logy*]

en|oph|thal|mus or **en|oph|thal|mos** (en′of-thal′məs), *n. Medicine.* an abnormal sinking of the eyeball into the orbit. [< New Latin *enophthalmus, enophthalmos* < Greek *en-* in + *ophthalmós* eye]

e|norm (i nôrm′), *adj. Archaic.* abnormally large; fat; monstrous; enormous.

e|nor|mi|ty (i nôr′mə tē), *n., pl.* **-ties. 1** extreme wickedness; outrageousness: *the enormity of religious persecution. The enormity of his crime made it probable that the man was not sane.* **2** an extremely wicked crime; outrageous offense. **3** *Informal.* great size, especially of a problem, job, etc.; enormousness: *The enormity of the task is staggering.* [< Old French *enormite* < Latin *ēnormitās* < *ēnormis;* see etym. under **enormous**]

e|nor|mous (i nôr′məs), *adj.* **1** very, very large; huge: *Long ago, enormous, shaggy mammoths lived on the earth. The glutton had an enormous appetite.* **SYN:** immense, colossal, gigantic, vast, mammoth, prodigious, stupendous. See syn. under **huge. 2** extremely wicked; outrageous: *enormous crimes.* **SYN:** abominable, atrocious. [< Latin *ēnormis* (with English *-ous*) < *ex-* out of + *norma* pattern, rule] —**e|nor′mous|ness,** *n.*

e|nor|mous|ly (i nôr′məs lē), *adv.* in or to an enormous degree; extremely; vastly; beyond measure: *enormously wealthy.*

E|nos (ē′nəs), *n.* a son of Seth and grandson of Adam (in the Bible, Genesis 5:3-11).

e|no|sis (e nō′sis), *n.* **1** union, especially the union of Cyprus with Greece. **2** a movement of Greek Cypriots for such union. [< Greek *hénōsis* union]

en|os|to|sis (en′os tō′sis), *n., pl.* **-ses** (-sēz). a bony growth in the interior of a bone.

e|nough (i nuf′), *adj., n., adv., interj.* —**adj.** as much or as many as needed or wanted; sufficient: *Buy enough food for the picnic. Are there enough seats for all?*
—***n.*** a quantity or number needed or wanted; sufficient amount: *Has he had enough to eat? There were just enough of the apples to have one each.* **SYN:** sufficiency, plenty.
—***adv.* 1** sufficiently; adequately; until no more is needed or wanted: *Have you played enough?* **2** quite; fully: *He was willing enough to go.* **3** rather; fairly: *She talks well enough for a baby.* **SYN:** passably, tolerably.
—***interj.*** stop! no more! *Lay on, Macduff! And damn'd be him that first cries "Hold, enough!"* (Shakespeare).
sure enough. See under **sure.**
[Old English *genōg*]
—***Syn.*** *adj.* **Enough, sufficient, adequate** mean as much as is needed. **Enough,** and its more formal equivalent, **sufficient,** mean as much as will fully satisfy a desire or need: *A growing boy never has enough* (or *sufficient*) *time to play. I have enough* (or *sufficient*) *money to pay the bill. She is not eating enough* (or *sufficient*) *food.* **Adequate** means as much as is needed to meet special, sometimes minimum, requirements: *To be healthy, one must have an adequate diet.*
► **enough** may be preceded by a plural or singular verb: *Five boxes of apples are* (or *is*) *enough for the camp. Enough* often follows the word it modifies: *We have room enough.* [*Her*] *sewing is good enough for me. You don't get up early enough.*

e|nounce (i nouns′), *v.t.*, **e|nounced, e|nouncing. 1** to announce; declare; proclaim. **2** to state (a proposition or opinion) definitely. **3** to pronounce; enunciate: *The student should be able to enounce these* [*sounds*] *independently* (A. M. Bell). [< Latin *ēnuntiāre* (see etym. under **enunciate**); influenced by English *announce,* or French *annoncer*]

E|nov|id (e nov′id), *n. Trademark.* a drug derived from various hormones, such as estrogen, used in ovulation control and especially as an oral contraceptive; norethynodrel.

e|now (i nou′), *adj., n., adv. Archaic.* enough. [Middle English *ynowe,* Old English *genōge,* plural < *genōg* enough]

en pan|tou|fles (äɴ päɴ tü′flə), *French.* **1** in slippers: *Then came the French, shuffling along as if en pantoufles* (New Yorker). **2** *Figurative.* easy, casual, or informal: *The authority and erudition he can pack into eight pages on "The North-East in the Eighteenth Century," for instance, is yet one more proof that he is never en pantoufles* (London Times).

en pas|sant (äɴ pä säɴ′), *French.* **1** in passing; by the way; incidentally: *If I could drop a word en passant into the Sultan's ear, the syndicate would be overjoyed to set aside a few shares of stock for both of us* (New Yorker). **2** a form of pawn capture in chess. If a pawn in its first move passes over a square controlled by an opposing pawn, the opposing pawn has the right to capture it immediately while advancing to that square. *Why, you're so rusty you've forgotten the rules about castling and pawn taking pawn en passant* (Punch).

en pen|sion (äɴ päɴ syôɴ′), *French.* as a boarder; in a boarding house or boarding school: *The other remarkable film is ... taken from Jules Barbey d'Aurevilly's notable tale of a young officer en pension in the provincial château of a dull couple* (New Yorker).

en|phy|tot|ic (en′fī tot′ik), *adj. Botany.* recurrent among plants throughout a region: *an enphytotic disease.* [< *en-*[2] + Greek *phytón* plant + *-ōtikos,* an adjective suffix]

en|plane (en plān′), *v.i., v.t.* **-planed, -plan|ing.** to go or put aboard an airplane: [*She*] *enplanes to work* (Saturday Evening Post). Also, **emplane.**

en plein (äɴ plaɴ′), *French.* in full; fully; entirely: *I would have liked to stake all our troubles en plein and to lose them* (Harper's).

en plein air (äɴ ple ner′), *French.* in the open air: *Terraces and gardens ... provide space for ninety patrons, en plein air* (New Yorker).

en plein jour (äɴ plaɴ zhür′), *French.* in open daylight; in the open; not concealed.

***en pointe** or **en pointes** (äɴ pwaɴt′), *French.* (in ballet) on the toe or toes: *A ballet dancer was ... turning from side to side on the stiffened ends of the flesh-pink satin slippers that keep her en pointe* (Newsweek).

***en pointe**

en poste (äɴ pôst′), *French.* on duty: *It* [*a newspaper*] *must keep something like 20 highly experienced foreign correspondents en poste throughout the world: a highly expensive operation* (London Times).

en prince (äɴ praɴs′), *French.* as a prince; in princely style.

en prin|cipe (äɴ praɴ sēp′), *French.* in principle: *He will also be attempting ... to get some sort of agreement en principe as to the future shape and limits of the cold war* (New Yorker).

en prise (äɴ prēz′), *French.* in a grip; in a position for capture in chess.

en queue (äɴ kœ′), *French.* as a tail; in a line; following.

en|quire (en kwīr′), *v.t., v.i.*, **-quired, -quir|ing.** = inquire.

en|quir|y (en kwīr′ē, en′kwər-), *n., pl.* **-quir|ies.** = inquiry.

en|rage (en rāj′), *v.t.*, **-raged, -rag|ing.** to make very angry; make furious; madden: *The dog was enraged by their teasing. Their refusal to come enraged him.* **SYN:** infuriate, exasperate, incense, anger. [< Old French *enrager* < *en-* in (< Latin *in-*) + *rage* rage]

en|ra|gé (äɴ rà zhā′), *n. French Slang.* **1** a militant radical: *Members of Occident, an extreme-right-wing student group, waiting in the street to beat up Nanterre enragés, start fighting with police when they see enragés arrested* (Mavis Gallant). **2** (literally) enraged one.

en|raged (en rājd′), *adj.* angered; infuriated; furious: *With an enraged roar, the elephant charged.*

en|rage|ment (en rāj′mənt), *n.* **1** the act of enraging. **2** the state of being enraged.

en|rank (en rangk′), *v.t.* to arrange in a rank or row, or in ranks.

en rap|port (äɴ rà pôr′), *French.* in sympathy; in agreement: *a process by which man puts himself en rapport with his environment* (New Yorker).

en|rapt (en rapt′), *adj.* filled with great delight; rapt; enraptured.

en|rap|ture (en rap′chər), *v.t.*, **-tured, -tur|ing.** to move to rapture; fill with great delight; entrance: *The audience was enraptured by the singer's beautiful voice.*

en|rap|tur|er (en rap′chər ər), *n.* a person or thing that enraptures.

en|reg|is|ter (en rej′ə stər), *v.t.* to register; record.

en rè|gle (äɴ re′glə), *French.* according to rule; in order.

Pronunciation Key: hat, āge, cãre, fär; let, ēqual, tėrm; it, īce; hot, ōpen, ôrder; oil, out; cup, pu̇t, rüle; child; long; thin; ᴛʜen; zh, measure; ə represents **a** in about, **e** in taken, **i** in pencil, **o** in lemon, **u** in circus.

en ré|su|mé (äɴ rā zʏ mā′), *French.* to sum up; on the whole.

en re|traite (äɴ rə tret′), *French.* **1** in retreat; retreating. **2** in retirement; on the retired list.

en re|vanche (äɴ rə vänsh′), *French.* by way of retaliation; in return.

en|rich (en rich′), *v.t.* **1** to make rich or richer: *Decorations enrich a room.* (*Figurative.*) *An education enriches your mind.* (*Figurative.*) *Many foreign words and phrases have enriched the English language.* **2** to raise the nutritive value of (a food) by adding vitamins and minerals in processing: *enriched milk.* **3** to make fertile; fertilize: *Fertilizer enriches the soil.* **4** to decorate; ornament; adorn: *The coat was enriched with silver buttons.* **5** to make (a radioactive element) more fissionable by increasing the content of fissionable material: *Uranium that has its content of the isotope U^{235} increased is called enriched uranium.* **6** *Education.* to improve (a curriculum or program) by providing students with more varied and intensive material of study: *Ordinarily, these "enriched" courses are reserved for selected students but some schools do give enrichment subjects to all students, in foreign languages for elementary students, for example* (Wall Street Journal).
[< Old French *enrichir* < *en-* in + *riche* rich] —**en|rich′er**, *n.*

en|rich|en (en rich′ən), *v.t.* to make rich or richer; enrich: *The Canadian north is the present frontier of North America and its winning cannot but enrichen and strengthen the Canadian people* (Wall Street Journal). (*Figurative.*) *... the enrichening perspectives provided by great literature* (Ralph Ellison).

en|rich|ment (en rich′mənt), *n.* **1** the act of enriching or condition of being enriched: (*Figurative.*) *the enrichment of life by knowledge.* **2** a thing that enriches: (*Figurative.*) *Books are an enrichment of life.*

en|ridge (en rij′), *v.t.*, **-ridged, -ridg|ing.** to form into ridges.

en|ring (en ring′), *v.t.*, **-ringed, -ring|ing.** **1** to form a ring or circle about; encircle. **2** to put a ring or rings on; adorn with a ring.

en|robe (en rōb′), *v.t.* **-robed, -rob|ing.** to clothe with or as if with a robe; dress; attire.

en|robe|ment (en rōb′mənt), *n.* the process of enrobing or state of being enrobed.

en|rob|er (en rō′bər), *n.* **1** a machine for coating candy. **2** a person who enrobes.

en|roll or **en|rol** (en rōl′), *v.*, **-rolled, -roll|ing.**
—*v.t.* **1** to make a member: *He enrolled his son in a music school. The school enrolled 200 students.* **2** to enlist in the armed forces: *After graduation, he was enrolled for military service.* **3** to write in a list: *The secretary enrolled our names.* **4** to put in a record; record. **5** to roll or wrap up. **6** *Obsolete.* to engross (a document).
—*v.i.* **1** to become a member: *Her mother enrolled in a sewing class.* **2** to join the armed forces; enlist: *He enrolled in the navy after graduation.* **3** to have one's name written in a list: *We checked to see if he enrolled among the voters of our district.* [< Old French *enroller* < *en-* in (< Latin *in-*) + *roller* roll] —**en|roll′er**, *n.*

en|roll|ee (en rō′lē′), *n.* a person who enrolls in a group as a member: *A class of 157 students, all brimming with hope and ambition, is ... in an unusual school, designed especially to prepare enrollees for final exams* (Wall Street Journal).

en|roll|ment or **en|rol|ment** (en rōl′mənt), *n.* **1** the act or process of enrolling: *Enrollment took place in the fall.* **2** the number enrolled: *The school has an enrollment of 200 students.* **3** a roll, register, or record.

en|root (en rüt′, -rủt′), *v.t.* **1** to fix by the root. **2** *Figurative.* to implant deeply; fix firmly.

en route (än rüt′), on the way: *En route to California, he stopped off in Colorado.* [< French *en route* on the way]

ens (enz), *n., pl.* **en|ti|a.** *Philosophy.* **1** being, considered in the abstract. **2** something that is; an entity. [< Late Latin *ēns*, present participle of Latin *esse* be]

Ens., ensign.

en|sam|ple (en sam′pəl, -säm′-), *n. Archaic.* an example; instance. [< Anglo-French *ensample*, Old French *essample;* see etym. under **example**]

en|san|guine (en sang′gwin), *v.t.*, **-guined, -guin|ing.** to stain with blood: *The pirate waved an ensanguined sword.*

en|sate (en′sāt), *adj. Biology.* sword-shaped; ensiform. [< New Latin *ensatus* < Latin *ēnsis* sword]

en|sconce (en skons′), *v.t.*, **-sconced, -sconc|ing.** **1** to shelter safely; hide: *The soldiers were ensconced in strongly fortified trenches. We were ensconced in the cellar during the tornado.* **2** to settle comfortably and firmly: *The cat ensconced itself in the armchair.* [< *en-*[1] + *sconce*[3] fortification, probably < Dutch *schans*]

en|scroll (en skrōl′), *v.t.* = inscroll.

en|seal (en sēl′), *v.t.* **1** to close up with a seal; seal up. **2** *Archaic.* to put a seal or stamp on.

en|se et ar|a|tro (en′sē et ar′ə trō), *Latin.* with sword and with plow; with service both in war and in peace.

en|sel|lure (en sel′yər), *n. Anthropology.* a strongly marked curve of the lower back, inward at the waist and outward below. [< French *ensellure* < *en-* in + *selle* saddle]

en|sem|ble (än säm′bəl), *n., adv.* —*n.* **1** all the parts of a thing considered together; the general effect: *Its members have a commendable knack of subordinating themselves as parts of the total ensemble* (New Yorker). **2** *Music.* **a** a united performance of the full number of singers, players, or performers: *After the solo, all the singers joined in the ensemble.* **b** the group of musicians or the musical instruments used in such a performance: *Two violins, a cello, and a harp made up the string ensemble.* **3** a complete, harmonious costume: *Her dress and coat made an attractive ensemble.*
—*adv. Obsolete.* together; at the same time.
[< Old French *ensemble* < Latin *īnsimul* < *in-* + *simul* at the same time]

ensemble playing or **acting**, a unity of artistic purpose by the entire cast in a theatrical production: *Ensemble playing results when every actor adjusts himself to the needs of the play, and remains aware of the methods, strengths, and weaknesses of his fellow performers* (Oscar G. and Lenyth Brockett).

en|se pe|tit pla|ci|dam sub li|ber|ta|te qui|e|tem (en′sē pē′tit plas′ə dam sub lib′ər tā′tē kwī ē′tem), *Latin.* by the sword we seek peace, but peace only under liberty (the motto of Massachusetts).

en|sep|ul|cher (en sep′əl kər), *v.t.* to put into a sepulcher or tomb; entomb.

en|sep|ul|chre (en sep′əl kər), *v.t.*, **-chred, -chring.** = ensepulcher.

en|serf (en sėrf′), *v.t.* to make a serf or serfs of: *the enserfed peasants of czarist Russia.*

en|sheathe (en shēᴛʜ′), *v.t.*, **-sheathed, -sheath|ing.** = insheathe.

en|shield (en shēld′), *v.t.* = shield.

en|shrine (en shrīn′), *v.t.*, **-shrined, -shrin|ing.** **1** to enclose in a shrine: *A fragment of the Cross is enshrined in the cathedral.* **2** *Figurative.* to keep sacred; cherish: *Memories of happier days were enshrined in the old man's heart.*

en|shrine|ment (en shrīn′mənt), *n.* **1** the act of enshrining. **2** anything that enshrines or surrounds.

en|shroud (en shroud′), *v.t.* to cover with a shroud: (*Figurative.*) *Fog enshrouded the ship, but we could hear its whistle.*

en|si|form (en′sə fôrm), *adj. Biology.* sword-shaped; ensate; xiphoid. [< New Latin *ensiformis* < Latin *ēnsis* sword + *forma* form]

en|sign (en′sīn, -sən *for 1, 3-6;* en′sən *for 2*), *n.* **1** a flag or banner: *The ensign of the United States is the Stars and Stripes.* **2** a navy officer ranking next below a lieutenant junior grade and next above a warrant officer. An ensign is the lowest commissioned officer in the United States Navy. *Abbr:* Ens. **3** a former British army officer whose duty was carrying the flag; standard-bearer. **4** the sign of one's rank, position, or power; symbol of authority: *The ensign of the queen was her crown and scepter.* **5** a sign; emblem; badge. **6** *Obsolete.* a signal. [< Old French *enseigne* < Latin *īnsignia*, plural. See etym. of doublet **insignia.**]

en|sign|cy (en′sən sē), *n., pl.* **-cies.** = ensignship.

ensign fly, a parasitic hymenopterous insect whose abdomen is held up high like a flag by a long, stalklike foot.

en|sign|ship (en′sən ship), *n.* the rank or position of an ensign in the navy or army.

ensign staff, the staff at the stern of a ship from which an ensign is flown.

en|si|lage (en′sə lij), *n., v.*, **-laged, -lag|ing.** —*n.* **1** the preservation of green fodder by packing it in a silo or pit. **2** green fodder preserved in this way; silage. Ensilage is used to feed cattle in winter.
—*v.t.* = ensile.
[< French *ensilage* < *ensiler;* see etym. under **ensile**]

en|sile (en sīl′, en′sīl), *v.t.*, **-siled, -sil|ing.** **1** to preserve (green fodder) in a silo. **2** to make into ensilage. [< French *ensiler* < Spanish *ensilar* < *en-* in (< Latin *in-*) + *silo* silo]

en|sky (en skī′), *v.t., v.i.* **-skied** or **-skyed, -sky|ing.** **1** to place or be placed in the sky or heaven: *I hold you as a thing enskied, and sainted* (Shakespeare). **2** *Figurative.* to raise or be placed very high; make or be lofty: *No other place I know has a ... castle enskied over its principal shops* (Harold Hobson). *Secluded in the yard, the lady looked even more commandingly rapt and enskied* (Sylvia Townsend Warner).

en|sky|ment (en skī′mənt), *n.* the state of being enskied: *What a sublime end of one's body, what an enskyment; what a life after death* (Robinson Jeffers).

en|slave (en slāv′), *v.t.*, **-slaved, -slav|ing.** to make a slave of; take away freedom from: *Education makes a people ... easy to govern but impossible to enslave* (Lord Brougham).

en|slav|ed|ness (en slā′vid nis), *n.* the condition of being enslaved.

en|slave|ment (en slāv′mənt), *n.* **1** the act of enslaving. **2** the condition of being enslaved.

en|slav|er (en slā′vər), *n.* a person or thing that enslaves.

ens le|gis (enz lē′jis), *Latin.* a person or thing created by law, such as a corporation.

en|snare (en snãr′), *v.t.*, **-snared, -snar|ing.** to catch in a snare; snare; trap: *She ensnared mankind with her fair looks* (Milton). **SYN:** entrap, entangle. Also, **insnare.**

en|snare|ment (en snãr′mənt), *n.* the act of ensnaring or state of being ensnared; entrapment. Also, **insnarement.**

en|snar|er (en snãr′ər), *n.* a person or thing that ensnares. Also, **insnarer.**

en|snarl (en snärl′), *v.t.* to catch or entangle (in): (*Figurative.*) *ensnarled in the web of prejudice.*

en|sor|cell or **en|sor|cel** (en sôr′səl), *v.t.*, **-celled, -cell|ing.** to bewitch; enchant: *The mice creep out, ensorcelled by that high, uncertain tremolo* (New Yorker). [< Old French *ensorceler* < *en-* in (< Latin *in-*) + *sorceler* to bewitch < *sorcier* sorcerer]

en|soul (en sōl′), *v.t.* **1** to put or take into the soul. **2** to endow with a soul. Also, **insoul.**

en|sphere (en sfir′), *v.t.*, **-sphered, -spher|ing.** to enclose in a sphere; make into a sphere; encircle.

Ens Su|pre|mum (enz sủ prē′məm), *Latin.* the Supreme Being; God.

en|sta|tite (en′stə tīt), *n. Mineralogy.* a variety of pyroxene, occurring in gray, green, or brown colors. *Formula:* $MgSiO_3$ [< Greek *enstátēs* adversary + English *-ite*[1] (because of its refractory nature)]

en|stool (en stül′), *v.t.* (in western Africa) to place (a chief) in office: *He [spoke] to one newly enstooled chief* (Time). [< *en-*[1] + *stool*]

en|sue (en sü′), *v.*, **-sued, -su|ing.** —*v.i.* **1** to come after; follow. The ensuing year means the year following this year. **SYN:** succeed. **2** to happen as a result: *In his anger he hit the man, and a fight ensued. I spent my allowance the first day, and a lean week ensued.* **SYN:** result. See syn. under **follow.**
—*v.t. Obsolete.* to follow; pursue: *Let him seek peace, and ensue it* (I Peter 3:11).
[< Old French *ensivre, ensuivre* < Latin *īnsequi* < *in-* upon + *sequī* follow] —**en|su′ing|ly**, *adv.*

en suite (än swēt′), *French.* in succession; in a connected series: *The salons of the Sorbonne are ... arranged en suite for exhibitions and academic receptions* (New Yorker).

en|sure (en shủr′), *v.t.*, **-sured, -sur|ing.** **1** to make sure or certain: *Careful planning and hard work ensured the success of the party.* **2** to make sure of getting; secure: *A letter of introduction will ensure you an interview.* **3** to make safe; protect: *Proper clothing ensured us against suffering from the cold.* **4** to guarantee against risk; insure. **5** *Obsolete.* to inform (a person) positively. [< Anglo-French *enseurer* < *en-* (< Latin *in-*) + *seür* sure]

▶ **ensure, insure.** Although *ensure* and *insure* are interchangeable in most meanings, prevailing usage tends to differentiate them. *Ensure* is the usual spelling for "make sure or certain"; *insure* for "arrange for money payment in case of loss, accident, or death": *These letters ensure your claims. He insured his car against theft.*

en|swathe (en swāᴛʜ′), *v.t.*, **-swathed, -swath|ing.** to bind or wrap in a bandage; swathe. Also, **inswathe.**

en|swathe|ment (en swāᴛʜ′mənt), *n.* the act of enswathing or condition of being enswathed.

-ent, *suffix added to verbs.* **1** (*to form adjectives*) that _____s; _____ing: *Absorbent = that absorbs or absorbing. Indulgent = that indulges or indulging.*
2 (*to form nouns*) one that _____s: *Correspondent = one that corresponds. President = one that presides.*
3 (*to form adjectives*) other meanings, as in *competent, confident.*
See also **-ant.**
[< Latin *-ēns, -entis,* present participle endings of Latin verbs in *-ēre, -ere, -īre*]
▶ See **-ance** for usage note.

ent., entomology.

ENT (no periods), ear, nose, and throat.

***en|tab|la|ture** (en tab′lə chủr, -chər), *n. Architecture.* a part of a building resting on the top of columns. A classical entablature consisted of an architrave, frieze, and cornice. [< Italian *intavolatura* < *intavolare* arrange < *in-* on + *tavola* board, tablet < Latin *tabula*]

cornice
frieze
architrave
***entablature**

en|ta|ble|ment (en tā′bəl mənt), *n.* **1** = entablature. **2** the part of a pedestal above the dado.
en|tad (en′tad), *adv. Anatomy, Zoology.* on or towards the inner side or interior; in or into a position nearer to the center. [< Greek *entós* within + Latin *ad* toward]
en|tail (en tāl′), *v., n.* —*v.t.* **1** to impose or require: *Owning an automobile entailed greater expense than he had expected.* **2** to limit the inheritance of (property or right) to a specified line of heirs so that it cannot be left to anyone else. An entailed estate usually passes to the eldest son.
—*n.* **1** the act or process of entailing. **2** an entailed inheritance. **3** the order of inheritance settled for an estate: *Though the nobleman had quarreled with his heir, he could not break the entail and leave the estate to someone else.*
[< *en-*[1] + Old French *taille* tax, a cutting < *tailler* to cut; limit] —**en|tail′er**, *n.*
en|tail|ment (en tāl′mənt), *n.* the action of entailing.
en|tal (en′təl), *adj. Anatomy, Zoology.* inner; internal. [< Greek *entós* within + English *-al*[1]]
en|tame (en tām′), *v.t.*, **-tamed**, **-tam|ing.** to tame; subdue.
ent|a|me|ba or **ent|a|moe|ba** (en′tə mē′bə), *n., pl.* **-bas**, **-bae** (-bē). = endameba.
en|tan|gle (en tang′gəl), *v.t.*, **-gled**, **-gling.** **1** to get twisted up and caught; tangle: *Threads are easily entangled. He entangled his feet in the coil of rope and fell down.* SYN: snarl, knot, mat.
2 *Figurative.* to get into difficulty; involve: *entangling alliances. Do not entangle my brother in your schemes.* SYN: implicate, ensnare. **3** to make tangled: *The kitten entangled the ball of yarn.*
4 *Figurative.* to perplex; confuse: *My mind is entangled by this mass of data.* SYN: bewilder, embarrass. —**en|tan′gling|ly**, *adv.*
en|tan|gle|ment (en tang′gəl mənt), *n.* **1** the act of entangling or condition of being entangled: (*Figurative.*) *George Washington warned against entanglement with foreign countries.* **2** a thing that entangles; snare; something hard to get out of or get through: *The trenches were protected by barbed-wire entanglements.*
en|tan|gler (en tang′glər), *n.* a person or thing that entangles or ensnares.
en|ta|sia (en tā′zhə, -zhē ə), *n.* a constrictive spasm, such as in a cramp or in lockjaw. [< New Latin *entasia* < Greek *éntasis;* see etym. under **entasis**]
en|ta|sis (en′tə sis), *n. Architecture.* a slight, gradual swelling and tapering of the shaft of a column between the base and capital. [< New Latin *entasis* < Greek *éntasis* < *enteínein* strain, stretch out]
en|té (äɴ tā′), *adj. Heraldry.* divided from the rest of the field by a wedge-shaped or chevronlike outline.
en|tel|e|chy (en tel′ə kē), *n., pl.* **-chies.** *Philosophy.* a thing that is real or actual, and not simply a potentiality. [< Greek *enteléchia* (coined by Aristotle) < *entelés* complete, full (< *en-* in + *télos* perfection) + *échein* have]
en|tel|lus (en tel′əs), *n.* an Indian monkey having a long tail, a full beard, and a caplike growth of hair. The Hindus regard it as a sacred animal. [< New Latin *entellus* the species name < Latin *Entellus* an old man, a famous pugilist, in Virgil's "Aeneid"; allusion unknown]
en|tel|o|dont (en tel′ə dont), *n.* any one of a family of giant pigs that lived during the Oligocene and early Miocene epochs. They attained a height of six feet. [< New Latin *Entelodontidae* the family name < Greek *entelês* complete, full + *odoús, odóntos* tooth]
en|tem|ple (en tem′pəl), *v.t.*, **-pled**, **-pling.** to enclose as in a temple; enshrine.
en|tente (än tänt′), *n.* **1** an understanding; agreement between two or more governments: *Two powerful groups are ... to fix the basis for an entente* (London Times). **2** the parties to an understanding; governments that have made an agreement. [< French *entente* < *entendre* understand < Latin *intendere.* See etym. of doublet **intent**[1].]
en|tente cor|diale (äɴ täɴt′kôr dyȧl′), *French.* a friendly understanding or agreement, especially between two or more governments: *Between the Greeks and the Turks ... there is an entente cordiale* (New Yorker).
En|tente Cor|diale (äɴ täɴt′kôr dyȧl′), the agreement between France and Great Britain in 1904, which became the Triple Entente when Russia joined it in 1907.
en|ter (en′tər), *v.t.* **1** to go into; come into: *He entered the house. The bullet entered his heart.* (*Figurative.*) *The idea ... had never entered her head* (Anthony Trollope). **2** to become a part or member of; join: *to enter a contest. He entered the university at seventeen. The men entered the army.* **3** to cause to join or enter; enroll: *Parents enter their children in school.* **4** *Figurative.* to begin; start: *After years of training, the doctor entered the practice of medicine.* **5** to write or print in a book, list, or other place for holding data: *In a dictionary words are entered in alphabetical order.* **6** *Law.* to put in regular form; make a record of; record: *The teller entered the deposit in my bank book. The injured man entered a complaint in court.* **7** to report (a ship or its cargo) at the custom house: *The cargo having been entered in due form, we began trading* (Richard Henry Dana). **8** *Obsolete.* to initiate; introduce; train.
—*v.i.* to go in; come in: *Let them enter. The actor's cue to enter was after the first speech.*
enter into, a to take part in; join in; form a part of: *The two speakers entered into a debate. Lead enters into the composition of pewter. The principle of nuclear fission enters into the operation of a nuclear reactor.* **b** to consider; discuss: *to enter into a question of law. Let's enter into the subject of taxes.*
enter on (or **upon**) **a** to begin; start: *He entered on his professional duties as soon as he finished law school.* **b** to take possession of: *The heir entered upon the estate the first of the following year.*
[< Old French *entrer* < Latin *intrāre* < *intrā* within] —**en′ter|er**, *n.*
enter-, *combining form.* the form of **entero-** before vowels, as in *enteritis.*
en|ter|a|ble (en′tər ə bəl), *adj.* that can be entered.
en|ter|al (en′tər əl), *adj.* = intestinal. [< *enter-* + *-al*[1}] —**en′ter|al|ly**, *adv.*
en|ter|al|gi|a (en′tə ral′jē ə), *n.* spasmodic pain in the intestines or stomach; colic. [< Greek *énteron* intestine + *-algiā* < *álgos* pain]
en|ter|ate (en′tər it), *adj.* having an enteron; provided with an alimentary canal.
en|ter|ec|to|my (en′tə rek′tə mē), *n., pl.* **-mies.** the surgical removal of a portion of the intestine. [< *enter-* + *-ectomy*]
Entered Apprentice, the first degree granted to a man who joins the Blue Lodge, the basic organization of Freemasonry.
en|ter|ic (en ter′ik), *adj.* = intestinal. [< Greek *enterikós* < *éntera,* plural of *énteron* intestine]
enteric fever, = typhoid fever.
en|ter|ing chisel (en′tər ing), a bent chisel with a bezel on each side, used by sculptors.
en|ter|i|tis (en′tə rī′tis), *n.* inflammation of the intestines, usually accompanied by diarrhea and fever. [< *enter-* + *-itis*]
entero-, *combining form.* intestine; intestines: *Enterology = the study of diseases of the intestines.* Also, **enter-** before vowels. [< Greek *énteron*]
en|ter|o|bac|te|ri|a (en′tər ō bak tir′ē ə), *n. pl. of* **en|ter|o|bac|te|ri|um** (en′tər ō bak tir′ē əm). intestinal bacteria, especially those belonging to a large family of rod-shaped bacteria that includes E. coli and klebsiella.
en|ter|o|bac|tin (en′tər ō bak′tin), *n.* a substance produced by enterobacteria that has an inhibiting effect on other bacteria.
en|ter|o|bi|a|sis (en′tər ō bī′ə sis), *n.* infestation of the intestines with pinworms. [< New Latin *Enterobius* the genus name of the pinworm + *-iasis* diseased condition]
en|ter|o|cele (en′tər ō sēl), *n.* a hernia containing part of the intestines. [< *entero-* + Greek *kḗlē* tumor]
en|ter|o|coc|cal (en′tər ō kok′əl), *adj.* having to do with an enterococcus or a disease caused by enterococci.
en|ter|o|coc|cus (en′tər ō kok′əs), *n., pl.* **-coc|ci** (-kok′sī). a streptococcus usually found in the human intestine.
en|ter|o|coele (en′tər ō sēl), *n. Embryology.* the coelom formed by eversion of the wall of the archenteron. [< *entero-* + Greek *koîlos* hollow]
en|ter|o|co|li|tis (en′tər ō kə lī′tis), *n.* inflammation of the intestines.
en|ter|o|gas|trone (en′tər ō gas′trōn), *n.* a hormone of the intestinal mucosa that inhibits gastric movement and secretions: *Fat entering the duodenum releases a hormone* (*enterogastrone*), *which also inhibits gastric peristalsis* (New Scientist). [< *entero-* + *gastr*(ic) + (horm)*one*]
en|ter|o|graph (en′tər ō graf, -gräf), *n.* an instrument for recording the peristaltic movements of the intestines.
en|ter|og|ra|phy (en′tə rog′rə fē), *n., pl.* **-phies.** a description of the intestines.
en|ter|o|hep|a|ti|tis (en′tər ō hep′ə tī′tis), *n.* **1** inflammation of the liver and intestines. **2** an infectious disease of poultry, especially turkeys, with lesions of the liver and intestines; blackhead disease.
en|ter|oid (en′tə roid), *adj.* shaped like a bowel or intestine.
en|ter|o|ki|nase (en′tər ō kī′nās, -kin′ās), *n.* an enzyme secreted by the intestine that changes inactive trypsinogen to active trypsin.
en|ter|o|lith (en′tər ō lith), *n.* an intestinal stone; bezoar. [< *entero-* + Greek *líthos* stone]
en|ter|ol|o|gy (en′tə rol′ə jē), *n.* the study of diseases of the intestines.
en|ter|on (en′tə ron), *n.* = alimentary canal. [< Greek *énteron* intestine]
en|ter|o|path|o|gen|ic (en′tər ō path′ə jen′ik), *adj.* producing intestinal disease.
en|ter|op|a|thy (en′tər op′ə thē), *n.* any disease of the intestines.
en|ter|op|neust (en′tər op′nüst, -nyüst), *n.* = acorn worm. [< New Latin *Enteropneusta* the class name < *entero-* + Greek *pneustós* having breath]
en|ter|op|to|sis (en′tər op tō′sis), *n.* a prolapse or sinking down of the intestines or other abdominal viscera. [< *entero-* + *ptosis*]
en|ter|os|to|my (en′tə ros′tə mē), *n., pl.* **-mies.** the making of an artificial opening in the intestine by surgery. [< *entero-* + Greek *stóma* mouth]
en|ter|ot|o|my (en′tə rot′ə mē), *n., pl.* **-mies.** surgical incision into the intestine.
en|ter|o|tox|i|gen|ic (en′tər ō tok′sə jen′ ik), *adj.* creating or producing enterotoxins: *... obtained from cultures of enterotoxigenic staphylococci* (Science).
en|ter|o|tox|in (en′tər ō tok′sən), *n.* an intestinal toxin produced by certain bacteria that causes symptoms of food poisoning.
en|ter|o|vi|rus (en′tər ō vī′rəs), *n.* a virus living in the intestine that sometimes causes diseases of the nervous system: *The poliomyelitis virus is an enterovirus.*
en|ter|prise (en′tər prīz), *n.* **1** an important, difficult, or dangerous plan to be tried; great or bold undertaking: *A trip into space is a daring enterprise. Quixotic is his enterprise and hopeless his adventure is* (William S. Gilbert). **2** any undertaking; project: *a business enterprise. He has two enterprises—raising chickens and collecting butterflies.* SYN: plan, venture. **3** readiness to start projects; willingness to undertake great or bold projects: *The explorers of America were men of great enterprise. The enterprise and energy of the new manager were all in his favor.* SYN: boldness. **4** the carrying on of enterprises; a taking part in enterprises: *Private enterprise is the business of a person or company of making and selling things, as contrasted with government control.* [< Old French *entreprise,* feminine past participle of *entreprendre* undertake < *entre-* between (< Latin *inter-*) + *prendre* take < Latin *prehendere*]
en|ter|pris|er (en′tər prī′zər), *n.* **1** a person who carries on or takes part in enterprises. **2** = entrepreneur. **3** = adventurer.
enterprise zone, = urban enterprise zone.
en|ter|pris|ing (en′tər prī′zing), *adj.* likely to start projects; ready to face difficulties: *an enterprising young businessman.* SYN: bold, venturesome.
—**en′ter|pris′ing|ly**, *adv.*
en|ter|tain (en′tər tān′), *v.t.* **1** to keep pleasantly interested; please or amuse: *The circus entertained the children.* SYN: divert, beguile, delight. See syn. under **amuse.** **2** to have as a guest: *She entertained ten people at dinner.* **3** to take into the mind; consider: *I refuse to entertain such a foolish idea.* SYN: harbor. **4** to hold in the mind; maintain: *Even after failing twice, we still entertained a hope of success. We had always entertained the kindest feelings toward his family.*
5 *Archaic.* to maintain; keep up. **6** *Obsolete.* to take into or retain (a person) in one's service.
—*v.i.* to have guests; provide entertainment for guests: *She entertains a great deal.* [< Old French *entretenir* < *entre-* among (< Latin *inter-*) + *tenir* hold < Latin *tenēre*]
en|ter|tain|a|ble (en′tər tā′nə bəl), *adj.* that can be entertained.
en|ter|tain|er (en′tər tā′nər), *n.* **1** a person who entertains: *The people next door are great enter-*

Pronunciation Key: **hat, āge, cãre, fär; let, ēqual, tėrm; it, īce; hot, ōpen, ôrder; oil, out; cup, pu̇t, rüle; child; long; thin; ᴛʜen; zh,** measure;
ə represents **a** in about, **e** in taken, **i** in pencil, **o** in lemon, **u** in circus.

tainers; they are always having a party. **2** a singer, musician, actor, dancer, or other performer before the public, especially as a profession.

en·ter·tain·ing (en′tər tā′ning), *adj.* interesting, pleasing, or amusing: *The explorer told many entertaining tales of his experiences.* —**en′ter·tain′·ing·ly**, *adv.* —**en′ter·tain′ing·ness**, *n.*

en·ter·tain·ment (en′tər tān′mənt), *n.* **1** something that interests, pleases, or amuses. A show or a circus is an entertainment. **SYN:** amusement, diversion, recreation, pastime. **2** the act of entertaining: *The hostess devoted herself to the entertainment of her guests. Some expenses of entertainment are tax deductible.* **3** the condition of being entertained: *She played the piano for our entertainment.* **4** attention to the comfort and desires of guests; hospitality: *That hotel is famous for its good entertainment.* **5** *Obsolete.* maintenance in service; employment; pay.

en·tê·té (äɴ te tā′), *adj. French.* possessed by a notion or opinion; very obstinate; infatuated.

en·thal·pi·met·ric (en thal′pə met′rik), *adj.* of or having to do with enthalpimetry.

en·thal·pi·met·ry (en thal′pə met′rē), *n.* the measurement of total heat content generated or absorbed by a substance, used especially to follow the progress of a chemical reaction: *Enthalpimetry depends on the fact that almost all reactions are associated with the evolution or absorption of heat* (New Scientist). [< *enthalpy* + *-metry*]

en·thal·py (en thal′pē, en′thəl-), *n.* the heat content per unit mass of substance. [< Greek *enthálpein* to warm (in)]

en·thet·ic (en thet′ik), *adj.* introduced from without; exogenous: *A disease produced by inoculation is an enthetic disease.* [< Greek *enthetikós* < *entithénai* to place within < *en-* in + *tithénai* to place]

en·thrall or **en·thral** (en thrôl′), *v.t.*, **-thralled, -thrall·ing.** **1** to captivate; fascinate; charm: *The explorer enthralled the audience with the story of his exciting adventures.* **2** to make a slave of; enslave: *The captive Incan peoples were enthralled by their Spanish conquerors.* Also, **inthrall.** —**en·thrall′er**, *n.*

en·thrall·ing (en thrô′ling), *adj.* captivating; fascinating; charming. —**en·thrall′ing·ly**, *adv.*

en·thrall·ment or **en·thral·ment** (en thrôl′mənt), *n.* **1** the act of enthralling: *the enthrallment of captives.* **2** the state of being enthralled. **3** anything that enthralls or subjugates.

en·throne (en thrōn′), *v.t.*, **-throned, -thron·ing.** **1** to set on a throne. **2** *Figurative.* to place highest of all; exalt: *George Washington is enthroned in the hearts of his countrymen.* **3** to invest with authority, especially as a sovereign or a bishop.

en·throne·ment (en thrōn′mənt), *n.* **1** the act of enthroning: *a ceremonial enthronement.* **2** the state of being enthroned: *Enthronement is as rigorous as imprisonment.*

en·thron·i·za·tion (en thrō′nə zā′shən), *n.* = enthronement.

en·thron·ize (en thrō′nīz), *v.t.*, **-ized, -iz·ing.** = enthrone.

en·thuse (en thüz′), *v.*, **-thused, -thus·ing.** *Informal.* —*v.i.* to show enthusiasm; grow enthusiastic: *She enthused over the idea of a picnic.* —*v.t.* to fill with enthusiasm. [American English; back formation < *enthusiasm*]

▶Although **enthuse** is in common use, it is still objectionable in formal writing.

en·thu·si·asm (en thü′zē az əm), *n.* **1** eager interest; zeal: *The pep talk filled us with enthusiasm. Nothing great was ever achieved without enthusiasm* (Emerson). **SYN:** eagerness, ardor, fervor. **2** *Archaic.* extreme or extravagant religious emotion. **3** *Archaic.* possession or inspiration by a god. [< Late Latin *enthūsiasmus* < Greek *enthousiasmós* < *éntheos* god-possessed < *en-* in + *theós* god]

en·thu·si·ast (en thü′zē ast), *n.* **1** a person who is filled with enthusiasm: *a baseball enthusiast. The world belongs to the enthusiast who keeps cool* (William McFee). **2** a person who is carried away by his feelings for a cause, principle, or belief: *It is unfortunate . . . that so few enthusiasts can be trusted to speak the truth* (Arthur Balfour). **SYN:** zealot, fanatic, devotee. **3** *Archaic.* a person filled with religious enthusiasm.

en·thu·si·as·tic (en thü′zē as′tik), *adj.* full of enthusiasm; eagerly interested: *My little brother is very enthusiastic about going to kindergarten. The idiot who praises with enthusiastic tone, All centuries but this, and every country but his own* (William S. Gilbert). **SYN:** zealous, eager.

en·thu·si·as·ti·cal (en thü′zē as′tə kəl), *adj.* = enthusiastic.

en·thu·si·as·ti·cal·ly (en thü′zē as′tə klē), *adv.* with enthusiasm: *New theories and discoveries in physics, chemistry, and biology are enthusiastically heralded* (Atlantic).

en·thy·meme (en′thə mēm), *n. Logic.* a syllogism in which one premise is not expressed. [< Latin *enthȳmēma* < Greek *enthȳmēma* thought, reasoning < *enthȳméesthai* think < *en-* in + *thȳmós* mind, soul, spirit]

en·ti·a (en′shē ə), *n.* plural of **ens.**

en·tice (en tīs′), *v.t.*, **-ticed, -tic·ing.** to attract by arousing hopes or desires; tempt: *The smell of food enticed the hungry children into the house. My son, if sinners entice thee, consent thou not* (Proverbs 1:10). **SYN:** inveigle, decoy. See syn. under **lure.** [< Old French *enticier* stir up, incite < *en-* in (< Latin *in-*) + Latin *tītiō* firebrand] —**en·tic′ing·ly**, *adv.*

en·tice·a·ble (en tī′sə bəl), *adj.* that can be enticed.

en·tice·ment (en tīs′mənt), *n.* **1** the act of enticing or condition of being enticed. **2** a thing that entices: *Enticements of milk and meat brought the frightened cat down from the tree.*

en·tic·er (en tī′sər), *n.* a person or thing that entices; tempter; seducer.

en·tire (en tīr′), *adj., adv., n.* —*adj.* **1** having all the parts; whole; complete: *The entire platoon was rewarded for bravery. The entire creation was at peace with man* (John Wesley). **SYN:** total, full. See syn. under **complete.** **2** not broken; in one piece; having an unbroken outline: *The original property is still entire, though it has had many owners.* **SYN:** intact, unimpaired. **3** *Biology.* (of leaves, shells, and other structures) having an even margin; without notches. **4** not castrated or gelded: *an entire horse.* **5** *Obsolete.* unmixed; pure.

—*adv.* entirely; wholly: *. . . its resolve to grasp the sorry scheme entire* (Saturday Review).

—*n.* **1** the whole; entirety. **2** an entire horse. **3** *British.* a kind of malt liquor; porter.

[< Old French *entir* < Latin *integer* < *in-* not + unrecorded root *tag-* touch, related to *tangere* touch. See etym. of doublet **integer.**] —**en·tire′·ness**, *n.*

en·tire·ly (en tīr′lē), *adv.* **1** to the whole amount or extent; completely; fully: *He is entirely wrong. The house is entirely surrounded by trees.* **2** wholly and exclusively; solely: *He did it entirely for money. What you do is entirely your business.*

en·tire·ty (en tīr′tē, -tīr′ə-), *n., pl.* **-ties.** **1** the state of being entire; wholeness; completeness. **2** a complete thing; the whole.

in its entirety, wholly; completely: *He enjoyed the concert in its entirety.*

en·ti·ris (en tī′ris), *n.* the posterior pigmented layer of the iris of the eye.

en·ti·ta·tive (en′tə tā′tiv), *adj.* having to do with or of the nature of an entity; having existence as an entity.

en·ti·tle (en tī′təl), *v.t.*, **-tled, -tling.** **1** to give a claim or right (to); provide with a reason to ask or get something: *The one who wins is entitled to first prize. A ticket will entitle you to admission.* **SYN:** empower, qualify, enable. **2** to give the title of; name: *The author entitled his book "Treasure Island." The Queen of England is also entitled "Defender of the Faith."* **SYN:** denominate, designate. **3** to give or call by an honorary title. Also, **intitle.** [< Old French *entituler,* learned borrowing from Late Latin *intitulāre* < Latin *in-* in + *titulus* title, inscription, claim]

en·ti·tle·ment (en tī′təl mənt), *n.* something to which one is entitled; a privilege: *A careful campaign . . . must be developed to enable older people fully to understand their entitlements under the new law* (New York Times).

en ti·tre (äɴ tē′trə), *French.* in title; officially: *Chargé d'Affaires ad interim in Peking since February, 1969, [he] has now been appointed Chargé d'Affaires en titre* (London Times).

en·ti·ty (en′tə tē), *n., pl.* **-ties.** **1** something that has a real and separate existence. Persons, mountains, languages, and beliefs are distinct entities. **2** being; existence: *In his unhappiness he had come even to question his entity.* [< Medieval Latin *entitas* < Latin *ēns,* present participle of *esse* be]

en·to·blast (en′tə blast), *n.* **1** = endoderm. **2** any one of the blastomeres from which the endoderm develops. [< Greek *entós* within + *blastós* sprout]

en·to·blas·tic (en′tə blas′tik), *adj.* of or having to do with the entoblast.

en·to·con·dyle (en′tə kon′dəl), *n.* the inner condyle of a bone, on the side next to the body.

en·to·cra·ni·al (en′tə krā′nē əl), *adj.* within the cranium.

en·to·derm (en′tə dėrm), *n.* = endoderm.

en·to·der·mal (en′tə dėr′məl), *adj.* = endodermal.

en·to·der·mic (en′tə dėr′mik), *adj.* = endodermal.

en·to·gas·tric (en′tə gas′trik), *adj.* of or having to do with the interior of the stomach.

en·toil (en toil′), *v.t.* to ensnare; entrap.

en·tomb (en tüm′), *v.t.* **1** to place in a tomb; bury: *Mankind has developed many fashions of entombing its dead.* **2** to serve as a tomb for: *The cave where he perished entombed him.* Also, **intomb.** [< Old French *entomber* < *en-* in (< Latin *in-*) + *tombe* tomb < Late Latin *tumba*]

en·tomb·ment (en tüm′mənt), *n.* the act of entombing or state of being entombed.

en·tom·ic (en tom′ik), *adj.* of or having to do with insects.

en·to·mog·e·nous (en′tə moj′ə nəs), *adj.* (of fungi) growing upon or in insects.

entomol. or **entom.,** entomology.

en·tom·o·lite (en tom′ə līt), *n.* a fossil insect. [< Greek *éntoma* insects + English *-lite*]

en·to·mo·log·ic (en′tə mə loj′ik), *adj.* = entomological.

en·to·mo·log·i·cal (en′tə mə loj′ə kəl), *adj.* of or having to do with entomology. —**en′to·mo·log′i·cal·ly**, *adv.*

en·to·mol·o·gist (en′tə mol′ə jist), *n.* a person who studies entomology: *An entomologist deals with insects, though he is never an expert in all the orders* (A. Franklin Shull).

en·to·mol·o·gize (en′tə mol′ə jīz), *v.i.*, **-gized, -giz·ing.** **1** to study entomology. **2** to collect specimens or observe the habits of insects.

en·to·mol·o·gy (en′tə mol′ə jē), *n.* **1** *no pl.* the branch of zoology that deals with insects. **2** *pl.* **-gies.** a treatise on insects. [< Greek *éntoma* insects + English *-logy*]

en·to·moph·a·gous (en′tə mof′ə gəs), *adj.* feeding on insects; insectivorous. [< Greek *éntoma* insects + *phageîn* eat + English *-ous*]

en·to·moph·i·lous (en′tə mof′ə ləs), *adj. Botany.* pollinated by insects, as the flowers of orchids and irises. [< Greek *éntoma* insects + *philos* (with English *-ous*) fond]

en·to·moph·i·ly (en′tə mof′ə lē), *n. Botany.* pollination by insects.

en·to·mos·tra·can (en′tə mos′trə kən), *adj., n.* —*adj.* of or having to do with a group of crustaceans of simple structure, usually of comparatively small size, including the branchiopods, copepods, and cirripeds.

—*n.* an entomostracan crustacean.

[< New Latin *Entomostraca* the order name < Greek *éntoma* insects + *óstrakon* shell < *ostéon* bone]

en·to·mot·o·mist (en′tə mot′ə mist), *n.* a person who studies the interior structure of insects; an entomological anatomist.

en·to·mot·o·my (en′tə mot′ə mē), *n.* the science of the dissection of insects to study their structure.

en·to·phyte (en′tə fīt), *n. Botany.* a plant growing inside an animal or another plant, usually as a parasite. [< Greek *entós* within + *phytón* plant]

en·to·phyt·ic (en′tə fit′ik), *adj.* of or like an entophyte.

ent·op·tic (ent op′tik), *adj.* having to do with or originating in the interior of the eye. [< Greek *entós* within + *optikós* optic]

ent·op·tics (ent op′tiks), *n.* the study of the phenomena connected with the interior of the eye.

ent·op·to·scope (ent op′tə skōp), *n.* an instrument for testing the transparency of the interior of the eye.

en·to·ret·i·na (en′tə ret′ə nə), *n., pl.* **-nas, -nae** (-nē). the inner layer of the retina.

ent·or·gan·ism (ent ôr′gə niz əm), *n.* an internal parasite. [< Greek *entós* within + English *organism*]

ent·o·tic (ent ō′tik, -ot′ik), *adj.* having to do with or originating in the inner ear. [< Greek *entós* within + *ōtikós* relating to the ear, otic]

en·tou·rage (än′tü räzh′), *n.* **1** a group of attendants or people usually accompanying a person; retinue: *the queen and her entourage.* **2** surroundings; environment. [< Middle French *entourage* < *entourer* surround < Old French *entour* that which surrounds < *en-* (< Latin *in-*) + *tour* circuit, tour]

en tout (äɴ tü′), *French.* in all; wholly.

en tout cas (äɴ tü kä′), *French.* in any case.

en-tout-cas (äɴ tü kä′), *adj.* all-weather; having a surface of quick-drying material: *The club has three en-tout-cas tennis courts.* [< French *en tout cas* in any case, at all events]

en·to·zo·an (en′tə zō′ən), *adj., n.* —*adj.* of or having to do with the entozoa.

—*n.* = entozoon.

en·to·zo·ic (en′tə zō′ik), *adj.* = entozoan.

en·to·zo·ol·o·gist (en′tə zō ol′ə jist), *n.* a person who studies entozoology.

en·to·zo·ol·o·gy (en′tə zō ol′ə jē), *n.* the branch of zoology dealing with entozoa.

en·to·zo·on (en′tə zō′on), *n., pl.* **-zo·a** (-zō′ə). an internal parasite, such as an intestinal worm. [< Greek *entós* within + *zôion* animal]

en·tr'acte (än trakt′), *n.* **1** the interval between two acts of a play, ballet, or opera: *During the entr'acte the star received her friends.* **2** music, dancing, or any entertainment performed during this interval; interlude: *The entr'acte consisted of a short ballet, "The Flying Saucer."* [< French *entr'acte* < *entre* between (< Latin *inter*) + *acte* act]

en|trails (en′trālz, -trəlz), *n.pl.* **1** the inner parts of a human being or animal: *Before a chicken can be cooked, the entrails are removed.* **2** the intestines; bowels. **3** any inner parts. [< Old French *entrailles* < Late Latin *intrālia* intestines < Latin *interānea* (originally) things inside < *inter* within, between]

en|train¹ (en trān′), *v.i.* to get on a train. —*v.t.* to put on a train: *The soldiers were secretly entrained at night.*
[< *en-*¹ + *train,* noun]

en|train² (en trān′), *v.t.* **1** to draw away or on; carry along: *He suggested that as a growing cumulus cloud rises, it "entrains" air from the outside* (Scientific American). **2** *Chemistry.* to carry (particles) along in the flow of a fluid. [< Middle French *entraîner* < *en-* away (< Latin *inde*) + *traîner* to drag] —**en|train′er,** *n.*

en train (äɴ traɴ′), *French.* in progress; in good spirits.

en|train|ment (en trān′mənt), *n.* the process of entraining or state of being entrained: *The trouble this year was gas entrainment in the molten metal (an alloy of sodium and potassium) used to cool the reactor* (New Scientist).

en|tram|mel (en tram′əl), *v.t.,* **-meled, -mel|ing** or (*especially British*) **-melled, -mel|ling.** to trammel; hamper; restrain: *The assumption . . . that the appropriation of the means of production by the proletariat will release a new flow of wealth now entrammeled by capitalism is totally unfounded* (Bulletin of Atomic Scientists). [< *en-*¹ + *trammel*]

en|trance¹ (en′trəns), *n.* **1** the act of entering: *The actor's entrance was greeted with applause.* **SYN:** entry, ingress. **2** a place by which to enter; door; passageway: *The entrance to the hotel was blocked with baggage.* **SYN:** opening, inlet, gate, portal. **3** the right to enter; permission to enter; admission: *Entrance to the exhibit is on weekdays only.* **4** *Nautical.* the bow or forepart of a ship under the water line. [< Old French *entrance* < *entrer* enter]

en|trance² (en trans′, -träns′), *v.t.,* **-tranced, -tranc|ing.** **1** to fill with joy; delight; charm: *From the first note the singer's voice entranced the audience. Poets whose effusions entranced my soul* (Mary Shelley). **2** to put into a trance. —**en|tranc′ing|ly,** *adv.*

entrance cone, a conical projection formed by the protoplasm of an egg cell at the point of entrance of the sperm in fertilization; fertilization cone.

en|tranc|ed|ly (en tran′sid lē, -trän′-), *adv.* in the manner of someone entranced: *. . . stretching out an arm entrancedly toward a snake charmer* (New Yorker).

en|trance|ment (en trans′mənt, -träns′-), *n.* **1** the act or process of entrancing or the state of being entranced. **2** a thing that entrances.

en|trance|way (en′trəns wā′), *n.* a place by which to enter: *We walked through an entranceway into the central hall* (Atlantic).

en|trant (en′trənt), *n.* **1** a person who enters: *Every entrant was handed a court summons.* **2** a person who takes part in a contest: *Five girls were entrants in the beauty contest.* **3** a new member in a profession, club, association, or other group: *A banquet honored the entrants of the current year.* [< French *entrant,* present participle of *entrer* enter]

en|trap (en trap′), *v.t.,* **-trapped, -trap|ping.** **1** to catch in a trap. **SYN:** ensnare. **2** *Figurative.* to bring into difficulty or danger; deceive; trick: *By clever questioning, the lawyer entrapped the witness into contradicting herself.* **SYN:** ensnare. [< Old French *entrapper* < *en-* in (< Latin *in-*) + *trape* trap]

en|trap|ment (en trap′mənt), *n.* **1** the act of entrapping: (*Figurative.*) *Maybe the Federal judges will overlook revenooers bearing false witness and practicing entrapment against people* (Wall Street Journal). **2** the condition of being entrapped: *She expresses a few major themes, of which the entrapment of the spirit in the flesh and the shadow cast by eternity upon time are two* (New Yorker).

en|trap|per (en trap′ər), *n.* a person or thing that entraps.

en|treas|ure (en trezh′ər, -trā′zhər), *v.t.,* **-ured, -ur|ing.** to store up in or as if in a treasury.

en|treat (en trēt′), *v.t.* **1** to keep asking earnestly; beg and pray; implore: *She entreated her father not to send her to summer camp. The prisoners entreated their captors to let them go.* **SYN:** beseech, supplicate. **2** *Archaic.* to treat; deal with. **3** *Obsolete.* **a** to persuade by pleading. **b** to induce. Also, **intreat.** [< Old French *entraitier* < *en-* in (< Latin *in-*) + *traitier* to treat < Latin *tractāre*] —**en|treat′ing|ly,** *adv.*

en|treat|ment (en trēt′mənt), *n.* **1** *Archaic.* treatment. **2** *Obsolete.* something entreated, such as a favor.

en|treat|y (en trē′tē), *n., pl.* **-treat|ies.** an earnest request; prayer: *Her father gave in to her entreaties. The savages paid no attention to their captives' entreaties for mercy.* **SYN:** supplication, appeal, solicitation, suit, petition.

en|tre|chat (äɴ trə shä′), *n.* a leap in ballet in which the dancer points his feet and crosses them a number of times: *It was Nigel who, for my benefit, attempted entrechats that made the lampshades tingle* (Harper's). [< French *entrechat,* a respelling of Italian (*capriola*) *intrecciata* complicated (caper) < *intrecciare* intertwine < *in-* in + *treccia* tress, plait]

en|tre|côte (äɴ trə kōt′), *n. French.* a steak cut from between the ribs: *It became a habit with my husband to . . . eat the bit of cake sitting on a ruffled doily or the leftover entrecôte sprinkled with crumbled egg yolk* (New Yorker).

en|tre|deux (äɴ trə dœ′), *n., pl.* **-deux** (-dœ′). a narrow strip of lace, embroidery, or other decorative material, used between pieces being joined, as in dresses and blouses; insertion: *The ruffled jabot of a white organdie blouse with a high, ruffled collar, connected by entredeux . . .* (New Yorker).

en|tre deux vins (äɴ trə dœ vaɴ′), *French.* **1** half drunk. **2** (literally) between two wines.

en|tree or **en|trée** (än′trā), *n.* **1** freedom or right to enter; access: *The principal's son has entree to his father's office that the rest of the students don't have.* **2** the main dish of food at dinner or lunch. **3** *British.* a dish of food served before the roast or between the main courses at dinner. **4** an appetizer served as the first course. [< French *entrée* < Old French, feminine past participle of *entrer* enter]

en|tre|mets (än′trə mā; *French* äɴ trə me′), *n., pl.* **-mets** (-māz; *French* -me′). a relish or side dish served between the principal courses at dinner. [< Old French *entremes* (literally) between courses < *entre* between + *mes* course, mess]

en|trench (en trench′), *v.t.* **1** to surround with a trench; fortify with trenches: *Our soldiers were entrenched opposite the enemy.* **2** *Figurative.* to establish firmly: *Exchanging gifts at Christmas is a custom entrenched by long tradition.* —*v.i.* to trespass; encroach; infringe: *Do not entrench upon the rights of others.* Also, **intrench.**

en|trenched clause (en trencht′), *Politics.* a legal or constitutional clause that may only be altered or repealed by an act of the legislature or with the approval of all the states of a country: *The Smith government moved to amend the constitution without regard to entrenched clauses* (Atlantic).

★en|trench|ment (en trench′mənt), *n.* **1** the act of entrenching. **2** an entrenched position. **3** a defense consisting of a trench and a rampart of earth or stone. Also, **intrenchment.**

★entrenchment definition 3

en|tre nous (äɴ trə nü′), *French.* between ourselves; confidentially: *He came around eventually, but, entre nous, the man will never be the same* (New Yorker).

en|tre|pôt or **en|tre|pot** (än′trə pō), *n.* **1** a place where goods are stored; warehouse. **2** a place where goods are sent for distribution; commercial center: *Antwerp . . . had now become the principal entrepôt . . . of Europe* (John Lothrop Motley). [< French *entrepôt,* patterned on *dépôt* depot]

en|tre|pre|nant (äɴ trə prə näɴ′), *adj.* enterprising; pushing; bold.
[< French *entreprenant* < Old French *entreprendre;* see etym. under **enterprise**]

en|tre|pre|neur (än′trə prə nėr′), *n.* a person who organizes and manages a business or industrial undertaking. An entrepreneur takes the risk of not making a profit and gets the profit when there is one: *In the uppermost executive echelons of TV, there is not one recognized major theatrical entrepreneur* (New York Times). [< Old French *entrepreneur* < *entreprendre* undertake; see etym. under **enterprise**]

en|tre|pre|neur|i|al (än′trə prə nėr′ē əl), *adj.* of or having to do with an entrepreneur or entrepreneurs: *the entrepreneurial class, entrepreneurial income. Texas businessmen are supplying capital, entrepreneurial vigor and acumen in nearly every area of the U.S. economy* (Time).

en|tre|pre|neur|ship (än′trə prə nėr′ship), *n.* **1** the state of being an entrepreneur: *New patterns of entrepreneurship have unfolded both in the United States and in Europe* (Bulletin of Atomic Scientists). **2** entrepreneurs collectively.

en|tre|salle (äɴ trə sȧl′), *n. French.* an anteroom.

en|tre|sol (en′tər sol, än′trə-), *n.* a low story between the first two floors of a building; mezzanine: *Only the entresol and the ground floor were in use* (New Yorker).
[< French *entresol* < *entre* between (< Latin *inter*) + Old French *sole* < Vulgar Latin *sola,* for Latin *solea* floor, plank, sole]

en|trez (äɴ trā′), *v.i. French.* enter; come in (used as a command or request).

en|tro|chite (en′trə kīt), *n.* one of the wheel-shaped joints of an encrinite. Entrochites occur abundantly in certain limestones.

en|tro|chus (en′trə kəs), *n., pl.* **-chi** (-kī). = entrochite.

en|tro|pic (en′trə pik), *adj.* of or characterized by entropy: *. . . the entropic, increasing disorderly expansion of physical universe* (Buckminster Fuller).

en|tro|pi|on (en trō′pē on), *n. Medicine.* an abnormal turning or rolling inward of the eyelid, so that the lashes come in contact with the eyeball.
[< New Latin *entropion* < Greek *entropḗ;* see etym. under **entropy**]

en|tro|pi|um (en trō′pē əm), *n.* = entropion.

en|tro|py (en′trə pē), *n.* **1** *Physics.* **a** a measure of the unavailability of energy for conversion into mechanical work in a thermodynamic system, due to the random motion of the molecules which comprise the system. It is directly proportional to the quantity of heat in a body and inversely proportional to its absolute temperature. It vanishes at absolute zero. **b** a measure of the degree of disorder of a system. The total entropy of an isolated system cannot decrease with change. It can only remain constant, in a reversible process; or increase, in an irreversible process. The entropy of the universe is increasing. An increase in entropy with change signifies a reduced amount of available energy. **2** *Communication and Electronics.* the measure of the unpredictability, or unexpectedness, in a message source in a signal system; specifically, the average number of choices a message source has in producing information, measured in bits (binary digits) per symbol, per unit of time, or per message. [< German *Entropie,* probably influenced by Greek *entropíā, entropḗ* a turning in < *en-* in + *tropḗ* a turning < *trépein* to turn]

en|trust (en trust′), *v.t.* **1** to charge with a trust; trust: *The club entrusted the treasurer with all its money.* **2** to give (something or somebody) in trust; hand over for safekeeping: *She entrusted the children to the care of a baby sitter. He entrusted his life to his doctor.* **SYN:** See syn. under **commit.** Also, **intrust.**

en|trust|ment (en trust′mənt), *n.* the act of entrusting or fact of being entrusted.

en|try (en′trē), *n., pl.* **-tries.** **1** the act of entering: *His sudden entry startled me.* **2** a place by which to enter; way to enter. A vestibule is an entry. *The entry to the hotel was blocked with luggage so that no one could enter or leave. The floor of the entry was slate.* **3** the act of entering or recording something in a book, register, list, or other place for data. **4** a thing written or printed in a book, list, or other place for data. Each word explained in a dictionary is an entry. **5** a person or thing that takes part in a contest: *The car race had nine entries.* **6** *Law.* the act of taking possession of lands or buildings by entering or setting foot on them. **7** a giving of an account of a ship's cargo at customs to obtain permission to land the goods.
[< Old French *entree,* (originally) feminine past participle of *entrer* enter]

en|try-lev|el (en′trē lev′əl), *adj.* of or for a basic level at which one begins to learn a skill or use: *an entry-level job.*

en|try|man (en′trē mən), *n., pl.* **-men.** a person who enters upon a tract of public land with intent to acquire it under the provisions of the law.

en|try|way (en′trē wā′), *n.* a place by which to enter; entry.

entry word, **1** the word at the head of an article in a reference book; head word. **2** the word under which a book is entered in a catalog.

en|twine (en twīn′), *v.,* **-twined, -twin|ing.** —*v.t.* **1** to twine together: *She entwined two hearts on the valentine she made.* **SYN:** plait, interweave. **2** to twine around: *Roses entwined the little cottage.* —*v.i.* to be or become twined. Also, **intwine.**

en|twine|ment (en twīn′mənt), *n.* the act of entwining or state of being entwined.

en|twist (en twist′), *v.t.* to twist together; twist about. Also, **intwist.**

e|nu|cle|ate (*v.* i nü′klē āt, -nyü′-; *adj.* i nü′klē āt, -nyü′-; -it), *v.,* **-at|ed, -at|ing,** *adj.* —*v.t.* **1** *Surgery.* to remove (a tumor, eyeball, or other structure) from its capsule or cover without cutting.

Pronunciation Key: **hat, āge, cãre, fär; let, ēqual, tėrm; it, īce; hot, ōpen, ôrder; oil, out; cup, pu̇t, rüle; child; long; thin; ᴛʜen; zh,** measure;
ə represents **a** in about, **e** in taken, **i** in pencil, **o** in lemon, **u** in circus.

2 *Biology.* to take away the nucleus of. 3 *Figurative.* to bring out; make clear; explain.
—*adj.* without a nucleus.
[< Latin *ēnucleāre* (with English *-ate*[1]) < *ex-* out + *nucleus* kernel, nucleus]

e|nu|cle|a|tion (i nü′klē ā′shən, -nyü′-), *n.* the act or process of enucleating.

e|nu|mer|a|ble (i nü′mər ə bəl, -nyü′-), *adj.* that can be enumerated.

e|nu|mer|ate (i nü′mə rāt, -nyü′-), *v.t.*, **-at|ed, -at|ing.** 1 to name one by one; list: *He enumerated the capitals of the 50 states.* SYN: recount, rehearse, detail. 2 to find the number of; count. [< Latin *ēnumerāre* (with English *-ate*[1]) < *ex-* out + *numerus* number]

e|nu|mer|a|tion (i nü′mə rā′shən, -nyü′-), *n.* 1 the act or process of enumerating; listing or counting: *A census is an official enumeration of the people of a country.* 2 a list or catalog: *a long enumeration of the articles needed.*

e|nu|mer|a|tive (i nü′mə rā′tiv, -nyü′-), *adj.* that enumerates; having to do with enumeration.

e|nu|mer|a|tor (i nü′mə rā′tər, -nyü′-), *n.* 1 a person who enumerates. 2 = census taker. 3 an election official in Canada who compiles lists of eligible voters in urban constituencies.

e|nun|ci|a|bil|i|ty (i nun′sē ə bil′ə tē, -shē-), *n.* the quality of being enunciable.

e|nun|ci|a|ble (i nun′sē ə bəl, -shē-), *adj.* that can be enunciated.

e|nun|ci|ate (i nun′sē āt, -shē-), *v.*, **-at|ed, -at|ing.** —*v.i.* to pronounce words and syllables; articulate: *Radio and television announcers must enunciate very clearly.* —*v.t.* 1 to speak or pronounce; articulate. 2 to state definitely; announce: *After performing many experiments, the scientist enunciated a new theory.* [< Latin *ēnūntiāre* (with English *-ate*[1]) < *ex-* out + *nūntius* messenger]

e|nun|ci|a|tion (i nun′sē ā′shən, -shē-), *n.* 1 the manner of pronouncing words and syllables; articulation: *The enunciation of the various singers was gratifyingly clear* (New Yorker). 2 a definite statement; announcement.

e|nun|ci|a|tive (i nun′sē ā′tiv, -shē-), *adj.* 1 serving to enunciate; declaratory. 2 having to do with enunciation. —**e|nun′ci|a′tive|ly,** *adv.*

e|nun|ci|a|tor (i nun′sē ā′tər, -shē-), *n.* a person or thing that enunciates.

e|nun|ci|a|to|ry (i nun′sē ə tôr′ē, -tōr′-; -shē-), *adj.* = enunciative.

en|ure (en yůr′), *v.t., v.i.*, **-ured, -ur|ing.** *Law.* to inure.

en|u|re|sis (en′yů rē′sis), *n. Medicine.* the inability to control urination; bed-wetting. [< New Latin *enuresis* < Greek *enoureîn* urinate in]

en|u|ret|ic (en′yů ret′ik), *adj.* of or having to do with enuresis.

en|ur|ny (en ėr′nē), *adj., n. Heraldry.* —*adj.* (of a bordure) charged with beasts.
—*n.* a charge of this kind on a bordure. [< Anglo-French *enourne,* Old French *aourne* adorned]

env., envelope.

en|va|por (en vā′pər), *v.t.* to surround with vapor.

en|veil (en vāl′), *v.t.* to cover with a veil; place a veil upon.

en|vel|op (en vel′əp; *for n. also* en′və lōp, än′-), *v., n.* —*v.t.* 1 to wrap or cover: *The baby was so enveloped in blankets that we could hardly see its face.* SYN: enfold. 2 *Figurative.* to hide; conceal: *Fog enveloped the village.* 3 to surround: *Our soldiers enveloped the enemy and captured them.* SYN: encompass, encircle.
—*n.* an envelope.
[< Old French *enveloper,* or *envoluper* < *en-* in + *voluper* to wrap] —**en|vel′op|er,** *n.*

en|ve|lope (en′və lōp, än′-), *n.* 1 a paper cover in which a letter or anything flat and fairly thin can be mailed. It can usually be folded over and sealed by wetting a gummed edge. 2 a wrapper; covering. 3 *Figurative.* something enveloping; an outer cover: *The envelope of a man's behavior is his response to his surroundings through the arts* (Burton Rothleder). 4 *Botany.* a surrounding or enclosing part: *an envelope of leaves.* 5 *Biology.* any enclosing covering, such as a membrane or shell; integument. 6 *Geometry.* a curve or surface touching a continuous series of curves or surfaces. 7 *Astronomy.* a nebulous mass surrounding the nucleus of a comet on the side nearest the sun: *Coggia's Comet displayed magnificent envelopes* (Bernhard, Bennett, and Rice). 8a the bag that holds the gas in a balloon or airship. b the outer covering of a rigid airship: *Concealed within the envelope or "bag" is the largest revolving radar antenna ever carried by an aircraft* (Science News Letter). [< French *enveloppe* < Old French *enveloper;* see etym. under **envelop**]

en|vel|op|ment (en vel′əp mənt), *n.* 1 the act of enveloping. 2 the state of being enveloped. 3 something that envelops; wrapping; covering.

en|ven|om (en ven′əm), *v.t.* 1 to make poisonous: *an envenomed arrow.* 2 *Figurative.* to fill with bitterness, hate, or malice: *The wicked boy envenomed his father's mind against his stepbrother.* [< Old French *envenimer* < *en-* in (< Latin *in-*) + *venim* venom]

en vé|ri|té (äɴ vā rē tā′), *French.* in truth.

en|vi|a|ble (en′vē ə bəl), *adj.* to be envied; desirable; worth having: *She has an enviable school record.* —**en′vi|a|ble|ness,** *n.*

en|vi|a|bly (en′vē ə blē), *adv.* in an enviable manner: *Whatever he may say, he strikes me as enviably brave* (Sunday Times).

en|vi|er (en′vē ər), *n.* a person who envies.

en vi|gueur (äɴ vē gœr′), *French.* in force, as a law.

en ville (äɴ vēl′), *French.* in town; away from home; out.

en|vi|ous (en′vē əs), *adj.* 1 feeling or showing discontent because of a wish to have something that someone else has; full of envy: *The weak are often envious of the strong. He was envious of his cousin's success.* 2 *Obsolete.* a malicious; spiteful. b enviable. [< Anglo-French *envious,* Old French *envieus* < Latin *invidiōsus* < *invidia;* see etym. under **envy**] —**en′vi|ous|ly,** *adv.* —**en′vi|ous|ness,** *n.*

en|vi|ron (en vī′rən), *v., n.* —*v.t.* to hem in; surround; enclose.
—*n. Informal.* surrounding parts; environs: *After all, the environ was teeming with illegally parked cars"* (Alan Coren).
[< Old French *environner* < *environ* around < *en-* in (< Latin *in-*) + *viron* circle < *virer* to turn < Latin *gȳrāre* to circle < Greek *gyros* circle]

en|vi|ron|al (en vī′rə nəl), *adj.* environmental.

en|vi|ron|ment (en vī′rən mənt), *n.* 1 all of the surrounding things, conditions, and influences affecting the growth or development of living things: *A child's character is greatly influenced by his home environment. Differences in environment often account for differences in plants of the same kind found in different places.* 2 *Figurative.* surroundings: *Abraham Lincoln grew up in an environment of poverty.* 3 the condition of the air, water, soil, plants, and animals; natural surroundings: *a rabies-free environment.* 4 the act or fact of surrounding: *The environment of his troops by enemy ambushers forced his surrender.* 5 a work of environmental art: *... the $2.5 million Pepsi-Cola pavilion at the Osaka World's Fair in Japan ... will include among its features environments that can be manipulated by the viewer* (Benjamin de Brie Taylor).

en|vi|ron|men|tal (en vī′rən men′təl), *adj.* 1 having to do with environment: *Important as environmental factors are for the shaping of human destiny, we now see clearly that man's influence on his environment [is] ... no less important than is the environment* (Science News). 2 of or having to do with environmental art: *From the desire to be totally encompassed by the work came the wall-size dimensions of the drip canvases, so suggestive to later "environmental" painters and sculptors* (Harold Rosenberg). —**en|vi′ron|men′tal|ly,** *adv.*

environmental art, a form of art that seeks to enlarge the aesthetic experience by surrounding the spectator with an artistic interior or exterior display of objects, instead of confronting him with a fixed object or image within a standard space: *Luminal, minimal, and three-dimensional pop art have contributed to the development of environmental art in rejecting fixed walls and standard spaces and in becoming concerned with the commercial and urban world beyond the galleries* (Benjamin de Brie Taylor).

environmental impact statement, a review of the possible consequences that a proposed idea or project may have on the environment: *A group of middle-class whites in Newark had been able to block a highly controversial low-income housing project by bringing a long series of challenges to the project's environmental impact statements* (Harper's).

en|vi|ron|men|tal|ism (en vī′rən men′tə liz əm), *n.* the view that the environment, rather than hereditary factors or individual initiative, is the dominating force in effecting change.

en|vi|ron|men|tal|ist (en vī′rən men′tə list), *n.* 1 a person concerned with problems of the environment and especially with the effects of uncontrolled pollution on the earth's atmosphere: *Some environmentalists reject all of modern technology and call for a return to a simple, pastoral life free of fumes, artificial chemicals and any noise but the chirping of birds and the croaking of frogs* (Science News). 2 an advocate or supporter of environmentalism: *Sometimes it seems as if any single life were no more than a leaf borne along by whatever stream it happened to fall upon, and such was the argument of the environmentalists in their heyday* (Harper's). 3 an artist who creates environmental art: *Other environmentalists see their works as means to engage the viewer in a new kind of emotional release ... "People become part of the art object," [Tony] Martin explains* (Time).

en|vi|ron|men|tal|is|tic (en vī′rən men′tə lis′tik), *adj.* having to do with or based on environmentalism.

environmental science, the study of environmental problems, especially those created by pollution: *As a group of marine biologists, we are actively involved in various facets of environmental science—a less emotive and more encompassing term than pollution studies* (J. R. Lewis).

en|vi|rons (en vī′rənz, en′vər ənz), *n.pl.* surrounding districts or areas; vicinity; surroundings: *the beautiful environs of Hudson Bay. We visited Boston and its environs.* [< French *environs* < Old French *environ* around; see etym. under **environ**]

en|vis|age (en viz′ij), *v.t.*, **-aged, -ag|ing.** 1 to form a mental picture of; visualize: *The architect looked at the plans and envisaged the finished house.* 2 to look in the face of; face: *He envisaged an old age of loneliness and discontent.* [< French *envisager* < *en-* (Latin *in-*) + *visage* face, visage]

en|vis|age|ment (en viz′ij mənt), *n.* the act of envisaging.

en|vi|sion (en vizh′ən), *v.t.* to see as if in a vision; envisage: *The mother envisioned her little girl as a prima ballerina.*

en|voi (en′voi, än′-), *n.* = envoy[2].

en|voûte|ment (äɴ vüt mäɴ′), *n.* sympathetic magic in which a doll or other image of a person is used, usually to do him harm. [< French *envoûtement* < *envoûter* to cast a spell on]

en|voy[1] (en′voi), *n.* 1 a messenger or representative: *The next envoy was given the same curt answer.* SYN: agent, deputy. 2 a diplomat ranking next below an ambassador and next above a minister: *Contrary to expectation, the two French envoys have not yet left Antsirabe, Madagascar* (London Times). 3 any person sent to represent a government or ruler for diplomatic purposes. [< French *envoyé,* past participle of *envoyer* send < Old French *envoier;* see etym. under **envoy**[2]]

en|voy[2] (en′voi, än′-), *n.* 1 a short concluding stanza, especially to a ballade. 2 a postscript to a literary work, often addressed to a friend or patron of the author. Also, **envoi.** [< Old French *envoy* < *envoier* send < *en-* on (< Latin *in-*) + *voie* way < Latin *via*]

en|voy|ship (en′voi ship), *n.* the position or function of an envoy.

en|vy (en′vē), *n., pl.* **-vies,** *v.*, **-vied, -vy|ing.** —*n.* 1 discontent or ill will at another's good fortune because one wishes it had been his; dislike for a person who has what one wants: *Some boys were full of envy when they saw my new bicycle, but my friends were glad for me. The nightingale ... provoketh envy of the lesser songsters* (Robert Bridges). 2 the object of such feeling; person who is envied: *She was the envy of the younger girls in school.* 3 *Obsolete.* malice; ill will; ill repute.
—*v.t.* 1 to feel envy toward: *Poor people envy the rich; sometimes the rich envy the poor.* 2 to feel envy because of: *He envied his friend's success.* 3 *Obsolete.* to begrudge.
—*v.i. Obsolete.* to feel or show envy: *But now I envy at their liberty* (Shakespeare).
[< Old French *envie* < Latin *invidia,* ultimately < *invidēre* look with enmity at < *in-* against + *vidēre* see] —**en′vy|ing|ly,** *adv.*
—*Syn. v.t.* 1 **Envy, covet** mean to feel discontent about the good fortune of others. **Envy** implies resentment, jealousy, or even hatred directed toward them: *He envies famous people.* **Covet** implies a craving for the good fortune that is rightfully theirs: *He covets the fame that his brother has earned.*

en|wall (en wôl′), *v.t. Archaic.* to enclose within a wall; inwall.

en|wind (en wīnd′), *v.t.*, **-wound** or **-wind|ed, -wind|ing.** to wind or coil about; encircle. Also, **inwind.**

en|womb (en wüm′), *v.t.* to enclose in or as if in a womb.

en|wrap (en rap′), *v.t.*, **-wrapped, -wrap|ping.** = wrap. Also, **inwrap.**

en|wreathe (en rēᴛʜ′), *v.t.*, **-wreathed, -wreath|ing.** to wreathe around; encircle; surround: (*Figurative.*) *Enwreathed in smiles of satisfaction, she greeted her guests.* Also, **inwreathe.**

en|write (en rīt′), *v.t.*, **-wrote, -writ|ten, -writ|ing.** *Poetic.* to write upon something; inscribe; imprint: *What wild heart histories seemed to lie enwritten upon those crystalline, celestial spheres* (Edgar Allan Poe).

E|nyo (i nī′ō), *n. Greek Mythology.* a goddess of war, associated with Ares.

en|zo|ot|ic (en′zō ot′ik), *adj., n.* —*adj.* (of diseases) continuously prevalent among animals in a certain region. —*n.* an enzootic disease.
[< Greek *en-* in + *zôion* animal; patterned on *epizootic*]

en|zym (en′zim), *n.* = enzyme.

en|zy|mat|ic (en′zī mat′ik, -zē-), *adj.* of or having to do with an enzyme or enzymes: *Having completed their whole enzymatic journey in a fraction of a second, the hydrogen electrons join the hydrogen protons* (Life).

en|zy|mat|i|cal|ly (en′zī mat′ə klē, -zē-), *adv.* in the manner of an enzyme or enzymes.

en|zyme (en′zīm, -zim), *n.* a protein substance produced in living cells, that influences a chemical reaction within a plant or animal without being changed itself; an organic catalyst. Enzymes help break down food so that it can be digested. Pepsin is an enzyme. *The biologic catalysts (enzymes) differ from the inorganic catalysts in that they are sensitive to heat and light* (Heber W. Youngken). [< Greek *énzymos* leavened < *en-* in + *zýmē* leaven]

enzyme detergent, a detergent containing water-soluble enzymes that break down protein and are derived from bacteria. The enzymes dissolve most stains, but are commonly regarded as dangerous skin and respiratory irritants. *In Britain, failing any voluntary and urgent action, a total ban on the manufacture of enzyme detergents might well be in the public interest* (New Scientist).

enzyme inhibitor, a chemical substance which specifically prevents or lessens the activity of a particular enzyme.

en|zy|mic (en zī′mik, -zim′ik), *adj.* = enzymatic: *Enzymes are proteins, and therefore an increase in the cell's enzymic activity means that it is synthesizing these proteins* (Scientific American).

en|zy|mi|cal|ly (en zī′mə klē), *adv.* = enzymatically.

en|zy|mo|log|i|cal (en′zī mə loj′ə kəl, -zē-), *adj.* of or having to do with enzymology: *enzymological procedures.*

en|zy|mol|o|gist (en′zī mol′ə jist, -zē-), *n.* a person who studies enzymology.

en|zy|mol|o|gy (en′zī mol′ə jē, -zē-), *n.* the study of enzymes, their composition, and activity.

en|zy|mol|y|sis (en′zī mol′ə sis, -zē-), *n.* the chemical change activated by an enzyme.

en|zy|mot|ic (en′zī mot′ik, -zē-), *adj.* = enzymatic.

E|o|an|thro|pus (ē′ō an thrō′pəs, -an′thrə-), *n.* the anthropological genus to which the so-called Piltdown man was assigned when the remains were believed genuine. [< New Latin *Eoanthropus* < Greek *ēōs* dawn + *ánthrōpos* man]

E|o|cene (ē′ə sēn), *n., adj.* —*n.* **1** the second epoch of the Tertiary period of the Cenozoic era, after the Paleocene and before the Oligocene, when the lowest rocks and the ancestors of many modern mammals appeared. **2** the earliest epoch of the Tertiary period, now more commonly divided into two periods, the Paleocene and the Eocene. **3** the rocks formed in either of these epochs.
—*adj.* of or having to do with these epochs or their rocks.
[< Greek *ēōs* dawn + *kainós* new, recent]

E|o|gene (ē′ə jēn), *n., adj.* —*n.* **1** a division of the Tertiary period (comprising the Paleocene, Eocene, and Oligocene epochs); Paleogene. **2** the strata formed in this division.
—*adj.* of or having to do with the Eogene division or its rocks.
[< Greek *ēōs* dawn + *-genēs* born < *gígnesthai* be born]

e|o|hip|pus (ē′ō hip′əs), *n.* any one of an extinct genus of horses that were the ancestors of modern horses; dawn horse. It was about 15 inches high at the shoulder and 3½ feet long and had, instead of hoofs, four toes on each front foot and three on each hind foot. Eohippus lived about 65,000,000 years ago in North America and Europe. [< New Latin *Eohippus* < Greek *ēōs* dawn + *hippos* horse]

e|o ip|so (ē′ō ip′sō), *Latin.* by itself: *Everything new is not eo ipso good and everything old inferior* (Saturday Evening Post).

EOKA (no periods), or **E|o|ka** (ā ō′kə), *n.* Ethniki Organosis Kypriakon Agonos (National Organization of Cypriot Struggle, the party or movement which sought to free Cyprus from British rule and to unite it with Greece before the country gained independence in 1961).

e|o|li|an (ē ō′lē ən), *adj.* = aeolian.

E|o|li|an (ē ō′lē ən), *adj., n.* = Aeolian.

E|ol|ic (ē ol′ik), *n., adj.* = Aeolic.

e|o|li|enne (ā ō′lē en′), *n.* a fine dress fabric of silk and wool. [< French *éolienne*]

e|o|li|pile or **e|o|li|pyle** (ē′ə lə pīl, ē ol′ə-), *n.* = aeolipile.

e|o|lith (ē′ə lith), *n.* a roughly shaped stone instrument, especially of flint, characteristic of a very early stage of human culture. [< Greek *ēōs* dawn + *líthos* stone]

e|o|lith|ic or **E|o|lith|ic** (ē′ə lith′ik), *adj., n.* —*adj.* having to do with a very early stage of human culture, characterized by the use of eoliths.
—*n.* this stage or period.

E.O.M., **1** end of the month. **2** a discount dating term indicating that the discount becomes effective from the end of the month in which goods were purchased. "2/10/E.O.M." means that a 2 per cent discount is allowed on bills that are paid within 10 days after the end of the month in which goods were purchased.

e|on (ē′ən, -on), *n.* **1** a very long period of time; many thousands of years: *Eons passed before life existed on the earth.* **2** *Geology, Astronomy.* one billion years: *Eon [is] geologic shorthand for a period of one billion years* (James E. Oberg). *"Aeon" is being increasingly used by earth and planetary scientists as a convenient short synonym for "billion years"* (Science News). Also, **aeon**. [< Latin *aeōn* < Greek *aiôn* lifetime, age]

e|o|ni|an (ē ō′nē ən), *adj.* = aeonian.

e|o no|mi|ne (ē′ō nom′ə nē), *Latin.* by that name; on that claim.

e|o|no|so|mi|a (ē′ə nə sō′mē ə), *n.* a method of preserving a corpse from decay by a form of crystallizing process: *He [Dr. Katsusaburo Miyamoto] said the system, which he called eonosomia, consisted of crystallizing the blood and keeping open the pores of the body* (London Times). [apparently < Greek *aiôn* age + *sôma* corpse, body]

e|o|phyte (ē′ə fīt), *n.* a fossil plant found in Eozoic rocks. [< Greek *ēōs* dawn + *phytón* plant]

e|o|phyt|ic (ē′ə fit′ik), *adj.* of or having to do with eophytes.

E|os (ē′os), *n. Greek Mythology.* the goddess of the dawn, identified with the Roman goddess Aurora. [< Latin *Eōs* < Greek *ēōs* dawn]

e|o|sin (ē′ə sin), *n.* **1** a rose-red dye or stain made from coal tar, used in dyeing textiles, making red ink, and the like. *Formula:* $C_{20}H_8Br_4O_5$ **2** its reddish-brown potassium or sodium salt. **3** any one of various similar dyestuffs. [< Greek *ēōs* dawn + English *-in*] —**e′o|sin|like′**, *adj.*

e|o|sine (ē′ə sin, -sēn), *n.* = eosin.

e|o|sin|ic (ē′ə sin′ik), *adj.* of or containing eosin.

e|o|sin|o|pe|ni|a (ē′ə sin′ə pē′nē ə), *n.* an abnormal decrease of eosinophils in the blood. [< *eosin* + Greek *peniā* poverty]

e|o|sin|o|phil (ē′ə sin′ə fil), *n., adj.* —*n.* a cell containing granules that are easily stained by eosin or other acid dyes, especially a type of white blood cell: *The number of one kind of white blood cells, called eosinophils, increased in their blood* (Science News Letter).
—*adj.* easily stained by eosin or other acid dyes: *eosinophil leucocytes.* [< *eosin* + *-phil*(e)]

e|o|sin|o|phile (ē′ə sin′ə fīl, -fil), *n., adj.* = eosinophil.

e|o|sin|o|phil|i|a (ē′ə sin′ə fil′ē ə), *n.* an abnormal increase of eosinophils in the blood.

e|o|sin|o|phil|ic (ē′ə sin′ə fil′ik), *adj.* **1** of or having to do with eosinophils or eosinophilia: *eosinophilic meningitis.* **2** having an affinity for eosin or other acid dyes: *eosinophilic granulocytes.*

e|o|sin|o|phil|ous (ē′ə sin′ə fil′əs), *adj.* = eosinophilic.

E|os|tra or **E|os|tre** (ā′os trə), *n.* the Teutonic goddess of spring, originally of dawn: *To delight children, Eostre is said to have magically changed her pet bird into the familiar Easter bunny* (New York Times). [< Old English *Eostre.* Compare Old English *ēastre* Easter.]

E|o|zo|ic (ē′ə zō′ik), *n., adj.* —*n.* **1** a geological time when life first appeared, preceding the Paleozoic. **2** the rock strata formed during this time. —*adj.* of or having to do with this time or its rocks.
[< Greek *ēōs* dawn + *zôion* animal + English *-ic*]

ep-, *prefix.* the form of **epi-** before vowels and *h*, as in *epode, eponym, ephemeral.*

Ep., Epistle.

EP (no periods), **1** European plan. **2** extreme pressure.

EPA (no periods), Environmental Protection Agency (of the United States): *The Environmental Protection Agency will determine applicable water quality standards and make findings regarding compliance with these standards in particular cases. In turn, the EPA will consult with state or interstate agency water quality officials in making these determinations* (Science News).

E.P.A. or **e.p.a.**, *British.* educational priority area (an area requiring extra educational facilities).

ep|ac|me (ep ak′mē), *n. Biology.* the period of evolution preceding the acme of development in the history of organisms.

e|pact (ē′pakt), *n.* **1** the number of days by which a solar year exceeds 12 lunar months, or a lunar year. **2** the age in days of the moon at the beginning of the year (on January 1). [< Late Latin *epactae*, plural < Greek *epaktaí* (*hēmérai*) intercalated (days) < *epágein* to intercalate < *epi-* upon, in + *ágein* bring, lead]

ep|a|go|ge (ep′ə gō′jē), *n.* a rhetorical argument by induction; the use of a number of particular instances to lead to a general conclusion. [< Greek *epagōgê* < *epi-* upon, in + *agōgê* guide]

ep|a|gog|ic (ep′ə goj′ik), *adj.* having to do with induction; of an inductive nature.

ep|a|gom|e|nal days (ep′ə gom′ə nəl), in the Egyptian calendar, 5 or 6 days intercalated, not included in any month. [< Greek *epágomenos* (< *epágein* to intercalate) + English *-al*[1]; see etym. under **epact**]

ep|a|na|lep|sis (ep′ə nə lep′sis), *n.* a figure of speech in which the same word or phrase is repeated after one or more intervening words or on returning to the same subject after a digression. [< New Latin *epanalepsis* < *ep-* upon + *ana-* back + Greek *lêpsis* a taking]

ep|a|naph|o|ra (ep′ə naf′ər ə), *n.* = anaphora.

ep|a|nas|tro|phe (ep′ə nas′trə fē), *n.* = anadiplosis.

ep|a|ni|sog|na|thous (ep′ə ni sog′nə thəs), *adj.* having the upper teeth narrower than the lower ones. [< *ep-* + *aniso-* unequal + Greek *gnáthos* jaw + English *-ous*]

ep|an|or|tho|sis (ep′ə nôr thō′sis), *n.* an immediate revocation of a word or statement in order to correct, justify, weaken, or intensify it. *Example:* "A very brave act. Brave, did you say? A very heroic act." [< Greek *epanorthōsis* < *ep-* upon + *ana-* back + *orthós* straight]

ep|an|thous (ep an′thəs), *adj.* growing upon flowers: *an epanthous fungus.* [< *ep-* + Greek *ánthos* flower + English *-ous*]

ep|arch (ep′ärk), *n.* **1** the prefect or governor of an eparchy. **2** the bishop of an eparchy in the Greek Orthodox Church; metropolitan. [< Greek *éparchos* < *epi-* over + *archós* leader]

ep|ar|chi|al (ep är′kē əl), *adj.* of or having to do with an eparch.

ep|ar|chy (ep′är kē), *n., pl.* **-chies**. **1** an administrative subdivision of modern Greece, smaller than a province. **2** a district or province in ancient Greece. **3** a diocese or archdiocese of the Greek Orthodox Church.

ep|ar|te|ri|al (ep′är tir′ē əl), *adj. Anatomy.* situated above the pulmonary artery.

é|pa|tant (ā pá täɴ′), *adj. French.* amazing; startling.

é|pa|ter le bour|geois (ā pá tā′ lə bür zhwä′), *French.* to shock the bourgeois: *He was an establishment figure but found it a pleasure and . . . a duty to épater le bourgeois* (London Times).

e|paule (e pôl′), *n.* (in fortifications) the shoulder or angle where the face and flank of a bastion meet. [< French *épaule* shoulder; see etym. under **epaulet**]

e|paule|ment (e pôl′mənt), *n.* an earthwork or other screen for protecting a battery, troops, or the like, as from flanking fire. [< French *épaulement*]

é|paule|ment (ā pōl mäɴ′), *n. French.* the movement in ballet of twisting the body from the waist up, so as to bring one shoulder forward.

∗**ep|au|let** or **ep|au|lette** (ep′ə let, ep′ə let′), *n.* **1** an ornament worn on the shoulder of a uniform. In the armed forces epaulets are usually worn only as part of a military dress uniform. **2** a similar ornament worn on uniforms of theater ushers, doormen, and the like. **3** a similar ornamental piece in women's dress. **4** any one of various pieces or coverings for protecting the shoulder in a suit of armor. [< French *épaulette* (diminutive) < *épaule* shoulder < Old French *espaule, espalle* < Latin *spatula* blade]

∗**epaulet**
definition 1

epaulette tree, a tree native to China and Japan, having slender, spreading branches with oblong, alternate leaves and hanging clusters of white fragrant flowers.

ep|ax|i|al (ep ak′sē əl), *adj. Anatomy.* situated on or above the axis of the body. [< *ep-* + *axi*(s) + *-al*[1]] —**ep|ax′i|al|ly**, *adv.*

EPB (no periods), Environmental Protection Board (of Great Britain): *The EPB has three main divisions—air, water, and nature in general (primarily landscape and wildlife care) —and has two main tasks. One is to grant subsidies to industries and communities in constructing pollution-control apparatus . . . the other is to serve, in a sense, as an environmental watchdog* (New Scientist).

Pronunciation Key: hat, āge, cãre, fär; let, ēqual, tėrm; it, īce; hot, ōpen, ôrder; oil, out; cup, pu̇t, rüle; child; long; thin; ᴛʜen; zh, measure; ə represents a in about, e in taken, i in pencil, o in lemon, u in circus.

é|pée or **e|pee** (ā pā′), *n.* **1** a type of sword used in fencing and dueling, having a thin, pointed blade without a cutting edge: *His style, both with the foil and the épée, was a joy to watch* (London Times). **2** a tournament or competition using the épée: *Qualifiers from the Atlantic Coast division will compete for championships in épée, foil, and saber* (New York Times). [< French *épée* < Old French *espee* < Latin *spatha* < Greek *spáthē* blade, sword. See etym. of doublets **spade**[2], **spathe**.]

é|pée|ist or **e|pee|ist** (ā pā′ist), *n.* a person skilled in the use of the épée.

e|pei|ro|gen|e|sis (i pī′rō jen′ə sis), *n.* epeirogeny.

e|pei|ro|ge|net|ic (i pī′rō jə net′ik), *adj.* epeirogenic.

e|pei|ro|gen|ic (i pī′rō jen′ik), *adj.* of the nature of epeirogeny. Also, **epirogenic**.

ep|ei|rog|e|ny (ep′ī roj′ə nē), *n.* the wide changes of level of the earth's crust by which continents and ocean basins are produced. Also, **epirogeny**, **epeirogenesis**. [< Greek *ēpeiros* land, mainland + English *-gen* + *-y*[3]]

ep|en|ce|phal|ic (ep′en sə fal′ik), *adj.* of or having to do with the epencephalon.

ep|en|ceph|a|lon (ep′en sef′ə lon), *n., pl.* **-la** (-lə). = hindbrain. [< *ep-* upon + *encephalon*]

ep|en|the|sis (ep en′thə sis), *n., pl.* **-ses** (-sēz). **1** the insertion of one or more sounds within a word. *Example:* dialectal *chimbley* for *chimney. A sound may be inserted by epenthesis or it may be omitted by elision* (Simeon Potter). **2** the transposition of a semivowel to the syllable preceding that in which it originally occurred. [< Late Latin *epenthesis* < Greek *epénthesis* insertion, ultimately < *epi-* in addition, upon + *en-* in + *tithénai* set, place]

ep|en|thet|ic (ep′ən thet′ik), *adj.* (of a sound or letter) inserted by or resulting from epenthesis.

e|pergne (i pėrn′, ā pärn′), *n.* an ornamental dish for the center of a table, usually with several tiers, branches, or divisions, to hold fruit, candy, cakes, or flowers: *An epergne of unusual design, with a large circular basket in the centre and eight branches supporting four oval and four circular dishes ...* (London Times). [perhaps < French *épargne* saving, economy]

ep|ex|e|ge|sis (ep ek′sə jē′sis), *n.* **1** the addition of a word or words to explain a preceding word or sentence. **2** a word or words added for this purpose. [< Greek *epexḗgēsis,* ultimately < *epi-* upon + *ex-* out + *ágein* lead]

ep|ex|e|get|ic (ep ek′sə jet′ik), *adj.* having to do with or of the nature of an epexigesis. —**ep|ex′e|get′i|cal|ly**, *adv.*

ep|ex|e|get|i|cal (ep ek′sə jet′ə kəl), *adj.* = epexegetic.

Eph., Ephesians (a book of the Bible).

e|pha (ē′fə), *n.* = ephah.

e|phah (ē′fə), *n.* an ancient Hebrew unit of dry measure equal to a little more than a bushel (in the Bible, Ezekiel 45:11). [< Hebrew *'ēphāh*]

eph|apse (ef aps′, ef′aps), *n. Physiology.* the place where two lateral axons (processes carrying impulses away) touch each other. [< Greek *ephapsis* a touching < *epháptein* to touch < *epi-* upon + *háptein* to fasten]

eph|ap|tic (ef ap′tik), *adj.* having to do with an ephapse: *The section on neuron physiology includes chapters on ... synaptic and ephaptic transmission* (Science).

e|phebe (e fēb′, ef′ēb), *n.* **1** a youth in ancient Greece just entering upon manhood or just enrolled as a citizen. **2** any youth or young man: *Staff are generationally divided between the older type of don ... and the younger tough-minded ephebes who have worked hard, but often in specialised and limited areas* (Malcolm Bradbury). [< Latin *ephēbus* < Greek *éphēbos* < *epi-* upon + *hḗbē* puberty, youth]

eph|e|be|um (ef′ə bē′əm), *n., pl.* **-be|a** (-bē′ə). a building or court in ancient Greece, devoted to the exercise or recreation of ephebes.

e|phe|bic (e fē′bik), *adj.* of or having to do with ephebes.

ephebic oath, **1** (in ancient Greece) the oath by which ephebes bound themselves to the service and defense of their country. **2** any solemn promise made by young men to become good citizens.

e|phe|bos (e fē′bos), *n., pl.* **-boi** (-boi). an ephebe of ancient Greece.

e|phe|bus (e fē′bəs), *n., pl.* **-bi** (-bī). an ephebe of ancient Greece.

e|phe|dra (i fē′drə, ef′ə-), *n.* any one of a group of leafless gymnospermous shrubs found in arid regions of the New and Old Worlds. Ephedrine is obtained from several Asiatic varieties. [< New Latin *Ephedra* < Latin < Greek *ephédra* horsetail (plant) < *epi-* upon + *hédra* a seat]

e|phed|rin (i fed′rin; *in Chemistry* ef′ə drin), *n.* = ephedrine.

e|phed|rine (i fed′rin; *in Chemistry* ef′ə drēn, -drin), *n.* a drug used to treat allergic disorders, hay fever, asthma, and head colds. Ephedrine constricts mucous membranes and stimulates the heart and the central nervous system. It is obtained from ephedra or produced synthetically. *Formula:* $C_{10}H_{15}NO$ [< *ephedr*(a) + *-ine*[2]]

e|phe|lis (e fē′lis), *n., pl.* **-li|des** (-lə dēz). *Medicine.* a freckle. [< Greek *éphēlis*]

e|phem|er|a (i fem′ər ə), *n., pl.* **-er|ae** (-ə rē), **-er|as**. **1** a person or thing that has a transitory existence: *These papers of a day, the ephemerae of learning* (Samuel Johnson). **2** = ephemerid; May fly. **3** a fever lasting but a day or a very short time. [< Greek *ephḗmeros* living only a day < *epi-* upon + *hēméra* the day]

e|phem|er|al (i fem′ər əl), *adj., n.* —*adj.* **1** lasting for only a very short time; very short-lived; transitory: *By summoning a little patience, science can deal with rare and ephemeral phenomena* (Science). **SYN:** evanescent, transient. **2** lasting for only a day.

—*n.* anything that lasts or lives but for a day or a very short time. —**e|phem′er|al|ly**, *adv.*

e|phem|er|al|i|ty (i fem′ə ral′ə tē), *n., pl.* **-ties**. **1** the quality or state of being ephemeral. **2** something ephemeral; transient trifle.

e|phem|er|id (i fem′ər id), *n.* any one of an order of insects having a soft, delicate body and two pairs of membranous wings, the forewings being much larger than the rear wings, and usually three long, delicate tails; May fly. Ephemerids live only a day or two in the adult form, but spend a few months to two years in the immature stage. [< New Latin *Ephemeridae* the family name < Greek *ephḗmeros;* see etym. under **ephemera**]

e|phem|er|is (i fem′ər is), *n., pl.* **eph|e|mer|i|des** (ef′ə mer′ə dēz). **1a** a table showing the daily positions of a heavenly body. **b** an astronomical almanac containing such tables. **2** an almanac or calendar. **3** *Obsolete.* a diary. [< Latin *ephēmeris* daybook < Greek *ephēmerís* diary, calendar < *ephḗmeros;* see etym. under **ephemera**]

ephemeris second, *Astronomy.* the fundamental unit of ephemeris time, adopted in 1956 by the International Bureau of Weights and Measures, based upon a particular fraction of the solar year 1900: *The ... ephemeris second is accurate within a few parts per billion* (Scientific American).

ephemeris time, *Astronomy.* a standard measure of time, derived from the time required by the moon and the planets to move around their orbits: *At present ephemeris time is gaining on universal time by about a third of a second per year* (R. W. Clarke).

e|phem|er|on (i fem′ə ron, -ər ən), *n., pl.* **-er|a** (-ər ə), **-er|ons**. **1** = ephemerid. **2** anything that is ephemeral. [< Greek *ephḗmeron,* neuter of *ephḗmeros;* see etym. under **ephemera**]

e|phem|er|ous (i fem′ər əs), *adj.* = ephemeral.

Ephes., Ephesians (a book of the Bible).

E|phe|sian (i fē′zhən), *adj., n.* —*adj.* of Ephesus, an ancient city of Asia Minor, famous for its temple to Artemis or Diana, or of its people.

—*n.* **1** a native or inhabitant of Ephesus. **2** *Obsolete.* a boon companion.

E|phe|sians (i fē′zhənz), *n.pl.* (*sing. in use*). a book of the New Testament. It consists of a letter thought to have been written by the Apostle Paul to the Christians at Ephesus. *Abbr:* Eph.

Eph|e|sine (ef′ə sin), *adj.* = Ephesian.

Eph|i|al|tes (ef′ē al′tēz), *n.* **1** a demon supposed to cause nightmares. **2** the nightmare itself. [< Greek *ephiáltēs*]

e|phip|pi|al (e fip′ē əl), *adj.* having to do with the ephippium: *There are also fertilized, so-called, ephippial eggs which contain no haemoglobin* (H. Munro Fox).

e|phip|pi|um (e fip′ē əm), *n., pl.* **e|phip|pi|a** (e fip′ē ə). a thickened part of the shell of certain crustaceans which, under certain circumstances, is employed as an egg case, and molted together with the eggs, which may lie dormant over the winter before developing: *Females which produce ephippia can return to normal egg production when conditions improve* (J. Green). [< Latin *ephippium* saddle, horse blanket < Greek *ephíppios* that is for putting on a horse < *epi* upon + *híppos* horse (because of the similar appearance of a horse saddle and the thickened shell)]

eph|od (ef′od, ē′fod), *n.* a vestment worn by the ancient Hebrew priests, especially the high priest, in performing sacred duties. [< Hebrew *'ēphōdh*]

eph|or (ef′ôr, -ər), *n., pl.* **-ors, -o|ri** (-ə rī). **1** an official in various ancient Doric states, especially one of five leading magistrates of ancient Sparta, elected yearly by the people to advise the king. **2** an official supervisor of public works in modern Greece, especially one in charge of archaeological excavations: *Born in Athens in 1905, he has held a number of government posts, including that of ... ephor of antiquities of central Macedonia and chief of the department of archaeology* (Scientific American). [< Latin *ephorus* < Greek *éphoros* < *epi-* upon, over + *horân* to see]

eph|or|al (ef′ər əl), *adj.* of or belonging to the office of ephor.

eph|or|ate (ef′ər āt), *n.* the office or position of an ephor.

eph|or|ship (ef′ər ship), *n.* the term of office of an ephor.

E|phra|im (ē′frē əm, -frəm; ef′rəm), *n.* **1** the younger son of Joseph (in the Bible, Genesis 41:51-52). **2** the tribe of Israel descended from him (in the Bible, Joshua 16:5-10). **3** the ancient northern kingdom of Israel, so called because Ephraim was its leading tribe.

E|phra|im|ite (ē′frē ə mīt, -frə mīt; ef′rə-), *n., adj.* —*n.* **1** a member of the tribe of Ephraim. **2** an inhabitant of the ancient northern kingdom of Israel.

—*adj.* of or belonging to the tribe or kingdom of Ephraim.

eph|y|ra (ef′ər ə), *n., pl.* **-y|rae** (-ə rē). an embryo jellyfish. See picture under **alternation of generations**. [< New Latin *ephyra* < Latin *Ephyrē,* a Nereid]

e|phyr|u|la (i fir′ə lə, -yə-), *n., pl.* **-lae** (-lē). = ephyra. [< New Latin *ephyrula* (diminutive) < *ephyra* ephyra]

epi-, *prefix.* on; upon; above; in addition; toward; among: *Epicalyx = on the calyx. Epidermis = upon or above the dermis.* Also, **ep-** before vowels and *h.* [< Greek *epi-,* related to *epí* on, upon, besides, toward]

ep|i|ben|thic (ep′ə ben′thik), *adj.* of the epibenthos: *epibenthic fauna.*

ep|i|ben|thos (ep′ə ben′thos), *n.* the whole body of plant and animal organisms living just above the sea floor. [< *epi-* + *benthos*]

e|pib|i|ont (i pib′ē ont), *n.* a plant or animal that lives on the surface of another organism without feeding parasitically upon its host: *Many mosses and lichens are epibionts.* [< *epi-* + *bio-* + Greek *ón, ontós* being]

e|pib|i|o|sis (i pib′ē ō′sis), *n.* a harmless parasitism in which a plant or animal derives support but not nutrition from its host. [< *epi-* + (sym) *biosis*]

ep|i|blast (ep′ə blast), *n.* the outermost of the three layers of the wall of a blastoderm when fully formed; ectoderm. [< *epi-* + Greek *blastós* sprout, germ]

ep|i|blas|tic (ep′ə blas′tik), *adj.* of, having to do with, or of the nature of an epiblast.

ep|i|bol|ic (ep′ə bol′ik), *adj.* of, having to do with, or of the nature of epiboly.

e|pib|o|ly (i pib′ə lē), *n. Embryology.* the inclusion of one set of dividing cells within another during gastrulation by reason of the more rapid division of the latter. [< Greek *epibolḗ* < *epi-* upon + *bállein* to throw]

ep|ic (ep′ik), *n., adj.* —*n.* **1** a long poem that tells of the adventures of one or more great heroes; epopee. An epic is written in a dignified, majestic style, and often gives expression to the characters and ideals of a nation or race. Homer's *Iliad* and *Odyssey, Beowulf,* Milton's *Paradise Lost,* Virgil's *Aeneid,* and the German *Nibelungenlied* are epics. **2** any writing, drama, motion picture, or artistic work resembling or suggesting an epic. Some very long novels are called epics. *He would like to film an epic of ancient Egypt instead of one-reelers about cowboys, Indians, and pirates* (New Yorker). **3** *Figurative.* a story or series of events worthy of being the subject of an epic: *The heroic resistance of the French is a living epic.*

—*adj.* **1** of or like an epic: *an epic poem, epic poetry, epic sonority.* **2** grand in style; heroic: *epic deeds. Flying over the Atlantic for the first time was an epic achievement.* **3** very great or large: *an epic snowstorm. A stay-at-home protest would have to be of epic proportions to produce a victory* (New York Times).

[< Latin *epicus* < Greek *epikós* < *épos* story, word] —**ep′i|cal|ly**, *adv.*

ep|i|cal (ep′ə kəl), *adj.* = epic.

***ep|i|ca|lyx** (ep′ə kā′liks, -kal′iks), *n.* a ring of bracts at the base of a flower that looks like an outer calyx, such as that of the mallow; calycle.

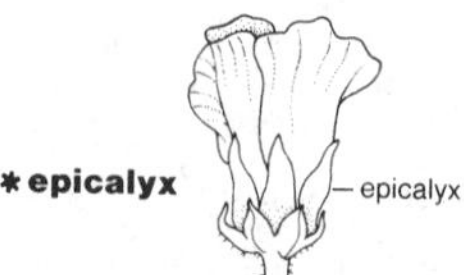

***epicalyx**

ep|i|can|thic fold (ep′ə kan′thik), a fold of skin extending from the eyelid over the inner and sometimes outer corner of the eye; epicanthus: *The Mongolian "slant," "slit," or "oblique" eye is* *due to an overdeveloped epicanthic fold ... partially covering the lash-bearing edge of the lid* (Alfred L. Kroeber). [< *epicanth*(us) + *-ic*]

ep|i|can|thus (ep′ə kan′thəs), *n., pl.* **-thi** (-thī). = epicanthic fold. [< New Latin *epicanthus* < *epi-* + *canthus*]

ep|i|car|di|ac (ep′ə kär′dē ak), *adj.* = epicardial.

ep|i|car|di|al (ep′ə kär′dē əl), *adj.* having to do with the epicardium.

ep|i|car|di|um (ep′ə kär′dē əm), *n., pl.* **-di|a** (-dē ə). the innermost layer of the pericardium, which adheres to the heart. [< *epi-* over + (peri)*cardium*]

ep|i|carp (ep′ə kärp), *n.* the outer layer of the wall (pericarp) of a fruit or ripened ovary of a plant; exocarp: *The skin of a pear is its epicarp.* See picture under **fruit**. [< *epi-* + Greek *karpós* fruit]

ep|i|ce|di|um (ep′ə sē′dē əm, -sə dī′-), *n., pl.* **-ce|di|a** (-sē′dē ə, -sə dī′-). a funeral song; dirge; elegy. [< Latin *epicēdium* < Greek *epikḗdeion*, neuter of *epikēdeiós* of or for a funeral < *epi-* upon + *kôdos* mourning]

ep|i|cene (ep′ə sēn), *adj., n.* —*adj.* **1** belonging to or partaking of the characteristics of both sexes. **2a** of no definite sex or kind. **b** = effeminate. **3** *Grammar.* having but one form to denote both genders, as certain Greek and Latin nouns.
—*n.* a person who is epicene.
[< Latin *epicoenus* < Greek *epíkoinos* common gender < *epi-* upon + *koinós* common]

ep|i|cen|ism (ep′ə sē niz′əm), *n.* epicene quality or character.

ep|i|cen|ter (ep′ə sen′tər), *n.* **1** the point on the earth's surface from which earthquake waves seem to radiate, situated directly above the true center of the earthquake: *Grand Banks Earthquake caused a turbidity current that broke cables as far as 300 miles away from the epicenter of the disturbance* (Scientific American). **2** any central or focal point: *the epicenter of a revolt. The bedroom suburb, the new epicenter of U.S. population, owes its existence to the highway which whisks the suburbanite from home to downtown job* (Time).

ep|i|cen|tral (ep′ə sen′trəl), *adj.* having to do with an epicenter.

ep|i|cen|tre (ep′ə sen′tər), *n. Especially British.* epicenter.

ep|i|cen|trum (ep′ə sen′trəm), *n., pl.* **-tra** (-trə). = epicenter.

é|pice|rie (ā pēs rē′), *n. French.* **1** spices. **2** groceries. **3** a grocer's shop: *Eventually they would buy a shop—an épicerie, a charcuterie, or a bakery* (New Yorker).

ep|i|chile (ep′ə kil, -kīl), *n.* = epichilium.

ep|i|chil|i|um (ep′ə kil′ē əm), *n., pl.* **-i|a** (-ē ə). *Botany.* the terminal lobe of the divided lip of an orchid.

ep|i|chlor|o|hy|drin (ep′ə klôr′ə hī′drin, -klōr′-), *n.* a colorless liquid used as a solvent in the manufacture of various chemical products such as paint, varnish, and adhesives. *Formula:* C_3H_5ClO

ep|i|chon|dro|sis (ep′ə kon drō′sis), *n., pl.* **-ses** (-sēz). a growth of cartilage upon the periosteum, as that producing the antlers of a deer.

ep|i|chon|drot|ic (ep′ə kon drot′ik), *adj.* of or having to do with an epichondrosis or epichondroses.

ep|i|cho|ri|al (ep′ə kôr′ē əl, -kōr′-), *adj.* peculiar to a particular country or district.

ep|i|cho|ris|tic (ep′ə kə ris′tik), *adj.* = epichorial.

ep|i|cist (ep′ə sist), *n.* a writer of epic poetry.

ep|i|cle|sis (ep′ə klē′sis), *n.* a part of the prayer of consecration in liturgies of the Eastern Church, in which the presence of the Holy Spirit is invoked to bless the gifts on the altar and the worshippers. [< Greek *epíklēsis* invocation < *epikaleîn* to invoke < *epi-* upon + *kaleîn* to call]

ep|i|con|dyle (ep′ə kon′dəl), *n. Anatomy.* the rounded part at the end of the long bone in the upper part of the arm, at the elbow; the condyle at the distal end of the humerus. [< *epi-* + *condyle*]

ep|i|con|dy|li|tis (ep′ə kon′də lī′tis), *n.* inflammation of the elbow: *Epicondylitis, a chronic and painful inflammation of the lateral or medial condyle at the distal end of the humerus, is commonly known as tennis elbow* (New Yorker).

ep|i|con|ti|nen|tal (ep′ə kon′tə nen′təl), *adj.* resting upon a continent: *Those shallow portions of the sea which lie upon the continental shelf, and those portions which extend into the interior of the continent with like shallow depths, ... may be called epicontinental seas* (Chamberlin and Salisbury).

ep|i|cor|mic (ep′ə kor′mik), *adj.* (of a shoot or branch) growing from a dormant bud which has been suddenly exposed to the light and air. [< *epi-* + *corm* + *-ic*]

ep|i|cot|yl (ep′ə kot′əl), *n.* the part of the stem or axis that is above the cotyledons in the embryo of a plant. See picture under **cotyledon**. [< *epi-* + Greek *kotýlē* small vessel, a hollow]

ep|i|cra|ni|al (ep′ə krā′nē əl), *adj.* of or having to do with the epicranium.

ep|i|cra|ni|um (ep′ə krā′nē əm), *n., pl.* **-ni|a** (-nē ə). **1** the upper surface of an insect's head: *The mouth parts are attached to the ventral side of the epicranium* (Hegner and Stiles). **2** the covering of the cranium or vertebrate skull, especially the muscular and tendinous parts below the skin; scalp.

ep|i|crit|ic (ep′ə krit′ik), *adj.* of or having to do with sensory nerve fibers in the skin and mouth that can make fine distinctions in touch and temperature. [< Greek *epikritikós* determining < *epíkrisis* judgment < *epikrínein* decide < *epi-* on + *krínein* to judge]

epic simile, a long or elaborate simile, especially of a kind that extends over a number of lines in a poem, as in the epic poetry of Homer.

epic theater, a form of theater or drama, associated especially with the works of Bertolt Brecht, that uses many techniques of the epic poem, such as condensing the action and mixing narrative with dialogue: *The epic theater ... aims to make one think rather than feel* (Howard Taubman).

ep|i|cure (ep′ə kyůr), *n.* **1a** a person who enjoys eating and drinking and who is very particular in choosing fine foods, wines, and other things to eat and drink; gourmet: *Serenely full, the epicure would say Fate cannot harm me, I have dined today* (Sydney Smith). **b** a person who is discriminating in all matters of taste; connoisseur. **c** a person who is fond of pleasure and luxury: *The old epicure tasted the exquisiteness of romance* (Lytton Strachey). **2** *Obsolete.* a person who gives himself up to sensual pleasure, especially eating; glutton. [Anglicized variant of Latin *Epicurus*, founder of the Epicurean philosophy]

ep|i|cu|re|an (ep′ə kyů rē′ən), *adj., n.* —*adj.* **1** of or like an epicure; fond of pleasure and luxury: *epicurean tastes.* **2** fit for an epicure: *an epicurean banquet.*
—*n.* a person who is fond of pleasure and luxury; epicure. **SYN:** sybarite.

Ep|i|cu|re|an (ep′ə kyů rē′ən), *adj., n.* —*adj.* of or having to do with Epicurus or his philosophy, which holds that pleasure is the proper end of man's efforts, but also that true pleasure depends upon self-control, moderation, and honorable behavior: *... the sober majesties Of settled, sweet, Epicurean life* (Tennyson).
—*n.* a believer in the philosophy of Epicurus: *He appears, also, as an Epicurean who scorned idealism and loved reality with an energy which never flagged* (Atlantic).

Ep|i|cu|re|an|ism (ep′ə kyů rē′ə niz əm), *n.* **1** the philosophy or principles of Epicurus or his followers. **2** Also, **epicureanism**. belief in or practice of this philosophy. **3** Also, **epicureanism**. the habits or tastes of an epicure; epicurism.

ep|i|cur|ism (ep′ə kyů riz′əm), *n.* the habits or tastes of an epicure.

Ep|i|cur|ism (ep′ə kyů riz′əm), *n.* = Epicureanism.

ep|i|cu|ti|cle (ep′ə kyü′tə kəl), *n.* the outermost layer of a cuticle or an exoskeleton.

ep|i|cu|tic|u|lar (ep′ə kyü tik′yə lər), *adj.* having to do with or serving as an epicuticle: *Insects and arachnids possess a discrete epicuticular layer of wax and do not lose much water by evaporation* (New Scientist).

***ep|i|cy|cle** (ep′ə sī′kəl), *n.* **1** a small circle, the center of which moves round in the circumference of a larger circle (formerly used in astronomy to explain the motions of planets). **2** *Geometry.* a circle that rolls around the inside or outside of the circumference of another circle. [< Late Latin *epicyclus* < Greek *epíkyklos* < *epi-* on + *kýklos* circle]

***epicycle**
definition 1

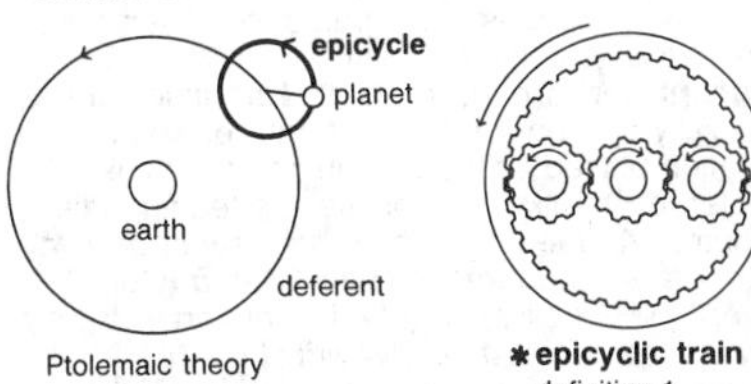

Ptolemaic theory

***epicyclic train**
definition 1

ep|i|cy|clic (ep′ə sī′klik, -sik′lik), *adj.* of or having to do with an epicycle.

ep|i|cy|cli|cal (ep′ə sī′klə kəl, -sik′lə-), *adj.* = epicyclic.

***epicyclic train**, **1** a group of gears or wheels whose axes revolve about a common center. **2** such a group in which the axis of one wheel revolves around the circumference of another fixed or moving wheel.

ep|i|cy|cloid (ep′ə sī′kloid), *n. Geometry.* a curve traced by a point moving on the circumference of a circle that rolls upon the convex side of a fixed circle. [< *epicycl*(e) + *-oid*]

ep|i|cy|cloi|dal (ep′ə sī kloi′dəl), *adj.* in the form of an epicycloid.

epicycloidal wheel, a gear or wheel in an epicyclic train.

ep|i|deic|tic (ep′ə dīk′tik), *adj.* serving for exhibition or display: *an epideictic ovation.* [< Greek *epideiktikós* < *epi-* around + *deiknýnai* to show]

ep|i|dem|ic (ep′ə dem′ik), *n., adj.* —*n.* **1** the rapid spreading of a disease so that many people have it at the same time: *All the schools in the city were closed because of an epidemic of flu.* **2** *Figurative.* the rapid spread of an idea, fashion, or the like: *an epidemic of buying goods on the installment plan. The city suffered from an epidemic of strikes by different labor unions all through the winter.*
—*adj.* affecting many people at the same time; widespread: *An outbreak of flu became epidemic last winter.* (*Figurative.*) *The idea of two cars in every garage has become epidemic.*
[< French *épidémique* < Old French *epidemie*, learned borrowing from Medieval Latin *epidemia* < Greek *epidēmía* a stay, visit, prevalence (of a disease) < *epi-* among, upon + *dêmos* people, district] —**ep′i|dem′i|cal|ly**, *adv.*

ep|i|dem|i|cal (ep′ə dem′ə kəl), *adj.* = epidemic.

epidemic cerebrospinal meningitis, = cerebrospinal meningitis.

ep|i|de|mic|i|ty (ep′ə də mis′ə tē), *n.* the quality of being epidemic.

epidemic tremor, an acute, viral infection of young chicks characterized by ataxia and tremor of the head and neck; avian encephalomyelitis.

ep|i|de|mi|o|log|ic (ep′ə dē′mē ə loj′ik), *adj.* **1** of or having to do with epidemiology. **2** having the character of an epidemic. —**ep′i|de′mi|o|log′i|cal|ly**, *adv.*

ep|i|de|mi|o|log|i|cal (ep′ə dē′mē ə loj′ə kəl), *adj.* = epidemiologic: *Typhoid fever in Devonshire could have been prevented if Dr. William Budd's epidemiological observations had not been ridiculed by the clinicians of his time* (Atlantic).

ep|i|de|mi|ol|o|gist (ep′ə dē′mē ol′ə jist), *n.* a person who studies epidemic diseases: *On a world-wide basis epidemiologists now recognise many instances of diseases related to geographical factors like climate, insect vectors, or socioultural pressures* (New Scientist).

ep|i|de|mi|ol|o|gy (ep′ə dē′mē ol′ə jē), *n.* the branch of medicine dealing with the causes, distribution, and control of the spread of diseases in a community, especially of infectious diseases.

ep|i|den|dron (ep′ə den′dron), *n.* = epidendrum.

ep|i|den|drum (ep′ə den′drəm), *n.* any one of a genus of epiphytic orchids native to South America and the West Indies. [< New Latin *Epidendrum* the genus name < Greek *epi-* upon + *déndron* tree]

ep|i|der|mal (ep′ə dėr′məl), *adj.* of or having to do with the epidermis: *During the formation of the leaf epidermis of certain plant species, there occur modifications resulting in the formation of epidermal hairs* (Harbaugh and Goodrich).

ep|i|der|mic (ep′ə dėr′mik), *adj.* = epidermal.

ep|i|der|mis (ep′ə dėr′mis), *n.* **1** the outer, protective layer of the skin of vertebrate animals, that covers the true skin or dermis; cuticle. See picture under **skin**. **2** the outer covering on the shells of many mollusks. **3** any one of various other outer layers of invertebrates. **4** a skinlike layer of cells in seed plants and ferns: *In most respects, however, the epidermis of a stem is like that of the leaves and is continuous with it* (Fred W. Emerson). **5** *Embryology.* = ectoderm. [< Late Latin *epidermis* < Greek *epidermis* < *epi-* on + *dérma* skin]

ep|i|der|mi|za|tion (ep′ə dėr′mə zā′shən), *n. Medicine.* skin grafting.

ep|i|der|moid (ep′ə dėr′moid), *adj.* resembling epidermis.

ep|i|der|moi|dal (ep′ə dėr moi′dəl), *adj.* = epidermoid.

ep|i|der|mol|y|sis (ep′ə dėr mol′ə sis), *n.* a loosened state of the epidermis.

ep|i|di|a|scope (ep′ə dī′ə skōp), *n.* a projector which throws the images of transparent or opaque objects on a screen. [< *epi-* + Greek *diá* through + English *-scope*]

ep|i|dic|tic (ep′ə dik′tik), *adj. Obsolete.* epideictic.

ep|i|did|y|mal (ep′ə did′ə məl), *adj.* having to do with the epididymis: *epididymal ducts, epididymal tissue.*

Pronunciation Key: hat, āge, cãre, fär; let, ēqual, tėrm; it, īce; hot, ōpen, ôrder; oil, out; cup, půt, rüle; child; long; thin; ᴛʜen; zh, measure; ə represents **a** in about, **e** in taken, **i** in pencil, **o** in lemon, **u** in circus.

ep|i|did|y|mis (ep′ə did′ə mis), *n., pl.* **-did|y|mi-des** (-did′ə mə dēz′). an elongated oblong body, composed chiefly of convoluted tubes, resting upon and alongside the testicle. [< Greek *epididymís* < *epi-* on + *dídymoi* testicles]

ep|i|did|y|mi|tis (ep′ə did′ə mī′tis), *n.* inflammation of the epididymis.

e|pid|o|site (i pid′ə sīt), *n.* a rock composed chiefly of epidote, with quartz and some other minerals in variable amounts: *Epidosite is granular to schistose . . . and commonly is very tough as well as hard* (Fenton and Fenton). [< Greek *epidósis* an increase (< *epididónai* to increase) + English *-ite* [1]]

ep|i|dote (ep′ə dōt), *n.* a mineral consisting largely of aluminum, iron, and lime silicate, usually occurring in yellowish-green, needle-shaped crystals. *Formula:* $Ca_2(Al, Fe)_3Si_3O_{12}OH$ [< French *épidote* < Greek *epididónai* to increase < *epi-* over + *didónai* give (because it is longer in the base of the crystal than allied minerals)]

ep|i|dot|ic (ep′ə dot′ik), *adj.* of or like epidote.

ep|i|do|ti|za|tion (ep′ə dō′tə zā′shən), *n.* alteration into epidote.

ep|i|do|tized (ep′ə dō tīzd), *adj.* (of a rock) changed into epidote.

ep|i|du|ral (ep′ə dùr′əl, -dyùr′-), *adj. Anatomy.* situated upon or outside the dura mater.

ep|i|fau|na (ep′ə fô′nə), *n., pl.* **-nas, -nae** (-nē). the animals living on the surface of sediments, plants, or objects on the sea floor; infauna.

ep|i|fau|nal (ep′ə fô′nəl), *adj.* of or having to do with epifauna; belonging to the epifauna: *epifaunal organisms.*

ep|i|fo|cal (ep′ə fō′kəl), *adj.* above the focus, or true center of disturbance, of an earthquake; epicentral.

ep|i|gam|ic (ep′ə gam′ik), *adj. Zoology.* that serves to attract the opposite sex: *epigamic coloring.* [< Greek *epígamos* for marriage (< *epi-* upon + *gámos* marriage) + English *-ic*]

ep|i|gas|tric (ep′ə gas′trik), *adj.* of or having to do with the region immediately above the stomach. [< *epigastr*(ium) + *-ic*]

ep|i|gas|tri|um (ep′ə gas′trē əm), *n.* the epigastric region. [< New Latin *epigastrium* < Greek *epigástrion* < *epi-* over + *gastêr, gastrós* belly, stomach]

ep|i|ge|al (ep′ə jē′əl), *adj.* **1** living close to the ground, as some insects. **2** *Botany.* epigeous.

ep|i|ge|an (ep′ə jē′ən), *adj.* = epigeal.

ep|i|gene (ep′ə jēn), *adj. Geology.* formed or originating on the earth's surface (contrasted with *hypogene*) : *epigene rocks, epigene deposits.* [< Greek *epi-* over, above + *-genēs* born < *gígnesthai* be born]

ep|i|gen|e|sis (ep′ə jen′ə sis), *n.* **1** *Biology.* the development of the embryo by a series of new formations or successive differentiations from the substance of the fertilized egg. **2** *Geology.* the formation of ore deposits after the origin of the rocks in which they occur. **3** *Medicine.* occurrence of formations of tissue built on existing material. [< *epi-* + Greek *génesis* generation]

ep|i|gen|e|sist (ep′ə jen′ə sist), *n.* a person who holds the theory of epigenesis.

ep|i|ge|net|ic (ep′ə jə net′ik), *adj.* **1** having to do with or produced by epigenesis: *It is an axiom of embryology that development is epigenetic* (S. A. Barnett). **2** = epigene. **—ep′i|ge|net′i|cal|ly,** *adv.*

ep|i|ge|net|i|cist (ep′ə jə net′ə sist), *n.* a person who studies epigenetics.

ep|i|ge|net|ics (ep′ə jə net′iks), *n.* the study of the processes by which organisms develop.

ep|i|gen|ic (ep′ə jen′ik), *adj.* = epigene.

e|pig|e|nist (i pij′ə nist), *n.* = epigenesist.

e|pig|e|nous (i pij′ə nəs), *adj. Botany.* growing on the surface, especially the upper surface, as fungi on leaves.

ep|i|ge|ous (ep′ə jē′əs), *adj. Botany.* **1** (of plants) growing on or close to the ground. **2** (of cotyledons) borne above ground in germination. [< Greek *epígeios* (with English *-ous*) < *epi-* upon + *gê* earth]

ep|i|glot|tal (ep′ə glot′əl), *adj.* of or having to do with the epiglottis.

ep|i|glot|tic (ep′ə glot′ik), *adj.* = epiglottal.

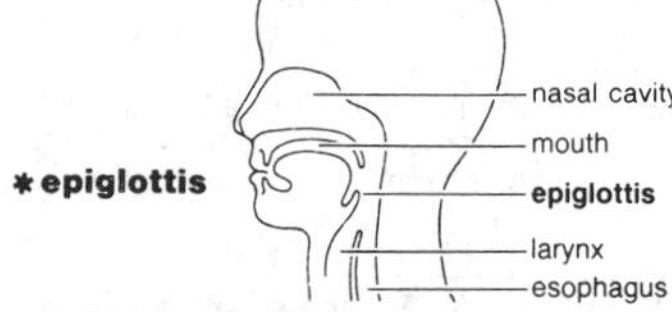

***epiglottis**

***ep|i|glot|tis** (ep′ə glot′is), *n.* a thin, triangular plate of cartilage that covers the entrance to the windpipe during swallowing, so that food and drink do not get into the lungs. [< Late Latin *epiglōttis* < Greek *epiglōttís* < *epi-* on + *glôtta* tongue]

e|pig|na|thous (i pig′nə thəs), *adj.* (of birds) having the end of the upper mandible decurved over and beyond that of the lower one, as a bird of prey, parrot, petrel, or gull. [< *epi-* + Greek *gnáthos* jaw + English *-ous*]

ep|i|gone (ep′ə gōn), *n.* a person who belongs to a later generation; a successor or descendant, especially one who tries unsuccessfully to emulate his forerunners: *He is one of a small group of epigones left over from the dying enthusiasms of the first decade or two of this century* (Architectural Forum). [< French *epigones,* plural < Latin *epigonī, Epigonī;* see etym. under **Epigoni**]

E|pig|o|ni (i pig′ə nī), *n.pl. Greek Legend.* the seven sons of the seven Argive chiefs who unsuccessfully attacked Thebes. They avenged their fathers just before the Trojan War. [< Latin *Epigonī* < Greek *epígonoi,* plural of *epígonos* born afterwards < *epi-* upon + a root of *gígnesthai* be born]

ep|i|gon|ic (ep′ə gon′ik), *adj.* of an epigone or epigones; tending to emulate or imitate; emulative: *The energetic aggressiveness characteristic of Mill has been replaced in much modern liberal thinking by a sort of eclectic, epigonic complacency* (Listener).

e|pig|o|nism (i pig′ə niz əm), *n.* the state of belonging to a later and less distinguished generation: *Is it reasonable to reduce all the living composers of our day, old and young, to a dead level of epigonism?* (New York Times).

ep|i|gram (ep′ə gram), *n.* **1** a short, pointed, or witty saying. *Examples:* "Speech is silver, but silence is golden." "The only way to get rid of a temptation is to yield to it" (Oscar Wilde). **2** a short poem ending in a witty or clever, and often a satirical, turn of thought.

Example: "Here lies our sovereign lord, the king,
Whose word no man relies on,
Who never said a foolish thing,
Nor ever did a wise one."

3 epigrammatic expression. **4** *Obsolete.* an inscription. [< Latin *epigramma* < Greek *epígramma* < *epigráphein* < *epi-* on + *gráphein* write]

▶**epigrams.** An *epigram* is a short, pointed, or witty saying. A special type of epigram is the *paradox,* which makes a statement that, as it stands, contradicts fact or common sense or itself, and yet suggests a truth or at least a half truth: *All generalizations are false, including this one.* Closely related to epigrams are *aphorisms* —pithy statements, but more likely to be abstract and not necessarily witty: *Fools rush in where angels fear to tread. Proverbs* are the often-quoted, concrete expressions of popular wisdom. They are likely to make observations on character or conduct: *Still waters run deep.*

ep|i|gram|mar|i|an (ep′ə grə mãr′ē ən), *n.* a maker of epigrams: *Soviet Ambassador Pyotr Abrasimov's pithy reports on the progress of the secret sessions ("What is long is good"; "Where there are roses, there are also thorns") have won him a reputation among newsmen as the leading epigrammarian among the Big Four* (Time).

ep|i|gram|mat|ic (ep′ə grə mat′ik), *adj.* **1** like an epigram; short and witty. **2** of epigrams; full of epigrams: *smart epigrammatic speeches* (Emerson). **—ep′i|gram|mat′i|cal|ly,** *adv.*

ep|i|gram|mat|i|cal (ep′ə grə mat′ə kəl), *adj.* = epigrammatic.

ep|i|gram|ma|tism (ep′ə gram′ə tiz əm), *n.* epigrammatic character or style.

ep|i|gram|ma|tist (ep′ə gram′ə tist), *n.* a maker of epigrams.

ep|i|gram|ma|tize (ep′ə gram′ə tīz), *v.,* **-tized, -tiz|ing.** **—*v.i.*** to make epigrams.
—*v.t.* to express by epigrams.

ep|i|gram|ma|tiz|er (ep′ə gram′ə tī′zər), *n.* a person who composes epigrams, or writes epigrammatically; epigrammatist.

ep|i|graph (ep′ə graf, -gräf), *n.* **1** an inscription, especially one on a building, tomb, or statue. **2** a quotation placed at the beginning of a book, chapter, or the like, to indicate the leading idea or theme: *As the epigraph to his new book, Mr. Hyams takes a quotation from Conrad* (Observer). [< Greek *epigraphê* inscription < *epigráphein* < *epi-* on + *gráphein* write]

e|pig|ra|pher (i pig′rə fər), *n.* = epigraphist.

ep|i|graph|ic (ep′ə graf′ik), *adj.* of or having to do with an epigraph or epigraphy. **—ep′i|graph′i-cal|ly,** *adv.*

ep|i|graph|i|cal (ep′ə graf′ə kəl), *adj.* = epigraphic.

e|pig|ra|phist (i pig′rə fist), *n.* a person skilled in epigraphy.

e|pig|ra|phy (i pig′rə fē), *n.* **1** inscriptions. **2a** the branch of knowledge that deals with the deciphering and interpretation of inscriptions. **b** the paleography of inscriptions.

e|pig|y|nous (i pij′ə nəs), *adj.* **1** situated on the edge of the receptacle, just above the pistil: *epigynous stamens, sepals, or petals.* **2** (of a flower) having its parts so arranged, as the apple. [< *epi-* + Greek *gynê* female + English *-ous*]

e|pig|y|num (i pij′ə nəm), *n.* **1** the opening of the female genital organs in the arachnids. **2** a flat plate covering this opening in a spider. [< New Latin *epigynum* < Greek *epi-* on, over + *gynê* female]

e|pig|y|ny (i pij′ə nē), *n.* the state or condition of being epigynous.

ep|i|la|tion (ep′ə lā′shən), *n.* removal or loss of hair, especially by destruction of the roots: *Epilation . . . was common, mainly on the scalp, among those who survived for more than two weeks after the explosion* (Los Alamos Scientific Laboratory). [< French *épilation* < *épiler* to remove hair < Latin *ex-* out + *pilus* hair]

ep|i|lep|sy (ep′ə lep′sē), *n.* a chronic disorder of the nervous system characterized by partial or complete loss of consciousness and sometimes convulsions. It is caused by a disturbance in the normal electrical rhythm of brain cells. [< Late Latin *epilēpsia* < Greek *epilēpsiā* seizure < *epi-* upon + *lêpsis* a seizure < *lambánein* seize, take]

ep|i|lep|tic (ep′ə lep′tik), *adj., n.* **—*adj.*** **1** of or having to do with epilepsy: *an epileptic attack, epileptic fits.* **2** having epilepsy.
—*n.* a person who has epilepsy: *A deficiency of glutamic acid in brains of epileptics has been clearly demonstrated* (Newsweek). **—ep′i|lep′ti-cal|ly,** *adv.*

ep|i|lep|ti|form (ep′ə lep′tə fôrm), *adj.* = epileptoid.

ep|i|lep|to|gen|ic (ep′ə lep′tə jen′ik), *adj.* producing or produced by epilepsy: *epileptogenic areas of the brain, epileptogenic lesions.*

ep|i|lep|toid (ep′ə lep′toid), *adj.* resembling epilepsy.

ep|i|lim|ni|on (ep′ə lim′nē ən), *n., pl.* **-ni|a** (-nē ə). the warm, aerated upper layer of water in a lake: *The thermocline is the zone in which the warm temperatures of the epilimnion drop rapidly to the cold ones of the hypolimnion* (Scientific American). [< *epi-* + Greek *límnion,* diminutive of *límnē* marsh, lake]

e|pil|o|gist (i pil′ə jist), *n.* the writer or speaker of an epilogue.

ep|i|logue or **ep|i|log** (ep′ə lôg, -log), *n.* **1** a concluding part added to a novel, poem, film, or other literary or dramatic work. An epilogue may be used to round out or interpret the work. **2a** a speech or poem after the end of a play. It is addressed to the audience and spoken by one of the actors: *No epilogue, I pray you; for your play needs no excuse* (Shakespeare). **b** the actor who speaks an epilogue. **3** *Figurative.* any concluding act or event. [< Old French *epilogue,* learned borrowing from Latin *epilogus* < Greek *epílogos* < *epi-* in addition + *lógos* a speaking < *légein* speak]

ep|i|loi|a (ep′ə loi′ə), *n.* an abnormal congenital condition characterized by mental deficiency, epileptic attacks, and tumors on the kidneys and other organs. [< New Latin *epiloia;* origin uncertain]

ep|i|mer (ep′ə mər), *n. Chemistry.* an isomeric compound, common in certain sugars, that differs from its corresponding isomer in the relative positions of an attached hydrogen and hydroxyl. [< *epi-* + (iso)*mer*]

ep|i|mere (ep′ə mir), *n. Embryology.* the dorsal part of a mesodermal section in chordates. [< *epi-* + *-mere*]

ep|i|mer|ic (ep′ə mer′ik), *adj. Chemistry.* having the characteristics of an epimer; related as epimers: *epimeric compounds.*

ep|i|mer|i|za|tion (ep′ə mə rə zā′shən), *n.* the process by which a chemical is changed to an epimeric form.

ep|i|mer|ize (ep′ə mə rīz), *v.t.,* **-ized, -iz|ing.** to change into an epimer.

Ep|i|me|theus (ep′ə mē′thüs, -thē əs), *n. Greek Mythology.* the brother of Prometheus and husband of Pandora, whom he accepted as a gift of Zeus, though warned by Prometheus.

ep|i|mor|phic (ep′ə môr′fik), *adj.* of or having to do with epimorphosis.

ep|i|mor|pho|sis (ep′ə môr′fə sis), *n.* **1** the regeneration of a part of an organism by cell proliferation at the cut or injured surfaces. **2** (in arthropods) growth without a marked change in the form. [< New Latin *epimorphosis,* from Greek *epi-* upon + *morphê* form]

ep|i|my|si|um (ep′ə mis′ē əm), *n., pl.* **-my|si|a** (-mis′ē ə). the sheath of connective tissue around a muscle. [< New Latin *epimysium* < *epi-* over + Greek *mŷs, myós* mouse, muscle]

ep|i|nas|tic (ep′ə nas′tik), *adj.* having to do with or of the nature of epinasty.

ep|i|nas|ty (ep′ə nas′tē), *n.* the bending downward of a part or organ, caused by more rapid growth along the upper surface, as in a leaf. [<

Greek *epi-* on, over + *nastós* compact, tight (< *nássein* squeeze) + English *-y*[3]]

ep|i|neph|rin (ep′ə nef′rin), *n.* = epinephrine.

ep|i|neph|rine (ep′ə nef′rin, -rēn), *n.* a hormone secreted by the inner part of the adrenal gland, which enables the body to meet conditions of physical stress; adrenalin. [< *epi-* + Greek *nephrós* kidney + English *-ine*[2]]

ep|i|neu|ral (ep′ə nůr′əl, -nyůr′-), *adj., n.* — ***adj.*** lying upon a neural arch, as a spine of a fish's backbone.
— ***n.*** a spine attached to a neural arch.

ep|i|neu|ri|al (ep′ə nůr′ē əl, -nyůr′-), *adj.* having to do with or consisting of epineurium: *epineurial sheaths.*

ep|i|neu|ri|um (ep′ə nůr′ē əm, -nyůr′-), *n., pl.* **-neu|ri|a** (-nůr′ē ə, -nyůr′-). the thick sheath of connective tissue surrounding the trunk of a nerve. [< New Latin *epineurium* < Greek *epi-* on + *neûron* sinew, nerve]

ep|i|op|ti|con (ep′ē op′tə kon), *n.* the second of the three ganglionic swellings in each of the optic ganglia of an insect.

ep|i|pet|al|ous (ep′ə pet′ə ləs), *adj.* **1** (of flowers) having stamens attached to the corolla. **2** (of stamens) borne upon the petals of a flower. [< *epi-* + *petalous*]

Epiph., Epiphany.

ep|i|phan|ic (ep′ə fan′ik), *adj.* characterized by epiphany; providing insight; revealing: *Now and then, characteristically, Godard's black world will light up with an epiphanic flash of something better* (Penelope Gilliatt).

e|piph|a|nous (i pif′ə nəs), *adj.* **1** = epiphanic. **2** resplendent; showy.

E|piph|a|ny (i pif′ə nē), *n.* January 6, the anniversary of the coming of the Three Wise Men to honor the infant Jesus at Bethlehem; Twelfth-day; Little Christmas. [< Old French *epiphany* < Late Latin *epiphanīa* < Greek *epipháneia* < *epi-* upon + *phaínein* to show]

e|piph|a|ny (i pif′ə nē), *n., pl.* **-nies. 1** an appearance or manifestation, especially of a deity. **2** *Figurative.* **a** a sudden revelation or perception; an insight into the essence of a thing: *"Inadmissible Evidence" progresses through what James Joyce called "epiphanies": episodes of cumulative revelation* (Time). **b** a poem, sketch, or other literary work recording an epiphany. [< Greek *epipháneia;* see etym. under **Epiphany**]

ep|i|phe|nom|e|nal (ep′ə fə nom′ə nəl), *adj.* of the nature of an epiphenomenon; having to do with epiphenomena. — **ep′i|phe|nom′e|nal|ly,** *adv.*

ep|i|phe|nom|e|nal|ism (ep′ə fə nom′ə nə liz′əm), *n.* = automatism.

ep|i|phe|nom|e|non (ep′ə fə nom′ə non, -nən), *n., pl.* **-na** (-nə). **1** something additional that appears: *If biology is just complicated physics, then life is an epiphenomenon, no more* (Listener). **2** a secondary or additional symptom or complication arising during the course of a disease.

ep|i|phragm (ep′ə fram), *n.* **1** *Zoology.* the dried mucus with which a snail closes the aperture of its shell during estivation. **2** *Botany.* a membrane closing the mouth of the spore case in certain mosses and fungi. [< New Latin *epiphragma* < Greek *epíphragma* covering, ultimately < *epi-* upon + *phrágma* fence]

ep|i|phyl|lous (ep′ə fil′əs), *adj. Botany.* growing upon a leaf, as certain parasitic fungi and the floral parts of some plants. [< *epi-* + Greek *phýllon* leaf + English *-ous*]

ep|i|phyl|lum (ep′ə fil′əm), *n.* any one of a group of spineless, branching cactuses of tropical America, often cultivated for their large, showy, red, yellow, or white flowers.

ep|i|phys|e|ol|y|sis (ep′ə fiz′ē ol′ə sis), *n.* the separation of an epiphysis from the shaft of the related bone.

ep|i|phys|i|al or **ep|i|phys|e|al** (ep′ə fiz′ē əl), *adj.* having to do with or having the nature of an epiphysis.

e|piph|y|sis (i pif′ə sis), *n., pl.* **-ses** (-sēz). *Anatomy.* **1** the spongy end of a bone which, originally separated from the main bone by a layer of cartilage, ossifies and becomes united to the main bone. **2** = pineal body. [< New Latin *epiphysis* < Greek *epíphysis* growth of bone to bone < *epi-* upon + *phýsis* growth]

epiphysis cer|e|bri (ser′ə brī), the pineal body of the brain. [< New Latin *epiphysis cerebri*]

e|piph|y|si|tis (i pif′ə sī′tis), *n.* inflammation of an epiphysis or of the cartilage which separates it from the main bone.

ep|i|phy|tal (ep′ə fī′təl), *adj.* = epiphytic.

ep|i|phyte (ep′ə fīt), *n.* **1** any one of various plants that grow on other plants for support but draw nourishment from the air and rain instead of from their host; air plant; aerophyte. Many mosses, lichens, and orchids are epiphytes. **2** *Medicine.* a vegetable parasite living on the surface of the body.

ep|i|phyt|ic (ep′ə fit′ik), *adj.* growing as an epiphyte; having the characteristics of an epiphyte: *Most of the orchids here are of the epiphytic type, which require no earth* (New Yorker). — **ep′i|phyt′i|cal|ly,** *adv.*

ep|i|phyt|i|cal (ep′ə fit′ə kəl), *adj.* = epiphytic.

ep|i|phy|tol|o|gy (ep′ə fī tol′ə jē), *n.* the study of epiphytotic diseases.

ep|i|phy|tot|ic (ep′ə fī tot′ik), *adj., n.* — ***adj.*** occurring or spreading widely among plants, such as an epidemic disease: *an epiphytotic disease.*
— ***n.*** any widely occurring disease among plants: *The delay of an epiphytotic reduces damage within a given field and the amount of inoculum available to infect other fields* (J. Artie Browning).

ep|i|plank|ton (ep′ə plangk′tən), *n.* the part of the plankton which occurs between the surface of the sea and a depth of about one hundred fathoms.

e|pip|lo|on (i pip′lō ən), *n., pl.* **-lo|a** (-lō ə). *Anatomy.* = great omentum. [< Greek *epíploon* < *epipleîn* to float on (from its location over the intestines)]

e|pip|o|dite (i pip′ə dīt), *n.* a process on the basal part of the leg of certain crustaceans. [< *epi-* + Greek *poús, podós* foot + English *-ite*[1]]

ep|ip|ter|ic (ep′ip ter′ik), *adj., n.* — ***adj.*** *Anatomy.* of or designating a small, irregular bone sometimes present in the human skull, between the parietal and the great wing of the sphenoid.
— ***n.*** an epipteric bone.

e|pi|ro|gen|ic (i pī′rō jen′ik), *adj.* = epeirogenic.

ep|i|rog|e|ny (ep′ī roj′ə nē), *n.* = epeirogeny.

Epis., **1a** Episcopal. **b** Episcopalians. **2** Epistle.

Episc., Episcopal.

e|pis|ci|a (i pish′ē ə), *n.* a tropical American plant of the gesneria family, with hairy leaves and scarlet or purplish flowers, frequently cultivated as a house plant. [< New Latin *Episcia* the genus name < Greek *episkios* shaded < *epi-* over + *skiā́* shadow]

ep|i|scle|ra (ep′ə sklir′ə), *n.* the layer of connective tissue covering the sclerotic coat of the eyeball. [< New Latin *episclera* < *epi-* + *sclera*]

ep|i|scle|ri|tis (ep′ə skli rī′tis), *n.* inflammation of the episclera. [< *episclera* + *-itis*]

e|pis|co|pa|cy (i pis′kə pə sē), *n., pl.* **-cies. 1** government of a church by bishops; the form of church government in which there are three distinct orders of ministers, namely bishops, priests or presbyters, and deacons. **2** bishops as a group. **3** the position, rank, or term of office of a bishop; episcopate.

e|pis|co|pal (i pis′kə pəl), *adj., n.* — ***adj.*** **1** of or having to do with a bishop or bishops. **2** Sometimes, **Episcopal.** governed by bishops. **3** Sometimes, **Episcopal.** recognizing the office of a bishop as a ministerial rank.
— ***n.*** = episcopalian.
[< Late Latin *episcopālis* < Latin *episcopus* bishop, overseer < Greek *epískopos* overseer < *epi-* over + *skopós* watcher. See related etym. at **bishop.**] — **e|pis′co|pal|ly,** *adv.*

E|pis|co|pal (i pis′kə pəl), *adj.* of or having to do with the Church of England or the Protestant Episcopal Church of the United States.

e|pis|co|pa|lian (i pis′kə pāl′yən, -pā′lē ən), *adj., n.* — ***adj.*** having to do with bishops or episcopacy; episcopal.
— ***n.*** a person who belongs to an episcopal church, or adheres to the episcopal form of church government.

E|pis|co|pa|lian (i pis′kə pāl′yən, -pā′lē ən), *n., adj.* — ***n.*** a member of the Protestant Episcopal Church.
— ***adj.*** of or having to do with an Anglican church; Episcopal.

E|pis|co|pa|lian|ism (i pis′kə pāl′yə niz əm, -pā′lē ə niz′-), *n.* **1** the doctrines, organization, and manner of worship of Episcopalians. **2** adherence to the Episcopal Church or Episcopal principles.

e|pis|co|pal|ism (i pis′kə pə liz′əm), *n.* the theory of church polity according to which the supreme ecclesiastical authority is vested in the episcopal order as a whole, and not in any individual except by delegation.

episcopal stork, a black stork of Africa and India with a white neck and long white feathers which project beyond the true tail feathers.

e|pis|co|pate (i pis′kə pit, -pāt), *n.* **1** the position, rank, or term of office of a bishop. **2** the district under the charge of a bishop; bishopric; see. **3** bishops as a group. [< Latin *episcopātus* < *episcopus* bishop]

e|pis|co|pa|ture (i pis′kə pə chůr), *n.* **1** bishops as a group. **2** the term of office of a bishop.

ep|i|sco|tis|ter (ep′ə skō tis′tər), *n.* an apparatus for admitting light into a darkened area and varying its intensity by means of rotating discs. [< Greek *episkotízein* throw a shadow over (< *epi-* over + *skótos* darkness, shadow) + English *-er*[1]]

ep|i|se|mat|ic (ep′ə sə mat′ik), *adj. Biology.* (of natural colors, markings, scent, or the like) that assist animals of the same species to recognize each other.

e|pi|si|ot|o|my (i piz′ē ot′ə mē, i pē′sē-), *n., pl.* **-mies.** surgical incision of the vulva to facilitate childbirth. [< Greek *epísion* pubic region + English *-tomy*]

ep|i|sod|al (ep′ə sō′dəl), *adj.* = episodic.

ep|i|sode (ep′ə sōd), *n.* **1** an incident or experience that stands out from others: *Being named the best athlete of the year was an important episode in the baseball player's life. His meeting with Matisse was an important episode in the artist's year in France.* **2a** a set of events or actions separate from the main plot of a novel, story, or other literary work. **b** *Music.* a passage separated from and in contrast to the principal themes, especially in a sonata or fugue. **3** the part in a Greek tragedy between two choric songs. [< Greek *epeisódion* addition, neuter of *epeisódios* coming in besides < *epi-* in addition + *eís* into + *hodós* way]

ep|i|sod|ic (ep′ə sod′ik), *adj.* **1** like an episode; incidental; occasional. **2** consisting of a series of loosely related episodes; unintegrated: *an episodic plot.* — **ep′i|sod′i|cal|ly,** *adv.*

ep|i|sod|i|cal (ep′ə sod′ə kəl), *adj.* = episodic.

ep|i|so|mal (ep′ə sō′məl), *adj.* of or having to do with an episome or episomes: *The "virus" can exist in integrated and nonintegrated states which parallels the behaviour of the episomal determinants of bacteria* (New Scientist).

ep|i|some (ep′ə sōm), *n.* a genetic particle found in bacteria, that may either be integrated in a chromosome or exist independently: *A different kind of episome ... conveys multiple resistance to antibiotics from one bacterial cell to another* (London Times). [< *epi-* + *-some*[3]]

ep|i|spas|tic (ep′ə spas′tik), *adj., n. Medicine.* — ***adj.*** raising a blister when applied to the skin.
— ***n.*** a blistering agent or remedy; vesicatory.
[< Late Latin *epispasticus* < Greek *epispastikós* + *epispân* attract < *epi-* to + *spân* draw out]

ep|i|sperm (ep′ə spėrm), *n. Botany.* the outer integument of a seed; testa.

e|pis|ta|sis (i pis′tə sis), *n.* the ability of a gene to affect the expression of a character controlled by a nonallelic gene. [< Greek *epístasis* a deterrent]

ep|i|stat|ic (ep′ə stat′ik), *adj.* able to affect the expression of a character controlled by a nonallelic gene.

ep|i|stax|is (ep′ə stak′sis), *n. Medicine.* bleeding from the nose. [< Greek *epístaxis* < *epistázein* bleed at the nose < *epi-* over, upon + *stázein* spill in drops]

ep|i|ste|mic (ep′ə stē′mik, -stem′ik), *adj.* of or having to do with knowledge or learning: *Epistemic behavior is prompted by the desire for new information* (Science Journal). [< Greek *epistḗmē* knowledge + English *-ic*] — **ep′i|ste′mi|cal|ly,** *adv.*

e|pis|te|mo|log|i|cal (i pis′tə mə loj′ə kəl), *adj.* of or having to do with epistemology: *Einstein's work has changed our whole concept of physics and its epistemological background* (Bulletin of Atomic Scientists). — **e|pis′te|mo|log′i|cal|ly,** *adv.*

e|pis|te|mol|o|gist (i pis′tə mol′ə jist), *n.* an expert in epistemology.

e|pis|te|mol|o|gy (i pis′tə mol′ə jē), *n.* the part of philosophy that deals with the origin, nature, and limits of knowledge. [< Greek *epistḗmē* knowledge (< *epístasthai* be able < *epi-* upon + *histánai* stand) + English *-logy*]

ep|i|ster|nal (ep′ə stėr′nəl), *adj., n.* — ***adj.*** of or having to do with the episternum.
— ***n.*** an episternal process.

ep|i|ster|num (ep′ə stėr′nəm), *n., pl.* **-na** (-nə). **1a** (in mammals) the upper part of the sternum; manubrium. **b** (in lower vertebrate animals) the interclavicle. **2** a division of the thorax of an insect.

e|pis|tle (i pis′əl), *n.* **1** a letter. Epistles are usually long, instructive letters written in formal or elegant language. **SYN:** See syn. under **letter. 2** a literary work, usually in verse, written in the form of a letter. [< Old French *epistle,* learned borrowing from Latin *epistola* < Greek *epistolḗ,* ultimately < *epi-* to + *stéllein* send]

E|pis|tle (i pis′əl), *n.* **1** a letter written by one of Christ's Apostles to various churches and individuals. The canonical Epistles make up 21 books of the New Testament. The Epistles to Timothy and Titus are often known as the *Pastoral Epistles,* those of James, Peter, John, and Jude as *General* or *Catholic Epistles.* **2** a selection from one of these, read as part of the Mass or the Anglican service of Holy Communion. [< *epistle*]

Pronunciation Key: hat, āge, cãre, fär; let, ēqual, tėrm; it, īce; hot, ōpen, ôrder; oil, out; cup, půt, rüle; child; long; thin; ᴛʜen; zh, measure; ə represents a in about, e in taken, i in pencil, o in lemon, u in circus.

e|pis|tler (i pis′lər), *n.* **1** the writer of an epistle. **2** *Ecclesiastical.* epistoler.

epistle side, the south side of the altar, at which the Epistle is read.

e|pis|to|lar|y (i pis′tə ler′ē), *adj.* **1** carried on by letters; contained in letters: *an epistolary correspondence.* **2** of letters; suitable for writing letters: *an epistolary style.* **3** given to writing letters: *The female . . . is by nature a much more epistolary animal than the male* (C. S. Lewis). **4** written in the form of a series of letters: *an epistolary novel.*

e|pis|to|ler (i pis′tə lər), *n.* the person who reads the Epistle in the Mass or the Communion Service.

e|pis|to|log|ra|phy (i pis′tə log′rə fē), *n.* the art or practice of letter writing.

e|pis|to|ma (i pis′tə mə), *n., pl.* **ep|i|sto|ma|ta** (ep′ə stō′mə tə). = epistome.

e|pis|to|mal (i pis′tə məl), *adj.* having to do with or consisting of an epistome.

ep|i|stome (ep′ə stōm), *n. Zoology.* any part, region, or organ lying upon or before the mouth, such as the prostomium of polyzoans or the clypeus of insects.

e|pis|tro|phe (i pis′trə fē), *n. Rhetoric.* a figure in which successive clauses or sentences end with the same word. [< Greek *epistrophē* < *epi-* upon + *strophē* a turning < *stréphein* to turn]

ep|i|stro|phe|al (ep′ə strō′fē əl), *adj.* of or having to do with the epistropheus.

ep|i|stro|phe|us (ep′ə strō′fē əs), *n., pl.* **-phe|i** (-fē ī). the second cervical vertebra, having a tooth or process upon which the head is turned; axis. [< Greek *epistropheús* (literally) turning on a pivot]

ep|i|stroph|ic (ep′ə strof′ik), *adj.* of or having to do with an epistrophe.

ep|pis|tro|phy (i pis′trə fē), *n. Botany.* the reversion of an abnormal form or type to the normal one.

ep|i|style (ep′ə stīl), *n.* the part of a building resting directly on top of columns; architrave. [< Latin *epistȳlium* < Greek *epistylion* < *epi-* on + *stylos* pillar]

ep|i|taph (ep′ə taf, -täf), *n., v.,* —*n.* **1** a short statement in memory of a dead person. It is often put on a gravestone or tomb. *Let no man write my epitaph* (Robert Emmet). **2** *Figurative.* any writing resembling such an inscription: *The extraordinary thing about this biography is that it reads . . . as an epitaph to that second phase in Canadian history which ended in 1957* (Canadian Saturday Night).

—*v.t.* to commemorate in an epitaph: *After he is dead and buried, And epitaphed* (James Russell Lowell).

[< Latin *epitaphium* < Greek *epitáphion,* neuter, funeral oration < *epi-* at + *táphos* tomb, funeral rites]

ep|i|taph|ic (ep′ə taf′ik), *adj.* **1** having the form or character of epitaphs. **2** relating to epitaphs.

Ep|i|taph|i|os (ep′ə taf′ē ōs), *n.* a ceremony in the Greek Catholic Church held on Good Friday, commemorating the burial of Christ. [< Greek *epitáphios* being at a tomb]

ep|i|taph|ist (ep′ə taf′ist), *n.* a writer of epitaphs.

e|pit|a|sis (i pit′ə sis), *n.* the part of the play in classical drama in which the action leading up to the catastrophe is developed. The epitasis follows the protasis. [< New Latin *epitasis* < Greek *epítasis* a stretching < *epiteínein* stretch over < *epi-* over + *teínein* stretch]

ep|i|tax|i|al (ep′ə taks′ē əl), *adj.* of or containing a crystal, as of silicon, that is homogeneous with the substrate from which it is grown: *an epitaxial transistor.* —**ep′i|tax′i|al|ly,** *adv.*

ep|i|tax|y (ep′ə tak′sē), *n.* the growth of crystals of one material on the crystal face of another, in an orientation which retains the structure of the underlying material. [< *epi-* + Greek *táxis* arrangement]

ep|i|tha|la|mi|on (ep′ə thə lā′mē ən), *n., pl.* **-mi|a** (-mē ə). = epithalamium.

ep|i|tha|la|mi|um (ep′ə thə lā′mē əm), *n., pl.* **-mi-ums, -mi|a** (-mē ə). a poem or song in honor of a bride, bridegroom, or newly married couple. [< Latin *epithalamium* < Greek *epithalámion* < *epi-* at + *thálamos* bridal chamber]

ep|i|the|ca (ep′ə thē′kə), *n., pl.* **-cae** (-sē). *Zoology.* a continuous thin sheath or layer surrounding the theca or skeleton in some corals. [< Latin *epithēca* addition < *epi-* over, upon + *thēca* case, sheath]

ep|i|the|ci|um (ep′ə thē′shē əm, -sē-), *n., pl.* **-ci|a** (-shē ə, -sē-). *Botany.* the surface of the fruiting disk in certain lichens and fungi. [< New Latin *epithecium* < *epi-* over + Greek *thēkion* (diminutive) < *thēkē* case]

ep|i|the|li|al (ep′ə thē′lē əl), *adj.* of or having to do with the epithelium: *In a piece of skin, for example, the epithelial cells migrate round over the surface normally exposed to the air, enclosing it in a capsule* (New Scientist).

ep|i|the|li|oid (ep′ə thē′lē oid), *adj.* resembling epithelium.

ep|i|the|li|o|ma (ep′ə thē′lē ō′mə), *n., pl.* **-mas, -ma|ta** (-mə tə). a tumor derived from and consisting chiefly of epithelial cells, especially such a tumor when malignant or cancerous. [< *epitheli-*(um) + *-oma*]

ep|i|the|li|o|ma|tous (ep′ə thē′lē ō′mə təs, -om′ə-), *adj.* having do do with or of the nature of epithelioma.

ep|i|the|li|o|mus|cu|lar (ep′ə thē′lē ō mus′kyə-lər), *adj.* having to do with epithelial cells with muscular processes: *The epitheliomuscular cells of coelenterates are generally considered to be the most primitive type of muscle cells* (Hegner and Stiles).

ep|i|the|li|um (ep′ə thē′lē əm), *n., pl.* **-li|ums, -li|a** (-lē ə). **1** a thin layer or layers of cells forming a tissue that covers surfaces of the body and lines hollow organs. Epithelium is compactly arranged with little intercellular substance. It performs protective, secretive, and other functions. **2** *Botany.* **a** a delicate layer of cells lining certain internal cavities. **b** the thin epidermis of petals. [< New Latin *epithelium* < Greek *epi-* on + *thēlē* nipple]

ep|i|the|li|za|tion (ep′ə thē′lə zā′shən), *n.* the process of becoming covered with epithelium.

ep|i|the|lize (ep′ə thē′līz), *v.t.,* **-lized, -liz|ing.** to cover with epithelium.

ep|i|them (ep′ə them), *n.* a group of water-secreting cells in the leaf of a plant.

ep|i|the|ma (ep′ə thē′mə), *n., pl.* **-ma|ta** (-mə tə). = epithem.

ep|i|ther|mal (ep′ə thėr′məl), *adj.* (of ore deposits) formed at shallow depths and at low temperatures and pressures: *Shallow, or epithermal, vein deposits were made at depths of less than 4000 feet* (Fenton and Fenton).

ep|i|thet (ep′ə thet), *n.* **1** a descriptive expression; a word or phrase expressing some quality or attribute. In "crafty Ulysses," "Richard the Lion-Hearted," and "Honest Abe," the epithets are "crafty," "Lion-Hearted," and "Honest." *Such epithets like pepper, Give zest to what you write* (Lewis Carroll). **2** a word or phrase (sometimes insulting or contemptuous) used in place of a person's name. **3** that part of the scientific name of an animal or plant which denotes a species, variety, or other division of a genus. *Example:* In *Canis familiaris* (the dog), *familiaris* is the specific epithet. In *Prunus persica* (the peach), *persica* is the specific epithet. **4** *Obsolete.* a phrase or expression. [< Latin *epitheton* < Greek *epítheton* < *ep-* on, in addition + *tithénai* to place]

ep|i|thet|ic (ep′ə thet′ik), *adj.* **1** having to do with or of the nature of an epithet. **2** *Obsolete.* abounding with epithets.

ep|i|thet|i|cal (ep′ə thet′ə kəl), *adj.* = epithetic.

e|pit|o|me (i pit′ə mē), *n.* **1** a condensed account; summary. An epitome contains only the most important points of a book, essay, article, or other literary work. *In general nothing is less attractive than an epitome* (Macaulay). SYN: compendium. **2** *Figurative.* a person or thing that is typical or representative of something: *Solomon is often spoken of as the epitome of wisdom. [She] is rated the epitome of fashion elegance* (Eugenia Sheppard). *The rubber plant and the antimacassar were the epitome of good taste* (New York Times Magazine). SYN: embodiment.

in epitome, in a diminutive form; in miniature: *The characteristics and pursuits of various ages and races of men are always existing in epitome in every neighborhood* (Thoreau).

[< Latin *epitomē* < Greek *epitomē* < *epitémnein* cut short < *epi-* into + *témnein* cut]

ep|i|tom|ic (ep′ə tom′ik), *adj.* representative; typical: *The Packers, who, as charter members of the N.F.L. [are] its most epitomic team . . .* (New Yorker).

e|pit|o|mise (i pit′ə mīz), *v.t.,* **-mised, -mis|ing.** *Especially British.* epitomize.

e|pit|o|mist (i pit′ə mist), *n.* a person who writes epitomes.

e|pit|o|mize (i pit′ə mīz), *v.t.,* **-mized, -miz|ing.** **1** to make a summary of: *to epitomize a long report.* SYN: abridge, condense. **2** *Figurative.* to be typical or representative of: *Galahad and Lancelot epitomize the knighthood of ancient Britain. Helen Keller epitomizes the human ability to overcome handicaps. John Finley epitomized the sensible attitudes for oldsters to take by his witty motto, "Nothing succeeds like successors"*(Harper's). **3** to contain in a brief form: *His problems epitomize the problems of the entire neighborhood.* SYN: concentrate. —**e|pit′o|miz′er,** *n.*

ep|i|tope (ep′i tōp), *n.* the part of an antigen molecule to which a specific antibody molecule becomes attached: *The specific patterns that are recognized by antibody molecules are epitopes* (Scientific American). [< *epi-* into + Greek *tópos* place]

ep|i|tox|oid (ep′ə tok′soid), *n.* a toxoid which has less affinity than the toxin for the corresponding antitoxin.

ep|i|trich|i|um (ep′ə trik′ē əm), *n.* a thin membrane which overlies the epidermis and hair during fetal life, usually disappearing before birth.

ep|i|trite (ep′ə trīt), *n.* a foot of verse consisting of three long syllables and one short one, called first, second, third, or fourth epitrite, according as the short syllable is the first, second, third, or fourth. [< Latin *epitritos* < Greek *epítritos* greater by one third < *epi-* in addition + *trítos* one third]

ep|i|tym|pa|num (ep′ə tim′pə nəm), *n.* the upper portion of the tympanic cavity of the ear.

ep|i|zeux|is (ep′ə zük′sis), *n. Rhetoric.* immediate or almost immediate repetition of a word or phrase for the sake of emphasis. Example: *Alone, alone, all all alone, Alone on a wide, wide sea* (Samuel Taylor Coleridge). [< Greek *epízeuxis* a fastening upon < *epí* upon + *zeugnýnai* to yoke]

ep|i|zo|ic (ep′ə zō′ik), *adj.* living as an external parasite or commensal.

ep|i|zo|ite (ep′ə zō′īt), *n.* an epizoic animal; epizoon.

ep|i|zo|on (ep′ə zō′on, -ən), *n., pl.* **-zo|a** (-zō′ə). an animal living on the outer surface of another animal, often as a parasite or as a commensal. [< *epi-* + Greek *zôion* animal]

ep|i|zo|ot|ic (ep′ə zō ot′ik), *adj., n.* —***adj.*** occurring or spreading widely among animals, such as an epidemic disease. —***n.*** an epizootic disease. [< French *épizootique,* ultimately < Greek *epi-* among + *zôion* animal]

ep|i|zo|ot|i|ol|o|gy (ep′ə zō ot′ē ol′ə jē), *n.* the study of epizootic diseases.

ep|i|zo|o|tol|o|gy (ep′ə zō′ə tol′ə jō), *n.* = epizootiology.

ep|i|zo|o|ty (ep′ə zō′ə tē), *n., pl.,* **-ties.** an epidemic disease affecting animals.

e plu|ri|bus u|num (ē plůr′ə bəs yü′nəm), *Latin.* out of many, one. It is the motto inscribed on the official seal of the United States. It was once the official motto of the United States, but since 1956 the official motto has been "In God We Trust."

ep|och (ep′ək; *especially British* ē′pok), *n.,* **1** a period of time; era: *an epoch of extravagance, an epoch of strange manifestations. There were few peaceful epochs in the history of our country.* SYN: age. **2** a period of time in which striking things happened: *The years of the Civil War were an epoch in the history of the United States.* **3** the starting point of such a period: *The invention of the steam engine marked an epoch in the growth of industry.* **4** one of the divisions of time into which a geological period is divided: *the Recent epoch of the Quaternary period.* **5** *Astronomy.* **a** an arbitrarily fixed instant of time or date (usually the beginning of a century or half-century) used as a reference point in giving the elements of a planetary orbit or the like. **b** the longitude of a planet seen from the sun at such an instant or date. [< Latin *epochē* < Greek *epochē* a stopping, fixed point in time < *epéchein* to stop < *epi-* on, upon + *échein* to hold]

ep|och|al (ep′ə kəl), *adj.* **1** of or having to do with an epoch or epochs. **2** of the nature of an epoch; very important or significant: *Marriage is an epochal event in life.* —**ep′och|al|ly,** *adv.*

ep|och-mak|ing (ep′ək mā′king; *especially British* ē′pok mā′king), *adj.* beginning an epoch; causing important changes; epochal: *an epoch-making discovery.*

ep|ode (ep′ōd), *n.* in classical verse: **1** a lyric poem in which a long line is followed by a shorter one, a form used by Horace. **2** the part of a lyric ode following the strophe and antistrophe. [< French *épode,* learned borrowing from Latin *epōdos* < Greek *epōidós* < *epi-* after + *ōidē* song < *aeídein* sing]

ep|od|ic (e pod′ik), *adj.* having to do with or containing an epode.

e|pol|li|cate (i pol′ə kāt), *adj. Zoology.* having no pollex or thumb.

é|ponge (āpôɴzh′), *n. French.* a thick, nubby, spongy fabric having a loose but firm weave, used as a dress material.

e|po|nych|i|um (ep′ə nik′ē əm), *n.* **1** the horny embryonic structure from which the nail is developed. **2** the skin of the nail; a film of epidermis which covers part of the body of the nail.

ep|o|nym (ep′ə nim), *n.* **1** a person, real or imaginary, from whom a nation, tribe, or place gets or is reputed to get its name: *Romulus is the eponym of Rome.* **2** a person whose name is a

Pronunciation Key: hat, āge, cãre, fär; let, ēqual, tėrm; it, īce; hot, ōpen, ôrder; oil, out; cup, pu̇t, rüle; child; long; thin; ᴛʜen; zh, measure; ə represents **a** in about, **e** in taken, **i** in pencil, **o** in lemon, **u** in circus.

synonym for something: *Ananias is the eponym of liar.* [< Greek *epônymos* < *epi-* upon + dialectal *ónyma* name]

ep·o·nym·ic (ep′ə nim′ik), *adj.* relating to or having to do with an eponym: *an eponymic name, an eponymic legend.*

ep·on·y·mist (e pon′ə mist), *n.* an eponymous ancestor or founder.

ep·on·y·mous (e pon′ə məs), *adj.* giving one's name to a nation, tribe, or place: *George Washington is the eponymous leader after whom our capital city is named.*

ep·on·y·my (e pon′ə mē), *n., pl.* **-mies**. the derivation of names from eponyms.

ep·o·pee (ep′ə pē, ep′ə pē′), *n.* **1** = epic. **2** epic poetry. [< French *épopée* < Greek *epopoiïā* < *epopoiós* maker of epics < *épos* epos + *-poios* maker < *poíein* make]

ep·o·poe·ia (ep′ə pē′ə), *n.* = epopee.

ep·opt (ep′opt), *n., pl.* **ep·op·tae** (e pop′tē). **1** a seer. **2** a person fully initiated into the Eleusinian mysteries. **3** an initiate in any secret system. [< Late Latin *epopta* < Greek *epóptēs,* ultimately < *epi* upon + *op-* to see]

ep·op·tic (e pop′tik), *adj.* **1** having the character or faculty of an epopt or seer. **2** perceived by an epopt: *an epoptic vision.*

ep·os (ep′os), *n.* = epopee. [< Latin *epos* < Greek *épos* song, word < *ep-,* stem of *eipeîn* say]

ep·ox·ide (ep ok′sīd), *n.* any epoxy compound.

ep·ox·i·dize (ep ok′sə dīz), *v.t.,* **-dized, -diz·ing.** to combine (oils, plastics, or other substance) with epoxy.

ep·ox·ied (ep ok′sēd), *adj.* made with epoxy resin: *epoxied plastics, epoxied earrings.*

ep·ox·y (ep ok′sē), *adj., n., pl.* **-ox·ies**. **—*adj.*** of or designating a large group of compounds containing oxygen as a bridge between two different atoms or radicals in a chain: *epoxy compounds.* **—*n.*** = epoxy resin. [< *ep-* + *oxy*(gen)]

epoxy resin, any one of various synthetic resins derived by polymerization of an epoxy compound and made to become hard and permanently shaped under application of heat. Epoxy resins are widely used in the manufacture of plastics, adhesives, and coating materials. *Epoxy resins . . . are tough, hard, dimensionally stable, solvent resistant, chemical resistant, heat resistant, and rigid* (Scientific American).

é·pris (ā prē′), *adj. French.* enamored; in love.

e·pru·i·nose (ē prü′ə nōs), *adj. Botany, Zoology.* not covered with a whitish powdery substance; not pruinose.

***epsilon**

E	ϵ
capital letter	lower-case letter

***ep·si·lon** (ep′sə lon; *especially British* ep sī′lən), *n.* the fifth letter of the Greek alphabet, corresponding to short *e* in English. [< Medieval Greek *epsilon* < Greek *e psīlón* simple *e*]

Ep·som Downs (ep′səm dounz′), a course near Epsom, England, where England's famous annual horse race, the Derby, is run.

ep·som·ite (ep′sə mīt), *n.* a mineral consisting of hydrated magnesium sulfate; native Epsom salt.

Epsom salts or **salt**, a bitter, white crystalline powder taken in water as a laxative or as an antidote for poisons, or used to reduce inflammation; hydrated magnesium sulfate. *Formula:* $MgSO_4\ 7H_2O$ [< *Epsom,* Surrey, England, where it was originally obtained]

Ep·stein-Barr virus (ep′stīn bär′), a virus found to be associated with various types of human cancers. It was first isolated by the British virologists M. A. Epstein and Y. M. Barr in 1964. *A recent development in the study of infectious mononucleosis is the evidence indicating that its cause may be a herpes-like virus, called the Epstein-Barr virus* (Alfred S. Evans).

ept (ept), *adj.* capable; clever; effective: *It is different because it is inept, and those other businesses are very ept indeed. They are eptest at getting what they want from the Administration* (Atlantic). [back formation < *inept*]

EPT (no periods), **E.P.T.**, or **e.p.t.**, excess-profits tax.

ept·i·tude (ep′tə tüd, -tyüd), *n.* ability; cleverness; effectiveness: *What makes Huntford's Anglo-Saxon hackles rise is less the cleverness and thoroughgoing eptitude of the Social Democratic persuasion*-cum-*administration machine . . . than the supine attitude of the Swede-in-the-street* (New York Times Book Review). [back formation < *ineptitude*]

ep·u·lar·y (ep′yə ler′ē), *adj.* of or having to do with a feast or banquet. [< Latin *epulāris* < *epulum* feast]

ep·u·lis (e pu′lis), *n.* a small elastic tumor of the gums.

ep·u·lo·sis (ep′yə lō′sis), *n.* cicatrization. [< Greek *époulōsis* < *epí* upon + *oulḗ* scar + *-ōsis* condition]

ep·u·lot·ic (ep′yə lot′ik), *adj., n.* **—*adj.*** healing; cicatrizing. **—*n.*** a medicine or an application that tends to dry, and heal wounds or ulcers.

e·pu·pil·late (ē pyü′pə lāt), *adj. Zoology.* having no pupil (applied to a color spot when it is surrounded by a ring of another color, but is without a central dot or pupil).

ep·u·ral (ep yu̇r′əl), *adj., n.* **—*adj.*** situated upon the tail. **—*n.*** a piece of bone or cartilage, as on the end of the axial column of fishes. [< *ep-* + Greek *ourā́* tail + *-al*[1]]

e·pure (e pu̇r′), *n. Architecture.* the plan of a building, or part of a building, traced on a wall or horizontal surface, on the same scale as the work to be constructed. [< French *épure* diagram < *épurer* purify < Latin *ex-* out of + *purāre* purify]

e pur si muo·ve! (ā pür′sē mwô′vā), *Italian.* and yet it does move! (attributed to Galileo, just after his recantation of the doctrine of the earth's movement round the sun).

e·pyl·li·on (e pil′ē ən), *n., pl.* **-pyl·li·a** (-pil′ē ə), **-pyl·li·ons.** a short narrative poem using some of the conventions of epic poetry. Several ancient Greek poets wrote epyllia. [< Greek *epyllion,* diminutive of *épos* epic poem]

eq., **1** equal. **2** equalizer. **3** equation. **4** equivalent.

eq·ua·bil·i·ty (ek′wə bil′ə tē, ē′kwə-), *n.* equable condition or quality; continued regularity or uniformity.

eq·ua·ble (ek′wə bəl, ē′kwə-), *adj.* changing little; uniform; even; tranquil: *The good-natured policeman had an equable disposition. The Gulf Stream makes England's climate fairly equable.* SYN: unvarying, steady, smooth. See syn. under **even**. [< Latin *aequābilis* < *aequāre* make uniform < *aequus* even, just] **—eq′ua·ble·ness**, *n.*

eq·ua·bly (ek′wə blē, ē′kwə-), *adv.* in an equable manner; evenly: *an equably tempered person. Laws should be equably enforced.*

e·qual (ē′kwəl), *adj., n., v.,* **-qualed, -qual·ing** or (*especially British*) **-qualled, -qual·ling.** **—*adj.*** **1** the same in amount, size, number, value, degree, or rank; as much; neither more nor less: *Ten dimes are equal to one dollar. All men are considered equal in a court of law.* **2** the same throughout; even; uniform: *an equal mixture.* **3** evenly matched; with no advantage on either side: *an equal contest.* **4** *Archaic.* level: *an equal plain.* **5** *Archaic.* unperturbed; unruffled: *Let us swear an oath, and keep it with an equal mind* (Tennyson). **6** *Archaic.* just; fair.

—*n.* **1** a person or thing that is equal to another, as in rank, ability, age, or strength: *In spelling she has no equal. She is no equal for his birth* (Shakespeare). SYN: peer, match. **2** an equal amount or number: $7 + 3$ *is the equal of* 5×2.

—*v.t.* **1** to be or become the same as: *Four times five equals twenty.* **2** to make or do something equal to (something else); match: *Our team equaled the other team's score, and the game ended in a tie.* **3** to give, do, feel, or show in return: *. . . who answered all her cares and equaled all her love* (John Dryden). **4** *Archaic.* to equalize.

equal to, able to; strong enough for; brave enough for: *One horse is not equal to pulling a load of five tons.*

[< Latin *aequālis* < *aequus* even, just] **—e′qual·ness**, *n.*

—*Syn.* *adj.* **1 Equal, equivalent, tantamount** mean being the same or as much as. **Equal** applies to things that are exactly the same in size, amount, value, or any other quality that can be measured or weighed: *The pieces of pie are equal.* **Equivalent** applies to things otherwise different but equal in value or in a quality that cannot be physically measured, such as meaning, importance, or effect: *A one-year course in high school may be regarded as equivalent to a college semester course.* **Tantamount**, applying only to immaterial things, means equivalent to another in effect: *His answer was tantamount to an insult.*

***e·qual-ar·e·a** (ē′kwəl ãr′ē ə), *adj. Cartography.* homolographic; showing or preserving the relative areas of countries or regions on a map, but not necessarily their true shapes. See picture of *equal-area projection* at bottom of page.

e·qual·ise (ē′kwə līz), *v.t.,* **-ised, -is·ing.** *Especially British.* equalize.

e·qual·is·er (ē′kwə lī′zər), *n. Especially British.* **1** equalizer. **2** a score in a game that makes both sides even.

e·qual·i·tar·i·an (i kwol′ə tãr′ē ən), *adj., n.* **—*adj.*** having to do with or believing in the doctrine that all human beings are equal in the social and

***equal-area**

view of the globe

equal-area projection

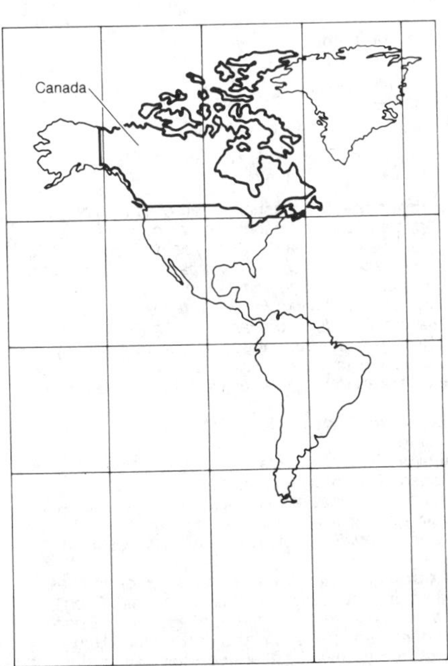

projection with area distorted

political realms; egalitarian.
—*n.* a believer in or supporter of this doctrine.

e|qual|i|tar|i|an|ism (i kwol′ə tãr′ē ə niz′əm), *n.* the doctrine that every human being is equal socially and politically: *The dominant liberal ideas were freedom and a certain vague equalitarianism* (H. G. Wells).

e|qual|i|ty (i kwol′ə tē), *n., pl.* **-ties.** the condition or quality of being equal; exact likeness in amount, size, number, value, degree, or rank: *I do not believe in equality of capacity, but I do believe in equality of opportunity* (Listener).

Equality State, a nickname for Wyoming.

e|qual|i|za|tion (ē′kwə lə zā′shən), *n.* **1** the act or process of equalizing. **2** the condition of being equalized.

e|qual|ize (ē′kwə līz), *v.t.,* **-ized, -iz|ing. 1** to make equal. **2** to make even or uniform. **3** *Obsolete.* to be or become equal to.

e|qual|iz|er (ē′kwə lī′zər), *n.* **1** a person or thing that equalizes. **2** a device for equalizing forces, strains, pressures, etc. **3a** any network of coils, capacitors, or resistors introduced into a circuit to change its response, especially its frequency response, in a specified way. **b** a conductor of low resistance used to connect two points of the same potential on the armature of an electrical machine. **4** *U.S. Slang.* a pistol.

e|qual|iz|ing gear (ē′kwə lī′zing), **1** any device for making each of the driving parts of a machine do its share of the work. **2** = differential gear.

e|qual|ly (ē′kwə lē), *adv.* in equal shares; in an equal manner; to an equal degree; so as to be equal: *to deal equally between man and man* (Thomas Hobbes). *The sun shines equally on all. The two sisters are equally pretty.*
►**Equally as** (*good, rare,* or the like) is a blend of *equally* and *just as.* Though the idiom is used by reputable writers, it is sometimes suggested that it be avoided.

e|qual-op|por|tu|ni|ty (ē′kwəl op′ər tü′nə tē, -tyü′-), *adj. U.S.* not allowing or practicing discrimination in employment because of race, color, religion, sex, or national origin; giving an equal opportunity to all employees or applicants for jobs: *A city could effectively enforce equal-opportunity laws* (New York Times). *Hughes is an equal-opportunity employer* (Scientific American).

Equal Rights Amendment, a proposed amendment to the United States Constitution providing for equal rights of both sexes: *The Equal Rights Amendment. . . cannot go into effect until 38 states have ratified it* (Milton Greenberg). *Abbr.:* ERA (no periods).

equal sets, *Mathematics.* sets that have the same members, regardless of their arrangements. (2, 7, 9) and (7, 9, 2) are equal sets. The set of even whole numbers and the set of whole numbers whose squares are even are equal sets.

***equal sign,** a sign used especially in mathematics and logic to show the equality or sameness of two quantities or things. *Examples:* 5 + 5 = 10 means that 10 and 5 + 5 are equal in quantity. The statement A = B means that A and B are identical things. The equal sign is used in this dictionary to show equivalent terms in the language.

***equal sign**

= 4 + 2 = 6

equal time, 1 an equal period of time allotted to opposing political candidates or parties to air their views on a radio or television broadcast: *The Senator's campaign manager . . . announced his intention of requesting the three national television networks for equal time for the Senator before Tuesday's primary election* (New York Times). **2** an equal opportunity to reply to any charge or opposing view.

e|quan|gu|lar (ē kwang′gyə lər), *adj.* = equiangular.

E|qua|nil (ē′kwə nəl), *n. Trademark.* = meprobamate.

e|qua|nim|i|ty (ē′kwə nim′ə tē, ek′wə-), *n.* evenness of mind or temper; calmness; composure: *The speaker bore the insults of the heckler with equanimity.* SYN: self-possession. [< Latin *aequanimitās* < *aequus* even + *animus* mind, temper]

e|quan|i|mous (i kwan′ə məs), *adj.* of an even temper; not easily elated or depressed: *Everything withered under the gentle touch of Beerbohm's equanimous depreciation* (John Updike).

e|quant (ē′kwant), *n.* (in the Ptolemaic system of astronomy) a circle around whose center the epicycle of a planet supposedly describes equal angles at equal times. Equants were conceived for the purpose of making planetary movements consistent with the hypothesis that celestial motion must be uniform in velocity.

e|qua|ta|ble (i kwā′tə bəl), *adj.* capable of being equated: *Spending money isn't equatable with the good life* (Sunday Times).

e|quate (i kwāt′), *v.t.,* **-quat|ed, -quat|ing. 1** to state to be equal; put in the form of an equation: *He equated inches to feet when buying lumber to make a bookcase.* **2** *Figurative.* to consider, treat, or represent as equal: *From the time of Francis Bacon on, forward-looking people had been inclined to equate mechanical invention with civilization itself* (New Yorker). **3** to make equal. **4** to reduce to an average. [< Latin *aequāre* (with English *-ate*[1]) make equal < *aequus* equal]

***e|qua|tion** (i kwā′zhən, -shən), *n.* **1** a statement of equality between two quantities, indicated by using the equal sign (=) between them. *Examples:* 4 + 5 = 9. (4 × 8) + 12 = 44. C = 2πr. **2** an expression using chemical formulas and symbols to show quantitatively the substances used and produced in a chemical change. In "HCl + NaOH = NaCl + H_2O," HCl and NaOH are the reacting substances, and NaCl and H_2O are the resulting products, the sign = being read "produces" or "gives." **3** the act of making equal. **4** the state of being equally balanced; equilibrium; equality. **5** a condition involving some equivalence or relation: *The supply-demand equation . . . is indicative of still higher prices* (Wall Street Journal).

***equation**
definitions 1, 2

mathematics:

$$(x + 3)^2 = x^2 + 6x + 9$$

chemistry:

$$Na_2CO_3 + CaSO_4 = Na_2SO_4 + CaCO_3$$

e|qua|tion|al (i kwā′zhə nəl, -shə-), *adj.* **1** having to do with or involving equations. **2** designating a type of sentence in Latin and certain other languages, consisting of two nominal expressions with no verb. —**e|qua′tion|al|ly,** *adv.*

e|qua|tion|ism (i kwā′zhə niz əm, -shə-), *n.* the principle of solving problems equationally.

equation of state, *Physics.* an equation that relates the temperature, volume, and pressure of a gas, taking into account the forces between the molecules of the gas.

equation of time, *Astronomy.* the difference between mean solar time and apparent solar time.

***e|qua|tor** (i kwā′tər), *n.* **1** an imaginary circle around the middle of the earth, halfway between the North Pole and the South Pole: *The United States is north of the equator; Australia is south of it. Crossed the equator . . . I now for the first time felt at liberty . . . to call myself a son of Neptune* (Richard Henry Dana). **2** a similarly situated circle on any heavenly body. **3** a great circle (celestial equator) of the celestial sphere, the plane of which is perpendicular to the axis of the earth. **4** *Aeronautics.* the horizontal circle about a balloon at the place of its greatest width. **5** *Biology.* = equatorial plane. [< Medieval Latin *aequator* (*diei et noctis*) equalizer (of day and night) < Latin *aequāre;* see etym. under **equate**]

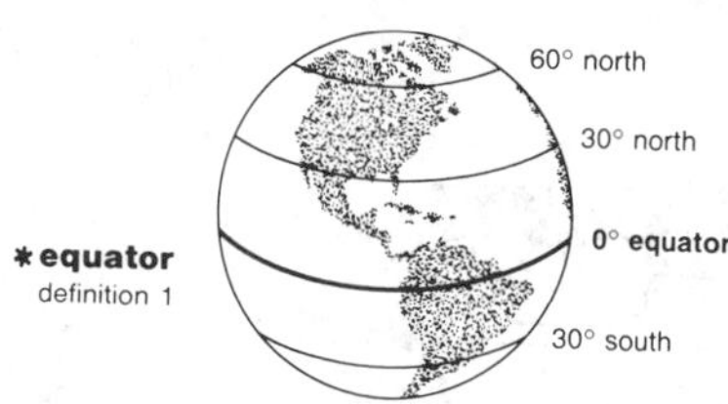

***equator**
definition 1

e|qua|to|ri|al (ē′kwə tôr′ē əl, -tōr′-; ek′wə-), *adj., n.* —*adj.* **1** of, at, or near an equator, especially the earth's equator: *Ecuador is an equatorial country. Another countercurrent . . . was found flowing from Asia toward Panama in the equatorial region* (Science News Letter). **2** like conditions at or near the equator: *The weather this week was hot and humid; it was almost equatorial.* **3** like the equator; extending in a plane or horizontally: *an equatorial arch or line. The bonds extending to hydrogen are . . . "equatorial" (or near horizontal)* (New Scientist).
—*n.* Also, **equatorial telescope.** a telescope having two axes of motion, one parallel to the earth's axis, and the other at right angles to it.
—**e′qua|to′ri|al|ly,** *adv.*

equatorial belt, the regions near the earth's equator; doldrums.

equatorial low, a long, narrow region nearly encircling the earth near the equator, over which low barometric pressure, with warm showery weather and light winds or calms, prevails.

equatorial plane, 1 *Astronomy.* the plane of the celestial equator which is perpendicular to the axis of the earth. **2** *Biology.* the plane lying midway between the poles of a dividing cell: *During this phase of mitosis [metaphase] the split chromosomes become located in the equatorial plane of the spindle* (Hegner and Stiles).

equatorial plate, *Biology.* the site or position of the chromosomes in the equatorial plane during metaphase.

e|qua|tor|ward (i kwā′tər wərd), *adv., adj.* toward the equator: *cold water from the polar seas sinks and creeps equatorward along the bottom* (White and Renner).

eq|uer|ry (ek′wər ē), *n., pl.* **-ries. 1** an officer of a royal or noble household who has charge of the horses or who accompanies his master's carriage. **2** an attendant on a royal or noble person. **3** an attendant upon a member of the British royal household. [short for *groom of the equerry;* < French *écurie* stable, ultimately < Germanic (compare Old High German *scūra* < *scur* protection); influenced by Latin *equus* horse)]

e|ques|tri|an (i kwes′trē ən), *adj., n.* —*adj.* **1** having to do with horseback riding, horses, or horseback riders: *Cowboys have equestrian skill.* **2** on horseback; mounted on a horse. An equestrian statue shows a person riding a horse. *the antique equestrian statue of Marcus Aurelius* (Joseph Addison). **3** having to do with or composed of knights: *an equestrian order.* **4** (in Roman history) of or having to do with the equites.
—*n.* a rider or performer on horseback.
[< Latin *equestris* of a horseman (< *equus* horse) + English *-an*]

e|ques|tri|an|ism (i kwes′trē ə niz′əm), *n.* the art or practice of an equestrian; horsemanship.

e|ques|tri|enne (i kwes′trē en′), *n.* a woman rider or performer on horseback. [< *equestri*(an) + French feminine suffix *-enne*]

equi-, *combining form.* **1** equal ___: *Equidistance = equal distance.*
2 equally ___: *Equidistant = equally distant.*
[< Latin *aequi-* < *aequus* equal]

e|qui|an|gu|lar (ē′kwē ang′gyə lər), *adj.* having all angles equal: *A square is equiangular.*

e|qui|axed (ē′kwə akst′), *adj. Crystallography.* **1** having about the same dimensions on all sides; regular in shape: *equiaxed crystal grains.* **2** consisting of equiaxed grains formed in the center of an alloy casting: *an equiaxed zone.* [< *equi-* + *ax*(is) + *-ed*[2]]

eq|uid (ek′wid), *n.* any animal of the family of mammals which includes horses, asses, mules, and zebras. [< New Latin *Equidae* the family name < Latin *equus* horse]

e|qui|dis|tance (ē′kwə dis′təns), *n.* equal distance.

e|qui|dis|tant (ē′kwə dis′tənt), *adj.* equally distant: *All points of the circumference of a circle are equidistant from the center.* —**e′qui|dis′tant|ly,** *adv.*

e|qui|gla|cial lines (ē′kwə glā′shəl), lines drawn on a map connecting those points on the earth's surface at which the condition of the ice formation is the same in thickness or amount on any given day in the year.

***e|qui|lat|er|al** (ē′kwə lat′ər əl), *adj., n.* —*adj.* having all sides equal: *an equilateral triangle.*
—*n.* **1** a figure having all sides equal. **2** a side equal to others.
[< Late Latin *aequilaterālis* < Latin *aequus* equal + *latus, -eris* side] —**e′qui|lat′er|al|ly,** *adv.*

***equilateral**
definition 1

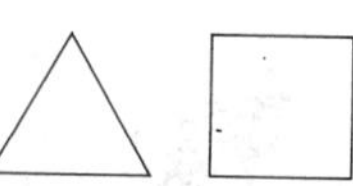

e|quil|i|brant (i kwil′ə brənt), *n. Physics.* a force or set of forces that counterbalances another force or set of forces.

e|qui|li|brate (ē′kwə lī′brāt, i kwil′ə-), *v.,* **-brat|ed, -brat|ing.** —*v.t.* **1** to bring into or keep in a state of equipoise or equilibrium; balance. **2** to be in equilibrium with; counterpoise.
—*v.i.* to be in equilibrium.
[< Latin *aequilībrātus* in equilibrium < Latin *aequus* equal + *lībra* a balance, scales]

e|qui|li|bra|tion (ē′kwə lī brā′shən, i kwil′ə-), *n.* **1** the act of balancing evenly. **2** the state of being evenly balanced.

e|qui|li|bra|tor (ē′kwə lī′brā tər, i kwil′ə brā′-), *n.* a mechanical device for securing equilibrium, as in a balloon.

e|qui|li|bra|to|ry (ē′kwə lī′brə tôr′ē, -tōr′-), *adj.* tending to produce equilibrium or balance.

e|quil|i|brist (i kwil′ə brist), *n.* a person who is skilled in feats of balancing, especially a ropewalker or acrobat.

e|quil|i|bris|tic (i kwil′ə bris′tik), *adj.* of or having to do with an equilibrist.

e|qui|lib|ri|um (ē′kwə lib′rē əm), *n., pl.* **-ri|ums,**

-ri|a (-rē ə). **1** balance; condition in which opposing forces exactly balance or equal each other: *The acrobat in the circus maintained equilibrium on a tightrope. Scales are in equilibrium when the weights on each side are equal.* **2** the state of a chemical system when no further change occurs in it. **3** *Figurative.* balance between powers of any kind; equality of importance or effect among the various parts of any complex unity: *After a time which varies from a few to many years an equilibrium is established between parasite and host, so that both continue to survive* (Fenner and Day). **4** mental poise: *My mother does not let quarrels between my brother and me upset her equilibrium.* SYN: stability. [< Latin *aequilībrium* < *aequus* equal + *lībra* balance]

equilibrium price, *Economics.* the price at which supply equals demand.

e|quil|i|brize (i kwil′ə brīz), *v.t.,* **-brized, -briz|ing.** = balance.

e|qui|mo|lal (ē′kwə mō′ləl), *adj. Chemistry.* having equivalent molal concentrations: *an equimolal mixture of rhenium and osmium.*

e|qui|mo|lar (ē′kwə mō′lər), *adj. Chemistry.* having equivalent molar concentrations: *an equimolar amount of methanol and water.*

e|qui|mo|lec|u|lar (ē′kwə mə lek′yə lər), *adj.* having an equal number of molecules.

e|qui|mo|men|tal (ē′kwə mō men′təl), *adj. Physics.* having equal moments of inertia about parallel axes.

e|qui|mul|ti|ple (ē′kwə mul′tə pəl), *adj., n.* **—*adj.*** produced by multiplication by the same number or quantity.
—*n.* one of the products obtained by multiplying two or more numbers or quantities by the same number or quantity.

e|quine (ē′kwīn), *adj., n.* **—*adj.*** **1** of horses: *The mule is apt to forget all but the equine side of his pedigree* (James Russell Lowell). **2** like a horse; like that of a horse.
—*n.* a horse.
[< Latin *equīnus* < *equus* horse]

equine encephalitis or **encephalomyelitis,** a serious virus disease of horses and other animals and, to a lesser extent, humans, attacking the brain and spinal cord, transmitted by the mosquito.

equine variola, a contagious viral disease of horses, marked by the eruption of pocks similar to those of smallpox in man, horsepox.

e|quin|i|a (i kwin′ē ə), *n.* **1** glanders; a serious contagious disease of horses, mules, or the like. **2** farcy; a form of the same disease mainly affecting the skin. [< New Latin *equinia* < Latin *equīnus;* see etym. under **equine**]

e|qui|noc|tial (ē′kwə nok′shəl), *adj., n.* **—*adj.*** **1** having to do with an equinox, or with a state when day and night are of equal length in all parts of the earth. **2** occurring at the time of an equinox: *equinoctial storms. The equinoctial seasons* (*when the sun is directly over the Equator*) *are usually rainier than other parts of the year* (White and Renner). **3** at or near the earth's equator: *Borneo is an equinoctial island.* **4** (of a flower) opening regularly at a certain hour.
—*n.* **1** = celestial equator. **2** a storm or gale occurring at or near an equinox.

equinoctial circle, = celestial equator.

equinoctial colure, the great circle passing through the poles and equinoctial points.

equinoctial line, *Astronomy.* = celestial equator.

equinoctial points, two imaginary points in the sky where the sun crosses the celestial equator.

equinoctial year, = astronomical year.

***equinox**
definition 1

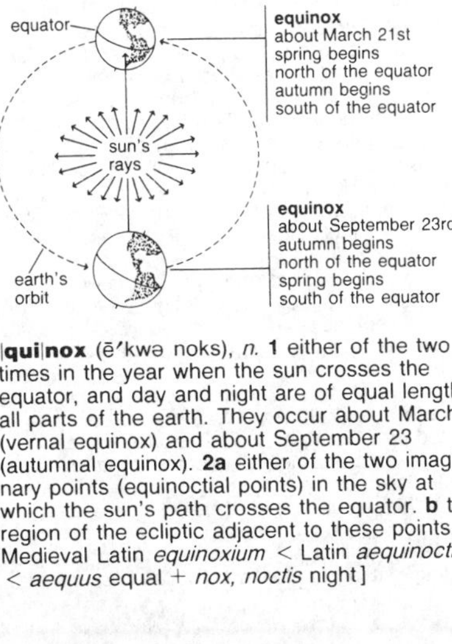

equator
equinox
about March 21st
spring begins
north of the equator
autumn begins
south of the equator
sun's rays
equinox
about September 23rd
autumn begins
north of the equator
spring begins
south of the equator
earth's orbit

***e|qui|nox** (ē′kwə noks), *n.* **1** either of the two times in the year when the sun crosses the equator, and day and night are of equal length in all parts of the earth. They occur about March 21 (vernal equinox) and about September 23 (autumnal equinox). **2a** either of the two imaginary points (equinoctial points) in the sky at which the sun's path crosses the equator. **b** the region of the ecliptic adjacent to these points. [< Medieval Latin *equinoxium* < Latin *aequinoctium* < *aequus* equal + *nox, noctis* night]

e|quip (i kwip′), *v.t.,* **e|quipped, e|quip|ping. 1** to supply with all that is needed; fit out; provide: *The expedition was fully equipped with food, tents, medical and other supplies. Is the ship fully equipped for its voyage?* SYN: See syn. under **furnish. 2** *Figurative.* to furnish with the physical or mental qualifications necessary for any task: *A college degree made him well equipped for teaching.* **3** to array; dress. [< French *équiper* < Old French *esquiper,* probably < Scandinavian (compare Old Icelandic *skipa* to man a ship < *skip* ship)]

eq|ui|page (ek′wə pij), *n.* **1** a carriage. **2** a carriage with its horses, driver, and servants: *Here roll and rumble all kind of equipages* (Hawthorne). **3a** equipment; outfit: *80 sailors and 100 arquebusiers formed the equipage* [*of three small ships*] (Walter Besant). **b** the apparatus of war, such as artillery, or means of transport. **c** the tackle of a ship. **4** a set of small household articles, such as china, glassware, or earthenware. **5** articles for personal ornament or use. **6** *Obsolete.* retinue; following.

e|quipe or **é|quipe** (ā kēp′), *n.* a sports or racing crew and its equipment; team: *a motorcycle equipe, a Grand Prix equipe.* [< French *équipe* gang, crew]

e|quip|ment (i kwip′mənt), *n.* **1** the act of equipping; fitting out; providing: *The equipment of the expedition took six months.* **2** the state of being equipped: *The equipment of the second expedition was vastly superior to that of the first.* **3** outfit; what a person or thing is equipped with; furnishings; supplies: *expensive equipment. A dentist must keep his equipment in order.* SYN: matériel, paraphernalia. **4** *Figurative.* knowledge or skill; ability: *His equipment for the job, in experience and skill, was outstanding.* SYN: qualification. **5** *U.S.* the rolling stock of a railroad.

e|qui|poise (ē′kwə poiz, ek′wə-), *n., v.,* **-poised, -pois|ing. —*n.*** **1** equal distribution of weight or force; even balance; equilibrium. **2** a balancing force; counterbalance. SYN: counterpoise.
—*v.t.* **1** to bring into a state of equipoise or balance; hold in equipoise. **2** to counterbalance.

e|qui|pol|lence (ē′kwə pol′əns), *n.* the condition of being equipollent.

e|qui|pol|len|cy (ē′kwə pol′ən sē), *n.* = equipollence.

e|qui|pol|lent (ē′kwə pol′ənt), *adj., n.* **—*adj.*** **1** equal in power, effectiveness, or validity; equivalent. **2** *Logic.* (of propositions) having the same logical force, notwithstanding formal diversity.
—*n.* something equal in power, weight, force, effect, importance, or significance; equivalent.
[< Old French *equipolent* < Latin *aequipollēns, -entis* < *aequus* equal + *pollēre* be strong]

e|qui|pon|der|ance (ē′kwə pon′dər əns), *n.* equality of weight; equilibrium.

e|qui|pon|der|an|cy (ē′kwə pon′dər ən sē), *n.* = equiponderance.

e|qui|pon|der|ant (ē′kwə pon′dər ənt), *adj.* of equal weight or importance; evenly balanced.

e|qui|pon|der|ate (ē′kwə pon′də rāt), *v.,* **-at|ed, -at|ing. —*v.t.*** to equal or offset as to power, weight, force, effect, importance, or significance; counterbalance.
—*v.i.* to be of equal power, weight, force, effect, importance, or significance.
[< Medieval Latin *aequiponderare* (with English *-ate*[1]) < Late Latin *aequipondus* < Latin *aequus* equal + *pondus, -eris* weight, related to *pendēre* hang]

e|quip|o|tent (i kwip′ə tənt), *adj.* equal in power.

e|qui|po|ten|tial (ē′kwə pə ten′shəl), *adj.* **1** *Physics.* possessing the same or equal potential: *The potential distribution in an electric field may be represented graphically by equipotential surfaces* (Sears and Zemansky). **2** *Obsolete.* of equal power or authority.

e|qui|po|ten|ti|al|i|ty (ē′kwə pə ten′shē al′ə tē), *n.* **1** the quality or condition of being equipotential. **2** *Psychology.* the principle that certain small areas of the brain can take on the function of larger, related areas that have been destroyed.

e|quip|per (i kwip′ər), *n.* a person who equips.

e|qui|prob|a|bil|ism (ē′kwə prob′ə bə liz əm), *n. Theology.* the opinion or belief that where the reasons for either of two opposed courses of action are equally balanced, one may use his liberty to follow either.

e|qui|prob|a|bil|i|ty (ē′kwə prob′ə bil′ə tē), *n.* the quality or fact of being equally probable.

e|qui|prob|a|ble (ē′kwə prob′ə bəl), *adj.* equally probable or likely to occur: *The human operator can take about 20 binary decisions a second, or choose between about one million equiprobable alternatives* (Science Journal).

e|qui|ro|tal (ē′kwə rō′təl), *adj.* having the front and rear wheels of the same size or diameter, especially on a vehicle. [< *equi-* + Latin *rota* wheel + English *-al*[1]]

eq|ui|se|ta|ceous (ek′wə si tā′shəs), *adj.* belonging to the family of plants typified by the horsetail. [< *equiset*(um) + *-aceous*]

eq|ui|se|tum (ek′wə sē′təm), *n., pl.* **-tums, -ta** (-tə). any one of a genus of flowerless plants with jointed, green, cylindrical stems, either simple or branched, rough to the touch, and having scalelike leaves at each joint; horsetail. In a former geological period some equisetums grew in great, treelike forms. [< New Latin *Equisetum* the genus name < Latin *equisaetum* the plant name < *equus* horse + *saeta* (coarse) hair]

eq|ui|ta|ble (ek′wə tə bəl), *adj.* **1** fair; just: *It is equitable to pay a man or woman the same good wages for work well done.* SYN: right, reasonable. **2** *Law.* having to do with or dependent upon equity; valid in equity, as distinguished from common law and statute law. **—eq′ui|ta|ble|ness,** *n.*

eq|ui|ta|bly (ek′wə tə blē), *adv.* in an equitable manner; fairly; justly; impartially.

eq|ui|tant (ek′wə tənt), *adj. Botany.* overlapping, as certain leaves whose bases successively overlap the leaves above or within them, such as those of the iris. [< Latin *equitāns, -antis,* present participle of *equitāre* to ride < *eques, -itis* horseman < *equus* horse]

eq|ui|ta|tion (ek′wə tā′shən), *n.* horseback riding; horsemanship. [< Latin *equitātiō, -ōnis* < *equitāre;* see etym. under **equitant**]

eq|ui|tes (ek′wə tēz), *n.pl.* in Roman history: **1** (originally) the body of citizens comprising the cavalry. **2** (later) a privileged class of citizens. [< Latin *equitēs,* plural of *eques, -itis* horseman, knight < *equus* horse]

eq|ui|ty (ek′wə tē), *n., pl.* **-ties. 1** fairness; justice: *The judge was noted for the equity of his decisions.* SYN: impartiality. **2** what is fair and just: *In all equity, he should pay for the damage he did.* SYN: justice, right. **3a** a system of rules and principles as to what is fair or just. Equity supplements common law and statute law in the United States and the Commonwealth by covering cases in which fairness and justice require a settlement not covered by the common law. In the United States, law and equity are usually administered by the same court. **b** a claim or right according to equity. **c** fairness in the adjustment of conflicting interests. **d** = equity of redemption. **4a** the amount that a property is worth beyond what is owed on it. **b** a share in the ownership of a business; stock: *Leading industrial equities were fairly firm on selective demand today, although the best prices were not always maintained* (New York Times). [< Old French *equite,* learned borrowing from Latin *aequitās* < *aequus* even, just]

equity capital, 1 the funds in a business which have been invested by the owners and not loaned by others. **2** any security or stock representing ownership in a business.

equity of redemption, the privilege extended to the mortgager of redeeming the mortgaged property by payment of mortgage and interest even after his default.

equiv., equivalent.

e|quiv|a|lence (i kwiv′ə ləns), *n.* **1** the condition of being equivalent; equality in value, force, power, weight, effect, importance, or significance: *Einstein's recognition of the equivalence of mass and energy should prove an invaluable guide in the exploration of atomic phenomena* (Scientific American). **2** *Chemistry.* **a** the quality of having equal valence. **b** = valence. **3** *Geometry.* the fact of being equal in extent, but not in form.

equivalence point, a condition in which the substances required for a chemical reaction are all present in precisely the amounts required for a complete reaction.

e|quiv|a|len|cy (i kwiv′ə lən sē), *n.* = equivalence.

e|quiv|a|lent (i kwiv′ə lənt), *adj., n.* **—*adj.*** **1** equal; the same in value, measure, force, effect, meaning, power, importance, or significance: *Nodding your head is equivalent to saying yes.* SYN: tantamount. See syn. under **equal. 2** *Geometry.* equal in extent, but not having the same form: *A triangle and a square of equal area are equivalent.* **3** *Chemistry.* equal in combining or reacting value to a (stated) quantity of another substance. **4** *Obsolete.* equal in power, rank, authority, efficacy, or excellence.
—*n.* **1** something equal in value or worth: *Five pennies are the equivalent of a nickel. Pay me for the suit or give me its equivalent in trade at your store.* **2** a word, expression, sign, or the like, of equal meaning or import. **3** *Chemistry.* **a** equal-

Pronunciation Key: hat, āge, cãre, fär; let, ēqual, tėrm; it, īce; hot, ōpen, ôrder; oil, out; cup, pu̇t, rüle; child; long; thin; ᴛʜen; zh, measure;
ə represents **a** in about, **e** in taken, **i** in pencil, **o** in lemon, **u** in circus.

ity in combining value to a (stated) quantity of another substance. **b** = equivalent weight. [< Late Latin *aequivalēns, -entis,* present participle of *aequivalēre* to be equivalent < Latin *aequus* equal + *valēre* be worth] —**e|quiv′a|lent|ly,** *adv.*

equivalent principle, (in Einsteinian physics) the principle that mass and energy are related by a specified conversion factor and are measures of the same physical quantity.

equivalent sets, *Mathematics.* sets that have the same number of members and which can be put into a one-to-one correspondence with each other. If the number of desks in a classroom is the same as the number of students, the set of desks and the set of students are equivalent sets.

equivalent weight, *Chemistry.* the weight of a substance which will combine with or can replace one-half gram atom of oxygen or one gram atom of hydrogen; the atomic weight divided by the valence; combining weight: *An equivalent weight of one element will react with exactly one equivalent weight of any other element with which it is capable of combining, or it will liberate one equivalent weight of any element which it is active enough to displace* (W. N. Jones).

e|qui|valve (ē′kwə valv′), *adj., n.* —*adj. Zoology.* having both valves alike in shape and size. —*n.* a bivalve mollusk with both valves alike.

e|quiv|o|cal (i kwiv′ə kəl), *adj.* **1** having two or more meanings; ambiguous: *His equivocal answer was so vague that we could not tell what his real opinion was.* SYN: doubtful. **2** undecided; uncertain: *Nothing was decided because the result of the experiment was equivocal.* **3** rousing suspicion; questionable: *There was something equivocal about his long and secret trips.* SYN: dubious, suspicious. [< Late Latin *aequivocus* ambiguous (< Latin *aequus* equal + *vocāre* call < *vōx, vocis* voice) + English *-al*[1]] —**e|quiv′o|cal|ly,** *adv.* —**e|quiv′o|cal|ness,** *n.*

e|quiv|o|cal|i|ty (i kwiv′ə kal′ə tē), *n., pl.* **-ties.** **1** the quality or condition of being equivocal. **2** something equivocal; an equivoque.

e|quiv|o|cate (i kwiv′ə kāt), *v.i.,* **-cat|ed, -cat|ing.** **1** to use expressions of double meaning in order to mislead: *When asked if he had finished his arithmetic, he equivocated by saying, "I was working on that an hour ago."* SYN: quibble. **2** to lie consciously; prevaricate. [< Late Latin *aequivocāre* (with English *-ate*[1]) call by the same name < *aequivocus;* see etym. under **equivocal**] —**e|quiv′o|cat′ing|ly,** *adv.*

e|quiv|o|ca|tion (i kwiv′ə kā′shən), *n.* **1** the use of expressions with double meaning in order to mislead. **2** an equivocal expression. **3** conscious lying; prevarication. **4** *Logic.* a fallacy depending on the double significance of a word.

e|quiv|o|ca|tor (i kwiv′ə kā′tər), *n.* a person who equivocates.

e|quiv|o|ca|to|ry (i kwiv′ə kə tôr′ē, -tōr′-), *adj.* characterized by equivocation.

eq|ui|voque or **eq|ui|voke** (ek′wə vōk), *n.* **1** an expression capable of more than one meaning; a play upon words, often of a humorous nature; pun. **2** ambiguity of speech. **3** = equivocation. [< Latin *aequivocus;* see etym. under **equivocal**]

E|quu|le|i (i kwü′lē ī), *n.* genitive of **Equuleus.**

E|quu|le|us (i kwü′lē əs), *n., genitive* **E|quu|le|i.** a northern constellation near Aquila. [< Latin *equuleus* a colt (diminutive) < *equus* horse]

-er[1], *suffix forming nouns.* **1** (*added to verbs*) a person or thing that ___s: *Climber = a person, animal, or plant that climbs. Admirer = a person who admires.*
2 (*added to nouns*) a person living in ___: *New Yorker = a person living in New York. Villager = a person living in a village.*
3 (*added to nouns*) a person who makes or works with ___: *Hatter = a person who makes hats.*
4 (*added to nouns*) a person or thing that is or has ___: *Six-footer = a person who is six feet tall. Rancher = a person who has a ranch.*
[Old English *-ere,* ultimately < Latin *-ārius* having to do with]

▶**-er, -or.** Names of persons or things performing an act (nouns of agent) and some other nouns are generally formed in English by adding *-er* to a verb (*doer, killer, painter, heater, thinker*), but many, chiefly nouns taken from Latin or French (*assessor, prevaricator*), end in *-or.* Since the two endings are pronounced the same (ər), it is sometimes hard to remember whether *-er* or *-or* should be written. A dictionary will settle such questions.

-er[2], *suffix forming nouns from other nouns.* a person or thing connected with ___: *Officer = a person connected with an office.* [< Anglo-French *-er,* Old French *-ier* < Latin *-ārius, -ārium* having to do with]

-er[3], *suffix forming the comparative degree of adjectives.* more: *Softer = more soft.* [Middle English *-er, -ere,* Old English *-ra* (masculine), *-re* (feminine, neuter)]

-er[4], *suffix forming the comparative degree of adverbs.* more: *Slower = more slow.* [Old English *-or*]

-er[5], *suffix.* the action or process of ___ing, as in *waiver, supper.* [< Old French *-er* (originally, an infinitive ending) < Latin *-āre*]

-er[6], *suffix.* ___frequently; ___again and again, as *to flicker, patter.* [Middle English *-eren,* Old English *-rian*]

Er (no period), erbium (chemical element).

E.R., **1** King Edward (Latin, *Eduardus Rex*). **2** Queen Elizabeth (Latin, *Elizabeth Regina*).

e|ra (ir′ə, ē′rə), *n.* **1** an age in history; historical period: *the Napoleonic era, the Romantic era. The years from 1817 to 1824 in United States history are often called the Era of Good Feeling.* **2** a period of time starting from some important or significant happening or date: *the postwar era.* **3** a system of reckoning time starting from some important or significant happening or given date: *The Christian Era is the period of time reckoned from about four years after the birth of Christ. We live in the 20th century of the Christian Era.* **4** one of the five very large divisions of time in geological history: the Cenozoic, Mesozoic, Paleozoic, Proterozoic, and Archeozoic. An era is usually divided into periods. **5** the period of time to which anything belongs or is to be assigned: *'Twas in November, but I'm not so sure About the day—the era's more obscure* (Byron). [< Late Latin *era,* variant of *aera* number, epoch; probably same word as Latin *aera* counters (for reckoning), plural of *aes, aeris* brass]

ERA (no periods) or **E.R.A.,** **1** earned run average. **2** Emergency Relief Administration. **3** Equal Rights Amendment (a proposed constitutional amendment stating that "equality of rights under the law shall not be denied or abridged by the United States or any state on account of sex"): *Proponents of ERA redoubled efforts to . . . make it law* (Caroline Bird).

e|ra|di|ate (i rā′dē āt), *v.t.,* **-at|ed, -at|ing.** to send forth, as rays of light. [< Latin *ē* out + *radiate*]

e|ra|di|a|tion (i rā′dē ā′shən), *n.* emission of rays or beams, as of light; radiation.

e|rad|i|ca|ble (i rad′ə kə bəl), *adj.* that can be eradicated.

e|rad|i|cant (i rad′ə kənt), *n.* = eradicator.

e|rad|i|cate (i rad′ə kāt), *v.t.,* **-cat|ed, -cat|ing.** **1** to get rid of entirely; destroy completely; extirpate: *Yellow fever has been eradicated in the United States but it still exists in some countries.* SYN: eliminate. **2** to pull out by the roots: *The gardener eradicated weeds from the garden.* [< Latin *ērādīcāre* (with English *-ate*[1]) < *ex-* out + *rādīx, rādīcis* root]

e|rad|i|ca|tion (i rad′ə kā′shən), *n.* the act of eradicating or state of being eradicated; complete destruction or uprooting. SYN: extirpation, extermination.

e|rad|i|ca|tive (i rad′ə kā′tiv), *adj.* tending to eradicate.

e|rad|i|ca|tor (i rad′ə kā′tər), *n.* a person or thing that roots out or removes utterly.

e|ra|dic|u|lose (ir′ə dik′yə lōs), *adj. Botany.* without rootlets.

e|ras|a|ble (i rā′sə bəl), *adj.* that can be erased: *Erasable X-ray pictures are printed in a new machine* (Scientific American).

e|rase (i rās′), *v.t.,* **e|rased, e|ras|ing.** **1** to rub out; remove by rubbing or scraping: *He erased the wrong answer and wrote in the right one.* **2** to remove all trace of; blot out: *Unwanted recordings may simply be erased by demagnetizing and the tape reused almost indefinitely* (New Yorker). (*Figurative.*) *The blow on his head erased the details of the accident from his memory.* [< Latin *ērāsus,* past participle of *ērādere* < *ex-* out + *rādere* scrape]
—*Syn.* **1, 2 Erase, expunge, efface** mean to remove something from a record of some kind. **Erase** means to remove all trace of it by or as if by scraping or rubbing, literally as from paper or figuratively as from memory: *I erased the faulty recording from the tape. I erased him from my mind.* **Expunge** means to blot it out so that it seems never to have existed: *The judge ordered certain charges expunged from the record.* **Efface** means to wipe out its identity or existence by or as if by rubbing away its face: *Rain and wind had effaced the inscription on the stone.*

erase head, the device on a tape recorder that erases previous recordings on a tape by demagnetizing the tape; erasing head.

e|rase|ment (i rās′mənt), *n.* = erasure.

e|ras|er (i rā′sər), *n.* something used to erase marks made with pencil, ink, or chalk: *My pencil is equipped with an eraser made of rubber.*

e|ras|ing head (i rā′sing), = erase head.

e|ra|sion (i rā′shən, -zhən), *n.* = erasure.

E|ras|mi|an (i raz′mē ən), *adj., n.* —*adj.* of or having to do with the Dutch scholar and humanist Desiderius Erasmus or with his writings and work. —*n.* a follower or imitator of Erasmus.

e|ras|or|y (i rā′sər ē), *adj.* involving erasure or obliteration (of a wart or other neoplasm): *No known compound has an effect upon the polyoma virus which spreads verrucae [warts], and the orthodox doctor is left still with only the erasory treatments of cauterization, freezing or electrosurgery* (New Scientist).

E|ras|tian (i ras′chən, -tē ən), *adj., n.* —*adj.* **1** of or having to do with Thomas Erastus, a Swiss-German theologian, a follower of Zwingli, or his doctrine. **2** advocating the doctrine of state supremacy in ecclesiastical matters.
—*n.* an advocate of the doctrine of state supremacy in ecclesiastical matters.

E|ras|tian|ism (i ras′chə niz əm, -tē ə niz′-), *n.* Erastian doctrines or advocacy of them.

e|ra|sure (i rā′shər, -zhər), *n.* **1** the act of erasing; a scraping or rubbing out: *the erasure of a typing error.* **2** an erased word, letter, or the like: *He questioned her about the erasure.* **3** the place where a word, letter, or the like, has been erased: *The erasure was obvious.*

Er|a|to (er′ə tō), *n. Greek Mythology.* the Muse of poetry about love.

***er|bi|um** (ėr′bē əm), *n.* a grayish, rare-earth metallic chemical element of the yttrium group. It is soft and lustrous, occurs as a minute part of various minerals, and is used in nuclear research. [< New Latin *erbium* < (Ytt)*erby,* a town in Sweden, where gadolinite (which contains erbium) was found]

***erbium**

symbol	atomic number	atomic weight	oxidation state
Er	68	167.26	3

ERDA (ėr′də), *n.* Energy Research and Development Administration (of the United States, from 1974 to 1977).

ere (ãr), *prep., conj. Archaic.* —*prep.* before: *He will come ere long. Sent to the devil somewhat ere his time* (Byron). —*conj.* **1** before: *How long will it be ere they believe me* (Numbers 14:11). *Ere sin could blight or sorrow fade, Death came with friendly care* (Samuel Taylor Coleridge). **2** sooner than; rather than: *You shall want ere I want* (motto of a Border family). [Old English *ǣr*]

Er|e|bus (er′ə bəs), *n. Greek Mythology.* **1** a dark, gloomy place through which the dead passed on their way to Hades. **2** one of the sons of Chaos. He represented darkness.

Er|ech|thei|on (er′ək thī′on), *n.* = Erechtheum.

Er|ech|the|um (er′ək thē′əm), *n.* an Ionic temple on the Acropolis at Athens, built about 400 B.C., famous for its technical perfection and architectural variety.

E|rech|theus (i rek′thüs), *n. Greek Legend.* a king and guardian divinity of Athens: *King Erechtheus of Athens was usually said to be the king in whose reign Demeter came to Eleusis and agriculture began* (Edith Hamilton).

e|rect (i rekt′), *adj., v.* —*adj.* **1** straight up; not tipping or bending; upright: *an erect tree. A telephone pole stands erect. A soldier holds his body erect.* SYN: See syn. under **upright.** **2** raised or directed upward; bristling; stiff: *The cat faced the dog with fur erect.* **3** *Botany.* vertical throughout; not spreading: *an erect stem, an erect leaf or ovule.* **4** *Obsolete.* **a** (of the hands) uplifted. **b** (of the mind) alert or attentive.
—*v.t.* **1** to put straight up; set upright: *They erected a television antenna on the roof. The pole was erected on a firm base.* **2** to put up; build: *The house was erected forty years ago.* SYN: construct. **3** to put together: *When the missing parts arrived, we erected the machine.* SYN: assemble. **4** *Figurative.* to set up; establish; found: *to erect an institution.* **5** to form (into): *to erect a territory into a state.* **6** *Geometry.* to draw or construct (a line or figure) upon a given line, base, or the like. **7** *Optics.* to change (an inverted image) to a normal position. **8** *Physiology.* to raise a tissue by distention. **9** *Archaic.* to lift up; exalt; elevate.
[< Latin *ērēctus,* past participle of *ērigere* < *ex-* up + *regere* to direct, keep straight] —**e|rect′ly,** *adv.* —**e|rect′ness,** *n.*

e|rect|a|ble (i rek′tə bəl), *adj.* that can be erected.

e|rect|er (i rek′tər), *n.* = erector.

e|rec|tile (i rek′təl), *adj.* **1** capable of being erected or set upright. **2** *Physiology.* that can become erect and rigid by distention, as certain animal tissues.

e|rec|til|i|ty (i rek′til′ə tē, ē′rek-), *n.* erectile quality.

e|rec|tion (i rek′shən), *n.* **1** the act or process of erecting; setting up; raising: *The erection of the* *tent took only a few minutes.* **2** the condition of being erected. **3** the thing erected; building or other structure. **4** *Physiology.* the state of the penis, clitoris, or other bodily organ or part in which the erectile tissue has become distended and rigid by the accumulation of blood.

e|rec|tive (i rek′tiv), *adj.* setting upright or tending to erect.

e|rec|tor (i rek′tər), *n.* **1** a person or thing that erects. **2** *Physiology.* a muscle that erects a part.

E region, = E layer.

ere|long (ãr′lông′, -long′), *adv. Archaic.* before long; soon.

e|re|mic (i rē′mik), *adj. Zoology.* inhabiting deserts; living in dry, sandy places.

er|e|mite (er′ə mīt), *n.* a hermit, especially a religious one: *Like nature's patient, sleepless eremite* (Keats). [< Old French *eremite,* learned borrowing from Late Latin *ērēmīta* < Greek *erēmītēs* < *erêmos* uninhabited. See etym. of doublet **hermit**.]

er|e|mit|ic (er′ə mit′ik), *adj.* **1** having to do with or characteristic of a hermit, especially a religious one. **2** inhabited by or containing hermits: *We follow their adventures in eremitic Ireland, Ethelred's troublous England,* [and] *Normandy* (Observer).

er|e|mit|i|cal (er′ə mit′ə kəl), *adj.* = eremitic.

er|e|mit|ish (er′ə mī′tish), *adj.* like or befitting a hermit: *By a basin, under a small portico cut in the solid wall, sat a priest, old, bearded, wrinkled, cowled—never being more perfectly eremitish* (Lew Wallace).

er|e|mit|ism (er′ə mə tiz′əm), *n.* the condition or way of life of a hermit, especially a religious one.

er|e|mu|rus (er′ə myůr′əs), *n., pl.* **-ri** (-rī). any one of a group of plants of the lily family, native in Asia, including species cultivated for their tall flower stalks (sometimes 8 feet high) topped with a spike of white, yellow, pink, or red flowers; foxtail lily. [< New Latin *Eremurus* the genus name < Greek *erêmos* solitary + *ourá* tail (because of the bare stalk)]

ere|now (ãr′nou′), *adv. Archaic.* before this time.

e|rep|sin (i rep′sin), *n.* an enzyme complex found in the intestinal and pancreatic juices, that breaks down protein molecules into amino acids. [< Latin *ereptus,* past participle of *eripere* to set free + English (pep)*sin*]

er|e|thism (er′ə thiz əm), *n.* an excessive or abnormal amount of irritability or stimulation in an organ or tissue. [< Greek *erethismós* irritation < *erethízein* irritate]

ere|while (ãr′hwīl′), *adv. Archaic.* a while before; a short time ago: *All his armour stain'd, erewhile so bright* (Milton).

ere|whiles (ãr′hwīlz′), *adv. Archaic.* erewhile.

Er|e|whon (er′ə hwon, -won), *n.* **1** a form of utopia described by Samuel Butler in his novel *Erewhon* (1872). **2** any place or state resembling this utopia: *Touré turned instinctively to the Soviet bloc, whose economic embrace rapidly made Guinea a kind of cold-war Erewhon* (Time). [< partial reversal of *Nowhere*]

Er|e|who|ni|an (er′ə hwō′nē ən, -wō′-), *adj., n.* **—*adj.*** of or having to do with Erewhon: *... the Erewhonian paradox of imprisoning the invalid* (Observer). **—*n.*** an inhabitant of Erewhon.

erf (ėrf), *n., pl.* **er|ven.** (in South Africa) a small piece of ground; plot: *The erven will be taken over by the Pretoria City Council ... and the owners have been given 30 days to state the amounts they claim for their erven* (Cape Times). [< Afrikaans *erf* < Dutch]

erg[1] (ėrg), *n.* a unit for measuring work or energy in the centimeter-gram-second system. It is equivalent to the amount of work done by a force of one dyne acting through a distance of one centimeter. *An erg is a very small amount of energy: it is about the amount that a moderately slow mosquito transfers when it collides with your forehead—and this does not include the sting* (New Astronomy). [< Greek *érgon* work]

erg[2] (ėrg), *n.* a desert area of shifting sand dunes, especially in the Sahara Desert. [< French *erg* < Arabic (North Africa) *'irj*]

erg-, *combining form.* the form of **ergo-** before vowels, as in *ergal.*

ERG (no periods), electroretinogram.

er|gal (ėr′gəl), *n.* = potential energy.

er|gas|to|plasm (ėr gas′tə plaz əm), *n. Biology.* cytoplasmic material that stains readily with a basic dye, especially the endoplasmic reticulum. [< French *ergastoplasme* < Greek *ergastikós* able to work + *plásma* something formed, plasma]

er|gas|tu|lum (ėr gas′chə ləm), *n., pl.* **-la** (-lə). (in ancient Rome) a private prison or house of correction for slaves. [< Latin *ergastulum*]

er|ga|tan|drous (ėr′gə tan′drəs), *adj.* (of ants) having wingless males resembling workers. [< Greek *ergátēs* worker + *anêr, andrós* man]

er|gat|a|ner (ėr gat′ə nər), *n.* a wingless male ant resembling a worker. [< Greek *ergátēs* worker + *anêr, andrós* man]

er|gate (ėr′git), *n.* an ergates; worker.

er|ga|tes (ėr′gə tēz), *n., pl.* **-tes.** a neuter ant or sterile female ant; worker. [< Greek *ergátēs* worker]

er|ga|to|gyne (ėr′gə tə jīn), *n.* a potentially fertile female ant that is wingless like a worker. [< Greek *ergátēs* worker + *gynê* woman]

er|ga|tog|y|nous (ėr′gə toj′ə nəs), *adj.* (of ants) having potentially fertile females that are wingless like workers.

er|ga|toid (ėr′gə toid), *n., adj.* **—*n.*** an ant of either sex that is not sterile but wingless like a worker. **—*adj.*** having the characteristics of an ergatoid.

erg|me|ter (ėrg′mē′tər), *n.* an apparatus for measuring work or energy in ergs.

er|go (ėr′gō), *adv., conj. Latin.* therefore.

ergo-, *combining form.* work: *Ergometer = device for measuring work.* Also, **erg-** before vowels. [< Greek *érgon* work]

er|god|ic (ėr god′ik), *adj.* of or having to do with a theory of probability maintaining that in a closed system every elementary state is as likely to occur as every other and no new state is likely to appear in place of an elementary state: *the ergodic hypothesis, an ergodic theorem.* [< *erg-* + Greek *hodós* way + English *-ic*]

er|go|dic|i|ty (ėr′gō dis′ə tē), *n.* ergodic property or character; probability of the occurrence of every elementary state in a closed system.

er|go|gram (ėr′gə gram), *n.* a record made by an ergograph.

er|go|graph (ėr′gə graf, -gräf), *n.* a device for measuring and recording muscular work done, rate of fatigue, and the like.

er|gom|e|ter (ėr gom′ə tər), *n.* a device for measuring work done, as by a muscle.

er|go|met|ric (ėr′gō met′rik), *adj.* of an ergometer or ergometry.

er|go|met|rics (ėr′gō met′riks), *n.* = ergometry.

er|go|met|rine (ėr′gə met′rin), *n.* = ergonovine.

er|gom|et|ry (ėr gom′ə trē), *n.* the measurement of work done or energy expended.

er|gon (ėr′gon), *n.* **1** = erg. **2** work measured by its equivalent in heat. [< Greek *érgon* work]

er|go|nom|ic (ėr′gə nom′ik), *adj.* of or having to do with ergonomics. **—er′go|nom′i|cal|ly,** *adv.*

er|go|nom|ics (ėr′gə nom′iks), *n.* the study of the relationship between individuals and their work or working environment, especially with regard to fitting jobs to the needs and abilities of workers: *The essential nature of ergonomics is the convergence of the disciplines of human biology* (*especially anatomy, physiology, and psychology*) *on the problems of Man at work* (New Scientist). [< *ergo-* + (eco)*nomics*]

er|gon|o|mist (ėr gon′ə mist), *n.* a student or advocate of ergonomics.

er|go|no|vine (ėr′gə nō′vin, -vēn), *n.* an alkaloid drug extracted from ergot and used to contract the uterus during childbirth and in the treatment of migraine headache. *Formula:* $C_{19}H_{23}N_3O_2$ [< *ergot* + Latin *novus* new + *-ine*[2]]

er|go|pho|bi|a (ėr′gə fō′bē ə), *n.* an aversion to or fear of work (in humorous use).

er|go|sphere (ėr′gə sfir), *n. Astronomy.* an outer layer of high energy below the surface of and surrounding a black hole: *A body that enters this ergosphere can be influenced by the black hole without being completely captured by it* (Science News). [< *ergo-* + *sphere*]

er|gos|ter|ol (ėr gos′tə rōl, -rol), *n.* a steroid alcohol originally derived from ergot and now obtained chiefly from yeast. When exposed to ultraviolet light, it is turned into vitamin D and can be used for the prevention or curing of rickets. *Formula:* $C_{28}H_{44}O$ [< *ergo*(t) + *sterol*]

er|got (ėr′gət, -got), *n.* **1** a disease of rye and other cereals in which the grains are replaced by blackish fungous growths. **2** any fungus producing this disease. **3** the growth produced by this disease. **4** medicine made from these growths, used to contract the uterus during childbirth. [< Old French *argot* cock's spur (from the shape of the diseased grain)]

er|got|a|mine (ėr got′ə mēn, -min), *n.* an alkaloid drug extracted from ergot, used chiefly in its tartrate form to relieve migraine headaches and to prevent hemorrhage after childbirth. *Formula:* $C_{33}H_{35}N_5O_5$ [< *ergot* + *amine*]

er|got|ed (ėr′gə tid), *adj.* diseased by the attack of ergot.

er|got|ic (ėr got′ik), *adj.* having to do with or derived from ergot.

er|got|in or **er|got|ine** (ėr′gə tin), *n.* an extract of ergot, used therapeutically.

er|got|ism (ėr′gə tiz əm), *n.* **1** the disease in rye and other cereals causing the formation of ergot. **2** a disease caused by eating food made with grain affected with ergot or by prolonged use of the drug ergot.

er|got|ize (ėr′gə tīz), *v.t.,* **-ized, -iz|ing.** to affect with ergot.

er|go|tox|ine (ėr′gə tok′sin, -sēn), *n.* an alkaloid drug obtained from ergot, used chiefly to stimulate the contraction of the uterus during childbirth. *Formula:* $C_{35}H_{39}N_5O_5$

er|ic (er′ik), *n.* a fine formerly paid, according to old Irish law, by a person who murdered another, or by his relatives, to the family of his victim. [< Irish *eiric*]

ERIC (no periods), Educational Research Information Center (a computerized information network of the United States Office of Education).

er|i|ca (er′i kə), *n.* any species of heath: *The ericas ... need an annual hard trim after flowering to keep them low and bushy* (London Times). [< New Latin *Erica* the genus name < Latin *erīca* heath < Greek *ereíkē*]

er|i|ca|ceous (er′ə kā′shəs), *adj.* belonging to the heath family. [< New Latin *Erica* the heath genus + English *-aceous*]

Er|ich|tho|ni|us (er′ik thō′nē əs), *n. Greek Legend.* a king of Athens, son of Hephaestus and grandfather of Erechtheus.

er|i|coid (er′ə koid), *adj.* resembling a genus of plants that includes the heath.

E|rid|a|ni (i rid′ə nī), *n.* genitive of **Eridanus.**

E|rid|a|nus (i rid′ə nəs), *n., genitive* (for def. 1) **E|rid|a|ni. 1** a southern constellation containing Achernar, a star of the first magnitude. **2** *Greek Legend.* a large river in northern Europe associated with the myth of Phaëthon: *The mysterious river Eridanus, which no mortal eyes have ever seen, received him* [*Phaëthon*] *and put out the flames and cooled the body* (Edith Hamilton).

E|rie (ir′ē), *n.* a member of an Iroquoian tribe of American Indians formerly living along the southern and eastern shores of Lake Erie.

e|rig|e|ron (i rij′ə ron), *n.* **1** any one of a group of plants of the composite family, having flower heads like those of the aster but with narrower and usually more numerous rose, white, or purple rays. **2** the dried leaves and tops of the horseweed, used in medicine to treat diarrhea and dropsy and to stop the flow of blood; fleabane. [< Latin *ērigeron* groundsel < Greek *ērigérōn* < *êri* early + *gérōn* old man (because it bears a hoary down in spring)]

Er|in (er′ən, ir′-), *n.* Ireland. [< Old Irish *Erinn,* dative of *Eriu* Ireland]

er|i|na|ceous (er′ə nā′shəs), *adj.* having to do with or similar to a hedgehog; bristly. [< Latin *ērīnāceus* hedgehog + English *-ous*]

e|rin|e|um (i rin′ē əm), *n., pl.* **-e|a** (-ē ə). *Botany.* an abnormal growth of hairlike structures on leaves, caused by certain mites. [< New Latin *erineum* < Greek *eríneos* woolly < *érion* wool]

e|rin|go (i ring′gō), *n., pl.* **-goes, -gos.** = eryngo.

E|rin|y|es (i rin′ē ēz), *n. pl. of* **Erinys.** = Furies.

E|rin|ys (i rin′is, -rī′nis), *n., pl.* **E|rin|y|es.** one of the Furies.

e|ri|om|e|ter (ir′ē om′ə tər), *n.* an optical instrument for measuring the diameters of minute particles and fibers from the size of the colored rings produced by the diffraction of the light in which the objects are viewed. [< Greek *érion* wool + English *-meter*]

e|ri|o|phyl|lous (ir′ē ə fil′əs), *adj. Botany.* having woolly leaves.

Er|i|phy|le (er′ə fī′lē), *n. Greek Legend.* the sister of Adrastus, slain by her son for inciting her husband to join the fatal expedition against Thebes.

E|ris (ir′is, er′-), *n. Greek Mythology.* the goddess of strife and discord.

er|is|tic (e ris′tik), *adj., n.* **—*adj.*** of or having to do with controversy or disputation; controversial: *The eristic art is greatly enhanced by a background of listeners and hecklers* (Atlantic). **—*n.* 1** a controversialist. **2** the art of disputation. [< Greek *eristikós* < *erízein* wrangle < *éris* discord]

er|is|ti|cal (e ris′tə kəl), *adj.* = eristic.

Er|i|tre|an (er′ə trē′ən), *adj., n.* **—*adj.*** of or having to do with Eritrea, a former Italian colony in northeastern Africa and (since 1962) a province of Ethiopia. **—*n.*** a native or inhabitant of Eritrea.

erk (ėrk), *n. British Slang.* **1** an aircraftsman. **2** a simple-minded person. [origin uncertain]

Er|len|mey|er flask (ėr′lən mī′ər, er′-), a cone-shaped flask with a flat bottom, used in laboratory work: *We immersed each sample in an Erlenmeyer flask containing a litre of distilled water and a drop or two of detergent* (New Yorker). [< Emil *Erlenmeyer,* 1825-1909, a German chemist]

erl|king (ėrl′king′), *n. German and Scandinavian Legend.* a spirit or personification of natural

---

Pronunciation Key: hat, āge, cãre, fär; let, ēqual, tėrm; it, īce; hot, ōpen, ôrder; oil, out; cup, pů̇t, rüle; child; long; thin; ᴛʜen; zh, measure; ə represents **a** in about, **e** in taken, **i** in pencil, **o** in lemon, **u** in circus.

forces, such as cold or storm, that does harm, especially to children. [partial translation of German *Erlkönig* alder-king, mistranslation of Danish *ellerkonge* < *elverkonge* king of the elves]

ERMA (no periods), Electronic Recording Method of Accounting.

★**er|mine** (ėr′mən), *n., pl.* **-mines** or (*collectively*) **-mine.** **1a** any one of several kinds of weasel of northern regions that are brown in summer but white in winter, except for a black tip on the tail. **b** its soft, white fur, used on the robes of English judges and for women's garments. The ermine trimming on judges' robes is a symbol of purity and fairness. **2** *Figurative.* the position, rank, or duties of a judge. [< Old French *ermine,* perhaps < Germanic (compare Old High German *harmo*)]

★**ermine**
definition 1a

er|mined (ėr′mənd), *adj.* **1** lined or trimmed with ermine. **2** clothed in ermine: *Ermined and minked and Persian-lambed ... The women of the better class* (Oliver Hereford). **3** *Figurative.* made a judge or a peer.

erne or **ern** (ėrn), *n. Especially Poetic or Dialect.* a kind of white-tailed European eagle that lives near the sea. [Old English *earn*]

Er|nie (ėr′nē), *n. British Informal.* an electronic device used to select winning numbers in the weekly national lottery: *Ernie is regularly tested ... and the prize lists are constantly analysed to ensure that the distribution of prizes is statistically fair* (London Times). [alteration of *ERNI,* abbreviation of *Electronic Random Number Indicator*]

e|rode (i rōd′), *v.,* **e|rod|ed, e|rod|ing.** —*v.t.* **1** to eat into; eat away; wear away gradually: *Acid erodes metal. Running water erodes soil and rocks.* **2** to form by a gradual eating or wearing away: *The stream eroded a channel in the solid rock.*
—*v.i.* to be worn away or eaten out: *The channel had probably eroded for a million years.*
[< Latin *ērōdere* < *ex-* away + *rōdere* gnaw]

e|rod|ent (i rō′dənt), *adj.* eroding; erosive.

e|rod|i|ble (i rō′də bəl), *adj.* subject to erosion.

er|o|gen|ic (er′ə jen′ik), *adj.* = erogenous.

e|rog|e|nous (i roj′ə nəs), *adj.* giving rise to sexual desire. [< Greek *érōs* sexual desire + English *-gen* + *-ous*]

E|ros (ir′os, er′-), *n.* **1** *Greek Mythology.* the god of love, son of Aphrodite. The Romans called him Cupid. **2** an asteroid which passes less than 14,000,000 miles from the orbit of the earth at its closest approach: *Eros, discovered in 1898, is 105 million miles from the sun at perihelion* (Robert H. Baker). **3** the Freudian instinct of sexual desire and self-preservation manifested as the libido.

e|rose (i rōs′), *adj.* (of leaves) having the margin irregularly indented, as if gnawed away. [< Latin *ērōsus,* past participle of *ērōdere;* see etym. under **erode**]

e|ro|sion (i rō′zhən), *n.* **1** the act or process of gradual eating into or wearing away by glaciers, temperature changes, running water, waves, ice, or wind: *Trees help prevent the erosion of soil by running water.* **2** the condition of being eaten into or worn away: *The face of the cliff had suffered erosion from wind and sea.* [< Latin *ērōsiō, -ōnis* < *ērōdere;* see etym. under **erode**]

e|ro|sion|al (i rō′zhə nəl), *adj.* **1** causing erosion: *The wind is an erosional agent.* **2** produced by erosion: *Agassiz recognized the former existence of a great ice sheet in North America by the presence, on a grand scale, of depositional and erosional features strikingly similar to those of the mountain glaciers he had observed in action* (Robert M. Garrels). —**e|ro′sion|al|ly,** *adv.*

e|ro|sive (i rō′siv), *adj.* eroding; causing erosion.

e|ros|trate (i ros′trāt), *adj. Botany.* having no beak. [< *e-* without + *rostrate*]

er|o|te|sis (er′ə tē′sis), *n. Rhetoric.* the use of a question or questions for oratorical purposes, such as when implying a negative. *Example:* Should man give up freedom for security? [< Greek *erṓtēsis* < *erōtâein* to question]

e|rot|ic (i rot′ik), *adj., n.* —*adj.* **1** of or having to do with sexual passion or love: *an erotic poem.* **SYN:** amatory. **2** arousing or tending to arouse sexual desire: *an erotic dance.* **3** subject to strong sexual desire: *an erotic person.*
—*n.* an erotic person or thing.
[< Greek *erōtikós* of Eros] —**e|rot′i|cal|ly,** *adv.*

e|rot|i|ca (i rot′ə kə), *n.pl.* books and pictures that emphasize erotic activities. [< New Latin *erotica*]

e|rot|i|cal (i rot′ə kəl), *adj.* = erotic.

e|rot|i|cism (i rot′ə siz əm), *n.* erotic character or tendency: *The degree of wit renders the eroticism* [*of the book*] *aseptic and—except to prudes and prurients—innocuous* (Saturday Review).

e|rot|i|cize (i rot′ə sīz), *v.t.,* **-cized, -ciz|ing.** to make, or make more, erotic.

er|o|tism (er′ə tiz əm), *n.* **1** sexual excitement. **2** the sexual instinct in any of its manifestations.

e|rot|o|gen|ic (i rot′ə jen′ik), *adj. Psychoanalysis.* **1** erogenous. **2** originating in sex; sexual.

er|o|tol|o|gist (ir′ə tol′ə jist), *n.* a student of erotology.

er|o|tol|o|gy (ir′ə tol′ə jē), *n.* erotic literature and art; erotica.

e|rot|o|ma|ni|a (i rot′ə mā′nē ə), *n.* **1** excessive sexual desire. **2** an exaggerated passion for another person. **3** *Psychoanalysis.* the delusion of being greatly loved. [< Greek *érōs, érōtos* sexual love + *maniā* madness]

e|rot|o|ma|ni|ac (i rot′ə mā′nē ak), *n.* a person who suffers from erotomania.

ERP (no periods) or **E.R.P.,** **1** European Recovery Program (the Marshall Plan). **2** early receptor potential (an extremely rapid electrical change recorded in the eye after exposure to light): *The ERP may well stimulate the much larger late receptor potential that eventually reaches the optic nerve* (Science News).

err (ėr, er), *v.i.* **1** to be wrong; be mistaken or incorrect; blunder: *to err in an opinion or belief.* **2** *Figurative.* to do wrong; sin: *To err is human; to forgive, divine.* **SYN:** trespass. **3** to go wrong; fail; miss: *Everyone errs at some time or other. The Arrows ... err not from their aim* (Robert Southey).
[< Old French *errer,* learned borrowing from Latin *errāre* wander]
▶ **Err** was in the past regularly pronounced (ėr); but there is some tendency to pronounce it (er), from analogy with *error* (er′ər).

er|ran|cy (er′ən sē), *n.* the tendency to do wrong; waywardness: *Frank's errancy consisted mostly of pranks* (Time).

er|rand (er′ənd), *n.* **1** a trip to do something, especially a short trip to get or do something or deliver a message for someone else: *She has gone on an errand to the store for her mother.* **2** what one is sent to do: *She did ten errands in one trip.* **3** the purpose or object of a trip: *an errand to take her father his lunch.* [Old English *ǣrende* message, mission]

errand boy, **1** a boy who does errands. **2** *Informal.* a person who acts under instructions and not on his own initiative: *In matters of importance, the Foreign Secretary is the Premier's errand boy.*

er|rant (er′ənt), *adj.* **1** traveling in search of adventure; wandering; roving: *He was an errant knight seeking adventures.* **SYN:** wayfaring. **2** straying from the proper course or place; astray: *errant sheep.* **3** wrong; mistaken; incorrect. **4** *Obsolete.* arrant. [< Old French *errant,* present participle of *errer* travel (< Vulgar Latin *iterāre* < Latin *iter* journey), fused with *errant,* present participle of *errer* err (< Latin *errāre* wander)] —**er′rant|ly,** *adv.*

er|rant|ry (er′ən trē), *n., pl.* **-ries.** **1** conduct or action like that of a knight-errant. **2** the condition of being errant.

er|ra|re hu|ma|num est (e rãr′ē hyü mā′nəm est), *Latin.* to err is human.

er|ra|ta (ə rā′tə, -rä′-), *n.* **1** the plural of **erratum.** **2** errors and corrections in printing listed and inserted in a book; corrigenda: *He sought a list of errata at the back* (New Yorker).

er|rat|ic (ə rat′ik), *adj., n.* —*adj.* **1** not steady; uncertain; irregular: *An erratic clock is not dependable. An erratic mind jumps from one idea to another.* **2** queer; odd: *erratic ideas, erratic behavior.* **SYN:** eccentric. **3** having no certain course; wandering: *an erratic star or planet.* **4** *Medicine.* moving from point to point; changeable: *erratic rheumatic pains.* **5** *Geology.* having to do with boulders, blocks, or masses of rock that have been transported from their original site to an unusual location as by glacial action.
—*n.* **1** a wanderer. **2** an eccentric person. **3** *Geology.* an erratic block or boulder: *a glacial erratic ... scratched and smoothly abraded on one face by ice action* (Raymond Cecil Moore).
[< Latin *erráticus* < *errāre* err, wander] —**er|rat′i|cal|ly,** *adv.*

er|rat|i|cism (ə rat′ə siz əm), *n.* an erratic quality or tendency.

er|ra|tum (ə rā′təm, -rä′-), *n., pl.* **-ta.** an error in writing or printing: *His early papers are paralyzingly beautiful, but there are many errata* (Robert Oppenheimer). [< Latin *errātum,* neuter past participle of *errāre* err]

er|rhine (er′īn, -in), *n.* a medicine causing or tending to cause nasal discharges and sneezing, especially so as to clear the nasal passages. [< New Latin *errhinum* < Greek *érrhīnon* < *en* in + *rhīs, rhīnos* nose]

err|ing (ėr′ing, er′-), *adj.* going astray; in error; wrong; sinning: *an erring child, erring faiths.* —**err′ing|ly,** *adv.*

erron., **1** erroneous. **2** erroneously.

er|ro|ne|ous (ə rō′nē əs), *adj.* **1** containing error; mistaken; incorrect; wrong: *Years ago many people held the erroneous belief that the earth is flat.* **SYN:** false. **2** *Archaic.* misguided. **3** *Obsolete.* wandering. [< Latin *errōneus* (with English *-ous*) < *errō, -ōnis* wanderer < *errāre* err] —**er|ro′ne|ous|ly,** *adv.* —**er|ro′ne|ous|ness,** *n.*

er|ror (er′ər), *n.* **1** something done that is wrong; something that is not as it ought to be; mistake: *I failed my test because of errors in spelling. There is an error in the date of his birth.* **2** the condition of being wrong, mistaken, or incorrect: *You are in error; your answer is wrong. All men are liable to error* (John Locke). **3** wrongdoing; sin: *Into the second* [*tabernacle*] *went the high priest ... not without blood which he offered ... for the errors of the people* (Hebrews 9:7). **4** *Baseball.* a faulty play in catching or throwing that permits a batter who should have been put out to reach base or allows a runner to advance. **5** *Bowling.* = break[1] (*n.* def. 15). **6** *Mathematics.* the difference between the observed or approximate amount and the correct amount. **7** *Archaic.* the action of wandering or roving: *The damsel's headlong error thro' the wood* (Tennyson). [< Old French *error* < Latin *error* < *errāre* err] —**er′ror|less,** *adj.*
—*Syn.* **1 Error, mistake** mean something incorrect or wrong. **Error** applies to any incorrect or wrong act; unimportant or serious, careless or intentional, easily excused or deserving blame: *The typist failed to get the job because of errors in spelling.* **Mistake** applies to an error in judgment or understanding or to something done thoughtlessly or by oversight: *My mistake was failing to buy land when it was cheap.*

error in principle, *Bookkeeping.* an error in placing an entry, especially in an incorrect account.

er|ror|ist (er′ər ist), *n.* a person who encourages and propagates error: *It is one thing to refuse joint prayer to heretics and persistent errorists; it is not quite the same thing to refuse joint prayer to the victims ... of heretics and errorists* (Martin H. Franzmann).

error signal, (in a servosystem) a signal, usually in the form of a voltage, indicating the amount of error between the controlling and controlled mechanisms. The error signal is used to operate a servo device.

er|satz (er zäts′, -sats′), *n., adj.* —*n.* a substitute or imitation, especially something inferior: *The coffee ... will be ... tempered with a judicious mixture of ersatz* (Observer).
—*adj.* substitute: *ersatz leather, ersatz coffee.*
[< German *Ersatz*]

Erse (ėrs), *n., adj.* —*n.* **1** the Celtic language of the Scottish Highlanders; Scottish Gaelic. **2** the Celtic language of Ireland; Irish Gaelic.
—*adj.* of or in either of these languages.
[Scottish variant of *Irish*]

erst (ėrst), *adv. Archaic.* **1** before the present time. **2** long ago. **3** a little while ago. [Old English *ǣrest,* superlative of *ǣr* ere]

erst|while (ėrst′hwīl′), *adj., adv.* —*adj.* former; past: *an erstwhile companion. Our erstwhile foe returns to the fold of the freedom-loving nations of the world as a friend and ally* (New York Times). —*adv. Archaic.* in time past; formerly.

Er|te|bol|le (er′tə bol′ə), *adj.* belonging to or denoting a late Mesolithic culture based on the Maglemosian culture, represented by huge kitchen middens found in Denmark. [< *Ertebolle,* a town in Denmark]

ERTS (ėrts), *n.* Earth Resources Technology Satellite (a United States artificial satellite for studying earth resources, renamed *Landsat* in 1975): *The observations made aboard ERTS will be applied to agriculture, cartography, geology, geography, hydrology, hydrography, and oceanography* (Science News).

er|u|bes|cence (er′ů bes′əns), *n.* a redness of the skin or other surface; blush.

er|u|bes|cent (er′ů bes′ənt), *adj.* reddening; blushing. [< Latin *ērubēscēns, -entis,* present participle of *ērubēscere* blush < *ex-* out + *rubēscere* redden < *rubēre* be red < *rubor, -ōris* red]

e|ru|ca (i rü′kə), *n., pl.* **-cae** (-sē). the larva of a butterfly or similar insect; caterpillar.

e|ru|cic acid (i rü′sik), an unsaturated fatty acid occurring as glycerides in rape oil and other vegetable oils. *Formula:* $C_{22}H_{42}O_2$ [< Latin *ērūca* a kind of cabbage + English *-ic*]

e|ruct (i rukt′), *v.t., v.i.* = belch. [< Latin *ēructāre* < *ex-* out + *ructāre* belch]

e|ruc|tate (i ruk′tāt), *v.t., v.i.,* **-tat|ed, -tat|ing.** = belch.

e|ruc|ta|tion (i ruk′tā′shən, ē′ruk-), *n.* **1** the act of belching. **2** that which is belched up.

e|ruc|ta|tious (i ruk′tā′shəs, ē′ruk-), *adj.* belching.

er|u|dite (er′ů dīt, -yů-), *adj.* having much knowledge; scholarly; learned: *an erudite teacher, an erudite book.* [< Latin *ērudītus,* past participle of *ērudīre* instruct < *ex-* away, out of + *rudis* rude, unskilled] **—er′u|dite′ly,** *adv.* **—er′u|dite′ness,** *n.*

er|u|dit|i|cal (er′ů dit′ə kəl, -yů-), *adj.* characterized by erudition.

er|u|di|tion (er′ů dish′ən, -yů-), *n.* scholarship; learning: *The professor's erudition came from long years of study. It is packed with historical and legal erudition and characterized by hard thinking* (Wall Street Journal).

er|u|di|tion|al (er′ů dish′ə nəl, -yů-), *adj.* of or having to do with erudition.

e|rum|pent (i rum′pənt), *adj.* **1** bursting forth. **2** *Botany.* prominent, as if bursting through the epidermis. [< Latin *ērumpēns, -entis,* present participle of *ērumpere* erupt < *ex-* out + *rumpere* burst]

e|rupt (i rupt′), *v.i.* **1** to burst forth: *Lava and ashes erupted from the volcano.* (*Figurative.*) *Headlines erupted around the world* (Time). **2** to break out in a rash: *Her skin erupted when she had measles.* **3** to break through the gums: *When the baby was 7 months old, his teeth started to erupt.* **—*v.t.*** to throw forth: *The volcano erupted lava and ashes.* **SYN:** eject. [< Latin *ēruptus,* past participle of *ērumpere* < *ex-* out + *rumpere* burst]

e|rup|tion (i rup′shən), *n.* **1** the act of bursting forth; outbreak; outburst: *A careless smoker may cause the eruption of a disastrous forest fire.* (*Figurative.*) *His mounting irritation led to a sudden eruption of anger.* (*Figurative.*) *Wise men deplore eruptions of racial or national hatred.* **2** a throwing forth of lava, etc., from a volcano or of hot water from a geyser: *The eruption of Mount Vesuvius in* A.D. *79 buried Pompeii.* **3** *Medicine.* **a** a breaking out with many small red spots on the skin; rash. **b** red spots on the skin or mucous membranes; rash: *In measles, there is an eruption on the body.* **4** the act of breaking through the gums: *The eruption of teeth made the baby fretful.*

e|rup|tion|al (i rup′shə nəl), *adj.* of eruptions; like or having to do with eruptions; eruptive.

e|rup|tive (i rup′tiv), *adj., n.* **—*adj.* 1** bursting forth; tending to burst forth. **2** causing the skin to break out: *Measles is an eruptive disease.* **3** *Geology.* of or formed by volcanic eruptions. **—*n.*** *Geology.* a rock formed or forced up by eruption: *Basalts, rhyolites, andesites, and tuffs are examples of eruptives* (White and Renner). **—e|rup′tive|ly,** *adv.*

e|ruv or **e|rub** (ā′rüv), *n.* an area that is not considered a public place but is enclosed, as by a fence in the form of beams, cords, or telephone lines, etc., so that Orthodox Jews may carry objects or engage in some activities otherwise prohibited on the Sabbath. [< Hebrew *ērūbh,* literally, amalgamation]

E.R.V., *U.S.* English Revised Version (of the Bible).

er|ven (ėr′vən), *n.* plural of **erf.**

ERW (no periods), enhanced radiation weapon.

-ery, *suffix forming nouns.* **1** (*added to verbs*) a place for ____ing: *Cannery = a place for canning.* **2** (*added to nouns*) a place for ____s: *Nunnery = a place for nuns.* **3** (*added to nouns*) the art or occupation of a ____: *Cookery = the art or occupation of a cook.* **4** (*added to nouns*) the condition of a ____: *Slavery = the condition of a slave.* **5** (*added to nouns*) the qualities or actions of a ____: *Knavery = the qualities or actions of a knave.* **6** (*added to nouns*) a group of ____s: *Machinery = a group of machines.* [< Old French *-erie* < *-ier* (< Latin *-ārius*) + *-ie* < Late Latin *-ia* < Greek *-ĭā*]

Er|y|ci|na (er′ə sī′nə), *n.* a surname of Aphrodite.

Er|y|man|thi|an boar (er′ə man′thē ən), *Greek Legend.* a savage boar captured by Hercules as the fourth of his twelve labors. [< Latin *Erymanthēus* of Mount Erymanthus, in Arcadia, home of the beast + English *-ian*]

e|ryn|go (i ring′gō), *n., pl.* **-goes, -gos. 1** any plant of a group of coarse herbs of the parsley family, with toothed or spiny leaves and heads or spikes of small white or blue flowers, such as the sea holly. **2** *Obsolete.* the candied root of the sea holly. Also, **eringo.** [perhaps < Italian *eringio* < Latin *ēryngion* < Greek *ērýngion* (diminutive) < *ēryngos* the plant eryngo; (literally) a goat's-beard]

er|y|ops (er′ē ops), *n.* any one of a genus of extinct reptiles from the Permian rocks of North America, having an elongated triangular skull with somewhat tapering snout and cranial bones with indistinct sutures. [< New Latin *Eryops* the genus name < Greek *eryein* draw out + *ōps, ōpós* eye]

er|y|sip|e|las (er′ə sip′ə ləs, ir′-), *n.* **1** an acute infectious disease that causes fever and chills, and a rapidly spreading, deep-red inflammation of the skin, caused by a streptococcus. **2** an acute or chronic bacterial disease of swine, and less commonly of turkeys and sheep, characterized by enteritis, red patches on the skin, and arthritis: *Fresh outbreaks of swine erysipelas may cause heavy losses among the farmer's hogs* (Science News Letter). [< Late Latin *erysipelas* < Greek *erysípelas*]

er|y|si|pel|a|tous (er′ə si pel′ə təs, ir′-), *adj.* **1** resembling erysipelas. **2** having erysipelas.

er|y|sip|e|loid (er′ə sip′ə loid, ir′-), *n.* an infectious disease, resembling erysipelas but not attended with fever, contracted by people who handle animals infected with erysipelas.

er|y|the|ma (er′ə thē′mə), *n.* a severe redness of the skin associated with some local inflammation. [< Greek *erýthēma* reddening < *erythaínein* be red < *erythrós* red]

er|y|the|mat|ic (er′ə thi mat′ik), *adj.* **1** of erythema. **2** accompanied by erythema.

er|y|them|a|tous (er′ə them′ə təs), *adj.* = erythematic.

er|y|the|mic (er′ə thē′mik), *adj.* = erythematic.

erythr-, *combining form.* the form of **erythro-** before vowels, as in *erythrasma, erythrin.*

er|y|thras|ma (er′ə thraz′mə), *n.* a chronic, contagious skin disease attacking especially the armpits and groin, caused by certain bacteria and controlled by the use of antibiotics, especially erythromycin. [< New Latin *erythrasma* < *erythr-* red + *-asma* (noun suffix)]

e|ryth|rin (i rith′rin), *n. Chemistry.* **1** a colorless substance that is a constituent of various lichens. *Formula:* $C_{20}H_{22}O_{10}$ **2** a red dye formerly used to color silk. [< Greek *erythrós* red + English *-in*]

e|ryth|rism (i rith′riz əm), *n.* an abnormal redness, as of plumage or hair.

er|y|thris|mal (er′ə thriz′məl), *adj.* characterized by erythrism.

er|y|thris|tic (er′ə thris′tik), *adj.* = erythrismal.

e|ryth|rite (i rith′rīt), *n.* **1** a hydrous, usually red-colored cobalt arsenate; cobalt bloom. *Formula:* $Co_3(AsO_4)_2 \cdot 8H_2O$ **2** = erythritol.

e|ryth|ri|tol (i rith′rə tōl, -tol), *n.* a colorless, crystalline compound, an alcohol, obtained from various lichens or synthetically. *Formula:* $C_4H_{10}O_4$

erythro-, *combining form.* **1** red: *Erythrophobia = fear of red.* **2** red blood cell: *Erythrogenic = producing red blood cells.* Also, **erythr-** before vowels. [< Greek *erythrós* red]

e|ryth|ro|blast (i rith′rō blast), *n.* a nucleated cell, found in bone marrow, from which red corpuscles develop. [< *erythro-* + Greek *blastós* sprout, germ]

e|ryth|ro|blas|to|sis (i rith′rō blas tō′sis), *n.* **1** an often fatal blood condition of the fetus and newborn infant that occurs when antibodies produced in the blood of an Rh negative mother react against the blood of an Rh positive fetus. **2** the presence of erythroblasts in the blood.

erythroblastosis fe|tal|is (fi tal′is), erythroblastosis of the fetus: *Erythroblastosis fetalis occurs in about 10 per cent of the cases when an Rh negative mother is pregnant with an Rh positive baby* (New York Times). [< New Latin *erythroblastosis fetalis* fetal erythroblastosis]

e|ryth|ro|blas|tot|ic (i rith′rō blas tot′ik), *adj.* of or having erythroblastosis.

e|ryth|ro|car|pous (i rith′rō kär′pəs), *adj. Botany.* having or bearing red fruit. [< *erythro-* + Greek *karpós* fruit + English *-ous*]

e|ryth|ro|chro|ism (i rith′rō krō′iz əm), *n.* = erythrism.

e|ryth|ro|cyte (i rith′rō sīt), *n.* = red blood cell.

e|ryth|ro|cyt|ic (i rith′rō sit′ik), *adj.* of or having to do with erythrocytes.

e|ryth|ro|cy|tom|e|ter (i rith′rō sī tom′ə tər), *n.* an instrument for counting red corpuscles.

e|ryth|ro|cy|to|sis (i rith′rō sī tō′sis), *n., pl.* **-ses** (-sēz). an excessive formation of red blood cells.

e|ryth|ro|gen|ic (i rith′rō jen′ik), *adj.* producing or giving rise to red blood cells.

er|y|throid (er′ə throid), *adj.* of or having to do with erythrocytes.

e|ryth|ro|me|lal|gi|a (i rith′rō mə lal′jē ə), *n.* a painful condition of the feet, and occasionally of the hands, caused by a swelling of the blood vessels and marked by a purplish coloration and a burning discomfort and tenderness in the soles or palms. [< New Latin *erythromelalgia* < *erythro-* + Greek *mélos* limb + *álgos* pain]

e|ryth|ro|my|cin (i rith′rō mī′sin), *n.* a drug related to streptomycin, used against certain bacterial infections. *Formula:* $C_{37}H_{67}NO_{13}$ [< *erythro-* + (strepto)*mycin*]

er|y|thro|ni|um (er′ə thrō′nē əm), *n.* **1** = dog-tooth violet. **2** the former name of vanadium.

er|y|throph|i|lous (er′ə throf′ə ləs), *adj. Biology.* (of a cell, etc.) readily staining in a red dye. [< *erythro-* + Greek *phílos* loving + English *-ous*]

e|ryth|ro|pho|bi|a (i rith′rō fō′bē ə), *n.* **1** a fear of the color red. **2** a fear of blushing.

e|ryth|ro|phyll (i rith′rō fil), *n.* = anthocyanin. [< *erythro-* + Greek *phyllon* leaf]

er|y|thro|pi|a (er′ə thrō′pē ə), *n.* = erythropsia.

e|ryth|ro|poi|e|sis (i rith′rō poi ē′sis), *n.* the production of red blood cells. [< *erythro-* + Greek *poíēsis* production]

e|ryth|ro|poi|et|ic (i rith′rō poi et′ik), *adj.* having to do with the production of red blood cells.

e|ryth|ro|poi|e|tin (i rith′rō poi′ə tin), *n.* a hormone, produced by the kidneys, that controls the production of red blood cells.

er|y|throp|si|a (er′ə throp′sē ə), *n.* defective vision in which all objects appear to be tinged with red. [< *erythro-* + Greek *ópsis* vision]

e|ryth|ro|sine (i rith′rō sīn), *n.* a brown powder obtained from fluorescein by the action of iodine, used as a dye in fabrics, foods, and cosmetics. *Formula:* $C_{20}H_6I_4Na_2O_5$ [< *erythro-* + (eo)*sine*]

-es¹, *suffix.* the form of **-s¹** used chiefly after *s, z, sh, ch,* as in *asses, whizzes, bushes, witches;* in the plural of nouns ending in *-y* after a consonant, as in *dandies, duties, rubies;* and in some cases after *o,* as in *mosquitoes, potatoes, tomatoes.*

-es², *suffix.* the form of **-s²** used after *s, z, sh, ch,* as in *dresses, buzzes, washes, touches,* and after certain vowels, as in *does, goes, hurries, magnifies.*

Es (no period), einsteinium (chemical element).

ESA (no periods), European Space Agency (which replaced ESRO in 1975).

E|sa|ki diode (ē sä′kē), = tunnel diode. [< Leo *Esaki,* a Japanese electronics researcher, who developed it in 1957]

E|sau (ē′sô), *n.* the older son of Isaac and Rebecca, who sold his birthright to his twin brother Jacob (in the Bible, Genesis 25:21-34).

es|bat (es′bat), *n.* a meeting of witches: *Apart from the festivals, the covens meet once a month as near as possible to the time of the full moon to celebrate a less important ceremony known as the esbat* (Atlantic). [probably < Old French *esbat* a frolic, gambol (French *ébats*) < *esbatre* to frolic, ultimately < Latin *ex-* out + *battere* to beat]

es|ca|drille (es′kə dril′), *n.* a former unit of airplanes or warships, together with the equipment and men needed to keep them in use. In World War I an escadrille commonly consisted of six airplanes. [< French *escadrille* < Spanish *escuadrilla* (diminutive) < *escuadra* squadron]

es|ca|lade (es′kə lād′), *n., v.,* **-lad|ed, -lad|ing.** **—*n.*** a scaling of or attack over the walls of a fort, castle, or the like, by means of ladders. **—*v.t.*** to scale or attack over (a wall or rampart) by means of ladders. [< Middle French *escalade* < Italian *scalata* < *scala* ladder < Latin *scālae,* plural, ladder]

es|ca|lad|er (es′kə lā′dər), *n.* a person who escalades.

es|ca|late (es′kə lāt), *v.,* **-lat|ed, -lat|ing. —*v.t.*** **1** to increase or decrease (prices, wages, or benefits), especially automatically, in proportion to some index, such as cost of living. **2** to expand or increase (something) by stages: *The general escalated the war by sending in more troops.* **—*v.i.* 1** to increase or decrease in proportion to some index: *As prices go up, costs escalate.* **2** to increase or expand by stages: *The commotion in the sports arena almost escalated into a riot. The greater the number of nuclear Powers, the greater the chances that a limited attack might escalate into a full-scale nuclear war* (Manchester Guardian). **3** to move on, or as if on, an escalator. [back formation < *escalator*]

es|ca|la|tion (es′kə lā′shən), *n.* **1** an automatic price increase or decrease: *This price is subject to escalation reflecting changes in labor, material and other costs* (Wall Street Journal). **2** the act or process of escalating or state of being escalated; increase or expansion by stages: *We should consider the risks if we fail, particularly of the possibility of escalation of a military struggle in a place of danger* (John F. Kennedy).

escalation clause, = escalator clause.

es|ca|la|tor (es′kə lā′tər), *n., adj.* **—*n.* 1** a continuous moving stairway made on the endless chain principle, so that the steps ascend or descend continuously, for carrying passengers up or down: *Many department stores have escalators to carry the customers from one floor to another.* **2** a person or thing that escalates: *... the mobility of the social escalator* (New Yorker). *... to halt the escalators of war by policing cease-fires*

(Maclean's). **3** = escalator clause.
—***adj.*** of or having to do with an escalator clause or clauses: *escalator provisions, an escalator adjustment of prices and wages.*
[American English, earlier *Escalator,* trademark of the Otis Elevator Company < *escal*(ade) + (elev)-*ator*]

escalator clause, a provision in a contract or treaty allowing an increase or decrease in wages, prices, royalties, or benefits, under specified conditions: *To protect themselves against increased costs, producers wrote in escalator clauses permitting gas price increases* (Time).

es|ca|la|to|ry (es'kə lə tôr'ē, -tōr'-), *adj.* leading to or involving escalation: *Simply to carry on as things stood was bound to lead to defeat; the U.S. had to make some sort of escalatory move* (Sunday Times).

es|ca|lier (es ká lyā'), *n. French.* stairs.

es|cal|lo|ni|a (es'kə lō'nē ə), *n.* any one of a group of mostly evergreen shrubs and small trees of the saxifrage family, having white, pink, or red flowers, and found in the temperate parts of South America. [< New Latin *Escallonia* the genus name < *Escallon,* a Spanish traveler in South America in the 1700's]

es|cal|lop[1] or **es|cal|op[1]** (es kol'əp, -kal'-), *n.* = scallop. [< Old French *escalope* shell < Germanic (compare Middle Dutch *scelpe, scolpe*)]

es|cal|lop[2] or **es|cal|op[2]** (es kol'əp, -kal'-), *v.t.* = scallop (def. 1). [American English; variant of *scallop,* probably on analogy of *escallop*[1]]

es|cal|loped or **es|cal|oped** (es kol'əpt, -kal'-), *adj.* scalloped.

es|cam|bi|o (es kam'bē ō), *n., pl.,* **-bi|os.** a license formerly necessary to empower an English merchant to draw bills of exchange on persons living or traveling abroad. [< Italian *escambio* < Medieval Latin *excambium* exchange]

es|cap|a|ble (es kā'pə bəl), *adj.* that can be escaped.

es|ca|pade (es'kə pād, es'kə pād'), *n.* an act of breaking loose from rules or restraint; wild or mischievous adventure or prank: *He was saddened by the escapade of his wayward son* (Newsweek). [< French *escapade* < Spanish *escapada* (< *escapar*) or < Italian *scappata* < *scappare* to escape < Vulgar Latin *excappāre;* see etym. under **escape**]

es|cape (es kāp'), *v.,* **-caped, -cap|ing,** *n., adj.*
—***v.i.*** **1** to get free; get out and away: *The soldier escaped from the enemy's prison. The bird escaped from its cage.* SYN: flee. **2** to avoid capture, trouble, punishment, or any threatened evil: *Up to this time the thief has escaped.* **3** to come out or find a way out from a container; leak: *Gas had been escaping from the cylinder all night.* **4** *Botany.* to grow wild.
—***v.t.*** **1** to get free from: *He thinks he will never escape hard work. Escape me? Never—Beloved! While I am I, and you are you* (Robert Browning). **2** to keep free or safe from: *We all escaped the measles.* **3** *Figurative.* to come out of without being intended: *A cry escaped her lips.* **4** to fail to be noticed or remembered by: *The pin escaped my eye. I knew his face, but his name escaped me.*
—***n.*** **1** the act of escaping: *His escape was aided by the thick fog.* **2** a way of escaping: *a fire escape. There was no escape from the trap.* **3** *Figurative.* relief from boredom, trouble, tension, responsibility, or other burden: *Some people find escape in mystery stories.* **4** an outflow or leakage, as of gas or water. **5** *Botany.* a plant that was once cultivated, but is now growing wild in fields or roadsides; wilding.
—***adj.*** **1** providing a way of escape or avoidance: *The fugitive looked for an easy escape route. Detective stories are escape literature.* **2** *Figurative.* skilled in escaping or freeing oneself from restraints: *an escape artist.*
[< Old North French *escaper* < Vulgar Latin *excappāre* get out of one's cape < Latin *ex-* out of + Late Latin *cappa* cloak, cape[1]]
—***Syn.*** *v.t.* **1, 2 Escape, evade, elude** mean to keep free from someone or something. **Escape** implies avoiding danger or unpleasantness: *He escaped the fire in the house by jumping out of the window when he smelled smoke.* **Evade** suggests cleverness or trickery in managing to stay free: *He used forged papers to evade military service.* **Elude** suggests slipperiness and quickness in getting away from trouble that is close: *The bandit eluded the posse that was following him.*

escape clause, a clause that frees a signer of a contract from certain responsibilities under specified circumstances: *The "escape clause" permits the U.S. to alter reductions previously agreed upon if imports are injuring a domestic industry* (Wall Street Journal).

es|cap|ee (es kā'pē', -kā'pē), *n.* a person or, less commonly, an animal, that has escaped: *Police were warned to be on the lookout for two escapees from the Arkansas state penitentiary* (Time).

escape hatch, **1** a hatch or door in a closed structure, such as an aircraft, elevator, or submarine, to permit those within to get out in an emergency: *The capsule would contain escape hatches as well as equipment for bringing the men back to earth safely in the event of a booster malfunction* (Science News Letter). **2** *Figurative.* any route or means of escape: *To many people television is an escape hatch from routine.*

escape mechanism, *Psychology.* a course of thought or action, taken usually unconsciously to avoid unpleasant reality, responsibility, or other burden. Daydreaming is an escape mechanism.

***es|cape|ment** (es kāp'mənt), *n.* **1** a device that gives a watch or clock its regular movement. The motion of the wheels and of the pendulum or balance wheel are accommodated to each other by the escapement. One tooth of the wheel escapes at each swing of the pendulum. **2** the mechanism that controls the movement of a typewriter carriage. **3** a means of escape; outlet. **4** the action of escaping. **5** the number of fish that are allowed to spawn in each stream, as in salmon conservation.

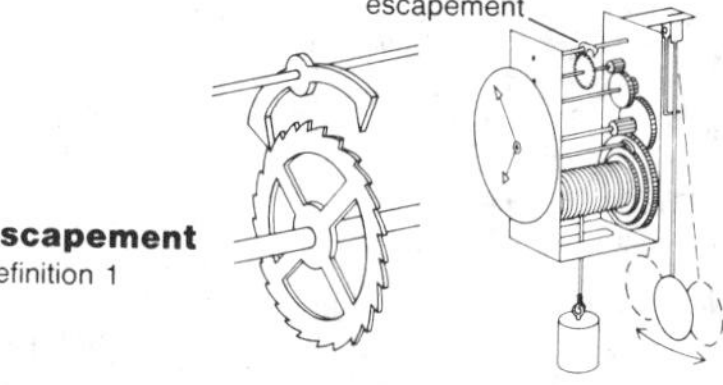

***escapement**
definition 1

es|cape|proof (es kāp'prüf'), *adj.* safe from escape; secure: *Zookeepers too readily describe their animals' quarters as "escapeproof"* (New Yorker).

es|cap|er (es kā'pər), *n.* a person or thing that escapes or has escaped; escapee: *The cadets met former members of the underground movement who assisted escapers* (London Times).

escape velocity, the minimum velocity that a moving body must reach to break away from the gravitational field of the earth or other attracting body. To overcome the gravitational pull of the earth a speed of approximately 25,000 miles per hour is needed. *To make a Moon satellite, some sort of brake has to be provided to slow down the vehicle below the escape velocity* (New Scientist).

es|cap|ism (es kā'piz əm), *n.* the habit of avoiding unpleasant things by daydreaming or by entertainment, such as motion pictures or reading light fiction: *This "management by escapism" is usually a manifestation of a fearful and insecure society* (Atlantic).

es|cap|ist (es kā'pist), *n., adj.* —***n.*** a person who habitually seeks escape from unpleasant reality in daydreams or entertainment: *Escapists ... will find things here that make the idea of life on a South Sea island charming and repellent by turns* (Newsweek).
—***adj.*** of or for escapists: *escapist fiction.*

es|cap|ol|o|gist (es kā'pol'ə jist), *n. Especially British.* **1** a performer who escapes or frees himself from specially devised restraints: *It took ... an escapologist only 50 sec. to escape from a straitjacket while hanging upside down from a crane 75 ft. above Blackpool promenade* (London Times). **2** *Figurative.* a person who is adept at extricating himself from difficult situations.

es|cap|ol|o|gy (es kā'pol'ə jē), *n. Especially British.* **1** the art or methods of an escapologist: *Every week there's that advertisement from the man in Cheshire offering handcuffs, leg-irons and manacles. It's too late now to try escapology* (Punch). **2** (*Figurative.*) *No beginner when it comes to shooting himself out of a tight corner, this was one of his finest moments in the art of parliamentary escapology* (London Times).

es|car|bun|cle (es kär'bung kəl), *n. Heraldry.* a charge representing a carbuncle with its rays. [< Old French *escarbuncle*]

es|car|got (es kár gō'), *n. French.* a snail, especially when edible or served as food.

es|ca|role (es'kə rōl), *n.* a kind of endive that has broad leaves, used for salads. [< Middle French *scariole* < Italian *scariola* < Late Latin *escariola* < Latin *escārius* pertaining to food < *ēsca* food, victuals]

es|carp (es kärp'), *n., v.* —***n.*** escarpment.
—***v.t.*** to make into an escarp; give a steep slope to. [< French *escarpe* < Italian *scarpa*]

es|carp|ment (es kärp'mənt), *n.* **1** a steep slope; cliff: *a naked escarpment of ice, 1,200 feet high* (Elisha K. Kane). See picture under **mountain**. **2** ground made into a steep slope as part of a fortification.

es|car|te|lé (es'kär tə lā'), *adj. Heraldry.* broken by a square projection or depression: *an escartelé line serving as the division between two parts of the field.* [< Old French *escartelé,* past participle of *escarteler* to quarter < *quartier* fourth, quarter]

-escent, *suffix.* coming to be or do something; in the process of ___ing, as in *adolescent, convalescent.*
[< Latin *-ēscēns, -ēscentis,* present participle ending of verbs in *-ēscere*]

esch|a|lot (esh'ə lot, esh'ə lot'), *n.* = shallot.

es|char (es'kär, -kər), *n. Medicine.* a hard crust or scab, as from a burn or caustic. [< Old French *eschare,* learned borrowing from Late Latin *eschara* scab, scar < Greek *eschárā* scar; (originally) hearth. See etym. of doublet **scar.**]

es|cha|rot|ic (es'kə rot'ik), *adj., n. Medicine.*
—***adj.*** producing a dry crust; caustic.
—***n.*** a caustic substance or agent.
[< Late Latin *escharōticus* < Greek *escharōtikós* < *eschárā* scar; (originally) hearth]

es|chat|o|col (es kat'ə kol, -kôl), *n.* the concluding section of a charter or similar document, containing the attestation, date, and other legal fixtures; a concluding clause or formula. [< French *eschatocole* < Greek *éschatos* last + *kólla* glue]

es|cha|to|log|i|cal (es'kə tə loj'ə kəl), *adj.* of or having to do with eschatology. —**es'cha|to|log'i|cal|ly,** *adv.*

es|cha|tol|o|gist (es'kə tol'ə jist), *n.* an expert in or student of eschatology.

es|cha|tol|o|gy (es'kə tol'ə jē), *n.* **1** a doctrine of the last or final things, especially death, judgment, heaven, and hell: *Every eschatology, Brandon concludes, is an effort by man to provide himself with "spiritual security" against the passage of time* (Time). **2** the branch of theology dealing with these doctrines. [< Greek *éschatos* last, final + English *-logy*]

es|cheat (es chēt'), *n., v. Law.* —***n.*** **1** a reverting of the ownership of property to the state or to the lord of the manor when there are no legal heirs: *Abandoned property laws ... are an outgrowth of the ancient law of escheat, which permits states to seize and confiscate unclaimed property* (New York Times). **2** property whose ownership has so reverted.
—***v.i.*** to revert to the state or the lord of the manor: *The lands must escheat unless the present owner made a will* (James Fenimore Cooper).
—***v.t.*** to transfer (ownership of property) to the state; confiscate.
[< Old French *eschete,* (originally) past participle of *escheoir* to fall to one's share, ultimately < *ex-* from + *cadēre* fall] —**es|cheat'a|ble,** *adj.*

es|cheat|age (es chē'tij), *n.* the right to appropriate by escheat.

es|cheat|ment (es chēt'mənt), *n.* a loss or forfeiture by escheat.

es|cheat|or (es chē'tər), *n.* (formerly, in England) an officer appointed to register escheats.

es|cheat|or|ship (es chē'tər ship), *n.* (formerly in England) the office of escheator.

Esch|e|rich|i|a co|li (esh'ə rik'ē ə kō'lī), = E. coli.

es|chew (es chü'), *v.t.* to keep away from; avoid; shun: *to eschew rich foods. A wise person eschews bad company.* [< Old French *eschiver,* or *eschever* < Germanic (compare Old High German *sciuhen* to fear)] —**es|chew'er,** *n.*

es|chew|al (es chü'əl), *n.* the act of eschewing; avoidance.

esch|scholt|zi|a (e shōlt'sē ə), *n.* any one of a group of plants of the poppy family, native in the western United States, such as the California poppy, with finely divided, light bluish-green leaves and showy yellow or orange flowers. [< New Latin *Eschscholtzia* the genus name < Johann F. von *Eschscholtz,* 1793-1831, a German naturalist]

es|clan|dre (es klän'drə), *n. French.* a circumstance that causes scandal; scene.

Es|cof|fier (es kof yā'), *n.* an expert cook or chef: *Competition, of course, is traditional in American cookery at the church bazaar or county-fair level ... and there is more than one housewife trying desperately to keep up with the local Escoffier* (Harper's). [< Georges A. *Escoffier,* 1846-1935, a famous French chef]

es|co|lar (es'kō lär'), *n.* a fish that resembles the mackerel, having an elongate body and swift movements, found in temperate waters; oilfish. It is valued as food and for its oil, which is used as a cathartic. [< Spanish *escolar* scholar (because of an assumed resemblance)]

es|co|pe|ta (es'kō pā'tä), *n.* a carbine, or short-barreled rifle, formerly common in Mexico and the southwestern United States. [American English < Spanish *escopeta,* ultimately < Latin *stloppus* a slap]

es|co|pette (es′kō pet′), *n.* = escopeta. [< French *escopette*]

Es|co|ri|al (es kôr′ē əl, -kōr′-), *n.* a huge structure in central Spain near Madrid, containing a palace and tomb for the kings of Spain, a church, a convent, and a monastery. Also, **Escurial**. [< Spanish *escorial* (literally) slag heap]

es|cort (*n.* es′kôrt; *v.* es kôrt′), *n., v.* **—*n.*** **1** a person or a group going with another person or persons, or with valuable goods, to see that they are kept safe or to honor them: *An escort of ten airplanes greeted the famous aviator. Her escort to the party was a tall young man.* **2** one or more ships or airplanes serving as a guard: *During World War II Canada's destroyers served as escorts to many convoys.* **3** the act of going with another as an escort.
—***v.t.*** to go with to keep safe or to honor: *Warships escorted the troopship. He enjoyed escorting his cousin to the movies.* **SYN:** See syn. under **accompany**.
[< Middle French *escorte* < Italian *scorta* < *scorgere* to guide < Vulgar Latin *excorrigere* < Latin *ex-* out + *corrigere* set right, correct]

escort carrier, an aircraft carrier of the smallest type: *For two years the Kalinin Bay escort carrier steamed through the thick of it, in the Marianas, the China Sea, the Battle of Leyte Gulf* (Time).

escort fighter, a long-range fighter plane used to escort and protect bombers.

es|crime (es krēm′), *n. French.* fencing.

* **es|cri|toire** (es′krə twär′, es′krə twär), *n.* a writing desk. [< Middle French *escritoire* < Old French *escriptoire* < Late Latin *scrīptōrium* place for writing or study < Latin *scrībere* write].

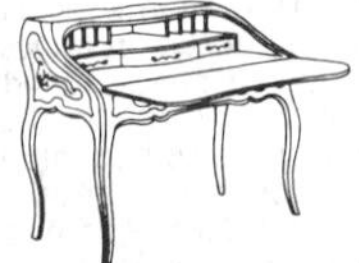

***escritoire**

es|croll or **es|crol** (es krōl′), *n. Heraldry.* a ribbonlike appendage to a coat of arms, on which the motto of a family or house is inscribed. [< Old French *escroele* (diminutive) < *escroue;* see etym. under **escrow**]

es|crow (es′krō, es krō′), *n.* a deed, bond, or other written agreement held by a third person until certain conditions are met by other parties.
in escrow, in the care of a third party in accordance with an agreement: *The SEC will tighten its small-securities regulations by requiring brokers to . . . place a certain amount of stock-sale proceeds in escrow to insure that investment money will be used for legitimate business purposes* (Time).
[< Anglo-French *escrowe,* Old French *escroue* scrap, scroll < Germanic (compare Old High German *scrōt* scrap, shred)]

es|cu|age (es′kyů ij), *n.* in feudal law: **1** military service due a lord from a tenant. **2** a tax levied instead of such military service. [< Anglo-French *escuage* < Old French *escu* shield < Latin *scūtum*]

es|cu|do (es kü′dō), *n., pl.* **-dos. 1** the unit of money of Portugal, a coin equal to 100 centavos. **2** the former unit of money of Chile, replaced by the peso in 1975. **3** the former unit of money of Angola, Guinea-Bissau, and Mozambique. **4** a former gold or silver coin of Spain, Portugal, and their colonies. [< Spanish, Portuguese *escudo* < Latin *scūtum* shield]

es|cu|lent (es′kyə lənt), *adj., n.* **—*adj.*** suitable for food; edible. **—*n.*** anything that is fit for food, especially vegetables.
[< Latin *ēsculentus* < *ēsca* food]

es|cu|lin (es′kyů lin), *n.* a white, crystalline glucoside obtained from the leaves and bark of the horse chestnut, used in cosmetics to prevent sunburn. *Formula:* $C_{15}H_{16}O_9$ Also, **aesculin**. [< New Latin *Aesculus* the horse chestnut genus + English *-in*]

Es|cu|ri|al (es kyůr′ē əl), *n.* = Escorial.

es|cutch|eon (es kuch′ən), *n.* **1** a shield on which a coat of arms is put. **2** a protective metal plate around a keyhole. **3** the panel on a ship's stern bearing her name.
blot on the escutcheon. See under **blot**[1].
[< Old North French *escuchon,* Old French *escusson* < *escut* shield < Latin *scūtum*]

es|cutch|eoned (es kuch′ənd), *adj.* **1** having a coat of arms. **2** marked with or as if with an escutcheon.

escutcheon of pretense, *Heraldry.* a small escutcheon bearing the arms of an heiress placed in the center of her husband's shield.

e|scu|tel|late (ē skyü′tə lāt), *adj. Zoology.* having no visible scutellum.

Esd., Esdras (either of two books of Apocrypha).

Es|dras (ez′drəs), *n.* **1** either of the first two books, I Esdras and II Esdras, of the Protestant Apocrypha. **2** either of two books, I Esdras and II Esdras, in the Douay Bible; called Ezra and Nehemiah in the Protestant and Jewish Bibles.

-ese, *suffix added to nouns.* **1** (*to form adjectives*) of or having to do with ____: *Japanese = of or having to do with Japan.*
2 (*to form nouns*) a person born or living in ____: *Portuguese = a person born or living in Portugal.*
3 (*to form nouns*) the language of ____: *Chinese = the language of China.*
4 (*to form nouns*) the typical style or vocabulary of ____: *Journalese = the typical style of journalists. Pentagonese = the typical style or vocabulary of the Pentagon.*
[< Old French *-eis* < Latin *-ēnsis* of, from (a place)]

ESE (no periods), **E.S.E., ESE.**, or **e.s.e.**, east-southeast.

es|em|plas|tic (es′em plas′tik), *adj.* having the function of molding diversified matter into unity; unifying: . . . *the imagination, or esemplastic power* (Samuel Taylor Coleridge). [< Greek *es* into + *én,* neuter of *eîs* one + *plastikós* fit for moulding < *plássein* to mould]

e|sep|tate (ē sep′tāt), *adj. Botany, Zoology.* without septa or partitions.

es|er|ine (es′ə rēn, -ər in), *n.* = physostigmine. [< French *ésérine* < *éséré* the Calabar bean (source of the substance)]

Esh|mun (esh′mən), *n.* a Phoenician divinity, companion of the goddess Astarte.

es|ker or **es|kar** (es′kər), *n.* a winding ridge of gravelly and sandy drift, believed to have been formed by streams flowing under or in glacial ice. See picture under **glacier**. [< Irish *eiscir*]

Es|ki|mau|an (es′kə mō′ən), *adj., n.* = Eskimoan.

Es|ki|mo (es′kə mō), *n., pl.* **-mos** or **-mo**, *adj.* **—*n.*** **1** a member of a people living in the arctic regions of North America and northeastern Asia. Eskimos are short and stocky, and have broad, flat faces, yellowish skin, and black hair. *In spite of their squat, Mongolian frame, the Eskimos are handsome, less dark-skinned than one expects* (Harper's). **2** the language of the Eskimos: . . . *willing to learn Eskimo, a language with ten thousand parts to the verb* (Manchester Guardian Weekly). **—*adj.*** of or having to do with the Eskimos, their language, or their culture.
[American English < French *Esquimaux,* plural, probably < Algonkian (Abnaki *esquimantsec* or Ojibwa *askimeq* "eaters of raw meat")]

Es|ki|mo|an (es′kə mō′ən), *adj., n.* **—*adj.*** = Eskimo. **—*n.*** a family of languages that includes Eskimo and Aleut.

Eskimo curlew, a small, brownish curlew, now almost extinct, formerly common in northern North America.

Eskimo dog, **1** any one of a breed of large, strong, broad-chested dogs much used by the Eskimos to pull their sleds; husky. Eskimo dogs have furry outer hair with another coat of fine hair near the skin. **2** = Siberian husky. **3** = Alaskan malamute.

Es|ki|moid (es′kə moid), *adj., n.* **—*adj.*** resembling the Eskimos; having the physical characteristics of Eskimos: *The Aleuts [are] an Eskimoid people who occupied the Aleutian Islands* (Ernest Gruening). **—*n.*** member of an Eskimoid people.

Es|ki|mol|o|gist (es′kə mol′ə jist), *n.* a person who studies the Eskimo language and customs; person skilled in Eskimology.

Es|ki|mol|o|gy (es′kə mol′ə jē), *n.* the study of Eskimo language and customs.

Eskimo Pie, *Trademark.* a chocolate-covered ice-cream bar.

es|ky (es′kē), *n., pl.* **-kies.** *Australian.* **1** a portable container for keeping drinks cold: *No less popular is Rugby League football, where raucous fans with well-stocked "eskies"—beer coolers—scream and swill and brawl* (National Geographic). **2 Esky**, a trademark for such a container. [probable < *Eskimo*]

ESL (no periods), English as a second language: *ESL texts. ESL programs.*

ESN (no periods) or **e.s.n.**, *British.* educationally subnormal: *Since scientists have to classify, they have drawn a line, inevitably a wavy one, at an IQ of fifty. Above that, up to seventy-five, children are classified as ESN* (Elspeth Huxley).

es|ne (ez′nē), *n.* a slave or servant among the Anglo-Saxons. [Old English *esne*]

e|sod|ic (i sod′ik), *adj.* carrying inward to a central point; afferent: *esodic nerves.* [< Greek *ésō* within + *hodós* way + English *-ic*]

es|o|nar|thex (es′ō när′theks), *n. Architecture.* the inner vestibule of a Greek church, opening onto the nave. [< Greek *ésō* within + *narthex*]

ESOP (ē′sop), *n.* any one of various plans that promote stock ownership among company employees: *ESOP's have become increasingly popular . . . as a combination of an employee bonus plan and as a source of inexpensive capital for the company* (New York Times). [< *E*(mployee) *S*(tock) *O*(wnership) *P*(lan)]

e|soph|a|gal (ē sof′ə gəl), *adj.* = esophageal.

e|so|phag|e|al (ē′sə faj′ē əl), *adj.* of or connected with the esophagus.

e|so|phag|e|an (ē′sə faj′ē ən), *adj.* esophageal.

e|soph|a|gi|tis (ē sof′ə jī′tis), *n.* inflammation of the esophagus.

e|soph|a|go|scope (ē sof′ə gə skōp), *n.* an instrument for visual examination of the inside of the esophagus.

e|soph|a|go|scop|ic (ē sof′ə gə skop′ik), *adj.* having to do with esophagoscopy.

e|soph|a|gos|co|py (ē sof′ə gos′kə pē), *n.* the visual examination of the inside of the esophagus.

* **e|soph|a|gus** (ē sof′ə gəs), *n., pl.* **-gi** (-jī). **1** the passage for food from the mouth to the stomach in vertebrates; gullet. **2** an analogous tube in the lower animals such as insects. Also, **oesophagus**. [< New Latin *oesophagus* < Greek *oisophágos,* perhaps < *oiso-,* a root of *phérein* to carry + *phágein* eat]

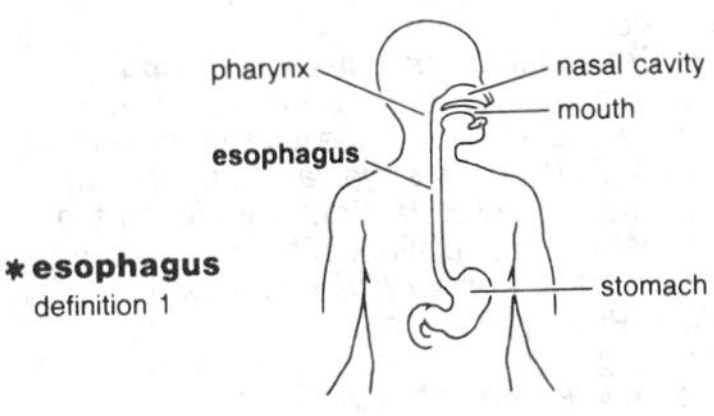

***esophagus**
definition 1

E|so|pi|an (ē sō′pē ən), *adj.* = Aesopian.

es|o|ter|ic (es′ə ter′ik), *adj.* **1** understood only by a select few; intended for an inner circle as of disciples or scholars; abstruse: *esoteric literature.* **2** belonging to such an inner circle, as a disciple: *an esoteric writer.* **3** private; secret; confidential.
[< Greek *esōterikós* < *esōtérō,* comparative of *ésō* within] **—es′o|ter′i|cal|ly,** *adv.*

es|o|ter|i|ca (es′ə ter′ə kə), *n.pl.* esoteric things; matters involving highly specialized or abstruse knowledge. [< New Latin *esoterica*]

es|o|ter|i|cal (es′ə ter′ə kəl), *adj.* esoteric.

es|o|ter|i|cism (es′ə ter′ə siz əm), *n.* esoteric doctrine or tendency: *The statistician finds great difficulty in explaining to a layman the scope of his job . . . chiefly because of the barrier caused by the esotericism of the language of statistics* (J. A. Nelder).

es|o|ter|i|cist (es′ə ter′ə sist), *n.* a person who holds esoteric doctrines.

es|o|ter|ics (es′ə ter′iks), *n.pl.* esoteric doctrines; esoteric treatises: *I must, in my esoterics, stand aloof from all controversies* (Samuel Parr).

e|sot|er|ism (e sot′ə riz əm), *n.* esotericism.

e|sot|er|ist (e sot′ər ist), *n.* esotericist.

esp., especially.

ESP (no periods), extrasensory perception.

es|pa|drille (es′pə dril; *French* es pȧ drē′yə), *n.* a kind of flat sandal, usually with a canvas upper and a sole of rope or rubber, used for casual wear: *Lena was wearing a blue straw hat, a red-and-white striped cotton jersey, a blue summer skirt, and a pair of blue espadrilles* (Christopher Rand). [< French *espadrille*]

es|pa|gno|lette (es pan′yə let′), *n.* a bolt for French windows, made of a rod reaching from top to bottom of the window with hooks at each end, which engage fixtures when the rod is rotated by a handle. [< French *espagnolette* < *espagnol* Spanish]

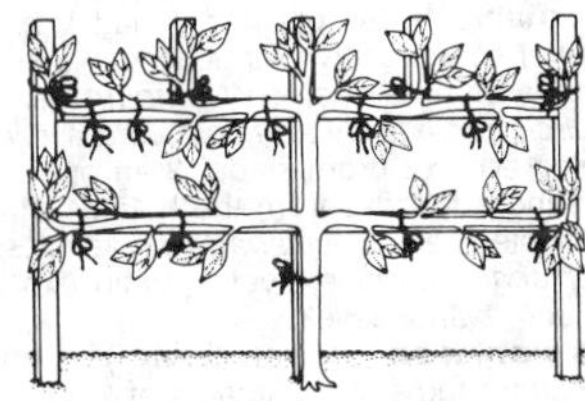
***espalier**
definition 1

* **es|pal|ier** (es pal′yər), *n., v.* **—*n.*** **1** a trellis or framework of stakes upon which fruit trees or ornamental shrubs are trained to grow in flattened form. **2** a tree, plant, or row of plants trained to

Pronunciation Key: hat, āge, cãre, fär; let, ēqual, tėrm; it, īce; hot, ōpen, ôrder; oil, out; cup, pu̇t, rüle; child; long; thin; ᴛʜen; zh, measure; ə represents a in about, e in taken, i in pencil, o in lemon, u in circus.

grow up a wall or on an espalier: *The ... espaliers ... had pulled their stakes out of the ground* (Thomas Hardy)
—***v.t.*** to train on or furnish with an espalier: *to espalier a pear tree.*
[< French *espalier* < Italian *spalliera* support < *spalla* shoulder < Latin *spatula* spatula]

Es·pa·ña (es pä′nyä), *n.* the Spanish name of Spain.

es·par·to (es pär′tō), *n., pl.* **-tos**. any one of several tough grasses of southern Spain and northern Africa, used to make printing paper, brooms, mats, nets, baskets, rope, and shoes. [< Spanish *esparto* < Latin *sparton* < Greek *spárton*, neuter of *spártos* grown from seed < *speirein* to sow]

esparto grass, = esparto.

espec., especially.

es·pe·cial (es pesh′əl), *adj.* special; chief; more than others: *of no especial value. Your birthday is an especial day for you.* SYN: particular, exceptional. [< Old French *especial* < Latin *speciālis*. See etym. of doublet **special**.]

es·pe·cial·ly (es pesh′ə lē, -pesh′lē), *adv.* specially; more than others; chiefly; unusually: *This book is especially designed for students. Youngsters today are especially interested in space travel. Abbr:* esp.
— ***Syn.*** **Especially, particularly, principally** mean in a manner or degree that is exceptional. **Especially** implies that it is exclusive or singular: *This book is designed especially for family use with an encyclopedia.* **Particularly** implies that it is foremost or most distinct: *The visitors admired all his paintings, but particularly the portrait of his daughter.* **Principally** implies that it is prominent or prevailing: *Robberies occur principally at night.*

es·per·ance (es′pər əns), *n. Obsolete.* hope. [< Old French *esperance* < *esperer* < Latin *spērāre* to hope < *spēs, spēī* hope]

Es·pe·ran·tic (es′pə rän′tik, -ran′-), *adj.* of or resembling Esperanto.

Es·pe·ran·tism (es′pə rän′tiz əm, -ran′-), *n.* the use of Esperanto.

Es·pe·ran·tist (es′pə rän′tist, -ran′-), *n.* an advocate or user of Esperanto.

Es·pe·ran·to (es′pə rän′tō, -ran′-), *n.* a simple artificial language for international use, whose vocabulary and grammar are based on root words and forms common to the principal European languages: *It is perhaps not surprising that in multilingual regions like Belgium and Switzerland, Czechoslovakia and Poland, Esperanto finds its most enthusiastic adherents* (Simeon Potter). [< the pseudonym, "Doctor *Esperanto*" (in Esperanto, "one who hopes"), used by its inventor, Doctor Ludovic Lazarus Zamenhof, 1859-1917, a Polish physician and language scholar]

es·pi·al (es pī′əl), *n.* **1** the act of spying. **2** the act of watching; observation. **3** = discovery (def. 1). **4** *Obsolete.* a spy.

es·piè·gle (es pye′glə), *adj. French.* frolicsome; roguish.

es·piè·gle·rie (es pye glə rē′), *n. French.* **1** frolicsomeness; roguishness: *Bertie Wooster's young female acquaintances still have oomph, not to say espièglerie, and motor round the countryside in scarlet roadsters* (Manchester Guardian). **2** a roguish or playful trick.

es·pi·er (es pī′ər), *n.* a person who espies.

es·pi·o·nage (es′pē ə nij, -näzh), *n.* **1** the use of spies; spying. Nations use espionage to find out other countries' military, political, and other secrets. **2** the use of spies to obtain secret information from another or others: *industrial espionage.* **3** the activities of those who do this; spying. [< French *espionnage* < Middle French *espionner* to spy < Old French *espion* spy < Italian *spione* < *spia* < Germanic (compare Old High German *spëha* spying)]

es·pla·nade (es′plə nād′, -näd′), *n.* **1** any open, level space used for public walks or drives, especially along a shore: *Weymouth Beach is a semicircle rimmed by an esplanade a mile long* (New Yorker). SYN: promenade. **2** an open space separating a fortress from the houses of a town. [< Middle French *esplanade* < Italian *spianata* < *spianare* to make level < Latin *explānāre* < *ex-* out + *plānus* level]

Es·plan·di·an (es plän′dē än′), *n.* (in medieval romance) the son of Amadis of Gaul and Oriana, called "the Black Knight."

es·plees (es plēz′), *n.pl. Law.* **1** the products which land yields. **2** the lands themselves. [< Anglo-French *esplez*, plural of Old French *esplet* revenue < Vulgar Latin *explicāre* extract < Latin, unfold]

es·pous·al (es pou′zəl), *n., adj.* —***n.*** **1** the act of espousing; adoption or support: *The candidate's espousal of the campaign for a new park made him very popular. Political reasons forbid the open espousal of his cause* (Horace Walpole). **2** the ceremony of becoming engaged or married.
—***adj.*** having to do with the ceremony of becoming engaged or married: *The nightingale ... practiseth every phrase of his espousal lay* (Robert Bridges).

espousals, **a** a betrothal; a betrothal ceremony: *[He] tells us the distinction which there is between espousals and matrimony* (William Maskell). **b** a marriage; wedding: *Is not the day then fixed for your espousals?* (Edward Young).
[< Old French *espousailles*, plural < Latin *spōnsālia*, neuter plural of *spōnsālis* having to do with betrothal < *spōnsus;* see etym. under **espouse**]

es·pouse (es pouz′), *v.t.,* **-poused, -pous·ing.** **1** to take up or make one's own; adopt: *Late in life he espoused a new religion.* SYN: embrace. **2** to marry. **3** to promise, engage, or bestow in marriage; betroth. [< Old French *espouser* marry, betroth < Latin *spōnsāre* betroth < *spondēre* betroth]

es·pous·er (es pouz′ər), *n.* a person who espouses or adopts.

es·pres·si·vo (es′pre sē′vō), *adv. Music.* with expression (used as a direction). [< Italian *espressivo* expressive]

es·pres·so (es pres′ō), *n., pl.* **-sos**. a very strong black coffee made of coffee beans roasted black, and brewed under steam pressure, usually in a special machine; caffè espresso: *Afterward, order an espresso—the straight coffee tastes like betel nut on the half-shell* (Maclean's). [< Italian *espresso*, past participle of *esprimere* < Latin *exprimere;* see etym. under **express**]

espresso bar, a coffee shop that specializes in serving espresso: *The schoolchildren from homes with television, particularly the girls over 13, are more likely to be members of youth clubs, to visit espresso bars, go to dances* (New Yorker).

espresso coffee, = espresso.

es·prin·gal (es pring′əl), *n.* a military engine used in medieval times for throwing stones, bolts, or other missiles; catapult; springald: *... in the espringal fix the brass-winged arrows* (Robert Southey). [< Old French *espringalle* < *espringer* to spring. Compare etym. under **springald**[2].]

es·prit (es prē′), *n.* lively wit; spirit; intelligence: *a woman of beauty and esprit.* [< Middle French *esprit* < Old French *espirit*, learned borrowing from Latin *spīritus, -ūs* spirit, (originally) breath < *spīrāre* breathe. See etym. of doublets **spirit, sprite.**]

es·prit de corps (es prē′ də kôr′), group spirit; sense of union and of common interests and responsibilities in some group; comradeship: *The club's strong esprit de corps showed itself in the intense loyalty, devotion, and enthusiasm of its members.* [< French *esprit de corps*]

es·prit fort (es prē′ fôr′), *French.* **1** a strong-minded person; freethinker. **2** (literally) strong spirit.

es·py (es pī′), *v.t.,* **-pied, -py·ing.** **1** to see at a distance; catch sight of: *He espied the castle from afar.* SYN: spy, descry. **2** *Archaic.* to spy on: *Now question me no more; we are espied* (Shakespeare). [< Old French *espier* < Germanic (compare Old High German *spëhōn*)]

Esq. or **Esqr.**, Esquire.
▶**Esq., Esquire**. Following a person's name in the inside and outside address of a letter, *Esq.* or *Esquire* is formal. In the United States it is not often used except when addressing letters to professional men, and women, especially lawyers, architects, engineers, and journalists. When it is used, other titles (such as *Mr., Dr., Hon.*) are omitted: *Harry A. Kinne, Esq.*

e·squa·mate (ē skwā′māt), *adj. Zoology.* having no scales. [< *e-*[1] + *squamate*]

-esque, *suffix forming adjectives from other adjectives or from nouns.* **1** in the ______ style; resembling the ______ style: *Romanesque = resembling the Roman style.* **2** like a ______; like that of a ______: *Statuesque = like a statue.* [< French *-esque* < Italian *-esco* < Germanic (compare Old English *-isc* -ish)]

Es·qui·line (es′kwə līn), *n.* one of the seven hills of Rome.

Es·qui·mau (es′kə mō), *n., pl.* **-maux** (-mō, -mōz), **-mau**, *adj.* = Eskimo. [< French *Esquimau*]

es·quire (es kwīr′, es′kwīr), *n., v.,* **-quired, -quir·ing.** —***n.*** **1** (in the Middle Ages) a young man of noble family who attended a knight until he himself was made a knight; squire. **2a** an Englishman ranking next below a knight. **b** any Englishman who practices a profession or belongs to the upper middle class; a gentleman. **3** *Archaic.* an English country gentleman; a squire. **4** a gentleman who attends or escorts a lady in public.
—***v.t.*** **1** to raise to the rank of esquire. **2** to address as Esquire. **3** to escort (a lady) as an esquire.
[< Old French *esquier* < Latin *scūtārius* shield-bearer < *scūtum* shield]

Es·quire (es kwīr′, es′kwīr), *n.* a title of respect placed after a person's last name instead of *Mr.* (or *Mrs., Ms.*) before the name: *John Jones, Esquire = Mr. John Jones; Mary May, Esquire = Ms. or Mrs. Mary May. Abbr:* Esq. or Esqr.
▶See **Esq.** for usage note.

ESR (no periods), electron spin resonance (a technique for detecting and identifying radicals by the magnetic properties of their odd electron): *In ... ESR, a strong magnetic field is applied to the sample and the energy absorption is measured when the odd electrons flip their spins from being aligned in the same direction as the field to being aligned in the opposite direction* (Scientific American).

ESRO (no periods), European Space Research Organization (a group of ten European countries engaged in joint space research), replaced by ESA in 1975.

es·rog (es′rōg), *n., pl.* **es·rogs, es·ro·gim** (es rō′gim). = ethrog.

ess (es), *n.* **1** the 19th letter of the alphabet (S, s). **2** anything shaped like an S.

-ess, *suffix added to nouns to form other nouns.* a female ______: *Lioness = a female lion. Hostess = a female host. Stewardess = a female steward. Sculptress = a female sculptor.* [< Old French *-esse* < Latin *-issa* < Greek *-issa*]
▶A number of nouns containing the feminine suffix **-ess** are in use. Several, however, have acquired derogatory connotations. *Jewess* and *Negress* are now generally avoided as likely to give offense. *Authoress* is sometimes objected to as carrying in its use a certain male condescension. Similar objections have been raised to *poetess* and *sculptress*, the terms *poet* and *sculptor* being applied to both male and female.
▶The suffix is pronounced (-is) or (-əs), but in this dictionary only the former is listed. The pronunciation (-es) occurs in *princess* and in words where the suffix has secondary stress.

ESSA (no periods), Environmental Science Services Administration (absorbed into the National Oceanic and Atmospheric Administration).

es·say (*n. 1, 3, 4* es′ā; *n. 2* es′ā, e sā′; *v.* e sā′), *n., v.* —***n.*** **1** a literary composition on a particular subject. An essay is usually shorter and more personal but less methodical than a treatise. **2** a try; an attempt: *He made an ineffective essay at conversation, then lapsed into silence.* SYN: effort, endeavor. **3** a sample or trial design of a postage stamp considered but not used for issue. **4** *Obsolete.* a testing or experiment: *I hope ... he wrote this but as an essay or taste of my virtue* (Shakespeare).
—***v.t.*** **1** to try; attempt: *The student essayed his first solo flight.* **2** to put to the test.
[< Old French *essai* < Latin *exagium* a weighing < *ex-* out + *agere* do, act] —**es·say′er**, *n.*

es·say·ette (es′ā et′), *n.* a short essay.

es·say·i·cal (e sā′ə kəl), *adj.* of the nature of an essay.

es·say·ist (es′ā ist), *n.* a writer of essays.

es·say·is·tic (es′ā is′tik), *adj.* **1** of or in the style of the essay: *essayistic prose, essayistic literature.* **2** digressive in the manner of an essay: *With Professor Williams, who had the truly essayistic mind, one thing invariably suggested another* (Wall Street Journal).

essay question, a question in a written test that must be answered in the form of a composition: *Some educators deplored the passing of the old essay question ("Discuss the consequences of the Dred Scott decision") in favor of the objective type ("The chief justice in the Dred Scott Case was: 1. John C. Calhoun, 2. Roger B. Taney, 3. William Lloyd Garrison, 4. Salmon P. Chase, 5. Stephen A. Douglas")* (Time).

es·se (es′ē), *n. Latin.* existence; being.

Es·se·le·ni·an (es′ə lē′nē ən), *n.* a linguistic stock of North American Indians, formerly inhabiting a narrow strip of coast in California.

es·sence (es′əns), *n.* **1** that which makes a thing what it is; necessary part or parts; important feature or features: *Being thoughtful of others is the essence of politeness. History is the essence of innumerable biographies* (Thomas Carlyle). SYN: heart, substance. **2** any concentrated preparation that has the characteristic flavor, fragrance, or effect of the plant, fruit, drug, or the like, from which it was obtained: *Atropine is the essence of the belladonna plant.* SYN: extract. **3** a solution of such a substance in alcohol: *Essence of peppermint is oil of peppermint dissolved in alcohol.* **4** a perfume. SYN: scent. **5** *Figurative.* something that is, especially a spiritual or immaterial entity: *that ineffable essence which we call spirit* (Emerson). **6** *Philosophy.* the inward nature or true substance of anything.

in essence, essentially: *In essence, the U.S. agreed to exempt new issues of Canadian securities from excise taxes* (Wall Street Journal).

of the essence, essential; of great importance: *Time is of the essence.*

[< Latin *essentia* < *esse* to be]

es|sence d'o|ri|ent (es'əns dōr'ē ənt; *French* e säNS dô ryäN'), = pearl essence. [< French *essence d'orient* (literally) essence of the Orient]

Es|sene (es'ēn, e sēn'), *n.* a member of a brotherhood or monastic order of Jews in ancient Palestine, from about 100 B.C. to about 100 A.D., characterized by asceticism, celibacy, and strict observance of the non-Levitical portion of the Mosaic law. [< plural *Essenes* < Latin *Essēnī* < Greek *Essēnoí*]

Es|se|ni|an (e sē'nē ən), *adj.* of or having to do with the Essenes.

Es|sen|ic (e sen'ik), *adj.* = Essenian.

Es|sen|i|cal (e sen'ə kəl), *adj.* = Essenian.

Es|se|nism (es'ə niz əm), *n.* the doctrines, principles, or practices of the Essenes: *There were elements in Essenism that sound as if they had come from Persia or Babylonia: the non-Jewish rite of baptism and the early morning practice of sun worship* (New Yorker).

es|sen|tial (ə sen'shəl), *adj., n.* —*adj.* **1** needed to make a thing what it is; very important; necessary: *Good food and enough rest are essential to good health.* SYN: indispensable, requisite, vital. See syn. under **necessary**. **2** of or making up the essence of a substance: *the essential coldness of ice. Essential color is the color of a mineral without any impurities in it.* See also **essential oil**. **3** being or containing the essence, or fragrance, flavor, and medicinal qualities, of a plant or other material: *essential odors.* **4** being such by its essence or very nature, or in the highest sense: *essential happiness, essential poetry.*

—*n.* an absolutely necessary element or quality; fundamental feature: *Learn the essentials first; then learn the details.*

[< Late Latin *essentiālis* < Latin *essentia;* see etym. under **essence**] —**es|sen'tial|ness**, *n.*

essential hypertension, *Medicine.* hypertension when its cause is unknown.

es|sen|tial|ism (ə sen'shə liz əm), *n.* **1** *Education.* the theory that basic cultural ideals and attitudes should be identified and taught systematically to all students. **2** *Philosophy.* a theory or belief that emphasizes the essence of things.

es|sen|tial|ist (ə sen'shə list), *n.* a person who believes in or practices essentialism.

es|sen|ti|al|i|ty (ə sen'shē al'ə tē), *n., pl.* **-ties.** **1** essential quality: *Transcribing hubby's convention jottings or going with him to luncheon and dinner meetings isn't enough to establish a wife's essentiality, the Internal Revenue Service held* (Wall Street Journal). **2** an essential element or point.

es|sen|tial|ize (ə sen'shə līz), *v.t.,* **-ized, -iz|ing.** to raise to essential character; express the essential form of.

es|sen|tial|ly (ə sen'shə lē), *adv.* in essence; in essentials; in an essential manner.

essential oil, a volatile oil that has the characteristic flavor or fragrance of the plant or fruit from which it is extracted. It is used in making perfume and flavorings.

essential proposition, *Logic.* a proposition which predicates of a subject something that is implied in its definition.

es|se quam vi|de|ri (es'ē kwam vi dir'ī), *Latin.* to be rather than to seem (the motto of North Carolina).

Es|sex (es'iks), *n.* any one of a small, black breed of hogs valued chiefly for rapid growth and early maturity, originating in Essex, England.

es|soin (e soin'), *n.* **1** a former practice in English law courts of accepting certain excuses for not appearing in court at the appointed time. **2** the excuse itself. Essoins of pilgrimage or of illness were often accepted. [< Old French *essoine,* ultimately < Latin *ex-* out + Late Latin *sonium* care, worry]

es|so|nite (es'ə nīt), *n.* a cinnamon-colored variety of garnet. Also, **hessonite**. [< Greek *hḗssōn* less + English *-ite*[1] (because it is less hard than some similar minerals)]

es|so|rant (es'ər ant), *adj. Heraldry.* (of an eagle or other bird) about to soar; standing with the wings lifted up as if about to rise on the wing. [< Old French *essorant,* present participle of *essorer* soar]

est (est), *n.* a method of training people to achieve self-realization by combining Zen Buddhist concepts with austere exercises, including exposure to harsh treatment, verbal abuse, and the like. [< *E*(rhard) *S*(eminar) *T*(raining)]

-est, *suffix forming the superlative degree of adjectives and adverbs.* most: *Warmest = most warm. Slowest = most slow.*

[Old English *-est-, -ost-*]

▶ The suffix is pronounced (-ist) or (-əst), but in this dictionary only the former is listed. The pronunciation (-est) is sometimes used in reading verse, particularly when the suffix rhymes with a stressed syllable, as in *best-loveliest.*

est., an abbreviation for the following:
1 established.
2 estate.
3 estimated.
4 estuary.

E.S.T., EST (no periods), or **e.s.t.**, **1** Eastern Standard Time. **2** electric shock therapy.

estab., established.

es|tab|lish (es tab'lish), *v.t.* **1** to set up on a firm or lasting basis: *to establish a government or a business. The English established colonies in America.* SYN: found, institute. See syn. under **fix**. **2a** to settle in a position; set up in business: *A new doctor has established himself on this street.* **b** to settle (oneself) in a place or position: *He established himself near the fire.* **3** to cause to be accepted and used for a long time: *to establish a custom.* SYN: enact, ordain. **4** to show beyond dispute; prove: *to establish a claim. He established his innocence by showing that he was in another city when the theft was committed.* SYN: verify, substantiate. **5** to bring about (a more or less settled state of affairs): *It has been hard work to establish order here* (Dickens). **6** to make (a church) a national institution recognized and supported by the government. **7** in card games: **a** to obtain such control of (a suit) that a player can count on taking all the remaining tricks of it. **b** to make (a card) the highest remaining in its suit by causing higher cards to be played. [< Old French *establiss-,* stem of *establir* < Latin *stabilīre* make stable < *stabilis* stable, steady < *stāre* to stand] —**es|tab'lish|er**, *n.*

es|tab|lish|a|ble (es tab'li shə bəl), *adj.* that can be established.

es|tab|lished church (es tab'lisht), a church that is a national institution, recognized and supported by the government; state church.

Established Church, = Church of England.

es|tab|lish|ment (es tab'lish mənt), *n.* **1** the act or process of establishing: *The establishment of the business took several years.* **2** the condition of being established: *The custom has already achieved establishment.* **3** something established. A household, business, church, or army is an establishment. **4** Often, **the Establishment**. **a** the ruling groups or institutions of a country; a nation's power structure: *If the Establishment means anything, it means big government and big business, and between them they pay most of the bills for big science* (Atlantic). **b** the ruling circle of any institution (usually preceded by a modifier): *A sizable minority of senators tried unsuccessfully to reduce the size and influence of the military establishment by cutting the weapons procurement requests of the Department of Defense* (Robert M. Lawrence). **c** conventional society: *The revival of pearls, downgraded in past years for representing the tired chic of the establishment, was one of the big accessory events ...* (Ruth Mary DuBois). **5a** the recognition by the state of a church as the official church. **b** a church thus recognized by the state. **6** Usually, **the Establishment**. the Church of England or the Presbyterian Church of Scotland. **7** a settled income; secure livelihood. **8** settlement in life; steady or permanent position, formerly usually by marriage: *... their anxiety for the establishment of their daughters* (Edward G. Bulwer-Lytton). **9** *Obsolete.* a settled constitution or government.

es|tab|lish|men|tar|i|an (es tab'lish men tãr'ē ən), *n., adj.* —*n.* **1** a person who supports the principle of an established church. **2** an adherent of the Established Church. **3** a person who belongs to or favors the Establishment: *[He] has defined the true Establishmentarians as the pivotal Republicans who are given top posts in Democratic Administrations* (David Halberstam).
—*adj.* **1** advocating the principle of an established church. **2** belonging to the Established Church. **3** of or favoring the Establishment.

es|tab|lish|men|tar|i|an|ism (es tab'lish men tãr'ē ə niz'əm), *n.* the tenets of an establishmentarian; attachment to the principle of a state church.

es|ta|cade (es'tə kād', -käd'), *n.* a dike or barrier of piles or the like set in the sea, a bay, a river, or lake, to check the approach of an enemy or protect against floating objects. [< French *estacade* < Spanish *estacada* < *estaca* stake]

es|ta|fette (es'tə fet'), *n.* a mounted courier. [< French *estafette* < Italian *staffetta* (diminutive) < *staffa* stirrup]

es|ta|mi|net (es tá mē ne'), *n. French.* **1** a small restaurant or coffee house. **2** a taproom.

es|tam|page (es tam'pij), *n.* an impression on paper of an inscription. [< French *estampage* < *estamper* to stamp]

es|tan|cia (es tän'syä), *n.* a large ranch or estate in Latin America: *One of the estancias visited by the writer—San José de la Tinta near Tandil—is 12,000 hectares and is just one of several estancias owned by the Santamarina family* (New York Times). [< Spanish *estancia* (literally) station < Medieval Latin *stantia* < Latin *stāre* stand]

es|tan|cie|ro (es tän'sye'rō), *n., pl.* **-ros.** a farmer in Latin America. [< Spanish *estanciero* < *estancia;* see etym. under **estancia**]

es|tate (es tāt'), *n., v.,* **-tat|ed, -tat|ing.** —*n.* **1** a large piece of land belonging to a person; landed property: *He has a beautiful estate 40 miles from New York with a country house and a swimming pool on it.* **2** that which a person owns; property; possessions: *When the rich man died, he left an estate of two million dollars. Land and buildings are real estate.* **3** *British.* **a** an area of land, usually near a city or town, used for a building development. **b** such an area together with the houses, shops, and other facilities, built on it. **4** a condition or stage in life: *A boy reaches man's estate at the age of 21.* **5** a class or group of people in a nation forming a social or political division: *We know your tenderness of heart ... to all estates* (Shakespeare). **6** *Archaic.* rank; status; standing: *O that estates, degrees, and offices were not derived corruptly* (Shakespeare). **7** *Obsolete.* display of grandeur.

—*v.t.* to establish (a person) in an estate; provide with an estate: *Then would I ... estate them with large land and territory* (Tennyson).

the three estates, the clergymen, noblemen, and common people, especially in France at the time of the French Revolution: *The French legislative assembly representing the three estates, called the States-General, was summoned only in emergencies; the last began the revolution of 1789.*

[< Old French *estat,* learned borrowing from Latin *status, -ūs* state < *stāre* stand. See etym. of doublets **state, status.**]

estate agent, *British.* a person who conducts business in real estate; a real-estate agent or broker.

estate car, *British.* a station wagon.

estate duty, *British.* = estate tax.

Es|tates-Gen|er|al (es tāts'jen'ər əl, -jen'rəl), *n.* = States-General.

estate tax, *U.S.* a tax placed on an estate before it is divided among the heirs: *Both inheritance and estate taxes are direct and progressive* (Charles J. Gaa).

estate wagon, *Especially British.* station wagon.

es|teem (es tēm'), *v., n.* —*v.t.* **1** to have a very favorable opinion of; think highly of: *We esteem courage.* SYN: See syn. under **value**. **2** to think; consider: *He esteemed the slowest way to be the safest way. Men have often esteemed happiness the greatest good.* **3** to estimate the value of; assess the merit of; appraise (at).

—*n.* **1** a very favorable opinion; high regard: *Courage is held in esteem.* SYN: estimation, respect, favor, admiration, honor. **2** *Archaic.* opinion; judgment. **3** *Archaic.* account; worth; reputation: *a man of great esteem.*

[< Old French *estimer,* learned borrowing from Latin *aestimāre* to value. See etym. of doublet **aim.**]

es|ter (es'tər), *n.* a compound produced by the reaction between an acid and an alcohol by the elimination of a water molecule. In such a reaction the acid hydrogen of the acid is replaced by the hydrocarbon radical of the alcohol. Animal and vegetable fats and oils are esters. *Many esters have extremely pleasant fruity odors* (Monroe M. Offner). [< German *Ester,* probably contraction of *Essigäther* < *Essig* vinegar + *Äther* ether; coined by L. Gmelin, 1788-1853, a German chemist, to contrast with *ether*]

es|ter|ase (es'tə rās), *n.* any ferment or enzyme that can decompose an ester into an acid and alcohol (with the addition of a molecule of water).

es|ter|i|fi|a|ble (es ter'ə fī'ə bəl), *adj.* that can be changed into an ester or esters.

es|ter|i|fi|ca|tion (es ter'ə fə kā'shən), *n.* **1** the process of esterifying. **2** the state of being esterified.

es|ter|i|fy (es ter'ə fī), *v.t., v.i.,* **-fied, -fy|ing.** to change or be changed into an ester.

es|ter|i|za|tion (es'tər ə zā'shən), *n.* = esterification.

es|ter|ize (es'tə rīz), *v.t., v.i.,* **-ized, -iz|ing.** = esterify.

Esth (est), *n.* an Estonian.

Esth., Esther (book of the Bible).

Es|ther (es'tər), *n.* in the Bible: **1** the Jewish wife of Ahasuerus, a Persian king, who saved her people from a massacre plotted by Haman. **2** the book of the Old Testament that tells her story.

Pronunciation Key: hat, āge, cãre, fär; let, ēqual, tėrm, it, īce; hot, ōpen, ôrder; oil, out; cup, pu̇t, rüle; child; long; thin; ᴛʜen; zh, measure; ə represents **a** in about, **e** in taken, **i** in pencil, **o** in lemon, **u** in circus.

The scroll of Esther is read at the Jewish festival of Purim.

es|the|sia (es thē′zhə, -zhē ə), *n.* = aesthesia.

es|the|si|om|e|ter (es thē′zē om′ə tər, -sē-), *n.* an instrument for measuring the degree of sensitivity to touch, especially by finding how close two points pressed against the skin can be to each other and yet be felt as distinct points. Also, **aesthesiometer**.

es|the|si|o|met|ric (es thē′zē ə met′rik, -sē-), *adj.* having to do with the esthesiometer or its use.

es|the|sis (es thē′sis), *n.* = aesthesis.

es|thete (es′thēt), *n.* = aesthete.

es|thet|ic (es thet′ik), *adj., n.* = aesthetic: *No culture is known in which some form of esthetic expression does not occur* (Beals and Hoijer).

es|thet|i|cal (es thet′ə kəl), *adj.* = aesthetical.

es|thet|i|cal|ly (es thet′ə klē), *adv.* = aesthetically.

es|the|ti|cian (es′thə tish′ən), *n.* = aesthetician.

es|thet|i|cism (es thet′ə siz əm), *n.* = aestheticism.

es|thet|ics (es thet′iks), *n.* = aesthetics.

Es|tho|ni|an (es tō′nē ən, -thō′-), *n., adj.* = Estonian.

es|ti|ma|ble (es′tə mə bəl), *adj.* **1** worthy of esteem; deserving high regard: *a hardworking, thrifty, estimable young man. Unselfishness is an estimable trait.* SYN: reputable, respectable, meritorius, excellent. **2** capable of being estimated or calculated: *The value of a friend is not estimable.* SYN: calculable, computable. **3** *Obsolete.* valuable: *A pound of man's flesh ... Is not so estimable ... As flesh of muttons, beefs, or goats* (Shakespeare). **—es′ti|ma|ble|ness**, *n.*

es|ti|ma|bly (es′tə mə blē), *adv.* in an estimable manner.

es|ti|mate (*n.* es′tə mit, -māt; *v.* es′tə māt), *n., v.,* **-mat|ed, -mat|ing.** **—*n.*** **1** a judgment or opinion about how much, how many, how good, etc.: *My estimate of the length of the room was 15 feet; it actually measured 14 feet, 9 inches.* **2** a statement of what certain work will cost, made by one willing to do the work: *The painter's estimate for painting the house was $1,500.*

—*v.t.* **1** to form a judgment or opinion about (how much, how many, how good, or the like): *The gardener estimated that it would take him four hours to weed the garden.* **2** to fix the worth, size, amount, quality, or condition of, especially in a rough way; calculate approximately: *to estimate one's losses, estimate the cost of a trip. He estimated his time as worth twice what he received.* SYN: reckon, gauge. **3** *Obsolete.* to assign a value to; appraise; value.

—*v.i.* to draw up or submit a statement of the cost of doing a specified piece of work or the price at which a contractor is prepared to undertake it.

[< Latin *aestimāre* (with English *-ate*[1]) to value]

— *Syn.* *v.t.* **1, 2 Estimate, appraise, evaluate** mean to judge the measure, weight, or value of someone or something. **Estimate** means to make a judgment regarding amount, number, value, or the like, under such circumstances that the result is not likely to be exactly right: *They estimated the tree to be thirty feet high.* **Appraise** means to make an expert judgment about some thing or things, and implies that the result given is correct or cannot be questioned: *The stolen necklace had been appraised at $15,000.* **Evaluate** suggests a judgment in terms of something besides money: *She evaluates people by their clothes.*

es|ti|ma|tion (es′tə mā′shən), *n.* **1** opinion or judgment: *In my estimation, your plan will not work.* **2** esteem; respect: *The doctor was held in high estimation by the community.* SYN: regard. **3** the act or process of estimating. SYN: valuation.

es|ti|ma|tive (es′tə mā′tiv), *adj.* having to do with or capable of estimating.

es|ti|ma|tor (es′tə mā′tər), *n.* a person who estimates or judges.

e|stip|u|late (ē stip′yə lit, -lāt), *adj.* = exstipulate.

es|ti|val (es′tə vəl, es tī′-), *adj.* of or having to do with summer. Also, **aestival.** [< Latin *aestīvālis* < *aestīvus*, adjective to *aestās* summer]

es|ti|vate (es′tə vāt), *v.i.,* **-vat|ed, -vat|ing. 1** *Zoology.* to spend the summer in a dormant or torpid condition. Some snakes and rodents estivate. **2** to spend the summer. Also, **aestivate.** [< Latin *aestivāre* (with English *-ate*[1]) to reside during the summer]

es|ti|va|tion (es′tə vā′shən), *n.* **1** *Zoology.* the act of remaining dormant during the summer. **2** *Botany.* the disposition of the parts of a flower in the bud. Also, **aestivation.**

es|ti|va|tor (es′tə vā′tər), *n.* an estivating animal. Also, **aestivator.**

es|ti|vo-au|tum|nal (es′tə vō ô tum′nəl), *adj.* of, occurring in, or having to do with both summer and autumn: *estivo-autumnal malaria.*

✱es|toile (es toil′, -twäl′), *n. Heraldry.* a star-shaped figure, continually having six points and wavy rays. [< Old French *estoile* < Latin *stella* star]

✱estoile

Es|to|ni|an (es tō′nē ən), *n., adj.* **—*n.*** **1** one of a Finnish people inhabiting Estonia and the neighboring parts of the Soviet Union. **2** the Finno-Ugric language of this people.

—*adj.* of or having to do with Estonia, the Estonians, or their language. Also, **Esthonian.**

es|top (es top′), *v.t.,* **-topped, -top|ping. 1** *Law.* to prevent from asserting or doing something contrary to a previous assertion or act. **2** *Rare.* to stop; prevent. **3** *Archaic.* to bar; obstruct. [< Anglo-French *estopper* < Late Latin *stuppāre* cram with tow or wax < Latin *stuppa* tow, oakum < Greek *stýppē.* See etym. of doublet **stop.**]

es|to per|pe|tu|a (es′tō pər pech′ü ə), *Latin.* may she endure forever (the motto of Idaho).

es|top|page (es top′ij), *n.* **1** the act or process of estopping. **2** the condition of being estopped.

es|top|pel (es top′əl), *n.* **1** *Law.* an impediment that prevents a person from asserting or doing something contrary to his own previous assertion or act. **2** the act or process of estopping. [apparently < Old French *estouppail* < *estopper;* see etym. under **estop**]

es|to|que (es tō′kā), *n. Spanish.* a short sword used for killing the bull in bullfighting.

es|to|vers (es tō′vərz), *n.pl.* **1** the necessary supplies, especially wood and timber, allowed by law to a tenant for repairs. **2** (in common law) alimony. [noun use of Old French *estover, estovoir* be necessary, ultimately < Latin *est opus* it is necessary]

es|trade (es träd′, -trād′), *n.* a raised platform; dais: *I mounted the estrade ... where stood the teacher's desk and chair* (Charlotte Brontë). [< French *estrade* < Spanish *estrado* carpeted part of a room, ultimately < Latin *sternere* spread with carpets]

es|tra|di|ol (es′trə dī′ōl, -ol), *n.* a crystalline estrogen related to estrone, used medicinally in the treatment of disorders of the sexual organs and certain malignancies. *Formula:* $C_{18}H_{24}O_2$: *Male embryos of the toad had been changed into egg-laying females by giving them estradiol, a female hormone* (Science News Letter). Also, **oestradiol.** [< *estrus* + *di-*[1] + *-ol*[1]]

es|tra|gon (es′trə gon), *n.* = tarragon. [< Middle French *estragon* < earlier *targon;* see etym. under **tarragon**]

es|tral (es′trəl), *adj.* = estrous: *estral cycle.*

es|trange (es trānj′), *v.t.,* **-tranged, -trang|ing. 1** to turn (a person) from affection to indifference, dislike, or hatred; make unfriendly; separate: *A quarrel had estranged him from his family.* SYN: alienate. **2** to keep apart; keep away: *estranged from politics* (Alexander Pope). **3** to divert to a new or different use: *They ... have estranged this place, and have burned incense in it unto other gods* (Jeremiah 19:4). [< Old French *estrangier* < Latin *extrāneāre* < *extrāneus* foreign; see etym. under **extraneous.** See related etym. at **strange.**] **—es|trang′er**, *n.*

es|tran|ge|lo (es strang′gə lō), *n.* an archaic form of the Syriac alphabet. [< Syriac *estrangelō*]

es|trange|ment (es trānj′mənt), *n.* **1** the act or process of estranging; turning away in feeling: *Their gradual estrangement began when they started to live such different lives.* **2** the condition of being estranged; becoming distant or unfriendly: *A misunderstanding had caused the estrangement of the two friends.*

es|tray (es trā′), *n., v.* **—*n.*** **1** a stray person, animal, or thing. **2** *Law.* a stray domestic animal whose owner is not known.

—*v.i.* *Archaic.* to stray.

[< Anglo-French *estray* < Old French *estraier* to stray]

es|treat (es trēt′), *n., v.* in English Law: **—*n.*** a true copy or extract of an original record or writing on the rolls of a court, especially of a fine.

—*v.t.* **1** to make an extract of (a fine or bail) from the records of a court, for prosecution. **2** to exact under an estreat, or as a fine or levy.

[< Anglo-French *estrete,* Old French *estraite* < *estraire* < Latin *extrahere* to extract]

es|treat|ment (es trēt′mənt), *n.* the act or process of estreating.

es|trepe (es trēp′), *v.t.,* **-treped, -trep|ing.** to spoil or waste (land); cause estrepement to; destroy needlessly.

es|trepe|ment (es trēp′mənt), *n.* **1** the spoiling of lands, especially by a tenant. **2** making land barren by continual ploughing.

Es|trild (es′trild), *n.* Estrildis.

Es|tril|dis (es tril′dis), *n.* the mythical daughter of a German king, loved by Locrine and the mother by him of Sabrina.

es|trin (es′trin), *n.* **1** = estrone. **2** = estrogen. Also, **oestrin.**

es|tri|ol (es′trē ōl, -ol), *n.* a crystalline hormone, an estrogen that causes or promotes estrus, found in the urine of pregnant females. It is a phenol alcohol. *Formula:* $C_{18}H_{24}O_3$ Also, **oestriol.** [< *estrus* + *-ol*[1]]

es|tro|gen (es′trə jən), *n.* any one of various hormones that induce a series of physiological changes in females, especially in the reproductive or sexual organs. Also, **oestrogen.** [< New Latin *estrus* (see etym. under **estrus**) + English *-gen*]

es|tro|gen|ic (es′trə jen′ik), *adj.* **1** causing or promoting estrus. **2** of an estrogen or estrogens.

Es|tron (es′tron), *n. Trademark.* a synthetic yarn and fiber of cellulose acetate that in addition to its use in textiles is useful especially in the making of electrical insulation, oilcloth, and linoleum: *Estron ... looks and feels like a nubby linen knit and can be washed by hand* (New Yorker).

es|trone (es′trōn), *n.* **1** a female hormone, an estrogen, that causes or promotes estrus and stimulates growth of the reproductive organs. *Formula:* $C_{18}H_{22}O_2$ Also, **oestrone. 2** an extract of this hormone used to relieve ailments accompanying menopause; theelin. [< *estr*(us) + *-one*]

es|trous (es′trəs), *adj.* having to do with or causing the estrus. Also, **oestrous.**

estrous cycle, the recurrent bodily changes in the sexual and other organs connected with estrus (def. 1) in the female of the lower mammals. Also, **oestrous** or **oestrus cycle.**

es|tru|al (es′trü əl), *adj.* = estrous.

es|trum (es′trəm), *n.* = estrus. Also, **oestrum.**

es|trus (es′trəs), *n.* **1** a periodically recurring state of sexual activity in most female mammals during which mating may take place; heat. **2** = estrous cycle. Also, **oestrus.** [< New Latin *estrus* < Latin *oestrus* frenzy; gadfly < Greek *oîstros* gadfly]

es|tu|ar|i|al (es′chü ãr′ē əl), *adj.* of or having to do with an estuary; estuarine.

es|tu|a|rine (es′chü ər in), *adj.* **1** of or having to do with an estuary: *... the romantically wild estuarine haunts of the wild fowl round our coasts* (Listener). **2** formed or deposited in an estuary.

es|tu|ar|y (es′chü er′ē), *n., pl.* **-ar|ies. 1** a broad mouth of a river, into which the tide flows: *An estuary is a semi-enclosed, coastal body of water which has free connection with the open sea and within which sea water is measurably diluted with fresh water derived from land drainage* (D. W. Pritchard). **2** an inlet of the sea. SYN: firth. [< Latin *aestuārium* < *aestus, -ūs* boiling (of the sea), tide]

es|tu|fa (es tü′fä), *n.* an underground chamber, in which a fire is kept constantly burning; used by the Pueblo Indians of Spanish North America as a place of assembly; kiva.

e.s.u., esu (no periods), or **E.S.U.,** electrostatic unit or units.

e|su|ri|ence (i sůr′ē əns), *n.* hunger; appetite.

e|su|ri|en|cy (i sůr′ē ən sē), *n.* = esurience.

e|su|ri|ent (i sůr′ē ənt), *adj.* hungry; greedy: *an esurient unprovided advocate: Danton* (Thomas Carlyle). [< Latin *ēsuriēns, -entis,* present participle of *ēsurīre* to be hungry] **—e|su′ri|ent|ly,** *adv.*

-et, *suffix forming nouns from other nouns.* little ______: *Owlet = a little owl. Islet = a little isle.* This meaning has, however, disappeared in most words formed by adding *-et,* as in *turret, tablet.* [< Old French *-et* < Vulgar Latin; origin uncertain]

▶The suffix is pronounced (-it) or (-ət), but in this dictionary only the former is listed.

Et (no period), *Chemistry.* ethyl.

e.t., elapsed time.

E.T. or **ET** (no periods), **1** Eastern Time. **2** electrical transcription. **3** ephemeris time.

✱e|ta[1] (ā′tə, ē′-), *n.* the seventh letter of the Greek alphabet, corresponding to English long a (ā). [< Greek *ēta* (originally H) < Hebrew *hēth*]

✱eta[1]

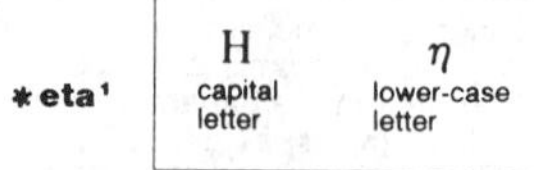

e|ta[2] (e′tä), *n.* **1** a former Japanese caste consisting of laborers and workers living in segregated slums and held to be inferior to the rest of the population. **2** a member of the eta caste. [< Japanese *eta*]

ETA (no periods) or **E.T.A.,** estimated time of arrival.

e|taac (ā tāk′), *n.* = blaubok.

E|ta Ca|ri|nae (ā′tə kə rī′nē), a star in the southern constellation Carina noted for its periodic explosions and the increased brightness they produce. [< Greek *êta* eta[1] + Latin *carīnae,* genitive of *carīna* keel]

e|tae|ri|o (i tir′ē ō), *n. Botany.* a fruit consisting of a mass of achenes, drupelets, or follicles, such as the strawberry. Also, **hetaerio.** [< New Latin *etaerio* < Greek *hetaîros* an associate]

é|tage (ā tȧzh′), *n. French.* a story or floor of a house.

***é|ta|gère** (ā tȧ zher′), *n. French.* a stand with open shelves for small ornaments or bric-a-brac; whatnot: *Antique apothecary jars were arranged on the gilded shelves of a slim étagère* (New Yorker).

***étagère**

et al. (*often pronounced* et al, ôl), **1** and others (Latin, *et alii*): *I moved back to Manhattan—wife, kids, lawn furniture, dog, et al.* (Esquire). **2** and elsewhere (Latin, *et alibi*): *By the thousands, young and old Cubans are trekking to Prague, Moscow, Leningrad et al. to learn fishing, technology, Russian, and of course, Marxist-Leninism* (Look).

► **Et alii** means "and other (people)," but is now frequently used to mean "and other things," though *etc.* is the usual abbreviation.

et|a|lon (et′ə lon), *n.* an interferometer used in physics and astronomy to measure wave lengths of light, producing fringes by reflection rather than by transmission: *High resolving power can be obtained with etalons* (New Scientist). [< French *etalon* standard of values]

e|ta meson (ā′tə, ē′-), a meson of zero electric charge, having a mass 1072 times that of the electron. Eta mesons decay to form pi-mesons and gamma rays.

Et|a|min (et′ə min′), *n.* a star of the second magnitude in the constellation Draco.

et|a|mine (et′ə min, -mēn), *n.* **1** a light cotton or worsted fabric with a loose weave, used for clothing. **2** a kind of embroidered canvas. **3** a worsted fabric with a highly twisted yarn in an open weave. [< French *étamine*]

é|tape (ā tȧp′), *n. French.* **1** a public storehouse. **2a** an allowance of supplies for soldiers on the march. **b** the halting place at the end of a march. **c** the distance marched by troops during one day. **3** (in old Russia) a stockade used to confine and shelter exiles or refugees going from one place to another.

é|tat (ā tȧ′), *n., pl.* **é|tats** (ā tȧ′). *French.* **1** state; condition. **2** position, rank, or calling. **3** an estate or social order. **4** a government; a commonwealth or nation.

e|tat|ism (ā tät′iz əm), *n.* **1** extreme development of the power of the state over the individual citizen: *Where is the antithesis between etatism and liberalism here, or between collectivism and individualism, for that matter?* (Manchester Guardian Weekly). **2** a form of socialism in which the state uses its power to improve social conditions; state socialism. [< French *étatisme*]

é|ta|tisme (ā tȧ tēz′mə), *n. French.* etatism.

e|ta|tist or **é|ta|tist** (ā tät′ist), *adj.* characterized by or favoring etatism: *an etatist society, an étatist structure of industry.* [< French *étatiste,* adjective and noun]

etc., et cetera: *Symbolism plays a much greater role in the Japanese mentality—in language, gesture, sensibility, dress, etc.—than in Western consciousness* (Saturday Review).

► **etc., et cetera.** *Etc.,* usually read *"and so forth,"* is a convenient abbreviation, widely current in reference and business usage: *The case is suitable for carrying prints, maps, blueprints, etc. Etc.* in this and similar sentences shows that the sentence applies to other similar items in addition to the ones mentioned. It is inappropriate however, in a sentence like this: *A student's professors can be of immense aid to him because of their knowledge of boys and their habits, customs, needs, ideals, etc.* Writing out *et cetera* now seems an affectation, and in consecutive writing is usually replaced by *and so forth. And etc.* is a gross error, indicating that the writer does not realize that the *et* of *etc.* means *and* and thus is really saying *"and and so forth."*

et cet|er|a (et set′ər ə, set′rə), and others; and the rest; and so forth; and so on; and the like. *Abbr:* etc. [< Latin *et cētera* and other things]

► See **etc.** for usage note.

et|cet|er|as (et set′ər əz, -set′rəz), *n.pl.* extra things; usual additions: *the hundred etceteras of travelling baggage* (Charles J. Lever).

etch (ech), *v., n.* —*v.t.* **1** to engrave (a design) on metal, glass, wood, mineral, or plastic by acid or heat that burns lines into it. Filled with ink, the lines of the design will reproduce a copy on paper. **2** to engrave (metal, glass, mineral, wood, or plastic) by this process: *The artist etched only a few copperplates.* **3** *Figurative.* to impress deeply; fix firmly; engrave: *Her face was etched in my memory. The author ... can etch a flying moment with a sharpness denied Dreiser* (Manchester Guardian Weekly).

—*v.i.* to use this method of producing designs and pictures; practice the art of etching.

—*n.* **1** the act or process of etching. **2** a substance used for etching; etchant.

[< Dutch *etsen* < German *ätzen*] —**etch′er,** *n.*

etch|ant (ech′ənt), *n.* a solution used to etch, especially metal or glass: *The etchant is a mixture based on hydrochloric, nitric, and phosphoric acids, containing a high proportion of dissolved stainless steel to facilitate control* (Science News Letter).

etch|ing (ech′ing), *n.* **1** a picture or design printed from an etched plate: *All that I own is a print, An etching, a mezzotint* (Robert Browning). **2** an etched plate; etched drawing or design. **3** the art or process of engraving a drawing or design on metal, glass, wood, mineral, or plastic, by means of acid or heat.

etching ground, the varnish or coating used in etching to protect the surface of the metal plate from the action of the acid, except where the artist scrapes the ground away. The etching ground is usually a composition of wax, gum, resin, and bitumen.

Etch|mi|ad|zin (ech′mē äd′zin), *n.* a monastery in Vagharshapad, Russian Armenia, the residence of the primate of the Armenian Church.

et cum spir|i|tu tu|o (et kum spir′ə tü tü′ō), *Latin.* and with thy spirit (the response to the salutation *Dominus vobiscum*).

ETD (no periods) or **e.t.d.,** estimated time of departure.

E|te|o|cles (i tē′ə klēz), *n. Greek Legend.* a son of Oedipus and Jocasta, and the King of Thebes who defended the city against seven heroes (the Seven Against Thebes) who sought to restore the rights of Polynices, his brother.

E|te|o|clus (i tē′ə kləs), *n. Greek Legend.* one of the Seven against Thebes, according to some accounts.

Et|e|o|cre|tan (et′ē ō krē′tən, ē′tē-), *n., adj.* —*n.* an ancient language used in Crete and found on stone inscriptions. The script uses a form of the Greek alphabet.

—*adj.* of or having to do with this language or script.

[< Greek *eteós* true + English *Cretan*]

e|tern (i tėrn′), *adj.* = eterne.

e|ter|nal (i tėr′nəl), *adj., n.* —*adj.* **1** without beginning or ending; lasting throughout all time; timeless: *Eternal Father! strong to save, Whose arm has bound the restless wave* (William Whiting). **2** always and forever the same: *the eternal truths.* **SYN:** immutable. **3** seeming to go on forever; occurring very frequently: *When will we have an end to this eternal noise?* **SYN:** constant, perpetual, incessant, interminable. **4** independent of time conditions; timeless: *the eternal fitness of things* (Henry Fielding). **5** that has, or is thought of as having, always existed: *the eternal granite of the mountains.*

—*n.* **eternals,** eternal things: *A certain stock of eternals transmigrates through various forms* (James Martineau).

the Eternal, God: *His trust was with the Eternal to be deemed equal in strength, and rather than be less cared not to be at all* (Milton).

[< Latin *aeternālis* < *aeternus,* earlier *aeviternus* < *aevum* age] —**e|ter′nal|ness,** *n.*

—*Syn. adj.* **1 Eternal, everlasting** mean lasting forever. **Eternal** emphasizes having neither a beginning nor an end: *Because a circle has no beginning or end, the wedding ring is a symbol of eternal love.* **Everlasting** does not imply the absence of a beginning but emphasizes having no end: *We wish for everlasting peace.*

Eternal City, Rome.

e|ter|nal|ize (i tėr′nə līz), *v.t.,* **-ized, -iz|ing.** to make eternal; perpetuate; immortalize; eternize: *Is it as maiden, matron, or crone that the females will be eternalized?* (New Yorker).

eternal light, 1 a continuously burning flame, used as a memorial. A perpetual flame burns in the Eternal Light Peace Memorial at Gettysburg. **2** a light hanging above and in front of the ark in synagogues as a symbol of the Torah.

e|ter|nal|ly (i tėr′nə lē), *adv.* **1** without beginning or ending; throughout all time. **2** always and forever. **3** constantly; incessantly: *There's a pleasure eternally new* (Andrew Lang).

e|ter|nals (i tėr′nəlz), *n.pl.* See under **eternal.**

e|terne (i tėrn′), *adj. Archaic.* eternal. Also, **etern.**

e|ter|ni|ty (i tėr′nə tē), *n., pl.* **-ties. 1** all time; all the past and all the future; time without beginning or ending. **SYN:** timelessness. **2** the endless period after death; future life: *All that lives must die, Passing through nature to eternity* (Shakespeare). **SYN:** immortality. **3** a period of time that seems endless: *The injured man waited an eternity for the ambulance to arrive.* **4** eternal quality; endlessness. [< Old French *eternite,* learned borrowing from Latin *aeternitās* < *aeternus;* see etym. under **eternal**]

eternity ring, a ring for the finger set with a circle of small diamonds or other stones.

e|ter|ni|za|tion (i tėr′nə zā′shən), *n.* the act of eternizing.

e|ter|nize (i tėr′nīz), *v.t.,* **-nized, -niz|ing.** to make eternal; perpetuate; immortalize.

e|te|sian (i tē′zhən), *adj.* (of certain Mediterranean winds) recurring annually. [< Latin *etēsius* (< Greek *etēsios* annual < *étos* year) + English *-an*]

eth (eᴛʜ), *n.* = edh.

-eth[1], *suffix.* the form of **-th** when the cardinal number to which it is attached ends in *-y,* as in *twentieth, fiftieth.*

-eth[2], *Archaic or Poetic.* a suffix used to form the third person singular of verbs in the present indicative active, as in *the iceman cometh, the wind bloweth, the fire consumeth. One is uneasily conscious of the injunction that he that girdeth his harness on should not boast like him who taketh his harness off* (Harold Hobson). [Middle English *-eth,* Old English *-ath*]

Eth., Ethiopia.

eth|a|cryn|ic acid (eth′ə krin′ik), a potent diuretic drug, effective in congestive heart failure and pulmonary edema. *Formula:* $C_{13}H_{12}Cl_2O_4$ [< (m)*eth*(ylene) + *ac*(etic) + (buty)*ry*(l) + (phe)*n*-(ol)*ic*]

eth|am|bu|tol (eth am′byu̇ tôl, -tōl), *n.* a synthetic drug that inhibits the growth of tuberculosis bacilli. *Formula:* $C_{10}H_{24}N_2O_2$ [< *eth*(ylenedi)-*am*(ine) + *but*(an)ol]

eth|ane (eth′ān), *n.* a colorless, odorless, gaseous hydrocarbon of the methane series, found in natural gas, coal gas, and crude petroleum. It is used as a refrigerant and as a fuel. *Formula:* C_2H_6 [< *eth*(er) + *-ane*]

eth|a|nol (eth′ə nōl, -nol), *n.* = ethyl alcohol. [< *ethan*(e) + *-ol*[1]]

eth|a|nol|a|mine (eth′ə nol′ə mēn′, -nə lam′in), *n.* a colorless liquid produced from petroleum gases, used as a cleaning agent and in making soap. *Formula:* C_2H_7NO

Eth|ba|al (eth bā′əl, eth′bā-), *n.* a king of Tyre, the father of Jezebel (in the Bible).

eth|ene (eth′ēn), *n.* = ethylene.

e|ther (ē′thər), *n.* **1** a colorless, sweet-smelling liquid that burns and evaporates readily; ethyl ether; diethyl ether. Its fumes cause unconsciousness when deeply inhaled. Ether is produced by the action of sulfuric acid on ethyl alcohol and is used as an anesthetic, as a solvent for fats and resins, and as a refrigerant. *Formula:* $C_4H_{10}O$ **2** the upper regions of space beyond the earth's atmosphere; clear sky; aether. **3** the invisible, elastic substance formerly supposed to fill all space and to conduct light waves, electric waves, etc.; aether. **4** any one of a group of organic compounds consisting of two hydrocarbon groups linked by an oxygen atom. Ethers are formed by the action of acids on alcohols. [< Latin *aether* < Greek *aithēr* upper air]

e|the|re|al (i thir′ē əl), *adj.* **1** light; airy; delicate: *the ethereal beauty of a butterfly. Her ethereal beauty made her seem more like a goddess than a human being.* **2** not of the earth; heavenly: *An angel is an ethereal messenger. She longed for an ethereal home. Where thy footstep gleams —In what ethereal dances, By what eternal streams* (Edgar Allan Poe). **SYN:** celestial. **3** of or having to do with the upper regions of space. **4** of or having to do with the ether diffused through space. **5** *Chemistry.* of or like ether or one of the ethers: *Esters are called ethereal salts because they often have ether-like odors* (Monroe M. Offner). Also, **aethereal** (for defs. 1-4). —**e|the′re|al|ly,** *adv.* —**e|the′re|al|ness,** *n.*

e|the|re|al|i|ty (i thir′ē al′ə tē), *n.* ethereal quality.

e|the|re|al|i|za|tion (i thir′ē ə lə zā′shən), *n.* the act or the result of etherealizing.

Pronunciation Key: hat, āge, cãre, fär; let, ēqual, tėrm, it, īce; hot, ōpen, ôrder; oil, out; cup, pu̇t, rüle; child; long; thin; ᴛʜen; zh, measure; ə represents **a** in about, **e** in taken, **i** in pencil, **o** in lemon, **u** in circus.

e|the|re|al|ize (i thir′ē ə līz), *v.t.,* **-ized, -iz|ing.** to make ethereal.
e|the|re|ous (i thir′ē əs), *adj.* = ethereal.
e|the|ri|al (i thir′ē əl), *adj.* = ethereal.
e|ther|ic (i ther′ik, ē′thər-), *adj.* **1** of or belonging to the ether group of compounds. **2** of or belonging to the chemical substance ether: *etheric wave transmission.*
e|ther|i|fi|ca|tion (i ther′ə fə kā′shən, ē′thər-), *n.* the formation of the chemical substance ether.
e|ther|i|fy (i ther′ə fī, ē′ther-), *v.t.,* **-fied, -fy|ing.** to change into ether or one of the ethers.
e|ther|i|za|tion (ē′thər ə zā′shən), *n.* **1** the condition of the system when under the anesthetic influence of ether. **2** the act or process of giving ether as an anesthetic. **3** *Chemistry.* the process of producing ether; etherification.
e|ther|ize (ē′thə rīz), *v.t.,* **-ized, -iz|ing. 1** to make unconscious with ether fumes: *When the evening is spread out against the sky Like a patient etherized upon a table* (T. S. Eliot). **2** to change into ether; etherify.
e|ther|iz|er (ē′thə rī′zər), *n.* a person or thing that etherizes.
eth|ic (eth′ik), *adj., n.* **—*adj.*** = ethical.
—*n.* system of ethics; ethics: *From her grandfather, a one-time Lutheran minister . . . she inherited a sense of compassion and a strong personal ethic* (Time).
[< Latin *ethicus* < Greek *ēthikós* < *êthos* moral character, related to *éthos* custom, habit]
eth|i|cal (eth′ə kəl), *adj., n.* **—*adj.* 1** having to do with standards of right and wrong; of ethics or morals: *ethical standards.* **SYN:** See syn. under **moral. 2** morally right: *ethical conduct.* **3** in accordance with formal or professional rules of right and wrong: *It is not considered ethical for a doctor to repeat a patient's confidences.* **4** of or having to do with ethical drugs: *ethical products, an ethical consultant firm.*
—*n.* Usually, **ethicals.** a drug that cannot be obtained without a doctor's prescription; ethical drug: *The proprietary industry is not growing as fast as the ethicals* (Wall Street Journal). **—eth′i|cal|ly,** *adv.* **—eth′i|cal|ness,** *n.*
Ethical Culture, 1 a chiefly American movement founded in 1876 which holds the ethical factor in life to be paramount and above all theological and other considerations. **2** the beliefs and practices of this movement.
Ethical Culturist, a person who believes in and observes the tenets of Ethical Culture.
ethical dative, *Grammar.* the dative case used to indicate a person who has a sympathetic interest in the statement, as *mihi* in *Quid mihi Celsus agit?* (How does my Celsus?) or *me* in "He plucked me ope his doublet and offered them his throat to cut."
ethical drug, a drug that cannot be dispensed by a pharmacist without a doctor's prescription. Antibiotics and narcotics are ethical drugs.
eth|i|cal|i|ty (eth′ə kal′ə tē), *n., pl.* **-ties.** ethical standard or principle; ethics: *the ethicality of business.*
eth|i|cals (eth′ə kəlz), *n.pl.* See under **ethical,** *n.*
e|thi|cian (e thish′ən), *n.* a person who studies ethics.
eth|i|cism (eth′ə siz əm), *n.* **1** devotion to ethics or ethical ideals. **2** a tendency to moralize: *Their art . . . was marred by the intense ethicism that pervaded the New England mind for two hundred years* (William Dean Howells).
eth|i|cist (eth′ə sist), *n.* a person versed in ethics; ethician.
eth|i|cize (eth′ə sīz), *v.t.,* **-cized, -ciz|ing.** to make ethical.
eth|ics (eth′iks), *n.* **1** (*sing. in use*) **a** the study of standards of right and wrong; that part of philosophy dealing with moral conduct, duty, and judgment: *Ethics is concerned with morality. From the poetry of Lord Byron they drew a system of ethics compounded of misanthropy and voluptuousness* (Macaulay). **b** a book about ethics. **2** (*pl. in use*) **a** formal or professional rules of right and wrong; system of conduct or behavior: *It is against medical ethics for doctors to advertise.* **b** moral principles by which a person is guided: *The seat of ethics is in our hearts, not in our minds* (Atlantic). **SYN:** morality, morals.
eth|i|on|a|mide (eth′ē on′ə mīd), *n.* a synthetic drug that inhibits the growth of tuberculosis bacilli. *Formula:* $C_8H_{10}N_2S$ [< *eth*(yl) + (th)*ion*(ic) + *amide*]
eth|i|o|nine (eth ī′ə nīn, -nin, -nēn), *n.* an amino acid which inhibits the production of protein by tissue cells. The synthetic drug has been used experimentally in the treatment of cancer and to prevent the development of certain viruses. [< *eth*(yl) + (th)*ion*(ic) + *-ine*[2]]
E|thi|op (ē′thē op), *adj., n. Archaic or Poetic.* Ethiopian: *Like a rich jewel in an Ethiop's ear* (Shakespeare). [< Latin *Aethiops* < Greek *Aithíops* said to mean "sunburned" < *aíthein* to burn + *óps* face]
E|thi|ope (ē′thē ōp), *adj., n.* = Ethiopian.
E|thi|o|pi|an (ē′thē ō′pē ən), *adj., n.* **—*adj.* 1** of or having to do with Ethiopia, a country in northeastern Africa, or its people. **2** having to do with the region that includes Africa south of the Sahara, and Madagascar. **3** *Archaic.* Black.
—*n.* 1 a native or inhabitant of Ethiopia. **2** *Ethnology.* a member of one of the five races into which mankind was formerly divided, including the African Black and the Negrito. **3** *Archaic.* a Black.
Ethiopian lily, = calla lily.
E|thi|op|ic (ē′thē op′ik, -ō′pik), *adj., n.* **—*adj.* 1** of or having to do with the ancient Semitic language of Ethiopia or the church using this language. **2** = Ethiopian.
—*n.* the ancient Semitic language of Ethiopia.
eth|moid (eth′moid), *adj., n.* **—*adj.*** having to do with a bone situated in the walls and septum of the nose and containing numerous perforations for the filaments of the olfactory nerve.
—*n.* the ethmoid bone.
[< Greek *ēthmoeidēs* < *ēthmós* sieve + *eîdos* form]
eth|moi|dal (eth moi′dəl), *adj.* = ethmoid.
eth|narch (eth′närk), *n.* the governor of a nation, people, or province.
[< Greek *ethnárchēs* < *éthnos* nation + *archós* ruler < *árchein* to rule]
eth|nar|chy (eth′när kē), *n., pl.* **-chies.** the government, jurisdiction, or rank of an ethnarch.
eth|nic (eth′nik), *adj., n.* **—*adj.* 1** having to do with the various racial and cultural groups of people and the characteristics, language, and customs of each; of, having to do with, or peculiar to a people: *The diverse ethnic and economic interests that make up the political machines frequently clash* (Harper's). **2** of or having to do with people of foreign birth or descent: *There are many ethnic groups in our large cities.* **3** having to do with nations not Christian or Jewish; heathen; pagan: *These are ancient ethnic revels, Of a faith long since forsaken* (Longfellow). **4** of or for ethnics: *Ethnic [Christmas] cards with black, brown or yellow Santas testify to the fact that the American melting pot is still bubbling.* (Time).
—*n.* a member of a racial, cultural, or national minority; a member of an ethnic group: *All sports are now saturated with ethnics* (Harper's).
[< Latin *ethnicus* < Greek *ethnikós* < *éthnos* nation] **—eth′ni|cal|ly,** *adv.*
eth|ni|cal (eth′nə kəl), *adj.* = ethnic.
eth|nic|i|ty (eth nis′ə tē), *n.* ethnic status, quality, or character: *There are vast differences among American families, differences related to . . . ethnicity and social class, to region and religion* (American Scholar).
ethno-, *combining form.* race; people; nation: *Ethnology = the science of races of people.*
[< Greek *éthnos* nation]
eth|no|ar|chae|ol|o|gy or **eth|no|ar|che|ol|o|gy** (eth′nō är′kē ol′ə jē), *n.* a branch of archaeology dealing with the tools, artifacts, and other resources of existing cultures and societies: *Ethnoarchaeology [is] seeking some methodological stability in an effort to link human behavior and material residues within the context of living societies* (Scientific American). **—eth′no|ar|chae|ol′o|gist,** *n.* **—eth|no|ar|che|ol′o|gist,** *n.*
eth|no|as|tron|o|my (eth′nō ə stron′ə mē), *n.* the study of astronomy as used by different cultures and civilizations: *Ethnoastronomy . . . includes prescientific astronomy . . . [and] the astronomy of modern peoples who have not been influenced by advanced scientific culture* (Scientific News). **—eth′no|as|tron′o|mer,** *n.*
eth|no|bo|tan|i|cal (eth′nō bə tan′ə kəl), *adj.* having to do with the relation between plants and man.
eth|no|bot|a|nist (eth′nō bot′ə nist), *n.* a person who studies ethnobotany.
eth|no|bot|a|ny (eth′nō bot′ə nē), *n.* the branch of botany which deals with the relation between plants and man.
eth|no|cen|tric (eth′nō sen′trik), *adj.* characterized by ethnocentrism.
eth|no|cen|trism (eth′nō sen′triz əm), *n.* the practice of regarding one's own race or culture as superior to others.
eth|no|cide (eth′nəsīd), *n.* the systematic destruction of an ethnic culture: *Those missionaries who, by the verdict of Bishop Alejo Ovelar, "are implicated in the grave crime of ethnocide" . . . would see nothing wrong in the destruction of the racial identity of Indians* (Sunday Times Magazine).
[< *ethno-* + *-cide*[2]]
eth|noc|ra|cy (eth nok′rə sē), *n., pl.* **-cies.** rule by a race. [< *ethno-* + *-cracy,* as in *democracy*]
eth|nod|i|cy (eth nod′ə sē), *n.* the comparative study of systems of law as a branch of ethnology.
[< Greek *éthnos* nation + *díkē* justice]
ethnog., 1 ethnographic. **2** ethnography.
eth|no|gen|ic (eth′nə jen′ik), *adj.* having to do with ethnogeny.
eth|nog|e|ny (eth noj′ə nē), *n.* the branch of ethnology which treats of the origin of races, nations, and peoples.
eth|nog|ra|pher (eth nog′rə fər), *n.* a person who studies ethnography.
eth|no|graph|ic (eth′nə graf′ik), *adj.* having to do with ethnography. **—eth′no|graph′i|cal|ly,** *adv.*
eth|no|graph|i|cal (eth′nə graf′ə kəl), *adj.* = ethnographic.
eth|nog|ra|phist (eth nog′rə fist), *n.* = ethnographer.
eth|nog|ra|phy (eth nog′rə fē), *n.* the branch of anthropology that deals with the description of various racial and cultural groups of people.
eth|no|his|to|ri|an (eth′nō his tôr′ē ən, -tōr′-), *n.* a person who studies ethnohistory.
eth|no|his|tor|i|cal (eth′nō his tôr′ə kəl, -tor′-), *adj.* of or having to do with ethnohistory.
eth|no|his|to|ry (eth′nō his′tər ē, -his′trē), *n.* the collection and evaluation of materials that shed light on the history of ethnic groups.
ethnol., 1 ethnological. **2** ethnology.
eth|no|lin|guist (eth′nō ling′gwist), *n.* a specialist in ethnolinguistics.
eth|no|lin|guis|tic (eth′nō ling gwis′tik), *adj.* of or having to do with ethnolinguistics.
eth|no|lin|guis|tics (eth′nō ling gwis′tiks), *n.* a branch of linguistics that deals with the relationship between language and culture, especially the effect of social, economic, and similar factors on language.
eth|nol|o|ger (eth nol′ə jər), *n.* an ethnologist.
eth|no|log|ic (eth′nə loj′ik), *adj.* = ethnological.
eth|no|log|i|cal (eth′nə loj′ə kəl), *adj.* of or having to do with ethnology.
eth|no|log|i|cal|ly (eth′nə loj′ə klē), *adv.* from the point of view of ethnology.
eth|nol|o|gist (eth nol′ə jist), *n.* a person who studies ethnology: *In another special field ethnologists are concerned with the lifeways of living peoples—how people are born and trained to live in their society, how they choose their mates, marry, make a living, and organize their relations with their fellow men* (Beals and Hoijer).
eth|nol|o|gy (eth nol′ə jē), *n.* the branch of anthropology that deals with the various racial or cultural groups of ancient or contemporary people, their origin and distribution, and their distinctive characteristics, customs, institutions, and culture.
eth|no|mu|si|col|o|gist (eth′nō myü′zə kol′ə jist), *n.* a person who studies ethnomusicology.
eth|no|mu|si|col|o|gy (eth′nō myü′zə kol′ə jē), *n.* the branch of musicology dealing with the native or folk music of various peoples and cultures.
eth|no|my|co|log|i|cal (eth′nō mī′kə loj′ə kəl), *adj.* of or having to do with ethnomycology.
eth|no|my|col|o|gist (eth′nō mī kol′ə jist), *n.* a person who studies ethnomycology.
eth|no|my|col|o|gy (eth′nō mī kol′ə jē), *n.* the study of the use of hallucinogenic mushrooms and other fungi among various peoples and cultures.
eth|no|phar|ma|col|o|gy (eth′nō fär′mə kol′ə jē), *n.* use of traditional medicinal substances by a particular culture; folk medicine.
eth|no|psy|cho|log|i|cal (eth′nō sī′kə loj′ə kəl), *adj.* of or having to do with ethnopsychology.
eth|no|psy|chol|o|gy (eth′nō sī kol′ə jē), *n.* the investigation of the psychology of races and peoples.
eth|nos (eth′nos), *n.* a race, tribe, or nation.
[< Greek *éthnos*]
e|tho|gram (ē′thə gram), *n.* a detailed description of the behavior of an animal: *This "looking away" gesture of the gull is only one of many in its total "ethogram" of postures* (Robin Fox).
e|thog|ra|phy (i thog′rə fē), *n.* the study and description of human characteristics and morals.
[< Greek *êthos* character + English *-graphy*]
eth|o|log|i|cal (eth′ə loj′ə kəl), *adj.* of or having to do with ethology (def. 1).
e|thol|o|gist (i thol′ə jist), *n.* a person who studies ethology.
e|thol|o|gy (i thol′ə jē), *n.* **1** the individual and comparative study of animal behavior, including that of man: *In ethology we have valuable objective descriptions of overt behaviour in a number of species observed in their normal surroundings, and of the specific external stimuli which influence behaviour* (S. A. Barnett). **2** the study of ethical and moral systems. [< Latin *ēthologia* < Greek *ēthologiā,* ultimately < *êthos* character + *légein* speak]
e|tho|pro|pa|zine (ē′thə prō′pə zēn), *n.* a drug used in its hydrochloride form in the treatment of Parkinson's disease. *Formula:* $C_{19}H_{24}N_2S$
e|thos (ē′thos), *n.* **1** the characteristic spirit, as of a people or institution: *the ethos of democracy.* **2** the distinctive features of a particular culture or group. **3** (in ancient Greek aesthetics) an ideal or universal quality as distinguished from the subjective or emotional. [< New Latin *ethos* < Greek *êthos* character, nature]

eth|ox|yl (eth ok′səl), *n.* a univalent radical, —C_2H_5O [< *eth*(yl) + *ox*(ygen) + *-yl*]

Eth|rel (eth′rel), *n. Trademark.* a compound of ethane, chlorine, and phosphoric acid, used to regulate the growth of certain plants: *Ethrel controls flower formation, ripening time, and time of fruit fall in a number of crops, including cucumbers and pineapples* (Sylvan H. Wittwer).

eth|rog (es′rōg, et rōg′), *n., pl.* **eth|rogs, eth|ro|gim** (es rō′gim, et rō gēm′). *Judaism.* a citron used with a palm branch during the Sukkoth service in observance of a Biblical commandment (Leviticus 23:40). Also, **esrog, etrog.** [< Hebrew *ethrōg*]

eth|yl (eth′əl), *n.* a univalent radical present in many organic chemical compounds. Ordinary alcohol contains ethyl. *Formula:* —C_2H_5 [< *eth*(er) + *-yl*]

Eth|yl (eth′əl), *n. Trademark.* **1** a poisonous, colorless compound usually containing tetraethyl lead, used in gasoline to reduce knocking. *Formula:* $Pb(C_2H_5)_4$ **2** a gasoline containing this compound. [< *ethyl*]

ethyl acetate, a colorless, pleasant-smelling liquid obtained by the action of acetic acid on ethyl alcohol in the presence of sulfuric acid, used in medicine, as a solvent, and in organic synthesis. *Formula:* $C_4H_8O_2$

ethyl alcohol, ordinary alcohol, a colorless, volatile liquid made by fermentation, as of grain or sugar; ethanol: *Ethyl alcohol is an excellent solvent and as such finds extensive use in industry and in medicine* (Monroe M. Offner). *Formula:* C_2H_5OH

eth|yl|ate (eth′ə lāt), *v.,* **-at|ed, -at|ing,** *n.* **—*v.t.*** to treat (a compound) so as to add one or more ethyl radicals.
—*n.* a compound derived from ethyl alcohol by the replacement of the hydroxyl hydrogen with a metal.

eth|yl|ben|zene (eth′əl ben′zēn, -ben zēn′), *n.* a colorless, flammable liquid derived from ethylene and benzene, used as a solvent and as an intermediate in the production of styrene. *Formula:* C_8H_{10}

ethyl cellulose, a white, granular solid made from cellulose and ethyl alcohol in the presence of dehydrating agents, used especially as a toughening agent for plastics, adhesives, and coatings.

ethyl chloride, a gas that liquefies under pressure, used as a local anesthetic, a refrigerant, and a solvent or agent in various chemical reactions. *Formula:* C_2H_5Cl

eth|yl|ene (eth′ə lēn), *n.* a colorless, flammable gas with a faint, sweet, but not pleasant odor. It is the diatomic hydrocarbon of the olefin series, an important constituent of coal gas, and is used as an anesthetic, in making organic compounds, and for coloring and ripening citrus fruits. *Formula:* C_2H_4 Also, **ethene.**

eth|yl|ene|di|a|mine (eth′ə lēn dī′ə mēn′, -dī-am′in), *n.* a colorless, alkaline liquid obtained by distillation of a mixture of ethylene dichloride and ammonia, used in the preparation of various chemical products and as a solvent in the treatment of bone for grafting. *Formula:* $C_2H_8N_2$

ethylenediamine tet|ra-a|ce|tic acid (tet′rə-ə sē′tik, -set′ik), a colorless, crystalline acid used as a metal chelating agent, as an anticoagulant, and in the treatment of chlorosis, calcinosis, lead poisoning, and other conditions. *Formula:* $C_{10}H_{16}N_2O_8$ *Abbr:* EDTA (no periods).

ethylene dibromide, a colorless, poisonous liquid having an odor like that of chloroform, used especially as a solvent for oils, fats, and resins, as a fumigant and insecticide, and as a gasoline purifier. *Formula:* $C_2H_4Br_2$

ethylene dichloride, an oily liquid used as a fumigant, cleansing agent, and solvent in various chemical processes. *Formula:* $C_2H_4Cl_2$

ethylene glycol, = glycol.

ethylene oxide, a colorless gas which liquefies at low temperatures, used as an insecticide and fumigant, and in the manufacture of antifreeze, plastics, and other chemical products. *Formula:* C_2H_4O

ethylene series, a series of compounds of carbon and hydrogen having the general formula C_nH_{2n}.

ethyl ether, = ether (def. 1).

e|thyl|ic (i thil′ik), *adj.* **1** of or containing ethyl. **2** made from ethyl.

ethyl mercaptan, a compound with an odor like that of garlic, sometimes used as a warning signal in mines or elsewhere where a sound might not be heard. *Formula:* C_2H_6S

et|ic (et′ik), *adj. Linguistics.* not distinctive or contrastive; generalized: *etic syllables, etic sounds.* [abstracted < *phonetic*] **—et′i|cal|ly,** *adv.*

e|ti|o|late (ē′tē ə lāt), *v.,* **-lat|ed, -lat|ing. —*v.t.*** to make (a plant) pale or white through loss of normal color, as from lack of sunlight; blanch: *to etiolate celery.*
—*v.i.* to grow pale or colorless from absence of the normal amount of chlorophyll following exclusion of sunlight, as plants.
[< French *étioler* (with English *-ate*[1]) blanch, perhaps < Old French *esteuler* become slender, puny]

e|ti|o|la|tion (ē′tē ə lā′shən), *n.* **1** a becoming pale or colorless through loss of natural coloring matter as a result of the exclusion of light or of disease. **2** the making of plants, especially certain market vegetables, white, crisp, and tender by excluding the action of light from them.

e|ti|o|log|ic (ē′tē ə loj′ik), *adj.* = etiological: *There is little or no evidence that tobacco is an etiologic (causative) factor in . . . diseases of the upper gastrointestinal tract* (Science News Letter).

e|ti|o|log|i|cal (ē′tē ə loj′ə kəl), *adj.* of or having to do with etiology. Also, **aetiological. —e′ti|o-log′i|cal|ly,** *adv.*

e|ti|ol|o|gist (ē′tē ol′ə jist), *n.* a person who studies etiology. Also, **aetiologist.**

e|ti|ol|o|gy (ē′tē ol′ə jē), *n.* **1** the science that deals with origins or causes. **2a** the theory of the causes of disease. **b** the cause or causes of a disease. **3** the act or process of assigning a cause. Also, **aetiology.** [< Late Latin *aetiologia* < Greek *aitiologiā* < *aitiā* cause + *légein* speak]

et|i|quette (et′ə ket), *n.* **1** the customary rules for behavior in polite society: *a book of etiquette. Etiquette requires a man to rise when a woman enters the room.* SYN: manners, decorum, propriety. **2** formal rules governing behavior, especially in a profession or official ceremony: *medical etiquette. Ambassadors observe diplomatic etiquette.* **3a** the prescribed ceremonial of a court. **b** the formalities required by usage in international diplomacy. [< Old French *estiquette* ticket, label < *estiquier* to stick (on) < Germanic (compare Low German *sticke* tag)]

et|na (et′nə), *n.* a small vessel for heating water or other liquid, consisting of a cup for the liquid, with a fixed saucer surrounding it in which alcohol is burned. [< Mount *Etna,* a volcano in Sicily]

ETO (no periods), European Theater of Operations.

é|toile (ā twȧl′), *n. French.* a star.

E|ton (ē′tən), *n.* = Eton College.

Eton blue (ē′tən), a light blue color, the school color of Eton College.

∗**Eton collar**, a wide, round, stiff collar, worn over the coat collar.

∗**Eton collar**
∗**Eton jacket**
definition 1

Eton College, a famous English school for boys, at Eton, a town near London.

E|to|ni|an (ē tō′nē ən), *adj., n.* **—*adj.*** of or having to do with Eton College: *Tory pattern of leadership . . . is Anglican, Etonian, and upper-class* (Time).
—*n.* a student or former student at Eton College: *Thomas Arne, an Etonian, was intended for the law* (Punch).

∗**Eton jacket** or **coat**, **1** a short, black coat with broad lapels. The jacket comes to the waist and is not made to button. **2** a similar jacket worn by women and girls.

e|tor|phine (ē tôr′fēn, -fin), *n.* a synthetic drug related to morphine, used as a narcotic and analgesic: *Etorphine was first synthesised in 1963 and has been widely employed to immobilize game animals in Africa* (New Scientist). *Formula:* $C_{25}H_{33}NO_4$ [< *et-* (perhaps < *ether*) + (m)*orphine*]

et|rog (et rōg′, es′rōg), *n., pl.* **et|rogs, et|ro|gim** (et rō gēm′, es rō′gim), = ethrog.

E|tru|ri|an (i trůr′ē ən), *adj., n.* = Etruscan.

E|trus|can (i trus′kən), *adj.* of or having to do with Etruria, an ancient country in central western Italy, its people, or their language, art, or customs: *The Etruscan civilization bloomed in central Italy from the seventh to the first century B.C.* (Scientific American). **—*n.*** **1** a person who was born or lived in Etruria: *For centuries the Etruscans had been the shadowy forerunners of the Romans* (Time). **2** the language of the ancient Etruscans. [< Latin *Etruscus* + English *-an*]

E|trus|col|o|gist (ē′trus kol′ə jist), *n.* a student of Etruscan history and antiquities.

E|trus|col|o|gy (ē′trus kol′ə jē), *n.* the study of Etruscan history and antiquities: *For today the Etruscans still elude us, and . . . "Etruscology" seems to have remained as highly controversial as the days of the Classical Dictionary* (New Scientist).

ETS (no periods) or **E.T.S.**, Educational Testing Service (a United States educational service that develops school and college examinations): *E.T.S. is the author of the familiar College Boards tests and the somewhat less familiar Advanced Placement Examinations, which let able high school students skip certain required freshman courses* (Time).

et seq. (*sometimes pronounced* et sek), and the following; and that which follows: *These thoughts, and others, kept me so busy that I just climbed aboard page 91, et seq., this morning* (New Yorker). [< Latin *et sequēns* and following; *sequēns,* present participle of *sequī* follow]

et seqq., and those following.

et sic de cet|er|is (et sik dē set′ər is), *Latin.* and so concerning the rest.

et sic de si|mi|li|bus (et sik dē si mil′ə bəs), *Latin.* and thus concerning (all) similar things.

et sqq., and those following (Latin, *et sequentes, et sequentia*).

-ette, *suffix added to nouns to form new nouns.*
1 little ____: *Kitchenette = a little kitchen.*
2 female ____: *Usherette = a female usher.*
3 a substitute for ____: *Leatherette = a substitute for leather.* [< French *-ette,* feminine of *-et* -et]

et|tle (et′əl), *n., v.,* **-tled, -tling.** *Scottish.* **—*n.*** aim; intent; purpose: *Nannie . . . flew at Tam wi′ furious ettle* (Robert Burns). **—*v.t.*** to intend or purpose. **—*v.i.*** to direct one's course.
[< Scandinavian (compare Old Icelandic *aetla* think)]

et tu, Bru|te! (et tü brü′tē, -tyü), *Latin.* and thou, Brutus! (the exclamation of reproach that Julius Caesar is said to have uttered when he saw his friend Brutus among his assassins).

é|tude (ā tüd′, -tyüd′), *n.* **1** a piece of music intended to develop skill in technique. **2** a composition of similar type, having artistic quality and intended for public performance: *a Chopin étude.* [< French *étude* study < Latin *studium.* See etym. of doublets **studio, study.**]

e|tui (ā twē′, e-; et′wē), *n., pl.* **e|tuis.** a small case, usually ornamental, for small articles, as needles or toilet articles. [< French *étui* < Old French *estui* (originally) prison < *estuier* guard, enclose, ultimately < Latin *studēre* attend to, to study < *studium* study]

et ux., and wife (Latin, *et uxor*).

ETV or **etv** (no periods), educational television.

e|twee (e twē′, et′wē), *n.* = etui.

etym. or **etymol.**, **1** etymological. **2** etymology.

et|y|ma (et′ə mə), *n.* a plural of **etymon.**

et|y|mo|log|ic (et′ə mə loj′ik), *adj.* = etymological.

et|y|mo|log|i|cal (et′ə mə loj′ə kəl), *adj.* of or having to do with the origin and history of words; in accordance with etymology.

et|y|mo|log|i|cal|ly (et′ə mə loj′ə klē), *adv.* according to etymology; by etymology; with respect to origin and history: *Etymologically, ecology is the "science of the house." Scientifically, it is the "science of the environment"* (J. J. De Gryse).

et|y|mo|log|i|con (et′ə mə loj′ə kon), *n.* an etymological dictionary. [< Greek *etymologikón,* neuter of *etymologikós* etymological < *etymologiā;* see etym. under **etymology**]

et|y|mol|o|gist (et′ə mol′ə jist), *n.* a person who studies etymology, especially an expert in etymology: *By modern standards Johnson knew too little of early English to be a thorough etymologist* (Time).

et|y|mol|o|gize (et′ə mol′ə jīz), *v.,* **-gized, -giz|ing. —*v.t.*** to trace or give the history of (words).
—*v.i.* **1** to study etymology. **2** to provide or suggest etymologies for words.

et|y|mol|o|gy (et′ə mol′ə jē), *n., pl.* **-gies. 1** the derivation of a word. **2** an account or explanation of the origin and history of a word. **3** the study dealing with the origin and history of words. [< Latin *etymologia* < Greek *etymologiā* < *étymon* the original sense or form of a word, neuter of *étymos* true, real (< *etázein* prove < *etós* true, genuine) + *-logos* treating of]

et|y|mon (et′ə mon), *n., pl.* **-mons, -ma.** a primary word or form from which other words are derived. [< Latin *etymon* < Greek *étymon;* see etym. under **etymology**]

e|typ|ic (ē tip′ik), *adj. Biology.* diverging or divergent from a given type.

e|typ|i|cal (ē tip′ə kəl), *adj.* = etypic.

Et|zel (et′səl), *n. Germanic Legend.* a king identified with Atli of the Volsungs and sometimes with the historical Attila.

Pronunciation Key: hat, āge, cãre, fär; let, ēqual, tėrm; it, īce; hot, ōpen, ôrder; oil, out; cup, půt, rüle; child; long; thin; ᴛʜen; zh, measure; ə represents **a** in about, **e** in taken, **i** in pencil, **o** in lemon, **u** in circus.

eu-, *prefix.* good; well; true, as in *eugenic, eucalyptus, eulogy, euphoria, euglobulin.* [< Greek *eu-* < *eús* good]

Eu (no period), europium (chemical element).

E.U.B. or **EUB** (no periods), Evangelical United Brethren.

Eu|boe|an (yü bē′ən), *adj. n.* —*adj.* of or having to do with Euboea, a large island in the Aegean Sea, belonging to Greece, or its inhabitants. —*n.* a native or inhabitant of Euboea.

Eu|bo|ic (yü bō′ik), *adj.* = Euboean.

eu|caine (yü kān′), *n.* a crystalline, synthetic organic compound, used in the form of its hydrochloride as a local anesthetic; betaeucaine. *Formula:* $C_{15}H_{21}NO_2$ [< *eu-* + (co)*caine*]

eu|ca|lypt (yü′kə lipt), *n.* = eucalyptus.

eu|ca|lyp|tic (yü′kə lip′tik), *adj.* of or having to do with a eucalyptus.

eu|ca|lyp|tol (yü′kə lip′tōl, -tol), *n.* cineole; the chief constituent of the oil of eucalyptus. [< *eucalpyt*(us) + *-ol*[2]]

eu|ca|lyp|tole (yü′kə lip′tōl), *n.* = eucalyptol.

***eu|ca|lyp|tus** (yü′kə lip′təs), *n., pl.* **-tus|es, -ti** (-tī). any one of a group of very tall evergreen trees that grow mainly in Australia and neighboring islands, such as the blue gum; gum tree. Many species are valued for their hard timber and for their leaves from which a medicinal oil is made. The eucalyptus belongs to the myrtle family. It has been naturalized in the United States, especially in California and Florida. [< New Latin *eucalyptus* < Greek *eu-* well + *kalyptós* covered < *kalýptein* to cover (from the covering on the bud)]

***eucalyptus**

eucalyptus oil, any one of various oils obtained from the leaves of eucalyptus trees, used chiefly as antiseptics, deodorants, and stimulants.

eu|car|y|ote (yü kar′ē ōt), *n.* a cell or organism having a visible nucleus or nuclei: *If the first eucaryotes arose 1.2 to 1.4 billion years ago, there would be about half this time available for the evolution of soft-bodied multicellular organisms, since the first fossil animal skeletons were deposited around 600 million years ago at the beginning of the Cambrian period* (Scientific American). Also, **eukaryote**. [< *eu-* good, true + Greek *káryon* nut, kernel]

eu|car|y|ot|ic (yü kar′ē ot′ik), *adj.* containing a visible nucleus or nuclei: *eucaryotic cells.* Also, **eukaryotic**.

eu|cha|ris (yü′kər is), *n.* any one of a group of South American plants of the amaryllis family, bearing large, fragrant, bell-shaped, white flowers. [< Greek *eúcharis* pleasing < *eu-* good + *cháris* grace]

Eu|cha|rist (yü′kər ist), *n.* **1** the sacrament of the Lord's Supper; Holy Communion. **2** the consecrated bread and wine used in this sacrament, especially the bread. [< Late Latin *eucharistia* < Greek *eucharistiā* thankfulness, the Eucharist < *euchár̄istos* grateful < *eúcharis;* see etym. under **eucharis**]

Eu|cha|ris|tic (yü′kə ris′tik), *adj.* of, having to do with, or treating of the Eucharist. —**Eu′cha|ris′ti|cal|ly**, *adv.*

Eu|cha|ris|ti|cal (yü′kə ris′tə kəl), *adj.* = Eucharistic.

Eucharistic congress, an assembly of Catholics, both clerics and laymen, from all countries to promote the religious way of life. Public processions are held in honor of the Eucharist.

Eu|chite (yü′kīt), *n.* a member of an eastern sect of the 300's that attached supreme importance to prayer and the presence of the Holy Spirit. [< Late Latin *euchīta* < Greek *euchitēs* < *euchē* prayer]

eu|chre (yü′kər), *n., v.,* **-chred, -chring.** —*n.* **1** a simple card game for two, three, or four players, using the 32 (or 24) highest cards in the pack, in which the bowers are high trumps, and the object is to win a majority of the five tricks. **2** the failure of the side making the trump in this game to win three tricks.
—*v.t.* **1** to prevent (the side making the trump in this game) from winning three tricks. **2** *Informal, Figurative.* to outwit; best.

euchre out of, *Informal.* to do out of by trickery: *He was not disposed to accept second place from the men who four years before had euchred him out of first place* (Wall Street Journal). [American English; origin uncertain]

eu|chro|ma|tin (yü krō′mə tin), *n.* the chromatin of a chromosome containing the genes.

eu|chro|mo|some (yü krō′mə sōm), *n.* any chromosome except a sex chromosome; autosome.

eu|clase (yü′klās), *n.* a brittle mineral, a silicate of aluminum and beryllium, occurring in prismatic crystals, usually light-green. [< *eu-* + Greek *klásis* breaking < *klân* break (from its easy cleavage)]

Eu|clid (yü′klid), *n.* **1** the works of Euclid, a Greek mathematician, especially his *Elements* (treatise on geometry). **2** = geometry.

Eu|clid|e|an or **Eu|clid|i|an** (yü klid′ē ən), *adj.* of Euclid; in accordance with the principles of Euclid's geometry. By fixing the admission of certain propositions as more elementary than others, Euclidean geometry has greatly influenced the mode of presentation of mathematical theories.

eu|coe|lo|mate (yü sē′lə māt, -mit), *adj., n.* —*adj.* having a body cavity (coelom), as the frog does. —*n.* an animal having a coelom.

eu|cone (yü′kōn′), *adj.* having a well-developed or true cone as in the eyes of certain crustaceans and insects. [< *eu-* + *cone*]

eu|crite (yü′krīt), *n.* a variety of gabbro composed essentially of anorthite and augite. [< German *Eukrit* < Greek *eúkritos* easily distinguished < *eu-* well, easily + *krínein* to discern, judge]

eu|crit|ic (yü krit′ik), *adj.* of or resembling eucrite: *a eucritic meteorite.*

eu|cy|clic (yü sī′klik, -sik′lik), *adj.* having petals, stamens, or other parts, equal in number on each whorl and alternate with one another.

eu|dae|mon or **eu|de|mon** (yü dē′mən), *n.* a benevolent or protective spirit. [< *eu-* + Greek *daimōn* guardian spirit]

eu|dae|mon|ic or **eu|de|mon|ic** (yü′də mon′ik), *adj.* having to do with or conducive to happiness.

eu|dae|mon|i|cal or **eu|de|mon|i|cal** (yü′də-mon′ə kəl), *adj.* = eudaemonic.

eu|dae|mon|ics or **eu|de|mon|ics** (yü′də mon′-iks), *n.* **1** the science of happiness. **2** = eudaemonism.

eu|dae|mon|ism or **eu|de|mon|ism** (yü dē′mə-niz əm), *n.* the system of ethics that holds that the basis of moral obligations lies in their relation to the production of happiness.

eu|dae|mon|ist or **eu|de|mon|ist** (yü dē′mə-nist), *n.* a believer in eudaemonism.

eu|dae|mon|is|tic or **eu|de|mon|is|tic** (yü dē′-mə nis′tik), *adj.* of or having to do with eudaemonism.

eu|dae|mon|is|ti|cal or **eu|de|mon|is|ti|cal** (yü-dē′mə nis′tə kəl), *adj.* = eudaemonistic.

eu|di|a|lyte (yü dī′ə līt), *n.* a brownish-red mineral, a silicate of zirconium, iron, manganese, sodium, and other elements, occurring in Greenland. [< Greek *eudiálytos* easily dissolved < *eu-* good + *dialýein* dissolve]

eu|di|om|e|ter (yü′dē om′ə tər), *n.* a device, generally a graduated glass tube, used in volumetric analysis and measurement of gases, and formerly used for testing the purity of the air or the quantity of oxygen contained in it. [< Greek *eúdios* fair weather + English *-meter*]

eu|di|o|met|ric (yü′dē ə met′rik), *adj.* of or having to do with a eudiometer or with eudiometry. —**eu′di|o|met′ri|cal|ly**, *adv.*

eu|di|o|met|ri|cal (yü′dē ə met′rə kəl), *adj.* = eudiometric.

eu|di|om|e|try (yü′dē om′ə trē), *n.* the art or practice of using the eudiometer.

eu|di|pleu|ral (yü′də plůr′əl), *adj. Anatomy, Zoology.* having two equal and symmetrical halves; bilaterally symmetrical.

eu|ge|nes|ic (yü′jə nes′ik), *adj.* (especially of hybrids) capable of breeding freely.

eu|gen|e|sis (yü jen′ə sis), *n.* the quality of breeding freely, especially among hybrids; fertility.

eu|gen|ic (yü jen′ik), *adj.* **1** having to do with eugenics; improving the offspring produced; improving the race: *a eugenic mating.* **2** coming of good stock. [< Greek *eugenēs* well-born, of good stock (< *eu-* good + *génos* stock, race)]

eu|gen|i|cal (yü jen′ə kəl), *adj.* = eugenic.

eu|gen|i|cal|ly (yü jen′ə klē), *adv.* in a eugenic manner; with respect to racial improvement.

eu|gen|i|cist (yü jen′ə sist), *n.* **1** a person who studies eugenics. **2** an advocate of eugenics.

eu|gen|ics (yü jen′iks), *n.* **1** the science of improving the human race. Eugenics would apply the same principles of careful selection of parents that have long been applied to animals and plants, and theoretically develop healthier, more intelligent, and better children. **2** the science of improving offspring.

eu|ge|nist (yü′jə nist), *n.* = eugenicist.

eu|ge|nol (yü′jə nōl, -nol), *n.* a colorless, aromatic compound, a constituent of oil of cloves and certain other essential oils, used in dentistry as a mild anesthetic and in the compounding of various aromatics. *Formula:* $C_{10}H_{12}O_2$ [< New Latin *Eugenia* genus of tropical trees (< *Eugene,* 1663-1736, a Prince of Savoy) + English *-ol*[1]]

eu|ge|o|syn|cli|nal (yü jē′ō sin klī′nəl), *adj.* of or having to do with a eugeosyncline.

eu|ge|o|syn|cline (yü jē′ō sin′klīn), *n. Geology.* a long, narrow geosyncline in which volcanic rocks abound. [< *eu-* + *geosyncline*]

***eu|gle|na** (yü glē′nə), *n., pl.* **-nas** or **-na**. any one of a genus of microscopic, one-celled organisms, usually green, that move by a whiplike tail. It is easily grown for study. Euglenas are protistans classified as flagellates. *The tiny one-celled animals called euglena have a reddish spot which is thought to be sensitive to changes in light* (Matthew Luckiesh). [< New Latin *Euglena* the genus name < Greek *eu-* good + *glēnē* pupil of the eye]

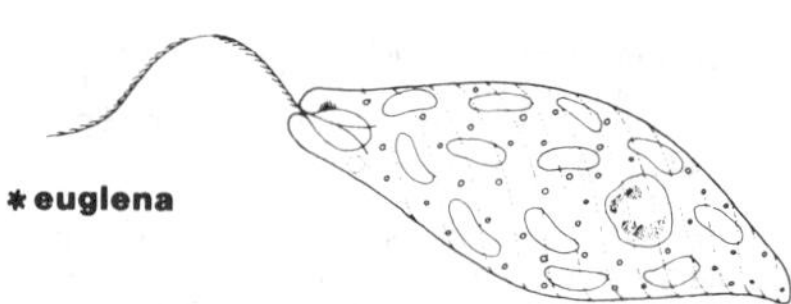

***euglena**

eu|gle|nid (yü glē′nid), *n.* = euglenoid.

eu|gle|noid (yü glē′noid), *adj., n.* —*adj.* having to do with or like a euglena: *It exhibited wormlike euglenoid movements.*
—*n.* a euglenoid organism.

eu|glob|u|lin (yü glob′yə lin), *n.* any true globulin, soluble in saline solutions but insoluble in water, unlike the pseudoglobulins.

eu|he|mer|ism (yü hē′mə riz əm, -hem′ə-), *n.* **1** the theory held by Euhemerus, an ancient Greek writer, that the gods were merely deified men and women. **2** the method of mythological interpretation that regards myths as traditional accounts of actual history.

eu|he|mer|ist (yü hē′mər ist, -hem′ər-), *n., adj.* —*n.* a believer in the doctrine of euhemerism. —*adj.* = euhemeristic.

eu|he|mer|is|tic (yü hē′mə ris′tik, -hem′ə-), *adj.* of or having to do with euhemerism. —**eu|he′mer-is′ti|cal|ly**, *adv.*

eu|he|mer|ize (yü hē′mə rīz, -hem′ə-), *v.t.,* **-ized, -iz|ing.** to explain (myths) as traditional accounts of actual events.

eu|hom|i|nid (yü hom′ə nid), *n. Anthropology.* a true member of the family of man.

eu|kar|y|ote (yü kar′ē ōt), *n.* = eucaryote.

eu|kar|y|ot|ic (yü kar′ē ot′ik), *adj.* = eucaryotic.

eu|la|chon (yü′lə kon), *n.* = candlefish. [variant of *oolakon,* a native American Indian word]

Eu|len|spie|gel (oi′lən shpē′gəl), *n.* **Till** or **Tyll** (til), a German of the 1300's, about whose name have been grouped popular tales of the mischievous pranks of a vagabond peasant.

***Eu|ler's circles** (oi′lərz), circles that show relationships and solve problems between mathematical sets, first developed by Leonhard Euler, 1707-1783, a Swiss mathematician.

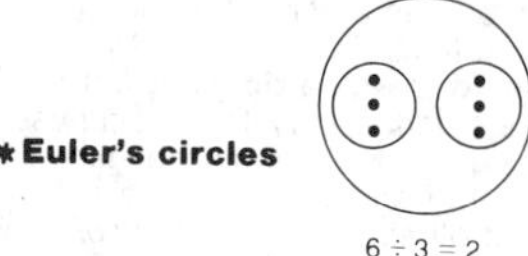

***Euler's circles**

6 ÷ 3 = 2

Euler's diagram, a graphic representation of logical relations first given by the Swiss mathematician Leonhard Euler in the 1700's. Circles or ovals are used to represent, each by its contained surface, the aggregate of possible individuals to which a certain predicate applies.

eu|lo|gi|a (yü lō′jē ə), *n.* **1** a plural of **eulogium**. **2** unconsecrated bread, blessed and distributed among the congregation after the Eucharist to those members who did not commune though they had the right (a custom, emblematic of brotherly love, still observed in the Greek Orthodox Church). [< Late Latin *eulogia* < Greek *eulogiā* blessing; praise, eulogy]

eu|lo|gist (yü′lə jist), *n.* a person who eulogizes. SYN: encomiast, panegyrist.

eu|lo|gis|tic (yü′lə jis′tik), *adj.* of or like a eulogy; praising very highly; commendatory; laudatory: *an article highly eulogistic about modern art.* SYN: panegyrical. —**eu′lo|gis′ti|cal|ly**, *adv.*

eu|lo|gis|ti|cal (yü′lə jis′tə kəl), *adj.* = eulogistic.

eu|lo|gi|um (yü lō′jē əm), *n., pl.* **-gi|ums** or **-gi|a**. eulogy; praise: *Paradoxically enough, [Queen] Victoria received the highest eulogiums for assenting to a political evolution, which, had she completely realised its import, would have filled her with supreme displeasure* (Lytton Strachey). [< Medieval Latin *eulogium,* variant of Late Latin *eulogia* < Greek *eulogiā;* see etym. under **eulogy**]

eu|lo|gize (yü′lə jīz), *v.t.*, **-gized, -giz|ing.** to praise very highly; extol. **SYN:** laud, panegyrize, commend.

eu|lo|giz|er (yü′lə jī′zər), *n.* a person who eulogizes; eulogist.

eu|lo|gy (yü′lə jē), *n., pl.* **-gies. 1** a speech or writing in praise of a person or thing, especially a set oration in honor of a deceased person. **2** high praise; commendation. **SYN:** laudation, panegyric, encomium. [< Greek *eulogiā* < *eu-* well + *lógos* word < *légein* speak]

Eu|mae|us (yü mē′əs), *n.* the faithful swineherd of Odysseus in Homeric legend, who helped his master slay the suitors of Penelope.

Eu|men|i|des (yü men′ə dēz), *n.pl. Greek and Roman Mythology.* the Furies; Erinyes. Literally, the kindly (goddesses), a name for the Furies used to avoid offending them.

eu|mi|to|sis (yü′mī tō′sis), *n. Biology.* true or typical mitosis. [< *eu-* + *mitosis*]

Eu|mol|pus (yü mol′pəs), *n. Greek Mythology.* a priestly bard, reputed founder of the Eleusinian mysteries.

Eu|no|mi|a (yü nō′mē ə), *n. Greek Mythology.* one of the Horae.

eu|nuch (yü′nək), *n.* **1** a castrated man. **2** a castrated man in charge of a harem or the household of an Oriental ruler. [< Latin *eunūchus* < Greek *eunoûchos* (literally) guard of the bedchamber, attendant < *eunḗ* bed + *échein* to keep]

eu|nuch|ism (yü′nə kiz əm), *n.* **1** the condition of a castrated male. **2** the former practice of castrating males to preserve their soprano singing voices or to prepare them for the priesthood, guardianship of harems, and similar duties: *Eunuchism, which persisted at the Chinese court until this century, never got a foothold in Japan* (Alfred L. Kroeber).

eu|nuch|oid (yü′nə koid), *adj.* **1** affected by eunuchoidism. **2** *Figurative.* emasculated; womanish; henpecked: *Nevertheless, shading into the new image is the old Clerk of Oxford—prim, vaguely eunuchoid, and cloistered* (David Boroff).

eu|nuch|oid|ism (yü′nə koi diz′əm), *n.* a condition in which the testes are present but have become atrophied and inactive.

eu|on|y|mus (yü on′ə məs), *n.* any one of a genus of evergreen shrubs and small trees, native of northern temperate regions, having loose clusters (cymes) of small purplish flowers, followed by (usually) crimson capsules that on opening disclose the seed wrapped in an orange-colored covering (aril), as the wahoo and spindle tree. Also, **evonymus.** [< Latin *euōnymus* < Greek *euonymos* (literally) of good name < *eu-* good + dialectal *ónyma* name]

eu|pa|to|ri|um (yü′pə tôr′ē əm, -tōr′-), *n.* any one of a large genus of composite plants, mostly perennial and native of America, with white or purplish flowers, as thoroughwort, joe-pye weed, and hemp agrimony, and especially a cultivated species, the mistflower. [< New Latin *Eupatorium* < Greek *eupatórion* < (Mithridates) *Eupátōr,* King of Pontus, who first used the plants as medicine]

eu|pat|rid (yü pat′rid, yü′pə trid), *n., adj.* —*n.* **1** one of the hereditary aristocrats (eupatridae) of ancient Athens and other Greek states, in whom were vested the powers of making and administering the law. **2** *Rare.* a patrician.
—*adj.* of or having to do with the eupatrids.
[< Greek *eupatrídēs* one of noble ancestry < *eu-* good + *patḗr* father]

eu|pat|ri|dae (yü pat′rə dē), *n.pl.* the eupatrids.

eu|pep|si|a (yü pep′sē ə, -shə), *n.* good digestion (contrasted with *dyspepsia*). [< New Latin *eupepsia* < Greek *eupepsiā* < *eúpeptos;* see etym. under **eupeptic**]

eu|pep|tic (yü pep′tik), *adj.* **1** having or characteristic of good digestion. **2** aiding digestion. **3** *Figurative.* gay; optimistic: *The company would employ eupeptic scoundrels of this sort* (New Yorker). [< Greek *eúpeptos* having a good digestion < *eu-*well + *péptein* digest] —**eu|pep′ti|cal|ly,** *adv.*

eu|pep|tic|i|ty (yü′pep tis′ə tē), *n.* the state of feeling resulting from good digestion.

eu|phau|sid (yü fô′zəd), *n., adj.* —*n.* any one of a numerous group of small shrimplike crustaceans found in all oceans, important as food for whales, seals, and similar animals.
—*adj.* of or belonging to the euphausids.
[< New Latin *Euphausia* the typical genus, apparently < Greek *eu-* good + *phôs* light + *ousiā* substance]

eu|phau|si|id (yü fô′zē əd), *n., adj.* = euphausid.

eu|phe|mism (yü′fə miz əm), *n.* **1** the use of a mild or indirect expression instead of one that is harsh or unpleasantly direct. **2** a word or expression used in this way. "Pass away" is a common euphemism for "die." [< Greek *euphēmismós* < *euphēmízein* speak with fair words < *eu-* good + *phḗmē* speaking < *phánai* speak]

eu|phe|mist (yü′fə mist), *n.* a person who uses euphemisms.

eu|phe|mis|tic (yü′fə mis′tik), *adj.* of or showing euphemism; using mild or indirect words instead of harsh or unpleasant ones.

eu|phe|mis|ti|cal (yü′fə mis′tə kəl), *adj.* = euphemistic.

eu|phe|mis|ti|cal|ly (yü′fə mis′tə klē), *adv.* by way of euphemism; using euphemism: *Teachers wondered what to do with those in their classes whom we euphemistically call "slow learners"* (Atlantic).

eu|phe|mize (yü′fə mīz), *v.,* **-mized, -miz|ing.**
—*v.t.* to express by euphemism.
—*v.i.* to make use of euphemisms.

eu|phe|miz|er (yü′fə mī′zər), *n.* a person who speaks euphemistically.

eu|phen|ic (yü fen′ik), *adj.* of or having to do with euphenics.

eu|phen|ics (yü fen′iks), *n.* a science dealing with ways of improving the human race after birth, especially by technological means such as organ transplantation and prosthetics: *Attempts to control the basic characteristics of the organisms which develop under the influence of defective genetic constitutions have been spoken of ... as 'euphenics', in contrast to 'eugenics', which tries to change the genetic constitution itself* (John Newell). [< *eu-* good + *phen*(otype) + *-ics* (coined by Joshua Lederberg, born 1925, American geneticist)]

eu|pho|ne (yü fō′nē), *n.* a 16-foot organ stop with free reeds, giving a sweet, subdued, clarinetlike tone.

eu|phon|ic (yü fon′ik), *adj.* **1** of or having to do with euphony. **2** = euphonious. —**eu|phon′i|cal|ly,** *adv.* —**eu|phon′i|cal|ness,** *n.*

eu|phon|i|cal (yü fon′ə kəl), *adj.* = euphonic.

eu|pho|ni|ous (yü fō′nē əs), *adj.* pleasing to the ear; sounding agreeable; harmonious: *Our door chimes have a euphonious sound. Lionel Trilling, someone once remarked, is the owner of the most euphonious name in American letters today* (Newsweek). —**eu|pho′ni|ous|ly,** *adv.* —**eu|pho′ni|ous|ness,** *n.*

eu|pho|nism (yü′fə niz əm), *n.* the use of euphonious words.

eu|pho|nis|tic (yü′fə nis′tik), *adj.* characterized by euphonism.

eu|pho|ni|um (yü fō′nē əm), *n.* a brass musical instrument like a tuba, but having a mellower, deeper tone. [< New Latin *euphonium* < Greek *eúphōnos* well-sounding; see etym. under **euphony**]

eu|pho|nize (yü′fə nīz), *v.t.,* **-nized, -niz|ing.** to make euphonious.

eu|pho|ny (yü′fə nē), *n., pl.* **-nies. 1** pleasing effect to the ear; agreeableness of sound, especially agreeableness of speech sounds as uttered or combined in utterance. **SYN:** consonance. **2** a tendency to change sounds so as to favor ease of utterance. [< Late Latin *euphōnia* < Greek *euphōniā* < *eúphōnos* well-sounding < *eu-* good + *phōnḗ* sound]

eu|phor|bi|a (yü fôr′bē ə), *n.* any one of a group of plants of the spurge family, with acrid, milky juice and small, inconspicuous flowers; spurge. Some euphorbias, especially African species, resemble cactuses. [< Latin *euphorbea* < *Euphorbus* (< Greek *Eúphorbos*) a Greek physician to Juba, king of Mauretania, where the herb was first found]

eu|phor|bi|a|ceous (yü fôr′bē ā′shəs), *adj.* belonging to the spurge family.

eu|phor|bi|um (yü fôr′bē əm), *n.* an extremely bitter gum resin obtained from a species of euphorbia, used as a plaster in veterinary medicine and formerly as a cathartic.

Eu|phor|bus (yü fôr′bəs), *n. Greek Mythology.* a brave Trojan, slain by Menelaus. Pythagoras professed to be animated by his soul.

eu|pho|ri|a (yü fôr′ē ə, -fōr′-), *n.* a feeling of happiness and bodily well-being: *... a few months after the armistice, in the early euphoria of peace* (New Yorker). [< Greek *euphoriā* ease of bearing, fertility < *eúphoros* (literally) well-bearing < *eu-* good + *phérein* to bear]

eu|phor|i|ant (yü fôr′ē ənt, -fōr′-), *n.* a drug used to relieve depression and induce a feeling of well-being: *Besides the hallucinogens there are, for instance, euphoriants. They incapacitate by making their victim so witlessly optimistic about everything that he is no good for anything* (Robert Coughlan).

eu|phor|ic (yü fôr′ik, -for′-), *adj.* having to do with or characterized by euphoria: *We're glad to bring such good tidings* [*of a business boom*], *but the euphoric glow shouldn't blind us to some perils* (Life). —**eu|phor′i|cal|ly,** *adv.*

eu|pho|ri|gen|ic (yü fôr′ə jen′ik, -fōr′-), *adj.* inducing euphoria.

eu|phot|ic layer or **zone** (yü fot′ik), the relatively thin surface of a body of water that receives sunlight and in which photosynthesis and consequent production of organic matter can take place: *During the summer in these latitudes, the euphotic zone is steadily depleted of nutrient, and this limits the production* (New Scientist). [< *eu-* + Greek *phôs, phōtós* light + English *-ic*]

eu|phra|sy (yü′frə sē), *n., pl.* **-sies.** = eyebright (a plant): *Then purged with euphrasy and rue The visual nerve, for he had much to see* (Milton). [< Medieval Latin *euphrasia* < Greek *euphrasíā* (literally) cheerfulness < *euphraínein* to cheer up < *eu-* good + *phrḗn, phrenós* mind]

Eu|phra|te|an (yü frā′tē ən), *adj.* of or having to do with the Euphrates River or the region around it: *Euphratean routes.*

eu|phroe (yü′frō), *n. Nautical.* a block having holes through which the ropes of a crowfoot are passed and spread, from which an awning is suspended. Also, **uphroe.** [< Dutch *juffrouw* (literally) maiden]

Eu|phros|y|ne (yü fros′ə nē), *n. Greek Mythology.* one of the three Graces. Euphrosyne means joy.

eu|phu|ism (yü′fyů iz əm), *n.* **1** an affected style of speaking and writing English that was fashionable in England in the late 1500's, characterized by long series of antitheses, frequent similes, and alliteration. *Example:* Be valiant but not too venturous. Let thy attire be comely but not costly (John Lyly). **2** *Figurative.* any affected, elegant style of writing; flowery, artificial language. **3** a euphuistic phrase or composition. [< *Euphues,* main character in two works of John Lyly, 1554?-1606, an English dramatist and romance writer + *-ism*]

eu|phu|ist (yü′fyů ist), *n.* a person who uses euphuism.

eu|phu|is|tic (yü′fyů is′tik), *adj.* using or containing euphuism; like euphuism. —**eu′phu|is′ti|cal|ly,** *adv.*

eu|phu|is|ti|cal (yü′fyů is′tə kəl), *adj.* euphuistic.

eu|plas|tic (yü plas′tik), *adj., n.* —*adj.* that can easily be transformed into permanent organized tissue, as the cells that differentiate into organs of the body embryologically.
—*n.* euplastic matter.
[< Greek *eúplastos* easy to mold (< *eu-* good + *plastós* molded < *plássein* to mold, shape) + English *-ic*]

eu|ploid (yü′ploid), *adj. Genetics.* having a number of chromosomes which is a multiple of the haploid number for the species. [< *eu-* + (ha)*ploid*]

eup|ne|a or **eup|noe|a** (yüp nē′ə), *n. Medicine.* natural or normal breathing; easy respiration. [< New Latin *eupnea* < Greek *eúpnoia* < *eúpnoos* breathing easily < *eu-* well + *pneîn* breathe]

eu|py|rene (yü pī′rēn), *adj.* (of certain spermatozoa) having a well-developed nucleus. [< *eu-* + Greek *pyrḗn* nucleus]

Eur-, *combining form.* the form of **Euro-** before vowels, as in *Eurafrican.*

Eur., **1** Europe. **2** European.

Eur|af|ri|can (yů raf′rə kən), *adj., n.* —*adj.* **1** having to do with Europe and Africa taken together. **2** of mixed European and African descent.
—*n.* a person of mixed European and African descent.

Eu|rail|pass (yůr′āl pas′, -päs′), *n.* a pass permitting unlimited railroad transportation for a specified period of time in countries of the Western European continent. [< *Eu*(ropean) *rail*(road) *pass*]

Eur|a|mer|i|can (yůr′ə mer′ə kən), *adj., n.* —*adj.* **1** having to do with Europe and America taken together: *The technological equipment of Euramerican culture allows a far greater latitude in ways of living in the tropics than could ever be dreamed of without them* (Melville J. Herskovits). **2** native to both Europe and America: *The best known of the northern floras is the "Euramerican flora," represented by the fossils of the great coal basins of Europe and eastern North America* (W. G. Chaloner).
—*n.* a person of mixed European and American descent.

Eur|a|sia (yů rā′zhə, -shə), *n.* Europe and Asia, thought of as a single continent. The Soviet Union is the largest country in Eurasia.

Eur|a|sian (yů rā′zhən, -shən), *n., adj.* —*n.* a person of mixed European and Asian descent.
—*adj.* **1** of or having to do with Europe and Asia taken together, or its people. **2** of mixed European and Asian descent.

Eur|a|si|at|ic (yů rā′zhē at′ik, -shē-), *adj.* = Eurasian.

Eur|at|om (yů rat′əm), *n.* the European Atomic Energy Community, an organization that pools nuclear-power developments. The original mem-

Pronunciation Key: hat, āge, cãre, fär; let, ēqual, tėrm, it, īce; hot, ōpen, ôrder; **oi**l, **ou**t; cup, půt, rüle; **ch**ild; lo**ng**; **th**in; **ᴛʜ**en; **zh**, measure; **ə** represents **a** in about, **e** in taken, **i** in pencil, **o** in lemon, **u** in circus.

bers were Belgium, France, Italy, Luxembourg, the Netherlands, and West Germany.

eu|re|ka (yu̇ rē′kə), *interj., n.* **1** the reputed exclamation ("I have found it") uttered by Archimedes when he discovered the means of determining (by specific gravity) the proportion of base metal in King Hiero's golden crown. **2** an exclamation of triumph at any discovery. **3** the motto of California. [< Greek *heúrēka*, 1st singular perfect active indicative of *heurískein* find]

eu|rhyth|mic (yu̇ riᴛʜ′mik, -rith′-), *adj.* **1** of or having to do with eurhythmics. **2** of or having to do with well-arranged proportion, especially in architecture. Also, **eurythmic**. **—eu|rhyth′mi|cal|ly,** *adv.*

eu|rhyth|mi|cal (yu̇ riᴛʜ′mə kəl, -rith′-), *adj.* = eurhythmic. Also, **eurythmical**.

eu|rhyth|mics (yu̇ riᴛʜ′miks, -rith′-), *n.* the art of interpreting in graceful bodily movements the rhythm of musical compositions.

eu|rhyth|my (yu̇ riᴛʜ′mē, -rith′-), *n.* **1** *Architecture.* harmony in the proportions of a building. **2** *Medicine.* regularity of the pulse. **3a** rhythmical order or movement. **b** graceful proportion and carriage of the body. Also, **eurythmy**. [< Latin *eurhythmia* < Greek *eurythmíā* < *eúrythmos* well-proportioned < *eu-* well + *rhythmós* proportion]

Eu|rip|i|de|an (yu̇ rip′ə dē′ən), *adj.* of, having to do with, or in the style of the Greek tragic poet Euripides, 480?-406? B.C.

eu|ri|pus (yu̇ rī′pəs), *n.* a strait, especially one in which the flow of water in both directions is violent, as that of the Euripus, between Euboea and the mainland in Greece. [< Latin *eurīpus* < Greek *eúrīpos* < *eu-* well + *ripē* a rapid motion]

eu|ro (yu̇r′ō), *n., pl.* **-ros.** a large kangaroo of Australia; wallaroo. [origin uncertain]

Euro-, *combining form.* **1** of Europe, especially western Europe, as in *Europort, Eurocean.* **2** of or having to do with the European money market, as in *Eurobond, Eurocurrency.* **3** of or having to do with the European Economic Community or Common Market, as in *Eurocrat, Euromarket.* Also, **Eur-** before vowels.

Eu|ro-Af|ri|can (yu̇r′ō af′rə kən), *adj., n.* = Eurafrican.

Eu|ro-A|mer|i|can (yu̇r′ō ə mer′ə kən), *adj., n.* = Euramerican.

Eu|ro|bank (yu̇r′ō bangk′), *n.* a European bank, especially one holding deposits from various European and other countries: *It is not only American companies which obtain finance from Eurobanks: many European concerns in the high-interest countries also have recourse to this "fountain of short-term money"* (London Times). **—Eu′ro|bank|er,** *n.*

Eu|ro|bond (yu̇r′ō bond′), *n.* a bond issued by an American or other non-European corporation for sale in European countries: *Issued abroad by both U.S. and foreign companies and usually payable in dollars, Eurobonds are used to tap the $60 billion in American money that is sloshing around Europe* (Time).

Eu|ro|cean (yu̇r′ō shən), *n.* an organization of six European nations, including France, the United Kingdom, the Netherlands, West Germany, Italy, and Sweden, set up to study the exploitation of the deep sea.

Eu|ro|cheque (yu̇r′ō chek′), *n. British.* a credit card used for obtaining goods and services in various European countries.

Eu|roc|ly|don (yu̇ rok′lə don), *n.* **1** a stormy northeast wind of the Mediterranean. Acts 27:14. **2** *Rare.* any tempestuous wind. [< Greek *eurok-lýdōn* < *eûros* east wind + *klýdōn* billow, wave]

Eu|ro|com|mu|nism (yu̇r′ō kom′yə niz əm), *n.* a theory popular in Western European Communist parties that Marxist goals can be achieved by democratic methods. **—Eu′ro|com′mu|nist,** *n., adj.*

Eu|roc|ra|cy (yu̇ rok′rə sē), *n.* the officials or administrators of the European Economic Community or Common Market. [< *Euro-* + *-cracy*, as in *bureaucracy*]

Eu|ro|crat (yu̇r′ə krat), *n.* an official or representative of the European Economic Community or Common Market.

Eu|ro|crat|ic (yu̇r′ə krat′ik), *adj.* of or having to do with the Eurocrats or Eurocracy.

Eu|ro|cur|ren|cy (yu̇r′ō kėr′ən sē), *n., pl.* **-cies.** U.S. dollars and some other currencies held by foreign interests, especially by European banks, and used as a medium of international credit.

Eu|ro|dol|lar (yu̇r′ō dol′ər), *n.* a U.S. dollar held by a foreign interest and involved in a transaction outside of the United States, especially in Europe: *The growth of the Eurodollar market is causing rising concern in European banking circles* (London Times).

Eu|ro|mar|ket (yu̇r′ō mär′kit), *n.* the European Common Market.

Eu|ro|mon|ey (yu̇r′ō mun′ē), *n., pl.* **-eys** or **-ies.** = Eurocurrency.

Eu|ro|pa (yu̇ rō′pə), *n.* **1** *Greek Mythology.* a Phoenician princess loved by Zeus. He took the form of a white bull and carried her off on his back to Crete. **2** the third satellite of Jupiter.

Eu|ro|par|lia|ment (yu̇r′ō pär′lə mənt), *n.* = European Parliament.

Eu|ro|par|lia|men|tar|i|an (yu̇r′ō pär′lə men tãr′ē ən), *n.* a member of the European Parliament.

Eu|ro|par|lia|men|ta|ry (yu̇r′ō pär′lə men′tər ē), *adj.* of or having to do with the European Parliament.

Eu|ro|pe|an (yu̇r′ə pē′ən), *adj., n.* **—adj.** **1** of or having to do with Europe or its people. **2** originating in or native to Europe.
—n. **1** a person who was born in or lives in Europe. The French, Germans, and Spaniards are Europeans. **2** a person of European descent. **3** a person who favors joining the European Economic Community or Common Market.

European chafer, a beetle of Europe that has spread to the United States, where its larva destroys lawns, pasture, hay, and small grains.

European char, a trout of the cold lakes and mountain streams of northern Europe.

European Common Market, = European Economic Community.

European Community, = European Economic Community. *Abbr.:* EC (no periods).

European corn borer, = corn borer.

European cowslip, a cowslip with showy, fragrant clusters of large yellow or purple flowers that grows in meadows throughout Europe.

European cranberry, a small cranberry with red berries, found in swamps of cold regions in Europe, Asia, and North America; bogberry.

European cranberry bush, = cranberry tree (def. 2).

European Economic Community, an organization of European states formed to operate a common market and eventually a complete customs union; Common Market. *Abbr.* EEC

European goldfinch, a small, brownish, red-faced finch with yellow on the wings, native to Europe and parts of Asia and Africa; It has been introduced into North America.

Eu|ro|pe|an|ism (yu̇r′ə pē′ə niz əm), *n.* **1** European characteristics, ideas, methods, etc. **2** a European trait or practice. **3** the neutralization or union of European countries: *... the powerful trend toward Europeanism and the towering strength of the European Common Market* (James M. Gavin).

Eu|ro|pe|an|ist (yu̇r′ə pē′ə nist), *n.* a person supporting Europeanism or Europeanization.

Eu|ro|pe|an|i|za|tion (yu̇r′ə pē′ə nə zā′shən), *n.* **1** the process of making or becoming European. **2** the process of Europeanizing, free of any particular nation.

Eu|ro|pe|an|ize (yu̇r′ə pē′ə nīz), *v.t.,* **-ized, -iz|ing.** **1** to make European in appearance, habit, way of life, or the like. **2** to put under the rule of a neutral commission so as to make (a territory claimed by two or more countries) part of all Europe.

European larch, a cone-bearing tree native to the Alps, largely cultivated in the United States for ornament and in Europe for its tough and durable timber.

Eu|ro|pe|an|ly (yu̇r′ə pē′ən lē), *adv.* in a European way or style: *He was Europeanly precise in his movements* (Harold Brodkey).

European mole, a mole native to Europe that builds as its nest a central chamber connected to other smaller rooms, instead of building tunnels.

European Monetary System, a monetary system to stabilize exchange rates of the currencies of member countries in the European Economic Community.

European mountain ash, a tree of the rose family, native to Europe and Asia, often cultivated for its bright-red, berrylike fruit; rowan.

Eu|ro|pe|an|ness (yu̇r′ə pē′ən nis), *n.* the quality or condition of being European in character, outlook, ideas, or manners: *Russia's essential Europeanness.*

European Parliament, the legislative and advisory branch of the European Economic Community, consisting of 410 members elected by the voters of member nations.

European partridge, = Hungarian partridge.

European plan, *U.S.* a system of charges to guests in a hotel by which the price covers the room, but not the meals (distinguished from *American plan*).

European plum, any one of several varieties of blue or red plums with medium to very large fruits and a high sugar content, often dried as prunes; garden plum.

European Recovery Program, a plan adopted by the United States for financial aid to European Nations after World War II. It was originally called the Marshall Plan because it was formally proposed by U.S. Secretary of State George C. Marshall in 1947. It began in April, 1948.

European white birch, the weeping birch of northern Europe.

European wildcat, a large, powerful wildcat resembling the tabby in color, found in Scotland, parts of the European continent, and in central Siberia. It is possibly an ancestor of the domestic cat.

***eu|ro|pi|um** (yu̇ rō′pē əm), *n.* a soft, grayish, chemical element of the same group as cerium. It is a rare-earth, metallic element that occurs only in combination with other elements. Europium compounds are used in coating color television screens and in control rods in atomic power plants. [< New Latin *Europium* < Latin *Europa* Europe]

***europium**

symbol	atomic number	atomic weight	oxidation state
Eu	63	151.96	3,2

Eu|ro|po|cen|tric (yu̇r′ə pə sen′trik), *adj.* having Europe as its center: *He [a historian] knows that for half a millennium the nations of Western Europe were destined to predominate. Thus, it is natural for him to have a Europocentric view of the modern world* (Benjamin Quarles).

Eu|ro|port (yu̇r′ə pôrt′, -pōrt′), *n.* a European port serving as a major import and export harbor, especially for the Common Market countries. [< Dutch *Europoort*]

Eu|ro|vi|sion (yu̇r′ō vizh′ən), *n.* a television network linking most of the countries of Western Europe. [< *Euro*(pe) + (tele)*vision*]

Eu|rus (yu̇r′əs), *n.* the east or southeast wind. [< Latin *Eurus* < Greek *Eûros* the East Wind]

eury-, *combining form.* wide; broad: *Eurycephalic* = broad-headed. [< Greek *eurýs* wide]

Eu|ry|a|le (yu̇ rī′ə lē), *n. Greek Legend.* one of the Gorgons.

eu|ry|bath|ic (yu̇r′ə bath′ik), *adj.* = eurybenthic. [< *eury-* + Greek *báthos* depth + English *-ic*]

eu|ry|ben|thic (yu̇r′ə ben′thik), *adj. Biology.* able to live in a broad range of depths of water. [< *eury-* + Greek *bénthos* depth + English *-ic*]

eu|ry|ce|phal|ic (yu̇r′ə sə fal′ik), *adj.* broad-headed.

eu|ry|ceph|a|lous (yu̇r′ə sef′ə ləs), *adj.* = eurycephalic.

Eu|ry|cle|a (yu̇r′ə klē′ə), *n.* the nurse of Odysseus in Homeric legend, who after twenty years identified him by a scar.

Eu|ryd|i|ce (yu̇ rid′ə sē), *n. Greek Legend.* the wife of Orpheus. He freed her from Hades by the charm of his music, but lost her again because he disobeyed the orders of Pluto and turned back to see if she was following.

eu|ryg|nath|ic (yu̇r′ig nath′ik), *adj.* eurygnathous.

eu|ryg|na|thism (yu̇ rig′nə thiz əm), *n.* eurygnathous feature or characteristic.

eu|ryg|na|thous (yu̇ rig′nə thəs), *adj.* having a broad upper jaw. [< *eury-* + Greek *gnáthos* jaw + English *-ous*]

eu|ry|ha|line (yu̇ rī′hə lin, -līn), *adj. Biology.* capable of living in water of any degree of saltiness within a wide range. [< *eury-* + Greek *háls* brine + English *-ine*[1]]

Eu|ryn|o|me (yu̇ rin′ə mē), *n. Greek Mythology.* a daughter of Oceanus, and mother by Zeus of the Graces.

eu|ry|on (yu̇r′ē on), *n.* the point of either end of the greatest crosswise diameter of the skull. [< New Latin *euryon* < Greek *eurýs* wide]

eu|ryph|a|gous (yu̇ rif′ə gəs), *adj. Zoology.* living on a wide variety of foods. [< *eury-* + Greek *phageîn* eat + English *-ous*]

eu|ry|prog|na|thous (yu̇r′ə prog′nə thəs), *adj. Anthropology.* having wide cheekbones and upper jaws, combined with prognathism. [< *eury-* + *prognathous*]

eu|ryp|ter|id (yu̇ rip′tər id), *n.* any one of an extinct order of crustaceans of the Paleozoic era, varying in size from a few inches to six feet, related to the king crabs. [< New Latin *Eurypteridae* the order name < Greek *eurýs* broad + *pterón* wing]

eu|ryp|ter|us (yu̇ rip′tər əs), *n.* a large, scorpion-like eurypterid. [< New Latin *Eurypterus* the genus name]

eu|ry|py|lous (yu̇r′ə pī′ləs), *adj. Zoology.* having or characterized by one or more large, wide openings. [< *eury-* + Greek *pýlē* gate + English *-ous*]

Eu|rys|theus (yu̇ ris′thüs, -thē əs), *n. Greek Legend.* the king at whose bidding Hercules performed his twelve labors.

eu|ry|stom|a|tous (yu̇r′ə stom′ə təs), *adj. Zoology.* having a wide or distensible mouth: *an eurystomatous snake.* [< *eury-* + Greek *stóma, -atos* mouth + English *-ous*]

eu|ry|therm (yu̇r′ə thėrm′), *n. Biology.* a eurythermal organism.

eu|ry|ther|mal (yu̇r′ə thėr′məl), *adj. Biology.* able

to live in any temperature within a broad range.

eu|ry|ther|mic (yůr′ə thėr′mik), *adj.* = eurythermal.

eu|ryth|mic (yů rɪᴛʜ′mik, -rith′-), *adj.* = eurhythmic. —**eu|ryth′mi|cal|ly**, *adv.*

eu|ryth|mi|cal (yů rɪᴛʜ′mə kəl, -rith′-), *adj.* = eurhythmic.

eu|ryth|mics (yů rɪᴛʜ′miks, -rith′-), *n.* = eurhythmics.

eu|ryth|my (yů rɪᴛʜ′mē, -rith′-), *n.* = eurhythmy.

eu|ry|top|ic (yůr′ə top′ik), *n. Biology.* able to tolerate a wide range of variations in environmental conditions. [< *eury-* + Greek *tópos* place]

Eu|se|bi|ans (yü sē′bē ənz), *n.pl.* the followers of Eusebius of Nicomedia, an Arian bishop of Constantinople in the 300's.

Eus|ka|ra or **Eus|ke|ra** (yüs′kər ə), *n.* the Basque language: *The Basques of Northern Spain ... proudly tell visitors that no foreigner has ever been able to master their complex language, Euskara* (Saturday Review). [< Basque *Euskara*]

eu|sol (yü′sōl, -sol), *n.* an antiseptic solution containing hypochlorous acid. [< *E*(dinburgh) *U*(niversity) *sol*(ution); because it was developed there]

eu|spo|ran|gi|ate (yü′spə ran′jē āt), *adj. Botany.* having sporangia formed from a group of epidermal cells.

Eu|sta|chi|an tube (yü stā′kē ən, -shən), a slender canal between the pharynx and the middle ear. It equalizes the air pressure on the two sides of the eardrum. *The stuffy sensation in the ears and the dizziness he found came from pressure on the Eustachian tube* (Science News Letter). See picture under **ear**[1]. [< *Eustachius*, Latinized form of Bartolommeo *Eustachio*, an Italian anatomist of the 1500's + *-ian*]

eu|sta|sy (yü′stə sē), *n.* world-wide changes in sea level caused by the melting of icecaps, deposition of sediments, and similar or related phenomena.

eu|stat|ic (yü stat′ik), *adj.* **1** of or characterized by eustasy: *That eustatic fall in level laid bare the bed of the North Sea* (London Times). **2** (of a land area) not undergoing depression or elevation [< German *eustatisch* < Greek *eu-* good + *statikós* causing to stand + German *-isch* -ic]

eu|tec|tic (yü tek′tik), *adj., n.* —*adj.* that may be easily melted, as an alloy or mixture whose melting point is lower than that of any other alloy or mixture composed of the same ingredients.
—*n.* a eutectic substance.
[< Greek *eútēktos* easily melting (< *eu-* well + *tēkein* melt) + English *-ic*]

eu|tec|toid (yü tek′toid), *adj., n.* —*adj.* like a eutectic.
—*n.* a mixture produced by decomposition of a solid solution at a relatively low temperature, which is constant for any one alloy.

Eu|ter|pe (yü tėr′pē), *n. Greek Mythology.* the Muse of music and lyric poetry.

Eu|ter|pe|an (yü tėr′pē ən), *adj.* **1** having to do with or relating to Euterpe. **2** having to do with music.

eu|tex|i|a (yü tek′sē ə), *n.* the quality of melting easily; eutectic quality. [< Greek *eutexiā* < *eu-* well + *tēkein* melt]

eu|tha|na|sia (yü′thə nā′zhə), *n.* **1** a painless killing, especially to end a painful and incurable disease; mercy killing. **2** an easy, painless death. **3** *Figurative.* a painless end or extinction: *Removing the exchange risk in holding sterling ... leaves the French in a very weak position to impose a slow euthanasia on the pound, and they know it* (Anthony Harris). [< Greek *euthanasiā* < *eu-* good + *thánatos* death]

eu|tha|na|siac (yü thə nā′zhək), *adj.* **1** of euthanasia; euthanatic. **2** *Figurative.* painless; merciful: *Abie's Irish Rose* [*a play*] *finally died a slow, lingering, and euthanasiac death six years and 2326 performances after ... opening night* (Alexander Woollcott).

eu|tha|nat|ic (yü′thə nat′ik), *adj., n.* —*adj.* of or having to do with euthanasia.
—*n.* an advocate or supporter of euthanasia.

eu|tha|nize (yü′thənīz), *v.t.*, **-nized, -nizing.** to put to death painlessly; perform euthanasia on: *Dysart said lay people make decisions about euthanizing animals "at every animal control organization that I know of in the world"* (New Orleans States-Item). *Even if the patient wishes to die, he has no right to being "euthanized"* (Lorne E. Rozovsky). —**eu′tha|ni|za′tion**, *n.*

eu|then|ics (yü then′iks), *n.* the science or art of improving the human race by controlling the environment or living conditions. [< Greek *euthēneîn* thrive, flourish + English *-ics*]

eu|ther|i|an (yü thir′ē ən), *adj.* of or having to do with placental mammals. [< New Latin *Eutheria* the group name (< Greek *eu-* well + *thērion* beast) + English *-an*]

eu|to|mous (yü′tə məs), *adj.* (of a mineral formation) having distinct cleavages; cleaving readily. [< Greek *eútomos* (with English *-ous*) well divided < *eu-* well + *témnein* cut]

eu|troph|ic (yü trof′ik), *adj., n.* —*adj.* **1** (of lakes and other waters) rich or excessively rich in accumulated phosphates, nitrates, and other nutrients that promote the growth of algae, which deplete the water of oxygen and cause the extinction of other organisms: *Often the low species diversity of the phytoplankton in eutrophic lakes is a result of high population of blue-green algae* (Arthur D. Hasler). **2** *Medicine.* tending to promote nutrition.
—*n.* a eutrophic medicine.
[< Greek *eútrophos* thriving, nourishing < *eu-* well + *tréphein* nourish]

eu|tro|phi|cate (yü trof′ə kāt), *v.i.*, **-cat|ed, -cat|ing.** to be or become eutrophic; undergo eutrophication: *The increased growth of vegetation in the water and the proliferation of algae in huge blotches of green slime ... causes lakes to eutrophicate, or age, before their time* (New York Times).

eu|tro|phi|ca|tion (yü′trə fə kā′shən), *n.* the accumulation of nutrients in lakes and other bodies of water, causing rapid growth of algae, which deplete the water of oxygen: *Eutrophication literally means "nourishing well," but in current usage it refers to the inadvertent nourishing of algae in lakes to the detriment of other living things* (Scientific American).

eu|tro|phied (yü′trə fēd), *adj.* eutrophicated; eutrophic: *... phosphates did the damage to the severely eutrophied Lake Washington, near Seattle* (John F. Henahan).

eu|tro|phy (yü′trə fē), *n. Physiology.* healthy nutrition.

eu|trop|ic (yü trop′ik), *adj. Botany.* revolving with the sun; dextrorse. [< Greek *eútropos* (< *eu-* well + *trépein* to turn) + English *-ic*]

Eu|tych|i|an (yü tik′ē ən), *adj., n.* —*adj.* of or having to do with, or adhering to the doctrine of Eutyches, a monk of Constantinople living in the 400's, who opposed the Nestorians, maintaining that Christ has only one nature, the divine.
—*n.* an adherent or follower of Eutyches.

Eu|tych|i|an|ism (yü tik′ē ə niz′əm), *n.* the doctrine or belief of the Eutychians.

eux|e|nite (yük′sə nīt), *n.* a brownish-black mineral found in Norway, containing yttrium, columbium, titanium, uranium, and other elements. [< Greek *eúxenos* hospitable (< *eu-* good + *xénos* stranger) + English *-ite*[1] (from its numerous constituents)]

Eux|ine (yük′sin), *adj., n.* —*adj.* of or having to do with the Black Sea, the sea between Europe and the Middle East.
—*n.* an ancient name for the Black Sea.
[< Latin (*Pontus*) *Euxinus* friendly (Sea) < Greek *eúxenos* hospitable < *eu-* good + *xénos* stranger]

e.v. or **ev** (no periods), electron volt or volts.

E.V., **1** electron volt or volts. **2** English Version (of the Bible).

EVA (no periods), extravehicular activity: *In their first EVA the astronauts took conventional and stereo pictures, gathered rock and soil samples, and made visual and photographic geological surveys* (Frederick I. Ordway and Mitchell R. Sharpe, Jr.).

e|vac|u|a|ble (i vak′yů ə bəl), *adj.* that may be readily evacuated: *an evacuable furnace, an evacuable city.*

e|vac|u|ant (i vak′yů ənt), *adj., n. Medicine.* —*adj.* evacuating, especially from the bowels; cathartic; purgative.
—*n.* an evacuant medicine or remedy, especially a purgative.

e|vac|u|ate (i vak′yů āt), *v.*, **-at|ed, -at|ing.** —*v.t.* **1** to leave empty; withdraw from: *After surrendering, the soldiers evacuated the fort.* **SYN:** quit, vacate. **2** to remove; withdraw: *The government evacuated all civilians from the war zone.* **3** to clear out the contents of; empty (a container). **4** to make empty: *to evacuate the stomach.*
—*v.i.* to withdraw from a place in danger or that has undergone some disaster: *We will have to evacuate if the flood gets any worse.*
[< Latin *ēvacuāre* (with English *-ate*[1]) empty the bowels < *ex-* out + *vacuus* empty]

e|vac|u|a|tion (i vak′yů ā′shən), *n.* **1** the act or process of evacuating; leaving empty; withdrawal from occupation or possession: *The first scene in the withdrawal of the troops had been the evacuation of ... Antwerp* (John Lothrop Motley). **2** removal; withdrawal. **3** a making empty. **4** a discharge.

Evacuation Day, the anniversary of the day on which the British troops evacuated the city of New York, November 25, 1783.

e|vac|u|a|tor (i vak′yů ā′tər), *n.* a person or thing that evacuates, empties, or makes void.

e|vac|u|ee (i vak′yů ē, -vak′yů ē′), *n.* a person who is removed to a place of greater safety: *The evacuees from the flood were housed in the schools and churches. As the boats filled and pulled away, some evacuees helped pull the oars, some sat stunned and silent* (Time).

e|vad|a|ble (i vā′də bəl), *adj.* that can be evaded.

e|vade (i vād′), *v.*, **e|vad|ed, e|vad|ing.** —*v.t.* **1** to get away from by trickery; avoid by cleverness: *The thief evaded his pursuers and escaped.* **SYN:** elude, avoid. See syn. under **escape.** **2** to avoid by indefinite or misleading statements: *When Father asked who broke the window, I tried to evade the question by saying, "I wonder who!" The witness tried to evade an embarrassing question by saying he couldn't remember.* **SYN:** parry, prevaricate, equivocate. **3** to elude or baffle (efforts or plans).
—*v.i.* **1** to practice evasion. **2** *Rare.* to get away; escape. [< Latin *ēvādere* leave; go out < *ex-* away + *vādere* go]

e|vad|er (i vā′dər), *n.* a person or thing that evades.

e|vad|i|ble (i vā′də bəl), *adj.* = evadable.

e|vad|ing|ly (i vā′ding lē), *adv.* in an evading manner; evasively.

E|vad|ne (i vad′nē), *n. Greek Legend.* the wife of Capaneus. When her husband was killed by Zeus, she threw herself on his funeral pyre.

e|vag|i|na|ble (i vaj′ə nə bəl), *adj.* that can be evaginated.

e|vag|i|nate (i vaj′ə nāt), *v.t.*, **-nat|ed, -nat|ing.** to turn inside out or cause to protrude by eversion, as a tubular organ. [< Latin *ēvāgīnāre* (with English *-ate*[1]) < *ex-* out + *vagīna* sheath, vagina]

e|vag|i|na|tion (i vaj′ə nā′shən), *n.* **1** the act of evaginating. **2** the state of being evaginated. **3** what is evaginated.

e|val|u|a|ble (i val′yů ə bəl), *adj.* that can be evaluated.

e|val|u|ate (i val′yů āt), *v.t.*, **-at|ed, -at|ing.** **1** to find out the value or the amount of; estimate the worth or importance of; appraise: *An expert will evaluate the old furniture you wish to sell. The expedition has now returned, and its members are beginning to evaluate and integrate the facts gathered in the field and at the base* (E. F. Roots). **SYN:** See syn. under **estimate.** **2** *Mathematics.* to find a numerical expression for. [< Middle French *évaluer* (with English *-ate*[1]) < *é-* out (< Latin *ex-*) + *value* value]

e|val|u|a|tion (i val′yů ā′shən), *n.* **1** the act or process of evaluating: *The detective began his evaluation of the evidence.* **2** an estimated value; valuation.

e|val|u|a|tive (i val′yů ā′tiv), *adj.* of or capable of evaluation: *Mr. Priestley has written an evaluative account of Dickens' literary contribution that is sensible, just, and perceptively critical* (New Yorker).

e|val|u|a|tor (i val′yů ā′tər), *n.* a person or thing that evaluates.

E|van|der (i van′dər), *n. Greek Legend.* a son of Hermes, and founder of an Arcadian colony on the Palatine before the Trojan War.

ev|a|nesce (ev′ə nes′), *v.i.*, **-nesced, -nesc|ing.** to disappear gradually; fade away; vanish. [< Latin *ēvānēscere* < *ex-* out + *vānēscere* vanish < *vānus* insubstantial, empty]

ev|a|nes|cence (ev′ə nes′əns), *n.* **1** a gradual disappearance; fading away; vanishing: *The gradual evanescence of dogmatic teaching* (W. E. H. Lecky). **2** a tendency to disappear or fade away; inability to last long: *This evanescence and lubricity of all objects ... lets them slip through our fingers* (Emerson).

ev|a|nes|cent (ev′ə nes′ənt), *adj.* gradually disappearing; soon passing away; vanishing: *the evanescent beauty of the sunset.* **SYN:** transitory, ephemeral. [< Latin *ēvānēscens, -entis* present participle of *ēvānēscere;* see etym. under **evanesce**]

evang. or **Evang.**, evangelical.

e|van|gel[1] (i van′jəl), *n.* **1** the Gospel; the good news of the saving of mankind through Christ (in Christian belief). **2** any good news: *We wait for thy coming, sweet Wind of the South ... For the yearly evangel thou bearest from God* (John Greenleaf Whittier). [< Late Latin *evangelium* < Greek *evangélion* good tidings, ultimately < *eu-* good + *angéllein* announce < *ángelos* messenger]

e|van|gel[2] (i van′jəl), *n.* = evangelist. [< Greek *euángelos* bringing good news]

E|van|gel (i van′jəl), *n.* one of the four Gospels; Matthew, Mark, Luke, or John.

e|van|gel|ic (ē′van jel′ik, ev′ən-), *adj.* = evangelical.

Pronunciation Key: hat, āge, cãre, fär; let, ēqual, tėrm; it, īce; hot, ōpen, ôrder; oil, out; cup, půt, rüle; child; long; thin; ᴛʜen; zh, measure; ə represents a in about, e in taken, i in pencil, o in lemon, u in circus.

e|van|gel|i|cal (ē'van jel'ə kəl, ev'ən-), *adj., n.* —*adj.* **1** of or according to the four Gospels or the New Testament. **2** of or having to do with the Protestant churches that emphasize Christ's atonement and man's salvation by faith as the most important parts of Christianity. Methodists and Baptists are evangelical; Unitarians and Universalists are not. **3** having to do with a movement in Protestantism during the 1700's and 1800's that placed emphasis on the need for deep personal religious experience, especially a realization of personal sin and the approach to God through Christ. **4** = evangelistic.
—*n.* **1** a person who maintains evangelical doctrines; Protestant. **2** a member of an evangelical church or party, especially a low churchman in the Church of England: *At his theological college, Ridley Hall, Cambridge, he was thought a strong "evangelical"* (Manchester Guardian Weekly). —**e'van|gel'i|cal|ly**, *adv.* —**e'van|gel'i|cal|ness**, *n.*

E|van|gel|i|cal (ē'van jel'ə kəl, ev'ən-), *adj.* **1** designating those Protestant churches deriving from Lutheranism rather than Calvinism (contrasted with *Reformed*). **2** (in some parts of Europe) Protestant.

Evangelical Alliance, an association of Christians belonging to the Evangelical denominations, to promote more effective cooperation in Christian work.

e|van|gel|i|cal|ism (ē'van jel'ə kə liz'əm, ev'ən-), *n.* **1** the doctrines of an evangelical church. **2** adherence to such doctrines.

Evangelical United Brethren, a Protestant church formed in 1946 in the United States by the merger of two churches which had been formed in the 1800's by German settlers in Pennsylvania and Maryland. In 1968 the Evangelical United Brethren united with the Methodist Church.

e|van|gel|i|cism (ē'van jel'ə siz əm, ev'ən-), *n.* = evangelicalism.

E|van|ge|line (i van'jə lin), *n.* an idyllic poem by Henry Wadsworth Longfellow, based on the deportation of the Acadians by the British in 1755.

e|van|gel|ise (i van'jə līz), *v.t., v.i.,* **-ised, -is|ing.** *Especially British.* evangelize.

e|van|gel|ism (i van'jə liz əm), *n.* **1** the preaching of the Gospel; earnest effort for the spread of the Gospel: *An aggressive program of evangelism has been undertaken in the postwar period* (Atlantic). **2** belief in the doctrines of an evangelical church or party; evangelicalism. **3** the work of an evangelist.

e|van|gel|ist (i van'jə list), *n.* **1** a preacher of the Gospel. **2a** a traveling preacher who stirs up religious feeling in a revival service or camp meeting. SYN: revivalist. **b** a person who brings the Gospel to pagan peoples or nonbelievers; missionary.

E|van|gel|ist (i van'jə list), *n.* **1** the writer of one of the four Gospels; Matthew, Mark, Luke, or John. **2** (in the Mormon Church) a patriarch, one of the higher order of priests.

e|van|gel|is|tar|i|on (i van'jə lis tãr'ē on), *n., pl.* **-i|a** (-ē ə). = evangelistary.

e|van|gel|is|tar|i|um (i van'jə lis tãr'ē əm), *n., pl.* **-i|a** (-ē ə). = evangelistary.

e|van|gel|is|ta|ry (i van'jə lis'tər ē), *n., pl.* **-ries.** **1** a book containing passages from the Gospels, used at services in the Greek and Roman Catholic churches as part of the liturgy. **2** a copy of the four Gospels. [< Medieval Latin *evangelistarium*]

e|van|gel|is|tic (i van'jə lis'tik), *adj.* **1** of or by an evangelist or evangelists. **2** = evangelical (def. 2). **3** Sometimes, **Evangelistic.** of or having to do with the four Evangelists. —**e|van'gel|is'ti|cal|ly**, *adv.*

e|van|gel|i|za|tion (i van'jə lə zā'shən), *n.* the act of evangelizing.

e|van|gel|ize (i van'jə līz), *v.,* **-ized, -iz|ing.** —*v.t.* **1** to preach the Gospel to. **2** to convert to Christianity by preaching.
—*v.i.* to preach the Gospel; act as an evangelist.

e|van|gel|iz|er (i van'jə lī'zər), *n.* a person who evangelizes.

e|van|ish (i van'ish), *v.i. Poetic.* **1** to vanish; disappear: *... like the rainbow's lovely form Evanishing amid the storm* (Robert Burns). **2** to cease to be; die: *and cares evanish, like a morning dream* (Allan Ramsay). [< Old French *evaniss-*, stem of *evanir* < Latin *ēvānēscere;* see etym. under **evanesce**]

e|van|ish|ment (i van'ish mənt), *n.* the act of vanishing; disappearance.

ev|ans|ite (ev'ən zīt), *n.* a hydrous phosphate of aluminum occurring in white reniform masses. [< Brooke *Evans*, who brought it from Hungary in 1855 + *-ite*[1]]

e|vap|o|ra|bil|i|ty (i vap'ər ə bil'ə tē), *n.* the quality of being evaporable.

e|vap|o|ra|ble (i vap'ər ə bəl), *adj.* that can be evaporated; volatile.

e|vap|o|rate (i vap'ə rāt), *v.,* **-rat|ed, -rat|ing.** —*v.i.* **1** to turn into vapor; change from a liquid or solid into a vapor: *Boiling water evaporates rapidly. Some solids, such as moth balls and dry ice, evaporate without melting.* SYN: volatilize, vaporize. **2** to give off moisture. **3** *Figurative.* to vanish; disappear: *His good resolutions evaporated after New Year.* SYN: dissipate.
—*v.t.* **1** to remove water or other liquid from, for example by heat, in order to dry or to reduce to a more concentrated state: *Heat is used to evaporate milk.* **2** to cause to change from a liquid (or less often, solid) into a vapor; drive off in the form of vapor: *Heat evaporates water.*
[< Latin *ēvapōrāre* (with English *-ate*[1]) < *ex-* out + *vapor* vapor, steam]

e|vap|o|rat|ed milk (i vap'ə rā'tid), a thick, unsweetened, canned milk, prepared by evaporating some of the water from ordinary milk.

e|vap|o|ra|tion (i vap'ə rā'shən), *n.* **1** the act or process of changing a liquid or a solid into vapor; an evaporating: *Wet clothes on a line become dry by evaporation of the water in them.* **2** the state of being changed into vapor. **3** the removal of water or other liquid. **4a** the product of the evaporating process. **b** the amount evaporated. **5** *Figurative.* disappearance.

e|vap|o|ra|tive (i vap'ə rā'tiv), *adj.* causing or having to do with evaporation: *In climates where sweating for evaporative heatloss is unnecessary, dietary intake of salt is usually greatly in excess of human requirements* (New Scientist).

e|vap|o|ra|tor (i vap'ə rā'tər), *n.* an apparatus for removing water or other liquid from a substance: *an evaporator for drying fruits.*

e|vap|o|rim|e|ter (i vap'ə rim'ə tər), *n.* an instrument for measuring the quantity of a liquid evaporated in a given time.

e|vap|o|rite (i vap'ə rīt), *n.* a sedimentary deposit formed as a result of the evaporation of seawater: *The rich Middle East and Texan oil fields are closely associated with formations bearing thick deposits of salt and related evaporites* (New Scientist).

e|vap|or|o|graph (i vap'ər ə graf, -gräf), *n.* a device for taking crude pictures in darkness, by means of focusing infrared radiation on a heat-sensitive film of oil, spread on a plastic sheet. It is thought to have possible military use.

e|vap|o|rom|e|ter (i vap'ə rom'ə tər), *n.* = evaporimeter.

e|vap|o|tran|spi|ra|tion (i vap'ō tran'spə rā'shən), *n.* the return of water from the soil and from plants to the atmosphere by evaporation and transpiration. [< *evapo*(ration) + *transpiration*]

e|vap|o|tran|spire (i vap'ō tran spīr'), *v.t.,* **-spired, -spir|ing.** to cause the return of (water) to the atmosphere by evaporation and transpiration: *Water-use efficiency can be expressed in a variety of ways, such as tons of hay or bushels of potatoes per acre-inch of water evapotranspired, crates of marketable lettuce per acre-foot of water, or as a weight ratio, kilogram per kilogram* (E. G. Viets, Jr.). [back formation < *evapotranspiration*]

é|va|sé (ā vá zā'), *adj. French.* (of the neck of a vase, the capital of a column, or similar object) spreading or flaring outward.

e|va|si|ble (i vā'sə bəl), *adj.* that can be evaded; evadable.

e|va|sion (i vā'zhən), *n.* **1** the act of getting away from something by trickery; avoiding by cleverness: *He had no excuse for the evasion of his responsibilities.* SYN: avoidance, dodging. **2** an attempt to escape an argument, a charge, a question, or the like: *The prisoner's evasions of the lawyer's questions convinced the jury he was guilty.* **3** a means of evading; trick or excuse used to avoid something: *His evasions and delays prevented us from getting to know the truth.* SYN: subterfuge, prevarication, equivocation, quibble.
[< Late Latin *ēvāsiō, -ōnis* < Latin *ēvādere;* see etym. under **evade**]

e|va|sive (i vā'siv, -ziv), *adj.* tending or trying to evade: *"I really haven't given it much thought" is an evasive answer. The witness has been very evasive in his testimony.* SYN: shifty, misleading.
—**e|va'sive|ly**, *adv.* —**e|va'sive|ness**, *n.*

eve[1] (ēv), *n.* **1** the evening or day before a holiday or special day: *New Year's Eve, Christmas Eve, the eve of my birthday.* **2** *Figurative.* the time just before something happens: *Everything was quiet on the eve of the battle. The campaign ended on the eve of the election.* **3** *Archaic.* evening. [short form of *even*[2]]

eve[2] (ēv), *v.i.,* **eved, ev|ing.** *British Dialect.* to become moist or damp. [short for obsolete *geve*, dialectal variant of *give*]

Eve (ēv), *n.* the first woman, the wife of Adam (in the Bible, Genesis 2:21-25; 3:20). **a daughter of Eve.** See under **daughter.**

e|vec|tion (i vek'shən), *n. Astronomy.* the largest of the oscillatory disturbances of the moon's orbit, caused by changes in the sun's attraction. The time required for a complete oscillation is about 32 days. [< Latin *ēvectiō, -ōnis* a carrying away < *ēvehere* carry out < *ex-* out + *vehere* carry]

e|vec|tion|al (i vek'shə nəl), *adj.* relating or belonging to the evection.

e|ven[1] (ē'vən), *adj., v., adv.* —*adj.* **1** level; flat; smooth: *The country is even, with no high hills.* SYN: plane. See syn. under **level.** **2** at the same level; in the same plane or line: *The snow was even with the window.* SYN: parallel. **3** keeping about the same; regular; uniform: *The car goes with an even motion.* **4** equal; no more or less than: *They divided the money in even shares. The score was even.* **5** that can be divided by two without leaving a remainder: *2, 4, 6, 8, and 10 are even numbers.* **6** neither more nor less; exact: *Twelve apples make an even dozen.* **7** owing nothing: *When he paid all his debts, he was even.* SYN: square. **8** equally balanced; in equilibrium. **9** not easily disturbed or angered; calm: *A person with an even temper is seldom excited.* SYN: placid, unruffled. **10** not favoring one more than another; fair: *Justice is even treatment.* SYN: just. **11** *Obsolete.* straightforward; direct: *Be even and direct with me, whether you were sent for or no* (Shakespeare). **12** *Obsolete.* equal in rank, dignity, power, or the like.
—*v.t.* **1** to make even; make equal or level: *She evened the edges by trimming them.* **2** to make (accounts) balance; square: *My brother beat me in the broad jump but I evened accounts by beating him in the high jump.* **3** *Chiefly Scottish.* to treat as equal; put on the same level. **4** *Dialect.* to liken; compare.
—*v.i.* to become equal or comparable.
—*adv.* **1** in an even manner; evenly. **2** just; exactly: *She left even as you came.* **3** indeed: *He is ready, even eager, to go.* **4** fully; quite: *He was faithful even unto death.* **5** though one would not expect it; as one would not expect: *Even young children can understand it. Even the last man arrived on time.* **6** still; yet: *You can do even better if you try.* **7** *Archaic.* exactly; precisely: *Even so have I also sent them into the world* (John 17:18).
break even, *Informal.* to have equal gains and losses: *This flood insurance program should be ... designed to permit the Government to break even* (New York Times).
even if, in spite of the fact that; although: *I will come, even if it rains.*
even out, to become level; balance: *Things get a little slow for a while but they always pick up and even out* (Wall Street Journal).
even though, although: *Even though I was tired, I went to the party.*
get even. See under **get.**
[Old English *efen*] —**e'ven|er**, *n.* —**e'ven|ness**, *n.*
—*Syn. adj.* **3 Even, uniform, equable** mean always the same. **Even** emphasizes being regular and steady, never changing in motion, action, sound, quality, etc.: *The even hum of the motor stopped.* **Uniform** emphasizes sameness in form or character throughout all parts of a substance, series, course, etc.: *We should have uniform traffic laws.* **Equable** suggests freedom from sudden alterations: *A watch has equable movement.*

e|ven[2] (ē'vən), *n. Archaic.* evening. [Old English *ǣfen*]

e|ven|age or **e|ven-age** (ē'vən āj'), *adj.* made up of plants of the same age: *Vast even-age plant communities are often very vulnerable to insects* (New Scientist).

e|ven|aged or **e|ven-aged** (ē'vən ājd'), *adj.* = evenage.

é|vé|ne|ment (ā ven mäɴ'), *n. French.* event; incident (in the sense of a major social and political development): *Clouds of acrid tear gas hung over the chestnut trees of Left Bank boulevards, just as they had during the shattering événements of May 1968 that tore France apart* (Time).

e|ven|fall (ē'vən fôl'), *n.* the beginning of evening; dusk.

e|ven|hand|ed or **e|ven-hand|ed** (ē'vən han'did), *adj.* impartial; fair; just: *evenhanded justice. The press associations do an even-handed job of straight reporting* (Time). SYN: equitable. —**e'ven-hand'ed|ly**, *adv.* —**e'ven|hand'ed|ness**, *n.*

eve|ning (ēv'ning), *n., adj.* —*n.* **1** the last part of day and early part of night; time between sunset and bedtime: *We spent the evening watching television.* **2** *Figurative.* the last part: *Old age is the evening of life.* **3** an evening spent in a particular way, especially an evening devoted to the entertainment of friends.
—*adj.* in the evening; of the evening; for the evening: *evening prayers, evening clothes.*

[Old English *ǣfnung* < *ǣfnian* become evening < *ǣfen* evening, even[2]]

evening bat, a brown bat common in the southern United States.

evening dress, **1** formal clothes worn in the evening. **2** = evening gown.

evening gown, a woman's evening dress.

evening grosbeak, a large, thick-billed finch with a yellow body and black and white wings, most common in central North America.

evening prayer, a church service of the late afternoon or early evening; evensong.

evening primrose, any one of a genus of tall American herbs with spikes of fragrant white, yellow, or pink flowers that open in the evening.

eve|ning-prim|rose family (ēv′ning prim′rōz′), a group of dicotyledonous herbs, or, rarely, shrubs and trees, mostly natives of temperate North America. The family includes the fuchsia, willow herb, and clarkia.

eve|nings (ēv′ningz), *adv.* during the evening; in the evening: *She is happiest evenings, when she can meet her friends.*

eve|ning-snow (ēv′ning snō′), *n.* a delicate herb of California, with white flowers that open about four o'clock in the afternoon and close in the morning, and are so abundant on open slopes that they whiten the ground.

evening star, a bright planet seen in the western sky after sunset. Venus or Mercury is often the evening star. The Greeks called Venus *Hesperus* as an evening star and the Romans called it *Vesper.*

evening stock, = Grecian stock.

evening wear, = evening dress.

e|ven|ly (ē′vən lē), *adv.* **1** smoothly; at the same level: *Spread the frosting evenly on the cake.* **2** at about the same speed. **3** equally: *Divide the money evenly.*

e|ven|mind|ed or **e|ven-mind|ed** (ē′vən mīn′did), *adj.* having equanimity; calm; composed.

even money, **1** paying exactly as much as bet: *I had the winner, a filly named Lamina. She was second choice but paid only twenty francs, which means even money* (New Yorker). **2** *Figurative.* with estimated chances of success or failure equal: *The Democratic incumbent . . . expects to win, but he's really no better than an even money bet* (Newsweek).

even page, the left-hand page of a book, marked by an even number.

e|ven|song (ē′vən sông′, -song′), *n.* **1** a church service said or sung in the late afternoon or early evening; vespers. In the Roman Catholic Church evensong is the sixth of the seven canonical hours. In the Church of England evensong is the evening prayer, combining the vespers and complin services. **2** any song sung at evening. **3** *Archaic.* evening. [Old English *ǣfensang* vespers < *ǣfen* even[2] + *sang* song]

even Ste|ven or **Ste|phen** (stē′vən), *U.S. Slang.* even; with the chances even; as likely to go one way as another: *It's even Stephen whether the innocent floor show or . . . the merengue is more fun* (New Yorker).

e|vent (i vent′), *n.* **1** a happening, especially an important happening: *The discovery of America was a great event. The discovery of polio vaccine was a great-event in medicine.* **2** result; outcome: *We made careful plans and awaited the event.* SYN: consequence. **3** an item or contest in a program of sports: *There was a possibility that the four relays would be held tomorrow but now the full programme of 30 events will be held on Sunday* (London Times).

at (or **in**) **all events**, in any case; whatever happens: *Civil war . . . must in all events prove calamitous to the nation* (David Hume).

in any event, in any case; anyhow: *In any event, you can always count on my friendship. Emerson had intended to halt them there for the night, in any event* (Harper's).

in the event of, in case of; if there is; if there should be: *In the event of rain, the party will be held indoors.*

in the event that, if it should happen that: *In the event that the roads are icy, we shall not come.*

[< Old French *event*, learned borrowing from Latin *ēventus, -ūs* < *ēvenīre* < *ex-* out + *venīre* come]

— ***Syn.*** **1 Event, incident, occurrence** mean a happening. **Event** applies particularly to a happening of some importance, usually resulting from what has gone before: *Her graduation from college was an event I did not want to miss.* **Incident** applies to a happening of little importance or of less importance than an event: *My unexpected meeting with a boy I used to know was an amusing incident.* **Occurrence** is the general word for any happening, event, or incident: *Getting up is an everyday occurrence.*

e|ven|tem|pered or **e|ven-tem|pered** (ē′ven-tem′pərd), *adj.* not easily disturbed or angered; calm.

e|vent|ful (i vent′fəl), *adj.* **1** full of events; having many unusual events: *The class spent an eventful day touring the new zoo.* **2** having important results; important: *The discovery of atomic energy began an eventful period in history.*
—**e|vent′ful|ly**, *adv.* —**e|vent′ful|ness**, *n.*

event horizon, *Astronomy.* the inner surface of a black hole, below the ergosphere, from which no energy can escape.

e|ven|tide (ē′vən tīd′), *n. Archaic.* evening.

e|vent|ing (i ven′ting), *n. Especially British.* equestrian competition including dressage, cross-country riding, and show jumping: *Eventing is a comparatively new sport, but . . . the number of people watching show jumping on television is second only to soccer* (London Times). —**e|vent′er**, *n.*

e|vent|less (i vent′lis), *adj.* uneventful: *August seemed an eventless month to the idlers loafing on the beaches* (New York Times).

e|ven|tog|nath (i ven′təg nath), *n.* any of a large group of freshwater fishes which includes the carps, distinguished by the peculiar development of the lower pharyngeal bones. [< New Latin *Eventognathi* the suborder name < Greek *eugood* + *entós* within + *gnáthos* jaw]

ev|en|tog|na|thous (ev′ən tog′nə thəs), *adj.* of or like the eventognaths.

e|ven|tra|tion (ē′ven trā′shən), *n.* a protruding of the intestine, stomach, or other digestive organ through the wall of the abdomen.

event tree, a diagram showing possible consequences of an event: *An event tree can be constructed showing the initial failure of a pipe break and . . . possible choices of success (up) and failure (down) of the functions shown* (Saul Levine).

e|ven|tu|al (i ven′chů əl), *adj.* **1** coming in the end; final: *After several failures, his eventual success surprised us.* SYN: ultimate. **2** depending on uncertain events; possible. SYN: contingent.

e|ven|tu|al|i|ty (i ven′chů al′ə tē), *n., pl.* **-ties.** a possible occurrence or condition; possibility: *We hope for rain, but we are ready for the eventuality of a drought.* SYN: contingency.

e|ven|tu|al|ly (i ven′chů ə lē), *adv.* in the end; finally: *We waited more than an hour for him but eventually we had to leave without him.*

e|ven|tu|ate (i ven′chů āt), *v.i.,* **-at|ed, -at|ing.** to come out in the end; happen finally; result: *In the event of hostilities (which we trust will not eventuate), these warheads could not be used operationally* (Canadian Saturday Night). [American English < Latin *ēventus* (see etym. at **event**)]

e|ven|tu|a|tion (i ven′chů ā′shən), *n.* the act of eventuating.

ev|er (ev′ər), *adv.* **1** at any time: *Is she ever at home?* **2** at all times; always: *A mother is ever ready to help her children.* SYN: forever, eternally, perpetually, constantly, continuously, incessantly. **3** at all; by any chance; in any case: *What did you ever do to make him so angry?*

ever and again (or **anon**), every now and then; again and again: *And ever and anon, with rosy red, The bashful blood her snowy cheeks did dye* (Edmund Spenser). *Ever and anon some falling bolt proves his divinity* (Milton).

ever so, *Informal.* very: *The ocean is ever so deep.*

for ever and a day, always: *Farewell for ever and a day* (Shakespeare).

[Middle English *evere*, Old English *ǣfre*]

ev|er|bear|ing (ev′ər bãr′ing), *adj.* producing flowers without regard to the length of its exposure to light; bearing continuously: *everbearing roses.*

ev|er|bloom|ing (ev′ər blü′ming), *adj.* = everbearing.

Ev|er|est (ev′ər ist, ev′rist), *n.* **1** a great height; summit; pinnacle: *He possessed the sheer muscular authority and drive to tackle music's Everests* (London Times). **2** something resembling a great mountain in size or amount. [< Mount *Everest*, the world's highest peak]

ev|er|glade (ev′ər glād), *n.* a large tract of low, wet ground partly covered with tall grass; large swamp or marsh; glade.

everglade kite, a hawk, now nearly extinct, that lives on snails, found in the Florida Everglades.

Everglade State, a nickname for Florida.

ev|er|green** (ev′ər grēn′), *adj., n.* —adj.*** **1** having green leaves or needles all the year round. In trees of this kind, the leaves of the past season remain on the tree until the new ones are completely formed, for example in the holly or the pine. *The vast majority of the conifers are evergreen* (Fred W. Emerson). **2** lasting until the next season: *evergreen leaves.* **3** *Figurative.* always fresh; never failing; perennial: *The Post sang the song of evergreen optimism* (Atlantic).
—***n.*** **1** an evergreen plant or tree. Pine, spruce, cedar, ivy, box, and many rhododendrons are evergreens. **2** *Figurative.* something enduring or perennial: *Spencer Williams . . . wrote "Basin Street Blues" and "I found a New Baby" among a score of evergreens* (New York Times).

evergreens, evergreen twigs or branches used for decoration, especially at Christmas.

***evergreen**
definition 1

evergreen trees:

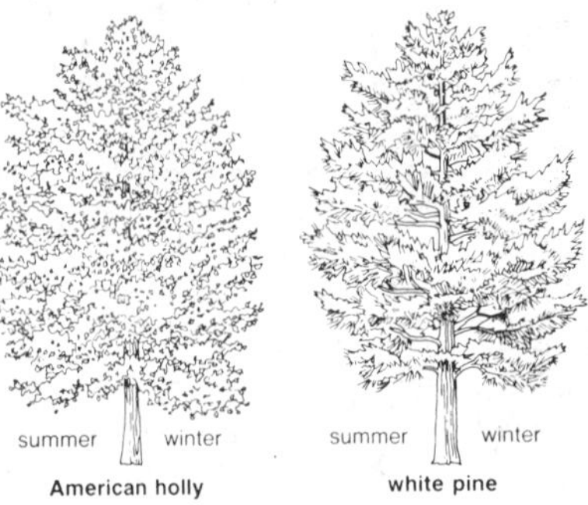

American holly   white pine

deciduous trees:

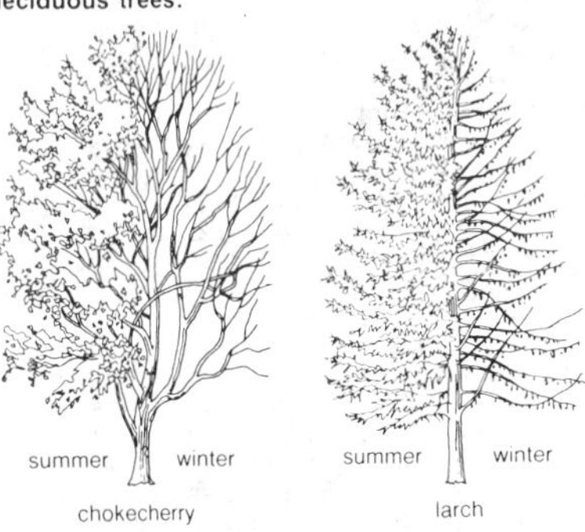

chokecherry   larch

evergreen blackberry, a variety of blackberry with large sweet berries and evergreen leaves, grown on the Pacific coast of the United States.

evergreen candytuft, a perennial border plant that grows about 12 inches high, has small narrow leaves, and pure white flowers borne on upright heads.

Evergreen State, a nickname for Washington.

ev|er|last|ing (ev′ər las′ting, -läs′-), *adj., n.*
—***adj.*** **1** lasting forever; never stopping: *the everlasting beauty of nature. See Cromwell, damn'd to everlasting fame* (Alexander Pope). SYN: See syn. under **eternal**. **2** lasting a long time; unceasing: *everlasting propaganda.* **3** lasting too long; repeated too often; tiresome: *Her everlasting complaints annoyed me.* **4** indefinitely durable; that will never wear out: *O! so light a foot Will ne'er wear out the everlasting flint* (Shakespeare).
—***n.*** **1** eternity. **2a** any one of various plants, chiefly composites, whose flowers keep their shape and color when dried; immortelle. **b** the flower of any of these plants; everlasting flowers. **3** a durable twilled woolen fabric, used especially for women's shoes; lasting.

the Everlasting, God: *O . . . that the Everlasting had not fix'd His canon 'gainst self-slaughter!* (Shakespeare).
—**ev′er|last′ing|ly**, *adv.* —**ev′er|last′ing|ness**, *n.*

everlasting flower, any one of various strawlike flowers that keep their shape and color for some time after they are picked and dried. The immortelle and the globe amaranth are everlasting flowers.

everlasting pea, any one of various plants of the pea family, especially those cultivated for their handsome flowers.

ev|er|liv|ing (ev′ər liv′ing), *adj.* that lives or will live forever; immortal.

ev|er|more (ev′ər môr′, -mōr′), *adv.* always; forever; for always: *I shall evermore remember this narrow escape from death. The mind of man desireth evermore to know the truth* (Richard Hooker).

for evermore, for all time; for eternity: *They swore to love each other for evermore. Life shall live for evermore* (Tennyson).

ev|er|pres|ent (ev′ər prez′ənt), *adj.* always or continuously present: *Perhaps the dread of can-*

Pronunciation Key: hat, āge, cãre, fär; let, ēqual, tėrm; it, īce; hot, ōpen, ôrder; oil, out; cup, pút, rüle; child; long; thin; ᴛʜen; zh, measure; ə represents a in about, e in taken, i in pencil, o in lemon, u in circus.

cer is everpresent (Ladies' Home Journal).

Ev|er-Read|y (ev′ər red′ē), *n., pl.* **-Read|ies**. *British.* a member of the Territorial Army's emergency reserve unit: *One hundred Ever-Readies . . . will leave on Saturday for a fortnight's exercise in Aden* (London Times).

e|ver|si|ble (i vėr′sə bəl), *adj.* that can be everted or turned inside out. [< Latin *ēversus,* past participle of *ēvertere* (see etym. under **evert**) + English *-ible*]

e|ver|sion (i vėr′zhən, -shən), *n.* **1** the action of turning an organ or structure inside out. **2** the condition of being turned inside out. [< Latin *ēversiō, -ōnis* < *ēvertere;* see etym. under **evert**]

e|vert (i vėrt′), *v.t.* to turn inside out or outward: *to evert an eyelid, evert the feet.* [< Latin *ēvertere* < *ex-* out + *vertere* turn]

e|ver|te|bral (i vėr′tə brəl), *adj.* not vertebral; not of or connected with the vertebral column.

e|ver|tile (i vėr′təl), *adj.* = eversible.

e|ver|tor (i vėr′tər), *n.* a muscle that turns a part of the body outward.

ev|er|y (ev′rē), *adj.* **1** each one of the entire number of: *Read every word on the page. Every boy must have his own book.* **SYN:** See syn. under **each.** **2** all possible: *We showed him every consideration.*

every last, *Informal.* absolutely all or every one: *I know it is with me—every last sentence of it* (Mark Twain).

every now and then, from time to time; again and again: *Every now and then we have a frost that ruins the crop.*

every other, every second; alternate: *The milkman makes deliveries every other day.*

every which way. See under **way.**

[Middle English *everich, everilc,* Old English *ǣfre ǣlc; ǣfre* ever + *ǣlc* each]

▶**every.** The adjective *every* modifies singular nouns: *Every child was vaccinated.* Since plurality is implied, however, there is sometimes a shift to the plural further on in the sentence: *Every book has been cataloged and they are now ready to be shelved.* This sort of shift is more common in spoken than in written English. See **everyone** for another usage note.

ev|er|y|bod|y (ev′rē bod′ē), *pron.* every person; everyone: *Everybody likes the new principal.*

▶**everybody.** The pronoun everybody is grammatically singular: *Everybody was thrilled when our troops marched past.* In informal speech, *everybody* is sometimes used as a collective. A verb immediately following is usually singular, but a pronoun referring back to it from a little distance is likely to be plural: *Everybody dresses in their best clothes.* To make such expressions conform to formal written usage, it is often better to change the *everybody* to a more accurate plural or collective than to change the later pronoun.

ev|er|y|day (ev′rē dā′), *adj.* **1** of every day; daily: *Accidents are everyday occurrences.* **2** for every ordinary day; not for Sundays or holidays: *She wears everyday clothes to work.* **3** not exciting; usual: *She had only an everyday story to tell.*

▶**Everyday** is one word when it is an adjective, two words when *day* is a noun modified by *every: This was an everyday occurrence. Every day seemed a year.*

ev|er|y|day|ness (ev′rē dā′nis), *n.* the state of being prosaic or common; commonplaceness.

Ev|er|y|man (ev′rē man′), *n.* **1** an English morality play of the early 1500's, in which man's journey through life is symbolically described. **2** the main character in this play, representing humanity. **3** the ordinary or typical human being.

ev|er|y|one (ev′rē wun, -wən), *pron.,* or **every one,** every person; each person; everybody: *Everyone took his purchases home.*

▶**everyone. a** The pronoun *everyone* is grammatically singular: *Everyone who wishes to attend is invited.* In informal speech, *everyone* is sometimes used as a collective. A verb immediately following is usually singular, but a pronoun referring back to it from a little distance is likely to be plural: *Everyone contributes their share.* **b** *Everyone* is usually one word, but when *one* is stressed or emphasized, it is written as two: *Everyone wants to attend the concert. Winning this game depends upon every one of the players in the team.*

ev|er|y|place (ev′rē plās), *adv. Informal.* in every place; everywhere: *We went everyplace on our trip.*

ev|er|y|thing (ev′rē thing), *pron., n.* —*pron.* every thing; all things: *She does everything she can to help her mother.*

—*n.* something extremely important; a very important thing: *This news means everything to us.*

▶**Everything** is one word when it is a noun or pronoun, two words when *thing* is stressed or emphasized: *Everything was in its place. She meant everything to him. Food, water, clothes —every thing that Midas touched turned to gold.*

ev|er|y|way (ev′rē wā), *adv.* in every direction, manner, or respect.

ev|er|y|when (ev′rē hwen), *adv.* at all times: *We ourselves are living here and now, but if we are generous enough, we can stretch our souls everywhere and everywhen else* (New Scientist).

ev|er|y|where (ev′rē hwãr), *adv., n.* —*adv.* in every place; in all places or lands: *A smile is understood everywhere. We looked everywhere for our lost dog.*

—*n.* **(the) everywhere,** that which is infinite; limitless space: *For love, all love, . . . makes one little room, an everywhere* (John Donne).

ev|er|y|whith|er (ev′rē hwiтн′ər), *adv.* to every place; in every direction.

e|vict (i vikt′), *v.t.* **1** to expel by law from land, a building, or the like; eject (a tenant): *The tenant was evicted by the sheriff for not paying his rent.* **SYN:** dispossess, oust. **2** to recover (property) by a legal process or by having superior title. [< Latin *ēvictus* overcome, eject; past participle of *ēvincere;* see etym. under **evince**]

e|vict|ee (i vik′tē′), *n.* a person who is evicted.

e|vic|tion (i vik′shən), *n.* the act or process of evicting or the state of being evicted; expulsion: *The tenant who refused to pay his rent was served with a notice of eviction.*

e|vic|tor (i vik′tər), *n.* a person who evicts.

ev|i|dence (ev′ə dəns), *n., v.,* **-denced, -dencing.** —*n.* **1** anything that shows or makes clear what is true or what is not; facts; proof: *The jam on his face was evidence that he had been in the kitchen.* **2** *Law.* **a** facts established and accepted in a court of law: *Before deciding a case, the judge and the jury heard all the evidence given by both sides.* **b** a person who gives testimony in a court of law: *state's evidence.* **3** an indication; sign: *A smile is evidence of pleasure.*

—*v.t.* **1** to make easy to see or understand; show clearly; prove: *His smiles, evidenced his pleasure.* **2** to support by one's testimony.

in evidence, easily seen or noticed: *Poverty is much in evidence in the city slums.*

turn (state's, king's, queen's) evidence, (of an accomplice in a crime) to offer oneself as a witness against the others implicated: *One of the gang, to save his own life, has turned evidence* (Daniel Defoe).

—*Syn. n.* **1, 2a Evidence, testimony, proof** mean that which tends to demonstrate the truth or falsity of something. **Evidence** applies to any facts that point toward, but do not fully prove, the truth or falsehood of something: *Running away was evidence of his guilt.* **Testimony** means something said or done to show or prove something true or false: *His testimony contradicted that of the preceding witness.* **Proof** means evidence so full and convincing as to leave no doubt: *The signed receipt is proof that the letter was delivered.*

ev|i|dent (ev′ə dənt), *adj.* easy to see or understand; clear; plain: *The little girl's joy was evident when she saw the kitten her father had brought her.* **SYN:** apparent. See syn. under **obvious.** [< Latin *ēvidēns, -entis* < *ex-* out + *vidēns,* present participle of *vidēre* see, seem]

ev|i|den|tial (ev′ə den′shəl), *adj.* **1** serving as evidence; of evidence; based on evidence: *He had once asked a famous researcher his opinion on what was the most evidential fact in favour of survival* (Psychic News). **2** like evidence; giving evidence. —**ev′i|den′tial|ly,** *adv.*

ev|i|den|tia|ry (ev′ə den′shər ē), *adj.* = evidential.

ev|i|dent|ly (ev′ə dənt lē), *adv.* plainly; clearly; apparently: *If he hasn't arrived yet he evidently missed his train.*

ev|i|dent|ness (ev′ə dənt nis), *n.* clearness; plainness.

e|vil (ē′vəl), *adj., n., adv.* —*adj.* **1** morally bad; wrong; sinful; wicked: *an evil life, an evil character. There is some soul of goodness in things evil* (Shakespeare). **SYN:** iniquitous, depraved, vicious, corrupt. See syn. under **bad.** **2** that does harm: *an evil plan.* **SYN:** harmful, pernicious, bad. **3** unfortunate: *They have fallen on evil days.* **4** due to bad character or conduct: *an evil reputation.*

—*n.* **1** something bad; sin; wickedness; evil quality or act: *There is no evil in that child. This heart, all evil shed away . . . gives somewhere back the thoughts by England given* (Rupert Brooke). **SYN:** iniquity, depravity, unrighteousness. **2** a thing that does harm: *Crime and poverty are some of the evils of society.* **3** misfortune; harm; mischief; damage: *Yea, though I walk through the valley of the shadow of death, I will fear no evil* (Psalms 23:4). **SYN:** disaster, calamity. **4** = king's evil (scrofula).

—*adv.* in an evil manner; harmfully; maliciously. [Old English *yfel*] —**e′vil|ly,** *adv.* —**e′vil|ness,** *n.*

e|vil|do|er (ē′vəl dü′ər), *n.* a person who does evil.

e|vil|do|ing (ē′vəl dü′ing), *n.* the act of doing evil.

evil eye, the power that some people are supposed to have of causing harm or bringing bad luck to others by looking at them.

e|vil-eyed (ē′vəl īd′), *adj.* **1** looking with malice or envy. **2** supposed to possess the evil eye.

e|vil-mind|ed (ē′vəl mīn′did), *adj.* **1** having an evil mind; wicked; malicious. **2** = salacious. —**e′vil-mind′ed|ly,** *adv.* —**e′vil-mind′ed|ness,** *n.*

Evil One, the Devil; Satan.

e|vince (i vins′), *v.t.,* **e|vinced, e|vinc|ing.** **1** to show clearly: *The dog evinced its dislike of strangers by growling.* **SYN:** exhibit, manifest. See syn. under **display.** **2** to show that one has (a certain quality or trait): *The new manager evinced a commendable desire to please.* **3** *Obsolete.* to overcome; subdue. [< Latin *ēvincere* overcome; eject, evict < *ex-* out + *vincere* conquer]

e|vince|ment (i vins′mənt), *n.* the act of evincing.

e|vin|ci|ble (i vin′sə bəl), *adj.* capable of proof; demonstrable.

e|vin|cive (i vin′siv), *adj.* giving indications of proof; indicative.

e|vi|rate (ē′və rāt, ev′ə-), *v.t.,* **-rat|ed, -rat|ing.** to castrate; emasculate. [< Latin *ēvirāre* (with English *-ate*[1]) < *ex* out + *vir* man]

e|vi|ra|tion (ē′və rā′shən, ev′ə-), *n.* = castration.

e|vis|cer|ate (i vis′ə rāt), *v.,* **-at|ed, -at|ing,** *adj.* —*v.t.* **1** to remove the bowels from; disembowel: *The butcher eviscerated a chicken.* **2** *Figurative.* to deprive of something essential.

—*adj.* having the viscera protruding through an abdominal incision after an operation.

[< Latin *ēviscerāre* (with English *-ate*[1]) < *ex-* out + *vīscera* viscera]

e|vis|cer|a|tion (i vis′ə rā′shən), *n.* the act of eviscerating.

ev|i|ta|ble (ev′ə tə bəl), *adj.* that can be avoided; avoidable: *The War of 1812 appears to have been entirely evitable* (New Yorker). [< Latin *ēvītābilis* < *ēvītāre* avoid; see etym. under **evite**]

ev|i|tate (ev′ə tāt), *v.t.,* **-tat|ed, -tat|ing.** *Obsolete.* to evite. [< Latin *ēvītāre* (with English *-ate*[1]); see etym. under **evite**]

ev|i|ta|tion (ev′ə tā′shən), *n. Archaic.* an avoiding; a shunning.

e|vite (i vīt′), *v.t.,* **e|vit|ed, e|vit|ing.** *Archaic.* to avoid; shun. [< Latin *ēvītāre* < *ex-* away + *vītāre* shun]

e|vit|tate (i vit′āt), *adj.* (of the fruit of some plants) having no vittae or oil canals.

ev|o|ca|ble (ev′ə kə bəl), *adj.* that can be evoked or called forth.

ev|o|cate (ev′ə kāt), *v.t.,* **-cat|ed, -cat|ing.** = evoke. [< Latin *ēvocāre* (with English *-ate*[1]); see etym. under **evoke**]

ev|o|ca|tion (ev′ə kā′shən), *n.* **1** the act of evoking or calling forth. **2** *Law.* the transferring of a case from a lower to a higher court.

e|voc|a|tive (i vok′ə tiv, -vō′kə-), *adj.* tending to evoke: *The whole is a skillful and robustly unsentimental piece of evocative writing* (New Yorker). —**e|voc′a|tive|ly,** *adv.* —**e|voc′a|tive|ness,** *n.*

ev|o|ca|tor (ev′ə kā′tər), *n.* a person who evokes.

e|voc|a|to|ry (i vok′ə tôr′ē, -tōr′-), *adj.* having the function of evoking.

e|voke (i vōk′), *v.t.,* **e|voked, e|vok|ing.** **1** to call forth; bring out: *A good joke evokes a laugh.* **SYN:** elicit. **2** *Law.* to transfer (a case) from a lower to a higher court. [< Latin *ēvocāre* < *ex-* out + *vocāre* call]

evoked potential, the electrical response arising from the cortex of the brain upon stimulation of a sense organ: *Evoked potentials can be used to detect deafness in infants, which is otherwise quite difficult to diagnose* (Scientific American).

e|vok|er (i vō′kər), *n.* one that evokes.

é|vo|lu|é (ā vô ly ā′), *n. French.* an educated or advanced African native: *Since World War II, a new social group had appeared in the Congo—the évolués* (Atlantic).

***evolute**

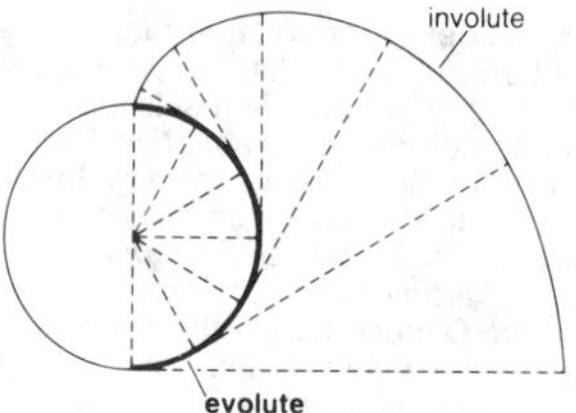

***ev|o|lute** (ev′ə lüt), *n. Geometry.* a curve that is the locus of the center of curvature of another

Pronunciation Key: hat, āge, cãre, fär; let, ēqual, tėrm; it, īce; hot, ōpen, ôrder; oil, out; cup, pu̇t, rüle; child; long; thin; тнen; zh, measure; ə represents **a** in about, **e** in taken, **i** in pencil, **o** in lemon, **u** in circus.

curve (the involute), or the envelope of the normals to the latter; the curve from which an involute is formed by the unwrapping of a flexible and inextensible string. [< Latin *ēvolūtus,* past participle of *ēvolvere* roll out; see etym. under **evolve**]

*** ev|o|lu|tion** (ev′ə lü′shən), *n.* **1** any process of formation or growth; gradual development: *the evolution of the flower from the bud, the evolution of the modern steamship from the first crude boat.* **2** something evolved; product of development; not a sudden discovery or creation. **3** the theory that all living things developed from a few simple forms of life through a series of physical changes. According to evolution, the first mammal developed from a type of reptile, and ultimately all forms are traced back to a simple, perhaps single-celled, organism. See picture below. **4a** a movement of ships or soldiers, planned beforehand; deployment. **b** any movement into a new formation, especially in marching. **5** a movement that is a part of a definite plan, design, or series: *A clumsy person could never achieve the graceful evolutions of that ballet dancer.* **6** a releasing; giving off; setting free, especially by chemical or physical change: *the evolution of heat from burning coal.* **7** *Mathematics.* the extraction of roots from powers. Finding the square root of a number is an example of evolution. **8** one of the regulated and recurring movements of a portion of a machine. **9** *Philosophy.* the theory that a process or progressive change, with the development of more complex entities, characterizes all force and matter in the universe: *Evolution is advance from the simple to the complex* (Edward Clodd). [< Latin *ēvolūtiō, -ōnis* < *ēvolvere;* see etym. under **evolve**]

ev|o|lu|tion|al (ev′ə lü′shə nəl), *adj.* = evolutionary. **—ev′o|lu′tion|al|ly,** *adv.*

ev|o|lu|tion|ar|i|ly (ev′ə lü′shə ner′ə lē), *adv.* in an evolutionary manner; in accordance with the theory of evolution: *Each [human population] becomes a separate race evolutionarily affected by technological and other cultural factors* (John J. Honigmann). *Evolutionarily speaking, brains —of a sort, at least—are a fairly early development* (Listener).

ev|o|lu|tion|ar|y (ev′ə lü′shə ner′ē), *adj.* **1** having to do with evolution; evolutional. **2** in accordance with the theory of evolution. **3** performing evolutions; having to do with evolutions.

ev|o|lu|tion|ism (ev′ə lü′shə niz əm), *n.* the biological doctrine of evolution: *Herbert Spencer's evolutionism, Alfred Tennyson's poems, the fashion of geologizing—all were the expression of a general movement* (Scientific American).

ev|o|lu|tion|ist (ev′ə lü′shə nist), *n., adj.* **—*n.*** a person who believes in and supports the theory of evolution. **—*adj.*** = evolutionistic.

ev|o|lu|tion|is|tic (ev′ə lü′shə nis′tik), *adj.* **1** tending to support the theory of evolution. **2** that produces evolution. **—ev′o|lu′tion|is′ti|cal|ly,** *adv.*

ev|o|lu|tive (ev′ə lü′tiv), *adj.* having to do with or tending to evolution or development; promoting evolution: *To establish a comparative and evolutive physiology of the heart, we must try to create a technique with any kind of vertebrate animal which will allow the heart to survive for long periods wide open* (New Scientist).

e|volv|a|ble (i vol′və bəl), *adj.* that can be evolved.

e|volve (i volv′), *v.,* **e|volved, e|volv|ing.** **—*v.t.*** **1** to develop gradually; work out; unfold: *The boys evolved a plan for earning money during their summer vacation.* **2** *Biology.* to develop by a process of growth and change to a more highly organized condition. **3** to release; give off; set free, as gases.
—*v.i.* **1** to be developed by evolution: *Buds evolve into flowers. The modern automobile evolved from the horse and buggy.* **2** to become an évolué: *To "evolve," an African must reach a certain educational and economic level* (Wall Street Journal).
[< Latin *ēvolvere* < *ex-* out + *volvere* roll]

e|volve|ment (i volv′mənt), *n.* **1** the act or process of evolving. **2** the condition of being evolved.

e|volv|ent (i vol′vənt), *adj., n.* **—*adj.*** that evolves. **—*n.*** the involute of a curve.

e|volv|er (i vol′vər), *n.* a person or thing that evolves.

e|von|y|mus (e von′ə məs), *n.* = euonymus.

e|vo|vae (ē vō′vē), *n.* in Gregorian music: **1** the trope at the end of the melody for the lesser doxology. **2** any trope.

EVR (no periods), electronic video recording (a system of cassette television in which miniaturized film coiled in cartridges is inserted in a converter unit connected to the antenna terminals of a television set).

e|vulse (i vuls′), *v.t.,* **e|vulsed, e|vuls|ing.** to pluck or pull out; tear away. [< Latin *ēvulsus,* past participle of *ēvellere* pluck out < *ex-* out + *vellere* pluck]

e|vul|sion (i vul′shən), *n.* the act of plucking or pulling out; forcible extraction.

*** ev|zone** (ev′zōn), *n.* a member of a special corps of infantrymen in the Greek army, known for its great valor and picturesque uniform: *A kilted evzone hobnobbed with a philosopher in a white toga* (Harper's). [< Greek *eúzōnos* dressed for exercise < *eu-* well + *zōnē* girdle]

***evzone**

EW (no periods), emergency ward (in a hospital): *As they saw it, the first duty of the EW residents was to lower that fever by every possible means, even if this hampered further diagnostic efforts* (Michael Crichton).

ew|der (yü′dər), *n. Scottish.* smoke; fume.

ewe (yü), *n.* a female sheep. [Old English *ēowu*]

E|we (ā′vā), *n.* **1** an African tribe inhabiting both sides of the border of Ghana and Togo. **2** a member of this tribe. **3** the Kwa language of this tribe.

ewe lamb, 1 a female lamb. **2** a parent's only child.

ewe|lease (yü′lēz′), *n.* a pasture for ewes.

ewe-neck (yü′nek′), *n.* a thin neck like that of a ewe, hollowed instead of arched, as of a horse.

ewe-necked (yü′nekt′), *adj.* having a ewe-neck.

ew|er (yü′ər), *n.* a wide-mouthed water pitcher: *The ewer and basin are on the wash-stand.* [< Old French *eviere,* or *aiguiere* < Vulgar Latin *aquāria* < Latin *aquārius* for drawing water < *aqua* water]

ew|est (yü′ist), *adj. Scottish.* close at hand.

E|wig|keit (ā′viH kīt), *n. German.* eternity.

E|wig-Weib|li|che (ā′viH vīp′li Hə), *n. German.* the eternal feminine (as used in Goethe's *Faust*).

ex[1] (eks), *prep.* **1** out of. "Ex elevator" means free of charges until the time of removal from the grain elevator. **2** without; not including. Ex dividend stocks are stocks on which the purchaser will not receive the next dividend to be paid.
3 *U.S.* in the class of, but not as a graduate: *ex '54.* [< Latin *ex* out of, away from; except for]

ex[2] (eks), *n.* **1** the 24th letter of the alphabet (x, X). **2** anything shaped like an X. [spelling of *X*]

ex[3] (eks), *n. Informal.* a person who formerly occupied some position, as a former spouse or beau: *She has been seen dating her ex again.* [short for *ex-wife, ex-fiancée, ex-president,* etc.]

ex-[1], *prefix.* **1** former; formerly: *Ex-president* = *former president.*
2 out of; from; out: *Express* = *press out.*
3 thoroughly; utterly: *Exterminate* = *terminate* (*finish* or *destroy*) *thoroughly.*
4 removing; freeing from; lacking, as in *expatriate, exonerate.* Also: **e-** before consonants except *c, f, p, q, s, t;* **ef-** before *f.*
[< Latin *ex-,* related to *ex,* or *ē,* out of, from]

ex-[2], *prefix.* from; out of, as in *exarch, exodus.* Also, **ec-** before consonants. [< Greek *ex-,* related to *ex-* from, out of]

ex-[3], *prefix.* the occasional form of **exo-** before vowels, as in *exoccipital.*

ex., an abbreviation for the following:
1 examined.
2 example.
3 exception.
4 exchange.
5 excursion.
6 executed.
7 executive.

Ex., Exodus (book of the Bible).

exa-, *combining form.* one quintillion (10^{18}) ______: *Exavolt* = *one quintillion volts.* [perhaps alteration of Greek *exō-* outside, exo-]

ex|ac|er|bate (eg zas′ər bāt, ek sas′-), *v.t.,* **-bat|ed, -bat|ing. 1** to make worse (pain, disease, anger); aggravate: *to exacerbate the growing moodiness of his temper* (Edgar Allan Poe). SYN: embitter. **2** to irritate (a person's feelings): *His physical awareness of her was so keen that she could exacerbate his nerves with perfume* (Atlantic). SYN: provoke. [< Latin *exacerbāre* (with English *-ate*[1]) < *ex-* (intensive) + *acerbus* harsh, bitter]

ex|ac|er|ba|tion (eg zas′ər bā′shən, ek sas′-), *n.* the act or process of exacerbating or condition of being exacerbated; aggravation or irritation: *The exacerbation of the friction between the two friends ended their friendship for good.*

ex|act (eg zakt′), *adj., v.* **—*adj.*** **1** without any error or mistake; strictly correct; accurate; precise: *an exact measurement, the exact amount.* SYN: See syn. under **correct. 2** strict; severe; rigorous. **3** characterized by or using strict accuracy: *A scientist should be an exact thinker. Writing [maketh] an exact man* (Sir Francis Bacon).
—*v.t.* **1** to demand and get; force to be paid: *If he does the work, he can exact payment for it.* SYN: extort. **2** to call for; need; require: *Hard work exacts effort and patience.*
[< Latin *exactus,* past participle of *exigere* weigh (out) accurately; drive out < *ex-* out + *agere* weigh]

ex|ac|ta (eg zak′tə), *n. U.S. and Canada.* a form of betting on a horse or dog race in which the bettor must pick the winners of the first and second place in their exact order; perfecta: *Since exacta wagering calls for the bettor to pick the precise 1, 2 finish (unlike in quiniela gambling, in which 1, 2 or 2, 1 do not matter) two payoffs were in order to the holders of winning ninth-race exacta tickets* (Louis Efrat). [< American Spanish *exacta,* short for *quiniela exacta* exact quiniela]

ex|act|a|ble (eg zak′tə bəl), *adj.* that can be exacted.

ex|act|er (eg zak′tər), *n.* = exactor.

ex|act|ing (eg zak′ting), *adj.* **1** requiring much; making severe demands; hard to please: *An exacting teacher will not permit careless work.* **2** requiring effort, care, or attention: *Flying an airplane is exacting work.* **—ex|act′ing|ly,** *adv.* **—ex|act′ing|ness,** *n.*

ex|ac|tion (eg zak′shən), *n.* **1** the act or process of exacting; demanding and getting; forcing to be paid: *The ruler's repeated exactions of money left the people very poor.* **2** the condition of being exacted; extortion. **3** the thing exacted. Taxes, fees, etc., forced to be paid are exactions.

ex|act|i|tude (eg zak′tə tüd, -tyüd), *n.* = exactness.

ex|act|ly (eg zakt′lē), *adv.* **1** without any error; in an exact manner; accurately; precisely: *The clerk figured the bill exactly.* **2** just so; quite right: *Do you mean I can go? Exactly!*

ex|act|ness (eg zakt′nis), *n.* the condition of being exact: *He recalled the story with exactness, down to every detail.*

ex|ac|tor (eg zak′tər), *n.* a person or thing that exacts.

exact science, a science in which facts can be

***evolution**
definition 3

evolution of the horse

eohippus

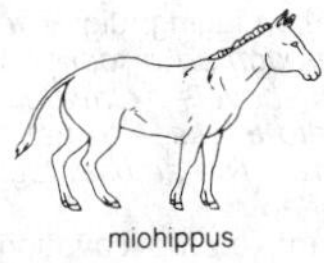
miohippus

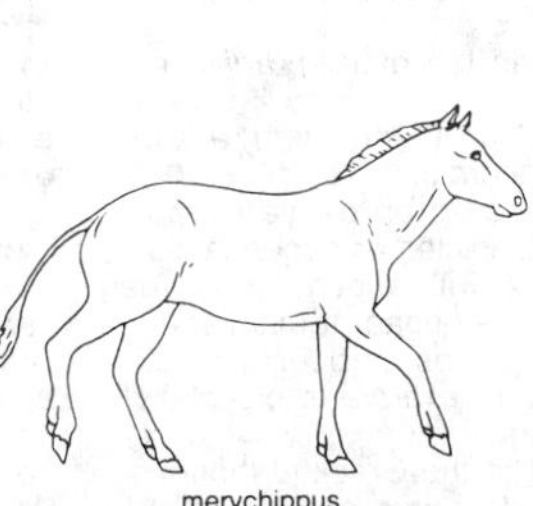
merychippus

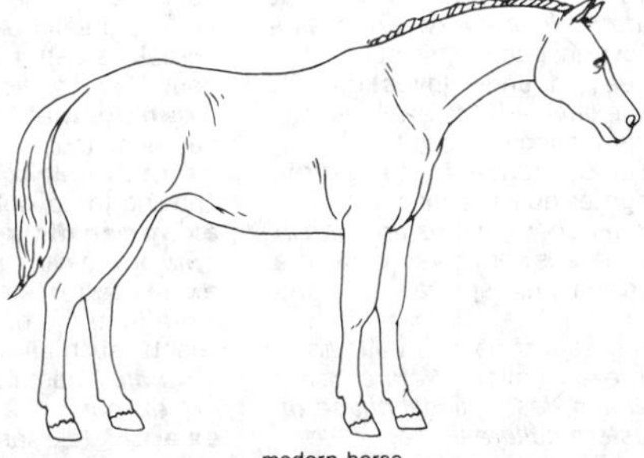
modern horse

accurately observed and results can be accurately predicted: *Mathematics and physics are exact sciences.*

ex ae|quo et bo|no (eks ē′kwō et bō′nō), *Latin.* according to what is fair and good.

ex|ag|ger|ate (eg zaj′ə rāt), *v.,* **-at|ed, -at|ing.** —***v.t.*** **1** to make too large; say or think (something) greater than it is; overstate: *He exaggerated the dangers of the trip in order to frighten them into not going. A friend exaggerates a man's virtues* (Joseph Addison). **SYN:** stretch, magnify, color. **2** to increase or enlarge beyond what is normal: *The artist exaggerated parts of the drawing to make them clearer.*
—***v.i.*** to say or think something is greater than it is; go beyond the truth: *The little boy exaggerated when he said there were a million cats in the backyard.*
[< Latin *exaggerāre* (with English *-ate*[1]) < *ex-* out, up + *agger* heap] —**ex|ag′ger|at′ing|ly,** *adv.*

ex|ag|ger|at|ed (eg zaj′ə rā′tid), *adj.* **1** magnified beyond the limits of fact or truth; excessive: *She has an exaggerated idea of her importance.* **2** *Zoology.* larger, more conspicuous, or more positive than is normal. —**ex|ag′ger|at|ed|ly,** *adv.* —**ex|ag′ger|at′ed|ness,** *n.*

ex|ag|ger|a|tion (eg zaj′ə rā′shən), *n.* **1** a statement that goes beyond the truth; overstatement: *It is an exaggeration to say that you would rather die than touch a snake.* **SYN:** hyperbole. **2** the act of going beyond the truth: *His constant exaggeration made people distrust him.* **3** the condition of being exaggerated.

ex|ag|ger|a|tive (eg zaj′ə rā′tiv), *adj.* **1** tending to exaggerate. **2** marked by exaggeration. **SYN:** hyperbolical.

ex|ag|ger|a|tor (eg zaj′ə rā′tər), *n.* a person who exaggerates.

ex|ag|ger|a|to|ry (eg zaj′ər ə tôr′ē, -tōr′-), *adj.* containing exaggeration.

ex|a|late (eks ā′lāt), *adj. Botany.* not alate.

ex|al|bu|mi|nose (ek′sal byü′mə nōs), *adj.* = exalbuminous.

ex|al|bu|mi|nous (ek′sal byü′mə nəs), *adj. Botany.* lacking albumen, as seeds.

ex|alt (eg zôlt′), *v.t.* **1** to make high in rank, honor, power, character, or quality: *We exalt a man when we elect him President of our country.* **SYN:** elevate, ennoble. **2** to fill with pride, joy, or noble feeling: *He was exalted by success.* **SYN:** elevate, ennoble. **3** to praise; honor; glorify: *God shall be exalted.* **4** to raise in degree; intensify; heighten, as a color. **5** to raise or set up on high; lift up; elevate: *I shall not lower but exalt the subjects I treat upon* (Sir Richard Steele). [< Latin *exaltāre* < *ex-* out, up + *altus* high] —**ex|alt′er,** *n.*

ex|al|ta|tion (eg′zôl tā′shən), *n.* **1** the act of exalting. **2** the condition of being exalted. **3** lofty emotion; rapture; an elation of mind or feeling. It is sometimes abnormal or morbid in character. **4** *Medicine.* abnormal increase in the action of an organ. **5** *Archaic.* a group of larks flying together.

ex|alt|ed (eg zôl′tid), *adj.* **1** elevated, as in rank or character: *exalted powers* (Emerson). **2** dignified; lofty; noble: *An exalted mood is one in which we think noble thoughts.* **SYN:** sublime, grand. —**ex|alt′ed|ly,** *adv.* —**ex|alt′ed|ness,** *n.*

ex|am (eg zam′), *n. Informal.* an examination: *After she receives her A.B. from Wisconsin this June, she will hurry back to Athens to take July law exams* (Newsweek).

exam., **1** examination. **2** examined.

ex|a|men (eg zā′mən), *n. Ecclesiastical.* a formal examination of the conscience, as of a candidate for ordination. [< Latin *exāmen* means of weighing, tongue of a balance, ultimately < *exigere;* see etym. under **exact**]

ex|am|in|a|ble (eg zam′ə nə bəl), *adj.* that can be examined.

ex|am|i|nant (eg zam′ə nənt), *n.* a person who examines.

ex|am|i|nate (eg zam′ə nit), *n.* a person undergoing examination.

ex|am|i|na|tion (eg zam′ə nā′shən), *n.* **1** the act of examining: *The doctor made a careful examination of my eyes.* **SYN:** inspection, scrutiny, search, research. See syn. under **investigation. 2** the state of being examined: *My examination took three hours.* **SYN:** inspection, scrutiny, search, research. See syn. under **investigation. 3** a test of knowledge or qualifications; list of questions; test: *The teacher gave us an examination in arithmetic.* **4** the answers given in such a test. **5** *Law.* an interrogation, especially of a witness.

ex|am|i|na|tion|al (eg zam′ə nā′shə nəl), *adj.* of or having to do with examination: *We are now ... in the examinational and destructional phase of the evolution of Western culture* (Time).

ex|am|i|na|tion|ism (eg zam′ə nā′shə niz əm), *n.* the habit of relying upon examinations as the test of fitness, knowledge, or the like.

ex|am|i|na|tion|ist (eg zam′ə nā′shə nist), *n.* a person who upholds or practices examinationism.

ex|am|i|na|tor (eg zam′ə nā′tər), *n.* a person who examines; examiner.

ex|am|i|na|to|ri|al (eg zam′ə nə tôr′ē əl, -tōr′-), *adj.* of or having to do with an examiner or an examination.

ex|am|ine (eg zam′ən), *v.t.,* **-ined, -in|ing. 1** to look at closely and carefully: *The doctor examined the wound. She examined the lining of the coat.* **SYN:** scrutinize, inspect, investigate. **2** to test the knowledge or qualifications of; ask questions of; test: *The teacher examined the students on the book they read.* **SYN:** interrogate. **3** to question formally: *The lawyer examined the witness.* **SYN:** interrogate. **4** to subject (an organ, a person, or an animal) to autopsy. [< Old French *examiner,* learned borrowing from Latin *exāmināre* < *exāmen* a weighing < *exigere;* see etym. under **exact.**]

ex|am|i|nee (eg zam′ə nē′), *n.* a person who is being examined.

ex|am|in|er (eg zam′ə nər), *n.* a person who examines: *a medical examiner.*

ex|am|in|ing|ly (eg zam′ə ning lē), *adv.* in an examining or scrutinizing manner.

ex|am|plar (eg zam′plər, -zäm′-), *n. British Archaic.* exemplar.

ex|am|ple (eg zam′pəl, -zäm′-), *n., v.,* **-pled, -pling.** —***n.*** **1** one thing taken to show what others are like; a case that shows something; sample: *New York is an example of a busy city.* **2** a person or thing to be imitated; model; pattern: *Abraham Lincoln is a good example for boys to follow.* **SYN:** paragon, ideal, archetype, prototype. **3** a problem devised to illustrate a rule in arithmetic, mathematics, or a science: *She wrote the example on the blackboard.* **SYN:** precedent, illustration, case. *Abbr:* ex. **4** a warning to others: *The captain made an example of the soldiers who shirked by making them clean up the camp.*
—***v.t.*** **1** to be an example of; exemplify. **2** to set an example to.
for example, as an example; by way of illustration; for instance: *Many flowers are fragrant; lilacs, for example. ... countries tied to the United States such as, for example, Venezuela* (Harper's).
set an example, to give, show, or be a model or pattern of conduct: *She set an example for the rest of the class by having a perfect record of attendance. If you will set me that example, I promise to follow it* (Dickens).
without example, with nothing like it before; unprecedented: *Such cold weather in July is without example in our town.*
[< Old French *example, essample,* learned borrowing from Latin *exemplum* (originally) that which is taken out (a sample) < *eximere;* see etym. under **exempt.** See etym. of doublet **ensample.**]
— ***Syn.*** *n.* **1 Example, sample** mean a part or thing selected to show the nature of the whole. **Example** applies to any person or thing that shows what the type or kind is like or how a general rule works: *This chair is an example of period furniture.* **Sample** applies to one thing, part, or piece taken out of a group or class to show the quality of the whole, which is considered to be exactly like it: *She looked carefully at all the samples of material before buying.*

ex|an|i|mate (eg zan′ə mit, ek san′-), *adj.* **1** lifeless; inanimate; dead. **2** lifeless in appearance; spiritless. [< Latin *exanimātus,* past participle of *exanimāre* deprive of life or spirit < *ex-* away + *anima* breath, life]

ex a|ni|mo (eks an′ə mō), *Latin.* from the mind or heart; sincerely: *He writes with detached, honest scholarship, but he also writes ex animo* (New York Times).

ex|an|them (ek san′thəm), *n.* = exanthema.

ex|an|the|ma (ek′san thē′mə), *n., pl.* **-ma|ta** (-mə tə). *Medicine.* **1a** an eruption or rash on the skin. **b** a disease characterized by such an eruption, especially one attended with fever, such as smallpox or measles. **2** = vesicular exanthema. [< Late Latin *exanthēma* < Greek *exánthēma* a breaking out < *exanthein* burst into bloom < *ex-* out + *ánthos* flower]

ex|an|the|mat|ic (ek san′thə mat′ik), *adj.* = exanthematous.

ex|an|them|a|tous (ek′san them′ə təs), *adj.* of or having to do with exanthema.

ex|ap|pen|dic|u|late (eks ap′ən dik′yə lit), *adj. Biology.* having no appendicles or appendages.

ex|a|rate (ek′sə rāt), *adj.* with appendages largely free from the body, as the pupae of many insects, such as beetles, wasps, or bees. [< Latin *exarātus,* past participle of *exarāre* to plough up < *ex-* out + *arāre* plough]

ex|arch[1] (ek′särk), *n.* **1** in the Greek Orthodox Church: **a** a patriarch's deputy. **b** a bishop ranking below a patriarch and above a metropolitan. **c** (originally) a patriarch. **2** the ruler of a province in the Byzantine Empire. [< Latin *exarchus* < Greek *éxarchos* leader, chief < *exárchein* take the lead < *ex-* out + *árchein* rule, begin]

ex|arch[2] (ek′särk), *adj. Botany.* having the protoxylem developing toward the center: *exarch vascular tissue.* [< *ex-*[3] outside + Greek *archē* beginning]

ex|ar|chal (ek sär′kəl), *adj.* of or having to do with a political or ecclesiastical exarch.

ex|ar|chate (ek′sär kāt; ek sär′kāt, -kit), *n.* the office, rank, or jurisdiction of an exarch.

ex|ar|chy (ek′sär kē), *n., pl.* **-chies.** = exarchate.

ex|ar|te|ri|tis (eks är′tə rī′tis), *n.* inflammation of the outer layer of the wall of an artery. [< *ex-*[3] + *arter(y)* + *-itis*]

ex|ar|tic|u|late (ek′sär tik′yə lit), *adj. Zoology.* not jointed.

ex|ar|tic|u|la|tion (ek′sär tik′yə lā′shən), *n.* amputation at a joint.

ex|as|per|ate (*v.* eg zas′pə rāt, -zäs′-; *adj.* eg zas′pə rit, -zäs′-), *v.,* **-at|ed, -at|ing,** *adj.* —***v.t.*** **1** to irritate very much; annoy greatly; make angry: *The little boy's constant noise exasperated his father.* **SYN:** incense, anger, nettle, vex, provoke. See syn. under **irritate. 2** to increase the intensity or violence of (ill feeling, pain, passions, or the like); intensify: *... tribes whose native ferocity was exasperated by [debasing forms of] superstition* (Thomas De Quincey). *... a temper exasperated by disease* (William H. Prescott).
—***adj.*** **1** *Botany.* rough; covered with short, stiff points. **2** *Archaic or Poetic.* irritated; exasperated: *Why art thou then exasperate?* (Shakespeare). *Swallows which the exasperate dying year Sets spinning in black circles* (Elizabeth Barrett Browning).
[< Latin *exasperāre* (with English *-ate*[1]) < *ex-* thoroughly + *asper* rough]

ex|as|per|at|ed|ly (eg zas′pə rā′tid lē, -zäs′-), *adv.* in an exasperated manner.

ex|as|per|at|er or **ex|as|per|a|tor** (eg zas′pə rā′tər, -zäs′-), *n.* provoker.

ex|as|per|at|ing|ly (eg zas′pə rā′ting lē, -zäs′-), *adv.* in an exasperating manner.

ex|as|per|a|tion (eg zas′pə rā′shən, -zäs′-), *n.* **1** extreme annoyance; anger; irritation: *His exasperation caused him to lash out in angry words.* **2** the act of exasperating: *The dog's exasperation of his master was the result of constant barking.*

exc., **1** excellent. **2a** except. **b** excepted. **3** exception.

Exc., Excellency.

ex|ca|late (eks′kə lāt), *v.t.,* **-lat|ed, -lat|ing.** to remove from a series. [< *ex-*[1] out + (inter)*calate*]

ex|ca|la|tion (eks′kə lā′shən), *n.* **1** the omission, absence, or elimination of a part from the middle of a series. **2** *Zoology.* the absence of any part of an organism, such as one of the middle digits.

Ex|cal|i|bur (ek skal′ə bər), *n.* the magic sword of King Arthur in Arthurian legends. [< Old French *Escalibor* < Medieval Latin *Caliburnus,* probably < a Celtic word]

ex|camb (ek skamb′), *v.t.* (in Scottish law) to exchange (land); barter. [< Medieval Latin *excambiare* < Latin *ex-* out + *cambiāre* to change]

ex|camb|er (ek skam′bər), *n.* (in Scottish law) a person who excambs; a party to excambion.

ex|cam|bi|on (ek skam′bē on), *n.* (in Scottish law) exchange or barter of land.

ex|car|di|nate (eks′kär′də nāt), *v.t.,* **-nat|ed, -nat|ing.** to transfer (a priest, deacon, or other functionary) from a particular church or diocese to another: *The documents state specifically that he was properly excardinated from Baltimore* (New York Times). [< *ex-*[1] + Late Latin *cardināre* assign to a church (with English *-ate*[1]); see etym. under **incardinate**]

ex|car|di|na|tion (eks′kär də nā′shən), *n.* **1** the act or process of excardinating. **2** the condition of being excardinated.

ex ca|the|dra (eks kə thē′drə, -kath′ə-), **1** with authority; from the seat of authority: *an ex cathedra judgment.* **2** spoken with authority; authoritative: *Teresa Wright played ... Louella to near-perfection ... delivering ex cathedra pronouncements on Louella's likes* (Time). [< New Latin *ex cathedra* < Latin *ex* out of, *cathedra* armchair]

ex|ca|the|dral (eks′kə thē′drəl), *adj.* official; authoritative.

ex|cau|date (eks kô′dāt), *adj.* tailless; acaudal.

ex|ca|vate (eks′kə vāt), *v.,* **-vat|ed, -vat|ing.** —***v.t.*** **1** to make hollow; hollow out: *The tunnel was made by excavating the side of a mountain.* **2** to make by digging; dig: *The tunnel was excavated through solid rock.* **3** to dig out; scoop out: *Steam shovels excavated the dirt and loaded it into trucks.* **4** to get or uncover by digging; unearth: *The archaeologists excavated an ancient buried city.*
—***v.i.*** **1** to make an excavation; dig. **2** *Figurative.*

to search carefully: *creditors, after more than a year of excavating, are still not at all certain where all the money went* (New York Times). [< Latin *excavāre* (with English *-ate*[1]) < *ex-* out + *cavāre* to hollow < *cavus* hollow]

ex|ca|va|tion (eks′kə vā′shən), *n.* **1** the act or process of digging out or up; digging; an excavating: *The excavation for the basement of our new house took three days.* [*Crete*] *whose magnificent prehistory was brought to light only 50 years ago by the excavations* (Newsweek). **2** a hole made by digging; excavated space: *The excavation for the new building was fifty feet across.* **SYN:** cavity, pit.

ex|ca|va|tor (eks′kə vā′tər), *n.* a person or thing that excavates. A steam shovel is an excavater.

ex|ca|va|to|ri|al (eks′kə və tôr′ē əl, -tōr′-), *adj.* = excavatory.

ex|cav|a|to|ry (ek skav′ə tôr′ē, -tōr′-), *adj.* having to do with excavation: *excavatory archaeology.*

ex|ceed (ek sēd′), *v.t.* **1** to be more or greater than: *The sum of five and seven exceeds ten. To lift a heavy trunk exceeds a child's strength.* **2** to do more than; go beyond: *Drivers are not supposed to exceed the speed limit.* **3** to surpass; outdo; be superior to: *The honor student exceeded all his classmates.* **4** *Archaic.* **a** to pass out of (boundaries). **b** to project beyond. *—v.i.* to be more, greater, or better than others; excel: *Justice must punish the rebellious deed; Yet punish so, as pity may exceed* (John Dryden). [< Old French *exceder,* learned borrowing from Latin *excēdere* < *ex-* out + *cēdere* go] **—ex|ceed′er,** *n.*

ex|ceed|ing (ek sē′ding), *adj., adv.* ***—adj.*** very great; unusual: *She is a girl of exceeding beauty.* **SYN:** extreme, excessive, surpassing.

—adv. exceedingly: *My heart is exceeding heavy* (Shakespeare). *But within that ten-minute limit, he is exceeding droll* (Esquire).

ex|ceed|ing|ly (ek sē′ding lē), *adv.* more than others; unusually; extremely; very: *The middle of summer has some exceedingly hot days.*

ex|cel (ek sel′), *v.,* **-celled, -cel|ling.** ***—v.t.*** to be better than; do better than; outdo; surpass: *He excelled his class in spelling.*

—v.i. to be better than others; do better than others: *Solomon excelled in wisdom.*

[< Latin *excellere* < *ex-* out from + *-cellere* rise]

—Syn. *v.t., v.i.* **Excel, surpass, outdo** mean to be better in quality or action. **Excel** suggests being outstanding in merit or achievement: *He excels in mathematics.* **Surpass** suggests being better than someone else in some specified way: *She surpasses her sister in history.* **Outdo** suggests doing better than others, or better than has been done before: *The runner outdid his previous record for the race.*

ex|cel|lence (ek′sə ləns), *n.* the condition of being better than others; unusually good quality; superiority: *His teacher praised him for the excellence of his report. The inn was famous for the excellence of its food. Excellence in arithmetic requires patience and great care.* **SYN:** preeminence.

Ex|cel|lence (ek′sə ləns), *n.* Excellency; Your Excellency.

ex|cel|len|cy (ek′sə lən sē), *n., pl.* **-cies.** = excellence.

Ex|cel|len|cy (ek′sə lən sē), *n., pl.* **-cies. 1** a title of honor used in speaking to or of a prime minister, governor, bishop, ambassador, or other high official: *Your Excellency. His Excellency, the British Ambassador.* **2** a person having this title.

ex|cel|lent (ek′sə lənt), *adj.* **1** very, very good; better than others: *Excellent work deserves high praise.* **SYN:** superior, meritorious, worthy, estimable, choice. **2** *Archaic.* extraordinary: ... *The excellent impostors of this earth* (Shelley). **3** *Obsolete.* excelling, especially in rank or dignity. [< Latin *excellēns, -entis,* present participle of *excellere;* see etym. under **excel**] **—ex′cel|lent|ly,** *adv.*

ex|cel|si|or (*adj.* ek sel′sē ôr; *n.* ek sel′sē ər), *adj., n.* ***—adj.*** ever upward; higher. "Excelsior" is the motto of New York State.

—n. **1** short, fine, curled shavings of soft wood used for packing dishes, glassware, and other breakable articles or as stuffing for cushions and mattresses. **2** a size of printing type (3 point). [American English < Latin *excelsior,* comparative of *excelsus* high, past participle of *excellere;* see etym. under **excel**]

Excelsior State, a nickname for New York State.

ex|cen|tral (ek sen′trəl), *adj. Botany.* out of the center.

ex|cen|tric (ek sen′trik), *adj.* = excentral.

ex|cept (ek sept′), *prep., v., conj.* ***—prep.*** leaving out; other than; with the exception of; but: *He works every day except Sunday.*

—v.t. to leave out; exclude: *Those who passed the first test were excepted from the second.*

—v.i. to make objection; object.

—conj. **1** only; but: *I would have had a perfect score except I missed the last question. The last time a tiger had me down, I wouldn't have gotten up except a lion attacked the tiger* (Newsweek). **2** *Archaic.* unless.

except for, a were it not for: *I would go with you except for my headache.* **b** with the exception of: *Everyone came to my party except for John.*

[< Latin *exceptus,* past participle of *excipere* < *ex-* out + *capere* take] **—ex|cept′er,** *n.*

—Syn. *prep.* **Except, but** mean leaving out. **Except** emphasizes the idea of leaving out, keeping out, or even shutting out: *Everyone was invited to the party except me.* **But** is unemphatic, and suggests more the idea of not taking in than of keeping out: *Everyone was invited but me.*

▶See **accept** for usage note.

ex|cep|tant (ek sep′tənt), *adj., n.* ***—adj.*** that excepts; taking exception. ***—n.*** a person who takes exception, as to a ruling of a court.

ex|cept|ing (ek sep′ting), *prep., conj.* ***—prep.*** leaving out; except; with the exception of; other than; but: *School is open every day excepting Saturday and Sunday.*

—conj. *Archaic.* unless.

ex|cep|tion (ek sep′shən), *n.* **1** a leaving out; excepting: *I like all my studies with the exception of arithmetic.* **SYN:** omission, exclusion. **2** a person or thing left out: *She praised the pictures with two exceptions.* **3** a thing that is different from the rule: *He comes on time every day; today is an exception. My short brother was the exception to our family tradition of tall men.* **SYN:** anomaly. **4** an objection: *a statement liable to exception.*

above (or **beyond**) **exception,** above or beyond criticism, reproach, or the like: *I produce two witnesses beyond exception* (John Bramhall).

take exception, a to object: *Several teachers and students took exception to the plan of having classes on Saturdays. There were not two persons ... who did not take some exception to it* (Edward H. Clarendon). **b** to be offended: *She took exception to his rude remark. Some of the more haughty of the aristocracy did take exception at his neglecting to raise his cap to them* (William H. Prescott).

ex|cep|tion|a|ble (ek sep′shə nə bəl), *adj.* liable to exception; objectionable. **—ex|cep′tion|a|ble|ness,** *n.* **—ex|cep′tion|a|bly,** *adv.*

ex|cep|tion|al (ek sep′shə nəl), *adj.* out of the ordinary; unusual: *This warm weather is exceptional for January. That bright little girl is an exceptional student.* **SYN:** uncommon, singular, extraordinary. **—ex|cep′tion|al|ly,** *adv.* **—ex|cep′tion|al|ness,** *n.*

exceptional child, *Education.* any child who deviates from mental, physical, or behavioral norms to the extent of needing special schooling, training, or treatment: *The state also is planning to help school systems meet the needs of the exceptional child. Under this category would fall those who are mentally deficient on the one end, and the "genius" upper level* (New York Times).

ex|cep|tion|al|i|ty (ek sep′shə nal′ə tē), *n., pl.* **-ties. 1** exceptional character or quality. **2** an exceptional thing.

ex|cep|tious (ek sep′shəs), *adj.* disposed to make objection; captious: *It is the character of country ladies to be exceptious and suspicious of slights* (Lord Chesterfield).

ex|cep|tis ex|ci|pi|en|dis (ek sep′tis ek sip′ē-en′dis), *Latin.* the necessary exceptions being made.

ex|cep|tive (ek sep′tiv), *adj.* **1** that excepts. **2** inclined to object; captious.

ex|cep|tor (ek sep′tər), *n.* a person who excepts.

ex|cerpt (*n.* ek′sėrpt; *v.* ek sėrpt′), *n., v.* ***—n.*** a passage taken out of a book or other source; quotation; extract: *The news announcer read several excerpts from the President's speech.*

—v.t. to take out (passages) from a book or other source; quote: *In his report on President Lincoln, he included some passages excerpted from Lincoln's speeches. This article is excerpted from a lecture delivered at Bowdoin College* (Wall Street Journal). **SYN:** select.

—v.i. to make extracts.

[< Latin *excerptus,* past participle of *excerpere* pluck out < *ex-* out + *carpere* pluck]

ex|cerpt|i|ble (ek sėrp′tə bəl), *adj.* that can be excerpted; suitable to make extracts or selections from.

ex|cerp|tion (ek sėrp′shən), *n.* **1** the act of excerpting. **2** an excerpt.

ex|cerp|tive (ek sėrp′tiv), *adj.* **1** inclined to excerpt. **2** characterized by excerption.

ex|cerp|tor (ek sėrp′tər), *n.* a person who excerpts or extracts.

ex|cess (*n., v.* ek ses′; *adj.* ek′ses, ek ses′), *n., adj., v.* ***—n.*** **1** more than enough; part that is too much: *Pour off the excess. We had an excess of snow last month.* **SYN:** surplus. **2** the condition of exceeding what is usual or necessary; superabundance. **SYN:** superfluity. **3** the amount by which one thing is more than another: *The excess of 7 over 5 is 2.* **4** an action that goes beyond what is necessary or just: *The gangster movie has an excess of violence. The enemy burned houses and committed other excesses.* **5** eating or drinking too much; overindulgence; intemperance: *His excesses shortened his life.* **SYN:** dissipation, immoderation.

—adj. **1** beyond the usual amount; extra: *Passengers must pay for excess baggage on an airplane.* **2** beyond what is necessary, proper, or right: *The fat man went on a diet to get rid of his excess weight.*

—v.t. *U.S.* to transfer or dismiss (a teacher or civil servant) from a position that has been eliminated or declared overstaffed: *According to a spokesman for the Board of Education, 243 supervisors were "excessed" last November and transferred out of their districts* (New York Times).

in excess of, more than: *The contributions received were in excess of $5,000. The quantity we receive is in excess of the quantity lost* (John Tyndall).

to excess, too much: *That fat man eats candy to excess.*

[< Latin *excessus, -ūs* < *excēdere;* see etym. under **exceed**]

ex|ces|sive (ek ses′iv), *adj.* too much; too great; going beyond what is necessary or right; extreme: *Ten dollars is an excessive price for five pounds of sugar. Many teen-agers spend an excessive amount of time on the telephone.* **—ex|ces′sive|ly,** *adv.* **—ex|ces′sive|ness,** *n.*

—Syn. **Excessive, exorbitant, inordinate** mean exceeding a right or proper limit. **Excessive** means going beyond what is right or normal in amount or extent: *They spend an excessive amount of time watching television.* **Exorbitant** applies particularly to unreasonable prices or demands: *He asked an exorbitant rent for the house.* **Inordinate** emphasizes lack of restraint in desires: *He has an inordinate appetite.*

ex|cess-prof|its tax (ek′ses prof′its), a tax on profits above the average profit for a given number of years or above a certain percentage of capital.

exch., 1 exchange. **2** exchequer.

ex|change (eks chānj′), *v.,* **-changed, -chang|ing,** *n.* ***—v.t.*** **1** to give (one thing) for another; change: *She would not exchange her house for a palace.* **2** to give in trade for something regarded as equivalent; barter; swap: *I will exchange two dimes for twenty pennies.* **3** to give and receive (things of the same kind): *to exchange letters. You two boys exchange places. The two boxers exchanged blows.* **4** to replace or have replaced (a purchase): *We can exchange no yard goods.*

—v.i. **1** to make an exchange. **2** to pass or be taken in exchange or as an equivalent.

—n. **1** a giving up of one thing and receiving or taking another for it; an exchanging: *Ten pennies for a dime is a fair exchange. During the truce there was an exchange of prisoners.* **2** a person or thing given or received in exchange for another, or as a substitute. **3** a place where things are exchanged. Stocks are bought, sold, and traded in a stock exchange. **4** a central station or office. A telephone exchange handles telephone calls. **5a** a system of settling accounts in different places by exchanging bills of exchange that represent money instead of exchanging money itself. **b** the payment of debts or obligations in different places by this method. **6** a changing of the money of one country into the money of equivalent value of another. **7** the fee charged for settling accounts, for changing money, or for transferring funds. **8a** the rate of exchange; a varying rate or sum in one currency given for a fixed sum in another currency. **b** the amount of the difference in rates of exchange. **9a** the checks, drafts, or bills exchanged in a clearing house. **b** = bill of exchange. **10** *British.* a labor exchange.

[< Old French *eschangier* to exchange < Vulgar Latin *excambiāre* < Latin *ex-* out + *cambiāre* to change < a Gaulish word]

—Syn. *v.t.* **1,2,3 Exchange, interchange** mean to give and take. **Exchange** implies trading, giving one thing and getting back something else: *He exchanged his independence for the chance to make more money.* **Interchange** implies trading evenly, giving and receiving by turn and in equal amount or value: *People of different countries interchange ideas.*

ex|change|a|bil|i|ty (eks chān′jə bil′ə tē), *n.* the condition of being exchangeable.

Pronunciation Key: hat, āge, cãre, fär; let, ēqual, tėrm; it, īce; hot, ōpen, ôrder; oil, out; cup, pu̇t, rüle; child; long; thin; ᴛʜen; zh, measure; ə represents **a** in about, **e** in taken, **i** in pencil, **o** in lemon, **u** in circus.

ex|change|a|ble (eks chān′jə bəl), *adj.* that can be exchanged.

exchangeable value, the value of a thing measured by what may be produced in exchange.

ex|change|a|bly (eks chān′jə blē), *adv.* in an exchangeable manner.

exchange control, the control of foreign exchange transactions, such as the transfer of gold and currency, by government agencies.

ex|chang|ee (eks′chān jē′; eks chān′jē, -chān′jē′), *n.* a person or thing exchanged, especially an exchange student.

exchange editor, an editor who selects extracts from other publications for reproduction in his own publication.

ex|chang|er (eks chān′jər), *n.* **1a** a person who exchanges. **b** a person who practices exchange: *Thou oughtest therefore to have put my money to the exchangers* (Matthew 25:27). **2** = heat exchanger. **3** a material, such as a resin or zeolite, used in an ion exchange process, as in the purification of water.

exchange rate, rate of exchange especially of one country's money for another's: *With a new exchange rate for the franc the balance of trade changed from deficit to surplus* (Manchester Guardian).

exchange reaction, *Chemistry.* a process whereby atoms of the same element in two different molecules, or in two different positions in the same molecule, exchange places. It is usually studied by means of a tracer or tagged atom.

exchange student, a student participating in a program of trading students between countries or institutions.

exchange teacher, a teacher participating in a program of exchanging teachers between institutions.

Ex|cheq|uer (eks chek′ər, eks′chek-), *n.* **1a** the department of the British government in charge of its finances and the public revenue. **b** the offices of this department. **2** the funds of the British government. **3** the Court of Exchequer, now merged in the Queen's Bench Division of the High Court of Justice. [Middle English *escheker* <Old French *eschequier* chessboard (accounts apparently were reckoned with counters on a table cover marked with squares)]

ex|cheq|uer (eks chek′ər, eks′chek-), *n.* **1** a treasury, especially of a state or nation. **2** *Informal.* finances; funds.

Exchequer bill, a negotiable bill of credit, bearing interest at a current rate, formerly issued by the British Exchequer for raising money to meet some emergency.

Exchequer bond, a bond issued by the British Exchequer at a fixed rate of interest and for a fixed period.

ex|cide (ek sīd′), *v.t.*, **-cid|ed, -cid|ing.** to cut out. [<Latin *excīdere;* see etym. under **excise**[2]]

ex|ci|mer (ek′sə mər), *n. Chemistry.* a substance formed by atoms in an excited state: *The term excimer means that atoms that are energetically excited come together and form molecules, and the molecules then emit the laser light. "Two excimer" means that molecules of two different elements are involved* (Science News). [<*exci*(ted) + (di)*mer*]

ex|cip|i|ent (ek sip′ē ənt), *n.* **1** any inert drug substance used as a medium or carrier for an active drug, such as the syrup in a cough medicine. **2** one that takes up or receives. [<Latin *excipiēns, -entis,* present participle of *excipere;* see etym. under **except**]

ex|ci|ple (ek′sə pəl), *n.* a layer of cells partially enclosing lichens. [<Latin *excipulum* receptacle <*excipere* take out; see etym. under **except**]

ex|ci|plex (ek sī′pleks, ek′sə-), *n.* a complex or aggregate of excited states, especially one produced in a dye laser: *Exciplexes . . . are believed to play an important role in many photochemical systems* (Nicholas J. Turro). [<*exci*(ted state) + (com)*plex*]

ex|cip|u|lar (ek sip′yə lər), *adj.* having to do with an exciple.

ex|ci|pule (ek′sə pyül), *n.* = exciple.

ex|cip|u|li|form (ek sip′yə lə fôrm), *adj.* like an exciple; having a rim.

ex|cip|u|lum (ek sip′yə ləm), *n., pl.* **-la** (-lə). = exciple.

ex|cis|a|ble[1] (ek sī′zə bəl), *adj.* subject to excise duty. [<*excise*[1] + *-able*]

ex|cis|a|ble[2] (ek sī′zə bəl), *adj.* that can be removed. [<*excise*[2] + *-able*]

ex|cise[1] (*n.* ek′sīz, -sīs; ek sīz′; *v.* ek sīz′), *n., v.,* **-cised, -cis|ing.** —*n.* **1** a tax on the manufacture, sale, or use of certain articles made, sold, or used within a country: *There is an excise on tobacco.* **2** a tax for a license to follow or practice certain trades or sports. **3** *British.* the division of the civil service in the Customs and Excise Department charged with collecting excises.
—*v.t.* to force (a person) to pay an excise. [apparently <Middle Dutch *excijs* <Old French *acceis* tax, ultimately <Latin *ad-* to + *census* tax]

ex|cise[2] (ek sīz′), *v.t.*, **-cised, -cis|ing.** to cut out; remove: *The editor excised passages from the book.* SYN: expunge. [<Latin *excīsus,* past participle of *excīdere* <*ex-* out + *caedere* cut]

ex|cise|man (ek sīz′mən), *n., pl.* **-men.** an official of the British government who collects excises and enforces the laws having to do with excises: *Of all the manifold ills in the train of smuggling, surely the exciseman is the worst* (Oliver Goldsmith).

ex|cise|man|ship (ek sīz′mən ship), *n.* the position or office of exciseman.

ex|ci|sion (ek sizh′ən), *n.* **1** the act or process of cutting out; removal: *Through the processes of excision and sloughing of certain structures . . . plants get rid of wastes* (Harbaugh and Goodrich). **2** the state of being excised. **3** exclusion, as from a religious society; excommunication. **4** extirpation or destruction.

ex|ci|sion|al (ek sizh′ə nəl), *adj.* of or having to do with an excision: *excisional therapy.*

ex|cit|a|bil|i|ty (ek sī′tə bil′ə tē), *n.* **1** the quality of being easily excited. **2** *Physiology.* the capacity to respond to a stimulus; irritability.

ex|cit|a|ble (ek sī′tə bəl), *adj.* **1** easily excited: *Young children and puppies are very excitable.* **2** *Physiology.* sensitive to or capable of responding to stimuli. —**ex|cit′a|ble|ness,** *n.* —**ex|cit′a|bly,** *adv.*

ex|ci|tan|cy (ek′sə tən sē), *n.* the property of exciting or calling into activity.

ex|cit|ant (ek sī′tənt), *n., adj.* —*n.* an agent or drug that excites; stimulant. **1** the liquid that produces a magnetic field in an electric cell.
—*adj.* that excites or stimulates.

ex|ci|ta|tion (ek′sī tā′shən), *n.* **1** the act or process of exciting. **2** the state of being excited; excitement. **3a** the production of a magnetic field by electricity. **b** the current producing the magnetic field in a generator or motor. **4** the raising of an electron, atom, nucleus, or molecule to a higher state of energy.

ex|cit|a|tive (ek sī′tə tiv), *adj.* **1** tending to excite. **2** characterized by excitement.

ex|cit|a|tor (ek sī′tə tôr, -tōr), *n.* a person or thing that produces excitation.

ex|cit|a|to|ry (ek sī′tə tôr′ē, -tōr′-), *adj.* **1** tending to or producing excitation: *These larvae have an excitatory effect on the worker* [*ants*] (Science News Letter). **2** characterized or produced by excitation.

ex|cite (ek sīt′), *v.t.*, **-cit|ed, -cit|ing. 1** to stir up the feelings of; move to strong emotion: *The news of war excited everybody.* SYN: rouse, animate, kindle. **2** to arouse: *Her new dress excited envy among the other girls.* **3** to stir to action; stimulate: *Do not excite the dog; keep away from him.* **4** *Physiology.* to affect (an organ or tissue) so that its usual activity is aroused or intensified; stimulate. **5** to produce an electric or magnetic field in (a generator or particle accelerator). **6** to raise one or more electrons of (an atom) or an atom, nucleus, or molecule to a higher state of energy. [<Latin *excitāre* (frequentative) <*exciēre* set in motion <*ex-* out + *ciēre* set in motion]

ex|cit|ed (ek sī′tid), *adj.* **1** stirred up; aroused: *The excited mob rushed into the mayor's office.* SYN: disturbed, agitated. **2** electrified. **3** magnetized. **4** having one or more electrons raised to a higher state of energy; raised to an excited state: *an excited atom, an excited nucleus.* —**ex|cit′ed|ly,** *adv.*

excited state, *Physics.* a state of higher energy than the ground state; that state of energy in which the electrons have been displaced to a more distant orbit than in the ground state.

ex|cite|ment (ek sīt′mənt), *n.* **1** an excited condition: *The baby's first step caused great excitement in the family.* SYN: agitation, perturbation, commotion, ado. **2** something that excites: *The circus was an excitement to every boy in town.* **3** the act of exciting; arousing: *The excitement of nations to war is foolish.*

ex|cit|er (ek sī′tər), *n.* **1** a person or thing that excites. **2** a generator, battery, or other apparatus that supplies the current for producing a magnetic field in another dynamo or in a motor. **3** a device for producing hertzian waves.

ex|cit|ing (ek sī′ting), *adj.* causing excitement; arousing; stirring: *an exciting story about pirates.* —**ex|cit′ing|ly,** *adv.* —**ex|cit′ing|ness,** *n.*

ex|ci|tive (ek sī′tiv), *adj.* tending to excite; excitatory.

ex|ci|to|mo|tor (ek sī′tō mō′tər), *adj.* **1** exciting muscular action. **2** having to do with reflex action. [<*excito*(r) + *motor*]

ex|ci|ton (ek sī′ton, ek′sə-), *n. Physics.* an excited state formed by the association of an electron and a positively charged hole, which together disperse energy in a semiconductor or other crystal. *Solid-state physicists . . . have witnessed the splitting of an exciton, a conceptual entity consisting of the temporary union of a negative electron and a positive electron "hole" in an excited crystal lattice* (Scientific American). [<*excit*(ed) + *-on*]

ex|ci|ton|ic (ek′sī ton′ik, -sə-), *adj.* of or having to do with excitons: *There is a variety of excitonic processes, however, that give rise to electrical conductivity* (Martin Pope).

ex|ci|ton|ics (ek′sī ton′iks, -sə-), *n.* the study of excitons: *The recent developments in excitonics could have an important bearing on the study of energy-transfer mechanisms such as those involved in photosynthesis by living plants* (Scientific American).

ex|ci|tor (ek sī′tər), *n.* **1** a nerve whose stimulation excites greater action in the part supplied. **2** = exciter.

ex|ci|to|ry (ek sī′tər ē), *adj.* fitted to excite; instrumental in exciting.

ex|ci|to|se|cre|to|ry (ek sī′tō si krē′tər ē), *adj. Physiology.* causing increased secretion.

excl., **1** exclamation. **2a** exclusive. **b** exclusively.

ex|claim (ek sklām′), *v., n.* —*v.i., v.t.* to say or speak suddenly in surprise or strong feeling; cry out: *"Here you are at last!" exclaimed his mother.* SYN: shout, ejaculate.
—*n. Archaic.* an exclamation or outcry: *cursing cries and deep exclaims* (Shakespeare).
[<Middle French *exclamer,* learned borrowing from Latin *exclamāre* <*ex-* out + *clamāre* cry out] —**ex|claim′er,** *n.*

exclam., **1** exclamation. **2** exclamatory.

ex|cla|ma|tion (eks′klə mā′shən), *n.* **1** something said suddenly as the result of feeling; interjection. *Oh! Hurrah! Well! Look!* and *Listen!* are common exclamations. **2** the action of exclaiming or crying out suddenly. **3** = exclamation mark.

***exclamation mark** or **point**, a mark of punctuation used after a word, phrase, or sentence to show that it was exclaimed. *Example:* Hurrah! We are going to the circus. The exclamation mark is also used within parentheses, to suggest that some statement or situation is remarkable, absurd, or the like: *"The poet John Milton was born in Connecticut"* (!).

***exclamation mark**

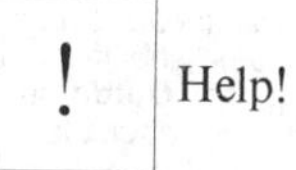

ex|clam|a|tive (ek sklam′ə tiv), *adj.* = exclamatory.

ex|clam|a|to|ry (ek sklam′ə tôr′ē, -tōr′-), *adj.* using, containing, or expressing exclamation; noisy; outspoken: *exclamatory shouts from the audience.*

ex|clave (eks′klāv), *n.* a part of a country surrounded by foreign territory. Such a part is an exclave in relation to the nation to which it belongs, and is an enclave in relation to the surrounding nation. *West Berlin is an exclave of West Germany.* [<*ex-*[1] + (en)*clave*]

ex|clud|a|bil|i|ty (ek sklü′də bil′ə tē), *n.* the condition of being excludable: *His excludability was due to his criminal record.*

ex|clud|a|ble (ek sklü′də bəl), *adj.* that can be excluded: *The payments were excludable from the widow's gross income* (Wall Street Journal).

ex|clude (ek sklüd′), *v.t.*, **-clud|ed, -clud|ing. 1** to shut out; keep (something) from entering: *Curtains exclude light.* **2** to drive out and keep out; expel; banish: *Perfect faith excludes doubt.* SYN: eject, exile. **3a** to give no place to; prevent the existence, occurrence, or use of. **b** to reject from consideration, notice, or use. [<Latin *exclūdere* <*ex-* out + *claudere* shut]
—*Syn.* **1 Exclude, eliminate** mean to keep out. **Exclude** emphasizes keeping someone or something from coming into a place, into consideration, etc.: *Closing the windows excludes street noises. The government excludes immigrants who have certain diseases.* **Eliminate** emphasizes putting out something already in, by getting rid of it or shutting it off from attention: *He eliminated fear from his thinking.*

excluded middle, *Logic.* the premise that, since every proposition must be true or false, there can be no third alternative or middle ground between true and false, or between contradictions.

ex|clud|er (ek sklü′dər), *n.* a person or thing that excludes or shuts out.

ex|clu|sion (ek sklü′zhən), *n.* **1** the act or process of excluding: *We voted for exclusion from the club of children over ten years of age.* **2** the state of being excluded: *Her exclusion from the meeting hurt her feelings.* **3** *Physiology.* the process of expelling or keeping out.

to the exclusion of, so as to shut out or keep out: *He spoke in the singular number to the express exclusion of Eugene* (Dickens). [< Latin *exclusiō, -ōnis* < *exclūdere* exclude < *ex-* out + *claudere* shut]

ex|clu|sion|ar|y (ek sklü′zhə ner′ē), *adj.* of or having to do with exclusion: *an exclusionary rule.*

exclusionary rule, *U.S. Law.* the rule that evidence obtained by unlawful means cannot be introduced in the trial of a criminal case: *The primary purpose of the exclusionary rule is to deter police misbehavior. Without the rule, the U.S. Supreme Court has held, lawmen could violate—with impunity—citizens' Fourth Amendment rights to be free of unreasonable searches and seizures* (Newsweek).

exclusion clause, a provision in an insurance policy that excludes coverage for certain risks.

ex|clu|sion|er (ek sklü′zhə nər), *n.* = exclusionist.

ex|clu|sion|ism (ek sklü′zhə niz əm), *n.* the principle, policy, or practice of exclusion, as from rights or privileges.

ex|clu|sion|ist (ek sklü′zhə nist), *n., adj.* —***n.*** a person who favors exclusion; a person who would exclude another from some right or privilege. —***adj.*** of or having to do with exclusionists: *They have established rigid import quotas and other exclusionist devices to protect their product in their own markets* (Atlantic).

exclusion principle, *Physics.* the principle that no two electrons of an atom can have the same four quantum numbers; Pauli's principle.

ex|clu|sive (ek sklü′siv, -ziv), *adj., n.* —***adj.*** **1** each shutting out the other. "Tree" and "animal" are exclusive terms; a thing cannot be both a tree and an animal. **2** shutting out all or most others: *She gave her exclusive attention to the teacher's instructions.* **3** not divided or shared with others; single; sole: *An inventor has an exclusive right for a certain number of years to make what he has invented and patented.* **4a** very particular about choosing friends, members, patrons, clientele, or other associates; select: *It is hard to get admitted to an exclusive club. The literary class is usually proud and exclusive* (Emerson). **b** barring persons thought of as outside the group, especially for social or economic reasons; snobbish. SYN: clannish, undemocratic.
—***n.*** **1** an article exclusively contributed to a particular newspaper or magazine: *The Times had been granted the interview as an exclusive.* **2** some unique item, plan, or other design, offered by a particular store, company, or the like: *Our new insurance plan is a company exclusive.*
exclusive of, excluding; leaving out; not counting or considering: *There are 26 days in that month, exclusive of Sundays.*
—**ex|clu′sive|ness**, *n.*

Exclusive Brethren, the Plymouth Brethren, a Protestant religious sect, especially those particularly strict in their views.

exclusive economic zone, = economic zone.

exclusive enunciation or **proposition**, *Logic.* a proposition which asserts something to be true of a certain class of things and to be false of everything else.

ex|clu|sive|ly (ek sklü′siv lē, -ziv-), *adv.* **1** with the exclusion of all others: *That selfish girl looks out for herself exclusively.* **2** with the exclusion of the part or parts specified: *We accept the contract as set forth exclusively.*

ex|clu|siv|ism (ek sklü′sə viz əm), *n.* the principle or practice of being exclusive; systematic exclusiveness: *Historian Arnold Toynbee, in A Study of History, referred to ... the Old Testament's exclusivism* (Time).

ex|clu|siv|ist (ek sklü′sə vist), *adj., n.* —***adj.*** that excludes outsiders; discriminatory: *exclusivist nationalism.* —***n.*** a person who excludes or favors excluding certain people, doctrines, practices, etc.: *The Chinese are not exclusivists in religion but may profess two or more at the same time.*

ex|clu|siv|is|tic (ek sklü′sə vis′tik), *adj.* = exclusivist.

ex|clu|siv|i|ty (eks′klü siv′ə tē), *n.* **1** exclusiveness; exclusive rights: *Our record company does not have exclusivity over the titles we sell.* **2** availability to very few or only one: *women to whom fashion and exclusivity are important* (New Yorker).

ex|clu|so|ry (ek sklü′sər ē), *adj.* **1** having the power or the function of excluding. **2** tending to exclude.

ex|cog|i|tate (eks koj′ə tāt), *v.t.*, **-tat|ed, -tat|ing.** to think out; devise; contrive. [< Latin *excōgitāre* (with English *-ate*[1]) discover by thinking < *ex-* out + *cōgitāre* think, cogitate]

ex|cog|i|ta|tion (eks koj′ə tā′shən), *n.* **1** the act of excogitating. **2** a plan; contrivance; invention.

ex|cog|i|ta|tive (eks koj′ə tā′tiv), *adj.* of or having to do with excogitation.

ex|cog|i|ta|tor (eks koj′ə tā′tər), *n.* a person who excogitates.

ex|com|mu|ni|ca|ble (eks′kə myü′nə kə bəl), *adj.* **1** that may or should be excommunicated. **2** punishable by excommunication, as an offense.

ex|com|mu|ni|cant (eks′kə myü′nə kənt), *n.* an excommunicated person: *The excommunicants professed to be shocked by the order* (Time).

ex|com|mu|ni|cate (eks′kə myü′nə kāt), *v.*, **-cat|ed, -cat|ing**, *n., adj.* —***v.t.*** **1** to cut off from membership in a church; shut out from communion with the church; prohibit from participating in any of the rites of a church: *The Pope excommunicated King John.* **2** *Figurative.* to exclude or expel from the fellowship of any group: *He [Tito] was excommunicated from the international Communist society* (William Henry Chamberlin).
—***n.*** an excommunicated person: *Thus, an individual whose guilt is known only to himself is ipso facto an excommunicate* (New York Times).
—***adj.*** excommunicated.
[< Latin *excommūnicāre* (with English *-ate*[1]) < *ex-* out of + *commūnis* common]

ex|com|mu|ni|ca|tion (eks′kə myü′nə kā′shən), *n.* **1a** the action of cutting off from membership in a church and from any part in its ceremonies; prohibition from participating in any of the rites of a church or from association with its members. **b** *Figurative.* a similar exclusion or expulsion from any group. **2** an official statement announcing this: *The following day came the Vatican excommunication* (Time). **3** the condition or state of a person who has been excommunicated.

excommunication by candle, an obsolete form of excommunication in which the offender was allowed time to repent only while a candle burned out.

ex|com|mu|ni|ca|tive (eks′kə myü′nə kā′tiv), *adj.* **1** inclined or serving to excommunicate. **2** containing a sentence of excommunication.

ex|com|mu|ni|ca|tor (eks′kə myü′nə kā′tər), *n.* a person who excommunicates.

ex|com|mu|ni|ca|to|ry (eks′kə myü′nə kə tôr′ē, -tōr′-), *adj.* having to do with or causing excommunication.

ex|con|ju|gant (eks kon′jə gənt), *n.* a protozoan that has conjugated and again become an independent organism.

ex-con|vict (eks′kon′vikt), *n.* a former convict.

ex|co|ri|a|ble (ek skôr′ē ə bəl, -skōr′-), *adj.* that can be excoriated; censurable: *excoriable actions.*

ex|co|ri|ate (ek skôr′ē āt, -skōr′-), *v.t.*, **-at|ed, -at|ing.** **1** to strip or rub off the skin of; make raw and sore; abrade; chafe: *The corpse ... was much bruised and excoriated* (Edgar Allan Poe). SYN: gall. **2** *Figurative.* to denounce violently; censure: *In a sarcastic speech the candidate excoriated his opponent. It is more likely to strike a reader as being like a hell-fire sermon—excoriating sin, not sinners* (James Boylan). [< Late Latin *excoriāre* (with English *-ate*[1]) < *ex-* off + *corium* hide, skin] —**ex|co′ri|at′ing|ly**, *adv.*

ex|co|ri|a|tion (ek skôr′ē ā′shən, -skōr′-), *n.* **1** the act of excoriating. **2** the state of being excoriated. **3** an excoriated place on the body.

ex|co|ri|a|tive (ek skôr′ē ā′tiv, -skōr′-), *adj.* violently denunciatory: *excoriative sermons.*

ex|cor|ti|cate (ek skôr′tə kāt), *v.t.*, **-cat|ed, -cat|ing.** to strip off the bark, rind, or coating, from. [< *ex-*[1] + Latin *cortex, -icis* bark + *English -ate*[1]]

ex|cor|ti|ca|tion (ek skôr′tə kā′shən), *n.* the act of stripping off or peeling the bark from (a tree).

ex|cre|ment (eks′krə mənt), *n.* waste matter that is discharged from the body, especially from the bowels. [< Latin *excrēmentum* < stem of *excrētus;* see etym. under **excrete**]

ex|cre|men|tal (eks′krə men′təl), *adj.* of or like excrement.

ex|cre|men|ti|tious (eks′krə men tish′əs), *adj.* = excremental.

ex|cres|cence (ek skres′əns), *n.* **1** an unnatural growth; disfiguring addition. A corn or wart is an excrescence. (*Figurative.*) *Many new office buildings are unsightly excrescences upon the city's landscape.* **2** a natural outgrowth. Hairs and fingernails are excrescences. **3** an abnormal increase; overflow (of anything).

ex|cres|cen|cy (ek skres′ən sē), *n., pl.* **-cies.** = excrescence.

ex|cres|cent (ek skres′ənt), *adj.* **1** forming an unnatural growth or a disfiguring addition; superfluous. **2** *Phonetics.* (of a sound) present for no historical or grammatical reason, as *b* in *thimble,* derived from Old English *thymle.* [< Latin *excrēscēns, -entis,* present participle of *excrēscere* grow out of < *ex-* out + *crēscere* grow]

ex|cres|cen|tial (eks′krə sen′chəl), *adj.* having to do with or of the nature of an excrescence.

ex|cre|ta (ek skrē′tə), *n.pl.* waste matter discharged from the body, such as urine or sweat: (*Figurative.*) *We're fouling our nest with social and industrial excreta—residues of pesticides, effluent of factories* (Elspeth Huxley). [< Latin *excrēta,* neuter plural of *excrētus;* see etym. under **excrete**]

ex|cre|ta|ble (ek skrē′tə bəl), *adj.* that can be excreted.

ex|cre|tal (ek skrē′təl), *adj.* having to do with or of the nature of excrement.

ex|crete (ek skrēt′), *v.t.*, **-cret|ed, -cret|ing.** to discharge (waste matter) from the body; separate (waste matter) from the blood or tissues of an animal or from the system of a plant: *The sweat glands excrete sweat.* [< Latin *excrētus,* past participle of *excernere* discharge < *ex-* out + *cernere* sift]

ex|cret|er (ek skrē′tər), *n.* a person or thing that excretes: *One day Shakespeare denounced a critic as an "excreter of ink"* (Time).

ex|cre|tion (ek skrē′shən), *n.* **1** the discharging of waste matter from the body; separation of waste matter from the blood or tissues. **2** the waste matter that is separated and discharged: *Sweat is an excretion.*

ex|cre|tion|ar|y (ek skrē′shə ner′ē), *adj.* of or having to do with excretion.

ex|cre|tive (ek skrē′tiv), *adj.* excreting; serving to excrete.

ex|cre|to|ry (eks′krə tôr′ē, -tōr′-), *adj., n.* —***adj.*** **1** excreting; having the function of excreting; that excretes: *The kidneys are excretory organs.* **2** of or having to do with excretion or excretions: *excretory products. No animal can live long with an impairment of its excretory function* (A. M. Winchester). —***n.*** an excretory organ or duct.

ex|cru|ci|ate (ek skrü′shē āt), *v.t.*, **-at|ed, -at|ing.** to cause great suffering to; pain very much; torture: (*Figurative.*) *Her presence used to excruciate Osborn* (Thackeray). [< Latin *excruciāre* (with English *-ate*[1]) < *ex-* out + *cruciāre* torture, crucify < *crux, crucis* cross]

ex|cru|ci|at|ing (ek skrü′shē ā′ting), *adj.* **1** causing great suffering; very painful; torturing: *"While you were away, I strained my back again, reaching for a hatbox," she said. "The pain is excruciating"* (New Yorker). SYN: agonizing, tormenting. **2** *Figurative.* excessively elaborate; extreme: *excruciating politeness.* —**ex|cru′ci|at′ing|ly**, *adv.*

ex|cru|ci|a|tion (ek skrü′shē ā′shən), *n.* **1** the act of causing extreme pain. **2** great suffering; extreme pain. **3** an instance of this.

ex|cru|ci|a|tor (ek skrü′shē ā′tər), *n.* a person who excruciates; a tormentor.

ex|cu|bi|to|ri|um (ek skyü′bə tôr′ē əm, -tōr′-), *n., pl.* **-to|ri|a** (-tôr′ē ə, -tōr′-). a gallery in some churches for watchers on the eve of a festival, within view of the shrines. [< Medieval Latin *excubitorium* < Latin *excubitōrium* guardhouse < *excubāre* to lie out on guard < *ex-* out + *cubāre* lie down]

ex|cu|dit (ek skyü′dit), *Latin.* (the person specified) struck out, fashioned, or engraved it.

ex|cul|pa|ble (ek skul′pə bəl), *adj.* that can be freed from blame or accusation.

ex|cul|pate (eks′kul pāt, ek skul′-), *v.t.*, **-pat|ed, -pat|ing.** to free from blame; prove innocent: *The driver was exculpated by the testimony of several witnesses.* SYN: exonerate, clear. [< Medieval Latin *exculpare* (with English *-ate*[1]) < Latin *ex-* out + *culpa* guilt]

ex|cul|pa|tion (eks′kul pā′shən), *n.* **1** the act of freeing from blame; a proving innocent. **2** vindication; proof of innocence; excuse.

ex|cul|pa|to|ri|ly (ek skul′pə tôr′ə lē, -tōr′-), *adv.* in an exculpatory manner.

ex|cul|pa|to|ry (ek skul′pə tôr′ē, -tōr′-), *adj.* that clears or tends to clear from blame; exculpating.

ex cu|ri|a (eks kyůr′ē ə), *Latin.* out of court.

ex|cur|rent (ek skėr′ənt), *adj.* **1** giving exit: *the excurrent siphon of an oyster or clam.* **2** having the axis prolonged so as to form an undivided main trunk, as the spruce tree does. **3** projecting beyond the tip or margin, as the midrib does in certain leaves. **4** running out. [< Latin *excurrēns, -entis* < *excurrere* run out < *ex-* out + *currere* run]

ex|curse (ek skėrs′), *v.i.*, **-cursed, -curs|ing.** **1** to run out or off. **2** *Figurative.* to digress. **3** to make an excursion. [< Latin *excursus,* past participle of *excurrere;* see etym. under **excursion**]

ex|cur|sion (ek skėr′zhən, -shən), *n., adj., v.* —***n.*** **1** a trip, especially a short trip taken for interest or pleasure, often by a number of people together: *Our club went on an excursion to the mountains. He [the astronaut] never did get all the way to the command module during the excursion* (Science News). (*Figurative.*) *Preliminary excursions into the systematic study of patterns of science* (New Scientist). SYN: expedition, tour,

Pronunciation Key: hat, āge, cãre, fär; let, ēqual, tėrm; it, īce; hot, ōpen, ôrder; oil, out; cup, půt, rüle; child; long; thin; ᴛʜen; zh, measure; ə represents **a** in about, **e** in taken, **i** in pencil, **o** in lemon, **u** in circus.

jaunt. **2** a trip on a train, ship, airplane, or the like, at fares lower than are usually charged: *The Pennsylvania Railroad announced yesterday that it would begin excursions to Philadelphia ... that will allow a mother and father and two children to travel round-trip for a family rate of $10* (New York Times). **3** a group of people who go on an excursion. **4** *Figurative.* a deviation or wandering from the subject; digression. **5** *Physics.* the departure of a body from its main position or proper course. **6** the range of stroke of any moving part. **7** a sally; sortie; raid.
—*adj.* of or having to do with a trip, especially a short trip, taken for pleasure; excursional: *an excursion train. The Wilson Line had been operating excursion boats in local waters since 1800* (New Yorker).
—*v.i.* to make an excursion: *Within limits, almost any reason will justify a trip off campus. But with six-hour homework loads, much excursioning is unlikely* (Newsweek).
[< Latin *excursiō, -ōnis* < *excurrere* run out < *ex-* out + *currere* run]

ex|cur|sion|al (ek skėr′zhə nəl, -shə-), *adj.* of or having to do with an excursion.

ex|cur|sion|ar|y (ek skėr′zhə ner′ē, -shə-), *adj. British.* excursional.

ex|cur|sion|ist (ek skėr′zhə nist, -shə-), *n.* a person who goes on an excursion: *Scarborough has welcomed both day excursionists and resident holidaymakers in greater numbers than ever before* (London Times).

ex|cur|sion|ize (ek skėr′zhə nīz, -shə-), *v.,* **-ized, -iz|ing.** —*v.t.* to make excursions through.
—*v.i.* to make excursions or an excursion.

excursion ticket, a round-trip ticket, usually at a reduced fare.

excursion train, a train carrying persons on a trip, especially a short trip taken for pleasure, usually at a reduced fare.

ex|cur|sive (ek skėr′siv), *adj.* **1** off the subject; wandering; rambling. **SYN**: erratic, digressive. **2** of the nature of an excursion. **3** *Figurative.* desultory: *excursive reading.* —**ex|cur′sive|ly,** *adv.*
—**ex|cur′sive|ness,** *n.*

ex|cur|sus (ek skėr′səs), *n., pl.* **-sus|es** or **-sus. 1** a detailed discussion of some point, inserted at the end of a book or chapter. **2** a digression: *This brief personal excursus may help to explain something of the fascination that keeps the categorisers at their self-appointed task* (Punch).
[< Latin *excursus, -ūs* < *excurrere;* see etym. under **excursion**]

ex|cur|vate (eks kėr′vit), *adj. Zoology.* excurved.

ex|cur|vat|ed (eks kėr′vā tid), *adj. Zoology.* excurved.

ex|cur|va|tion (eks′kėr vā′shən), *n.* = excurvature.

ex|cur|va|ture (eks kėr′və chər), *n. Zoology.* **1** the state of being excurved. **2** a part of a margin, mark, or the like, curved outwardly, or away from the center of the body or organ. [< *excurvate* + *-ure,* as in *curvature*]

ex|curved (eks kėrvd′), *adj. Zoology.* curved outward, or away from the disk or center of a part or organ: *an excurved margin, an excurved mark.*

ex|cus|a|ble (ek skyü′zə bəl), *adj.* that can be excused; deserving pardon. —**ex|cus′a|ble|ness,** *n.*

ex|cus|a|bly (ek skyü′zə blē), *adv.* in a manner open to excuse; so as to deserve being excused.

ex|cus|al (ek skyü′zəl), *n.* **1** the action of excusing. **2** an instance of this.

ex|cus|a|tive (ek skyü′zə tiv), *adj.* tending to excuse.

ex|cus|a|to|ry (ek skyü′zə tôr′ē, -tōr′-), *adj.* serving or intended to excuse.

ex|cuse (*v.* ek skyüz′; *n.* ek skyüs′), *v.,* **-cused, -cus|ing,** *n.* —*v.t.* **1** to offer an apology for; try to remove the blame of: *She excused her own faults by blaming others.* **2** to be a reason or explanation for; clear of blame: *Sickness excuses absence from school.* **SYN**: justify, extenuate, exculpate. **3** to overlook (a fault, offense, or other defect); pardon; forgive: *Excuse me, I have to go now. This time he excused my carelessness in upsetting the ink.* **4** to free from duty; let off: *Those who passed the first test are excused from the second one.* **5** to agree to do without; not demand or require; dispense with: *We will excuse your presence.* **6** to seek exemption or release for. **7** to obtain exemption or release for.
—*n.* **1** a real or pretended reason that is given; explanation: *Sickness was his excuse for being absent from school.* **SYN**: justification. **2** an apology given. **3** the act of excusing.
excuse oneself, a to ask to be pardoned: *He excused himself for bumping into me by saying that he was in a hurry.* **b** to ask permission to leave: *I excused myself from the table.* **c** to ask to be let off: *He excused himself from participation in the card game because he wanted to watch television.*
[< Old French *excuser,* learned borrowing from Latin *excūsāre* < *ex-* away + *causa* cause, accusation]
—*Syn. v.t.* **3 Excuse, pardon, forgive** mean to free from blame or punishment. **Excuse** means to overlook, or let off with only disapproval, less important errors and faults: *She excused our failure to reply.* **Pardon** is used in a similar manner, but it can also mean to free from punishment due for serious faults, wrongdoing, or crimes: *The governor pardoned him and restored his civil rights.* **Forgive** suggests more personal feeling, and emphasizes giving up all wish to punish for wrong done: *I am sure his rudeness was unintentional, and I forgive him for it.*
—*n.* **1 Excuse, apology** mean something said to explain an offense or failure. **Excuse** suggests trying to justify a mistake or failure or to make it seem less serious, in order to escape blame or punishment: *He is always late, and always has an excuse.* **Apology** suggests admitting a wrong and regretting it: *He offered his apology for damaging my car.*
▶ **excuse, pardon.** As conventional expressions of regret, both *Excuse me* and *Pardon me* are equally proper. *Pardon me* or *I beg* (*your*) *pardon* is also a standard formula meaning "I didn't hear what you said." *Excuse me* also has the special meaning "I must leave."

ex|cuse|less (ek skyüs′lis), *adj.* **1** having no excuse. **2** = inexcusable.

ex|cus|er (ek skyü′zər), *n.* a person who excuses.

ex|cus|ing (ek skyü′zing), *adj.* that excuses, or makes excuse; containing an excuse.

ex|cus|ing|ly (ek skyü′zing lē), *adv.* in an excusing tone or manner; by way of excuse.

ex|cyst (ek sist′), *v.i.* to come out from a cyst or sac.

ex|cys|ta|tion (ek′sis tā′shən), *n.* **1** the process of coming out from a cyst or sac. **2** the state of being excysted.

ex de|lic|to (eks di lik′tō), *Latin.* from an offense or wrong.

ex-di|rec|to|ry (eks′də rek′tər ē, -dī-; -trē), *adj. British.* not in the telephone directory; unlisted: *Manager Harry Catterick has the League's best kept ex-directory phone number* (Sunday Times).

ex div or **ex d.,** without the dividend.

ex-div|i|dend (eks′div′ə dend), *adv., adj.* without the dividend next to be paid included in the sale price of stocks or shares.

ex do|no (eks dō′nō), *Latin.* by gift; as a present.

ex do|no De|i (eks dō′no dē′ī), *Latin.* by the gift of God.

ex|e|at (ek′sē at), *Latin.* let him go out or depart.

ex|ec (eg zek′), *n. U.S. Informal.* executive: *We have a new ad exec in the office.*

exec., **1** executive. **2** executor.

ex|e|cra|ble (ek′sə krə bəl), *adj.* **1** abominable; detestable: *an execrable villain.* **SYN**: damnable, accursed. **2** of wretched quality: *an execrable pun. Her French had always been execrable* (Atlantic). —**ex′e|cra|ble|ness,** *n.*

ex|e|cra|bly (ek′sə krə blē), *adv.* in an execrable manner; abominably; detestably.

ex|e|crate (ek′sə krāt), *v.,* **-crat|ed, -crat|ing.** —*v.t.* **1** to feel intense loathing for; abhor; detest. **SYN**: abominate. **2** to curse or damn; denounce; excoriate: *Time* [*magazine*] *has been execrated but also imitated more than any other English-language publication on earth* (Alistair Cooke).
—*v.i.* to curse.
[< Latin *exsecrārī* < *ex-* completely < *sacrāre* to curse < *sacer, sacrī* reserved religiously as untouchable]

ex|e|cra|tion (ek′sə krā′shən), *n.* **1** abhorrence; loathing; detestation. **2** a cursing. **3** a curse: *The mob shouted angry execrations at the assassin.* **4** a person or thing execrated.

ex|e|cra|tive (ek′sə krā′tiv), *adj.* having to do with or of the nature of execration. —**ex′e|cra′tive|ly,** *adv.*

ex|e|cra|tor (ek′sə krā′tər), *n.* a person who execrates or pronounces an execration.

ex|e|cra|to|ry (ek′sə krə tôr′ē, -tōr′-), *adj.* = execrative.

ex|e|cut|a|ble (ek′sə kyü′tə bəl), *adj.* that can be executed.

ex|ec|u|tan|cy (eg zek′yə tən sē), *n.* the qualification of an executant; power and skill in performance, especially of music: ... *such music lying hardly within the sphere of amateur executancy* (London Times).

ex|ec|u|tant (eg zek′yə tənt), *n., adj.* —*n.* a person who executes or performs, especially a musical performer: *The performance confirmed that* [*his*] *genius as an executant is unimpaired* (London Times).
—*adj.* that executes or performs, especially as a musician: [*He*] *is the greatest ... executant genius ever thrown up by music in Britain* (Cyril Connolly).

ex|e|cute (ek′sə kyüt), *v.t.,* **-cut|ed, -cut|ing. 1** to put to death according to an order, especially according to a sentence determined by law: *The murderer was executed.* **SYN**: kill, hang, electrocute. **2** to put into effect; enforce: *Congress makes the laws; the President executes them.* **3** to carry out; do: *The nurse executed the doctor's orders.* **SYN**: accomplish, fulfill, complete. See syn. under **perform. 4** to make according to a plan or design: *An artist executes a painting or statue.* **5** to perform or play (a piece of music). **6** to make (a deed, lease, contract, will, or other document) legal by signing, sealing, or doing whatever is necessary. [< Medieval Latin *exsecutare* < Latin *exsecūtus,* past participle of *exsequī* < *ex-* out + *sequī* follow]

ex|e|cut|er (ek′sə kyü′tər), *n.* a person who carries out or executes plans, laws, or the like; executor.

ex|e|cu|tion (ek′sə kyü′shən), *n.* **1** a putting to death according to law: *His execution, scheduled for the week of Jan. 23, was stayed last week when he filed an appeal* (Newsweek). **2** a carrying out; a doing; a performing: *He was prompt in the execution of his duties. His intention and execution are not very near each other* (Samuel Johnson). **SYN**: accomplishment. **3** a putting into effect; an enforcing: *The execution of local laws is carried out by the city police.* **4** the way of carrying out or doing; skill: *The artist's execution is a mark of his greatness.* **5** the manner of performing or playing a piece of music. **6** a making according to a plan or design. **7** a making legal by signing, sealing, or doing what is necessary: *the execution of a deed or contract.* **8** a written order from a court of law directing a judgment to be carried out. **9** effective action, especially of weapons: *His brandish'd steel, which smoked with bloody execution* (Shakespeare).
do execution, a to have a destructive effect: *The shot, probably from the distance of the ships, did no great execution* (William H. Prescott). **b** to be effective: *Black eyes, which might have done some execution had they been placed in a smoother face* (Thackeray).

ex|e|cu|tion|er (ek′sə kyü′shə nər), *n.* a person who puts someone to death according to an order, especially according to law.

ex|ec|u|tive (eg zek′yə tiv), *adj., n.* —*adj.* **1a** having to do with carrying out or managing affairs: *the executive committee, an executive council. An executive job is a job at managing something. The head of a school has an executive position. The executive director or secretary of an organization manages or directs the organization's affairs.* **b** for or by an executive or executives: *an executive suite.* **2a** having the duty and power of putting the laws into effect: *The President of the United States is the head of the executive branch of the government.* **b** coming from or having to do with that branch of a government which has this duty and power: *The Department of Justice is one of the executive departments of the government.*
—*n.* **1** a person who carries out what he (or another) has decided should be done; manager: *The president of a company is an executive. A good executive usually gets on well with people.* **2** the person, group, or branch of government that has the duty and power of putting the laws into effect: *the chief executive. The highest executive of a state is the governor.*
the Executive, *U.S.* the executive branch of the government: *Apart from the fact that he* [*the President*] *is rapidly adding to ... the expansion of the Executive, he impresses most of the nation as a man of restraint* (Wall Street Journal).
—**ex|ec′u|tive|ly,** *adv.*

executive agreement, *U.S.* an agreement between the President as head of the Executive and the government of a foreign country, usually dealing with matters of administration. An executive agreement has the force of a treaty in international law, but it does not require Senate approval.

Executive Council, (in Canada) the cabinet of a provincial government, consisting of the premier and his ministers.

Executive Mansion, *U.S.* **1** the official residence of the President of the United States; the White House in Washington, D.C. **2** the official residence of the governor in some states.

executive order or **Executive Order,** *U.S.* an order or directive issued by the President of the United States or by someone acting under his authority and having the force of law. Executive orders are based on the powers granted to the President by either the Congress or the Constitution. [*President*] *Kennedy issued an Executive Order barring racial discrimination in new housing financed with mortgages insured by the Federal Housing Administration* (Wall Street Journal).

executive privilege, *U.S.* the theoretical right invoked by members of the executive branch of the government to refuse to appear or testify before a court of law or a Congressional committee: *Administration spokesmen argued that withholding information deemed by the President or his delegates not in the public interest was a proper exercise of executive privilege, a right intrinsic in the doctrine of separation of powers* (Paul Fisher).

executive session, a meeting or session of a legislative body, usually closed to the public, in which it serves as a council to the executive, as such a session of the United States Senate when it considers the ratification of treaties or the confirmation of executive appointments: *After the adjournment of Congress, the senate went into executive session* (Harper's).

ex|ec|u|tive|ship (eg zek′yə tiv ship), *n.* **1** the office or power of an executive. **2** executives of a government or organization or the executive branch of a government: *In the early days of our republic Alexander Hamilton succinctly expressed his fears too about a weak government executiveship* (Harper's).

ex|ec|u|tor (eg zek′yə tər *for 1;* ek′sə kyü′tər *for 2*), *n.* **1** a person chosen to carry out what another person has said shall be done with his money and other belongings after his death: *The man named his lawyer as his executor.* **2** a person who performs or carries out something. [< Anglo-French *executour,* learned borrowing from Latin *exsecūtor* < *exsequī;* see etym. under **execute**]

executor dative, *Law.* an executor appointed by the court.

ex|ec|u|to|ri|al (eg zek′yə tôr′ē əl, -tōr′-), *adj.* = executive.

executor nominate, *Law.* an executor named in a person's will.

ex|ec|u|tor|ship (eg zek′yə tər ship), *n.* the office or duty of an executor: *the affairs of his executorship* (Samuel Richardson).

ex|ec|u|to|ry (eg zek′yə tôr′ē, -tōr′-), *adj.* **1** = executive. **2** = operative. **3** drawn up or ready to take effect only on a future contingency: *If a man leaves his estate to his wife in trust for his children, it is an executory contract.*

ex|ec|u|trix (eg zek′yə triks), *n., pl.* **ex|ec|u|trixes, ex|ec|u|tri|ces** (eg zek′yə trī′sēz). a woman executor.

ex|ec|u|try (eg zek′yə trē), *n., pl.* **-tries**. executorship.

ex|e|dra (ek′sə drə, ek sē′-), *n., pl.* **-drae** (-drē). **1** a semicircular outdoor bench. **2** a portico or open room with seats in ancient Greece. Also, **exhedra.** [< Latin *exedra* < Greek *ex-* out + *hédra* a sitting place]

ex|e|ge|sis (ek′sə jē′sis), *n., pl.* **-ses** (-sēz). **1** a scholarly explanation or interpretation of the Bible or of a passage in the Bible: *The minister gave an exegesis of the parable of the Good Samaritan.* **2** any explanation or interpretation of a word, sentence, or other passage; explanatory note: *Before she could turn and ask for an exegesis, I was making for a piano, at which I sat for some time* (New Yorker). [< Greek *exḗgēsis* < *exēgéesthai* interpret < *ex-* out + *hēgéesthai* to lead, guide]

ex|e|ge|sist (ek′sə jē′sist), *n.* = exegete.

ex|e|gete (ek′sə jēt), *n.* a person skilled in exegesis; interpreter: *an articulate exegete of the new art movement.*

ex|e|get|ic (ek′sə jet′ik), *adj.* having to do with exegesis; explanatory; interpretative; expository. [< Greek *exēgētikós* < *exēgéesthai;* see etym. under **exegesis**]

ex|e|get|i|cal (ek′sə jet′ə kəl), *adj.* = exegetic.

ex|e|get|i|cal|ly (ek′sə jet′ə klē), *adv.* by or by way of exegesis; as explanation.

ex|e|get|ics (ek′sə jet′iks), *n.* the branch of theology that deals with the exposition and interpretation of the Bible.

ex|e|get|ist (ek′sə jet′ist), *n.* = exegete.

ex|e|gi mo|nu|men|tum ae|re pe|ren|ni|us (ek sē′jī mon′yu̇ men′təm ir′ē pə ren′ē əs), *Latin.* I have made a monument more lasting than bronze (Horace).

ex|em|pla (eg zem′plə), *n.* the plural of **exemplum.**

ex|em|plar (eg zem′plər, -plär), *n.* **1** a person or thing worth imitating; good model or pattern: *Justice Oliver Wendell Holmes was the exemplar of the humane jurist.* SYN: standard. **2** = archetype. **3** a typical case; example. [< Latin *exemplar* < *exemplum;* see etym. under **example**]

ex|em|pla|ri|ly (eg zem′plər ə lē, eg′zəm pler′-), *adv.* in an exemplary manner.

ex|em|pla|ri|ness (eg zem′plər ē nis, eg′zəmpler′-), *n.* exemplary quality.

exemplar proposition, *Logic.* a proposition which states something to be true of an example of a class.

ex|em|pla|ry (eg zem′plər ē, eg′zəm pler′-), *adj.* **1** worth imitating; being a good model or pattern: *exemplary conduct.* SYN: commendable. **2** serving as a warning to others: *exemplary punishment of the ringleaders.* **3** serving as an example; typical: *an exemplary incident.* SYN: illustrative. [< Latin *exemplāris* < *exemplum;* see etym. under **example**]

exemplary damages, damages beyond the actual financial loss sometimes awarded as a punishment of the defendant, as an example to others, and as an adequate recompense for the entire injury sustained.

ex|em|pli|fi|ca|tion (eg zem′plə fə kā′shən), *n.* **1** the act or process of showing by example or the state of being an example. **2** an example: *That old village is an exemplification of peaceful charm.* **3** *Law.* a certified copy of a deed, record, etc.

ex|em|pli|fi|ca|tion|al (eg zem′plə fə kā′shə nəl), *adj.* of or having to do with exemplification.

ex|em|pli|fi|ca|tive (eg zem′plə fə kā′tiv), *adj.* serving to exemplify.

ex|em|pli|fi|er (eg zem′plə fī′ər), *n.* a person who exemplifies.

ex|em|pli|fy (eg zem′plə fī), *v.t.,* **-fied, -fy|ing.** **1** to show by example; be an example of: *Knights exemplified courage and courtesy.* SYN: illustrate. **2** *Law.* to make a certified copy of under seal. **3** to transfer or copy. [< Medieval Latin *exemplificare* < Latin *exemplum* example + *facere* make]

ex|em|pli gra|ti|a (eg zem′plī grā′shē ə), *Latin.* for example; for instance. *Abbr:* e.g.

ex|em|plum (eg zem′plum), *n., pl.* **-pla.** **1** a model or pattern worth imitating: *It is unlikely that he will be any more successful in creating an exemplum of love for our times* (Saturday Review). **2** an anecdote used to illustrate a moral lesson or truth: *So in the Middle Ages did priests relate exempla to make their point* (Richard Dorson). [< Latin *exemplum;* see etym. under **example**]

ex|empt (eg zempt′), *v., adj., n.* — *v.t.* **1** to make free (from a duty, obligation, rule, or other binding restriction); release: *Students who get very high marks will be exempted from the final examination.* **2** *Obsolete.* to except.
— *adj.* **1** freed from a duty, obligation, rule, or other binding restriction; released: *School property is exempt from all taxes.* **2** *Obsolete.* removed: *And this our life, exempt from public haunt, Finds tongues in trees, books in the running brooks* (Shakespeare).
— *n.* an exempt person, especially one freed from a duty or other tax.
[< Latin *exēmptus,* past participle of *eximere* take out < *ex-* out + *emere* take]

ex|empt|ee (eg zemp′tē′, -zemp′tē), *n.* a person exempt from a duty, especially military duty: *The review of present exemptees will proceed apace, to replenish the manpower drain to date* (Time).

ex|emp|ti|ble (eg zemp′tə bəl), *adj.* **1** that can be exempted. **2** that can be easily removed.

ex|emp|tion (eg zemp′shən), *n.* **1** the act of exempting. **2** freedom from a duty, obligation, rule, or other binding restriction; release: *Churches have exemption from taxes.* **3** an instance of such a release or a cause permitting one: *income-tax exemptions.*
— *Syn.* **2 Exemption, immunity** mean freedom from obligations, duties, rules, etc., imposed on others. **Exemption** implies freeing a person or thing from a legal obligation or rule: *exemption from jury duty.* **Immunity** implies freedom from restrictions and penalties to which other people are liable: *Ambassadors have immunity from prosecution under the laws of the United States.*

ex|emp|tive (eg zemp′tiv), *adj.* of or having to do with exemption; exempting: *A Senate Banking and Currency subcommittee today will begin hearings on proxy solicitations, increasing the exemptive limit for registration of securities* (Wall Street Journal).

ex|en|te|rate (ek sen′tə rāt), *v.t.,* **-rat|ed, -rat|ing.** **1** to remove by surgery. **2** to disembowel; eviscerate. [< Latin *exenterāre* (with English *-ate*[1]) < *ex-* out + Greek *énteron* intestine]

ex|en|te|ra|tion (ek sen′tə rā′shən), *n.* the act or process of exenterating.

ex|e|qua|tur (ek′sə kwā′tər), *n.* **1** a written recognition of a consul or commercial agent by the government to which he is accredited, authorizing him to exercise his powers. **2** an authorization granted by a secular ruler for the publication of papal bulls or other ecclesiastical enactments. [< Latin *exsequātur* he may execute, 3rd singular present subjunctive of *exsequī*]

ex|e|qui|al (ek sē′kwē əl), *adj.* of or having to do with a funeral.

ex|e|quies (ek′sə kwēz), *n.pl.* a funeral rite or ceremony.

ex|e|quy (ek′sə kwē), *n., pl.* **-quies.** **1** a funeral procession. **2** = exequies. [< Old French *exequies,* plural < Latin *exsequiās,* accusative of *exsequiae* funeral procession < *exsequī* follow out (to the grave) < *ex-* out + *sequī* follow]

ex|er|cis|a|ble (ek′sər sī′zə bəl), *adj.* that can be exercised: *The option is exercisable by either party* (Wall Street Journal).

ex|er|cise (ek′sər sīz), *n., v.,* **-cised, -cis|ing.**
— *n.* **1** active use to give practice and training or to cause improvement: *Exercise of the body is good for the health.* **2** something that gives practice and training or causes improvement: *He performs physical exercises each day to strengthen his body. Study the lesson, and then do the exercises at the end.* **3** active use; application: *Safety requires the exercise of care. Voting is the exercise of a civil right.* SYN: employment.
— *v.t.* **1** to make use of; use actively; employ: *It is wise to exercise caution in crossing the street. When you vote you exercise your right as a citizen.* SYN: apply. **2** to give exercise to; train: *The Army exercises new recruits with long marches.* SYN: discipline, drill. **3** to carry out in action; perform: *The mayor exercises the duties and powers of his office.* **4** to bring into effect; wield; exert: *What others think exercises a great influence on most of us.* **5** to occupy the attention of; keep busy; tax the capacity of: *Managing the household of twelve exercised them both, to the exclusion of all other interests.* **6** *Figurative.* to make uneasy; worry, trouble, or annoy: *When her plan failed, she was greatly exercised.* SYN: harass.
— *v.i.* to take exercise; go through exercises: *I exercise for ten minutes each morning.* SYN: drill.
exercises, procedures; activities; ceremony: *The opening exercises in our Sunday school are a song and a prayer.*
[< Old French *exercice,* learned borrowing from Latin *exercitium* < *exercitāre* to exercise (frequentative) < *exercēre* keep busy < *ex-* out + *arcēre* keep away, prevent]
— *Syn. n.* **1 Exercise, practice, drill** mean active use of physical or mental power for training or improvement. **Exercise** implies repeated use of mental or physical powers to develop strength, health, and energy: *Exercise of the mind increases its power.* **Practice** implies action repeated often and regularly to develop skill or gain perfection, especially in the use of a particular power: *Learning to play the piano well takes much practice.* **Drill** implies constant repetition of a particular kind of exercise to discipline the body or mind and develop correct habits: *Children need drill in spelling.*

exercise bone, a deposit of bony matter in a tendon, muscle, or fascia, supposedly as a result of overexercise or pressure.

exercise book, *Especially British.* a notebook: *No free pencils and exercise books could be issued, so the students came to school for a week without pencils and exercise books* (Observer).

exercise boy, a person who warms up and exercises race horses.

ex|er|cis|er (ek′sər sī′zər), *n.* **1** a person or thing that exercises. **2** a piece of gymnastic equipment.

ex|er|cis|es (ek′sər sī′ziz), *n.pl.* See **exercise.**

exercise yard, a yard in a prison where the inmates relax or take their exercise: *There is a 16-ft. brick wall around the exercise yards* (Manchester Guardian).

ex|er|ci|tant (eg zėr′sə tənt), *n.* a person engaged in spiritual exercises.

ex|er|ci|ta|tion (eg zėr′sə tā′shən), *n.* **1** exercise; exertion: *the exercitation of will power.* **2** practice; training. **3** a performance. **4** a discourse; disquisition. [< Latin *exercitātiō, -ōnis* < *exercitāre;* see etym. under **exercise**]

ex|er|ci|tor (eg zėr′sə tər), *n. Law.* the person to whom the profits of a ship belong; the owner or charterer of a ship.

ex|er|ci|to|ri|al (eg zėr′sə tôr′ē əl, -tōr′-), *adj.* of or having to do with an exercitor.

∗exercycle definition 1

∗ex|er|cy|cle (ek′sər sī′kəl), *n., v.,* **-cled, -cling.** *U.S.* — *n.* **1** a stationary bicycle used for physical exercise indoors: *Now in his Seattle pad, Beck can't shake the stirborn routine of stretching his*

Pronunciation Key: hat, āge, cãre, fär; let, ēqual, tėrm, it, īce; hot, ōpen, ôrder; oil, out; cup, pu̇t, rüle; child; long; thin; ᴛʜen; zh, measure; ə represents **a** in about, **e** in taken, **i** in pencil, **o** in lemon, **u** in circus.

legs without going anywhere, so he's bought an exercycle for a fast, 15-minute spin every morning (Time). **2 Exercycle.** a trademark for such a device.
— ***v.i.*** to use an exercycle: *You can "exercycle," lift modest weights, swing from bars and steam at the Andrews Health Club* (Maclean's).

ex|er|gon|ic (ek′sər gon′ik), *adj. Biochemistry.* releasing energy: *This movement of electrons liberates energy (is exergonic), part of which is conserved as ATP* (Trevor W. Goodwin). [< *ex-*[3] outside + Greek *érgon* work + English *-ic*]

ex|er|gual (eg zėr′gəl, ek sėr′-), *adj.* having to do with the exergue.

ex|ergue (eg zėrg′, ek′sėrg), *n.* **1** the small space below the principal figure or pattern on the reverse of a coin or medal, for an engraver's mark, date, or the like. **2** the inscription or mark in this space: ... *stamped upon memory in lines as vivid ... as the exergues of the Carthaginian medals* (Edgar Allan Poe). [< French *exergue,* apparently learned borrowing from New Latin *exergum* < Greek *ex-* outside + *érgon* work]

ex|ert (eg zėrt′), *v.t.* **1** to put into use; use fully: *A clever fighter exerts both strength and skill. A ruler exerts authority.* **SYN:** exercise. **2** *Obsolete.* **a** to thrust forth. **b** to exhibit; reveal.
exert oneself, to make an effort; try hard; strive: *You will really have to exert yourself to make up the work you missed. Every individual ... is under obligation to exert himself for the general good* (Henry Hunter).
[< Latin *exsertus,* past participle of *exserere* thrust out < *ex-* out + *serere* attach]

ex|er|tion (eg zėr′shən), *n.* **1** strenuous action; effort: *The exertions of the firemen kept the fire from spreading.* **SYN:** endeavor, struggle, attempt. **2** the act of putting into use; full use: *Unwise exertion of authority may cause rebellion.*

ex|er|tive (eg zėr′tiv), *adj.* causing exertion.

ex|es (ek′siz), *n.pl. British Slang.* expenses.

ex|e|unt (ek′sē ənt), *v.i. Latin.* they go out (a stage direction for actors to leave the stage).

ex|e|unt om|nes (ek′sē ənt om′nēz), *Latin.* all go out (a stage direction for all the actors to leave the stage at the same time).

ex fa|ci|e (eks fā′shē ē), *Latin.* from or on the face (of a document, coin, or the like).

ex fi|de for|tis (eks fī′dē fôr′tis), *Latin.* strong by faith.

ex|fil|trate (eks fil′trāt, eks′fil trāt), *v.t., v.i.,* **-trat|ed, -trat|ing.** *U.S. Military Slang.* to get out of a hostile area stealthily or unnoticeably; slip out through the enemy lines: *During the night, the Viet-cong remnants tried to "exfiltrate" ... but ran up against the blocking force and were turned back after an exchange of fire* (David Bonavia). [< *ex-*[1] out + (in)*filtrate*] — **ex′fil|tra′tion,** *n.*

ex|fo|li|ate (eks fō′lē āt), *v.,* **-at|ed, -at|ing.** — ***v.i.*** **1** to come off in scales or layers; peel. **2** to become scaly or layered: *Gypsum exfoliates when placed before a blowpipe.* **3** to throw off scales.
— ***v.t.*** **1** to throw off in scales or layers. **2** to remove the surface of: *to exfoliate a diseased bone.* **3** to cut out; excise (leaves or pages).
[< Late Latin *exfoliāre* (with English *-ate*[1]) strip of leaves < Latin *ex-* away + *folium* leaf]

ex|fo|li|a|tion (eks fō′lē ā′shən), *n.* **1** the process of scaling or peeling. **2** scaly or peeling condition. **3** the bark, skin, or bone that is coming off in scales or peeling in layers.

ex|fo|li|a|tive (eks fō′lē ā′tiv), *adj.* having the power or tendency to cause exfoliation: *Sir George points to the procedure of exfoliative cytology as a way to reduce the toll of cervical cancer* (Manchester Guardian).

ex. gr., exempli gratia. Also, **e.g.**

ex gra|ti|a (eks grā′shē ə), *Latin.* from grace or favor, rather than from legal right: *an ex gratia payment. Eventually the United States presented the Japanese government with two million dollars' compensation—ex gratia* (Harper's).

ex|hal|a|ble (eks hā′lə bəl), *adj.* that can be exhaled.

ex|hal|ant (eks hā′lənt), *adj.* exhaling; emitting.

ex|ha|la|tion (eks′hə lā′shən), *n.* **1** the act of exhaling: *Breathing out is an exhalation of air.* **2** something exhaled; air, vapor, or an odor.

ex|hale (eks hāl′), *v.,* **-haled, -hal|ing.** — ***v.t.*** **1** to breathe out: *We exhale air from our lungs.* **2** to give off (air, vapor, smoke, or odor). **SYN:** emit, discharge. **3** to change into vapor; evaporate.
— ***v.i.*** **1** to breathe out air or vapor. **2** to pass off into the air as vapor; rise like vapor: (*Figurative.*) *Sweet odors exhale from the flowers.*
[< Old French *exhaler,* learned borrowing from Latin *exhālāre* < *ex-* out + *hālāre* breathe]

ex|hale|ment (eks hāl′mənt), *n.* = exhalation.

ex|haust (eg zôst′), *v., n.* — ***v.t.*** **1** to empty completely; drain: *to exhaust an oil well.* **SYN:** deplete. **2** to use up; expend: *to exhaust one's money, exhaust the supply of water, exhaust one's strength.* **SYN:** consume. **3** to tire very much: *The climb up the hill exhausted us.* **SYN:** fatigue. **4** to drain of strength or resources: *to exhaust the soil. The long war exhausted the country.* **5** to draw off: *to exhaust the air in a jar.* **6** to create a vacuum in. **7** to find out or say everything important about; explain fully: *Her book about tulips exhausted the subject.* **8** to deprive of ingredients by the use of solvents.
— ***v.i.*** to be discharged; go forth: *Gases from an automobile exhaust through a pipe.*
— ***n.*** **1** the escape of used steam, spent gases, or fluid, from an engine or turbine. **2a** the pipe or other means through which steam, spent gases, or fluid escape from an engine or turbine. **b** the duct through which used air passes, especially in an air-conditioning system. **3a** the used steam, spent gases, or fluid, that escape: *The exhaust from an automobile engine is poisonous.* **b** the hot gases emitted from the nozzle of a jet engine or rocket. **4a** the production of an air current by the creation of a partial vacuum. **b** an apparatus for this purpose, such as a fan or pump.
[< Latin *exhaustus,* past participle of *exhaurīre* draw out < *ex-* out, off + *haurīre* draw] — **ex|haust′er,** *n.*

ex|haust|ed (eg zôs′tid), *adj.* **1** used up: *Mother's patience was exhausted from the constant fighting between the boys.* **2** worn out; very tired: *The exhausted soldiers stopped to rest after their long march.* **SYN:** See syn. under **tired.** — **ex|haust′ed|ly,** *adv.* — **ex|haust′ed|ness,** *n.*

ex|haust|ee (eg′zôs tē′, eg zôs′-), *n.* a person who has used up a resource, such as unemployment insurance or credit: *Temporary extension of benefits for exhaustees was voted in Colorado, Connecticut, Illinois, Ohio, and Wisconsin* (Eugene Skotzko).

ex|haust|i|bil|i|ty (eg zôs′tə bil′ə tē), *n.* the quality of being exhaustible; capability of being exhausted.

ex|haust|i|ble (eg zôs′tə bəl), *adj.* that can be exhausted.

ex|haust|ing (eg zôs′ting), *adj.* **1** that exhausts. **2** that exhausts the strength; wearying; tiring; enfeebling: *a long exhausting day at work.* — **ex|haust′ing|ly,** *adv.*

ex|haus|tion (eg zôs′chən), *n.* **1** the act of exhausting: *The heavy exhaustion of gas from a truck or bus pollutes the air.* **2** the condition of being exhausted: *Britain suffers from an exhaustion of natural resources as a result of intense participation in the industrial revolution.* **3** extreme fatigue, especially from exertion: *Combat fatigue is an example of nervous exhaustion.* **SYN:** weariness, lassitude, languor.

ex|haus|tive (eg zôs′tiv), *adj.* **1** tending to exhaust or use up (strength or resources). **2** leaving out nothing important; thorough; complete; comprehensive: *The new policemen were given an exhaustive examination covering every point of their training.* — **ex|haus′tive|ly,** *adv.* — **ex|haus′tive|ness,** *n.*
▶ **Exhaustive, exhausting** are not synonymous: An *exhaustive* lecture on vitamin A would be *exhausting* to an eighth-grade class, but welcome in a medical school.

ex|haust|less (eg zôst′lis), *adj.* that cannot be exhausted; inexhaustible. — **ex|haust′less|ly,** *adv.* — **ex|haust′less|ness,** *n.*

exhaust manifold, the pipe or set of pipes in an internal-combustion engine that conveys the spent gases from the cylinders to the exhaust pipe.

***exhaust pipe,** the pipe in an engine which carries away used steam or spent gases such as the pipe in an automobile engine from the manifold to the muffler, and sometimes including the tail pipe.

***exhaust pipe**

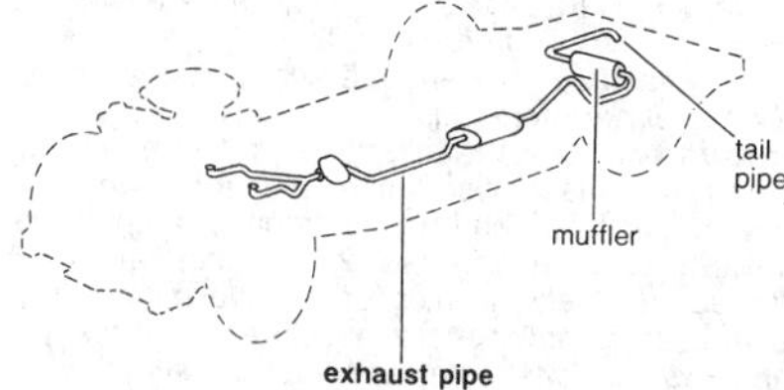

exhaust steam, steam which has performed its work, such as that allowed to escape from the cylinder of a steam engine after it has moved the piston.

exhaust stream, *Aerospace.* the high-speed current of gaseous or other particles emitted from a rocket or other reaction engine.

exhaust valve, a valve in an engine that opens to let the steam or spent gases escape: ... *every time the cylinder fires, the exhaust valve must open to let the burned gas out* (Automotive Encyclopedia).

exhaust velocity, the speed at which burning gases leave the combustion chamber of a rocket.

ex|he|dra (ek′sə drə, eks hē′-), *n., pl.* **-drae** (-drē). = exedra.

ex|her|e|date (eks her′ə dāt), *v.t.,* **-dat|ed, -dat|ing.** = disinherit. [< Latin *exhērēdāre* (with English *-ate*[1]) < *ex-* from + *hēres, hērēdis* heir]

ex|her|e|da|tion (eks her′ə dā′shən), *n.* the act or process of exheredating or condition of being exheredated.

ex|hib|it (eg zib′it), *v., n.* — ***v.t.*** **1** to show; display; indicate: *The child exhibited a bad temper at an early age. He exhibits interest whenever you talk about dogs.* **SYN:** manifest, evince, reveal, disclose. See syn. under **display. 2** to show publicly; put on display: *He hopes to exhibit his paintings in New York.* **3** to show in court as evidence; submit for consideration or inspection. **4** to administer (a drug or remedy).
— ***v.i.*** to show works of art or other objects publicly; hold an exhibition; give a performance: *A group of artists will exhibit next year.*
— ***n.*** **1a** a showing; display: *an exhibit of books.* **b** a showing of a document or other evidence: *The dishonest accountant was forced into an exhibit of his account books.* **2** a thing or things shown publicly: *Her exhibit of roses won first prize at the flower show. Some emperor penguins were the exhibit that attracted the most people.* **3** a document or other thing shown in court as evidence: *The accused man's knife was labeled Exhibit A.*
[< Latin *exhibitus,* past participle of *exhibēre* hold forth < *ex-* out + *habēre* hold]
— ***Syn.*** *n.* **1, 2. Exhibit, exhibition** mean a public show. **Exhibit** applies particularly to any object or collection of things put on view that is usually part of a larger show: *His calf was part of the school's exhibit at the county fair.* **Exhibition** applies to a large or small showing of art or art objects or to a large public show of any kind having many parts: *There is an exhibition of early Dutch painting at the National Art Gallery. The city holds an exhibition of all its different products every year.*

exhibit A, the first or principal evidence produced in a law court: (*Figurative.*) *In jail they* [*defendants charged with conspiracy to incite a riot*] *will be martyrs, fueling the militant protest, serving as exhibit "A" in every radical propagandist's case* (John H. Collins).

ex|hib|it|a|ble (eg zib′ə tə bəl), *adj.* that may be exhibited; capable of being exhibited: *They are all ... exhibitable powers* (Samuel Taylor Coleridge).

ex|hib|it|er (eg zib′ə tər), *n.* = exhibitor.

ex|hi|bi|tion (ek′sə bish′ən), *n.* **1** a showing; display: *I never saw such an exhibition of bad manners before.* **SYN:** manifestation. **2** a public show: *The art school holds an exhibition of paintings every year.* **SYN:** exposition. See syn. under **exhibit. 3** a thing or things shown publicly; exhibit. **4** the administration of a drug or remedy. **5** *British.* a scholarship, especially one awarded as the result of a competitive examination.

ex|hi|bi|tion|al (ek′sə bish′ə nəl), *adj.* of or having to do with an exhibition.

ex|hi|bi|tion|er (ek′sə bish′ə nər), *n.* **1** = exhibitor. **2** *British.* a student who holds a scholarship at a college or university. **3** *Obsolete.* a person who provides maintenance.

ex|hi|bi|tion|ism (ek′sə bish′ə niz əm), *n.* **1** an excessive tendency to show off one's abilities; extravagant behavior to attract attention. **2** a tendency to show what should not be shown, especially the indecent display of the body.

ex|hi|bi|tion|ist (ek′sə bish′ə nist), *n., adj.* — ***n.*** a person who tends to show off or behave in an unusual way in order to attract attention.
— ***adj.*** = exhibitionistic: *The heart of the paper and very likely where its treasure lies also, is in the serials, the hideous life stories of people either so cornered by poverty, so avaricious, or so painfully exhibitionist that they will sell any detail of their lives* (Punch).

ex|hi|bi|tion|is|tic (ek′sə bish′ə nis′tik), *adj.* **1** of or having to do with exhibitionism: *I knew it was wrong—the exhibitionistic behavior of someone who was trying to resolve the conflict in himself* (New Yorker). **2** tending toward exhibitionism: *The men ... are startling, frequently extravagant and exhibitionistic* (Wall Street Journal). — **ex′hi|bi′tion|is′ti|cal|ly,** *adv.*

ex|hib|i|tive (eg zib′ə tiv), *adj.* **1** serving for exhibition. **2** tending to exhibit. — **ex|hib′i|tive|ly,** *adv.*

ex|hib|i|tor (eg zib′ə tər), *n.* a person, company, or group that exhibits. Also, **exhibiter.**

ex|hib|i|to|ry (eg zib′ə tôr′ē, -tōr′-), *adj.* **1** of or having to do with exhibition. **2** intended for exhibition.

ex|hil|a|rant (eg zil′ər ənt), *adj., n.* — ***adj.*** that exhilarates. — ***n.*** something that exhilarates.

ex|hil|a|rate (eg zil′ə rāt), *v.t.*, **-rat|ed, -rat|ing.** to cheer; make merry; make lively: *The joy of the holiday season exhilarates us all.* **SYN:** elate, stimulate. [< Latin *exhilarāre* (with English *-ate*[1]) < *ex-* thoroughly + *hilarāre* make cheerful < *hilarus* merry]

ex|hil|a|rat|ing (eg zil′ə rā′ting), *adj.* enlivening; inspiriting: *an exhilarating gallop. We enjoy an exhilarating swim.* —**ex|hil′a|rat′ing|ly,** *adv.*

ex|hil|a|ra|tion (eg zil′ə rā′shən), *n.* **1** a being or feeling exhilarated; high spirits; lively joy. **SYN:** stimulation. **2** an exhilarating. **3** a cheering or enlivening influence: *The exhilaration of success lent wings to our sorely battered feet* (Robert Edwin Peary).

ex|hil|a|ra|tive (eg zil′ə rā′tiv), *adj.* tending to exhilarate.

ex|hil|a|ra|tor (eg zil′ə rā′tər), *n.* a person or thing that exhilarates.

ex|hil|a|ra|to|ry (eg zil′ər ə tôr′ē, -tōr′-), *adj.* exhilarative; tending to exhilarate.

ex|hort (eg zôrt′), *v.t.* to urge strongly; advise or warn earnestly: *The preacher exhorted his congregation to live better lives. Industry was exhorted to stand fast against excessive wage demands* (Anthony Lewis). **SYN:** admonish. —*v.i.* to give earnest advice or warning; make an exhortation. [< Latin *exhortārī* < *ex-* (intensive) + *hortārī* urge strongly]

ex|hor|ta|tion (eg′zôr tā′shən, ek′sôr-), *n.* **1** strong urging; earnest advice or warning. **2** a speech or sermon that exhorts.

ex|hor|ta|tive (eg zôr′tə tiv), *adj.* = exhortatory. —**ex|hor′ta|tive|ly,** *adv.*

ex|hor|ta|to|ry (eg zôr′tə tôr′ē, -tōr′-), *adj.* intended to exhort; exhorting; urging; admonitory: *Most people resent an exhortatory style of advice.*

ex|hort|er (eg zôr′tər), *n.* one who exhorts, especially a person who delivers religious exhortation.

ex|hu|mate (eks hyü′māt, eks′hyü-), *v.t.*, **-mat|ed, -mat|ing.** = exhume. [< Medieval Latin *exhumare* (with English *-ate*[1]); see etym. under **exhume**]

ex|hu|ma|tion (eks′hyü mā′shən), *n.* the act of exhuming.

ex|hu|ma|tor (eks′hyü mā′tər), *n.* a person who exhumes; exhumer.

ex|hume (eks hyüm′, eg zyüm′), *v.t.*, **-humed, -hum|ing. 1** to take (a dead body) out of the grave or the ground; dig up. **SYN:** disinter. **2** *Figurative.* to bring to light; reveal. [< Medieval Latin *exhumare* < Latin *ex-* out of + *humāre* bury < *humus* ground]

ex|hum|er (eks hyü′mər, eg zyü′-), *n.* a person who exhumes.

ex hy|po|the|si (eks hī poth′ə sī), *Latin.* in terms of the hypothesis; hypothetically: *It is the natural right of man to be policed by forces over which he has control and not by those of an alien Power (which ex hypothesi he cannot control)* (Manchester Guardian). [< Late Latin *ex hypothesi*]

ex|i|geant (ek′sə jənt; *French* eg zē zhäN′), *adj.* requiring much or too much; exacting: *the jealous, exigeant, selfish type of affection* (R. H. Hutton). [< French *exigeant,* present participle of *exiger* to exact, learned borrowing from Latin *exigere;* see etym. under **exact**]

ex|i|gence (ek′sə jəns), *n.* = exigency.

ex|i|gen|cy (ek′sə jən sē), *n., pl.* **-cies. 1** a situation demanding prompt action or attention; urgent case; emergency: *The curtains caught fire, but she proved equal to the exigency and put out the flames with a heavy blanket.* **2** exigent state or character; urgency.

exigencies, urgent needs; demands for action or attention: *The exigencies of business kept him from taking a vacation.*

ex|i|gent (ek′sə jənt), *adj.* **1** demanding prompt action or attention; pressing; urgent: *The exigent pangs of hunger sent the bear on a search for food.* **2** demanding a great deal or more than is reasonable; exacting: *A busy doctor has an exigent occupation.* [< Latin *exigēns, -entis,* present participle of *exigere;* see etym. under **exact**] —**ex′i|gent|ly,** *adv.*

ex|i|gi|ble (ek′sə jə bəl), *adj.* that can be demanded or required.

ex|i|gu|i|ty (ek′sə gyü′ə tē), *n.* scantiness; smallness.

ex|ig|u|ous (eg zig′yü əs, ek sig′-), *adj.* scanty in measure or number; extremely small: *Many public servants suffer from exiguous pay and great responsibility.* **SYN:** diminutive, minute. [< Latin *exiguus* (with English *-ous*) scanty; (originally) weighed out (sparingly) < *exigere;* see etym. under **exact**] —**ex|ig′u|ous|ly,** *adv.* —**ex|ig′u|ous|ness,** *n.*

ex|il|arch (ek′sə lärk), *n.* one of a line of Jewish princes or rulers in Babylon who exercised authority over, and received tribute from, Jews in all countries from about the 200's to the 1200's. [< *exil*(e) + Greek *archós* ruler]

ex|il|ar|chate (ek′sə lär′kit), *n.* **1** the period during which there were exilarchs. **2** the people over whom the exilarch had power.

ex|ile[1] (eg′zīl, ek′sīl), *v.,* **-iled, -il|ing,** *n.* —*v.t.* **1** to make (a person) leave home or country, often by law as a punishment; banish: *The traitor was exiled from his country for life. Thucydides failed to relieve the siege of Amphipolis, and was exiled for 20 years* (C. Bradford Welles). **SYN:** expel, expatriate. See syn. under **banish. 2** to remove (oneself) from one's country or home for a long time: *Many artists and musicians and writers have exiled themselves to protest harsh and unjust government at home.*

—*n.* **1** a being exiled; banishment: *The traitor was sent into exile for life.* **SYN:** expulsion, expatriation. **2** a person who is banished: *He has been an exile for ten years.* (*Figurative.*) *An exile from the paternal roof* (Washington Irving). **3** any prolonged absence from one's own country.

[< Old French *exilier,* learned borrowing from Latin *exiliāre* < *exilium* period (or place) of exile < *exul* an exile]

ex|ile[2] (eg′zīl, ek′sīl), *adj. Archaic.* **1** thin; slender. **2** meager. **3** poor; barren: *exile soil.* **4** very subtle; finespun. **5** overrefined. [< Latin *exīlis*]

Ex|ile (eg′zīl, ek′sīl), *n.* the Babylonian captivity of the Jews in the 500's B.C. [< *exile*[1], noun]

ex|ile|ment (eg′zīl mənt, ek′sīl-), *n. Obsolete.* banishment.

ex|il|i|an (eg zil′ē ən, ek sil′-), *adj.* = exilic.

ex|il|ic (eg zil′ik, ek sil′-), *adj.* of or having to do with exile, or a time of exile, especially the period of the Babylonian captivity of the Jews.

ex|il|i|ty (eg zil′ə tē, ek sil′-), *n. Archaic.* **1** thinness. **2** meagerness. **3** tenuity. **4** subtlety.

Ex|im|bank (eks′im′bangk′), *n.,* or **Ex-Im Bank,** *U.S.* the Export-Import Bank, a bank created by Congress in 1934 to facilitate trade with foreign countries by extending easy credit to importers and exporters of American goods.

ex|im|i|ous (eg zim′ē əs), *adj.* excellent; distinguished; eminent. [< Latin *eximius* (with English *-ous*) select, choice < *eximere;* see etym. under **exempt**]

ex|in|a|ni|tion (eg zin′ə nish′ən, ek sin′-), *n.* **1** the act of complete emptying. **2** exhaustion or enfeeblement, as from being emptied. **3** abasement or humiliation. [< Latin *exinānītiō, -ōnis* < *exinānīre* to make empty < *ex-* from + *inānis* empty]

ex|ine (ek′sēn, -sīn), *n.* = extine.

ex|in|gui|nal (eks ing′gwə nəl), *adj., n.* —*adj.* situated outside the groin.

—*n.* the second joint of a spider's leg, the first of the two forming the thigh.

ex int., ex interest (without interest).

ex in|te|gro (eks in′tə grō), *Latin.* anew; afresh.

ex|ist (eg zist′), *v.i.* **1** to have being; be: *The world has existed a long time. It might be necessary to assert that mind exists, but that it is nowhere in space, and perhaps does not exist in time either* (R. Hadekel). **2** to be real: *Do fairies exist or not?* **3** to continue to be; have life; live: *We cannot exist without air.* **4** to be found; occur: *Cases exist of persons who cannot smell anything.* [< Middle French *exister,* learned borrowing from Latin *exsistere* < *ex-* forth + *sistere* to stand < *stāre* to stand] —**ex|ist′er,** *n.*

ex|ist|ence (eg zis′təns), *n.* **1** the fact or state of existing; being: *When we are born, we come into existence.* **2** the fact or state of being real: *Most people do not now believe in the existence of ghosts.* **3** continued being; living; life: *Drivers of racing cars lead a dangerous existence.* **4** occurrence; presence: *The newspapers report the existence of many new cases of flu in the city.* **5** all that exists. **6** a thing that exists; a being.

ex|ist|ent (eg zis′tənt), *adj.* **1** that exists; existing. **2** now existing; of the present time. **SYN:** current.

ex|is|ten|tial (eg′zis ten′shəl, ek′sis-), *adj.* **1** of or having to do with existentialism: *an existential novel, an existential point of view.* **2** of or having to do with existence.

ex|is|ten|tial|ism (eg′zis ten′shə liz əm, ek′sis-), *n.* a philosophy holding that reality consists of living and that man makes himself what he is and is responsible personally only to himself for what he makes himself. Modern existentialism was developed by a group of contemporary writers, such as Gabriel Marcel, Karl Jaspers, and especially Jean Paul Sartre, out of the works of Sören Kierkegaard, Friedrich Nietzsche, and other existentialist philosophers and writers of the 1800's. *Existentialism, as expounded by Sartre, is not pessimistic in the nihilist sense, but is a doctrine of fortitude and even hope* (New York Times). [probably < French *existentialisme*]

ex|is|ten|tial|ist (eg′zis ten′shə list, ek′sis-), *adj., n.* —*adj.* **1** having to do with existentialism: *His somber estimate of the human condition has led him not to existentialist nausea but to melancholy compassion* (Atlantic). **2** like existentialism.

—*n.* a person who believes in the philosophy of existentialism: *To the existentialists' obsession with man's degradation Malraux again proposes man's essential greatness* (Time).

ex|is|ten|tial|is|tic (eg′zis ten′shə lis′tik, ek′sis-), *adj.* = existential (def. 1).

ex|is|ten|tial|ly (eg′zis ten′shə lē, ek′sis-) , *adv.* in an existential manner.

ex|it (eg′zit, ek′sit), *n., v.* —*n.* **1** a way out: *The theater had six exits.* **2** the act of going out; departure: *When the cat came in, the mouse made a hasty exit.* **3** the opportunity to go out. **4** the act of leaving the stage: *The actor made a graceful exit.* **5** *Figurative.* death: *Wheresoever, whensoever, or howsoever we shall be called upon to make our exit, we will die free men* (Josiah Quincy).

—*v.i.* **1** to go out; leave: *He exited in a hurry.* **2** *Latin.* goes out; leaves; departs (a stage direction for an actor to leave the stage). **3** *Figurative.* to die. —*v.t. Informal.* to leave; depart: *He exits the stage dripping with perspiration* (Show).

[< Latin *exit* he goes out, and < *exitus, -ūs* a going out, both < *exīre* go out < *ex-* out + *īre* go]

ex|ite (ek′sīt), *n. Zoology.* each of the processes on the outer side of the limb of a phyllopod crustacean. [< *ex-*[3] + *-ite*[1]]

exit poll, a poll taken of voters as they leave the voting place: *Some of the networks' "exit-polls" on primary days showed that Democrats favored Kennedy on the questions of who would handle the economy better* (New Yorker).

ex|i|tus (ek′sə təs), *n., pl.* **ex|i|tus. 1** death, especially as the outcome of a disease: *The thick tenacious material in the lumina of bronchi ... is the main cause of exitus* (Morris Fishbein). **2** *Law.* issue; offspring. **3** *Obsolete.* a going out; departure: *The period between the flood and the exitus of the people out of Egypt was about 800 years* (Mathew Hale). [< Latin *exitus, -ūs;* see etym. under **exit**]

ex|i|tus ac|ta pro|bat (ek′sə təs ak′tə prō′bat), *Latin.* the outcome justifies the acts (George Washington's motto).

ex le|ge (eks lā′gā), *Latin.* from the law; arising from the law.

ex|lex (eks′leks′), *adj. Latin.* beyond the law; outside the law.

ex lib., ex libris.

ex li|bris (eks lī′bris, lē′-), **1** *Latin.* from the library (of). **2** an inscription or device in or on a book to indicate the owner; bookplate.

ex-li|brism (eks lī′briz əm), *n.* the collecting of bookplates. [< *ex libr*(is) + *-ism*]

ex-li|brist (eks lī′brist), *n.* a person who collects specimens of bookplates.

ex me|ro mo|tu (eks mē′rō mō′tü, mō′tyü), *Latin.* of his (her, its) own accord; by mere impulse.

Ex|moor (eks′mu̇r, -mōr), *adj.* of or designating any one of certain breeds of ponies and sheep native to the region of Exmoor, in southwestern England.

ex mo|re (eks mō′rē), *Latin.* according to custom; from custom.

ex ne|ces|si|ta|te re|i (eks nə ses′ə tā′tē rē′ī), *Latin.* from the necessity of the case.

ex ni|hi|lo (eks nī′hə lō), *Latin.* from or out of nothing: *It is impossible to create ex nihilo a union of this kind* (Bulletin of Atomic Scientists).

ex ni|hi|lo ni|hil fit (eks nī′hə lō nī′hil fit), *Latin.* **1** you cannot make something out of nothing. **2** (literally) from nothing, nothing is made.

exo-, *prefix.* outside; outside of; outer: *Exoskeleton = outer skeleton.* Also, **ex-** before vowels. [< Greek *exō-,* related to *éxō* outside < *ex-* out]

ex|o|at|mos|phere (ek′sō at′mə sfir), *n.* the outermost region of the earth's atmosphere; exosphere: *The larger Spartan's [an antiballistic missile] job would be to provide an "area defence" by engaging enemy warheads in the exoatmosphere—roughly 300,000 ft. up* (New Scientist).

ex|o|at|mos|pher|ic (ek′sō at′mə sfir′ik), *adj.* of the exoatmosphere; designed for the exoatmosphere: *Some experts say the Moscow part of the Soviet missile defense system is based upon what is called an "exoatmospheric" rocket, or a defensive missile designed to intercept incoming missiles above the atmosphere* (Hanson W. Baldwin).

ex|o|bi|o|log|i|cal (ek′sō bī′ə loj′ə kəl), *adj.* of or having to do with exobiology.

ex|o|bi|ol|o|gist (ek′sō bī ol′ə jist), *n.* a person who studies exobiology.

ex|o|bi|ol|o|gy (ek′sō bī ol′ə jē), *n.* the study of life on other planets or celestial bodies.

ex|o|bi|o|ta (ek′sō bī ō′tə), *n. pl.* animal and plant life outside of or originating away from the earth

---

Pronunciation Key: hat, āge, cãre, fär; let, ēqual, tėrm; it, īce; hot, ōpen, ôrder; oil, out; cup, pu̇t, rüle; child; long; thin; ᴛʜen; zh, measure; ə represents **a** in about, **e** in taken, **i** in pencil, **o** in lemon, **u** in circus.

and its atmosphere; extraterrestrial life: *Such exobiota might do better on earth than native living creatures do* (Time). [< *exo-* + *biota*]

ex|o|bot|a|ny (ek'sō bot'ə nē), *n.* the study of possible plant life, in living or fossil form, outside the earth.

ex|o|can|ni|bal|ism (ek'sō kan'ə bə liz'əm), *n.* the custom of eating the flesh of persons belonging to another tribe.

ex|o|car|di|a (ek'sō kär'dē ə), *n.* displacement of the heart. [< *exo-* + Greek *kardiā* heart]

ex|o|carp (ek'sō kärp), *n.* = epicarp. [< *exo-* + Greek *karpós* fruit]

ex|oc|cip|i|tal (eks'ok sip'ə təl), *adj., n.* —*adj.* outside the occipital bone. —*n.* those parts of the occipital bone which form the sides of the foramen magnum and support the condyles.

ex|o|cen|tric (ek'sō sen'trik), *adj.* not belonging to the same form class as one of the immediate constituents of a grammatical construction. *Example:* The phrase *in the house* is an exocentric construction, since it does not belong to (i.e., it does not function the same way as) any of the form classes to which its immediate constituents belong.

ex|o|cho|ri|on (ek'sō kôr'ē on, -kōr'-), *n.* the outer layer of the membrane that encloses the fetus of higher vertebrates. [< *exo-* + *chorion*]

ex|o|cli|nal (ek'sō klī'nəl), *adj. Geology.* of or having to do with an exocline.

ex|o|cline (ek'sō klīn), *n. Geology.* an inverted fan fold. [< *exo-* + Greek *klínein* to fold]

ex|o|coe|lar (ek'sō sē'lər), *adj.* having to do with the outer side of the coelom or body cavity.

ex|o|crine (ek'sə krīn, -krin), *adj.* **1** secreting outwardly, through a duct or into a cavity: *exocrine cells. The pancreas is both an exocrine and endocrine gland.* **2** of or having to do with the exocrine glands: *exocrine secretions.* [< *exo-* + Greek *krínein* to separate]

exocrine gland, any one of various glands that discharge their products through ducts or into a cavity; gland of external secretion. The exocrine glands include the salivary, lachrymal, sweat, mammary, and sebaceous glands as well as many others.

ex|oc|u|la|tion (eks ok'yə lā'shən), *n.* the act of putting out the eyes, as formerly in execution of a judicial sentence; blinding. [< Latin *exoculāre* to put out the eyes (< *ex-* out + *oculus* eye) + English *-ation*]

ex|o|cy|clic (ek'sō sī'klik, -sik'lik), *adj. Chemistry.* situated outside a ring: *exocyclic atoms.*

ex|o|cy|to|sis (ek'sō sī tō'sis), *n.* the process by which cells release or secrete substances. [< *exo-* + (endo)*cytosis*]

Exod., Exodus.

ex|ode (ek'sōd), *n.* **1** (in Greek drama) the concluding part of a play. **2** (in Roman drama) a farce or satire, played as an afterpiece or as an interlude. [< French *exode* < Late Latin *exodium* < Greek *exódion* < *exódios* of an exodus or exit < *éxodos* exodus, exit]

ex|o|derm (ek'sō dėrm), *n.* = ectoderm. [< *exo-* + Greek *dérma* skin]

ex|o|der|mis (ek'sə dėr'mis), *n.* the outer layer of cortex in roots, just under the epidermis, corresponding to the hypodermis of stems. [< *exo-* + (epi)*dermis*]

ex|o|di|um (ek sō'dē əm), *n., pl.* **-di|a** (-dē ə). = exode. [< Late Latin *exodium;* see etym. under **exode**]

ex|o|don|tia (ek'sə don'shə), *n.* the branch of dentistry that deals with the extraction of teeth. [< New Latin *exodontia* < Greek *ex-* out + *odoús, odóntos* tooth]

ex|o|don|tist (ek'sə don'tist), *n.* a dentist who specializes in the extraction of teeth.

Ex|o|dus (ek'sə dəs), *n.* **1** the departure of the Israelites from Egypt under the leadership of Moses. **2** the second book of the Old Testament, containing an account of this departure. *Abbr:* Exod. [< Latin *exodus* < Greek *éxodos* < *ex-* out + *hodós* way]

ex|o|dus (ek'sə dəs), *n.* **1** a going out; departure: *Every June there is an exodus of students from the college.* **2** a departure or emigration, usually of a large number of people. [< *Exodus*]

ex|o|e|lec|tron (ek'sō i lek'tron), *n.* an electron emitted from surface atoms under conditions associated with such factors as heat, wear, cracks, and friction.

ex|o|en|zyme (ek'sō en'zīm, -zim), *n.* an enzyme which acts outside the cell.

ex off., ex officio.

ex of|fi|ci|is (eks ə fish'ē ēs), = ex officio. [< Late Latin *ex officiis*]

ex of|fi|ci|o (eks ə fish'ē ō), **1** because of one's office: *The Vice-President is, ex officio, the presiding officer of the Senate. The latter would ex officio succeed to the Presidency* (Newsweek). **2** proceeding from office or authority; in an official capacity: *All members of the Executive Council who are not elected as delegates shall be ex officio delegates to the convention* (New York Times). [< Late Latin *ex officio* < Latin *ex* out of, in accordance with, *officiō,* ablative of *officium* office]

ex|o|gam|ic (ek'sə gam'ik), *adj.* = exogamous.

ex|og|a|mous (ek sog'ə məs), *adj.* of or having to do with exogamy.

ex|og|a|my (ek sog'ə mē), *n.* **1** the custom of marrying only outside of one's own tribe or group. **2** the union of two protozoan gametes of different descent. [< *exo-* + *-gamy*]

ex|o|gen (ek'sə jen), *n.* a plant whose stem grows by successive concentric layers on the outside (an old plant classification of the dicotyledons). [< New Latin *exogena* growing on the outside, feminine of *exogenus;* see etym. under **exogenous**]

ex|og|e|nous (ek soj'ə nəs), *adj.* **1** *Botany.* **a** having stems that grow by the addition of layers of wood on the outside under the bark. **b** of exogens. **2** *Figurative.* originating from the outside; caused by external conditions: *Disorders of old age are generally not exogenous.* [< New Latin *exogenus* (with English *-ous*) growing on the outside < Greek *éxō* outside + *-genes* born, produced < *gígnesthai* be born] —**ex|og'e|nous|ly,** *adv.*

ex|o|hor|mone (ek'sō hôr'mōn), *n.* a pheromonal secretion which affects the olfactory organ of another animal, causing it to alter its behavior in a certain way: *If a goat's kid is taken away for only two hours from birth, the mother will reject it when it is returned. They probably become conditioned to its smell, or exohormones, at this time* (Science Journal).

ex|o|lin|guis|tic (ek'sō ling gwis'tik), *adj.* = metalinguistic.

ex|o|lin|guis|tics (ek'sō ling gwis'tiks), *n.* = metalinguistics.

ex|o|mi|on (ek sō'mē on), *n.* = exomis.

ex|o|mis (ek sō'mis), *n.* a vest without sleeves, leaving the shoulders bare, worn by workmen and slaves in ancient Greece. [< Greek *exōmis* < *ex-* out + *ômos* shoulder]

ex|o|mor|phic (ek'sō môr'fik), *adj. Geology.* having to do with changes in surrounding rocks by the intrusion of igneous matter. [< *exo-* + Greek *morphḗ* form]

ex|o|mor|phism (ek'sō môr'fiz əm), *n. Geology.* the state of being exomorphic.

ex|om|pha|los (ek som'fə ləs), *n.* a hernia at the navel. [< Greek *exómphalos* < *ex-* out + *ómphalos* navel]

ex|on¹ (ek'son), *n.* a segment of DNA that specifies the genetic code for a protein, as distinguished from an intervening sequence (intron): *In general the introns of split genes are longer than the exons* (Scientific American). [< *ex-* outer, outside + *-on*]

ex|on² (ek'son), *n.* each of four officers (originally corporals) of the yeomen of the royal English bodyguard, who in turn command in the absence of their superior officers. [Anglicization of French *exempt*]

ex|on|er|ate (eg zon'ə rāt), *v.t.,* **-at|ed, -at|ing.** **1** to free from blame; prove or declare innocent; exculpate: *Witnesses to the accident completely exonerated the truck driver.* SYN: vindicate. **2** to relieve from a duty, task, or obligation. **3** *Obsolete.* to remove a burden from. [< Latin *exonerāre* (with English *-ate*¹) < *ex-* off + *onus, -eris* burden]

ex|on|er|a|tion (eg zon'ə rā'shən), *n.* **1** the act or process of exonerating. **2** the state of being exonerated.

ex|on|er|a|tive (eg zon'ə rā'tiv), *adj.* tending to exonerate.

ex|on|er|a|tor (eg zon'ə rā'tər), *n.* a person who exonerates.

ex|o|nu|cle|ase (ek'sō nü'klē ās, -nyü'-), *n.* an enzyme that breaks up the strands of DNA segmented by the enzyme endonuclease.

ex|o|nu|mi|a (ek'sō nü'mē ə, -nyü'-), *n.pl.* catalogs, handbills, commemorative tokens, or the like, that are not considered true numismatic objects, such as coins, paper money, and medals are. [< New Latin *exonumia* < *exo-* + Latin *numisma* coin]

ex|o|nu|mist (ek'sō nü'mist, -nyü'-), *n.* a numismatist who specializes in exonumia.

ex|o|path|ic (ek'sə path'ik), *adj.* having its origin outside the body. [< *exo-* + Greek *páthos* pain + English *-ic*]

ex|o|pep|ti|dase (ek'sō pep'tə dās), *n. Biochemistry.* any one of various proteolytic enzymes that break down terminal peptide bonds.

ex|o|pe|rid|i|um (ek'sō pə rid'ē əm), *n.* the outer peridium of a fungus.

ex|oph|a|gous (ek sof'ə gəs), *adj.* practicing exophagy.

ex|oph|a|gy (ek sof'ə jē), *n.* the custom of eating the flesh of persons, but only of those belonging to other tribes; exocannibalism. [< *exo-* + Greek *phageîn* eat + English *-y*³]

ex|o|pho|ri|a (ek'sō fôr'ē ə, -fōr'-), *n.* a tendency of the lines of vision to diverge outwards so that they are no longer parallel. [< New Latin *exophoria* < Greek *exō-* outside + *phérein* to bear]

ex|oph|thal|mi|a (ek'sof thal'mē ə), *n.* abnormal protrusion of the eyeball from the orbit, especially because of disease or suffocation. [< New Latin *exophthalmia* < Greek *exóphthalmos* < *ex-* out + *ophthalmós* eyeball]

ex|oph|thal|mic (ek'sof thal'mik), *adj.* characterized by protrusion of the eyeballs.

ex|oph|thal|mos or **ex|oph|thal|mus** (ek'sof-thal'məs), *n.* = exophthalmia.

ex|o|plasm (ek'sə plaz əm), *n.* = ectoplasm.

ex|o|plas|mic (ek'sə plaz'mik), *adj.* = ectoplasmic.

ex|op|o|dite (ek sop'ə dīt), *n.* the outer branch of a two-branched appendage in crustaceans. [< *exo-* + Greek *poús, podós* foot + English *-ite*¹]

ex|op|o|dit|ic (ek sop'ə dit'ik), *adj.* of or having to do with the exopodite of a crustacean.

ex|o|ra|bil|i|ty (ek'sər ə bil'ə tē), *n.* the quality or condition of being exorable.

ex|o|ra|ble (ek'sər ə bəl), *adj.* that can be persuaded; easily influenced by request. [< Latin *exōrābilis* < *exōrāre* pray earnestly < *ex-* (intensive) + *ōrāre* pray < *ōs, ōris* mouth]

ex|or|bi|tance (eg zôr'bə təns), *n.* **1** the state of being exorbitant, especially outrageous excessiveness. **2** *Archaic.* misconduct.

ex|or|bi|tan|cy (eg zôr'bə tən sē), *n., pl.* **-cies.** = exorbitance.

ex|or|bi|tant (eg zôr'bə tənt), *adj.* **1** exceeding what is customary, proper, or reasonable; very excessive; much too high: *One dollar is an exorbitant price for a pack of gum.* SYN: See syn. under **excessive**. **2** not coming within the intended scope of the law: *an exorbitant case* [< Latin *exorbitāns, -antis,* present participle of *exorbitāre* go out of the track]

ex|or|bi|tant|ly (eg zôr'bə tənt lē), *adv.* **1** = extravagantly. **2** in an excessive degree or amount; beyond reasonable limits.

ex|or|cise (ek'sôr sīz), *v.t.,* **-cised, -cis|ing.** **1** to drive out (an evil spirit) by prayers, ceremonies, or the like: *I . . . wandered up and down, like an exorcised spirit that had been driven from its old haunts* (Hawthorne). **2** to free (a person or place) from an evil spirit; purify. **3** to conjure up (a spirit). [< Late Latin *exorcīzāre* < Greek *exorkīzein* exorcise, bind by oath < *ex-* + *horkízein* adjure < *hórkos* oath]

ex|or|cise|ment (ek'sôr sīz'mənt), *n.* = exorcism.

ex|or|cis|er (ek'sôr sī'zər), *n.* **1** a person who casts out evil spirits by adjurations and conjuration; exorcist. **2** *Obsolete.* a person who calls up spirits; a conjurer.

ex|or|cism (ek'sôr siz əm), *n.* **1** the process of exorcising. **2** the prayers, ceremonies, or the like, used in exorcising.

ex|or|cist (ek'sôr sist), *n.* **1** a person who exorcises: *The priestly exorcists of the later Christian period were more interested in producing spectacular convulsions and other physical symptoms in their subjects than in putting them into trances* (The Listener). **2** a member of the second of the minor orders in the Roman Catholic Church, next below that of acolyte.

ex|or|cis|tic (ek'sôr sis'tik), *adj.* **1** of or having to do with an exorcist. **2** of or having to do with an exorcism.

ex|or|cize (ek'sôr sīz), *v.t.,* **-cized, -ciz|ing.** = exorcise.

ex|or|di|al (eg zôr'dē əl, ek sôr'-), *adj.* **1** of an exordium. **2** = introductory.

ex|or|di|um (eg zôr'dē əm, ek sôr'-), *n., pl.* **-di|ums, -di|a** (-dē ə). **1** the beginning. **2** the introductory part of a speech, treatise, or the like. SYN: preamble. [< Latin *exōrdium* < *ex-* + *ōrdīrī* begin (originally) a web]

ex|or|gan|ic (ek'sôr gan'ik), *adj.* having ceased to be organic or organized.

ex|or|na|tion (ek'sôr nā'shən), *n. Rhetoric.* decoration; embellishment. [< Latin *exornātiō, -ōnis* < *exornāre* adorn < *ex-* out + *ornāre* adorn]

ex|o|skel|e|tal (ek'sō skel'ə təl), *adj.* of or having to do with the exoskeleton.

ex|o|skel|e|ton (ek'sō skel'ə tən), *n.* any hard, external, covering or structure that protects or supports the body, such as the shells of turtles and lobsters; ectoskeleton. [< *exo-* + *skeleton*]

ex|os|mic (ek soz'mik, -sos'-), *adj.* = exosmotic.

ex|os|mose (ek'soz mōs, -sos-), *n.* = exosmosis.

ex|os|mo|sis (ek'soz mō'sis, -sos-), *n.* osmosis from within outward.

ex|os|mot|ic (ek'soz mot'ik, -sos-), *adj.* **1** having to do with exosmosis. **2** of the nature of exosmosis.

ex|o|sphere (ek'sə sfir), *n.* the outermost region of the atmosphere, beyond the ionosphere. It begins about 300 miles above the earth's surface and contains so little air that there is hardly any atmospheric resistance. [< *exo-* + (atmo)*sphere*]

ex|o|spher|ic (ek′sə sfir′ik), *adj.* of the exosphere; exoatmospheric: *exospheric temperatures.*

ex|os|po|ral (ek sos′pər əl), *adj.* of or having to do with an exospore.

ex|o|spore (ek′sə spôr, -spōr), *n.* **1** *Botany.* the outer coat or wall of a spore of certain plants. **2** *Bacteriology.* a spore borne outside of the parent cell of certain bacteria.

ex|o|spo|ri|um (ek′sō spôr′rē əm, -spōr′-), *n., pl.* **-spo|ri|a** (-spôr′ē ə, -spōr′-). the outer coat of a spore; exospore; extine. [< New Latin *exosporium* < Greek *éxō* outside + *sporá* a sowing]

ex|os|to|sis (ek′sos tō′sis), *n., pl.* **-ses** (-sēz). a bony tumor on a bone or cartilage. [< New Latin *exostosis* < Greek *exóstōsis* outgrowth of bone < *ex-* out + *ostéon* bone + *-ōsis* condition]

ex|o|ter|ic (ek′sə ter′ik), *adj.* **1** that can be understood by the general public. **2** not belonging or restricted to an inner circle of disciples or scholars. **3** popular; well-known; commonplace: *Nowadays cheeses must be produced for large numbers of townsfolk and in these circumstances must be necessarily exoteric in flavour, not for the gourmet* (J. A. Barnett). [< Latin *exōtericus* < Greek *exōterikós* < *exōtérō*, comparative of *éxō* outside < *ex* out of] **—ex′o|ter′i|cal|ly,** *adv.*

ex|o|ter|i|cal (ek′sə ter′ə kəl), *adj.* = exoteric.

ex|ot|e|ries (eg zot′ər ēz), *n.pl.* exotic substances; exotica: *"From these exoteries, gentlemen, I have selected two products that will serve your purpose admirably. First, Stud's "Creme de caresse ..."* (New Scientist). [< *exot*(ic) + *-ery*]

ex|o|the|ci|um (ek′sə thē′shē əm, -sē-), *n., pl.* **-ci|a** (-shē ə, -sē-). the outer covering of an anther. [< New Latin *exothecium* < Greek *éxō-* outside + *thēkē* a covering]

ex|o|ther|mal (ek′sō thėr′məl), *adj.* = exothermic.

ex|o|ther|mic (ek′sō thėr′mik), *adj.* of or indicating a chemical change accompanied by a liberation of heat. [< *exo-* + Greek *thermē* heat + English *-ic*] **—ex′o|ther′mi|cal|ly,** *adv.*

ex|ot|ic (eg zot′ik), *adj., n.* **—*adj.*** **1** from a foreign country; not native: *We saw many exotic plants at the flower show.* **2** fascinating or interesting because strange or different: *an exotic tropical island.* **3** (of a rocket propellant) new, experimental, and high-energy; using an unconventional oxidizer, such as fluorine: *exotic fuels. Listed as "exotic" and thus presumably further in the future are such systems as a rocket propelled by controlled nuclear explosions* (New York Times). **4** *Nuclear Physics.* highly unstable and hard to capture: *exotic nuclear particles, exotic resonances.*
—*n.* an exotic person or thing: *Mr. Buckley is an American exotic of the far right* (New York Times). *Mr. Amati's re-enactment of village life and culture in the Italian Alps, from neolithic times to the first century* AD *... is another archaeological exotic* (Punch).
[< Latin *exōticus* < Greek *exōtikós* < *éxō* outside < *ex* out of] **—ex|ot′i|cal|ly,** *adv.*

ex|ot|i|ca (eg zot′ə kə), *n.pl.* exotic things: *Americans ... avid for the exotica of bullfights, jai alai* (Newsweek). [< Latin *exōtica,* neuter plural of *exōticus* exotic]

ex|ot|i|cism (eg zot′ə siz əm), *n.* **1** exotic quality or character: *orchestral and choral color, rather Byzantine both in its exoticism and in its spirit of monumentality* (New Yorker). **2** anything exotic, such as a foreign word or idiom. **3** a tendency to adopt what is exotic.

ex|ot|i|cist (eg zot′ə sist), *n.* a person who favors anything exotic.

ex|ot|i|cize (eg zot′ə sīz), *v.t.,* **-cized, -ciz|ing.** to make exotic; cause to appear strange or different: *Exoticized by Lytton Strachey and André Maurois, ... he* [*Disraeli*] *rarely appears in all his dimensions, living and breathing* (Saturday Review).

ex|o|tox|ic (ek′sō tok′sik), *adj.* of or having to do with an exotoxin.

ex|o|tox|in (ek′sō tok′sən), *n.* a toxin secreted into the substance surrounding the organsim that produces it.

ex|o|tro|pi|a (ek′sō trō′pē ə), *n. Medicine.* an exaggerated turning out of one or both eyes, amounting to actual divergent strabismus or wall-eye. [< New Latin *exotropia* < Greek *éxō-* out + *trépein* turn]

ex|o|trop|ic (ek′sō trop′ik), *adj. Botany.* (of lateral roots) tending to grow away; divergent in relation to the main root or to the next higher root in order. [< *exo-* + Greek *tropē* a turning + English *-ic*]

ex|ot|ro|pism (ek sot′rə piz əm), *n. Botany.* the property of being exotropic.

exp., an abbreviation for the following:
1 expenses.
2a export. **b** exported.
3 exportation.
4 express.

ex|pand (ek spand′), *v.t.,* **1** to make grow larger; increase in size; enlarge; swell: *A man may expand his business or his chest. Heat expanded the metal.* **2** to spread out; open out; unfold: *A bird expands its wings before flying. Expand thy sails ... and catch the nimble gales* (Alexander Pope). SYN: unfurl, expand. **3** *Figurative.* to express in fuller form or greater detail: *to expand a mathematical equation. The writer expanded one sentence into a paragraph.* **—*v.i.*** **1** to grow or become larger; swell: *A balloon expands when it is blown up. Our country expanded by adding new territory.* **2** to unfold; open out: *As the plant grew, its leaves and flowers gradually expanded.* SYN: unfurl, extend.
[< Latin *expandere* < *ex-* out + *pandere* spread. See etym. of doublet **spawn.**] **—ex|pand′er,** *n.* **—ex|pand′ing|ly,** *adv.*
—*Syn.* *v.t.* **1,** *v.i.* **1 Expand, swell, dilate** mean to make or become larger. **Expand** implies spreading out or opening out in any or all directions: *Heat expands metal.* (*Figurative.*) *Our interests expand as we grow.* **Swell** implies growing bigger, usually from pressure inside or from having something added: *His abscessed tooth made his face swell.* **Dilate** implies widening, and applies particularly to circular or hollow things: *The doctor dilates the pupils of your eyes when he examines them.*

ex|pand|a|bil|i|ty (ek span′də bil′ə tē), *n.* the capacity for expanding.

ex|pand|a|ble (ek span′də bəl), *adj.* that can be expanded: *He can design an expandable airport terminal for a bustling city, or plan a charming home shaped to a busy doctor's needs* (Newsweek).

ex|pand|ed (ek span′did), *adj.* **1** increased in area or bulk; enlarged: *Foamed, or expanded, plastics ... are as hard or soft as the original plastic, but ... many times lighter* (Atlantic). **2** spread open; outspread: *Sicily then lay expanded like a map beneath our eyes* (Leigh Hunt). **3** (of type) unusually wide for its height; extended. **—ex|pand′ed|ly,** *adv.*

expanded cinema, = mixed media.

expanded metal, sheet metal slit and stretched into a lattice. It is used for making screens and lockers, and for reinforcing concrete.

ex|pand|ing bullet (ek span′ding), a bullet with a soft nose that spreads out when it strikes, as a dumdum bullet.

expanding universe, a theory of the universe in which the galaxies are viewed as constantly moving apart from one another. They recede from the earth at a speed proportionate to their distance from it, those farthest away moving the fastest.

ex|panse (ek spans′), *n.* **1** an open or unbroken stretch; wide, spreading surface: *The Pacific Ocean is a vast expanse of water.* **2** the amount or distance of expansion. [< Latin *expānsum,* neuter past participle of *expandere;* see etym. under **expand**]

ex|pan|si|bil|i|ty (ek span′sə bil′ə tē), *n.* capacity for expanding.

ex|pan|si|ble (ek span′sə bəl), *adj.* that can be expanded.

ex|pan|sile (ek span′səl), *adj.* **1** capable of expanding; dilatable. **2** of or having to do with expansion. **3** tending to expansion.

ex|pan|sion (ek span′shən), *n.* **1** the act or process of expanding: *Heat causes the expansion of gas.* **2** the state of being expanded; increase in size, volume, or other dimension: *The expansion of the factory made room for more machines.* **3a** an expanded part or form: (*Figurative.*) *That book is an expansion of a magazine article.* **b** anything that is spread out; an expanse. **4** the amount or degree of expansion. **5** *Mathematics.* the fuller development of an indicated operation: *The expansion of* $(a+b)^3$ *is* $a^3 + 3a^2b + 3ab^2 + b^3$. **6** the increase in bulk of the power medium which takes place in a cylinder of an engine, especially of steam after communication with the boiler is cut off or of gasoline after explosion in an internal-combustion engine. [< Late Latin *expānsiō, -ōnis* < Latin *expandere;* see etym. under **expand**]

ex|pan|sion|ar|y (ek span′shə ner′ē), *adj.* **1** having to do with or tending toward expansion. **2** *Figurative.* inflationary: *The economy is in a long-term expansionary trend* (Wall Street Journal).

expansion attic, an attic that can be readily changed into a room or rooms in which to live.

✱expansion bolt

✱expansion bolt, a cylindrical bolt device which can be expanded by turning a screw.

ex|pan|sion|ism (ek span′shə niz əm), *n.* a policy of expansion, for example of territory or currency: *Present-day economics ... propagates a philosophy of unlimited expansionism, without any regard to the true and genuine needs of man, which are limited* (The Observer).

ex|pan|sion|ist (ek span′shə nist), *n., adj.* **—*n.*** a person who advocates a policy or a theory of expansion, especially an advocate of expansion of the territory or currency of a country.
—*adj.* of or having to do with expansionism; favoring expansion.

ex|pan|sion|is|tic (ek span′shə nis′tik), *adj.* = expansionist.

✱expansion joint, a corrugated, sliding, or bent fitting that allows expansion in a structure due to temperature changes.

✱expansion joints

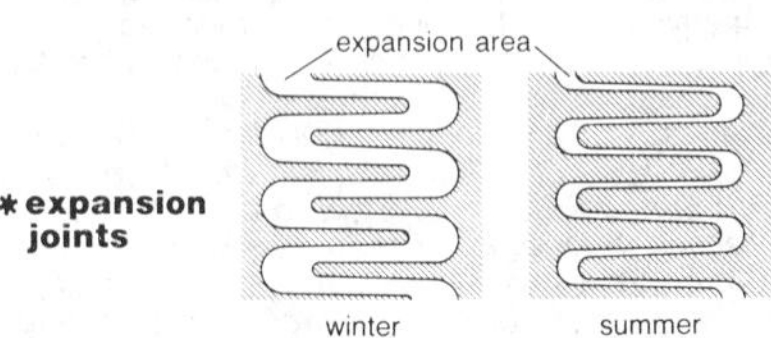

expansion team, *U.S. and Canada.* a sports team formed by buying a franchise from a professional league and drafting available players from the league's established teams: *Expansion teams ..., are typically launched with fourth-class flotsam—arthritic veterans and immature, unskilled rookies* (Maclean's).

ex|pan|sive (ek span′siv), *adj.* **1** capable of expanding; tending to expand: *expansive gases.* SYN: dilatable. **2** capable of causing expansion: *the expansive force of heat.* **3** expanding over or occupying a large surface or space; wide; spreading: *an expansive lake.* SYN: broad, extensive. **4** *Figurative.* taking in much or many things; having a wide range; comprehensive: *an expansive view of history.* SYN: broad, extensive. **5** *Figurative.* showing one's feelings freely and openly; unrestrained; demonstrative; effusive: *Her expansive personality made it easy for her to make friends.* **6** of or having to do with expansion, especially (of an engine, process, or economy) involving or depending upon the principle of expansion: (*Figurative.*) *During the expansive phase, the growth of construction is little affected by a general decline in business* (Atlantic). **7** *Psychiatry.* (of mood or behavior) characterized by excessive euphoria, self-confidence, talkativeness, or other indication of a feeling of security. **—ex|pan′sive|ly,** *adv.* **—ex|pan′sive|ness,** *n.*

ex|pan|siv|i|ty (ek′span siv′ə tē), *n.* the quality, condition, or degree of being expansive: *... local variations of expansivity, viscosity, and surface tension* (Scientific American).

ex par|te (eks pär′tē), **1** *Law.* from one side only: *an ex parte testimony or affidavit. In ex parte Quirin ... the Supreme Court found no constitutional objection to the trial by a military commission of nine saboteurs* (New York Times). **2** in the interest of only one side: *... the B.B.C. do not allow broadcast discussions or ex parte statements on issues about to be debated in either House of Parliament* (London Times). [< Latin *ex parte; ex* out of, from; *parte,* ablative of *pars, partis* side, part, share]

ex|pat (eks′pāt), *n. British Informal.* an expatriate.

ex|pa|ti|ate (ek spā′shē āt), *v.i.,* **-at|ed, -at|ing.** **1** to write or talk much; enlarge (on): *She expatiated on the thrills of her trip to Hawaii.* SYN: descant. **2** to roam without restraint; wander at will: *Winter-flies ... crawl out ... to expatiate in the sun* (James Russell Lowell). [< Latin *exspatiārī* (with English *-ate*[1]) < *ex-* out + *spatiārī* to walk < *spatium* space]

ex|pa|ti|a|tion (ek spā′shē ā′shən), *n.* **1** the process of writing or talking too much. **2** an extended talk or description.

ex|pa|ti|a|tor (ek spā′shē ā′tər), *n.* a person who expatiates.

ex|pa|ti|a|to|ry (ek spā′shē ə tôr′ē, -tōr′-), *adj.* characterized by or indulging in expatiation.

ex|pa|tri|ate (*v.* eks pā′trē āt; *n., adj.* eks pā′trē-it, -āt), *v.,* **-at|ed, -at|ing,** *n., adj.* **—*v.t.*** **1** to force to leave one's country; banish; exile. **2a** to withdraw (oneself) from one's native country or renounce one's citizenship: *Some Americans expatriate themselves and live in Europe.* **b** to force (someone) to give up his citizenship: *A*

Pronunciation Key: hat, āge, cãre, fär; let, ēqual, tėrm, it, īce; hot, ōpen, ôrder; oil, out; cup, pu̇t, rüle; child; long; thin; ᴛʜen; zh, measure; ə represents **a** in about, **e** in taken, **i** in pencil, **o** in lemon, **u** in circus.

naturalized citizen may also be expatriated ... because of acts he committed after he became a citizen (Robert Rienow).
— ***v.i.*** to expatriate oneself: *Aetolus ... having been forced to expatriate from Peloponnesus* (George Grote).
— ***n.*** an expatriated person; exile: *a famous meeting place for American expatriates* (Atlantic).
— ***adj.*** expatriated: *The chief purveyors of capital and skills have in all cases been the expatriate companies* (Atlantic).
[< Late Latin *expatriāre* (with English *-ate*[1]) < Latin *ex-* out of + *patria* fatherland < *pater, patris* father]

ex|pa|tri|a|tion (eks pā′trē ā′shən), *n.* **1** banishment; exile. **2** withdrawal from one's country or renunciation of citizenship.

ex|pect (ek spekt′), *v.t.* **1** to think (something) will probably come or happen; look forward to: *We expect hot days in summer.* **2** to look forward to with reason or confidence; desire and feel sure of getting: *I shall expect to find that job finished by Saturday. Poetry will return to the stage ... when the audience is brought to expect it and, expecting it, to need it* (Atlantic). **SYN**: hope. **3** to count on as necessary or right: *Parents usually expect too much of their children. A nation expects support from its allies.* **4** *Informal.* to think; suppose; guess: *I expect you are right about that.* **5** *Obsolete.* to wait for; await. — ***v.i.*** to look forward; anticipate.
be expecting, to be pregnant: *Our cat is expecting and stays pretty close to home now.*
[< Latin *exspectāre* < *ex-* + *spectāre* (frequentative) < *specere* to look]
— ***Syn.*** *v.t.* **1 Expect, anticipate** mean to look forward to a future event. **Expect** implies some certainty or confidence that it will occur: *He expects to take a vacation in May.* **Anticipate** means to look forward with pleasure or dread to something one expects to occur: *He anticipates a wonderful vacation.*

ex|pect|a|bil|i|ty (ek spek′tə bil′ə tē), *n.* the quality or state of being expectable: *One of the charms of archeology in the great rain forest ... in Middle America is the expectability of the unexpected* (New Yorker).

ex|pect|a|ble (ek spek′tə bəl), *adj.* that can be expected: *The expectable snarl developed this morning over the public's tickets to the conference sessions* (New York Times). — **ex|pect′a|ble|ness,** *n.*

ex|pect|a|bly (ek spek′tə blē), *adv.* in an expectable manner; as anticipated: *Sinatra, despite spit-curl bangs and a put-on accent, expectably works hardest* [*and*] *acts best* (Time).

ex|pect|ance (ek spek′təns), *n.* = expectation.

ex|pect|an|cy (ek spek′tən sē), *n., pl.* **-cies.** **1** = expectation: *There was an atmosphere of expectancy in the family on Christmas Eve.* **2** something expected or that can be expected: *Increased expectancy of life, even without any increase in the birth rate, effects a rapid population growth* (Science News). **3** the state or condition of being expected or looked forward to.

ex|pect|ant (ek spek′tənt), *adj., n.* — ***adj.*** **1** thinking something will come or happen; looking for; expecting; waiting: *An expectant mother is soon to have a baby.* **2** showing expectation: *Mary opened her package with an expectant smile.*
— ***n.*** a person who expects something. — **ex|pect′ant|ly,** *adv.*

expectant method or **treatment,** a method of treating certain diseases by letting them run their normal course without attempting more than the checking of certain symptoms and conditions: *Cholera is treated by the expectant method.*

ex|pec|ta|tion (eks′pek tā′shən), *n.* **1** the act of expecting or state of being expected; anticipation: *the expectation of a good harvest.* **SYN**: hope. **2** something expected or looked forward to.
expectations, good reasons for expecting something; prospects: *He has expectations of money from a rich uncle.*

expectation of life, the average number of years that a person of a certain age can expect to live, as indicated by mortality statistics; life expectancy.

Expectation Week, the interval of ten days between Ascension Day and Whitsunday, in commemoration of the season of the apostles' earnest prayer for and expectation of the Holy Ghost.

ex|pec|ta|tive (ek spek′tə tiv), *adj.* **1** of or having to do with expectation. **2** = expectant.

expectative grace, the bestowal of the expectation or right of succession to a benefice not yet open.

ex|pect|ed|ly (ek spek′tid lē), *adv.* in a way that is expected; in the manner looked for: *The Labour Party reaction was expectedly hostile to what they regarded as a philosophy "of slump and unemployment"* (Observer).

ex|pect|ed|ness (ek spek′tid nis), *n.* the quality or state of being expected or anticipated: *For sheer expectedness the holy man's edifying death isn't likely to be surpassed in our time* (New Yorker).

ex|pect|ing|ly (ek spek′ting lē), *adv.* with expectation: *Prepar'd for fight, expectingly he lies* (John Dryden).

ex|pec|to|rant (ek spek′tər ənt), *adj., n.* — ***adj.*** causing or helping the discharge of phlegm.
— ***n.*** a medicine that promotes expectoration.

ex|pec|to|rate (ek spek′tə rāt), *v.,* **-rat|ed, -rat|ing.** — ***v.t.*** to cough up and spit out (phlegm); spit.
— ***v.i.*** = spit.
[< Latin *expectorāre* (with English *-ate*[1]) < *ex-* out of + *pectus, -oris* breast]
► As a substitute for the plain English word *spit,* **expectorate** is a vulgarly genteel euphemism.

ex|pec|to|ra|tion (ek spek′tə rā′shən), *n.* **1** the act of expectorating. **2** expectorated matter. **SYN**: sputum.

ex|pec|to|ra|tive (ek spek′tə rā′tiv), *adj., n.*
— ***adj.*** **1** of or having to do with expectoration. **2** = expectorant.
— ***n.*** = expectorant.

ex|pec|to|ra|tor (ek spek′tə rā′tər), *n.* a person who expectorates or spits.

ex|pede (ek spēd′), *v.t.,* **-ped|ed, -ped|ing.** (in Scottish law) to send out or issue officially (a document or letter). [< Latin *expedīre;* see etym. under **expedient**]

ex pe|de Her|cu|lem (eks pē′dē hėr′kyə lem), *Latin.* **1** from a part you may judge the whole. **2** (literally) from the foot (one may know) Hercules.

ex|pe|di|ence (ek spē′dē əns), *n.* = expediency.

ex|pe|di|en|cy (ek spē′dē ən sē), *n., pl.* **-cies.** **1** the act or process of helping to bring about a desired result; fitness; usefulness: *There was little doubt about the expediency of postponing our picnic until after the rain stopped. Consider expediency as well as truth in what you say.* **2a** the consideration of what is selfishly expedient, to the neglect of what is just or right; personal advantage; self-interest: *The salesman was influenced more by the expediency of making a sale than by the needs of the buyer.* **b** the consideration of what is expedient as a motive or rule of action: *No man is justified in doing evil on the ground of expediency* (Theodore Roosevelt).

ex|pe|di|ent (ek spē′dē ənt), *adj., n.* — ***adj.*** **1** useful; helping to bring about a desired result; desirable or suitable under the circumstances: *It is expedient to be friendly and pleasant if you want to have friends. All things are lawful unto me, but all things are not expedient* (I Corinthians 6:12). **SYN**: advantageous, profitable, advisable. **2** giving or seeking personal advantage; based on self-interest without regard to what is just or right: *No honest judge would make a decision that was expedient rather than fair and just.* **3** studious of expediency.
— ***n.*** a way of getting something; contrivance or device adopted for attaining an end; resource; shift: *The prisoner tied sheets together and escaped by this expedient.*
[< Latin *expediēns, -entis,* present participle of *expedīre* to free from a net, set right < *ex-* out + *pēs, pedis* foot] — **ex|pe′di|ent|ly,** *adv.*

ex|pe|di|en|tial (ek spē′dē en′shəl), *adj.* **1** having to do with expediency. **2** regulated by expediency. — **ex|pe′di|en′tial|ly,** *adv.*

ex|pe|dite (eks′pə dīt), *v.,* **-dit|ed, -dit|ing,** *adj.*
— ***v.t.*** **1** to make easy and quick; help forward; hurry along; speed up: *Airplanes expedite travel. The telephone expedites business. If everyone will help, it will expedite matters.* **SYN**: accelerate, hasten, quicken. **2** to do quickly: *The manager had the ability to expedite all tasks assigned him.* **3** to issue officially; dispatch.
— ***adj.*** **1** (of a place, road, or way) clear of obstacles or impediments. **2** (of an action or motion) unrestricted; unembarrassed; easy; free. **3** (of persons) ready for action; prompt; alert; ready. **4** (of contrivances or instruments) ready for immediate use; conveniently serviceable; handy. **5** (of an action or process, a means, or remedy) prompt; speedy; expeditious.
[< Latin *expedītus,* past participle of *expedīre;* see etym. under **expedient**]

ex|pe|dit|er (eks′pə dī′tər), *n.* **1** a person who is responsible for supplying raw materials or delivering finished products on schedule: *To keep material and equipment moving on time from subcontractors,* [*the company*] *maintains a large staff of expediters around the world* (Wall Street Journal). **2** a person who issues official statements and decisions.

ex|pe|di|tion (eks′pə dish′ən), *n.* **1** a journey made for some special purpose. A voyage of discovery or a march against the enemy is an expedition. *It was intended that the success of the expedition should be judged solely on what was brought back in its notebooks and specimen boxes* (E. F. Roots). **SYN**: trip. **2** a group of people, ships, vehicles, or beasts, that make such a journey. **3** the act of sending or setting forth on such a journey. **4** prompt action; speed: *He not only did the job well, he did it with expedition.* **SYN**: promptness, haste, quickness. **5** *Obsolete.* **a** an expediting. **b** a being expedited.

ex|pe|di|tion|ar|y (eks′pə dish′ə ner′ē), *adj.* of an expedition; having to do with or making up an expedition: *The United States sent an expeditionary force of soldiers to Europe in World War II.*

ex|pe|di|tion|ist (eks′pə dish′ə nist), *n.* a person who goes on an expedition.

ex|pe|di|tious (eks′pə dish′əs), *adj.* efficient and prompt; quick; speedy: *an expeditious method of packing.* — **ex′pe|di′tious|ly,** *adv.* — **ex′pe|di′tious|ness,** *n.*

ex|pe|di|tor (eks′pə dī′tər), *n.* = expediter.

ex|pel (ek spel′), *v.t.,* **-pelled, -pel|ling.** **1** to drive out with much force; force out: *When the gunpowder exploded, the bullet was expelled from the gun. When we exhale we expel air from our lungs.* **SYN**: eject. **2** to put (a person) out; dismiss permanently: *A pupil who cheats or steals may be expelled from school.* [< Latin *expellere* < *ex-* out + *pellere* drive]

ex|pel|la|ble (ek spel′ə bəl), *adj.* **1** that can be expelled. **2** that justifies being expelled.

ex|pel|lant or **ex|pel|lent** (ek spel′ənt), *adj., n.*
— ***adj.*** expelling; tending to expel.
— ***n.*** a medicine that expels.

ex|pel|lee (eks′pe lē′), *n.* a person expelled, especially one forced, as by a law or government action, to leave his country of residence for political reasons: *It was also imperative to create a new existence for the ten million expellees and refugees from the East* (Atlantic).

ex|pel|ler (ek spel′ər), *n.* a person or thing that expels.

ex|pend (ek spend′), *v.t.* to spend; use up: *He expended thought, work, and money on his project.* **SYN**: disburse, consume. See syn. under **spend.** [< Latin *expendere* < *ex-* out + *pendere* weigh (out), pay. See etym. of doublet **spend.**]
— **ex|pend′er,** *n.*

ex|pend|a|bil|i|ty (ek spen′də bil′ə tē), *n.* the quality or state of being expendable: *The Army believes that this ratio of expendability among its best qualified fighters is more to be honored than deplored* (Harper's).

ex|pend|a|ble (ek spen′də bəl), *adj., n.* — ***adj.*** **1** that can be expended or used up. **2** *Military.* **a** that is or may be normally used up in service, battle, or other function. **b** worth giving up or sacrificing to the enemy or to destruction for strategic reasons, such as to prevent greater loss.
— ***n.*** **expendables,** expendable persons or things: *Spare parts of machinery are some of the expendables in a military operation.*

ex|pend|i|ture (ek spen′də chůr, -chər), *n.* **1** the act or process of spending; a using up or paying out: *A large piece of work requires the expenditure of money, time, and effort.* **2** the amount of money, time, or effort, spent; expense: *Her expenditures for Christmas presents were $25 and several hours of work.*

ex|pense (ek spens′), *n., v.,* **-pensed, -pens|ing.**
— ***n.*** **1** cost; charge: *The expense of the trip for the youngest child was very slight. He traveled at his uncle's expense.* (*Figurative.*) *We had many a laugh at his expense.* **SYN**: price. **2** the act or process of expanding; paying out of money; outlay: *A boy at college puts his father to considerable expense.* **3** a cause or occasion of spending: *Running an automobile is an expense.* **4** *Figurative.* loss or sacrifice: *The town was captured at great expense to the victors.* **5** *Obsolete.* money expended.
— ***v.t.*** to charge or deduct as an expense: *Rails, for instance, are not depreciated but are carried at full value ... When the rail is replaced, it is expensed, reducing earnings* (New York Times).
at the expense of, a so as to be paid for by: *I declined to have dinner at the expense of my friends and insisted on treating them instead.* **b** *Figurative.* with the loss or sacrifice of: *Taney favored states' rights but not at the expense of basic national powers* (Jerre S. Williams).
expenses, a charges incurred in doing something: *The expenses for storing our piano were in the neighborhood of $15.* **b** money to repay a person for what he has to spend to do his job: *A traveling salesman gets expenses away from home besides his salary.*
[< Anglo-French *expense,* learned borrowing from Late Latin *expēnsa,* (originally) feminine past participle of Latin *expendere;* see etym. under **expend**]

expense account, a record of expenditure for travel, hotel accommodations, entertainment, and food, in connection with business, charged to or reimbursed by an employer or company.

ex|pens|es (ek spen′siz), *n.pl.* See under **expense.**

ex|pen|sive (ek spen′siv), *adj.* costly; dear; high-priced: *He wore an expensive necktie which cost $10. Women are such expensive things* (George Meredith). **—ex|pen′sive|ly,** *adv.* **—ex|pen′sive-ness,** *n.*

—Syn. **Expensive, costly, dear** mean high-priced. **Expensive** implies that the price is more than one can afford or than the thing is worth, and applies to the cost in money, time, effort, or the like: *The book was very expensive, costing over $500.* **Costly** implies that the price, though very high, is justified by the worth of the article: *A diamond is costly.* **Dear** implies that the price is higher than usual: *Meat is dear this week.*

ex|pe|ri|ence (ek spir′ē əns), *n., v.,* **-enced, -enc-ing.** ***—n.*** **1** what happens to a person; what is seen, done, felt, or lived through: *Battle is a shattering experience to many men. We had several pleasant experiences on our trip.* **2** all of the actions, events, or states which make up the life of a person, a community, a race, etc.: *Nothing in human experience has prepared man for space travel.* **3** knowledge or skill gained by doing, observing, or living through things: *Have you had any experience in this kind of work? He has had little business experience.* **4** the act or process of observing, doing, or living through things: *People learn by experience. Experience is the name everyone gives to his mistakes* (Oscar Wilde).

—v.t. **1** to have happen to one; meet with; feel; live through: *In life you experience pain, joy, and sorrow.* **2** to learn by experience; find: *I have experienced that a landscape and the sky unfold the deepest beauty* (Hawthorne).

experience religion. See under **religion.**

[< Old French *experience,* learned borrowing from Latin *experientia* < *experīrī* to test < *ex-* out + unrecorded root *peri-* to try] **—ex|pe′ri|enc-er,** *n.*

—Syn. *v.t.* **1 Experience, undergo** mean to go through something in life. **Experience** applies whether it is pleasant or unpleasant, brief or long-lasting, important or unimportant: *Visiting Washington was the greatest thrill I ever experienced.* **Undergo** applies if it is unpleasant, painful, or dangerous: *I had to undergo disappointment and failure before experiencing success.*

ex|pe|ri|enced (ek spir′ē ənst), *adj.* **1** having had experience; taught by experience: *The job calls for a man experienced in driving a truck.* **2** skillful or wise because of experience: *an experienced teacher, an experienced nurse.* **SYN:** expert, practiced.

ex|pe|ri|ence|less (ek spir′ē əns lis), *adj.* without experience.

experience meeting, a meeting, as of members of a church, for the telling of religious experiences.

experience table, a record of the length of life among people having life insurance, used by actuaries to evaluate risks, premiums, etc.

ex|pe|ri|ent (ek spir′ē ənt), *n., adj.* ***—n.*** an experienced person: *She assumes the role of experient and sets out to describe her experiences* (Fay Lezard).

—adj. experienced.

ex|pe|ri|en|tial (ek spir′ē en′shəl), *adj.* **1** having to do with experience. **2** based on or coming from experience. **SYN:** empirical. **—ex|pe′ri|en′-tial|ly,** *adv.*

ex|pe|ri|en|tial|ism (ek spir′ē en′shə liz əm), *n.* the theory or doctrine that all knowledge is derived from experience.

ex|pe|ri|en|tial|ist (ek spir′ē en′shə list), *n.* a person who believes in or supports the theory of experientialism.

ex|per|i|ment (*v.* ek sper′ə ment; *n.* ek sper′ə-mənt), *v., n.* ***—v.i.*** to try in order to find out; make trials or tests: *A baby experiments with his hands. The painter is experimenting with different paints to get the color he wants.*

—n. **1** a test or trial to find out something: *a cooking experiment.* **SYN:** See syn. under **trial.** **2** a conducting of such tests or trials: *Scientists test out theories by experiment.* **SYN:** experimentation. **3** an apparatus or instrument used in an experiment: *On Apollo 11 was a package of three experiments—a passive seismometer, laser reflector, and solar wind sensor* (Science Journal).

[< Latin *experīmentum* < *experīrī;* see etym. under **experience**] **—ex|per′i|ment′er,** *n.*

ex|per|i|men|tal (ek sper′ə men′təl), *adj.* **1** based on experiments: *Chemistry is an experimental science.* **2** used for experiments: *A new variety of wheat was developed at the experimental farm.* **3** for testing or trying out: *a young bird's experimental attempts to fly. This trip in the model of the new car will be only experimental. Youth is wholly experimental* (Robert Louis Stevenson). **4** based on experience, not on theory or authority: *experimental knowledge.* **SYN:** empirical.

ex|per|i|men|tal|ism (ek sper′ə men′tə liz əm), *n.* the doctrine or practice, especially in the fine arts, of experimenting freely with new techniques, forms, media, or the like: *His literary experimentalism, his frank use of the stream-of-consciousness technique, sits a little oddly with his north-country material* (Punch).

ex|per|i|men|tal|ist (ek sper′ə men′tə list), *n.* a person who makes experiments: *Abstract examples of statement of form for its own sake without further "meaning" in a literary or representational sense are shown by such fertile experimentalists as Boris Margo* (New York Times).

ex|per|i|men|tal|ize (ek sper′ə men′tə līz), *v.i.,* **-ized, -iz|ing.** = experiment.

ex|per|i|men|tal|ly (ek sper′ə men′tə lē), *adv.* **1** by making experiments. **2** as an experiment.

ex|per|i|men|ta|tion (ek sper′ə men tā′shən), *n.* the act or process of experimenting: *A cure for the disease was found by experimentation on animals.*

ex|per|i|men|ta|tive (ek sper′ə men′tə tiv), *adj.* = experimental.

ex|per|i|ment|ist (ek sper′ə men′tist), *n.* a systematic experimenter.

ex|per|i|ment|ize (ek sper′ə men tīz), *v.i.,* **-ized, -iz|ing.** to try experiments.

experiment station, a place where experiments in a particular line of research or activity, such as agriculture, are systematically carried on.

ex|pert (*n., v.* eks′pėrt; *adj.* ek spėrt′, eks′pėrt), *n., adj., v.* ***—n.*** a person who has much skill or who knows a great deal about some special thing; authority; specialist: *She is an expert at fancy skating.*

—adj. **1** having much skill; knowing a great deal about some special thing: *an expert painter. He is an expert chemist.* **2** requiring or showing special skill: *expert workmanship, expert testimony.*

—v.t. *Especially U.S. Informal.* to study or examine as an expert: *to expert the accounts of a company.* ***—v.i.*** *Especially U.S. Informal.* to be or act as an expert: *The millionaire ... devoted much of his life thereafter to playing and experting at bridge* (Time).

[< Latin *expertus,* past participle of *experīrī;* see etym. under **experience**] **—ex|pert′ly,** *adv.* **—ex-pert′ness,** *n.*

—Syn. *adj.* **1 Expert, proficient, skilled** mean having the training and knowledge to do a special thing well. **Expert** implies having mastery or unusual ability as the result of experience in addition to training and practice: *The secretary was an expert typist.* **Proficient** implies being very good at doing something, especially as the result of training and practice, but not having complete mastery or unusual ability: *She is proficient at sewing.* **Skilled** implies knowing thoroughly how to do something, usually because of training and practice, and being competent at doing it: *He is a skilled mechanic.*

ex|pert|ise (*n.* eks′pėr tēz′; *v.* eks′pėr tīz), *n., v.,* **-ised, -is|ing.** ***—n.*** **1** expert opinion or knowledge, often expressed on some matter submitted to consideration by experts: *connoisseurs full of mumbo-jumbo and expertise.* **2** the quality or state of being an expert; skill or expertness in a particular study or sport: *His expertise was not equal to the task.* ***—v.i., v.t.*** = expertize.

[< French *expertise* < *expert* expert < Latin *expertus;* see etym. under **expert**]

ex|pert|ism (eks′pėr tiz əm), *n.* = expertise (def. 2).

ex|pert|ize (eks′pėr tīz), *v.,* **-ized, -iz|ing.** ***—v.i.*** to give opinions as or in the manner of an expert. ***—v.t.*** to bring expertise to bear on: *Yet few Presidents have not used their personal influence and the publicity processes of government, as these were enlarged, perfected, and expertized* (Arthur Krock).

ex|pert|iz|er (eks′pėr tī′zər), *n.* a person who expertizes.

ex|per|to cre|di|te (eks pėr′tō kred′ə tē), *Latin.* believe the expert; trust him who knows by experience.

expert system, a computer program that incorporates the knowledge of an expert in an area such as medicine or finance: *Among the best-known expert systems are programs that contain medical information that can help doctors diagnose illnesses* (G. Kolata).

ex|pi|a|ble (eks′pē ə bəl), *adj.* that can be expiated: *an expiable sin.*

ex|pi|ate (eks′pē āt), *v.,* **-at|ed, -at|ing.** ***—v.t.*** to pay the penalty for (a wrong, sin, or crime); atone for: *The thief expiated his theft by giving back twice as much as he stole.* ***—v.i.*** to make amends; atone: *His success in sieges did not expiate ... for the loss in men* (Robert Southey).

[< Latin *expiāre* (with English *-ate*[1]) < *ex-* completely + *piāre* appease < *pius* devout]

ex|pi|a|tion (eks′pē ā′shən), *n.* **1** a making amends for a sin, wrong, or crime; atonement: *He made a public apology in expiation of his error.* **2** the means of atonement; amends: *His apology was considered a suitable expiation.*

ex|pi|a|tion|al (eks′pē ā′shə nəl), *adj.* having to do with or for the purpose of expiation.

ex|pi|a|tive (eks′pē ə tiv), *adj.* = expiatory.

ex|pi|a|tor (eks′pē ā′tər), *n.* a person who expiates.

ex|pi|a|to|ri|ness (eks′pē ə tôr′ē nis, -tōr′-), *n.* expiatory quality.

ex|pi|a|to|ry (eks′pē ə tôr′ē, -tōr′-), *adj.* intended or serving to expiate; expiating; atoning.

ex|pi|rate (eks′pər it), *adj. Phonetics.* that results from or is accompanied by exhaling.

ex|pi|ra|tion (eks′pə rā′shən), *n.* **1** a coming to an end; termination: *We shall move at the expiration of our lease.* **2a** a breathing out; exhalation: *The expiration of used air from the lungs is part of breathing.* **b** the sound made in breathing out. **3** *Obsolete.* the action of breathing one's last; death. **4** *Obsolete.* a giving off as if by breathing; evaporation.

ex|pi|ra|tor (eks′pə rā′tər), *n.* an instrument for forcing out air, gas, etc.

ex|pir|a|to|ry (ek spīr′ə tôr′ē, -tōr′-), *adj.* of or having to do with breathing out air from the lungs.

expiratory accent, *Phonetics.* an accent consisting in variation of stress.

ex|pire (ek spīr′), *v.,* **-pired, -pir|ing.** ***—v.i.*** **1** to come to an end; terminate: *You must obtain a new automobile license when your old one expires.* **2** to breathe one's last; die. **SYN:** perish. **3** to breathe out; exhale.

—v.t. **1** to breathe out (air); exhale: *Used air is expired from the lungs.* **2** *Obsolete.* to give off (a perfume or vapor); emit.

[< Latin *exspīrāre* < *ex-* out + *spīrāre* breathe]

ex|pi|ree (eks′pə rē′), *n.* one of the British criminals who were formerly transported and imprisoned in Australia, after the completion of his sentence; an ex-convict.

ex|pir|er (ek spīr′ər), *n.* a person who expires.

ex|pir|ing|ly (ek spīr′ing lē), *adv.* in an expiring or dying manner.

ex|pir|y (ek spīr′ē, eks′pər-), *n., pl.* **-ries. 1** expiration; termination; end: *Current subscriptions renewed by this date will be extended for one year from their next date of expiry* (Encounter). **2** dying; death.

ex|plain (ek splān′), *v.t.* **1** to make plain or clear; tell how to do: *The teacher explained long division to the class.* **2** to tell the meaning of; interpret: *Will you explain this poem to me? Shakespeare's plays have been explained in many different ways.* **3** to give reasons for; account for: *Can somebody explain her absence?* **4** to give an explanation of: *Even scientists have not been able to explain life so far.* ***—v.i.*** to give an explanation.

explain away, to nullify or deprive of force by giving reasons: *It is not scientific to invent theories to explain away that which you do not like* (Psychic News).

explain oneself, a to make one's meaning plain or clear: *Explain yourself, lovely Adeline* (Ann Radcliffe). **b** to give reasons for one's behavior: *His actions would not be so mysterious if he would only explain himself.*

[< Latin *explānāre* < *ex-* out + *plānus* flat] **—ex-plain′er,** *n.*

—Syn. *v.t.* **1, 2 Explain, interpret** mean to make plain or understandable. **Explain** means to make clear and plain something that is not understood: *He explained the problem in arithmetic.* **Interpret** means to explain or bring out more than the obvious meaning of something by using special knowledge or, sometimes, unusual understanding or imagination: *She interpreted the poem for us.*

ex|plain|a|ble (ek splā′nə bəl), *adj.* that can be explained.

ex|plain|ing|ly (ek splā′ning lē), *adv.* by way of explanation; so as to explain oneself.

ex|pla|nate (eks′plə nit), *adj.* Botany, Zoology. flattened; spread out. [< Latin *explānātus,* past participle of *explānāre* to spread out; see etym. under **explain**]

ex|pla|na|tion (eks′plə nā′shən), *n.* **1** the act or process of explaining; clearing up a difficulty or mistake: *He did not understand the teacher's explanation of long division.* **SYN:** elucidation, exposition, definition. **2** something that explains: *This*

Pronunciation Key: hat, āge, cãre, fär; let, ēqual, tėrm; it, īce; hot, ōpen, ôrder; oil, out; cup, pu̇t, rüle; child; long; thin; ᴛʜen; zh, measure; ə represents **a** in about, **e** in taken, **i** in pencil, **o** in lemon, **u** in circus.

diagram is a good explanation of how an automobile engine works. **3** a mutual declaration of the sense of spoken words, motives of actions, or the like, in order to adjust a misunderstanding and reconcile differences: *We had an explanation and agreed to quarrel no more.*

ex|plan|a|tive (ek splan′ə tiv), *adj.* explanatory; serving to explain.

ex|plan|a|to|ri|ly (ek splan′ə tôr′ə lē, -tōr′-), *adv.* in an explanatory manner; by way of explanation.

ex|plan|a|to|ry (ek splan′ə tôr′ē, -tōr′-), *adj.* that explains; helping to make clear; containing an explanation: *Read the explanatory part of the lesson before you try to do the problems.* **SYN:** explicatory, interpretative.

ex|plant (*v.* eks plant′, -plänt′; *n.* eks′plant, -plänt), *v., n.* —***v.t.*** to remove (living tissue) from the body to some other medium for scientific study: *In his original experiments,* [*he*] *explanted small pieces of parathyroid gland from man, mouse, and chicken* (Honor B. Fell).
—***n.*** living tissue taken from the body for scientific study: *Dr. Kao also tried to culture brain material taken from humans in brain surgery, but the explant wouldn't grow* (Science News).
[< *ex-*[1] + *plant*]

ex|plan|ta|tion (eks′plan tā′shən), *n.* the act or process of explanting.

ex|ple|tive (eks′plə tiv), *n., adj.* —***n.*** **1** a word or phrase used for filling out a sentence or a line of verse, without adding to the sense. In "There is a book on the table," *there* is an expletive. **2** an oath or meaningless exclamation standing by itself. "Damn!" and "My goodness!" are expletives. **SYN:** interjection.
—***adj.*** filling out a sentence or line of verse; completing.
[< Late Latin *explētīvus* < Latin *explēre* fill up < *ex-* out + *-plere* fill] —**ex′ple|tive|ly,** *adv.*

ex|ple|to|ry (eks′plə tôr′ē, -tōr′-), *adj.* = expletive.

ex|pli|ca|ble (eks′plə kə bəl, ek splik′ə-), *adj.* that can be explained or accounted for. —**ex′pli|ca|ble|ness,** *n.*

ex|pli|cate (eks′plə kāt), *v.t.,* **-cat|ed, -cat|ing. 1** to develop (a principle, doctrine, or theory). **2** to make clear the meaning of (anything); remove difficulties or obscurities from; clear up; explain. [< Latin *explicāre* (with English *-ate*[1]) < *ex-* out + *plicāre* to fold]

ex|pli|ca|tion (eks′plə kā′shən), *n.* **1** an explanation; interpretation. **2** a detailed statement or description.

ex|pli|ca|tion de texte (eks plē kä syôɴ′ də tekst′), *French.* **1** a formal analysis of the language, style, and content of a literary work or passage: *Impressed by Milton's "Lycidas," my teacher gave me John Ruskin's analysis of the poem, an early and excellent example of what the French call explication de texte* (Granville Hicks). **2** (literally) explanation of text.

ex|pli|ca|tive (eks′plə kā′tiv, ek splik′ə-), *adj., n.* —***adj.*** that explains.
—***n.*** an explanatory term.

ex|pli|ca|tor (eks′plə kā′tər), *n.* a person who explains or expounds; interpreter.

ex|pli|ca|to|ry (eks′plə kə tôr′ē, -tōr′-), *adj.* that explains.

ex|plic|it (ek splis′it), *adj.* **1** clearly expressed; distinctly stated; definite: *He gave such explicit directions that everyone understood them.* **SYN:** precise, exact, unequivocal. **2** not reserved; frank; outspoken. [< Latin *explicitus,* variant past participle of *explicāre* unfold, explain < *ex-* un- + *plicāre* to fold] —**ex|plic′it|ly,** *adv.* —**ex|plic′it|ness,** *n.*

explicit faith or **belief,** the acceptance of a religious doctrine with distinct understanding of all that is logically involved in it.

explicit function, *Mathematics.* a function whose value is given in terms of the independent variable or variables.

ex|plod|a|ble (ek splō′də bəl), *adj.* **1** that can be exploded: *The explodable compound suddenly burst into flame.* **2** that can be rejected or discredited: *Mr. Christopher Scott's latest exposition of his supposed queuing paradox ... is easily explodable* (New Scientist).

ex|plode (ek splōd′), *v.,* **-plod|ed, -plod|ing.** —***v.i.*** **1a** to blow up; burst with a loud noise: *The building was destroyed when the defective boiler exploded.* **b** to burst or expand violently because of the pressure produced by the sudden generation of one or more gases, for example by gunpowder, nitroglycerin, or a nuclear reaction: *A firecracker explodes.* **2** *Figurative.* to burst forth noisily or violently: *The speaker's mistake was so funny the audience exploded with laughter. Racial tensions exploded into riots. The Madagascar crisis exploded suddenly this month* (New York Times). **3** to undergo a sudden or rapid increase, growth, or expansion: *As China's population explodes, is it not natural for Mao Tse-tung to look longingly at the vast unpopulated areas of Siberia?* (Canada Month). *It is not easy to maintain the traditional role of the liberal university in a century of exploding knowledge* (Atlantic). **4** *Phonetics.* (of stops) to be articulated with audible release of the breath at the end.
—***v.t.*** **1** to cause to explode; blow up: *Many boys explode firecrackers on the Fourth of July.* **SYN:** detonate. **2** *Figurative.* to cause to be rejected; destroy belief in; discredit; disprove: *Columbus and other navigators helped to explode the theory that the earth is flat.* **3** *Phonetics.* to end the articulation of (a stop) by audibly releasing the breath. The first *p* in *pop* is always exploded, the final *p* is often not. **4** *Obsolete.* to drive (an actor, singer, etc.) off the stage by hoots and yells of disapproval.
[< Latin *explōdere* drive out by clapping < *ex-* out + *plaudere* clap]

***ex|plod|ed view** (ek splō′did), a drawing or diagram of a mechanism, construction, or apparatus showing the parts separated but so placed as to indicate their relative positions: *an exploded view of the fan and water pump assembly of an automobile.*

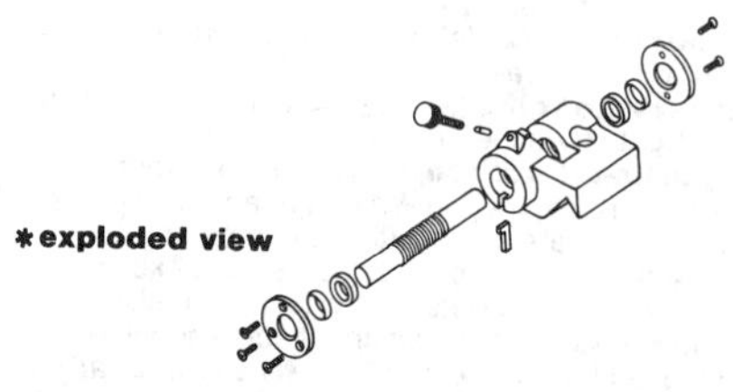

***exploded view**

ex|plod|ent (ek splō′dənt), *n. Phonetics.* an explosive.

ex|plod|er (ek splō′dər), *n.* **1** a person or thing that explodes. **2** a device for setting off, or detonating, an explosive charge.

ex|ploit (*n.* eks′ploit, ek sploit′; *v.* ek sploit′), *n., v.* —***n.*** a bold, unusual act; daring deed: *the exploits of Robin Hood against the evil Prince John and his wicked sheriff.*
—***v.t.*** **1** to make use of; turn to practical account: *A mine is exploited for its minerals. The Communist press exploited the first two points, which the Soviet Union favors, and ignored the third, which the U.S. considers essential* (Time). **2** to make unfair use of; use selfishly for one's own advantage: *Nations used to exploit their colonies, taking as much wealth out of them as they could.*
[< Anglo-French *espleit,* Old French *esploit* < Vulgar Latin *explicitum* achievement < Latin *explicāre* unfold; see etym. under **explicit**] —**ex|ploit′er,** *n.*
—***Syn.*** ***n.*** **Exploit, feat, achievement** mean a great or unusual deed. **Exploit** emphasizes daring or great courage or bravery in accomplishing something in the face of danger or against odds: *The sergeant won the Medal of Honor for his exploits in Korea.* **Feat** emphasizes use of great skill or strength in accomplishing something unusual: *Climbing Mount Everest is a feat.* **Achievement** emphasizes continued hard work in spite of difficulties and obstacles in accomplishing something outstanding: *Ralph Bunche won the Nobel Prize for his achievement in Palestine.*

ex|ploit|a|bil|i|ty (ek sploi′tə bil′ə tē), *n.* openness to exploitation.

ex|ploit|a|ble (ek sploi′tə bəl), *adj.* that can be exploited.

ex|ploit|age (ek sploi′tij), *n.* = exploitation.

ex|ploi|ta|tion (eks′ploi tā′shən), *n.* **1** use: *the exploitation of the ocean as a source of food.* **SYN:** utilization. **2** selfish or unfair use: *There are laws against the exploitation of child labor.*

ex|ploit|a|tive (ek sploi′tə tiv), *adj.* **1** concerned with exploiting. **2** tending to exploit; exploiting: *... the policies of the restrictive and exploitative industrialists of Europe* (Harper's).

ex|ploi|tive (ek sploi′tiv), *adj.* = exploitative.

ex|ploi|ture (ek sploi′chər), *n.* the act of exploiting; exploitation.

ex|plo|ra|tion (eks′plə rā′shən), *n.* **1** the act of traveling in little-known lands or seas for the purpose of discovery: *Returning to St. Petersburg, he persuaded the government to sponsor a second exploration* (Atlantic). **2** the act or process of going over carefully; looking into closely; examining. **3** *Medicine.* the examination of parts or organs concealed within the body.

ex|plo|ra|tion|al (eks′plə rā′shə nəl), *adj.* having to do with or for exploration.

ex|plor|a|tive (ek splôr′ə tiv, -splōr′-), *adj.* **1** = exploratory. **2** inclined to make explorations. —**ex|plor′a|tive|ly,** *adv.*

ex|plor|a|to|ry (ek splôr′ə tôr′ē, -splōr′-; -tōr′-), *adj.* **1** of or having to do with exploration for discovery: *He is ... far from the exploratory spirit that distinguished Marx and Engels* (Edmund Wilson). **2** undertaken for the sake of exploration: (*Figurative.*) *Exploratory experiments were carried out on specimens mounted between two silver chloride disks* (Science).

ex|plore (ek splôr′, -splōr′), *v.,* **-plored, -plor|ing.** —***v.t.*** **1** to travel in (little-known lands or seas) for the purpose of discovery: *Admiral Byrd explored much of Antarctica.* **2** to go over carefully; look into closely; examine: *to explore a possibility. The children explored the new house from attic to cellar.* **SYN:** investigate, scrutinize. See syn. under **search. 3** *Medicine.* to examine by touch, for example with a probe: *The surgeon explored the wound.* **4** *Obsolete.* to search for; search out: *Let some prophet ... Explore the cause of great Apollo's rage* (Alexander Pope).
—***v.i.*** to carry out a methodical searching operation; engage in exploration: *Some geologists explore for oil.*
[< Latin *explōrāre* investigate, spy out, (originally) cry out (at the sight of game or an enemy) < *ex-* out + *plōrāre* weep, cry]

ex|plor|er (ek splôr′ər, -splōr′-), *n.* **1** a person who explores. **2** any instrument for exploring a wound, a dental cavity, or other hole.

Explorer Scout or **explorer scout,** a boy who takes part in the exploring program of the Boy Scouts. Explorer Scouts are 14 years old or over.

ex|plor|ing coil (ek splôr′ing, -splōr′-), *Electricity.* a small flat coil of insulated wire connected with a galvanometer, used for exploring magnetic fields and for other purposes.

ex|plor|ing|ly (ek splôr′ing lē, -splōr′-), *adv.* in an exploring manner.

ex|plo|si|bil|i|ty (ek splō′zə bil′ə tē), *n.* **1** ability to explode. **2** liability to explode.

ex|plo|si|ble (ek splō′zə bəl), *adj.* **1** that can be exploded. **2** liable to explode.

ex|plo|sim|e|ter (eks′plō sim′ə tər), *n.* a device for measuring the gas content of an enclosed space relative to the exploding point of the gas.
[< *explosi*(on) + *-meter*]

ex|plo|sion (ek splō′zhən), *n.* **1** the action of bursting (of something) with a loud noise; an exploding; blowing up: *The explosion of the bomb shook the whole neighborhood.* **2** a loud noise caused by this: *People five miles away heard the explosion.* **3** *Figurative.* a noisy bursting forth into sudden activity; outbreak; outburst: *explosions of anger, an explosion of laughter.* **4** *Figurative.* a sudden or rapid increase or growth that causes a great turmoil: *The explosion of the world's population has created a shortage of food in many countries. ... the critical problem of controlling the urban explosion* (New York Times). *To cope with the current culture explosion ... museums sprout wings like seraphim* (Time). **5** *Phonetics.* the sudden audible release of the breath at the end of the articulation of a stop.
[< Latin *explōsiō, -ōnis* < *explōdere;* see etym. under **explode**]

explosion bomb, a form of calorimeter used to determine the heat of combustion of substances.

explosion shot, a golf shot used to hit the ball out of a trap, in which the club cuts into the sand under and around the ball and throws up a considerable amount along with the ball.

ex|plo|sive (ek splō′siv, -ziv), *adj., n.* —***adj.*** **1** of or for explosion: *an explosive sound. The idea developed that it might be possible to convert explosive energy into heat* (Bulletin of Atomic Scientists). **2** tending to explode: *Gunpowder is an explosive compound.* **3** *Figurative.* tending to burst forth noisily: *The grouchy old man had an explosive temper.* **4** *Phonetics.* (of a stop consonant) pronounced with a slight pop or explosion of breath. The consonants *p, b, t, d, k,* and *g* as in *"go"* are explosive.
—***n.*** **1** an explosive substance: *Explosives are used in making fireworks.* **2** *Phonetics.* **a** a stop: *Stops are also called plosives, or explosives, because the explosive release is often a prominent mark of the presence of these sounds.* (John S. Kenyon). **b** an exploded stop. —**ex|plo′sive|ly,** *adv.* —**ex|plo′sive|ness,** *n.*

explosive bolt, a bolt which can be exploded by remote control to separate two components, such as one stage of a guided missile from its booster.

explosive decompression, the decompression of an area that has been under increased air pressure, causing the air to be released suddenly and with great force: *An explosive decompression ... comparable with the bursting of a toy balloon* (New York Times).

explosive forming, the process of shaping sheet metal by forcing it into a die of the desired shape with a controlled explosion.

explosive train, a series of explosives arranged so that one charge of explosive sets fire to the next one until the main explosive is set off.

Ex|po (eks′pō), *n., pl.* **-pos.** a large public show

or exhibition: *Canada's Expo '67, Japan's Expo '70.* [< *Expo*(sition)]

∗ex|po|nent (ek spō′nənt), *n.* **1** a person or thing that explains or interprets. **2** a person or thing that stands as an example, type, or symbol of something: *Abraham Lincoln is a famous exponent of self-education.* **3** a person who argues for a policy, program, etc.; advocate. **4** *Algebra.* a small number written above and to the right of a symbol or quantity to show how many times the symbol or quantity is to be used as a factor; index. *Examples:* $2^2 = 2 \times 2$; $a^3 = a \times a \times a$. [< Latin *expōnēns, -entis,* present participle of *expōnere;* see etym. under **expound**]

$$a^2 = a \times a$$

∗exponent definition 4

$$2^4 = 2 \times 2 \times 2 \times 2$$

$$2^3a^2 = 2 \times 2 \times 2 \times a \times a$$

ex|po|nen|tial (eks′pō nen′shəl), *adj., n.* —*adj.* having to do with algebraic exponents; involving unknown or variable quantities as exponents.
—*n.* an exponential quality or function. —**ex′po|nen′tial|ly,** *adv.*

exponential curve or **equation,** a curve or an equation depending on an exponential function.

exponential function, *Mathematics.* a function involving the variable or unknown quantity as an exponent or part of an exponent.

exponential horn, a horn or tube used in certain loudspeakers, having a variable rate of size increases to improve performance on a low-frequency level.

ex|po|nen|ti|a|tion (eks′pō nen′shē ā′shən), *n.* the act of providing with an exponent.

exponent proposition, *Logic.* a proposition setting forth the meaning of an exponible, and stating it in regular form.

ex|po|ni|ble (ek spō′nə bəl), *adj., n.* —*adj.* that can be explained.
—*n.* a proposition in logic that requires restatement in order to be used in a syllogism.
[< Latin *expōnere* (see etym. under **expound**) + English *-ible*]

ex|port (*v.* ek spôrt′, -spōrt′; eks′pôrt, -pōrt; *n., adj.* eks′pôrt, -pōrt), *v., n., adj.* —*v.t.* **1** to send (products) out of one country for sale and use in another (opposed to *import*): *The United States exports many kinds of machinery to countries of Europe, Asia, and Africa.* **2** *Figurative: As befits the world's major dance power, the United States exports many dancers, choreographers, and touring companies* (William Livingstone). *His efforts to export revolution to the rest of the Americas never had less success* (Jeremiah O'Leary).
—*v.i.* to send products out of one country for sale or use in another: *That company exports only when it gets an order from a foreign buyer. Our films do well in Sweden, but they don't export* (Goeran Gentele).
—*n.* **1** a thing exported (opposed to *import*): *Cotton is an important export of the United States.* **2** the act or fact of exporting; exportation: *the export of wool from Great Britain.*
—*adj.* of exportation; having to do with or adapted to exportation: *Exporters stated that prospective export business includes 150,000 tons of U.S. hard wheat* (Wall Street Journal).
[< Latin *exportāre* < *ex-* away + *portāre* carry]

ex|port|a|bil|i|ty (ek spôr′tə bil′ə tē, -spōr′-), *n.* the quality or condition of being exportable: *The potential exportability of British aero-engines was colossal* (London Times).

ex|port|a|ble (ek spôr′tə bəl, -spōr′-), *adj.* that can be exported: *Exportable wheat stocks in the four major shipping countries promise to rise further* (Wall Street Journal).

ex|por|ta|tion (eks′pôr tā′shən, -pōr-), *n.* **1** the act of exporting: *the exportation of wheat from Canada to India.* **2** an article exported; export: *Machinery and vehicles are among the major exportations of the United States.*

ex|port|er (ek spôr′tər, -spōr′-; eks′pôr-, -pōr-), *n.* a person or company whose business is exporting.

ex|pos|al (ek spō′zəl), *n.* exposure; exposition.

ex|pose (ek spōz′), *v.t.,* **-posed, -pos|ing. 1** to lay open; uncover: *The excavation exposed some ancient ruins.* **2** to lay open to a specified risk or chance; make liable or open (to): *Soldiers in an open field are exposed to the enemy's fire. Foolish actions expose a person to ridicule. The children had all been exposed to scarlet fever.* **3** to leave bare: *These costumes exposed the greater part of the body.* **4** to put in plain sight; display: *Goods are exposed for sale in a store.* **SYN:** exhibit. **5** to make known; show up; reveal: *He exposed the plot to the police.* **SYN:** disclose, unmask. **6** to put out without shelter; abandon: *The ancient Spartans exposed babies they did not want.* **7** to allow light to reach and act on (a photographic film or plate). [< Old French *exposer* < *ex-* forth (< Latin) + *poser* < Latin *pausāre* stop, but influenced by Old French *espondre* < Latin *expōnere* set forth; see etym. under **expound**]

ex|po|sé or **ex|po|se** (eks′pō zā′), *n.* **1** a showing up of crime, dishonesty, or fraud: *a public exposé of graft. After Mr. Keating's exposé four men were arrested and are awaiting trial for ... wiretapping* (New York Times). **2** a detailed explanation or statement of facts; exposition: *This lucid exposé of the various experimental methods, and of what one can learn from them, is likely to be extremely helpful to workers in the field* (Scientific American). [< French *exposé,* (originally) past participle of *exposer;* see etym. under **expose**]

ex|posed (ek spōzd′), *adj.* **1** left unsheltered or unprotected from the elements or from hostile attack: *exposed boards on an unpainted house.* **2** disclosed to view; not concealed; displayed: *Exposed beams in a ceiling have a rustic charm.*

ex|pos|ed|ness (ek spō′zid nis), *n.* the state of being exposed.

ex|pos|er (ek spō′zər), *n.* a person who exposes, uncovers, or lays bare: *an exposer of fraud.*

ex|pos|it (ek spoz′it), *v.t.* to reveal; exhibit; show clearly.

ex|po|si|tion (eks′pə zish′ən), *n.* **1** a public show or exhibition. A world's fair is an exposition. **SYN:** display, fair. **2** a detailed explanation. **3** a speech or writing explaining a process, thing, or idea. **SYN:** commentary. **4** *Music.* **a** the first section of a movement, for example of a sonata, in which the principal themes are presented. **b** the first entry, in a fugue, of the theme or themes in each part or voice. **5** = exposure (def. 5).

ex|pos|i|tive (ek spoz′ə tiv), *adj.* = expository.

ex|pos|i|tor (ek spoz′ə tər), *n.* **1** a person or thing that explains; expounder: *The speaker was a powerful expositor of his convictions.* **2** = interpreter. [< Old French *expositour,* learned borrowing from Late Latin *expositor* one that puts forth or lays open < Latin *expōnere;* see etym. under **expound**]

ex|pos|i|to|ri|al (ek spoz′ə tôr′ē əl, -tōr′-), *adj.* = expository.

ex|pos|i|to|ri|um (ek spoz′ə tôr′ē əm, -tōr′-), *n.* a monstrance; a receptacle for showing the consecrated Host. [< New Latin *expositorium* < Late Latin *expositor*]

ex|pos|i|to|ry (ek spoz′ə tôr′ē, -tōr′-), *adj.* = explanatory.

ex post fac|to (eks′ pōst′ fak′tō), made or done after something, but applying to it. An ex post facto law applies to actions done before the law was passed. *Balanced history is always ex post facto; it must represent judgment of past events* (Atlantic). [< Medieval Latin *ex* from, *postfacto* what is done afterwards < Latin *ex* from, *post* after + *factō,* ablative of *factum* deed, fact]

ex|pos|tu|late (ek spos′chə lāt), *v.i.,* **-lat|ed, -lat|ing.** to reason earnestly with a person, protesting against something he means to do or has done; remonstrate in a friendly way: *The father expostulated with his son about the foolishness of leaving school.* [< Latin *expostulāre* (with English *-ate*[1]) < *ex-* from + *postulāre* to demand]

ex|pos|tu|lat|ing|ly (ek spos′chə lā′ting lē), *adv.* in an expostulatory manner.

ex|pos|tu|la|tion (ek spos′chə lā′shən), *n.* earnest protest; friendly remonstrance: *The teacher's expostulations were wasted, for the boy made no effort to improve his work.*

ex|pos|tu|la|tive (ek spos′chə lā′tiv), *adj.* expostulating; expostulatory.

ex|pos|tu|la|tor (ek spos′chə lā′tər), *n.* a person who expostulates.

ex|pos|tu|la|to|ry (ek spos′chə lə tôr′ē, -tōr′-), *adj.* of or containing expostulation.

ex|po|sure (ek spō′zhər), *n.* **1** the act or process of exposing; laying open: *The exposure of the real criminal cleared the innocent man. Anyone would dread public exposure of all his faults.* **2** the state of being exposed: *Exposure to the rain has spoiled this machinery.* **3** position in relation to the sun and wind. A house with a southern exposure is open to sun and wind from the south. **4** *Photography.* **a** the time taken to get an image on a photographic film or plate. **b** the part of a photographic film for one picture. **c** the total amount of light on a film in making a picture. **5** the act of putting out without shelter; abandoning: *the exposure of the infant Moses.* [< *expose,* probably patterned on *enclose, enclosure*]

exposure meter, an instrument, usually containing a photoelectric cell, that helps a photographer determine the best exposure by measuring the light on a given scene.

exposure suit, a suit made of an insulated rubberized material to protect a person from extreme temperatures, freezing water, or other unnatural conditions: *In case you're told during the flight that you're going to ditch the plane, first put on your exposure suit ... and then your inflatable life jacket* (New Yorker).

ex|pound (ek spound′), *v.t.* **1** to make clear; explain or interpret: *to expound the Scriptures. The teacher expounds each new rule or principle in arithmetic to the class.* **2** to set forth or state in detail: *The Senator expounded his objections to the bill.* —*v.i.* to make a comment or comments; remark: *They are apt to talk to the French ... and to expound on the character of President de Gaulle* (New York Times). [< Anglo-French *espoundre,* Old French *espondre* < Latin *expōnere* < *ex-* forth + *pōnere* put. Compare etym. under **expose.**] —**ex|pound′er,** *n.*

ex-pres|i|dent (eks′prez′ə dənt, -prez′dənt), *n.* a former president; a living person who once was a president, but no longer is.

ex|press (ek spres′), *v., adj., n., adv.* —*v.t.* **1** to put into words: *Try to express your ideas clearly.* **SYN:** utter, declare, state, say. **2** to show by look, voice, or action; reveal: *A smile expresses joy.* **3** to show by a sign or figure; indicate: *The sign X expresses multiplication. Flowers express sentiments, tastefully, eloquently—their fragrant beauty brings comfort to those who grieve* (London Times). **SYN:** signify, denote, designate, represent, mean. **4a** *U.S.* to send by some quick means: *Express your baggage to Chicago.* **b** *British.* to send (a letter or parcel) by special delivery. **5** to press out; squeeze: *to express the juice from grapes to make wine.* **6** *Genetics.* to cause (a gene) to produce the specific protein or effect it codes for: *When a gene is to be expressed ... its bases act as a template, or pattern* (Jerald C. Ensign). **7** to emit as a secretion; exude. **8** *Archaic.* to portray in sculpture or painting. **9** *Obsolete.* to elicit; extort.
—*adj.* **1** clear and definite: *It was his express wish that we should go without him.* **SYN:** plain, unmistakable, explicit. **2** for a particular purpose; special: *She came for the express purpose of seeing you.* **3** exact: *He is the express image of his father.* **SYN:** precise. **4** having to do with express: *an express agency or company.* **5** traveling fast and making few stops; quick: *an express elevator.* **6** for fast traveling: *an express highway.*
—*n.* **1** a quick or direct means of sending things. Packages and money can be sent by express in trains or airplanes. **2** a system or company that carries packages or money. **3** things sent by express. **4** a train, bus, elevator, or other vehicle, traveling from one point to another without making intermediate stops. **5** a special messenger or message sent for a particular purpose. **6** an express rifle.
—*adv.* **1** by express; directly: *Please send this package express to Boston.* **2** on purpose; specially: *He has come here express to visit his old friends.*
express oneself, to say what one thinks: *A good speaker must be able to express himself clearly and effectively. He was just expressing himself on the subject when the train whistle blew and some soldiers came in* (Edmund Wilson).
[< Medieval Latin *expressare* (frequentative) < Latin *expressus,* past participle of *exprimere* < *ex-* out + *premere* press] —**ex|press′er,** *n.*

ex|press|age (ek spres′ij), *n. Especially U.S.* **1** the business of carrying parcels or money by express. **2** the charge for carrying parcels or money by express.

express bullet, an expanding bullet for use with an express rifle.

express car, a railroad car for carrying packages sent by express.

ex|press|ed|ly (ek spres′id lē), *adv.* = expressly.

ex|press|i|ble (ek spres′ə bəl), *adj.* that can be expressed.

ex|pres|sion (ek spresh′ən), *n.* **1** the act of putting into words; expressing: *the expression of an idea. His clear expression of the plan made it easier for us to understand.* **SYN:** utterance, statement. **2** a word or group of words used as a unit: *"Wise guy" is a slang expression.* **3** the act of showing by look, voice, or action: *Her sigh was an expression of her sadness.* **4** the manner or form in which a thing is expressed: *Gyp ... gave a short bark ... he had not a great range of expression* (George Eliot). **SYN:** language, diction, phraseology. **5** a look that shows feeling: *A grin is a happy expression.* **SYN:** look, aspect, air. **6** the act of bringing out the meaning or beauty of something read, spoken, played, sung, painted, or sculptured: *Try to read with more ex-*

Pronunciation Key: hat, āge, cãre, fär; let, ēqual, tėrm, it, īce; hot, ōpen, ôrder; oil, out; cup, pu̇t, rüle; child; long; thin; ᴛʜen; zh, measure; ə represents **a** in about, **e** in taken, **i** in pencil, **o** in lemon, **u** in circus.

pression. **7** the act of showing by a sign or figure. **8** any combination of constants, variables, and symbols expressing some mathematical process or quantity. **9** manifestation in action, condition, or otherwise of any fact, quality, or feeling; declaration: *an expression of God's will.* **10** the act of pressing out: *the expression of oil from plants.* **11** *Genetics.* the manner or degree in which a gene produces the protein or effect it codes for.

ex|pres|sion|al (ek spresh′ə nəl), *adj.* of or having to do with expression.

ex|pres|sion|ism (ek spresh′ə niz əm), *n.* the tendencies, doctrines, methods, and style of painters, writers, sculptors, and other artists who believe that art should represent the artist's own reactions and be free of tradition, often distorting nature or reality. Expressionism was a revolt against impressionism and naturalism.

ex|pres|sion|ist (ek spresh′ə nist), *n., adj.* — ***n.*** an artist, writer, sculptor, or other artist whose work follows the principles of expressionism.
— ***adj.*** of or having to do with expressionism: *In passing, I must ask you to note that expressionist plays ... seem inevitably to cast a particular kind of shadow* (Atlantic). **2** like expressionism.

ex|pres|sion|is|tic (ek spresh′ə nis′tik), *adj.* of or having to do with expressionism or expressionists: *His [Franz Werfel's] first prose work, "Not the Murderer" (1937) introduced the expressionistic movement in the German novel* (G. F. Merkel). — **ex|pres′sion|is′ti|cal|ly,** *adv.*

ex|pres|sion|less (ek spresh′ən lis), *adj.* without expression: *an expressionless face, an expressionless voice.* — **ex|pres′sion|less|ly,** *adv.* — **ex|pres′sion|less|ness,** *n.*

expression mark, a sign or direction indicating the desired way of rendering a musical phrase or passage.

ex|pres|sive (ek spres′iv), *adj.* **1** serving as a sign or indication; expressing: *"Alas" is a word expressive of sadness.* **SYN:** indicative. **2** full of expression; having much feeling or meaning: *"His skin hung on his bones" is a more expressive sentence than "He was very thin."* **3** of or having to do with expression. — **ex|pres′sive|ly,** *adv.* — **ex|pres′sive|ness,** *n.*
— *Syn.* **1 Expressive, significant, suggestive** mean full of meaning. **Expressive** emphasizes showing in a strikingly clear or lively way the meaning or feeling in what is described: *She gave an expressive shrug.* **Significant** emphasizes being full of meaning, which may be expressed, but often is only pointed to: *Graduation Day is a significant day in every student's life.* **Suggestive** emphasizes conveying meaning in an indirect way, by expressing part of the meaning or by hinting: *The teacher gave an interesting and suggestive list of composition topics.*

expressive riot, *Sociology.* a riot in which members of a minority group use violence to express dissatisfaction with their living conditions (contrasted with *instrumental riot*).

ex|pres|siv|i|ty (ek′spre siv′ə tē), *n.* **1** the quality or state of being expressive; expressiveness. **2** *Genetics.* the ability of a gene to manifest itself or its effects within the organism.

ex|press|less (ek spres′lis), *adj. Archaic.* inexpressible.

ex|press|ly (ek spres′lē), *adv.* **1** clearly; plainly; definitely: *The package is not for you; you are expressly forbidden to touch it.* **2** on purpose; specially: *You ought to talk to her, since she came expressly to see you.*

ex|press|man (ek spres′mən), *n., pl.* **-men.** *Especially U.S.* a worker who collects or delivers articles for an express company.

ex|press|ness (ek spres′nis), *n.* **1** the quality of being express. **2** = definiteness. **3** = explicitness.

Ex|pres|so (ek spres′ō), *n.* = caffè espresso.

express rifle, a sporting rifle for hunting big game at short range, using a heavy charge of powder and a light bullet, and designed to fire with high velocity.

express train, a railroad or subway train that travels at a high speed and makes few or no stops between terminals.

express wagon, a wagon formerly used for collecting and delivering articles sent by express.

ex|press|way (ek spres′wā′), *n.* a divided highway for traveling by motor vehicle at high speeds; an express highway: *A northbound motorist can take the New Hampshire and Maine Turnpikes, which are expressways, as far as Portland* (Harper's).

ex|pro|mis|sion (eks′prō mish′ən), *n. Law.* the acceptance by a creditor of an expromissor or new debtor in place of the former debtor.

ex|pro|mis|sor (eks′prō mis′ər, -ôr), *n. Law.* a person who takes over the debt of another.

ex|pro|pri|ate (eks prō′prē āt), *v.t.,* **-at|ed, -at|ing.** **1** to take (land, mineral rights, or other property) out of the owner's possession, especially for public use. A city can expropriate land for a public park. **2** to put (a person) out of possession; dispossess. [< Medieval Latin *expropriare* (with English *-ate*[1]) < *ex-* away from + Late Latin *propriāre* to appropriate < Latin *proprius* one's own]

ex|pro|pri|a|tion (eks prō′prē ā′shən), *n.* **1** the taking of land or other property from the owner, especially for public use, for example by right of eminent domain. **2** the taking of property into public ownership, without compensation, such as the property of foreign investors or foreign industry in a country.

ex|pro|pri|a|tor (eks prō′prē ā′tər), *n.* a person who expropriates.

ex pro|pri|o mo|tu (eks prō′prē ō mō′tü, -mō′tyü), *Latin.* of one's own accord.

ex|pul|sa|to|ry (ek spul′sə tôr′ē, -tōr′-), *adj.* of or having to do with expulsion.

ex|pulse (ek spuls′), *v.t.,* **-pulsed, -puls|ing.** *Obsolete.* to drive out; expel: *For ever should they be expulsed from France* (Shakespeare). [< Latin *expulsāre* (frequentative) < *expellere;* see etym. under **expel**]

ex|pul|sion (ek spul′shən), *n.* **1** the act or process of expelling; forcing out: *Expulsion of used air from the lungs is part of breathing.* **2** the condition of being expelled; being forced out: *Expulsion from school is a punishment for bad behavior.* [< Latin *expulsiō, -ōnis* < *expellere;* see etym. under **expel**]

ex|pul|sive (ek spul′siv), *adj.* forcing out; expelling: *a passion so potent ... so expulsive of other loves* (Cardinal Newman).

ex|punc|tion (ek spungk′shən), *n.* the act of expunging; erasure. [< Latin *expūnctiō, -ōnis* < *expungere;* see etym. under **expunge**]

ex|punge (ek spunj′), *v.t.,* **-punged, -pung|ing.** to remove completely; blot out; erase: *The secretary was directed to expunge certain remarks from the record.* **SYN:** See syn. under **erase.** [< Latin *expungere* < *ex-* out + *pungere* to prick, mark]

ex|punge|ment (ek spunj′mənt), *n.* the act of expunging; expunction.

ex|pung|er (ek spun′jər), *n.* a person who expunges.

ex|pur|gate (eks′pər gāt), *v.t.,* **-gat|ed, -gat|ing.** to remove objectionable passages or words from (a book, play, film, letter, or the like); purify. [< Latin *expūrgāre* (with English *-ate*[1]) < *ex-* out + *pūrgāre* to purge]

ex|pur|ga|tion (eks′pər gā′shən), *n.* the removing or removal from a book, play, film, letter, or the like, of something that seems objectionable.

ex|pur|ga|tor (eks′pər gā′tər), *n.* a person who expurgates (especially books).

ex|pur|ga|to|ri|al (ek spėr′gə tôr′ē əl, -tōr′-), *adj.* having to do with an expurgator or expurgation.

ex|pur|ga|to|ry (ek spėr′gə tôr′ē, -tōr′-), *adj.* **1** of or having to do with expurgation. **2** serving to expurgate.

Expurgatory Index, the Index Expurgatorius.

ex|qui|site (eks′kwi zit, ek skwiz′it), *adj., n.* — ***adj.*** **1** very lovely; delicate; beautifully made: *Those violets are exquisite flowers.* **SYN:** dainty, fine, beautiful. See syn. under **delicate.** **2** sharp; intense: *exquisite joy. A toothache causes exquisite pain. Chiggers, called red bugs down South, cause the most exquisite itching* (Science News Letter). **SYN:** acute, keen. **3** of highest excellence; most admirable: *She has exquisite taste and manners. In German he was an exquisite stylist, and he brought to that language a new sensitivity in the art of storytelling* (Time). **4** keenly sensitive: *an exquisite ear for music.* **5** *Obsolete.* carefully chosen or devised: *I have no exquisite reason for't, but I have reason good enough* (Shakespeare).
— ***n.*** a person (usually a man) who is too fastidious in dress; dandy; fop.
[< Latin *exquīsītus,* past participle of *exquīrere* < *ex-* out + *quaerere* seek]

ex|qui|site|ly (eks′kwi zit lē, ek skwiz′it lē), *adv.* in an exquisite manner or degree: *A people exquisitely sensitive on points of national honor* (Macaulay).

ex|qui|site|ness (eks′kwi zit nis, ek skwiz′it nis), *n.* the quality of being exquisite.

exr., *Law.* executor.

ex-rights (eks′rīts′), *adj., adv.,* or **ex rights,** without the right to purchase new or additional shares of stock: *Exchange contracts unless specifically made for cash will be ex-rights contracts* (Wall Street Journal). (adj.) *The old shares are now quoted ex-rights* (Economist). (adv.)

exrx., *Law.* executrix.

ex|san|gui|nate (eks sang′gwə nāt), *v.t.,* **-nat|ed, -nat|ing.** to make bloodless. [< Latin *exsanguināre* (with English *-ate*[1]) < *ex-* from + *sanguis, sanguinis* blood]

ex|san|gui|na|tion (eks sang′gwə nā′shən), *n.* the process of exsanguinating.

ex|san|guine (eks sang′gwin), *adj.* bloodless; deficient in blood; anemic. [< *ex-*[1] + Latin *sanguis, sanguinis* blood]

ex|san|guin|i|ty (eks′sang gwin′ə tē), *n.* a deficiency of blood; anemia.

ex|scind (ek sind′), *v.t.* to cut out; cut off; excise. [< Latin *exscindere* < *ex-* away + *scindere* cut, shear]

ex|sculp|tate (ek skulp′tāt), *adj. Zoology.* covered with irregular and varying depressions, so that it appears like carved work.

ex|sect (ek sekt′), *v.t.* to cut out: *to exsect a tumor from the lung.* [< Latin *exsectus,* past participle of *exsecāre* < *ex-* out + *secāre* to cut]

ex|sec|tion (ek sek′shən), *n.* a cutting out.

ex|sert (ek sėrt′), *v., adj.* — ***v.t.*** to thrust out; protrude.
— ***adj.*** = exserted.
[< Latin *exsertus,* past participle of *exserere* put forth < *ex-* out + *serere* bind, entwine]

ex|sert|ed (ek sėr′tid), *adj.* projecting beyond the surrounding parts: *an exserted stamen or sting.*

ex|ser|tile (ek sėr′təl), *adj.* capable of being exserted.

ex|ser|tion (ek sėr′shən), *n.* the act of exserting or state of being exserted.

ex-serv|ice (eks′sėr′vis), *adj.* having formerly served in the armed forces.

ex-serv|ice|man (eks′sėr′vis mən), *n., pl.* **-men.** a former member of the armed forces; veteran.

ex|sic|cant (ek sik′ənt), *adj., n.* — ***adj.*** having the power of drying up, as a medicine.
— ***n.*** an exsiccant medicine or agent.
[< Latin *exsiccāns, -antis,* present participle of *exsiccāre;* see etym. under **exsiccate**]

ex|sic|cate (ek′sə kāt), *v.,* **-cat|ed, -cat|ing.** — ***v.t.*** to remove all moisture from; make utterly dry.
— ***v.i.*** to dry up; lose all moisture.
[< Latin *exsiccāre* (with English *-ate*[1]) < *ex-* up, away + *siccāre* make dry < *siccus* dry]

ex|sic|ca|tion (ek′sə kā′shən), *n.* the act of drying what is moist; absolute dryness.

ex|sic|ca|tive (ek′sə kā′tiv, ek sik′ə-), *adj.* tending to dry.

ex|sic|ca|tor (ek′sə kā′tər), *n.* a drying agent or apparatus.

ex|so|lu|tion (eks′sə lü′shən), *n.* the process by which a pair of minerals in solid solution separate from one another at certain temperatures.

ex|solve (eks solv′), *v.i.,* **-solved, -solv|ing.** to undergo exsolution.

ex|stip|u|late (eks stip′yə lit, -lāt), *adj.* without stipules. Also, **estipulate.**

ex|stro|phy (ek′strə fē), *n., pl.* **-phies.** the process of turning inside out a part, such as a congenital malformation of the bladder. [< *ex-*[2] + Greek *strophē* a turning]

ex|suc|cous (eks suk′əs), *adj.* without juice or sap; dry. [< Latin *exsuccus* (with English *-ous*) < *ex-* from + *sūcus* juice]

ex|suc|tion (ek suk′shən), *n.* the act of drawing or sucking out, especially the removal of air by means of a pump.

ex|suf|flate (eks suf′lāt), *v.t.,* **-flat|ed, -flat|ing.** **1** to blow out or away. **2** *Ecclesiastical.* to drive off (an evil spirit) by blowing. [< Latin *exsufflāre* (with English *-ate*[1]) < *ex-* out + *sufflāre* inflate < *sub-* under + *flāre* to blow]

ex|suf|fla|tion (eks′su flā′shən), *n.* the act or process of exorcising the devil or evil by blowing, especially by or upon a person being baptized.

ext., an abbreviation for the following:
1 extension.
2a external. **b** externally.
3 extinct.
4 extra.
5 extract.

ex|tant (eks′tənt, ek stant′), *adj.* **1** still in existence; still existing; not destroyed or lost: *Some of George Washington's letters are extant. The roach is the oldest extant winged insect, dating back more than 300 million years* (Robert W. Stock). **2** *Archaic.* standing out or above any surface. **3** *Archaic.* prominent; conspicuous. [< Latin *exstāns, -antis,* present participle of *exstāre* stand forth < *ex-* out, forth + *stāre* to stand]

ex|tem|po|ral (ek stem′pər əl), *adj. Archaic.* extemporaneous. [< Latin *extemporālis* arising at the moment < *ex tempore;* see etym. under **extempore**] — **ex|tem′po|ral|ly,** *adv.*

ex|tem|po|ra|ne|ous (ek stem′pə rā′nē əs), *adj.* **1** spoken or done without preparation; offhand: *The chairman made a few extemporaneous remarks. I prefer the give and take of extemporaneous talk to formal lecturing* (Harper's). **2** made for the occasion: *an extemporaneous shelter against the storm.* **3** carefully prepared, though usually not written out and never committed to memory: *an extemporaneous speech.* **4** inclined and able to make speeches without preparation. [< Late Latin *extemporaneus* extemporal < Latin *ex tempore;* see etym. under **extempore**] — **ex|tem′po|ra′ne|ous|ly,** *adv.* — **ex|tem′po|ra′ne|ous|ness,** *n.*

ex|tem|po|rar|i|ly (ek stem′pə rer′ə lē), *adv.* without previous study or preparation.

ex|tem|po|rar|i|ness (ek stem′pə rer′ē nis), *n.* extemporary quality.

ex|tem|po|rar|y (ek stem′pə rer′ē), *adj.* **1** = extemporaneous. **2** *Obsolete.* sudden.

ex|tem|po|re (ek stem′pər ē, -pə rē), *adv., adj.* —***adv.*** on the spur of the moment; without preparation; offhand: *Each pupil will be called on to speak extempore. They could deliver, extempore, long, inflammatory speeches* (Sonia Shiragian). —***adj.*** made, done, or said on the spur of the moment; impromptu: *There is a good deal of talk going on now about the Prime Minister's dramatic extempore explanation* (New Yorker).
[< Latin *ex tempore* according to the moment < *ex-* out of, from, *tempore,* ablative of *tempus, -oris* time]

ex|tem|po|ri|za|tion (ek stem′pər ə zā′shən), *n.* **1** the act of extemporizing; improvisation: *He dislikes detailed work; he is impatient, eager for quick results, and capable of brilliant extemporizations* (Atlantic). **2** anything extemporized, especially a musical performance, either vocal or instrumental.

ex|tem|po|rize (ek stem′pə rīz), *v.i., v.t.,* **-rized, -riz|ing.** **1** to speak, play, sing, or dance, composing as one goes along; improvise: *The pianist was extemporizing instead of following the score.* **2** to prepare offhand; make for the occasion: *The campers extemporized a shelter for the night.*

ex|tem|po|riz|er (ek stem′pə rī′zər), *n.* a person who extemporizes.

ex|tend (ek stend′), *v.t.* **1** to stretch out: *to extend your hand.* **2** to continue or prolong in time, space, or direction: *He is extending his vacation another week.* **SYN**: See syn. under **lengthen.** **3** to widen; enlarge: *The works have been extended several times.* **4** to enlarge the scope or application of; increase: *They plan to extend their research in this field.* **5** to hold out to others; offer; give; grant: *This organization extends help to poor people.* **6a** to exert (oneself); strain. **b** to cause to put out greater or maximum effort: *The competition was not strong enough to extend him.* **7** to increase the time allowed for (the payment of a debt) beyond the date originally agreed to. **8** *Law.* **a** *Especially British.* to assess or value (lands, etc.). **b** to take possession of (land) by a writ of extent; levy upon. **9** *Obsolete.* to take possession of by force. **10** *Obsolete.* to exaggerate. —***v.i.*** **1** to stretch out in one or all directions; continue in time, space, or direction: *a road that extends to New York. The beach extends for miles in both directions. The conference extends from Wednesday to Saturday.* **2** to become longer or larger; increase in length or size: *The area of desert is extending.* **3** to have a specified range, scope, or application: *His kindness extends to all.* [< Latin *extendere* < *ex-* out + *tendere* stretch]

ex|tend|a|ble (ek sten′də bəl), *adj.* = extensible.

ex|tend|ed (ek sten′did), *adj.* **1** extensive; widespread. **2** stretched out; prolonged: *an extended visit.* **3** widened. **4** stretched out fully; spread out; outstretched. **5** (of type) expanded. —**ex|tend′ed|ly,** *adv.* —**ex|tend′ed|ness,** *n.*

extended coverage, the extension of an insurance policy to afford protection not only against a primary hazard, such as fire, but also against other specified risks, such as explosion or windstorm: *An owner may have an adequate amount of fire insurance, but he will not be protected against other hazards unless the fire insurance policy carries an extended coverage or other suitable endorsement* (New York Times).

extended family, a family and its near relatives, such as grandparents and married sons and their families, living together usually under the authority of the eldest male. Extended families are common among the nomadic and farming peoples of southwestern Asia.

ex|tend|er (ek sten′dər), *n.* **1** a person or thing that extends. **2** a cheap, plentiful material added to an expensive or scarce material to make it last longer: *Extenders or fillers are mixed with paint bases to make them go further.* **3** a chemical added to an insecticide in order to increase the period of its effectiveness: *When one of these extenders, methyl ethyl ketone, was used as a solvent for DDT, spray residues on foliage killed flies for 60 days and longer, compared to less than 15 days when the DDT was in an oil solution* (Science News Letter).

ex|tend|i|ble (ek sten′də bəl), *adj.* = extensible.

ex|tense (ek stens′), *adj. Archaic.* **1** extended. **2** extensive. [< Latin *extēnsus,* past participle of *extendere;* see etym. under **extend**]

ex|ten|si|bil|i|ty (ek sten′sə bil′ə tē), *n.* the quality of being extensible: *the extensibility of a fiber or of a plate of metal.*

ex|ten|si|ble (ek sten′sə bəl), *adj.* that can be extended. —**ex|ten′si|ble|ness,** *n.*

ex|ten|sile (ek sten′səl), *adj.* **1** that can be stuck out: *extensile claws.* **2** = extensible.

ex|ten|sim|e|ter (eks′ten sim′ə tər), *n.* = extensometer.

ex|ten|sion (ek sten′shən), *n.* **1** the act or process of stretching out; extending: *the extension of one's arm, the extension of a road.* (*Figurative.*) *For the last three centuries, Western civilization has dedicated a good part of its energies to the invention of machines and the extension of their operations into every corner of life* (New Yorker). **SYN**: expansion, enlargement. **2** the condition of being extended. **3** an extended part; addition: *The new extension to our school will make room for more students.* **SYN**: projection. **4** range; extent. **5** a telephone connected with the main telephone or with a switchboard but in a different location; extension telephone. **6** the provision of courses of study by a university or college to people unable to take courses in the regular session. **7** a written engagement given by a creditor, granting a debtor additional time in which to pay a debt. **8** *Physics.* that property of a body by which it occupies a portion of space. **9a** the straightening of a part by the action of an extensor muscle. **b** the condition of being straightened in this way. **10** *Logic.* the subclasses of things included in a given term or concept: *In its extension "clothing" includes "coat," "dress," and "shoes."* **11** the pulling or stretching of a fractured or dislocated part to enable the bones to be restored to their natural relative positions. [< Late Latin *extēnsiō, -ōnis* < Latin *extendere;* see etym. under **extend**]

ex|ten|sion|al (ek sten′shə nəl), *adj.* **1** having to do with or having extension or extent. **2** existing in space. —**ex|ten′sion|al|ly,** *adv.*

ex|ten|sion|al|i|ty (ek sten′shə nal′ə tē), *n.* the quality or condition of being extensional.

extension cord, a length of electric cord fitted with a plug and a socket, used to connect a short cord to an outlet or other source of power.

extension courses, courses of instruction offered by some universities or colleges to persons who are not regular students, in evening classes, or by correspondence.

ex|ten|sion|ist (ek sten′shə nist), *n.* a person who favors extension or expansion of any kind; an expansionist.

extension ladder, a ladder having one or more movable sections that can be raised to extend above the main section when greater height is needed.

extension lens, a lens that may be used in combination to increase its focal length.

ex|ten|sion|less (ek sten′shən lis), *adj.* without extension: *an extensionless moment of time* (Alfred North Whitehead).

extension phone, = extension telephone.

extension spring, a spiral spring designed to resist a pull or strain in line with its length.

extension table, a table whose frame can be extended in length for the insertion of additional leaves to make the top larger; drawing table.

extension telephone, = extension (def. 5).

ex|ten|si|ty (ek sten′sə tē), *n.* **1** spatial quality. **2** *Psychology.* a spatial attribute of sense data or sensation on which spatial perception is said to depend.

ex|ten|sive (ek sten′siv), *adj.* **1** of great extent; wide; broad; large: *an extensive park.* **SYN**: extended, ample. **2** far-reaching; affecting many things; comprehensive: *extensive changes.* **3** depending on the use of large areas: *extensive agriculture.* **4** large in amount: *extensive expenditures.* **5** of or having to do with extension. —**ex|ten′sive|ly,** *adv.* —**ex|ten′sive|ness,** *n.*

ex|ten|som|e|ter (eks′ten som′ə tər), *n.* an instrument for measuring minute degrees of expansion, contraction, or deformation, as in a bar of metal. Also, **extensimeter.**

ex|ten|sor (ek sten′sər, -sôr), *n.* a muscle that when contracted extends or straightens out a limb or other part of the body: *The contraction of one group of muscles, the flexors, diminishes the angle between the skeletal segments, while the contraction of the opposite group, the extensors, increases the angle between the segments* (Harbaugh and Goodrich). [< Late Latin *extēnsor* one who stretches < *extēndere;* see etym. under **extend**]

ex|tent (ek stent′), *n.* **1** the size, space, length, amount, or degree to which a thing extends: *Freight trains and motor trucks carry goods through the whole extent of the country. The extent of a judge's power is limited by law. I agree with your plans, but only to a certain extent.* **SYN**: magnitude, area, scope, compass, range. **2** something extended; extended space: *a vast extent of prairie.* **3** *Physics.* anything that has extension; an object or body having length, area, or volume. **4** *Mathematics.* a continuous magnitude of dimensions: *A plane figure is 2-extent.* **5** (in the United States) a writ or levy by which a creditor may have his debtor's lands valued and transferred to himself. **6** in Great Britain: **a** a writ to recover debts recorded as due to the Crown. **b** a seizure of lands or other property, in execution of such a writ. **c** a valuation of land, usually for taxation; assessment. **7** *Logic.* = extension. **8** *Obsolete.* an attack or assault: *This uncivil and unjust extent Against thy peace* (Shakespeare). [< Anglo-French *extente, estente,* noun use of feminine past participle of *estendre* extend < Latin *extendere;* see etym. under **extend**]

ex|ten|u|ate (ek sten′yu̇ āt), *v.t.,* **-at|ed, -at|ing.** **1** to make the seriousness of (guilt, a fault, or an offense) seem less; excuse in part: *The hunger of his children extenuated his crime of stealing a loaf of bread. His foreign upbringing extenuates his faulty pronunciation.* **2** to make thin or weak; diminish. **3** *Obsolete.* **a** to diminish in size, number, or amount. **b** to lessen in degree. **4** *Obsolete.* to diminish in honor: *Righteous are thy decrees on all thy works: Who can extenuate thee?* (Milton).
[< Latin *extenuāre* (with English *-ate*[1]) < *ex-* out + *tenuis* thin]

ex|ten|u|at|ing circumstances (ek sten′yu̇ ā′ting), circumstances that tend to diminish culpability: *The young criminal's unsatisfactory home conditions were regarded by the judge as extenuating circumstances.*

ex|ten|u|at|ing|ly (ek sten′yu̇ ā′ting lē), *adv.* in an extenuating manner; by way of extenuation.

ex|ten|u|a|tion (ek sten′yu̇ ā′shən), *n.* **1** the act or process of extenuating: *The lawyer pleaded his client's youth in extenuation of the crime.* **2** extenuated condition. **3** something that lessens the seriousness of guilt, a fault, or an offense; a partial excuse.

ex|ten|u|a|tive (ek sten′yu̇ ā′tiv), *adj.* **1** having to do with or like extenuation. **2** tending to extenuate; extenuating.

ex|ten|u|a|tor (ek sten′yu̇ ā′tər), *n.* a person who extenuates.

ex|ten|u|a|to|ry (ek sten′yu̇ ə tôr′ē, -tōr′-), *adj.* that extenuates.

ex|te|ri|or (ek stir′ē ər), *n., adj.* —***n.*** **1** an outer surface or part; outward appearance; outside: *I saw only the exterior of the house, not the interior. The exterior of the house was made of brick.* (*Figurative.*) *The gruff old man has a harsh exterior but a kind heart.* **2a** an outdoor scene on the stage. **b** a motion picture made outdoors. —***adj.*** **1** on the outside; outer: *The skin of an apple is its exterior covering.* **SYN**: outward, external. **2** coming from without; happening outside: (*Figurative.*) *exterior influences.* **SYN**: extrinsic. **3** *Obsolete.* foreign.
[< Latin *exterior,* comparative of *exterus* outside < *ex* out of] —**ex|te′ri|or|ly,** *adv.*

***exterior angle,** **1** any one of the four angles formed outside of two parallel lines intersected by a straight line. **2** an angle formed by a side of a closed polygon and the extension of an adjacent side.

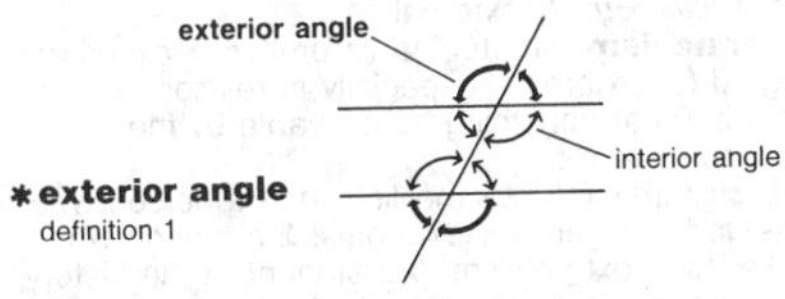

***exterior angle** definition 1

exterior galaxy, = extragalactic nebula.

ex|te|ri|or|i|ty (ek stir′ē ôr′ə tē, -or′-), *n., pl.* **-ties.** **1** the state or fact of being exterior. **2** something exterior. **3** an outward circumstance.

ex|te|ri|or|i|za|tion (ek stir′ē ər ə zā′shən), *n.* the process of making exterior or external.

ex|te|ri|or|ize (ek stir′ē ə rīz), *v.t.,* **-ized, -iz|ing.** **1** to make exterior: *The war dances, chants and witch doctors of primitive societies may all serve a useful purpose in exteriorizing stress—getting rid of it* (Atlantic). **2** to externalize (a conception).

ex|ter|mi|nate (ek stėr′mə nāt), *v.t.,* **-nat|ed, -nat|ing.** to destroy completely: *This poison will exterminate rats.* **SYN**: extirpate, eradicate, annihilate. [< Latin *extermināre* (with English *-ate*[1]) drive out (in Late Latin, destroy) < *ex-* out of + *termināre* to bound < *terminus* boundary]

ex|ter|mi|na|tion (ek stėr′mə nā′shən), *n.* complete destruction: *Poison and traps are useful for the extermination of rats.*

extermination camp, a concentration camp, especially one established by the Nazis in various European countries for the mass destruction

---

Pronunciation Key: hat, āge, cãre, fär; let, ēqual, tėrm, it, īce; hot, ōpen, ôrder; oil, out; cup, pu̇t, rüle; child; long; thin; ᴛʜen; zh, measure; ə represents **a** in about, **e** in taken, **i** in pencil, **o** in lemon, **u** in circus.

of prisoners in gas chambers and crematories; death camp.

ex|ter|mi|na|tive (ek stėr′mə nā′tiv), *adj.* tending to exterminate.

ex|ter|mi|na|tor (ek stėr′mə nā′tər), *n.* **1** a person or thing that exterminates. **2** a person whose business is exterminating fleas, cockroaches, lice, bedbugs, rats, and other pests.

ex|ter|mi|na|to|ry (ek stėr′mə nə tôr′ē, -tōr′-), *adj.* serving or tending to exterminate.

ex|ter|mine (ek stėr′mən), *v.t.,* **-mined, -min|ing.** *Obsolete.* to exterminate.

ex|tern (eks′tėrn, ek stėrn′), *n., adj.* **—*n.*** a person connected with a hospital or other institution, but not residing in it. Also, **externe.**
—*adj.* *Poetic.* outside; outward; external.
[< Latin *externus* belonging to the outside; see etym. under **external**]

ex|ter|nal (ek stėr′nəl), *adj., n.* **—*adj.*** **1** on the outside; outer: *An ear of corn has an external husk.* **SYN:** outward, exterior. **2** entirely outside; coming from without: *the external air.* **3** to be used only on the outside of the body: *Liniment and rubbing alcohol are external remedies.*
4 having existence outside one's mind. **5** *Figurative.* easily seen but not essential; superficial: *Going to church is an external act of worship. His art criticism had external brilliance but no substance.*
6 having to do with international affairs; foreign: *War affects a nation's external trade.* **7** *Zoology, Anatomy.* situated toward or on the outer surface; remote from the median line or center. **8** *British.* (of a student) having studied elsewhere than in the university where he is examined: *Once a year he returned to London to sit for his exams as an external student after pirating the appropriate learning from half a dozen different universities* (Manchester Guardian).
—*n.* an outer surface or part; outside.
externals, clothing, manners, or other outward acts or appearances: *He judges people by mere externals rather than by their character.*
[< Latin *externus* outside (< *exterus* outside < *ex* out of) + English *-al*^{1}] **—ex|ter′nal|ly,** *adv.*

ex|ter|nal-com|bus|tion engine (ek stėr′nəl-kəm bus′chən), an engine in which the pressure is produced by fuel ignited outside the cylinder, as a steam engine.

external ear, the outer part of the ear, including the passage leading to the middle ear; auricle and meatus; outer ear.

external fertilization, the fertilization of an egg, especially a human ovum, outside the body, usually by the introduction of sperm into an egg cell surgically removed from an ovary: *The so-called test-tube babies were of course not monsters but simply ordinary babies produced by external fertilization* (John Newell). *Some clergymen saw no ethical problems in external fertilization: others called it interference with nature* (Albin Krebs).

external galaxy, = extragalactic nebula.

ex|ter|nal|ise (ex stėr′nə līz), *v.t.,* **-ised, -is|ing.** *Especially British.* externalize.

ex|ter|nal|ism (eks tėr′nə liz əm), *n.* **1** excessive regard for externals, especially in religion. **2** the doctrine that only things observable by the senses have reality.

ex|ter|nal|ist (ek stėr′nə list), *n.* **1** a person who has undue regard for externals. **2** a person who believes in externalism. **3** a student of the history of science and the social effects of science.

ex|ter|nal|is|tic (ek stėr′nə lis′tik), *adj.* of or having to do with externalism; regarding what is merely external and not essential.

ex|ter|nal|i|ty (eks′tėr nal′ə tē), *n., pl.* **-ties. 1** the quality or condition of being external. **2** an external thing.

ex|ter|nal|i|za|tion (ek stėr′nə lə zā′shən), *n.* **1** the act or process of externalizing. **2** the fact or condition of being externalized.

ex|ter|nal|ize (ek stėr′nə līz), *v.t.,* **-ized, -iz|ing.** to make external; embody in an outward form.

external respiration, the exchange of oxygen and carbon dioxide between the environment and the respiratory organs; breathing.

ex|ter|nals (ek stėr′nəlz), *n.pl.* See **external.**

external screw, a cylindrical metal pin with a thread winding around the outside; male screw.

external senses, the senses that are stimulated by things outside the body, such as the senses of hearing, sight, smell, taste, and touch; the exteroceptive senses.

external world, *Philosophy.* everything that exists outside the conscious mind; the world of external objects.

ex|terne (eks′tėrn, ek stėrn′), *n.* = extern.

ex|ter|ni|za|tion (ek stėr′nə zā′shən), *n.* = externalization: *The Universe is the externization of the soul* (Emerson).

ex|ter|nize (ek stėr′nīz, eks′tər-), *v.t.,* **-nized, -niz|ing.** = externalize.

ex|ter|no|me|di|an (ek stėr′nō mē′dē ən), *adj. Zoology.* exterior to the central line.

ex|ter|o|cep|tive (eks′tər ō sep′tiv), *adj.* having to do with or aroused by stimuli from outside the body: *Vision is an exteroceptive sense.*

ex|ter|o|cep|tor (eks′tər ō sep′tər), *n.* a sense organ stimulated from outside the body, such as the eye or ear. [< Latin *exter* outside < English (re)*ceptor*]

ex|ter|res|tri|al (eks′tə res′trē əl), *adj.* = extraterrestrial.

ex|ter|ri|to|ri|al (eks′ter ə tôr′ē əl, -tōr′-), *adj.* = extraterritorial. **—ex′ter|ri|to′ri|al|ly,** *adv.*

ex|ter|ri|to|ri|al|i|ty (eks′ter ə tôr′ē al′ə tē, -tōr′-), *n.* = extraterritoriality.

ex|tinct (ek stingkt′), *adj.* **1** no longer existing: *The dinosaur is an extinct animal.* **SYN:** dead.
2 no longer active; extinguished: *an extinct volcano.* **3** (of offices, titles, or the like) obsolete; having no living possessor or qualified claimant: *With his death the family name became extinct.*
[< Latin *exstīnctus,* past participle of *exstinguere;* see etym. under **extinguish**]

ex|tinc|teur (eks tᴀɴk tœr′), *n. French.* a fire extinguisher.

ex|tinc|tion (ek stingk′shən), *n.* **1** the act or process of extinguishing: *The sudden extinction of the lights left us in darkness.* **2** the condition of being extinguished; extinct condition: *Regression or devolution and extinction are quite as much a part of the total record as is progression* (Beals and Hoijer). **3** the act or process of doing away with completely; wiping out; destruction; suppression: *Physicians are working for the extinction of diseases.*

ex|tinc|tive (ek stingk′tiv), *adj.* tending or serving to extinguish.

ex|tine (eks′tin, -tīn), *n. Botany.* the outer coat of a pollen grain. Also, **exine.** [< Latin *extimus,* most outward, superlative of *exter* outward + English *-ine*^{1}]

ex|tin|guish (ek sting′gwish), *v.t.* **1** to put out; quench: *Water extinguished the fire.* **2** to bring to an end; do away with; wipe out; destroy: (*Figurative.*) *One failure after another extinguished her hope. The authority of the ... government is everywhere extinguished* (Edmund Burke). **SYN:** obliterate, annihilate, exterminate. See syn. under **abolish. 3** to eclipse or obscure by superior brilliancy; outshine. **4** to annul (a right or claim); nullify. [< Latin *exstinguere* (< *ex-* out + *stinguere* quench) + English *-ish*^{2}]

ex|tin|guish|a|ble (ek sting′gwi shə bəl), *adj.* that can be extinguished.

ex|tin|guish|er (ek sting′gwi shər), *n.* **1** a person or thing that extinguishes. **2** an apparatus for putting out fires: *Using extinguishers, single-handed, he put out the fire and did not leave the vehicle until all danger was passed* (London Times).
3 a conical cap with which to extinguish a lighted candle.

ex|tin|guish|ment (ek sting′gwish mənt), *n.* **1** the act of extinguishing, especially the putting an end to, as a law, or the wiping out of, as a debt.
2 the fact of being extinguished.

ex|tir|pate (eks′tər pāt, ek stėr′-), *v.t.,* **-pat|ed, -pat|ing. 1** to remove completely; destroy totally; root out; eradicate: *We look forward to the day when disease and poverty will be extirpated.* **SYN:** exterminated. **2** to tear up by the roots; remove root and branch. [< Latin *exstirpāre* (with English *-ate*^{1}) < *ex-* out + *stirps, stirpis* a root, stock]

ex|tir|pa|tion (eks′tər pā′shən), *n.* **1** complete removal; total destruction: *Experiments on rats involving the extirpation of portions of the cortex have shown that particular memories are not located in one particular region ...* (S. A. Barnett).
2 the act of tearing up by the roots.

ex|tir|pa|tive (eks′tər pā′tiv), *adj.* tending to extirpate.

ex|tir|pa|tor (eks′tər pā′tər), *n.* a person or thing that extirpates.

ex|tir|pa|to|ry (ek stėr′pə tôr′ē, -tōr′-), *adj.* extirpating; serving to extirpate.

ex|tis|pex (ek stis′peks), *n., pl.* **-pi|ces** (-pə sēz). an ancient Roman who inspected the entrails of sacrificial animals for the purpose of divination; haruspex. [< Latin *extispex* < *exta* entrails + *specere* look at]

ex|tis|pi|cy (ek stis′pə sē), *n.* the practice of an extispex; haruspicy.

ex|tol or **ex|toll** (ek stōl′, -stol′), *v.t.,* **-tolled, -tol|ling.** to raise high with praise; praise highly; commend: *the newspapers extolled the brave soldiers. Critics of the American medical system are always extolling the virtues of Britain's National Health Service* (Franklin S. Ward). **SYN:** laud, eulogize. [< Latin *extollere* < *ex-* up + *tollere* raise]

ex|tol|ler (ek stō′lər, -stol′ər), *n.* a person who extols; a praiser or eulogizer.

ex|tol|ling|ly (ek stō′ling lē, -stol′ing-), *adv.* in an extolling manner; in commendation or praise: *A celebrated physician spoke to me extollingly of Bath* (Argosy).

ex|tol|ment or **ex|toll|ment** (ek stōl′mənt, -stol′-), *n.* the act of extolling or praising; eulogy.

ex|tor|sion (ek stôr′shən), *n.* an outward turning or rotation, as of the eye. [< *ex-*^{1} + *torsion*]

ex|tor|sive (ek stôr′siv), *adj.* = extortive.

ex|tort (ek stôrt′), *v.t.* **1** to obtain (money, a promise, or other commitment) by threats, force, fraud, or wrong use of authority: *Blackmailers try to extort money from their victims.* **SYN:** See syn. under **extract. 2** to take unlawfully by using one's official position. [< Latin *extortus,* past participle of *extorquēre* twist out < *ex-* out + *torquēre* twist] **—ex|tort′er,** *n.*

ex|tor|tion (ek stôr′shən), *n.* **1** an extorting; obtaining of money, a promise, or other commitment, by threats, force, fraud, or illegal use of authority: *Collecting very high interest on loans is considered extortion and is forbidden by law.*
2 something extorted; money, a promise, or other commitment, obtained in this way. **3** *Law.* the crime of using one's official position to obtain money or other thing of value unlawfully.

ex|tor|tion|ar|y (ek stôr′shə ner′ē), *adj.* = extortionate.

ex|tor|tion|ate (ek stôr′shə nit), *adj.* **1** much too great; exorbitant: *International oil companies ... are currently being publicized sensationally ... as monopolists who fix prices to gain extortionate profits* (Wall Street Journal). **2** characterized by extortion: *extortionate demands.* **—ex|tor′tion|ate|ly,** *adv.*

ex|tor|tion|er (ek stôr′shə nər), *n.* = extortionist.

ex|tor|tion|ist (ek stôr′shə nist), *n.* a person who is guilty of extortion.

ex|tor|tive (ek stôr′tiv), *adj.* tending to extort; extortionate.

ex|tra (eks′trə), *adj., n., adv.* **—*adj.*** beyond what is usual, expected, or needed; additional: *extra fare, extra pay, extra favors.* **SYN:** supplemental, supplementary.
—*n.* **1** something extra; anything beyond what is usual, expected, or needed; *a new car equipped with many extras. Her bill for extras was $30.*
2 an additional charge: *Practically all steel products carry extras of one kind or another* (Wall Street Journal). **3** a special edition of a newspaper: *The paper published an extra to announce the end of the war.* **4** something of superior excellence or quality. **5** a person who is employed by the day to play minor parts in motion pictures: *Two hundred extras were hired for the battle scene.* **6** *Informal.* an additional worker: *We were Christmas extras in the toy department, Santa Claus's helpers* (Saul Bellow). **7** *Cricket.* a run scored other than from a hit, such as a bye, wide, or no-ball.
—*adv.* **1** more than usually: *extra fine quality. With railroads extra busy some mills face shipping delays due to boxcar shortages* (Wall Street Journal). **SYN:** unusually. **2** in addition to the usual amount: *The larger edition contains three maps extra. I wouldn't care if I did go a little extra for it* (Harriet Beecher Stowe).
[probably short for *extraordinary*]

extra-, *prefix.* outside; beyond; besides, as in *extraordinary.* [< Latin *extra-* < *extrā* outside of]

ex|tra|al|i|men|ta|ry (eks′trə al′ə men′tər ē), *adj.* outside the alimentary canal.

ex|tra|ar|tis|tic (eks′trə är tis′tik), *adj.* out of the range of art; having nothing to do with art.

ex|tra-base hit (eks′trə bās′), *Baseball.* a two-base hit, three-base hit, or home run. *Bolin took over in the eighth inning after the Pirates had scored twice off Marichal, getting three extra-base hits during the inning* (New York Times).

ex|tra|bold (eks′trə bōld′), *n.* a style of type with very thick lines; very heavy boldface type.

ex|tra|bran|chi|al (eks′trə brang′kē əl), *adj., n.* **—*adj.*** *Anatomy.* outside of the branchial arches.
—*n.* an extrabranchial cartilage.

ex|tra|bron|chi|al (eks′trə brong′kē əl), *adj.* outside of the bronchial tubes.

ex|tra|ca|non|i|cal (eks′trə kə non′ə kəl), *adj.* not included in the canon of Scripture.

ex|tra|car|pal (eks′trə kär′pəl), *adj.* outside the carpal region.

ex|tra|cel|lu|lar (eks′trə sel′yə lər), *adj.* situated or taking place outside of a cell or cells: *The weight loss is due mainly to loss of fat and extracellular body fluid* (Science News Letter).
—ex′tra|cel′lu|lar|ly, *adv.*

ex|tra|chance (eks′trə chans′, -chäns′), *adj.* beyond the normal range of chance; not accidental: *The findings ... are dependent on clerical and statistical errors ... all extrachance results not so explicable are dependent on deliberate fraud* (Time).

ex|tra|chro|mo|so|mal (eks′trə krō′mə sō′məl), *adj.* occurring or operating outside the chromosomes: *extrachromosomal particles or elements, extrachromosomal mechanisms of heredity.*

ex|tra|con|densed (eks′trə kən denst′), *adj.* (of type) having a very narrow face.

ex|tra|con|sti|tu|tion|al (eks′trə kon′stə tü′shə-nəl, -tyü′-), *adj.* beyond the control or influence of the constitution of a nation; not included in or provided for by the national constitution: *The cabinet of the President of the United States is extraconstitutional.*

ex|tra|cor|po|re|al (eks′trə kôr pôr′ē əl, -pōr′-), *adj.* outside the body: *He is being honored for his pioneering efforts in the field of extracorporeal circulation, which resulted in the development of a heart-lung apparatus* (Science).

extra cover, *Cricket.* **1** a fieldsman whose position is between cover-point and mid-off, but more distant than either from the batsman's wicket. **2** his position in the field: *Dollery had batted for two hours when he drove Marlar to extra cover* (London Times).

ex|tra|cra|ni|al (eks′trə krā′nē əl), *adj.* lying or situated outside of the skull. [< *extra-* + *cranial*]

ex|tract (*v.* ek strakt′; *n.* eks′trakt), *v., n.* —*v.t.* **1a** to draw out, usually with some effort; *to extract a tooth,* (*Figurative.*) *to extract a confession, to extract iron from the earth.* **b** *Figurative.* to force (money, a promise, or other commitment) from; extort. **2** to obtain by pressing, squeezing, or distillation: *to extract oil from olives.* **3** to deduce, especially from some data; infer: *to extract a principle from a collection of facts.* **4** to derive; obtain; secure: (*Figurative.*) *to extract pleasure from a party.* **5** to take out (a passage) from a book, speech, play, or other literary work; make extracts from; excerpt: *He extracted several sections from the article to read at the meeting.* **6** to calculate or find (the root of a number or expression).

—*n.* **1** something drawn out or taken out; a passage taken from a book, speech, play, or other literary work; quotation; excerpt: *He read several extracts from the poem.* SYN: citation, selection. **2a** a concentrated preparation of a substance: *Vanilla extract, made from vanilla beans, is used as flavoring.* **b** *Pharmacy.* a dry substance made from a plant, drug, or substance, by dissolving the active ingredients and then evaporating the solvent: *extract of malt.*

[< Latin *extractus,* past participle of *extrahere* draw out < *ex-* out + *trahere* draw]

—*Syn. v.t.* **1a, b Extract, extort** mean to draw out with force. **Extract** implies pulling out something hard to get loose: *The dentist extracted her wisdom tooth.* **Extort** suggests wringing something from a person who does not want to give it up: *Not even torture could extort from him the names of his companions.*

ex|tract|a|ble (ek strak′tə bəl), *adj.* that can be extracted: *Here* [*in the Santa Cruz Basin*] *the extractable organic content is at least three to four times as great as in the Grande Isle core, and more aromatics than paraffin-naphthenes were found* (P. V. Smith).

ex|tract|ant (ek strak′tənt), *n.* a substance capable of extracting a mineral or other substance from solution: *Fused salts dissolved in liquid bismuth look promising as extractants of fission products from the fuel* (Scientific American).

ex|tract|i|ble (ek strak′tə bəl), *adj.* = extractable.

ex|trac|ti|form (ek strak′tə fôrm), *adj.* having the nature or appearance of an extract.

ex|trac|tion (ek strak′shən), *n.* **1** the act or process of extracting; pulling, drawing, or taking out: *the extraction of a tooth.* **2** the state of being extracted. **3** racial, national, or family origin; lineage; descent: *Miss Del Rio is of Spanish extraction; her parents came from Spain.* **4** an extracted substance or object; extract.

extraction unit, a machine that removes impurities, such as dust, sulphur, and water, from natural gas.

ex|trac|tive (ek strak′tiv), *adj., n.* —*adj.* **1** extracting; tending to extract. **2** that can be extracted. **3** deriving products from nature, as agriculture or mining does. **4** of the nature of an extract.

—*n.* an extractive substance. —**ex|trac′tive|ly,** *adv.*

extractive industry, an industry that derives its products from nature, as agriculture or mining.

extractive metallurgy, the first stage of refining metals, including mineral dressing, electrolysis, amalgamation, smelting, and leaching; recovery metallurgy.

ex|trac|tor (ek strak′tər), *n.* **1** a person or thing that extracts. **2** the part of a gun or rifle which pulls the cartridge or shell case out of the chamber so that it may be ejected after firing.

extract wool, wool that is recovered from rags of various cloths in which cotton and wool are woven together.

ex|tra|cu|ri|al (eks′trə kyůr′ē əl), *adj.* arranged, settled, or made outside a court of law. [< *extra-* + Latin *cūria* place of assembly; court + English *-al*[1]]

ex|tra|cur|ric|u|lar (eks′trə kə rik′yə lər), *adj.* **1** outside the regular course of study; of or having to do with activities such as sports, dramatics, or clubs, usually supervised by the faculty: *Football, dramatics, and debating are extracurricular activities in our high school.* **2** *Figurative.* outside the regular limits, usual capacity, or normal conduct of a job, profession, or activity: *extracurricular campaign fund collections. There should not be an assortment of extracurricular activities going on in the kitchen while the housewife is trying to prepare a meal* (New York Times). —**ex′tra|cur|ric′u|lar|ly,** *adv.*

ex|tra|cur|ric|u|lar|ism (eks′trə kə rik′yə lər iz′əm), *n.* extracurricular tendencies or activities.

ex|tra|cur|ric|u|lum (eks′trə kə rik′yə ləm), *adj.* = extracurricular.

ex|tra|cu|ta|ne|ous (eks′trə kyü tā′nē əs), *adj.* outside the true skin. [< *extra-* + New Latin *cutaneus* (with English *-ous*) < Latin *cutis* skin]

ex|tra|dit|a|ble (eks′trə dī′tə bəl), *adj.* **1** that can be extradited: *A person accused of murder in one state is extraditable if he is caught in another state.* **2** for which a person can be extradited: *Murder is an extraditable crime.*

ex|tra|dite (eks′trə dīt), *v.t.,* **-dit|ed, -dit|ing. 1** to give up or deliver (a fugitive or prisoner) to another state, nation, or authority: *If an escaped prisoner of the state of Ohio is caught in Indiana, he can be extradited from Indiana to Ohio.* **2** to obtain the surrender of (such a person). [back formation < *extradition*]

ex|tra|di|tion (eks′trə dish′ən), *n.* the surrender of a fugitive or prisoner by one state, nation, or legal authority to another. [< French *extradition* < Latin *ex-* out + *trāditiō, -ōnis* a delivering up < *trādere* trade < *trāns-* over + *dare* give]

ex|tra|dos (ek strā′dos), *n., pl.* **-dos** or **-dos|es.** the exterior curve or surface of an arch or vault. [< French *extrados* < Latin *extrā* outside + French *dos* back < Latin *dorsum*]

extra dry cider, = hard cider.

ex|tra|ga|lac|tic (eks′trə gə lak′tik), *adj.* outside of our own galaxy: *the measurement of extragalactic distances.*

extragalactic nebula, a nebula or galaxy present outside of our own galaxy; exterior galaxy; external galaxy: *The Magellanic Clouds are extragalactic nebulae visible to the naked eye.*

ex|tra|gov|ern|men|tal (eks′trə guv′ərn men′təl), *adj.* outside the jurisdiction of a government: *Europe is gradually uniting in extragovernmental and supernational organizations* (Harper's).

ex|tra|haz|ard|ous (eks′trə haz′ər dəs), *adj.* involving more than ordinary hazard, risk, or peril: *A steeplejack has an extrahazardous occupation.*

ex|tra|he|pat|ic (eks′trə hi pat′ik), *adj.* situated outside the liver: *extrahepatic bile ducts.*

ex|tra|his|tor|i|cal (eks′trə his tôr′ə kəl, -tor′-), *adj.* beyond the range of history.

ex|tra-il|lus|trate (eks′trə il′ə strāt, -i lus′trāt), *v.t.,* **-trat|ed, -trat|ing.** to add illustrations to (a book) after it is printed or published, by pasting or binding them in.

ex|tra|ju|di|cial (eks′trə jü dish′əl), *adj.* beyond the action or authority of a law court; occurring outside a court: *an extrajudicial settlement.* —**ex′tra|ju|di′cial|ly,** *adv.*

ex|tra ju|di|ci|um (eks′trə jü dish′ē əm), *Latin.* beyond the judicial field or scope.

ex|tra|ju|ral (eks′trə jůr′əl), *adj.* = extrajudicial.

ex|tra|lat|er|al (eks′trə lat′ər əl), *adj.* **1** placed or extending beyond the sides. **2** having to do with the right of a mine owner to a part of his vein or lode extending beyond the side lines of his claim.

ex|tra|le|gal (eks′trə lē′gəl), *adj.* outside the control or influence of law: *Partly by their own desire to cluster together and partly by extralegal confinement, the Negroes are concentrated in ghettos* (Atlantic). —**ex′tra|le′gal|ly,** *adv.*

ex|tra|lim|it|al (eks′trə lim′ə təl), *adj.* beyond the limits of a country or district.

ex|tra|lin|guis|tic (eks′trə ling gwis′tik), *adj.* outside the province of language or linguistics: *Thus the MEANING relation, particularly in the case of lexical designation—for example, that the English word table designates "table", has seemed to some not to be part of linguistics, since it involves references to extralinguistic events* (Harvey B. Sarles). —**ex′tra|lin|guis′ti|cal|ly,** *adv.*

ex|tra|lit|er|ar|y (eks′trə lit′ə rer′ē), *adj.* outside the scope of literature: *If literature is to be called on for all manner of extraliterary functions . . . to order our lives or to become our effective religion . . . gaps in the literary attitude are likely to become serious* (Listener).

ex|tral|i|ty (ek stral′ə tē), *n. Informal.* extraterritoriality.

ex|tra|lu|nar (eks′trə lü′nər), *adj.* coming from or existing outside the moon: *A small fraction* [*of lunar breccias*] *is an extralunar component of meteoritic or cometary origin* (Scientific American).

ex|tra|mar|gin|al (eks′trə mär′jə nəl), *adj. Psychology.* outside the field of consciousness.

ex|tra|mar|i|tal (eks′trə mar′ə təl), *adj.* outside the bonds of marriage: *extramarital sexual relations.* —**ex′tra|mar′i|tal|ly,** *adv.*

ex|tra|men|tal (eks′trə men′təl), *adj.* beyond the mind; independent of mental apprehension.

ex|tra mo|dum (eks′trə mō′dəm), *Latin.* **1** beyond measure. **2** to excess.

ex|tra|mo|lec|u|lar (eks′trə mə lek′yə lər), *adj.* outside the molecule.

ex|tra|mo|rain|ic (eks′trə mō rā′nik), *adj. Geology.* of glacial origin though occurring in regions beyond the outermost terminal moraine.

ex|tra|mun|dane (eks′trə mun′dān), *adj.* beyond our world or the material universe: *For a youth in search of identification, the urgency to life, which he finds in jazz, becomes a vital symbol of hope and extramundane aspiration* (Atlantic).

ex|tra|mu|ral (eks′trə myůr′əl), *adj.* **1a** occurring outside the boundaries of a college, school, or other institution: *extramural activities.* **b** having to do with informally arranged competition between colleges: *extramural sports.* **c** *Especially British.* of or having to do with lectures or courses offered by a university to persons not students in the university. **2** outside the walls or boundaries of a city or town. [< Latin *extrā mūrōs* outside the walls + English *-al*[1]] —**ex′tra|mu′ral|ly,** *adv.*

ex|tra|mu|si|cal (eks′trə myü′zə kəl), *adj.* outside the field or sphere of music: *extramusical sounds, such as the trumpeting of geese.*

ex|tra|nat|u|ral (eks′trə nach′ər əl), *adj.* outside the operation of natural law.

ex|tra|ne|ous (ek strā′nē əs), *adj.* **1** from outside; not belonging; foreign: *Sand and some other extraneous matter had got into the butter and ruined it.* **2** not part of what is under consideration; not essential; external: *The speaker made many extraneous remarks.* [< Latin *extrāneus* (with English *-ous*) < *extrā* outside < *ex* out of. See etym. of doublet **strange.**] —**ex|tra′ne|ous|ly,** *adv.* —**ex|tra′ne|ous|ness,** *n.*

ex|tra|neu|ral (eks′trə nůr′əl, -nyůr′-), *adj.* outside a nerve, neuron, or the nervous system: *extraneural tissue.*

ex|tra|nu|cle|ar (eks′trə nü′klē ər, -nyü′-), *adj.* existing or acting outside the nucleus: *The chemical properties of an atom depend chiefly on the number of extranuclear electrons.*

ex|tra|oc|u|lar (eks′trə ok′yə lər), *adj.* situated or occurring outside the eyes: *the extraocular muscles of the eyeball.*

ex|tra|of|fi|cial (eks′trə ə fish′əl), *adj.* outside of the ordinary duties, rights, or privileges of an office.

ex|traor|di|naire (ek′strôr di nãr′), *adj.* remarkable; extraordinary: *In a cluttered rear corner is the unprepossessing Tudor City Meat Market, presided over for the last four years by Ralph Annibale, butcher extraordinaire* (New York Times). [< French *extraordinaire* extraordinary]

ex|traor|di|nar|i|ly (ek strôr′də ner′ə lē, -strôr′dəner′-), *adv.* in an extraordinary manner; to an extraordinary degree; most unusually.

ex|traor|di|nar|i|ness (ek strôr′də ner′ē nis), *n.* the character of being extraordinary; uncommonness; remarkableness.

ex|traor|di|nar|y (ek strôr′də ner′ē; *especially for 2* eks′trə ôr′-), *adj.* **1** beyond what is ordinary; very unusual or remarkable: *Eight feet is an extraordinary height for a person.* SYN: uncommon, exceptional, singular. **2** ranking below the regular class of officials; special. An envoy extraordinary is one sent on a special mission; he ranks below an ambassador. [< Latin *extraordinārius* < *extrā ōrdinem* out of the (usual) order < *extrā* out + *ōrdō, -inis* order, rank]

ex|tra or|di|nem (eks′trə ôr′də nem), *Latin.* **1** beyond the usual order. **2** in an extraordinary manner, measure, or degree.

ex|tra|o|vate (eks′trə ō′vāt), *adj. Biology.* exterior to the egg.

ex|tra|pa|ren|tal (eks′trə pə ren′təl), *adj.* beyond the action or authority of parents.

ex|tra|par|lia|men|ta|ry (eks′trə pär′lə men′tər ē, -trē), *adj.* beyond the action or authority of parliament.

ex|tra|pa|ro|chi|al (eks′trə pə rō′kē əl), *adj.* **1** outside of a parish. **2** not included in any parish. **3** exempt from liability to parish obligations.

ex|tra|phys|i|cal (eks′trə fiz′ə kəl), *adj.* not subject to physical laws or methods.

ex|trap|o|la|bil|i|ty (ek strap′ə lə bil′ə tē, eks′trəpə-), *n., pl.* **-ties.** the ability to extrapolate or infer possibilities from available data: *We explored many traditional processes and sites, and from our observations are now trying to extrapolate what we can about ancient methodology. Obviously the degree of extrapolability from evidence*

Pronunciation Key: hat, āge, cãre, fär; let, ēqual, tėrm; it, īce; hot, ōpen, ôrder; oil, out; cup, pu̇t, rüle; child; long; thin; ᴛʜen; zh, measure; ə represents a in about, e in taken, i in pencil, o in lemon, u in circus.

or [from] crafts extant today must vary enormously from case to case (Theodore A. Wertime).

ex|trap|o|late (ek strap′ə lāt, eks′trə pə-), *v.t., v.i.,* **-lat|ed, -lat|ing.** to calculate or infer from what is known something that is possible but unknown; predict from facts: *Science fiction writers often extrapolate from today's trends. The unconscious tendency of most forecasters is to "extrapolate" the recent business curve* (Newsweek). [< *extra-* + (inter)*polate*]

ex|trap|o|la|tion (ek strap′ə lā′shən, eks′trə pə-), *n.* the action or method of extrapolating: *If these extrapolations are true, then 2,000,000 of the Kennedy margin came from television's impact on the American mind* (Theodore H. White).

ex|trap|o|la|tive (ek strap′ə lā′tiv), *adj.* extrapolating; based on extrapolation: *extrapolative planning.*

ex|trap|o|la|tor (ek strap′ə lā′tər), *n.* a person who extrapolates: *The advent of atomic power is at hand, and ... fission machines will multiply rather more rapidly than cautious extrapolators prophesy* (Bulletin of Atomic Scientists).

ex|trap|o|la|to|ry (ek strap′ə lə tôr′ē, -tōr′-), *adj.* that extrapolates: *The atomic theory, once termed extrapolatory reasoning, is now accepted as fact.*

ex|tra|pro|fes|sion|al (eks′trə prə fesh′ə nəl, -fesh′nəl), *adj.* beyond the ordinary limits of professional interest or duty.

ex|tra|pu|ni|tive (eks′trə pyü′nə tiv), *adj.* inflicting punishment upon all but oneself; having the tendency to blame misfortune on others: *The bigot ... is extrapunitive rather than intropunitive and overtly glorifies his parents and himself* (Urie Bronfenbrenner). [< *extra-* + *punitive*] —**ex′tra-pu′ni|tive|ness,** *n.*

ex|tra|py|ram|i|dal (eks′trə pə ram′ə dəl), *adj.* outside the pyramidal tract of the spinal cord: *an extrapyramidal disorder, the extrapyramidal motor system.*

ex|tra|red (eks′trə red′), *adj.* = infrared.

ex|tra|sci|en|tif|ic (eks′trə sī′ən tif′ik), *adj.* outside the scope or range of science: *Nor for that matter can the young scientist really spend much time on extrascientific affairs and still do outstanding work in his subject* (Edward Shils).

ex|tra|sen|so|ry (eks′trə sen′sər ē), *adj.* beyond the normal range of the sense organs: *The great majority of scientists remain unconvinced by extrasensory research* (Scientific American).

extrasensory perception, the perceiving of thoughts or actions through other than the normal senses; thought transference; mental telepathy: *Extrasensory perception does not often reach a forum for serious debate among scientists* (Scientific American). *Abbr:* ESP (no periods).

ex|tra|so|lar (eks′trə sō′lər), *adj.* found or existing outside the solar system: *The search for extrasolar planets has been going on for 32 years, slowly, painstakingly, with none of the excitement of more glamorous fields of science* (Peter van de Kamp).

ex|tra|sys|to|le (eks′trə sis′tə lē), *n.* an abnormal contraction in the normal rhythmical beat of the heart.

ex|tra|sys|tol|ic (eks′trə sis tol′ik), *adj.* of or characterized by abnormal contractions of the heart.

ex|tra|tel|lu|ri|an (eks′trə te lůr′ē ən), *adj.* beyond or away from the earth; not belonging to the earth.

ex|tra|tel|lu|ric (eks′trə te lůr′ik), *adj.* = extratellurian.

ex|tra|ter|res|tri|al (eks′trə tə res′trē əl), *adj., n.* —*adj.* outside or originating away from the earth and its atmosphere: *extraterrestrial radiations, extraterrestrial regions. Study of lunar organic matter should throw light on such problems as the ... possibility of extraterrestrial life* (Scientific American).

—*n.* a creature from another planet: *... widespread popular interest in the possibility of contact with intelligent extraterrestrials* (Saturday Review). —**ex′tra|ter|res′tri|al|ly,** *adv.*

ex|tra|ter|ri|to|ri|al (eks′trə ter′ə tôr′ē əl, -tōr′-), *adj.* **1** having to do with freedom from the jurisdiction of the country that a person is in. Any ambassador to the United States has certain extraterritorial privileges. **2** beyond territorial limits or jurisdiction. Also, **exterritorial.** —**ex′tra|ter′ri-to′ri|al|ly,** *adv.*

ex|tra|ter|ri|to|ri|al|i|ty (eks′trə ter′ə tôr′ē al′ə tē, -tōr′-), *n.* **1** the privilege of having extraterritorial rights: *I should have had to explain about the Opium Wars and the Boxer Rebellion and the Unequal Treaties, the extraterritoriality whereby the white man walked the earth free from arrest by a Chinese authority* (Harper's). **2** lack of association with any particular country or territory; international character; cosmopolitanism: *... such contemporary cultural developments as ... the "extraterritoriality" (or multitonguedness) of such literary masters as Vladimir Nabokov, Jorge Luis Borges and Samuel Beckett* (Christopher Lehmann-Haupt). Also, **exterritoriality.**

ex|tra|the|cal (eks′trə thē′kəl), *adj. Zoology, Botany.* situated outside the theca.

ex|tra|the|is|tic (eks′trə thē is′tik), *adj.* beyond the range of theism; outside of theistic study.

ex|tra|trop|i|cal (eks′trə trop′ə kəl), *adj.* outside or originating outside the tropics; occurring in middle and higher latitudes of either hemisphere: *The uncertainties of weather forecasting were forcibly dramatized in the extratropical cyclone that brought killer floods to the Northeast last weekend* (New York Times).

ex|tra|u|ni|ver|si|ty (eks′trə yü′nə vėr′sə tē), *adj.* of or having to do with matters outside the university.

ex|tra ur|bem (ek′strə ėr′bəm), **1** *Latin.* outside the city (Rome). **2** chosen from among the clergy of places outside Rome: *Chamberlain of Honor (to the Pope) extra urbem.*

ex|tra|u|ter|ine (eks′trə yü′tər in, -tə rīn), *adj.* outside the uterus.

ex|trav|a|gance (ek strav′ə gəns), *n.* **1** careless and lavish spending; wastefulness of funds or resources: *His extravagance kept him always in debt.* **SYN**: dissipation. **2** the act of going beyond the bounds of reason; excess; absurd exaggeration: *The extravagance of his story made us doubt him.* **3** an extravagant action, idea, or purchase; unreasonable excess; absurdity: *Her mink coat is an extravagance.*

ex|trav|a|gan|cy (ek strav′ə gən sē), *n., pl.* **-cies.** = extravagance.

ex|trav|a|gant (ek strav′ə gənt), *adj.* **1** spending carelessly and lavishly; wasteful: *An extravagant person has extravagant tastes and habits.* **SYN**: prodigal, lavish. **2** beyond the bounds of reason; fantastically absurd; excessive: *an extravagant price, extravagant praise. A hat for $75 is extravagant. To call a poodle "the sweetest thing alive" is extravagant.* **SYN**: immoderate, inordinate, exorbitant. **3** *Obsolete.* wandering out of bounds; straying: *The extravagant and erring spirit hies To his confine* (Shakespeare). [< Medieval Latin *extravagans, -antis,* present participle of *extravagari* wander outside limits < Latin *extrā-* outside + *vagārī* wander < *vagus* wandering, unfixed] —**ex|trav′a|gant|ly,** *adv.* —**ex|trav′a|gant-ness,** *n.*

ex|trav|a|gan|za (ek strav′ə gan′zə), *n.* a fantastic play, piece of music, or literary composition. Musical comedies having elaborate scenery and gorgeous costumes are extravaganzas. [alteration of earlier Italian *estravaganza* peculiar behavior, after English *extravagance*]

ex|trav|a|gate (ek strav′ə gāt), *v.i.,* **-gat|ed, -gat|ing.** **1** to wander; stray. **2** to go beyond what is proper or reasonable. [< Medieval Latin *extravagari* (with English *-ate*[1]); see etym. under **extravagant**]

ex|trav|a|sate (ek strav′ə sāt), *v.,* **-sat|ed, -sat|ing,** *n.* —*v.t.* **1** to force out from the proper vessels through the surrounding parts, as of blood or lymph. **2** *Geology.* to force (petroleum) to the surface.

—*v.i.* **1** to escape from the proper vessels: *A hard blow may cause blood to extravasate, creating a bruise.* **2** *Geology.* to pour forth.

—*n.* any fluid which has been extravasated.

[< Latin *extrā* outside + *vās* vessel + English *-ate*[1]]

ex|trav|a|sa|tion (ek strav′ə sā′shən), *n.* **1** the act of extravasating: *If there is a tendency to cough, a large pad and a firm chest binder should be used in order to minimise extravasation of air* (Beaumont and Dodds). **2** extravasated matter.

ex|tra|vas|cu|lar (eks′trə vas′kyə lər), *adj.* **1** outside of the proper vessels. **2** not contained in vessels: *the extravascular circulatory system of insects.* **3** not vascular; having no blood vessels: *Skin is an extravascular structure.*

ex|tra|ve|hic|u|lar (eks′trə vi hik′yə lər), *adj.* **1** outside a vehicle in outer space; beyond an orbiting spacecraft: *Only by means of rendezvous, docking, and extravehicular activity can the astronauts venture onto the moon* (New York Times). **2** of or for activity outside a spacecraft: *Called the "Extravehicular Mobility Unit," the suit consists of a number of layers* (Science News Letter).

ex|tra|ven|tric|u|lar (eks′trə ven trik′yə lər), *adj.* not within a ventricle of either the heart or the brain.

ex|tra|ver|sion (eks′trə vėr′zhən), *n.* = extroversion.

ex|tra|vert (eks′trə vėrt), *n., v.t.* = extrovert.

ex|tra|vert|ed (eks′trə vėr′tid), *adj.* = extroverted.

ex|tra|vi|o|let (eks′trə vī′ə lit), *adj.* outside the visible spectrum just beyond the violet; ultraviolet.

ex|tra|vis|cer|al (eks′trə vis′ər əl), *adj.* outside the viscera.

ex|tra|zon|al (eks′trə zō′nəl), *adj.* outside a zone: *extrazonal facilities.*

ex|tre|mal (ek strē′məl), *adj. Mathematics.* of or having to do with extreme values; involving maximum and minimum values: *extremal problems.* [< *extrem*(um) + *-al*[1]]

ex|treme (ek strēm′), *adj.,* **-trem|er, -trem|est,** *n.* —*adj.* **1** much more than usual; very great or unusual: *extreme joy, extreme peril. Their surprise at his escape was therefore extreme* (Scott). **SYN**: immoderate. **2** going to the greatest possible lengths; very severe; very strong or violent: *an extreme case. The police took extreme measures to stop the riot.* **SYN**: radical, fanatical, excessive. **3** farthest from the center; outermost: *the extreme outlying districts of the city.* **4** at the very end; farthest possible: *The extreme north stops at the North Pole.* **SYN**: utmost. **5** last or final: *thy extreme hope, the loveliest and the last* (Shelley). **SYN**: ultimate.

—*n.* **1** something extreme; one of the two things as far or as different as possible from each other: *Love and hate are two extremes of feeling.* **2** the highest degree; beyond the ordinary or average: *Joy is happiness in the extreme. The extreme of coldness is absolute zero. Life in the East is fierce, short, hazardous, and in extremes* (Emerson). **3** an action or policy of excess; extreme measure. **4** *Mathematics.* the first or last term in a proportion or series: *In the proportion, 2 is to 4 as 8 is to 16, 2 and 16 are the extremes; 4 and 8 are the means.* **5** *Logic.* the major or minor term of a syllogism or the subject or predicate of a conclusion. **6** *Obsolete.* the utmost point of anything; end.

go to extremes, to do or say too much: *She goes to extremes of fashion and always overdresses.*

[< Old French *extreme,* learned borrowing from Latin *extrēmus,* superlative of *exterus* outside < *ex* out of] —**ex|treme′ness,** *n.*

ex|treme|ly (ek strēm′lē), *adv.* much more than usual; very: *It is extremely cold in the Arctic. Their house is extremely beautiful. All I can say further is that I still hope extremely to do some more* (Harper's).

extremely high frequency, = EHF.

extremely low frequency, = ELF.

extreme unction or **Extreme Unction,** a sacrament of the Roman Catholic Church and the Eastern Orthodox Churches, given by a priest to a person who is very sick, dying, or in danger of death; anointing of the sick. It consists of anointing with oil and reciting special prayers.

ex|trem|ism (ek strē′miz əm), *n.* a tendency or disposition to go to extremes: *The enemy is extremism—revolutionary or reactionary* (Scientific American).

ex|trem|ist (ek strē′mist), *n., adj.* —*n.* **1** a person who goes to extremes. **2** a supporter of extreme doctrines or practices: *Hemmed in between such extremists, French democracy this week faced the problem of erecting a government on the shifting sands* (Newsweek).

—*adj.* **1** belonging to or having to do with extremists: *Outside the four rebellious states, little extremist talk was heard* (Newsweek). **2** = radical.

ex|trem|i|ty (ek strem′ə tē), *n., pl.* **-ties.** **1** the very end; farthest possible place; last part or point; the tip: *Explorers have traveled to the extremities of the earth.* **2** very great danger or need: *In their extremity the people on the sinking ship bore themselves bravely.* **3** an extreme degree; that which reaches the utmost point: *Joy is the extremity of happiness.* **4** an extreme action or measure: *The soldiers were forced to the extremity of firing their rifles to scatter the angry mob. His business reverses forced him to the extremity of declaring himself bankrupt.*

extremities, a the hands and feet: *As the hunter sat in the open boat his extremities began to grow numb with cold.* **b** a person's last moments before death: *The king being in extremities, the priest was called to administer the last rites.*

ex|tre|mum (ek strē′məm), *n., pl.* **-ma** (-mə). *Mathematics.* a maximum or minimum value of a function. [< New Latin *extremum* < neuter of Latin *extrēmus* extreme]

ex|tri|ca|ble (eks′trə kə bəl), *adj.* that can be extricated.

ex|tri|cate (eks′trə kāt), *v.t.,* **-cat|ed, -cat|ing.** **1** to set free (from entanglements, difficulties, embarrassing situations, or the like); release: *He extricated the kitten from the net.* **2** to set free (as gas or heat) from a state of combination, for example during a chemical process. [< Latin *extrīcāre* (with English *-ate*[1]) < *ex-* out of + *trīcae* perplexities]

ex|tri|ca|tion (eks′trə kā′shən), *n.* **1** the act of extricating. **2** the condition of being extricated.

3 the act or process of setting free, as gas or heat, from something containing it.

ex|trin|sic (ek strin′sik), *adj.* **1** not essential or inherent; caused by external circumstances; accessory; additional: *extrinsic differences.* **2** being outside of a thing; coming from without; external; extraneous: *extrinsic influences.* **3** originating outside the part on which it acts: *the extrinsic muscles of the legs.* [< Late Latin *extrīnsicus* external, for *extrīnsecus* from outside < unrecorded Old Latin *extrim* from outside (< *exterus* outside) + *secus* following]

ex|trin|si|cal (ek strin′sə kəl), *adj.* = extrinsic.

ex|trin|si|cal|i|ty (ek strin′sə kal′ə tē), *n.* the state of being extrinsical.

ex|trin|si|cal|ly (ek strin′sə klē), *adv.* from without; externally.

ex|trin|si|cal|ness (ek strin′sə kəl nis), *n.* = extrinsicality.

extrinsic factor, = vitamin B_{12}.

ex|trorse (ek strôrs′), *adj. Botany.* turned or facing outward. Anthers that open away from the axis of the flower are extrorse. [< Late Latin *extrorsus* in an outward direction < *extrā* outside + *versus* turned (toward), past participle of *vertere* turn] —**ex|trorse′ly,** *adv.*

ex|tro|ver|sion (eks′trə vėr′zhən, -shən), *n.* **1** a tendency to be more interested in what is going on around one than in one's own thoughts and feelings. **2** the condition of being turned inside out, especially such a condition of the bladder. Also, **extraversion.**

ex|tro|ver|sive (eks′trə vėr′siv), *adj.* of extroversion; characterized by or inclined to extroversion; extrovertive: *Gruenther himself had once said he was too introverted for so extroversive a job as supreme commander* (Time).

ex|tro|vert (*n.* eks′trə vėrt; *v.* eks′trə vėrt′), *n., v.* —*n.* **1** a person more interested in what is going on around him than in his own thoughts and feelings; person tending to act rather than think. **2** a sociable person; person who makes friends easily. [< verb]
—*v.t.* to run outward; turn inside out. Also, **extravert.**
[< alteration of *extra-* + Latin *vertere* turn]

ex|tro|vert|ed (eks′trə vėr′tid), *adj.* characterized by extroversion; sociable: *He lived and breathed politics, and he felt most at home in the company of robust, extroverted cronies* (New Yorker). Also, **extraverted.**

ex|tro|ver|tish (eks′trə vėr′tish), *adj.* of an extrovert; having to do with or like an extrovert: *an affable, extrovertish manner.*

ex|tro|ver|tism (eks′trə vėr′tiz əm), *n.* extroverted quality or character; outgoingness; sociability: *... the extrovertism of a group of performers consistently more involved with their audience than with their footwork* (Dan Sullivan).

ex|tro|ver|tive (eks′trə vėr′tiv), *adj.* tending to extroversion: *Actors are not the extrovertive creatures they are generally considered* (Wall Street Journal).

ex|tro|vert|ly (eks′trə vėr′tlē), *adv.* in an extroverted manner: *to act extrovertly.*

ex|trude (ek strüd′), *v.,* **-trud|ed, -trud|ing.** —*v.t.* **1** to thrust out; push out; force out; expel: *He extruded toothpaste from the tube. In building the cocoon the caterpillar extruded more than a mile of silk* (Scientific American). **2** to shape (metal, plastics, rubber, or ceramics) by forcing through dies: *Pipe will be extruded for the oil and gas utilities fields* (Fortune).
—*v.i.* to stick out; protrude.
[< Latin *extrūdere* < *ex-* out + *trūdere* thrust]

ex|trud|er (ek strü′dər), *n.* a person or thing that extrudes.

ex|tru|si|ble (ek strü′zə bəl), *adj.* that can be extruded; capable of extrusion.

ex|tru|sion (ek strü′zhən), *n.* **1** the process of extruding. **2** the state of being extruded; expulsion. **3** the thing extruded. **4** a mass of lava or volcanic material which has reached the earth's surface. [< Latin *extrūsus,* past participle of *extrūdere* (see etym. under **extrude**) + English *-ion*]

extrusion press, a machine that extrudes metals, plastics, rubber, or ceramics: *The plant shapes metal products in an extrusion press* (Wall Street Journal).

ex|tru|sive (ek strü′siv), *adj., n.* —*adj.* **1** tending to extrude or thrust outward. **2** resulting from or characterized by extrusion. **3** that can be extruded. **4** (of igneous rock) having been forced out in a molten or plastic condition at the surface of the earth.
—*n.* igneous rock that has been forced to the surface of the earth; extrusion.

ex|u|ber|ance (eg zü′bər əns), *n.* **1** the fact or condition of being exuberant; great abundance. **2** luxuriant growth: *an exuberance of tropic vegetation.* **3** an extravagance; excessive outburst: *the exuberance of the dog's joy at our return.* **4** an overflowing amount or quantity; a superabundance: *There is an exuberance of fancy in him* (William Gilpin).

ex|u|ber|an|cy (eg zü′bər ən sē), *n., pl.* **-cies.** = exuberance.

ex|u|ber|ant (eg zü′bər ənt), *adj.* **1** very abundant; overflowing; lavish: *exuberant health, good nature, or joy. The astronaut received an exuberant welcome when he returned to his hometown.* **2** profuse in growth; luxuriant: *the exuberant vegetation of the jungle.* **3** abounding in health and spirits; overflowing with good cheer: *an exuberant young man.* [< Latin *exūberāns, -antis,* present participle of *exūberāre* grow luxuriantly < *ex-* thoroughly + *ūber, -eris* fertile] —**ex|u′ber|ant|ly,** *adv.*

ex|u|ber|ant|ness (eg zü′bər ənt nis), *n.* = exuberance.

ex|u|ber|ate (eg zü′bə rāt), *v.i.,* **-at|ed, -at|ing.** to be exuberant; abound; overflow. [< Latin *exūberāre* (with English *-ate*[1]); see etym. under **exuberant**]

ex|u|date (eks′yů dāt), *v.,* **-dat|ed, -dat|ing,** *n.* —*v.i., v.t.* = exude.
—*n.* something exuded.

ex|u|da|tion (eks′yů dā′shən), *n.* **1** the action of exuding; an oozing out. **2** something exuded, such as sweat.

ex|u|da|tive (eks yü′də tiv), *adj.* having to do with or characterized by exudation.

ex|ude (eg züd′, ek süd′), *v.,* **-ud|ed, -ud|ing.** —*v.i.* to come out in drops; ooze: *Sweat exudes from the pores in the skin.*
—*v.t.* **1** to send out in drops: *Some trees exude sap in the spring.* **2** *Figurative.* to give forth; emit: *Some successful men exude self-confidence. A woman of almost nebulous personality ... somehow exudes more force than anyone else in the book* (New Yorker).
[< Latin *exsūdāre* < *ex-* out + *sūdāre* to sweat < *sūdor* sweat]

ex|ul|cer|a|tion (eks ul′sə rā′shən), *n.* **1** ulceration. **2** an ulcerated place; sore.

ex|ult (eg zult′), *v.i.* **1** to be very glad; rejoice greatly: *The winners exulted in their victory.* **2** *Obsolete.* to spring or leap up; leap for joy: *The sea ... Exults and owns the monarch of the main* (Alexander Pope). [< Latin *exsultare* < *exsultus,* past participle of *exsilīre* leap out or up < *ex-* forth + *salīre* leap]

ex|ult|ance (eg zul′təns), *n.* = exultation.

ex|ult|an|cy (eg zul′tən sē), *n.* = exultation.

ex|ult|ant (eg zul′tənt), *adj.* rejoicing greatly; exulting; triumphant: *The troops in the besieged town gave an exultant shout at the sight of new troops advancing to help them.* —**ex|ult′ant|ly,** *adv.*

ex|ul|ta|tion (eg′zul tā′shən, ek′sul-), *n.* the act of exulting; great rejoicing; triumph: *There was exultation over our team's overwhelming victory.*

ex|ult|ing|ly (eg zul′ting lē), *adv.* in an exulting or triumphant manner.

ex|um|bral (eks um′brəl), *adj.* = exumbrellar.

ex|um|brel|la (eks′um brel′ə), *n. Zoology.* the aboral or outer surface of the umbrella of a jellyfish.

ex|um|brel|lar (eks′um brel′ər), *adj.* of or having to do with the exumbrella.

ex un|gue le|o|nem (eks un′gwē lē ō′nəm), *Latin.* **1** a part can tell us all. **2** (literally) from the claw (one may know) the lion.

ex|urb (eks′ėrb), *n.* a town or area in exurbia: *All over the U.S., the cities are losing their middle-class populations to the suburbs and the exurbs* (Newsweek).

ex|ur|ban (eks ėr′bən), *adj.* of or having to do with exurbia; in exurbia: *For his exurban retreat, he chose a soft-blue-and-white stucco house seven miles east of the capital* (Time). [< *ex-*[1] + Latin *urbs, urbis* city + English *-an*]

ex|ur|ban|ite (eks ėr′bə nīt), *n., adj.* —*n.* a person who has moved out of a large city to exurbia, and whose way of living is a mixture of urban and rural elements: *Fairfield County "exurbanites" are New Yorkers in all but voting* (Wall Street Journal).
—*adj.* = exurban.

ex|ur|bi|a (eks ėr′bē ə), *n.* a region between the suburbs and the country inhabited by exurbanites: *One feels that he carried not only a notebook but a tape recorder with him on his safari into Exurbia* (Phyllis McGinley). [< *ex-*[1] + Latin *urbs, urbis* city, patterned on *suburbia*]

ex|u|vi|a|bil|i|ty (eg zü′vē ə bil′ə tē, ek sü′-), *n.* **1** the ability to slough or cast off. **2** the susceptibility of being exuviated or shed.

ex|u|vi|a|ble (eg zü′vē ə bəl, ek sü′-), *adj.* capable of being exuviated or sloughed off.

ex|u|vi|ae (eg zü′vē ē, ek sü′-), *n.pl.* the castoff skins, shells, antlers, or other coverings of animals. [< Latin *exuviae* stuffed skins, garments < *exuere* divest oneself of]

ex|u|vi|al (eg zü′vē əl, ek sü′-), *adj.* having to do with or like exuviae.

ex|u|vi|ate (eg zü′vē āt, ek sü′-), *v.i., v.t.,* **-at|ed, -at|ing.** to cast off or shed skin, shell, feathers, or antlers; molt: *The young crayfish exuviate two or three times in the course of the first year* (Thomas H. Huxley). [< Latin *exuviae* (see etym. under **exuviae**) + *-ate*[1]]

ex|u|vi|a|tion (eg zü′vē ā′shən, ek sü′-), *n.* the act or process of exuviating.

ex-vo|to (eks vō′tō), *n., pl.* **-tos,** *adj.* —*n.* an offering in fulfillment of a vow or as an expression of gratitude for a miraculous cure or deliverance: *He hung the dagger, as an ex-voto, in his monastery church* (New Yorker).
—*adj.* of or having to do with an ex-voto: *ex-voto tokens and inscriptions, ex-voto offerings.* [< *ex voto*]

ex vo|to (eks vō′tō), *Latin.* from a vow; in carrying out a vow.

ex-works (eks′wėrks′), *adv. British.* directly from the factory: *It may be that some clerk has developed the habit of putting down the value ex-works and not the price at which it is being sold* (London Times).

-ey, *suffix forming adjectives from nouns.* full of; containing; like ____: *Clayey = like or containing clay. Gooey = like goo.* [variant of *-y*[1]]

e|ya|let (ā′yä let′), *n.* = vilayet.

ey|as (ī′əs), *n.* **1** a young hawk taken from the nest for training. **2** a very young or unfledged bird; nestling. Also, **eyess.** [misdivision of Middle English *a neyas* < Old French *niais* nestling < Vulgar Latin *nīdāx* < Latin *nīdus* nest]

***eye** (ī), *n., v.,* **eyed, ey|ing** or **eye|ing.** —*n.* **1** the organ of the body by which people and animals see; organ of sight: *The sensitive elements in the retina of the vertebrate eye are of two kinds: rods and cones* (J. L. Cloudsley-Thompson). **2** the colored part of the eye; iris: *He has brown eyes.* **3** the region and structures surrounding the eye: *The blow gave him a black eye.* **4** any organ that is sensitive to light. **5** Often, **eyes.** the sense of seeing; vision; sight: *A jet pilot must have good eyes.* **6** the ability to see small differences in things: *A good artist must have an eye for color. He has ... an eye for the rich parade of human eccentricity* (Newsweek). **7** a look; glance: *He cast an eye at the pretty girl.* **8** a watchful look; careful regard: *an eye for detail.* **9** Often, **eyes.** *Figurative.* a way of thinking or considering; point of view; opinion; judgment: *Stealing is a crime in the eyes of the law.* **10** a thing shaped like, resembling, or suggesting an eye. The little buds on potatoes, the hole for thread in a needle, the hole in the head of an ax for a wooden handle, and the loop to which a hook fastens are all called eyes. **11** the

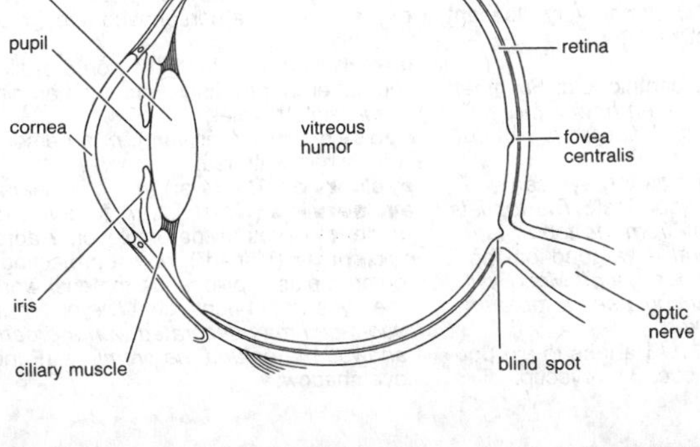

lens
pupil
cornea
iris
ciliary muscle
sclera
choroid
retina
vitreous humor
fovea centralis
optic nerve
blind spot

***eye**
definition 1

Pronunciation Key: hat, āge, cãre, fär; let, ēqual, tėrm, it, īce; hot, ōpen, ôrder; oil, out; cup, pu̇t, rüle; child; long; thin; ᴛʜen; zh, measure; ə represents a in about, e in taken, i in pencil, o in lemon, u in circus.

relatively calm, clear area at the center of a hurricane: *As with a whirlpool, there is a hole in the center—the "eye" of the storm* (New York Times). **12** the angle from which a graphic image is viewed on a computer screen: *In addition to three-dimensional manipulation of an object, the program offers separate but simultaneous manipulation of the "eye," the viewing point* (Popular Computing).
—*v.t.* **1** to look at; watch; observe: *The dog eyed the stranger.* **2** to make an eye or eyes in.
—*v.i. Obsolete.* to look or appear to the eye.
an eye for an eye, punishment as severe as the injury: *The revengeful man insisted on an eye for an eye.*
be all eyes, *Informal.* to look eagerly; watch attentively: *The children were all eyes at the circus.*
catch one's eye, to attract one's attention: *Her bright red hat caught my eye.*
clap eyes on, *Informal.* to look at; see: . . . *you might never have clapped eyes upon the boy* (Dickens).
cry one's eyes (or **heart**) **out,** to shed many tears: *She cries her eyes out whenever her mother leaves her with a baby sitter.*
easy on the eyes, *Informal.* pleasant to look at; attractive; beautiful: *The landscape was easy on the eyes.*
give one the eye, *Slang.* to look at one in a flirting way; make eyes at a person: *He blushed when the pretty girl gave him the eye.*
have an eye to, to look out for; pay attention to: *Almost everyone has an eye to his advantage.*
have eyes only for, a to love or want a person or thing to the exclusion of all others: *Monk . . . only has eyes for Nellie* (Time). **b** to look at or consider a particular thing or point of view to the exclusion of all others: *He has eyes only for that with which he is familiar.*
in a pig's eye, See under **pig.**
in the eye of the wind. See under **wind**[1].
in the public eye, a often seen in public; noticed by the public: *The suit is much in demand by beauty contestants and others who wear suits in the public eye* (Wall Street Journal). **b** widely known: *The Senator is in the public eye.*
keep an eye on, to look after; watch carefully: *Keep an eye on the baby while I go out.*
keep one's eyes open, to be watchful or alert: *The reporter kept his eyes open for any news.*
keep one's eyes peeled, *U.S. Informal.* to be on the alert: *I kept my eyes peeled, but I didn't see her in the afternoon crowd* (Munsey's Magazine).
knock one's eyes out, *U.S. Slang.* to overwhelm with wonder: *Bad roads in there, but my God Almighty, the little part of the river I've seen would knock your eyes out* (James Dickey).
lay eyes on, to look at; see; notice: *I never laid eyes on this man until today.*
make eyes at, to look at with liking or love; flirt with: *He was making eyes at the girl across the room.*
my eye, *Slang.* an expression used to show disagreement or disbelief: *"New" my eye; these are just revivals* (Lois Long).
open one's eyes, to make one see what is really happening: *Overhearing his neighbors' conversation opened his eyes.*
pipe one's (or **the**) **eye,** to shed tears; weep; cry: *The rest [of the smoke] eddied about the house, and kept us coughing and piping the eye* (Robert Louis Stevenson).
put one's eyes out, *U.S. Dialect.* to overwhelm with wonder: *"In all our number we didn't have but one with the looks to put your eyes right out, and that was our baby brother Sam Dale"* (Eudora Welty).
see eye to eye, to agree entirely; have exactly the same opinion: *My father and I do not see eye to eye on my weekly allowance.*
set eyes on, to see; look at: *I never set eyes on this man till today.*
shut one's eyes to, to refuse to see or consider; ignore: *He shut his eyes to the faults of his friends.*
turn a blind eye, to ignore; overlook; disregard: *There is a feeling that the police turn a blind eye to this problem* (London Times).
with an eye to, for; considering: *With an obvious eye to the new importance of the women's vote . . .* (New York Times).
with one's eyes open, aware of the risks or consequences: *They did it with their eyes open, knowing that the publication of military secrets is a punishable offense.*
without batting an eye, with no external show of emotion: *Fitzsimmons sat through the race without batting an eye* (New York Times).
[Old English *ēge, ēage*] —**eye'like',** *adj.*

eye|a|ble (ī'ə bəl), *adj.* **1** visible. **2** pleasing to the eye.

eye agate, a variety of agate having the layers in concentric circles.

eye appeal, *U.S. Informal.* pleasantness of appearance; attractiveness.

eye-ap|peal|ing (ī'ə pē'ling), *adj. U.S. Informal.* attractive; good-looking.

eye|ball (ī'bôl'), *n., v.* —*n.* the eye without the surrounding lids and bony socket. It is shaped like a ball.
—*v.t. U.S. Slang.* to watch intently; eye sharply: *Poker is a game . . . in which you either eyeball the other fellow or he eyeballs you* (Springfield Leader and Press).
eyeball to eyeball, *Informal.* face to face in a conflict; in direct opposition: *There the adversaries stood, eyeball to eyeball* (Newsweek).
to the eyeballs, *Informal.* to the hilt; completely: *Never mind that the [grape] grower was mortgaged to the eyeballs, strangling on 9 and 10 per cent interest payments* (John Gregory Dunne).

eye bank, a place for the storage of human eyes, to be used in transplanting the corneas to persons who are blind from diseases causing scarring of the cornea.

eye|beam (ī'bēm'), *n.* a beam or glance of the eye.

*****eye|bolt** (ī'bōlt'), *n.* a bolt having an eye at one end to receive a hook, ring, or rope.

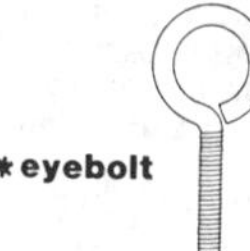
***eyebolt**

eye|bright (ī'brīt'), *n.* **1** a European herb of the figwort family, formerly used as a remedy for weak eyes and diseases of the eye; euphrasy. **2** = scarlet pimpernel.

eye|brow (ī'brou'), *n.* **1** the strip of hair above the eye. **2** the bony ridge that the hair above the eye grows on.
raise an eyebrow (or **eyebrows**), to elicit or express doubt, disapproval, or wonder: *An American caparisoned in woolly Western chaps might raise an eyebrow or two* (New York Times).

eyebrow pencil, a pencil used to accentuate the eyebrows in making up.

eye candy, something or someone pleasing to look at: *But most actresses are accessories, used for supportive warmth or eye candy* (Vanity Fair).

eye-catch|ing (ī'kach'ing), *adj. Informal.* **1** attractive; appealing: *We found ourself surrounded by gay and eye-catching things, ranging from tapestries to eggs dressed up as dolls* (New Yorker). **2** clearly visible; noticeable; conspicuous: *an eye-catching career.*

eye chart, a chart with printed letters, numbers, or pictures of decreasing sizes, used for testing sight.

eye contact, a meeting of eyes; visual contact between two individuals: *Subordinates are constantly attentive to the leader, and as soon as eye contact is made, they [wolves] submissively avert their eyes* (New Yorker).

eye|cup (ī'kup'), *n.* a small cup with a rim shaped to fit over the eye, used in washing the eyes or putting medicine in them.

eyed (īd), *adj.* marked or ornamented with eyelike spots; spotted.

-eyed, *combining form.* having a ____ eye or eyes: *One-eyed = having one eye. Green-eyed = having green eyes.*

eye dialect, *Linguistics.* the phonetic respelling of words to represent pronunciations that suggest dialect or some form of nonstandard speech, as *sez* for *says* or *wuz* for *was* or *axed* for *asked.*

eye doctor, an optometrist or ophthalmologist; doctor specializing in the care and treatment of the eyes.

eye|drop (ī'drop'), *n.* = tear.

eye|drop|per (ī'drop'ər), *n.* = dropper (def. 1).

eye drops, liquid medicine administered to the eyes in drops to ease eyestrain.

eye-fill|ing (ī'fil'ing), *adj. Informal.* very pleasant to look upon; highly attractive.

eye fly, eye gnat.

eye|fold (ī'fōld'), *n.* an epicanthic fold: *Bushmen are like the Asian peoples, often having Mongolian eyefolds and rather broad, flat faces* (Atlantic).

eye|ful (ī'fu̇l), *n.* **1** as much as the eye can see at one time. **2** *Informal.* a good look: *The tourists will get an eyeful of the city from the top of that tall building.* **3** *Slang, Figurative.* a good-looking person: *If you could take your eye off Mrs. Bliss, who is quite an eyeful, you could see a table in the background* (New Yorker).

eye|glass (ī'glas', -gläs'), *n.* **1** a lens to aid poor vision; monocle. **2** = eyepiece. **3** = eyecup.

eyeglasses, a pair of lenses, mounted in a frame, to help vision; glasses; spectacles: *The lenses of her shell-rimmed eyeglasses were fogged with thumbprints* (New Yorker).

eye gnat, a small, disease-carrying fly which hovers around the face and eyes of human beings and domestic animals; eye fly.

eye|ground (ī'ground'), *n.* the fundus of the eye, as viewed through an ophthalmoscope; the back part of the interior of the eyeball: *More emphasis is being placed upon the examination of the eyegrounds . . . as an index of the general arteriolar pattern* (Morris Fishbein).

eye|hole (ī'hōl'), *n.* **1** = eye socket. **2** a hole in a mask or fence to look through; peephole. **3** a round opening for a pin, hook, rope, or the like, to go through.

eye|lash (ī'lash'), *n.* **1** one of the hairs on the edge of the eyelid. **2** the fringe of such hairs.
by an eyelash, by a narrow margin; by very little: *The General lost the state, but only by an eyelash* (New York Times).

eye lens, the lens nearest the eye in an optical instrument.

eye|less (ī'lis), *adj.* **1** without eyes. **2** blind; sightless: *Eyeless in Gaza, at the mill with slaves* (Milton). —**eye'less|ly,** *adv.*

eye|let (ī'lit), *n., v.* —*n.* **1** a small, round hole for a lace or cord to go through, as in most shoes. **2** a metal ring around such a hole to strengthen it. **3** a hole to look through; peephole. **4** a small, round hole with stitches around it, used to make a pattern in embroidery. **5** a small eye. —*v.t.* to make eyelets in. [< Old French *oeillet* (diminutive) < *oeil* eye < Latin *oculus;* influenced by *eye, -let*]

eye|let|eer (ī'lə tir'), *n.* a small, pointed instrument for making eyelets.

eyelet hole, an eyelet, or small hole; loophole.

eye|lid (ī'lid'), *n.* the movable fold of skin, upper or lower, containing muscles by means of which we can shut and open our eyes: *[Her] eyelids are bluer with intellectual fatigue than with eye shadow* (Punch).

eye|lin|er (ī'lī'nər), *n.* **1** a cosmetic preparation for drawing a line over the eyelashes to accentuate the eyes: *Eyeliner is applied sparingly, close to the lashes and not extended beyond the corner of the eye* (Which). **2** a pencil or crayon for drawing such a line.

eye-mind|ed (ī'mīn'did), *adj.* having a mental constitution chiefly or exclusively visual, so that thoughts and memories take the form of visual images: *Most consumers are "eye-minded": they must see an article to appreciate its merit* (Bernice Chambers). —**eye'-mind'ed|ness,** *n.*

ey|en (ī'ən), *n.* obsolete or dialectal plural of **eye.**

eye opener, or **eye-o|pen|er** (ī'ō'pə nər), *n. Informal.* **1** a surprising happening or discovery; startling piece of information: *This is often an eye opener to parents who insist that little Susie may be thirty pounds overweight but she hardly eats a thing* (Maclean's). **2** *U.S.* a drink of alcoholic liquor taken early in the day.

eye-o|pen|ing (ī'ō'pə ning), *adj.* revealing; illuminating: *eye-opening statistics, an eye-opening book.*

eye|patch (ī'pach'), *n.* a pad, usually of black cloth or leather, worn over a blind or injured eye.

eye|piece (ī'pēs'), *n.* the lens, or set of lenses in a telescope or microscope that is nearest the eye of the user. See diagram at **microscope.**

eye|point (ī'point'), *n.* the point at which the rays from the eyepiece of a telescope, microscope, or other instrument with lenses, converge, and to which the eye is applied to view an object.

eye-pop|per (ī'pop'ər), *n. Informal.* something eye-popping; an astonishing thing or event; a marvel: *The service structure for the newest Saturn launch facility at Canaveral is an eye-popper* (Wall Street Journal).

eye-pop|ping (ī'pop'ing), *adj. Informal.* causing great surprise or wonder; amazing; astonishing: *Santana polished off . . . the Australian veteran who has dominated amateur tennis for the last three years by the eye-popping score of 6-1, 6-1, 6-4* (New Yorker).

eye purple, = visual purple.

ey|er (ī'ər), *n.* a person who eyes, or watches closely.

eye rhyme, the rhyme of words of similar spelling but different pronunciation, such as *near* and *bear;* sight rhyme.

eye|serv|ant (ī'sėr'vənt), *n.* a person who works only when watched.

eye|serv|er (ī'sėr'vər), *n.* = eyeservant.

eye|serv|ice (ī'sėr'vis), *n.* **1** service done only under the eyes of the employer. **2** admiring looks.

eye|shade (ī'shād'), *n.* **1** a projecting visor of colored plastic or opaque material worn to protect the eyes from bright light: *The editor, Mr. Bigley, a sad-faced man decorated with a green eyeshade, showed me around the premises* (Punch). **2** = eye shadow.

eye shadow, a cosmetic used for coloring the eyelids, so as to beautify the eyes.
eye|shot (ī′shot′), *n.* **1** the range of vision; view: *in eyeshot of the parade.* **2** a glance; prospect.
eye|sight (ī′sīt′), *n.* **1** the power of seeing; sight: *A hawk has keen eyesight. The old man's eyesight is failing.* **2** the range of vision; view: *The water was within eyesight.*
eye socket, the bony cavity in which the eyeball is set.
eyes-on|ly (īz′ōn′lē), *adj. U.S.* (of confidential or secret information) intended to be read only by the recipient: *[J. Edgar] Hoover sent the ... letter to six senior bureau officials on an "eyes-only" basis* (Washington Post).
eye|sore (ī′sôr′, -sōr′), *n.* something unpleasant to look at; an ugly mark or feature: *That garbage heap is an eyesore.*
eye splice, a splice made by splicing the end of a rope into itself to form a circle or an eye.
eye|spot (ī′spot′), *n.* **1** the simplest kind of organ for seeing, found in many lower animals, such as the euglena and starfish. It consists of a group of pigmented cells. *Near the base of the flagella is an eyespot* (Fred W. Emerson). **2** a spot or marking resembling an eye.
eye-spot|ted (ī′spot′id), *adj.* having spots resembling eyes.
eyes right or **eyes left** (īz), a military order to turn the head to the right or to the left as a salute while marching.
ey|ess (ī′əs), *n.* = eyas.

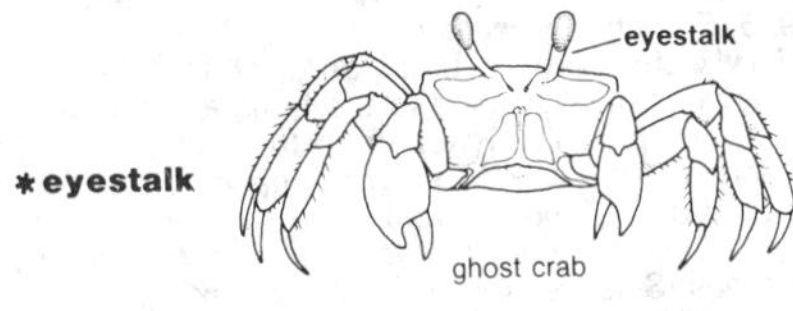

***eyestalk**

***eye|stalk** (ī′stôk′), *n. Zoology.* the stalk or peduncle that bears the eye in crabs, lobsters, and shrimps.

eye|stone (ī′stōn′), *n.* a smooth bit of shell, flat on one side and convex on the other, passed between the eye and the eyelid to remove cinders and the like.
eye|strain (ī′strān′), *n.* a tired or weak condition of the eyes caused especially by using them too much or reading in a dim light.
eye|strings (ī′stringz′), *n.pl.* the muscles, tendons, or nerves of the eye, formerly supposed to break at death or on loss of sight.
eye|tooth (ī′tüth′), *n., pl.* **-teeth**. either of the two pointed, upper teeth between the incisors and the bicuspids; an upper canine tooth.
cut one's eyeteeth, to grow out of babyhood: *... like progress that is made by a boy when he cuts his eyeteeth* (Emerson).
give one's eyeteeth, to surrender something extremely valuable: *He would give his eyeteeth to get his hands on a car.*
eye-view (ī′vyü′), *n. British.* a point of view; viewpoint; view: *... a passenger's eye-view of a flight in a supersonic airliner* (London Times). *My last novels, you could say, took the conventional god's eye-view, dipping into the minds of a number of characters* (Christine Brooke-Rose).
eye|wall (ī′wôl′), *n.* a layer of turbulent, funnel-shaped clouds around the eye of a storm; wall cloud: *Hurricane Debbie ... was some 800 miles east of Puerto Rico. Planes flew there to drop their crystals, in hopes of causing supercooled water droplets in the hurricane's eyewall to condense* (Science News).
eye|wash (ī′wosh′, -wôsh′), *n.* **1** a liquid preparation to clean or heal the eyes. **2** *Slang.* deceiving flattery; an insincere excuse. **3** *Slang.* nonsense: *This notion is romantic eyewash* (Maclean's).
eye|wa|ter (ī′wôt′ər, -wot′-), *n.* **1** liquid eyewash. **2** natural fluid in the eye; a tear.
eye|wink (ī′wingk′), *n.* **1** a wink of the eye. **2** an instant. **3** a glance.
eye|wink|er (ī′wing′kər), *n.* an eyelash or an eyelid.
eye|wit|ness (ī′wit′nis), *n., v.* **—n.** a person who actually sees or has seen some act or happening, and thus can give testimony concerning it: *Eyewitnesses counted about 25 bomb explosions in all* (London Times).
—*v.t.* to witness; see: *He was one of three foreign correspondents who eyewitnessed the recent riots in Kashmir* (Time).
eye|wit|ness|er (ī′wit′nə sər), *n. Informal.* a report by an eyewitness, usually a newspaper correspondent: *He sent out a fast-moving 2,000-word eyewitnesser* (Time).
eye worm, a small, parasitic roundworm found in certain areas of Africa. The adult causes irritation by moving about in the subcutaneous tissue and the eyes.
ey|ot (ī′ət, āt), *n. British.* a small island. [variant of *ait*[1]]
ey|ra (ār′ə, ī′rə), *n.* = jaguarundi. [< American Spanish *eyra* < an American Indian word]
eyre (ãr), *n.* **1** a journey in circuit: *Justices in eyre were English judges who rode a circuit to hold court until 1285.* **2** the court held by justices in eyre. [< Old French *eire, oirre* journey < *errer,* chiefly < Late Latin *iterāre,* for Latin *iterfacere* make a journey, but influenced by *errāre* err]
ey|rie or **ey|ry** (ãr′ē, ir′-), *n., pl.,* **-ries**. **1** the nest of an eagle or other bird of prey in a high place. **2** the young of an eagle or other bird of prey. **3** a lofty position. **4** a house or castle built in a high place. Also, **aerie** or **aery**. [variant of *aerie*]
ey|rir (ā′rir), *n., pl.* **au|rar**. an Icelandic coin, worth 1/100 of a króna. [< Icelandic *eyrir*]
Ez. or **Ezr.**, Ezra (a book of the Bible).
E|ze|chi|el (i zē′kē əl, -zēk′yəl), *n.* (in the Douay Bible) Ezekiel.
Ezek., Ezekiel (a book of the Bible).
E|ze|ki|el (i zē′kē əl, -zēk′yəl), *n.* **1** a Hebrew prophet of the 500's B.C., considered one of the major prophets. **2** a book of the Old Testament containing his prophecies. *Abbr:* Ezek.
Ez|ra (ez′rə), *n.* **1** a Hebrew priest and scribe of the 400's or 300's B.C. who returned to Palestine from Babylonia to lead a revival of Judaism. **2** a book of the Old Testament that tells about him. *Abbr:* Ez. or Ezr.

✱F[1] or **f** (ef), *n., pl.* **F's** or **Fs, f's** or **fs. 1** the sixth letter of the English alphabet: *There are two f's in offer.* **2** any sound represented by this letter. **3** (used as a symbol for) the sixth (of an actual or possible series): *row F in a theater.* **4** the lowest or failing grade (in schools and colleges): *to get an F in physics.* **5** *Music.* **a** the fourth tone in the scale of C major. **b** a symbol representing this tone. **c** a key, string, etc., that produces this tone. **d** the scale or key that has F as its keynote: *a sonata in F.*

✱F[1]
definition 5b

F[2] (ef), *n., pl.* **F's.** anything shaped like the letter F.

F1 layer (ef′wun′), one of the ionosphere's layers, about 90 to 150 miles above the earth's surface. It reflects radio waves.

F2 layer (ef′tü′), one of the ionosphere's layers, occurring from about 125 miles to over 250 miles above the earth's surface. It reflects radio waves.

f (no period), an abbreviation for the following:
1 farad.
2 femto-.
3 focal length (used especially in F numbers to express the effective diameters of lenses in terms of their focal lengths).
4 *Music.* forte (loud).
5 frequency.

f., an abbreviation for the following:
1 fathom.
2 female.
3 feminine.
4 (of lead pencils or pens) fine.
5 florin.
6 fluid (ounce).
7 folio.
8 following.
9 franc or francs.

F (no period), fluorine (chemical element).

F (no period), an abbreviation for the following:
1 Fahrenheit: *32°F = 32 degrees on the Fahrenheit scale.*
2 *Genetics.* a filial generation (used with a subscript number, as F_1 or the first generation of offspring of a mating, F_1 or second, and so on).
3 (of lead pencils or pens) fine.
4 *Photography.* focal length.
5 franc or francs.
6 *Physics.* free energy.
7 French: *OF = Old French.*
8 Friday.
9 *Mathematics.* function.

F., an abbreviation for the following:
1 Fahrenheit.
2 February.
3 Fellow (of), as in F.R.S. = Fellow of the Royal Society: *Sir Isaac Newton, F.R.S.*
4 fluid (ounce).
5 folio.
6 France.
7 French.

F-, fighter (in the U.S. Air Force): *the swing-wing F-111.*

fa (fä), *n.* the fourth tone of the diatonic scale. Do, re, mi, fa, sol, la, ti, do are the names of the tones of the scale. [< Italian *fa* < Medieval Latin *fa(muli)*; see etym. under **gamut**]

FA (no periods) or **F.A., 1** field artillery. **2** freight agent.

f.a.a., free of all average.

FAA (no periods) or **F.A.A.,** Federal Aviation Administration (an agency in the U.S. Department of Transportation whose director has the authority to control civilian and military air traffic and regulate air lines).

F.A.A.A.S., 1 Fellow of the American Academy of Arts and Sciences. **2** Fellow of the American Association for the Advancement of Science.

fab (fab), *adj. British Informal.* fabulos; wonderful: *We want our pop stars to be fab, of course, but not so fab they can't be copied* (Punch).

fa|ba bean (fā′bə), = broad bean. [< Latin *faba* bean]

fa|ba|ceous (fə bā′shəs), *adj.* belonging to the pea family: *Peas, lentils, broom, and locust trees are fabaceous plants.* [< Latin *fabāceus* (with English *-ous*) < *faba* bean]

Fa|bi|an (fā′bē ən), *adj., n.* —*adj.* **1** using stratagem and delay to wear out an opponent; cautious; slow: *By recognizably Fabian tactics, then, socialism has recaptured Labour* (Canadian Saturday Night). **2** of the Fabian Society: *He gave hundreds of lectures, at least as much for Shavian as for Fabian causes* (New Yorker).
—*n.* a member of or sympathizer with the Fabian Society.
[< Latin *Fabiānus* of the family of *Quintus Fabius Maximus,* Roman general and statesman, surnamed *Cunctator* (Delayer), who sought to wear out the enemy (Hannibal) by harassing tactics without risking a decisive battle]

Fa|bi|an|ism (fā′bē ə niz′əm), *n.* a moderate type of socialism; the principles of economic and social reform advanced by the Fabian Society: *Marxism deeply penetrated into the consciousness of the German working class—as deeply at least as Methodism and Fabianism impressed themselves on British Labour* (Listener).

Fa|bi|an|ist (fā′bē ə nist), *n., adj.* = Fabian.

Fa|bi|an|is|tic (fā′bē ə nis′tik), *adj.* of or having to do with Fabianism.

Fabian Society, an English socialist society, founded in 1884, that favors the adoption of socialism by gradual reform rather than revolution.

fa|ble (fā′bəl), *n., v.,* **-bled, -bling.** —*n.* **1** a story that is made up to teach a lesson. Fables are often about animals who can talk, as in *The Hare and the Tortoise* and *The Fox and the Crow.* **SYN:** apologue. **2** an untrue story; falsehood; fabrication: *What is said . . . on this subject in the Courier d'Europe is entirely fable* (Thomas Jefferson). **3** legend or myth: *Greek fable.* **4** the plot of a drama or epic poem.
—*v.i.* **1** to tell or write fables: *Vain now the tales which fabling poets tell* (Matthew Prior). **2** to tell false stories; lie.
—*v.t.* **1** to make up falsely; fabricate: *I fabled nothing fair, But . . . told her all* (Tennyson). **2** to tell or represent in a fable: *I pray you sit not fabling here old tales* (Ben Jonson).
[< Old French *fable* < Latin *fābula* narrative, tale < *fārī* speak]
▶See **allegory** for usage note.

fa|bled (fā′bəld), *adj.* **1** told about in fables, legends, or myths; legendary: *Zeus was chief of the fabled Greek gods.* **2** not real; made-up; fictitious.

fa|bler (fā′blər), *n.* **1** = fabulist. **2** = falsifier.

fab|li|au (fab′lē ō), *n., pl.* **-aux** (-ōz). a medieval poem, usually French or English, relating a short tale that deals with real or possible (often comic) incidents of ordinary human life. [< Old North French *fabliau,* Old French *fablel* (diminutive) < *fable;* see etym. under **fable**]

fab|ric (fab′rik), *n.* **1** woven, knitted, or felted material; cloth. Velvet, canvas, linen, flannel, jersey, and tricot are fabrics. **SYN:** textile. **2a** texture, whether smooth or rough, loose or close: *suits and dresses made of cloths of different fabric.* **b** *Figurative.* the way in which a thing is put together; method of construction: *The fabric of a person's character may be weak or strong.* **3** *Figurative.* **a** a thing constructed of combined parts; framework: *Unwise loans weakened the financial fabric of the bank. Sultan Said ibn Taymur elaborated a program for improving the living conditions of his people, but he moved cautiously to avoid disrupting the old fabric of society* (George Rentz). **b** something constructed; a structure; edifice; building: *We build with what we deem eternal rock: A distant age asks where the fabric stood* (William Cowper). [< Middle French *fabrique,* learned borrowing from Latin *fabrica* workshop < *faber* worker. See etym. of doublet **forge[1]**.]

fab|ri|cant (fab′rə kənt), *n.* = manufacturer.

fab|ri|cate (fab′rə kāt), *v.t.,* **-cat|ed, -cat|ing. 1** to make (anything that requires skill); build; construct. **2** to make by putting parts together; manufacture: *Automobiles are fabricated from parts made in different factories.* **3** to make up; invent (stories, lies, excuses, or accomplishments). **SYN:** devise. **4** to forge (a document). [< Latin *fabricāre* (with English *-ate[1]*) build < *fabrica* workshop < *faber* worker]

fab|ri|cat|ed food (fab′rə kā′tid), = engineered food.

fab|ri|ca|tion (fab′rə kā′shən), *n.* **1** a fabricating; manufacture; construction: *the fabrication of a government* (Edmund Burke). **2** something fabricated; story, lie, excuse, or accomplishment: *The account of his exploration was a complete fabrication.* **SYN:** fiction, falsehood, figment.

fab|ri|ca|tive (fab′rə kā′tiv), *adj.* fabricating; constructive: *There are the fabricative industries, such as smelting, refining, processing, and manufacturing* (White and Renner).

fab|ri|ca|tor (fab′rə kā′tər), *n.* **1** a maker; manufacturer: *Fabricators have been reluctant to commit themselves to all-out use of titanium* (Newsweek). **2** = falsifier.

Fab|ri|koid (fab′rə koid), *n. Trademark.* a waterproof fabric made to look like leather, used for bindings of books, for traveling bags, for automobile upholstery, and the like. [< *fabric* + *-oid*]

Fa|bry-Pe|rot (fä brē′pā rō′), *adj.* of or having to do with a type of interferometer developed by Charles Fabry, 1867-1945, and A. Pérot, 1863-1925, French physicists.

Fa|bry's disease (fä′brēz), an enzyme deficiency genetically linked to the female chromosome and passed by women to their male offspring: *A hereditary disorder attacking the heart, kidneys and central nervous system, Fabry's disease usually kills its victims in their early twenties* (Science News). [< Johannes *Fabry,* 1860-1930, a German dermatologist]

fab|u|lar (fab′yə lər), *adj.* of a fable or fables.

fab|u|list (fab′yə list), *n.* **1** a person who tells, writes, or makes up fables: *Fabulists always endow their animals with the passions and desires of men* (James Russell Lowell). **2** = liar. [< French *fabuliste* < Latin *fābula;* see etym. under **fable**]

fab|u|lize (fab′yə līz), *v.i.,* **-lized, -liz|ing.** to make up or tell fables.

fab|u|lous (fab′yə ləs), *adj.* **1a** too extraordinary to seem possible; beyond belief; amazing: *Ten dollars is a fabulous price for an ordinary pencil.* **SYN:** incredible, astonishing. **b** *Informal.* very good; wonderful or exciting: *a fabulous party.* **2** of a fable or fables; belonging to fable; imaginary; mythical: *The centaur is a fabulous monster.* **SYN:** legendary. **3** like a fable. [< Latin *fābulōsus* < *fābula;* see etym. under **fable**]
—**fab′u|lous|ly,** *adv.* —**fab′u|lous|ness,** *n.*

fac., 1 facsimile. **2** factor. **3** factory.

fa|cade or **fa|çade** (fə säd′), *n.* **1** the front part of a building: *. . . by the justice symbol on the courthouse façade* (Esquire). **2** any side of a building that faces a street or other open space: *. . . the colored spotlights at night playing on its glossy facades* (Saturday Review). *The owner of the doomed buildings . . . decided to demolish from the inside, leaving the old façades up for a while* (Forum). **3** *Figurative.* a front or outward part of anything, especially when thought of as concealing something, such as an error, weakness, or scheme; outward appearance: *a facade of honesty. The impressive façade of progress has collapsed* (Newsweek). [< French *façade* < Italian *facciata* < *faccia* face < Vulgar Latin *facia;* see etym. under **face**]

✱face (fās), *n., v.,* **faced, fac|ing.** —*n.* **1** the front part of the head. Your eyes, nose, and mouth are parts of your face. See the picture opposite on the following page. **2** a look; expression: *His face was sad. With . . . haggard face to his last field he came* (Macaulay). **3** an ugly or funny look made by twisting the face: *The boy made a face at his sister.* **SYN:** grimace. **4a** the front part; right side; surface: *the whole face of the earth, the face of a coin or card. The face of a clock or watch has numbers on it.* **b** front; facade; vertical or steep side: *the face of a house, the face of a cliff.* **5** outward appearance: **a** physical form or character: *the face of nature* (Washington Irving); *the face of the fields* (Dallas Lore Sharp). **b** the

✱F[1]
definition 1

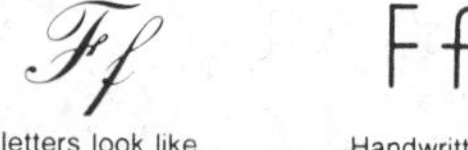

Script letters look like examples of fine penmanship. They appear in many formal uses, such as invitations to social functions.

Ff *Ff*

Handwritten letters, both manuscript or printed (left) and cursive (right), are easy for children to read and to write.

Ff *Ff*

Roman letters have *serifs* (finishing strokes) adapted from the way Roman stonecutters carved their letters. This is *Times Roman* type.

Ff ***Ff***

Sans-serif letters are often called *gothic.* They have lines of even width and no serifs. This type face is called *Helvetica.*

Ff *Ff*

Between roman and gothic, some letters have thick and thin lines with slight flares that suggest serifs. This type face is *Optima.*

F

Computer letters can be sensed by machines either from their shapes or from the magnetic ink with which they are printed.

apparent or obvious meaning of a thing: *An unprejudiced eye, upon the face of the letter, would condemn the writer of it* (Samuel Richardson). **6** *Figurative.* assumed appearance; disguise; pretense: *... there will be time To prepare a face to meet the faces that you meet* (T. S. Eliot). **7** *Figurative.* boldness; impudence: *He had the face to insult his father.* **SYN**: assurance, effrontery, audacity. **8** *Figurative.* self-respect; personal importance; dignity: *to lose face. To most people, loss of face is humiliating. Saving face is the strongest motive in the world* (John Galsworthy). **9** the stated value: *The face of the note was $100, but $73 was all that anybody would pay for it.* **10** any of the planes or surfaces that bound a solid figure. A cube has six faces. **11** the acting or working surface of a tool, tooth, or other implement or device: *the face of a chisel.* **12** *Mining.* the end of a tunnel, drift, or other excavation, especially where work is in progress: *Today, operators figure the miners actually spend only about 6½ hours "at the face"* (Wall Street Journal). **13** *Printing.* **a** the printing surface of a plate or piece of type. **b** the style of the printing surface of type, especially its thickness, serifs, and other such characteristics: *Janson is such an open face that the larger fonts will give a hazy look if, as in this case, the composition is close-set on a full page and not well leaded* (Poetry). **14a** the part of a wall between two neighboring bastions or salients in a fortification. **b** either of the two most forward sides of a bastion coming together at an angle. **15** *Military.* any side of a square formation of soldiers. **16** the loose net at the end of the racket or crosse used in the game of lacrosse. **17** *Archaic or Literary.* sight; presence: *driven out an exile from the face of Saul* (William Cowper).
—*v.t.* **1** to have the front toward; be opposite to: *The house faces the street. The picture faces page 60 in my book.* **2** to turn the face toward: *Jews face the east when they pray.* **3** to cause to face: *He faced the clock toward the wall.* **4** to meet face to face; stand before: *The teacher faced the class.* **SYN**: front, confront. **5** *Figurative.* to meet bravely or boldly; oppose and resist: *to face a challenge. The soldiers faced the enemy. How can man die better than facing fearful odds?* (Macaulay). **SYN**: brave, defy. **6** to present itself to: *A crisis faced us.* **7** *Figurative.* to deal with in a practical manner: *A realist faces reality.* **8** to cover or line with a different material: *That wooden house is being faced with brick.* **9** to cover the edges of (parts of a garment, such as cuffs or collar), inside or out, with the same or different material; for protection or trimming; trim: *robes of scarlet faced with white* (Scott). *She faced the lapels with velvet.* **10** to smooth the surface of (stone); dress: *The stones used in the building had all been faced by hand.* **11** *Military.* to order (troops) to turn to the right, left, or in the opposite direction. **12a** to turn (a playing card) face upward; expose. **b** to stack (letters) face upward ready for postmarking and sorting.
—*v.i.* **1** to have the face (toward); look: (*Figurative.*) *He steadfastly faced towards peace* (Alexander W. Kinglake). **2** to be situated; lie; front in a specified direction: *Our house faces north.* **3** *Military.* to execute a turn to the right, left, or in the opposite direction, from a stationary position.
face down, a to face fearlessly; meet boldly: *Mao and his associates ... faced down the worst the Russians could do to them* (Atlantic). **b** to put down (a person) with effrontery; browbeat: *Here's a villain that would face me down* (Shakespeare).
face off, a to confront in a test of strength, will, endurance, etc.: *to face off an opponent.* **b** to make a face-off in ice hockey, lacrosse, etc.: *I skated over to face off the puck to run the final two minutes of play* (Maclean's).
face out, a to put or force (a person) down or out by assuming a bold front; defeat by mere effrontery or audacity: *... you would face our Saviour out of the blessed sacrament* (Sir Thomas More). **b** to persist in maintaining (an assertion or a position which is not true): *A madcap ruffian, and a swearing Jack, That thinks with oaths to face the matter out* (Shakespeare).
face the music. See under **music.**
face to face, a with faces toward each other: *The enemies stood face to face.* **b** in the actual presence: *face to face with danger.*
face up to, to meet boldly; take full cognizance of: *Charity is not giving people things which will only encourage them to postpone facing up to the necessities under which they are going to have to live in the long run* (Atlantic).
fall (flat) on one's face, *Informal.* to fail utterly: *The system ... is only now embarking on its practical tests in operational use. "It could fall flat on its face," a senior official* [*said*] (London Times).
fly in the face of, to disobey openly; defy: *Any decision by a judge to lock up a man as a "public menace" ... would fly in the face of our whole system* (New York Times).
in (the) face of, a in the presence of: *No one wanted to surrender even in the face of invasion.* **b** in spite of: *He insisted he was right in the face of facts that proved he was wrong.*
on the face of it, by its own evidence; obviously: *His action, on the face of it, looks bad.*
pull a long face, to look sad, unhappy, or disapproving: *He pulled a long face when he was told to clean up the mess his brother had made.*
set one's face against, to oppose and resist: *Set your faces ... against a whole faction of vice* (Bishop Joseph Hall).
show one's face, to appear; be seen: *I should be ashamed to show my face in public* (Samuel Richardson).
stare one in the face, a to be very evident to one; force itself on one's notice: *The contradiction stared them in the face.* **b** to seem very likely or certain to happen soon to one: *Ruin and bankruptcy were staring him in the face* (Edward L. Ellenborough).
to one's face, a in one's presence: *Sharp ... read to their faces the whole service as it stood in the book* (Macaulay). **b** openly; boldly: *Thy very children ... curse thee to thy face* (William Cowper).
[< Old French *face* < Vulgar Latin *facia* < Latin *faciēs* form, related to *facere* make. See etym. of doublet **facies.**]
—*Syn. n.* **1, 2 Face, countenance, visage** mean the front part of the head. **Face,** the common word, emphasizes the physical nature or the features: *That girl has a pretty face.* **Countenance,** a more formal word, emphasizes the looks, especially as they reveal a person's thoughts, feelings, or character: *He has a cheerful countenance.* **Visage,** a distinctly literary term for either face or countenance, emphasizes the general look of the face: *We think of the visage of Abraham Lincoln.*

***face**
definition 1

bones of the face:

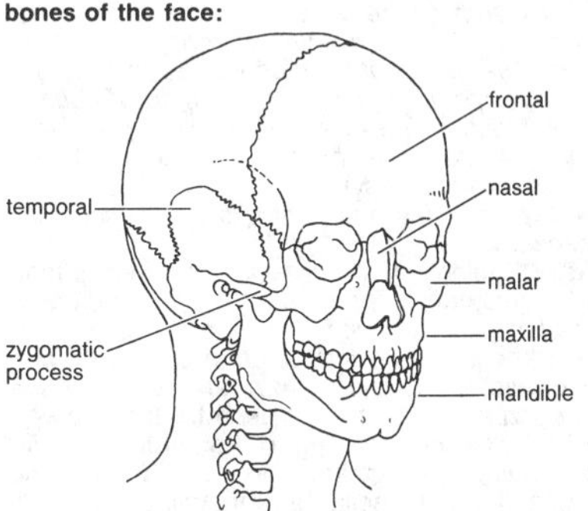

muscles of the face:

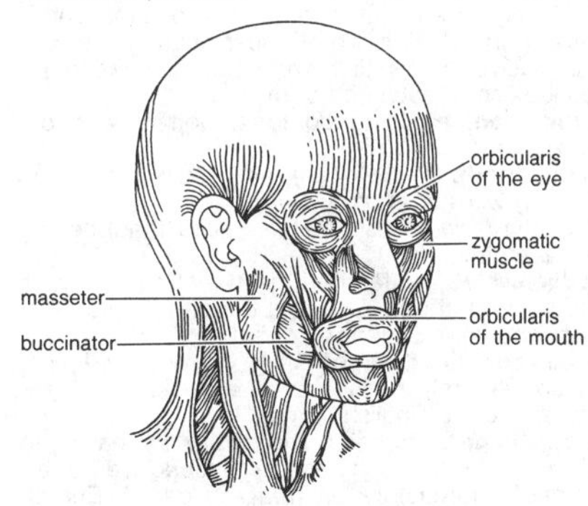

face|a|ble (fā′sə bəl), *adj.* that can be faced or approached.
face brick, a compact brick of clay or shale, used especially on the exterior part of a wall.
face card, a king, queen, or jack of playing cards.
face-cen|tered (fās′sen′tərd), *adj. Physics.* (of crystalline structures) having cubic crystals with an atom at each corner and an atom in the center of each face.
face|cloth (fās′klôth′, -kloth′), *n.* a cloth to wash the face with: *She found me a clean towel and facecloth and took the candles and tablecloth away* (New Yorker).
face cord, a unit for measuring cut firewood. A pile of wood 4 feet high, 8 feet long, and often 2 feet wide (but varying in width) is a face cord.
face cream, a cosmetic cream for the face.
faced (fāst), *adj.* having a special finish on the face or surface: *faced cloth.*
-faced, *combining form.* having a —— face or look: *Round-faced = having a round face. Satin-faced garments = garments having a satin face.*
face|down (*adv.* fās′doun′; *n.* fās′doun′), *adv., n.* —*adv.* with the face downward: *Only two cards remain facedown, one of which is red* (Scientific American).
—*n. Informal.* a direct confrontation or showdown between rivals or enemies: *The other cowboy in the electoral facedown ... will no doubt make* [*a*] *political counterblow* (Punch).
face flannel, *Especially British.* facecloth.
face fly, an insect similar to the common housefly that feeds on the fluid around the eyes, nose, and mouth of livestock. The face fly was discovered in Nova Scotia in 1952 but has since spread throughout most of North America.
face|ful (fās′fu̇l), *n., pl.* **-fuls.** as much as covers a person's face: *a faceful of freckles.*
face gear, a wheel having teeth on the face, instead of on the rim.
face guard, a covering or mask to protect the face and eyes from injury, as in factory work or in fencing.
face hammer, 1 a hammer having a flat face. **2** a hammer with a cutting end and a blunt end, used in masonry.
face-hard|en (fās′här′dən), *v.t.* to harden the surface of (a metal), especially by chilling or casting.
face joint, *Architecture.* a division between stones or bricks which shows on the finished side of the wall.
face|less (fās′lis), *adj.* **1** without a face: *a faceless clock.* **2** without individuality or personality; impersonal: *This book ... trumpets its concern for faceless collectives* (New York Times). —**face′less|ly,** *adv.* —**face′less|ness,** *n.*
face-lift (fās′lift′), *n., v.* —*n.* **1** an operation to tighten the skin of the face to remove wrinkles, fat deposits, and otherwise change the features. **2** *Informal.* a superficial change to improve appearance or modernize: *The Right has called for a face-lift to give the party a more attractive image* (Manchester Guardian).
—*v.t. Informal.* **1** to change in appearance superficially, to make more attractive: *To loosen consumer purse strings Chrysler spent $150 million to face-lift its cars* (Time). **2** to tighten the skin of the face of, by an operation. —**face′-lift′er,** *n.*
face-lift|ing (fās′lift′ing), *n.* = face-lift.
face mask, 1 a covering of plastic or other material worn over the face for protection: *The diver adjusted his face mask before submerging.* **2** a mask in the likeness of a person's face.
face-off (fās′ôf′, -of′), *n.* **1** the act of placing the puck or ball between the sticks or crosses of two players from opposing sides as a way of beginning or resuming a game of hockey or lacrosse. **2** *Figurative.* a confrontation between opponents: *How elemental the face-off* [*between generations*] *can become was demonstrated ... when the state unemployment-insurance office ruled that jobless men with long hair can no longer collect unemployment benefits* (Time).
face pack, a cosmetic paste for the face.
face|plate (fās′plāt′), *n.* **1** a cover for the front, such as the metal or plastic sheet covering a light switch. **2** a round plate attached to the spindle of a lathe, for securing work to be turned.
face powder, a cosmetic powder for the face: *A makeup artist arrived at Sandringham to advise Elizabeth on such problems as foundation creams, face powder, and eye shadow* (Time).
fac|er (fā′sər), *n.* **1** a person or thing that faces. **2** *Informal.* a blow in the face. **3** *Informal.* a violent check; sudden serious difficulty.
facer canceller, a machine that automatically stacks letters with the side having the stamp face up and then postmarks the letters.
face-sav|er (fās′sā′vər), *n. Informal.* something that saves from humiliation and serves to preserve self-respect and importance.
face-sav|ing (fās′sā′ving), *adj. Informal.* serving to prevent humiliation or embarrassment: *a face-saving solution.*
***fac|et** (fas′it), *n., v.,* **-et|ed, -et|ing** or (*especially British*) **-et|ted, -et|ting.** —*n.* **1** any one of the small, polished, flat surfaces of a cut gem. **2** anything like the facet of a gem. See the picture above on the following page. **3** *Figurative.* any

Pronunciation Key: hat, āge, cãre, fär; let, ēqual, tėrm; it, īce; hot, ōpen, ôrder; oil, out; cup, pu̇t, rüle; child; long; thin; ᴛʜen; zh, measure; ə represents **a** in about, **e** in taken, **i** in pencil, **o** in lemon, **u** in circus.

one of several sides or views; a distinct part; phase; aspect: *a facet of the mind, a facet of a problem. Selfishness was a facet of his character that we seldom saw.* **4** *Zoology.* one of the individual external visual units of a compound eye: *The eyes of certain insects have facets.* **5** *Architecture.* the vertical band or strip between the flutes of a column. **6** *Anatomy.* a small, smooth, flat surface, especially on a bone.
—***v.t.*** **1** to cut facets on: *Next, we visited the rooms in which the diamonds were faceted* (New Yorker). **2** *Geology.* to grind off flat surfaces on (ridges, stones, or the like).
—***v.i.*** *Geology.* to be ground off by glacial action, winds, or water.
[< French *facette* (diminutive) < Old French *face;* see etym. under **face**]

facets

***facet**
definition 1

fa·cete (fə sēt′), *adj. Archaic.* facetious. [< Latin *facētus* witty, pleasing]
fa·ce·ti·ae (fə sē′shē ē), *n.pl.* **1** humorous sayings or writings; witticisms. **2** books of a coarse or indecent humor. [< Latin *facētiae,* plural of *facētia* jest < *facētus* witty]
fa·ce·tious (fə sē′shəs), *adj.* **1** having the habit of joking; being slyly humorous. SYN: waggish, jocular, jocose. **2** said in fun; not to be taken seriously: *facetious remarks.* [< Middle French *facétieux* (with English *-ous*) < Latin *facētia* jest < *facētus* witty] —**fa·ce′tious·ly,** *adv.* —**fa·ce′tious·ness,** *n.*
face-to-face (fās′tə fās′), *adj., adv.* —***adj.*** direct; personal: *a face-to-face talk.*
—***adv.*** in direct contact; face to face: *face-to-face with danger.*
face·up (fās′up′), *adv.* with the face upward.
face value, 1 the value stated on a bond, check, note, bill, or other paper security; par value: *When a foreigner asks for stamps they . . . offer to sell their rarities at 40 to 50 times face value* (New York Times). **2** the apparent worth or meaning: *Honest advertisements can be taken at their face value. The reader would be well advised to take nothing in the book at face value* (New Yorker).
face·work (fās′wėrk′), *n.* the part of a wall or the like, that forms the exterior, especially of the side exposed to view; facing.
fa·ci·a (fash′ē ə), *n., pl.* **fa·ci·ae** (fash′ē ē). *British.* fascia; a long, flat part, or band.
fa·cial (fā′shəl), *adj., n.* —***adj.*** **1** of the face: *a facial artery, the facial nerves.* **2** for the face: *a facial ointment.*
—***n.*** a massage or treatment of the face: *So you thought a facial and a finger wave would help you hold him, eh?* (S. J. Perelman).
[< French *facial* < Medieval Latin *facialis* < Latin *faciēs;* see etym. under **face**]
facial angle, the angle formed by two lines, one passing backward from the nostril to the center of the ear, and the other from the nostril upward to the forehead.
facial disk, the flat, feathered area surrounding the eyes of an owl.
facial index, the ratio of the length of the face to its width, usually obtained by multiplying the length by 100 and dividing by the width.
fa·cial·ly (fā′shə lē), *adv.* **1** in a facial manner; with reference to the face. **2** face to face; vis-à-vis.
facial tissue, a square of thin, soft, absorbent paper used to wipe the nose or face.
facial vision, the awareness, especially in blind persons, of nearby objects, apparently felt by having a certain sensation on the forehead.
fa·ci·end (fā′shē end), *n. Mathematics.* a number or quantity to be multiplied by another; multiplicand. [< Latin *faciendum* (thing) to be worked (on), neuter gerundive of *facere* do, make]
fa·cient (fā′shənt), *n.* **1** a doer; a person who does anything, good or bad. **2** *Mathematics.* a variable of a quantic. [< Latin *faciēns, -entis,* present participle of *facere* do]
fa·ci·es (fā′shē ēz), *n.* **1** *Geology.* the particular character of a formation in a given region with respect to fossils of animals and plants, rock structure, and other characteristics. **2** the general appearance or aspect, as of a species or group.
3 *Medicine.* the expression or appearance of the face, especially as indicating a particular disorder or condition.
[< Latin *faciēs* form, related to *facere* make. See etym. of doublet **face.**]
fac·ile (fas′əl), *adj.* **1** easily done or used; taking little effort: *Lazy people seek facile tasks. Facile methods speed up work.* **2** moving, acting, or working easily or rapidly: *The gossip has a facile tongue. He writes in a facile style.* SYN: ready, expert, dexterous. **3** of easy manners or temper; gentle; agreeable; yielding: *Her facile nature adapted itself to any group of people without effort. Since Adam and his facile consort Eve lost Paradise* (Milton). SYN: flexible, mild. **4** *Obsolete.* easy to understand.
[< Old French *facile,* learned borrowing from Latin *facilis* easy < *facere* do] —**fac′ile·ly,** *adv.* —**fac′ile·ness,** *n.*
fa·ci·le prin·ceps (fas′ə lēprin′seps), *Latin.* easily the first or foremost.
fa·ci·lis de·scen·sus A·ver·no or **A·ver·ni** (fas′ə-lis di sen′səs ə vėr′nō, ə vėr′nī), *Latin.* easy is the descent to Avernus (or of Avernus); the path to hell is easy (Virgil, *Aeneid* 6:126).
fa·cil·i·tate (fə sil′ə tāt), *v.t.,* **-tat·ed, -tat·ing. 1** to make easy; lessen the labor of; help forward (a process): *Mother's vacuum cleaner facilitates her housework. Removing a splinter from a wound facilitates healing.* SYN: expedite. **2** to assist (a person). —**fa·cil′i·ta·tor,** *n.*
fa·cil·i·ta·tion (fə sil′ə tā′shən), *n.* **1** the act or process of facilitating. **2** *Psychology.* greater ease of performance of an action resulting from simultaneous performance of another action, from increased ease of transmission of nerve impulse, or prior performance of the same action.
fa·cil·i·ta·tive (fə sil′ə tā′tiv), *adj.* facilitating; helpful.
fa·cil·i·ta·to·ry (fə sil′ə tə tôr′ē, -tōr′-), *adj.* = facilitative.
fa·cil·i·ty (fə sil′ə tē), *n., pl.* **-ties. 1** absence of difficulty; ease: *Long practice enabled the storekeeper to add up long columns of figures with facility. The facility of communication is far greater now than it was a hundred years ago.* easiness.
2 the power to do anything easily, quickly, and smoothly; skill in using the hands or mind: *The boy ran and dodged with such facility that no one could catch him.* SYN: knack, readiness, aptitude, dexterity. **3** Usually, **facilities.** something that makes an action easy; an aid; a convenience: *Ropes, swings, and sand piles are facilities for play. The new hospital's research facilities are excellent.* **4** a place built or set aside to provide a special service: *the mental hygiene facility of a hospital. A regional computer facility . . . will serve as a research centre for affiliated bodies* (London Times). **5** easygoing quality; tendency to yield to others: *The facility of Charles was such as has perhaps never been found in any man of equal sense* (Macaulay). SYN: affability, pliancy. [< Middle French *facilité,* learned borrowing from Latin *facilitās* < *facilis* easy]
fa·ci·ne·ri·ous (fas′ə nir′ē əs), *adj. Obsolete.* facinorous.
fac·ing (fā′sing), *n.* **1** a covering of different material for ornament or protection: *A wooden house sometimes has a brick facing.* **2** a material put around the inside or outside edge of cloth to protect or trim it: *a blue coat with red facings on the collar and cuffs.* **3** anything used for these purposes. **4** *Military.* a turning to the right, left, or in the opposite direction in response to a command. **facings,** the cuffs, collar, and trimmings of a military coat: *. . . your tawny coats with greasy facings* (Lodowick Barry).
facing machine, a machine that lines up letters uniformly for automatic sorting and postmarking.
facing slip, *U.S.* a slip of paper bearing particulars such as destination and date, attached in a post office to each bag of mail.
facing tool, a cutting tool for smoothing work on a lathe.
fa·cin·or·ous (fə sin′ər əs), *adj. Archaic.* extremely wicked; atrocious; vile.
[< Latin *facinorōsus* < *facinus, -oris* (bad) deed < *facere* make]
fa·ci·o·bra·chi·al (fā′shē ō brā′kē əl), *adj.* having to do with both the face and the arm. [< Latin *faciēs* face + English *brachial*]
fa·ci·o·cer·vi·cal (fā′shē ō sėr′və kəl), *adj.* having to do with both the face and the neck. [< Latin *faciēs* face + English *cervical*]
fa·ci·o·lin·gual (fā′shē ō ling′gwəl), *adj.* having to do with both the face and the tongue (used of a form of paralysis). [< Latin *faciēs* form + English *lingual*]
fa·ckel·tanz (fäk′əl tänts′), *n.* **1** a torchlight procession held formerly at some of the German courts on the marriage of a member of the royal family. **2** a musical composition designed for such a procession.
[< German *Fackeltanz* < *Fackel* torch + *Tanz* dance]
fa·çon (fà sôN′), *n. French.* **1** make; style. **2** workmanship.
fa·çon d'a·gir (fà sô Ndà zhēr′), *French.* way of acting; behavior.
fa·çon de par·ler (fà sô N′də pàr lā′), *French.* way of speaking.
facsim., facsimile.
fac·sim·i·le (fak sim′ə lē), *n., v.,* **-led, -le·ing,** *adj.* —***n.*** **1** an exact copy or likeness; perfect reproduction: *A coupon or reasonable facsimile is required to enter the contest.* SYN: duplicate, counterpart. **2** an electronic process for transmitting images, such as printed matter or photographs, by electrical means over wire or radio, and reproducing them on paper at the receiving set.
—***v.t.*** to make a facsimile of.
—***adj.*** **1** being a facsimile: *a facsimile signature.*
2 producing facsimiles: *facsimile transmission.*
in facsimile, exactly; in exact counterpart: *The inscription is produced in facsimile* (Daniel Wilson).
[(originally) two words < Latin *fac* make! + *simile,* neuter of *similis* similar, like]
facsimile machine, = fax machine.
facsimile mail, mail sent by facsimile transmission.
facsimile telegraph, a telegraphic device for transmitting facsimiles of written messages, drawings, or photographs.
fact (fakt), *n.* **1** a thing known to be true; thing known to have happened: *scientific facts. It is a fact that the Pilgrims sailed to America on the Mayflower in 1620. Nobler than any fact My wish that failed of act* (John Greenleaf Whittier). **2** what is true; what has happened; state of things; truth; reality: *The fact is, I did not want to go to the dance. Time dissipates to shining ether the solid angularity of facts* (Emerson). SYN: actuality. **3** a thing said or supposed to be true or to have really happened: *We doubted his facts.* **4** *Law.* **a** a crime or offense: *an accessory after the fact.*
b anything that is known or alleged to have occurred in connection with a case (as distinguished from a principle or rule): *A question of fact is decided by the jury, a question of law by the court.*
5 *Obsolete.* a deed; act.
as a matter of fact, in point of actual fact; indeed: *He and I have met before; as a matter of fact, we were once on the same football team.*
in fact, as a matter of fact; truly; really: *He was touched by a feeling of awe as if he had in fact been given his death sentence by the doctor* (Graham Greene). *All of Britain, in fact, seems a sort of Old Curiosity Shop* (Harper's).
[< Latin *factum* (thing) done, neuter past participle of *facere* do. See related etym. at **factum.** See etym. of doublet **feat**[1].]
►**fact.** *The fact that* is often used where *that* alone would suffice: *He was quite conscious* [*of the fact*] *that his visitor had some other reason for coming.*
fac·ta (fak′tə), *n.* the plural of **factum.**
fact-find·er (fakt′fīn′dər), *n.* **1** an investigator; researcher. **2** a person selected to find, arrange, and evaluate issues and their background in a dispute, and sometimes to recommend a plan to settle it: *Steel-strike fact-finders failed in an attempt to get a last-minute settlement* (Wall Street Journal).
fact-find·ing (fakt′fīn′ding), *n., adj.* —***n.*** **1** = investigation. **2** = mediation.
—***adj.*** **1** of or having to do with investigation; investigating: *a fact-finding study of immigration.*
2 having to do with mediation; mediating: *a fact-finding panel.*
fac·tic·i·ty (fak tis′ə tē), *n.* factuality; factualness: *It was known all over the church that a man had denied the facticity of certain miracles* (Time).
fac·tion[1] (fak′shən), *n.* **1** a group of people in a political party, church, club, neighborhood, or other body or organization who stand up for their side or act together for some common purpose against the rest of a larger group: *A faction in our club tried to make the president resign. Public tranquility was disturbed by a discontented faction* (Edward Gibbon). SYN: party, group. **2** a selfish or unscrupulous group. SYN: clique, cabal. **3** strife or quarreling among the members of a political party, church, club, neighborhood, or other body or organization: *Faction almost broke up the club.* SYN: dissension. **4** *Obsolete.* a set of persons; class; sort.
[< Latin *factiō, -ōnis* party, class; (originally) a doing < *facere* do. See etym. of doublet **fashion.**]
fac·tion[2] (fak′shən), *n.* a story, description or other narrative based on facts but written as fiction; writing that combines fact and fiction: [*Alex*] *Haley maintained that he had created a work of "faction," historical material made readable by fictional embellishment* (Philip Kopper). [blend of *fact* and *fiction*]
fac·tion·al (fak′shə nəl), *adj.* **1** having to do with factions; partisan: *Both . . . know how to keep from getting embroiled in factional fights* (Newsweek). **2** causing faction or strife. —**fac′tion·al·ly,** *adv.*
fac·tion·al·ism (fak′shə nə liz′əm), *n.* a condition characterized by faction; tendency to factional differences: *Whether . . . pleas for less factionalism will succeed in reuniting the party will not be clear for some weeks* (London Times).
fac·tion·ist (fak′shə nist), *n.* **1** a member of a faction. **2** a person who stirs up strife.

fac|tious (fak′shəs), *adj.* **1** fond of stirring up disputes; given to causing faction: *Many of the old Puritan colonists retained their factious temperaments in the New World.* **SYN**: quarrelsome. **2** of or caused by faction. [< Latin *factiōsus* < *factiō;* see etym. under **faction**] – **fac′tious|ly**, *adv.* – **fac′tious|ness**, *n.*

fac|ti|tious (fak tish′əs), *adj.* developed by effort; not natural; forced; artificial: *His factitious smile convinced me that he was not sincere. Extensive advertising can cause a factitious demand for an article.* [< Latin *factīcius* (with English *-ous*) < *facere* do, make. See etym. of doublet **fetish**.] – **fac|ti′tious|ly**, *adv.* – **fac|ti′tious|ness**, *n.*

fac|ti|tive (fak′tə tiv), *adj. Grammar.* **1** (of a verb) giving a certain character to a person or thing. Such a verb takes both a direct object and an objective complement. *Examples:* They *made* him captain. They *called* him a fool. We *painted* the door green. **2** having to do with a verb of this kind. [< New Latin *factitivus* < Latin *factitāre* make or declare to be < *factāre* make (frequentative) < *facere* make, do] – **fac′ti|tive|ly**, *adv.*

fac|to (fak′tō), *adv. Law.* in fact; in deed; by the fact.

fact of life, a fact that cannot be disputed or changed, however undesirable it may be: *It was a "fact of life" that nations which could not pay their way in the world did not have any influence on the course of events* (Manchester Guardian Weekly). See also **facts of life**.

fac|toid (fak′toid), *n.* a contrived fact; something having no existence except as an item reported in the news media: *Juggling facts, guesses, and factoids as suits his fancy, ... he loses authority as both biographer and novelist* (George P. Elliott). [American English (coined by Norman Mailer) < *fact* + *-oid*]

fac|tor (fak′tər), *n., v.* – *n.* **1** any one of the causes that help to bring about a result; one element in a situation: *Ability, industry, and health are factors of his success in school. Endurance is an important factor of success in sports.* **2** any one of the numbers or expressions which produce a given number or quantity when multiplied together: *5 and 2 are factors of 10.* **3a** a person who does business for another; an agent; commission merchant. **b** an agent managing a trading post: *[He] so impressed Hudson's Bay officials in London that he was transferred out of Labrador to Montreal as the company's chief factor* (Maclean's). **4** *Biology.* a gene: *The terms gene, factor, and determiner will be used as synonyms to designate the units responsible for the transmission of hereditary characters* (Harbaugh and Goodrich). **5** *Scottish.* a person who manages an estate; steward; bailiff. **6** *Law.* a person appointed to manage property that is forfeited or taken away. **7** an agent or company that lends money to a firm which has not yet collected its bills. When the bills are collected, the firm pays the factor a commission on the bills paid and interest on the loan.
– *v.t.* **1** to separate or resolve into factors; factorize. **2** to buy and collect the receivable accounts of (a business).
– *v.i.* to be a factor; act or serve as a factor.
[< Latin *factor, -ōris* doer < *facere* make, do. See etym. of doublet **faitour**.]

fac|tor|a|ble (fak′tər ə bəl), *adj. Mathematics.* that can be separated or resolved into factors.

fac|tor|age (fak′tər ij), *n.* **1** the business of a factor or agent; buying and selling on commission. **2** the commission paid to a factor or agent.

factor analysis, *Statistics.* any one of various methods for correlating a set of values by analyzing the smallest possible number of factors.

***fac|to|ri|al** (fak tôr′ē əl, -tōr′-), *adj., n.* – *adj.* **1** *Mathematics.* of or having to do with a factor or a factorial: *n! is a factorial notation.* **2** of or having to do with a factory.
– *n. Mathematics.* the product of an integer multiplied by all its lower integers. *Example:* The factorial of 4 is 4 X 3 X 2 X 1 = 24, and is symbolized 4!.

***factorial**
definition 1

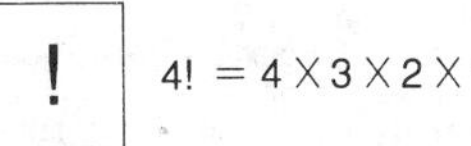

factorial series, *Mathematics.* a series proceeding by factorials instead of powers of the variable.

fac|tor|ing (fak′tər ing), *n.* **1** the business of buying bills, accounts receivable, or other obligations, and collecting them to one's own account. **2** *Mathematics.* process of resolving into factors.

fac|tor|i|za|tion (fak′tər ə zā′shən), *n.* the act or process of factorizing.

fac|tor|ize (fak′tə rīz), *v.t.,* **-ized, -iz|ing. 1** *Mathematics.* to resolve into factors. **2** *U.S. Law.* to garnishee.

fac|tor|ship (fak′tər ship), *n.* the office or business of a factor.

fac|to|ry (fak′tər ē, fak′trē), *n., pl.* **-ries. 1** a building or group of buildings where things are manufactured. A factory usually has machines in it. *Everywhere there sprang up factories using first water then steam power* (H. G. Wells). **SYN**: mill, plant. **2** a trading post in a foreign country for merchants and factors. [< Medieval Latin *factoria,* or Late Latin *factōrium* oil press or mill < Latin *factor;* see etym. under **factor**] – **fac′to|ry|less**, *adj.*

factory farm, a farm using many of the methods of a factory.

factory farming, a system of farming using many of the methods of a factory, especially in the processing of livestock.

factory ship, a ship equipped for whaling and the processing of captured whales.

fac|to|tum (fak tō′təm), *n., pl.* **-tums. 1** a person employed to do all kinds of work: *He is our factotum; he does many odd jobs. Saunders was a model valet and factotum* (Charles Reade). **2** *Obsolete.* a busybody. [< Medieval Latin *factotum* < Latin *fac* do! + *tōtum,* accusative of *tōtus* all; the whole]

fac|trix (fak′triks), *n.* a woman factor or agent.

fact sheet, a printed form issued by a government agency or business, listing the facts and data about anything.

facts of life, **1** facts that cannot be disputed or changed, however undesirable they may be: *He reminded the party of the hard political facts of life.* **2** the basic facts about sex and reproduction: *to teach children the facts of life.*

fac|tu|al (fak′chů əl), *adj.* **1** concerned with fact; consisting of facts; of the nature of fact: *The explorer kept a factual account of the trip in his diary. While the script may do violence to factual accuracy, the film catches magnificently the spirit of a unique historical moment* (Reporter). **2** real; actual. – **fac′tu|al|ly**, *adv.* – **fac′tu|al|ness**, *n.*

fac|tu|al|ism (fak′chů ə liz′əm), *n.* emphasis on or extensive use of facts. – **fac′tu|al|ist**, *n., adj.*

fac|tu|al|i|ty (fak′chů al′ə tē), *n.* the state of being factual; factualness.

fac|tum (fak′təm), *n., pl.* **-ta.** a statement of the facts of a case or controversy; memorial. [< Latin *factum;* see etym. under **fact**]

fac|ture (fak′chər), *n.* **1** the act, process, or manner of making anything; construction. **2** the thing made. [< Latin *factūra* a making; thing made < *facere* make]

fac|u|la (fak′yə lə), *n., pl.* **-lae** (-lē). *Astronomy.* one of the bright patches on the surface of the sun. [< Latin *facula* (diminutive) < *fax, facis* torch]

fac|u|lar (fak′yə lər), *adj.* of or having to do with a facula.

fac|ul|ta|tive (fak′əl tā′tiv), *adj.* **1** giving a faculty, privilege, or permission; giving the power of doing or not doing something: *a facultative order or decree.* **2** left to one's choice; optional. **3** that may or may not take place or assume a specified character. **4** *Biology.* having the power to exist under different conditions of life, as an organism which is usually a parasite but which can also grow as a saprophyte. – **fac′ul|ta′tive|ly**, *adv.*

fac|ul|ty (fak′əl tē), *n., pl.* **-ties. 1** a power of the mind or body: *the faculty of hearing, the faculty of memory. Old people sometimes lose their faculties.* **SYN**: capacity, capability. **2** the power to do some special thing, especially a power of the mind: *She has a great faculty for arithmetic. ... that faculty of beholding at a hint the face of his desire and the shape of his dream* (Joseph Conrad). **SYN**: knack, talent. **3** the teachers of a school, college, or university. **4** a department of learning in a university: *the faculty of theology, faculty of law. The faculty of medicine is made up of doctors, surgeons, etc., who teach and do research.* **5** the members of a learned profession: *The medical faculty is made up of many doctors including surgeons, internists, and pathologists.* **6** *Ecclesiastical.* a permission, authorization, or right granted by an authority, as the permission granted by a bishop to a priest to hear confession within the diocese. **7** a power or privilege given by some authority. **8** one of the powers into which the mind was formerly believed to be divided, such as the reason, will, or memory. **9** *Archaic.* a trade; profession. [< Latin *facultās* < *facilis;* see etym. under **facile**]

faculty adviser, *U.S.* a member of a college or university faculty who advises students on academic and related matters.

fac|ul|ty|man (fak′əl tē mən), *n., pl.* **-men.** *U.S.* a member of the faculty of a school, college, or university.

faculty psychology, the explanation of mental facts by the operation of general powers, especially of attention, memory, and reasoning.

faculty tax, a tax based on the ability to pay. The Colonies levied faculty taxes.

faculty theory, a theory of taxation maintaining that every man should help to carry the public burdens according to his ability.

fac|und (fak′ənd, fə kund′), *adj. Archaic.* eloquent. [< Old French *facond,* learned borrowing from Latin *fācundus* < *fārī* speak]

fad (fad), *n.* something everybody is very much interested in for a short time; fashion or craze; rage: *No one plays that game anymore; it was only a fad. Most doctors do not believe in food fads* (Sarah R. Riedman). [origin unknown]

FAD (no periods), flavin adenine dinucleotide.

fad|a|yeen (fad′ə yēn′), *n.* = fedayeen.

fad|dish (fad′ish), *adj.* **1** inclined to follow fads. **2** like a fad. – **fad′dish|ly**, *adv.* – **fad′dish|ness**, *n.*

fad|dism (fad′iz əm), *n.* devotion to fads: *environmental faddism, fact and fiction* (Electrical World).

fad|dist (fad′ist), *n., adj.* – *n.* a person devoted to a fad; person who takes up new fads: *[He] was a health faddist, and for a time lived on a massive diet of carrots washed down with turnip juice* (Time).
– *adj.* inclined to follow fads: *Some of the designers of cars have become increasingly faddist.*

fad|dle (fad′əl), *v.,* **-dled, -dling.** *Dialect.* – *v.i.* to trifle. – *v.t.* to dandle. [origin uncertain; perhaps related to **fad, fondle**]

fad|dy (fad′ē), *adj.,* **-di|er, -di|est.** = faddish.

fade¹ (fād), *v.,* **fad|ed, fad|ing,** *n.* – *v.i.* **1** to become less bright; lose color; dim: *Daylight fades when the sun sets. My blue dress faded when it was washed.* **SYN**: blanch, bleach, pale. **2** to lose freshness or strength; wither: *The flowers in her garden faded at the end of summer.* **SYN**: droop. **3** to die away; weaken; disappear little by little: *The sound of the train faded after it went by. Princes and lords may flourish or may fade* (Oliver Goldsmith). **SYN**: See syn. under **disappear. 4** *Sports.* to move or drift to the rear; retreat: *He faded back to pass.*
– *v.t.* **1** to cause to fade: *Sunlight faded the new curtains.* **SYN**: bleach. **2** *Slang.* to match all or part of the bet of (the person shooting dice).
– *n.* **1** a fading in or out: *Not since Chaplin's tramp made his great exit, has there been so melancholy a fade* (Newsweek). **2** = brake fade.
fade in, (in motion pictures, radio, and television) to become slowly more distinct or louder: *... fade in to the much-publicised naked chariot-race sequence where ... Ozymandias is challenging Ambrosius, Emperor of Malta* (Punch).
fade out, (in motion pictures, radio, and television) to diminish in sound or distinctness; become gradually less perceptible: *As the scene fades out, the hero and the heroine walk away from each other.*
[< Old French *fader* < *fade* pale, weak, perhaps a blend of Latin *fatuus* silly, tasteless, and *vapidus* flat, vapid]

fade² (fȧd), *adj. French.* flat; commonplace; dull.

fade|a|way (fād′ə wā′), *n. Baseball.* a slow ball thrown with the motion of a fast pitch, having an inside curve with some drop.

fad|ed (fā′did), *adj.* that has lost its color, freshness, or strength: *faded flowers, faded cheeks, a faded metaphor.* – **fad′ed|ly**, *adv.* – **fad′ed|ness**, *n.*

fade-in (fād′in′), *n.* (in motion pictures, radio, and television) the gradual brightening of a picture or increasing of a sound.

fade|less (fād′lis), *adj.* not fading; permanent: *fadeless colors.* – **fade′less|ly**, *adv.*

fade|om|e|ter (fā dom′ə tər), *n.* **1** an instrument that subjects colored materials to controlled amounts of light to determine their resistance to fading. **2 Fade-Ometer.** a trademark for this instrument.

fade-out (fād′out′), *n.* **1** a scene in a motion picture, radio or television show that slowly diminishes in sound and brightness until it is imperceptible: *To conform with the screen's moral code, I was always repentant at the final fade-out* (Tallulah Bankhead). **2** a gradual disappearance: *The fade-out of the moderates leaves the foes of integration firmly in control* (Wall Street Journal).

fade|proof (fād′prüf′), *adj.* resistant to fading; that will not fade: *fadeproof colors.*

fadge (faj), *v.i.,* **fadged, fadg|ing.** *Obsolete.* **1** to fit or suit; agree. **2** to get on; thrive; succeed. [origin uncertain]

fad|ing (fā′ding), *n.* **1** gradual loss of color, freshness, or vigor. **2** the periodic variation in the in-

Pronunciation Key: hat, āge, cãre, fär; let, ēqual, tėrm; it, īce; hot, ōpen, ôrder; **oi**l, **ou**t; cup, pu̇t, rüle; **ch**ild; lo**ng**; **th**in; **ᴛʜ**en; **zh**, measure; **ə** represents **a** in about, **e** in taken, **i** in pencil, **o** in lemon, **u** in circus.

tensity of the sound of a radio or the picture on a television screen.

fa|do (fä′dü), *n., pl.* **-dos.** **1** a Portuguese folk song, usually sad: *The fados are unique in their compelling sour-sweetness; and they are still being freshly composed today in their best tradition, an unusual survival in a jazz-influenced world* (Harper's). **2** a folk dance performed to this music. [< Portuguese *fado* (literally) fate < Latin *fātum*]

fae|cal (fē′kəl), *adj.* = fecal.

fae|ces (fē′sēz), *n.pl.* = feces.

fae|cu|la (fek′yə lə), *n.* = fecula.

fa|e|na (fä ā′nä), *n. Spanish.* an outstanding performance during a bullfight, a boxing match, or other contest.

Fa|en|za (fä en′tsä), *adj.* having to do with or designating the type of colorfully decorated, enameled pottery made in Faenza, Italy, in the 1500's.

fa|er|ie (fā′ər ē, fãr′ē), *n., pl.* **-er|ies,** *adj. Archaic.* —*n.* **1** fairyland. **2** a fairy. —*adj.* fairy. [variant of *fairy*]

fa|ër|ie (fā′ər ē, fãr′ē), *n., pl.* **-ies.** = faerie.

Faer|o|ese (fãr′ō ēz′, -ēs′), *adj., n., pl.* **-ese.** —*adj.* of or having to do with the Faeroe Islands, the people living there, or their language. —*n.* **1** a native or inhabitant of the Faeroe Islands. **2** the Scandinavian language of the Faeroe Islands. Also, **Faroese.**

Faer|o|ish (fãr′ō ish), *n.* = Faeroese (the language).

fa|er|y (fā′ər ē, fãr′ē), *n., pl.* **-er|ies,** *adj.* = faerie.

fa|ër|y (fā′ər ē, fãr′ē), *n., pl.* **-ër|ies.** = faery.

Faf|nir (fäv′nir, fäf′-), *n. Norse Mythology.* the dragon that guarded the Nibelung's treasure until he was slain by Sigurd.

fag[1] (fag), *v.,* **fagged, fag|ging,** *n.* —*v.t.* **1** to tire by work; weary: *After climbing to the top of the mountain he was completely fagged. The horse was fagged by the heavy load.* **SYN:** fatigue, exhaust. **2** *British.* (in certain public schools) to compel to be a fag: *A curtailment was introduced by the authorities to a monitor's powers of fagging juniors* (Observer).
—*v.i.* **1** to work hard or until wearied: *I fagged away at German* (Charlotte Brontë). **SYN:** toil. **2** *British.* (in certain public schools) to act as a fag.
—*n.* **1** hard, uninteresting work; drudgery. **2** a person who does hard work; drudge. **3** *British.* a student who waits on an older boy in certain public schools: *His lordship ... talked much of my uncle ... whose fag he had been at Eton* (Charles J. Lever).
fag out, *Informal.* to tire completely; exhaust: *He really looked fagged out—as if he hadn't slept for a week* (John Stephen Strange).
[apparently variant of *flag*[3]] —**fag′ger,** *n.*

fag[2] (fag), *n. Especially British.* **1** *Slang.* a cigarette. **2** a fag end. [probably short for *fag end*]

fag[3] (fag), *n. Slang.* a male homosexual. [origin unknown]

fa|ga|ceous (fə gā′shəs), *adj.* belonging to the beech family of trees and shrubs: *The beech, chestnut, and oak are fagaceous trees.* [< New Latin *Fagaceae* the family name < *Fagus* the genus name (< Latin *fāgus* beech tree) + English *-ous*]

fag end, 1 the last part or remnant of anything after the best part has been used: *the fag end of a cigar.* **2** the coarse, unfinished end of a piece of cloth. **3** an untwisted end of rope. **4** *Informal.* the worse end of a bargain or other arrangement: *The poor man, as usual, got the fag end of the deal.* **5** *British Informal.* **a** a cigarette or cigar butt. **b** a cigarette.

fag|ger|y (fag′ər ē), *n.* the system of fagging at certain English public schools.

fag|got[1] (fag′ət), *n., v.t.* = fagot.

fag|got[2] (fag′ət), *n. Slang.* a male homosexual. [origin unknown]

fag|got|ing (fag′ə ting), *n. Especially British.* fagoting.

fag|got|ry (fag′ə trē), *n. Slang.* male homosexuality.

faggot vote, *British.* a vote arranged dishonestly for party purposes, as by transferring to persons without voting qualifications the property or documents required to qualify them as electors.

fag|got|y (fag′ə tē), *adj. Slang.* effeminate; homosexual.

fag|gy (fag′ē), *adj.* = faggoty.

Fa|gin (fā′gən), *n.* **1** a criminal in Charles Dickens' novel *Oliver Twist,* who trained boys to be thieves. **2** any criminal who trains children to break the law.

fag|mas|ter (fag′mas′tər, -mäs′-), *n. British.* (in certain public schools) a student who has a younger boy waiting on him: *Boys found it quite agreeable to be back in school, especially if they were fagmasters* (Manchester Guardian Weekly).

fag|ot (fag′ət), *n., v.* —*n.* **1** a bundle of sticks or twigs tied together for fuel: *He built the fire with fagots. In dinner talk it is perhaps allowable to fling on any fagot rather than let the fire go out* (James M. Barrie). **2** a bundle of iron rods or pieces of iron or steel to be welded.
—*v.t.* **1** to tie or fasten together into bundles; make into a fagot or fagots. **2** to ornament with fagoting.
[< Old French *fagot* < Vulgar Latin *facellum* < Greek *phákelos* bundle]

***fag|ot|ing** (fag′ə ting), *n.* **1** an ornamental, open, zigzag stitch used for loosely joining two finished edges. **2** an ornamental stitch made by drawing horizontal threads out of the cloth and tying groups of the cross threads together in the middle.

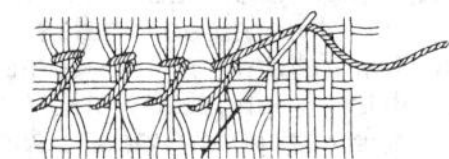
***fagoting** definition 2

fa|ham (fä′əm, fā′-), *n.* **1** an orchid grown in Réunion and Mauritius, whose leaves are used as a substitute for tea leaves. **2** the leaves so used. [origin uncertain]

fahl|band (fäl′band), *n. Mining.* a belt or zone of rock filled with metallic sulfides. [< German *Fahlband* < *fahl* pale + *Band* stripe, band]

fahl|un|ite (fä′lə nīt), *n.* a hydrated silicate of aluminum and iron resulting from an alteration of iolite. [< *Fahlun,* a city in Sweden, near where it is found + *-ite*[1]]

Fahr., Fahrenheit.

***Fahr|en|heit** (far′ən hīt), *adj., n.* —*adj.* of, based on, or according to a scale for measuring temperature, on which 32 degrees marks the freezing point of water and 212 degrees the boiling point, at standard atmospheric pressure. *Abbr:* F, F. or Fahr.
—*n.* the Fahrenheit thermometer or its scale.
[< Gabriel D. *Fahrenheit,* 1686-1736, a German physicist, who introduced it]

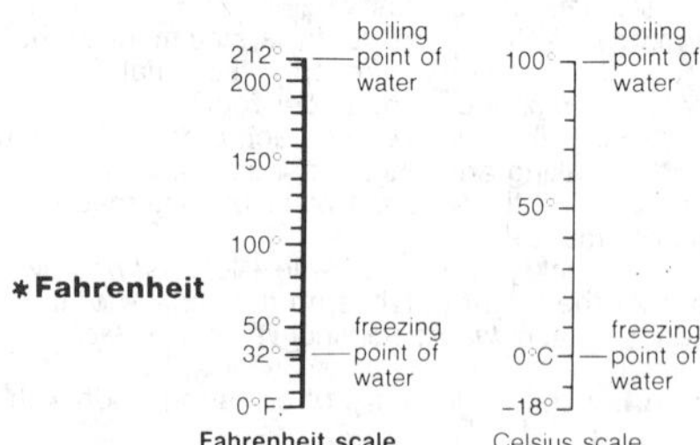

***Fahrenheit**

fai|ence or **fa|ïence** (fī äns′, fā-), *n.* a glazed, highly colored and decorated earthenware usually of fine quality. [< French *faïence,* earlier *faenze* < *Faenza,* near Ravenna, Italy, from where it was imported]

fail (fāl), *v., n.* —*v.i.* **1** to not succeed; be unable to do or become what is wanted, expected, or attempted; come out badly: *After a long drought, the crops failed. He tried hard to learn to sing, but he failed. Our envious foe hath failed* (Milton). **SYN:** miscarry, default. **2** to be missing; be not enough; fall short: *The wind failed, so we could not sail home. When our supplies failed, we had no food. His speech failed in persuasiveness and proof.* **3** to lose strength; become weak; die away: *The sick man's heart was failing.* **SYN:** decline, sink, wane, deteriorate. **4** to be unable to pay what one owes; become bankrupt: *The company lost all its money and failed in business.* **5** to be unsuccessful in an examination or course; receive a mark of failure: *He failed because he didn't study hard enough.*
—*v.t.* **1** to not do; neglect: *He failed to follow our advice.* **2** to be of no use to when needed: *When we needed his help, he failed us.* **3** to become weak or faint within: *The old man's memory failed him.* **4** to be unsuccessful in (an examination or course); receive a mark of failure in: *Bill failed two examinations and did not pass into his senior year.* **5** to give a mark of failure to (a student).
—*n.* **1** a failure: *Some college courses are graded in terms of either a pass or a fail.* **2** the failure of a stockbroker to deliver purchased stock within a specified period: *Fails generally occur because brokers are unable to obtain stock certificates within the five-day period ... allotted for payment and delivery after every securities transaction* (Time).
fail of, to be unable to have or get; lack: *The debater's argument failed of logical connection.*
without fail, without failing to do, happen, etc.; surely; certainly: *You must do your homework without fail. I will pay my bill next week without fail.*
[< Old French *faillir* < Vulgar Latin *fallīre* be cheated of; be lacking, for Latin *fallere* deceive] —**fail′er,** *n.*

failed (fāld), *adj.* that did not succeed; unsuccessful: *a failed attempt, a failed actor. These twin compositions ... certainly constitute examples of failed satire* (Louise Bogan).

fail|ing (fā′ling), *n., prep., adj.* —*n.* **1** = failure. **2** a fault; weakness; defect: *She is a charming girl in spite of her failings. His bigotry, the failing of age* (William H. Prescott). **SYN:** shortcoming. See syn. under **fault.**
—*prep.* **1** in the absence of; lacking; without: *Failing good weather, the tennis match will be played indoors.* **2** in the event of failure in: *Failing election, he will return to his law practice.*
—*adj.* that fails: *failing health, a failing grade.* —**fail′ing|ly,** *adv.*

faille (fīl, fāl), *n.* a soft, ribbed cloth of silk, rayon, cotton, or acetate with a plain or printed weave.

fail-safe (fāl′sāf′), *adj., v.,* **-safed, -saf|ing.** or **failed-, fail|ing-.** —*adj.* **1** having a built-in safety device that is automatically activated to protect the operator from injury or its parts from damage, in case of power failure or malfunction of some part of the machine: *A fail-safe reel brake prevents accidental spilling of tape in case of power failure* (Science News). *The authority said that subway trains were equipped with a fail-safe device that halts the train automatically if the brakes fail* (New York Times). **2** guaranteed not to fail; safe from failure; foolproof: *A master plan was worked out, beautifully turned and fail-safe on paper* (Manchester Guardian Weekly).
—*v.i.* to stop or alter an operation automatically in case of some malfunction or power failure: *Those with gas central heating will have cursed the irony of a system which fails-safe when the electrical power supply is severed* (Anthony Tucker).
—*v.t.* to make or cause to be fail-safe.
[< *Fail Safe*]

Fail Safe, a procedure of the U.S. Strategic Air Command in which a bomber may not proceed toward its target beyond a certain point until a final affirming order has been issued: *And even beyond Fail Safe point and all the way to bombdrop point, the war order can be reversed and the aircraft called home* (Time).

fail spot, (in forestry) a place where natural or artificial reproduction has failed.

fail|ure (fāl′yər), *n.* **1** the fact of failing; lack of success; the fact of being unable to do or become what is wanted, expected, or attempted: *failure in one's work. When disappointment trips you up or failure barks your shin* (Grantland Rice). **2** the act or fact of not doing; neglecting: *Failure to obey orders on a ship is mutiny.* **3** the fact of lacking or being absent; being not enough; falling short: *a failure of crops, failure of supplies.* **4** the fact or condition of losing strength; becoming weak; dying away: *a failure of eyesight.* **SYN:** decline, decay, deterioration. **5** the condition of being unable to pay what one owes; bankruptcy: *There were many bank failures during the depression.* **SYN:** insolvency. **6** a person or thing that has failed: *The picnic was a failure because it rained. The teacher announced that there had been only one failure in the final examination.*

fain (fān), *adv., adj. Archaic.* —*adv.* by choice; gladly; willingly: *I would fain die a dry death* (Shakespeare).
—*adj.* **1** willing, but not eager. **2** forced by circumstances; obliged: *Men were fain to eat horseflesh* (William Gouge). **3** glad; willing. **4** eager; desirous: *Love coming towards me, fair and fain* (Dante Gabriel Rossetti).
[Middle English *fein,* Old English *fægen*] —**fain′ness,** *n.*

fai|naigue (fə nāg′), *v.,* **-naigued, -nai|guing.** *British Dialect.* —*v.i.* **1** to fail to play a card of the suit that is led, when you have one; revoke; renege. **2** to break one's word; evade duty; shirk. **3** to use guile.
—*v.t.* to get by guile. —**fai|nai′guer,** *n.*

fai|ne|ance (fā′nē əns), *n.* = faineancy.

fai|ne|an|cy (fā′nē ən sē), *n.* fainéant quality or condition.

fai|né|ant (fā′nē ənt; *French* fe nā äN′), *adj., n.* —*adj.* that does nothing; idle: *Perhaps he was more industrious than the obligation to appear fainéant allows him to disclose* (Manchester Guardian Weekly).
—*n.* a person who does nothing; idler.
[< French *fainéant* < Old French *faignant* idler, present participle of *feindre* be idle, feign. Compare etym. under **faint.**]

faint (fānt), *adj., v., n., adv.* —*adj.* **1** not clear or plain; dim; hardly perceptible: *faint colors, a faint idea.* **SYN:** indistinct, faded. **2** weak; feeble: *a faint*

voice. **3** done feebly or without zest; half-hearted: *a faint attempt. Damn with faint praise* (Alexander Pope). SYN: faltering, languid. **4** ready to faint; about to faint; dizzy and weak: *He felt faint at the sight of blood.* **5** lacking courage; cowardly: *Faint heart never won fair lady* (William S. Gilbert). **6** oppressive.
—***v.i.*** **1** to lose consciousness temporarily; fall into a faint: *He fainted at the sight of his own blood.* **2** *Archaic.* to grow weak; lose courage: *"Ye shall reap, if ye faint not."* **3** *Archaic.* to lose brightness or vividness.
—***n.*** a temporary loss of consciousness caused by a lessening of the flow of blood to the brain. It is often caused by great hunger, sudden fear, illness, or exhaustion. In a faint, the person lies as if asleep and does not know what is going on around him. SYN: swoon.
—***adv.*** feebly; dimly: *Calling as he used to call, faint and far away* (Alfred Noyes).
faints, the weak and impure spirit that is produced first and last in the distillation of whiskey, etc. Also, **feints**.
[< Old French *faint*, or *feint* sluggish, feigned, past participle of *faindre*, or *feindre;* see etym. under **feign**] —**faint′er**, *n.* —**faint′ing|ly**, *adv.* —**faint′ly**, *adv.* —**faint′ness**, *n.*

faint|heart (fānt′härt′), *n.* a fainthearted person.

faint|heart|ed (fānt′här′tid), *adj.* lacking courage to carry a thing through; cowardly; timid: *She had no use for her fainthearted suitor.* SYN: feeble, timorous. —**faint′|heart′ed|ly**, *adv.* —**faint′-heart′ed|ness**, *n.*

faint|ish (fān′tish), *adj.* rather faint. —**faint′ish-ness**, *n.*

faints (fānts), *n.pl.* See under **faint**.

fair[1] (fãr), *adj., adv., n., v.* —***adj.*** **1** not favoring one more than any other; just; honest: *a fair judge. He is fair even to the people he dislikes. Every person is entitled to a fair hearing in court. By fair exchange, not robbery* (Byron). **2** according to the rules: *fair play.* **3** not good and not bad; average: *There is a fair crop of wheat this year.* SYN: middling, passable, tolerable. **4** considerable: *He made a fair sum of money on the stock market.* **5** giving promise of success; favorable; likely; promising: *a fair prospect. He is in a fair way to succeed.* SYN: propitious. **6** light; not dark: *A blond person has fair hair and skin.* **7** not cloudy or stormy; clear or sunny: *The weather will be fair today.* **8** pleasing to see; beautiful: *a fair lady.* SYN: pretty, comely, attractive. **9** smooth; even: *That ship has fair lines.* **10** gentle; civil; courteous: *fair words.* **11** without spots or stains; clean: *She made a fair copy of her letter and threw the dirty one away.* SYN: spotless, untarnished, pure. **12** easily read; plain: *fair handwriting.* **13** not blocked up; open: *a fair view of the ocean.* SYN: unobstructed. **14** seeming good at first, but not really so: *His fair promises proved false.* **15** *Obsolete.* desirable; elegant.
—***adv.*** **1** in a fair manner; honestly: *fair spoken, to play fair.* **2** directly; straight: *The stone hit him fair in the head.*
—***n.*** **1** a thing that is fair. **2** *Archaic.* a woman; sweetheart. **3** *Obsolete.* beauty; fairness.
—***v.i.*** **1** to become fair. **2** (of the weather) to clear. **3** to become flush; fit according to the curvature: *In normal flight the doors fair into the fuselage.*
—***v.t.*** to make fair.
bid fair. See under **bid**.
fair and square, a just; honest: *As a businessman, he was fair and square.* **b** justly; honestly: *She won the game fair and square.*
fair to middling, moderately good; average: *Costuming is fair to middling, and the settings ... do not seem worthy of Texas millions* (Wall Street Journal).
for fair, *U.S.* **a** *Informal.* completely; altogether: *What you say is true, for fair!* **b** playing the game of marbles for fun, returning the marbles won after each game.
[Old English *fæger*]
—***Syn.*** *adj.* **1 Fair, just, impartial** mean not showing favor in making judgments. **Fair** emphasizes putting all on an equal footing, not favoring one because of personal feelings or interests: *The umpire is fair even to players he dislikes.* **Just** emphasizes acting only according to what is right or lawful, leaving out personal leanings or anything favoring one side: *A judge's decisions must be just, equal, and exact for all men.* **Impartial** emphasizes complete absence of prejudices regarding the matter at issue: *We need someone impartial to settle this quarrel.*

fair[2] (fãr), *n.* **1** a showing of products and manufactured goods for the purpose of helping people see what has been done, and urging them to buy better seeds, stock, and machinery: *At the county fair last year, prizes were given for the best farm products and livestock.* SYN: exhibit, exhibition. **2** a gathering of people for the buying and selling of goods, often held in a certain place at regular times during the year: *a horse fair.* **3** an entertainment and sale of articles; bazaar: *Our church held a fair to raise money for charity.* [< Old French *feire* < Vulgar Latin *fēria* holiday, market fair, for Latin *fēriae*, plural, festal days, (religious) festival]

fair ball, *Baseball.* a batted ball that is not foul, permitting the batter to start around the bases.

fair catch, *Football.* a catch of a kicked ball after the receiver has given a certain signal that he will not run with it. Interference with him brings a penalty.

fair comment, *Law.* **1** criticism that expresses one's honest opinion and does not maliciously distort facts. **2** the right to make such criticism: *The defendants denied that the words complained of were defamatory of the plaintiffs and pleaded, inter alia, fair comment* (London Times).

fair copy, a copy of a document made after final correction.

Fair Deal, the name given by President Harry S. Truman to his domestic policy, particularly during and after the 1948 presidential campaign. —**Fair Dealer**.

fair dinkum, *British and Australian Slang.* very good; dinkum.

fair employment, the hiring and treatment of workers without discrimination against race, religion, sex, or national origin.

faire sui|vre (fer swē′vrə), *French.* (of mail) please forward.

fair-faced (fãr′fāst′), *adj.* **1** having a fair or beautiful face. **2** having a fair or light complexion. **3** seeming to be fair; plausible; specious.

Fair|field (fãr′fēld′), *n.* a decorative printing type of the old style.

fair game, **1** animals or birds that it is lawful to hunt. **2** *Figurative.* a suitable object of pursuit or attack: *The bully thought I was fair game. Government departments and national marketing boards generally are considered fair game by both members of the Opposition and private humorists* (Manchester Guardian).

fair|ground (fãr′ground′), *n.* a place outdoors, usually with equipment for exhibitions and entertainment, where fairs are held.

fair-haired (fãr′hãrd′), *adj.* having light-colored hair.

fair-haired boy, *Informal.* a favorite.

fair housing, the sale or rental of private housing without discrimination against race, religion, or national origin.

fair|ies′-horse (fãr′ēz hôrs′), *n.* = ragwort.

fair|ies′-ta|ble (fãr′ēz tā′bəl), *n.* **1** = mushroom. **2** any similar fungus.

fair|i|ly (fãr′ə lē), *adv.* in a fairylike manner.

fair|ing[1] (fãr′ing), *n.* an outer structure or surface of an aircraft or ship which reduces air or water resistance. [< *fair*[1], verb + *-ing*[1]]

fair|ing[2] (fãr′ing), *n. Archaic.* **1** a present given at or brought from a fair: *Fairings were what would now be called souvenirs—ribbons, trinkets, and cakes cut into the form of animals* (Edward J. Lee). **2** any present or gift. [< *fair*[2] + *-ing*[1]]

fair|ish (fãr′ish), *adj.* fairly good, well, or large.

Fair Isle, **1** any one of various woolen articles of wear with colorful designs, originally knitted on Fair Isle, one of the Shetland Islands, near Scotland. **2** of or designating such articles of wear: *Fair Isle mittens, a Fair Isle sweater.*

fair-lead (fãr′lēd′), *n. Nautical.* a strip of board having holes in it, or a ring, thimble, or block, through which running rigging is passed to be guided and kept clear.

fair-lead|er (fãr′lē′dər), *n.* = fair-lead.

fair|ly (fãr′lē), *adv.* **1** in a fair manner: *fairly matched.* **2** not extremely; to a fair degree; moderately; passably: *He rides fairly well.* SYN: tolerably. **3** justly; honestly: *That salesman deals fairly with his customers. He came by his fortune fairly by wise investments.* SYN: impartially. **4** rather; somewhat; moderately: *She is a fairly good pupil, about average.* **5** absolutely; positively; actually; completely: *He was fairly beside himself with anger.* **6** clearly. SYN: legibly, distinctly, plainly. **7** *Obsolete.* gently; softly; courteously.

fair maid, **1** *U.S. Dialect.* a scup or porgy. **2** *British Dialect.* a dried or smoked pilchard.

Fair Maid of February, = snowdrop.

fair market value, a value established by a buyer with a clear intention to buy and a seller with a clear intention to sell, both of whom are acquainted with market conditions.

fair-mind|ed (fãr′mīn′did), *adj.* not prejudiced; just; impartial: *a fair-minded judge.* —**fair′-mind′ed|ly**, *adv.* —**fair′-mind′ed|ness**, *n.*

fair|ness (fãr′nis), *n.* the condition of being fair; justice: *Our teacher is known for her fairness in grading pupils.*

fairness doctrine, *U.S.* the principle of providing equal radio and television broadcasting time for different points of view in a controversial public issue: *The Federal Communications Commission ruled that under the so-called "fairness doctrine," all broadcasters who carry cigarette advertising must also carry announcements and programs telling of the possible perils of smoking* (New York Times).

fair play, fair action or treatment, as in a game or in business: *... the spirit of competition, which is not something to be deplored if kept in bounds by a spirit of fair play* (Newsweek).

fair sex, women.

fair shake, *U.S. Informal.* fair treatment or arrangement: *But we're right proud of the principle that everybody is entitled to a fair shake in court* (Wall Street Journal).

fair-spo|ken (fãr′spō′kən), *adj.* speaking smoothly and pleasantly; civil; courteous: *a fair-spoken young man.*

fair trade, the marketing of trademarked goods in accordance with a fair trade agreement.

fair-trade (fãr′trād′), *v.t.*, **-trad|ed, -trad|ing**. **1** to set a minimum retail price on (a trademarked product). **2** to sell (a trademarked product) in accordance with a fair trade agreement. —**fair′-trad′er**, *n.*

fair trade agreement, *U.S.* an agreement which permits manufacturers to set minimum price levels on products. In states that have legalized this agreement, retailers must hold to the price levels set by the manufacturers.

fair value, the value of something as estimated for purposes of sale or taxation based on market value, earning power, good will, and other assets.

fair|way (fãr′wā′), *n.* **1** an unobstructed passage or way: *The fairway in a harbor is the channel for ships.* **2** the part in a golf course between the tee and putting green, where the grass is kept short: *He hooked his drive off the high tee into thick, impossible rough to the left of the fairway* (Time). See picture under **golf course**.

fair-weath|er (fãr′weᴛʜ′ər), *adj.* **1** of or fitted for fair weather: *fair-weather clothing.* **2** *Figurative.* weakening or failing in time of need: *a fair-weather friend.*

fair|y (fãr′ē), *n., pl.* **fair|ies**, *adj.* —***n.*** **1** a supernatural being with magic powers who could help or harm human beings. In recent legend, fairies have been pictured as very small, and sometimes very lovely and delicate. In medieval stories, however, fairies were often of full human size. SYN: elf, fay, sprite, brownie. **2** fairies; fairyland: *Her ears are pointed at the tips, She stayed so long in Fairy* (Stephen Vincent Benét). **3** *Slang.* a male homosexual.
—***adj.*** **1** of fairies: *fairy voices.* **2** like a fairy; lovely and delicate: *a fairy shape.*
[< Old French *faerie* < *fae;* see etym. at **fay**[1]]

fairy bird, the smallest tern, about nine inches long, having a white crescent on its black cap, a yellow bill tipped with black, and yellow or orange feet; least tern.

fairy bluebird, any one of several East Indian passerine birds that are a brilliant blue and black.

fair|y-cake (fãr′ē kāk′), *n. British.* a small sponge cake, often iced or decorated.

fairy creeper, a delicate climbing vine of the fumitory family of eastern North America, having panicles of drooping white or purplish flowers.

fairy cup, any one of a group of bright-red, cuplike or disklike fungi, growing on the ground and on decaying wood.

fairy dahlia, = pompon (def. 3).

fairy fly, a hymenopterous insect whose larvae feed on destructive bugs.

fairy gold, **1** = fairy money. **2** money or wealth lacking real substance or value.

fair|y|hood (fãr′ē hu̇d), *n.* **1** fairy state or nature. **2** fairies collectively.

fair|y|ism (fãr′ē iz əm), *n.* **1** the state, character, or action of a fairy. **2** fairylike quality. **3** belief in fairies.

fair|y|land (fãr′ē land′), *n.* **1** a place where the fairies are supposed to live. **2** *Figurative.* an enchanting and pleasant place: *The garden was a fairyland of beautiful flowers and sweet odors.*

fairy lantern, = mariposa lily.

fair|y|like (fãr′ē līk′), *adj.* resembling or suggesting a fairy.

fairy lily, = zephyr lily.

fairy money, money that in old legends and fairy tales is given by the fairies, only to turn into withered leaves or rubbish.

fairy ring, a ring of grass differing in color from the grass surrounding it, formed by the growth of certain fungi. People used to think the fairies made it when dancing.

fair|y-ring mushroom (fãr′ē ring′), a mushroom

Pronunciation Key: ha**t, ā**ge, c**ã**re, f**ä**r; l**e**t, **ē**qual, t**ė**rm; **i**t, **ī**ce; h**o**t, **ō**pen, **ô**rder; **oi**l, **ou**t; c**u**p, p**u̇**t, r**ü**le; **ch**ild; lo**ng**; **th**in; **ᴛʜ**en; **zh**, measure; **ə** represents **a** in about, **e** in taken, **i** in pencil, **o** in lemon, **u** in circus.

that grows in fairy rings and has a flavor like nuts. It is often dried and preserved as a food.

fairy rose, miniature red rose, derived from the China rose, with flowers about an inch across growing on bushes about a foot high.

fairy shrimp, a small crustacean with a semitransparent, pinkish inner shell that swims on its back and is common to freshwater pools.

fairy stone, **1** a fossil sea urchin of the Cretaceous period. **2** a clay concretion; clay stone. **3** a staurolite in the form of cruciform twins. **4** an arrowhead of stone.

fairy tale, **1** a story about fairies, pixies, elves, or other beings with magic powers. **2** *Informal, Figurative.* something said that is not true; falsehood; lie.

fair|y-tale (fãr′ē tāl′), *adj.* out of or as if out of a fairy tale: *a fairy-tale wedding dress. This book has no fairy-tale ending, and ... seems an attempt at a more serious study* (New Yorker).

fairy tern, a small, pure white tern of the islands of the Southern Hemisphere that lays a single egg in a hollow place without making a nest; love tern.

fait ac|com|pli (fe tȧ kôN plē′), *pl.* **faits ac|com|plis** (fe tȧ kôN plē′), *French.* **1** a thing done and therefore no longer worth opposing: *Wilson had no preconceived ideas about the future boundaries of Europe and was faced with the dissolution of the Hapsburg Empire virtually as a fait accompli* (Economist). **2** (literally) an accomplished fact.

faith (fāth), *n., interj., v.* —*n.* **1** a believing without proof; trust; confidence: *We have faith in our friends. Faith is the substance of things hoped for, the evidence of things not seen* (Hebrews 11:1). **SYN**: reliance. **2** belief in God or in God's promises, religion, or spiritual things: *Faith without works is dead* (James 2:26). **3** what a person believes: *Faith that he was on the right track supported him through all his research.* **SYN**: doctrine, tenet, creed. **4** a system of religion: *the Christian faith, the Jewish faith.* **5** a being loyal; faithfulness: *Good faith is honesty of intention; bad faith is intent to deceive.* **SYN**: fidelity, loyalty, constancy.

—*interj.* truly; indeed: *I'd rather be in old John's chimney corner, faith* (Dickens).

—*v.t. Archaic.* to put faith in; trust.

break faith, to break one's promise: *If you break faith once, you won't be believed the next time.*

in bad faith, dishonestly; insincerely: *The swindler's offer was in bad faith as he never expected to honor the agreement.*

in faith, truly; indeed: *In faith, man ... I was never so sorry* (Sir Thomas More).

keep faith, to keep one's promise: *She promised to pay her debt next day and she kept faith.*

keep the faith, *U.S. Informal.* to remain faithful to one's convictions; refuse to retreat or give up: *The Journal ... explained rather lamely that it had been concerned about libel charges. "The Journal couldn't keep the faith," retorted the mayor* (Time).

[< Old French *feit* < Latin *fidēs* < *fīdere* to trust. See etym. of doublet **fay**².]

faith cure, **1** a method of attempting to cure disease by prayer and religious faith alone. **2** a cure effected by this method.

faith|ful (fāth′fəl), *adj., n.* —*adj.* **1** worthy of trust; doing one's duty; keeping one's promise; loyal: *A faithful friend keeps his promises. A faithful servant is reliable and can be depended on to do his work. His faithful dog shall bear him company* (Alexander Pope). **2** true to fact; accurate: *The witness gave a faithful account of what happened.* **SYN**: precise, exact. **3** *Archaic.* full of faith; trusting; believing.

—*n.* those who are faithful.

the faithful, a true believers, especially: (1) those who have been baptized as members of a Christian church; Christians: *The faithful turned out in large numbers for the outdoor Easter dawn service.* (2) the adherents of the Moslem faith: *The caliph rallied the faithful against the foe.* **b** loyal followers or supporters: *All these as well as most of the old festival faithfuls will be competing* (New Statesman).

—**faith′ful|ly**, *adv.* —**faith′ful|ness**, *n.*

—*Syn. adj.* **1 Faithful, loyal, constant** mean true to a person or thing. **Faithful** emphasizes being true to a person, group, belief, duty, or trust to which one is bound by a promise, pledge, honor, or love: *He is a faithful friend.* **Loyal** adds to *faithful* the idea of wanting to stand by and fight for the person or thing, even against heavy odds: *She was loyal during his trial.* **Constant** implies steadfast devotion to friends or loved ones: *The dog is her constant protector. Men were deceivers ever; ... To one thing constant never* (Shakespeare).

faith healer, a person who professes to cure the sick by means of prayer and other expressions of faith.

faith healing, = faith cure.

faith|less (fāth′lis), *adj.* **1** not true to duty or to one's promises; not loyal: *That traitor was faithless to his country.* **SYN**: disloyal, false, inconstant, fickle, perfidious. **2** that cannot be trusted; not reliable: *a faithless coward. Yonder faithless phantom flies to lure thee to thy doom* (Oliver Goldsmith). **SYN**: unstable. **3a** without faith, especially religious faith; unbelieving: *He lived a faithless life.* **SYN**: incredulous, skeptical, doubting. **b** (among Christians) without Christian faith.

—**faith′less|ly**, *adv.* —**faith′less|ness**, *n.*

fai|tour or **fai|tor** (fā′tər), *n. Archaic.* an impostor; rogue. [< Anglo-French *faitour,* Old French *faitor* doer < Latin *factor.* See etym. of doublet **factor**.]

faits di|vers (fe dē ver′), *n.pl. French.* news items; trivial happenings.

fa|ja (fä′Hä, fä′hä), *n. Spanish.* a kind of colored sash worn instead of belts by men in Spain and Latin America.

fake¹ (fāk), *v.,* **faked, fak|ing,** *n., adj.* —*v.t.* **1** to make up to seem satisfactory; falsify; counterfeit: *to fake an answer. The picture was faked by pasting together two photographs.* **2** to give intentionally a false impression of; pretend; feign: *to fake illness.* **SYN**: simulate. **3** *Sports.* **a** to mislead or outmaneuver (an opponent). **b** to pretend to make (a play or movement) to mislead or outmaneuver an opponent. **4** (in jazz) to improvise: *to fake the harmony, to fake the clarinet part.*

—*v.i.* **1** to practice deception; produce a fake: *He isn't really hurt; he's only faking.* **2** *Sports.* to fake an opponent, movement, or play: *I faked to the sideline and hooked back* (Gene Williams). **3** (in jazz) to improvise.

—*n.* **1** anything made to seem other than what it actually is; a fraud; deception: *The beggar's limp was a fake.* **SYN**: cheat. **2** a person who fakes: *Anyone who says he can fly like a bird is a fake.* **3** *Sports.* a throw, kick, pass, or any play or movement intended to outmaneuver an opponent. **4** a relatively elaborate contrivance or apparatus used by a stage magician to deceive his audience; a kind of gimmick.

—*adj.* intended to deceive; false: *a fake telegram. The spy used a fake passport to get in and out of the enemy country.*

fake out, *U.S. Informal.* to mislead by a fake: *Lest they be faked out, they learn like any linebacker that when the offensive linemen charge, it is usually a run* (Time).

[origin uncertain; perhaps variant of earlier *feak,* or *feague* do (for), work (on) someone or thing, perhaps < German *fegen* clean up, furbish]

fake² (fāk), *n., v.,* **faked, fak|ing.** *Nautical.* —*n.* one circle or winding of a rope or cable, that is laid in a coil so that it may be easily run out.

—*v.t.* to lay or wind (a rope or cable) in fakes; coil. [origin uncertain]

fake book, *U.S.* a book reproducing the melodies or similar shorthand versions of copyrighted popular songs without permission of the copyright owners.

fa|keer (fə kir′), *n.* = fakir.

fake|ment (fāk′mənt), *n.* a fake.

fak|er (fā′kər), *n. Informal.* **1** a person who fakes. **2** a petty swindler. **3** = peddler.

fak|er|y (fā′kər ē), *n., pl.* **-er|ies.** *Informal.* deceit; fraud.

fa|kir (fə kir′, fā′kər), *n.* **1a** a Moslem holy man who lives by begging. **b** = dervish. **2** a Hindu ascetic, who sometimes performs extraordinary feats, such as lying upon sharp knives or nails. [< Arabic *faqīr* poor (man)]

fa|kir|ism (fə kir′iz əm, fā′kər-), *n.* **1** religious mendicancy, especially as practiced among Moslem dervishes. **2** the ascetic practices of Hindu fakirs.

fa-la (fä′lä′), *n. Music.* **1** a meaningless refrain in old songs and madrigals. **2** a kind of madrigal or part song of the 1500's and 1600's. Also, **fal-la.**

fa|la|fel (fə lä′fəl), *n.* = felafel.

fa|la|na|ka (fä′lə nä′kə), *n.* a carnivorous animal of Madagascar, of the same family as the civet cat, that subsists on insects and fruit. [< the Malagasy name]

Fa|lange (fā′lanj; *Spanish* fä läng′hä), *n.* a Spanish fascist group holding power in Spain since the Spanish civil war of 1936-1939: *The first to manifest its discontent was the Falange, Spain's only official political party and one of the pillars of the National Movement, as Franco calls his regime* (Atlantic).

Fa|lan|gism (fə lan′jiz əm), *n.* the fascism of the Falange.

Fa|lan|gist (fə lan′jist), *n., adj.* —*n.* a member of the Falange.

—*adj.* of or representing the Falange and its policies: *Falangist ranks have been infiltrated by extremists of both right and left* (Atlantic).

[< Spanish *Falangista* < *falange* phalanx < Latin *phalanx*]

Fa|la|sha (fä lä′shə), *n.* an Ethiopian sect that practices a form of Judaism and claims descent from Hebrew immigrants who followed the Queen of Sheba.

fal|ba|la (fal′bə lə), *n.* a flounce; furbelow. [< French *falbala*]

fal|cate (fal′kāt), *adj.* curved like a sickle; hooked; falciform: *a falcate cartilage.* [< Latin *falcātus* < *falx, falcis* sickle]

fal|cat|ed (fal′kā tid), *adj.* = falcate.

fal|ca|tion (fal kā′shən), *n.* **1** falcate condition. **2** a falcate part or appendage.

fal|chion (fôl′chən), *n.* **1** a broad, short sword with an edge that curves sharply to a point. **2** any sword. [< Old French *fauchon* < Vulgar Latin *falciō, -ōnis* < Latin *falx, falcis* sickle. See related etym. at **falcon**.]

fal|ci|form (fal′sə fôrm), *adj.* sickle-shaped; falcate. [< New Latin *falciformis* < Latin *falx, falcis* sickle + *forma* form]

fal|cip|a|rum malaria (fal sip′ər əm), a very severe form of malaria which runs its course in a relatively short time and without relapses. [< New Latin *falciparum* the species name of the transmitting mosquito < Latin *falx, falcis* sickle + *parere* to bear (because of the shape of the organism)]

***fal|con** (fôl′kən, fal′-, fô′-), *n.* **1** any one of various hawks, especially the female, trained to hunt and kill birds and small game. In the Middle Ages, hunting with falcons was a popular sport. **2** the female peregrine. **3** any one of a family of birds of prey that hunt in the daytime, especially a swift-flying hawk having a short tail, a short, curved, notched bill, and long wings and claws. Falcons take their quarry as it moves. **4** a short, light cannon of the 1400's through the 1600's. [< Old French *faucon* < Late Latin *falcō, -ōnis* < Latin *falx, falcis* sickle (because of its hooked talons). See related etym. at **falchion**.] —**fal′con|like′**, *adj.*

***falcon**
definition 1

fal|con|er (fôl′kə nər, fal′-, fô′-), *n.* **1** a person who hunts with falcons; hawker. **2** a person who breeds and trains falcons for hunting.

fal|co|net¹ (fôl′kə net, fal′-, fô′-), *n.* a little falcon, especially any one of various Asiatic species.

fal|co|net² (fôl′kə net, fal′-, fô′-), *n.* a smaller and lighter falcon (def. 4). [< Italian *falconetto* (diminutive) < *falcone* falcon < Late Latin *falcō;* see etym. under **falcon**]

fal|con-gen|tle (fôl′kən jen′təl, fal′-, fô′-), *n.* **1** the female of the peregrine falcon. **2** the female of any falcon. [< Middle French *faucon gentil*]

fal|co|nid (fal′kə nid), *n.* any one of a family of diurnal birds of prey, now especially a hawk but formerly also including eagles and buzzards.

fal|con|i|form (fal′kə nə fôrm), *adj.* of or having to do with the order that comprises all birds of prey except the owls.

fal|con|ry (fôl′kən rē, fal′-, fô′-), *n.* **1** the sport of hunting with falcons or hawks; hawking. **2** the training of falcons or hawks for hunting.

fal|cu|la (fal′kyə lə), *n., pl.* **-lae** (-lē). a sharp, sickle-shaped claw, as that of a cat. [< Latin *falcula* (diminutive) < *falx, falcis* sickle]

fal|cu|late (fal′kyə lit), *adj. Zoology.* having the form of a falcula; falcate.

fal|dage (fôl′dij), *n.* an old English law under which the lord of a manor required a tenant's sheep to pasture on his fields as a means of manuring the land, he in turn being bound to provide a fold for the sheep. [Middle English *faldage* < *fald* fold² + *-age*]

fal|de|ral (fal′də ral), *n.* **1** a flimsy thing; trifle; gewgaw. **2** foolish talk or ideas; nonsense; rubbish. Also, **folderol.** [< *fal-de-ral,* a meaningless refrain in songs]

fal|de|rol (fal′də rol), *n.* = falderal.

fald|stool (fôld′stül′), *n.* **1** a chair, armless and, formerly, folding, used by a bishop or other prelate when officiating in his own church away from the throne, or in a church not his own. **2a** a movable folding stool or desk at which worshipers kneel during certain acts of devotion. **b** such a stool used by the sovereigns of Great Britain at the ceremony of coronation. **c** (in the Church of England) a small desk at which the litany is said or sung. [< Medieval Latin *faldistolium,* perhaps

< Germanic (compare Old Saxon *faldistōl* (literally) folding seat < *faldan* to fold + *stōl* seat, stool)]

fal|le (fä′lə), *n.* (in Samoa) a house, especially a house with open sides and a thatched roof supported by poles with palm-leaf blinds that can be rolled down. [< Samoan *fale*]

fall (fôl), *v.*, **fell, fall|en, fall|ing,** *n., adj.* —*v.i.* **1** to drop or come down from a higher place: *The snow falls fast. Leaves fall from the trees.* **SYN:** descend, sink. **2** to come down suddenly from a standing position: *He fell on his knees. My baby brother often falls now that he is learning to walk. The walls of the burning building fell.* **3** to hang down: *Her curls fell upon her shoulders.* **4** to be directed downward: *She blushed and her eyes fell. The light falls on my book.* **5** *Figurative.* to do wrong; become bad or worse; sin: *Adam was tempted and he fell. It is their husbands' faults if wives do fall* (Shakespeare). **6** *Figurative.* to lose position, power, or dignity; be taken by any evil: *The President fell from the people's favor.* **7** *Figurative.* to be captured, overthrown, or destroyed: *The city has fallen into the power of its enemies. The government fell to the rebels.* **8** to drop wounded or dead; be killed: *Many men fell in that battle.* **9a** to pass into some condition or position; become: *He fell sick. The baby fell asleep. The boy and girl fell in love. The rent falls due on Monday. The buildings of ancient Rome fell into ruins. He fell heir to his uncle's riches. ... liberalism fell into discredit with the country* (Lytton Strachey). **b** *Figurative.* to come as if by stumbling or slipping; become involved; be drawn (into): *to fall into a bad habit, to fall into an argument.* **10a** to come as if by dropping: *When night falls the stars appear. He listened to every word that fell from her lips. His conclusion fell wide of the answer.* **b** (of the young of certain animals) to be born: *The lambs should fall in May.* **11a** to come by chance or lot: *Our choice fell on him. The sovereignty will fall upon Macbeth* (Shakespeare). **b** to be thrown (on); happen (upon), usually by chance: *fallen upon evil times.* **12** to come to pass; happen; occur: *Christmas fell on Sunday that year.* **13** to pass by inheritance: *The money fell to the only son.* **14** to have proper place or position: *The accent of "farmer" falls on the first syllable.* **15a** to become lower or less; decrease: *The water in the river has fallen two feet. Prices are falling. The voice often falls at the end of a statement. The wind fell after the storm blew over.* **SYN:** diminish, abate, subside. **b** to become lower in price or value: *Wheat has fallen. The stock market fell in 1957.* **16** to be divided: *His story falls into five parts.* **17** to look sad or disappointed; lose animation: *His face fell at the bad news.* **18** to slope downward: *The land falls gradually to the beach. The river fell into the sea.* **19** *Obsolete.* to come as a result (of).
—*v.t. U.S. Dialect.* to cut down (trees); fell.
—*n.* **1** a falling; dropping from a higher place: *The fall from his horse broke his arm.* **2** the amount that comes down: *We had a heavy fall of snow last winter.* **3** the distance that anything drops or comes down: *The fall of the river here is two feet. He survived a fall of 40 feet.* **4** = waterfall. **5** a coming down suddenly from a standing position: *He had a bad fall on the ice.* **6** a hanging down; dropping. **7** *Figurative.* the condition of becoming bad or worse: *Adam's fall. He blamed his fall on bad companions.* **8** *Figurative.* **a** capture; overthrow; destruction: *the fall of Troy.* **b** a descent from power or high rank; downfall: *The Decline and Fall of the Roman Empire* (Edward Gibbon). **9** the proper place or position: *The fall of the accent on "farmer" is on the first syllable.* **10a** a becoming lower or less: *a fall of the barometer. The rise and fall of the tides.* **b** a reduction in price or value; depreciation: *a fall in prices, a fall in the market.* **11** a downward slope: *the fall of the hills toward the sea.* **12a** a coming as if by dropping: *at the fall of evening.* **b** the birth of the young of certain animals. **c** the number of animals born at a particular time or season: *We have had our largest fall of lambs this year.* **13** the season of the year between summer and winter; autumn. **14** *Wrestling.* **a** a way of throwing or being thrown on one's back so that both shoulders are simultaneously on the floor. **b** a contest in wrestling: *The final falls will be wrestled next week.* **15** (in surfing) a dumper. **16** death in battle. **17a** the loose end of the rope, etc., in a tackle, to which the power is applied in hoisting. **b** a hoisting tackle for cargo, etc. **18** the movable front of a piano that covers the keyboard. **19** a kind of trap for catching animals. **20** a flock (of woodcock). **21a** a band or collar, lying flat around the neck, fashionable during the 1600's: *a fall of lace.* **b** a kind of veil, especially one hanging from the back of a hat, worn by women. **22** a woman's wig that fastens to the top of the head and falls straight down the back to give the appearance of long hair: *After dark, many a coiffure has a dangling addition that ... is called a "fall"* (New Yorker).
—*adj.* of or having to do with fall or autumn: *fall weather, fall plowing, fall hats.*

fall aboard, a *Nautical.* (of a ship) to have a collision with: *Steer carefully or you'll fall aboard that coal barge.* **b** to quarrel: *He falls aboard with him for her, to have her for his servant* (Francis Thynne). **c** to attack: *The horse again refused the grass, and fell aboard the hemlock, greedily eating it up* (John Ray).

fall across (or **among**), to come upon or among by chance; meet with: *I happened to fall across Estmere ... in the park* (Hugh Conway). *The honest country boy fell among thieves.*

fall (all) over oneself, to make every effort; go all-out: *Southern moderates are falling all over themselves trying to postpone the inevitable* (New York Times).

fall apart, to crumble; break down; disintegrate: *Feudalism was falling apart and the new city republics were rising* (Edmund Wilson).

fall away, a to become lean or emaciated: *He delights, like a fat, overgrown man, to see himself fall away* (Samuel Butler). **b** to decline gradually; languish; fade: *The breeze has fallen away to nothing* (A. C. Doyle). **c** to renounce allegiance or faith; backslide; desert: *Large numbers of the Normans ... fell away from Christianity* (Edward A. Freeman).

fall back, to go toward the rear; retreat; recede: *The enemy fell back as our army advanced.*

fall back on (or **upon**), to turn to (something or someone) when other things fail: *They had to fall back on a German aunt, who had instructed her in languages and music* (Edmund Wilson).

fall behind, to fail to keep up; lose ground: *Recorded times of horses and cyclists show that after about twenty miles the horse slowly but surely falls behind* (Bury and Hillier).

fall down, *Informal.* to prove a failure; fail: *He fell down on the job. That is where Pap fell down—he eschewed irony* (Donald Barthelme).

fall flat, to fail completely; have no effect or interest: *The poor performance fell flat.*

fall for, *Slang.* **a** to be taken in by: *European critics, for ever falling for new things, would fall most certainly for this* (Rose Macaulay). **b** to fall in love with; be captivated by: *Francis Wilmot? Oh! he's "fallen for" Marjorie Ferrar* (John Galsworthy).

fall foul, a to come into conflict; quarrel: *If they be any ways offended they fall foul* (Robert Burton). **b** *Nautical.* to come into collision with: *The principal Galleon ... falling foul of another ship, had her foremast broken* (Richard Hakluyt). **c** *Rare.* to make an assault: *You fall foul upon our miracles and our saints* (Walter S. Landor).

fall from, *Obsolete.* **a** to disagree with: *Galen ... in some things hath fallen from him [Hippocrates]* (Sir Thomas Browne). **b** to forsake allegiance to: *England, I will fall from thee* (Shakespeare). **c** to give up; depart from: *Thieves ... never fall from their craft* (Sir Thomas More).

fall from grace. See under **grace**.

fall in, a to take a place in line or a military formation and come to a position of attention: *"Fall in!" said the officer to the soldiers.* **b** to meet: *On our trip we fell in with some interesting people.* **c** to agree: *They fell in with our plans. The cagetory of liberals must be exploited by making them believe that one falls in with their programs and then compromising them by involving them with one's own* (Edmund Wilson). **d** to collapse toward the inside: *The building fell in.*

fall off, a to become less; drop: *The profits from the business fell off last month.* **b** to drop off; become separated: *His hat fell off.* **c** (of health) to deteriorate. **d** to move away: *They fell off one by one* (Dickens). **e** to become estranged; part company: *Were I always grave, one half of my readers would fall off from me* (Joseph Addison). **f** *Nautical.* (of a ship) to turn or break off to leeward of the course intended because of a heading wind: *Let her have a plenty of helm, to come and fall off freely with the sea* (Richard Henry Dana, Jr.).

fall on, a to attack: *The thieves fell on the traveler and stole his money.* **b** to come across; light on: *The Romans fell on this model by chance* (Jonathan Swift).

fall out, a to leave a place in line or a military formation: *"Fall out!" said the officer to the soldiers.* **b** to stop being friends; quarrel: *He has fallen out with his friends and family.* **c** to turn out; happen: *As it fell out, I was able to help them.*

fall over backward. See under **backward**.

fall over oneself. See under **oneself**.

falls, a a waterfall; cataract; cascade: *Niagara Falls.* **b** the loose end of the tackle to which power is applied in lowering or raising a lifeboat, a yard, or the like: *The ends or falls of the tackle ... being ... held by the Arabs* (Austen H. Layard). **c** tackle used in lowering or raising a lifeboat, a yard, or the like: *The port boat's falls were ... provided with patent hooks, which sprang open and released the boat the moment she touched the water* (W. C. Russell). **d** Also, **fall.** the change in the surface of a deck from a higher to a lower level: *The falls gave height to the captain's cabin.* **e** those parts or petals of a flower that bend downward: *Silver Flame, the second introduction, has even more sharply contrasted coloring, with pure white standards and rich yellow falls* (New York Times).

fall short, a to fail to come up to a standard or requirement: *We fall far short in applying what we know* (Saturday Review). **b** (of a shot) to miss the mark aimed at: *The Fort fired at us, but their balls fell short* (Nicholas H. Nicolas). **c** to give out; become insufficient: *The corn falls short.*

fall short of, a to fail to perform; fail to reach or obtain: *He fell lamentably short of his duty* (H. S. Merriman). **b** to fail to equal: *The party wasn't a failure, but it did fall short of the success we had expected.*

fall through, to fail: *His plans fell through.*

fall to, a to begin: *They fell to and worked with a will.* **b** to begin to attack, eat, or otherwise address: *They fell to with their bare fists. When the food was served, they fell to.* **c** to go into place; close by itself: *The trap door fell to.*

fall under, a to belong under; be classified as: *Whales fall under the class of mammals.* **b** to come under (treatment, observation, or the like); be subjected to: *His "Revolt of Islam" ... fell under the lash of the "Quarterly"* (Thomas Medwin).

fall upon, to attack: *The pirates fell upon the city.*

ride for a fall, to act so as to invite danger or trouble: *If he keeps up his reckless spending, he is riding for a fall.*

the Fall or **the Fall of Man,** the sin of Adam and Eve in yielding to temptation and eating the forbidden fruit: *Though Scripture gives no definition of the idea of sin, it ... gives a full account of how sin penetrated into human nature by the Fall of Man* (Schaff and Herzog).

[Old English *fallan, feallan*]

► **Falls,** though plural in form, is really singular (or collective) in meaning. We speak of a *falls* but ordinarily use it with a plural verb: *The falls are almost dry in August.* In proper names, *falls* is frequently used with a singular verb: *Niagara Falls is receding.*

fal|la (fäl′yä′), *n., pl.* **-las.** a celebration in Spain that honors a patron saint. Fallas include parades, fireworks, and street dancing. [< Spanish dialect *falla*]

fal-la (fäl′lä′), *n.* = fa-la.

fal|la|cious (fə lā′shəs), *adj.* **1** that causes disappointment; deceptive; misleading: *a fallacious peace. Yet how fallacious is all earthly bliss* (William Cowper). **SYN:** delusive, false. **2** logically unsound; erroneous: *It is fallacious reasoning to base a general rule on just two or three instances.* **SYN:** sophistical. —**fal|la′cious|ly,** *adv.* —**fal|la′cious|ness,** *n.*

fal|la|cy (fal′ə sē), *n., pl.* **-cies. 1** a false idea; mistaken belief; an error: *It is a fallacy to suppose that riches always bring happiness.* **SYN:** delusion. **2** a mistake in reasoning; misleading or unsound argument. **SYN:** sophistry. **3** unsoundness; falsity; delusive or deceptive character. **4** *Logic.* any one of a number of errors in reasoning that make an argument unsound and any conclusion untrustworthy or false. [< Old French *fallace,* learned borrowing from Latin *fallācia* < *fallāx, -ācis* deceptive < *fallere* deceive]

fal|lal or **fal-lal** (fal′lal′), *n., adj.* —*n.* a useless bit of finery.
—*adj.* affected; foppish. Also, **fallol.** [a coined word]

fal|lal|er|y (fal′lal′ər ē), *n.* fallals collectively; finery: *dancing and flirting and fallalery* (George Meredith).

fall|back (fôl′bak′), *n.* **1** the act or process of falling back or behind; lag. **2** some person or thing to turn to for help or support; recourse; resort: *As a fallback, the liberals cling to the hope that Rep. Brooks [might] accept an appointment* (Wall Street Journal).

fall cankerworm, the caterpillar of a geometrid moth, widespread in the northern United States, that hatches in the early spring from eggs laid on trees the preceding fall. It is very destructive to

Pronunciation Key: hat, āge, cãre, fär; let, ēqual, tėrm; it, īce; hot, ōpen, ôrder; oil, out; cup, pu̇t, rüle; child; long; thin; ᴛʜen; zh, measure; ə represents **a** in about, **e** in taken, **i** in pencil, **o** in lemon, **u** in circus.

fruit and shade trees.

fall dandelion, a fall-blooming composite plant with flowers like the spring dandelion, naturalized in the United States from Europe.

fall·en (fô′lən), *v., adj.* —*v.* the past participle of **fall**: *Much rain has fallen.*

—***adj.*** **1** dropped: *fallen arches, a fallen market.* **SYN:** decreased, depreciated. **2** down on the ground; down flat: *a fallen tree.* **SYN:** prostrate. **3** that has become bad or worse; degraded: *a fallen woman.* **SYN:** debased. **4** *Figurative.* overthrown; ruined; destroyed: *a fallen fortress, a fallen dynasty.* **5** dead: *fallen heroes.* **6** shrunken; decreased: *fallen cheeks.*

fallen angel, any one of the angels who were cast out of heaven when Lucifer rebelled against God.

fall·er (fô′lər), *n.* **1** a person who falls. **2** a part of a machine that operates by falling, as in certain stamping or spinning machines. **3** a man who cuts down trees, especially in logging.

fall·fish (fôl′fish′), *n., pl.* **-fish·es** or (*collectively*) **-fish.** any one of several freshwater, cyprinoid fishes, especially one of the eastern United States; silver chub.

fall flower, = white wreath aster.

fall-front (fôl′frunt′), *adj.* = drop-front.

fall guy, *Informal.* a person left to face blame or consequences of something; scapegoat: *Things go all wrong, comically, thanks to the influence of a seedily incompetent fall guy* (London Times).

fal·li·bi·lism (fal′ə bə liz′əm), *n. Philosophy.* the principle that no statement can be completely verified and therefore accepted as true beyond all doubt.

fal·li·bi·list (fal′ə bə list), *n., adj.* —***n.*** a person who believes in or supports the principle of fallibilism. —***adj.*** = fallibilistic.

fal·li·bi·list·ic (fal′ə bə lis′tik), *adj.* of or having to do with or based on fallibilism.

fal·li·bil·i·ty (fal′ə bil′ə tē), *n.* a fallible condition or quality.

fal·li·ble (fal′ə bəl), *adj.* **1** liable to be deceived or mistaken; liable to err. **2** liable to be erroneous, inaccurate, or false; unreliable: *Strong emotion can make human judgment fallible.* [< Medieval Latin *fallibilis* < Latin *fallere* deceive] —**fal′li·ble·ness,** *n.*

fal·li·bly (fal′ə blē), *adv.* in a fallible manner; mistakenly; deceptively.

fall·ing band (fô′ling), **1** a type of band or collar made to turn over and lie upon the shoulders, worn especially by the Puritans in the 1600′s. **2** a kind of veil worn by women, especially one hanging from the front of a bonnet.

falling diphthong, a diphthong that receives the main stress on the first element, as the element *o* of the diphthong *oi* in the word *oil.*

falling door, = flap door.

fall·ing-off (fô′ling ôf′, -of′), *n., pl.* **fall·ings-off.** = fall-off.

fall·ing-out (fô′ling out′), *n., pl.* **fall·ings-out.** a disagreement; quarrel: *The boys had a falling-out but soon made up.*

falling sickness or **evil**, = epilepsy.

falling star, = meteor.

fall line, **1** a line which marks the end of layers of hard rock of a plateau and the beginning of a softer rock layer of the coastal plain. There are many waterfalls and rapids along this line. **2** a natural downhill course in skiing; the straight line from the skier to the bottom of a slope.

Fall Line, a fall line running north and south to the east of the Appalachian Mountains. Philadelphia, Baltimore, and Richmond were built along the Fall Line to take advantage of the available water power.

fall-off (fôl′ôf′, -of′), *n.* a decrease: *a fall-off in production.*

fal·lol (fal′lol′), *n., adj.* = fallal.

***Fal·lo·pi·an tubes** (fə lō′pē ən), a pair of slender tubes through which ova from the ovaries pass to the uterus. [< Gabriel *Fallopio,* 1523-1562, Italian anatomist, who described them + *-an*]

Fal·lot's tetralogy (fa lōz′), a combination of four congenital defects of the heart interfering with the passage of blood: *One of the commonest forms of blue-baby disorder* [*is*] *Fallot's tetralogy* (Time). [< Étienne-Louis Arthur *Fallot,* 1850-1911, a French physician]

fall·out (fôl′out′), *n.* **1** the radioactive particles or dust that fall to earth after a nuclear explosion. Fallout may be assumed always to be dangerously radioactive. *Fallout sifting down ... will affect every living person* (Stuart Chase). **2** the falling of these particles to the earth, especially in a widening pattern immediately surrounding, or downwind from, the point of explosion. **3** a byproduct or residue of something, usually unexpected; spin-off: *A sublime piece of technological fallout from space technology is a means of purifying foul-smelling sewage and converting it into sterile drinking water* (New Scientist).

fallout shelter, an underground shelter to protect occupants from radioactive fallout.

fal·low¹ (fal′ō), *adj., n., v.* —***adj.*** **1** plowed but not seeded for a season or more: *We'll let the north forty acres lie fallow next spring.* **2** *Figurative.* (of the mind) uncultivated; inactive.

—***n.*** **1** land plowed and left without planting it for a season or more. **2** the plowing of land without seeding it for a season to destroy weeds or improve the soil: *Your fallow adds to your fertility* (Edmund Burke).

—***v.t.*** to plow and break up (land) without seeding; lay fallow.

[Old English *fealh* fallow land] —**fal′low·ness,** *n.*

fal·low² (fal′ō), *adj.* pale yellowish-brown: *a fallow dog.* [Old English *fealu*]

fallow chat, = wheatear.

fallow deer, a small deer of Europe and Asia, having a yellowish-brown coat that is spotted with white in the summer.

falls (fôlz), *n.pl.* See under **fall.**

fall trap, a trap which operates by falling, such as a deadfall.

fall wind, = katabatic wind.

FALN, Puerto Rican Armed Forces of National Liberation (Spanish, *Fuerzas Armadas de Liberación Nacional Puertoriqueño).*

false (fôls), *adj.,* **fals·er, fals·est,** *adv., v.,* **falsed, fals·ing.** —***adj.*** **1** not true; not correct; wrong: *false statements.* **SYN:** erroneous, mistaken, incorrect. **2** not truthful; lying: *a false witness, a false accusation.* **SYN:** untruthful, mendacious. **3** not loyal; not faithful; deceitful: *a false friend, a man false to his promise.* **SYN:** disloyal, unfaithful, inconstant, treacherous, traitorous. **4** used to deceive; deceiving: *false weights, false signals.* **SYN:** misleading, deceptive, fallacious. **5** *Music.* not true in pitch: *a false note.* **6** not real; artificial: *false diamonds, false hair, false eyelashes, false grief.* **7** based on wrong notions; ill-founded: *False pride kept the poor man from accepting money from his rich brothers.* **8** improperly called or named, especially in popular or vernacular names, usually because of some resemblance: *One name for the locust tree is "false acacia."* **9** substituted for or supplementing, especially temporarily, something properly or primarily denoted by the name: *false supports for a bridge under construction.*

—***adv.*** in a false manner; improperly; wrongly: *to interpret something false, to judge a person false.*

—***v.t.*** *Obsolete.* **1** to make false; corrupt; falsify. **2** to counterfeit; forge. **3** to prove false to.

play (one) false, to deceive, cheat, trick, or betray: *His memory played him false when he grew old. They had their fears that Lewis might be playing false* (Macaulay).

[< Old French *fals* < Latin *falsus* < *fallere* deceive] —**false′ly,** *adv.* —**false′ness,** *n.*

—***Syn.*** *adj.* **6 False, counterfeit** mean not real or genuine. **False,** describing something made to look like the real thing, does not necessarily suggest that it is intended to decieve: *The false front of the building partially hid its pitched roof. Most false teeth are made to look natural.* **Counterfeit** always suggests a dishonest attempt to make the imitation closely resemble the genuine: *Much counterfeit money is in circulation.*

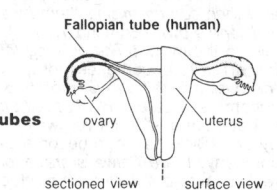

Fallopian tube (human)

ovary

uterus

sectioned view

surface view

***Fallopian tubes**

false acacia, the locust tree.

false alarm, **1** a warning signal, as of fire, given when no danger actually exists. **2** a person or thing that falls far short of expectations: *The Cripple Creek gold rush in the '80s was only a false alarm.*

false arrest, *Law.* the arrest of a person contrary to law: *to sue for false arrest.*

false bittersweet, = bittersweet (def. 2).

false bottom, a bottom in a trunk or drawer that forms a secret or a supplementary compartment.

false card, a card played to mislead the opponents, especially as to the player's holding in a suit.

false-card (fôls′kärd′), *v.i.* to play a false card.

false cast, a fishing cast made in the air without permitting the fly or line to touch the water.

false-col·or (fôls′kul′ər), *adj.* of or having to do with a photographic process using infrared radiation to show images in unnatural hues and increase color differentiation: *Special, false-color processing of some of the new photos suggest large-scale* (*though subtle*) *variations, implying ... that Callisto's surface "is not of uniform composition"* (Science News).

false colors, **1** the flag of another country. **2** *Figurative.* false pretenses.

false coltsfoot, = wild ginger.

false dawn, **1** a transient light that precedes the true dawn by about an hour. **2** *Figurative: Group psychotherapy ... had a false dawn as far back as 1905, when a tuberculosis specialist found that his patients benefited from regular meetings* (Time).

false face, a funny or ugly mask; mask.

false foxglove, any plant of a group of herbs of the figwort family, resembling the foxglove but usually having yellow flowers.

false-heart·ed (fôls′här′tid), *adj.* treacherous; deceitful.

false hellebore, any plant of a group of perennial herbs of the lily family, such as the American hellebore.

false·hood (fôls′hu̇d), *n.* **1** a false statement; lie: *His oral reports to the F.B.I. were laced with falsehoods* (New York Times). **SYN:** untruth, fib. See syn. under **lie. 2** the quality of being false; falsity: *the scandalous falsehood of the charges now circulated against them* (Cardinal Newman). **SYN:** falseness, untruthfulness, mendacity. **3** something false; an untrue proposition, doctrine, or belief: *Each age has to fight with its own falsehoods* (Sir Arthur Helps). **4** the act of making false statements; lying.

false horizon, = artificial horizon.

false imprisonment, *Law.* the restraint or imprisonment of a person contrary to law.

false indigo, = wild indigo.

false keel, a narrow timber attached below the main keel of a ship to protect the bottom or decrease leeway.

false key, **1** = picklock. **2** = skeleton key. **3** a duplicate key.

false lily of the valley, = bead-ruby.

false nettle, a plant related to the nettle but without its stinging hairs, which grows as a wild flower in moist, shady areas throughout the eastern United States and from Florida to Texas.

false pregnancy, = pseudocyesis.

false pretenses, *Law.* misrepresentations or untrue statements made to defraud.

false relation, = cross relation.

false ribs, ribs not attached to the breastbone. Human beings have five pairs of false ribs.

false Solomon's-seal, a perennial herb of the lily family native to North America and Asia, resembling the Solomon's-seal but having small, white flowers.

false start, **1** a wrong start in a race. **2** *Figurative.* any unsuccessful beginning: *After ... a series of false starts, orders were issued ... for construction to begin "as quickly as possible"* (New York Times).

false step, **1** a wrong step; stumble. **2** *Figurative.* a blunder; mistake: *You are on probation: one false step, and you will be expelled from school.*

false strawberry, = cinquefoil (def. 1).

false teeth, artificial teeth used to replace the real teeth. **SYN:** denture.

false topaz, a yellow variety of quartz; citrine.

fal·set·to (fôl set′ō), *n., pl.* **-tos,** *adj., adv.* —***n.*** **1** an artificially high-pitched voice, especially in a man. **2** a person who sings with such a voice. —***adj.*** of or for a falsetto; that sings in a falsetto. —***adv.*** in a falsetto. [< Italian *falsetto* (diminutive) < *falso* false < Latin *falsus;* see etym. under **false**]

false vampire, a tropical American leaf-nosed bat, erroneously believed to suck blood.

false vocal cords, the upper of the two pairs of vocal cords; superior vocal cords.

false·work (fôls′wėrk′), *n.* a temporary structure used as a support during construction, as of a building or bridge; scaffolding.

fal·sid·i·cal (fôl sid′ə kəl), *adj.* lying; false; illusory. [< Latin *falsidicus* falsehood telling (< *falsum* falsehood + *dīcere* speak) + English *-al*¹]

fal·sie (fôl′sē), *n. Informal.* a false beard, mustache, or sideburns.

fal·sies (fôl′sēz), *n.pl. Informal.* padding or pads for a brassiere to give the breasts a fuller appearance.

fal·si·fi·a·bil·i·ty (fôl′sə fī′ə bil′ə tē), *n.* openness to falsification.

fal·si·fi·a·ble (fôl′sə fī′ə bəl), *adj.* that can be falsified.

fal·si·fi·ca·tion (fôl′sə fə kā′shən), *n.* **1** the act of falsifying; change made to deceive. **2** the fact of

Pronunciation Key: hat, āge, cãre, fär; let, ēqual, tėrm; it, īce; hot, ōpen, ôrder; oil, out; cup, pu̇t, rüle; child; long; thin; ᴛʜen; zh, measure; ə represents **a** in about, **e** in taken, **i** in pencil, **o** in lemon, **u** in circus.

being falsified: *The falsification of the will was not discovered for three months.*

fal|si|fi|er (fôl′sə fī′ər), *n.* **1** a person who falsifies, especially one who makes counterfeit money: *a willful falsifier of history* (North American Review). **2** a liar.

fal|si|fy (fôl′sə fī), *v.,* **-fied, -fy|ing.** —*v.t.* **1** to make false; change in order to deceive; misrepresent: *The cheat falsified his bowling score when no one was looking.* SYN: counterfeit. **2** to prove to be false; disprove. —*v.i.* to make false statements; lie. SYN: prevaricate.
[< Middle French *falsifier,* learned borrowing from Late Latin *falsificāre* < Latin *falsificus* acting falsely < *falsus* false + *facere* make]

fal|sism (fôl′siz əm), *n.* a statement so obviously false as not to require discussion; self-evident falsehood.

fal|si|ty (fôl′sə tē), *n., pl.* **-ties. 1** the fact or condition of being false; incorrectness: *Education showed him the falsity of his superstitions.* SYN: falseness. **2** untruthfulness; deceitfulness; treachery. SYN: fraud. **3** something false; falsehood.

Fal|staff (fôl′staf, -stäf), *n.* Sir **John,** a fat, jolly, swaggering soldier, brazen and without scruples, in three of Shakespeare's plays.

Fal|staff|i|an (fôl staf′ē ən), *adj.* characteristic of or like Falstaff or his group of ragged soldiers.

falt|boat (fält′bōt′), *n.* a light, collapsible boat, similar to a kayak; foldboat. [half-translation of German *Faltboot* folding boat]

fal|ter (fôl′tər), *v., n.* —*v.i.* **1** to not go straight; lose courage; draw back or hesitate; waver: *The soldiers faltered for a moment as their captain fell.* SYN: vacillate, flinch. See syn. under **hesitate. 2** to become unsteady in movement; stumble; totter: *The old man faltered up the path.* SYN: stagger, tremble. **3** to come forth in hesitating, broken sounds: *The child's voice faltered as she described her fall from the bicycle.*
—*v.t.* to speak in hesitating or broken words; stammer: *Greatly embarrassed, he faltered out his thanks.* SYN: stutter.
—*n.* **1** an act of faltering. **2** a faltering sound.
[Middle English *faltren,* perhaps < Scandinavian (compare Old Icelandic *faltrask* be cumbered)]
—**fal′ter|er,** *n.*

fal|ter|ing (fôl′tər ing), *adj.* that falters: *a faltering hand.* —**fal′ter|ing|ly,** *adv.*

fam., 1 familiar. **2** family.

fame (fām), *n., v.,* **famed, fam|ing.** —*n.* **1** a having much said or written about one; being very well known: *the fame of George Washington.* SYN: notoriety, celebrity, renown, eminence. **2** what is said about one; reputation: *Success is in the silences Though fame is in the song* (Bliss Carman). **3** *Archaic.* **a** a public report; common talk: *The fame . . . was heard in Pharaoh's house, saying, Joseph's brethren are come* (Genesis 45:16). **b** a rumor.
—*v.t.* **1** to spread the fame of. **2** *Archaic.* to tell or spread abroad.
[< Old French *fame,* learned borrowing from Latin *fāma* < *fārī* speak]

famed (fāmd), *adj.* made famous; celebrated; well-known: *Ay, this is the famed rock, which Hercules and Goth and Moor bequeathed us. At this door England stands sentry* (Wilfred Scawen Blunt). SYN: renowned.

Fa|meuse (fə myüz′; *French* fȧ mœz′), *n.* a variety of red apple ripening in the late autumn; snow apple. [American English < French *fameuse,* feminine of *fameux* < Old French *fameus;* see etym. under **famous**]

fa|mil|ial (fə mil′yəl), *adj.* **1** of or characteristic of a family. **2** genetically transmitted: *The familial jauntiness appeared in every generation.*

fa|mil|iar (fə mil′yər), *adj., n.* —*adj.* **1** known from constant association; well-known: *a familiar face. French is as familiar to him as English.* **2** of everyday use; common; ordinary: *A knife is a familiar tool.* **3** well-acquainted: *He is familiar with French and English.* SYN: conversant, versed. **4** close; personal; intimate: *Those familiar friends know each other very well.* **5** not formal; friendly: *a familiar attitude.* SYN: unceremonious, informal, easy. **6** too friendly; presuming; forward: *It is considered to be too familiar for a pupil to call his teacher by her first name.* **7** (of animals) domesticated; tame. **8** *Archaic.* of or having to do with one's family or household.
—*n.* **1** a familiar friend or acquaintance: *Labor's staunch old familiars ranged out onto the hustings last week to address a country which seemed to be basking in a kind of prosperous complacency* (Time). **2** a spirit or demon supposed to serve a particular person. A black cat was thought to be a witch's familiar. **3** a person who belongs to the household of a bishop in the Roman Catholic Church and renders domestic, though not menial, service. **4** an officer of the Inquisition whose chief duty was to arrest the accused or suspected. **5** *Obsolete.* a member of a person's family or household.
[< Old French *familier,* learned borrowing from Latin *familiāris* < *familia* family < *famulus* servant]
—**fa|mil′iar|ly,** *adv.* —**fa|mil′iar|ness,** *n.*
—*Syn. adj.* **4 Familiar, intimate, confidential** mean personally near or close. **Familiar** suggests an easy, informal relationship that comes of long or close acquaintance: *I feel very familiar with my cousin.* **Intimate** suggests a very close personal relationship based on affection or common interests: *They have been intimate friends since childhood.* **Confidential** suggests mutual trust and willingness to share personal secrets or private affairs: *The twin sisters had always lived on the most intimate and confidential terms. She is the manager's confidential secretary.*

fa|mil|iar|i|ty (fə mil′yar′ə tē), *n., pl.* **-ties. 1** close acquaintance; knowledge: *The Indian scout's familiarity with the rugged countryside was helpful to the explorers.* SYN: intimacy, friendship, fellowship. **2** a thing done or said in a familiar way: *She dislikes such familiarities as the use of her first name by people she has just met.* **3** freedom of behavior suitable only to friends; lack of formality or ceremony. SYN: informality.

fa|mil|iar|ize (fə mil′yə rīz), *v.t.,* **-ized, -iz|ing. 1** to make (a person) well acquainted with something: *Before playing the new game, familiarize yourself with the rules.* SYN: accustom. **2** to make well known; bring into common knowledge or use: *Exploration in space has familiarized the word "astronaut."* SYN: popularize. **3** to habituate. **4** *Archaic.* to make familiar; divest of strangeness. —**fa|mil′iar|i|za′tion,** *n.*

familiar spirit, a demon or spirit supposed to serve a particular person; familiar.

fam|i|lism (fam′ə liz əm), *n.* the feeling existing between members of a family; fraternity.

fam|i|lis|tic (fam′ə lis′tik), *adj.* of or characteristic of a family or familism: *He loves the South's piety toward the land, its sense of the past, its respect for manners, its familistic loyalties* (Time).

fa|mille de robe (fȧ mē′yə də rôb′), *French.* **1** a lawyer's family: *He belongs to a respectable famille de robe.* **2** (literally) family of the robe (the legal profession).

fam|i|ly (fam′ə lē, fam′lē), *n., pl.* **-lies,** *adj.* —*n.* **1** a father, mother, and their children, as a group: *Our town has about a thousand families.* **2** the children of a father and mother; offspring. *They have a family of three boys and two girls.* **3** a group of people living in the same house or under one head, including parents, children, relatives, and servants; household. **4** all of a person's relatives: *After many years the man's wife finally met all of his family.* **5** a group of related people; tribe or clan; race: *The Roosevelt family produced two Presidents, Theodore Roosevelt and Franklin D. Roosevelt.* **6** *Especially British.* good or noble descent; descent: *They are people of family.* SYN: ancestry, stock, lineage. **7** a group of related animals or plants. Lions, tigers, and leopards belong to the cat family. A family ranks below an order and above a genus. In zoology, the names of families end in *-idae,* for example *Felidae,* the cat family; in botany, the names of families usually end in *-aceae,* for example *Rosaceae,* the rose family. **8** any group of related or similar things: *We all belong to the human family.* **9** a group of genetically related languages: *Linguists customarily divide the languages of the world into stocks or families* (Beals and Hoijer). **10** *Chemistry.* a group of elements having similar properties. **11** *Geometry.* a group of related curves or surfaces. **12** a unit of the Mafia, operating in a geographical area: *A Mafia family is a group of individuals who are not necessarily blood relations* (New York Times).
—*adj.* **1** of or having to do with the family or household; domestic: *family life.* **2** belonging to or shared by a whole family: *the family car.*
in the family way, pregnant: *The wives will have a fine easy time when they are in the family way* (Benjamin Jowett).
[< Latin *familia* < *famulus* servant]
▶**Family,** though usually construed as a singular, may take a plural verb when the emphasis is on the individual members: *Her family is opposed to the marriage. The family were gathered in the living room.*

family allowance, 1 an allowance paid to a worker or person in the military service on the basis of the number of dependents in his family, usually to cover living expenses overseas. **2** (in Great Britain and Canada) a subsidy paid periodically by the government to parents for each of their children under a stipulated age.

family Bible, a large copy of the Bible for use at family prayers, often containing a register in which family events, especially the births of children, can be recorded.

family circle, 1 the adults and children in a particular household, thought of as sharing certain customs, pleasures, and experiences: *I was welcomed to the family circle.* **2** = circle (def.6).

family court, = court of domestic relations.

family doctor, a general practitioner who is the doctor for all the members of a family.

fam|i|ly|ish (fam′ə lē ish, fam′lē-), *adj.* **1** displaying strong family ties; closely united: *They're a very familyish sort of family* (Harper's). **2** having a domestic atmosphere: *a familyish hotel.*

family man, 1 a man with a family. **2** a man who enjoys domestic life and strives to fulfill his domestic obligations: *Vincent had reformed, is now a steady worker, a family man* (Time).

family medicine, general practice medicine for families and individuals: *Family medicine—a newly emerging medical discipline devoted to the holistic approach to the patient* (New York Times Magazine).

family name, the name of all the members of a certain family; surname. In America and Europe, Africa, and large parts of Asia, it is one's last name, but in some other societies, such as Chinese, the family name comes first. *The boy's given name is John; his family name is Smith.*

family planner, a person who advocates or actively promotes family planning.

family planning, regulation or limitation of the size of a family by birth control; planned parenthood: *India has struggled . . . for years to promote family planning* (Time).

family practice, = family medicine.

family room, *U.S.* an informal room for general family use.

fam|i|ly-size (fam′ə lē sīz′, fam′lē-), *adj.* of a large size suitable for a family: *family-size bottles of soda, a family-size car.*

family skeleton, a cause of shame that a family tries to keep secret.

fam|i|ly-style (fam′ə lē stīl′, fam′lē-), *adj.* **1** appealing to or suitable for the whole family: *a family-style humorist.* **2** (of a meal) served from dishes at the table.

***family tree, 1** a diagram showing how all the members and ancestors of a family are related;

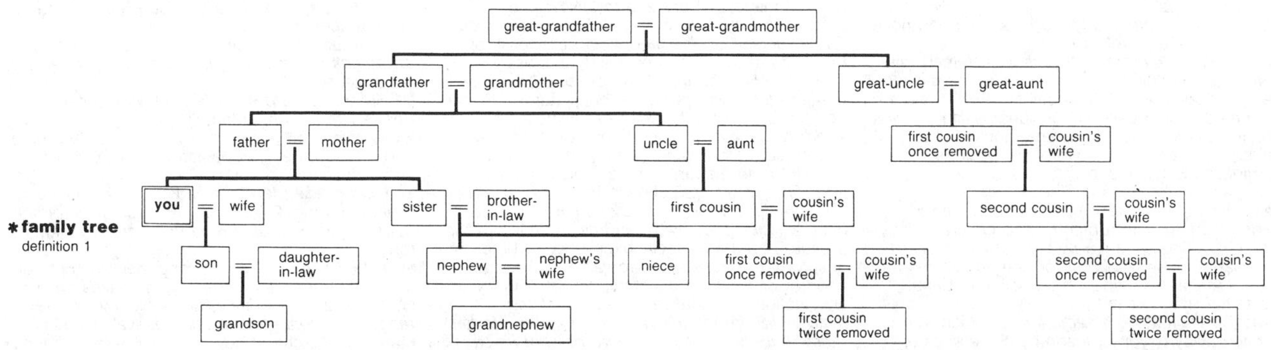

***family tree**
definition 1

genealogical tree. **2** all the members of a family line; line of descent; lineage; genealogy: *Even today surprisingly little is known of man's own family tree* (Walter Sullivan).

fam|ine (fam′ən), *n.* **1** lack of food in a place; time of starving: *Many people died during the famine in India.* **2** starvation: *Many people died of famine.* **3** *Figurative.* a very great lack of anything; scarcity; shortage: *a coal famine.* SYN: insufficiency, deficiency, dearth. [< Old French *famine* < *faim* hunger < Latin *famēs*]

famine fever, = typhus.

fam|ish (fam′ish), *v.t.* **1** to make extremely hungry; starve: *He hadn't eaten for ten hours and said he was famished.* **2** to starve to death; kill with hunger: *to famish to death.* —*v.i.* **1** to be very hungry: *I am famished.* SYN: See syn. under **hungry. 2** to die of starvation. [alteration (influenced by *perish,* etc.) of Middle English *famen* famish < Latin *famēs* hunger]

fam|ish|ment (fam′ish mənt), *n. Obsolete.* the pain of extreme hunger or thirst.

fa|mous (fā′məs), *adj.* **1** very well known; much talked about or written about; noted; celebrated: *a region famous for its scenery. A great crowd of people greeted the famous hero.* **2** *Informal.* first-rate; excellent: *That wooded park would be a famous place for a picnic.* **3** *Archaic.* notorious. [< Anglo-French *famous,* Old French *fameus,* learned borrowing from Latin *fāmōsus* < *fāma;* see etym. under **fame**] —**fa′mous|ly,** *adv.* —**fa′mous|ness,** *n.*

—***Syn.* 1 Famous, renowned, noted** mean very well known. **Famous** implies being widely and usually favorably known: *A great crowd of people greeted the famous statesman.* **Renowned** implies great and enduring fame, glory, and honor: *Marie Curie was a renowned scientist. Shakespeare is renowned.* **Noted** implies being well known or especially noticed for some particular thing: *A noted architect designed the store.*

▶ See **notorious** for usage note.

fam|u|lus (fam′yə ləs), *n., pl.* **-li** (-lī). an attendant or servant, especially of a scholar or magician. [< Latin *famulus* servant]

fan¹ (fan), *n., v.,* **fanned, fan|ning.** —*n.* **1** a hand implement for producing a current of air to cool the face and body. A fan is often made so that it can be folded or spread out into part of a circle. **2** anything that is flat and spread out like an open fan, such as the tail of a bird. **3** *Machinery.* **a** any one of various devices consisting essentially of a series of radiating flat or curved blades attached to and revolving with a central hublike part. **b** such a device turned by a belt from the crankshaft for cooling the radiator of an automobile. **c** such a device turned by an electric motor for cooling a room. **4** a small guiding vane or combination of vanes used to keep the large sails of a windmill pointed into the wind. **5a** a machine for winnowing grain. **b** a shallow basket or broad shovel formerly used to fling grain into the air so that the chaff, being much lighter, might be blown away. **6** *Geology.* = fan delta.

—*v.t.* **1** to stir (the air) with a fan. **2** to direct a current of air toward with a fan or anything like a fan: *She fanned herself with a newspaper to keep from fainting. Fan the fire to make it burn faster.* **3** to drive away with a fan or anything like a fan: *She fanned the flies from the sleeping child with her hand.* **4** *Figurative.* to stir up; arouse: *Bad treatment fanned their dislike into hate.* **5** to spread out like an open fan: *He fanned the cards.* **6** to blow gently and refreshingly upon; cool: *The breeze fanned their hot faces.* **7** to winnow (grain). **8** *Baseball.* to strike out (a batter). **9** *Rare.* to breathe upon.

—*v.i.* **1** *Baseball.* to strike out or to be struck out: *Andy Carey had fanned and Yogi Berra had flied out to Johnny Groth, retiring the side* (New York Times). **2** to assume a fanlike shape.

fan out, to spread out or be spread out like an open fan: *The posse fanned out to cover several hundred yards.*

[Old English *fann* < Latin *vannus* fan for winnowing grain] —**fan′like′,** *adj.*

fan² (fan), *n. Informal.* **1** a person extremely interested in something, such as a sport, the movies, radio, or television. A baseball fan thinks, talks, and reads about baseball besides seeing as many games as he can. **2** an enthusiastic admirer, as of an actor or writer. SYN: devotee. [American English, short for *fanatic*]

Fan (fan), *n., pl.* **Fans** or **Fan.** = Fang.

Fa|na|ko|lo (fä′nä kō′lō), *n., pl.* **-los.** a mixed form of Bantu, with a much-simplified grammar, used as a lingua franca by the natives of different Bantu tribes who work on the gold mines of South Africa. [probably an alteration of Bantu *ifana nalo* it is like this]

fa|nat|ic (fə nat′ik), *n., adj.* —*n.* a person who is carried away beyond reason by his feelings or beliefs: *My friend was such a fanatic about fresh air that he would not stay in any room with the windows closed.* SYN: zealot.

—*adj.* enthusiastic or zealous beyond reason, especially in religion or politics: *a fanatic follower of some leader or belief.*

[< Latin *fānāticus,* adjective, inspired by divinity; (originally) of a temple < *fānum* temple, fane]

fa|nat|i|cal (fə nat′ə kəl), *adj.* unreasonably enthusiastic; extremely zealous. SYN: rabid. —**fa|nat′i|cal|ly,** *adv.* —**fa|nat′i|cal|ness,** *n.*

fa|nat|i|cism (fə nat′ə siz əm), *n.* excessive or unreasonable enthusiasm; extreme zeal, especially in matters of religion or politics.

fa|nat|i|cize (fə nat′ə sīz), *v.,* **-cized, -ciz|ing.** —*v.t.* to make a fanatic of. —*v.i.* to act like a fanatic.

✱**fan belt,** a reinforced rubber belt behind the radiator of an automobile engine that is rotated by the crankshaft and serves to turn the generator and radiator fan.

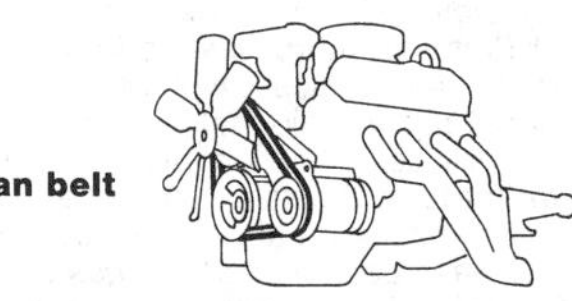

✱**fan belt**

fan|cied (fan′sēd), *adj.* **1** imagined; imaginary: *a fancied insult.* **2** liked: *He beat the two most fancied runners* (London Times).

fan|ci|er (fan′sē ər), *n.* **1** a person who has a liking for or is especially interested in something: *an art fancier. A dog fancier is interested in breeding and raising dogs.* **2** a person who fancies or imagines: *those people who in their speculations on politics, are not reasoners but fanciers* (Macaulay).

fan|ci|ful (fan′si fəl), *adj.* **1** showing fancy; quaint; odd; fantastic: *Fanciful decorations are made up, not patterned after something.* SYN: curious. **2** led by fancy; using fancies; imaginative: *Hans Christian Andersen was a fanciful writer.* SYN: whimsical. **3** suggested by fancy; imaginary; unreal: *A story about fairyland is fanciful.* —**fan′ci|ful|ly,** *adv.* —**fan′ci|ful|ness,** *n.*

fan|ci|fy (fan′sə fī), *v.t., v.i.,* **-fied, -fy|ing.** to make fanciful; embellish.

fan|ci|less (fan′sē lis), *adj.* lacking in fancy; unimaginative.

fan|ci|ly (fan′sə lē), *adv.* in a fancy manner: *He back-pedaled fancily, like a young acrobat giving out with the footwork before actually stepping on the tight wire* (Harper's).

fan|ci|ness (fan′sē nis), *n.* the fact of being fancy, especially in ornamentation or decorativeness.

fan club, a club organized by the admirers of a celebrity and usually named after him.

Fan|co|ni's anemia (fan kō′nēz), a constitutional anemia of children, resembling pernicious anemia. [< Guido *Fanconi,* 1882-1940?, a Swiss pediatrician, who first described the disease]

fan|cy (fan′sē), *n., pl.* **-cies,** *v.,* **-cied, -cy|ing,** *adj.,* **-ci|er, -ci|est,** *adv.* —*n.* **1a** the power to imagine; imagination: *Dragons, fairies, and giants are creatures of fancy.* SYN: fantasy. See syn. under **imagination. b** the ability to create illustrative or decorative imagery, especially in literature. SYN: fantasy. See syn. under **imagination. c** something imagined; mental image: *the fancies of the storyteller.* SYN: fantasy. See syn. under **imagination. 2** something supposed; idea; notion: *Is it fancy, or do I hear a sound? That's just a fancy; don't believe it.* SYN: conception. **3a** delusive imagination; hallucination. **b** an instance of this. **4a** a liking; fondness: *They took a great fancy to each other. He has a fancy for bright ties. Tell me where is fancy bred, Or in the heart or in the head?* (Shakespeare). **b** a liking that lasts only a short time. **5a** changefulness of mood; caprice. **b** an instance of this. SYN: whim. **6** critical judgment in matters of art, and the like; taste.

—*v.t.* **1** to picture to oneself; imagine: *Can you fancy yourself on the moon?* SYN: conceive, picture. **2** to have an idea or belief; suppose: *I fancy that is right, but I am not sure. I fancy she is about forty.* SYN: presume, conjecture. **3** to like; be fond of: *I fancy the idea of having a picnic.*

—*adj.* **1** made or arranged specially to please; decorated; ornamental: *a fancy blouse, fancy trimming.* SYN: elegant, fine. **2** requiring much skill: *fancy skating.* **3** chosen to please the fancy or one's special taste: *fancy fruit.* **4** much too high: *a fancy price.* **5** (of an animal, fruit, or other produce) bred for special excellence of grade or quality: *fancy fruits and vegetables.* **6** based upon or drawn from conceptions of the fancy or imagination; imaginative: *a fancy picture.*

—*adv. U.S. Informal.* in a fancy manner: *He talks fancy, but don't believe a word of what he says.*

fancy up, *U.S. Informal.* to make showy or attractive; decorate; embellish: *We'd like to talk to you about ... how to fancy up a house or apartment* (New Yorker). *Demonstrations actually lose their power, in many cases, when fancied up with high artistic pretensions* (New York Times).

the fancy, *Rare.* those who fancy a particular amusement or pursuit, especially the prize ring: *Among leaders of the fancy, it is an unhesitating belief that pluck and endurance are the highest of attributes* (Herbert Spencer).

[contraction of *fantasy*]

fancy ball, a ball at which fancy dress is worn.

fan|cy|dan (fan′sē dan′), *n., adj.* —*n.* an athlete who displays intricate or showy maneuvers rather than effectiveness.

—*adj.* showy rather than effective: *fancydan footwork.*

fancy diving, competitive diving in which the contestants use varied and elaborate diving techniques.

fancy dress, 1 a costume worn at a masquerade. **2** such costumes collectively.

fan|cy-dress (fan′sē dres′), *adj., v.* —*adj.* of or having to do with fancy dress.

—*v.t.* to dress in a fancy dress.

fancy-dress ball, = masquerade.

fan|cy-free (fan′sē frē′), *adj.* **1** not in love; not bound to anyone; able to center one's affection and attention upon whomever one wishes. **2** not restrained; free of care: *The man may be in relative comfort, but he is far from fancy-free* (Time).

fancy goods, 1 goods or articles of trade serving for ornament or show, or merely to please the fancy rather than for common, necessary use. **2** miscellaneous goods, such as novelties or luxurious accessories.

fancy man, 1 a man supported as a lover by a woman, especially by a prostitute. **2** one of the fancy. **3** *Archaic.* a man who is fancied; sweetheart.

fancy pants, *U.S. Slang.* a person who puts on airs; a dandy.

fan|cy-talk (fan′sē tôk′), *n. U.S.* **1** unnatural or affected speech. **2** technical language; jargon.

fan|cy-talk|ing (fan′sē tô′king), *adj. U.S.* using unnatural or affected speech.

fancy woman, a mistress or prostitute.

fan|cy|work (fan′sē wėrk′), *n.* ornamental needlework; embroidery, crocheting, or the like.

fan dancer, a woman dancer who performs wearing very little clothing and covering herself with a fan or fans.

fan|dan|gle (fan dang′gəl), *n. Informal.* **1** fantastic ornament. **2** nonsense; tomfoolery. [perhaps an alteration of *fandango*]

fan|dan|go (fan dang′gō), *n., pl.* **-gos. 1** a lively Spanish or Spanish-American dance in three-quarter time. **2** the music for such a dance. [< Spanish *fandango,* perhaps < Portuguese *fado* fado]

fan delta, a fan-shaped alluvial deposit.

fan|dom (fan′dəm), *n.* the world of enthusiasts for some sport or amusement.

fane¹ (fān), *n. Archaic.* a temple; church. [< Latin *fānum* temple]

fane² (fān), *n. Scottish.* an elf; fairy.

fa|ne|ga (fä nā′gä), *n.* **1** a Spanish dry measure, about a bushel and a half. **2** a Mexican area measure, about eight and four fifths acres. [< Spanish *fanega* < Arabic *fanīqa* (literally) big sack]

fa|ne|ga|da (fä′nā gä′ᴛʜä), *n.* a Spanish area measure, about one and three fifths acres. [< Spanish *fanegada* < *fanega;* see etym. under **fanega**]

fan|fare (fan′fãr), *n., v.,* **-fared, -far|ing.** —*n.* **1** a short tune played on trumpets, bugles, hunting horns, or the like: *Queen Elizabeth, hailed by fanfares, passed through the nave* (Newsweek). **2** a loud show, as of activity or talk; showy flourish; showy parade: *The hero was welcomed with great fanfare by the mayor and city officials. The Soviet Union, with great fanfare, formally gave up the Porkkala naval base outside Helsinki* (Joachim Joesten).

—*v.t.* to announce with a fanfare: *Fanfared by an orchestra, he strode to the stage and began his speech.*

[< French *fanfare* < *fanfarer* blow a fanfare < Spanish *fanfarrón* fanfaron]

fan|fa|ron (fan′fə ron), *n.* **1** a noisy boaster; braggart. **2** = fanfare. [< Spanish *fanfarrón;* apparently imitative]

fan|fa|ron|ade (fan′fər ə nād′), *n.* **1** a boastful assertion; brag. **2** = fanfare. [< French *fanfaronnade* < Spanish *fanfarronada* < *fanfarrón* fanfaron]

✱**fang** (fang), *n., v.* —*n.* **1** a long, pointed tooth of a dog, wolf, or snake. Poisonous snakes have hollow or grooved fangs for injecting venom. *His fangs like spears in him uprose* (Walter de la Mare). See picture above on next page. **2** a long, slender, tapering part of anything. The root of a tooth or the prong of a fork is called a fang. —*v.t. Obsolete.* to lay hold of; grasp; seize. [earlier, a catching, Old English *fang* booty, prey]

***fang**
definition 1

Fang (fang), *n., pl.* **Fangs** or **Fang. 1** a member of a people of Gabon, Cameroon, and Equatorial Guinea, noted for their artwork and elaborate mythology. **2** the Bantu language of this people. Also, **Fan.**

fanged (fangd), *adj.* having fangs.

fan·gle (fang′gəl), *n.* a new fashion or invention; novelty: *new fashions and fangles of dress* (Grant White).

fan·gled (fang′gəld), *adj.* = newfangled. [apparently back formation < *newfangled*]

fang·less (fang′lis), *adj.* without fangs.

fan·ion (fan′yən), *n.* a small flag carried with the baggage of a military brigade, or used to mark positions in surveying. [< French *fanion, fanon* < Old French < Medieval Latin *fano, -onis* banner, napkin < Germanic (compare Old High German *fano*)]

fan-jet (fan′jet′), *n.* **1** = turbofan. **2** an aircraft powered by a turbojet.

fan·kle (fang′kəl), *n. Scottish.* tangle; entanglement. [< earlier verb *fankle* to tangle, entangle < *fank* a noose, variant of *fang*]

fan letter, a letter to a celebrity from a fan.

***fan·light** (fan′līt′), *n.* **1** a semicircular window over a door, or the like, with bars or mullions spread out like an open fan. **2** any semicircular or other window over a door. **3** *Especially British.* a transom.

***fanlight**
definition 1

fan mail, the mail received by a celebrity from fans.

fan·ner (fan′ər), *n.* **1** a person or thing that fans. **2** a machine for winnowing grain.

Fan·nie Mae or **Fan·ny May** (fan′ē mā′), the Federal National Mortgage Association (a government-chartered private organization, established to buy and sell mortgages to create a revolving fund for mortgage lending). [< spelling for pronunciation of its abbreviation, *FNMA*]

fan·nings (fan′ingz), *n.pl.* a grade of tea consisting of particles or siftings only a degree larger than dust, size having no relation to its quality.

fan·ny (fan′ē), *n., pl.* **-nies.** *Slang.* the buttocks: *She has never been willing to slink into an automobile fanny first* (New Yorker).

fan·on (fan′ən), *n.* **1** a maniple or napkin worn by the celebrant and deacons at Mass. **2** a striped scarflike vestment worn over the alb by the Pope at pontifical Mass. [< Old French *fanon.* See related etym. at **fanion.**]

***fan palm**, any palm having fan-shaped leaves, such as the talipot and cabbage palmetto.

***fan palm**
***fantail**
definition 2

palmetto

fantail pigeon

fan-shaped (fan′shāpt′), *adj.* like a fan in shape.

***fan·tail** (fan′tāl′), *n.* **1** a tail, end, or part spread out like an open fan. **2** a pigeon, goldfish, or other animal whose tail spreads out like an open fan. An Australian flycatcher has such a tail. **3** the slender, overhanging part of the stern of some ships. **4** *Architecture.* **a** a fan-shaped structure or part, especially a centering for an arch made of radial struts. **b** one of the radial struts.

fan-tailed (fan′tāld′), *adj.* having a fan-shaped tail.

fan-tan (fan′tan′), *n.* **1** a Chinese gambling game played by betting on the number of coins under a bowl. **2** a card game in which the player who gets rid of his cards first wins the game. [< Chinese *fan t'an* repeated divisions]

fan·ta·si·a (fan tā′zhē ə, -zhə, -zē ə), *n.* **1** a musical or literary composition following no fixed form or style. **2** a medley of well-known airs connected by interludes. [< Italian *fantasia* < Latin *phantasia.* See etym. of doublet **fantasy.**]

fan·ta·sied (fan′tə sēd, -zēd), *adj.* imaginary; fancied: *a fantasied illness.*

fan·ta·sist (fan′tə sist, -zist), *n.* **1** a composer or creator of fantasies or fantasias, in art, literature, or music: *Often he writes realistically; but he thinks like a fantasist or a poet* (Harper's). **2** = fantast.

fan·ta·size (fan′tə sīz), *v.,* **-sized, -siz·ing.** —*v.t.* to imagine; fancy: *For Genet the theater is an instrument of the outcast's fantasized revenge* (Time). —*v.i.* to engage in fantastic speculation; daydream: *Only when they listened to the other could one fantasize about their mood* (Manchester Guardian Weekly).

fan·tasm (fan′taz əm), *n.* = phantasm.

fan·tas·mo (fan taz′mō), *adj. Informal.* supremely fantastic: *The figures that populate his [Richard Condon's] books are . . . fantasmo embodiments of various sorts of foaming mania* (Time). *Antioch College, Yellow Springs, Ohio, [is] the absolute fantasmo super-pinnacle of academic liberalism* (National Review). [< *fantas*tic + *-mo,* as in *supremo*]

fan·tast (fan′tast), *n.* an impractical person; dreamer; visionary: *There's a bit of a fantast in Mr. Baldwin and his extravaganzas are attractive* (New Statesman).

fan·tas·tic (fan tas′tik), *adj., n.* —*adj.* **1** very odd or queer; strange and wild in shape or manner; showing unrestrained fancy: *The firelight cast weird, fantastic shadows on the walls. Come and trip it, as you go, On the light fantastic toe* (Milton). SYN: freakish, bizarre, grotesque. **2** very fanciful; capricious; eccentric; irrational: *Many of her dreams are fantastic. The idea that machines could be made to fly seemed fantastic a hundred years ago.* SYN: fabulous. **3** existing only in imagination; unreal: *She saw fantastic things in her dream. Superstition causes fantastic fears. . . . filled me with fantastic terrors never felt before* (Edgar Allan Poe). SYN: imaginary. **4** *Informal.* unbelievably good, quick, high, etc.: *That store charges fantastic prices.*

—*n.* a person who has fantastic ideas, mannerisms, etc.: *The inhabitants of . . . Stepney are fantastics: You won't find their originals in the documentary or in the music hall* (Listener).

[< Late Latin *phantasticus* < Greek *phantastikós* < *phantázesthai* imagine < *phaínesthai* appear] —**fan·tas′ti·cal·ness,** *n.*

fan·tas·ti·cal (fan tas′tə kəl), *adj.* = fantastic.

fan·tas·ti·cal·i·ty (fan tas′tə kal′ə tē), *n., pl.* **-ties. 1** fantastic quality. **2** something fantastic; a whim; crotchet.

fan·tas·ti·cal·ly (fan tas′tə klē), *adv.* **1** according to one's fancy; capriciously; arbitrarily. **2** in a fanciful or odd manner; oddly; strangely: *beads and feathers, fantastically arranged* (Jedidiah Morse).

fan·tas·ti·cate (fan tas′tə kāt), *v.t.,* **-cat·ed, -cat·ing.** to make fantastic: *Mr. Salmi does not act realistically. He fantasticates an imagined character* (New York Times). —**fan·tas′ti·ca′tion,** *n.*

fan·ta·sy (fan′tə sē, -zē), *n., pl.* **-sies,** *v.,* **-sied, -sy·ing.** —*n.* **1** a play of the mind; product of the imagination; fancy. Many stories, such as *Gulliver's Travels* and *Alice in Wonderland,* are fantasies. **2** a picture existing only in the mind; any strange mental image or illusion. Fantasies seem real to a delirious person. *A daydream is a fantasy. I talk of dreams, Which are the children of an idle brain, Begot of nothing but vain fantasy* (Shakespeare). **3** a wild, strange fancy: *Many were sure the scheme to put a man on the moon was a fantasy doomed to failure.* **4** a caprice; whim. **5** *Music.* = fantasia. **6** a coin of questionable origin or purpose, especially one issued by a country for sale to coin collectors rather than for use as legal tender: *Partly because of the appeal of the advertising and partly because so many collectors want to believe the claims, the "fantasy coin" business has grown to sizable proportions* (New York Times). Also, **phantasy.**

—*v.t.* **1** to imagine; fancy: *He fantasies himself a hero. . . . to discuss their views—frequently fantasied—of their parents, college, and society* (New York Times Magazine). **2** *Archaic.* to affect or sway by fancy.

—*v.i.* to engage in fantastic speculation; daydream: *In a time of anxiety, fantasying increases* (Wall Street Journal). [< Old French *fantasie* < Latin *phantasia* < Greek *phantasíā* appearance, image; imagination < *phaínesthai* appear < *phaínein* to show. Compare etym. under **fancy.** See etym. of doublet **fantasia.**]

fan·ta·sy·land (fan′tə sē land′, -zē-), *n.* = dreamland.

Fan·ti (fan′tē), *n., pl.* **-ti. 1** a member of a tribe inhabiting the coastal areas of Ghana. **2** the Kwa language of this tribe.

fan·tigue, fan·teague, or **fan·teeg** (fan tēg′), *n. British Dialect.* a state of anxiety; excitement. [earlier *fantique,* perhaps contraction of *fantastic*]

fan·toc·ci·ni (fan′tə chē′nē), *n.pl.* **1** puppets made to move by hidden strings or wires: *awkward as a pair of fantoccini* (Besant and Rice). **2** a puppet show. [< Italian *fantoccini,* plural of *fantoccino* (diminutive) < *fantoccio* puppet < *fante* boy < Latin *īnfāns, -antis* child, infant]

fan·tod (fan′tod), *n. Dialect.* an uneasy or uncomfortable state of mind or body; a fidget: *Nice pictures, I reckon, but . . . they always give me the fantods* (Mark Twain). [perhaps variant of *fantigue*]

fan·tom (fan′təm), *n., adj.* = phantom.

fan tracery, *Architecture.* tracery used to decorate fan vaulting, consisting of diverging ribs like those of an opened fan.

fan tree, 1 = fan palm. **2** a tree spread out in the form of a fan.

fan vault, *Architecture.* an elaborate type of vault in which the ribs flare out like a fan, used in the late Gothic architecture of England.

***fan vaulting,** *Architecture.* fan vaults collectively; vaulting in which the ribs flare out like a fan.

***fan vaulting**

fan window, a fan-shaped window with bars spread out like an open fan; fanlight.

fan·wise (fan′wīz′), *adv.* spread out like an open fan: *The plans and model show that the auditorium will provide 500 seats radiating fanwise from a screen* (London Times).

fan worm, an annelid with a crown of feathery tentacles for gathering food particles. Fan worms live in tubes imbedded in sand and mud flats.

fan·wort (fan′wėrt′), *n.* a plant of the water-lily family with floating leaves and white flowers, growing in ponds and streams; water shield.

fan·zine (fan′zēn′), *n.* a magazine or newsletter published by and for fans, especially of fantasy and science fiction. [< *fan*[2] + (*maga*)*zine*]

FAO (no periods), Food and Agriculture Organization (of the United Nations).

fa·qih (fä kē′), *n.* an authority on Moslem religious law. [< Arabic *faqīh*]

fa·quir (fə kir′, fā′kər), *n.* = fakir.

far (fär), *adj., adv.* **far·ther, far·thest.** —*adj.* **1** not near; distant: *He lives in a far country. The moon is far from the earth. Your birthday is not far from mine.* SYN: remote. See syn. under **distant. 2** more distant: *He lives on the far side of the hill.* **3** extending to a great distance; long: *a far look ahead, a far journey. Over all the sky—the sky! far, far out of reach* (Walt Whitman). **4** advanced: *An old person is far in years.*

—*adv.* **1** a long way off in time or space: *Far in the past, the Norsemen began sailing westward.* **2** very much: *It is far better to go by train. The job was far more difficult than he had imagined.* **3** to an advanced point, distance, or degree: *He studied far into the night. The explorers penetrated far into the jungle.*

as far as, to the distance, point, or degree that: *As far as might be, to carve out free space for every human doubt* (Tennyson).

by far, very much: *She is by far the best-looking girl. And the bride-maidens whispered, "'Twere better by far to have matched our fair cousin with young Lochinvar"* (Scott).

far and away, very much: *This is far and away the best story I have read this year.*

far and near, everywhere: *We searched far and near for the lost dog.*

far and wide, everywhere; even in distant parts: *This incident made headlines far and wide* (Listener).

far be it from. See under **be.**

far from it, by no means; not at all: *"For heaven's sake!" he said, "I'm not a pessimist—far from it"* (New Yorker).

Pronunciation Key: hat, āge, cãre, fär; let, ēqual, tėrm; it, īce; hot, ōpen, ôrder; oil, out; cup, pu̇t, rüle; child; long; thin; ᴛʜen; zh, measure; ə represents **a** in about, **e** in taken, **i** in pencil, **o** in lemon, **u** in circus.

far out, *Informal.* far away from the ordinary or the conventional; avant-garde: [*His*] *innovations in orchestral programming ... have not been that far out* (London Times). See also **far-out**.
from far, from a distance: *But now the trumpet, terrible from far, In shriller clangours animates the war* (Joseph Addison).
how far. See under **how**.
in so far as. See under **insofar**.
so far. See under **so**[1].
so far as. See under **so**[1].
thus far. See under **thus**.
[Old English *feorr*]

far|ad (far′əd, -ad), *n.* a unit of electrical capacitance. It is the capacitance of a body that, when charged with one coulomb, has an electrical potential of one volt. *Abbr:* f (no period). [< Michael *Faraday;* see etym. under **faraday**]

far|a|day (far′ə dā, -dē), *n.* a unit of quantity of electricity equivalent to about 96,500 coulombs. It is the quantity that, in electrolysis, is necessary to deposit one gram atom of a univalent element. [< Michael *Faraday*, 1791-1867, an English physicist and chemist]

Faraday cage, a grounded metal screen put around laboratory apparatus to insulate it from stray electrical interference.

Faraday effect, the effect produced when a beam of polarized light passes through a magnetic field and is rotated in the direction of the lines of magnetic force.

Faraday's law, any one of several laws of electrolysis formulated by Michael Faraday, especially one that states the relationship between electricity and the valence.

fa|rad|ic (fə rad′ik), *adj.* of or having to do with induced currents of electricity or with phenomena connected with them. [< French *faradique* < Michael *Faraday;* see etym. under **faraday**]

far|a|dism (far′ə diz əm), *n.* **1** *Medicine.* the use of induced currents of electricity in treating disease. **2** induced currents of electricity.

far|a|dize (far′ə dīz), *v.t.*, **-dized, -diz|ing.** *Medicine.* to stimulate or treat (a muscle or other part of the body) with induced currents of electricity.
— **far′a|di|za′tion**, *n.*

far|ad|me|ter (far′əd mē′tər), *n.* an instrument for determining, in farads, the electrostatic capacity of a condenser.

far|an|dole (far′ən dōl), *n.* **1** a lively Provençal dance in 6/8 time in which dancers hold hands and do various steps. **2** music for this dance. [< French *farandole* < Provençal *farandoulo*]

far|a|way (fär′ə wā′), *adj.* **1** distant; far away; remote: *He read of faraway places in geography books.* **2** directed to a distance; absent; dreamy: *A faraway look in her eyes showed that she was thinking of something else.* SYN: absent, abstracted.

far-back (fär′bak′), *adj.* ancient; remote: *a far-back poet, a far-back place.*

farce (färs), *n., v.,* **farced, farc|ing.** — *n.* **1** a play full of ridiculous happenings, absurd actions, and unreal situations, meant to be very funny. **2** such plays as a class; branch of drama concerned with such plays. **3** the kind of humor found in such plays; broad humor. **4** a ridiculous mockery; absurd pretense; sham: *The lazy boy's attempts to find hard work were a farce.* **5** *Obsolete.* stuffing for a fowl, roast, etc.; forcemeat.
— *v.t.* **1** to spice (a composition or speech); season: *He farced his essay with anecdotes.* **2** *Obsolete.* to stuff (a fowl or roast).
[< Old French *farce* comic interlude in a mystery play; (literally) stuffing < *farcir* to stuff < Latin *farcīre*]

farce|meat (färs′mēt′), *n. Obsolete.* forcemeat.

far|ceur (får sœr′), *n. French.* **1** a person who is fond of telling jokes; joker; wag. **2** an author or actor of farces.

far|ceuse (får sœz′), *n. French.* the feminine form of **farceur**.

far|ci (fär sē′), *adj.* stuffed for cooking.

far|cial (far′shəl), *adj.* = farcical.

far|ci|cal (fär′sə kəl), *adj.* of or like a farce; ridiculous; absurd; improbable: *But even when the action has wildly farcical overtones, one feels that no caricature is involved* (Atlantic). SYN: ludicrous.
— **far′ci|cal|ness**, *n.*

far|ci|cal|i|ty (fär′sə kal′ə tē), *n.* **1** farcical quality or character. **2** something farcical; absurdity.

far|ci|cal|ly (fär′sə klē), *adv.* in a farcical manner; ridiculously.

far cry, a long way; great distance: *a far cry from home, a far cry from what we had hoped. The kind of thinking he must do is a far cry from the quiet reflection that is possible at a university* (New Yorker).

far|cy (fär′sē), *n.* a usually fatal bacterial disease of horses, mules, etc., a form of glanders that affects the lymphatics and causes lesions of the skin. [< Old French *farcin* < Latin *farcīmen, -inis* tubercle; sausage < *farcīre* to stuff]

fard (färd), *n., v. Obsolete.* — *n.* paint for the face.
— *v.t.* **1** to paint (the face). **2** to gloss over.
[< Middle French *farder* < Old French *farde,* feminine < Germanic (compare Old High German *faro* colored)]

far|del (fär′dəl), *n. Archaic.* a bundle; burden. [< Old French *fardel* (diminutive) < *farde* bundle, burden < Arabic *farda* bale]

far-dis|tant (fär′dis′tənt), *adj.* very distant: *far-distant stars.*

fare (fãr), *n., v.,* **fared, far|ing.** — *n.* **1** the money that a person pays to ride in a train, taxi, bus, ship, or aircraft. **2** a passenger in a train, taxi, bus, ship, or aircraft. **3** food provided or eaten: *dainty fare, slim fare.* **4** *Archaic.* the state of things; fortune. [blend of Old English *fær* and *faru* journey]
— *v.i.* **1** to eat food; be fed: *We fared very well at Grandmother's Thanksgiving dinner.* **2** to get along; get on; do: *He is faring well in school. If you fare well, you have good luck or success.* **3** to turn out; happen: *It will fare hard with the thief if he is caught.* **4** *Archaic.* to go; travel: *to fare forth on a journey.*
[Old English *faran*]

Far Eastern, of, having to do with, or in the Far East (China, Japan, and other parts of eastern Asia, including Korea and eastern Siberia).

fare|box (fãr′boks′), *n. Especially U.S.* a box in a subway, bus, or other vehicle of public transportation, into which the fare is put.

far|er (fãr′ər), *n.* = traveler.

fare-thee-well (fãr′ᴛʜē wel′), *n.* **to a fare-thee-well**, to the last point or utmost degree; completely: *The book is illustrated, indexed, and appendixed to a fare-thee-well* (New Yorker). Also, **fare-you-well**.

fare|well (fãr′wel′), *interj., n., adj., v.* — *interj.* **1** good-by; good luck. **2** an expression of good wishes at parting. [contraction of *fare-you-well*]
— *n.* **1** good-by; good luck. **2** good wishes at parting. **3** departure; leave-taking: *The poor exiles ... fondly look'd their last, And took a long farewell* (Oliver Goldsmith).
— *adj.* of farewell; parting; last: *a farewell kiss. The singer gave a farewell performance.*
— *v.t., v.i.* to give or wish farewell: *One of the most popular photographs ... showed a young Catholic nun farewelling her brother* (Punch). *"Shoo!" farewelled Mrs. Otter and fended off the cat* (Sylvia Townsend Warner).
[< earlier phrase *fare* (thou, or ye) *well*]

fare|well-sum|mer (fãr′wel′sum′ər), *n. U.S.* any one of various late-blooming asters, such as the heath aster.

fare|well-to-spring (fãr′wel′tə spring′), *n.* an annual herb of western North America, especially of California, that blooms in the summer and is grown for its showy purple or rose-colored flowers.

fare-you-well (fãr′yů wel′), *n.* = fare-thee-well.

far-famed (fär′fāmd′), *adj.* widely celebrated; well-known.

far|fel (fär′fəl), *n. Jewish Cookery.* noodle dough cut into small pellets or grains. [< Yiddish *farfl* < Middle High German *varveln* noodles]

far-fetched (fär′fecht′), *adj.* **1** not closely related to the topic; remotely connected; forced; strained: *a far-fetched comparison. His excuse was too far-fetched for anyone to believe.* **2** *Archaic.* brought from afar.

far-flung (fär′flung′), *adj.* covering a large area; widely spread: *Many American banks have far-flung operations in Europe, Asia, and South America. ... this far-flung vista of the land he loved* (Harry Emerson Fosdick).

far|forth (fär′fôrth′, -fōrth′), *adv. Archaic.* to a definite degree, extent, or distance.

far-gone (fär′gôn′, -gon′), *adj.* advanced to a great extent: *the far-gone night, a far-gone romance.*

fa|ri|na (fə rē′nə), *n.* **1** a flour or meal made from grain, potatoes, beans, nuts, or starchy root, and used especially as cereal or in puddings. **2** starch. **3** a coarse, white corn meal. **4** *Biology.* a mealy, powdery substance, such as the pollen of flowers or the powder found on certain insects. [< Latin *farīna* < *far, farris* grits, spelt]

far|i|na|ceous (far′ə nā′shəs), *adj.* consisting or made of flour or meal; starchy; mealy: *Cereals, bread, and potatoes are farinaceous foods.*
— **far′i|na′ceous|ly**, *adv.*

fa|rin|ha de man|di|o|ca (fə rēn′yə də man dē-ō′kə), a coarse meal resembling corn meal, ground from the cassava root. It is the main food for many Brazilians in the farming regions. [< Portuguese *farinha de mandioca* meal of manioc (cassava)]

far|i|nose (far′ə nōs), *adj.* **1** yielding farina. **2** like farina or meal. **3** *Biology.* covered with a white, mealy substance.

Far|ish (fãr′ish), *adj.* = Faeroese.

far|kle|ber|ry (fär′kəl ber′ē), *n., pl.* **-ries.** a shrub or small tree of the heath family, growing in the southern United States, and bearing small, inedible black berries. [American English; origin uncertain]

farl or **farle** (färl), *n. Scottish.* a small, thin cake made of oatmeal or flour. [originally, quarter of a cake, Middle English *fardel* a quarter, Old English *fēortha dǣl* fourth part]

farm (färm), *n., v.* — *n.* **1** a piece of land which a person uses to raise crops or animals: *a potato farm, a chicken farm.* **2** anything like a farm. A tract of water for cultivating oysters is an oyster farm. **3** *U.S.* a minor-league baseball team belonging to or associated with a major-league club. Young players are usually sent to a farm to gain experience. **4** *Archaic.* **a** a fixed yearly amount payable in the form of rent, taxes, or the like. **b** a fixed yearly amount accepted from a person instead of taxes, or the like, that he is authorized to collect. **5a** the letting out of the collection of public taxes. **b** the condition of being let out at a fixed amount: *a district in farm.* **c** a district let out for the collection of taxes.
— *v.i.* to raise crops or animals on a farm either to eat or to sell; be a farmer: *Her father farms for a living.*
— *v.t.* **1** to cultivate (land); till: *He farms forty acres.* **2** to take proceeds or profits of (a tax or undertaking) on paying a fixed sum. **3** to let the labor or services of (a person) for hire: *He farmed his pickers to work in the beet fields.* **4** to let out (taxes, revenues, or an enterprise) to another for a fixed sum or percentage: *Mr. Bell farms the right to pick berries on his land.* **5** to contract for the maintenance of (paupers, children, or other indigents): *The parish authorities ... resolved that Oliver should be "farmed"* (Dickens).
farm out, **a** to let for hire or subcontract: *He farms out the right to pick berries on his land. The principal issues in dispute are the unions' demands the Pennsy quit farming out ... repair and construction work* (Wall Street Journal). **b** *Baseball.* to assign to a minor-league team: *The Cardinals farmed out a rookie pitcher.* **c** to live for a time; stay during the duration of: *... a laconic realist determined to farm out the war in an edgy Southern community* (New York Times). *The actors don't have enough money to live elsewhere so they farm out in whatever community they are playing* (Harper's).
[Middle English *ferme* fixed rent or charge < Old French, lease < *fermer* fasten, fix (on), decide < Latin *firmāre* < *firmus* firm] — **farm′a|ble**, *adj.*

Farm Belt, a region of the United States consisting of the Midwestern agricultural states.

farm bloc, a group in Congress from different political parties that favors laws to help the farmers.

farm|er (fär′mər), *n.* **1** a person who raises crops or animals on a farm. SYN: agriculturist. **2** a person who takes a contract for the collection of taxes by agreeing to pay a certain sum to the government.

farmer cheese, *U.S.* a soft, white cheese made from whole or partly skimmed milk.

farm|er|ess (fär′mər is), *n.* **1** = farmerette. **2** a farmer's wife.

farm|er|ette (fär′mə ret′), *n. U.S. Informal.* a woman or girl who farms or works on a farm.

farm|er-gen|er|al (fär′mər jen′ər əl, -jen′rəl), *n., pl.* **farm|ers-gen|er|al.** a person who paid a fixed sum for the right to collect certain taxes in France before the Revolution. [< French *fermier-général* (literally) general farmer]

farmer's lung, a disease of the lungs caused by inhalation of the dust of moldy hay or other vegetable produce: *Farmer's lung is widespread throughout the central part of the United States and Canada* (Science News Letter).

farm|er|y (fär′mər ē), *n., pl.* **-er|ies**, *adj.* — *n.* the buildings, yards, and the like, of a farm.
— *adj.* like a farmer: [*He*] *makes his cheese with farmery care* (George W. Thornbury).

farm hand, a person who works on a farm.

farm|hold (färm′hōld′), *n.* a quantity of land held and cultivated as a farm.

farm|house (färm′hous′), *n.* a house in which a farmer and his family live.

farm|ing (fär′ming), *n., adj.* — *n.* **1** the occupation or business of raising crops or animals on a farm; agriculture. SYN: husbandry, tillage. **2** the practice of letting out the collection of public revenue. **3** the condition of being let out at a fixed sum.
— *adj.* of or for farms or farming.

farm|land (färm′land′, -lənd), *n.* land used or suitable for raising crops or grazing: *In the grain lands of the Vojovdina, Yugoslavia's richest farmland, I saw rolling acres of splendid maize* (Manchester Guardian).

farm|stead (färm′sted), *n.* a farm with its buildings.

farm|stead|ing (färm′sted′ing), *n. Especially British.* a farmstead.

farm system, 1 *U.S.* the system of farming out or assigning young baseball players to a minor-league team. 2 (in Canada) a similar system for training hockey players.

farm|wife (färm′wīf′), *n., pl.* **-wives.** 1 a farmer's wife; farmeress. 2 a woman who farms; woman farmer.

farm|work|er (färm′wėr′kər), *n. British.* a farm hand.

farm|yard (färm′yärd′), *n.* 1 a yard connected with farm buildings or enclosed by them. 2 *Especially British.* a barnyard.

far|ne|sol (fär′nə sol, -sōl), *n.* a colorless liquid found in many flowers and essential oils. It has a delicate floral odor and is used in perfumes. *Formula:* $C_{15}H_{25}OH$
[< Odoardo *Farnese,* an Italian cardinal of the 1600's + English *-ol*[1]]

far|o (fãr′ō), *n.* a gambling game played by betting on the order in which certain cards will appear in the dealer's pack. [apparently alteration of *Pharaoh;* allusion uncertain]

faro bank, an establishment where faro is played.

Far|o|ese (fãr′ō ēz′, -ēs′), *adj., n., pl.* **-ese.** = Faeroese.

far-off (fär′ôf′, -of′), *adj.* distant; far away. SYN: remote.

fa|rouche (fȧ rüsh′), *adj. French.* 1 shy; unsociable. 2 wild; fierce.

far-out (fär′out′), *adj. Informal.* 1a far away from the ordinary; very unconventional; experimental; avant-garde: *What began a few seasons ago as a real far-out and rather random sport has achieved formal status and regular schedules* (New York Times Magazine). b extreme: *a far-out reactionary.* 2 far away from common experience; highly theoretical; abstruse: *far-out research.* 3 transported; inspired: *a far-out look, far-out jazz fans.* 4 far removed in space; very distant in space: *Although Pluto, the solar system's most far-out planet, has appeared to be growing slightly dimmer for the past ten years, this is not a permanent change* (Science News). **—far′-out′-ness,** *n.*

far-out|er (fär′ou′tər), *n. Informal.* a person who is far-out; very unconventional person: *Only the most hardy far-outers wear them [overcoats] as short or shorter than their skirts* (Sunday Times).

far point, *Optics.* the point farthest from the eye at which an image is clearly formed on the retina when accommodation is relaxed.

far|rag|i|nous (fə raj′ə nəs), *adj.* consisting of various materials; confused; jumbled: *A farraginous concurrence of all conditions, tempers, sexes, and ages* (Thomas Browne). [< Latin *farrāgō, -inis* (see etym. under **farrago**) + English *-ous*]

far|ra|go (fə rā′gō, -rä′-), *n., pl.* **-goes.** a confused mixture; hodgepodge; jumble: *a confounded farrago of doubts, fears, hopes, wishes* (Richard Brinsley Sheridan).
[< Latin *farrāgō* medley; (originally) mixed fodder < *far, farris* grits, spelt]

far|rand (far′ənd), *adj. Scottish.* having a specified appearance or nature. [Middle English *farrand,* good-looking; (literally) present participle of *faren* to fare (well)]

far-rang|ing (fär′rān′jing), *adj.* 1 extending over a great space or distance: *far-ranging missiles, a far-ranging inspection tour.* 2 covering a great deal; broad: *The debate was, nevertheless, sharp, far-ranging, and unusually outspoken* (Atlantic).

far-reach|ing (fär′rē′ching), *adj.* having a wide influence or effect; extending far: *The use of atomic energy is having far-reaching effects today.* SYN: extensive.

far-red light (fär′red′), the reddish-purple part of the red band of the spectrum. Far-red light inhibits the growth of plants by counteracting the effect of red light on the enzyme phytochrome.

far|ri|er (far′ē ər), *n. Especially British.* 1 a blacksmith who shoes horses. 2 *Archaic.* a horse doctor or veterinarian. [< Middle French *ferrier* < Latin *ferrārius* of iron < *ferrum* iron]

far|ri|er|y (far′ē ər ē), *n., pl.* **-er|ies.** *Especially British.* 1 the work of a farrier. 2 the place where a farrier works. 3 *Archaic.* the care and treatment of horses.

far|row[1] (far′ō), *n., v.* **—n.** 1 a litter of pigs. 2 *Obsolete.* a young pig.
—v.t., v.i. to give birth to (a litter of pigs).
[Old English *fearh*]

far|row[2] (far′ō), *adj. Scottish.* (of cows) not calving in a certain year or season. [origin uncertain. Compare Flemish *verwekoe,* earlier *verrekoe* barren cow.]

far|ru|ca (fär rü′kä), *n.* an Andalusian Gypsy dance. [< Spanish *farruca,* ultimately (diminutive) < *Francisco* Francis, a man's name]

farse (färs), *n., v.,* **farsed, fars|ing.** **—n.** an interpolation made in a liturgy, especially the liturgy of the Mass.
—v.t. to interpolate a farse in (a liturgy or a certain part of it).
[< Medieval Latin *farsa* (literally) stuffing, ultimately < past participle of Latin *farcīre* to stuff]

far-see|ing (fär′sē′ing), *adj.* 1 able to see far; far-sighted. 2 *Figurative.* looking ahead; planning wisely for the future; far-sighted: *His keen and far-seeing judgment perceived clearly his true interest* (William Lecky). SYN: prudent, prescient.

Far|si or **Far|see** (fär′sē), *n.* the language of Iran; Persian.

far-sight (fär′sīt′), *n.* the ability to see far.

far-sight|ed or **far|sight|ed** (fär′sī′tid), *adj.* 1 seeing distant things more clearly than near ones; not seeing nearby objects clearly; hyperopic; hypermetropic. The condition occurs when parallel light rays entering the eye come to a focus behind, rather than on, the retina. 2 *Figurative.* looking ahead; planning wisely for the future; shrewd; prudent: *The far-sighted man is saving money while his wages are high.* SYN: sagacious. 3 able to see far. **—far′-sight′ed|ly,** *adv.* **—far′-sight′ed|ness,** *n.*

fart (färt), *v., n. Slang.* (*often considered vulgar*).
—v.i. to expel gas in the stomach or intestines from the anus; break wind.
—n. a discharge of such gas; a breaking wind.
[Middle English *farten*]

far|ther (fär′ᴛʜər), *adj., adv., comparative of* **far,** *v.* **—adj.** 1 more far; more distant: *Three miles is farther than two.* 2 more; additional: *Do you need farther help?*
—adv. 1 at or to a greater distance: *We walked farther than we meant to.* 2 at or to a more advanced point: *He has investigated the subject farther than any other man.* 3 in addition; also. SYN: besides, moreover.
—v.t. *Obsolete.* to further.
[Middle English *ferther,* variant of *further* (originally) more, forward]
▶**farther** and **further.** In formal English a distinction is occasionally made between *farther* and *further. Farther* is confined to expressions of physical distance: *He lives farther from town than I do. Further* refers to abstract relationships of degree or quantity: *She needs further schooling.* In informal English, the distinction is not usually kept.

far|ther|most (fär′ᴛʜər mōst), *adj.* most distant; farthest: *He has traveled to the farthermost points of the earth.*

far|thest (fär′ᴛʜist), *adj., adv., superlative of* **far.**
—adj. 1 most distant: *the farthest reaches of the universe. Ours is the farthest house down the road.* 2 longest: *the farthest journey of Magellan.*
—adv. 1 to or at the greatest distance: *The last golfer hit the ball farthest and it landed almost on the green.* 2 most: *His ideas were the farthest advanced of his time.*
[Middle English *ferthest,* variant of *furthest*]

far|thing (fär′ᴛʜing), *n.* 1 a former British coin, worth ¼ of a British penny or about 2/5 of a United States cent. 2 *Figurative.* something of very small value; very little bit.
not care a farthing, not to care a single bit: *The gentleman . . . has told her he does not care a farthing for her* (Sir Richard Steele).
[Old English *fēorthung,* also *fēorthling* < *fēortha* fourth + *-ling* -ling]

***far|thin|gale** (fär′ᴛʜing gāl), *n.* a hoop skirt or framework for expanding a woman's skirt or petticoat, worn in England from about 1550 to about 1650. [earlier *verdyingale* < Middle French *verdugale,* alteration of Spanish *verdugado* hoop skirt < *verdugo* rod, ultimately < Latin *viridis* green]

***farthingale**

Far West, 1 the part of the United States from the Rocky Mountains to the Pacific Ocean. 2 *Historical.* the Middle West, especially the section of the United States west of the Mississippi.

Far Western, of or having to do with the Far West.

f.a.s., free alongside ship (delivery to the ship without charge to the buyer).

FAS (no periods), 1 Fetal Alcohol Syndrome: *The original estimates of FAS suggested that there were about 1,500 FAS babies in the U.S.* (Wall Street Journal). 2 free alongside ship (delivery to the ship without charge to the buyer).

fasc., fascicle.

***fas|ces** (fas′ēz), *n.pl. of* **fas|cis.** a bundle of rods or sticks containing an ax with the blade projecting, carried before a Roman magistrate as a symbol of authority.
[< Latin *fascēs,* plural of *fascis* bundle]

***fasces**

Fa|sching (fäsh′ing), *n. German.* carnival.

fas|ci (fä′shē), *n.* plural of **fascio.**

fas|ci|a (fash′ē ə), *n., pl.* **fas|ci|ae** (fash′i ē). 1 a band; fillet; long, flat strip. 2 *British.* the dashboard of a motor vehicle: *For parking, there is a foot-operated brake, released by a spring lever under the fascia* (London Times). 3 *Anatomy.* a a usually thin band of fibrous connective tissue covering, supporting, or binding together a muscle, part, or organ. b tissue of this kind. 4 (in surgery) a bandage. 5 *Architecture.* a long, flat part or band, especially a horizontal division of an architrave. 6 *Botany, Zoology.* a wide and distinct band of color. [< Latin *fascia* band, girdle. See etym. of doublet **fess.**]

fas|ci|al (fash′ē əl), *adj.* 1 having to do with a fascia. 2 consisting of fasciae. 3 of the fasces.

fas|ci|ate (fash′ē āt), *adj.* 1 *Botany.* compressed into a band or bundle; grown together: *fasciate stems.* 2 *Zoology.* marked with wide bands or stripes; striped. 3 bound with a band, fillet, or bandage. [< Latin *fasciātus,* past participle of *fasciāre* swathe; bind up < *fascia* fascia] **—fas′ci-ate′ly,** *adv.*

fas|ci|at|ed (fash′ē ā′tid), *adj.* = fasciate.

fas|ci|a|tion (fash′ē ā′shən), *n.* 1 the act or process of binding up or bandaging. 2 a fasciate condition. 3 *Botany.* a malformation in plants, in which a stem or branch becomes expanded into a flat, ribbonlike shape.

fas|ci|cle (fas′ə kəl), *n.* 1 a small bundle. 2 *Botany.* a close cluster, especially of flowers, leaves, or roots. 3 *Anatomy.* = fasciculus (def. 1). 4 a single part of a printed work issued in installments; fasciculus. [< Latin *fasciculus* (diminutive) < *fascis* bundle. See etym. of doublet **fascicule.**]

fas|ci|cled (fas′ə kəld), *adj.* arranged in a fascicle; fasciculate: *Some plants, notably the dahlia, have fascicled root systems* (Hardy and Perrin).

fas|cic|u|lar (fə sik′yə lər), *adj.* of or like a fascicle.

fas|cic|u|late (fə sik′yə lit, -lāt), *adj.* arranged in a fascicle or fascicles. **—fas|cic′u|late|ly,** *adv.*

fas|cic|u|lat|ed (fə sik′yə lā′tid), *adj.* = fasciculate.

fas|cic|u|la|tion (fə sik′yə lā′shən), *n.* 1 the state of being fasciculate. 2 a thing that is fasciculate.

fas|ci|cule (fas′ə kyül), *n.* 1 a fascicle, especially of a book; fasciculus. 2 = fasciculus (def. 1).
[< Middle French *fascicule,* learned borrowing from Latin *fasciculus.* See etym. of doublet **fascicle.**]

fas|cic|u|lus (fə sik′yə ləs), *n.* 1 *Anatomy.* a set of nerve or muscle fibers bound closely together; fascicle. 2 a fascicle of a book. [< Latin *fasciculus* (diminutive) < *fascis* bundle]

fas|ci|nate (fas′ə nāt), *v.,* **-nat|ed, -nat|ing.** **—v.t.** 1 to attract very strongly; enchant by charming qualities; charm: *The actress's beauty and cleverness fascinated everyone.* SYN: entrance, enrapture, captivate. 2 to hold motionless by strange power or by terror: *Snakes are said to fascinate small birds.* 3 *Obsolete.* to put under a spell; bewitch.
—v.i. to be very strongly attractive; hold a person spellbound: *[In] his detective novels . . . it is what emerges unsummed that fascinates* (Observer).
[< Latin *fascināre* (with English *-ate*[1]) < *fascinum* a spell]

fas|ci|nat|ed|ly (fas′ə nā′tid lē), *adv.* in a fascinated manner.

fas|ci|nat|ing (fas′ə nā′ting), *adj.* irresistibly attractive; enchanting; charming: *a fascinating woman. Gardening is a fascinating hobby.* SYN: captivating, bewitching. **—fas′ci|nat′ing|ly,** *adv.*

fas|ci|na|tion (fas′ə nā′shən), *n.* 1 the act of fascinating or state of being fascinated. 2 a very strong attraction; charm; enchantment: *Youth, full*

Pronunciation Key: **hat, āge, cãre, fär; let, ēqual, tėrm; it, īce; hot, ōpen, ôrder; oil, out; cup, pu̇t, rüle; child; long; thin; ᴛʜen; zh,** measure;
ə represents **a** in about, **e** in taken, **i** in pencil, **o** in lemon, **u** in circus.

of grace, force, fascination, Do you know that Old Age may come after you with equal grace, force, fascination? (Walt Whitman).

fas|ci|na|tor (fas′ə nā′tər), *n.* **1** a person or thing that fascinates: *What she had was charm, and she's worth reading about—if not as a doer, then as a fascinator* (New Yorker). **2** a crocheted scarf worn as a head covering by women.

fas|cine (fa sēn′), *n.* a bundle of sticks tied together, used to line trenches, strengthen earthworks, dams, and the like. [< French *fascine,* learned borrowing from Latin *fascīna* bundle (of sticks) < *fascis* bundle]

fa|scio (fä′shō), *n., pl.* **fas|ci.** *Italian.* **1** the fasces, especially as the official emblem of the Italian Fascist party. **2** a local branch of this party.

fas|ci|o|li|a|sis (fə sē′ə lī′ə sis, -sī′-), *n.* a disease of mammals, especially cattle and sheep, caused by infestation with liver flukes. [< New Latin *fascioliasis* < *Fasciola* the genus name of trematodes including the liver fluke (< Latin *fascis* bundle) + *-iasis*]

fas|cis (fas′is), *n.* singular of **fasces.**

Fas|cism (fash′iz əm), *n.* **1** the form of government in Italy from 1922 to 1943, under the leadership of Benito Mussolini. It was ruled by a dictator, with strong control of industry and labor by the central government, great restrictions upon the freedom of individuals, and extreme nationalism and militarism. It was opposed to radical socialism and communism. **2** the doctrines, principles, or methods of the Fascists. [< Italian *fascismo* < *fascio* bundle (as political emblem) < Latin *fascis* bundle]

▶**Fascism** is capitalized when it refers to the Italian Fascist party and movement, as we capitalize *Republican* and *Democrat* in this country. When the word refers to a movement in another country in which the party has a different name, it need not be capitalized but often is. When it refers to the general idea of fascist politics, or to an organized fascist tendency, it is not capitalized.

fas|cism (fash′iz əm), *n.* **1** any system of government in which property is privately owned, but all industry and labor are regulated by a strong national government, while all opposition is rigorously suppressed: *A basic idea of fascism was: Everyone shall work, but no one shall work against the state* (Emory S. Bogardus). **2** the doctrines, principles, or methods of such a government or of a political party favoring such a government. **3** any movement favoring such a system of government. **4** = Fascism. [< *Fascism*]
▶See **Fascism** for usage note.

Fa|scis|mo (fä shēz′mō), *n. Italian.* Fascism.

Fas|cist (fash′ist), *n., adj.* **—*n.*** a member of a strongly nationalistic political party that seized control of the Italian government in 1922 under the leadership of Benito Mussolini.
—*adj.* of or having to do with Fascism or Fascists.

fas|cist (fash′ist), *n., adj.* **—*n.*** **1** a member of a political party favoring the principles and methods of fascism. **2** a person who favors and supports fascism.
—*adj.* of or having to do with fascism or fascists: *Since fascist politicians have been extremely opportunistic in their efforts to secure support, such movements have often encompassed groups with conflicting interests and values* (Seymour Martin Lipset).
[< *Fascist*]

Fa|scis|ti (fə shis′tē; *Italian* fä shē′stē), *n.pl. of* **Fa|scis|ta** (fə shis′tə; *Italian* fä shē′stä). **1** the political party of the Fascists. **2** a similar party in other countries.

Fas|cis|tic (fa shis′tik), *adj.* = Fascist. **—Fas|cis′ti|cal|ly,** *adv.*

fas|cis|tic (fa shis′tik), *adj.* = fascist. **—fas|cis′ti|cal|ly,** *adv.*

Fas|cis|tize (fash′is tīz), *v.t.,* **-tized, -tiz|ing.** to make Fascist; change into a Fascist. **—Fas′cis|ti|za′tion,** *n.*

fas|cis|tize (fash′is tīz), *v.t.,* **-tized, -tiz|ing.** to make fascist; change into a fascist. **—fas′cis|ti|za′tion,** *n.*

fash (fash), *n., v. Scottish.* **—*n.*** **1** trouble; bother. **2** a troublesome person or thing. [< verb]
—*v.t., v.i.* to annoy or be annoyed; trouble: *Don't fash yourself about me; a cup of tea will do nicely.*
[< Middle French *fascher,* ultimately < Latin *fastīdīre* annoy < *fastīdium* annoyance; see etym. under **fastidious**]

fash|ion (fash′ən), *n., v.* **—*n.*** **1** the way a thing is shaped or made or done; manner: *He walks in a peculiar fashion. Subjects serious in themselves, but treated after my fashion, nonseriously* (Charles Lamb). **2** the current custom in dress, manners, or speech; style: *It is no longer the fashion for women to wear hoop skirts. Fashion has many odd vagaries* (G. M. Trevelyan). **3** polite society; fashionable people. **4** make; form; shape: *Madame—if I know your sex, From the fashion of your bones* (Tennyson). **5** kind; sort: *You can fix it with a tool—a drill or something of that fashion.* **6** *Obsolete.* the act or process of making; workmanship.
—*v.t.* **1** to make, shape, or form: *He fashioned a whistle out of a piece of wood. Take her up tenderly, Lift her with care; Fashioned so slenderly, Young, and so fair!* (Thomas Hood). SYN: frame, construct. See syn. under **make. 2** to adapt: *By doctrines fashioned to the varying hour* (Oliver Goldsmith). SYN: accommodate. **3** *Obsolete.* to contrive; manage: *You and Douglas ... as I will fashion it, Shall happily meet* (Shakespeare).
after (or **in**) **a fashion,** in some way or other; not very well: *He played the violin, after a fashion. Providence ... has made me a lady after a fashion* (Anthony Trollope).
set the fashion, to fix the fashion, method, etc., for others to follow: *... the fashion being of course set by the upper class* (Dickens).
[< Old French *façon* < Latin *factiō, -ōnis* a doing or making. See etym. of doublet **faction**[1].]
—*Syn. n.* **2 Fashion, style** mean custom in dress, manners, living arrangements, speech, etc. **Fashion** applies to the custom prevailing at a particular time or among a particular group: *It is no longer the fashion to curtsy in greeting people.* **Style** is often used in place of *fashion,* but also applies to a distinctive fashion or to a fashion based on good taste rather than custom: *That dress is such a good style it will be fashionable for years.*

fash|ion|a|bil|i|ty (fash′ə nə bil′ə tē, fash′nə-), *n., pl.* **-ties.** fashionable quality or status; fashionableness: *A Latin-American rhythm called the bossa nova, a sort of loose-jointed jazz samba ... acquired a sudden fashionability* (Harper's).

fash|ion|a|ble (fash′ə nə bəl, fash′nə-), *adj., n.* **—*adj.*** **1** following the fashion; in fashion; stylish: *Her hats are always fashionable, but they do not always suit her. It has become fashionable to blame America for sins that are the common heritage of mankind* (William McFee). SYN: modish, chic. **2** of, like, or used by people who set the styles: *They are members of a fashionable club. Fashionable and momentary things we need not see or speak of* (Robinson Jeffers). **3** *Obsolete.* that can be fashioned.
—*n.* a fashionable person. **—fash′ion|a|ble|ness,** *n.* **—fash′ion|a|bly,** *adv.*

fashion book, a book describing and illustrating new fashions in dress.

fashion coordinator, a person who coordinates or harmonizes the styles, colors, materials, etc., of wearing apparel in a department store, garment factory, or similar establishment.

fashion designer, a person who creates and develops new styles of wearing apparel.

-fashioned, *combining form.* ____in fashion or style: *Old-fashioned = old in fashion or style.*

fash|ion|er (fash′ə nər), *n.* **1** a person or thing that fashions; creator; maker. **2** *Archaic.* a tailor or dressmaker.

fash|ion|less (fash′ən lis), *adj.* without fashion; formless.

fash|ion|mon|ger (fash′ən mung′ger, -mong′-), *n.* a person who faithfully studies and follows what is fashionable.

fashion plate, 1 a person who follows the latest style in dress. **2** a picture of the latest style of dress.

fashion show, an exhibition of wearing apparel, usually of the latest styles for women, worn and displayed by models.

fas|sa|ite (fas′ē īt), *n.* a mineral consisting of a dark-green variety of pyroxene containing a little alumina. [< *Fassa,* a region in the Tyrol, where it was found + *-ite*[1]]

fast[1] (fast, fäst), *adj., adv.* **—*adj.*** **1** moving, acting, or doing with speed; quick; rapid; swift: *A fast runner can beat a slow one. As fast years flow away, The smooth brow gathers* (Shelley). SYN: fleet, speedy, hasty. See syn. under **quick. 2** showing a time ahead of the correct time: *My watch is fast.* **3** not restrained in pleasures; too gay or wild: *He led a fast life, drinking and gambling.* SYN: dissipated, dissolute, profligate, immoral. **4** firm and secure; tight: *a fast hold on a rope.* SYN: fixed, immovable, tenacious. **5** loyal; faithful; steadfast: *They have been fast friends for years.* **6** that will not fade easily: *Good cloth is dyed with fast color.* **7** adapted for speed; helping to produce or increase speed: *a fast track.* **8** with greater than average speed, force, etc.: *a fast pitcher.* **9** firmly fixed or attached; tightly shut or locked: *a fast window or door.* **10** *Photography.* (of a film or lens) making a short exposure possible. **11** *Physics.* of high energy: *Certain important questions could only be answered by experimenting with beams of high-energy, or fast, protons* (Scientific American).
—*adv.* **1** quickly; rapidly; swiftly: *Airplanes go fast. Faster than springtime showers comes thought on thought* (Shakespeare). **2** firmly; securely; tightly: *Bolt the door fast. He held fast as the sled went on down the hill. The fox was caught fast in the trap.* **3** thoroughly; soundly; completely: *The baby is fast asleep.* **4** *Archaic.* close; near.
play fast and loose, to say one thing and do another; be tricky, insincere, or unreliable: *Obviously, [he] has been playing fast and loose with the public welfare for his own purposes* (Time).
pull a fast one, *U.S. Slang.* to play a trick: *"Kennedy pulled a fast one on us politically, but this thing could boomerang," one GOP leader said* (Wall Street Journal).
[Old English *fæst* firmly fixed]

fast[2] (fast, fäst), *v., n.* **—*v.i.*** **1** to go without food: *Jesus fasted in the wilderness. If man has enough water, he can fast from 40 to 50 days without suffering permanent injury* (Ewald E. Selkurt). **2** to eat little or nothing; go without certain kinds of food: *Members of that church fast on certain days.*
—*n.* **1** the act of fasting. **2** a day or time of fasting.
break one's fast, to eat the first food of the day; breakfast: *My purpose is to be at Hodsden ... before I break my fast* (Izaak Walton).
[Old English *fæstan*]

fast[3] (fast, fäst), *n. Nautical.* a rope or chain by which a ship is secured, as to a pier or wharf. [Middle English *fest* < Scandinavian (compare Old Icelandic *festr*)]

fast|back (fast′bak′, fäst′-), *n. U.S.* **1** an automobile roofline that slopes down the rear in an unbroken convex curve. **2** an automobile with such a roofline: *Ford's new racer is a sleek fastback with a 200-m.p.h. top speed and a 375-h.p. engine* (Time).

Fast Back, an economical breed of pigs first produced in 1971 in Great Britain.

fast ball, *Baseball.* a pitched ball delivered at high speed and without a curve.

fast ball|er (bôl′ər), *Baseball.* a pitcher who delivers fast balls; speedballer.

fast break, *Sports.* a rush to score after gaining possession of the ball or puck to prevent the opposing team from establishing a defense: *By half time, relying on a collapsing zone defense that stalled Illinois' fast break, Northwestern had a 34-28 lead* (Time).

fast-break|ing (fast′brā′king, fäst′-), *adj.* occurring suddenly in a rapid sequence of events: *a fast-breaking news story, a fast-breaking political crisis.*

fast breeder, or **fast-breed|er reactor** (fast′-brē′dər, fäst′-), an atomic power plant that utilizes fast neutrons to produce its own plutonium fuel as well as generate power with almost no loss of fissionable material: *Two different breeder systems are involved, depending on which raw material is being transmuted. The thermal breeder, employing slow neutrons, operates best on the thorium 232-uranium 233 cycle (usually called the thorium cycle). . The fast breeder, employing more energetic neutrons, operates best on the uranium 238-plutonium 239 cycle (the uranium cycle)* (Glenn T. Seaborg and Justin L. Bloom). *Abbr:* FBR (no periods).

fast buck, *U.S. Slang.* **1** money earned on the side for performing a quick or easy task: *After he quit college, while he polished up his pitching, he also earned a fast buck playing professional basketball with the Boston Celtics* (Time). **2** money obtained by playing on circumstance, often improperly: *[He] condemns what he calls the whole gray flannel suit psychology, the terrible drive for the fast buck* (Wall Street Journal).

fast-can|ning (fast′can′ing, fäst′-), *adj.* of or having to do with a method of preserving foods by using high temperatures, between 250°F. and 280°F., for short periods of time. Commercial foods processed by fast-canning methods include baby foods, cream-style corn, potted meats, and sauces.

fast day, a day observed by fasting, especially a day regularly set apart by a church.

fas|ten (fas′ən, fäs′-), *v.t.* **1** to tie, lock, or make hold together in any way; fix firmly in place: *to fasten a dress, to fasten a door.* SYN: link, hook, clasp, clamp, secure, bind. **2** *Figurative.* to attach; connect: *He tried to fasten the blame upon me.* **3** to fix; direct intently: (*Figurative.*) *The dog fastened his eyes on the stranger.* **—*v.i.*** **1** to become fixed or fastened together. **2** to become firm; set.
fasten on (or **upon**), **a** to take hold of; seize: *I will fasten on this sleeve of thine* (Shakespeare). *Riemann fastened at once on the axiom that a straight line is infinite* (Scientific American). **b** to

fix on (a person); impute or attach to: *Those very Londoners . . . now fastened on the prince . . . the nickname of Butcher* (Macaulay).
[Old English *fæstnian* make fast, firm < *fæst* fast, firm]
fas|ten|er (fas′ə nər, fäs′-), *n.* **1** a person who fastens. **2** an attachment, device or the like, used to fasten anything, such as a door, garment, or dog leash; fastening. A zipper is a fastener. *Four kinds of . . . fasteners are regularly used: buttons, hooks and eyes, snaps, and mechanical or slide fasteners* (Bernice G. Chambers).
fas|ten|ing (fas′ə ning, fäs′-), *n.* a thing used to fasten something. Locks, bolts, clasps, zippers, hooks, buttons, and the like, are all fastenings.
fast|er (fas′tər, fäs′-), *n.* a person who fasts.
fast-food (fast′füd′, fäst′-), *adj.* serving foods that can be prepared quickly, such as hamburgers, frankfurters, and fried chicken.
fast-for|ward (fast′fôr′wərd, fäst′-), *v., n.* —*v.t., v.i.* to wind a cassette tape rapidly forward: . . . *the mechanism of a hypersensitive tape-recorder that could fast-forward or rewind* (New York Times). —*n.* the process of fast-forwarding.
fast ice, sea ice frozen securely to rocks along the shore.
fas|tid|i|ous (fas tid′ē əs), *adj.* hard to please, often because one is dainty in taste or easily disgusted; extremely refined or critical: *a fastidious dresser, a fastidious eater.* SYN: squeamish, overnice. [< Latin *fastīdiōsus* < *fastīdium* loathing, probably < *fastus* contempt + *taedium* disgust] —**fas|tid′i|ous|ly**, *adv.* —**fas|tid′i|ous|ness**, *n.*
fas|tig|i|ate (fas tij′ē it, -āt), *adj.* **1** rising or tapering to a pointed top. **2** *Botany.* **a** pointing upward and parallel, as the branches of the Lombardy poplar. **b** having branches like this. **3** *Zoology.* fastened together in a cone-shaped bunch. [< Latin *fastīgium* apex of a gable; summit]
fas|tig|i|at|ed (fas tij′ē ā′tid), *adj.* = fastigiate.
fas|tig|i|um (fas tij′ē əm), *n. Medicine.* the acme or highest state of intensity of a disease. [< Latin *fastīgium* apex of a gable; summit]
fast|ing (fas′ting, fäs′-), *n.* the act of abstaining from food; a fast: *And she . . . departed not from the temple, but served God with fastings and prayers night and day* (Luke 2:37).
fast|ish (fas′tish, fäs′-), *adj.* somewhat fast.
fast lane, *U.S. Informal.* a style of living that is socially active and often unrestrained: *life in the fast lane.*
fast-mov|ing (fast′mü′ving, fäst′-), *adj.* **1** that moves fast: *a fast-moving radioactive particle.* **2** rapidly advancing; progressive: *a fast-moving business.*
Fast|nacht (fäst′näнt′), *n.* **1** a German festival celebrating the last day before Lent. **2** the last day before Lent; Shrove Tuesday. [German *Fastnacht* < *Fast* fast + *Nacht* night]
fast|ness[1] (fast′nis, fäst′-), *n.* **1** a strong, safe place; stronghold: *The bandits hid in their mountain fastness.* SYN: refuge. **2** a being fast or firm; firmness. [< *fast*[1] secure + *-ness*]
fast|ness[2] (fast′nis, fäst′-), *n.* **1** the fact or condition of being quick or rapid; swiftness. **2** the fact or condition of being fast in behavior or way of life. [< *fast*[1] rapid + *-ness*]
fast neutron, a neutron of relatively high energy, usually of more than 10,000 electron volts: *Bombardment of U^{238} with fast, or high-energy, neutrons will cause fission* (R. L. Thornton).
Fast of Esther, a fast observed by Jews on the day before the holiday of Purim, in remembrance of the three days' fast of Queen Esther before she pleaded with King Ahasuerus to save her people. Esther 4:16.
Fast of Ged|a|li|ah (ged′ə lī′ə, gə däl′yə), a fast observed by Jews on the third of Tishri, the day after Rosh Hashanah, in remembrance of the murder of Gedaliah, governor of Judah under Nebuchadnezzar; Tzom Gedaliah. Jeremiah 41:2.
fast-paced (fast′pāst′, fäst′-), *adj.* filled with action or activity: *the tense, fast-paced atmosphere of most television studios* (Atlantic).
fast reactor, a reactor using fast neutrons without a moderator.
fast-step|ping (fast′step′ing, fäst′-), *adj.* rapidly advancing; swift: *a fast-stepping horse.*
fast-talk (fast′tôk′, fäst′-), *v. U.S. Slang.* —*v.t.* to trick, allure, or mislead by means of high-pressure salesmanship or quick answers: *The car dealer fast-talked me into signing an order.* —*v.i.* to talk fast so as to evade an issue or an explanation.
fast-track (fast′track′), *adj.* rapid; accelerated: *The Government has approved the use of fast-track planning procedures, which minimise the scope for public scrutiny and debate* (Manchester Guardian Weekly).
fas|tu|ous (fas′chü əs), *adj.* haughty; arrogant; ostentatious: *Also to be cleaned by autumn are the three long, richly pilastered, and fastuous garden façades of the Palais-Royal* (New Yorker). [< Latin *fastuōsus* < *fastus* haughtiness] —**fas′tu|ous|ly**, *adv.* —**fas′tu|ous|ness**, *n.*

fat[1](fat), *n., adj.,* **fat|ter, fat|test,** *v.,* **fat|ted, fat|ting.** —*n.* **1** a type of white or yellow, oily substance formed in the body of animals. Fat is also found in plants, especially in some seeds. Fats are made up chiefly of carbon, hydrogen, and oxygen. **2** this substance from animal or plant tissues used in cookery. **3** animal tissues composed mainly of such a substance. **4** any one of a class of organic chemical compounds of which the natural fats are mixtures, comprising an important group of animal foods. Fats contain carbon, hydrogen, and oxygen, but no nitrogen, and are chiefly glycerides, compound esters of several acids. They are insoluble in water but dissolve in ether, chloroform, and benzine. **5** something inessential or superfluous; excess: . . . *slicing the fat from military outlays* (Wall Street Journal). **6** the richest, best, or most nourishing part of anything: *Not of the princes and prelates . . . Riding triumphantly laurelled to lap the fat of the years* (John Masefield). **7** corpulence; obesity.
—*adj.* **1** consisting of or containing fat; oily: *fat meat.* SYN: greasy, unctuous. **2** having much flesh; fleshy; plump; well-fed: *a fat pig. The boy is fatter than his brother, but his father is fattest of all.* **3** too fat; corpulent; obese: *Sweep on, you fat and greasy citizens* (Shakespeare). **4** containing much of some constituent; fertile: *fat land.* SYN: rich. **5** yielding much money; profitable: *That fat job pays well. His sordid way he wends, An incarnation of fat dividends* (Charles Sprague). SYN: lucrative, remunerative. **6** affording good opportunities. **7** full of good things; plentiful: *A fat kitchen makes a lean will* (Benjamin Franklin). **8** thick; broad. **9** dull; stupid. **10** *Slang.* not much; little; small: *A fat chance you have of catching him now. A fat lot of help you are to me.* **11** *Archaic.* prosperous; wealthy.
—*v.t.* to make fat; fatten: *fatting pigs for market.* —*v.i.* to become fat: *The pigs fatted on corn.*
chew the fat, *Slang.* to talk at length: *He [likes] to chew the fat with his cronies* (Manchester Guardian).
live off the fat of the land, to have the best of everything: *That rich boy lived off the fat of the land.*
the fat is in the fire, it is too late to prevent unpleasant results; matters have been made worse: . . . *farewell riches, the fat is in the fire* (John Heywood). *Once the Chinese began to criticize the Russians openly for going too far in courting nationalist governments, the fat was in the fire* (Listener).
[Old English *fǣtt,* (originally) past participle, fatted] —**fat′less**, *adj.* —**fat′like′**, *adj.* —**fat′ness**, *n.*
—*Syn. adj.* **2**, **3**. **Fat, stout, portly** mean having too much flesh. **Fat**, the general word, commonly applies to any degree from healthy, well-fed plumpness to ugly, unhealthy excess of weight: *The fat man had difficulty walking up the flight of stairs.* **Stout** emphasizes thickness and bulkiness, suggesting firm rather than flabby flesh, but is often used as a euphemism for "too fat": *She calls herself stylishly stout.* **Portly** suggests stately stoutness: *The retired admiral is a portly old gentleman.*
fat[2] (fat), *n. Archaic or Dialect.* a vessel; tub or vat: *The fats shall overflow with wine and oil* (Joel 2:24). [Old English *fæt.* Compare etym. under **vat.**]
fa|tal (fā′təl), *adj.* **1** causing death: *Careless drivers cause many fatal accidents.* **2** causing destruction or ruin: *The loss of all our money was fatal to our plans.* SYN: destructive, disastrous, ruinous. **3** important; fateful; decisive: *At last the fatal day for the contest arrived.* **4** influencing fate. The three goddesses who controlled the fate of mankind were called the fatal sisters. **5** *Archaic.* fated; doomed. **6** *Obsolete.* foreboding or associated with death or disaster; ominous: *the black and fatal ravens* (Christopher Marlowe). [< Latin *fātālis* < *fātum;* see etym. under **fate**]
—*Syn.* **1** **Fatal, deadly, mortal** mean causing death or capable of causing death. **Fatal** emphasizes the idea of certain death and applies to anything that is sure to cause death or that has caused it: *Many diseases are no longer fatal.* **Deadly** applies to something that is likely to cause death and usually does: *Cyanide is a deadly poison.* **Mortal** applies to something that is the direct cause of death, but cannot apply to the weapon used to cause the injury that actually killed the person: *His wound was mortal.*
fa|tal|ism (fā′tə liz əm), *n.* **1** the belief that fate controls everything that happens. **2** acceptance of everything that happens because of this belief: *A major worry is public apathy—fatalism bred of stories about the all-destroying horror of the H-bomb* (Wall Street Journal).
fa|tal|ist (fā′tə list), *n.* a believer in fatalism.
fa|tal|is|tic (fā′tə lis′tik), *adj.* **1** of or having to do with fatalism or fatalists: *Are you a Christian, and talk about a crisis in that fatalistic sense?* (Samuel Taylor Coleridge). **2** believing that fate controls everything; accepting things and events as inevitable. —**fa′tal|is′ti|cal|ly**, *adv.*
fa|tal|i|ty (fā tal′ə tē, fə-), *n., pl.* **-ties. 1** a fatal accident or happening; death: *Careless drivers cause thousands of fatalities every year.* **2** fatal influence or effect; deadliness: *Doctors are trying to reduce the fatality of heart disease.* **3** liability to disaster: *His fatality predestined his early death.* **4** the condition of being controlled by fate; inevitable necessity: *We struggle against fatality in vain.* SYN: destiny, lot. **5** the belief that everything is predestined; fatalism: *the pessimistic doctrine of fatality.*
fa|tal|ize (fā′tə līz), *v.,* **-ized, -iz|ing.** —*v.i.* to incline to fatalism. —*v.t.* to render subject to fate; yield to the inevitable.
fa|tal|ly (fā′tə lē), *adv.* **1** in a manner leading to death or disaster: *The soldier was fatally wounded in battle.* SYN: mortally. **2** according to fate.
fa|ta mor|ga|na (fä′təmôr gä′nə), a kind of mirage seen most frequently in the Strait of Messina. [< Italian *fata* fairy; *Morgana* Morgan le Fay; allusion uncertain]
fat|back (fat′bak′) *n.* **1** salt pork from the upper part of a side of pork. **2** = menhaden.
fat|bird (fat′bėrd′), *n.* **1** = guacharo. **2** = pectoral sandpiper.
fat body, **1** fatty tissue in insects that serves as a reserve food supply. **2** a mass of fatty tissues next to the genital glands in frogs and toads.
fat cat, *U.S. Slang.* **1** a wealthy contributor to a political campaign: *Money has given labor a louder voice in politics, although it contends that its political spending is petty cash in comparison with that of industrial fat cats* (Atlantic). **2** a person who expects special comforts or privileges because of wealth or position: *No one of management calibre in the firm can be a "fat cat"—but must hunger for money or personal success* (Wall Street Journal).
fat|cat or **fat-cat** (fat′kat′), *adj. U.S. Slang.* **1** of or belonging to fat cats. **2** smug or complacent because of wealth or position.
fat cell, a cell containing fat. Fat cells make up the adipose tissue.
fat city, *U.S. Slang.* a very good, comfortable, or successful state or condition.
fate (fāt), *n., v.,* **fat|ed, fat|ing.** —*n.* **1** the power supposed to fix beforehand and control everything that happens. Fate is thought by some to be beyond one's control. *He does not believe in fate. There is no armour against fate; Death lays his icy hand on kings* (James Shirley). **2** what is caused by fate: *Drowning was his sad fate.* **3** one's lot or fortune; what happens to a person or group: *In every game it is her fate to get caught. He deserved a better fate.* **4** what becomes of a person or thing: *The jury decided the fate of the accused.* **5** death or ruin; destruction.
—*v.t.* to be selected or destined by fate: *All men are fated to die. He was fated to be a great leader. Thereby thinks Acrisius to forego This doom that has been fated long ago, That by his daughter's son he shall be slain* (William Morris). [< Latin *fātum* (thing) spoken (that is, by the gods), one's destiny, neuter past participle of *fārī* speak]
—*Syn. n.* **1**, **3**. **Fate, destiny, doom** mean a person's fortune or lot in life. **Fate** suggests some determining power or force, and implies that the outcome cannot be avoided, escaped, or changed: *The fate of Joan of Arc was death.* **Destiny**, often used interchangeably with *fate,* suggests a fate all laid out beforehand: *Washington's destiny was to be President.* **Doom** applies to an unhappy or awful end: *The condemned man went to his doom.*
Fate (fāt), *n.* a goddess of fate or destiny. See **Fates.**
fat|ed (fā′tid), *adj.* **1** controlled by fate: *Many people today still believe they lead a fated life.* **2** destined; predestined. **3** doomed to destruction: *A blazing comet may cross this fated planet* (Thomas Chalmers).
fate|ful (fāt′fəl), *adj.* **1** controlled by fate: *The fateful course of the ship toward the rocks was not changed in spite of the crew's frantic efforts.* **2** determining what is to happen; important; decisive: *a fateful decision. Yorktown was the site of a fateful battle of the American Revolution.* **3** showing what will happen according to fate;

Pronunciation Key: hat, āge, cãre, fär; let, ēqual, tėrm; it, īce; hot, ōpen, ôrder; oil, out; cup, pu̇t, rüle; child; long; thin; ᴛʜen; zh, measure; ə represents **a** in about, **e** in taken, **i** in pencil, **o** in lemon, **u** in circus.

prophetic: *the fateful words of the prophet.* **4** causing death, destruction, or ruin; disastrous: *a fateful blow. The soldier's fateful steel* (Joel Barlow). **—fate′ful·ly,** *adv.* **—fate′ful·ness,** *n.*

Fates (fāts), *n.pl. Greek and Roman Mythology.* the three goddesses who controlled human life; Parcae. They were Clotho, who spun the thread of life; Lachesis, who decided how long it should be; and Atropos, who cut it off. [< Latin *Fāta,* plural of *fātum;* see etym. under **fate**]

fat farm, *U.S. Slang.* a health resort or spa for overweight people.

fat-free (fat′frē′), *adj.* without fat; lean: *fat-free livestock.*

fath., fathom.

fat·head (fat′hed′), *n.* **1** *Slang.* a dull and stupid person; dolt. **2** a richly colored red fish of southern California, with a thick body and a fatty lump on its blunt forehead.

fat·head·ed (fat′hed′id), *adj. Slang.* dull and stupid. **—fat′head′ed·ness,** *n.*

fat hen, = pigweed (def. 1).

fa·ther (fä′ᴛʜər), *n., v.* **—*n.*** **1** a male parent: *The father of a family tries to take good care of his wife and children.* **2** a person who is like a father. **3a** a male ancestor; forefather: *the customs of our fathers. Four score and seven years ago our fathers brought forth on this continent a new nation* (Abraham Lincoln). **b** *Figurative.* a thing that is a cause or source: *The wish is father to the thought.* **4** *Figurative.* a man who did important work as a maker or leader: *the founding father of an organization. George Washington is called the father of his country.* **5 Father,** a title of respect used in addressing a priest or other clergyman. *Abbr:* Fr. **6** a clergyman having this title. **7** a title of respect for an old man. **8** a senator of ancient Rome: *The Fathers of the City Are met in high debate* (Macaulay).

—*v.t.* **1** to be the father of: *He fathered eleven sons.* **2** to take care of as a father does; act as a father to: *to father an orphan.* **3** *Figurative.* to be the cause of; make; originate: *Edison fathered many inventions. . . . the fine delight that fathers thought* (Gerard Manley Hopkins). **4** to acknowledge oneself as the father of.

be gathered to one's fathers, to die and be buried: *No change was to be made till MacFinnan Dhu had been gathered to his fathers* (James A. Froude).

father upon, to attribute to: *Opponents have fathered upon me the slogan: "Better red than dead"* (Bertrand Russell).

the Father, a God: *Love and honour be to the Father of heaven* (Sir Thomas Malory). **b** the First Person of the Trinity: *Honour, laud, and praise addressing To the Father and the Son* (John M. Neale).

(the) fathers, a the leading men of a city or an assembly: *With the civic fathers of Los Angeles and San Francisco offering slightly less than the Santa Anita race track . . . to attract them, the Brooklyn Dodgers and the New York Giants sped west* (Maclean's). **b** the chief writers and teachers of the Christian Church during the first six centuries A.D.: *Of Fathers, by custom so call'd, they quote Ambrose, Augustin, and some other ceremonial Doctors of the same leven* (Milton).

[Middle English *fader,* Old English *fæder*]

Father Christmas, *British.* the personification of Christmas; Santa Claus.

father confessor, 1 a priest to whom one confesses. **2** a person to whom one confides everything.

father figure, 1 *Psychoanalysis.* a person imaginatively substituted for one's real father and made the object of responses originally developed toward the father: *The scene is . . . presided over by a man who is both the perfect boss and a perfect father figure* (Harper's). **2** a paternal figure; a respected or venerable person: *At the top of our hierarchy was that bearded, jovial, rotund, elegant father figure, His Majesty King Edward VII* (Sean O'Faolain).

fa·ther·hood (fä′ᴛʜər hu̇d), *n.* the condition of being a father.

father image, = father figure.

fa·ther-in-law (fä′ᴛʜər in lô′), *n., pl.* **fa·thers-in-law. 1** the father of one's husband or wife. **2** *British Informal.* a stepfather.

fa·ther·land (fä′ᴛʜər land′, -lənd), *n.* **1** one's native country. **2** the land of one's ancestors.

fa·ther·less (fä′ᴛʜər lis), *adj.* **1** without a father living: *fatherless children.* SYN: orphaned. **2** without a known father. SYN: illegitimate.

Pronunciation Key: hat, āge, cãre, fär; let, ēqual, tėrm; it, īce; hot, ōpen, ôrder; oil, out; cup, pu̇t, rüle; child; long; thin; ᴛʜen; zh, measure; ə represents **a** in about, **e** in taken, **i** in pencil, **o** in lemon, **u** in circus.

fa·ther·like (fä′ᴛʜər līk′), *adj., adv.* = fatherly.

fa·ther·li·ness (fä′ᴛʜər lē nis), *n.* fatherly quality.

father longlegs, = crane fly.

fa·ther·ly (fä′ᴛʜər lē), *adj., adv.* **—*adj.*** **1** of a father. **2** like a father; like a father's: *The old gentleman gave the boy a fatherly smile.*

—*adv. Archaic.* in a fatherly manner.

Father of Waters, *U.S.* the Mississippi River.

father right, the supremacy of the father in a family in which descent follows the male line.

father rule, the rule or authority of the father in a family in which descent follows the male line.

fa·thers (fä′ᴛʜərs), *n.pl.* See under **father.**

Father's Day, the third Sunday in June set apart in the United States and Canada in honor of fathers.

fa·ther-sib (fä′ᴛʜər sib′), *n. U.S. Anthropology.* a group or clan whose members trace their descent from a common ancestor through the line of the father.

father substitute, = father figure.

***Father Time,** time personified, usually as a bald and bearded old man carrying a scythe and an hourglass.

***Father Time**

fath·om (faᴛʜ′əm), *n., pl.* **fath·oms** or (*collectively*) **fath·om,** *v.* **—*n.*** a unit of measure equal to 6 feet. It is used mostly in measuring the depth of water and the length of ships' ropes or cables: *The ship sank in 10 fathoms. Full fathom five thy Father lies* (Shakespeare). *Abbr:* f.

—*v.t.* **1** to find the depth of; sound: *to fathom the ocean.* **2** *Figurative.* to get to the bottom of; understand fully: *I can't fathom what you mean. I tried to fathom the motives for his behavior.* SYN: comprehend.

—*v.i.* **1** to take soundings: *to fathom with a plumb line.* **2** *Figurative.* to delve; search: *The philosopher . . . went fathoming on . . . in the very abysses of human thought* (Henry Hart Milman).

[Middle English *fadum* or *fathum,* Old English *fæthm* width of the outstretched arms; grasp] **—fath′om·er,** *n.*

fath·om·a·ble (faᴛʜ′ə mə bəl), *adj.* **1** that can be fathomed or measured. **2** *Figurative.* understandable.

fa·thom·e·ter (fa ᴛʜom′ə tər), *n.* **1** a device for determining depth of water by sending sound waves through the water and timing their return from the bottom. **2 Fathometer,** *Trademark.* a name for such a device.

fath·om·less (faᴛʜ′əm lis), *adj.* **1** too deep to be measured; bottomless: *The stream disappeared into a fathomless abyss.* **2** *Figurative.* impossible to be fully understood: *the fathomless riddle of the origin of the universe.* SYN: incomprehensible. **—fath′om·less·ly,** *adv.* **—fath′om·less·ness,** *n.*

fa·tid·ic (fə tid′ik), *adj.* = prophetic. [< Latin *fātidicus* < *fātum* fate + *dīcere* speak, tell]

fa·tid·i·cal (fə tid′ə kəl), *adj.* = fatidic.

fat·i·ga·bil·i·ty (fat′ə gə bil′ə tē), *n.* the condition of becoming easily tired.

fat·i·ga·ble (fat′ə gə bəl), *adj.* easily fatigued or tired.

fat·i·gate (fat′ə gāt), *adj., v.,* **-gat·ed, -gat·ing.** *Obsolete.* **—*adj.*** fatigued.

—*v.t.* to fatigue.

[< Latin *fatīgātus,* past participle of *fatīgāre* to tire]

fa·tigue (fə tēg′), *n., v.,* **-tigued, -ti·guing,** *adj.* **—*n.*** **1** weariness caused by hard work or effort: *Studying for two hours caused him as great fatigue as a game of football.* SYN: lassitude, languor, exhaustion. **2** a task or exertion producing weariness: *The doctor has not yet recovered from the fatigues of the epidemic.* **3** a weakening (of metal) caused by long-continued use or strain. **4** *Physiology.* a temporary reduction in the capacity to respond to stimuli on the part of cells or organs after excessive activity. **5** *Psychology.* a decrease in the ability to do work due to the tiring effects of recent previous work. **6** *Military.* = fatigue duty.

—*v.t.* **1** to make weary or tired. SYN: tire, exhaust. **2** to weaken (metal) by much use or strain: *Valleys or "intrusions" form on the surface of copper after it has been fatigued at liquid helium temperatures* (New Scientist).

—*v.i.* to become fatigued: *I saw her without expression, like a kid asleep on the excursion train, fatigued at night from picnicking* (Saul Bellow). SYN: tire, exhaust.

—*adj.* having to do with fatigue.

fatigues, *Military.* = fatigue clothes.

[< Middle French *fatigue* < *fatiguer,* learned borrowing from Latin *fatīgāre* to tire] **—fa·ti′guing·ly,** *adv.*

fatigue clothes, military clothes of herringbone twill worn with boots for fatigue duty; fatigues.

fatigue duty, nonmilitary work done by members of the armed services. Cleaning up the camp or repairing roads is fatigue duty.

fatigue party, a detail of soldiers engaged in fatigue duty.

fa·tigues (fə tēgz′), *n.pl.* = fatigue clothes.

fatigue strength, the maximum stress that a metal can endure without weakening or breaking: *The fatigue strength of metal bars is increased by as much as 25 per cent when a thin surface layer of metal is removed by machining* (New Scientist).

fa·ti·hah or **fa·ti·ha** (fä′ti hä), *n.* the first chapter of the Koran, greatly revered by Moslems and used as a prayer. [< Arabic *fātiha* start, beginning]

fat·ling (fat′ling), *n.* a calf, lamb, kid, or pig fattened for slaughter. [< *fat*[1] + *-ling*]

fat lip, *Slang.* a swollen lip, usually caused by a blow received in the mouth.

fat liquor, a mixture of oils and alkali for oiling hides or skins to make them soft.

fat-liq·uor (fat′lik′ər), *v.t.* to treat or coat (a hide or skin) with fat liquor.

fat·ly (fat′lē), *adv.* **1** in a fat manner; plumply. **2** like a fat person; clumsily.

fat-mouth (fat′mouᴛʜ′), *v.i. U.S. Slang.* to talk excessively, especially without taking action.

fats·hed·er·a (fats hed′ər ə), *n.* a hybrid plant with dark-green shiny, lobate leaves, grown for its decorative foliage. It is a cross of the English ivy and a related plant. [< New Latin *Fats*(ia) + *Hedera,* the genus names of the crossed plants, both of the ginseng family]

fat·so (fat′sō), *n., pl.* **-sos** or **-soes.** *U.S. Slang.* a fat person.

fat-sol·u·ble (fat′sol′yə bəl), *adj.* that can be dissolved in fats, or in solvents for fats.

fat·stock (fat′stok′), *n. British.* fattened livestock: *Fatstock can best repay the feedbills by being brought precociously to the butcher's scale* (New Scientist).

fat-tailed sheep (fat′tāld′), one of a breed of sheep raised in Asia and North Africa, having fatty tails much esteemed as a food.

fat·ted (fat′id), *adj. Archaic.* fattened: *And bring hither the fatted calf, and kill it; and let us eat, and be merry* (Luke 15:23).

fat·ten (fat′ən), *v.t.* **1** Also, **fatten up.** to make fat; feed (animals) for market: *The farmer fattened his pigs for market.* **2** to make productive; enrich (soil). **3** *Figurative.* to fill or build up; increase in size: *to fatten one's income or stock.* **4** (in poker) to put more chips in (a pot); sweeten. **—*v.i.*** to become fat: *The pigs fattened on corn. The meanest worm That . . . fattens on the dead* (Shelley). **—fat′ten·er,** *n.*

fat·ti mas·chi·i, pa·ro·le fe·mi·ne (fät′tē mä′skē ē, pä rô′lā fā′mē nā), *Italian.* deeds (are) masculine, words (are) feminine (the motto of Maryland).

fat·tish (fat′ish), *adj.* somewhat fat.

fat·ty (fat′ē), *adj.,* **-ti·er, -ti·est,** *n., pl.* **-ties. —*adj.*** **1** of fat; containing fat: *fatty tissue.* SYN: adipose. **2** like fat; oily; greasy: *Some plastics made of nylon have a fatty feel to them.* **3** *Medicine.* marked by abnormal deposits of fat; tending to produce fat.

—*n. Informal.* a fat person or animal. **—fat′ti·ly,** *adv.* **—fat′ti·ness,** *n.*

fatty acid, *Chemistry.* any one of a group of organic acids, such as oleic acid, palmitic acid, and stearic acid, found in animal and vegetable fats and oils. *Formula:* $C_nH_{2n}O_2$

fatty degeneration, the accumulation of fat in or around the heart, arteries, liver, and other organs.

fatty tissue, = adipose tissue.

fatty tumor, a tumor composed of fat; lipoma.

fa·tu·i·tous (fə tü′ə təs, -tyü′-), *adj.* characterized by fatuity.

fa·tu·i·ty (fə tü′ə tē, -tyü′-), *n., pl.* **-ties. 1a** self-satisfied stupidity; folly; silliness: *O strange fatuity of youth!* (Thackeray). SYN: inanity. **b** something exceedingly foolish. **2** *Archaic.* imbecility; idiocy. [< Latin *fatuitās* < *fatuus* foolish]

fat·u·ous (fach′ů əs), *adj.* **1** stupid but self-satisfied; foolish; silly: *a fatuous smile, a fatuous empty-headed conversation. These poor Might-Have-Beens, These fatuous, ineffectual Yesterdays!* (William Ernest Henley). SYN: See syn. under **foolish. 2** not real; illusory: *A fatuous light that shall lead him astray* (Edmund Hamilton Sears). **3** *Archaic.* idiotic; imbecile. [< Latin *fatuus* (with English *-ous*) foolish, insipid] **—fat′u·ous·ly,** *adv.* **—fat′u·ous·ness,** *n.*

fat-wit·ted (fat′wit′id), *adj.* dull; stupid: *If they are endowed, professors become fat-witted* (Sydney Smith).

fau|bourg (fō′bůr, fō′bůrg; *French* fō bür′), *n.* in France: **1** a suburb. **2** a district in a city. [< Middle French *faux bourg* < Old French *fors bourg* suburb < Latin *forīs* outside + Late Latin *burgus* bourg]

fau|cal (fô′kəl), *adj., n.* **—*adj.*** of or produced in the fauces; faucial.
—*n.* *Phonetics.* a sound produced in the fauces. [< Latin *faucēs* throat + English *-al*[1]]

fau|ces (fô′sēz), *n.pl. Anatomy.* the cavity at the back of the mouth, leading into the pharynx. [< Latin *faucēs* throat]

***fau|cet** (fô′sit), *n. Especially U.S.* **1** a device for turning on or off a flow of liquid from a pipe or a container holding it by opening or closing a valve; tap; spigot. **2** the enlarged end of a pipe into which the end of another pipe enters to form a joint. [< Old French *fausset,* probably < *fausser* bore through; (originally) break < Late Latin *falsāre* corrupt, falsify < *falsa* false]
▶**Faucet** is now the term in most general use in the United States. **Spigot** is still widely used, particularly in the South. **Tap** is chiefly British.

***faucet**
definition 1

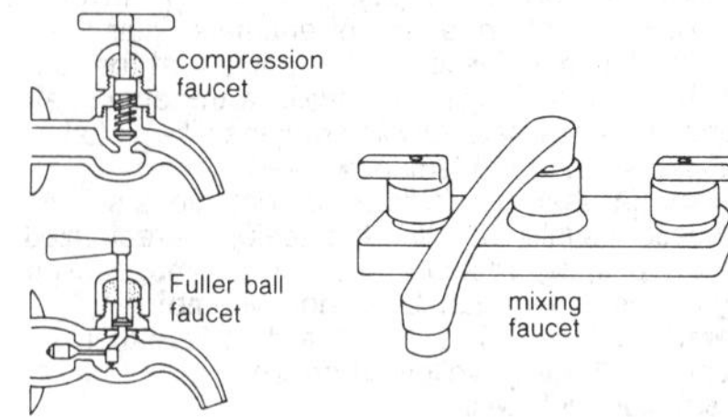

fau|cial (fô′shəl), *adj.* = faucal.

faugh (fô), *interj.* an exclamation of disgust: *A monkey! faugh! . . . I hate the nauseous animal* (Washington Irving).

Faulk|ner|i|an (fôk nir′ē ən), *adj.* of or like William Faulkner, American writer (1897-1962) or his writings, ideas, or style: *There are many styles in the book, ranging from Faulknerian rhetoric to flat journalese* (Saturday Review).

fault** (fôlt), *n., v.* **—*n. **1** something that is not as it should be; defect; flaw: *Her dog has two faults; it eats too much, and it howls at night. Sloppiness is his greatest fault. A fault in wiring started the fire. The fault, dear Brutus, is not in our stars, But in ourselves that we are underlings* (Shakespeare). **2** a mistake; error; failure in what is attempted: *a fault in the answer to an arithmetic problem.* **SYN:** slip, lapse. **3** a misdeed or offense: *Cleanse thou me from secret faults* (Psalms 19:12). **SYN:** transgression. **4** cause for blame; responsibility: *Whose fault was it?* **SYN:** culpability. **5** a break in the earth's crust, with the mass of rock on one side of the break pushed up, down, or sideways. **6a** a failure to serve the ball properly or into the right place in tennis and similar games. **b** a served ball that does not fall in the proper court. **7** an accidental defect in an electric circuit. **8** a break in the line of scent in hunting; loss of the scent. **9** *Archaic.* lack; want: *. . . one it pleases me, for fault of a better, to call my friend* (Shakespeare). **10** *Obsolete.* default; failing; neglect.
—*v.i.* **1** *Geology.* (of rock strata) to undergo a fault or faults. **2** to commit a fault. **—*v.t.*** **1** *Geology.* to cause a fault in. **2** to find fault with: *We could not fault him on his knowledge of algebra. It is difficult . . . to fault the logic which leads to these gloomy conclusions* (Stewart Alsop).
at fault, a deserving blame; wrong: *Nature . . . has been at fault* (Leslie Stephen). *Whether it's the church or the state (or both) that's at fault . . . , the result is the same* (Maclean's). **b** uncertain: *His theory was entirely at fault and was therefore unacceptable.* **c** unable to pick up a lost scent in hunting: *They [bloodhounds] are at fault . . . by overrunning the line* (London Times).
find fault, to find mistakes; complain: *Why do you find fault so much?*
find fault with, to object to; criticize: *He found fault with very small and unimportant details and overlooked the main idea.*
in fault, deserving blame; wrong: *When weak poets go astray, The stars are more in fault than they* (Winthrop M. Praed).
to a fault, too much; excessively: *Grandmother is generous to a fault. The actor played his part to a fault and looked silly before the audience.*
[< Old French *faulte* < Vulgar Latin *fallita* a falling < *fallitus* for Latin *falsus* false, (originally) past participle of *fallere* deceive]
—*Syn.* *n.* **1 Fault, failing** mean a defect in character, mental attitude, personality, conduct, or habits. **Fault** suggests a lack of something essential to perfection, but not necessarily a cause for blame: *Laziness is his greatest fault.* **Failing** suggests a falling short of perfection, and applies particularly to a weakness which may be excusable: *Her slowness in reading is a failing that can be corrected.*

fault block, *Geology.* a mass of displaced rock between two faults, lifted above or sunk below the general level.

fault breccia, *Geology.* a breccia formed by the crushing of rock along a fault.

fault|find|er (fôlt′fīn′dər), *n.* **1** a person who finds fault; person who complains. **2** a device for locating defects, such as one in an electric circuit.

fault|find|ing (fôlt′fīn′ding), *n., adj.* **—*n.*** the act of finding fault. **—*adj.*** finding fault; complaining; pointing out faults. **SYN:** captious, critical.

fault|ful (fôlt′fəl), *adj.* **1** full of faults; faulty: *faultful carelessness.* **2** = culpable.

fault|ing (fôl′ting), *n. Geology.* the formation of a fault.

fault|less (fôlt′lis), *adj.* without a single fault or defect; free from blemish or error; perfect: *Faultless beauty is rare. Whoever thinks a faultless piece to see, Thinks what ne'er was, nor is, nor e'er shall be* (Alexander Pope). **SYN:** unblemished, flawless, blameless, impeccable, irreproachable. **—fault′less|ly,** *adv.* **—fault′less|ness,** *n.*

fault line, *Geology.* a line which marks the intersection of a fault plane with the earth's surface.

fault plane, *Geology.* the plane along which faulting occurs.

fault scarp, a steep slope resulting from movement along a fault.

fault|y (fôl′tē), *adj.,* **fault|i|er, fault|i|est. 1** having faults; containing blemishes or errors; wrong; imperfect; defective: *a faulty design, a faulty principle. The leak in the faucet was caused by a faulty valve. Faulty friends* (Robert Browning). **SYN:** incomplete, unsound. **2** blamable. **SYN:** culpable, reprehensible, censurable. **—fault′i|ly,** *adv.* **—fault′i|ness,** *n.*

fault zone, 1 *Engineering.* a pocket of shattered rock encountered in building a mountain tunnel. **2** *Geology.* an area containing many small faults.

***faun** (fôn), *n.* a minor god in Roman myths that lived in fields and woods and helped farmers and shepherds. A faun was supposed to look like a man, but to have the ears, horns, tail, and sometimes the legs, of a goat. [< Latin *Faunus* Faunus, a rural deity] **—faun′like′,** *adj.*

***faun**

fau|na (fô′nə), *n., pl.* **-nas, -nae** (-nē). **1** the animals or animal life of a given region or time: *the fauna of Australia. The lands around the polar sea . . . contain a rich flora and fauna including such land animals as the reindeer, the polar bear, and the musk ox* (Gabriele Rabel). **2** a treatise on the animals of any geographical area or geological period. [< New Latin *fauna* < Late Latin *Fauna,* wife of *Faunus*]

fau|nal (fô′nəl), *adj.* of or having to do with a fauna or faunas. **—fau′nal|ly,** *adv.*

faunal analysis, *Archaeology.* the study of animal bones to identify, date, and trace them back to their source.

fau|nis|tic (fô nis′tik), *adj.* of a fauna; faunal: *Each continental area has in fact three main floristic and faunistic elements* (New Scientist). **—fau|nis′ti|cal|ly,** *adv.*

fau|no|log|i|cal (fô′nə loj′ə kəl), *adj.* = zoogeographic.

fau|nol|o|gy (fô nol′ə jē), *n.* the study of the geographical distribution of animals; zoogeography. [< *fauna* + *-logy*]

***Faunt|le|roy** (fônt′lə roi, fänt′-), *adj.* having to do with or resembling the appearance of Lord

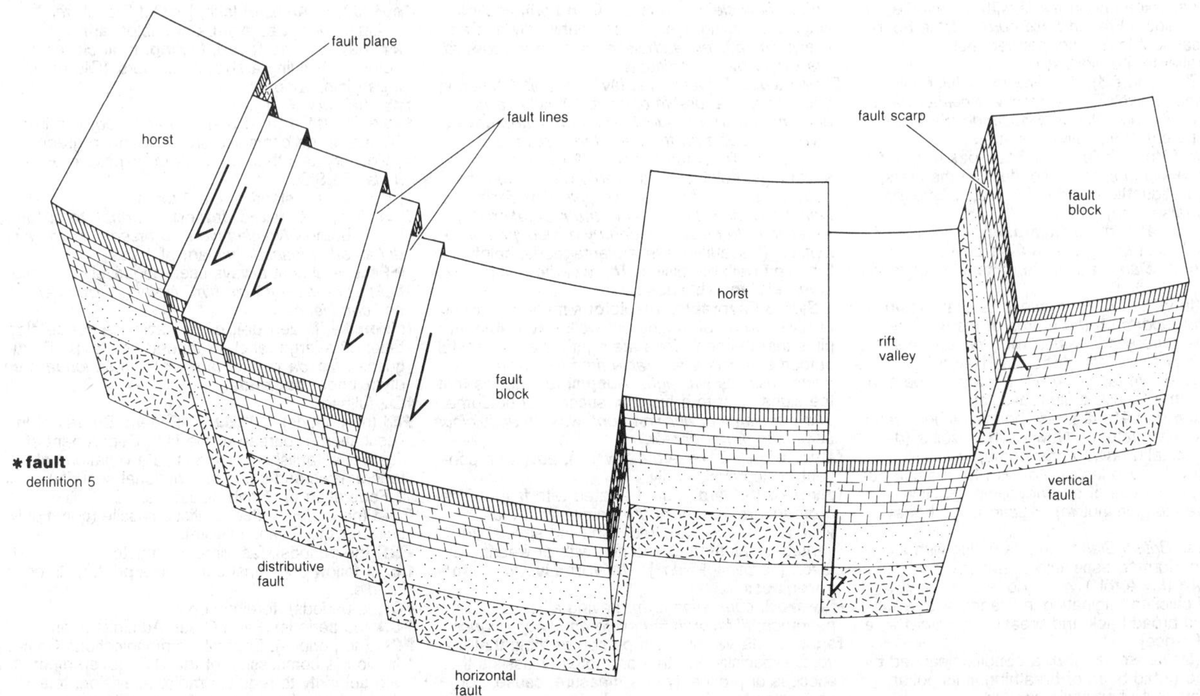

***fault**
definition 5

Fauntleroy, the seven-year-old hero of the novel *Little Lord Fauntleroy* (1886) by Frances Hodgson Burnett, who wears velvet suits, lace collars, and frilled shirts: *He dressed the boy in Fauntleroy clothes and kept his hair in curls* (New Yorker).

***Fauntleroy**

fau·nule (fô′nyül), *n.* a small fauna of fossils, especially a subdivision of a fauna consisting of a local group of fossils found in successive beds of a given rock formation. [< New Latin *faunula* (diminutive) < *fauna;* see etym. under **fauna**]

Fau·nus (fô′nəs), *n. Roman Mythology.* a rural deity, god of animals and plants, identified with the Greek Pan.

Faust (foust), *n. German Legend.* a man who sold his soul to the Devil in return for youth, knowledge, and magic powers.

Faus·ti·an (fous′tē ən), *adj.* of or having to do with Faust, especially with regard to his legendary relationship with the Devil: *A kind of Faustian legend involving a worker in the Hollywood vineyard who sacrifices his soul for assorted emoluments* (New Yorker).

Faus·tus (fôs′təs, fous′-), *n.* = Faust.

faute de mieux (fōt′dəmyœ′), *French.* for want of something better: *Many married couples grow close with age, in part faute de mieux* (New Yorker).

fau·teuil (fō tœ′yə; *Anglicized* fō′təl), *n. French.* **1** an armchair. **2** an official chair. **3** a seat or membership in the French Academy.

Fauve (fōv), *n., adj.* = Fauvist.

Fauves (fōvz), *n.pl.* a group of French artists, including Matisse and Braque, whose paintings represent a radical form of expressionism, using brilliant colors and bold designs. [< French *fauves* wild beasts (because of their vigor)]

Fau·vism (fō′viz əm), *n.* **1** the theories and style of painting of the Fauves, developed in France in the early 1900's. **2** the school or movement of the Fauves.

Fau·vist (fō′vist), *adj., n.* —***adj.*** of or in the style of the Fauves: *bright Fauvist landscapes.*
—***n.*** one of the Fauves.

faux (fō), *adj.* fake; imitation: *In Cleveland a plagiarism suit between two* faux *Elvises resulted in the defendant's singing "Burnin' Love" in an actual courtroom* (Spy Magazine). [< F *faux* fake]

faux·bour·don (fō′bùr dôɴ′), *n. Music.* a form of harmonic progression in three parts in which the lowest voice or bass moves in parallel sixths with the highest voice and in thirds with the middle voice. [< Middle French *fauxbourdon* false bourdon (because it is not independent but merely runs parallel to the highest voice)]

faux-na·ïf (fō′nä ēf′), *adj. French.* **1** feignedly naive; mock naive: *This simplicity is neither naive folksiness nor faux-naïf sophistication* (St. Louis Post-Dispatch). **2** (literally) false-naive.

faux pas (fō′pä′; fō′pä′), *pl.* **faux pas** (fō′päz′; fō′päz′), a slip in speech, conduct, or manners; breach of etiquette; blunder. [< French *faux pas* (literally) false step]

fa·va (fä′və, fā′-), *n.,* or **fava bean,** = broad bean. [< Italian *fava* < Latin *faba* bean]

fave (fāv), *n. Slang.* a favorite. [alteration of *favorite*]

fa·ve·la (fə ve′lə), *n. Portuguese.* a shantytown or slum: *She reports on the mores of the wealthy Brazilians, bitterly contrasted with the abysmal poverty in Rio's favelas* (Saturday Review).

fa·ve·la·do (fə ve lä′dō), *n. Portuguese.* a person who lives in a favela; a slum dweller.

fa·ve·o·late (fə vē′ə lāt), *adj.* honeycombed; cellular; pitted; alveolate. [< New Latin *faveolus* (diminutive < Latin *favus* honeycomb)]

fa·ve·o·lus (fə vē′ə ləs), *n., pl.* **-li** (-lī). a small depression, like a cell of a honeycomb. [< New Latin *faveolus* (diminutive) < Latin *favus* honeycomb]

fave rave, *British Slang.* an infatuation with a popular performer, especially a singer.

Fav·e·rolle (fav′ə rōl′), *n.* any one of a heavy breed of chicken originating in France, with a full beard and broad back and breast. [< *Faverolle,* a town in France]

fa·vism (fä′viz əm, fā′-), *n.* a condition caused by eating the broad bean or breathing in its pollen, marked by acute hemolytic anemia.

fa·vo·ni·an (fə vō′nē ən), *adj. Poetic.* **1** of or having to do with the west wind. **2** mild; favorable; propitious. [< Latin *Favōniānus* < *Favōnius* the west wind]

fa·vor (fā′vər), *n., v.* —***n.*** **1** an act of kindness: *Will you do me a favor?* **2** liking; approval: *They will look with favor on your plan.* **3** the condition of being liked, accepted, or approved: *A fashion in favor this year may be out of favor next year. Those who took part in the strike were out of favor with their employers.* **4a** exceptional kindness. **b** more than fair treatment; too great kindness: *He divided the candy among the children without favor to any one.* SYN: partiality, favoritism. **5a** a gift; token: *The knight wore his lady's favor on his arm.* **b** a small token given to every guest at a dinner or party: *Small hats were used as favors at the birthday party.* **c** a ribbon, badge, or the like, worn in evidence of good will or loyalty. **6** a letter; note: *your favor of the 15th.* **7** kind indulgence; leave; permission; pardon: *But, with your favor, I will treat it here* (John Dryden). **8** *Archaic.* appearance; look: *Folks don't use to meet for amusement with firearms . . . this has an angry favor* (Richard Brinsley Sheridan). **9** *Archaic.* the face; countenance. **10** *Archaic.* attractiveness; beauty; charm: *Thine eye desireth favor and beauty* (Ecclesiasticus 40:22).
—***v.t.*** **1** to show kindness to; treat kindly; oblige: *Favor us with a song.* **2** to like; approve; prefer: *We favor his plan.* **3** to give more than fair treatment to: *The teacher favors you.* **4** to be on the side of; support: *The town favors the new zoning plan.* **5** to be to the advantage of; help; aid: *The darkness of the night favored the enemy's approach. The silence and solitude of the place . . . favored his meditations* (Joseph Addison). SYN: facilitate. **6** to treat gently: *The dog favors his sore foot when he walks.* **7** *Informal.* to look like: *The girl favors her mother a great deal.*
curry favor, to seek a person's favor by insincere flattery, constant attentions, or the like: *Most students disliked him because he tried to curry favor with the teacher.* [*They*] *attempted to curry favor with the government by affronting members of the opposition* (Macaulay). *He curried favor with Crassus, the richest man in Rome* (Time).
in favor of, a on the side of; supporting: *The whole class voted in favor of visiting the firehouse instead of the post office. In China most of the trained people seem to be fundamentally in favor of the new regime* (New York Review of Books). **b** to the advantage of; helping: *The referee's decision was in favor of our team. There remains a balance of strength in favour of the bridge* (Howard Douglas). **c** to be paid to: *Write a check in favor of the bank.*
in one's favor, to one's advantage; to one's benefit: *His touchdown scored six points in our favor. With her youth, health, and good education, she has a lot in her favor.*
[< Old French *favor* < Latin < *favēre* show kindness to]
—*Syn. n.* **2 Favor, good will** mean an attitude of friendly approval. **Favor** applies when the feeling is not outwardly expressed: *The manager looked on the new clerk with favor.* **Good will** applies when the feeling is expressed outwardly and actively: *The audience showed its good will toward the singer by its applause.*

fa·vor·a·ble (fā′vər ə bəl, fāv′rə-), *adj.* **1** favoring; approving: *a favorable opinion. "Yes" is a favorable answer to a request. The committee gave a favorable report on the secretary's plan.* SYN: kindly, friendly, commendatory. **2** being to one's advantage; helping: *A favorable wind made the boat go faster. This is a favorable time for a trip. Nothing is more favorable to the reputation of a writer than to be succeeded by a race inferior to himself* (Macaulay). SYN: advantageous, helpful. **3** boding well; promising: *The weather looks favorable.* —**fa′vor·a·ble·ness,** *n.*
—*Syn.* **3 Favorable, auspicious** mean promising or giving signs of turning out well. **Favorable** implies that the conditions are right for a successful outcome: *It was a favorable time for our trip, since business was light.* **Auspicious** implies that the signs point to a lucky or successful outcome: *The popularity of her first book was an auspicious beginning of her career.*

fa·vor·a·bly (fā′vər ə blē, fāv′rə-), *adv.* with consent or approval; kindly.

fa·vored (fā′vərd), *adj.* **1** treated with favor: *Older brothers are forever of the opinion that the younger ones are favored.* **2** having special advantages; talented. **3** adorned with or wearing a favor. [< *favor* + *-ed*[1]] —**fa′vored·ly,** *adv.* —**fa′vored·ness,** *n.*

-favored, *combining form.* having a ______ appearance: *Ill-favored = having an ill appearance.*

fa·vor·er (fā′vər ər), *n.* a person or thing that favors, especially one that promotes or assists the success or prosperity of a measure, cause, person, or party.

fa·vor·ite (fā′vər it, fāv′rit), *adj., n.* —***adj.*** liked better than others; liked very much: *What is your favorite flower?*
—***n.*** **1** the one liked better than others; a person or thing liked very much: *He is a favorite with everybody.* **2** a person treated with special favor: *The king had his favorites at court.* **3** a person, horse, or other contestant, believed to have the best chance of winning. [< Middle French *favorit,* masculine, or *favorite,* feminine < Italian *favorire* to favor < *favore* favor < Latin *favor*]

favorite son, a political figure supported as a presidential candidate by his own state delegation in the party's national convention.

fa·vor·it·ism (fā′vər ə tiz′əm, fāav′rə tiz-), *n.* **1** the act of favoring a certain one or group more than others; having favorites: *He got his job through favoritism, not through ability.* SYN: partiality, nepotism. **2** the state of being a favorite.

fa·vose (fā′vōs, fā vōs′), *adj.* resembling a honeycomb. [< Latin *favus* honeycomb + English *-ose*[1]]

fav·o·site (fav′ə sīt), *n.* any one of a group of extinct corals having a structure that resembles a honeycomb; honeycomb coral. [< New Latin *Favosites* the genus name < Latin *favus* honeycomb]

fa·vour (fā′vər), *n., v.t. Especially British.* favor.

fav·rile (fav′rəl), *n.* a kind of enameled glass, having a rich, iridescent color, popular at the turn of the century. [originally *Favrile,* a trademark, alteration of obsolete *fabrile* craftsmanlike < Latin *fabrilis* < *faber* craftsman, worker]

fa·vus (fā′vəs), *n. Medicine.* a contagious skin disease, usually affecting the scalp, characterized by dry pustules resembling a honeycomb, caused by a fungus. [< Latin *favus* honeycomb]

fawn[1] (fôn), *n., adj., v.* —***n.*** **1** a deer less than a year old. **2** a light yellowish-brown.
—***adj.*** light yellowish-brown.
—***v.i.*** (of deer) to give birth to young.
[< Old French *faon* young animal < Vulgar Latin *fetō, -ōnis* < Latin *fētus, -ūs* fetus] —**fawn′-like′,** *adj.*

fawn[2] (fôn), *v., n.* —***v.i.*** **1** to try to get favor or notice by slavish acts: *Many flattering relatives fawned on the rich old man.* **2** to show fondness by crouching, wagging the tail, licking the hand, etc., as a dog does.
—***n.*** *Archaic.* an act of fawning; a servile cringe.
[Old English *fagnian* < *fagen,* variant of *fægen* fain] —**fawn′er,** *n.* —**fawn′ing·ly,** *adv.*

fawn lily, = dogtooth violet.

fax (faks), *n., pl.* **fax·es,** *v.* —***n.*** **1** = fax machine. **2** a copy of graphic material sent or received by a fax machine. —***v.t.*** to send by a fax machine: *Restaurant owners fax menus to nearby offices* (Woody Hochswender). [short for *facsimile*]

fax machine, an electronic device that transmits and receives facsimiles of graphic material over telephone lines; facsimile machine: *Corporate high-rollers fire off memos from the rear of limousines, using portable fax machines* (New York Times).

fay[1] (fā), *n.* = fairy (def. 1). [< Old French *fee,* also *fae* < Vulgar Latin *fāta* < Latin *fātum* fate]

fay[2] (fā), *n. Archaic.* faith. [< Old French *fei* < Latin *fidēs.* See etym. of doublet **faith.**]

fay[3] (fā), *v.t., v.i.,* **fayed, fay·ing.** to fit closely together in building a ship, as timbers. [Old English *fēgan* join, adapt]

fay[4] (fā), *adj.* = fey.

fay·al·ite (fā′ə līt, fī ä′-), *n. Mineralogy.* an iron silicate of the chrysolite group, found in greenish-yellow crystals that turn dark on exposure. *Formula:* Fe_2SiO_4
[< *Fayal,* an island of the Azores]

faze (fāz), *v.t.,* **fazed, faz·ing.** *Informal.* to disturb; worry; bother: *Nothing we said fazed her; she just did as she pleased.* [variant of *feeze*]
►**Faze** is almost always used negatively: *His original failure did not faze him. Nothing fazes her self-confidence.*

fa·zen·da (fə zen′də), *n.* in Brazil: **1** a coffee plantation. **2** a large ranch or landed estate. [< Portuguese *fazenda* estate; farm < Latin *facienda.* See etym. under **hacienda.**]

f.b., fullback.

FBI (no periods) or **F.B.I., 1** Federal Bureau of Investigation (a bureau of the U.S. Department of Justice, established to investigate violations of federal laws and safeguard national security). **2** Federation of British Industries.

FBM (no periods), fleet ballistic missile (commonly used for the Polaris missile).

FBR (no periods), fast-breeder reactor.

f.c., 1 follow copy (instruction to a printer). **2** footcandle.

FC (no periods), foreign consul.

FCA (no periods), Farm Credit Administration.

FCC (no periods), Federal Communications Commission (a commission of the U.S. government with authority to regulate radio, television, telephone, and other means of electronic communication).

F.C.C., first class certificate.
F clef, the bass clef in music.
fcp., foolscap.
fd (no period), ferredoxin.
F.D., Defender of the Faith (Latin, *Fidei Defensor*).
FDA (no periods), Food and Drug Administration.
FDIC (no periods), Federal Deposit Insurance Corporation (an agency of the U.S. government with the authority to insure depositors of member banks up to $100,000).
FDR (no periods) or **F.D.R.**, Franklin Delano Roosevelt.
Fe (no period), iron (chemical element). [for Latin *ferrum*]
feal (fēl), *adj. Archaic.* faithful; loyal. [< Old French *feal* < Latin *fidēlis*, related to *fīdere* to trust]
fe|al|ty (fē′əl tē), *n., pl.* **-ties. 1a** the loyalty and duty owed by a vassal to his feudal lord: *The nobles swore fealty to the king.* **b** the recognition of this obligation. **2** loyalty; faithfulness; allegiance. SYN: fidelity. [< Old French *feaulte* < Latin *fidēlitās.* See etym. of doublet **fidelity**.]
fear (fir), *n., v.* **—*n.* 1** the emotion or condition of being afraid; feeling that danger or evil is near; dread: *She screamed in fear and jumped away from the snake.* **2** cause for being afraid; danger; chance: *There is no fear of our losing. He will never leave her—no fear!* **3** an uneasy feeling; anxious thought; concern: *He went in fear of his life.* **4** awe; reverence: *In thy fear will I worship toward thy holy temple* (Psalms 5:7).
—*v.t.* 1 to be afraid of; regard with fear: *Our cat fears big dogs. A small baby fears loud noises. Men fear death as children fear to go in the dark* (Francis Bacon). SYN: dread, apprehend. **2** to feel concern for or about: *She fears that the child will be sick. Many may, I fear, maintain that I have been merely arguing in a circle* (Listener). **3** to have awe or reverence for: *Fear God. Honour the king* (I Peter 2:17). SYN: revere, venerate. **4** *Archaic.* to frighten: *a scarecrow ... to fear the birds of prey* (Shakespeare).
—*v.i.* 1 to feel fear. **2** to have an uneasy feeling or idea; feel concern: *The captain feared for his men's safety. I'll find the occasion, never fear!* (Edward George Bulwer-Lytton).
for fear of, in order to prevent something from occurring: *Must we not wish, for fear of wishing ill?* (John Dryden).
I fear me, *Archaic.* I am afraid: *I fear me he is slain* (Christopher Marlowe).
without fear or favor, impartially; justly: *In this company, promotions are given without fear or favor.*
[Old English *fǣr* peril] **—fear′er**, *n.*
—*Syn.* *n.* 1 Fear, dread, alarm mean the painful feeling that comes over a person when danger or harm threatens. **Fear** is the general word meaning a being afraid: *The knight felt no fears in the midst of battle.* **Dread** applies to great fear that comes from knowing something unpleasant or frightening will or might happen or from expecting danger, often unknown or uncertain: *He has a dread of losing his job.* **Alarm** applies to startled or excited fear, coming from the sudden appearance of danger: *The explosion caused alarm.*
feared (fird), *adj. Dialect.* frightened; afraid; timid.
fear|ful (fir′fəl), *adj.* **1** causing fear; terrible; dreadful: *a fearful explosion, a fearful dragon. At midnight's fearful hour* (Samuel Rogers). SYN: awful, frightful, horrible. **2a** feeling fear; frightened: *fearful of the dark.* SYN: afraid, alarmed, apprehensive, cowardly, craven, pusillanimous. **b** full of awe or reverence: *The savages thought the explorers were gods and, fearful, knelt before them.* **3** showing fear; caused by fear: *fearful cries. Adeline ... threw a fearful glance around* (Ann Radcliffe). **4** *Informal.* very bad, difficult, or unpleasant: *I have a fearful cold. If he does not run for Governor, he confronts a fearful task in maintaining party primacy* (New York Times Magazine). **—fear′ful|ly**, *adv.* **—fear′ful|ness**, *n.*
fear|less (fir′lis), *adj.* without fear; afraid of nothing; brave; daring: *Joyous we too launch out on trackless seas, Fearless for unknown shores* (Walt Whitman). SYN: intrepid, courageous, dauntless. **—fear′less|ly**, *adv.* **—fear′less|ness**, *n.*
fear|mon|ger (fir′mung′gər, -mong′-), *n.* a person who voices and spreads fear.
fear|some (fir′səm), *adj.* **1** causing fear; frightful; dreadful: *a fearsome sight.* **2** afraid; timid; apprehensive: *She was fearsome of danger.* **3** to be dreaded; formidable: *[His] mien and manner lend credence to his fearsome reputation* (Saturday Evening Post). *His [Babe Ruth's] presence turned the New Yorkers into the most fearsome team in baseball* (Time). **—fear′some|ly**, *adv.* **—fear′some|ness**, *n.*
fea|sance (fē′zəns), *n. Law.* a doing or performance, as of a condition, obligation, or duty. [< Anglo-French *fesaunce*, Old French *faisance* < *faire* do, make < Latin *facere*]
►**Feasance**, the proper performance of a duty, is not now much used, in contrast to related words indicating improper performance or nonperformance, **malfeasance** or **nonfeasance**.
fea|si|bil|i|ty (fē′zə bil′ə tē), *n.* the quality or condition of being feasible: *Data are being collected in Panama's jungle hills to determine the feasibility of excavating a new canal at sea level* (New York Times).
feasibility study, a study to determine the desirability and practicability of adopting a plan or system: *The scientists won't decide on conducting the large-scale project until they know the outcome of the feasibility study* (Wall Street Journal).
fea|si|ble (fē′zə bəl), *adj.* **1** that can be done easily; possible without difficulty or damage; practicable: *Of the many plans submitted, the committee selected the plan that seemed most feasible. Today, most of these fine old houses are dilapidated almost beyond feasible repair* (St. Louis Post-Dispatch). SYN: See syn. under **possible**. **2** likely; probable: *The witness's explanation of the accident sounded feasible.* **3** suitable; convenient: *The road was too rough to be feasible for travel by automobile.* [< Old French *faisable* or *faisible* < *faire* do, make < Latin *facere*] **—fea′si|ble|ness**, *n.* **—fea′si|bly**, *adv.*
feast (fēst), *n., v.* **—*n.* 1** a rich meal prepared for some special occasion, usually a joyous one, and for a number of guests; banquet: *We went to the wedding feast.* **2** an unusually delicious or abundant meal. **3** *Figurative.* something that gives pleasure or joy: *a feast for the eyes, a feast of toys. Two ... voices, that were a perfect feast to ears that had heard nothing but French operas for a year* (Thomas Gray). **4** a religious festival or celebration: *Christmas and Easter are the most important Christian feasts.*
—*v.i.* 1 to eat a rich meal; have a feast: *They feasted on goose.* **2** *Figurative.* to take delight; delight: *Let your eyes feast on this.*
—*v.t.* 1 to provide a rich meal for: *The king feasted his friends.* **2** to entertain sumptuously: *How shall I feast him?* (Shakespeare). **3** *Figurative.* to give pleasure or joy to; delight: *We feasted our eyes on the beautiful sunset.*
[< Old French *feste* < Vulgar Latin *festa*, feminine singular < Latin, neuter plural, festal ceremonies < *fēstus* festal. See related etym. at **fête**. See etym. of doublet **fiesta**.] **—feast′er**, *n.*
—*Syn.* *n.* 1 Feast, banquet mean an elaborate meal with many guests. **Feast** emphasizes the abundance, fineness, and richness of the food and drink, served to a large number in celebration of a special occasion: *The king and his nobles celebrated the birth of his heir with a feast.* **Banquet** emphasizes the formality of the celebration and applies particularly to a formal dinner given in rich surroundings: *A banquet was given to honor the retiring president.*
feast day, **1** a day set aside for a celebration or festivity. **2** a religious festival: *Moslem feast days.*
feast|ful (fēst′fəl), *adj.* **1** festive; joyful. **2** filled with feasting.
Feast of Booths, = Sukkoth.
Feast of Dedication, = Hanukkah.
Feast of First Fruits, = Shabuoth.
Feast of Fools, a festival celebrated in many countries of Europe, especially in France, during the Middle Ages, in late December or early January, close to January first, in which minor clergy were elevated to mock office as bishop, archbishop, and pope of fools, and ritual was often burlesqued.
Feast of Ingathering, = Sukkoth.
Feast of Lanterns, = Bon.
Feast of Lights, = Hanukkah.
Feast of Lots, = Purim.
Feast of Orthodoxy, a festival celebrated in the Greek Orthodox Church on the first Sunday in Lent in commemoration of the final overthrow of the iconoclasts of the 700's and 800's.
Feast of Tabernacles, = Sukkoth.
Feast of Unleavened Bread, = Passover.
Feast of Weeks, = Shabuoth.
feast-or-fam|ine (fēst′ər fam′ən), *adj.* fluctuating between extremes of gain and loss, success and failure, etc.: *the [textile] industry's age-old feast-or-famine cycle* (Time).
feat[1] (fēt), *n.* **1** a great deed; act showing great skill, strength, or daring; tour de force: *He could, perhaps, have passed the Hellespont, As once (a feat on which ourselves we prided) Leander, Mr. Ekenhead and I did* (Byron). SYN: achievement, stunt. See syn. under **exploit**. **2** *Archaic.* an action; deed. [< Old French *fait* or *fet* < Latin *factum* (thing) done. See etym. of doublet **fact**.]
feat[2] (fēt), *adj. Archaic.* **1** skillful; apt; adroit. **2** fitting; suitable. **3** neat. [< Old French *fet* or *fait* made < Latin *factus*, past participle of *facere* do, make] **—feat′ness**, *n.*
***feath|er** (fe*th*′ər), *n., v.* **—*n.* 1** one of the light, thin growths that cover a bird's skin. A feather consists typically of a hollow, horny tube, the quill, attached to the body of the bird and passing into a squarish, tapering central midrib, the shaft or rachis, that is fringed on either side with parallel filaments or processes, barbs, each bearing a secondary barb or barbule, all of which unite to form the vane or web. Because certain kinds of feathers are soft and light, they are used to fill pillows. **2a** plumage: *a bird in full feather.* **b** *Figurative.* attire: *in full clerical feather* (Thackeray). **c** *Figurative.* kind; character: *birds of a feather.* **3** something like a feather in shape or lightness. **4a** the fringe of hair on the back of the legs, on the neck, on the tail, or on the ears of some breeds of dogs, such as setters. **b** a sort of natural frizzling of a horse's hair, which in some places rises above the smooth coat, and makes a figure resembling the tip of an ear of wheat. **c** any featherlike tuft or fringe of hair. **5** the act of feathering an oar. **6** a projection, rib, or flange on a shaft or other mechanical part. **7** one of the two wedges between which a plug is driven to split rock. **8** *Archery.* **a** a feather or feathers attached to the end of an arrow to direct its flight. **b** the end of an arrow to which the feathers are attached. **9** a featherlike flaw, such as one in a precious stone or the eye. **10** a projection on a board, or the like, for fitting into a groove. **11** a single layer of the grain of the wood of the yew.
—*v.t.* 1 to supply or cover with or as if with feathers: *to feather an arrow.* **2a** to turn (an oar or paddle) after a stroke so that the blade is flat and keep it that way until the next stroke begins. **b** to turn (the blade of an airplane propeller) to decrease wind resistance when its motor is not operating. **3** to touch (the strings of a violin) very lightly with the bow. **4** to join (boards, concrete slabs, or sheets of plastic) by tonguing and grooving.
—*v.i.* 1 to move like feathers. **2** to grow like feathers. **3** to be or become feathery in appearance. **4** to feather an oar.
feather in one's cap, a mark of honor; something to be proud of: *Winning the essay contest is a feather in his cap.*
feather one's nest. See under **nest**.
feather out, *U.S.* to taper off: *Inflation is expected to feather out as manufacturing increases.*
feathers, wings: *Fleet-wing'd duty with thought's feathers flies* (Shakespeare).
feather up to, *U.S. Slang.* to court: *His son ... was feathering up to Nina* (Carl Carmer).
in fine (good or **high) feather**, in good health, high spirits, etc.: *Never was Mr. Rigsby in finer feather than at Court Royal* (Sabine Baring-Gould).
make feathers fly, to cause trouble: *Old cronies feathering their nests appear alongside the young rebels hell-bent on making feathers fly* (New York Times).
ruffle (someone's) feathers, to irritate; upset mildly: *Smoothly, discreetly, rarely ruffling feathers, Reston not only preserved the bureau's autonomy but also increased its prestige within a very few years* (Gay Talese).
smooth (someone's) feathers, to placate: *Whether he can keep so calm, and smooth the feathers of all the provincial Premiers, when the next federal-provincial constitutional conference is held, is another matter* (Clyde Sanger).
[Old English *fether*] **—feath′er|less**, *adj.* **—feath′er|like′**, *adj.*

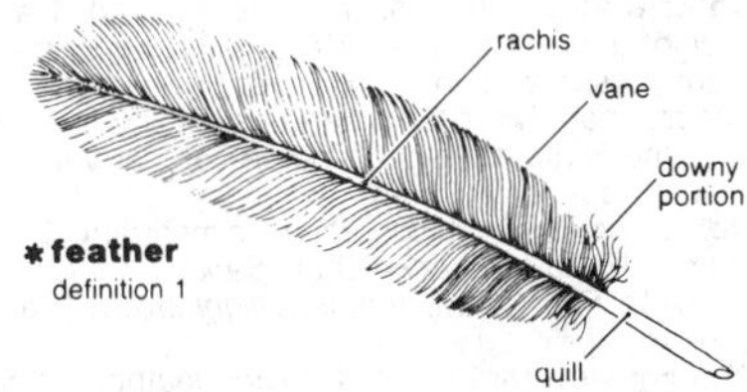

***feather**
definition 1

feath|er|bed (fe*th*′ər bed′), *v.*, **-bed|ded, -bed|ding**, *n.* **—*v.i.*** to practice featherbedding.
—*v.t.* 1 to arrange (work) under conditions of featherbedding. **2** to employ (workers) in addition to those needed: *... results in such frequent job changes that production is disrupted and laid-off employes often must be featherbedded* (Wall Street Journal).
—*n.* the practice or condition of featherbedding:

Pronunciation Key: hat, āge, cãre, fär; let, ēqual, tėrm; it, īce; hot, ōpen, ôrder; oil, out; cup, pu̇t, rüle; child; long; thin; *th*en; zh, measure; ə represents **a** in about, **e** in taken, **i** in pencil, **o** in lemon, **u** in circus.

They [railroad unions] cannot call an immediate strike to bring back the featherbed (New York Times). —**feath'er|bed'der**, *n.*

feather bed, 1 a soft, warm mattress, quilt, or bedcovering stuffed with feathers. 2 a bed with such a mattress.

feath|er|bed|ding (feᴛʜ'ər bed'ing), *n.* the practice on the part of some labor unions of forcing employers to hire more men than are needed for a particular job.

feather boa, a boa for the neck. See picture under **boa**.

feath|er|brain (feᴛʜ'ər brān'), *n.* a silly, foolish, weak-minded person.

feath|er|brained (feᴛʜ'ər brānd'), *adj.* silly, foolish, or weak-minded.

feath|er|cut (feᴛʜ'ər kut'), *n.* a style of arranging the hair, created by cutting the hair short and unevenly to form small curls with feather-shaped, upturned tips.

feather duster, a brush consisting of feathers attached to a handle, used for dusting.

feath|ered (feᴛʜ'ərd), *adj.* 1 having feathers; covered with feathers: *He calls birds "our fine-feathered friends."* 2 swift; rapid: *Youth now flees on feathered foot* (Robert Louis Stevenson). SYN: fleet, winged. 3 fitted with a feather or feathers: *a feathered arrow.*

feath|er|edge (feᴛʜ'ər ej'), *n.* a very thin, easily damaged edge.

feath|er|edged (feᴛʜ'ər ejd'), *adj.* having a very thin, easily damaged edge.

feather fern, an ornamental branching herb of Japan, belonging to the saxifrage family and bearing white flowers in erect panicles.

feather grass, a North American grass having a long plumy beard.

feath|er|head (feᴛʜ'ər hed'), *adj.* a silly, empty-headed person; featherbrain.

feath|er|head|ed (feᴛʜ'ər hed'id), *adj.* = featherbrained.

feath|er|ing (feᴛʜ'ər ing), *n.* 1 a very light application of the violin bow to the strings. 2 = feather (*n.* def. 4).

feath|er|let (feᴛʜ'ər lit), *n.* a small feather.

feather palm, any palm having featherlike (pinnate) leaves.

feath|ers (feᴛʜ'ərz), *n.pl.* See under **feather**.

feather star, a free-swimming crinoid; comatulid.

***feath|er|stitch** (feᴛʜ'ər stich'), *n., v.* —*n.* a zigzag embroidery stitch.
—*v.i.* to make zigzag embroidery stitches.
—*v.t.* to decorate with such stitches.

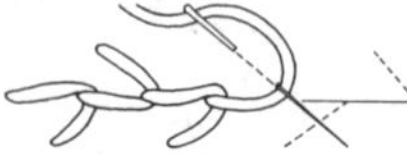

***featherstitch**

feath|er|stitch|ing (feᴛʜ'ər stich'ing), *n.* = featherstitch.

feather tree, 1 = smoke tree. 2 a tree of the mahogany family growing in valleys and on mountain slopes of the western United States; valley mahogany.

feath|er-veined (feᴛʜ'ər vānd'), *adj. Botany.* having a series of veins branching from each side of the midrib of a leaf toward the margin.

feath|er|weed (feᴛʜ'ər wēd'), *n.* 1 one of a group of red algae, common on the Atlantic and Pacific coast. 2 the common American everlasting, a fragrant plant that retains its appearance when dried.

feath|er|weight (feᴛʜ'ər wāt'), *n., adj.* —*n.* 1 a very light thing or person. 2 *Figurative.* an unimportant person or thing. 3 a boxer who weighs not more than 126 pounds and usually more than 118. 4 the lightest weight a horse can carry in a handicap race.
—*adj.* 1 very light. 2 *Figurative.* unimportant. 3 of or classed with featherweights: *Sandy Saddler ... beat Willie Pep for the featherweight crown* (Sam Nisenson).

feath|er|y (feᴛʜ'ər ē), *adj.* 1 having feathers; covered with feathers; feathered: *feathery birds, a feathery flock of geese.* 2 like feathers; soft: *a feathery flower, feathery clouds, feathery snow.* 3 light; flimsy. —**feath'er|i|ness**, *n.*

feat|ly (fēt'lē), *adv., adj.* —*adv. Archaic.* 1 nimbly; skillfully. 2 suitably; properly. 3 neatly; elegantly.
—*adj.* (of a garment) neat; well-fitting.
[< *feat*[2] + *-ly*[1]] —**feat'li|ness**, *n.*

fea|tur|al (fē'chər əl), *adj.* of or having to do with the features: *There was no featural resemblance between the two faces* (George Macdonald). —**fea'tur|al|ly**, *adv.*

fea|ture (fē'chər), *n., adj., v.,* **-tured, -tur|ing.**
—*n.* 1 a part of the face. The eyes, nose, mouth, chin, and forehead are features. *There was daring ... in the dark eye, but the other features seemed to express a bashful timidity* (Scott). 2 the form or cast of the face. 3 a distinct part or quality; thing that stands out and attracts attention: *Your plan for the picnic has many good features and some bad ones. The main features of southern California are the climate and the scenery.* 4 a long motion picture; feature film: *They are showing a good feature this week.* 5 a special article, column, comic strip, or the like, in a newspaper. 6 *Archaic.* make, form, or shape.
—*adj.* 1 of or having to do with a feature: *[She] was a feature writer for Effluvia, a periodical circulated gratis by supermarkets* (New Yorker). 2 being the main part of a program: *Six finalists had been chosen who would be the feature performers in the show* (Esquire).
—*v.t.* 1 to be a feature of. 2 to make a feature of; give prominence to: *The local newspapers featured the President's visit.* 3 *Informal.* to be like in features; favor: *All the sisters feature their mother.* 4 to affect or mold the features of. 5 to sketch the features of; portray.
—*v.i.* to be a feature or attraction; play a major or prominent part: *The former candidate hasn't featured in any news lately. My favorite actress is featuring in a new movie.*
features, the face: *pleasing features.*
[< Anglo-French *feture,* Old French *faiture* < Latin *factūra* < *factus;* see etym. under **feat**[2]]
—*Syn. n.* 3 **Feature, characteristic, trait** mean a distinguishing quality. **Feature** applies to a quality or detail that stands out and attracts attention: *the striking geological features of the Grand Canyon.* **Characteristic** applies to a quality or feature that expresses or shows the character or nature of a person, thing, or class, or distinguishes it from others: *The use of slang is a characteristic of his writing.* **Trait** applies particularly to a distinguishing feature of mind or disposition: *Cheerfulness is his finest trait.*

fea|tured (fē'chərd), *adj.* 1 *Informal.* made a feature of; given prominence to: *the featured actors in a motion picture, a featured painting at an exhibition, a featured newspaper story.* 2 having a certain kind of features: *hard-featured.* 3 *Obsolete.* formed; shaped.

-featured, *combining form.* having ___ features: *Hard-featured = having hard features.*

feature film, the main attraction at a motion-picture theater, especially the longest of several films shown in one program.

fea|ture-length (fē'chər length'), *adj.* (of a motion picture, newspaper or magazine article, or column) of the length of a feature; of full or standard length.

fea|ture|less (fē'chər lis), *adj.* without features; not interesting or impressive; not distinctive; uneventful: *The more featureless and commonplace a crime is, the more difficult to bring it home* (Sir Arthur Conan Doyle). *When we travel over these featureless waters we tend to assume that the bottom is an equally smooth plain* (Scientific American). —**fea'ture|less|ly**, *adv.* —**fea'ture|less|ness**, *n.*

fea|tures (fē'chərz), *n.pl.* See under **feature**.

fea|tur|ette (fē'chə ret'), *n.* a short motion picture, such as a cartoon or newsreel; short: *[The film company] will release five technicolor feature films and six, three-reel featurettes* (Wall Street Journal).

feaze[1] (fēz), *v.t., v.i.,* **feazed, feaz|ing.** *Nautical.* to unravel. [origin uncertain; perhaps related to Low German *fäsen* frayed edge, or to Old English *fæs* fringe]

feaze[2] (fēz, fāz), *n., v.t., v.i.,* **feazed, feaz|ing.** = feeze.

feaz|ings (fē'zingz), *n.pl. Nautical.* the unlaid end of a rope.

Feb., February.

feb|ri|fa|cient (feb'rə fā'shənt), *adj., n. U.S.*
—*adj.* producing fever.
—*n.* something that produces fever. [< Latin *febris* fever + *faciēns, -entis,* present participle of *facere* do, make]

fe|brif|er|ous (fi brif'ər əs), *adj.* producing fever.

fe|brif|ic (fi brif'ik), *adj.* 1 producing fever. 2 = feverish.

fe|brif|u|gal (fi brif'yə gəl, feb'rə fyü'gəl), *adj.* curing or lessening fever.

feb|ri|fuge (feb'rə fyüj), *n., adj.* —*n.* 1 a medicine to reduce fever. 2 a cooling drink.
—*adj.* curing or lessening fever.
[< French *fébrifuge,* learned borrowing from Late Latin *febrifugia.* See etym. of doublet **feverfew**.]

fe|brile (fē'brəl, feb'rəl), *adj.* 1 of fever; feverish: *to toss in febrile restlessness.* 2 caused by fever: *a febrile flush.* [< Medieval Latin *febrilis* < Latin *febris* fever]

fe|bril|i|ty (fi bril'ə tē), *n.* = feverishness.

Feb|ru|ar|y (feb'rü er'ē, feb'yü-), *n., pl.* **-ar|ies.** the second month of the year. It has 28 days except in leap years, when it has 29. *Abbr:* Feb. [< Latin *Februārius* < *februa, -ōrum,* plural, the Roman feast of purification celebrated on February 15]

fec., he or she made it (Latin, *fecit*).

fe|cal (fē'kəl), *adj.* having to do with feces. Also, **faecal**.

fe|ces (fē'sēz), *n.pl.* 1 waste matter discharged from the intestines; excrement. 2 dregs; sediment. Also, **faeces**. [< Latin *faecēs* dregs, plural of *faex, faecis*]

fe|cit (fē'sit), *v. Latin.* he (or she) made (it), often inscribed on a work of art after the name of the artist.

feck (fek), *n. Scottish.* 1a effect; value. b vigor; energy. 2 amount; quantity. [variant of *fect,* short for *effect*]

feck|less (fek'lis), *adj.* 1 futile; ineffective; *Rip Van Winkle was an idle, feckless character.* 2 *Scottish.* spiritless; worthless. [< *feck* + *-less*] —**feck'less|ly**, *adv.* —**feck'less|ness**, *n.*

feck|ly (fek'lē), *adv. Scottish.* for the most part; mostly; almost.

fec|u|la (fek'yə lə), *n., pl.* **-lae** (-lē). any form of starch obtained as a sediment by washing the pulverized roots, grains, or other parts of plants in water. Also, **faecula**. [< Latin *faecula* sediment in wine (diminutive) < *faex, faecis* dregs]

fec|u|lence (fek'yə ləns), *n.* 1 the fact or condition of being feculent; foulness. 2 filth; dregs.

fec|u|lent (fek'yə lənt), *adj.* like or containing dregs or foul matter; muddy; turbid. [< Latin *faeculentus* < *faex, faecis* dregs]

fe|cund (fē'kənd, fek'ənd), *adj.* 1 able to produce much; fruitful; productive; fertile: *Edison had a fecund mind.* 2 capable of producing offspring or vegetable growth abundantly; prolific: *the fecund earth of the tropical jungles.* [< Old French *fecond,* learned borrowing from Latin *fēcundus*]

fe|cun|date (fē'kən dāt, fek'ən-), *v.t.,* **-dat|ed, -dat|ing.** 1 to make fruitful or productive. 2 *Biology.* to fertilize. [< Latin *fēcundāre* (with English *-ate*[1]) < *fēcundus* fecund, fruitful] —**fe'cun|da'tion**, *n.*

fe|cun|di|ty (fi kun'də tē), *n.* 1 the condition of being fertile; fruitfulness; productiveness; fertility: *Thomas Edison is remembered for the fecundity of his inventive mind.* 2 the ability, especially in female animals, to produce young in great numbers: *The slaughter, mostly by trapping, of some hundred million rabbits every year has, because of the animal's fecundity, little appreciable effect on their numbers in lush seasons* (Science News).

fed[1] (fed), *v.* the past tense and past participle of **feed**: *We fed the birds yesterday. Have they been fed today?*
fed up, *Informal.* bored or disgusted; surfeited: *... a major relief to a frankly fed up and frustrated nation* (London Times). *I've been a shipping clerk for a whole ... year, and I'm fed up with it* (James T. Farrell).

fed[2] (fed), *n. U.S. Informal.* a Federal investigator or detective: *The cops and the feds swooped down [and] caught the terrified Waxey with a pound of heroin* (Time).

Fed (fed), *n. U.S. Informal.* 1 Federal Reserve System. 2 Federal Reserve Bank. 3 Federal Reserve Board of Governors.

fed. or **Fed.**, 1 federal. 2 federation.

fed|a|i or **fed|a|yee** (fed'ä yē'), *n.* = fedayeen.

fed|a|yeen (fed'ä yēn'), *n., pl.* **-yeen.** an Arab commando or guerrilla. Also, **fadayeen**. [< Arabic *fidā'īn,* plural of *fidā'ī* (literally) one who sacrifices himself < *fidā'* redemption; sacrifice]

fed|a|yin (fed'ä yēn'), *n., pl.* **-yin.** = fedayeen.

fed|dan (fe dän'), *n.* a measure of land in Egypt and the Sudan, equivalent to 1.038 acres. [< Arabic *faddān*]

fed|er|al (fed'ər əl, fed'rəl), *adj., n.* —*adj.* 1 formed by an agreement of states or groups establishing a central organization to handle their common affairs while the states or groups keep separate control of local affairs: *Switzerland and the United States both became nations by federal union. The American Federation of Labor is a federal organization of labor unions.* 2 of or having to do with the central government formed in this way: *Coining money is a federal power. Congress is the federal lawmaking body of the United States.*
—*n.* a supporter of federation or federalism.
[< Latin *foedus, foederis* compact, league (< *fīdere* to trust) + English *-al*[1]] —**fed'er|al|ly**, *adv.*

Fed|er|al (fed'ər əl, fed'rəl), *adj., n.* —*adj.* 1 of or having to do with the central government of the United States, not of any state alone: *a Federal office building. The Federal courts are managed by the national government.* 2a of or having to do with the Federal Party. b supporting the Union during the Civil War.
—*n.* 1 a supporter or soldier of the Union during the Civil War: *The front lines were close, and the Federals threw hand grenades into the Confederate works* (ROTC Manual of American Military History). 2 = Federalist.
[< *federal*] —**Fed'er|al|ly**, *adv.*

Federal aid, *U.S.* financial assistance given by

the Federal government to a state, a local government or a private institution.

Federal case, *U.S.* a matter for a Federal agency or law court to investigate or to decide.
make a Federal case, *U.S. Informal.* to make a great fuss; make an issue: *I was only a little late, but she made a Federal case out of it.*

Federal Constitution, the Constitution of the United States.

federal district or **Federal District**, land which a country sets apart and administers as its national capital, such as the District of Columbia in the United States. Australia, Brazil, Mexico, and Venezuela are among the countries which have federal districts.

fed\|er\|al\|ese (fed′ər ə lēz′, -lēs′; fed′rə-), *n. U.S.* the jargon commonly used in government publications, reports, and letters.

fed\|er\|al\|ise (fed′ər ə līz, fed′rə-), *v.t.*, **-ised, -is\|ing**. *Especially British.* federalize.

Fed\|er\|al\|ism (fed′ər ə liz′əm, fed′rə liz-), *n.* the principles of the Federalist Party in the United States.

fed\|er\|al\|ism (fed′ər ə liz′əm, fed′rə liz-), *n.* **1** the federal principle of government. **2** support of this principle.

Fed\|er\|al\|ist (fed′ər ə list, fed′rə-), *n., adj. U.S. History.* —*n.* **1** a member or supporter of the Federalist Party in the United States. **2** a series of 85 essays by Alexander Hamilton, James Madison, and John Jay, issued chiefly in 1787-1788 in support of the proposed Constitution of the United States.
—*adj.* of or supporting the Federalists: *The congressional caucus developed out of semiofficial meetings held by the Federalist members of Congress* (Ernst C. Meyer).

fed\|er\|al\|ist (fed′ər ə list, fed′rə-), *n., adj.* —*n.* a person who favors the federal principle of government.
—*adj.* of or supporting federalism.

fed\|er\|al\|is\|tic (fed′ər ə lis′tik, fed′rə-), *adj.* = federalist.

Federalist Party, *U.S. History.* a political party in the United States that favored the adoption of the Constitution and, later, the establishment of a strong central government. It existed from about 1791 to about 1816.

fed\|er\|al\|i\|za\|tion (fed′ər ə lə zā′shən, fed′rə-), *n.* **1** the act of federalizing. **2** the state of being federalized.

fed\|er\|al\|ize (fed′ər ə līz, fed′rə-), *v.t.*, **-ized, -iz\|ing**. **1** to unite into a federal union. **2** to put under the control of the federal government: *Once the Guard is "federalized," the Governor no longer has control* (New York Times).

Federal Party, = Federalist Party.

Federal Reserve Bank, *U.S.* any one of twelve district banks of the Federal Reserve System of the United States established to regulate and help member banks in each district.

Federal Reserve Board, *U.S.* a group of seven men appointed by the President of the United States to supervise the Federal Reserve System. *Abbr:* FRB (no periods).

Federal Reserve System, *U.S.* the federal system of banks consisting of twelve Federal Reserve Banks and supervised by the Federal Reserve Board. The Federal Reserve System regulates the loans and reserves of member banks and influences the flow of credit and currency in the country. It loans money only to banks in the system and adjusts the amount of money in the country to the needs by changing the rate of interest on its loans. *Abbr:* FRS (no periods).

fed\|er\|ate (*v.* fed′ə rāt; *adj., n.* fed′ər it, fed′rit), *v.*, **-at\|ed, -at\|ing**, *adj., n.* —*v.t., v.i.* **1** to form into a union or federation: *a plan to federate the provinces. The provinces federated in order to facilitate trade between them and strengthen their defense. The recently created African states are engaged in federating* (Rómulo Betancourt). **2** to organize on a federal basis: *to federate a country or an empire.*
—*adj.* formed into a union or federation; federated; allied.
—*n.* a member of a union or federation.
[< Latin *foederāre* (with English *-ate*[1]) league together < *foedus*; see etym. under **federal**]

fed\|er\|at\|ed city (fed′ə rā′tid), a unit of government in a metropolitan area with authority to finance projects of the area by taxes.

fed\|er\|a\|tion (fed′ə rā′shən), *n.* **1** the act of federating or uniting into a league: *A federation of all humanity ... would mean such a release and increase of human energy as to open a new phase in human history* (H. G. Wells). **2** formation of a political unity out of a number of separate states or districts, each of which retains control of its own internal affairs: *The United States is a federation.* **3** a league; a union by agreement, often a union of states or nations: *the American Federation of Labor, a federation of students. Each member of the federation controls its own affairs.*

fed\|er\|a\|tive (fed′ə rā′tiv), *adj.* of or having to do with a federation; like a federation; forming a federation. —**fed′er\|a′tive\|ly**, *adv.*

***fe\|do\|ra** (fə dôr′ə, -dōr′-), *n.* a man's low, soft felt hat with a curved brim. The crown is creased lengthwise: *He was in ... a freshly blocked fedora, dented like a soft bread by the fingers* (Saul Bellow). [American English; apparently < *Fédora*, a play by Victorien Sardou, 1831-1908, a French playwright]

***fedora**

fed-up\|ness (fed′up′nis), *n. Informal.* utter boredom, weariness, or disgust: *... a mood of fed-upness with the world* (New Yorker); *... Hamlet's fed-upness with a corrupt court* (Time).

fee (fē), *n., v.*, **feed, fee\|ing**. —*n.* **1** a sum of money asked or paid for some service or privilege; charge; payment: *an admission fee, a license fee. Doctors and lawyers receive fees for their services.* **SYN:** pay, compensation, recompense. **2** a small present of money; tip. **SYN:** gratuity. **3** in feudal law: **a** the right to keep and use land. **b** = fief. **4** a territory held in fee: *My lute and I are lords of more Than thrice this kingdom's fee* (James Russell Lowell). **5** ownership; possession. **6** *Law.* an estate in land capable of passing to the owner's heirs, either an estate that belongs to the owner and his heirs forever with no restrictions on the class of heirs (fee simple) or an estate restricted to some particular class of heirs (fee tail).
—*v.t.* **1** to give a fee to. **2** to tip. **3** *Scottish.* to engage or employ for a fee; hire.
hold in fee, to own: *Once did she hold the gorgeous East in fee* (Wordsworth).
[< Anglo-French *fee*, Old French *fieu, fief*, apparently < Germanic (compare Old Frisian *fio* money; property; cattle). Compare etym. under **feu, feud**[2], **fief**.]

Fee\|bie (fē′bē), *n. U.S. Slang.* a member of the FBI. [< irregular pronunciation of *FBI*]

fee\|ble (fē′bəl), *adj.*, **-bler, -blest**. **1** lacking strength; weak; frail: *a feeble barrier. An old or sick person is often feeble. This way and that the feeble stem is driven, weak to sustain the storms and injuries of heaven* (John Dryden). **SYN:** infirm, doddering. See syn. under **weak**. **2** weak intellectually or morally: *a feeble mind.* **3** lacking in force or effectiveness: *a feeble resistance. A feeble attempt is liable to fail.* **SYN:** ineffective. **4** lacking in volume, loudness, brightness, or distinctness: *a feeble cry, a feeble light.* **SYN:** slight, faint. [< Old French *feble* < Latin *flēbilis* lamentable < *flēre* weep. Compare etym. under **foible**.] —**fee′ble\|ness**, *n.*

fee\|ble-mind\|ed (fē′bəl mīn′did), *adj.* **1** weak in mind; lacking normal intelligence. **2** indecisive: *Comfort the feeble-minded* (I Thessalonians 5:14). —**fee′ble-mind′ed\|ly**, *adv.* —**fee′ble-mind′ed\|ness**, *n.*

fee\|blish (fē′blish), *adj.* somewhat feeble.

fee\|bly (fē′blē), *adv.* in a feeble manner; without strength; weakly; faintly.

feed (fēd), *v.*, **fed, feed\|ing**, *n.* —*v.t.* **1** to give food to: *We feed a baby who cannot feed himself. And He that doth the ravens feed ... Be comfort to my age!* (Shakespeare). (*Figurative.*) *He has fed his people with a steady diet of "blood, sweat, and tears" speeches* (New York Times). **2** to give as food: *Feed this grain to the chickens.* **3** to cause to grow; nourish: *He fed his anger with thoughts of revenge.* **SYN:** sustain. **4** *Figurative.* **a** to satisfy; gratify: *Praise fed his vanity.* **b** to comfort (someone) with false hopes. **5a** to supply (material to be used up) as to a fire or reservoir: *to feed kerosene to a lamp, to feed information into a computer.* **b** to provide or supply (anything): *"I've had to keep feeding money into my broker so I wouldn't get sold out"* (James T. Farrell). **6** to supply with material: *to feed a machine. Feed the fire with more logs.* **7** to yield or serve as food for: *Grass feeds cows.* **SYN:** sustain. **8** to use (land) for grazing. **9** *Theater.* to supply (another actor) with cues. **10** *Sports.* to pass or give (the puck or ball) to a teammate.
—*v.i.* **1** (of animals) to eat: *We put cows to feed in the pasture. Cattle and horses feed on hay.* **2** to go into a machine or the like for processing or other use: *information feeding into the computer.*
—*n.* **1a** food for animals; fodder: *Give the chickens their feed.* **b** the allowance of food for an animal. **2** *Informal.* a meal for a person: *What a feed we had last night!* **3** the act of feeding. **4** the act or process of supplying a machine, or the like, with material. **5** the material supplied. **6** a part of a machine that supplies material. **7** *Theater.* **a** a line or cue to which a comedian replies with a line that gets a laugh. **b** = feeder. **8** *Sports.* a pass or hand-off of the puck or ball: *He gave him a pretty feed near the Vermonter's cage* (New York Times). **9** *Obsolete.* pasture ground: *His flocks and bounds of feed Are now on sale* (Shakespeare).
feed on (or **upon**), **a** to live at the expense of; prey on: *All feed on one vain patron* (Alexander Pope). **b** to derive satisfaction or support from: *Grant me to feed on beauty's rifled charms* (Robert Pollok).
[Old English *fēdan* < *fōda* food] —**feed′a\|ble**, *adj.*
—*Syn. n.* **1a Feed, fodder** mean food for animals. **Feed** is the general word applying to food for animals or fowls: *That store supplies feed to the dairy farms and poultry farms.* **Fodder** applies to coarse or dried feed, like alfalfa, hay, corn, or other plants fed to horses, cattle, pigs, or sheep: *Put some fodder in the bins.*

feed\|back (fēd′bak′), *n., adj.* —*n.* **1** a process by which a system or device regulates itself by feeding back to itself part of its output. **2** *Biology.* a process whereby the course of a reaction is controlled by the activity of some of the products of the reaction. **3** a reciprocal effect of one person or thing upon another, especially as a reaction that affects the behavior of whatever produced the reaction: *Primitives treat things and animals as people, and experience feedback from them* (Manchester Guardian Weekly). *Outsiders are unable to penetrate the continuing feedback between the [Army Engineers] Corps and the congressional committees* (Elizabeth B. Drew).
—*adj.* characterized by or using feedback: *a feedback amplifier, a feedback oscillator. No array of feedback arguments is the product of team activity* (Merle A. Ture).

feedback inhibition, *Biochemistry.* a form of cellular control by which a mechanism producing a particular substance in the cell is inhibited at a certain level of accumulation of that substance, thereby balancing the amount produced with the amount needed.

feedback loop, the path through a feedback system or device from input to output and back to input.

feed\|bag (fēd′bag′), *n.* a bag for holding food, hung on a horse's head; nose bag.
put on the feedbag, *Slang.* to eat: *Let's stop talking and put on the feedbag.*

feed\|box (fēd′boks′), *n.* **1** a box used in feeding livestock. **2** a box containing a feed motion and related apparatus for feeding a machine.

feed crop, a crop grown as feed for livestock, as distinguished from a cash crop.

feed\|er (fē′dər), *n.* **1** a person or thing that feeds: *a heavy feeder.* **2** a person or device that supplies food to a person or animal. **3** a thing that supplies something else with material: *These brooks are feeders of the big river. That branch railroad that brings traffic to the main line is a feeder.* **4** a steer, lamb, or other livestock, to be or being fattened for slaughtering. **5** a person or device that supplies material to a machine, fuel to a furnace, or similar device, such as a mechanical device for producing and delivering molten glass to a glass-forming unit. **6** a wire or cable used to conduct electricity from a source to a distribution point. **7** *Theater.* **a** a comedian's straight man, who feeds him cues for his comic lines; feed. **b** a part that supplies such cues.

feeder line, a branch airline or railroad.

feeder road, a secondary road that leads traffic to a major road such as a turnpike or an expressway: *Feeder roads are considered essential to connect the proposed ferry terminal ... with U.S. 13 and State Route 113* (New York Times).

feed\|for\|ward (fēd′fôr′wərd), *n.* the control of a feedback process by anticipating any defects in the process before it is carried out: *This more "intelligent" type of control is known as "feedforward" as opposed to feedback, and essentially it involves locating the sensor at the input end* (Kenneth Owen).

feed grain, grain used as livestock feed: *Corn, wheat, and sorghum are feed grains.*

feed-in (fēd′in′), *n.* a gathering of people to receive free food: *Even food, modest but nourish-*

ing, was provided for penniless but hungry travelers at the two or three daily "feed-ins" (New York Times).

feed|ing frenzy (fē′ding), *U.S. Informal.* the frantic pursuit of anything, as of profit, markets, art, or the like: *Charles Saatchi . . . was soon buying Chia [paintings], and other collectors quickly went into a feeding frenzy* (Anthony Haden-Guest).

feeding grounds, any area of land or water where birds, fish, or wild animals gather to eat, usually for an extended period each year.

feed|ing|stuff (fē′ding stuf′), *n. British.* feedstuff.

feed lot, or **feed|lot** (fēd′lot′), *n.* an establishment, often a farm, near a slaughtering center, where cattle shipped from a distance are fattened for the market.

feed mill, a mill in which feed for livestock is prepared.

feed|stock (fēd′stok′), *n.* oil, methane, or other principal materials in a chemical process producing petroleum products such as synthetic rubber.

feed|stuff (fēd′stuf′), *n.* feed for livestock: *They could qualify for cheap feedstuffs provided under the Federal program* (Wall Street Journal).

feed trough, **1** *U.S.* a trough in which the feed for domestic animals is placed. **2** a tank or trough containing a supply of water for a steam-driven locomotive.

feed|wa|ter (fēd′wôt′ər, -wot′-), *n.* a supply of water for a boiler, reactor, or the like.

fee-faw-fum (fē′fô′fum′), *n.* **1** nonsense fitted only to terrify children; absurdity; humbug. **2** a bloodthirsty person. [from the first word spoken by the giant in the tale *Jack the Giant Killer*]

fee-fo-fum (fē′fō′fum′), *n.* = fee-faw-fum.

feel (fēl), *v.,* **felt, feel|ing,** *n.* **—*v.t.*** **1** to put the hand or some other part of the body on or against; touch: *Feel this cloth.* **SYN:** handle. **2** to try to find or make (one's way) by touch: *He felt his way across the room when the lights went out.* **3** to test or examine by touching: *to feel a person's pulse, to feel a child's forehead to see if he has a fever.* **4** to find out by touching: *Feel how cold my hands are.* **5** to be aware of: *He feels the cool breeze. She felt the heat. He felt the blood run down his arm.* **6** to have in one's mind; experience: *They feel pity. I felt pain. He felt fear of the thunder.* **7** *Figurative.* to be influenced or affected by: *The ship feels her helm.* **8** to think; believe; consider: *I feel he will come.*
—*v.i.* **1** to search by touch; grope: *He felt in his pocket for a dime.* **2** to have the feeling of being; be: *She feels glad. He feels angry. We feel hot. She felt sure. How do you feel about this?* **3** to give the feeling of being; seem: *The air feels cold. Your dress feels wet.* **SYN:** appear. **4** to have a feeling, especially pity or sympathy: *She feels for all who suffer. Try to feel more kindly toward her.* **5** to have or be capable of sensations: *From sense of grief and pain we shall be free; We shall not feel, because we shall not be* (John Dryden).
—*n.* **1** touch: *I like the feel of silk.* **2** a way something seems; the quality sensed by touch, intellect, or emotion; feeling: *Wet soap has a greasy feel. The winner had a satisfying feel of accomplishment. She has a feel for music. Men visited production plants . . . to get the feel of things* (London Times). **3** the sense of touch. **4** the act of feeling.
feel like, *Informal.* to have a desire or inclination for: *After your letter came, I felt like a ride* (Elizabeth Custer).
feel like oneself. See under **oneself.**
feel out, to try to find out from or about in a cautious way: *Feel him out on this matter.*
feel up to, *Informal.* to feel able or ready to (do something): *I don't feel up to taking such a long trip.*
[Old English *fēlan*]

feel|er (fē′lər), *n.* **1** a special part of an animal's body for sensing by touch. A cat's whiskers are its feelers. The long feelers on the heads of insects help them find their way. **2** *Figurative.* a suggestion, remark, hint, question, or the like, made to find out what others are thinking or planning: *The new regime has been putting out feelers in almost every direction . . . for assistance in getting the country on to its feet again* (Sunday Times). **3** a person or thing that feels: *He [Thoreau] was not a strong thinker, but a sensitive feeler* (James Russell Lowell).

feeler gauge, a strip of metal of known thickness used to measure the desired distance between two surfaces, as between a piston and cylinder, in making adjustments; thickness gauge.

feel|good (fēl′gu̇d′), *n., adj. U.S. Slang.* **—*n.*** **1** Also, **Feelgood.** a quack doctor: *to guard against Feelgoods and charlatans is for the medical profession* (Newsweek). **2** a blissful state; perfect contentment: *psychic feelgood.*
—*adj.* providing well-being or contentment.

feel|ie (fē′lē), *n.* an art object or medium which the spectator can feel as well as see, smell, and sometimes hear.

feel|ing (fē′ling), *n., adj.* **—*n.*** **1** the act or condition of one that feels. **2** the sense of touch. By feeling we tell what is hard from what is soft. **3** a sensation; condition of being aware; awareness: *a feeling of security. She had no feeling of heat, cold, or pain.* **SYN:** impression. **4** an emotion. Joy, sorrow, fear, and anger are feelings. *The loss of the ball game stirred up much feeling.* **5** the capacity for emotion; sensibility: *She was guided by feeling rather than thought. Is he not a man of honour and feeling?* (Jane Austen). **6a** sensitivity to the higher or more refined emotions: *His work shows both feeling and taste.* **b** pity; sympathy: *Have you no feeling for that poor, sick creature?* **7** an opinion; sentiment: *He had no feeling about our plan, one way or the other. Her feeling was that right would win.* **SYN:** idea. **8** the quality felt to belong to anything: *There is a weird feeling about the place.* **9a** the emotional or sympathetic perception revealed by an artist in his work. **b** the general tone of a work of art. **c** sympathetic appreciation of a work of art, or of something thought of in similar terms: *a feeling for music.* **10** *Psychology.* consciousness, awareness, or sensation in itself, isolated from anything thought or perceived.
—*adj.* **1** that feels; full of feeling; sensitive; emotional: *a feeling heart.* **2** deeply felt: *feeling sorrows* (Shakespeare).
feelings, the sensitive side of one's nature: *You hurt his feelings when you yell at him.*
—feel′ing|ly, *adv.* **—feel′ing|ness,** *n.*
—Syn. *n.* **4 Feeling, emotion, passion** means a pleasant or painful mental state produced in a person in reaction to a stimulus of some kind. **Feeling** is the general word: *He had some feeling of hope.* **Emotion** means a strong and moving feeling such as love, fear, sorrow, or joy: *She was overwhelmed with emotion and couldn't speak for a moment.* **Passion** means violent emotion, usually overcoming the power to think clearly and taking complete possession of a person: *In a passion of rage he killed her.*

feel|ing|less (fē′ling lis), *adj.* without feeling; devoid of feeling. **—feel′ing|less|ly,** *adv.*

feel|ings (fē′lings), *n.pl.* See under **feeling.**

fee patent, a first grant of title to public land, issued by the government to an individual with the right to sell or give it to anyone.

fee simple, ownership of land with the right to sell or give it to anyone.

fee-split|ting (fē′split′ing), *n.* an unethical practice in which a professional man refers a client or patient to a second man and receives a part of the latter's fee in return.

feet (fēt), *n.* plural of **foot**; more than one foot: *A dog has four feet. He is six feet tall.*
carry (or **sweep**) **off one's feet, a** to make very enthusiastic: *The speech carried the audience off its feet and there was prolonged applause.* **b** to impress or overwhelm: *He was certainly not a man to sweep a young girl off her feet* (Winston Churchill).
die on one's feet, to collapse, fail, or break down: *Now this most promising of African economies is liable to die on its feet, even if it does not disintegrate into chaos* (Manchester Guardian Weekly).
drag one's feet, to move sluggishly or wearily; act in a slow and hesitant manner: *A vague uneasiness . . . caused German nuclear scientists to drag their feet* (Bulletin of Atomic Scientists).
keep one's feet, to stand or walk upright without falling: *He could not keep his feet in a breeze* (Macaulay).
put on one's feet, to put into an established or settled position: *The man who put the Museum on its feet . . . first had to put himself on his own feet* (New Yorker).
sit at one's feet, to be one's pupil or admirer: *He sat at his professor's feet and tried to emulate him in every way.*
stand on one's own feet, to be independent: *In time he stopped his dependence on his father and learned to stand on his own feet.*
think on one's feet, to be mentally alert; think quickly: *A good teacher has to be able to think on his feet.*
vote with one's feet, to show one's disapproval of a condition by leaving or escaping from it: *Some continue to "vote with their feet" by climbing over, digging under or slipping through the Wall* (New York Times).

fee tail, ownership of land limited to a certain class of heirs. [< Anglo-French *fee* fee; *taile,* past participle of Old French *taillier* to fix, limit]

feet of clay, human flaws or shortcomings, especially in a great or idealized person: *A boy's love for his mother is not affected by discovering . . . that she had feet of clay* (Atlantic). *The same impulse is seen everywhere, . . . to question standards, to puncture complacency, to reveal the idol's feet of clay* (Manchester Guardian). [in allusion to the idol whose feet were partly of iron and partly of clay, in Daniel 2:33]

feeze (fēz, fāz), *n., v.,* **feezed, feez|ing.** **—*n.*** **1** *Dialect.* **a** a rush. **b** a violent impact. **c** a rub. **2** *U.S. Informal.* a state of alarm or perturbation: *I am in a feeze half the time* (James Russell Lowell). [< verb]
—*v.t. Dialect.* **1** to frighten; faze. **2** to beat; flog; drive.
—*v.i. Dialect or Informal.* to fret; worry. Also, **feaze.**
[Old English *fēsian*]

feh (fā), *n.* a fricative form of *peh,* the seventeenth letter of the Hebrew alphabet.

Feh|ling's solution (fā′lingz), a solution composed of copper sulfate and a tartrate, used in testing a substance for the presence of sugar. [< Herman von *Fehling,* 1812-1885, a German chemist]

feign (fān), *v.t.* **1** to put on a false appearance of; make believe; pretend: *Some animals feign death when in danger.* **SYN:** assume, affect, simulate, sham. **2** to make up to deceive; invent falsely: *to feign an excuse.* **3** to represent fictitiously: *Things . . . worse than fables yet have feign'd* (Milton). **4** to imagine (what is unreal). **5** *Obsolete.* to dissemble: *Both doth strive their fearfulness to feign* (Edmund Spenser). **—*v.i.*** **1** to make oneself appear; pretend (to be): *He isn't sick; he is only feigning.* **SYN:** assume, affect, simulate, sham. **2** *Obsolete.* to indulge in fiction.
[< Old French *feign-,* stem of *feindre* < Latin *fingere* to form] **—feign′er,** *n.* **—feign′ing|ly,** *adv.*

feigned (fānd), *adj.* **1** pretended; sham: *Mortal enemies . . . came every day to pay their feigned civilities* (Macaulay). **2** *Archaic.* fictitiously invented; related in fiction: *The phoenix is a feigned bird.* **—feign′ed|ly,** *adv.*

fei|jo|a (fā jō′ə, fē-), *n.* a shrub or small tree of the myrtle family cultivated in South America for its edible fruit. [< New Latin *Feijoa* the genus name < J. da Silva *Feijo,* director of the Natural History Museum at San Sebastian, Spain]

fei|jo|a|da (fā′zhō ä′dä), *n.* a Brazilian dish consisting of black beans, rice, and sausage or pork. [< Portuguese *feijoada* < *feijão* bean]

fein|schmeck|er (fīn′shmek′ər), *n. U.S. Slang.* a person devoted to cultural matters, especially one who is self-conscious or conspicuous in his devotion. [< German *Feinschmecker* epicure, gourmet; (literally) fine taster]

feint (fānt), *n., v., adj.* **—*n.*** **1** a false appearance; pretense: *The boy made a feint of studying hard, though actually he was listening to the radio.* **2** a movement made with the purpose of deceiving, especially: **a** (in war) a sham attack: *A single regiment made a feint on the front of the fortress while the rest of the division prepared to attack from the rear.* **SYN:** stratagem. **b** (in fencing and boxing) a pretended thrust or blow: *The fighter made a feint at his opponent with his right hand and struck with his left.* **SYN:** stratagem.
—*v.t.* **1** to feign an attack, hit, or other offensive act, upon: *The Israeli troops fanned out to feint at the Egyptian flanks* (Time). **2** to maneuver (someone) by a feint: *He feinted the pitcher off balance.*
—*v.i.* to make a pretended blow or sham attack: *The fighter feinted with his right hand and struck with his left.*
—*adj. Now Rare.* feigned.
[< French *feint* < Old French *feinte,* feminine past participle of *feindre;* see etym. under **feign.**]

feints (fānts), *n.pl.* = faints.

feir|ie (fir′ē), *adj. Archaic Scottish.* nimble; vigorous: *O hold your tongue, my feirie old wife* (Robert Burns).
[Middle English *fery,* perhaps related to Old English *fōr* going]

feis (fesh), *n.* **1** (in Ireland) a festival. **2** *U.S.* any celebration by the Irish. [< Irish *feis,* or *fess* meeting, assembly]

feist (fīst), *n. U.S. Dialect.* a small dog: *In our lodge were three huge curs and four cross feists* (L. H. Garrard). Also, **fice, fist.**
[American English, apparently < dialectal English *fisting (cur)* (literally) stinking (cur) < Middle English *fysta* stink]

feist|y (fīs′tē), *adj.,* **feist|i|er, feist|i|est.** *U.S. Dialect.* full of life or high spirits: *That there feisty bay mare jumped straight upwards and broke the tongue outen the plow* (Elizabeth Roberts).

fe|la|fel (fə lä′fəl), *n.* a kind of pancake filled with fried peas, onions, and spices: *The fondness of little boys [in] Jerusalem for felafel is at least as strong as the popularity of hamburgers in America* (Milwaukee Journal). Also, **falafel.** [< Hebrew *felāfəl* < Arabic *falafīl*]

feld|sher (feld′shər), *n.* in Russia: **1** a surgeon's assistant or hospital orderly. **2** an army surgeon. [< Russian *fel'dsher* < German *Feldscher,* short for *Feldscherer* field surgeon < *Feld* field + *Scherer* barber, surgeon]

feld|spar (feld′spär′, fel′-), *n.* any one of several

crystalline minerals composed of silicate of aluminum, combined with potassium, sodium, calcium, and barium. Feldspars are found in igneous rocks and are the most abundant minerals near the surface of the earth. They are used in making glass and pottery. Also, *especially British,* **felspar**. [half-translation of German *Feldspat,* or *Feldspath* (literally) field spar]

feld|spath (feld′spath, fel′-), *n.* = feldspar.

feld|spath|ic (feld spath′ik, fel-), *adj.* of the nature of or containing feldspar: *Feldspathic rocks have produced a clayey soil* (Charles Darwin).

feld|spath|ize (feld′spath īz, fel′-), *v.t.,* **-ized, -iz|ing**. *Geology.* to change to feldspar through metamorphism. — **feld′spath|i|za′tion**, *n.*

feld|spath|oid (feld′spa thoid, fel′-), *n.* any one of a group of aluminum silicates related to the feldspars, especially nephelite and leucite.

fe|li|cif|ic (fē′lə sif′ik), *adj.* tending to make happy. [< Latin *fēlīx, -īcis* happy + English *-fic*]

felicific calculus, *Philosophy.* a utilitarian method for calculating the best course of action by determining the preponderance of pleasure over pain in any act or decision; hedonic calculus.

fe|lic|i|tate (fə lis′ə tāt), *v.,* **-tat|ed, -tat|ing,** *adj.*
— ***v.t.*** **1** to express good wishes to formally; congratulate: *The young man's friends felicitated him on his engagement to marry.* **2** to cause to be happy: *Since I cannot make myself happy, I will have the glory to felicitate another* (John Dryden).
— ***adj.*** *Obsolete.* made happy.
[< Late Latin *fēlīcitāre* (with English *-ate*[1]) < *fēlīx, -īcis* happy] — **fe|lic′i|ta′tor**, *n.*

fe|lic|i|ta|tion (fə lis′ə tā′shən), *n.* **1** a formal expression of good wishes; congratulation: *... my best respects and felicitations* (Wilkie Collins). **2** the act of congratulating.

fe|lic|i|tous (fə lis′ə təs), *adj.* **1** well chosen for the occasion; appropriate; well-worded: *a felicitous speech of thanks. The poem was full of striking and felicitous similes.* **SYN:** fitting, apt. **2** having a gift for apt speech. — **fe|lic′i|tous|ly**, *adv.* — **fe|lic′i|tous|ness**, *n.*

fe|lic|i|ty (fə lis′ə tē), *n., pl.* **-ties. 1** great happiness; bliss: *that perfect bliss and sole felicity* (Christopher Marlowe). **SYN:** See syn. under **happiness**. **2** a particular instance or kind of happiness: *by a rare felicity of accident* (Samuel Taylor Coleridge). **3** a source of happiness; good fortune; blessing: *the felicity of good health. Her spring of felicity was ... in the warmth of her heart* (Jane Austen). **4** a pleasing ability in expression; appropriateness or gracefulness: *The famous writer phrased his ideas with felicity.* **SYN:** grace. **5** an unusually appropriate or graceful expression; well-chosen phrase: *Those felicities which cannot be produced at will by wit and labour* (Samuel Johnson). **6** a piece of good fortune. **7** prosperity; success. [< Old French *felicite,* learned borrowing from Latin *fēlīcitās* < *fēlīx, -īcis* happy]

fe|lid (fē′lid) *n.* = feline (*n.* def. 2). [< New Latin *Felidae* the family name < Latin *fēlēs, fēlis* wild cat]

fe|line (fē′līn), *adj., n.* — ***adj.*** **1a** of a cat; catlike in form or structure: *feline eyes, a feline tail.* **b** like that of a cat: *feline grace or stealth. The Indian stalked the deer with noiseless, feline movements.* **2** of or belonging to the family which includes the cats.
— ***n.*** **1** a cat. **2** any animal belonging to the family of meat-eating animals including cats, lions, tigers, leopards, and panthers.
[< Latin *fēlēs, fēlis* wild cat + English *-ine*[1]] — **fe′line|ly**, *adv.* — **fe′line|ness**, *n.*

feline enteritis or **distemper**, a contagious virus disease of cats, usually fatal, characterized especially by diarrhea; cat distemper.

fe|lin|i|ty (fi lin′ə tē), *n.* feline quality or disposition.

fell[1] (fel), *v.* past tense of **fall**: *Snow fell last night.*

fell[2] (fel), *v., n.* — ***v.t.*** **1** to cause to fall; cut, knock, or strike down: *One blow felled him to the ground.* **2** to cut down (a tree): *The lumberman will fell these great trees.* **3** to turn down and stitch one edge of (a seam) over the other.
— ***n.*** **1** all the trees cut down in one season. **2** a seam made by felling.
[Old English *fellan* (causative) < *feallan* fall] — **fell′a|ble**, *adj.*

fell[3] (fel), *adj., adv.* — ***adj.*** **1** extremely bad; cruel; fierce; terrible: *a fell blow.* **SYN:** savage, ruthless. **2** *Archaic.* deadly; destructive: *a fell disease, the murderer's fell plans.* **SYN:** dire. **3** intensely painful. **4a** keen; eager. **b** *Scottish.* (of taste) keen; pungent. **5** *Dialect.* sturdy; doughty **6** *Scottish.* huge; mighty.
— ***adv.*** *Dialect.* **1** cruelly; fiercely. **2** eagerly; vigorously.
[< Old French *fel* < Vulgar Latin *fellō* fellon[1]] — **fell′ness**, *n.*

fell[4] (fel), *n.* the skin or hide of an animal. **SYN:** pelt. [Old English *fell.* See related etym. at **film**.]

fell[5] (fel), *n. Scottish.* **1** a stretch of high moorland; down. **2** a hill; mountain (now only in names). [< Scandinavian (compare Old Icelandic *fjall*)]

fel|la (fel′ə), *n. Slang.* fellow: *He has a gray flannel suit and he looks like one of those Madison Avenue advertising fellas* (New Yorker).

fel|la|gha (fə lä′gə), *n., pl.* **-ghas** or **-gha**. a Moslem nationalist guerrilla fighter in Algeria or Tunisia. [< Arabic *fallāq* (literally) outlaw]

fel|lah (fel′ə), *n., pl.* **fel|la|hin** or **fel|la|heen** (fel′ə-hēn′), **fel|lahs**. a peasant or laborer in Egypt and other Arabic-speaking countries. [< Arabic *fallāh*]

fel|la|ti|o (fə lā′shē ō, -lä′tē ō), *n.* oral stimulation of the male genital organs. [< New Latin *fellatio, -onis* < Latin *fellātus,* past participle of *fellāre, felāre* to suck]

fell|er[1] (fel′ər), *n.* **1** a person or thing that fells. **2** a part attached to a sewing machine to fell seams. [< *fell*[2] + *-er*[1]]

fell|er[2] (fel′ər), *n. Dialect.* fellow: *There was a feller here once by the name of Jim Smiley, in the winter of '49* (Mark Twain).

fell|mon|ger (fel′mung′gər, -mong′-), *n.* a person who deals in animal skins, especially sheepskins. [< *fell*[4] + *-monger*]

fell|mon|ger|ing (fel′mung′gər ing, -mong′-), *n.* the craft or occupation of a fellmonger.

fell|mon|ger|y (fel′mung′gər ē, -mong′-), *n.* = fellmongering.

fel|loe (fel′ō), *n.* the circular rim of a wheel into which the outer ends of the spokes are inserted. Also, **felly**. See picture under **spoke**[2]. [variant of *felly*[1]]

fel|low (fel′ō; *often* fel′ə *for n. 1-4*), *n., adj., v.*
— ***n.*** **1** a male person; man or boy: *Never mind, old fellow. Poor fellow!* **2** *Informal.* a young man courting a young woman; beau. **3** a person; anybody; one: *What can a fellow do? Have pity on a fellow.* **4** a friendly term of address for a dog, horse, or other domestic animal, or sometimes, another person. **5** a contemptible person: *Worth makes the man, and want of it the fellow* (Alexander Pope). **6** companion; associate; comrade: *He was cut off from his fellows.* **7** one of the same class or rank; equal; peer: *The world has not his fellow.* **8** the other one of a pair; mate; match: *I have the fellow of your glove.* **9** a person or graduate student who has a fellowship from a university or college. **10** a member of a learned society: *a Fellow of the Royal Society. Abbr:* F. **11** an incorporated member of certain British colleges. **12** a trustee in certain universities and colleges. **13** a member, as of a company or party. **14** *Obsolete.* a colleague; co-worker.
— ***adj.*** being of the same or like condition; belonging to the same class; united by the same work, interests, or aims: *fellow citizens, fellow sufferers, fellow workers. He was like a man who meets a fellow countryman in a strange continent* (Graham Greene).
— ***v.t.*** **1** to make, or represent as, an equal or match with another. **2** to produce a fellow to; match.
hail fellow well met, a very friendly: *She is not hail fellow well met; nor is she one to whom the round of committee work and administration comes ... readily* (New Scientist). **b** on intimate or overly familiar terms: *Palavering rascals, who come hail fellow well met* (Leigh Hunt). **c** a person who is unduly intimate or familiar: *Associates describe him as a good companion without being a hail fellow well met* (New York Times).
[Old English *fēolaga* < Scandinavian (compare Old Icelandic *fēlagi* partner; (literally) fee layer)]

fellow commoner, one of a former privileged class of undergraduates in certain British colleges who were permitted to dine at the table occupied by fellows or incorporated members.

Fel|low|craft (fel′ō kraft′, -kräft′), *n.* a Freemason of the second rank, above an Entered Apprentice and below a Master Mason.

fellow creature, a fellow human being.

fellow feeling, **1** = sympathy. **2** a sense of joint interest: *A fellow feeling makes one wondrous kind* (David Garrick).

fel|low|ly (fel′ō lē), *adj. British Dialect.* **1** companionable; sociable. **2** familiar.

fellow man, a fellow or kindred human being; fellow creature: *Love of one's fellow man ... is associated with an abiding sense of the dignity and worth of every individual* (Will Herberg).

fellow servant rule, the common-law principle that an employer is not to be held accountable for harm or injury done to one servant or worker because of the negligence of another.

fellow servants, **1** workers employed by the same person and engaged in and about a common undertaking. **2** servants employed by the same person.

fel|low|ship (fel′ō ship), *n., v.,* **-shiped, -ship|ing** or (*especially British*) **-shipped, -ship|ping.**
— ***n.*** **1a** companionship; friendliness; comradeship: *But keep the grasp of fellowship which warms us more than wine* / Julia Ward Howe). **b** community of interest, sentiment, or aim. **2** the state or condition of being one of a group; membership; sharing: *I have enjoyed fellowship in this club.* **3a** a group of people having the same tastes, interests, etc.; association or union of any kind; brotherhood: *the fellowship of human beings.* **b** any body of friends or equals; company. **c** a guild; corporation. **4a** a position or sum of money given to a student in a university or college to enable him to go on with his studies. **b** a foundation for the maintenance of a fellow at a university or college. **c** *Archaic.* (in Great Britain) the body of fellows collectively. **5** the relationship existing among those holding the same religious beliefs; communion. **6** *Obsolete.* the membership of a society. **7** *Obsolete.* dealing; intercourse.
— ***v.t.*** *Especially U.S.* to admit (someone) to religious fellowship.
— ***v.i.*** *Especially U.S.* to join in religious fellowship.

fellow traveler, a person sympathizing with a political movement or party, especially the Communist Party, or supporting its program, though not a member. [translation of Russian *poputchik* < *po-* along + *put′* journey, way + *-chik,* a personal suffix]

fel|low-trav|el|ing (fel′ō trav′ə ling, -trav′ling), *adj., n.* — ***adj.*** sympathizing with a movement or party, especially the Communist Party, and following its program or a similar one, without belonging to it.
— ***n.*** the attitudes, support, or other activities of a fellow traveler.

fell|side (fel′sīd′), *n. British.* the side of a high moor. [< *fell*[5] + *side*]

fel|ly[1] (fel′ē), *n., pl.* **-lies**. = felloe. [Old English *felgi,* dative of *felg*]

fel|ly[2] (fel′lē), *adv.* fiercely; cruelly. [< *fell*[3] + *-y*[1]]

fe|lo-de-se (fē′lō dē sē′, fel′ō-), *n., pl.* **fe|los-de-se** (fē′lōz dē sē′, fel′ōz-), **fe|lo|nes-de-se** (fē lō′-nēz dē sē′, fe lon′ēz-). *Law.* **1** a person who kills himself; a suicide. **2** suicide; self-murder. [< Medieval Latin (England) *felo* murderer, felon + *de se* of (him)self]

fel|on[1] (fel′ən), *n., adj.* — ***n.*** **1** a person who has been convicted of a felony; criminal. Murderers and thieves are felons. **2** *Archaic.* a villain.
— ***adj.*** cruel; fierce; wicked: *a felon blow.* [< Old French *felon* < Vulgar Latin *fellō;* uncertain origin]

fel|on[2] (fel′ən), *n.* a very painful inflammation of a finger or toe, usually near the nail; whitlow. [perhaps < unrecorded Old French *felon* ulcer < Latin *fel* gall]

felon grass, = black hellebore.

felon herb, **1** a woody, perennial, bitter herb; wormwood. **2** a weedy herb, with small summer and autumn flowers; hawkweed.

fe|lo|ni|ous (fə lō′nē əs), *adj.* **1** of or involving a felony; criminal: *to break into a house with felonious intent. A felonious homicide may be either murder or manslaughter.* **2** very wicked; villainous: *A bloody murderer, or foul felonious thief* (Shakespeare). — **fe|lo′ni|ous|ly**, *adv.* — **fe|lo′ni|ous|ness**, *n.*

fel|on|ry (fel′ən rē), *n.* **1** felons as a class. **2** the convict population of a penal colony (originally, the convict population of Australia).

fel|on|weed (fel′ən wēd), *n.* = tansy ragwort.

fel|o|ny (fel′ə nē), *n., pl.* **-nies**. any crime more serious than a misdemeanor, usually punishable in the United States by imprisonment for more than a year in a state prison, or by death. Murder, burglary, and blackmail are felonies.
compound a felony, to accept money or other payment not to prosecute a crime: *Law enforcement officials who compound a felony are subject to the full penalty of the law.*

fel|site (fel′sīt), *n.* a compact igneous rock consisting of feldspar and quartz in minute crystals. [< *fels*(par) + *-ite*[1]]

fel|sit|ic (fel sit′ik), *adj.* consisting of or containing felsite.

fel|spar (fel′spär′), *n. Especially British.* feldspar.

felt[1] (felt), *v.* past tense and past participle of **feel**: *He felt the cat's soft fur. It was felt that the picnic should be postponed.*

felt[2] (felt), *n., adj., v.* — ***n.*** **1** a cloth made by rolling and pressing together wool, hair, or fur. Felt is used to make hats, slippers, and pads. **2** something made of felt, especially a hat: *a red felt. The old man sleeping on the bed of rugs*

Pronunciation Key: hat, āge, cãre, fär; let, ēqual, tėrm; it, īce; hot, ōpen, ôrder; oil, out; cup, pu̇t, rüle; child; long; thin; ᴛʜen; zh, measure; ə represents **a** in about, **e** in taken, **i** in pencil, **o** in lemon, **u** in circus.

and felts (Matthew Arnold). **3** any material that resembles felt.
—***adj.*** made of felt: *a felt hat.*
—***v.t.*** **1** to make into felt; mat or press (fibers or threads) together. **2** to cover with felt.
—***v.i.*** to become matted together: *a felted mane.* [Old English *felt*]

felt|board (felt′bôrd′, -bōrd′), *n.* = flannel board.

felt|ed (fel′tid), *adj.* **1** matted together by or as if by felting. **2** *Botany.* composed of closely interwoven filaments or hyphae.

felt|ing (fel′ting), *n.* **1** felted cloth. **2** the act or process of making felt. **3** the materials of which felt is made.

felt pen, = felt-tip pen.

felt-tip pen (felt′tip′), a pen with a small felt tip: *[He] underlined the most compelling passages with a yellow felt-tip pen for future reference* (Time).

felt|wort (felt′wėrt′), *n.* a weed of the figwort family, with coarse, woolly leaves; mullein.

***fe|luc|ca** (fə luk′ə), *n.* a long, narrow, relatively fast ship moved by oars or lateen sails, or both, often with three masts, used for voyages along the coast in the Mediterranean and Red Seas. [< Italian *felucca* < Arabic *fulūka*]

***felucca**

fem (fem), *adj. U.S. Slang.* **1** effeminate. **2** female or feminine.

fem., **1** female. **2** feminine.

fe|male (fē′māl), *n., adj.* —***n.*** **1** a woman or girl; person of the sex that brings forth young. See syn. under **woman**. **2** an animal belonging to the sex that produces eggs or brings forth young. **3** *Botany.* **a** a flower having a pistil or pistils and no stamens. **b** a plant bearing only flowers with pistils.
—***adj.*** **1** of or having to do with women or girls: *female education. Sewing is usually a female occupation.* **2** of or belonging to the sex that produces eggs or brings forth young. Mares, cows, and hens are female animals. **3** consisting of women and girls: *female company.* **4** peculiar to or characteristic of womankind: *female charm.* **5** *Botany.* **a** (of seed plants) having flowers which contain a pistil or pistils but not stamens; pistillate. **b** denoting or having to do with any reproductive structure that produces or contains elements that need fertilization from the male element. **6** designating some part of a machine or connection into which a corresponding (male) part fits. **7** *Archaic.* womanish; weakly; effeminate: *Boys ... clap their female joints In stiff unwieldy arms* (Shakespeare).
[< Old French *femelle* < Latin *fēmella* (diminutive) < *fēmina* woman; spelling influenced by English *male*] —**fe′male|ness**, *n.*

female rhyme, = feminine rhyme.

female screw, a hollow cylindrical part having an interior spiral thread adapted to receive the thread of a male screw; internal screw.

female suffrage, = woman suffrage.

feme (fem), *n.* **1** *Law.* a woman. **2** a wife. Also, **femme**. [< Anglo-French, Old French *feme* < Latin *fēmina* woman]

fem|e|rell (fem′ə rel), *n.* a turret or lantern constructed on a roof, as in medieval architecture, to supply ventilation or for the escape of smoke; louver.

fem|i|na|cy (fem′ə nə sē), *n., pl.* **-cies**. = femininity.

fem|i|nal|i|ty (fem′ə nal′ə tē), *n., pl.* **-ties**. = femininity.

fem|i|ne|i|ty (fem′ə nē′ə tē), *n., pl.* **-ties**. = womanliness. [< Latin *fēmineus* (< *fēmina* woman) + English *-ity*]

fem|i|nie (fem′ə nē), *n. Archaic.* **1** women collectively. **2** the Amazons. **3** the country of the Amazons. [< Old French *feminie* < Latin *fēmina* woman]

fem|i|nin (fem′ə nin), *n.* = estrone. [< Latin *fēmina* woman + English *-in*]

fem|i|nine (fem′ə nin), *adj., n.* —***adj.*** **1** of women or girls; having to do with a woman or women; consisting of or carried on by women: *feminine society, feminine discussion. Jewelry and lace are mostly feminine belongings.* **2** like a woman; womanly; gentle: *feminine sympathy or intuition.* **3** like that of a woman; not suited to a man; womanish; effeminate; weak. **4** of or belonging to the female sex. **5** *Grammar.* of the gender to which certain nouns and pronouns belong. In Modern English it includes all words referring to females. "Actress," "queen," "tigress," and "cow" are feminine nouns.
—***n.*** **1** the feminine gender. **2** a word or form in the feminine gender. *Abbr:* fem.
[< Old French *feminin*, learned borrowing from Latin *fēminīnus* < *fēmina* woman] —**fem′i|nine|ly**, *adv.* —**fem′i|nine|ness**, *n.*

feminine ending, **1** an ending in which a line of verse closes with an extra unaccented syllable instead of the normal accented syllable. *Example:* "O Cassius, Brutus gave the word too earl(y)." **2** *Grammar.* a termination proper to the feminine gender.

feminine rhyme, a rhyme of two syllables of which the second is unstressed, as in *motion, notion,* or of three syllables of which the second and third are unstressed, as in *happily, snappily.*

feminine sign, one of the even signs of the zodiac, as the second (Taurus), fourth (Cancer), or sixth (Virgo).

fem|i|nin|ism (fem′ə nə niz′əm), *n.* **1** the state of being feminine. **2** a feminine or women's word or expression.

fem|i|nin|i|ty (fem′ə nin′ə tē), *n., pl.* **-ties**. **1** feminine quality or condition; womanliness: *As the car is a symbol of masculinity, so is the house a symbol of femininity* (Harper's). **2** women; womankind.

fem|i|nism (fem′ə niz əm), *n.* **1** the doctrine that favors more rights and activities for women in their economic, social, political, and private lives. **2** a movement to secure these rights. **3** the qualities of females. **4** the presence of specifically feminine characteristics in the male.

fem|i|nist (fem′ə nist), *n., adj.* —***n.*** a person who believes in or favors feminism.
—***adj.*** believing in or favoring feminism.

fem|i|nis|tic (fem′ə nis′tik), *adj.* = feminist.

fe|min|i|ty (fi min′ə tē), *n.* **1** the doctrine favoring extension of the activities of women in social and political life. **2** the qualities of females.

fem|i|ni|za|tion (fem′ə nə zā′shən), *n.* the act of making feminine or womanish.

fem|i|nize (fem′ə nīz), *v.t.,* **-nized, -niz|ing.** to make effeminate or womanish: *The art of poetry, historically one of the most masculine of pursuits, has, to an alarming degree, become feminized in the American consciousness* (Wall Street Journal).

Fem Lib, or **Fem|lib** (fem′lib′), *n. Informal.* the Women's Liberation movement: *Should the conditions of Femlib take over, the cultural fallout will be stupendous* (Fred Saidy).

femme (fâm), *n.* **1** *French.* **a** a woman. **b** a wife. **2** = feme.

femme de cham|bre (fâm′ də shäɴ′brə), *French.* **1** a chambermaid. **2** a lady's maid.

femme fa|tale (fâm′ fâ tâl′), *pl.* **femmes fa|tales** (fâm′ fâ tâl′). *French.* a seductive woman for whom men are willing to abandon careers, ties, and responsibilities and who feels no pity or compunction in return; seductress: *... the femme fatale operating on the hapless male* (New York Times).

fem|o|ra (fem′ər ə), *n.* a plural of **femur**.

fem|o|ral (fem′ər əl), *adj.* of or in the region of the femur or thigh: *a femoral artery.* [< Latin *femur, femoris* thigh + English *-al*[1]]

fem|o|ro|tib|i|al index, (fem′ər ō tib′ē əl), *Anthropology.* the length of the tibia expressed in percentage of the length of the femur.

femto-, *combining form.* one quadrillionth (10^{-15}) of a ______: *Femtogram = one quadrillionth of a gram.* [< Danish *femten* fifteen]

fe|mur (fē′mər), *n., pl.* **fe|murs, fem|o|ra** (fem′ər ə). **1** = thighbone. **2** a corresponding bone in the leg or hindlimb of other animals. **3** the third section (from the body) of the leg of an insect. [< Latin *femur, femoris* thigh]

fen[1] (fen), *n.* low, wet land; marsh. It is covered wholly or partially with shallow, often stagnant water. *The margin of the broad, reedy fen* (Robert Louis Stevenson). **SYN:** swamp, bog. [Old English *fenn*]

fen[2] (fun), *n., pl.* **fen**. a Chinese unit of money equal to 1/10 of a chiao, or about 1/2 cent. [< Chinese *fen*]

fen|ber|ry (fen′ber′ē, -bər-), *n., pl.* **-ries**. the small cranberry.

fence** (fens), *n., v.,* **fenced, fenc|ing.** —n.*** **1** a railing or wall put around a yard, garden, field, farm, or building area, to show where it ends or to keep people or animals out or in. Most fences are made of wood, wire, or metal. A stone fence is a wall. A fence of growing bushes is a hedge. *Good fences make good neighbors* (Robert Frost). **2a** a person who buys and sells stolen goods. **b** a place where stolen goods are bought and sold. **3** a guard, guide, or gauge designed to regulate the movements of a tool or machine. **4** a low vertical fin on the upper surface of a swept-back wing on certain aircraft to prevent a lateral flow of air along the wing, and to increase stability at high speeds. **5** = fencing. **6** skill or adroitness in argument or repartee. **7** *Archaic.* a defense; bulwark.
—***v.t.*** **1** to put a fence around; enclose with a fence; keep out or in with a fence. **2** *Figurative.* to separate as by a fence; keep apart or at a distance: *The patents were used to fence in and block off other manufacturers.* **3** to defend; protect; guard. **4** to buy or sell (stolen goods); dispose of (a stolen item or items): *Convinced that money is the problem, [she] hatches a ... plot to rob a jewelry store, fence the proceeds through her favorite newsboy* (Time). **5** *Informal.* (in ice hockey) to send (a player) to the penalty box for breaking a rule. **6** *British.* to declare (a forest, river, or other area) closed against hunting or fishing. **7** *Archaic.* to keep out; ward off; exclude. —***v.i.*** **1a** to practice the use of foils or swords as an art or sport. **b** to fight with swords or foils. **2** *Figurative.* to deal with a debater or questioner in the manner of a fencer, by evading or parrying the other's moves: *The hostile witness kept fencing with the questions put to him by the cross-examiner.* **3** to buy or sell stolen goods. **4** *Obsolete.* to provide a defense.

come (or **get**) **off the fence**, to stop being neutral; take sides: *Within the Communist bloc, Peiping is already backed by Albania, North Korea, and North Vietnam, although Ho Chi Minh may have come off the fence only because of geographical necessity* (Atlantic).

mend one's fences, a to look after one's political interests at home, as in preparation for renomination: *An early adjournment is deemed essential in order that the members may go home to mend their fences* (H. L. West). **b** to improve one's relations and popularity in any area: *Even most critics conceded that he did much to mend U.S. fences in Latin America* (Newsweek).

on both (or **opposite**) **sides of the fence**, on the two sides of a dispute or controversy: *A campaign by political, financial, and commercial groups in Salisbury on both sides of the UDI [Unilateral Declaration of Independence] fence is bringing pressure on the British Government to settle with Mr. Smith before the end of the year* (Manchester Guardian Weekly).

on the fence, not having made up one's mind which side to take; doubtful; hesitating; uncommitted: *Editors for a long time on the fence ... occasionally undertake ... to sit as censors upon their fatigued and dusty brethren* (Richmond Whig).

refuse one's fences, *British.* to avoid danger or risk: *It was time that Britain stopped refusing its fences and really got down to solving its problems at home and not looking for escape routes* (London Times).

ride (the) fence, *Western U.S.* to ride along the fence of a ranch to inspect and keep it in repair: *The cowboys roped and branded cattle and rode fence for the rancher.*

rush one's fences, *British.* to proceed too hurriedly: *He [an organist] unfolded the argument with exemplary clarity and discipline, never rushing his fences or playing for obvious dramatic effect* (Joan Chissell).

straddle (or **walk**) **the fence**, to be on the fence; not make up one's mind which side to take: *The Russians have tried to straddle the fence—sending military equipment to Hanoi while only verbally chilling their relations with Washington* (New York Times). *If [he] attempts to walk the fence and says nothing, the Parliament will surely have something to say* (New York Times). [variant of *defence*] —**fence′less**, *adj.* —**fence′less|ness**, *n.*

***fence**
definition 1

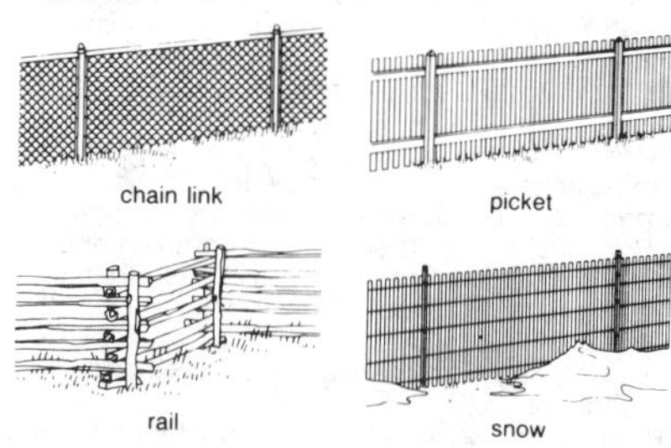

fence lizard, either of two varieties of small North American lizards with dark bands or stripes and, in the male, blue throat and sides.

fence-mend|ing (fens′men′ding), *n., adj. U.S. Informal.* —***n.*** the restoration or repair of good relations, friendship, or popularity in a political constituency, with a foreign country, or group: *The ambassador's job was chiefly fence-mending.*

—*adj.* restoring or intended to restore good relations with a political constituency, foreign nation, or group: *The Senator made a fence-mending trip across his state.*

fence-off (fens′ôf′, -of′), *n. Fencing.* an additional match to break a tie.

fen|cer (fen′sər), *n.* **1** a person who knows how to fight with a sword or foil. **2** *Australian.* a person who makes or mends fences. **3** a horse that jumps fences; steeplechaser.

fence row, *U.S.* a fence with the line of shrubs and other vegetation growing in its protection.

fence season, *British.* a closed season for hunting and fishing; fence time.

fence-sit|ter (fens′sit′ər), *n. Informal.* a person, group, or nation reserving decision to join either side in a controversy.

fence-sit|ting (fens′sit′ing), *adj., n. Informal.* **—*adj.*** uncommitted: **—*n.*** the position or policy of a fence-sitter.

fence-strad|dler (fens′strad′lər), *n. U.S. Informal.* a person who tries to get along with both sides in a controversy.

fence-strad|dling (fens′strad′ling), *n., adj. U.S. Informal.* **—*n.*** the attempt to get along with both sides in a controversy: *The motives behind neutrality are noble or realistic according as one views neutralism as a moral force ... or as a policy of fence-straddling, pure and simple* (Atlantic). **—*adj.*** pleasing or intended to please both sides in a controversy.

fence time, = fence season.

fen|chene (fen′chēn), *n.* an oil of the terpene series resembling camphene. It is prepared by boiling fenchyl chloride with aniline. *Formula:* $C_{10}H_{16}$

fen|chone (fen′chōn), *n.* a ketone, isomeric with camphor, which it resembles in general chemical properties. The dextro-form occurs in fennel oil, the levo-form in thuja oil. *Formula:* $C_{10}H_{16}O$ [< *fench*(yl) + *-one*]

fen|chyl (fen′chəl), *n.* the levo-form of fenchone. [< German *Fenchel* fennel + English *-yl*]

fen|ci|ble (fen′sə bəl), *adj., n.* **—*adj.*** **1** that can be defended. **2** capable of making defense. **—*n.*** a soldier enlisted for defensive service in his own country only.

fencibles, British volunteer regiments of the late 1700's and early 1800's organized for local emergency defense: *Officers of the fencibles and the militia ... rank together* (General Regulations and Orders for the Army).

***fenc|ing** (fen′sing), *n.* **1** the art or sport of fighting with swords or foils: *Fencing was a popular form of dueling in France when men carried swords.* SYN: swordplay. **2** *Figurative.* the act or practice of parrying the points of one's opponent in a debate, discussion, or argument. **3** material for fences: *A pile of fencing lay about the yard ready to be erected.* **4** fences: *Beautiful white fencing enclosed the pastures.*

***fencing**
definition 1

fencing master, a person who gives instruction in fencing.

fencing stick, a stick, as of hickory with a basketwork guard for the hand, used in fencing.

fen cress, = water cress.

fend (fend), *v., n.* **—*v.i.*** **1** to make an effort; strive to do something: *We may strive ... and fend, but it's little we can do* (George Eliot). **2** to defend oneself. **—*v.t.*** *Archaic.* to defend; resist. **—*n.*** *Scottish.* a shift or effort which one makes for oneself.

fend for oneself, to provide for oneself; get along by one's own efforts: *Most baby fishes have to fend for themselves.*

fend off, to ward off; keep off: *He fended off blows with his arm. New nations cling to nationalism as an ideological weapon to fend off the encroachments of the great powers* (Richard J. Barnet).

[variant of *defend*]

fend|er (fen′dər), *n.* **1** a guard or protection over the wheel of a car, truck, bicycle, or other wheeled vehicle, that protects the wheel and reduces splashing in wet weather; mudguard. **2** a rope pad or cushion, log, piece of plastic, or rubber tire, put between a boat and a pier, wharf, or other vessel to prevent damage to the side of the boat when docking, towing, or pushing. **3** a metal guard, frame, or screen in front of a fireplace to keep hot coals and sparks from the room. **4** a cowcatcher or other device at the front of a locomotive or streetcar, to reduce injury should an animal or person be struck. **5** *Especially British.* a metal bar or frame on the front or rear of a locomotive or streetcar, to lessen damage in case of collision. **6** a piece of leather attached to a saddle to protect the rider's legs. **7** anything that protects by being between or keeping something off. [probably < *fend* + *-er*[1]]

fender bar, a long fender of wood hung over a ship's side just above the water line to prevent chafing against a dock.

fend|er-bend|er (fen′dər ben′dər), *n. Slang.* **1** a driver involved in an automobile collision: *Compensating those who have suffered injuries in car accidents—by trying to figure out which fender-bender was at fault* (Fred P. Graham). **2** an automobile collision.

fen|dil|late (fen′də lāt), *v.t.*, **-lat|ed, -lat|ing.** to split or crack slightly in many places. [< French *fendiller* (with English *-ate*[1]) < *fendre* split < Latin *findere*] —**fen′dil|la′tion**, *n.*

fen|es|tel|la (fen′ə stel′ə), *n., pl.* **-es|tel|lae** (-ə stel′ē). a small window. [< Latin *fenestella* (diminutive) < *fenestra* window]

fe|nes|tra (fə nes′trə), *n., pl.* **-trae** (-trē). **1** a small opening in a bone. **2** a transparent spot on the wings of moths and certain other insects. **3** any opening resembling a window. [< Latin *fenestra* window]

fe|nes|tral (fə nes′trəl), *adj.* of or having to do with a fenestra; like a window.

fenestra ovalis, an opening on the inner wall of the tympanum of the ear, leading into the vestibule. [< New Latin *fenestra ovalis* oval window]

fenestra rotunda, an opening on the inner wall of the tympanum of the ear, leading into the cochlea. [< New Latin *fenestra rotunda* round window]

fe|nes|trate (fə nes′trāt), *adj.* **1** having windows. **2** having fenestrae. [< Latin *fenestrāre* (with English *-ate*[1]) to furnish with windows < *fenestra* window]

fe|nes|trat|ed (fə nes′trā tid), *adj.* = fenestrate.

fenestrated membrane, the outer layer of the inner coat of an artery.

fen|es|tra|tion (fen′ə strā′shən), *n.* **1a** the arrangement of windows in a building, especially for the purpose of providing light for the interior. **b** the use of windows as decorative elements of a facade. **2** *Medicine.* the operation of making an opening into the labyrinth or semicircular canal of the ear to eliminate deafness caused by obstruction of sound waves. **3** *Anatomy.* the process or condition of being perforated.

fen fire, = will-o'-the-wisp.

feng|shui or **feng-shui** (fung′shwā′), *n.* **1** (in Chinese folklore) a system of spirit influences, good and evil, which inhabit the natural features of landscapes. **2** a kind of geomancy for dealing with these influences in determining sites for houses and graves. [< Chinese *feng-shui* < *feng* wind + *shui* water]

Fe|ni|an (fē′nē ən, fēn′yən), *n., adj.* **—*n.*** **1** a member of the Fenian Brotherhood. **2** a member of the Fianna. **—*adj.*** of or having to do with the Fenians. [< Irish *fēinn*, alteration of *fiann* the Fianna]

Fenian Brotherhood, an Irish secret organization founded in the United States about 1858 for the purpose of overthrowing English rule in Ireland.

Fenian cycle, a mass of legends about a group of Irish warriors of the 300's and 400's, comparable to the Arthurian cycle of legends.

fen|land (fen′land′), *n.* a swampy area.

fen|man (fen′mən), *n., pl.* **-men.** an inhabitant of fens or marshes.

fen|nec or **fen|nek** (fen′ek), *n.* a small, pale orange-brown, desert fox of North Africa and Syria, having large, pointed ears. [< Arabic *fanak*]

fen|nel (fen′əl), *n.* **1** a tall perennial plant with yellow flowers. It belongs to the parsley family. Its aromatic seeds and leaves have a licorice taste and are used in medicine and cooking. **2** its seeds. **3** any one of several similar plants of other genera, such as the giant fennel. [Old English *finul, fenol* < Vulgar Latin *fēnuclum* for Latin *fēniculum* < *fēnum*, earlier *faenum* hay (apparently because of its odor)]

fen|nel|flow|er (fen′əl flou′ər), *n.* **1** any plant of a genus of herbs of the crowfoot family, especially a species whose seeds are used in the Orient as a seasoning and medicine. **2** its flower.

fennel giant, a tall plant of the parsley family; giant fennel.

fennel oil, a colorless or yellowish, aromatic, volatile oil distilled from the seed of the fennel, used in medicine, perfumes, liqueurs, and as a flavoring.

fennel seed, **1** the seed of the fennel. **2** the seed of the fennelflower.

fen|ny (fen′ē), *adj.* **1** marshy; swampy; boggy. **2** growing or living in fens: *a fenny snake* (Shakespeare). [Old English *fennig* < *fenn* fen]

Fen|rir (fen′rir), *n. Norse Mythology.* the wolflike monster, son of Loki, that killed Odin.

fent (fent), *n.* **1** a remnant (of cloth). **2** *Especially British Dialect.* = placket (def. 1). [< Old French *fente* < *fendre* to split < Latin *findere*]

fen thrush, = missel thrush.

fen|u|greek (fen′yu̇ grēk), *n.* an annual Asian and southern European plant of the pea family, having aromatic, mucilaginous seeds which are used in making curry, and also in medicine. [< Old French *fenugrec* < Latin *fēnugraecum*, for *fēnum Graecum* Greek hay < *fēnum* hay (apparently because of its odor)]

feoff (*n.* fēf; *v.* fef, fēf), *n., v.* **—*n.*** = fief. **—*v.t.*** to put in legal possession of a fief or fee; enfeoff: *When Arthur had thus his Knights feoffed* (William Caxton). [< Anglo-French *feoffer*, Old French *fieuffer* < *fieu*, or *fieff* a fief; see etym. under **fee**]

feoff|ee (fef ē′, fēf-), *n.* a person who is invested with a feudal estate.

feoff|fer (fef′ər, fē′fər), *n.* a person who grants a fief or fee.

feoff|ment (fef′mənt, fēf′-), *n.* the act of investing with a fief or fee.

feof|for (fef′ər, fē′fər), *n.* = feoffer.

FEPA (no periods), Fair Employment Practices Act.

FEPC (no periods), Fair Employment Practices Committee.

FERA (no periods), Federal Emergency Relief Administration.

fe|ra|cious (fə rā′shəs), *adj.* bearing abundantly; fruitful; prolific: *a world so feracious, teeming with endless results* (Thomas Carlyle). [< Latin *ferāx, -ācis* (with English *-ous*) < *ferre* bear]

fe|rac|i|ty (fə ras′ə tē), *n.* fruitfulness; productiveness.

fe|rae na|tu|rae (fir′ē nə tůr′ē, -tyůr′-), *Law.* animals, such as deer or pheasants, living in a wild state, as contrasted with domesticated animals, such as cows or horses. [< Latin *ferae nātūrae* (literally) of a wild nature]

Fer|a|ghan (fer′ə gon), *n.* a finely woven Persian rug, usually small, with soft colors and a complex design. [< *Feragana, Ferghana*, a region in central Asia, where it originated]

fe|ral[1] (fir′əl), *adj.* **1** having reverted from domestication back to the original wild or untamed state: *The dovecot pigeon ... has become feral in several places* (Charles Darwin). **2** wild; untamed; uncultivated: *A corresponding variability is as normal to some purely feral animals as to the semidomesticated species* (Coues and Allen). **3** characteristic of wild beasts; brutal; savage: *feral hostility.* [< Latin *fera* beast (< *ferus* wild) + English *-al*[1]]

fe|ral[2] (fir′əl), *adj.* **1** of or having to do with the dead; funereal; gloomy. **2** deadly; fatal: *feral diseases* (Thomas Burton). [< Latin *fērālis* funereal]

fe|rash (fə räsh′), *n.* a servant in the East Indies employed to spread carpets, pitch tents, and the like, and in a house to do the work of a chambermaid. [Anglo-Indian < Hindi *farrāsh* < Arabic]

fer|bam (fėr′bam), *n.* an iron carbamate used as a spray to kill fungus, especially on roses and peach trees. [< Latin *ferrum* iron + English (dimethyldithiocar)*-bam*(ic acid), a chemical substance (because it is the iron salt of the acid)]

fer|ber|ite (fėr′bə rīt), *n.* a tungsten ore consisting of compounds of tungsten with iron. *Formula:* $FeWO_4$ [< German *Ferberit* < Rudolf *Ferber*, a German mineralogist of the 1800's + *-it* -ite[1]]

fer-de-lance (fãr′də läns′), *n.* a large, very poisonous snake of tropical America, related to the rattlesnake and growing up to eight feet long. [< French *fer-de-lance* iron (tip) of a lance]

fere[1] (fir), *n. Archaic.* **1** a companion; comrade: *Ha' we lost the goodliest fere of all ...?* (Ezra Pound). **2** a husband or wife; mate: *Paris ... took thee, the widow, as his fere* (Bayard Taylor). [Old English *gefēra* < *gi-* together + base of *faran* go, travel]

fere[2] (fir), *adj. Scottish.* able; strong; sound; healthy: *I trust to find ye baith hale and fere* (Scott). [< Scandinavian (compare Old Icelandic *fœrr*)]

fer|e|to|ry (fer′ə tôr′ē, -tōr′-), *n., pl.* **-ries.** **1** a portable shrine for relics. **2** a room or chapel set aside for such a shrine or shrines. **3** = bier. [alteration of Middle English *fertre* < Old French *fiertre* < Latin *feretrum* < Greek *phéretron* bier <

Pronunciation Key: hat, āge, cãre, fär; let, ēqual, tėrm; it, īce; hot, ōpen, ôrder; oil, out; cup, pu̇t, rüle; child; long; thin; ᴛʜen; zh, measure; ə represents a in about, e in taken, i in pencil, o in lemon, u in circus.

phérein to bear]

fer|e|trum (fer′ə trəm), *n., pl.* **-tra** (-trə). a portable shrine for relics; feretory.

fer|gu|son|ite (fėr′gə sə nīt), *n.* a mineral containing yttrium and other rare elements, occurring in pegmatites. [< Robert *Ferguson,* of Raith, Scotland + *-ite*[1]]

fe|ri|a[1] (fir′ē ə), *n., pl.* **-ri|as**. *Ecclesiastical.* an ordinary weekday as opposed to a holiday or festival. [< Late Latin *fēria* day of the week < Latin, holiday]

fe|ri|a[2] (fer′ē ə; *Spanish* fe′rē ä), *n., pl.* **-ri|as**. a local fair in Spain or Latin America, usually held in connection with a church festival or holiday: *... the revelry following the feria at Seville* (Time). [< Spanish *feria* < Vulgar Latin *fēria* holiday, market fair < Late Latin *fēria;* see etym. under **feria**[1]]

fe|ri|ae (fir′ē ē), *n.pl. Latin.* (in ancient Rome) holidays; festival days.

fe|ri|al (fir′ē əl), *adj.* **1** having to do with a holiday. **2** *Ecclesiastical.* having to do with weekdays not set apart as festivals.

fe|rine (fir′īn, -in), *adj.* wild; feral. [< Latin *ferīnus* < *fera* wild beast < *ferus* wild] **—fer′ine|ly**, *adv.*

Fe|rin|gi or **Fe|rin|ghee** (fə ring′gē), *n.* a European or a person of European descent in India, especially a Portuguese born in India (usually used in an unfriendly way). [< Persian *Firangī,* or < Arabic *Firanjī* < *firanj* < Old French *Franc* a Frank]

fer|i|ty (fer′ə tē), *n.* **1** wild or savage state. **2** ferocity; savagery. [< Latin *feritās* < *ferus* wild, savage]

fer|ly (fėr′lē), *n., pl.* **-lies**. *Scottish.* something wonderful; marvel: *Where ye gaun, ye crawlin' ferly?* (Robert Burns). [Old English *fǣrlic* sudden < *fǣr* peril; (later) fear]

fer|ma|ta (fer mä′tä), *n. Music.* **1** a pause or rest of indefinite length. **2** the sign for this; hold. [< Italian *fermata*]

fer|ment (*v.* fər ment′; *n.* fėr′ment), *v., n.* **—*v.i.*** **1** to undergo a gradual chemical change in which substances, especially bacteria or yeast, change sugar into alcohol and produce carbon dioxide. Vinegar is formed when cider ferments. **2** to be excited; seethe with agitation or unrest: *His mind was fermenting with plans for the vacation.*
—*v.t.* **1** to cause to ferment. Enzymes help ferment animal and vegetable matter. *Yeasts often ferment food, or make it alcoholic* (John T. R. Nickerson). **2** to act on as a ferment. **3** *Figurative.* to cause unrest in; excite; agitate: *the Christianity which fermented Europe* (Emerson). **4** *Figurative.* to inflame; foment; exacerbate.
—*n.* **1** a substance that causes others to ferment. Ferments are of two kinds: organized ferments and unorganized ferments. Yeast is a ferment. Enzymes are ferments. **2** the act or process of fermenting; fermentation. **3** *Figurative.* excitement; agitation; unrest; tumult: *The school was in a ferment. Rumors of war caused ferment throughout the country.*
[< Latin *fermentāre* < *fermentum* leaven, related to *fervere* to boil]

fer|ment|a|bil|i|ty (fər men′tə bil′ə tē), *n.* the quality of being fermentable.

fer|ment|a|ble (fər men′tə bəl), *adj.* that can be fermented: *The first step in brewing beer is "malting," a procedure which partly converts barley starch into fermentable sugar* (Scientific American).

fer|men|ta|tion (fėr′men tā′shən), *n.* **1** the act or process of fermenting: *Fermentation causes milk to sour and bread to rise.* SYN: effervescence. **2** a chemical change in an organic compound caused by a ferment: *The fermentation of milk is necessary in the making of cheese.* **3** *Figurative.* excitement; agitation; unrest; ferment. SYN: commotion.

fermentation tube, a tube filled with a culture medium inoculated with bacteria, in which the gases that are formed collect in a closed arm of the tube where they can be measured and tested for composition.

fer|men|ta|tive (fər men′tə tiv), *adj.* **1** tending to cause or undergo fermentation. **2** developed by fermentation: *... with the bacteria we have to use a good microscope and examine some fermentative reactions* (N. W. Pirie). **—fer|men′ta|tive|ly**, *adv.*

fer|ment|er (fər men′tər), *n.* **1** a vessel in which a ferment is raised. **2** a substance causing fermentation; ferment.

fer|men|tum (fər men′təm), *n.* in the medieval church, a portion of a consecrated wafer reserved by a bishop and brought to a priest about to say Mass, as a token of Christian communion.

fer|mi (fėr′mē), *n. Physics.* a unit of length, 10^{-13} centimeters. [< Enrico *Fermi,* 1901-1954, an Italian-born American nuclear physicist]

Fer|mi-Di|rac statistics (fėr′mē də rak′), a statistical theory in quantum mechanics which holds that in the distribution of nuclear particles of a given type, only one of a set of identical particles may occupy a particular quantum-mechanical state. [< Enrico *Fermi,* 1901-1954 + Paul *Dirac,* born 1902, a British physicist]

fer|mi|on (fėr′mē on), *n.* (in quantum mechanics) any of a class of elementary particles, including protons, neutrons, and electrons, only one of which can occupy a given state at one time. [< Enrico *Fermi* + *-on,* as in *electron*]

***fer|mi|um** (fėr′mē əm), *n.* a rare, radioactive, chemical element. It is a metallic element produced artifically from plutonium or uranium. [< New Latin *fermium* < Enrico *Fermi;* see etym. under **fermi**]

***fermium**

symbol	atomic number	mass number
Fm	100	257

***fern** (fėrn), *n.* any one of a group of plants that have roots, stems, and feathery leaves, but do not have flowers or seeds. The plant reproduces by means of spores, which grow in little brown clusters on the backs of the leaves. *Maidenhair, adder's-tongue, spleenwort, osmund, and brake are ferns.* [Old English *fearn*] **—fern′like′**, *adj.*

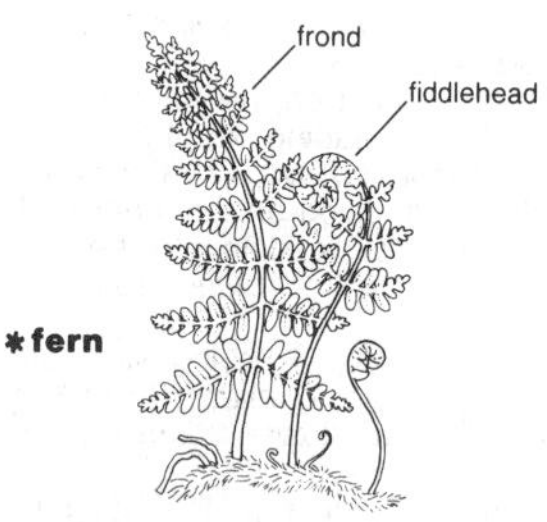

***fern**

Fer|nan|di|no (fėr′nän dē′nō), *n., pl.* **-nos**. an inhabitant of Fernando Po, an island near the coast of western Africa.

fern|bird (fėrn′bėrd′), *n.* a small perching bird of New Zealand, usually placed with the warblers of the Old World.

fern brake, a thicket of ferns.

ferned (fėrnd), *adj.* abounding in ferns.

fern|er|y (fėr′nər ē, fėrn′rē), *n., pl.* **-er|ies**. **1** a place where ferns grow. **2** a container in which ferns are grown for ornament.

fern seed, the spores of ferns, formerly supposed to produce an invisible seed that had the power to make persons invisible.

fern-tree jacaranda (fėrn′trē′), a tall jacaranda, popular in the southern United States, that produces clusters of small, fernlike leaves which it sheds in early spring. In late spring, it produces large clusters of bluish-violet flowers.

fern|wort (fėrn′wėrt′), *n.* any one of the pteridophytes.

fern|y (fėr′nē), *adj.* **1** of ferns. **2** like ferns. **3** overgrown with ferns: *a ferny dell.*

fe|ro|cious (fə rō′shəs), *adj.* **1** very cruel; fierce; savage: *The bear's ferocious growl terrified the hunter.* SYN: ruthless, brutal, murderous, pitiless, barbarous. See syn. under **fierce**. **2** *Informal, Figurative.* intense: *a ferocious headache.* [< Latin *ferōx, -ōcis* (with English *-ous*) fierce < *ferus* wild] **—fe|ro′cious|ly**, *adv.* **—fe|ro′cious|ness**, *n.*

fe|roc|i|ty (fə ros′ə tē), *n., pl.* **-ties**. **1** the quality or state of being ferocious; great cruelty; savage behavior; fierceness: *The wolves fought with bloodthirsty ferocity.* SYN: brutality, inhumanity. **2** a savage or cruel act. [< Latin *ferōcitās* < *ferōx, -ōcis* fierce < *ferus* wild]

-ferous, *suffix added to nouns to form adjectives.* producing; containing; conveying, as in *metalliferous, odoriferous.* [< Latin *-fer* (< *ferre* to bear) + English *-ous*]

Fer|ra|rese (fer′ə rēz′, -rēs′), *adj., n.* **—*adj.*** of or having to do with the city of Ferrara in Italy, noted as the center of a school of Renaissance painting.
—*n.* a native or inhabitant of Ferrara.

fer|rate (fer′āt), *n. Chemistry.* a salt of ferric acid. [< *ferr*(ic) + *-ate*[2]]

fer|re|dox|in (fer′ə dok′sin), *n.* an iron-rich protein present in anaerobic bacteria and in green plants, and thought to be the agent of primary energy-transfer process, especially in photosynthesis. [< Latin *ferrum* iron + Greek *dóxa* glory + English *-in*]

fer|re|ous (fer′ē əs), *adj.* of or consisting of iron; having to do with or resembling iron. [< Latin *ferreus* (with English *-ous*) < *ferrum* iron]

fer|ret[1] (fer′it), *n., v., adj.* **—*n.*** **1a** a white or yellowish-white animal related to the weasel, domesticated and used for killing rats and driving rabbits from their holes, found in Europe. It is the domesticated form of the European polecat. **b** = black-footed ferret. **2** *Figurative.* a person who ferrets or searches out, such as a detective or investigator: *The Treasury ... decided to put its ferrets in to look at the whole setup* (Sunday Times).
—*v.t.* **1** to hunt with ferrets. **2** *Figurative.* to drive from, off, or out of a place: *Measures were accordingly taken ... to ferret this vermin brood [buccaneers]out of the colonies* (Washington Irving). **3** *Figurative.* to hunt; search out; discover: *It took the detectives over a year to ferret out the criminal.*
—*v.i.* **1** to hunt with ferrets. **2** *Figurative.* to search about; rummage: *to ferret among the ruins.*
—*adj.* designed to search or pry with antennas and other electronic equipment: *a ferret ship, ferret cars, a ferret satellite. "Ferret" orbiters ... listen to each other's radio messages* (Science News).
[< Old French *furet,* or *fuiret* (diminutive) < *fuiron* < Late Latin *fūrō, -ōnis* ferret, probably < Latin *fūr* thief] **—fer′ret|er**, *n.*

fer|ret[2] (fer′it), *n.* a stout, narrow tape, used for bindings and shoestrings. [alteration of obsolete Italian *fioretto* floss silk (diminutive) < *fiore* flower < Latin *flōs, flōris*]

ferret badger, a small omnivorous mammal of southern and eastern Asia, having an elongated body and short tail.

fer|ret|ing (fer′ə ting), *n.* a stout, narrow tape; ferret.

fer|ret|like (fer′it līk′), *adj.* resembling or suggesting a ferret; ferrety.

fer|ret|y (fer′ə tē), *adj.* = ferretlike.

fer|ri|age (fer′ē ij), *n.* **1** the act or business of ferrying. **2** the charge for ferrying.

fer|ric (fer′ik), *adj.* **1** of or containing iron, especially trivalent iron. **2** of or extracted from iron. [< Latin *ferrum* iron + English *-ic*]

ferric chloride, a water-soluble, crystalline compound used widely in industry, especially in photography and the manufacturing of pigments. It is also used in the treatment of certain skin disorders. *Formula:* $FeCl_3 \cdot 6H_2O$

ferric hydroxide, hydrated ferric oxide; a brown precipitate obtained by the addition of ferrous sulfate to an ammonia solution, used in the manufacture of pigments and in medicines. *Formula:* $Fe(OH)_3$

ferric oxide, a compound occurring naturally as the mineral hematite and produced synthetically as a reddish or brown powder; iron oxide. It is used as a pigment (rouge or Venetian red) and as an abrasive. *Formula:* Fe_2O_3

ferric sulfate, a grayish-white or yellow powder used in water purification, as a textile dye, and as a disinfectant. *Formula:* $Fe_2O_{12}S_3$

fer|ri|cy|an|ic acid (fer′i sī an′ik), an acid occurring in the form of its salts (ferricyanides). *Formula:* $H_3Fe(CN)_6$ [< Latin *ferrum* iron + English *cyanic*]

fer|ri|cy|a|nide (fer′i sī′ə nīd), *n.* a salt of ferricyanic acid that contains the trivalent group $Fe(CN)_6$.

fer|rif|er|ous (fe rif′ər əs), *adj.* containing iron; producing or yielding iron. [< Latin *ferrum* iron + English *-ferous*]

fer|ri|mag|net (fer′i mag′nit), *n.* a ferrimagnetic substance or material.

fer|ri|mag|net|ic (fer′i mag net′ik), *adj., n.* **—*adj.*** of or characteristic of ferrimagnetism or a substance that exhibits ferrimagnetism: *a ferrimagnetic crystal. Because ferrimagnetic substances are electrically nonconducting ... they have proved highly useful material for the coating of magnetic tape, computer memory cores, and other important Electronic Age components* (Time). **—*n.*** a substance that exhibits ferrimagnetism.

fer|ri|mag|net|ism (fer′i mag′nə tiz əm), *n.* a form of magnetism displayed by ferrites and certain other compounds in which neighboring ions align in an antiparallel manner in a magnetic field. Ferrimagnetism is similar to but not identical with ferromagnetism.

Fer|ris wheel (fer′is), a large, revolving wheel with seats hanging from its rim, used in carnivals and amusement parks, and at fairs. [American English < George W. G. *Ferris,* 1859-1896, an American engineer, the inventor]

fer|rite (fer′īt), *n.* **1** a mixed oxide of iron and other elements that is a poor conductor of electricity, used especially where magnetic materials are needed in which eddy current losses are small. **2** almost pure metallic iron, separated out from iron carbides in the cooling of steel. **3** *Geology.* a substance, not analyzable but probably containing iron, that occurs in red or yellow particles in certain rocks. [< Latin *ferrum* iron]

fer|rit|ic (fe rit′ik), *adj.* containing or resembling ferrite: *ferritic stainless steel.*

fer|ri|tin (fer′ə tin), *n.* a protein containing iron, synthesized in the liver for use by the body. [< Latin *ferrum* iron + English *-ite*[1] + *-in*]

fer|ri|ti|za|tion (fer′ə tə zā′shən), *n.* alteration of a mineral into ferrite.

ferro-, *combining form.* **1** alloy of iron and ——: *Ferrochromium = an alloy of iron and chromium.* **2** that contains iron: *Ferroconcrete = concrete that contains iron.* [< Latin *ferrum* iron]

fer|ro|al|loy (fer′ō al′oi), *n.* an alloy of iron with another element such as tungsten, manganese, chromium, or vanadium, for use as a means of introducing one or more of these elements into molten steel in order to remove impurities and harden the steel.

fer|ro|a|lu|mi|num (fer′ō ə lü′mə nəm), *n.* an alloy of iron and aluminum.

fer|ro|cal|cite (fer′ō kal′sīt), *n.* a variety of calcite that contains carbonate of iron and turns brown on exposure.

fer|ro|cene (fer′ō sēn), *n.* an orange, water-insoluble, crystalline compound, used especially to improve the burning qualities of petroleum fuels. *Formula:* $(C_5H_5)_2Fe$ [< *ferro-* + *c*(yclopentadi)*ene*]

fer|ro|ce|ri|um (fer′ō sir′ē əm), *n.* = misch.

fer|ro|chrome (fer′ō krōm′), *n.* an alloy of iron and 60 or 70 per cent chromium, used for introducing chromium into steel.

fer|ro|chro|mi|um (fer′ō krō′mē əm), *n.* = ferrochrome.

fer|ro|con|crete (fer′ō kon′krēt, -kon krēt′), *n.* concrete strengthened by a metal framework embedded in it; reinforced concrete.

fer|ro|cy|an|ic acid (fer′ō sī an′ik), an acid occurring in the form of its salts (ferrocyanides). *Formula:* $H_4Fe(CN)_6$

fer|ro|cy|a|nide (fer′ō sī′ə nīd), *n.* a salt of ferrocyanic acid.

fer|ro|e|lec|tric (fer′ō i lek′trik), *adj., n.* —*adj.* exhibiting electrical qualities analogous to the magnetic qualities of ferromagnetic materials, such as the ability to hold an electric charge.
—*n.* a nonconducting material having ferroelectric qualities.

fer|ro|e|lec|tric|i|ty (fer′ō i lek′tris′ə tē, -ē′lek-), *n.* ferroelectric quality or condition.

fer|ro|mag|ne|sian (fer′ō mag nē′shən, -zhən), *adj.* containing iron and magnesium silicates: *ferromagnesian minerals.*

fer|ro|mag|net (fer′ō mag′nit), *n.* a ferromagnetic substance or material.

fer|ro|mag|net|ic (fer′ō mag net′ik), *adj., n.*
—*adj.* of, having to do with, or characteristic of ferromagnetism or a substance that exhibits ferromagnetism; able to become highly magnetic in a relatively weak magnetic field, as iron, steel, cobalt, and nickel.
—*n.* a substance that exhibits ferromagnetism.

fer|ro|mag|net|ism (fer′ō mag′nə tiz əm), *n.* a form of magnetism in which a substance tends to take a position with the longer axis parallel to the lines of force in a magnetic field. Very high magnetic permeability and hysteresis are characteristics of ferromagnetism.

fer|ro|man|ga|nese (fer′ō mang′gə nēs, -nēz), *n.* an alloy of iron, containing about 80 per cent manganese and small amounts of carbon, used for making tough steel.

fer|ro|mo|lyb|de|num (fer′ō mə lib′də nəm, -mol′ib dē′-), *n.* an alloy of iron and 55 to 75 per cent of molybdenum, used in making a type of steel.

fer|ro|nick|el (fer′ō nik′əl), *n.* an alloy of iron and 25 per cent or more of nickel.

fer|ro|pseu|do|brook|ite (fer′ō sü′dō brůk′īt), *n.* a lunar form of the mineral pseudobrookite (a titanium iron oxide): *Three new minerals were found in the lunar rocks. They are pyroxmangite, ferropseudobrookite and a chromium-titanium spinel, and they differ only in detail from terrestrial minerals* (Science Journal).

fer|ro|sil|i|con (fer′ō sil′ə kən), *n.* an alloy of iron, silicon, and carbon, used in deoxidizing steel, and for making a steel high in silicon.

fer|ro|ti|ta|ni|um (fer′ō tī tā′nē əm, -tē-), *n.* an alloy of iron and titanium used to some extent in steel making.

fer|ro|tung|sten (fer′ō tung′stən), *n.* an alloy of iron and 70 to 80 per cent of tungsten, used in making high-speed steel tools.

fer|ro|type (fer′ō tīp), *v.,* **-typed, -typ|ing,** *n.*
—*v.t.* to add a glossy surface to (a photographic print) by pressing it while wet onto a smooth metal sheet.
—*n.* **1** a photograph taken as a positive on a sheet of enameled iron or tin; tintype. **2** the process used.

ferrotype tin or **plate,** a smooth, enameled sheet of metal on which photographs are pressed and dried to add a glossy surface.

fer|rous (fer′əs), *adj.* **1** of or containing iron, especially divalent iron. **2** obtained from iron.

ferrous oxide, a highly oxidizable black powder, obtained by reduction of higher oxides; iron monoxide. *Formula:* FeO

ferrous sulfate, = copperas.

fer|ro|va|na|di|um (fer′ō və nā′dē əm), *n.* an alloy of iron and about 40 per cent vanadium, used in the manufacture of tool steels, high-strength structural steels, and wear-resistant iron.

fer|ru|gi|nate (fə rü′jə nāt), *v.t.,* **-nat|ed, -nat|ing.** to give (rock) the color or properties of the rust of iron. —**fer|ru′gi|na′tion,** *n.*

fer|ru|gin|e|ous (fer′ů jin′ē əs), *adj.* = ferruginous.

fer|ru|gi|nous (fə rü′jə nəs), *adj.* **1** of or containing iron; like that of iron: *ferruginous sandstone.* **2** reddish-brown like rust. [< Latin *ferrūginus* (with English *-ous*), variant of *ferrūgineus* < *ferrūgō, -inis* iron rust < *ferrum* iron]

ferruginous rough|leg (ruf′leg′), a rough-legged hawk of the western United States and Canada, noted for its large size. It has a black-and-white streaked head, white underparts, and black and brown body.

fer|rule (fer′əl, -ül), *n., v.,* **-ruled, -rul|ing.**
—*n.* **1** a metal ring or cap put around the end of a cane, wooden handle, umbrella, or the like, for strength and protection. The metal band holding the eraser in a pencil is a ferrule. **2** a ring-shaped bushing to protect the end of a pipe or tube.
—*v.t.* to furnish with a ferrule. Also, **ferule.** [alteration of earlier *verrel* < Old French *virelle,* and *virole* < Latin *viriola* (diminutive) < *viriae* bracelets]

fer|ry (fer′ē), *v.,* **-ried, -ry|ing,** *n., pl.* **-ries.**
—*v.t.* **1** to carry (people, vehicles, and goods) back and forth across a river or narrow stretch of water: *In Greek mythology, Charon ferried the souls of the dead over the River Styx.* **2** to go across in a ferryboat: *We ferried the river on a small boat.* **3a** to carry back and forth in an airplane: *The plane ferries passengers across the straits in half an hour.* **b** to fly (an airplane) to a destination for delivery. —*v.i.* to travel by ferryboat: *I intended to remain until the weather cleared before I ferried back* (Theodore Hook). [Old English *ferian* < *fær* a journey]
—*n.* **1** a place where boats carry people and goods across a river or narrow stretch of water: *He went down to the ferry but found the boat on the other side.* **2** the boat used; ferryboat: *He drove onto the ferry when the boat returned.* **3** a franchise or license to operate a ferry and charge a fare or toll. **4** a system for flying aircraft to a destination for delivery; air ferry. [probably < Scandinavian (compare Old Icelandic *ferja*)]

***fer|ry|boat** (fer′ē bōt′), *n.* a boat that carries people, animals, vehicles, and goods across a river or narrow stretch of water.

***ferryboat**
***ferry bridge**

***ferry bridge,** the landing platform of a ferry, hinged at one end to the wharf, the other end being raised or lowered to the level of the incoming boat.

fer|ry|man (fer′ē mən), *n., pl.* **-men. 1** a man who owns or has charge of a ferry. **2** a man who runs or works on a ferry.

fer|tile (fėr′təl), *adj.* **1** able to produce seeds, fruit, young, etc.: *a fertile animal or plant.* **2** able to develop into a new individual; fertilized: *Chicks hatch from fertile eggs.* **3a** able to produce much; producing crops easily; rich in things that aid growth and development: *Fertile soil yields good crops.* **b** producing many offspring. **4** *Botany.* **a** fruiting or capable of producing fruit; having a perfect pistil: *a fertile flower.* **b** capable of fertilizing, as an anther with well-developed pollen. **c** producing organs that bear spores, as a fern. **5** *Physics.* not fissionable, but capable of becoming fissionable through the action of bombarding neutrons in a reactor. **6** *Figurative.* producing ideas; creative: *Keats had a fertile imagination. Einstein had a fertile mind.* **7** *Figurative.* producing abundance (in or of): *A mind fertile in schemes. A reforming age is always fertile of impostors* (Macaulay). **8** promoting fertility or productivity: *fertile showers.* **9** *Obsolete.* abundant. [< Old French *fertil,* learned borrowing from Latin *fertilis* < *ferre* to bear] —**fer′tile|ly,** *adv.* —**fer′tile|ness,** *n.*
—*Syn.* **1, 6 Fertile, productive** mean able to produce much. **Fertile** emphasizes the power of producing and applies to things in which seeds or ideas can take root and grow: *The seed fell on fertile ground. He has a fertile imagination.* **Productive** suggests bringing forth in abundance: *Those fruit trees are very productive. He is a productive writer.*

fer|ti|lise (fėr′tə līz), *v.t.,* **-lised, -lis|ing.** *Especially British.* fertilize.

fer|til|i|ty (fėr til′ə tē), *n.* **1** the bearing, or abundant bearing, of seeds, fruits, crops, or young. SYN: fecundity, productiveness. **2** the power to produce: (*Figurative.*) *The fertility of an inventor's mind usually exceeds that of the average mind.* SYN: fecundity, productiveness.

fertility cult, 1 a cult whose members seek to render game, crops, and similar things, or themselves more fertile through rites usually involving a particular deity. **2** the members of a cult who practice such rites.

fertility drug or **pill,** a drug in tablet form consisting of synthesized hormones that release ova in women who do not ovulate normally. Fertility drugs have sometimes caused multiple births. *Fertility drugs are useful when infertility is caused by failure of the woman's body to produce an egg each month that is capable of being fertilized* (New York Times).

fer|ti|liz|a|bil|i|ty (fėr′tə lī′zə bil′ə tē), *n.* **1** the state or condition of being fertilized. **2** the ability to fertilize.

fer|ti|liz|a|ble (fėr′tə lī′zə bəl), *adj.* that can be fertilized.

fer|ti|li|za|tion (fėr′tə lə zā′shən), *n.* **1** the act or process of fertilizing. **2** the condition of being fertilized. **3a** the union of a male and a female reproductive cell to form a cell that will develop into a new individual. **b** impregnation; fecundation. **4** *Botany.* **a** the process by which the pollen reaches and acts upon the ovules, and assures the production of fruit. **b** the corresponding process in cryptogams. **5** the process of increasing the productivity of the soil by adding fertilizer.

fer|ti|li|za|tion|al (fėr′tə lə zā′shə nəl), *adj.* of or having to do with fertilization.

fertilization cone, = entrance cone.

fertilization membrane, an extension of the membrane surrounding an egg, which prevents the entry of additional sperm after fertilization has occurred.

fer|ti|lize (fėr′tə līz), *v.t.,* **-lized, -liz|ing. 1a** to make fertile; make able to produce much: *A crop of alfalfa fertilizes the soil by adding nitrates to it.* **b** to make (a thing) start to grow; enrich: (*Figurative.*) *Our knowledge of the large molecules might fertilize biochemistry as much as Heisenberg's* [*uncertainty*] *principle fertilized physics* (N. W. Pirie). **2a** to unite with (an egg cell) in fertilization. **b** to impregnate; fecundate. **3** to make (the soil) richer by adding manure or other fertilizer: *to fertilize a lawn.*

fer|ti|liz|er (fėr′tə lī′zər), *n.* **1** manure, or any organic substance, or a chemical that makes soil richer in plant foods when it is spread over or put into soil. Prepared chemical mixtures commonly contain nitrogen, phosphorus, and potassium in varying proportions, and sometimes other ingredients. **2** a person or thing that fertilizes.

fer|ti|li|zin (fėr′tə lī′zin, fėr′tə lī′-), *n.* a soluble gelatinous substance that surrounds certain ova and appears to activate, attract, and finally bunch sperm.

fer|u|la (fer′yů lə, -ů-), *n., pl.* **-lae** (-lē). **1** any one of a large group of plants of the parsley family, found chiefly in the Mediterranean region and central Asia. Many of the Asiatic species yield strongly scented gum resins, such as asafetida and galbanum. **2** = ferule (def. 1). [< Latin *ferula* the giant fennel; rod]

fer|u|la|ceous (fer′yů lā′shəs, -ů-), *adj.* like or having to do with reeds or canes.

fer|ule[1] (fer′əl, -ül), *n., v.,* **-uled, -ul|ing.** —*n.* **1** a stick or ruler for punishing children by striking them, especially on the hand. **2** *Figurative.* school discipline; punishment: *to learn at the point of the ferule* (Frederick W. Farrar). —*v.t.* to punish with a stick or ruler. [< Latin *ferula* (because, since Roman times, the ferula has been used to whip schoolboys); see etym. under **ferula**]

fer|ule[2] (fer′əl, -ül), *n., v.t.,* **-uled, -ul|ing.** = ferrule.

fer|ven|cy (fėr′vən sē), *n.* warmth of feeling; great earnestness; fervor: *She would never have*

Pronunciation Key: hat, āge, cãre, fär; let, ēqual, tėrm; it, īce; hot, ōpen, ôrder; oil, out; cup, pu̇t, rüle; child; long; thin; ᴛʜen; zh, measure; ə represents **a** in about, **e** in taken, **i** in pencil, **o** in lemon, **u** in circus.

known the fervency of your love (Charles Kingsley). SYN: zeal, ardor, eagerness.

fer·vent (fėr′vənt), *adj.* **1** showing warmth of feeling; very earnest: *The coach made a fervent plea for greater loyalty to the team.* SYN: ardent, zealous, passionate, eager. **2** hot; glowing; intense: *The elements shall melt with fervent heat* (II Peter 3:10). SYN: warm, burning, fervid, fiery. [< Old French *fervent,* learned borrowing from Latin *fervēns, -entis,* present participle of *fervere,* or *fervēre* to boil] **—fer′vent·ly,** *adv.* **—fer′vent·ness,** *n.*

fer·vid (fėr′vid), *adj.* **1** full of strong feeling; very emotional; ardent; spirited; impassioned: *The orator's fervid speech stirred the crowd to action.* **2** intensely hot: *The mounted sun shot down his fervid rays* (Milton). [< Latin *fervidus* < *fervere;* see etym. under **fervent**] **—fer′vid·ly,** *adv.* **—fer′vid·ness,** *n.*

fer·vid·i·ty (fėr vid′ə tē), *n.* = fervency.

Fer·vi·dor (fer vē dôr′), *n.* the 11th month of the French Revolutionary calendar, beginning July 19. [< French *Fervidor* < Latin *fervidus* fervid]

fer·vor (fėr′vər), *n.* **1a** great warmth of feeling; intense emotion, enthusiasm, or earnestness: *The patriot's voice trembled from the fervor of his emotion.* SYN: passion, vehemence, zeal, ardor. **b** an instance of this: *a fervor unique even in the history of American enthusiasms* (Adolphus W. Ward). **2** intense heat. [< Old French *fervour,* learned borrowing from Latin *fervor* < *fervere;* see etym. under **fervent**]

fer·vour (fėr′vər), *n. Especially British.* fervor.

Fes·cen·nine (fes′ə nīn, -nin), *adj.* licentious; obscene; scurrilous. [< Latin *Fescennīnī versūs* Fescennine verses < *Fescennia,* a town in Etruria, where a vulgar type of verse is supposed to have originated]

fes·cue (fes′kyü), *n.* **1** Also, **fescue grass.** any one of a genus of tough perennial grasses growing in tufts, found in temperate regions and used for pasture or lawns: *The fescues, now so much in the news, were European pasture grasses* (New York Times). **2** a small stick, straw, or the like, for pointing out the letters in teaching a child to read. [alteration of Middle English *festu* < Old French < Latin *festūca* straw, stalk]

fess[1] or **fesse** (fes), *n. Heraldry.* a wide, horizontal band across the middle of a shield.
in fess, lying in the middle of the fess, horizontally across the middle of the field.
per fess, (of the shield) divided by a horizontal line through the middle: *an ordinary per fess argent and sable.*
[< Old French *fesse,* or *faisse* < Latin *fascia* band. See etym. of doublet **fascia.**]

fess[2] or **'fess** (fes), *v.t., v.i. Slang.* to confess.
fess up, to admit the truth of something: *The joke is on him and he may as well fess up to it* (Randolph Enterprise).

fess point or **fesse point,** *Heraldry.* the exact center of a shield; heart point.

fess·wise or **fesse·wise** (fes′wīz′), *adv. Heraldry.* horizontally.

-fest, *combining form.* meeting, occasion, contest, or game, characterized by ______, as in *songfest, slugfest, talkfest.* [< German *Fest*]

fes·ta (fes′tä), *n. Italian.* **1** holiday; festival. **2** party; feast.

fes·tal (fes′təl), *adj.* of or having to do with a feast, festival, or holiday; gay; festive; joyous: *A wedding or a birthday is a festal occasion.* [< Old French *festal* < Late Latin *fēstālis* < Latin *fēstum* feast] **—fes′tal·ly,** *adv.*

fes·ter (fes′tər), *v., n.* **—*v.i.*** **1** to form pus; suppurate: *The neglected wound festered and became very painful.* **2** to poison or inflame the surrounding parts progressively, as a disease does. **3** *Figurative.* to cause soreness or pain; rankle: *Resentment at the unkind remark festered in his mind.* **4** to decay; rot: *Lilies that fester smell far worse than weeds* (Shakespeare).
—*v.t.* **1** to cause pus to form in. **2** *Figurative.* to cause soreness or pain in; cause to rankle: *Time festered the insult to his pride.*
[< noun]
—*n.* a sore that forms pus; small ulcer.
[< Old French *festre* < Latin *fistula* pipe, ulcer. See etym. of doublet **fistula.**]

fes·ti·na len·te (fes tī′nə len′tē), *Latin.* make haste slowly.

fes·ti·nate (*v.* fes′tə nāt; *adj.* fes′tə nit), *v.,* **-nat·ed, -nat·ing,** *adj.* **—*v.t.*** = hasten.
—*adj.* = hasty.
[< Latin *festīnāre* (with English *-ate*[1])]

fes·ti·na·tion (fes′tə nā′shən), *n.* **1** *Medicine.* an involuntary hurrying in gait, such as observed in Parkinson's disease and other nervous diseases. **2** *Obsolete.* haste.

fes·ti·val (fes′tə vəl), *n., adj.* **—*n.*** **1** a day or special time of rejoicing or feasting, often in memory of some great happening: *Christmas and Easter are two festivals of the Christian Church; Purim and Hanukkah are two festivals of the Jewish religion.* **2** a celebration or entertainment, often at recurring periods: *a strawberry festival. Every year the city has a summer music festival. Just returned from a film festival in Acapulco, he sported a healthy bronze glow* (Rex Reed). **3** merrymaking; revelry: *The morning trumpets festival proclaim'd through each high street* (Milton).
—*adj.* **1** of or having to do with a festival. **2** *Obsolete.* joyful.
[< Medieval Latin *festivalis* < Latin *fēstīvus* < *fēstum* feast]

fes·ti·val·go·er (fes′tə vəl gō′ər), *n.* a person who attends a festival or festivals.

Festival of Freedom, = Passover.

Festival of Lanterns, = Bon.

Festival of Lights, = Hanukkah.

festival seating, *U.S.* unreserved seating, especially at a rock music concert.

fes·tive (fes′tiv), *adj.* of or suitable for a feast, festival, or holiday; gay; merry; joyous: *Her birthday was a festive occasion. Flags and flowers made the hall look festive.* SYN: festal. **—fes′tive·ly,** *adv.* **—fes′tive·ness,** *n.*

fes·tiv·i·ty (fes tiv′ə tē), *n., pl.* **-ties.** **1** the act of rejoicing and feasting; festive activity; thing done to celebrate: *The festivities on the Fourth of July included a parade and fireworks.* **2** gaiety; merriment: *Come, join in the festivity!* **3** = festival.

fes·ti·vous (fes′tə vəs), *adj.* = festive.

fes·toon (fes tün′), *n., v.* **—*n.*** a string or chain of flowers, leaves, ribbons, or the like, hanging in a curve between two points: *Bunting was draped on the walls in colorful festoons.* **1** a carved or molded ornament like this on furniture, pottery, or a building: *a design of grape leaves in plaster festoons.*
—*v.t.* **1** to decorate with or as if with festoons: *The Christmas tree was festooned with tinsel.* **2** to form into festoons; hang in curves like festoons: *Draperies were festooned over the windows.* **3** to connect by festoons: *Growths of jasmine turned their humid arms festooning tree to tree* (Tennyson).
[< Middle French *feston* < Italian *festone* < *festa* < Latin *fēsta;* see etym. under **feast**]

fes·toon·er·y (fes tü′nər ē), *n., pl.* **-er·ies.** **1** a decoration of festoons; festoonlike arrangement. **2** festoons collectively.

Fest·schrift or **fest·schrift** (fest′shrift′), *n., pl.* **-schrif·ten** (-shrif′tən), **-schrifts.** a volume usually containing original essays by several different students or colleagues of a scholar, published in his honor, and often formally presented to him. [< German *Festschrift* (literally) festival writing]

fet (fet), *v.t.,* **fet, fet·ting.** *British Dialect.* to fetch. [Old English *fetian*]

FET (no periods), field effect transistor.

fet·a (fet′ə), *n.* a Greek cheese made from sheep's or goat's milk, cured in brine. Also, **fetta.** [< New Greek *pheta*]

fe·tal (fē′təl), *adj.* **1** of or having to do with a fetus: *Fetal hemoglobin differs chemically from normal hemoglobin.* **2** like that of a fetus: *a rolled-up, fetal posture.* Also, **foetal.**

fetal alcohol syndrome, a group of physical and mental defects in a newborn, including retardation, resulting from the consumption of too much alcohol by the mother during pregnancy: *French researchers first identified what has come to be called the "fetal alcohol syndrome" (malformations and behavioral damage)* (New Scientist).

fe·ta·tion (fē tā′shən), *n.* the formation of a fetus; pregnancy.

fetch[1] (fech), *v., n.* **—*v.t.*** **1** to go and get; bring: *Please fetch me my glasses.* SYN: See syn. under **bring.** **2** to cause to come; succeed in bringing: *Her call fetched him at once.* **3** to be sold for: *These eggs will fetch a good price.* **4** *Informal.* to attract; charm: *A little flattery will fetch him.* **5** *Informal.* to deal or strike (a blow, etc.); hit. **6a** to draw or take (a breath): *to fetch a deep breath.* **b** to give (a groan, sigh, or other sign of emotion): *In answer he only fetched a sigh.* **7** (of a ship) to arrive at; reach. **8** to draw or derive (from or out of): *to fetch examples from history.*
—*v.i.* **1a** to go and bring a thing or things back. SYN: See syn. under **bring.** **b** (of hunting dogs) to retrieve killed or wounded game. **2** of ships: **a** to take or hold a course; move; go. **b** to veer.
—*n.* **1** an act of fetching. **2** the distance something is fetched. **3** the distance across which the wind blows with the same direction and speed. **4** a long stretch: *The day was half gone and it was a far fetch to Stepney* (Jack London). **5** a trick; stratagem: *This excuse . . . though true in part, was principally a fetch* (James Fenimore Cooper).
fetch and carry, to do small jobs: *All he's good for is to fetch and carry.*
fetch up, *Informal.* **a** to arrive; stop: *We fetch up around three o'clock in a grimy cul-de-sac behind a prison* (Manchester Guardian). **b** *U.S.* to bring up or rear (a child): *I was fetchin' on her up to work for her livin' as I was fetched up* (Harriet Beecher Stowe).
[Old English *feccan,* apparently variant of *fetian.* Compare etym. under **fet.**] **—fetch′er,** *n.*

fetch[2] (fech), *n.* the apparition of a living person; wraith: *She believed she had seen his fetch as a forerunner of his death* (Mary Leadbeater). [origin uncertain]

fetch·ing (fech′ing), *adj. Informal.* attractive; charming: *She wore a fetching hat.* **—fetch′ing·ly,** *adv.*

fete (fāt; *French* fet), *n., v.,* **fet·ed, fet·ing.** **—*n.*** a festival or party, especially an elaborate one and often one held outdoors: *A large fete was given for the benefit of the town hospital.*
—*v.t.* to give parties for; honor with a fete; entertain: *The bride-to-be was feted by her friends.*
[< French *fête* feast < Old French *feste.* See etym. of doublets **feast, fiesta.**]

fête (fāt; *French* fet), *n., v.t.,* **fêt·ed, fêt·ing.** = fete.

fête cham·pê·tre (fet′ shäN pe′trə), *pl.* **fêtes cham·pê·tres** (fet′ shäN pe′trə). *French.* a garden party; outdoor festival.

fete or **fête day,** **1** = name day. **2** = birthday.

fet·e·ri·ta (fet′ə rē′tə), *n.* a tall, African variety of grain sorghum, related to durra, grown for fodder in the Southwestern United States. [< Arabic (Sudan) *feterīta*]

fe·tial (fē′shəl), *adj., n.* **—*adj.*** **1** of or having to do with the fetiales. **2** concerned with declarations of war and treaties of peace. **3** = heraldic.
—*n.* one of the fetiales.

fe·ti·a·les (fē′shē ā′lēz), *n.pl.* a body of priests in ancient Rome who acted as heralds and as representatives of the people in disputes with foreign nations and in the declaration of war and the conclusion of peace.
[< Latin *fētiālis,* plural *-ālēs*]

fe·tich (fē′tish, fet′ish), *n.* = fetish.

fe·tich·ism (fē′ti shiz əm, fet′i-), *n.* = fetishism.

fe·tich·ist (fē′ti shist, fet′i-), *n.* = fetishist.

fe·tich·is·tic (fē′ti shis′tik, fet′i-), *adj.* = fetishistic.

fe·ti·cid·al (fē′tə sī′dəl), *adj.* of feticide; having to do with or used in feticide.

fe·ti·cide (fē′tə sīd), *n.* the killing of a fetus; aborticide. [< Latin *fētus* fetus + English *-cide*[2]]

fet·id (fet′id, fē′tid), *adj.* smelling very bad; stinking. SYN: malodorous, noisome. Also, **foetid.** [< Latin *foetidus* < *foetēre* to smell] **—fet′id·ly,** *adv.* **—fet′id·ness,** *n.*

fetid buckeye, = Ohio buckeye.

fetid horehound, = black horehound.

fe·tid·i·ty (fe tid′ə tē, fē-), *n.* the quality or state of being fetid.

fetid shrub, = papaw.

fetid wood witch, = stinkhorn.

fe·tif·er·ous (fē tif′ər əs), *adj. Zoology.* producing offspring.

fe·tip·a·rous (fē tip′ər əs), *adj.* giving birth to incompletely developed young, as marsupial mammals. [< Latin *fētus* fetus + *parere* give birth to + English *-ous*]

fe·tish (fē′tish, fet′ish), *n.* **1** any material object supposed to have magic power: *The tribe worshiped a fetish that was a hideous snake carved out of stone.* SYN: talisman, amulet. **2** *Figurative.* anything regarded with unreasoning reverence or blind devotion: *Some people make a fetish of stylish clothes.* **3** an object or a part of the body that arouses abnormal erotic feeling. Also, **fetich.** [< French *fétiche* < Portuguese *feitiço* charm; (originally) artificial < Latin *factīcius,* or *factītius.* See etym. of doublet **factitious.**]

fe·tish·ism (fē′ti shiz əm, fet′i-), *n.* **1** belief in fetishes; worship of fetishes. **2** an abnormal attachment of erotic feeling to an object (such as an article of clothing) or part of the body.

fe·tish·ist (fē′ti shist, fet′i-), *n.* **1** a person who worships or believes in fetishes. **2** a person who has erotic feelings for nonsexual objects, such as an article of clothing.

fe·tish·is·tic (fē′ti shis′tik, fet′i-), *adj.* of fetishism; having to do with or characterized by fetishism. **—fe′tish·is′ti·cal·ly,** *adv.*

fe·tish·ize (fē′ti shīz, fet′i-), *v.t.,* **-ized, -iz·ing.** to worship as a fetish; make a fetish of: (*Figurative.*) *[His] description . . . of existentialism as a "permanent carnival of fetishized inwardness" touched a raw nerve* (Listener).

fet·lock (fet′lok), *n.* **1** the tuft of hair above a horse's hoof on the back part of the leg. **2** the part of a horse's leg where this tuft grows. See picture under **horse.** **3** the joint at this spot. [Middle English *fetlak,* and *fitlok;* origin uncertain; taken as *feet* (or *foot*) *lock*]

fet·locked (fet′lokt′), *adj.* **1** having a fetlock. **2** hobbled or fastened by the fetlock; hampered; shackled.

fet·low (fet′lō), *n.* a whitlow or felon in cattle.

fe·tol·o·gist (fē tol′ə jist), *n.* a person who studies fetology.

fe·tol·o·gy (fē tol′ə jē), *n.* the branch of medicine

dealing with the growth, development, and diseases of fetuses.

fe|to-pla|cen|tal (fē′tə plə sen′təl), *adj.* of the fetus and placenta: *the feto-placental unit.*

fe|tor (fē′tər), *n.* a strong, offensive smell: *This flesh of the female seal . . . has not the fetor of her mate's* (Elisha K. Kane). **SYN:** stench, stink. [< Latin *foetor* < *foetēre* to smell]

fe|to|scope (fē′tə skōp), *n.* an instrument that permits direct visual observation of a fetus inside the womb: *Looking through a fetoscope, Yale's Dr. John Hobbins guides a hairlike needle into a blood vessel on a pregnant woman's placenta* (New York Times Magazine). [< *feto-* (< Latin *fētus* fetus) + English *-scope*]

fet|ta (fet′ə), *n.* = feta.

fet|ter (fet′ər), *n., v.* **—*n.*** a chain or shackle for the feet to prevent escape.
—*v.t.* **1** to bind with fetters; chain the feet of; shackle. **2** *Figurative.* to bind; restrain: *Fetter your temper. . . . to set wild The fettered hope* (Witter Bynner). **SYN:** confine, hamper, impede.
fetters, a shackles: *Fetters prevented the prisoner's escape. Antony presented [him] . . . to Cleopatra in golden fetters* (Henry N. Humphreys). **b** *Figurative.* anything that shackles or binds; restraint: *Here the free spirit of mankind, at length, Throws its last fetters off* (William Cullen Bryant).
[Old English *feter.* See related etym. at **foot.**]
—fet′ter|er, *n.* **—fet′ter|less,** *adj.*

fet|ter|bush (fet′ər bu̇sh′), *n.* **1** an evergreen shrub of the heath family, with fragrant, white or pink flowers, that grows in the southern United States. **2** a similar and related shrub, bearing nodding, white, bell-shaped flowers. **3** any one of various other shrubs of the heath family found in the eastern United States.

fet|ter|lock (fet′ər lok), *n.* **1** = fetlock. **2** a shackle for a horse's leg or foot.

fet|ters (fet′ərz), *n.pl.* See under **fetter.**

fet|tle (fet′əl), *n., v.,* **-tled, -tling.** **—*n.*** **1** condition; state of readiness for action; trim: *The horse is in fine fettle and should win the race.* **2** *Northern British Dialect.* a scouring; a polishing; a thorough cleaning.
—*v.t.* **1** *Dialect.* to make ready; put in order; arrange. **2** *Northern British Dialect.* to scour; polish; clean: *to fettle a room, to fettle the pans, to fettle the gas cooker.* **3** *Dialect.* to beat; thrash. **4** to line or cover (the hearth of a puddling furnace or open-hearth furnace) with sand, ore, etc.
[probably Middle English *fettelen* prepare, gird up < Old English *fetel* belt]

fet|tling (fet′ling), *n.* the sand or ore used to line the hearth of a puddling furnace. [< *fettle* + *ing*[1]]

fet|tuc|cine or **fet|tu|ci|ne** (fet′ə chē′nē), *n.* **1** Italian noodles, made in strips or ribbons; flat, thin noodles. **2** a dish of such noodles, prepared with butter, cheese, and sometimes cream. [< Italian *fettuccine,* plural of *fettuccina* (diminutive) < *fetta* ribbon, slice]

fet|tuc|ci|ni or **fet|tu|ci|ni** (fet′ə chē′nē), *n.* = fettucine.

fe|tus (fē′təs), *n.* an animal embryo during the later stages of its development in the womb or in the egg, especially a human embryo about three months old. Also, **foetus.** [< Latin *fētus*]

fet|wa (fet′wə), *n.* a decision, usually in writing, given by a Mufti or other Moslem authority on religious law. [< Arabic *fetwa*]

feu (fyü), *n., v. Scottish.* **—*n.*** **1** an estate in land capable of passing by inheritance; fee. **2a** a feudal tenure in which the holder makes a return in money or other commodity, in place of military service. **b** a grant of land held under these conditions. **c** (in modern use) a perpetual lease for a fixed rent. **3** land held in any of these ways.
—*v.t.* to grant (land) in feu.
[< Anglo-French *feu,* Old French *fieu,* or *fief;* see etym. under **fee**]

feud[1] (fyüd), *n., v.* **—*n.*** **1** a long and deadly quarrel between two families or tribes. Feuds are often passed on from father to son. . . . *seeds of lasting feuds and animosities* (Bishop Gilbert Burnet). **2** bitter hatred between two persons or groups. **3** a quarrel: *frequently torn by intramural feuds* (Newsweek). **SYN:** See syn. under **quarrel.**
—*v.i.* to carry on a feud: *Their families have been feuding for three generations.*
[variant of Middle English *fede* < Old French *feide* < Old High German *fēhida* enmity] **—feud′er,** *n.*

feud[2] (fyüd), *n.* a grant of land held on condition of giving military and other services to the lord owning it in return for protection and the use of the land; feudal estate; fief; fee: *The Conqueror conferred the estates . . . on his principal followers as strict feuds* (William A. Guise). [< Medieval Latin *feudum,* or *feodum,* alteration of Germanic (compare Old Frisian *fio* money; cattle). Compare etym. under **fee.**]

feu|dal[1] (fyü′dəl), *adj.* of or having to do with a feud or feuding. [< *feud*[1] + *-al*[1]]

feu|dal[2] (fyü′dəl), *adj.* **1** of or having to do with feudalism: *feudal law. The remaining feudal monarchies in the Middle East, such as Jordan and Saudi Arabia* (Wall Street Journal). **2** of or having to do with feuds or fiefs: *feudal lands.* **3** having to do with the holding of land in fee: *a claim under feudal tenure.* [< Medieval Latin *feudalis* < *feudum;* see etym. at **feud**[2]] **—feu′dal|ly,** *adv.*

feu|dal|ism (fyü′də liz əm), *n.* **1** the social, economic, and political system of Europe in the Middle Ages; feudal system. Under this system, vassals gave military and other services to their lord in return for his protection and the use of the land. **2** any social, economic, or political system or doctrine, thought of as resembling the feudal system in subordinating people to the dictates of a leader or system.

feu|dal|ist (fyü′də list), *n.* **1** a supporter of the feudal system. **2** a person who is learned in feudal law; feudist.

feu|dal|is|tic (fyü′də lis′tik), *adj.* **1** of or having to do with feudalism. **2** tending toward feudalism; favoring feudalism.

feu|dal|i|ty (fyü dal′ə tē), *n., pl.* **-ties.** **1** = feudalism. **2** a feudal estate; fief.

feu|dal|ize (fyü′də līz), *v.t.,* **-ized, -iz|ing. 1** to bring under the feudal system. **2** to give a feudal character to. **—feu′dal|i|za′tion,** *n.*

feudal system, the system of feudalism: *The exchange of land for services prevailed from top to bottom of the feudal system, including the manorial organization which was its economic base* (Wallace K. Ferguson).

feu|da|to|ry (fyü′də tôr′ē, -tōr′-), *adj., n., pl.* **-ries.**
—*adj.* **1** owing feudal services to a lord. **2** holding or held as a feudal estate or fief. **3** (of a kingdom or state) under the overlordship of the sovereign of another state. **4** of vassals or retainers.
—*n.* **1** a feudal vassal: *The duke summoned his feudatories to aid him in war.* **2** a feudal estate; fief. **3** a feudatory kingdom, state, country, or other territory.

feu de joie (fœ′ də zhwä′), *pl.* **feux de joie** (fœ′ də zhwä′). *French.* **1** fire of joy; a bonfire kindled in rejoicing or celebration. **2** a salute of rifle fire fired in rapid succession along a rank of men so as to make one long, continuous sound.

feud|ist[1] (fyü′dist), *n. U.S.* a person engaging in a feud. [< *feud*[1] + *-ist*]

feud|ist[2] (fyü′dist), *n.* an authority on feudal law. [< *feud*[2] + *-ist*]

feu duty, annual rent paid for tenure of a feu.

feuil|le|té (fœ yə tā′), *n. French.* a pie, the crust of which separates in rising into a number of very thin, flat layers like the leaves of a book.

feuil|le|ton (fœ yə tôɴ′), *n.* **1** a part of one or more pages of a newspaper containing miscellaneous articles, serial stories, verse, and the like. Originally, feuilletons of French and other European newspapers appeared at the bottom of the page, marked off from the rest of the page by a rule. **2** an article or other work, especially a part of a serial story, printed in the feuilleton. **3** a light, informal essay or similar journalistic writing: *His bent, in the undergraduate years, was poetic, and he had issued feuilletons on Villon and Edwin Arlington Robinson* (New Yorker). [< French *feuilleton* < *feuillet* (diminutive) *feuille* leaf, sheet]

feuil|le|ton|ism (fœ′yə tə niz′əm), *n.* an aptitude for writing feuilletons.

feuil|le|ton|ist (fœ′yə ton′ist), *n.* a writer for a newspaper feuilleton.

feuil|le|ton|is|tic (fœ′yə tə nis′tik), *adj.* characteristic of a feuilleton.

Feul|gen reaction (foil′gən), a method of staining for microscopic examination, which colors a nucleic acid purple and leaves the remainder of a cell colorless, used in the study of the nuclei of cells, especially to determine the presence and location of deoxyribonucleic acid. [< Robert *Feulgen,* 1844-1955, a German biochemist]

fe|ver (fē′vər), *n., v.* **—*n.*** **1a** an unhealthy condition of the body in which the temperature is higher than normal (98.6 degrees Fahrenheit or 37 degrees centigrade), often accompanied by rapid pulse and weakness. **b** a body temperature that is greater than normal; pyrexia: *Let fever sweat them till they tremble* (W. H. Auden). **2** any one of various sicknesses that heat the body and make the heart beat fast: *scarlet fever, typhoid fever, or yellow fever.* **3** *Figurative.* an excited, restless condition; agitation: *When gold was discovered, the miners were in a fever of excitement. Passion is a sort of fever in the mind* (William Penn). **SYN:** ferment. **4** *Figurative.* a current fad or enthusiasm for something or for some person. **SYN:** furor.
—*v.t.* to affect with fever; heat: *The scorching blast . . . fevers the blood* (Alexander W. Kinglake). **—*v.i.*** to become feverish. [Old English *fefer* < Latin *febris*] **—fe′ver|less,** *adj.*

fever blister, = cold sore.

fe|ver|bush (fē′vər bu̇sh′), *n.* **1** = spicebush. **2** = black alder.

fe|vered (fē′vərd), *adj.* **1** having fever. **2** *Figurative.* excited; restless: *In spite of the fevered consultations of the past two days, the affair is not finished with* (London Times).

fe|ver|few (fē′vər fyü), *n.* a bushy, perennial European herb of the composite family with small, white and yellow, daisylike flowers, formerly used as a febrifuge. It is a species of chrysanthemum. [Old English *feferfugie,* and < Anglo-French *fewerfue,* both < Late Latin *febrifugia* < Latin *febris* fever + *fugāre* drive away. See etym. of doublet **febrifuge.**]

fever fly, an English fly whose larva eats the roots of the hop plant. The coincidence of its swarming in enormous numbers in certain years when fever among humans was prevalent led to a false conclusion.

fe|ver|gum (fē′vər gum′), *n.* = blue gum.

fever heat, 1 the high temperature of the body in fever. **2** *Figurative.* great intensity of emotional excitement.

fe|ver|ish (fē′vər ish, fēv′rish), *adj.* **1a** having an abnormally high temperature; having fever. **b** having some fever but not much. **2** caused by fever: *a feverish thirst.* **3** causing fever: *a feverish climate.* **4** infested with fever: *a feverish swamp.* **5** *Figurative.* excited; restless: *a feverish glance. He packed his bags in feverish haste.* **—fe′ver|ish|ly,** *adv.* **—fe′ver|ish|ness,** *n.*

fe|ver|ous (fē′vər əs, fēv′rəs), *adj.* = feverish. **—fe′ver|ous|ly,** *adv.*

fever pitch, a high degree of excitement or activity: *an economy at fever pitch* (Wall Street Journal).

fe|ver|root (fē′vər rüt′, -ru̇t′), *n.* any plant of a group of coarse North American herbs of the honeysuckle family whose roots are sometimes used for medicine, said to have been used by the Indians as a remedy for fevers; feverwort; horse gentian.

fever sore, = cold sore.

fe|ver|trap (fē′ver trap′), *n.* a place where a person is liable to catch fever.

fever tree, any one of several trees yielding, or reputed to yield, febrifuges, especially: **a** the blue gum tree, thought to prevent malaria. **b** a tree of the madder family growing in the southeastern United States, whose bark is used as a tonic and a febrifuge.

fe|ver|twig (fē′vər twig′), *n.* = false bittersweet.

fe|ver|weed (fē′vər wēd′), *n.* any one of several plants that are used medicinally, especially a West Indian species of eryngo.

fe|ver|wort (fē′vər wėrt′), *n.* **1** = feverroot. **2** = boneset or thoroughwort.

few (fyü), *adj., n.* **—*adj.*** not many; amounting to a small number: *There are few men in our neighborhood over six feet tall. If few their wants, their pleasures are but few* (Oliver Goldsmith).
—*n.* a small number: *Winter in New England has not many warm days, only a few. Few will rise, for few are the places to fill at the top* (Vannevar Bush).
quite a few, *Informal.* a good many: *Quite a few of us went to the game.*
the few, the minority: *The favour of the few may silence the clamour of the many* (Joseph Priestley).
[Old English *fēawe*] **—few′ness,** *n.*
▶**fewer, less.** *Fewer* refers to number, *less* to degree or quantity: *Fewer cars were on the road. There were fewer than sixty present. There was a good deal less tardiness in the second term.* The distinction is not always observed, especially before *than,* where *less* often replaces *fewer: In the making of the present book no less than 100,000 words were critically examined.*

fey (fā), *adj.* **1** fairylike; elfin. **2** pert; gamin. **3** visionary: *The villagers thought the girl was fey and might even have the second sight.* **4a** behaving as if doomed or enchanted. **b** mentally unbalanced; crazy. **5a** fated to die. **b** dying. Also, **fay.** [Old English *fǣge*] **—fey′ness,** *n.*

Feyn|man diagram (fān′mən), a graphic representation of the interactions of elementary particles: *Electromagnetic and weak processes exhibit striking similarities when depicted in the form of Feynman diagrams. Such diagrams symbolize the interactions that underlie subnuclear phenomena, for example the collision between two particles, which physicists refer to as a scattering event* (Scientific American). [< Richard P. *Feynman,* born 1918, an American nuclear physicist who devised this type of diagram]

***fez** (fez), *n., pl.* **fez|zes.** a brimless felt cap with a flat top, usually red and ornamented with a long, black tassel, worn by men in Egypt and some other

---

Pronunciation Key: **hat, āge, cãre, fär; let, ēqual, tėrm; it, īce; hot, ōpen, ôrder; oil, out; cup, pu̇t, rüle; child; long; thin; ᴛʜen; zh,** measure;
ə represents **a** in about, **e** in taken, **i** in pencil, **o** in lemon, **u** in circus.

countries in the Middle East. It was formerly the national headdress of the Turks. [< French *fez* < Turkish *fes* < *Fez,* a town in Morocco]

***fez**

ff (no period), fortissimo (a direction in music).

ff., **1** folios. **2** and the following pages, sections, or other parts; and what follows. **3** fortissimo (a direction in music).

FFA (no periods), Future Farmers of America (a national organization of students of vocational agriculture).

F.F.A. or **f.f.a.,** free from alongside (ship).

F.F.V., *U.S.* First Families of Virginia.

FHA (no periods), **1** Federal Housing Administration (an agency of the federal government that insures loans made by private individuals or companies for approved home construction or improvement). **2** Future Homemakers of America (a national organization of high-school girls studying or interested in homemaking).

F-head engine (ef′hed′), a type of internal-combustion engine with the inlet valve in the cylinder head and the outlet valve on the side of the cylinder.

***f-hole** (ef′hōl′), *n.* one of the two openings in the top of the body of the violin and similar instruments, resembling the italic letter *f.*

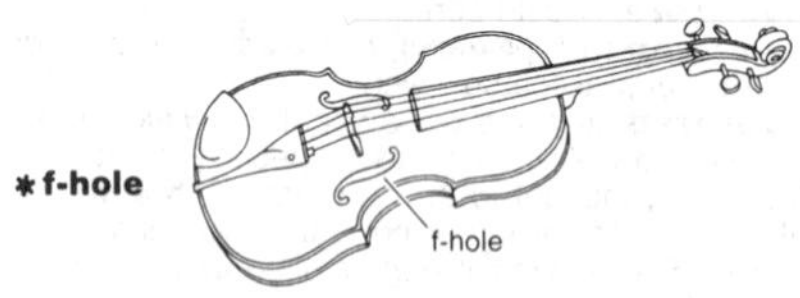

***f-hole**

fi (fī), *n. Slang.* **1** hi-fi. **2** fidelity of sound reproduction: *wretchedly low in fi.*

fi·a·cre (fē ä′kər; *French* fyȧ′krə), *n.* four-wheeled carriage for hire; horse-drawn cab. [< French *fiacre,* because of the sign with the image of St. *Fiacre* over the Paris inn where they were hired]

fi·an·cé or **fi·an·ce** (fē′än sā′, fē′än sā), *n.* a man engaged to be married. [< French *fiancé,* past participle of *fiancer* betroth < Old French < *fiance* a promise, a trust < *fier* to trust]

fi·an·cée or **fi·an·cee** (fē′än sā′, fē′än sā), *n.* a girl or woman engaged to be married. [< French *fiancée,* feminine of *fiancé* fiancé]

fi·an·chet·to (fē′ən ket′ō -chet′ō), *n., pl.* **-toes,** *v.,* **-toed, -to·ing.** *Chess.* **—*n.*** the advancing or development of a bishop by moving it to the second square along the diagonal: *Portisch . . . develops his opening along modern lines, characterized by the fianchetto of the king's bishop* (Al Horowitz).
—*v.t., v.i.* to advance or develop (a bishop) in this way.
[< Italian *fianchetto* (diminutive) < *fianco* flank, side]

Fi·an·na (fē′ə nə), *n.,* or **Fianna Éireann** (ãr′in), a group of Irish warriors famous in Irish legend, especially as the defenders of Ireland in the 300's and 400's; Fenians. [< Old Irish *Fianna* (literally) the bands; the permanent militia in ancient Ireland]

Fianna Fáil (fäl), an Irish political party, founded in 1926 by Eamon de Valera, that advocated the complete separation of Ireland from Great Britain. [< Irish *Fianna Fāil* the Fenians of Ireland; *Fāil,* genitive of *fāl* the Stone of Destiny; (originally) a sod, a barrier]

fiard (fyärd), *n.* an inlet somewhat like a fiord but broader and set among low hills, as in eastern Canada and Newfoundland. [< Swedish *fjärd.* See related etym. at **fiord.**]

fi·as·co¹ (fē as′kō), *n., pl.* **-cos** or **-coes.** a complete or ridiculous failure; humiliating breakdown: *The play was a fiasco and closed after only three performances.* [< French *fiasco* < Italian *fiasco* < a Germanic word]

fia·sco² (fyä′skō), *n., pl.* **-schi** (-skē). *Italian.* a flask; wine bottle.

fi·at (fī′ət, -at; fē′at), *n., v.* **—*n.*** **1** an authoritative order or command; decree: *to determine by the fiat of the king alone the course of national policy* (William Stubbs). **2** an authoritative sanction; authorization.
—*v.t.* **1** to attach a fiat to; sanction. **2** to declare by a fiat.
[< Latin *fīat* let it be done < *fierī,* passive of *facere* do]

fi·at jus·ti·ti·a, ru·at coe·lum (fī′at jus tish′ē ə, rü′at sē′ləm), *Latin.* let justice be done, though the heavens fall.

fi·at lux (fī′at luks′), *Latin.* let there be light.

fiat money, *U.S.* paper currency made legal tender by decree of the government, but not based on or convertible into coin.

fib¹ (fib), *n., v.,* **fibbed, fib·bing.** **—*n.*** a lie about some small matter: *Ask me no questions, and I'll tell you no fibs* (Oliver Goldsmith). **SYN:** See syn. under **lie¹.**
—*v.i.* to lie about some small matter.
[perhaps < obsolete *fibble-fable,* a reduplication of *fable*] **—fib·ber,** *n.*

fib² (fib), *v.t., v.i.,* **fibbed, fib·bing.** *Slang.* to strike or beat, especially with the fists. [origin unknown]

fi·ber (fī′bər), *n.* **1a** a thread; threadlike part; any one of the very fine, long, threadlike pieces of which many organic and some inorganic materials consist; filament: *A muscle is made up of many fibers.* **b** a similar structure of artificial origin: *a fiber of rayon, a fiber of glass.* **2** a substance made up of threads or threadlike parts: *Hemp fiber can be spun into rope or woven into coarse cloth.* **3** texture: *a cloth of coarse fiber.* **4** *Figurative.* character; nature: *He was a person of strong moral fiber and could resist temptation.* **5** one of the narrow elongated cells found in the bast of plants. **6** a slender, threadlike root of a plant. **7** one of the most slender twigs of a tree or bush: *to the last fiber of the loftiest tree* (Shelley). **8** = vulcanized fiber. **9** = dietary fiber: *Some types of fiber bind bile salts and acids, cholesterol, and other sterols, enhancing their elimination and thereby lowering their level in the blood* (Mina W. Lamb). Also, **fibre.** [< Old French *fibre,* learned borrowing from Latin *fibra*] **—fi′ber·less,** *adj.*

fi·ber·board (fī′bər bôrd′, -bōrd′), *n.* **1** a building material made by compressing fibers, especially of wood, into flat sheets. **2** a board or sheet of this material. Also, **fibreboard.**

fi·bered (fī′bərd), *adj.* having fibers: *a cashmere type of wool, though much longer fibered* (Atlantic). Also, **fibred.**

fi·ber-faced (fī′bər fāst′), *adj.* **1** having a facing or coat of fiber. **2** *U.S.* (of paper) having a surface composed of visible fibers.

fi·ber·fill (fī′bər fil′), *n.* a synthetic fiber used for filling or padding cushions, mattresses, etc.

Fi·ber·glas (fī′bər glas′, -gläs′), *n. Trademark.* = fiberglass.

fi·ber·glass (fī′bər glas′, -gläs′), *n.* very fine, flexible filaments of glass; spun glass. Fiberglass can be used, especially when combined with plastic, to make a wide variety of products, such as textiles, automobile bodies, swimming pools, insulating materials, boats, and fishing rods.

fi·ber·ize (fī′bə rīz), *v.t.,* **-ized, -iz·ing.** to break down to fibers; make fibrous.

fi·ber·op·tic (fī′bər op′tik), *adj.* of or having to do with fiber optics: *fiberoptic scanners, a fiberoptic light tube.*

fiber optics, **1** a bundle of very thin glass or plastic fibers enclosed in a tube, one end of which is at a light source and the other fronting a camera lens, used for conducting or transmitting light and images around bends and corners. The bundle may be bent or twisted without distorting the image. *Fiber optics have been fabricated from materials that transmit light in the ultraviolet to the infrared region; the frequent dependence of scientific instrumentation on responses in this spectral region should give impetus to using such fibers in the design of this equipment* (Morton Beroza). **2** the branch of optics using optical fibers to conduct or transmit light: *Technological progress in fiber optics, especially during the past ten years, has given the engineer an important additional tool for transferring information by means of light* (Science).

fiber plant, any plant which produces a fiber of commercial value, such as cotton, hemp, or straw.

fi·ber·scope (fī′bər skōp), *n.* an instrument for photographing, in color, small interiors, as of the stomach, consisting of a flexible tube containing a bundle of very thin glass fibers, which conduct the light, a mirror, and a lighting device at the end of the tube to be inserted.

fiber silk, an artificial material like silk made from cellulose.

Fi·bo·nac·ci numbers, series, or **sequence** (fē′bə nä′chē), the continuous series or sequence of numbers 1, 1, 2, 3, 5, 8, 13, 21, 34, 55, 89, 144, in which each number is the sum of the preceding two numbers: *The number of spiral floret formations visible in many sunflowers . . . and segments on the surface of a pineapple have been found to match Fibonacci numbers* (Time). *To make a C-major chord, you can play the third note of the octave* (*E*)*, the fifth note* (*G*)*, and the eighth note* (*C*)*. So your chord is made up of notes 3, 5, and 8, a Fibonacci series* (Diane Sherman). [< Leonardo *Fibonacci,* an Italian mathematician of the 1200's]

fi·bre (fī′bər), *n.* = fiber.

fi·bre·board (fī′bər bôrd′, -bōrd′), *n.* = fiberboard.

fi·bred (fī′bərd), *adj.* = fibered.

fi·bre·glass (fī′bər glas′), *n.* = fiberglass.

fi·bre·ize (fī′bə rīz), *v.t.,* **-ized, -iz·ing.** = fiberize.

fi·brid (fī′brid), *n.* any one of various synthetic polymers in fibrous form used as bonding materials.

fi·bri·form (fī′brə fôrm), *adj.* of the form of a fiber or fibers.

fi·bril (fī′brəl), *n.* **1** a small or very slender fiber. **2** one of the hairs on the roots of some plants. [< New Latin *fibrilla* (diminutive) < Latin *fibra* fiber]

fi·bril·la (fī bril′ə), *n., pl.* **-bril·lae** (-bril′ē). = fibril.

fi·bril·lar (fī′brə lər), *adj.* of fibrils; having to do with or of the nature of fibrils.

fi·bril·lar·y (fī′brə ler′ē), *adj.* **1** of fibrils; having to do with or of the nature of fibrils. **2** of or having to do with fibrillation: *The fibrillary threshold, however, is markedly reduced by hypothermia* (Scientific American).

fi·bril·late (fī′brə lāt), *adj., v.,* **-lat·ed, -lat·ing.**
—*adj.* **1** having fibrils. **2** finely fibrous.
—*v.i.* **1** to suffer fibrillation: *Hearts cooled to an average 28 degrees centigrade during hypothermia also become highly irritable; they may fibrillate and cause death* (Time). **2** to turn into fibrillae; form fibrils or fibers.
—*v.t.* to form fibrils or fibers from: *to fibrillate a film to form the warp of a synthetic fabric.*

fi·bril·la·tion (fī′brə lā′shən), *n.* **1** *Medicine.* a shivering or tremor in a muscle or nerve, especially a condition of the heart characterized by independent and irregular action of the muscle fibers. **2a** the act or process of forming fibrils or fibers. **b** the condition of being fibrillated.

fi·bril·li·form (fī bril′ə fôrm), *adj.* of the form of a fibril or fibrils.

fi·bril·lose (fī′brə lōs), *adj.* made of or furnished with fibrils.

fi·brin (fī′brən), *n.* **1** a white, tough, elastic, fibrous protein formed when blood clots by the action of thrombin on fibrinogen: *The fibrin forms a meshwork of strands which, with the entrapped red blood cells, comprises the clot* (Harbaugh and Goodrich). **2** a similar substance found in some plants; gluten in plants. [< Latin *fibra* fiber + English *-in*]

fi·bri·nate (fī′brə nāt), *v.t.,* **-nat·ed, -nat·ing.** to add fibrin to (the blood). **—fi′bri·na′tion,** *n.*

fi·brin·bi·o·plast (fī′brən bī′ō plast), *n.* a synthetic fibrous tissue used to replace missing human tissue in surgical operations: *The Hungarian biochemical invention "fibrinbioplast" . . . also stimulates regeneration of the body's own tissue* (Richard A. Pierce).

fibrin foam, a soft, spongy substance made of fibrinogen which is activated by dipping into or spraying with thrombin and used as a pad or filling to close wounds and promote clotting of blood. It is not necessary to remove the foam, as it will be absorbed by the body.

fi·brin·o·gen (fī brin′ə jən), *n.* a protein, found especially in the blood and lymph, that interacts with thrombin, an enzyme, to yield fibrin in the coagulation of blood. [< *fibrin* + *-gen*]

fi·bri·no·gen·ic (fī′brə nō jen′ik), *adj.* = fibrinogenous.

fi·bri·nog·e·nous (fī′brə noj′ə nəs), *adj.* producing fibrin.

fi·bri·noid (fī′brə noid), *adj., n.* **—*adj.*** having the characteristics of fibrin: *a fibrinoid material.*
—*n.* *Biology.* a homogeneous substance that stains like fibrin, found normally in the placenta and also in diseased connective tissue.

fi·bri·no·ly·sin (fī′brə nō lī′sin, -nol′ə-), *n.* an enzyme that can cause fibrin to dissolve, formed by the action of certain bacteria.
[< *fibrin* + *lysin*]

fi·bri·nol·y·sis (fī′brə nol′ə sis), *n.* the dissolving of fibrin by enzymatic action. Fibrinolysis resulting from an imbalance of enzymes may cause severe bleeding, especially during surgery and childbirth.
[< *fibrin* + *lysis*]

fi·bri·no·lyt·ic (fī′brə nō lit′ik), *adj.* of or produced by a fibrinolysin.

fi·bri·no·pep·tide (fī′brə nō pep′tīd), *n.* a protein substance formed in blood clotting: *The fact that the genes of man and of the chimpanzee specify identical fibrinopeptides implies that the two species shared a common ancestor comparatively recently* (London Times).

fi·bri·no·sis (fī′brə nō′sis), *n.* a condition marked by excess of fibrin in the blood.

fi·bri·nous (fī′brə nəs), *adj.* **1** of or composed of fibrin. **2** like fibrin.

fi·bro (fī′brō), *n.* (in Australia) asbestos cement. [shortened < *fibro-cement*]

fibro-, *combining form.* fiber; fibers; fibrous tissue: *Fibroid = made up of fibers. Fibroplasia = creation of fibrous tissue.* [< Latin *fibra* fiber]

fi|bro|blast (fī′brə blast), *n.* one of the cells from which fibrous tissue is immediately formed after an injury: *In the dermis ... the cells called fibroblasts enter the wound and build scar tissue by manufacturing collagen fibers and other proteins* (Scientific American).

fi|bro|blas|tic (fī′brə blas′tik), *adj.* of or having to do with fibroblasts.

fi|bro|car|ti|lage (fī′brō kär′tə lij), *n.* a very resistant cartilage found between vertebrae and at other points of articulation of the bones.

fi|bro-ce|ment (fī′brō sə ment′), *n. British.* = asbestos cement.

fi|bro|crys|tal|line (fī′brō kris′tə lin), *adj.* crystallized in fibrous form: *Many calcareous organic forms, such as the skeletons of the corals, are fibrocrystalline.*

fi|bro|cyte (fī′brə sīt), *n.* a fibroblast that is normally inactive but that begins to proliferate following tissue injury.

fi|bro|cyt|ic (fī′brə sit′ik), *adj.* of or having to do with fibrocytes.

fi|bro|gen|ic (fī′brə jen′ik), *adj.* producing fibers: *The great fibrogenic activity of quartz compared with other minerals makes dust composition of equal importance* (New Scientist).

fi|broid (fī′broid), *adj., n.* **—*adj.*** **1** made up of fibers or fibrous tissue: *a fibroid tumor.* **2** of fiberlike structure.
—*n.* a tumor made up of fibers or fibrous tissue.

fi|bro|in (fī′brō in), *n.* a protein forming the principal constituent of raw silk and cobwebs. [< *fibro* + *-in*]

fi|bro|lite (fī′brə līt), *n.* a fibrous white or gray mineral consisting chiefly of aluminum silicate; sillimanite.

fi|bro|lyt|ic (fī′brə lit′ik), *adj.* having the ability to break down fibrous tissue, as certain enzymes.

fi|bro|ma (fī brō′mə), *n., pl.* **-mas, -ma|ta** (-mə tə). *Medicine.* a fibrous tumor, usually benign. [< New Latin *fibroma* < Latin *fibra* fiber + New Latin *-oma* tumor]

fi|brom|a|tous (fī brom′ə təs), *adj.* having to do with or of the nature of a fibroma.

fi|bro|pla|sia (fī′brə plā′zhə), *n.* the creation of fibrous tissue, occurring normally in the healing of wounds, and abnormally in certain diseases. [< New Latin *fibroplasia* < Latin *fibra* fiber + Greek *plássein* to mold]

fi|bro|sar|co|ma (fī′brō sär kō′mə), *n.* a tumor intermediate in character between a fibroma and a sarcoma.

fi|brose (fī′brōs), *v.i.,* **-brosed, -bros|ing.** to form fibrous tissue, as in cirrhosis or in cicatrization.

fi|bro|sis (fī brō′sis), *n.* excessive growth of fibrous connective tissue in an organ or part of the body. [< New Latin *fibrosis* < Latin *fibra* fiber + *-osis* -osis]

fi|bro|si|tis (fī′brə sī′tis), *n.* inflammation of fibrous tissue in the muscle sheaths.

fi|brot|ic (fī brot′ik), *adj.* of or having to do with fibrosis.

fi|brous (fī′brəs), *adj.* **1** made up of fibers; having fibers. **2** like fiber; stringy. **3** having a splintery or threadlike surface when fractured: *fibrous minerals.* **—fi′brous|ly,** *adv.* **—fi′brous|ness,** *n.*

fibrous root, one of a group of slender roots of nearly equal size found on plants such as corn, wheat, and grass. See picture under **root**[1].

fi|bro|vas|cu|lar (fī′brō vas′kyə lər), *adj. Botany.* consisting of woody fibers and ducts: *the fibrovascular tissue in a plant.*

fibrovascular bundle, a vascular bundle surrounded by elongate fibers. Leaf veins are fibrovascular bundles.

fib|ster (fib′ster), *n. Informal.* a fibber: *You silly little fibster* (Thackeray).

fib|u|la (fib′yə lə), *n., pl.* **-lae** (-lē), **-las. 1** the outer and thinner of the two bones in the lower leg of a human being. It extends from knee to ankle and articulates with the tibia and talus. See picture under **leg. 2** the corresponding bone in the hind leg of animals. **3** *Archaeology.* a clasp, buckle, or brooch, often highly ornamented. [< Latin *fībula* clasp, brooch]

fib|u|lar (fib′yə lər), *adj.* of or having to do with the fibula: *a fibular ridge, fibular osteomyelitis.*

-fic, *suffix forming nouns from nouns, adjectives, and adverbs.* making; causing: *Pacific = making peace. Terrific = causing terror.* [< Latin *-ficus* < *-ficere,* variant in compounds of *facere* do, make]

FICA (no periods), Federal Insurance Contributions Act (a federal act dealing with the tax paid toward social security).

-fication, *suffix forming nouns, usually corresponding to verbs ending in* **-fy.** a making or doing: *Falsification = a falsifying or making false.* [< Latin *-ficātiō, -ōnis* < *-ficāre* < *facere* do, make]

fice (fīs), *n. U.S. Dialect.* feist.

fiche (fēsh), *n., pl.* **fich|es** or **fiche. 1** a card, slip of paper, or strip of film, used in indexing or cataloging: *There is a strong possibility that a uniform, computer-supported fiche system will be developed over the next few years to prevent gaps from appearing in the records—not to "lose" people, as it were* (Science Journal). **2** a microfiche or ultrafiche. [< French *fiche*]

***fich|u** (fish′ü), *n.* a three-cornered piece of muslin, lace, or other soft material worn by women about the neck, throat, and shoulders, the ends being drawn together or crossed on the breast. It was formerly worn also on the head. [< French *fichu* neckerchief]

***fichu**

fi|cin (fī′sin), *n.* a protein-splitting enzyme extracted from fig trees, used especially as a milk coagulant and meat tenderizer. [< Latin *fīcus* fig + English *-in*]

fick|le (fik′əl), *adj.* **1** changing; not constant; likely to change without reason: *fickle fortune, a fickle lover.* **SYN:** inconstant, unstable, unsteady, capricious, volatile. **2** likely to change in aspect or nature; uncertain: *fickle weather, winds, etc.* [Old English *ficol* deceitful] **—fick′le|ness,** *n.*

fi|co (fē′kō), *n., pl.* **-coes.** *Obsolete.* a fig. [< Italian *fico* < Latin *fīcus.* See etym. of doublet **fig.**]

fict., fiction.

fic|tile (fik′təl; *especially British* fik′tīl), *adj.* **1** that can be molded. **2** molded into form by art. **3** made of earth or clay by a potter: *The Etruscans, who were famous potters, used to make fictile coffins* (Thomas D. Fosbroke). **4** having to do with pottery or earthenware. [< Latin *fictilis* < *fingere* to form, fashion]

fic|tion (fik′shən), *n.* **1** a story that is not fact; novels, short stories, and other prose writings that tell about imaginary people and happenings. "Robinson Crusoe" is fiction. *Modern fiction lacks the long descriptive passages so characteristic of Victorian writing. Most of our nautical fictions seem to be caulked with hokum* (William McFee). *Abbr:* fict. **SYN:** tale, romance, fable. **2** something made up: *The explorer exaggerated so much in telling about his adventures that it was impossible to separate fact from fiction.* **3** an imaginary account or statement; made-up story: *The book was supposed to be an authentic diary, but it was, obviously, an improbable fiction.* **SYN:** fabrication, figment. **4** an inventing of imaginary incidents, accounts, or stories; a feigning: *Her noble birth was just a fiction of the mind.* **SYN:** falsehood, fib. **5** *Law.* something acted upon as a fact in spite of its possible falsity; legal fiction. It is a fiction that a corporation is a person. [< Latin *fictiō, -ōnis* < *fingere* to form, fashion]

fic|tion|al (fik′shə nəl), *adj.* of or having to do with fiction: *Robinson Crusoe is a fictional character. Fictional writing differs from factual writing. Some fictional characters seem very real.* **—fic′tion|al|ly,** *adv.*

fic|tion|al|ist (fik′shə nə list), *n.* a writer of fiction; fictionist.

fic|tion|al|i|za|tion (fik′shə nə lə zā′shən), *n.* **1** the presentation in a dramatic or literary work of actual persons, events, or both, with imaginative invention: *"Inherit the Wind" ... is a fictionalization of the [Scopes] Trial and the surrounding events* (New York Times). **2** the conversion of a factual account into a fictional account.

fic|tion|al|ize (fik′shə nə līz), *v.t.,* **-ized, -iz|ing.** to give a fictitious form to; make fiction out of: *The famous trial was fictionalized in this novel.* **—fic′tion|al|iz′er,** *n.*

fic|tion|eer (fik′shə nir′), *n.* a writer of fiction: *The scientific fictioneers who look into the future may be awfully right or awfully wrong, but they are valuable men* (Newsweek).

fic|tion|eer|ing (fik′shə nir′ing), *n.* the writing of fiction.

fic|tion|ist (fik′shə nist), *n.* a writer of fiction.

fic|tion|ize (fik′shə nīz), *v.,* **-ized, -iz|ing.** **—*v.i.*** to write fiction.
—*v.t.* to give a fictitious form to; fictionalize.

fic|ti|tious (fik tish′əs), *adj.* **1** not real; imaginary; made-up: *The characters in "Alice in Wonderland" are fictitious.* **2** of fiction; having to do with or of the nature of fiction; originating in the imagination. **3** assumed in order to deceive; false: *The criminal used a fictitious name.* **SYN:** counterfeit, sham, feigned. [< Latin *fictīcius* (with English *-ous*) artificial < *fingere* to form, fashion] **—fic|ti′tious|ly,** *adv.* **—fic|ti′tious|ness,** *n.*

fictitious planet, the hypothetical center of an epicycle, formerly used in astronomy to explain the motion of planets.

fic|tive (fik′tiv), *adj.* **1** concerned with or having to do with the creation of fiction. **2** originating in fiction; created by the imagination; fictitious. **3** sham; assumed. **—fic′tive|ly,** *adv.*

***fid**[1] (fid), *n.* **1** a heavy square bar used to support a topmast. **2** a wooden or metal bar or pin, used to support or steady anything. **3** a hard pin like a spike, for separating strands of rope in splicing. [origin uncertain]

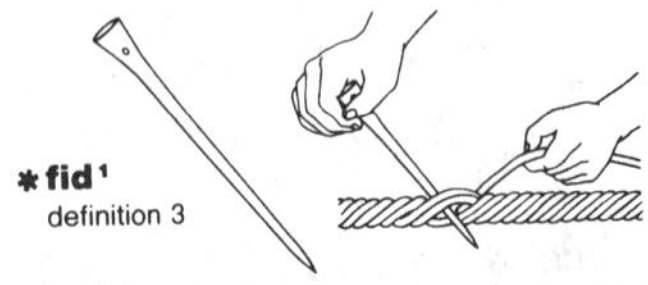

***fid**[1]
definition 3

fid[2] (fid), *n. British Informal.* a pile; heap: *Each would always return with a fid of manuscript written on board* (Nigel Nicolson). [probably < English dialect *fid* a handful of straw]

-fid, *suffix.* split; cleft; lobed, as in *bifid.* [< Latin *-fidus,* noun suffix related to *findere* cleave, split]

fid., fiduciary.

FID (no periods), Fédération Internationale de Documentation (French, International Federation of Documentation).

fi|date (fī′dāt), *v.t.,* **-dat|ed, -dat|ing.** to give (a chess piece) immunity from capture. [< Latin *fīdus* sure + English *-ate*[1]] **—fi|da′tion,** *n.*

fid|dle (fid′əl), *n., v.,* **-dled, -dling. —*n.*** **1** *Informal.* a violin: *When I play on my fiddle in Dooney, Folk dance like a wave of the sea* (William Butler Yeats). **2** something resembling a violin. **3** *Nautical.* a low railing on the edge of a table to prevent dishes from sliding off when the ship rolls or pitches. **4** *Slang.* deception; fraud; swindle.
—*v.i.* **1** *Informal.* to play on a violin. **2** to make aimless movements; play nervously; toy: *The embarrassed boy fiddled with his hat.* **3** to fool around; tamper: *Such a notice might discourage anyone tempted to fiddle with the investment company's funds* (Wall Street Journal).
—*v.t.* **1** *Informal.* to play (a piece of music) on a violin. **2** to trifle: *He fiddled away the whole day doing absolutely nothing.* **3** *Slang.* to cheat; swindle; falsify.
be (or **play**) **second fiddle (to).** See under **second fiddle.**
fit as a fiddle, in excellent physical condition: *I arrived at my destination feeling ... fit as a fiddle* (Harrington O'Reilly).
[Middle English *fidele,* perhaps ultimately < Medieval Latin *vitula.* Compare etym. under **viol.**]

fid|dle|back (fid′əl bak′), *n.* **1** a back shaped like a violin, especially the splat of a chair. **2** *Informal.* a chasuble having a fiddle-shaped back. **3** = fiddler beetle.

fiddleback figure, a pattern in the grain of wood which produces an appearance of waviness.

fiddle block, *Nautical.* a long block having a larger sheave above a smaller one.

fiddle bow, a slender rod with horsehairs stretched on it for playing a violin, cello, or other stringed instrument.

fid|dle-de-dee (fid′əl dē dē′), *interj., n.* = nonsense.

fid|dle-fad|dle (fid′əl fad′əl), *n., interj., v.,* **-dled, -dling.** *Informal.* **—*n.*** trifling talk or action; nonsense.
—*interj.* = nonsense!
—*v.i.* to be busy with trivial matters; fuss: *The women spent more time ... fiddle-faddling with lace and silk and colored beads* (Harper's).
fiddle-faddles, trivial matters: *Come leave your fiddle-faddles* (Roger North).
[perhaps humorous reduplication of *fiddle* to make aimless movements]

fiddle fig, = fiddle-leaf fig.

fid|dle-foot|ed (fid′əl fu̇t′id), *adj. U.S. Informal.* moving back and forth; restless: *a fiddle-footed traveler, fiddle-footed journalists.*

fid|dle|head (fid′əl hed′), *n.* **1** a scroll-shaped ornament at the bow of a ship, resembling the head of a violin. **2** a young frond of a fern.

fid|dle-leaf fig (fid′əl lēf′), a fig tree native to tropical Africa, with large, thick, shiny fiddle-shaped leaves. It is often cultivated as a house plant.

fid|dler (fid′lər), *n.* **1** a person who plays a violin. **2** = fiddler crab. **3** a trifler.

fiddler beetle, a black, scarabaeid beetle of Australia, with green markings that form the shape of a violin on the elytra; fiddleback.

***fiddler crab,** a small, burrowing crab, common

Pronunciation Key: hat, āge, cãre, fär; let, ēqual, tėrm; it, īce; hot, ōpen, ôrder; oil, out; cup, pu̇t, rüle; child; long; thin; ᴛʜen; zh, measure; ə represents **a** in about, **e** in taken, **i** in pencil, **o** in lemon, **u** in circus.

along the Atlantic Coast of the United States; calling crab; fiddler. The male has an enlarged claw.

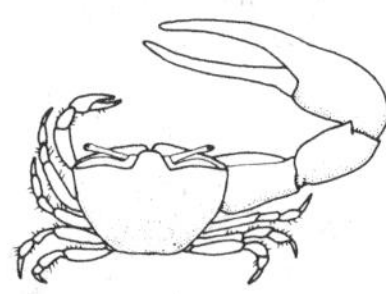
***fiddler crab**

fid|dler|fish (fid′lər fish′), *n., pl.* **-fish|es** or (*collectively*) **-fish.** a ray similar to and related to the guitarfish.
fid|dle-shaped (fid′əl shāpt′), *adj.* having the form of a violin; panduriform: *a fiddle-shaped leaf, a fiddle-shaped chasuble.*
fid|dle|stick (fid′əl stik′), *n.* **1** *Informal.* a violin bow. **2** a mere nothing; trifle.
fid|dle|sticks (fid′əl stiks′), *interj. Informal.* nonsense! rubbish!
fid|dle|wood (fid′əl wu̇d′), *n.* **1** the heavy, hard wood of various tropical American trees. **2** any one of these trees.
fid|dling (fid′ling), *adj.* **1** petty; trifling; unimportant: *fiddling work.* **2** contemptible; futile: *fiddling criticism.*
fid|dly (fid′lē), *adj. Informal.* requiring much handling and fussing: *fiddly paperwork. In electronics, men's hands lack the dexterity for "fiddly" jobs* (London Times). [< *fiddle,* verb + *-y* [1]]
fi|de|i|com|mis|sar|y (fī′dē ī kom′ə ser′ē), *n., pl.* **-sar|ies,** *adj.* **—*n.*** a person who is the beneficiary of a fideicommissum.
—*adj.* of or like a fideicommissum.
fi|de|i|com|mis|sor (fī′dē ī kə mis′ər), *n.* a person who makes or leaves a fideicommissum.
fi|de|i|com|mis|sum (fī′dē ī kə mis′əm), *n., pl.* **-mis|sa** (-mis′ə). a request in a will that an heir give something to a third person. [< Latin *fideicommissum,* neuter past participle of *fidei-committere* < *fideī,* dative of *fidēs* faith + *committere* entrust, commit]
Fi|de|i De|fen|sor (fī′dē ī di fen′sôr), *Latin.* Defender of the Faith (a title held by English kings and queens from Henry VIII to the present).
fi|de|ism (fī′dē iz əm), *n.* a mode of philosophical or theological thought according to which knowledge depends upon a fundamental act of faith.
fi|de|ist (fī′dē ist), *n.* a believer in fideism.
fi|de|is|tic (fī′dē is′tik), *adj.* of or having to do with fideism or fideists.
Fi|del|ism (fə del′iz əm), *n.* = Fidelismo.
Fi|de|lis|mo (fi′de lēz′mō), *n.* Communist revolutionary activity in Latin America based on the theories and practices of Fidel Castro, born 1927, premier of Cuba; Castroism: *The incident served to underline the widening differences between the traditional Latin-American Moscow-based Communism and the Cuban variety, often referred to as Fidelismo* (David Huelin). [< Spanish *Fidelismo* < *Fidel* Castro + *-ismo* -ism]
Fi|de|lis|ta (fi′de lēs′tə), *n., adj.* **—*n.*** a supporter of Fidel Castro or Fidelismo.
—*adj.* favoring or supporting Fidelismo.
[< Spanish *Fidelista* < *Fidel* Castro + *-ista* -ist]
fi|del|i|ty (fī del′ə tē, fə-), *n., pl.* **-ties. 1** steadfast faithfulness; loyalty: *a dog's fidelity to his master. Fidelity to engagements is a virtue* (Jeremy Bentham). **SYN:** constancy, allegiance, fealty. **2** strictness or thoroughness in the performance of duty: *His fidelity and industry brought him speedy promotion.* **3** exactness, as in a copy; accuracy: *The reporter wrote his story with absolute fidelity. The only critics who have expressed our convictions with any adequate fidelity* (Emerson). **4** the ability of a radio transmitter or receiver or other device to transmit or reproduce an electric signal or sound accurately: *The fidelity of tape reproduction is considered equal to that of discs* (Wall Street Journal). [< Latin *fidēlitās* < *fidēlis* faithful < *fidēs* faith. See etym. of doublet **fealty.**]
fidelity bond, a bond issued as fidelity insurance.
fidelity insurance, insurance against losses due to the dishonesty or negligence of an employee.
fidge (fij), *n., v.,* **fidged, fidg|ing.** *Dialect.* **—*n.*** **1** the act or habit of fidgeting. **2** the state of being fidgety. **3** a restless person.
—*v. i.* to twitch: *Look, Jim, how my fingers fidge . . . I can't keep 'em still* (Robert Louis Stevenson).
[apparently variant of *fike*]
fidg|et (fij′it), *v., n.* **—*v. i.*** to move about restlessly; be uneasy: *My little brother fidgets if he has to sit still a long time.*
—*v. t.* to make uneasy; worry.
—*n.* **1** a condition of being restless or uneasy. **2** a person who moves about restlessly or worries unnecessarily, or who causes the fidgets in others: *No fidget and no reformer, just A calm observer of ought and must* (Bliss Carman).
the fidgets, a fit of restlessness or uneasiness: *The long, tiresome speech gave us the fidgets.*
[apparently < *fidge,* in the sense of "move restlessly"]—**fidg′et|er,** *n.*
fidg|et|y (fij′ə tē), *adj.* restless; uneasy: *That fidgety girl keeps twisting her fingers and moving her feet.* —**fidg′et|i|ness,** *n.*
fi|dic|i|na|lis (fi dis′ə nā′lis), *n., pl.* **-les** (-lēz). one of the four little lumbrical muscles in the palm of the hand, the action of which facilitates quick motion of the fingers, as in playing the violin. [< New Latin *fidicinalis* < Latin *fidicen, -inis* a lyre or lute player]
fi|do or **FIDO**[1] (fī′dō), *n., pl.* **-dos** or **-DOS.** a coin minted with an error or defect. [< *f*(reaks), *i*(rregulars), *d*(efects), *o*(ddities); coined by Edward V. Wallace, an American numismatist]
FIDO[2] (fī′dō), *n.* dispersal of fog at a runway of an airfield by the use of heat. [< *F*(og) *I*(nvestigation) (and) *D*(ispersal) *O*(peration)]
fi|du|cial (fə dü′shəl, -dyü′-), *adj.* **1** (especially of a line or point) assumed as a fixed basis of reference or comparison. **2** = fiduciary. **3** *Theology.* of or having to do with trust or reliance. [< Late Latin *fīdūciālis* < Latin *fīdūcia* a trust < *fīdere* to trust]—**fi|du′cial|ly,** *adv.*
fiducial edge, the thin edge of a ruler.
fi|du|ci|ar|i|ly (fə dü′shē er′ə lē, -dyü′-), *adv.* **1** in trust. **2** with confidence.
fi|du|ci|ar|y (fə dü′shē er′ē, -dyü′-), *adj., n., pl.* **-ar|ies. —*adj.*** **1** held in trust: *fiduciary estates.* **2** holding in trust. A fiduciary possessor is legally responsible for what belongs to another. **3** of a trustee; of trust and confidence: *A guardian acts in a fiduciary capacity.* **4** depending upon public trust and confidence for its value: *Paper money that cannot be redeemed in gold or silver is fiduciary currency.* **—*n.*** = trustee.
[< Latin *fīdūciārius* (holding) in trust < *fīdūcia* a trust < *fīdere* to trust]
fiduciary bond, a bond issued to insure against losses due to the dishonesty or negligence of a person appointed by a court to be responsible for another's property, such as an executor or guardian.
fi|dus A|cha|tes (fī′dəs ə kā′tēz), *Latin.* **1** (literally) faithful Achates (the trusted friend of Aeneas). **2** a trusted friend.
fie (fī), *interj.* for shame! shame!: *Fie upon you!* [Middle English *fi* < Old French *fi,* or *fy* < Latin *fī* an expression of disgust at a disagreeable odor]
▶**Fie,** in early use, expressed disgust or indignant reproach. More recently it was said to children to shame them for some unbecoming action, but is now used to express humorous pretense of feeling shocked.
fief (fēf), *n.* **1** a piece of land held on condition of giving military and other services to the feudal lord owning it, in return for his protection and the use of the land; feudal estate; feud; fee. **2** a territory held in fee: *proprietors who received their land as an hereditary fief* (Thomas Arnold). **3** *Figurative.* domain; realm: *Bergen County, for instance, is cut up into seventy municipalities, each with its multitude of police chiefs, dog catchers, and health officers. Each guards its tiny fief jealously* (Harper's). Also, **feoff.** [< Old French *fief,* variant of *fieu;* see etym. under **fee**]
fief|dom (fēf′dəm), *n.* = fief.
field (fēld), *n., v., adj.* **—*n.*** **1** Often, **fields.** a piece of land with few or no trees; stretch of open land; open country: *They rode through forests and fields.* **2** a piece of land used for crops or pasture, usually cleared and enclosed by hedges, fences, boundary stones, or the like. **3** a piece of land used for some special purpose: *a flying field, a baseball field.* **4** land yielding some product: *the coal fields of Pennsylvania, the gold fields of South Africa.* **5** *Military.* **a** the place where a battle is or has been fought; battlefield: *the field of Gettysburg.* **b** a battle: *a hard-fought field. What though the field be lost? All is not lost* (Milton). **c** the region or area other than a post or camp, where military or other operations are carried on. **6a** an area or place away from the usual location where something is done or handled: *a hospital emergency operation in the field.* **b** an area away from the base of operation of a school, company, or other organization: *The salesman called on his customers in the field.* **7** a flat space; broad surface: *A field of ice surrounds the North Pole.* **8** the surface on which something is pictured or painted; background: *the field of a coat of arms.* **9** range of interest; sphere of activity: *the field of politics, the field of art, the field of science.* **10** *Physics.* the space throughout which a force operates. A magnet has a field of force around it. **11a** (in an electric motor or generator) the magnetic field. **b** (in a generator) a field magnet. **c** a field winding. **12** the space or area in which things can be seen through a telescope, microscope, or other optical instrument, without moving it. **13** *Television.* the entire screen area occupied by an image. **14a** an area set aside for sports or games: *the playing fields of Eton.* **b** the center of such an area, especially when circled by a track where contests such as in jumping or throwing are held. **c** the sports contested in this area (contrasted with *track*). **d** all the contestants in a game, contest, or outdoor sport. **e** the players active on the field, for example in football. **f** all those in a game or contest except one or more specified: *to bet on one horse against the field.* **g** the defensive team, especially in cricket or baseball, as distinguished from the one trying to score. **15** *Baseball.* **a** the playing area, especially as divided into infield and outfield. **b** the outfield, generally divided into right field, center field, and left field. **16** the ground of each division of a flag: *Their flag was a red circle on a white field.* **17** *Mathematics.* any set of elements, such as the set of all real numbers, which has two operations called addition and multiplication. For each operation the set is closed, associative, and commutative, has an identity element and inverses (the zero element being excluded for multiplication), and is distributive of multiplication over addition.
—*v. t.* **1** (especially in baseball or cricket) to stop or catch (a batted ball) and throw it in. **2** to send (a player, team, troops, or other individual or group) to the field. **3** *Informal, Figurative.* to answer skillfully (difficult or controversial questions): *The President fielded fast ones on everything from the civil rights controversy to his personal finances* (Newsweek). **4** to protect; defend: *He fielded his political position gracefully.*
—*v. i.* to act as a fielder in baseball, cricket, etc.
—*adj.* **1** of or having to do with a field or fields; used in the field. **2** inhabiting or growing in open country or fields. **3** *Sports.* of or contested on a field: *Athletic events such as polevaulting and discus throwing are called field events.* **4** of or used for combat, as distinguished from service or staff: *a field operation.* **5** having to do with or in an area away from a base of operation or a location where something is usually done: *a field call by the company salesman.*
play the field, a to take a broad sphere of action or operation: *He played the field academically, obtaining doctorates from several universities.* **b** *U.S. Slang.* to go with many different persons of the opposite sex: *The brothers will be uncomfortable, the pattern will be upset, and it is all Susie's fault for trying to play the field a bit* (Atlantic).
take the field, to begin a battle, campaign, game, or other contest: *They will. . . learn the strength of the rebels, before they dare take the field* (Robert Cecil).
[Old English *feld.* See related etym. at **veld.**]
field ambulance, an ambulance used to pick up and treat the sick and wounded on the battlefield.
field army, the largest tactical unit consisting typically of a headquarters, two or more corps, and auxiliary troops, commanded by a general.
field artillery, artillery mounted on carriages for easy movement by armies in the field and used against ground forces and installations.
Field Artillery, a combat branch of the U.S. Army equipped with mobile artillery and attached in units to various units of ground forces. *Abbr:* FA (no periods).
field bag, = musette bag.
field battery, a set of guns mounted on carriages for use in the field.
field bean, any of various beans whose edible seeds are removed from the pod before cooking; shell bean.
field bed, 1 a usually portable bed for use in the open. **2** a bed with four posts supported by an arched canopy.
field bindweed, a bindweed native to Europe and now commonly found on the eastern coast of Canada and the United States and in the Middle Western United States.
field book, a book used in field work for recording observations, as by surveyors, geologists, or naturalists.
field brome grass, = brome grass.
field coil, an insulated coil of wire that serves to produce by its flow of current the magnetic field of any electrical device.
field colors, *Military.* small flags for indicating the positions of squadrons or other groupings, and the location of headquarters.
field commander, a military officer whose duty is to direct combat action.
field corn, a type of corn grown primarily as feed

for livestock or to be ground as meal. The kernels are tough and not sweet.

field cornet, a minor official having jurisdiction within a district in South Africa, charged with inquiring into and reporting crime, and with other duties.

field|craft (fēld′kraft′, -kräft′), *n. Especially British.* **1** skills appropriate to the battlefield: *The cadets have been practising command, tactics, radio, map-reading, and fieldcraft in the Kyrenia Mountains area* (Manchester Guardian). **2** knowledge about wildlife, woods, and outdoor activities; skill in hunting, camping, and similar activities; woodcraft: *The object of the hunt is the trophy, with the attendant fieldcraft and sportsmanship* (New Scientist).

field cricket, **1** a black cricket of North America, commonly found in the fields. **2** a black or brown European cricket with long, threadlike antennae. It is larger and makes a louder noise than the house cricket. It lays its eggs in the soil.

field crop, any crop, such as grain or hay, grown on a large scale, usually for feeding livestock.

field day, **1** a day for outdoor sports, games, and athletic contests. **2** a day when soldiers or airmen perform drills, mock fights, or flyovers. **3** *Figurative.* a day of unusual activity, display, or success: *The children were having a field day at the beach, swimming and digging in the sand. The rally provided a field day for the new fashion of lapel buttons* (Alistair Cooke). **4** a day when explorations, scientific investigations, or the like, such as of a learned society, are carried on in the field.

field effect transistor, a transistor in which the effect of a transverse electric field is used to control the current. *Abbr:* FET (no periods).

field emission, the release of electrons from the surface of a conductor, caused by a strong electric field.

field-e|mis|sion microscope (fēld′i mish′ən), a microscope which uses the electrons emitted from the surface of a conductor under the influence of a strong electric field to produce a magnified image of the emitting surface on a fluorescent screen. The more powerful field-ion microscope was developed from this device.

field|er (fēl′dər), *n.* **1** a baseball player who is stationed around or outside the diamond to stop the ball and throw it in. **2** a similar player in a game of cricket.

fielder's choice, a play in which a baseball fielder tries to put out a runner already on base rather than the batter, though the latter could have been put out at first base.

field|fare (fēld′fãr′), *n.* a European thrush with a gray head, black tail, and brown and white body. [Middle English *feldefare*, apparently altered spelling of *feldeware*, perhaps field dweller]

field glasses or **field glass**, small binoculars for use outdoors.

field goal, **1** *American Football.* a goal counting three points, made by a place kick or drop kick. **2** *Basketball.* a basket scored while the ball is in play, counting two points, or counting three points when scored from beyond the 3-point line.

field-grade officer (fēld′grād′), = field officer.

field gun, a cannon mounted on a carriage for use in the field; fieldpiece.

field hand, *U.S.* **1** a person who is hired to work in the fields; farm laborer: *The huge machines ... are capable of picking as much cotton in one day as from 40 to 70 good field hands* (Wall Street Journal). **2** (formerly) a slave who worked on a plantation.

field hockey, a game similar to ice hockey but played on a field with eleven players on a side.

field hospital, a temporary hospital on or near a battlefield.

field house, **1** a building near an athletic field used for storing equipment, and often having dressing rooms. **2** a building used principally for athletic contests indoors, as basketball, or track and field events.

field ice, ice formed in fields or large flat tracts in the polar seas.

field|ing average (fēl′ding), a decimal fraction indicating a baseball player's record as a fielder. It is obtained by dividing the number of put-outs and assists by the number of chances, and carrying it to three decimal places.

field intensity, = field strength.

field-i|on microscope (fēld′ī′on, -ən), an extremely powerful microscope similar to the field-emission microscope but using, instead of electrons, the ions of a gas near the emitting surface to produce a magnified image of the emitting surface on a flourescent screen; ion microscope: *In the field-ion microscope, it is possible not only to observe the positions of individual atoms on a metal surface at low temperatures, but also to follow the movement of the atoms when the specimen is heated* (New Scientist).

***field jacket**, a military jacket designed to be worn under combat conditions.

***field jacket**

field judge, *U.S.* a person who assists the referee at a football game. His chief function is timing the game and starting and stopping the clock between plays.

field kitchen, **1** mobile kitchen equipment to provide meals for military personnel in the field. **2** any kitchen set up outdoors to serve a considerable number of people.

field lark, = meadow lark.

field lens, the lens furthest from the eye in the eyepiece of a microscope or telescope.

field magnet, a magnet used to produce or maintain a magnetic field, especially a magnet in a generator or electric motor.

field marshal, an army officer ranking next below the commander in chief in the British, French, German, and some other armies.

field mouse, any variety of mouse living in fields and meadows; meadow mouse.

field mushroom, = meadow mushroom.

field music, **1** the musicians attached to a military unit to provide music during active operations when the band is not present, as drummers, fifers, buglers, and pipers. **2** the music produced by such a group.

field officer, an army officer ranking above a captain and below a brigadier general. Colonels, lieutenant colonels, and majors are field officers. Also, **field-grade officer**.

field of force, = field (def. 10).

field of honor, the site of armed conflict, as in a battle or duel.

field of play, *U.S.* playing field; the area officially marked off for play.

field of vision, the space over which objects can be discerned, especially the space or range within which objects are visible to an eye looking through a telescope or microscope; visual field.

field painter, an abstract expressionist who produces field paintings; imagist.

field painting, a style of abstract expressionism restricted to painting simple, luminous expanses of closely related colors; imagism.

field pea, a valuable forage plant related to the cultivated pea.

field|piece (fēld′pēs′), *n.* = field gun.

field pine, a small heathlike herb related to the rockrose, found near the Atlantic coast from Nova Scotia to Virginia.

field poppy, the European corn poppy.

field ration, a food ration provided for troops in the field.

field round, a round in archery of four arrows shot at each of 14 targets on a woodland or other open course.

field scabious, a plant with long, tough stems and dense flower heads of various colors.

field service, service, especially by civil servants and social workers, performed away from the main office or center: *All the executive departments have headquarters in Washington, but about 90 of every 100 employees work elsewhere in field services* (William G. Carleton).

fields|man (fēldz′mən), *n., pl.* **-men.** a cricket fielder.

field spaniel, any one of a breed of hunting dogs with a flat, glossy, usually black coat and weighing from 35 to 50 pounds.

field sparrow, a North American sparrow with a rusty crown and pink bill, found in overgrown pastures and brushy areas.

field sport, an outdoor sport, especially hunting or games and athletic contests played or held outdoors.

field station, an experiment station: *Their ramshackle laboratory building is part of the university's engineering research field station* (Wall Street Journal).

field|stone (fēld′stōn′), *n.* rough stone used in the construction of houses and walls.

field strength, *Physics.* the strength of a field at a given point, as measured by the force generated on a unit charge, unit mass, or the like, at that point; field intensity.

field-strip (fēld′strip′), *v.t.,* **-stripped, -strip|ping.** *U.S. Military.* **1** to take apart (a rifle, machine gun, or other firearm) for cleaning, repair, or inspection. **2** to take apart and scatter the tobacco of (a cigarette butt) so as to dispose of it neatly: *After smoking, the men "field-strip" their cigarettes except for filter tips, which must be placed in their pockets* (Harper's).

field structure, the part of a generator that acts as a magnet and sets up the magnetic lines of force. The coils for the field structure are usually insulated copper wire wound around iron cores.

field test, the field trial of a new product.

field-test (fēld′test′), *v.t.* to put (a new product) into field trial: *A live virus measles vaccine ... will soon be field-tested on 100,000 children* (Wall Street Journal).

field theorist, a person who studies field theory: *Field theorists like to start work by writing down a mathematical summary ... which expresses the energies of a general group of particles under the influence of whatever force is being considered* (Science News).

field theory, **1a** *Physics.* any theory about physical phenomena that takes into account the effects of one or more fields: *... quantum electrodynamics and other field theories* (New Scientist). See also **unified field theory**. **b** the branch of physics dealing with such theories: *Field theory begins from a prejudice in favor of mathematical depth ... The emphasis is on a rigorous mathematical understanding of the theory* (Scientific American). **2** *Psychology.* any theory or system, such as Gestalt psychology, that regards behavior as the result of the interaction of complex forces.

field trial, **1** a test of hunting dogs for their performance under working conditions in the field. **2** the testing of the efficiency and usefulness of a newly developed product under the conditions it would encounter in actual use.

field trip, a trip away from school to give students the opportunity to see things or places closely and at first hand: *The class went on a field trip to the fire department to observe the fire prevention methods they had been reading about.*

field winding, the coils in a generator or motor, connected in series, forming the circuit conducting the electrical current that produces the magnetic field.

field|work (fēld′wėrk′), *n.* **1** = field work. **2** a temporary fortification for defense made by soldiers in the field.

field work, **1** scientific or technical work done in the field, as by surveyors, geologists, or naturalists. **2** plowing, planting, or hoeing, or other work on the fields of a farm.

field|work|er (fēld′wėr′kər), *n.* a person who does field work.

fiend (fēnd), *n.* **1** an evil spirit; devil: *The natives thought the explorer was possessed by a fiend.* SYN: demon. **2** *Figurative.* a very wicked or cruel person: *a fiend in human form.* SYN: monster. **3** *Informal, Figurative.* a person who gives himself up to some habit, practice, game, or other activity: *A heroin fiend cannot get along without heroin. The free lunch fiend ... is one who makes a meal off what is really provided as a snack* (John S. Farmer). SYN: addict. **4** *U.S. Slang.* a student devoted to or unusually proficient in some study.

the Fiend, the Devil; Satan: *Gates ... belching outrageous flame ... since the Fiend passed through* (Milton).

[Old English *fēond*, (originally) present participle of *fēogan* to hate] —**fiend′like**, *adj.*

fiend|ish (fēn′dish), *adj.* very cruel or wicked; devilish; characteristic of a fiend: *fiendish tortures, a fiendish yell. The savages took fiendish delight in torturing their prisoners.* SYN: diabolical, demoniacal. —**fiend′ish|ly**, *adv.* —**fiend′ishness**, *n.*

fiend|ly (fēnd′lē), *adj. Obsolete.* devilish; fiendish.

fierce (firs), *adj.,* **fierc|er, fierc|est.** **1** savage; wild; ferocious: *A wounded lion can be fierce.* **2** *Figurative.* raging; violent: *fierce anger, a fierce attack. A fierce wind blows very hard. Moloch ... the strongest and the fiercest spirit That fought in heaven, now fiercer by despair* (Milton). **3** *Figurative.* very eager or active; ardent: *fierce determination to win, fierce efforts to get ahead.* **4** *Slang, Figurative.* very bad, unpleasant, or harmful: *This heat is really fierce.* [< Old French *fers*, or *fiers* < Latin *ferus* wild] —**fierce′ly**, *adv.* —**fierce′ness**, *n.*

—*Syn.* **1 Fierce, ferocious, savage** mean wild and cruel. **Fierce** suggests violence of feeling, manner, or action: *He was a fierce fighter.* **Ferocious** suggests a very cruel or brutal appearance or disposition: *That man looks ferocious.* **Savage** suggests the lack of all civilized restraint or compassion: *He has a savage temper.*

Pronunciation Key: hat, āge, cãre, fär; let, ēqual, tėrm; it, īce; hot, ōpen, ôrder; oil, out; cup, pu̇t, rüle; child; long; thin; ᴛʜen; zh, measure; ə represents **a** in about, **e** in taken, **i** in pencil, **o** in lemon, **u** in circus.

fi|e|ri cu|ra|vit (fī′ə rī kyů rā′vit), *Latin.* (the person specified) caused this to be made (used in inscriptions on monuments and works of art).

fi|e|ri fa|ci|as (fī′ə rī fā′shē as), a writ issued after the award of a judgment for a sum of money, commanding the sheriff to levy upon the goods or the lands of the debtor for the collection of the amount due. [< Latin *fierī facias* cause it to be made!]

fier|y (fīr′ē, f ī′ər-), *adj.,* **fier|i|er, fier|i|est. 1** containing fire; burning; flaming: *a burning fiery furnace* (Daniel 3:6). **2** like fire; very hot; flashing; glowing: *a fiery red, fiery heat.* **3** *Figurative.* full of feeling or spirit; ardent: *a fiery speech.* **SYN:** fervent, fervid, spirited, passionate. **4** *Figurative.* easily aroused or excited: *a fiery temper.* **5a** highly inflammable; liable to take fire, as gas in a mine. **b** (especially of a mine) containing large quantities of inflammable gas. **6** inflamed: *a fiery sore.* **7** *Figurative.* producing a burning sensation; pungent: *the fiery taste of raw whiskey.* [< *fire* + *-y*[1]] **—fier′i|ly,** *adv.* **—fier′i|ness,** *n.*

fiery cross, 1 *U.S.* a large cross set up and usually fired by Ku Klux Klanners to signal their presence in a locality. **2** = fire cross.

fi|es|ta (fē es′tə), *n.* **1** a religious festival; saint's day. In Spain and Latin-American countries fiestas are held with colorful ceremonies and festivities. **2** a holiday or festivity. [American English < Spanish *fiesta* feast < Vulgar Latin *festa.* Compare etym. under **fiesta.**]

fi fa (fī′fā′), *Law.* = fieri facias.

fife (fīf), *n., v.,* **fifed, fif|ing.** **—*n.*** a small, shrill musical instrument like a flute, played by blowing. Fifes are used with drums to make music for marching. See picture under **flute.**
—*v.t.* , ***v.i.*** to play on a fife.
[perhaps < German *Pfeife* pipe, probably ultimately < Latin *pīpāre* to chirp, to pipe]

fif|er (fī′fər), *n.* a person who plays the fife.

fife rail, a rail around the foot of a mast in which belaying pins are set.

FI|FO (fī′fō), *n.,* first in, first out (a method of valuing inventory which assumes items in stock are those purchased latest and values them at prices charged in most recent orders).

fif|teen (fif′tēn′), *n., adj.* **—*n.* 1** five more than ten; 15. **2** a team of fifteen players, such as the team in Rugby. **—*adj.*** being five more than ten. [Old English *fīftēne*]

fif|teenth (fif′tēnth′), *adj., n.* **1** next after the 14th; last in a series of 15: *Bills must be paid by the fifteenth of the month.* **2** one, or being one, of 15 equal parts.

fifth (fifth), *adj., n.* **—*adj.* 1** next after the fourth; last in a series of 5: *He is the fifth person to ask me what happened.* **2** being one of 5 equal parts: *This is the fifth and last part.*
—*n.* 1 next after the fourth; last in a series of 5. **2** one of 5 equal parts: *Twenty cents is a fifth of a dollar.* **3a** *U.S.* a unit of liquid measure for alcoholic beverages, equal to one fifth of a gallon. **b** a bottle of an alcoholic beverage holding this quantity. **4a** a musical tone five diatonic degrees from a given tone. **b** the interval between such tones. **c** the harmonic combination of such tones. **d** the fifth tone of a diatonic scale, five degrees above the tonic; dominant.
[alteration (on analogy of *fourth*) of earlier *fift,* Old English *fīfta*]

Fifth Amendment, an amendment to the United States Constitution and a part of the Bill of Rights, containing provision that no person "shall be compelled in any criminal case to be a witness against himself."

fifth column, 1 persons living within a country who secretly aid its enemies, especially by sabotage or espionage. **2** (originally) the Franco sympathizers within Madrid in the Spanish Civil War, who were said by the insurgent General Mola to constitute a fifth column which would join the four columns he was leading against the city.

fifth columnist, a member of a fifth column. **SYN:** quisling.

fifth disease, a virus disease of children marked by a reddish rash. [< the fact that it is one of five common childhood fevers]

fifth estate, any important class or group of people other than the nobility, the clergy, the middle class, and the press: *Unions were now the fifth estate of the realm* (London Times).

fifth force, *Physics.* a hypothetical force in nature intermediate in range between the gravitational and electromagnetic forces, which are infinite in range, and the strong and weak nuclear forces, which do not extend beyond the radius of an atomic nucleus: *The fifth force . . . is quite weak, and is in practice detectable only on scales of about 200 metres, at which it appears as a modification of the usual gravitational force* (New Scientist).

fifth|ly (fifth′lē), *adv.* in the fifth place.

fifth monarchy, the last of the five great kingdoms mentioned in the prophecy of Daniel (in the Bible, Daniel 2:44).

Fifth Republic, the government of France established in 1958 under Charles de Gaulle.

fifth wheel, 1 *Informal.* a person or thing that is not needed. **2** an extra wheel for a four-wheeled vehicle. **3** a horizontal ring, placed above the forward axle of a carriage and designed to support the forepart of the body while allowing it to turn freely in a horizontal plane.

fif|ti|eth (fif′tē ith), *adj., n.* **1** next after the 49th; last in a series of 50: *This is our fiftieth customer today.* **2** one, or being one, of 50 equal parts: *a fiftieth share in the profit.*

fif|ty (fif′tē), *n., pl.* **-ties,** *adj.* five times 10; 50: *I got change of five dimes for my fifty-cent piece.* [Old English *fīftig*]

fif|ty-fif|ty (fif′tē fif′tē), *adj., adv. Informal.* half-and-half; in two equal parts; with equal shares; even: *a fifty-fifty chance of winning* (adj.), *to go fifty-fifty on expenses* (adv.).

fig[1] (fig), *n.* **1** a small, soft, sweet, oblong or pear-shaped fruit that grows in warm regions. It grows on certain trees and shrubs belonging to the mulberry family. Figs are sometimes eaten fresh or canned, but usually are dried like dates and raisins. *We ate a whole box of figs.* **2** any one of the trees that figs grow on: *We broke several branches off the fig trying to climb it.* **3** any one of several plants whose fruit is somewhat like the fig. **4** a very small amount: *I don't care a fig for your opinion.* [< Old French *figue* < Old Provençal *figa* < Vulgar Latin *fīca* < Latin *fīcus* fig. See etym. of doublet **fico.**]

fig[2] (fig), *n., v.,* **figged, fig|ging.** *Informal.* **—*n.* 1** dress; equipment. **2** condition; form.
—*v.t.* fig out, to dress; get up: *Landsmen . . . figged out as fine as Lord Harry* (Frederick Marryat).
fig up, to furbish up; make smart: *[The house] wants a little figging up* (Punch).
in full fig, fully dressed or equipped: *The broad, red-carpeted steps . . . are bordered by ten more Republican Guards in full fig* (Atlantic).
[perhaps abbreviation of *figure*]

fig., 1a figurative. **b** figuratively. **2** figure or figures.

Fig|a|ro (fig′ə rō), *n.* an original and witty liar, a stock character in drama and opera.

fig banana, a small variety of the banana.

fig|eat|er (fig′ē′tər), *n.* a large, green beetle of the southern United States that feeds on grasses, young corn, and ripe fruit.

fig finch, = beccafico.

fig|gy (fig′ē), *adj.,* **-gi|er, -gi|est. 1** made or filled with figs: *a figgy cake.* **2** resembling figs.

fight (fīt), *n., v.,* **fought, fight|ing.** **—*n.* 1** a violent struggle; combat or conflict; battle; contest: *a street fight, a dog fight, a long fight for justice. A fight ends when one side gives up.* **2** an angry dispute; quarrel: *Their fights were always over money.* **3** the power or will to fight; fighting spirit: *There is fight in the old dog yet.* **SYN:** pugnacity. **4** a boxing match: *The champion had not had a fight for over a year.* [Middle English *fiht,* Old English *feoht*]
—*v.i.* 1 to take part in a fight: *When boys fight they hit one another. Soldiers fight by shooting with guns. Countries fight with armies.* **2** to dispute angrily; contend; struggle: (*Figurative.*) *We may fight against our own feelings and desires. For modes of faith let graceless zealots fight* (Alexander Pope).
—*v.t.* 1 to take part in a fight against; war against: *to fight disease.* (*Figurative.*) *She will not fight her fear of the dark. For some were sunk . . . and so could fight us no more* (Tennyson). **2** to carry on (a fight, conflict, or struggle); engage in: *to fight a duel.* **3** *Figurative.* to exert oneself in support of (a cause, case at law, or the like); maintain: *He fought the case clear up to the Supreme Court.* **4** to get or make by fighting: (*Figurative.*) *He had to fight his way through the crowd.* **5** to cause to fight: *The nobles and gentry had fought cocks* (Scott). **6** to use, command, or manage (troops, ships, guns, or aircraft) in battle.
fight back, to offer resistance; show fight: *They had no heart to fight back.*
fight it out, to fight until one side wins: *I propose to fight it out on this line, if it takes all summer* (Ulysses S. Grant).
fights, *Obsolete.* a protective screen for sailors on warships during battle: *Fights . . . hang round about the ship, to hinder men from being seen in fight* (John Phillips).
fight shy of, to keep away from; avoid: *I have . . . had to fight shy of invitations that would exhaust time and spirits* (Washington Irving).
show fight, to resist; be ready to fight: *Until . . . something or another happens to make little Eleanor show fight* (Henry Kingsley).
[Middle English *fihten,* Old English *feohtan*]
—fight′a|ble, *adj.*
—*Syn. n.* 1 Fight, combat, conflict mean battle or struggle. **Fight** means a struggle for victory or mastery between two or more people, animals, or forces, and often suggests hand-to-hand fighting: *The boys of the gang had a big fight.* **Combat** applies particularly to a battle between armed men or forces: *The marines went into combat against the enemy entrenched along the shore.* **Conflict** emphasizes clashing or collision between opposing forces, often drawn out and hard to resolve: *The UN General Assembly discussed the conflict in the Middle East. We all undergo mental conflicts.*

fight|back (fīt′bak′), *n. British.* a return attack; counteroffensive.

fight|er (fī′tər), *n.* **1** a person or thing that fights, especially as a soldier or boxer: *Our dog is a real fighter and is leader among the neighborhood dogs. The sergeants were tough fighters. Nobody thought the young fighter would win until he had more experience boxing.* **SYN:** combatant, belligerent, warrior, champion, gladiator, pugilist. **2** a highly maneuverable and heavily armed airplane, used mainly for attacking enemy airplanes or strafing ground forces. **3** a pugnacious person.

fight|er-bomb|er (fī′tər bom′ər), *n.* an airplane that functions as both a fighter and a bomber.

fighter escort, (in Great Britain) one or more aircraft assigned to fly with and protect friendly bombers; bomber escort.

fight|er-in|ter|cep|tor (fī′tər in′tər sep′tər), *n.* an airplane that functions as both a fighter and an interceptor: *They are supposed to be able to take off in their fighter-interceptors within 60 seconds after they receive warning from the Aircraft Warning Service* (Science News Letter).

fighter plane, = fighter (def. 2).

fight|ing (fī′ting), *adj.* **1** that fights or is trained for fighting: *a fighting force, a fighting man.* **2** of or having to do with fighting: *fighting gear, the fighting field; . . . so long as the two halves of the divided world maintain their fearful fighting trim* (Atlantic). **3a** warlike; hostile: *fighting words, a fighting mood.* **b** courageous; bold: *She met adversity with a fighting spirit.*

fighting chair, *U.S.* a chair fixed to the deck of a boat, used by an angler in sports fishing to catch large fish at sea.

fighting chance, *Informal.* the possibility of success after a long, hard struggle: *Observers give him only a fighting chance in his campaign against the incumbent Senator.*

fighting cock, 1 = gamecock. **2** *Informal.* a pugnacious person.

fighting fish, a brightly colored Siamese freshwater fish, often kept in aquariums; betta.

fight|ing|ly (fī′ting lē), *adv.* in a fighting manner; pugnaciously.

fighting top, a platform on or near the head of a mast of a warship, from which sharpshooters or rapid guns fire.

fight-off (fīt′ôf′, -of′), *n.* a contest to decide a tie, especially in a boxing match.

fights (fīts), *n.pl.* See under **fight.**

fig insect, 1 any one of various insects inhabiting the hollow interior of the immature fig. **2** a small hymenopterous insect serving as an important agent in cross-pollination of the fig.

fig leaf, 1 the leaf of a fig tree (chiefly in reference to the first covering of Adam and Eve). Genesis 3:7. **2** *Figurative.* a device for concealing something shameful or improper; flimsy disguise: *They tore off . . . even the fig leaves of decent reticence* (Charles Kingsley).

fig marigold, any one of various low-growing plants of the carpetweed family, bearing showy pink, white, or yellow flowers.

fig|ment (fig′mənt), *n.* something made up, feigned, or imagined; a made-up story: *I don't believe it; it's just a figment of your imagination.* **SYN:** fiction. [< Latin *figmentum* < *fingere* to form, fashion]

fig|men|tar|y (fig′mən ter′ē), *adj.* fictitious; imaginary; not real: *figmentary fears.*

fig paste, Turkish confection, consisting of a semitransparent, sweetened, and flavored fig paste cut into small blocks and dusted with fine sugar; loukoum.

Fig Sunday, the Sunday before Easter Sunday; Palm Sunday. [because it was formerly customary to eat figs on this occasion]

fig|u|line (fig′yů lin, -līn), *n.* **1** a piece of pottery. **2** = potter's clay. [< Latin *figulīnus* < *figulus* potter]

fig|ur|a|ble (fig′yər ə bəl), *adj.* that can take or keep a definite figure or shape.

fig|ur|al (fig′yər əl), *adj.* **1** having to do with figures, or delineation by figures: *A collection of Lalique glass in the sale will include jardinieres, bowls and figural pieces* (New York Times). **2** *Music.* figurate.

fig|u|rant (fig′yə rant), *n.* **1** a ballet dancer, especially one who dances only as one of a group. **2** *Theater.* a character who appears in any scene without taking a prominent part; supernumerary. [< French *figurant*, present participle of *figurer* to make a figure < Old French *figure* figure]

fig|u|rante (fig′yə rant′), *n.* a female figurant. [< French *figurante*, feminine of *figurant;* see etym. under **figurant**]

fig|ur|ate (fig′yər it), *adj.* **1** having definite form or shape. **2** formed into figures or patterns. **3** distinguished by the use of passing tones or other ornaments of a piece of music; florid. [< Latin *figūrātus*, past participle of *figūrāre* to fashion, form < *figūra;* see etym. under **figure**] —**fig′ur|ate|ly**, *adv.*

figurate number, any one of the numbers occurring in a series that has been derived from an arithmetical progression whose first term is 1 and whose difference is a whole number. By taking for the consecutive terms of the derived series the first term, the sum of the first two terms, the sum of the first three terms, and so on, of the simple progression, the units of such a number can be arranged symmetrically in the form of a figure, as a triangle, characteristic of the series to which it belongs.

fig|ur|a|tion (fig′yə rā′shən), *n.* **1** a form; shape. SYN: contour, outline. **2** the action or process of forming; shaping. **3** representation by a likeness or symbol. **4** the act of marking or adorning with figures or designs. **5** *Music.* **a** the use of passing tones, ornaments, or the like. **b** the action of indicating harmonics with figures above the bass part.

fig|ur|a|tive (fig′yər ə tiv), *adj.* **1** using words out of their literal meaning to add beauty or force. Many words are indicated in their figurative sense in this dictionary by labeling the meaning or the sentence *Figurative.* SYN: metaphorical. **2** having many figures of speech. Poetry is frequently figurative. **3** representing by a likeness or symbol; symbolic: *Baptism is a figurative ceremony; it represents cleansing by washing away sin.* SYN: emblematical. **4** representing by means of a figure or likeness, as in drawing or sculpture; representational. —**fig′ur|a|tive|ly**, *adv.* —**fig′ur|a|tive-ness**, *n.*

fig|ure (fig′yər; *see note below*), *n., v.,* **-ured**, **-ur-ing**. —*n.* **1** a symbol for a number. 1, 2, 3, 4, and so on, are figures. **2** an amount or value given in figures; price; estimate: *His figure for that house is very high.* **3** a form enclosing a surface or space: *Circles, triangles, squares, cubes, and spheres are geometrical figures.* **4a** the form of anything as determined by the outline; external form; shape generally: *The cloud had the figure of an outstretched hand.* SYN: conformation, outline. See syn. under **form**. **b** a person considered as a human shape or form: *I could see the figure of a woman against the window.* SYN: conformation, outline. See syn. under **form**. **5** the human form; way in which a person looks or appears; build: *He has a scholar's figure, tall, thin, a little stooped.* **6** the impression which a particular person or thing produces by his character, behavior, or deportment; appearance of a specified quality: *It is my wish . . . to have my boy make some figure in the world* (Richard Brinsley Sheridan). **7** a person or character noted or remembered: *George Washington is a well-known figure in American history. Hamlet is the most enigmatic figure in Shakespeare.* **8** an artificial representation of the human form in sculpture, painting, or drawing, usually of the whole or greater part of the body: *They passed like figures on a marble urn* (Keats). SYN: effigy, statue. **9** a person, animal, or thing that stands for or represents another person, thing, quality, or accomplishment; image; likeness: *He is their standard figure of perfection* (Edmund Burke). **10** a picture, drawing, diagram, or other illustration: *My science book has many figures to help explain the lessons. Abbr:* fig. **11** a design or pattern: *the figures in the wallpaper.* **12** an outline traced by movements: *The airplane's maneuvers wrote intricate figures in the air.* **13** a set of movements in dancing or skating coordinated to form a pattern. **14** a figure of speech; form or mode of expression, differing from the normal, and resorted to for ornament, emphasis, vividness, or the like; simile, metaphor, hyperbole, or the like. **15** an emblem; symbol: *Learning is normally represented by the figure of a torch.* **16** a short series of musical notes or chords forming a complete phrase, theme, or other unit and conveying a particular impression: *The opening eight-note figure gives the theme of the whole composition.* **17** *Logic.* any one of the forms of a syllogism that differ only in the position of the middle term. **18** the curve needed on the surface of the mirror of a reflecting telescope. **19** *Psychology.* any shape or form perceived as standing out or apart from its surroundings: *an ambiguous figure-ground relationship in a picture.* **20** *Obsolete.* a phantom; delusion.

—*v.t.* **1** to use figures to find (the answer to a problem); reckon; compute: *Please figure my bill so that I may pay you.* SYN: calculate, cipher. **2** to indicate or express in figures: *Your draft is worded for twenty pounds and figured for twenty-one* (William Cowper). **3** to show by a figure; represent in a diagram. **4** to decorate with a figure or pattern; ornament with a design: *crimson satin, figured with velvet flowers.* **5** to portray by speech or action; represent: *[My heart] is figured in my tongue* (Shakespeare). **6** to express by a metaphor or other figure of speech. **7** to represent by an emblem or symbol; be an emblem or symbol of: *You, lord archbishop . . . whose white investments figure innocence* (Shakespeare). **8** *Informal.* to think; consider; form the opinion: *I figured I should stop where I was.* **9** *Music.* **a** to write figures over and under (the bass) to indicate the intended harmony. **b** to use passing tones, ornaments, or the like, in; embellish. **10** to picture mentally; imagine: *Figure to yourself a happy family, secure in their own home.* **11** *Obsolete.* to give figure to; form; shape.

—*v.i.* **1** to use numbers to find the answer to some problem; compute: *The bookkeeper wrote and figured well.* **2** to be conspicuous; appear; be notable: *The names of great leaders figure in the story of human progress.* **3** to perform a dancing figure (often with *away* or *down*): *The squire himself figured down several couples with a partner* (Washington Irving).

figure in, *U.S. Informal.* to count in; take into account: *The car is quite expensive if you figure in the insurance and upkeep.*

figure on, *Informal.* **a** to depend on; count on; rely on; expect: *I can figure on my father's help to pay my way through college. The engineers figured on one-way traffic to relieve the congestion west of the bridge.* **b** to consider as part of a plan or undertaking: *I had not figured on that.*

figure out, **a** to estimate; calculate; find out by using figures: *Please figure out how much I owe you. He has figured out how many men he is likely to need.* **b** to think out; understand; make out: *Even the repairman couldn't figure out what had gone wrong with the washer.*

figures, calculations using figures; arithmetic: *She was never very good at figures.*

[< Old French *figure*, learned borrowing from Latin *figūra* a shape, form < *fingere* to form] —**fig′ure|less**, *adj.* —**fig′ur|er**, *n.*

▶The pronunciation fig′ər is dialectal or jocular in the United States, and standard in England.

fig|ured (fig′yərd), *adj.* **1** decorated with a design or pattern; not plain: *figured silk.* **2** shown by a figure, diagram, or picture: *The model figured is one sixth of the full size.* **3** = figurative. **4** *Music.* **a** having accompanying chords of the bass part indicated by figures. **b** florid; figurate.

figure dance, a dance consisting of elaborate figures.

figure dancer, a performer in a figure dance.

figured bass, = thorough bass.

figured syllogism, a syllogism so expressed as to belong to a definite figure.

figure eight, **1** a flight maneuver in which an aircraft flies a path resembling a horizontal 8. **2** an evolution in figure skating in which the skater traces a single line resembling an 8.

***fig|ure|head** (fig′yər hed′), *n.* **1** a person who is the head in name only, without real authority: *The old man is just a figurehead; his son really runs the business.* **2** a statue or carving placed for ornament on the bow of a ship.

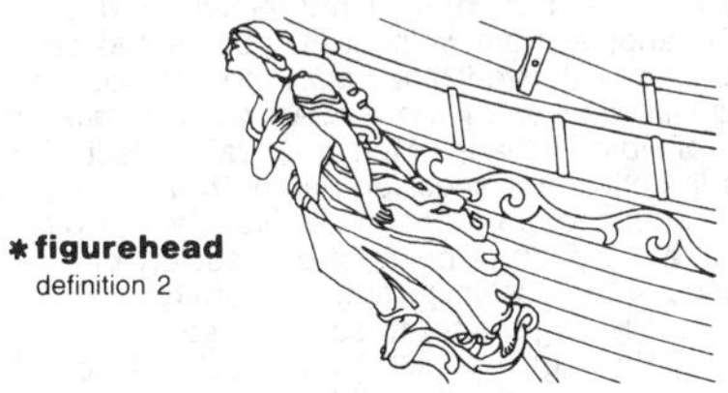

***figurehead**
definition 2

figure of eight, a kind of knot or loop made in the end of a rope to keep it from running out of a block, resembling the figure 8. See picture under **knot**[1].

figure of speech, an expression in which words are used out of their literal meaning or in striking combinations to add beauty or force. "The eye of an eagle" (a metaphor) and "as brave as a lion" (a simile) are figures of speech.

fig|ures (fig′yərz), *n.pl.* See under **figure**.

figure skate, an ice skate with a slight toothed curve on the point of the blade and a high shoe, used for figure skating.

fig|ure-skate (fig′yər skāt′), *v.i.,* **-skat|ed**, **-skat-ing**. to engage in figure skating.

fig|ure-skat|er (fig′yər skā′tər), *n.* a person engaged in figure skating; a performer who figure-skates.

***figure skating**, **1** the art or practice of describing certain figures and of performing feats of grace and agility to music on skates, somewhat resembling ballet. **2** a competition in the display of this art.

***figure skating**
definition 1

figure stone, = agalmatolite.

fig|ur|ette (fig′yə ret′), *n.* = figurine.

fig|ur|ine (fig′yə rēn′), *n.* a small ornamental figure made of stone, pottery, metal, or other material; statuette. [< French *figurine* < Italian *figurina* (diminutive) < *figura* figure, learned borrowing from Latin *figūra;* see etym. under **figure**]

fig wasp, a wasp that lives in caprifigs and carries pollen from the male flowers to the female flowers of the Smyrna figs.

fig|wort (fig′wėrt′), *n.* **1** any one of a genus of tall, coarse herbs with small, greenish-purple or yellow, bell-shaped flowers, divided into two lips, that have a disagreeable odor. **2** any similar plant.

***figwort family**, a group of dicotyledonous herbs and shrubs or small trees having alternate leaves, bisexual flowers, and bearing (commonly) a capsule as the fruit. The family includes the toadflax, digitalis, snapdragon, and mullein.

***figwort family**

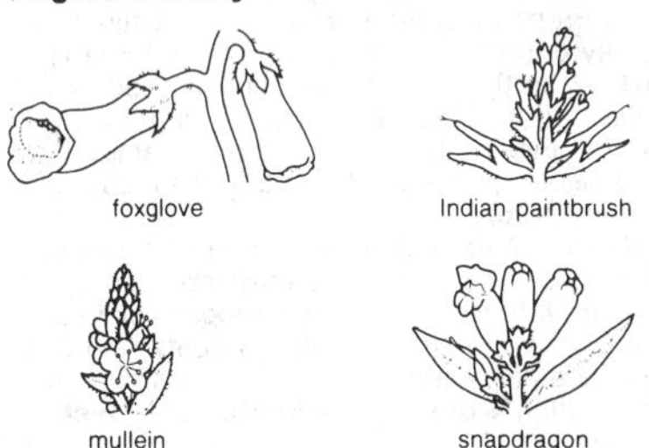

Fi|ji (fē′jē), *n.* a native of the Fiji Islands in the South Pacific; Fijian.

Fi|ji|an (fē′jē ən, fi jē′-), *adj., n.* —*adj.* of or having to do with the Fiji Islands, their people, or their language.

—*n.* **1** a native or inhabitant of the Fiji Islands. **2** the Melanesian language of the Fijians.

fike[1] (fīk), *n., v.,* **fiked**, **fik|ing**. *Scottish.* —*n.* **1** a restless movement. **2** anxiety about what is trifling; fuss.

—*v.i.* to fidget.

[< Scandinavian (compare Middle Swedish *fīkja* move briskly)]

fike[2] (fīk), *n.* = fyke.

fil|a|gree (fil′ə grē), *n., v.t.,* **-greed**, **-gree|ing**, *adj.* = filigree.

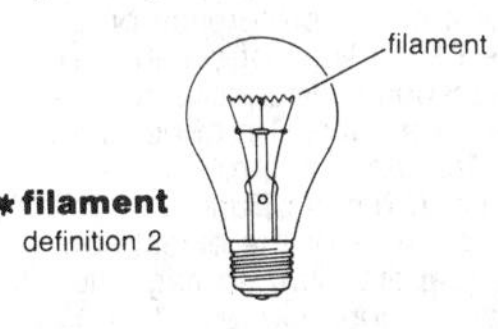

***filament**
definition 2

***fil|a|ment** (fil′ə mənt), *n.* **1** a very fine thread; very slender part that is like a thread: *the delicate filaments of a spider's web.* **2** the threadlike wire that gives off light in an electric light bulb. **3** the heated wire that acts as a negative electrode in a vacuum tube. In some vacuum tubes, the filament also acts as the cathode. **4** *Botany.* **a** the stalklike part of a stamen that supports the anther, usually slender and threadlike, but quite variable in form. **b** a very long, thin cell or a series of very long, thin cells, especially in various algae and fungi. **5** one of the fine barbs of a

Pronunciation Key: hat, āge, cãre, fär; let, ēqual, tėrm; it, īce; hot, ōpen, ôrder; oil, out; cup, pu̇t, rüle; child; long; thin; ᴛʜen; zh, measure; ə represents a in about, e in taken, i in pencil, o in lemon, u in circus.

down feather. **6** a continuous strand of yarn of a synthetic, such as acetate, which may be used in weaving without spinning. [< Late Latin *fīlāmentum* < *fīlāre* spin < Latin *fīlum* thread]

fil|a|men|ta|ry (fil′ə men′tər ē), *adj.* having to do with or of the nature of a filament or filaments.

fil|a|ment|ed (fil′ə men′tid), *adj.* provided with a filament or filaments.

fil|a|men|tous (fil′ə men′təs), *adj.* **1** threadlike. **2** having filaments.

fi|lar (fī′lər), *adj.* **1** of or having to do with a thread. **2** having threads or wires across its field of view: *a filar microscope.* [< Latin *fīlum* thread + English *-ar*[1]]

fi|lar|i|a (fi lãr′ē ə), *n., pl.* **-lar|i|ae** (-lãr′ē ē). any one of a family of threadlike, parasitic nematode worms, whose larvae are transmitted by mosquitoes and other arthropods. The filariae live in the blood and tissues of man and other vertebrates, causing such diseases as elephantiasis and onchocerciasis. [< New Latin *Filaria* the genus name < Latin *fīlum* thread]

fi|lar|i|al (fi lãr′ē əl), *adj.* **1** of or belonging to the filariae. **2** of the nature of or caused by filariae: *filarial disease.*

fil|a|ri|a|sis (fil′ə rī′ə sis), *n.* a diseased condition caused by the presence of filariae in the blood, tissues, and especially lymph vessels. [< New Latin *filariasis* < *Filaria* filaria]

fi|lar|i|id (fi lãr′ē id), *adj., n.* **—*adj.*** of or caused by filariae. **—*n.*** = filaria.
[< New Latin *Filariidae* the family name < *Filaria* filaria]

fi|lasse (fi las′), *n.* vegetable fiber prepared for the process of manufacture. [< French *filasse* tow, flax]

fi|late (fī′lit), *adj. Zoology.* straight and without a lateral bristle or process: *filate antennae.*

fil|a|ture (fil′ə chər), *n.* **1** the act or process of forming or spinning into threads. **2a** a reel for drawing off silk from cocoons. **b** the reeling of silk from cocoons. **c** an establishment for reeling silk. [< French *filature* < *filer* < Late Latin *fīlāre* spin, pay out a long line < Latin *fīlum* thread]

fil|bert (fil′bərt), *n.* **1** a sweet, thick-shelled kind of cultivated hazelnut. **2** the tree or shrub it grows on. Filberts belong to the birch family. [< Saint *Philibert* (because the nuts ripen near his day, August 20)]

filch (filch), *v.t.* to steal in small quantities; pilfer: *He filched apples from the pantry.* **SYN:** See syn. under **steal.** [origin uncertain. Compare Middle English *filchen* to snatch, take as booty, Old English *gefylce* band, army, *gefylcian* to marshal an army] **—filch′a|ble,** *adj.* **—filch′er,** *n.* **—filch′ing|ly,** *adv.*

file[1] (fīl), *n., v.,* **filed, fil|ing.** **—*n.*** **1a** a place for keeping papers in order; container in or on which papers may be placed or arranged for convenient reference or storage: *Put this letter in the main file.* **b** a cabinet, shelves, or the like, for storing film or magnetic tape containing recorded information. **2a** a set of papers kept in order: *a file of receipts.* **b** film or magnetic tape containing recorded information. **3** a row of persons, animals, or things one behind another: *a file of soldiers marching in time. The hypocrite Days ... marching single in an endless file* (Emerson). **4** *Military.* **a** a single line or row of men arranged one behind another from front to rear. **b** the man in front of, or the man behind, another, especially in a two-deep formation: *Always keep level with your file.* **c** a small detachment of soldiers. **d** a numerical position or order of preference on a promotion list. **5** one of the lines of squares extending across a chessboard or checkerboard from player to player. **6** a collection of news stories sent by wire. **7** *Archaic.* a list; roll: *catalogued files of murders* (Edmund Burke). **8** *Heraldry.* the label or mark of the eldest son.
—*v.t.* **1** to put away (papers, film, or magnetic tape) in order: *Please file those letters.* **2** to place (a document) among the records of a court, public office, or legislature: *to file a petition, file a bill. The deed to our house is filed with the county clerk.* **3** to send (a news story) by wire: *The reporter immediately filed his story of the explosion.*
—*v.i.* **1** to march or move in a file: *The pupils filed out of the room during the fire drill. A party of Americans filed into his studio* (Hawthorne). **2** *U.S.* to make written application for a position, as a candidate, etc.
file on (or **upon**), *U.S.* to enter on or occupy (unclaimed land): *Having filed on the quarter of vacant land adjoining me, of course I had to move over there* (W. F. Drannan).
in file, one after another; in succession: *Ships sailing in file. The men were standing in silent file on each side of it* (Elisha K. Kane). *The ants ... changed their course, and in narrow file reascended the wall* (Charles Darwin).
on file, in a file; put away and kept in order: *The principal keeps all our school reports on file.*
[partly < Old French *fil* thread < Latin *fīlum;* partly < Middle French *file* row < Old French *filer* < Late Latin *fīlāre* spin a thread < Latin *fīlum*]

file**[2] (fīl), *n., v.,* **filed, fil|ing.** **—*n. a tool of steel or other metal with many small ridges or teeth on it. Its rough surface is used to smooth or wear away hard substances. *The carpenter's file made a pile of sawdust as he used it to smooth down the edge of a door.*
—*v.t.* to smooth or wear away (hard substances) with a file: *to file the teeth of a saw, to file the fingernails.*
[Old English *fīl*]

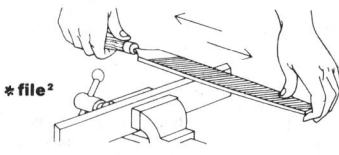

***file**[2]

file[3] (fīl), *v.t.,* **filed, fil|ing.** *Dialect.* to pollute; defile. [Old English *fȳlan* defile. See related etym. at **foul.**]

file[4] (fīl), *n.* a cunning, shrewd, or artful person. [origin unknown]

file clerk, a person whose work is taking care of the files in an office.

***file|fish** (fīl′fish′), *n., pl.* **-fish|es** or (*collectively*) **-fish.** a fish whose skin is covered with many very small spines instead of scales, and whose front dorsal fin is a long spine, such as the triggerfish and various related fishes.

***filefish**

fil|er[1] (fī′lər), *n.* = file clerk.

fil|er[2] (fī′lər), *n.* a person who cuts, smooths, or polishes with a file.

fi|let (fi lā′, fil′ā), *n., v.* **—*n.*** **1** a fillet of fish or meat. **2** Also, **filet lace.** a net or lace having a square mesh.
—*v.t.* to fillet (fish or meat).
[< French *filet* < Old French. See related etym. at **fillet.**]

file 13, *U.S. Slang.* a wastebasket.

fi|let mi|gnon (fi lā′ mēn′yon, min yon′; *French* fē le′ mē nyôɴ′), *pl.* **fi|lets mi|gnons** (fi lā′ mēn′yon, min yon′). a thick, round slice of beef tenderloin, often larded with bacon before cooking. [< French *filet mignon* (literally) dainty filet]

fil|i|al (fil′ē əl), *adj.* **1** of a son or daughter; due from a son or daughter toward a mother or father: *filial affection. The children treated their parents with filial respect.* **2** *Genetics.* of any generation of offspring of a hybrid. *Symbol:* F (no period). F_1 is the first filial generation, F_2, the second filial generation, and so on. [< Late Latin *fīliālis* < Latin *fīlius* son, and *fīlia* daughter] **—fil′i|al|ly,** *adv.* **—fil′i|al|ness,** *n.*

fil|i|al|i|ty (fil′ē al′ə tē), *n.* the state of being filial.

fil|i|a|tion (fil′ē ā′shən), *n.* **1** the relation of one thing to another from which it may be said to be descended or derived: *The institutions of modern Europe are derived by more direct filiation from those of Rome* (Charles Merivale). **2a** the fact of being the child of a specified parent. **b** a person's parentage. **3a** formation of branches or offshoots. **b** a branch or offshoot of a society or language. **4** the assigning of the paternity of a child (usually illegitimate) to some person.

fil|i|beg (fil′ə beg), *n.* = kilt. [< Scottish Gaelic *feileadhbeag* < *feileadh* a fold; pleated stuff + *beag* little]

fil|i|bus|ter (fil′ə bus′tər), *n., v.* **—*n.*** **1** *U.S.* **a** the act or process of deliberately hindering the passage of a bill in a legislature by long speeches or other means of delay: *There was a three-hours' filibuster against the Civil Service Clause* (E. F. Wyatt). **b** a member of a legislature who deliberately hinders the passage of a bill by long speeches or other means of delay. **c** any hindering by delaying actions or speeches: *A male stockholder told* [*him*] *that by repeatedly calling upon certain predictable filibusterers in the room he was in effect conducting a filibuster himself* (New Yorker). **2** any person, especially a citizen of the United States, who unlawfully initiated or supported a revolt against South American and Central American governments during the 1800's in order to enrich himself. **3** a person who fights against another country without the authorization of his government; a freebooter.
—*v.i.* **1** *U.S.* to deliberately hinder the passage of a bill by long speeches or other means of delay. **2** to hinder progress by delaying actions or speeches: *It figured that he'd stay in there filibustering for Morris's book* (Saturday Review). **3** to act as a filibuster or freebooter; fight against another country without the authorization of one's government.
—*v.t.* to deliberately hinder the passage of (a bill) by long speeches or other means of delay: *Many House members are in a churlish mood, having passed last year's bill ... only to see the Senate filibuster it to death* (New York Times).
[< Spanish *filibustero,* perhaps < French *flibustier* < Dutch *vrijbuiter.* See etym. of doublet **freebooter.**] **—fil′i|bus′ter|er,** *n.*

fil|i|cau|line (fil′ə kô′lin), *adj. Botany.* having a threadlike stem. [< Latin *fīlum* thread + English *cauline*]

fi|lic|ic acid (fi lis′ik), a crystalline compound found in the rhizome of the common male fern; filicin. *Formula:* $C_8H_{10}O_3$ [< Latin *filex, filicis* fern + English *-ic*]

fil|i|cid|al (fil′ə sī′dəl), *adj.* having to do with the slaughter of sons and daughters.

fil|i|cide[1] (fil′ə sīd), *n.* a person who kills his child. [< Latin *fīlius* son, or *fīlia* daughter + English *-cide*[1]]

fil|i|cide[2] (fil′ə sīd), *n.* the act of killing one's child. [< Latin *fīlius* son, or *fīlia* daughter + English *-cide*[2]]

fil|i|cin (fil′ə sin), *n.* = filicic acid.

fi|lif|er|ous (fi lif′ər əs), *adj.* producing threads, or bearing threadlike growths, as some plants, insects, and mollusks.

fil|i|form (fil′ə fôrm), *adj.* threadlike. [< Latin *fīlum* thread + English *-form*]

fil|i|gree** (fil′ə grē), *n., v.,* **-greed, -gree|ing,** *adj.* **—*n. **1** very delicate, lacelike ornamental work of gold or silver wire. **2** any similar ornamental work. **3a** a lacy, delicate, or fanciful pattern in any material: *The frost made a beautiful filigree on the windowpane.* **b** *Figurative.* anything very delicate or fanciful: *Guarantees, he said, were mere filigree, pretty to look at but too brittle to bear the slightest pressure* (Macaulay).
—*v.t.* **1** to decorate (especially jewelry) with filigree. **2** to form (gold, silver, or other metal) into filigree.
—*adj.* **1** ornamented with or as if with filigree; made into filigree: *filigree earrings.* **2** *Figurative.* delicate. Also, **filagree.**
[earlier *filigrane* < French < Italian *filigrana* < *fili,* plural, threads (< Latin *fīlum*) + *grana* grain < Latin *grānum*]

***filigree**
definition 1

fil|i|gree|work (fil′ə grē wėrk′), *n.* work in filigree; filigree.

fil|ings (fī′lingz), *n.pl.* small pieces removed by a file: *iron filings, nail filings.*

fil|i|o|pi|e|tis|tic (fil′ē ō pī′ə tis′tik), *adj.* marked by an excess of filial piety. [< Latin *fīlius* son + *pietistic*]

fil|i|o|que (fil′ē ō′kwē), *n.* the Latin word, meaning "and from the Son," inserted in the Western version of the Niceno-Constantinopolitan Creed to assert the doctrine that the Holy Spirit proceeds not only from the Father, as the Eastern Church believes, but from both the Father and the Son.

fil|i|pin (fil′ə pin), *n.* an antibiotic effective against various fungous diseases, obtained from a moldlike soil microorganism discovered in the Philippines. *Formula:* $C_{30}H_{50}O_{10}$ [< *Filip*(pines), variant of Philippines + *-in*]

Fil|i|pine (fil′ə pēn), *adj.* = Philippine.

Fil|i|pi|nism (fil′ə pē′niz əm), *n.* Philippine nationalism.

Fil|i|pi|no (fil′ə pē′nō), *n., pl.* **-nos,** *adj.* **—*n.*** a person born or living in the Philippines.
—*adj.* = Philippine.

fill[1] (fil), *v., n.* **—*v.t.*** **1** to put something into until there is room for nothing more; make full: *to fill a cup. Fill this bottle with water. Fill this hole with something.* **2a** to take up all the space in: *The crowd filled the hall. Smoke filled the room.* **b** to occupy all the time of: *She filled her days with trivial tasks. Solemn marches fill the nights* (Julia Ward Howe). **3** to satisfy the hunger or appetite of: *to fill one's needs. A poor man finds that a starchy diet will fill his family at least expense.* **4** to supply with all that is needed for: *The store filled her order by selling what she asked for. The druggist filled the doctor's prescription.* **5** to stop up or close by putting something in: *After*

the dentist had taken out the decay, he filled my tooth. **6** to hold and do the duties of (a position or office): *to fill a diplomatic post. Can he fill the office of vice-president?* **SYN:** occupy. **7** to supply a person for or appoint a person to (a position or office): *to fill a judgeship.* **8** to stock or supply abundantly: *to fill a stream with trout.* **9** to adulterate: *to fill fabrics.* **10** to make delivery on or execute (an order): *When can you fill this order for lumber?* **11a** (of the wind) to stretch out (a sail) by blowing fully into it. **b** to set (a yard) so that the wind will blow into the sail fully from behind. **12** to build up or make an embankment in (a gully, hollow, or other depression) with fill. **13** in poker: **a** to complete (a full house, flush, straight, or other combination) by drawing the necessary cards. **b** to improve (one's hand) by drawing complementary cards.
—***v.i.*** **1** to become full: *The well filled with water. The hall filled rapidly. Her heart filled with joy.* **2** in poker: **a** to make a flush or other combination. **b** (of the flush or other combination) to become complete.
—***n.*** **1** enough to fill something: *a fill of tobacco for a pipe.* **2** *Figurative.* all that is needed or wanted: *Eat and drink your fill; there is plenty for all of us.* **3** something that fills, such as earth or gravel for building up a gully, hollow, or other depression, or making an embankment.
fill away, *Nautical.* to catch the wind by setting the yards or trimming the sails: *Each vessel filled away, and kept on her course* (Richard Henry Dana).
fill in, a to fill with something; put in: *Fill in the cracks with putty.* **b** to complete by filling: *to fill in a traffic ticket.* **c** to put in to complete something; insert: *to fill in the date of an application.* **d** to supply (a person) with new or additional items of information; brief: *A spokesman filled in reporters on the properties of the vaccine.* **e** to be a substitute: *The understudy filled in for the vacationing star.*
fill one's shoes. See under **shoe.**
fill out, a to make larger; grow larger; swell: *to fill out a tire with air.* **b** to make rounder; grow rounder: *Good food and exercise filled out his skinny frame. Her cheeks have filled out.* **c** to complete by filling: *to fill out an application.* **d** to supply what is needed in: *The clerk added a sack of potatoes to fill out the order.*
fill the bill. See under **bill**[1].
fill up, to fill; fill completely: *Come, fill up my cup, come, fill up my can* (Scott). *They have passed very decisive laws for filling up their regiments for the war* (A. McDougall).
[Old English *fyllan* < *full* full]

fille (fē′yə), *French.* **1** a daughter. **2** a girl; maid. **3** a spinster.

filled (fild), *adj.* **1** = full. **2** made with a filling, or an addition, of a different, usually inferior, material: *filled cloth.*

fille de cham|bre (fē′yə də shäɴ′brə), *French.* a lady's maid.

fille de joie (fē′yə də zhwä′), *French.* a prostitute.

filled gold, cheap metal, commonly brass, covered with a layer of gold, used as a substitute for solid gold, as for jewelry.

fille d'hon|neur (fē′yə dô nœr′), *French.* a maid of honor.

filled milk, skim milk to which vegetable oils have been added to increase the fat content.

fill|er (fil′ər), *n.* **1** a person or thing that fills. **2** a thing put in to fill something. A pad of paper for a notebook is a filler. **3a** a liquid or paste used to coat the pores or cracks of a surface, especially wood, before applying paint, varnish, or other protective covering. **b** sizing of starch or soluble glue used to fill the threads of cloth and thus give it more weight and body. **4** an item or ornament used to fill a vacant space, such as a short item used on a newspaper, magazine, or book page to fill space for which no news, stories, or advertisements are available: *to use a short poem as a filler on a magazine page.* **5** a sheet or plate inserted to fill the space between two solid portions or parts of a structure. **6** = extender (def. 2). **7** the inner part of a cigar, forming the body, around which the binder and wrapper are rolled. **8** an implement used in filling, as a funnel. [< *fill*[1] + *-er*[1]]

fil|lér (fēl′lār), *n., pl.* **-lér** or **lérs.** a Hungarian bronze coin, formerly worth 1/100 of a pengö, but now worth 1/100 of a forint. [< Hungarian *fillér*]

filler metal, the metal used in welding to strengthen a welded joint. Filler metal is usually in the form of a welding rod or a wire electrode that melts during the welding.

fil|let (fil′it; *n. 6, v. 2, usually* fi lā′, fil′ā), *n., v.* —***n.*** **1** a narrow band, ribbon, or the like, worn around the head to hold the hair in place, often as an ornament: *a belt her waist, a fillet binds her hair* (Alexander Pope). **2** a narrow band or strip of metal or other material: *The blanks for silver coins are punched out of a fillet of silver.* **3** any kind of strip used for binding anything. **4** *Bookbinding.* **a** a decorative line impressed upon the cover of a book. **b** a rolling tool used to make such lines. **5** *Architecture.* **a** a narrow, flat band or strip of any material, especially a plane molding often used between curved moldings. **b** one of the flat vertical strips between flutes on the shaft of a column. **6a** a thin slice of fish or meat without bones or fat; filet. **b** a heavy slice of lean beef, mutton, or other meat, cooked especially by broiling. **c** a long, flat piece of lean meat rolled up and tied, cooked especially by roasting. **7** *Anatomy.* a band of fibers, especially a white nerve tract in the brain; lemniscus. **8** a raised rim or edge, especially around the muzzle of a gun. **9** *Heraldry.* a horizontal portion of an escutcheon, equal to one fourth of the chief, of which it is the lowest part.
—***v.t.*** **1** to bind or decorate with a narrow band, ribbon, strip, or molding. **2a** to cut (fish or meat) into fillets. When a fish is filleted, the flesh is cut away from the skeleton. **b** to slice fillets off of (a meat carcass, or part of one).
[< Old French *filet* (diminutive) < *fil* thread < Latin *fīlum*]

fil|let|ing (fil′ə ting), *n.* **1** the material of which fillets are made. **2** fillets collectively. **3** mortar or plaster used in a building to fill up a close joint where one surface meets another.

fil|li|bus|ter (fil′ə bus′tər), *n., v.i., v.t.* = filibuster.

fil|li|gree (fil′ə grē), *n., v.t.,* **-greed, -gree|ing,** *adj.* = filigree.

fill-in (fil′in′), *n.* **1** a briefing: *an up-to-the-minute fill-in on the Berlin crisis ...* (Baltimore Sun). **2** a replacement, as for an employee on vacation or for goods sold in a store: *Stores are urged to anticipate normal requirements and avoid last minute fill-ins* (New York Times). **3** an activity or attraction to occupy the time between more important events or the like.

fill|ing (fil′ing), *n.* **1** a thing put in to fill something: *cake filling, a custard filling for pie.* **2** a substance, such as gold, amalgam, or any one of various plastics, used by a dentist to fill a cavity in a decayed tooth. **3a** threads running from side to side across a woven fabric; woof. **b** one of the threads for the woof. **4** the action of making full. **5** the condition of becoming full.
fillings, fill; woof: *Much of* [*the wool*] *may be wrought into ... worsted chain or warp for woolen weft or fillings* (Niles' Weekly Register).

filling station, a place where gasoline and oil for motor vehicles are sold; gas station; service station.

fil|lip (fil′əp), *n., v.* —***n.*** **1** a thing that rouses, revives, or stimulates: *The relishes serve as a fillip to my appetite.* **2** a quick, light blow given by striking with the fingernail as it is snapped quickly from the end of the thumb.
—***v.t.*** **1** to rouse, revive, or stimulate. **2** to strike with the fingernail as it is snapped quickly from the end of the thumb. **3** to toss or cause to move by striking in this way: *He filliped a speck of lint from the sleeve of his coat.*
—***v.i.*** to make a fillip.
[probably imitative. Compare etym. under **flip**[1].]

fil|li|peen (fil′ə pēn′), *n.* = philopena.

fil|lis|ter (fil′ə stər), *n.* **1** a plane used in cutting rabbets or grooves. **2** a rabbet or groove, especially one on a window sash in which the glass is inserted. [origin unknown]

fil|ly (fil′ē), *n., pl.* **-lies. 1** a young female horse; a mare less than four or five years old. **2** *Informal.* a young, lively girl. [perhaps < Scandinavian (compare Old Icelandic *fylja*). See related etym. at **foal.**]

film (film), *n., v.* —***n.*** **1** a very thin layer, sheet, surface, or coating, often of liquid. Oil poured on water will spread and make a film. *A film of fog covered the hills. An icy gale ... o'er the pool Breathes a blue film* (James Thomson). **2a** a roll or sheet of thin, flexible material, such as cellulose nitrate or cellulose acetate, with a coating that is changed by light, used to take photographs: *He bought two rolls of film for his camera.* **b** such a roll or sheet used as a coating on a photographic plate. **3a** motion-picture film. **b** a motion picture: *We saw a film about animals.* **4** a thin skin or membranous layer. **5** a very thin sheet or leaf of metal or other material. **6a** a very fine thread; fiber; filament: *like films of silk blown by the wind* (Charles Darwin). **b** a delicate web of filaments or fine threads: *From the twig a film of cobweb hung.* **7a** a dimness in the eye, as from tears: *As sheathes A film the mother-eagle's eye When her bruised eaglet breathes* (Robert Browning). **b** a growth forming an opaque spot on the eye.
—***v.t.*** **1** to cover with or as if with a film; coat; cover: *Tears filmed her eyes.* **2a** to make a motion picture of (another dramatic form); screen: *They filmed "Hamlet."* **b** to photograph for motion pictures: *They filmed the scene three times.*
—***v.i.*** **1** to be or become covered with or as if with a film: *Her eyes filmed with tears.* **2a** to be (well or ill) suited for acting or reproduction in motion pictures; be photographed for motion pictures. **b** to take or make a motion picture.
films, motion pictures: *The great majority of heroic and patriotic films shown here make United States sailors and roughriders the heroes* (London Times).
[Old English *filmen.* See related etym. at **fell**[4].]
—**film′like′,** *adj.*
▶The pronunciation fil′əm is nonstandard.

film|a|ble (fil′mə bəl), *adj.* that can be filmed or adapted to motion pictures.

film badge, a badge containing photographic film that records amounts of radiation exposure. It is worn by a person at an atomic plant or wherever there is a danger of exposure to radiation.

film|card (film′kärd′), *n.* a heavy paper or plastic card or sheet containing a strip of microfilm; microfiche. A filmcard usually measures about 4 by 6 inches.

film clip, a short reel of film, usually clipped from a motion picture or taped telecast, used to blend in with a live television program, or for other purposes.

film|craft (film′kraft′, -kräft′), *n.* the art of making motion pictures; cinematographic art or skill.

film|dom (film′dəm), *n.* all the people and companies engaged in or with the production and presentation of motion pictures.

film gate, a device that aligns and secures motion-picture film while it is being projected or exposed.

film|go|er (film′gō′ər), *n.* a person who goes often to see motion pictures.

film|ic (fil′mik), *adj.* **1** of or having to do with motion pictures: *The same newspaper headlined a story "Richard Egan's Career at Filmic High Point"* (TV Guide). **2** through the medium of motion pictures: *The latest to achieve a filmic incarnation is James T. Farrell's inflammatory "Studs Lonigan"* (Saturday Review). —**film′i|cal|ly,** *adv.*

film|i|za|tion (fil′mə zā′shən), *n.* a motion picture adapted from a play, story, or other literary form: *These filmizations ... are too reverential* (Dwight MacDonald).

film|land (film′land′, -lənd), *n.* = filmdom.

film|let (film′lit), *n.* a short motion picture, sometimes made as a film loop: *Students, most of whom borrow their parents' 8-mm. equipment, are required to make one filmlet a week which is subjected ... to scathing professional criticism* (Time).

film library, a library consisting of material on film: **a** a collection of photographic copies of rare or very large printed works, especially on microfilm. **b** a collection of motion pictures, as documentary films or silent films.

film loop, 1 a short, continuous film, for use in small desk projectors at schools, at museum exhibits, and the like: *The future will see more cine projectors developed to use film loops which can be repeated on the screen continuously and without attention* (New Scientist). **2** = filmstrip.

film|mak|er (film′mā′kər), *n.* a person who produces motion pictures; moviemaker.

film|mak|ing (film′mā′king), *n.* the production of motion pictures; moviemaking.

film|og|ra|phy (fil mog′rə fē), *n., pl.* **-phies. 1** a list or record of the films of a particular actor or director: *... complete filmographies of such performers as Bogart, Chaplin, Bette Davis, W. C. Fields* (Saturday Review). **2** writings dealing with motion pictures: *This important book ... is essential for any real followers of the cinema to add to their bookcase of filmography* (Manchester Guardian Weekly). **3** a book or article dealing with the films of a particular actor or director: *Books about the movies are tumbling from the presses ... : star autobiographies, illustrated filmographies of their careers* (Harper's). [< *film* + *-ography,* as in *bibliography, biography*]

film pack, a package of photographic film for a camera.

film recorder, a device used for recording sound on a motion-picture sound track.

films (filmz), *n.pl.* See under **film.**

film|script (film′skript′), *n.* = screenplay.

film|set (film′set′), *n., v.,* **-set, -set|ting.** —***n.*** the set for a motion picture.
—***v.t.*** = photocompose.

film star, a person who stars in motion pictures; a movie star.

film|strip (film′strip′), *n.* a related series of still

Pronunciation Key: hat, āge, cãre, fär; let, ēqual, tėrm; it, īce; hot, ōpen, ôrder; **oi**l, **ou**t; cup, pu̇t, rüle; **ch**ild; lo**ng**; **th**in; **ᴛʜ**en; **zh**, measure; ə represents **a** in about, **e** in taken, **i** in pencil, **o** in lemon, **u** in circus.

pictures made up on a reel of 35-millimeter film, used to project each picture separately on a screen, as in teaching or lecturing.

film|y (fil′mē), *adj.,* **film|i|er, film|i|est.** **1** of or like a film; very thin: *a filmy gown.* **2** SYN: gossamer. **3** covered with or as if with a film; dim; hazy. —**film′i|ly,** *adv.* —**film′i|ness,** *n.*

filmy dome spider, a spider that spins a tangle of threads around a dome-shaped silk sheet, and hangs under the dome. Insects that drop onto the dome are pulled through the webbing by the spider.

filmy fern, a fern whose blade is only a single cell thick, found on moist rocks and in copses.

Fi|lo|fax (fī′lō faks), *n. Trademark.* a leather-bound datebook that includes tables, maps, check lists, and other items.

fil|o|plume (fil′ə plüm, fī′lə-), *n.* a threadlike or hairlike feather with only a minute tuft of barbs at the tip, occurring at the base of a contour feather. [< New Latin *filopluma* < Latin *fīlum* thread + *plūma* feather]

fi|lo|po|di|um (fil′ə pō′dē əm, fī′lə-), *n., pl.* **-di|a** (-dē ə). a threadlike pseudopodium found in certain protozoans. [< Latin *fīlum* + Greek *poús, podós* foot]

fi|lose (fī′lōs), *adj.* threadlike; ending in a threadlike process. [< Latin *fīlum* + English *-ose*[1]]

fils[1] (fils), *n., pl.* **fils.** a unit of money in Iraq, Jordan, Kuwait, Yemen (Aden), and Bahrain, equal to 1/1000 dinar. [< Arabic *fils*]

fils[2] (fēs), *n. French.* son (often used after a name to distinguish a son from his father): *Dumas fils. Rockefeller père informed Rockefeller fils that if the river plot could be purchased, he was prepared to donate it to the United Nations* (New Yorker).

fil|ter (fil′tər), *n., v.* —*n.* **1** a device for passing a liquid or gas slowly through paper, sand, charcoal, felt, or other porous media. A filter is used to remove impurities from drinking water. **2** paper, sand, charcoal, felt, or other porous material used in such a device. **3** any one of various devices for removing dust, smoke, germs, or other pollutant from the air. **4** the tip on a filter cigarette, designed to trap nicotine and tars before the smoke is inhaled; filter tip. **5** a screen of colored gelatin or glass used before a camera lens to absorb entirely or partially certain rays of light: *Putting a yellow filter in front of a camera lens causes less blue light to reach the film.* **6** *Physics.* **a** a device for permitting only waves of particular frequencies to pass, eliminating or reducing the others. **b** an electric circuit which permits a particular range of frequencies to be transmitted while eliminating other frequencies. **c** a substance or device for absorbing or reflecting rays of light of particular wave lengths. **7** *British.* a lane for motor vehicles turning or moving away from the main flow of traffic, especially at an intersection.
—*v.t.* **1** to pass through a filter; strain: *We filter this water for drinking.* **2** to act as a filter for: *Charcoal filters many gases.* **3** to remove or control by a filter: *Filter the dirt out of the drinking water.*
—*v.i.* **1** to pass or flow very slowly: *Water filters through the sandy soil and into the well.* (*Figurative.*) *All the news about the party that has filtered East in recent years has been good* (New Yorker). **2** *British.* to turn or move away from the main flow of traffic, especially at an intersection: *A traffic light with a green arrow allows drivers to filter to the left or the right.*
[< Medieval Latin *filtrum* felt < Germanic (compare Old Saxon *filt.* See related etym. at **felt**[2].] —**fil′ter|er,** *n.* —**fil′ter|less,** *adj.*

fil|ter|a|bil|i|ty (fil′tər ə bil′ə tē), *n.* the quality of being filterable.

fil|ter|a|ble (fil′tər ə bəl), *adj.* **1** that can be filtered. **2** capable of passing through a filter that arrests most microorganisms: *a filterable virus.* Also, **filtrable.**

filter alum, a salt used to remove suspended sediment from natural water; aluminum sulfate. Filter alum is a common water-purifying agent.

filter bed, a pond or tank with a false bottom covered with sand or gravel, serving as a filter for water, sewage, or the like.

filter center, the point in an information network to which all reports come for sorting, evaluation, and, when indicated, forwarding to appropriate points.

filter cigarette, a cigarette containing a section of filtering material such as cellulose, which removes undesirable elements from the smoke.

filter factor, the amount of time by which a photographic exposure must be increased when a given filter is used.

filter feeder, any animal that gets its food by filtering the water going into and out of its body. Oysters and clams are filter feeders.

filter paper, porous paper used by chemists and others for filtering.

filter passer, a pathogenic microorganism, such as that of influenza, that is so small that it passes through a filter.

fil|ter-pass|ing (fil′tər pas′ing), *adj.* passing through a filter, as a microorganism or virus.

filter tip, 1 = filter cigarette. **2** the section of filtering material in a filter cigarette.

fil|ter-tip (fil′tər tip′), *adj.* having a filter tip: *a filter-tip cigarette.*

fil|ter-tipped (fil′tər tipt′), *adj.* = filter-tip.

filth (filth), *n.* **1** foul, disgusting dirt: *The alley was filled with garbage and other filth.* SYN: muck. **2** *Figurative.* obscene words or thought; vileness; moral corruption. [Old English *fȳlth* < *fūl* foul]

filth disease, a disease resulting from uncleanliness or from unsanitary conditions.

filth|y (fil′thē), *adj.,* **filth|i|er, filth|i|est,** *adv.* —*adj.* **1a** full of filth; disgustingly dirty; foul; unclean: *an alley filthy with rotting garbage.* SYN: squalid, nasty. See syn. under **dirty. b** (in a weakened sense) very dirty: *a filthy dress. My hands are filthy from working in the garden.* **2** *Figurative.* morally foul; vile; obscene: *a filthy story.* SYN: corrupt, indecent.
—*adv. Informal.* extremely; utterly: *to be filthy rich.* —**filth′i|ly,** *adv.* —**filth′i|ness,** *n.*

filthy lucre, 1 *Informal.* money. **2** *Obsolete.* dishonorable gain.

fil|tra|bil|i|ty (fil′trə bil′ə tē), *n.* = filterability.

fil|tra|ble (fil′trə bəl), *adj.* = filterable.

fil|trate (fil′trāt), *n., v.,* **-trat|ed, -trat|ing.** —*n.* the liquid that has been passed through a filter. [< verb]
—*v.t., v.i.* to pass through a filter.
[< Medieval Latin *filtrum* filter + English *-ate*[1]]
—**fil|tra′tion,** *n.*

fi|lum (fī′ləm), *n., pl.* **-la** (-lə). *Anatomy.* a filament or threadlike part. [< Latin *fīlum*]

fim|ble (fim′bəl), *n.* the male or staminate plant of hemp that ripens before the female plant and is picked first. It produces a weaker and shorter fiber than the female plant. [< Middle Dutch *femel* < Old French (*chanvre*) *femelle* (literally) female hemp (because it was thought to be the female plant since it produced the weaker and shorter fiber)]

fim|bri|a (fim′brē ə), *n. pl.* **-bri|ae** (-brē ē). *Biology.* Often, **fimbriae.** a fringe or fringed border. [< Latin *fimbriae* fringe]

fim|bri|al (fim′brē əl), *adj.* having a fimbria or fimbriae.

fim|bri|ate (fim′brē āt), *v.,* **-at|ed, -at|ing,** *adj.*
—*v.t.* to finish with a border.
—*adj. Biology.* bordered with hairs or filiform processes; fringed, as the petals of certain flowers.
[< Latin *fimbriātus* fringed < *fimbriae* fimbria, fringe] —**fim′bri|a′tion,** *n.*

fim|bril|la (fim bril′ə), *n., pl.* **-bril|lae** (-bril′ē). *Biology.* a single division or tooth of a minute or fine fringe. [< New Latin *fimbrilla* (diminutive) < Latin *fimbriae* fringe]

fim|bril|late (fim bril′āt), *adj. Biology.* bordered with a very fine fringe.

***fin**[1] (fin), *n., v.,* **finned, fin|ning.** —*n.* **1** one of the movable, winglike or fanlike parts of the body of a fish or other aquatic animal. By moving its fins a fish can swim and balance itself in the water. The large fins of a flying fish unfold like a fan and can carry it a little way through the air. **2** a thing shaped or used like a fin. Some aircraft have fins as part of the tailpiece to help balance them in flight. **3** a rubber, paddlelike attachment for the feet, worn by swimmers to gain added propulsion. **4** any one of certain thin, flat, lateral projections in various mechanisms: *the cooling fins of a radiator.* **5a** a finlike projection on a boat, especially on a submarine. **b** = fin keel. **6** *Slang.* the hand.
—*v.t.* to cut off the fins from (a fish).
—*v.i.* **1** to move the fins. **2** lash the water with the fins when dying, as a whale.
[Old English *finn*] —**fin′less,** *adj.* —**fin′like′,** *adj.*

***fin**[1]
definition 1

spiny dorsal fin
soft dorsal fin
pectoral fin
pelvic fin
anal fin
caudal fin

fin[2] (fin), *n. U.S. Slang.* a five-dollar bill. [< Yiddish *finf* five]

fin., 1 financial. **2a** finish. **b** finished (Latin, *finis*).

Fin., 1 Finland. **2** Finnish.

fin|a|ble (fī′nə bəl), *adj.* **1** (of a person or an offense) liable to be punished by a fine. **2** (of a tenure or a tenant) subject or liable to the payment of a fine on renewal.

fi|na|gle (fə nā′gəl), *v.,* **-gled, -gling.** *Informal.*
—*v.t.* **1** to get (something) by trickery or fraud. **2** to cheat; swindle: *He finagled me out of my property.*
—*v.i.* to use trickery; practice fraud: *He's a finagling rascal.*
[apparently variant of *fainaigue* renege at cards]

fi|na|gler (fə nā′glər), *n.* a person who finagles.

fi|nal (fī′nəl), *adj., n.* —*adj.* **1** at the end; with no more after it; coming last: *the final syllable of a word, a final effort, the final moment. The book was interesting from the first to the final chapter. The last day of school each year is the final one for graduating seniors.* SYN: ultimate, eventual, terminal. See syn. under **last**[1]. **2** the last possible; beyond which no other may be expected; ultimate: *Oh yet we trust that somehow good Will be the final goal of ill* (Tennyson). **3** deciding completely; settling the question; not to be changed: *The one with the highest authority makes the final decisions. A decision of the Supreme Court is final.* SYN: definitive. **4** having to do with or expressing end or purpose: *a final clause.*
—*n.* **1** something final. The last examination of a school term is a final. SYN: end, termination. **2** the last trial, heat, game, or set, in a contest: *Miss A. S. Haydon . . . reached the final of the girls' singles* (London Times).
finals, the last or deciding set in a series, as of games or examinations: *If you pass your finals at the end of the term, you will be promoted.*
[< Latin *fīnālis* < *fīnis* end]

final drive, the mechanism in the rear axle of an automobile by which power is transmitted from the engine to the wheels.

fi|na|le (fə nä′lē), *n.* **1** the last part of a piece of music or a play: *As a finale, Miss Pons . . . sang four more arias and an encore* (Newsweek). **2** the last part; end. SYN: conclusion, termination. [< Italian *finale* final < *fine* end < Latin *fīnis*]

fi|nal|ise (fī′nə līz), *v.t.,* **-ised, -is|ing.** *British Informal.* finalize.

fi|nal|ism (fī′nə liz əm), *n.* the belief that all things in nature are the final results of a plan or design; belief in final causes.

fi|nal|ist (fī′nə list), *n.* **1** a person who takes part in the last or deciding set in a series, such as a series of contests or examinations. **2** a person who believes in finalism.

fi|nal|is|tic (fī′nə lis′tik), *adj.* of or characterized by finalism.

fi|nal|i|ty (fī nal′ə tē, fə-), *n., pl.* **-ties. 1** the quality, condition, or fact of being final, finished, or settled: *Father refused with finality; we knew that he would not change his mind. The accused man seemed crushed by the finality of his conviction.* SYN: conclusiveness, decisiveness. **2** something final; a final act, state, or statement. **3** belief that change or progress in man or nature cannot occur; assumption as doctrine of a static universe.

fi|nal|ize (fī′nə līz), *v.t.,* **-ized, -iz|ing.** *Informal.* **1** to make final or conclusive: *The President likes to get a wide variety of opinions discussed before a decision is finalized* (Wall Street Journal). **2** to complete. —**fi′nal|i|za′tion,** *n.*

fi|nal|ly (fī′nə lē), *adv.* **1** at the end; at last: *The lost dog finally came home.* SYN: eventually. **2** in such a way as to decide or settle a question; with finality: *They must tackle the issue finally.* SYN: decisively.

fi|nals (fī′nəlz), *n.pl.* See under **final.**

Final Solution, 1 the Nazi code name for the mass extermination of Jewry: *Why was almost nothing done by the free countries to save Europe's Jewish population from the Nazi extermination machine between 1933 and the end of 1943, when the Final Solution was about nine-tenths completed?* (Listener). **2** Also, **final solution.** a systematic plan for the destruction of any people; genocide: *Objectively, one knew that no one in Lagos had consciously plotted a "final solution" to the Ibo question, however much the Ibo was detested* (New York Times). [translation of German *endgültige Lösung*]

fi|nance (fə nans′, fī-; fī′nans), *n., v.,* **-nanced, -nanc|ing.** —*n.* **1** money matters; the science or conduct of monetary business or affairs: *The millionaire boasted of his skill in finance.* **2** the system by which money matters, such as of a nation, state, or corporation, are managed. Management of government revenue and expenditure is called public finance.
—*v.t.* **1** to provide money or credit for: *His father financed his way through college. His friends helped him finance a new business.* **2** to manage the finances of.
—*v.i.* to conduct or engage in financial operations: *He financed with the aid of a loan from his bank.*
finances, money matters; money; funds; revenues: *New taxes were needed to increase the nation's finances. Their finances were quite low.*

[< Old French *finance* ending, settlement of a debt < *finer* bring to an end, alteration of *fenir* < Latin *fīnīre* < *fīnis* end. See related etym. at **fine[2]**.]

finance bill, **1** a legislative bill to appropriate money for governmental expenses. **2** a bill of exchange drawn by one bank on another as part of a financial transaction between them.

finance company, a business firm that loans money on interest, especially to finance the purchase of goods on credit or installment payments.

fi|nan|cial (fə nan′shəl, fī-), *adj.* **1** having to do with money matters: *His financial affairs are in bad condition. Like many artists, he has little financial sense.* **2** having to do with the management of large sums of public or private money. *Abbr:* fin.

—*Syn*. Financial, monetary, fiscal mean having to do with money. **Financial** means having to do with money matters in general: *the nation's financial policy.* **Monetary** applies to coined or printed money as such: *The United States has a decimal monetary system.* **Fiscal** means having to do with the funds and financial affairs of a government, institution, or corporation: *The fiscal year in the United States government begins on July 1.*

fi|nan|cial|ly (fə nan′shə lē, fī-), *adv.* in relation to finances; with respect to money matters.

financial statement, a report of financial data, consisting of a statement of profit and loss (with supporting schedules), and a balance sheet, showing assets, liabilities, and net worth for a specified period of time.

financial year, *British.* fiscal year.

fin|an|cier (fin′ən sir′, fī′nən-), *n., v.* **—*n.*** **1** a person occupied with or skilled in finance. Bankers are financiers. **2** a person who is active in matters involving large sums of money.

—*v.t.* = finance.

—*v.i.* **1** to act as a financier; conduct financial operations. **2** *Especially U.S.* to swindle.

[< Middle French *financier* < Old French *finance*; see etym. under **finance**]

fi|nanc|ing (fə nan′sing, fī-), *n.* **1** the raising of money to back or manage an enterprise. **2** the money raised: *The rest of the financing would come from bank borrowings* (Wall Street Journal).

fi|nan|cist (fə nan′sist, fī-), *n.* = financier.

fin|back (fin′bak′), *n.*, or **finback whale**, any one of a group of baleen whales with prominent dorsal fins, especially a species averaging about 60 feet long; rorqual.

fin|ca (fēng′kä), *n. Spanish.* a farm, ranch, or plantation in Spanish-American countries.

finch (finch), *n.* **1** any one of a group of numerous small songbirds that have strong, cone-shaped bills for cracking seeds. Sparrows, cardinals, canaries, goldfinches, buntings, and grosbeaks are finches. **2** any one of certain other perching (passerine) birds. [Old English *finc*]

find (fīnd), *v.*, **found, find|ing**, *n.* **—*v.t.*** **1** to meet with; come upon by chance; happen on: *He found a dollar on the road. They found trouble everywhere.* **2** to look for and get; discover by searching: *Please find my hat for me. The surgeon probed the wound to find the bullet.* **3** to learn; discover: *We found that he could not swim. He finds rest more agreeable than motion* (Sir Richard Steele). **4** to see; know; feel; perceive: *He found that he was growing sleepy. He found himself in a dilemma.* **5** to get the use of; get: *Can you find the time to do this?* **6** to arrive at; reach: *The arrow found its mark. Water finds its level.* **7a** to decide and declare: *The jury found the accused man guilty.* **b** to agree upon and deliver (a verdict): *The jury found a verdict of guilty.* **8a** to recover (something lost): *to find one's wallet.* **b** to gain or recover the use of: *to find one's tongue.* **9** to provide; supply; furnish: *Can you find food and lodging for my friend?* **10** to come to have; receive: *The book found many readers.*

—*v.i.* **1** to arrive at a judgment or verdict: *The jury found against the accused man.* **2** *British.* to discover game in hunting.

—*n.* **1** an act or instance of finding; discovery. **2** something found, especially something valuable: *The company believes it has a "find" in the new alloy* (Wall Street Journal).

find fault. See under **fault**.

find oneself, to learn one's abilities and how to make good use of them: *Browning may be said almost to have found himself in the delight he took in reading other persons' souls* (Spectator).

find out, to learn about; come to know; discover: *Canst thou by searching find out God?* (Job 11:7).

[Old English *findan*] **—find′a|ble**, *adj.*

find|er (fīn′dər), *n.* **1** a person or thing that finds. **2** a small, extra lens on the outside of a camera that shows what is being photographed; view finder. **3** a small telescope attached to a larger one to help find objects more easily. **4** a device for measuring distances; range finder (especially in military use).

find|er's fee (fīn′dərz), a fee paid for bringing together two or more persons or companies in a business transaction, such as the borrowing and lending of money.

fin-de-siè|cle (faɴ′də sye′klə), *adj.* **1** of or characteristic of the closing years of the 1800's; characteristically enlightened, sophisticated, overelegant, precious, or decadent: *a fin-de-siècle boulevardier.* **2** resembling or suggesting any one of the qualities or characteristics of this period: *a fin-de-siècle [attitude] of cultivated fatigue and bored aestheticism* (New Yorker). [< French *fin de siècle* end of the century]

find|ing (fīn′ding), *n.* **1** a discovery; find: *"You speak as though my misfortunes had been of my own seeking." "They have been of your own finding"* (Mrs. J. H. Riddell). **2** a thing found: *Such a finding as this exquisite painted tomb is rare indeed.* **3** a decision reached after an examination or inquiry. The verdict of a jury is its finding. SYN: judgment. **4** *U.S.* an authorization for covert governmental action: *a Presidential "finding" to justify C.I.A. logistical help to the operation* (William Safire).

findings, a tools, materials, and supplies (other than the basic materials) provided by a worker or craftsman: *A dressmaker's findings include pins, thread, and tape. A jeweler's findings include swivels, clasps, and wire. A shoemaker's findings include thread and wax.* **b** the results of any research or inquiry: *the census takers' findings.*

finding list, a list or catalogue of the books in a library without any description as to contents, date of publication, or size of volume.

fine[1] (fīn), *adj.*, **fin|er, fin|est**, *adv.*, *v.*, **fined, fin|ing.** **—*adj.*** **1** of very high quality; very good; excellent: *a fine sermon, a fine view, a fine scholar. Everybody praised her fine singing. Lee was a fine general.* **2** very small or thin: *fine wire. Thread is finer than rope.* SYN: slender, minute. **3** sharp; keen: *a fine sword, a tool with a fine edge, to be in a fine frenzy.* **4a** not coarse or heavy; delicate: *fine linen, fine lace.* SYN: dainty. **b** in very small particles: *fine dust, fine flour. Sand is finer than gravel.* **5** refined; elegant: *fine manners.* SYN: polished. **6** subtle: *The law makes fine distinctions.* **7** too highly decorated; showy: *fine language or writing.* SYN: ornate. **8** good-looking; handsome: *a fine young man. His wife ... had much pretension to beauty, and is still a very fine woman* (Henry Fielding). **9** clear; bright: *fine weather.* **10** free from imperfections; without impurities. Fine gold is gold not mixed with any other metal. **11** having a stated proportion of gold or silver in it. A gold alloy that is 925/1000 fine is 92.5 per cent gold. **12** (of an athlete, horse, or other contestant) trained to the maximum degree of efficiency. **13** *Obsolete.* clever; ingenious.

—*adv.* **1** *Informal.* very well; excellently: *"How are you?" "I'm doing fine."* **2** (in billiards and pool) so that the ball struck just grazes the object ball.

—*v.t.* **1** to make fine or finer. **2** to refine; clarify: *To bring out all its native clarity, [the sherry] is fined with the whites of eggs* (New Yorker).

—*v.i.* to become fine or finer.

cut it fine, *Informal.* to allow a very fine margin of time or space: *He gave himself only ten minutes to get to work, which was cutting it fine.*

[< Old French *fin* perfected, ultimately < Latin *fīnīre* to finish < *fīnis* end; epitome]

—Syn. *adj.* **1 Fine, choice, elegant** mean of very high quality. **Fine** is the general word: *He does fine work.* **Choice** applies to something that seems fine to a discriminating taste: *He selected a choice piece of jade.* **Elegant** applies to something that is both choice and rich or luxurious: *The designer was noted for his elegant styles.*

fine[2] (fīn), *n.*, *v.*, **fined, fin|ing.** **—*n.*** **1** a sum of money paid as a punishment, especially for breaking a law or regulation. **2a** a fee paid by the tenant at the beginning of his tenancy or for the renewal of the lease. **b** a fee paid by a feudal tenant to the landlord on some alteration of the tenancy. **3** (in English law) a settlement of a fictitious suit by means of which the ownership of land was formerly transferred. **4a** *Obsolete.* a sum of money offered or paid for exemption from punishment or by way of compensation for an injury. **b** a penalty of any kind. **5** *Obsolete.* an end; termination; conclusion.

—*v.t.* to cause to pay a fine: *The judge fined the driver twenty dollars for speeding.*

in fine, a finally: *He sent me a challenge, ... which I restored, and in fine we met (Ben Jonson).* **b** in a few words; briefly: *In fine, the Government may do its will* (Thomas Brown).

[< Old French *fin* < Latin *fīnis* end (in Medieval Latin *finis* settlement, payment)]

fi|ne[3] (fē′nā), *n.* the end (a direction on a score in music marking the end of a musical passage that has to be repeated)[< Italian *fine* < Latin *fīnis* end. See etym. of doublet **finis.**]

fine arts, **1** the arts depending upon taste and appealing to the sense of beauty; painting, drawing, sculpture, and architecture. Literature, music, dancing, and acting are also often included in the fine arts. **2** (*sing. in use*) the fine arts as constituting a department of practice or study.

fine champagne (fēn), a French brandy made from grape wine of Grande Champagne, in western France. [< French *fine champagne*, short for *eau-de-vie fine de la Champagne* fine brandy of Champagne]

fine-comb (fīn′kōm′), *v.t.* to search through in great detail: *Records in that office were fine-combed* (Birmingham News).

fine-cut (fīn′kut′), *adj.*, *n.* **—*adj.*** (of tobacco) cut into shreds for chewing or pipe smoking.

—*n.* tobacco cut into shreds.

fine|draw (fīn′drô′), *v.t.*, **-drew, -drawn, -draw|ing.** **1** to sew together so carefully that the joining can hardly be seen. **2** to draw out to extreme fineness or subtlety.

fine-drawn (fīn′drôn′), *adj.* **1** drawn out until very small or thin. **2** very subtle: *Fine-drawn distinctions are difficult to understand.*

fine-grained (fīn′grānd′), *adj.* having a fine grain.

fine|ly (fīn′lē), *adv.* **1** closely; carefully: *Those estimates must be finely figured.* **2** elegantly; excellently: *a finely dressed woman.*

fine|ness (fīn′nis), *n.* **1** thinness: *the fineness of a line, thread, needle, or wire.* **2** sharpness: *the fineness of an edge or point.* **3** clearness: *the fineness of the weather.* **4** fine quality; perfection: *the fineness of materials.* **5** the proportion of pure gold or silver contained in an alloy, commonly expressed by number of parts in 1,000: *the fineness of a metal.*

fine ounce, an ounce of a metal containing not more than a specified proportion of impurities, used as a unit of weight in valuation.

fine print, the portion of a printed contract that states in small type, usually at the lower margin of the document, the various reservations or limiting conditions attached to the agreement.

fin|er (fī′nər), *n.* = refiner.

fin|er|y[1] (fī′nər ē), *n.*, *pl.* **-er|ies. 1** showy clothes or ornaments. **2** fineness, smartness, or elegance. [< *fin(e)*[1] + *-ery*]

fin|er|y[2] (fī′nər ē), *n.*, *pl.* **-er|ies.** a hearth where cast iron is made malleable, or in which steel is made from pig iron. [apparently short for French *affinerie* < Old French *affiner* refine]

fines (fīnz), *n.pl. Mining.* **1** broken material capable of going through a sieve. **2** small particles of rock, wood, or other material, that are left when larger pieces are broken up.

fines herbes (fēn zerb′), *French.* a mixture of herbs, especially tarragon, chervil, parsley, and chives, usually cut fine, used in omelets, sauces, and other dishes.

fine|spun (fīn′spun′), *adj.* **1** spun or drawn out until very small or thin; delicate in texture: *finespun linens.* **2** very subtle: *The materialist ... mocks at finespun theories* (Emerson).

fi|nesse (fə nes′), *n.*, *v.*, **-nessed, -ness|ing. —*n.*** **1** delicacy of execution; skill: *That young artist shows wonderful finesse.* **2** the skillful handling of a delicate situation to one's advantage; subtle or tactful strategy: *A successful diplomat must be a master of finesse.* SYN: artifice, strategem, craft. **3** an attempt to take a trick in bridge, whist, or some other card games, with a lower card while holding a higher card, in the hope that the card or cards between may not be played.

—*v. i.* **1** to use finesse. **2** to make a finesse in card playing. **—*v. t.*** **1** to bring or change by finesse: *He finessed his small inheritance into a substantial fortune.* **2** to make or attempt a finesse with (a card).

[< French *finesse* < Old French *fin*; see etym. under **fine[1]**]

fi|ness|er (fə nes′ər), *n.* a schemer; strategist.

fin|est (fī′nist), *n. U.S. Informal.* police force; police officers: *Tied to the vehicle was an illegal parking ticket, signed, with a flourish, by one of the Fourteenth Precinct's finest* (New Yorker).

fine-tooth comb, (fīn′tüth′), = fine-toothed comb.

fine-tooth-comb (fīn′tüth′kōm′), *v.t.* to go over with a fine-toothed comb; fine-comb: *It would be squalid to fine-tooth-comb the volume for contra-*

Pronunciation Key: hat, āge, cãre, fär; let, ēqual, tėrm; it, īce; hot, ōpen, ôrder; oil, out; cup, pu̇t, rüle; child; long; thin; ᴛʜen; zh, measure;
ə represents **a** in about, **e** in taken, **i** in pencil, **o** in lemon, **u** in circus.

dictions (New York Times).

fine-toothed comb (fīn′tütht′, -tüᴛʜd′), a comb having fine, closely set teeth.

go over with a fine-toothed comb, to examine closely or hunt through carefully.

fine-tune (fīn′tün′, -tyün′), *v.t.*, **-tuned, -tun|ing.** to make fine adjustments in the operation or performance of; regulate.

fine wool, wool of the highest quality from the Merino or other related breeds of sheep.

fin|fish (fin′fish′), *n.* = finback.

fin|fold (fin′fōld′), *n.* a fold on the skin of an embryo fish from which fins are developed.

fin|foot (fin′fůt′), *n., pl.* **-foots.** any one of various lobate or web-footed aquatic birds related to the rails and coots.

fin|foot|ed (fin′fůt′id), *adj.* being web-footed or having lobate toes, as certain aquatic birds.

fin|ger (fing′gər), *n., v.* —*n.* **1** one of the five end parts of the hand, especially the four besides the thumb: *My pen slips out of my fingers* (William Cowper). *God's fingers touched him and he slept* (Tennyson). **2** the part of a glove that covers a finger. **3** *Figurative.* **a** anything shaped or used like a finger; a thing that reaches out and touches: *a long finger of light. Spires whose solemn finger points to Heaven* (Wordsworth). **b** a part of an instrument resembling a finger in form or function; indicator: *the finger of a clock* (William Cowper). **c** a projecting part, tongue, pawl, etc., of a machine or implement. **4a** the breadth of a finger, about ¾ inch: *two fingers of whiskey.* **b** the length of a finger, about 4½ inches. **5** *Music.* skill in fingering a musical instrument.
—*v.t.* **1** to touch or handle with the fingers; use the fingers on: *to finger a piece of cloth, to finger a gun.* **2a** to play upon (musical instruments) with the fingers: *to finger the keys of a piano.* **b** to play (a passage of music) with the fingers used in a given way. **c** to mark (a piece of music) with figures indicating a certain way of playing. **3** *U.S. Slang.* to point out (a prospective victim or loot) to a criminal: *to finger a bank for a holdup.* **4** to pilfer; filch; steal. **5** *Slang.* to point out; betray; inform upon: *. . . fled to Canada after fingering four others in the plot* (Wall Street Journal).
—*v.i.* **1** to use the fingers in playing a musical instrument. **2** to make vague grasping movements with the fingers: *She flung her on her face, And fingered at the grass* (Charles Kingsley). **3** to touch or handle something with the fingers. **4** to be capable of or suited for manipulation by the fingers.

burn one's fingers, a to get into trouble by meddling: *The busybody burns his own fingers* (Samuel Palmer). **b** to lose money through speculation: *Gold shares on the Stock Exchange also fell back quite sharply after the United States gold warning that speculators' fingers would be burnt if they gambled on a higher price of gold* (London Times).

cross one's fingers, a to put one finger over another to keep trouble away or when saying something but keeping back part of it. **b** to try to soften or annul the act of uttering a lie (by this action): *If he has done something wrong, he is apt to deny it, though he might cross his fingers when he does* (Time).

fingers, the hands (as the parts of the body with which work is done): *fingers used to hard work.*

have a finger in the pie, *Informal.* **a** to take part or have a share in doing something: *Susie . . . liked to have a finger in every pie* (Henrietta Keddie). **b** to meddle; interfere: *Lusatia . . . must needs . . . have her finger in the pie* (Bartholomew Harris).

keep (or **have**) **one's fingers crossed**, to curl one finger over another in the belief that this will ward off misfortune: *The optimists in Washington will keep their fingers tightly crossed until the Moscow conversations have come down to the essentials* (New York Times).

lift a finger, to make some effort, however slight: *"I've just this minute stopped worrying," she said, and folded her hands in her lap with the air of one who is not going to lift a finger* (New Yorker).

point the (or **a**) **finger at**, to single out for fault or blame; accuse: *[The] leader of the Christian Democratic party's Bundestag delegation declared that other countries "have no right to point the finger at us—we do not have a race problem, we are not fighting a war in Asia"* (New York Times).

pull one's finger out, *British Slang.* to stop obstructing some process or operation: *If people will pull their fingers out over the Heathrow extension . . . we can stay in the lead* (London Times).

put (or **lay**) **a finger on**, to touch; meddle with: *He wished he'd . . . never laid a finger on him to save his life* (R.S. Hawker).

put (or **lay**) **one's finger on**, to point out exactly: *The doctor could not put his finger on the cause of the pain.*

put the finger on, *U.S. Slang.* to single out for slaying (by a gang): *Once the finger was put on a mobster, his days were usually numbered.*

slip through one's fingers, to go by unnoticed or ignored, unheeded, or unused: *It would be tragic if we let this opportunity slip through our fingers, because it would be gone for this century and for some years into the next* (London Times).

twist around (or **round**) **one's** (**little**) **finger**, to manage easily; control completely: *Women may twist me round their fingers at their pleasure* (Dickens).
[Old English *finger*] —**fin′ger|er**, *n.* —**fin′ger-less**, *adj.* —**fin′ger|like′**, *adj.*

finger alphabet, an alphabet consisting of signs made with the fingers as a means of communication between deaf-mutes; manual alphabet.

finger board, **1** a strip of wood on the neck of a violin, guitar, or other instrument like them, against which the strings are pressed by fingers. **2** the keyboard of a piano, organ, or other instrument like them.

finger bowl, a small bowl to hold water for rinsing the fingers after or during a meal.

fin|ger|breadth (fing′gər bredth′, -bretth′), *n.* the breadth of a finger, about ¾ inch.

finger coral, a corallike hydrozoan bearing finger-shaped tentacles; millepore.

fin|gered (fing′gərd), *adj.* **1** having fingers. **2** *Botany.* digitate. **3** designed for playing upon with the fingers, as a clarinet or organ.

finger exercise, **1** a sequence of notes, scales, or chords performed on a musical instrument chiefly to strengthen or exercise the fingers. **2** an exercise in the techniques of any art or skill.

fin|ger|fish (fing′gər fish′), *n., pl.* **-fish|es** or (*collectively*) **-fish.** = starfish.

fin|ger|hold (fing′gər hōld′), *n.* **1** a grip with the fingers only. **2** something that offers a grip only to the fingers. **3** a weak grip or support.

finger hole, **1** one of a series of holes in a wind instrument which are closed or opened by the fingers in playing in order to alter the pitch of the tone. **2** any one of the holes on the dialing disk of a telephone. **3** one of a pair of holes in a bowling ball for grasping it with the fingers.

fin|ger|ing (fing′gər ing, -gring), *n.* **1** the act of touching or handling with the fingers; way of using the fingers. **2a** the action or way of using the fingers in playing a musical instrument. **b** the figures or signs marked on a piece of music to show how the fingers are to be used in playing it.

finger lake, any one of a group of lakes which diverge like the fingers of an open hand.

fin|ger|ling (fing′gər ling), *n.* **1** a small fish no longer than a finger, especially a small salmon or trout less than a year old. **2** something very small. [< *finger* + *-ling*]

finger man, *Slang.* a person who fingers: *He had been a "finger man"—one who points out places or persons to be robbed* (New York Times).

fin|ger|mark (fing′gər märk′), *n.* a mark, especially a smudge or stain, made by a finger.

fin|ger|nail (fing′gər nāl′), *n.* a hard layer of horn at the end of a finger.

finger nut, = wing nut.

finger paint, any of the thickened water colors used with the fingers or hands in finger painting.

fin|ger|paint (fing′gər pānt′), *v.i.* to paint with finger paint using fingers or hands instead of brushes.

finger painting, **1** a method of painting pictures or designs with thickened water colors on large sheets of paper, with fingers or hands instead of brushes, used especially by children. **2** a picture or design painted in this way.

finger pier, one of two or more adjacent piers extending into the water and suggesting the fingers of a hand.

finger plate, a plate of metal or piece of glass or plastic on a door as a protection from finger-marks.

fin|ger|poll (fing′gər pōl), *n.* a South African plant belonging to the spurge family, characterized by fingerlike growths, and used as food for cattle. [<Afrikaans *vingerpol* < *vinger* finger + *pol* shrub]

finger post, a guidepost having a sign shaped like a finger or hand to show the direction.

fin|ger|print (fing′gər print′), *n., v.* —*n.* **1** an impression of the markings on the inner surface of the last joint of the thumb or a finger. A person's fingerprints can be used to identify him because no two fingers have identical markings. **2** *Figurative: Szell's musical memory, his knowledge of style and the composers' personal fingerprints, was quite remarkable* (Manchester Guardian Weekly). **3** = DNA fingerprint: *Fingerprints obtained from different tissues or body fluids of a particular individual are identical* (Peter Gill).
—*v.t.* **1** to take the fingerprints of: *At the police station, the burglary suspect was fingerprinted and photographed.* **2** *Figurative: A convenient, foolproof method was devised for "fingerprinting" missiles and other metal objects. In this method a photomicrograph or a replica of the metallic microstructure is used as a positive and unique means of identification* (A. V. Astin).

fin|ger|print|ing (fing′gər prin′ting), *n.* the art or technique of taking fingerprints and using them as a means of identification.

finger puppet, a very small hand puppet that fits over a finger.

fin|gers (fing′gərz), *n.pl.* See under **finger**.

fin|ger-shaped (fing′gər shāpt′), *adj.* **1** shaped like a finger. **2** slenderly oblong.

fin|ger-spell (fing′gər spel′), *v.i., v.t.* to communicate by means of a finger alphabet.

finger sponge, any one of various slender, finger-shaped, branching sponges of commercially poor quality found on the Atlantic coast of America and Europe.

fin|ger|stall (fing′gər stôl′), *n.* a sheath, as of leather, worn to protect a finger.

fin|ger|tip (fing′gər tip′), *n., adj.* —*n.* the outer end or tip of a finger.
—*adj.* **1** requiring only a light touch to operate or manage. **2** (of a garment) extending downward to the point on the thigh reached by the fingertips when the arm is relaxed. **3** *Archaeology.* of or having to do with ornamentation made with the tips of the fingers: *the fragment of a typical fingertip urn* (Crawford and Keiller).

be at one's fingertips, to have immediately available: *Thanks to his wealth, the best schools and tutors are at his fingertips.*

have at one's fingertips, to have thorough familiarity with; know well: *He has at his fingertips every stroke of the game* (Strand Magazine).

to the fingertips, through a person's whole body; throughout; completely: *She is a lady to the fingertips.*

finger wave, a wave set in the hair by the fingers, without the use of any other instruments or heat.

fin|ger|work (fing′gər wėrk′), *n.* the way of using the fingers in playing a musical instrument: *Careless fingerwork is the worst enemy of the average Wigmore Hall pianist* (London Times).

Fin|go (fing′gō), *n., pl.* **-gos** or **-goes.** a member of a South African people who are descendants of wandering Bantu tribes driven out of Natal by the Zulus and other natives.

***fin|i|al** (fin′ē əl, fī′nē-), *n. Architecture.* **1** an ornament, such as one on top of a roof, the corner of a tower, end of a pew, or top of a bedpost. **2** the highest point.
[(originally) variant of *final*]

***finial**
definition 1

fin|i|cal (fin′ə kəl), *adj.* too dainty or particular; too precise; fussy. SYN: mincing, overnice, fastidious, squeamish. [apparently < *fine*¹ + *-ic* + *-al*¹] —**fin′i|cal|ly**, *adv.* —**fin′i|cal|ness**, *n.*

fin|i|cal|i|ty (fin′ə kal′ə tē), *n., pl.* **-ties.** **1** finical quality; finicalness. **2** something finical.

fin|ick (fin′ik), *v.i.* to do something in a fastidious manner, wasting time over unnecessary details; to mince; affect airs: *Stop finicking with that dress!* [back formation < *finical*]

fin|ick|ing (fin′ə king), *adj.* = finical. [probably < *finick* + *ing*²] —**fin′ick|ing|ly**, *adv.* —**fin′ick-ing|ness**, *n.*

fin|ick|y (fin′ə kē), *adj.* too fussy or particular; finical: *He is very finicky about the clothes he wears.* [variant of *finical*] —**fin′ick|i|ness**, *n.*

fin|i|kin (fin′ə kin), *adj.* = finical. [variant of *finicking*]

fin|ing (fī′ning), *n.* **1** the process by which air or other gas is removed from glass. **2** the process of clarifying especially wine and beer.

finings, a preparation consisting chiefly of isinglass, used to clarify beer.

fi|nis (fī′nis, fin′is), *n.* the end; conclusion; a word occasionally, and in former times commonly, placed at the end of a book. SYN: finale. [< Latin *fīnis.* See etym. of doublet **fine**³.]

fin|ish (fin′ish), *v., n.* —*v.t.* **1** to bring (action, speech, work, affairs, or any other enterprise) to an end; reach the end of; complete; end: *to finish one's dinner, to finish sewing a dress. He started the race but did not finish it.* SYN: See syn. under **end**. **2** to use up completely: *to finish a bottle of milk, to finish a spool of thread.* **3** to prepare the surface of in some way: *to finish cloth with a nap.* **4** to perfect in detail; polish. **5** to complete

or perfect the education or social graces of (a person): *She was finished at an exclusive school.* **6** *Informal.* **a** to overcome completely: *The climb finished him. My answer finished him.* **b** to destroy; put an end to; kill: *to finish a wounded animal. God hath numbered thy kingdom, and finished it* (Daniel 5:26).
—*v.i.* **1** to come to an end: *There was so little wind that the sailing race didn't finish until after dark.* **2** *Obsolete.* to die: *Who with wet cheeks were present when she finished* (Shakespeare).
—*n.* **1** the conclusion; end; close: *the finish of a day, to fight to a finish. The fit and worthy finish of such a life* (Robert Southey). **2** the way in which a surface is prepared: *a smooth finish on furniture.* **3** polished condition or quality; perfection: *the finish of a person's manners. His singing lacks finish.* **4** a thing that completes or perfects anything: *to have an American finish put to her education and manners* (Century Magazine). **5** a material used in completing or perfecting a job: *Bands of ebony provided the perfect finish for the cabinet.* **6** cultivated manners or speech; social polish: *Though he lacked finish, even the Bostonians liked him.* **7a** work done on a building after the main structure is completed, especially on the interior, such as window and door trim, paneling, and other features added chiefly to improve appearance. **b** material used for such work, especially high-grade lumber.
finish off, a to complete: *Plutarch finishes off the story in his usual manner* (Henry N. Coleridge). **b** to overcome completely; defeat, destroy, or kill: *He then won the championship by knocking out Jersey Joe Wolcott with about the only punch landed in their bout at Chicago. Next, he finished off Roland La Starza* (London Times).
finish up, a to complete: *to finish up a job.* **b** to use up completely: *I've finished up all the paint.*
finish with, a to complete: *to finish with one's work.* **b** to stop being friends with; have nothing further to do with: *to finish with a person.*
in at the finish, present at the end: *The old squire was determined to be in at the finish* (W. Stephens Hayward).
[< Old French *feniss-*, stem of *fenir* < Latin *fīnīre* < *fīnis* an end] **—fin′ish|er**, *n.*

fin|ished (fin′isht), *adj.* **1** ended or completed. **2** brought to the highest degree of excellence; perfected; polished: *It takes years of study and practice to become a finished musician.*

finished cattle, cattle fat enough to be marketed before they reach full growth. Finished cattle may be as young as 8 months and weigh only 600 pounds.

fin|ish|ing (fin′i shing), *n.* that which completes or gives a finished appearance to any kind of work: **a** *Textiles.* hemming, bleaching, dyeing, and the like: *Finishing involves all the handwork on a dress* (Bernice G. Chambers). **b** *Building.* ornamental work; decoration: *The house is ... of a pale cream color, with white finishings* (Harper's). **c** *Bookbinding.* the lettering and ornamental work on the covers.

finishing nail, a slender nail with a small round head, designed to be set below the surface of the wood with a countersink and concealed by the exterior finish. See picture under **nail**.

finishing school, a private school that prepares young women for social life rather than for business or a profession, and gives chiefly arts courses.

finishing touch, any small change or addition tending to complete or perfect something: *Soon he was putting his characteristic finishing touches on the number—a little accent here, a ritardando there* (New Yorker).

finish line, the line that marks the end of a race.

fi|nite (fī′nīt), *adj.*, *n.* **—*adj.*** **1a** having limits or bounds; not infinite: *Human understanding is finite.* SYN: bounded, limited. **b** not too great or too small to be measured. **2** of or having to do with a finite verb. **3** *Mathematics.* **a** (of a number) capable of being reached or passed in counting. **b** (of a magnitude) less than infinite and greater than infinitesimal. **c** (of a set) having a limited number of elements.
—*n.* what is finite; something finite.
[< Latin *fīnītus*, past participle of *fīnīre* to finish < *fīnis* end] **—fi′nite|ly**, *adv.* **—fi′nite|ness**, *n.*

finite canon, *Music.* a canon whose theme comes to a definite end, instead of perpetually returning into itself.

fin|i|tes|i|mal (fin′ə tes′ə məl), *adj. Mathematics.* distinguished by a finite ordinal. [< *finite;* patterned on *millesimal*]

finite verb, a verb form that has grammatical person, number, tense, and mood; not an infinitive, participle, or gerund. In the following example *stopped* is a finite verb; *going* and *to mail* are not: *Before going to work, he stopped to mail the letter.*

fin|i|tude (fin′ə tüd, -tyüd; fī′nə-), *n.* the condition or state of being finite.

fink (fingk), *n.*, *v. U.S. Slang.* **—*n.*** **1** a spy or informer, especially on union activities. **2** = strikebreaker. **3** an undesirable or inferior person: *He was not dangerous but pathetic. A fink* (Norman Mailer).
—*v.i.* *Slang.* to act as an informer: *As long as an inmate ... minds his own business and doesn't ever fink on others, he will not be molested* (Canadian Saturday Night).
fink out, *U.S. Slang.* **a** to back out; retreat: *Naturally, ARENA* [*a Brazilian political party*] *dominated Congress and so when Castella Branco decreed that the next President would be elected by Congress, the opposition finked out* (Time). **b** to fail; flop: *If this fellow had really been a magician he would have finked out, busted. Instead, he's a success* (New Yorker).
[origin uncertain]

fin keel, a heavy, finlike projection from the keel of a boat, especially a sailboat, which reduces leeway and increases stability by lowering the center of gravity; fin.

fink-out (fingk′out′), *n. U.S. Slang.* an act or instance of backing out; retreat: *The cop-out is like a fink-out, but only more graceful* (New Yorker).

fink|y (fing′kē), *adj.*, **fink|i|er, fink|i|est.** *Slang.* unpleasant; obnoxious; undesirable: *a finky character. Students ... are tired of all these finky rules* (Maclean's).

Fin|land|er (fin′lən dər), *n.* a native or inhabitant of Finland; Finn.

Fin|land|i|za|tion (fin′lən də zā′shən), *n.* the adoption by a European country of a foreign policy like that of Finland, which seeks to maintain friendly relations with the Soviet Union, usually by acceding to pressure from the Soviet government: *There is a foreign policy called Finlandization, which allows more independence than Rumania has* (Manchester Guardian Weekly).

fin|let (fin′lit), *n.* a small fin.

Fin|mark (fin′märk′), *n.* = Finnmark.

Finn (fin), *n.* **1** a person born or living in Finland. **2** a member of those peoples that speak Finnish or a related language; a Lapp or Estonian.

fin|nan had|die (fin′ən had′ē) or **haddock**, smoked and dried haddock. [originally *Findhorn haddock* < a river name later taken as *Findon,* a town in Scotland; *haddie* (diminutive) < *haddock*]

finned (find), *adj.* having a fin or fins.

fin|ner (fin′ər), *n.* = finback.

fin|nes|ko (fə nes′kō), *n.*, *pl.* **-ko.** a boot, originally of Norway, made of birch-tanned reindeer skin with the hair left on.

Fin|nic (fin′ik), *adj.* **1** of or having to do with the Finns or the languages spoken by them. **2** of or having to do with the division of Finno-Ugric languages to which Finnish, Estonian, and Lapp belong.

fin|nip (fin′əp), *n. British Slang.* a five-pound note. [perhaps < Yiddish pronunciation of German *fünf* five]

Fin|nish (fin′ish), *adj.*, *n.* **—*adj.*** **1** of or having to do with Finland, its people, or their language. **2** Finnic (def. 2).
—*n.* **1** *pl. in use.* the people of Finland. **2** the Finno-Ugric language of Finland. *Abbr:* Fin.

Finn|mark (fin′märk′), *n.* the unit of money of Finland; markka. Also, **Finmark**.

fin|nock or **fin|noc** (fin′ək), *n.* a sea trout, especially a white variety of the north and west of Scotland. [< Gaelic *fionnag* < *fionn* white]

Fin|no-U|gri|an (fin′ō ü′grē ən), *adj.*, *n.* = Finno-Ugric.

Fin|no-U|gric (fin′ō ü′grik), *adj.*, *n.* **—*adj.*** **1** of or having to do with the Finns and the Ugrians. **2** designating or having to do with a family of languages of eastern Europe and western Asia, including Finnish, Estonian, Lapp, and Hungarian.
—*n.* this family of languages.

fin|ny (fin′ē), *adj.*, **-ni|er, -ni|est. 1a** filled with fish: *the finny deep* (Oliver Goldsmith). **b** of or having to do with fish. **2** having fins; finned. **3** like a fin: *a finny shape.*

fi|no (fē′nō), *n.*, *pl.* **-nos.** *Spanish.* dry sherry wine.

fi|noc|chi|o (fi nō′kē ō), *n.* a variety of fennel, grown for its edible stalks similar to celery and tasting like anise. [< Italian *finocchio* < Vulgar Latin *fēnuclum.* See etym. of doublet **fennel**.]

fin ray, a rod of cartilage or horny tissue which stiffens the fin of a fish.

fin. sec., financial secretary.

Fin|sen light (fin′sən), light composed of violet and ultraviolet rays, used in the treatment of cutaneous diseases. [< Niels R. *Finsen,* 1860-1904, a Danish physician, who won the Nobel prize for the treatment]

fin|ta (fēn′tä), *n.* **1** a fixed contribution paid by Sephardic Jews to the synagogue. **2** a land tax or contribution, formerly paid in Spain and Portugal by every subject in time of special emergency. [< Spanish, and Portuguese *finta*]

fin whale, = finback.

f.i.o., (in shipping) free in and out.

fiord (fyôrd, fyōrd), *n.* a long, narrow bay of the sea bordered by steep cliffs. Norway has many fiords. See picture under **bay**[1]. Also, **fjord.** [< Norwegian *fiord,* earlier *fjorthr.* See related etym. at **fiard, firth.**]

fio|ri|tu|ra (fyō′rē tü′rä), *n.*, *pl.* **-tu|re** (-tü′rā). a musical ornamentation, such as a trill or run, either instrumental or vocal. [< Italian *fioritura* < *fiorire* to flower]

fip (fip), *n. U.S.* a fippenny bit.

fip|pence (fip′əns), *n. Informal.* fivepence.

fip|pen|ny bit (fip′ə nē, fip′nē), **1** = fivepence. **2** the name formerly used in Pennsylvania and several southern states for the Spanish half real, a silver coin then worth about 6 cents. [American English, variant pronunciation of *fivepenny bit*]

fip|ple (fip′əl), *n.* a plug at the mouth of certain wind instruments, such as recorders and flageolets, with a narrow slit through which the breath is led toward the edge of a side opening. [earlier, hanging lip, perhaps < Scandinavian (compare Icelandic *flipi* a horse's lip)]

fipple flute, a flageolet, recorder, or other flutelike instrument utilizing a fipple.

fir (fėr), *n.* **1** any one of a group of evergreen trees somewhat like a spruce. Firs belong to the pine family. The needles of fir trees are distributed evenly around the branch and have a pleasant smell. Small firs are often used for Christmas trees. Some firs reach a height of 300 feet and are valued for their timber. **2** any one of certain other evergreen trees, such as the Douglas fir. **3** the wood of any of these trees. [Middle English *firre,* Old English *fyrh*]

fir., firkin.

fir apple, the fruit of the fir tree; a fir cone.

fir balsam, = balsam fir.

Fir|bolgs (fir′bul əgz), *n.pl.* a legendary aboriginal race of Ireland, akin to the Silures.

fir club moss, a club moss of North America resembling a little fir tree; foxfeet.

fire (fīr), *n.*, *v.*, **fired, fir|ing. —*n.*** **1** flame, heat, and light caused by something burning. SYN: blaze, combustion, conflagration. **2** something burning. **3** destruction by burning: *A cigarette thrown into the woods in dry weather may start a fire.* **4** fuel burning or arranged so that it will burn quickly: *Please light the fire.* **5a** a preparation that will burn: *Red fire is used in signaling.* **b** *Archaic.* an inflammable composition used for starting fires or for display; firework: *Greek fire.* **6a** something that suggests a fire because it is hot, glowing, brilliant, or light: *the fire of lightning, the fire of a diamond, an insane fire in his eye. His sparkling eyes, replete with wrathful fire* (Shakespeare). **b** *Poetic.* a star: *the fires of heaven.* **7** *Figurative.* heat of feeling; readiness to act; passion, fervor, enthusiasm, or excitement: *a man full of fire and courage. Their hearts were full of patriotic fire. Wake in our breasts the living fire, the holy faith that warmed our sires* (Oliver Wendell Holmes). SYN: ardor, zeal, spirit. **8** *Figurative.* liveliness of imagination; inspiration: *poetic fire; fantasy's hot fire* (Scott). **9** burning pain; fever; inflammation: *the fire of a wound. ... the raging fire of fever* (Shakespeare). **10** severe trial or trouble: *And run through fire I will for thy sweet sake* (Shakespeare). SYN: ordeal, danger, hardship. **11a** the discharge of a weapon using an explosive charge; shooting; firing: *rifle fire, to cease fire. The soldiers advanced under the enemy's fire.* **b** the destructive effect of the missiles discharged by a weapon or weapons; firepower: *Our artillery fire wiped out the target.* **12** *Figurative.* the action of plying with questions, criticisms, protests, or the like: *He was subjected to a fire of reproaches.* **13** *Historical.* torture or death by burning; exposure to fire by way of ordeal. **14** the heating effect of alcoholic liquors: [*He*] *was of a cold nature, and needed perhaps the fire of wine to warm his blood* (Thackeray). **15** lightning; thunderbolt: *from whose solid atmosphere black rain, and fire, and hail will burst* (Shelley).
—*v.t.* **1** to cause to burn; set on fire: *The Scottish foe has fired his tent* (Scott). **2** to supply with fuel; tend the fire of: *to fire a furnace or a boiler.* **3** to dry with heat, especially to bake (as pottery or bricks) in a kiln: *Bricks are fired to make them hard. ... the kiln in which our glazed ware is fired* (Josiah Wedgwood). **4** to dry, preserve, or cure (as tea or tobacco) by heating: *For green tea, the leaf is fired within two hours of picking.* **5** to cause to glow as with fire; make hot, red, or glowing: *When* [*the sun*] *... fires the proud tops*

Pronunciation Key: hat, āge, cãre, fär; let, ēqual, tėrm; it, īce; hot, ōpen, ôrder; oil, out; cup, pu̇t, rüle; child; long; thin; ᴛʜen; zh, measure; ə represents a in about, e in taken, i in pencil, o in lemon, u in circus.

of the eastern pines (Shakespeare). **6** *Figurative.* to arouse; excite; inflame: *Stories of adventure fire the imagination.* **7a** to discharge (a gun, bomb, gas mine, or cannon): *He fired his rifle four times.* **b** to discharge (a missile) from or as if from a gun or launch pad; shoot: *to fire a rocket. The hunter fired small shot at the birds.* **8** to ply with questions, criticism, protests, or the like: *The newspaper reporters fired questions at the mayor about his plans for city traffic.* **9** *Informal.* to throw: *If you wish to see the professor, fire a pebble at his window.* **10** *Informal.* to dismiss from a job or position: *Fire him at once!* **11** to cauterize. **12** *Obsolete.* to drive (a person) from a place with fire.
—*v.i.* **1** to begin to burn; burst into flame: *Gunpowder will readily fire with a spark* (Oliver Goldsmith). **2** to grow hot, red, or glowing: *watching ... the dawn as it fir'd* (Andrew Lang). **3** to become inflamed with anger or passion; get excited: *I should have fired and fumed* (Dickens). **4** to be filled with enthusiasm; be inspired: *His heart swells, and his imagination fires.* **5a** to shoot; discharge a gun or guns, cannon, or rocket: *The soldiers fired from the fort. "Fire when ready, Gridley"* (George Dewey). **b** to be discharged; go off with an explosion: *This gun won't fire.* **6** (of grain) to turn yellow before ripening as a result of drought or disease. **7** (of pottery or bricks) to respond in a specified manner to baking in a kiln: *This clay fires a deep red.*
between two fires, attacked from both sides: *He was about to find himself placed between two fires—viz. the Mahdi and the reinforced garrison of Metammeh* (London Times).
catch fire, **a** to begin to burn: *Air and water ... never catch fire* (Henry Hunter). **b** to arouse enthusiasm; gain widespread or enthusiastic support: *The ideas of the revolutionaries caught fire in the colonies.*
fire away, **a** to proceed to fire guns as ordered: *"Fire away!" shouted the captain from the bridge.* **b** to use up (ammunition) by shooting: *There is a tendency in the soldiers ... to fire away their ammunition in a reckless and aimless manner* (A. McDougall). **c** *Informal.* to begin doing anything, especially to talk rapidly or ask repeated questions; start; go ahead: *Then Edgeworth fires away about the odes of Pindar* (Edward FitzGerald).
fire off, **a** to discharge (guns): *to fire off the port battery.* **b** to launch (a rocket or space vehicle): *Sputnik I, the first artificial satellite, was fired off on October 4, 1957.* **c** to send in haste and anger: *to fire off a memo to the chairman.*
fire up, **a** to start a fire in a furnace, boiler, etc.: *In the depth of winter ... it is quite enough to fire up twice in the twenty-four hours* (Sabine Baring-Gould). **b** to become angry; lose one's temper: *If I were to hear any one speak slightingly of you, I should fire up in a moment* (Jane Austen). **c** to start a machine or other device in operation: *The time required to "fire up," and set the engine again in motion, delayed the arrival* (E. M. Stone). **d** to set into motion; stimulate: *to fire up the imagination.*
go through fire and water, to endure many troubles or dangers: *The loyal soldiers were ready to go through fire and water for their king.*
hang fire, **a** to be slow in going off: *The bomb hung fire long enough for those nearby to escape.* **b** to be slow in acting; be delayed: *He ... was sure the jury would not hang fire in giving him a verdict* (Sporting Magazine). **c** to remain unsettled or unfinished: *A book produced anonymously hung fire for six weeks* (Literary World).
lay a fire, to arrange the fuel for a fire ready to be lit: *He laid a fire in the fireplace, ready to light in the morning.*
miss fire, **a** to fail to fire or go off; misfire: *May my pistols miss fire* (John Gay). **b** to go wrong; fail to do what was attempted: *All his schemes seem to miss fire. He got up half way about three times, and missed fire and fell every time* (Mark Twain).
on fire, **a** burning: *To the North I saw the town on fire* (Shelley). **b** full of a feeling or spirit like fire; excited; enthusiastic; eager: *They were all on fire to fall on [the enemy]* (Daniel Defoe).
open fire, to begin shooting or throwing: *The boys with the water pistols opened fire as soon as the girls rounded the corner.*
play with fire, to meddle with something dangerous: *There is no sort of use in playing with fire, even for fun* (Rudyard Kipling).
set fire to, to cause to burn: *The Indians set fire to the ranch.*
set on fire, **a** to cause to burn: *Water poured on lime sets it on fire* (Stephen Charnock). **b** to fill with a feeling or spirit like fire: *Enough was carried beyond the sea to set on fire the minds of all* (Edward Freeman).
take fire, to begin to burn: *The soot took fire* (Tobias Smollett).
under fire, **a** exposed to shooting from the enemy's guns: *Soldiers are under fire in a battle.* **b** attacked; blamed: *The prime minister was under fire in Parliament for his handling of the budget.*
[Old English *fȳr*]

fire alarm, **1** a signal that a fire has broken out. **2** a device that gives such a signal.

fire altar, an altar for burnt sacrifices, as distinguished from one for incense only.

fire and brimstone, **1** the fires and tortures of hell; hellfire. **2** any severe punishment or trial. **3** angry or violent denunciation or recrimination: *[The] hearings did not produce the same fire and brimstone over the subject that might have occurred some years ago* (New York Times).

fire-and-brim|stone (fīr′ən brim′stōn′), *adj.* raising visions of fire and brimstone; hellfire: *a fire-and-brimstone sermon.*

fire ant, a very destructive, poisonous ant native to South America and now very common in the southeastern United States, and spreading to other sections.

fire|arm (fīr′ärm′), *n.* a gun, pistol, or similar weapon to shoot with. It is usually one that can be carried and used by a single person. *The law imposes a tax on the sale or transfer of firearms.*

fire arrow, an arrow with combustible matter attached, formerly used, by shooting from a handbow or an engine, for incendiary purposes.

fire|ball (fīr′bôl′), *n.* **1** the great, luminous cloud of hot gases, water vapor, and dust produced by a nuclear explosion. **2** anything that looks like a ball of fire, such as a ball of lightning. **3** a large, brilliant meteor. **4** a ball filled with a preparation to cause burning or an explosion, formerly thrown from a catapult or similar device. **5** a very fast pitch to the batter in baseball. **6** *Informal, Figurative.* a person who possesses great energy and enthusiasm.

fire|ball|er (fīr′bô′lər), *n. Baseball.* a pitcher who relies principally on speed.

fire|ball|ing (fīr′bô′ling), *adj.* **1** (of a baseball pitcher) throwing very fast pitches. **2** *Figurative.* characterized by great energy and enthusiasm: *his fireballing years, a fireballing politician.*

fire balloon, **1** a balloon made buoyant by air heated by a fire attached beneath an opening at the bottom. **2** a balloon sent up at night with fireworks that ignite at a regulated height.

fire|base (fīr′bās′), *n.* a military base established especially to deliver heavy gunfire against an enemy.

fire bay, *British.* one of the sections of a fire trench, manned usually by a single rifle squad.

fire bean, = scarlet runner.

fire beetle, any one of certain elaterid beetles, especially a genus of tropical America, capable of producing light; cucuyo.

fire bell, a loud bell for sounding a fire alarm.

fire|belt (fīr′belt′), *n.* = firebreak.

fire bill, a bill showing the proper distribution of the officers and crew on board a vessel in case of a fire alarm.

fire|bird (fīr′bėrd′), *n.* any one of certain small birds having brilliant plumage, such as the Baltimore oriole or scarlet tanager.

fire|blende (fīr′blend′), *n.* = pyrostilpnite.

fire blight, a disease of apple and pear trees, caused by a bacterium that attacks blossoms, leaves, and twigs.

fire|board (fīr′bôrd′, -bōrd′), *n.* a board used to close a fireplace.

***fire|boat** (fīr′bōt′), *n.* a vessel equipped with apparatus for putting out fires on a dock, ship, or land bordering a waterway.

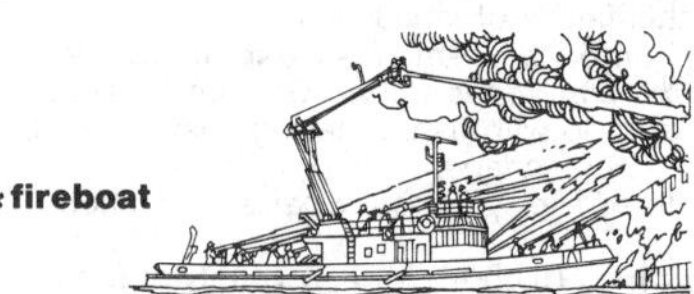
***fireboat**

fire bomb, an incendiary bomb, such as one containing napalm.

fire|bomb (fīr′bom′), *v.t.* to attack with a fire bomb or bombs: *In the meantime, attempts to firebomb the floating oil and burn it up were proving as unsuccessful as local efforts to dissolve it with detergents* (Science News).

fire boss, a mine official who examines the mine for explosive gas and inspects safety lamps taken into the mine.

fire|box (fīr′boks′), *n.* **1** the grate and surrounding walls of firebrick, etc., in which the fuel is burned in a furnace. **2** the furnace of a steam boiler, especially that of a steam locomotive. **3** a box with a device for giving the alarm in case of fire. **4** *Archaic.* a tinderbox.

fire|brand (fīr′brand′), *n.* **1** a piece of burning wood or other material: *I took up a great firebrand and in I rushed ... with the stick flaming in my hand* (Daniel Defoe). **2** *Figurative.* a person who arouses angry feelings in others; one who stirs up unrest, strife, rebellion, etc. SYN: agitator, incendiary.

fire|brat (fīr′brat′), *n.* a light-brown, wingless insect closely related to the silverfish, which lives around furnaces and steam pipes, emerging to eat starchy substances, especially in books, clothing, and wallpaper paste.

fire|break (fīr′brāk′), *n. U.S.* a strip of land in a forest or on a prairie that has been cleared of trees or on which the sod has been turned over as a means of checking the progress of a fire.

fire|brick (fīr′brik′), *n., pl.* **-bricks** or (*collectively*) **-brick.** a brick made of fire clay that can stand great heat without fusion, used to line furnaces, kilns, and fireplaces; refractory brick.

fire brigade, **1** a group of people organized to put out fires. **2** *British.* a body of firemen; fire department. **3** a highly mobile military unit organized to handle emergency outbreaks or attacks: *These units will serve as "fire brigades," taking advantage of their mobility to rush to any location where it appears that the [Army] is in trouble* (Time).

fire|bug (fīr′bug′), *n. U.S. Informal.* a person who purposely sets houses or property on fire; arsonist. SYN: pyromaniac, incendiary.

fire chief, the official in charge of a fire department.

fire clay, a clay capable of resisting high temperatures, used for making crucibles, firebricks, etc.

fire company, **1** a group of men organized to put out fires; fire brigade. **2** a fire-insurance company.

fire control, control of the aim, range, time, and volume of fire of projectiles or rockets, now commonly by automatic tracking and computing devices: *The jet plane was equipped with a radar system for fire control.*

fire|crack|er (fīr′krak′ər), *n.* a paper roll containing gunpowder and a fuse. Firecrackers explode with a loud noise.

firecracker flower, a perennial plant of the amaryllis family that grows in California, has a slender stalk, low, narrow leaves that look like blades of grass, and scarlet, tube-shaped flowers tipped with green.

fire|crest (fīr′krest′), *n.* = fire-crested wren.

fire-crest|ed wren (fīr′kres′tid), a kinglet of central Europe and parts of the Mediterranean, having a bright gold crown and a black stripe across the eye; firecrest.

fire cross, a wooden cross of light wood set on fire at one end and dipped in the blood of an animal at the other, used anciently in Scotland as a signal sent from place to place to summon men to arms; fiery cross.

fire-cure (fīr′kyůr′), *v.t.*, **-cured**, **-cur|ing.** to dry and thus to prepare (tobacco) for use by hanging over open fires. Fire-cured tobacco is usually dark in color and has a noticeably smoky flavor.

fire|damp (fīr′damp′), *n.* **1** a gas formed in coal mines that is dangerously explosive when mixed in certain proportions with air. It consists chiefly of methane. **2** the explosive mixture thus formed.

fire department, **1** a city, town, or community department organized and equipped to put out and prevent fires. **2** the body of men in such a department or other organization. In some fire departments they are municipal employees; in others they are unpaid volunteers.

fire|dog (fīr′dôg′, -dog′), *n.* an andiron, often one without the ornamental shaft in front.

fire|drake (fīr′drāk′), *n.* a fiery dragon in Germanic mythology. [Old English *fȳr-draca* < *fȳr* fire + *draca* dragon, drake]

fire drill, a drill for firemen, a ship or airplane crew, pupils in a school, or others in a building, to train them for duties or for orderly exit in case of fire.

fired-up (fīrd′up′), *adj. Slang.* enthusiastic: *a fired-up football team.*

fire-eat|er (fīr′ē′tər), *n.* **1** an entertainer who eats or pretends to eat fire: *Richardson, the famous fire-eater, devoured ... glowing coals* (John Evelyn). **2** *Figurative.* a person who is too ready to fight or quarrel: *The newcomer proved to be, ... as he pleasantly acknowledged, a Southern Fire-Eater* (Hawthorne).

fire-eat|ing (fīr′ē′ting), *adj.* of or having to do with a fire-eater.

fire engine, a truck or other vehicle that carries equipment for putting out fires and making rescues, especially one that carries ladders and pumps and hose for spraying water and chemicals; fire truck.

fire escape, a stairway or series of steel ladders in or on a building, used when a building is on fire.

✱fire extinguisher, a container filled with water or chemicals to spray on fire to put it out.

✱fire extinguisher

fire|fang (fīr′fang′), *v.i.* to deteriorate by oxidation that results from extreme heat, as manure, barley, and cheese do.
fire|fight (fīr′fīt′), *n.* a military engagement between opponents who shoot at each other without either opponent making a direct assault on the other.
fire fighter, a person employed to put out fires, especially on forest lands.
fire fighting, **1** the act of putting out a fire. **2** the occupation of a fire fighter. —**fire′-fight′ing**, *adj.*
fire|fish (fīr′fish′), *n., pl.* **-fish|es** or (*collectively*) **-fish**. a fish of the tropical waters of the East Indies, having a striped body, a collar of long pectoral fins, and a row of venomous dorsal spines.
fire|fly (fīr′flī′), *n., pl.* **-flies**. any one of the small beetles that give off flashes of light when they fly at night; lightning bug; glowfly. The larvae and wingless females of some species are commonly called glowworms. See picture under **beetle**[1].
fire foam, a foamy substance consisting of alumina and carbon dioxide, used to blanket and smother fires, especially of oil or gasoline.
fire gilding, a gilding process in which the gold is put on in the form of an amalgam of gold and mercury, and then heated in a muffle. The mercury escaping leaves a film of gold.
fire-god (fīr′god′), *n.* a spirit or deity that in certain cultures personifies or rules over the power of fire.
fire|guard (fīr′gärd′), *n.* **1** a metal screen placed before an open fireplace; fire screen. **2** a firebreak.
fire hangbird, = Baltimore oriole.
fire hook, **1** a strong iron hook used at fires in tearing away burning timbers, thatch, and the like. **2** a hook with a long handle, for raking or stirring a furnace fire.
fire hose, a flexible tube to convey water, used especially for putting out fires.
fire|house (fīr′hous′), *n.* a building where apparatus for putting out fires is kept, or one forming the headquarters of a fire company; fire station. Paid firemen usually live there when on duty.
fire hunt, *U.S.* **1** a hunt in which a torch or other light is used to reveal or attract the game. **2** a hunt in which animals are trapped in a fire set to part of a forest and killed as they try to escape.
fire-hunt (fīr′hunt′), *v.t. U.S.* to hunt (animals) in a fire hunt. —*v.i.* to carry out a fire hunt.
fire hydrant, = hydrant.
fire insurance, insurance against damage or loss caused by fire.
fire irons, implements for tending a fire in a fireplace, as shovel, tongs, and poker.
fire lane, **1** = firebreak. **2** a traffic lane, usually in a city, to be kept unblocked for use of fire engines.
fire|less (fīr′lis), *adj.* **1** without a fire. **2** *Figurative.* without life or animation.
fireless cooker, an insulated container heated by electric coils or by preheated disks of soapstone, that stays hot a long time without additional heating, used to cook food or keep it hot.
fire|light (fīr′līt′), *n.* the light from a fire, such as that on a hearth.
fire|line (fīr′līn′), *n.* **1** a strip of forest land cleared to prevent the spread of fire; firebreak. **2** a police line around the scene of a fire.
fire|lock (fīr′lok′), *n.* **1a** any one of the early guns, such as the flintlocks, fired by a spark falling on the gunpowder. **b** the gunlock of such a weapon. **2** a soldier whose principal weapon was such a gun.
fire main, a pipe for water to be used in case of fire.
fire|man (fīr′mən), *n., pl.* **-men**. **1** a man whose work is putting out fires; man who is employed by or belongs to a fire department. **2** a man whose work is taking care of the fire in a furnace, boiler, or locomotive; stoker.
fire marshal, the head of a fire department in a city or state.
fire|mas|ter (fīr′mas′tər, -mäs′-), *n. British.* the chief of a fire brigade.
fire office, *British.* an office for issuing policies for fire insurance; a fire-insurance company.
fire opal, = girasol (def. 1).
fire patrol, a salvage corps maintained by insurance companies, and working with the fire department of a city.
fire pink, a plant of the pink family, having scarlet flowers, found in the eastern United States; catchfly.
fire pit, an open volcanic crater, or pitlike part of a larger crater, where hot lava is in frequent or continuous activity.
fire|place (fīr′plās′), *n.* a place built to hold a fire. Fireplaces are sometimes made of stones out of doors, but usually of brick or stone in a room, with a chimney leading up from them. Cooking used to be done over the fire in a big fireplace. **SYN**: grate.
fire plug, = hydrant.
fire pot, the part of a stove or furnace that holds the fire.
fire|pow|er (fīr′pou′ər), *n.* **1** the ability to deliver effective, accurate, and destructive fire: *The artillery has more firepower than the infantry.* **2** the amount of fire delivered by a military unit or a particular weapon.
fire|proof (fīr′prüf′), *adj., v.* —*adj.* **1** that will not burn, or will not burn easily: *Asbestos is fireproof.* **SYN**: incombustible. **2** that is relatively hard to set fire to; not easily destroyed by fire: *A building made entirely of steel and concrete is fireproof.*
—*v.t.* to make so that it will not burn, or not burn easily: *to fireproof a theater curtain.*
fire|proof|ing (fīr′prü′fing), *n.* material for use in making anything fireproof.
fir|er (fīr′ər), *n.* **1** a person or thing that fires. **2** a firearm of a particular method, style, or process of firing.
fire-rais|er (fīr′rā′zər), *n. British.* an arsonist.
fire-rais|ing (fīr′rā′zing), *n. British.* arson.
fire-re|sist|ant (fīr′ri zis′tənt), *adj.* = fire-retardant.
fire-re|tard|ant (fīr′ri tär′dənt), *adj.* having or providing a considerable but incomplete resistance to combustion or damage from fire.
fire|room (fīr′rüm′, -rům′), *n.* **1** a room containing a fireplace. **2** a space in front of a furnace or steam boiler, from which coal is supplied. **3** = stokehold (def. 1).
fire sale, a sale at very low prices of goods that have been damaged in a fire.
fire screen, a screen to be placed in front of a fire as protection against heat or flying sparks. **SYN**: fender.
fire setting, an excavation in a mine with the preliminary aid of a fire built against the working face.
fire ship, a ship loaded with combustibles and explosives, that is set adrift among an enemy's ships to destroy them.
fire|side (fīr′sīd′), *n., adj.* —*n.* **1** the space around a fireplace or hearth: *All our adventures were by the fireside and all our migrations from the blue bed to the brown* (Oliver Goldsmith). **2** *Figurative.* **a** home; hearth: *The soldier longed to be back at his own fireside. There is no fireside, howsoe'er defended, But has one vacant chair* (Longfellow). **b** home life: *a happy fireside.*
—*adj.* beside the fire; informal: *fireside comfort.*
fireside chat, **1** a conversation marked by the intimate informality of a small group sitting around a fire. **2** a speech by a political leader, especially over radio or television, marked by a similar informality.
fire station, = firehouse.
fire stick, **1** a lighted stick or brand; firebrand. **2** a stick used to obtain fire by friction, either by rubbing it against another stick or by twirling it between the hands with the point in a hole in a flat piece of wood.
fire sticks, a pair of sticks used for lifting coals out of the fire or for rearranging burning faggots: *In the same plate are included a pair of wooden fire sticks or tongs* (Annual Report of the Smithsonian Institution).
fire|stone (fīr′stōn′), *n.* **1** a stone that resists the action of fire, especially a kind of sandstone formerly much used for lining furnaces, ovens, etc. **2** *Obsolete.* a stone capable of being used in striking fire, especially iron pyrites or flint. [Old English *fȳrstān* flint < *fȳr* fire + *stān* stone]
fire storm or **fire|storm** (fīr′stôrm′), *n.* **1** an immense blaze, such as that created by an atomic explosion, that fans its own flames by creating its own draft. **2** *Figurative.* a violent outburst or outpouring; flood; storm: *The White House was inundated by a "firestorm" of indignation* (National Review).
fire test, **1** a test to determine the temperature at which kerosene or other oils begin to burn. **2** the process of subjecting pottery, concrete, or brick to various degrees of heat to test their relative hardness or fire-resistant properties.
fire|thorn (fīr′thôrn′), *n.* any one of a group of thorny, red-fruited, evergreen shrubs of the rose family found in Asia, Europe, and America, and often cultivated as a hedge.
fire tower, a tower from which forest rangers can watch for forest fires and give the alarm.
fire|trap (fīr′trap′), *n.* **1** a building that would be hard to get out of if it were on fire. **2** a building that could burn very easily.
fire trench, a trench composed of connected bays in which men are protected while firing.
fire truck, = fire engine.
fire tube, a tube or flue in a steam boiler, used for the passage of the flame and heated gas.
fire wall, **1** a wall of fire-resistant material in or around a building or other structure. **2** a plate of fireproof material behind the engine of an aircraft or automobile to confine a possible fire.
fire|ward|en (fīr′wôr′dən), *n. U.S.* an official whose duty is preventing and putting out fires in towns, forests, camps, and buildings.
fire|wa|ter (fīr′wôt′ər, -wot′-), *n. Informal.* strong alcoholic drink.
fire|weed (fīr′wēd′), *n.* any one of various weeds that often appear on land recently burned over, especially a tall plant of the evening-primrose family, with magenta flowers, found all over the United States and in Canada. It is the official flower of the Yukon Territory.
fire wheel, a gaillardia; blanketflower.
fire|wood (fīr′wůd′), *n.* wood to make a fire.
fire|work (fīr′wėrk′), *n.* a firecracker, skyrocket, or other pyrotechnic device, that makes a loud noise or a beautiful fiery display at night: *It was a firework, mate, a Bengal light* (Punch).
fire|works (fīr′wėrks′), *n.pl.* **1** firecrackers, skyrockets, and other things that make a loud noise or a beautiful fiery display at night. **2** a fireworks display. **3** *Informal, Figurative.* an outburst or display of fiery emotions, such as a heated controversy. **4** *Informal.* any spectacular display: *the soprano's coloratura fireworks.*
fire|worm (fīr′wėrm′), *n.* **1** the larva of a small North American moth that feeds on cranberry leaves. **2** = glowworm.
fir|ing (fīr′ing), *n.* **1** the act or process of setting on fire; catching fire: *Those meetings led to the firing and pulling down of houses* (William Cobbett). **2** the act, process, or effect of discharging a gun, mine, or other explosive device. **3** preparation, baking, or curing by heat: *The firing of the pottery took a full 24 hours.* **4** the feeding and tending of a fire or furnace. **5** = cauterization. **6** material for a fire; fuel: *I . . . brought home firing sufficient for . . . several days* (Mary Shelley).
firing glass, a wineglass made in England and elsewhere from 1740 to 1800 which had a heavy base to rap on the table in response to a toast. It made a sound like a gun firing.
firing line, **1** a line where soldiers are stationed to shoot at the enemy or target. **2** the soldiers on such a line. **3** the foremost position in a controversy, campaign for a cause, or the like.
firing party, = firing squad.
firing pin, the part of the mechanism of a firearm, cannon, mine, or other explosive device, that sets off the detonator to explode the charge.
firing range, **1** an area used for practice in shooting or in firing guns or missiles. **2** the distance within which a gun is effective: *the enemy was within firing range.*
firing squad, a detachment of troops, usually a squad, designated to fire the salute at a military burial service or to shoot to death a person condemned to be shot.
fir|kin (fėr′kən), *n.* **1** a quarter of a barrel, used in Great Britain as a measure of capacity. A firkin equals either about 9 imperial gallons or about 56 pounds. **2** a small wooden cask for liquids, fish, butter, and other commodity. [Middle English *ferdekin*, perhaps < unrecorded Middle Dutch *verdelkijn* (diminutive) < *verdel* (literally) fourth part]
firm[1] (fėrm), *adj., v.* —*adj.* **1** not yielding easily when pressed; solid; hard: *firm flesh, firm ground.* **2** not easily shaken or moved; fixed in place: *a tree firm in the earth. Hope, as an anchor firm and sure, holds fast the Christian vessel and defies the blast* (William Cowper). **SYN**: fast, secure, immovable, stable. **3** steady in motion or action: *a firm step, a firm grasp.* **4** not easily changed; determined; resolute; positive: *a firm purpose, a firm character, a firm belief.* **5** not changing; staying the same; stable: *a firm price.* **SYN**: enduring, constant, steady.
—*v.t.* **1** to make firm; solidify: *to firm the soil around a newly planted tree.* **2a** to set or fix firmly in place: *to firm a flagpole in its socket.*

Pronunciation Key: hat, āge, cãre, fär; let, ēqual, tėrm; it, īce; hot, ōpen, ôrder; oil, out; cup, pů́t, rüle; child; long; thin; ᴛʜen; zh, measure; ə represents **a** in about, **e** in taken, **i** in pencil, **o** in lemon, **u** in circus.

b to hold (a thing) fast. 3 *Obsolete.* **a** to establish, settle, or confirm (a person, etc.). **b** to encourage. —*v.i.* to become firm.
[Middle English *ferm* < Old French *ferme* < Latin *firmus*] —**firm'ly**, *adv.* —**firm'ness**, *n.* —*Syn. adj.* 1 **Firm, hard, solid** mean not yielding easily to pressure or force. **Firm** implies being so tough, compact, or stiff that it can not be easily bent, squeezed, or pulled out of shape: *His muscles are firm.* **Hard** implies a surface difficult to dent or penetrate: *The ground is too hard to dig.* **Solid** implies being so strongly built or uniformly dense as to withstand all pressure or force: *We build houses on solid ground.*

firm² (fėrm), *n.* 1 a company of two or more persons in business together. It is distinguished from a corporation in that it is not considered a legal person. 2 the name or title used by such a company or partnership: *the firm of Black and Sons.* 3 any business concern. [< Italian *firma* signature < Latin *firmāre* strengthen, establish < *firmus* firm, solid]

fir|ma|ment (fėr'mə mənt), *n.* the arch or vault of the heavens; sky. [< Latin *firmāmentum* < *firmāre* strengthen < *firmus* firm, solid]

fir|ma|men|tal (fėr'mə men'təl), *adj.* having to do with the firmament or upper regions; celestial.

fir|man (fėr'mən, fər män'), *n., pl.* **-mans.** an order issued by an Oriental ruler, especially by a Turkish sultan. [< Turkish *ferman* < Persian *fermān*]

firm bid, a commitment to buy a specified amount at a specified price within a specified time.

firm|er (fėr'mər), *adj., n.* —*adj.* of or having to do with chisels, gouges, and other woodworking tools driven by blows of a mallet.
—*n.* a firmer chisel.
[< French *fermoir*, alteration of earlier *formoir* chisel < *former* to form, mold]

firmer chisel, a chisel for use with wood, having a broad, thin blade with a sharp edge.

firm offer, a commitment to sell a specified amount at a specified price within a specified time.

firm power, electric power supplied, or to be supplied, at all times by a generating unit, in contrast to power which may be interrupted in times of adverse generating conditions.

firm|ware (fėrm'wãr'), *n.* computer programs that are stored permanently, usually in a read-only memory.

firn (firn), *n.* 1 = névé. 2 *Skiing.* granular snow. [< Swiss German *Firne* snow above glaciers, (literally) old snow]

firn|i|fi|ca|tion (fir'nə fə kā'shən), *n.* conversion of snow into névé; process which results in firn.

fir parrot, = crossbill.

fir rape, 1 = pinesap. 2 = beechdrops.

fir|ry (fėr'ē), *adj.* 1 of or having to do with a fir. 2 made of fir. 3 abounding in firs.

first (fėrst), *adj., adv., n.* —*adj.* **1a** coming before all others; before anything else: *Sunday is the first day of the week. First* is used as the ordinal of *one*, in which it may be written *1st.* SYN: earliest, original, initial, chief, foremost, principal, leading. **b** foremost in position, rank, or importance: *He is first in his class.* **2a** playing or singing the part highest in musical pitch: *first violin, first soprano.* **b** highest in musical pitch. 3 designating the lowest gear ratio of a standard automobile transmission; low.
—*adv.* 1 before all others; before anything else: *We eat first and then feed the cat. The good die first* (Wordsworth). 2 before some other thing or event: *First bring me the chalk.* 3 for the first time: *When first I met her, she was a child.* 4 rather; sooner: *The soldiers said they would never give up their flag, but would die first.*
—*n.* 1 a person, thing, or place that comes before all others; first number or member of a series: *We were the first to get here. Boswell is the first of biographers* (Macaulay). 2 the winning position in a race or contest. 3 the first day of the month: *I'll see you on the first.* 4 *Baseball.* first base. 5 the beginning: *the first of a storm.* 6 the first gear; low gear. 7 the voice or instrument of its class taking the highest part. 8 *British.* **a** a place in the first class in an examination: *a first in physics.* **b** a person who has taken a place in the first class.
at (the) first, in the beginning: *At first he did not like school.*
first and last, taking all together: *[In] the Bay of Campeachy ... I lived first and last about 3 years* (William Dampier).
first off, in the first place: *Men of science ... no longer admit first off what simple good sense shows to us* (Nation).
first or last, at one time or another; sooner or later: *All are fools and lovers first or last* (John Dryden).
firsts, articles of the best quality: *The "firsts" or best grains, and the "seconds" or poorer grains, were put into separate sacks* (Chase and Clow).
from first to last, from beginning to end: *Mr. Gladstone was ... in his place from first to last* (Strand Magazine).
from the first, since the beginning: *Their practice, from the first, is ill grounded* (Henry Bracken).
of the first water. See under **water**.
[Old English *fyrst*]
▶**first, last, latest**. *First* and *last* refer to items in a series, usually of more than two: *His first act in office was to appoint a new secretary. We felt let down at the end of the last act. Last* refers either to a completed or to a continuing series: *His last jump proved fatal. I was pleased with the last election. Latest* refers to a series that is still continuing: *Have you read the latest installment of the Evening News story?*

first aid, emergency treatment given to a person who is injured or suddenly ill before a doctor comes.

first-aid (fėrst'ād'), *adj.* of or for first aid: *a first-aid kit.*

first base, *Baseball.* 1 the base that must be touched first by a runner. 2 the position of the fielder covering the area near this base.
get to first base, *U.S. Informal.* to make the first step, of several, successfully: *This girl will never get to first base the way she is* (New Yorker).
—**first baseman**.

first-born (fėrst'bôrn'), *adj., n.* —*adj.* born first; oldest.
—*n.* the first-born child.

First Cause, *Theology.* God as the original and uncaused cause of the universe.

first-chair (fėrst'chãr'), *adj.* 1 occupying a first chair in an orchestra; leading a section or group of instruments in an orchestra: *The concertmaster of an orchestra is usually the first-chair violinist.* 2 having to do with or for the outstanding performer on a particular instrument.

first class, 1 the best and most expensive passenger accommodations offered for travel by ship, airplane, or train. Some ships and many trains now lack a first class. 2 the class of mail that includes letters, post cards, and small packages, sealed against postal inspection.

first-class (fėrst'klas', -kläs'), *adj., adv.* —*adj.* 1 of the highest class or best quality; excellent: *a first-class writer.* 2 of or having to do with first class.
—*adv.* by the best and most expensive passenger accommodations offered by ship, airplane, or train: *We could not afford to travel first-class.*

first-class matter (fėrst'klas', -kläs'), (in the postal system of the United States) letters, post cards, and small packages, sealed against inspection.

first|com|er (fėrst'kum'ər), *n.* a person who is first to arrive somewhere.

First Communion, the ceremony in which a child receives the sacrament of the Eucharist for the first time in the Roman Catholic Church: *First Communion is generally held at age seven* (Maclean's).

first cousin, a child of one's uncle or aunt; cousin-german. See diagram under **family tree**.

first day, = Sunday.

first-day cover (fėrst'dā'), an envelope that bears a commemorative stamp canceled on its first day of issue by the post office that issued it, much sought after by stamp collectors.

first-de|gree burn (fėrst'di grē'), a burn in which the surface of the skin is red and painful, but not broken or blistered.

first-degree murder, *Law.* homicide committed intentionally, or unintentionally while committing robbery, arson, or another felony.

first-desk (fėrst'desk'), *adj.* ranking among the foremost performers in an orchestra; first-chair.

first down, *Football.* 1 the first of four chances for a team to move the ball forward from the line of scrimmage. 2 the right to move the ball in this way: *If a team advances the ball 10 yards during the course of a series of four downs, or plays, it received a first down, or a new series of four plays* (Forest Evashevski).

first estate or **First Estate**, the clergy, as distinguished from the nobility and the common people, especially in French history.

first family, *U.S.* 1 the family of the President of the United States. 2 a family descending from one of the original American colonists.

first finger, the finger next to the thumb; forefinger; index finger.

first floor, 1 *U.S.* the floor or story built on or just above the ground; ground floor. 2 *British.* the floor or story of a building next above the ground floor.

first-foot (fėrst'fu̇t), *n.* in Scotland and northern England: 1 the person who first enters a house after the coming in of the new year. 2 the first person or object met on setting out on any important journey or undertaking.

first fruits, 1 the earliest fruits of the season. 2 *Figurative.* the first products or results.

first|hand (fėrst'hand'), *adj., adv.* from the original source; direct: *This is firsthand information* (adj.). *We got our information firsthand* (adv.).

first in, first out, FIFO.

first intention, the healing of a wound by direct union of the wounded parts without granulations.

First International, an international socialistic organization formed in London in 1864 under the leadership of Karl Marx to promote the interests of workers, dissolved in 1876.

first lady, *U.S.* the official hostess of the President of the United States or of the governor of a state. She is usually the wife, but occasionally, in the absence of a wife, the daughter or other close relative.

first lieutenant, *U.S.* a commissioned army, air force, or marine officer ranking next below a captain and next above a second lieutenant.

first|ling (fėrst'ling), *n.* 1 the first of its kind. 2 the first product or result. 3 the first offspring of an animal.

first|ly (fėrst'lē), *adv.* in the first place; before anything else; first.

first mortgage, a mortgage giving its holder legal claim ahead of all other liens on property.

first name, a person's given name: *Her first name is Mary Anne; her last name is Stone.*

first-name (fėrst'nām'), *v.,* **-named, -nam|ing,** *adj.* —*v.t.* to address (someone) by his first or given name: *Guards appeared, were first-named by their employer, and waved us through* (New Yorker).
—*adj.* allowing a person to be addressed by his first name; familiar or informal: *Few of the convicts were on a first-name basis with the guards* (Maclean's). *Artists and audience are on first-name terms within hours* (Time).

first night, the initial public performance in a run of a play or the like.

first-night|er (fėrst'nī'tər), *n.* a person who makes a practice of attending the theater on the nights of the first public performance of plays.

first offender, a person who has been found guilty of a violation of law for the first time.

first papers, the initial documents in the process of naturalization, in which an alien formally declares his intention of becoming a citizen of the United States.

first person, a form of a pronoun or verb used to refer to the speaker or writer and those he includes with himself. *I, me, my* and *we, us, our* are pronouns of the first person.

first quarter, 1 the period of time between the new moon and the first half moon. 2 the phase of moon represented by the first half moon after the new moon. 3 the first fourth of any period of time; the first quarter of the year.

first-rank (fėrst'rangk'), *adj.* = first-rate.

first-rate (fėrst'rāt'), *adj., adv.* —*adj.* 1 of the highest class: *The question is one of first-rate importance* (John Bright). 2 excellent; very good.
—*adv.* excellently; very well: *I did first-rate on the test.*

First Reich, = Holy Roman Empire.

First Republic, the government of France from 1792 to 1804.

first-run (fėrst'run'), *adj.* 1 (of a new motion picture) shown for the first time: *First-run movies and television were used to lure more passengers aboard [airplanes]* (Leslie A. Bryan). 2 (of a theater) featuring first-run motion pictures.

firsts (fėrsts), *n.pl.* See under **first**.

first sergeant, a master sergeant in the U.S. Army or Marine Corps in direct charge of a company or similar unit under the commissioned officer in command. A first sergeant is below a sergeant major in the Army and below a master sergeant in the Marine Corps.

First State, a nickname for Delaware.

first-strike (fėrst'strīk'), *adj., n.* —*adj.* 1 (of a nuclear weapon or force) designed or intended for use only in an initial attack: *Weapons openly deployed and susceptible to annihilation by the enemy who strikes first can be used only as first-strike weapons. Second-strike weapons are hidden or protected so that they cannot easily be destroyed and can remain available for retaliation* (Atlanta Constitution). 2 limited to the power to strike first; not retaliatory: *first-strike capability.*
—*n.* an attack by first-strike weapons: *The Soviet ICBMs are certain to be vulnerable to a US first-strike* (New Republic).

first string, *Sports.* the players, collectively, who usually comprise the starting line-up in a game, distinguished from alternates or substitutes.

first-string (fėrst'string'), *adj.* 1 of or having to do with a first string: *a first-string quarterback.* 2 of or having to do with the foremost or best available; first-rate: *a first-string diplomat.*

first-string|er (fėrst′string′ər), *n.* a member of a first string, in any activity.
first-term|er (fėrst′tėr′mər), *n. U.S.* one serving his first term (at a school, in prison, as a soldier, or Congressman).
first-tim|er (fėrst′tī′mər), *n. Informal.* **1** a person who does something for the first time; novice: *Some first-timers will burn their fingers by building in the wrong positions* (Sunday Times). **2** a person who comes to a place for the first time; newcomer: *To first-timers still harboring old border-town images, Mexico City comes as a happy shock* (Time).
First World, the developed or industrialized countries of the world: *He tries to prick the conscience of the First World for its complicity in the Third World's troubles* (Time).
First World War, the World War of 1914-1918; World War I.
firth (fėrth), *n.* **1** a narrow arm of the sea. See picture under **bay**[1]. **2** the estuary of a river. [Scottish, probably < Scandinavian (compare Old Icelandic *fjörthr*). Compare etym. under **fiord**.]
FIS (no periods), Fédération Internationale de Ski (French, International Ski Federation).
fisc (fisk), *n.* a royal or state treasury; exchequer. [< Latin *fiscus* purse, imperial treasury; (originally) basket woven of twigs]
fis|cal (fis′kəl), *adj., n.* —*adj.* **1** = financial. **SYN:** See syn. under **financial**. **2** having to do with public finance: *Important changes were made in the government's fiscal policy.*
—*n.* a public prosecutor in some countries: *cited before the fiscal of the empire* (Sarah Austin).
[< Latin *fiscālis* < *fiscus* purse; see etym. under **fisc**] —**fis′cal|ly**, *adv.*
fiscal agent, a representative of another in matters of finance; financial agent.
fiscal year, the time between one yearly settlement of financial accounts and another. The fiscal year of the United States government begins on July 1 and ends June 30. In Great Britain and Canada it begins on April 1 and ends on March 31.
Fisch|er-Tropsch process (fish′ər trōpsh′), = gas synthesis. [Franz *Fischer* + Hans *Tropsch*, German chemists of the 1900's]
***fish** (fish), *n., pl.* **fish|es** or (*collectively*) **fish**, *v., adj.* —*n.* **1** an animal that lives in water, is covered with scales, has gills to breathe with, and has a long backbone for support. Fish are cold-blooded and usually have fins for swimming. Some fishes lay eggs in the water; others produce living young. **2** any one of numerous other animals living in water, such as shellfish or whales. **3** the flesh of fish used for food. **4** *Informal, Figurative.* a person; fellow: *He is an odd fish.* **5a** a long strip of iron or wood used to strengthen a mast, spar, or joint. **b** = fish tackle.
—*v.i.* **1** to catch fish; try to catch fish: *Though we sat in the boat and fished for hours we didn't catch anything.* **2** to try for something as if with a hook: *He fished with a stick for his watch, which had fallen through a grating.* **3** *Figurative.* to search: *She fished in her purse for a coin.* **4** to search by dredging, dragging, diving, or otherwise for objects under water, mud, or refuse: *to fish for pearls.* **5** *Figurative.* to try to get by means of cunning: *She fished for compliments.*
—*v.t.* **1** to catch (fish); try to catch (fish): *to fish trout. Thou hast fished salmon a thousand times* (Scott). **2** to try to catch fish in: *He fished the stream for trout.* **3** *Figurative.* to search through as by fishing: *The sheriff's men fished the whole stream for the body but failed to find it.* **4** *Figurative.* to find and pull: *He fished the map from the drawer.* **5** *Nautical.* **a** to reinforce (a strained mast, spar, or joint) by lashing wood or iron bars along the strained part: *All hands were now employed ... fishing the spritsail yard* (Richard Henry Dana). **b** to hoist the flukes of (an anchor) to the gunwale with fish tackle.
—*adj.* of or having to do with fishes, fishing, or the sale of fish.
fish in troubled waters. See under **troubled waters**.
fish or cut bait, *U.S.* to make a choice; make up one's mind; stop vacillating: *One of the attributes of an administrator is his ability to stick his neck out, ... to decide what side of the fence he is on and to take a stand there, to fish or cut bait* (Time).
fish out, **a** to use up the supply of fish in: *That stream is completely fished out.* **b** *Figurative.* to get (information) by careful inquiry or subtle methods: *... an admirable knack of fishing out the secrets of his customers* (Joseph Addison).
fish out of water, a person who is out of his element; stranger: *Is there a chance of his finding a kindred soul at Newell Hall, so that he will not be a fish out of water?* (London Times).
have other fish to fry, *Informal.* to have other things to do: *I've got other things in hand ... I've got other fish to fry* (Margaret Oliphant).
make fish of one and flesh (or **fowl**) **of another**, to treat two persons differently; show partiality or favor: *This is making fish of one and fowl of another with a vengeance* (Manchester Examiner).
neither fish nor fowl, a person or thing that does not fit into any group or class: *Four years after college, the man with an M.D. is neither fish nor fowl; if he wants to do clinical work he needs another three to five years hospital experience; if he wants to do research, he probably has to go back to school* (Michael Crichton).
[Old English *fisc*] —**fish′less**, *adj.* —**fish′like′**, *adj.*
▶**fish.** The usual plural is *fish* except in speaking of different kinds or species: *He has a string of eight fish. Most of the income of the island is from these fishes: cod, halibut, and swordfish.*

***fish**
definition 1

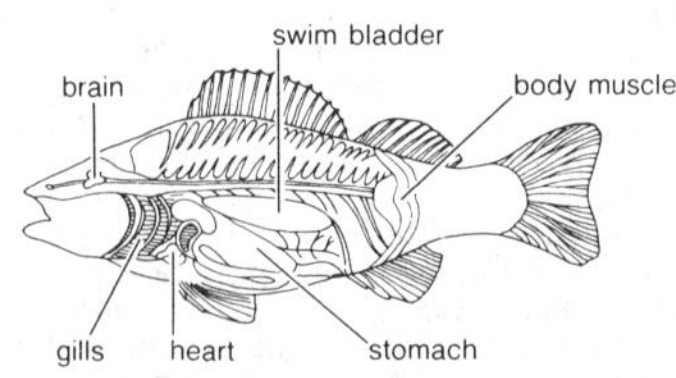

fish|a|ble (fish′ə bəl), *adj.* **1** that can be fished in: *a fishable stream.* **2** lawful to be fished in.
fish and chips, *British.* fried slabs of cod, haddock, or other fish, and French fried potatoes.
fish ball, shredded cooked fish and mashed potatoes, shaped into a ball and fried.
fish-bel|lied (fish′bel′id), *adj.* shaped like the belly of a fish; swelling downward.
fish|bolt (fish′bōlt′), *n.* a bolt used to secure a fishplate.
fish|bone (fish′bōn′), *n.* a bone or the skeleton of a fish.
fish|bowl (fish′bōl′), *n.* **1** a glass bowl for keeping and displaying live fish. **2** anything resembling a fishbowl. **3** *Figurative: "Can't conduct diplomacy in a fishbowl," the Secretary said* (Atlantic).
fish cake, shredded cooked fish and mashed potatoes, shaped into a cake and fried.
fish crow, a shellfish-eating crow of the Atlantic and Gulf coastal region of the United States, slightly smaller than the common crow.
fish culture, the artificial breeding of fish; pisciculture.
fish day, a day on which fish is eaten customarily, or in observance of religious regulations forbidding the eating of meat.
fish eagle, **1** = eagle vulture. **2** = osprey.
fish|er (fish′ər), *n.* **1a** a slender mammal like a weasel but larger, living in forested regions of Canada and northern United States. It belongs to the same family as the weasel. **b** its dark-brown fur. **2** an animal that catches fish for food. **3** *Archaic.* a fisherman (def. 1): *And he saith unto them, Follow me, and I will make you fishers of men* (Matthew 4:19).
fish|er|folk (fish′ər fōk′), *n.pl.* people who earn their livelihood by fishing.
fish|er|man (fish′ər mən), *n., pl.* **-men**. **1** a man who fishes, especially one who makes his living by catching fish: *Each day the fishermen climb into their boats to fish the sea, and each night they return.* **2** a ship used for fishing.
fisherman's bend, a kind of knot tied in a rope, especially to secure it to a link of cable, anchor, or fishhook; anchor bend.
fisherman's ring, the Pope's ring, bearing his name and a picture of Saint Peter in a boat, used as a signet for papal documents.
fisher spider, a spider with a large body and long, thin legs that lives near water and hunts water insects, small fish, and tadpoles. Because of its light weight, it can walk on the water without sinking.
fish|er|y (fish′ər ē), *n., pl.* **-er|ies**. **1** a place for breeding fish, especially a government-operated fish-culture station: *At the fishery we saw long trays of fish eggs under water that will turn into trout.* **2** a place for catching fish, especially commercially; fishing ground: *The birds watch for the boats returning with their catch from the fishery.* **3** the occupation of catching fish or of taking other products of the sea or streams from the water. **4** the legal right or the license to fish in certain waters in a certain way; piscary.
Fish|es (fish′iz), *n.pl.* = Pisces.
fish|eye (fish′ī′), *n. U.S. Slang.* a fishy glance; look of suspicion.
fish-eye (fish′ī′), *adj. Photography.* **1** covering a very wide angle of view, usually approaching 180 degrees, and curving outward so that a distorted image is created. **2** using or made with a fish-eye lens: *The 160° "fish-eye" cameras were synchronized to less than a tenth of a second for each pair of eight-second exposures* (New Scientist).
fish farm, a pond or irrigated tract in which fish are stocked and grown to be sold commercially.
fish farmer, a person who owns a fish farm.
fish farming, the stocking and growing of fish on a fish farm.
fish finger, *British.* fish stick.
fish flour, a flour obtained by pulverizing the dried bodies of fish.
fish fork, a pitchfork with a short handle and two or three tines, used in pitching fish into or out of a boat.
fish fry, a picnic at which fried fish is the main dish.
fish|garth (fish′gärth′), *n.* a garth or weir on a river or on the seashore for the taking and retaining of fish; fishweir.
fish guano, a manure or fertilizer made from the dried bodies of fish; fish manure.
fish hatchery, a hatchery for fish raised to stock lakes, rivers, streams, ponds, and reservoirs.
fish hawk, a large bird that feeds on fish; osprey.
fish|hook (fish′hu̇k′), *n.* **1** a hook used for catching fish. Most fishhooks are barbed near the point so that the fish cannot easily slip off the hook. **2** *Nautical.* a large metal hook forming part of a pendant at the lower end of a fish tackle, used in hoisting an anchor to the gunwale of a vessel.
fishhook cactus, a cactus of the southwestern United States and Mexico, with hooked spines and white and rose flowers.
fish|i|fy (fish′ə fī), *v.t.,* **-fied**, **-fy|ing**. **1** to change to fish: *O flesh, flesh, how art thou fishified* (Shakespeare). **2** to supply with fish: *In about a week the Round Pond will be full, as well as fishified, and Kensington Gardens will have its focal point again* (London Times).
fish|ing (fish′ing), *n.* **1** the catching of fish for a living or for pleasure. **2** a place or facilities for catching fish; fishing ground; fishery.
fishing banks, a fishing ground of comparatively shallow water in the sea.
fishing cat, a semiaquatic spotted cat resembling the civet that lives in marshes, where it catches fish with its paws. It ranges from Ceylon (Sri Lanka) through India to China and is considered extremely fierce.
fishing eagle, = osprey.
fishing expedition, *U.S. Informal.* any official investigation conducted without clearly defined objectives or guidelines.
fishing float, a raft or scow with a small house on it, designed to be floated and anchored wherever desired, for use in fishing with a seine.
fishing ground, a place where fish are plentiful.

***fishing rod**

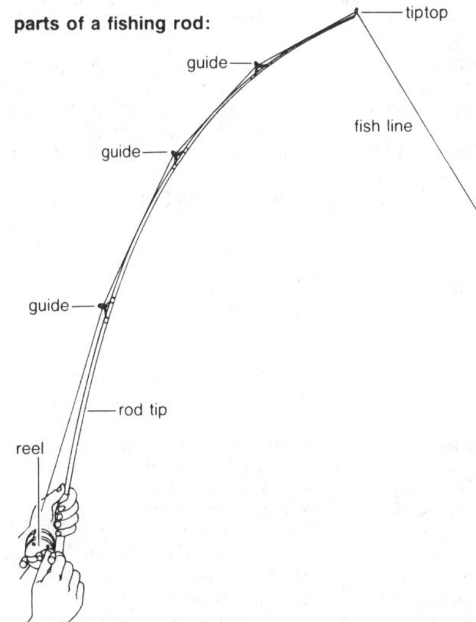

***fishing rod**, a long, light, slender pole with a line and hook attached to it, and often having a reel, used in catching fish.
fishing tackle, rods, lines, hooks, and other

Pronunciation Key: hat, āge, cãre, fär; let, ēqual, tėrm; it, īce; hot, ōpen, ôrder; oil, out; cup, pu̇t, rüle; child; long; thin; ᴛʜen; zh, measure; ə represents a in about, e in taken, i in pencil, o in lemon, u in circus.

equipment used in catching fish.
fish joint, a joint formed by bolting a fishplate across a butt-joint.
***fish ladder**, an arrangement of successive ascending pools enabling fish to pass over a fall or dam on their way to spawning grounds upstream; fishway.

***fish ladder**

fish line, a cord used with a fishhook for catching fish.
fish louse, any one of various small crustaceans that are parasitic on the surface of fish.
fish manure, = fish guano.
fish maw, the air bladder of a fish.
fish meal, a mealy substance obtained by pulverizing the dried bodies of fish not usable as food for humans, and also the heads and entrails of food fish. Fish meal is used as fertilizer or as an ingredient of feed for poultry and stock.
fish|mon|ger (fish′mung′gər, -mong′-), *n.* a dealer in fish.
fish|net (fish′net′), *n.* **1** a net for catching fish. **2** a meshed fabric that resembles netting, used especially for women's beachwear and stockings.
fish oil, oil obtained from fish and other marine animals.
fish|plate (fish′plāt′), *n.* a plate used to fasten two rails or beams together end to end.
fish poison, any one of a large number of plants having the property of killing or stupefying fish in water.
fish pole, = fishing rod.
fish pomace, the refuse of fish, such as menhaden, after the oil has been pressed out, used as a fertilizer; fish scrap.
fish|pond (fish′pond′), *n.* a pond containing fish, especially one in which fish are stocked to be sold commercially.
fish|pot (fish′pot′), *n.* a pot or trap for catching fish, crabs, lobsters, or crayfish.
fish protein concentrate, a tasteless, odorless, durable fish flour made by pulverizing dried whole hake and similar species, used as food or as a dietary supplement. *Abbr:* FPC (no periods).
fish scrap, = fish pomace.
fish|skin disease (fish′skin′), = ichthyosis.
fish slice, **1** an implement for turning fish in the pan. **2** *Especially British.* a knife for carving fish at the table.
fish spear, a spear or lance, often having more than one tine, for spearing fish.
fish stick, a boneless piece of cod, haddock, perch, or other food fish, cooked or uncooked, dipped in batter and breaded, usually sold in frozen form.
fish story, *Informal.* an exaggerated, unbelievable story.
fish tackle, the heavy tackle for raising and lowering an anchor to and from the gunwale.
fish|tail (fish′tāl′), *adj., v., n.* **—*adj.*** like a fish's tail in shape or action.
—*v.i.* *Informal.* to swing the tail of an airplane from side to side to reduce its speed.
—*n.* *Informal.* a fishtailing movement or maneuver.
fishtail bit, a wedge-shaped steel bit used to drill oil wells through soft underground formations.
fish trap, a trap for catching fish, having a funnel-shaped entrance through which fish pass, with a barrier of stakes or other obstacles to prevent their escape.
fish warden, *U.S.* an officer who has jurisdiction over fishing in any particular locality.
fish|way (fish′wā′), *n.* = fish ladder.
fish|weir (fish′wir′), *n.* = fishgarth.
fish|wheel (fish′hwēl′), *n. U.S.* = salmon wheel: *A good number of chum salmon end their inward migration up the Tanana river in fishweels* (Fairbanks, Alaska Daily News-Miner).
fish|wife (fish′wīf′), *n., pl.* **-wives. 1** a woman who uses very coarse and abusive language; termagant. **2** *British.* a woman who sells fish.
fish|wom|an (fish′wu̇m′ən), *n., pl.* **-wom|en.** a woman who sells fish.
fish|wood (fish′wu̇d′), *n.* = strawberry bush.
fish|works (fish′wėrks′), *n.pl.* **1** the appliances and devices used in fish culture for the artificial propagation of fish. **2** a place where the products of fisheries are used for a specific purpose, such as the manufacture of oil or guano.
fish|worm (fish′wėrm′), *n.* a worm, especially an earthworm, used as bait in angling.

fish|y (fish′ē), *adj.,* **fish|i|er, fish|i|est. 1** like a fish in smell, taste, or shape: *The apartment had a fishy smell after we had codfish for dinner.* **2** of fish. **3** full of fish: *the fishy flood* (Alexander Pope). **4** *Informal.* not probable; doubtful; unlikely; suspicious: *a fishy story. His excuse sounds fishy; I don't believe it.* **5** without expression or luster; dull: *fishy eyes.* **—fish′i|ly,** *adv.* **—fish′i|ness,** *n.*
fish|y|back (fish′ē bak′), *n., adj. Slang.* **—*n.*** the transportation of loaded truck trailers and railroad freight cars by ship.
—*adj.* by means of or having to do with the moving of truck trailers or containers, by ship: *fishyback shipping.*
fis|sile (fis′əl), *adj.* **1** easily split or divided. SYN: cleavable. **2** capable of nuclear fission; fissionable. [< Latin *fissilis* < *findere* to split, cleave]
fis|si|lin|gual (fis′i ling′gwəl), *adj. Zoology.* **1** having the tongue cleft. **2** of or having to do with a group of saurian reptiles having forked tongues.
fis|sil|i|ty (fi sil′ə tē), *n.* the quality of being fissile.
fis|sion (fish′ən), *n., v.* **—*n.* 1** the splitting of atoms which releases tremendous amounts of energy and is used to start the chain reaction of an atomic explosion; nuclear fission. It occurs when the nucleus of an atom is bombarded by neutrons, absorbs a neutron, and then divides into two nearly equal parts. *Atomic power plants and nuclear submarines are powered by the energy of fission* (Ralph E. Lapp). **2** a method of reproduction in which the body of the parent divides to form two or more independent individuals. Many simple plants and animals reproduce by fission. **3** a splitting apart; division into parts: *The appearance in Kenya of tendencies to political fission along tribal lines was of greater concern than similar developments in . . . other countries* (Arthur C. Turner).
—*v.t., v.i.* to split or divide: *Although it will not fission, U-238 can absorb a neutron to become U-239, an unstable element which decays in several days to a new element, plutonium* (Science News). *The McCarthy "new politics movement . . . fissioned the state party, the Democratic-Farmer Labor Party* (Austin C. Wehrwein).
[< Latin *fissiō, -ōnis* < *findere* cleave]
fis|sion|a|bil|i|ty (fish′ə nə bil′ə tē), *n.* the quality or state of being fissionable.
fis|sion|a|ble (fish′ə nə bəl), *adj., n.* **—*adj.*** capable of nuclear fission; fissile: *The element plutonium . . . is highly fissionable* (Willard F. Libby).
—*n.* a fissionable atom or element: *Private exploitation of the atom was limited by a ban on patents except for nonmilitary uses of fissionables* (Scientific American).
fission bomb, an atomic bomb that derives its force solely from the splitting of atoms. The original atomic bombs were fission bombs; the newer hydrogen bombs are fusion bombs.
fis|sion-track dating (fish′ən trak′), a method of determining age of rocks and other geological formations by counting the characteristic tracks left by spontaneous fission of uranium 238 during the lifetime of each sample. The number of tracks is proportional to the age of the sample. *Fission-track dating is direct and visual and has proved to be applicable to many materials and over an enormous range of ages. The critical factor is the uranium content of the material to be dated. A concentration of one part per million—which is common in rocks—provides enough tracks to date an object older than some 100,000 years easily* (Scientific American).
fis|sip|a|rism (fi sip′ə riz əm), *n. Biology.* reproduction by fission.
fis|sip|a|rous (fi sip′ər əs), *adj.* **1** *Biology.* reproducing by fission. **2** splitting or tending to split apart; divisive: *French democracy . . . faced the problem of erecting a government on the shifting sands of its fissiparous center parties* (Newsweek). [< Latin *fissus,* past participle of *findere* cleave + *parere* to give birth + English *-ous*] **—fis·sip′a|rous|ness,** *n.*
fis|si|ped (fis′i ped), *adj., n.* **—*adj.*** having the toes cleft; cloven-footed.
—*n.* an animal having its toes cleft or divided.
fis|si|ros|tral (fis′ə ros′trəl), *adj.* **1** having a broad beak or bill with a deep cleft, as the swifts or swallows. **2** (of a bill) broad and deeply cleft. [< Latin *fissus* (see etym. under **fission**) + English *rostral*]
fis|sive (fis′iv), *adj.* having to do with or of the nature of fission.
fis|sur|al (fish′ər əl), *adj.* of or having to do with a fissure.
fis|sure (fish′ər), *n., v.,* **-sured, -sur|ing. —*n.*** **1** a long, narrow opening; split or crack: *Water dripped from a fissure in a rock.* **2** a splitting apart; division into parts. **3** a natural cleft or opening in an organ or part, as those separating the convolutions of the brain, or that on the lower surface of the liver.

—*v.t.* to split apart; divide into parts.
—*v.i.* to become split or cleft.
[< Old French *fissure,* learned borrowing from Latin *fissūra* < *findere* cleave]
fissure of Ro|lan|do (rō lan′dō), a deep groove separating the frontal and parietal lobes of each hemisphere of the brain; central fissure. [< Luigi *Rolando,* 1773-1831, an Italian anatomist]
fissure of Syl|vi|us (sil′vē əs), the largest and deepest groove of each hemisphere of the brain, separating the frontal and parietal lobes from the temporal lobe; lateral fissure. [< Franciscus *Sylvius,* 1614-1672, a German anatomist]
***fist¹** (fist), *n., v.* **—*n.* 1** a tightly closed hand: *He shook his fist at me.* **2** *Informal.* the hand. **3** *Informal.* handwriting. **4** *Informal.* grasp; grip; clutches. **5** the index symbol used in printing.
—*v.t.* 1 to strike with the fist; beat; punch: *We have been down together . . . fisting each other's throat* (Shakespeare). **2** *Especially Nautical.* to grasp or seize; handle.
[Old English *fȳst*] **—fist′like′,** *adj.*

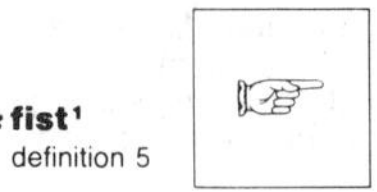
***fist¹**
definition 5

for departure at 11:00.
☞ Members must board the bus…

fist² (fīst), *n. U.S. Dialect.* feist.
-fisted, *combining form.* having ____ fists: *Two-fisted = having two fists.*
fist|fight (fist′fīt′), *n.* a fight in which the opponents use their fists: *Her husband has got into a fistfight defending her good name* (New Yorker).
fist|ful (fist′fu̇l), *n., pl.* **-fuls.** a handful: *a fistful of money.*
fis|ti|a|na (fis′tē ā′nə, -ä′nə, -an′ə), *n.pl.* matters relating to boxing; the realm of pugilism.
fist|ic (fis′tik), *adj. Informal.* having to do with fighting with the fists; done with the fists: *A boxing match is a fistic encounter.* SYN: pugilistic.
fist|i|cuff (fis′tə kuf′), *n., v.* **—*n.*** a blow with the fists: *It now and then happened that the literary gladiators came to actual fisticuffs* (John Symonds).
—*v.t.* to strike (someone) with the fists.
—*v.i.* to fight or strike blows with the fists.
fisticuffs, a fight with the fists; boxing bout: *The big boys say that the little boys must not engage in fisticuffs but must stick to name-calling* (Atlantic).
[< *fist¹* + *cuff²*]
fist|i|cuff|er (fis′tə kuf′ər), *n.* a person who fights with his fists, especially a boxer.
fist|note (fist′nōt′), *n.* a note in printed matter to which attention is drawn by the symbol of a fist with an extended index finger.
fis|tu|la (fis′chu̇ lə), *n., pl.* **-las, -lae** (-lē). **1** a reed or pipe; tube. **2** a deep passage connecting a sore on the skin with some internal cavity or organ. It is caused by a wound, abscess, or disease. **3** *Veterinary Medicine.* a pus-generating inflammation especially affecting the withers of a horse. **4** *Obsolete.* a primitive flute. [< Latin *fistula* pipe, ulcer. See etym. of doublet **fester**, n.]
fis|tu|lar (fis′chu̇ lər), *adj.* = fistulous.
fis|tu|li|form (fis′chu̇ lə fôrm), *adj.* fistulous in form; tubular.
fis|tu|lize (fis′chu̇ līz), *v.t., v.i.,* **-lized, -liz|ing. 1** to form a fistula. **2** to form or implant by surgical means, especially in the treatment of glaucoma, a structure resembling a fistula and intended to facilitate drainage.
fis|tu|lous (fis′chu̇ ləs), *adj.* **1** tubelike; tubular. **2** made up of tubes or tubelike parts. **3** *Medicine.* having to do with or of the nature of a fistula.
fist|y (fis′tē), *adj.,* **fist|i|er, fist|i|est.** = fistic.
fit¹ (fit), *adj.,* **fit|ter, fit|test,** *v.,* **fit|ted** or **fit, fit|ting,** *n., adv.* **—*adj.* 1** having the necessary qualities; well adapted for a purpose; suitable: *a man fit to be president. Grass is a fit food for cows; it is not fit for men.* **2** right; proper: *It is fit that we give thanks.* SYN: seemly, becoming. **3** healthy and strong: *He is now recovered from his illness and fit again.* **4** qualified or competent: *Choose the fittest candidate.* **5** ready; prepared: *land fit for a crop, fit for active service.* **6** *Informal.* liable or likely: *to walk until one is fit to drop.*
—*v.t.* 1 to make right, proper, or suitable; suit: *to fit the action to the word.* **2** to be fit for; suit: *a punishment that fits the crime.* **3** to have the right size or shape for: *The dress fitted her.* **4** to make or try to make fit; adjust: *to fit a key in a lock. The salesman was fitting new seat covers on our car. He fit the words to the music.* **5** to make ready; prepare; qualify: *to fit men for active duty in the army.* **6** to supply with what is needed; equip: *to fit a store with counters.* SYN: furnish, provide.

—*v.i.* **1** to have the right size or shape: *Does this glove fit?* **2** *Archaic.* to be fit, seemly, proper, or suitable: *It fits to aske ye, what your native shore, and whence your race?* (Alexander Pope). **3** to be harmonious or appropriate; belong; agree: *At camp I didn't fit anywhere. She fits in well with her age group. He fit perfectly into the new teaching system.*
—*n.* **1** the way something fits: *the fit of a coat, a tight fit.* **2** a thing that fits: *The coat was not a very good fit; it was too tight.* **3** the process of fitting or making fit.
—*adv.* **see** (or **think**) **fit**, to prefer and decide; choose: *If God sees fit . . . that I should marry, in his due time he will provide me with a worthy husband* (Mary Sherwood).
fit out (or **up**), to provide with what is needed: *to fit out a room.*
fit to be tied, *U.S. Informal.* very angry or annoyed: *I was fit to be tied when three-quarters of an hour had elapsed without any sign of Barney* (S. J. Perelman).
fit to kill, *U.S. Informal.* very showily or strikingly: *And here you people come, all dressed up fit to kill, and with God knows how much baggage* (Dudley Fitts).
[Middle English *fyt;* origin uncertain] —**fit′ness**, *n.*
—*Syn. adj.* **1 Fit, suitable, appropriate** mean having the right qualities for something. **Fit** emphasizes having all the necessary qualities: *That shack is not fit to live in.* **Suitable** suggests having the particular qualities right or proper for a definite occasion, position, condition, or situation: *The lawyer found a suitable office.* **Appropriate** suggests special readiness or fitness for a purpose or activity: *The verdict of the jury was announced with appropriate solemnity. A tailored suit is appropriate for a secretary.*
▶Besides *fitted* (the standard past tense form), *fit* also occurs: *The coat fit me badly.* In the eastern United States, for which evidence is available, *fit* is particularly common in the Middle Atlantic States and in the South, both in cultivated and in non-standard speech.

fit[2] (fit), *n.* **1** a sudden, sharp attack of disease: *a fit of colic.* **2** a sudden attack characterized by loss of consciousness or by convulsions: *a fainting fit, a fit of epilepsy.* **3** *Figurative.* any sudden, sharp attack: *In a fit of anger, he hit his friend.* **4** *Figurative.* a short period of doing some one thing; spell: *a fit of coughing, a fit of laughing.*
by (or **in**) **fits and starts**, starting, stopping, beginning again, and so on; irregularly: *He does his homework by fits and starts instead of steadily. Jane was . . . more hopeful by fits and starts than continuously so* (Ellen Wood). *She talked about herself and her family, in fits and starts, as if unaware of . . . time* (Mavis Gallant).
throw (or **have**) **a fit**, *Informal.* to get very angry or excited: *You can give them a steak and apple pie, but if they don't get that rice, they'll throw a fit* (New York Times).
[Old English *fitt* conflict]

fit[3] (fit), *n. Archaic.* a part or section of a poem, song, or story; canto. [Old English *fitt.* Perhaps related to **fit[2]**.]

fitch[1] (fich), *n.* **1** the polecat of Europe. **2** its fur, nearly black with a purplish gloss. [perhaps < Middle Dutch *fisse,* or *vitsche*]

fitch[2] (fich), *n.* = vetch.

fitch|é or **fitch|ée** (fich′ā, -ē), *adj.* designating a cross whose lower end is sharpened or cut to a point, as if intended to be fixed in the ground. See picture under **cross.** [< French *fiché, fichée,* masculine and feminine past participles of *ficher* to fix]

fitch|er (fich′ər), *Mining.* —*v.t.* to cause (a drill) to stick, by drilling without a rotary motion.
—*v.i.* (of a drill) to stick fast.
[apparently < French *ficher* to stick]

fitch|et (fich′it), *n.* **1** a fitch; the polecat of Europe. **2** its fur.
[< Old French *fissau, fissel* polecat fur (< Germanic; compare Middle Dutch *fisse* fitch) + English *-et.* Compare etym. under **fitch[1]**.]

fitch|ew (fich′ü), *n.* = fitchet.

fit|ful (fit′fəl), *adj.* going on and then stopping for a while; irregular: *fitful conversation. She had a fitful sleep during the storm. After life's fitful fever he sleeps well* (Shakespeare). SYN: spasmodic. [< *fit*[2] + *-ful*] —**fit′ful|ly**, *adv.* —**fit′ful|ness**, *n.*

fit|ly (fit′lē), *adv.* **1** in a suitable manner: *A word fitly spoken is like apples of gold in pictures of silver* (Proverbs 25:11). **2** at a proper time.

fit|ment (fit′mənt), *n.* a fitting; fixture: *The chief fitments are in Australian walnut, of a pleasantly rich dark brown* (London Times).

fitness center, a gymnasium.

fit|root (fit′rüt′, -růt′), *n.* = Indian pipe.

fit|ter (fit′ər), *n.* **1** a person whose work is fitting clothes on people. **2** a person who supplies and fixes anything necessary for some purpose: *a pipe fitter. The gas fitter installed our new gas stove.* **3** a man who adjusts parts of machinery. **4** a person or thing that fits.

fit|ting (fit′ing), *adj., n.* —*adj.* right, proper, or suitable: *In some countries it is not fitting for a girl to be seen in public without a chaperon.*
—*n.* **1** the action of trying on unfinished clothes to see if they fit: *She will go for her final fitting on Monday.* **2** anything with which something is fitted by way of furnishing or equipping.
fittings, things used in fitting up permanently; furnishings; fixtures: *gas fittings. Desks, chairs, and files are office fittings.*
—**fit′ting|ly**, *adv.* —**fit′ting|ness**, *n.*
—*Syn. adj.* **Fitting, becoming, seemly** mean right and proper. **Fitting** means suiting the purpose, nature of a thing, the character or mood of a person, and the atmosphere or spirit of an occasion, etc.: *Christmas is a fitting time to bring joy to underprivileged children.* **Becoming** implies fitting in looks, conduct, or speech, suiting a person's appearance, position, or personal standards: *Gentleness is becoming in a nurse.* **Seemly** implies fitting or becoming, as judged by rules for conduct or behavior, as well as by good taste: *Swearing and coarse language is hardly seemly in polite company.*

fit-up (fit′up′), *n. British.* **1** a stage or other theatrical accessory fitted up for the occasion. **2** a member of a traveling theatrical company using fit-ups.

five (fīv), *n., adj.* —*n.* **1** one more than four; 5: *Three and two make five.* **2** a set of five things. **3** a playing card, throw of the dice, domino, billiard ball, or other part of a game with five spots or a "5" on it. **4** a team of five basketball players.
—*adj.* being one more than four.
[Old English *fīf*]

five-and-dime (fīv′ən dīm′), *n. U.S. Informal.* a dime store.

five-and-ten (fīv′ən ten′), *n. U.S. Informal.* a dime store.

Five Civilized Nations or **Tribes**, the Cherokee, Chickasaw, Choctaw, Creek, and Seminole tribes of eastern Oklahoma.

five-fin|ger (fīv′fing′gər), *n.* **1** any one of various plants, such as the cinquefoil, bird's-foot trefoil, oxlip, and Virginia creeper. The five-finger fern has broad, slightly cut pinnules folded so the edges point upwards. **2** a starfish having five rays.

five-fin|gered jack (fīv′fing′gərd), **1** = starfish. **2** = cinquefoil.

five-fin|gers (fīv′fing′gərz), *n.* five-finger.

five|fold (fīv′fōld′), *adj., adv.* —*adj.* **1** five times as much or as many: *Last year yielded a fivefold increase in profits.* **2** having five parts.
—*adv.* five times as much or as many: *The firm's profits increased fivefold over a three-month period.*

five hundred, a card game resembling euchre, using a joker and widow, in which 500 points make game.

five-leaf (fīv′lēf′), *n.* = cinquefoil.

five|ling (fīv′ling), *n.* a twin crystal consisting of five individuals.

Five Nations, a former confederacy of Iroquois Indian tribes, consisting of the Mohawk, Oneida, Onondaga, Cayuga, and Seneca tribes.

five o'clock shadow or **5 o'clock shadow**, a short growth of beard; stubble, especially toward the end of the day: *[He] sported a heavy 5 o'clock shadow for his role as Captain Ahab in Herman Melville's "Moby Dick"* (Newsweek).

five|pence (fīv′pəns, fip′əns), *n.* **1** a sum of money of the value of five British pennies. **2** a British coin having this value.

five|pen|ny (fīv′pə nē, fip′ə-), *adj.* of the amount or value of fivepence: *a fivepenny tax. A fivepenny nail is 1¾ inches long, and it is so called because originally the nails cost fivepence per hundred.*

five per|cent|er (pər sen′tər), *U.S.* a person who obtains government contracts for others in return for a 5 per cent fee (used to discredit a person).

five-pins (fīv′pinz′), *n.* (in Canada) a game played with five wooden pins at which a ball is bowled to knock them down.

fiv|er (fī′vər), *n. Informal.* **1** *British.* a five-pound note. **2** *U.S.* a five-dollar bill.

fives (fīvz), *n.* an English game like handball. [< *five* + *-s*[1] (perhaps because there are five fingers on a hand)]

five|score (fīv′skôr′, -skōr′), *adj.* being five times twenty; a hundred.

fives|court (fīvz′kôrt′, -kōrt′), *n.* a court where the game of fives is played.

five-shoot|er (fīv′shü′tər), *n.* a revolver having five cartridge chambers.

five|some (fīv′səm), *n.* **1** a group of five; a set of five things. **2** a game or round in which five players take part.

five-spice (fīv′spīs′), *n.* a powdery mixture of five common spices, sold commercially.

five-spot (fīv′spot′), *n.* **1** *U.S. Informal.* a five-dollar bill; fiver. **2** a playing card, domino, or part of a game having five spots or a "5" on it.

five-star (fīv′stär′), *adj.* **1** of a rank indicated by five stars on the insignia of one's uniform: *a five-star general or admiral.* **2** of the highest class; first-rate: *a five-star play or motion picture.*

five|stones (fīv′stōnz′), *n.pl.* the game of jackstones played with five stones.

five-year plan (fīv′yir′), any one of a series of government plans listing the economic goals of a country to be reached in five years.

Five-Year Plan (fīv′yir′), **1** any one of the government plans for the economic development of the Soviet Union, the first of which was adopted in 1928. In 1958, a Seven-Year Plan replaced the Five-Year Plan. **2** any one of various similar plans in other countries, such as in India.

fix (fiks), *v.,* **fixed** or **fixt, fix|ing,** *n.* —*v.t.* **1** to make firm; fasten tightly: *Her image was fixed in his mind. The man fixed the post in the ground. He fixed the spelling lesson in his mind.* **2** to settle; set: *He fixed the price at one dollar. Did you fix a day for the picnic?* **3** to direct or hold steadily (eyes, attention, a camera, telescope, or a light); look at with a steady gaze. **4** to attract and hold (the eye, attention, a camera, telescope, or a light). **5** to make rigid. **6** to put or place definitely: *She fixed the blame on the person who did the damage.* **7** to treat to prevent fading or otherwise changing: *A dye or photograph is fixed with chemicals.* **8** to set right; put in order; arrange: *to fix one's hair.* **9** to mend; repair: *He fixed the broken watch.* **10** *U.S.* to prepare (a meal or food): *to fix dinner.* **11** to give someone money, etc., to decide something favorable to you instead of deciding for your opponents: *to fix a jury, to fix a game.* **12** *Informal.* to get revenge upon; get even with; punish. **13** *Chemistry.* to make stable by decreasing or destroying volatility, fluidity, etc. To fix nitrogen is to change it from a gas into a compound that can be used, such as a fertilizer or explosive. **14** to prepare or preserve (an organism or tissue) for microscopic study. **15** to castrate or spay (an animal).
—*v.i.* **1** to become firm; be fastened tightly. **2** to be directed or held steadily. **3** to become stiff or rigid: *eyes fixed in death.* **4** *U.S. Dialect.* to make ready; intend: *He is fixing to go fishing.*
—*n. Informal.* **1** a position hard to get out of; an awkward state of affairs: *The boy who cried "Wolf" got himself into a bad fix. If we get left on this wreck we are in a fix* (Mark Twain). **2** the position of a ship, aircraft, satellite, radio transmitter, or stellar body, as determined by obtaining radio or other signals from two or more known points. **3** the determining of such a position. **4** a fixed condition; repair: *"They have elevators in public housing, and they're constantly getting out of fix," she said* (New Yorker). **5** *U.S. Slang.* a bribe. **6a** *Slang.* a dose of a narcotic drug: *These prowlers are narcotic addicts. Office thievery is the source of their next fix* (Time). **b** *Informal, Figurative: My addiction to the Sunday crossword puzzles was out of control. I desperately needed a "fix"* (Phyllis R. Johnson). **7** a determined position or opinion: *to get a fix on the villain's identity.*
fix on (or **upon**), to decide on; choose; select: *Have you fixed on the date for your wedding?*
fix up, *Informal.* **a** to mend; repair: *Fix up the hole in your stocking. They moved to the country and fixed up an old farmhouse.* **b** to put in order; arrange: *to fix up the house.* **c** to make oneself neat and well-dressed: *Wait until I get fixed up—you won't recognize me.*
[< Old French *fixer* < *fixe* fixed < Latin *fīgere* to fix, attach]
—*Syn. v.t.* **1, 2 Fix, establish, settle** mean to set something or someone firmly in position. **Fix** (most often used of things) emphasizes setting some thing so firmly, solidly, or definitely in a position, place, or condition that it is hard to change or move: *We fixed the stove in place.* **Establish** (most often used of groups, foundations, businesses, etc.) means to set up or fix firmly or permanently: *They established a partnership.* **Settle** (used of people or affairs) means to put in a steady, ordered, or permanent position, place, or condition: *He settled his daughter in Chicago. They settled their father's estate.*

fix|a|ble (fik′sə bəl), *adj.* that can be fixed.

fix|ate (fik′sāt), *v.,* **-at|ed, -at|ing.** —*v.t.* **1** to make fixed so as to establish a habit. **2** to concentrate (one's attention) on something.
—*v.i.* **1** to become fixed or fixated. **2** to have or develop an abnormal attachment or prejudice.
[back formation < *fixation*]

fix|a|tion (fik sā′shən), *n.* **1** the act of fixing or

Pronunciation Key: hat, āge, cãre, fär; let, ēqual, tėrm; it, īce; hot, ōpen, ôrder; oil, out; cup, pu̇t, rüle; child; long; thin; ᴛʜen; zh, measure; ə represents **a** in about, **e** in taken, **i** in pencil, **o** in lemon, **u** in circus.

condition of being fixed. **2** a treatment to prevent something from fading or otherwise changing: *the fixation of a photographic film.* **3a** the process of making stable, especially by decreasing or destroying volatility or fluidity. **b** the process of combining nitrogen with hydrogen under high pressure to form ammonia, used in making fertilizers and explosives. **4a** a strong emotional attachment which results in a halt at an early stage in the development of sexual desire. **b** *Psychology.* an abnormal attachment or prejudice. [< Medieval Latin *fixatio, -onis* < *fixare* to fix, attach < Latin *fīgere*]

fix|a|tive (fik′sə tiv), *n., adj.* **—n. 1** a substance used to prevent something from fading or otherwise changing. **2** a liquid sprayed on pastels, charcoal drawings, collages, glossy ink prints, and the like, to fix the loose particles or keep ink from smearing. **3** = hypo[1].
—adj. that prevents fading or change.

fixed (fikst), *adj.* **1** not movable; made firm: *The seats in some modern classrooms are not fixed.* SYN: stationary. **2** definitely assigned; settled; set: *fixed charges for taxicabs.* SYN: definite. **3** steady; not moving: *a fixed gaze.* **4** made stiff or rigid: *She stood fixed in horror.* **5** *Figurative.* prearranged privately or dishonestly: *a fixed horse race.* **6** *Chemistry.* **a** entered in a stable compound. **b** not volatile: *a fixed acid.* **7** provided, especially with money: *The widow was left comfortably fixed.* **—fix′ed|ly,** *adv.* **—fix′ed|ness,** *n.*

fixed asset, a piece of land, building, or other immovable fixture, of a business; capital asset.

fixed bayonet, a bayonet attached to the muzzle end of a rifle.

fixed capital, capital in the form of land, buildings, or machinery which can be used recurrently without change of form or possession.

fixed charge, any of certain charges or expenses, such as rent, upkeep, taxes, and depreciation, that occur regularly or continuously in the operation of a business.

fixed idea, a very persistent thought or idea, especially an obsession or delusion from which a person cannot escape. It is characteristic of certain forms of insanity.

fixed-in|come (fikst′in′kum), *adj.* earning at a fixed or nearly constant rate.

fixed liability, an obligation which does not mature for at least a year.

fixed oil, a nonvolatile natural oil, such as lard oil or linseed oil, found in the cellular membranes of animals and in the seeds, capsules, or pulp surrounding the seeds in plants.

fixed-pitch propeller (fikst′pich′), a propeller in which the pitch, or blade angle, is not adjustable and not variable.

fixed-point (fikst′point′), *adj.* of or designating a computation in a digital computer in which numbers are represented by a sequence of digits with a fixed location of the decimal point or the binary point.

fixed price, 1 a uniform price set for all buyers of a product. **2** a price set by a manufacturer under a fair trade agreement. **3** a price set under price control or through price fixing. **—fixed′-price′,** *adj.*

fixed star, a star whose position in relation to other stars appears not to change. Fixed stars are so far from earth that many thousands of years must pass before man can see that they have moved.

fixed trust, an investment trust in which members are allowed to make investments only in a small number of specified securities; unit trust.

fixed-wing aircraft (fikst′wing′), an aircraft with wings attached to the fuselage, as distinguished from an aircraft with rotating wings, such as a helicopter or one with adjustable or movable wings.

fix|er (fik′sər), *n.* **1** a person who fixes something. **2** a thing which fixes or makes permanent; fixative. **3** *Informal.* a person who dishonestly arranges beforehand the result of a game, event, or other circumstance of chance. **4** = hypo[1].

fix|ing (fik′sing), *n.* **1** the action of a person or thing that fixes. **2** the process by which anything is fixed.
fixings, *Informal.* trimmings or furnishings: *We had turkey and all the fixings for Thanksgiving dinner.*

fixing bath, = hypo[1].

fix-it (fiks′it′), *adj. U.S. Informal.* of or for fixing things; doing or involving small repairs: *a fix-it man, a fix-it job. The fourth will open a fix-it shop in a small town* (Birmingham News).

fix|i|ty (fik′sə tē), *n., pl.* **-ties. 1** fixed condition or quality; permanence; steadiness; firmness: *The fixity of her gaze disturbed him. The translation of the Bible ... gave fixity to the tongue of the new religion* (William Taylor). SYN: stability. **2** something fixed.

fixt (fikst), *v.* fixed; a past tense and a past participle of **fix.**

fix|ture (fiks′chər), *n.* **1** a thing put in place to stay: *bathroom fixtures. A chandelier is a lighting fixture.* **2** a person or thing that stays in one place, job, or other situation: *He is a fixture in the office.* **3** *Law.* anything, such as a furnace, sink, or water pipe, that is part of the more or less permanent equipment of a house or property. **4** an event, such as a music festival, international games, tournament, special dramatic performance, or the like, held at regular intervals, as annually: *a mile-and-a-half grass fixture scheduled for Ascot Heath on July 16* (New York Times). **5** a clamping device for holding a piece of work while it is being machined. **6** the act or process of fixing. **7** the condition of being fixed. [variant of earlier *fixure;* influenced by English *mixture*]

fix|ure (fik′shər), *n. Archaic.* fixed position or condition. [< Latin *fīxūra* act of or place of fixing < *fīgere* to fix, attach]

fiz (fiz), *v.,* **fizzed, fiz|zing,** *n.* = fizz.

fiz|gig (fiz′gig), *n.* **1** a light, frivolous woman: *My husband ... prefers to me ... this fizgig called Fifine* (Robert Browning). **2** a small, sputtering firework; squib. **3** a spinning toy that whirs noisily. **4** = fish spear. [probably < *fizz* + *gig*[1] frivolous person]

fizz (fiz), *v.,* **fizzed, fizz|ing,** *n.* **—v.i. 1** to make a hissing sound. **2** *Figurative.* to bubble; effervesce: *Grigson's "Poets and Poems" ... fizzed with critical insights* (John Raymond).
—n. 1 a hissing sound; bubbling: *the fizz of soda water.* **2** a bubbling drink, such as champagne or soda water. **3** *Figurative.* ebullience; liveliness; effervescence: *Some of the fizz has gone from Shaw's conversational fireworks of 1909, but there are still brilliantly amusing passages* (Punch). [imitative] **—fizz′er,** *n.*

fiz|zle (fiz′əl), *v.,* **-zled, -zling,** *n.* **—v.i. 1** to make a hissing sound that dies out weakly: *The firecracker fizzled instead of exploding with a bang.* **2** *Figurative.* to droop; flag; lose vitality: *His poems start with an engaging bounce or a grave statement; then they fizzle* (New York Times). **3** *Informal, Figurative.* to make a fiasco of something, especially after a good start.
—n. 1 the action of fizzling or hissing: *The chicken and ham had a cheerful fizzle in the pan* (Harriet Beecher Stowe). **2** *Informal, Figurative.* a failure: *The whole project was a fizzle.* SYN: fiasco.
fizzle out, *Informal.* to come to a poor end; fail: *The picnic fizzled out when it began to look like rain. The left-wing rebellion ... which had threatened a full-scale crisis, fizzled out today as the rebel group recanted unconditionally* (London Times).
[perhaps < *fizz* + *-le* (frequentative)]

fizz|y (fiz′ē), *adj.,* **fizz|i|er, fizz|i|est.** that fizzes; fizzing.

fjeld (fyeld), *n.* a high, rocky, almost barren plateau on the Scandinavian peninsula. [< Dano-Norwegian *fjeld.* See related etym. at **fell**[5].]

fjord (fyôrd, fyōrd), *n.* = fiord.

fl., 1 florin. **2** flourished. **3** fluid.

Fl (no period), fluorine (chemical element).

Fl., 1 Flanders. **2** Flemish.

FL (no periods), Florida (with postal Zip Code).

Fla., Florida.

flab (flab), *n. U.S. Informal.* **1** anything flabby, especially flesh; excessive weight: *His muscles, long gone to flab, knotted again with every pull* (Esquire). **2** *Figurative.* an excess of anything: *to cut the flab out of a story, executive flab in the company administration. The law covering lobbying activity is more flab than muscle* (Harper's). [back formation < *flabby*]

flab|ber|gast (flab′ər gast), *v.t. Informal.* to make speechless with surprise; astonish greatly; amaze: *The aldermen ... were ... flabbergasted; they were speechless from bewilderment* (Benjamin Disraeli). SYN: dumfound. [origin uncertain]

flab|by (flab′ē), *adj.,* **-bi|er, -bi|est. 1** lacking firmness; soft; flaccid: *flabby cheeks.* SYN: See syn. under **limp**[2]. **2** *Figurative.* lacking force; feeble: *a flabby nature, a flabby will, flabby arguments.* SYN: See syn. under **limp**[2]. [perhaps variant of earlier *flappy* < *flap*] **—flab′bi|ly,** *adv.* **—flab′bi|ness,** *n.*

fla|bel|late (flə bel′it, -āt), *adj. Botany, Zoology.* fan-shaped; flabelliform. [< Latin *flābellum* a fan + English *-ate*[1]]

flab|el|la|tion (flab′ə lā′shən), *n.* the act of cooling by the use of a fan.

fla|bel|li|fo|li|ate (flə bel′ə fō′lē it), *adj.* having a fanlike arrangement of leaves.

fla|bel|li|form (flə bel′ə fôrm), *adj.* = flabellate.

fla|bel|li|nerved (flə bel′ə nėrvd′), *adj.* having a fanlike arrangement of nerves.

fla|bel|lum (flə bel′əm), *n., pl.* **-bel|la** (-bel′ə). **1** a fan-shaped part. **2** a fan, especially one used for some ecclesiastical purpose, as the large fans borne before the Pope in certain ceremonies. [< Latin *flābellum* (diminutive) < *flābrum* breath, breeze < *flāre* to blow]

fla|brum (flā′brəm), *n., pl.* **-bra** (-brə). = flabellum (def. 2).

flac|cid (flak′sid), *adj.* **1** hanging or lying loose or in wrinkles; flabby: *flaccid muscles. Flaccid threads of ivy, in the still And sultry air depending motionless* (Wordsworth). **2** *Figurative.* limp or weak: *a flaccid will.* [< Latin *flaccidus* < *flaccus* flabby] **—flac′cid|ly,** *adv.* **—flac′cid|ness,** *n.*

flac|cid|i|ty (flak sid′ə tē), *n.* flaccid quality or condition.

flache|rie (flâsh rē′), *n. French.* a disease of silkworms.

flack[1] (flak), *n., v. Slang.* **—n.** a press agent.
—v.i. to act as a press agent: *Maney no longer flacks ..., and therefore is not found to compose compliments* (Maclean's). [variant of *flak* (supposedly because of his blustery nature)]

flack[2] (flak), *n.* = flak.

flack|er|y (flak′ər ē), *n. Slang.* press-agentry; publicity; promotion: *There were also slogans minted by a Manhattan advertising agency and mimeographed press releases that smacked of big-city flackery* (Time).

fla|con (flȧ kôɴ′; *Anglicized* fla kon′), *n.* a small bottle with a stopper, used for perfume, smelling salts, etc.: *A flacon of Russia's finest perfume, "The Spirit of the Red Army," was waiting in her hotel room* (Time). [< French *flacon* < Old French *flascon.* See related etym. at **flagon.**]

***flag**[1] (flag), *n., v.,* **flagged, flag|ging.** **—n. 1** a piece of cloth with a pattern or picture on it that stands for some country, city, party, club, or other group, or that gives some information or signal. Flags are hung on poles over buildings, ships, army camps, etc. They vary in design but are frequently oblong or square and attached by one edge to a staff or halyard. *the flag of the United States, the white flag of truce, the red flag showing danger. Weather flags are flown to show what kind of weather is coming.* SYN: ensign, standard, banner. **2** something that suggests or resembles a flag, such as the tail of a deer or of a setter dog. **3** a large cloth used to keep lights from interfering with a television camera. **4** *Music.* = hook (def. 18). **5** the name of a newspaper printed across the top of the front page.
—v.t. 1 to put a flag or flags over or on; decorate with flags. **2** to stop or signal (a person, train, bus, ship, airplane, etc.) by a flag: *to flag down a cab. The train was flagged at the bridge.* **3** to call attention to: *He is ... refreshingly ready to flag his mistakes as well as his achievements* (Listener). **4** *U.S. Military.* to put a tab of special color on a file folder or card to stop it from being altered or processed in any way: *Wilson was able to order [the colonel], chief of staff at Fort Benning, to "flag" [the lieutenant's] records, an Army procedure freezing any promotion or transfer for a soldier* (Harper's). **5** to communicate by a flag: *to flag a message.* **6** to decoy (game) by waving a flag or something like it to excite attention or curiosity.
break the flag, to unfurl the flag at the top of the staff: *After ceremonies commissioning the ship her new captain broke the flag.*
flag down, to signal to stop: *A policeman flagged down a motorist ... for making an illegal left turn* (Maclean's).
flags, a the long feathers on the lower parts of certain birds' legs. **b** the feathers on the second joint of a bird's wing: *Like ... the haggard, cloistered in her mew ... to renew her broken flags* (Francis Quarles).
keep the flag flying, to keep up an endeavor; carry on despite difficulties: *Yet Freud, after valiant efforts to keep the flag flying, had to admit before 1900, that neither he nor anybody else could yet correlate all mental disturbances with demonstrable physical processes in the brain or nervous system* (Atlantic).
wave the flag, to stir up patriotic or similar sentiments: *The industry gets together annually to wave the flag in a pocket-sized exhibition* (London Times).
[perhaps < *flag*[3]] **—flag′ger,** *n.* **—flag′less,** *adj.*

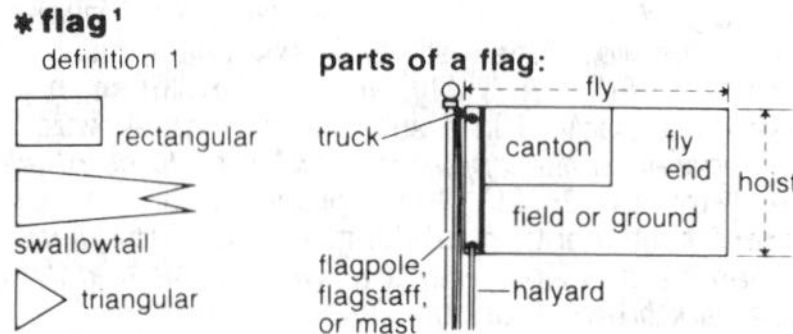

flag[2] (flag), *n.* **1** an iris with blue, purple, yellow, or white flowers and sword-shaped leaves. **2** = sweet flag. **3** = cattail. **4** the flower of any one of these plants. **5** the leaf of any one of these plants. [perhaps < Scandinavian (compare Danish *flaeg*)]

flag[3] (flag), *v.i.,* **flagged, flag|ging. 1** to get tired; grow weak; droop: *My horse was flagging, but I urged him on. After you do the same thing for a long time, your interest flags.* **SYN**: decline, languish, fail, slacken. **2** to hang down; flap about loose. [perhaps variant of Middle English *flacken* to flap, perhaps < Scandinavian (compare Old Icelandic *flakka* flutter, flicker)]

flag[4] (flag), *n., v.,* **flagged, flag|ging.** *—n.* = flagstone.
—v.t. to pave with flagstones.
[< Scandinavian (compare Old Icelandic *flaga* slab)]

flag|bear|er (flag′bãr′ər), *n.* the leader of a movement; standardbearer: *The coalition Prime Minister ... is regarded as an anti-Market flagbearer* (Manchester Guardian Weekly).

flag boat, a boat, recognizable by a flag or flags, moored so as to mark the course to be followed in a sailing or rowing race.

flag captain, the commanding officer of a flagship.

flag code, a set of rules for displaying and honoring a flag, especially a national flag.

flag day, *British.* a day on which money is raised for a cause by the sale of small paper flags which are worn as evidence that the wearer has contributed: *A small licensing fee is to be introduced for persons selling flags on flag days* (Punch).

Flag Day, June 14, the anniversary of the day in 1777 when the Second Continental Congress adopted the Stars and Stripes as the flag of the United States.

fla|gel|la (flə jel′ə), *n.* a plural of **flagellum**.

flag|el|lant (flaj′ə lənt, flə jel′ənt), *n., adj.* *—n.* **1** a person who whips or is whipped. **2** a religious fanatic who whips himself for religious discipline or for penance.
—adj. having the habit of whipping.
[< Latin *flagellāns, -antis,* present participle of *flagellāre* to flog; see etym. under **flagellate**]

flag|el|lant|ism (flaj′ə lən tiz′əm), *n.* the habit or practice of a flagellant.

fla|gel|lar (flə jel′ər), *adj.* having to do with a flagellum or flagella.

flag|el|late (flaj′ə lāt), *v.,* **-lat|ed, -lat|ing,** *adj., n.*
—v.t. to whip; flog. **SYN**: scourge, drub, thrash.
—adj. **1** flagelliform. **2** having flagella: *... complex forms of flagellate infusoria* (W. B. Carpenter). **3** *Botany.* having runners or runnerlike branches.
—n. any one of a class of protistans that have one or more flagella serving as organs of locomotion and for obtaining food. Euglenas belong to this class.
[< Latin *flagellāre* (with English *-ate*[1]) < *flagellum* (diminutive) < *flagrum* whip] **—flag′el|la′tor,** *n.*

flag|el|lat|ed (flaj′ə lā′tid), *adj.* = flagellate.

flag|el|la|tion (flaj′ə lā′shən), *n.* a whipping; flogging: (*Figurative.*) *Chiang made his decisions by introspection amounting almost to spiritual flagellation* (Time).

flag|el|la|to|ry (flaj′ə lə tôr′ē, -tōr′-), *adj.* of or having to do with flagellation.

fla|gel|li|form (flə jel′ə fôrm), *adj.* like a whip; long, thin, and flexible; flagellate. [< Latin *flagellum* (see etym. under **flagellum**) + English *-form*]

fla|gel|lu|la (flə jel′yə lə), *n., pl.* **-lae** (-lē). a spore or sporule with a flagelliform appendage. [< New Latin *flagellula* < Latin *flagellum* flagellum]

fla|gel|lum (flə jel′əm), *n., pl.* **-la** or **-lums. 1** a long, whiplike tail or part. Certain bacteria, sperm cells, and protozoans have flagella to enable them to move. **2** a runner of a plant. **3** a whip. [< Latin *flagellum* (diminutive) < *flagrum* whip]

flag|eo|let (flaj′ə let′), *n.* a small wind instrument somewhat like a flute, with a mouthpiece at one end, usually six finger holes, and sometimes keys. See picture under **flute**. [< French *flageolet* (diminutive) < Old French *flageol,* or *flajol* flute < Vulgar Latin *flābeolum* < Latin *flāre* to blow]

flag-fall (flag′fôl′), *n.* the falling or dropping of a flag to indicate the start of a race.

flag|ger (flag′ər), *n. Dialect.* an iris; flag.

flag|ging[1] (flag′ing), *adj.* drooping; tired; weak: *Flagging spirits mark the end of the long day.* [< *flag*[3] + *-ing*[2]] **—flag′ging|ly,** *adv.*

flag|ging[2] (flag′ing), *n.* **1** flagstones. **2** a pavement made of flagstones. [< *flag*[4] + *-ing*[1]]

flag|gy[1] (flag′ē), *adj.,* **-gi|er, -gi|est. 1** hanging down limply; drooping. **2** soft and flabby; having no firmness; flaccid. [< *flag*[3] + *-y*[1]]

flag|gy[2] (flag′ē), *adj.* of or like flagstone. [< *flag*[4] + *-y*[1]]

flag|gy[3] (flag′ē), *adj.* abounding in or resembling the plants called flags. [< *flag*[2] + *-y*[1]]

flag hoist, a group of signal flags attached to the same halyard and hoisted as a unit.

flag|i|tate (flaj′ə tāt), *v.t.,* **-tat|ed, -tat|ing.** to entreat earnestly; importune. [< Latin *flāgitāre* (with English *-ate*[1]) demand earnestly < *flag-,* root of *flagrāre* to burn]

fla|gi|tious (flə jish′əs), *adj.* scandalously wicked; shamefully vile: *Crimes shall whelm in ruin yon flagitious town* (Alexander Pope). **SYN**: infamous, heinous, nefarious. [< Latin *flāgitiōsus* < *flāgitium* shame] **—fla|gi′tious|ly,** *adv.* **—fla|gi′tious|ness,** *n.*

flag|leaf (flag′lēf′), *n.* = flag[2] (def. 1).

flag lieutenant, an officer on an admiral's staff who acts as the admiral's aide-de-camp.

flag|man (flag′mən), *n., pl.* **-men. 1** a person who signals with a flag or lantern at railroad crossings or to train crews. **2** a person who has charge of or carries a flag.

flag of convenience, the flag of a foreign country under which the owner of a merchant vessel registers and sails his ship, for a variety of reasons, such as less rigid regulation or differences in taxation.

flag officer, a naval officer entitled to display a flag on his ship indicating his rank or command. Fleet admiral, admiral, vice-admiral, rear admiral, and commodore are the U.S. ranks that are flag officers.

flag of truce, a white flag used as a sign of surrender or of a desire to confer with the enemy.

flag|on (flag′ən), *n.* **1** a container for liquids, usually having a handle and a spout, and often a cover. **2** a large bottle, holding about two quarts. **3** the contents of a flagon.
flinch the flagon, to let the bottle pass without taking a drink: *He kept himself sober by always flinching the flagon.*
[< Old French *flacon* < *flascon* < Late Latin *flascō, -ōnis.* See related etym. at **flacon**.]

flag|pole (flag′pōl′), *n.* a pole from which a flag is or may be flown; flagstaff.

flagpole sitter, a person who sits atop a flagpole for a long time, sometimes longer than a month, as a stunt, usually to get publicity.

fla|grance (flā′grəns), *n.* = flagrancy.

fla|gran|cy (flā′grən sē), *n.* flagrant nature or quality.

flag rank, the rank of a naval officer above the grade of captain; a flag officer's rank.

fla|grant (flā′grənt), *adj.* **1** glaringly offensive; notorious; outrageous; scandalous: *a flagrant crime. You're an old flagrant heathen* (John Millington Synge). **2** glaring: *a flagrant error.* [< Latin *flagrāns, -antis,* present participle of *flagrāre* to burn] **—fla′grant|ly,** *adv.*

fla|gran|te de|lic|to (flə gran′tē di lik′tō), *Law.* = in flagrante delicto.

flag root, the root of the sweet flag.

flags (flagz), *n.pl.* See under **flag**[1].

flag|ship (flag′ship′), *n.* the ship that carries the officer in command of a fleet or squadron and displays his flag: *From the flagship they saw the modern Navy put on an impressive, well-run drill* (Time).

flag smut, a smut infecting wheat and other grasses, causing dwarfing and the appearance of dark lines on the leaf blades: *Flag smut occurs on wheat in most of the world's major wheat countries but has caused heavy losses only in Australia* (Holton and Tapke).

flag|staff (flag′staf′, -stäf′), *n.* = flagpole.

flag station, *U.S.* a railroad station where trains stop only when a signal is given, often by waving a flag, or to discharge passengers.

flag|stick (flag′stik′), *n. Golf.* the pole bearing a flag that marks the location of the hole on a putting green.

flag|stone (flag′stōn′), *n.* **1** a large, flat slab of stone, used especially for paving paths. **2** any highly stratified, hard rock that is easily broken into slabs.
flagstones, a pavement made with flagstones; flagging: *She turned and, noiseless in her sneakers, padded across the flagstones toward the house* (Atlantic).

flag stop, a place where a bus or train stops for passengers or freight when flagged.

flag-wav|er (flag′wā′vər), *n.* a person who engages in flag-waving to stir up popular sentiment.

flag-wav|ing (flag′wā′ving), *n.* **1** the waving of the flag of one's country to excite patriotic feelings in others. **2** any similar attempt to arouse popular enthusiasm for a cause.

flag|worm (flag′wėrm′), *n.* a worm found in the roots of iris or flags, used as bait by anglers.

***flail**
definition 1

***flail** (flāl), *n., v.* *—n.* **1** an instrument for threshing grain by hand. A flail consists of a wooden handle with a short, heavy, freely swinging stick fastened at one end by a thong. **2** a medieval weapon somewhat resembling this.
—v.t. **1** to strike with a flail; thresh. **2** to beat; thrash. **SYN**: whip, scourge.
[perhaps < Old French *flaiel* < Latin *flagellum* whip, flagellum. Compare Old English *fligel.*]

flair (flãr), *n.* **1** natural talent: *The poet had a flair for making clever rhymes.* **2** keen perception: *That trader had a flair for bargains.* [< Old French *flair* scent < *flairer* to smell < Late Latin *flagrāre,* for Latin *fragrāre* exhale an odor]

flak (flak), *n.* **1** the exploding shells fired from antiaircraft cannon. **2** antiaircraft cannon. **3** *U.S. Informal, Figurative.* **a** criticism; censure: *We now have a tough anti-pollution law, and the city is taking a lot of flak because its own incinerators won't be upgraded in time for the deadline set by that law* (Jeff Greenfield). **b** exchange of criticism; heated discussion or argument: *Concludes one Pentagon official: "There's been a lot of flak about civilian know-it-alls, but ... he [a civilian] has forced the services to do their homework"* (Wall Street Journal). [< German *Fl*(*ieger*)-*a*(*bwehr*)*k*(*anone*) antiaircraft cannon]

flak|age (flā′kij), *n. Anthropology.* the flakes chipped off in the making of flint arrowheads and other implements of stone.

flake[1] (flāk), *n., v.,* **flaked, flak|ing.** *—n.* **1** a small, light mass; soft, loose bit: *a flake of snow.* **2** a thin, flat piece or layer, usually not very large: *flakes of rust, flakes of ice floating on the pond.* **SYN**: chip, scale. **3** a carnation whose petals are marked by stripes of a single color. **4** *U.S. Slang.* a very unconventional or eccentric person: *For kicks, [he] races fast cars and jumps from airplanes; he has tried his hand at bullfighting, and he has a well-deserved reputation as something of a flake* (Time). **5** *U.S. Slang.* an arrest to meet a quota or to satisfy pressure for police action.
—v.i. **1** to come off in flakes; separate into flakes: *Dirty, gray spots showed where the paint had flaked off.* **2** to fall in flakes, as snow does.
—v.t. **1** to break or separate into flakes: *to flake a piece of fish for salad.* **2** to cover or mark with flakes; make spotted. **3** to break flakes or chips from; chip: *Men of the Stone Age flaked flint to make tools.* **4** to form into flakes.
[Middle English *flake,* perhaps < Scandinavian (compare Old Icelandic *flakna* to chip or scale off)] **—flake′like′,** *adj.* **—flak′er,** *n.*

flake[2] (flāk), *n.* a frame for drying produce, especially fish. [perhaps < Scandinavian (compare Old Icelandic *flaki,* or *fleki* a hurdle, wicker shield)]

flake[3] (flāk), *n.* one layer or circle of a cable, hawser, or the like, laid in a coil; fake. [probably variant of *fake*[2]]

flake[4] (flāk), *v.i.,* **flaked, flak|ing.** *U.S. Slang.* **1** to fall asleep or collapse from fatigue. **2** to get out; leave; disappear: *Take our advice: state the right facts or flake out!"* (Time).
flake out, to faint or collapse, as from fatigue or intoxication: *What is the Greek national drink anyway?—oh, yeah, ouzo, and everybody eventually flakes out* (Maclean's).
[perhaps special use of *flake*[3]]

flake|board (flāk′bôrd′, -bōrd′), *n.* a pressed fiberboard in which there are relatively large particles of wood.

flake|let (flāk′lit), *n.* a small flake.

flake tool, a paleolithic tool consisting of a flake broken off from a core of stone (often distinguished from *core tool*)

flake white, a pigment made from the flakes or scales of pure white lead.

flak jacket, a padded jacket with small steel plates sewn in place to protect the wearer from bullets or shrapnel, originally used by air force pilots.

fla|ko (flā′kō), *adj. U.S. Slang.* drunk. [< *flake*[4]]

flak vest, = flak jacket.

flak|y (flā′kē), *adj.,* **flak|i|er, flak|i|est. 1** consisting of flakes: *Mica is a flaky substance.* **2** easily broken or separated into flakes: *Shale is a flaky rock.* **3** *U.S. Slang.* very unconventional; eccentric or crazy: *We can now talk to the kid who was punching me and ask why he acts so flaky* (Atlantic). **—flak′i|ly,** *adv.* **—flak′i|ness,** *n.*

flam[1] (flam), *n., v.,* **flammed, flam|ming.** *—n.* **1** a fabrication; falsehood. **2** deception; humbug; blarney.
—v.t., v.i. Dialect. to deceive or be deceived by a flam; delude; cheat.

Pronunciation Key: hat, āge, cãre, fär; let, ēqual, tėrm, it, īce; hot, ōpen, ôrder; oil, out; cup, pu̇t, rüle; child; long; thin; ᴛʜen; zh, measure; ə represents **a** in about, **e** in taken, **i** in pencil, **o** in lemon, **u** in circus.

[perhaps back formation < *flimflam*]

flam[2] (flam), *n.* a drumbeat made by the two sticks striking the head almost at the same time, but still heard separately. [perhaps imitative]

flam|ant or **flam|mant** (flam′ənt), *adj. Heraldry.* flaming.

flamb (flam), *v.t. Scottish.* to baste.

flam|bé (flän bā′), *adj., pl.* **-bés** or **-bées**, *v.,* **-béd** or **-béed, -bé|ing.** —*adj.* **1** (of a dish, especially a dessert) served in flames, by pouring brandy, rum, or other alcoholic liquor over the food and lighting it: *Bing cherries flambées* (New Yorker). **2** (of chinaware) iridescent from the irregular application of glaze: *a flambé vase, flambé ware.*
—*v.t.* to pour liquor over and set aflame: *For dessert I sautéd some bananas and flambéd them with Spanish-made vodka* (Maclean's).
[< French *flambé* (literally) passed through a flame < *flamber* to flame < Old French *flambe;* see etym. under **flame**]

flam|beau (flam′bō), *n., pl.* **-beaux** or **-beaus** (-bōz). **1** a flaming torch. **2** a large, decorated candlestick. [< French *flambeau* < Old French *flambe,* or *flamble;* see etym. under **flame**]

flam|berg (flam′bérg), *n.* = flamberge.

flam|berge (flän berzh′), *n.* a type of fencing sword or rapier: *The third, fifth and sixth Henrys sported seventeenth-century cuirassier armour and flamberge swords of the same vintage* (Manchester Guardian). [< Old French *flamberge* the sword of Roland; a sword]

flam|boy|ance (flam boi′əns), *n.* flamboyant nature or quality.

flam|boy|an|cy (flam boi′ən sē), *n.* = flamboyance.

flam|boy|ant (flam boi′ənt), *adj., n.* —*adj.* **1** flaming, gorgeous, or striking in a showy way: *flamboyant colors, a flamboyant sunset.* SYN: brilliant. **2** very ornate; much decorated; florid: *flamboyant architecture.* **3** given to display; ostentatious; showy; swaggering: *a flamboyant person, a flamboyant speech. That flamboyant but egotistical figure, Alexander the Great* (H. G. Wells). **4** having wavy lines or flamelike curves: *flamboyant designs. With massive face, flamboyant hair* (George Eliot). **5** *Architecture.* characterized by lines that spiral and wave in flamelike patterns: *flamboyant tracery of French architecture in the 1400's.*
—*n.* = royal poinciana.
[< French *flamboyant,* present participle of *flamboyer* to flame < Old French *flambe;* see etym. under **flame**] —**flam|boy′ant|ly,** *adv.*

flam|doo|dle (flam′dü′dəl), *n. Informal.* nonsense. [variant of *flapdoodle*]

flame (flām), *n., v.,* **flamed, flam|ing.** —*n.* **1** one of the glowing tongues of light, usually red or yellow, that come when a fire blazes up: *The burning house went up in flames.* **2** a burning gas or vapor: *an oxidizing flame.* **3** a burning with flames; blaze; fire: *The dying fire suddenly burst into flame.* **4** *Figurative: Love is indestructible, Its holy flame forever burneth* (Robert Southey). **5** brilliance; luster; sparkle: *that jewel of the purest flame* (William Cowper). **6** a bright light: *When the moon began to show her silver flame* (Longfellow). **7** *Figurative.* a burning feeling; passion; ardor; zeal: *Ah youth, ungrateful to a flame like mine* (Alexander Pope). **8** a streak or patch of color: *The horse had a flame on its forehead.* **9** *Informal.* a sweetheart: *Euphelia serves to grace my measure; But Chloe is my real flame* (Matthew Prior). **10** = flame color.
—*v.i.* **1** to rise up in flames; burst into flames; blaze. SYN: flare, glow, flash. **2** to grow hot or red; flush with color: *Her cheeks flamed.* **3** to shine brightly; give out a bright light; flash: *Her eyes flamed with rage.* SYN: gleam. **4** *Figurative.* **a** have or show a burning feeling: *The rage of James flamed high* (Macaulay). **b** to burst out quickly and hotly; be or act like a flame: *The mob flamed through the streets.*
—*v.t.* **1** to subject to a flame; heat in a flame: *to flame a test tube. The fact that the pancakes are flamed is undoubtedly why they have an irresistible appeal for diners* (New York Times). **2** to send (messages) by means of flames.
flame out, a (of a jet engine) to suddenly fail to function, because the flame has gone out: [*They*] *have successfully conducted tests with fuels which ignite on contact with air and ... can relight jet engines which have flamed out at high altitudes* (Wall Street Journal). **b** to burst out quickly: *The fire flamed out, enveloping the wrecked car.*
flame up (or **forth**), to burst out quickly and hotly: *She felt the color flame up in her cheeks* (Edna Lyall).
the flames, fire, with reference to destruction or death by burning: *condemned to the flames.*
[< Anglo-French *flaumbe,* Old French *flambe,* or *flamble* < Latin *flammula* (diminutive) < *flamma* flame] —**flame′less,** *adj.* —**flame′like′,** *adj.*
—*Syn. n.* **1, 3 Flame, blaze** mean a bright burning or fire. **Flame** applies to either a single glowing tongue of fire, such as that of a candle, or a fire burning brightly and quickly, and is often used in the plural to suggest a fire with many bright tongues darting or shooting up: *The house burst into flames.* **Blaze** applies to a hotter, brighter, and more steady fire: *The whole room was lighted by the blaze in the fireplace.*

flame azalea, a brilliant, showy azalea that bears orange or scarlet flowers, found in the eastern United States.

flame cell, an excretory cell in flatworms, rotifers, or the like, containing a group of cilia that beat with a flamelike motion and move waste products into excretory tubes.

flame color, a bright reddish-yellow or reddish-orange color; the color of flame.

flame-col|ored (flām′kul′ərd), *adj.* of the color of flame.

flame cultivation, the clearing of fields for cultivation by destroying weeds or insects with a flame thrower.

flame cultivator, = flame thrower (def. 2).

flame-cut (flām′kut′), *v.t.,* **-cut, -cut|ting.** to cut (metal) by means of a gas flame.

flamed (flāmd), *adj.* **1** furnished with flames. **2** (of a tulip) bearing flamelike marks.

flame flier, *U.S. Slang.* the pilot of a jet plane.

flame flower, a climbing perennial nasturtium with showy vermilion flowers.

flame gun, = flame thrower (def. 2).

flame holder, a ring, grid, or other device in certain jet engines which keeps the flame from being blown out by the incoming air.

flame|keep|er (flām′kē′pər), *n.* a person who acts as a caretaker: *No one seemed overly impressed by his car, his haberdashery, or his pretensions as the flamekeeper of Western Culture* (Time).

flame|let (flām′lit), *n.* a little flame.

fla|men (flā′men), *n.* a priest devoted to one particular Roman god: *a flamen of Jupiter.* [< Middle French *flamine,* learned borrowing from Latin *flāmen, -inis* a Roman priest devoted to one certain deity]

***fla|men|co** (flə meng′kō), *n., adj.* —*n.* **1** a style of Spanish Gypsy dance, originally of Andalusia, with much twirling, hand-clapping, and foot-stamping, performed with castanets to fast, fiery, vigorous rhythms. **2** a song or piece of music to which the dance is performed: *It was like a flamenco—first guttural and then falsetto* (New Yorker).
—*adj.* of or in the style of the dance or music: *flamenco rhythms.*
[< Spanish *flamenco* (originally) Flemish; a Fleming (the gypsies dance to celebrate their leaving Germany, later confused with Flanders). See etym. of doublet **flamingo.**]

***flamenco**
definition 1

flame|out (flām′out′), *n.* the sudden failure of a jet engine to function, because the flame has gone out, especially while in flight.

flame photometer, an instrument used to measure the concentration of certain elements in solution, such as the amount of sodium and potassium salts in the blood. When the solution is sprayed into a very hot flame, the relative intensities of the emission spectra of the elements present in the solution can be measured.

flame photometry, quantitative analysis done by flame photometer.

flame projector, = flame thrower.

flame|proof (flām′prüf′), *adj., v.* —*adj.* free from the danger of combustion; not liable to burn when exposed to flames: *flameproof coveralls.*
—*v.t.* to make flameproof: *This resin flameproofs the cotton permanently without harming the other qualities of the fabric* (Science News Letter). —**flame′proof′er,** *n.*

flam|er (flā′mər), *n.* a person or thing that uses or works with flames.

flame-re|sist|ant (flām′ri zis′tənt), *adj.* not easily burned; holding back fire: *The interior decorating is done in spun glass, plastics, and the special flame-resistant fiber Dynel* (Newsweek).

flames (flāmz), *n.pl.* See under **flame.**

flame scarlet, = flame color.

flame stability, the ability of the fuel in a jet engine to burn steadily over a wide range of temperatures and pressures.

flame stitch, a pattern in bargello needlework that suggests rows of flames, used especially in upholstery fabrics and pillow covers.

flame test, a test to identify certain chemical elements by the color of their salts when heated in the flame of a Bunsen burner.

flame tetra, a tropical fish of the upper Amazon region, about two inches long, yellow in front, and bright red in back; red tetra. It makes a colorful aquarium fish.

flame thrower, or **flame|throw|er** (flām′thrō′ər), *n.* **1** a weapon that throws a stream of burning fuel through the air from the nozzle of a metal tube connected to tanks of fuel and compressed air: *U.S. marines, landing from 30 helicopters, fought a mock battle against "enemy" strongpoints with flame throwers and satchel charges* (Time). **2** a device similar to this, used especially to clear fields infested with weeds or insects; flame cultivator; flame gun. **3** a person who operates either of these. **4** *U.S. Slang.* a jet plane. [translation of German *Flammenwerfer*]

flame tree, or **flame-tree** (flām′trē′), *n.* **1** an ornamental tree of the sterculia family grown in warm climates for its showy, scarlet flowers; Chinese parasol tree. **2** any one of various trees with showy, red flowers.

flame|ware (flām′wãr′), *n.* kitchenware treated to withstand the heat of an open flame.

fla|min|e|ous (flə min′ē əs), *adj.* of or having to do with a flamen.

flam|ing (flā′ming), *adj.* **1** burning with flames; on fire: *a flaming house.* **2** like a flame; very bright; brilliant: *flaming eyes, a flaming field of poppies.* **3** *Figurative.* showing or arousing strong feeling; violent; vehement: *flaming anger, flaming youth.* **4** *British Slang.* cursed; confounded: *a flaming fool.* —**flam′ing|ly,** *adv.*

fla|min|go (flə ming′gō), *n., pl.* **-gos** or **-goes.** a large, web-footed tropical wading bird with very long and slender legs and neck, a heavy, bent bill, and feathers that vary from pink to deep red. [< Portuguese *flamingo* < Spanish *flamenco* (originally) Flemish; a Fleming (< Middle Dutch *Vlâming*); later, flamingo, associated by popular etymology with Spanish *flama* flame, because of the ruddy complexion of the Flemings, and the red color of the bird. See etym. of doublet **flamenco.**]

flamingo plant, a tropical American plant of the arum family, grown for its bright-scarlet spathe and showy flowers.

flam|ma|bil|i|ty (flam′ə bil′ə tē), *n.* flammable quality or condition; inflammability: *The material has a flammability similar to kerosine* (Occupational Health Newsletter).

flam|ma|ble (flam′ə bəl), *adj., n.* —*adj.* easily set on fire; inflammable: *Hair and beards are extremely flammable in the oxygen-rich atmosphere of a spacecraft* (Science News).
—*n.* something flammable: *The majority of home fires could be prevented ... if portable heaters were kept away from curtains and other flammables* (New York Times).
▶**Flammable, inflammable** are synonymous, not antonymous. The *in-* of *inflammable* is an intensive prefix, not a negative.

flam|mu|lat|ed (flam′yə lā′tid), *adj.* (of birds) reddish; ruddy.

flam|mu|la|tion (flam′yə lā′shən), *n. Zoology.* a small flamelike marking. [< Latin *flammula* flame (diminutive < *flamma*) + English *-ation*]

flam|y (flā′mē), *adj.* of or like flame: *And look! that flash of flamy wings, the fireplumed oriole!* (Oliver Wendell Holmes).

flan (flan), *n.* **1** *British.* an open tart filled with custard, cream, or fruit: *large fresh strawberry flans, dripping with juice* (Manchester Guardian). **2** a piece of metal shaped to make a coin but not yet stamped. [< Old French *flaon* a tart < Germanic (compare Old High German *flado*)]

flanch[1] (flanch, flänch), *n. Heraldry.* a subordinary formed on each side of the shield by a line arched or convex toward the center. [perhaps < Old French *flanche,* feminine of *flanc;* see etym. under **flank**]

flanch[2] (flanch, flänch), *v.i.* to spread; widen out; flare: *The sides of the boat flanch outwards.* [see etym. under **flange**]

flanched (flancht, flänchd), *adj. Heraldry.* having a flanch.

Flan|ders brick (flan′dərz), = Bath brick. [< *Flanders,* part of Belgium and France, where it was made]

Flanders poppy, the common field poppy of European cornfields; corn poppy; coquelicot. The Flanders poppy is a historic emblem or symbol of those who were killed in World War I.

flâ|ne|rie (flän rē′), *n. French.* idleness.

flâ|neur (flä nœr′) *n. French.* an idler.

***flange** (flanj), *n., v.,* **flanged, flang|ing.** —*n.* **1** a raised edge, collar, or rim on a wheel, pulley,

pipe, or other object. It is used to keep an object in place, fasten it to another object, or strengthen it. Railroad cars and locomotives have wheels with flanges to keep them on the track. **2** a tool used in making flanges.
— ***v.t.*** to provide with a flange: *"With flanged and battering tail ..." He said, "Let there be Whale!"* (William Rose Benét).
— ***v.i.*** to project like, or take the form of, a flange. [variant of earlier *flanch,* noun, perhaps < Old French *flanchir* bend, apparently < a Germanic word] — **flang'er,** *n.*

***flange**
definition 1

flank (flangk), *n., v.* — ***n.*** **1** the side of an animal or person between the ribs and the hip. **2** the strip of flesh and muscle forming this part. **3** a piece of beef cut from this part. **4** the outer part of the thigh. **5** the side of a mountain, building, or similar large object: *Mountains have arisen since With cities on their flanks* (Tennyson). **6a** the far right or the far left side of an army, fleet, or other military formation; wing. **b** the right or left side of a fortification or one of its projecting parts. **c** the section of a fortification that protects an adjacent part by gunfire. **d** the wall of a bastion between the curtain and the face on either side.
— ***v.t.*** **1** to be at the side of: *A garage flanked the house. High buildings flanked the dark, narrow alley.* **2** to get around the far right or left side of; march past the flank of: *Did they flank the snow and go around to the right?* **3a** to attack from or on the side. **b** to protect, control, or guard the side of. **4** to present the flank to (waves or other opposing object or force): *Again to flank the tempest she might reel* (William Falconer).
— ***v.i.*** **1** to occupy a position on a flank or side. **2** to present the flank or side.
[< Old French *flanc* < Germanic (compare Old High German *hlanca* loin, side). See related etym. at **lank.**]

flan|ken (fläng'kən), *n. Jewish Cookery.* cooked ribs of beef cut from the flank, usually eaten with horseradish. [< Yiddish *flanken* < German *Flanken* flanks, sides]

flank|er (flang'kər), *n.* **1** a person or thing that flanks. **2** = flankerback.

flank|er|back (flang'kər bak'), *n. American Football.* a back who lines up for a flanking position closer to the sidelines than his opponent.

flank speed, 1 a ship's maximum prescribed speed: *They turned out to be three Indonesian torpedo boats racing at flank speed (40 knots) toward the Dutch New Guinea coast* (Time). **2** a very great speed; top speed: *Seventh Avenue was filled with cabs, all rushing past at flank speed* (Russell Baker).

flank steak, a boneless cut of beef from the underside of the flank. Broiled and sliced flank steak is called *London broil.*

flan|nel (flan'əl), *n., adj., v.,* **-neled, -nel|ing** or (*especially British*) **-nelled, -nel|ling.** — ***n.*** **1** a soft, warm, woolen cloth. Flannel has a nap on both sides. **2** a similar fabric made of cotton, especially a strong fabric with a long, soft nap, usually on one side only. **3** = flannelette. **4** *British Slang.* insincere talk or action used to cover up or deceive; bluff; blarney: *The Government wanted the power to put the troops in. The rest was all fairy tale and flannel* (London Times).
— ***adj.*** made of flannel.
— ***v.t.*** **1** to wrap in or rub with flannel. **2** *British Slang.* to cover up or deceive by insincere talk or action; bluff: *I ... believed that I could flannel my way through by a combination of Parliamentary sleight-of-hand and spur-of-the-moment decisions* (Punch).
— ***v.i.*** *British Slang.* to talk or act insincerely; bluff: *Some of the cast, I suspect, were flanneling; but there are two spellbinding performances* (Irving Wardle).
flannels, a clothes, especially trousers, made of flannel: *[He] changed to a costume of white flannels, white shirt of silk, and white leather shoes* (L. J. Vance). **b** woolen underwear: *Mother made the children wear flannels in winter.*
[perhaps < Welsh *gwlanen*]

flannel board, a flannel or felt-covered board to which material with a similar backing will adhere without glue, widely used for displaying visual aids in teaching.

flannel cake, a thin, soft-textured pancake.

flan|nel|ette or **flan|nel|et** (flan'ə let'), *n.* a soft, warm cotton cloth with a nap that looks like flannel.

flan|nel|ly (flan'ə lē), *adj.* characteristic of or like flannel; suggesting the quality or texture of flannel: *a thick, muffled, flannelly voice; a downy, flannelly cloth.*

flan|nels (flan'əlz), *n.pl.* See under **flannel.**

flap** (flap), *v.,* **flapped, flap|ping,** *n.* — ***v.i. **1** to swing or sway about loosely and with some noise: *The sails flapped in the wind. Curtains flapped in the open windows.* **2** to move up and down, as a bird's wings do; produce noise by beating of wings: *While o'er them flapped the sea birds' dewy wing* (Byron). **3** to fly by moving wings up and down: *The goose flapped heavily away through the air.* **4** to strike with something broad and flat: *The clown's big shoes flapped along the ground.* **5** to throw oneself flat (down): *Soldiers flap down to drink it from the puddles* (Thomas Carlyle). **6** *Slang.* to become excited, confused, or alarmed: *The Navy flapped when Congress asked why it stored 886,020 pounds of canned hamburger, plus 812,179 gallons of ketchup* (New York Times).
— ***v.t.*** **1** to cause to swing or sway loosely, especially with noise: *The wind is flapping the shade.* **2** to move (wings, arms, or the like) up and down; beat: *The ostrich flapped its wings but could not rise from the ground.* **3** to strike noisily with a broad, flat object; drive away thus: *Then let me flap this bug with gilded wings* (Alexander Pope). **4** *Informal.* to toss (a flat, flexible object) with a smart movement; throw; cast; turn: *He flapped the cover back.*
— ***n.*** **1** a flapping motion: *the flap of the banners, that flit as they're borne* (Byron). **2** the noise caused by flapping: *the flap of a bird's wing.* **3** a blow from something broad and flat: *a flap from a beaver's tail.* **4** a broad, flat, piece usually hanging or fastened at one edge only: *His coat had flaps on the pockets.* **5** a hinged or sliding section, usually at the trailing edge of a wing of an aircraft, that can be extended or tilted to assist a take-off or a landing. **6** *Slang.* excitement or anger; commotion: *Congress is in a flap about the budget proposals.* **7** (in surgery) a piece of flesh partially detached from adjacent tissue, such as one for later use in grafting. **8** *Phonetics.* a type of trill in which the vibrating organ gives only a single tap, as in the London English pronunciation of *merry, very.* **9** a concentration of sightings of unidentified flying objects in a small area within a short period: *We talked the Michigan flap over with three local ufologists and found them both elated and alarmed* (New Yorker).
[perhaps imitative. Compare East Frisian *flappen.*]

***flap**
n., definition 5

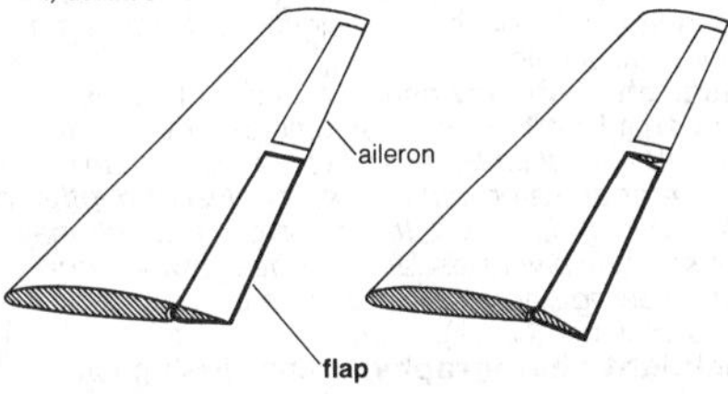

flap|doo|dle (flap'dü'dəl), *n. Informal.* nonsense; bosh; humbug. [a coined word]

flap door, a door with the hinges on the lower side, so that it opens downward and outward; falling door.

flap-eared (flap'ird'), *adj.* having broad, loose, flapping ears.

flap|jack (flap'jak'), *n.* = pancake.

flap|less (flap'lis), *adj.* without a flap or flaps: *The Army wanted its pockets flapless* (Wall Street Journal).

flap-mouthed (flap'mouᴛʜd', -moutht'), *adj.* having loose, hanging lips, as a dog.

flap|pa|bil|i|ty (flap'ə bil'ə tē), *n. Informal.* flappable quality or condition.

flap|pa|ble (flap'ə bəl), *adj. Informal.* tending to become excited, alarmed, or confused: *As he demonstrated for a nationwide audience while he was being questioned by newsmen after the assassination attempt, Chief Reddin is not easily flappable* (New York Times). [back formation < *unflappable*]

flap|per (flap'ər), *n., v.* — ***n.*** **1** something that flaps. A broad fin is sometimes called a flapper. **2** a broad, flat, hanging piece; flap. **3** a young bird just able to fly. **4** *Informal.* **a** a young girl. **b** a rather forward and unconventional girl of the 1920's.
— ***v.i.*** to move with a loose, flapping motion.

flap|per-bag (flap'ər bag'), *n.* = burdock.

flap|per|ish (flap'ər ish), *adj. Informal.* having to do with or characteristic of a flapper or flappers of the 1920's.

flap|py (flap'ē), *adj.,* **-pi|er, -pi|est.** that flaps; flapping: *flappy curtains.*

flare (flãr), *v.,* **flared, flar|ing,** *n.* — ***v.i.*** **1** to flame up briefly or unsteadily, sometimes with smoke: *A gust of wind made the torches flare.* **2** to shine; glow: *Lo! the blood-red light of dawn flared on her face* (Tennyson). **3** to spread out in the shape of a bell: *This skirt flares at the bottom. The sides of a ship flare from the keel to the deck.*
— ***v.t.*** **1** to signal by lights: *The rockets flared a warning.* **2** to cause (a lamp, lantern, or torch) to burn with a swaying or variable flame: *He flared the candle at me again, smoking my face and hair* (Dickens). **3** to spread out to view; make a display of; flourish: *We ... began ... to make every signal in our power, by flaring the shirts in the air* (Edgar Allan Poe). **4** to give an outward-curving shape to: *The skirt should be flared at the bottom.* **5** *Metallurgy.* to heat (brass containing a large amount of zinc) to the temperature at which the zinc vapors start burning.
— ***n.*** **1** a bright, unsteady light or blaze that lasts only a short time: *The flare of a match showed us his face.* **2** a dazzling light that burns for a short time, used for signaling, lighting up a battlefield or rescue area, or the like: *The police put up flares on the road to warn motorists of the accident. The Coast Guard vessel responded to the flare sent up from the lifeboat.* **3** a sudden eruption of gases on the surface of the sun; solar flare. **4** a burst into sudden action or feeling. **5** the act of spreading out into a bell shape. **6** the part that spreads out: *the flare of a skirt.* **7** *Optics.* a spot of light or a blurred area in an image or film caused by reflection of light between lens surfaces.
flare out, a to flame up; burst into sudden anger or violence: *Tempers flared out at court during the final argument.* **b** to bring an aircraft down in a smooth curve preparatory to touching down: *Should the pilot flare out too soon, the airplane may overshoot the runway.*
flare up, a to burst into flames: *The California forest fires, which were regarded yesterday as almost under control, flared up again during the night* (London Times). **b** *Figurative.* to burst into sudden anger or violence: *Their quarrel flared up all over again when the two angry boys met in the hall.*
[origin uncertain. Compare Norwegian *flara* blaze, flaunt.]

flare|back (flãr'bak'), *n.* **1** a burst of flame from unburned powder that shoots back from the breech of a howitzer or other heavy gun when it is opened after firing. **2** *Figurative: a flareback of winter.*

flare-out (flãr'out'), *n.* the final glide position of an aircraft in which power is reduced and the nose is raised to decrease the steepness of its approach before touchdown.

flare star, a star that exhibits a sudden, intense increase in brightness followed by return to normal within a few minutes.

flare-up (flãr'up'), *n.* **1** an outburst of flame. **2** *Informal, Figurative.* a sudden outburst of anger or violence: *The two boys had frequent flare-ups but remained friends.*

flar|ing (flãr'ing), *adj., n.* — ***adj.*** **1** burning with a broad, irregular flame; flaming: *flaring tapers brightening as they waste* (Oliver Goldsmith). **2** *Figurative.* showy; gaudy: *The modern building had a sort of flaring beauty.* **3** spreading or curving gradually outward in form: *a flaring skirt, a flaring bow.*
— ***n.*** the practice of burning unwanted natural gas that has been piped off from an oil well during oil production. — **flar'ing|ly,** *adv.*

flar|y (flãr'ē), *adj.* flaring; gaudy; showy.

flash (flash), *n., v., adj.* — ***n.*** **1** a sudden, brief light or flame: *a flash of lightning.* **2** *Figurative.* a sudden, short feeling or display: *a flash of hope, a flash of wit, a flash of unforeseen remembrance.* **3** a very short time; an instant: *It all happened in a flash.* **4** a showy display: *Pedants ... are apt to decry the writings of a polite author, as flash and froth* (Joseph Addison). **5** a news report sent by teletype, telegraph, radio, or other means of communication: *The same flash that recommended the sale of General Telephone urged the purchase of Western Union, which jumped 3⅜ points* (Wall Street Journal). **6** = flashbulb. **7** *Informal.* a flashlight. **8a** a rush of water, such as that produced by a dam or sluiceway, used to float a boat over shoals or for other

---

Pronunciation Key: hat, āge, cãre, fär; let, ēqual, tėrm, it, īce; hot, ōpen, ôrder; oil, out; cup, pu̇t, rüle; child; long; thin; ᴛʜen; zh, measure; ə represents **a** in about, **e** in taken, **i** in pencil, **o** in lemon, **u** in circus.

purposes. **b** the device, such as a lock or sluice, used for this purpose. **9** *Informal.* the jargon of thieves, tramps, etc. **10** a preparation of cayenne and caramel used for tinting liquors.
—*v.i.* **1a** to give out a sudden, brief light or flame: *Lightning flashed in the sky.* **b** *Figurative.* to give out like a flash; gleam: *Her eyes flashed with happiness.* **2** to come suddenly; pass quickly: *A train flashed by.* (*Figurative.*) *A thought flashed across his mind.* **3** *U.S. Slang.* to experience the effects of a psychedelic drug. **4** *Informal.* to make a showy display: *She was flashing around with a big diamond.* **5** *Archaic.* to splash or dash: *The tortured wave ... Now flashes o'er the scattered fragments* (James Thomson).
—*v.t.* **1a** to give out by flashes: *The lighthouse flashes signals twice a minute.* **b** *Figurative.* to send out like a flash: *Her eyes flashed defiance. Stern is the tyrant's mandate, red the gaze that flashes desolation* (Shelley). **2** to cause to flash: *to flash a lamp in a person's face, to flash one's sword.* **3** to communicate by flashes; send by teletype, telegraph, radio, or other means of communication: *to flash the news across the country.* **4** to flood or flush with water. **5** to display shortly or quickly: *to flash a card,* (*Figurative.*) *to flash one's wit.* **6** *Informal.* to make a great display of; show off: *to flash one's jewelry.* **7** *Archaic.* to dash or splash (water): *With his raging arms he rudely flashed The waves about* (Edmund Spenser). **8** to protect from water by providing with a flashing. **9a** to coat (glass or a glass article) with a film of colored glass. **b** to apply (a film of colored glass) to glass.
—*adj.* **1** flashy: *The new car has a flash appearance.* **2** very sudden and rapid: *a flash fire, flash heating.* **3** *Slang.* shrewdly knowing; smart; sly. **4** *Informal.* of or having to do with thieves, tramps, or other groups, or their cant or jargon: *flash language.*

flash in the pan, a sudden, showy attempt or effort that fails or is not followed by further efforts: *The Kuwait oil strike was no flash in the pan; ... the country's known reserves will last more than a century* (New Yorker).

flash on, *U.S. Slang.* to appreciate immediately; understand quickly: *If you "dig" something, you "flash on it," ... "get into it"* (Sara Davidson).
[apparently imitative]
—*Syn. n.* **1 Flash, glitter, sparkle** mean a sudden or briefly gleaming light. **Flash** means a sudden, bright light that disappears immediately: *We saw a single flash of light from the signal tower.* **Glitter** means a bright and wavering light reflected from a shining, hard surface: *the glitter of coins on the table.* **Sparkle** means light shooting out in many tiny, brief, brilliant flashes like sparks: *We looked at the sparkle of little dancing waves in the sunlight.*

flash|back (flash′bak′), *n., v.* —*n.* **1** a break in the course of a motion picture, novel, or the like, to show some event or scene of a previous time; cutback: *One is sometimes confused about where the flashbacks end and the present begins* (Harper's). **2** the recurrence of a hallucination originally experienced under the influence of a hallucinogenic drug: *This decline [in the use of LSD] has been due, in part, to the bad "trips" that terrified many users, the frequency of disturbing "flashbacks"* (Sidney Cohen). **3** a sudden backward flash of fire or electricity, as from a burner: *to be burned by a flashback.*
—*v.i.* **1** to become visible in the form of flashbacks: *While he convalesces at the home of his Quaker foster aunt outside Philadelphia, his whole life flashbacks before his eyes* (Time). **2** to return (to) in the form of flashbacks: *We then flashback to 1903 and the Mayfair bonbonnière where the tiny Dunglass first entered Debrett* (Alan Coren).
—*v.t.* to show in the form of flashbacks: *In the flashbacked past, the reader can observe Pennington's speedily remarried wife* (New York Times).

flash|board (flash′bôrd′, -bōrd′), *n.* a board set up on edge upon a milldam, when the water is low, to throw a larger quantity of water into the millrace.

flash|bulb (flash′bulb′), *n.* an electric bulb which gives out a brilliant flash of light for a very short time; photoflash lamp. It is used in taking photographs indoors or at night. It consists of a glass bulb containing a wire filament and aluminum or zirconium foil.

flash burn, a severe burn caused by instantaneous thermal radiation, such as that from an atomic bomb.

flash|card (flash′kärd′), *n.* a card bearing a letter, word, number, simple problem, or picture. In drills in elementary reading, arithmetic, and other skills, the teacher displays a flashcard briefly and the student gives an answer.

flash-cook (flash′ku̇k′), *v.t.* to cook by a very short exposure to intense heat, such as infrared radiation: *[This custard] is the first test of ... aseptic canning, which gives a fresher tasting product because cans are flash-cooked for six seconds rather than sterilised for 60 minutes* (Sunday Times).

flash|cube (flash′kyüb′), *n.* a small, plastic cube containing four miniature flashbulbs, which revolve into place as each photograph is taken.

flash distillation, a method of distilling salt water by heating and then releasing it into a low-pressure chamber, causing part of the water to turn quickly into stream, which is then condensed into fresh water.

flash|er (flash′ər), *n.* **1** a person or thing that flashes. **2** *U.S. Slang.* a person who exposes himself indecently in public: *a compulsiver flasher.*

flash fire, a very sudden, violent fire, especially one that spreads rapidly through underbrush.

flash flood, a very sudden, violent flooding of a river, stream, or lake.

flash-for|ward (flash′fôr′wərd), *n.* a break in the course of a motion picture, novel, or the like, to show some future event or scene ahead of its occurrence. [patterned on *flashback*]

flash gun, *Photography.* an attachment to a camera that sets off a flashbulb and opens the camera's shutter in synchronization.

flash heating, very rapid heating: *They say the descriptions of the glassy patches do not tally with what is expected for material melted by flash heating* (London Times).

***flash|ing** (flash′ing), *n., adj.* —*n.* **1** pieces of sheet metal, such as copper or aluminum, used around windows or chimneys, and in roof joints, to make them watertight. **2** the process of suddenly letting in a rush of water so as to produce an artificial flood, as for cleaning a sewer.
—*adj.* that flashes or looks like flashing: *And all should cry Beware! Beware! His flashing eyes, his floating hair!* (Samuel Taylor Coleridge).

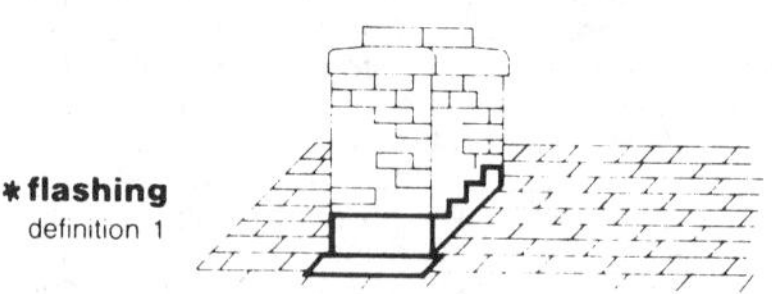
***flashing** definition 1

flash|ing|ly (flash′ing lē), *adv.* **1** very brightly; flashily: *a flashingly red automobile.* **2** brilliantly.

flashing point, = flash point (def. 1).

flash lamp, *Photography.* = flashbulb.

flash|light (flash′līt′), *n.* **1** a portable electric light, operated by batteries. It produces a light by the pressure of a button. **2** a light that flashes, used in a lighthouse or for signaling. **3** *Photography.* = flashbulb.

flashlight fish, any one of a family of fishes that emit light from special luminescent organs: *The Atlantic flashlight fish lives in more than 500 feet of water and only enters lesser depths to feed during darkness. Its light organs, which may be seen by divers as far as 50 feet away, contain glowing bacteria and can be covered with a lid* (Science News).

flashlight photography, = photoflash photography.

flash|me|ter (flash′mē′tər), *n.* = tachistoscope.

flash|o|ver (flash′ō′vər), *n., v.* —*n.* an unintended arc between two conducting parts of a machine or electrical device, or between a part and the ground.
—*v.i.* to have a flashover.

flash|pan (flash′pan′), *n.* a receptacle in a flintlock for holding the priming.

flash point. **1** the temperature at which the vapor given off from a flammable substance, such as an oil or hydrocarbon, will ignite momentarily in air, in the presence of a small flame. **2** *Figurative: The conflict between Southern Rhodesia's four million Africans and quarter million Europeans has now reached its flash point* (Manchester Guardian).

flash powder, a mixture of aluminum or magnesium with certain other substances that produces a bright flash when ignited, commonly used before the invention of the flashbulb to supply artificial light for taking photographs.

flash spectrum, (in a total solar eclipse) a bright-line spectrum that flashes out for a few seconds from the edge of the sun at the beginning and end of the time when all of its direct light is cut off.

flash synchronizer, a device on a camera that causes the greatest brightness of the flashbulb's light to occur at the instant when the shutter reaches its full opening.

flash test, a test to determine the flash point of kerosene or other substance; fire test.

flash tube, a glass discharge tube filled with an inert gas, used to produce very short and intense flashes of light. Flash tubes are used in lasers, high-speed photography, and in various optical systems.

flash|y (flash′ē), *adj.,* **flash|i|er, flash|i|est.** **1** very bright for a short time; flashing. SYN: glittering, dazzling, sparkling. **2** *Figurative.* showy; gaudy: *He tries to impress the girls by wearing flashy socks and jackets.* SYN: tawdry. See syn. under **gaudy**. **3** transitory; momentary. —**flash′i|ly**, *adv.* —**flash′i|ness**, *n.*

***flask**[1] (flask, fläsk), *n., v.* —*n.* **1** any bottle-shaped container. Thin glass flasks are used in chemical laboratories for heating liquids, etc. **2** a small glass, plastic, or metal bottle with flat sides, especially one with a narrow neck, made to be carried in the pocket for use on a journey: *a flask of whiskey.* **3** a box or frame consisting of two halves, for holding the sand, used as a mold in a foundry. **4** a bottle-shaped iron vessel for shipping mercury, holding 76 lbs.
—*v.t.* to put into a flask.
[Old English *flasce,* also *flaxe,* probably < Late Latin *flasca;* origin uncertain]

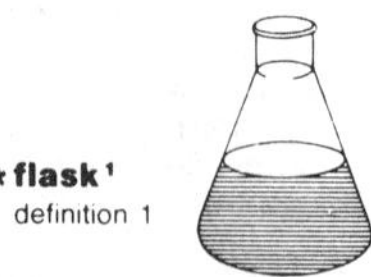
***flask**[1] definition 1

flask[2] (flask, fläsk), *n.* **1** the side of the trail of a gun carriage, formed of metal plates. **2** *Obsolete.* the bed or platform of a gun carriage. [< Middle French *flasque,* variant of *flaque* plank, perhaps < Germanic (compare German *flach* level, flat). Compare etym. under **flasket**.]

flask|et (flas′kit, fläs′-), *n.* **1** a long, shallow basket. **2** a small flask: *a flasket richly chased* (Scott). [< Old North French *flasquet,* Old French *flachet* (diminutive) < *flasque* < Late Latin *flasca* flask; origin uncertain]

***flat**[1] (flat), *adj.,* **flat|ter, flat|test,** *n., adv., v.,* **flat|ted, flat|ting.** —*adj.* **1** smooth and level; even: *flat land. This floor is flat.* SYN: plane. **2** leveled with the ground; horizontal; at full length; overthrown: *The storm left the trees flat on the ground.* SYN: prone, supine. **3** close to an even surface; touching such a surface throughout its length: *The ladder was flat against the wall.* **4** not very deep or thick: *A plate is flat.* **5** with little air in it; deflated; collapsed: *A nail or sharp stone can cause a flat tire.* **6a** unfolded; opened, as an unrolled map is: *The brute earl ... with flat hand ... smote her on the cheeks* (Tennyson). **b** (of feet) having the arches fallen. **c** lacking the normal or natural projection, elevation, roundness, or other shape: *the broad, flat face of the Eskimo.* **7** *Figurative.* not to be changed: **a** without qualification; positive; downright: *A flat refusal is complete.* SYN: absolute. **b** not varied; fixed: *We paid a flat rate with no extra charges.* **8** *Figurative.* neither more nor less; exact: *a flat ten seconds.* **9** *Figurative.* dull: **a** without much life, interest, flavor, or emotion: *a flat voice. Plain food tastes flat.* SYN: plain, monotonous, uninteresting. **b** having little business activity; without significant changes in price: *a flat market in grain futures.* **10** *Figurative.* **a** not shiny or glossy: *a flat yellow.* **b** (of a color or tint) of uniform depth or shade. **c** without appearance of relief or projection in a painting. **11** *Figurative.* not clear or sharp in sound. **12** *Music.* **a** below the true pitch; too low in pitch: *Her voice tends to go flat.* **b** one half step or half note below natural pitch: *music written in B flat.* **c** marked with flats; having flats in the signature. **d** minor, as an interval. **13** *Phonetics.* **a** (of the letter *a*) having the sound it has in *man,* as contrasted with the *a* in *father.* **b** (of consonants) voiced. **14** *Grammar.* not distinguished by a characteristic ending, as an adverb which has the same form as an adjective or noun, or a noun used as an adjective: *"Fast," "slow," "cheap," "dear" are flat adverbs. Many nouns have given us flat adjectives.* **15** of a sail: **a** trimmed very nearly fore and aft, as for sailing into the wind. **b** not receiving the wind. **c** taut. **16** (of loans or other financial arrangements) without interest. **17** *British.* producing no electric current; dead: *The battery was flat, so I had to push [the car] from the back* (Punch).
—*n.* **1** something flat. **2** a flat surface: *with the flat of the sword. The palm of an open hand is the flat.* **3** *Informal.* a tire with little air in it: *On examining the flat, Riar discovered a slash in the tread* (Atlantic). **4a** land that is smooth and level; plain. **b** land covered with shallow water; marsh; swamp: *The naked shore, Wide flats, where nothing but coarse grasses grew* (Tennyson). **c** a nearly level tidal area; shallow; shoal. **5** *Music.*

a a tone or note that is one half step or half note below natural pitch: *music written in B flat.* **b** the sign that shows such a tone or note. **6** a shallow box or basket in which seeds are planted for growing under shelter until large enough to be set out in the garden. **7** a piece of theatrical scenery, usually consisting of canvas mounted on a wooden frame. **8** = flatcar. **9** = flatboat. **10** a stupid person; simpleton: *You wouldn't be such a flat as to let three thousand a year go out of the family?* (Thackeray). **11** *Horse Racing.* **a** a race on a flat course in contrast to a steeplechase or other jumping race: *Pari-mutuel betting at the flats is taxed 11 per cent by the state* (New York Times). **b** flat racing, on a track without jumps or obstacles.
—adv. **1** in or into a flat position; horizontally: *He fell flat on the floor.* **2** *Music.* below the true pitch: *He was singing very flat.* **3** *Figurative.* in a flat manner; positively; absolutely: *flat broke.* **4** *Figurative.* directly; exactly: *His time for the race was two minutes flat. He contradicted his father flat.* **5** *Finance.* without interest.
—v.t. **1** to make flat; flatten: *Suppose that the earth was flatted near the poles* (Thomas G. Fessenden). **2** *Music.* to lower (a note), especially by one half step. **3** to draw in (a sail) nearly to the line of the keel.
—v.i. **1** to become gradually flat or level: *The bank flatted off for the last ten miles* (Thoreau). **2** *Music.* to sound below the true pitch. **3a** to sink down; subside (out): *The great surge of numbers rolls up noisily and imposingly, but flats out on the shore* (Edward Bushnell). **b** to prove a failure; collapse.
fall flat, to fail completely; have no effect or interest: *His attempts at clowning fell flat.*
flat out, at maximum speed or effort: *Then in 1954 came the decision that Britain must go flat out in the making of the hydrogen bomb* (New Scientist).
flats, a pair of women's shoes without built-up heels.
that's flat, I mean it: *I'll not march through Coventry with them, that's flat* (Shakespeare).
[< Scandinavian (compare Old Icelandic *flatr*)]
—**flat'ly,** *adv.* —**flat'ness,** *n.*

***flat[1]**
n., definition 5b

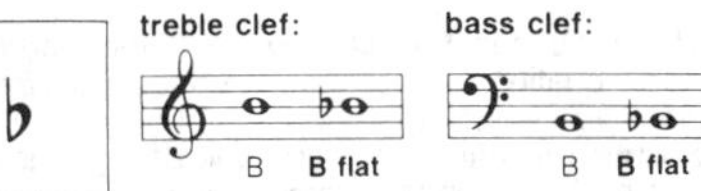

flat[2] (flat), *n.* an apartment or set of rooms on one floor. [alteration of Old English *flet, flett*]
▶In present American use, **flat** survives chiefly in "cold-water flat," a set of rooms not furnished with heat or hot water, in a residential building of a poorer sort, such as one in a city slum. In England the word has not acquired this sense and may be applied to a luxurious apartment.

flat back, **1** a book whose back is flat when it is closed. **2** the flat binding of such a book.

flat-bed (flat'bed'), *adj.* (of a truck or wagon) having a strong, low body without back or sides.

flat-bed cylinder press, a printing press in which the paper is pressed between a revolving cylinder and a reciprocating flat surface holding the type or printing plates.

***flat|boat** (flat'bōt'), *n., v.* *—n.* a large boat with a flat bottom and squared off at both ends, formerly much used for carrying goods on a river or canal: *Down the Ohio drifted the flatboats and rafts* (Atlantic).
—v.t. to transport in a flatboat: *The supplies are flatboated through the canal.*

***flatboat**

flat|boat|man (flat'bōt'mən), *n., pl.* **-men.** a person who works on a flatboat.

flat-bot|tomed (flat'bot'əmd), *adj.* having a flat bottom: *Flat-bottomed ... boats carry 24 cars and have a top deck for pedestrians* (Sunset).

flat bread, a hard, dry, unleavened Norwegian bread baked on top of a stove and resembling hardtack.

flat|cap (flat'kap'), *n.* **1** a round cap with a low, flat crown, worn in the 1500's and 1600's by Londoners. **2** a person wearing such a cap; a London citizen.

flat|car (flat'kär'), *n. U.S.* a railroad freight car without a roof or sides; platform car.

flat-coat|ed retriever (flat'kō'tid), any of a breed of hunting dogs most common in Great Britain, having a dense, usually solid, black or reddish-brown coat and weighing 60 to 70 pounds.

flat|ette (flə tet'), *n.* a small apartment in Australia and New Zealand; flatlet.

flat fell seam, a seam made by stitching once, trimming one edge of the seam close to the stitching, and turning the other edge over this and stitching it flat, used on pajamas, shirts, and the like; fell.

flat|fish (flat'fish'), *n., pl.* **-fish|es** or (*collectively*) **-fish.** any one of a group of fishes that live in the sea and are much used for food; fluke. Flatfish have a flat body, and swim on one side. Their eyes are on the same side of the head. Halibut, flounder, sole, and turbot are flatfishes.

flat|foot (flat'fu̇t'), *n., pl.* **-feet** (for defs. 1 and 2), **-foots** (for def. 3). **1** a foot with a flattened arch so that the entire sole touches the ground. **2** a condition in which the feet have flattened arches. **3** *U.S. Slang.* a policeman.

flat-foot|ed (flat'fu̇t'id), *adj., adv.* *—adj.* **1** having feet with flattened arches. **2** *Informal, Figurative.* not to be changed or influenced; firm; uncompromising: *He gave me a flat-footed refusal.*
—adv. Informal. plainly, openly, or directly and often with no stated reason or no preparation: *to come out flat-footed for a new constitution.*
catch one flat-footed, to catch one unprepared; take one by surprise: *They had worked out a bold tactical move that caught us flat-footed* (Saturday Review).
—**flat'-foot'ed|ly,** *adv.* —**flat'-foot'ed|ness,** *n.*

flat glass, glass that is drawn out or rolled into flat sheets, such as sheet glass and plate glass.

flat-grain (flat'grān'), *adj.* (of lumber) sawed at less than right angles to the annual rings.

flat-hat (flat'hat'), *v.i.,* **-hat|ted, -hat|ting.** *U.S. Slang.* to fly needlessly or dangerously low: *[He] was flat-hatting along Highway 1, only 100 ft. off the [surface], at 500 m.p.h.* (Time). —**flat'-hat'ter,** *n.*

Flat|head (flat'hed'), *n.* **1** a member of a tribe of North American Indians of Salishan speech in western Montana. **2** a Chinook Indian. [American English < a mistaken idea that the tribe had the practice of flattening the heads of their children]

flathead adder, = hognose snake.

flat-head|ed (flat'hed'id), *adj.* having a flat head or top.

-flation, *combining form.* inflation: *slumpflation, hesiflation, stagflation. Armstrong said that when inflation hits the tax system—taxflation, he calls it—it penalizes the poor* (Memphis Press-Scimitar). *Oilflation breeds huge trade and balance-of-payments deficits* (New York Times).

flat|i|ron (flat'ī'ərn), *n.* **1** an iron with a flat bottom surface, which is heated and used for smoothing wrinkles out of cloth; iron. **2** *Geology.* a ridge of rocks with a ragged and angular crest caused by erosion removing the softer rocks above the harder ones.

flat knot, = square knot.

flat|land (flat'land'), *n.* level land, not broken by hills and valleys.

flat|land|er (flat'lan'dər), *n.* an inhabitant of a flatland.

flat|let (flat'lit), *n. British.* a small apartment.

flat|ling (flat'ling), *adv., adj.* *—adv. Archaic.* **1** with the flat or broad side, especially of a sword. **2** in a prostrate position; at full length; flat.
—adj. Obsolete. (of a blow) dealt with the flat side of a weapon. [< *flat*[1], adjective + Old English *-ling,* an adverbial suffix]

flat|lings (flat'lingz), *adv. Archaic.* flatling: *The blade struck me flatlings* (Scott).

flat|man (flat'mən), *n., pl.* **-men.** a person who works on a flatboat; flatboatman.

flat|mate (flat'māt'), *n. British.* a person who shares a flat or apartment with another or others.

flat-out (flat'out'), *adj.* **1** absolute; outright: ... *half-truths, which were worse than direct, flat-out lies* (London Times). **2** at maximum speed or effort: *Meanwhile the war brought flat-out work on production* (New Scientist)

flat pad, a stable platform for launching a missile in contrast to a launch pad on a ship, affected by the motion of the ship.

flat-plate collector (flat'plāt'), a device for using the sun's rays principally for heating and generating low-pressure steam. It consists of a metal plate covered by glass or plastic, with tubes in the back through which water or some other fluid circulates.

flat race, a race, especially a horse race, on a track without jumps or obstacles, in contrast to a steeplechase.

flat racing, racing, especially horse racing, on a track without jumps or obstacles.

flat-rolled (flat'rōld'), *adj.* rolled between cylinders so as to be flat in form: *flat-rolled steel.*

flats (flats), *n.pl.* See under **flat**[1].

flat silver, silver knives, forks, and spoons.

flat|ten (flat'ən), *v.t., v.i.* **1** to make flat or become flat: *Use a rolling pin to flatten the pie dough. Michelangelo's nose was flattened by a blow from a jealous artist.* **2** (of a wind) to die out; drop off.
flatten out, a to spread out flat: *Wrinkled silk will flatten out again if you iron it.* **b** *Aeronautics.* to return to a level position from a dive or climb; level off. —**flat'ten|er,** *n.*

flat|ter[1] (flat'ər), *v.t.* **1** to praise too much or beyond the truth; praise insincerely: *He was only flattering her when he said that she sang well; he didn't really mean it.* **2** to show as more beautiful or better looking than what is true; exaggerate the good points of: *This picture flatters her.* **3** to try to win over or please by words or actions; fawn upon: *He flattered her with flowers and expensive gifts.* SYN: cajole, blandish, court. **4** to cause to be pleased or feel honored: *You flatter me with your concern for my welfare.* **5** *Archaic.* to beguile; charm away: *Music's golden tongue Flatter'd to tears this aged man* (Keats). *—v.i.* to use flattery.
flatter oneself, a to be pleased to know or think: *[The] people ... flatter themselves that things are not so bad as they really are* (Joseph Addison). **b** to overestimate oneself: *He flattereth himself in his own eyes* (Psalms 36:2).
[Middle English *flateren* to float, fawn upon; influenced by Old French *flaterie,* or *flatir* caress with the flat of the hand. See related etym. at **flutter.**] —**flat'ter|er,** *n.*

flat|ter[2] (flat'ər), *n.* **1** a person or thing that makes something flat. **2** a tool used in making things flat, especially a hammer used by smiths. **3** a drawplate with a flat hole through which flat metal strips, such as watch springs, may be drawn.

flat|ter|a|ble (flat'ər ə bəl), *adj.* that can be flattered.

flat|ter|ing|ly (flat'ər ing lē), *adv.* in a flattering manner; in a manner to gratify or soothe.

flat|ter|y (flat'ər ē), *n., pl.* **-ter|ies. 1** the act of flattering: *Be sure the salve of flattery soaps all you do or say* (Eugene Field). **2** words of praise, usually untrue or exaggerated: *Some people use flattery to get favors. Can ... flatt'ry soothe the dull cold ear of death?* (Thomas Gray). SYN: adulation, blandishment. [< Old French *flaterie* < *flatir* stroke (with the flat of the hand) < unrecorded Frankish *flat* a caress]

flat|tie (flat'ē), *n.* **1** *Informal.* a flat-soled shoe; one of a pair of flats. **2** *Informal.* = flatfish. **3** *U.S. Slang.* a two-dimensional motion picture. **4** *Slang.* a policeman; flatfoot (def. 3).

flat|ting (flat'ing), *n.* **1** the act or process of laying, beating, or pressing out flat. **2** the process of covering a surface with paint which has no gloss or luster. **3a** a method of preserving unburnished gilding, by touching it with size. **b** the coating of size laid over the gilding. **4** the process of rolling metal into sheets. **5** *Music.* the act of depressing a tone below a true or given pitch.

flat|tish (flat'ish), *adj.* somewhat flat.

flat|top (flat'top'), *n. Informal.* **1** an aircraft carrier. **2** a haircut similar to a crew cut but completely flat across the top.

flat|u|lence (flach'ə ləns), *n.* **1** excessive gas in the stomach or intestines. **2** *Figurative.* pompous speech or behavior; vanity; emptiness.

flat|u|len|cy (flach'ə lən sē), *n.* = flatulence.

flat|u|lent (flach'ə lənt), *adj.* **1** having excessive gas in the stomach or intestines. **2** causing gas in the stomach or intestines, as certain foods may. **3** *Figurative.* pompous in speech or behavior; vain; empty. [< French *flatulent* < Latin *flātus, -ūs* a blowing < *flāre* to blow] —**flat'u|lent|ly,** *adv.*

fla|tus (flā'təs), *n., pl.* **-tus|es. 1** gas accumulated in the stomach, intestines, or other cavity of the body. **2** a puff of wind. [< Latin *flātus, -ūs;* see etym. under **flatulent**]

flat|ware (flat'wãr'), *n.* **1** knives, forks, and spoons, especially of silver or silver plate. SYN: cutlery. **2** plates, platters, saucers, and other flat or nearly flat dishes.

flat water, a lake or similar body of water without turbulence or much current:

flat|ways (flat'wāz'), *adv.* with the flat side forward, upward, or touching another surface: *A drawer is replaced flatways.*

flat|wise (flat'wīz'), *adv.* = flatways.

flat|woods (flat'wu̇dz'), *n. pl. U.S.* a level, low-

Pronunciation Key: hat, āge, cãre, fär; let, ēqual, tėrm; it, īce; hot, ōpen, ôrder; oil, out; cup, pu̇t, rüle; child; long; thin; ᴛʜen; zh, measure; ə represents **a** in about, **e** in taken, **i** in pencil, **o** in lemon, **u** in circus.

lying timberland, usually having poor natural drainage.

flat|work (flat′wėrk′), *n.* household linens, such as sheets and napkins, that do not require hand ironing but can be ironed on a mangle.

***flat|worm** (flat′wėrm′), *n.* any one of a group of worms with thin flat bodies, that live in water or as parasites in or on some animals; platyhelminth. Tapeworms and planarians are flatworms.

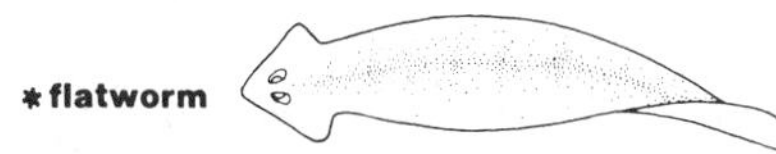
***flatworm**

Flau|ber|ti|an (flō ber′tē ən), *adj.* of or characteristic of Gustave Flaubert, his novels, or his style of writing: *the stark Flaubertian dogma that the writer must not voice opinions about his characters and story* (New York Times).

flaunt (flônt, flänt), *v., n.* **—*v.t.*** to show off; try to impress others with; display ostentatiously or obtrusively: *She flaunts her riches before her friends.* **SYN:** flourish, obtrude.
—*v.i.* **1** to parade oneself boastfully, impudently, or defiantly on the public view. **2a** to wave proudly or gaily: *Flags and pennants flaunted from the masts of the ships.* **b** (of plants) to wave so as to display their beauty.
—*n.* **1** the act of flaunting. **2** *Obsolete.* showy dress; finery.
[origin uncertain. Compare Norman French *flâneur* idler.] **—flaunt′er,** *n.* **—flaunt′ing|ly,** *adv.*
▶Because of partial similarity of sound, **flaunt** and **flout** are sometimes confused. *Flaunt* means to display boldly and brazenly, regardless of what people may think: *to flaunt one's vices, to flaunt one's wealth. Flout* means to mock or treat with contempt: *to flout school rules.* Confusion arises because one may *flaunt* one thing in order to *flout* another: *She flouted the custom of wearing simple dresses to the office by flaunting her red satin cocktail dress.*

flaunt|y (flôn′tē, flän′-), *adj.* flaunting; showy. **—flaunt′i|ly,** *adv.* **—flaunt′i|ness,** *n.*

flau|tan|do (flou tän′dō), *adj. Music.* like a flute; flautato. [< Italian *flautando,* present participle of *flautare* to play the flute < *flauto* flute]

flau|ta|to (flou tä′tō), *adj. Music.* like a flute (used as a direction). [< Italian *flautato,* past participle of *flautare;* see etym. under **flautando**]

flau|ti|no (flou tē′nō), *n., pl.* **-nos.** *Italian.* **1** a small flute; piccolo. **2** a small accordion. [< Italian *flautino* (diminutive) < *flauto* flute]

flau|tist (flô′tist), *n.* = flutist. [< Italian *flautista* < *flauto* flute]

fla|va|none (flā′və nōn), *n.* a colorless derivative of flavone, found in various plants. *Formula:* $C_{15}H_{12}O_2$

fla|ve|do (flə vē′dō), *n., pl.* **-dos.** the outer rind of a citrus fruit, made up of small glands that contain an essential oil. [< New Latin *flavedo* < Latin *flāvus* yellow]

fla|ves|cent (flə ves′ənt), *adj.* turning a pale yellow; yellowish. [< Latin *flāvēscēns, -entis,* present participle of *flāvēscere* become yellow < *flāvēre* be yellow < *flāvus* yellow]

Fla|vi|an (flā′vē ən), *adj., n.* **—*adj.*** having to do with members of the Flavius gens or clan of ancient Rome, especially the three Roman emperors, Vespasian and his sons Titus and Domitian.
—*n.* any one of the Flavian emperors.

fla|vin (flā′vin), *n.* **1** any of the flavoproteins. **2** a heterocyclic ketone occurring in the flavoproteins. *Formula:* $C_{10}H_6N_4O_2$ **3** = riboflavin. **4** a yellow dyestuff obtained from quercitron bark; quercetin. [< Latin *flāvus* yellow + English *-in*]

flavin adenine dinucleotide, a compound of adenosine diphosphate and flavin mononucleotide that constitutes the nonprotein part, or coenzyme, of various flavoproteins. *Formula:* $C_{27}H_{33}N_9O_{15}P_2$ *Abbr:* FAD (no periods).

fla|vine (flā′vēn), *n.* **1** = acriflavine. **2** = flavin.

flavin mononucleotide, a phosphoric ester of riboflavin that constitutes the nonprotein part, or coenzyme, of various flavoproteins. *Formula:* $C_{17}H_{21}N_4O_9P$ *Abbr:* FMN (no periods).

fla|vo|bac|te|ri|um (flā′vō bak tir′ē əm), *n., pl.* **-te|ri|a** (-tir′ē ə). any of a group of rod-shaped bacteria that form yellow pigments, found in water and soil. [< New Latin *Flavobacterium* the genus name < Latin *flāvus* yellow + English *bacterium*]

fla|von (flā′von), *n. Nuclear Physics.* a hypothetical constituent of quarks that determines electric charge: *If there are only two flavons and if they are the sole carriers of electric charge, not all of the charge values observed in nature can be reproduced* (Scientific American). [< *flav*(or), def. 5 + *-on*]

fla|vone (flā′vōn), *n.* **1** a colorless, crystalline compound found in various plants and also produced synthetically. It is used as the basis of several yellow dyes. *Nectar . . . draws ethereal oils and flavones from the flower to obtain its characteristic taste, perfume and colour* (New Scientist). *Formula:* $C_{15}H_{10}O_2$ **2** any derivative of this substance. [< Latin *flāvus* yellow]

fla|vo|noid (flā′və noid), *n.* any one of a group of natural organic compounds found chiefly as coloring matter in fruits and flowers.

fla|vo|nol (flā′və nol, -nōl), *n.* any one of various plant pigments or dyes derived from flavone.

fla|vo|pro|te|in (flā′vō prō′tēn, -tē ən), *n.* any of a group of yellow respiratory enzymes containing riboflavin. The flavoproteins are conjugated proteins of a special type called chromoproteins. [< Latin *flāvus* yellow + English *protein*]

fla|vo|pur|pu|rin (flā′vō pėr′pyər in), *n.* a yellow, crystalline substance obtained from commercial alizarin, and used in dyeing. *Formula:* $C_{14}H_8O_5$ [< Latin *flāvus* yellow + English *purpurin*]

fla|vor (flā′vər), *n., v.* **—*n.*** **1** a taste, especially a characteristic taste: *Chocolate and vanilla have different flavors.* **SYN:** savor, smack, tang. See syn. under **taste.** **2** a thing used to give a certain taste to food or drink; flavoring. **3** *Figurative.* a special quality: *Stories about ships and sailors have a flavor of the sea. Variety's the very spice of life, That gives it all its flavor* (William Cowper). **4** a smell; aroma; odor: *the flavor of onions. A general flavor of mild decay* (Oliver Wendell Holmes). **5** *Nuclear Physics.* a hypothetical property, such as strangeness, that distinguishes one subatomic particle from another: *The different kinds of quarks or leptons are known technically as flavors* (Robert H. March).
—*v.t.* **1** to give an added taste to; season: *We use salt, pepper, and spices to flavor food. The onion flavors the whole stew.* **2** *Figurative.* to give an exciting quality to: *Many exciting adventures flavor an explorer's life.*
[alteration of Old French *flaur,* perhaps ultimately < Latin *fragrāre* emit odor] **—fla′vor|er,** *n.* **—fla′vor|less,** *adj.*

fla|vor|ful (flā′vər fəl), *adj.* having flavor and interest; tasty: (*Figurative.*) *She had tasted the simple life and found it flavorful* (New Yorker). **—fla′vor|ful|ly,** *adv.*

fla|vor|ing (flā′vər ing), *n.* something used to give a certain taste to food or drink: *vanilla flavoring, chocolate flavoring.*

fla|vor|ous (flā′vər əs), *adj.* full of flavor; pleasant to the smell or taste.

fla|vor|some (flā′vər səm), *adj.* full of flavor; flavorful.

fla|vor|y (flā′vər ē), *adj.,* **-vor|i|er, -vor|i|est.** = flavorsome.

fla|vour (flā′vər), *n., v.t. Especially British.* flavor. **—fla′vour|er,** *n.*

flaw[1] (flô), *n., v.* **—*n.*** **1** a defective place; crack: *A flaw in the dish caused it to break.* **SYN:** chink, rent, breach. **2** a fault; defect; blemish: *His nasty temper is a flaw in his character.* **SYN:** imperfection. See syn. under **defect.** **3** a defect in a legal document, procedure, or the like, that makes it invalid.
—*v.t., v.i.* to make or become defective; crack: *The wood flaws and splinters easily. The pottery jug flawed when it was fired. She avoided flawing the role with more than the necessary touches of sentimentality and melodrama* (Time).
[Middle English *flawe* a flake, fragment < Scandinavian (compare Swedish *flaga* flake, flaw)]

flaw[2] (flô), *n.* **1** a gust of wind; sudden squall: *The hulk flew . . . before rapidly succeeding flaws of wind* (Edgar Allan Poe). **2** a short period of rough weather. **3** *Obsolete.* a sudden uproar or tumult. [perhaps unrecorded Old English *flagu*]

flawed (flôd), *adj.* having flaws; imperfect: *The cut in the diamond showed that it was flawed. Man is a flawed creature* (Eric Larrabee).

flaw|less (flô′lis), *adj.* without a flaw; perfect: *a flawless diamond, flawless reasoning.* **SYN:** faultless, unblemished. **—flaw′less|ly,** *adv.* **—flaw′less|ness,** *n.*

flaw|y[1] (flô′ē), *adj.* having flaws or cracks; broken; defective; faulty. [< *flaw*[1] + *-y*[1]]

flaw|y[2] (flô′ē), *adj.* coming in gusts, as wind. [< *flaw*[2] + *-y*[1]]

flax (flaks), *n., v.* **—*n.*** **1** a slender, upright plant from whose stems linen is made. Flax has small, narrow leaves, blue flowers, and slender stems about two feet tall. Linseed oil is made from its seeds. **2** the threadlike parts into which the stems of this plant separate. Flax is spun into linen thread and made into linen cloth. **3** any of certain plants resembling flax.
—*v.t.* *U.S. Informal.* to beat; thrash.
—*v.i.* *U.S. Informal.* to bustle about; be busy.
[Old English *fleax*]

flax bellflower, = harebell.

flax|bush (flaks′bůsh′), *n.* a New Zealand plant of the agave family, with erect, sword-shaped leaves that yield a strong fiber.

flax comb, an instrument for cleansing and straightening flax fibers; hatchel.

flax dodder, a dodder injurious to flax.

flax drop, = flax dodder.

flax|en (flak′sən), *adj.* **1** made of flax: *flaxen thread.* **2** like the color of flax; pale-yellow: *Flaxen hair is very light.* **3** of or having to do with flax as a commercial product.

flax plant, **1** = flax. **2** = flaxbush.

flax|seed (flaks′sēd′), *n.* the seed of flax; linseed, used to make linseed oil and in medicine.

flax|tail (flaks′tāl′), *n.* = cattail.

flax|weed (flaks′wēd′), *n.* = toadflax.

flax|y (flak′sē), *adj.* = flaxen.

flay (flā), *v.t.* **1** to strip off the skin or outer covering of; skin: *Whole deer were often brought in to be . . . flayed* (George James). **2** *Figurative.* to scold severely; criticize without pity or mercy. **3** to rob; cheat. **4** *Rare.* to inflict acute pain or torture upon. [Old English *flēan*] **—flay′er,** *n.*

F layer, the two layers of the ionosphere above, or outside, the E layer, which reflect high-frequency radio waves; Appleton layer; F region. The altitude of the F layer varies according to the time of day and time of year and other factors such as hydrogen flares from the sun.

fld., **1** field. **2** (of plants) flowered.

fl. dr., fluid dram.

***flea** (flē), *n.* **1** a small, jumping insect without wings. Fleas live in the fur of dogs, cats, and monkeys or under the clothing of human beings and feed on their blood. **2** any one of various small beetles or crustaceans that jump like a flea, such as the beach flea.
flea in one's ear, **a** a severe scolding; sharp hint; rebuff: *We, being stronger than they, sent them away with a flea in their ear* (John Arbuthnot). **b** secret information intended to cause action: *I was hurrying out with a "flea in my ear," as the saying is* (Samuel Richardson).
[Old English *flēa,* or *flēah*]

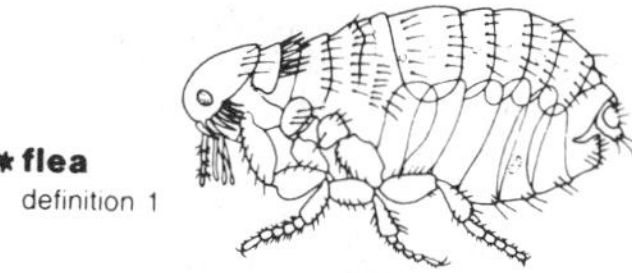
***flea**
definition 1

flea|bag (flē′bag′), *n. U.S. Slang.* a very cheap and low-quality hotel or rooming house: *a Times Square fleabag* (Harper's).

flea|bane (flē′bān′), *n.* **1** any one of a genus of plants of the composite family, supposed to drive away or destroy fleas. **2** = erigeron (def. 2).

flea beetle, any one of various small, jumping leaf beetles which damage certain plants.

flea|bite (flē′bīt′), *n.* **1** the bite of a flea. **2** the red spot caused by it. **3** a mark resembling that caused by the bite of a flea. **4** *Figurative.* a hurt or loss of very small consequence or importance; mere trifle: *The proposed $500 million, claims one backer, would be "a fleabite when we consider all the needs"* (Wall Street Journal).

flea-bit|ten (flē′bit′ən), *adj.* **1** bitten by or infested with fleas. **2** having reddish-brown spots on a light-colored hide: *a flea-bitten horse.* **3** *Figurative.* shabby; miserable; squalid: *a flea-bitten kingdom in the Middle East* (Maclean's). *a flea-bitten acting school* (Time).

flea bug, *U.S.* a flea beetle.

flea circus, a show in which trained fleas perform various acts, such as racing against each other and pulling tiny wagons.

flea|dock (flē′dok′), *n.* = butterbur.

flea|hop|per (flē′hop′ər), *n.* a small jumping bug that is destructive to garden and cotton plants.

flea market, *Informal.* a market, often a street market, dealing in all sorts of cheap antiques, junk, and odd items: *Any guidebook will tell you how to find the antique shops and flea markets* (Harper's). [supposedly because of the fleas found in second-hand articles; apparently translation of French *marché aux puces*]

flea|mint (flē′mənt), *n.* = pennyroyal.

flea|pit (flē′pit′), *n. British Slang.* a motion-picture theater; cinema.

flea|wort (flē′wėrt′), *n.* **1** any one of various plants thought to destroy fleas, especially a European composite herb having rough leaves and yellow flowers. **2** a plantain of southern Europe, used medicinally as a laxative; psyllium.

flea|y (flē′ē), *adj.* full of fleas: *a fleay kennel.*

flèche (flāsh; *French* flesh), *n.* **1** *Architecture.* **a** a spire, especially a slender spire surmounting a roof. **b** a slender spire placed over the junction of the nave and transept of a church or cathedral: *Ideally, the narthex should be surmounted by a flèche* (London Times). **2** (in a fortification) an arrow; a defensive work shaped somewhat like an arrowhead. [< French *flèche* arrow < Old French *fleche;* origin uncertain]

flé|chette (flā shet′), *n.* a steel dart thrown from an airplane during World War I as a weapon against troops. [< French *fléchette* (diminutive) < *flèche* arrow: see etym. under **flèche**]

fleck (flek), *n., v.* —*n.* **1** a spot or patch of color, light, or the like: *Freckles are brown flecks on the skin.* **SYN:** speckle. **2** a small particle; flake; speck: *a fleck of dust.*
—*v.t.* to mark with spots of color, light, or the like; speckle: *The bird's breast is flecked with brown. Sunlight coming through the branches flecked the shadow cast by the tree.* **SYN:** dapple, spot.
[perhaps < Scandinavian (compare Old Icelandic *flekkr*)]

flecked (flekt), *adj.* sprinkled with spots or patches of color, light, or the like; speckled: *When a banana ripens it is flecked with brown.*

fleck|less (flek′lis), *adj.* = spotless.

fleck|y (flek′ē), *adj.,* **fleck|i|er, fleck|i|est.** full of flecks; spotted; streaked. —**fleck′i|ness,** *n.*

flec|tion (flek′shən), *n.* **1** a bending: *the flection of a reed in the wind. Every flection of his arm caused the muscles to bulge.* **2** a bent part; bend. **3** *Physiology.* = flexion. **4** *Grammar.* = inflection. [spelling alteration of *flexion* < Latin *flexiō, -ōnis* < *flectere* to bend] —**flec′tion|less,** *adj.*

flec|tion|al (flek′shə nəl), *adj.* of or having to do with flection.

fled (fled), *v.* past tense and past participle of **flee**: *The enemy fled when we attacked. The clouds fled before the wind. The chicken has fled the coop.*

fledge (flej), *v.,* **fledged, fledg|ing,** *adj.* —*v.i.* (of a young bird) to grow the feathers needed for flying; become fully plumed.
—*v.t.* **1** to provide or cover with feathers; fletch: *The Indian fledged his arrows with eagles' feathers.* **2** to bring up (a young bird) until it is able to fly.
—*adj. Obsolete or Dialect.* (of young birds) ready to fly; fledged.
[unrecorded Old English *flicge.* Compare Old English *unfligge* unfledged, unfit to fly, related to *flēogan* to fly.]

fledge|less (flej′lis), *adj.* unfledged, especially undeveloped or immature.

fledg|ling or **fledge|ling** (flej′ling), *n., adj.* —*n.* **1** a young bird just able to fly. **2** *Figurative.* a young, inexperienced person.
—*adj.* just beginning; inexperienced or new: *The fledgling producers could hardly be regarded as nonentities any longer* (New Yorker).

fledg|y (flej′ē), *adj.* feathered.

flee (flē), *v.,* **fled, flee|ing.** —*v.i.* **1** to run away; try to get away by running: *The robbers tried to flee but they were caught. He fled to the seashore to escape the heat.* **SYN:** decamp, fly. **2** to withdraw or go hastily (to or into) for refuge or protection: *To whom will ye flee for help?* (Isaiah 10:3). **3** to go quickly; move swiftly: *The clouds are fleeing before the wind.* **4** to pass away quickly and suddenly; cease to be; disappear; vanish: *The shadows flee as day breaks.*
—*v.t.* **1** to run away from; try to get away from by running: *He fled the burning house. He fled the town. I fled Him, down the nights and down the days* (Francis Thompson). **2** to avoid by flight; shun.
[Old English *flēon*] —**fle′er,** *n.*

fleece (flēs), *v.,* **fleeced, fleec|ing,** *n.* —*v.t.* **1** to strip of money or belongings; rob or cheat: *The gamblers fleeced him of all his money.* **SYN:** plunder, victimize. **2** to cut the fleece from. **3** to dapple or fleck with fleecelike masses: *stones ... fleeced with moss* (Wordsworth).
—*n.* **1** the wool that covers the skin of a sheep or similar animal: *Spring clipping of sheep cleans the animals of their long fleece worn through the winter.* **2** the amount of wool cut off or shorn from a sheep at one time. **3** *Figurative.* something like a fleece: *a fleece of hair, the fleece of new-fallen snow.* **4a** a fabric with a soft, silky pile, used for lining outer garments. **b** the pile of such a fabric.
[Old English *flēos*] —**fleece′a|ble,** *adj.* —**fleece′like,** *adj.* —**fleec′er,** *n.*

fleece-lined (flēs′līnd′), *adj.* lined with cloth having a soft, silky pile.

fleech (flēch), *Scottish.* —*v.t.* to cajole; wheedle; beseech.
—*v.i.* to speak in a cajoling or beseeching manner. [origin uncertain]

fleec|y (flē′sē), *adj.,* **fleec|i|er, fleec|i|est.** **1** like fleece; soft and white: *Fleecy clouds floated in the blue sky.* **2** covered with fleece or wool. **3** made of fleece; woolly: *The change to long, fleecy underwear was a wise precaution against winter ills* (Time). —**fleec′i|ly,** *adv.* —**fleec′i|ness,** *n.*

fleer (flir), *v., n.* —*v.i.* **1** to laugh or smile mockingly; jeer: *They're actually sneering at us, fleering at us, jeering at us!* (Gilbert and Sullivan). **2** to laugh in a coarse, impudent, or unbecoming manner. —*v.t.* to laugh mockingly at; ridicule.
—*n.* a mocking look or speech; sneer; jibe.
[Middle English *fleryen, fliren.* Compare Norwegian *flira* grin.] —**fleer′er,** *n.* —**fleer′ing|ly,** *adv.*

fleet¹ (flēt), *n.* **1a** a group of warships, naval aircraft, personnel, and bases under one command: *The sixth fleet is based in San Francisco.* **b** a group of warships engaged in a single mission. **c** the entire navy of a nation or allied nations: *the United States fleet.* **2** any group of ships or boats sailing together: *a fleet of fishing boats. I must go Where the fleet of stars is anchored* (James Elroy Flecker). **SYN:** flotilla. **3** a group of airplanes, automobiles, or the like, moving or working together: *Each large Post Office has a fleet of trucks to help carry the mail.* [Old English *flēot* ship, vessel < *flēotan* to float. Compare etym. under **fleet³**.]

fleet² (flēt), *adj., v.* —*adj.* **1** swiftly moving; rapid: *a fleet horse. The fairest things have fleetest end* (Francis Thompson). **2** not lasting; evanescent. **3** *Dialect.* having little depth; shallow.
—*v.i.* **1** to pass swiftly; move rapidly. **2** (of a crew or vessel) to alter in station or position; move; shift. **3a** (of a vessel) to sail. **b** *Obsolete.* to float. **c** *Obsolete.* to swim. **4** *Obsolete.* to drift. **5** *Obsolete.* **a** to dissolve or waste away; fall to pieces. **b** (of immaterial things) to fade away; vanish. —*v.t.* **1** *Rare.* to pass or while away (time). **2** to alter the station or position of (a crew or vessel); move; shift.
[probably < Scandinavian (compare Old Icelandic *fliōtr* swift)] —**fleet′ly,** *adv.* —**fleet′ness,** *n.*

fleet³ (flēt), *n. Obsolete or Dialect.* **1** an inlet, especially an inlet from the sea; a tidal creek (surviving chiefly as an element in place names). **2** a drain; sewer. [Old English *flēot* estuary, bay; water < *flēotan* to float, flow]

fleet admiral, **1** the naval officer of the highest rank in the United States Navy, entitled to an insigne or flag bearing five stars. **2** *British.* = Admiral of the Fleet.

fleet-foot|ed (flēt′fu̇t′id), *adj.* running or able to run rapidly: *Fleet-footed outfielder Bruton ranges centerfield like a hawk* (Time).

fleet|ful (flēt′fu̇l), *n., pl.* **-fuls.** **1** as many as would make a fleet: *a fleetful of ships.* **2** any large number: *The fleetfuls of foreign students who came to attend surprisingly advanced teaching ...* (Stephen L. Gwynn).

fleet|ing (flē′ting), *adj.* passing swiftly; moving rapidly; soon gone: *a fleeting smile, the fleeting beauty of youth. Art is long and Time is fleeting* (Longfellow). **SYN:** transitory, momentary, temporary. —**fleet′ing|ly,** *adv.* —**fleet′ing|ness,** *n.*

Fleet Street, **1** a very old street in London, now a center for many newspaper offices. **2** *British.* newspapers generally; the press.

Fleet Street|er (strē′tər), a London newspaperman or journalist.

fleet train, the service or auxiliary ships that support the fighting ships of a country's navy.

flei|shig (flā′shik), *adj.* (in Jewish dietary law) restricted to meat or meat products: *a fleishig meal, fleishig dishes.* [< Yiddish *fleishig* (literally) meaty]

Flem., Flemish.

Flem|ing (flem′ing), *n.* **1** a person born or living in Flanders. **2** a Belgian whose native language is Flemish.

Fleming valve, *Electronics.* an early form of diode used to detect wireless telegraph messages: *This so-called Fleming valve later became an amplifier by the addition of Lee De Forest's grid* (H. H. Skilling). [< Sir John Ambrose *Fleming,* 1849-1945, an English electrical engineer]

flem|ish (flem′ish), *v.t. Nautical.* to coil (a rope) in a Flemish coil; flemish-coil.

Flem|ish (flem′ish), *adj., n.* —*adj.* of or having to do with Flanders, its people, or their language.
—*n.* **1** the people of Flanders. **2** their language, formerly one of the official languages of Belgium. Flemish is a form of Low German closely related to Dutch.

***Flemish bond**

***Flemish bond,** a bond in bricklaying, in which each course consists of alternate headers and stretchers, with the headers centered on the stretchers of the courses above and below.

Flemish coil, *Nautical.* a coil of rope in which each turn is laid down flat on the deck, forming a sort of mat.

flem|ish-coil (flem′ish koil′), *v.t.* to coil (a rope) in a Flemish coil.

Flemish Giant, any one of a breed of very large rabbits of Flemish origin, raised for meat and fur.

Flemish knot, a form of knot much used by sailors, shaped like the figure 8.

Flemish stitch, a stitch used for the filling in of some kinds of point lace.

flense (flens), *v.t.,* **flensed, flens|ing.** to strip blubber or skin from (a whale or seal). [probably < Dutch *flensen* cut a dead whale to pieces] —**flens′er,** *n.*

flesh (flesh), *n., v.* —*n.* **1** the soft substance of the body that covers the bones and is covered by skin. Flesh consists mostly of muscles and fat. **2** meat; the tissue or muscles of animals, regarded as an article of food. **3** fatness; plumpness: *He has lost flesh.* **4** the body, not the soul or spirit: *O! that this too too solid flesh would melt* (Shakespeare). **5** *Figurative.* the physical side of human nature, as distinguished from the spiritual or moral side: *The spirit indeed is willing, but the flesh is weak* (Matthew 26:41). **6** *Figurative.* the human race; mankind: *the thousand natural shocks that flesh is heir to* (Shakespeare). **7** *Figurative.* living creatures collectively: *All flesh must die.* **8** *Figurative.* family or relatives by birth: *He is our brother and our flesh* (Genesis 37:27). **9** the soft part of fruits or vegetables; the part of fruits that can be eaten: *The flesh of apples is white. The flesh of a pineapple has an exotic flavor.* **10** a pinkish-white color with a little yellow. **11** the surface of the body, especially with reference to color.
—*v.t.* **1** to feed (a hound or hawk) with flesh of the game killed, in order to excite his eagerness in the chase. **2** to excite (to passion, bloodshed, or other action) by a foretaste: *to flesh raw soldiers.* **3** to plunge (a weapon, etc.) into the flesh: *Impatient strait to flesh his virgin sword* (Alexander Pope). **4** to harden (in wrongdoing); inure. **5** to make fleshy; fatten. **6** to remove flesh or tissue from (hides) before making leather.
—*v.i. Informal.* to become fleshy.
flesh out, to give body or substance to; fill or round out; complete: *I found him dictating speeches for his staff to flesh out* (Harper's).
in the flesh, a living; alive: *We all know in the flesh liberal Catholics and latitudinarian Protestants* (John Morley). **b** really present, not merely thought of; in person: *St. Paul ... did speak there of seeing Christ in the flesh* (Daniel Defoe).
press the flesh, *Especially U.S. Informal.* to shake hands: [*He*] is a diffident public speaker who prefers to press the flesh with individual voters in a kind of Western one-on-one campaign (Time).
[Old English *flǣsc*] —**flesh′less,** *adj.*

flesh and blood, **1** the body; the material of which man's physical frame is composed. **2** *Figurative.* an individual man or men; mankind. **3** *Figurative.* human nature with its emotions and infirmities.
one's own flesh and blood, family or relatives by birth; a child or relative by birth: *Athanasius ... had not spared his own flesh and blood* (Henry Milman).

flesh-and-blood (flesh′ən blud′), *adj.* having actual human existence; real: *the lives of flesh-and-blood people* (New York Times).

flesh-col|ored (flesh′kul′ərd), *adj.* pinkish-white with a tinge of yellow; of the color of a white person's skin.

flesh crow, = carrion crow.

flesh-eat|er (flesh′ē′tər), *n.* = carnivore.

flesh-eat|ing (flesh′ē′ting), *adj.* = carnivorous.

-fleshed, *combining form.* having flesh: *Pink-fleshed = having pink flesh. Firm-fleshed = having firm flesh.*

flesh|er (flesh′ər), *n.* **1** a person who fleshes hides. **2** a knifelike tool used for fleshing. **3** *Scottish.* a butcher.

fle|shette (flə shet′), *n.* one of a spray of darts exploded as an antipersonnel weapon: *The canister round ... exploded on impact and distributed 9800 "fleshettes," which look like little roofing nails with barbs on the end* (Atlantic). [alteration (influenced by *flesh*) of *fléchette*]

flesh flea, = chigoe.

flesh fly, a fly whose larvae feed on decaying flesh, garbage, and other rot; blowfly.

flesh|hook (flesh′hu̇k′), *n.* **1** a hook for removing meat from a pot. **2** a hook to hang meat on.

Pronunciation Key: hat, āge, cãre, fär; let, ēqual, tėrm; it, īce; hot, ōpen, ôrder; **oi**l, **ou**t; cup, pu̇t, rüle; **ch**ild; lo**ng**; **th**in; ᴛʜen; **zh**, measure; ə represents **a** in about, **e** in taken, **i** in pencil, **o** in lemon, **u** in circus.

flesh|ing (flesh′ing), *n.* the distribution of the flesh on an animal: *It had good fleshing and was a good butcher's beast* (London Times). See also **fleshings**.

fleshing knife, a blunt-edged, convex knife with two handles, used in the making of leather to scrape the hair and loose flesh from the hides.

flesh|ings (flesh′ingz), *n.pl.* **1** flesh-colored tights. **2** flesh scraped from hides, used in making glue.

flesh|li|ness (flesh′lē nis), *n.* **1** the state of being fleshly. **2** *Figurative.* carnal appetites and passions.

flesh|ly (flesh′lē), *adj.*, **-li|er**, **-li|est**. **1** of the flesh; bodily; corporeal. **2** *Figurative.* of man's physical nature; sensual: *pretty lyrics of fleshly love* (Joseph Slater). **SYN:** carnal, lascivious. **3** *Figurative.* worldly. **4** of or having to do with the material body; mortal; human. **5** *Obsolete.* fat; plump.

flesh|ment (flesh′mənt), *n. Obsolete.* the excitement resulting from a first success. [< *flesh, verb transitive* + *-ment*]

flesh|pot (flesh′pot′), *n.* a pot for cooking meat. **fleshpots**, **a** good food and living; luxuries: *He might have been a saint had he been able to forego the fleshpots.* **b** *Figurative.* establishments where these are offered for sale: *I expect to hear the two ladies lamenting the fleshpots of Cavan Street* (Jonathan Swift).

flesh-print|ing (flesh′prin′ting), *n.* an electronic tracing or recording of the protein patterns found in the flesh of fish, used to match any species of fish with its birth waters and thus help to chart its migrations and control or increase its population.

flesh worm, a worm that burrows in and feeds on flesh, especially the larva of the flesh fly.

flesh wound, a wound that merely injures the flesh; slight wound.

flesh|y (flesh′ē), *adj.*, **flesh|i|er**, **flesh|i|est**. **1** having much flesh; fat; plump. **SYN:** corpulent, stout. **2** of flesh; like flesh. **3** composed of juicy, cellular tissue; pulpy: *a fleshy peach.* **–flesh′i|ly**, *adv.* **–flesh′i|ness**, *n.*

fletch (flech) *v.t.* to feather, as an arrow; fledge. [probably back formation < *fletcher*]

fletch|er (flech′ər), *n.* a person who makes or deals in arrows, or bows and arrows. See also **bowyer**. [< Old French *flechier* < *fleche* arrow; see etym. under **flèche**]

Fletch|er|ism (flech′ə riz əm), *n.* the practice of chewing food very thoroughly, advocated as an aid to health. [< Horace *Fletcher*, 1849-1919, an American nutritionist + *-ism*]

Fletch|er|ize (flech′ə rīz), *v.t.*, **-ized**, **-iz|ing**. to chew (food) very thoroughly.

fleth|er (fleᴛʜ′ər), *v., n. Scottish.* **–*v.i.*** to flatter; use blarney.
–*n.* flattering talk; blarney.

flet|ton (flet′ən), *n.* a type of brick made from a moist clay found in the area of Fletton, a town in central England.

fleur d'a|mour (flėr′ də mür′), *pl.* **fleur d'a|mour** or **fleurs d'a|mour** (flėr′ də mür′). a plant of the dogbane family, having small cymes of white or yellowish flowers. [< French *fleur d'amour* (literally) flower of love]

fleur de coin (flėr′ də kwaɴ′), *Numismatics.* of the highest grade; in mint condition: *a fleur de coin gold coin or medal.* [< French *fleur de coin* (literally) flower of die]

***fleur-de-lis** (flėr′də lē′, -lēs′), *n., pl.* **fleurs-de-lis** (flėr′də lēz′). **1** a design or device used in heraldry to represent a lily (originally supposed by some to represent an iris). The fleur-de-lis is part of the Boy Scout badge. **2a** the royal coat of arms of France. **b** the French royal family or nation. **3** = blue flag. [< Middle French *fleur-de-lis* lily flower]

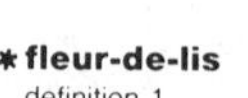

***fleur-de-lis**
definition 1

fleur du mal (flėr′ dʏ mȧl′), *pl.* **fleurs du mal** (flėr′ dʏ mȧl′). a shocking or decadent work of art, literature, or the like. [< French *fleur du mal* (literally) flower of evil]

fleu|ret (flü ret′, flėr′it), *n.* **1** a small flower; floweret. **2** an ornament like a small flower. **3** a light foil used in fencing. [< French *fleurette* (diminutive) < *fleur* flower]

fleu|ron (flœ rôɴ′), *n. French.* a flower-shaped ornament, used especially in architectural decoration and on coins, medals, or armor.

fleu|ry (flür′ē), *adj. Heraldry.* **1** decorated with fleur-de-lis. **2** (of a cross) having each arm ending in a fleur-de-lis, or the upper part of one. See the diagram under **cross**. Also, **flory**. [< Old French *floure* < *fleur* flower]

flew[1] (flü), *v.* past tense of **fly[2]**: *The bird flew away.*

flew[2] (flü), *n.* = flue[3].

flewed (flüd), *adj.* (of dogs) having flews.

flews (flüz), *n.pl.* the pendulous part of the upper lip of certain dogs, especially hounds. [origin uncertain]

flex (fleks), *v., n.* **–*v.t., v.i.*** **1** to bend (a joint or limb) by the action of the flexor muscles: *He flexed his stiff arm slowly.* **2** to bend or contract (a muscle or muscles). **3** to bend without breaking: *New spring-steel supports . . . flex to help absorb minor impacts* (Saturday Review).
–*n.* **1** flexible quality; flexibility: *The rubber is used to protect the cord, to provide a wearing surface and to provide the flex in a tire* (Wall Street Journal). **2** a bend or contraction of a muscle. **3** *Especially British.* flexible insulated wire used to connect electric appliances or lamps; cord.
[< Latin *flexus,* past participle of *flectere* bend]

flex|a|gon (flek′sə gon), *n.* a polygonal figure made with folded paper strips, having the property of changing faces when flexed: *Flexagon playhouse provides hours of constructive fun for children* (Science News Letter). [< *flex* + *-agon,* as in *hexagon*]

flex|i|bil|i|ty (flek′sə bil′ə tē), *n.* flexible quality: *The flexibility of a man's muscles usually lessens as he becomes old.*

flex|i|ble (flek′sə bəl), *adj.* **1** that can be bent without breaking; not stiff; easily bent in all directions: *Leather, rubber, and wire are flexible.* **2** *Figurative.* easily adapted to fit various conditions: *The actor's flexible voice accommodated itself to every emotion. Important principles may and must be flexible* (Abraham Lincoln). **3** *Figurative.* easily managed; willing to yield to influence or persuasion; tractable: *Can you conceive that the people . . . will long submit to be governed by so flexible a House of Commons?* (Junius Letters). [< Latin *flexibilis* < *flexus;* see etym. under **flex**] **–flex′i|ble|ness**, *n.* **–flex′i|bly**, *adv.*
–*Syn.* **1, 3. Flexible, pliant, limber** mean easily bent. **Flexible** means capable of being bent or twisted easily and without breaking, or, used figuratively of people and their minds, etc., of being adaptable and able to turn easily from one situation or subject to another: *Great thinkers have flexible minds.* **Pliant** means inherently tending to bend, or, figuratively, to yield easily to an influence: *He was too weak and pliant to make up his own mind.* **Limber**, used chiefly of the body, means having flexible muscles and joints and suggests easy movement: *A dancer has limber legs.*

flex|ile (flek′səl), *adj.* = flexible.

flex|il|i|ty (flek sil′ə tē), *n.* = flexibility.

flex|ion (flek′shən), *n.* **1** *Physiology.* **a** the bending of a joint in the body by the action of the flexors. **b** a being bent in this way. **2** *Especially British.* = flection (defs. 1,2). [earlier spelling of *flection*] **–flex′ion|less**, *adj.*

flex|ion|al (flek′shə nəl), *adj.* of or having to do with flexion.

flex|i|place (flek′sē plās′), *n.* a workplace at home connected by a computer to an office. [< *flexi*(ble) + (work)*place*]

flex|o|graph|ic (flek′sə graf′ik), *adj.* of or characteristic of flexography.

flex|og|ra|phy (flek sog′rə fē), *n.* a method of printing with aniline inks impressed by plates, usually of rubber, in relief as in letterpress printing, used especially in the printing of packaging materials such as cellophane or foils. [< *flex-*(ible) + *-graphy*]

flex|or (flek′sər, -sôr), *n.* any muscle that when contracted bends a joint of the body. [< New Latin *flexor* < Latin *flexus;* see etym. under **flex**]

flex|time (fleks′tīm′), *n.* a method of staggering working hours to enable each employee to work full-time but at his own convenience: *The company has incorporated "flextime," which allows employees to set their own work schedule whenever possible* (Newsweek). [< *flex*(ible) *time*]

flex|u|os|i|ty (flek′shü os′ə tē), *n., pl.* **-ties**. **1** the quality or condition of being flexuous. **2** an instance of this; a winding.

flex|u|ous (flek′shü əs), *adj.* **1** full of bends or curves; winding; sinuous. **2** waving; undulating. [< Latin *flexuōsus* < *flexus, -ūs* a bending < *flectere* to bend] **–flex′u|ous|ly**, *adv.*

flex|u|ra (flek shür′ə), *n.* **1** *Anatomy.* a flexure. **2** (in veterinary medicine) the articulation of the knee of a horse, corresponding to the human wrist. [< New Latin *flexura* < Latin *flexūra;* see etym. under **flexure**]

flex|ur|al (flek′shər əl), *adj.* of or having to do with flexure.

flex|ure (flek′shər), *n.* **1** the action of flexing or bending; curving. **2** the state of being flexed or bent. **3** a bent part or thing; bend; curve. [< Latin *flexūra* < *flexus;* see etym. under **flex**]

fley (flā), *v., n. Scottish.* **–*v.t.*** to frighten; scare; terrify. **–*n.*** a fright. Also, **fly**, or **flye**. [unrecorded Old English *flīgan*]

flib|ber|ti|gib|bet (flib′ər tē jib′it), *n.* **1** a frivolous, flighty person. **2** a chatterbox. [perhaps imitative]

flib|ber|ti|gib|bet|y (flib′ər tē jib′ə tē), *adj.* flighty; frivolous; senseless.

flic (flik, *French* flēk), *n. Informal.* a French policeman. [< French *flic*]

flic|flac (flik′flak′), *n.* **1** a dance step in which one foot is brushed twice against the other. **2** a backward somersault used by acrobatic dancers. [< French *flicflac;* imitative]

flick (flik), *n., v.* **–*n.*** **1** a sudden, light blow or stroke: *The farmer drove the fly from the horse's head by a flick of the whip.* **2** the light, snapping sound of such a blow or stroke: *the flick of a light switch.* **3** a streak or splash; fleck. **4** *Slang.* a motion picture.
–*v.t.* **1** to strike lightly with a quick, snapping blow: *He flicked the dust from his shoes with a handkerchief.* **2** to make a sudden, snapping stroke with: *The boys flicked wet towels at each other.* **–*v.i.*** to move quickly and lightly; flutter. [probably imitative]

flick|er[1] (flik′ər), *v., n.* **–*v.i.*** **1** to shine or burn with a wavering, unsteady light: *A dying fire flickered on the hearth.* **2** to move lightly and quickly in and out, or back and forth; quiver: *The tongue of a snake flickers.* **3** to flutter; hover: *We heard the birds flicker in the leaves.* **–*v.t.*** to cause to flicker: *The wind flickered the candlelight.*
–*n.* **1** a wavering, unsteady light or flame: *the flicker of an oil lamp.* **2** a brief flash; spark. **3** *Figurative: a flicker of enthusiasm.* **4** a quick, light movement: *the flicker of an eyelash.* **flickers**, *Slang.* motion pictures; movies: *A number of American film companies . . . intend to make three-dimensional flickers in quantity* (Wall Street Journal).
[Old English *flicorian*] **–flick′er|ing|ly**, *adv.*

flick|er[2] (flik′ər), *n.* **1** a large, common woodpecker of North America with brownish back, yellow markings on its tail, and white rump, wing and tail feathers; yellowhammer; yellow-shafted flicker. **2** = red-shafted flicker. [American English; perhaps imitative of its call]

flicker fusion, *Psychology.* the perception of an intermittently flashing light as if continuous when the flashes occur above a certain frequency.

flick|er|less (flik′ər lis), *adj.* without flickers; producing no flicker.

flicker photometer, a device to compare light intensity by alternate flashes from two sources.

flick|ers (flik′ərz), *n.pl.* See under **flicker[1]**.

flick|er|tail (flik′ər tāl′), *n.* a destructive ground squirrel of the northern central United States.

Flick|er|tail (flik′ər tāl′), *n.* a nickname for a native or inhabitant of North Dakota.

flick|er|y (flik′ər ē), *adj.* wavering.

flick-knife (flik′nīf′), *n., pl.* **-knives**. *British.* a switchblade knife.

flicks (fliks), *n.pl. Slang.* motion pictures; movies. [short for *flickers*]

flied (flīd), *v.* a past and past participle of **fly[2]** (*v.i.* def. 8): *The batter flied to center field.*

fli|er (flī′ər), *n.* **1** a person or thing that flies: *That eagle is a high flier.* **2** the pilot of an airplane; aviator. **3** a very fast train, ship, or bus. **4** *Informal.* a reckless financial venture: *a flier in foreign bonds.* **5** a small handbill. **6** a mechanical part that moves or revolves quickly. **7** *Architecture.* a single one of a straight flight of steps. **8** a device to make the bait spin in fishing. Also, **flyer**. **fliers**, stairs laid out in straight flights, as opposed to winding stairs: *Fliers and winders are . . . steps without any landing place* (Stephen Primatt).

flies[1] (flīz), *n.* the plural of **fly[1]** and **fly[2]**: *There are many flies on the window. Both batters hit flies to the outfield.*

flies[2] (flīz), *v.* third person singular, present tense of **fly[2]**: *A bird flies. He flies an airplane.*

flies[3] (flīz), *n.pl.* See under **fly[2]**.

flight[1] (flīt), *n., v.* **–*n.*** **1** the act or manner of flying: *the flight of a bird through the air.* **2** the distance a bird, bullet, airplane, missile, or other projectile can fly: *Because the Heron soars upward in the sky Above the arrow's flight* (Robert Southey). **3** a group of things flying through the air together: *a flight of pigeons, a flight of angels, a flight of arrows.* **4** *U.S.* a tactical unit of the Air Force consisting of two or more airplanes. **5** a trip in an aircraft, especially a scheduled trip on an airline: *He took the three o'clock flight to Boston.* **6** travel beyond the earth or into outer space by means of a spacecraft: *a rocket flight, a lunar flight.* **7** a swift movement: *a flight of the clouds.* **8** *Figurative.* the act or fact of soaring above or beyond what is ordinary: *a flight of fancy, a flight of imagination.* **9** a set of stairs or steps from

one landing or story of a building to the next. **10** the passing of time, especially when it seems to pass very quickly: *I call the lone night good, Though thy sweet wishes wing its flight* (Shelley). **11a** = flight arrow. **b** a contest at shooting for distance. **12a** a series of adjacent locks on a canal: *descending from the hill-tops by a flight of locks* (Samuel Smiles). **b** one of a series of conveyor belts in a conveyor system. **13** a set of fishhooks appended to a spinner. **14** *Cricket.* the course of a bowled ball.
–***v.i.*** **1** (of birds) to fly or travel in flights: *The wild geese are flighting* (Rudyard Kipling). **2** *Obsolete.* to migrate. –***v.t.*** **1** to shoot (wild fowl) in flight. **2** to feather (an arrow).
[Old English *flyht.* See related etym. at **fly**[2].]

flight[2] (flīt), *n.* **1** the act of running away; escape: *The flight of the prisoners was discovered.* **2** the act of absconding.
put to flight, to force to run away: *Our soldiers put the enemy to flight.*
take to flight, to flee: *The remainder [of a herd of whales] took to flight when their companions were harpooned* (F. D. Bennet).
[Middle English *fliht.* See related etym. at **flee.**]

flight arrow, **1** a light and well-feathered arrow, for long-distance shooting. **2** any long-shafted, light arrow to be shot from a bow.

flight attendant, a steward or stewardess on an airplane.

flight bag, a small, lightweight bag, usually made of canvas or plastic and fastened with a zipper, originally used for air travel.

flight control, **1** the control of aircraft in flight, especially by radio or electronically from the ground. **2** Usually, **flight controls.** the system of levers, cables, control surfaces, and navigational devices, used to control the attitude and movement of an aircraft.

flight deck, the large, flat, upper deck of an aircraft carrier, from which aircraft take off and on which they land.

flight director, a computer used on large aircraft to furnish information needed to fly through poor weather conditions.

flight engineer, a member of the crew of certain aircraft responsible for the craft's mechanical performance in flight: *The pilot and copilot are assisted by a flight engineer* (Wall Street Journal).

flight feather, one of the rigid feathers that compose a bird's wing and are essential to flight.

flight formation, the arrangement, as in an echelon, of two or more airplanes flying together.

flight instrument, any instrument in an aircraft that indicates the altitude, attitude, air speed, climb, drift, or direction of an aircraft.

flight|less (flīt′lis), *adj.* unable to fly. Emus and kiwis are flightless birds. *An ostrich is flightless but it can run with great speed.*

flight lieutenant, a commissioned officer in the Australian Air Force, British Royal Air Force, or Royal Canadian Air Force, corresponding in rank to a captain in the United States Air Force.

flight line, **1** the portion of an airfield which includes hangars and service buildings, but not runways or their approaches: *the thunder of her departure ricocheting off the buildings along the flight line* (Harper's). **2** the flight path of an airplane.

flight path, *Aeronautics.* the path (with reference to the earth) taken by the center of gravity of an aircraft or missile: *The guidance equipment failed to put the satellite on the planned flight path* (New Scientist).

flight pay, = flying pay.

flight plan, a statement of the destination, route, altitude, and other details of a proposed flight which a pilot usually must submit to a controlling agency.

flight recorder, a tightly sealed electronic device installed in an aircraft to keep a continuous graphic record of the craft's speed, course, and other data for purposes of analysis in the event of a crash.

flight shooting, **1** (in archery) distance-shooting with flight arrows. **2** the sport or practice of shooting wild fowl as they fly over.

flight|shot (flīt′shot′), *n.* **1** the distance to which a flight arrow is shot; bowshot. **2** a shot taken at wild fowl in flight.

flight simulator, a device that simulates any or all of the conditions of actual flight, used especially for training purposes.

flight status, = flying status.

flight strip, an auxiliary landing strip running parallel to a highway.

flight surgeon, a doctor in the U.S. Air Force or Navy who specializes in aviation medicine.

flight-test (flīt′test′), *v.t.* to test in or by actual flight.

flight test, a test in or by actual flight.

flight|wor|thy (flīt′wėr′ᴛʜē), *adj.,* **-thi|er, -thi|est.** capable of flight or of being used in flight: *Shepard underwent surgery, and examination by National Aeronautics and Space Administration physicians found his condition flightworthy* (Science News). –**flight′wor′thi|ness,** *n.*

flight|y (flī′tē), *adj.,* **flight|i|er, flight|i|est.** **1** likely to have sudden fancies; full of whims; frivolous. SYN: fickle, inconstant. **2** slightly crazy; light-headed. **3** swift; quick; fleet. [< *flight*[1] + *-y*[1]] –**flight′i|ly,** *adv.* –**flight′i|ness,** *n.*

flim|flam (flim′flam′), *n., v.,* **-flammed, -flam|ming,** *adj. Informal.* –***n.*** **1** nonsense; rubbish: *I tell thee 'tis all flimflam* (Henry Fielding). **2** a low trick; deception.
–***v.t.*** *U.S.* to cheat (a person) out of money or other thing of value by glib and confusing talk or other maneuver; trick. SYN: defraud.
–***adj.*** **1** intended to trick or deceive; sham. **2** nonsensical.
[origin uncertain; *flim* perhaps < Scandinavian (compare Old Icelandic *flim* a lampoon, *flimska* mockery). Compare etym. under **flam.**]

flim|flam|mer (flim′flam′ər), *n. U.S.* a person who flimflams; cheater; trickster.

flim|flam|mer|y (flim′flam′ər ē), *n. U.S.* actions or practices intended to trick or deceive: *commercial flimflammery.*

flim|sy (flim′zē), *adj.,* **-si|er, -si|est,** *n., pl.* **-sies.**
–***adj.*** **1** light and thin; slight; frail; without strength; easily broken: *The tissue paper she used to wrap my present was flimsy and tore off. Muslin is too flimsy to be used for sails. The Great Crash revealed that scores of apparently sound consolidations rested on the flimsiest of foundations* (New York Times). SYN: unsubstantial. **2** lacking seriousness or sense; feeble; shallow; trivial: *Her excuse was so flimsy that everybody laughed at her.* SYN: weak.
–***n.*** **1a** a thin paper used by reporters. **b** a newspaper report on this paper. **2** *Slang.* a piece of paper money.
[probably alteration of *film* + *-sy,* as in *clumsy*] –**flim′si|ly,** *adv.* –**flim′si|ness,** *n.*

flinch (flinch), *v., n.* –***v.i.*** **1** to draw back (from a difficulty, danger, or duty): *to flinch from the responsibilities of life.* SYN: quail. See syn. under **shrink.** **2** to shrink under physical pain; wince: *The baby flinched when he touched the hot radiator.* SYN: quail. See syn. under **shrink.** **3** to permit the foot to lose its hold on the ball in croqueting.
–***v.t.*** to withdraw from.
–***n.*** **1** the act of drawing back. **2** a game played with cards bearing numbers from 1 to 14.
[probably < Old French *flenchir,* probably < *flechier,* ultimately < Latin *flectere* to bend] –**flinch′er,** *n.* –**flinch′ing|ly,** *adv.*

flin|der (flin′dər), *n.* a small piece; fragment; splinter: *The box was smashed into flinders.* SYN: shred. [origin uncertain. Compare Norwegian *flindra.*]

fling (fling), *v.,* **flung, fling|ing,** *n.* –***v.t.*** **1** to throw with force; throw: *to fling a stone.* **2** to put suddenly or violently; send forcibly: *to fling someone into jail.* **3** to throw aside; discard; abandon: *He has flung us off; and leaves us to poverty* (Thackeray). **4** send forward suddenly and rapidly: *to fling fresh troops into a battle.* **5** *Figurative.* to cast scornfully (a look or glance) in a certain direction. **6** to direct or apply: *She had flung all her energies into her work.* **7** to emit; diffuse; project: *The huge trees fling their cool shade over the grass.* **8a** to throw to the ground, as in wrestling or from horseback: *Never a man could fling him; for Willy stood like a rock* (Tennyson). *His horse started, flung him, and fell upon him* (Horace Walpole). **b** *Figurative.* to cause to fall; overthrow: *to fling the ministry.*
–***v.i.*** **1** to move hastily; rush; dash: *She flung out of the room.* **2** to move violently; plunge or kick: *The excited horse flung about in the stall.* **3** (of a sword, lance, or knife) to be thrown or driven quickly or with force. **4** to break out in a violent attack of words; start scolding; curse.
–***n.*** **1** a sudden throw. **2** a plunge or kick; cast. **3** a time of doing as one pleases: *He had his fling when he was young; now he must work.* **4** *Figurative.* a scornful remark or critical attack on a person, institution, or convention of society; jibe: *The editor took another fling at the city fathers today.* **5** a lively Scottish dance: *the Highland fling.*
have a fling at, a to try; attempt: *He had a fling at acting, but discovering that he had no talent he returned to his law studies.* **b** to make scornful remarks about: *Not one king hath been in England ... but they have ... had their false flings at him* (John Bale). **c** to attack: *I mean ... to have a fling at magicians for their abominable lies* (Philemon Holland).
[perhaps < Scandinavian (compare Icelandic *flengja* to flog)] –**fling′er,** *n.*

flint (flint), *n., v.* –***n.*** **1** a very hard, gray or brown, granular quartz that makes a spark when struck against steel; silex: *Indians used flint for arrowheads.* **2** a piece of this used with steel to light fires or explode gunpowder. **3** *Figurative.* anything very hard or unyielding: *The miser had a heart of flint.*
–***v.t.*** **1** to fit (a gun) with a flint. **2** to furnish or provide (a person) with a flint or flints for a firearm.
[Old English *flint*] –**flint′like′,** *adj.*

flint corn, a variety of corn having very hard-coated kernels that do not shrink: *Flint corn can be shipped and stored with less spoilage than other kinds* (G. F. Sprague). See picture under **corn**[1].

flint-dried (flint′drīd′), *adj.* dried in the sun to a flinty hardness: *flint-dried hides.*

flint-eyed (flint′īd′), *adj.* **1** having keen or piercing eyes; sharp-eyed: *a flint-eyed scout.* **2** = hard-hearted.

flint glass, a brilliant, heavy glass, containing lead, potassium or sodium, and silicon, used especially for lenses and dishes. See also **crown glass.**

flint|head (flint′hed′), *n.* = wood ibis.

flint-heart|ed (flint′här′tid), *adj.* unfeeling; cruel; hard-hearted.

*__flint|lock__ (flint′lok′), *n.* **1** a gunlock in which a flint striking against steel makes sparks that explode the gunpowder. It is a firelock. **2** an old-fashioned gun with such a gunlock.

***flintlock**
definition 1

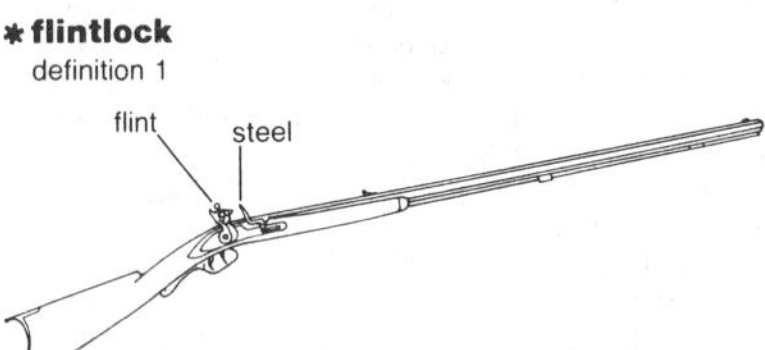

flint mill, a mill in which calcined flints are ground to powder for mixing with clay to form slip for porcelain.

flint|y (flin′tē), *adj.,* **flint|i|er, flint|i|est.** **1** made of flint; containing flint: *... some flinty concretions of Late Cretaceous age* (Raymond Cecil Moore). **2** *Figurative.* like flint; very hard; unyielding: *flinty stubbornness. Her answer struck him unpleasantly as having a flinty little edge on it* (Atlantic). SYN: adamant, obdurate. **3** having a taste suggesting the metallic smell of flint struck against steel: *The Valais also produces a fine red wine ...; it is known for its "flinty" taste, and is smooth and pungent at the same time* (London Times). –**flint′i|ly,** *adv.* –**flint′i|ness,** *n.*

FLIP (no periods), Floating Instrument Platform (a manned oceanographic research vessel): *The FLIP ... can be towed to a suitable site and up-ended by partial flooding* (New Scientist).

flip[1] (flip), *v.,* **flipped, flip|ping,** *n.* –***v.t.*** **1** to toss or move with a snap of the finger and thumb; flick: *He flipped a coin on the counter.* **2** to turn or move quickly or with a jerk: *She flipped her fan shut. I flipped the pages of the magazine to find an interesting article.* **3** *U.S. Slang.* to please; arouse enthusiasm in: *"Dark of the Moon" ... absolutely flipped me, with all that witch-doctor stuff* (New Yorker).
–***v.i.*** **1** to flick: *The stagecoach driver flipped at a fly with his whip.* **2** to turn or move with a jerk: *The branch flipped back and scratched his face. He flipped through the pages of the book, looking for pictures.* **3** to step lightly and nimbly: *She flipped gaily down the path.* **4** *U.S. Slang.* to get excited; go wild: *He just flipped. He made a racket in the middle of the night and ... started throwing things* (New Yorker).
–***n.*** **1** a smart tap; snap: *The cat gave the kitten a flip on the ear.* **2** a sudden jerk or movement: *Since there was a tie, the winner was picked by the flip of a coin.* **3** a dive in which the body turns completely over before striking the water: *a back flip.*
flip out, *Slang.* **a** to lose one's mind; go crazy: *Kingsley Hall ... an anti-hospital in London where "people who flipped out, or near to it, could stay and go through whatever they had to go through without drugs [or] electric shocks"* (Manchester Guardian Weekly). **b** to get mildly excited: *The British rock trio ... has poured into the U.S. for its American debut, and the faithful are flipping out* (Time).
flip up, to flip a coin in the air to decide a

Pronunciation Key: hat, āge, cãre, fär; let, ēqual, tėrm; it, īce; hot, ōpen, ôrder; oil, out; cup, pu̇t, rüle; child; long; thin; ᴛʜen; zh, measure; ə represents **a** in about, **e** in taken, **i** in pencil, **o** in lemon, **u** in circus.

chance: *The two great men could flip up to see which should have the second place* (New York Herald Tribune). [probably imitative]

flip[2] (flip), *n.* a hot drink containing beer, cider, or the like, with sugar, egg, and spice, usually nutmeg. [noun use of *flip*[1], verb (because of the mixing necessary for its preparation)]

flip[3] (flip), *adj. Informal.* flippant: *She's a flip young thing.* [perhaps short for *flippant*]

flip chart, a chart consisting of several sheets that are turned over to show different types of information.

flip chip, a microcircuit chip with an adhesive pad for fastening the chip to other components.

flip-flap (flip′flap′), *adv., n., v.,* **-flapped, -flapping.** **—*adv.*** with a repeated flapping movement. **—*n.*** a flip-flop. **—*v.i.*** to go flip-flap.

flip-flop (flip′flop′), *n., v.,* **-flopped, -flop|ping,** *adj.* **—*n.*** **1** *Informal.* a turnabout; reversal: *Early last year, officials did a complete flip-flop and endorsed a nationwide shelter program* (Wall Street Journal). **2** an acrobatic stunt of jumping forward and backward, landing alternately upon hands and feet: *By the time Alfredo was four years old, he was doing handstands, back bends, flip-flops* (New Yorker). **3** a switching unit used in electronic equipment, which changes physical states, frequencies, and the like, upon certain impulses. **4** Often **flip-flops.** flat sandal made of rubber, held on the foot by a thong between the first and second toes and over the instep.
—*v.i.* to turn about; reverse: *The Communists flip-flopped and agreed to resume their explanations to prisoners* (Newsweek).
—*adj.* of or having to do with a flip-flop: *a flip-flop circuit, a flip-flop stunt.*

flip glass, a large glass tumbler used for mixing and heating flip.

flip|ness (flip′nis), *n.* = flippancy.

flip|pan|cy (flip′ən sē), *n., pl.* **-cies. 1** flippant quality or behavior: *Beneath the surface flummery and flippancy, one has to recognize the story's underlying seriousness* (Atlantic). **2** flippant speech or conduct.

flip|pant (flip′ənt), *adj.* **1** smart or pert in speech or manner; not respectful: *The boy gave a flippant answer.* **SYN:** impertinent, saucy. **2** *Obsolete.* **a** nimble; limber; pliant. **b** talkative; voluble. [apparently < *flip*[1], verb + *-ant*] **—flip′pant|ly,** *adv.* **—flip′pant|ness,** *n.*

flip|per (flip′ər), *n.* **1** a broad, flat limb especially adapted for swimming. Seals have flippers. **2** a molded rubber attachment for the human foot, shaped like a large frog's foot, used as an aid to swimming: *A professional frogman gives you expert advice on how to explore the silent underwater world with mask, flippers, aqualung, and spear* (New York Times). **3** a stabilizing fin on an ocean liner. **4** *Slang.* the hand.

flip|ping (flip′ing), *adj. Slang.* (used as a mild intensive) confounded; blooming.

flip side, **1** the reverse side of a phonograph record, especially the side with the less important or less popular piece of recorded music: *"I'm Mad Again" . . . is the next-to-last number on the flip side of their first album* (New Yorker).
2 *Figurative.* the opposite or reverse: *She is the flip side of Cinderella—the homely girl who made it* (Time).

flip-top (flip′top′), *adj., n.* **—*adj.*** provided with a hinged top, lid, or cover that can be flipped open: *a flip-top box, a flip-top table.*
—*n.* a flip-top item or product: *The box, a flip-top, is described as the first major innovation in cigarette packaging since the soft-paper pack was put on the market toward the close of World War I* (New York Times).

flirt (flėrt), *v., n.* **—*v.i.*** **1** to play at making love; make love without meaning it: *Every man likes to flirt with a pretty girl, and every pretty girl likes to be flirted with* (George Eliot). **2** *Figurative.* to trifle; toy: *He flirted with the idea of going to Europe, even though he couldn't afford it. In Mexico City, 50,000 people often turn out to see bullfighters flirt with death in the afternoon* (Newsweek). **3** to move quickly; spring; dart: *The bird flirted from one branch to another.* **SYN:** flutter. **—*v.t.*** **1** to give a brisk, sudden motion to; flutter: *She flirted her fan impatiently.* **2** to propel or throw with a jerk; toss.
—*n.* **1** a person who plays at making love; person who flirts. **2** a quick movement or flutter: *With a flirt of her apron she turned and ran.* **3** a toss; jerk.
[probably ultimately imitative] **—flirt′er,** *n.* **—flirt′ing|ly,** *adv.*

flir|ta|tion (flėr tā′shən), *n.* **1** the action of making love without meaning it. **2** a love affair that is not serious. **3** *Figurative.* the act of flirting or toying: . . . *a brief flirtation with the notion that the Russian village organization—the mir—could be built into a Socialist state* (Harper's).

flir|ta|tion|al (flėr tā′shə nəl), *adj.* of or having to do with flirtation.

flir|ta|tious (flėr tā′shəs), *adj.* **1** inclined to flirt: *a flirtatious girl.* **2** having to do with flirtation: *a flirtatious glance.* **—flir|ta′tious|ly,** *adv.* **—flir|ta′tious|ness,** *n.*

flir|tish (flėr′tish), *adj.* characteristic of a flirt; somewhat flirtatious.

flirt|y (flėr′tē), *adj.,* **flirt|i|er, flirt|i|est.** = flirtatious.

flisk (flisk), *v., n. British Dialect.* **—*v.i.*** **1** to move or dance about in a frolicsome manner; frisk. **2** to be restive. **—*v.t.*** to make restive. **—*n.*** **1** a fillip with the fingers. **2** = whisk. **3** a large-toothed comb. [imitative]

flit (flit), *v.,* **flit|ted, flit|ting,** *n.* **—*v.i.*** **1** to fly lightly and quickly; flutter: *Birds flitted from tree to tree.* **2** *Figurative.* to pass lightly and quickly; dart: *Many idle thoughts flitted through his mind as he lay in the sun.* **3** *Obsolete.* to depart or swerve from a custom or law. **—*v.t.*** *Scottish.* to remove, transport, or take away to another place; transfer from one position to another.
—*n.* a light, quick movement, such as that of a bird's wing; flutter; light touch.
[perhaps < Scandinavian (compare Old Icelandic *flytja*)]

flitch (flich), *n., v.* **—*n.*** **1** the side of a hog, salted and cured; side of bacon. **2** a steak cut from a halibut. **3** one of the planks of a beam constructed by fastening two or more planks together. **4** a slab cut lengthwise from a log.
—*v.t.* to cut into flitches or as a flitch is cut.
[Old English *flicce*]

flite (flīt), *v.,* **flit|ed, flit|ing,** *n. Dialect.* **—*v.i.*** **1** to dispute, especially in words; wrangle; rail. **2** to scold. **—*v.t.*** to berate; scold; jeer at. **—*n.*** **1** a dispute; contention; strife. **2** abuse. Also, **flyte.** [Old English *flītan* strive, dispute]

*** flit gun**, a light, small, hand-operated sprayer used especially to spray an insecticide. [< *Flit,* a trademark for an insecticide]

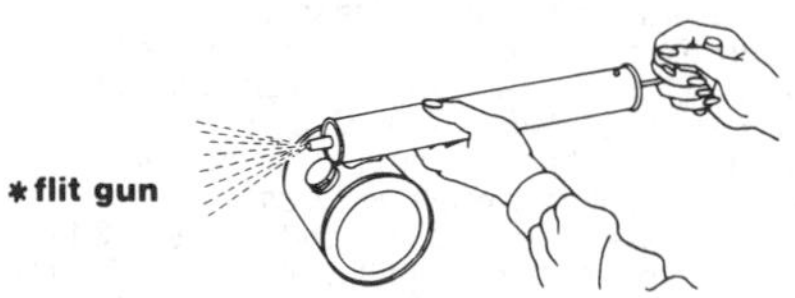

*** flit gun**

flit|ing (flī′ting), *n.* a kind of contest practiced by Scottish poets in the 1500's in which two persons assailed each other alternately with tirades of abusive verse. Also, **flyting.** [< *flit*(e) + *-ing*[1]]

flit|ter[1] (flit′ər), *v.i., v.t., n.* = flutter. [perhaps frequentative of *flit*]

flit|ter[2] (flit′ər), *n.* a person who flits. [< *flit* + *-er*[1]]

flit|ter[3] (flit′ər), *n.* **1** a minute square of thin metal used in decoration. **2** such squares collectively. [< German *Flitter*]

flit|ter|mouse (flit′ər mous′), *n., pl.* **-mice.** = bat. [< *flitter*[1], verb + *mouse*]

flit|ters (flit′ərz), *n.pl. Dialect.* fragments; bits; shreds. [alteration of *fitters;* influenced by *flitter*[1], verb]

flit|ting (flit′ing), *adj.* moving lightly and swiftly; passing quickly; fluttering. **—flit′ting|ly,** *adv.*

fliv|ver (fliv′ər), *n., v. Slang.* **—*n.*** **1** a small, cheap automobile, especially one that is no longer new. **2** any small vehicle thought of as resembling this. **3** a failure or bungle; fizzle.
—*v.i.* **1** to fail shamefully; fizzle. **2** to go in a flivver. [American English; perhaps a coined word]

flix (fliks), *n.* **1** fluffiness or waviness, as of hair or fur. **2** *Archaic.* down; fur. [origin unknown]

float (flōt), *v., n.* **—*v.i.*** **1** to stay on top of or be held up by air, water, or other liquid. A cork will float, but a stone sinks. *Ice floats on water.* **2** to move with a moving liquid; drift: *The boat floated out to sea.* **3** to rest or move in a liquid or in the air or other gas: *Clouds floated in the sky.*
4 *Figurative.* to move or hover before the eyes or in the mind: *Faded ideas float in the fancy like half-forgotten dreams* (Richard Brinsley Sheridan). **5** *Figurative.* to move aimlessly; pass from person to person: *The rumor floated through the town.* **6a** (of a company) to be supported by the public; be launched. **b** (of an acceptance) to be in circulation. **7** (of a currency) to rise and fall in value according to supply and demand instead of through government regulation: *Other countries, such as Switzerland and Japan, are allowing their currencies to float* (Newsweek).
—*v.t.* **1** to cause to float: *to float a ship.* **2** to cover with liquid; flood. **3** to set going (a company, scheme, or other venture); launch: *to float a loan.* **4** to put on the market; sell (securities): *to float an issue of stock. To get money the government floated an issue of bonds.* **5** to allow (a currency) to change in value according to supply and demand: *The Germans are angry with the French for floating the franc and thus trying to underprice German exports* (Time). **6** to refine (pigments) by causing them to pass through a stream of water. **7** to make smooth or level, as the surface of plaster.
—*n.* **1** anything that stays up or holds up something else in water. A raft or a life preserver is a float. **2** a piece of wood, cork, or quills on a fish line that supports the line and bobs when a fish bites the hook; bobber. **3** an air-filled organ that supports a fish or other aquatic animal or an aquatic plant. **4** an air-filled, watertight part on an aircraft for landing or floating on water; pontoon. **5** a hollow, metal ball that regulates the level, supply, or outlet of a liquid in a tank, boiler, or the like. **6** a milkshake or ice-cream soda, with ice cream floating in it. **7** a low, flat car that carries something to be shown in a parade. **8** a flat board of a water wheel or paddle wheel. **9** a tool for smoothing or leveling, such as a trowel for smoothing plaster. **10** *Banking.* **a** checks that are in transit, as by mail, and have not yet been collected. **b** *U.S.* credit automatically extended by Federal Reserve banks to member banks covering checks delayed in collection. **11** *Finance.* the floating of a currency on the monetary market: *It seems possible that a growing number of currencies will follow the Canadian example of a fairly relaxed float* (National Review). **12** *British.* a sum of small change with which a shopkeeper, tradesman, peddler, or one who takes transportation fares, begins the day's work: *"What's that, then?" I asked, pointing at the drawer. "That's my float," she grunted. "I'm not parting with that"* (Sunday Times). **13a** the passing of the weft over a part of the warp without being interwoven with it. **b** the loose mass of thread resulting from this action. **14** *Archaic.* act of floating.
floats, footlights in a theater: *The floats are operated from the main instrument panel offstage.*
[Old English *flotian* < *flot* body of water. See related etym. at **fleet**[1].]

float|a|bil|i|ty (flō′tə bil′ə tē), *n.* floating ability.

float|a|ble (flō′tə bəl), *adj.* **1** that can float or be floated. **2** that can be floated on: *a floatable river.*

float|age (flō′tij), *n.* = flotage.

float|a|tion (flō tā′shən), *n.* = flotation.

float|a|tive (flō′tə tiv), *adj.* = flotative.

float|board (flōt′bôrd′, -bōrd′), *n.* **1** one of the boards of an undershot water wheel. **2** one of the boards or paddles at the circumference of a paddle wheel.

float chamber, the part of a carburetor which holds the fuel before it is vaporized and drawn into the cylinders. It contains one or more floats that regulate the inflow of fuel.

floa|tel (flō tel′), *n.* an excursion boat with sleeping and eating accommodations.

float|er (flō′tər), *n.* **1** a person or thing that floats. **2** *Informal.* a person who often changes his place of living or working: *A Cleveland restaurant chain operator bemoans the number of "floaters" who won't stick to a job* (Wall Street Journal). **3** *Informal.* = floating voter. **4** *U.S.* a person who votes illegally in several places. **5** *Sports.* a ball thrown or hit so as to travel slowly and appear to hang in the air, usually on a slightly arched course: *The girl from Ohio was playing a shrewdly calculated match, keeping the ball deep down the middle with high floaters* (New York Times). **6** an insurance policy covering a category of goods, such as household effects, whether at a fixed location or in transit: *The small percentage of homeowners who had all-risk personal-property floaters also can collect for damage to belongings* (Time).

float-feed (flōt′fēd′), *n., adj.* **—*n.*** a device, such as a carburetor, that regulates the flow of a liquid by means of a float. **—*adj.*** that regulates the flow of a liquid by means of a float.

float glass, a flat glass of very smooth, brilliant finish, produced by flowing molten glass upon a bed of molten metal under controlled temperatures.

float|ing (flō′ting), *adj.* **1** that floats: *The floating ice shelf was found to abut the grounded ice inland* (E. F. Roots). **2** not fixed; not staying in one place; moving around: *a floating poulation.* **3** *Finance.* **a** in use or circulation; not permanently invested: *floating capital.* **b** not funded; changing. The floating debt of a business consists of notes, drafts, etc., payable within a short time. **4** of or having to do with a machine part, such as a connecting rod or coupler, connected or hung so that it functions without causing vibration. **5** *Medicine.* not in the normal position; displaced: *a floating kidney.* **—float′ing|ly,** *adv.*

*** floating bridge**, **1** a bridge supported by boats, rafts, or pontoons. See the picture above on the following page. **2** the part of certain swing bridges, supported by a caisson or pontoon, which can swing away. **3** a kind of double bridge whose upper member projects beyond the lower and can be moved forward by ropes, formerly used for carrying troops over narrow moats.

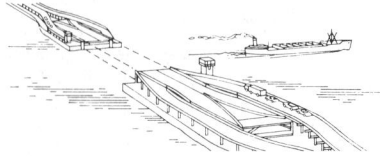

***floating bridge**
definition 1

floating capital, = circulating capital.
floating dock or **dry dock**, a type of movable dry dock that is raised above the water after a ship has entered, and lowered after repairs are completed.
floating garden, an artificially made island that floats on the surface of a lake and consists of a long strip of woven rushes covered with mud and weeds upon which vegetables and flowers are grown.
floating heart, an aquatic plant of the gentian family that has floating, heart-shaped leaves.
floating island, **1** a floating mass of earth held together especially by driftwood or roots. **2** a dessert made of boiled custard with meringue or whipped cream on it.
floating light, **1** = lightship. **2** a lifebuoy with a lantern, for use in rescue work at night.
float|ing-point (flō′ting point′), *adj.* of or designating a computation in a digital computer in which the location of the decimal point or the binary point may vary from number to number.
floating ribs, ribs not attached to the breastbone; the last two pairs of ribs. See picture under **chest**. See also **false ribs**.
floating stock, stock available for speculation rather than for investment, and thus not held permanently.
floating supply, the quantity of goods or securities immediately available in a market.
floating vote, the group of voters without known party affiliation or preference.
floating voter, a voter who is not committed to any political party, candidate, or issue; an undecided voter; floater: *What [the Prime Minister] is after is the floating voter . . . to win the floater's respect by getting tough with the unions, and by securing a balance of payments surplus* (Punch).
float|plane (flōt′plān′), *n.* an airplane with floats in place of wheels.
float process, a process for making float glass.
floats (flōts), *n.pl.* See under **float**.
float|stone (flōt′stōn′), *n.* **1** a stone used by bricklayers for smoothing the surfaces of bricks used in curved work. **2** a whitish-gray, spongy variety of opal, so light as to float upon water.
float|y (flō′tē), *adj.*, **float|i|er, float|i|est.** **1** that can float; buoyant. **2** (of a ship) needing very little water to float.
floc (flok), *n.* a light, loose mass that looks like a tuft of wool, such as in a chemical precipitate. Also, **flock**. [probably short for *floccule*]
floc|ci (flok′sī), *n.* plural of **floccus**.
floc|cil|la|tion (flok′sə lā′shən), *n.* = carphology. [< Latin *floccus* a flock of wool + *-illus*, a diminutive suffix + English *-ation*]
floc|cose (flok′ōs), *adj.* **1** *Botany.* composed of or bearing tufts of woolly hairs. **2** *Obsolete.* woolly. [< Late Latin *floccōsus* < *floccus* flock of wool]
floc|cu|lant (flok′yə lənt), *n., adj.* —*n.* an agent which causes or promotes flocculation: *Flocculants . . . cause particles in the water to precipitate to the bottom* (Matt Clark).
—*adj.* causing or promoting flocculation: *flocculant polymers.*
floc|cu|late (flok′yə lāt), *v.*, **-lat|ed, -lat|ing,** *n.* —*v.t.*, *v.i.* to form into flocculent masses; form compound masses of particles, such as a cloud or a chemical precipitate: *Humus, mixed with the mineral parts of the soil, causes the finer particles to flocculate* (Fred W. Emerson).
—*n.* a flocculated formation or mass.
[< *floccul*(us) + *-ate*[1]]
floc|cu|la|tion (flok′yə lā′shən), *n.* the process of flocculating; formation into flocculent masses.
floc|cule (flok′yül), *n.* something that looks like a small flock or tuft of wool, as in a liquid. [< Latin *flocculus;* see etym. under **flocculus**]
floc|cu|lence (flok′yə ləns), *n.* the state of being woolly or flocculent.
floc|cu|lent (flok′yə lənt), *adj.* **1** like bits of wool. **2** made up of soft, woolly masses. **3** covered with a soft, woolly substance. **4** having a soft, waxy coating, as certain insects do. —**floc′cu|lent|ly**, *adv.*
floc|cu|lous (flok′yə ləs), *adj.* resembling flocculi.
floc|cu|lus (flok′yə ləs), *n., pl.* **-li** (-lī). **1** a small flock of wool or something that looks like it; floccule. **2** one of the cloudy masses of very hot gases which cover the surface of the sun, as photographed by the spectroheliograph. **3** *Anatomy.* a small lobe on the underside of the cerebellum. [< Late Latin *flocculus* small flock (of wool) < Latin, woollike tuft (of clouds) (diminutive) < *floccus* tuft]
floc|cus (flok′əs), *n., pl.* **floc|ci.** something that looks like a flock of wool. [< Latin *floccus* tuft of wool]
flock[1] (flok), *n., v.* —*n.* **1** a group of animals of one kind keeping, feeding, or herded together, especially sheep, goats, or birds: *a flock of geese. A flock can mean lions in Africa, sheep in Australia, goats in Ireland, and geese in the United States* (Science News Letter). **SYN:** herd, drove. **2** a large group; crowd: *Visitors came in flocks to the zoo to see the new gorrilla.*
3 *Figurative.* people of the same church group; band; company: *The pastor reproved his flock for fishing on Sunday.*
—*v.i.* **1** to go or gather in a flock; keep in groups: *Sheep usually flock together.* **SYN:** congregate. **2** to come crowding; crowd: *The children flocked around the ice-cream stand.* **SYN:** congregate.
[Old English *flocc*] —**flock′less**, *adj.*
flock[2] (flok), *n., v.* —*n.* **1** a tuft of wool or cotton. **2** waste wool or cotton used to stuff mattresses and cushions. **3** finely powdered wool or other fiber used to form a velvety pattern or surface on wallpaper or fabric. **4** = floc.
—*v.t.* **1** to stuff with flock. **2** to cover or coat with flock.
[probably < Old French *floc* lock of wool < Latin *floccus* tuft of wool. Compare etym. under **floccus.**]
flock|ing (flok′ing), *n.* **1** a pattern or design made with flock. **2** the bunching together of wet wool fibers to form a shrunken mass.
flock|mas|ter (flok′mas′tər, -mäs′-), *n. British.* an owner or overseer of a flock; sheep farmer.
flock|pa|per (flok′pā′pər), *n.* wallpaper coated or decorated with flock or powdered wool.
flock pigeon, a kind of pigeon found in Australia in very large flocks.
flock printing, a form of decoration on wallpaper, greeting cards, or the like, in which the design is outlined with glue and then finely chopped bits of silk and wool are sprinkled on.
flock|y (flok′ē), *adj.*, **flock|i|er, flock|i|est.** **1** like flocks or tufts. **2** covered with flocks or tufts.
floe (flō), *n.* **1** a field or sheet of floating ice. **2** a floating piece broken off from such a field or sheet. [compare Icelandic *flō*]
floe|berg (flō′bėrg′), *n.* a large mass of ice formed from floes heaped up by the action of the wind and waves.
floe rat, = ringed seal.
flog (flog, flôg), *v.*, **flogged, flog|ging.** —*v.t.* **1** to beat or whip hard: *The inhuman flogging of disobedient soldiers and sailors was stopped years ago. Trees were seen to flog the ground with their branches* (Sir John Herschel). **SYN:** drub, flagellate. **2** to cast a fly line over (a stream) repeatedly in fishing. **3** to tire out; exhaust: *After the hike I was flogged out.* **4** *British Slang.* to sell; offer for sale (originally something not belonging to the seller): *One of them tried to flog me second-hand cotton machinery* (Punch).
—*v.i.* to beat or flap heavily, as of a sail.
flog a dead horse. See under **dead horse**.
[origin uncertain. Compare Latin *flagellāre* to whip.] —**flog′ger**, *n.*
flog|ging (flog′ing, flôg′-), *n.* **1** the practice of beating or whipping as punishment. **2** a beating or whipping; chastisement.
flong (flong), *n.* a prepared sheet of thick, composite paper, used for making a stereotype mold. [variant of *flan*]
flood (flud), *n., v.* —*n.* **1** a great flow of water over what is usually dry land; inundation: *The heavy rains caused a serious flood near the river.* **2** a large amount of water; ocean, sea, lake, or river: *She will to her peaceful woods return, and to her murmuring floods* (Wordsworth). **3** *Figurative.* a great outpouring of anything: *a flood of light, a flood of words.* **4** a flowing of the tide toward the shore; rise of the tide.
—*v.t.* **1** to flow over; cover with a great flow of water: *The river flooded our fields.* **SYN:** inundate. **2** to fill much fuller than usual. **3** to put much water on: *A wave flooded the holes I had dug in the sand.* **4** *Figurative.* to fill, cover, or overcome like a flood: *The room was flooded with moonlight. The rich man was flooded with requests for money.* **SYN:** overwhelm, deluge. **5** to cause or allow too much fuel to flow into (the carburetor of a motor), so that the motor fails to start: *He flooded the carburetor when he tried to start the car.*
—*v.i.* **1** to pour out or stream like a flood. **2** *Figurative.* to flow like a flood; overflow: *Sunlight flooded into the room.* **3** to become covered or filled with water: *During the thunderstorm, our cellar flooded.* **4** to receive too much fuel into the carburetor: *He tried to start the car, but he was nervous and the motor flooded* (New Yorker). **5** *Medicine.* **a** to suffer from uterine hemorrhage. **b** to have an excessive menstrual flow.
the Flood, the waters that covered the earth in the time of Noah; the Deluge (in the Bible, Genesis 7): *Your ancient but ignoble blood has crept through scoundrels ever since the Flood* (Alexander Pope).
[Old English *flōd*] —**flood′a|ble**, *adj.* —**flood′er**, *n.*
—***Syn.*** *n.* **1 Flood, deluge, inundation** mean a great flow of water. **Flood** applies particularly to a great flow of water over land usually dry, caused by the rising and overflowing of a river or other body of water: *Floods followed the melting of mountain snow.* **Deluge** applies to a great flood that washes away everything in its path, or, sometimes, to a heavy, continuous rain that causes a flood: *Livestock drowned in the deluge.* **Inundation**, a formal term, means an overflow, not necessarily harmful, covering everything around: *Crops were destroyed by the inundation of the fields.*
flood control, the practice of attempting to prevent or lessen damage caused by floods especially by the use of dams, levees, dikes, and extra outlets, or by reforestation.
flood current, the movement of water toward the coast or inland due to the movement of the tide.
flood|gate (flud′gāt′), *n.* **1** a gate in a canal, river, stream, or dam, to control the flow of water. **2** *Figurative.* a thing that controls the flow or passage of anything: *More important, if the West yields to terrorism in one place, the floodgates are open* (New York Times).
flood lamp, = floodlight (def. 1).
flood level, **1** the highest mark reached by a flood. **2** the level above which high water in a river is regarded as in flood, usually the level at which water overflows its natural banks.
flood|light (flud′līt′), *n., v.*, **-light|ed** or **-lit, -light|ing.** —*n.* **1** a lamp that gives a broad beam of light: *Silhouetted by its own 98 floodlights, the Capitol is white and serene against the winter night sky* (Newsweek). **2** a broad beam of light from such a lamp: *We could see the whole yard in the floodlight.*
—*v.t.* to light by a floodlight or floodlights: *The baseball field was brightly floodlighted for the night game.*
flood plain, a plain bordering a river and made of soil deposited by floods.
flood tide, the flowing of the tide toward the shore; rise of the tide.
flood|time (flud′tīm′), *n.* the period during which a river is in flood.
flood|wall (flud′wôl′), *n.* a wall erected for protection against flooding waters.
flood|wa|ter (flud′wôt′ər, -wot′-), *n.* water flooding dry land: *Floodwaters began receding in some areas of Kentucky* (Wall Street Journal).
flood|way (flud′wā′), *n.* a natural or artificial pathway by which excess water drains off in floodtime.
flood|wood (flud′wu̇d′), *n.* pieces of wood brought down by a flood.
floo|ey (flü′ē), *adj. U.S. Slang.* out of order; askew: *Our combustion control just went flooey* (New Yorker). [probably alteration of *blooey*]
floor (flôr, flōr), *n., v.* —*n.* **1** the part of a room to walk or stand on; inside bottom covering of a room: *The floor of this room is made of wood.* **2** a flat surface at the bottom: *They dropped their net to the floor of the ocean.* **3a** a story of a building: *Five families live on the fifth floor.* **b** the level supporting surface in other structures: *the floor of a bridge or elevator.* **4** any large level surface: *a forest floor of pine needles and cones.* (*Figurative.*) *For Lycidas your sorrow is not dead, Sunk though he be beneath the watery floor* (Milton). **5** the part of a room or hall where members of a lawmaking body, convention, or the like, sit, and from which they speak. **6** *Figurative.* the right to speak in a lawmaking body, convention, or the like: *"You may have the floor," said the chairman.* **7** the main part of an exchange, where buying and selling of stocks, bonds, or commodities, is done. **8** *Informal.* the lowest level (of prices or amounts). **9** *Mining.* an underlying stratum on which a seam of coal, or other mineral, lies. **10** *Nautical.* the part of the bottom of a ship that

Pronunciation Key: hat, āge, cãre, fär; let, ēqual, tėrm; it, īce; hot, ōpen, ôrder; oil, out; cup, pu̇t, rüle; child; long; thin; ᴛʜen; zh, measure; ə represents **a** in about, **e** in taken, **i** in pencil, **o** in lemon, **u** in circus.

is almost level on each side of the keelson.
—***v.t.*** **1** to put a floor in or on: *The carpenter will floor this room with oak.* **2** to knock down; shoot-down: *He floored the boy with one blow.* **3** *Informal, Figurative.* to beat or defeat. **4** *Informal, Figurative.* to confuse or puzzle completely: *The last question on the examination was a problem that completely floored us.* SYN: nonplus, confound. **5** to press against the floorboard: *To start the car, turn on the ignition and floor the accelerator.* **6** to place upon a floor; base.
cross the floor, to change political parties: *Churchill crossed the floor of the House and became a Liberal* (Atlantic).
wipe the floor with, to inflict a crushing defeat on: *The Gaullists had won a resounding victory, wiping the floor with all their opponents* (London Times).
[Old English *flōr*] —**floor′less,** *adj.*

floor|age (flôr′ij, flōr′-), *n.* **1** the amount of floor, usually measured in square feet, available in a building or part of a building; floor space. **2** = flooring (def. 2).

floor|board (flôr′bôrd′, flōr′bōrd′), *n., v.* —*n.* **1** one of the boards of a wooden floor. **2** Usually, **floorboards.** the floor of an automobile, especially of the driver's compartment: *Then the green flag fell and 33 big feet pushed 33 throttles to the floorboards* (Time).
—*v.t. Informal.* to push (the accelerator) down to the floorboard of an automobile.

floor broker, a member of a stock exchange who executes orders for other members. He does not deal directly with the public.

floor|cloth (flôr′klôth′, flōr′-; -kloth′), *n.* **1** a cloth or other material for covering a floor, such as linoleum. **2** a cloth for washing or wiping floors.

floor|er (flôr′ər, flōr′-), *n.* **1** a person who lays floors. **2** a person or thing that strikes someone or something to the floor. **3** *Informal, Figurative.* something that confuses, puzzles, or embarrasses one, as a decisive retort or a hard question.

floor girl, *U.S.* a girl or woman who does odd jobs in a store, workshop, etc.

floor|ing (flôr′ing, flōr′-), *n.* **1** a floor. **2** floors. **3** material for making or covering floors, such as wood, linoleum, or tile.

floor lamp, a tall lamp that stands on the floor.

floor leader, *U.S.* the member of a lawmaking body chosen to direct the members who belong to his political party: *The floor leader has the responsibility of managing legislation on the floor of the Senate.*

floor-length (flôr′lengkth′, flōr′-; -length′), *adj.* reaching down to the floor: *floor-length draperies.*

floor man, a representative of a brokerage house who operates on an exchange floor.

floor-man|age (flôr′man′ij, flōr′-), *v.t.,* **-aged, -ag|ing.** *U.S.* to direct as a floor manager or floor leader: *Within two years he was floor-managing major New Deal legislation* (Harper's).

floor manager, 1 the manager of a particular floor in a hotel or department store: *[The] key would not open the door, so the porter got a passkey from the floor manager* (Time). **2** *U.S.* **a** the campaign manager for a political candidate at a nominating convention. **b** = floor leader.

***floor plan,** a diagram, drawn to scale, of a horizontal section of a room, or rooms, on the same level, showing the thickness of walls, the positions of openings, as doorways, and, often, other features.

***floor plan**

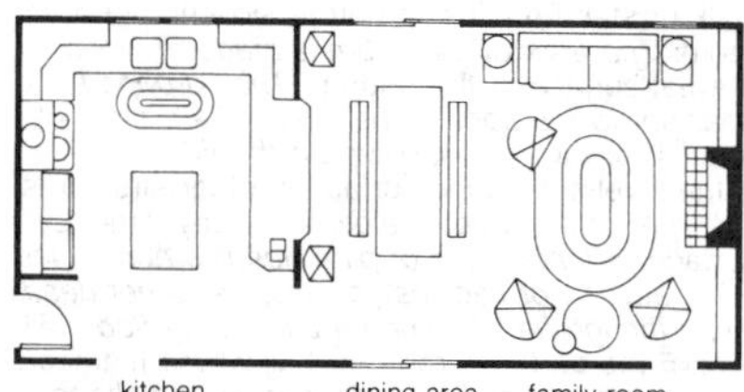

floor show, an entertainment consisting of music, singing, dancing, or comedy acts, presented at a night club, hotel, or club.

floor space, the horizontal surface area of a room, floor, or building: *It will be a one-story structure with 12,000 square feet of floor space* (Wall Street Journal).

floor-through (flôr′thrü′, flōr′-), *n. U.S.* an apartment that takes up an entire floor.

floor trader, a member of a stock exchange who usually buys and sells for his own account only.

floor|walk|er (flôr′wô′kər, flōr′-), *n.* a person employed in a large store to direct the work of salesclerks and give assistance to customers.

floor|ward (flôr′wərd, flōr′-), *adv., adj.* —***adv.*** toward the floor: *The glass spun floorward, hit, and splintered.* —***adj.*** directed toward the floor: *a floorward glance of bashfulness and modesty.*

floor|wards (flôr′wərdz, flōr′-), *adv.* = floorward.

flooz|ie or **flooz|y** (flü′zē), *n., pl.* **flooz|ies,** *adj. Slang.* —*n.* **1** a girl or woman of loose morals: *To his current floozie he is an elderly bore with a useful wallet* (Punch). **2** a girl or woman of not much intelligence or taste.
—***adj.*** of or characteristic of a floozie: *with a mincing, floozy strut* (Time).
[perhaps variant of *Flossie,* a nickname for *Florence*]

flop (flop), *v.,* **flopped, flop|ping,** *n., adv.* —*v.i.* **1** to move loosely or heavily; flap around clumsily: *The fish flopped helplessly on the deck.* SYN: flounder, wriggle. **2** to fall or move heavily or clumsily; plump down suddenly; come down with a flop: *The tired boy flopped down into a chair.* **3** *Figurative.* to change or turn suddenly: *He flopped over to the other point of view.* **4** *Informal.* to fail: *His first business venture flopped completely.* **5** *Slang.* to sleep: *The west end has ... stucco "motor courts," where a tired family can flop overnight* (Harper's). —*v.t.* **1** to drop or throw with a sudden bump or thud. **2** to flap (wings) heavily and clumsily. **3** to strike with a sudden blow. **4** to reverse (a picture or image).
—*n.* **1** the action of flopping: *Every stop caused a flop of the wide brim of her hat.* **2** a dull, heavy sound made by flopping. **3** *Informal.* a failure: *His last book was a flop.* **4** = flophouse.
—***adv.*** straight; directly: *He dropped the package flop on the couch.* [variant of *flap*]

flop|house (flop′hous′), *n. U.S.* a cheap, rundown hotel or rooming house for vagrant and homeless persons, usually in a very poor section of a city.

flop|o|ver (flop′ō′vər), *n. U.S.* **1** *Informal.* a turning over; turnover. **2** a television image that appears as a series of frames running down the screen, due to faulty reception.

flop|per (flop′ər), *n.* one that flops.

flop|py (flop′ē), *adj.,* **-pi|er, -pi|est,** *n., pl.* **-pies.** *Informal.* —***adj.*** tending to flop; flopping: *a floppy hat.* —*n.* = floppy disk. —**flop′pi|ly,** *adv.* —**flop′pi|ness,** *n.*

floppy disk or **disc,** a small, flexible, magnetically coated disk in which data is stored in digital form: *A one-ounce floppy disk can contain as much information as 3,000 punch cards* (John R. Rice).

flops (flops), *n.* a unit of speed in the operation of a computer, often used in combination, as in *megaflops* (one million flops) and *gigaflops* (one billion flops). [< *f*(loating) *l*(ogical) *o*(perations) *p*(er) *s*(econd)]

Flo|ra (flôr′ə, flōr′-), *n.* the Roman goddess of flowers. [< Latin *Flōra* goddess of flowers < *flōs, flōris* flower]

flo|ra (flôr′ə, flōr′-), *n., pl.* **flo|ras, flo|rae** (flôr′ē, flōr′-). **1** plants of a particular region or time: *the flora of the West Indies, the flora of the Carboniferous period.* **2** a work that systematically describes such plants. [< *Flora*]
▶**Flora** is a collective singular: *The flora of this desert region is more varied than we supposed.*

flo|ral (flôr′əl, flōr′-), *adj.* **1** of or having to do with flowers: *floral decorations.* **2** resembling flowers: *floral patterns.* [< Latin *flōs, flōris* flower + English *-al*[1]] —**flo′ral|ly,** *adv.*

floral circle, *Botany.* a ring of like organs, such as petals, around the axis of a flower; one of the whorls of a flower.

floral emblem, a flower or plant used as a symbol of a country, state, city, or organization.

floral envelope, *Botany.* the floral leaves (petals or sepals, or both) of a flower.

flo|ral|ize (flôr′ə līz, flōr′-), *v.t.,* **-ized, -iz|ing.** to make floral; adorn with flowers.

Flo|ré|al (flô rā àl′), *n. French.* the eighth month, from April 20 to May 19, in the calendar of the first French republic. [< French *Floréal* < Latin *flōrēus* of flowers < *flōs, flōris* flower]

flo|re|at (flôr′ē at, flōr′-), *Latin.* may it (or he or she) flourish.

Flor|ence fennel (flôr′əns, flor′-), = finocchio.

Florence flask, 1 a globular bottle of thin transparent glass with a long neck, usually covered with straw or similar material, used for holding olive oil or wine. **2** a bottle of similar shape, usually of heat-resistant glass, used in a laboratory for heating chemicals.

flor|en|tine (flôr′ən tēn, flor′-), *n.* a twilled silk cloth, used for wearing apparel. [< Latin *Flōrentīnus* of or having to do with *Flōrentia* Florence, a city in Italy, where it was made]

Flor|en|tine (flôr′ən tēn, flor′-), *adj., n.* —***adj.*** of or having to do with Florence, Italy.
—*n.* a person born or living in Florence, Italy.

flo|res|cence (flô res′əns, flō-), *n.* **1** the act of blossoming. **2** the condition of blossoming. **3** the period of blossoming. **4** flowers. [< New Latin *florescentia* < Latin *flōrēscere* begin to flower < *flōrēre* to flower, flourish < *flōs, flōris* flower]

flo|res|cent (flô res′ənt, flō-), *adj.* blossoming. SYN: flowering, blooming, efflorescent.

flo|ret (flôr′it, flōr′-), *n.* **1** a small flower; floweret: *acres of houstonia whose innumerable florets whiten and ripple before the eye* (Emerson). **2** *Botany.* one of the small flowers in a flower head of a composite plant, such as the dandelion or aster. [< Old French *florete* (diminutive) < *flor* flower < Latin *flōs, flōris*]

flo|ri|at|ed (flôr′ē ā′tid, flōr′-), *adj.* decorated with floral ornamentation: *floriated tracery.*

flo|ri|a|tion (flôr′ē ā′shən, flōr′-), *n.* floral decoration.

flor|i|bun|da (flôr′ə bun′də, flōr′-), *n.* a type of hybrid polyantha rose which bears many blossoms upon a low, bushy plant. [< New Latin *floribunda* < Latin *flōs, flōris* flower]

flo|ri|cul|tur|al (flôr′ə kul′chər əl, flōr′-), *adj.* having to do with floriculture. —**flo′ri|cul′tur|al|ly,** *adv.*

flo|ri|cul|ture (flôr′ə kul′chər, flōr′-), *n.* the cultivation of flowers or flowering plants, especially ornamental plants. [< Latin *flōs, flōris* flower + English *culture*]

flo|ri|cul|tur|ist (flôr′ə kul′chər ist, flōr′-), *n.* an expert in floriculture.

flor|id (flôr′id, flor′-), *adj.* **1** highly colored; ruddy: *a florid complexion.* SYN: rubicund. **2** *Figurative.* much ornamented; flowery; showy; ornate: *florid language, a florid piece of music, florid architecture.* **3** *Obsolete.* full of flowers; covered with flowers. [< Latin *flōridus* < *flōs, flōris* flower] —**flor′id|ly,** *adv.* —**flor′id|ness,** *n.*

Flor|i|da gallinule (flôr′ə də, flor′-), a slate-colored gallinule with a red bill tipped with yellow, found in wet, marshy areas of tropical and temperate America.

Florida grackle, a grackle that lives in the southern parts of the United States.

Florida jay, a blue and gray jay without a crest, found only in the state of Florida.

Florida moss, = Spanish moss.

Flor|i|dan (flôr′ə dən, flor′-), *adj., n.* = Floridian.

Flo|rid|i|an (flô rid′ē ən, flō-), *adj., n.* —***adj.*** of or having to do with Florida.
—*n.* a native or inhabitant of Florida.

flo|rid|i|ty (flô rid′ə tē, flō-), *n.* the quality or state of being florid: (*Figurative.*) *He deprecated the floridity of Trotsky's style, but predicted that he would outgrow it* (Edmund Wilson).

flo|rif|er|ous (flô rif′ər əs, flō-), *adj.* bearing flowers: *One of the most floriferous varieties I have ever grown is ... a single-fringed white petunia with golden throat* (New York Times). [< Latin *flōrifer* flower-bearing (< *flōs, flōris* + *ferre* to bear) + English *-ous*] —**flo|rif′er|ous|ness,** *n.*

flor|i|gen (flôr′ə jen, flōr′-), *n.* a hypothetical hormone in plants which is supposed to stimulate the production of flowers. [< Latin *flōs, flōris* flower + English *-gen*]

flo|ri|le|gi|um (flôr′ə lē′jē əm, flōr′-), *n., pl.* **-gi|a** (-jē ə). **1** = anthology. **2a** a collection of flowers. **b** a descriptive list of a flower collection. [< New Latin *florilegium* < Latin *flōrilegus* flower culling < *flōs, flōris* flower + *legere* gather]

flor|in (flôr′ən, flor′-), *n.* **1** a British silver coin worth ten pence or 2 shillings. **2** a gold coin issued at Florence in 1252. **3** any one of various gold or silver coins used in different countries of Europe since then, such as the Dutch guilder. [< Old French *florin* < Italian *fiorino* Florentine coin marked with a lily < *fiore* flower < Latin *flōs, flōris.* Compare etym. under **forint.**]

flo|rist (flôr′ist, flōr′-, flor′-), *n.* a person who raises or sells flowers.

flo|ris|tic (flô ris′tik, flō-), *adj.* **1** of a flora or floristics. **2** of flowers. —**flo|ris′ti|cal|ly,** *adv.*

flo|ris|tics (flô ris′tiks, flō-), *n.* study of the abundance and geographical distribution of plants.

flo|rist|ry (flôr′ə strē, flōr′-, flor′-), *n.* the art or skill of raising flowers.

flo|ri|su|gent (flôr′ə sü′jənt, flōr′-), *adj.* sucking honey from flowers: *florisugent birds or insects.* [< Latin *flōs, flōris* flower + *sūgens, -entis* present participle of *sūgere* suck]

flo|ru|it (flôr′ů it, flōr′-; flor′yů-), *Latin.* he (or she) flourished (used in giving the date of the most successful or accepted period of a person's life and activity): *Kenya last week was like Dakota Territory in the days of Sitting Bull (floruit 1876)* (Time).

flo|ry (flôr′ē, flōr′-), *adj.* = fleury.

Flo|ry temperature (flôr′ē, flōr′-), a specific temperature at which any one polymer exists in an ideal state for study of its properties in comparison with those of other polymers: *The Flory temperature ... became the basis for the development of hundreds of different plastics and synthetics* (Time). [< Paul J. Flory, born 1910, an American chemist, who discovered it]

flos|cu|lar (flos′kyə lər), *adj.* of or having to do with a floscule.

flos·cule (flos′kyül), *n.* = floret (def. 2). [< French *floscule* < Latin *flōsculus* (diminutive) < *flōs, flōris* flower]
flos·cu·lous (flos′kyə ləs), *adj.* = floscular.
floss (flôs, flos), *n., v.* —*n.* **1** a shiny, silk thread that has not been twisted, made from short, loose, silk fibers. Floss is used for embroidery. Waxed floss is used for cleaning between the teeth. **2** soft, silky fluff or fibers. Milkweed pods contain white floss. Ears of corn have brownish floss. **3** short, loose, silk fibers.
—***v.t., v.i.*** to clean (the teeth) with dental floss: *Brushing, flossing, and irrigation of the teeth pry loose . . . dental plaque* (Samuel W. Rosenberg).
[origin uncertain]
floss silk, **1** silk in untwisted filaments or strands. **2** the floss spun by silkworms.
floss·y (flôs′ē, flos′-), *adj.,* **floss·i·er, floss·i·est.** **1** of floss. **2** like floss. **3** *Informal, Figurative.* fancy; glamorous; highly decorated: *One of the flossiest office buildings in this or any other city may be ready this month* (New York Times).
floss yarn, a soft, slightly twisted yarn made from floss silk.
flo·ta (flō′tä), *n. Spanish.* a fleet of ships.
flo·tage (flō′tij), *n.* **1** the act or state of floating. **2** floating power; buoyancy. **3** anything that floats, such as ships floating on a river, or flotsam. **4** the portion of a ship above the water line. Also, **floatage.** [earlier *floatage* < *float* + *-age.* Compare French *flottage.*]
flo·ta·tion (flō tā′shən), *n.* **1** the act or process of floating or launching. **2** the condition of keeping afloat. **3** the act or process of getting started or established: *the flotation of a business.* **4** the act or fact of selling or putting on sale: *a flotation of bonds.* **5** a process of obtaining a specific mineral from crushed ore by agitating it in water mixed with oils and chemicals, causing one group of particles to attach itself to the oily froth and float to the surface of the water, where it may be skimmed off. Also, **floatation.** [variant of *floatation* < *float* + *-ation;* spelling influenced by French *flottaison*]
flotation bag, an inflatable bag to keep afloat or stabilize a craft in water.
flotation collar, a ring-shaped buoyant device attached to something in the water to keep it afloat until it is recovered, especially a spacecraft after a splashdown.
flotation gear, **1** a landing gear for aircraft, incorporating floats rather than wheels. **2** any buoyant gear serving to keep an airplane or persons afloat after an emergency landing on water.
flo·ta·tive (flō′tə tiv), *adj.* of or having to do with flotation; having the quality of floating. Also, **floatative.**
flo·til·la (flō til′ə), *n.* **1** a small fleet. **2** a fleet of small ships.
[< Spanish *flotilla* (diminutive) < *flota* fleet < Old French *flote* < Scandinavian (compare Old Icelandic *floti* fleet)]
flot·sam (flot′səm), *n.* the wreckage of a ship or its cargo found floating on the sea. Legally it belongs to the original owner, though finders may claim salvage.
flotsam and jetsam, a wreckage or cargo found floating on the sea or washed ashore: *To the Lord High Admiral belongs . . . a share of all lawful prizes, lagan, flotsam and jetsam* (John Chamberlayne). **b** *Figurative.* odds and ends; useless things: *a mind stored with a mass of flotsam and jetsam of useless information. "The flotsam and jetsam of a slum clearance project"* (John Stephen Strange). **c** people without steady work or permanent homes: *The slums are filled with the flotsam and jetsam of humanity.*
[< Anglo-French *floteson,* Old French *flotaison* < *floter* to float, perhaps < Old English *flotian*]
flot·san (flot′sən), *n.* = flotsam.
flounce¹ (flouns), *v.,* **flounced, flounc·ing,** *n.*
—*v.i.* **1** to go with an angry or impatient fling of the body: *She flounced out of the room in a rage.* **2** to make floundering movements; twist and turn; jerk.
—***n.*** **1** an angry or impatient fling of the body. **2** a floundering movement; twisting and turning.
[perhaps < Scandinavian (compare dialectal Swedish *flunsa* plunge, fall with a splash)]
flounce² (flouns), *n., v.,* **flounced, flounc·ing.** —*n.* a wide strip of cloth, gathered along the top edge and sewed to a dress, skirt, or other clothing, for trimming; a wide ruffle.
—***v.t.*** to trim with a flounce or flounces: *The bouffant skirt floats over a flounced white petticoat* (New Yorker).
[variant of *frounce;* perhaps spelling influenced by *flounce¹*]
flounc·ey (floun′sē), *adj.,* **flounc·i·er, flounc·i·est.** = flouncy.
flounc·ing (floun′sing), *n.* **1** material for flounces. **2** a flounce or flounces.
flounc·y (floun′sē), *adj.,* **flounc·i·er, flounc·i·est.** **1** fluffed out; bouffant: *blonde and redhead girls, flouncy skirts flying* (Wall Street Journal). **2** trimmed with a flounce or flounces: *flouncy lampshades and period furniture* (London Times).
floun·der¹ (floun′dər), *v., n.* —*v.i.* **1** to struggle awkwardly without making much progress; plunge about: *The horses were floundering in the deep snowdrifts.* **2** *Figurative.* to be clumsy or confused and make mistakes: *The girl was frightened by the audience and floundered through her song.*
—***n.*** the act or fact of floundering.
[perhaps < *flounder²* (because of the fish's habit of flopping when caught)]
floun·der² (floun′dər), *n., pl.* **-ders** or (*collectively*) **-der.** any one of a group of flatfish that live in salt water and are much used for food. The flounder has a large mouth, a nearly white underside and an upper side that takes on the color of the sea floor where it lives. [< Anglo-French *floundre,* perhaps < Scandinavian (compare Norwegian *flundra*)]
flour (flour), *n., v.* —*n.* **1** a fine, powdery meal made by grinding and sifting the kernels of wheat or other grain. Flour is used to make bread, rolls, cake, and other baked goods. **2** any fine, soft powder.
—*v.t.* **1** to cover or sprinkle with flour. **2** *U.S.* to grind and sift (grain) into flour.
—*v.i.* (of mercury) to break up into dull particles coated with some sulfide and incapable of coalescing with other metals.
[variant of *flower* as "flower (that is, the finest part) of meal²"]
flour beetle, any one of various beetles that live on flour or mealy substances.
flour corn, a type of corn with soft, starchy kernels grown by the Indians in the Southwestern United States and in the warm areas of South America; soft corn.
flour·ish (flėr′ish), *v., n.* —*v.i.* **1** to grow or develop with vigor; do well; be prosperous; thrive: *Your radishes are flourishing. His newspaper business grew and flourished. The stars shall fade away, the sun . . . Grow dim . . . But thou shalt flourish in immortal youth* (Joseph Addison). SYN: succeed, prosper. **2** *Figurative.* to be in the best time of life or activity: *Shakespeare flourished during Queen Elizabeth's reign.* **3** *Figurative.* to make a showy display. **4** *Obsolete.* to blossom; flower.
—*v.t.* **1** to wave (a sword, stick, arm, or other object) in the air: *He flourished the letter at us when he saw us.* SYN: brandish. **2** *Figurative.* to make a showy display of; flaunt: *to flourish one's wealth.* **3** to decorate or ornament with color or designs.
—***n.*** **1** the act of waving about in the air: *He gave a flourish of his hat. The donkey gave a flourish of his heels.* **2** an extra ornament or curve in handwriting; flowing curves made with the pen: *He ended his signature with a flourish.* **3** *Music.* a showy trill or passage: *a flourish of trumpets.* **4** a showy display: *The agent showed us about the house with much flourish.* **5** *Figurative.* the condition of being in the best time of life: *in full flourish.* **6** an expression used for effect in speech or writing. **7** *Obsolete.* the state of blooming.
[< Old French *floriss-,* stem of *florir* < Vulgar Latin *flōrīre,* for Latin *flōrēre* to bloom < *flōs, flōris* a flower] —**flour′ish·er,** *n.*
flour·ish·ing (flėr′i shing), *adj.* that flourishes; thriving; prospering: *a flourishing garden,* (*Figurative.*) *a flourishing career.* —**flour′ish·ing·ly,** *adv.*
flour mill, **1** a machine for grinding wheat or other grain into flour. **2** a place or establishment where there is such a machine or machines.
flour moth, a small, grayish-black moth whose larvae feed on flour, found in many parts of the world, especially in Mediterranean countries; Mediterranean flour moth.
flour·y (flour′ē), *adj.* **1** of or like flour. **2** covered or white with flour or powder.
flout (flout), *v., n.* —*v.t.* to treat with contempt or scorn; mock; scoff at: *The foolish boy flouted his mother's advice.* SYN: taunt.
—*v.i.* to show contempt or scorn; mock; scoff: *Ah, you may flout and turn up your faces* (Robert Browning). SYN: jeer.
—***n.*** a contemptuous speech or act; insult; mockery; scoffing: *Bruise me with scorn, confound me with a flout* (Shakespeare). SYN: taunt, jeer.
[special use of variant of *flute* (play the flute)]
—**flout′er,** *n.* —**flout′ing·ly,** *adv.*
►See **flaunt** for usage note.
flow (flō), *v., n.* —*v.i.* **1** to run like water; move in a current or stream: *A stream flows past the house. Blood flows through our bodies. Flow gently, sweet Afton, among thy green braes* (Robert Burns). **2** to pour out; pour along: (*Figurative.*) *The crowd flowed out of the town hall and down the main street.* **3** *Figurative.* to move easily or smoothly; glide: *Light traffic flowed along the highway.* **4** to hang loosely and waving: *flowing robes, a flowing tie. Her long hair flowed in the wind.* **5** to be plentiful; be full and overflowing: *a land flowing with milk and honey* (Exodus 3:8). **6** (of the tide) to flow in; rise. **7** *Obsolete.* to be overfull.
—***v.t.*** **1** to cause to flow. **2** to cover with water or other liquid; flood.
—***n.*** **1** a thing that flows; current; stream: *There is a constant flow of water from the spring.* **2** *Figurative.* any smooth, steady movement like that of water in a river: *a rapid flow of speech, the flow of traffic. A bird sings the self-same song with never a fault in its flow* (Thomas Hardy). **3** the act or way of flowing: *a flow of blood. From farm to farm the Concord glides, and trails my fancy with its flow* (James Russell Lowell). **4** the rate of flowing: *a flow of two feet per second.* **5** the flowing of the tide toward the shore; rise of the tide: *Each wavelet on the ocean toss'd Aids in the ebb-tide or the flow* (Charles Mackay). **6** an overflowing; flooding: *the flows of the Nile.* **7** *Physics.* the directional movement in a current or stream that is a characteristic of all fluids, such as air or electricity: *The flow of cosmic ray energy is just about the same as the energy-flow in starlight* (E. P. George).
[Old English *flōwan*]
—***Syn.*** *v.i.* **1, 2 Flow, gush, stream** mean to run or pour out or along. **Flow** emphasizes the continuous forward movement of running or pouring water, whether fast or slow, in great or small quantity: *Water flowed over the sidewalks.* **Gush** means to rush out or flow forth suddenly in considerable quantity from an opening: *Water gushed from the broken pipe.* **Stream** means to pour forth steadily from a source, or flow steadily, always in the same direction: *Tears streamed from her eyes.*
flow·age (flō′ij), *n.* **1** the act or process of flowing; flow. **2** the state of being flooded. **3** the fluid that flows or floods. **4** the gradual internal alteration in structure of a viscous solid, such as asphalt, by intermolecular movement.
flow·back (flō′bak′), *n.* backflow; return.
***flow chart**, a diagram or chart showing the flow of supplies, equipment, or information, in an industrial, military, or other operation; flow sheet.

***flow chart**

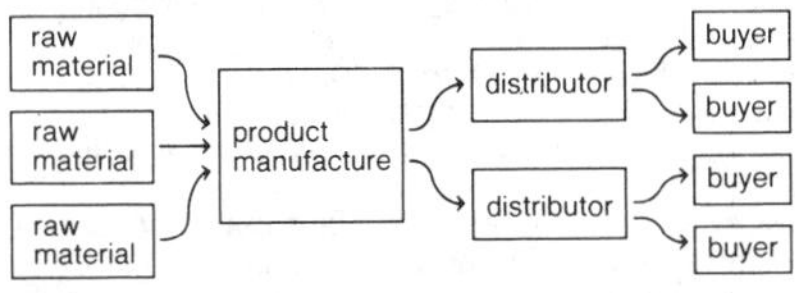

flow diagram, = flow chart.
***flow·er** (flou′ər), *n., v.* —*n.* **1** a blossom; the part of a plant that produces the seed. A flower is a shortened branch with modified leaves called petals. In botanical use, a flower consists normally of pistil, stamens, corolla, and calyx in regular series, any one or more of which may be absent. Flowers are often beautifully colored or shaped. *Bees gather nectar from flowers. The earliest known flowers were relatively simple, with small carpels, simple stamens, and flat or cup-shaped receptacles* (Fred W. Emerson). See the picture above on the next page. **2** a plant grown for its blossoms: *Her hobby is raising flowers.* **3** any one of several kinds of reproductive structures in lower plants, such as the mosses. **4** *Figurative.* the finest part: *the flower of the country's youth. The flower of high society was present at the royal ball. Lancelot the flower of bravery* (Tennyson). SYN: cream. **5** *Figurative.* the time when a thing is at its best; prime: *He is a man in the flower of life, about thirty* (Scott). **6** an ornament representing a flower; ornament; adornment: *A diamond flower glittered in her hair.*
—*v.i.* **1** to have flowers; produce flowers; bloom: *Most fruit trees flower in the spring.* **2** *Figurative.* to be at one's or its best; come into or be in one's prime: *Italian culture flowered in the Renaissance.* SYN: flourish.
—***v.t.*** **1** to cover or decorate with flowers. **2** to cause to blossom or bloom.
flowers, a chemical substance in the form of a fine powder, obtained especially as the result of condensation after sublimation: *flowers of sulfur.*
in flower, in the condition or time of having flowers; flowering: *An orchard in flower looks . . . more delightful than . . . the most finished parterre* (Joseph Addison).

Pronunciation Key: hat, āge, cãre, fär; let, ēqual, tėrm; it, īce; hot, ōpen, ôrder; oil, out; cup, pu̇t, rüle; child; long; thin; ᴛʜen; zh, measure; ə represents **a** in about, **e** in taken, **i** in pencil, **o** in lemon, **u** in circus.

in full flower, at the peak of attainment: *The young leader was in full flower when he was struck down by a crippling disease.*
[< Old French *flour* < Latin *flōs, flōris*] —**flow′er-like′**, *adj.*

★flower
definition 1

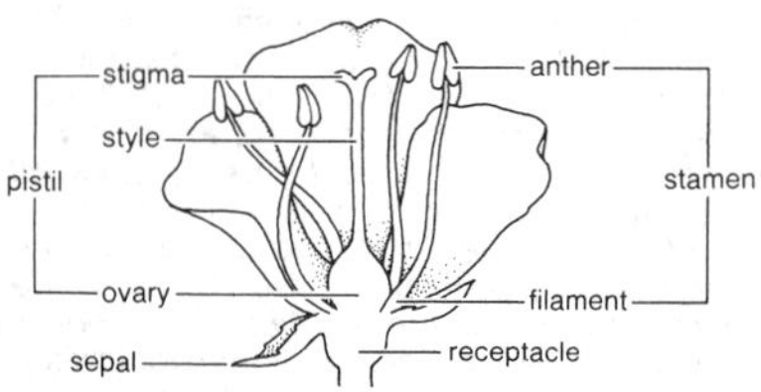

flow|er|age (flou′ər ij), *n.* **1** flowers. **2** a display of flowers; floral decoration. **3** a flowering or flowering state.
flower bed, **1** a plot of soil set aside for the growing of flowers. **2** a plot of flowers.
flower box, a box of wood or metal, filled with soil, in which flowers can be grown. It is often fixed to a window ledge or porch railing.
flower bug, any one of various small true bugs or hemipterous insects which frequent the blossoms of flowering plants.
flower child, **1** a hippie who proclaims love and peace, especially by carrying around or handing out flowers: *A long-haired flower child was cleared here of charges of "throwing a flower, to wit, a daisy" at a city police car* (New York Times). **2** any hippie.
flower clock, an arrangement of flowers that open and close at certain hours, such as the four-o'clock, in order to tell the approximate time of day.
flower cup, **1** = calyx. **2** the cup-shaped receptacle formed by certain flowers.
Flower Day, April 8, a day set aside by the Japanese to honor the birthday of Buddha. They decorate temples with flowers and pour sweet tea over small statues of the infant Buddha.
flow|er-de-luce (flou′ər də lüs′), *n.* **1** = iris. **2** *Archaic.* the heraldic fleur-de-lis. [spelling for variant pronunciation of *fleur-de-lis*]
flow|ered (flou′ərd), *adj.* **1** having flowers: *a flowered border of the garden.* **2** covered or decorated with flowers: *a flowered bowl, flowered silk.*
flow|er|er (flou′ər ər), *n.* a plant that flowers in a certain way or at a certain time: *The lilac is a spring flowerer.*
flow|er|et (flou′ər it), *n.* **1** a small flower. **2** = floret (def. 2).
flower fence, a leguminous, tropical shrub having large, showy, orange or red flowers, sometimes used for hedges.
flower girl, **1** a young girl carrying flowers before the bride at some weddings: *Susan Allen, a niece of the bride, served as flower girl* (New York Times). **2** a girl who sells flowers, usually on the street.
flower head, a dense cluster of florets growing from the shortened summit of a stem, such as that on the dandelion, chrysanthemum, sunflower, or other composite plants. A flower head is also called a capitulum, anthodium, or compound flower.
flow|er|ing (flou′ər ing), *adj., n.* —***adj.*** having flowers: *Many flowering plants blossom in the spring.*
—***n.*** a coming into flower; a ripening: (*Figurative.*) *Inside Japan a flowering called by historians the "Japanese Renaissance" took place in the 17th Century* (Atlantic).
flowering almond, a shrub of the rose family grown for its pink or white flowers.
flowering dogwood, a small North American tree covered in the spring with large white or pink flowers. Its flower is the state flower of Virginia and North Carolina. See also **dogwood**.
flowering maple, = abutilon.
flowering quince, = Japanese quince.
flowering spurge, a hardy spurge of eastern North America, grown for the showy white appendages of its flower cluster; emetic root.
flowering tobacco, = nicotiana.
flow|er|less (flou′ər lis), *adj.* **1** having no flowers. **2** *Botany.* = cryptogamic.
flower of an hour, = bladder ketmia.
flower people, = flower children.
flower piece, **1** a specially designed arrangement of flowers. **2** a picture with flowers as its subject. **3** a particular shape worked in flowers.
flow|er|pot (flou′ər pot′), *n.* **1** a pot to hold soil for a plant to grow in. **2** a form of fireworks: *The kind of fireworks that we call a flowerpot throws colored balls into the air* (Ralph Ingersoll).
flower power, power sought by flower children to achieve social change through love and nonviolence.
flow|ers (flou′ərz), *n.pl.* See under **flower**.
flowers of sulfur, a yellow powder formed by condensing the vapor of sulfur, used especially as a fungicide and in medicine.
flower stalk, the peduncle supporting the flower or flower head.
flow|er|y (flou′ər ē), *adj.*, **-er|i|er, -er|i|est.** **1** having many flowers: *flowery plants.* **2** *Figurative.* full of fine words and fanciful expressions; florid: *a flowery speech.* **3** decorated with a design of flowers: *a flowery fabric.* —**flow′er|i|ly**, *adv.* —**flow′er|i|ness**, *n.*
flow|ing (flō′ing), *adj.* **1** moving in a current or stream: *flowing water.* **2** *Figurative.* moving easily or smoothly: *flowing verse, a flowing movement in a dance.* **3** hanging loosely: *flowing robes.* —**flow′ing|ly**, *adv.* —**flow′ing|ness**, *n.*
flowing tracery, *Architecture.* tracery which is characterized by lines branching into flowing curves, forming leaves, arches, or the like.
flow line, **1** = assembly line. **2** (in igneous rocks) a band of color or an arrangement of crystals that indicates the differential flow of the molten mass before solidification.
flow|me|ter (flō′mē′tər), *n.* any one of various devices for measuring the volume or rate of flow of a liquid or gas.
flown¹ (flōn), *v.* past participle of **fly²**: *The bird has flown. The flag is flown on all national holidays. Flown* also occurs as an element of compound adjectives: *far-flown, high-flown, new-flown.*
flown² (flōn), *adj.* **1** *Archaic.* filled to excess: *The sons of Belial, flown with insolence and wine* (Milton). **2** *Obsolete.* swollen, as a river in flood. [obsolete past participle of *flow*]
flow sheet, a chart or diagram showing materials, operations, apparatus, and, sometimes, labor involved at various stages in a process, such as in manufacturing or construction.
flow|stone (flō′stōn′), *n.* a large cave formation resulting from deposits of calcium carbonate upon walls where water flows from the rock.
flow structure, the structure in igneous rock produced by the flow of the molten mass before solidification.
fl. oz., fluid ounce or ounces.
fl. pt., flash point.
F.L.S., Fellow of the Linnean Society (in London).
flu (flü), *n.* = influenza.
flub (flub), *v.*, **flubbed, flub|bing,** *n. Informal.*
—***v.t.*** to do (something) very clumsily; spoil; botch: *Poor foul-shooting also hurt the Knicks, who flubbed fifteen free throws* (New York Times).
—***v.i.*** to perform badly; fail: *He spent a miserable time as a mill hand, flubbed at newspaper work* (Time).
—***n.*** a failure in performance; botch; mistake; error.
[origin uncertain]
flub|dub (flub′dub), *n. Dialect.* pretentious nonsense or show; airs. [varied reduplication of *flub*]
fluc|tu|ant (fluk′chü ənt), *adj.* fluctuating; varying. [< Latin *flūctuāns, -antis,* present participle of *flūctuāre;* see etym. under **fluctuate**]
fluc|tu|ate (fluk′chü āt), *v.*, **-at|ed, -at|ing.** —***v.i.*** **1** to rise and fall; change continually; vary irregularly; waver: *Prices fluctuate. The temperature fluctuates from day to day. The needle on the scale fluctuates between 125 and 126 pounds.* (*Figurative.*) *His emotions fluctuated between hopefulness and despair.* **SYN**: oscillate, vacillate. **2** to move in waves.
—***v.t.*** to cause to fluctuate: *A breeze began to … fluctuate all the still perfume* (Tennyson).
[< Latin *flūctuāre* (with English *-ate¹*) < *flūctus, -ūs* wave < *fluere* to flow]
fluc|tu|a|tion (fluk′chü ā′shən), *n.* **1** the act or process of rising and falling; continual change; irregular variation; wavering. **SYN**: vacillation. **2** a wavelike motion.

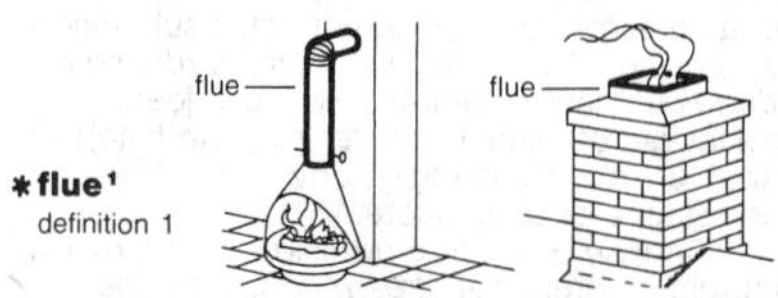

★flue¹
definition 1

★flue¹ (flü), *n.* **1** a tube, pipe, or other enclosed passage for conveying smoke, hot air, or other exhaust, outside a structure or from one part of it to another. A chimney often has several flues. **2** a pipe or tube for conveying heat to water in certain kinds of steam boilers. **3** a flue pipe in an organ. **4** the air passage in such a pipe. [origin uncertain]
flue² (flü), *n.* downy matter; fluff. [earlier *flew.* Compare Middle Dutch *vloe,* and Flemish *vluwe.*]
flue³ (flü), *n.* a kind of fishing net. Also, **flew.** [< Middle Dutch *vluwe,* or *vlouwe*]
flue⁴ (flü), *n.* **1** either arm of an anchor; fluke. **2** the barb of a harpoon, feather, etc. [origin uncertain. Compare Swedish *fly.*]
flue-cured (flü′kyůrd′), *adj.* cured by hanging for several days in a barn heated through flues, without smoke: *flue-cured tobacco.*
flued (flüd), *adj.* having a flue or flues.
flu|en|cy (flü′ən sē), *n.* **1** a smooth, easy flow: *The orator had great fluency of speech.* [*She*] *danced with her usual fine fluency* (New York Times). **2** easy, rapid speaking or writing: *His fluency had no great depth.* **SYN**: volubility.
flu|ent (flü′ənt), *adj.* **1** flowing smoothly or easily: *Long practice enabled the American to speak fluent French.* **2** speaking or writing easily and rapidly: *a fluent speaker. Fluent children are often also good readers.* **3** not fixed or stable; fluid; liquid. [< Latin *fluēns, -entis,* present participle of *fluere* to flow] —**flu′ent|ly**, *adv.* —**flu′ent|ness**, *n.*
—***Syn.*** **2 Fluent, glib, voluble** mean speaking easily. **Fluent** suggests speaking or writing both easily and well: *He is a fluent lecturer.* **Glib** suggests speaking so easily and so smoothly that it is not trustworthy: *He is a glib liar.* **Voluble** suggests speaking so much and continuously that it is boring: *Detained by a voluble talker, I was late.*
flue pipe, an organ pipe in which the sound is made by a current of air striking the mouth or opening in the pipe.
flu|er|ic (flü′ər ik), *adj.* = fluidic. [< Latin *fluere* to flow + English *-ic*]
flue stop, a stop controlling a series of flue pipes.
flue|y (flü′ē), *adj.* covered with flue; fluffy; downy. [< *flue²* + *-y¹*]
fluff (fluf), *n., v.* —***n.*** **1** soft, light, downy particles: *Woolen blankets often have fluff on them.* **2** a soft, light, downy mass: *The little kitten looked like a fluff of fur.* **3** *Informal.* a mistake in reading, speaking, or performing, on the stage or on radio or television: *As the kindly nurse,* [*she*] *is fine and her performance easily survives several minor fluffs in speaking her lines* (New York Herald-Tribune).
—***v.t.*** **1** to shake or puff out (hair, feathers, or nap) into a soft, light, downy mass: [*He*] *fluffed his hair before the wind with his hand, that it might dry* (Atlantic). **2** to buff (leather). **3** *Slang.* to make a mistake in reading, speaking, etc.: *He begins to drink and to fluff his announcements* (New York Times).
—***v.i.*** **1** to become fluffy. **2** to move or float softly like fluff. **3** *Informal.* to make a mistake in reading, speaking, or performing: *A bad reader of speeches, he fluffed frequently* (Wall Street Journal).
[perhaps variant of *flue²* downy matter; perhaps influenced by *puff*]
fluff|y (fluf′ē), *adj.*, **fluff|i|er, fluff|i|est.** **1** soft and light like fluff: *a fluffy shawl. Whipped cream is fluffy.* **2** covered with fluff; filled with fluff; downy: *fluffy baby chicks, a fluffy pillow.* **SYN**: fleecy. —**fluff′i|ly**, *adv.* —**fluff′i|ness**, *n.*
flü|gel|horn or **flu|gel|horn** (flü′gəl hôrn′), *n.* a brass wind instrument whose valves and shape resemble a cornet. [< German *Flügelhorn* < *Flügel* wing + *Horn* horn]
flu|gel|man (flü′gəl mən), *n., pl.* **-men.** = fugleman.
flu|id (flü′id), *n., adj.* —***n.*** any liquid or gas; something that will flow. Water, mercury, air, and oxygen are fluids. **SYN**: See syn. under **liquid.**
—***adj.*** **1** like a liquid or gas; flowing: *She poured the fluid mass of hot candy into a dish to harden.* **2** of or having to do with fluids. **3** *Figurative.* changing easily; not fixed, firm, or stable: *The general reported that the situation on the battlefield was still fluid.* **4** *Figurative.* flowing smoothly; fluent. **5** liquid: *fluid assets.*
[< Latin *fluidus* < *fluere* to flow] —**flu′id|ly**, *adv.* —**flu′id|ness**, *n.*
fluid amplifier, any one of various control and switching devices that run on compressed air, gas, or liquid without requiring moving parts.
fluid bed, a layer of solid material so finely pulverized that it has some of the characteristics of a fluid, utilized in the refining of iron and other ores, especially in nuclear reactors.
fluid cat cracking, the use of a powdered catalyst to flow through petroleum like a fluid in catalytic cracking.
fluid clutch, = fluid coupling.
fluid coupling, a device for transmitting power from one shaft to another, in which an oil or other fluid serves as the only connection between a pair of bladed rotors. An engine turning the first rotor forces fluid against the blades of the second rotor, causing it to turn.
fluid drachm (dram), = fluid dram.

fluid dram, one eighth of a fluid ounce or 3.6966 milliliters.
fluid drive, a system which utilizes a fluid coupling to transmit power from the engine to the drive shaft.
fluid dynamics, the study of gases and liquids in motion, including both aerodynamics and hydrodynamics.
flu|id|ex|tract (flü′id eks′trakt), *n.* a tincture or solution of a vegetable drug of such strength that one cubic centimeter represents (in therapeutic effect) one gram of the standardized drug in dry form.
*__fluid flow__, *Physics.* any characteristic movement of fluid particles, such as laminar flow and turbulent flow: *Using this method, scientists can study what they call "fluid flow," such as water running out of faucets or through pipes in your house, or the meandering of rivers and streams* (Science News Letter).

***fluid flow**

kinds of flow:

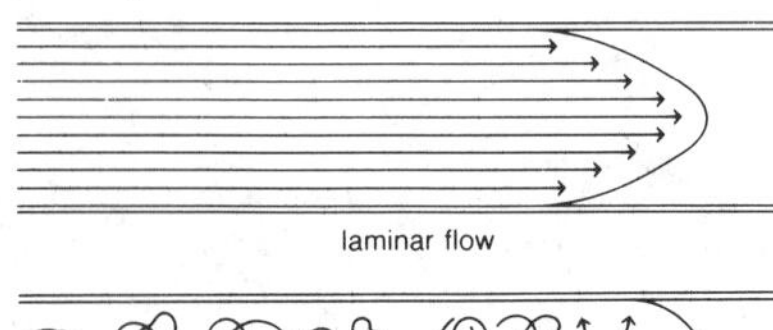

laminar flow

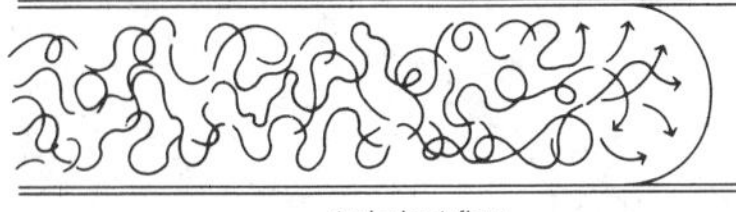

turbulent flow

fluid flywheel, a type of fluid coupling used in certain automobiles in connection with an automatic or semiautomatic transmission.
fluid fuel, liquid, gas, and chemical fuels: *Throughout the world fluid fuels are replacing solid fuels because their technical advantages in transport, handling, storage, processing and use have a large monetary value* (London Times).
flu|id|ic (flü id′ik), *adj.* **1** of or having to do with fluids or fluidics. **2** using the interaction of fluid streams of gas, air, or liquid to perform functions of instrumentation and control, which would otherwise be performed by mechanical or electrical mechanisms; flueric: *The signal in fluidic devices is carried by the flow of a liquid, just as the signal in electronic circuits is carried by the flow of the electrons* (Foster P. Stockwell).
fluidic circuit, fluid amplifiers connected to form circuits that can be used instead of mechanical devices or electrical circuits in performing industrial processes involving timing and counting and in controlling parts of airplanes and spacecraft.
flu|id|ics (flü id′iks), *n.* the science or technology of using fluid streams or fluidic devices instead of mechanical or electrical mechanisms to perform functions of instrumentation, the control of machinery, or the processing of information: *Where electronics uses streams of electrons, the growing technology of fluidics employs liquids or gases, which operate more reliably in certain environments* (New Scientist).
flu|id|ise (flü′ə dīz), *v.t.*, **-ised, -is|ing.** *British.* fluidize.
flu|id|i|ty (flü id′ə tē), *n.* fluid condition or quality: (*Figurative.*) *The play moved forward with an always professional fluidity* (Harper's).
flu|id|i|za|tion (flü′ə də zā′shən), *n.* **1** the process of making fluid or liquid. **2** the process in which a solid is so finely ground as to take on most of the properties of a liquid.
flu|id|ize (flü′ə dīz), *v.t.*, **-ized, -iz|ing. 1** to make fluid or liquid. **2** to give fluid properties to (a solid) by means of fluidization, so that it flows when in contact with a liquid or gaseous stream. **—flu′i|diz|er**, *n.*
flu|id|ized bed (flü′ə dīzd), = fluid bed.
fluid measure, = apothecaries' measure.
fluid mechanics, an applied science based on the principles of the flow of gases and liquids; fluid dynamics and fluid statics.
fluid ounce, or **flu|id|ounce** (flü′id ouns′), *n.* a measure for liquids. In the United States, 16 fluid ounces = 1 pint and a fluid ounce equals about .0295 liter; in Great Britain, 20 fluid ounces = 1 imperial pint.
fluid pressure, the pressure exerted by a confined fluid in static equilibrium, equal in all directions and perpendicular to the surfaces confining it.
flu|i|drachm (flü′ə dram′), *n.* = fluid dram.
flu|i|dram (flü′ə dram′), *n.* = fluid dram.
fluid statics, the study of gases and liquids at rest. Hydrostatics is a part of fluid statics.
fluid transmission, = fluid drive.

fluke[1] (flük), *n.* **1** the flat, three-cornered piece at the end of each arm of an anchor, which catches in the ground and holds it fast. **2** the barbed head of an arrow, harpoon, etc. **3** either of the two halves of a whale's tail. [perhaps special use of *fluke*[3] (because of its shape)]
fluke[2] (flük), *n., v.,* **fluked, fluk|ing.** *Informal.* **—*n.* 1** a lucky shot in billiards or pool. **2** a lucky chance; fortunate accident. **3** a chance or accident.
—*v.t.* 1 to make or hit by a lucky shot in billiards or pool. **2** to get by chance or accident.
—*v.i.* to make a fluke.
[origin uncertain]
fluke[3] (flük), *n.* **1** a flatfish, especially a common flounder. **2** a parasitic flatworm shaped somewhat like a flatfish; trematode: *They may be found in many parts of an animal body; there are blood flukes, lung flukes, liver flukes, intestinal flukes, and even some that cling to the external surface of some water animals* (A. M. Winchester). [Old English *flōc* flatfish]
fluke disease, an often fatal disease of the liver, especially in cattle and sheep, characterized by anemia, weakness, and swollen jaws; fascioliasis. It is caused by a liver fluke that lives as a larva in snails and then encysts on grass.
fluk|ey (flü′kē), *adj.*, **fluk|i|er, fluk|i|est.** = fluky.
flu|ki|cide (flü′kə sīd), *n.* a chemical substance that kills parasitic flatworms or flukes. [< *fluke*[3] + *-cide*[1]]
fluk|y (flü′kē), *adj.*, **fluk|i|er, fluk|i|est.** *Informal.* **1** like a fluke; obtained by chance rather than by skill: *a fluky victory.* **2** uncertain: *fluky weather.* **—fluk′i|ness**, *n.*
flume (flüm), *n., v.,* **flumed, flum|ing. —*n.* 1** a deep, narrow valley with a stream running through it. **2** a large, inclined trough or chute for carrying water. Flumes are used to transport logs or to furnish water for power.
—*v.t.* 1 to move (logs or timber) in a flume. **2** to divert (a river, etc.) by a flume.
[< Old French *flum* < Latin *flūmen, -inis* river < *fluere* to flow]
flum|mer|y (flum′ər ē), *n., pl.* **-mer|ies. 1a** a pudding made of milk, eggs, flour, sugar, etc. **b** a heavy pudding made of oatmeal or flour boiled with water. **2** *Figurative.* an empty compliment; empty trifling; nonsense: *a fine flummery about the . . . eminent genius of the person whom they are addressing* (Thackeray). SYN: froth, frivolity. [< Welsh *llymru*]
flum|mox (flum′əks), *v.t. Informal.* to bring to confusion; confound; bewilder. [apparently from dialectal *flummocks* to maul, mangle] **—flum′mox|er**, *n.*
flump (flump), *v., n. Informal.* **—*v.i., v.t.*** to move heavily with a dull noise.
—*n.* the act or sound of flumping. [perhaps imitative]
flung (flung), *v.* past tense and past participle of **fling:** *The boy flung the ball. The paper was flung away.*
flunk (flungk), *v., n. Informal.* **—*v.t.* 1** to fail (a test, course, or grade) in schoolwork: *He flunked his history examination but passed all the others.* **2** to cause to fail: *His answers on the final exam flunked him.* **3** to mark or grade as having failed.
—*v.i.* 1 to fail in a test, course, or grade in school. **2** to give up; back out.
—*n.* a flunking; failure.
flunk out, *Informal.* to dismiss or be dismissed from school, college, or the like, for failing work: *When I nearly flunked out, a number of my classmates and I discovered that studies were important* (New York Times).
[American English; apparently variant of *funk*]
flunk|ee (flung kē′), *n. U.S. Informal.* a person who flunks out.
flunk|er (flung′kər), *n. U.S.* **1** a student who fails in an examination. **2** a teacher who marks or grades such a student.
flunk|ey (flung′kē), *n., pl.* **-eys.** = flunky.
flunk-out (flungk′out′), *n. U.S. Informal.* a person who flunks out; flunkee: *a college flunk-out.*
flunk|y (flung′kē), *n., pl.* **flunk|ies. 1** a flattering, fawning person; toady. SYN: sycophant. **2** a manservant who wears livery; footman: *His flunkies answer at the bell* (Robert Burns). SYN: lackey. [perhaps alteration of *flanker* an outrider, one posted on the *flank* of a person or group]
flunk|y|ism or **flunk|ey|ism** (flung′kē iz əm), *n.* the actions or conduct of a flunky; being flattering and fawning.
Flu|on (flü′on), *n. Trademark, British.* polytetrafluoroethylene, a chemically inert plastic; Teflon.
flu|o|phos|phate (flü′ə fos′fāt), *n.* a phosphate containing fluorine as an essential constituent. [< *fluo*(rine) + *phosphate*]
flu|or (flü′ôr), *n.* = fluorite. [< Latin *fluor, -ōris* a flowing < *fluere* to flow]
flu|or|a|cet|a|mide (flü′ər ə set′ə mīd, -mid), *n.* the amide of fluoroacetic acid, used in Great Britain as a pesticide.

flu|or|ap|a|tite (flü′ər ap′ə tīt), *n.* a form of the mineral apatite containing fluorine. It is a major constituent of fossilized bones and is used as a measure of anthropological dating. *Formula:* $Ca_5(PO_4)_3F$ [< *fluor*(ine) + *apatite*]
flu|or|car|bon (flü′ər kär′bən), *n.* = fluorocarbon.
flu|o|rene (flü′ə rēn), *n.* a crystalline hydrocarbon extracted from coal tar, fluorescent when impure. *Formula:* $C_{13}H_{10}$
flu|o|resce (flü′ə res′), *v.i.*, **-resced, -resc|ing.** to give off light by fluorescence; become fluorescent. [back formation < *fluorescence*]
flu|o|res|ce|in (flü′ə res′ē in), *n.* an orange-red, crystalline powder that forms a greenish-yellow, fluorescent alkaline solution, used in making dyes. *Formula:* $C_{20}H_{12}O_5$ [< *fluoresce* + *-in* (because of its fluorescence in a solution)]
flu|o|res|ce|ine (flü′ə res′ē ēn, -in), *n.* = fluorescein.
flu|o|res|cence (flü′ə res′əns), *n.* **1** a giving off of light by a substance exposed to X rays, ultraviolet rays, or certain other rays, which continues only as long as exposure to these rays continues. The wave length of the radiation emitted is greater than that of the radiation absorbed. **2** the property of a substance that causes this. It is an ability to transform radiation so as to emit rays of a different wave length or color. **3** the light given off in this way. See also **phosphorescence.** [< *fluor*(spar) + *-escence,* as in *phosphorescence*]
flu|o|res|cent (flü′ə res′ənt), *adj., n.* **—*adj.* 1** that gives off light by fluorescence. Fluorescent substances glow in the dark when exposed to X rays. **2** *Figurative: a fluorescent youth.*
—*n.* = fluorescent light. **—flu′o|res′cent|ly**, *adv.*
fluorescent lamp, an electric lamp consisting of a tube in which a coating of fluorescent powder exposed to ultraviolet rays gives off a light that is cooler and less glaring than incandescent light.
fluorescent light, the light produced by a fluorescent lamp.
fluorescent screen, a screen coated on one side with a fluorescent substance such as calcium sulfide which gives off light when struck by X rays or cathode rays.
flu|o|res|cer (flü′ə res′ər), *n.* a chemical substance which absorbs ultraviolet radiation and emits it in the form of visible light: *Fluorescers . . . were incorporated in detergents to "add brightness to whiteness"* (New Scientist).
flu|or|ic (flü ôr′ik, -or′-), *adj.* of or having to do with fluorite or fluorine. [< *fluor* + *-ic*]
flu|o|rid (flü′ər id), *n.* = fluoride.
fluor|i|date (flůr′ə dāt, flü′ər ə-), *v.t.*, **-dat|ed, -dat|ing.** to add small amounts of a fluorine compound to (drinking water), especially to decrease tooth decay. [back formation < *fluoridation*]
fluor|i|da|tion (flůr′ə dā′shən, flü′ər ə-), *n.* the act or process of fluoridating. [< *fluorid*(e) + *-ation*]
flu|o|ride (flü′ə rīd, -ər id), *n.* a compound of fluorine and another element or radical.
fluor|i|di|za|tion (flůr′ə də zā′shən, flü′ər ə-), *n.* the application of a fluoride to the teeth.
fluor|i|dize (flůr′ə dīz, flü′ər ə-), *v.t.*, **-dized, -diz|ing.** *Dentistry.* to apply a fluoride locally to (the teeth) to decrease decay.
flu|o|ri|met|ric (flü′ər ə met′rik), *adj.* = fluorometric.
flu|o|rim|e|try (flü′ə rim′ə trē), *n.* = fluorometry.
flu|o|rin (flü′ər in), *n.* = fluorine.
fluor|i|nate (flůr′ə nāt, flü′ər ə-), *v.t.*, **-nat|ed, -nat|ing. 1** = fluoridate. **2** *Chemistry.* to combine or cause to react with fluorine. [< *fluorin*(e) + *-ate*[1]]
fluor|i|na|tion (flůr′ə nā′shən, flü′ər ə-), *n.* **1** the treatment of a water supply with fluorine. **2** the chemical combination or reaction of fluorine with another substance.
*__flu|o|rine__ (flü′ə rēn, -ər in), *n.* a greenish-yellow, bad-smelling, poisonous gas which occurs only in combination with certain other elements. It is the most active of all the chemical elements and is used in small amounts to purify water and to decrease tooth decay. [< *fluor* + *-ine*[2]]

***fluorine**

symbol	atomic number	atomic weight	oxidation state
F	9	18.9984	-1

flu|o|rite (flü′ə rīt), *n.* a transparent, translucent, crystalline mineral composed of calcium and fluorine that occurs in many colors; calcium fluoride; fluor; fluorspar. It is used especially for fusing metals and making glass and is an important

Pronunciation Key: hat, āge, cãre, fär; let, ēqual, tėrm; it, īce; hot, ōpen, ôrder; oil, out; cup, půt, rüle; child; long; thin; ᴛʜen; zh, measure; ə represents **a** in about, **e** in taken, **i** in pencil, **o** in lemon, **u** in circus.

source of fluorine. *Formula:* CaF_2 [< *fluor* + *-ite*[1]]

flu|o|ro|ac|e|tate (flü′ər ə as′ə tāt), *n.* a salt or ester of fluoroacetic acid, used chiefly as a rat poison.

flu|o|ro|a|ce|tic acid (flü′ər ə ə sē′tik, -set′ik), a highly poisonous acid in the form of colorless crystals, made synthetically or obtained from the gifblaar (a South African plant). *Formula:* CH_2FCOOH

flu|o|ro|car|bon (flü′ər ə kär′bən), *n.* any one of a group of compounds of fluorine and carbon that are chemically stable, used as solvents, lubricants, and refrigerator gases: *The outstanding quality of most fluorocarbons is their tremendous stability; they resist heat, acids, alkalis, insects, fungi and weathering* (Scientific American). [< *fluor*(ine) + *carbon*]

flu|o|ro|chem|i|cal (flü′ər ə kem′ə kəl), *n., adj.* —*n.* any one of various chemicals containing fluorine, such as the fluorocarbons: *Fluorochemicals are highly resistant to oxidation and heat, two of the worst enemies of paint and oil* (Wall Street Journal).
—*adj.* of or having to do with fluorochemicals.

flu|o|ro|chrome (flü′ər ə krōm), *n.* a fluorescent substance used to stain biological specimens.

flu|o|ro|form (flü′ər ə fôrm), *n.* a colorless, odorless gas analogous to chloroform, used as a refrigerant. *Formula:* CHF_3

fluor|o|graph|ic (flůr′ə graf′ik, flü′ər ə-), *adj.* of or having to do with fluorography.

fluo|rog|ra|phy (flü rog′rə fē, flü′ə rog′-), *n.* a technique for taking pictures giving a fluoroscopic view, that uses a camera requiring only one-sixth of the amount of X-ray exposure required by a fluoroscope. [< *fluoro*(scope) + *-graphy*]

flu|o|ro|hy|dro|cor|ti|sone (flü′ər ə hī′drə kôr′tə zōn), *n.* synthetic hormone much used in dermatology to relieve skin allergies. *Formula:* $C_{21}H_{29}FO_5$

flu|o|rom|e|ter (flü′ə rom′ə tər), *n.* an instrument which measures the fluorescence given off by a substance. [< *fluor*(escence) + *-meter*]

flu|o|ro|met|ric (flü′ər ə met′rik), *adj.* of, having to do with, or using a fluorometer. Also, **fluorimetric**. —**flu′o|ro|met′ric|al|ly**, *adv.*

flu|o|rom|e|try (flü′ə rom′ə trē), *n.* the measurement of fluorescent radiation with a fluorometer. Also, **fluorimetry**.

fluor|o|scope (flůr′ə skōp, flü′ər ə-), *n., v.,* **-scoped, -scop|ing.** —*n.* a device containing a fluorescent screen for examining the inner parts of an object by exposing it to X rays or other radiations; roentgenoscope. The parts of the object not penetrated by the rays cast shadows on the screen. *One important tool doctors have been using to detect cancers of the digestive tract has been the fluoroscope* (Science News Letter).
—*v.t.* to examine with a fluoroscope.
[American English < *fluor*(escence) + *-scope*]

fluor|o|scop|ic (flůr′ə skop′ik, flü′ər ə-), *adj.* of or having to do with the fluoroscope or with fluoroscopy. —**fluor′o|scop′i|cal|ly**, *adv.*

fluo|ros|co|pist (flü ros′kə pist, flü′ə ros′-), *n.* a person trained in the use of the fluoroscope.

fluo|ros|co|py (flü ros′kə pē, flü′ə ros′-), *n.* the use of a fluoroscope; examination of an object by X rays or other radiations.

flu|o|ro|sis (flü′ə rō′sis), *n.* a diseased condition, especially a mottled tooth enamel, caused by too much fluorine in drinking water. [< *fluor*(ine) + *-osis*]

flu|o|ro|u|ra|cil (flü′ər ə yůr′ə səl), *n.* a compound of fluorine and uracil, used as an antimetabolite in the palliative treatment of certain types of cancer.

flu|or|spar (flü′ər spär′), *n.* = fluorite.

flu|o|sil|i|cate (flü′ə sil′ə kit), *n.* a salt of fluosilicic acid.

flu|o|si|lic|ic acid (flü′ə sə lis′ik), a colorless, poisonous, highly corrosive liquid used in electroplating, as a disinfectant, and in hardening ceramics and cement. *Formula:* H_2SiF_6 [< *fluo*(rine) + *silicic*]

flu|phen|a|zine (flü fen′ə zēn, -zin), *n.* a long-acting tranquilizing drug given by injection, especially to schizophrenic and other mentally disturbed persons. *Formula:* $C_{22}H_{26}F_3N_3OS$ [< *flu*(orine) + *phenazine*]

flurr (flėr), *v.i.* to fly up; fly with whirring or fluttering wings. —*v.t.* to scatter; throw about.

flur|ry (flėr′ē), *n., pl.* **-ries**, *v.,* **-ried, -ry|ing.** —*n.* **1** a sudden gust: *A flurry of wind upset the small sailboat.* **2** a light fall of rain or snow: *flurries of snow.* **3** *Figurative.* **a** a sudden burst or round of activity: *a flurry of conferences, a flurry of rumors.* **b** a sudden excitement, confusion, or disturbance: *the flurry of last-minute preparations, a flurry of alarm. In the past year the flurry of public attention and headlines involving Fort Monmouth has faded away* (Bulletin of Atomic Scientists). SYN: commotion. **4** a sudden fluctuation of trading and prices on a stock or commodity exchange. **5** the spasmodic movements of a dying whale.
—*v.t.* to fluster; excite; make nervous; agitate: *Noise in the audience flurried the actor so that he forgot his lines.* SYN: confuse, disturb.
—*v.i.* **1** to become flustered or excited. **2** to come down in a flurry: *He stared out the window at the snow flurrying lightly through the sunless Christmas day* (James T. Farrell).
[perhaps related to *flurr* throw about (as dust); whir, flutter]

flush[1] (flush), *v., n.* —*v.i.* **1** to become red suddenly; blush; glow: *Her face flushed when they laughed at her.* SYN: redden. **2** to rush suddenly; flow rapidly: *Embarrassment caused the blood to flush to her cheeks.* **3** (of a plant) to send out shoots.
—*v.t.* **1** to cause to blush or glow: *Exercise flushed his face.* SYN: redden. **2a** to send a sudden rush of water over or through: *The city streets were flushed every night to make them clean.* **b** to empty out; drain: *to flush water from flooded land, to flush the stomach of a poisoned person.* **3** to make joyful and proud; excite: *The team was flushed with its first victory. Armies flushed with conquest* (Joseph Addison).
—*n.* **1** a rosy glow or blush: *The flush of sunrise was on the clouds.* **2** a sudden rush; rapid flow. **3** the action of draining water: *Don't dump ashes in the toilet; every flush uses 5 to 8 gallons* (New York Times). **4** an excited condition or feeling, especially as in a sudden rush of joyous pride: *in the flush of victory.* SYN: elation, thrill. **5a** a sudden, fresh growth: *April brought the first flush of grass.* **b** a tender young shoot of a tea plant. **6** glowing vigor; freshness: *the first flush of youth.* **7** a fit of feeling very hot.
[perhaps blend of *flash* and *blush*]

flush[2] (flush), *adj., adv., v.* —*adj.* **1a** even; level; in the same plane: *The edge of the new shelf must be flush with the old one. The column of a newspaper page is flush.* **b** having a flat surface all on one level: *a flush deck of a ship.* **2** well supplied; having plenty: *The rich man was always flush with money. The banks still are far from flush with funds* (Wall Street Journal). **3** abundant; plentiful: *Money is flush when times are good.* SYN: copious. **4** liberal; lavish: *He was always flush in tipping.* SYN: generous. **5** prosperous: *If times ever again come smooth and flush with me* (Washington Irving). **6** glowing; ruddy: *flush with health.* **7** direct; square: *a flush blow on the jaw.* **8** full of vigor; lusty. **9** very full; flooded: *The reservoir was flush.*
—*adv.* **1** so as to be level; evenly: *The two edges met flush.* **2** directly; squarely: *The boxer hit his opponent flush on the nose.*
—*v.t.* to make even; level.
[perhaps special use of *flush*[1]]

flush[3] (flush), *v., n.* —*v.i.* to fly or start up suddenly: *The bird flushed from its cover under the bush.*
—*v.t.* **1** to cause to fly or start up suddenly: *The hunter's dog flushed a partridge in the woods.* **2** to bring out of hiding; dig up: *Four bewildered shepherd boys* [*were*] *flushed from the caves* (Newsweek). *The government troops have . . . to flush out snipers* (London Times).
—*n.* **1** the act of flushing. **2** a flushed bird or flock of birds.
[Middle English *flusshen;* origin uncertain]
—**flush′er**, *n.*

flush[4] (flush), *n., adj.* —*n.* a hand of cards all of one suit. In poker, a flush is next above a straight and next below a full house.
—*adj.* consisting of cards of one suit.
[origin uncertain. Compare Old French *flus* or *flux* a flowing (in sense of "run"), learned borrowing < Latin *flūxus;* see etym. under **flux**.]

flush gate, a gate, sluice, or valve placed in a dam or reservoir, used to flush out the channel below the reservoir, the pipe system, or the like.

flus|ter (flus′tər), *v., n.* —*v.t.* to make nervous and excited; confuse: *The honking of horns flustered the driver, and he stalled his automobile. She was flustered by her surprise party.*
—*v.i.* to become nervous and excited; become confused.
—*n.* nervous excitement; confusion.
[Middle English *flostyrynge* a flustering < Scandinavian (compare Old Icelandic *flaustr* bustle)]

flus|ter|ate (flus′tə rāt), *v.t., v.i.,* **-at|ed, -at|ing.** *Informal.* flustrate.

flus|ter|a|tion (flus′tə rā′shən), *n. Informal.* flustration.

flus|trate (flus′trāt), *v.t., v.i.,* **-trat|ed, -trat|ing.** *Informal.* to fluster. [< *fluster* + *ate*[1]] —**flus|tra′tion**, *n.*

***flute** (flüt), *n., v.,* **flut|ed, flut|ing.** —*n.* **1** a long, slender, pipelike musical instrument. A flute is played by blowing across a hole near one end. Different notes are made by covering different holes along the tube with the fingers or with keys. *Rang the pure music of the flutes of Greece* (Algernon Charles Swinburne). **2** an organ stop with a flutelike tone. **3** a long, round or elliptical groove, especially one of a parallel series. Some columns have flutes. See picture under **Corinthian**. **4** a decorative fine groove or crimp pressed into a fabric, such as one in a ruffle or pleating on a garment. **5** a very tall, thin wineglass.
—*v.t.* **1** to make long, round grooves in: *to flute a pillar in Ionic style.* **2** to play (a melody) on a flute. **3** to sing, whistle, say, etc., in flutelike tones: *The redwing flutes his o-ka-lee* (Emerson). **4** to press (a ruffle) in flutes.
—*v.i.* **1** to play on a flute. **2** to sing or whistle so as to sound like a flute: *The thrushes are in song there, fluting from the nest* (John Masefield).
[< Old French *fleüte*, or *flaüte* < Provençal *flauta*, perhaps ultimately < Latin *flāre* to blow]
—**flute′like′**, *adj.* —**flut′er**, *n.*

***flute**
definition 1

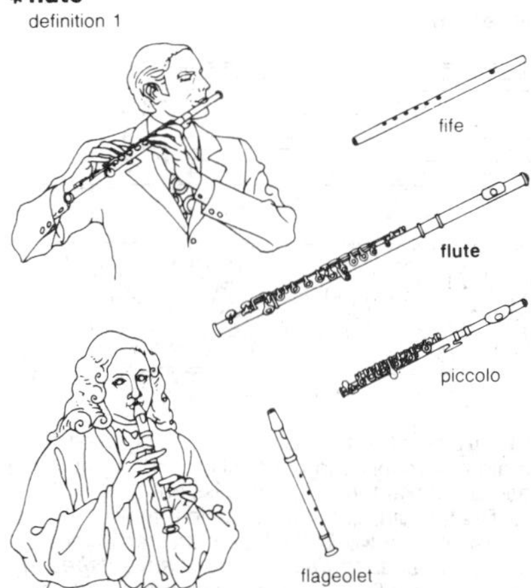

flut|ed (flü′tid), *adj.* **1** having long, round grooves: *fluted columns.* **2** *Figurative.* clear, thin, and soft; flutelike: *the fluted notes of the blackbird.*

flut|ing (flü′ting), *n.* **1** decoration made of long, round grooves. **2** a decorative groove; flute. **3** fluted work. **4** a flutelike sound. **5** the act of a person who makes fluting or plays the flute.

fluting iron, an iron with grooves in the surface for fluting ruffles.

flut|ist (flü′tist), *n.* a person who plays a flute. Also, **flautist**. [< *flute* + *-ist*]

flut|ter (flut′ər), *v., n.* —*v.i.* **1** to wave back and forth quickly and lightly; quiver: *A small flag fluttered in the breeze.* **2** to move or flap the wings without flying or with short flights: *The chickens fluttered excitedly when they saw the dog.* **3** to come or go with a trembling or wavy motion: *The young birds fluttered to the ground.* SYN: hover, flicker, flit. **4** *Figurative.* to move (about) restlessly; flit: *She fluttered about making preparations for the party.* **5** *Figurative.* to move quickly and unevenly; tremble: *Her hands fluttered. With this my lady swept out of the room, fluttering with her own audacity* (Thackeray). **6** to beat feebly and irregularly: *The patient's pulse fluttered.*
—*v.t.* **1** to cause to flutter. **2** *Figurative.* to throw into confusion; excite. SYN: confuse, agitate, ruffle.
—*n.* **1** the act or condition of fluttering: *the flutter of curtains in a breeze.* **2** *Figurative.* a confused or excited condition; agitation: *The appearance of the queen caused a great flutter in the crowd. He immediately . . . fell into a great flutter* (Dickens). **3** *British.* a small bet made for the excitement. **4** = flutter kick. **5** unstable vibration of some part of an aircraft: *wing flutter.* **6** an abnormal fluttering of some part of the body: *a heart flutter.* **7** a rapid rise and fall in pitch of a phonograph, film, or tape recording caused by slight variations in the speed at which the recording is played. Also, **flitter**.
[Middle English *floteren*, Old English *flotorian*. See related etym. at **flatter**[1], **fleet**[1].] —**flut′ter|a|ble**, *adj.* —**flut′ter|er**, *n.* —**flut′ter|ing|ly**, *adv.* —**flut′ter|less**, *adj.*

flutter board, = kick board.

flutter kick, a swimming movement in which the legs are moved alternately in short, rapid up-and-down kicks, as in the crawl; the thrash.

flut|ter|some (flut′ər səm), *adj.* inclined to flutter; fluttery.

flut|ter|y (flut′ər ē), *adj.* apt to flutter; fluttering.

flu|tu|an|te (flü′tü än′tä), *n. Portuguese.* **1** a floating house on the Rio Negro near its junction with the Amazon. **2** (literally) floater.

flut|y (flü′tē), *adj.* flutelike in tone or some other quality.

flu|vi|al (flü′vē əl), *adj.* of or found in a river: *A delta is a fluvial deposit.* [< Latin *fluviālis* < *fluvius* river < *fluere* to flow]

flu|vi|at|ic (flü′vē at′ik), *adj.* growing or living in streams; fluvial.

flu|vi|a|tile (flü′vē ə təl), *adj.* = fluvial. [< French *fluviatile,* learned borrowing from Latin *fluviātilis* < *fluvius* river < *fluere* to flow]

flu|vi|o|gla|cial (flü′vē ō glā′shəl), *adj.* of or having to do with the combined action of rivers and glaciers; glaciofluvial.

flu|vi|ol|o|gy (flü′vē ol′ə jē), *n.* the science of rivers and streams. [< Latin *fluvius* river + English *-logy*]

flu|vi|o|ma|rine (flü′vē ō mə rēn′), *adj. Geology.* of or having to do with deposits produced by action of the sea and a stream emptying into it. [< Latin *fluvius* river + English *marine*]

flu|vi|om|e|ter (flü′vē om′ə tər), *n.* an apparatus for determining the height of water in a river. [< Latin *fluvius* river + English *-meter*]

flu|vi|o|ter|res|tri|al (flü′vē ō tə res′trē əl), *adj.* having to do with the land surface of the earth and its fresh waters.

flux (fluks), *n., v.* **—*n.*** **1** the action of flowing; flow. **2** the action of the tide flowing in. **3** *Figurative.* continuous change: *New words and meanings keep the English language in a state of flux.* **4** an abnormal and excessive discharge of liquid matter from the body. **5** rosin or other substance used in soldering, welding, or brazing, to clean the surfaces of metals and help them join. **6** the rate of flow of a fluid, heat, or force, across a certain surface or area. **7** *Chemistry.* any substance that lowers the melting point of a substance to which it is added.
—*v.t.* **1** to cause an abnormal discharge of blood or liquid matter in; purge. **2** to heat with a substance that helps metals or minerals melt together.
—*v.i.* **1** to melt together. **2** to flow. **3** *Figurative.* to change.
[< Latin *flūxus, -ūs* < *fluere* to flow]

flux density, *Physics.* the magnetic flux or other quantity of flow of a fluid or of energy for a unit of area.

flux gate, a device used in gyrocompasses to detect the direction of the earth's magnetic field.

flux|ion (fluk′shən), *n.* **1** the action of flowing; flow. **2** a discharge. **3** *Mathematics.* the rate of change of a continuously varying quantity; differential. [< Middle French *fluxion,* ultimately < Latin *fluere* to flow]

flux|ion|al (fluk′shə nəl), *adj.* **1** subject to flux or change; variable; inconstant. **2** *Mathematics.* having to do with or solved by the method of fluxions. **—flux′ion|al|ly,** *adv.*

flux line, any one of the imaginary lines of a magnetic field that curve from the north pole to the south pole of a magnet.

flux|me|ter (fluks′mē′tər), *n. Physics.* an instrument for measuring magnetic flux.

flux tube, a flow of charged particles producing large bursts of radio energy, occuring at a point along the magnetic field between the planet Jupiter and its satellite Io: *The craft* [*Voyager 1*] *had to undergo a trip through ... the 400,000-volt "flux tube" connecting Jupiter with its moon Io, providing data for the mission's more than 100 scientists* (Science News).

flux unit, a unit used in radio astronomy to measure the intensity of radio waves, equal to 10^{-26} watts per square meter per hertz: *By the standards of radio astronomy 22 flux units is an extremely strong signal* (London Times).

flux valve, = flux gate.

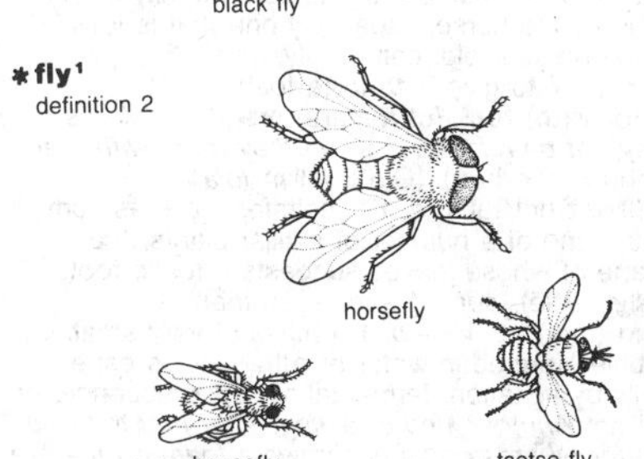

***fly**[1] (flī), *n., pl.* **flies. 1** = housefly. **2** any one of a large group of insects that have two wings, including houseflies, mosquitoes, and gnats. The wings are transparent. There are many different kinds of flies. **3** any insect with transparent wings, such as a May fly. **4** a fishhook with feathers, silk, or tinsel on it to make it look like an insect. **5** *Printing.* **a** a device for removing printed sheets from a press. **b** the person who formerly did this by hand.

fly in the ointment, a small thing that spoils something else or lessens its value: *The one fly in the ointment is, as the chairman puts it, the cloudy economic horizon* (London Times).
[Old English *flēoge,* related to *flēogan* to fly[2]]

fly[2] (flī), *v.,* **flew, flown, fly|ing; flied, fly|ing** *for 8; n., pl.* **flies. —*v.i.*** **1** to move through the air with wings: *These birds fly long distances. The shell must break before the bird can fly* (Tennyson). **2** to float or wave in the air; flutter: *Our flag flies every day.* **3** to travel in an aircraft or spacecraft. **4** to pilot an aircraft or spacecraft: *The pilot has to fly long hours.* **5** to move swiftly; go rapidly: *The ship flies before the wind. Time flies, and friends must part* (Leigh Hunt). **6** to run away; flee; abscond: *to fly from one's enemies. For those that fly may fight again, Which he can never do that's slain* (Samuel Butler). **7** to move through the air in bits or shreds: *The bottle flew into a thousand pieces.* **8** *Baseball.* to hit a ball high in the air with a bat. **9a** to hunt with a falcon. **b** to attack by flying, as a hawk does. **10** *Slang.* to be under the euphoric influence of a narcotic or psychedelic drug.
—*v.t.* **1** to cause to float or wave in the air: *Our boys are flying kites.* **2** to travel over in an aircraft or spacecraft: *We flew the Pacific in record time.* **3** to pilot (an aircraft or spacecraft). **4** to carry in an airplane or airship: *They flew a large number of rare birds from Africa.* **5** to flee from; shun. **6** to chase with or like a hawk. **7** to change (stage scenery) by raising or lowering units suspended overhead.
—*n.* **1** *Baseball.* a ball hit high in the air with a bat. **2** a flap to cover buttons, a zipper, or hooks, on clothing. **3** the flap forming the door of a tent. **4** a piece of canvas forming an extra, outer top for a tent. **5a** the width of a flag from the staff to the end. **b** the part of a flag farthest from the staff. **6** *British.* a light, public carriage for passengers: *She came ... driving up from the station in a fly* (John Galsworthy). **7** = flywheel. **8** a speed-regulating device, usually consisting of vanes on a rotating axis, chiefly used in the strikers or chimes of clocks. **9** = flyleaf. **10** an act of flying; flight.

flies, the space above a stage in a theater: *Persons on the stage saw flames creeping along the edge of the flies* (Harper's).

fly at, to attack violently: *The two dogs flew at each other.*

fly high. See under **high.**

fly in the face of. See under **face.**

fly off, to leave suddenly; break away: *I was ... ready to fly off if any one knocked at the street-door* (Frances Burney).

fly out, a to burst out in bad temper or passion: *"I was crazy," he thought. "What made me fly out like that? I've lost a friend"* (Graham Greene). **b** *Baseball.* to go out by hitting a fly caught in the air by a fielder.

let fly, a to shoot or throw: *The hunter let fly an arrow.* **b** *Figurative.* to speak or say violently: *The opposing candidates let fly with a host of mutual insults.*

on the fly, a while still in the air; before touching the ground: *If the ball he hits should be caught by any one of the fielders ... on the fly ... he is out* (Henry Chadwick). **b** *Informal, Figurative.* hurriedly: *I had my lunch on the fly.*
[Old English *flēogan*]

fly[3] (flī), *adj. Slang.* **1** knowing; sharp; smart. **2** dexterous; nimble; skillful. [perhaps < *fly*[2]]

fly[4] or **flye** (flī), *v.t., n. Scottish.* fley.

fly|a|bil|i|ty (flī′ə bil′ə tē), *n.* flyable quality or condition; ability to fly.

fly|a|ble (flī′ə bəl), *adj.* **1** that can be flown. **2** suitable for flying: *The weather ... was not good but was flyable* (Atlantic).

fly agaric, a very poisonous mushroom with a red to orange or yellow top. It is sometimes used as a poison for flies.

fly amanita, = fly agaric.

fly ash, 1 the fine ash or residue that is produced by the industrial use of pulverized coal as fuel. **2** the unburned residue of any solid fuel.

fly|a|way (flī′ə wā′), *adj.* **1** fluttering; streaming: *flyaway sleeves.* **2** frivolous; flighty. **3** out of control; runaway: *flyaway food costs.* **4** that flee; fugitive: *flyaway pigeons.*

flyaway kit, an assembly of airplane parts, supplies, and tools carried by two or more airplanes, to enable an air unit, especially a squadron, to maintain its own airplanes when cut off from outside contact for a considerable length of time.

fly|back (flī′bak′), *n. Electronics.* **1** the return of the tracing beam in a cathode-ray tube to its starting point after having completed its trace. **2** the time required for this return.

flyback transformer, a transformer used in television receivers to supply the high voltage necessary for flyback.

fly ball, *Baseball.* = fly.

fly|ball governor (flī′bôl′), an apparatus for governing an engine's speed by linking the governor with the valve that controls the input of steam: *Flyball governor ... one of the earliest automatic control devices, was invented by James Watt* (Scientific American).

fly|belt (flī′belt′), *n.* a region of Africa overrun with tsetse flies.

fly|blow (flī′blō′), *n., v.,* **-blew, -blown, -blow|ing. —*n.*** the egg or young larva of a blowfly deposited especially in or on meat.
—*v.t.* **1** to deposit eggs or larvae in or on (especially meat). **2** *Figurative.* to spoil; taint; corrupt.
—*v.i.* to deposit eggs or larva in or on meat.

fly|blown (flī′blōn′), *adj.* **1** tainted by the eggs or larvae of flies. **2** *Figurative.* spoiled; tainted; corrupted.

fly|boat (flī′bōt′), *n.* any fast sailing ship or boat. [apparently < Dutch *vlieboot* (originally) boat used on the *Vlie,* a channel from the Zuider Zee]

fly book, a small case somewhat like a wallet for carrying artificial fishing flies.

fly|boy (flī′boi′), *n. U.S. Informal.* a flier, especially one in the Air Force.

fly bridge, a platform on top of a cabin cruiser equipped with duplicate controls. Also, **flying bridge.**

fly-by (flī′bī′), *n., pl.* **-bys. 1** a flight of a space vehicle close to a planet or other heavenly body. **2** = flyover.

fly-by-night (flī′bī nīt′), *adj., n.* **—*adj.*** not to be trusted; not reliable; irresponsible: *a fly-by-night real-estate speculator.*
—*n.* *Informal.* **1** a person who avoids paying his debts by leaving secretly at night. **2** an unreliable or irresponsible person.

fly-by-night|er (flī′bī nī′tər), *n.* an unreliable or irresponsible person, especially one who misrepresents merchandise: *Once only fly-by-nighters in dingy back streets offered fake bargains* (Time).

fly-by-wire (flī′bī wīr′), *adj.* of or having to do with an electronic guidance system that adjusts the path of a space capsule automatically after it is turned on manually.

fly-cast|er (flī′kas′tər, -käs′-), *n.* a person who casts for fish with rod and line, using an artificial fly as bait.

fly-cast|ing (flī′kas′ting, -käs′-), *n., adj.,* or **fly casting. —*n.*** the sport of fishing with rod and line, using an artificial fly as bait.
—*adj.* of or having to do with fly-casting: *a fly-casting rod.*

fly|catch|er (flī′kach′ər), *n.* **1** any one of a family of songless, American perching birds that catch flies and other insects while flying. The tyrant flycatcher has small, weak feet, a short neck, and a large head with a broad, flattened bill hooked at the tip. The kingbird, phoebe, and crested flycatcher are common examples. **2** any one of a family of Old World perching birds related to the thrush.

fly-cruise (flī′krüz′), *n., v.,* **-cruised, -cruis|ing. —*n.*** a pleasure cruise using air travel to reach the cruise ship's port of embarkation and to return from the port of landing.
—*v.i.* to go on a fly-cruise.

fly|er (flī′ər), *n.* **1** = flier. **2** *Informal.* a try; an experimental venture into something: *He finally got back to Massachusetts by way of lecturing at Harvard and taking a flyer at magazine editing* (Wall Street Journal). **3** an aerialist who swings from a trapeze through the air to another performer or to another trapeze: *The circus ... is sunning itself here on the Gulf of Mexico, where the flyers are flying through the warm winter air* (Saturday Review). **4** a vagrant, light wind: *We had to row all-out to keep up with the little flyers when the puffs hardened* (Atlantic).

fly-fish (flī′fish′), *v.i.* to fish with flies, natural or artificial, as bait; fly-casting.

fly-fish|ing (flī′fish′ing), *n.* fishing with natural or artificial flies as bait.

fly-front (flī′frunt′), *adj.* having a fly covering buttons or fastenings.

fly gallery, a high, narrow platform at the side of the stage in a theater, from which scenery is lowered and raised.

fly-half (flī′haf′, -häf′), *n. Rugby Football.* a stand-off halfback.

fly-in (flī′in′), *adj.* having a landing field for airplanes or helicopters.

fly|ing (flī′ing), *adj., n.* **—*adj.*** **1** that flies; moving

Pronunciation Key: hat, āge, cãre, fär; let, ēqual, tėrm; it, īce; hot, ōpen, ôrder; oil, out; cup, pu̇t, rüle; child; long; thin; ᴛʜen; zh, measure; ə represents **a** in about, **e** in taken, **i** in pencil, **o** in lemon, **u** in circus.

through the air: *the handsome young man on the flying trapeze* (George Leybourne). **2** floating or waving in the air. **3** swift; rapid: *Earth rolls back beneath the flying steed* (Alexander Pope). **4** short and quick; hasty: *a flying visit.* **5** fleeing; running away. **6** organized for rapid movement or prompt action: *a flying squad.*

—*n.* **1** the act of a person or thing that flies. SYN: flight. **2** *Theater.* **a** a method of changing scenery by raising and lowering units suspended overhead as they are needed on the stage. **b** a drop, curtain, border, ceiling, or other unit used in flying.

flying boat, a seaplane with a watertight body that floats in the water like the hull of a ship.

flying bomb, an unmanned, winged, guided missile, such as a buzz bomb.

flying boxcar, a large transport and cargo-carrying airplane.

flying bridge, **1** the highest bridge of several on a ship, located next to the control tower. **2** = fly bridge. **3** a pontoon or other temporary bridge.

flying buttress, an arched support or brace built between the wall of a building and a supporting column to bear some of the outward pressure of the weight of the roof.

flying circus, **1** a circular formation of aircraft in which each follows another, protecting its rear, used in World War I. **2a** an organized group of aircraft which gives exhibitions of acrobatics. **b** an exhibition by such a group.

flying colors, **1** success; victory: *The team finished the tournament with flying colors.* **2** flags flying.

flying column, a military force, now usually an armored force supported by motorized infantry and some artillery, that can move swiftly ahead or on the side of the main body.

flying disk, = flying saucer.

flying doctor, a doctor, especially in Australia, who tends the sick and injured in outlying areas by flying in to treat them: *In May 1928 Dr. K. St. Vincent Welch, the first flying doctor, set up practice at Cloncurry in Queensland* (Lancet).

flying dragon, = flying lizard.

Flying Dutchman, **1** a legendary Dutch sea captain condemned to sail the seas until the Day of Judgment. **2** his ghostlike ship, supposed to appear to mariners near the Cape of Good Hope in storms, and regarded by sailors as a bad omen.

flying field, a small tract of land where aircraft can land or take off. It is much smaller and has fewer facilities than an airport.

***flying fish**, a tropical sea fish that has pectoral fins like wings and can leap for some distance through the air.

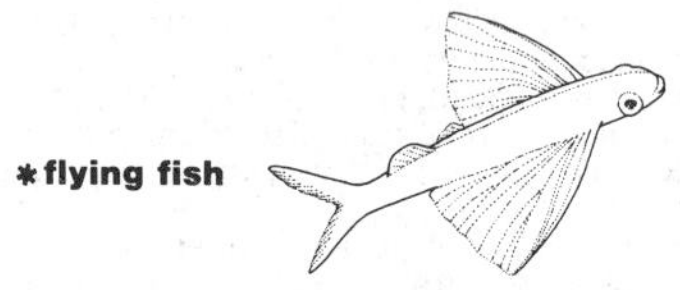

***flying fish**

flying fortress or **Flying Fortress**, a large, armored bomber, used extensively by the United States during World War II.

flying fox, a large, fruit-eating bat of tropical countries of the Old World. It has a foxlike head.

flying frog, an East Indian frog with large, webbed toes that help it to glide through the air.

flying gurnard, a marine fish with winglike pectoral fins, that can fly short distances.

flying jib, a small, triangular sail set in front of the regular jib. See picture under **jib**[1].

flying lemur, an East Indian mammal that resembles a lemur and has a broad fold of skin on each side of its body which it spreads and glides from tree to tree; colugo.

flying line, the string from which a kite is flown.

***flying lizard**, any one of the small, brightly colored lizards living in the trees of southeastern Asia and having a broad, winglike membrane on each flank covering extended ribs, that enables them to glide some distance through the air; flying dragon.

***flying lizard**

flying machine, **1** an airplane or helicopter: *The challenge of the missile does not mean that the flying machine is outdated. On the contrary there will always be great need for the work of the manned aircraft, which it alone can perform* (London Times). **2** an airship.

flying mare, *Wrestling.* a move made by seizing the opponent's wrist, turning, and throwing him forward and down across the shoulder.

flying mouse, a small Australian flying phalanger.

flying officer, a commissioned officer in the Australian, British, or Canadian air force, corresponding in rank to first lieutenant in the U.S. Air Force. *Abbr:* F.O.

flying pay, additional pay given to members of an air force who participate in regular authorized flights; flight pay.

flying phalanger, a phalanger (marsupial quadruped) of Australia and South Pacific islands with a fold of skin along each side of the body which it extends to glide through the air.

flying saucer, an unidentified, disklike object reported in the sky over many different parts of the world, especially since 1947; unidentified flying object; UFO: *When Kenneth Arnold saw something from his airplane near Mount Rainier in June 1947, he gave them the happy name of flying saucers* (New Society).

flying spot, a moving beam of light which produces a succession of thin lines against a surface containing an image. The areas of lightness and darkness are electronically picked up and transmitted to television receiving sets where the image is reproduced.

flying squad, *Especially British.* **1** a police squad trained and equipped for rapid pursuit: *In 1920 . . . he* [*Hambrook*] *was put in charge of a team of three inspectors, four sergeants, and four detective constables, together with two drivers . . . Within a few days the team had been named the Flying Squad* (Guardian). **2** any highly mobile group organized for special tasks: *a flying squad of teachers.*

flying squirrel, a squirrel that can make long, gliding leaps through the air. Its front and hind legs are connected by winglike folds of skin (called *parachutes* or *patagia*).

flying start, **1** (in a race) a start in which the competitors pass the starting point at full speed. **2** *Figurative: He climbed slowly in Elizabeth's reign despite his flying start as the son of a Lord Keeper* (Listener). *How are the likes of you and me to get a good flying start with nothing to kick off from?* (L.A. Stong).

flying status, the status of a member of an air force who participates in regular authorized flights; flight status.

flying wedge, **1** an arrangement or formation of soldiers or policemen in the form of a wedge: *The police burst out, and with flying wedge techniques dispersed the crowd* (New York Times). **2** an old offensive formation in football similar to this.

flying wing, a type of airplane in which the fuselage and motors are inside the wing structure. Every exposed portion contributes to the lift in return for the drag it causes.

fly-kick (flī′kik′), *n., v. Rugby.* —*n.* a kick made while running.

—*v.t., v.i.* to kick (the ball) while running.

fly|leaf (flī′lēf′), *n., pl.* **-leaves.** a blank sheet of paper at the beginning or end of a book.

fly|less (flī′lis), *adj.* without flies.

fly line, a line used in fly-fishing.

fly|man (flī′mən), *n., pl.* **-men.** a stage hand who works in the flies.

fly mushroom, = fly agaric.

fly|ness (flī′nis), *n. Slang.* the quality or fact of being fly; smartness; alertness.

fly net, a net to keep away flies.

fly|off (flī′ôf′, -of′), *n.* a contest in flying between two or more aircraft.

fly|o|ver (flī′ō′vər), *n.* **1** a mass flight of aircraft in formation over a city, reviewing stand, or other designated area, usually as a review or as a display of air power; fly-by. **2** *British.* a highway overpass.

fly|pa|per (flī′pā′pər), *n.* paper covered with a sticky or poisonous substance, used to catch or kill flies.

fly|past (flī′past′, -päst′), *n.* = flyover.

fly|post (flī′pōst′), *v.t. British.* to post with bills or notices in haste, especially to avoid detection.

fly reel, a fishing reel used for storing the line and pulling in the cast fly.

fly rod, a very light fishing rod made of fiberglass, cane, or other materials and usually jointed. It is designed for use with light lures, as artificial flies.

flysch (flish), *n. Geology.* a partly Tertiary, partly Cretaceous formation. It consists chiefly of sandstones, soft marls, and sandy shales, and is found in the Alps and other places. [< dialectal Swiss *flysch*]

fly sheet, **1** a loose sheet of paper forming a single leaf, as one on which a handbill or broadside is printed. **2** a cover made of lightweight cloth, used to keep flies off a horse.

fly|speck (flī′spek′), *n., v.* —*n.* **1** a tiny spot left by a fly. **2** any tiny speck. **3** *Figurative.* a small error or imperfection: *There are only a few small matters of fact which I should like to point out . . . for they could not have been generally known . . . by your readers. Nevertheless, they represent flyspecks, which you might wish to avoid* (Robert B. Livingston).

—*v.t.* **1** to mark with flyspecks. **2** to examine closely or pick at small errors or imperfections; nit-pick: *The interest-group leaders are not going to break their backs to renominate Jimmy Carter . . . They've been flyspecking him for the last two years, and you can't expect them to turn around and work for him with enthusiasm* (David Broder).

fly|speck|ing (flī′spek′ing), *n.* the act or process of examining for small errors or imperfections: *These discussions range from tedious flyspecking about trivia to disapproving comments on such subjects as the high recidivism rate* (Fred P. Graham).

fly|strike (flī′strīk′), *n. Australian.* a condition in sheep caused by infestation of blowflies.

fly swatter, a square sheet of wire, plastic, or rubber mesh attached to a handle, used as a swatter to kill insects.

fly|tail (flī′tāl′), *n. U.S.* a small gill net without sinkers formerly used for catching perch, etc.

flyte (flīt), *v.i., v.t.,* **flyt|ed, flyt|ing,** *n.* = flite.

fly-ti|er (flī′tī′ər), *n.* **1** a maker of artificial flies for anglers. **2** a person who ties flies on hooks.

flyt|ing (flī′ting), *n.* = fliting.

fly|trap (flī′trap′), *n.* **1** any one of several plants that trap insects, especially Venus's-flytrap and the pitcher plant. **2** a trap to catch flies.

fly-ty|ing (flī′tī′ing), *n.* the construction of artificial flies for fly-casting.

fly-up-the-creek (flī′up ᴛʜə krēk′), *n.* = little green heron.

fly|way (flī′wā′), *n.* a route usually followed by migrating birds: *Wildfowl are abundant in the prairie provinces on the central flyway* (London Times).

fly|weight (flī′wāt′), *n.* a boxer who weighs not more than 112 pounds.

fly|wheel (flī′hwēl′), *n.* a heavy wheel attached to a machine that has revolving motion to keep it and its parts moving at an even speed. See picture at **steam engine.**

fly whisk, a small bunch of twigs, feathers, grass, or similar material, tied to a handle, used to brush off flies, crumbs, and the like.

fm., **1** fathom. **2** from.

Fm (no period), fermium (chemical element).

FM (no periods), **1** field manual (of the U.S. Army). **2** frequency modulation.

F.M., **1** field manual (of the U.S. Army). **2** field marshal. **3** frequency modulation.

FMC (no periods), Federal Maritime Commission.

FMCS (no periods), Federal Mediation and Conciliation Service.

FM-CW (no periods), frequency modulation-continuous wave.

FMD (no periods), foot-and-mouth disease.

FMN (no periods), flavin mononucleotide.

fn., footnote.

FNMA (no periods) or **F.N.M.A.**, Federal National Mortgage Association.

f number, *Photography.* the focal length of a lens divided by its effective diameter. An f/4 lens is one in which the diameter of the widest effective opening is ¼ of its focal length (f).

fo., folio.

f°, folio.

F.O., **1** field officer. **2** flying officer. **3** (the British) Foreign Office.

foal (fōl), *n., v.* —*n.* a young horse, donkey, zebra, or other member of the same family of animals as the horse, especially one that is less than one year old; colt or filly.

—*v.t., v.i.* to give birth to (a foal).

in (or **with**) **foal**, (of a mare) pregnant: *Mares may not be ridden . . . when they* [*are*] *with foal* (John Fitzherbert). [Old English *fola*]

foal|foot (fōl′fu̇t′), *n.* **1** = coltsfoot. **2** = asarum. **3** any one of a number of similar plants, the shape of whose leaves suggests a foal's foot.

foal|y (fō′lē), *adj.* (of a mare) in foal.

foam (fōm), *n., v.* —*n.* **1** a mass of very small bubbles formed in water or other liquids especially by agitation, fermentation, effervescence, or boiling: *Another kind of extinguisher that is valuable for oil fires pours or throws a foam on the fire* (Beauchamp, Mayfield, and West). **2** the frothy saliva formed in the mouth in epilepsy or rabies. **3** the frothy white perspiration covering a horse or other animal as the result of hard labor. **4** a spongy, flexible, or semirigid material made from various plastics or rubber by solidification of the basic material around air bubbles: *polyurethane foam, latex foam.*

— *v.i.* **1** to form or gather foam; froth: *The soda foamed over the glass.* **2** to break into foam; emit foam: *The stream foams over the rocks.* (*Figurative.*) *The angry old man foamed for quite a while about the insulting behavior of his grandchildren.*
— *v.t.* **1** to cause to foam: *The boy foamed the soap in the water.* **2** to cover with foam: *Children love to foam their hands with soap.* **3** to fill with foaming liquor. **4** to give (plastic or rubber) a spongy, flexible texture by solidifying it around trapped air or gas bubbles.
[Old English *fām*] — **foam′er**, *n.* — **foam′ing|ly**, *adv.* — **foam′less**, *adj.* — **foam′like′**, *adj.*

foam|bow (fōm′bō′), *n.* a bow, similar to a rainbow, formed by sunlight upon foam or spray.

foamed (fōmd), *adj.* made with foam; spongy: *Foamed plastics come in two distinct kinds—rigid and flexible* (Manchester Guardian).

foam|flow|er (fōm′flou′ər), *n.* a North American spring-blooming herb of the saxifrage family, having white flowers.

foam glass or **foamed glass**, a lightweight, porous glass, used especially as a heat insulator in buildings and a substitute for cork.

foam rubber, a soft, spongy rubber used especially for mattresses and cushions; sponge rubber. It is made by beating thickened latex into foam or by using a vacuum to cause gas to generate, and then stabilizing the foam with chemicals.

foam|y (fō′mē), *adj.*, **foam|i|er**, **foam|i|est**. **1** covered with foam; foaming: *foamy surf.* **2** made of foam. **3** like foam. — **foam′i|ly**, *adv.* — **foam′i-ness**, *n.*

fob[1] (fob), *n.* **1** a short watch chain or ribbon that hangs out of a watch pocket. **2** an ornament worn on the end of such a chain or ribbon. **3** a small pocket for holding a watch, ticket stubs, or change. [perhaps < Low German *fobke* little pocket]

fob[2] (fob), *v.*, **fobbed**, **fob|bing**, *n.* — *v.t.* to deceive by a trick; cheat: *While everyone else he is fobbing, He still may be honest to me* (Henry Fielding).
— *n.* a trick; an artifice.
fob off, a to put off or deceive by a trick: *Inquiries from children should never be fobbed off* (Punch). **b** to palm off or get rid of by a trick: *It is an outrage to fob off such elementary stuff as higher education* (Saturday Evening Post).
[perhaps back formation < Middle English *fobbe*, variant of *foppe* a fool]

f.o.b. or **FOB** (no periods), free on board. The price $850, f.o.b. Detroit, means that the $850 does not include freight or other expenses after the article has been put on board a freight car at Detroit.

fob chain, a watch chain hanging free from a pocket and usually carrying a seal, key, or other ornament.

FOBS (fobz), *n.* Fractional Orbital Bombardment System (a nuclear-weapon system in which warheads are delivered to targets on earth from an orbiting space vehicle in order to escape detection by conventional radar).

fo|cal (fō′kəl), *adj.* of a focus; having to do with a focus. See also **focal length**. — **fo′cal|ly**, *adv.*

focal infection, an infection in a particular area, as in a tooth or a gland, from which infection spreads or can spread to other parts.

fo|cal|ize (fō′kə līz), *v.*, **-ized**, **-iz|ing**. — *v.t.* **1** to focus: **a** to bring (rays of light, heat, or other radiation) into focus. **b** *Figurative:* *The information about sales is focalized in the company's main office and put before the sales manager.* **2** to localize (an infection or other danger) at a particular site of activity.
— *v.i.* to come to a focus. — **fo′cal|i|za′tion**, *n.*

focal length or **distance**, **1** the distance from the optical center of a lens or mirror to the principal point of focus: *The simple astronomical telescope, which is the basis of modern refracting telescopes, contains two double convex lenses at a distance apart equal to the sum of their focal lengths* (Robert H. Baker). **2** the distance between the objective of a telescope and the image that is mirrored.

focal plane, **1** *Optics.* a plane through the focal point of a lens. **2** *Photography.* the plane where the object image is brought into sharp focus.

fo|cal-plane shutter (fō′kəl plān′), *Photography.* a shutter that is mounted close to the focal plane of the lens.

focal point, **1** *Optics.* the point where rays of light are focused: *When an image strikes the objective, the light waves are bent by the lens until they come to one bright point, known as the focal point* (R. William Shaw). **2** the center of attention; interest, or other attraction: *Our company seems to be the focal point of many rumors involving alleged mergers* (Wall Street Journal).

fo|ci (fō′sī), *n.* focuses; a plural of **focus**.

fo|co (fō′kō), *n.*, *pl.* **-cos**. a small guerrilla center radiating revolutionary activity throughout a country. [< Spanish *foco* focus]

fo′c′sle (fōk′səl), *n. Nautical.* = forecastle.

***fo|cus** (fō′kəs), *n.*, *pl.* **-cus|es** or **-ci**, *v.*, **-cused**, **-cus|ing** or (*especially British*) **-cussed**, **-cussing**. — *n.* **1** a point at which rays of light, heat, or other radiation, meet after being reflected from a mirror or bent by a lens or lenslike or mirrorlike device. **2a** the distance from a lens, mirror, or lenslike or mirrorlike device, to a point where rays from it meet; focal length: *A near-sighted eye has a shorter focus than a normal eye.* **b** a point at which rays of light (or their prolongations) that diverge from (or converge toward) one point meet and form an image after being bent by a lens, curved mirror, or other reflecting or refracting device. **c** the correct adjustment of a lens, the eye, or lenslike device, to make a clear image: *If my camera is not brought into focus, the photograph will be blurred.* **d** that point or position of an object necessary to produce a clear image. **e** the clear and well-defined state of an image. **3** *Figurative.* a central point of attention, activity, disturbance, or other attraction: *The new baby was the focus of attention.* **4** *Geometry.* **a** a fixed point used in determining a conic section. A parabola has one focus, while an ellipse or a hyperbola has two foci. **b** a point having a similar relation to some other curve. **5** the point where an earthquake originates. **6** *Medicine.* the principal site of a pervasive disease or the area where a disease's activity is localized: *The focus of a disease is the part of the body where it is most active.*
— *v.t.* **1** to bring (rays of light, heat, or other radiation) to a point: *The lens focused the sun's rays on a piece of paper and burned a hole in it.* **2** to adjust (a lens, the eye, or lenslike device) to make a clear image: *A near-sighted person cannot focus accurately on distant objects. His eyes were so tired that he had difficulty focusing them.* **3** to make (an image or focus of rays) clear by adjusting a lens, the eye, or lenslike device. **4** *Figurative.* to concentrate or direct: *When studying, he focused his mind on his lessons.*
— *v.i.* **1** to converge to a focus. **2** to adjust the eye or an optical instrument for clear vision: *Focus upon some distinct object.*
in focus, clear; distinct: *After a certain distance all objects will be in focus* (Walter Woodbury).
out of focus, blurred; indistinct: *In the course of a* [*song*] *he might ... execute a perfect, slightly out of focus scale* (Whitney Balliett).
[< New Latin *focus* < Latin, hearth] — **fo′cuser**, *n.*

light rays
lens
focus
focal length

***focus**
definition 1

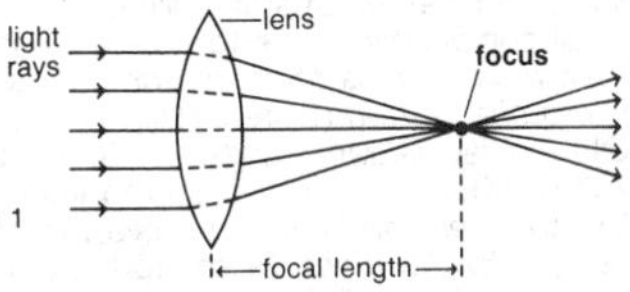

fod|der (fod′ər), *n.*, *v.* — *n.* coarse food for horses, cattle, and similar domestic animals. Hay and cornstalks with their leaves are fodder. **SYN:** See syn. under **feed**.
— *v.t.* to give fodder to (horses, cattle, or the like).
— *v.i.* to obtain feed or fodder: *Swine at all time —unless a sow was in trouble farrowing— ... foddered for themselves* (London Times).
[Old English *fōdor*, related to *fōda* food]

fodg|el (foj′əl), *adj. Scottish.* squat and plump. [< obsolete *fodge*, variant of obsolete *fadge* a short, fat person + *-el*, a diminutive suffix]

foe (fō), *n.* **1** = enemy. **SYN:** See syn. under **enemy**. **2** *Figurative.* anything that harms or is likely to injure. [Old English *fāh*hostile. See related etym. at **feud**.]

F.O.E., Fraternal Order of Eagles.

foehn (fān; *German* fœn), *n.* a warm, dry south wind that blows down the leeward slope of a mountain, especially in the Alps. Also, **föhn**. [< dialectal German *Föhn*, ultimately < Latin *Favōnius* the west wind]

foe|man (fō′mən), *n.*, *pl.* **-men**. *Archaic.* an enemy in war; adversary.

foe|tal (fē′təl), *adj.* = fetal.

foe|tid (fē′tid, fet′id), *adj.* = fetid.

foe|tus (fē′təs), *n.* = fetus.

fog[1] (fog, fôg), *n.*, *v.*, **fogged**, **fog|ging**. — *n.* **1** a cloud of fine drops of water or ice crystals just above the earth's surface; a low cloud or thick mist: *The fog comes on little cat feet* (Carl Sandburg). *The cooling of air which causes the formation of fog most frequently occurs when relatively warm, moist air passes over a colder surface* (George F. Taylor). **2** a darkened condition of the atmosphere, or a substance in the atmosphere that causes this. **3** *Figurative.* a state of intellectual darkness; confused or puzzled condition: *a fog of ignorance, a fog of doubt.* **4** *Photography.* a grayish cloud or veil obscuring part or all of a developed film, plate, or print. **5** *Chemistry.* particles of liquid dispersed in a gas; a type of colloidal system.
— *v.t.* **1** to cover with fog: *The dog fogged the window with his panting.* **2** to darken; dim; blur. **3** *Figurative.* to confuse; puzzle; perplex. **4** to make misty or cloudy; obscure (a film, plate, or print) with fog: *Something fogged six of our photographs.* **5** *U.S. Slang.* to pitch (a ball) fast and hard: *He has been fogging the ball past enemy batters ever since* (Time).
— *v.i.* **1** to become covered or filled with fog: *My breath caused the window to fog.* **2** to become misty or cloudy; be obscured by fog.
[perhaps back formation < *foggy*]

fog[2] (fog, fôg), *n.*, *v.*, **fogged**, **fog|ging**. — *n.* **1** the grass that grows after mowing. **2** the long grass left standing in fields during winter. **3** *Scottish.* moss.
— *v.t.* **1** to leave (land) with long grass standing. **2** to pasture or feed (cattle) on the grass grown after mowing.
— *v.i. Scottish.* to become overgrown with moss.
[apparently < Scandinavian (compare Norwegian *fogg* long grass on damp ground)]

fog bank, a dense mass of fog seen at a distance.

fog|bound (fog′bound′, fôg′-), *adj.* kept from sailing or moving by fog.

fog|bow (fog′bō′, fôg′-), *n.* a phenomenon like the rainbow, sometimes seen in fog.

fog|broom (fog′brüm′, -brům′; fôg′-), *n.* a device to thin or disperse fog: *He set up a research group, which finally evolved a "fogbroom," a 30-in. by 48-in. aluminum frame strung with a half mile of nylon thread and rotated at 86 r.p.m. by a base-mounted motor* (Time).

fog|dog (fog′dôg′, -dog′; fôg′-), *n.* a bright spot sometimes seen in a fog bank; sea dog.

fog|eat|er (fog′ē′tər, fôg′-), *n.* **1** = fogdog. **2** = fogbow. **3** a break in a fog bank, presaging clearing weather.

fo|gey (fō′gē), *n.*, *pl.* **-geys**. = fogy.

fo|gey|ism (fō′gē iz əm), *n.* = fogyism.

fog|fruit (fog′früt′, fôg′-), *n.* a plant that lies on the ground without putting forth roots and has elongated spikes of small, pale-blue sessile flowers.

fog|ger[1] (fog′ər, fôg′-), *n. British.* a person who places fog signals on railroad tracks.

fog|ger[2] (fog′ər, fôg′-), *n. British Dialect.* a person who cares for cattle on a farm.

fog|gy (fog′ē, fôg′-), *adj.*, **-gi|er**, **-gi|est**. **1** having much fog; misty; murky: *If it is cloudy, rainy, or foggy, the water vapor in the air is condensing* (Beauchamp, Mayfield, and West). **2** not clear; dim; blurred: (*Figurative.*) *I haven't the foggiest idea of what you mean.* **3** *Figurative.* confused; puzzled. **4** *Photography.* fogged; indistinct. — **fog′gi|ly**, *adv.* — **fog′gi|ness**, *n.*

Foggy Bottom, *Informal.* the U.S. State Department: *Somewhere deep in the office caverns of official Washington, the officials of Foggy Bottom and the Pentagon are at odds concerning United States foreign policy* (New York Times). [originally a local name applied to Hamburgh, a town which became part of Washington, D.C., and especially to its swampy southern portion, on which government buildings, including the headquarters of the State Department, were later built]

fog|horn (fog′hôrn′, fôg′-), *n.* **1** a horn or other device that warns ships in foggy weather. See picture under **beacon**. **2** a large, harsh voice.

fo|gle (fō′gəl), *n. Slang.* a handkerchief or neckerchief, usually of silk.

fog|less (fog′lis, fôg′-), *adj.* free from fog: *the starry ocean sky of the fogless night.*

fog light, a special light on an automobile for use in heavy fog. Its beam, of low intensity and position, causes less reflection and glare than that of the white headlight.

fo|go (fō′gō), *n. Informal.* stench.

fog signal, a bell, siren, horn, or other easily identifiable signal, used in fog or darkness to guide a ship or railroad train.

fo|gy (fō′gē), *n.*, *pl.* **-gies**. an old-fashioned person; one who is behind the times or who lacks enterprise: *My part ... is always that of the old Fogy who sees nothing to admire in the young folks* (George Eliot). [originally Scottish *foggie;* origin uncertain, perhaps < *foggy* in the sense of "moss-grown"]

Pronunciation Key: hat, āge, cãre, fär; let, ēqual, tėrm, it, īce; hot, ōpen, ôrder; oil, out; cup, pu̇t, rüle; child; long; thin; ᴛʜen; zh, measure; ə represents a in about, e in taken, i in pencil, o in lemon, u in circus.

fo|gy|ish (fō′gē ish), *adj.* inclined to be a fogy.
fo|gy|ism (fō′gē iz əm), *n.* the habits or practices of a fogy.
foh (fō), *interj.* an exclamation of disgust. [variant of *faugh*]
föhn (fān; *German* fœn), *n.* = foehn.
foi|ble (foi′bəl), *n.* **1** a weak point; weakness: *Talking too much is one of her foibles. The accidental consequences of some human frailty or foible* (Henry Fielding). **SYN:** failing, frailty. **2** the flexible part of a sword blade, between the middle and the point. [< Old French *foible,* earlier *faible;* see etym. under **feeble**]
foie gras (fwä′ grä′), *French.* liver, rich in fat, especially goose liver.
foil¹ (foil), *v., n.* — ***v.t.*** **1** to prevent from carrying out plans or attempts; get the better of; turn aside or hinder; defeat; outwit: *Quick thinking by the bank clerk foiled the robbers, and they were captured.* **SYN:** balk, baffle, frustrate. **2** to prevent (a plan or attempt) from being carried out or from succeeding. **3** to spoil (a trace or scent) by crossing it.
— ***n.*** **1** *Archaic.* a repulse; defeat; frustration. **2** the track of a hunted animal.
[< Old French *fouler* trample, to full (cloth) < Medieval Latin *fullare*] — **foil′er,** *n.*
foil² (foil), *n., v.* — ***n.*** **1** metal beaten, hammered, or rolled into a very thin sheet: *Candy is sometimes wrapped in tin foil to keep it fresh.* **2** *Figurative.* anything or person that makes something else or another person look or seem better by contrast: *The green dress was a foil for her red hair.* **3** a very thin layer of polished metal, placed under a gem, especially an inferior or imitation gem, to give it more color or sparkle. **4** a metallic sheet applied to glass to produce a reflecting surface in making a mirror. **5** *Architecture.* a leaflike ornament; an arc or rounded space between cusps, as in medieval tracery. **6** the leaf of a plant. **7** = hydrofoil (def. 1).
— ***v.t.*** **1** to coat or back with foil. **2** *Figurative.* to set off by contrast. **3** *Architecture.* to decorate with foils.
[< Old French *foille* < Latin *folia* leaves]
foil³ (foil), *n.* a long, narrow sword, with a knob or button on the point to prevent injury, used in fencing.
foils, the sport or skill of fencing with such a sword: *It makes him ... fight ... as though he were but at foils amongst his fellows* (Thomas Nashe).
[origin uncertain, perhaps related to **foil¹**]
foil|borne (foil′bôrn′, -bōrn′), *adj., adv.* — ***adj.*** **1** supported by hydrofoils: *a foilborne craft.* **2** involving the use of hydrofoils: *foilborne speeds.*
— ***adv.*** on hydrofoils: *It is designed to be operated foilborne in waves up to 15 feet* (London Times).
foil|ist (foi′list), *n.* = foilsman.
foils|man (foilz′mən), *n., pl.* **-men.** a person who fences with a foil.
foin (foin), *n., v. Archaic.* — ***n.*** a thrust, as with a sword.
— ***v.i.*** to thrust with a weapon: *You foin only at your own shadow* (John Jewel).
[perhaps < Old French *fouisne* fish spear < Latin *fuscina* trident]
foi|son (foi′zən), *n.* **1** *Archaic.* an abundance; a plentiful supply. **2** *Archaic.* a plentiful crop or harvest: *Earth's increase, foison plenty, Barns and garners never empty* (Shakespeare). **3** *Scottish.* **a** vigor; vitality; strength. **b** nourishment, as in food.
foisons, *Scottish.* resources: *Scotland hath foisons to fill up your will* (Shakespeare).
[< Old French *foison* < Vulgar Latin *fusiō, -ōnis,* alteration of Latin *fūsiō, -ōnis* outpouring. See etym. of doublet **fusion.**]
foist (foist), *v.t.* **1** to palm off as genuine; impose by fraud: *The dishonest clerk foisted inferior goods on his customers.* **2** to put in secretly or slyly: *The author discovered that the translator had foisted several passages into his book.* [perhaps < dialectal Dutch *vuisten* take in hand < *vuist* fist]
fol., **1** folio. **2** following.
fol|a|cin (fol′ə sin), *n.* = folic acid.
fo|late (fō′lāt), *adj., n.* — ***adj.*** of or having to do with folic acid: *Folate deficiency.*
— ***n.*** = folic acid.
fold¹** (fōld), *v., n.* — ***v.t. **1** to bend or double over on itself: *You fold a letter or your napkin.* **2** to bring together with the parts in or around one another: *You fold your arms.* **3** to bring (the wings) close to the body: *A bird folds its wings.* **4** to put the arms around and hold tenderly; embrace: *A mother folds her child to her breast.* **SYN:** clasp. **5** to wrap; enclose: *He folded the pills in a blue paper.* **6** *Poetic.* to surround; cover: *Light and shadow ever wander O'er the green that folds thy grave* (Tennyson). **7** *Informal.* to bring to a halt; close up; terminate: *They folded the business after only two months and with great loss.*
— ***v.i.*** **1** to become folded. **2** to fail in business or other such endeavor; close up; fold up: *In eight years, 3,000 mines have folded and more than 200,000 miners have lost their jobs* (Wall Street Journal). **3** to pass or wind about something.
— ***n.*** **1** a layer of something folded; pleat: *a fold of linen.* **SYN:** plait. **2** a mark or line made by folding. **3** the act or process of folding: *A fold gives two sheets of paper for one.* **4** an enveloping layer or thickness of something: *to wrap a mummy in many folds of cloth.* **5** something that is or can be folded. **6a** a slight hill or hollow: *the folds of the mountains.* **b** *Geology.* a bend or flexure occurring in a layer of rock after its stratification, having varying sizes and positions, including anticlines, synclines, and monoclines. See picture below.
fold in, to add (an ingredient) to a mixture in cooking by gently turning one part over another with strokes of a spoon: *to fold in beaten egg whites.*
fold up, a to make or become smaller by folding: *Many new products can be folded up or disassembled for space-saving storage.* **b** to break down; collapse: *It is less clear why the society folded up so tamely, with hardly a trace left behind* (Manchester Guardian Weekly). **c** *Informal.* to fail completely; come to a halt; close up: *Then the business folds up and she is back where she started* (Listener).
[Old English *faldan, fealdan*] — **fold′a|ble,** *adj.*
fold² (fōld), *n., v.* — ***n.*** **1** a pen to keep sheep in: *The shepherd and his dog drove the sheep into the fold for the night.* **2a** sheep kept in a pen. **b** a flock of sheep. **3** *Figurative.* **a** a church group; congregation. **b** a church. **4** *Figurative.* any group of people having common goals or interests: *A number of party regulars ... have returned to the fold* (London Times).
— ***v.t.*** to put or keep (sheep) in a pen.
[Old English *falod*]
-fold, *suffix forming adjectives and adverbs.* **1** ___ times as many; ___ times as great: *Tenfold = ten times as many.*
2 formed or divided into ___ parts: *Manifold = formed in many parts.*
[Middle English *-fōld,* Old English *-feald*]
fold-a|way (fōld′ə wā′), *adj.* that can be folded out of sight or out of the way when not in use: *portable models with fold-away legs* (Wall Street Journal).
fold-back (fōld′bak′), *adj., n.* — ***adj.*** that can be folded back: *a fold-back dome in an auditorium to let the sky in for open-air spectacles.* — ***n.*** something that can be folded back: *the fold-back of a car's front seat.*
fold|boat (fōld′bōt′), *n.* = faltboat.
folded mountain, a mountain formed when the earth's crust folds into great waves, somewhat like the folds of a washboard. An example of folded mountains is the Jura range on the French-Swiss border.
fold|er (fōl′dər), *n.* **1** a holder for papers, made by folding a piece of stiff paper: *Stacks of papers lay neatly sorted in labeled folders on his desk.* **2** a pamphlet, usually made of one folded sheet: *The policeman handed out colorful folders about bicycle safety.* **3** a person or thing that folds.
fol|de|rol (fol′fə rol), *n.* = falderal.
fold|ing carton or **box** (fōl′ding), a paperboard carton that can be folded flat: *June shipments of folding cartons from manufacturing plants to packagers were above June a year ago* (Wall Street Journal).
folding chair, a chair that can be folded up for easier handling or storage: *Rows of folding chairs on sidewalk to accommodate hundred or more guests* (New Yorker).
folding doors, doors having one part attached to another by hinges so that they open and close by folding and unfolding.
folding money, *Informal.* paper money; bills: *a pocketful of folding money.*
fold|out (fōld′out′), *n.* an illustrated page that is extra long and has to be folded to fit into a book or magazine, and unfolded to be read.
fo|li|a (fō′lē ə), *n.* a plural of **folium.**
fo|li|a|ceous (fō′lē ā′shəs), *adj.* **1** of or having to do with leaves; leaflike; leafy. **2** made of leaflike plates or thin layers. **3** *Zoology.* shaped or arranged like leaves. [< Latin *foliāceus* (with English *-ous*) < *folium* leaf]
fo|li|age (fō′lij, -lē ij, -lə-), *n.* **1** the leaves of a plant, especially growing leaves: *These naked shoots ... Shall put their graceful foliage on again* (William Cowper). **SYN:** leafage. **2** a decoration made of carved or painted leaves or flowers. [alteration of earlier *fuelage* < Middle French *feuillage* < Old French *feuille* leaf < Latin *folium*]
fo|li|aged (fō′lijd, -lē ijd), *adj.* **1** having foliage. **2** decorated with foliage.
fo|li|a|geous (fō′lē ā′jəs), *adj.* containing representations of foliage.
foliage plant, any plant cultivated for ornament for the sake of its foliage rather than its flowers.
fo|li|al (fō′lē əl), *adj.* = foliar.
fo|li|ar (fō′lē ər), *adj.* of or having to do with a leaf or leaves.
fo|li|ate (*adj.* fō′lē it, -āt; *v.* fō′lē āt), *adj., v.,* **-at|ed, -at|ing.** — ***adj.*** **1** having leaves; covered with leaves. **2** resembling a leaf; leaflike.
— ***v.i.*** **1** to put forth leaves. **2** to split into leaflike plates or thin layers.
— ***v.t.*** **1** to decorate with leaflike ornaments. **SYN:** leaf. **2** to furnish with leaves. **3** to number the folios or leaves of (a volume). **4** to shape like a leaf. **5** to foil (glass); silver.
[< Latin *foliātus* < *folium* leaf]
fo|li|at|ed (fō′lē ā′tid), *adj.* **1** having leaves. **2** shaped like a leaf or leaves. **3** consisting of thin, leaflike layers or laminae. **4** backed with foil, as glass. **5** *Architecture.* ornamented with foils, or

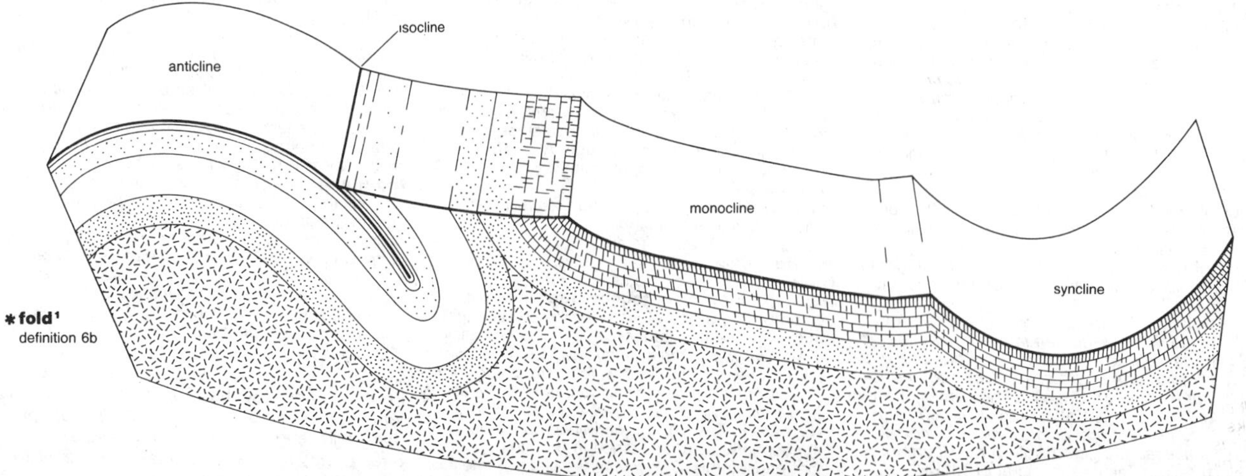

***fold¹**
definition 6b

with foliage. **6** (of a volume) numbered consecutively.

fo|li|a|tion (fō′lē ā′shən), *n.* **1** the process of growing leaves; putting forth of leaves: *foliation of trees in the spring.* **2** the state of being in leaf. **3** leafage; foliage. **4** decoration with leaflike ornaments or foils. **5a** the arrangement and numbering of the folios or leaves of a volume. **b** the total number of such folios or leaves. **6** *Geology.* **a** the property of splitting up into leaflike layers. **b** the leaflike plates or layers into which crystalline rocks are divided. **7** the beating of metal into foil. **8** the application of foil to glass to form a mirror.

fo|li|a|ture (fō′lē ə chər), *n.* a cluster of leaves; foliage.

fo|lic acid (fō′lik), *Biochemistry.* a constituent of the vitamin B complex, found in green leaves and animal tissue, thought to be useful in treating anemia. *Formula:* $C_{19}H_{19}N_7O_6$ [< Latin *folium* leaf + English *-ic*]

fo|lie (fô lē′), *n. French.* delusion; mania; insanity.

fo|lie à deux (fô lē′ à dœ′), *pl.* **fo|lies à deux (fô lē′à dœ′).** *Psychiatry.* a mental disorder shared by two closely associated persons, such as man and wife. [< French *folie à deux* double delusion]

fo|li|ic|o|lous (fō′lē ik′ə ləs), *adj.* (of fungi, etc.) growing parasitically on leaves.

fo|li|if|er|ous (fō′lē if′ər əs), *adj.* bearing leaves or leaflike appendages.

fo|lin|ic acid (fō lin′ik), = citrovorum factor. [< *fol* (ic acid) + *-in* + *-ic*]

fo|li|o (fō′lē ō), *n., pl.* **-li|os,** *adj., v.,* **-li|oed, -li|o-ing.** **—*n.*** **1** a large sheet of paper folded once to make two leaves, or four pages, of a book or magazine. **2a** a book having pages made by folding large sheets of paper once; volume having pages of the largest size. A folio is usually any book more than 11 inches in height. *I do not care for a First Folio of Shakespeare* (Charles Lamb). **b** the size of a folio book. **3** *Printing.* a page number of a book. **4** a leaf of a book or manuscript, numbered on the front side only. **5** a page of an accounting record, or both a left-hand page and the right-hand page facing it, marked with the same serial number. **6** a case for loose papers. **7** *Law.* a certain number of words (usually 100 in the United States and 72-90 in England) in a document, used as a unit of measurement or reference. *Abbr:* fol.

—*adj.* having to do with or having the form of a folio: *The encyclopedia was in twenty volumes folio.*

—*v.t.* **1** to number the pages or folios of (a book, magazine, or accounting record); page. **2** *Law.* to mark each folio in (a pleading) with the proper number.

in folio, of folio size or form: *The more usual form of books printed in the 15th century is in folio* (Henry Hallam).

[< Latin *foliō,* ablative of *folium* leaf]

fo|li|o|late (fō′lē ə lāt; fō lī′ə lit, -lāt), *adj.* having to do with or consisting of leaflets (used chiefly in composition, as in *bifoliolate, trifoliolate*). [< *foliole* + *-ate* [1]]

fo|li|ole (fō′lē ōl), *n.* **1** *Botany.* a division of a compound leaf; leaflet. **2** *Zoology.* a small leaflike part or organ. [< French *foliole,* learned borrowing from Late Latin *foliolum* (diminutive) < Latin *folium* leaf]

fo|li|ose (fō′lē ōs), *adj. Botany.* having or abounding in leaves; leafy. [< Latin *foliōsus* < *folium* leaf]

fo|li|o ver|so (fō′lē ō vėr′sō), *Latin.* on the back of the leaf (of a book or other bound printed matter). *Abbr:* f.v.

fo|li|um (fō′lē əm), *n., pl.* **-li|a** or **-li|ums.** **1** a thin layer, as in a rock. **2** a leaf or sheet, as of paper: *protocols and memoranda in ten thousand folia* (John Lothrop Motley). **3** *Geometry.* a loop. [< Latin *folium* leaf]

fo|li|vore (fō′lə vôr, -vōr), *n.* a folivorous animal: *The three-toed sloth is ... classified as an "arboreal folivore"* (Science News).

fo|liv|o|rous (fō liv′ər əs), *adj.* eating or feeding on leaves: *Presbytis entellus and Gorilla gorilla are the only folivorous primates that do forage extensively on the ground* (Science). [< Latin *folium* leaf + *vorāre* devour + English *-ous*]

folk (fōk), *n., pl.* **folk** or **folks,** *adj.* **—*n.*** **1a** people in general: *All the folk I write about have died* (Rudyard Kipling). **b** people of a particular class or group: *poor folk, country folk. Most city folk know very little about farming.* **2** a tribe or nation. **3** the common people of a nation or other group.

—*adj.* of or having to do with the common people, their beliefs, legends, customs, and the like: *folk culture, folk heroes, folk tunes.*

folks, a people: *Hawaii, which has almost no billboards at all, seems to be surviving this lack, and most folks will agree that it does a pretty good tourist business* (St. Louis Post-Dispatch). **b** *Informal.* the members of one's own family; one's relatives: *How are all your folks? For his vacation he went home to see his folks.*

[Old English *folc*]

folk art, a simple, unsophisticated form of art based upon traditional beliefs and methods.

folk|craft (fōk′kraft′, -kräft′), *n.* **1** the art or craftsmanship of the people of a country or region; native handicraft: *Eskimo folkcraft.* **2** a work of native art or handicraft: *clay and ceramic folkcrafts by anonymous Mexican and Latin-American artists.*

folk dance, **1** a dance originating and handed down among the common people. **2** the music for it.

folk dancer, a person who performs or takes part in folk dances.

folk dancing, the dancing of folk dances.

Fol|ke|ting or **Fol|ke|thing** (fōl′kə ting′), *n.* **1** the unicameral parliament of Denmark. **2** the lower house of Denmark's former bicameral parliament. [< Danish *Folketing* (literally) folk assembly]

folk etymology, a popular misconception of the origin of a word that often results in a modification of its sound or spelling. *Examples:* Old French *crevice* became English *crayfish,* influenced by *fish. Cape Despair* came from *Cape d'espoir, Welsh rarebit* from *Welsh rabbit,* and *sparrowgrass* from *asparagus.*

folk|ie (fō′kē), *n. Slang.* a folk singer.

folk|ish (fōk′ish), *adj.* of or resembling the common or native people of a region or country: *folkish naiveté.* **—folk′ish|ness,** *n.*

folk|like (fōk′līk′), *adj.* = folkish.

folk|lore (fōk′lôr′, -lōr′), *n.* **1** the beliefs, legends, customs, and the like, of a people, tribe, or other group: *The literate peoples of antiquity left a ... folklore; the Greek stories of the origins of fire and of agriculture are examples* (Beals and Hoijer). **2** the study of these.

folk|lor|ic (fōk′lôr′ik, -lōr′-), *adj.* suggestive of or giving rise to folklore: *I remembered a verse from a folkloric poem* (New Yorker).

folk|lor|ique (fōk′lô rēk′, -lō-), *adj. French.* folkloric.

folk|lor|ish (fōk′lôr′ish, -lōr′-), *adj.* somewhat folkloric: *folklorish music.*

folk|lor|ism (fōk′lôr′iz əm, -lōr′-), *n.* a piece of folklore.

folk|lor|ist (fōk′lôr′ist, -lōr′-), *n.* a person who studies folklore: *It was in the bayou country that Alfred Pouinard, French folklorist, found the largest number of French folk songs still extant in the U.S.* (Newsweek).

folk|lor|is|tic (fōk′lô ris′tik, -lō-), *adj.* of or having to do with folklore. **—folk′lor|is′ti|cal|ly,** *adv.*

folk mass, a Mass using folk music and often involving audience participation.

folk medicine, the traditional medical maxims, remedies, and methods prevalent among the people of a region.

folk|moot (fōk′müt′), *n.* (in English history) a general assembly of the people of a town, city, or shire. [modern revival of Old English *folkgemōt* < *folk* people + *gemōt* a meeting]

folk|mot or **folk|mote** (fōk′mōt′), *n.* = folkmoot.

folk music, **1** music originating and handed down among the common people. **2** music imitating real folk music.

folk|nik (fōk′nik), *n. Slang.* **1** a person who is very enthusiastic about folk singing. **2** = folk singer. [< *folk* (singer) + *-nik,* as in *beatnik*]

folk psychology, **1** the psychology of ethnic groups or peoples, especially of non-literate or primitive cultures. **2** the study of the mental characteristics and behavior of such groups or peoples.

folk|right (fōk′rīt′), *n.* (in English history) the common law or right of the people, especially as distinguished from that of the privileged classes.

folk rock , a type of rock'n'roll music with elements of folk-song melody and lyrics.

folk-rock|er (fōk′rok′ər), *n.* a person who sings or plays folk rock.

folks (fōks), *n.pl.* See under **folk.**

folk|say (fōk′sā′), *n.* the traditional speech and sayings of a people or social group: *Carl Sandburg ... fashioned the speech, history, and folkways of the Midwest—what he called "folksay"—into a sparse, lean, rhythmic, free verse* (C. Hugh Holman).

folk singer, a person who sings folk songs.

folk singing, the singing of folk songs.

folk song, **1** a song originating and handed down among the common people. **2** a song imitating a real folk song: *"Oh! Susanna" is a folk song written by Stephen Foster.* **3** the music for either of these.

folk speech, the dialect spoken by the common people of a country or district.

folk state, a political state embracing only one homogeneous folk or people.

folk|ster (fōk′stər), *n. U.S. Informal.* a folk singer.

folk story, = folk tale.

folk|sy (fōk′sē), *adj.,* **-si|er, -si|est.** *U.S. Informal.* **1** sociable; friendly; affable: *the column's blend of folksy humor and sage observation* (Newsweek). **2** simple; unpretentious; common: *all, to judge from the pictures, very folksy people, plain as old shoes but nice* (New Yorker). **3** apparently or affectedly simple and friendly: *I ... would rather get my old-fashioned, homemade this or that off a chainstore shelf, without any folksy buildup* (New Yorker). **—folk′si|ly,** *adv.* **—folk′si-ness,** *n.*

folk tale, a story or legend originating and handed down among the common people.

folk|way (fōk′wā′), *n.* a custom or habit that has grown up within a social group and is very common among the members of this group.

folk|y (fō′kē), *adj.,* **folk|i|er, folk|i|est.** *Informal.* **1** folksy. **2** commonplace.

foll., following.

***fol|li|cle** (fol′ə kəl), *n.* **1** a small cavity, sac, or gland in the body. Hair grows from follicles. **2** *Botany.* a one-celled seed vessel; a dry fruit, formed of a single carpel, that splits open along one seam only: *Milkweed pods are follicles.* [< Latin *folliculus* (diminutive) < *follis* a bellows; (literally) leather bag]

***follicle**
definition 2

follicle mite, any one of various tiny mites that lodge in hair follicles.

fol|li|cle-stim|u|lat|ing hormone (fol′ə kəl-stim′yə lā′ting), a hormone which is secreted by the anterior part of the pituitary gland and stimulates the growth of the ovary during the menstrual cycle. *Abbr:* FSH (no periods).

fol|lic|u|lar (fə lik′yə lər), *adj.* **1** having to do with, consisting of, or like a follicle or follicles. **2** *Medicine.* (of a disease) affecting the follicles of a particular organ. [< Latin *folliculus* (see etym. under **follicle**) + English *-ar*]

fol|lic|u|late (fə lik′yə lāt), *adj.* provided with or consisting of a follicle or follicles.

fol|lic|u|lat|ed (fə lik′yə lā′təd), *adj.* = folliculate.

fol|lic|u|lin (fə lik′yə lin), *n.* = estrone.

fol|lic|u|li|tis (fə lik′yə lī′tis), *n.* inflammation of a follicle or follicles.

fol|lic|u|lose (fə lik′yə lōs), *adj.* **1** full of or containing follicles. **2** characteristic of or resembling a follicle.

fol|lies (fol′ēz), *n.* **1** plural of **folly. 2** a theater revue.

fol|low (fol′ō), *v., n.* **—*v.t.*** **1** to go or come after: *Night follows day. Sheep follow a leader. A farmer used to follow a plow.* **2** *Figurative.* to come after as a consequence or effect; result from: *Misery follows war.* **3** to go along: *Follow this road to the corner.* **4** to go along with; accompany: *My dog followed me to school.* **5** to go in pursuit of; pursue: *The dogs followed the fox.* **6** to act according to; take as a guide; use; obey: *Follow her advice.* **7** *Figurative.* to accept (a person) as a guide or leader; accept the authority or example of: *The house of Judah followed David.* **8** to keep the eyes or attention on: *I could not follow that bird's flight.* **9** to keep the mind on; keep up with and understand: *to follow an argument. Try to follow my meaning.* **10** to take as one's work; be concerned with: *Fred expects to follow the profession of lawyer. A sailor follows the sea.* **11** *Figurative.* to attempt to reach; strive after: *I follow fame* (Tennyson). *Follow peace with all men* (Hebrews 12:14). **12** *Obsolete.* to imitate or copy; take after.

—*v.i.* **1** to go or come after something or someone else: *He leads; we follow.* **2** to occur as a consequence; result: *If you eat too much candy, a stomach ache will follow.* **3** to attend: *Behind the principals, the chorus followed.* **4** to pursue: *Up, follow after the men* (Genesis 44:4). **5** *Figurative.* to strive for attainment: *Some have failed; will he dare to follow?* **6** to understand: *Jack said, "I come out on Dexter." "I don't follow," said Judge Moody* (Eudora Welty).

—*n.* **1** an act of following. **2** *Billiards.* a stroke that causes the player's ball to roll on after the ball struck by it.

Pronunciation Key: hat, āge, cãre, fär; let, ēqual, tėrm; it, īce; hot, ōpen, ôrder; oil, out; cup, pu̇t, rüle; child; long; thin; ᴛʜen; zh, measure; ə represents **a** in about, **e** in taken, **i** in pencil, **o** in lemon, **u** in circus.

as follows, the following: *The list of people to be invited is as follows: John, Mary, Bill, Hattie, Clem, and Virginia.*
follow on, *Cricket.* to go in again at once after completing the first innings in consequence of having made a prescribed number of runs less than the opponents in the first innings: *Being left in a minority of 93 they had to follow on* (Leeds Mercury).
follow one's nose. See under **nose**.
follow out, to carry out to the end: *The general followed out his plan of attack in spite of opposition from members of his staff.*
follow suit. See under **suit**.
follow through, to continue a stroke, motion, plan, policy, or reasoning through to the end: *In following through, the club or racket acts upon the ball for the longest possible time and therefore the ball travels faster* (E. A. Fessenden).
follow up, **a** to follow closely and steadily: *The Forest bylaws . . . make no provision for wounded deer being followed up* (London Times). **b** *Figurative.* to carry out to the end: *The author planned the book carefully, but he found it hard to follow up the plan.* **c** to act upon with energy: *to follow up a suggestion. The Romans followed up their success by an attack on Olbia* (Bosworth Smith).
[Old English *folgian*]
—***Syn.*** *v.t.* 1, *v.i.* **1 Follow, succeed, ensue** mean to come or go after. **Follow** is the general word: *He has come to take his new position, but his wife will follow later. April follows March.* **Succeed** means to come next in order of time, and usually suggests taking the place of someone or something: *to succeed to a title. He succeeded his father as president of the company.* **Ensue**, a formal word, means to follow as a result or conclusion and does not take a direct object: *A lasting friendship ensued from our working together during the war.*
▶**follow**. The idiom is *followed by,* not *followed with: Supper was followed by games and dancing.*

fol|low|a|ble (fol′ō ə bəl), *adj.* that can be followed.

fol|low|er (fol′ō ər), *n.* **1** a person or thing that follows: *By slipping into a side street the man was able to get away from his followers.* **2** a person who follows the ideas or beliefs of another: *Christians are followers of Christ.* **3** a member of the household of a king or nobleman; attendant or servant: *The King's baggage was carried on the backs of his followers.* **4** a gear, wheel, or other machine part that is given motion by another part. **5** *Informal.* a man who courts a young woman.
—***Syn.*** **2 Follower, adherent, disciple** mean someone who follows another, his beliefs, a cause, or the like. **Follower** is the general word: *Men who promise riches always find followers among unthinking people.* **Adherent**, more formal, implies active and loyal support of a belief, cause, or party, and sometimes personal devotion to the leader: *Adherents of a political party will rarely switch over to another party.* **Disciple** emphasizes both devotion to a person as leader and teacher and firm belief in his teachings: *The disciples of Karl Marx spread his ideas throughout Europe.*

fol|low|er|ship (fol′ō ər ship), *n.* **1** the ability to follow or to be a follower. **2** a group of followers; a following.

fol|low|ing (fol′ō ing), *n., adj.* —***n.*** **1** a group of followers; attendants. **2** admirers; supporters.
—***adj.*** **1** that follows; next after: *If that was Sunday, then the following day must have been Monday.* SYN: subsequent, ensuing. **2** that now follows; that is immediately to be named, related, or described. *Abbr:* ff.
the following, the persons, things, or items now to be named, related, or described: *The winners of the three contests are the following: Smith, Johnson, and Moore.*

fol|low-on (fol′ō on′, -ôn′), *n., adj.* —***n.*** **1** *Cricket.* the act of a player who follows on. **2** something that follows or develops from an earlier thing or action; successor: *The Jupiter was a follow-on, more sophisticated than earlier rockets.*
—***adj.*** following; succeeding: *a follow-on project, contract, or order.*

fol|low-the-lead|er (fol′ō ᴛʜə lē′dər), *n.* a children's game in which each player must completely copy every action of the leader.

fol|low-through (fol′ō thrü′), *n., adj.*
—***n.*** **1** *Sports.* the continuation of a movement or stroke after its climax has been reached: *A good tennis player or golfer knows that follow-through is important in striking the ball* (E. A. Fessenden). **2** the continuation of a development, trend, plan, or other action once started: *There was no follow-through to the demand and the market subsequently gave ground* (Wall Street Journal).
—**adj.** continuing: *follow-through support.*

fol|low-up (fol′ō up′), *n., adj.* —***n.*** **1** the act of following up. **2** any action or thing, such as a second or subsequent visit, advertising appeal, or letter, designed to be a further effort in achieving some goal. **3** a newspaper story after an initial story of an event, adding new facts or background.
—***adj.*** sent or used as a follow-up: *a follow-up circular.*

fol|ly (fol′ē), *n., pl.* **-lies**. **1** the fact or state of being foolish; lack of sense; unwise conduct: *It was folly to eat too much on the picnic. My only books Were women's looks, and folly's all they taught me* (Thomas Moore). *Where ignorance is bliss, 'Tis folly to be wise* (Thomas Gray). **2** a foolish act, practice, or idea; something silly. **3** a costly but foolish undertaking. **4** *Obsolete.* **a** wickedness. **b** wantonness.
[< Old French *folie* < *fol* foolish; see etym. under **fool**]

Fol|som man (fol′səm), a Stone Age man thought to have lived in North America at the end of the most recent glacial period. [< *Folsom,* a town in New Mexico, where relics were discovered]

Folsom point, a thin, chipped stone somewhat like an arrowhead, one of many found at Folsom, New Mexico, and associated with the culture of the Folsom man: *New methods of dating Folsom points have pushed the human occupation of America back to 14,000 B.C. or earlier* (Allan Nevins).

Fo|mal|haut (fō′məl hôt), *n.* one of the twenty brightest stars in the sky, near Capricorn in the Southern Hemisphere. [< Arabic *fam al-khūt* (literally) mouth of the fish (because it is in the constellation *Piscis Australis,* literally, Southern Fish)]

fo|ment (fō ment′), *v.t.* **1** to foster (trouble, rebellion, or other turmoil); promote: *Three sailors were fomenting a mutiny on the ship.* SYN: encourage, instigate. **2** to apply warm water, hot cloths, or other sources of heat to (a hurt or pain). [< Late Latin *fōmentāre* < Latin *fōmentum* a warm application < *fovēre* to warm] —**fo|ment′er**, *n.*

fo|men|ta|tion (fō′men tā′shən), *n.* **1** the act of stirring up; instigation; encouragement. **2** application of moist heat. **3** a hot, moist application.

fo|mes (fō′mēz), *n., pl.* **fom|i|tes** (fom′ə tēz, fō′mə-). any porous substance capable of absorbing and retaining contagious germs: *Bedding, books, curtains, and clothes are common fomites.* [< Latin *fōmes* tinder]

Fon (fon), *n., pl.* **Fon**. **1** a member of a West African people of Benin. **2** the Kwa language of this people.

fonc|tion|naire (fôɴk syô ner′), *n. French.* a civil servant or government official: *The fonctionnaires, as they retired on pension, took to farming* (New Yorker).

fond[1] (fond), *adj.* **1** loving; affectionate; tender: *a fond look.* SYN: amorous. **2** cherished or entertained strongly or unreasoningly: *fond hopes.* **3** loving foolishly or too much; over-affectionate; doting: *She was fond and foolish of the cat carrying it everywhere.* **4** *Archaic.* foolishly ready to believe or hope; foolish.
fond of, having a liking for: *fond of children. I am not fond of uttering platitudes In stained-glass attitudes* (William S. Gilbert).
[< Middle English *fonned,* past participle of *fonnen* be foolish, perhaps < *fonne* fool; origin uncertain]

fond[2] (fond; *French* fôɴ), *n.* **1** a background or foundation: *There is no early French literature of any value in which the Teutonic blood did not supply the fond* (James Russell Lowell). **2** a stock; fund. [< French *fond,* spelling variant of *fonds* fonds]

fon|da (fôn′dä), *n. Spanish.* an inn or hotel.

fon|dant (fon′dənt), *n.* **1** a creamy confection used as a filling or coating for other candies. **2** a candy consisting mainly of fondant. [< French *fondant* (literally) melting, present participle of *fondre* melt < Latin *fundere* pour]

fon|dle (fon′dəl), *v.,* **-dled, -dling**. —***v.t.*** **1** to handle or treat with fondness; pet; caress: *The mother fondled her baby.* **2** *Obsolete.* to coddle; pamper.
—***v.i.*** to behave, play, or speak fondly. [< *fond*[1], in obsolete use as verb + *-le*] —**fon′dler**, *n.*

fon|dling (fond′ling), *n.* **1** a person or thing treated fondly; pet. **2** *English Dialect.* a fool; simpleton. [< *fond*[1] + *-ling*]

fond|ly (fond′lē), *adv.* **1** affectionately; lovingly; tenderly: *The mother murmured fondly to her baby.* **2** with self-pleasing or affectionate credulity. **3** *Obsolete.* foolishly.

fond|ness (fond′nis), *n.* **1** strong inclination, desire, or liking: *a fondness for travel. She has a fondness for sweets.* **2** affectionateness; tenderness. **3** foolish affection; unreasoning tenderness **4** *Obsolete.* foolishness; folly.

fonds (fondz; *French* fôɴ), *n.pl.* **1** ground. **2** land; capital; stock; fund. [< French *fonds* < Old French *fons,* or *fonz* < Latin *fundus*]

fon|du (fon′dü, fon dü′), *adj.* **1** blended; softened. **2** characterized by the blending of colors, one into another, through delicate gradations. [< French *fondu,* past participle of *fondre;* see etym. under **fondant**]

fon|due (fon′dü, fon dü′; *French* fôɴ dʏ′), *n.* **1** a dish chiefly made of melted cheese, eggs, butter, etc., into which crackers or small pieces of toast are dipped before eating them. **2** any dish of heated sauce into which small pieces of food are dipped before eating: *beef fondue, chocolate fondue.* [< French *fondue* (originally) feminine of *fondu* fondu]

fon|io (fôn′yō), *n.* a crab grass whose seeds are used as a cereal in Upper Volta. [< a native name]

***font**[1] (font), *n.* **1** a basin holding water for baptism. **2** a basin for holy water; stoup. **3** a fountain; source. SYN: fount, spring. **4** the reservoir for oil in a lamp. [Old English *font,* ultimately < Latin *fōns, fontis* spring, fount. Compare etym. under **fount**[1].]

***font**[1]
definition 1

font[2] (font), *n.* **1** *Printing.* a complete set of type of one size and style. **2** the act or process of founding or casting. Also, *especially British,* **fount**. [< Middle French *fonte* < *fondre* melt; see etym. under **fondant**]

fon|tal (fon′təl), *adj.* having to do with a font, fountain, source, or origin. [< Medieval Latin *fontalis* < Latin *fōns, fontis* spring, fount]

fon|ta|nel or **fon|ta|nelle** (fon′tə nel′), *n.* **1** one of the soft spots, closed by membrane and later to be filled by bone, on the head of an infant or fetus. **2** *Obsolete.* an opening for the discharge of pus. [< French *fontanelle,* alteration of Old French *fontenele* (originally diminutive) < *fontaine* fountain]

fon|tange (fôɴ tänzh′), *n., pl.* **-tanges** (-tänzh′). = commode (def. 4). [< French *fontange* < the Duchess of *Fontanges,* the mistress of Louis XIV]

Fon|té|che|vade man (fôɴ tā shə vȧd′), an early form of Homo sapiens who presumably lived about 100,000 years ago, according to the evidence of fossil remains found in France. [< *Fontéchevade,* a town in France, where remains were found]

fon|ti|na (fon tē′nə), *n.* a soft, creamy Italian cheese with a nutty flavor, usually made from sheep's milk. [< Italian *fontina (d'Aosta)* fontina (from Aosta) < *Aosta,* a valley in northern Italy, where the cheese is made]

fon|ti|nal (fon′tə nəl), *adj.* growing in or about springs, as certain plants. [< Latin *fontinālis* having to do with springs < *fōns, fontis* spring, fount]

food (füd), *n.* **1** anything that animals or people eat or drink that makes them live and grow; nourishment: *Milk and green vegetables are valuable foods for young people.* **2** what is eaten: *Give him food and drink.* **3** anything that plants take in that enables them to live and grow. **4** a particular kind or article of food: *breakfast foods.* **5** *Figurative.* anything that causes growth: *Books are food for the mind.* **6** *Figurative.* anything that sustains or serves for consumption in any way: *food for thought. If music be the food of love, play on* (Shakespeare). [Old English *fōda*] —**food′less**, *adj.* —**food′less|ness**, *n.*
—***Syn.*** **1, 3 Food, provisions, rations** mean that which is intended to be eaten. **Food** is the general word for anything that nourishes people, animals, or plants: *healthful foods, plant food.* **Provisions**, usually having to do with human food only, means a supply of food, either for immediate use or stored away: *I must buy provisions for the holidays.* **Rations**, also usually restricted to human food, means fixed allowances of food for a particular period or that amount of food allowed under some system of rationing: *a weekly ration of meat, rations for a company of soldiers.*

food additive, any substance, natural or synthetic, that is added to food to preserve, enrich, or color it: *Benzoic acid and sodium benzoate [are] chemicals used as food additives* (Wall Street Journal).

food|a|hol|ic (füd′ə hôl′ik, -hol′-), *n.* a person having an obsessive need to eat; compulsive eater: *Lynn admits that she once had a weight problem. "At 23 . . . I was a foodaholic," she said* (New York Sunday News). [< *food* + *a*(lco)*holic*]

∗**food chain**, *Ecology.* a group of organisms so interrelated that each member of the group feeds upon the one below it and is in turn eaten by the organism above it.

∗**food chain**

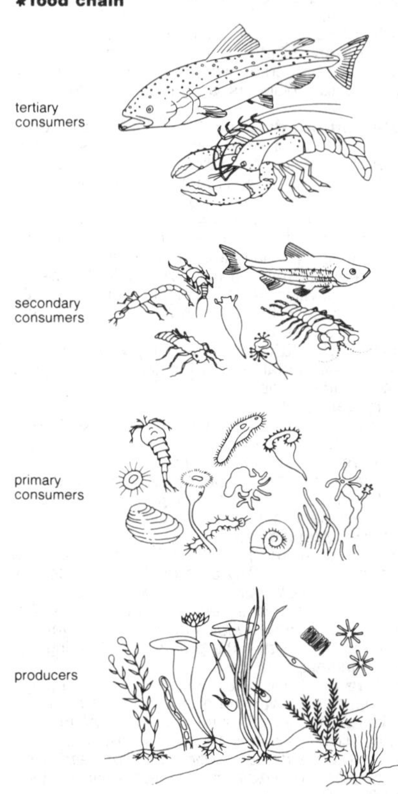

food cycle, *Ecology.* a group of interrelated food chains in a particular community; food web.

food faddist, a person who attributes special therapeutic properties to certain foods.

food fish, a fish suitable for and used as food.

food-gath|er|er (füd′gaᴛʜ′ər ər), *n. Anthropology.* a primitive or prehistoric type of man who obtained food by gathering wild plants and fruits and hunting animals instead of raising crops or livestock.

food|grain (füd′grān′), *n.* wheat, corn, oats, and other grain grown for human consumption.

food|lift (füd′lift′), *n.* the transportation of food by air in an emergency; an airlift of food: *Massive foodlift to starving Yemen* (London Times).

food poisoning, a poisoning caused by consuming foods that are poisonous in themselves or that contain certain bacteria or bacterial toxins, or certain chemicals. Botulism is a severe form of food poisoning.

food processor, **1** an individual or company that converts agricultural products into the form in which they are sold as food, or prepares them for sale, as by packing, canning, or freezing. **2** an electric appliance that cuts slices, chops, shreds, minces, and otherwise processes food at high speed: *A food processor may be less expensive to manufacture than a blender, but the Cuisinart food processor does not come cheap* (New York Daily News).

food pyramid, *Ecology.* the gradually narrowing structure representing the amount of food passed along a food chain, as at each upward link or step the quantity of food passed on becomes smaller.

food science, the technical study of the preparation and processing of foods (sometimes including the science of nutrition and dietetics).

food stamp, a stamp to buy food with, issued by the U.S. Department of Agriculture, usually in return for some payment, to people without enough money to maintain the minimum standard of living set by the U.S. government.

food|stuff (füd′stuf′), *n.* **1** material for food. Grain and meat are foodstuffs. **2** any nutritionally valuable element in food, such as protein or carbohydrate.

food vacuole, a vacuole containing food particles, found in certain protozoans such as amebas. It serves as a simple digestive system.

food web, = food cycle.

food yolk, the portion of the yolk of an egg that nourishes the embryo, as distinguished from the germinative portion.

foo|fa|raw or **foo|fe|raw** (fü′fə rô), *n.* **1** ornaments, as fringes, knots, or frills. **2** *Slang.* a noisy commotion over something unimportant. [perhaps alteration of *fanfaron*]

fool[1] (fül), *n., v., adj.* —*n.* **1** a person without sense or judgment; person who acts unwisely; simpleton: *The young man who has not wept is a savage, and the old man who will not laugh is a fool* (George Santayana). **2** a clown formerly kept by a king or lord to amuse people; jester: *How ill white hairs become a fool and jester* (Shakespeare). **3** a person who has been deceived or tricked; dupe. **4** a feeble-minded or idiotic person.
—*v.i.* to act like a fool for fun; joke; play; pretend: *I was only fooling.*
—*v.t.* to make a fool of; deceive; trick; dupe: *You can't fool all of the people all of the time* (Abraham Lincoln).
—*adj. Informal.* foolish; silly: *They're always bringing up a shell or some other fool thing* (Saturday Evening Post).
be nobody's fool. See under **nobody**.
fool around, *Informal.* to waste time foolishly; trifle; idle: *He spent his best years just fooling around.*
fool away, *Informal.* to waste foolishly: *He fools away his time, his money, and his health* (C. Cowden Clarke).
fool with, *Informal.* to meddle foolishly with: *Stop fooling with that machine. The accused . . . began fooling with a loaded gun* (Manchester Examiner).
play the fool, to act the part of a fool or jester; act like a fool: *I advise you not to play the fool with me any longer* (Daniel Defoe).
[< Old French *fol* madman, probably < Late Latin *follis* empty-headed < Latin, bag, bellows]
—*Syn. n.* **1 Fool, idiot, imbecile,** in nontechnical use, mean a foolish person. **Fool** suggests absence of any sign of intelligence, and expresses contempt for someone who acts without good sense or judgment: *She is a fool to leave school in order to get a job.* **Idiot** is used of someone acting as if he were totally feeble-minded: *I should call her an idiot if she walked in the deep snow without her boots.* **Imbecile** is used of someone the speaker considers half-witted: *Look at that imbecile grinning at nothing.*

fool[2] (fül), *n. British.* a dessert of stewed fruit and cream. [probably < *fool*[1]]

fool duck, *U.S.* the ruddy duck.

fool|er|y (fü′lər ē), *n., pl.* **-er|ies. 1** a foolish action, performance, or thing: *We've had about enough of this foolery* (Robert Louis Stevenson). **2** the habit or practice of acting foolishly.

fool|fish (fül′fish′), *n., pl.* **-fish|es** or (*collectively*) **-fish. 1** a small-scaled, small-mouthed plaice of the eastern United States, noted for the readiness with which it takes any bait. **2** a short, rough-skinned, dull-greenish or brownish filefish of the eastern United States, having long fins and an irregular, wriggling swimming motion.

fool|har|di|hood (fül′här′dē hůd), *n.* foolish boldness; rashness.

fool|har|dy (fül′här′dē), *adj.,* **-di|er, -di|est.** foolishly bold; rash: *The man made a foolhardy attempt to go over Niagara Falls in a barrel.* **SYN:** reckless. —**fool′har′di|ly**, *adv.* —**fool′har′di-ness**, *n.*

fool hen, the spruce grouse of the western United States and Canada, which is notoriously unwary and easily killed.

fool|ing (fü′ling), *n.* **1** the speech or actions of one who fools; frivolity; nonsense. **2** ridiculous or absurd behavior. **3** playful actions; play; sport.

fool|ish (fü′lish), *adj.* **1** like a fool; without sense or judgment; unwise; silly: *It is foolish to keep late hours every night.* **SYN:** stupid. **2** ridiculous; absurd: *foolish notions.* **3** *Archaic or Dialect.* humble; paltry; insignificant: *a trifling foolish banquet* (Shakespeare). —**fool′ish|ly**, *adv.* —**fool′-ish|ness**, *n.*
—*Syn.* **1 Foolish, silly, fatuous** mean without sense. **Foolish** means showing lack of common sense and judgment: *The foolish girl insists on having her own way.* **Silly** means seeming weak-minded, doing or saying things without sense or point, often making oneself laughed at unkindly: *Being called silly is not a compliment.* **Fatuous** means silly and stupid, but completely self-satisfied: *After his boring speech, the fatuous speaker received almost no applause.*

foolish guillemot, the common murre, a large, brown and white oceanic bird of northern seas.

fool|proof (fül′prüf′), *adj.* so safe or simple that even a fool can use or do it: *a foolproof device, a foolproof scheme.*

fools|cap (fülz′kap′), *n.* **1** writing or printing paper in sheets from 12 to 13½ inches wide and 15 to 17 inches long, originally watermarked with a fool's cap. **2** = fool's cap.

fool's cap, **1** a cap or hood, usually with bells on it, worn by the fool or jester of a king or lord. **2** = dunce cap.

fool's errand, a foolish or useless undertaking.

fool's gold, a mineral that looks like gold, especially a pyrite or a chalcopyrite.

fool's mate, a checkmate of the white king by the black queen after only four moves have been made, the shortest ending to a game of chess.

fool's paradise, a condition of happiness based on false beliefs or hopes: *Taking advantage of their freedom from prosecution during the past 14 weeks, they've been living in a fool's paradise* (Wall Street Journal).

fool's parsley, a poisonous native European weed that resembles parsley.

∗**foot** (fůt), *n., pl.* **feet**, *v.* —*n.* **1** the end part of a leg; part that a person, animal, or thing stands on: *I misplaced a shoe and was walking about with one foot bare.* See picture opposite on the following page. **2** an organ present in some invertebrates, especially the muscular, ventral protuberance of the mollusks, used for locomotion. **3** the part opposite the head of something; end toward which the feet are put: *the foot of a bed.* **4** the lowest part; bottom; base: *the foot of a column, the foot of a hill, the foot of a page.* **5** the part of a stocking that covers the foot. **6** soldiers that go on foot; infantrymen; infantry. **7** a measure of length; 12 inches or 30.48 centimeters. 3 feet = 1 yard. *Abbr:* ft. See picture opposite on the following page. **8** one of the parts into which a line of poetry is divided. This line has four feet: "The boy/ stood on/ the burn/ing deck." **9** the lower edge or bottom of a sail. **10a** a thing or part resembling an animal's foot in function: *the foot of a chair.* **b** a small spring-loaded plate in a sewing machine that holds the cloth in position. **11** the last of a list or series. **12** a thing that is written at the bottom, such as the total of a column of figures. **13a** step; pace; speed: *Death, which I did think with slower foot came on* (Shakespeare). **b** *Obsolete.* the power of walking or running. **14** *Printing.* either of two parts of the base of a piece of type; the surface opposite the face, on either side of the groove.
—*v.t.* **1** to walk; cross on foot; walk over: *The boys footed the whole ten miles.* **2** to add up; total: *Foot this column of numbers.* **3** *Informal.* to pay (a bill or costs): *Father foots the bill.* **4** to walk or dance on; set foot on; tread. **5** to make or renew the foot of: *to foot a stocking.* **6** to settle or establish: *What confederacy have you with the traitors Late footed in this kingdom?* (Shakespeare). **7** to seize or clutch with the talons, as a bird of prey does. **8** *Obsolete.* to kick.
—*v.i.* Also, **foot it. 1** to go on foot; walk: *We're footing it instead of riding today.* **2** to dance. **3** to move or sail at a good pace.
feet. For **drag one's feet, put on one's feet, sit at one's feet, think on one's feet, vote with one's feet**, and others, see under **feet**.
foots, a thing that sinks to and lies upon the bottom; the refuse in refining or distilling; sediment: *This here cider don't suit me; there's too much foots in it!* (Frederick T. Elworthy).
get a foot in the door, to make a successful entry into something desirable: [*This oil company*] *was the first to get a foot in the door, with a 35-year contract in the upper Amazon* (Newsweek).
my foot, *Slang.* an expression used to show disagreement or disbelief: *Purporting to be about pollution* (*my foot*), *the show is visually quite resourceful* (Edith Oliver).
one foot in the grave, almost dead; near death: *He has twenty thousand a year . . . and one foot in the grave* (James Payn).
on foot, **a** on one's feet; standing or walking: *Treading the crude consistence, half on foot, half flying* (Milton). **b** going on; in progress: *There's mischief on foot.*
put one's best foot forward, **a** to do one's best: *Some say that our Atomic Energy Commission is actually discouraging industry in this country from putting its best foot forward* (New York Times). **b** to try to make a good impression: *A good salesman always puts his best foot forward with his clients.* **c** to walk or run as fast as possible: *Put your best foot forward, or I fear that we shall miss the mail* (Tennyson).
put one's foot down, make up one's mind and act firmly: *She . . . put her foot down . . . upon the least symptoms of an unpleasantry* (James Payn).
put one's foot in it, *Informal.* to get into trouble

Pronunciation Key: hat, āge, cãre, fär; let, ēqual, tėrm; it, īce; hot, ōpen, ôrder; oil, out; cup, půt, rüle; child; long; thin; ᴛʜen; zh, measure; ə represents **a** in about, **e** in taken, **i** in pencil, **o** in lemon, **u** in circus.

by meddling; be very tactless in words or actions; blunder: *I put my foot in it ..., for I was nearly killed* (Frederick Marryat).

put one's foot in (or **into**) **one's mouth**, *Informal.* to say something very tactless or embarrassing; make a verbal blunder: [*He*] *is a behind-the-scenes politician who knows that one way to avoid putting his foot into his mouth is to keep it shut* (Time).

shoot oneself in the foot, *U.S. Informal.* to hurt oneself; bungle: *Said* [*the*] *publisher of the Milling and Baking News in Kansas City, of the grain embargo: "America has just shot itself in the foot"* (Time).

trample under foot, to treat cruelly, harshly, or scornfully: *He protested that his rights were being trampled under foot.*

under foot, a in the way: *She complains that her small children are always under foot when she is doing her housework.* **b** *Figurative.* in one's power; in subjection: *The dictator kept the masses of people under foot.*

[Old English *fōt*] —**foot′like′**, *adj.*

***foot**
definitions 1, 7

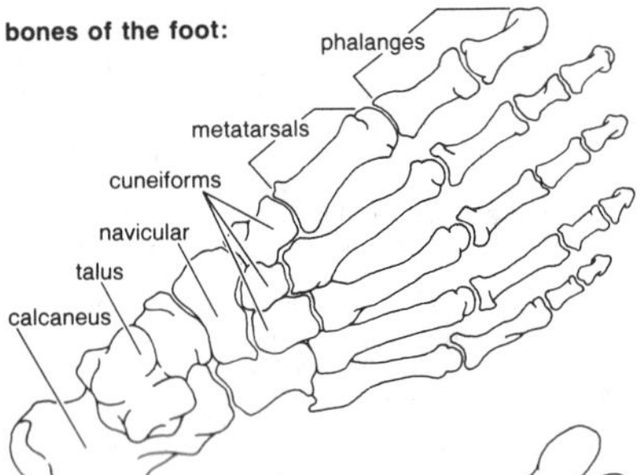

bones of the foot: phalanges, metatarsals, cuneiforms, navicular, talus, calcaneus

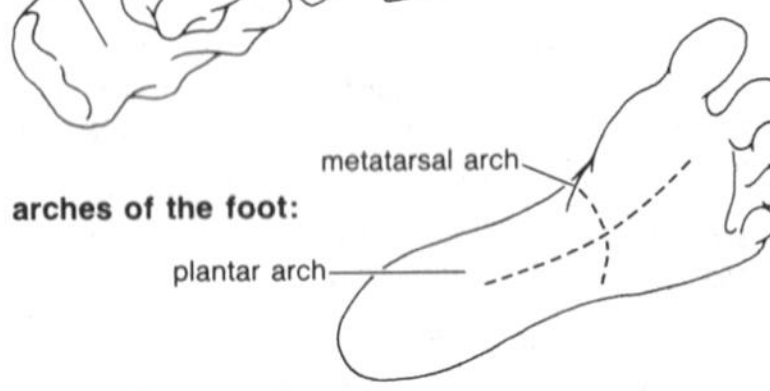

arches of the foot: metatarsal arch, plantar arch

definition 7

1 foot = 12 inches

1 yard = 3 feet or 36 inches

1 meter = 3.28 feet or 39.37 inches

foot|age (fu̇t′ij), *n.* **1** length in feet: *How much footage is left on the movie film?* **2** a quantity of lumber expressed in board feet. **3** *Mining.* **a** a piecework system of paying miners by the running foot of work. **b** the amount paid. **4** one or more sequences of motion pictures: *A French-Algerian cameraman ... took extensive and dramatic footage* (Newsweek).

foot-and-mouth disease (fu̇t′ən mouth′), an acute, contagious virus disease of cattle and some other hoofed animals, causing fever and blisters in the mouth and around the hoofs. It rarely occurs in man.

***foot|ball** (fu̇t′bôl′), *n.* **1** a game played with a large, inflated, leather ball by two teams of eleven players each, on a field with a goal at each end; American football. The players try to score by carrying the ball past the goal line by a run or pass, or by kicking it through the goal posts. **2** the inflated, oval ball used in this game or in Rugby. **3** the spherical ball used in soccer. **4** *British.* Rugby. **5** *British.* soccer. **6** *Figurative.* a person or thing that is kicked or tossed about: *The pollution issue became a political football in the election campaign.*

foot|ball|er (fu̇t′bô′lər), *n.* a person who plays football.

foot|bath (fu̇t′bath′, -bäth′), *n.* **1** the act of bathing the feet. **2** a vessel for bathing the feet.

foot|beat (fu̇t′bēt′), *n.* = footstep.

foot-bind|ing (fu̇t′bīn′ding), *n.* the ancient Chinese custom of tightly binding the feet of infant girls in order to keep the feet small.

foot|board (fu̇t′bôrd′, -bōrd′), *n.* **1** a board or small platform on which to support the feet or to stand. **2** an upright piece across the foot of a bed. **3** = treadle.

foot|boy (fu̇t′boi′), *n.* a boy in livery employed as a servant; pageboy.

foot brake, a brake worked by pressing with the foot, as on an automobile.

foot|bridge (fu̇t′brij′), *n.* a bridge for people on foot only.

foot-can|dle (fu̇t′kan′dəl), *n.* a unit for measuring illumination; candle-foot. It is the amount of light produced by a candle on a surface at a distance of one foot, and equal to one lumen per square foot. *Abbr:* ft.-c. or f.c.

foot|cloth (fu̇t′klôth′, -kloth′), *n.* **1** a carpet or rug. **2** *Obsolete.* a large, richly ornamented cloth draped over a horse.

foot dirt, = foots. See under **foot**.

foot-drag|ging (fu̇t′drag′ing), *n. U.S. Informal.* sluggishness, hesitation, or delay.

foot|ed (fu̇t′id), *adj.* having a foot or feet: *an animal footed like a goat.*

-footed, *combining form.* having a ___ foot or feet: *Club-footed = having a club foot. Four-footed animal = an animal having four feet.*

foot|er (fu̇t′ər), *n. Rare.* a person who goes on foot; pedestrian.

-footer, *combining form.* a person or thing of ___ feet in height or length: *Six-footer = a person or thing six feet in height or length.*

foot|fall (fu̇t′fôl′), *n.* **1** the sound of steps coming or going. **2** a footstep; tread.

foot fault, (in lawn tennis) a fault committed by the server if he fails to maintain contact with the ground or if he brings either foot across the base line before hitting the ball.

foot|fault (fu̇t′fôlt′), *v.i.* to make a foot fault. —*v.t.* to record a foot fault against (a player).

foot|gear (fu̇t′gir′), *n.* shoes, boots, or other covering for the feet.

foot guard, **1** a boot or pad worn by a horse to prevent wounding the feet. **2** one of a body of infantry soldiers forming a guard.

foot|hill (fu̇t′hil′), *n.* a low hill at the base of a mountain or mountain range. See picture under **mountain**.

foot|hold (fu̇t′hōld′), *n.* **1** a place to put a foot; support for the feet; surface to stand on: *He climbed the steep cliff by getting footholds in cracks in the rock.* **2** *Figurative.* a firm footing or position: *It is hard to break a habit after it has a foothold.*

foot|ie (fu̇t′ē), *n. U.S. Slang.* footsie; a surreptitious flirtation.

***football**
definitions 2,3

football

Rugby

soccer

foot|ing (fu̇t′ing), *n.* **1** a firm placing or position of the feet: *He lost his footing and fell down on the ice.* **2** a place or support for the feet; surface to stand on; foothold: *The steep cliff gave us no footing.* **3** *Figurative.* a secure position; status: *The newly rich family struggled for a footing in society.* **4** *Figurative.* condition; position; relationship: *The United States and Canada are on a friendly footing.* SYN: standing. **5** the projecting base of a foundation, wall, monument, or the like, that distributes the load. The footing for the foundation of a house extends below ground which might be affected by frost. **6a** the process of adding up a column of figures. **b** the amount found by adding; sum; total. **7** the act of moving on the feet; walking, dancing, or the like. **8** the manner of placing or using the feet; footwork. **9** the act of sewing or knitting a foot on a stocking or sock. **10** material for making feet for boots, stockings, or other footgear. **11** a narrow width of net.

footing beam, the tie beam of a roof.

foot-in-mouth (fu̇t′in mouth′), *adj. Informal.* characteristic of a person who makes very tactless or embarrassing blunders: *a foot-in-mouth comment.*

foot-in-mouth disease, the habit or condition of saying tactless or embarrassing things: ... *film clips of well-known speakers in the throes of foot-in-mouth disease* (Time). [humorously patterned on *foot-and-mouth disease*]

foot jaw, one of the anterior limbs of crustaceans and other arthropods that are modified into accessory mouthparts; maxilliped.

foot-lam|bert (fu̇t′lam′bərt), *n.* a unit of luminance, equivalent to the luminance of a perfectly diffused surface that emits or reflects one lumen per square foot.

foo|tle (fu̇t′əl, fü′təl), *v.*, **-tled, -tling**, *n.*, *adj. Slang.* —*v.i.* to talk or act foolishly; trifle. —*n.* twaddle; nonsense. —*adj.* paltry; trifling. [perhaps < *footer,* variant of *fouter*] —**foo′tler**, *n.*

foot|less (fu̇t′lis), *adj.* **1** without a foot or feet. **2** *Figurative.* without support; not substantial: *footless fancies.* **3** *Informal, Figurative.* awkward; helpless; inefficient. —**foot′less|ly**, *adv.* —**foot′less|ness**, *n.*

foot|lights (fu̇t′līts′), *n.pl.* **1** a row of lights at the front of a stage, nearly on a level with the feet of the actors: *Footlights ... have receded to the status of old-fashioned encumbrances, since they often cast dismal shadows on the stage* (New Yorker). **2** *Figurative.* the profession of acting; stage; theater.

foot|line (fu̇t′līn′), *n.* **1** the bottom line of a page of type. **2** the lower line of a fishing net or seine.

foo|tling[1] (fu̇t′ling, füt′ling), *adj. Informal.* trifling; trivial; silly: *The things Mr. Morris observed ... prove to be quite astonishing and not nearly as footling as the cynical may expect* (Atlantic). [< *footle* + *-ing*[2]]

foot|ling[2] (fu̇t′ling), *adv., adj.* (in obstetrics) with the feet foremost. [< *foot* + *-ling*]

foot|lock|er (fu̇t′lok′ər), *n.* a small chest for personal belongings, usually kept at the foot of one's bed, as in a barracks: *With him he has only a footlocker full of khaki work clothes* (Wall Street Journal).

foot|loose (fu̇t′lüs′), *adj.* free to go anywhere or anything: *The real Roger Tichborne was a melancholy, footloose sort who left England and was unheard of for 13 years* (Wall Street Journal).

foot|man (fu̇t′mən), *n., pl.* **-men**. **1** a male servant who answers the bell, waits on the table, goes with a carriage or car to open the door, and has similar duties. Footmen usually wear a kind of uniform. **2** *Rare.* a foot soldier. **3** a stand to support a kettle or pot before a fire. **4** *Archaic.* a pedestrian. **5** *Obsolete.* a footpad. [< *foot* + *man*]

foot|mark (fu̇t′märk′), *n.* = footprint.

foot|note (fu̇t′nōt′), *n., v.,* **-not|ed, -not|ing.** —*n.* **1** a note at the bottom of a page about something on the page. **2** something appended as an explanation, reference, or comment: *The new Yalta papers also added a small, bright footnote to history* (Newsweek). **3** *Figurative.* something incidental or anticlimactic: ... *a man who wrote a courageous and imperishable page of history in his youth, then found that everything else he might ever do could be no more than a footnote* (Manchester Guardian Weekly). —*v.t.* **1** to furnish with a footnote or footnotes: *If he reads the most recent Catholic Scriptural studies, he will find them liberally footnoted with references to Protestant works* (Harper's). **2** to comment on in a footnote: *Just let it be footnoted that these crimes are controlled by social, psychotic, and economic factors* (Maclean's).

foot|pace (fu̇t′pās′), *n.* **1** the speed of ordinary walking; a walking pace. **2** a half landing, such as a step having a broader tread, on a staircase; halfpace.

foot|pad (fu̇t′pad′), *n.* **1** a highway robber who goes on foot only. **2** one of the cushioned or padded feet of a soft-landing spacecraft: *The footpads, about 37 inches in diameter, are made of 2 layers of spun aluminum bonded to an aluminum-honeycomb core* (Steven Moll).

foot page, a boy attendant or servant; footboy.

foot|path (fu̇t′path′, -päth′), *n., v.* —*n.* a path for people on foot only. —*v.t.* to make a footpath or footpaths across.

foot|plate (fůt′plāt′), *n.* **1** the step of a carriage. **2** a platform on certain early types of locomotives on which the engineer and fireman stood.
foot|plate|man (fůt′plāt′mən), *n., pl.* **-men.** *British.* a locomotive engineer or fireman.
foot post, **1** a postman or messenger who travels on foot. **2** postal delivery by means of mailmen on foot.
foot-pound (fůt′pound′), *n.* a unit of work or energy. It is equal to the quantity of energy needed to raise a weight of one pound avoirdupois to a height of one foot, or the work done by a force of one pound that moves an object one foot in the direction of the force applied. *Abbr:* ft.-lb.
foot-pound|al (fůt′poun′dəl), *n.* a unit of work or energy, equivalent to the work done by a force of one poundal acting through a distance of one foot. It is equal to a foot-pound divided by the acceleration due to gravity, or about 32.2 feet per second per second.
foot-pound-sec|ond system (fůt′pound′sek′ənd), a system of units in which the foot, pound, and second are considered as the basic units of length, mass, and time.
foot|print (fůt′print′), *n., v.* —*n.* **1a** a mark made by a foot. **SYN:** track, footmark, footstep. **b** *Figurative: Other aboriginal languages and groups have left shadows of their phonetic footprints* (John Hollander). **2** the track of a tire. **3** *Aerospace.* the predetermined landing area of a spacecraft: *A corkscrew course ... is the procedure needed to reach most sites within the "footprint," or region accessible to the astronauts* (Walter Sullivan).
—*v.t.* to mark with footprints.
foot pump, a portable pump, operated by hand, that has a bracket or stirrup for holding it in place by the pressure of the foot.
foot|race (fůt′rās′), *n.* a race on foot; running race.
foot|rac|er (fůt′rā′sər), *n.* a person who competes in a running contest.
foot|rail (fůt′rāl′), *n.* **1** a rail, especially a crosspiece connecting the legs of a table or seat, upon which the feet are rested; footrest. **2** a crosspiece on or near the floor, as in some chairs and tables.
foot|rest (fůt′rest′), *n.* a support on which to rest the feet.
foot|rope (fůt′rōp′), *n. Nautical.* **1** the part of the boltrope sewed along the lower edge of a sail. **2** a rope suspended under a yard or bowsprit, on which sailors stand while working on the sails.
foot rot, an inflammatory disease of the foot in cattle and sheep, caused by the presence of bacteria.
foot rule, a wooden, metal, or plastic ruler one foot long.
foot-run|ner (fůt′run′ər), *n.* a man in parts of Africa and Asia appointed to deliver messages and news by running on foot from village to village.
foots (fůts), *n.pl.* See under **foot**.
foot-sec|ond (fůt′sek′ənd), *n.* **1** *Physics.* a unit of velocity equal to one linear foot per second, used in stating the velocity of a projectile. **2** a unit for measuring the flow of liquids, equal to a flow of one cubic foot per second. *Abbr:* f.s.
foot|sie (fůt′sē), *n. U.S. Slang.* a surreptitious flirtation.
play footsie with, to carry on or start a flirtation with; ally or cooperate with in a covert manner: *The movies played footsie with television for years before finally embracing it.*
foot|slog (fůt′slog′), *v.i.,* **-slogged, -slog|ging.** to go on foot; tramp; march.
foot|slog|ger (fůt′slog′ər), *n.* a person who footslogs, especially a foot soldier.
foot soldier, a soldier who fights on foot; infantryman.
foot|sore (fůt′sôr′, -sōr′), *adj.* having sore feet, especially from much walking: *The hike left us footsore and hungry.* **SYN:** footworn.
foot|stalk (fůt′stôk′), *n.* **1** *Botany.* the stem of a leaf, flower, or flower cluster. **2** *Zoology.* a stemlike supporting or attaching part of an animal; peduncle.
foot|stall (fůt′stôl′), *n.* **1** the stirrup of a woman's saddle. **2** *Architecture, Rare.* the base or pedestal of a pillar, or statue.
foot|step (fůt′step′), *n.* **1** a person's step; tread: *The hikers made deep footsteps in the mud.* **2** the distance covered in one step: *Grown-ups sometimes forget that their footstep is about twice as long as a little child's.* **3** the sound of steps coming or going; footfall: *We thought we heard some footsteps in the hall.* **4** the mark made by a foot; footprint: *It was easy to follow the hunter's footsteps in the snow.* **5** a step on which to go up or down: *the footsteps of a throne* (Wordsworth).
follow in someone's footsteps, to do as somebody else has done: *Johnson proposed to follow in Lincoln's footsteps, but for a cautious experiment he substituted a dogmatic theory* (George S. Merriam).
foot|stone (fůt′stōn′), *n.* a stone placed at the foot of a grave.
foot|stool (fůt′stül′), *n.* a low stool on which to place the feet when seated.
foot stove, a perforated tin box with a wooden frame, containing a pan with live coals in a bed of ashes, formerly used in cold weather as a foot warmer.
foot-ton (fůt′tun′), *n.* a unit of work or energy equivalent to the energy that can raise a long ton (2,240 pounds) against gravity to a height of one foot.
foot|wall (fůt′wôl′), *n.* **1** *Mining.* the wall or side of rock that is under a vein or lode. **2** *Geology.* the mass of rock under a fault plane.
foot warmer, any device, such as a foot stove, for keeping the feet warm.
foot washing, the washing of another's feet as a religious observance, especially in some Christian churches in commemoration of Christ's washing of the feet of his disciples after the Last Supper (John 13:4-17).
foot|way (fůt′wā′), *n.* a path for people on foot only; sidewalk.
foot|wear (fůt′wãr′), *n.* shoes, slippers, stockings, gaiters, or footgear.
foot|well (fůt′wel′), *n.* the space for the feet of the driver and passengers in the front seat of a motor vehicle.
foot|work (fůt′wėrk′), *n.* the way of using the feet: *Footwork is important in boxing and dancing.*
foot|worn (fůt′wôrn′, -wōrn′), *adj.* **1** worn by the feet: *a footworn path.* **2** having tired feet; footsore.
foo|ty (fůt′ē, fü′tē), *adj.,* **-ti|er, -ti|est,** *n., pl.* **-ties.** *Informal.* —*adj.* poor; worthless; trashy.
—*n.* a worthless person or thing. [variant of obsolete *foughty* musty < Old English *fūht* damp]
foo|zle (fü′zəl), *v.,* **-zled, -zling,** *n.* —*v.t.* to do clumsily; bungle (especially a stroke in golf).
—*v.i.* to act or play clumsily.
—*n.* **1** a clumsy failure, especially a badly played stroke in golf. **2** *Informal.* a dull, old-fashioned person; fogy. **3** *Informal.* a man who is easily fooled.
[origin uncertain. Compare dialectal German *fuseln* work badly or slowly.]
fop (fop), *n., v.,* **fopped, fop|ping.** —*n.* **1** a vain man who is very fond of fine clothes and has affected manners; dandy: *We used to sit ... and watch the fops and dandies of the campus go strolling and strutting by* (New Yorker). **SYN:** macaroni. **2** *Obsolete.* a conceited person. **3** *Obsolete.* a fool.
—*v.t.* to make a fool of; cheat; dupe.
[origin uncertain]
fop|ling (fop′ling), *n.* a petty fop.
fop|per|y (fop′ər ē), *n., pl.* **-per|ies.** **1** the behavior or dress of a fop. **2** *Obsolete.* folly.
fop|pish (fop′ish), *adj.* **1** of a fop; suitable for a fop: *foppish dress.* **2** vain; affected: *foppish manners.* **SYN:** empty-headed. **3** *Obsolete.* foolish; silly: *Wise men are grown foppish* (Shakespeare).
—**fop′pish|ly,** *adv.* —**fop′pish|ness,** *n.*
for (fôr; *unstressed* fər), *prep., conj.* —*prep.* **1** in place of; instead of: *We used boxes for chairs. He gave me a new book for the old one.* **2** in support of; in favor of: *He stands for honest government. I am for giving everyone an equal opportunity.* **3** representing; in the interest of: *A lawyer acts for his client.* **4** in return for; in consideration of: *These apples are eight for a dollar. We thanked him for his kindness.* **5** with the object or purpose of: *He went for a walk.* **6a** in order to obtain: *a suit for damages. She looks for happiness.* **b** in order to become: *The navy trains men for sailors.* **c** in order to keep or save: *He ran for his life.* **7** in search of: *She is hunting for her cat.* **8** in order to get to: *He has just left for New York.* **9a** meant to belong to or be used with: *a box for gloves, a present for you, money for traveling.* **b** suited to; adapted to: *books for children.* **10** because of; by reason of: *to shout for joy. He was punished for stealing. This coat is the worse for wear.* **11** in honor of: *A party was given for her.* **12** with a feeling toward: *love for friends. She has an eye for beauty. We longed for home.* **13** with regard or respect to: *It is warm for April.* **14** as affecting (a person or thing): *Eating too much is bad for one's health. It is all for her good.* **15** as far as: *We walked for a mile.* **16** as long as; throughout; during: *He worked for an hour.* **17** as being: *They know it for a fact.* **18** in spite of: *For all his faults, we like him still.* **19** in proportion to; considering: *For one poisonous snake there are many harmless ones.* **20a** to the amount of: *His father gave him a check for $20.* **b** showing equality or proportion between objects: *word for word, one sunny day for six rainy ones. The prisoners were exchanged man for man.*
—*conj.* **1** because: *We can't go, for it is raining.* **2** seeing that; since.
be for it, *British Informal.* to be in trouble: *No one can sit on the same side of the room as Madame, and you're for it if she sees you leaning on the piano* (Sunday Times).
for (one) to, that one will, should, or must: *A secretary writes letters for her employer to sign. It is time for us to go.*
Oh, for, I wish that I might have: *Oh, for a swim! Oh, for a lodge in some vast wilderness* (William Cowper).
[Old English *for*]
▶ **for**. A comma is usually needed between two coordinate clauses joined by *for;* without it the *for* might be read as a preposition: *He was glad to go, for Mr. Crane had been especially good to him.* (Not: *He was glad to go for Mr. Crane. ...*)
▶ See **because** and **like** for other usage notes.
for-, *prefix.* away; opposite; completely (often in a wrong or negative sense), as in *forbid, forswear.* [Old English *for-* forth, away]
for., **1** foreign. **2a** forest. **b** forestry.
f.o.r. or **F.O.R.**, free on rail.
fo|ra (fôr′ə, fōr′ə), *n.* a plural of **forum**.
for|age (fôr′ij, for′-), *n., v.,* **-aged, -ag|ing.**
—*n.* **1** hay, grain, or other food for horses, cattle, or other domestic animals; fodder: *Forage for the cattle is in the hayloft.* **SYN:** provender. **2** a hunting or searching for food or provisions.
—*v.i.* **1** to hunt or search for food: *Rabbits forage in our garden.* **2** to search about; hunt; rummage: *The boys foraged for old metal.* **3** to make a raid.
—*v.t.* **1** to supply with food; feed. **2** to get by hunting or searching about; root out. **3** to get or take food from. **4** to plunder; ravage: *The soldiers foraged nearby villages.*
[< Old French *fourage* < *fuerre* fodder < unrecorded Frankish *fōdr* food] —**for′ag|er,** *n.*
***forage cap**, a small undress cap worn by soldiers.

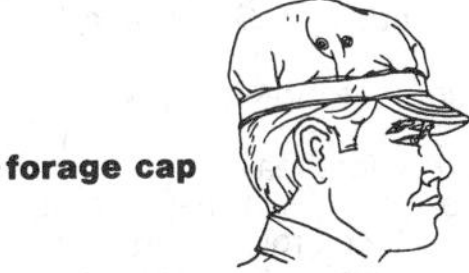
***forage cap**

for|ag|ing ant (fôr′ə jing, for′-), any species of ant that goes hunting for food in vast numbers, especially the driver ant or army ant.
for|a|lite (fôr′ə līt, for′-), *n. Geology.* a tubelike marking in sandstone and other strata, which resembles the burrow of a worm. [< Latin *forāre* bore a hole + English *-lite*]
fo|ram (fôr′əm, for′-), *n., pl.* **-rams** or **-ram.** one of the foraminifera; a foraminifer: *Some thirty thousand species of foram are known to exist* (New Yorker).
fo|ra|men (fə rā′mən), *n., pl.* **fo|ram|i|na** or **fo|ra|mens.** an opening, orifice, or short passage, such as one in a bone or in the covering of the ovule of a plant. [< Latin *forāmen, -inis* (originally) aperture < *forāre* bore a hole]
foramen mag|num (mag′nəm), *Anatomy.* the opening in the skull for the passage of the spinal cord to the cranial cavity.
foramen o|va|le (ō vā′lē), *Anatomy.* **1** an opening between the right and left auricle of the heart, found in the fetus but usually closed soon after birth. **2** an opening in the greater wing of the sphenoid bone for the passage of one of the divisions of the fifth cranial nerve.
fo|ram|i|na (fə ram′ə nə), *n.* a plural of **foramen**.
fo|ram|i|nate (fə ram′ə nit, -nāt), *adj.* furnished with foramina; perforated.
fo|ram|i|nat|ed (fə ram′ə nā′tid), *adj.* = foraminate.
for|a|min|i|fer (fôr′ə min′ə fər, for′-), *n.* one of the foraminifera.
fo|ram|i|nif|er|a (fə ram′ə nif′ər ə), *n.pl.* an order of usually marine protozoans that have calcareous or chitinous shells with tiny holes in them: *The foraminifera ... construct a perforated shell, usually of calcium carbonate, through which slender pseudopodia project* (Hegner and Stiles). [< New Latin *Foraminifera* the order name < Latin *forāmen* (see etym. under **foramen**) + *ferre* to bear]
fo|ram|i|nif|er|al (fə ram′ə nif′ər əl), *adj.* **1** consisting of or containing foraminifera. **2** having to

---

Pronunciation Key: hat, āge, cãre, fär; let, ēqual, tėrm, it, īce; hot, ōpen, ôrder; oil, out; cup, pů̇t, rüle; child; long; thin; ᴛʜen; zh, measure; ə represents a in about, e in taken, i in pencil, o in lemon, u in circus.

do with the foraminifera.

fo|ram|i|nif|er|an (fə ram′ə nif′ər ən), *adj.* = foraminiferal.

fo|ram|i|nif|er|ous (fə ram′ə nif′ər əs), *adj.* **1** having perforations or pores (foramina). **2** = foraminiferal.

fo|ram|i|nous (fə ram′ə nəs), *adj.* full of holes or foramina.

fo|ram|i|nule (fə ram′ə nyül), *n.* a very small foramen. [< New Latin *foraminule* (diminutive) < Latin *forāmen;* see etym. under **foramen**]

for|a|min|u|lous (fôr′ə min′yə ləs, for′-), *adj.* pierced with fine holes or pores.

for|as|much as (fôr′əz much′ az), in view of the fact that; because; since.

for|ay (fôr′ā, for′-), *n., v.* **—*n.*** **1** a raid for plunder: *Armed bandits made forays on the villages and took away cattle.* **2** any incursion into another's domain: *The Court could therefore withstand the attacks of those critics who charged that its opinion was an unprecedented foray into the sociological rather than the legal* (Atlantic).
—*v.i.* to make a raid.
—*v.t.* to lay waste; plunder; pillage.
[perhaps back formation < Middle English *forreyour* forager < Old French *forrier* to forage < *fuerre* food] **—for′ay|er,** *n.*

forb (fôrb), *n.* any herb, excluding grasses and plants resembling grasses. [probably < Greek *phorbê* pasture, food]

for|bade or **for|bad** (fər bad′), *v.* the past tenses of **forbid**: *The doctor forbade the sick boy to leave his bed.*

for|bear¹ (fôr bãr′), *v.,* **-bore, -borne, -bear|ing.**
—*v.i.* **1** to hold back; keep from doing, saying, or using: *The boy forbore to hit back because the other boy was smaller. I forbore telling her the truth because I knew it would upset her.* **2** to be patient; control oneself: *The kindest and the happiest pair will find occasion to forbear* (William Cowper).
—*v.t.* **1** to abstain or refrain from: *I had much ado to forbear laughing* (Ben Jonson). **2** to refrain from doing, saying, or using; withhold; keep back. **3** *Obsolete.* to endure. **4** *Obsolete.* **a** to lose. **b** to avoid; shun.
[Old English *forberan*] **—for|bear′er,** *n.* **—for|bear′ing|ly,** *adv.*

for|bear² (fôr′bãr), *n.* = forebear.

for|bear|ance (fôr bãr′əns), *n.* **1** the act of forbearing. **2** patience; self-control. **SYN:** See syn. under **patience**. **3** a refraining from enforcing the payment of a debt after it is due.

forbes|ite (fôrb′zīt), *n.* a mineral, a hydrated arsenate of nickel and cobalt, occurring in grayish-white crystalline masses. [< David *Forbes,* 1828-1876, a British mineralogist + *-ite*¹]

Forbes log (fôrbz), a type of patent log consisting of a small rotator in a tube that projects through the ship's bottom. [< Robert B. *Forbes,* 1804-1889, an American shipowner and inventor of nautical equipment]

for|bid (fər bid′), *v.,* **-bade** or **-bad, -bid|den** or **-bid, -bid|ding.** **—*v.t.*** **1** to not allow; say one must not do something; make a rule against; prohibit; ban: *The teacher forbade us to leave our seats. If my father had known that I was going, he would have forbidden it.* **2** to keep from happening; prevent: *God forbid it!* **3** to command to keep away from; exclude from: *I forbid you the house.*
—*v.i.* to utter a prohibition: *Forbid who will, none shall from me withhold Longer thy offer'd good* (Milton). [Old English *forbēodan*] **—for|bid′der,** *n.*
—*Syn.* *v.t.* **1 Forbid, prohibit** mean to not allow to do something. **Forbid** implies an order or rule that is often direct or personal and suggests that obedience is expected: *His father forbade him to smoke.* **Prohibit** implies a formal regulation against something, usually by law or official action, and suggests power to enforce it: *Picking flowers in this park is prohibited.*

for|bid|dance (fər bid′əns), *n.* **1** the act of forbidding. **2** a prohibition; interdiction.

for|bid|den (fər bid′ən), *adj., v.* **—*adj.*** not allowed; against the law or the rules; prohibited: *Eve ate the forbidden fruit. Forbidden crossings of the border continued.*
—*v.* a past participle of **forbid:** *My father has forbidden me to go swimming in that river.*

forbidden fruit, 1 the fruit of the tree of the knowledge of good and evil that Adam and Eve ate (in the Bible, Genesis 2:17 and Genesis 3). **2** *Figurative.* unlawful pleasure, especially illicit love.

forbidden lines, *Physics.* spectral lines of radiation produced by changes in energy level that occur within an atom only when the interval between atomic collisions is exceptionally long: *They are the so-called forbidden lines—colors which an atom is extremely reluctant to radiate and will not radiate at all unless left undisturbed by collisions for seconds or minutes at a time* (Armin J. Deutsch).

for|bid|ding (fər bid′ing), *adj.* causing fear or dislike; looking dangerous or unpleasant; grim: *The coast was rocky and forbidding. . . . an elderly man of remarkably hard features and forbidding aspect* (Dickens). **SYN:** disagreeable, repulsive, repellent. **—for|bid′ding|ly,** *adv.* **—for|bid′ding|ness,** *n.*

for|bore (fôr bôr′, -bōr′), *v.* the past tense of **forbear**¹: *He forbore from showing his anger.*

for|borne (fôr bôrn′, -bōrn′), *v.* the past participle of **forbear**¹: *We have forborne from vengeance.*

for|by or **for|bye** (fôr bī′), *prep., adv. Archaic.*
—*prep.* **1** besides. **2** close by; near.
—*adv.* **1** besides; in addition. **2** aside.

force¹ (fôrs, fōrs), *n., v.,* **forced, forc|ing.**
—*n.* **1** active power; strength: *The speeding car struck the tree with great force. He chews gum through force of habit. A policeman should have great force of character.* **SYN:** might, vigor, energy. See syn. under **power**. **2** strength used against a person or thing; violence: *The robber had to use force to get into the house. Who overcomes By force hath overcome but half his foe* (Milton). **SYN:** coercion, compulsion, constraint. **3** the power to control, influence, persuade, or convince; effectiveness; vividness: *He writes with force. Let not her cries or tears have force to move you* (Joseph Addison). **SYN:** power. **4** power or might, especially military power or the power of a ruler or realm: *an army superior in fighting force.* **5** a group of people who work or act together: *our office force. The whole legal force of the company set to work on the case.* **6** a group of soldiers, sailors, policemen, wardens, or others: *The force moved in for a showdown, each marshal looking for bandits.* **7a** any cause that produces, changes, or stops the motion of a body: *the force of gravitation, electric force, magnetic force.* **b** the intensity of such an influence as a measurable quantity. **8** the meaning or significance (of a word, sentence, paragraph, or entire literary piece). **9** binding power; validity, as of a law or contract: *The force of some laws has to be tested in court.* **10** *Figurative.* an agency, influence, or source of power likened to a physical force: *social forces.* **11** (in card games) an act of forcing.
—*v.t.* **1** to make (a person) act against his will; make do by force: *Give it to me at once, or I will force you to. Art thou King, and wilt be forced?* (Shakespeare). **2** to get or take by force; make or drive by force: *He forced his way in.* **3** to impose or impress by force: *to force one's views on another.* **4** to break open by force; break through: *to force a lock, to force a door.* **5** to urge to violent effort. **6** to make by an unusual or unnatural effort; strain: *The unhappy child forced a smile.* **7** to hurry the growth or development of by artificial means: *to force hothouse vegetables.* **8** *Baseball.* **a** to cause (a runner) to be put out by requiring him to try to advance to the next base. **b** (of a pitcher) to cause (a run or a runner) to score by giving a base on balls or by hitting the batter with a pitch when the bases are full: *to force in a run.* **9** in card games: **a** to compel (a player) to trump or to play so as to indicate the strength of his hand. **b** to compel a player to play (a certain card). **c** (of a bid) to require (the bidder's partner) to bid in response. **10** to use violence on (a woman); violate; ravish. **11** *Obsolete.* **a** to enforce (a law or decree). **b** to strengthen; reinforce. **c** to attach importance to; care for; regard.
—*v.i.* to use force; make one's way by force.
by force of, by dint of; by virtue of; by means of: *It is not by the force of long attention and inquiry that we find any object to be beautiful* (Edmund Burke).
by main force, by using full strength: *The invaders conquered the country by main force.*
force one's hand. See under **hand**.
forces, the army, navy, or air force; armed forces; soldiers; troops: *The enemy forces tried to take the city but our forces drove them back.*
in force, a in use; in effect or operation; binding; valid: *The old rules are still in force.* **b** in large numbers; with full strength; strongly: *The enemy attacked us in force.* **c** in large numbers: *The television boys were out in force the other day, trying to entice him [a celebrity] into the studios* (Manchester Guardian Weekly).
[< Old French *force,* ultimately < Latin *fortis* strong]

force² (fôrs, fōrs), *n. Northern England.* a waterfall. [< Scandinavian (compare Old Icelandic *fors*)]

force bill, *U.S.* any of several bills or acts of Congress which authorized the use of military power to enforce federal law. The first force bill, in 1833, enforced the collection of customs under the tariff bills of 1828 and 1832. Three force bills were passed during Reconstruction to enforce the Fourteenth and Fifteenth Constitutional amendments.

forced (fôrst, fōrst), *adj.* **1** made or driven by force: *The work of slaves is forced labor. The damaged plane had to make a forced landing.* **SYN:** enforced, compulsory. **2** done by unusual effort: *The soldiers made a forced march of three days.* **3** *Figurative.* not natural; strained; not spontaneous: *She hid her dislike with a forced smile.* **SYN:** affected. **—forc′ed|ly,** *adv.*

forced draft, a draft produced by forcing air through a burner in order to accelerate combustion: *In the immense modern forced-draft furnaces, relatively cheap and low-grade coal can be burned efficiently* (Atlantic).

force de dis|sua|sion (fôrs də dē swȧ zyôɴ′), *French.* **1** = force de frappe. **2** (literally) force of dissuasion.

force de frappe (fôrs də fräp′), *French.* **1** an atomic stockpile for use as a deterrent against enemy attack: *. . . the embryonic beginning of a European force de frappe* (New York Times). **2** (literally) striking force.

forced march, an unusually long, fast march.

force feed, a system that forces a lubricant into bearings in an engine.

force-feed (fôrs′fēd′, fōrs′-), *v.t.,* **-fed, -feed|ing.** to feed by force: *If a patient will not eat, he may be force-fed* (Atlantic).

force field, *Physics.* the space throughout which a force operates; field of force.

force|ful (fôrs′fəl, fōrs′-), *adj.* having much force; powerful, vigorous, or effective; strong: *a forceful manner. We persist in hoping that there is some forceful, simple, final way of winning or giving to others the freedom of which Mrs. Stowe wrote* (New Statesman). **—force′ful|ly,** *adv.* **—force′ful|ness,** *n.*

force-land (fôrs′land′, fōrs′-), *v.i.* to make a forced landing: *Two men . . . spent nine days wandering through the Kalahari desert in Botswana after their aircraft force-landed* (Sunday Times).

force|less (fôrs′lis, fōrs′-), *adj.* without force; impotent; feeble.

force ma|jeure (fôrs mȧ zhœr′), *pl.* **forces majeures** (fôrs mȧ zhœr′). *French.* **1** a superior or overpowering force. **2** *Law.* an irresistible force; act of God that permits a party to refuse to perform a contract.

force|meat (fôrs′mēt′, fōrs′-), *n.* finely chopped and seasoned meat or fish, used chiefly for stuffing or as a garnish; farcemeat. [< *force,* variant of *farce,* in obsolete sense "to stuff" + *meat*]

force-out (fôrs′out′), *n. Baseball.* a putout resulting from a force play.

force play, a play in which a base runner is forced to leave his base to the runner behind him and is put out by the fielder with the ball stepping on the next base before the base runner can reach it.

***for|ceps** (fôr′seps, -səps), *n., pl.* **-ceps.** small pincers or tongs used especially by surgeons, dentists, etc., for seizing and holding. Dentists use forceps for pulling teeth. [< Latin *forceps* tongs < *formus* hot + *capere* take]

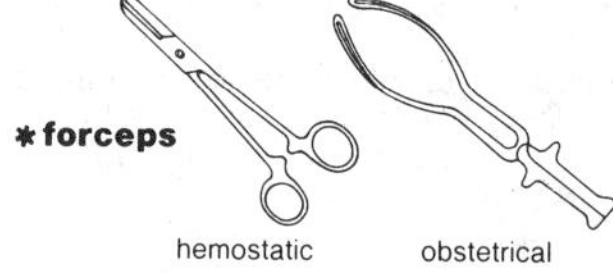

***forceps**

force pump, any pump that delivers liquid under pressure, especially a pump with a valveless piston whose action forces liquid through a pipe.

forc|er (fôr′sər, fōr′-), *n.* a person or thing that forces.

forc|es (fôr′siz, fōr′-), *n.pl.* See under **force**.

for|ci|ble (fôr′sə bəl, fōr′-), *adj.* **1** made or done by force; using force: *a forcible entrance into a house.* **2** *Figurative.* having or showing force; strong; powerful or effective; convincing: *a forcible speaker.* **—for′ci|ble|ness,** *n.*

forcible detainer, (in law) a violent withholding from a person of his lands or goods.

for|ci|bly (fôr′sə blē, fōr′-), *adv.* in a forcible manner: *What struck me first and forcibly after an absence of six years was the relaxed elegance of Dublin* (New Statesman).

forc|ing house (fôr′sing, fōr′-), **1** a hothouse or greenhouse to force the growth of plants and flowers. **2** any place favorable for rapid growth. **3** a school with a narrow or restricted curriculum.

forcing pump, = force pump.

for|ci|pate (fôr′sə pāt), *adj. Botany, Zoology.* formed like a forceps; deeply forked; furcate: *forcipate claws.* [< Latin *forceps, -ipis* forceps + English *-ate*¹]

for|cip|i|form (fôr sip′ə fôrm), *adj. Zoology.* having the form of a forceps.

for|cip|u|late (fôr sip′yə lit), *adj.* shaped like a small forceps, as the pedicellariae of echinoderms. [< New Latin *forcipulatus* (ultimately diminutive) < Latin *forceps, -ipis* forceps]

for|cite (fôr′sīt, fōr′-) *n.* a powerful explosive containing nitroglycerin, soluble gun-cotton, and potassium nitrate. [< *force*[1] + *-ite*[1]]

ford (fôrd, fōrd), *n., v.* —*n.* a place where a river, stream, or other body of water is not too deep to cross by walking or driving through the water.
—*v.t.* to cross (a river) by walking or driving through the water: *The streams rose so rapidly that we could hardly ford them* (Francis Parkman). [Old English *ford*] —**ford′a|ble**, *adj.*
—**ford′less**, *adj.*

for|do (fôr dü′), *v.t.,* **-did, -done, -do|ing.** *Archaic.* **1** to destroy; ruin: *This is the night That either makes me or fordoes me quite* (Shakespeare). **2** to kill. Also, **foredo.** [Old English *fordōn* < *for-* for- + *dōn* do]

for|done (fôr dun′), *adj., v. Archaic.* —*adj.* worn out; exhausted.
—*v.* the past participle of **fordo:** *With Indian heats at last fordone* (Matthew Arnold). Also, **foredone.**

fore[1] (fôr, fōr), *adj., adv., n., prep.* —*adj.* **1** at the front; toward the beginning or front; forward: *The fore wall of a house faces the street.* **2** *Archaic.* earlier.
—*adv.* **1** at or toward the bow or front: *Several of the crew went fore.* **2** *Obsolete.* formerly; previously.
—*n.* **1** the forward part; front. **2** *Nautical.* **a** the bow of a ship. **b** the foremast.
—*prep. Dialect.* (in oaths) before: *'Fore George, I'm vastly puzzled what to do* (Richard Harris Barham).
to the fore, a to the front; into full view; into a conspicuous place or position: *The question of new taxes will come to the fore at the next session of Congress.* **b** at hand; ready; available: *If he hasn't me to the fore to prove what I said, he can do nothing* (Charles J. Lever). **c** alive: *The steward . . . though stricken in years—was still to the fore* (James Payn).
[adjective use of *fore-*, Old English, (originally) adverb]

fore[2] (fôr, fōr), *interj. Golf.* a shout of warning to persons ahead on the fairway who are liable to be struck by the ball. [perhaps short for *before*]

Fore (fôr, fōr), *n., pl.* **Fore.** a member of a tribe living in the highlands of eastern New Guinea, characterized by a Stone Age culture in which cannibalism was formerly practiced.

fore-, *prefix.* **1** front; in front; at or near the front: *Forepaw = a front paw. Foremast = mast near the front of a ship.*
2 before; beforehand: *Foregoing = going before. Forearm = to arm beforehand.*
[Old English *fore-*, unstressed form of adverb *fore*]

fore-and-aft (fôr′ən aft′, -äft′; fōr′-), *adj.* lengthwise on a ship; from bow to stern; placed lengthwise.

fore and aft, 1 at or toward both bow and stern of a ship. **2** lengthwise on a ship; from bow to stern.

fore-and-af|ter (fôr′ən af′tər, -äf′-; fōr′-), *n.* any ship or boat having fore-and-aft sails, such as a schooner.

fore-and-aft rig, the arrangement of one or more fore-and-aft sails with any number of masts.

fore-and-aft-rigged (fôr′ən aft′rigd′, -äft′-; fōr′-), *adj.* having fore-and-aft sails. A fore-and-aft-rigged ship has the sails set lengthwise.

fore-and-aft sail, a sail extending from the center line to the lee side of a ship or boat, generally set on a stay or gaff.

fore|arm[1] (fôr′ärm′, fōr′-), *n.* that part of the arm between the elbow and the wrist.

fore|arm[2] (fôr ärm′, fōr-), *v.t.* to prepare for trouble ahead of time; arm beforehand.

fore|bay (fôr′bā′, fōr′-), *n.* the part of a millrace where the water flows on the wheel.

fore|bear (fôr′bãr, fōr′-), *n.* an ancestor; forefather: *Other things to be seen in Northants include Sulgrave Manor, ancestral home of the Washingtons and of George Washington's forebears* (Punch). Also, **forbear.**

fore|bode (fôr bōd′, fōr-), *v.,* **-bod|ed, -bod|ing.**
—*v.t.* **1** to give warning of; predict: *Black clouds forebode a storm.* SYN: foretell, portend. **2** to have a feeling that (something bad is going to happen); anticipate: *My heart forebodes Danger or death awaits thee on this field* (Matthew Arnold).
—*v.i.* **1** to forecast; prophesy: *If the Gypsy foreboded truly, they would inherit a fortune the next year.* SYN: conjecture. **2** to have a feeling that something bad is going to happen: *The house itself seemed to be foreboding.* —**fore|bode′ment**, *n.* —**fore|bod′er**, *n.*

fore|bod|ing (fôr bō′ding, fōr-), *n., adj.* —*n.* **1** a prediction; warning: *She disregarded the Gypsy's foreboding that she would regret marrying.* SYN: omen, portent. **2** a feeling that something bad is going to happen: *The sailor's wife had a foreboding that he would not return.* SYN: presentiment.
—*adj.* that forebodes; ominous; portentous: *foreboding signs.* —**fore|bod′ing|ly**, *adv.*

fore|bod|y (fôr′bod′ē, fōr′-), *n., pl.* **-bod|ies.** the part of a ship which lies forward of the midship section.

fore|brace (fôr′brās′, fōr′-), *n. Nautical.* a brace or rope attached to a foreyard.

fore|brain (fôr′brān′, fōr′-), *n.* the front part of the brain, composed of the telencephalon and the diencephalon; prosencephalon. It includes the cerebrum, thalamus, and hypothalamus.

fore|cad|die (fôr′kad′ē, fōr′-), *n.* a caddie who goes ahead of the players to locate the balls on the course.

fore|cast (fôr′kast′, -käst′; fōr′-), *v.,* **-cast** or **-cast|ed, -cast|ing,** *n.* —*v.t.* **1** to tell what is coming; predict on the basis of observations, study, or experience; prophesy: *Cooler weather is forecast for tomorrow.* **2** to be a prophecy or prediction of; foreshadow: *Clouds do not necessarily forecast rain.* **3** to plan or decide ahead; foresee: *How could I have forecast such a dilemma?* SYN: prearrange. —*v.i.* to plan ahead; make a forecast: *The weatherman forecasts on the basis of atmospheric conditions.*
—*n.* **1** a statement of what is coming; prophecy; prediction: *stock-market forecasts. What is the forecast about the weather for today?* **2** the act or process of planning ahead; foresight: *evils which no forecast could avert* (William Hickling Prescott). **3** the act or fact of foreshadowing: *Summer styles are often a forecast of winter fashion.*

fore|cast|a|ble (fôr′kas′tə bəl, -käs′-; fōr′-), *adj.* that can be forecast; predictable.

fore|cast|er (fôr′kas′tər, -käs′-; fōr′-), *n.* a person who forecasts, especially one who predicts what the weather will be.

fore|cast|ing (fôr′kas′ting, -käs′-; fōr′-), *n.* the act or process of predicting, on the basis of present trends, of probable conditions or events to come, as forthcoming weather or business activity: *Daily forecasting is a matter of charting current atmospheric conditions . . . to be able to foresee the state of the weather for a short period in the future* (Thomas A. Blair).

***fore|cas|tle** (fōk′səl; fôr′kas′əl, -käs′-; fōr′-), *n.* **1** the upper deck in front of the foremast. **2** the quarters for sailors in a merchant ship, formerly in the forward part of the ship.

forecastle

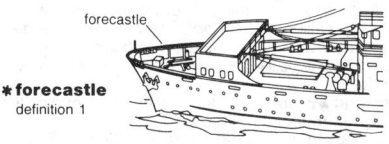

***forecastle**
definition 1

forecastle deck or **head**, the small, raised deck behind the bow of ships of former times.

fore|cas|tle|man (fōk′səl mən; fôr′kas′əl-, -käs′-; fōr′-), *n., pl.* **-men.** a sailor stationed on the forecastle.

fore|check (fôr′chek′, fōr′-), *v.i.* to check an opposing ice-hockey player in his own defensive zone. —**fore′check′er**, *n.*

fore|cit|ed (fôr′sī′tid, fōr′-), *adj.* previously cited.

fore|clos|a|ble (fôr klō′zə bəl, fōr-), *adj.* that can be foreclosed.

fore|close (fôr klōz′, fōr-), *v.,* **-closed, -clos|ing.**
—*v.t.* **1** to shut out; prevent; exclude: *to foreclose objections. The club voted to foreclose further discussion of the subject.* SYN: bar. **2a** to take away the right to redeem (a mortgage). **b** to take away the right of (a mortgager) to redeem his property. —*v.i.* to take away the right to redeem a mortgage: *When the conditions of the mortgage were not met, the holder of the mortgage foreclosed and took possession of the house.* [< Old French *forclos,* past participle of *forclore* exclude < *for-* out (< Latin *forīs* out; influenced by Germanic *fora-* before) + *clore* shut < Latin *claudere*]

fore|clo|sure (fôr klō′zhər, fōr-), *n.* the act of foreclosing a mortgage; taking away the right of a mortgager to redeem his property.

fore|con|scious (fôr′kon′shəs, fōr′-), *adj., n.* = preconscious.

fore|course (fôr′kôrs′, fōr′kōrs′), *n. Nautical.* the square sail attached to the lowest yard of the forward mast of a square-rigged vessel; foresail.

fore|court (fôr′kôrt′, fōr′kōrt′), *n.* **1** a front or outer court. **2a** the part of a tennis court near the net. **b** the part of a basketball court near the offensive basket.

fore|date (fôr′dāt′, fōr′-), *v.t.,* **-dat|ed, -dat|ing.** = antedate.

fore|deck (fôr′dek′, fōr′-), *n. Nautical.* the part of the main deck nearest the bow.

fore|des|tine (fôr des′tən, fōr-), *v.t.,* **-tined, -tin|ing.** = predestine.

fore|do (fôr dü′, fōr-), *v.t.,* **-did, -done, -do|ing.** *Archaic.* fordo.

fore|done (fôr dun′, fōr-), *adj., v. Archaic.* fordone; exhausted.

fore|doom (fôr düm′, fōr-), *v., n.* —*v.t.* to doom beforehand: *Fate foredoomed him to be an invalid most of his life.* —*n.* = destiny.

fore|dune (fôr′dün′, fōr′-; -dyün′), *n.* the part of a dune closest to the sea: *. . . the precipitous edge of a foredune* (Harper's).

fore edge, the front or outer edge of a leaf in a book or of the book itself.

fore-end (fôr′end′, fōr′-), *n.* **1** the fore part of the stock of a gun, which supports the barrel. **2** *Nautical.* the fore part; front: *the fore-end of the poop.* **3** *Dialect.* **a** the beginning or early part, as of a month or year. **b** the season of spring.

fore|fa|ther (fôr′fä′ᴛʜər, fōr′-), *n.* an ancestor: *Think of your forefathers! Think of your posterity* (John Quincy Adams). SYN: forebear, progenitor.

fore|fa|ther's-cup (fôr′fä′ᴛʜərz kup′, fōr′-), *n.* = pitcher plant.

Forefathers' Day, December 21, the anniversary of the landing of the Pilgrims at Plymouth, Massachusetts in 1620.

fore|feel (fôr fēl′, fōr-), *v.,* **-felt, -feel|ing,** *n.*
—*v.t.* to feel beforehand; have a foreboding of.
—*n.* a feeling beforehand.

fore|feel|ing (fôr fē′ling, fōr-), *n.* a feeling beforehand; foreboding: *a strong forefeeling that much of my destined life . . . was yet to come* (Alexander W. Kinglake).

fore|fend (fôr fend′, fōr-), *v.t.* = forfend.

fore|fin|ger (fôr′fing′gər, fōr′-), *n.* the finger next to the thumb; first finger; index finger.

fore|flank (fôr′flangk′, fōr′-), *n.* **1** the front part of the flank. **2** *British Dialect.* a projection of fat upon the ribs near the shoulder of sheep.

fore|foot (fôr′fu̇t′, fōr′-), *n., pl.* **-feet. 1** one of the front feet of an animal having four or more feet. **2** *Nautical.* the forward end of a ship's keel.

fore|front (fôr′frunt′, fōr′-), *n.* the foremost part, such as the place of greatest importance or activity or the extreme front: *The captain led his soldiers to the forefront of battle.* (*Figurative.*) *the forefront of a reform movement.* SYN: vanguard.

fore|gang|er (fôr′gang′ər, fōr′-), *n.* a short piece of rope connecting the towline with the shank of a whaling harpoon; foregoer.

fore|gath|er (fôr gaᴛʜ′ər, fōr-), *v.i.* = forgather.

fore|glance (fôr′glans′, fōr′-; -gläns′), *n.* **1** the act of glancing forward. **2** a view or glance beforehand: *How . . . interesting it would be to have a foreglance into a science textbook of a century hence* (James J. Hissey).

fore|glimpse (fôr′glimps′, fōr′-), *n.* a glimpse or revelation of the future.

fore|go[1] (fôr gō′, fōr-), *v.t.,* **-went, -gone, -go|ing.** to forgo; do without; give up.

fore|go[2] (fôr gō′, fōr-), *v.i., v.t.,* **-went, -gone, -go|ing.** to go before; precede. [Old English *foregān*]

fore|go|er (fôr gō′ər, fōr-), *n.* **1** a person or thing that goes in front or leads the way. **2** a person who has gone before; forerunner; predecessor. **3** = foreganger.

fore|go|ing (fôr gō′ing, fōr-; fôr′gō′-, fōr′-), *adj.* preceding; going before; previous: *There have been many pictures in the foregoing pages.* SYN: antecedent.

fore|gone (fôr gôn′, -gon′; fōr-; fôr′gôn, -gon; fōr′-), *adj., v.* —*adj.* **1** known or decided beforehand. See also **foregone conclusion. 2** that has gone before; previous.
—*v.* past participle of **forego**[1] and **forego**[2].
—**fore|gone′ness**, *n.*

▶**foregone.** The adjective is stressed either on the first or last syllable, depending largely on the rhythm: *fore′gone* in *foregone conclusion,* but *foregone′* in *the conclusion was foregone.* The verb, however, is always stressed on the last syllable.

foregone conclusion, 1 a safe assumption about some future event: *It is a foregone conclusion that the one good student in the class will win the prize.* **2** an inevitable result.

fore|ground (fôr′ground′, fōr′-), *n.* the part of a picture or scene nearest the observer; part toward the front: *The foreground of the picture shows a cottage, while mountains loom in the background.*
in the foreground, conspicuous: *The young*

Pronunciation Key: hat, āge, cãre, fär; let, ēqual, tėrm; it, īce; hot, ōpen, ôrder; oil, out; cup, pu̇t, rüle; child; long; thin; ᴛʜen; zh, measure; ə represents **a** in about, **e** in taken, **i** in pencil, **o** in lemon, **u** in circus.

secretary always manages to be in the foreground at every conference.

fore|gut (fôr′gut′, fōr′-), *n.* 1 *Embryology.* the front section of the digestive canal of an embryo. The pharynx, esophagus, stomach, part of the duodenum, and liver develop from it. 2 *Zoology.* the front section of the digestive tract of an insect.

fore|hand** (fôr′hand′, fōr′-), *n., adj., adv.* **—*n. 1 a stroke in tennis and other games played with a racket or paddle, made with the palm of the hand turned forward and the arm sideways to the body. 2 the side of the body on which a forehand is hit. 3 the position in front or above; advantage: *The great Achilles ... The sinew and the forehand of our host.* (Shakespeare). 4 the part of a horse in front of the rider.
—*adj.* 1 done or made with the palm of the hand turned forward: *a forehand stroke in tennis.* 2 foremost; leading: *Our auld forehand ox* (Scott). 3 done beforehand; given or made in advance.
—*adv.* with a forehand stroke or motion.

***forehand** definition 1

fore|hand|ed (fôr′han′did, fōr′-), *adj.* 1 providing for the future; prudent; thrifty: *an early and forehanded care* (Jeremy Taylor). 2 done beforehand; early; timely. 3 in easy circumstances; well-to-do. 4 = forehand. **—fore′hand′ed|ly,** *adv.* **—fore′hand′ed|ness,** *n.*

fore|hatch (fôr′hach′, fōr′-), *n.* the hatch on the foredeck; the hatch closest to the bow.

fore|head (fôr′id, for′-; fôr′hed′, for′-), *n.* 1 the part of the face above the eyes: *His forehead was noble, but his mouth was cruel.* SYN: brow. 2 *Figurative.* a front part: *Even to the teeth and forehead of our faults* (Shakespeare). [Old English *forhēafod* < *fore-* fore- + *hēafod* head]

for|eign (fôr′ən, for′-), *adj.* 1 outside one's own country: *She has traveled much in foreign countries.* 2 coming from outside one's own country: *a foreign ship, a foreign language, foreign money.* 3 having to do with other countries; carried on or dealing with other countries: *foreign trade, foreign service.* 4 not belonging; not related; unfamiliar; strange: *Sitting still is foreign to a healthy boy's nature. The customs of Australian bushmen seem foreign to us.* 5 not related to the matter that is being discussed or considered. SYN: irrelevant. 6 not belonging naturally to the place where found: *a foreign object in the eye, a foreign substance in the blood.* 7 *Law.* falling outside the jurisdiction of a particular country. 8 belonging to or coming from other persons or things: *a statement supported by foreign testimony.*
[< Old French *forain* < Late Latin *forānus* on the outside, exterior < Latin *forās* outside < *foris* door] **—for′eign|ly,** *adv.* **—for′eign|ness,** *n.*

foreign affairs, a country's relations with other countries.

foreign aid, financial or technical assistance given by one nation to another in order to further its development and supply some or most of its needs. **—for′eign-aid′,** *adj.*

foreign bill or **draft,** a bill or draft drawn in one country, state, or other location, and payable in another.

for|eign-born (fôr′ən bôrn′, for′-), *adj.* born in another country: *These foreign-born scientists were familiar with the way dictatorships are set up* (New Yorker). SYN: alien.

foreign correspondent, a reporter sent by a newspaper, magazine, or television network to report on events and trends in one or more foreign nations.

for|eign|er (fôr′ə nər, for′-), *n.* 1 a person from another country; alien: *We are all foreigners in other countries. They spell it Vinci and pronounce it Vinchy; foreigners always spell better than they pronounce* (Mark Twain). 2 *Informal, Figurative.* a person from another section, state, province, or other location; outsider. 3 a foreign ship.

foreign exchange, 1 the system of settling accounts between people in different countries by giving and receiving bills of exchange, letters of credit, traveler's checks, or other commercial paper. 2 bills of exchange or other commercial paper drawn on persons or organizations in a foreign country. 3 holdings, especially by a central bank, of currencies of foreign countries.

for|eign-flag (fôr′ən flag′, for′-), *adj.* (of a ship or aircraft) registered in a country other than one's own.

for|eign|ism (fôr′ə niz əm, for′-), *n.* 1 foreign quality. 2 a foreign custom, trait, expression, or the like.

foreign legion, a part of an army made up largely of soldiers who are volunteers from other countries.

Foreign Legion, a part of the French Army made up largely of volunteers from other countries. It fought especially in colonial wars, and in Indochina, 1946-1954, and in the Korean War.

foreign minister, a person who is appointed to manage the foreign affairs of his nation and government, corresponding to the Secretary of State in the United States and the Foreign Secretary in Great Britain. France, West Germany, and many other countries have foreign ministers.

foreign office, *British.* the government department in charge of foreign affairs. *Abbr:* F.O.

foreign policy, the policy followed by a nation or its government in conducting its relations with one or more foreign nations.

Foreign Secretary, the foreign minister of Great Britain: [*The President*] *and ... the Foreign Secretary agreed at their White House conference today that the situation in Cuba merited the urgent and continued attention of the British and American Governments* (Manchester Guardian).

Foreign Service, a division of the United States Department of State, supplying the personnel for American embassies, consulates, and other missions, in other countries. It also trains young men and women for the diplomatic service.

foreign trade zone, a port or area where foreign goods may be unloaded, stored, and shipped without being subject to customs duties or taxes; free trade area; free port.

fore|judge[1] (fôr juj′, fōr-), *v.t., v.i.,* **-judged, -judg|ing.** to judge beforehand; prejudge.

fore|judge[2] (fôr juj′, fōr-), *v.t.,* **-judged, -judg|ing.** *Law.* to forjudge; exclude by a judgment.

fore|judg|ment (fôr juj′mənt, fōr-), *n.* a judgment formed or given beforehand.

fore|keel (fôr′kēl′, fōr′-), *n.* the part of the keel nearest the bow.

fore|knew (fôr nü′, -nyü′; fōr-), *v.* the past tense of **foreknow.**

fore|know (fôr nō′, fōr-), *v.t.,* **-knew, -known, -know|ing.** to know beforehand.

fore|know|a|ble (fôr nō′ə bəl, fōr-), *adj.* that can be foreknown.

fore|knowl|edge (fôr′nol′ij, fōr′-; fôr nol′-, fōr-), *n.* knowledge of a thing before it exists or happens; prescience: *This persistent foreknowledge, this queer ability to outguess my betters, began to have a vaguely dispiriting effect on me.* (New Yorker).

fore|known (fôr nōn′, fōr-), *v.* the past participle of **foreknow.**

fore|la|dy (fôr′lā′dē, fōr′-), *n., pl.* **-dies.** *U.S.* a forewoman.

fore|land (fôr′land′, fōr′-), *n.* 1 a cape; headland. SYN: promontory. 2 land or territory lying in front.

fore|lay (fôr lā′, fōr-), *v.t.,* **-laid, -lay|ing.** 1 to lay obstacles in the way of; plot against; hinder; frustrate: *I prevailed on his distraught widow to forelay and defeat the commercial passions and academic intrigues that were bound to come swirling around her husband's manuscript* (Harper's). 2 *Archaic or Dialect.* to lie in wait for; waylay: *An ambushed thief forelays a traveller* (John Dryden). 3 *Archaic or Dialect.* to plan beforehand; prearrange: *In all his works of art* [*he*] *has forelaid in his mind a perfect model of his intended fabric* (Robert South).

fore|leg (fôr′leg′, fōr′-), *n.* one of the front legs of an animal having four or more legs.

fore|limb (fôr′lim′, fōr′-), *n.* one of the front limbs of an animal having four or more limbs.

fore|lock[1] (fôr′lok′, fōr′-), *n.* 1 a lock of hair that grows just above the forehead. 2 a lock that hangs down over the forehead, as of a horse.
take time by the forelock. See under **time.**
[Old English *forelocc* < *fore-* fore- + *locc* lock]

fore|lock[2] (fôr′lok′, fōr′-), *n., v.* **—*n.*** a wedge or pin passed through a hole in the end of a bolt to keep it in place; cotter pin.
—*v.t.* to fasten with a forelock.
[< *fore-* + *lock*[1]]

fore|man (fôr′mən, fōr′-), *n., pl.* **-men.** 1 a man in charge of a group of workers; man in charge of the work in some part of a factory: *The foreman was inspecting the work on the production line.* SYN: overseer. 2 the chairman of a jury, who announces the verdict: *The foreman stated that the jury found the defendant "not guilty."*

fore|man|ship (fôr′mən ship, fōr′-), *n.* the position, work, or duties of a foreman.

fore|mast (fôr′mast′, -mäst′; fōr′-; *Nautical* fôr′məst, fōr′-), *n.* the mast nearest the bow of a ship, except in two-masted vessels in which the forward mast is the principal mast. See picture under **mast.**[1]

fore|mast|man (fôr′mast′mən, fōr′-; *Nautical* fôr′məst mən, fōr′-), *n., pl.* **-men.** a common sailor; a man before the mast.

fore|men|tioned (fôr men′shənd, fōr-), *adj.* mentioned before; forenamed: *Take the forementioned ingredients and mix with water.*

fore|milk (fôr′milk′, fōr′-), *n.* = colostrum.

fore|most (fôr′mōst, fōr′-), *adj., adv.* **—*adj.*** 1 first: *I am foremost in line.* 2 chief; leading; most notable: *Einstein is regarded as one of the foremost scientists of this century.*
—*adv.* 1 first: *He stumbled and fell head foremost.* 2 in the first place; firstly.
first and foremost, before everything else; above all: *The atmospheric sciences must, first and foremost, grow in the scale and ... quality of work carried on* (Saturday Review).
[Old English *formest;* spelling influenced by *fore*[1], and *most*]

fore|moth|er (fôr′muᴛʜ′ər, fōr′-), *n.* a female ancestor.

fore|name (fôr′nām′, fōr′-), *n.* a first name.

fore|noon (fôr′nün′, fōr′-), *n., adj.* **—*n.*** the time between early morning and noon; the part of the day from sunrise to noon.
—*adj.* between early morning and noon: *The morning watch passed into a forenoon watch and brought a welcome end to the gale* (Maclean's).

fo|ren|sic (fə ren′sik), *adj., n.* **—*adj.*** 1 oratorical; suitable for public debate: *forensic arguments, a forensic gift of speech.* 2 having to do with or belonging to a court of law; like that used in a law court: *a forensic expert in weapons, forensic medical scientists. A "forensic" psychiatrist ... works with court cases* (Science News Letter).
—*n.* a spoken or written exercise in argumentation, as in a college or high-school class in speech or rhetoric.
forensics, the art or study of public argumentation or debate.
[< Latin *forēnsis* (< *forum* forum) + English *-ic*] **—fo|ren′si|cal|ly,** *adv.*

forensic medicine, the science that deals with the application of medical knowledge to certain questions of civil and criminal law; medical jurisprudence.

forensic psychiatry, the application of psychiatry to questions of law, especially those involving mental responsibility, abnormal behavior, and insanity.

fore|or|dain (fôr′ôr dān′, fōr′-), *v.t.* to ordain beforehand; determine beforehand; predestine. SYN: predetermine. **—fore′or|dain′ment,** *n.*

fore|or|di|nate (fôr ôr′də nāt, fōr-), *v.t.,* **-nat|ed, -nat|ing.** = foreordain.

fore|or|di|na|tion (fôr′ôr də nā′shən, fōr′-), *n.* the act of ordaining beforehand; predestination.

fore|pale (fôr′pāl′, fōr′-), *v.t., v.i.,* **-paled, -pal|ing.** to protect (an excavation or a work in progress) from falling debris, quicksand, or the like, by timbers driven in front. [< *fore-* + *pale*[2] enclose with a fence]

fore|par|ent (fôr′pãr′ənt, fōr′-), *n. U.S. Dialect.* a person from whom one is descended; ancestor: *For more than two centuries our foreparents labored in this country without wages* (Martin Luther King, Jr.).

fore|part (fôr′pärt′, fōr′-), *n.* the front part; first or early part.

fore|passed or **fore|past** (fôr past′, -päst′; fōr-), *adj. Archaic.* (of time) that has passed; passed.

fore|paw (fôr′pô′, fōr′-), *n.* a front paw.

fore|peak (fôr′pēk′, fōr′-), *n.* the part of the hold of a ship in the angle formed by the bow.

fore|piece (fôr′pēs′, fōr′-), *n.* 1 the first or front piece of anything. 2 *Theater.* a curtain raiser. 3 a flap attached to the forepart of a sidesaddle, to protect the rider's clothing.

fore|play (fôr′plā′, fōr′-), *n.* amorous play or stimulation preceding coitus.

fore|pole (fôr′pōl′, fōr′-), *v.t., v.i.,* **-poled, -pol|ing.** = forepale.

fore|post (fôr′pōst′, fōr′-), *n.* an advanced post; outpost.

fore|quar|ter (fôr′kwôr′tər, fōr′-), *n.* the front leg, shoulder, and nearby ribs of beef, lamb, pork, or other animal with four legs; front quarter.

fore|ran (fôr ran′, fōr-), *v.* the past tense of **forerun.**

fore|reach (fôr rēch′, fōr-), *v.i.* to make headway quickly against the wind, or gain distance, as a ship does after coming into the wind. **—*v.t.*** 1 to move ahead of; pass. 2 *Figurative.* to get the better of.

fore|roy|al mast, sail, or **yard** (fôr′roi′əl, fōr′-), *Nautical.* the uppermost mast, sail, or yard of the forward mast of a square-rigged ship.

fore|run (fôr run′, fōr-), *v.t.,* **-ran, -run, -run|ning.** 1 to run in front of; precede. 2 to be a sign or warning of (something to come): *These signs* *forerun the death or fall of Kings* (Shakespeare). **SYN:** foreshadow. **3** to forestall; anticipate. **4** *Figurative.* to outrun; outstrip.

fore|run|ner (fôr′run′ər, fōr′-), *n.* **1** a person or thing that goes before or is sent ahead to show that another or something more is coming; herald: *John the Baptist was the forerunner of Christ. The old tintype was a forerunner of today's modern photograph.* **SYN:** harbinger, precursor. **2** a sign or warning of something to come: *Black clouds are forerunners of a storm.* **SYN:** omen, prognostic. **3** a predecessor or ancestor. **SYN:** forefather.

fore|sad|dle (fôr′sad′əl, fōr′-), *n.* the front part of a saddle, as of mutton or venison.

fore|said (fôr′sed′, fōr′-), *adj.* aforesaid; forementioned.

fore|sail (fôr′sāl′, fōr′-; *Nautical* fôr′səl, fōr′-), *n.* **1** the principal sail on the foremast of a schooner. **2** the lowest sail on the foremast of a square-rigged ship; forecourse. See picture under **sail**. **3** = forestaysail.

fore|saw (fôr sô′, fōr-), *v.* past tense of **foresee:** *Mother foresaw our hunger and put up a big picnic lunch.*

fore|see (fôr sē′, fōr-), *v.*, **-saw, -seen, -see|ing.** —*v.t.* to see or know beforehand: *We didn't take our bathing suits, because we could foresee that the water would be cold.* **SYN:** anticipate, divine. —*v.i.* to use foresight. [Old English *foresēon*]

fore|see|a|bil|i|ty (fôr sē′ə bil′ə tē, fōr-), *n.* a foreseeable quality or condition.

fore|see|a|ble (fôr sē′ə bəl, fōr-), *adj.* that can be foreseen: *Machine tool prices are stable, a condition most companies contend will hold for the foreseeable future* (Wall Street Journal). —**fore-see′a|bly,** *adv.*

fore|see|ing|ly (fôr sē′ing lē, fōr-), *adv.* with foresight; with forethought.

fore|seen (fôr sēn′, fōr-), *v.* past participle of **foresee:** *Nobody could have foreseen how cold it would be. Interdependence absolute, foreseen, ordained, decreed* (Rudyard Kipling).

fore|se|er (fôr sē′ər, fōr-), *n.* a person who foresees; one who exercises foresight.

fore|shad|ow (fôr shad′ō, fōr-), *v., n.* —*v.t.* to indicate beforehand; be a warning of; prefigure: *Those black clouds foreshadow a storm. Rousseau ... invented a system for behavioral control that foreshadowed some modern theories of psychological conditioning and behavior* (Lester G. Crocker). —*n.* an indication of something to come: *to impart some outline or foreshadow of this doctrine* (Thomas Carlyle). *A truce is often the foreshadow of a peace* (J. M. Ludlow). —**fore|shad′ow|er,** *n.*

fore|shad|ow|ing (fôr shad′ō ing, fōr-), *n.* a foreshadow: *At Wormwood, each season carries a hundred foreshadowings of the season that is to follow ...* (New Yorker).

fore|shank (fôr′shangk′, fōr′-), *n.* the meat on the upper part of the forelegs of cattle.

fore|sheet (fôr′shēt′, fōr′-), *n.* one of the ropes used to trim and hold a foresail in place.

foresheets, the space in the forward part of an open boat: *We sat in the foresheets, the spray blowing in our face.*

fore|ship (fôr′ship′, fōr′-), *n.* forepart of a ship.

fore|shock (fôr′shok′, fōr′-), *n.* a lesser shock preceding the main shock of an earthquake.

fore|shore (fôr′shôr′, fōr′-), *n.* **1** the part of the shore between the high-water mark and low-water mark. **2** the area adjoining the beach or shore.

fore|short|en (fôr shôr′tən, fōr-), *v.t.* **1** to shorten (lines or objects) in a drawing or painting in order to give the impression of depth and distance to the eye. Foreshortening helps give perspective to a drawing or painting. **2** *Figurative.* to shorten or condense: *It has developed a heavy-duty truck model with a foreshortened hood* (New York Times).

***fore|short|en|ing** (fôr shôr′tə ning, fōr-), *n.* the representation of figures in a drawing or painting in perspective in order to give to the eye an impression of their three dimensions and their distance.

***foreshortening**

fore|show (fôr shō′, fōr-), *v.t.*, **-showed, -shown, -show|ing.** to show beforehand; foretell; foreshadow: *Astrologers that future fates foreshow* (Alexander Pope). [Old English *forescēawian*]

fore|shown (fôr shōn′, fōr-), *v.* past participle of **foreshow.**

fore|side (fôr′sīd′, fōr′-), *n.* **1** the front side or edge. **2** the upper side. **3** a piece of land facing the sea.

fore|sight (fôr′sīt′, fōr′-), *n.* **1** the power to see or know beforehand what is likely to happen: *No one had enough foresight to predict the winner.* **SYN:** prevision. **2** careful thought for the future; prudence: *A spendthrift does not use foresight. His foresight had provided for his family in case of his death.* **SYN:** See syn. under **prudence. 3** a looking ahead; view into the future: *Foresight now tells us that space travel is not impossible.* **SYN:** prospect. **4** *Surveying.* sight or reading taken in a forward direction. **5** the sight nearest the muzzle of a firearm.

fore|sight|ed (fôr′sī′tid, fōr′-), *adj.* having or showing foresight; foreseeing. **SYN:** provident. —**fore′sight′ed|ly,** *adv.* —**fore′sight′ed|ness,** *n.*

fore|skin (fôr′skin′, fōr′-), *n.* the fold of skin that covers the end of the penis; prepuce.

fore|speak (fôr spēk′, fōr-), *v.t.*, **-spoke** or (*Archaic*) **-spake, -spo|ken** or (*Archaic*) **-spoke, -speak|ing.** *Rare.* **1** to foretell; predict. **2** to ask for in advance, bespeak.

fore|spend (fôr spend′, fōr-), *v.t.*, **-spent, -spend|ing.** = forspend.

for|est (fôr′ist, for′-), *n., adj., v.* —*n.* **1a** a large area of land covered with trees; thick woods; woodland: *We wandered in the forest looking at its mighty trees. ... primeval forests undefaced by the hand of man* (Charles Darwin). **b** the trees themselves: *an oak forest, a pine forest.* **2** *Figurative.* a thick mass of anything: *A forest of supporting posts and pillars was put in beneath the house* (New Yorker). *Stretford is ... a Manchester suburb with forests of semidetached houses* (Manchester Guardian Weekly). **3** (in English law) a tract of woods and pasture, usually owned by the Crown, and set apart for game. —*adj.* of a forest; in a forest: *Help prevent forest fires. It will be found that all forest and game laws were introduced into Europe at the same time and by the same policy as gave birth to the feudal system* (William Blackstone). —*v.t.* to plant with trees; change into a forest: *The farmer forested the old pasture with pine trees.*
[< Old French *forest* < Late Latin *forestis* (*silva*) outer woods < Latin *forīs* outside < *foris* door] —**for′est|less,** *adj.*

fore|stage (fôr′stāj′, fōr′-), *n.* the area of a theater stage in front of the curtain; proscenium: *a movable forestage.*

for|es|tal (fôr′is təl, for′-), *adj.* of or having to do with a forest.

fore|stall (fôr stôl′, fōr-), *v.t.* **1** to prevent by acting first: *The mayor forestalled a strike by starting to negotiate early with the union.* **2** to act sooner than and so get the better of; get ahead of; anticipate: *By settling the deal by telegraph, he had forestalled all his competitors.* **3** to buy up (goods or other commodities) in advance in order to increase the price. **4** *Obsolete.* **a** to lie in wait for; intercept. **b** to obstruct by force. [Middle English *forstallen* < Old English *foresteall* prevention] —**fore|stall′er,** *n.*

fore|stall|ment or **fore|stal|ment** (fôr stôl′mənt, fōr-), *n.* the act of forestalling.

for|est|a|tion (fôr′ə stā′shən, for′-), *n.* the act of planting or taking care of forests.

fore|stay (fôr′stā′, fōr′-), *n.* a rope or cable reaching from the top of a ship's foremast to the bowsprit. The forestay helps to support the foremast.

fore|stay|sail (fôr′stā′sāl′, fōr′-; *Nautical* fôr′stā′səl, fōr′-), *n.* a triangular headsail attached to the forestay of a sloop, cutter, or other sailing vessel. It is the first sail in front of the forward (or single) mast.

for|est|ed (fôr′ə stid, for′-), *adj.* covered with trees; thickly wooded.

for|est|er (fôr′ə stər, for′-), *n.* **1a** a person in charge of a forest, who looks after the trees and guards against fires. **b** a person trained in forestry who manages forestland. **2** a person, bird, or animal that lives in a forest. **3** = giant kangaroo. **4** any one of a variety of moths having scaly wings, especially a black moth with large yellow spots, whose larva eats the foliage of grapevines.

forest fire, a fire burning woods or timber, often very destructive.

forest green, a dark green.

forest horse, a wild horse native to Europe and similar to Przhevalski's horse. It probably had the same ancestor as the tame horse today.

fo|res|tial (fə res′chəl), *adj.* = forestal.

fore|stick (fôr′stik′, fōr′-), *n. U.S.* the front stick lying on the andirons in a wood fire.

for|est|ine (fôr′ə stin, -stīn; for′-), *adj.* of or belonging to the forest.

for|est|land (fôr′ist land′, for′-; -lənd), *n.* land consisting of forests.

Forest Negro, a member of any one of the native peoples of western Africa, especially those inhabiting the tropical forests of equatorial Africa, characterized by typical Negroid features.

forest preserve, = forest reserve.

forest ranger, *U.S.* **1** an officer of the Forest Service in charge of a unit of forestland. **2** any person employed to guard and patrol a tract of forest; ranger; forester.

forest reserve, a tract of wooded land set aside by the government as a natural park and protected from wasteful cutting, fires, and other ravages.

for|est|ry (fôr′ə strē, for′-), *n.* **1** the science of planting and taking care of forests. **2** the art of making and managing forests. **3** = forestland.

forest school, a school for giving instruction and training in forestry.

Forest Service, a division of the United States Department of Agriculture in control of the national forests.

forest tent caterpillar, a black, hairy caterpillar with blue spots on both sides and a row of yellow spots along its back, common in eastern and central North America.

fore|tack (fôr′tak′, fōr′-), *n. Nautical.* the rope by which the windward corner of the foresail is kept in place.

fore|taste (*n.* fôr′tāst′, fōr′-; *v.* fôr tāst′, fōr-), *n., v.*, **-tast|ed, -tast|ing.** —*n.* a taste beforehand; anticipation: *He got a foretaste of business life by working during his vacation from school.* —*v.t.* to taste beforehand; anticipate. —**fore-tast′er,** *n.*

fore|tell (fôr tel′, fōr-), *v.t.*, **-told, -tell|ing.** to tell beforehand; predict; prophesy: *Who can foretell what a baby will do next?* **SYN:** prognosticate, forecast. —**fore|tell′a|ble,** *adj.* —**fore|tell′er,** *n.*

fore|think (fôr thingk′, fōr-), *v.t.*, **-thought, -think|ing.** *Obsolete.* to think of beforehand. —**fore|think′er,** *n.*

fore|thought (*n., adj.* fôr′thôt′, fōr′-; *v.* fôr thôt′, fōr-), *n., adj., v.* —*n.* **1** previous thought or consideration; planning beforehand. **SYN:** anticipation. **2** careful thought for the future; prudence; foresight: *His children are grateful for his forethought in saving the money to pay for their education.* **3** a thinking out beforehand: *His good was mainly an intent, His evil not of forethought done* (John Greenleaf Whittier). —*adj.* thought of beforehand. —*v.* past tense and past participle of **forethink.**

fore|thought|ful (fôr thôt′fəl, fōr-), *adj.* full of forethought; having forethought. **SYN:** provident. —**fore|thought′ful|ly,** *adv.* —**fore|thought′ful-ness,** *n.*

fore|time (fôr′tīm′, fōr′-), *n.* past time; the past.

fore|to|ken (*v.* fôr tō′kən, fōr-; *n.* fôr′tō′kən, fōr′-), *v., n.* —*v.t.* to indicate beforehand; be an omen of. **SYN:** foreshadow. [probably < noun] —*n.* an indication of something to come; omen. [Old English *foretācn* < *fore-* fore- + *tācn* token]

fore|told (fôr tōld′, fōr-), *v.* past tense and past participle of **foretell:** *The Weather Service foretold the cold wave. He had foretold the depression.*

fore|tooth (fôr′tüth, fōr′-), *n., pl.* **-teeth.** one of the front teeth.

fore|top (fôr′top′, fōr′-; *Nautical* fôr′təp, fōr′-), *n.* **1** the platform at the top of the bottom section of a foremast. **2** *U.S.* the front seat on the top of a vehicle. **3** the forelock of a horse. **4** *Obsolete.* the forelock of a person or on a wig: *a periwig with an high foretop* (Sir Richard Steele).

fore-top|gal|lant (fôr′top gal′ənt, fōr′-; *Nautical* fôr′tə gal′ənt, fōr′-), *adj.* of or belonging to the mast, sails, or yards next above the fore-topmast on the forward mast of a square-rigged ship. The fore-topgallant mast is the third section of mast from the deck of the ship. See picture under **mast.**[1]

fore|top|man (fôr′top′mən, fōr′-; *Nautical* fôr′təp-mən, fōr′-), *n., pl.* **-men.** *Nautical.* a sailor whose work aloft is on the foretop or above it.

fore-top|mast (fôr′top′mast′, -mäst′; fōr′-; *Nautical* fôr′top′məst, fōr′-), *n.* the mast next above the foremast. See picture under **mast.**[1]

fore-top|sail (fôr′top′sāl′, fōr′-; *Nautical* fôr′top′-səl, fōr′-), *n.*, or **fore-topsail yard.** the sail or yard set on the fore-topmast and next above the foresail. See pictures at **sail** and **mast**[1].

fore|type (fôr′tīp′, fōr′-), *n.* a preceding or earlier type; antetype.

for|ev|er (fər ev′ər), *adv.* **1** for always; without

Pronunciation Key: hat, āge, cãre, fär; let, ēqual, tėrm; it, īce; hot, ōpen, ôrder; oil, out; cup, pu̇t, rüle; child; long; thin; ᴛʜen; zh, measure; ə represents **a** in about, **e** in taken, **i** in pencil, **o** in lemon, **u** in circus.

ever coming to an end: *Nobody lives forever. Forever honour'd and forever mourned* (Alexander Pope). SYN: ever, evermore, eternally, everlastingly. **2** all the time; always: *Some girls in my class are forever talking. She is forever telling me that I should take more exercise.* SYN: continually. [(originally) *for ever*] —**for|ev'er|ness**, *n.*

for|ev|er|more (fər ev'ər môr', -mōr'), *adv.* = forever.

fore|warn (fôr wôrn', fōr-), *v.t.* to warn beforehand: *We should have been forewarned of his illness when he began to lose weight.* SYN: caution. —**fore|warn'er**, *n.*

fore|warn|ing (fôr wôr'ning, fōr-), *n., adj.* —*n.* a warning beforehand: *He had ample forewarning of the reception his report would get* (P.C. Woodyatt).
—*adj.* that forewarns. —**fore|warn'ing|ly**, *adv.*

fore|went (fôr went', fōr-), *v.* past tense of **forego:** *She forewent dessert.*

fore|wing (fôr'wing', fōr'-), *n.* one of the front wings of an insect having four wings.

fore|wom|an (fôr'wu̇m'ən, fōr'-), *n., pl.* **-wom|en.** **1** a woman in charge of a group of workers or of some part of a factory. **2** the chairwoman of a jury.

fore|word (fôr'wėrd', fōr'-), *n.* an introduction or preface to a book or other literary or dramatic work, or to a speech. SYN: See syn. under **introduction.**

fore|worn (fôr wôrn', fōr-), *adj.* = forworn.

fore|yard¹ (fôr'yärd, fōr'-), *n.* the yard or court in front of a building.

fore|yard² (fôr'yärd', fōr'-), *n.* the lower yard on the foremast of a ship.

for|feit (fôr'fit), *v., n., adj.* —*v.t.* to lose or have to give up by one's own act, neglect, or fault: *to forfeit a bond. He forfeited his life by his careless driving.* [< noun]
—*n.* **1** a thing lost or given up because of some act, neglect, or fault; penalty; fine: *Good health was the forfeit he paid for staying up late every night.* **2** the loss or giving up of something as a penalty; forfeiture. **3** anything given up by a player in a game because of a mistake and redeemed by some penalty or fine: *And here I took pleasure to take forfeits Of the ladies* (Samuel Pepys).
—*adj.* lost or given up as a penalty; forfeited: *Thy wealth being forfeit to the state, Thou hast not left the value of a cord* (Shakespeare).
forfeits, a game in which things are forfeited and redeemed by paying a penalty: *We ... beguile the time with forfeits and old stories* (Dickens).
[< Old French *forfait;* past participle of *forfaire* transgress < *for-* wrongly (< Latin *forīs* out) + *faire* do < Latin *facere*] —**for'feit|a|ble**, *adj.* —**for'feit|er**, *n.*

for|fei|ture (fôr'fə chər), *n.* **1** loss by forfeiting. **2** a thing forfeited; penalty; fine.

for|fend (fôr fend'), *v.t.* **1** *Especially U.S.* to defend, secure, or protect: *It is the duty of the courts also to forfend the rights of citizens.* **2** *Archaic.* to ward off; avert; prevent. **3** *Obsolete.* to forbid; prohibit. Also, **forefend.**

for|fi|cate (fôr'fə kit, -kāt), *adj.* deeply forked, as the tail of certain birds. [< Latin *forfex, -icis* shears + English *-ate*¹]

for|fi|ca|tion (fôr'fə kā'shən), *n.* **1** the state of being forficate. **2** a deep forking or furcation.

for|fic|u|late (fôr fik'yə lit), *adj. Zoology.* shaped like a pair of small scissors. [< Latin *forficula* (diminutive) < *forfex, -icis* shears + English *-ate*¹]

for|gat (fər gat'), *v. Archaic.* forgot; a past tense of **forget.**

for|gath|er (fôr gaᴛʜ'ər), *v.i.* **1** to gather together; assemble; meet: *Our families usually forgather at Christmas time.* SYN: convene. **2** to meet by accident. **3** to be friendly; associate (with). Also, **foregather.**

for|gave (fər gāv'), *v.* past tense of **forgive:** *She forgave my mistake.*

***forge**¹ (fôrj, fōrj), *n., v.,* **forged, forg|ing.** —*n.* **1** a place with a fire where metal is heated very hot and then hammered into shape; an open fireplace or hearth with a bellows attached. A blacksmith uses a forge. See picture above. **2** a blacksmith's shop; smithy: *The blacksmith came out of the forge to fit the horseshoe.* **3** a place where iron or other metal is melted and refined.
—*v.t.* **1** to heat (metal) very hot and then hammer into shape: *The blacksmith forged a bar of iron into a big hook.* **2** *Figurative.* to make, shape, or form: *Yet do the songsmiths Quit not their forges; Still on life's anvil Forge they the rhyme* (Sir William Watson). SYN: fashion, frame, construct. **3** to make or write (something false) to deceive; sign falsely to deceive: *to forge a check, to forge a passport.* SYN: counterfeit, falsify. **4** to sign (another's name) falsely to deceive: *to forge a signature.*
—*v.i.* **1** to work at a forge. **2** to commit forgery: *But pens can forge, my friend, that cannot write* (Alexander Pope). **3** (of horses) to strike the forward shoe with the rear one in walking or running; overreach.
[< Old French *forge,* earlier *faverge* < Latin *fabrica* workshop < *faber* workman. See etym. of doublet **fabric.**]

***forge**¹
definition 1

forge² (fôrj, fōrj), *v.i.,* **forged, forg|ing. 1** to move forward slowly but steadily: *One runner forged ahead of the others and won the race.*
2 (of a vessel) to move along by momentum or the pressure of tide. [origin uncertain]

forge|a|bil|i|ty (fôr'jə bil'ə tē, fōr'-), *n.* the quality or property of being forgeable.

forge|a|ble (fôr'jə bəl, fōr'-), *adj.* that can be forged.

forge|mas|ter (fôrj'mas'tər, -mäs'-; fōrj'-), *n.* **1** a person in charge of a forge. **2** a master forger.

forg|er (fôr'jər, fōr'-), *n.* **1** a person who forges another person's name or makes any fraudulent imitation. **2** a person who forges metals; a smith.

for|ger|y (fôr'jər ē, fōr'-), *n., pl.* **-ger|ies. 1** the act of forging a signature, or making or writing something false. Forgery is a crime and is punishable by law. **2** something made or written falsely to deceive: *The painting was a forgery. The signature on the check was not mine but a forgery.* SYN: counterfeit. **3** *Poetic.* invention; fiction.

for|get (fər get'), *v.,* **-got** or (*Archaic*) **-gat, -got|ten** or **-got, -get|ting.** —*v.t.* **1** to let go out of the mind; fail to remember; be unable to remember: *He forgot the poem which he had memorized. He has forgotten more than I ever learned.* **2** to fail to think of; fail to do without meaning to: *I forgot to call the dentist.* **3** to fail to take; leave behind: *He had forgotten his umbrella.* **4** to neglect to mention; pass over in silence; disregard; slight: *Let us not forget the Constitution when we discuss civil liberties.*
—*v.i.* to be forgetful; fail to remember; be unable to remember: *Wear your hat if it's cold; don't forget.*
forget it, *U.S. Informal.* to take no notice of it; not mention it: *He was going to thank me, but I told him to forget it.*
forget oneself, a to think of others before oneself; put the interests of others before one's own interests; be unselfish: *The miser forgot himself for once, and gave the beggar a coin.* **b** to fail to consider what one should do or be; say or do something improper: *The angry man forgot himself and started to shout in front of everybody in the bus. Urge me no more, I shall forget myself* (Shakespeare). **c** to become absentminded: *Forgetting himself, the daydreaming child almost got lost in the park.* **d** to lose consciousness, as if in sleep: *Though cold like you, unmov'd and silent grown, I have not yet forgot myself* (Alexander Pope).
[Middle English *forgeten,* alteration of *foryeten,* Old English *forgietan;* spelling influenced by Middle English *geten* get]

for|get|ful (fər get'fəl), *adj.* **1** apt to forget; having a poor memory: *Old people sometimes become forgetful.* **2** neglecting; heedless: *forgetful of the law.* SYN: neglectful, oblivious, unmindful.
3 causing to forget: *The sound of that forgetful shore* (Tennyson). —**for|get'ful|ly**, *adv.* —**for|get'ful|ness**, *n.*

for|ge|tive (fôr'jə tiv, fōr'-), *adj. Archaic.* inventive; creative. [perhaps < *forge*¹, verb; perhaps patterned on *creative*]

for|get-me-not (fər get'mē not'), *n.* **1** any one of several small plants with hairy stems, light green leaves, and clusters of small blue, pink, or white flowers. It belongs to the borage family and is frequently regarded as a symbol of friendship. **2** any one of several similar plants. **3** the flower of any one of these plants.

for|get|ta|bil|i|ty (fər get'ə bil'ə tē), *n.* the quality of being forgettable.

for|get|ta|ble (fər get'ə bəl), *adj.* that can or is likely to be forgotten; not memorable: *a forgettable face, forgettable characters.* —**for|get'ta|ble|ness**, *n.*

for|get|ter (fər get'ər), *n.* a person who forgets.

for|get|ter|y (fər get'ər ē), *n. U.S. Dialect or Informal.* a capacity or aptitude for forgetting; inability to remember.

forge water, water in which hot irons have been dipped, formerly in popular use as a medicine. [because such irons are used in a *forge*]

For|ghan or **For|gan** (fôr'gən), *n.* a Moslem organization in Iran opposing the revolutionary government established in 1979: *As Khomeini pressed through his ideas on the Islamic government of Iran, ... the ultra-Muslim Forghan terrorist group perpetrated a series of assassinations against the senior clergy* (H.V. Hodson).
[< a Persian name for the Koran]

forg|ing (fôr'jing, fōr'-), *n.* **1** something forged; a piece of metal that is forged. **2** the act or process of shaping metal on a forge. **3** = forgery.

forging press, a machine which presses down vertically on hot metal to shape it under pressure between dies.

for|giv|a|ble (fər giv'ə bəl), *adj.* that can be forgiven; excusable; pardonable: *An irremissible sin, an inexcusable sin; yet to him that will truly repent, it is forgivable* (Hugh Latimer).

for|giv|a|bly (fər giv'ə blē), *adv.* in a forgivable manner; pardonably.

for|give (fər giv'), *v.,* **-gave, -giv|en, -giv|ing.**
—*v.t.* **1** to give up the wish to punish or get even with; not have hard feelings at or toward; pardon; excuse: *She forgave her brother for breaking her doll. Please forgive my mistake.* SYN: absolve. See syn. under **excuse. 2** to give up all claim to; not demand payment for: *to forgive a debt.*
—*v.i.* to give forgiveness; pardon: *To err is human, to forgive, divine* (Alexander Pope).
[Middle English *forgiven,* alteration of *foryiven, foryeven,* Old English *forgiefan;* spelling influenced by Middle English *given* give] —**for|giv'er**, *n.*

for|giv|en (fər giv'ən), *v.* the past participle of **forgive:** *Your mistakes are forgiven, but be more careful.*

for|give|ness (fər giv'nis), *n.* **1** the act of forgiving; pardon: *Prayer can be a plea for forgiveness that would otherwise remain unuttered.* **2** willingness to forgive: *His forgiveness made her realize how unselfish he was.* **3** remission of a debt, obligation, or penalty: *Republicans urge a 20% "forgiveness" for the first $100 of tax* (Wall Street Journal).

for|giv|ing (fər giv'ing), *adj.* that forgives; willing to forgive. SYN: remissive. —**for|giv'ing|ly**, *adv.* —**for|giv'ing|ness**, *n.*

for|go (fôr gō'), *v.t.,* **-went, -gone, -go|ing. 1** to do without; give up: *She decided to forgo the movies and do her lessons.* SYN: surrender, relinquish, sacrifice. **2** *Archaic.* **a** to go or pass by. **b** to neglect; overlook. **3** *Archaic.* to leave; quit: *I wish I might this weary life forgo, And shortly turn unto my happy rest* (Edmund Spenser). Also, **forego.** [Old English *forgān*] —**for|go'er**, *n.*

for|gone (fôr gôn', -gon'), *v.* the past participle of **forgo:** *She has forgone dessert for a month in an effort to lose weight.*

for|got (fər got'), *v.* a past tense and a past participle of **forget:** *He was so busy that he forgot to eat his lunch.*

for|got|ten (fər got'ən), *v.* a past participle of **forget:** *He has forgotten much of what he learned.*

forgotten man, *U.S. Politics.* a person belonging to the middle class or working class: *Buckley's most ardent supporters ... were mostly "the forgotten men"—office clerks, construction workers, taxicab drivers* (New Yorker). [< its use by President Franklin D. Roosevelt in the 1930's as a symbol of the victims of the depression]

for-hire (fôr'hīr'), *adj.* for use or work in return for payment; hireable or rentable: *for-hire trucks.*

for-in|stance (fər in'stəns), *n. U.S. Informal.* an example: *Just to give you a for-instance, we're cloud-seeding the Rockies* (New Yorker).

for|int (fôr'int), *n.* the basic unit of money of Hungary, worth 100 fillér. [< Hungarian *forint,* probably Italian *fiorino* florin]

for|judge (fôr juj'), *v.t.,* **-judged, -judg|ing.** *Law.* to exclude or deprive by a judgment. Also, **forejudge.** [< Old French *forjugier* < *fors* out (< Latin *forīs*) + *jugier* to judge]

fork (fôrk), *n., v.* —*n.* **1** an instrument with a handle and two or more long, pointed parts at one end: *A small fork is used to lift food. A much larger fork, called a pitchfork, is used for such purposes as to lift and throw hay.* **2** anything shaped like a fork, such as a tuning fork or a divining rod. **3** the place where a tree, road, or stream divides into two branches: *They parted at the fork of the road.* **4** one of the branches into which anything is divided: *Take the right-hand fork.* SYN: ramification. **5** *Especially U.S.* a branch or tributary stream: *Let's go fishing in the north fork.* **6** *Obsolete.* the barbed head of an arrow. **7** *Obsolete.* a choice of alternatives; dilemma.
—*v.t.* **1** to lift, throw, or dig with a fork: *to fork hay into a wagon, fork weeds.* **2** to make in the shape or form of a fork. **3** to attack (two or more chess pieces) at once with the same piece.
—*v.i.* to have a fork or forks; divide into branches: *There is a garage where the road forks.*
fork over (out or **up),** *Slang.* to hand over; pay out: *He forked over the money. Fork out your balance in hand* (Dickens).

[Old English *forca* pitchfork < Latin *furca*]
—**fork'less**, *adj.* —**fork'like'**, *adj.*

fork ball, *Baseball.* a pitch in which the ball is gripped with the first and second fingers of the pitching hand spread considerably apart, permitting an extra spin when it is released.

forked (fôrkt; *Archaic and Poetic* fôr'kid), *adj.* 1 having a fork or forks; divided into branches; branching: *a forked stick.* 2 zigzag: *forked lightning.* —**fork'ed|ly**, *adv.* —**fork'ed|ness**, *n.*

forked chain, *Chemistry.* two smaller chains branching in a forked manner from the end of a straight chain.

forked tongue, stinging or virulent language: ... *the forked tongue that contributed so much to the venomous delight of "Virginia Woolf"* (Time).
speak with a forked tongue, to lie; say something deceitful or in an insincere way: *The Indians would not bargain with the dishonest trader who they said spoke with a forked tongue.*

fork|ful (fôrk'fúl), *n., pl.* **-fuls.** as much as a fork will hold: *The summer's last harvesters winnowed the wheat by throwing forkfuls in the air* (Time).

fork|head (fôrk'hed'), *n.* an arrowhead having two points directed forward.

***fork lift**, a device with horizontal metal prongs that can be inserted under a load to lift it or put it down, and is attached to the front of a small three- or four-wheeled tractor.

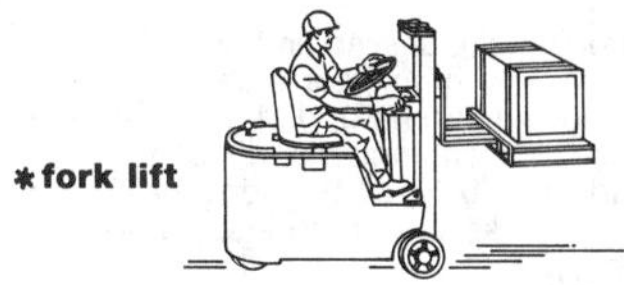
***fork lift**

fork-lift truck (fôrk'lift'), a small three- or four-wheeled tractor equipped with a fork lift.

fork|tail (fôrk'tāl'), *n.* 1 a fish with a forked tail, such as the salmon and swordfish. 2 a bird with a forked tail, such as the kite.

fork-tailed (fôrk'tāld'), *adj.* having a forked tail; scissor-tailed; swallow-tailed.

fork-tongued (fôrk'tungd'), *adj.* stinging; caustic; virulent: *a fork-tongued character, a fork-tongued play.*

fork truck, = fork-lift truck.

fork|y (fôr'kē), *adj.* shaped like a fork; forked.

for|la|na (fôr lä'nä), *n.* = furlana.

for|lorn (fôr lôrn'), *adj.* 1 left alone; neglected; deserted: *The lost kitten, a forlorn little animal, was wet and dirty.* SYN: abandoned, forsaken. 2 wretched and miserable in feeling or looks; unhappy. 3 hopeless; desperate. 4 bereft (of): *forlorn of hope. Dreamland lies forlorn of light* (Dante Gabriel Rossetti). [Old English *forloren* lost, past participle of *forlēosan*] —**for|lorn'ly**, *adv.* —**for|lorn'ness**, *n.*

forlorn hope, 1 a dangerous or desperate enterprise. 2 an undertaking almost sure to fail. 3 *Figurative.* a party of soldiers selected for a very dangerous job. 4 *Figurative.* a member of such a party. [alteration of Middle Dutch *verloren hoop* (literally) lost troop]

form (fôrm), *n., v.* —*n.* 1 appearance apart from color or materials; shape: *The pupils learned that circles and triangles are simple forms.* 2 shape of body; body of a person or animal, considered with regard to its shape or external appearance. 3 the way in which a thing exists, takes shape, or shows itself; condition; character; manifestation: *sulfur in the crystalline or the amorphous form, a mild form of a disease, a novel in the form of a diary. Ice, snow, and steam are forms of water.* 4 kind; sort; variety: *Electricity is a form of energy.* 5 the way of doing something; manner; method: *He is a fast runner, but his form in running is bad.* 6 a set way of behaving according to custom or rule; formality; ceremony: *He said "good morning" as a matter of form, although he hardly noticed me. Shaking hands is a form. For who would keep an Ancient form Through which the spirit breathes no more?* (Tennyson). SYN: conventionality, convention. 7 a set order of words; customary wording; formula: *A written agreement to buy, sell, or do something follows a certain form.* 8 merely outward observance; empty ceremony. 9 a document with printing or writing on it and blank spaces to be filled in: *To get a license to drive an automobile you must fill out a form.* 10 an orderly arrangement of parts: *In what form did he put the list of words? Some proverbs are in verse form. The effect of a work of literature, art, or music comes from its form as well as its content.* 11 a thing that gives shape to something; mold; pattern: *Ice cream is often made in forms.* 12 good condition of body or mind: *Athletes exercise to keep in form.* 13 *Grammar.* any one of the ways in which a word is spelled, pronounced, or inflected to show its different meanings. *Boys* is the plural form of *boy. Saw* is the past form of *see. My* and *mine* are the possessive forms of *I.* 14 a grade in school: *He is now in the fifth form.* 15 a long seat; bench. 16 *Printing.* type fastened in a frame ready for printing or making plates. 17 *Crystallography.* the combination of all the like faces possible on a crystal of given symmetry. 18 *Philosophy.* the element or quality in a thing that makes it what it is. Some philosophers maintain that the form of a thing can be separated from the content and analyzed in terms of itself; others maintain that form is inseparable from content or substance, and that the one is meaningless without the other. 19 the bed or lair of a hare: *Despite the mother hare's wiles, he found a leveret, and was a little hurt when it was taken from him and put back in its "form"* (London Times). 20 *Obsolete.* beauty; comeliness.
—*v.t.* 1 to give shape to; make in a certain form: *Bakers form dough into loaves.* SYN: fashion. 2 to become: *Water forms ice when it freezes.* 3 to make up; compose: *Parents and children form a family.* SYN: constitute. 4 to organize; establish: *We formed a club.* 5 to develop: *He formed the good habit of getting his lessons done each day before looking at television.* 6 to arrange in some order: *The soldiers formed themselves into lines.* 7 to mold by discipline; educate: *The most skillful masters ... had labored to form the mind and body of the young prince* (Edward Gibbon). 8 *Grammar.* to construct or develop (a new word) by adding a prefix, suffix, or word element. A noun is often formed by adding *-ness* to an adjective. 9 to conceive in the mind; arrive at: *They formed a poor opinion of him.*
—*v.i.* 1 to be formed; take shape: *Clouds form in the sky. Ice formed in the pail.* 2 to assume a certain form: *The dancers formed into three groups.* 3 to come into existence.
bad form, behavior contrary to accepted customs: *It is considered bad form to be a poor loser.*
good form, behavior in accordance with accepted customs: *It is good form to thank your hostess when leaving.*
[< Old French *forme,* learned borrowing from Latin *forma* form, shape] —**form'a|ble**, *adj.*
—*Syn. n.* 1 **Form, shape, figure** mean the appearance of something apart from the color or the material of which it consists. **Form** suggests an appearance dependent on a certain distribution and arrangement of parts: *the form of a leaf.* **Shape** suggests both the outline and the bulk of something: *the shape of the head.* **Figure** applies only to the outline of an object: *geometrical figures. He drew figures of animals.*

-form, *suffix forming adjectives.* 1 having the form of ___: *Cruciform = having the form of a cross.* 2 having ___ form or forms: *Multiform = having many forms.*
[< Latin *-formis* < *forma* form, shape]

form|a|bil|i|ty (fôr'mə bil'ə tē), *n.* the capability of being shaped or formed: *Cerium is a rare earth which improves the formability of certain forms of stainless steel* (New York Herald Tribune).

for|mal (fôr'məl), *adj., n.* —*adj.* 1 with strict attention to outward forms and ceremonies; not familiar and homelike; stiff: *a formal greeting, a formal bow.* 2 according to set customs or rules: *a formal invitation. The new ambassador paid a formal call on the President.* 3 done, used, said, or otherwise employed, as a formality only; routine. 4 done with the proper forms; clear and definite: *A written contract is a formal agreement to do something.* 5 very regular; symmetrical; orderly: *a formal arrangement of furniture, a formal poem. A cold-looking formal garden, cut into angles and rhomboids* (Washington Irving). 6 having to do with the form, not the content: *formal criticism, a formal analysis.* 7 (of language) conforming to established convention in grammar, syntax, and pronunciation. 8 *Philosophy.* having to do with form; essential.
—*n.* 1 a formal dance, party, or other affair. 2 a gown worn to a formal affair: *She was dressed in her first formal. Women's apparel items likely to be popular this fall include knit dresses, beaded cocktail dresses, and long formals* (Wall Street Journal).
[< Latin *formālis* < *forma* form, shape] —**for'mal|ly**, *adv.* —**for'mal|ness**, *n.*
—*Syn. adj.* 1, 2 **Formal, conventional** mean in keeping with outward forms and rules. **Formal** implies paying strict attention to prescribed forms and procedures, and suggests lack of warmth and naturalness: *A judge has a formal manner in a law court.* **Conventional** implies paying attention to generally accepted forms and customs of social behavior, and often suggests lack of originality: *She wrote a conventional note of sympathy.*

form|al|de|hyde or **form|al|de|hyd** (fôr mal'də hīd), *n.* a colorless gas with a sharp, irritating odor. It is used in water solution to disinfect and to preserve. *Formula:* CH_2O [< *form*(ic acid) + *aldehyde*]

formal fallacy, *Logic.* an argument in which the statements used as evidence fail to justify or support the conclusion; an illogical argument; paralogism. *Example:* If some students in a class are good at geometry and some students are handsome, it does not necessarily follow that some students good at geometry are handsome.

for|ma|lin (fôr'mə lin), *n.* a solution of formaldehyde in water.

for|mal|ise (fôr'mə līz), *v.t., v.i.,* **-ised, -is|ing.** *Especially British.* formalize.

for|mal|ism (fôr'mə liz əm), *n.* 1 strict observance of outward forms, as in art, literature, and religion: *Formalism is the hallmark of the national culture* (H. L. Mencken). 2 = Gestalt psychology.

for|mal|ist (fôr'mə list), *n., adj.* —*n.* a person inclined to formalism.
—*adj.* = formalistic.

for|mal|is|tic (fôr'mə lis'tik), *adj.* of formalism or formalists; inclined to formalism: *a formalistic approach to the study of language.* —**for'mal|is'ti|cal|ly**, *adv.*

for|mal|i|ty (fôr mal'ə tē), *n., pl.* **-ties.** 1 a procedure required by custom or rule; outward form; ceremony: *At a wedding there are many formalities.* SYN: ritual. 2 something done for the sake of form; something required by etiquette or custom. SYN: conventionality. 3 strict attention to forms and customs: *Visitors at the court of a king are received with formality.* 4 stiffness of manner, behavior, or arrangement: *The formality of the party made her shy.*

for|mal|ize (fôr'mə līz), *v.,* **-ized, -iz|ing.** —*v.t.* 1 to make formal. 2 to give a definite form to: *He began to formalize his ideas on architecture into definite designs.* 3 to raise careful objections to.
—*v.i.* to be formal; act with formality. —**for'mal|iz|a|ble**, *adj.* —**for'mal|i|za'tion**, *n.*

for|mal|iz|er (fôr'mə lī'zər), *n.* 1 a person who formalizes. 2 = formalist.

formal logic, the branch of logic that studies the structure of propositions and of deductive reasoning. Formal logic deals only with the logical form of propositions, not their content.

formal theory, an aesthetic theory which holds that a thing is beautiful if it has a well-knit internal unity, an orderly arrangement of parts, and a capacity for manifesting its pattern.

form|am|ide (fôr'mə mīd), *n.* a colorless, oily liquid, the amide of formic acid, used as a solvent: *Formamide is the only molecule found in interstellar clouds which contains atoms of hydrogen, carbon, nitrogen and oxygen, a fact of importance for pre-biological chemistry* (New Scientist). *Formula:* $HCONH_2$ [< *form*(ic acid) + *amide*]

for|mant (fôr'mənt), *n. Phonetics.* the characteristic pitch of a vowel sound: *The front vowels with their high acoustic formants are associated with smaller magnitudes than the back vowels with their lower formants* (Roger Brown). [< German *Formant* < Latin *formāns, -antis,* present participle of *formāre* to form]

for|mat (fôr'mat), *n., v.,* **-mat|ted, -mat|ting.** —*n.* 1 the shape, size, binding, type face, and general arrangement of a book, magazine, or other printed matter: *She established a new paper in 1940 out in Nassau County, choosing big-city tabloid format* (New York Times). 2 the design, plan, or arrangement of anything: *the format of a television show.*
—*v.t.* to lay out or specify the style or format of: *The signal processor formats the position data for readout in a manner similar to the technique used in the automatic position-determination system for Omega* [*a satellite navigation system*] (Eugene Ehrlich).
[< French *format* < Latin (*liber*) *formātus* (book) formed (in a special way), past participle of *formāre* to form < *forma* form]

for|mate (fôr'māt), *n.* a salt or ester of formic acid.

for|ma|tion (fôr mā'shən), *n.* 1 the act or process of forming, making, or shaping (something): *Heat causes the formation of steam from water.* SYN: production. 2 the condition of being formed. 3 the way in which a thing is formed; arrangement; order: *Football players line up in various formations for their plays. The logical formation of his ideas made him a clear lecturer.* SYN: structure. 4 the thing formed: *Clouds are formations of tiny drops of water in the sky.* 5 an assembling or arrangement of troops in a certain way: *battle* formation. *The soldiers marched in perfect parade formation.* 6 *Geology.* a series of layers or deposits of the same kind of rock or mineral: *the siliceous formation around a geyser.*

for|ma|tion|al (fôr mā′shə nəl), *adj.* of or having to do with formation or formations.

form|a|tive (fôr′mə tiv), *adj., n.* —***adj.*** **1** having to do with formation or development; forming; molding: *Home and school are the chief formative influences in a child's life.* **2** *Grammar.* used to form words. Words are often made from other words by adding formative endings, such as *-ly* and *-ness.* **3** *Biology.* that can produce new cells or tissues: *formative tissue, formative yolk.*
—***n.*** *Grammar.* **1** a formative element of a word. **2** a word formed by adding a formative element. —**form′a|tive|ly**, *adv.* —**form′a|tive|ness**, *n.*

formative element, *Grammar.* an element, such as a prefix or suffix, that is used to form words; morpheme. Words are made from other words by adding suffixes, such as *-ly* and *-ness,* or prefixes, such as *pre-* and *com-.*

form book, *British.* a book which records the performances of a race horse, issued yearly.

form class, *Linguistics.* a class of words or other forms in a language which share some grammatical feature, such as all nouns, or all plural feminine nouns, or all third person singular verbs.

form criticism, a method of analyzing the Bible, especially the New Testament, in terms of the homilies, parables, elegies, and other literary forms used by compilers of the original texts.

forme (fôrm), *n. British Printing.* form.

for|mé or **for|mée** (fôr′mā), *adj. Heraldry.* (of a cross) narrow in the center and broad at the ends. See the diagram under **cross**. [< French *formé,* past participle of *former* to form]

for|mer¹ (fôr′mər), *adj.* **1** the first mentioned of two: *When she is offered ice cream or pie, she always chooses the former because she likes ice cream better.* **2** earlier; past; long past: *In former times, cooking was done in fireplaces instead of stoves.* SYN: bygone. **3** *Obsolete.* forward; foremost. [Middle English *formere,* a comparative patterned on *formost* foremost]

form|er² (fôr′mər), *n.* **1** a person or thing that forms. **2** *British.* a student who is in a certain grade at school: *a sixth former.* [< *form* + *-er*¹]

for|mer|ly (fôr′mər lē), *adv.* in the past; some time ago: *Our teacher formerly taught at a different school.* SYN: previously, once.

form factor, (in forestry) the proportion which exists between the volume of a tree and the volume of a regularly shaped body, such as a cylinder, which has the same base and height as the tree.

form-fit|ting (fôrm′fit′ing), *adj.* fitting closely the body's contour; close-fitting: *a form-fitting dress.*

form|ful (fôrm′fəl), *adj.* **1** showing good performing style; excelling in form: *The average U.S. skier has already become more able and more formful than his European counterpart* (Newsweek). **2** shapely: *formful statues.*

form genus, *Biology.* a group of animals or plants with no clear genetic relationship but classed together as a genus because they show similarities of form or structure.

for|mic (fôr′mik), *adj.* of or derived from ants; having to do with ants. [< Latin *formīca* ant]

For|mi|ca (fôr mī′kə), *n. Trademark.* a laminated plastic covering resistant to water, heat, and most chemicals, much used on kitchen and bathroom surfaces, tables, and other furniture. **1 formica,** any similar plastic covering. [< Latin *formīca* ant (because of the hard exoskeleton)]

formic acid, (fôr′mik), a colorless, pungent liquid that is irritating to the skin. It occurs in ants, bees, wasps, spiders, and nettles, and is now made synthetically for use as a reagent, especially in dyeing and finishing textiles. *Formula:* CH_2O_2 [< Latin *formīca* ant (because it was first obtained from red ants)]

for|mi|car|y (fôr′mə ker′ē), *n., pl.* **-car|ies.** an ants' nest. [< Medieval Latin *formicarium,* neuter < Latin *formīca* ant]

for|mi|cate (fôr′mə kāt), *v.i.,* **-cat|ed, -cat|ing.** **1** to crawl like ants. **2** to swarm with moving beings. [< Latin *formīcāre* (with English *-ate*¹) crawl like (or, as with) ants < *formīca* ant]

for|mi|ca|tion (fôr′mə kā′shən), *n.* **1** the act or process of formicating. **2** an abnormal sensation, as of ants creeping over the skin.

for|mi|cide (fôr′mə sīd), *n.* a substance that kills ants. [< Latin *formīca* ant + English *-cide*¹]

for|mi|da|bil|i|ty (fôr′mə də bil′ə tē), *n.* formidable quality; formidableness.

for|mi|da|ble (fôr′mə də bəl, fôr mid′ə-), *adj.* hard to overcome; hard to deal with; to be dreaded: *a formidable opponent. A long examination is more formidable than a short test.* [< Latin *formīdābilis* < *formīdāre* dread < *formīdō* terror, dread] —**for′mi|da|ble|ness**, *n.*

for|mi|da|bly (fôr′mə də blē), *adv.* in a formidable manner.

form|ing tool (fôr′ming), a shaped cutter or similar tool used in a lathe or other machine to give a special shape to a piece of work.

form|less (fôrm′lis), *adj.* without definite or regular form; shapeless: *Marlowe's play is formless, lacking in characterization and emotion* (Newsweek). SYN: amorphous. —**form′less|ly**, *adv.* —**form′less|ness**, *n.*

form letter, a letter copied from a pattern so that copies may be made easily and sent to many different people; circular letter.

form master, *British.* a teacher in charge of a form.

for|mol (fôr′mōl, -mol) *n.* a solution of formaldehyde, used as an antiseptic.

For|mo|san (fôr mō′sən), *adj., n.* —***adj.*** of or having to do with Formosa.
—***n.*** a person born or living in Formosa.

form sheet, **1** a publication giving the horses entered in a day's races, with jockeys, records of past performance, weights carried, and other information; racing form. **2** a detailed record of the participants in any contest.

***for|mu|la** (fôr′myə lə), *n., pl.* **-las** or **-lae.** **1** a set form of words, especially one which by much use has partly lost its meaning: *"How do you do?" is a polite formula.* **2** a statement of religious belief or doctrine: *The Apostles' Creed is a formula of Christian faith.* **3** *Figurative.* a rule or method for doing something, especially when followed slavishly, unintelligently, or mechanically: *The basic formula was: boy meets girl, boy loses girl, boy gets girl* (Russell Baker). **4** a recipe or prescription: *a formula for making soap.* **5** a mixture, especially of milk, water, and sugar prepared for feeding an infant, made according to a recipe or prescription: *He must prepare the baby's formula . . . which goes into the bottle and which no American mother would alter without the doctor's sanction* (Harper's). **6** *Chemistry.* an expression showing by symbols and figures the composition of a compound: *The formula for water is H_2O.* An empirical formula indicates the kind of atoms in each molecule and their proportions. *Example:* methanol or methyl alcohol, CH_4O. A structural formula, in addition to this, shows the interrelationships of the atoms. *Example:* CH_3OH or
H
HC-OH. **7** an expression showing by algebraic
H
symbols a rule, principle, etc.: *$(a + b)^2 = a^2 + 2ab + b^2$ is an algebraic formula.* **8** a clearly formulated concept, plan, or method: *a formula for settling a strike.* **9** the mechanical specifications of a racing car, especially the capacity of the engine: *the Grand Prix formula.* [< Latin *formula* (literally, diminutive) < *forma* form]

definition 6
H_2O — empirical   H—O—H — structural

***formula** definitions 6, 7
definition 7
$(a + b)^2 = a^2 + 2ab + b^2$ — mathematical

for|mu|lae (for′myə lē), *n.* a plural of **formula**.

for|mu|la|ic (fôr′myə lā′ik), *adj.* based on or consisting of formulas; formulistic. —**for′mu|la′i|cal|ly**, *adv.*

Formula One or **Formula I**, a racing car with a single seat, open cockpit, and exposed wheels, powered by an engine of from 1,500 to 3,000 cubic centimeters displacement.

for|mu|lar (fôr′myə lər), *adj.* of or having to do with a formula.

for|mu|lar|i|za|tion (fôr′myə lər ə zā′shən), *n.* a formularizing or formulating.

for|mu|lar|ize (fôr′myə lə rīz), *v.t.,* **-ized, -iz|ing.** **1** = formulate. **2** to make flat or stereotyped by reducing too much to a formula.

for|mu|lar|y (fôr′myə ler′ē), *n., pl.* **-lar|ies,** *adj.* —***n.*** **1** a collection of formulas. **2** a set form of words; formula. **3** *Pharmacy.* a book of formulas for standard preparations used in medicines.
—***adj.*** having to do with formulas.

for|mu|late (fôr′myə lāt), *v.t.,* **-lat|ed, -lat|ing.** **1** to state definitely or systematically: *Our country formulates its laws according to its constitution. A church may formulate its doctrines in a creed.* **2** to express in a formula; reduce to a formula. —**for′mu|la′ter**, *n.*

for|mu|la|tion (fôr′myə lā′shən), *n.* **1** a definite expression or statement: *After conceiving the theory, he spent weeks on its formulation.* **2** an expression in a formula.

for|mu|la|tive (fôr′myə lā′tiv), *adj.* of or having to do with formulation; formulating.

for|mu|la|tor (fôr′myə lā′tər), *n.* a person who formulates: *Many of the President's advisors are formulators of national policy.*

for|mu|lise (fôr′myə līz), *v.t.,* **-lised, -lis|ing.** *Especially British.* formulize.

for|mu|lism (fôr′myə liz əm), *n.* **1** adherence to or dependence upon formulas. **2** a system of formulas.

for|mu|list (fôr′myə list), *n.* a person inclined to formulism.

for|mu|lis|tic (fôr′myə lis′tik), *adj.* of or having to do with formulas; fond of formulas.

for|mu|lize (fôr′myə līz), *v.t.,* **-lized, -liz|ing.** = formulate. —**for′mu|li|za′tion**, *n.*

for|mu|liz|er (fôr′myə lī′zər), *n.* a person or thing that constructs formulas.

form word, *Linguistics.* = function word.

form|work (fôrm′wėrk′), *n.* a form or mold used in construction.

for|myl (fôr′məl), *n.* the univalent radical occurring in formic acid and formaldehyde. *Formula:* CHO- [< *form*(ic acid) + *-yl*]

For|na|cis (fôr nā′sis), *n.* genitive of **Fornax**.

For|nax (fôr′naks), *n., genitive* **For|na|cis.** *Astronomy.* a southern constellation near Eridanus. [< Latin *fornax* furnace]

for|nent (fər nent′), *prep. Scottish.* **1** opposite to; facing. **2** in the direction of. **3** with regard to. [< *for*(e) + (a)*nent*]

for|ni|cal (fôr′nə kəl), *adj.* of or having to do with a fornix.

for|ni|cate¹ (fôr′nə kāt), *v.i.,* **-cat|ed, -cat|ing.** to commit fornication. [< Latin *fornicārī* (with English *-ate*¹) < *fornix, -icis* brothel; (originally) arch, vault (because brothels were often situated in underground vaults)]

for|ni|cate² (fôr′nə kit), *adj.* arched; vaulted. [< Latin *fornicātus* < *fornix, -icis* arch]

for|ni|ca|tion (fôr′nə kā′shən), *n.* **1** voluntary sexual intercourse between unmarried persons. **2** in the Bible: **a** adultery. **b** *Figurative.* idolatry.

for|ni|ca|tor (fôr′nə kā′tər), *n.* a person who commits fornication.

for|ni|ca|to|ry (fôr′nə kə tôr′ē, -tōr′-), *adj.* having to do with or characterized by fornication.

for|nix (fôr′niks), *n., pl.* **-ni|ces** (-nə sēz). *Anatomy.* any one of several structures resembling an arch, such as the arched formation of fibers connecting the two cerebral hemispheres of the brain. [< Latin *fornix* arch, vaulted place]

for-prof|it (fər prof′it), *adj. U.S.* organized or existing to make profit; profit-making: *By . . . direct competition the for-profit chains have driven many nonprofit hospitals also to combine into chains* (Scientific American).

for|rad|er or **for|rard|er** (fôr′ə dər), *adj. British Informal.* more forward; further ahead: *to get no forrader.* [alteration of *forwarder,* comparative of *forward*]

for|rit (fôr′it, for′-), *adv. Scottish.* forward.

for|sake (fôr sāk′), *v.t.,* **-sook, -sak|en, -sak|ing.** to give up; leave alone; leave; abandon: *At fourteen he ran away, forsaking his home and friends.* SYN: renounce. See syn. under **desert²**. [Old English *forsacan* < *for-* for- + *sacan* dispute, deny] —**for|sak′er**, *n.*

for|sak|en (fôr sā′kən), *v., adj.* **a** past participle of **forsake**: *She has forsaken her old friends.* —***adj.*** deserted; abandoned; forlorn: *We found an old forsaken graveyard out in the country.* —**for|sak′en|ly**, *adv.*

for|see|a|ble (fôr sē′ə bəl, fōr-), *adj.* = foreseeable.

for|sook (fôr sůk′), *v.* past tense of **forsake**: *He forsook his family.*

for|sooth (fôr süth′), *adv. Archaic.* in truth; indeed. [Old English *forsōth, for sōth* < *for* for + *sōth* truth, sooth]

for|speak (fôr spēk′), *v.t.,* **-spoke, -spo|ken** or **-spoke, -speak|ing.** *Scottish.* to bewitch.

for|spend (fôr spend′), *v.t.,* **-spent, -spend|ing.** to wear out or exhaust (rare except for the past participle): *Into the woods my Master came Forspent with love and shame* (Sidney Lanier).

for|spoke (fôr spōk′), *v.* past tense and a past participle of **forspeak**.

for|spo|ken (fôr spō′kən), *v.* a past participle of **forspeak**.

For|ster's tern (fôrs′tərz), a white tern with a grayish mantle, deeply forked tail, and silvery wing tips, which nests in marshes of western North America and along the coast of the southeastern United States. [< Johann R. *Forster,* 1729-1798, a German naturalist]

for|swear (fôr swār′), *v.,* **-swore, -sworn, -swear|ing.** —***v.t.*** **1** to swear solemnly to give up; renounce on oath: *The coach asked the team to forswear smoking.* **2** to deny solemnly or on oath. **3** to perjure (oneself); swear (something) falsely; break (an oath): *purest faith unhappily forsworn* (Shakespeare).
—***v.i.*** to be untrue to one's sworn word or promise; swear falsely; commit perjury. [Old English *forswerian*] —**for|swear′er**, *n.*

for|swore (fôr swôr′, -swōr′), *v.* past tense of **forswear**: *The team forswore smoking.*

for|sworn (fôr swôrn′, -swōrn′), *adj., v.* —***adj.*** untrue to one's sworn word or promise; perjured.

—*v.* the past participle of **forswear**: *He has forsworn his bad habits.*

for|syth|i|a (fôr sith′ē ə, -sī′thē-), *n.* **1** a shrub having many bell-shaped, yellow flowers in early spring before its leaves come out; golden bell. It belongs to the olive family. See picture under **olive family**. **2** its flower.
[American English < New Latin *Forsythia* the genus name < William *Forsyth,* 1737-1804, a Scottish horticulturist]

fort (fôrt, fōrt), *n., v.* —*n.* **1** a strong building or place that can be defended against an enemy; fortified place; fortress. SYN: fortification, stronghold. **2** a permanent U.S. Army post: *Fort Benning, Georgia, is the site of the United States Army Infantry Center, and Fort Bragg, North Carolina, is the home of airborne combat units.* **3** (in North America) a frontier trading post.
—*v.t.* to fortify; enclose in a fort.
hold the fort, a to make a defense: *The ambushed party held the fort desperately till reinforcements arrived.* **b** to carry on: *Our colleagues . . . having had their holidays earlier in the year, were holding the fort in our absence* (London Times).
[< French *fort,* noun use of Old French, adjective < Latin *fortis* strong] —**fort′like′**, *adj.*

fort., **1** fortification. **2** fortified.

for|ta|lice (fôr′tə lis), *n.* **1** a small fort; outwork. **2** *Obsolete.* a fortress. [< Old French *fortelesse* (< *fort* strong) or < Medieval Latin *fortalitia* < Latin *fortis* strong. See etym. of doublet **fortress**.]

forte¹ (fôrt, fōrt; *also* fôr′tā *for 1*), *n.* **1** something a person does very well; strong point: *Playing the piano is her forte.* **2** the stronger part of the blade of a sword, between the middle and the hilt. [earlier *fort* < French *fort* strong (see etym. under **fort**); later a feminine *-e* was added on the analogy of *locale, morale*]

***for|te²** (fôr′tā), *adj., adv., n. Music.* —*adj.* loud; strong.
—*adv.* loudly; strongly.
—*n.* a passage or tone played loudly or strongly. *Abbr:* f (no period).
[< Italian *forte* strong < Latin *fortis*]

***forte²**

for|te-pi|a|no (fôr′tā pē ä′nō), *adj., adv., n. Music.* —*adj.* suddenly and briefly loud, then immediately soft.
—*adv.* loudly, then softly (used as a direction).
—*n. Archaic.* a pianoforte.

forth (fôrth, fōrth), *adv., prep.* —*adv.* **1** forward; onward: *From that day forth he lived alone.* **2** into view or consideration; out: *The sun came forth from behind the clouds.* **3** away: *Go forth and seek your fortune.* **4** *Obsolete.* abroad.
—*prep. Archaic.* away from; out of: *Steal forth thy father's house to-morrow night* (Shakespeare).
and so forth, and so on; and the like: *We ate cake, candy, nuts, and so forth. The anthology contains poems by Chaucer, Shakespeare, Pope, Byron, Shelley, Keats, and so forth.*
[Old English *forth*]

FORTH or **Forth** (fôrth, fōrth), *n.* a computer language that uses common English words, used especially for computer games and real-time applications involving control of machinery.

forth|com|ing (fôrth′kum′ing, fōrth′-), *adj., n.* —*adj.* **1** about to appear; approaching: *The forthcoming week will be busy.* **2** coming forth; ready when wanted: *She needed help, but none was forthcoming.* SYN: available. **3** ready to meet or make advances; accommodating: *They can afford to be forthcoming or coy just as his attitude warrants* (Manchester Guardian).
—*n.* appearance; approach.

forth|go|ing (fôrth′gō′ing, fōrth′-), *n., adj.* —*n.* a going forth; a proceeding from or out.
—*adj.* **1** that goes forth. **2** disposed to make advances; friendly; outgoing.

forth|put|ting (fôrth′pu̇t′ing, fōrth′-), *adj. U.S.* **1** that puts forth. **2** putting oneself forward; presumptuous; meddlesome.

forth|right (*adj., n.* fôrth′rīt′, fōrth′-; *adv. also* fôrth′rīt′, fōrth′-), *adj., adv., n.* —*adj.* **1** frank and outspoken; straightforward; direct: *The speaker did not like the plan and made forthright objections to it.* SYN: unswerving. **2** proceeding in a straight course.
—*adv.* **1** straight ahead; directly forward. **2** at once; immediately: *No more he spake, But thitherward forthright his ready way did make* (Edmund Spenser). SYN: straightway.
—*n.* a straight course or path. —**forth′right′ly**, *adv.* —**forth′right′ness**, *n.*

forth|with (fôrth′with′, -wiᵺ′; fōrth′-), *adv.* at once; without delay; immediately: *The judge's summons ordered the witness to appear forthwith in court.* SYN: instantly.

for|ti|eth (fôr′tē ith), *adj., n.* **1** next after the 39th; last in a series of 40. **2** one, or being one, of 40 equal parts.

for|ti|fi|a|ble (fôr′tə fī′ə bəl), *adj.* that can be fortified.

for|ti|fi|ca|tion (fôr′tə fə kā′shən), *n.* **1** the act of making strong; process of adding strength to; fortifying: *The general was responsible for the fortification of the town.* **2** a wall, fort, ditch, or other defense built to make a place strong. **3** a place made strong by building walls, forts, ditches, or other defenses. SYN: stronghold, citadel. **4** the art or science of building military defenses. **5** the enriching of foods with vitamins and minerals.

for|ti|fied wine (fôr′tə fīd), any wine to which an alcoholic liquor, usually brandy, is added for strength. Many dessert wines, such as port and Madeira, are fortified wines.

for|ti|fi|er (fôr′tə fī′ər), *n.* a person or thing that fortifies: *Low-income households must rely on food fortifiers—say flour, wheat germ, etc.* (New York Times).

for|ti|fy (fôr′tə fī), *v.,* **-fied, -fy|ing.** —*v.t.* **1** to protect (a place) against attack; strengthen against attack; provide with forts, walls, ditches, or other defenses: *The soldiers fortified their position on the hill by building earthworks and erecting log walls.* **2** to give support to; strengthen: *They fortified each other against the coming ordeal.* **3** to enrich with vitamins and minerals: *to fortify bread.* **4** to strengthen (a wine) with alcohol.
—*v.i.* to build forts, walls, ditches, or other defenses; protect a place against attack.
[< Middle French *fortifier,* learned borrowing from Late Latin *fortificāre* < Latin *fortis* strong + *facere* make]

for|tis (fôr′tis), *adj., n. Phonetics.* —*adj.* uttered with muscular tension and force.
—*n.* a fortis consonant.
[< Latin *fortis* strong]

For|ti|san (fôr′tə san), *n. Trademark.* a sturdy synthetic acetate fiber used for draperies, upholstery, and other purposes. [probably < Latin *fortis* strong]

***for|tis|si|mo** (fôr tis′ə mō), *adj., adv., n., pl.* **-mos, -mi** (-mē). *Music.* —*adj.* very loud (used as a direction).
—*adv.* very loudly.
—*n.* a very loud passage or movement: *from lucid fortissimos to a sort of dry, understated pianissimo* (New Yorker). *Abbr:* ff (no periods), ff.
[< Italian *fortissimo,* superlative of *forte* strong < Latin *fortis*]

***fortissimo**

for|ti|tude (fôr′tə tüd, -tyüd), *n.* **1** courage in facing pain, danger, or trouble; firmness of spirit: *She could bear the disappointments of other people with tolerable fortitude* (Dickens). *Adamantine fortitude, which sustained without flinching a mountain of responsibility* (John Lothrop Motley). SYN: endurance, bravery, resolution. See syn. under **patience**. **2** *Obsolete.* physical strength. [< Latin *fortitūdō* < *fortis* strong]

for|ti|tu|di|nous (fôr′tə tü′də nəs, -tyü′-), having or characterized by fortitude.

fort|night (fôrt′nīt, -nit), *n.* two weeks: *A new administration . . . will take control at Washington in less than a fortnight's time* (Saturday Review). [Middle English *fourtenight,* contraction of Old English *fēowertīene niht* fourteen nights]

fort|night|ly (fôrt′nīt lē), *adv., adj., n., pl.* **-lies.**
—*adv.* once in every two weeks.
—*adj.* appearing or happening once in every two weeks: *The establishment of a new Cominform fortnightly journal is reported* (Observer).
—*n.* a magazine published every two weeks.

FORTRAN or **For|tran** (fôr′tran), *n.* a computer language using algebraic notation for programming a computer, especially one involved in scientific and algebraic computations: *A computer is no better than the software that controls its operation. The BESM-6 can be programmed in Fortran and Algol, the two universal languages for scientific computer work* (Scientific American).
[< *For*(mula) *tran*(slation)]

for|tress (fôr′tris), *n., v.* —*n.* a place built with walls and defenses; large fort or fortification. SYN: citadel.
—*v.t.* to provide or protect with a fortress; fortify.
[< Old French *forteresse,* variant of *fortelesse* < *fort* strong; see etym. under **fort**. See etym. of doublet **fortalice**.] —**for′tress|like′**, *adj.*

for|tu|i|tism (fôr tü′ə tiz əm, -tyü′-), *n. Philosophy.* the doctrine or belief that adaptations in nature occur by chance, and not by design or plan.

for|tu|i|tous (fôr tü′ə təs, -tyü′-), *adj.* happening by chance; accidental: *a fortuitous meeting, a fortuitous acquaintance. The fortuitous falling of an apple led Newton to formulate the law of gravitation.* SYN: casual.
[< Latin *fortuītus* (with English *-ous*) < *fortē* by chance < *fors, fortis* chance] —**for|tu′i|tous|ly**, *adv.* —**for|tu′i|tous|ness**, *n.*

for|tu|i|ty (fôr tü′ə tē, -tyü′-), *n., pl.* **-ties. 1** the fact or condition of being accidental; accidental character. **2** chance; accident: *Fortuity brought the sisters together.*

For|tu|na (fôr tü′nə, -tyü′-), *n. Roman Mythology.* the goddess of chance, fortune, or luck, identified with the Greek goddess Tyche.

for|tu|nate (fôr′chə nit), *adj.* **1** having good luck; lucky: *You are fortunate in having such a fine family.* **2** bringing good luck; having favorable results: *a fortunate occurrence.* [< Latin *fortūnātus,* past participle of *fortūnāre* give (good) fortune to < *fortūna* fortune] —**for′tu|nate|ly**, *adv.* —**for′tu|nate|ness**, *n.*
—*Syn.* **1, 2 Fortunate, lucky** mean having or bringing good luck. **Fortunate** suggests being favored by circumstances rather than mere chance: *He made a fortunate decision when he went into advertising.* **Lucky**, less formal, suggests the idea of pure chance or accident: *He is lucky that he missed his train the day it was wrecked.*

Fortunate Islands, = Islands of the Blessed.

for|tune (fôr′chən), *n., v.,* **-tuned, -tun|ing.** —*n.* **1** a great deal of money or property; riches; wealth: *He made a fortune in oil.* **2** what happens; luck; chance: *Fortune was against us; we lost. . . . the vicissitudes of fortune which spares neither man nor the proudest of his works* (Edward Gibbon). **3** good luck; success; prosperity: *May fortune attend you!* **4** what is going to happen to a person; fate: *Gypsies often claim that they can tell people's fortunes.* SYN: destiny, lot. **5** position in life as determined by wealth; standing: *A youth to fortune and to fame unknown* (Thomas Gray). **6** *Archaic.* a woman of fortune; heiress: *He is secretly married to a great fortune* (Sir Richard Steele).
—*v.t.* to provide with a fortune.
—*v.i. Archaic.* to happen by chance.
[< Old French *fortune,* learned borrowing from Latin *fortūna* < *fors, fortis* chance]

For|tune (fôr′chən), *n.* the personification of chance, usually regarded as a goddess who distributes good and bad luck to people without plan: *I care not, Fortune, what you me deny* (James Thomson).

fortune cookie, a cookie served in Chinese restaurants containing a piece of paper on which is written a fortune or other message.

fortune hunter, **1** a person who tries to get a fortune by marrying someone rich. **2** anybody who seeks wealth.

for|tune-hunt|ing (fôr′chən hun′ting), *n., adj.* trying to get a fortune by marrying someone rich.

for|tune|tell|er (fôr′chən tel′ər), *n.* a person who claims to be able to tell what will happen to people. SYN: soothsayer.

for|tune|tell|ing (fôr′chən tel′ing), *n., adj.* telling or claiming to tell what will happen in the future.

for|ty (fôr′tē), *n., pl.* **-ties**, *adj.* four times ten; 40. [Old English *fēowertig*]

for|ty-eight|mo (fôr′tē āt′mō), *n., pl.* **-mos**, *adj.* —*n.* **1** a size of a book, or of its pages, made by folding a sheet of paper forty-eight times to form leaves about 2½ × 4 inches. *Abbr:* 48mo or 48°. **2** a book having pages of this size.
—*adj.* of this size; having pages of this size.
[< *forty-eight* + *-mo,* as in *decimo*]

for|ty-five (fôr′tē fīv′), *n.* **1** a .45 caliber revolver or automatic pistol. **2** a phonograph record which revolves at 45 revolutions per minute.

for|ty|ish (fôr′tē ish), *adj.* about forty years of age; looking forty years old.

For|ty-Nin|ers or **for|ty-nin|ers** (fôr′tē nī′nərz), *n.pl.* the people who went to California in 1849 to seek gold during the gold rush that had started there in 1848.

forty winks, *Informal.* a short nap.

fo|rum (fôr′əm, fōr′-), *n., pl.* **-rums** or **-ra. 1** the public square or market place of an ancient Roman city. There business was done and courts and public assemblies were held. **2** *Figurative.* an assembly for discussing questions of public interest: *An open forum was held last Tuesday eve-*

ning. **3** *Figurative.* a law court; tribunal. [< Latin *forum*]

for|ward (fôr′wərd), *adv., adj., v., n.* **—*adv.*** **1** onward; ahead: *Forward march! From this time forward, do your homework every night.* **2** to the front: *Come forward.* **3** in consideration; out: *In his talk, he brought forward several new ideas.*
—*adj.* **1** to the front: *the forward part of a ship.* **2** far ahead; advanced: *A child of four years that can read is forward for his age.* SYN: precocious. **3** ready; eager: *He knew his lesson and was forward with his answers. I killed a seafowl or two . . . but was not very forward to eat them* (Daniel Defoe). SYN: prompt. **4** *Figurative.* impudent; bold: *Don't be so forward as to interrupt the speaker. Your cousin Sophy is a forward, impertinent gipsy* (Richard Brinsley Sheridan). SYN: pert, impertinent, presumptuous. See syn. under **bold**. **5** directed ahead; onward: *a forward movement.* **6** having to do with the future; prospective: *Most cotton mills don't expect much additional forward buying until the goods ordered . . . are used up* (Wall Street Journal). **7** *Figurative.* radical; extreme: *a forward view of politics.*
—*v.t.* **1** to help on: *He tried to forward his friend's plan.* SYN: promote, advance. **2** to send on farther: *Please forward my mail to my new address.* **3** *Bookbinding.* to prepare (a book) for the finisher, especially by fitting it with back and covers.
—*n.* a player whose position is in the front line in team games such as basketball, hockey, or soccer: *The forwards play near the basket their team is attacking, so they can maneuver into good positions for shooting and rebounding* (A. W. Haarlow).
[Old English *foreweard*]
—*Syn.* *adv.* **1 Forward, onward** mean toward the front or a point ahead. **Forward** suggests looking or moving toward what lies ahead, or in the future: *We must look forward, not backward.* **Onward**, often interchangeable with *forward,* suggests moving or progressing toward a definite point, place, or goal: *The boat sailed onward toward the shore.*

for|ward|er (fôr′wər dər), *n.* **1** a person or thing that forwards. **2** a person who accepts goods for transportation and turns them over on behalf of their owner to a carrier.

for|ward|ing (fôr′wər ding), *n. Bookbinding.* fitting a book with back and covers and preparing it for the finisher.

forwarding agent, a firm or individual that receives and ships goods for others for a fee.

for|ward-look|ing (fôr′wərd lu̇k′ing), *adj.* **1** anticipating or preparing for probable future developments; progressive: *a forward-looking educator or writer.* **2** foretelling; foreshowing: *a forward-looking indicator of future business conditions.*

for|ward|ly (fôr′wərd lē), *adv.* **1** readily; eagerly. SYN: promptly. **2** *Figurative.* pertly; boldly. SYN: presumptuously. **3** *U.S.* in a forward direction; toward the front.

for|ward|most (fôr′wərd mōst), *adj.* most to the front; foremost; nearest.

for|ward|ness (fôr′wərd nis), *n.* **1** the state of being far ahead. **2** readiness; eagerness. SYN: promptness, zeal. **3** *Figurative.* impudence; boldness; pertness.

forward pass, throwing a football to a player on the same team in the direction of the opponents' goal.

forward play, *Cricket.* a batting stroke with the bat set forward and away from the wicket.

for|wards (fôr′wərdz), *adv.* = forward.

forward scatter, the scattering of radio waves which pass into the troposphere or ionosphere by a combination of reflection, refraction, and diffraction. It tends to direct the waves forward and downward, thus enabling the transmission of radio waves over long distances.

for|went (fôr went′), *v.* past tense of **forgo**: *She forwent the movies in order to do her lessons.*

for|why (fôr hwī′), *adv., conj. Obsolete.* **—*adv.*** why; wherefore. **—*conj.*** because.

for|worn (fôr wôrn′, -wōrn′), *adj. Archaic.* worn out; exhausted. Also, **foreworn.**

for|zan|do (fôr tsän′dō), *adj.* = sforzando. [< Italian *forzando,* gerund of *forzare* to force < Vulgar Latin *fortiāre,* ultimately < Latin *fortis* strong]

for|za|to (fôr tsä′tō), *adj.* = sforzando.

Fos|bur|y flop (foz′bėr ē, -brē), a style of high jumping in which the jumper goes over the bar backwards and lands on his shoulders and back. [< Dick *Fosbury,* an American athlete, who introduced it at the 1968 Olympic Games]

FOS|DIC or **Fos|dic** (foz′dik), *n.* an electronic scanning device built by the United States Bureau of Standards to translate data into a digital computer. It is used in large-scale statistics, such as the census. [< *F*(ilm) *O*(ptical) *S*(ensing) *D*(evice for) *I*(nput to) *C*(omputers)]

fos|sa[1] (fos′ə), *n., pl.* **fos|sae** (fos′ē). *Anatomy.* a usually elongated shallow depression or cavity, especially in a bone. [< Latin *fossa* ditch, properly feminine of *fossus,* past participle of *fodere* to dig. See etym. of doublet **fosse**.]

fos|sa[2] (fos′ə), *n.* a slender, catlike carnivore of Madagascar that reaches an overall length of five feet; galet. It is the only species of its genus and appears to be a connecting link between the cats and the civets. [< New Latin *Fossa* the genus name < Malagasy *fossa* fossa]

fos|sage (fos′ij), *n.* (in old English law) a duty levied on the inhabitants of a fortified town for the purpose of cleaning the moat or ditch surrounding it. [< Medieval Latin *fossagium* < Latin *fossa* ditch]

fosse (fos), *n.* a ditch, trench, canal, or moat. [< Old French *fosse* < Latin *fossa* ditch. See etym. of doublet **fossa.**]

fos|sette (fo set′), *n.* a small hollow; depression; dimple. [< French *fossette* (diminutive) < *fosse* fosse]

fos|sick (fos′ik), *Australia.* **—*v.i.*** **1** *Mining.* **a** to search for gold by digging in crevices, washing places, abandoned workings, etc. **b** to take gold from someone else's claim. **2** *Figurative.* to search about; rummage.
—*v.t.* to dig; hunt.
[apparently < dialectal *fussick* or *fussock* to putter about < *fuss,* verb + *-ock*] **—fos′sick|er,** *n.*

fos|sil (fos′əl), *n., adj.* **—*n.*** **1** the hardened remains or traces of an animal or plant of a former age. Fossils of ferns are found in coal. **2** *Figurative.* a very old-fashioned person, set in his ways: *That lecturer is an old fossil—a century behind the times!* **3** *Obsolete.* any rock or mineral dug out of the earth.
—*adj.* **1** forming a fossil; of the nature of a fossil: *the fossil remains of a dinosaur.* **2** dug out of the earth: *fossil fuels.* **3** *Figurative.* belonging to the outworn past; very old-fashioned; not modern: *fossil ideas.* SYN: antiquated.
[< French *fossile* < Latin *fossilis* < *fodere* to dig]
—fos′sil|like′, *adj.*

fossil fuel, coal, oil, or natural gas.

fos|sil|if|er|ous (fos′ə lif′ər əs), *adj.* bearing or containing fossils.

fos|sil|ise (fos′ə līz), *v.t., v.i.,* **-ised, -is|ing.** *Especially British.* fossilize.

fossil ivory, ivory from the tusks of walruses or mammoths, preserved in good condition from prehistoric times in the ice of the north polar region.

fos|sil|ize (fos′ə līz), *v.,* **-ized, -iz|ing.** **—*v.t.*** **1** to make into a fossil. **2** *Figurative.* to make antiquated, set, stiff, or rigid: *His conventional training as a youth fossilized him.*
—*v.i.* **1** to change into a fossil; turn into stone: *Only the relatively few plants and animals that are covered by water or are in some other way protected from bacterial action can fossilize* (Fred W. Emerson). **2** *Figurative.* to become antiquated, set, stiff, or rigid. **3** *Informal.* to search for fossils.
—fos′sil|i|za′tion, *n.*

fossil radiation, the energy trapped by prehistoric plants from the sun and released when the coal formed from these plants is burned.

fossil water, water deposited underground in geological ages: *Fossil water . . . apparently accumulated during heavy rains associated with the last Ice Age* (Walter Sullivan). *Fossil water below the desert's surface can be pumped to relieve its aridity* (Scientific American).

fos|so|ri|al (fo sôr′ē əl, -sōr′-), *adj.* **1** digging or burrowing: *a fossorial animal.* **2** adapted for digging or burrowing: *the fossorial feet of a mole.* [< Latin *fossōrius* (< *fossor, -ōris* digger < *fodere* to dig) + English *-al*[1]]

fos|so|ri|ous (fo sôr′ē əs, -sōr′), *adj. Zoology.* fossorial.

fos|su|la (fos′yə lə), *n., pl.* **-lae** (-lē). **1** a small fossa. **2** a vacant space representing one of the primitive septa of certain corals.

fos|su|late (fos′yə lit), *adj. Zoology.* grooved; slightly excavated or hollowed out; having a small or shallow fossa.

foss|way (fos′wā′), *n.* one of the great Roman roads in England, built with a ditch on each side of the roadway.

fos|ter (fôs′tər, fos′-), *v., adj., n.* **—*v.t.*** **1** to help the growth or development of; encourage: *Our city fosters libraries, parks, and playgrounds.* SYN: promote, further. **2** to care for fondly; cherish: *to foster hope in an invalid. He gave them charge about the Queen, To guard and foster her forevermore* (Tennyson). SYN: See syn. under **cherish.** **3** to bring up; help to grow; make grow; rear. **4** *Obsolete.* to feed; nourish: *foster'd with cold dishes* (Shakespeare).
—*adj.* **1** in the same family, but not related by birth: *a foster daughter, foster siblings.* **2** of or for a foster child or foster children: *foster care.*
—*n. Archaic.* a foster parent.
[Old English *fōstrian* nourish < *fōstor* nourishment. See related etym. at **food.**]

fos|ter|age (fôs′tər ij, fos′-), *n.* **1** the act of bringing up another's child as one's own. **2** the state of being a foster child. **3** the custom of putting a child under the care of foster parents. **4** the act of encouraging or promoting.

foster brother, a boy brought up with another child or children of different parents.

foster child, a child brought up by persons who are not his parents.

foster daughter, a girl who is brought up as a daughter by a foster parent or parents.

fos|ter|er (fôs′tər ər, fos′-), *n.* **1** = foster parent. **2** a person or thing that encourages or promotes. **3** a patron; protector.

foster father, a man who brings up another person's child.

foster home, a home in which one or more foster children are placed or brought up.

fos|ter|ling (fôs′tər ling, fos′-), *n.* = foster child. [Old English *fōstorling* < *fōstor* nourishment + *-ling* -ling[1]]

foster mother, a woman who brings up another person's child.

foster parent, a person who brings up another person's child; foster father or foster mother.

foster sister, a girl brought up with another child or children of different parents.

foster son, a boy who is brought up as a son by a foster parent or parents.

foth|er (fo**th**′ər), *v.t.* **1** to cover (a sail) with oakum, rope yarn, or the like, for placing over and stopping a leak in a ship. **2** to stop (a leak) with a sail prepared in this way. [perhaps < Middle Dutch *voederen*]

fou[1] (fü), *adj. Scottish.* drunk. [variant of Scottish *fow* full[1]]

fou[2] (fü), *n., adj. French.* **—*n.*** a fool.
—*adj.* foolish.

***Fou|cault pendulum** (fü kō′), a pendulum used by Foucault in 1851 to demonstrate the earth rotates on its axis. The plane of its swing slowly wheeled, a phenomenon explained only by the earth's rotation. The deviation is clockwise north of the equator, counterclockwise south of it, the rate varying with latitude.

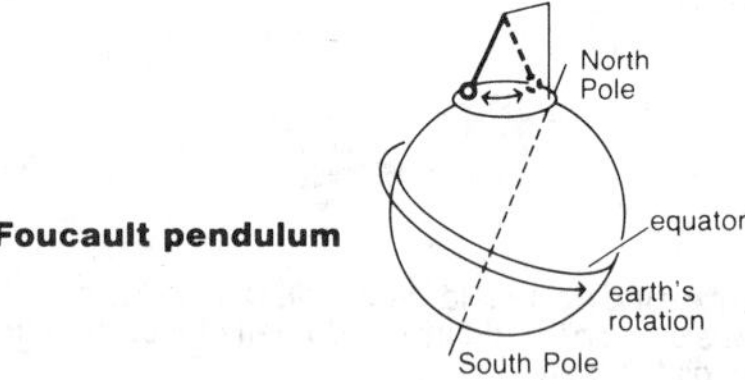

***Foucault pendulum**

foud (foud), *n.* a bailiff or magistrate in Orkney, Shetland, and the Faeroe Islands. [< Scandinavian (compare Old Icelandic *fōguti*)]

fou|droy|ant (fü droi′ənt), *adj.* **1** sudden and overwhelming; stunning; dazzling. SYN: flashing. **2** *Medicine.* beginning very suddenly and severely: *a foudroyant disease.* [< French *foudroyant,* present participle of *foudroyer* strike like lightning < Old French *fouldre* lightning < Late Latin *fulgere* to flash < Latin *fulgur* lightning]

fouet|té (fwe tā′), *n., v.,* **-téd, -té|ing.** **—*n.*** a snap turn in ballet in which one leg is thrown out to the side and then brought back with the foot bent in toward the knee of the other leg, while the other foot acts as a pivot, often done in a continuous movement.
—*v.i.* to perform a fouetté.
[< French *fouetté* (literally) a whipped step, past participle of *fouetter* to whip, beat]

fou|gasse (fü gas′), *n. Military.* a small mine resembling a well sunk in the ground. [< French *fougasse*]

fought (fôt), *v.* past tense and past participle of **fight:** *He fought bravely yesterday. A battle was fought there.*

fought|en (fô′tən), *v., adj.* **—*v.*** an archaic past participle of **fight.**
—*adj. Archaic.* that has been the scene of fighting: *a foughten field.*

foul (foul), *adj., v., n., adv.* **—*adj.*** **1** containing filth; covered with filth; very dirty, nasty, or smelly: *We opened the windows to let out the foul air.* SYN: soiled, polluted, unclean. See syn. under **dirty.** **2** very wicked; vile: *a victim of foul play. Murder is a foul crime.* SYN: abominable. **3** offending modesty or decency; obscene; profane: *foul language, a foul joke.* **4** against the rules; unfair: *a foul play, a foul stroke at billiards.* **5** hitting against: *One boat was foul of the other.* **6** tangled up; caught: *The sailor cut the foul rope.* **7** (of a ship) having the bottom covered with seaweed, barnacles, or other debris. **8** clogged up: *The fire will not burn because the chimney is foul.* **9** unfavorable; stormy: *Foul weather delayed the ship.* **10** contrary: *a foul*

wind. **11** *Informal.* very unpleasant or objectionable: *I had a foul time last evening.* **12** *Baseball.* of or having to do with the foul lines or foul balls. **13** *Printing.* having many mistakes or correction marks: *foul proofs.* **14** *Archaic.* ugly; unattractive. **15** *Obsolete.* disfigured: *My face is foul with weeping* (Job 16:16).
—***v.t.*** **1** to make dirty; soil; defile: *Mud fouls things.* **2** *Figurative.* to dishonor; disgrace: *a name fouled by misdeeds.* **3** to make a foul against: *The short guard fouled his tall opponent in trying to block a shot.* **4** *Baseball.* to hit (a ball) outside the foul lines: *He fouled the first three pitches.* **5** to hit against: *Their boat fouled ours.* **6** to get tangled up with; catch: *The rope they threw fouled the anchor chain.* **7** to clog up: *Grease fouled the drain.* **8** to cover (a ship's bottom) with seaweed, barnacles, or other debris.
—***v.i.*** **1** to become dirty; soil. **2** to make a foul: *The clumsy player fouls too much.* **3** *Baseball.* to hit a ball so that it falls outside the foul lines. **4** to get tangled up; catch: *The anchor fouled on the seaweed.* **5** to become clogged up.
—***n.*** **1** (in football, baseball, horse racing, and other sports) a thing done contrary to the rules; an unfair play: *However, a foul was claimed because in taking the lead in the stretch she swerved and bumped . . . Gandharva, who finished second* (New Yorker). **2** a baseball hit so that it falls outside the foul lines; foul ball. **3** a collision or entanglement.
—***adv.*** **1** *Baseball.* so that it is foul: *The line drive curved foul at the last minute.* **2** in a foul manner; foully; unfairly.
foul out, a *Baseball.* to be put out by hitting a ball that is caught on the fly outside the foul lines: *Given a green light to swing at the 3-0 pitch with two out and two on in the eighth of the curtain-raiser, [he] fouled out* (New York Times). **b** *Basketball.* to be removed from a game for committing too many fouls: *[He] got 19 points before fouling out with a little over a minute to go in the overtime session* (New York Times).
foul up, *U.S. Informal.* to make a mess of; bungle: *This first operation in Giron went smoothly enough, but at the beach and on the water nearby the invasion was fouled up* (Life).
run (go or **fall) foul of, a** to hit against and get tangled up with: *Two of the transports, in tacking, ran foul of each other* (George Anson). **b** *Figurative.* to get into trouble or difficulties with: *to run foul of the law. For they knew, as everyone who occasionally fell foul of him knew, that however hard he drove others he drove himself ten times harder still* (Manchester Guardian Weekly).
[Old English *fūl*] —**foul′ly,** *adv.* —**foul′ness,** *n.*

foul anchor, 1 an anchor that is entangled, especially with another anchor or a cable. **2a** an anchor with the slack of its cable twisted round its stock or one of its flukes. **b** a representation of such an anchor, used as a badge, insigne, colophon, or the like.

fou|lard (fü lärd′, fə-), *n.* **1** a soft, thin fabric made of silk, rayon, or cotton, usually with a printed pattern. It is used for neckties, dresses, scarfs, and handkerchiefs. **2** a necktie, scarf, or handkerchief made from this material. [<French *foulard* <Swiss French *foulat* cloth that has been cleansed and thickened <French *fouler* to full]

foul ball, *Baseball.* batted ball that lands outside the foul lines. A foul ball is counted as a strike unless the batter has two strikes against him.

foul|brood (foul′brüd′), *n.* a severe disease of larval bees, caused by a bacterium.

foul line, 1 *Baseball.* either one of two straight lines extending from home plate through first base and third base to the limits of the field. **2** *Basketball.* a line within the circle in front of each basket from which foul shots are made; free throw line. **3** a line or mark which may not be stepped on or over in bowling, in the broad jump, in throwing the javelin, and in other sports and games.

foul-mind|ed (foul′mīn′did), *adj.* foul or unclean in mind or thoughts.

foul-mouthed or **foul|mouthed** (foul′mouᵺd′, -moutht′), *adj.* using obscene, profane, or vile language.

foul play, 1 an unfair play; a thing or things done against the rules. **2** treachery or violence.

foul shot, *Basketball.* **1** an unhindered shot from the foul line awarded to a player or team after a foul by an opponent has been called; free throw. **2** one point scored by putting such a shot into the basket.

foul-spo|ken (foul′spō′kən), *adj.* = foul-mouthed.

foul tip, *Baseball.* a ball deflected by the bat directly back to the catcher, which if caught with two strikes on the batter is the third strike.

foul-tongued (foul′tungd′), *adj.* = foul-mouthed.

foul-up (foul′up′), *n. U.S. Informal.* a muddle or mess that seriously interferes with an operation or movement: *a shipping foul-up, a foul-up in diplomatic relations.*

fou|mart (fü′märt), *n.* the European polecat. [Middle English *fulmard* <Old English *fūl* foul + *mearth* marten]

found[1] (found), *v., adj., n.* **a** past tense and past participle of **find:** *We found the treasure. The lost child was found.* —***adj.*** **1** (of artistic works or materials) appropriated from nature or the environment; not fashioned by the artist but taken as found and adapted for artistic value or effect: *A branch of "found art," derelict sculptures are built . . . from driftwood, discarded tires, broken toys, beer cans, jugs and other rubbish* (Time). **2** *Especially British.* furnished; equipped: *Gipsy Moth IV is probably the best found yacht ever to undertake a voyage as testing as this* (London Times).
—***n.*** free board and room in exchange for services: *The agency has jobs for domestics willing to work for weekly wages and found.*

found[2] (found), *v.t.* **1** to set up; establish: *The Pilgrims founded a colony at Plymouth. John Wesley founded the Methodist Church.* SYN: settle, originate, create, initiate. **2** to rest for support; base: *He founded his claim on facts.* SYN: ground. **3** to build on a firm base or ground: *a house founded upon a rock.* —***v.i.*** **1** to be founded or based. **2** to base one's opinion (on or upon).
[<Old French *fonder* <Latin *fundāre* <*fundus* bottom]

found[3] (found), *v.t.* to melt and mold (metal); make of molten metal; cast: *He designs and founds the type with which he prints his own writings* (Atlantic). [<Old French *fondre* <Latin *fundere* melt, cast, pour]

foun|da|tion (foun dā′shən), *n., v.* —***n.*** **1** a part on which the other parts rest for support; base: *The foundation of a house is built first.* SYN: See syn. under **base. 2** *Figurative.* a basis or groundwork: *This report has no foundation of fact.* **3** the act or process of founding; establishing: *The foundation of the United States began in 1776.* **4** the condition of being founded; being established. **5** an institution established and endowed for its maintenance: *A foundation for research was set up in 1936.* **6** a fund given to support an institution: *Nearly every university today has a foundation for research.* **7** a part on which other parts are overlaid, such as a material used for stiffening a garment. **8** = foundation garment. **9** a cosmetic, usually a liquid or cream, applied as a base before using face powder or rouge: *You apply the new Scandia foundation, which merits the word "fabulous" in my book, and then powder* (New Yorker).
—***v.t.*** to put a foundation on; cover with a foundation.

foun|da|tion|al (foun dā′shə nəl), *adj.* of or having to do with a foundation; fundamental.

foun|da|tion|er (foun dā′shə nər), *n. Especially British.* a person who is supported by the foundation or endowment of a college or school.

foundation garment, a woman's girdle, corset, or similar garment often with an attached brassiere.

foundation member, *British.* a charter member.

foundation stone, 1 a large stone or the like, serving as part of the foundation of a structure. **2** the basis or groundwork: *The very concept of collective security, the foundation stone of all our actions now, was then strange doctrine* (New York Times).

foun|der[1] (foun′dər), *v., n.* —***v.i.*** **1** to fill with water and sink: *The ship foundered in the storm.* **2a** to fall down; stumble: *His horse foundered in the swamp.* **b** to be affected with laminitis. **3** *Figurative.* to break down; fail: *His business has foundered. In this point All his tricks founder* (Shakespeare).
—***v.t.*** **1** to cause to fill with water and sink: *The collision foundered the ship.* **2** to cause (a horse) to break down or fall lame. **3** *Golf.* to hit (the ball) into the ground.
—***n.*** an inflammation in the foot of a horse, mule, etc.; laminitis.
[<Old French *fondrer* <*fond* bottom <Latin *fundus*]

found|er[2] (foun′dər), *n.* a person who founds or establishes something: *His grandfather was the founder of the family fortune.* [Middle English *foundour* <Anglo-French *fundur* <Latin *fundātor* <*fundāre* establish]

found|er[3] (foun′dər), *n.* a person who casts metals. [Middle English *foundour* <Old French *fondeur;* see etym. under **found**[3]]

foun|der|ous (foun′dər əs), *adj.* causing foundering; full of ruts and holes; swampy.

founders' shares, shares of special stock given to the organizers or promoters of a corporation, in consideration for their services. Founders' shares sometimes carry special voting privileges.

founding father, a man who is or is regarded as a founder of a nation, institution, or the like: *H. G. Wells . . . remains with Verne one of the founding fathers of science fiction* (Manchester Guardian).

Founding Fathers, *U.S. History.* the leaders in the struggle to free the original 13 American colonies from Great Britain and in the formation of the United States, especially those instrumental in the writing and ratification of the Constitution.

found|ling (found′ling), *n.* a baby or little child found deserted. [Middle English *fundeling* <*funden,* past participle of *finden* find]

foundling hospital, an institution for receiving foundlings.

found object, = objet trouvé.

found poem, a piece of prose writing presented or reproduced in a form that makes it look or sound like poetry: *"Found poems" aren't a new idea: William Butler Yeats produced one thirty years ago from the prose of essayist Walter Pater. And the opposite process—presenting poetry as if it were prose—is as old as the Bible* (Maclean's).

foun|drous (foun′drəs), *adj.* = founderous.

found|ry (foun′drē), *n., pl.* **-ries. 1** a place where metal is melted and molded; place where things are made of molten metal. **2** the process of melting and molding metal; making things of molten metal. **3** things made of molten metal; castings.
[<Middle French *fonderie* <*fondre* found[3]]

found|ry|man (foun′drē mən), *n., pl.* **-men.** a worker in a foundry.

foundry proof, *Printing.* the final proof to be checked before plates are made.

fount[1] (fount), *n.* **1** = fountain. **2** *Figurative.* a source: *The fount of joy's delicious springs* (Byron). [probably short for *fountain,* influenced by Latin *fōns, fontis* spring, and English *mount*]

fount[2] (font), *n. Especially British.* font[2].

foun|tain (foun′tən), *n., v.* —***n.*** **1** water flowing or rising into the air in a spray: *The droplets of the fountain created a gleaming spray in the sunlight.* **2** the pipes through which this water is forced and the basin that receives it: *A beautiful stone fountain was set in the middle of the garden.* **3** a spring of water: *The fountain where the animals drank bubbled up from the ground under a stone.* **4** a place to get a drink: *a drinking fountain, a soda fountain.* **5** *Figurative.* a source; origin: *He found that his father was a fountain of information about football.* **6** a container to hold a steady supply of ink, oil, or other liquid similarly used.
—***v.i.*** to jet, spray, or flow as water from a fountain: *Spray fountained high and wide, and the first damp patch spread over a knee of my trousers* (Manchester Guardian).
[<Old French *fontaine* <Late Latin *fontāna,* (originally) feminine of *fontānus* of a spring <Latin *fōns, fontis* spring] —**foun′tain|less,** *adj.*

foun|tained (foun′tənd), *adj.* having a fountain or fountains.

foun|tain|head (foun′tən hed′), *n.* **1** the source of a stream; fountain or spring from which a stream flows. **2** *Figurative.* an original source of anything: *Latin is the fountainhead of the Romance languages.*

Fountain of Youth, a legendary spring whose waters were supposed to cure any sickness and restore youth. It was sought in the West Indies and Florida by Ponce de León and other explorers.

foun|tain|ous (foun′tə nəs), *adj.* **1** of, like, or having to do with a fountain. **2** containing fountains or springs of water.

fountain pen, a pen for writing which has a tube in which to store ink. A fountain pen gives a continuous flow of ink.

fountain shell, a large, spiral sea shell; conch.

fountain tree, = deodar.

fou|quier|i|a (fü kir′ē ə), *n.* = ocotillo. [<New Latin *Fouquieria* the genus name <Pierre Eloi *Fouquier,* 1776-1850, a French professor of medicine]

four (fôr, fōr), *n., adj.* —***n.*** **1** one more than three; 4: *A dog has four legs.* **2** a set of four things or persons, such as a team of four horses, or the crew of a four-oared boat. **3** a boat with four oars. **4** a playing card, domino, billiard ball, or other part of a game with four spots or "4" on it. **5** a hit in cricket for which four runs are scored.
—***adj.*** being one more than three.
on all fours. See under **all fours.**
[Old English *fēower*]

four-ale bar (fôr′āl′, fōr′-), *British.* **1** a bar where cheap ale (originally at fourpence a quart) is sold. **2** *Informal.* any bar or tavern; pub.

Pronunciation Key: hat, āge, cãre, fär; let, ēqual, tėrm; it, īce; hot, ōpen, ôrder; oil, out; cup, pu̇t, rüle; child; long; thin; ᵺen; zh, measure; ə represents **a** in about, **e** in taken, **i** in pencil, **o** in lemon, **u** in circus.

four-bag|ger (fôr′bag′ər, fōr′-), *n. U.S. Slang.* a home run in baseball.

four-ball (fôr′bôl′, fōr′-), *adj.* (in golf) of or designating a foursome in which four balls are used, the best ball on each side counting at each hole.

four-cant (fôr′kant′, fōr′-), *adj., n.* **—*adj.*** *Nautical.* consisting of four strands, as a rope.
—*n.* a four-stranded rope.

four-chan|nel (fôr′chan′əl, fōr′-), *adj.* = quadraphonic.

four|ché or **four|chée** (fůr shā′), *adj. Heraldry.* (of a cross) having arms that fork at the ends. See the diagram under **cross**. [< French *fourché* < Old French *fourche,* past participle of *fourcher* < *fourche* fork; see etym. under **fourchette**]

four|chette (fůr shet′), *n.* **1** a fork or something resembling a fork. **2** a small fold of membrane just inside the rear part of the vulva. **3** the wishbone of a bird. **4** the frog of the hoof of a horse, donkey, or the like. **5** a forked piece of material on a glove, joining the front and back parts of the finger: *The glove . . . has a chamois palm and a terry-cloth back, and the fourchettes—those little panels along the sides of the fingers—are of stretch nylon* (New Yorker). **6** a combination in one hand of a playing card and the next higher or lower one; tenace. [< French *fourchette* (diminutive) < Old French *fourche* fork < Latin *furca* pitchfork]

four-cy|cle (fôr′sī′kəl, fōr′-), *n.* a cycle in an internal-combustion engine in which one piston stroke out of every four is a working stroke.

four-di|men|sion|al (fôr′də men′shə nəl, fōr′-), *adj. Mathematics.* of or denoting a space, extent, set of magnitudes, or other measure or function, each of whose elements can be precisely determined only by four coordinates.

Four|drin|i|er (fůr drin′ē ər), *n.* a machine for making paper in a continuous strip or web. [< Henry and Sealy *Fourdrinier,* who developed the machine in England in the early 1800's]

four|er (fôr′ər, fōr′-), *n. Cricket.* a hit from which four runs are scored.

four-eyed fish (fôr′īd′, fōr′-), = anableps.

four-eyes (fôr′iz′), *n. Slang.* a person who wears eyeglasses.

4-F or **4F** (fôr′ef′, fōr′-), *n.* **1** a United States Selective Service classification for men who are physically, mentally, or morally unfit for military service. **2** a man who is classified as 4-F.

four flush, 1 a hand in poker with only four cards of the same suit, instead of the five needed to make a flush.
2 *Slang.* a mere bluff; empty pretense.

four-flush (fôr′flush′, fōr′-), *v.i.* **1** to bluff in poker on a four flush; bet as if one has a real flush.
2 *Slang.* to be a four-flusher; bluff.

four-flush|er (fôr′flush′ər, fōr′-), *n.* **1** a person who has or bets on a four flush. **2** *Slang.* a person who pretends to be more or other than he really is; bluffer. [American English < *four-flush* + *-er*[1]]

four|fold (fôr′fōld′, fōr′-), *adj., adv.* **—*adj.*** **1** four times as much or as many: *a fourfold increase in profits.* **2** having four parts: *a fourfold argument.*
—*adv.* four times as much or as many: *Profits increased fourfold.*

four-foot|ed (fôr′fůt′id, fōr′-), *adj.* having four feet; quadruped: *A dog is a four-footed animal.*

four freedoms, freedom of speech, freedom of worship, freedom from want, and freedom from fear (set forth by Franklin D. Roosevelt in 1941).

four|gon (für gôɴ′), *n. French.* **1** a long covered wagon for carrying baggage and military supplies, used in the 1800's. **2** *Rare.* a baggage car of a railroad train.

four-hand|ed (fôr′han′did, fōr′-), *adj.* **1** for four players: *four-handed bridge.* **2** *Music.* for four hands or two players: *a four-handed piano sonata.* **3** having four hands.

4-H club or **Four-H club** (fôr′āch′, fōr′-), *U.S. and Canada.* any one of a system of clubs to teach agriculture, home economics, and other subjects to young people in rural and suburban sections. Its aim is the improvement of head, heart, hands, and health.

4-H'er or **Four-H'er** (fôr′ā′chər, fōr′-), *n.* a member of a 4-H club.

four-horned antelope (fôr′hôrnd′), an antelope of India, the male having two pairs of horns.

four-horse (fôr′hôrs′, fōr′-), *adj.* drawn by four horses: *a four-horse coach.*

Four Horsemen of the Apocalypse, four horsemen, each riding a horse of a different color, the white horse representing Christ or Conquest, the red horse War, the black horse Famine, and the pale horse Death or Pestilence (in the Bible, Revelation 6:1-8).

four hundred, the most fashionable or exclusive social set. **SYN:** élite. [because the *Social Register* once listed only four hundred names]

Fou|ri|er analysis (fůr′ē ā, -ē ər), *Physics.* the breakdown of a periodic function, such as a sound wave, into the sum of its harmonic motions; harmonic analysis. [< Jean Baptiste Joseph *Fourier,* 1768-1830, a French mathematician and physicist]

Fou|ri|er|ism (fůr′ē ə riz′əm), *n.* the socialistic system developed by François Marie Charles Fourier, 1772-1837, a French socialist. It favored the creation of small, economically and socially self-sufficient communities whose members would own property in common.

Fou|ri|er|ist (fůr′ē ə rist), *n.* a follower of Fourierism.

Fourier series, *Mathematics.* an infinite series using combinations of sines and cosines of the first degree, used to approximate a function within a given domain.

four-in-hand** (fôr′in hand′, fōr′-), *n., adj.* **—*n. **1** a necktie tied in a slip knot with the ends left hanging. **2** a carriage pulled by four horses driven by one person. **3** a team of four horses driven by one person.
—*adj.* **1** (of a necktie) tied in a slip knot with the ends left hanging. **2** having four horses driven by one person: *a four-in-hand carriage.*

***four-in-hand**
definition 1

four-leaf clover (fôr′lēf′, fōr′-), a clover with four leaves instead of the usual three, supposed to bring good luck to the finder.

four-leaved (fôr′lēvd′, fōr′-), *adj.* having four leaves or leaflets.

four-let|ter word (fôr′let′ər, fōr′-), any word of a group of English profanities or obscenities spelled with four letters.

four-mast|ed (fôr′mas′tid, fōr′-; -mäs′-), *adj.* rigged with four masts.

four modernizations, a program to modernize China's agriculture, industry, national defense, and science and technology: *Peking's ambitious program for turning China into an industrial power by the end of the century is known as the "four modernizations"* (Fox Butterfield).

Four Noble Truths, *Buddhism.* the four fundamental beliefs that suffering is universal, that the cause of suffering is desire, that suffering can cease by eliminating desire, and that desire can be eliminated by following the eight virtues that lead to the cessation of pain.

four-o'clock (fôr′ə klok′, fōr′-), *n.* **1** a small plant with red, white, pink, yellow, or mixed, trumpet-shaped flowers that open late in the afternoon and close in the morning; marvel-of-Peru. **2** its flower. **3** = friarbird.

four-o'clock family, a group of plants of warm regions, but chiefly American, typically having brightly colored tubular calyxes, such as the bougainvillea, four-o'clock, and sand verbena.

four of a kind, a hand in poker with four cards of the same value, such as four tens or four queens. It is higher in value than a full house, but lower than a straight flush.

four-part (fôr′pärt′, fōr′-), *adj. Music.* having four voices or parts in the harmony.

four|pence (fôr′pəns, fōr′-), *n.* **1** four British pennies. **2** a British silver coin, the groat, not in common use but still issued as Maundy money, worth four British pennies.

four|pen|ny (fôr′pen′ē, fōr′-; -pə nē), *n., pl.* **-nies,** *adj.* **—*n.*** = fourpence.
—*adj.* worth fourpence; costing fourpence: *a fourpenny piece. A fourpenny nail is 1½ inches long, and it is so called because originally the nails cost fourpence per hundred.*

***four-post|er** (fôr′pōs′tər; fōr′-), *n.* a bed with four tall corner posts for supporting a canopy or curtains.

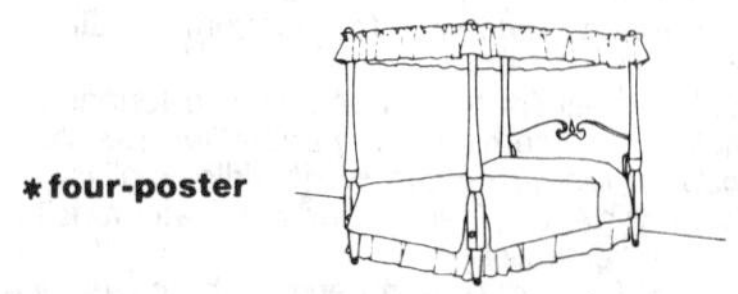

***four-poster**

four-pound|er (fôr′poun′dər, fōr′-), *n.* **1** a gun that shoots a projectile weighing four pounds. **2** a loaf weighing four pounds.

four|ra|gère (fü rá zher′), *n. Military.* a braided cord, of a different color for each branch of service, looped around the left shoulder. It is worn by members of a unit to indicate an award to the unit. [< French *fourragère,* noun use of feminine adjective < *fourrage,* noun, forage]

four|ré (fü rā′), *n.* a cream mixture in which nuts, fruit, and the like, are dipped to make fondants. [< French *fourré* (literally) thrust (into)]

four|score (fôr′skôr′, fōr′skōr′), *adj., n.* four times twenty; 80.

four seas, the waters bounding Great Britain.

four|some (fôr′səm, fōr′-), *n., adj.* **—*n.*** **1** a group of four people. **2** a game played by four people, two on each side. **3** the players.
—*adj.* *Especially Scottish.* **1** consisting of four. **2** performed by four persons together.

four|square (*adj., adv.* fôr′skwãr′, fōr′-; *n.* fôr′skwãr′, fōr′-), *adj., adv., n.* **—*adj.*** **1** = square. **2** frank; outspoken. **3** not yielding; firm.
—*adv.* **1** in a square form. **2** without yielding; firmly.
—*n.* = square.

four-star (fôr′stär′, fōr′-), *adj.* **1** (of an officer in the U.S. armed forces) wearing or entitled to wear four stars, the insignia of a full general or admiral. **2** *Figurative.* first-class: *The Carter Handicap will have four-star coverage by television and newsreel companies* (New York Times).

four-tailed bandage (fôr′tāld′, fōr′-), a strip of cloth cut to form two tails at each end to hold dressings especially on the nose and chin.

four|teen (fôr′tēn′, fōr′-), *n., adj.* four more than ten; 14. [Old English *fēowertēne*]

four|teen|er (fôr′tē′nər, fōr′-), *n.* a line of poetry of fourteen syllables.

four|teenth (fôr′tēnth′, fōr′-), *adj., n.* **1** next after the 13th; last in a series of 14. **2** one, or being one, of 14 equal parts.

fourth (fôrth, fōrth), *adj., n.* **—*adj.*** **1** next after the third; last in a series of 4: *Their fourth child was their last.* **2** being one of 4 equal parts; quarter: *The fourth part of a dollar is a quarter or a twenty-five-cent piece.*
—*n.* **1** the next after the third; last in a series of 4: *He was the fourth in that race.* **2** one of 4 equal parts; quarter: *Twenty-five cents is one fourth of a dollar.* **3** *Music.* **a** a tone on the fourth degree from a given tone that is counted as the first. **b** the interval between such tones. **c** the combination of such tones. **d** a tone on the fourth degree above the tonic; subdominant. **4** *Mathematics.* the fraction indicated by a unit in the fourth place in the sexagesimal, decimal, or any other system of fractional notation having a constant modulus. **5** a player completing a group of four: *a fourth at bridge.*
[Old English *fēowertha* < *fēower* four]

fourth-class matter, (fôrth′klas′, -kläs′; fōrth′-), (in the postal system of the United States) matter for mailing consisting of merchandise, or weighing over 16 ounces.

fourth dimension, a dimension in addition to length, width, and depth. Time has been thought of as a fourth dimension. In the theory of relativity, it is one of the four dimensions that form the space-time continuum.

fourth-di|men|sion|al (fôrth′də men′shə nəl, fōrth′-), *adj.* of or having to do with the fourth dimension.

fourth estate or **Fourth Estate,** newspapers or newspaper workers; the press.

fourth|ly (fôrth′lē, fōrth′-), *adv.* in the fourth place.

fourth market, *U.S.* the trading of unlisted securities directly between investors: *Often talking simultaneously over two telephones—one connected to a buyer, the other to a seller—Tomaso arranges direct trades between large institutional investors. He is one of the handful of entrepreneurs who run the "fourth market"* (Time).

Fourth of July, *U.S.* a holiday in honor of the adoption of the Declaration of Independence on July 4, 1776; Independence Day.

fourth proportional, *Mathematics.* the second extreme of a proportion having four variables: *In the proportion, 2 is to 4 as 8 is to 16, 16 is the fourth proportional.*

fourth quarter, = last quarter.

Fourth Republic, the government of France from 1946 to September, 1958.

Fourth World or **fourth world,** the poor countries of the world, as distinguished from the oil-rich countries of the Third World: *Called the "Fourth World" . . . they comprise nearly one billion people in some 40 undeveloped nations in Africa, Asia, and Latin America* (Time).

four-way (fôr′wā′, fōr′-), *adj.* having communication with four ways or passages: *a four-way valve.*

four-wheel (fôr′hwēl′, fōr′-), *adj.* = four-wheeled.

four-wheel drive, a system in which power is transmitted to all four wheels of a motor vehicle.

four-wheeled (fôr′hwēld′, fōr′-), *adj.* having four wheels; running on four wheels: *a four-wheeled landing gear.*

four-wheel|er (fôr′hwē′lər, fōr′-), *n.* **1** a vehicle with four wheels. **2** *British Informal.* a four-wheeled public carriage.

fou|ter or **fou|tre** (fü′tər), *n. Archaic.* a term of deep contempt applied to a person: *O'Brien declared that he was a liar, and a cowardly foutre* (Frederick Marryat).
a fouter for, *Archaic.* (to care not) a fig for: *A foutre for the world and worldlings base!* (Shakespeare).
[< French *foutre,* noun use of infinitive, to care nothing for < Old French, to copulate with < Latin *futuere*]

fo|ve|a (fō′vē ə), *n., pl.* **-ve|ae** (-vē ē). *Biology.* a small depression or pit: *The yellow spot on the retina of the eye has a fovea in the center. Vision is much more acute at the fovea than at other portions of the retina* (Sears and Zemansky). [< Latin *fovea* small pit, pitfall]

fovea cen|tra|lis (sen trā′lis), *Anatomy.* a small spot in the center of the retina of the eye, where vision is sharpest. See picture under **eye**. [< New Latin *fovea centralis* central fovea]

fo|ve|al (fō′vē əl), *adj.* **1** of or having to do with a fovea. **2** situated in a fovea.

fo|ve|ate (fō′vē āt, -it), *adj.* having foveae; pitted.

fo|ve|i|form (fō vē′ə fôrm), *adj.* having the shape of a fovea.

fo|ve|o|la (fō vē′ə lə), *n., pl.* **-lae** (-lē). *Biology.* a very small pit or depression. [< New Latin *foveola* (diminutive) < Latin *fovea* fovea]

fo|ve|o|late (fō′vē ə lāt), *adj.* having very small pits.

fowl (foul), *n., pl.* **fowls** or (*collectively*) **fowl**, *v.* —*n.* **1** any bird: *a wild fowl.* **2** any one of several kinds of large birds that nest on the ground. Most domestic fowl can fly only short distances. The chicken, turkey, duck, and goose are fowls. **3** a full-grown hen or rooster. **4** the flesh of a fowl used for food.
—*v.i.* to hunt, shoot, catch, or trap wild birds for sport or food: *They hunt all grounds, and draw all seas, Fowl every brook and bush to please Their wanton taste* (Ben Jonson).
neither fish nor fowl. See under **fish**.
[Old English *fugol*]

fowl cholera, a contagious, virulent, febrile disease of poultry, characterized by diarrhea and internal bleeding, and caused by a bacterium; chicken cholera.

fowl|er (fou′lər), *n.* a person who hunts, shoots, catches, or traps wild birds.

fowl|ing (fou′ling), *n.* the hunting of wild birds.

fowling piece, a light shotgun for shooting wild birds.

fowl paralysis, = Marek's disease.

fowl|pest (foul′pest′), *n.* an infectious virus disease of poultry, common in Europe, characterized by diarrhea, laying of soft-shelled eggs or loss of ability to lay eggs, respiratory difficulty, and discharge of mucus.

fowl plague, a very destructive, infectious disease of domestic poultry, caused by a virus: *Fowl plague strikes hardest in India and Middle East countries and Europe* (Science News Letter).

fowl pox, a virus disease of chickens and other birds, characterized by skin damage.

fox (foks), *n., v.* —*n.* **1** a wild animal related to the dog, having a pointed muzzle and bushy tail. Foxes are flesh-eating mammals smaller than wolves. In many stories the fox gets the better of other animals by his cunning. See picture under **dog**. **2** its fur. **3** an animal having some resemblance to the fox, such as the flying fox. **4** *Figurative.* a cunning or crafty person: *Don't you see how that old fox steals away your customers?* (John Arbuthnot). **5** *Nautical.* two or more rope yarns twisted together and smoothed out, used for seizing. **6** *Obsolete.* a kind of sword: *Put up your fox, and let us be jogging* (Scott).
—*v.t.* **1** *Informal.* to trick by being sly and crafty; deceive: *We are actually in the gallant British machine that foxes the enemy with its special thirty-times-more-powerful radar* (Punch). **2** to discolor; stain: *The book is still sound, but badly foxed.* **3** to befuddle; make drunk: *The last of whom I did almost fox with Margate ale* (Samuel Pepys). **4** to make (beer) sour. **5** to make or repair (a boot, shoe, or glove) by covering with or adding upper leather.
—*v.i.* **1** to act slyly and craftily: *To his mind everybody was dodging and foxing* (D. C. Murray). **2** to become discolored or stained. **3** (of beer) to turn sour. **4** to hunt the fox. **5** *Obsolete.* to get drunk.
[Old English *fox*] —**fox′like′**, *adj.*

Fox (foks), *n., pl.* **Fox|es** or **Fox**. **1** a member of an Algonkian tribe of Indians closely associated with the Sauk, formerly of Wisconsin but now living mainly in Iowa. **2** the Algonkian language of the tribe.

∗**fox and geese**, a game played on a cross-shaped board or a checkerboard with pins or checkers, one of which represents the fox, the rest the geese. The geese can move only forward, and win if they can surround the fox or drive him into a corner. The fox can move forward or backward, and wins if he jumps over and captures all the geese.

∗**fox and geese**

fox|bane (foks′bān′), *n.* = aconite.

fox bat, = flying fox.

fox|ber|ry (foks′ber′ē), *n., pl.* **-ries**. = bearberry.

foxed (fokst), *adj.* **1** drunk; befuddled. **2** discolored; stained: *a foxed book. The village had no public library; no foxed copies of Pascal* (New Yorker). **3** sour: *foxed beer.*

fox|feet (foks′fēt′), *n.* = fir club moss.

fox|fire (foks′fīr′), *n.* the phosphorescent light emitted by decaying timber, caused by fungi.

fox|glove (foks′gluv′), *n.* **1** any one of a group of plants with tall stalks having many large, drooping, bell-shaped, purple, yellow, or white flowers. It belongs to the figwort family. The drug digitalis is obtained from the leaves and the seeds of one variety. **2** its flower. [Old English *foxes glōfa*]

fox grape, any one of several varieties of North American wild grapes that have a musky or foxy scent.

fox|hole (foks′hōl′), *n.* a hole in the ground, large enough for one or two soldiers, dug for protection against enemy fire.

fox|hound (foks′hound′), *n.* a hound with a keen sense of smell, bred and trained to hunt foxes. There are two recognized breeds, the English foxhound and the American foxhound.

fox hunt, a sport in which hunters on horseback follow dogs that chase the fox.

fox-hunt (foks′hunt′), *v.i.* to hunt foxes with hounds.

fox|hunt|er (foks′hun′tər), *n.* one who hunts or pursues foxes with hounds.

fox-hunt|ing (foks′hun′ting), *n., adj.* —*n.* the sport of hunting the fox: *He inherited the family estate at Taynton and with it a taste for fox-hunting* (Manchester Guardian Weekly).
—*adj.* **1** relating to the hunting of the fox. **2** having the tastes or habits of a foxhunter: *Cowper himself . . . calls a fox-hunting squire Nimrod* (Macaulay).

fox|i|ly (fok′sə lē), *adv.* in a foxy manner.

fox|i|ness (fok′sē nis), *n.* foxy quality.

fox|ing (fok′sing), *n.* the piece or pieces of leather or other material with which a shoe is foxed.

fox shark, = thresher (def. 3).

fox snake, a large, harmless snake of the central United States, of a light-brown color with squarish dark-brown blotches.

fox sparrow, a large, reddish sparrow found chiefly in wooded regions of Canada and the United States.

fox squirrel, a North American tree squirrel noted for its large size.

fox|tail (foks′tāl′), *n.* **1** the tail of a fox. **2** any one of various grasses with soft, brushlike spikes of flowers.

foxtail lily, = eremurus.

foxtail millet, a grass native to Europe and Asia, grown in the United States for hay, pasture, and fodder.

foxtail pine, an evergreen tree or shrub with long, curving prickles on its cones; bristlecone pine.

fox terrier, a small, active dog kept as a pet, once trained to drive foxes from their holes. Fox terriers are white with brown or black spots and may have smooth or rough coats.

fox trot, **1** a ballroom dance in in time having both slow and quick steps. **2** the music for it. **3** a gait (of a horse or other four-footed animal) between a trot and a walk, made up of short steps.

fox-trot (foks′trot′), *v.i.,* **-trot|ted, -trot|ting.** to dance the fox trot.

Fox|trot (foks′trot′), *n. U.S.* a code name for the letter *f,* used in transmitting radio messages.

fox|wood (foks′wůd′), *n.* discolored or stained wood.

fox|y (fok′sē), *adj.,* **fox|i|er, fox|i|est.** **1** like a fox; sly; crafty; cunning: *With his neat pointed beard (not quite a goatee) he looks a bit more like that traditional turn-of-the-century character, "foxy grandpa"* (New York Times). **2** discolored; stained. **3** yellowish or reddish brown, like the common red fox. **4** (of beer, wine, or other alcoholic beverage) turned sour while fermenting. **5** musky, like the fox grape: *European "connoisseurs" have coined a derogatory term—'foxy'—for the flavor of some American grape varieties* (Maclean's).

foy (foi), *n. Dialect.* **1** a feast, present, cup of liquor, or other offering, given by or to a person starting out on a journey: *He did at the Dog give me, and some other friends of his, his foy, he being to set sail today* (Samuel Pepys). **2** a feast at the end of the harvest or fishing season. [< Middle Dutch *voye,* or *foye,* probably < Old French *voie* journey, way < Latin *via*]

foy|er (foi′ər, -ā), *n.* **1** an entrance hall used as a lounging room in a theater, apartment house, or hotel; lobby. **2** an entrance hall. [< French *foyer,* ultimately < Latin *focus* hearth, fireplace]

fo|zy (fō′zē, foz′ē), *adj. Scottish and Dialect.* **1** spongy; soft. **2** thick-witted; stupid. [origin uncertain. Compare Dutch *voos.*]

fp or **FP** (no periods), **1** foot-pound. **2** freezing point.

fp., foot-pound.

FPC (no periods) or **F.P.C.**, **1** Federal Power Commission (an agency that regulates natural gas and electric companies in interstate commerce and supervises Federal hydroelectric projects). **2** fish protein concentrate.

fpm (no periods) or **f.p.m.**, feet per minute.

FPO (no periods), *U.S. Navy.* Fleet Post Office.

fps (no periods) or **f.p.s.**, **1** feet per second. **2** *Physics.* foot-pound-second.

fr., **1** fragment. **2** franc. **3** from.

Fr (no period), francium (chemical element).

Fr., **1** father. **2** France. **3** Frau. **4** French. **5** friar.

Fra (frä), *n.* Brother. It is used as the title of a monk or friar. [< Italian *fra,* short form of *frate* brother < Latin *frāter*]

frab|jous (frab′jəs), *adj.* **1** very joyous or happy; fabulous: *a frabjous show, a frabjous comedian.* **2** very bad; outrageous; terrible: *a frabjous mistake.* [(coined by Lewis Carroll) probably < a blend of *fair, fabulous,* and *joyous*]

fra|cas (frā′kəs), *n.* a noisy quarrel or fight; disorderly noise; disturbance; uproar; brawl: *We have only the Wheelers' word for it that the Wheelers were right in every fracas and ruction they got into* (New Yorker). SYN: row, fray. [< French *fracas* < Italian *fracasso* < *fracassare* to smash < *fra* (intensive < Latin *infrā* below) + *cassare* break, shatter, quash]

frac|tal (frak′təl), *n.* any one of a class of highly irregular and fragmented shapes or surfaces not represented in classical geometry. [< Latin *frāctus,* past participle of *frangere* to break + English *-al*]

fractal geometry, the branch of geometry that deals with fractals: *The increasing popularity of fractal geometry . . . stems from the vast diversity of physical problems that can be viewed as variations on a similar theme* (Science News).

fract|ed (frak′tid), *adj. Heraldry.* having a part displaced, as if broken: *a fracted chevron.* [< Latin *frāctus,* past participle of *frangere* to break + English *-ed*[2]]

parts of a fraction:

$\frac{4}{5}$ numerator or dividend / denominator or divisor

kinds of fractions:

$\frac{2}{3}, \frac{5}{4}, \frac{6}{7}$ common fractions

$\frac{\frac{1}{3}}{7}, \frac{7}{\frac{1}{3}}, \frac{\frac{1}{3}}{\frac{1}{7}}$ complex fractions

$\frac{1}{3}, \frac{2}{5}, \frac{6}{7}$ proper fractions

$\frac{4}{3}, \frac{5}{4}, \frac{27}{23}$ improper fractions

∗**fraction** definition 1

∗**frac|tion** (frak′shən), *n., v.* —*n.* **1** *Mathematics.* **a** one or more of the equal parts of a whole number: $\frac{2}{3}$, $\frac{3}{4}$, $\frac{5}{6}$, and $\frac{7}{8}$ are fractions. **b** a division of one mathematical expression by another, indicated by a line with one quantity above it and another below it, such as $\frac{\frac{3}{8}+\frac{9}{16}}{7}$. **c** a similar expression in which the quantities are ex-

Pronunciation Key: hat, āge, cãre, fär; let, ēqual, tėrm; it, īce; hot, ōpen, ôrder; oil, out; cup, pu̇t, rüle; child; long; thin; ᴛʜen; zh, measure; ə represents **a** in about, **e** in taken, **i** in pencil, **o** in lemon, **u** in circus.

pressed in algebraic terms, such as $\frac{a}{b}$ and $\frac{xty^2}{x+2}$.
2 a very small part or amount; not all of a thing; fragment: *He has done only a fraction of his homework.* **3** *Chemistry.* a portion separated especially by fractional distillation or precipitation, for collection. **4** the act of breaking. **5** *Obsolete.* a broken state or place.
— ***v.t.*** **1** to separate into fractions. **2** to fractionate.
[< Late Latin *frāctiō, -ōnis* < Latin *frangere* to break]

frac|tion|al (frak′shə nəl), *adj.* **1** of or having to do with fractions. **2** forming a fraction: *440 yards is a fractional part of a mile.* **3** small by comparison; insignificant; partial: *Rent is only a fractional part of our household expense.* **4** *Chemistry.* of or designating a method for separating a mixture into its component parts, based on certain differences in boiling points, solubility, and other characteristics of these parts: *fractional crystallization, fractional oxidation.* **5** (in stock exchanges) being less than the amount used as a standard unit of measurement, as less than 100 shares of stock, or $10,000 of bonds. — **frac′tion|al|ly,** *adv.*

fractional currency, **1** coins or paper money having a value less than that of the basic monetary unit. **2** certain paper money issued by the United States (1862-76), and Canada, in values of from three to fifty cents.

fractional distillation, *Chemistry.* the separation of two or more volatile liquids having different boiling points, by heating them so as to vaporize them successively and collecting the more volatile first.

frac|tion|al|ism (frak′shə nə liz′əm), *n.* a tendency toward, or a policy of, division into parts or fractions: *No constitution can by itself eliminate political fractionalism and ensure a two or three party system* (Atlantic).

frac|tion|al|ize (frak′shə nə līz), *v.t.,* **-ized, -iz|ing.** to divide (an organization, system, or other structure) into parts or fractions: *Incident to these objectives is the attempt to fractionalize the North Atlantic Treaty Organization and the Southeast Asian defense organization* (New York Times). — **frac′tion|al|i|za′tion,** *n.*

frac|tion|ar|y (frak′shə ner′ē), *adj.* **1** = fractional. **2** having to do with or carried on by fractions; tending to divide into fractions.

frac|tion|ate (frak′shə nāt), *v.t.,* **-at|ed, -at|ing.** *Chemistry.* **1** to separate (a mixture) by distillation, crystallization, or other process, into its ingredients or into portions having different properties. **2** to obtain by this process. — **frac′tion|a′tion,** *n.*

frac|tion|a|tor (frak′shə nā′tər), *n.* a machine which fractionates, such as one which separates whole blood into plasma, red cells, and other useful components.

fraction bar, *Mathematics.* the line separating a numerator and a denominator.

frac|tion|ize (frak′shə nīz), *v.t., v.i.,* **-ized, -iz|ing.** to divide into fractions. — **frac′tion|i|za′tion,** *n.*

frac|tious (frak′shəs), *adj.* **1** easily made angry; cross; fretful; peevish: *in a fractious mood.* **SYN:** irritable, snappish. **2** hard to manage; unruly: *There were men ... struggling doubtfully with fractious cows and frightened sheep* (Lew Wallace). **SYN:** refractory, intractable. [< *fraction,* in obsolete sense of "discord, brawling"; patterned on *captious,* etc.] — **frac′tious|ly,** *adv.* — **frac′tious|ness,** *n.*

frac|to-cu|mu|lus (frak′tō kyü′myə ləs), *n., pl.* **-li** (-lī). a very low, ragged, slightly rounded cloud which often appears under nimbostratus clouds during precipitation. [< Latin *frāctus* broken + English *cumulus*]

frac|tog|ra|phy (frak tog′rə fē), *n.* the study of the surface of fractured metals.

frac|to-stra|tus (frak′tō strā′təs), *n., pl.* **-ti** (-tī). a very low, ragged, horizontally elongated cloud which often appears under nimbostratus clouds during precipitation. [< Latin *frāctus* broken + English *stratus*]

frac|tur|al (frak′chər əl), *adj.* having to do with or like a fracture; caused by a fracture.

frac|tur|a|tion (frak′chə rā′shən), *n.* the breaking or fracturing within a mass of rock.

frac|ture** (frak′chər), *n., v.,* **-tured, -tur|ing.** — ***n. **1** the act or fact of breaking a bone or cartilage: *In the comminuted fracture, the bone splinters* (Claude Lambert). **2** the act or fact of breaking or the state of being broken: *a fracture of the ice, a fracture of friendly relations.* **3** the result of breaking; break or crack: *The fracture in the foundation is widening.* **SYN:** division, split. See picture above. **4** *Mineralogy.* **a** the way in which a mineral breaks. **b** the appearance of the surface of a freshly broken mineral.
— ***v.t.*** **1** to break or crack. **2** to cause a fracture in (a bone or cartilage): *The boy fell from a tree and fractured his arm.* **3** *U.S. Slang.* to overwhelm with humor, feeling, magnificence, or the like: *Big receptions and honors just fracture me.*
— ***v.i.*** to undergo fracture; crack: *Then propellers bend, sometimes fracture, sometimes break, in the crush of hardpacked pack ice* (Newsweek).
[< Old French *fracture,* learned borrowing from Latin *frāctūra* < *frangere* to break] — **frac′tur|a|ble,** *adj.*

***fracture**
definition 3

kinds of fractures:

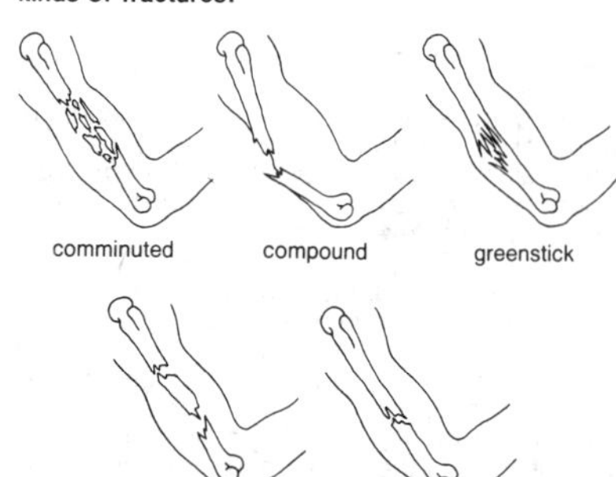

frac|tured (frak′chərd), *adj. U.S. Informal.* (of a language) spoken or written with disregard for conventional syntax, meanings, idiom, or the like: *the Yankee manager snapped in his best fractured English: "I ain't gonna comment about a guy which made $100,000 writin' how this club lost"* (New York Times).

frae (frā), *prep., adv. Scottish.* — ***prep.*** from.
— ***adv.*** fro.

frae|num (frē′nəm), *n., pl.* **-na** (-nə). = frenum.

frag (frag), *v.,* **fragged, frag|ging,** *n. U.S. Military Slang.* — ***v.t., v.i.*** to kill or injure (one's superior officer or a fellow soldier), especially by means of a fragmentation grenade.
— ***n.*** a fragmentation grenade: *When MPs were called in to quell the riot at Camp Baxter, they found ... sequestered about the camp stocks of frags* (Saturday Review).

frag|ile (fraj′əl), *adj.* easily broken, damaged, or destroyed; delicate; frail: *Be careful; that thin glass is fragile. She had a fragile beauty.* **SYN:** breakable, weak, perishable. [< Latin *fragilis,* related to *frangere* to break. See etym. of doublet **frail**[1].] — **frag′ile|ly,** *adv.* — **frag′ile|ness,** *n.*

fra|gil|i|ty (frə jil′ə tē) *n.* fragile quality; delicacy; frailness.

frag|ment (frag′mənt), *n., v.* — ***n.*** **1** a part broken off; piece of something broken: *When she broke the dish, she tried to put the fragments back together.* **SYN:** chip, scrap, bit. **2** *Figurative.* an incomplete or disconnected part: *Because of the noise he could hear only fragments of the conversation.* **3** *Figurative.* a part of an incomplete or unfinished work: *Many Old English poems exist as fragments.* **4** *Figurative.* a surviving part of something lost or no longer in existence: *A land of old ... where fragments of forgotten peoples dwelt* (Tennyson).
— ***v.t., v.i.*** to break or divide into fragments: *... a Europe fragmented by history* (London Times). *For years the Tecumseh [a sunk warship] was presumed lost beyond recovery, either buried too deep or fragmented hopelessly* (New York Times).
[< Latin *fragmentum,* related to *frangere* to break]

frag|men|tal (frag men′təl), *adj.* **1** = fragmentary. **2** *Geology.* formed from older rocks; clastic. — **frag|men′tal|ly,** *adv.*

frag|men|tar|y (frag′mən ter′ē), *adj.* **1** made up of fragments; incomplete or disconnected: *fragmentary remains of a temple,* (*Figurative.*) *fragmentary evidence.* (*Figurative.*) *The injured man could give only a fragmentary account of the accident.* **2** *Geology.* = fragmental. — **frag′men|tar′i|ly,** *adv.* — **frag′men|tar′i|ness,** *n.*

frag|men|tate (frag′mən tāt), *v.t., v.i.,* **-tat|ed, -tat|ing.** to break up; fragmentize.

frag|men|ta|tion (frag′mən tā′shən), *n., adj.* — ***n.*** **1** the act or process of breaking up into fragments or parts: (*Figurative.*) *I deplore nothing more than this fragmentation of our democratic society into special interest groups—labor, farmers, business* (Adlai E. Stevenson). **2** a bursting and scattering of certain bombs, grenades, or artillery shells.
— ***adj.*** that throws bits of metal in all directions as it bursts: *a fragmentation grenade.*

fragmentation bomb, a bomb or grenade that throws bits of metal in all directions as it bursts.

frag|ment|ed (frag′mən tid), *adj.* broken into fragments; incomplete; disconnected. — **frag′ment|ed|ly,** *adv.*

frag|ment|ist (frag′mən tist), *n.* a writer of fragments or of works which survive only in fragments.

frag|ment|ize (frag′mən tīz), *v.t., v.i.,* **-ized, -iz|ing.** to break into fragments: *The fortnight recess from studies fragmentizes the fall semester already burdened by the existing holidays* (New York Times). — **frag′ment|i|za′tion,** *n.* — **frag′ment|iz′er,** *n.*

fra|grance (frā′grəns), *n.* a sweet smell; pleasing odor: *the fragrance of flowers or of perfume.* **SYN:** aroma, perfume.

fra|gran|cy (frā′grən sē), *n., pl.* **-cies.** = fragrance.

fra|grant (frā′grənt), *adj.* **1** having or giving off a pleasant odor; sweet-smelling: *This rose is fragrant.* **2** *Figurative: Their fragrant memory will outlast the tomb* (William Cowper). [< Latin *fragrāns, -antis,* present participle of *fragrāre* emit (a sweet) odor] — **fra′grant|ly,** *adv.*

fraid|y cat (frā′dē), *U.S. Slang.* (used by children) a person who is easily frightened; timorous person.

frail[1] (frāl), *adj.* **1** slender and not very strong; weak: *a frail and sickly child. These words ... seem too soon from a frail memory fallen away* (R. Ellis). **SYN:** delicate. **2** easily broken, giving way, damaged, or destroyed: *Be careful; those branches are a very frail support.* **SYN:** brittle. **3** morally weak; liable to yield to temptation: *tales ... of frail and erring men* (Stoddard King). [< Old French *frele, fraile* < Latin *fragilis,* related to *frangere* to break. See etym. of doublet **fragile.**] — **frail′ly,** *adv.* — **frail′ness,** *n.*

frail[2] (frāl), *n.* **1** a flexible basket made of rushes, used for packing figs, raisins, and other delicate produce. **2** the quantity of figs, raisins, and other produce, packed in such a basket. A frail equals 30 to 75 pounds. [< Old French *fraiel* < Vulgar Latin *fragellum* < Latin *flagellum* rush, branch, whip. Compare etym. under **flail.**]

frai|le|jon (frī′lā hōn′), *n.* a growth of tall composite plants belonging to the paramos of the equatorial Andes. Their densely hairy leaves are as long as the arm and form rosettes. [< American Spanish *frailejón* < Spanish *fraile* friar]

frail|ish (frā′lish), *adj.* somewhat frail.

frail|ty (frāl′tē), *n., pl.* **-ties.** **1** the condition of being frail; weakness: *a sick person's physical frailty. The works of man inherit ... their author's frailty and return to dust* (William Cowper). **2** moral weakness; liability to yield to temptation: *His frailty of character caused him to yield to temptation.* **3** a fault or sin caused by moral weakness: *Laziness is his only frailty.*

frais (fre), *n.pl. French.* expenses; charges.

fraise (frāz), *n.* **1** a fortified position consisting of pointed, horizontal, or inclined stakes near the top of a rampart. **2** a ruff worn around the neck. [< French *fraise*]

fraises des bois (frez′ dā bwä′), *French.* wild strawberries native to France and often served as a delicacy with thick cream.

***Frak|tur** (fräk tür′), *n. German.* a style of printing type.

***Fraktur** The World Book Dictionary

fram|be|sia or **fram|boe|sia** (fram bē′zhə), *n.* = yaws. [< New Latin *frambesia* < French *framboise* raspberry (because of its appearance)]

fram|boise (fräɴ bwäz′), *n. French.* a liqueur made from raspberries.

frame** (frām), *n., v.,* **framed, fram|ing.** — ***n. **1** a support over which something is stretched or built; framework: *the frame of a house.* **2** anything made of parts fitted and joined together; structure or system: *His [Milton's] death dissolved the whole frame of society* (Macaulay). **3** the body; build of the body: *a man of heavy frame.* **4** a skeleton. **5** *Figurative.* **a** the way in which a thing is put together; structure; construction: *the frame of the Constitution.* **b** mental or emotional state. **6** an established order or plan: *Should the whole frame of Nature round him break ... He, unconcerned, would hear the mighty crack* (Joseph Addison). **7** shape or form: *Put your discourse into some frame* (Shakespeare). **8** the border in which a thing is set: *a window frame, a picture frame.* **9** one of the individual pictures on a strip of motion-picture film. **10** one image transmitted by television. **11** one of the units or steps in programmed instruction. Each frame requires some response from the student. **12** a machine constructed on or within a framework. **13** any one of the ten small squares for recording the score for each turn at bowling.

14 one turn at bowling, or one tenth of the game. **15** *Informal.* an inning in baseball. **16a** the triangular form used to arrange the balls at the start of a game of pool. **b** the triangle of balls thus placed. **c** the period of play between the placing of the balls. **17** one of the ribs forming the framework of a ship's hull, extending from the bilge or from the keel to the gunwale on either side. A square frame crosses each deck in a perpendicular plane; a cant frame crosses each deck in an oblique plane. **18** a box with a glass cover, used to protect seeds and young plants from cold; cold frame. **19** *U.S. Slang.* = frame-up. [< verb]
— ***v.t.*** **1** to shape or form: *to frame one's life according to a noble pattern. Nature hath framed strange fellows in her time* (Shakespeare). **SYN**: fashion. **2** to put together; plan; make: *to frame an answer to a difficult question. James Madison helped to frame the Constitution.* **SYN**: devise, fabricate. **3** to put a border around: *to frame a picture.* **4** *Slang.* to make seem guilty by some false arrangement: *to frame an innocent person.* **5** *Archaic.* to direct (one's steps).
— ***v.i.*** *Dialect.* **1** to prepare, attempt, or manage to do something. **2** to succeed; do well. **3** to betake oneself; go.
[Middle English *framen* to join or frame timber, Old English *framian* to profit < *fram* forth]
— **fram′a|ble, frame′a|ble,** *adj.* — **frame′less,** *adj.* — **fram′er,** *n.*

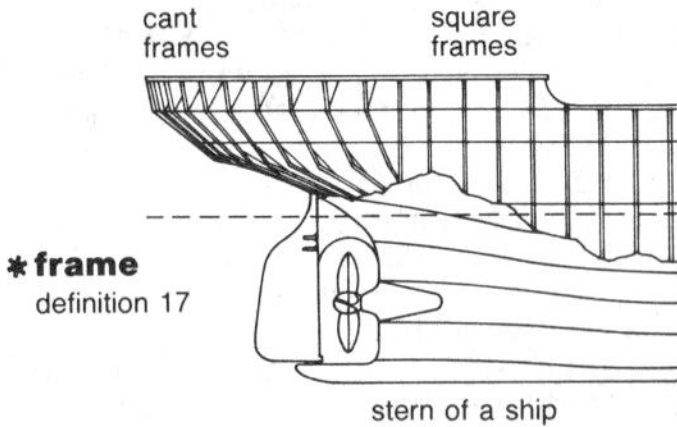

***frame**
definition 17

frame house, a house made of a wooden framework covered with boards.
frame of mind, way of thinking or feeling; disposition; mood.
frame of reference, 1 the standards by which a person compares something to form an attitude or make a judgment or analysis: *... the inability of the Congressional Committee, with its domestic orientation and limited frame of reference, to read the larger questions of international reality* (Bulletin of Atomic Scientists). **2** *Mathematics.* a set of lines or planes used as a reference for describing position, as of a point or line.
frame saw, a thin saw stretched in a frame to give it sufficient rigidity for working.
frame|shift (frām′shift′), *adj. Genetics.* having to do with or causing an insertion or deletion in a codon that results in an incorrect genetic message: *a frameshift mutation, a frameshift mutagen.*
frame-up (frām′up′), *n. Informal.* **1** a secret and dishonest arrangement made beforehand. **2** an arrangement made to have a person falsely accused.
frame|work (frām′wėrk′), *n., v.* — ***n.*** **1** a support or skeleton; stiff part that gives shape to a thing; frame: *The bridge had a steel framework.* **2** *Figurative.* the way in which a thing is put together; structure or system: *the framework of government.* **3** the branches of a fruit tree.
— ***v.t.*** to graft by inserting cuttings on the branches of (a fruit tree).
fram|ing (frā′ming), *n.* **1** framed work; a frame or system of frames. **2** the way in which a thing is put together; framework. **3** the action or process of making or shaping: *The framing of this letter calls for considerable diplomacy.*
franc (frangk), *n.* **1** the unit of money of France, Belgium, Switzerland, and some other European and African countries, equal to 100 centimes. **2** a coin or note worth one franc. **3** a former French silver coin. *Abbr:* fr. [< Old French *franc* < Latin *Francōrum Rēx* king of the Franks, an early gold coin first struck in 1360]
fran|chis|al (fran′chī zəl), *adj.* of or belonging to the franchise.
fran|chise (fran′chīz), *n., v.,* **-chised, -chis|ing.** — ***n.*** **1** a privilege or right, granted by a government: *The city granted the company a franchise to operate buses on the city streets.* **2** the right to vote: *The United States granted women the franchise in 1920.* **3** the privilege, often exclusive, of selling the products of a manufacturer in a given area. **4** *Obsolete.* an asylum; sanctuary.
— ***v.t.*** **1** to grant a franchise to or for: *to franchise a retail outlet, a franchised car dealer. The brothers decided ... to franchise the establishment of miniature tracks where the public could pay to take part in the racing* [*of*] *cars* (London Times). **2** to set free; enfranchise.
[< Old French *franchise* freedom; frankness < *franc* free; see etym. under **frank[1]**]
fran|chis|ee (fran′chī zē′), *n.* a person who is franchised by a company to operate a retail store or branch, a hotel, or other business: *Some* [*franchises*] *may require considerable capital on the part of the franchisee, as in setting up a hotel in the Holiday Inns chain, or none at all beyond one's time in becoming a franchisee of a hearing aid company* (London Times).
fran|chis|er (fran′chī zər), *n.* **1** = franchisee. **2** a person or company that grants a franchise.
fran|chis|or (fran′chī zôr′), *n.* = franchiser (def. 2).
Fran|cis|can (fran sis′kən), *adj., n.* — ***adj.*** of Saint Francis of Assisi or the religious order founded by him in 1209: *Franciscan abstinence, Franciscan cloisters.*
— ***n.*** a friar belonging to the Franciscan order; Gray Friar.
Fran|cis-type (fran′sis tīp′), *adj.* having spirally curved vanes: *a Francis-type reaction turbine.* [< *Francis water turbine,* a commonly used turbine of this type]
***fran|ci|um** (fran′sē əm), *n.* a rare radioactive chemical element produced artificially from actinium or thorium. It is one of the alkali metals. [< New Latin *francium* < *France*]

***francium**

symbol	atomic number	mass number	oxidation state
Fr	87	223	1

Fran|ci|za|tion (fran′sə zā′shən), *n.* the act or process of Francizing; Frenchification.
Fran|cize (fran′sīz), *v.t.,* **-cized, -ciz|ing.** to make French, as in ideas, style, or manners; Frenchify. [< French *franciser* < *français* French]
Franco-, *combining form.* **1** of France; of the French: *Francophile = friend of France or the French.*
2 French and ____: *Franco-German = French and German.*
[< Medieval Latin *Francus* a Frank]
Fran|co-A|mer|i|can (frang′kō ə mer′ə kən), *adj., n.* — ***adj.*** **1** of France and the United States; French and American: *Franco-American relations.* **2** of or having to do with Americans of French descent.
— ***n.*** an American of French descent.
Fran|co-Ger|man (frang′kō jėr′mən), *adj.* of France and Germany; French and German.
Fran|co|ism (frang′kō iz əm), *n.* the policies of Francisco Franco, (1892-1975), dictator of Spain, associated with the Falange.
Fran|co|ist (frang′kō ist), *n.* a supporter of Francisco Franco or his policies.
fran|co|lin (frang′kə lin), *n.* a partridge found in Africa, southern Asia, and southern Europe. It has a very loud whistle, and its meat is considered a great delicacy. [< Old French *francolin* < Italian *francolino* (perhaps diminutive) < *franco* free (in sense of "wild")]
fran|co|lite (frang′kə līt), *n.* a grayish-green or brown variety of apatite from Devonshire, England. It occurs in small rounded crystals grouped in stalactitic masses.
Fran|co|ni|an (frang kō′nē ən), *n.* the German dialect spoken by the Franks who lived along the Rhine.
Fran|co|phil (frang′kə fil), *adj., n.* = Francophile.
Fran|co|phile (frang′kə fīl, -fil), *adj., n.* — ***adj.*** friendly to the French or to France.
— ***n.*** a person friendly to the French or to France.
Fran|co|phil|i|a (frang′kə fil′ē ə), *n.* love or admiration for the French or France.
Fran|co|phobe (frang′kə fōb), *adj., n.* — ***adj.*** fearing or hating the French or France.
— ***n.*** a person who fears or hates the French or France.
Fran|co|pho|bi|a (frang′kə fō′bē ə), *n.* fear or hatred of the French or France: *There have been several serious French complaints here lately about growing Francophobia* (New Yorker).
Fran|co|phone or **fran|co|phone** (frang′kə fōn), *n., adj.* — ***n.*** a French-speaking native or inhabitant of a country in which French is one of two or more official languages.
— ***adj.*** = Francophonic.
[< French *Francophone* < *Franco-* + *-phone*]
Fran|co|phon|ic or **fran|co|phon|ic** (frang′kə-fon′ik), *adj.* of Francophones; French-speaking.
Fran|co-Prus|sian (frang′kō prush′ən), *adj.* of or having to do with France and Prussia: *the Franco-Prussian war.*
franc-ti|reur (frän tē rœr′), *n., pl.* **francs-ti|reurs** (frän tē rœr′). a member of a corps of light infantry, originating in the wars of the French Revolution, and having an organization distinct from that of the regular army. [< French *franc-tireur* (literally) free shooter < *franc* free + *tireur* shooter < *tirer* to shoot]
fran|gi|bil|i|ty (fran′jə bil′ə tē), *n.* the quality or state of being frangible.
fran|gi|ble (fran′jə bəl), *adj.* easily broken or breakable; fragile: *a delicate, irreplaceable, and most frangible set of antique china teacups.* [< Old French *frangible,* learned borrowing from Medieval Latin *frangibilis* < Latin *frangere* to break]
— **fran′gi|ble|ness,** *n.*
fran|gi|pane (fran′jə pān), *n.* **1** a cake of pastry made with cream, almonds, and spices. **2** = frangipani. [< French *frangipane,* variant of *frangipani* < Italian < *Frangipani* an Italian marquis of the 1500's, the supposed inventor of the perfume]
fran|gi|pan|i (fran′jə pan′ē), *n., pl.* **-pan|is. 1** a perfume made from, or imitating the odor of, the flower of the red jasmine. **2** the red jasmine, a tropical American shrub or tree of the dogbane family. [< Italian *frangipani;* see etym. under **frangipane**]
fran|gi|pan|ni (fran′jə pan′ē), *n., pl.* **-nis.** = frangipani.
fran|glais or **Fran|glais** (fräng glā′), *n., adj.* French spoken with many English words and expressions: *Franglais permits a Frenchman to do le planning et research on le manpowerisation of a complexe industrielle before taking off for le weekend in le country* (Time). [< French *franglais,* blend of *français* French and *anglais* English]
fran|gli|fi|ca|tion (frang′glə fə kā′shən), *n.* the introduction of English words and expressions into French. [< French *franglification* < *franglais* + *-fication*]
frank[1] (frangk), *adj., v., n.* — ***adj.*** **1** free in expressing one's real thoughts, opinions, and feelings; not hiding what is in one's mind; not afraid to say what one thinks; open: *She was frank in telling me she did not like my new hat.* **2** clearly manifest; undisguised; plain: *frank mutiny, a frank imitation.* **3** *Rare.* liberal; generous: *In such frank style the people lived* (James Anthony Froude). **4** *Obsolete.* without restriction or restraint; free: *The court of aldermen ... shall all have their places frank* (Alexander Pope).
— ***v.t.*** **1** to send (a letter, message, or package) without charge. **2** to mark to show that a letter, message, or package is to be sent without charge. **3** *Figurative.* to send or convey (a person) free of charge; enable to come and go freely: *English ... will now frank the traveller through the most of North America* (Robert Louis Stevenson). **4** to secure exemption for; make immune: *The abstract merits ... are almost franked from criticism* (George Saintsbury).
— ***n.*** **1** a mark to show that a letter, message, or package is to be sent without charge: *I must ... send this scrawl into town to get a frank ... it is not worthy of postage* (Scott). **2** the right to send letters, messages, or packages without charge. **3** a letter, message, or package sent without charge.
[< Old French *franc* free; sincere, (originally) a Frank, a freeman < Frankish *Frank* a Frank]
— **frank′ly,** *adv.* — **frank′ness,** *n.*
— ***Syn.*** *adj.* **1 Frank, outspoken, candid** mean not afraid to say what one thinks or feels. **Frank** suggests being willing to express oneself openly, hiding or keeping back nothing: *He was frank to admit that he had not studied the lesson carefully.* **Outspoken** suggests being ready or even eager to speak out, often bluntly: *He was outspoken in his criticism.* **Candid** suggests being unwilling to conceal the truth, however unpleasant it may be: *He was candid about his brother's dishonesty.*
frank[2] (frangk), *n. Informal.* a frankfurter.
Frank (frangk), *n.* **1** a member of a group of West Germanic tribes that conquered northern Gaul in the 400's and 500's A.D. **2** a Levantine name for any European. [apparently < Old French *franc;* see etym. under **frank[1]**]
frank|a|ble (frang′kə bəl), *adj.* that can be franked: *a frankable letter.*
Frank|en|stein (frang′kən stīn), *n.* **1** a scientist in a story written in the 1800's who creates a monster that he cannot control. **2** the monster itself. **3** *Figurative.* anything that causes the ruin of its creator. [< *Frankenstein,* a novel by Mary Shelley, 1797-1851]
frank|er (frang′kər), *n.* a person or machine that franks letters, messages, or packages.
frank|fort sausage (frangk′fərt), = frankfurter.
frank|furt (frangk′fərt), *n.* = frankfurter.
frank|furt|er (frangk′fər tər, -fėr′-), *n.* a reddish

Pronunciation Key: hat, āge, cãre, fär; let, ēqual, tėrm, it, īce; hot, ōpen, ôrder; oil, out; cup, pu̇t, rüle; child; long; thin; ᴛʜen; zh, measure; ə represents **a** in about, **e** in taken, **i** in pencil, **o** in lemon, **u** in circus.

smoked sausage made of beef and pork, or of beef alone; wiener. Frankfurters on buns are often called hot dogs. [American English < German *Frankfurter* (originally) of Frankfurt, Germany]

frank|in|cense (frang′kin sens), *n.* a fragrant gum resin from certain Asiatic or African trees of the same family as myrrh. It gives off a sweet, spicy odor when burned. It has been much used from ancient times, especially for burning as incense in religious observances. [< Old French *franc encens* pure incense]

frank|in|censed (frang′kin senst), *adj.* perfumed with frankincense.

Frank|ish (frang′kish), *adj., n.* **—*adj.*** of or having to do with the Franks. **—*n.*** the Germanic language of the Franks (def. 1).

frank|lin (frangk′lən), *n.* in England: **1** a freeholder. **2** (in the 1300's and 1400's) a landowner of free but not noble birth, who ranked next below the gentry. [Middle English *frankelein,* ultimately < Medieval Latin *francus* free, (originally) a Frank]

Frank|lin|i|an (frangk lin′ē ən), *adj., n.* **—*adj.*** **1** of or having to do with Benjamin Franklin. **2** following his views or example in politics.
—*n.* a follower of Franklin.

frank|lin|ite (frangk′lə nīt), *n. Mineralogy.* an oxide of iron, manganese, and zinc, found in brilliant black crystals, used as a zinc ore and in the manufacture of spiegeleisen, a kind of pig iron. [American English < *Franklin,* New Jersey, the site of its discovery + *-ite*[1]]

Franklin's grouse, a grouse found in the spruce regions of the northwestern U.S. [< Sir John *Franklin,* 1786-1847, an English arctic explorer]

Franklin's gull, a small white gull with gray mantle, black and white wing tips, and in the summer a black head; prairie pigeon. It is one of the few gulls not found along seacoasts, nesting in the prairies and marshy lakes of interior North America. [see etym. under **Franklin's grouse**]

***Franklin stove**, *U.S.* **1** a stove for heating a room, resembling an iron fireplace, devised by Benjamin Franklin. **2** any one of certain open stoves.

***Franklin stove**
definition 1

Franklin tree, a small tree of the tea family that once grew wild in Georgia, now cultivated for its showy white flowers. [< Benjamin *Franklin,* 1706-1790 (named in his honor)]

frank|pledge (frangk′plej′), *n.* in Old English Law: **1** a system by which the members of a tithing (a group of ten inhabitants of a community) were made responsible for one another's conduct. **2** each of these mutually responsible members. **3** the tithing itself. [< Anglo-French *fraunke plege* < *franc* free + *plege* pledge; perhaps mistranslation of Old English *frith-borh* peace pledge]

fran|tic (fran′tik), *adj.* **1** very much excited; wild with rage, fear, pain, grief, etc.: *frantic with anxiety. The trapped animal made frantic efforts to escape. For frantic boast and foolish word Thy mercy on thy people Lord* (Rudyard Kipling). **SYN:** mad, distracted. **2** *Archaic.* affected with mental disease; lunatic; insane. [< Old French *frenetique,* learned borrowing from Latin *phrenēticus* < Greek *phrenītikós* < *phrenītis* inflammation of the brain, frenzy < *phrēn* mind. See etym. of doublet **phrenetic**.] **—fran′tic|ness**, *n.*

fran|ti|cal|ly or **fran|tic|ly** (fran′tə klē), *adv.* in a frantic manner; with wild excitement: *The fox pulled frantically at the trap to escape.*

frap (frap), *v.t.,* **frapped, frap|ping. 1** *Nautical.* **a** to bind (as a sail) securely. **b** to draw taut the ropes of (as tackle). **2** *British Dialect.* to strike. [< Old French *fraper* shoot, dart out, apparently < a Germanic word]

frappe (frap), *n.* **1** a flavored milk drink into which ice cream has been beaten. **2** = frappé.

frap|pé (fra pā′), *adj., n., v.,* **-péed, -pé|ing.** *U.S.* **—*adj.*** iced; cooled.
—*n.* **1** a fruit juice sweetened and partially frozen or shaken with finely cracked ice. **2** any frozen or iced food or drink.
—*v.t.* to ice; cool: *The daiquiris were served frappéed.*
[American English < French *frappé,* past participle of *frapper* chill, beat < Old French *fraper;* see etym. under **frap**]

F.R.A.S., Fellow of the Royal Astronomical Society.

Fras|ca|ti (frä skä′tē), *n.* a sweet white wine made in Latium, central Italy. [< *Frascati,* a town in Latium]

Fra|ser fir (frā′zhər), a small fir that grows in the mountains of North Carolina, Virginia, and Tennessee, having dense foliage and small cones with a rough surface, and often used as a Christmas tree; she-balsam. [< John *Fraser,* an English botanist of the 1700's]

fra|sier (frā′zhər), *n. Heraldry.* cinquefoil. [< French *fraisier* strawberry plant < *fraise* strawberry]

frass (fras), *n.* **1** the refuse left behind by boring insects. **2** the excrement of larvae. [< German *Frass* (literally) feed]

frat (frat), *n., v.,* **frat|ted, frat|ting. —*n.*** *U.S. Slang.* a fraternity.
—*v.i.* *Slang.* to fraternize: *... a little fratting with a certain ... lady, with an obvious eye to the main chance* (London Times).

fratch (frach), *v., n. Dialect.* **—*v.i.*** to disagree; quarrel. **—*n.*** a disagreement; quarrel. [perhaps imitative] **—fratch′er**, *n.*

fratch|y (frach′ē), *adj. Dialect.* quarrelsome; that scolds.

fra|ter[1] (frā′tər), *n.* **1** a brother or comrade. **2** *Obsolete.* a friar. [< Latin *frāter*]

fra|ter[2] (frā′tər), *n. Historical.* the refectory, or room where meals were eaten, of a monastery. [Middle English *freitore* < Old French *fraitur,* for *refreitor* < *refeitor* < Late Latin *refectōrium*]

fra|ter|nal (frə tėr′nəl), *adj.* **1** of or having to do with brothers or a brother; characteristic of brothers or a brother; brotherly: *a fraternal likeness, a fraternal feeling of responsibility.* **2** having to do with a group organized for mutual fellowship: *a fraternal affiliation.* **3** having to do with fraternal twins. [< Latin *frāternus* brotherly (< *frāter* brother) + English *-al*[1]] **—fra|ter′nal|ly**, *adv.*

fra|ter|nal|ism (frə tėr′nə liz əm), *n.* **1** the state or character of being fraternal. **2** the principle or practice of association in fraternal organizations.

fraternal order or **society**, a group organized for mutual aid and fellowship; fraternity.

fraternal twins, twins of the same or opposite sex coming from two separately fertilized egg cells rather than from one egg cell as identical twins do.

frat|er|nise (frat′ər nīz), *v.i., v.t.,* **-nised, -nis|ing.** *Especially British.* fraternize.

fra|ter|ni|ty (frə tėr′nə tē), *n., pl.* **-ties. 1** a group of men or boys joined together for fellowship or for some other purpose. There are student fraternities in many American colleges. They often have a name of two or three Greek letters, secret rites, and affiliated chapters at other schools. See also **sorority**. **2** *Figurative.* a group having the same interests, kind of work, or other common endeavor: *the musical fraternity, the engineering fraternity. Homebuilding had been an entirely private undertaking of a real estate fraternity* (Commentary). **3a** an ecclesiastical order. **b** an organization of laymen in the Roman Catholic Church for pious or charitable purposes. **4** fraternal feeling; brotherhood. [perhaps < Old French *fraternite,* learned borrowing from Latin *frāternitās* brotherhood < *frāternus* brotherly < *frāter* brother]

fraternity house, a house occupied by a college or school fraternity.

frat|er|ni|za|tion (frat′ər nə zā′shən), *n.* **1** the act of fraternizing. **2** the state or condition of fraternity; fraternal association.

frat|er|nize (frat′ər nīz), *v.,* **-nized, -niz|ing. —*v.i.*** **1** to associate in a brotherly way; be friendly (with). **2** to associate in a friendly way with the citizens of a hostile nation during occupation of their territory.
—*v.t.* to bring into fraternal association or sympathy; unite as brothers. **—frat′er|niz′er**, *n.*

frat house, *U.S. Slang.* a fraternity house.

frat|ri|cid|al (frat′rə sī′dəl, frā′trə-), *adj.* **1** having to do with fratricide. **2** having to do with the killing of relatives or fellow citizens: *A civil war is a fratricidal struggle.*

frat|ri|cide[1] (frat′rə sīd, frā′trə-), *n.* the act of killing one's own brother or sister. [< Latin *frātricīdium* < *frāter* brother + *-cīdium* act of killing, -cide[2]]

frat|ri|cide[2] (frat′rə sīd, frā′trə-), *n.* a person who kills his own brother or sister. [< Latin *frātricīda* < *frāter* brother + *-cīda* killer, -cide[1]]

frau (frou), *n., pl.* **fraus** (frouz). *Slang.* wife. [< *Frau*]

Frau (frou), *n., pl.* **Fraus** (frouz), *German* **Frau|en** (frou′ən). **1** Mrs. *Abbr:* Fr. **2** a wife. [< German *Frau*]

fraud (frôd), *n.* **1a** dishonest dealing; cheating; trickery: *to obtain a prize by fraud, to win an election by fraud.* **SYN:** deceit, dishonesty. **b** *Law.* any deliberate misrepresentation of the truth or a fact used to take money, rights, or other privilege or property away from a person or persons: *Any intent to deceive is proof of fraud.* **2** a dishonest act or statement; something which is not what it seems to be; trick: *The advertisement of a sale was a fraud to lure people into the store.* **SYN:** dodge, sham, fake. **3** *Informal.* a person who is not what he pretends to be: *You old fraud! Pretending to be stingy and yet donating so generously!* **SYN:** cheat, impostor. [< Old French *fraude,* learned borrowing from Latin *fraus, fraudis* cheating, deceit]

fraud|ful (frôd′fəl), *adj.* full of fraud; deceitful; treacherous; fraudulent. **—fraud′ful|ly**, *adv.*

fraud|u|lence (frô′jə ləns, frôd′yů-), *n.* the quality or fact of being fraudulent.

fraud|u|len|cy (frô′jə lən sē, frôd′yů-), *n., pl.* **-cies.** = fraudulence.

fraud|u|lent (frô′jə lənt, frôd′yů-), *adj.* **1** cheating; dishonest; deceitful: *a fraudulent dealer, a fraudulent schemer.* **2** intended to deceive: *a fraudulent offer.* **3** done by fraud; obtained by trickery: *fraudulent gains.* [< Old French *fraudulent* < Latin *fraudulentus* < *fraus, fraudis* cheating] **—fraud′u|lent|ly**, *adv.*

fraught (frôt), *adj., n., v.,* **fraught** or **fraught|ed, fraught|ing. —*adj.*** (of a vessel) laden.
—*n.* *Scottish.* a burden; load.
—*v.t.* *Obsolete.* to load (a ship) with cargo.
fraught with, loaded, filled, or stored with: *The attempt to climb Mount Everest was fraught with danger. A battlefield is fraught with horror.*
[< Middle Dutch or Middle Low German *vracht* freight]

fräu|lein (froi′līn), *n., pl.* **fräu|leins.** *Slang.* a young, unmarried German woman.

Fräu|lein (froi′līn), *n., pl.* **Fräu|leins,** *German* **Fräu|lein. 1** Miss. **2** an unmarried woman; young lady. **3** governess. [< German *Fräulein* (diminutive) < *Frau* lady]

Fraun|ho|fer lines (froun′hō′fər), the dark lines observed in the solar spectrum, caused by the absorption of some of the light by gaseous elements. [< Joseph von *Fraunhofer,* 1787-1826, a Bavarian optician and physicist]

frax|i|nel|la (frak′sə nel′ə), *n.* a plant of the rue family cultivated for its showy flowers; dittany. It is sometimes called *gas plant* or *burning bush* because, on a hot, windless summer night, the strong fumes from its foliage and flowers will ignite if a lighted match is held close. [< New Latin *fraxinella* the species name (diminutive) < Latin *frāxinus* ash tree]

fray[1] (frā), *n., v.* **—*n.*** a noisy quarrel, brawl, or fight: *The first blow makes the Wrong, but the second makes the Fray* (John Donne). (*Figurative.*) *always eager for the fray.* **SYN:** skirmish, conflict.
—*v.i.* *Archaic or Dialect.* to make a disturbance; quarrel or fight.
—*v.t.* *Archaic or Dialect.* to affect with fear; make afraid; frighten. [variant of *affray*]

fray[2] (frā), *v., n.* **—*v.t.*** **1** to cause to separate into threads (something woven or twisted); make ragged or worn along the edge: *Long wear had frayed the collar and cuffs of his old shirt.* (*Figurative.*) *His nerves were frayed by long hours and hard work.* **2** to wear away; rub: *A stag frays its horns against a tree to rub off the velvet.*
—*v.i.* to become ragged or worn along the edge: *His trousers are beginning to fray at the cuffs.*
—*n.* the result of fraying; frayed place.
[< Old French *freier* < Latin *fricāre* to rub]

fra|zil (frə zil′), *n. Canada and U.S.* fine crystals of ice that form in moving water, such as in the Arctic Ocean. [< Canadian French *frazil* < French *fraisil* cinders]

fraz|zle (fraz′əl), *v.,* **-zled, -zling,** *n.* **—*v.t., v.i.*** **1** to wear to shreds; fray; ravel; wear out: *The edges of the rug were completely frazzled.* (*Figurative.*) *Tempers are easily frazzled during a crisis of work and worry.* **2** to tire out; weary.
—*n.* *Informal.* a frazzled condition.
[perhaps a blend of *fray*[2], and obsolete *fazle,* Middle English *faselyn* unravel < Old English *fæs* a fringe]

FRB (no periods) or **F.R.B.**, Federal Reserve Board.

F.R.C.P., Fellow of the Royal College of Physicians.

F.R.C.S., Fellow of the Royal College of Surgeons.

freak[1] (frēk), *n., adj., v.* **—*n.*** **1a** something very queer or unusual: *A green leaf growing in the middle of a rose would be called a freak of nature.* **b** an animal, plant, or person that has developed in an abnormal way; monstrosity: *A circus often has a sideshow of freaks.* **2** a sudden change of mind without reason; odd notion or fancy: *a freak of fancy. Her nature was subject to freaks.* **SYN:** whim, vagary, caprice. **3** a sudden change of the wind. **4** capriciousness. **5** a capricious prank or trick; caper: *... expelled from Harrow for some boyish freak* (Anthony Trollope). **6** *Slang.* **a** a person who has broken away from conventional society, especially a hippie: *The number of freaks—people given to long hair, beads, and joss sticks—grows every year* (Harper's). **b** a drug addict: *Parental and official concern, and anger too, is focused in Canada on amphetamine abuse, on the growth of a depression-ridden community of "speed freaks"* (*methedrine addicts*) (London Times). **c** an addict of anything; devotee or enthusiast: *I am also a Black Coffee freak, and have been known to drink fifteen to twenty cups in a day* (Raymond Mungo).

—***adj.*** very queer or unusual: *a freak storm.*

—***v.i.*** **1** to indulge in freaks; caper; frolic. **2** *Slang.* to get or make extremely excited, as if under the influence of a hallucinogenic drug: *"They* [*a rock singing group*] *won't do an encore," one of the crew said. "The kids didn't freak enough"* (Atlantic).

freak out, *Slang.* **a** to come or put under the influence of hallucinogenic drugs: *The undergraduates attracted there might not be strong on scholarship but they would be ... more given to surfing than freaking out on drugs* (Manchester Guardian Weekly). **b** to experience or produce sensations or reactions similar to those induced by hallucinogenic drugs; make or become extremely excited: *As a matter of fact, it's nonsense to listen to most good west coast rock unless you're prepared to let yourself freak out emotionally and just wallow around in the sound* (Canadian Saturday Night). **c** to break away from the attitudes or institutions of conventional society; change radically: *There are two ways to react to a world you never made. You can 'freak out' or you can 'bend the wind'* (Jesse Unruh). *I have never known so many intelligent ... persons to be so freaked out by an election* (Michael J. Arlen).

[origin uncertain]

freak² (frēk), *v., n.* —***v.t.*** to fleck or streak whimsically or capriciously; variegate: *The pansy freak'd with jet* (Milton).

—***n.*** a splash, fleck, or streak of color.

[perhaps variant of *freck*]

freak|i|ness (frē'kē nis), *n.* the state or quality of being freaky or freakish.

freak|ish (frē'kish), *adj.* **1** full of freaks; very queer or unusual: *The famous actress had a freakish disposition.* **2** capricious; whimsical: *the bounds of freakish youth* (William Cowper). **3** of the nature of a freak; queer; grotesque: *Some forms of cactus appear freakish.* —**freak'ish|ly**, *adv.* —**freak'ish|ness**, *n.*

freak|out (frēk'out'), *n. Slang.* **1** the fact or state of being under the influence of a drug that distorts reality, such as LSD or other hallucinogenic drug. **2** a party where people use hallucinogenic drugs. **3** a person who is under the influence of a hallucinogenic drug. **4** the action or behavior of a freakout.

freak show, a sideshow of abnormally developed animals or people or very queer or unusual things at a circus, carnival, or the like.

freak|y (frē'kē), *adj.*, **freak|i|er, freak|i|est**, *n., pl.* **-freak|ies.** —***adj.*** **1** = freakish. **2** of or having to do with freaks or freakouts: *freaky rock music.*

—***n.*** a person who has freaked out; freak.

fream (frēm), *v.i.* (of a boar) to roar; rage; growl.

freck (frek), *v.t.* to mark with spots or freckles; dapple. [perhaps short for *freckle*]

freck|le (frek'əl), *n., v.*, **-led, -ling.** —***n.*** one of the small, light-brown spots that some people have on the skin; lentigo. They are sometimes produced by exposure to the sun.

—***v.t.*** to make freckles on; cover with freckles.

—***v.i.*** to become marked or spotted with freckles.

[probably alteration of Middle English *frecken*, perhaps < Scandinavian (compare Old Icelandic *frecknur*, plural)]

freck|led (frek'əld), *adj.* **1** marked with freckles. **2** spotted; dappled; variegated: *the freckled trout.* —**freck'led|ness**, *n.*

freck|le-faced (frek'əl fāst'), *adj.* having a face marked with freckles.

freck|ling (frek'ling), *n.* a mark like a freckle; a spot, fleck.

freck|ly (frek'lē), *adj.* covered with freckles.

free (frē), *adj.*, **fre|er, fre|est**, *adv., v.*, **freed, free|ing.** —***adj.*** **1** not under another's control; not a captive or slave: *a free man, a free people, a free nation, free speech.* **SYN:** independent. **2** not held back from acting or thinking as one pleases; having liberty: *She was free to come and go around the house. You are free to criticize my work.* **3a** not held back, fastened, or shut up; released; loose: *Let the captives go free.* **SYN:** movable, unfastened. **b** released from ties, obligations, work, or duty: *Free, madam! no ... He's bound unto Octavia* (Shakespeare). **4** not hindered; easy: *a free step, to get one's hand free.* **5** clear; open; unobstructed: *water having a free passage.* **6** open to all competitors: *a free contest.* **7** without anything to pay: *These tickets are free.* **SYN:** gratuitous. **8** having no tax, duty, or toll: *free trade, free importation of goods.* **9** *Figurative.* not following rules, forms, or words exactly; not strict: *free verse, a free translation.* **10a** not combined with something else: *Oxygen exists free in air.* **b** not in contact with or connected to some other body or surface: *at the free surface of the mucous membrane* (Ronald Knox). **11** done, given, or made willingly or spontaneously: *He made a free offer of his services.* **12** abundant; copious; profuse: *a rose that is a free bloomer.* **13** saying what one thinks; frank: *He is free to the point of being tactless.* **SYN:** ingenuous, open, unreserved. **14** not restrained enough by manners or morals: *For a stranger, his manner was entirely too free.* **SYN:** forward, familiar. **15** easily worked; loose and soft, as stone or land. **16** blowing in a favorable direction for sailing, not on the bow: *The breeze was fair and free.* **17** *Phonetics.* **a** (of a vowel or diphthong) occurring in an open syllable: *The vowel represented by "aw" is free in "law," but checked in "lawn."* **b** (of a vowel or diphthong) being a member of a class of vowels and diphthongs which may occur in an open syllable: *In English, the vowel of "law" is one of the free vowels.* **c** (of a syllable) ending in a vowel or diphthong; open: *The first syllable of "over" is free.* **d** (of word accent) not fixed on the same syllable in different inflectional forms of a word. **e** (of variation between allophones) not determined by position.

—***adv.*** **1** without cost or payment: *Children under 12 can attend free.* **2** in a free manner; freely: *The animals ran free around the farm.* **3** *Nautical.* with the wind blowing favorably, not on the bow.

—***v.t.*** **1** to relieve from any kind of burden, bondage, or slavery; make free: *Abraham Lincoln freed the slaves.* **SYN:** liberate, emancipate. **2** to let loose; release: *He freed his foot from the vine that tripped him.* **SYN:** disengage, disentangle. See syn. under **release**. **3** to clear: *to free gas of impurities. The judge freed him of this charge of stealing.*

for free, without charge or cost: *... train passengers who sleep past their destination and get trundled back home for free* (Punch).

free and clear, *Law.* (of real estate) not encumbered by any lien, as a mortgage: *He's met his mortgage payments promptly—and now his home is free and clear* (Wall Street Journal).

free and easy, **a** free from constraint; natural; unaffected: *a free and easy manner, to act free and easy.* **b** careless; slipshod: *He was criticized for his free and easy methods of research.*

free from (or **of**), without; having no; lacking: *free from fear, air free of dust. The industry has a statutory obligation to distribute gas free from hydrogen sulphide* (Times Literary Supplement).

free with, giving or using freely; generous, liberal, or lavish with: *free with one's money. He is too free with criticism.*

make free with, to use as if one owned or had complete rights: *Our uninvited guests made free with everything we owned.*

set free, to make free; let loose; release: *He set free the bear cub caught in the trap.*

[Old English *frēo, frīo*] —**free'ly**, *adv.*

free agent, *U.S.* a player, especially in football or baseball, who is not under contract to any professional team.

free alongside ship or **vessel**, delivered to a ship's side without charge to the buyer, but with all further transportation being at the buyer's expense. *Abbr:* f.a.s.

free-and-eas|y (frē'ən ē'zē), *adj., n., pl.* **-eas|ies.** —***adj.*** paying little attention to rules and customs: *For years, respectable, upper-register Palm Springs had prided itself on the fact that, unlike free-and-easy Las Vegas, it achieved its place among top-flight resort communities without surrendering its civic virtue* (Newsweek).

—***n.*** **1** a convivial gathering or party, as in a tavern. **2** a tavern.

free-as|so|ci|ate (frē'ə sō'shē āt), *v.i.*, **-at|ed, -at|ing.** to use or engage in free association: *"But you can free-associate to anything" said Polly. "The word 'fire' for instance. What does it make you think of?" "Water." "And water?" ...* (Mary McCarthy). [back formation < *free association*]

free association, *Psychoanalysis.* **1** a linkage or sequence of ideas, one suggesting another regardless of logical connection and without control or suggestion on the part of an analyst. **2** the psychoanalytic technique of evoking free associations from a patient as subjects for analysis and as a means of assisting the patient's conscious recall of feelings and experiences not consciously remembered.

free-as|so|ci|a|tion|al (frē'ə sō'sē ā'shə nəl, -shē-), *adj.* of or characterized by free association.

free atmosphere, the region that includes all of the atmosphere except a layer of about a mile thick next to the surface of the earth.

free|base (frē'bās'), *v.*, **-based, -bas|ing.** *n., adj.*

—***v.t.*** to remove the salts and other additives from (cocaine): *The comic was freebasing cocaine ... when the mixture exploded* (New York Post).

—***n.*** cocaine that has been freebased: *Freebase, made by treating the white powder with ether* (New York Times). —***adj.*** freebased.

free|bie or **free|bee** (frē'bē), *n. Especially U.S. Slang.* **1** something obtained free of charge; something gratis, especially free tickets or drinks: *Bartenders are enjoined from giving freebies to customers, no matter how much they spend* (Time). **2** a person who gets or gives something free of charge: [originally an adjective, *freebie* or *freeby* free of charge < *free* + *-bee* or *-by* (origin unknown)]

free|board (frē'bôrd', -bōrd'), *n.* **1** the vertical distance, or the surface of the hull, between the water line and the deck or gunwale. **2** the distance between the ground and the under part of the frame of an automobile.

free|boot (frē'büt'), *v.i.* to act as a freebooter.

free|boot|er (frē'bü'tər), *n.* a pirate; buccaneer: *In their veins flows the blood of those countless mariners, freebooters, fishermen, and traders who have sailed these seas* (Atlantic). [< Dutch *vrijbuiter* < *vrijbuiten* to rob, plunder < *vrij* free + *buit* booty. See etym. of doublet **filibuster**.]

free|boot|ing (frē'bü'ting), *n.* piracy; buccaneering.

free|born (frē'bôrn'), *adj.* **1** born free, not in slavery. **2** of or suitable for people born free: *freeborn rights.*

free chant, a form of recitative for the psalms and canticles, invented by John Crowdy. It consists of two chords only to each hemistich of the words.

free chapel, (in England) a chapel not subject to the jurisdiction of the ordinary, having been founded by the king or by a subject specially authorized by him.

free charge, *Physics.* the charge within a conductor that moves when a force is exerted on it by an electric field: *The free charges in a metallic conductor are negative electrons. The free charges in an electrolyte are ions, both positive and negative* (Sears and Zemansky).

free church, **1** *U.S.* a church in which the pews are not rented, but are open to all. **2** a church free from state control.

Free Church, **1** a Presbyterian Church in Scotland, organized in 1843 by secession from the established Presbyterian Church. **2** *British.* any church, especially a Protestant church, that is not in communion with the Church of England.

free city, a city having an independent government and forming an independent state: *During the life of Paul, Tarsus became one of the "free cities" of the Roman Empire* (Joseph W. Swain).

free coinage, the coinage of any amount of bullion (gold or silver), or other specified metal, into money acceptable as legal tender, at little or no charge, for anyone who brings it to the mint.

free companion, a member of a band of mercenary of the Middle Ages, who hired themselves to any ruler or nation; free lance; condottiere.

free company, a band of free companions.

free diver, = skin diver.

free diving, = skin diving.

freed|man (frēd'mən), *n., pl.* **-men.** a man freed from slavery; emancipated slave.

free|dom (frē'dəm), *n.* **1** the state or condition of being free: *In this then consists freedom ... in our being able to act or not to act, according as we shall choose or will* (John Locke). **2** not being under another's control; power to do, say, or think as one pleases; liberty: *freedom of religion, freedom of the press, political freedom.* **3** *Figurative.* free use: *We give a guest the freedom of our home.* **4** too great liberty; lack of restraint; frankness: *We did not like the freedom of his manner.* **SYN:** outspokenness. **5** ease of movement or action: *A fine athlete performs with freedom.* **6** exemption or release from unfavorable or undesirable conditions: *freedom from fear, freedom from want.* **7** a special immunity or privilege possessed by a city, corporation, or other group or individual. **8** exemption or immunity from a charge or burden: *freedom from taxation.* **9** boldness of conception or execution; fluency: *freedom of style in writing.* **10** *Philosophy.* the position of the will as an independent cause of human actions: *The power of relinquishing what one would keep; that is freedom* (Marianne Moore). **11** *Physics.* the capacity that a system

---

has for undergoing change without loss of equilibrium; the number of variables which fix the state of a system or substance. [Old English *frēodōm*]

— *Syn.* 1, 2 **Freedom, liberty, independence** mean being able to act without interference or control by another. **Freedom** emphasizes the power to exercise rights, powers, and the like: *Every person should have the freedom to worship as he chooses.* **Liberty** emphasizes absence of external restraint and compulsion on an individual: *Freedom of speech does not mean liberty to gossip and tell lies.* **Independence** emphasizes the power to stand alone, sometimes supported by, but never subject to or dependent on someone or something else: *Parents try to teach their children independence.*

Freedom Day, *U.S.* February 1, the anniversary of the day in 1865 when Abraham Lincoln signed a resolution proposing an amendment to the Constitution to outlaw slavery.

freedom fighter, a person who bears arms against or otherwise actively opposes a dictatorial government, such as those Hungarians who revolted against the Soviet-supported, Communist government in 1956.

Free|dom|ite (frē′də mīt), *n., adj.* **—*n.*** a member of the Sons of Freedom, a small sect of Doukhobors in Canada.
—***adj.*** of or having to do with this sect.

freedom march, *U.S.* freedom walk. **—freedom marcher.**

freedom of information, 1 freedom from governmental interference with the flow of information: *Scarcely one-fifth of UN member countries enjoyed what could genuinely be called freedom of information* (Harford Thomas). 2 unrestricted public access to government records and documents that do not violate an individual's privacy or endanger national security: *Legislation introduced [in Canada] during the first two months included a freedom of information Bill designed to allow greater access to government files* (Bruce Thordarson).

freedom of speech, = free speech.

freedom of the seas, the right of ships to come and go on the high seas, no state having any jurisdiction over foreign vessels except within its own territorial waters.

freedom ride, *U.S.* a bus ride taken to challenge racial segregation in interstate public travel.

freedom rider, *U.S.* a Negro or white person taking part in a freedom ride.

Freedom School, *U.S.* a special school to supplement the education of children in order for them to meet various legal requirements, such as a voting rights test.

freedom walk, *U.S.* a march undertaken to demonstrate against racial discrimination. **—freedom walker.**

freed|wom|an (frēd′wům′ən), *n., pl.* **-wom|en.** a woman freed from slavery.

free electron, an electron that is detached from an atom and can therefore move from atom to atom, as it does in a conductor of electricity.

free energy, *Physics.* the internal energy potential of a thermodynamic system.

free enterprise, the right of private business to select and operate undertakings for profit with little control or regulation by the government; private enterprise.

free enterpriser, *U.S. and Canada.* a person who favors free enterprise; capitalist.

free fall, 1 the motion of a body in flight through space when it is not acted upon by any force except the gravity of planetary bodies. A body is weightless during free fall. 2 *Aeronautics.* the part of a parachute jump before a parachute is opened.

free-fall|ing (frē′fô′ling), *adj.* in a state of free fall, as a ballistic missile after the termination of thrust.

free fight, *Informal.* a fight involving any number of people; free-for-all.

free-fire zone (frē′fīr′), *Military.* an area in which any moving thing may be fired upon or bombed.

free flight, 1 the flight of a rocket or missile after thrust has terminated. 2 the flight of a balloon or glider after release from restraining cables or towrope.

free-flight tunnel (frē′flīt′), a wind tunnel that tests the stability and control of an aircraft. An operator outside the tunnel controls the aircraft as it flies freely inside.

free-float|ing (frē′flō′ting), *adj.* 1 floating or moving without an attachment: *free-floating grass, a free-floating astronaut.* 2 not established; unfounded; unproven: *a free-floating theory.* 3 not bound or committed; independent: *It was less a school now than a free-floating group of individuals* (New Yorker).

free-for-all (frē′fər ôl′), *n., adj.* **—*n.*** a fight, race, or contest, open to all or in which everybody participates: *The bystanders engaged in a free-for-all.* **—*adj.*** open to all.

free-for-all|er (frē′fər ôl′ər), *n. British Slang.* a person that ignores rules and restrictions to gain advantage.

free form, 1 a linguistic form which occurs alone or independently, as distinguished from a bound form. *Examples:* cold, street, eaten. 2 a form not having a conventional or prescribed structure or shape, such as one in music, art, or design: *a free form that predates the Mozart fantasias* (New York Times). **—free′-form′,** *adj.*

Free French, the French people who continued resistance to Germany after the Franco-German armistice of 1940. They were later sometimes known as the Fighting French.

free gold, 1 *U.S.* treasury gold in excess of the amount needed to back or redeem currency in circulation. 2 natural pure gold, as in nuggets. 3 the free coinage of gold.

free goods, (in time of war) goods and merchandise not subject to capture.

free|hand (frē′hand′), *adj., adv.* **—*adj.*** done by hand without measurements or instruments: *freehand drawing.* **—*adv.*** in a freehand manner.

free hand, 1 freedom to do as one chooses: *The carriers ... have been adamant in their demands for a free hand on the revisions* (Wall Street Journal). 2 generosity; open-handedness: *to serve guests with a free hand.*

free|hand|ed (frē′han′did), *adj.* generous; liberal; open-handed.

free|heart|ed (frē′här′tid), *adj.* 1 frank; open; unreserved. 2 generous; liberal; bountiful. 3 unburdened with anxiety, guilt, or suspicion. **—free′-heart′ed|ly,** *adv.* **—free′heart′ed|ness,** *n.*

free|hold (frē′hōld′), *n., adj., adv. Law.* **—*n.*** 1 a piece of land held for life or with the right to transfer it to one's heirs, as distinguished from a leasehold, which is held for a specified number of years: *It need hardly be added that the club, who own the freehold, find the problem of repairs and maintenance more and more difficult to solve* (London Times). 2 the fact of holding land in this way. 3 a corresponding tenure of an office or position.
—***adj.*** 1 held by freehold. 2 of or of the nature of a freehold. **—*adv.*** by freehold; for an indefinite time: *Few Irish farmers held their property freehold* (New York Times Magazine).

free|hold|er (frē′hōl′dər), *n.* a person who has a freehold.

free kick, *Football.* an unhampered kick, the opponents being prohibited from advancing upon the kicker.

Free Kirk, *Scottish.* Free Church (def. 1).

free lance, 1 a writer, artist, or other independent craftsman, who sells his work to anyone who will buy it. 2 a mercenary, especially a knight in the Middle Ages who fought for any person or state that would pay him; free companion; condottiere. 3 *Figurative.* a person who fights or works for any cause that he chooses, as in politics.

free-lance (frē′lans′, -läns′), *v.,* **-lanced, -lanc|ing,** *adj.* **—*v.i.*** to work as an independent writer, artist, or other independent craftsman, who sells his work to anyone who will buy it; be a free lance: *He is one of the very few outstanding modern-jazz figures who prefer to free-lance on records rather than sign an exclusive contract with one of the record companies* (New Yorker).
—***adj.*** of or having to do with such a writer, artist, or other independent craftsman; done by a free lance: *free-lance journalism.*

free-lanc|er (frē′lan′sər, -län′-), *n.* = free lance.

free list, a list of things on which payment of duty is not required.

free liver, a person who gives free indulgence to his appetites.

free-liv|ing (frē′liv′ing), *adj.* 1 living in a free or unrestrained manner. 2 *Biology.* **a** living free from and independent of a host; not parasitic. **b** living free from and independent of the parent, such as a medusa bud separated from the polyp stock upon which it grew. **c** able to live and move about independently; not sessile: *Most animals not parasitic or sessile are free-living.*

free|load (frē′lōd′), *v.i. Informal.* 1 to get something at another's expense, such as a free trip or free tickets, accommodations, or food. 2 to take freely, without making any contribution or effort of one's own: *protesting that a ... TV and radio crew had no right to freeload on questions and answers developed by newspapermen* (Time). **—free′load′er,** *n.*

free love, the doctrine of the right of free choice in sexual relations, without the restraint of marriage or other legal obligation.

free lover, a person who advocates or practices free love.

free|man (frē′mən), *n., pl.* **-men.** 1 a person who is not a slave or serf; a man who could own land: *In Parthia did I take thee prisoner ... Now be a freeman* (Shakespeare). 2 a person who has civil or political freedom; citizen: *a freeman of Athens.*

free market, a market in which prices are controlled by supply and demand, without governmental regulation or restriction. **—free′-mar′ket,** *adj.*

free|mar|tin (frē′mär′tən), *n.* an imperfect or sterile female calf born twin with a male. [origin uncertain. Compare Gaelic *mart* heifer, fatted cow.]

free|ma|son (frē′mā′sən), *n. Historical.* a member of a class of skilled stoneworkers in the 1300's and later, who traveled from place to place and formed a society using a system of secret signs and passwords.

Free|ma|son (frē′mā′sən), *n.* a member of a world-wide secret society (the Free and Accepted Masons), whose purpose is mutual aid and fellowship; Mason.

free|ma|son|ry (frē′mā′sən rē), *n.* common understanding and sympathy based on similar experiences.

Free|ma|son|ry (frē′mā′sən rē), *n.* 1 the principles, practices, and institutions of the Freemasons; Masonry. 2 the members of this society.

Free Methodist, a member of a church that follows the Methodist teachings of John Wesley and the free will doctrine of the Arminians, founded in 1860.

free-mind|ed (frē′mīn′did), *adj.* having the mind free from care, trouble, or perplexity.

free mount, a kind of display mounting for skeletons, especially for fossil bones, consisting of a steel framework to which the bones are fastened to hide the steel, so that in the finished mount the skeleton seems to stand by itself.

free|ness (frē′nis), *n.* the quality or state of being free; freedom.

free on board, (of goods, etc.) placed on a freight car, truck, or other means of transportation at a point specified by the seller, without charge to the buyer, but with all further transportation being at the buyer's expense. *Abbr:* f.o.b., FOB (no periods).

free overside, *Commerce.* (of merchandise bought for import) free of all charges down to the moment of discharge, as from a ship.

free part, *Music.* 1 a part added to a canon or fugue to complete the harmony. 2 in a canon, any part not an antecedent or a consequent.

free pass, authority to travel on a railway or other public carrier or to enter a place of entertainment without payment.

free-pis|ton engine (frē′pis′tən), an internal-combustion engine which has pairs of opposing pistons not connected to a crankshaft. When the two pistons come together after ignition, the exhaust gases are forced out and turn a turbine.

free place, (in Great Britain) a scholarship paying tuition in a secondary school awarded to a scholar from an elementary school.

free port, 1 a port open to traders of all countries on the same conditions. 2 = foreign trade zone.

free press, the business of publishing newspapers, magazines, and books without censorship or control by the government.

fre|er[1] (frē′ər), *n.* a person who frees.

fre|er[2] (frē′ər), *adj.* the comparative of **free.**

free radical, *Chemistry.* an organic compound in which some of the valence electrons are not paired, such as triphenyl methyl, $(C_6H_5)_3C$-.

free rein, complete freedom to do as one chooses: *Although you may indulge your emotions in imagining a part, you must not allow them free rein until you have selected exactly what you want to show the audience* (Listener).

free reserve, *U.S.* the difference between a bank's total reserve and the required minimum reserve and its own borrowings.

free-re|turn trajectory (frē′ri tėrn′), the trajectory of a spacecraft toward a lunar or planetary orbit which provides for an automatic return to earth if the spacecraft is unable to enter the proper orbit.

free ride, 1 something obtained without cost or effort: *The argument that enemy bombers must not be given a free ride over North America is often used in support of maintaining some means of active air defence* (Canadian Saturday Night). 2 *U.S. Informal.* the practice of subscribing to securities in advance of issue to sell them at a profit before having paid for them; the activity engaged in by a free rider. 3 (in poker) the right to play in a jack pot without having to ante or bet.
give a free ride, to put up for all the others in a poker jack pot: *Usually you give a free ride as a penalty for drawing to false openers.*

free rider, *U.S. Informal.* a person who subscribes for securities in advance of issue in the hope of selling them at a profit before having paid for them.

free school, a privately operated school in which traditional methods of teaching are discarded in favor of the open classroom and other experimental forms of education.
free services, (in the feudal system) services becoming the character of a soldier or freeman to perform, such as to serve under his lord in the wars and to contribute money.
free|sia (frē′zhə), *n.* any one of a genus of South African plants of the iris family, grown for their clusters of fragrant, white, rose, salmon, or yellow flowers. Freesias are grown from corms. [< New Latin *Freesia* the genus name < F.H.T. *Freese,* about 1795-1876, a German botanist]
free silver, the free coinage of silver, especially at a fixed 16-to-1 ratio with gold; the making of silver into coins for anyone who brings it to the mint. **–free′-sil′ver**, *adj.*
free-skat|er (frē′skā′tər), *n.* a person engaged in free skating.
free skating, a competitive form of figure skating in which the skater creates a routine of jumps, spins, and patterns to music of his own choice.
free soil, *U.S. Historical.* **1** a territory in which slaveholding was prohibited before the Civil War. **2** also, **free-soil** or **Free-soil (frē′soil′),** *adj.* **a** having to do with or in favor of the nonextension of slavery into those parts of the country not yet admitted as states. **b** of or having to do with the Free Soil Party or its principles.
Free Soil|er (frē′soi′lər), a member of the Free Soil Party.
Free Soil Party, a U.S. political party that was opposed to extending slavery into territories not yet admitted as states. It existed from 1848 to 1856.
free speech, the freedom accorded by law to express opinions and facts publicly or privately, subject to reasonable restriction by the government, as where danger to the country or to people's lives, property, or good reputation is involved; freedom of speech.
free speech|er (spē′chər), *U.S.* a person who agitates for free speech, as at a college or university.
free-spend|er (frē′spen′dər), *n.* a person who spends money liberally and lavishly.
free-spend|ing (frē′spen′ding), *adj.* given to or characterized by liberal spending.
free-spo|ken (frē′spō′kən), *adj.* speaking freely; saying what one thinks; frank: *Some people are too free-spoken to be popular.* **–free′-spo′ken-ness**, *n.*
free spool reel, a bait-casting reel having a handle that does not turn until the spool is to be wound.
fre|est (frē′ist), *adj.* the superlative of **free**.
free-stand|ing or **free|stand|ing** (frē′stan′-ding), *adj.* standing or able to stand by itself; separate; independent: *a free-standing building.*
Free State, *U.S. Historical.* any state in which slavery did not exist before the Civil War.
free|stone (frē′stōn′), *n., adj.* **–*n.*** **1** any fine-grained stone, especially limestone or sandstone, that can easily be cut without splitting. **2a** a fruit having a stone that is easily separated from the pulp. Certain kinds of peaches and plums are freestones. **b** the stone of such a fruit.
–*adj.* having a stone that is easily separated from the pulp: *a freestone peach.*
free-style (frē′stīl′), *adj., adv., n.* **–*adj.*** unrestricted as to style, method, or manner: *a free-style race. A free-style swimmer is allowed to choose his own stroke.*
–*adv.* in an unrestricted style or manner.
–*n.* **1** a free-style race, figure-skating contest, or other athletic event. **2** = catch-as-catch-can.
free-styl|er (frē′stī′lər), *n.* a free-style swimmer, skater, or other athlete.
free-swim|mer (frē′swim′ər), *n.* a free-swimming animal.
free-swim|ming (frē′swim′ing), *adj. Zoology.* able to swim about freely, as a jellyfish.
free-swing|er (frē′swing′ər), *n.* a recklessly bold person: *He has always been a free-swinger, too outspoken to serve in the legislature for long* (Atlantic).
free-swing|ing (frē′swing′ing), *adj.* **1** suspended or mounted so as to swing without hindrance, as a pendulum is. **2** *Figurative.* unrestrained, as by caution or tact: *a free-swinging fight, a free-swinging article.*
free|think|er (frē′thing′kər), *n.* a person who forms his own opinions, especially on religion, independently of authority or tradition. Historically the term is applied to a group of deists of the early 1700's and it still has the sense of agnostic, skeptic, or even atheist. *A freethinker I will be, and Believe nothing but what I know and understand* (Charles Kingsley).
free|think|ing (frē′thing′king), *n., adj.* **–*n.*** = free thought.
–*adj.* **1** holding the principles of a freethinker. **2** having to do with or relating to freethinkers or free thought.
free thought, religious opinions formed independently of authority or tradition.
free throw, in basketball: **1** = foul shot. **2** one point for scoring a foul shot.
free throw circle, either of the two circles in front of each basket on a standard basketball court.
free throw lane, a lane, usually 12 feet wide, that extends onto a basketball court from either end line and ends in a semicircle; keyhole. Players are not permitted in this lane during a foul shot.
free throw line, = foul line.
free-tongued (frē′tungd′), *adj.* given to speaking freely and without reserve.
free trade, **1a** trade between nations or states free from protective duties and subject only to tariffs for revenue. **b** the system, principles, or practice of maintaining such trade. **2** trade unrestricted by taxes, customs, duties, or differences of treatment. **3** smuggling.
free-trade (frē′trād′), *adj.* of or having to do with free trade.
free trade area, = foreign trade zone.
free|trad|er (frē′trā′dər), *n.* a person who favors the system of free trade.
free-trad|ing (frē′trā′ding), *adj.* favoring free trade.
free union, cohabitation of a couple without marriage.
free university, an independent college or university organized chiefly by students to study subjects of interest to them without the usual academic restrictions of grades, credits, or prerequisite courses.
free verse, poetry not restricted by the usual conventions of meter, rhyme, and the like, and often emphasizing variation of cadence and rhythm; vers libre.
free-vers|er (frē′vėr′sər), *n.* = free-versifier.
free-ver|si|fi|er (frē′vėr′sə fī′ər), *n.* a composer of free verse.
free water, the excess water following protracted rains that is unable to attach itself to soil particles, so that it gravitates into the zone of ground water; gravitational water.
free|way (frē′wā′), *n.* a divided highway for fast traveling on which usually no tolls are charged; expressway.
free|wheel (frē′hwēl′), *n., v.* **–*n.*** **1** a clutchlike device in the transmission of an automobile that disengages when the drive shaft turns faster than the shaft from the engine and engages when the speeds are equal. **2** a device on a bicycle that allows the wheels to continue turning when the pedals are stopped, as in coasting.
–*v.i.* to coast: *"You could freewheel backwards down," suggested Purbright, "if we guided you"* (Punch).
free|wheel|er (frē′hwē′lər), *n. U.S. Slang.* **1** an independent person. **2** = free-spender.
free|wheel|ing (frē′hwē′ling), *adj., n.* **–*adj.*** **1** coasting freely; having or using a freewheel. **2** *Figurative.* acting freely or without restraint; untrammeled and independent: *a freewheeling pioneer, a freewheeling discussion.*
–*n.* the use of a freewheel; coasting.
free will, will free from outside restraints; voluntary choice; freedom of decision.
free|will (frē′wil′), *adj.* made or done freely or of one's own accord; voluntary: *a freewill offering to the Red Cross.*
Freewill Baptist or **Free Will Baptist**, a member of a sect of Arminian Baptists.
free-willed (frē′wild′), *adj.* having the faculty of free will.
free|will|er (frē′wil′ər), *n.* a person who believes in the doctrine of free will.
free world or **Free World**, the nations of the world that are not under communist control; the non-Communist nations: *Some may believe it is America's business to guard the free world from Communist domination* (Wall Street Journal). **–free′-world′**, **Free′-World′**, *adj.*
freeze (frēz), *v.,* **froze, fro|zen, freez|ing,** *n.*
–*v.i.* **1a** to be turned into ice; harden by cold. Water becomes ice when it freezes. *The water in the pipes froze. The ice cream soon froze.* **b** to be of the degree of cold at which water becomes ice: *It is freezing tonight.* **2** to become very cold: *We froze at the football game. The weather suddenly froze.* **3** to be killed or injured by frost: *The flowers froze last night.* **4** to become covered or clogged with ice: *The pipes froze.* **5** *Figurative.* to become fixed to something by freezing: *His fingers froze to the tray of ice cubes. My very lips might freeze to my teeth* (Shakespeare). **6** *Figurative.* to become stiff and unfriendly: *The shy boy froze up when I tried to be friendly. At my question he immediately froze.* **7** *Figurative.* to be chilled with fear: *She froze at the sight of the ghostly hand.* **8** to become motionless: *The baby rabbit learned to freeze at a strange sound or sudden movement.*
–*v.t.* **1a** to turn into ice; harden by cold; congeal: *to freeze ice cream.* **b** to subject (food for preservation) to a very low temperature, usually below 0 degrees Fahrenheit, so rapidly that the juices and flavor are retained; quick-freeze. **2** to make very cold; chill: *The north wind froze the spectators.* **3** to kill or injure by frost: *The cold weather will freeze the flowers.* **4** to cover or clog with ice: *The snow and hail will freeze the pond.* **5** to fix to something by freezing; set fast in ice: *The low temperature has frozen the milk bottles to the porch. For the centerpiece, flowers were frozen in a block of ice.* **6** *Figurative.* to make stiff and unfriendly: *The reporter's question to the governor froze him and he refused to answer.* **7** *Figurative.* to chill with fear: *The howling of the wolves froze him with terror.* **8** *Figurative.* to fix at a definite amount, usually by governmental decree: *to freeze prices, freeze rents.* **9** *Figurative.* **a** to make (funds, bank balances, and other holdings of foreign ownership) unusable and inaccessible by governmental decree. **b** *Informal.* to make (bank loans and other holdings) impossible to turn into cash: *The depression froze all his assets.* **10** *Figurative.* to prohibit the further production, use, or sale of (a raw material, weapon, etc.): *Cobalt was frozen during the war.* **11** *Medicine.* to chill (a part of the body) until anesthetized.
–*n.* **1** the act or process of freezing: (*Figurative.*) *Under the freeze, Marine Midland, which operates 11 banks over the state, has been barred from acquiring additional banks with its own stock or cash* (Wall Street Journal). *The House passed a nonbinding resolution ... for a "mutual and verifiable" freeze on the production of nuclear weapons* (W.S. Mossberg). **2** the state of being frozen: *The city was in the grip of a severe freeze.* **3** a period during which there is freezing weather.
freeze (on) to, to hold tightly to; become attached to; take to: *He's a lawyer and he might not freeze on to you* (H. Rider Haggard).
freeze out, *U.S. Informal.* to force out; exclude, as from business or society, by chilling behavior, severe competition, and the like: *to freeze the small advertiser out of prime time* (Sponsor).
[Old English *frēosan*] **–freez′a|ble**, *adj.*
▶Various nonstandard forms occur, such as **froze** for the past participle and *freezed, frozed, friz,* or *frez* for the past tense.
freeze-dry (frēz′drī′), *v.t.,* **-dried, -dry|ing.** to dehydrate (organic substances, such as foods or penicillin) by freezing the moisture content to ice and evaporating the ice by subjecting it to microwaves in a vacuum. Freeze-dried substances keep without refrigeration.
freeze-etch|ing (frēz′ech′ing), *n.* a method of preparing specimens for study under an electron microscope by freezing them and then breaking them up along natural planes of weakness to show their internal structure in three dimensions.
freeze frame, = frozen frame.
freeze|nik (frēz′nik), *n. U.S. Slang.* a person who supports a freeze on the production of nuclear weapons. [< *freeze,* n. + *-nik*]
freeze-out (frēz′out′), *n. U.S. Informal.* **1** the act of putting out by force, stratagem, or cold treatment; elimination. **2** the act or fact of keeping out; exclusion.
freez|er (frē′zər), *n.* **1** a machine to freeze ice cream: *We cranked the freezer for half an hour before the cream began to thicken.* **2** a large chest or refrigerator compartment for freezing or storing frozen foods: *Keep ice cream in freezer.* **3** anything that freezes.
freezer burn, a dull or dried-out appearance from loss of moisture in frozen foods that have been improperly protected during storage.
freeze-up (frēz′up′), *n.* **1** the condition of being stopped by frost; a frozen condition, as of a water tank or automobile engine. **2** weather causing or likely to cause such a condition.
freez|ing (frē′zing), *adj., n.* **–*adj.*** **1** very cold; chilling: *a freezing wind.* **2** tending to freeze; that freezes: *a freezing process.* **–*n.*** **1** the act of congealing: *the freezing of water.* **2** the method of preserving food by maintaining it at a very low temperature: [*The*] *production of vegetables for canning and freezing is expected to drop this year* (Wall Street Journal). **–freez′ing|ly**, *adv.*
freezing point, the temperature at which a liquid freezes. The freezing point of water at sea level

Pronunciation Key: hat, āge, cãre, fär; let, ēqual, tėrm; it, īce; hot, ōpen, ôrder; oil, out; cup, pu̇t, rüle; child; long; thin; ᴛʜen; zh, measure; ə represents **a** in about, **e** in taken, **i** in pencil, **o** in lemon, **u** in circus.

is 32 degrees Fahrenheit or 0 degrees centigrade. *Abbr:* f.p. or F.P.

free zone, an area or zone similar to a free port, maintained to facilitate shipping and handling of goods.

F region, = F layer.

freight (frāt), *n., v.* **—*n.*** **1** goods that a train, truck, ship, or aircraft carries; cargo: *When the trucks crashed, their freight was spread all over the road.* **2a** the transportation of goods on a train, truck, ship, or aircraft for a price based on weight, distance, etc.: *He sent the box by freight. Freight is usually slower and cheaper than express.* **b** such transportation afforded by a common carrier: *The machinery came by freight.* **3** the price paid for carrying goods: *The captains talk together about . . . how freights are in America* (Hawthorne). **4** a train or ship for carrying goods: *A freight of thirty cars collided with another train.* **5** *U.S. and Canada.* anything carried for pay by land, water, or air; goods in transit. **6** *Chiefly Figurative.* a load; burden: Taxpayers resist carrying the freight of big government.
—*v.t.* **1** to load with a cargo: *They freighted the boat with bananas.* **2** to carry as freight. **3** to send as freight. **4** to hire or let out (as a vessel) for the transportation of goods or conveyance of passengers. **5** *Figurative.* to load; burden; oppress: *Freighted with responsibility, he broke down.*
[< Middle Dutch or Middle Low German *vrecht, vracht.* Compare etym. under **fraught**, noun.]

freight|age (frā′tij), *n.* **1** the carrying of goods on a train, truck, ship, or aircraft. **2** the price paid for this. **3** the load carried; freight; cargo; lading.

freight agent, the person in the employ of a transportation company who has charge of the freight-carrying department of its business in his locality. *Abbr:* FA (no periods), F.A.

freight car, a railroad car for carrying freight.

freight elevator, *U.S.* an elevator for hoisting heavy loads; hoist.

freight engine, *U.S.* the locomotive of a freight train.

freight|er (frā′tər), *n.* **1** any ship or aircraft that carries mainly freight: *He arrived . . . to investigate the take-off crash of a Bristol freighter in which the crew of three had died* (Maclean's). **2** a person who loads a ship. **3** a person whose occupation is to receive and forward freight. **4** a person for whom freight is transported; a consignor. **5** the owner of, or agent responsible for, the cargo of a ship.

freight forwarder, a firm or individual that ships goods for others for a fee; forwarding agent; forwarder: *A freight forwarder collects goods for shipment, routes them most of the way by railroad, and delivers them by truck to their destination, with all the services covered by one rate* (Wall Street Journal).

freight house, *U.S.* a place where freight is received and stored; depot.

freight|less (frāt′lis), *adj.* lacking freight.

freight|lin|er (frāt′lī′nər), *n. British.* a freight train that carries goods packaged in containers.

freight ton, a unit of measure about equal to the space occupied by a ton's weight of the thing measured, usually about 40 cubic feet; measurement ton.

freight train, a railroad train of freight cars.

Frei|herr (frī′her′), *n., pl.* **Frei|her|ren** (frī′her′ən). *German.* a nobleman ranking below a Graf (or count), and corresponding to an English baron.

freit (frēt, frāt), *n. Scottish.* anything to which superstition attaches: **a** an omen **b** a superstitious formula or charm. **c** a superstitious observance or act of worship.

Fre|li|mo or **FRELIMO** (frā lē′mō), *n.* Frente de Libertação de Moçambique (Front of Liberation of Mozambique).

fremd (fremd), *adj. Scottish.* **1** foreign. **2** strange; unfamiliar; unknown. **3** hostile. [Old English *fremde* foreign, strange]

frem|i|tus (frem′ə təs), *n. Medicine.* a palpable vibration or tremor, as of the walls of the chest. [< Latin *fremitus, -ūs* roaring < *fremere* roar, murmur]

fre|na (frē′nə), *n.* plural of **frenum**.

fre|nate (frē′nāt), *adj. Zoology.* having a frenulum.

French (french), *adj., n., v.* **—*adj.*** of or having to do with France, its people, or their language: *The French government asks all voters of France to vote in the next election.*
—*n.* **1** the people of France collectively: *The French helped the Americans in our Revolutionary War.* **2** their language. French is a Romance language divided historically into Old French, Middle French, and Modern French. *Abbr:* Fr.
—*v.t.* **1** to prepare (rib chops) for cooking by cutting the meat away from the thin end and often decorating with a paper frill. **2** to prepare (green beans) by slicing lengthwise or diagonally.
[Old English *Francisc* Frankish < *Franca* Frank]

French bean, the common kidney bean or haricot.

French blue, **1** artificial ultramarine. **2** *British Slang.* **a** an amphetamine tablet. **b** = drinamyl.

French bread, a bread with a crisp, well-browned crust, baked in long, slender loaves.

French bulldog, any one of a breed of usually brindle or brindle-and-white dogs with a chunky body, loose skin, large square head, and batlike ears. French bulldogs weigh from 18 to 28 pounds.

French Canadian, **1** a Canadian whose ancestors came from France. **2** the variety of French spoken in Canada; Canuck. **3** any one of a breed of dairy cattle, similar to Jerseys. **—French-Ca|na′di|an**, *adj.*

French chalk, a variety of talc used especially for marking lines on cloth and removing grease stains.

French chop, a rib chop with the meat cut from the thin end. The thin end is often covered with a paper frill.

French Coach, any heavy harness or coach horse of a French breed popular in North America until the early 1900's; Normand.

French combing wool, wool fibers from about 1¼ to 2 inches long.

French Community, an association formed in 1958 that includes France, her overseas territories, and many of her former colonies. It is similar to the Commonwealth of Nations.

French cuff, a broad cuff on the sleeve of a shirt, doubled back to make a fold at the wrist, with four buttonholes to be fastened together with a cuff link.

French curve, a flat, finely curved device used as a template in drawing to make curves which are not true circles.

***French doors**, a pair of doors that have glass panes or panels and are hinged at the sides so that they open in the middle.

***French doors**

French dressing, a salad dressing made chiefly of olive oil, vinegar, salt, and spices.

French endive, = endive (def. 2).

French fried potatoes, potatoes cut into thin strips and fried in deep fat until crisp on the outside.

French fries (frīz), = French fried potatoes: *. . . a lunch of steak, French fries, and iced tea* (Newsweek).

French-fry (french′frī), *v.t.,* **-fried**, **-fry|ing**. to fry in deep fat: *to French-fry potatoes.*

French Guianan, **1** a native or inhabitant of French Guiana, an overseas department of France on the northeastern coast of South America. **2** of or having to do with French Guiana or its people.

French heel, a kind of curved high heel on a woman's dress shoe.

***French horn**, a brass wind instrument that has a mellow tone. It was derived from the hunting horn.

***French horn**

French ice cream, a rich ice cream, usually containing small bits of vanilla bean and enough eggs to give it a distinct yellow color.

French|i|fi|ca|tion (fren′chə fə kā′shən), *n.* the act of Frenchifying.

French|i|fy (fren′chə fī), *v.,* **-fied**, **-fy|ing**. **—*v.t.*** to make French or like the French: *The Russian court . . . for all its Frenchified airs, was a bear pit of intrigue and malevolence* (Time).
—*v.i.* to become French, as in ideas, style, or manners.

French|ism (fren′chiz əm), *n.* a French custom, idiom, or characteristic; Gallicism.

French kiss, an open-mouthed kiss in which the tongues touch.

French-kiss (french′kis′), *v.i., v.t.* to kiss with a French kiss.

French knot, a decorative stitch which is made by twisting the thread twice around the needle and inserting the needle where it originally came out.

French leave, **1** the act of leaving without ceremony, permission, or notice; secret or hurried departure: *Other times they would simply take French leave—firmly locking the headmaster in as they went* (Time). **2** (originally) the custom of going away from a reception or other social function without taking leave of the host or hostess.

French|man (french′mən), *n., pl.* **-men**. **1** a person born or living in France. **2** a French ship.

French marigold, a common variety of marigold having a yellow flower with red markings.

French|ness (french′nis), *n.* the quality or state of being French or of displaying French characteristics.

French overture, *Music.* a type of baroque overture having two or three movements in a slow-fast-slow tempo.

French pancake, a thin rolled pancake, covered with powdered sugar and often filled with jelly or jam.

French pastry, **1** tarts, éclairs, small fancy cakes, and other delicate pastries. **2** one of these.

***French Provincial**, (of furniture, fabric design, or other fashion) of or resembling a style used in the French provinces during the time of Louis XV and generally less ornate than the Louis Quinze style.

***French Provincial**

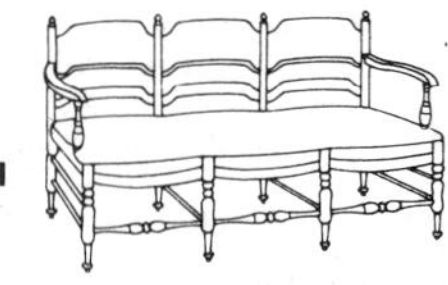

French Revolutionary calendar, = Revolutionary calendar.

French roof, a form of roof resembling a mansard roof.

French seam, a seam made by stitching once on the right side, turning, and stitching on the wrong side, thus covering the raw edges.

French toast, slices of bread dipped in a mixture of egg and milk or a batter and then fried usually in very little fat, often served with syrup.

French twist, a woman's hair style in which the hair is spiraled up from the back of the head and fastened into a vertical roll.

French walnut, **1** a variety of English walnut that is grown from central California to Oregon and resists extremes of heat and cold. **2** its edible nut.

French windows, a pair of long windows like doors, hinged at the sides and opening in the middle: *When the bailiffs broke into the house, they found the family had barricaded themselves in the back downstairs room and they had to force the French windows to get in* (Manchester Guardian).

French|wom|an (french′wům′ən), *n., pl.* **-women**. a woman born or living in France.

French|y (fren′chē), *adj., n., pl.* **French|ies**. *Informal.* **—*adj.*** characteristic or suggestive of the French: *a Frenchy tune, a theatrical and Frenchy hat.*
—*n.* a Frenchman.

fre|net|ic (frə net′ ik), *adj., n.* **—*adj.*** **1** excessively excited; frantic; frenzied: *frenetic gestures.* **2** insane (in nontechnical use).
—*n.* a madman. Also, **phrenetic**.
[Middle English variant of *phrenetic*] **—fre|net′i|cal|ly**, *adv.*

fre|net|i|cism (frə net′ə siz əm), *n.* feverish excitement; frenzy.

Fren|quel (freng′kwəl), *n. Trademark.* a tranquilizing drug, used especially in the treatment of schizophrenia; azacyclonol. *Formula:* $C_{18}H_{21}NO$

fren|u|lum (fren′yə ləm), *n., pl.* **-la** (-lə). **1** a small frenum. **2** a slender, stiff process extending from the hind wing of most moths and interlocking with a process on the front wing, keeping the two wings of a side together in flight. [< New Latin *frenulum* (diminutive) < *frēnum* bridle]

fre|num (frē′nəm), *n., pl.* **-na.** a ligament or fold of membrane which checks or restrains the motion of the organ to which it is attached, such as that which holds down the under side of the tongue; bridle. Also, **fraenum.** [< Latin *frēnum* bridle]

fren|zied (fren′zid), *adj.* **1** very much excited; frantic; wild: *the frenzied look of the mother of a lost child.* SYN: distracted. **2** crazy; mad. —**fren′zied|ly,** *adv.*

fren|zy (fren′zē), *n., pl.* **-zies,** *v.,* **-zied, -zy|ing.** —*n.* **1** near madness; frantic condition; mental derangement: *She was in a frenzy of grief when she heard that her child was missing. Demoniac frenzy, moping melancholy, And moon-struck madness* (Milton). **2** very great excitement: *a frenzy of haste. The crowd was in a frenzy after the home team scored the winning goal. The poet's eye, in a fine frenzy rolling, Doth glance from heaven to earth, from earth to heaven* (Shakespeare). SYN: furor, delirium.
—*v.t.* to drive (a person) to frenzy; infuriate.
[< Old French *frenesie,* learned borrowing from Medieval Latin *phrenesia* < Latin *phrenēsis* < Greek *phrēn* mind]

Fre|on (frē′on), *n. Trademark.* any one of a group of nearly odorless, colorless, gaseous carbon compounds, each of which has one or more atoms of fluorine, used as a refrigerant, aerosol propellant, solvent, and fire-extinguishing agent.

freq., **1** frequent. **2** frequentative. **3** frequently.

fre|quence (frē′kwəns), *n.* = frequency.

fre|quen|cy (frē′kwən sē), *n., pl.* **-cies. 1** the rate of occurrence: *The flashes of light came with a frequency of three per minute.* **2** the fact of occurring often or being repeated at short intervals: *The frequency of his visits began to annoy us.*
3 *Physics.* **a** the number of times that any regularly repeated event, such as a vibration, occurs in a given unit of time: *If the natural frequency of a particular blade corresponds to the frequency of the critical operating speed of the engine, the blade will vibrate* (New York Times). **b** the number of complete cycles per second of an alternating current or other electric wave. Sixty cycles per second is a commonly used frequency of current in a house. Different radio and television stations broadcast at different frequencies so that their signals can be received distinctly.
4 *Statistics.* the number of cases of the data under consideration falling within a particular class interval. **5** *Mathematics.* the ratio of the number of times an event actually occurs to the number of times it might occur in a given period. **6** *Obsolete.* **a** the state or condition of being crowded. **b** a crowd.

frequency band, a particular range of wave lengths in radio, television, or other electromagnetic transmission.

frequency distribution, *Statistics.* **1** an arrangement of data according to size, rather than time, location, or degree; an arrangement of data to show the number of times an event occurs in a particular way: *The basis of Yule's and Wake's method is the study of the frequency distribution of quite ordinary characters in a random sample* (Science News). **2** a table or graph depicting such an arrangement: *The values themselves, arranged in a table, form a frequency distribution* (A. E. Waugh).

frequency modulation, 1 a deliberate changing of the frequency of transmitting waves in order to agree with the changes in the sounds or images being transmitted. Frequency modulation reduces static. *Abbr:* FM, F.M. **2** a broadcasting system using this method of modulation.

frequency response, *Electronics.* the effectiveness of a circuit or device in transmitting the various frequencies applied to it; the range of frequencies transmitted by a circuit or device.

frequency shifting, *Electronics.* the shifting of the frequencies of signals so that several different signals may be sent without confusion along one line of transmission.

fre|quent (*adj.* frē′kwənt; *v.* fri kwent′), *adj., v.* —*adj.* **1** happening often, near together, or every little while: *In my part of the country, storms are frequent in March. The coast has frequent lighthouses.* **2** that does a thing often; constant; habitual; regular: *He is a frequent caller at our house.* **3** *Obsolete.* (of a place) filled; full; crowded.
—*v.t.* **1** to be often in; go to often: *Frogs frequent ponds, streams, and marshes.* **2** to visit or associate with: *He frequents Lord Pembroke, a man of quality as well as of pleasure* (New York Times Book Review).
—*v.i. Obsolete.* to associate (with).
[< Latin *frequēns, -entis* crowded] —**fre′|quent·ness,** *n.*

fre|quen|ta|tion (frē′kwən tā′shən), *n.* the act or habit of frequenting; visiting or resorting to frequently.

fre|quen|ta|tive (fri kwen′tə tiv), *adj., n. Grammar.* —*adj.* serving to express the frequent repetition of an action. "Waggle" is a frequentative verb from "wag."
—*n.* a frequentative verb or verbal form.

fre|quent|er (fri kwen′tər), *n.* a person who frequents or resorts to a place.

fre|quent|ly (frē′kwənt lē), *adv.* every little while; often; repeatedly: *He hardly ever saves and is frequently in debt* (Atlantic). SYN: See syn. under **often.**

frère (frer), *n. French.* **1** brother. **2** friar.

fres|co (fres′kō), *n., pl.* **-coes** or **-cos,** *v.,* **-coed, -co|ing.** —*n.* **1** the act or art of painting with water colors on the damp, fresh plaster of a wall or ceiling. The colors sink in and become very durable. *Fresco was used much oftener in the past than today.* **2** a picture or design so painted: *Beautiful frescoes covered the walls and ceiling of the cathedral.* **3** *Obsolete.* **a** cool, fresh air. **b** a fresh breeze.
—*v.t.* to paint with water colors on damp, fresh plaster.
[< Italian *fresco* cool, fresh < Germanic (compare Old High German *frisc*). See related etym. at **fresh.**] —**fres′co|er,** *n.*

fres|co|ing (fres′kō ing), *n.* **1** the process of painting in fresco: *Frescoing must be done very rapidly.* **2** frescoed decoration.

fresh[1] (fresh), *adj., adv., n.* —*adj.* **1** newly made, arrived, or gathered; recent: *fresh vegetables. On it were the fresh footmarks of a little animal* (John Tyndall). **2** not known, seen, or used before; new; recent: *Is there any fresh news from home?* SYN: novel. **3** another; additional; further: *After her failure, she made a fresh start. The dispute ... took a fresh turn today when 81 deputies ... handed in their notice* (London Times). **4** not salty: *Rivers are usually fresh water.* **5** not spoiled; not stale: *Is the milk fresh?*
6 not artificially preserved: *Fresh butter, fresh meat, fresh herring, and fresh vegetables usually have more flavor than when canned or frozen.*
7 not tired out; vigorous; lively: *Put in fresh horses.* **8** not faded or worn; bright: *The party was fresh in her memory. The spring time of her childish years Hath never lost its fresh perfume* (James Russell Lowell). SYN: undimmed, untarnished. **9** looking healthy or young: *Grandmother is as hale and fresh in appearance as she was ten years ago. He looked as fresh as a boy after his vacation.* SYN: blooming. **10** cool; refreshing; pure: *a fresh breeze. The desire of fresh air ... had carried her into the ... garden* (Scott). SYN: invigorating. **11** fairly strong; brisk: *A fresh wind is more than a breeze.* **12** not experienced; unsophisticated: *How green you are and fresh in this old world* (Shakespeare). SYN: untrained. **13** (of a cow) having recently calved and yielding a renewed or increased supply of milk. **14** *Informal.* tipsy; drunk.
—*adv.* freshly; newly: *She has a charming fresh colour—Yes, when it is fresh put on* (Richard Brinsley Sheridan).
—*n.* **1** the fresh or early part of a day, year, or other period of time or the beginning of something: *The robins ... keep on pretending it is the fresh of the year* (James Russell Lowell). **2** a pool, spring, or stream of fresh water: *I ... have found several delightful wood-alleys ... and quiet freshes* (Keats). **3a** a flood of fresh water flowing into the sea. **b** a freshet; flood. **4** a stream of fresh water running into tidewater; the part of a tidal river above the salt water. **5** *College Slang.* a freshman.
[Old English *fersc;* spelling probably influenced by Old French *freis,* masculine, *fresche,* feminine < Germanic (compare Old High German *frisc*)]
—**fresh′ness,** *n.*

fresh[2] (fresh), *adj. Informal.* too bold; impudent; forward: *She rose and in a loud voice cried: "Say, you're too fresh! Where d'ye think ye are?"* (Alan Dale). SYN: saucy, presumptuous, impertinent, obtrusive. [< German *frech* impudent]

fresh-air (fresh′ ãr′), *adj.* of or having to do with the outdoors or with outdoor living: *fresh-air sports and games. The fresh-air cure has been ... very much boomed of late years ... One result of this has been the evolution of what I may term the fresh-air maniac* (Daily Chronicle).

fresh breeze, wind having a velocity between 19 and 24 miles per hour (force 5 on the Beaufort scale).

fresh|en (fresh′ən), *v.t.* **1** to make fresh; renew; revive: *The rest freshened my spirits.* **2** to remove salt from; make less salty. **3** *Nautical.* to move (a rope) to a different position to distribute the wear and strain. —*v.i.* **1** to become fresh: *The air freshened after the storm.* **2** to clean, wash, or groom oneself: *to freshen up before dinner.* **3** to lose salt or saltiness. **4** of a cow: **a** to calve. **b** to produce more milk.

fresh|en|er (fresh′ə nər), *n.* something that freshens.

fresh|er (fresh′ər), *n. British Slang.* a freshman.

fresh|et (fresh′it), *n.* **1** a flood caused by heavy rains or melted snow: *Freshets usually occur in spring.* **2** a rush or stream of fresh water flowing into the sea. **3** *Obsolete.* a small stream of fresh water. [< *fresh* flood, stream, or pool of fresh water + *et*]

fresh gale, a wind with a velocity of 39-46 miles per hour (force 8 on the Beaufort scale).

fresh|ly (fresh′lē), *adv.* **1** in a fresh manner: *a freshly challenging air.* **2** recently: *freshly shaved.*

fresh|man (fresh′mən), *n., pl.* **-men,** *adj.* —*n.*
1 a student in the first year of high school or college: *Academically, he found himself in trouble as a freshman in 1953 principally because of his difficulty with English* (Newsweek). **2** a beginner: *I came to Congress as a freshman in the first Administration of Woodrow Wilson* (New York Times).
—*adj.* of first-year high school or college students: *the freshman team.*

freshman or **freshmen week,** *U.S.* a week, directly preceding the college year, in which freshmen become familiar with life at college, take intelligence and aptitude tests, and participate in other activities.

fresh|wa|ter (fresh′wôt′ər, -wot′-), *adj.* **1** of or living in water that is not salty: *The brook trout is a freshwater fish.* **2** not used to sailing on the sea: *a freshwater sailor.* **3** having little experience; unskilled: *freshwater critics.* SYN: untrained, raw. **4** *U.S.* provincial; not widely known: *a freshwater college.*

freshwater drumfish, a drumfish sometimes weighing over 50 pounds, found from the Great Lakes and the Mississippi Valley to Guatemala; gaspergou.

fres|nel (frā nel′), *n.* a unit of frequency equivalent to 10^{12} (one trillion) cycles per second. [< Jean Augustin *Fresnel,* 1788-1827, a French physicist]

Fresnel lens, a lens formed of a central plano-convex lens surrounded by many segmental lenses, all having the same focus. It is used especially in searchlights, spotlights, and headlights. [see etym. under **fresnel**]

fret[1] (fret), *v.,* **fret|ted, fret|ting,** *n.* —*v.i.* **1** to be peevish, unhappy, or discontented; worry: *Don't fret about your mistake. A baby frets in hot weather.* SYN: chafe, complain. **2** to become gnawed or corroded; waste away. SYN: decay, fray. **3** to form or make a passage by wearing away: *I love the Brooks which down their channels fret* (Wordsworth). **4** to be disturbed or agitated: *the mill-stream ... fretting with gnarled tree-roots* (Charlotte Brontë).
—*v.t.* **1** to make peevish, unhappy, or discontented; cause to worry: *Her failures fretted her. [He] then found himself doomed to live and work there with his mind always fretted by the problems of Russia* (Edmund Wilson). SYN: harass, vex, provoke, distress, irritate, annoy. **2** to eat away; wear; rub: *The river frets away the rocks along its banks* (Aldous Huxley). **3** to make or form by wearing away: *Till they have fretted us a pair of graves within the earth* (Shakespeare).
4 to roughen; disturb: *Not one gondola frets the lagoon* (Joaquin Miller). SYN: ruffle, agitate.
—*n.* **1** discontented condition; peevish complaining; worry: *She is in a fret about her examinations.* SYN: irritation, vexation. **2** the act or process of eating or wearing away: *Before ... the busy fret Of that sharpheaded worm begins* (Tennyson). SYN: erosion, corrosion. **3** an eaten or worn-away place; decayed spot: *galls, scabs, and frets.*
[Old English *fretan* eat]

fret[2] (fret), *n., v.,* **fret|ted, fret|ting.** —*n.* **1** an ornamental pattern made of straight lines bent or combined at angles; fretwork. **2** an ornamental net, especially a headdress consisting of jewels or flowers.
—*v.t.* **1** to decorate with fretwork. **2** *Obsolete.* to adorn with gold or silver embroidery or with gold, silver, or jewels.
[< Old French *frete* < Germanic (compare Old English *feter*)]

***fret[3]** (fret), *n., v.,* **fret|ted, fret|ting.** —*n.* any one of a series of ridges of metal, wood, or ivory across the finger board of a guitar, banjo, or other similar instrument played by plucking. By holding a string against a fret with the finger the tone of the string can be raised. *The violin, which once had six strings with guitar frets, was fortunately relieved of these superfluities* (Blackwood's Magazine). See picture on next page.

Pronunciation Key: hat, āge, cãre, fär; let, ēqual, tėrm, it, īce; hot, ōpen, ôrder; oil, out; cup, pu̇t, rüle; child; long; thin; ᴛʜen; zh, measure; ə represents **a** in about, **e** in taken, **i** in pencil, **o** in lemon, **u** in circus.

—*v.t.* to provide with frets. [origin uncertain]

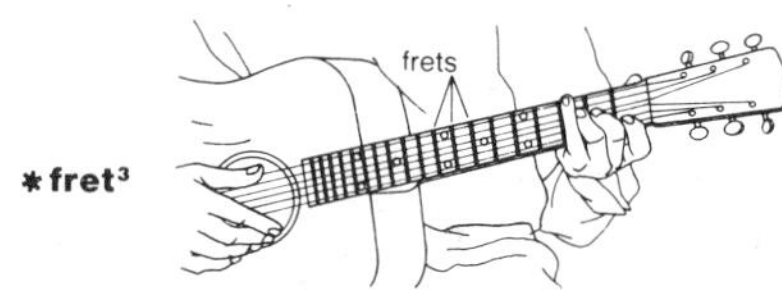

fret|ful (fret′fəl), *adj.* **1** ready to fret; peevish, unhappy, discontented, or worried: *My baby brother is fretful because he is cutting his teeth.* SYN: irritable. **2** agitated; seething: *the fretful sea.* **3** gusty: *the fretful wind.* **4** apt to produce fretting: *The fretful days Of prejudice and error* (James Thomson). —**fret′ful|ly**, *adv.* —**fret′ful-ness**, *n.*

fret|less (fret′lis), *adj.* free from worry or discontent; untroubled; unruffled: *fretless and free* (Robert Browning).

fret saw, a saw with a long, slender blade and fine teeth, used to cut thin wood into patterns.

fret|tage (fret′ij), *n.* **1** the process of shrinking on rings of metal about the breech of a gun to give additional strength. **2** the collection of rings so employed. [< French *frettage* < *fretter* to ring < *frette* a ring]

fret|ted (fret′id), *adj., v.* —*adj.* having frets. —*v.* past tense and past participle of **fret**[1], **fret**[2], and **fret**[3].

fret|ty (fret′ē), *adj.,* **-ti|er, -ti|est. 1** fretful; irritable: *O'Connell's speeches are the old thing: fretty, boastful, frothy* (Dickens). **2** (of a sore) inflamed; festering.

fret|work (fret′wėrk′), *n.* ornamental openwork or carving consisting largely of intersecting lines.

fret|worked (fret′wėrkt′), *adj.* ornamented with fretwork: *The tumbling residential villas, fretworked and pinnacled in the last excesses of chinoiserie ...* (Manchester Guardian Weekly).

Freud|i|an (froi′dē ən), *adj., n.* —*adj.* of or having to do with Sigmund Freud (1856-1939), his teachings, or the technique of psychoanalysis introduced by him and developed by his followers: *Some of them have married the interviewing methods of the pollsters to a Freudian process of interpretation of the subconscious* (Newsweek).
—*n.* a person who believes in Freud's teachings or follows his technique of psychoanalysis: *Freudians may have their own explanation of this* (Time).

Freud|i|an|ism (froi′dē ə niz′əm), *n.* Freudian theories or doctrines.

Freud|i|an|ize (froi′dē ə nīz), *v.t.,* **-ized, -iz|ing. 1** to describe or characterize (a person, event, or phenomenon) in Freudian terms: *Poor Poe, romanticized, sentimentalized, Freudianized, and vilified ...* (Atlantic). **2** to subject to Freudian influence or Freudianism.

Freud|i|an|ly (froi′dē ən lē), *adv.* in a Freudian manner; in accordance with Freud's theories.

Freudian slip, *Informal.* a slip of the tongue; lapsus linguae.

Freud|ism (froi′diz əm), *n.* = Freudianism.

Freud|ist (froi′dist), *n.* a follower of Freudian theories or doctrines; Freudian.

Freund's adjuvant (froindz), an emulsion containing killed bacteria, used to increase the production of antigens or to distribute antigen throughout the body. [< Jules *Freund,* 1890-1960, a Hungarian-born American bacteriologist]

Frey (frā), *n.* the Norse god of love, peace, plenty, and fertility and giver of wealth.

Frey|a (frā′ə), *n.* the Norse goddess of love and beauty.

Frey|ja (frā′yə), *n.* = Freya.

Freyr (frā′ər), *n.* = Frey.

F.R.G.S., Fellow of the Royal Geographical Society.

Fri., Friday.

fri|a|bil|i|ty (frī′ə bil′ə tē), *n.* the condition of being friable.

fri|a|ble (frī′ə bəl), *adj.* easily crumbled; crumbly: *Dry soil is friable. Coke is rather tiresome to handle, as it does not shovel well and is inclined to be friable* (London Times). [< Latin *friābilis* < *friāre* crumble]

fri|a|ble|ness (frī′ə bəl nis), *n.* = friability.

fri|ar (frī′ər), *n.* a man who belongs to one of certain religious brotherhoods of the Roman Catholic Church. The Franciscans, Dominicans, Carmelites, and Augustinians are the four great orders of friars. *The friar strives to be free of worldly goods that he may engage more efficiently in preaching, missionary work, or other charitable undertakings* (Fulton J. Sheen). *Abbr:* Fr. [Middle English *frere* < Old French < Latin *frāter* brother]
►See **monk** for usage note.

fri|ar|bird (frī′ər bėrd′), *n.* an Australasian bird, a variety of honey eater, which has a bare head and neck, and sucks nectar from flowers.

fri|ar|ly (frī′ər lē), *adj.* of friars; like that of a friar: *a friarly tonsure.*

Friar Minor, *pl.* **Friars Minor. 1** a friar of the Franciscan order who follows the original and strictest rule of the order. **2** any Franciscan friar; Gray Friar; Minorite.

Friar Minor Capuchin, = Capuchin.

Friar Minor Conventual, = Conventual.

fri|ar's-cap (frī′ərz kap′), *n.* = monkshood.

fri|ar's-cowl (frī′ərz kowl′), *n.* = wake-robin.

friar's lantern, the will-o'-the-wisp; ignis fatuus.

fri|ar|y (frī′ər-ē), *n., pl.* **-ar|ies. 1** the building or buildings where friars live; monastery. **2** a brotherhood of friars.

frib|ble (frib′əl), *v.,* **-bled, -bling,** *n., adj.* —*v.i.* **1** to behave frivolously; trifle: *Not as you treat those fools that are fribbling round about you* (Thackeray). **2** *Obsolete.* to falter; totter.
—*v.t.* to waste foolishly.
—*n.* **1** a frivolous person; trifler. **2** a trifling or frivolous thing. **3** frivolity; nonsense.
—*adj.* trifling; frivolous. —**frib′bler**, *n.*

fric|an|deau (frik′ən dō[ˆ]), *n.* veal or other meat larded, braised, or fried, and served with a sauce. [< French *fricandeau,* related to *fricassée;* see etym. under **fricassee**]

fric|as|see (frik′ə sē′), *n., v.,* **-seed, -see|ing.**
—*n.* **1** chicken or other meat cut up, stewed, and served in a sauce made with its own gravy. **2** *Figurative.* a hodgepodge: *Richard Ford found the portal [of Dos Aquas palace in Valencia, Spain] "grotesque ... a fricassee of palm trees, Indians, serpents and absurd forms"* (Kenneth Tynan).
—*v.t.* to prepare (meat) in this way.
[< Middle French *fricassée* < *fricasser* mince and cook in sauce < *frire* fry + *casser* break, cut up]

fric|a|tive (frik′ə tiv), *adj., n. Phonetics.* —*adj.* pronounced by forcing the breath through a narrow opening formed especially by placing the tongue or lips near or against the palate or teeth; spirant. *F, v, s,* and *z* are fricative consonants.
—*n.* a fricative consonant; spirant.
[< Latin *fricātus,* past participle of *fricāre* rub, scrape + English *-ive*]

fric|tion (frik′shən), *n.* **1** a rubbing of one object against another, such as hand against hand, skates on ice, or a brush on shoes; rubbing: *Matches are lighted by friction.* **2** resistance to motion of surfaces that touch; resistance of a body in motion to the air, water, or other medium through which it travels or to the surface on which it travels: *Oil reduces friction. Bodies moving through a vacuum encounter no friction. A sled moves more easily on smooth ice than on rough ground because there is less friction.* **3** *Figurative.* conflict of differing ideas or opinions; disagreement; clash: *Constant friction between the two brothers led to many fights and arguments.* [< Latin *frictiō, -ōnis* < *fricāre* rub]

fric|tion|al (frik′shə nəl), *adj.* **1** of or having to do with friction: *the frictional factor.* **2** moved or caused by friction: *If it is now assumed that ... the frictional resistance of the hull can be accurately estimated ...* (P. G. Morgan). —**fric′tion|al-ly**, *adv.*

frictional unemployment, *U.S.* short-term or temporary unemployment of workers arising from such circumstances as job changes and relocation.

friction brake, a brake operating by friction, usually applied to a revolving element such as a wheel or a drum: *A powerful friction brake on the winch prevents boats from slipping back* (Newsweek).

friction clutch or **coupling**, a device for transmitting motion by frictional contact. It is used where it is desirable to engage or disengage moving parts gradually and smoothly, as when shifting gears.

friction drive, a type of power transmission used in early automobiles, in which power is transmitted from the driving to the driven member by pressing one against the other at right angles, and different speed ratios are obtained by moving the driven member toward or away from the center of the driving member.

friction gear or **gearing**, a set of gears without teeth in which one wheel presses against another and causes it to turn. Friction gears provide uniform power, but not as much power as toothed gears.

fric|tion|ize (frik′shə nīz), *v.t.,* **-ized, -iz|ing.** to subject to friction; rub.

fric|tion|less (frik′shən lis), *adj.* free from friction: *In frictionless space, this electrical propulsion system uses tiny amounts of fuel to move payloads as large as jet-liners—at much higher speeds* (Wall Street Journal). —**fric′tion|less|ly**, *adv.*

friction match, a kind of match tipped with a compound that ignites by friction: *He listed "lucifer matches" (or friction matches) among the great inventions of his time* (Atlantic).

friction saw, a high-speed, usually toothless band saw or circular saw that melts and cuts steel and other metals by heat generated by the friction between the saw and the metal.

fric|tion-saw (frik′shən sô′), *v.t.,* **-sawed, -sawed** or **-sawn, -saw|ing.** to cut (steel or other metals) with a friction saw.

friction tape, *U.S.* a cotton tape saturated with an adhesive and moisture-repelling substance. It is used especially to protect electric wires and conductors and to wrap objects, such as handles, for strength and good grip.

fric|tion-tight (frik′shən tīt′), *adj.* fitting so tightly or closely that a desired effect of friction is produced: *A friction-tight joint prevents slipping.*

friction wheel, a wheel operating by friction, used to transmit the motion of one wheel to another by simple contact.

Fri|day (frī′dē, -dā), *n.* **1** the sixth day of the week, following Thursday. *Abbr:* Fri. **2** the servant of Robinson Crusoe. **3** any faithful servant or devoted follower. [Old English *Frīgedæg* Frigg's day < *Frīge,* genitive of *Frīg* Frigg + *dæg* day]

fridge (frij), *n. Informal.* a refrigerator: *Manufacturers say the country may buy perhaps 600,000 fridges of all types this year* (London Times). Also, **frig.** [short for *refrigerator*]

fried (frīd), *adj., v.* —*adj.* cooked in hot fat.
—*v.* past tense and past participle of **fry**[1]: *I fried the ham. The potatoes have been fried.*

fried cake, or **fried|cake** (frīd′kāk′), *n.* a small cake fried in deep fat. Doughnuts and crullers are fried cakes.

Fried|man|ite (frēd′mə nīt), *n.* a follower or supporter of the theories of Milton Friedman, born 1912, an American economist, especially the theory that economic growth depends chiefly on a country's money supply.

friend (frend), *n., v.* —*n.* **1** a person who knows and likes another: *A friend should bear his friend's infirmities* (Shakespeare). SYN: comrade, chum, crony, companion. **2** a person who favors and supports: *She was a generous friend to the poor.* SYN: supporter, patron, helper, advocate. **3** a person who belongs to the same side or group: *Are you friend or foe; speak out!*
—*v.t. Archaic.* to befriend.
be friends with, a to be a friend of: *Will you be friends with me again, Mary?* (John Wilson). **b** to be in a close relation to; like: *I shall never be friends again with roses* (Algernon Charles Swinburne).
make friends with, a to become a friend of: *He quickly made friends with the new boy on the block.* **b** to become accustomed to; get to like: *Nor could she make friends with the Danish teakwood coffee table I had got on sale; it was too low for playing solitaire* (New Yorker).
[Old English *frēond,* (originally) present participle of *frēogan* to love]

Friend (frend), *n.* a member of the Society of Friends; Quaker. Friends favor simplicity in clothes and manners and are opposed to war and to taking oaths. *Two Quakers of the district—Friends have never believed in a stated ministry—are among his helpers* (J. W. R. Scott).

friend at court, a person who can help one with others; influential friend.

friend|ed (fren′did), *adj.* having a friend or friends.

friend|less (frend′lis), *adj.* without friends; forlorn. —**friend′less|ness**, *n.*

friend|ly (frend′lē), *adj.,* **-li|er, -li|est,** *adv., n., pl.* **-lies.** —*adj.* **1** of a friend; having the attitude of a friend; kind: *a friendly teacher.* **2** like a friend; like that of a friend: *a friendly greeting. These I have loved ... the strong crust of friendly bread* (Rupert Brooke). *Neighbouring trees with friendly shade invite* (John Dryden). **3** on good terms; not hostile; amicable: *friendly relations between countries, friendly natives. In contrast with his arrogant behavior ... last summer, [he] was friendly, conciliatory, and even companionable* (New York Times). **4** wanting to be a friend: *a friendly dog.* **5** favoring and supporting; favorable: *His talk was friendly to labor.* SYN: kindly, propitious. **6** = user-friendly.
—*adv.* in a friendly manner; as a friend.
—*n.* **1** a person who is an ally or supporter: *The enemy kept pouring in that night, ... concealed sometimes in flowers, disguised as friendlies* (New Yorker). **2** *British.* a game or contest that is not part of a tournament for a prize or trophy: *Those games ... in the league have been no different from the old friendlies, with a strong defensive bias added* (London Times).
[Old English *frēondlīc*] —**friend′li|ly**, *adv.* —**friend′li|ness**, *n.*

friendly society, *British.* benefit society.

friend of the court, = amicus curiae.

friend|ship (frend′ship), *n.* **1** the condition of being friends: *And softly, through a vinous mist, My college friendships glimmer* (Tennyson). **2** a liking between friends. **3** friendly feeling or behavior; friendliness: *Hard by here is a hovel; some friendship will it lend you against the tempest* (Shakespeare).

fri|er (frī′ər), *n.* **1** a person or thing that fries. **2** a chicken intended for frying. Also, **fryer**.

fries (frīz), *n.* the plural of **fry**[1].

Frie|sian (frē′zhən), *adj., n.* **—adj.** = Frisian. **—n. 1** = Frisian. **2** *Especially British.* Holstein-Friesian, a breed of cattle.

***frieze**[1] (frēz), *n.* **1** a horizontal band of decoration around a room, building, mantel, or other structure. **2** a horizontal band, often ornamented with sculpture, between the cornice and architrave of a building: *the frieze of the Parthenon.* [< Middle French *frise;* origin uncertain] **—frieze′like′,** *adj.*

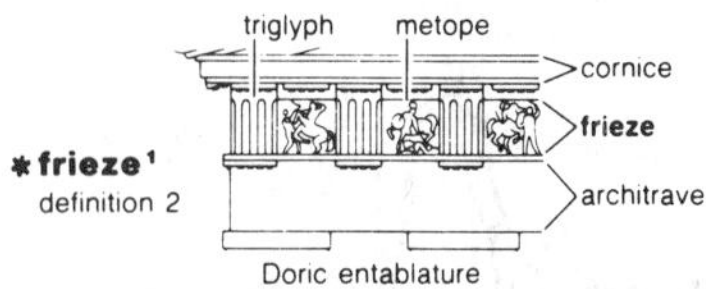

***frieze**[1] definition 2

Doric entablature

frieze[2] (frēz), *n., v.,* **friezed, friez|ing.** **—n.** a thick woolen cloth with a shaggy nap on one side.
—v.t. to raise a nap on (cloth).
[< French *frise,* probably < a Germanic word]

frig (frij), *n. British Informal.* fridge; a refrigerator.

***frig|ate** (frig′it), *n.* **1** a fast, three-masted, sailing warship of medium size. Frigates were much used between 1750 and 1860. **2** a small escort vessel equipped to destroy submarines. It belongs to the destroyer class. *Their light coastguard patrol boats were no match for the naval frigates protecting the British fishermen* (S. B. Fay). **3** *Poetic.* a light, fast ship moved by oars or sails. [< Middle French *frégate* < dialectal Italian *fregata;* origin uncertain]

***frigate** definition 1

frigate bird, a strong-flying, tropical sea bird that steals other birds' food; man-of-war bird; man-of-war hawk. It has a long, forked tail and a wingspread of over seven feet.

frig|ate-built (frig′it bilt′), *adj. Nautical.* having a quarterdeck and forecastle raised above the main deck.

frigate mackerel, a game fish found in warm and temperate waters on both sides of the Atlantic. It has widely separated dorsal fins and a wavy pattern on the upper sides.

frigate pelican, = frigate bird.

frig|a|toon (frig′ə tün′), *n.* a Venetian vessel with a square stern and two masts. [alteration of Italian *fregatone* (augmentative) < dialectal *fregata* frigate]

Frigg (frig), *n.* the wife of Odin, and Norse goddess of the sky.

Frig|ga (frig′ə) *n.* = Frigg.

fright (frīt), *n., v.* **—n. 1** sudden and extreme fear; sudden terror or alarm: *Fright seized the invaders. It might be said then that anxiety is a protection against fright* (Sigmund Freud). SYN: dismay, consternation. **2** *Informal.* a person or thing that is ugly, shocking, or ridiculous: *In her wig and make-up she looked a fright.* **3** *Obsolete.* anything that causes terror.
—v.t. *Poetic.* to frighten; terrify.
[Old English *fyrhto*]

fright|ed (frī′tid), *adj.* frightened; terrified.

fright|en (frī′tən), *v.t.* **1** to fill with fright; make afraid; scare or terrify: *Thunder and lightning frighten most children and many adults.* **2** to drive or force by terrifying: *The sudden noise frightened the deer away.* **—v.i.** to become afraid: *She frightens easily.* **—fright′en|a|ble,** *adj.* **—fright′en|er,** *n.*
—Syn. *v.t.* **1 Frighten, scare, alarm** mean to fill with fear. **Frighten** means to fill with a sudden, startling, often very great fear: *The rattlesnake frightened me.* **Scare,** often used as an informal substitute for *frighten,* particularly suggests suddenly giving sharp fear or terror to a timid person or animal, making him shrink and tremble or turn and run: *The firecrackers scared the puppy.* **Alarm** means to fill suddenly with excited fear and anxiety: *Her failure to come home at midnight alarmed us.*

fright|ened (frī′tənd), *adj.* filled with fright; afraid. SYN: See syn. under **afraid**.

fright|en|ing (frī′tə ning), *adj.* alarming: *It was a frightening reminder of how outnumbered the West is* (Canadian Saturday Night). **—fright′en|ing|ly,** *adv.*

fright|ful (frīt′fəl), *adj.* **1** that would frighten; causing fright or horror; dreadful; terrible: *a frightful explosion. . . . like one that . . . knows a frightful fiend Doth close behind him tread* (Samuel Taylor Coleridge). SYN: frightening, alarming. **2** ugly; shocking; revolting: *The victim's clothes were in frightful condition.* **3** *Informal.* disagreeable; unpleasant: *He has frightful manners.* **4** *Informal.* very great: *I'm in a frightful hurry.*

fright|ful|ly (frīt′fə lē), *adv.* **1** in a frightful manner; dreadfully; terribly. **2** *Informal.* intolerably; hideously. **3** *Informal.* exceedingly: *A dollar for a dozen eggs is frightfully expensive.*

fright|ful|ness (frīt′fəl nis), *n.* **1** frightful quality or state. **2** the military policy of terrorizing the enemy, especially the civilian population; terrorism.

fright wig, 1 an actor's or clown's wig with hair that stands on end, or that can be made to stand on end by pulling a string, to indicate sudden fright. **2** *Informal.* a wig or hairdo whose appearance suggests an actor's or clown's fright wig.

frig|id (frij′id), *adj.* **1** very cold: *Eskimos are used to living in a frigid climate.* SYN: See syn. under **cold**. **2** *Figurative.* cold in feeling or manner; stiff; chilling: *a frigid stare. He received a frigid greeting from the man he had insulted.* **3** (of females) sexually indifferent or not responsive; disliking sexual intercourse. [< Latin *frīgidus,* related to *frīgēre* be cold] **—frig′id|ly,** *adv.* **—frig′id|ness,** *n.*

Frig|i|daire (frij′ə dãr′), *n. Trademark.* an electric refrigerator.

frig|i|dar|i|um (frij′ə dãr′ē əm), *n., pl.* **-dar|i|a** (-dãr′ē ə). **1** the cooling apartment of the ancient Roman baths, usually furnished with a cold bath: *Like Catullus in the great pleasure dome at Sermione, he . . . steamed in the sudatorium, chilled in the frigidarium* (Harper's). **2** the cold bath. **3** any room kept at a low temperature. [< Latin *frīgidārium* < *frīgidus* cold]

fri|gid|i|ty (fri jid′ə tē), *n.* the condition of being frigid.

Frigid Zone, either of the two regions within the polar circles.

frig|o|rif|ic (frig′ə rif′ik), *adj. Physics.* causing or producing cold; freezing; cooling. [< Latin *frīgorificus* < *frīgus, -oris* cold(ness) + *facere* make]

fri|go|ri|fi|co (frig′ə rif′i kō; *Spanish* frē′gō rē′fē-kō), *n., pl.* **-cos.** a South American packing and freezing plant, especially for meats; a refrigerated meat-packing plant. [< Spanish *frigorífico* (literally) freezing < Latin *frīgorificus*]

fri|jol (frē′hōl; *Spanish* frē hōl′), *n., pl.* **fri|joles** (frē′hōlz, fri hō′liz; *Spanish* frē hō′lās). a bean, especially the kidney bean, much used for food in Mexico and the southwestern United States: *The government even granted the firm a license to import 4,000 metric tons of frijoles* (Time). [American English < Spanish *frijol* < Latin *faseolus* (diminutive) < *phaselus* < Greek *phásēlos* kidney bean]

fri|jole (frē′hōl, frē hō′lē; *Spanish* frē hōl′), *n., pl.* **fri|joles** (frē′hōlz, fri hō′liz; *Spanish* frē hō′lās). = frijol.

frill (fril), *n., v.* **—n. 1** a ruffle: *Her fancy blouse had frills around the neck and down the front.* **2** *Figurative.* a thing added merely for show; useless ornament; affectation, especially of dress, manner, or speech: *The poet rejected all the frills of modern society.* **3** a fringe of feathers, hair, or skin around the neck of a bird or animal. **4** *Photography.* a wrinkling of the edge of a film or plate.
—v.t. 1 to put a ruffle on; decorate with a ruffle; adorn with ruffles: *to frill a curtain.* **2** to form into a ruffle. **3** *Photography.* to cause to wrinkle.
—v.i. *Photography.* to become wrinkled at the edge.
[origin uncertain]

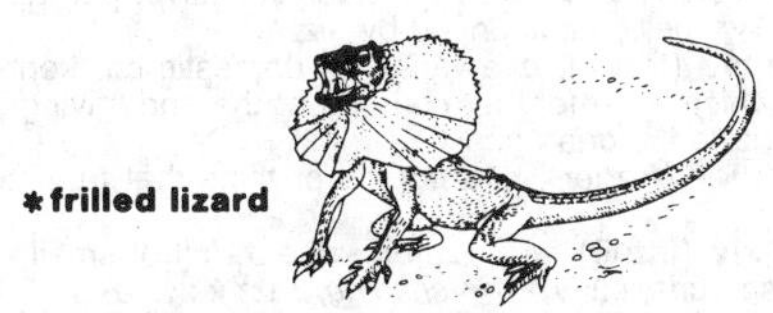
***frilled lizard**

***frilled lizard** (frild), an Australian lizard, about three feet long, that has a broad, rufflelike fold of skin about the neck. When startled, it runs on its hind legs.

frill|er|y (fril′ər ē), *n., pl.* **-er|ies.** an arrangement or mass of frills: *. . . a wealth of snowy frillery and lace* (Joseph Ashby-Sterry).

frill|ing (fril′ing), *n.* **1** frilled trimming. **2** frills.

frill lizard, = frilled lizard.

frill|y (fril′ē), *adj.* **frill|i|er, frill|i|est.** full of frills; like frills.

Fri|maire (frē mer′), *n.* the third month of the year, from November 21 to December 20, in the calendar of the first French republic. [< French *Frimaire* < Middle French *frimas* hoarfrost, probably < Germanic (compare Old Icelandic *hrim* rime[2])]

fringe (frinj), *n., v.,* **fringed, fring|ing,** *adj.* **—n. 1** a border or trimming made especially of threads or cords, either loose or tied together in small bunches: *The cat played with the strings of long fringe at the end of the rug.* **2** anything like this; border: *a fringe of trees about a field. A fringe of hair hung over her forehead.* **3** *Figurative.* anything thought of as marginal rather than central: *He belongs to the radical fringe of the labor movement.*
—v.t. 1 to make a fringe for: *to fringe a bedspread.* **2** to be a fringe for: *Bushes fringed the road.*
—adj. 1 of the border or outside: *a fringe district.* **2** *Figurative.* apart from the main purpose; secondary: *the fringe provisions of a contract.*
fringes, alternate light and dark or colored bands caused by the interference of light waves: *It is then found that the images presented to the observer's eye consist of coloured spots and haloes and fringes* (H. Hartridge).
[< Old French *frenge* < Vulgar Latin *frimbia,* for Latin *fimbria*]

fringe area, 1 the part of a city which is out near its edges: *The [plan] is to move tens of thousands in overpopulated fringe areas out of the town altogether* (Atlantic). **2** any district at a distance from a television or radio station, which makes it difficult to get good reception from the station: *So powerful, you get wonderfully clear reception and superb tone even in fringe areas* (New Yorker).

fringe benefit, any benefit given to employees in addition to wages and compensations required by law. Pension plans, paid holidays and vacations, and recreational facilities are fringe benefits.

fringed gentian (frinjd), an eastern North American gentian with a showy, sky-blue, delicately fringed corolla.

fringed orchis, any one of various North American orchids having a fringed lip.

fring|er (frin′jər), *n. Informal.* **1** a person belonging to the fringe of a party or movement or who is on the fringes of society or some group: *Bishop Sheil made himself just as unpopular with fringers on the right as with those on the left* (Time). **2** a person belonging to a lunatic fringe.

fring|es (frin′jiz), *n.pl.* See under **fringe**.

fringe|tail (frinj′tāl′), *n.* any one of a variety of goldfish having long, fringed fins.

fringe time, the hours of television viewing before or after prime time (in the United States, approximately from 5 to 7 p.m. and from 11 p.m. to 1 a.m.): *"We feel that original programming works best in fringe time," said Dick Ebersol, the head of NBC's late-night operations* (TV Guide).

fringe tree, a small tree or shrub of the olive family that bears drooping clusters of white flowers with long, narrow petals. It grows in the middle and southern United States.

frin|gil|line (frin jil′in, -īn), *adj.* of or belonging to a family of birds that includes the grosbeaks, finches, sparrows, towhees, and buntings. [< Latin *fringilla* finch, small bird + English *-ine*[1]]

fring|ing reef (frin′jing), a coral reef formed close to the shoreline with no navigable channel between.

fring|lish or **Fring|lish** (fring′glish), *n., adj.* English containing or spoken with French words and expressions: *If they did not watch out, they thought gloomily, they would soon descend to using fringlish words like cul-de-sac instead of the proper French term impasse* (Manchester Guardian Weekly). [alteration of earlier *Frenglish,* blend of *French* and *English*]

fring|y (frin′jē), *adj.* **1** like a fringe. **2** adorned with a fringe or fringes.

frip|per|ous (frip′ər əs), *adj.* of little worth; frivolous: *fripperous remarks.*

frip|per|y (frip′ər ē), *n., pl.* **-per|ies. 1** cheap, showy clothes; gaudy ornaments. **2** a cheap,

Pronunciation Key: hat, āge, cãre, fär; let, ēqual, tėrm; it, īce; hot, ōpen, ôrder; oil, out; cup, pu̇t, rüle; child; long; thin; ᴛʜen; zh, measure; ə represents **a** in about, **e** in taken, **i** in pencil, **o** in lemon, **u** in circus.

showy article of clothing; gaudy ornament. **3** a showing off; foolish display; pretended refinement: *Affectations of manner and speech are mere frippery. Listeners, saner and more perceptive, know it is solidly beautiful under its fripperies* (Atlantic). [< French *friperie* < Old French *freperie* < *frepe* rag < Late Latin *faluppa* fiber, thing without value. Compare etym. under **furbelow.**]

Fris|bee (friz′bē), *n. Trademark.* a saucer-shaped plastic disk for skimming into the air, used as a toy or in various games: *Kids flip Frisbees while their elders chat* (Time).

Fris|co (fris′kō), *n. Informal.* San Francisco.

fri|sé (fri zā′), *adj.* (of a fabric) made with a pile of uncut loops, or with uncut loops combined with cut loops. [< French *frisé,* past participle of *friser* to frizz, curl]

fri|sette (fri zet′), *n.* a fringe or band of small, usually artificial, curls, worn on the forehead by women. Also, **frizette.** [< French *frisette* < *friser* to frizz, curl]

fri|seur (frē zœr′), *n. French.* a hairdresser.

Fri|sian (frizh′ən), *adj., n.* —*adj.* of or having to do with Friesland (a district in the northern part of the Netherlands), its people, or their language.
—*n.* **1** a native or inhabitant of Friesland or certain nearby islands. **2** the language spoken in Friesland and certain nearby islands, a West Germanic dialect closely related to English. **3** a member of an ancient Germanic tribe of the Netherlands. Also, **Friesian.**

frisk (frisk), *v., n., adj.* —*v.i.* to run and jump about playfully; skip and dance joyously; frolic: *Our lively puppy frisks all over the house.* **SYN:** gambol.
—*v.t.* **1** to move (something) in a playful or lively manner. **2** to search (a person) for concealed weapons, stolen goods, drugs, or other illegal possessions, by running the hands quickly over his clothes or by a detecting device, as an X-ray machine, Geiger counter or metal detector. *The police frisked the prisoner.* **3** *Slang.* to steal from (a person) in this way: *The pickpocket frisked him of his wallet.*
—*n.* **1** a playful running and jumping; joyous skipping and dancing; frolic. **2** the frisking of a person for concealed weapons, stolen goods, drugs, or other illegal possessions: *Suspects may not be detained if the frisk or questioning fails to yield probable cause for actual arrest* (Time). **3** *Obsolete.* a caracole or curvet in horsemanship or dancing.
—*adj. Archaic.* lively; brisk; frisky.
[(originally) adjective < Middle French *frisque* frisky, perhaps < Germanic (compare Old High German *frisc*)] —**frisk′er,** *n.*

fris|ket (fris′kit), *n. Printing.* **1** a thin framework of iron hinged to the tympan of a hand press, for holding in place the sheet to be printed. **2** a sheet with parts cut out, or a frame for holding such a sheet, for placing over a form so that only certain parts may print. [< French *frisquette;* origin uncertain]

frisk|ful (frisk′fəl), *adj.* brisk; lively; frolicsome.

frisk|y (fris′kē), *adj.,* **frisk|i|er, frisk|i|est.** playful; lively: *The beach was teeming with people from frisky merry little children to decrepit old men just soaking up the sun.* —**frisk′i|ly,** *adv.* —**frisk′i|ness,** *n.*

fris|son (frē sôN′), *n. French.* a thrill; a shiver: *that frisson of horror in her voice* (John Stephen Strange).

fri|sure (frizh′ər), *n.* mode or fashion of curling the hair; hairdressing. [< French *frisure* < *friser* to curl, frizz]

frit (frit), *n., v.,* **frit|ted, frit|ting.** —*n.* **1** a calcined, partly fused mixture of sand and fluxes, used in making glass: *The new coating is composed of chromium, and a glass in the form known as frit* (Science News Letter). **2** *Ceramics.* **a** the pulverized vitreous composition from which soft-paste porcelain is made: *Soft-paste porcelain was made from combinations of a white-firing clay with a fusible silicate, such as a pulverized frit* (Eugene F. Bunker, Jr.) **b** any one of various mixtures of materials, especially fluxes, which have been fired and reground, used in the preparation of certain glasses and glazes.
—*v.t.* to produce frit from (materials for glass or a glaze); fuse partly. Also, **fritt.**
[< French *fritte* < Italian *fritta,* (originally) past participle of *friggere* fry < Latin *frīgere*]

frit fly, a small fly whose larva is harmful to grain.

frith (frith), *n.* a narrow arm of the sea; firth. [variant of *firth*]

frit|il|lar|i|a (frit′ə lãr′ē ə), *n.* = fritillary.

frit|il|lar|y (frit′ə ler′ē), *n., pl.* **-lar|ies. 1** any one of a genus of bulbous plants of the lily family with drooping, bell-shaped flowers usually spotted with dark green or purple: *If you have the patience to wait four or five years, it is best to raise fritillaries from seed* (Sunday Observer). **2** any one of several genera of butterflies with brown, pale, or, sometimes, blue spots on both the upper and under sides of their wings. [< New Latin *Fritillaria* the genus name < Latin *fritillus* dice box (because of the checkered markings on the petals)]

fritt (frit), *n., v.t.,* **frit|ted, frit|ting.** = frit.

frit|ter¹ (frit′ər), *v., n.* —*v.t.* **1** to waste little by little: *to fritter away one's savings. He frittered away both time and energy reading worthless books. The allies ... frittered away precious time in ... disputes* (H. G. Wells). **2** to cut or tear into small pieces; break into fragments.
—*v.i.* to waste or squander resources little by little: *On the stocks, he'd frittered around ... while they sank to seven bucks on each of his eighty shares* (James T. Farrell).
—*n.* a small piece; fragment.
[< Old French *freture, fraiture* < Latin *frāctūra;* see etym. under **fracture**] —**frit′ter|er,** *n.*

frit|ter² (frit′ər), *n.* a small cake of batter, containing fruit, meat, or other food, fried in fat: *corn fritters.* [< Old French *friture* < Late Latin *frīctūra,* for *frīxūra* < Latin *frīgere* fry]

fritz (frits), *n., v. U.S. Informal.*
fritz out, to go out of order; break down: *The television camera fritzed out on the lunar surface* (Time).
on the fritz, out of order; on the blink: *Today's diversion is that the plumbing went on the fritz* (Hamilton Basso).

Fritz (frits), *n. Slang.* **1** a German soldier. **2** a German shell, airplane, submarine, or other weapon or armament. [< German *Fritz,* a nickname for *Friedrich* Frederick, a man's name]

Fri|u|li|an (fri ü′lē ən), *n.* a Rhaeto-Romanic dialect spoken in northern Italy.

friv|ol (friv′əl), *v.,* **-oled, -ol|ing** or (*especially British*) **-olled, -ol|ling,** *n., adj. Informal.* —*v.i.* to behave frivolously; trifle: *She was advised not to frivol with the young heir.*
—*v.t.* to spend frivolously: *One generation frivoled away the fortune made by three.*
—*n.* a frivolous thing; trifle: *... homebodies too plain for cosmetics, too dowdy for bits of frivol* (Punch).
—*adj.* frivolous: *a frivol promise.*
[back formation < *frivolous*] —**friv′ol|er** or (*especially British*) **friv′ol|ler,** *n.*

fri|vol|i|ty (fri vol′ə tē), *n., pl.* **-ties. 1** the fact or condition of being frivolous; silly behavior; trifling: *The hare-brained chatter of irresponsible frivolity* (Benjamin Disraeli). **2** a silly thing or frivolous act.

friv|o|lous (friv′ə ləs), *adj.* **1** lacking in seriousness or sense; silly: *Frivolous behavior is out of place in church.* **SYN:** foolish. **2** of little worth or importance; trivial: *He wasted his time reading frivolous books.* **SYN:** trifling, unimportant, petty. [< Latin *frīvolus* (with English *-ous*)] —**friv′o|lous|ly,** *adv.* —**friv′o|lous|ness,** *n.*

friz (friz), *v.,* **frizzed, friz|zing,** *n., pl.* **friz|zes.**
—*v.t.* **1** to form into small, crisp curls; curl: *He wore his hair ... powdered and frizzed out* (Charles Lamb). **2** to form (the nap of cloth) into little tufts.
—*v.i.* to form into short, crisp curls; curl.
—*n.* **1** hair curled in small, crisp curls or a very close crimp. **2** a being frizzed.
[apparently < French *friser*]

fri|zette (fri zet′), *n.* = frisette.

frizz¹ (friz), *v.t., v.i., n.* = friz.

frizz² (friz), *v.t., v.i.* to fry with a hissing, sputtering noise. [< *fry* + imitative ending *-zz*]

friz|zi|ly (friz′ə lē), *adv.* in a frizzy manner.

friz|zi|ness (friz′ē nis), *n.* frizzy or curly quality or condition.

friz|zle¹ (friz′əl), *v.,* **-zled, -zling,** *n.* —*v.t., v.i.* to form (hair) in small, crisp curls; curl.
—*n.* **1** the condition of being frizzled. **2** a small, crisp curl. [probably < *friz* + *-le* (frequentative)] —**friz′zler,** *n.*

friz|zle² (friz′əl), *v.,* **-zled, -zling,** *n.* —*v.i.* to make a hissing, sputtering noise when cooking; sizzle: *The ham frizzled in the frying pan.*
—*v.t.* to fry or broil until crisp. —*n.* a hissing, sputtering noise; sizzle: *Flounders ... with their tails jerking Flip, flap in the frizzle of the pan* (Samuel R. Crockett). [probably imitative, perhaps < *fry;* spelling influenced by *sizzle*]

Friz|zle (friz′əl), *n.* a variety of domestic chicken in which each feather curls up at the end, giving a frizzled appearance.

friz|zler (friz′lər), *n.* a person or thing that frizzles hair.

friz|zly (friz′lē), *adj.,* **-zli|er, -zli|est.** full of small, crisp curls; curly: *The crisping, frizzly waves glide in snaky folds* (Longfellow).

friz|zy (friz′ē), *adj.,* **-zi|er, -zi|est.** curly; frizzly.

Frl., *German.* Fräulein.

fro (frō), *adv., prep.* —*adv.* from; back.
—*prep. Scottish.* from.
to and fro, first one way and then back again; back and forth: *A rocking chair goes to and fro.*
[< Scandinavian (compare Old Icelandic *frā*)]

frock (frok), *n., v.* —*n.* **1** a woman's or girl's dress; gown: *... a lavender blue lightweight summer frock and a nylon nightdress* (London Times). *The east wind whistled into every open crevice of her afternoon frock* (Angus Wilson). **2** a loose outer garment; smock. **3** a robe worn by a clergyman. **4** the position or authority of clergymen; ministry. **5** a woolen jersey worn by sailors. **6** a long coat, tunic, or mantle. **7** = frock coat.
—*v.t.* **1** to provide with or clothe in a frock. **2** to invest with clerical position or authority.
[< Old French *froc* < Frankish (compare Old High German *hroc* cloak)]

***frock coat,** a man's coat, usually double-breasted, reaching about to the knees, and equally long in front and in back.

***frock coat**

frock-coat|ed (frok′kō′tid), *adj.* wearing a frock coat: *a frock-coated ambassador.*

frock|ing (frok′ing), *n.* material for making frocks.

frock|less (frok′lis), *adj.* without a frock.

froe (frō), *n. Especially U.S.* a wedge-shaped tool having a handle in the plane of the blade, set at right angles to the back, used especially for cleaving and riving staves and shingles. Also, **frow.** [earlier *frower,* perhaps < *froward* (literally) turned away (with reference to the position of the handle)]

Froe|bel|i|an (frœ bel′ē ən), *adj.* of or having to do with Friedrich Fröbel, (1782-1852), a German educational reformer, or his kindergarten system.

***frog¹** (frog, frôg), *n., v.,* **frogged, frog|ging.**
—*n.* **1** a small, leaping amphibian with webbed feet that lives in or near water. They are usually tailless and have a smooth skin and powerful hind legs for leaping. A frog is more agile than a toad. Frogs lay jellylike clusters of eggs in the water which develop into tadpoles in the larval stage until they grow legs. Some common North American frogs are the bullfrog, the pickerel frog, the leopard frog, and the wood frog. **2** an animal like this. A tree frog lives in trees. **3** an arrangement of a rail where a railroad track crosses or branches from another, which guides the flanges of the wheels over the gaps, thus helping a train to stay on its track. **4** a triangular pad of elastic, horny substance in the middle of the bottom of a foot of a horse, donkey, or related animal. **5** a perforated or spiky holder for flower stems, placed at the bottom of a vase or bowl. **6** the nut of a violin bow. **7** the frame of a plow, to which the plowshare, moldboard, and landside are attached.
—*v.i.* to catch or hunt frogs.
frog in one's (or **the**) **throat,** a slight hoarseness caused by soreness or swelling in the throat: *While singing the Liebestod, I sang with frogs in my throat because she wasn't feeling well* (Time).
[Old English *frogga*] —**frog′like′,** *adj.*

***frog¹**
definitions 1,3

leopard frog

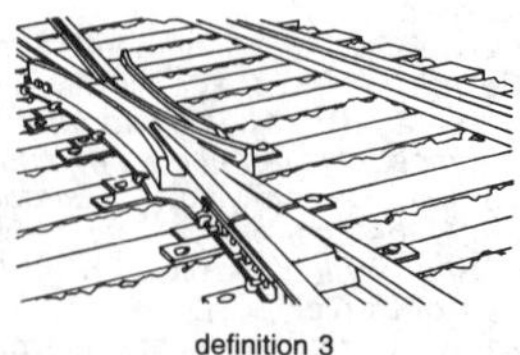
definition 3

***frog²** (frog, frôg), *n.* **1** an ornamental fastening for a coat or dress. It usually consists of a loop and a button which passes through it. See the picture above on the opposite page. **2** a loop or attachment on a belt for carrying a sword, bayonet, billy club, or other weapon or tool: *I made him a* *belt with a frog hanging to it, such as in England we wear hangers in* (Daniel Defoe). [perhaps < Portuguese *froco* < Latin *floccus* flock, tuft]

***frog²** definition 1

frog|bit (frog′bit′, frôg′-), *n.* **1** a floating aquatic plant of Europe, with white flowers. **2** a similar plant of the United States.
frogbit family, a widely distributed group of monocotyledonous aquatic herbs which either grow below the water or float on the surface. The family includes the waterweed, tape grass, and eelgrass.
frog breathing, glossopharyngeal breathing; a method of forcing small amounts of air into the lungs by using the back of the tongue as a pump. It is practiced especially by polio patients who are not able to use their diaphragms.
frog|eye (frog′ī′, frôg′-), *n.* a disease of tobacco plants caused by a fungus that produces small white spots on the leaves.
frog|eyed (frog′īd′, frôg′-), *adj.* affected with frogeye.
frog|face (frog′fās′, frôg′-), *n.* a deformity, caused by the presence of an intranasal tumor, in which the face assumes a fancied resemblance to that of a frog.
frog|fish (frog′fish′, frôg′-), *n., pl.* **-fish|es** or (*collectively*) **-fish**. **1** a fish with a wide, froglike mouth and broad, leglike fins. **2** = angler (def. 3).
frogged (frogd, frôgd), *adj.* fastened or ornamented with frogs: *lackeys in powdered wigs and frogged liveries.*
frog|ger|y (frog′ər ē, frôg′-), *n., pl.* **-ger|ies**. **1** a place where frogs are raised or kept for sale as bait. **2** a place with many frogs.
frog|gi|ness (frog′ē nis, frôg′-), *n.* froggy character or nature.
frog|ging (frog′ing, frôg′-), *n.* fastenings or ornamentation consisting of frogs.
frog|gish (frog′ish, frôg′-), *adj.* like a frog.
frog|gy (frog′ē, frôg′-), *adj.,* **-gi|er, -gi|est**. **1** full of frogs. **2** of, having to do with, or like a frog or frogs: *a gruff, froggy voice.*
frog|hop|per (frog′hop′ər, frôg′-), *n.* a small, leaping, homopterous insect whose young cover themselves with a foamy secretion known as cuckoo spit; spittle insect; spittlebug.
frog kick, a swimming movement in which the legs are moved simultaneously, being first bent outward at the knees, then extended, then brought together, as in the breast stroke.
frog|let (frog′lit, frôg′-), *n.* a small or young frog.
frog lily, = spatterdock.
frog|ling (frog′ling, frôg′-), *n.* a little frog.
frog|man (frog′man, frôg′-), *n., pl.* **-men**. a person trained and equipped with aqualungs for underwater operations of various kinds. Most of the world's navies now have frogmen.
frog-march (frog′march′, frôg′-), *v., n. Especially British.* **—*v.t.*** to march (a person) forward by pinning his arms from behind and pushing him along. **—*n.*** an act of frog-marching.
frog|mouth (frog′mouth′, frôg′-), *n.* a goatsucker (bird) of the East Indies and Australia.
frog plant, = orpine.
frog|pond (frog′pond′, frôg′-), *n. Especially U.S.* a pond frequented by frogs.
frog's-bit (frogz′bit′, frôgz′-), *n.* = frogbit.
frog's-bit family, = frogbit family.
frog's-mouth (frogz′mouth′, frôgz′-), *n.* = frogmouth.
frog spawn, **1** = frog spit (def. 2). **2** a microorganism that causes fermentation and the formation of slimy masses in saccharine solutions.
frog spit or **spittle**, **1** = cuckoo spit. **2** any one of various freshwater algae that form green and slimy floating masses on the surfaces of ponds and ditches.
frog|stool (frog′stül′, frôg′-), *n.* = toadstool.
frog|wort (frog′wėrt′, frôg′-), *n.* = buttercup.
froi|deur (frwä dœr′), *n. French.* coldness; cold indifference; unfriendliness.
frol|ic (frol′ik), *n., v.,* **-icked, -ick|ing,** *adj.* **—*n.*** **1** a merry prank; play; fun: *He ... often filled whole pages ... with the gay frolics of his pencil* (James Russell Lowell). **2** a merry game or party: *The children had a frolic on the lawn.*
—*v.i.* to play about joyously; have fun together; make merry: *Children frolicked with the puppy.*
—*adj.* full of fun; merry.
[(originally) adjective < Middle Dutch *vrolyc* < *vro* glad + *lyc* like]
frol|ick|er (frol′ə kər), *n.* a person who frolics.
frol|ick|y (frol′ə kē), *adj.* = frolicsome.
frol|ic|some (frol′ik səm), *adj.* full of fun; playful; merry: *... the frolicsome little prairie dog* (Science News Letter). **—frol′ic|some|ly**, *adv.* **—frol′ic|some|ness**, *n.*
from (from, frum; *unstressed* frəm), *prep.* **1** out of: *a train from New York. Steel is made from iron.* **2** out of the possession or control of: *Take the book from her.* **3** beginning with; starting at: *from that time forward. Three weeks from today is a holiday.* **4** because of; caused by; by reason of: *to act from a sense of duty. He is suffering from a cold. The cut in his finger was from a knife.* **5** as distinguished from; as being unlike: *Anyone can tell apples from oranges.* **6** off of; away from: *He took a book from the table.* **7** left at a distance or left behind: *to escape from a fire.* [Old English *fram, from*]
fro|mage (frô mäzh′), *n. French.* cheese.
fro|men|ty (frō′mən tē), *n.* = frumenty.
frond (frond), *n.* **1a** the divided leaf of a fern, palm, or cycad. See picture under **fern**. **b** a leaflike part that includes both stem and foliage, such as the thallus of a seaweed or lichen. **2** *Zoology.* a leaflike expansion in certain animal organisms. [< Latin *frōns, frondis* leaf] **—frond′less**, *adj.*
frond|age (fron′dij), *n.* **1** fronds. **2** = foliage.
frond|ed (fron′did), *adj.* having fronds: *fronded palms.*
fron|des|cence (fron des′əns), *n.* **1** the process or period of coming into leaf. **2** leaves; foliage.
fron|des|cent (fron des′ənt), *adj.* putting forth leaves or fronds.
fron|dif|er|ous (fron dif′ər əs), *adj.* bearing leaves or fronds.
fron|dose (fron′dōs, fron dōs′), *adj.* leafy; frondiferous; frondlike. [< Latin *frondōsus* < *frōns, frondis* leaf]
frons (fronz), *n. Anatomy, Zoology.* the forehead; front part of the head. [< Latin *frōns, frontis.* See etym. of doublet **front**.]
front** (frunt), *n., adj., v.* **—*n. **1** the first part; foremost part: *the front of a car, the front of the tongue.* **2** the part that faces forward: *the front of a dress.* **3** the face or part of a building that faces toward something: *the garden front.* **4** a thing fastened or worn on the front, such as a shirt front. **5a** the foremost part of the ground occupied or of the field of operations: *Anatole France ... had been declared unfit for service at the front and, as a member of the National Guard, had been reading Virgil on the fortifications* (Edmund Wilson). **b** the foremost line or part of an army, column, battalion, or other formation. **c** a place where fighting is going on; line of battle: *This, along with Germany, remains one of the few spots where U.S. forces face Red troops on a definite "front"* (Wall Street Journal). **6** a sphere of activity combining different groups in a political or economic battle: *The educational front called for cooperation on all levels.* **7** the forces fighting for some political or social aim: *Liberal Socialists, who formerly supplied most council members, won only seven of 32, and the Labour front, which forms the present Government, won four of sixteen* (Manchester Guardian). **8** land facing a street, river, field, or other specific area: *The store is on the street front.* **9** a promenade of a seaside resort. **10** manner of looking or behaving: *a genial front.* **11** *Informal.* an outward appearance, as of wealth, importance, or happiness: *The newcomer put up an impressive front.* **12** *Informal.* a person appointed to add respectability or prestige to an enterprise: *He was the kind of despot who needed a front, and this was Gil Bucknam's job* (New Yorker). **13** *Informal.* a person or thing that serves as a cover for illegal activities, or for a pressure group: *The club was just a front for gangster activities.* **14** the dividing surface between two dissimilar air masses: *A cold front is moving toward this area from Canada.* See picture above in next column. **15** the forehead. **16** the face. **17** *Theater.* those parts in front of the stage, especially the auditorium. **18** a call to a bellboy to come to the main part of the hotel lobby or to the desk. **19** *Rare.* impudence; cool assurance.
—*adj.* **1** of, on, in, or at the front: *a front room, the front line of battle. The front side of a lens is the side from which the light comes, and the back side is the side from which the light emerges* (Shortley and Williams). **2** *Phonetics.* pronounced by raising the tongue against or near the forward part of the hard palate. The *e* in *bee* is a front vowel.
—*v.t.* **1** to have the front toward; face: *Our house fronts the park.* **2** to be in front of: *A small boy fronted the line to the water fountain.* **3** to meet face to face; confront; oppose; defy: *With stupidity and sound digestion a man may front much* (Thomas Carlyle). **4** to furnish with a front. **5** to be at the head of; lead: *An able blues guitarist ... fronts a blues band* (New Yorker).
—*v.i.* **1** to have the front in a certain direction: *Most houses front on the street.* **2** *Informal.* to serve as a cover for a pressure group, an illegal activity, or the like: *Some claimed that the dockers' union fronted for the smuggling ring.*
change front, to turn in another direction: *The platoon changed front on command.*
in front of, in a place or position before (a person or thing); before: *Standing in front of the blackboard, their blond teacher wrote, 1 + 0 = 1* (Harper's).
up front, *U.S. Informal.* **a** in advance: *The book then went to thirty other publishers ... One offered $40,000 up front if all the proper changes were made* (Harper's). **b** in an open or straightforward manner: *He ... held that it would be better to finance such projects "up front"—that is, with Government appropriations or other means that permitted full and clear public knowledge of the total costs* (New York Times). **c** in the open or foreground: *Vanocur is at ABC as an executive ... and Chancellor works up front, using his face muscles more than his leg muscles* (New Yorker).
[< Old French *front* < Latin *frōns, frontis* (literally) forehead. See etym. of doublet **frons**.]

***front** definition 14

weather map symbols:
cold front — warm front — stationary front

front., frontispiece.
front|age (frun′tij), *n.* **1** the front of a building or of a lot. **2** the length of this front. **3** the direction that the front of a building or lot faces. **4** the land facing a street, river, etc.: *France, with its five great rivers, with its frontage on three seas—with its wheat ... and everywhere almost, the wine* (Edmund Wilson). **5** the land between a building and a street, river, etc.
front|ag|er (frun′ti jər), *n.* a person who owns land fronting on a road, shore, or stream.
frontage road, a road paralleling an expressway or freeway to provide access to local traffic.
fron|tal¹ (frun′təl), *adj., n.* **—*adj.*** **1** of, on, in, or at the front: *The soldiers charged straight ahead and made a frontal attack on the enemy.* **2** of the forehead: *frontal bones.* **3** *Phonetics.* pronounced with the front of the tongue.
—*n.* a bone of the forehead. See picture at **face**.
[< New Latin *frontalis* < Latin *frōns, frontis* (literally) forehead] **—fron′tal|ly**, *adv.*
fron|tal² (frun′təl), *n.* **1** the facade of a building. **2** a movable cover or hanging for the front of an altar. **3** a band or ornament worn on the forehead. [< Old French *frontal, frontel* < Late Latin *frontāle* < Latin *frōns, frontis* (literally) forehead]
frontal fog, *Meteorology.* fog that forms at a front as a result of moisture evaporating from rain which falls from the warmer air mass and saturates the colder air mass below.
fron|tal|is (frun tal′əs, -täl′-), *n.* the muscle of the face that elevates the eyebrows and causes the transverse wrinkles of the forehead. [< New Latin *frontalis;* see etym. under **frontal¹**]
fron|tal|i|ty (frun tal′ə tē), *n.* composition in painting and sculpture in which the figure is viewed from the front; frontal attitude or representation.
frontal lobe, the anterior part of either lobe of the cerebrum. See picture under **brain**.
frontal lobotomy, = prefrontal lobotomy.
front bench, *British.* **1** the front bench on either side of the Houses of Commons and Lords, where ministers and leading members of the Opposition sit. **2** the leaders who occupy a front bench: *On so many of the great issues of the day it is to the interest of both front benches to prevent the most important things from being said* (Manchester Guardian).
front bencher, *British.* a party leader in Parliament who occupies a front bench.
front burner, on the front burner, in a primary place; taking precedence or priority over others: *The most influential man on the labor scene ... for obvious reasons normally keeps the jobs picture on the front burner* (Washington Post).
front cloth, a painted stage curtain in front of which a scene is played: *Its gold front cloth showing a riverboat ... then lifts to reveal a plushy red and gold setting for the minstrel show itself* (Clive Barnes).
front court, the half of the court of the offensive team in basketball.

Pronunciation Key: hat, āge, cãre, fär; let, ēqual, tėrm; it, īce; hot, ōpen, ôrder; oil, out; cup, pu̇t, rüle; child; long; thin; ᴛʜen; zh, measure; ə represents a in about, e in taken, i in pencil, o in lemon, u in circus.

front door, 1 the main entrance of a house or dwelling. 2 *Figurative.* the main approach to a place or objective: . . . *Lanchow, an ancient city on the Silk Route around the Tibetan mountains into Russia and western Asia: classical China's "front door"* (New Scientist). 3 *Figurative.* an open and aboveboard approach to any objective: [*He*] *is hoping to get by the back door what* [*he*] *failed to obtain through the front door of the House of Lords last year* (London Times).

front|ed (frun′tid), *adj.* having a front; formed with a front.

front-end (frunt′end′), *adj.* provided or paid in advance, especially to start a project: *The report advocates front-end support which would involve large payments for R & D at the start* (New Scientist).

front-end load, the sales and commission charges that make up part of the early payments of an investor or buyer under certain long-term investment or purchasing plans.

fron|ten|is (fron ten′is), *n.* a Latin-American ball game resembling handball and consisting essentially of jai alai or pelota played with tennis rackets. [< American Spanish *frontenis,* blend of Spanish *frontón* jai alai court, and *tenis* tennis]

front|er (frun′tər), *n. U.S. Informal.* a member of a front group: *a Red fronter.*

front foot, *U.S.* a foot in length along the front of a lot.

front group, an organization that serves as a cover for illegal activities; front: *The inquiries relate to Communist . . . front groups and* [*their*] *activities* (Bulletin of Atomic Scientists).

fron|tier (frun tir′; frun′tir, fron′-), *n., adj.* —*n.* 1 the last edge of settled country, where the wilds begin; border of inhabited regions: *James Bowie . . . pushed west with the widening frontier to the plains of Texas* (Saturday Review). 2 the part of one country that touches the edge of another; boundary line between two countries; border: *These four Powers are guarantors of the 1942 Ecuador-Peru treaty, which was intended to settle the long-standing quarrel over the Peru frontier with Ecuador* (London Times). SYN: boundary. 3 *Figurative.* an uncertain or undeveloped region: *to explore the frontiers of science.* 4 *Obsolete.* a fortress; border town.
—*adj.* of or on the frontier: *a frontier post.*
[< Old French *frontiere* < *front* < Latin *frōns, frontis* (literally) forehead]

frontier pants or **trousers**, *U.S.* close-fitting, reinforced trousers of a heavy material, worn especially in the Western United States.

fron|tiers|man (frun tirz′mən), *n., pl.* **-men.** a man who lives on the frontier: *As the frontiersmen pushed west into the new land, Baptist preachers were never far behind them* (Time).

fron|tis|piece (frun′tis pēs′, fron′-), *n., v.,* **-pieced, -piec|ing.** —*n.* 1 a picture facing the title page of a book or of a division of a book. 2 *Architecture.* **a** the main part or the decorated entrance of a building. **b** a pediment over a door, window, gate, or vent. 3 *Obsolete.* the title page or first page of a book.
—*v.t.* 1 to furnish (a book) with a frontispiece. 2 to represent on a frontispiece. 3 to provide as a frontispiece.
[< French *frontispice* front of a building < Late Latin *frontispicium* (literally) looking at the forehead < Latin *frōns, frontis* forehead + *specere* look]

front|lash (frunt′lash′), *n. U.S. Informal.* a reaction that offsets or reverses an unfavorable reaction. [< *front* + (back)*lash*]

front|less (frunt′lis), *adj.* without a front.

front|let (frunt′lit), *n.* 1 a band or ornament worn on the forehead. 2 a phylactery bound on the forehead during prayer. 3 the forehead of an animal. 4 the forehead of a bird when of a different color or texture of plumage. [< Old French *frontlet* (diminutive) < *frontel* frontal]

front line, the most advanced line occupied by troops, nearest to enemy positions.

front-line (frunt′līn′), *adj.* 1 of or at the front line: *The general sent* [*the band*] *into the nearby combat areas, in a two-and-a-half-ton truck, to play for the front-line troops* (New Yorker). 2 of or having to do with any country which borders on or is closest to an enemy country or area of conflict: *Iraq still seemed caught between feeling left out of the ranks of "front-line" states with Israel and being deeply involved in Gulf affairs* (Manchester Guardian).

front man, 1 a person who publicly represents a group or organization: *Their party began to go places only after it found a glamorous front man* (Time). 2 a person who fronts for another or others.

front matter, *Printing.* those pages that precede the main text in a book, including the title page, preface, and table of contents.

front-of|fice (frunt′ôf′is, -of′-), *adj.* executive; administrative: *Professionally they are hamstrung by front-office pressure and fear of community wrath* (Time).

fron|to|gen|e|sis (frun′tə jen′ə sis), *n. Meteorology.* the formation of a front, as by the convergence of dissimilar air masses.

fron|tol|y|sis (frun tol′ə sis), *n. Meteorology.* the dissolution of a front, as by the divergence or mingling of dissimilar air masses.

fron|ton (fron′ ton), *n.* 1 a court for jai alai or pelota. 2 a building where jai alai games are played [< Spanish *frontón* < *frente* forehead < Latin *frōns, -frontis*]

front-page (frunt′pāj′), *adj., v.,* **-paged, -pag|ing.** —*adj.* on or suitable for the front page of a newspaper; important: *front-page news.*
—*v.t.* to put on the front page; emphasize.

front-porch campaign (frunt′pôrch′, -pōrch′), *U.S.* a presidential election campaign in which a candidate makes all his political speeches in his home district instead of engaging in a speaking tour across the country: *William McKinley in 1896 and 1900 and Warren G. Harding in 1920 conducted front-porch campaigns.*

front quarter, = forequarter.

front-rank (frunt′rangk′), *adj.* of the first or foremost rank; first-class: *Ideally, no doubt, young conductors should learn their jobs on fully professional orchestras, though not necessarily front-rank ones* (London Times).

front room, the parlor or living room of a house.

front-run|ner (frunt′run′ər), *n.* 1 a horse, not necessarily the eventual winner, that leads or takes the lead in a race. 2 *Figurative.* the leading contender at a given moment in any contest: *A dark horse might win the nomination if the two front-runners should trip each other.*

front-run|ning (frunt′run′ing), *adj.* leading in a race or contest.

front-steer|er (frunt′stir′ər), *n.* an iceboat steered by the runner at the front.

front|ward (frunt′wərd), *adv.* toward or near the front.

front|wards (frunt′wərdz), *adv.* = frontward.

front-wheel drive (frunt′hwēl′), a system in which power is transmitted to the front wheels of a motor vehicle.

frore (frôr, frōr), *adj.* 1 *Archaic or Dialect.* frozen. 2 *Poetic.* intensely cold; frosty. [Middle English *froren* < Old English *frēosan* freeze]

frosh (frosh), *n., pl.* **frosh.** *U.S. Informal.* a freshman at a college or school. [perhaps < German *Frosch* (literally) frog; (in informal use) university freshman]

frost (frôst, frost), *n., v.* —*n.* 1 a freezing condition; very cold weather; temperature below the point at which water freezes: *Frost came early last winter. Frosts occur most readily in low places, especially if there is no outlet* (Thomas A. Blair). 2 the act or process of becoming frozen: *If the secret ministry of frost Shall hang them in silent icicles* (Samuel Taylor Coleridge). 3 moisture frozen on or in a surface; feathery crystals of ice formed when water vapor in the air condenses at a temperature below freezing; white frost; hoarfrost: *frost on windows. On cold fall mornings, there was frost on the grass. The only difference between dew and frost is that the frost occurs at sub-freezing temperatures* (Neuberger and Stephens). 4 *Figurative.* coldness of manner or feeling; frigidity: *One of those moments of intense feeling when the frost of the Scottish people melts like a snow wreath* (Scott). 5 *Slang.* a failure; flop: *One small meeting can be a frost and another a crashing success* (New Yorker). 6 *Informal, Figurative.* a falling off of, or coolness in, friendship; estrangement: *A slight frost has since settled over Belgrade's friendship with Ankara* (New York Times).
—*v.t.* 1 to cover with frost: *Delicate traceries frosted the windowpanes.* 2 to cover with anything that suggests frost: *The baker frosted the cake with a mixture of sugar and beaten whites of eggs.* 3 to give a frostlike surface to (glass or metal). 4 to kill or injure by frost or freezing: *The drop in temperature frosted the tomato plants.*
—*v.i.* to freeze; become covered with frost.
[Old English *forst.* See related etym. at **freeze.**]
—**frost′less,** *adj.* —**frost′like′,** *adj.*

Frost Belt or **Frost|belt** (frôst′belt′, frost′-), *n. U.S.* 1 the northern region of the United States extending east to west that regularly has frost in colder seasons. 2 = Snowbelt (def. 2a).

frost|bite (frôst′bīt′, frost′-), *n., v.,* **-bit, -bit|ten, -bit|ing.** —*n.* an injury to a part of the body caused by exposure to severe cold. Frostbite is characterized by severe burning pain, the rupturing of blood vessels, and gangrene: *Frostbite may, however, cause local death, so that fingers and toes and ears swell, then blacken and shrivel and eventually drop off* (New Scientist).
—*v.t.* to injure (a part of the body) by exposure to frost; harm by severe cold: *The trapper's feet were frostbitten when he was lost in the arctic snow.* —*v.i.* to take part in a frostbite race.

frostbite boating, *U.S.* = frostbiting.

frost|bit|er (frôst′bī′tər, frost′-), *n. U.S. Informal.* 1 a sailboat used in frostbiting. 2 a person sailing such a boat.

frostbite race or **regatta**, *U.S.* a race between sailboats in the winter months.

frost|bit|ing (frôst′bī′ting, frost′-), *n. U.S.* the sport of sailing or racing a sailboat in the winter months.

frost|bit|ten (frôst′bit′ən, frost′-), *adj., v.* —*adj.* 1 injured by severe cold: *frostbitten fingers.* 2 coldly impassive; having an ice-cold or frigid personality. **a** the past participle of **frostbite**: *My ears were frostbitten.*

frost|bound (frôst′bound′, frost′-), *adj.* 1 covered with frost; in a frozen condition: *The birds are much more cheerful and vocal than they were when the countryside was frostbound* (Manchester Guardian). 2 *Figurative.* lacking in warmth; frigid: *Relations with France seemed as frostbound as ever* (Annual Register of World Events).

frost|ed (frôs′tid, fros′-), *adj., n.* —*adj.* 1 covered with frost: *a frosted window.* 2 having a surface like frost: *Frosted glass has a rough surface.* (*Figurative.*) *When I, with frosted hairs, Should look at what I was* (George Daniel). 3 covered with frosting; iced: *a frosted cake.* 4 frozen; frostbitten: *frosted fingers.* 5 = quick-frozen.
—*n.* a beverage made by shaking or beating milk, flavoring, and ice cream until frothy.

frost|fish (frôst′fish′, frost′-), *n., pl.* **-fish|es** or (*collectively*) **-fish.** 1 the tomcod, which appears along the New England coast as the frost sets in. 2 the American smelt.

frost heave, an uplift of the ground in winter, caused by the freezing of water beneath the surface: *Frost heave caused burst and buckled road surfaces all over Lincolnshire* (London Times).

frost|ing (frôs′ting, fros′-), *n.* 1 a mixture of sugar and some liquid, with flavoring, to cover cakes or cookies; icing. Sometimes frosting also contains the beaten whites of eggs. 2 a dull, rough finish on glass or metal. 3 a coarse powdered glass used to decorate signs, lamp shades, etc. 4 *Figurative.* an embellishment: *The stock market rose again yesterday, adding frosting to Tuesday's advance* (New York Times).
frosting on the cake, something added as an embellishment; trimming: *Most other features are . . . frosting on the cake* (*as remote speaker switches*) *that are handy if you need them, but can be done without* (Saturday Review).

frost|line (frôst′līn′, frost′-), *n.* the maximum depth to which frost penetrates into the ground in a given locality, as measured during winter.

frost plant, any one of various plants on whose stems crystals of ice form in autumn, such as the frostweeds or the North American dittany.

frost point, the point at which frost begins to form from air saturated with water vapor and cooled to a temperature below freezing.

frost|weed (frôst′wēd′, frost′-), *n.* any of the woody herbs or low shrubs notable for the crystals of ice which shoot from the bursting bark near the base of the stems in autumn.

frost|work (frôst′wėrk′, frost′-), *n.* 1 the delicate tracery formed by frost on a surface, especially of glass. 2 ornamentation in imitation of this.

frost|y (frôs′tē, fros′-), *adj.,* **frost|i|er, frost|i|est.** 1 cold enough for frost; freezing: *a frosty morning.* 2 covered with frost; consisting of frost: *The glass is frosty.* 3 covered with anything like frost. 4 *Figurative.* cold and unfriendly; with no warmth of feeling: *a frosty greeting, a frosty manner.* SYN: frigid, chilling. 5 *Figurative.* hoary; gray: *He was frosty at the temples.* 6 of or like old age: *the frosty blood of many years.* —**frost′i|ly,** *adv.* —**frost′i|ness,** *n.*

froth (frôth, froth), *n., v.* —*n.* 1 foam; spume: *The froth of the waves collected on the beach.* SYN: lather, scum, suds. 2 foaming saliva coming from the mouth, caused especially by disease or exertion: *There was froth on the mad dog's lips.* 3 *Figurative.* something light and trifling; unimportant talk: *a froth of fleeting joy* (Shakespeare). *Society is froth above and dregs below* (Walter Savage Landor).
—*v.i.* to give out froth; foam: *The ginger ale frothed up in the glass.*
—*v.t.* 1 to cause to foam, as by beating or pouring. 2 to give out or emit like froth or foam. 3 to cover with foam. 4 *Figurative.* to cover or invest with something light and trifling: *The Church of Santa Maria della Salute . . . is frothed with baroque winged statues* (Atlantic).
[Middle English *frothe,* perhaps < Scandinavian (compare Old Icelandic *frotha*)]

froth flotation, = flotation.

froth|y (frôth′ē, froth′-), *adj.,* **froth|i|er froth|i|est.** 1 of, like, or having froth; foamy: *frothy soapsuds, frothy ruffles.* 2 *Figurative.* light and trifling; shallow; unimportant: *frothy conversation. Instru-*

mentalists were seated in niches around the stage and played frothy music as the performers spoke and sang (Time). SYN: vain, empty, unsubstantial. **—froth′i|ly,** *adv.* **—froth′i|ness,** *n.*

frot|tage (frô tȧzh′), *n. French.* **1** (especially in surrealistic art) a method of reproducing textures by placing paper on a surface (of weathered wood, rough cloth, or the like) and rubbing charcoal or pencil over the paper. **2** a work produced by this method. **3** sexual stimulation produced by rubbing against a person or thing.

frot|té (frô tā′), *n. French.* a picture, or part of a picture, executed by means of very slight and more or less transparent washes of color, as in producing hazy effects of atmosphere in landscape.

frot|teur (frô tœr′), *n. French.* a person who practices frottage.

frou|frou (frü′frü′), *n.* **1** *Informal.* fancy or fussy trimmings or the like; frills. **2** a rustling or swishing sound, like that of a silk dress. [< French *frou-frou;* imitative]

frounce (frouns), *v.,* **frounced, frounc|ing,** *n.*
—*v.t.* **1** to frizz or curl (the hair or a wig): *Not trick'd and frounc'd as she was wont* (Milton). **2** *Obsolete.* to gather into creases or pleats; pleat.
—*v.i.* *Obsolete.* to fall in folds or pleats.
—*n.* **1** foppish display. **2** *Obsolete.* a fold, crease, or pleat.
[< Old French *froncir* fold, pleat, wrinkle. See etym. of doublet **flounce².**]

frous|y (frou′zē), *adj.,* **frous|i|er, frous|i|est.** = frowzy.

frouz|y (frou′zē), *adj.,* **frouz|i|er, frouz|i|est.** = frowzy.

frow¹ (frō), *n.* = froe.

frow² (frou), *n.* **1** a woman. **2** a wife (used especially with reference to the Dutch or Germans). [< Dutch *vrouw*]

fro|ward (frō′wərd, -ərd), *adj.* **1** not easily managed; willful; contrary: *My uncle's mule is a froward animal. Human life is ... but like a froward child ... that must be played with and humoured ... till it falls asleep, and then the care is over* (Sir William Temple). SYN: perverse, obstinate, refractory. **2** *Obsolete.* adverse; unfavorable; untoward. [< *frō* (or *from*) + *-ward*] **—fro′ward|ly,** *adv.* **—fro′ward|ness,** *n.*

frown (froun), *n., v.* **—*n.*** **1** a wrinkling of the forehead in deep thought, anger, or disapproval: *a frown of concentration.* **2** any expression or show of disapproval: *Her very frowns are fairer far Than smiles of other maidens are* (Hartley Coleridge).
—*v.i.* **1** to wrinkle the forehead in deep thought, anger, or disapproval; scowl: *The more he wrestled with his homework, the more he frowned in concentration.* **2** *Figurative.* to look displeased or angry: *The heavens ... are angry and frown upon us* (Shakespeare). **3** to look with disapproval: *The principal frowned on our plan for a picnic just before examinations.* **4** to have a threatening aspect; lower.
—*v.t.* **1** to express by a frown: *He frowned his disapproval. She smiles preferment or she frowns disgrace* (Richard Brinsley Sheridan). **2** to drive or force with a frown (down, off, away): *He frowned down all his opponents.*
[< Old French *froignier,* probably < a Germanic word] **—frown′er,** *n.* **—frown′ing|ly,** *adv.* **—frown′less,** *adj.*
—*Syn.* *v.i.* **1, 2 Frown, scowl** mean to produce a forbidding look by lowering or drawing the eyebrows together. **Frown** suggests a stern look indicating strong anger, mild displeasure, or merely concentration: *The teacher frowned when the boy came in late.* **Scowl** suggests a sullen look indicating bad humor: *He is a disagreeable person, always scowling.*

frowst (froust), *n., v. Especially British.* **—*n.*** a close, fusty atmosphere.
—*v.i.* to stay in a close, fusty atmosphere: *The cure for this ill is not to sit still, or frowst with a book by the fire* (Rudyard Kipling). [back formation < *frowsty*]

frowst|y (frous′tē), *adj. Especially British.* fusty; having an unpleasant smell. [origin uncertain. Compare Old French *frouste* decayed.] **—frowst′i|ly,** *adv.*

frows|y (frou′zē), *adj.,* **frows|i|er, frows|i|est.** = frowzy.

frow|y (frō′ē), *adj. Dialect.* (of food) musty; stale. [apparently related to **frowsty**]

frowz|y (frou′zē), *adj.,* **frowz|i|er, frowz|i|est. 1** dirty and untidy; slovenly: *My study was so frowzy I couldn't sit in it* (Thomas Hughes). SYN: dingy, slatternly, unkempt, soiled. **2** smelling bad; musty: *a thousand frowzy steams which I could not analyze* (Tobias Smollett). SYN: fusty. Also, **frousy, frouzy, frowsy.** [apparently related to **frowsty**] **—frow′zi|ly,** *adv.* **—frow′zi|ness,** *n.*

froze (frōz), *v.* the past tense of **freeze:** *The water in the pond froze last week.*

fro|zen (frō′zən), *adj., v.* **—*adj.*** **1** hardened with cold; turned into ice; subjected or exposed to extreme cold: *a river frozen over, frozen sherbet, frozen carbon dioxide. The hare limped trembling through the frozen grass* (Keats). **2** very cold: *My hands are frozen; I need some gloves. Antarctica is a frozen continent.* **3** preserved by being subjected to low temperatures: *frozen foods.* **4** killed or injured by frost: *frozen flowers.* **5** covered or clogged with ice: *frozen water pipes.* **6** *Figurative.* cold and unfeeling: *a frozen heart, a frozen stare, a frozen smile.* **7** too frightened or stiff to move: *frozen to the spot in horror.* **8** made temporarily impossible to sell or exchange; made impossible to liquidate, as by business conditions: *frozen assets, frozen loans.* **9** (of a price, rent, wage, or other financial matter) fixed at a particular amount or level; unchanged: *These dwellings ... suffered inevitably during the war and, subsequently, when frozen rents and rising costs progressively reduced owners' resources for repairs* (London Times). **10** *U.S., Figurative.* hard; solid: *frozen facts, the frozen truth.*
—*v.* the past participle of **freeze:** *The water has frozen to ice.* **—fro′zen|ness,** *n.*

frozen custard, a soft, creamy ice cream.

frozen daiquiri, a daiquiri thoroughly blended with crushed ice and sipped through a straw.

frozen food, food preserved by quick-freezing and storage in a freezer until it is prepared for use by defrosting or cooking.

frozen frame, a single image held still in the midst of a motion-picture sequence; freeze frame: *... the frozen frame, when the camera makes its point by stopping and holding a motionless shot of Sophia Western laughing* (Maclean's).

fro|zen|ly (frō′zən lē), *adv.* **1** in a frozen manner; with a cold look. **2** *U.S.* stubbornly.

frozen sleep, = hypothermia.

frs., francs.

FRS (no periods), Federal Reserve System.

F.R.S., Fellow of the Royal Society.

frt., freight.

Fruc|ti|dor (fryk tē dôr′), *n.* the twelfth month of the French Revolutionary calendar, from August 18 to September 16. [< French *Fructidor* < Latin *frūctus, -ūs* fruit (literally) an enjoyment (see etym. under **fruit**) + Greek *dôron* gift]

fruc|tif|er|ous (fruk tif′ər əs), *adj.* bearing or producing fruit. [< Latin *frūctifer* (< *frūctus, -ūs* fruit + *ferre* to bear) + English *-ous*]

fruc|ti|fi|ca|tion (fruk′tə fə kā′shən), *n.* **1** the act or fact of forming or bearing fruit. **2** the fruit of a plant. **3** the organs of fruiting or reproduction in lower plants, such as the reproductive parts of ferns and mosses.

fruc|ti|fy (fruk′tə fī), *v.,* **-fied, -fy|ing.** **—*v.i.*** to bear fruit: (*Figurative.*) *After many years of perseverance his plan fructified.*
—*v.t.* to make fruitful or productive; cause to bear fruit; fertilize: (*Figurative.*) *The trace of genius on the air ought to be fructifying, or at any rate heady; but somehow it is nothing of the kind* (London Times).
[< Old French *fructifier,* learned borrowing from Latin *frūctificāre* < *frūctus, -ūs* fruit + *facere* make]

fruc|tiv|o|rous (fruk tiv′ər əs), *adj.* feeding on fruits; frugivorous: *Some vertebrates are herbivorous ... some fructivorous, and a few even omnivorous* (White and Renner). [< Latin *frūctus* fruit + *vorāre* devour + English *-ous*]

fruc|tose (fruk′tōs), *n.* a sugar present in many fruits and in honey; fruit sugar; levulose. In honey it is present as one of the two products of the hydrolysis of sucrose. Fructose is much sweeter than glucose or sucrose. *Formula:* $C_6H_{12}O_6$ [< Latin *frūctus, -ūs* fruit + English *-ose²*]

fruc|tu|ous (fruk′chů əs), *adj.* **1** producing fruit. **2** *Figurative.* productive of results; profitable. SYN: advantageous, beneficial. [< Latin *frūctuōsus* producing fruit < *frūctus, -ūs* fruit]

frug (früg), *n., v.,* **frugged, frug|ging.** **—*n.*** a rock'n'roll dance performed with little or no movement of the feet but with rhythmic motions of the hips, arms, head, and shoulders: *One of the most popular discotheque dances in Europe was the frug, which ... derived from the older twist* (Robert Jarvis).
—*v.i.* to dance the frug. [origin unknown] **—frug′ger,** *n.*

fru|gal (frü′gəl), *adj.* **1** without waste; not wasteful; saving; using things well: *My aunt is a frugal housekeeper who buys and uses food carefully. Though on pleasure she was bent, She had a frugal mind* (William Cowper). SYN: sparing, thrifty. See syn. under **economical. 2** costing little; barely enough: *He ate a frugal supper of bread and milk.* [< Latin *frūgālis* < *frūgī* temperate, useful, ultimately < *frūctus;* see etym. under **fruit**] **—fru′gal|ly,** *adv.* **—fru′gal|ness,** *n.*

fru|gal|i|ty (frü gal′ə tē), *n., pl.* **-ties.** an avoidance of waste; tendency to save money; thrift: *Riches are gotten with industry and kept by frugality* (Thomas Hobbes).

fru|gi|vore (frü′jə vôr, -vōr), *n.* a frugivorous animal: *folivores ... are distinguished from frugivores, which cannot utilize cellulose* (Science).

fru|giv|o|rous (frü jiv′ər əs), *adj.* eating or feeding on fruit. [< Latin *frūgis* fruit + *vorāre* devour]

fruit** (früt), *n., v.* **—*n. **1** a juicy or fleshy product of a tree, bush, shrub, vine, or fleshy-stemmed plant that is good to eat. Apples, oranges, bananas, and berries are sweet fruits; a lemon is a sour fruit. **2** *Botany.* the part of a plant in which the seeds are. A fruit is the ripened ovary of a flower and the tissues connected with it. Complete pea pods, acorns, cucumbers, and grains of wheat are fruits. **3** *Figurative.* a useful product of plant growth: *The fruits of the earth are used mostly for food.* **4** the result of anything; product: *The fairs enable man to display the fruits of his invention to the rest of the world* (Science News Letter). SYN: return, profit.
—*v.i., v.t.* to bear or bring to bear fruit; have or produce fruit: *The crop in the lower Rio Grande Valley was fruiting heavily during the past week* (Wall Street Journal).
fruit of the body (loins or **womb),** offspring; progeny (especially as a Biblical archaism): *The Lord withheld the fruit of the womb ... so that by her he had no issue* (William Hinde).
[< Old French *fruict* < Latin *frūctus, -ūs* fruit, produce < *fruī* enjoy, make use of] **—fruit′like′,** *adj.*

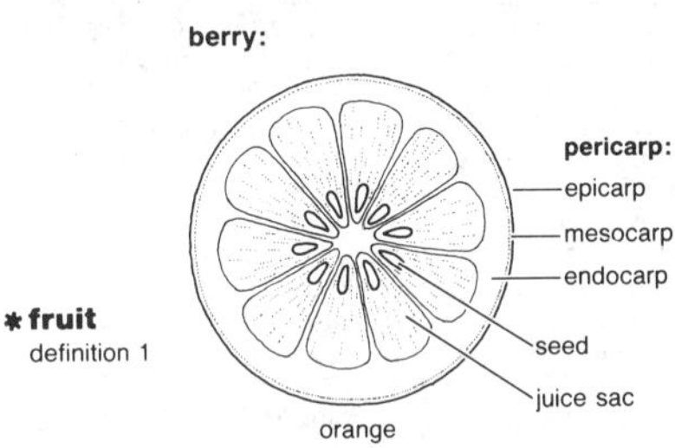

***fruit**
definition 1

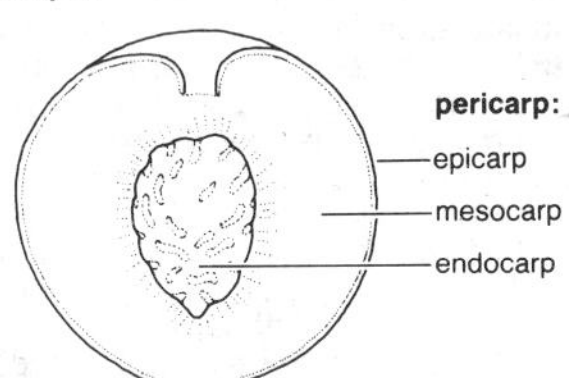

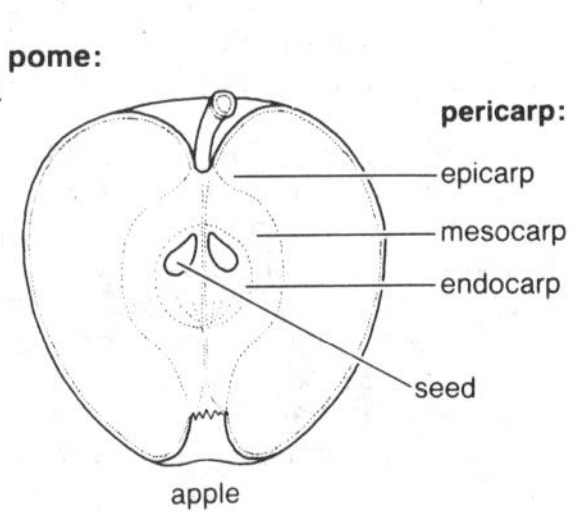

fruit|age (frü′tij), *n.* **1** a having or producing fruit. **2** a crop of fruit; fruit: *Greedily they pluck'd the fruitage fair to sight* (Milton). **3** product; result. [< Old French *fruitage* < *fruit;* see etym. at **fruit**]

fruit bat, any one of various fruit-eating bats found in warm regions of the world. One variety, the flying fox, is one of the largest of all bats.

fruit body, = fruiting body.

fruit|cake (früt′kāk′), *n.,* or **fruit cake,** a rich cake usually containing raisins, currants, and other fruits and sometimes nuts and spices.

fruit cocktail, a fruit cup served as an appetizer.

fruit cup, mixed fruits served in a cup or glass as an appetizer or dessert.

fruit|ed (frü′tid), *adj.* **1** having or containing fruit. **2** laden with fruit.

fruit|er (frü′tər), *n.* **1** a cargo ship for carrying fruit. **2** a tree that produces fruit. **3** a fruit grower.

fruit|er|er (frü′tər ər), *n.* **1** a dealer in fruit. **2** = fruiter (def. 1).

Pronunciation Key: hat, āge, cãre, fär; let, ēqual, tėrm; it, īce; hot, ōpen, ôrder; oil, out; cup, pu̇t, rüle; child; long; thin; ᴛʜen; zh, measure; ə represents **a** in about, **e** in taken, **i** in pencil, **o** in lemon, **u** in circus.

fruit|er|y (frü′tər ē), *n., pl.* **-er|ies. 1** a place for raising or storing fruit. **2** fruit collectively.

fruit fly, any one of various small flies whose larvae feed on fruits and vegetables. Fruit flies are used in scientific studies of heredity, because of the large size of the chromosomes and the rapidity of generation.

fruit|ful (früt′fəl), *adj.* **1** producing much fruit; bearing plenty of fruit. **2** *Figurative.* producing much of anything; prolific: *a fruitful mind.* SYN: productive, fertile. **3** *Figurative.* having good results; bringing benefit or profit: *a fruitful subject for discussion. A successful plan is fruitful.* SYN: profitable, beneficial, remunerative. **4** favorable to the growth of fruit or useful vegetation in general, as soil or showers. **—fruit′ful|ly,** *adv.* **—fruit′ful-ness,** *n.*

fruit|ing body (frü′ting), any part of a plant that produces spores; spore fruit; fruit body.

fru|i|tion (frü ish′ən), *n.* **1** the condition of having results; fulfillment; attainment: *After years of hard work, his plans came to fruition.* SYN: realization. **2** the pleasure that comes from possession or use; enjoyment: *An object of desire placed out of the possibility of fruition* (Joseph Addison). **3** the condition of producing fruit. [< Old French *fruission, fruition,* learned borrowing from Late Latin *fruītiō, -ōnis* enjoyment < *fruī* enjoy, use]

fruit jar, a large-mouthed jar, usually of glass, which can be sealed airtight to preserve fruit and other canned produce.

fruit|less (früt′lis), *adj.* **1** having no results; useless; unsuccessful: *Our search was fruitless; we could not find the lost book.* SYN: abortive, futile, vain, ineffectual, unprofitable, empty, idle. **2** producing no fruit; barren: *a fruitless orchard.* SYN: sterile. **—fruit′less|ly,** *adv.* **—fruit′less|ness,** *n.*

fruit|let (früt′lit), *n.* a small fruit.

fruit loop, *U.S. Slang.* **1** an unconventional or eccentric person. **2** unconventional; eccentric: *This is no fruit loop, artsy-craftsy refuge for students looking for a degree in pottery making* (Christian Science Monitor).

fruit machine, *British.* a coin-operated gambling device in which balls of different colors are used; slot machine.

fruit pigeon, any one of various small, fruit-eating, brightly colored pigeons of southern Asia, Australia, and the South Pacific islands.

fruit ranch, a ranch or farm where fruit is raised.

fruit salad, 1 fruits, usually uncooked, cut up and mixed in a bowl with sugar, cream, etc. **2** *U.S. Slang.* an array of ribbons and decorations worn on a uniform.

fruit stand, a small store or stand where fruit is sold.

fruit sugar, = fructose.

fruit tree, a tree whose fruit is good to eat.

fruit|wood (früt′wu̇d′), *n., adj.* **—*n.*** the wood of a fruit tree, used in furniture and veneers: *Cherry is the finest and most popular of fruitwoods.* **—*adj.* 1** of fruitwood: *a fruitwood side chair.* **2** of the color and pattern of fruitwood: *a fruitwood finish.*

fruit|y (frü′tē), *adj.,* **fruit|i|er, fruit|i|est. 1** tasting or smelling like fruit: *the rich fruity odor of jam.* **2** (of wine) having the taste of the grape: *The Madeira . . . is a trifle too fruity for my taste* (F. H. Smith). **3** *Informal, Figurative.* full of rich or strong quality; highly interesting, attractive, or suggestive: *His description was fruity but embarrassing.* **4** *Informal, Figurative.* excessively or cloyingly sentimental. **—fruit′i|ly,** *adv.* **—fruit′i-ness,** *n.*

fru|men|ta|ceous (frü′men tā′shəs), *adj.* **1** made of wheat or other cereals. **2** resembling wheat or other cereals. [< Late Latin *frūmentāceus* (with English *-ous*) < *frūmentum* grain < *fruī* enjoy, use]

fru|men|ty (frü′mən tē), *n.* hulled wheat boiled in milk and flavored with sugar, cinnamon, and other spices: *And we are going to have real frumenty and yule cakes* (Juliana H. Ewing). Also, **fromenty, furmenty, furmety.** [< Old French *frumentee* < *frument* grain < Latin *frūmentum* < *fruī* enjoy]

frump (frump), *n.* a woman who is shabby and out of style in dress.

frumps, *Dialect.* sulks; ill humor: *Why should you be in your frumps, Pug, when I design only to oblige you?* (John Dryden).

[origin uncertain; perhaps short for Middle English *frumple* wrinkle]

frump|ish (frum′pish), *adj.* **1** shabby and out of style in dress; dowdy: *Most of the women looked like frumpish dairymaids, their faces unsullied by make-up* (Atlantic). **2** ill-natured; cross. **—frump′-ish|ly,** *adv.* **—frump′ish|ness,** *n.*

frump|y (frum′pē), *adj.,* **frump|i|er, frump|i|est.** = frumpish. **—frump′i|ly,** *adv.* **—frump′i|ness,** *n.*

frus|trate (frus′trāt), *v.,* **-trat|ed, -trat|ing,** *adj.* **—*v.t.* 1** to bring to nothing; make useless or worthless; foil; defeat: *Heavy rain frustrated our plans for a picnic.* **2** to thwart; oppose; prevent from accomplishing: *The struggling artist was often frustrated in his ambition to paint.*

—*adj.* 1 defeated; disappointed; balked: *frustrate hopes.* **2** futile; vain: *frustrate attempts.* SYN: ineffectual, fruitless, unavailing, useless.

[< Latin *frūstrārī* (with English *-ate*[1]) < *frūstrā* in vain] **—frus′trat|er,** *n.*

—*Syn.* *v.t.* **2 Frustrate, thwart, baffle** mean to keep someone from accomplishing some purpose. **Frustrate** implies making a person's efforts and plans seem useless: *The police frustrated the bandits' attempt to rob the bank.* **Thwart** implies blocking his efforts: *The sudden storm thwarted the men trying to reach the wrecked plane.* **Baffle** implies puzzling or confusing him so that he can proceed no further: *The absence of clues baffled the police.*

frus|trat|ed (frus′trā tid), *adj.* having a feeling of frustration; disappointed; discouraged: *. . . the miseries of frustrated teen-agers* (Manchester Guardian Weekly). **—frus′trat|ed|ly,** *adv.*

frus|trat|ing (frus′trā ting), *adj.* causing frustration; discouraging; dispiriting: *frustrating experiences. The roads from New Jersey to New York were . . . perilous—and frustrating* (New York Times). **—frus′trat|ing|ly,** *adv.*

frus|tra|tion (frus trā′shən), *n.* the act of frustrating or condition of being frustrated: *One of the many aspects of growing up is the increasing ability to deal with frustration, to tolerate disappointment, and to draw from a thwarting experience some positive result* (Sidonie M. Gruenberg).

frus|tra|tive (frus′trā tiv, -trə-), *adj.* tending to frustrate, balk, or defeat; disappointing.

frus|tule (frus′chül, -tyül), *n. Botany.* the siliceous, bivalve shell of a diatom: *The frustule is really a box, composed of an upper and lower lid, each fitted with a girdle band around the edge* (N. Ingram Hendey). [< French *frustule* < Late Latin *frustulum* (diminutive) < Latin *frustum* a piece broken off]

***frus|tum** (frus′təm), *n., pl.* **-tums, -ta** (-tə). *Geometry.* **1** the part of a cone-shaped solid left after the top has been cut off by a plane parallel to the base. **2** the part of a solid between two parallel cutting planes. [< Latin *frustum* piece broken off]

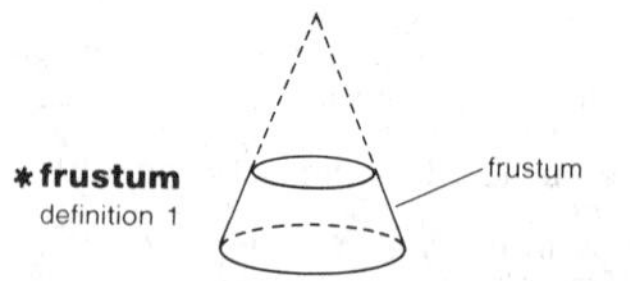

***frustum** definition 1

fru|tes|cence (frü tes′əns), *n.* a frutescent condition; shrubbiness.

fru|tes|cent (frü tes′ənt), *adj.* having the appearance or habit of a shrub; shrubby, or becoming shrubby. [< Late Latin *frutēscēns, -entis,* present participle of *frutēscere* put out shoots < Latin *frutex, -icis* shoot, runner, bush]

fru|ti|cose (frü′tə kōs), *adj.* having the form of a shrub; shrubby: *Fruticose lichens look like moss or tiny shrubs* (Rolla M. Tryon). [< Latin *fruticōsus* full of bushes, shrubby < *frutex, -icis* bush, shrub]

fry[1] (frī), *v.,* **-fried, fry|ing,** *n., pl.* **fries. —*v.t.*** to cook in hot fat or oil in a deep or shallow pan, often over a flame: *She is frying potatoes.*

—*v.i.* 1 to be cooked in hot fat or oil, especially in a pan over a flame: *These fish are small and will soon fry.* **2** *Figurative.* to burn with strong feeling or emotion: *I let him fry in his own fat.* **3** *Obsolete.* (of water) to be agitated; boil; seethe; foam.

—*n.* 1 a dish of something fried: *Cook promises a little fry for supper* (Dickens). **2** an outdoor social gathering at which food is fried and eaten: *a fish fry.* **3** Often, **fries.** *Dialect.* any one of various internal parts of animals, usually eaten fried. [< Old French *frire* < Latin *frīgere* to fry]

fry[2] (frī), *n., pl.* **fry. 1a** young fishes: *salmon fry.* **b** the young of other creatures produced in very large numbers, such as oysters or shellfish. **2** small adult fish living together in large groups or schools. **3** young or insignificant persons: *. . . all the fry who feed on the little weaknesses of humanity* (C. Fleet). *"You are saying that although he is one of the lesser fry, he started the whole thing?"* (London Times). See **small fry.** [< Anglo-French *frei,* Old French *frai, froi* spawn < *frayer* rub, probably < Scandinavian (compare Old Icelandic *frjōr* seed)]

fry|er (frī′ər), *n.* **1** a chicken intended for frying. **2** a person or thing that fries. **3** a pan used for frying. Also, **frier.**

fry|ing pan (frī′ing), a shallow pan with a long handle, used for frying food.

out of the frying pan into the fire, from one danger or difficulty into a worse one: *If they thought they could get away from the State by disestablishment, they would find that they were jumping out of the frying pan into the fire* (Manchester Guardian).

fry|pan (frī′pan′), *n.* = frying pan.

fry-up (frī′up′), *n. British.* a fried dish, especially one quickly prepared in a frying pan.

f.s., foot-second.

FSA (no periods), Farm Security Administration.

F.S.A., *British.* **1** Fellow of the Society of Antiquaries. **2** Fellow of the Society of Arts.

f-set|ting (ef′set′ing), *n.* f-stop.

FSH (no periods), follicle-stimulating hormone.

FSLIC (no periods), Federal Savings and Loan Insurance Corporation (a public corporation of the United States government).

f-stop (ef′stop′), *n.* the aperture to which a camera is adjusted.

ft., 1 foot or feet. **2** fort. **3** fortification.

Ft., Fort (usually in proper names).

ft. b. m., feet board measure (of lumber).

ft.-c., foot-candle.

FTC (no periods), Federal Trade Commission (a commission of five members appointed by the President to investigate and enforce laws against unfair business practices and violations of Federal laws regulating trade).

fth. or fthm., fathom.

F.T.I., federal tax included.

ft.-l., foot-lambert.

ft.-lb., foot-pound.

ft sec (no periods), foot-second; feet per second.

fu (fü), *n.* in China: **1** a prefecture or department. **2** the chief city of a department. [< Chinese *fu*]

fu′ (fü), *adj.* the Scottish form of **full**[1].

fub[1] (fub), *v.t.,* **fubbed, fub|bing.** = fob[2].

fub[2] (fub), *n. Obsolete.* a small, chubby person. [origin uncertain]

fubs (fubz), *n. Obsolete.* fub[2].

fub|sy (fub′zē), *adj.,* **-si|er, -si|est.** *British Dialect.* chubby; short and fat or thick. [< *fub*[2] + *-sy,* as in *clumsy*]

fuch|sia (fyü′shə), *n.* **1** any one of various ornamental shrubs or trees with handsome, pink, white, red, or purple flowers that droop from the stems. Fuchsias belong to the evening-primrose family. **2** a purplish red like that of the flower. **3** a related perennial plant having large scarlet flowers; California fuchsia. **—*adj.*** purplish-red. [< New Latin *Fuchsia* the genus name < Leonhard *Fuchs,* 1501-1566, a German botanist]

fuch|sin (fu̇k′sin), *n.* a coal tar occurring as a greenish solid which forms deep-red or purplish-red solutions, formerly used as a dye; magenta. [< *fuchs*(ia) + *-in* (because of its color)]

fuch|sine (fu̇k′sin, -sēn), *n.* = fuchsin.

fu|ci (fyü′sī), *n.* a plural of **fucus.**

fu|coid (fyü′koid), *adj., n.* **—*adj.* 1** having to do with seaweeds, especially the fuci. **2** resembling or related to seaweeds, especially the fuci. **3** characterized by or containing impressions of or markings like seaweeds, as sandstone. **—*n.*** a seaweed of the fucus type.

fu|cose (fyü′kōs), *n.* a type of crystalline sugar found in fucus (seaweed) and in human milk. *Formula:* $C_6H_{12}O_5$ [< *fuc*(us) + *-ose*[2]]

fu|co|xan|thin (fyü′kō zan′thēn, -thin), *n.* the brown carotenoid pigment characteristic of brown algae. [< *fucus* + *xanthin*]

fu|cus (fyü′kəs), *n., pl.* **-ci** or **-cus|es. 1** any one of a group of olive-brown seaweeds having flat, leathery branching fronds and often having air bladders; rockweed. **2** *Obsolete.* a paint, dye, or coloring. [< Latin *fūcus* rock lichen; orchil, rouge < Greek *phykos* seaweed; rouge]

fud (fud), *n. Informal.* a fuddy-duddy.

fud|dle (fud′əl), *v.,* **-dled, -dling,** *n. Informal.* **—*v.t.* 1** to make stupid with drink; intoxicate: *The inhabitants . . . get fuddled with mint-julep and apple-toddy* (Washington Irving). **2** to confuse; muddle; stupefy: *He once fuddled a group of government mediators with a speech urging "a program for planned pragmatism"* (Newsweek). **—*v.i.*** to have a drinking bout; tipple; booze. **—*n.* 1** = intoxication. **2** the state of being muddled or confused. [origin uncertain. Compare dialectal German *fuddeln* to swindle.] **—fud′dler,** *n.*

fud|dy (fud′ē), *n., pl.* **-dies,** *adj.,* **-di|er, -di|est,** *Informal.* fuddy-duddy: *. . . a fuddy old psychoanalyst* (New York Times).

fud|dy-dud|dy (fud′ē dud′ē), *n., pl.* **-dies,** *adj.,* **-di|er, -di|est.** *Informal.* **—*n.*** a fussy or stuffy, usually elderly, person who has outmoded tastes and manners: *This extraordinary mid-Victorian fuddy-duddy . . .* (Punch). **—*adj.*** out-of-date; stuffy: *a fuddy-duddy old maid, fuddy-duddy architecture.* [perhaps varied reduplication of *fuddle*]

fudge[1] (fuj), *n.* a soft candy made of sugar, milk, chocolate, and butter. [American English; origin unknown]

fudge[2] (fuj), *v.,* **fudged, fudg|ing,** *n.* **—*v.t.*** to put together in a clumsy, makeshift, or dishonest

way; fake: *Not for a moment had* [*he*] *considered fudging his figures to keep the crowd-pleasing champion in the race* (Time).
—*v.i.* **1** to be dishonest; cheat; fake. **2** to evade the fulfillment of an obligation; welsh: *Pentagon policy makers vow there's no thought of fudging on their intentions* (Wall Street Journal).
—*n.* **1** a made-up story; lie. **2** a patch or small insert by means of which late news or print of a different color can be added to a printing plate or type page for a newspaper without remaking the whole. **3** the material added. **4** a machine or part of a press for printing such material.
[apparently variant of *fadge* in sense of "patch out, to make fit"] —**fudg'er**, *n.*

fudge[3] (fuj), *n., interj.* —*n.* nonsense; stuff; bosh: *There comes Poe with his raven like Barnaby Rudge, Three fifths of him genius, and two fifths sheer fudge* (James Russell Lowell).
—*interj.* nonsense! bosh! *Mr. Burchell, who . . . at the conclusion of every sentence would cry out Fudge!* (Oliver Goldsmith).
[origin uncertain]

Fu|e|gi|an (fyü ē'jē ən, fwā'jē-), *adj., n.* —*adj.* of or having to do with Tierra del Fuego or its natives. —*n.* an Indian of Tierra del Fuego.

Fueh|rer (fʏ'rər), *n.* = Führer.

fu|el (fyü'əl), *n., v.,* **-eled, -el|ing** or (*especially British*) **-elled, -el|ling.** —*n.* **1a** anything that can be burned to make useful heat or power. Coal, wood, and oil are fuels. SYN: combustible. **b** a substance oxidized in a rocket engine to produce heat and a rapid expansion of gases. **c** atomic matter producing heat by fission or fusion, as in a nuclear reactor. **2** *Figurative.* something that keeps up or increases a feeling: *His insults were fuel to her hatred of him. Each party is always laying up fuel for dissension* (Sir Richard Steele).
—*v.t.* **1** to supply with fuel: *The Atomic Energy Commission asked architect-engineering firms to propose design studies for a heavy water-moderated nuclear reactor fueled by natural uranium* (Wall Street Journal). **2** *Figurative.* to act as a driving force for; support: *Fueling the pool-building boom are a number of things* (Wall Street Journal).
—*v.i.* to get fuel: *The ship will have to fuel at the nearest port.*
[< Old French *feuaile* < Vulgar Latin *focālia,* neuter plural adjective < Latin *focus* hearth, fire] —**fu'el|er, fu'el|ler,** *n.* —**fu'el|less,** *adj.*

fuel cell, a device which produces electricity directly from a chemical reaction between oxygen and a gaseous fuel such as hydrogen or carbon monoxide.

fuel element, the radioactive material and mechanical devices of the core in a complete unit ready to be incorporated in a nuclear reactor.

fuel injection, the pumping of vaporized fuel under pressure into the cylinders of an internal-combustion engine, either to increase the force of combustion, or to achieve a more economical rate of fuel consumption. Fuel injection is widely used in rockets and aircraft and has replaced the carburetor in certain automobiles. *Fuel injection is becoming more popular with manufacturers as better designs make the system more dependable* (Science News Letter).

fuel|ish (fyü'lish), *adj.* using excessive fuel: *A word to the fuelish: Beginning Labor Day weekend, Canadians will again be bombarded by an advertising campaign urging energy conservation* (Maclean's). [< *fuel* + *ish* as a pun on *foolish*] —**fu'el|ish|ly,** *adv.*

fuel oil, an oil used for fuel, especially one used as a substitute for coal, made from crude petroleum.

fuel pump, a pump in an engine that forces the liquid fuel from the tank to the carburetor or combustion chamber.

fuel rod, a long rod of nuclear fuel used in a nuclear reactor.

fuel slug, a lump or short rod of nuclear fuel used in a nuclear reactor.

fuff (fuf, fůf), *n., v. Scottish.* —*n.* **1** a puff; whiff; sputter. **2** an angry fume of huff.
—*v.t., v.i.* to puff; whiff. [probably imitative]

fuff|y (fuf'ē, fůf'-), *adj. Scottish.* light; fluffy.

fug (fug), *n., v.,* **fugged, fug|ging.** *Especially British.* —*n.* **1** stuffiness and discomfort: *. . . the fug and cramp of being locked with two other men for thirteen hours a day . . . in a cell 13 ft. long by 7 ft. wide* (Manchester Guardian). **2a** warmth and comfort: *Because of the lowness of ceilings it was possible to maintain a good cosy fug with a minimum of fuel* (Manchester Guardian).
b warmth of feeling: *No warm gush of parental fug follows her pronouncements* (Punch).
—*v.t.* to render close or stuffy; fill with smoke or steam: *The rich lady coughed at the smoke from the cigarettes the men had lit, which was mingling with the steam from the kettle to fug up the room* (Maclean's).
[origin uncertain]

fu|ga|cious (fyü gā'shəs), *adj.* **1** passing quickly; tending to flee; fleeting; transitory: *the fugacious nature of life and time* (Harriet Martineau). SYN: transient, fugitive, evanescent. **2** *Botany.* falling or fading early: *If the calyx falls very early, it is called fugacious* (Heber W. Youngken). **3** = volatile. [< Latin *fugāx, -ācis* (with English *-ous*) fleeting, tending to flee < *fugere* fly, flee] —**fu|ga'cious|ly,** *adv.* —**fu|ga'cious|ness,** *n.*

fu|gac|i|ty (fyü gas'ə tē), *n.* **1** the quality of being fugacious; instability; transitoriness: *the fugacity of pleasure, the fragility of beauty* (Samuel Johnson). **2** (of a material substance) volatility.

fu|gal[1] (fyü'gəl), *adj. Music.* **1** in the style of a fugue. **2** of or having to do with a fugue. —**fu'gal|ly,** *adv.*

fu|gal[2] (fyü'gəl), *n. Australian.* any centrifugal machine. [short for *centrifugal*]

fu|ga|to (fü gä'tō), *n., pl.* **-tos.** *Music.* a piece or part of a piece composed in fugue style but not in strict fugue form. [< Italian *fugato* < *fuga* a fugue]

fug|gy (fug'ē), *adj.,* **-gi|er, -gi|est.** *Especially British.* **1** (of the air in a room) close, stuffy, and smelly, from lack of ventilation: *Truth to tell, they enjoy the fuggy, slightly choked atmosphere, pungent with cigar smoke* (New York Times). **2** (of persons) accustomed to living in such an atmosphere: *The artists are rather a fuggy lot indoors* (Silberrad). —**fug'gi|ly,** *adv.* —**fug'gi|ness,** *n.*

fu|ghet|ta (fyü get'ə; *Italian* fü get'tä), *n. Music.* a short, condensed fugue, especially a fugue in which the subjects are introduced in succession, without discussion or stretto; free fugue. [< Italian *fughetta* (diminutive) < *fuga* fugue]

Fu|gi|o cent (fyü'jē ō), the first coin issued by Congress in 1787, a copper showing the sun and the Latin inscription *Fugio* (I fly) and the motto, "Mind your business." On the reverse 13 interlocking rings are around the motto, "We are one."

fu|gi|tive (fyü'jə tiv), *n., adj.* —*n.* **1** a person who is running away or has run away from danger, an enemy, or justice: *The escaped convict became a fugitive from justice.* **2** a person who intends flight: *The fugitive had already packed and bought his ticket.* **3** a person who leaves or is banished from his country; exile; refugee: *Fugitives crossed the border by night to escape arrest.* **4** *Figurative.* something fleeting or elusive: *that airy fugitive called wit. His dream remained a fugitive, always eluding his grasp.* **5** *Obsolete.* a deserter.
—*adj.* **1** running away or having run away; runaway: *a fugitive slave. A fugitive and gracious light he seeks. Shy to illumine* (Matthew Arnold).
2 *Figurative.* lasting only a very short time; passing swiftly; fleeting: *fugitive bliss.* SYN: evanescent. **3** moving from place to place; shifting; roving. **4** *Figurative.* dealing with subjects of temporary interest; occasional: *They indulged in fits of fugitive conversation.* **5** quickly fading: *fugitive colors.* **6** readily escaping: *fugitive odors.* **7** soon falling: *fugitive flowers or petals.*
[< Middle French *fugitive,* learned borrowing from Latin *fugitīvus* < *fugere* to flee] —**fu'gi|tive|ly,** *adv.* —**fu'gi|tive|ness,** *n.*

fu|gle (fyü'gəl), *v.i.,* **-gled, -gling.** to serve as a fugleman; act as guide or director; make signals. [back formation < *fugleman*]

fu|gle|man (fyü'gəl mən), *n., pl.* **-men. 1** a soldier expert in military skills, formerly placed in front of a company as a model for the others during a drill. **2** *Figurative.* a person or thing serving as a model or leader. Also, **flugelman.** [alteration of German *Flügelmann* file leader < *Flügel* wing (in an army) + *Mann* man]

fugue (fyüg), *n.* **1** a musical composition based on one or more short themes in which different voices or instruments follow one another in counterpoint, sometimes seemingly in the manner of a flight or chase, repeating the same melody with slight variations: *But remember that the preludes and fugues were first of all reverie pieces used in the church service* (Atlantic). **2** *Psychology.* a form of hysteria characterized by an amnesia of indefinite duration, and in many cases by running away from home: *Examples of the third common form of clinical hysteria—fugue—are equally apparent* (Bulletin of Atomic Scientists). [< French *fugue* < Italian *fuga,* learned borrowing from Latin *fuga* flight < *fugere* to flee]

fugued (fyügd), *adj.* composed in the style of a fugue.

fu|guing (fyü'ging), *adj.* consisting of or performing a fugue or fugues: *fuguing music.*

fu|guist (fyü'gist), *n.* **1** a composer of fugues. **2** a performer of fugues.

Füh|rer (fʏ'rər), *n. German.* leader. It was the title given to Adolf Hitler, the dictator of Nazi Germany. Also, **Fuehrer.**

fu|ji (fü'jē), *n.* **1** a lightweight, close-woven, silk fabric used especially for blouses or shirts. **2** = Japanese wisteria. [< *Fuji,* a mountain in southern Japan]

Ful (fůl), *n., pl.* **Ful** or **Fuls. 1** a language belonging to the Niger-Congo group, spoken by the Fula and Fulani. **2** one of the Fula or Fulani.

-ful, *suffix added to nouns to form adjectives or other nouns.* **1** full of ___: *Cheerful = full of cheer.*
2 showing ___: *Careful = showing care.*
3 having a tendency to ___: *Harmful = having a tendency to harm.*
4 enough to fill a ___: *Cupful = enough to fill a cup.*
5 that can be of ___: *Useful = that can be of use.*
6 having the qualities of ___: *Masterful = having the qualities of a master.*
[Old English *-ful,* use of adjective *full* full[1]]
►Nouns ending in **-ful** take the plural suffix at the end: *cupfuls, handfuls, spoonfuls.*

Fu|la or **Fu|lah** (fü'lä), *n., pl.* **-la** or **-las, -lah** or **-lahs. 1** one of a Moslem people of the Sudan and adjacent territories, probably of mixed Hamitic and Negro origin. They are mainly shepherds and the ruling class over a large area along the southern border of the Sahara. **2** their language; Ful.

Fu|la|ni (fü lä'nē), *n., pl.* **-ni** or **-nis. 1a** a member of the Fula or northern Nigeria. **b** = Fula. **2** the language of this people; Ful. **3** a kind of cattle of western Africa similar to the brahma of India. It has a large hump, wide-spreading horns, and is mostly white.

Ful|bright (fůl'brīt), *n.* **1** = Fulbright scholarship. **2** a student or scholar awarded a Fulbright scholarship.

Fulbright scholarship, a grant of money made by the United States government to help American students continue studies in other lands or to help foreign students to study in the United States. [< James W. *Fulbright,* born 1905, United States Senator from Arkansas, who initiated legislation for this plan]

***ful|crum** (ful'krəm, fůl'-), *n., pl.* **-crums, -cra** (-krə), *v.,* **-crumed, -crum|ing.** —*n.* **1** the support on which a lever turns or is supported in moving or lifting something: *The distance from the weight to the fulcrum is the weight-arm, and the distance from the force* (*your hand*) *to the fulcrum is the forcearm* (Beauchamp, Mayfield, and West). **2** *Figurative.* any prop or support.
—*v.t.* **1** to furnish with a fulcrum. **2** to place (something) on, as a fulcrum. **3** to establish as a fulcrum.
[< Latin *fulcrum* bedpost < *fulcīre* to support]

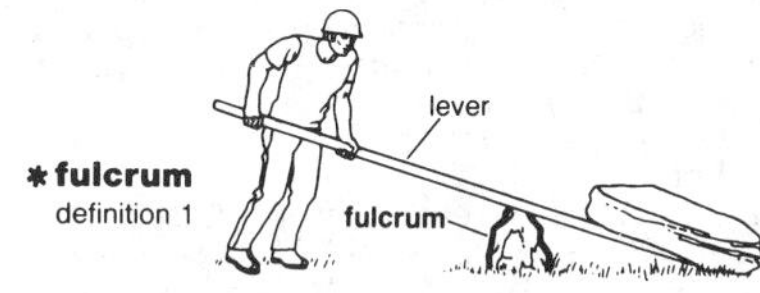

***fulcrum** definition 1

ful|fill or **ful|fil** (fůl fil'), *v.t.,* **-filled, -fill|ing. 1a** to carry out (a promise or prophecy); cause to happen or take place. SYN: accomplish. **b** (reflexively) to realize or develop fully: *My desire . . . By its own energy fulfill's itself* (Tennyson). *We shall never be able to fulfill ourselves truly unless we are working for the welfare of our fellows: then only shall our burdens not break us* (Edmund Wilson). SYN: accomplish. **2** to perform or do (a duty or command): *She fulfilled all the teacher's requests.* SYN: execute, discharge. **3** to satisfy (a requirement or condition): *This diet will fulfill your needs in food. The new cleanser completely fulfilled its purpose.* **4** to bring to an end; finish or complete (a period of time or work): *to fulfill a contract.* **5** *Archaic.* to fill full or make full: *I hear it now, that tender strain Fulfilled with all of sorrow save its pain* (R. W. Gilder). [Old English *fullfyllan* < *full* full[1] + *fyllan* to fill] —**ful|fill'er,** *n.*

ful|fill|ment or **ful|fil|ment** (fůl fil'mənt), *n.* a fulfilling; completion; accomplishment; performance: *the fulfillment of a wish or requirement.*

ful|gent (ful'jənt), *adj.* shining brightly; brilliant; glittering; resplendent: *Then issued Vesper from the fulgent West* (Wordsworth). [< Latin *fulgēns, -entis,* present participle of *fulgēre* shine, be bright; (originally) flash, related to *fulgor* splendor, brightness] —**ful'gent|ly,** *adv.*

ful|gid (ful'jid), *adj.* flashing; glittering; shining: *Through the brown shade the fulgid weapons shined* (Alexander Pope). [< Latin *fulgidus* < *fulgēre* to shine]

Pronunciation Key: hat, āge, cãre, fär; let, ēqual, tėrm; it, īce; hot, ōpen, ôrder; oil, out; cup, půt, rüle; child; long; thin; ᴛʜen; zh, measure; ə represents **a** in about, **e** in taken, **i** in pencil, **o** in lemon, **u** in circus.

ful|gor or **ful|gour** (ful′gər), *n. Archaic.* dazzling brightness; splendor. [< Latin *fulgor*]

ful|gu|ral (ful′gyər əl), *adj.* of or having to do with lightning.

ful|gu|rant (ful′gyər ənt), *adj.* flashing like lightning: *That erect form, flashing brow, fulgurant eye* (Robert Browning). [< Latin *fulgurāns, -antis,* present participle of *fulgurāre* flash like lightning < *fulgur* lightning, related to *fulgēre* to shine] **—ful′gu|rant|ly,** *adv.*

ful|gu|rate (ful′gyə rāt), *v.,* **-rat|ed, -rat|ing.** **—*v.i.*** to emit vivid flashes like lightning.
—*v.t.* *Medicine.* to destroy (a tumor or the like) with electric sparks.
[< Latin *fulgurāre* (with English *-ate*[1]) < *fulgur* lightning, related to *fulgēre* to shine] **—ful′gu|ra′tion,** *n.*

ful|gu|rite (ful′gyə rīt), *n.* **1** a bore or tube formed in sand or rock by lightning. **2** a rocky substance that has been fused or vitrified by lightning: *Fulgurite is partially fused sand lying on the surface of sand dunes in the form of rods and tubes* (Carroll Lane Fenton).

ful|gu|rous (ful′gyər əs), *adj.* resembling lightning; full of or charged with lightning.

ful|ham (fu̇l′əm), *n. Slang.* a die loaded at the corner: *There is no loading of the dice, or throwing of fulhams* (Arthur Conan Doyle). [perhaps < *Fulham,* once a gambling section of London]

fu|lig|i|nous (fyü lij′ə nəs), *adj.* resembling soot; sooty; smoky; dusky. [< Latin *fūlīginōsus* < *fūlīgō, -inis* soot] **—fu|lig′i|nous|ly,** *adv.*

full[1] (fu̇l), *adj., adv., n., v.* **—*adj.*** **1a** that can hold no more; with no empty space; filled. Anything is full when it holds all that it is intended to hold. *a full cup. I have eaten so much that I am full.* **SYN:** replete, sated. **b** *Figurative.* ready to overflow, especially overcharged with emotion: *His heart was so full, he could say no more* (Daniel Defoe). **2** complete; entire: *a full supply of clothes. He ran a full mile. She is in full possession of her senses. The two countries established full diplomatic relations.* **SYN:** whole. **3a** of the greatest size, amount, extent, volume, or quality: *a full moon.* **b** not limited or qualified: *a full professor, a full colonel.* **4** more than enough to satisfy; well supplied; abundant: *a full purse. He ate three full meals a day.* **SYN:** ample, plentiful, copious. **5** well filled out; plump; round: *a full face.* **6** made with wide folds or much cloth: *a full skirt.* **7** strong, rich, and distinct: *An orator should have a full voice.* **8** (of wines) having much body. **9** (of brothers and sisters) born of the same father and mother: *He is full brother to the present king.* **10** fitting a term or description in every respect: *a full scholar, if I ever met one.* **11a** (of sails) filled with wind. **b** (of a ship) having its sails filled: *We ... kept full, and started boldly out to sea* (Edgar Allan Poe).
—*adv.* **1** completely; entirely; fully: *Fill the pail full.* **2** directly; straight; exactly: *The ball hit him full in the face.* **3** very; exceedingly: *A sailor knows full well the fury of the sea. Full many a flower is born to blush unseen* (Thomas Gray).
—*n.* **1** completeness; greatest degree: *He satisfied his ambition to the full. We discussed the matter to the full.* **2** the central portion or height of a period: *in the full of the London season.* **3** (of a moon) the period or phase of complete illumination of the disk.
—*v.t.* to make with wide folds or much cloth.
—*v.i.* to become full: *The eclipse occurs when the moon fulls.*
at full, at full length; completely: *Thus said the bull ... published at full* (Chaucer).
at the full, at full length; completely: *The power of the house of commons ... is great; and long may it be able to preserve its greatness ... at the full* (Edmund Burke).
full and by, as close as possible to the wind with the sail or sails well filled: *They held on after us nevertheless, sailing full and by* (William C. Russell).
full of, a filled with: *Her bedroom is full of dolls.* **b** absorbed by; completely taken up with: *The speaker was full of his subject.*
in full, a to or for the complete amount: *They expect payment in full without delay.* **b** written or said with all the words; not abbreviated or shortened: *a document reproduced in full.*
to the full, completely; entirely: *I must expect my right to the full* (William Penn).
[Old English *full*]

full[2] (fu̇l), *v.t.* to clean and thicken (cloth) by beating and washing or a similar process: *In this manner a girl can full twenty pair of hose in four or five hours* (Robert Southey). **—*v.i.*** (of cloth) to become compacted or felted. [perhaps < Old French *fouler* < Medieval Latin *fullare,* related to Latin *fullō* fuller[1]]

full|back (fu̇l′bak′), *n.* **1** a football player who is a member of the offensive backfield and usually lines up between the halfbacks. **2** a player in field hockey, soccer, or Rugby who is responsible for the defense of the goal and whose position is behind the other backs.

full binding, a style of bookbinding in which only one material, especially leather, is used for the back, corners, and sides of the book.

full blast, *Informal.* in full operation; at highest speed or largest capacity: *The factory was operating at full blast.*

full blood, 1 pure or unmixed race, breed, or strain. **2** an individual of such ancestry. **3** relationship through both parents.

full-blood (fu̇l′blud′), *adj.* **1** born of the same parents: *a full-blood brother.* **2** full-blooded: *His mother [was] a full-blood Potawatomie squaw* (Columbus (Ohio) Dispatch).

full-blood|ed (fu̇l′blud′id), *adj.* **1** of pure or unmixed race, breed, or strain; thoroughbred: *a full-blooded Indian.* **2** *Figurative.* vigorous; hearty. **3** having plenty of blood. **—full′-blood′ed|ly,** *adv.* **—full′-blood′ed|ness,** *n.*

full-blown (fu̇l′blōn′), *adj.* **1** in full bloom: *a full-blown rose.* **2** *Figurative.* completely developed or matured: *Those [persons] showing the early signs may later develop the full-blown condition* (Laurence H. Snyder). **3** filled with wind; puffed out.

full-bod|ied (fu̇l′bod′ēd), *adj.* **1** having considerable strength and flavor: *full-bodied wine or coffee.* **2** having full or ample proportions: *She is a full-bodied woman who shows every one of her 33 years* (Time). **3** having a face value equal to its intrinsic value: *full-bodied money, a full-bodied silver coin.*

full-bound (fu̇l′bound′), *adj.* (of a book) bound in full binding.

full bridle, = double bridle.

full circle, having completed a cycle and returned to the starting point: *Here we are back full circle to theories long familiar to philosophers* (Marjorie Nicholson).

full cock, 1 a position of the hammer of a gun when it is pulled back completely. At full cock, the gun is ready to be fired. **2** *Informal.* a position of readiness: *[He] is one of those writers who face life, however trivial its manifestations, perpetually at full cock* (Francis King).

full-court press (fu̇l′kôrt′, -kōrt′), **1** *Basketball.* a defensive tactic in which strong pressure is applied on the offensive players on both sides of the court: *The Nets' ... full-court press had shaken the ball loose from the Knicks a number of times* (New York Times). **2** *Figurative.* a vigorous, full-scale effort to achieve something: *At the beginning of the year, [he] seemed to be pulling back from some of his most controversial proposals. But now he has gone to a full-court press* (London Times).

full-di|men|sion|al (fu̇l′də men′shə nəl), *adj.* **1** completely developed or realized: *a novel with full-dimensional characters.* **2** covering all sides and aspects: *full-dimensional journalism.*

full dress, the formal clothes worn in the evening or on important occasions.

full-dress (fu̇l′dres′), *adj.* **1** of or characterized by the wearing of full dress: *a full-dress parade.* **2** *Figurative.* formal: *a full-dress inquiry. The United Nations agreed to resume full-dress Korean truce talks* (Atlanta Constitution). **3** using all resources; complete; all-out: *We learnt later that this was a full-dress raid by the local gendarmerie* (Lord Mountbatten). **4** formally detailed; exhaustive: *a full-dress analysis. An Englishwoman, Elizabeth Sprigge, has given us the full-dress biography of Miss Stein* (Atlantic).

full|er[1] (fu̇l′ər), *n.* a person whose work is cleaning and thickening cloth. [Old English *fullere* < Latin *fullō*]

full|er[2] (fu̇l′ər), *n., v.* **—*n.*** **1** a tool for grooving and spreading iron, used in blacksmithing, etc. **2** a groove made by a fuller.
—*v.t.* to stamp with a fuller. [< *full*[1], verb + *-er*[1]]

Fuller ball faucet or **Fuller faucet,** a faucet in which a soft rubber ball attached to a lever is used to start or stop the flow of liquid. [< *Fuller,* a trademark]

fuller's earth, a soft, claylike mixture used for removing grease from cloth and in refining mineral, vegetable, and animal oils: *Fuller's earth, a kind of clay now used mainly as a filter and a catalyst in chemical reactions* (Science News Letter).

fuller's teasel, a tall, prickly European and Asian plant which has become naturalized in the United States, grown for the ripe heads (teasels) which are used to raise the nap on woolen cloth.

full|face (fu̇l′fās′), *n. Printing.* boldface type, such as that for headings of entries in this dictionary.

full-faced (fu̇l′fāst′), *adj.* **1** having a full or plump face: *a full-faced, portly man.* **2** having the face turned fully on the spectator or in some specified direction: *He was full-faced toward the camera in the best view.* **3** boldface: *full-faced printing type.*

full faith and credit, *U.S. Law.* the obligation of each state under the Constitution to recognize the public acts, records, and judicial proceedings of every other state.

full-fash|ioned (fu̇l′fash′ənd), *adj.* (of hose, sweaters, or other garments) knitted to fit the shape of the foot, leg, or body.

full-fledged (fu̇l′flejd′), *adj.* **1** fully developed: *a full-fledged robin. At the same time, the subject undergoes a full-fledged psychotic experience* (Newsweek). **2** *Figurative.* of full rank or standing: *He is now a full-fledged Boy Scout.*

full gainer, = gainer (def. 2).

full-grown (fu̇l′grōn′), *adj.* fully grown; mature.

full hand, (in poker) = full house.

full-heart|ed (fu̇l′här′tid), *adj.* **1** full of courage and confidence. **2** zealous. **3** full of emotion. **—full′-heart′ed|ly,** *adv.*

full house, a poker hand made up of three cards of one kind and two of another, such as three sixes and two kings.

full-length (fu̇l′lengkth′, -length′), *adj., adv.* **—*adj.*** **1** showing the entire human body: *a full-length portrait. Stand in front of a full-length mirror, so that you can judge how much bulk you can carry at the top* (New Yorker). **2a** (of a gown) almost touching the floor: *Many full-length evening gowns have strapless bodices and skirts that fall out sweeping folds at the back* (New York Times). **b** (of a coat) reaching to the bottom of a dress: *A full-length wrappy number of black Hudson seal has a raccoon collar and cuffs* (New Yorker). **3** of considerable length or duration: *Last night we watched a full-length movie on television. I may not write another full-length play now for three or four months* (William Saroyan).
—*adv.* in a straight or erect position; not folded or bent; lengthwise: *I would lie full-length around the house* (New Yorker).

full marks, *Especially British Informal.* complete credit; praise; compliments: *Moreno, who rode the winner, deserves full marks for horsemanship* (Audax Minor).

full moon, 1 the moon seen from the earth as a whole circle: *When the earth is between the sun and the moon, you see the full moon because the light from the sun shines over the earth and on to the moon* (Beauchamp, Mayfield, and West). **2** the period when this occurs: *All the moon's first quarter, half of the illuminated hemisphere is visible, just as it is a week after full moon* (Science New Letter).

full-mouthed (fu̇l′mouᴛʜd′, -moutht′), *adj.* **1** having the mouth full of teeth; having the full complement of teeth: *full-mouthed cattle.* **2** produced with a loud sound; uttered in a loud voice: *a full-mouthed laugh.* **—full′-mouth′ed|ly,** *adv.*

full nelson, a wrestling hold from behind, both arms being thrust under the arms of the opponent and the hands on the nape of his neck.

full|ness (fu̇l′nis), *n.* the condition of being full: *The bag bulged because of its fullness.* (*Figurative.*) *Fullness to such a burden is, That go on pilgrimage* (John Bunyan). **SYN:** repletion. Also, **fulness.**
fullness of (the) time, the proper or destined time: *When the fullness of the time was come, God sent forth his Son* (Galatians 4:4).

full-out (fu̇l′out′), *adj.* total; all-out: *a full-out attack.*

full-pres|sure lubrication (fu̇l′presh′ər), a lubricating system for an internal-combustion engine in which oil is pumped to the pistons.

full-rigged (fu̇l′rigd′), *adj.* **1** having three or four masts all completely square-rigged. **2** *Figurative.* completely equipped.

full sail, 1 with all sails set. **2** with all possible power and energy.

full-scale (fu̇l′skāl′), *adj.* **1** having the same size and proportion as the original: *a full-scale reproduction of a painting.* **2** built to the full size (usually in contrast with an experimental model or blueprint): *The work was conducted ... in a full-scale building used in other architectural experiments* (Science News Letter). **3** *Figurative.* not limited; using all resources; complete; all-out: *It is difficult to believe that any governments fail to appreciate that if full-scale nuclear war developed, their peoples and territories would share in the general decimation* (Bulletin of Atomic Scientists). **SYN:** total.

full score, a musical score in which the parts for all voices and instruments are given on separate staves.

full-size (fu̇l′sīz′), *adj.* **1** of full size; full-grown: *When he was small he was very cute, but now that he had become a full-size bulldog, we didn't think he was so cute.* **2** = full-length (def. 1): *a full-size mirror.* **3** = full-scale (def. 2): *a full-size house, a full-size working nuclear reactor.*

full-sized (fu̇l′sīzd′), *adj.* = full-size.

full steam, *Informal.* at highest power or effectiveness; full blast: *The industry would continue full steam through October* (Wall Street Journal).

full stop, *Especially British.* the point marking the

end of a sentence; period.

full-throat|ed (fu̇l′thrō′tid), *adj.* **1** loud and noisy; vociferous: *full-throated approval, a full-throated protest.* **2** sonorous; resounding: *Lanza ... burst into full-throated song* (New Yorker).
—**full′-throat′ed|ly,** *adv.*

full tilt, at full speed; with full force: *In times of heavy demand, steel mills run full tilt through holiday periods* (Wall Street Journal).

full-time (fu̇l′tīm′), *adj., adv.* for all of the usual or normal length of working time: *a full-time job* (adj.). *It occupies hundreds of men full-time* (New York Times) (adv.).

full-tim|er (fu̇l′tīm′ər), *n.* a full-time employee or worker.

ful|ly (fu̇l′ē), *adv.* **1** completely; entirely: *Was he fully satisfied? The soldiers were fully armed. ... a fully automatic office copying machine* (New Yorker). **2** abundantly; plentifully: *The gymnasium was fully equipped with ropes and rings.* **SYN:** amply. **3** quite; exactly: *fully cognizant. He could not fully describe what he had seen.*

ful|mar (fu̇l′mər), *n.* **1** a sea bird related to the petrel, about the size of the common gull, inhabiting northern regions: *The fulmar, a grey and white seabird of northern oceans, spits out an oily fluid at intruders approaching its nest* (Science News Letter). **2** a related large bird of the Antarctic; giant petrel. [probably < Scandinavian (compare Old Icelandic *fūlmārr* < *fūll* foul + *mār* sea gull)]

ful|mi|nant (ful′mə nənt), *adj.* **1** that fulminates; fulminating. **2** (of a disease) developing suddenly. [< Latin *fulminans, -antis,* present participle of *fulmināre* flash like lightning]

ful|mi|nate (ful′mə nāt), *v.,* **-nat|ed, -nat|ing,** *n.*
—*v.t.* **1** to thunder forth; utter or publish (condemnation, censure, threats, decrees, or the like). **2** *Figurative.* to denounce violently; censure strongly: *to fulminate such vain and impious wretches* (Edmund Burke). **3** to cause to explode violently.
—*v.i.* **1** *Figurative.* to denounce violently; thunder: *The newspapers fulminated against the crime wave.* **2** to explode violently; detonate; go off. **3** (of a disease) to develop suddenly and severely. **4** to thunder and lighten.
—*n. Chemistry.* **1** a violent explosive. **2** a salt of fulminic acid. The fulminates, chiefly mercury and silver, are very unstable compounds, exploding with great violence by percussion or heating.
[< Latin *fulmināre* (with English *-ate*[1]) < *fulmen* lightning, related to *fulgēre* to shine] —**ful′mi|na′tor,** *n.*

ful|mi|nat|ing compound (ful′mə nā′ting), *Chemistry.* = fulminate (*n.* def. 2).

fulminating powder, any explosive powder, especially one of the fulminates.

ful|mi|na|tion (ful′mə nā′shən), *n.* **1** a violent denunciation; strong censure. **2** a violent explosion.

ful|mi|na|to|ry (ful′mə nə tôr′ē, -tōr′-), *adj.* fulminating; denunciatory.

ful|mine (ful′mən), *v.t., v.i.,* **-mined, -min|ing.** = fulminate.

ful|min|ic (ful min′ik), *adj.* having to do with detonation. [< Latin *fulmen, -inis* thunder + English *-ic*]

fulminic acid, an acid known only in its salts (the fulminates), which are extremely explosive. *Formula:* CNOH

ful|mi|nous (ful′mə nəs), *adj.* of or having to do with thunder and lightning; fulminating.

ful|ness (fu̇l′nis), *n.* = fullness.

ful|some (fu̇l′səm, ful′-), *adj.* **1** so much as to be disgusting; offensive to good taste, especially from being overdone: *He was offended by the fulsome flattery of his work.* **SYN:** excessive. **2** *Archaic.* repulsive; odious. **3** *Obsolete.* lustful; obscene. [< *full*[1] + *-some*[1]; meaning influenced by *foul*] —**ful′some|ly,** *adv.* —**ful′some|ness,** *n.*

ful|vous (ful′vəs), *adj.* reddish-yellow; dull yellowish-brown or tawny: *A Nemean lion, fulvous, torrid-eyed* (James Russell Lowell). [< Latin *fulvus* (with English *-ous*) tawny]

fulvous tree duck, a tawny brown duck with a long neck and long legs, found in marshy areas of the southern United States south to Argentina and in parts of Africa and Asia.

fu|ma|gil|lin (fyü′mə gil′in), *n.* an antibiotic derived from a fungus, used especially against amebic infections. *Formula:* $C_{26}H_{34}O_7$ [< New Latin *fum*(igatus) + (Asper)*gill*(us), a reversal of *Aspergillus fumigatus,* the fungus from which it is derived + English *-in*]

fu|ma|rase (fyü′mə rās), *n.* an enzyme found in many plants and animals, especially in the muscles and liver of higher animals. Fumarase causes the conversion of fumaric acid to malic acid in the Krebs cycle.

fu|ma|rate (fyü′mə rāt), *n.* a salt or ester of fumaric acid.

fu|mar|ic acid (fyü mar′ik), a whitish, dicarboxylic acid found in all cells and essential to their respiration. Fumaric acid is prepared industrially by the action of fungi on glucose. *Formula:* $C_4H_4O_4$ [< New Latin *Fumaria* the fumitory genus, in which it is found + English *-ic*]

fu|ma|role (fyü′mə rōl), *n.* a hole or vent in the earth's crust in a volcanic region, from which steam and hot gases issue. [< French *fumerolle* < Italian *fumaruolo* vent in a chimney < Latin *fūmāriolum* flue, vent (diminutive) < *fūmārium* smoke chamber < *fūmus* smoke]

fu|ma|rol|ic (fyü′mə rol′ik), *adj.* of or formed by a fumarole.

fu|ma|to|ri|um (fyü′mə tôr′ē əm, -tōr′-), *n., pl.* **-to|ri|a** (-tôr′ē ə, -tōr′-). an airtight structure in which plants are fumigated to destroy insects or fungi. [< New Latin *fumatorium* < Latin *fūmāre* to smoke < *fūmus* smoke]

fum|ble (fum′bəl), *v.,* **-bled, -bling,** *n.* —*v.i.* **1** to feel or grope about clumsily; search awkwardly: *He fumbled in the darkness for the doorknob.* **2** to handle something awkwardly: *He fumbled and dropped his teacup.* **3** *Sports.* to drop a ball unintentionally, especially in attempting to catch or hold onto it.
—*v.t.* **1** to handle (something) awkwardly or with nervous clumsiness: *He fumbled the latch.* **2** *Sports.* to let (a ball) drop instead of catching and holding onto it: *The first baseman fumbled the ball, and two runs were scored. The halfback fumbled the ball, and the other team recovered it.* **3** to speak uncertainly; miss (words): *The actor fumbled his lines.*
—*n.* **1** an awkward attempt to find or handle something: *Unfortunately the fumble allowed the other team to make a goal.* **2** *Sports.* a failure to catch and hold onto a ball.
[earlier *fumyll.* Compare Low German *fummeln.*]
—**fum′bler,** *n.* —**fum′bling|ly,** *adv.*

fum|bly (fum′blē), *adj.* awkward; bumbling.

fume (fyüm), *n., v.,* **fumed, fum|ing.** —*n.* **1** Often, **fumes.** a vapor, gas, or smoke, especially if harmful, strong, or odorous: *The strong fumes of the automobile exhaust nearly choked him. The designs of his bright imagination were never etched by the sharp fumes of necessity* (Francis Thompson). **2** an odorous exhalation, such as that from flowers. **3a** odorous smoke, such as that of incense or tobacco: *Tobacco fumes filled the air in the room.* **b** *Archaic.* smoke. **4** *Figurative.* something comparable to smoke or vapor as being unsubstantial, transient, or imaginary: *Love is a smoke raised with the fume of sighs* (Shakespeare). **5** *Figurative.* a fit of anger; irritable or angry mood: *in a fume.*
—*v.i.* **1** to give off vapor, gas, or smoke: *The candle fumed, sputtered, and went out. Staggering off, he fumed with brandy.* **SYN:** smoke. **2** to pass off in fumes. **3** *Figurative.* to show anger or irritation; let off one's rage in angry complaints: *He fumed about the slowness of the trains.* **SYN:** chafe, fret.
—*v.t.* **1** to treat with smoke or fumes; fumigate: *to fume oak.* **2** *Archaic.* to send forth or emit as vapor.
[< Old French *fum* < Latin *fūmus* smoke]

fumed oak (fyümd), oak darkened and colored by exposure to ammonia fumes.

fume hood, a laboratory ventilating system composed of a shaft or flue connected to a canopy of metal or glass, designed to carry off fumes.

fum|er (fyü′mər), *n.* a person or thing that fumes.

fu|met (fyü′met), *n.* an extract of game meat used to flavor food. [< French *fumet* < Old French *fumer* to fume < Latin *fūmāre* to smoke]

fu|mette (fyü met′), *n.* = fumet.

fu|met|to (fü met′tō), *n., pl.* **-ti** (-tē). *Italian.* **1** a cartoon balloon. **2** a comic book with photographs using cartoon balloons.

fu|mi|gant (fyü′mə gənt), *n.* a substance used in fumigating: *Fumigants have been successfully used in field tests and actual farming* (Science News Letter).

fu|mi|gate (fyü′mə gāt), *v.t.,* **-gat|ed, -gat|ing.** **1** to disinfect or purify with fumes; expose to fumes: *They fumigated the building to kill the cockroaches.* **2** to scent with fumes; perfume: *The Cathedral had been thoroughly fumigated with frankincense* (John L. Motley). [< Latin *fūmigāre* (with English *-ate*[1]) to smoke < *fūmus* smoke, fume + *agere* to drive]

fu|mi|ga|tion (fyü′mə gā′shən), *n.* **1** the act of fumigating, as in disinfecting. **2** the generation of odorous smoke or fumes, as in magic rites: *On these the sorcerer threw tobacco, producing a stifling fumigation* (Francis Parkman). **3** the smoke or fumes generated in fumigating. **4** a preparation used for fumigating.

fu|mi|ga|tor (fyü′mə gā′tər), *n.* **1** a person or thing that fumigates. **2** an apparatus in which something is burned for the purpose of fumigating or perfuming rooms, etc.

fu|mi|ga|to|ry (fyü′mə gə tôr′ē, -tōr′-), *n., pl.* **-ries,** *adj.* —*n.* a room or apparatus for fumigating.
—*adj.* serving to fumigate.

fum|ing (fyü′ming), *adj.* that fumes: (*Figurative.*) *a fuming mood.* —**fum′ing|ly,** *adv.*

fuming nitric acid, a corrosive, liquid acid used in nitration and as an oxidizer in liquid rocket propellants.

fuming sulfuric acid, = pyrosulfuric acid.

fu|mi|to|ry (fyü′mə tôr′ē, -tōr′-), *n., pl.* **-ries.** any plant of a group of herbs of the fumitory family, especially a delicate, annual plant having finely dissected leaves and spikes of small flesh-colored flowers tipped with crimson. It is common in England, has been introduced into the southern and western United States, and was formerly used in medicine as a tonic, alterative, and diaphoretic. [earlier *fumiter* (with *-ory*) < Old French *fumeterre* < Medieval Latin *fumus* smoke, *terrae* of the earth]

*** fumitory family,** a group of dicotyledonous erect or climbing herbs, closely allied to the poppy family. The family includes the corydalis, Dutchman's-breeches, and bleeding heart.

*** fumitory family**

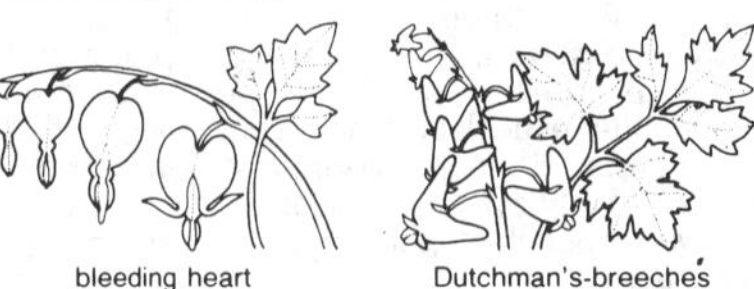

fum|y (fyü′mē), *adj.,* **fum|i|er, fum|i|est.** full of fumes; fuming; fumelike.

fun (fun), *n., adj., v.,* **funned, fun|ning.** —*n.* playfulness; merry play; amusement; joking: *The children had a lot of fun at the birthday party.* **SYN:** sport, enjoyment, diversion, gaiety, drollery.
—*adj. U.S. Informal.* giving fun; amusing; entertaining: *You said they were fun people* (New Yorker). [apparently < verb]
—*v.i. Informal.* to make fun or sport; indulge in fun; fool; joke: *The fellow was just funning, anyhow, and so are we* (Birmingham Post-Herald).
for (or **in**) **fun,** playfully; as a joke: *Just for fun, let's put a necktie on the snowman.*
make fun of or **poke fun at,** to laugh at; ridicule: *He [François Villon] poked fun at lawyers, churchmen, and merchants, and laughed at the tricks, shady dealings, and bawdy jokes of sharpsters* (Joel A. Hunt).
[probably variant of obsolete *fon* befool]

fun|a|bout (fun′ə bout′), *n.* any one of various small motor vehicles used to drive about for pleasure or sport: *Beach buggies those curious bathtub-shaped funabouts* (London Times). [< *fun* + (run)*about*]

fu|nam|bu|lism (fyü nam′byə liz əm), *n.* tightrope walking.

fu|nam|bu|list (fyü nam′byə list), *n.* a performer on a tightrope. [< Latin *fūnambulus* (< *fūnis* rope + *ambulāre* walk) + English *-ist*]

fun and games, (often used ironically) playful or lighthearted activity, as at a party: *"There's been a lot of fun and games today," [the Assemblyman] declared during the Assembly debate, "but we still don't have a budget"* (New York Times).

Fun City, a nickname for New York City.

func|tion (fungk′shən), *n., v.* —*n.* **1a** proper work; normal action or use; purpose: *The function of the stomach is to help digest food. The great general functions of plant parts ... are conduction, support, storage, protection, and secretion* (Fred W. Emerson). **b** a duty or office; employment. **SYN:** province, task. **2** a formal public or social gathering for some purpose: *The hotel ballroom is often used for weddings, anniversaries, and other functions. He ... set out to attend the last gathering of the season at Valleys House, a function ... almost perfectly political* (John Galsworthy). **3a** *Mathematics.* a quantity whose value depends on the value given to one or more related quantities: *The area of a circle is a function of its radius; as the radius increases so does the area.* **b** anything likened to a mathematical function. **4** *Grammar.* the way in which a word or phrase is used in a sentence.
—*v.i.* to work; act; perform a function or one's functions: *One of the older students can function as teacher. This old fountain pen does not function very well.* **SYN:** operate.
[< Latin *fūnctiō, -ōnis* < *fungī* perform]

func|tion|al (fungk′shə nəl), *adj., n.* —*adj.* **1** of a

Pronunciation Key: hat, āge, cãre, fär; let, ēqual, tėrm; it, īce; hot, ōpen, ôrder; oil, out; cup, pu̇t, rüle; child; long; thin; ᴛʜen; zh, measure; ə represents **a** in about, **e** in taken, **i** in pencil, **o** in lemon, **u** in circus.

function or functions: *His mathematical work has been concerned with ... functional analysis* (Scientific American). **2a** having a function; carrying out a function; working; acting: *The functional wings of an insect are those used for flying.* **b** having function as the primary basis of design: *functional furniture, a functional support of a building.* **3** useful in many ways; adaptable. **4** *Medicine.* of or having to do with the function of an organ rather than its structure; having no apparent organic cause: *functional psychosis, functional heart murmur. Functional disease involves changes of activity, but without change in the body, as in such mental diseases as hysteria* (Justina H. Hill).
—n. *Mathematics.* a function whose value depends on all the values assumed by another function. **—func'tion|al|ly,** *adv.*

functional analysis, 1 *Mathematics.* the study or analysis of functionals. **2** *Linguistics.* the analysis of the elements in a sentence or phrase according to their function rather than form.

functional calculus, the branch of symbolic logic that deals with propositional functions and relations and with quantifiers; predicate calculus.

functional group, *Chemistry.* a group of atoms responsible for the common properties of certain compounds, especially organic compounds, such as the carboxyl group present in organic acids.

functional illiteracy, the inability to read or write well enough to perform any but the most basic tasks.

functional illiterate, a person having the basic skills of reading or writing, but little ability in using those skills.

func|tion|al|ism (fungk'shə nə liz'əm), *n.* **1** regard for the function and purpose of something, such as a building or piece of furniture, as the primary factor in regulating its design. **2** *Anthropology.* the ways in which different parts of a culture are interrelated.

func|tion|al|ist (fungk'shə nə list), *n., adj.* ***—n.*** **1** a person who believes that the function and purpose of a building, piece of furniture, or device should determine its style. **2** a person who builds or designs functional buildings, furniture, or devices.
—adj. = functionalistic.

func|tion|al|is|tic (fungk'shə nə lis'tik), *adj.* of or having to do with functionalism: *He disagreed with the functionalistic American's plan to use the Stoa as a museum* (Time).

func|tion|al|i|ty (fungk'shə nal'ə tē), *n.* functional quality or condition.

func|tion|al|i|za|tion (fungk'shə nə lə zā'shən), *n.* **1** the act or process of dividing into functions: *Mr. Healey ... has started the process of greater functionalization in his department by giving his three Service Ministers new responsibilities* (London Times). **2** the result of such dividing: *Functionalization has brought with it basic changes in the structure of industrial organization* (R. H. Lansburgh).

functional shift, *Linguistics.* a change in the function of a word or phrase, as from one part of speech to another. *Examples:* He is an *author* (noun); He *authored* a book (verb). To *transplant* flowers (verb); a heart *transplant* (noun). The workers *walked out* (verb phrase); The workers staged a *walkout* (noun).

functional therapy, = physical restoration.

func|tion|ar|y (fungk'shə ner'ē), *n., pl.* **-ar|ies,** *adj.* ***—n.*** a person who has certain functions or duties to perform; an official: *a government functionary, a church functionary.*
—adj. official.

func|tion|ate (fungk'shə nāt), *v.i.,* **-at|ed, -at|ing.** = function.

func|tion|less (fungk'shən lis), *adj.* having no function.

function word, a word that expresses mainly a relationship between the grammatical elements of a sentence. Prepositions, conjunctions, and auxiliary verbs are function words.

func|tus of|fi|ci|o (fungk'tus ə fish'ē ō), having fulfilled one's office; out of office. [< Latin *functus officio* < *fungī* perform, *officiō,* ablative of *officium* office]

fund (fund), *n., v.* ***—n.*** **1** a sum of money set aside for a special purpose: *The school has a library fund of $2000 to buy books.* **2** a stock or store ready for use; supply; a permanent stock that can be drawn upon: *There is a fund of information in our new library.*
—v.t. **1** to set aside a sum of money to pay the interest on (a debt). **2** to change (a debt) from a short term to a long term, at a fixed rate of interest. **3** to put into a fund or store; collect; store up. **4** to finance: *The centers are to be funded jointly by the Office and sponsoring colleges, universities, or State departments of education* (J. N. Hook).

funds, a money ready for use: *We took $10 from the club's funds to buy a flag. Their funds were so low in 1917 that Lenin tried to get his brother-in-law in Russia to arrange for the publication of a "pedagogical encyclopedia"* (Edmund Wilson). **b** money: *If you wouldn't use up your entire allowance, you wouldn't always be low in funds.*
the (public) funds, *British.* the stock of the national debt, considered as a mode of investment: *Look what the funds were on the 1st of March* (Thackeray).
[Latinization of *fond*[2]; spelling influenced by Latin *fundus* bottom, piece of land] **—fund'a|ble,** *adj.*

fun|da|ment (fun'də mənt), *n.* **1** foundation; basis: *Life and liberty should be no dearer to us than their fundament, the welfare of our people* (Wall Street Journal). **2** = buttocks. **3** = anus. **4** *Obsolete.* the base of a wall, building, or other structure. [< Old French *fondement,* learned borrowing from Latin *fundāmentum* < *fundāre* to found[2]]

fun|da|men|tal (fun'də men'təl), *adj., n.* ***—adj.*** **1** of or forming a foundation or basis; essential: *Reading is a fundamental skill. The ideas of strict law and order were fundamental to all his political teaching* (George Eliot). **SYN:** basic, indispensable, underlying, elementary. **2** *Music.* **a** having to do with the lowest note of a chord. **b** designating a chord of which the root is the lowest note. **c** having to do with the first note or tone of an overtone series. **3** *Physics.* of or denoting a fundamental.
—n. **1** something fundamental; essential part: *the fundamentals of grammar. Every year thousands of teen-agers learn the fundamentals of our American economy* (Newsweek). **2** *Music.* **a** = fundamental tone. **b** = fundamental bass. **3** *Physics.* that component of a wave which has the greatest wave length or lowest frequency.
[< Late Latin *fundāmentālis* < Latin *fundāmentum;* see etym. under **fundament**] **—fun'da|men'tal|ly,** *adv.*

fundamental bass, *Music.* a low note or series of notes forming the root or roots of a chord or succession of chords.

fun|da|men|tal|ism (fun'də men'tə liz əm), *n.* **1** the belief that the words of the Bible were inspired by God and should be believed and followed literally. **2** Often, **Fundamentalism.** the movement in certain Protestant churches in the United States upholding this belief. **3** the position or status of believing in this doctrine.

fun|da|men|tal|ist (fun'də men'tə list), *n., adj.* ***—n.*** a person who believes in fundamentalism. Fundamentalists refuse to accept any teaching which conflicts with the literal interpretation of the Bible.
—adj. of or having to do with fundamentalism.

fun|da|men|tal|is|tic (fun'də men'tə lis'tik), *adj.* adhering to fundamentalism.

fun|da|men|tal|i|ty (fun'də men tal'ə tē), *n.* the quality of being fundamental.

fundamental particle, = elementary particle.

fundamental tone, *Music.* **1** the lowest note of a chord. **2** the first or primary tone of an overtone series.

fundamental unit, *Physics.* one of the independent units (especially those of mass, length, and time) taken as a basis for a system of units: *The centimeter is the fundamental unit of length in the centimeter-gram-second system.*

fund|ed debt (fun'did), a debt that exists in the form of long-term obligations.

fun|di[1] (fun'dē), *n.* a West African grass, related to the crab grass, cultivated for its seed, which resembles millet. [< the native name]

fun|di[2] (fun'dī), *n.* plural of **fundus.**

fun|dic (fun'dik), *adj.* of or having to do with the fundus.

fund|ing (fun'ding), *n.* financial backing; funds: *Overselling ... is combined with a tendency to promise more than a project can really deliver in order to get funding* (New Scientist). *Important manpower programs ... will unfortunately have their funding cut in the coming fiscal year* (Time).

fund|less (fund'lis), *adj.* without funds; moneyless: *Many parents are naturally anxious at the idea of their fundless young setting off into the blue* (London Times).

fun|do (fün'dō), *n., pl.* **-dos.** a large farm, plantation, or ranch in Chile. [< Spanish *fundo* rural property < Latin *fundus* bottom, a piece of land]

fund-rais|er (fund'rā'zər), *n.* **1** a person who raises funds. **2** a gathering to raise funds; fund-raising function.

fund-rais|ing (fund'rā'zing), *n., adj.* ***—n.*** **1** the soliciting of cash contributions or pledges to support a nonprofit organization or activity, often one devoted to the distribution of charity: *political campaign fund-raising, philanthropic fund-raising.* **2** the field of organized charity and philanthropy: *Fund-raising is a fairly new profession.*
—adj. of or having to do with soliciting contributions for nonprofit organizations, or with the field of fund-raising: *philanthropic fund-raising campaigns.*

funds (fundz), *n.pl.* See under **fund.**

fun|dus (fun'dəs), *n., pl.* **-di.** the bottom of an organ, or the part opposite or farthest from the opening: *the fundus of the stomach, eye, or uterus.* [< Latin *fundus* bottom, (piece of) ground]

fu|ner|al (fyü'nər əl, fyün'rəl), *n., adj.* ***—n.*** **1** the ceremonies that are performed at the burial or burning of a dead body. A funeral usually includes a religious service and taking the body to the place where it is buried or burned. **SYN:** obsequies. **2** a procession taking a dead person's body to the place where it is buried or burned: *A funeral, with plumes and lights, And music, went to Camelot* (Tennyson).
—adj. of a funeral; suitable for a funeral: *a funeral procession. The funeral march was very slow.*
[< Middle French *funérailles,* learned borrowing from Medieval Latin *funeralia,* neuter plural of Late Latin *fūnerālis,* adjective < Latin *fūnus, -eris* funeral]

funeral director, *U.S.* a person who prepares the dead for interment and conducts burials; undertaker.

funeral home or **parlor,** a place of business having rooms for embalming and for funeral services.

funeral pile, a pile of wood or other combustible material upon which a dead body is burned.

fu|ner|ar|y (fyü'nə rer'ē), *adj.* of or for a funeral or burial: *A funerary urn holds the ashes of a dead person's body.*

fu|ne|re|al (fyü nir'ē əl), *adj.* **1** of or suitable for a funeral: *funereal garb, funereal gloom. The sad funereal feast* (Alexander Pope). **2** *Figurative.* like a funeral; sad; gloomy; dismal. **SYN:** solemn, dark, melancholy, mournful. [< Latin *fūnereus* (< *fūnus, -eris* funeral) + English *-al*[1]] **—fu|ne're|al|ly,** *adv.*

fu|nest (fyü nest'), *adj. Rare.* causing or portending death or evil; fatal; deadly; disastrous. [< French *funeste,* learned borrowing from Latin *fūnestus* < *fūnus* funeral]

fun fair, 1 a local fair with many activities for children, often held by a church or the like to raise funds. **2** *British.* an amusement park.

fun fur, a garment made of an inexpensive or imitation fur or assembled furs, usually for casual wear.

Fung (füng), *n., pl.* **Fung** or **Fungs.** = Funj.

fun|gal (fung'gəl), *adj., n.* ***—adj.*** = fungous.
—n. = fungus.

fun|gate (fung'gāt), *v.i.,* **-gat|ed, -gat|ing. 1** to grow up with a fungous form or appearance. **2** to grow rapidly like a fungus. **—fun|ga'tion,** *n.*

fun|gi (fun'jī), *n.* a plural of **fungus.**

fun|gi|bil|i|ty (fun'jə bil'ə tē), *n.* the quality of being fungible.

fun|gi|ble (fun'jə bəl), *adj., n. Law.* ***—adj.*** of such a nature that one instance or portion may be replaced by another in respect of function, office, or use. Grain is fungible in that the identical grain placed in storage need not be returned; delivery may be in other grain of the same kind and quality.
—n. a fungible substance or object, as grain or wine.
[< Medieval Latin *fungibilis* < Latin *fungī* take the place of, perform]

fun|gi|cid|al (fun'jə sī'dəl), *adj.* that destroys fungi.

fun|gi|cide (fun'jə sīd), *n.* any substance that destroys fungi or retards the growth of the spores: *It is primarily a fungicide, and the experimenters demonstrated that it could control a fungus-incited disease* (Scientific American). [< Latin *fungus* fungus + English *-cide*[1]]

fun|gi|ci|din (fun'jə sī'din), *n.* = nystatin.

fun|gif|er|ous (fun jif'ər əs), *adj.* bearing or supporting growth of fungi.

fun|gi|form (fun'jə fôrm), *adj.* having the form of a fungus or mushroom.

fun|gi|nert (fun'jə nėrt), *n.* a material that will not support the growth of fungus. [< *fungus* + *inert*]

fun|gi|stat (fun'jə stat'), *n.* a substance that stops the development or growth of fungi. [< *fungi* + *-stat*]

fun|gi|stat|ic (fun'jə stat'ik), *adj.* stopping the development or growth of a fungus without killing it.

fun|giv|o|rous (fun jiv'ər əs), *adj.* feeding on mushrooms or fungi, as certain insects. [< *fungi* + Latin *vorāre* devour + English *-ous*]

fun|go (fung'gō), *n., pl.* **-goes.** a fly ball batted for baseball players to catch in practice, by a coach or player who tosses the ball up and hits it before it falls. [origin unknown]

fun|goid (fung'goid), *adj., n.* ***—adj.*** **1** resembling a fungus or its qualities; of the nature of a fungus. **2** *Medicine.* having spongy, unhealthful growths.
—n. a fungoid plant.

fun·gose (fung′gōs), *adj.* = fungous.

fun·gos·i·ty (fung gos′ə tē), *n., pl.* **-ties.** **1** the quality or condition of being fungous. **2** a fungous growth.

fun·gous (fung′gəs), *adj.* **1** of a fungus or fungi; like a fungus; spongy. **2** *Figurative.* growing or springing up suddenly like a mushroom, but not lasting or substantial. **3** caused by a fungus: *Wheat rust is a fungous disease.* [< Latin *fungōsus* < *fungus* fungus]

fun·gus** (fung′gəs), *n., pl.* **-gi** or **-gus·es,** *adj.* **—*n. **1** any one of a group of plants without flowers, leaves, or chlorophyll. Fungi get their nourishment from dead or living organic matter. They reproduce by spores and division. Fungi belong to the thallophytes. Mushrooms, toadstools, molds, smuts, rusts, mildews, and yeasts are fungi. **2** *Figurative.* something that grows or springs up rapidly like a mushroom. **3** a diseased, spongy, growth on the skin, such as granulation in a wound. **—*adj.*** = fungous. [< Latin *fungus*]

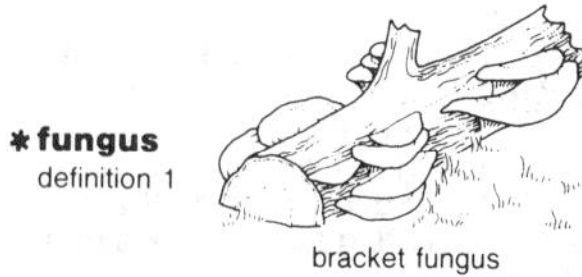
***fungus** definition 1

bracket fungus

fungus beetle, any one of various beetles that feed on fungi.

fun house, a building at a carnival or amusement park, with devices that stun or surprise those who enter, such as mirrors that distort the image, unexpectedly sliding floors, and sudden blasts of air.

fu·ni·cle (fyü′nə kəl), *n.* **1** a small cord or cordlike part. **2** = funiculus. [< Latin *fūniculus* funiculus]

fu·ni·cu·laire (fʏ nē kʏ ler′), *n. French.* a funicular railway.

fu·nic·u·lar (fyü nik′yə lər), *n., adj.* **—*n.*** = funicular railway.
—*adj.* **1a** hanging from a rope; depending on or worked by a rope. **b** of a rope or its tension. **2** of a funiculus; like a funiculus. **3** consisting of a funiculus.

***funicular railway,** a type of railway used on steep grades, in which two counterbalanced cars or trains are linked by a cable so that when one moves down the other moves up: *To get the magazine to the summit, he carried a copy up a funicular railway from St. Moritz to Corviglia* (Newsweek).

***funicular railway**

fu·nic·u·late (fyü nik′yə lāt), *adj.* having a funiculus.

fu·nic·u·lus (fyü nik′yə ləs), *n., pl.* **-li** (-lī). **1** *Anatomy.* a cordlike structure, such as the umbilical cord or the spermatic cord, or a bundle of nerve fibers. **2** *Botany.* the stalk by which a seed or ovule is attached to the placenta. [< Latin *fūniculus* little rope (diminutive) < *fūnis* rope]

Funj (fünj), *n., pl.* **Funj** or **Funjs.** **1** one of an African people occupying the wooded and mountainous region south of Sennar, between the White Nile and the Blue Nile. **2** the language of this people. Also, **Fung.**

Fun·ji (fün′jē), *n., pl.* **-ji, -jis** or **-jes.** = Funj.

funk¹ (fungk), *n., v. Informal.* **—*n.*** **1** a condition of panic or fear: *to be in a blue funk.* SYN: terror. **2** = coward.
—*v.t.* **1** to be afraid of. **2** to shrink from; shirk. SYN: evade. **3** to frighten or scare.
—*v.i.* to flinch or shrink through fear; try to back out of anything: *He always funked when competition grew too keen.*
[origin uncertain. Compare Middle Dutch *fonck* perturbation, or Old French *funicle* wild, mad.]
—funk′er, *n.*

funk² (fungk), *n., v.* **—*n.*** **1** a strong, offensive smell, especially of smoke. **2** = funk art.
[< verb]
—*v.t.* **1** to blow smoke upon; annoy with smoke. **2** to smoke (a pipe).
—*v.i.* to smoke: *But there my triumph's straw-fire flared and funked* (Robert Browning).
[perhaps < Old French *funkier, fungier,* ultimately < Latin *fūmus* smoke]

funk³ (fungk), *n. Jazz Slang.* a type of earthy blues with origins in gospel singing and African rhythms; funky jazz: *Funk was a deeper reach into Negro culture than jazz had taken before* (Time). [probably special use of *funk²*]

funk art, a type of pop art created from strange or bizarre objects, usually of a recognizable form, such as a huge toothbrush or a typewriter with finger-shaped keys.

funk artist, a person who produces funk art.

funk hole, **1** a rough shelter dug in the ground for protection against the enemy's fire; dugout. **2** *Informal.* a safe situation for a person shirking military duty.

fun·ki·a (fung′kē ə, füng′-), *n.* = plantain lily. [< New Latin *Funkia* the genus name < H. C. *Funck,* 1771-1839, a German botanist]

funk money, *British.* hot money (def. 1).

funk·y (fung′kē), *adj.,* **funk·i·er, funk·i·est.** **1** shrinking in fear; timid. **2** having a strong, offensive smell: *Lord, but this hallway was funky* (Louise Meriwether). **3** *U.S. Slang.* **a** having a flavor or sound like that of the blues; wistful and sad: *funky jazz.* **b** earthy; unpretentious; authentic: *a funky style of singing.* **c** elegant; fine; fashionable: *"That's a funky jacket, Kit Carson"* (Time). **—funk′i·ly,** *adv.* **—funk′i·ness,** *n.*

fun·less (fun′lis), *adj.* without fun; joyless.

fun·nel** (fun′əl), *n., v.,* **-neled, -nel·ing** or (*especially British*) **-nelled, -nel·ling.** **—*n. **1** a tapering tube with a wide mouth shaped like a cone. A funnel is used to prevent spilling in pouring liquids, powder, grain, or the like into containers with small openings. **2** anything shaped like a funnel: *a funnel of smoke.* **3** a round metal chimney; smokestack: *The steamship had two funnels. The steam locomotive had one funnel.* **4** a flue or stack for carrying off smoke or for ventilation or lighting. **5** the narrow cloud of a tornado that extends downward from a heavy, dark mass of cumulonimbus clouds: *A tornado has a strong lifting force due to the updraft of air in the funnel* (James E. Miller).
—*v.t., v.i.* to pass or feed through or as if through a funnel or other narrow opening: *to funnel gasoline into a can. The crowd funneled through the gate.* (*Figurative.*) *She funneled all of her efforts into her career.*
[< Old French *fonel* < Late Latin *fundibulum* < Latin *infundibulum* < *in-* in + *fundere* pour]

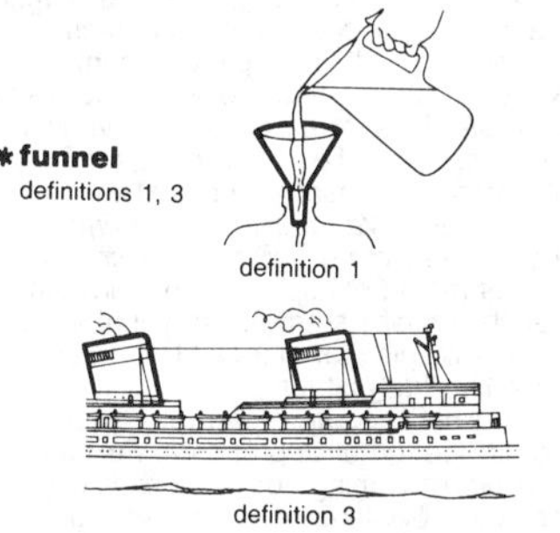
***funnel** definitions 1, 3

definition 1

definition 3

funnel chest, a malformed depression of the sternum and anterior portions of the ribs, often associated with rickets.

fun·neled (fun′əld), *adj.* **1** having a funnel or funnels: *the double-funneled stem of whirling mist* [*of a waterspout*] (D. Pidgeon). **2** = funnel-shaped.

fun·nel·form (fun′əl fôrm′), *adj. Botany.* having the form of a funnel, or inverted shallow cone.

fun·nel-shaped (fun′əl shāpt′), *adj.* **1** shaped like a funnel: *From the base of a thundercloud a funnel-shaped cloud extends a violently twisting spout toward the earth* (Scientific American). **2** having a tubelike corolla slowly enlarging upward and spreading widely at the top; infundibuliform.

fun·nel-web spider (fun′əl web′), a spider which builds a horizontal web with a funnel-shaped retreat at one side. It is found especially in grass, low bushes, or houses.

fun·nies (fun′ēz), *n.pl.* See under **funny.**

fun·ny (fun′ē), *adj.,* **-ni·er, -ni·est,** *n., pl.* **-nies.** **—*adj.*** **1** causing laughter; comical; amusing: *The clown's funny jokes kept us laughing.* **2** *Informal.* **a** strange; queer; odd: *It's funny that he is so late.* SYN: curious. **b** tricky or underhanded: *You'll be sorry if you try anything funny in class.* **c** impertinent; saucy: *I warned that boy not to get funny with the boss.* **3** *U.S.* having to do with the part of a newspaper containing comic strips.
—*n.* *Informal.* **1** a joke: *I hear he's a lawyer now, restricted, I suppose, to sneaking in a funny now and then in his summation to the jury* (New Yorker). **2** an amusing show, performance, or the like: *In 1935 "One Pair of Hands," Miss Dickens's account of her life as a maid and cook, turned out a real funny and brought her unsinkable fame* (London Times). **3** something peculiar, queer, or strange.
the funnies, a comic strips; comics: *Dad likes to read the funnies.* **b** the section of a newspaper carrying comic strips.
[< *fun* + *-y¹*] **—fun′ni·ly,** *adv.* **—fun′ni·ness,** *n.*
—*Syn.* *adj.* **1 Funny, laughable** mean such as to cause laughter or amusement. **Funny** implies almost any degree of amusement from a hearty laugh to a faint smile: *The funny little man and his funny little children keep our neighborhood smiling. Funny peculiar or funny ha-ha?* (Ian Hay). **Laughable** implies laughter, but often laughter that is scornful rather than hearty: *His fine airs are laughable.*

funny bone, **1** a sensitive place at the bend of the elbow where a nerve lies between the skin and bone; crazy bone. **2** *Figurative.* sense of humor: *The sophisticated, satirical irony is aimed at the mind and the funny bone, seldom the emotions* (Bosley Crowther).

funny book, = comic book.

funny business, *Informal.* questionable or underhanded activity; monkey business.

funny car, a type of drag-racing car with the body of a conventional automobile, a supercharged engine, and the driver's seat in the back.

funny farm, *Slang.* an insane asylum: *He eventually had to be removed to the funny farm by the men in the white coats* (Bernard Levin).

fun·ny·man (fun′ē man′), *n., pl.* **-men.** *U.S. Informal.* an actor or writer noted for being funny; comedian; humorist.

funny money, *U.S. and Canada. Informal.* **1** money that is not stable or redeemable. **2** money to promote an unsound or impractical venture.

funny paper, the section of a newspaper devoted to comic strips; funnies.

fun run, a running race that acknowledges participation rather than performance.

fun·some (fun′səm), *adj.* having or loving fun; given to amusement: *She signed on to replace Jennilee Harrison as the third member of the funsome threesome in "Three's Company"* (Maclean's).

fun·ster (fun′stər), *n.* a person who tries to amuse with funny talk or actions; comedian: *The men of Lincolnshire, it turns out, are great funsters* (Manchester Guardian). [after *punster*]

fuo·ri le mu·ra (fwô′rē lāmü′rä), *Italian.* outside the walls (used in the names of certain churches of Rome): *In the eleventh and twelfth centuries there was some Romanesque building, including . . . the nave and cloister of San Lorenzo fuori le mura* (Harper's).

fur (fėr), *n., adj., v.,* **furred, fur·ring.** **—*n.*** **1** the hair covering the skin of certain animals. Fur grows on many mammals and usually consists of a short, soft, thick undercoat thinly covered by a longer, coarser outer coat. **2** skin with such hair on it, dressed and treated. Fur is used to make, cover, trim, or line clothing. SYN: pelt. **3** any coating like fur, as on a plant. **4** a coating of foul or waste matter like fur. A sick person often has fur on his tongue. **5** *Heraldry.* one of three kinds of tincture (the other two being *color* and *metal*).
—*adj.* made of fur.
—*v.t.* **1a** to make, line, trim, or cover with fur. **b** to clothe or adorn with fur. **2** to coat with foul or waste matter like fur: *The walls on all sides* [*were*] *furred with mouldy damps* (Joseph Addison). **3** *Carpentry.* to put furring on (beams or walls). **—*v.i.*** **1** to grow fur: *In February the pussy willow furs in the chill wind* (New Yorker). **2** to become furred or fuzzy: *His voice doesn't vary from a monotonous mumble furring round the vowels* (Sunday Times).
furs, a a garment made of fur: *Mother's furs keep her warm. Underneath is the picture of Sir William Cecil, after Lord Burleigh, in his gown and furs* (Daniel Waterland). **b** skins of animals with the fur on them: *Some furs are imported from Canada.*
make the fur fly, *Informal.* to cause trouble; quarrel; fight: *I knew very well that I was in a devil of a hobble, for my father had been taking a few horns, and was in a good condition to make the fur fly* (David Crockett).
rub (or **stroke**) **one's fur the wrong way,** to irritate one: *With his persistent questions Tom ended up rubbing somebody's fur the wrong way.*
[Middle English *furre* < Old French *fourrer* to line with skins, encase < *feurre* sheath, case < Germanic (compare Gothic *fōdr*)] **—fur′less,** *adj.* **—fur′like′,** *adj.*

fur., **1** furlong. **2** furnished.

fu·ran (fyůr′an, fyů ran′), *n.* a colorless liquid prepared from furfural, used especially in tanning

Pronunciation Key: hat, āge, cãre, fär; let, ēqual, tėrm; it, īce; hot, ōpen, ôrder; oil, out; cup, pùt, rüle; child; long; thin; ᴛʜen; zh, measure; ə represents a in about, e in taken, i in pencil, o in lemon, u in circus.

and as a solvent for certain plastics; furfuran; furfurane. *Formula:* C_4H_4O [short for *furfurane* < German *Furfuran* < Latin *furfur* bran]

fu|rane (fyůr′ān), *n.* = furan.

fu|ra|nose (fyůr′ə nōs), *n.* a sugar having a ring structure of five atoms. Hexoses may sometimes occur in the form of a furanose.

fur|a|zol|i|done (fyůr′ə zol′ə dōn), *n.* a nitrofuran drug used in the treatment of various bacterial disorders and in protozoan diseases of poultry such as coccidiosis. *Formula:* $C_8H_7N_3O_5$

fur-bear|er (fėr′bãr′ər), *n.* **1** any animal having fur: *[the area] provides dense cover, as well as some food, for songbirds, bobwhite quail, and the small fur-bearers* (Harper's). **2** an animal having fur that is used commercially.

fur-bear|ing (fėr′bãr′ing), *adj.* having fur: *Fur-bearing animals start the long process of change to winter pelage when the season is hottest* (Sterling B. Hendricks).

fur|be|low (fėr′bə lō), *n., v.* **—*n.*** a bit of elaborate trimming.
—*v.t.* to trim in a fussy, elaborate way.
furbelows, showy ornaments or trimming, especially in women's dress: *There were too many frills and furbelows on her dress.*
[< Provençal *farbélla,* variant of French *falbala,* perhaps ultimately < Late Latin *faluppa* fiber, valueless thing]

fur|bish (fėr′bish), *v.t.* **1** to brighten by rubbing or scouring; polish; burnish: *He furbished the rusty sword until it shone like new.* **2** to restore to good condition; make usable again: (*Figurative.*) *Before going to France, he furbished up his half-forgotten French.* SYN: renovate, revive. [< Old French *forbiss-,* stem of *fourbir* to polish < Germanic (compare Old High German *furben* sweep clean)] **—fur′bish|er,** *n.* **—fur′bish|ment,** *n.*

Fur|bish lousewort (fėr′bish), a rare species of lousewort discovered in Maine in 1880 and thought to be extinct until rediscovered in 1976: *The Furbish lousewort, despite its unprepossessing name is . . . delicate and fernlike* (Philip Shabecoff). [< Kate *Furbish,* its discoverer]

fur|cal (fėr′kəl), *adj.* = forked.

fur|cate (*adj.* fėr′kāt, -kit; *v.* fėr′kāt), *adj., v.,* **-cat|ed, -cat|ing.** **—*adj.*** = forked. **—*v.i.*** to form a fork; divide into branches. [< Late Latin *furcātus* forked, cloven < Latin *furca* pitchfork] **—fur′cate|ly,** *adv.* **—fur|ca′tion,** *n.*

fur|cu|la (fėr′kyə lə), *n., pl.* **-lae** (-lē). the fused clavicles or wishbone of a bird; fourchette. [< Latin *furcula* forked support (diminutive) < *furca* pitchfork]

fur|cu|lar (fėr′kyə lər), *adj.* of or like a furcula: *a furcular bone.*

fur|cu|lum (fėr′kyə ləm), *n., pl.* **-la** (-lə). = furcula. [< New Latin *furculum,* variant of Latin *furcula;* see etym. under **furcula**]

fur farm, a farm or ranch on which fur farming is done.

fur farming, the business of raising fur-bearing animals such as fox and mink for their fur.

fur|fur (fėr′fər), *n., pl.* **-fur|es.** dandruff; scurf.
furfures, scales or particles of scurf.
[< Latin *furfur* bran]

fur|fu|ra|ceous (fėr′fyə rā′shəs), *adj.* **1** resembling bran; scurfy; scaly. **2** *Botany.* covered with branlike scales. [< Late Latin *furfurāceus* (with English *-ous*) branlike < Latin *furfur* bran]

fur|fur|al (fėr′fə ral, fėr′fə ral′), *n.* an oily, aromatic liquid aldehyde prepared by the distillation of oat hulls, corncobs, or wood, with sulfuric acid. It is used as a solvent, in refining lubricating oils, and in making plastics. *Formula:* $C_5H_4O_2$ [< *furfur*(ane) + *al*(dehyde)]

fur|fur|al|de|hyde (fėr′fə ral′də hīd), *n.* = furfural.

fur|fur|an (fėr′fə ran, fėr′fə ran′), *n.* = furan.

fur|fur|ane (fėr′fə rān, fėr′fə rān′), *n.* = furan.

fur|fur|es (fėr′fyə rēz), *n.pl.* See under **furfur.**

fur|fur|yl (fėr′fər əl), *n.* a monovalent radical, C_5H_5O-, derived from furfural.

fu|ri|bund (fyůr′ə bund), *adj.* raging; furious. [< Latin *furibundus* < *furere* to rage]

Fu|ries (fyůr′ēz), *n.pl. Greek and Roman Mythology.* the three spirits of revenge who pursued those who had not atoned for their crimes; Eumenides; Erinyes. They were Alecto, Megaera, and Tisiphone.

fu|ri|o|so (fyůr′ē ō′sō), *adv., adj., n., pl.* **-sos.** **—*adv.*, *adj.*** *Music.* with vehemence or great force; passionate (used as a direction).
—*n.* **1** *Music.* a furioso piece or part. **2** a person filled with violence or fury; fanatic.
[< Italian *furioso* < Latin *furiōsus* furious]

fu|ri|ous (fyůr′ē əs), *adj.* **1** full of wild, fierce anger; frantic: *The owner of the house was furious when he learned of the broken window.* SYN: mad, enraged. **2** violent, raging: *A hurricane is a furious storm.* SYN: tempestuous, turbulent. **3** of unrestrained energy, speed, or intensity: *furious activity, a furious pace or gallop.* **4** unrestrainedly boisterous: *The fun grew fast and furious.* [< Latin *furiōsus* < *furia* fury] **—fu′ri|ous|ly,** *adv.* **—fu′ri|ous|ness,** *n.*

furl (fėrl), *v., n.* **—*v.t.*** to roll up or fold up: *to furl a sail, to furl a flag. The boys broke up camp and furled the tent.* (*Figurative.*) *The birds furled their wings.* **—*v.i.*** to become rolled or gathered up in a spiral or twisted form; curl (up).
—*n.* **1** the act of furling or state of being furled. **2** a roll, coil, or curl of anything furled. **3** the manner in which a thing is furled.
[probably < French *ferler;* origin uncertain]
—furl′er, *n.*

fur|la|na (für lä′nä), *n. Italian.* **1** a lively Italian dance in sextuple rhythm, common especially among Venetian gondoliers. **2** a piece of music written for, or in the rhythm of, this dance.

fur|long (fėr′lông, -long), *n.* a measure of distance equal to one eighth of a mile; 220 yards or 201.168 meters. [Old English *furlang* < *furh* furrow + *lang* long]

fur|lough (fėr′lō), *n., v.* **—*n.*** a leave of absence, especially for a soldier: *The soldier has two weeks' furlough.*
—*v.t.* **1** to give a leave of absence to. **2** to lay off (a worker): *[The company] said the employees were furloughed for two weeks* (Wall Street Journal).
[earlier *foreloof,* and *vorloffe* < Dutch *verlof*]

fur|men|ty (fėr′mən tē), *n.* = frumenty.

fur|me|ty (fėr′mə tē), *n.* = frumenty.

furn., **1** furnished. **2** furniture.

fur|nace (fėr′nis), *n., v.,* **-naced, -nac|ing.** **—*n.*** **1** something to make a very hot fire in. Furnaces are used to heat buildings, melt metal, and make glass. A furnace has an enclosed chamber or box for the fire. **2** *Figurative.* a very hot place. **3** *Figurative.* a severe test: *the furnace of affliction* (Isaiah 48:10).
—*v.t.* **1** to subject to the heat of a furnace. **2** *Figurative.* to emit like a furnace: *He furnaces The thick sighs from him* (Shakespeare).
[< Old French *fornais, fornaise* < Latin *fornāx, -ācis* kiln, oven, related to *fornus* oven]

fur|nace|man (fėr′nis man′), *n., pl.* **-men.** a man who maintains a furnace or repairs furnaces.

fur|nish (fėr′nish), *v.t.* **1** to supply with something necessary, useful, or wanted; provide: *to furnish an army with blankets, to furnish a person with information or money. The sun furnishes heat.* **2** to supply (a room, house, or the like) with furniture and equipment: *We furnished the living room. He had taken more pains to furnish his house than his mind* (Bishop Connop Thirlwall).
[< Old French *furniss-,* stem of *furnir* furnish, accomplish < Germanic (compare Old High German *frummen*)] **—fur′nish|er,** *n.*
—*Syn.* **1, 2 Furnish, equip** mean to provide or supply what is needed or appropriate. **Furnish** applies particularly to things or services which are necessary for existence or wanted for use or comfort: *One donor furnished money, another, labor. That caterer furnishes both food and help. Furnish one good reason for your decision.* **Equip** applies particularly to whatever is needed to do work or to work with: *We equipped the kitchen with new appliances. He is not equipped to translate Latin.*

fur|nish|ing (fėr′ni shing), *n.* **1** the act of a person or thing that furnishes: *The furnishing took us three weeks.* **2** an instance of this: *Furnishing the transportation was our share.* **3** decoration.
furnishings, a furniture or equipment for a room, house, or the like: *Carpets from Fontainebleau, furnishings from Saint Cloud* (London Daily News). **b** accessories of dress; articles of clothing: *That store sells men's furnishings.*

fur|nish|ment (fėr′nish mənt), *n.* **1** the act of furnishing. **2** the state of being furnished. **3** something furnished.
furnishments, supplies: *Purveyor for the army . . . vastly rich; grown so as contractor of furnishments which he never furnishes* (Lewis Wallace).

fur|ni|ture (fėr′nə chər), *n.* **1** movable articles needed in a house or room, such as tables, chairs, beds, or desks. **2** articles needed; equipment: *God's residence is next to mine, His furniture is love* (Emily Dickinson). **3** apparatus, appliances, or instruments for work, now especially the tools, utensils, rigging, stores, and tackle of a ship. **4** the covers and linen of a bed. **5** strips or blocks of wood or metal, lower than type-high, set in and about pages of type to fill out large white areas such as margins. **6** (in the Middle Ages) the harness and ornamental coverings for a horse. **7** *Archaic.* the condition of being equipped in body or mind; equipment; preparedness. **8** *Archaic.* the act of furnishing. [< French *fourniture* < Old French *fournir;* see etym. under **furnish**]

fu|role (fyůr′ōl), *n.* = St. Elmo's fire. [< French *furole* < Middle French *fuirole*]

fu|ror (fyůr′ôr), *n.* **1** an outburst of wild enthusiasm or excitement: *The aviator who first flew over the ocean was received with furor.* **2** a craze; mania: *A furor of jogging swept the campus. The modern furor for organized sport has its roots in city life.* **3** a rage; fury; inspired madness; frenzy: *poetic furor.* [< Middle French *fureur,* learned borrowing from Latin *furor,* related to *furere* to rage. See etym. of doublet **furore.**]

fu|rore (fyůr′ôr; fyů rôr′ē, -rōr′-), *n.* = furor. [< Italian *furore* < Latin *furor.* See etym. of doublet **furor.**]

fur|o|sem|ide (fyůr′ə sem′īd, fyů rō′sə mīd), *n.* a diuretic drug, used especially for refractory edemas. *Formula:* $C_{12}H_{11}ClN_2O_5S$

fur|phy (fėr′fē), *n., pl.* **-phies.** *Australian Slang.* a story not based on fact; wild rumor: *A furphy is the exact equivalent of the good U.S. Navy . . . word scuttlebutt* (Time). [origin uncertain]

fur|piece (fėr′pēs′), *n.* a collar or stole of fur: *I see that's a nice furpiece you have on, Mrs. Arizona* (Thornton Wilder).

fur ranch, = fur farm.

furred (fėrd), *adj.* **1** having fur. **2** made of, lined, trimmed, or covered with fur. **3** wearing fur. **4** coated with foul or waste matter: *a furred tongue.* **5** *Carpentry.* with furring on it.

fur|ri|er (fėr′ē ər), *n.* **1** a dealer in furs. **2** a person whose work is preparing furs or making and repairing fur garments.

fur|ri|ered (fėr′ē ərd), *adj.* dressed by a furrier: *a furriered skin.*

fur|ri|er|y (fėr′ē ər ē), *n., pl.* **-er|ies.** **1** the business or work of a furrier. **2** furs. **3** a fur store.

fur|rin (fur′ən), *adj. Dialect.* foreign.

fur|rin|er (fur′ə nər), *n. Dialect.* foreigner.

fur|ring (fėr′ing), *n.* **1** fur used to make, cover, trim, or line clothing. **2** the act of lining, trimming, or clothing with fur. **3** a coating of foul or waste matter like fur, for example on the tongue or the inside of a boiler. **4** *Carpentry.* **a** the use of thin strips of wood or other material fastened to beams or walls to make a level support for laths, plaster, or other finish, or to provide air spaces. **b** the strips or other material so used.

fur|row (fėr′ō), *n., v.* **—*n.*** **1** a long, narrow groove or track cut in the ground by a plow. **2** any long, narrow groove or track: *the furrows between waves of the sea. Heavy trucks made deep furrows in the muddy road.* **3** *Figurative.* a wrinkle: *a furrow in one's brow.* **4** *Archaic.* **a** arable land. **b** a piece of plowed land. **c** a field or fields.
—*v.t.* **1** to cut furrows in; plow. **2** to make furrows in: (*Figurative.*) *Fair cheeks were furrowed with hot tears* (Byron). **3** *Figurative.* to make wrinkles in; wrinkle: *The old man's face was furrowed with age.* **4** *Figurative.* to cleave (as the sea): *to furrow large space of stormy seas* (Henry Howard, Earl of Surrey).
—*v.i.* to make a furrow or furrows.
[Old English *furh*] **—fur′row|er,** *n.* **—fur′row|less,** *adj.*

furrow slice, a narrow slice of earth turned up by a plow.

fur|row|y (fėr′ō ē), *adj.* full of furrows.

fur|ry (fėr′ē), *adj.,* **-ri|er, -ri|est.** **1** of fur; consisting of fur: *a little cat with a furry coat.* **2** covered with fur; wearing fur: *a little furry animal.* **3** soft like fur: *a furry nap.* **4** *U.S. Slang.* hair-raising; horrible: *[He] misses the whole point of the "furry fear" that gripped America after the murders* (Harper's). **—fur′ri|ness,** *n.*

furs (fėrz), *n.pl.* See under **fur.**

fur seal, any one of various species of eared seal that have a thick, soft underfur of great value, such as the northern fur seal. See picture under **seal.**[2]

Fürst (fyrst), *n., pl.* **Für|sten** (fyr′stən). *German.* a nobleman ranking below a Herzog and above a Graf. The word is commonly represented in English by *prince.*

fur|ther (fėr′ᴛʜər), *compar. adj. and adv., superl.* **fur|thest,** *v.* **—*adj.*** **1** more distant; farther: *on the further side.* **2** additional; more: *Do you need further help? Have you any further need of me?*
—*adv.* **1** at or to a greater distance: *Go no further than a mile and you will find it. Seek no further for happiness.* **2** to a greater extent; more: *Inquire further into the matter.* **3** in addition; also; besides: *His father told him to clean his room and said further that he must make his bed.* SYN: additionally, moreover.
—*v.t.* to help forward; promote; forward: *Mother furthered our plans for a picnic. Let us further the cause of peace.* SYN: See syn. under **promote.**
[Old English *furthra,* adjective, *furthor,* adverb < *forth* forth] **—fur′ther|er,** *n.*
▶See **farther** for usage note.

fur|ther|ance (fėr′ᴛʜər əns), *n.* **1** the act of furthering; helping forward; advancement; promotion. SYN: aid, assistance. **2** a means or source of help.

further education, *British.* education or training

other than in a college or university offered as a supplement to that received in primary or secondary schools. Further education includes part-time or full-time technical, vocational, or cultural instruction for teen-agers and adults.

fur|ther|more (fėr′ᴛʜər môr, -mōr), *adv.* in addition; moreover; also; besides; further: *He wants to leave for home; furthermore, he wants to go right now.*

fur|ther|most (fėr′ᴛʜər mōst), *adj.* most distant or remote; furthest: *Explorers have gone to the furthermost corners of the world.*

fur|thest (fėr′ᴛʜist), *superl. adv. and adj.* **—adv.** most distant; farthest: *He who travels fastest travels furthest.*
—*adj.* **1** most distant; farthest: *the furthest reaches of the continent.* **2** to the greatest degree or extent; most: *Those who are poor and starving are in the furthest need.*
[Middle English *furthest,* apparently patterned on *further*]

fur|tive (fėr′tiv), *adj.* **1** done by stealth to avoid being noticed; secret: *a furtive snatch at the candy, a furtive glance into the forbidden room.* **SYN:** clandestine, surreptitious. **2** sly; stealthy; shifty: *The thief had a furtive manner.* [< Latin *fūrtīvus* < *fūrtum* theft < *fūr, fūris* thief] **—fur′tive|ly,** *adv.* **—fur′tive|ness,** *n.*

fu|run|cle (fyůr′ung kəl), *n. Medicine.* a boil; inflammatory sore. [< Latin *fūrunculus* (originally) little thief (diminutive) < *fūr, fūris* thief]

fu|run|cu|lar (fyů rung′kyə lər), *adj.* **1** of or having to do with furuncles or boils. **2** characterized by furuncles.

fu|run|cu|lo|sis (fyů rung′kyə lō′sis), *n. Medicine.* a condition characterized by the appearance of numerous furuncles or boils.

fu|run|cu|lous (fyů rung′kyə ləs), *adj.* = furuncular.

fu|ry (fyůr′ē), *n., pl.* **-ries. 1** wild, fierce anger; storm of anger; rage: *Heaven has no rage like love to hatred turned Nor Hell a fury like a woman scorned* (William Congreve). **SYN:** ire, wrath. See syn. under **rage. 2** violence; fierceness: *the fury of a battle, the fury of a hurricane.* **SYN:** vehemence. **3** a raging or violent person, especially a ferociously angry woman: *He had a fury for a wife.* **4** a course or period of great violence: *The Spanish Fury at Antwerp, in 1576, was characterized by plundering, burning, and massacre by Spanish soldiers.* **5** unrestrained force, such as of energy or speed: *to work with fury.* **6** *Archaic.* inspired frenzy, as of one possessed by a god or demon: *A sibyl . . . in her prophetic fury sew'd the work* (Shakespeare).
like fury, *Informal.* violently; furiously; very rapidly: *She worked like fury to prepare for the trip.*
[< Latin *furia,* related to *furere* to rage]

Fu|ry (fyůr′ē), *n., pl.* **-ries.** *Greek and Roman Mythology.* **1** any one of the three Furies. **2** an avenging or tormenting infernal spirit that pursues its victim: *She seemed possessed by a Fury.*

furze (fėrz), *n.* **1** a low, prickly evergreen shrub with yellow flowers, and common on waste lands in Europe; gorse; whin. It belongs to the pea family. **2** its flower. [Old English *fyrs*]

furze|chat (fėrz′chat′), *n.* = whinchat.

furze lark, *British Dialect.* titlark; pipit.

furz|y (fėr′zē), *adj.* **1** of or like furze. **2** covered with furze: *the furzy hills of Braid* (Scott).

fu|sain (fyü zān′, *French* fʏ zaɴ′ *for 1,2;* fyü′zān, fyü zān′ *for 3*), *n.* **1** a fine charcoal used in drawing, made of the wood of the spindle tree. **2** a drawing done with this. **3** a constituent of bituminous coal, often forming a characteristic dull-black band, very similar to charcoal in appearance, consisting of plant remains which have been converted into soft, dusty coal. [< French *fusain* (originally) spindle tree < Old French < Vulgar Latin *fūsāgō, -inis* < Latin *fūsus* spindle]

fu|sar|i|um (fyü sãr′ē əm), *n., pl.* **-i|a.** (-ē ə). any one of a group of common soil-borne fungi which attack the roots, stems, and fruit of plants, causing decay and blight, especially in such crops as tomatoes, cereal grains, and melons. [< New Latin *Fusarium* the genus name < Latin *fūsus* spindle]

fusarium wilt, a common disease of such plants as tomatoes, melons, cotton, and tobacco, caused by fusarium.

fus|cous (fus′kəs), *adj.* of a dark or somber hue; brown tinged with gray; dusky; swarthy. [< Latin *fuscus* (with English *-ous*) dark, dusky]

fuse[1]** (fyüz), *n., v.,* **fused, fus|ing. —*n. **1** a part of an electric circuit that melts and breaks the circuit if the current becomes dangerously strong. A fuse consists of a wire or strip of metal that is easily melted. See picture above. **2** = fuze (def. 1).
—*v.i.* *Informal.* (of an electric light) to be extinguished because of the melting of a fuse.
—*v.t.* **1** *Informal.* to extinguish by the melting of a fuse: *A professional photographer had fused the lights, engulfing the entire house in darkness* (Maclean's). **2** to put a fuse into (a circuit).
blow a fuse, *Informal.* to get very angry: *I'm afraid he'll blow a fuse when he hears that you lost the money.*
have a short fuse, *U.S. Informal.* to get excited or angry easily; to blow up easily or quickly: *He is famous for his nasty temper. He has a very short fuse* (New York Times).
[< Italian *fuso* tube < Latin *fūsus* spindle]

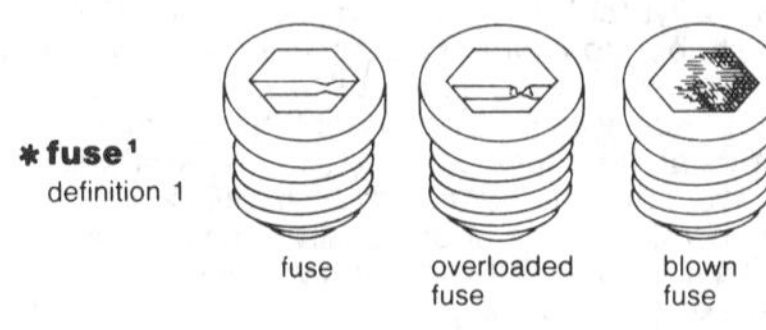

***fuse[1]** definition 1

fuse[2] (fyüz), *v.,* **fused, fus|ing. —*v.t.*** **1** to join together by melting; melt: *Copper and zinc are fused to make brass. A quantity of silver which had been fused in a ladle was allowed to solidify* (John Tyndall). **2** to blend; unite: *to fuse the various ingredients into glass. The intense heat fused the rocks together.*
—*v.i.* **1** to become melted; melt together: *The wax from the two candles fused as they burned.* **2** to become blended; unite: (*Figurative.*) *Two political parties fused to form a new party.*
[< Latin *fūsus,* past participle of *fundere* pour, melt]

fuse box, a box mounted in or on a wall, containing electrical fuses.

fused quartz or **silica** (fyüzd), = quartz glass.

fu|see (fyü zē′), *n.* **1** a large-headed match that will burn in a wind; lucifer; vesuvian. **2** a flare used on railroads and highways as a warning signal. A fusee burns with a red or yellow light. **3** a spirally grooved, conical pulley between the barrel and the central pinion of a watch or clock to keep the power of the mainspring constant. **4** = fuse. Also, **fuzee.** [< French *fusée* spindleful of tow < Medieval Latin *fusata* < Latin *fūsus* spindle]

fu|sel (fyü′zəl, -səl), *n.* = fusel oil.

fu|se|lage (fyü′zə läzh, -lij; -se-), *n.* the body of an airplane, helicopter, or glider to which the wings, tail, and other parts are fastened. The fuselage holds the pilot, passengers, and cargo. [< French *fuselage* < *fuselé* spindle-shaped < Old French *fusel* (diminutive) < Latin *fūsus* spindle]

fuse link, *Electricity.* the part of a fuse which melts when the current becomes dangerously strong.

fusel oil, 1 an acrid, poisonous, oily liquid consisting mainly ofamyl alcohol, that occurs in alcoholic liquors when they are not distilled enough. It is much used as a solvent. **2** = amyl alcohol. [< German *Fusel* bad liquor]

fu|si|bil|i|ty (fyü′zə bil′ə tē), *n.* **1** the condition or quality of being fusible. **2** the degree to which a substance possesses this quality, especially as given in terms of a particular scale.

fu|si|ble (fyü′zə bəl), *adj., n.* **—*adj.*** that can be fused or melted.
—*n.* a fabric that can be joined together or to another fabric through pressure. **—fu′si|ble|ness,** *n.* **—fu′si|bly,** *adv.*

fusible metal or **alloy,** any alloy, usually containing bismuth, lead, tin, or cadmium which melts at a low temperature and can be used for making various safety devices.

fu|si|form (fyü′zə fôrm), *adj.* rounded and tapering from the middle toward each end; shaped like a spindle: *A milkweed pod is somewhat fusiform.* [< Latin *fūsus* spindle + English *-form*]

fu|sil[1] (fyü′zəl), *n.* a light flintlock musket. [< Old French *fuisil,* later *fusil* steel for a tinder box < Vulgar Latin *fōcilis* < Latin *focus* hearth, fire]

fu|sil[2] (fyü′zəl, -səl), *adj.* **1** formed by melting or casting; founded. **2** fused; molten: *and o'er the silver pours the fusil gold* (Alexander Pope). **3** fusible. [< Latin *fūsilis* < *fūsus;* see etym. under **fuse[2]**]

fu|sile (fyü′zəl, -səl, -sīl), *adj.* = fusil[2].

fu|sil|ier or **fu|sil|eer** (fyü′zə lir′), *n.* **1** (formerly), a soldier armed with a light flintlock musket. **2** a soldier belonging to any of several British regiments who were formerly so armed. The members of these regiments wear tall fur hats called *busbies.* [< French *fusilier* < *fusil* musket, fusil[1]]

fu|sil|lade (fyü′zə lād′), *n., v.,* **-lad|ed, -lad|ing. —*n.*** **1** a rapid or continuous discharge of many firearms at the same time. **2** *Figurative.* something that resembles a fusillade: *The reporters greeted the mayor with a fusillade of questions.*
—*v.t.* to attack or shoot down by a fusillade.
[< French *fusillade* < *fusiller* to shoot < *fusil* musket, fusil[1]]

fu|sil|ly (fyü′zə lē), *adj. Heraldry.* covered with elongated lozenges. [< Old French *fuselé* < *fusel* a fusilly bearing, ultimately < Latin *fūsus* spindle]

fus|ing disk (fyü′zing), a flat, circular plate of steel mounted on an axis and rotated very rapidly to cause fusion, used for cutting metal bars.

fusing point, = melting point.

fu|sion (fyü′zhən), *n.* **1** the action or process of fusing; melting; melting together: *Bronze is made by the fusion of copper and tin.* **2** the action or process of blending; union; coalition: *A third party was formed by the fusion of independent Republicans and Democrats. The fusion of many nationalities is found in the United States. She is a fusion of the dreamer and the doer.* **3** a fused mass. **4** the action or process of combining two atomic nuclei to produce a nucleus of greater mass; nuclear fusion. The fusion of the atomic nuclei of elements of low atomic number requires a very high temperature and releases tremendous amounts of energy. Fusion is used to produce the reaction in the hydrogen bomb. **5** a blend of jazz and other popular musical styles; crossover: *Fusion enjoys a crucial advantage over mainstream and avant-garde jazz: it "crosses over" a wide range of formats* (Rolling Stone). [< Latin *fūsiō, -ōnis* < *fundere* pour, melt] **—fu′sion|a|ble,** *adj.*

fu|sion|al (fyü′zhə nəl), *adj.* having to do with fusion: *Fusional language expresses relations . . . by adding prefixes or suffixes that cannot stand alone* (Alfred L. Kroeber).

fusion bomb, = hydrogen bomb.

fu|sion|ism (fyü′zhə niz əm), *n.* the principle of supporting a coalition between political parties.

fu|sion|ist (fyü′zhə nist), *n., adj.* **—*n.*** a person who advocates or supports a coalition of political parties or factions.
—*adj.* advocating or supporting a coalition of political parties or factions.

fusion reaction, *Nuclear Physics.* a reaction in which fusion takes place.

fu|so|bac|te|ri|um (fyü′zō bak tir′ē əm), *n., pl.* **-te|ri|a** (-tir′ē ə). any of a group of rod-shaped bacteria that are parasites of man and animals. [< New Latin *Fusobacterium* the genus name < Latin *fūsus* spindle + New Latin *bacterium* bacterium]

fuss (fus), *n., v.* **—*n.*** **1** much bother about small matters; useless talk and worry; attention given to something not worth it: *She got under weigh with very little fuss* (Richard Henry Dana). *The king and queen meant to treat this fuss about the national finance as a terrible bore* (H. G. Wells). **SYN:** ado, commotion. **2** a person who fusses too much.
—*v.i.* to make a fuss; be in a bustle; busy oneself restlessly about trifles: *She fussed about with her work in a nervous manner.*
—*v.t.* to put into a fuss; make nervous or worried; bother: *Don't fuss me while I'm doing this experiment.* **SYN:** agitate, worry.
[origin uncertain; probably imitative] **—fuss′er,** *n.*

fuss and feathers, *Informal.* an excessive display; fuss: *We give you comfortable shelter at a moderate price, with an absolute minimum of fuss and feathers* (New Yorker).

fuss-budg|et (fus′buj′it), *n. Informal.* a fussy or fidgety person.

fuss-budg|et|y (fus′buj′ə tē), *adj. Informal.* characterized by fussiness; very fussy or particular.

fus|sock (fus′ək), *n. British Dialect.* a large, fat woman.

fuss|pot (fus′pot′), *n. Informal.* a fussy person.

fuss|y (fus′ē), *adj.,* **fuss|i|er, fuss|i|est. 1a** hard to please; hard to satisfy; very particular: *A sick person is likely to be fussy about his food; nothing suits him.* **b** moving and acting with fuss; habitually busy about trifles. **2** much trimmed; elaborately made: *Some girls like fussy dresses with many bows and much lace.* **3** full of details; requiring much care: *a fussy job.* **—fuss′i|ly,** *adv.* **—fuss′i|ness,** *n.*

fust (fust), *n., v. Obsolete or Dialect.* **—*n.*** **1** mold. **2** a moldy smell.
—*v.i.* **1** to become moldy or musty. **2** to smell moldy or musty.
[< Old French *fust* wine cask < Latin *fustis* cudgel, stick of wood]

fus|ta|nel|la (fus′tə nel′ə), *n.* a kind of skirt or kilt of white cotton or linen, very full and stiffened, worn by men in modern Greece. [< Italian *fustanella* (apparently diminutive) < *fustagno* fustian]

fus|ter|ic (fus′tər ik), *n.* the yellow dye obtained from fustet.

fus|tet (fus′tit), *n.* **1** a European smoke tree from which a yellow coloring matter is extracted. **2** the wood of this tree. [< French *fustet,* ultimately < Arabic *fustuq;* see etym. under **fustic**]

Pronunciation Key: hat, āge, cãre, fär; let, ēqual, tėrm; it, īce; hot, ōpen, ôrder; oil, out; cup, pu̇t, rüle; child; long; thin; ᴛʜen; zh, measure; ə represents **a** in about, **e** in taken, **i** in pencil, **o** in lemon, **u** in circus.

fus|tian (fus′chən), *n., adj.* **—*n.*** **1** a coarse, heavy cloth made of cotton and flax. Fustian was used for clothing in Europe throughout the Middle Ages. **2** a thick cotton cloth like corduroy or velveteen. It is twilled and has a short pile or nap. **3** *Figurative.* speech or writing made up of pompous, high-sounding words and phrases: *Between fustian in expression and bathos in sentiment* (William Hazlitt). **SYN:** bombast.
—*adj.* **1** made of fustian. **2** *Figurative.* pompous and high-sounding; inflated; bombastic: *Then comes he out with his fustian eloquence* (Robert Greene). **3** worthless.
[< Old French *fustaigne* < Medieval Latin *fustaneum* < Latin *fūstis* stick of wood]

fus|tic (fus′tik), *n.* **1** the wood of a large tropical American tree that yields a yellow dye. **2** the tree itself. It belongs to the mulberry family. **3** the dye. **4** any one of various other dyewoods. [< French *fustoc* < Spanish < Arabic *fustuq*, probably < Greek *pistákē* pistachio (tree)]

fus|ti|gate (fus′tə gāt), *v.t.*, **-gat|ed, -gat|ing.** to cudgel; beat (now only in humorously pedantic use). [< Late Latin *fūstīgāre* (with English *-ate*[1]) cudgel (to death) < Latin *fūstis* stick, staff] **—fus′ti|ga′tion,** *n.* **—fus′ti|ga′tor,** *n.*

fust|i|ly (fus′tə lē), *adv.* in a fusty manner.

fust|i|ness (fus′tē nis), *n.* **1** the state or quality of being fusty; a bad smell from moldiness. **2** = moldiness.

fust|y (fus′tē), *adj.*, **fust|i|er, fust|i|est.** **1** having a stale smell; musty; moldy; stuffy: *the fusty atmosphere of an unventilated sickroom.* **2** *Figurative.* too old-fashioned; out-of-date: *We regarded him as a fusty old man who was always reading fusty old books.* [< *fust* + *-y*[1]]

fu|su|line (fyü′zə līn, -lin), *n.* any one of a group of fossil foraminifera that provide an extensive geological record of late Paleozoic time; fusulinid. [< New Latin *Fusulina* the genus name < Latin *fūsus* spindle]

fu|su|lin|id (fyü zə lī′nid), *n.* = fusuline.

fu|su|ma (fü′sü mä), *n.* a sliding screen, covered with paper, used to separate room from room in a Japanese house. [< Japanese *fusuma*]

fut., future.

fu|ta or **fu|tah** (fü′tä), *n.* a kind of loincloth resembling a kilt, worn by men in Arab countries. [< Arabic *fūṭta*]

fu|tharc or **fu|thark** (fü′thärk), *n.* the runic alphabet. [< *f, u, th, a, r, c,* the first six letters]

fu|thorc or **fu|thork** (fü′thôrk), *n.* = futharc.

fu|tile (fyü′təl), *adj.* **1** not successful; useless; vain: *He fell down after making futile attempts to keep his balance. Many people have made futile attempts to swim from England to France. An instance of futile classicism ... is the conventional spelling of the English language* (Thorstein Veblen). **SYN:** ineffectual, profitless. See syn. under **vain.** **2** not important; trifling: *futile tasks.* **SYN:** frivolous, idle, trivial. **3** occupied with things of no value or importance; addicted to trifling; lacking in purpose: *a futile life.* [< Latin *fūtilis* pouring easily; worthless < *fundere* to pour] **—fu′tile|ly,** *adv.* **—fu′tile|ness,** *n.*

fu|til|i|tar|i|an (fyü til′ə tãr′ē ən), *adj.*, n. **—*adj.*** devoted to futility or futile pursuits.
—*n.* a person who is devoted to futility. [< *futility*, humorously patterned on *utilitarian*]

fu|til|i|tar|i|an|ism (fyü til′ə tãr′ē ə niz′əm), *n.* futilitarian policy.

fu|til|i|ty (fyü til′ə tē), *n., pl.* **-ties.** **1** uselessness; ineffectiveness: *The chief characteristic of her existence seemed to be a tragic futility* (Arnold Bennett). **2** unimportance; frivolity. **3** something futile, such as an action or event.

fu|ton (fü′ton), *n.* a padded Japanese floor mattress, used as a bed. [< Japanese *futon*]

fut|tock (fut′ək), *n.* one of the curved timbers that form part of a compound rib or frame in the framework of a ship's hull. [perhaps contraction of *foot hook*]

futtock plates, iron plates near the top of a lower mast or the top of a topmast, having holes into which the upper ends of the futtock shrouds are hooked.

futtock shrouds, the shrouds, or iron rods, in bigger ships, connecting the lower rigging with the rigging of the tops, set up to an iron band on the lower mast.

Fu|tu|ra (fyü chůr′ə), *n.* a style of sans-serif printing type.

fu|tu|ram|a (fyü′chə ram′ə, -rä′mə), *n.* a display of things to come; a projection of the future: *a futurama of life in the 21st century.* [< *Futurama*, an exhibit at the 1939 New York World's Fair < *future* + (pano)*rama*]

fu|tu|ram|ic (fyü′chə ram′ik, -rä′mik), *adj.* of or like a futurama: *New York teachers will go in for some futuramic training with the course in radioisotopes* (Time).

fu|ture (fyü′chər), *n., adj.* **—*n.*** **1a** time to come; time to be: *You cannot change the past, but you can do better in the future. Oh blindness to the future! Kindly given* (Alexander Pope). **b** the events of the future; what is to come; what will be: *We hope your future will be happy.* **2** a chance of success or prosperity: *a young man with a future.* **3a** the verb form with *shall* or *will* that expresses something taking place in time to come. "I shall go" or "I will go" is the future of "I go." **b** = future tense. *Abbr:* fut. **4** a memo kept by a newspaper editor of a future event or a lead on a story.
—*adj.* **1** that is to come; that will be; coming: *future events, a future hope. We hope your future years will be happy.* **SYN:** prospective. **2** *Grammar.* of or expressing the future tense. In English, the future is usually expressed by the auxiliary verbs *shall* or *will*, as in *We shall go tomorrow. They will go tomorrow.* **3** occurring or experienced after death: *our future state.*
futures, a commodities or stocks bought or sold to be received or delivered at a future date: *Cotton futures at New York fell to $1.50 a bale* (Wall Street Journal). **b** a buying or selling of commodities or stocks for future delivery: *On futures, the Committee are, on the whole, inclined to look with a lenient eye, and do not see their way to compelling merchants by law to deliver everything they sell, and to acquire possession of it before they sell it* (The Nation).
[< Old French *future* future, learned borrowing from Latin *futūrus*, future participle of *esse* to be] **—fu′ture|ly,** *adv.* **—fu′ture|ness,** *n.*

future estate, a freehold that is owned but cannot be enjoyed until some time in the future, such as property that is to go to a wife after her husband's death.

fu|ture|less (fyü′chər lis), *adj.* without a future; having no future before one; without prospects.

future life, life after death.

future perfect, *Grammar.* **1** designating or belonging to a tense that expresses or indicates past time with respect to some point in future time, as in *Next month he will have left.* **2** such a tense. **3** a verb form or phrase in such a tense.

fu|tures, *n.pl.* See under **future.**

future shock, a state of stress and disorientation brought on by too quick a succession of changes in society: *What brings on future shock ... is a rate of social change that has become so fast as to be impossible for most human beings to assimilate* (Time).

future tense, 1 the tense that expresses action taking place in the future, constructed in English with *shall* or *will.* **2** a verb form or phrase in this tense.

fu|tur|i|an (fyü chůr′ē ən, -tůr′-; -tyůr′-), *n.* an individual of the future; person belonging to posterity.

fu|tur|ism (fyü′chə riz əm), *n.* **1** a movement in art that originated and flourished in Italy in the early 1900's, characterized by attempts to express the sensation of movement and growth in objects and not the objects' appearance at some particular moment. The themes and forms are an attempt to attune the fine arts to an age of violence, machines, and speed. **2** a similar tendency in literature and music.

fu|tur|ist (fyü′chər ist), *n., adj.* **—*n.*** **1** a person who favors futurism. **2** = futurologist.
—*adj.* **1** following the principles of futurism. **2** like futurism.

fu|tur|is|tic (fyü′chə ris′tik), *adj.* **1** of or like futurism: *The whole picture is a swirl of swift, circular movement, and there is something almost futuristic in the violent stylizations* (New Yorker). **2** of or for the future; not traditional; advanced; radical in design. **—fu′tur|is′ti|cal|ly,** *adv.*

fu|tu|ri|ty (fyü tůr′ə tē, -tyůr′-), *n., pl.* **-ties.** **1** the future: *These events were still in the womb of futurity* (Scott). **2** a future state or event. **3** the quality or fact of being future. **4** = futurity race.

futurity race, a race to be run long after the entries have been made, especially a race for two-year-old horses nominated as starters before their birth.

futurity stakes, 1 the stakes run for in a futurity race. **2** = futurity race.

fu|tur|o|log|i|cal (fyü′chə rə loj′ə kəl), *adj.* of or having to do with futurology.

fu|tur|ol|o|gist (fyü′chə rol′ə jist), *n.* a person who studies or makes forecasts about the future developments in science and technology and their effect upon society.

fu|tur|ol|o|gy (fyü′chə rol′ə jē), *n.* the art or practice of making forecasts about future developments in science and technology and their effect upon society.

futz (futs), *v.i.* Usually, **futz around.** *U.S. Slang.* to putter around; waste time; dawdle.

fuze (fyüz), *n., v.*, **fuzed, fuz|ing.** **—*n.*** **1** a slow-burning wick or other device used to set off a shell, bomb, or blast of gunpowder. Also, **fuse.** **2** = fuse[1] (def. 1). **—*v.i., v.t.*** to furnish with a fuze. [variant of *fuse*[1]]

fu|zee (fyü zē′), *n.* = fusee.

fuzz (fuz), *n., v.* **—*n.*** **1** loose, light fibers or hair; fine down: *Caterpillars and peaches are covered with fuzz.* **2** a mass of such matter. **3a** *Slang.* a policeman or detective: *... he learned to call a cop a "fuzz," a lawyer a "patch"* (Robert Lewis Taylor). **b** the police: *The militant young ... now expect the worst from the fuzz* (Manchester Guardian Weekly). **—*v.t.*** to make fuzzy; cover with fine fibers or particles. **—*v.i.*** **1** to become fuzzy. **2** to fly out in fuzz. [perhaps imitative]

fuzz|ball (fuz′bôl′), *n.* **1** = puffball. **2** *U.S. Slang.* a derogatory term for a police officer: *"Ten years ago, police were pigs," said Moell, who works at criminal hearings. "Now they are fuzzballs ... "* (Fort Wayne Journal-Gazette).

fuzz|box (fuz′boks′), *n.* an attachment on an electric guitar that gives a fuzzy quality to the sound.

fuzz|bust|er (fuz′bus′tər), *n. U.S. Slang.* an electronic device to detect a police radar unit monitoring the speed of vehicles on a street or highway. [< *fuzz* policeman + *buster* (because it destroys the effectiveness of police radar)]

fuzz|i|fy (fuz′ə fī), *v.t.*, **-fied, -fy|ing.** *Informal.* to muddle or confuse. **—fuzz′i|fi|ca′tion,** *n.*

fuzz|i|ly (fuz′ə lē), *adv.* in a fuzzy manner; so as to appear curled or frizzed.

fuzz|i|ness (fuz′ē nis), *n.* the quality of being fuzzy.

fuzz|y (fuz′ē), *adj.*, **fuzz|i|er, fuzz|i|est.** **1** of fuzz: *the fuzzy down of a chick.* **2** like fuzz: *fuzzy chin whiskers.* **3** covered with fuzz: *a fuzzy little chick.* **4** blurred; indistinct: *This photograph is too fuzzy for me to identify the people in it. The legal situation is deliberately fuzzy* (Time).

fuzzy logic, a form of logic which tries to take into account ill-defined or vague terms such as "very," "somewhat," and "mostly": *Fuzzy logic ... avoids the abrupt changes that might result from the either-or, all-or-nothing judgments inherent in classical logic* (Kevin McKean and Tom Dworetzky). **—fuzzy logician.**

fuzzy set, *Mathematics.* a set whose elements converge or overlap with those of other sets: *a class or classes (that is, fuzzy sets) that do not possess sharply defined boundaries* (Science).

Fuzz|y-Wuzz|y (fuz′ē wuz′ē), *n., pl.* **Fuzz|y-Wuzzies.** *British Slang.* a Sudanese soldier, especially a warrior opposing the Anglo-Egyptian forces in the 1800's.

f.v., on the back of the page (Latin, *folio verso*).

fwd., forward.

FWPCA (no periods), Federal Water Pollution Control Administration.

-fy, *suffix forming verbs chiefly from adjectives.* **1** make ___ cause to be ___ : *Simplify = to make simple.* **2** become ___ Solidify = *to become solid.* **3** other meanings, as in *modify, qualify.* [< French *-fier* < Latin *-ficāre* < *-ficus* making < *facere* do, make]

FY (no periods), fiscal year.

FYI (no periods), for your information.

fyke (fīk), *n.* a bag-shaped net used for catching fish, especially shad. [American English < Dutch *fuik* a bow net]

fyl|fot (fil′fot), *n* = swastika. [< earlier phrase *fill foot*, as a design for filling the foot of a painted window]

fyrd (fẽrd), *n.* the military forces of England before the Norman Conquest. [Old English *fyrd, ferd* army < *faran* to go]

F.Z.S., Fellow of the Zoological Society (London).

Gg

***G**[1] or **g** (jē), *n., pl.* **G's** or **Gs, g's** or **gs. 1** the seventh letter of the English alphabet. There are two *g*'s in *egg*. **2** any sound represented by this letter. **3** (used as a symbol for) the seventh (of an actual or possible series): *row G in a theater*. **4** a grade in some schools that stands for *good*, usually equivalent to a B. **5** *Music.* **a** the fifth tone of the scale of C major. **b** a symbol representing this tone. **c** a key, string, etc., that produces this tone. **d** the scale or key that has G as its keynote: *a concerto in G*. **6** *Physics.* acceleration of gravity (about 32 feet per second per second, the unit of force exerted on a body by the pull of gravity. The force exerted on a body at rest at the earth's surface is 1 G). An accelerating body may experience a force of several Gs. *As the sled decelerated,* [*he*] *was subjected to more than 40 times the pull of gravity (40 gs); his normal weight of 168½lbs. momentarily shot up to 6,740 lbs.* (Time).

G in the treble clef

***G**[1]
definition 5b

G in the bass clef

G[2] (jē), *n., pl.* **G's.** anything shaped like the letter G.
G[3] (jē), *n., pl.* **G's** or **Gs.** *U.S. Slang.* a thousand dollars: *His phone bill alone last year must have come to twenty Gs* (Maclean's). [< *g* (rand) a thousand dollars]
g (no period), an abbreviation or symbol for the following:
1 *Electricity.* conductance.
2 *Psychology.* general intelligence.
3 giga-.
4 gilbert or gilberts.
5 grain.
6 gram or grams.
g., an abbreviation or symbol for the following:
1 gauge.
2 gender.
3 genitive.
4 goalie.
5 grain.
6 gram or grams.
7 gravity.
8 guide.
9 *British.* guinea or guineas.
G (no period), an abbreviation for the following:
1 *Electricity.* conductance.
2 General (a symbol used in the United States for motion pictures recommended to the general public).
3 German.
4 the universal constant of gravitation (6.67 $\times 10^{-8}$ dyne cm.^{2} gram^{-2}).
5 guanine.
6 specific gravity.
G., an abbreviation for the following:
1 gauge.
2 German.
3 *British.* guinea or guineas.
4 gulf.
g.a., general average.
Ga (gä), *n.* **1** a member of a people in West Africa, speaking a Sudanese language. **2** the language.
Ga (no period), gallium (chemical element).
Ga., **1** Gallic. **2** Georgia.
GA (no periods), **1** General American: *For convenience the following abbreviations will be used for the major speech areas: ... GA for General American* (C. K. Thomas). **2** Georgia (with postal Zip code).
G.A., **1** general agent. **2** General Assembly. **3** *Insurance.* general average.
gab[1] (gab), *v.,* **gabbed, gab|bing,** *n. Informal.* —*v. i.* to talk too much; chatter; gabble. SYN: prattle. —*n.* idle talk; chatter; gabble.
gift of (the) gab. See under **gift.**
[probably < *gabble*]—**gab'ber,** *n.*
gab[2] (gab), *n. Scottish.* the mouth. [variant of *gob*[3]]
gab[3] (gab), *n.* (in machines) a hook, especially on the rod transmitting the motion of an eccentric. [origin uncertain]
GABA (gab'ə), *n.* an amino acid occurring in the central nervous system, associated with the transmission of nerve impulses. [< *G*(amma)-*A*(mino)-*B*(utyric) *A*(cid)]
gab|ar|dine (gab'ər dēn, gab'ər dēn'), *n.* **1** a closely woven, woolen, cotton, or rayon cloth used for raincoats, suits, dresses, slacks, and other garments. Gabardine has small, diagonal ribs on its surface. **2** = gaberdine (def. 1). [variant of *gaberdine*]
gab|bai (gä bī'), *n.* **1** an official in a synagogue. **2** the treasurer of a synagogue. [< Hebrew *gabbai*]
gab|bart (gab'ərt), *n. Dialect.* a barge; lighter. [< French *gabare* < Portuguese *gabarra*]
gab|ble (gab'əl), *v.,* **-bled, -bling,** *n.* —*v. i.* **1** to talk rapidly and noisily with little or no meaning; jabber: *We were nervous of Mr. Cookeem, feeling we had not the correct entrée or visa as he waited while customers were served and he and they gabbled in some unrecognizable tongue* (London Times). **2** to make rapid, meaningless sounds; cackle: *the noisy geese that gabbled o'er the pool* (Oliver Goldsmith). —*v. t.* to utter rapidly with little or no meaning; babble: *At times the words were so gabbled that it was impossible to catch them* (Manchester Guardian).
—*n.* **1** rapid and noisy talk with little or no meaning; babble: *Richards' ... dialogue carries conviction, particularly the snatched gabbles of a man whose thoughts are elsewhere being overheard on the telephone* (Punch). **2** rapid, meaningless noises made by animals: *The turtles stun one with their yawning gabble* (Leigh Hunt).
[probably imitative]—**gab'bler,** *n.*
gab|bro (gab'rō), *n., pl.* **-bros.** any one of a group of granular igneous rocks, greenish-gray to black, containing pyroxene and triclinic feldspar. [< Italian *gabbro,* perhaps dialectal alteration of Latin *glaber, -brī* smooth]
gab|bro|ic (gə brō'ik), *adj.* of the nature of gabbro: *gabbroic rocks.*
gab|broid (gab'roid), *adj.* resembling gabbro.
gab|by (gab'ē), *adj.,* **-bi|er, -bi|est.** *Informal.* very talkative; garrulous. —**gab'bi|ness,** *n.*
ga|belle (gə bel'), *n.* a tax, especially a tax on salt in France before the Revolution of 1789. [< Middle French *gabelle* < Italian *gabella* < Arabic (*al-*) *qabāla* (the) impost]
gab|er|dine (gab'ər dēn, gab'ər dēn'), *n.* **1** a man's long, loose, outer garment or cloak. Gaberdines were worn in the Middle Ages. *You ... spit upon my Jewish gaberdine* (Shakespeare). **2** = gabardine (def. 1). [< Spanish *gabardina* < Middle French *gaverdine, galvardine;* origin uncertain]
gab|er|lun|zie (gab'ər lun'zē, -lün'yē), *n. Scottish.* **1** a wallet or pouch carried by beggars for receiving contributions. **2** a strolling beggar; mendicant: *barking at a gaberlunzie* (Scott). [origin uncertain]
gab|fest (gab'fest'), *n. Especially U.S. Informal.* an informal talk; a chat.
ga|bi|on (gā'bē ən), *n.* **1** a cylinder of wicker filled with earth, formerly used as a military defense. In modern warfare, sandbags are used in place of gabions. **2** a metal cylinder filled with stones, used in building dams, supporting bridge foundations, or the like.
[< Middle French *gabion* < Italian *gabbione* large cage < *gabbia* cage < Latin *cavea* cage, cave < *cavus* hollow]
ga|bi|on|ade (gā'bē ə nād'), *n.* a work made of or with gabions. [< French *gabionnade* < Middle French *gabion* gabion]
ga|bi|oned (gā'bē ənd), *adj.* having gabions or something resembling gabions; protected with or as with gabions.
***ga|ble** (gā'bəl), *n., v.,* **-bled, -bling.** —*n.* **1** the end of a ridged roof, with the three-cornered piece of wall that it covers: *Thatched were the roofs, with dormer windows; and gables projecting Over the basement below protected and shaded the doorway* (Longfellow). **2** an end wall with a gable. **3** a triangular ornament or canopy over a door, window, or the like.
—*v. t.* to make (a roof) end with a gable or gables.
—*v. i.* to form gables.
[< Old French *gable,* perhaps < Scandinavian (compare Old Icelandic *gafl*)]—**ga'ble|like',** *adj.*

***gable**
definition 1

ga|bled (gā'bəld), *adj.* built with a gable or gables; having or forming gables: *the gabled ends of a house.*
gable end, an end wall with a gable.
gable roof, a roof that forms a gable at one or both ends.
gable window, 1 a window built in or under a gable. **2** a window with its upper part shaped like a gable.
gab line, *U.S.* a telephone service that provides a person with another party or parties to have a conversation for a fixed charge per minute; talk line: *He might have ... the opportunity to listen in on 976-MEET, ... or almost any of the other so-called gab lines* (Philadelphia Inquirer).
Gab|o|nese (gab'ə nēz', -nēs'), *adj., n., pl.* **-nese.** —*adj.* of Gabon, its people, or their languages. —*n.* a native of Gabon, a country in Central Africa.
Ga|boon viper (gə bün'), a poisonous African snake related to the puff adder, often growing as long as six feet. [< *Gabon,* a country in Central Africa, where it is found]
Ga|bri|el (gā'brē əl), *n.* the archangel who acts as God's messenger in Jewish, Christian, and Moslem tradition. He is the angel of comfort and good news and of the Annunciation (in the Bible, Daniel 8-9; Luke 1:26-38).
ga|by (gā'bē), *n., pl.* **-bies.** *Informal.* a fool; simpleton. [origin uncertain]
GAC (no periods), General Advisory Committee (of the Atomic Energy Commission).
gad[1] (gad), *v.,* **gad|ded, gad|ding,** *n.* —*v. i.* **1** to move about restlessly or idly; go about looking for pleasure or excitement; ramble; wander: *She was out all day gadding about town. He was always gadding up and down the world* (William Camden). SYN: roam. **2** to straggle in growth: *Now gads the wild vine o'er the pathless ascent* (Wordsworth).
—*n.* **1** the act of gadding. **2** = gadabout.
on (or **upon**) **the gad,** *Informal.* on the move; going about: *He is always on the gad.*
[probably back formation < *gadling* wanderer, Old English *gædeling* (originally) companion (in arms)]—**gad'der,** *n.*
gad[2] (gad), *n., v.,* **gad|ded, gad|ding.** —*n.* **1** = goad. **2** a pointed mining tool for breaking up rock, coal, or ore.
—*v.t.* **1** = goad. **2** to break up (rock or ore) with a gad.
[< Scandinavian (compare Old Icelandic *gaddr* spike)]
Gad[1] or **gad**[3] (gad), *n., interj.* a variant of *God,* used as a mild oath or exclamation: *By gad, sir ... I never will give you a shilling* (Thackeray).
Gad[2] (gad), *n.* **1** the seventh son of Jacob (in the Bible, Genesis 30:9-11). **2** the tribe of Israel that claimed to be descended from him. **3** a Hebrew prophet and chronicler at the court of David (in the Bible, II Samuel 24:11-19).
gad|a|bout (gad'ə bout'), *n., adj. Informal.* —*n.* a person who moves about restlessly or goes about looking for pleasure or excitement; person fond of going from place to place.
—*adj.* given to gadding; rambling; wandering: *Gadabout Northerners are moving south in increasing numbers* (Newsweek).
Gad|a|rene (gad'ə rēn'), *adj.* **1** of or having to do with Gadara, a town in ancient Palestine. **2** characteristic of the Gadarene swine, described in the Bible (Matthew 8:28-32) as having rushed into the sea to their death after devils were cast

***G**[1]
definition 1

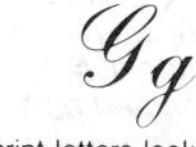
Script letters look like examples of fine penmanship. They appear in many formal uses, such as invitations to social functions.

Handwritten letters, both manuscript or printed (left) and cursive (right), are easy for children to read and to write.

Gg *Gg*
Roman letters have *serifs* (finishing strokes) adapted from the way Roman stonecutters carved their letters. This is *Times Roman* type.

Gg *Gg*
Sans-serif letters are often called *gothic.* They have lines of even width and no serifs. This type face is called *Helvetica.*

Gg *Gg*
Between roman and gothic, some letters have thick and thin lines with slight flares that suggest serifs. This type face is *Optima.*

G
Computer letters can be sensed by machines either from their shapes or from the magnetic ink with which they are printed.

into them by Jesus; violently hasty; reckless; impetuous.

gad|di (gə dē′), *n.* = gadi.

gad|fly (gad′flī′), *n., pl.* **-flies.** **1** a fly that bites cattle, horses, and other animals, and sucks their blood. The horsefly and botfly are two kinds. **2** *Figurative.* a person who constantly irritates or annoys, especially to bring about changes in the way things are: *Adams stood for free speech, free press, free debate. He spoke so often, so raspingly, and tried to introduce so many petitions representing so many thousands of people, that he became perhaps the most colossal gadfly in political history* (Newsweek). [< *gad*[2] + *fly*]

gadg|et (gaj′it), *n. Informal.* **1** a small mechanical device or contrivance; any ingenious device: *A cookie cutter and a can opener are kitchen gadgets. They have installed decent cooking ranges and gas, and the men have already made themselves all sorts of handy little labour-saving gadgets* (Rudyard Kipling). **2** a trivial thing; knicknack. [perhaps < French *gâchette* piece of mechanism (diminutive) < *gâche* staple of a lock]

gadg|et|ar|y (gaj′ə ter′ē), *adj.* having to do with gadgets: *a gadgetary industry.*

gadg|et|ed (gaj′ə tid), *adj.* furnished with gadgets: *a gadgeted car.*

gadg|e|teer (gaj′ə tir′), *n. Informal.* a person who makes or is fond of gadgets.

gadg|e|teer|ing (gaj′ə tir′ing), *n.* the invention, design, or making of gadgets.

gadg|et|ize (gaj′ə tīz), *v.,* **-ized, -iz|ing.** *—v.t.* to provide, treat, or fill with gadgets: *Instead of stressing technology and gadgetizing the course, he emphasizes principles.*
—v.i. to deal or play with gadgets.

gadg|et|ry (gaj′ə trē), *n.* **1** gadgets: *the latest electronic gadgetry.* **2** the making or using of gadgets: *mildly important with those who equate gadgetry and science* (Saturday Review).

gadg|et|y (gaj′ə tē), *adj.* **1** full of gadgets: *bigger and more gadgety boats.* **2** that tends to have gadgets: *"What the public wants" is being translated into the flashy, the gadgety, the spectacular* (Atlantic).

Ga|dhel|ic (gə del′ik, -dē′lik), *adj., n.* = Goidelic.

ga|di (gə dē′), *n.* **1** the cushioned throne of an Indian ruler. **2** the position or state of being the ruler. Also, **gaddi.** [< Marathi *gādī,* Hindustani *gaddī* (literally) cushion]

ga|did (gā′did), *n.* a gadoid fish. [< New Latin *Gadidae* the cod family < *Gadus;* see etym. under **gadoid**]

gad|i|nine (gad′ə nēn, -nin), *n.* a ptomaine formed in the putrefaction of fish and the bacterial cultures of human feces. [< New Latin *Gadus* (see etym. under **gadoid**) + English *-ine*]

Gad|ite (gad′īt), *n.* a member of the tribe of Gad.

ga|doid (gā′doid), *adj., n.* *—adj.* of or having to do with a family of marine food fishes having long, tapering bodies, large mouths, and soft fins: *The cod, haddock, and hake are gadoid fishes.*
—n. a gadoid fish.
[< New Latin *Gadus* the codfish genus (< Greek *gádos* a fish) + English *-oid*]

gad|o|lin|ite (gad′ə lə nīt), *n.* a silicate of iron, yttrium, cerium, and other rare-earth metals, found in black or brown crystals; ytterbite. [< Johann *Gadolin,* 1760-1852, a Finnish chemist, who discovered it]

*__gad|o|lin|i|um__ (gad′ə lin′ē əm), *n.* a magnetic, metallic chemical element. Gadolinium occurs in combination with certain minerals and is one of the rare-earth metals. [< New Latin *gadolinium* < Johann *Gadolin;* see etym. under **gadolinite**]

***gadolinium**

symbol	atomic number	atomic weight	oxidation state
Gd	64	157.25	3

ga|droon (gə drün′), *n.* one of a set of rounded beadings or flutings used as decoration, especially on molding or silverware. Also, **godroon.** [< French *godron* < Middle French *goderon* < Old French *godet* < Middle Dutch *codde* cylindrical piece of wood]

ga|drooned (gə dründ′), *adj.* ornamented with gadroons.

ga|droon|ing (gə drü′ning), *n.* ornamentation consisting of gadroons.

gad|wall (gad′wôl), *n., pl.* **-walls** or (*collectively*) **-wall.** a rare river duck of the Northern Hemisphere and Africa, with mottled, grayish-brown plumage. [origin unknown]

Gad|zooks (gad′züks′), *interj. Archaic.* a word used as a mild oath or exclamation.

gae[1] (gā), *v.i.,* **gaed** (gād), **gaen** (gān), **gae|ing.** *Scottish.* **1** to go. **2** (of animals) to graze.

gae[2] (gā), *v. Scottish.* gave.

Gae|a (jē′ə), *n. Greek Mythology.* the earth goddess whose children were the Titans; Terra. Also, **Gaia.**

gaek|ke|brev (gā′kə bref′), *n.* a kind of Danish valentine in which the sender writes an original rhyme and signs his name in a code of dots. If the recipient guesses the name, he rewards her with an Easter egg. [< Danish *gaekkebrev* joking letter]

Gaek|war (gīk′wär), *n.* the title of the ruler of Baroda, a former native state in western India. Also, **Gaikwar.** [< Marathi *Gāekwār* (literally) cowherd]

Gael (gāl), *n.* **1** a Scottish Highlander. **2** a Celt born or living in Scotland or the Isle of Man, or in Ireland. [< Scottish Gaelic *Gaidheal* < Old Irish *Góidhot*]

Gael., Gaelic.

Gael|dom (gāl′dəm), *n.* **1** the land of the Gaels. **2** Gaelic culture or civilization.

Gael|ic (gā′lik), *adj., n.* *—adj.* **1** of or having to do with the Gaels of the Scottish Highlands or their language. **2** = Irish. **3** = Goidelic.
—n. **1** the Celtic language of the Highlanders of Scotland; Erse. **2** = Irish. **3** = Goidelic.

Gaelic football, a form of football played in Ireland by two teams of fifteen players each, in which dribbling, kicking, and punching the ball is allowed but not throwing or running with it.

Gael|i|cise or **gael|i|cise** (gā′lə sīz), *v.t.,* **-cised, -cis|ing.** *Especially British.* Gaelicize.

Gael|i|cist (gā′lə sist), *n.* **1** a student of Gaelic. **2** a person who advocates the study and use of Gaelic.

Gael|i|cize or **gael|i|cize** (gā′lə sīz), *v.t.* **-cized, -ciz|ing.** to make Gaelic in form, pronunciation, habits, customs, or character: *Gaelicized names.*

gaff[1] (gaf), *n., v.* **1** a strong hook on a handle or a barbed spear for pulling large fish out of the water. **2** a spar or pole used to extend the upper edge of some fore-and-aft sails. **3** a sharp metal spur fastened to the leg of a gamecock. **4** something uncomfortable or hard to take.
—v.t. to hook or pull (a fish) out of the water with a gaff.
bring to gaff, to draw (a hooked fish) with the line within reach of the gaff: *When a fish is beat and is being brought to gaff, much caution is necessary* (Quarterly Review).
stand the gaff, *Slang.* to hold up well under strain or punishment of any kind: *It was dead white of you to stand the gaff and keep your mouth shut* (R. D. Paine).
throw a gaff into, *U.S. Slang.* to break up; disrupt: *The new increase threw a complete gaff into my tax picture.*
[< Old French *gaffe* boat hook, probably < a Celtic word]

gaff[2] (gaf), *n., v.* *—n.* **1** *British Slang.* a cheap theater or music hall. **2** *Slang.* a carnival performer who does freakish acts.
—v.t. Slang. to arrange to cheat or deceive; rig: *The roulette wheels were all gaffed.*
[earlier, a fair; origin unknown]

gaff[3] (gaf), *n. British Slang.* foolish talk.
blow the gaff, to let out a secret; reveal a plot; give convicting evidence: *So long as Nazism remained a German disease the world could shrug it off; the annexation of Austria blew the gaff* (Manchester Guardian Weekly).

gaffe (gaf), *n. French.* a blunder; faux pas: *Knowing nothing, you might easily make a bad gaffe* (Compton Mackenzie).

gaff|er[1] (gaf′ər), *n.* a person who gaffs fish.

gaf|fer[2] (gaf′ər), *n.* **1** an old man. **2** *British.* the foreman of a gang of workmen. **3** a person in charge of a shop of glass blowers: *For the last 10 years he has been a gaffer . . . fashioning vases, bowls, or candlesticks out of red-hot crystal glass* (Wall Street Journal). **4** a person who supervises the control and proper lighting of motion-picture or television sets and actors. [alteration of *godfather*]

gaf|fle (gaf′əl), *n.* **1** a lever for bending a crossbow. **2** an artificial spur for a gamecock. [probably < Dutch *gaffel*]

gaff-rigged (gaf′rigd′), *adj.* having one or more sails extended at the top by gaffs: *a gaff-rigged schooner.*

gaff-top|sail (gaf′top′sāl′; *Nautical* gaf′top′səl), *n.* a topsail set above a gaff by which its foot is extended.

gaff-topsail catfish, a marine catfish of Atlantic shore waters.

gag (gag), *n., v.,* **gagged, gag|ging.** *—n.* **1** something put in a person's mouth to keep him from talking or crying out: *Untie his feet; pull out his gag; he will chocke else* (Fletcher and Shirley). **2** *Figurative.* anything used to silence a person or persons; a restraint or hindrance to free speech: *Imagine, if you can, his indignant eloquence had England offered to put a gag upon his lips* (Wendell Phillips). **3** *Informal.* an amusing remark or trick; joke: *The clown's gags made the audience laugh.* **4** *U.S., Figurative.* (in a legislative body) a law or ruling designed to restrict or prevent discussion on a particular sublect. **5** a device for keeping the jaws open during surgery.
—v.t. **1** to stop up the mouth of with a gag; keep from talking or crying out with a gag: *The robbers tied the watchman's arms and gagged his mouth.* **2** *Figurative.* to force to keep silent; restrain or hinder from free speech: *The time was not yet come when eloquence was to be gagged* (Macaulay). SYN: silence, suppress. **3** to cause to choke or strain in an effort to vomit. **4** to put a device into (the mouth) to keep the jaws open. **5** to choke up (a valve or other opening). **6** *Informal.* to introduce additional gags into (a performance or script).
—v.i. **1** to strain in an effort to vomit; retch: *Badtasting medicines made him gag.* **2** *Informal.* **a** to tell or make gags; joke: *Even when he quit gagging, his audience sometimes kept on laughing* (Time). **b** to introduce additional gags in a performance or script. **c** to make fun of a person's readiness to believe by telling false stories.
[probably imitative] *—***gag′ger,** *n.*

ga|ga (gä′gä), *adj. Slang.* **1** silly; foolish; doting: *The conventional pictures of a young man and a young woman looking gaga at each other* (Sunday Express). **2** very enthusiastic; crazy: *They were thoroughly gaga about the show.*

ga|ga|ku (gä gä′kü), *n.* the classical ceremonial or court music of Japan. [< Japanese *gagaku* < *ga* graceful + *gaku* music]

gag|bit (gag′bit′), *n.* a powerful bit for breaking horses.

gag cartoon, a humorous cartoon consisting of a single picture with or without a gag line: *The gag cartoon is primarily a literary and not a visual trick* (Harper's).

gage[1] (gāj), *n., v.,* **gaged, gag|ing.** *—n.* **1** a pledge to fight; challenge: *The knight threw down his gauntlet as a gage of battle.* **2** a glove or other object thrown down as a challenge to combat. **3** a pledge; security: *The knight left a diamond as a gage for the horse and armor he borrowed.*
—v.t. Archaic. to offer as a pledge or security; wager: *I'll gage my silver wand of state* (Scott).
[< Old French *gage,* gauge < Germanic (compare Gothic *ga-wadjon, wadi* pledge). See etym. of doublet **wage.**]

gage[2] (gāj), *n.* any of several varieties of plum, especially the greengage. [short for *greengage*]

gage[3] (gāj), *n., v.t.,* **gaged, gag|ing.** = gauge.

gage block, = gauge block.

G-a|gent (jē′ā′jənt), *n.,* or **G agent,** a nerve gas: *They are often called G-agents because the original compounds came from Germany* (Science News Letter).

gag|gle (gag′əl), *v.,* **-gled, -gling,** *n.* *—v.i.* to make the cry of a goose; cackle.
—n. **1** the cry of a goose; cackle. **2** a flock of geese. **3** *U.S. Informal, Figurative.* a group of persons or things: *A gaggle of glorious young ladies* (New Yorker). [probably imitative]

gag|gy (gag′ē), *adj.,* **-gi|er, -gi|est.** *U.S.* having many, especially too many, gags or jokes.

gag law = gag rule.

gag line, a brief humorous statement or text, such as the caption of a cartoon, or a punch line.

gag|man (gag′man′), *n., pl.* **-men.** **1** a person who makes up jokes or comic situations for comedians. **2** = comedian.

gag order, *U.S.* a court order prohibiting reporting or public comments on a case before a court of law: *The Supreme Court . . . refused to interfere with a judge's gag order on lawyers and other participants in a criminal trial* (C. Herman Pritchett).

gag rule, *U.S.* a rule or law for preventing or restricting debate of a particular subject, especially in a legislative body; gag law.

gag|ster (gag′stər), *n. U.S. Informal.* **1** a person fond of gags and jokes; humorist. **2** an inventor of gags.

gag strip, a comic strip without a continuous story.

gag|writ|er (gag′rī′tər), *n.* = gagman (def. 1).

gahn|ite (gä′nīt), *n.* a dark-colored mineral containing aluminum and zinc in octahedral crystals. *Formula:* $ZnAl_2O_4$ [< Johann G. *Gahn,* 1745-1818, a Swedish chemist]

Gai|a (gā′ə, gī′-), *n.* = Gaea.

Gaia hypothesis or **theory,** the theory that the planet earth is the core of a unified living system which regulates itself much like an organism does: *It is the Gaia theory's insistence that the earth is a self-controlling, whole system, not a conglomeration of disconnected parts and discontinuous functions, that has drawn the interests of scientists* (Lawrence E. Joseph).

gai|e|ty (gā′ə tē), *n., pl.* **-ties.** **1** the state or quality of being gay; cheerful liveliness; merriment; joyousness: *Her gaiety helped to make the party a success.* SYN: jollity, joviality. **2** gay entertainment: *the gaieties of a country fair.* **SYN**: merrymaking. **3** a bright appearance; finery; showiness: *gaiety of dress.* Also, **gayety.** [< Middle French *gaieté* < Old French *gai* gay]

gai|jin (gī′jin), *n., pl.* **-jin.** *Japanese.* a foreigner; alien.

Gaik|war (gīk′wär), *n.* = Gaekwar.

gail|lar|di|a (gā lär′dē ə), *n.* **1** any one of a group of hardy plants of the composite family whose showy flowers have purple centers and red or yellow rays, often with purple bases. **2** any one of their large daisylike flowers. [< New Latin *Gaillardia* the genus name < *Gaillard* de Marentonneau, a French botanist]

gai|ly (gā′lē), *adv.* **1** in a gay manner; happily; merrily; cheerfully: *Addison wrote his papers as gaily as if he was going out for a holiday* (Thackeray). **SYN**: joyously, festively. **2** brightly; showily: *She was gaily dressed in a colorful costume.* Also, **gayly.**

gain¹ (gān), *v., n.* — ***v.t.*** to come to have; get; obtain; secure: *The king gained possession of more lands.* **SYN**: acquire, earn. **2** to get as an increase, addition, advantage, or profit: *How much do I gain by that? What does he have to gain?* **3** to be the victor in; win: *The stronger army gained the battle.* **4** to get to; arrive at; reach: *The swimmer gained the shore.* **SYN**: attain. **5** to run too fast by; make an increase of: *The clock gains a minute a day.*
— ***v.i.*** **1** to make a gain or profit; benefit: *He has obviously gained by the change.* **2** to make progress; become better; advance; improve: *The sick child is gaining and will soon be well.* **3** to improve in effect.
— ***n.*** **1** the act of gaining or getting anything: *The haughty man was blinded by the gain of success.* **2** what one gains; increase, addition, or advantage; profit: *a gradual gain in speed, a gain of ten percent over last year's earnings.* **SYN**: benefit, acquisition. **3** getting wealth: *Greed is love of gain.* **4** *Electronics.* **a** amplification of a signal, expressed as the ratio of the output of an amplifier to its input: *a voltage gain, a power gain.* **b** amplification of the volume of sound or brightness of a picture, as in a radio or phonograph or in a television set.
gain ground. See under **ground.**
gain on (or **upon**), to come closer to; get nearer to: *One boat is gaining on another.*
gain over, to persuade to join one's side: *He did not try to gain him over by smooth representations* (J. H. Newman).
gains, profits, earnings, or winnings: *They [the merchants] see gains of 5 to 10 per cent this spring* (Newsweek).
[< Middle French *gagner,* Old French *gaaignier* < Germanic (compare Old High German *weidenen* to hunt, pasture)]

gain² (gān), *adj.* **1** straight; direct: *Roundabout is sometimes gainest* (Midlands proverb). **2** convenient; advantageous; suitable. **3** handy; skillful. **4** active; graceful. [< Scandinavian (compare Old Icelandic *gegn*)]

gain³ (gān), *n., v.* — ***n.*** a groove or notch in a board; mortise.
— ***v.t.*** **1** to cut a gain or gains in. **2** to unite or fasten (boards) by a gain or gains. [origin uncertain]

gain|a|ble (gā′nə bəl), *adj.* that can be gained: *Greatness in art ... is not a teachable or gainable thing, but the expression of the mind of a God-made great man* (John Ruskin).

gaine (gān), *n.* **1** the lower part of a sculptured figure, below the bust or the head, having the appearance of a quadrangular sheath enclosing the body and contracting toward the feet. **2** a kind of pedestal of the same general shape, for holding a statuette or other art object. [< French *gaine* < Latin *vāgīna* sheath]

gain|er (gā′nər), *n.* **1** a person or thing that gains: *Wilt thou, after the expense of so much money, be now a gainer?* (Shakespeare). **2** a fancy dive in which the diver faces the water and turns a back somersault in the air.

gain|ful (gān′fəl), *adj.* bringing in money or advantage; profitable: *a gainful occupation.* **SYN**: lucrative, remunerative. — **gain′ful|ly,** *adv.* — **gain′ful|ness,** *n.*

gain|giv|ing (gān′giv′ing), *n.* a feeling of anxiety; misgiving. [Old English *gegn-* against + *giving*]

gain|ings (gā′ningz), *n.pl.* **1** something gained, especially through labor, diligence, or enterprise. **2** profits.

gain|less (gān′lis), *adj.* unprofitable; useless. — **gain′less|ness,** *n.*

gain|li|ness (gān′lē nis), *n.* gracefulness; shapeliness.

gain|ly (gān′lē), *adj.* **1** graceful; shapely; comely: *a gainly lad.* **2** *Dialect.* proper; suitable; becoming. [< *gain*² + *-ly*¹]

gains (gānz), *n.pl.* See under **gain¹.**

gain|said (gān′sed′), *v.* a past tense and a past participle of **gainsay**: *Most people gainsaid Columbus' contention that the earth is round. The champion's athletic ability cannot be gainsaid.*

gain|say (*v.* gān′sā′; *n.* gān′sā′), *v.,* **-said** or **-sayed, -say|ing,** *n.* — ***v.t.*** **1** to deny; contradict; dispute: *There is no gainsaying the fact that society rests upon the sanctity of the law, and that when ordinary citizens come to disdain it we all suffer an evil of consequence* (Wall Street Journal). **2** to act against; oppose. **SYN**: hinder.
— ***n.*** denial; contradiction: *He ... was the umpire in all disputes ... giving his decisions with an air and tone admitting of no gainsay or appeal* (Washington Irving).
[Old English *gegn-* against + *say*] — **gain′say′er,** *n.*

gainst or **'gainst** (genst; *British also* gānst), *prep., conj. Archaic.* against.

gair|ish (gãr′ish), *adj.* = garish.

gait** (gāt), *n., v.* — ***n. **1a** the kind of steps used in going along: *He has a lame gait because of an injured foot.* **b** *Figurative: Our great writers generally settle down to a stately but monotonous gait* (Leslie Stephen). **2** any one of the various manners of stepping or running of horses, such as the gallop, trot, or pace.
— ***v.t.*** **1** to train (a horse) to a certain gait. **2** to walk (a dog, horse, or farm animal) so as to judge the gait and appearance: *[He] devoted considerable time to appraising the boxer, the Pekingese and the English cocker spaniel. He gaited them a second time* (New York Times).
gang one's gait, *Scottish.* to go or take one's own way in a matter: *Put up your pipes and gang your gait* (Scott).
[Scottish spelling of *gate*³ way, road]

***gait**
definition 2

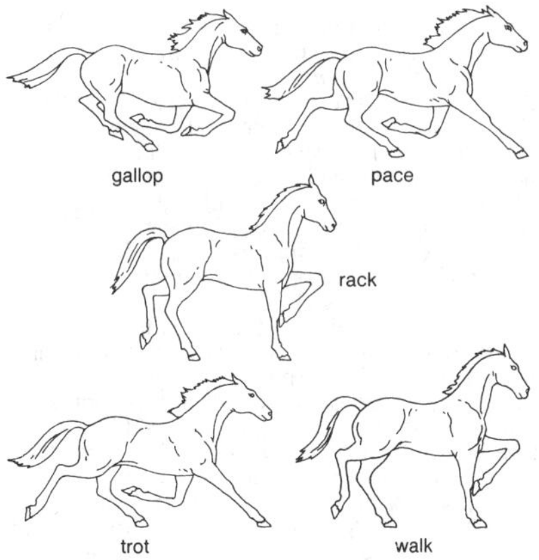

gai|ta (gī′tä), *n.* a musical instrument resembling a bagpipe, originally from Galicia, Spain. [< Spanish *gaita*]

gait|ed (gā′tid), *adj.* trained when to use different gaits; having a certain gait: *a gaited horse, heavy-gaited oxen.*

***gai|ter** (gā′tər), *n.* **1** an outer covering for the leg below the knee or for the ankle, made usually of cloth or leather, for outdoor wear. **2** a cloth or leather shoe usually with an elastic strip in each side. **3** an overshoe with a cloth top [< French *guêtre* < Middle French *guietre*]

***gaiter**
definition 2

gai|tered (gā′tərd), *adj.* wearing a gaiter or gaiters.

Gait|skell|ite (gāt′skə līt), *n.* a supporter of the policies of Hugh Gaitskell, 1906-1963, former leader of the British Labour Party, 1955-1963.

gaize (gāz), *n.* a fine-grained, micaceous sandstone found in the Mesozoic rocks of France and England. [< French *gaize*]

gal¹ (gal), *n. U.S. Informal.* a girl.

gal² (gal), *n.* a unit for measuring the acceleration of gravity, equal to one centimeter per second per second: *Since the variation of gravity from place to place helps geodesists determine the earth's shape and size, the Navy measures gals in order to pin down the location of remote islands too far from the mainland to be located accurately any other way* (Life). [< *Galileo,* 1564-1642, an Italian astronomer and physicist]

gal., gallon or gallons.

Gal., Galatians (a book of the New Testament).

ga|la (gā′lə, gal′ə, gä′lə), *adj., n.* — ***adj.*** of festivity; festive: *gala dress. In our family, Christmas and the Fourth of July are ga′la days.*
— ***n.*** **1** a festive occasion; festival. **SYN**: fete. **2** *Obsolete.* festivity; rejoicing. [< French *gala* gala attire < Italian < Old French *gale* merriment < *galer* make merry; origin uncertain]

ga|la|bi|a or **ga|la|bi|yah** (gä lä′bē ə), *n.* a flowing robe worn chiefly by Moslems in Egypt and many parts of Africa. [< Arabic *jallābīya*]

galact-, *combining form.* the form of **galacto-** before vowels, as in *galactose.*

ga|lac|ta|gogue (gə lak′tə gôg, -gog), *adj., n.* — ***adj.*** that stimulates or increases the flow of milk.
— ***n.*** an agent or medicine that stimulates or increases the flow of milk.
[< Greek *gála, -aktos* milk + *-agōgós* a leading < *ágein* lead]

ga|lac|tan (gə lak′tan), *n.* a polysaccharide found in plants during the germinative period, yielding galactose on hydrolysis.

ga|lac|tic (gə lak′tik), *adj.* **1** of or having to do with the Milky Way or with other galaxies: *It is because of the shape of the galaxy that we see the Milky Way, which is the concentration of stars as we look out toward the edge, in the galactic plane* (Science News Letter). **2** of milk; obtained from milk; lactic. [< Late Latin *galacticus* milky < Greek *gála, -aktos* milk]

galactic center, the theoretical gravitational center of our galaxy, located in the direction of Sagittarius.

galactic circle, the great circle inclined at an angle of 62 degrees to the celestial equator, whose plane nearly coincides with the central line of the Milky Way.

galactic cluster, a diffuse group of stars usually numbering over a hundred, such as the Pleiades: *The galactic clusters we observe are all within 20,000 light years from the sun, but they are doubtless as abundant in other parts of the spiral arms of our galaxy as they are in our own neighborhood* (Robert H. Baker).

galactic equator, = galactic circle.

galactic latitude, the angular distance of a celestial body from the galactic plane.

galactic longitude, the angular distance of a celestial body measured eastward along the galactic circle from its intersection with the celestial equator.

galactic nebula, any nebula that belongs to our galaxy, classified as either bright or dark depending on its illumination.

galactic noise, the radio noise emanating from the stars and interstellar matter of our galaxy; cosmic noise.

galactic plane, the plane of the galactic circle.

galactic poles, the two opposite points on the celestial sphere, 90 degrees from the galactic circle.

galacto-, *combining form.* milk: *Galactophorous = carrying milk.* Also, **galact-** before vowels. [< Greek *gála, -aktos*]

ga|lac|to|lip|id (gə lak′tō lip′id, -lī′pid), *n.* **1** a compound of galactose and a fatty substance found in tissues. **2** = cerebroside. [< *galacto*(se) + *lipid*]

gal|ac|tom|e|ter (gal′ak tom′ə tər), *n.* an instrument for determining the richness of milk by its specific gravity.

gal|ac|toph|o|rous (gal′ak tof′ər əs), *adj.* carrying or producing milk.

ga|lac|to|poi|e|sis (gə lak′tō poi ē′sis), *n.* the flow or production of milk. [< *galacto-* + Greek *poíēsis* a making < *poieîn* make]

ga|lac|to|poi|et|ic (gə lak′tō poi et′ik), *adj., n.* — ***adj.*** **1** having to do with galactopoiesis. **2** that stimulates or increases the flow of milk.
— ***n.*** an agent that stimulates or increases the flow of milk.

ga|lac|tor|rhe|a or **ga|lac|tor|rhoe|a** (gə lak′tə rē′ə), *n.* an excessive flow of milk. [< *galacto-* + Greek *rhoiā* a flowing]

ga|lac|tos|a|mine (gə lak tōs′ə mēn′, -tōs am′in), *n.* an amino sugar derived from galactose, found in large amounts in mucopolysaccharide. *Formula:* $C_6H_{13}O_5N$

ga|lac|tose (gə lak′tōs), *n.* a white, crystalline monosaccharide, found in combined form in lactose, pectins, gums, and certain other substances. *Formula:* $C_6H_{12}O_6$ [< *galact-* + *-ose*]

ga|lac|to|se|mi|a (gə lak′tə sē′mē ə), *n.* a disease of infants caused by the lack of the enzyme

Pronunciation Key: hat, āge, cãre, fär; let, ēqual, tėrm; it, īce; hot, ōpen, ôrder; oil, out; cup, pu̇t, rüle; child; long; thin; ᴛʜen; zh, measure; ə represents **a** in about, **e** in taken, **i** in pencil, **o** in lemon, **u** in circus.

necessary for the digestion of galactose: *For years, pediatricians have been baffled by galactosemia, an inherited blood disease which menaces thousands of newborn babies* (Newsweek). [< *galactos*(e) + *-emia*]

ga|lac|to|se|mic (gə lak′tə sē′mik), *adj.* affected or caused by galactosemia.

ga|lac|to|si|dase (gə lak′tə sī′dās), *n.* an enzyme that breaks down galactosides by hydrolysis. [< *galactosid*(e) + *-ase*]

ga|lac|to|side (gə lak′tə sīd), *n.* galactose in chemical combination with a nonsugar, a form in which it is sometimes found in nature: *Digitonin is a galactoside.*

ga|lac|to|zy|mase (gə lak′tə zī′mās), *n.* an enzyme system that ferments galactose, found in some strains of yeast.

ga|lac|tu|ron|ic acid (gə lak′tyù ron′ik), an aldehyde acid, formed by the hydrolysis of pectins, and related to galactose. *Formula:* $C_6H_{10}O_7$

ga|la|go (gə lā′gō), *n., pl.* **-gos.** any one of several species of small, furry, nocturnal primates of the African forests; bush baby; ojam. They move very nimbly on trees and have a childlike cry. [< New Latin *Galago* the genus name < a native name]

ga|lah (gə lä′), *n.* **1** a grayish cockatoo of Australia with a pinkish-red breast: *It was a magical experience to see a "mob" of galahs rise screeching from the khaki-colored plains* (New Yorker). **2** *Australian Slang.* a fool; nincompoop. [< a native name]

Gal|a|had (gal′ə had), *n.* **1 Sir,** *Arthurian Legend.* the son of Lancelot and Elaine, the noblest and purest knight of King Arthur's Round Table. He sought and finally saw the Holy Grail. **2** a man as noble and pure as Galahad.

ga|lan|gin (gə lan′jin), *n.* a yellow, crystalline substance allied to flavone, found in galingale. *Formula:* $C_{15}H_{10}O_5$ [< *galang*(ale), variant of *galingale,* + *-in*]

ga|lant (gȧ län′), *adj. French.* light; elegant: ... *new galant, Mozart-like trends* (Harper's).

ga|lan|te|rie (gȧ län tə rē′), *n. French.* gallantry.

gal|an|tine (gal′ən tēn), *n.* **1** veal, chicken, or other white, boned meat, tied up, boiled, and then served cold in its own jelly. **2** *Obsolete.* a kind of sauce usually for fish. [< Old French *galantine*]

ga|lan|ty show (gə lan′tē), a pantomime in which the shadows of tiny puppets are projected on a wall or screen. [perhaps < Italian *galanti,* plural of *galante* gallant]

gal|a|te|a (gal′ə tē′ə), *n.* a strong, striped cotton cloth used for clothing. [< Her Majesty's Ship *Galatea,* a British man-of-war in the 1800's (because the cloth was used in children's sailor suits)]

Gal|a|te|a (gal′ə tē′ə), *n. Greek Legend.* **1** an ivory statue of a maiden, carved by Pygmalion. He fell in love with the statue, and Aphrodite gave it life. **2** a Nereid who was loved by Polyphemus but gave herself to Acis. Polyphemus crushed Acis with a rock and his blood was changed into a stream.

Ga|la|tian (gə lā′shən), *adj., n.* **—adj.** of or having to do with the ancient country of Galatia, in Asia Minor, or its people.
—n. a native or inhabitant of Galatia.

Ga|la|tians (gə lā′shənz), *n. pl.* (*sing. in use*). a book of the New Testament. It is a letter written by the Apostle Paul to the Christians of Galatia. *Abbr:* Gal.

gal|a|vant (gal′ə vant), *v.i.* = gallivant.

ga|lax (gā′laks), *n.* a stemless, evergreen herb of the southeastern United States, having clusters of small, white flowers and shiny leaves. [American English < New Latin *Galax* the genus name < Greek *gála* milk (because of its white flower clusters)]

gal|ax|i|id (gal ak′sē id), *adj.* of or belonging to a family of scaleless, salmonlike fishes of New Zealand, Australia, and South America. [< New Latin *Galaxiidae* the family name < Greek *galaxías* a kind of fish, probably the lamprey]

Gal|ax|y (gal′ək sē), *n.* = Milky Way. [< Late Latin *galaxias* (in Latin, milkstone) < Greek *galaxías* < *gála, -aktos* milk]

***gal|ax|y** (gal′ək sē), *n., pl.* **-ax|ies. 1** a group of billions of stars forming one system. A galaxy is a system or aggregate of stars, cosmic dust, and gas, held together by gravitation, often thousands of light-years in diameter. The earth and the sun are part of one galaxy. Each galaxy holds many solar systems, and there are billions of galaxies in the universe. Many galaxies outside our own can be seen with a telescope. **2** *Figurative.* a brilliant or splendid group, especially of beautiful women or distinguished persons: *The queen was followed by a galaxy of brave knights and fair ladies.* **3** *Figurative.* any impressive group of things: *the new galaxy of hydrogen weapons* (Newsweek). *The place has a galaxy of mausoleums* (New Yorker). [< *Galaxy*]

***galaxy**
definition 1

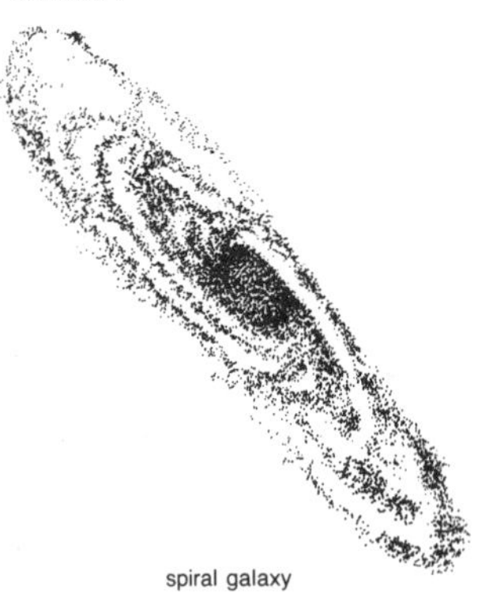

spiral galaxy

gal|ba|num (gal′bə nəm), *n.* a gum resin with an odd, disagreeable odor, obtained from various Asiatic plants of the parsley family, used in medicine as a stimulant and expectorant and in the arts as a plaster. [< Latin *galbanum* < Greek *chalbánē* < Hebrew *ḥelbənā*]

Gal|brai|thi|an (gal brā′thē ən), *adj., n.* **—adj.** of or having to do with John Kenneth Galbraith, born 1908, an American economist, or his ideas and theories: ... *the Galbraithian diagnosis of private affluence within public squalor* (Manchester Guardian Weekly).
—n. a follower or supporter of Galbraith or his theories.

gale[1] (gāl), *n.* **1** a very strong wind: *The weather report was of strong winds over the North Sea, rising at times to gale force* (Household). **2** *Meteorology.* any wind with a velocity of 32 to 63 miles per hour. **3** a breeze: *Wanton gales along the valleys play* (William Collins). **4** *Figurative.* a noisy outburst: *gales of laughter.* **5** *U.S. Informal, Figurative.* a mood of high spirits: *On the way, Wint was in a great gale, his spirits high, his hopes bouyant, his gaiety of heart overflowing* (Southern Literary Messenger). [earlier *gaile;* origin uncertain]

gale[2] (gāl), *n.* a shrub of the same family as the wax myrtle. It has fragrant leaves and grows in marshy places. [Old English *gagel*]

gale[3] (gāl), *n. British.* a periodical payment of rent, interest, etc. [perhaps < *gavel*[2]]

ga|le|a (gā′lē ə), *n., pl.* **-le|ae** (-lē ē), *Biology.* a structure or part that looks like a helmet, such as the upper part of a labiate flower, the membrane covering the jaws of certain insects, and a horny cap on the head of a bird. [< Latin *galea* helmet]

ga|le|ate (gā′lē āt), *adj.* **1** helmet-shaped. **2** having or covered with a galea. [< Latin *galeātus* < *galea* helmet]

ga|le|at|ed (gā′lē ā′tid), *adj.* = galeate.

ga|lee|ny (gə lē′nē), *n., pl.* **-nies.** = guinea fowl. [< Spanish *gallina* (*morisca*) (Moorish) hen]

ga|le|i|form (gə lē′ə fôrm), *adj.* helmet-shaped. [< Latin *galea* helmet + English *-form*]

Ga|len (gā′lən), *n.* a physician. [< Claudius *Galenus,* a Greek physician and writer of the 100's A.D.]

ga|le|na (gə lē′nə), *n.* a metallic, gray mineral containing lead and sulfur. It is the chief source of lead. *Formula:* PbS [< Latin *galēna* lead ore]

ga|len|ic (gə len′ik, -lē′nik), *adj.* **1** of or containing galena. **2** of or having to do with galenics: *galenic pharmacists.*

Ga|len|ic (gə len′ik, -lē′nik), *adj.* of or having to do with Galen, his medical principles, or his method of treating diseases.

ga|len|i|cal (gə len′ə kəl, -lē′nə-), *n.* a medicine or drug derived from materials of vegetable origin: *The business is principally concerned in the extraction of galenicals for the pharmaceutical industry* (London Times). [< *Galen*(ism) + *-ical*]

Ga|len|i|cal (gə len′ə kel, -lē′nə-), *adj.* = Galenic.

ga|len|ics (gə len′iks, -lē′niks), *n.* **1** the art or science of preparing galenicals. **2** the art or science dealing with the optimum form of drugs and medicines.

Ga|len|ism (gā′lə niz əm), *n.* the practice of preparing medicines from natural rather than synthetic sources. [< *Galen* + *-ism*]

ga|le|nite (gə lē′nīt), *n.* = galena.

ga|lè|re (gȧ ler′), *n. French.* a set or circle of people; coterie; clique.

ga|le|rie (gȧl rē′), *n. French.* gallery.

ga|le|ro (gä le′rō), *n. Italian.* the broad-brimmed red hat of cardinals: *The new cardinals will take the galero with them, but will never wear it. Ceremonially, it is used only once—when it rests on the cardinal's bier* (Time).

ga|let (gā′lit), *n.* = fossa[2]. [alteration of Greek *galeē* weasel]

ga|lette (gə let′), *n.* a broad, thin cake of bread or pastry. [< French *galette*]

gale warning, a display along a seacoast or lakeshore predicting the approach of a gale. A gale warning usually consists of two red pennants during the day or of a white light over a red light at night.

gal Friday, = girl Friday.

Ga|li|bi (gə lē′bē), *n., pl.* **-bis** or **-bi. 1** a member of an Indian people of French Guiana. **2** their Cariban language.

Ga|li|cian (gə lish′ən), *adj., n.* **—adj. 1** of or having to do with Galicia, a region in central Europe, its people, or their language. **2** of or having to do with Galicia, a region in northwestern Spain, its people, or their language.
—n. 1 a native or inhabitant of Galicia. **2** a Portuguese dialect spoken in Spanish Galicia.

gal|i|dic|tis (gal′ə dik′tis), *n.* a carnivorous quadruped of Madagascar, of the same family as the civet. [< New Latin *Galidictis* the genus name < Greek *galideús* young weasel + *íktis* yellow-breasted marten]

Gal|i|le|an[1] or **Gal|i|lae|an** (gal′ə lē′ən), *adj., n.* **—adj.** of or having to do with Galilee, the northernmost division of Palestine in the time of Christ, or its people.
—n. 1 a person born or living in Galilee. **2** a Christian.
the Galilean, Jesus: *The pagans called Christ the Galilean or the Nazarene because Jesus lived as a boy in Nazareth, a town which is in Galilee.*
[< *Galile*(e) + *-an*]

Gal|i|le|an[2] (gal′ə lē′ən), *adj.* of Galileo (1564-1642) or discovered by him: *the Galilean satellites of Jupiter.* [< *Galile*(o) + *-an*]

gal|i|lee (gal′ə lē), *n.* a porch or chapel at the west entrance of some medieval English churches. [< Old French *galilee* < Medieval Latin *Galilea* < Latin, a Roman province < Greek *Galilaîā* (because it was regarded as less sacred, as was Galilee by the Jews)]

gal|i|ma|ti|as (gal′ə mā′shē əs, -mat′ē-), *n.* confused or meaningless talk; gibberish; nonsense. [< Middle French *galimatias;* origin uncertain]

gal|in|gale (gal′ən gāl), *n.* **1** the aromatic rootstock of various Chinese and East Indian plants of the ginger family, formerly used in medicine and cooking. **2** a southern English sedge with an aromatic tuberous root. [< Old French *galingal* < Arabic *khalanjān,* probably < Chinese]

gal|i|ot (gal′ē ət), *n.* **1** a small, fast galley moved with oars and sails that was used until the end of the 1700's. **2** a heavy, single-masted, Dutch cargo or fishing boat. **3** *Obsolete.* an ancient Roman galley. Also, **galliot.** [< Old French *galiote* (diminutive) < *galie, galee;* see etym. under **galley**]

gal|i|pot (gal′ə pot), *n.* a kind of turpentine or resin that hardens on the stems of certain pines. Also, **gallipot.** [< French *galipot,* perhaps < Middle French *garipot* kind of pine tree]

gall[1] (gôl), *n.* **1** a bitter yellow, brown, or greenish liquid secreted by the liver and stored in the gall bladder; bile. **2** = gall bladder. **3** *Figurative.* anything very bitter or harsh. **4** *Figurative.* bitterness; hate: *Neither envy nor gall hath entered me upon this controversy* (Milton). **5** *Informal, Figurative.* too great boldness; impudence. SYN: effrontery.
dip one's pen in gall. See under **pen**[1].
[Old English *gealla*]

gall[2] (gôl), *v., n.* **—v.t. 1** to make sore by rubbing: *The rough strap galled the horse's skin.* SYN: chafe. **2** to damage the surface of by rubbing: *I am loath to gall a new-healed wound* (Shakespeare). **3** *Figurative.* to annoy; irritate: *The child was galled by being scolded so much. The sarcasms of the king soon galled the sensitive temper of the poet* (Voltaire). **4** *Figurative.* to harass: *Where bowmen might in ambush wait ... To gall an entering foe* (Scott).
—v.i. 1 to become sore by rubbing: *Thou'lt gall between the tongue and the teeth, with fretting* (Ben Jonson). **2** *Figurative.* to make galling or irritating remarks. [< noun]
—n. 1 a local sore on the skin caused by rubbing, especially one on a horse's back. **2** *Figurative.* a cause of annoyance or irritation: *They have left a perpetual gall in the minds of that people* (Edmund Spenser). **3** *Southern U.S.* a spot where the soil has been washed away or is unfit for planting. **4** a bare spot; blemish; flaw produced by rubbing.
[Old English *gealla* painful swelling, influenced by Old French *galle,* and *galer* chafe]

gall[3] (gôl), *n.* a lump or ball that forms usually on the leaves, stems, or roots of plants where they have been injured by insects, fungi, or parasitic bacteria. The galls of oak trees contain tannin, used in making ink and tanning leather, and in medicine. [< Old French *galle* < Latin *galla* oak apple, gallnut]

Gal|la (gal′ə), *n.* **1** *pl.* **-las** or **-la.** a member of one of the Hamitic tribes of Ethiopia and other countries of northeast Africa. **2** their language.

gal|lant (*adj. 1-4* gal′ənt, *5, 6* gə lant′, gal′ənt; *n.* gal′ənt, gə lant′; *v.* gə lant′), *adj., n., v.* —***adj.*** **1** noble in spirit or in conduct: *King Arthur was a gallant knight.* **SYN**: valiant. **2** brave and high-spirited; heroic: *a gallant antagonist.* **3** grand; fine; stately: *A ship with all its sails spread is a gallant sight.* **4** gay; showy: *Our garden was made gallant with tulips.* **5** very polite and attentive to women: *The general attended her himself to the street door, saying everything gallant as they went down stairs* (Jane Austen). **SYN**: chivalrous, courtly. **6** = amorous.
—***n.*** **1** a spirited or courageous man. **2** a man who is very polite and attentive to women: *How few nowadays use the word 'gallant' to describe a lady's man* (Matthew Arnold). **3** a man who wears showy, stylish clothes: *Gallants gambled away a fortune at a sitting* (John R. Green). **4** a lover; paramour.
—***v.t.*** **1** to pay court to (a woman). **2** to be an escort to; escort: *The little black steamer ... sometimes gallanting a tall ship in and out* (Hawthorne).
—***v.i.*** to be a gallant; flirt.
play the gallant, to flirt; pay court (to): *She waited for him to play the gallant, but he showed no interest.*
[< Old French *galant,* properly present participle of *galer* make a show; origin uncertain] —**gal′lant|ly,** *adv.* —**gal′lant|ness,** *n.*

gal|lant|ry (gal′ən trē), *n., pl.* **-ries. 1** noble spirit or conduct; bravery; dashing courage: *the gallantry of a soldier. Gallantry is part of the great heritage—part of the strength—of the American people* (New Yorker). **SYN**: heroism. **2** great politeness and attention to women: *Conscience has no more to do with gallantry than it has with politics* (Richard Brinsley Sheridan). **SYN**: chivalry. **3** a gallant act or speech; courtesy: *The prince ... said a thousand gallantries* (John Dryden). **4** *Archaic.* gay appearance; showy display; magnificence.

gal|late (gal′āt), *n.* a salt of gallic acid.

***gall bladder,** a sac attached to the liver, in which excess gall or bile is stored until needed.

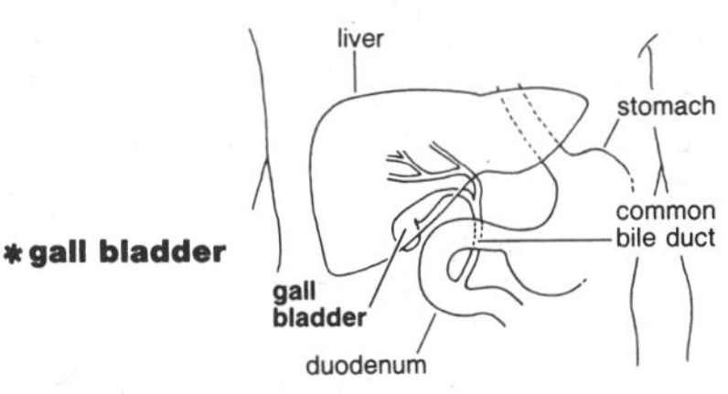

***gall bladder**

gal|le|ass (gal′ē as), *n.* a heavy, low-built warship larger than a galley and moved by both oars and sails. It was used on the Mediterranean in the 1500's and 1600's. Also, **galliass.** [< Middle French *galéace* < Italian *galeazza* < *galea* galley < Medieval Latin < Medieval Greek]

gal|le|gan (gəl yā′gən), *adj.* of or having to do with Spanish Galicia; Galician: *gallegan dishes.*

gal|le|go (gəl yā′gō), *n.* a native or inhabitant of Spanish Galicia; Galician. [< Spanish *gallego*]

gal|le|in (gal′ē ən), *n.* brownish-red or greenish-yellow crystals obtained by heating pyrogallol and phthalic anhydride, used as a dye or as an indicator. *Formula:* $C_{20}H_{12}O_7$ [< *gal*(lic acid) + (phtha)*lein*]

***gal|le|on** (gal′ē ən, gal′yən), *n.* **1** a large, high, fighting ship, usually with three or four decks and square sails, first used by the Italians in the 1400's as an armed merchant ship, and later developed by Henry VIII into a strictly fighting ship: *three very great galleons, or Spanish ships from the south seas* (Daniel Defoe). **2** an early Italian armed merchant ship. [< Old French *galion* (< *galie*), and < Spanish *galeón* < *galea* galley, both < Medieval Greek]

***galleon** definition 1

gal|ler|ied (gal′ər ēd, gal′rēd), *adj.* having a gallery or galleries: *galleried balconies.*

gal|ler|y (gal′ər ē, gal′rē), *n., pl.* **-ler|ies,** *v.,* **-ler|ied, -ler|y|ing.** —***n.*** **1a** a long, narrow room or passage, often with windows along one side; hall: *The armor is displayed in a long gallery outside the bedrooms.* **b** a long, narrow platform or open passage projecting from the wall of a building. **2** a balcony looking down into a large hall or room, especially in a church, theater, or hall, with seats or room for part of the audience: *Visitors to the Senate sit in the gallery and are not permitted on the floor when it is in session.* **3** the highest balcony in a theater. It contains the cheapest seats. *We had to pay $3 apiece for gallery seats* (Time). **4** the people who sit there: *The gallery is a critical judge of acting.* **5** a group of people watching or listening; spectators; audience. **6** a covered walk or porch. **SYN**: loggia. **7a** *Mining.* an underground passage; level or drift. **b** a covered underground passage in a fortification. **8** a passageway made or dug by an animal. **9a** a building or room used to show collections of pictures, statues, or other works of art: *The pictures were hung on the walls of the gallery.* **SYN**: museum. **b** a commercial company or firm which specializes in the sale of works of art. **10** a collection of works of art. **11** a room or building used for a particular purpose, such as taking photographs or practicing shooting. **12** a balcony or platform at the stern or quarters of older ships. **13** a jewelry setting with perforated sides.
—***v.t.*** to provide with a gallery; arrange like a gallery.
—***v.i.*** to make an underground passage.
play to the gallery, to try to get the praise or favor of the common people by doing or saying what will please them: *We hope that ... advocates will be courteous to judges, to opposing counsel, and to witnesses, and not play to the gallery* (Law Times).
[< Old French *galerie* < Italian *galleria* < Medieval Latin *galeria;* origin uncertain] —**gal′ler|y|less,** *adj.*

gallery forest, a forest that grows alongside a body of water without spreading inland. Gallery forests may be seen in small groves and along streams on the Great Plains of the United States and in central South America and Africa.

gal|ler|y|go|er (gal′ər ē gō′ər, gal′rē-), *n.* a person who visits art galleries.

gallery hit, play, or **shot,** a showy or flashy play in a game, intended to gain applause from the spectators.

gal|ler|y|ite (gal′ər ē īt, gal′rē-), *n. Informal.* a person who sits in the gallery of a theater, stadium, etc.

gal|let|a (gə yet′ə), *n.* a coarse, dry grass used for hay in the southwestern United States. [< Spanish *galleta* biscuit]

***gal|ley** (gal′ē), *n., pl.* **-leys. 1** a long, narrow ship of former times having oars and sails, used in the Mediterranean in ancient and medieval times. Galleys were often rowed by slaves, prisoners of war, or convicts. **2** a large rowboat, especially one for the captain's use on a British warship. **3** the kitchen of a ship or airplane: *The gleaming galley has most of the comforts of modern living, including ... a garbage grinder that should frustrate gulls and porpoises* (Time). **4** *Printing.* **a** a long, narrow tray for holding type that has been set. **b** = galley proof. **5** a state or pleasure barge. [< Old French *galee, galie* < Medieval Latin *galea* < Medieval Greek]

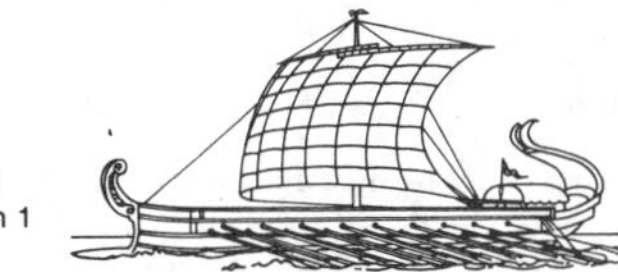
***galley** definition 1

galley proof, *Printing.* a proof printed from type in a galley. Galley proofs are usually made on long, narrow sheets with wide margins for marking corrections.

galley slave, 1 a person forced or condemned to row a galley. **2** *Figurative.* a drudge.

gal|ley-west (gal′ē west′), *adv. Informal.* into utter confusion or ruin: *A Justice Department official said last week that if the Government lost the Peters case, "it would knock the whole [security] program galley-west"* (New York Times). [American English < dialectal English *colly-west*]

gall|fly (gôl′flī′), *n., pl.* **-flies.** an insect that deposits its eggs in plants, causing galls to form; gall midge, gall moth, or gall wasp.

Gal|li|a (gal′ē ə), *n.* Latin name of Gaul, an ancient country in western Europe.

gal|liard (gal′yərd), *n., adj.* —***n.*** **1** a lively dance in triple time for two people, common in the 1500's and 1600's. **2** the music for it. **3** *Archaic.* a sturdy, hardy, or valiant man.
—***adj.*** *Archaic.* **1** lively; gay. **2** sturdy; hardy; valiant.
[Middle English *gaillard* < Old French, origin uncertain]

gal|liard|ise (gal′yər dīz), *n. Archaic.* **1** gaiety; merriment; revelry. **2** a gay joke or trick.

gal|li|ass (gal′ē as), *n.* = galleass.

gal|lic (gal′ik), *adj. Chemistry.* **1** of gallium. **2** containing gallium, especially with a valence of three.

Gal|lic (gal′ik), *adj.* **1** of or having to do with Gaul or its people: *Caesar's Gallic Wars.* **2** French: *Gallic wit.* [< Latin *Gallicus* Gaulish < *Gallī* the Gauls] —**Gal′li|cal|ly,** *adv.*

gallic acid, a white, crystalline, organic acid, obtained especially from galls on plants, used in making ink and dyes and in tanning. *Formula:* $C_7H_6O_5{\cdot}H_2O$ [< French *gallique* < Latin *galla* gall[3]]

Gal|li|can (gal′ə kən), *adj., n.* —***adj.*** **1** Gallic; French. **2** of or having to do with the Roman Catholic Church in France, especially a party among French Roman Catholics who wanted to restrict papal authority in favor of the authority of general councils.
—***n.*** a member of the Gallican party in the French Roman Catholic Church.

Gal|li|can|ism (gal′ə kə niz′əm), *n.* the spirit or policy of the Gallicans with respect to papal authority over the Roman Catholic Church in France.

Gal|li|ce (gal′ə sē), *adv.* **1** in French. **2** in the French style. [< Medieval Latin *Gallice* in French < Latin, in the Gaulish (tongue)]

Gal|li|cism or **gal|li|cism** (gal′ə siz əm), *n.* a French idiom or expression.

Gal|li|cize or **gal|li|cize** (gal′ə sīz), *v.t., v.i.,* **-cized, -ciz|ing.** to make or become French in form, pronunciation, habits, customs, or character.

gal|li|gas|kins (gal′ə gas′kinz), *n.pl.* **1** a kind of loose hose or breeches worn in the 1500's and 1600's. **2** loose breeches. **3** *British Dialect.* leggings; gaiters. [formerly *garragascoynes* < Middle French *garguesque,* variant of (*à la*) *greguesque* < Italian *alla grechesca* in the Greek fashion < *greco* Greek < Latin *Graecus;* influenced by earlier English *Gascoyne* Gascon]

gal|li|mau|fry (gal′ə mô′frē), *n., pl.* **-fries. 1** a mixture of unlike things; confused jumble; hodgepodge: *So now they have made our English tongue a gallimaufry or hodge-podge of all other speeches* (Edmund Spenser). **2** a meat stew or hash; ragout. [< Middle French *galimafrée*]

gal|li|na|cean (gal′ə nā′shən), *adj., n.* —***adj.*** = gallinaceous. —***n.*** a gallinaceous bird.

gal|li|na|ceous (gal′ə nā′shəs), *adj.* **1** of or belonging to an order of birds that nest on the ground and fly only short distances. Chickens, turkeys, pheasants, grouse, and partridges are gallinaceous birds. **2** having to do with or like domestic fowl. [< Latin *gallīnāceus* (with English *-ous*) of poultry < *gallīna* hen < *gallus* rooster]

gall|ing[1] (gô′ling), *adj.* that galls; chafing; irritating: *As stubborn steers ... joined reluctant to the galling yoke* (Alexander Pope). **SYN**: annoying, vexatious. [< *gall*[2], verb + *-ing*[2]] —**gall′ing|ly,** *adv.*

gall|ing[2] (gô′ling), *n.* the wearing off of a surface when two metals, pieces of leather, or other material rub against each other. [< *gall*[2], noun + *-ing*[1]]

gal|li|nip|per (gal′ə nip′ər), *n. Informal.* **1** an insect that bites or stings, especially a large mosquito. **2** any one of various similar insects that do not bite or sting, such as a crane fly. [American English; origin uncertain]

gall insect, any insect that causes galls, such as a gallfly.

gal|li|nule (gal′ə nül, -nyül), *n.* any one of certain long-toed, wading marsh birds related to the rails and coots, such as the purple gallinule. [< New Latin *Gallinula* the genus name < Latin *gallīna* hen < *gallus* rooster]

Gal|li|o (gal′ē ō), *n.* **1** an official who refuses to take action upon matters outside of his immediate jurisdiction (in the Bible, Acts 18:12-17). **2** *Figurative: Unhappily, Scotland was ruled, not by pious Josiahs, but by careless Gallios* (Macaulay).

gal|li|ot (gal′ē ət), *n.* = galiot.

gal|li|pot[1] (gal′ə pot), *n.* **1** a small pot or jar of glazed earthenware used especially by druggists to hold medicine, salve, or the like. **2** a druggist. [< *galley* + *pot,* perhaps because brought in galleys]

Pronunciation Key: hat, āge, cãre, fär; let, ēqual, tėrm; it, īce; hot, ōpen, ôrder; oil, out; cup, pu̇t, rüle; child; long; thin; ᴛʜen; zh, measure; ə represents **a** in about, **e** in taken, **i** in pencil, **o** in lemon, **u** in circus.

gal|li|pot² (gal′ə pot), *n.* = galipot.

gal|li|size (gal′ə sīz), *v.t.*, **-sized**, **-siz|ing**. = gallize.

***gal|li|um** (gal′ē əm), *n.* a grayish-white chemical element with a melting point slightly above room temperature but a high boiling point. Gallium is used in thermometers. It is a rare, shining metal occurring as a minute part of bauxite and other minerals, and is similar to aluminum in its chemical properties. [< New Latin *gallium* < *Gallia* France < Latin; or perhaps < Latin *gallus* cock, translation of *Lecoq* de Boisbaudran, the discoverer]

***gallium**

symbol	atomic number	atomic weight	oxidation state
Ga	31	69.72	3

gallium arsenide, a crystalline compound of gallium and arsenic, used as a semiconducting device in tunnel diodes and lasers. *Formula:* GaAs

gal|li|vant (gal′ə vant), *v.i.* **1** to go about seeking pleasure; gad about: *You were out all day yesterday, and gallivanting somewhere* (Dickens). **2** to flirt. Also, **galavant**. [apparently < dialectal French *galvauder*]

gal|li|wasp (gal′ē wosp, -wôsp), *n.* **1** a harmless lizard of Central America and the West Indies, that resembles a small alligator, and is usually about a foot long. **2** a fish of the Atlantic Coast of North America, with a lizardlike head. [origin uncertain]

gal|lize (gal′īz), *v.t.*, **-lized**, **-liz|ing**. to add water and sugar to (unfermented grape juice) to increase the quantity of the wine produced. [< Dr. *Gall,* of Trier, West Germany, a German scientist, who perfected the process + *ize*] — **gal′li|za′tion**, *n.*

gall-less (gôl′lis), *adj.* **1** having no gall. **2** *Figurative.* free from bitterness or hate; not easily roused to anger.

gall midge, a very small insect, such as a gnat, that causes galls on plants.

gall mite, any one of various mites that form small lumps, or galls, on leaves and twigs.

gall moth, a moth which causes galls on plants, especially on the goldenrod.

gall|nut (gôl′nut′), *n.* a nutlike gall on plants, especially on oaks.

Gallo-, *combining form.* Gallic; French; France; French things: *Gallophile = a friend or admirer of the French.* [< Latin *Gallus* a Gaul]

Gal|lo-A|mer|i|can (gal′ō ə mer′ə kən), *adj.* of combined French and American character, descent, or the like; Franco-American.

Gal|lo-Brit|on (gal′ō brit′ən), *n.* a person who is partly French and partly British by birth or in his sympathies.

gal|lo|glass (gal′ō glas), *n.* = gallowglass.

Gal|lo|ma|ni|a (gal′ə mā′nē ə), *n.* a craze for French institutions and customs, especially for imitating them.

***gal|lon** (gal′ən), *n.* **1** a measure for liquids, equal to 4 quarts. The United States gallon equals 231 cubic inches or 3.7853 liters. The British gallon equals 277.420 cubic inches or 4.546 liters. The United States gallon is also called a *wine gallon,* and the British gallon, an *imperial gallon.* **2** a dry measure equal to one-eighth of a bushel. *Abbr:* gal. [< Old French *galon*]

***gallon**
definition 1

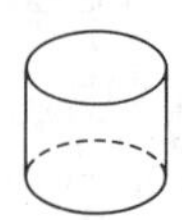
1 U.S. gallon = 231 cu. in.

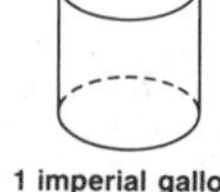
1 imperial gallon = 277.420 cu. in.

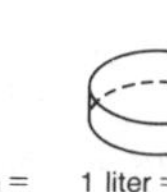
1 liter = 61.02 cu. in.

gal|lon|age (gal′ə nij), *n.* the amount (of a liquid) in gallons.

gal|loon (gə lün′), *n.* **1** a narrow, close-woven braid or ribbon of gold, silver, or silk thread, used in trimming uniforms, furniture, and draperies. **2** a trimming of this material. [< French *galon* < Old French *galonner* dress the hair with ribbons < *gale* merriment; see etym. under **gala**]

gal|looned (gə lünd′), *adj.* trimmed with galloon: *a gallooned dress uniform.*

gal|loot (gə lüt′), *n.* = galoot.

gal|lop (gal′əp), *n., v.* — *n.* **1** the fastest gait of a horse or other four-footed animal. In a gallop, all four feet are off the ground together once in each stride. See picture under **gait**. **2** a ride at a gallop: *Much more interesting were some of the winding-up gallops for the Champagne Stakes* (New Yorker). **3** *Figurative.* a rapid rate: *Sports announcers often speak at a gallop.*
— *v.i.* **1** to ride at a gallop: *The hunters galloped after the hounds. Up the hill galloped the gallant three hundred* (Tennyson). **2** to go at a gallop: *The wild horse galloped off when he saw us.* **3** *Figurative.* to go very fast; hurry: *to gallop through a book.* **SYN:** race.
— *v.t.* **1** to cause to go at a gallop: *He galloped his horse down the road.* **2** to gallop along or through: *The golden sun ... Gallops the Zodiac in his glistering coach* (Shakespeare).
[< Old French *galop* < *galoper,* unrecorded Old North French *waloper.* See etym. of doublet **wallop**.]

gal|lo|pade (gal′ə pād′), *n., v.,* **-pad|ed**, **-pad|ing**. — *n.* **1** a lively dance of Hungarian origin. **2** the music for it. **3** a sidelong or curvetting kind of gallop.
— *v.i.* to dance a gallopade.
[< French *galopade* < *galoper* to gallop]

gal|lop|er (gal′ə pər), *n.* **1** an animal or a person that gallops. **2** *Military.* **a** an aide-de-camp. **b** a light field gun.

Gal|lo|phile (gal′ə fīl, -fil), *n., adj.* — *n.* a friend or admirer of the French.
— *adj.* friendly to the French. **SYN:** Francophile.

gal|lop|ing (gal′ə ping), *adj.* **1** that gallops; going at a gallop. **2** *Figurative.* making rapid progress: *galloping inflation.*

galloping consumption, pulmonary tuberculosis that runs an extremely rapid course.

Gal|lo-Ro|mance (gal′ō rō mans′), *n.* the language spoken in France from about 600-900 A.D., developed from Latin.

gal|lous (gal′əs), *adj. Chemistry.* containing gallium, especially with a valence of 2.

gal|low (gal′ō), *v.t. British Dialect.* to frighten. [variant of *gally*]

Gal|lo|way (gal′ə wā), *n.* **1** any one of a breed of small, strong horses first raised in Galloway, Scotland. **2** a small horse. **3** any one of a breed of stocky, hornless beef cattle first raised in or near Galloway.

gal|low|glass (gal′ō glas), *n.* a soldier or armed retainer of a chief in ancient Ireland or Scotland. Also, **galloglass**. [< Irish and Scottish Gaelic *gall-óglách* < *gall* foreigner + *óglách* youth, retainer]

gal|lows (gal′ōz), *n., pl.* **-lows|es** or **-lows**, *adj., adv.* — *n.* **1** a wooden frame made of a crossbar on two upright posts, used for hanging criminals. **SYN:** gibbet. **2** punishment by hanging: *The judge sentenced the murderer to the gallows.* **3** a gallows bird; a rascal: *"Now, young gallows!" This was an invitation for Oliver to enter through a door ... which led into a stone cell* (Dickens). **4** a structure like a gallows, especially one used in gymnastics.
— *adj. Archaic or Slang.* **1** deserving to be hanged; villainous. **2** mischievous or wild: *gallows children.* **3** fine; great.
— *adv. Dialect or Slang.* extremely; very.
cheat the gallows, to escape punishment, such as the gallows, due for a capital crime: *... the greatest thief that ever cheated the gallows* (Dickens).
gallowses, *Dialect.* galluses: *It must be very handy to have shoulder straps instead of gallowses,—besides, gallows is an ugly name* (Baltimore Spirit Public Journals).
have the gallows in one's face, to have the look of a person doomed to or deserving the gallows: *Hold him fast, the dog; he has the gallows in his face* (Oliver Goldsmith).
[Old English *galga*]

gallows bird, *Informal.* a person who deserves to be hanged.

gallows bitts, a frame on the deck of a ship for supporting spare topmasts, spars, and the like.

gallows humor, a bitter, morbid form of humor, as of those condemned to the gallows.

gal|lows-ripe (gal′ōz rīp′), *adj.* ready for hanging.

gallows tree, = gallows (def. 1).

gall|stone (gôl′stōn′), *n.* a pebblelike mass, chiefly of cholesterol and mineral salts, that sometimes forms in the gall bladder or one of its ducts. When one or more gallstones stop the flow of bile, there is usually pain, and sometimes jaundice results.

gal|lumph (gə lumf′), *v.i.* = galumph.

gal|lup (gal′əp), *v.i., v.t.* to make a poll; to poll: *Several languages that had no word for polling, including Greek, acquired a new verb for it: to gallup* (Newsweek). [< *Gallup* (poll)]

Gallup poll, a poll of public opinion on a political or social topic or issue, as developed by George H. Gallup, born 1901, an American statistician.

gal|lused (gal′əst), *adj. U.S. Informal.* wearing suspenders: *Clustered beneath shady oaks on the lawn of the country courthouse were 50 ... gallused townspeople* (Time).

gal|lus|es (gal′ə siz), *n.pl. U.S. Dialect or Informal.* suspenders; braces: *He raved and ranted and snapped his galluses until people got ashamed of him* (Harper's). [variant of *gallowses,* plural of *gallows*]

gall wasp, any one of a family of wasps which cause galls on plants.

gal|ly (gal′ē), *v.t.*, **-lied**, **-ly|ing**. *Especially Dialect.* **1** to frighten or scare. **2** to frighten away. [Old English *a-gælwan* to alarm]

gal|ly|gas|kins (gal′ə gas′kinz), *n.pl.* = galligaskins.

Ga|lois field (gal′wä, gal wä′), a mathematical field with a finite number of elements: *Although conceived as an abstract mathematical exercise, Galois fields ... have been studied in connection with error-free codes for the transmission of information by high-speed machines* (Scientific American). [< Évariste *Galois,* 1811-1832, a French mathematician]

ga|loot (gə lüt′), *n. U.S. Slang.* an awkward or uncouth person. Also, **galloot**. [origin unknown]

gal|op (gal′əp), *n., v.* — *n.* **1** a lively dance in two-four time. **2** the music for it.
— *v.i.* to dance a galop.
[< French *galop,* also *galope* < Old French; see etym. under **gallop**]

ga|lore (gə lôr′, -lōr′), *adv., adj., n.* — *adv.* in abundance: *Every town we visited had automobiles galore.*
— *adj.* many; abundant: *Problems galore confront us.*
— *n.* abundance or plenty.
[< Irish *go leór* to sufficiency]

ga|losh or **ga|loshe** (gə losh′), *n.* **1** a rubber overshoe covering the ankle, worn in wet or snowy weather. **2** *Obsolete.* **a** a wooden shoe or sandal; clog: *He were worthy to unbuckle his galosh* (Chaucer). **b** any boot or shoe. Also, **galoche**, **golosh**. **galoshes**, rubber or plastic overshoes covering the ankles, worn in wet or snowy weather: *We wear galoshes in wet weather.* [< Old French *galoche* < Old Provençal *galocha*]

gals., gallons.

Gals|wor|thi|an (gôlz wėr′ᴛʜē ən), *adj.* of or characteristic of the novels and plays of John Galsworthy (1867-1933): *a nice bit of sentimental Galsworthian social drama* (Angus Wilson).

galt (gôlt), *n.* = gault.

Gal|to|ni|an (gôl tō′nē ən), *adj.* of or having to do with Francis Galton (1822-1911), English scientist, his writings, or his theories of eugenics.

ga|lumph (gə lumf′), *v., n.* — *v.i.* **1** to gallop in a clumsy way: *cows galumphing home.* **2** to gallop, prance, or go in or as if in triumph: *He left it dead and with its head He went galumphing back* (Lewis Carroll).
— *n.* an awkward person. Also, **gallumph**.
[(coined by Lewis Carroll), perhaps < *gallop* + *triumph*] — **ga|lumph′ing|ly**, *adv.*

gal|van|ic (gal van′ik), *adj.* **1** producing an electric current by chemical action; voltaic. **2** of or caused by an electric current. **3** *Figurative.* affecting or affected as if by galvanism; startling; galvanizing: *galvanic activity. ... a sort of galvanic grin* (Hawthorne). [< *galvan*(ism) + *-ic*] — **gal|van′i|cal|ly**, *adv.*

galvanic battery, a battery consisting of two or more galvanic cells; voltaic battery.

galvanic cell, an electrolytic cell for the production of electricity by chemical action; voltaic cell.

galvanic pile, a series of plates of two unlike metals, such as copper and zinc, arranged alternately with layers of cloth or paper moistened with acid between them, for producing an electric current; voltaic pile.

galvanic skin response, a change or variation in the skin's electrical conductivity due to excitement, fear, or other emotional stimulus: *The galvanic skin response measures the ability of the skin to conduct electricity, which is a function of the autonomic nervous system. The latter is intimately hooked up with those mechanisms regulating the body's ability to cope with stress* (Thomas P. Hackett). *Abbr:* GSR (no periods).

gal|va|nise (gal′və nīz), *v.t.*, **-nised**, **-nis|ing**. *Especially British.* galvanize.

gal|va|nism (gal′və niz əm), *n.* **1** electricity produced by chemical action. **2** the branch of physics dealing with this. **3** the use of such electricity for medical purposes. **4** any force suggesting such a chemical reaction: *There is some galvanism in this picture that either strongly attracts or repels* (New York Times). [< French *galvanisme* < Luigi *Galvani,* 1737-1798, an Italian scientist + *-isme* -ism]

gal|va|ni|za|tion (gal′və nə zā′shən), *n.* the process of galvanizing or condition of being galvanized.

gal|va|nize (gal′və nīz), *v.t.*, **-nized**, **-niz|ing**. **1** to apply an electric current produced by chemical action to. **2** *Figurative.* to stimulate as if by an electric current; arouse suddenly; startle: *The ringing of the alarm bell galvanized the dozing* *firemen into action. Everything seemed to be galvanized by a fresh spirit of vigor and infinite care* (New Yorker). **3** to cover (iron or steel) with a thin coating of zinc to prevent rust. **—gal′va|niz′er**, *n.*

gal|va|nized iron (gal′və nīzd), iron covered with a thin coating of zinc, which resists rust.

galvano-, *combining form.* connected with galvanism; galvanic in nature: *Galvanothermy = the production of heat by electricity.* [< *galvanism*]

gal|va|no|cau|ter|y (gal′və nō kô′tər ē, gal-van′ō-), *n., pl.* **-ter|ies. 1** a cautery consisting of a wire heated by resistance to an electric current. **2** cauterization by such means. [< *galvano + cautery*]

gal|va|nom|e|ter (gal′və nom′ə tər), *n.* an instrument for detecting an electric current, measuring its strength, and determining its direction.

gal|va|no|met|ric (gal′və nə met′rik, gal van′ə-), *adj.* **1** having to do with a galvanometer or galvanometry. **2** measured by a galvanometer.

gal|va|no|met|ri|cal (gal′və nə met′rə kəl, gal-van′ə-), *adj.* = galvanometric.

gal|va|nom|e|try (gal′və nom′ə trē), *n.* the detection, measurement, and determination of the strength of electric currents by a galvanometer.

gal|va|no|plas|tic (gal′və nə plas′tik, gal van′ə-), *adj.* having to do with galvanoplastics.

gal|va|no|plas|tics (gal′və nə plas′tiks, gal-van′ə-), *n.* the process of coating things with metal by electrolysis; electrotypy.

gal|va|no|plas|ty (gal′və nə plas′tē, gal van′ə-), *n.* = galvanoplastics.

gal|va|no|scope (gal′və nə skōp, gal van′ə-), *n.* an instrument for detecting very small electric currents and showing their direction.

gal|va|no|scop|ic (gal′və nə skop′ik, gal van′ə-), *adj.* of or having to do with a galvanoscope or galvanoscopy.

gal|va|nos|co|py (gal′və nos′kə pē), *n.* the use of the galvanoscope, especially in medicine.

gal|va|no|tax|is (gal′və nə tak′sis), *n. Biology.* movement in response to an electric current; electrotaxis.

gal|va|no|ther|my (gal′və nə thėr′mē, gal-van′ə-), *n.* the production of heat by electricity. [< *galvano-* + Greek *thermē* heat]

gal|va|not|ro|pism (gal′və not′rə piz əm), *n. Botany.* movements in growing organs caused by passing electric currents through them.

Gal|ves|ton plan or **system** (gal′və stən), = commission plan. [< *Galveston,* a city in Texas where it was originated]

Gal|ways (gôl′wāz), *n.pl. U.S. Slang.* thin whiskers following the jaw line from ear to ear. [perhaps < *Galway,* a county and bay in Ireland]

Gal|we|gian (gal wē′jən), *adj., n.* **—*adj.*** of or having to do with Galloway, a district in Scotland, or its people.

—*n.* a native or inhabitant of Galloway.

gal|yak or **gal|yac** (gal′yak), *n.* a flat, smooth fur from the pelts of kids or lambs. [ultimately < Russian *goljak* pauper < *golyj* naked]

gam¹ (gam), *n., v.,* **gammed, gam|ming. —*n.* 1** *Nautical.* a herd, pod, or school of whales. **2** *Nautical.* a visit or conference between the crews of ships, especially whalers, at sea. **3** *U.S. Dialect.* a social meeting or visit.

—*v.i.* 1 *Nautical.* to form a gam; have a visit or conference at sea. **2** *U.S. Dialect.* to have a social meeting or visit; call.

—*v.t.* *U.S. Dialect.* to have a social visit with. [origin uncertain; perhaps < Scandinavian (compare Danish *gammen* sport)]

gam² (gam), *n. Slang.* a leg, especially a woman's leg: *Those thin gams, those thin arms, and that wonderful face* (Time). [perhaps variant of *gamb*]

ga|ma grass (gä′mə), a tall, perennial grass found chiefly on moist land in the Great Plains and western United States, used for forage and fodder, and in soil conservation. [perhaps alteration of *grama*]

Ga|ma|li|el (gə mā′lē əl, -māl′yəl), *n.* **1** a Jewish scholar and teacher of Saul of Tarsus, who became the Apostle Paul (in the Bible, Acts 5:34). **2** a ruler of Manasseh (in the Bible, Numbers 10:23).

ga|mash|es (gə mash′iz), *n.pl. Archaic or Dialect.* a kind of leggings or gaiters, worn for protection against mud and wet by horseback riders. [< dialectal French *gamache*]

gamb (gamb), *n.* **1** a leg; shank. **2** the leg of an animal represented on a coat of arms. Also, **gambe**. [< Old North French *gambe,* Old French *jambe* < Late Latin *gamba, camba,* apparently < Greek *kampē* a bend]

gam|ba (gam′bə), *n.* **1** = viola da gamba. **2** an organ stop resembling a violin or cello in tone. [< Italian *gamba* leg < Late Latin; see etym. under **gamb** (because it is held between the legs)]

gam|bade (gam bād′), *n.* **1** a leap, as of a horse. **2** *Figurative.* a freakish action; caper; prank: **gambado**. [< French, Middle French *gambade;* see etym. under **gambol**]

gam|ba|do¹ (gam bā′dō), *n., pl.* **-dos** or **-does. 1** Often, **gambados**. a kind of large boot or gaiter, attached to a saddle instead of stirrups, for protecting the rider's feet against wet or cold. **2** any long gaiter or legging. [< Italian *gambado* < *gamba* leg; see etym. under **gambol**]

gam|ba|do² (gam bā′dō), *n., pl.* **-dos** or **-does**. = gambade.

gam|bang (gäm′bäng), *n.* a Javanese and Balinese musical instrument similar to a xylophone, consisting of a number of strips of resonant wood or metal fastened loosely on strings, and mounted on a concave wooden box or frame. [< Javanese *gambang*]

gambe (gamb), *n.* = gamb.

Gam|bel's quail (gam′bəlz), a buff and bluish-gray quail with a black and brown crest and white markings, found in desert regions of the southwestern United States and of Mexico. [< William *Gambel,* 1821-1849, an American ornithologist]

gam|be|son (gam′bə sən), *n.* a medieval military coat of leather or cloth worn for protection without other armor. [< Old French *gambeison*]

Gam|bi|an (gam′bē ən), *adj., n.* **—*adj.*** of or having to do with The Gambia, a country in West Africa.

—*n.* a native or inhabitant of The Gambia.

gam|bier or **gam|bir** (gam′bir), *n.* an astringent extract prepared from the leaves and young shoots of a tropical Asiatic shrub of the madder family, used in dyeing, tanning, and medicine. [< Malay *gambir,* the plant]

gam|bit (gam′bit), *n.* **1** a way of opening a game of chess by purposely sacrificing a pawn or a piece to gain some advantage. **2** *Figurative.* any opening move or action, especially one intended to gain some advantage: *These opening gambits were clearly designed to test Western firmness in the face of a new Communist threat* (Robert Strausz-Hupé). [< French *gambit* < Spanish *gambito* < *gamba* leg < Italian; see etym. under **gambol**]

gam|ble (gam′bəl), *v.,* **-bled, -bling,** *n.* **—*v.i.* 1** to play games of chance for money or other valuable stakes: *to gamble at cards, to gamble on the result of a race.* **2** to take great risks in business or speculation; take a risk: *Only a rich man can afford to gamble in stocks and bonds.* (*Figurative.*) *Gambling against the world for life or death* (Thomas Carlyle).

—*v.t.* to risk (money or other things of value) in gambling; bet; wager: *to gamble one's fortune on a turn of the cards.* (*Figurative.*) *The prisoner gambled his life on the chance he could escape without being shot.*

—*n.* 1 a risky act or undertaking: *Putting money into a new business is often a gamble.* (*Figurative.*) *If the Nazis discovered our course, they might move to close in on us through Spain. It was a terrible gamble* (Newsweek). **2** an act of gambling; a gambling transaction.

gamble away, to lose or squander by gambling: *He recklessly gambled away a fortune in one night. Men who had gambled away their liberty* (William Lecky).

[probably a back formation < *gambler, gambling* < earlier *gamler, gameling* < Middle English *gamen* to game]

gam|bler (gam′blər), *n.* **1** a person who gambles or takes risks a great deal. **2** a person whose occupation is gambling.

gam|bling (gam′bling), *n.* **1** the playing of games of chance for money: *Gambling is legal in some states.* **2** betting; wagering; taking great risks in business or speculation.

gambling house or **hall**, a house in which gambling is carried on as a business.

gambling room, a room set aside for gambling, especially in a hotel, casino, or night club.

gambling table, a table used, or adapted for use, in gambling; gaming table.

gam|bly (gam′blē), *adj.* depending on chance; risky.

gam|boge (gam bōj′, -büzh′), *n.* **1** a gum resin obtained from certain tropical trees of southeastern Asia belonging to the same family as the garcinia, used as a bright-yellow pigment for staining wood and also medicinally as a cathartic; cambogia. **2** a yellow or yellowish-orange color: *He had just purchased a big, square, gamboge country castle ... in Provence* (New Yorker). [< New Latin *gambogium* < *Cambodia* former name of Kampuchea]

gam|bol (gam′bəl), *n., v.,* **-boled, -bol|ing** or (*especially British*) **-bolled, -bol|ling. —*n.*** the act of running and jumping about in dancing or play; caper; frolic.

—*v.i.* to frisk about; run and jump about in play; frolic: *Lambs gamboled in the meadow.* [alteration of Middle French *gambade* < Italian *gambata* < *gamba* leg < Late Latin *gamba,* apparently < Greek *kampē* a bend]

gam|brel (gam′brəl), *n.* **1** the hock of a horse or other animal. **2** *U.S.* = gambrel roof. **3** a curved frame of metal or wood used by butchers for hanging slaughtered animals. [< Middle French *gamberel* < Old North French *gambe* leg; see etym. under **gamb**]

∗gambrel roof, a roof having two slopes on each side. The lower slope is usually steeper than the upper one.

∗gambrel roof

gam|brel-roofed (gam′brəl rüft′, -rúft′), *adj.* having a gambrel roof.

gam|bu|si|a (gam byü′zē ə, -sē-), *n.* a small American freshwater fish of the same order as the guppy; mosquito fish. The gambusia feeds largely on mosquito larvae, and is used in various parts of the world in the control of malaria.

game¹ (gām), *n., adj.,* **gam|er, gam|est,** *v.,* **gamed, gam|ing. —*n.* 1** a way of playing; pastime; amusement; diversion: *a game of tag, a game with bat and ball, children's games.* **SYN:** See syn. under **play**. **2** the things needed to play a game: *This store sells games.* **3** a contest with certain rules, which one side or person tries to win: *a football game.* **4** a single round in a game: *The winner won three games out of five.* **5** the condition of the score in a game: *At the end of the first quarter the game was 6 to 3 in our favor.* **6** the number of points needed to win: *Game is 100 points.* **7** a particular manner of playing a game: *Our right fielder is playing a good game today.* **8** *Figurative.* an activity or undertaking that is carried on under set rules like a game: *the game of diplomacy, to play a waiting game.* **9** *Informal, Figurative.* any activity or vocation in which there is competition: *He is in the insurance game.* **10** *Figurative.* a plan; scheme: *They tried to trick us, but we saw through their game.* **11** wild animals, birds, or fish hunted or caught for sport or for food. **12** the flesh of wild animals or birds when used for food. **13** *Figurative.* what is hunted or pursued: *Widows are ... the great game of fortune hunters* (Joseph Addison). **14** the spirit for fighting; pluck; endurance. **15** *Archaic.* fun; mirth; sport.

—*adj.* 1 having to do with game, hunting, or fishing: *Game laws protect wildlife. He knew his hunting grounds thoroughly, every game trail, every animal burrow* (Harper's). **2** *Figurative.* showing fight; brave; plucky; spirited: *The losing team put up a game fight.* **3** *Figurative.* daring to do a thing; having spirit or will enough: *The explorer was game for any adventure. Are you game to swim across the river?*

—*v.i., v.t.* to gamble: *He gamed away his inheritance. 'Tis a great pity he ... games so deep* (Richard Brinsley Sheridan).

ahead of the game, *U.S. Informal.* winning rather than losing: *Let us get out of the stock market while we are still ahead of the game.*

be off one's game, to be out of form; play badly: *What am I doing wrong, Tom? I'm quite off my game* (H. G. Hutchinson).

be on one's game, to be in form; play well: *Their disregard of the recognised rules was accentuated by the fact that neither man was on his game* (Westminster Gazette).

die game, to die bravely; maintain one's spirit to the end: *Good-bye, captain ... die game, captain* (John Gay).

games, athletic contests or exercises: *the Olympic games.*

give the game away, *Informal.* to act against one's own interest; defeat one's purpose: *Accused of misusing campaign funds ... both are in trouble because they went too far and gave the game away* (James Reston).

make game of, to make fun of; laugh at; ridicule: *She had all the talents which qualified her ... to make game of his scruples* (Macaulay).

play games, to avoid facing up to a task in earnest; act evasively: *He declared that this was no time for "playing games, political or otherwise, at the expense of the people"* (New York Times).

play (someone's) **game**, to act so as to secure someone's advantage or interest: *It is playing the enemy's game to draw him to attack our armies*

Pronunciation Key: hat, āge, cãre, fär; let, ēqual, tėrm; it, īce; hot, ōpen, ôrder; oil, out; cup, pút, rüle; child; long; thin; ᴛʜen; zh, measure; ə represents **a** in about, **e** in taken, **i** in pencil, **o** in lemon, **u** in circus.

in rotation (James C. Moore).
play the game, *Informal.* **a** to be fair; follow the rules; be a good sport: *Cheating in a test is not playing the game.* **b** to act or behave in one's relations with others: *The way the Communists play the game, there is no give and take* (Time).
the game is up, the plan or scheme has failed: *The universal opinion is that the game is irrecoverably up, and that the Tory party will be in power for fifty years to come* (Stephen Dowell).
the game is worth (or **not worth**) **the candle**, the advantage gained is worth (or not worth) the trouble or effort: *Syria . . . will eventually accept that the game of guerrillas is not worth the candle* (London Times).
[Old English *gamen* joy] —**game′ly**, *adv.* —**game′ness**, *n.*

game[2] (gām), *adj. Informal.* lame; crippled; injured: *He limps because of a game leg.* [origin uncertain. Compare Welsh *cam* and *gam* bent, crooked, wrong.]

game bag, a bag for carrying game that has been killed.

game bantam, any one of a breed of chickens identical with the game chicken but much smaller, weighing about 22 ounces when full grown.

game bird, a bird hunted for sport or food.

game chicken, any one of a breed of chickens with long legs, slender head and neck, and a compact, streamlined body, developed for fighting and exhibition. The males are more brightly colored than the females.

game|cock (gām′kok′), *n.* **1** a rooster bred and trained for fighting. **2** a plucky, brave, spirited person: *I consoled myself with the feeling that, at all events, he was an old gamecock, and would do his country credit if he went into action* (Lord Clarence Paget).

game fish, a fish that fights to get away when hooked.

game fowl, **1** = game chicken. **2** a fowl of any species regarded as game for hunting.

game|keep|er (gām′kē′pər), *n.* a person whose work is taking care of the wild animals and birds on an estate or in a certain district and preventing anyone from stealing them or killing them without permission.

game|keep|ing (gām′kē′ping), *n.* the protection of wild animals and birds on an estate, especially from poaching.

***gam|e|lan** (gum′ə län), *n.* **1** a Balinese or Javanese orchestra, consisting chiefly of a variety of chimes made of wood, bronze, bamboo, and metal. **2** the music produced by a gamelan. **3** the xylophone of a Balinese or Javanese orchestra. [< Javanese *gamelan*]

***gamelan**
definition 3

game|land (gām′land′, -lənd), *n.* a place or region in which game can be hunted.

game law, **1** a law to protect wild animals, birds, and fish by restricting hunting and fishing to certain seasons and by limiting the size and number of animals, birds, and fish that can be killed or caught. **2** a law that allows only certain persons to fish and shoot certain kinds of game.

game license, a license allowing a person to hunt, catch, and sometimes sell game under specified conditions.

gam|e|lin (gum′ə lin), *n.* = gamelan.

game of chance, a game depending on luck, not skill.

game pie, a meat pie made of venison, rabbit, or other meat from a wild animal.

game plan, *U.S.* **1** the strategy used by a football team in a particular game. **2** any carefully planned course of action; strategy: *Now that there are signs of a change in the trend of the economy, it is timely to make a preliminary judgment on how the so-called "game plan"—The Administration's strategy for overcoming inflation without recession—has been going* (New York Times).

game point, the final or winning point in a game, especially in tennis, volleyball, and other net games.

game preserve or **preserves**, an area of land set aside for the breeding and protection of wild animals, which is occasionally opened to hunters under strict regulations.

game preserver, a person who maintains a game preserve.

game protector, = game warden.

game ranger, a person who guards the game and enforces the game laws on a game preserve, in certain countries.

game reserve or **reserves**, = game preserve.

game room, = playroom.

games (gāmz), *n.pl.* See under **game**[1].

game show, *U.S.* a television program built around a game or contest in which the players or contestants are scored and the winners are given prizes: *Currently there are 30 hours of game shows on the networks' daytime schedules* (Time).

games|man (gāmz′mən), *n., pl.* **-men.** *Informal.* a person who uses gamesmanship.

games|man|ship (gāmz′mən ship), *n. Informal.* the skill of using ploys to gain an advantage in a game or other contest: *But in the . . . world of politics, doing voluntarily what you have to do anyway can be a sound piece of gamesmanship* (Wall Street Journal). [(coined by Stephen Potter, born 1900, an English author)]

games master, *British.* a teacher who directs and teaches the playing of games.

game|some (gām′səm), *adj.* full of play; ready to play; sportive; playful: *a hearty, jocund, rubicund, gamesome wag* (Washington Irving). **SYN:** frolicsome. —**game′some|ly**, *adv.* —**game′some|ness**, *n.*

game|ster (gām′stər), *n.* **1** a gambler: *The gamester . . . Oft risks his fortune on one desperate throw* (Oliver Goldsmith). **2** a courageous competitor in athletics.

gam|e|tal (gam′ə təl, gə mē′-), *adj.* having the character of a gamete; reproductive; generative.

gam|e|tan|gi|um (gam′ə tan′jē əm), *n., pl.* **-gi|a** (-jē ə). *Botany.* the cell or organ in which gametes are produced. [< New Latin *gametangium* < *gameta* (see etym. under **gamete**) + Greek *angeîon* vessel]

gam|ete (gam′ēt, gə mēt′), *n.* a mature reproductive cell capable of uniting with another cell to form a fertilized cell that can develop into a new plant or animal; an egg or sperm cell; germ cell. [< New Latin *gameta* < Greek *gametē* wife, *gamétēs* husband < *gameîn* marry < *gámos* marriage]

game theory, = theory of games.

ga|met|ic (gə met′ik), *adj.* of or having to do with gametes.

ga|met|i|cal|ly (gə met′ə klē), *adv.* as regards gametes; as a gamete.

ga|me|to|cide (gə mē′tə sīd), *n.* a chemical that destroys or stops the growth of pollen in certain plants, as in cotton.

ga|me|to|cyte (gə mē′tə sīt), *n.* a cell that produces gametes by division.

gam|e|to|gen|e|sis (gam′ə tə jen′ə sis), *n.* the formation or development of gametes.

gam|e|to|gen|ic (gam′ə tə jen′ik), *adj.* of or having to do with gametogenesis.

gam|e|tog|e|nous (gam′ə toj′ə nəs), *adj.* = gametogenic.

gam|e|tog|e|ny (gam′ə toj′ə nē), *n.* = gametogenesis.

gam|e|tog|o|ny (gam′ə toj′ə nē), *n.* sexual reproduction; gamogenesis.

ga|me|toid (gə mē′toid), *n.* a gamete having a number of nuclei instead of a single one.

ga|me|to|phore (gə mē′tə fôr, -fōr), *n.* a modified branch or filament bearing gametes, as in certain liverworts.

ga|me|to|phor|ic (gə mē′tə fôr′ik, -fōr′-), *adj.* having to do with a gametophore.

ga|me|to|phyte (gə mē′tə fīt), *n.* the individual plant or generation of a plant which produces gametes. See picture under **alternation of generations.** [< *gamete* + Greek *phytón* plant]

gam|e|to|phyt|ic (gam′ə tə fit′ik), *adj.* having to do with a gametophyte.

game warden, an official whose duty it is to enforce the game laws in a certain district.

gam|ey (gā′mē), *adj.,* **gam|i|er, gam|i|est.** = gamy.

gam|ic (gam′ik), *adj. Biology.* sexual. [< Greek *gamikós* relating to marriage < *gámos* marriage]

gam|in (gam′ən), *n., adj.* —*n.* **1** a neglected child, especially a boy, left to roam about the streets: *There are the little gamins mocking him* (Thackeray). **2** a small, lively person of either sex.
—*adj.* **1** of or like that of a gamin: *a gamin haircut, gamin-faced. In June she will follow her records to the U.S. and try out her calculated gamin style in Manhattan* (Time). **2** lively; pert.
[< French *gamin*] —**gam′in|like′**, *adj.*

gamin cut, a short hair style for women arranged to simulate natural disorder.

ga|mine (gȧ mēn′), *n. French.* **1** a neglected girl, left to roam about the streets. **2** a small, lively girl.

gam|ing (gā′ming), *n.* the playing of games of chance for money; gambling.

gaming house, = gambling house.

gaming room, = gambling room.

gaming table, = gambling table.

***gam|ma** (gam′ə), *n., pl.* **-mas** *for 1, 2, 4, 5 and 6,* **-ma** *for 3.* **1** the third letter of the Greek alphabet. It corresponds to English *G, g.* **2** the third in any series or group (used especially in scientific classification). **3** = microgram. **4** *Photography.* the ratio between the densities in a developed negative and the light values in its subject. **5** a unit of magnetic field intensity, equal to 10^{-5} oersted. **6** one of several positions of atoms or groups of atoms which are substituted in a chemical compound. [< Greek *gámma*]

***gamma**
definition 1

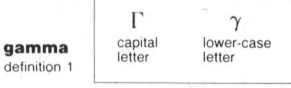

Γ	γ
capital letter	lower-case letter

gam|ma|di|on (gə mā′dē ən), *n., pl.* **-di|a** (-dē ə). a figure formed by combinations of the shape of the Greek letter gamma (Γ), such as a swastika. [< Medieval Greek *gammádion* (diminutive) < Greek *gámma* gamma]

gamma globulin, a part of human blood. Gamma globulin contains many antibodies which protect against measles and chicken pox, and some other infectious diseases.

gamma iron, a nonmagnetic, allotropic form of iron produced by raising the temperature of alpha iron above 900 degrees centigrade (Celsius).

gamma radiation, = gamma rays.

gamma radiography, the technique or act of making radiographic pictures with gamma rays.

gam|ma-ray camera (gam′ə rā′), an instrument for rapidly forming a radiographic image by scanning.

gamma-ray laser, = graser.

gamma rays, penetrating, electromagnetic radiation of very high frequency, given off spontaneously by radium and other radioactive substances. Gamma rays are like X rays, but have a shorter wave length. Deadly gamma rays are emitted by the nuclei of excited atoms in atomic explosions.

gamma ray spectrometer, an instrument for detecting gamma rays or other types of electromagnetic radiation, used to locate and identify radioactive materials.

gam|mar|us (gam′ər əs), *n.* any one of a group of small, whitish, aquatic crustaceans that swim in freshwater ponds and streams. [< New Latin *Gammarus* the genus name]

gam|ma|sonde (gam′ə sond), *n.* a radiosonde designed to measure the intensity of gamma rays in the upper atmosphere.

gamma surgery, a surgical operation in which gamma rays from pellets of radioactive cobalt are used to destroy cancerous cells and relieve Parkinson's disease.

gamme (gam), *n.* **1** the whole series of notes on the musical scale; gamut: *He keeps his bow arm close to his side, produces a gamme of sounds that are beautiful* (New Yorker). **2** the whole range or series of anything: *a broad gamme . . . from dark brown to bright orange* (New Yorker). [< Old French *gamme* < Italian *gamma* < Greek *gámma.* Compare etym. under **gamut.**]

gam|mel|ost (gäm′əl ôst), *n.* a strong Norwegian cheese made of skim milk. [< Norwegian *gammelost* < *gammel* old + *ost* cheese]

gam|mer (gam′ər), *n. Archaic.* an old woman: *Gammer Gurton's Needle* (the title of a celebrated English comedy published in 1575). [alteration of *godmother*]

gam|mon[1] (gam′ən), *n., v.* —*n.* **1** the lower end of a side of bacon. **2** a smoked or cured ham.
—*v.t.* to cure by salting and smoking; make into bacon.
[< Old North French *gambon* < *gambe* leg < Late Latin *gamba*] —**gam′mon|er**, *n.*

gam|mon[2] (gam′ən), *n., v.* in the game of backgammon: —*n.* a victory in which the winner throws off all his men before his opponent throws off any.
—*v.t.* to defeat (one's opponent) by a gammon.
[compare Middle English *gamen* a game[1]]

gam|mon[3] (gam′ən), *n., v.* —*n. British Informal.* nonsense; humbug.
—*v.i.* **1** to talk nonsense, especially to deceive. **2** to feign; pretend: *I got up in a temper, and told him to leave me. He laughed, and said I was gammoning* (Elizabeth A. Murray).
—*v.t.* to deceive; hoax: *to go and gammon old Mackenzie into the belief that he can read poetry* (William Black).
[perhaps related to **gammon**[2]]

gam|mon[4] (gam′ən), *v.t. Nautical.* to fasten (a bowsprit) close down to the stem of a ship. [perhaps < *gammon*[1] (referring to the tying up of hams)]

gam|mon|ing (gam′ə ning), *n. Nautical.* the arrangement of ropes, chains, or iron bands serving to gammon a bowsprit.
gam|o|gen|e|sis (gam′ə jen′ə sis), *n.* sexual generation or reproduction. [< Greek *gámos* marriage + English *genesis*]
gam|o|ge|net|ic (gam′ə jə net′ik), *adj.* producing or produced by gamogenesis.
gam|o|ge|net|i|cal|ly (gam′ə jə net′ə klē), *adv.* in a gamogenetic manner; by gamogenetic means.
gam|ont (gam′ont), *n.* a gametocyte stage in certain sporozoans; sporont. [< *gam*(ete) + Greek *ōn, ontós* being, present participle of *eînai* be]
gam|o|pet|al|ous (gam′ə pet′ə ləs), *adj. Botany.* having the petals united; monopetalous. [< Greek *gámos* marriage + English *petal* + *-ous*]
gam|o|phyl|lous (gam′ə fil′əs), *adj. Botany.* having the leaves united; monophyllous. [< Greek *gámos* marriage + *phýllon* leaf + English *-ous*]
gam|o|sep|al|ous (gam′ə sep′ə ləs), *adj. Botany.* having the sepals united; monosepalous. [< Greek *gámos* marriage + English *sepal* + *-ous*]
-gamous, *combining form.* **1** marrying: *Bigamous = marrying twice.*
2 joined or joining: *Heterogamous = having to do with the joining of unequal gametes.*
[< Greek *-gamos* (with English *-ous*) < *gámos* marriage]
gamp (gamp), *n. British Informal.* an umbrella, especially one tied up in a loose, untidy fashion. [< Mrs. Sarah *Gamp,* in Dickens' novel *Martin Chuzzlewit,* who carried a large umbrella]
gam|ut (gam′ət), *n.* **1** the whole range of anything: *During the day I ran the gamut of feeling from hope to despair.* **2** the whole series of notes on the musical scale. **3** the major diatonic scale. **4** the lowest note on the medieval scale of music. [contraction of Medieval Latin *gamma ut* < *gamma G,* the lowest tone + *ut* (later *do*), the first note; notes of the scale were named from syllables in a Latin hymn: *Ut* queant laxis *re*sonare fibris, *Mi*ra gestorum *fa*muli tuorum, *Sol*ve polluti *la*bii reatum, *Sa*ncte *I*ohannes]
gam|y (gā′mē), *adj.,* **gam|i|er, gam|i|est.** **1** having a strong taste or smell like the flesh of wild animals or birds, especially when kept until slightly tainted. **2** abounding in game. **3** brave; plucky; mettlesome: *a gamy little fellow.* **4** *Slang.* somewhat improper; racy: *This Was Burlesque ... is comic in an earthy kind of way, but it is also awfully gamy* (New Yorker). Also, **gamey.** —**gam′i|ly**, *adv.* —**gam′i|ness**, *n.*
-gamy, *combining form.* **1** marriage: *Polygamy = plural marriage.*
2 the condition of being joined together: *Allogamy = the condition of being joined in cross-fertilization.*
[< Greek *-gamiā* < *gámos* marriage]
gan or **'gan** (gan), *v. Archaic.* past tense of **gin**⁴.
Gan|da (gan′də), *n.* **1** = Baganda. **2** = Luganda.
gan|der (gan′dər), *n., v.* —*n.* **1** a male goose, especially one that has reached its full growth. **2** *Figurative.* a fool; simpleton. **3** *Slang.* a long look, like that of a gander: *Don't take our word for it! Just take a gander at this* (Wall Street Journal).
—*v.i. Slang.* to look: *We spent the day gandering around the town.*
[Old English *gandra.* See related etym. at **gannet.**]
Gan|dhar|vas (gun dėr′vəz), *n.pl. Hinduism.* the heavenly singers at the banquets of the gods.
Gan|dhi|an (gän′dē ən, gan′-), *adj.* of or having to do with Mahatma Gandhi (1869-1948) or his political and social outlook: *the Gandhian philosophy of nonviolence.*
∗**Gan|dhi cap** or **hat** (gän′dē, gan′-), a small, white cap without a brim or visor, worn in India.

∗**Gandhi cap**

Gan|dhi|ism (gän′dē iz əm, gan′-), *n.* **1** the philosophy and teachings of Mahatma Gandhi. **2** the doctrine of nonviolence as advocated by Gandhi.
Gan|dhi|ite (gän′dē īt, gan′-), *n., adj.* —*n.* a follower of Gandhi.
—*adj.* of or having to do with Gandhi.
Gan|dhist (gan′dist), *n.* a supporter or adherent of Gandhiism.
G & N (no periods), guidance and navigation.
G & S (no periods), Gilbert and Sullivan: *G&S discography.*
gan|du|rah (gän dü′rə), *n.* a silk blouse worn by Moslem Arabs. [< Arabic *ghandūrah*]
gan|dy dancer (gan′dē), *U.S. Slang.* **1** a member of a railroad section gang; railroad track worker; section hand. **2** a seasonal or itinerant laborer. [origin uncertain]
ga|nef (gä′nəf), *n. Slang.* a thief; crook; pickpocket. Also, **gonoph, gonof.** [< Yiddish *ganef* < Hebrew *ganābh*]
Gan|e|lon (gan′ə lən; *French* gȧ nə lôɴ′), *n.* (in medieval romances about Charlemagne) a treacherous paladin who caused the death of Roland and the loss of the battle of Roncesvalles.
Ga|ne|sha (gə nā′shə), *n. Hinduism.* **1** the lord of the troops of inferior deities. **2** the Hindu god of success and wisdom, represented as a small, fat creature with the head of an elephant.
gang¹ (gang), *n., v.* —*n.* **1** a group of people acting or going around together, especially a group engaged in some improper, unlawful, or criminal activity: *a political gang. Criminals often form gangs. A gang of crazy heretics* (Macaulay). **2a** a group of people working together under one foreman or overseer: *Two gangs of workmen were mending the road.* **b** a company of convicts, slaves, or the like. **3a** a set of similar tools or machines arranged to work together: *a gang of saws, a gang of plows.* **b** a set of things such as are ordinarily taken together: *a gang of oars.* **4** *U.S.* a herd, as of elk or buffalo. **5** *Scottish.* **a** a walk or pasture for cattle. **b** the right of pasturing.
—*v.i. Informal.* **1** to form a gang: *The boys ganged together to make plans for the summer.* **2** to attack in a gang. **3** to move as a gang: *The group ganged into the ice cream parlor and had sodas.* —*v.t.* **1** *Informal.* to attack (a person or thing) in or as if in a gang. **2** to arrange (tools or machines) in gangs: *to gang plows.*
gang up on, *Informal.* to oppose or attack as a group: *Owls are hated by other birds, which gang up on them whenever they find one by daylight in an exposed place* (Science News Letter).
[earlier, a (manner or way of) going, Old English *gang* a going] —**gang′like′**, *adj.*
gang² (gang), *n.* = gangue.
gang³ (gang), *v.i. Scottish.* to walk or go: *The best laid schemes o' mice an' men Gang oft agley* (Robert Burns). [Old English *gangan*]
gang|board (gang′bôrd′, -bōrd′), *n.* a board or plank with cleats for steps, used in getting on or off a ship, a low scaffolding, or the like.
gang|bust|er (gang′bus′tər), *n. U.S. Informal.* an investigator, prosecutor, or other agent of the law concerned with the breaking up of criminal gangs.
gang|bust|ing (gang′bus′ting), *n. U.S. Informal.* the work, activities, or criminal prosecution carried on by gangbusters.
gang cultivator, a cultivator having several sets of blades that operate simultaneously.
gang days, *Obsolete.* Rogation Days.
gang|dom (gang′dəm), *n.* = gangsterdom.
gang drill, a machine having several drills so arranged that they may be operated together or independently.
gange (ganj), *v.t.,* **ganged, gang|ing.** **1** to protect (a fishhook) with fine wire. **2** to fasten (a fishhook) to the end of the ganging.
gang|er¹ (gang′ər), *n.* the foreman of a gang of workmen.
gang|er² (gang′ər), *n.* **1** a fast horse. **2** *Dialect.* a walker.
Gan|ges shark (gan′jēz), a shark of India that frequents lakes and rivers: *One maneater, the Ganges shark, ... long has been known to attack bathers in India's Ganges and Hugli Rivers* (Science News Letter).
Gan|get|ic (gan jet′ik), *adj.* of or along the river Ganges in India: *the Gangetic plain.*
gang hook, two or three fishhooks joined at their shanks and attached to the same line.
gang|in (gang′in), *n.* a short piece of special line to which a fishhook is attached; snell.
gang|ing (gan′jing), *n.* **1** the act of fastening a fishhook to the line. **2** a section or part of a fishing line to the free end of which a hook is ganged.
gang|land (gang′land′, -lənd), *n., adj. Especially U.S.* —*n.* **1** the world of gangsters. **2** an area or territory occupied by gangsters.
—*adj.* of, from, or having to do with gangland.
gan|gle (gang′gəl), *v.i.,* **-gled, -gling.** to move awkwardly or loosely. [back formation < *gangling*]
gang|lead|er (gang′lē′dər), *n.* the head of a gang.
gan|gli|a (gang′glē ə), *n.* a plural of **ganglion.**
gan|gli|ate (gang′glē it, -āt), *adj.* = gangliated.
gan|gli|at|ed (gang′glē ā′tid), *adj.* having ganglia.
gan|gli|form (gang′lə fôrm), *adj.* having the form of a ganglion; like a ganglion.
gan|gling (gang′gling), *adj.* **1** awkwardly tall and slender; lank and loosely built: *He looks like a young, black-haired, rather gangling intellectual* (New Yorker). **2** straggling: *gangling weeds.* [perhaps < present participle of unrecorded *gangle* (frequentative) < *gang*¹, verb]
gan|gli|on (gang′glē ən), *n., pl.* **-gli|a** or **-gli|ons.** **1** a group of nerve cells forming a nerve center, especially outside of the brain or spinal cord. **2** *Figurative.* a center of force, activity, or interest. **3** a tumor, swelling, or cyst in the sheath of a tendon. [< Greek *ganglíon* (originally) a type of swelling (ganglia were compared to tumors)]
gan|gli|on|at|ed (gang′lē ə nā′tid), *adj.* = gangliated.
gan|gli|on|ec|to|my (gang′glē ə nek′tə mē), *n., pl.* **-mies.** the surgical removal of a ganglion.
gan|gli|on|ic (gang′glē on′ik), *adj.* **1** having to do with a ganglion or ganglia. **2** having or characterized by ganglia.
ganglionic or **ganglion block**, a drug-induced blocking of the ganglia that prevents nerve impulses from causing constriction of the blood vessels, used in the treatment of hypertension.
ganglionic blocker, a drug that induces a ganglionic block.
gan|gli|o|side (gang′glē ə sīd′), *n.* a cerebroside containing neuraminic acid. [< *ganglio*(n) + (cerebro)*side*]
gan|gly (gang′glē), *adj.,* **-gli|er, -gli|est.** = gangling (def. 1).
gang|man (gang′mən), *n., pl.* **-men.** *British.* a member of a working gang or crew.
gang of four, a faction within the Chinese Communist party, that attempted to gain control of government after the death of Mao Tse-tung: *The "gang of four" was ... accused of ... sabotaging production with calls for more efforts to modernize revolution* (Mark Gayn). [in reference to Chiang Ching and three of her allies]
gang|plank (gang′plangk′), *n.* a movable bridge used in getting on and off a ship; gangway.
gang plow, *U.S.* a plow or set of plows having several plowshares that operate simultaneously.
gan|grel (gang′grəl), *n. Archaic.* **1** a wandering beggar. **2** a lanky, loosely built person. [apparently < *gang*¹ + *-rel,* as in *wastrel*]
gan|grene (gang′grēn, gang grēn′), *n., v.,* **-grened, -gren|ing.** —*n.* the decay and death of tissue when the blood supply of a living person or animal is interfered with by injury, infection, or freezing; mortification; necrosis.
—*v.t.* to cause gangrene in. —*v.i.* to be or become affected with gangrene; decay: *The wounded leg gangrened and had to be amputated.*
[< Latin *gangraena* < Greek *gángraina,* probably < *grân* gnaw, eat]
gan|gre|nous (gang′grə nəs), *adj.* of or having gangrene; decaying.
gang|sa (gang′sə), *n.* a Balinese xylophone having metal keys which are struck with hardwood hammers. [compare Indonesian *gangsa* brass]
gang saw, one of a group of saws in a lumber mill, each mounted in a frame and acting simultaneously to cut a log into several boards in one operation.
gang|ster (gang′stər), *n.* a member of a gang of criminals or roughs: *finding the three Brighton gangsters guilty of murder* (London Daily Express). [American English < *gang*¹, noun + *-ster*]
gang|ster|dom (gang′stər dəm), *n.* **1** the realm of gangsters: *Natural death is a rarity in gangsterdom.* **2** = gangsterism.
gang|ster|ism (gang′stə riz əm), *n.* **1** the commission of crimes by or as if by members of an organized gang: *Racketeering and gangsterism were widespread in the twenties.* **2** gangsters or their crimes: *The fight against gangsterism never stops.* **3** crime; delinquency: *I was hesitant about car stealing ... the police couldn't overlook gangsterism of this sort* (Geoffrey Household).
gangue (gang), *n.* the worthless earthy or stony matter in a mineral deposit; matrix in which an ore is found. Also, **gang.** [< French *gangue,* alteration of German *Gang* lode, vein of metal; (literally) a going]
gang-up (gang′up′), *n. U.S. Informal.* a ganging up (on or against); attack.
gang war, a fight between two or more gangs, usually for the control of a district or territory.
gang|way (gang′wā′), *n., interj.* —*n.* **1** a passageway through or in a building: *The monument ... used to be in the gangway of the nave* (J. C. Cox). **2a** an aisle or passageway on a ship: *The ship has a gangway between the rail and the cabins.* **b** = gangplank. **c** an opening for the gangplank in the rail of a ship. **3** in England: **a** an aisle in a theater. **b** a cross aisle about halfway down in the House of Commons, just above which ministers, ex-ministers, and party members closely associated with policy sit. **4** a level in a

Pronunciation Key: hat, āge, cãre, fär; let, ēqual, tėrm; it, īce; hot, ōpen, ôrder; oil, out; cup, pu̇t, rüle; child; long; thin; ᴛʜen; zh, measure; ə represents **a** in about, **e** in taken, **i** in pencil, **o** in lemon, **u** in circus.

mine. **5** the incline on which logs are moved up into a sawmill from the water; a logway.
—interj. Informal. get out of the way! stand aside and make room!
above (or **below**) **the gangway**, the seating position of ministers and other members of the House of Commons in relation to the gangway.
[Old English *gangweg* a passage < *gang* a going + *weg* way]

gan|is|ter (gan′ə stər) *n.* **1** a close-grained, siliceous rock occurring in some English coal seams. **2** an artificial mixture resembling this, made of ground quartz and fire clay, used in lining furnaces. [origin uncertain]

gan|ja (gän′jä), *n.* Indian hemp prepared for smoking; marijuana; hashish. [< Hindi *gānjhā* a preparation of Indian hemp]

gan|net (gan′it), *n.* **1** any one of a group of large, fish-eating sea birds resembling a goose, but with a sharper bill, long, pointed wings, and a shorter tail. Gannets belong to the same family as the booby. The common variety of the North Atlantic is a large, white bird with black-tipped wings. **2** = wood ibis. [Old English *ganot.* See related etym. at **gander**.]

gan|net|ry (gan′it rē), *n., pl.* **-ries.** a place where gannets breed.

gan|oid (gan′oid), *adj., n.* *—adj.* (of fishes) having hard scales of bone overlaid with enamel.
—n. a ganoid fish. Sturgeons and gars are ganoids. [< Greek *gános* brightness + English *-oid*]

gan|te|lope (gan′tə lōp), *n. Archaic.* gantlet¹.

gant|let¹ (gônt′lit, gant′-, gänt′-), *n., v.* *—n.* **1** a former punishment or torture in which the offender had to run between two rows of men who struck him with clubs or other weapons as he passed. **2** an overlapping arrangement of two railroad tracks with the inner rail of each within the rails of the other so as to form a narrower bed over a bridge, through a tunnel, or the like, without the use of a switch.
—v.t. to lay or arrange (railroad tracks) to form a gantlet. Also, **gauntlet**.
run the gantlet, a to pass between two rows of men, each of whom strikes the victim as he passes: *One of the boatswain's mates ran the gantlet for stealing a shirt* (T. Pocock). **b** *Figurative.* to be exposed to unfriendly attacks or severe criticism; *proceed under attacks from both sides, or under any similar trying conditions: to run the gantlet of hostile or curious glances, or of criticism or ridicule. They have run the gantlet of the years* (Oliver Wendell Holmes).
[earlier *gantlope* < Swedish *gatlopp* < *gata* lane = *lopp* course; perhaps influenced by *gauntlet²*]

gant|let² (gônt′lit, gant′-, gänt′-), *n.* = gauntlet¹.

gant|line (gant′līn′), *n.* a rope passing through a block on the masthead, used to raise or lower rigging. [variant of *girtline*]

gant|lope (gant′lōp), *n. Archaic.* gantlet¹.

gan|try (gan′trē), *n., pl.* **-tries.** **1** a bridgelike framework that spans over something, for supporting a kind of suspended crane or block signals over railroad tracks. **2** = gantry crane. **3** a four-footed, wooden stand for barrels. Also, **gauntry**. [probably alteration of Old North French *gantier*, Old French *chantier* < Latin *canthērius* rafter, frame, related to Greek *kanthêlios* donkey]

***gantry crane**, a movable crane mounted on a gantry. It is used in servicing machines and vertically mounted rockets or missiles.

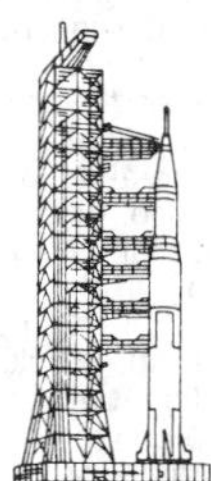
***gantry crane**

Gan|y|mede (gan′ə mēd), *n.* **1a** *Greek Mythology.* a beautiful youth carried off by Zeus to be cupbearer to the gods. **b** *Figurative: Lo! Ganymede appears with a foaming tankard of ale* (Punch). **2** the largest satellite of the planet Jupiter.

ganz|feld (gänts′felt), *n. Psychology. a blank surface, used to prevent interference with internally produced visual imagery: A ganzfeld can be a whitewashed wall or even, as in some experiments, halves of Ping-Pong balls taped over the eyes* (Marilyn Ferguson). [< German *Ganzfeld,* from *ganz* whole + *Feld* field]

GAO (no periods) or **G.A.O.**, *U.S.* General Accounting Office (a Congressional agency).

gaol (jāl), *n., v.t. British.* jail. [Middle English *gayhole* < Old North French gaiole < Vulgar Latin *gaviōla* < Latin *cavea* cage]—**gaol′er**, *n.*

gaol|bird (jāl′bėrd′), *n. British.* jailbird.

gaol-break (jāl′brāk′), *n. British Informal.* jailbreak.

gap (gap), *n., v.,* **gapped, gap|ping.** *—n.* **1** a broken place; opening: *The cows got out of the field through a gap in the fence.* SYN: break, breach. **2** an empty part; unfilled space; blank: *The record is not complete; there are several gaps in it. There still exists in general a wide gap between the empirical facts of chemistry on the one side, and the fundamental laws of physics on the other* (Science News). SYN: lacuna. **3** a wide difference of opinion, character, or the like. SYN: divergence. **4** a pass through mountains; gorge: *We passed the narrows or gaps of two ranges of high mountains* (M. Cutler). SYN: defile, ravine. See picture under **mountain.** **5** a space between two electrodes, such as that in the spark plug of a gasoline engine, across which an electric spark jumps.
—v.t. to make a gap or opening in: *Demolishing two-thirds of the houses and gapping . . . the remainder* (British Weekly).
—v.i. to have or show gaps: *The little boy's teeth gapped when he smiled.*
bridge the gap (**between**), *Especially British.* to do away with differences (between); effect harmony or uniformity: *. . . to help bridge the gap between rich and poor nations* (London Times).
stop (**fill** or **supply**) **a gap**, to make up a deficiency; supply a want; fill a vacant space: *We hope to fill the gap in our missile program very soon.*
[< Scandinavian (compare Old Icelandic *gap*). See related etym. at **gape**.]

GAPA (no periods), or **Gap|a** (gap′ə), *n.* ground-to-air pilotless aircraft.

gape (gāp, gap), *v.,* **gaped, gap|ing,** *n.* *—v.i.* **1** to open wide: *A deep hole in the earth gaped before us.* **2** to open the mouth wide; yawn: *Gape not too wide, lest you disclose your gums* (William Congreve). **3** to stare with the mouth open: *The crowd gaped at the daring tricks performed by the tightrope walkers.* **4** to be or become open wide: *May that ground gape and swallow me alive, Where I shall kneel to him that slew my father* (Shakespeare). **5** to desire eagerly (to do or have something): *He seeks no honours, gapes after no preferment* (Robert Burton).
—n. **1** a wide opening: *There was a gape in the seat of his pants where they had split.* **2** the act of opening the mouth wide; yawning. **3** an open-mouthed stare. **4** a state of eagerness or wonder: *The mind is not here kept in a perpetual gape after knowledge* (Joseph Addison). **5** *Zoology.* **a** the width of an open mouth or beak. **b** the line of compressure of the mandibles of a bird's beak.
the gapes, a a fit of yawning: *Another hour of music was to give delight or the gapes, as real or affected taste for it prevailed* (Jane Austen). **b** a disease of birds and poultry, caused by a roundworm: *A disease prevalent among the gallinaceous poultry in this country [is] the gapes* (British Medical Journal).
[< Scandinavian (compare Old Icelandic *gapa*)]
—**gap′ing|ly**, *adv.*

gape|mouthed (gāp′mouᴛʜd′, -moutht′), *adj.* open-mouthed; agape.

gap|er (gā′pər), *n.* **1** a person who gapes. **2** = broadbill (def. 1). **3** a bivalve mollusk, the shell of which is open at one end; soft clam. **4** = sea bass.

gapes (gāps, gaps), *n.pl.* See under **gape**.

gape|seed (gāp′sēd′), *n.* **1** something to gape or stare at. **2** the act of gaping or staring. **3** a person who gapes or stares.

gape|worm (gāp′wėrm′), *n.* a nematode worm that is parasitic in the trachea and bronchi of birds and causes the gapes.

gap|ey (gā′pē), *adj.* = gapy.

gap|o|sis (gə pō′sis), *n. U.S. Slang.* **1** a gap in the arrangement or matching of a person's clothing. **2** any conspicuous or abnormal gap, deficiency, or other lack: *Dollar gaposis between the U.S. and foreign countries is worse than ever* (Wall Street Journal). [< *gap* + *-osis*]

gapped scale (gapt), a musical scale derived from a more complete system of tones by the omission of some of the tones. The pentatonic is a gapped scale derived from the diatonic scale.

gap|py (gap′ē), *adj.* having gaps or breaks.

gap-toothed (gap′tütʜd′, -tütht′), *adj.* **1** having gaps in the rows of teeth. **2** having the teeth set wide apart.

gap|y (gā′pē), *adj.* affected with the gapes. Also, **gapey**.

gar¹ (gär), *n., pl.* **gars** or (*collectively*) **gar. 1** any one of a family of American freshwater fishes with a long, slender body covered with hard scales, and long, narrow jaws; garfish; gar pike. **2** = needlefish. [American English; short for *garfish*]

gar² (gär), *v.t. Scottish.* to make; cause; compel. [< Scandinavian (compare Old Icelandic *gera*)]

GAR (no periods), guided aircraft rocket.

G.A.R., Grand Army of the Republic.

ga|rage (gə räzh′, -räj′; *British also* gar′äzh, -ij), *n., v.,* **-raged, -rag|ing.** *—n.* **1** a place where automobiles are kept: *The city built a parking garage near the stores in town.* **2** a shop for repairing automobiles: *Our car, he told us, had been towed to a garage* (Newsweek).
—v.t. to put or keep in a garage: *He garages a Mercedes-Benz and a Cadillac* (Saturday Evening Post).
[< French *garage* < *garer* put in shelter < Germanic (compare Old High German *warōn*)]

ga|rage|man (gə räzh′man, -räj′-; *especially British* gar′ij mən), *n., pl.* **-men.** a person who works in a garage, especially an automobile mechanic.

garage sale, *U.S.* a private sale of used furniture, appliances, and other items, held in the garage or other part of a seller's home.

ga|rag|ist (gə rä′zhist, -jist; *British also* gar′ä-zhist, -jist), *n.* a garage owner or attendant. [< French *garagiste*]

Gar|a|mond (gar′ə mond), *n. Printing.* a style of type face based on one designed by Claude Garamond.

Gar|and rifle (gar′ənd, gə rand′), a semi-automatic rifle, .30 caliber, used by the United States Army from 1936 to 1960. [< John C. *Garand,* born 1888, an American inventor]

garb (gärb), *n., v.* *—n.* **1** the way one is dressed. **2** clothing: *official garb, military garb, priestly garb, peasant garb.* **3** *Figurative.* outward covering, form, or appearance: *. . . .false ruler prank'd in treason's garb* (Milton). **4** *Obsolete.* manner; style; fashion.
—v.t. to clothe; dress: *The doctor was garbed in white.*
[< Middle French *garbe* < Italian *garbo* grace, elegance]

gar|bage (gär′bij), *n.* **1** scraps of food to be thrown away; waste animal or vegetable matter, as from a kitchen, restaurant, or store: *We empty the garbage while Mother washes the dishes.* **2** *Informal, Figurative.* anything of no value, such as a trashy writing or painting. **3** any kind of waste matter. [origin uncertain; perhaps < Old North French *garbe* wheat sheaf + English *-age*]

garbage can, *U.S.* **1** a metal or plastic receptacle for the disposal of garbage. **2** *Slang.* a navy destroyer; can: *His new ship . . . looked like an old garbage can* (Time).

garbage disposal or **disposer**, an electric grinder, usually installed in the drain of a kitchen sink, that turns garbage into small pellets which pass into the sewage system.

gar|bage|man (gär′bij mən), *n., pl.* **-men.** *U.S.* a man who collects garbage for removal in a garbage truck.

garbage truck, *U.S.* a truck, usually equipped with a hopper, for collecting garbage and carrying it to a place of disposal.

gar|ban|zo (gär bän′thō, -sō), *n., pl.* **-zos** (-thōs, -sōs). *Spanish.* the chickpea: *We took the soup, which had a few garbanzos scattered around in it, and then ordered the chicken* (H. Allen Smith).

gar|ble (gär′bəl), *v.,* **-bled, -bling,** *n.* *—v.t.* **1** to confuse or mix up (facts, statements, words, or letters) unintentionally. **2** to make unfair or misleading selections from (facts, statements, or writings); omit parts of, often in order to misrepresent: *Foreign newspapers gave a garbled account of the President's speech.* SYN: distort, misquote. **3** to take out the best of; sort out: *to garble coins.*
—n. **1** the process of garbling. **2** something garbled, such as a writing or statement.
[< Old French *garbeler* to sift < Italian *garbellare* < Arabic *gharbala* he sifted, perhaps < Late Latin *crībellāre* < *crībellum* (diminutive) < Latin *crībrum* sieve]

gar|bler (gär′blər), *n.* a person or thing that garbles.

garble table, a table, chart, or other aid used to correct garbled messages or statements in a code or group of codes.

gar|bo (gär′bō), *n., pl.* **-bos.** (in Australia) a garbage or trash collector. [alteration of *garbage*]

gar|board (gär′bôrd′, -bōrd′), *n.,* or **garboard strake**, one of the planks or plates on a ship's bottom, next to the keel. [apparently < obsolete Dutch *gaarboord,* perhaps < *garen,* for *gaderan* gather + *boord* board]

Gar|bo|esque (gär′bō esk′), *adj.* having to do with or characteristic of the Swedish-American actress Greta Garbo: *a large-brimmed Garboesque hat. She may be Garboesque in her reclusiveness* (Time).

gar|boil (gär′boil), *n. Archaic.* a disturbance; tumult. [< Old French *garbouil* < Italian *garbuglio*]

gar|bol|o|gist (gär bol′ə jist), *n.* **1** *Chiefly Humor-*

ous. a garbage or trash collector. **2** a person who studies or is an expert in garbology. [< *garb* (age) + *-ologist,* as in *biologist, zoologist*]

gar|bol|o|gy (gär bol′ə jē), *n.* the study of a culture or society by examining and recording the contents of its garbage or refuse: *Among aficionados and practitioners of the new pop science of garbology . . . there's a saying: garbage doesn't lie* (Suburbia Today).

gar|bure (gär byr′), *n. French.* a vegetable soup made with cabbage and bacon.

gar|cin|i|a (gär sin′ē ə), *n.* any one of a group of tropical trees with thick, leathery leaves that yield resin. [< New Latin *Garcinia* the genus name < Laurent *Garcin,* 1683-1751, a French botanist]

gar|çon (går sôN′), *n., pl.* **gar|çons** (går sôN′). *French.* **1** a young man; boy. **2** a servant. **3** a waiter.

gar|çon d'hon|neur (går sôN′dô nœr′), *French.* a best man.

gar|çon|nière (går sô nyãr′), *n. French.* a bachelor's quarters.

gar|da (gor′də), *n., pl.* **gar|da|i** (gor′də ē). an Irish policeman or guard. [< Irish *gárda* (plural *gárdaí*)]

gar|da|loo (gär′də lü′), *n. Dialect.* gardyloo.

gar|dant (gär′dənt), *adj. Heraldry.* having the full face toward the spectator. [< French *gardant* guardant]

garde (gård), *n. French.* **1** guard, watch, or keeping; care or heed. **2** a body of troops or others, charged with guarding. **3** a guard, custodian, or keeper; guardsman.

garde-feu (gård′fœ′), *n. French.* a screen or fender for a fireplace.

garde-man|ger (gård′mäN zhā′), *n., pl.* **garde-man|gers** (gård′mäN zhā′). **1** a room in the kitchen of a hotel, restaurant, or the like, where cold foods and dishes are stored or prepared. **2** the person in charge of this room. [< French *garde-manger* (literally) food-keeper]

garde mo|bile (gård′mō bēl′), a member of a French military force acting as a state security police. [< French *Garde Mobile* the military police force; (literally) Mobile Guard]

gar|den (gär′dən), *n., v., adj.* **—*n.*** **1** a piece of ground used for growing vegetables, herbs, flowers, or fruits. **2** a park or place where people go for amusement or to see things that are displayed: *a beer garden, botanical gardens.* **3** a fertile and delightful spot; well-cultivated region: *Fruitful Lombardy, The pleasant garden of great Italy* (Shakespeare). **4** *Baseball Slang.* the outfield.

—*v.i.* to take care of a garden; make a garden; work in a garden: *He liked to garden because it kept him out of doors.*

—*v.t.* to cultivate, as one does a garden.

—*adj.* **1** growing or grown in a garden; for a garden. **2** common; ordinary. **3** = hardy[1] (def. 2).

lead up the garden path, *Slang.* to lead on; entice; mislead: *I fell for his scheme till I realized that he was leading me up the garden path.*

[< Old North French *gardin* < Germanic (compare Old High German *garto*)] **—gar′den|like′,** *adj.*

garden apartment, an apartment in a group or circle of low apartment houses, situated on the ground floor in a residential or suburban section of a city and having open lawns.

garden balsam, = balsam (def. 4).

garden center, a store that sells flowers, shrubbery, seeds, tools, and fertilizer and pesticides, for gardening.

garden centipede, a small centipede that often injures seeds and young shoots of sugar beets, asparagus, and other crops.

garden city, a suburban section of a town surrounded by gardens, parks, and open spaces, in which industry is restricted.

garden club, a club whose members share a common interest in gardening.

garden court, a suburban shopping center with landscaped surroundings.

garden cress, = peppergrass.

garden egg, the fruit of an eggplant.

gar|den|er (gärd′nər), *n.* **1** a person hired to take care of a garden, lawn, and other landscaping: *The gardeners were planting little trees in the park.* **2** a person who makes a garden or works in a garden: *My grandfather is quite a gardener and has many beds of flowers in the spring.*

garden flea, any one of a variety of springtails that damage young garden plants.

garden glass, a bell jar used for covering plants in a garden.

garden heliotrope, the common valerian.

garden house, **1** any small building in a garden. **2** a dwelling house situated in a garden or gardenlike surroundings. **3** *Dialect.* a small outhouse used as a toilet.

gar|de|nia (gär dēn′yə, -dē′nē ə), *n.* **1** a sweet-smelling, white or yellowish flower with smooth, waxy petals. It is somewhat like a rose. **2** an evergreen shrub or small tree that bears these flowers. It belongs to the madder family. See picture under **madder family.** [American English < New Latin *Gardenia* the genus name < Alexander *Garden,* 1730-1791, a Scottish naturalist]

gar|den|ing (gär′də ning, gärd′ning), *n.* **1** the cultivating of a garden. **2** the work of a gardener.

gar|den|ize (gär′dən īz), *v.,* **-ized, -iz|ing.** **—*v.t.*** to give a gardenlike appearance to; improve by introducing garden features: *to gardenize a public square.* **—*v.i.*** to act as a gardener; take care of a garden.

gar|den|less (gär′dən lis), *adj.* lacking a garden or gardens.

gar|den|ly (gär′dən lē), *adj.* characteristic of or like a garden; appropriate to a garden.

Garden of Eden, = Eden.

garden party, an informal gathering held on the lawn or in the garden of a house.

garden plum, = European plum.

garden sass, *U.S. Dialect.* vegetables from a garden, especially greens to be cooked and served with meat.

garden snail, a snail with a white lip and reddish markings that frequents gardens, where it often causes damage.

garden snake, = garter snake.

garden spot, **1** a piece of garden ground. **2** a place suggestive of a garden; a fertile or well-cultivated region.

Garden State, a nickname for New Jersey.

garden stuff, **1** plants grown in a garden. **2** vegetables for the table.

garden suburb or **village,** = garden city.

garden truck, the products of a vegetable garden, especially when grown for the market.

gar|den-va|ri|e|ty (gär′dən və rī′ə tē), *adj.* **1** of the ordinary kind that grows in a garden: *garden-variety tomatoes.* **2** ordinary; average; run-of-the-mill: *a garden-variety specimen of his breed* (Saturday Review).

garden warbler, any one of certain small birds mainly of Europe, considered as a table delicacy in Italy.

garde|robe (gärd′rōb), *n. Archaic.* **1** a room or place for keeping articles of clothing; wardrobe. **2** a private room; bedchamber. [< Old French *garderobe* < *garder* to keep, guard + *robe* robe]

gar|dez la foi (går dā lå fwå′), *French.* keep the faith; be loyal.

gar|dy|loo (gär′di lü′), *n. Dialect.* a warning cry uttered originally by people in Old Edinburgh before throwing slops from a window into the street. Also, **gardaloo.** [< French *gare* (*de*) *l'eau* beware of the water]

gare|fowl (gãr′foul′), *n., pl.* **-fowls** or (collectively) **-fowl.** = great auk.

Gar|eth (gar′əth), *n. Arthurian Legend.* a knight of the Round Table and nephew of King Arthur.

gar|fish (gär′fish′), *n., pl.* **-fish|es** or (*collectively*) **-fish.** **1** = gar. **2** = needlefish. [Middle English *garfish* < *gar,* Old English *gār* spear + *fish*]

gar|ga|ney (gär′gə nē), *n.* a small European duck. [apparently < dialectal Italian *garganey*]

Gar|gan|tu|a (gär gan′chů ə), *n.* **1** a good-natured giant in a satire by Rabelais. He was a tremendous eater and drinker. **2** *Figurative.* anything enormous, gigantic, or huge: *the undisputed Gargantua of the brokerage trade* (New Yorker).

Gar|gan|tu|an or **gar|gan|tu|an** (gär gan′chů ən), *adj.* enormous; gigantic; huge: *This building is built on a gargantuan scale, with a floor measuring 300 by 500 feet* (Walter Sullivan). **—Gar|gan′tu|an|ly** or **gar|gan′tu|an|ly,** *adv.*

gar|get (gär′git), *n.* **1** an inflamed condition of the head or throat of cattle and swine. **2** inflammation of the udder in cows, ewes, goats, and the like. **3** = pokeweed. [< Old French *gargate*]

gar|gle (gär′gəl), *v.,* **-gled, -gling,** *n.* **—*v.t.*** **1** to wash (the throat or mouth) with a liquid kept in motion by the outgoing breath. **2** to utter with a sound of gargling.

—*v.i.* **1** to use a gargle: *He gargled with hot salt water to relieve his sore throat.* **2** to make a sound in the throat as if gargling.

—*n.* a liquid used for gargling.

[probably < Old French *gargouiller* to gurgle, bubble < *gargouille* throat, waterspout, probably < Latin *gurguliō* windpipe]

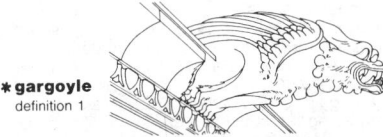

***gargoyle**
definition 1

***gar|goyle** (gär′goil), *n.* **1** a spout for carrying off rain water, ending in a grotesque figure of a head that projects from the gutter of a building. **2** a projection or ornament on a building resembling a gargoyle. Also, **gurgoyle, gurgoil.** [< Old French *gargouille* throat; waterspout; see etym. under **gargle**]

gar|goyled (gär′goild), *adj.* provided with gargoyles: *gargoyled eaves.*

gar|goyl|ish (gär′goi lish), *adj.* somewhat like a gargoyle in appearance; grotesque.

gar|goyl|ism (gär′goi liz əm), *n.* a hereditary condition characterized by mental deficiency, defective vision, a large head and abdomen, and short arms and legs.

gar|i|al (gär′ē əl), *n.* = gavial.

gar|i|bal|di (gar′ə bôl′dē), *n.* **1** a woman's blouse, originally red and later in other colors, made in imitation of the shirts worn by Garibaldi and his followers. **2** a red fish of the California coast. [< Giuseppe *Garibaldi,* 1807-1882, an Italian patriot]

Gar|i|bal|di|an (gar′ə bôl′dē ən), *adj., n.* **—*adj.*** of, having to do with, or supporting Giuseppe Garibaldi. **—*n.*** an adherent of Garibaldi.

ga|rigue (gə rēg′), *n.* = garrigue.

gar|ish (gãr′ish), *adj.* **1** unpleasantly bright; glaring: *the garish sun.* **2** showy; gaudy: *The circus performer was dressed in garish colors.* **SYN:** flashy. **3** adorned to excess. [apparently < obsolete *gaure* to stare] **—gar′ish|ly,** *adv.* **—gar′ish|ness,** *n.*

gar|land (gär′lənd), *n., v.* **—*n.*** **1** a wreath of flowers, leaves, or the like, worn on the head like a crown, or hung for decoration: *the poet's garland of laurels, a Christmas garland.* **2** *Figurative.* a collection of short poems, ballads, or the like; anthology. **3** *Nautical.* **a** a band, loop, or collar, as of rope, used on a mast for various purposes, such as to prevent chafing. **b** a net for holding provisions high up, away from rats or other animals.

—*v.t.* **1** to decorate with garlands: *The Duke passed a . . . garlanded bridegroom riding his ornamental horse* (Manchester Guardian Weekly). **2** to form into garlands.

[< Old French *garlande*]

gar|lic (gär′lik), *n., adj.* **—*n.*** **1** a plant of the same genus as the onion, whose strong-smelling bulb is composed of small sections called *cloves.* See picture under **amaryllis family.** **2** a bulb or clove of this plant, used to season meats, salads, or other foods.

—*adj.* flavored or seasoned with garlic: *garlic sausage, garlic salt, garlic bread.*

[Old English *gārlēac* < *gār* spear + *lēac* leek]

gar|lick|y (gär′lə kē), *adj.* **1** smelling or tasting of garlic. **2** (of wheat, barley, or other grain) growing or mixed with wild garlic.

Garm (gärm), *n. Norse Mythology.* the demon watchdog of Hel, the goddess of the realm of the dead.

gar|ment (gär′mənt), *n., v.* **—*n.*** **1** any article of clothing: *We took father's suit and some other garments to the dry cleaners.* **2** *Figurative.* an outer covering: *I am not weary of writing; it is the coarse but durable garment of my love* (John Donne).

—*v.t.* to dress or clothe: *A lovely Lady garmented in light* (Shelley).

[< Old French *garnement* < *garnir* fit out; see etym. under **garnish**] **—gar′ment|less,** *adj.*

garment bag, a flexible cover of paper, plastic, or other material, often open at the bottom and slotted at the top for the hook of a hanger, used to protect clothing.

garn (gärn), *interj. British Slang.* go on! (used to express disbelief or ridicule of a statement).

gar|ner (gär′nər), *v., n.* **—*v.t.*** **1** to gather and store away: *Wheat is cut and garnered at harvest time. Squirrels garner nuts in the fall.* **2** to collect or deposit: *Virtually the whole literature of England is garnered in this one library.*

—*v.i.* to store up; accumulate: *the wrath that garners in my heart* (Tennyson). [< noun]

—*n.* **1** a storehouse for grain; granary. **2** a store of anything.

[< Old French *gernier,* variant of *grenier* < Latin *grānārium* granary < *grānum* grain]

gar|net[1] (gär′nit), *n., adj.* **—*n.*** **1** a hard, glassy mineral, occurring in many varieties. Garnet is a silicate of which a deep-red, transparent variety is used for jewelry and as an abrasive. . . . *garnet, the dark red gem stone which occurs with the green mineral hornblende* (Science News Letter). **2** a deep red.

—*adj.* deep-red.

[Middle English *gernet* < Old French *grenat* of pomegranate color < (*pomme*) *grenate* pomegranate; see etym. under **grenade**] **—gar′net|like′,** *adj.*

Pronunciation Key: hat, āge, cãre, fär; let, ēqual, tėrm; it, īce; hot, ōpen, ôrder; oil, out; cup, pů́t, rüle; child; long; thin; ᴛʜen; zh, measure; ə represents **a** in about, **e** in taken, **i** in pencil, **o** in lemon, **u** in circus.

gar|net[2] (gär′nit), *n. Nautical.* a tackle rigged on the mainstay, used in raising and lowering cargo. [probably < Dutch *garnaat*]

gar|net|if|er|ous (gär′nə tif′ər əs), *adj.* yielding or containing garnets.

garnet paper, paper coated with finely crushed garnets held by glue, used like sandpaper for polishing.

gar|ni (gȧr nē′), *adj. French.* garnished.

gar|ni|er|ite (gär′nē ə rīt), *n.* a green mineral that occurs as a hydrous silicate of nickel and magnesium. It is an important ore of nickel. [< Jules *Garnier,* a French geologist of the 1800's, who discovered it + *-ite*[1]]

gar|nish (gär′nish), *n., v.* —*n.* **1** something laid on or around food as a decoration or to add flavor: *The turkey was served with a garnish of cranberries and parsley.* **2** decoration; trimming: (*Figurative.*) *to put on some garnish and dress of virtue to impose on the world* (Edward Hyde, 1st Earl of Clarendon). **3** *British Slang.* beer or the like bought by a new workman for his fellow workers. **4** *Historical.* a fee formerly paid in English jails by a new prisoner. **5** *Archaic.* an outfit; dress. [< verb]
—*v.t.* **1** to decorate or add flavor to (food). **2** to decorate; trim: *Her coat was garnished with fur.* (*Figurative.*) *Letters in very fair grammatical Latin, garnished with quotations* (William Stubbs). **SYN:** adorn. **3** *Law.* to warn or notify by a garnishment; garnishee.
[< Old French *garniss-,* stem of *garnir, guarnir, warnir* provide, furnish; defend < Germanic (compare Old High German *warnôn* provide, guard, warn)] —**gar′nish|er,** *n.*

gar|nish|ee (gär′ni shē′), *v.,* **-nish|eed, -nish|ee|ing,** *n.* —*v.t.* **1** to withhold (a person's money or property) by legal authority in payment of a debt. If a creditor garnishees a debtor's salary, a certain portion of the salary is withheld and paid to the creditor. **2** to notify (a person) not to hand over money or property belonging to the defendant in a lawsuit until the plaintiff's claims have been settled: *The debtor's employer was garnisheed.* [< noun]
—*n.* a person notified to hold the defendant's money or property as a trustee until the lawsuit is settled. [< *garnish* + *-ee*]

gar|nish|ment (gär′nish mənt), *n.* **1** decoration; trimming. **2** *Law.* **a** a legal notice warning a person to hold in his possession money or property that belongs to the defendant in a lawsuit until the plaintiff's claims have been settled. **b** the withholding of a person's money or property by legal authority in payment of a debt. **c** a summons to a third person to appear in court while a lawsuit between others is being heard.

gar|ni|ture (gär′nə chər), *n.* decoration; trimming; garnish: *that train of female garniture Which passeth by the name of accomplishments* (Charles Lamb). **SYN:** adornment, embellishment. [< Middle French *garniture* < *garnir* furnish; see etym. under **garnish**]

ga|rotte (gə rot′, -rōt′), *n., v.t.,* **-rot|ted, -rot|ting.** = garrote. —**ga|rot′ter,** *n.*

gar pike, = gar.

gar|ran (gar′ən), *n.* **1** a small, hardy horse bred in Ireland and Scotland. **2** a similar horse bred elsewhere. [< Irish, Scottish Gaelic *gearran*]

gar|ret (gar′it), *n.* **1** a space in a house just below a sloping roof; attic. **2** a room or apartment in such a place. [< Old French *garite* < *garir* defend; see etym. under **garrison**]

gar|ret|eer (gar′ə tir′), *n.* a person who lives in a garret, especially a very poor writer.

gar|ri (gär′ē), *n.* a staple food of Nigeria, made of ground cassava: *Garri is regarded by relief doctors* [*in Biafra*] *as a mere "filler" without real nutrient value* (Sunday Times). [< a native name]

gar|rigue (gə rēg′), *n.* an uncultivated land consisting of a calcareous soil overgrown with scrub oak and pine. Also, **garigue.** [< French *garrigue*]

gar|ri|son (gar′ə sən), *n., v.* —*n.* **1** a group of soldiers stationed in a fort or town to defend it: *The Japanese garrison on Wake surrendered at the end of World War II* (E. H. Bryan). **2** a place that has a garrison: *New York City was a garrison for British soldiers in the Revolutionary War.*
—*v.t.* **1** to station soldiers in (a fort or town) to defend it: *The captain commanding the Yankee troops garrisoned in the little town had been stationed in South Carolina for several years* (Atlantic). **2** to occupy (a fort or town) as a garrison: *the other towns, which were garrisoned by the Greek mercenaries, refused to receive him* (Connop Thirlwall). **3** to put (soldiers) on duty in a garrison.
in garrison, doing duty as a garrison or as one of a garrison: *Those in garrison at Goletta threatened to give up that important fortress* (William Robertson).
[< Old French *garison* < *garir* defend < Germanic (compare Gothic *warjan* protect, defend). See etym. of doublet **warison.**]

garrison belt, a wide belt with a large, heavy buckle.

garrison cap, *U.S. Military.* **1** a peaked dress hat of woolen or cotton cloth, with a visor. **2** a small, soft hat without a visor, usually with a colored braid around the side to indicate branch of service; overseas cap.

Garrison finish, *U.S. Informal.* a victory or success achieved at the last possible moment; an unexpected or spectacular finish: ... *a very young portmanteau revue, not entirely past the awkward stage but ending with a Garrison finish* (New Yorker). [< Snapper *Garrison,* an American jockey of the 1800's, famous for winning races at the last minute]

garrison flag, a large flag displayed at military posts in the United States on occasions of national importance.

garrison house, *U.S.* **1** a strongly built log house with a projecting upper story. **2** a fortified house like this, formerly used by settlers as a shelter during Indian raids.

garrison state, **1** a country organized in a military way in time of peace as well as of war: *As to the alleged virtues of the garrison state, we all know what happened to Hitler's vaunted totalitarian "efficiency" when the West took counter measures* (Wall Street Journal). **2** a country with strong central controls and regimentation.

gar|ron (gar′ən), *n.* = garran.

gar|rot (gar′ət), *n.* any sea duck, especially a goldeneye. [< French *garrot*]

gar|rote (gə rot′, -rōt′), *n., v.,* **-rot|ed, -rot|ing.** —*n.* **1** a method of executing a person by strangling him with an iron collar. The collar is fastened to a post and tightened by a screw. **2** the iron collar used for this. **3** strangulation, especially in order to rob. **4** any device used to strangle.
—*v.t.* **1** to execute by garroting. **2** to strangle and rob; strangle. **SYN:** throttle. Also, **garotte.** [< Spanish *garrote* stick for twisting cord] —**gar|rot′er,** *n.*

gar|rotte (gə rot′, -rōt′), *n., v.t.,* **-rot|ted, -rot|ting.** = garrote. —**gar|rot′ter,** *n.*

gar|ru|li|ty (gə rü′lə tē), *n., pl.* **-ties.** **1** the fact or quality of being garrulous; talkativeness: *His blunt, rough manners, garrulity and good humor won him attention* (Time). **2** garrulous remarks; wordiness.

gar|ru|lous (gar′ə ləs, -yə ləs), *adj.* **1** talking too much about trifles; talkative: *Age, garrulous, recounts The feats of youth* (James Thomson). **SYN:** loquacious. **2** using too many words; wordy: *garrulous comments.* **SYN:** long-winded. [< Latin *garrulus* (with English *-ous*) < *garrīre* to chatter] —**gar′ru|lous|ly,** *adv.* —**gar′ru|lous|ness,** *n.*

gar|tel (gär′təl), *n. Yiddish.* a black silk cord that Hasidic Jews tie around the waist to symbolize the separation between the spiritual and baser instincts of man.

gar|ter (gär′tər), *n., v.* —*n.* a band or strap to hold up a stocking or sock. It is usually elastic.
—*v.t.* to fasten with a garter: *Women used to the standard welt ... were gartering in the sheer part of the stocking and getting runs* (New York Times).
[< Old French *gartier* < *garet* band of the knee, perhaps < Celtic (compare Welsh *gār* leg)] —**gar′ter|less,** *adj.*

Gar|ter (gär′tər), *n.* **1 (Order of) the,** the oldest and most important order of knighthood in Great Britain, established about 1349. **2** a badge of this order. **3** membership in it. **4** = Garter King-of-Arms.

Garter King-of-Arms (king′əv ärmz′), the chief herald of the Order of the Garter.

garter snake, **1** a small, harmless, brownish or greenish snake with three yellow or white stripes that run along the body: *Garter snakes ... may be found in the back yards of city dwellers as well as in the fields and forests* (A. M. Winchester). **2** a South African snake conspicuously marked by alternate rings of black and red.

garter stitch, a simple knitting stitch, done without purling.

garth (gärth), *n.* **1** a dam or weir for catching fish. **2** the open space surrounded by a cloister; cloister garth. **3** a fence or hedge. **4** any enclosed or fenced area. **5** *Archaic.* a yard or garden. [< Scandinavian (compare Old Icelandic *garthr* yard, courtyard, fence)]

ga|ru|a (gə rü′ə; *Spanish* gä rü′ä), *n.* a heavy mist or fog along the coast of Peru and Chile; camanchaca. It occurs from May to October and plants of the region depend on it for their moisture. [< American Spanish *garúa*]

gas[1] (gas), *n., pl.* **gas|es,** *v.,* **gassed, gas|sing.** —*n.* **1** a substance that is not a liquid or a solid; any substance that has no shape or size of its own and can expand without limit. Oxygen and hydrogen are gases at ordinary temperatures. **2** any gas or mixture of gases except air. **3** any mixture of gases that can be burned, obtained from coal and other substances. Gas was once much used for lighting, but is now used chiefly for cooking and heating. *Much of the artificial gas now used in great areas of the United States to which natural gas is not delivered is made from coal* (Science News Letter). **4** any gas used as an anesthetic, such as nitrous oxide or laughing gas. **5** a substance that vaporizes and then poisons, suffocates, or stupefies, such as tear gas. Mustard gas has been used in warfare. **6** *Mining.* an explosive mixture of methane with air. **7** *Slang, Figurative.* empty or boasting talk. **8** Usually, **a gas.** *Slang.* a great pleasure; a delight; a joy: *As black Percussion Man Warren Duncan says, "It's a gas to ride the buses, see all the mountains and the jack rabbits and road runners"* (Time).
—*v.t.* **1** to supply with gas. **2** to treat with gas; use gas on. Some kinds of seeds are gassed to hasten sprouting. **3** to injure or kill by poisonous gas. **4** to kill in a gas chamber with poison gas: *The Nazis gassed millions of people.* **5** to pass (a thread or fabric) through a gas flame to remove superfluous fibers. **6** to impregnate (slaked lime) with chlorine, especially in the manufacture of bleaching powder. **7** *Slang.* **a** to deceive or impose upon by talking idly or boastingly. **b** to please; delight.
—*v.i.* **1** to give off gas. **2** *Slang.* to talk idly or in a boasting way: *I'm 'fraid I've been gassing awf'ly, sir* (Rudyard Kipling).
[(coined by Jean B. van Helmont, 1577-1644, a Flemish physician and chemist) probably alteration of Greek *cháos* chaos]

gas[2] (gas), *n., v.,* **gassed, gas|sing.** *U.S. Informal.* —*n.* **1** = gasoline. **2** = gas pedal.
—*v.t., v.i.* to supply with gasoline.
gas up, to fill up the gasoline tank of an automobile, truck, or airplane with gasoline: *to gas up the car. We gassed up at the service station for the long trip.*
step on the gas, *Slang.* **a** to make an automobile go faster by pressing down the gas pedal: *The engine roared as he stepped on the gas.* **b** to go faster; put on speed: *So as not to be late for classes, the boys stepped on the gas and ran all the way to school.*

gas attack, the release of asphyxiating or poisonous gases as a weapon of war.

gas bag, **1** a bag in which gas is kept for use. **2** an inflatable bag used as a plug in a gas pipe during repairs. **3** one of the separate containers of gas in a rigid airship. **4** *Slang.* an empty, voluble talker; windbag.

gas black, fine soot produced by turning a gas flame on metal, used as a paint and as a pigment; carbon black.

gas boat, a motorboat powered by an automobile engine converted for use in boats.

gas bottle, **1** = retort (def. 1). **2** a steel cylinder for holding compressed gas.

gas burner, the small nozzle of a gas fixture where gas comes out and is burned.

gas-cap drive (gas′kap′), a form of underground pressure exerted by natural gas on oil deposits, forcing the oil up the well.

gas carbon, a compact form of carbon deposited in the making of coal gas. It is used for electrodes in batteries and arc lamps.

gas chamber, a hermetically sealed room in which a poison gas is released. It has been used in some states to execute persons condemned to death and was one of the forms of extermination used in Nazi concentration camps.

gas chromatograph, the instrument used in gas chromatography for analyzing the substances in a mixture, especially mixtures found in petroleum products, essential oils, flavors, and the like.

gas chromatography, a method of separating the substances in a mixture by combining it with a gas such as nitrogen and passing it through a long column of packing, such as charcoal: *Gas chromatography is a procedure whereby a volatile mixture is separated into its components by a moving inert gas passing over a sorbent ... As a method of separating the individual components of a complex mixture gas chromatography has no equal* (Scientific American).

gas coal, bituminous coal used in making gas.

gas coke, coke produced from bituminous coal for use in the home.

Gas|con (gas′kən), *n., adj.* —*n.* a person born or living in Gascony, a region in southwestern France, whose people were famous in legend for their boastfulness.
—*adj.* of Gascony or its people.
[< Old French *gascon* < Latin *Vascō, -ōnis* Basque]

gas|con (gas′kən), *n., adj.* —*n.* a braggart; boaster. —*adj.* boastful.
[< *Gascon*]

gas|con|ade (gas′kə nād′), *n., v.,* **-ad|ed, -ad|ing.** —*n.* extravagant boasting; vainglorious fiction. —*v.i.* to boast extravagantly. [< French *gasconnade* < Old French *gascon;* see etym. under **Gascon**] —**gas′con|ad′er,** *n.*

gas-cooled reactor (gas′küld′), a nuclear reactor which uses air, carbon dioxide, or some other gas as its coolant.

gas|dy|nam|ic laser (gas′dī nam′ik), a gas laser in which the mixture of gases is energized by burning.

gas|e|i|ty (ga sē′ə tē), *n.* gaseous state.

gas|e|lier (gas′ə lir′), *n.* a chandelier for burning gas. Also, **gasolier.** [< *gas* + (chand)*elier*]

gas engine, 1 an internal-combustion engine run by illuminating gas, natural gas, or other gas supplied from an outside source or tank. **2** *U.S.* any internal-combustion engine.

gas|e|ous (gas′ē əs), *adj.* **1** in the form of gas; of or like gas: *Steam is water in a gaseous condition.* **2** relating to gases. **3** unsubstantial; lacking solidity. —**gas′e|ous|ness,** *n.*

gaseous diffusion, a method of separating isotopes, such as uranium 235 from the common nonfissionable type, by passing them in gas form through a great number of filters.

gas field, a region from which natural gas is obtained.

gas-fired (gas′fīrd′), *adj.* using gas as the source of heat or fuel: *a gas-fired boiler.*

gas fitter, a person whose work is putting in and repairing pipes and fixtures for the use of household gas.

gas fitting, occupation or work of a gas fitter.

gas fittings, fittings which conduct household gas for use in a building.

gas fixture, a permanent fixture attached to a gas pipe which burns household gas, especially for cooking or lighting.

gas furnace, 1 a furnace for manufacturing gas. **2** a furnace that burns gas.

gas gangrene, a kind of gangrene that develops in wounds, caused by bacteria which form gases in the muscles.

gas gland, a gland in the float of certain fishes and aquatic animals that secretes a gas consisting chiefly of nitrogen and oxygen.

gas guzzler, *U.S.* an automobile that has a motor that consumes large quantities of gasoline in excess of what is considered normal.

gas-guz|zling (gas′guz′ling), *adj.* consuming excessive quantities of gasoline: *"Gas-guzzling" cars will bear a tax penalty, while efficient ones will bring a tax rebate* (New Scientist).

gash¹ (gash), *n., v.* —*n.* a long, deep cut or wound: *When the knife slipped it made a gash in his thumb.* **SYN:** incision.
—*v.t.* to make a long, deep cut or wound in: (*Figurative.*) *The Atlantic terrace is gashed by many canyons, like the valleys of rivers with their tributaries* (Scientific American).
[< earlier *garsh,* variant of *garse* < Old North French *garser* scarify, Old French *jarser*]

gash² (gash), *adj. Scottish.* **1** sagacious; wise: *He was a gash an' faithful tyke* (Robert Burns). **2** well-dressed and dignified; trim. [origin unknown]

gash³ (gash), *adj. British Slang.* superfluous; wasted; worthless. [origin unknown]

gas helmet, = gas mask.

gas|hold|er (gas′hōl′dər), *n.* = gasometer.

gas|house (gas′hous′), *n.* = gasworks.

gas|i|fi|a|ble (gas′ə fī′ə bəl), *adj.* that can become or be converted into a gas.

gas|i|fi|ca|tion (gas′ə fə kā′shən), *n.* the process of converting into gas: *Experimenting with complete gasification processes, which make gas without coke, from oil or from coal* (Economist).

gas|i|fi|er (gas′ə fī′ər), *n.* **1** the portion of a free-piston engine that generates the gases used to run a turbine. **2** = free-piston engine. **3** a device for converting coal into gas.

gas|i|form (gas′ə fôrm), *adj.* having the form of a gas; gaseous.

gas|i|fy (gas′ə fī), *v.,* **-fied, -fy|ing.** —*v.t.* to produce gas from or change into gas.
—*v.i.* to become gas.

gas jet, 1 a small nozzle of a gas fixture. **2** a flame of gas.

gas|ket (gas′kit), *n.* **1** a ring, strip, or sheet of rubber, metal, plaited hemp, or other material packed around a piston, pipe joint, cylinder head, or other enclosed area under pressure, to keep steam, gas, and the like, from escaping. **2** *Nautical.* a cord or small rope used to tie a furled sail to a yard or boom. [origin uncertain. Compare Italian *gaschetta* rope end.]

gas|kin¹ (gas′kin), *n.* **1** the upper part of a horse's hind leg, between the stifle and the hock. See picture under **horse. 2** *Obsolete.* galligaskins. [perhaps short for *galligaskins*]

gas|kin² (gas′kin), *n.* = gasket.

gas lamp, a lamp containing one or more fixtures supplied with gas burners for giving light, especially on a street.

gas laser, a laser which produces its intense beam of light from a tube filled with a mixture of gases, such as neon and helium or carbon dioxide and nitrogen: *The energy generated by a gas laser increases as the volume increases* (New Scientist).

gas|less (gas′lis), *adj.* **1** without gas. **2** not lighted by gas.

gas|light (gas′līt′), *n.* **1** the light made by burning gas, usually coal gas. **2** a lamp or other fixture which burns gas. **3** a gas burner or gas jet.

gas-liq|uid chromatography (gas′lik′wid), a form of gas chromatography in which the mixture is passed through a liquid solvent instead of a porous solid.

gas|lit (gas′lit′), *adj.* **1** lit by gaslight: *gaslit streets.* **2** of or having to do with the period of the early 1900's; characteristic of that period, especially the manners, ideas, and theatrical entertainment of that age: *A lover not of antiquarianism but of genuine gaslit charm and hedge-hid privacy* (Time).

gas log, a piece of metal or other noninflammable material having the shape and appearance of a log, with a hollow center and small holes in its surface, used to burn gas in a fireplace.

gas main, a large underground pipe to carry household gas.

gas|man (gas′man), *n., pl.* **-men. 1** a person whose work is manufacturing or supplying gas. **2a** a collector of money due the gas company for gas supplied. **b** a man who reads gas meters. **3** a gas fitter: *A narrow alley full of delivery vans and gasmen with the road up* (Punch). **4** *U.S.* (in coal mining) a person who examines the mine for firedamp.

gas mantle, a lacelike tube around a gas flame that glows and gives off light when heated.

***gas mask,** a tight covering that fits over the mouth and nose to prevent breathing poisonous gas or smoke. A gas mask is a helmet or mask supplied with a filter so that the wearer breathes only filtered air.

***gas mask**

gas meter, an apparatus for measuring the amount of gas produced or consumed.

gas motor, = gas engine.

gas|o|gene (gas′ō jēn), *n.* = gazogene.

gas|o|hol (gas′ə hôl, -hol), *n.* **1** a mixture of gasoline and ethyl alcohol, used as a fuel in gasoline engines: *They say that widespread use of gasohol ... would do a lot to ease the energy crisis and cut pollution levels* (Tom Ferrel and Virginia Adams). **2 Gasohol,** a trademark for such a mixture. [< *gas²* + (alc)*ohol*]

gas oil, a distillate of petroleum that is heavier than kerosene but lighter than lubricating oil, used chiefly as an industrial or household fuel.

gas|o|lier (gas′ə lir′), *n.* = gaselier.

gas|o|line or **gas|o|lene** (gas′ə lēn, gas′ə lēn′), *n.* a colorless, liquid mixture of hydrocarbons which evaporates and burns very easily. It is made by distilling crude petroleum or from gas formed in the earth. Gasoline is used chiefly as a fuel for automobiles and other internal-combustion engines, and also as a solvent for fats and as a cleansing agent. [American English < *gas* + *-ol²* + *-ine²,* earlier *-ene*]

gasoline engine or **motor,** *U.S.* an internal-combustion engine using gasoline for fuel.

gas|om|e|ter (gas om′ə tər), *n.* **1** a container, such as a large cylindrical tank, for storing household gas. **2** *Chemistry.* a container for holding and measuring any gas. [< French *gazomètre* < *gaz* gas + *mètre* a measure < Greek *métron*]

gas|o|met|ric (gas′ə met′rik), *adj.* having to do with gasometry. —**gas′o|met′ri|cal|ly,** *adv.*

gas|o|met|ri|cal (gas′ə met′rə kəl), *adj.* = gasometric.

gas|om|e|try (gas om′ə trē), *n.* **1** the measurement of gases. **2** the science dealing with such measurements.

gas-op|er|at|ed (gas′op′ə rā′tid), *adj.* (of an automatic or semiautomatic weapon) utilizing part of the gas from the explosion in the barrel to unlock the bolt and activate the loading mechanism.

gasp (gasp, gäsp), *n., v.* —*n.* **1** a trying hard to get one's breath with open mouth, as if out of breath or surprised: *The fireman heard the gasps of the choking boy in the smoky room.* **2** a sudden, short utterance: *then Balin told him brokenly, and in gasps, All that had chanced* (Tennyson).
—*v.i.* **1** to try hard to get one's breath with open mouth. A person gasps when he is out of breath or surprised. *He has taken our breath away, and leaves us gasping* (John Ruskin). **2** to breathe with gasps; pant for air. **3** *Figurative.* to long (for); desire eagerly. —*v.t.* **1** to utter with gasps: *"Help! Help!" gasped the drowning man.* **2** to exhale or emit with convulsive breathings: *He ... lay gasping life away* (William Cowper).
at the (or **one's**) **last gasp, a** about to die. **b** about to come to an end: *The rebellion seems once more at its last gasp* (Horace Walpole).
gasp one's last. See under **last¹.**
gasp out (or **forth**), to utter with gasps: *She couldn't see even her children's faces, though we heard her gasping out their names* (Dickens).
[< Scandinavian (compare Old Icelandic *geispa* to yawn)]

Gas|par (gas′pər), *n.* (in medieval legend) one of the Three Wise Men. Also, **Kaspar.**

gas pedal, *U.S.* the pedal that controls the flow of gasoline to an automobile engine; accelerator.

gasp|er (gas′pər, gäs′-), *n.* **1** a person who gasps. **2** *Especially British Slang.* a cheap cigarette.

gas|per|gou (gas′pėr gü′), *n., pl.* **-gous** or **-gou.** = freshwater drumfish. [< Louisiana French *casburgot* < (dialectal) French *casse-burgot* < *casser* to break + *burgeau* a kind of shellfish]

gasp|ing (gas′ping, gäs′-), *n., adj.* —*n.* very difficult or convulsive breathing.
—*adj.* convulsive; spasmodic. —**gasp′ing|ly,** *adv.*

gas pipe, 1 a pipe for carrying gas. **2** *Informal.* a gun of low quality.

gas plant, 1 = fraxinella. **2** = gasworks.

gas producer, a furnace in which combustible gas is produced, to be used as fuel in another furnace.

gasp|y (gas′pē, gäs′-), *adj.,* **gasp|i|er, gasp|i|est.** out of breath; gasping.

gas range, a cooking stove in which household gas is used as the fuel.

gas ring, a hollow metal ring, with holes or jets through which gas is fed, usually used for simple cooking.

gassed (gast), *adj.* affected by poisonous gas: *Several thousands of other wounded and gassed men followed us* (E. M. Roberts).

gas|ser (gas′ər), *n.* **1** a person or thing that gasses. **2** a natural gas well or boring: *The gasser was brought in right in the middle of the oil field* (New York Times). **3** *U.S. Slang.* something extraordinary: *I wrote a piece of music ... just 28 bars ... It was a gasser—real great* (Time).

gas shell, an explosive shell filled with a poisonous gas, usually in liquid form, released when the shell explodes.

gas|sing (gas′ing), *n.* **1** the act of a person or thing that gasses. **2** the poisoning (of a person or animal) by exposure to toxic gas. **3** the production of gases during electrolysis. **4** the process by which a material is gassed.

gas station, a place where oil and gasoline are sold, especially for use in automobiles and trucks; service station.

gas stove, a stove that burns gas, for heating or cooking.

gas|sy (gas′ē), *adj.,* **-si|er, -si|est. 1** full of gas; containing gas: *Big gassy ... bubbles burst on the ooze* (John Masefield). **2** like gas. **3** *Informal.* characterized by or given to empty and boastful talk: *a gassy and overblown politician.* —**gas′si-ness,** *n.*

gas synthesis, a method of producing chemicals from coal in which the coal is changed into a gaseous mixture of carbon monoxide and hydrogen, which is then passed over various solid catalysts to change the mixture into useful products such as gasoline and diesel oil; Fischer-Tropsch process.

gas system, a gas-operated machine-gun mechanism.

gas tank, 1 a storage place for gas; gasometer. **2** *U.S.* the tank which holds gasoline in an automobile, truck, boat, or airplane.

gas tar, = coal tar.

Gast|ar|bei|ter (gäst′är′bī tər), *n. sing. or pl.* a worker in West Germany who has come from another country (mainly Italy, Yugoslavia, Turkey, Spain, or Pakistan) to supplement the labor shortage. [< German *Gastarbeiter* (literally) guest worker]

gas|ter|o|pod (gas′tər ə pod), *n.* = gastropod.

gas|ter|op|o|dous (gas′tə rop′ə dəs), *adj.* = gastropodous.

gast|ful (gast′fəl), *adj.* = ghastful.

Gast|haus (gäst′hous′), *n. German.* **1** an inn.

Pronunciation Key: hat, āge, cãre, fär; let, ēqual, tėrm; it, īce; hot, ōpen, ôrder; **oil, out;** cup, pu̇t, rüle; **ch**ild; lo**ng**; **th**in; **ᴛʜ**en; **zh,** measure; **ə** represents **a** in about, **e** in taken, **i** in pencil, **o** in lemon, **u** in circus.

2 (literally) guest house.
gas thermometer, a thermometer in which a column of gas is used as the medium of measurement. Changes in either pressure or volume indicate temperature changes.
Gast|hof (gäst′hōf′), *n. German.* **1** a hotel. **2** (literally) guest court.
gas|tight (gas′tīt′), *adj.* **1** so tight that no gas can enter or escape. **2** so made that a particular gas cannot enter under given pressure conditions. —**gas′tight′ness**, *n.*
gastr-, *combining form.* the form of **gastro-** before vowels, as in *gastritis.*
gas|trae|a (gas trē′ə), *n.* = gastrula.
gas|tral|gi|a (gas tral′jē ə), *n. Medicine.* pain in the stomach, especially neuralgia of the stomach.
gas|tral|gic (gas tral′jik), *adj., n.* —***adj.*** of, having to do with, or likely to have gastralgia.
—***n.*** a person who is subject to gastralgia.
gas trap, a device to prevent the escape of sewer gas.
gas|trec|to|my (gas trek′tə mē), *n., pl.* **-mies**. the surgical removal of all or part of the stomach.
gas|tric (gas′trik), *adj.* **1** of or having to do with the stomach. **2** near the stomach. [< Greek *gastêr, gastrós* stomach + English *-ic*]
gastric glands, the glands in the stomach lining that secrete gastric juice.
gastric juice, the thin, nearly clear digestive liquid secreted by glands in the lining of the stomach. It contains pepsin and other enzymes, water, salts, and hydrochloric acid. Gastric juice dissolves chiefly proteins. *Production of gastric juices for digesting food results from stimulation of the vagus nerves* (Science News Letter).
gastric mill, a framework consisting of movable calcareous or chitinous plates in the stomach of certain crustaceans.
gastric ulcer, *Medicine.* an ulcer affecting the mucous membrane of the stomach: *Gastric ulcers are caused by too much hydrochloric acid and pepsin* (Marguerite Clark).
gas|trin (gas′trin), *n.* a hormone that promotes secretion of gastric juice. [< *gastr*(ic) + *-in*]
gas|trit|ic (gas trit′ik), *adj. Medicine.* **1** having to do with gastritis. **2** like gastritis.
gas|tri|tis (gas trī′tis), *n. Medicine.* inflammation of the stomach, especially of its mucous membrane.
gastro-, *combining form.* **1** the stomach: *Gastrotomy = surgical incision into the stomach.*
2 the stomach and ___: *Gastrohepatic = of or having to do with the stomach and liver.* Also, **gastr-** before vowels.
[< Greek *gastêr, gastrós*]
gas|troc|ne|mi|us (gas′trok nē′mē əs), *n., pl.* **-mi|i** (-mē ī). the chief muscle of the calf of the leg, that gives it its bulging form. [< New Latin *gastrocnemius* < Greek *gastroknēmiā* calf < *gastêr, gastrós* belly + *knēmē* leg]
gas|tro|coel (gas′trə sēl), *n. Embryology.* the archenteron, or primitive cavity, in the gastrula.
gas|tro|col|ic (gas′trə kol′ik), *adj.* of or having to do with the stomach and the colon.
gas|tro|der|mal (gas′trō dėr′məl), *adj.* of or having to do with the gastrodermis.
gas|tro|der|mis (gas′trō dėr′mis), *n.* the inner cellular layer of the digestive tract of an invertebrate.
gas|tro|du|o|de|nal (gas′trō dü ə dē′nəl, -dü-od′ə nəl), *adj.* having to do with the stomach and the duodenum.
gas|tro|en|ter|it|ic (gas′trō en′tə rit′ik), *adj.* **1** having to do with gastroenteritis. **2** like gastroenteritis. **3** having gastroenteritis.
gas|tro|en|ter|i|tis (gas′trō en′tə rī′tis), *n. Medicine.* inflammation of the membranes lining the stomach and intestines.
gas|tro|en|ter|o|log|i|cal (gas′trō en′tə rə loj′ə-kəl), *adj.* of or having to do with gastroenterology.
gas|tro|en|ter|ol|o|gist (gas′trō en′tə rol′ə jist), *n.* an expert in gastroenterology.
gas|tro|en|ter|ol|o|gy (gas′trō en′tə rol′ə jē), *n.* the branch of medicine dealing with the stomach and intestines.
gas|tro|en|ter|os|to|my (gas′trō en′tə ros′tə mē), *n., pl.* **-mies**. the act or process of making an artificial opening connecting the stomach and the small intestine.
gas|tro|en|ter|ot|o|my (gas′trō en′tə rot′ə mē), *n., pl.* **-mies**. the opening by surgery of the intestine through the abdominal walls.
gas|tro|gen|ic (gas′trə jen′ik), *adj.* originating in the stomach.
gas|tro|he|pat|ic (gas′trō hi pat′ik), *adj.* of or having to do with the stomach and the liver.
gas|tro|in|tes|ti|nal (gas′trō in tes′tə nəl), *adj.* of or having to do with the stomach and intestines.
gas|tro|lith (gas′trə lith), *n. Medicine.* a calculus or stony concretion in the stomach. [< *gastro-* + Greek *lithos* stone]
gas|tro|log|i|cal (gas′trə loj′ə kəl), *adj.* of or having to do with gastrology.
gas|trol|o|gy (gas trol′ə jē), *n.* **1** the branch of medicine dealing with the stomach. **2** = gastronomy.
gas|tro|nom (gas′trə nom), *n.* a state-operated store for food and household supplies in the Soviet Union. [< Russian *gastronom* (literally) gastronome < French *gastronome*]
gas|tro|nome (gas′trə nōm), *n.* an expert in gastronomy; epicure: *For a gastronome there may be one day, and one day only, on which a cheese is right for eating* (J. A. Barnett). [< French *gastronome,* back formation < *gastronomie;* see etym. under **gastronomy**]
gas|tro|nom|ic (gas′trə nom′ik), *adj.* of or having to do with gastronomy: *A single Michelin rosette—the gastronomic beacon by which even the most parochial tourist now plots his course* (Harper's). —**gas′tro|nom′i|cal|ly**, *adv.*
gas|tro|nom|i|cal (gas′trə nom′ə kəl), *adj.* = gastronomic.
gas|tro|nom|ics (gas′trə nom′iks), *n.* = gastronomy.
gas|tron|o|mist (gas tron′ə mist), *n.* = gastronome.
gas|tron|o|my (gas tron′ə mē), *n.* the art or science of good eating; epicurism. [< French *gastronomie* < Greek *gastronomiā* (title of a poem) < *gastêr, gastrós* stomach + *nómos* law]
gas|tro|plas|ty (gas′trə plas′tē), *n.* plastic surgery of the stomach, used to treat obesity: *Gastroplasty ... involves sectioning off a small, upper portion of the stomach with a row of stainless steel staples* (Maclean's).
gas|tro|pod (gas′trə pod), *n., adj.* —***n.*** any one of a group of mollusks having eyes and feelers on a distinct head, usually a shell that is spiral or cone-shaped, and a muscular disklike foot organ on the under surface of its body used for locomotion. Snails, slugs, and limpets are gastropods.
—***adj.*** of such mollusks. Also, **gasteropod**. [< New Latin *Gastropoda* the class name < Greek *gastêr, gastrós* stomach + *poús, podós* foot]
gas|trop|o|dous (gas trop′ə dəs), *adj.* having to do with or like the gastropods.
gas|tro|scope (gas′trə skōp), *n.* an instrument for looking at the interior of the stomach.
gas|tro|scop|ic (gas′trə skop′ik), *adj.* of or having to do with gastroscopy.
gas|tros|co|pist (gas tros′kə pist), *n.* a person who does gastroscopy.
gas|tros|co|py (gas tros′kə pē), *n., pl.* **-pies**. an examination of the interior of the stomach with a gastroscope.
gas|tros|to|my (gas tros′tə mē), *n., pl.* **-mies**. an operation forming a new opening into the stomach for introducing food.
gas|trot|o|my (gas trot′ə mē), *n., pl.* **-mies**. surgical incision into the stomach.
gas|trot|rich (gas trot′rək, gas′trə trik), *n.* = gastrotrichan.
gas|trot|ri|chan (gas trot′rə kən), *n.* any one of various small, wormlike aquatic animals related to the rotifers, moving by means of cilia on the ventral surface. [< New Latin *Gastrotricha* the group name (< Greek *gastêr, gastrós* belly + *thríx, trichós* hair) + English *-an*]
gas|tro|vas|cu|lar (gas′trō vas′kyə lər), *adj. Zoology.* serving for both digestive and circulatory functions.
gas|tro|zo|oid (gas′trō zō′oid), *n.* a member of a hydrozoan colony having a mouth and digestive organs. [< *gastro-* + *zooid*]
gas|tru|la (gas′trů lə), *n., pl.* **-lae** (-lē). a stage in the development of all many-celled animals, when the embryo is usually saclike and composed of two layers of cells. See picture under **embryo**. [< New Latin *gastrula* (diminutive) < Greek *gastêr, gastrós* stomach]
gas|tru|lar (gas′trů lər), *adj.* having to do with a gastrula or gastrulation.
gas|tru|late (gas′trů lāt), *v.i.,* **-lat|ed, -lat|ing**. to be in or have a gastrula stage.
gas|tru|la|tion (gas′trů lā′shən), *n.* the act or process of forming a gastrula from a blastula, as by invagination.
gas turbine, a turbine which uses for its motive power the gas obtained by the combustion of a fuel.
***gas turbine engine**, an engine that utilizes a gas turbine to generate mechanical power, especially to turn the compressor in a jet engine or the generators used in a jet aircraft.
gas warfare, the use of poison gas and other harmful chemicals as weapons; chemical warfare.
gas welding, any process of joining two metal parts by means of the heat of an oxyacetylene torch or similar device.
gas well, a boring in the earth, tapping a supply of natural gas.
gas|work|er (gas′wėr′kər), *n.* a person employed in a gasworks.
gas|works (gas′wėrks′), *n.pl.* (*sing. in use*). an industrial plant which manufactures household gas; gashouse.
gat¹ (gat), *v. Archaic.* got; a past tense of **get**.
gat² (gat), *n. Especially British.* a channel between sandbanks; a natural or artificial opening between cliffs on a coast. [< Scandinavian (compare Old Icelandic *gat*)]
gat³ (gat), *n. Slang.* a revolver or automatic pistol. [American English; short for *Gatling* (gun)]
gat⁴ (gät), *n.* a complex rhythmic passage that usually marks the final movement or section of a raga, the traditional Hindu musical form. Also, **gath**. [< Sanskrit *gāth*]
ga|ta-nosed shark (gä′tə nōzd′), = nurse shark. [compare Spanish *gata,* feminine of *gato* cat]
gate¹ (gāt), *n., v.,* **gat|ed, gat|ing**. —***n.*** **1** a movable frame or door to close an opening in a wall or fence. It turns on hinges or slides open and shut. *The children liked to swing on the garden gate.* **2** an opening in a wall or fence where a gate is; gateway: *The big truck would not fit through the gate.* **3** the part of a building containing the gate or gates, with the adjoining towers, walls, and other structures. **4** *Figurative.* a way to go in or out; way to get to something: *Hard work is often the gate to success.* **5** a door or valve to stop or control the flow of water in a pipe, dam, canal, or lock. **6** *Informal.* the total number of people who pay to see a contest, exhibition, or performance: *He fought ... leading heavyweights, and attracted some of the richest gates ever known in his profession* (New Yorker). **7** the total amount of money received from people who pay to see a contest, exhibition, or performance: *The two teams divided a gate of $3250.* **8** a movable structure used to close any passageway, such as on a road or bridge. **9** a mountain pass: [*The ancients*] *used the word "gate" or "doors" of the mountain passes which gave an access to a land but which might be held against an enemy* (Edward B. Pusey). **10** = gatehouse (def. 1). **11a** = starting gate. **b** any one of the spaces between poles or buoys marking the course in a race. **12** a frame in which a saw or saws are placed when not in use. **13** an electronic circuit with two or more input terminals and one output terminal, used to connect printed circuits, etc. **14** one of the locations in the nervous system at which the sensation of pain is blocked: *This theory ... postulates the existence within the nervous system of "gates" that modulate or close off pain signals, either as a result of neurophysiological changes or through brain activity* (Emanuel M. Papper).
—***v.t.*** *British.* to punish (a student) by confinement to the grounds of a school: *The Dean gated him for a fortnight* (Thomas Hughes).
crash the gate, *Slang.* to attend a game or other entertainment without paying the admission fee or having a ticket: *The manager of the theatre stationed a guard in the lobby to prevent people from crashing the gate.*
get the gate, *Slang.* to be dismissed: *Plant managers, vice presidents, presidents, even board chairmen occasionally are getting the gate* (Wall Street Journal).
give (a person) the gate, *Slang.* to dismiss: *I guess his girl has given him the gate* (P. Marks).
[Old English *geat*] —**gate′less, gate′like′**, *adj.*
gate² (gāt), *n.* **1** the opening or channel through which the molten metal is poured into a mold; runner. **2** the waste piece of metal cast in it. [compare Old English *gēotan* to pour, cast]
gate³ (gāt), *n.* **1** *Scottish.* a street (now retained only locally in street names, as in *Kirkgate* and *Gallowgate*). **2** *Archaic.* a way of going; path.
3 *Archaic.* a way of behaving; peculiar habit. [< Scandinavian (compare Old Icelandic *gata*)]
-gate, *combining form.* a scandal associated with ___, as in *Hollywoodgate, Lancegate: The continually expanding scandal over the Park regime's influence peddling on Capitol Hill has already been called a "Koreagate"* (Manchester Guardian). [< (Water)*gate*]

***gas turbine engine**

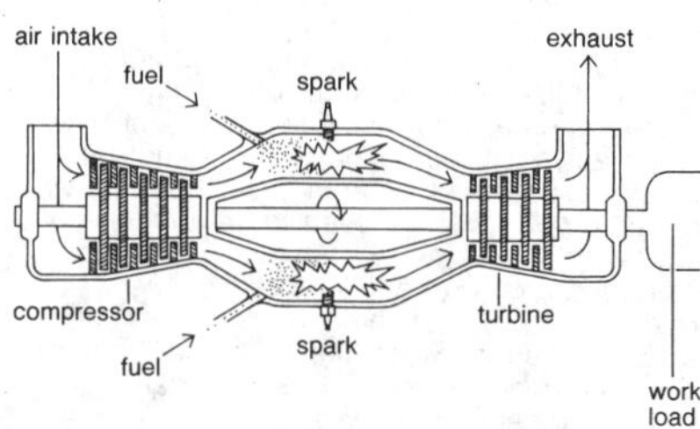

ga|te|a|do (gä tā′ä′dō), *n., pl.* **-dos**. a tree of the sumac family, native to Colombia and Venezuela, that yields a hard, durable, dark-colored cabinet-wood and a bark rich in tannin. [< American Spanish *gateado* < Spanish *gato* cat (because of its coloration)]

gâ|teau (gä tō′), *n., pl.* **-teaux** (-tō′). *French.* a cake.

gate-crash (gāt′krash′), *v.i., v.t. Slang.* to attend (a party, function, or other entertainment) without an invitation or ticket.

gate-crash|er (gāt′krash′ər), *n. Informal.* a person who attends parties or other gatherings, without an invitation; uninvited guest.

gat|ed (gā′tid), *adj. British.* punished by confinement to the grounds of a school.

-gated, *combining form.* having a ____ gate or gates: *Iron-gated = having an iron gate.*

gate|fold (gāt′fōld′), *n.* a folded page in a magazine, book, or other publication, that can be opened to display a large or continuous chart, illustration, or the like.

gate|house (gāt′hous′), *n.* **1** a house at or over a gate, used as the gatekeeper's quarters, a fortification, a prison, or the like; lodge. See picture under **castle**. **2** a structure at the gate of a reservoir, dam, lock, or other barrier, with machinery for regulating the flow of water.

gate|keep|er (gāt′kē′pər), *n.* a person who has charge of a gate.

gate-legged table (gāt′legd′), a gateleg table.

gate|leg table (gāt′leg′), a table with drop leaves supported by legs set in gatelike frames which may be swung back to allow the leaves to be shut down.

gate|man (gāt′mən), *n., pl.* **-men**. *Especially British.* a gatetender.

gate money, the money received for admission fees; gate.

gate position, the area at an airport assigned to an airliner for unloading or picking up passengers.

gate|post (gāt′pōst′), *n.* a post on either side of a gate. A swinging gate is fastened to one gatepost and closes against the other.

gate|tend|er (gāt′ten′dər), *n. U.S.* a gatekeeper at a railroad crossing.

gate valve, a valve with a sliding gate.

gate|way (gāt′wā′), *n.* **1** an opening in a wall or fence where a gate is: *Gateways between the fields were left open so that the horse got out.* **2** a frame or arch in which a gate is hung: *The sculptures of these gateways form a perfect picture Bible of Buddhism as it existed in India in the first century of the Christian Era* (James Fergusson). **3** a structure built at or over a gate: *A lofty massive front with three fortified and portcullised gateways* (Mark Pattison). **4** *Figurative.* a way to go in or out, especially to get to something: *A college education can be a gateway to success. Rostov-on-Don . . . is called the "gateway to the Caucasus" because of the extensive railroad system that runs from Rostov into the mountains* (Theodore Shabad).

gateway drug, a soft drug, such as alcohol, that often leads the user to turn to hard drugs: *Marijuana is often a gateway drug for other illicit use, specifically cocaine and heroin* (New York Times).

Gateway State, a nickname for Ohio.

gath (gäth), *n.* = gat⁴.

Gath (gath), *n.* one of the five confederate cities of the Philistines. It was the home of the giant Goliath, whom David killed with a sling (in the Bible, I Samuel 5:8, 9).

Ga|tha (gä′tä), *n.* any one of the seventeen hymns of the Avesta. The Gathas are arranged according to meter into five sections. [< Avestan *gāthā*]

gath|er (gaᴛʜ′ər), *v., n.* **—*v.t.*** **1** to bring into one place or group; collect; assemble; amass: *to gather sticks for a fire, to gather materials for a book. He gathered his books and papers and started to school. Gather the elders and all the inhabitants of the land into the house of the Lord* (Joel 1:14). *He at once gathered his forces and marched on Gloucester* (John R. Green). **2** to collect from the place of growth; pick and collect; glean and pluck: *The farmers gathered their crops.* **SYN:** harvest, garner. **3** to get or gain little by little; acquire gradually: *to gather a store of knowledge. The train gathered speed as it left the station. A rolling stone gathers no moss.* **4** to collect or assemble (oneself, one's strength, energies, thoughts, or other resources) for an effort or to meet some emergency: *He had almost gone by, before Hester . . . could gather voice enough to attract his observation* (Hawthorne). **5** *Figurative.* to put together in the mind; conclude; infer: *We gathered from his words that he was really much upset. We are anxious to help . . . because we gather that the information that will be obtained will be valuable* (London Times). **SYN:** deduce. **6** to pull together in little folds and stitch: *The skirt is gathered at the waist.* **7** to contract or wrinkle (the brow); pucker: *She gathered her brows into a frown.* **8** to draw together or closer: *Gather your robe around you.* **9** to take: *to gather a person into one's arms. Cast up the highway; gather out the stones* (Isaiah 62:10). **10** *Bookbinding.* to collect and place in order according to signatures (the printed, folded sheets of a book). **—*v.i.*** **1** to come together into one place or assembly; congregate; assemble: *A crowd gathered at the scene of the accident.* **2** to form by the coming together of material; form a mass; collect: *Tears gathered in her eyes. Clouds gathered as the storm approached.* **SYN:** accumulate. **3** to come to a head and form pus: *A boil is a painful swelling that gathers under the skin.* **4** to become contracted into wrinkles, as the brow does.

—*n.* **1** Often, **gathers**. one of the little folds between stitches when cloth is gathered. **2** a contraction; drawing together. **3** a blob of glass on the end of a blowpipe in glassmaking.

gather up, a to pick up: *The schoolmaster took the child . . . and bidding the old man gather up her little basket . . . bore her away* (Dickens). **b** to pull together; bring into a smaller space: *I mounted into the window seat; gathering up my feet, I sat cross-legged like a Turk* (Charlotte Brontë). **c** *Dialect.* to arrest; lead away: *"Gather him up, boys," said the judge, "the sentence of the law must be executed!"* (W. T. Thompson).

[Old English *gaderian,* probably < *gæd* fellowship or *gada* companion, mate] **—gath′er|a|ble**, *adj.* **—gath′er|er**, *n.*

—*Syn.* *v.t.* **1**, *v.i.* **1**, **2**. **Gather, collect, assemble** mean to bring or come together. **Gather**, the general word, suggests little or nothing as to plan or purpose: *I gathered the scattered papers. A crowd gathered on the corner.* **Collect** implies gathering together according to a definite plan: *She collected clothes for the fashion show.* **Assemble** implies gathering together for a definite purpose: *He assembled the slides for his illustrated lecture.*

▶ **gather together**. See usage note at **join**.

gath|er|ing (gaᴛʜ′ər ing, gaᴛʜ′ring), *n.* **1** the act of a person who gathers. **2** that which is gathered: *The book represents the gatherings of years.* **3** a group of people met together; meeting; assembly; party; crowd: *We had a great family gathering last Sunday.* **SYN:** meeting. **4** a swelling that comes to a head and forms pus: *A boil is a painful gathering.* **5** *Dialect.* a collection in money. **6** (in bookbinding) the sheets that are folded and stitched into a book as one section; a collation of signatures.

gathering coal, a large lump of coal or peat banked with embers at night to keep the fire until morning.

gathering line, a pipe for sending natural gas to an extraction unit.

gath|er|um (gaᴛʜ′ər əm), *n. Informal.* a miscellany: [*He*] *also instituted a saucily-written Monday-morning gatherum of gags, anecdotes, and other small bits that hadn't found their way into the previous week's news stories* (Harper's).

gat|ing (gā′ting), *n. British.* the punishment of a student by restricting him to the confines of the college.

***Gat|ling gun** (gat′ling), an early type of machine gun, consisting of a cluster of barrels revolving around a central axis by a hand crank. Each barrel was automatically loaded and fired during every revolution of the cluster. [American English < Richard J. *Gatling,* 1818-1903, an American inventor, who perfected it]

***Gatling gun**

'ga|tor (gā′tər), *n. U.S. Informal.* alligator.

Ga|tor|ade (gā′tər ād′), *n. Trademark.* a soft drink containing glucose, citric acid, sodium bicarbonate, potassium chloride, and similar substances, used by athletes instead of water to replenish rapidly lost body fluids and salts.

GATT (no periods), General Agreement on Tariffs and Trade: *GATT is an agreement through which . . . the world's major trading countries attempt to raise and lower tariffs on a reciprocal basis* (Wall Street Journal).

gat-toothed (gat′tütʜd′, -tütht′), *adj.* = gap-toothed. [*gat* apparently < Scandinavian *gat* gat²]

gau (gou), *n., pl.* **gau|e** (gou′e), **gaus**. **1** one of the political districts into which the Nazis divided Germany and other parts of Europe under their control. Each gau was governed by a Gauleiter. **2** a territorial and administrative division of ancient Germany which included several villages or communities. [< German *Gau*]

gauche (gōsh), *adj.* lacking grace or tact; awkward; clumsy: *His backhand is considered gauche* (Newsweek). **SYN:** gawky, maladroit. [< Middle French *gauche* left; (originally) awkward < Old French *gauchier* trample, walk clumsily < unrecorded Frankish *walkan*] **—gauche′ly**, *adv.* **—gauche′ness**, *n.*

gau|che|rie (gō′shə rē′, gō′shə rē), *n.* **1** awkwardness or tactlessness. **SYN:** clumsiness. **2** an awkward or tactless movement or act: *Structural gaucherie is relatively rare on our stage* (Harper's). **SYN:** blunder. [< French *gaucherie* < *gauche;* see etym. under **gauche**]

Gau|cher's disease (gō shāz′), a rare, inherited disease of infants and children, characterized by anemia and enlargement of the spleen. [< Philippe *Gaucher,* 1854-1918, French physician]

gau|ches|co (gou ches′kō), *adj.* of or having to do with a type of Spanish poetry whose character, language, and setting derive from the life of the gauchos of South America. [< American Spanish *gauchesco* < *gaucho* + Spanish *-esco* -esque]

gau|chist (gō′shist), *n.* = gauchiste.

gau|chiste (gō shēst′), *n. French.* a political radical; a leftist.

gau|cho (gou′chō), *n., pl.* **-chos**. a cowboy in the southern plains of South America, usually of mixed Spanish and Indian descent.

gauchos, baggy trousers usually reaching to, and often gathered at, the ankles, similar to those worn by South American gauchos. [American Spanish *gaucho* < Arawakan *cachu* comrade]

gaud (gôd), *n.* **1** a cheap, showy ornament; trinket; gewgaw: *The dancer wore many rings, bracelets, beads, and other gauds.* **2** a showy ceremony: *Among the gauds and gods of sinful Babylon . . .* (Time). [apparently < Anglo-French *gaude* < *gaudir* rejoice < Latin *gaudēre*]

gau|de|a|mus i|gi|tur (gou′dā ä′müs ig′i tür; gô′dē ā′məs ij′ə tər), *Latin.* let us therefore be merry (the first words of a famous student song, derived probably from a medieval Latin song).

gaud|er|y (gô′dər ē), *n., pl.* **-er|ies**. **1** ostentatious show; finery. **2** a piece of finery.

gaud|y¹ (gô′dē), *adj.,* **gaud|i|er**, **gaud|i|est**, *n., pl.* **gaud|ies**. **—*adj.*** **1** too bright and gay to be in good taste; cheap and showy: *gaudy jewelry. Costly thy habit as thy purse can buy, but not express'd in fancy; rich, not gaudy* (Shakespeare). **2** brilliantly fine or gay; showy: *Peacocks have gaudy plumage.* **—*n.*** *Obsolete.* a gaud. **—gaud′i|ly**, *adv.* **—gaud′i|ness**, *n.*

—*Syn.* *adj.* **1 Gaudy, flashy, showy** mean done for display. **Gaudy** suggests loud colors and overdone ornament: *a gaudy purple and orange dress. She would be attractive if she did not wear such gaudy jewelry.* **Flashy** suggests an eye-catching and dazzling but cheap display: *a flashy necktie.* **Showy** suggests a striking display, but not necessarily a flashy or gaudy one: *Peacocks are showy birds.*

gaud|y² (gô′dē), *n., pl.* **gaud|ies**. *British.* a festival or celebration, especially an annual college banquet. [< Latin *gaudium* joy, a rejoicing < *gaudēre* rejoice]

gaudy day, *British.* **1** a day of rejoicing; festival or gala day. **2** the day on which a college gaudy is held.

gaudy Dutch, a type of English earthenware of a colorful floral pattern, designed especially for the American market during the early 1800's.

gaudy night, *British.* a night for celebrating.

gauf|fer (gôf′ər), *v.t., n.* = goffer.

gauge** (gāj), *n., v.,* **gauged**, **gaug|ing**. **—*n. **1** Often, **gage**. a standard measure or scale of standard measurements; measure. There are gauges of the capacity of a barrel, the thickness of sheet iron, or the diameter of a wire. **2** Often, **gage**. an instrument for measuring or for regulating tools or parts to standard dimensions: *Gauges are used to measure such quantities as pressure, temperature, water level, and thickness* (Otto A. Uyehara). **3** *Figurative.* a means of estimating or judging: *The gauge of a pensioner's disability is always his unfitness to do manual work* (Century Magazine). **4** size; capacity; extent: *The broadening of gauge in crinolines seemed to demand an agitation* (George Eliot). **5** the diameter of the bore of a firearm, especially a shotgun, in terms of the number of lead balls of the same diameter that would weigh a pound. A 12-gauge shotgun requires 12 such balls. **6** the distance between rails of a railroad or between the right and left wheels of a wagon, automobile, or other vehicle. The standard gauge

Pronunciation Key: hat, āge, cãre, fär; let, ēqual, tėrm; it, īce; hot, ōpen, ôrder; oil, out; cup, pu̇t, rüle; child; long; thin; ᴛʜen; zh, measure; ə represents **a** in about, **e** in taken, **i** in pencil, **o** in lemon, **u** in circus.

between rails in the United States is 56½ inches. **7** the position of one sailing ship with reference to another and to the winds. A ship having the weather gauge of another is to the windward of it. **8** the fineness of a knitted fabric as expressed in the number of loops per 1½ inches: *51-gauge stockings.* **9** the depth to which a loaded ship sinks in the water. **10** the length of the exposed part of shingles, tiles, or the like, when laid in rows. **11** the proportion of plaster of Paris mixed with common plaster to speed up its setting. **12** a tool for marking lines parallel to an edge.
—*v.t.* **1** to measure accurately; find out the exact measurement of with a gauge: *The carpenter gauged the dowel with calipers.* **2** to determine the capacity or content of (a cask or similar vessel) by combined measurement and calculation. **3** *Figurative,* to estimate; judge: *It is difficult to gauge the character of a stranger.* **4** to render conformable to a standard. **5** to cut or rub (bricks or stones) accurately to the desired size. **6** to prepare (plaster) with a certain proportion of plaster of Paris to speed up its setting. **7** to gather in parallel rows in sewing. Also, **gage**.
take the gauge of, to figure the capacity, extent, dimensions, or proportions of: *to take the gauge of a man's ability.*
[< Old North French *gauger,* Old French *jauger;* origin uncertain] —**gauge'a|ble,** *adj.*

***gauge** definition 6
standard gauge rails

gauge block, a rectangular block of hard, precision-ground, polished metal, usually steel, used to set and control the tolerance of other gauges, such as micrometers.
gauge particle, *Nuclear Physics.* any of a group of elementary particles whose function is to transmit forces between other particles: *When the Sun lights the earth, the energy is transmitted . . . by photons, the gauge particles of electromagnetism. And when the Earth attracts the Moon, the two exchange gravitons, the gauge particles for gravity* (John Schwartz).
gauge pressure, the amount by which the pressure at a point in a fluid exceeds the pressure of the atmosphere.
gaug|er (gā'jər), *n.* **1** a person or thing that gauges. **2** an official who measures the contents of barrels of taxable liquor. **3** a collector of excise taxes.
gauge theory, *Physics,* any theory that attempts to establish relationships between fundamental forces such as gravity, electromagnetism, the weak force, and the like: *The existence of charm has been predicted by a powerful set of theories of the fundamental forces, the gauge theories, and this discovery established those theories* (New Scientist).
gaug|ing rod (gā'jing), an instrument for measuring the capacity or contents of a cask or barrel for purposes of excise or duty.
Gaul (gôl), *n.* **1** an ancient region in western Europe. It included what is now France, Belgium, Luxembourg, and parts of the Netherlands, Switzerland, Germany, and northern Italy. **2** one of the Celtic inhabitants of ancient Gaul. **3** a Frenchman. **4** France. [< Middle French *Gaule* < Medieval Latin *Gallia* France < Latin, Gaul < *Gallus* a Gaul]
gau|lei|ter (gou'lī'tər), *n.* **1** a high official of the Nazi Party who served as governor of a district in Germany or other parts of Europe under German control. The gauleiter was Hitler's chief deputy in a district. **2** *Figurative.* a subordinate who carries out unscrupulous or criminal orders; henchman: *In the murky world of politics and crime, he was . . . overlord of the rackets and American gauleiter* (Newsweek). [< German *Gauleiter* < *Gau* gau + *Leiter* Leader]
Gaul|ish (gô'lish), *adj. n.* —*adj.* of or having to do with ancient Gaul or the Gauls.
—*n.* the Celtic language of the ancient Gauls.
Gaull|ism (gô'liz əm), *n.* **1** the political doctrines and policies of Charles de Gaulle, 1890-1970. **2** support of Charles de Gaulle and his policies.
Gaull|ist (gô'list), *n. adj.* —*n.* a political follower and supporter of Charles de Gaulle.
—*adj.* of, having to do with, or supporting de Gaulle or Gaullism.
gault (gôlt), *n.* **1** *Geology,* a series of beds of clay and marl of the Cretaceous system, occurring in southern England. **2** *British,* a thick, heavy clay. [perhaps < Scandinavian (compare Old Swedish *galt,* neuter of *galder* barren)]
gaul|the|ria (gôl thir'ē ə), *n.* **1** any one of a large group of aromatic evergreen shrubs of the heath family, such as the wintergreen. **2** *Pharmacy,* oil of wintergreen. [< New Latin *Gaultheria* the genus name < M. *Gaultier,* a Canadian physician and botanist in the 1700's]
gaum¹ (gôm), *v.t.* to smear or daub with something greasy or sticky. [compare etym. under **coom²**]
gaum² (gôm), *v.t. British Dialect.* to understand; consider; distinguish. [< Scandinavian (compare Old Icelandic *gaumr* care, heed)]
gaum|less (gôm'lis), *adj. British Dialect,* without understanding; foolish.
gaunt (gônt, gänt), *adj. v.* —*adj.* **1** very thin and bony; with hollow eyes and a starved look: *Hunger and suffering had made the lost hikers gaunt.* SYN: lean, spare, lank. See syn. under **thin**. **2** such as to cause leanness or emaciation: *gaunt poverty.* **3** looking bare and gloomy; desolate; forbidding; grim: *the gaunt slopes of a high mountain in winter.* —*v.t.* to make lean or haggard: *. . . a woman with an eroded face, a body gaunted by diet* (John D. MacDonald).
[perhaps < Scandinavian (compare Norwegian *gand* thin pole or person), with influence of Old French *gant, gent* elegant] —**gaunt'ly,** *adv.* —**gaunt'ness,** *n.*
***gaunt|let¹** (gônt'lit, gänt'-), *n.* **1** an iron glove which was part of a knight's armor in the Middle Ages. A gauntlet was made usually of leather covered with plates of metal. **2** a stout, heavy glove with a deep, flaring cuff covering part of the arm, used especially in riding or fencing. **3** the wide, flaring cuff. Also, **gantlet**.
take (or **pick**) **up the gauntlet, a** to accept a challenge: *The champion took up the gauntlet of the challenger.* **b** to take up the defense of a person or viewpoint: *[She] had thrown down her gauntlet to him, and he had not been slow in picking it up* (Anthony Trollope).
throw down the gauntlet, to give a challenge. The medieval custom was to throw down a glove or gauntlet in challenging an opponent. *The gauntlet has been thrown down to the Democratic political machine* (Wall Street Journal).
[< Old French *gantelet* (diminutive) < *gant* glove, perhaps < a Germanic word]

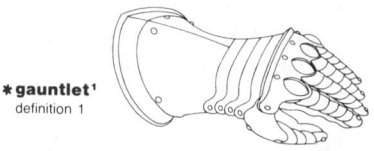

***gauntlet¹** definition 1

gaunt|let² (gônt'lit, gänt'-), *n., v.t.* = gantlet¹.
gaunt|let|ed (gônt'lə tid, gänt'-), *adj.* wearing or having a gauntlet.
gaun|try (gôn'trē), *n., pl.* **-tries.** = gantry.
gaup (gôp), *v.i.* = gawp.
gaur (gour), *n.* a large, wild ox of India, Burma, and Malaya, with a broad, protuberant forehead and long, curved, sharp horns, probably the wild stock of the gayal. [< Hindustani *gaur*]
gauss (gous), *n., pl.* **gauss|es** or **gauss.** *Physics.* **1** the unit of magnetic induction or magnetic flux density in the centimeter-gram-second system, equivalent to one maxwell per square centimeter: *The difficulty about the earth's field is that it is extremely weak—only about half a gauss* (Scientific American). **2** = oersted (def. 1). [< Karl F. *Gauss,* 1777-1855, a German mathematician]
gauss|age (gou'sij), *n.* the intensity of a magnetic field expressed in gausses.
Gauss|ian (gou'sē ən), *adj.* discovered or formulated by Karl Friedrich Gauss.
Gaussian curve or **distribution,** = normal curve or distribution.
gauss|iv|i|ty (gou siv'ə tē), *n.* the intensity of magnetizing force expressed in gilberts per square centimeter or in gausses.
gauss|me|ter (gous'mē'tər), *n.* an instrument for measuring the intensity of a magnetic field.
Gau|ta|ma (gô'tə mə, gou'-), *n.* = Buddha. Also, **Gotama**.
gauze (gôz), *n., adj.* —*n.* **1** a very thin, light cloth, easily seen through. Gauze is made of silk, linen, rayon, or cotton and is used as a fabric and often for bandages. **2** a thinly woven, open material resembling this fabric: *Wire gauze is used for screens.* **3** *Figurative,* a thin haze: *And in circles, Purple gauzes, golden hazes, liquid mazes, Flung the torrent rainbow round* (Tennyson).
—*adj.* like gauze; made of gauze: *gauze curtains fluttering before an open window.*
[< Middle French *gaze,* apparently < *Gaza,* a town in Palestine] —**gauze'like',** *adj.*
gauze weave, = leno (def. 1).
gauz|y (gô'zē), *adj.* **gauz|i|er, gauz|i|est,** like gauze, thin and light as gauze: *gauzy wings,* (*Figurative.*) *a gauzy mist. There are a number of pieces worth lingering over, including a wonderfully gauzy. "The Ballet School," by Degas* (New Yorker). (*Figurative.*) *A gauzy new moon sailed downward swiftly* (Katherine Anne Porter). SYN: diaphanous. —**gauz'i|ly,** *adv.* —**gauz'i|ness,** *n.*
ga|vage (gȧ vȧzh'), *n.* **1** forced feeding, as by a tube that passes down the throat to the stomach. **2** forced feeding of poultry to fatten them quickly. [< French *gavage* < *gaver* to gorge]
gave (gāv), *v.* past tense of **give**: *He gave me some candy. I gave the motor the gun to see what it could do* (New Yorker).
gav|el¹ (gav'əl), *n., v.,* **-eled, -el|ing** or (*especially British*) **-elled, -el|ling.** —*n.* a small mallet used by a presiding officer to signal for attention or order, or by an auctioneer to announce that the bidding is over: *The chairman rapped on the table twice with his gavel.*
—*v.t.* to enforce, effect, or bring about (a ruling or meeting) by using a gavel or resorting to its use instead of parliamentary procedure: *Both chambers were gaveled into session at noon* (Wall Street Journal). —*v.i.* to use or pound with a gavel: *The chairman gaveled for attention.*
gavel down, to disregard or rule out by gaveling: *The Senate's presiding officer . . . can gavel down a point of order on which normally no debate is permitted* (New York Times).
[American English; apparently < variant of *gable* a V-shaped hammer]
gav|el² (gav'əl), *n. Obsolete.* rent; tribute. [Old English *gafol*]
gav|el³ (gav'əl), *n.* a quantity of grain cut, especially by a cradle scythe, and ready to be made into a sheaf. [< Old North French *gavelle* heap]
gav|el|kind (gav'əl kīnd), *n.* in old English law: **1** a tenure of land, chiefly in Kent, in which at the age of fifteen a tenant in fee could dispose of his land, and in which at a tenant's death his land was divided equally among his sons or other heirs. **2** a tenure of land by the payment of rent or fixed services rather than by military service. **3** land held in this fashion. **4** the custom of dividing a deceased person's property equally among his sons. [Middle English *gavelikind* < Old English *gafol* tax + *gecynd* species, kind²]
gav|e|lock (gav'ə lok), *n. Archaic. or Dialect.* an iron crowbar or lever. [Old English *gafeluc*]
gav|el-to-gav|el (gav'əl tə gav'əl), *adj.* from the opening to the closing of a meeting, conference, or the like: *gavel-to-gavel television coverage of a political convention.*
ga|vi|al (gā'vē əl), *n.* any one of a family of large, harmless crocodilians of southern Asia that have long, extremely slender snouts. Also, **garial**. [< French *gavial* < Hindustani *ghariyāl*]
ga|vi|al|oid (gā'vē ə loid), *adj.* resembling or having the character of a gavial.
ga|votte or **ga|vot** (gə vot'), *n., v.,* **-vot|ted, -vot|ting.** —*n.* **1** an old French dance somewhat like a minuet but much more lively. **2** the music for it, in four-four time. —*v.i.* to dance a gavotte. [< French *gavotte* < Provençal *gavoto* < *Gavots,* an Alpine people]
G.A.W. or **Gaw** (no periods), guaranteed annual wage: *one of the union's proposals to meet the layoff problem has been some form of . . . G.A.W.* (New York Times).
Ga|wain (gä'win, -wān), *n. Arthurian legend.* a knight of the Round Table and nephew of King Arthur.
gawk (gôk), *v., n.* —*v.i.* to stare idly, rudely, or stupidly: *Foreign tourists . . . normally spend freely while gawking at the pyramids* (Wall Street Journal). —*n.* an awkward person; clumsy fool. [perhaps < obsolete *gaw* stare] —**gawk'er,** *n.*
gawk|ish (gô'kish), *adj.* = gawky. —**gawk'ish|ly,** *adv.* —**gawk'ish|ness,** *n.*
gawk|y (gô'kē), *adj.,* **gawk|i|er, gawk|i|est,** *n., pl.* **gawk|ies.** —*adj.* awkward; clumsy: *A lanky, gawky fellow . . . tumbles over everybody* (Thackeray). —*n.* an awkward person; gawk. —**gawk'i|ly,** *adv.* —**gawk'i|ness,** *n.*
gawp (gôp), *v.i.* to gape or yawn; stare with the mouth open. Also, **gaup**. [dialectal variant of obsolete *galp*] —**gawp'er,** *n.*
GAX (no periods), gaseous oxygen. Also, **GOX** (no periods).
gay (gā), *adj.,* **gay|er, gay|est,** *n. adv.* —*adj.* **1** happy and full of fun; merry: *a gay young girl, a gay dance, a gay laugh.* **2** bright-colored; showy: *a gay dress, gay with color, flowers, or ribbons.* **3** richly or showily dressed: *Seeing one so gay in purple silks* (Tennyson). **4** fond of pleasure; lively: *The place was merely a gay suburb of the capital* (Macaulay). **5** dissipated; immoral: *This elder Narcissa had led a gay and wild life while beauty lasted* (E. Peacock). **6** *Slang.* impertinent; forward; fresh: *I wouldn't get gay round her* (J. F. Wilson). **7** of or having to do with homosexuals; homosexual.
—*n.* a homosexual.

— *adv.* **1** *Scottish.* fairly; considerably; very. **2** *Obsolete.* in a bright or showy manner.
[< Old French *gai*] — **gay′ness**, *n.*
— *Syn. adj.* **1 Gay, merry** mean lively and lighthearted. **Gay** emphasizes being free from care and full of life, joy, and high spirits; **merry** emphasizes being full of laughter and lively pleasure and fun: *The gay young people were merry as they decorated the gym for the dance.*

gay|al (gā′əl, gə yäl′), *n.* a domesticated ox with slender horns and white legs, common in parts of India. It is believed to be a domesticated descendant of the gaur. [< Hindi *gayāl*]

Ga|ya|tri (gä′yə trē), *n.* an ancient Sanskrit meter of 24 syllables, generally arranged as a triplet of 3 divisions of 8 syllables each. [< Sanskrit *gāyatrī*]

gay dog, *Slang.* a person who seeks or indulges in extravagant pleasures and gaiety: *Hungary's "magnates" (the aristocratic heads of the great families) were Europe's most lavish hosts and its gayest dogs* (Time).

gay|e|ty (gā′ə tē), *n., pl.* **-ties.** = gaiety.

gay|feath|er (gā′feᴛʜ′ər), *n.* = button snakeroot.

Gay-Lus|sac's law (gā′lʏ sȧks′), = Charles's law. [< Joseph *Gay-Lussac,* 1778-1850, a French chemist and physicist]

gay|ly (gā′lē), *adv.* = gaily.

gay|o|la (gā ō′lə), *n. U.S. Slang.* undercover payments made by homosexual establishments for permission to operate without interference. [< *gay,* adjective, homosexual + *-ola,* on pattern of *payola*]

Gay-Pay-Oo (gā′pā′ü′; *Russian* ge′pe′ü′), *n.* = GPU (the official secret police of the Soviet Union during the 1920's). [attempted phonetic spelling for pronunciation of initials of the Russian name, *Gosudarstvennoe Politicheskoe Upravlenie* State Political Administration]

gay science, the art of poetry (so named with reference to the poetry of the troubadours).

gay|wings (gā′wingz′), *n.* a North American perennial herb having flowers with large, paired, rose-purple petals. Its foliage resembles that of the wintergreen.

gaz., **1** gazette. **2** gazetteer.

ga|za|bo (gə zā′bō), *n., pl.* **-bos. 1** a balcony; gazebo. **2** *Dialect.* a person gazed or stared at because of odd appearance. **3** *Slang.* a fellow; person.

Gaz|an (gäz′ən), *n., adj.* — *n.* a native either of the Gaza Strip, an area on the Mediterranean southwest of Jerusalem, or of Gaza, the largest city in the Strip.
— *adj.* of the Gaza Strip or Gaza.

ga|za|ni|a (gə zā′nē ə), *n.* any one of a group of South African herbaceous plants of the composite family, having large, showy heads of flowers with yellow or orange rays that expand only in bright weather. [< New Latin *Gazania* the genus name < Theodorus *Gaza,* a Greek scholar of the 1400's]

gaz|ar (gə zär′), *n.* a gauzy silk fabric, often sequined with shiny metal. [< French *gazar* < *gaze* gauze]

gaze (gāz), *v.,* **gazed, gaz|ing,** *n.* — *v.i.* to look long and steadily: *Ye men of Galilee, why stand ye gazing up into heaven* (Acts 1:11). *The mute rapture with which he would gaze upon her in company* (Washington Irving).
— *v.t.* to look long and steadily at: *Straight toward heaven my wondering eyes I turn'd, And gazed awhile the ample sky* (Milton).
— *n.* a long, steady look: *With secret gaze Or open admiration behold him* (Milton).
[compare Scandinavian (dialectal Norwegian) *gasa*] — **gaz′er**, *n.* — **gaze′less**, *adj.*
— *Syn. v.i.* **Gaze, stare** mean to look long and steadily at someone or something. **Gaze** emphasizes looking steadily and intently, chiefly in wonder, delight, or interest: *For hours he sat gazing at the stars.* **Stare** emphasizes looking steadily and directly at someone or something or off into space, chiefly in curiosity, rudeness, surprise, or stupidity: *The child stared at the stranger for a few minutes before answering his question.*

ga|ze|bo (gə zē′bō), *n., pl.* **-bos** or **-boes. 1** a summer house, balcony, projecting window, or the like, that overlooks a fine view. **2** a screened-in area with a cover, usually of canvas, for eating or relaxing outdoors. [supposedly < *gaze,* on pattern of Latin future tenses in *-bo.* Compare etym. under **placebo.**]

gaze|hound (gāz′hound′), *n.* a hunting dog that chases by sight rather than by scent; sight hound. Whippets and greyhounds are gazehounds.

ga|zel (gə zel′), *n.* = gazelle.

ga|zelle (gə zel′), *n., v.,* **-zelled, -zel|ling.** — *n.* any one of various small, swift, and graceful antelopes found in Africa and Asia. Gazelles have large, lustrous eyes.
— *v.i.* to leap like a gazelle does: *Gazelling over the nine hurdles faultlessly* (Newsweek).
[< Old French *gazel* < Arabic *ghazāl*] — **ga|zelle′like′**, *adj.*

gazelle hound, = saluki.

ga|zette (gə zet′), *n., v.,* **-zet|ted, -zet|ting.** — *n.* **1** a newspaper (now chiefly or only in the names of newspapers): *the "Emporia Gazette."* **2** an official government journal containing lists of appointments, promotions, bankruptcies, or other public announcements.
— *v.t.* to publish, list, or announce in a gazette: *The barony conferred in the Birthday Honours ... was gazetted last night by the name, style, and title* (London Times).
[< French *gazette* < Italian *gazzetta* < dialectal *gazeta* small coin, perhaps diminutive < *gaza* magpie, in sense of "gossipy"]

gaz|et|teer (gaz′ə tir′), *n., v.* — *n.* **1** a dictionary of geographical names. Names of places, seas, mountains, and other geographical locations, are arranged alphabetically in a gazetteer. **2** a writer for a gazette. **3** an official appointed to publish a gazette.
— *v.t.* to describe geographically in a gazetteer or gazetteers: *to gazetteer a country.*
[< French *gazettier* < *gazette;* see etym. under **gazette**]

gaz|o|gene (gaz′ə jēn), *n.* an apparatus for producing carbonated water. Also, **gasogene.** [< French *gazogène* < *gaz* gas + *-gène* -gen]

gaz|pa|cho (gäth pä′chō, gäs-), *n.* a spicy, cold soup that includes strained tomatoes, cucumbers, olive oil, and spices. [< Spanish *gazpacho*]

ga|zump (gə zump′), *v., n. British Slang.* — *v.t.* to demand from (the buyer of a house) a higher price after the original offer has been accepted by the seller or real estate agent: *The rapid increase in prices, the growing number of people with mortgages in their pockets, has meant that there is little time to be choosy before you are gazumped* (London Guardian).
— *n.* an act or instance of gazumping: *The brass-faced gazump is bad enough, but now the gazumpers are finding sneakier ways to dun the house-hungry* (News of the World).
[origin unknown] — **ga|zump′er**, *n.*

GB (no periods), the United States Army code name for the nerve gas sarin.

G.B., Great Britain.

G.B.E., (Knight or Dame) Grand Cross of the Order of the British Empire.

G.B.S., George Bernard Shaw.

gc., gigacycle.

GC (no periods), gas chromatography.

G.C., an abbreviation for the following:
1 George Cross.
2 Grand Chancellor.
3 Grand Chaplain.
4 Grand Chapter.
5 Grand Commander.
6 Grand Council.

GCA (no periods), **1** Girls Clubs of America. **2** ground-controlled approach (of aircraft).

G.C.B., (Knight) Grand Cross of the Bath.

GCD (no periods), General and Complete Disarmament.

G.C.D., g.c.d., or **gcd** (no periods), greatest common divisor.

GCE (no periods) or **G.C.E.**, General Certificate of Education.

G.C.F., g.c.f., or **gcf** (no periods), greatest common factor.

G clef, *Music.* the treble or violin clef.

G.C.L.H., (Knight) Grand Cross of the Legion of Honor.

G.C.M., g.c.m., or **gcm** (no periods), greatest common measure.

G.C.M.G., (Knight) Grand Cross of the Order of St. Michael and St. George.

G.C.T. or **GCT** (no periods), Greenwich Civil Time.

G.C.V.O., (Knight) Grand Cross of the (Royal) Victorian Order.

g.d., granddaughter.

Gd (no period), gadolinium (chemical element).

G.D., **1** grand duchess. **2** grand duchy. **3** grand duke.

gdn., garden.

GDP (no periods), gross domestic product.

GDR (no periods) or **G.D.R.**, German Democratic Republic (East Germany).

gds., goods.

Ge¹ (jē, gā), *n.* = Gaea.

Ge² (zhā), *n.* an important linguistic family of South American Indians; Tapuya.

Ge (no period), germanium (chemical element).

gean (gēn), *n.* a sweet wild cherry that is heart-shaped. [< Old French *guine*]

ge|an|ti|cli|nal (jē′an ti klī′nəl), *adj., n. Geology.* — *adj.* of or having to do with a geanticline.
— *n.* = geanticline.

ge|an|ti|cline (jē an′ti klīn), *n. Geology.* a general upward flexure of the earth's crust; a very broad anticline. [< Greek *gê* earth + English *anticline*]

***gear** (gir), *n., v., adj.* — *n.* **1** a wheel having teeth that fit into the teeth of another wheel to move it or be moved by it; cogwheel; gearwheel. If the wheels are of different sizes, they will turn at different speeds. **2** a set of such wheels working together to transmit power or change the direction of motion in a machine. Power is transmitted from the motor of an automobile to the wheels by means of gears. **3** any arrangement of gears or moving parts considered as a unit in a larger mechanism; machinery: *The car ran off the road when the steering gear broke.* **4** equipment needed for some purpose; implements; tackle; tools. Harness, clothing, household goods, tools, and rigging are various kinds of gear. *a carpenter's gear. Fishing gear includes a line, a pole, hooks, and a reel. Unless we provide researchers ... with really modern gear they will spend so long getting to the frontiers of knowledge that they will have only a tiny fraction of their time available for expanding them* (Listener). **SYN:** apparatus, paraphernalia. **5** clothes; apparel; attire; dress: *From every side came noisy swarms Of Peasants in their homely gear* (Wordsworth). **6** the diameter in inches of an imaginary wheel whose circumference is equal to the linear distance that a bicycle moves forward while the pedals make a single complete revolution. **7** *British Slang.* high quality; style; class: *"It was my sort of cafe, my sort of people—of course they had gear"* (London Times). **8** *Archaic.* armor; arms. **9** *Obsolete.* a material substance or stuff. **10** *Obsolete.* rubbish. **11** *Obsolete, Figurative.* a matter; affair; business. **12** *Obsolete Scottish.* possessions in general.
— *v.t.* **1** to connect by gears: *The motor is geared to the rear wheels of the automobile.* **2** to provide with gear; equip; harness. **3** *Figurative.* to make fit; adjust, adapt: *The old sea captain found it hard to abandon his ways and gear his life to the land. The steel industry was geared to the needs of war.* **4** to furnish with gears. **5** to put into gear.
— *v.i.* **1** to fit or work together; be in gear; mesh: *The cogs gear smoothly.* **2** *Figurative.* to prepare; arrange; plan: *The towns, in gearing to meet the need of their new neighbors, are moving cautiously* (Christian Science Monitor).
— *adj. British Slang.* **1** stylish; up-to-date: *The once stodgy city seems to possess ... the most gear combos* (London Times). **2** wonderful: *It's fab, Henchcliffe, it's gear, ... groovy, keen* (Punch).
in (or **into**) **gear, a** connected to the motor or mechanism: ... *the position of the eccentric pulley, relative to the crank when in gear* (R. S. Robinson). **b** *Figurative.* in or into working order: *In a week or two he began to get into gear and work better* (G. W. Thornbury).
out of gear, a not connected with the motor or mechanism: *The teeth of the wheel became disengaged and the machine, out of gear, stopped working.* **b** *Figurative.* out of working order, or out of smooth working order: *Only he among them had the class to throw England's bowlers out of gear and simplify batting for the rest of the side* (London Times).
shift gears, a to change from one gear to another; connect a motor or mechanism to a different set of gears: *Going up the steep hill, the truck shifted gears.* **b** to readjust one's attitude, approach, or style to meet new conditions: *Peiping policy has continued to be belligerent until the gear shifting last spring* (Wall Street Journal).
[apparently < Scandinavian (compare Old Icelandic *gervi, görvi*)]

***gear**
definition 2

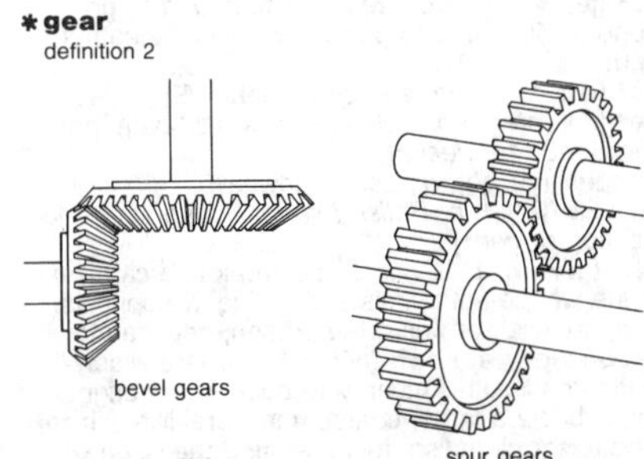

gear|box (gir′boks′), *n. Especially British.* an automobile or truck transmission.

Pronunciation Key: hat, āge, cãre, fär; let, ēqual, tėrm; it, īce; hot, ōpen, ôrder; oil, out; cup, pu̇t, rüle; child; long; thin; ᴛʜen; zh, measure; ə represents **a** in about, **e** in taken, **i** in pencil, **o** in lemon, **u** in circus.

gear|change (gir′chānj′), *n. Especially British.* gearshift.

gear-driven (gir′driv′ən), *adj.* driven by means of a toothed wheel or wheels.

gear|ing (gir′ing), *n.* **1** a set of gears, chains, or parts of machinery for transmitting motion or power; gears. **2** the act of fitting a machine with gears. **3** the way in which a machine is fitted with gears.

gear|less (gir′lis), *adj.* having no gear for the transmission of motion; acting directly.

gear pump, a type of pump with two meshing gears that rotate to move thick fluids such as oil on the gear teeth and through a housing to build up pressure to discharge the fluid.

gear ratio, the number of revolutions made by a driving gear for each revolution of the gear being driven: *Gear ratios can be determined by counting the teeth on a pair of gears. If the driving gear has 20 teeth and the driven gear 40 teeth, the ratio would be 2 to 1* (Toboldt and Purvis).

gear|shift (gir′shift′), *n.* a device for connecting a motor to any one of several sets of gears in a transmission.

gear|wheel (gir′hwēl′), *n.* **1** a wheel having teeth that fit into the teeth of another wheel of the same kind in order to move it or be moved by it; cogwheel; gear. **2** the larger of a set of meshing gears, distinguished from a pinion, the smaller.

ge|as|ter (jē as′tər), *n.* = earthstar. [< New Latin *Geaster* the genus name < Greek *gê* earth + *astḗr* star]

Geat (gēt, yät), *n.* a member of an ancient Germanic people of southern Scandinavia who were conquered by the Swedes in the 500's A.D. Beowulf was a prince of the Geats.

Geat|ish (gē′tish, yä′-), *adj.* of the Geats.

Geb (geb), *n.* the ancient Egyptian god of the earth, husband of the sky goddess Nut, and father of Osiris, Isis, and others. Also, **Keb, Seb.**

ge|bang (gə bang′, -bäng′), *n.* a Malayan fan palm. The leaves are used for basketwork and thatching and the pitch of the trunk yields a sago.

ge|bel (geb′əl, jeb′-), *n.* = djebel.

ge|bo|ren (gə bō′rən), *adj. German.* born with the name of: *Gary Goodspeed, geboren Julius Wolfbane, has learned his lesson* (S. J. Perelman).

geck (gek), *n., v.* —*n. Obsolete.* a dupe.
—*v.t. Scottish.* to mock; deceive; cheat.
—*v.i. Scottish.* **1** to use mocking language or gestures toward. **2** to toss the head, as in scorn.
[apparently < Low German (compare Middle Dutch *geck*)]

geck|o (gek′ō), *n., pl.* **geck|os** or **geck|oes.** any one of a group of small, insect-eating lizards, often having adhesive pads on the feet for climbing. Geckos are found in the temperate zone and are harmless to man. They are active chiefly at night. *Suddenly, a little gecko lizard jumped several inches along the white wall opposite me and gobbled up a fly* (New Yorker). [< Malay *gekok;* imitative of its cry]

ged or **gedd** (ged), *n. Scottish.* pike[3] (def. 1).
[< Scandinavian (compare Old Icelandic *gedda*)]

GED (no periods), General Educational Development (test).

ge|dunk (gē′dungk), *n. U.S. Slang.* ice cream, pudding, or the like, sold at a soda fountain. [origin unknown]

gee[1] (jē), *interj., v.,* **geed, gee|ing,** *n.* —*interj.* a word of command to horses or oxen directing them to turn to the right.
—*v.t., v.i.* to turn to the right.
—*n. British Informal.* a horse.
[origin uncertain]

gee[2] (jē), *v.i.,* **geed, gee|ing.** *Informal.* **1** to go properly; fit; suit. **2** to get on or go well together. [perhaps < *gee*[1]]

gee[3] (jē), *n., pl.* **gees** (jēz). the letter G.

gee[4] (jē), *interj.* an exclamation or mild oath; gee whiz. [short for *Jesus*]

gee|gaw (gē′gô), *n., adj.* = gewgaw.

gee|gee (jē′jē), *n. British Informal.* a horse. [reduplication of *gee*[1]]

geek (gēk), *n. U.S. Slang.* **1** a freak in a carnival troupe whose act consists of eating live animals. **2** any freakish or perverted person; degenerate.

geel|bec or **geel|bek** (gēl′bek′), *n.* **1** a widely-distributed South African wild duck with a bright yellow bill. **2** a large, coarse, mackerel-like fish related to the drumfish, found around the Cape of Good Hope. [< Afrikaans *geelbek* < *geel* yellow + *bek* beak]

geep (gēp), *n.* the offspring of a goat and a sheep; shoat. [blend of *goat* and *sheep*]

geese (gēs), *n.* plural of **goose.**

geest (gēst), *n. Geology.* **1** old alluvial matter on the surface of land; coarse drift or gravel. **2** similar material produced by the decay of rocks and remaining at the place where it was formed.
[< German *Geest* < Low German *geest* dry sandy land]

gee-string (jē′string′), *n.* **1** *U.S. Informal.* a string around the waist with a strip of cloth or the like between the legs, worn by dancers in a burlesque show. **2** string worn by American Indians around the waist with a strip of cloth between the legs. Also, **G string.** [origin uncertain]

gee|whil|li|kins (jē′whil′ə kins), *interj. U.S. Informal.* an exclamation expressing astonishment.

gee whiz or **whizz,** *U.S. Informal.* **1** an exclamation of surprise, wonder, or delight, sometimes used as an expletive or mild oath: *Gee whiz, do I have to go?* **2** something causing surprise, wonder, or delight.

gee-whiz (jē′hwiz′), *U.S. Informal.* characterized by or causing surprise, wonder, or delight: *a gee-whiz achievement, gee-whiz embellishments.*

geez (jēz), *interj.* = jeez.

Ge|ez (gē ez′, gēz), *n.* the ancient language of Ethiopia, still used as a liturgical language; Ethiopic.

gee|zer (gē′zər), *n. Slang.* **1** a rather odd person, especially an old one and nearly always a man. **2** any male; fellow; guy. [dialectal pronunciation of *guiser* queer character]

ge|fil|te fish (gə fil′tə), = gefüllte fish.

ge|füll|te fish (gə fil′tə), a cooked dish of boneless, freshwater fish minced, especially with eggs and breadcrumbs, and served hot or cold in the form of balls or cakes. [< Yiddish *gefilte fish* (literally) filled fish]

Ge|gen|schein (gā′gən shīn′), *n. German. Astronomy.* counterglow: *[He] offered this phenomenon in explanation of the Gegenschein—the faint diffuse glow sometimes observed at night at the antisolar point in the sky* (New Scientist).

Ge|hen|na (gə hen′ə), *n.* **1** the valley of Hinnom, southwest of Jerusalem. Because children had been sacrificed there to Moloch, it was defiled by Josiah and became a place where refuse was thrown and in which fires were kept burning to prevent pestilence (in the Bible, II Kings 23:10). **2** hell: *Down to Gehenna or up to the Throne, He travels fastest who travels alone* (Rudyard Kipling). **3** Also, **gehenna.** a place of torment or misery: *the "gehenna" or torture room [at Tournay]* (John Lothrop Motley). [< Latin *Gehenna* < Greek *Géenna* < Hebrew *Gē Hinnōm,* short for *gē ben Hinnōm* the valley of the son of Hinnom (see Jeremiah 19:6)]

Gei|ger (gī′gər) or **Gei|ger-Mül|ler counter** (gī′gər myl′ər), *Physics.* a device which detects and counts ionizing particles. It consists essentially of a tube with two electrodes between which a high potential difference is maintained. When a charged particle enters the tube, ionization occurs, setting up a current which actuates a loudspeaker or other indicating device. It is used especially to measure radioactivity and test cosmic-ray particles. [< Hans *Geiger,* 1882-1945, a German physicist, and W. *Müller,* a German physicist of the 1900's]

Gei|gers (gī′gərz), *n., Informal.* radioactive particles and radiation collectively.

gei|ger tree (gī′gər), a small tree of the West Indies, having heavy, hard, dark-brown wood. It belongs to the borage family. [< John *Geiger,* an American naturalist of the 1800's]

Geiger or **Geiger-Müller tube,** **1** the tube in a Geiger counter: *Cosmic rays and Geiger tubes have been combined in a new altimeter to tell pilots what their altitudes are* (Science News Letter). **2** = Geiger counter.

gei|sha (gā′shə, gē′-), *n., pl.* **-sha** or **-shas.** a Japanese girl trained to be a professional entertainer and companion for men: *Together with the hetaerae of ancient Greece and the courtesans of France, the geisha belongs to the aristocracy of dalliance* (Time). [< Japanese *geisha*]

Geiss|ler tube (gīs′lər), a sealed glass tube having two electrodes and containing a gas which becomes luminous after it is electrified. [< Heinrich *Geissler,* 1815-1879, a German physicist, who built it]

Geist (gīst), *n. German.* **1** soul or spirit, especially, in Kantian philosophy, the quality in a work of art that gives life to it and inspires the mind. **2** a disposition toward intellectual and artistic things. **3** a ghost.

gei|to|nog|a|my (gī′tə nog′ə mē), *n. Botany.* fertilization in which a flower is pollinated by pollen from another flower on the same plant. [< Greek *geítōn, -onos* neighbor + English *-gamy*]

GEK (no periods), geomagnetic electrokinetograph.

gel[1] (jel), *n., v.,* **gelled, gel|ling.** —*n.* a jellylike or solid material formed by the coagulation of a colloidal solution. When glue sets, it forms a gel. *Protoplasm in the gel state has the power of contraction, and this contractility enables the cell to change shape and to move* (Scientific American).
—*v.i.* **1** to form a gel. Egg white gels when it is cooked. SYN: thicken. **2** *Figurative.* to blend: *But the two just failed to gel in this programme* (Listener).
[short for *gelatin*]

gel[2] (gel), *n. British Slang.* a girl; gal.

ge|la|da (jel′ə də), *n.* an Ethiopian baboon notable for the long, heavy mane of the full-grown male. [perhaps < a native name]

ge|län|de|läu|fer (gə len′də loi′fər), *n., pl.* **-läu|fer** or **-läu|fers.** *Skiing.* a person engaged in cross-country skiing; langläufer. [< German *Geländeläufer* (literally) countryside runner]

ge|län|de|sprung (gə len′də shprůng′), *n. Skiing.* a vault, as over an obstacle, made by placing both poles in the snow in front, riding up on them with knees bent, and pushing out for distance.
[< German *Geländesprung* (literally) countryside jump]

gel|ate (jel′āt), *v.,* **-at|ed, -at|ing.** —*v.t.* to form into a gel.
—*v.i.* to form a gel; gel.

gel|a|tin (jel′ə tən), *n.* **1** an odorless, tasteless, protein substance like glue or jelly, obtained by boiling the bones, hoofs, and other waste parts of animals. It dissolves easily in hot water and is used in making jellied salads and desserts, camera film, and glue. **2** any one of various vegetable substances having similar properties: *A special kind of gelatin, developed as a plasma substitute, is being used at medical stations just behind the front* (Science News Letter). **3** the protein contained in these substances. **4** a preparation or product in which gelatin is the essential constituent. **5** a thin, transparent colored sheet used to change colors of stage lights. [< French *gélatine* < Italian *gelatina* < *gelata* jelly < *gelare* to jell < Latin *gelāre* freeze < *gelū* frost]

gel|a|tin|ase (jel′ə tə nās), *n.* an enzyme that liquefies gelatin, occurring among bacteria and yeasts.

ge|lat|i|nate (jə lat′ə nāt), *v.i., v.t.,* **-nat|ed, -nat|ing.** = gelatinize. —**gel′a|tin|a′tion,** *n.*

gel|a|tine (jel′ə tən, -tēn), *n.* = gelatin.

gel|a|ti|nif|er|ous (jel′ə tə nif′ər əs), *adj.* yielding gelatin.

ge|lat|i|nize (jə lat′ə nīz), *v.,* **-nized, -niz|ing.**
—*v.i.* to become gelatinous.
—*v.t.* **1** to make gelatinous or jellylike. **2** to coat with gelatin. —**ge|lat′i|ni|za′tion,** *n.*

ge|lat|i|noid (jə lat′ə noid), *adj., n.* —*adj.* resembling gelatin; jellylike; gelatinous.
—*n.* a substance resembling gelatin.

ge|lat|i|nous (jə lat′ə nəs), *adj.* **1** of or like jelly. **2** of or like gelatin. —**ge|lat′i|nous|ly,** *adv.* —**ge|lat′i|nous|ness,** *n.*

ge|la|tion (jə lā′shən), *n.* solidification by cooling; freezing. [< Latin *gelātiō, -ōnis* < *gelāre* freeze < *gelū* frost]

ge|la|to (jə lä′tō), *n., pl.* **-ti** (-tē). a rich, creamy Italian ice cream, often made with fruit. [< Italian *gelato,* from *gelare* to freeze < Latin *gelāre*]

gel|a|tose (jel′ə tōs), *n.* an albumose derived from gelatin.

geld[1] (geld), *v.t.,* **geld|ed** or **gelt, geld|ing.** to remove the male glands of (a horse or other animal); castrate.
[< Scandinavian (Old Icelandic *gelda* castrate < *geldr* barren)] —**geld′er,** *n.*

geld[2] (geld), *n.* the tax paid to the crown by landholders under the Anglo-Saxon and Norman kings. Also, **gelt, gheld.** [< Medieval Latin *geldum* < Old English *gield* payment, tribute. See related etym. at **yield.**]

geld|ing (gel′ding), *n.* **1** a castrated horse or other animal. **2** *Obsolete.* a eunuch. [< Scandinavian (compare Old Icelandic *geldingr* < *geldr* barren)]

ge|lech|i|id (jə lek′ē id), *adj., n.* —*adj.* of or having to do with a large family of moths related to the tineids and including such insects as the pink bollworm and the Angoumois grain moth.
—*n.* a gelechiid moth.
[< New Latin *Gelechiidae* the family name < Greek *gēlechḗs* sleeping upon earth]

ge|lée (zhə lā′), *n. French.* jelly: *gelée of fish stock.*

gel|id (jel′id), *adj.* cold as ice; frosty; frozen: (*Figurative.*) *a man of gelid reserve who had few intimates* (New Yorker). SYN: icy, glacial, frigid.
[< Latin *gelidus* < *gelū* frost, ice] —**gel′id|ly,** *adv.*

ge|lid|i|ty (jə lid′ə tē), *n.* extreme cold; frigidity.

gel|ig|nite (jel′ig nīt), *n.* a powerful explosive made with nitroglycerin, soluble guncotton, wood pulp, and potassium or sodium nitrate.
[perhaps < *gel*(atin) + Latin *ignis* fire + English *-ite*[1]]

gel|i|notte (gel′ə not), *n.* = hazel grouse.
[< French *gelinotte* (diminutive) < *geline* hen]

gelled paint (jeld), a jellylike paint made with a polyamide resin so as not to drip when used. The pigment does not settle and the paint requires no stirring.

ge|long (gā′lông), *n.* a monk in Tibet. [< Tibetan *gelon*]

gel|ose (jel′ōs, jə lōs′), *n.* a gelatinlike substance obtained from certain algae, much used in the East for soups and jellies.

gel|se|mi|um (jel sē′mē əm), *n.* **1** = yellow jasmine. **2** the root of the yellow jasmine. **3** a powerful and dangerous drug made from it, sometimes used to treat malaria, rheumatism, and neuralgia. [< New Latin *Gelsemium* the genus name < Italian *gelsomino* jasmine]

gelt[1] (gelt), *v.* gelded; a past tense and a past participle of **geld**[1].

gelt[2] (gelt), *n.* **1** *Dialect.* money: *All the gelt was gone* (Scott). **2** geld (a tax). [< German *Geld*]

***gem** (jem), *n., v.,* **gemmed, gem·ming.** —*n.* **1** a precious or semiprecious stone, especially when cut and polished for ornament; jewel. Diamonds and rubies are gems. One beautiful gem, the pearl, is not a stone, but is obtained from a mollusk. **2** *Figurative.* a person or thing that is very beautiful or precious: *The gem of his collection was a rare Italian stamp. . . . they have made me appreciate the gems of English literature* (Graham Greene). SYN: pearl. **3** a kind of muffin made of coarse flour: *graham gems.* **4** *Printing.* a size of type (4 point).
—*v.t.* **1** to set or adorn with gems: (*Figurative.*) *Stars gem the sky.* **2** to extract gems from; search for gems in: *The Government could have no objections to grant the right to gem the whole river* (Ceylon Observer). **3** *Obsolete.* to put forth in buds: *The stately trees . . . gemm'd Their blossoms* (Milton).
[< Old French *gemme,* learned borrowing from Latin *gemma* gem, bud] —**gem′like′,** *adj.*

***gem**
definition 1

gem cuts:

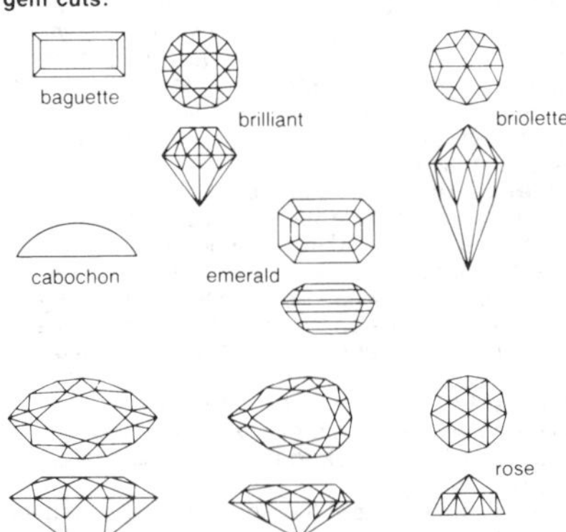

GEM (no periods), ground effect machine.

Ge·ma·ra (gə mä′rä, -mô′-), *n.* a rabbinical commentary on the Mishnah, and with it forming the Talmud. The Gemara is written in Aramaic. [< Aramaic *gemārā* completion]

Ge·ma·ric (gə mä′rik, -mô′-), *adj.* having to do with the Gemara.

Ge·ma·rist (gə mä′rist, -mô′-), *n.* a student of the Gemara.

ge·ma·tri·a (gə mā′trē ə), *n.* a cabalistic method of interpreting the Hebrew Scriptures by interchanging words whose letters have the same numerical value when added. [< Hebrew *gēmatriyā* < Greek *geometriā* geometry]

Ge·mein·schaft (gə mīn′shäft), *n. Sociology.* a group of people with an intimate relationship based on kinship, fellowship, or common traditions. [< German *Gemeinschaft* community]

gem·el (jem′əl), *n.* **1** = hinge. **2** = gemel ring. **3** a bottle with two or more heads, and with separate compartments for different liquids. [< Old French *gemel* < Latin *gemellus* (diminutive) < *geminus* a twin]

gem·el·lol·o·gist (je′mə lol′ə jist), *n.* a scientist who specializes in the study of twins: *Until their reunion took place, and those of other long-separated identical twins which consequently followed, gemellologists . . . had believed there to be fewer than a dozen such pairs of twins alive today* (New York Times Magazine). [< Latin *gemellus, geminus* twin + English *-ologist*]

gemel ring, a finger ring formed of two or more separable or interlocked circlets.

gem·i·nate (*v.* jem′ə nāt; *adj.* jem′ə nit, -nāt), *v.,* **-nat·ed, -nat·ing,** *adj.* —*v.t.* to make double; combine into pairs.
—*v.i.* to become double.
—*adj.* combined in a pair or pairs; coupled. SYN: twin, binate.
[< Latin *gemināre* (with English *-ate*[1]) < *geminus* twin] —**gem′i·nate·ly,** *adv.*

gem·i·na·tion (jem′ə nā′shən), *n.* **1** a doubling; duplication; repetition: *If the will be in the sense and in the conscience both, there is a gemination of it* (Francis Bacon). **2** *Phonetics.* the doubling of a single consonant sound. **3** a doubling in spelling. **4** *Rhetoric.* the immediate repetition of a word or phrase for rhetorical effect.

Gem·i·ni (jem′ə nī), *n.pl.* **1a** *genitive* **Gem·i·no·rum.** a northern constellation between Taurus and Cancer, containing the two bright stars Castor and Pollux; Twins. **b** the third sign of the zodiac. The sun enters Gemini about May 21. **c** a person born under the sign of Gemini. **2** *Greek Mythology.* Castor and Pollux, the twin sons of Zeus. [< Latin *Geminī* (literally, originally) twins < *geminus* a twin]

Gem·i·no·rum (jem′ə nôr′əm, -nōr′-), *n.* genitive of **Gemini.**

gem·ma (jem′ə), *n., pl.* **gem·mae** (jem′ē). **1** *Botany.* a bud: *Each gemma is a minute, thickened, flat, almost circular outgrowth from the bottom of the cup* (Fred W. Emerson). **2** a budlike reproductive body in some plants, such as liverworts and mosses, that becomes detached from the plant and can develop into a new individual. [< Latin *gemma* bud]

gem·ma·ceous (je mā′shəs), *adj.* of or like gemmae.

gem·mate (jem′āt), *v.,* **-mat·ed, -mat·ing,** *adj.* —*v.i.* to put forth buds; reproduce by budding.
—*adj.* having buds; reproducing by buds.
[< Latin *gemmāre* (with English *-ate*[1]) < *gemma* bud]

gem·ma·tion (je mā′shən), *n.* **1** reproduction by buds. **2** a putting forth of buds.

gem·ma·tive (jem′ə tiv), *adj.* having to do with the production of offspring by gemmation.

gem·maux (zhe mō′), *n.pl. French.* a work of art made of pieces of colored glass held together with a colorless enamel.

gem·mif·er·ous (je mif′ər əs), *adj.* **1** producing buds; increasing by gemmation. **2** producing or yielding gems. [< Latin *gemmifer* bearing gems (< *gemma* bud + *ferre* to bear) + English *-ous*]

gem·mip·a·rous (je mip′ər əs), *adj.* = gemmiferous (def. 1). —**gem·mip′a·rous·ly,** *adv.*

gem·mo·log·i·cal (jem′ə loj′ə kəl), *adj.* = gemological.

gem·mol·o·gist (je mol′ə jist), *n.* = gemologist.

gem·mol·o·gy (je mol′ə jē), *n.* = gemology.

gem·mu·la·tion (jem′yə lā′shən), *n.* the formation of gemmules.

gem·mule (jem′yül), *n.* **1** *Botany, Zoology.* a small bud. **2** a budlike reproductive body in sponges. **3** *Biology.* one of the living units thought by Charles Darwin to be the bearers of the hereditary characteristics of animals and plants. [< Latin *gemmula* (diminutive) < *gemma* bud]

gem·mu·lif·er·ous (jem′yə lif′ər əs), *adj.* bearing gemmules.

gem·my (jem′ē), *adj.,* **-mi·er, -mi·est.** **1** set with or as if with gems: *The gemmy bridle glitter'd free* (Tennyson). **2** gemlike; brilliant; glittering.

Gem of the Mountains, a nickname for Idaho.

gem·o·log·i·cal (jem′ə loj′ə kəl), *adj.* of or having to do with gemology.

gem·ol·o·gist (je mol′ə jist), *n.* a person who studies gemology.

gem·ol·o·gy (je mol′ə jē), *n.* the science of gems, their origins, uses, physical features, and other characteristics.

ge·mot or **ge·mote** (gə mōt′), *n.* an Anglo-Saxon meeting or assembly for judicial or legislative purposes. [a readoption in the 1600's of Old English *gemōt* < *ge-* with + *mōt* moot, a meeting]

gems·bok (gemz′bok′), *n.* a large antelope of southern Africa, having long, nearly straight horns and a long, tufted tail. [< Afrikaans *gemsbok* < German *Gemsbock* < *Gemse* chamois + *Bock* buck]

gems·buck (gemz′buk′), *n.* = gemsbok.

Gem State, a nickname for Idaho.

gem·stone (jem′stōn′), *n.* a precious or semiprecious stone that can be cut and polished to make a gem.

ge·müt·lich (gə mʏt′liʜ), *adj. German.* comfortable and contented; congenial; cozy. SYN: good-natured.

Ge·müt·lich·keit (gə mʏt′liʜ kīt), *n. German.* an atmosphere of comfort and kindliness; coziness: *Home was an island of Gemütlichkeit, snug and secure* (Harper's).

gen (jen), *n., v.,* **genned, gen·ning.** *British Slang.*
—*n.* inside information; low-down.
—*v.t.* to give inside information to.
[perhaps < *gen*(eral information)]

-gen, *combining form.* **1** something produced or growing, as in *acrogen.* **2** something that produces, as in *allergen, nitrogen.* [< French *-gène* < Greek *-genēs* born < *génos* a kind < *gígnesthai* be born]

gen., **1** gender. **2** genera. **3a** general. **b** generally. **4** genitive. **5** genus.

Gen., **1** General. **2** Genesis. **3a** Geneva. **b** Genevan.

ge·na (jē′nə), *n., pl.* **-nae** (-nē). *Zoology.* the cheek, or any part of the head resembling a cheek. [< Latin *gena* cheek]

ge·nappe (jə nap′), *n.* a worsted yarn used especially in manufacturing braids and fringes. Its smoothness allows combination with silk. [< *Genappe,* town in Belgium, where it was first made]

gen·ba·ku-sho (gen′bä′kü′shō′), *n. Japanese.* = radiation sickness.

gen·darme (zhän′därm), *n., pl.* **-darmes** (-därmz). **1** a policeman in France and several other European countries who has had military training: *A reformed jewel thief finds the gendarmes looking his way after a series of thefts break out in Cannes* (Newsweek). **2** any policeman. **3** an outcropping or tower of rock on a mountain. [< Middle French *gendarme* < Old French *gens d'armes* men of arms]

gen·darme·rie (zhäɴ dȧrm rē′; *Anglicized* zhän′där mər ē), *n. French.* a body of gendarmes; gendarmery.

gen·darm·er·y (zhän′där mər ē), *n., pl.* **-er·ies.** **1** the police force of France or of several other European countries. **2** any police force. [< Middle French *gendarmerie* < *gendarme;* see etym. under **gendarme**]

gen·der (jen′dər), *n., v.* —*n.* **1** the grouping of nouns into certain classes, such as masculine, feminine, and neuter. In English, except in pronouns (*him—her—it*) and a few nouns with endings such as *-ess* (*actress*), gender is now indicated only by the meaning of the word: *man—woman, nephew—niece, rooster—hen.* **2** one of such classes. *Abbr:* gen. **3** sex: *the female gender.* **4** *Archaic.* kind; sort; class.
—*v.t. Archaic.* to produce (offspring); procreate.
—*v.i. Archaic.* to be produced.
[< Old French *gendre,* learned borrowing from Latin *genus, generis* kind, sort; see etym. under **genus.** See etym. of doublet **genre.**]

►**gender.** Many languages have special endings for masculine, feminine, and neuter nouns and for adjectives modifying them, but English abandoned this system several hundred years ago, except for a few forms such as those ending in *-ess, -us, -a, -or, -trix, -e, -eur, -euse* (*actress, mistress, alumnus, alumna, actor, aviatrix, blonde, masseur, masseuse*).

gender gap, *U.S.* a credibility gap involving only women or only men, but not both: *The White House is opening the loophole to help close the "gender gap"—poll data that show women are disproportionately dubious about administration policies* (Newsweek).

gene (jēn), *n.* a minute part of a chromosome that influences the inheritance and development of some character; factor. Genes consist essentially of deoxyribonucleic acid (DNA) and are divisible into various functional units. The genes inherited from the parents determine what kind of a plant or animal will develop from a fertilized egg cell. *Located in the bands are the genes, . . . biological units that control specific chemical processes within the cell* (Earl Ubell). [< Greek *geneā* breed, kind]

geneal., **1** genealogical. **2** genealogy.

ge·ne·a·log·i·cal (jē′nē ə loj′ə kəl, jen′ē-), *adj.* having to do with genealogy. A genealogical chart is called a family tree. —**ge′ne·a·log′i·cal·ly,** *adv.*

genealogical tree, = family tree.

ge·ne·al·o·gist (jē′nē al′ə jist, -ol′-; jen′ē-), *n.* a person who makes a study of, or traces, genealogies.

ge·ne·al·o·gize (jē′nē al′ə jīz, -ol′-; jen′ē-), *v.,* **-gized, -giz·ing.** —*v.t.* to draw up a genealogy of.
—*v.i.* to trace descent; draw up genealogies.

ge·ne·al·o·gy (jē′nē al′ə jē, -ol′-; jen′ē-), *n., pl.* **-gies.** **1** an account of the descent of a person or family from an ancestor or ancestors. **2** the descent of a person or family from an ancestor; pedigree; lineage. SYN: ancestry. **3** the making or investigation of accounts of descent; study of pedigrees. [< Latin *geneālogia* < Greek *geneālogiā,* ultimately < *geneā* generation, race + *lógos* study of < *légein* speak]

gene deletion, the removal or loss of a gene or genes from the genetic inventory of a cell or animal.

gene flow, the diffusion of genes as a result of crossing with an unrelated group and from subsequent crossing within the hybrid group: *As they produced more and more food, the farmers and herdsmen overpopulated their territories and crowded each other along their frontiers, thus increasing the amount of mixture and the gene flow between populations* (Carleton S. Coon).

gene frequency, the degree to which a particular gene is present in the chromosomes of a group.

gene insertion, the insertion of missing genes in

Pronunciation Key: hat, āge, cãre, fär; let, ēqual, tėrm; it, īce; hot, ōpen, ôrder; oil, out; cup, pu̇t, rüle; child; long; thin; ᴛʜen; zh, measure;
ə represents **a** in about, **e** in taken, **i** in pencil, **o** in lemon, **u** in circus.

the genetic inventory of a cell or animal.
gene|like (jēn′līk′), *adj.* resembling a gene; like that of a gene.
gene mapping, the process of determining the arrangement of the genes of a chromosome: *Gene mapping may ... actually promise to correct many genetic disorders. If, for example, a defective gene could be removed and another gene inserted in its place on the map of human chromosomes, many genetic disorders could be prevented* (Dalma Heyn).
gene mutation, a sudden or dramatic change in the inherited characteristics of an organism, caused presumably by a chemical change in normal genes rather than by changes in chromosome structure: *radioactive fallout which could produce ... gene mutation affecting unborn generations* (Wall Street Journal).
gene pool, all of the genes contained in the genetic makeup of a species: ... *genetic stocks, or gene pools, have been carefully studied* (New Scientist).
gen|er|a (jen′ər ə), *n.* a plural of **genus**.
gen|er|a|ble (jen′ər ə bəl), *adj.* that can be generated or produced.
gen|er|al (jen′ər, əl, jen′rəl), *adj., n., v.,* **-aled**, **-al|ing** or (*especially British*) **-alled**, **-al|ling**. —*adj.* **1** of all; for all; from all: *A government takes care of the general welfare of its citizens.* **2** for many; from many; common to many or most; not limited to a few; widespread: *general principles, a general rule. There is a general interest in television.* **3** not detailed; sufficient for practical purposes: *The teacher gave us only general instructions. After we had answered the general questions they began to be more particular* (Daniel Defoe). **4** not special; not limited to one kind, class, department, or use: *a general magazine. A general reader reads different kinds of books.* **5** indefinite; vague: *She referred to her trip in a general way.* **6** of or for all those forming a group: *"Cat" is the general term for cats, lions, and tigers.* **7** of or having to do with a whole region or body: *a general election.* **8** in chief; of highest rank: *The Attorney General is the head of the legal department of the government.* **9** *Archaic.* whole: *the general body.*
—*n.* **1** a high officer in command of many soldiers in an army: *Washington was a famous general.* **2** *U.S.* **a** any officer ranking above a colonel and entitled to command a force larger than a regiment, such as a lieutenant general or a major general. **b** an officer ranking next below a General of the Army or a General of the Air Force and next above a lieutenant general, wearing the insignia of four stars; full general. **c** an officer of the highest rank in the United States Marine Corps. *Abbr:* Gen. **3** a British army officer ranking next below a field marshal and next above a lieutenant general. *Abbr:* Gen. **4** an officer holding the second or third highest rank in certain foreign armies. **5** a signal calling troops to prepare to march. **6** a general fact, idea, principle, or statement: *It is by means of our knowledge of particulars that we ascend to generals* (Henry Hallam). **7** the head of a religious order; superior general. **8** the head of the Salvation Army: *General William Booth.* **9** *Archaic.* people as a group; the general public: *The play ... pleased not the million; 'twas caviare to the general* (Shakespeare). **10** *Obsolete.* the total; whole.
—*v.t.* to serve as general to; command.
in general, **a** for the most part; usually; commonly: *He is friendly with me in general, but he was particularly friendly today.* **b** *Obsolete.* in all respects: *Thou art a grave and noble counsellor, Most wise in general* (Shakespeare).
[< Latin *generālis* of a (whole) class < *genus, -eris* class; see etym. under **genus**] —**gen′er|al|ness**, *n.*
—*Syn. adj.* **1, 2 General, common, popular** mean belonging or relating to all or to most. **General** means applying to or done by all of a group or class, or most of it: *As a general rule, male birds are more conspicuously marked than female birds. Laws are made for the general good.* **Common** means shared by all the members of a group or class, or most of them: *English is the common language in the United States.* **Popular** means belonging to or prevailing among the people: *Various polls are supposed to find out popular opinions.*
general adaptation syndrome, a series of changes by which the body responds to prolonged stress: *The general adaptation syndrome ... is considered a nonspecific reaction, for it is supposed to function in the same way regardless of the type of stressor confronting the individual. It consists of three stages: alarm, resistance, and exhaustion* (David C. Glass).
general agent, a person who represents a principal in all transactions of a particular business.
General American, the variety of English spoken in most of the United States, exclusive of New York City, the South, and New England. As a regional dialect, it is currently called *Midland* by most language scholars.
general anesthesia, the loss of sensation in the entire body, accompanied by loss of consciousness.
general assembly, an assembly of all the representatives or members of any organization: *The school held a general assembly.*
General Assembly, **1** the legislature of certain states of the United States. **2** the deliberative body of the United Nations, made up of delegates from every member nation. **3** the supreme legislative or governing body of a national church. **4** the lawmaking body of any country.
gen|er|al|ate (jen′ər ə lit, jen′rə-), *n.* **1** the office, headquarters, or jurisdiction of a general, especially of a religious order. **2** the term or period of office of a general.
general cargo, cargo of various kinds, such as that transported by a common-carrier ship.
General Certificate of Education, *British.* a certificate that a person has passed an examination on secondary-school subjects.
general circulation, *Meteorology.* the system formed by the prevailing world-wide movements of the atmosphere.
general classification test, *Psychology.* a test of general intelligence, intellectual achievement, and aptitude, used as a screening device in examining applicants for employment.
General Court, **1** the legislature of Massachusetts or New Hampshire. **2** any one of various colonial American legislatures that also had judicial powers.
general court-martial, a military or naval court consisting of five or more officers or enlisted men, including a law officer, before which a member of the armed services or other person subject to trial by military tribunal is brought.
gen|er|al|cy (jen′ər əl sē, jen′rəl-), *n., pl.* **-cies**. the office or rank of a general.
general delivery or **General Delivery**, the department of a post office that holds the mail of persons who come to the post office to collect it. A person who is not sure what his address will be in a city can have his mail directed to General Delivery.
general discharge, a discharge of a member of the armed forces given for honorable service, but for which all the conditions of an honorable discharge have not been met.
general editor, a supervisory editor in charge of other editors, as of a series of textbooks.
general education, a program of education for broad mental development and general knowledge, as distinguished from vocational education.
general election, **1** *U.S.* a local, state, or federal election in which every constituency elects candidates for public offices. **2** *British.* an election in which every constituency elects a representative for the House of Commons.
General Election Day, *U.S.* the day on which the election of public officials is held, the first Tuesday following the first Monday in November in most states; Election Day.
General Epistle, (in the Bible) one of the Epistles of James, Peter, John, or Jude, dealing with the church as a whole; Catholic Epistle.
general headquarters, the headquarters of a commander in chief. *Abbr:* GHQ (no periods).
general health, the ordinary health of the body as a whole, or of a community.
general hospital, **1** a hospital that accepts patients for all kinds of treatment. **2** a military hospital that receives the sick and wounded from field hospitals.
gen|er|al|ise (jen′ər ə līz, jen′rə-), *v.t., v.i.,* **-ised**, **-is|ing**. *Especially British.* generalize.
gen|er|al|ism (jen′ər ə liz′əm, jen′rə-), *n.* devotion to broad fields of study, business, or the like without becoming involved in details; the beliefs and practices of a generalist: ... *the preference for generalism over specialized training and professionalism in staffing the higher civil service* (T. J. O. Hickey).
gen|er|al|is|si|mo (jen′ər ə lis′ə mō, jen′rə-), *n., pl.* **-mos**. **1** the commander in chief of all the military forces in certain countries: *Generalissimo Chiang Kai-Shek.* **2** the commander in chief of several armies in the field. [< Italian *generalissimo,* superlative of *generale* general < Latin *generālis*]
gen|er|al|ist (jen′ər ə list, jen′rə-), *n.* a person who devotes himself to a broad field of study, business, or the like, without becoming involved in details.
gen|er|al|i|ty (jen′ə ral′ə tē), *n., pl.* **-ties**. **1** a general or vague statement; word or phrase not definite enough to have much meaning or value: *The candidate spoke only in generalities; not once did he say what he would do if elected.* **2** a general principle or rule: *"Nothing happens without a cause" is a generality.* SYN: generalization. **3** the greater part; main body; mass: *The generality of people must work for a living.* SYN: majority. **4** general quality or condition: *A rule of great generality has very few exceptions.*
gen|er|al|iz|a|bil|i|ty (jen′ər ə lī′zə bil′ə tē, jen′rə-), *n.* the quality of being generalizable.
gen|er|al|iz|a|ble (jen′ər ə lī′zə bəl, jen′rə-), *adj.* that can be summed up by a generalization: *generalizable data.*
gen|er|al|i|za|tion (jen′ər ə lə zā′shən, jen′rə-), *n.* **1** the act or process of generalizing: *Don't be hasty in generalization; be sure you have the necessary facts first.* **2** a general idea, statement, principle, or rule: *"Summer is warmer than winter" is a generalization based on long experience.*
gen|er|al|ize (jen′ər ə līz, jen′rə-), *v.,* **-ized**, **-iz|ing**. —*v.t.* **1** to make into one general statement; bring under a common heading, class, or law. **2** to infer (a general rule) from particular facts: *Knowledge is experience generalized* (John Stuart Mill). **3** to state in a more general form; extend in application: *The statement that $5 + 3 = 8$ and $50 + 30 = 80$ can be generalized to the form $5a + 3a = 8a$.* **4** to bring into general use or knowledge; popularize. **5** to make general; give a general form or character to.
—*v.i.* **1** to infer a general rule from particular facts; make general inferences: *If you have seen cats, lions, leopards, and tigers eat meat, you can generalize and say, "The cat family eats meat." It is a dangerous business to generalize about what the American voter will do* (Tom Wicker). **2** to talk or write indefinitely or vaguely; use generalities: *The news commentator generalized because he knew no details.* **3** to become general; spread: *This fear [of a dog] may generalize ... even more widely to other animals and to such objects as fur coats* (Walter Mischel).
—**gen′er|al|iz′er**, *n.*
gen|er|al|ized (jen′ər ə līzd, jen′rə-), *adj.* **1** *Biology.* representing a broad or general type of form or function; undifferentiated: *Man's brains, hands, and eyes ... are generalized features, even though they have developed enormously in complexity* (Beals and Hoijer). **2** *Medicine.* affecting many or all parts of the body: *a generalized disease.*
general ledger, *Accounting.* the main ledger that contains accounts of assets, liabilities, income, expenditures, and other financial data, of a business.
general linguistics, the study of language and linguistic phenomena in general, with reference to many languages and the various branches of linguistics.
gen|er|al|ly (jen′ər ə lē, jen′rə-), *adv.* **1** in most cases; usually: *He is generally on time.* SYN: commonly. **2** for the most part; widely: *It was once generally believed that the earth was flat.* SYN: extensively. **3** in a general way; without giving details; not specially: *Generally speaking, our coldest weather comes in January.*
general manager, the executive in charge of the day-to-day operation of a factory, business, or other enterprise.
general officer, an officer of the U.S. Army, Air Force, or Marine Corps holding a rank above colonel.
General of the Air Force, a general of the highest rank in the United States Air Force, wearing the insigne of five stars.
General of the Armies, *U.S.* a special military title created by Congress after World War I for General John J. Pershing.
General of the Army, a general of the highest rank in the United States Army, wearing the insigne of five stars.
general orders, a series of military publications issued by an authorized headquarters, each containing general announcements of official acts, such as citations of units, awards, important appointments, or other directive or informative matters. Some general orders have the force of regulations.
general paresis or **paralysis**, a condition characterized by mental and muscular deterioration, caused by a syphilitic infection of the brain and brain coverings; dementia paralytica.
general post, *British.* the first mail delivery in the morning.
general post office, a central post office for any city or district having branches.
general practice, the work of a general practitioner.
general practitioner, a physician who does not specialize in any single field of medicine. *Abbr:* GP (no periods) or G.P.
gen|er|al-pur|pose (jen′ər əl pėr′pəs, jen′rəl-), *adj.* of many or unlimited uses.
general quarters, (in the Navy) the stationing of all hands at battle stations, and the making of preparations, as for battle or an emergency.

general relativity, = general theory of relativity.
general retainer, 1 the securing of the services of a lawyer in all legal matters for a specified amount of time. **2** the fee paid for such services.
general semantics, a theory and a method intended to improve the quality of human experiences and relationships by training people to be more critical in their use of and reaction to words and symbols; developed by Alfred Korzybski.
general sessions, *U.S.* a court of law having general jurisdiction in criminal cases.
gen|er|al|ship (jen′ər əl ship, jen′rəl-), *n.* **1** ability as a general; skill in commanding an army: *He acknowledged . . . that his success . . . was to be attributed, not at all to his own generalship, but solely to the valour and steadiness of his troops* (Macaulay). **2** skillful management; leadership. **3** the rank, commission, authority, or term of office or function of a general.
general staff, a group of high army officers who assist a chief of staff of a division or larger unit in making plans for war or national defense.
general store, a store that carries a wide variety of goods for sale.
general strike, 1 a widespread strike in the essential industries of a country or in all the industries of a certain area. **2** a strike of all the workers of an industry.
general theory of relativity, an extension of Einstein's special theory of relativity, dealing with the equivalence of gravitational and inertial forces and related phenomena.
general trademark, a trademark that covers a general business or occupation and has no time limit.
gen|er|ant (jen′ər ənt), *adj., n.* —*adj.* generating; producing.
—*n.* a generator.
[< Latin *generāns, -antis,* present participle of *generāre;* see etym. under **generate**]
gen|er|ate (jen′ə rāt), *v.t.,* **-at|ed, -at|ing. 1** to cause to be; bring into being; produce: *Heating water can generate steam. The steam can generate electricity by turning an electric generator.* SYN: make. **2** to produce (offspring); procreate. SYN: beget. **3** *Mathematics.* to form (a line, surface, figure, or solid) especially by moving a point or line. **4** *Linguistics.* to derive or produce (a grammatical sentence) from more basic forms by a set of rules of operation or transformation: *Surface structures—the sentences we actually speak and hear—are not "like" the kernels from which they are generated by transformational rules* (New Yorker). [< Latin *generāre* (with English *-ate*[1]) < *genus, -eris* race; see etym. under **genus**]
gen|er|a|tion (jen′ə rā′shən), *n.* **1** all the people born in the same period of time. Your parents and their friends belong to one generation; you and your friends belong to the next generation. **2** about 20 or 30 years, or the time from the birth of one generation to the birth of the next generation: *The automobile was introduced in America during the generation before World War I.* **3** one step or degree in the descent of a family: *The picture showed four generations—great-grandmother, grandmother, mother, and baby.* **4** a group of things produced within the same period of time, often on the model of an earlier product: *The new computers are . . . much better priced in performance than the previous generation* (Wall Street Journal). **5** the production of offspring; procreation. **6** the act or process of producing; bringing into being; generating; production: *the generation of steam in a boiler. Steam and water power are used for the generation of electricity.* **7** *Biology.* a form or stage of a plant or animal, with reference to its method of reproduction: *the asexual generation of a fern.* **8** *Mathematics.* the formation of a line, surface, figure, or solid especially by moving a point or line. **9** *Obsolete.* offspring; descendants: *The book of the generation of Jesus Christ* (Matthew 1:1). **10** *Obsolete.* a class of persons; family; race.
gen|er|a|tion|al (jen′ə rā′shə nəl), *adj.* of or having to do with generations. —**gen′er|a′tion|al|ly,** *adv.*
generation gap, the difference in social values, behavioral attitudes, and personal aspirations of one generation and that of the next generation, especially the generation of adolescents or young adults and that of their parents: *In a day when the generation gap yawns ever wider . . . parents and children have become strangers to one another* (Time).
gen|er|a|tion|ism (jen′ə rā′shə niz əm), *n. Theology.* the theory that the soul originates with the body in generation, and not by a distinct act of creation; traducianism.
generation name, the second name customarily given in a Chinese family, taken from a brief poem adopted by each family.
gen|er|a|tive (jen′ə rā′tiv), *adj.* **1** having to do with the production of offspring. **2** having the power of producing: *generative cells, generative tissues.* **3** *Linguistics.* of or based on the derivation of grammatical sentences from more basic forms by operational or transformational rules: *generative phonology, generative semantics.* —**gen′er|a′tive|ly,** *adv.* —**gen′er|a′tive|ness,** *n.*
generative grammar, *Linguistics.* a system of rules of operation or transformation for deriving all the grammatical sentences of a language from more basic underlying strings of words.
gen|er|a|tiv|ist (jen′ə rā′tə vist), *n.* a follower or advocate of generative linguistics.
***gen|er|a|tor** (jen′ə rā′tər), *n.* **1** a machine that changes mechanical energy into electrical energy and produces either direct or alternating current; a dynamo. **2** an apparatus for producing gas or steam. **3** a person or thing that generates: . . . *the San Andreas Fault, a major generator of earthquakes* (New York Times). [< Latin *generātor* < *generāre;* see etym. under **generate**]

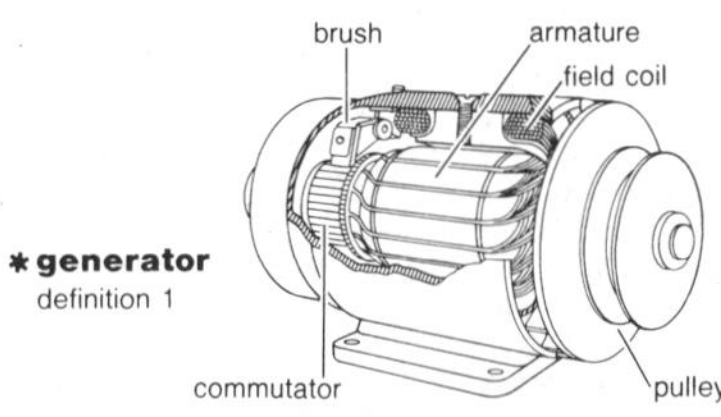

***generator**
definition 1

gen|er|a|trix (jen′ə rā′triks), *n., pl.* **gen|er|a|tri|ces** (jen′ər ə trī′sēz). **1** *Mathematics.* a point, line, or figure whose motion produces a line, surface, figure, or solid. **2** *Obsolete.* a female parent. [< Latin *generātrix,* feminine of *generātor;* see etym. under **generator**]
ge|ner|ic (jə ner′ik), *adj., n.* —*adj.* **1** having to do with or characteristic of a genus, kind, or class: *Cats and lions show generic differences. . . . a philanthropist in the generic sense of one who loves mankind* (Thomas Lask). **2** having to do with a class or group of similar things; general; not specific or special: *"Liquid" is a generic term, but "milk" is a specific term.* SYN: inclusive. **3** not registered as a trademark: *Drugs are always cheaper if ordered by the generic rather than the proprietary trade names* (Harper's).
—*n.* **1** a generic term: . . . *waterways with the generics* creek *and* run, *elevations with generics such as* hill, mount, *and* knob (Eugene Green). **2** a generic drug: *Indigents should purchase low-cost generics instead of more costly brand-name drugs* (Science News).
[< Latin *genus, -eris* kind (see etym. under **genus**) + English *-ic*] —**ge|ner′i|cal|ly,** *adv.*
ge|ner|i|cal (jə ner′ə kəl), *adj.* = generic.
ge|ner|ic|ness (jə ner′ək nis), *n.* generic nature or, quality.
gen|er|os|i|ty (jen′ə ros′ə tē), *n., pl.* **-ties. 1** the quality of being generous; willingness to share with others; unselfishness: *The millionaire was widely known for his generosity.* **2** nobleness of heart or mind; willingness to forgive; absence of meanness: *He accepted the apology with great generosity. Generosity is never a characteristic of political party warfare* (Sir Theodore Martin). **3** a generous act; generous behavior: *Giving money to the beggar was a generosity no one expected of the stingy old man.* **4** *Archaic.* nobility of birth or lineage.
gen|er|ous (jen′ər əs, jen′rəs), *adj.* **1** willing to share with others; unselfish: *Though he didn't have much to give, he was generous with his money.* SYN: liberal, bountiful, lavish. **2** noble and forgiving; not mean: *The generous soldiers treated their prisoners kindly.* SYN: high-minded, magnanimous. **3** large; plentiful: *A quarter of a pie is a generous piece.* SYN: ample, abundant, copious. **4** fertile: *generous fields.* **5** rich and strong: *a generous wine.* **6** *Archaic.* of noble lineage; highborn: *a generous race of horses* (Edward Gibbon). [< Latin *generōsus* of noble birth < *genus, -eris* race, stock; see etym. under **genus**] —**gen′er|ous|ly,** *adv.* —**gen′er|ous|ness,** *n.*
Gen|e|sis (jen′ə sis), *n.* the first book of the Old Testament. Genesis gives an account of the creation of the world. *Abbr:* Gen. [< Latin *genesis* < Greek *génesis* < *gígnesthai* be born]
gen|e|sis (jen′ə sis), *n., pl.* **-ses** (-sēz). a coming into being; origin; creation: *the genesis of an idea.* SYN: beginning, inception.
gene-splic|ing (jēn′splī′sing), *n. Informal.* the recombination of genetic material; production of recombinant DNA: *The basic process of . . . gene-splicing is . . . sufficiently developed to be a routine procedure in a properly equipped laboratory* (Edwin S. Weaver).
gen|et[1] (jen′it, jə net′), *n.* **1** any one of various flesh-eating mammals of southern Europe, Africa, and western Asia, related to the civets but lacking a scent pouch. A genet is about as large as a cat, with a sharper nose, shorter legs, and a longer tail. **2** the soft, brown fur of any of these animals. Also, **genette.** [< Old French *genette* < Arabic *jarnayt*]
gen|et[2] (jen′it), *n.* = jennet.
gene therapy, the treatment of a genetic disorder by replacing a defective gene on a chromosome with a normal one: *Other strategies of gene therapy . . . would be to implant normal cells (cells with the right genes and chromosomes in developing embryos)* (Joseph Fletcher).
ge|neth|li|ac (jə neth′lē ak), *adj., n.* —*adj.* **1** having to do with horoscopes. **2** having to do with a birthday.
—*n.* **1** a person skilled in genethlialogy; astrologer. **2** a birthday poem.
[ultimately < Greek *genethliakós* < *genéthlios* < *genéthlē* birth] —**gen′eth|li′a|cal|ly,** *adv.*
ge|neth|li|al|o|gy (jə neth′lē al′ə jē), *n.* the art of predicting the course of a person's life from the positions of the planets, etc., at the instant of birth; astrology.
ge|net|ic (jə net′ik), *adj.* **1** having to do with origin and natural growth. **2** of or having to do with genetics. **3** of or having to do with genes; genic: *genetic variation.*
[< Greek *genetês* begetter (< *génesis* origin; see etym. under **Genesis**) + English *-ic*] —**ge|net′i|cal|ly,** *adv.*
ge|net|i|cal (jə net′ə kəl), *adj.* = genetic.
genetic alphabet, the set of symbols for the four nucleic-acid bases that combine in various ways to form the genetic code: *Most DNA consists of sequences of only four nitrogenous bases: adenine (A), thymine (T), guanine (G) and cytosine (C). Together these bases form the genetic alphabet* (Scientific American).
genetic carrier, an individual who can transmit a heritable disease to offspring without himself having any symptoms of it.
genetic code, the various combinations of nucleotides which may occur in the DNA or RNA molecule of a chromosome. The genetic code determines the makeup of genes and is the biochemical code by which the four nucleic-acid bases combine, usually in units of three, to specify the synthesis of particular amino acids and proteins that determine the hereditary characteristics of an organism.
genetic copying, the duplication of a genetic inventory.
genetic counseling, the counseling of prospective parents on possible birth defects in their children on the basis of chromosomal tests and such medical procedures as amniocentesis.
genetic counselor, a person, usually a physician, who engages in genetic counseling.
genetic death, the inability of an organism to propagate its species due to a genetic defect: *Genetic death is not the death of any person—it is the extinction of a gene from the population* (Science).
genetic drift, change in genetic makeup of an isolated population, presumably due to the stabilization of random variations over a period of time.
genetic engineer, a person who specializes in genetic engineering.
genetic engineering, the scientific alteration of genes or genetic material to produce desirable new traits in organisms or to eliminate undesirable ones.
genetic fallacy, the fallacy or error of explaining anything in terms of its origin or genesis to the neglect of other factors.
genetic fingerprint, = DNA fingerprint.
genetic fingerprinting, = DNA fingerprinting.
ge|net|i|cist (jə net′ə sist), *n.* an expert in genetics.
genetic load, the accumulated mutations in the gene pool of a species: *We are learning more about the gene pool and genetic load, but many questions remain unanswered. We know very little about . . . the relative proportions of balanced and mutational load produced by the common mutagenic agents* (Scientific American).
genetic map, the way genes are arranged on a chromosome.
genetic marker, an inherited characteristic that can be followed from generation to generation: *Since the enzyme deficiency is transmitted from parents to children . . . it serves as a genetic marker* (Harper's).
genetic mutation, = gene mutation.
ge|net|ics (jə net′iks), *n.* **1** the branch of biology dealing with the principles of heredity and variation in animals and plants of the same or related

Pronunciation Key: hat, āge, cãre, fär; let, ēqual, tėrm; it, īce; hot, ōpen, ôrder; oil, out; cup, pu̇t, rüle; child; long; thin; ᴛʜen; zh, measure; ə represents **a** in about, **e** in taken, **i** in pencil, **o** in lemon, **u** in circus.

kinds. **2** genetic features or properties exhibited by an organism or any organic structure: *The genetics of the living cell is more remarkable than capsule statements allow* (Scientific American).

genetic screening, study of the genetic make-up of an individual to detect inheritable defects that may be transmitted to offspring.

genetic surgery, any experimental technique for altering whole blocks of genetic characteristics simultaneously.

Gen|e|tron (jen′ə tron), *n. Trademark.* a fluoride gas used as an aerosol dispersant, a refrigerant, and a solvent.

ge|nette (jə net′), *n.* = genet[1].

ge|ne|va (jə nē′və), *n.* an alcoholic liquor flavored with juniper berries; Hollands. [< Dutch *genever* < Old French *genevre* juniper < Latin *jūniperus* juniper (whose berries originally flavored it)]

Geneva bands, the clerical collar, with two strips hanging in front, originally worn by the Swiss Calvinist clergy.

Geneva Convention, any one of a series of agreements between nations establishing rules for humane treatment of prisoners of war, wounded, and sick and for handling of the dead, first formulated at Geneva, Switzerland, in 1864.

Geneva cross, a red Greek cross on a white background, used in wartime to distinguish ambulances, hospitals, and medical workers.

Geneva gown, a loose, large-sleeved black vestment originally used by the Swiss Calvinist clergymen.

Ge|ne|van (jə nē′vən), *adj., n.* —***adj.*** **1** of Geneva, Switzerland, or its people. **2** = Calvinistic. —***n.*** **1** a person born or living in Geneva. **2** = Calvinist.

Gen|e|vese (jen′ə vēz′, -vēs′), *adj., n., pl.* **-vese.** = Genevan.

gen|ial[1] (jēn′yəl), *adj.* **1** smiling and pleasant; cheerful and friendly; kindly: *She was glad to see us again and gave us a genial welcome.* **SYN:** jovial. **2** cheering; enlivening: *I hail thy genial loved return* (William Collins). **3** helping growth: *The soil is not genial to them* (Hawthorne). **4** pleasantly warming; comforting: *a genial climate. . . . a soft sunny morning in the genial month of May* (Washington Irving). **5** *Archaic.* **a** having to do with marriage; nuptial. **b** having to do with generation; generative. **6** *Archaic.* of or characterized by genius: *Great genial power, one would almost say, consists in not being original at all: in being altogether receptive* (Emerson). **7** *Obsolete.* natural; innate: *a theologue more by need than genial bent* (John Dryden). [< Latin *geniālis,* (literally) belonging to the genius (fostering spirit) < *genius*] —**gen′ial|ly,** *adv.* —**gen′ial|ness,** *n.*

ge|ni|al[2] (jə nī′əl), *adj. Anatomy.* of or having to do with the chin: *the lower genial process.* [< Greek *géneion* chin (< *génys* jaw) + English *-al*[1]]

ge|ni|al|i|ty (jē′nē al′ə tē), *n.* genial quality or behavior; cheerfulness; kindliness; mildness.

gen|ial|ize (jēn′yə līz), *v.t.,* **-ized, -iz|ing.** to make genial.

gen|ic (jen′ik), *adj. Biology.* of, produced by, or like a gene; genetic. —**gen′i|cal|ly,** *adv.*

-genic, *combining form.* **1** producing; having to do with production: *Carcinogenic = producing cancer.* **2** suitable for; suitable for production or reproduction by: *Photogenic = suitable for photography.* [< *-gen* + *-ic*]

ge|nic|u|lar (jə nik′yə lər), *adj. Botany.* growing on or at a node; occurring in the tissue of the node: *genicular cells.*

ge|nic|u|late (jə nik′yə lit, -lāt), *adj. Biology.* **1** having kneelike joints or bends. **2** bent at a joint like the knee. [< Latin *geniculātus* having knees, knots, past participle of *geniculāre* bend the knee < *geniculum* knot (diminutive) < *genū* knee] —**ge|nic′u|late|ly,** *adv.*

ge|nic|u|lat|ed (jə nik′yə lā′tid), *adj.* = geniculate.

ge|nic|u|la|tion (jə nik′yə lā′shən), *n. Biology.* **1** the state of being geniculate. **2** a geniculate formation or part.

ge|nic|u|lum (jə nik′yə lum), *n., pl.* **-la** (-lə). **1** *Botany.* a node or joint of a stem. **2** *Anatomy.* a sharp bend in any small organ, as that in the facial nerve where it passes through the temporal bone. [< Latin *geniculum* (diminutive) < *genū* knee]

ge|nie (jē′nē), *n., pl.* **-nies** or **-ni|i.** (in Moslem mythology) a powerful spirit; jinni: *When Aladdin rubbed his lamp, the genie came and did what Aladdin asked.* [< French *génie,* loan translation for Arabic *jinnī* jinni]

▶See **genius** for usage note.

ge|ni|i (jē′nē ī), *n.* **1** a plural of **genius**; spirits. **2** a plural of **genie**[1].

gen|i|pap (jen′ə pap), *n.* **1** the edible fruit of a tropical American tree of the madder family. It is about the size of an orange and has an agreeable winy flavor. **2** the tree itself. [< Portuguese *genipape* < Tupi (perhaps Brazil) *yanipaba*]

ge|nis|ta (jə nis′tə), *n.* any one of a group of shrubby plants of the pea family with striped, green, sometimes spiny branches and yellow or white flowers, such as the woadwaxen. [< New Latin *Genista* the genus name < Latin *genista* broom]

ge|nis|te|in (jə nis′tē in), *n.* a citrus flavonoid compound found in genista flowers, soybeans, and certain other leguminous plants. It has an effect similar to that of estrogen in animals. *Formula:* $C_{15}H_{10}O_5$

genit., genitive.

gen|i|tal (jen′ə təl), *adj.* having to do with reproduction or the sex organs. [< Latin *genitālis* < *genitus,* past participle of *gignere* beget, produce]

gen|i|ta|lia (jen′ə tāl′yə, -tā′lē ə), *n.pl.* = genitals. [< Latin *genitālia*]

gen|i|tals (jen′ə təlz), *n.pl.* the external sex organs, usually of the male.

gen|i|ti|val (jen′ə tī′vəl), *adj.* of or in the genitive case. —**gen′i|ti′val|ly,** *adv.*

gen|i|tive (jen′ə tiv), *adj., n.* —***adj.*** showing possession, source, or origin. *Mine, our, his,* and *their* are in the genitive case, or, as is usually said for English words, the possessive case. —***n.*** **1** the genitive case. **2** a word or construction in the genitive case. *Abbr:* gen. [< Latin *genitīvus,* for *genetīvus* pertaining to origin < *genitus* (see etym. under **genital**); mistranslation of Greek *genikė ptôsis* generic case] —**gen′i|tive|ly,** *adv.*

genitive absolute, a construction in Greek similar to the ablative absolute in Latin.

gen|i|tor (jen′ə tər, -tôr), *n. Archaic.* a male parent; father; progenitor.

gen|i|to|u|ri|nar|y (jen′ə tō yůr′ə ner′ē), *adj.* having to do with or denoting the genital and urinary organs or functions.

gen|i|ture (jen′ə chůr), *n.* **1** *Obsolete.* a begetting; generation; birth. **2** *Astrology.* nativity; horoscope.

gen|ius (jēn′yəs, jē′nē əs), *n., pl.* **gen|ius|es** *for 1-4, 7,* **ge|ni|i** *for 5, 6, 8.* **1** very great natural power of mind: *Important discoveries and inventions are usually made by men of genius. A man of genius . . . is a spring in which there is always more behind than flows from it* (James Froude). **2a** a person having such power: *Shakespeare, Benjamin Franklin, and Einstein were geniuses. Homer was the greater genius, Virgil the better artist* (Alexander Pope). **b** *Psychology.* a person with an IQ of 140 or more. **3** great natural ability of some special kind: *a task suited to one's genius. Beethoven played the piano well, but he had a genius for composing music. Walton had a genius for friendships* (James Russell Lowell). **4** the special character or spirit of a person, nation, age, language, concept, or place: *the genius of the age.* **5** a guardian spirit of a person, place, institution, or the like: *It seemed as if the Genius of the Weather sat in mournful meditation on the threshold* (Dickens). **6** either of two spirits, one good and one evil, supposed to influence a person's fate: *A fairy shield your Genius made, And gave you on your natal day* (Tennyson). **7** a person who strongly influences for good or evil the character, conduct, or destiny of another: *An evil genius had the princess under his spell.* **8** a spirit or jinni; genie. [< Latin *genius* tutelary spirit, male generative power < *gen-,* stem of *gignere* beget]

▶**genius, genie.** *Genius,* although in modern use most commonly meaning very great natural power of mind, also means a spirit giving a special character to a language, period, nation, concept, or place, or influencing or guarding the destiny of a person: *"Guardian angel" and "good genius" are much the same thing. Genie,* also meaning a spirit, applies specifically to a supernatural creature in Moslem mythology: *"The Arabian Nights" tells about the genie of Aladdin's lamp.*

Gen|ius (jēn′yəs, jē′nē əs), *n.* (in ancient Rome) a spirit attendant on a person or place: *Under him my Genius is rebuked, as it is said Mark Antony's was by Caesar* (Shakespeare).

ge|ni|us lo|ci (jē′nē əs lō′sī), *Latin.* **1** the guardian spirit of a place: *haunted by some baleful genius loci* (New York Times). **2** the spirit or character throughout a place or institution.

genl., general.

gen|o|a (jen′ō ə), *n.* = genoa jib.

genoa jib, a balloon jib, or a very tall balloon jib and topsail combined, used on yachts. [< *Genoa,* a seaport in Italy]

gen|o|cid|al (jen′ə sī′dəl), *adj.* having to do with genocide.

gen|o|cide (jen′ə sīd), *n.* the systematic extermination of a cultural or racial group: *The theoretical basis for the practice of genocide existed in the corroding Nazi doctrine of race* (Victor H. Bernstein). [American English (coined by R. Lemkin in 1944) < Greek *génos* race + English *-cide*[2]]

gen|o|cid|ist (jen′ə sī′dist), *n.* a person who uses or advocates genocide.

Gen|o|ese (jen′ō ēz′, -ēs′), *adj., n., pl.* **-ese.** —***adj.*** of or having to do with Genoa, Italy, or its people. —***n.*** a person born or living in Genoa.

gen|o|gram (jen′ə gram), *n.* a graph that traces the interplay of generations within a family to identify repetitive patterns of behavior: *A genogram of the family of Eugene O'Neill shows a pattern of estrangement between father and children over three generations* (Daniel Goleman). [from Greek *génos* race, stock + English *-gram*[1]]

gen|om (jē′nom), *n.* = genome.

gen|ome (jē′nōm), *n. Biology.* **1** the sum of all the chromosomes within each nucleus of any species. **2** a haploid set of chromosomes with their genes. [< *gen*(e) + Greek *-ōma* group]

ge|no|mic (jē nō′mik, -nom′ik), *adj.* of or having to do with a genome or genomes.

gen|o|type (jen′ə tīp), *n. Biology.* **1** the genetic make-up of an organism as distinguished from its appearance or phenotype: *The genotype determines how the developing individual will react to environment* (Scientific American). **2** a group of organisms each having the same combinations of hereditary characters; biotype. **3** such genes as expressed in a breeding formula. **4** the typical species of a genus; type species. [< Greek *génos* (see etym. under **genus**) + English *type*]

gen|o|typ|ic (jen′ə tip′ik), *adj.* of or having to do with a genotype. —**gen′o|typ′i|cal|ly,** *adv.*

gen|o|typ|i|cal (jen′ə tip′ə kəl), *adj.* = genotypic.

ge|nouil|lère (zhə nü yer′), *n.* a flexible piece of armor for covering the knee. [< French *genouillère* < Old French *genouil* knee < Vulgar Latin *genuclum* < Latin *genū* knee]

Gen|o|vese (jen′ə vēz′, -vēs′), *adj., n., pl.* **-vese.** = Genoese.

gen|re (zhäɴ′rə), *n.* **1** kind, sort, or style, especially in art or literature: *The novel and the drama are two literary genres. Poe was the originator of a genre of detective story.* **SYN:** class. **2** = genre painting. [< Old French *genre,* learned borrowing from Latin *genus, -eris* kind; see etym. under **genus**. See etym. of doublet **gender.**]

genre painting, a style of painting that shows scenes from ordinary life, often considered as stemming from Flemish tradition of the 1500's.

gen|ro (gen′rō), *n., pl.* **-ros. 1a** an elder statesman of Japan. **b** a group of such statesmen. **2** a former group of elder statesmen who were advisers to the emperor of Japan. [< Japanese *genrō*]

gens (jenz), *n., pl.* **gen|tes** (jen′tēz). **1** a group of families in ancient Rome that claimed the same ancestor and were united by a common name and common religious ceremonies: *Julius Caesar was a member of the Julian gens.* **2** *Anthropology.* persons claiming membership in the same group by virtue of descent by patrilineal links from a real or mythical ancestor. [< Latin *gēns, gentis* race, clan, ultimately < *gignere* beget]

gens du monde (zhäɴ′ dʏ mōɴd′), *French.* people of high society; fashionable people.

gent[1] (jent), *n. Informal.* man; gentleman: *An old gent . . . would spend his afternoons in the rear of a Tong house smoking a bamboo pipe* (Saturday Review). [< *gent*(leman)]

gent[2] (jent), *adj. Obsolete.* **1** noble; highborn. **2** graceful; elegant; pretty. [Middle English *gent* < Old French *gent* < Latin *genitus,* past participle of *gignere* beget]

Gent. or **gent.,** gentleman or gentlemen.

gen|ta|mi|cin or **gen|ta|my|cin** (jen′tə mī′sən), *n.* an antibiotic produced from the fermentation of an actinomycete, used especially against Gram-negative bacteria. [< *gent*(ian violet), the pigment produced by the actinomycete + (actino)*mycin*]

gen|teel (jen tēl′), *adj.* **1** belonging or suited to polite society: *Do now send a genteel conveyance for them, for . . . they were most of them used to ride in their own carriages* (Richard Brinsley Sheridan). **2** polite; well-bred; fashionable; elegant: *the genteelest dinner I have ever seen* (Samuel Pepys). **SYN:** refined. **3** trying to be aristocratic; artificially polite and courteous: *Her mannerisms were painfully genteel.* [< French *gentil* < Latin *gentīlis.* See etym. of doublets **gentile, gentle, jaunty.**] —**gen|teel′ly,** *adv.* —**gen|teel′ness,** *n.*

gen|teel|ism (jen tē′liz əm), *n.* a word or expression substituted for another in an effort to sound genteel; euphemism.

gen|tian (jen′shən), *n.* **1** any one of a large group of plants with funnel-shaped flowers, usually stemless leaves, and bitter juice, including the fringed gentian, the closed gentian, and the agueweed. Gentians have blue, white, red, or yellow flowers. **2** any one of certain similar plants of other genera. **3** the bitter root of one of these plants of southern and central Europe, or a preparation of this root, used in medicine as a tonic and a stomachic. [< Latin *gentiāna;* said by Pliny to be < *Gentius,* a king of ancient Illyria]

gen|tia|na|ceous (jen′shə nā′shəs), *adj.* belonging to the gentian family of plants.

gentian bitter, a tonic extracted from gentian root.

gentian blue, a reddish-blue color.

gen|tia|nel|la (jen′shə nel′ə), *n.* any one of several gentians, especially a dwarf species of the Alps, bearing large, intensely blue flowers. [< New Latin *gentianella* (diminutive) < Latin *gentiāna;* see etym. under **gentian**]

gentian family, a group of dicotyledonous plants, chiefly herbs, having showy, funnel-shaped flowers, stemless, opposite leaves, and bitter juice. The family includes the gentian, centaury, and buck bean.

gentian violet, a violet dye derived from rosaniline, used as a bactericide, as a stain in microscopy, and as a disinfectant crystal violet.

gen|til (zhäɴ tē′), *adj. French.* well-bred; refined.

gen|tile or **Gen|tile** (jen′tīl), *n., adj.* —*n.* **1** a person who is not a Jew, especially a Christian. **2** a heathen; pagan. **3** (among Mormons or Moslems) a person who is not a Mormon or Moslem.
—*adj.* **1a** not Jewish. **b** Christian (when directly distinguished from Jewish). **2** heathen; pagan. **3** (among Mormons or Moslems) of or having to do with those outside of the Mormon or Moslem community. **4** having to do with a nation, tribe, or other grouping: *gentile divisions, a gentile group.* **5** *Grammar.* (of a word) indicating the country, locality, or nation to which anything belongs: *"Arab," "Greek," and "Peruvian" are gentile nouns and adjectives.*
[< Late Latin *gentīlis* foreign < Latin, of a (or the) people, national. See etym. of doublets **genteel, gentle, jaunty.**]

gen|til|lesse (jen′tə les′), *n. Archaic.* **1** the quality of being gentle and courteous; well-bred politeness. **2** an example of courtesy. [< French *gentilesse* < *gentil;* see etym. under **genteel**]

gen|til|homme (zhäɴ tē yôm′), *n. French.* a gentleman.

gen|til|ic (jen til′ik), *adj.* tribal or national: *Sioux and Mohican are gentilic names for certain American Indians.* [< Latin *gentīlis* (see etym. under **gentile**) + English *-ic*]

gen|til|i|ty (jen til′ə tē), *n., pl.* **-ties. 1** gentle birth; a being of good family and social position. **2** good manners. **3** refinement: *shabby gentility. The gracious old lady had an air of gentility.* **4** *Archaic.* the gentry.
the gentilities, social superiority; pretended refinements: *My aunt . . . was a mighty cultivator of the gentilities, inward as well as outward* (Leigh Hunt).

gen|tis|ic acid (jen tis′ik), a crystalline substance found in the gentian and produced synthetically, used to relieve pain and induce sweating. *Formula:* $C_7H_6O_4$

gen|tle (jen′təl), *adj.,* **-tler, -tlest,** *n., v.,* **-tled, -tling.** —*adj.* **1** not severe, rough, or violent; mild: *a gentle tap.* **2** soft; low: *a gentle sound.* SYN: soothing. **3** not too much or too fast; not harsh or extreme; moderate: *gentle heat, a gentle slope.* **4** kindly; friendly: *a gentle disposition. For I have let men be, and have their way; Am much too gentle, have not used my power* (Tennyson). **5** easy to handle or manage: *a gentle dog.* SYN: docile, tame, quiet. **6** of good family and social position; wellborn. **7** having or showing good manners; refined; polite. **8** honorable; good; superior: *gentle birth, gentle blood, gentle breeding.* **9** (of a wind in the National Weather Service wind scale) having a velocity of 8-12 miles per hour (on the Beaufort scale, force 3). **10** *Archaic.* noble; gallant: *a gentle knight.* **11** *Archaic.* courteous; kind: *gentle reader.*
—*n. Archaic.* a person who is of gentle birth or rank: *Gentles, I would entreat you a courtesy* (Scott).
—*v.t.* **1** to treat in a soothing way; make quiet or gentle: *The rider gentled his excited horse. This is accomplished . . . through social controls and informal pressures which gentle down the extremists and prod along the laggards* (Harper's). **2** to tame; break in: *to gentle a colt.* **3** *Obsolete.* to raise from humble status; ennoble; dignify: *Be he ne'er so vile, This day shall gentle his condition* (Shakespeare).
—*v.t.* **1** to become gentle: *Some dogs gentle with age.* **2** to move in a gentle, quiet way: *Bottom up . . . the boat was another creature entirely . . . and he gentled cautiously against it* (Atlantic).
gentle and simple, *Archaic.* people of high and low degree: *Gentle and simple of every clan . . .* (William Dunbar).
[< Old French *gentil* < Latin *gentīlis* of the (same) family (later, of good family) < *gēns;* see etym. under **gens**. See etym. of doublets **genteel, gentile, jaunty.**] —**gen′tle|ness,** *n.*
—*Syn. adj.* **1 Gentle, mild, meek** mean agreeable, not harsh, rough, or violent. **Gentle** emphasizes control of strength or force, and suggests being pleasant or pleasing in some definite way, such as by being soft, tender, calm, or kindly: *The nurse is gentle in touch, manner, and voice.* **Mild** emphasizes being by nature agreeable and devoid of harshness, severity, and the like: *He is a mild man and seldom gets angry.* **Meek** emphasizes being patient and humble, and often suggests being afraid to act otherwise: *The meek little clerk tries to please everyone.*

gen|tle|folk (jen′təl fōk′), *n.pl.* people of good family and social position; gentry.

gen|tle|folks (jen′təl fōks′), *n.pl.* = gentlefolk.

gen|tle-heart|ed (jen′təl här′tid), *adj.* gentle in heart or disposition; mild; kindly.

gen|tle|hood (jen′təl hu̇d), *n.* the character or breeding proper to gentle birth.

gen|tle|man (jen′təl mən), *n., pl.* **-men. 1** a man who is honorable and well-bred: *With such true breeding of a gentleman, You never could divine his real thought* (Byron). **2** a man of fine feelings or instincts, shown by behavior and consideration for others: *It is almost a definition of a gentleman to say he is one who never inflicts pain* (Cardinal Newman). **3** a polite term for any man: *Being a gentleman who regards his own privacy as well as that of others as being inviolable, the author asks you not to expect any startling exposés* (New York Times Book Review). **4** a man of good family and social position. **5** (formerly) a man of gentle birth, especially, in England, one ranking above a yeoman and below the nobility. **6** *British.* an amateur competitor in sports, as distinguished from a professional: *In the program, gentlemen were entitled to have their initials listed before their names; not so the players who were listed only by their surnames* (Time).
gentlemen, a polite term of address to a company of men of whatever rank (corresponding to *Sir* in the singular): *"Aha!" exclaimed the director. ". . . This way, gentlemen!"* (Household Words).
—**gen′tle-man|like′,** *adj.*
▶See **man** for usage note.

gen|tle|man-at-arms (jen′təl mən ət ärmz′), *n., pl.* **gen|tle|men-at-arms.** (in England) one of forty gentlemen who act as guards or attendants to the sovereign on state occasions.

gen|tle|man-com|mon|er (jen′təl mən kom′ə nər), *n., pl.* **gen|tle|men-com|mon|ers.** one of a group of students who formerly had certain privileges at Oxford and Cambridge.

gentleman farmer, a man who owns a farm and directs it as an avocation, not for income.

gentleman in waiting, a man of good family who attends a king, prince, or other person of high rank.

gen|tle|man|ly (jen′təlm ənl ē), *adj.* like a gentleman; suitable for a gentleman; polite; well-bred. —**gen′tle|man|li|ness,** *n.*

gentleman of fortune, = pirate.

gentleman of the road, = highwayman.

gentleman ranker, *British Informal.* an enlisted man of aristocratic birth or background.

gentleman's or **gentlemen's agreement**, an informal agreement that is not legally binding. Because it is not written, the people or parties that make it are bound only by their promise to keep it. *Even though the state of the press is vital to the state of the nation, there is a . . . gentleman's agreement that no newspaper shall criticize or reflect upon another* (Harper's).

gentleman's gentleman, = valet.

gen|tle|man|ship (jen′təl mən ship), *n.* character or conduct of a gentleman; gentlemanliness.

gentleman usher, a gentleman employed as an usher at court or an attendant upon a person of rank.

gen|tle|men (jen′təl mən), *n. pl.* See under **gentleman.**

Gentle People, a term applied to any one of various groups of people noted for their nonviolent creed, such as the flower children and certain American Indians.

gen|tle|per|son (jen′təl pėr′sən), *n. U.S.* a polite term for a man or woman; gentleman or gentlewoman: *The ideological egalitarianism of these gentlepersons is uninhibited by thought . . . or by word refinement* (National Review).
▶**Gentleperson** eliminates reference to sex, and the form *Gentlepersons* is therefore a neutral salutation in letters.

gentle or **gen|tler sex** (jen′tlər), women collectively; womankind.

gen|tle|wom|an (jen′təl wu̇m′ən), *n., pl.* **-women. 1** a woman of good family and social position. **2** a well-bred woman; lady. **3** a woman attendant of a lady of rank.

gen|tle|wom|an|ly (jen′təl wu̇m′ən lē), *adj.* like or suitable for a gentlewoman. —**gen′tle|wom′an|li|ness,** *n.*

gen|tly (jen′tlē), *adv.* **1** in a gentle way; tenderly; softly: *Handle the baby gently. [His] face shone gently with sweat in the dusky room* (Graham Greene). **2** gradually: *a gently sloping hillside.*

gen|tly-born (jen′tlē bôrn′), *adj.* of gentle birth.

gen|too (jen tü′), *n., pl.* **-toos.** a penguin of the Falkland Islands. [perhaps special use of *Gentoo*]

Gen|too (jen tü′), *n., pl.* **-toos,** *adj.* —*n.* **1** a Hindu, especially, in southern India, one speaking Telugu. **2** the language of the Gentoos; Telugu.
—*adj.* of or having to do with the Gentoos.
[Anglo-Indian < Portuguese *gentio* gentile < Latin *gentīlis;* see etym. under **gentile**]

gen|trice (jen′tris), *n. Archaic or Scottish.* **1** gentle birth; noble descent or rank. **2** gentle or honorable feeling; courtesy. [< Old French *genterise;* see etym. under **gentry**]

gen|tri|fi|ca|tion (jen′trə fə kā′shən), *n.* the act or process of increasing the value of real estate in a neighborhood or other area by selling its houses to buyers of greater means than the present owners or tenants.

gen|tri|fy (jen′trə fī), *v.t.,* **-fied, -fy|ing.** to increase the value of real estate in (a neighborhood or other area) by gentrification.

gen|tro|gen|in (jen′trə jen′in), *n.* a chemical derived from a wild Mexican yam, used as a source of cortisone. *Formula:* $C_{27}H_{40}O_4$ [< Dr. Howard S. *Gentry,* born 1903, of the United States Department of Agriculture, + (boto)*genin*]

gen|try (jen′trē), *n.* **1** people of good family and social position, belonging to the upper class of society: *It is the church of the gentry; but it is not the church of the poor* (Emerson). **2** the class in England below the nobility and above the yeomanry. **3** the people of any particular group: *the sporting gentry.* **4** *Archaic.* rank by birth, especially high birth. **5** *Obsolete:* good breeding. [alteration of *gentrice* < Old French *genterise,* variant of *gentilise* noble birth < *gentil;* see etym. under **gentle**]

gents or **gents'** (jents), *n. pl. Slang.* a men's lavatory: *The "gents" appears to be the last sanctuary of male privilege* (Alistair Cooke). [< plural of *gent*[1]]

gen|ty (jen′tē), *adj. Scottish.* neat; pretty; graceful. [< Old French *gentil;* see etym. under **gentle**]

ge|nu (jē′nü, -nyü), *n., pl.* **gen|u|a** (jen′yu̇ ə). *Anatomy.* **1** a knee. **2** a kneelike bend or curved part, as in various organs of the body. [< Latin *genū* knee]

gen|u|al (jen′yu̇ əl), *adj.* of or having to do with the knee; kneelike.

gen|u|flect (jen′yu̇ flekt), *v.i.* to bend the knee as an act of reverence or worship. [< Medieval Latin *genuflectere* < Latin *genū* knee + *flectere* bend] —**gen′u|flec′tor,** *n.*

gen|u|flec|tion (jen′yu̇ flek′shən), *n.* the act of bending the knee in reverence or worship.

gen|u|flex|ion (jen′yu̇ flek′shən), *n. Especially British.* genuflection.

gen|u|ine (jen′yu̇ ən), *adj.* **1** actually being what it seems or is claimed to be; real; true: *genuine leather, genuine worth or benefit. The political correspondence of Machiavelli, first published in 1767, is unquestionably genuine* (Macaulay). **2** without pretense; sincere; frank: *genuine sorrow.* SYN: unaffected. **3** having to do with the original stock; purebred: *a genuine Celtic people.* **4** properly so called: *a case of genuine leprosy.* [< Latin *genuīnus* native, natural, ultimately < *gignere* beget] —**gen′u|ine|ly,** *adv.* —**gen′u-ine|ness,** *n.*
—*Syn.* **1 Genuine, authentic** mean being what it is claimed to be. **Genuine** emphasizes absence of artificiality, adulteration, or any spurious quality: *This table is genuine mahogany, not wood stained to look like it.* **Authentic** emphasizes absence of fraud or counterfeiting: *This is his authentic signature, not a forgery.*

ge|nus (jē′nəs), *n., pl.* **gen|e|ra** or **ge|nus|es. 1** any group of similar things; kind; sort; class: *Assuming, however, that there still exists the genus serious reader* (Hayden Carruth). **2** a group of related animals or plants. A genus ranks below a family or subfamily and above a species. A genus generally consists of two or more species, but sometimes of a single species, possessing certain common structural characteristics distinct from those of any other group. The scientific name of an animal or plant consists of the genus written with a capital letter and the species written with a small letter. *Example: Homo sapiens. Abbr:* gen. **3** *Logic.* a class or group of individuals divided into subordinate groups called species. [< Latin *genus, -eris* race, stock, kind < *gen-,* stem of *gignere* produce, beget]

geo-, *combining form.* **1** earth; of the earth: *Geology = science of the earth('s crust).*

Pronunciation Key: hat, āge, cãre, fär; let, ēqual, tėrm; it, īce; hot, ōpen, ôrder; oil, out; cup, pu̇t, rüle; child; long; thin; ᴛʜen; zh, measure; ə represents **a** in about, **e** in taken, **i** in pencil, **o** in lemon, **u** in circus.

2 geology *Geoplanetology = the geology of the planets.*
3 geographical: *Geopolitics = geographical politics.*
[< Greek *gê* the earth]

Geo., George.

ge|o|bi|o|log|ic (jē′ō bī′ə loj′ik), *adj.* = geobiological.

ge|o|bi|o|log|i|cal (jē′ō bī′ə loj′ə kəl), *adj.* of or having to do with geobiology. **—ge′o|bi′o|log′i|cal|ly,** *adv.*

ge|o|bi|ol|o|gist (jē′ō bī ol′ə jist), *n.* a person who studies geobiology.

ge|o|bi|ol|o|gy (jē′ō bī ol′ə jē), *n.* the study of the effects of the earth on animal and plant life.

ge|o|bo|tan|ic (jē′ō bə tan′ik), *adj.* = geobotanical.

ge|o|bo|tan|i|cal (jē′ō bə tan′ə kəl), *adj.* of or having to do with geobotany. **—ge′o|bo|tan′i|cal|ly,** *adv.*

ge|o|bot|a|nist (jē′ō bot′ə nist), *n.* a person who studies geobotany.

ge|o|bot|a|ny (jē′ō bot′ə nē), *n.* the study of the effect of the earth, or of geography, on plant life.

ge|o|car|py (jē′ō kär′pē), *n.* the production or growth of a fruit under the surface of the ground, exhibited by certain plants, such as the peanut.

ge|o|cen|tric (jē′ō sen′trik), *adj.* **1** as viewed or measured from the earth's center *the geocentric latitude of a planet.* **2** having or representing the earth as a center *a geocentric universe.* **—ge′o|cen′tri|cal|ly,** *adv.*

ge|o|cen|tri|cal (jē′ō sen′trə kəl), *adj.* = geocentric.

ge|o|cen|tric|i|ty (jē′ō sen tris′ə tē), *n.* = geocentrism.

geocentric parallax, the parallax of a heavenly body using the radius of the earth for measurement; diurnal parallax.

ge|o|cen|trism (jē′ō sen′triz əm), *n.* the belief that the earth is the center of the universe, or governed by a providential system.

ge|o|chem|i|cal (jē′ō kem′ə kəl), *adj.* of or having to do with geochemistry. **—ge′o|chem′i|cal|ly,** *adv.*

ge|o|chem|ist (jē′ō kem′ist), *n.* a person who studies geochemistry.

ge|o|chem|is|try (jē′ō kem′ə strē), *n.* the science dealing with the chemical changes in, and the composition of, the earth's crust.

ge|o|chron|o|log|i|cal (jē′ō kron′ə loj′ə kəl), *adj.* of or having to do with geochronology. **—ge′o|chron′o|log′i|cal|ly,** *adv.*

ge|o|chro|nol|o|gist (jē′ō krə nol′ə jist), *n.* a person who studies geochronology.

ge|o|chro|nol|o|gy (jē′ō krə nol′ə jē), *n.* the science of determining the time or length of existence of geological formations such as rocks and minerals, and of geological periods.

ge|o|chron|o|met|ric (jē′ō kron′ə met′rik), *adj.* of or having to do with geochronometry.

ge|o|chron|o|met|ri|cal (jē′ō kron′ə met′rə kəl), *adj.* = geochronometric.

ge|o|chro|nom|e|try (jē′ō krə nom′ə trē), *n.* the measurement of geologic time by means of geochronology.

ge|o|cide (jē′ə sīd), *n.* destruction of the whole earth.

ge|o|co|ro|na (jē′ō kə rō′nə), *n.* a region of very thin, ionized gas surrounding the earth at a height of between 9,000 and 18,000 miles.

ge|o|co|ro|nal (jē′ō kə rō′nəl), *adj.* of or having to do with the geocorona.

ge|o|crat|ic (jē′ō krat′ik), *adj.* of or having to do with the times or conditions in which land predominates or continents enlarge.

geod., **1** geodesy. **2** geodetic.

ge|o|dal (jē′ə dəl), *adj.* of or having to do with a geode or geodes.

ge|ode (jē′ōd), *n.* **1** a rock containing a cavity usually lined with crystals or other mineral matter. **2** the cavity itself. [< French *géode* < Latin *geōdes* < Greek *geōdēs* earthy < *gê*earth + *eîdos* form]

ge|o|des|ic (jē′ə des′ik), *adj., n.* **—*adj.*** **1** = geodetic. **2** having a curve like the curvature of the earth.
—*n.* = geodesic line.

ge|o|des|i|cal (jē′ə des′ə kəl), *adj.* = geodesic.

***geodesic dome**, a strong, lightweight dome, built on a framework of triangular segments. It has no internal supports.

geodesic line, the shortest possible line between two points on a surface.

ge|od|e|sist (jē od′ə sist), *n.* an expert in geodesy; geodetic surveyor.

ge|od|e|sy (jē od′ə sē), *n.* **1** the branch of applied mathematics dealing with the measurement of the earth and of large areas on the surface of the earth, with the variations in terrestrial gravity, and with the exact position of geographical points. **2** the branch of surveying dealing with such measurements. [< New Latin *geodesia* < Greek *geōdaisíā* < *gê* earth + *daíein* divide]

ge|o|det|ic (jē′ə det′ik), *adj.* having to do with geodesy; geodesic *a geodetic surveyor.* **—ge′o|det′i|cal|ly,** *adv.*

ge|o|det|i|cal (jē′ə det′ə kəl), *adj.* = geodetic.

geodetic line, = geodesic line.

ge|o|det|ics (jē′ə det′iks), *n.* = geodesy.

geodetic satellite, an earth satellite designed to make simultaneous observations of the earth's surface from two or more points in order to obtain data on the exact shape and size of the earth and the exact position of areas on the earth's surface.

ge|od|ic (jē od′ik), *adj.* of or like a geode.

ge|o|dim|e|ter (jē′ə dim′ə tər), *n.* **1** an electronic optical device for measuring distances on the ground, the measurements being based on the velocity of light. **2 Geodimeter.** a trademark for this device.

ge|o|duck (gü′ē duk), *n.* a large, edible clam of the Pacific Coast of North America; gweduc. [spelling alteration of *goeduck,* variant of *gweduc*]

ge|o|dy|nam|ic (jē′ō dī nam′ik), *adj.* of or having to do with geodynamics.

ge|o|dy|nam|i|cal (jē′ō dī nam′ə kəl), *adj.* = geodynamic.

ge|o|dy|nam|ics (jē′ō dī nam′iks), *n.* the science that deals with the forces inside the earth, especially those affecting the earth's structure.

ge|o|e|co|nom|ic (jē′ō ē′kə nom′ik, -ek′ə-), *adj.* of or having to do with geoeconomics.

ge|o|e|co|nom|ics (jē′ō ē′kə nom′iks, -ek′ə-), *n.* the study of the effects of geography on natural and human resources, population, and the like.

ge|o|eth|nic (jē′ō eth′nik), *adj.* of or having to do with the geographical relations of tribes and peoples.

geog., **1** geographer. **2a** geographic. **b** geographical. **3** geography.

ge|og|nost (jē′əg nost), *n.* a person who studies geognosy.

ge|og|nos|tic (jē′əg nos′tik), *adj.* of or having to do with geognosy. **—ge′og|nos′ti|cal|ly,** *adv.*

ge|og|no|sy (jē og′nə sē), *n.* the branch of geology that deals with the structure of the earth, the air and water that surround it, its surface, and the probable condition of its interior. [< French *géognosie* < Greek *gê* earth + *gnôsis* knowledge]

ge|o|gon|ic (jē′ə gon′ik), *adj.* of or having to do with geogony.

ge|og|o|ny (jē og′ə nē), *n.* a theory or account of the origin of the earth. Also, **geogeny**. [< *geo-* + Greek *-goníā* production]

ge|og|ra|pher (jē og′rə fər), *n.* a person who knows much about geography: *At every turn the geographer must have recourse to the findings of the geologist* (White and Renner).

ge|o|graph|ic (jē′ə graf′ik), *adj.* = geographical.

ge|o|graph|i|cal (jē′ə graf′ə kəl), *adj.* **1** of or having to do with geography *The challenge of geographical exploration has undergone several changes as human activities have gradually spread from hospitable and accessible to more remote regions* (E. F. Roots). **2** having to do with or characteristic of a particular place or region.
—ge′o|graph′i|cal|ly, *adv.*

geographical coordinate, either of two intersecting lines of latitude and longitude determining any geographical position on the surface of the earth.

geographical medicine, = geomedicine.

geographical mile, a measure of length equivalent to 1 minute of longitude on the equator, 6076.11549 feet; nautical mile.

geographic axis, the axis upon which the earth rotates, extending between the geographic poles.

geographic pole, one of the hypothetical points in the Arctic or Antarctic where the earth's rotational axis meets the surface. The North Pole and South Pole are the geographic poles.

geographic position, the position of a given celestial body in relation to the earth.

***geodesic dome**

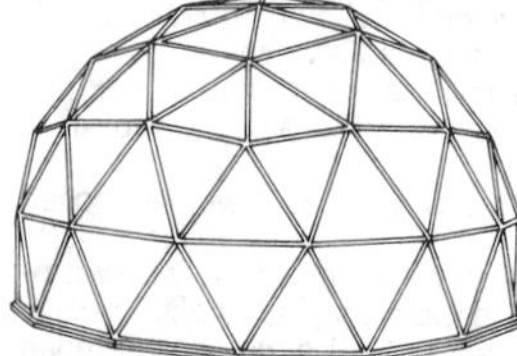

ge|og|ra|phy (jē og′rə fē), *n., pl.* **-phies**. **1** the study of the earth's surface, climate, continents, countries, peoples, industries, and products. *Abbr:* geog. **2** the surface features of a place or region: *the geography of New England.* **3** a book about geography. [< Latin *geographia* < Greek *gê* earth + *gráphein* describe, write (about), draw]

ge|o|hy|drol|o|gist (jē′ō hī drol′ə jist), *n.* a person who studies geohydrology.

ge|o|hy|drol|o|gy (jē′ō hī drol′ə jē), *n.* the science that deals with water formed or running underground.

geo|hy|giene (jē′ō hī′jēn, -jē ēn), *n.* hygiene of the people of the entire earth *The problem of geohygiene . . . is highly complex and closely tied to economic and social problems. This problem can therefore not be solved on a national and especially not on a local basis* (New York Times).

ge|oid (jē′oid), *n.* **1** an imaginary surface produced by extending the mean sea level of the earth over the oceans and under the continents *The geoid exists in the geodesist's imagination as a globe which bears only a partial resemblance to the earth as we know it* (Life). **2** the geometrical figure formed by this surface. [< Greek *geoeidês* earthlike < *gê* earth + *eîdos* form]

ge|oi|dal (jē oi′dəl), *adj.* of or having to do with a geoid.

geol., **1a** geologic. **b** geological. **2** geologist. **3** geology.

ge|o|log|ic (jē′ə loj′ik), *adj.* = geological.

ge|o|log|i|cal (jē′ə loj′ə kəl), *adj.* of or having to do with geology: *There is ample evidence in the geological record that major changes have occurred in the climate of at least some parts of the world* (W. G. Chaloner). **—ge′o|log′i|cal|ly,** *adv.*

geological or **geologic age**, a period in the history of the earth, earlier than the postglacial, or recent, that can be dated only by geological methods.

geological engineering, a branch of engineering that studies rocks, soils, and other components of the earth as building materials or as they affect construction.

geological survey, an investigation of an area to determine the distribution, composition, history, and other features, of its rock formations and mineral resources.

geological time, the time of existence of the earth before the ages of human history, as studied by historical geology.

geologic botany, the study of plants that existed early in the history of the earth, now known only as fossils; phytopaleontology.

geologic column, the succession of rocks, in order from oldest to youngest, that are known to exist on the earth as a whole or in any given region.

geologic map, a map that shows by various signs, colors, and symbols the geological features of a region, including the structure, composition, and age of the materials below the surface.

ge|ol|o|gist (jē ol′ə jist), *n.* a person who knows much about geology: *the geologist of an exploring expedition, a state geologist.*

ge|ol|o|gize (jē ol′ə jīz), *v.,* **-gized**, **-giz|ing**. **—*v.i.*** to make geological investigations.
—*v.t.* to study geologically.

ge|ol|o|gy (jē ol′ə jē), *n., pl.* **-gies**. **1** the science that deals with the earth's crust, the layers of which it is composed, and their history. **2** the features of the earth's crust in a place or region; rocks or rock formations of a particular area: *the geology of North America.* **3** the study of the surface structure, composition, or formation of any heavenly body: *planetary geology, the geology of the moon.* **4** a book about geology. *Abbr:* geol. [< Medieval Latin *geologia* < Greek *gê* earth + *lógos* study of < *légein* read, select]

geom., **1** geometer. **2a** geometric. **b** geometrical. **3** geometry.

ge|o|mag|net|ic (jē′ō mag net′ik), *adj.* of or having to do with the magnetism of the earth. **—ge′o|mag|net′i|cal|ly,** *adv.*

geomagnetic axis, the magnetic axis of the earth at an angle of 12 degrees with respect to the geographic axis.

geomagnetic equator, the great circle in a plane through the geomagnetic axis *Cosmic radiation measured close to earth is fairly weak near the geomagnetic equator and strongest near the magnetic poles* (Time).

ge|o|mag|ne|ti|cian (jē′ō mag′nə tish′ən), *n.* a specialist in geomagnetics.

geomagnetic pole, the hypothetical point in the Arctic or Antarctic where the earth's magnetic axis touches the earth's surface.

ge|o|mag|net|ics (jē′ō mag net′iks), *n.* the science of magnetics applied to earth phenomena.

ge|o|mag|net|ism (jē′ō mag′nə tiz əm), *n.* **1** the magnetism of the earth, measurable with magnetic instruments. **2** the science that deals with the magnetism of the earth, the effects of the earth's magnetic force, and the laws of magnetic attraction and repulsion.

ge|o|man|cer (jē′ə man′sər), *n.* a person who practices geomancy.

ge|o|man|cy (jē′ə man′sē), *n.* **1** the practice of foretelling the future by means of signs connected with the earth, such as the figure made by a handful of earth thrown down at random. **2** the practice of foretelling the future by means of lines or figures formed by a number of dots jotted down at random. [< Late Latin *geōmantīa* < Late Greek *geōmanteíā* < *gê* earth + *manteíā* divination]

ge|o|man|tic (jē′ə man′tik), *adj.* of or having to do with geomancy.

ge|o|man|ti|cal (jē′ə man′tə kəl), *adj.* = geomantic.

ge|o|man|ti|cal|ly (jē′ə man′tə klē), *adv.* in a geomantic manner; by geomancy.

ge|o|math|e|mat|ic (jē′ō math′ə mat′ik), *adj.* = geomathematical.

ge|o|math|e|mat|i|cal (jē′ō math′ə mat′ə kəl), *adj.* of or having to do with geomathematics. **–ge′o|math′e|mat′i|cal|ly**, *adv.*

ge|o|math|e|ma|ti|cian (jē′ō math′ə mə tish′ən), *n.* an expert in or student of geomathematics.

ge|o|math|e|mat|ics (jē′ō math′ə mat′iks), *n.* the science of calculating the dimensions of the earth.

ge|o|mat|i|cal (jē′ə mat′ə kəl), *adj.* of or having to do with geomatics. **–ge′o|mat′i|cal|ly**, *adv.*

ge|o|mat|ics (jē′ə mat′iks), *n.* geomathematics.

ge|o|med|i|cine (jē′ō med′ə sən), *n.* the branch of medicine that deals with the geographical distribution and occurrences of human disease and the influence of geographical and climatological factors on health: *This field of study, which deals essentially with such human adjustments, or maladjustments in the environment, is known usually as... geomedicine or the ecology of human disease* (New Scientist).

ge|om|e|ter (jē om′ə tər), *n.* **1** = geometrician. **2** a geometrid moth or its larva. [< Latin *geōmetra, geōmetrēs* < Greek *geōmétrēs* < *gê* earth + *métron* measure]

ge|o|met|ric (jē′ə met′rik), *adj.* **1** of geometry; according to the principles of geometry: *geometric proof.* **2** consisting of straight lines, circles, triangles, and other figures; regular and symmetrical: *a geometric design.* **–ge′o|met′ri|cal|ly**, *adv.*

ge|o|met|ri|cal (jē′ə met′rə kəl), *adj.* = geometric.

geometrical optics, the branch of optics that deals with the formation and structure of images, using geometric methods of description.

geometrical progression, = geometric progression.

ge|om|e|tri|cian (jē om′ə trish′ən, jē′ə mə-), *n.* an expert in geometry.

ge|o|met|ri|cism (jē′ə met′rə siz əm), *n.* the application of geometric principles to fields other than mathematics and science, especially in modern abstract art.

geometric mean, the mean of a number (*n*) of positive quantities produced by taking the nth root of their product: *The geometric mean of the two quantities of 16 and 4 is the square root of their product, or 8.*

geometric progression, a series of numbers in which each number is multiplied by the same factor in order to obtain the following number. 2, 4, 8, 16, and 32 form a geometric progression. See also **arithmetical progression.**

geometric proportion, an equation between ratios: *4:16 = 1:4 is a geometric proportion.*

geometric ratio, the constant ratio of a term of a geometric progression to the preceding term.

geometric series, = geometric progression.

geometric style, a style of art characterized by simple geometric patterns or stylized figures arranged in an orderly manner, found especially in some Greek vase paintings and some tracery in English architecture.

geometric tracery, tracery in some English architecture, characterized by delicate geometric patterns.

ge|om|e|trid (jē om′ə trid), *n., adj.* **–*n.*** any one of a family of slender gray or greenish moths whose larvae have legs at the ends of the body, causing them to travel with a looping motion and to be called *measuring worms* or *inchworms.* Geometrids move by bringing the rear end of the body forward, thus forming a loop, and then advancing the front end. *Some geometrid caterpillars are able to camouflage themselves by sticking out at an angle from a twig, like a twig* (New Yorker).
–*adj.* of or having to do with a geometrid.
[< New Latin *Geometridae* the family name < *Geometra* the typical genus < Latin *geōmetra*; see etym. under **geometer**]

ge|om|e|trism (jē om′ə triz əm), *n.* a movement in modern art, similar to cubism, that emphasizes the use of geometric lines and figures.

ge|om|e|trist (jē om′ə trist), *n.* = geometrician.

ge|om|e|trize (jē om′ə trīz), *v.,* **-trized, -triz|ing.** **–*v.i.*** to work by geometric methods. **–*v.t.*** to form geometrically.

ge|om|e|try (jē om′ə trē), *n., pl.* **-tries. 1** the branch of mathematics that measures and compares lines, angles, surfaces, and solids in space; mathematics of space. Geometry includes the definition, comparison, and measurement of squares, triangles, circles, cubes, cones, spheres, and other plane and solid figures. *Abbr:* geom. **2** a book about geometry. **3** shape or design: *the geometry of high white buildings.* [< Latin *geōmetria* < Greek *geōmetríā* < *gê* earth + *-metríā* measuring < *métron* measure]

ge|o|mor|phic (jē′ə môr′fik), *adj.* **1** of or having to do with the figure of the earth or the form of its surface. **2** resembling the earth. [< *geo-* + Greek *morphḗ* form + English *-ic*]

ge|o|mor|pho|log|i|cal (jē′ō môr′fə loj′ə kəl), *adj.* of or having to do with geomorphology: *One of the best geomorphological arguments for the stability of the present ice level...* (E. F. Roots). **–ge′o|mor′pho|log′i|cal|ly**, *adv.*

ge|o|mor|phol|o|gist (jē′ō môr fol′ə jist), *n.* a person who studies geomorphology.

ge|o|mor|phol|o|gy (jē′ō môr fol′ə jē), *n.* the study of the arrangement, origin, and changes of the earth's surface features.

ge|o|nav|i|ga|tion (jē′ō nav′ə gā′shən), *n.* = dead reckoning.

ge|oph|a|gism (jē of′ə jiz əm), *n.* = geophagy.

ge|oph|a|gist (jē of′ə jist), *n.* a person who eats earth.

ge|oph|a|gy (jē of′ə jē), *n.* the practice of eating earth. [< *geo-* + Greek *phageîn* eat]

ge|oph|i|lous (jē of′ə ləs), *adj.* **1** *Zoology.* living on or in the ground, as various snails or worms. **2** *Botany.* growing in the ground, as various plants with deep underground buds. [< *geo-* + Greek *phýllon* leaf + English *-ous*]

ge|o|phone (jē′ə fōn), *n.* an instrument that responds to vibrations of the earth. By timing seismic waves, set up artificially by explosives, it can be used in exploring the composition of the earth's crust through which the waves pass. It is used in locating fires in coal mines and in rescue operations there.

ge|o|phys|i|cal (jē′ō fiz′ə kəl), *adj.* of or having to do with geophysics: *The geophysical Earth is a huge, spinning, electromechanical rotor, intimately engaged in its immediate cosmic environment* (Bulletin of Atomic Scientists).

Geophysical Year, a year set aside for the study of the earth, especially its interior, the atmosphere, magnetic and gravitational phenomena, and the like. Scientists from all parts of the world participate. The International Geophysical Year, from July, 1957, to December, 1958, resulted in the most extensive geophysical investigations ever conducted.

ge|o|phys|i|cist (jē′ō fiz′ə sist), *n.* a person who studies geophysics.

ge|o|phys|ics (jē′ō fiz′iks), *n.* the science dealing with the relations between the physical features of the earth and the forces that change or produce them; physics of the earth. Geophysics includes geology, meteorology, seismology, and similar sciences.

ge|o|phyte (jē′ə fīt), *n. Botany.* a plant which grows in earth, especially one having deep underground buds. [< *geo-* + *-phyte*]

ge|o|plan|e|tol|o|gy (jē′ō plan′ə tol′ə jē), *n.* the study of the material composition and formation of the planets; the geology of the planets.

ge|o|po|lit|ic (jē′ō pə lit′ik), *adj.* = geopolitical.

ge|o|po|lit|i|cal (jē′ō pə lit′ə kəl), *adj.* having to do with or involved in geopolitics: *The new era would be a "geopolitical" era, for the conquest of space had rendered the old maritime empires obsolete* (Atlantic). **–ge′o|po|lit′i|cal|ly**, *adv.*

ge|o|pol|i|ti|cian (jē′ō pol′ə tish′ən), *n.* an expert in geopolitics.

ge|o|pol|i|tics (jē′ō pol′ə tiks), *n.* **1** the study of government and its policies as affected by physical geography. **2** the theory popular with the Nazis that politics is dependent on geography, and that expansion into new territories is justified by economic and political needs. [< German *Geopolitik*]

ge|o|pon|ic (jē′ə pon′ik), *adj.* **1** of or having to do with agriculture; agricultural. **2** rustic. [< Greek *geōponikós* husbandman, farmer < *gê* earth + a derivative of *pénesthai* to labor]

ge|o|pon|ics (jē′ə pon′iks), *n.* **1**the art or science of agriculture. **2** a book about geoponics. [< *geopon*(ic) + *-ics*]

ge|o|pres|sured (jē′ə presh′ərd), *adj.* under great pressure from geologic forces: *Success was also reported in tapping an unconventional source of natural gas—geopressured brine, or salt-containing water that has been subject to pressure from geological formations (Janet Raloff).*

ge|o|ram|a (jē′ə ram′ə, -rä′mə), *n.* a large, hollow globe which has a map of the earth's surface on the inside. It is to be viewed from within the globe. [< French *géorama* < Greek *gê* earth + *hórama* spectacle]

geor|die¹ (jôr′dē), *n. Scottish and Northern English.* a guinea (coin) bearing the figure of Saint George. [diminutive < Saint *George*]

geor|die² (jôr′dē), *n. Scottish and Northern English.* **1** a type of safety lamp used by coal miners. **2** a coal miner. [diminutive < *George* Stephenson, 1781-1848, who developed a safety lamp]

George (jôrj), *n.* **1** a part of the insigne of the Order of the Garter representing Saint George slaying the dragon. It may be a piece set with jewels or a single carved gem. *Look on my George; I am a gentleman* (Shakespeare). **2** *British Slang.* an automatic pilot of an airplane. **3** *Archaic.* any English coin bearing the image of Saint George, such as a half crown.
by George,an exclamation or mild oath: *I mean what I say, by George I do!* (F. Anstey).
let George do it, *Informal.* to relinquish personal responsibility and depend on another to accomplish an end: *... a tireless energy in serving humanity himself rather than letting George do it* (William Barrett).

George Cross or **Medal**, the highest award for civilian bravery presented by Great Britain. It was instituted in 1940 by George VI, and ranks second in distinction only to the Victoria Cross.

geor|gette (jôr jet′), *n.* a thin, fine, transparent silk cloth with a slightly wavy surface, used for dresses and other garments. [< French (*crêpe*) *georgette* < Madame *Georgette*, a French modiste]

Georgette crepe, = georgette.

Geor|gian** (jôr′jən), *adj., n.* **–*adj. **1** of or having to do with the four Georges, kings of England from 1714 to 1830. **2** having to do with the style of architecture, art, or decoration during this period: *One of Britain's most remarkable and characteristic contributions to European culture is her Georgian architecture* (London Times). **3** of or having to do with the state of Georgia or its people. **4** of or having to do with the Republic of Georgia in the Soviet Union, its people, or their language. **5** of or characteristic of the reign of George V, king of England from 1910 to 1936.
–*n.* **1** a person born or living in the state of Georgia. **2a** a person born or living in the Republic of Georgia in the Soviet Union. **b** the South Caucasian language of the Georgians. **3** a person, especially a writer, of the time of the first four Georges of England.

***Georgian**
definition 2

Geor|gian|ism (jôr′jə niz əm), *n.* a movement in British poetry characterized by attention to nature and pastoral life, as in the poems of Rupert Brooke, John Drinkwater, W. W. Gibson, and Harold Monro. [< *Georgian* (George V, in whose reign the anthologist Edward Marsh, 1872-1953, initiated it) + *-ism*]

Geor|gia pine (jôr′jə) = longleaf pine.

geor|gic (jôr′jik), *adj., n.* **–*adj.*** **1** of or having to do with agriculture. **2** rustic.
–*n.* a poem on agricultural matters.
[< Latin *georgicus* < Greek *geōrgikós* relating to farmers < *geōrgós* farmer < *gê* earth + *érgon* work]

ge|o|sci|ence (jē′ō sī′əns), *n.* any earth science dealing with solid earth, such as geology, geophysics, and geochemistry.

ge|o|sci|en|tist (jē′ō sī′ən tist), *n.* = earth scientist.

ge|o|sphere (jē′ō sfir), *n.* the solid part of the earth; lithosphere.

ge|o|stat|ic (jē′ə stat′ik), *adj.* **1** that can sustain the pressure of earth or the like: *a geostatic arch.* **2** having to do with pressure exerted by earth or the like.

ge|o|stat|ics (jē′ə stat′iks), *n.* the statics of rigid bodies.

Pronunciation Key: hat, āge, cãre, fär; let, ēqual, tėrm; it, īce; hot, ōpen, ôrder; oil, out; cup, pu̇t, rüle; child; long; thin; ᴛʜen; zh, measure; ə represents a in about, e in taken, i in pencil, o in lemon, u in circus.

ge|o|sta|tion|ar|y (jē′ō stā′shə ner′ē), *adj.* orbiting over a fixed position above the equator and therefore at the same rate as the earth moves: *The geostationary, or synchronous satellite's speed is . . . approximately 6,850 miles per hour* (Saturday Review).

geostationary orbit, the orbit of a synchronous satellite; an orbit in which an artificial satellite moves at the same rate as the earth does so that it can act as a fixed relay station.

ge|o|stra|te|gic (jē′ō strə tē′jik), *adj.* of or having to do with geostrategy.

ge|o|strat|e|gist (jē′ō strat′ə jist), *n.* an expert in geostrategy.

ge|o|strat|e|gy (jē′ō strat′ə jē), *n.* **1** the division of geopolitics concerned with strategy. **2** planning or management of affairs of state, especially military matters, by means of geopolitical strategy.

ge|o|stroph|ic (jē′ə strof′ik), *adj. Meteorology.* of or having to do with winds which are strongly deflected by the rotation of the earth. [< *geo-* + Greek *strophē* a turning + English *-ic*]

ge|o|syn|chro|nous orbit (jē′ō sing′krə nəs), = geostationary orbit.

ge|o|syn|cli|nal (jē′ō sin klī′nəl), *adj., n.* **—*adj.*** of or having to do with a geosyncline.
—*n.* = geosyncline.

ge|o|syn|cline (jē′ō sin′klīn), *n.* a broad, elongated, downward curve of the earth's crust.

ge|o|tac|tic (jē′ə tak′tik), *adj.* of or having to do with geotaxis.

ge|o|tac|ti|cal|ly (jē′ə tak′tə klē), *adv.* in a geotactic manner or direction.

ge|o|tax|is (jē′ə tak′sis), *n. Biology.* a movement of an organism toward or away from the center of the earth; tendency to move in response to the force of gravity. [< *geo-* + Greek *táxis* arrangement]

ge|o|tec|ton|ic (jē′ō tek ton′ik), *adj.* of or having to do with the structure or the arrangement of the materials composing the crust of the earth; structural. **—ge′o|tec|ton′i|cal|ly**, *adv.*

ge|o|tex|tile (jē′ō teks′təl, -tīl), *n.* a very strong, impermeable synthetic fabric, used in the construction of highways, bridges, railroad tracks, and the like: *Polypropylene fibers are finding a hot new market in what is called geotextiles* (Business Week).

ge|o|ther|mal (jē′ə thėr′məl), *adj.* of, having to do with, or produced by action of the internal heat of the earth: *geothermal electricity.* **—ge′o|ther′mal|ly**, *adv.*

geothermal gradient, *Geology.* the increase in the temperature of the earth from its surface downward to the core, estimated to be 1 degree Fahrenheit per 60 feet.

ge|o|ther|mic (jē′ə thėr′mik), *adj.* = geothermal.

ge|o|trop|ic (jē′ə trop′ik), *adj. Biology.* affected by geotropism; responding to gravity. **—ge′o|trop′i|cal|ly**, *adv.*

ge|ot|ro|pism (jē ot′rə piz əm), *n. Biology.* response by various parts of plants to the action of gravity. Positive geotropism is a tendency to move down into the earth, as roots do. Negative geotropism is a tendency to move upward, as stems do. [< German *Geotropismus* < Greek *geo-* + *tropē* a turning + German *-ismus* -ism]

Ger., **1a** German. **b** Germanic. **2** Germany.

ger., gerund.

ger (ger), *n.* = yurt. [< Mongolian *ger*]

ge|rah (gē′rə), *n.* an ancient Jewish weight and coin, equivalent to one twentieth of a shekel. [< Hebrew *gerāh*]

Ge|raint (jə rānt′), *n. Arthurian Legend.* a knight of the Round Table who married Enid.

ge|ra|ni|a|ceous (jə rā′nē ā′shəs), *adj.* of or belonging to the geranium family of plants. [< New Latin *Geraniaceae* the family name < Latin *geranium*; see etym. under **geranium**]

ge|ra|ni|al (jə rā′nē əl), *n.* = citral.

ge|ra|ni|ol (jə rā′nē ōl, -ol), *n.* an alcohol used in the making of perfumes, found in oil of rose, citronella, and other essential oils. *Formula:* $C_{10}H_{18}O$

ge|ra|ni|um (jə rā′nē əm), *n.* **1** any one of a group of plants with fragrant leaves and showy clusters of flowers of scarlet, pink, or white; stork's-bill; pelargonium. It is native of South Africa and often grown in gardens and window boxes. **2** any one of several similar wild plants with pink or purple flowers; crane's-bill; heron's-bill. **3** the flower of any one of these plants. **4** a vivid red. [< Latin *geranium* < Greek *gerániōn* (diminutive) < *géranos* crane (the seed pod resembles a crane's bill)]

geranium family, a group of dicotyledonous herbs and shrubs, widely distributed throughout temperate and subtropical regions. The family includes the geranium, pelargonium, alfilaria, and crane's-bill.

ge|rar|di|a (jə rär′dē ə), *n.* any one of a group of herbs of the figwort family found in eastern North America, having showy yellow, pink, or purple flowers. [< New Latin *Gerardia* the genus name < John *Gerard*, 1545-1612, an English botanist]

ger|a|tol|o|gy (jer′ə tol′ə jē), *n.* the study, especially of the late 1800's, of the phenomena of decadence, as of a species approaching extinction. [< Greek *gêras, -atos* old age + English *-logy*]

ger|be|ra (jėr bir′ə, gėr-), *n.* any one of a group of perennial herbs of the composite family, one variety being grown for its showy flowers of many colors. [< New Latin *Gerbera* the genus name < Traugott *Gerber*, German naturalist of the 1700's]

***ger|bil** or **ger|bille** (jėr′bəl), *n.* any one of a group of small rodents with short forelegs and long hind legs, native to desert regions of Africa, Asia, and eastern Europe. Gerbils are smaller than rats, are used in scientific research, and are kept as pets. [< French *gerbille*, learned borrowing from New Latin *Gerbillus* the genus name (diminutive) < *gerbo* or *jerbo* jerboa]

***gerbil**

ge|rent (jir′ənt), *n.* a manager; ruler. [< Latin *gerēns, -entis*, present participle of *gerere* manage, carry on]

ger|ent|o|crat|ic (jir′ən tə krat′ik), *adj.* of or having to do with administrators as a ruling class. [< *gerent* + *-cratic*, as in *bureaucratic*]

ge|re|nuk (ger′ə nu̇k), *n.* a reddish-brown antelope, native to East Africa, whose unusually long neck and legs enable it to reach the foliage which it eats. [< a native name]

ger|fal|con (jėr′fôl′kən, fal′-, -fô′-), *n.* = gyrfalcon.

ger|i|at|ric (jer′ē at′rik), *adj.* for or having to do with elderly people, old age, and geriatrics. [< Greek *gêras* old age (< *gérōn, -ontos* old man) + *īātrikós* -iatric]

ger|i|a|tri|cian (jer′ē ə trish′ən), *n.* an expert in geriatrics.

ger|i|at|rics (jer′ē at′riks), *n.* the branch of medicine dealing with the study of aging, old age, and its diseases: *In contrast to pediatrics which is concerned with the very young, geriatrics is the clinical application of knowledge to aging men and women toward maintaining their health and in treating their peculiar illnesses* (Edward J. Stieglitz). [< *geriatr*(ic) + *-ics*]

ger|i|at|rist (jer′ē at′rist), *n.* = geriatrician.

germ (jėrm), *n., adj.* **—*n.*** **1** a microscopic animal, plant, or other organism, especially one that causes disease; microbe: *the germ of scarlet fever.* There are many kinds of germs, including bacteria, viruses, and protozoa. **2** the earliest form of a living thing; early embryo; seed, bud, or spore. **3** = germ cell; gamete. **4** *Figurative.* the beginning of anything; origin: *Counting is the germ of arithmetic.*
—*adj.* **1** of or caused by disease germs. **2** *Figurative.* of or having to do with very early stages of development.
[< Old French *germe* < Latin *germen, -inis* sprout, bud] **—germ′like′**, *adj.*

Ger|man (jėr ′mən), *adj., n.* **—*adj.*** **1** of Germany, its people, or their language. **2** written or spoken in the German language. *Abbr:* Ger.
—*n.* **1** a person born or living in Germany. **2** the language of Germany, Austria, and parts of Switzerland, especially High German. [< Latin *Germānus*] **—Ger′man|ness**, *n.*

ger|man¹ (jėr′mən), *adj., n.* **—*adj.*** **1** having the same parents. Children of the same father or mother are brothers-german or sisters-german. **2** being a child of one's uncle or aunt. A cousin-german is a first cousin.
—*n.* a brother, sister, or first cousin.
[< Old French *germain* < Latin *germānus*, related to *germen, -inis* sprout, bud]

ger|man² (jėr′mən), *n.* **1** a dance with complicated steps and much changing of partners; cotillion. **2** a party at which it is danced. [short for *German cotillion*]

Ger|man-A|mer|i|can (jėr′mən ə mer′ə kən), *adj., n.* **—*adj.*** **1** having to do with Germany and America. **2** having to do with Americans of German birth or descent.
—*n.* an American of German birth or descent.

German band, an instrumental band of street musicians, originally of German extraction.

German camomile or **chamomile**, a camomile having conspicuously reflexed white ray flowers, brought to North America from its native habitat in Europe and northern Asia.

German Coach, any heavy harness horse of a German breed popular in North America until the early 1900's; Oldenburger.

German cockroach, a small cockroach, commonly found in houses; Croton bug; water bug.

ger|man|der (jėr man′dər), *n.* **1** any one of a genus of herbs or shrubs of the mint family with dense spikes of small flowers. **2** a species of speedwell, a plant with bright-blue flowers. [< Old French *germandree*, learned borrowing from Medieval Latin *calamendria*, alteration of *camidria* < Greek *chamaídrys* < *chamaí* on the ground + *drys* oak]

ger|mane (jėr mān′), *adj.* **1** closely connected; to the point; pertinent: *Your statement is not germane to the discussion.* SYN: appropriate, relevant. **2** *Obsolete,* german; akin. **—ger|mane′ly**, *adv.* **—ger|mane′ness**, *n.*

ger|man|ic (jėr man′ik), *adj. Chemistry.* of or containing germanium, especially with a valence of 4. [< *german*(ium) + *-ic*]

Ger|man|ic (jėr man′ik), *adj., n.* **—*adj.*** **1** of Germany or the Germans; German. **2** of the people of northwestern Europe, such as the Germans, Scandinavians, and English, and their Indo-European languages; Teutonic. **3** = Teutonic def. 1).
—*n.* a branch of the Indo-European language family, customarily divided into East Germanic (Gothic), North Germanic (the Scandinavian languages), and West Germanic (English, Frisian, Dutch, German). **—Ger|man′i|cal|ly**, *adv.*

Ger|man|ism (jėr′mə niz əm), *n.* **1** a German idiom used in some other language. **2** characteristic German quality, attitude, action, or belief. **3** attachment to or affection for what is German; tendency to adopt German ways.

Ger|man|ist (jėr′mə nist), *n.* a student of German or Germanic literature or culture.

***ger|ma|ni|um** (jėr mā′nē əm), *n.* a brittle, silver-white, metallic chemical element which occurs in zinc ores. It is used as a semiconductor in transistors and other electronic devices. Its compounds resemble those of tin. *In addition to transistors, industry uses germanium in such semiconductor devices as diodes and solar batteries* (J. Gordon Parr). [< New Latin *germanium* < Latin *Germānia* Germany < *Germānus* German]

***germanium**

symbol	atomic number	atomic weight	oxidation state
Ge	32	72.59	2,4

germanium oxide, a white powder slightly soluble in water, formerly used in medicine in treating pernicious anemia. *Formula:* GeO_2

Ger|man|ize (jėr′mə nīz), *v.,* **-ized, -iz|ing.** **—*v.t.*** **1** to make German in habits, customs, or character. **2** to translate into German.
—*v.i.* to become German in habits, customs, or character. **—Ger′man|i|za′tion**, *n.* **—Ger′man|iz′er**, *n.*

German measles, a contagious disease like measles, but less serious; rubella. It is caused by a virus.

Germano-, *combining form.* **1** of Germany; of the Germans: *Germanophobia = fear of Germany or the Germans.*
2 German and ____: *Germano-American cooperation = German and American cooperation.*

Ger|man|o|phile (jėr man′ə fīl, -fil), *adj., n.* **—*adj.*** friendly to or admiring Germany or the Germans. **—*n.*** a friend or admirer of Germany or the Germans.

Ger|man|o|phobe (jėr man′ə fōb), *n.* a person who hates or fears Germans or Germany.

Ger|ma|no|pho|bi|a (jėr′mə nə fō′bē ə), *n.* fear or hatred of Germany or the Germans.

ger|man|ous (jėr man′əs), *adj. Chemistry.* containing germanium with a valence of 2.

German police dog, = German shepherd.

German shepherd or **German shepherd dog**, any one of a breed of large, strong, intelligent dogs developed in Germany, often trained to work with soldiers and police or to guide blind persons; police dog.

German short-haired pointer, any one of a breed of sporting dogs used to point and retrieve game, especially birds.

German silver, a yellowish alloy of copper, zinc, and nickel, used for ornaments, utensils, and wire; nickel silver.

German text, a modern German style of type. It is sometimes used in English printing for headings and inscriptions.

German tinder, = amadou.

German wire-haired pointer, any one of a breed of liver-and-white hunting dogs with a wiry, weather-resistant coat and standing 24 to 26 inches high. It was developed in Germany as an all-purpose hunting dog and retrieves well on land or in water.

germ cell, **1** a cell that can produce a new individual, usually after union with another cell of the opposite sex; egg or sperm cell; gamete. **2** a primitive cell from which an egg or sperm cell develops. **3** a fertilized ovum or egg.

ger|men (jėr′mən), *n., pl.* **-mens, -mi|na** (-mə nə). *Archaic.* a germ. [< Latin *germen;* see etym. under **germ**]

germ|free (jėrm′frē′), *adj.* free of germs; sterile: *The phytoplankton were not only germfree; they were also actively antibiotic* (Scientific American).

ger|mi|cid|al (jėr′mə sī′dəl), *adj.* killing germs: *a germicidal spray. Germicidal lamps on the walls emit ultraviolet light rays* (New York Times).

ger|mi|cide (jėr′mə sīd), *n.* any substance that kills germs, especially disease germs. Disinfectants and fungicides are germicides.

ger|mi|cul|ture (jėr′mə kul′chər), *n.* the culture of germs; artificial cultivation of germs in studying diseases.

ger|mi|na|bil|i|ty (jėr′mə nə bil′ə tē), *n.* the condition of being germinable.

ger|mi|na|ble (jėr′mə nə bəl), *adj.* that can be germinated; ready to germinate.

ger|mi|nal (jėr′mə nəl), *adj.* **1** of or like germs or germ cells. **2** *Figurative.* in the earliest stage of development: *Those germinal ideas ... had been sprouting under cover* (George Eliot). **SYN:** elementary, rudimentary. [< New Latin *germinalis* < Latin *germen, -inis* sprout, bud] **—ger′mi|nal|ly,** *adv.*

Ger|mi|nal (zher mē nàl′, jer′mə nəl), *n.* (in the calendar of the first French Republic) the seventh month of the year, extending from March 21 to April 19. [< French *Germinal* < Latin *germen, -inis* sprout, bud]

germinal disk, 1 the part of the blastoderm of certain vertebrate eggs where the embryo appears. **2** = blastodisk.

germinal vesicle, 1 *Embryology.* the nucleus of an ovum before the polar bodies are formed. **2** *Botany.* an oosphere.

ger|mi|nant (jėr′mə nənt), *adj.* germinating.

ger|mi|nate (jėr′mə nāt), *v.,* **-nat|ed, -nat|ing.** **—*v.i.*** to begin to grow or develop; sprout: *Seeds germinate in the spring.* (*Figurative.*) *Many new ideas germinated from the invention of the telegraph.*
—*v.t.* to cause to grow or develop: *Warmth, moisture, and oxygen germinate seeds.*
[< Latin *germināre* (with English *-ate*[1]) < *germen, -inis* sprout, bud] **—ger′mi|na′tor,** *n.*

ger|mi|na|tion (jėr′mə nā′shən), *n.* a starting to grow or develop; sprouting. Germination takes place when seeds are warm and moist and have a supply of oxygen.

ger|mi|na|tive (jėr′mə nā′tiv), *adj.* **1** capable of germinating: *The germinative power of a seed ... is destroyed by fire* (F. Hall). **2** having to do with germination.

ger|mi|par|i|ty (jėr′mə par′ə tē), *n., pl.* **-ties.** reproduction by means of germs or germ cells. [< Latin *germen* germ + *parere* to produce + *-ity*]

germ layer, any one of the three primary layers of cells, the ectoderm, mesoderm, or endoderm, which become further differentiated as the embryo develops.

germ|less (jėrm′lis), *adj.* without germs.

ger|mon (jėr′mən), *n.* = albacore. [< French *germon*]

germ plasm or **plasma, 1** the germ cells of an organism. **2** the substance, now known to be the chromosomes, in germ cells that transmits hereditary characteristics to the offspring.

germ|proof (jėrm′prüf′), *adj.* not easily penetrated by germs; resistant to germs: *a germproof room.*

germ spot, an area about the size of a pinhead on the upper surface of the yolk of any egg; nucleus of an unfertilized egg.

germ theory, 1 the theory that infectious diseases are caused and spread by germs. **2** the theory that life develops from living germs.

germ|ule (jėr′myül), *n.* a small germ.

germ warfare, the spreading of germs to produce disease among the enemy in time of war.

germ|y (jėr′mē), *adj.* infected by germs: *Laundries need ... to keep washed and practically germfree articles from getting germy again while they dry* (Science News Letter).

ger|o|mor|phism (jer′ō môr′fiz əm), *n. Medicine.* the presence in a young or middle-aged person of the physical characteristics of old age.

Ge|ron|i|mo (jə ron′ə mō), *interj.* a battle cry of paratroopers, used especially in World War II as the paratrooper jumped from the airplane. [< *Geronimo,* 1829-1909, American Indian chief of a warring band of the Apache tribe]

ge|ron|tic (jə ron′tik), *adj.* of or having to do with old age; senile.

ge|ron|tics (jə ron′tiks), *n.* = gerontology.

ger|on|toc|ra|cy (jer′on tok′rə sē), *n., pl.* **-cies.** **1** government by old men: *We are in danger of engendering both a gerontocracy and a plutocracy* (William Ewart Gladstone). **2** a governing body consisting of old men. [< Greek *gérōn, -ontos* old man + *-kratiā* government]

ge|ron|to|crat (jə ron′tə krat), *n.* **1** a member of a gerontocracy. **2** an elderly person who is a leader in his field: *a labor gerontocrat.*

ge|ron|to|crat|ic (jə ron′tə krat′ik), *adj.* of, having to do with, or being a gerontocracy.

ge|ron|to|log|ic (jə ron′tə loj′ik), *adj.* = gerontological.

ge|ron|to|log|i|cal (jə ron′tə loj′ə kəl), *adj.* of or having to do with gerontology.

ger|on|tol|o|gist (jer′on tol′ə jist), *n.* an expert in gerontology.

ger|on|tol|o|gy (jer′on tol′ə jē), *n.* the branch of science dealing with the phenomena and problems of aging and old age. [< Greek *gérōn, -ontos* old man + English *-logy*]

ge|ron|to|mor|pho|sis (jə ron′tə môr′fə sis), *n. Biology.* evolution brought about by variations in adult organisms, characterized by increasing specialization with decreasing capacity for further evolution. [< Greek *gérōn, -ontos* old man + *morphōsis* process of forming]

ge|ron|to|pho|bi|a (jə ron′tə fō′bē ə), *n.* fear, dislike, or hatred of old age or old people: *Gerontophobia could be inflicted only upon the old. Ageism, on the other hand, is a social prejudice against people of any age* (New Republic). [< Greek *gérōn, -ontos* old man + *-phobia*]

-gerous, *combining form.* bearing; producing; containing, as in *crystalligerous, dentigerous.* [< Latin *gerere* to bear + English *-ous*]

ge|rou|si|a or **ge|ru|si|a** (jə rü′sē ə, gə-; -zhē-), *n.* a senate or council of elders in ancient Greece, especially the senate of Sparta, consisting of 28 members and the two hereditary kings who also served as generals. [< Greek *gerousía* < *gérōn, -ontos* old man]

ger|ry|man|der (ger′ē man′dər, jer′-), *v., n.* **—*v.t.*** **1** to arrange the political divisions of (a city, state, county, etc.) to give one political party an unfair advantage in elections: *Mack is durable; when another G.O.P. legislature gerrymandered his district a decade ago, he won anyway* (Time). **2** to manipulate unfairly: *The outgoing Executive managed to gerrymander the union's rules* (New Statesman).
—*n.* **1** the act of gerrymandering: [*The party*] *had made a partisan gerrymander of certain districts in order to retain power* (London Times). **2** an election district or other political division resulting from gerrymandering.
[American English < Elbridge *Gerry,* 1744-1814, a governor of Massachusetts, + (sala)*mander* (Governor Gerry's party redistricted Massachusetts in 1812, and Essex County was divided so that one district became roughly salamander-shaped)] **—ger′ry|man′der|er,** *n.*

gers|dorff|ite (gerz′dôr fīt, gers′-), *n.* a silver-white to steel-gray mineral with a metallic luster; a sulfarsenide of nickel occurring in cubic crystals. *Formula:* NiAsS [< H. von *Gersdorff,* proprietor of a nickel mine where it was discovered + *-ite*[1]]

ger|und (jer′ənd), *n.* **1** *English Grammar.* a verb form ending in *-ing* and used as a noun. In "Watching him carefully was hard work," *watching* is a gerund. See the usage note below. **2** *Latin Grammar.* a form of the verb occurring as a noun in all cases except the nominative. *Abbr:* ger. [< Late Latin *gerundium* < Latin *gerundum,* gerund of *gerere* to bear]
►The English **gerund** ends in *-ing.* It has the same form as the present participle but differs in use. Gerund: *"Running" a hotel appealed to him.* Participle: *"Running" around the corner, he bumped into a cop.* A gerund may take an object (*running a hotel*) or a complement (*being a hero*) and it may serve in any of the functions of a noun: Subject: *"Looking" for an apartment always fascinated her.* Object: *He taught "dancing."* Predicate noun: *Seeing is "believing."* Adjective use: *a "fishing" boat* (a boat for fishing, not a boat that fishes). When not in one of these constructions a gerund is related to the rest of the sentence by a preposition: *By "running," I was able to catch the bus.*

ge|run|di|al (jə run′dē əl), *adj.* **1** of a gerund. **2** used as a gerund.

ger|un|di|val (jer′ən dī′vəl), *adj.* of or having to do with a gerundive.

ge|run|dive (jə run′div), *n., adj.* **—*n.*** **1** a Latin verb form used as an adjective, frequently expressing the idea of necessity. **2** a similar form in other languages. **—*adj.*** having to do with or like a gerund. [< Late Latin *gerundīvus* like a gerund < *gerundium;* see etym. under **gerund**] **—ge|run′dive|ly,** *adv.*

Ge|ry|on (jir′ē ən, ger′-), *n. Greek Mythology.* a monster whom Hercules killed and whose red cattle he stole as one of his twelve labors.

Ge|ry|o|nes (jə rī′ə nēz), *n.* = Geryon.

Ge|samt|kunst|werk (gə zämt′künst′verk), *n. German.* a total work of art; a work combining a variety of art forms, such as music, poetry, and dance.

Ge|sell|schaft (gə zel′shäft), *n. Sociology.* a group of people organized on a formal or contractual basis and maintaining an impersonal relationship. [< German *Gesellschaft* society]

ges|ne|ri|a family (jes nir′ē ə), a large group of tropical plants, none native to the United States but a few grown for their showy flowers, such as the African violet and the gloxinia. [< New Latin *Gesneria* < Konrad von *Gesner,* a naturalist and scholar from Zurich, Switzerland, in the 1500's]

ges|so (jes′ō), *n., pl.* **-soes. 1** a plasterlike coating used especially to cover the surface of picture frames and furniture before painting or inlaying them. It is made by heating a mixture of glue and powdered chalk or whiting. **2** a plaster of Paris or gypsum preparation, especially for use in painting and sculpture. [< Italian *gesso* (originally) plaster, chalk < Latin *gypsum* gypsum]

gest[1] (jest), *n. Archaic.* **1** a story or romance in verse. **2** a story; tale. **3** a deed; exploit; feat: *The gests of kings, great captains, and sad wars* (Ben Jonson). Also, **geste.** [< Old French *geste,* learned borrowing from Latin *gesta* deeds, *gerere* carry on, accomplish]

gest[2] (jest), *n.* = geste[1].

gest., deceased; died (German, *gestorben*).

Ge|stalt (gə shtält′), *n., pl.* **-stal|ten** (-shtäl′tən), **-stalts.** *Psychology.* an integrated group of acts, experiences, etc., which functions as a whole over and above the sum of its parts; configuration. [< German *Gestalt* configuration]

ge|stal|tist (gə shtäl′tist), *n.* a student or follower of Gestalt psychology; configurationist.

Gestalt psychology, a school of psychology that emphasizes the fact that a whole may be something more than the sum of its parts, and that the parts of the whole are often modified by their relationships to it and to one another; configurationism.

Gestalt therapy, a form of psychological therapy stressing the unity of mind and body.

Ge|sta|po (gə stä′pō, -shtä′-), *n.* **1** an official organization of secret police in Germany during Hitler's regime. **2** Also, **gestapo.** any group or organization which, by its ruthlessness in carrying out its objectives and crushing all opposition, resembles the Nazi secret police: *Mr. Macmillan replied that ... "we do not want an independent security service—a gestapo, which is dangerous"* (Manchester Guardian Weekly). [< German *Ge*(*heime*) *Sta*(*ats*) *po*(*lizei*) secret state police]

ges|tate (jes′tāt), *v.,* **-tat|ed, -tat|ing.** **—*v.t.*** **1** to carry in the womb during pregnancy: *There are mammals ... whose progeny leave the womb half gestated* (Pall Mall Gazette). **2** *Figurative.* to form and develop (a project, idea, or plan) in the mind: *His mind was then gestating a work of the most original character* (Thomas Frost).
—*v.i.* to be in gestation: (*Figurative.*) [*Shirley*] *Jackson's stories gestated for some time in her mind and subconscious before she put them down.* (New York Times).
[< Latin *gestāre* (with English *-ate*[1]) carry (young in the womb) (frequentative) < *gerere* bear]

ges|ta|tion (jes tā′shən), *n.* **1** the act or process of having young developing in the uterus; pregnancy. **2** the period of pregnancy. **3** *Figurative.* the formation and development of a project, idea, or plan in the mind: *The transistor ... has now gone to work after a seven-year gestation in the Bell Telephone Laboratories* (Science News Letter). [< Latin *gestātiō, -ōnis* < *gestāre;* see etym. under **gestate**]

ges|ta|tion|al (jes tā′shə nəl), *adj.* = gestative.

ges|ta|tive (jes′tə tiv), *adj.* of or having to do with gestation: *the gestative process.*

geste[1] (jest), *n.* **1** a gesture: [*He*] *threw his head back and opened his eyes and his mouth wide—a characteristic geste with him when ideas began to bubble* (Atlantic). **2** *Archaic.* bearing; deportment. Also, **gest.** [< Middle French *geste* < Old French, learned borrowing from Latin *gestus, -ūs* gesture, bearing < *gerere;* see etym. under **gest**[1].]

geste[2] (jest), *n.* = gest[1].

ges|tic (jes′tik), *adj.* of or having to do with bodily motion, especially dancing. [< *geste*[1] + *-ic*]

ges|ti|cal (jes′tə kəl), *adj.* = geste[1].

ges|tic|u|lant (jes tik′yə lənt), *adj.* gesticulating.

ges|tic|u|late (jes tik′yə lāt), *v.,* **-lat|ed, -lat|ing.** **—*v.i.*** **1** to make or use gestures to help express an idea or feeling. **2** to make or use many vehement gestures: *The speaker gesticulated by rais-*

Pronunciation Key: hat, āge, cãre, fär; let, ēqual, tėrm; it, īce; hot, ōpen, ôrder; oil, out; cup, pu̇t, rüle; child; long; thin; ᴛʜen; zh, measure; ə represents **a** in about, **e** in taken, **i** in pencil, **o** in lemon, **u** in circus.

ing his arms and pounding the desk.
— *v.t.* to express by gesticulation: *He tried to gesticulate a message across the crowded room.* [< Latin *gesticulārī* (with English *-ate*[1]) < *gesticulus* (diminutive) < *gestus, -ūs;* see etym. under **geste**[1]] —**ges|tic'u|lat'ing|ly,** *adv.* —**ges|tic'u|la'tor,** *n.*

ges|tic|u|la|tion (jes tik'yə lā'shən), *n.* **1** the act of making lively or excited gestures: *Argument and rhetorical gesticulation are everywhere* (Atlantic). **2** a lively or excited gesture: *They fell into a magical dance, full of preposterous change and gesticulations* (Ben Jonson). **SYN:** See syn. under **gesture.**

ges|tic|u|la|tive (jes tik'yə lā'tiv), *adj.* making or using gestures: *He testifies to their disorderly and gesticulative fits of rage* (Frederic Farrar).

ges|tic|u|la|to|ry (jes tik'yə lə tôr'ē, -tōr'-), *adj.* making or using gestures: *He sprung up all lively ... and gesticulatory* (Harriet Beecher Stowe).

ges|tion (jes'chən), *n. Archaic.* conduct; management.

ges|tur|al (jes'chər əl), *adj.* of or having to do with a gesture or gestures: *By and large, the psychotherapists cannot be accused of neglecting the gestural, tonal, and other nonverbal aspects of their patients' acts* (Sebastian De Grazia).

ges|ture (jes'chər), *n., v.,* **-tured, -tur|ing.** —*n.* **1** a movement of the hands, arms, or any parts of the body, used instead of words or with words to help express an idea or feeling: *A speaker often makes gestures with his hands or arms to stress something he is saying.* **2** the use of such movements: *Gesture is the imitation of words* (Benjamin Jowett). **3** any action for effect or to impress others: *Her refusal was merely a gesture; she really wanted to go.* **4** *Obsolete.* the carriage or posture of the body.
— *v.i.* to make gestures; use gestures; gesticulate: *He brought out his tennis racket and gestured before the mirror like a star tennis player* (James T. Farrell). — *v.t.* to express by gestures. [< Medieval Latin *gestura* < Latin *gestus, -ūs;* see etym. under **geste**[1]] —**ges'ture|less,** *adj.*
—*Syn. n.* **1 Gesture, gesticulation** mean movement of the head, shoulders, hands, or arms to express thought or feeling. **Gesture** applies to any such movement used to take the place of words or add to their meaning: *He did not speak, but with a gesture told me to follow him.* **Gesticulation** applies to wild, excited, or clumsy gesture: *His gesticulations suggested he was losing his temper rapidly.*

gesture language or **system,** any language or system of communication that consists of gestures; sign language: *Wherever gesture systems occur, they appear to develop by reason of linguistic diversity, that is, to supply a rough means of communication between peoples who speak mutually unintelligible tongues* (Beals and Hoijer).

Ge|sund|heit (gə zůnt'hīt), *interj. German.* your health! People often say "Gesundheit" when someone sneezes.

get (get), *v.,* **got** or (*Archaic*) **gat, got** or (*especially U.S.*) **got|ten, get|ting,** *n.* —*v.t.* **1** to come to have; obtain; acquire: *I got a new coat yesterday. He got first prize in the spelling contest. He gets $5.00 a week for running errands.* **SYN:** receive, gain. **2a** to catch; get hold of: *I have got a bad cold. He got the heavy box by the end and hoisted it up.* **SYN:** seize. **b** to learn; commit to memory: *The student got by heart his history lesson.* **3** to bring: *Get me a drink of water.* **4** to find out by calculation or experiment: *He finally got the answer to the algebra problem.* **5** *Informal.* to stir up; move. **6** to cause to be or do: *He got his hair cut yesterday. Get the windows open. They got the fire under control. Mary got her work done. I must get the curtains washed.* **7** to persuade; influence: *Try to get him to come too.* **SYN:** induce. **8** to prepare; make ready: *She helped her mother get dinner.* **9** *Informal.* **a** to possess: *What have you got in your hand?* **b** to be obliged; need (with *have* and *had*): *We have got to win.* **10** *Informal.* to hit; strike: *The bullet got the soldier in the arm.* **11** *Informal.* to kill: *Once George got a deer with a .22-caliber rifle.* **12** *Informal.* to receive as punishment: *The thief got five years.* **13** *Informal.* to puzzle; annoy: *This question gets me.* **SYN:** irritate. **14** *Slang.* **a** to understand: *Do you get me? I don't get what you mean.* **b** to hear. **15** *Informal.* to have the opportunity; manage: *We didn't get to go to the circus this year.* **16** *U.S. Slang.* to gain mastery over: *Drink will finally get him.* **17** *Slang.* to put out (an opponent). **18** (of animals) to beget; procreate. **19** *Archaic.* to betake oneself: *Go get thee hence* (Shakespeare).
— *v.i.* **1** to reach; arrive: *I got home early last night. Your letter got here yesterday.* **2** to be; become: *to get sick. It is getting colder. Don't get nervous when you take the test.* **3** to come or go: *We finally get to feel that Michelet is the human spirit* (Edmund Wilson). **4** to gain; profit.
—*n.* **1** the return of a ball difficult to reach or hit, as in tennis: *Never applaud a difficult get in the middle of a rally* (London Daily Express). **2** the offspring of animals: *The term sire, incidentally, is applied only to a horse whose get have won races* (Atlantic). **3** a producing of offspring; procreation.

get about, a to go from place to place: *Not even a cab can get about in December for the snow* (F. C. Philips). **b** to become widely known; spread: *The rumour ... had got about that the timber was not his* (Frank Barrett).

get across (to), a *Informal.* to make clear, understood, or appreciated: *I sometimes wish I could get hold of some of you and shake you and get across to you that there is a way out* (Billy Graham). **b** *Slang.* to reach the audience or the public (originally "across the footlights" was implied); come across: *A politician who knows how to get across to the people succeeds.*

get after, a to scold: *The teacher gets after everyone who comes late to school.* **b** to urge: *You'd better get after him if you want his help.*

get ahead. See under **ahead.**

get along, a to go away: *Get along with you!* **b** to advance: *The farther he got along in his studies, the more difficult the work became.* **c** to manage: *The house isn't as large as I thought it would be, but we'll get along anyway.* **d** to succeed; prosper: *Do you think I'll be able to get along in a new business?* **e** to agree: *The partners don't get along in some ways.*

get around, a to go from place to place: *The new roads will allow people to get around faster.* **b** to become widely known; spread: *The news of the theft got around quickly.* **c** to overcome: *He found the problem hard to get around.* **d** to deceive; trick: *You can't get around that child; he's too smart to be fooled.*

get around to, to find time for; turn one's attention to: *He didn't get around to visiting the dentist until he got a toothache.*

get at, a to reach; arrive at: *The cat in the tree could not be got at without a ladder.* **b** to find out; learn: *The court will get at the facts on which its judgment is to hinge* (Law Times). **c** to talk about; explain: *What are you trying to get at?* **d** *Informal.* to tamper with; influence with money or threats; bribe: *... the electors [who] are to be got at by money* (J. S. Mill).

get away, a to go away: *Let's get away from here. Take whatever you like, and get away* (Jane Austen). **b** to escape: *The prisoner got away.* **c** to start, as in a race: *The hunting party was glad to get away at last.*

get away with, *Informal.* to take or do (something) and escape safely: *to get away with lying. It can be argued that for us to allow them to "get away with it" might cause us to lose prestige* (Wall Street Journal).

get back, a to return: *It is a moot point whether the family doctor "ousted from the hospital" really wants to get back* (Observer). **b** to recover: *Austria got back its hold on Italy* (Thomas F. Tout).

get back at (or **on**), *Slang.* to take revenge on: *You cannot afford to be rude to a journalist. Someday he will get back on you* (London Daily Chronicle).

get behind, a to support; endorse: *The district voters got firmly behind the incumbent congressman and reelected him.* **b** to fail to keep up: *to get behind in schoolwork.*

get by, *Informal.* **a** to pass: *Let him get by first, as he's in a great hurry.* **b** to not be noticed or caught by: *Somehow the escaping convicts got by the guards.* **c** *Figurative.* to make a living; manage: *He has just enough money to get by.*

get cracking. See under **cracking.**

get down, a to come down from; descend: *to get down a ladder.* **b** to depress: *Life got him down.* **c** to swallow: *Get down that medicine.*

get down to, a to attend or apply oneself to: *Sooner or later we shall have to get down to a sober appraisal of the economic possibilities of natural gas* (Manchester Guardian Weekly). **b** to make (something) into; bring to a condition of: *She has got her housework down to a science.*

get even, a to owe nothing. **b** to have revenge: *One should always "get even" in some way, else the sore place will go on hurting* (Mark Twain).

get even with, to get revenge on: *The angry townsmen swore to get even with the men who had tricked them out of their savings.*

get in, a to go in: *He hoped to get in without being seen.* **b** to put in: *She kept talking, and he couldn't get a word in.* **c** to arrive: *Our train should get in at about 9 P.M.* **d** to gather in (crops): *to get in hay.* **e** to become friendly or familiar (with): *I couldn't get in with him at all; ... he's tremendously reserved* (Sarah Fielding).

get into, a to find out about: *I endeavored to get, as well as I could, into the state of national credit there* (Thomas Jefferson). **b** to get control of: *A passion for sailing got into him.* **c** to come to be in; result in being in: *to get into trouble.* **d** to succeed in obtaining: *to get into office.*

get it, *Informal.* **a** to understand: [*He is*] *a dissenter* (*get it?*) *from Defense Department policies* (Time). **b** to be punished or scolded: *Not that it's so unusual, but the U.S. certainly is getting it from all sides* (Wall Street Journal).

get nowhere. See under **nowhere.**

get off, a to come down from or out of: *to get off a horse, train, or bus.* **b** to take off; remove: *Get your coat off.* **c** to escape punishment : *The leaders of the rebellion were powerful enough to get off lightly.* **d** to help to escape punishment: [*His*] *friends were powerful enough to get him off* (London Times). **e** to start: *The horses in the race got off well. We got off comfortably by the ten o'clock train* (Arthur Morrison). **f** to say or express: *He got off a few jokes.* **g** to deliver: *to get off a speech.* **h** to put out; issue: *They plan to get off 10,000 copies of the magazine.* **i** *U.S. Slang.* to begin feeling the effects of a narcotic; start to get high: *junkies getting off in hallways.*

get off on, a to start: *We finally got off on our vacation before summer was over.* **b** to pass onto without special intention; drift onto: *During a discussion of ocean life we got off on the subject of sharks.* **c** *U.S. Slang.* to get excited about or be thrilled with: *A lot of people get off on her* [*a jazz singer*] *... Her album was on the soul as well as middle-of-the-road charts* (New York Times Magazine).

get on, a to go up, on, or into: *to get on a ladder or a train.* **b** to put on: *Get on your rubbers; we have to go out in the rain.* **c** to advance: *to get on in years.* **d** *Figurative.* to manage: *We can't get on without their help.* **e** to succeed; prosper: *How are you getting on in your new job?* **f** to agree: *The two boys don't get on with each other very well.*

get one's goat. See under **goat.**

get on to, a to learn; grasp: *He will get on to calculus as he keeps on working at it.* **b** *British.* to communicate with: *I got on to the police* (London Times).

get out, a to go out: *Let's get out of here!* **b** to take out: *He got out his pencil and began to write.* **c** to go away: *You have nothing to do here* (*said she*): *Get out!* (Lord Molesworth). **d** to escape. **e** to help to escape. **f** to become known: *The secret got out.* **g** to publish: *She is getting out a new book.* **h** to find out: *They tried to get out his secret but he did not speak.*

get out of, a to escape from; evade: *He tried to ... get out of giving a direct reply* (Earl Dunmore). **b** to help to escape: *to get one out of a predicament.* **c** to draw out from; elicit: *to get money or information out of someone.*

get over, a to recover from: *She was a long time in getting over her illness.* **b** to overcome: *We have happily got over the prejudice of last century* (Tait's Magazine). **c** to make clear or convincing: *The speaker got his point over to the audience.* **d** to finish with; have done with: *Let's get over this once and for all.* **e** to stop being troubled or surprised by: *I can't get over his being married already.*

get over with, to come to grips with and dispose of (something unpleasant): *The Democrats view civil rights as a painful but inevitable issue which they might as well get over with as soon as possible so wounds will be healed before the ... election* (Newsweek).

get round, a to outwit: *This prince was clever enough to get round the Regent* (Lytton Strachey). **b** to wheedle; cajole: *The little boy always got round his grandmother by making a sad face.*

get set, to get ready; prepare: *On your mark, get set, go!*

get somewhere. See under **somewhere.**

get there, to succeed: *Being ambitious and diligent, he is sure to get there.*

get through, a to make oneself or something clear or understood: [*He*] *told the dealers that their advertising wasn't getting through* (New York Times). **b** to secure favorable action; finish: *The Irish Tithe Bill ... got through at last, though much cut about by the Opposition* (T. F. Tout).

get to, *Informal.* **a** to start: *When I got to thinking about the problem, I had an idea.* **b** to reach: *How are we going to get to the public without an advertising campaign?* **c** to affect or influence: *His honesty got to me.*

get together, *Informal.* **a** to bring or come together; meet; assemble: *Let's get together again next week.* **b** *Figurative.* to come to an agreement: *The jury was unable to get together* (New York Times).

get up, a to get out of bed; arise: *He got up at six o'clock.* **b** to stand up: *The old man fell and*

could not get up. **c** to prepare; arrange: *He has got up the legal aspect of the question* (Edmund Wilson). **d** to dress up: *Miss Willing was extremely well got up* (R. S. Surtees). **e** to go ahead: *"Get up!" he commanded the horse.* **f** to climb; ascend: *The coach stopped ... Passengers got up and passengers got down* (Dickens). **g** to work up (an emotion or feeling) in oneself: *She got up a strange affection for the little creature.*
get wind of. See under **wind**[1].
[Middle English *geten,* alteration of earlier *-yeten* (see etym. under **forget**), influenced by Scandinavian (compare Old Icelandic *geta*)]
—Syn. *v. t.* **1 Get, obtain, acquire** mean to come to have something. **Get,** the general word, applies whether or not one wants or tries to gain it: *I got a new car. He got a bad reputation.* **Obtain** usually suggests working hard or trying to get something one wants: *I obtained permission to go.* **Acquire** emphasizes getting possession of something by continued efforts or actions: *I acquired a reading knowledge of German.*
▶**Get** is increasingly used as an informal emphatic passive auxiliary: *We all got punished.*
▶**get up.** See **rise** for usage note.

***ge|ta** (ge'tə), *n., pl.* **ge|ta** or **ge|tas.** a wooden clog worn by the Japanese: *Some of the geta worn by little girls are painted in many colours* (London Daily Chronicle). [< Japanese *geta*]

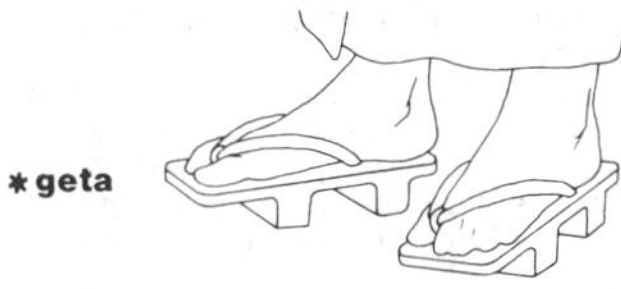
***geta**

get|a|ble (get'ə bəl), *adj.* = gettable.
get-at-a|ble (get'at'ə bəl), *adj.* that can be reached, or obtained; accessible.
get|a|way (get'ə wā'), *n. Informal.* **1** the act of getting away; escape: *Long jumps, quick getaways ... had helped Mr. Valentine to become noted as a successful dodger of retribution* (O. Henry). **2** a start from a complete stop: *a racing car's fast getaway. Most small cars, however, are at a serious disadvantage on the getaway* (Harper's). **3** the start of a race, dramatic performance, or other event: *[He] was in fourth place from the getaway to the stretch* (New York Times).
getaway day, *U.S.* the last day in a series of sports meets or events.
Geth|sem|a|ne (geth sem'ə nē), *n.* **1** a garden near Jerusalem, the scene of Jesus's agony, betrayal, and arrest (in the Bible, Matthew 26:36). **2** *Figurative: Racked by vertigo, melancholy, and nausea, he boards his Gethsemane—the Monday-morning 10:48* (John Cheever). [< Greek *Gethsēmanê* < Aramaic *gath shəmāni* oil press]
get-out (get'out'), *n. U.S. Informal.* a means of escape; a way out.
as all get-out, as can be; extremely: *amusing as all get-out* (Atlantic).
get-rich-quick (get'rich'kwik'), *adj. Informal.* **1** highly speculative: *get-rich-quick schemes.* **2** having the notion of acquiring wealth quickly: *The get-rich-quick people had better try oil or something other than timber* (Wall Street Journal).
get|ta|ble (get'ə bəl), *adj.* that can be got; obtainable.
get|ter (get'ər), *n.* **1** a person who gets. **2** a chemically active substance, such as magnesium, ignited in a vacuum tube to remove any remaining gases. **3** *U.S.* a device for killing destructive animals: *A "getter," designed primarily to kill coyotes, is a cyanide device with a scented wick. It is stuck in the ground, and it injects cyanide into the mouth of any animal that tugs at the wick* (New Yorker).
get|ter|ing (get'ər ing), *n.* the process by which residual gases are removed from a vacuum tube by means of a getter.
get|ter-up|per (get'ər up'ər), *n. U.S. Informal.* a person who gets up: *I'm a late getter-upper; I usually start working around 11* (Newsweek).
get-to|geth|er (get'tů geᴛʜ'ər), *n.* **1** an informal social gathering or party: *It was, in retrospect of their annual get-togethers, a circus* (Harper's). **2** a meeting; conference: *a political get-together.*
get-tough (get'tuf'), *adj. U.S. Informal.* having to do with or marked by resolute, forceful action, usually involving harsh practical measures: *an advocate of a get-tough policy with drug peddlers. Lenders are using several get-tough devices in their efforts to prevent borrowers from turning into delinquents* (Wall Street Journal).
get-up (get'up'), *n. Informal.* **1** the way a thing is put together; arrangement or style: *[They] are the sole owners and registered proprietors in India of the [product's] colour scheme, design and get-up* (Times of India). **2** dress or costume: *For Sardinians, traditional costumes are daily dress and not a holiday or touristic get-up* (Atlantic).
get-up-and-go (get'up'ən gō'), *n., adj. Informal.* *—n.* energy and readiness; initiative; spunk: *Guys love it ... for its road-ability and get-up-and-go!* (New Yorker).
—adj. full of spunk; enterprising; bold and dynamic: *get-up-and-go salesmanship.*
ge|um (jē'əm), *n.* = avens. [< Latin *geum*]
GeV or **Gev** (no periods), gigaelectron-volt (one billion electron volts).
GEV (no periods), ground effect vehicle.
gew|gaw (gyü'gô), *n., adj.* *—n.* a showy trifle; gaudy, useless ornament or toy; bauble: *The shops are filled with gewgaws for the dressing table, like fancy boxes, trays, and pincushions.*
—adj. showy but trifling: *Seeing his gewgaw castle shine New as his title* (Tennyson). Also, **geegaw.** [Middle English *giuegoue;* origin uncertain]
gew|gawed (gyü'gôd), *adj.* covered or adorned with gewgaws.
gew|gaw|ish (gyü'gô'ish) *adj.* gaudy; showy.
Ge|würz|tra|mi|ner (gə vʏrts'trä mē'nər), *n.* a spicy, dry, white table wine of Alsace. [< German *Gewürztraminer* < *Gewürz* spice + *Traminer* name of this type of wine]
gey (gā), *adj., adv. Scottish.* *—adj.* **1** considerable. **2** gay.
—adv. rather; somewhat.
[variant of *gay*]
***gey|ser** (gī'zər, -sər; *for 3 often* gē'zər, -sər), *n., v.* *—n.* **1** a spring that spouts a column of hot water and steam into the air at intervals. There are geysers in Iceland, New Zealand, and Yellowstone National Park. **2** any spouting or gushing column like that of this spring: *Great geysers of flaming gases are shot out into space not just by our sun, but by other stars in the heavens* (Science News Letter). **3** *British.* a water heater attached to a bath.
—v.i. to gush out like a geyser; shoot forth in a jet: *We would haul water to put in the radiator when it had stopped geysering* (New Yorker).
—v.t. to shoot out or cause to shoot out (a liquid or vapor) like a geyser.
[< Icelandic *Geysir,* the name of a hot spring < Old Icelandic *geysa* to gush]

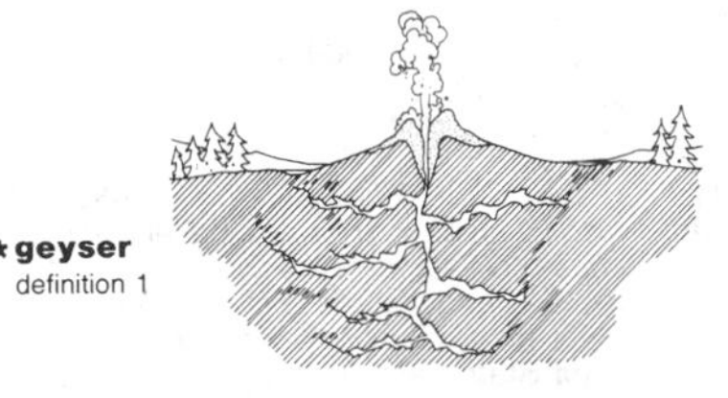
***geyser**
definition 1

gey|ser|ic (gī'zər ik, -sər-), *adj.* having to do with or like a geyser.
gey|ser|ite (gī'zə rīt, -sə-), *n.* a variety of opaline silica deposited about the openings of hot springs and geysers.
ge|zel|lig|heid (gə tsel'ig hīd), *n. Dutch.* good fellowship; conviviality.
g-fac|tor (jē'fak'tər), *n. Nuclear Physics.* the ratio of an elementary particle's magnetic moment to its angular momentum; gyromagnetic ratio: *The positron's ... g-factor was measured to one part in 100,000, the first accurate measurement of this basic constant of the atom* (Science News). [< *g*(yromagnetic) *factor*]
G.F.E., government-furnished equipment.
G-force (jē'fôrs', -fōrs'), *n.* the force exerted on a person or object by gravity, or by changes in speed or direction. [< *g*(ravity)]
GG (no periods) or **G.G.,** gamma globulin.
G gas, = nerve gas.
g.gr., great gross (144 dozen).
GH (no periods), growth hormone.
GHA (no periods), *Navigation.* Greenwich hour angle.
ghaf|fir (gä fir'), *n.* a native Egyptian guard or policeman. [< Arabic *ghafīr*]
ghaist (gāst), *n. Scottish.* ghost.
Gha|nai|an or **Gha|ni|an** (gä'nē ən), *adj., n.* *—adj.* of or having to do with Ghana or its people.
—n. a person born or living in Ghana.
Gha|nan (gä'nən), *adj., n.* = Ghanaian.
ghar|ry or **ghar|ri** (gar'ē), *n., pl.* **-ries.** a cart or carriage in India, especially one for hire: *The tender is alongside the ship, the canopied gharries are lined up on the quay* (Punch). [< Hindi *gārī*]
ghast (gast, gäst), *adj. Archaic.* ghastly. [back formation < *ghastly*]
ghast|ful (gast'fəl, gäst'-), *adj. Archaic.* **1** dreadful; terrible. **2** fearful; scared. Also, **gastful.**
ghast|ly (gast'lē, gäst'-), *adj.,* **-li|er, -li|est,** *adv.* *—adj.* **1** causing terror; horrible; frightful; shocking: *Murder is a ghastly crime.* **2a** like a dead person or ghost; deathly pale: *That very sick man looks ghastly. Faces ... ghastly with guilt and fear* (Hawthorne). SYN: deathlike, pallid. **b** (of light) lurid. **3** *Informal.* very bad; shocking: *a ghastly failure.* **4** *Obsolete.* terrified.
—adv. in a ghastly manner.
[Middle English *gastliche* frightening, perhaps < Old English *gāstlic* of the spirit, spiritual < *gāst* ghost + *-lic* -ly[1]] —**ghast'li|ly,** *adv.* —**ghast'li|ness,** *n.*
—Syn. *adj.* **1 Ghastly, grisly, horrible** mean such as to cause terror or dread. **Ghastly** suggests the dread caused by the sight of death or anything deathlike: *We saw a ghastly accident.* **Grisly** suggests terror of the kind that makes one shudder: *Robbing graves is grisly.* **Horrible** emphasizes the feeling of horror caused by what is described: *It was a horrible murder.*
ghat or **ghaut** (gôt), *n.* in India: **1** steps or a stairway leading down to a river; landing place. **2** a mountain pass. [Anglo-Indian < Hindi *ghāṭ* passage or path of descent, (originally) to a quay or ferry]
gha|wa|zi or **gha|wa|zee** (gə wä'zē), *n.pl.* public dancing girls in Egypt. [< Arabic *ghawazī*]
ghaz|al or **ghaz|el** (gaz'əl), *n.* a short Oriental poem of erotic character, in which the first two lines rhyme, with a corresponding rhyme in the second line of each succeeding couplet. [< Persian, Arabic *ghazal*]
gha|zi (gä'zē), *n., pl.* **-zis.** **1** a Moslem fanatic devoted to the destruction of infidels. **2** a title of honor given for distinguished military service against non-Moslems. [< Arabic *ghāzi* warrior]
Gha|zi (gä'zē), *n.* a Turkish title indicating highest rank, applied to the President of Turkey.
gha|zism (gä'ziz əm), *n.* fanatical fighting against infidels.
Ghe|ber or **Ghe|bre** (gā'bər, gē'-), *n.* a Persian fire worshiper; Zoroastrian. Also, **Gueber, Guebre.** [< French *guèbre* < Persian *gabr*]
ghee (gē), *n.* a liquid butter used in India, made by boiling and straining the milk of buffaloes and cows: *As an article of diet, ghee occupies a high status* (New York Times). Also, **ghi.** [< Hindustani *ghī*]
Gheg (geg), *n.* **1** an Albanian living north of the Shkumbin River. **2** the dialect spoken by such a person.
gheld (geld), *n.* = geld[2].
ghe|rao (ge rou'), *n., v.* *—n.* (in India and Pakistan) a coercive tactic used by striking workers, in which employers or managers are barricaded in their offices until they meet the workers' demands. *—v.t.* to subject to a gherao: *The directors of one steel concern were "gheraoed" next to the blast furnace* (New York Times).
[< Hindustani *gherao* encirclement, siege]
gher|kin (gėr'kən), *n.* **1** a small, prickly cucumber often used for pickles. **2** the plant it grows on. **3** any young, green cucumber used for pickles.
[< earlier Dutch *agurkje* (diminutive) < *agurk* < Slavic (compare Polish *ogurek*) < Medieval Greek *angourion*]
ghet|to (get'ō), *n., pl.* **-tos** or **-toes,** *v.,* **-toed, -to|ing.** *—n.* **1a** a part of a city where any racial or other minority group lives, especially because of economic or social restrictions: *Blacks and other minority groups, segregated in their urban ghettoes ..., refused to accept their continued status as second-class citizens* (Saturday Review). **b** *Figurative: "West Point is the beautiful ghetto. Everyone is healthy here, and if they are not healthy they are discharged"* (Atlantic). **2** the part of a city where Jews were required to live in former times.
—v.t. ghettoize: *If the immigrants are segregated, ghettoed, then they are apt to remain outsiders* (Punch).
[origin uncertain]
ghetto blaster, a large portable radio, often combined with a cassette tape player.
ghet|to|i|za|tion (get'ō ə zā'shən), *n.* the act or process of ghettoizing; segregation in a ghetto.
ghet|to|ize (get'ō īz), *v.t.,* **-ized, -iz|ing.** to segregate or enclose in a ghetto: *... the exclusive enclave of Riveredge, a millionaire subdivision [of estates], where a hundred of the best families have pridefully ghettoized themselves behind a wrought-iron gate* (New York Times).
ghi (gē), *n.* = ghee.
Ghib|el|line (gib'ə lin, -lēn), *n., adj.* *—n.* a member of the imperial and aristocratic political party of medieval Italy, that supported the German em-

Pronunciation Key: hat, āge, cãre, fär; let, ēqual, tėrm; it, īce; hot, ōpen, ôrder; oil, out; cup, pů̇t, rüle; child; long; thin; ᴛʜen; zh, measure;
ə represents **a** in about, **e** in taken, **i** in pencil, **o** in lemon, **u** in circus.

perors and was opposed to the Guelphs.
—adj. of or having to do with the Ghibellines.
[< Italian *Ghibellino* < German *Waiblingen,* name of an estate owned by the imperial family]

ghib|li (gib′lē), *n.* (in northern Africa, especially Libya) the khamsin or sirocco: *There is a ghibli rising, and the air is full of dust* (Agnes Newton Keith). [< Arabic *giblī*]

ghil|gai (gil′gī), *n.* (in Australia) a saucerlike depression forming a natural reservoir for rain water. Also, **gilgai**.

ghil|lie (gil′ē), *n.* **1** = gillie. **2** a low-cut sports shoe with fringed lace and no tongue.

Ghil|zai (gil′zī), *n., pl.* **-zai** or **-zais**. a member of a large Pathan tribe of Afghanistan.

Ghior|des (gyôr′dəs, gôr′-), *n.* a Turkish rug having a cotton web and an uneven woolen pile in which the two ends of piece of yarn appear at the surface between the two adjacent warps around which the yarn is knotted. [< *Gördes* (Ghiordes), a town in Turkey]

Ghoor|ka (gůr′kə), *n.* = Gurkha.

ghost (gōst), *n., v., adj.* *—n.* **1** the spirit of one who is dead. It is supposed to live in another world and appear to living people as a pale, dim, shadowy form. *The ghost of the murdered man haunted the house.* **2** *Figurative.* anything pale, dim, or shadowy like a ghost; a faint image; slightest suggestion: *a ghost of a smile. Our team didn't have a ghost of a chance to win the basketball game.* **3** the spirit, as distinct from the body; seat of feeling, thought, and moral action; soul: *It will be a good step towards the knowledge of what the world ought to be to us, who are body and ghost together* (N. Fairfax). **4** *Informal.* a ghost writer. **5** a secondary or multiple image resulting from the reflection of a transmitted television signal. **6** *Optics.* a bright spot or secondary image produced by some defect in the lens or instrument. **7** *Obsolete.* **a** a good spirit; angel. **b** an evil spirit; demon.
—v.t. **1** to haunt as a ghost does: *Julius Caesar, Who at Philippi the good Brutus ghosted* (Shakespeare). **2** *Informal.* to be a ghost writer for: *There was the case of a star performer who was being ghosted by sports editor John Barrington* (Harper's). **3** *Informal.* to ghostwrite: *A free-lance sports writer ... helped ghost the original manuscript into language for the layman* (Maclean's).
—v.i. **1** to go about or move like a ghost: *Other more elegant craft with neater lines than ours went ghosting by* (London Times). **2** *Informal.* to be a ghost writer: *All his life he ghosted for other writers.*
—adj. deserted; forsaken: *a ghost house.*
give up the ghost, a to die: *A tiger ... shot through the heart ... is still capable of killing half-a-dozen men before giving up the ghost* (FitzWilliam T. Pollok). **b** to cease to function; come to an end: *The Third Avenue "L" gave up the ghost ... in its seventy-seventh year, leaving no descendants* (New Yorker).
the ghost walks, (originally theatrical slang) payday: *This is the day the ghost walks.*
[spelling alteration of Middle English *goost,* Old English *gāst*] *—***ghost′less,** *adj.* *—***ghost′like′,** *adj.*
—Syn. n. **1 Ghost, specter, apparition** mean an appearance or visible form of someone or something not really present. **Ghost** applies chiefly to the spirit of a dead person: *He saw his father's ghost.* **Specter** applies to a ghostly, mysterious, usually frightening shape, sometimes appearing as if by magic: *A specter flitted through the graveyard.* **Apparition** applies especially to an appearance, often of someone dead or about to die, seeming very real to the person seeing it and impossible to explain or understand: *The apparition of his mother visited him.*

GHOST (gōst), *n.* Global Horizontal Sounding Technique (a system of collecting atmospheric data from radio-transmitting balloons set afloat at specified levels in the atmosphere).

ghost crab, a sand crab found commonly on beaches of the Atlantic Ocean from Long Island to Rio de Janeiro. It appears and suddenly disappears, ghostlike, in the sand. See picture under **eyestalk**.

ghost dance, a religious dance of certain North American Indians, especially a circle dance intended for communication with the dead.

ghost|dom (gōst′dəm), *n.* the region or domain of ghosts.

ghost gum, (in Australia) a stunted eucalyptus with white limbs and a few leaves.

ghost|hood (gōst′hůd), *n.* the state of being a ghost, a ghost town, a ghost writer, etc.: *Ghosthood decreed for a town in Italy* (New York Times).

ghost|ly (gōst′lē), *adj.,* **-li|er, -li|est. 1** like a ghost; pale, dim, and shadowy: *A ghostly form walked across the stage.* SYN: spectral. **2** of or having to do with a ghost: *ghostly legends.* **3** *Archaic.* spiritual; religious: *Both worldly and ghostly comfort* (Scott). *—***ghost′li|ness,** *n.*

ghost moth, any one of a family of lepidopterous, nocturnal insects with short antennae and long wings, whose larvae burrow in the roots or beneath the bark of trees.

ghost plant, = tumbleweed.

ghost shrimp, a slender, translucent shrimp that lives in burrows on sandy beaches of the western coast of North America.

ghost station, *British.* an unused or unstaffed railroad station.

ghost story, 1 a story about ghosts. **2** a story not to be believed.

ghost surgery, an unethical practice in which a surgeon operates on the patient of another surgeon with whom he has made this arrangement without the consent or knowledge of the patient.

ghost town, a once-flourishing town that has become empty and lifeless: *Then something went wrong, a lot of money was lost, and the place turned into a ghost town* (New Yorker).

ghost word, an apparent word found in manuscript or print, that owes its existence to the error of a scribe, editor, or printer.

ghost|write or **ghost-write** (gōst′rīt′), *v.t., v.i.,* **-wrote, -writ|ten, -writ|ing.** to write (something) for another who pretends to be the author: *This client telephoned my friend ... and asked that he ghost-write a letter to be sent to the head of the public relations firm* (Daniel J. Boorstin). [American English; back formation < *ghost writer*]

ghost writer, or **ghost|writ|er** (gōst′rī′tər), *n.* a person who writes something for another person who pretends to be the author: *Mencken had been mousetrapped into being a grievously unwitting Presidential ghost writer* (New York Times).

ghost|y (gōs′tē), *adj.,* **ghost|i|er, ghost|i|est.** of or like a ghost; ghostly. *—***ghost′i|ly,** *adv.*

ghoul (gül), *n.* **1** a horrible demon in Oriental stories, believed to rob graves and feed on corpses. **2** a person who robs graves or corpses. **3** *Figurative.* a person who enjoys what is revolting, brutal, and horrible. [< Arabic *ghūl*]

ghoul|ish (gü′lish), *adj.* like a ghoul; revolting, brutal, and horrible. *—***ghoul′ish|ly,** *adv.* *—***ghoul′ish|ness,** *n.*

GHQ (no periods), General Headquarters.

ghri|al (grē′əl), *n.* = garial.

Ghur|ka (gůr′kə), *n.* = Gurkha.

ghyll (gil), *n.* = gill³.

GHz (no periods), gigahertz.

gi., gill² or gills.

GI (jē′ī′), *adj., n., pl.* **GI's** (jē′īz′), *v.,* **GI'd, GI'ing.** *—adj.* **1** of United States government issue: *GI shoes, GI socks.* **2** *Informal.* conforming to regulations; standard: *GI uniforms.* **3** of, having to do with, or for a member, or former member, of the United States armed forces: *a GI loan, the GI Bill.*
—n. *Informal.* **1** an enlisted soldier in the United States Army; serviceman. **2** a member or former member of any one of the armed services of the United States.
—v.t., v.i. U.S. Informal. to clean, polish, or arrange in preparation for inspection by officers.
[< the initial letters of the phrase "Government Issue;" applied to general supplies issued to U.S. troops, earlier applied to specific military lists of issued equipment, and originally to army trash cans of galvanized iron coded GI on such lists]

GI (no periods) or **G.I., 1** gastrointestinal. **2** general issue. **3** government issue.

gial|lo an|ti|co (jäl′lō än tē′kō), a rich yellow marble found among ruins in Italy, used as a decoration. [< Italian *giallo antico* (literally) ancient yellow]

gi|ant (jī′ənt), *n., adj.* *—n.* **1** an imaginary being like a man but larger and more powerful. **2** *Figurative.* a person, animal, plant, or thing of unusual size, strength, importance, intellect, or other quality: *a circus giant, giants in the field of science.* **3** *Greek Mythology.* one of a race of imaginary beings having human form, but larger and more powerful than men. They were destroyed in a war with the gods. **4** a large nozzle used in placer mining to direct powerful streams of water.
—adj. **1** like a giant; unusually big or strong; huge: *a giant potato.* SYN: gigantic, monstrous. **2** *Figurative.* towering above others; distinguished; great. **3** indicating a variety or kind of plant or animal decidedly larger than others.
[Middle English *geaunt* < Old French *geant* < Vulgar Latin *gagas, gagantis,* alteration of Latin *gigās, gigantis* < Greek *gigās*]

giant anteater, the ant bear, or great anteater.

giant arbor vitae, 1 a tree of western North America often reaching a height of 200 feet; red cedar. It belongs to the cypress family. **2** its wood, often used for boats, poles, shingles, and siding.

giant bottle-nosed whale, any one of a variety of whales found in the North Pacific and Antarctic regions, having a snout that narrows into a round beak, a black or dark-gray color, and a maximum length of 42 feet and weight of 30 tons.

giant cactus, = saguaro.

giant cane, a bamboolike grass, found in the southern United States.

giant cell, an unusually large tissue or organ cell occurring naturally or associated with a pathological condition such as a tumor.

giant clam, a clam found on the coral reefs of the East Indies and off Australia, often weighing as much as 500 pounds and having shells 4 feet long.

giant crab, a spider crab of Japanese waters with extremely long legs; giant spider crab.

giant danio, a blue and yellow striped freshwater fish with orange-colored fins, often kept in aquariums.

gi|ant|esque (jī′ən tesk′), *adj.* = gigantesque.

gi|ant|ess (jī′ən tis), *n.* a woman giant.

giant fennel, a tall ornamental plant of the parsley family, grown for its finely divided leaves and umbels of yellow flowers.

giant frog, = goliath frog.

giant fulmar, = giant petrel.

giant hornet, a common hornet introduced in the United States from Europe.

giant hummer, the largest known hummingbird, native to the Andes Mountains, growing to a length of 9 inches.

gi|ant|ism (jī′ən tiz əm), *n.* **1** the condition of being a giant. **2** abnormally great bodily development; gigantism. **3** the tendency or trend of business to concentrate into an increasingly smaller number of companies of increasingly larger size.

giant kangaroo, a very large, grayish-brown kangaroo formerly common in Australia; great grey kangaroo.

giant kelp, a large seaweed of the Pacific coast of North and South America, having stems which sometimes grow more than 200 feet long. Algin is obtained from this seaweed.

giant killer, a person who opposes and defeats a powerful or important figure. [< Jack the *Giant Killer,* the hero who kills giants in an old children's tale]

gi|ant|like (jī′ənt līk′), *adj.* resembling a giant; gigantic.

giant panda, = panda (def. 1).

giant petrel, a large white or brownish bird of southern seas, up to 3 feet in length, related to the shearwaters and fulmars. It resembles a small albatross.

giant pigweed, a variety of pigweed having red roots; redroot. It belongs to the amaranth family.

giant powder, an explosive resembling dynamite, used in blasting.

giant ragweed, a kind of ragweed that sometimes grows 12 feet high; kinghead. Its pollen causes hay fever.

giant schnauzer, the largest of the three schnauzer dog breeds, standing up to 25 inches high. It was developed in Bavaria for use in herding cattle.

giant sequoia, a very large evergreen tree of California; sequoia; big tree; sierra redwood. The giant sequoia belongs to the same family as the redwood and often grows to a height of over 300 feet.

giant slalom, a slalom with a vertical descent of at least 1000 feet.

giant spider crab, = giant crab.

giant squid, a rarely seen squid, living in the ocean depths, that reaches a length of over fifty feet and is the largest known invertebrate animal. It is believed to be the basis for many of the sea serpent stories.

giant squirrel, a large tree squirrel, growing up to 18 inches long, with a tail of the same length. It lives in India and Malaysia.

giant stag, = stag beetle.

giant star, a very bright star of vast size and low density, such as Arcturus.

giant swallowtail, a large black-and-yellow butterfly of the southern United States, West Indies, and Central America, whose larvae feed on the leaves of citrus plants, prickly ash, Lombardy poplar, and rue.

giant tortoise, any one of various large land turtles of certain islands in the Pacific Ocean.

giaour (jour), *n.* a Moslem term for a person who does not believe in the Moslem religion. [< Turkish *gâvur* < Persian *gebr, gabr*]

gib¹ (gib), *n., v.,* **gibbed, gib|bing.** *—n.* **1** a piece of metal or wood fitted in a machine to hold parts together or in place. **2** a wedge that reduces the friction between parts of a machine that rub together.
—v.t. to secure with a gib or gibs.
[origin uncertain]

gib[2] (gib), *n.* **1** a cat, especially a male cat. **2** *Dialect.* a castrated cat. **3** *Obsolete.* a familiar name given to a cat. [contraction of *Gilbert,* a proper name]

Gib., Gibraltar.

gibbed (gibd), *adj.* (of a cat) castrated.

gib|ber[1] (jib′ər, gib′-), *v., n.* —*v.i.* to chatter senselessly; talk in a confused, meaningless way: *The monkeys gibbered angrily at each other.* **SYN:** babble, prattle.
—*n.* senseless chattering; confused, meaningless talking; gibberish. [perhaps imitative]

gib|ber[2] (jib′ər), *n.* (in Australia) a stone smoothed and rounded by the action of wind and water. [< a native name]

gib|ber|el|lic acid (jib′ə rel′ik), a plant hormone that increases size and the rate of growth. It was originally derived from a fungus which damages Japanese rice plants. *Formula:* $C_{19}H_{22}O_6$ [< New Latin *Gibberella* the genus name of the fungus + English *-ic*]

gib|ber|el|lin (jib′ə rel′in), *n.* any one of a group of hormones that are synthesized in the protoplasm of plants and that increase the rate and the amount of growth. Gibberellic acid is a gibberellin.

gib|ber|ish (jib′ər ish, gib′-), *n.* senseless chatter; confused, meaningless talk or writing; jargon. **SYN:** gabble, jabber. [probably < *gibber*]

gib|bet (jib′it), *n., v.,* **-bet|ed, -bet|ing.** —*n.* **1** an upright post with a projecting arm at the top, from which the bodies of criminals were in former times hung after execution. **2** = gallows.
—*v.t.* **1** to hang on a gibbet. **2** *Figurative.* to hold up to public scorn or ridicule: *Was he to be gibbeted in the press?* (Anthony Trollope). **3** to put to death by hanging.
[< Old French *gibet* (diminutive) < *gibe* club]

gib|ble-gab|ble (gib′əl gab′əl), *n.* senseless chatter; gibberish.

gib|bon (gib′ən), *n.* the smallest kind of ape, having very long arms and no tail. Gibbons live in trees in southeastern Asia and the East Indies. See picture under **ape.** [< French *gibbon*]

gib|bos|i|ty (gi bos′ə tē), *n., pl.* **-ties. 1** gibbous condition. **2** a protuberance; swelling.

gib|bous (gib′əs), *adj.* **1** curved out; humped. **2** so illuminated as to be convex on both margins. A gibbous moon is more than half full but less than full. **3** humpbacked. [< Latin *gibbōsus* < *gibbus* hump] —**gib′bous|ly,** *adv.* —**gib′bous-ness,** *n.*

gibbs|ite (gib′zīt), *n.* a whitish, crystalline or massive hydrate of aluminum oxide. It is an important component of bauxite, the principal ore of aluminum. *Formula:* $Al_2O_3 \cdot 3H_2O$ [< George *Gibbs,* 1766-1833, an American mineralogist + *-ite*[1]]

gibe (jīb), *v.,* **gibed, gib|ing,** *n.* —*v.i.* to speak in a sneering way; jeer; scoff; sneer: *My brother gibed at my efforts to paint a picture. He would familiarly gibe and jest with him* (Edmund Spenser). **SYN:** ridicule, deride. —*v.t.* **1** to taunt; mock. **2** to dismiss with taunts or jeers: *You ... with taunts Did gibe my missive out of audience* (Shakespeare). **SYN:** ridicule, deride.
—*n.* a jeer; taunt; sneer: *His gibes hurt his sister's feelings.* Also, **jibe.**
[perhaps < Old French *giber* jeer, handle roughly < *gibe* staff] —**gib′er,** *n.*

Gib|e|on|ite (gib′ē ə nīt), *n.* one of the inhabitants of Gibeon, an ancient city of Palestine, who tried to deceive Joshua and were punished by being made servants to the Israelites (in the Bible, Joshua 9).

gib|ing (jī′bing), *adj.* mocking; jeering; scoffing. —**gib′ing|ly,** *adv.*

gib|let (jib′lit), *n.* Usually, **giblets.** the heart, liver, and gizzard of a fowl: *The giblets were cut up and put in a giblet gravy.* [< Old French *gibelet* stew of game]

Gi|bral|tar (jə brôl′tər), *n.* a strongly fortified place; impregnable fortress or stronghold: *Canada's 11 chartered banks are Gibraltars of financial solidity.* [< *Gibraltar,* a British colony on the southern coast of Spain]

Gib|son (gib′sən), *n.* a cocktail consisting of gin or vodka with dry vermouth, served with a pickled onion. [< the name *Gibson*]

***Gibson girl,** **1** a typical, clean-cut, poised American woman of the outdoor type, as drawn by the illustrator, Charles Dana Gibson, 1867-1944: *Until replaced by the post-first-world-war flapper, the Gibson girl ... graced the calendars, the advertisements, the postcards, the embroidery—even the spoons—of a generation* (Newsweek). **2** a portable emergency radio transmitter, so called because of its curved shape, carrried aboard airplanes and lifeboats.

gi|bus (jī′bəs; *French* zhē bʏs′), *n.,* or **gibus hat,** = opera hat. [< *Gibus,* the original maker]

gid (gid), *n.* staggers in sheep due to infestation of the brain with a larval form of tapeworm; waterbrain. [short for *giddy*]

gid|dap (gi dap′), *interj.* = giddyup.

gid|di|fy (gid′ə fī), *v.t.,* **-fied, -fy|ing.** to daze.

gid|dup (gi dup′), *interj., n.* —*interj.* = giddyup. —*n. U.S. Slang.* get-up-and-go; spunk.

gid|dy (gid′ē), *adj.,* **-di|er, -di|est,** *v.,* **-died, -dy-ing.** —*adj.* **1** having a confused, whirling feeling in one's head; dizzy: *It makes me giddy to go on a merry-go-round.* **SYN:** light-headed. **2** likely to make dizzy; causing dizziness: *giddy precipices. The couples whirled and whirled in their giddy dance.* **3** rarely or never serious; living for the pleasure of the moment; in a whirl; frivolous; fickle: *That giddy girl thinks only of having a gay time.* **SYN:** flighty, heedless, inconstant. **4** nonsensical; absurd: *The giddy part of it is that our strike isn't up north at all* (A. J. Small).
—*v.t.* to make giddy. —*v.i.* to become giddy.
[Old English *gydig,* mad, possessed (by a spirit) < *god* a god] —**gid′di|ly,** *adv.* —**gid′di|ness,** *n.*

gid|dy|ap (gid′ē ap′), *interj.* = giddyup.

gid|dy|up (gid′ē up′), *interj.* a word of command to horses to start going or to go faster. [modification of *get up*]

Gid|e|on (gid′ē ən), *n.* **1** a hero of Israel who defeated the Midianites and was a judge of Israel for forty years (in the Bible, Judges 6-8). **2** a member of a Christian organization of American traveling salesmen, founded in 1899 for the purpose of placing Bibles in hotels, hospitals, prisons, and military bases.

gid|gee (gid′jē), *n.* a small, hard, close-grained acacia of eastern Australia, whose wood is much used for fence posts, walking sticks, and picture frames. [< a native name]

gie (gē), *v.t., v.i. Scottish and Dialect.* to give.

gier-ea|gle (jir′ē′gəl), *n.* an unclean bird, probably a vulture, mentioned in the Authorized Version of the Bible (Leviticus 11:18 and Deuteronomy 14:17). [< Dutch *gier* vulture + *eagle*]

gift (gift), *n., v.* —*n.* **1** something given; present: *a birthday gift, the gift of a million dollars to a university.* **2** the act of giving: *The house came to him by gift from an uncle.* **3** the power or right of giving: *The office is within his gift.* **4** a natural talent; special ability: *A great artist must have a gift for painting.* **SYN:** aptitude. **5** *Obsolete.* a bribe.
—*v.t.* **1** to present with a gift; endow. **2** *Especially Scottish.* to give as a gift.
[Middle English *gifte* < Scandinavian (compare Old Icelandic *gift* gift). Compare etym. under **give.**]
— *Syn. n.* **1 Gift, present** mean something given to express friendship, admiration, interest, or the like. **Gift** usually applies to what is given to a person, organization, or institution to benefit it: *The university received a gift of a million dollars.* **Present** always suggests a personal connection between giver and receiver, and applies to what is given a friend, relative, or other close person: *We bought a wedding present for our cousin.*

gift certificate, a certificate that a stated sum of money has been deposited at a store in payment for merchandise to be selected by the recipient, given as a gift.

gift|ed (gif′tid), *adj.* having natural talent or special ability; unusually able; talented: *Beethoven was gifted in music.* —**gift′ed|ly,** *adv.* —**gift′ed-ness,** *n.*

gifted child, 1 a child whose intelligence is generally in the top two to three per cent of his age level. **2** a child with an outstanding talent in a particular field.

gift horse, a gift, the value or significance of which is questionable.
look a gift horse in the mouth, to criticize and find fault with a gift: *He would be a fool ... to look such a gift horse in the mouth* (James Payn).

gift|less (gift′lis), *adj.* **1** having no gift to offer. **2** having received no gift. **3** lacking in natural gifts or abilities.

***Gibson girl**
definition 1

gift of gab or **gift of the gab,** fluency of speech; glibness: *It may be that* [*the author's*] *gift of gab has cut sharply into his literary output* (Newsweek).

gift of tongues, = glossolalia.

gift shop, a shop dealing in articles suitable for gifts.

gift tax, *U.S.* a tax levied on the value of a gift and assessed to the gift's donor.

gift-wrap (gift′rap′), *v.,* **-wrapped, -wrap|ping,** *n.* —*v.t.* to wrap (something) in fancy paper or with trimmings suitable for a gift.
—*n.* especially fancy wrappings.

gift-wrap|ping (gift′rap′ing), *n.* fancy paper and trimmings in which to wrap a gift.

***gig**[1] (gig), *n., v.,* **gigged, gig|ging.** —*n.* **1** a light, open, two-wheeled carriage drawn by one horse. **2** a long, light ship's boat moved by oars or sails: *The captain's gig was used to take him to and from the ship.* **3** a machine for raising nap on cloth.
—*v.i.* to travel in a gig.
—*v.t.* to raise the nap of (cloth).
[probably special use of *gig*[5]]

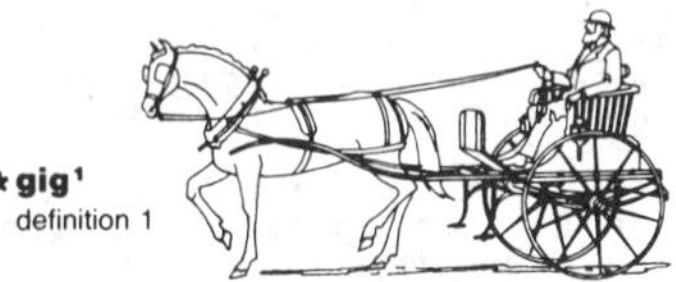

***gig**[1]
definition 1

gig[2] (gig), *n., v.,* **gigged, gig|ging.** —*n.* **1** a device for spearing fish; fish spear. **2** *U.S.* hooks for dragging in a school of fish to hook them through the body.
—*v.t.* to spear (fish) with a gig.
—*v.i.* to fish with a gig.
[short for *fishgig,* probably variant of *fizgig*]

gig[3] (gig), *n., v.,* **gigged, gig|ging.** *Military Slang.* —*n.* a demerit.
—*v.t.* to report for a breach of regulations.
[origin unknown]

gig[4] (gig), *n. Slang.* **1** a gathering or meeting of jazz or rock musicians. **2** a single engagement or playing time of a jazz or rock group, or solo entertainer. **3** any assignment or task; job: *a first gig as a reporter.* [origin uncertain]

gig[5] (gig), *n. Obsolete.* **1** something that whirls; a top. **2** a giddy girl. [Middle English *gigg*]

giga-, *combining form.* one billion: *Gigavolt = one billion volts.* [< Greek *gígās* giant]

gi|ga|bit (jig′ə bit′), *n.* a unit of information equivalent to one billion bits or binary digits.

gig|a|cy|cle (jig′ə sī′kəl), *n.* **1** a billion cycles. **2** a billion cycles per second.

gig|a|hertz (jig′ə hėrts′), *n.* one billion hertz.

gi|gan|tesque (jī′gan tesk′), *adj.* like a giant; suitable for a giant.

gi|gan|tic (jī gan′tik), *adj.* **1** of, having to do with, or like a giant: *a man of gigantic build. In folklore, Paul Bunyan was a gigantic lumberjack.* **2** huge; enormous: *a gigantic building project. An elephant is a gigantic animal.* **SYN:** immense, colossal. [< Greek *gigantikós* < *gígās, -antos* giant] —**gi|gan′ti|cal|ly,** *adv.*

gi|gan|tism (jī gan′tiz əm), *n.* **1** *Medicine.* a condition of overdeveloped growth of the body or part of the body, usually due to overactivity of the pituitary gland. **2** *Biology.* abnormally great vegetative growth. **3** a gigantic condition or tendency; giantism: *industrial gigantism.*

gi|gan|to|ma|chi|a (jī gan′tə mā′kē ə), *n.* **1** = gigantomachy. **2** a representation of this.

gi|gan|tom|a|chy (jī′gan tom′ə kē), *n., pl.* **-chies. 1** *Greek Mythology.* the war of the giants against the gods. **2** a contest resembling this. [< Late Latin *gigantomachia* < Greek *gigantomachíā* < *gígās, -antos* giant + *máchē* battle]

gi|gan|to|ma|ni|a (jī gan′tə mā′nē ə), *n.* a mania for bigness.

gi|gan|to|pith|e|cus (jī gan′tə pith′ə kəs), *n.* any one of a genus of extinct primates of the Pliocene, whose large fossil remains have been found in southern China and northern India. [< New Latin *Gigantopithecus* the genus name < Greek *gígās, -antos* + *píthēkos* ape]

gi|gan|to|sau|rus (jī gan′tə sôr′əs), *n., pl.* **-sau|ri** (-sôr′ī). an extremely large dinosaur whose remains have been found in eastern Africa. [< Greek *gígās, -antos* giant + *saûros* lizard]

gig|a|ton (jig′ə tun′), *n.* a measure of atomic power equivalent to the explosive force of one billion tons of TNT.

gig|a|volt (jig′ə vōlt′), *n.* one billion volts.

gig|a|watt (jig′ə wot′), *n.* one billion watts.

gig|gle (gig′əl), *v.,* **-gled, -gling,** *n.* —*v.i.* to laugh

Pronunciation Key: hat, āge, cãre, fär; let, ēqual, tėrm; it, īce; hot, ōpen, ôrder; oil, out; cup, pu̇t, rüle; child; long; thin; ᴛʜen; zh, measure; ə represents a in about, e in taken, i in pencil, o in lemon, u in circus.

in a silly or undignified way: *The girls whispered and giggled together.*
—*n.* **1** a silly or undignified laugh. **2** *Informal.* a joke: *"What a giggle," said Claudia. "Imagine Prescott-Clark as a captain"* (New Yorker). **3** *Informal.* a group of girls or women: . . . *a giggle of pretty undergraduates* (London Times).
[imitative] —**gig'gler**, *n.* —**gig'glingly**, *adv.*
giglish (gig'lish), *adj.* disposed to giggle.
giggly (gig'lē), *adj.*, **-glier**, **-gliest.** having the habit of giggling: *a giggly girl.* —**gig'gliness**, *n.*
gig lamp, **1** a lamp attached to a gig (carriage). **2** *Dialect.* a firefly.
giglet (gig'lit), *n.* **1** a giddy girl. **2** *Obsolete.* a wanton. [origin uncertain]
giglio (jē'lyō), *n., pl.* **-glios.** *Italian.* the lily on the coat of arms of Florence, resembling the fleur-de-lis, with two more petals.
giglot (gig'lət), *n.* = giglet.
GIGO (no periods), garbage in, garbage out: *New technology and curriculum changes, he says, can be beneficial, but "it's a matter of GIGO . . . You put garbage into a computer, you get garbage out." Simply investing money into new ideas isn't enough* (Science News).
gigolette (jig'ə let'; *French,* zhē gô let'), *n.* a woman hired as a dancing partner or escort for a man. [< French *gigolette*]
gigolo (jig'ə lō), *n., pl.* **-los.** a man hired as a dancing partner, escort, or lover for a woman. [< French *gigolo* < *gigolette*]
gigot (jig'ət), *n.* **1** a leg-of-mutton sleeve. **2** a leg of mutton, veal, venison, or other meat. [< Middle French *gigot*]
gigue (zhēg), *n.* **1** = jig[1]. **2** music, usually in 6/8 or 3/8 time, forming the last movement of a dance suite. [< French *gigue*]
***Gila monster** (hē'lə), **1** a large, poisonous lizard of the southwestern United States and northern Mexico, which has a thick tail and a heavy body covered with beadlike orange-and-black scales. **2** a closely related lizard of Mexico and Central America. [American English < *Gila* River, Arizona]

***Gila monster**
definition 1

Gila woodpecker, a woodpecker of southwestern U.S., that nests in giant cactuses.
gilbert (gil'bərt), *n.* unit of magnetomotive force, equivalent to 10/4 π ampere turns. [< William *Gilbert,* 1540-1603, English physician and physicist]
Gilbertese (gil'bər tēz', -tēs'), *n.* the Micronesian language of Kiribati (an island country in the southwestern Pacific including the Gilbert Islands).
Gilbertian (gil bėr'tē ən), *adj.* of, having to do with, or in the style of William S. Gilbert or his librettos; witty; satirical.
Gilbertines (gil'bər tinz, -tīnz), *n.* a religious order founded in England in the early 1100's by Saint Gilbert of Sempringham.
gild[1] (gild), *v.t.*, **gilded** or **gilt**, **gilding.** **1** to cover with a thin layer of gold or similar material; make golden: *to gild a picture frame with gold leaf.* **2** to color like gold: *The sun gilds the clouds.* **3** *Figurative.* to make (something) look bright and pleasing: *Love gilds the scene* (Sheridan). **4** *Figurative.* to make (something) seem better than it is. **5** *Archaic.* to smear (with blood).
gild the lily. See under **lily.**
[Old English *-gyldan* < *gold* gold]
gild[2] (gild), *n.* = guild.
gilded (gil'did), *adj.* **1** coated with or as if with gold. **2** colored like gold. **3** *Figurative.* made to appear better than it is. **4** wealthy.
Gilded Age, *U.S.* any period of wealth and growth of a nation or culture, especially the 35 years in America following the Civil War, marked by a shift to a complex, urban culture.
gilder[1] (gil'dər), *n.* a person who gilds, especially as a trade or art.
gilder[2] (gil'dər), *n. Obsolete.* guilder.
gilding (gil'ding), *n.* **1** a thin layer of gold or similar material with which a thing is gilded. **2** the act of covering with such a layer. **3** a gilded thing or surface. **4** *Figurative.* an attractive coating; veneer: *a gilding of politeness.*
gildsman (gildz'mən), *n., pl.* **-men.** = guildsman.
gild socialism, = guild socialism.
Gileadite (gil'ē ə dīt), *n.* **1** a native or inhabitant of Gilead, a region in ancient Palestine. **2** a member of a branch of the tribe of Manasseh.
gilgai (gil'gī), *n.* = ghilgai.
Gilgamesh (gil'gə mesh), *n.* a legendary Babylonian king, hero of the Gilgamesh Epic.
Gilgamesh Epic, a literary work predating the Old Testament, which tells the story of Gilgamesh and has an account similar to that of Noah and the Flood in Genesis.
gilgie (gil'gē), *n.* = yabbie.
gilguy (gil'gī), *n.* **1** *Nautical.* a temporary or makeshift device of rope, as for rigging. **2** a showy, useless trifle; gimcrack. [< *gil* (uncertain meaning) + *guy*[1]]
gilia (jil'ē ə), *n.* any one of a large group of plants related to the phlox, found chiefly in the western United States and often cultivated for their showy flowers. [< New Latin *Gilia* the genus name < Felipe Luis *Gil,* a Spanish botanist of the 1700's]
***gill**[1] (gil), *n., v.* —*n.* a part of the body of a fish, tadpole, crab, or other animal that lives in water, by which it breathes in water. Oxygen passes in and carbon dioxide passes out through the thin walls of the gills.
—*v.t.* **1** to catch (fish) by the gills in a gill net. **2** to clean (fish). **3** to cut away the gills of (a mushroom).
gills, a the fine, thin, leaflike structures on the underside of a mushroom. **b** the flesh under a person's jaws: *to look green around the gills.* **c** the red, hanging flesh under the throat of a fowl; wattles.
to the gills, very fully; to capacity: *The house is stuffed to the gills with food but it's all for Christmas* (Punch).
[perhaps < Scandinavian (compare Danish *gjelle*)]
—**gill'-like'**, *adj.*

***gill**[1]

***gills**
definition a

***gill**[2] (jil), *n.* a small liquid measure, equal 0.1183 to one fourth of a pint. One gill is half a cup or .1183 liter. [< Old French *gille* wine measure < Medieval Latin *gillo* cooling vessel]
gill[3] (gil), *n.* **1** a ravine; glen. **2** a stream in a ravine. Also, **ghyll.** [< Scandinavian (compare Old Icelandic *gil*)]
gill[4] (jil), *n.* **1** *Dialect.* the ground ivy. **2** *Obsolete.* a woman; girl. Also, **jill.** [contraction of *Gillian*]
gill arch, one of the cartilaginous arches supporting the gill of a fish or amphibian.
gill books, the leaflike gills through which a king crab breathes, borne on the second to sixth pairs of swimming organs.
gill cleft, one of the openings in the pharynx of a fish or amphibian that serve as channels for the passage of water to the exterior.
gilled (gild), *adj.* having gills, as fishes.
gill filament, the threadlike part of a gill filled with the blood vessels that absorb oxygen and give off carbon dioxide.
gillflirt (jil'flėrt'), *n. Archaic.* a giddy girl.
gill fungus (gil), = agaric.
gillie (gil'ē), *n.* **1** a man who goes with and helps a hunter or fisherman in the Scottish Highlands. **2** a follower; servant. **3** a sports shoe for women with laces that tie about the ankle. Also, **gilly, ghillie.** [< Scottish Gaelic *gille* lad, attendant]
gilliflower (jil'ē flou'ər), *n.* = gillyflower.
gill net, a net, suspended vertically in the water, to catch by the gills a fish that has thrust its head through.
gill-net (gil'net'), *v.t., v.i.*, **-netted**, **-netting.** to catch fish by means of a gill net.
gill netter, **1** a person who uses a gill net in fishing. **2** a boat used for gill-netting.
gill-over-the-ground (jil'ō'vər ᴛʜə ground'), *n.* = ground ivy.
gill raker, one of the series of bony processes on the inner edge of a gill arch to strain organic material from water passing to the gill.
gills (gilz), *n.pl.* See under **gill**[1].
gill slit, = gill cleft.
gilly (gil'ē), *n., pl.* **-lies.** = gillie.
gillyflower (jil'ē flou'ər), *n.* **1** any one of various flowers having a spicy, clovelike fragrance, such as the wallflower, the stock, the carnation, and the clove pink. **2** a variety of dark-red apple, of a delicate, spicy flavor. [alteration of Old French *gilofre,* ultimately < Greek *karyóphyllon* clove, the dried flower bud of the clove tree < *káryon* nut + *phýllon* leaf]
gilsonite (gil'sə nīt), *n.* a very pure form of asphalt; uintaite. [< S. H. *Gilson* of Utah, who introduced it + *-ite*[1]]
gilt[1] (gilt), *v., adj., n.* **a** gilded; a past tense and a past participle of **gild**[1]. —*adj.* gilded. —*n.* **1** a thin layer of gold or similar material with which a thing is gilded: *The gilt is coming off this frame.* **2** *Figurative.* gilding; veneer. **3** *Slang.* gold; money.
gilts, *British.* gilt-edged securities.
gilt[2] (gilt), *n.* a young sow or female pig, especially one less than a year old which has not given birth to pigs. [< Scandinavian (compare Old Icelandic *gyltr*)]
gilt-edge (gilt'ej'), *adj.* = gilt-edged.
gilt-edged (gilt'ejd'), *adj.* **1** having gilded edges. **2** *Figurative.* of the very best quality: *Gilt-edged securities are the safest kind to invest in.*
gilthead (gilt'hed'), *n.* any one of various fishes having golden markings on the head.
gimbal (jim'bəl, gim'-), *n., v.*, **-balled**, **-balling** or **-baled**, **-baling.** —*n.* = gimbals.
—*v.t.* to provide or support with gimbals.
—*v.i.* to swivel or rotate in or as if in gimbals.
[< *gimmal;* see etym. under **gimbals**]
gimbals (jim'bəlz, gim'-), *n.pl.* an arrangement for keeping an object horizontal, and giving it freedom to rotate about a fixed center. A ship's compass is supported on gimbals made of a pair of rings pivoted to swing, one within the other, on axes at right angles to each other. [< *gimmal* < Old French *gemel* twin < Latin *gemellus* (diminutive) < *geminus* a twin]
gimcrack (jim'krak'), *n., adj.* —*n.* a showy, useless trifle; knickknack. —*adj.* showy but useless. SYN: worthless. [origin uncertain]
gimcrackery (jim'krak'ər ē), *n., pl.* **-eries.** gimcracks collectively.
gimcracky (jim'krak'ē), *adj.* showy but useless: . . . *the gimcracky souvenirs that every fair inspires* (New Yorker).
gimel (gim'əl), *n.* the third letter of the Hebrew alphabet. [< Hebrew *gīmel* (literally) camel]
gimlet[1] (gim'lit), *n., v.*, **-leted**, **-leting** or (*especially British*) **-letted**, **-letting.** —*n.* a small tool with a screw point for boring holes.
—*v.t.* **1** to pierce with or as if with a gimlet: *He had dark, piercing black eyes that simply gimleted you.* **2** to turn around like a gimlet.
[< Old French *guimbelet*]
gimlet[2] (gim'lit), *n.* a cocktail of gin or vodka with sweetened lime juice. [perhaps < *gimlet*[1], coined as parallel to *screwdriver,* a similar drink]
gimlet eye, a sharp or piercing eye: *He is brought up under the gimlet eye and Puritan maxims of a crabby maiden aunt* (Time).
gimlet-eyed (gim'lit īd'), *adj.* having eyes that are sharp and piercing.
gimlety (gim'lə tē), *adj.* piercing like a gimlet.
gimmal (gim'əl, jim'-), *n.* two or more interlocking rings. [< Old French *gemel;* see etym. under **gimbals**]
gimme (gim'ē), *n., adj. Slang.* —*n.* the act or practice of asking for money, donations, gifts, or grants: *Santa . . . patron saint of gimme* (Canadian Saturday Night). —*adj.* characterized by gimme; asking for money, donations, or gifts: *gimme organizations.* [modification of *give me*]
gimme cap, *U.S.* a visored cap with a clasp for adjusting it to any head size: *You will not see his cowboys fixing a baler or wearing . . . gimme caps. They wear broad-rimmed hats* (Newsweek).
gimmick (gim'ik), *n., v. Slang.* —*n.* **1** any small device, especially one used secretly or in a tricky manner, such as one used by a magician in performing a trick or one attached to a wheel of chance: *These gadgets aren't gimmicks* (Wall Street Journal). **2** a hidden or tricky condition in a plan or the like; catch. **3** an idea, scheme, or stunt to attract attention: *The writer who attempts a new book on the subject tends to look for some gimmick to distinguish it from the others* (Observer). —*v.t.* to fit with gimmicks or gadgets: *Speakers' platforms are gimmicked up to catch both festival and brawl* (Time).
[American English; origin uncertain]
gimmickery (gim'ə krē), *n., pl.* **-eries.** *Slang.* gimmicks or the use of them.
gimmickry (gim'ə krē), *n., pl.* **-ries.** = gimmickery.
gimmicky (gim'ə kē), *adj. Slang.* using gimmicks: *nothing slick or gimmicky about this honest and perceptive story* (New York Times).
gimp[1] (gimp), *n.* a braidlike trimming made of silk, worsted, or cotton, sometimes stiffened with wire, used on garments, curtains, or furniture. [origin uncertain; compare Dutch *gimp*]
gimp[2] (gimp, gamp), *n.* = guimpe.
gimp[3] (gimp), *n. Informal.* energy; vigor. [origin unknown]
gimp[4] (gimp), *n., v.* —*n. Slang.* **1** a lame step or walk; limp. **2** a person who limps. —*v.i.* to walk with a limp; hobble. [perhaps related to Medieval German *Gimpel* limping person]
gimpy (gim'pē), *adj. Slang.* lame; limping; halting.
gin[1] (jin), *n.* a strong, colorless alcoholic drink, distilled mostly from grain and usually flavored with juniper berries. [alteration of *geneva* (liquor)]
gin[2] (jin), *n., v.*, **ginned**, **ginning.** —*n.* **1** a machine for separating cotton from its seeds; cotton gin. **2** a trap, snare, or net for catching game: *O Thou, who didst with Pitfall and with Gin Beset the Road I was to wander in* (Edward FitzGerald). **3** any one of various machines for pulling or lift-

ing objects, such as a winch. **4** *Obsolete.* **a** skill; cleverness. **b** trickery; cunning.
—***v.t.*** **1** to separate (cotton) from its seeds. **2** to trap; snare.
gin up, *U.S. Dialect or Informal.* to stir up: *gin up support for the President's ... policy* (Atlantic).
[Middle English *ginne* a contrivance, a result of skill, short for Old French *engin* engine]

gin³ (jin), *n., v.,* **ginned, gin|ning.** —***n.*** = gin rummy. —***v.i.*** to win a game in gin rummy; go gin.
go gin, to meld all of one's cards in gin rummy, except one for discarding; gin.

gin⁴ (gin), *v.t., v.i.,* **gan, gun, gin|ning.** *Archaic.* to begin. [short for Old English *aginnan,* variant of *onginnan,* partly perhaps for *beginnan* begin]

gin⁵ (gin), *conj. Scottish.* if; whether.

gin⁶ (jin), *n. Australian Slang.* a female aborigine.

gin and bitters (jin), a short alcoholic drink made with gin and angostura or other bitters.

gin and it, *British Informal.* a short drink consisting of gin and Italian vermouth. [*it* < *It*(alian)]

gin and tonic, an alcoholic drink consisting of gin and quinine water.

gin fizz, an alcoholic drink consisting of gin, lemon juice, sugar, and carbonated water.

gin|gal or **gin|gall** (jin'gôl), *n.* = jingal.

gin|ger¹ (jin'jər), *n., adj., v.* —***n.*** **1** a spice made from the pungent root of a cultivated tropical plant. It is used for flavoring and in medicine. **2** its root, often preserved in syrup or candied. **3** the plant, belonging to the ginger family. **4** *Informal, Figurative.* liveliness; energy. **5** a light, reddish or brownish yellow.
—***adj.*** light reddish- or brownish-yellow.
—***v.t.*** **1** to treat or flavor with ginger. **2** *Informal, Figurative.* to make spirited or lively; enliven: *New cadres were trained and sent out to ginger up timorous local committees* (Time).
[Middle English *gingere* < Old French *gingebre* < Late Latin *gingiber* < Latin *zingiberi* < Greek *zingīberis* < Prakrit *singabera* < Sanskrit *sṛñgavera*]

gin|ger² (jin'jər), *adj. Dialect.* gingerly.

ginger ale, a bubbling drink flavored with ginger. It contains no alcohol.

ginger beer, a drink similar to ginger ale, but made with fermenting ginger.

gin|ger|bread (jin'jər bred'), *n., adj.* —***n.*** **1** a kind of cake flavored with ginger and sweetened with molasses. Gingerbread is often made in fancy shapes. **2** *Figurative.* something showy and elaborate, but not in good taste; tasteless and useless ornamentation. Cheap carvings glued on furniture are gingerbread.
—***adj.*** showy; gaudy: *when architecture divested itself of the gingerbread frosting of the nineteenth century* (Atlantic).
[earlier, preserved ginger < Old French *gingembras,* ultimately < Late Latin *gingiber* (see etym. under **ginger**); influenced by *bread*]

gingerbread tree or **palm,** = doum palm.

gin|ger|bread|y (jin'jər bred'ē), *adj.* like gingerbread; having a trivial and showy style.

ginger family, a group of monocotyledonous herbs found chiefly in tropical regions of the Eastern Hemisphere. The family includes ginger, turmeric, and cardamom.

ginger group, *British.* an active, stimulating, and challenging group within an organization.

gin|ger|ly (jin'jər lē), *adv., adj.* —***adv.*** **1** with extreme care or caution; warily: *We live in an age when all men walk gingerly* (Esquire). **2** *Obsolete.* daintily; mincingly.
—***adj.*** **1** extremely cautious or wary: *Mahler's first symphony ... was given a loving but dangerously gingerly reading* (London Times). **2** *Obsolete.* dainty; mincing. —**gin'ger|li|ness,** *n.*

gin|ger|nut (jin'jər nut'), *n. Especially British.* gingersnap.

ginger oil, a thick, yellow, aromatic liquid with a somewhat burning taste, obtained from the rhizome of the ginger plant, and used as a flavoring, as an ingredient in soft drinks and liqueurs, and sometimes to relieve pain, as from a toothache; oil of ginger.

ginger pop, = ginger ale.

gin|ger|snap (jin'jər snap'), *n.* a thin, crisp cooky flavored with ginger and sweetened with molasses.

ginger tea, a tea brewed with ginger, used especially as a home remedy for stomachache.

ginger wine, *British.* an alcoholic drink made of green Jamaica ginger and sweet wine.

gin|ger|y (jin'jər ē), *adj.* **1** like ginger; hot and sharp; spicy. **2** light reddish- or brownish-yellow. **3** *Informal, Figurative.* spry; alert; peppery: *a gingery old man.*

ging|ham (ging'əm), *n., adj.* —***n.*** a cotton cloth made from colored threads, and used especially for dresses, aprons, or curtains. The patterns are usually in stripes, plaids, or checks.
—***adj.*** made of gingham: *a gingham dress.*
[< French *guingan* or *guingamp* < Malay *ginggang* striped]

gin|gi|li (jin'jə lē), *n., pl.* **-lis. 1** the sesame plant. **2** = sesame (def. 1a). **3** = sesame oil. [< Hindi *jinjalī*]

gin|gi|va (jin jī'və), *n., pl.* **-vae** (-vē). the flesh around the teeth; gum. [< Latin *gingīva* gum²]

gin|gi|val jin jī'vəl, jin'jə-), *adj.* **1** of or having to do with the gums. **2** *Phonetics.* alveolar. [< New Latin *gingivalis* < Latin *gingīva* gum²]

gin|gi|vi|tis (jin'jə vī'təs), *n.* inflammation of the gums.

ging|ko (ging'kō, jing'-), *n., pl.* **-koes.** = ginkgo.

gin|gly|mus (jing'glə məs, ging'-), *n., pl.* **-mi** (-mī). = hinge joint. [< New Latin *ginglymus* < Greek *gínglymos* hinge]

gink (gink), *n. Slang.* a fellow; person: *I saw the photo of her fiancé; he was a calm, responsible-looking gink* (James T. Farrell). [origin unknown]

gink|go (ging'kō, jing'-), *n., pl.* **-goes.** a large, ornamental tree native to China and Japan, with fan-shaped leaves and nuts that can be eaten; maidenhair tree. It is the only surviving species of a group that lived millions of years ago. Also, **gingko.** [< New Latin *Ginkgo* < Japanese *ginkyō*]

gin mill, *U.S. Slang.* a saloon or tavern.

gin|ner (jin'ər), *n.* a person who operates a cotton gin.

gin|ney (gin'ē), *n., pl.* **-neys.** an Italian; Guinea (an unfriendly use). [< *guinea*]

Gin|nie Mae jin'ē mā'), *U.S.* **1** the Government National Mortgage Association (a mortgage-lending agency of the Department of Housing and Urban Development). **2** a stock certificate issued by this agency: *A cautious market in interest-rate futures ... found long-term Ginnie Mae's and Treasury contracts finished slightly lower in price* (New York Times). [< spelling for pronunciation of its abbreviation, *GNMA*]

gin|nings (jin'ingz), *n.pl.* the output of a cotton gin: *Cotton crop news was favorable and new ginnings large* (Wall Street Journal).

gin|ny (jin'ē), *adj.,* **-ni|er, -ni|est.** smelling of gin: *ginny breath.*

gin pole, a pole, secured by guy ropes, to the top of which tackle for lifting heavy weights is fastened.

gin rummy, a kind of rummy, usually played by two persons. Players form sequences and matching combinations and may lay down their hands when their unmatched cards total ten points or less. [probably < *gin¹* as a pun on rummy²]

gin|seng (jin'seng), *n.* **1** a low plant of Asia and North America, grown chiefly in China, Korea, and the United States. It has a thick, branched, aromatic root and belongs to the ginseng family. **2** the root of this plant, much used in medicine by the Chinese. [< Chinese *jên shên; jên* man (from a frequent shape of the root)]

ginseng family, a widely distributed group of dicotyledonous herbs, shrubs, and trees usually having compound or lobed alternate leaves and small, regular flowers, usually in umbels, and bearing a berry as the fruit. The family includes the ginseng, English ivy, spikenard, and Hercules'-club.

gin|shop (jin'shop'), *n. Especially British.* a place serving alcoholic liquors; tavern; pub.

gin sling, an alcoholic drink consisting of gin, sugar, lemon or lime juice, and water.

gin|trap (jin'trap'), *n.* a trap for catching animals, especially rabbits, having two jaws with toothlike projections resembling those in a cotton gin.

gip¹ (jip), *n.* = Gypsy.

gip² (jip), *v.t., v.i.,* **gipped, gip|ping,** *n.* = gyp¹.

gi|pon (ji pon', jip'on), *n. Archaic.* jupon. [variant of *jupon*]

Gip|sy or **gip|sy** (jip'sē), *n., pl.* **-sies,** *adj. Especially British.* Gypsy or gypsy.

Gip|sy|dom (jip'sē dəm), *n. Especially British.* Gypsydom.

gipsy moth, = gypsy moth.

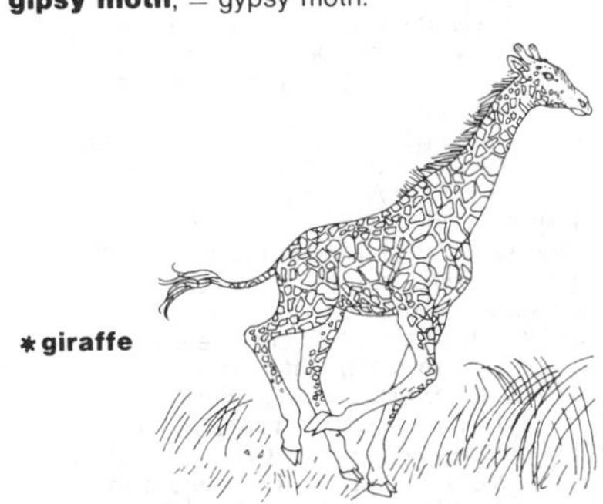
***giraffe**

***gi|raffe** (jə raf', -räf'), *n.* a large African animal with a very long neck and legs and a spotted skin; camelopard. Giraffes are mammals that chew their cud and are the tallest living animals. [< Middle French *giraffe* < Italian *giraffa* < Arabic *zarāfa*]

Gi|raffe (jə raf', -räf'), *n.* the northern constellation Camelopard.

gir|an|dole (jir'ən dōl), *n.* **1** a branched support or holder for candles or other lights, often one of several surrounding a mirror. **2** a rotating jet of water. **3** rotating fireworks. [< French *girandole* < Italian *girandola* fireworks circle (diminutive) < *giranda* fire circle < *girare* turn in a circle < Late Latin *gȳrāre* < Latin *gȳrus* circle < Greek *gyros*]

gir|a|sol or **gir|a|sole** (jir'ə sol, -sōl), *n.* **1** a whitish opal with fiery lights; fire opal. **2** = Jerusalem artichoke. Also, **girosol.** [< Italian *girasole* < *girare* (see etym. under **girandole**) + *sole* sun < Latin *sōl, sōlis*]

gird¹ (gėrd), *v.,* **girt** or **gird|ed, gird|ing.** —***v.t.*** **1** to put a belt or girdle around: *The pirate girded his waist with a broad belt and stuffed a knife in it.* **2** to fasten with a belt or girdle: *to gird up one's clothes.* **3** to equip with a sword or weapon suspended from the belt. **4** to surround; enclose. **5** *Figurative.* to get ready for action: *to gird oneself to face an examination. The soldiers girded themselves for battle.* **6** *Figurative.* to clothe; furnish; endue: *The Son On his great expedition now appear'd, Girt with omnipotence* (Milton).
—***v.i.*** *Figurative.* to get ready; prepare: *"It's an invisible enemy we face," said a police chief in the north, girding for what everyone believes will be new "troubles"* (New York Times).
gird (up) one's loins. See under **loin.**
[Old English *gyrdan*]

gird² (gėrd), *v., n. Especially British.* —***v.i.*** to jeer; sneer; scoff.
—***v.t.*** to sneer at; mock; taunt.
—***n.*** a sharp or biting remark.
[Middle English *girden, gurden;* origin uncertain]

***gird|er¹** (gėr'dər), *n.* a main supporting beam, made of steel, concrete, or wood. The weight of a floor is usually supported by girders. A tall building or big bridge often has steel girders for its frame. [< *gird¹* + *-er¹*]

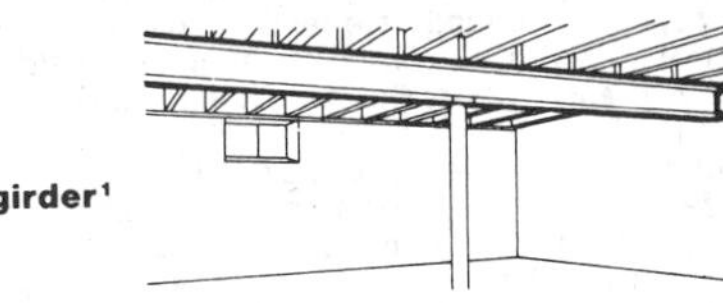
***girder¹**

gird|er² (gėr'dər), *n.* a person who girds or gibes. [< *gird²* + *-er¹*]

gir|dle¹ (gėr'dəl), *n., v.,* **-dled, -dling.** —***n.*** **1** a belt, sash, or cord worn around the waist. **2** *Figurative.* anything that surrounds or encloses: *a girdle of trees around a pond.* **3** a light corset worn about the hips and waist to support or shape the body. **4** a ring made around a tree trunk by cutting the bark: *All of them eventually die, provided the girdle be carefully cut through the sap into the heartwood of the tree* (J. Lorain). **5** *Anatomy.* a bony support for the limbs: *The shoulder girdle supports the arms, and the pelvic girdle, the legs.* **6** the rim around a diamond or other cut stone dividing upper and lower parts.
—***v.t.*** **1** to surround; encircle: *Wide roads girdle the city.* SYN: encompass. **2** to cut away the bark so as to make a ring around (a tree or branch). **3** to put a girdle on or around.
[Old English *gyrdel* < *gyrdan* gird¹]

gir|dle² (gėr'dəl), *n. Scottish.* a griddle.

gir|dler (gėr'dlər), *n.* **1** a person or thing that surrounds or encloses. **2** a beetle which cuts away bark around twigs. **3** a maker of girdles or belts.

girl (gėrl), *n.* **1** a female child from birth to about eighteen: *The new baby girl is adored by her brothers.* **2** a young unmarried woman: *Many girls hold a job before they get married.* SYN: maiden. **3** a female servant: *A girl comes in and cleans the room up each morning.* SYN: maid. **4** *Informal.* a sweetheart: *He is very much in love with his girl.* **5** *Informal.* a woman of any age. **6** *Informal.* any female animal. [Middle English *gurle, girle* child, young person; origin uncertain. Compare Low German *göre* child.]

girl|cott (gėrl'kot), *v.t. U.S.* to subject to a women's boycott. [< *girl* + (boy)*cott*]

girl Friday, *Informal.* a very versatile and loyal secretary: *Competition for these skilled girl Fridays has been about as intense as the corporate hunt for engineers* (Wall Street Journal). [patterned on *man Friday*]

Pronunciation Key: hat, āge, cãre, fär; let, ēqual, tėrm; it, īce; hot, ōpen, ôrder; oil, out; cup, pu̇t, rüle; child; long; thin; ᴛʜen; zh, measure; ə represents **a** in about, **e** in taken, **i** in pencil, **o** in lemon, **u** in circus.

girl|friend (gėrl′frend′), *n., or* **girl friend**, *Informal.* **1** a boy's sweetheart or a man's woman companion. **2** a female friend.

girl guide, a member of the Girl Guides.

Girl Guides, an international organization for girls between the ages of 7 and 18, originally founded in England, and similar to the Girl Scouts.

girl|hood (gėrl′hu̇d), *n.* **1** the time or condition of being a girl: *The old woman recalled her girlhood with pleasure.* **2** girls as a group: *the girlhood of the nation.*

girl|ie (gėr′lē), *n., adj.* **—*n.*** *Informal.* **1** a little girl. **2** any girl or woman: *Champagne, girlies, everything all polished . . .* (Vladimir Nabokov).
—*adj.* *Slang.* of or portraying girls in suggestive attire or poses: *a girlie magazine.*

girlie show, *Slang.* a burlesque show.

girl|ish (gėr′lish), *adj.* **1** of a girl: *The old woman liked to remember her girlish youth.* **2** like a girl: *The kerchief over his head made him look girlish.* **3** like that of a girl: *a slim girlish figure.* **4** suitable for girls. **—girl′ish|ly**, *adv.* **—girl′ish|ness**, *n.*

girl|less (gėrl′lis), *adj.* without a girl or girls: *It's a very girlless neighborhood* (John Masefield).

Girl Reserve, (until 1947) a Y-Teen.

girl scout, a member of the Girl Scouts.

Girl Scouts, an organization for girls that seeks to develop health, character, community participation, and skills in managing a home. It was formed as Girl Guides in 1912 at Savannah, Georgia, and became Girl Scouts the next year.

girl|y (gėr′lē), *adj.* = girlie.

girn (gėrn, girn), *v., n. Scottish.* **—*v.i.*** to show the teeth; snarl. **—*v.t.*** to utter in a snarling tone.
—*n.* a snarl; whine.
[variant of *grin*]

gi|ro[1] (jī′rō), *n., pl.* **-ros**. = autogiro.

Gi|ro or **gi|ro**[2] (jī′rō, zhir′ō), *n.* a post-office service in Great Britain and various European countries, which provides subscribers with a computerized system of money transfer similar to a checking account. [< German *Giro* < Italian *giro* circulation, ultimately < Greek *gyros* circle]

Gi|ron|dist (jə ron′dist), *n.* a member of a French political party of moderate republicans from 1791 to 1793. [< French *Girondiste* < *Gironde*, a district in France, where the party's leaders came from]

gir|o|sol (jir′ə sol, -sōl), *n.* = girasol.

girsh (girsh), *n.* an Ethiopian coin of small value. Also, **guerche**. [< Arabic *ghirsh*]

girt[1] (gėrt), *v.* a past tense and a past participle of **gird**[1]: *The knight girt himself for battle.*

girt[2] (gėrt), *v., n.* **—*v.t.*** **1** to put a belt, girdle, or girth around; gird. **2** to fasten with a belt, girdle, or girth. **—*v.i.*** to measure a certain amount in girth: *The tree 'girts' eighteen and a half feet, and spreads over a hundred* (Oliver Wendell Holmes). [< noun]
—*n.* **1** the measure around anything. **2** *Dialect.* a saddle girth. [variant of *girth*[1]]

girth[1] (gėrth), *n., v.* **—*n.*** **1** the measure around anything: *a man of large girth, the girth of a tree.* **SYN:** circumference. **2** a strap or band that keeps a saddle or pack in place on the back of a horse or other animal: *Always check the girth yourself before you get on a horse* (Harper's). **3** = girdle.
—*v.t.* **1** to fasten with a strap or band. **2** to surround; girdle; enclose. **SYN:** encircle.
—*v.i.* to measure a certain amount in girth.
[< Scandinavian (compare Old Icelandic *gjörth* girdle)]

girth[2] (gėrth), *n.* = grith. [variant of *grith*]

gi|sarme (gi zärm′), *n.* a medieval weapon consisting of a long pointed blade sharpened on both sides set at the end of the shaft. Often the blade had a hook on one side and a projecting point on the other. [< Old French *grisarme* or *gisarne*, perhaps < Germanic (compare Old High German *getan* weeding + *isarn* iron)]

gis|mo (giz′mō), *n., pl.* **-mos**. *U.S. Slang.* gizmo.

gist (jist), *n.* **1** the essential part; real point; main idea; substance of a longer statement: *The gist of his long speech was that we should build a new school.* **SYN:** essence, pith. **2** the basis for a legal action. [< Old French *gist* (it) consists (in), depends (on) < Latin *jacet* it lies, third person singular present indicative active of *jacēre*]

git (git), *v. Dialect.* get.

gi|ta|na (hē tä′nä), *n., pl.* **-nas** (-näs). *Spanish.* a Gypsy woman.

gi|ta|no (hē tä′nō), *n., pl.* **-nos** (-nōs). *Spanish.* a Gypsy man.

git|ter (git′ər), *n. Physics.* a diffraction grating. [< German *Gitter* lattice, grating]

git|tern (git′ərn), *n.* an old musical instrument with wire strings, somewhat like a guitar. [< Old French *guiterne*, apparently alteration of Latin *cithara* cithara]

give (giv), *v.*, **gave**, **giv|en**, **giv|ing**, *n.* **—*v.t.*** **1** to hand over as a present without pay: *to give money to charity. He likes to give books to his friends. My brother gave me his watch.* **2** to hand over; deliver: *to give a person into custody, give one's word. Give me that pencil. Please give me a drink.* **3** to hand over in return for something; pay: *He gave $3 for the wagon. I gave it to him for $3. This employer gives good wages.* **4** to let have; cause to have; grant: *Don't give the teacher any trouble. Give me permission to leave. Its deep seclusion gives it a peculiar charm* (John Tyndall). **SYN:** allow, cause, create. **5** to cause by some action of the body; deal; administer: *Some boys give hard blows, even in play.* **6** to offer; present: *to give a recital, give a lecture. This newspaper gives a full story of the game.* **SYN:** deliver. **7** to put forth; utter: *He gave a cry of pain.* **SYN:** emit, issue. **8** to furnish; supply: *to give more light, give a party, give aid to the enemy. This farm gives good crops. His reading gives him knowledge.* **SYN:** provide, produce. **9** to exhibit; show: *The house gave no sign of life.* **SYN:** manifest. **10** to make; do: *to give a start.* **11** to dedicate; devote: *Please give me your attention.* **12** to sacrifice; relinquish; surrender: *to give one's life, to give ground.*
—*v.i.* **1** to make a gift or present: *We give to several charities. It is more blessed to give than to receive* (Acts 20:35). **2** to yield to pressure or strain: *The lock gave under hard pushing against the door.* **3** to adapt oneself; adjust itself: *The passengers gave to the motion of the ship.* **4** to provide a view or passage; open; lead: *This window gives upon the courtyard.*
—*n.* **1** a yielding to force or pressure: *I could hear another sound—the slow sighing give of the floorboards* (Atlantic). **2** resilience; elasticity.
give away, *Informal.* **a** to give as a present: *She gave away her best toy.* **b** to hand over (a bride) to a bridegroom in marriage: *The bride was given away by her father.* **c** to cause to be known; reveal; betray: *A liar's eyes, breathing, heartbeat, and perspiration sometimes give him away* (Irving Younger). **d** to let slip (a secret) through carelessness or stupidity: *General Sherman would not be told a secret. He said he would give it away to the first person he met* (Boston Journal).
give back, to return; restore: *Give back the book you borrowed.*
give ground. See under **ground**[1].
give in, **a** to stop fighting and admit defeat; yield: *A stubborn person will not give in easily even when he's wrong.* **b** to hand in: *Names of competitors must be given in before the end of the month.*
give it the gun. See under **gun**[1].
give it to, *Informal.* to punish or scold: *His mother gave it to him for messing up the house.*
give off, to send out; put forth: *This lamp gives off a very bright light.*
give or take, to add or subtract (a part): *My income was $3,500, give or take the price of a beer* (Powell Smiley).
give out, **a** to send out; put forth: *The bomb fell, giving out a huge flash of fire.* **b** to distribute: *The supplies will be given out tomorrow.* **c** to make known; announce: *Who has given out this information? It was given out that Germany and Austria had the same policy in Europe* (Manchester Examiner). **d** to become used up or worn out: *His strength gave out after the long climb. Our money gave out.*
give over, **a** to hand over; deliver: *Colonel Lambert gave over the young Virginian to Mr. Wolfe's charge* (Thackeray). **b** to devote: *The main body of his book is given over to analyzing . . . three writers* (Listener). **c** to stop: *They ran hastily beside the carriage, but got nothing, and finally gave over* (Hawthorne).
give tongue. See under **tongue**.
give up, **a** to hand over; deliver; surrender: *He went to the police station to give himself up.* **b** to stop having or doing; abandon; relinquish: *We gave up the search when it got dark.* **c** to stop trying: *Don't give up so soon; try again and maybe you will succeed this time. They have been . . . very near giving up in despair* (Jonathan Swift). **d** to have no more hope for: *The doctors gave him up.* **e** to devote entirely: *She has given herself up to the study of music.*
give way. See under **way**.
what gives? *Informal.* what is happening? *"Hey, what gives?" demanded the men from security. "This is security!"* (Punch).
[Middle English *given*, alteration of earlier *yiven*, *yeven* (Old English *giefan*) influenced by Scandinavian (compare Old Danish *givæ*)]
—*Syn.* *v.t.* **1 Give**, **present**, **confer** mean to hand over or deliver as a gift. **Give** is the general word: *He gave me these books.* **Present** means to give in a formal way, often with ceremony: *The Chamber of Commerce presented a trophy to the football team.* **Confer** means to give in a kindly or courteous way, particularly as an honor or favor: *The university conferred an honorary degree on the distinguished journalist. She conferred her smiles on the admiring crowd.*

give-and-take (giv′ən tāk′), *n.* **1** an even or fair exchange; mutual concession. **2** good-natured banter; exchange of talk.

give|a|way (giv′ə wā′), *n., adj. Informal.* **—*n.*** **1** something revealed or made known unintentionally; exposure; betrayal. **2** something given away or sold at a cheap price to promote business or good relations: *Our sales drive features giveaways and discounts.* **3** a radio or television show in which contestants receive prizes. **4a** financial aid or subsidy without the requirement of repayment: *But when the four years were up the foreign giveaway continued* (Newsweek). **b** relinquishment of a right or property without compensation regarded as adequate: *a giveaway of the region's natural resources* (New York Times). **5** a game of checkers or the like in which the object is to lose.
—*adj.* of or having to do with a giveaway: *giveaway prices.*

give|back (giv′bak′), *n. U.S.* the cancellation of an employee benefit granted in a previous labor union contract, often in return for an increase in wages or other concession by management: *New York City and its Transit Authority are both demanding givebacks to compensate for pay increases sought by their unions* (New York Times).

giv|en (giv′ən), *adj., n., v.* **—*adj.*** **1** that has been stated; fixed; specified: *You must finish the test at a given time.* **2** having a fondness or habit; inclined; disposed: *A braggart is given to boasting.* **SYN:** addicted. **3** assigned as a basis of calculating, reasoning, etc.; assumed: *The given radius being 4 ft., find the circumference.* **4** executed, dated, and delivered: *This document given under my hand, February 1, 1787.*
—*n.* something fixed or specified as a premise; a given fact: *The need for organization, for a technical hierarchy . . . These are the "givens" of current civilization that cannot be dreamed, wished or shouted away* (Time).
—*v.* the past participle of **give**: *That book was given to me.*

given name, the name given to a person in addition to his family name; first name. *John* is the given name of *John Smith.*

giv|er (giv′ər), *n.* a person who gives; donor: *It is the giver, and not the gift, that engrosses the heart* (Henry Kollock).

give-up (giv′up′), *n.* **1** an announcement by a broker of the name of the person for whom he is acting, who is thereby obligated by custom to carry out the bargain. **2** *U.S.* a practice in the stock market in which a financial institution, such as a mutual fund, instructs its broker to yield part of a commission to another broker.

giz|mo (giz′mō), *n., pl.* **-mos**. *U.S. Slang.* a gadget; device; contraption. [origin unknown]

*****giz|zard** (giz′ərd), *n.* **1** a bird's second stomach where the food from the first stomach is ground up fine; ventriculus. The gizzard has thick, rough walls and usually contains bits of sand or gravel. **2** a muscular organ posterior to the crop in insects, earthworms, and some other animals, that serves to grind up the food. **3** *Informal.* a person's stomach or viscera. [Middle English *gyser* < Old French *guiser* < Latin *gigeria* or *gizeria* (cooked) entrails of a fowl]

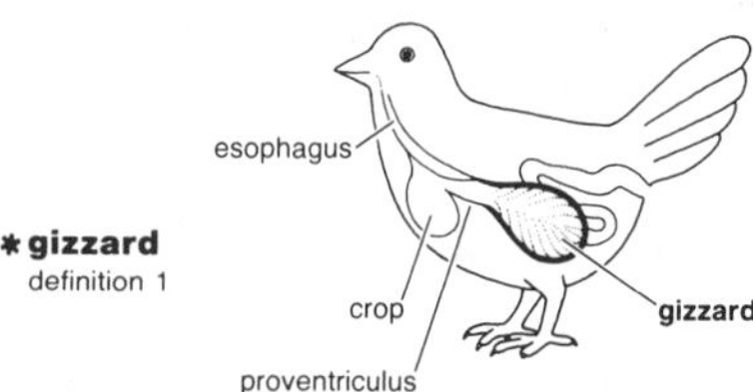

*** gizzard**
definition 1

gizzard shad, any one of various sluggish fishes inhabiting fresh and brackish waters of the Atlantic coast of North America and the eastern coasts of Asia and Australia. They feed in mud and have a muscular gizzard.

gje|tost (gā′tost, yā′-), *n.* a hard, sweet, brown Norwegian whey cheese made from goat's milk. [< Norwegian *gjetost* < *gjet* goat + *ost* cheese]

Gk., Greek.

Gl (no period), glucinum (beryllium).

gla|bel|la (glə bel′ə), *n., pl.* **-bel|lae** (-bel′ē). the small space on the forehead immediately above and between the eyebrows. [< New Latin *glabella*, special use of feminine of Latin *glabellus*, adjective (diminutive) < *glaber* smooth]

gla|bel|lar (glə bel′ər), *adj.* of or having to do with the glabella.

gla|brous (glā′brəs), *adj.* without hair or down; smooth: *Nasturtiums have glabrous stems.* [< Latin *glaber* smooth + English *-ous*]

gla|cé (gla sā′), *adj.* **1** covered with sugar, frosting, or icing; candied. **2** frozen. **3** finished with a glossy surface. [< French *glacé,* past participle of *glacer* to ice, impart a gloss to < Latin *glaciāre* < *glaciēs* ice]

gla|cial (glā′shəl), *adj.* **1** of ice or glaciers; having much ice or many glaciers: *During the glacial period, much of the Northern Hemisphere was covered with great ice sheets.* **2** of or having to do with a glacial epoch or period. **3** made by the pressure and movement of ice or glaciers. **4** like ice; very cold; icy: (*Figurative.*) *a distant glacial manner.* **SYN**: freezing, frigid. **5** *Figurative.* like that of a glacier; very slow: *Cars moved at glacial speed* (New York Times). **6** *Chemistry.* having an icelike form: *glacial acetic acid.* [< Latin *glaciālis* < *glaciēs* ice] —**gla′cial|ly**, *adv.*

glacial drift, clay, gravel, sand, or other rock material transported or deposited by a glacier.

glacial epoch, **1** any one of the times when much of the earth was covered with glaciers; ice age. **2** the most recent time when much of the Northern Hemisphere was covered with glaciers; Pleistocene.

glacial period, the period that includes the glacial epochs; ice age.

gla|ci|ar|i|um (glā′shē ãr′ē əm), *n., pl.* **-i|a** (-ē ə). a skating rink with a floor of artificial ice. [< Latin *glaciēs* ice + English *-arium,* as in *aquarium*]

gla|ci|ate (glā′shē āt), *v.t.,* **-at|ed, -at|ing. 1** to cover with ice or glaciers. **2** to act on or form by ice or glaciers: *a glaciated valley.* **3** to freeze. [< Latin *glaciāre* (with English *-ate*[1]) < *glaciēs* ice]

gla|ci|a|tion (glā′shē ā′shən), *n.* the act or process of covering or state of being covered with ice; glacial action or effect.

***gla|cier** (glā′shər), *n.* a large mass of ice formed from snow on high ground and moving very slowly down a mountain or along a sloping valley, or spreading slowly over a large area of land until it melts or breaks up. Glaciers can form wherever winter snowfall exceeds summer melting over many years. [< French *glacier* < *glace* ice, ultimately < Latin *glaciēs*]

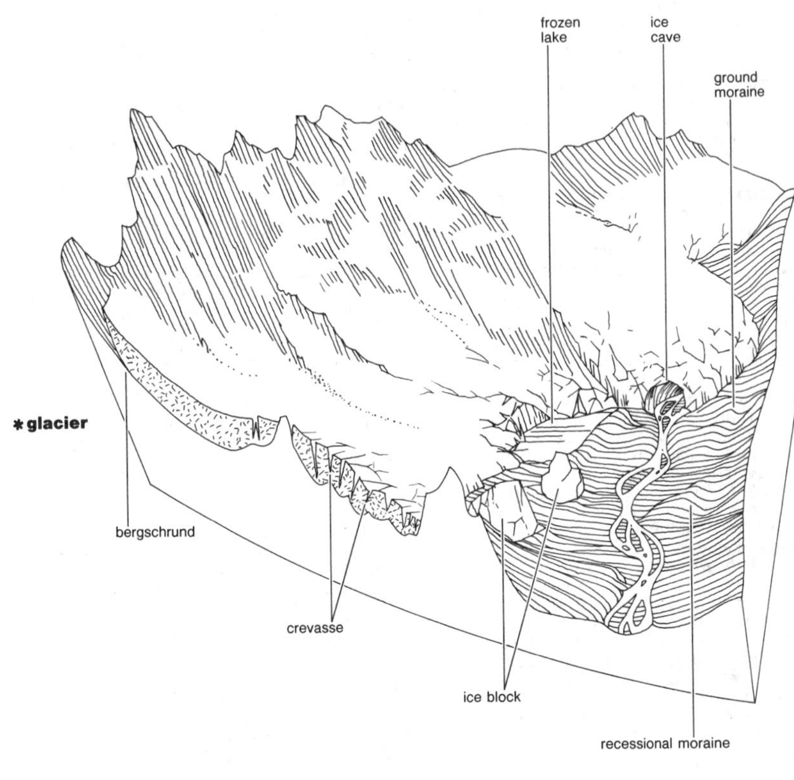

***glacier**

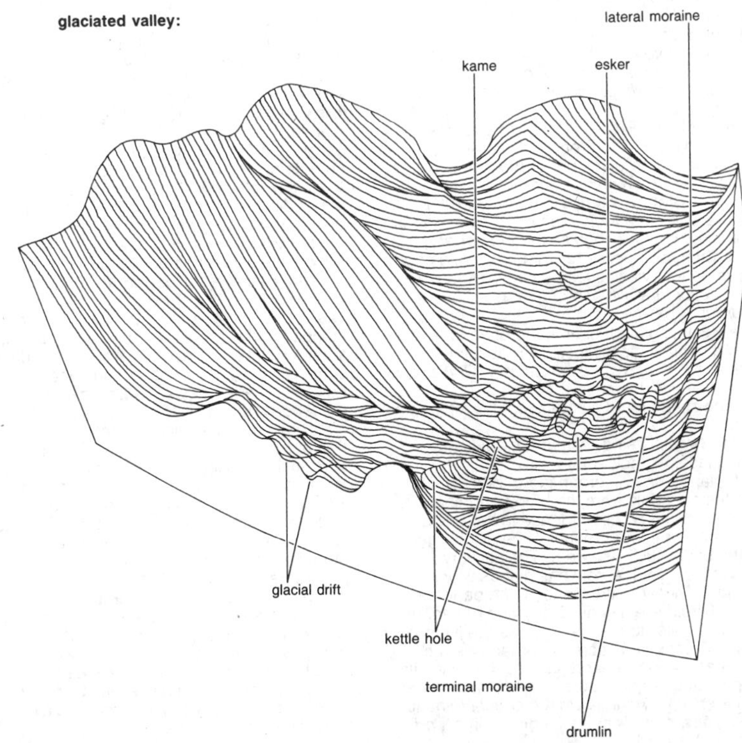

glaciated valley:

glacier bear, = blue bear.

gla|ciered (glā′shərd), *adj.* having glaciers.

gla|cier|ize (glā′shə rīz), *v.t.,* **-ized, -iz|ing.** = glaciate. —**gla′cier|i|za′tion**, *n.*

glacier lily, a dogtooth violet of the Rocky Mountains; snow lily.

glacier theory, *Geology.* the geological theory, now generally accepted, that large areas of the Northern Hemisphere were once covered by glacial ice that moved great masses of sand, gravel, and rock from one place to another.

gla|ci|o|flu|vi|al (glā′shē ō flü′vē əl, -sē-), *adj.* of or produced by glaciers and rivers: *a glaciofluvial plain.* [< Latin *glaciēs* ice + English *fluvial*]

gla|ci|o|la|cus|trine (glā′shē ō lə kus′trin, -sē-), *adj.* of or produced by glaciers and lakes: *glaciolacustrine deposits.* [< Latin *glaciēs* ice + English *lacustrine*]

gla|ci|o|log|ic (glā′shē ə loj′ik, -sē-), *adj.* = glaciological.

gla|ci|o|log|i|cal (glā′shē ə loj′ə kəl, -sē-), *adj.* of or having to do with glaciology: *The glaciological studies will also help to establish the earth's heat balance more accurately* (Science News Letter).

gla|ci|ol|o|gist (glā′shē ol′ə jist, -sē-), *n.* a person who studies glaciology.

gla|ci|ol|o|gy (glā′shē ol′ə jē, -sē-), *n.* the science that deals with glaciers and glacial action: *Glaciology is a relatively new subject for the U.S. to be concerned with; but in the Antarctic it, in effect, describes the continent* (Bulletin of Atomic Scientists).
[< Latin *glaciēs* ice + English *-logy*]

gla|cis (glā′sis, glas′is), *n., pl.* **-cis** or **-cis|es. 1** a gentle slope: *The entire edifice was surrounded by a glacis, or slope, which forced attackers to climb uphill to reach the fortress* (Scientific American). **2** a bank of earth in front of the counterscarp of a fortification, having a gradual slope toward the field or open country. [< French *glacis* (originally) slippery place < *glacer* freeze, make icy < Latin *glaciāre* < *glaciēs* ice]

glad[1] (glad), *adj.,* **glad|der, glad|dest,** *v.,* **glad|ded, glad|ding.** —***adj.*** **1** feeling joy, pleasure, or satisfaction; happy; pleased: *She is glad to see us.* **2** cheerful; merry: *a troop of damsels glad* (Tennyson). **SYN**: joyful, joyous. **3** bringing joy; pleasant: *The glad news made her happy.* **4** bright; gay: *The glad sunshine cheered us.* **5** willing; ready: *I will be glad to go if you need me.*
—***v.t.*** *Archaic.* to make glad: *The hour's gone by, When Albion's lessening shores could grieve or glad mine eye* (Byron).
—***v.i.*** *Obsolete.* to become glad.
[Old English *glæd* bright, joyous] —**glad′ly**, *adv.* —**glad′ness**, *n.*
—***Syn.*** *adj.* **1 Glad, happy** mean feeling pleasure or joy. **Glad**, which is not ordinarily used before the noun when describing people (as distinct from their looks, etc.), particularly suggests feeling pleasure or delight: *She was glad that everything was going so well.* **Happy** particularly suggests feeling deeply and fully contented and at peace: *He will never be happy until he has paid all his debts.*

glad[2] (glad), *n. Informal.* a gladiolus.

glad|den (glad′ən), *v.t.* to make glad: *He was gladdened by the good news.* **SYN**: enliven, delight. See syn. under **cheer**. —***v.i.*** *Archaic.* to become glad. —**glad′den|er**, *n.*

glade (glād), *n.* **1** a little open space in a wood or forest: *She guided them through the wood to a little open glade ... surrounded by trees and bushes* (Scott). **2** *U.S.* a marshy tract of low ground covered with grass; everglade. **3** *U.S. Dialect.* an opening in the ice of a river or lake. **4** *U.S. Dialect.* a stretch of smooth ice. [probably related to **glad**[1], in the sense of "bright"]

glad eye, *U.S. Slang.* a flirtatious look: *"She started giving me the glad eye, but I don't go for that obvious stuff"* (Time).

glad-hand (glad′hand′), *n., v. Informal.* —***n.*** a friendly or cheerful greeting; readiness to shake hands: ... *moved about with a big smile and glad-hand* (Time).
—***v.t.*** to greet in a cheerful and friendly manner: *The Foreign Office ... now sends a couple of bowler-hatted chappies to port and airport to glad-hand arriving American journalists* (Saturday Review).

Pronunciation Key: hat, āge, cãre, fär; let, ēqual, tėrm; it, īce; hot, ōpen, ôrder; oil, out; cup, pu̇t, rüle; child; long; thin; ᴛʜen; zh, measure; ə represents **a** in about, **e** in taken, **i** in pencil, **o** in lemon, **u** in circus.

–*v.i.* to give a friendly or cheerful greeting: *Some . . . forsook our birthday glad-handing for the ocean and the beaches* (Maclean's). –**glad′-hand′er**, *n.*

glad|i|ate (glad′ē āt, glā′dē-), *adj. Botany.* sword-shaped. [< Latin *gladius* sword + English *-ate*[1]]

glad|i|a|tor (glad′ē ā′tər), *n.* **1** a slave, captive, or paid fighter who fought at the public shows in the arenas in ancient Rome. **2** a skilled contender in any fight or struggle: (*Figurative.*) *Intellectual gladiators, each trying his strength against the rest* (Richard F. Burton). [< Latin *gladiātor* < *gladius* sword]

glad|i|a|to|ri|al (glad′ē ə tôr′ē əl, -tōr′-), *adj.* **1** of or having to do with gladiators or their combats. **2** *Figurative.* of or having to do with debates or disputes.

glad|i|o|la (glad′ē ō′lə, glə dī′ə-), *n.* = gladiolus. [variant of *gladiolus* (perhaps misunderstood as *gladiolas,* plural)]

glad|i|o|lus (glad′ē ō′ləs, glə dī′ə-), *n., pl.* **-li** (-lī), **-lus|es.** **1** a plant with spikes of large, silky, handsome flowers in various colors and with sword-shaped leaves growing from bulblike underground stems. It belongs to the iris family. See picture under **iris family. 2** the spike or flower of this plant. **3** *Anatomy.* the bladelike intermediate segments of the breastbone, as in man. [< Latin *gladiolus* iris (diminutive) < *gladius* sword]

glad rags, *Slang.* one's best or most elegant clothes.

glad|some (glad′səm), *adj.* **1** glad; joyful; cheerful: *like gladsome buds in May* (Wordsworth). **2** causing gladness; pleasant; delightful: *the gladsome light of Jurisprudence* (Sir Edward Coke). –**glad′some|ly**, *adv.* –**glad′some|ness**, *n.*

Glad|stone (glad′stōn, -stən), *n.* **1** a four-wheeled carriage with a folding top, two inside seats, and outside seats for the driver and footman. **2** = Gladstone bag. [< William Ewart *Gladstone,* 1809-1898, a British statesman]

***Gladstone bag,** a traveling bag that opens flat into two equal compartments.

***Gladstone bag**

Glad|sto|ni|an (glad stō′nē ən), *adj.* of or characteristic of William Ewart Gladstone, Prime Minister four times in the reign of Queen Victoria: . . . *the Gladstonian view that Britain has somehow a more moral conception of the world order than other selfish powers* (Listener).

Glag|o|lit|ic (glag′ə lit′ik), *adj.* denoting or having to do with an old Slavonic alphabet displaced by the Cyrillic but still used in the liturgy books of the Roman Catholics of Dalmatia. [< Serbo-Croatian *glagolica* < Old Church Slavic *glagolŭ* word]

glaik|it or **glaik|et** (glā′kit), *adj. Scottish and North English.* foolish; thoughtless; flighty.

glair (glãr), *n., v.* –*n.* **1** the raw white of an egg or any similar viscous substance. **2** a glaze or size made from it, used in bookbinding, etc. –*v.t.* to smear with glair. [< Old French *glaire* < Vulgar Latin *clāria* < Latin *clārus* clear]

glair|e|ous (glãr′ē əs), *adj.* = glairy.

glair|y (glãr′ē), *adj.,* **glair|i|er, glair|i|est. 1** like glair; sticky; viscous. **2** covered with glair. –**glair′i|ness**, *n.*

glaive (glāv), *n. Archaic.* a sword; broadsword. Also, **glave.** [< Old French *glaive* (originally) lance < Latin *gladius* sword]

glaived (glāvd), *adj.* armed with a glaive. Also, **glaved.**

glam (glam), *n. Informal.* glamour: *A champagne reception before the awards had the glitz and glam the Genies need, and the stars turned out in relative force* (Maclean's).

glam|or (glam′ər), *n.* = glamour.
▶See **glamour** for usage note.

glam|or|ise (glam′ə rīz), *v.t.,* **-ised, -is|ing.** *Especially British.* glamorize.

glam|or|ize (glam′ə rīz), *v.t.,* **-ized, -iz|ing. 1** to make (someone or something) glamorous; glorify: *This glamorizing of the presidency is the work of that bureaucratic elite which wants to rule the United States in the protecting shadow of a loved and trusted symbol* (Time). **2** to invest with glory or romance; glorify: *Bottom and his rustic cronies are not glamorized but appear to the strains of boisterous German band music* (Newsweek). –**glam′or|i|za′tion**, *n.* –**glam′or|iz′er**, *n.*

glam|or|ous (glam′ər əs, glam′rəs), *adj.* full of glamour; fascinating; charming: *a glamorous actress. That thought shone out . . . like a glamorous flower* (John Galsworthy). –**glam′or|ous|ly**, *adv.* –**glam′or|ous|ness**, *n.*

glam|our (glam′ər), *n., v., adj.* –*n.* **1** a mysterious fascination; alluring charm; magic attraction: *The glamour of Hollywood draws many young people there every year.* **2** a magic spell or influence; enchantment: *Like that maiden in the tale Whom Gwydion made by glamour out of flowers* (Tennyson). –*v.t.* to bewitch, charm.
–*adj.* having special appeal to investors: *Glamour and conglomerate issues continued to twitch erratically. Among the more active stocks, Republic rose 3⅝, to 61¾; Control Data declined 2⅛, to 122, and Whittaker Corporation rose 3¾, to 74* (New York Times).
glamours, shares of glamour stock: *Analysts said profit-taking was apparent in glamours* (London Times).
[originally Scottish, alteration of *grammar* or its variant *gramarye* occult learning; a spell]
▶The spelling **glamor** is making slow but steady headway. The adjective is usually *glamorous.*

glamour boy, *Informal.* a glamorous man; a very attractive and fashionable young man.

glamour girl, *Informal.* a glamorous girl or young woman; a very attractive and fashionable girl.

glam|our|ize (glam′ə rīz), *v.t.,* **-ized, -iz|ing.** = glamorize.

glam|our|ous (glam′ər əs, glam′rəs), *adj.* = glamorous. –**glam′our|ous|ly**, *adv.*

glam|our|puss (glam′ər pu̇s′), *n. Slang.* a glamorous person; person with a very attractive face.

glam|ours (glam′ərz), *n.pl.* See under **glamour.**

glamour stock, *U.S.* shares of stock having special public appeal, usually issued by small companies in fields such as electronics and aircraft.

glance[1] (glans, gläns), *n., v.,* **glanced, glanc|ing.** –*n.* **1** a quick look: *I gave him only a glance. He looked over the papers with a hasty glance. She was prettier than she had seemed at first glance.* **2** a flash of light; gleam: *The silver light, with quivering glance, Played on the water's still expanse* (Scott). **3** a glancing off; deflected motion; slanting movement: *the glance of a bullet after hitting a wall.* **4** *Figurative.* a passing reference; brief allusion. **5** *Cricket.* a stroke in which the ball is made to glance off the bat.
–*v.i.* **1** to look quickly: *I glanced out of the window to see if the rain had stopped.* **2** to flash with light; gleam: *glancing eyes. An insane light glanced in her heavy black eyes* (Harriet Beecher Stowe). **3** to hit and go off at a slant: *The spear glanced off his shield.* **4** *Figurative.* to make a short reference and go on to something else: *He had written verse, wherein he glanced at a certain reverend doctor, famous for dullness* (Jonathan Swift). –*v.t.* **1** to cause to look quickly: *glancing his severe eye around the group* (Hawthorne). **2** to catch a glimpse of; see at a glance: *The man glanced the burglar climbing out of the window.* **3** to reflect as a flash or gleam: *The bink [bench] glanced back the flame of the lamp merrily* (Scott). **4** to cause to hit and go off at a slant. **5** *Cricket.* to deflect (the ball) with a glance. **6** *Obsolete, Figurative.* to make a short reference to; suggest; hint: *Alone, it was the subject of my theme; In company, I often glanced it* (Shakespeare).
[variant of Middle English *glacen* to graze, strike a glancing blow < Old French *glacier* to slip, make slippery (see etym. under **glacis**); perhaps influenced by Dutch *glans* brightness]
–*Syn. n.* **1 Glance, glimpse** mean a quick look. **Glance** applies to a look directed at someone or something: *I could recognize the old car at a glance.* **Glimpse** applies to what is seen, a short, quick, imperfect view, such as can be seen in a glance: *I caught a glimpse of him as he turned the corner.*

glance[2] (glans, gläns), *n.* any one of various minerals with a high, glassy luster. [in obsolete *glance-ore* < Dutch *glans* < German *Glanz* (originally) brightness, luster]

glance coal, any hard, lustrous coal, such as anthracite.

glanc|ing|ly (glan′sing lē, glän′-), *adv.* in a glancing fashion; incidentally.

gland[1] (gland), *n.* **1** an organ in the body which separates materials from the blood and changes them into some secretion for use in the body, such as bile, or into a product to be discharged from the body, such as sweat. The salivary glands make saliva. A cow has glands which make milk. The liver, the kidneys, the pancreas and the thyroid are glands. **2** any one of various structures similar to glands, such as the lymph nodes. **3** *Botany.* **a** a secreting organ or structure, generally on or near a surface. **b** any similar swelling that does not secrete. [< French *glande* < Old French *glandre* < Latin *glandula* (diminutive) < *glāns, glandis* acorn] –**gland′like′**, *adj.*

gland[2] (gland), *n.* **1** the adjustable part of a stuffing box, by which the packing is compressed. **2** a device for clamping parts together. [< French *glande;* see etym. under **gland**[1]]

glan|dered (glan′dərd), *adj.* affected with glanders.

glan|ders (glan′dərz), *n.* a serious, contagious, bacterial disease of horses and mules, accompanied by fever, swellings beneath the lower jaw, and a profuse discharge from the nostrils. It can also be communicated to dogs, goats, sheep, and man. [< Old French *glandre;* see etym. under **gland**[1]. Compare Late Latin *glandulae* swollen glands.]

glan|des (glan′dēz), *n.* the plural of **glans.**

glan|dif|er|ous (glan dif′ər əs), *adj.* bearing acorns or other nuts. [< Latin *glandifer* acorn bearing (< *glāns, glandis* acorn + *ferre* to bear) + English *-ous*]

gland|i|form (glan′də fôrm), *adj.* **1** acorn-shaped. **2** like a gland.

gland|less (gland′lis), *adj.* without glands.

glan|du|lar (glan′jə lər, -dyə-), *adj.* **1** of or like a gland: *a glandular infection.* **2** having glands. **3** made up of glands: *glandular tissue.* –**glan′du|lar|ly**, *adv.*

glandular fever, = infectious mononucleosis.

glan|dule (glan′jül, -dyül), *n.* a small gland. [< Latin *glandula* (diminutive) < *glāns, glandis* acorn]

glan|du|lif|er|ous (glan′jə lif′ər əs, -dyə-), *adj.* bearing glandules.

glan|du|lose (glan′jə lōs, -dyə-), *adj.* = glandular.

glan|du|lous (glan′jə ləs, -dyə-), *adj.* = glandular. [< Latin *glandulōsus* < *glandula* gland of the throat (diminutive) < *glāns, glandis* acorn]

glans (glanz), *n., pl.* **glan|des.** *Anatomy.* the head of the penis or of the clitoris. [< Latin *glāns, glandis* acorn]

glare[1] (glãr), *n., v.,* **glared, glar|ing.** –*n.* **1** a strong, bright light; light that shines so brightly that it hurts the eyes: *When he began working with the torch . . . a few window-watchers seemed annoyed at the glare* (Newsweek). **2** a fierce, angry stare. **3** *Figurative.* too great brightness and showiness; gaudiness: *Private informal talks out of the public glare should be held* (New York Times). [< verb]
–*v.i.* **1** to give off a strong, bright light; shine so brightly as to hurt my eyes. **2** to stare fiercely and with anger: *Each upon his rival glared* (Scott). **3** *Figurative.* to be too bright or showy; be conspicuous: *These colors glare.*
–*v.t.* to express by a fierce, angry stare.
[Middle English *glaren,* perhaps < Middle Dutch *glaren* gleam]

glare[2] (glãr), *n., adj.* –*n.* a bright, smooth surface, such as a sheet of ice.
–*adj.* bright and smooth; glassy: *glare ice.*
[probably extended use of *glare*[1], noun]

glare|proof (glãr′prüf′), *adj.* permitting no glare; glareless: *a glareproof finish.*

glar|i|ness (glãr′ē nis), *n.* glary quality.

glar|ing (glãr′ing), *adj.* **1** very bright; shining so brightly that it hurts the eyes; dazzling. **SYN:** brilliant. **2** staring fiercely and angrily. **3** *Figurative.* too bright and showy: *glaring colors.* **4** *Figurative.* very easily seen; conspicuous: *The student made a glaring error in spelling.* **SYN:** obvious. –**glar′ing|ly**, *adv.* –**glar′ing|ness**, *n.*

glar|y[1] (glãr′ē), *adj.,* **glar|i|er, glar|i|est.** dazzling; glaring.

glar|y[2] (glãr′ē), *adj.,* **glar|i|er, glar|i|est.** *U.S.* smooth and slippery: *glary ice.*

glas|nost (gläs nôst′), *n.* a policy of open and public discussion of domestic issues encouraged by the Soviet government: *No explosion of glasnost in Moscow is going to allow Western scholars on-site inspection of all of Lenin's notes* (William Safire). [< Russian *glasnost'* public notice]

glass (glas, gläs), *n., adj., v.* –*n.* **1** a hard substance that breaks easily and can usually be seen through. It is made by melting sand with soda, potash, lime, or other substances. Windows are made of glass. *Glass is chemically inert; it does not rust, rot, decay, or react to most chemicals.* **2** any artificial or natural substance that has similar properties or chemical composition, such as fused borax or obsidian. **3** a container to drink from, usually made of glass: *Please fill my glass.* **4** the amount a glass can hold: *to drink a glass of water.* **5** a mirror: *Look at yourself in the glass.* **6** a lens, telescope, or other thing made of glass. A piece of glass for a picture frame, a windowpane, a watch crystal, a thermometer, a barometer, or an hourglass is a glass. **7** things made of glass; glassware: *a waggon full of fenders, fire-irons, and glass, and crockery* (Thackeray).
–*adj.* **1a** made of glass: *a glass dish.* **b** *Figurative: That boxer has a glass jaw.* **2** with glass put in; covered in glass: *a glass door.* **3** having to do with glass: *the glass trade.*

—*v.t.* **1** to put glass in; cover or protect with glass: *tranquil almost and careless as a flower glassed in a greenhouse* (Wordsworth). **2** to reflect; mirror: *Never more shall the lake glass her flying over it* (Matthew Arnold). **3** to make glassy. **4** *Obsolete.* to cover with a glasslike surface.
glasses, **a** a pair of lenses to correct defective eyesight; eyeglasses; spectacles. **b** field glasses; binoculars.
see (view, look at, or **behold) through rose-colored glasses** or **spectacles,** to regard (anything) in a highly favorable or attractive light: *Oxford was a sort of Utopia to the Captain . . . He continued to behold* [*it*] *through rose-colored spectacles* (Thomas Hughes).
[Old English *glæs*] —**glass′like′,** *adj.*

glass bell, = bell glass.

glass block, a block or brick of translucent glass used as a building material.

glass blower, a person who shapes glass by blowing while it is still hot and soft.

glass blowing, the art or process of shaping glass objects by blowing air from the mouth through a tube into a bulb of molten glass at the other end of the tube.

glass brick, = glass block.

glass ceiling, an intangible barrier that prevents a person's advancement to higher executive positions: *In climbing the corporate ladder they* [*women*] *collide with a "glass ceiling" of subtle discrimination* (New York Times).

glass-ce|ram|ic (glas′sə ram′ik, gläs′-), *n.* a material made from glass, but different from glass in having a crystallized structure. It is extremely strong and highly resistant to heat and acid.

glass cloth, cloth woven with glass fiber yarns and coated with synthetic rubber or resin.

glass|es (glas′iz, gläs′-), *n.pl.* See under **glass.**

glass eye, **1** an artificial eyeball made of glass or plastic for a person who has lost an eye. **2** a Jamaican thrush, the eye of which has a white iris. **3** = walleyed pike or perch.

glass fiber, a flexible, durable fiber made by pulling molten glass through a small opening. Glass fiber can be spun into yarns or combined with various plastics, and is used as insulation, for making such things as fabrics, boats, and fishing rods.

glass fish, any one of several small fishes, often kept in aquariums, having transparent flesh that makes the brain, gills, air bladder, and skeleton clearly visible; transparent fish.

glass|ful (glas′fu̇l, gläs′-), *n., pl.* **-fuls.** as much as a glass holds.

glass harmonica, a musical instrument consisting of a set of glasses played by rubbing a moistened finger on the rims.

glass|house (glas′hous′, gläs′-), *n.* **1** *Especially British.* a greenhouse or hothouse. **2** a factory where glass is made. **3** *British Army Slang.* a military prison.

glas|si|fy (glas′ə fī, gläs′-), *v.,* **-fied, -fy|ing.**
—*v.t.* to cover or surround with glass.
—*v.i.* to become glass or like glass: *A little sand will glassify on the cavity's sides* (Time).

glass|ine (gla sēn′, glä-), *n.* a thin but strong, nearly transparent, glazed paper, used for packaging.
[< *glass* + *-ine*[1]]

glass|less (glas′lis, gläs′-), *adj.* without glass or a glass: *a glassless window.*

glass|mak|er (glas′mā′kər, gläs′-), *n.* a person who makes glass.

glass|mak|ing (glas′mā′king, gläs′-), *n.* the art or process of making glass.

glass|man (glas′mən, gläs′-), *n., pl.* **-men. 1** = glassmaker. **2** a person who sells glassware. **3** = glazier.

glass|rope (glas′rōp′, gläs′-), *n.* the twisted, glasslike stem of a glass sponge.

glass snake, a legless, harmless, snakelike lizard of southeastern and central United States and Mexico, that grows about two feet long and has a tail twice as long as its body: *The lizard known as the glass snake escapes from its enemies by breaking off the end of its tail. It later grows a new one* (Ralph Buchsbaum).

glass sponge, any one of various sponges with glasslike, siliceous fibers: *The beautiful glass sponges live at depths of 1,500 to 15,000 feet off islands in the Pacific Ocean around the Philippines and Japan* (Science News Letter).

glass tank, a furnace in which glass is made by melting its component parts.

glas|steel (glas′stēl′, gläs′-), *adj.* made of glass and steel: *glassteel skyscrapers.*

glass|ware (glas′wãr′, gläs′-), *n.* articles made of glass.

glass wool, glass spun into very fine threads, with a texture resembling loose fibers of wool, used especially for insulation.

glass|work (glas′wėrk′, gläs′-), *n.* **1** the making of glass or glassware. **2** articles or ornaments made of glass; glassware. **3** the fitting of glass in windows, etc.; glazing.

glass|work|er (glas′wėr′kər, gläs′-), *n.* a person who works with glass.

glass|works (glas′wėrks′, gläs′-), *n.pl.* a factory where glass is made.

glass worm, = arrowworm.

glass|wort (glas′wėrt′, gläs′-), *n.* **1** a plant of the goosefoot family, with juicy, leafless stems, that grows in saltwater marshes. Its ashes were formerly used as a source of soda in making glass. **2** the common saltwort.

glass|y (glas′ē, gläs′-), *adj.,* **glass|i|er, glass|i|est,** *n., pl.* **glass|ies.** —*adj.* **1** like glass; smooth; easily seen through: *Pointing to the glassy water, which, as it rose and fell, reflected the golden glow of the sky* (Harriet Beecher Stowe). SYN: vitreous. **2** *Figurative.* having a fixed, stupid stare: *The dazed man's eyes were glassy.*
—*n.* a shooting marble; taw. —**glass′i|ly,** *adv.* —**glass′i|ness,** *n.*

glass|y-eyed (glas′ē īd′, gläs′-), *adj.* characterized by glassy eyes; dazed; stupefied.

Glas|we|gian (glas wē′jən, -jē ən; gläs-), *adj., n.* —*adj.* of Glasgow, Scotland.
—*n.* a person born or living in Glasgow.

glatt (glät), *adj.* (of kosher meat) ritually clean by the strictest standards: *a glatt kosher meal.*
[< Yiddish *glat* (literally) smooth (because of the unblemished surface of the animal's lung)]

Glau|ber salt or **salts** (glou′bər, glô′-), = Glauber's salt.

Glau|ber's salt or **salts** (glou′berz, glô′-), hydrated sodium sulfate used in dyeing and as a laxative and diuretic. *Formula:* $Na_2SO_4 \cdot 10H_2O$
[< Johann *Glauber,* 1604-1668, German chemist]

glau|ces|cent (glô ses′ənt), *adj.* somewhat glaucous. [< Latin *glaucus* bluish-green]

glau|co|ma (glô kō′mə, glou-), *n.* a disease of the eye, characterized by pressure within the eyeball, hardening of the eyeball, and gradual loss of sight. It is common in old age. [< Greek *glaukōma* an opacity of the crystalline lens; usually, cataract < *glaukós* gray, silvery]

glau|co|ma|tous (glô kō′mə təs, -kom′ə-; glou-), *adj.* having to do with or affected with glaucoma.

glau|co|nite (glô′kə nīt), *n.* a greenish mineral consisting essentially of a hydrous silicate of iron and potassium, occurring in greensand, clays, and seawater.
[< Greek *glaukón,* neuter of *glaukós* gray-green + English *-ite*[1]]

glau|co|nit|ic (glô′kə nit′ik), *adj.* like or containing glauconite.

glau|co|sis (glô kō′sis, glou-), *n.* = glaucoma.

glau|cous (glô′kəs), *adj.* **1** light bluish-green: *The glaucous caverns of old Ocean* (Shelley). **2** covered with a whitish, powdery or waxy substance, as plums and grapes are. [< Latin *glaucus* (with English *-ous*) < Greek *glaukós* gray-green, silvery]

glaucous gull, a large white gull with a bluish mantle, of circumpolar oceans; burgomaster.

Glau|cus (glô′kəs), *n. Greek Legend and Mythology.* **1** the steersman of the Argo. **2** a son of Sisyphus and father of Bellerophon. He was torn in pieces by his own mares. **3** a son of Minos and Pasiphaë. He was smothered in a jar of honey. **4** a Lycian prince, friend of Diomedes before the Trojan War. **5** a sea god who loved a nymph that later became the monster Scylla.

glave (glāv), *n.* = glaive.

glaved (glāvd), *adj.* = glaived.

glaze (glāz), *v.,* **glazed, glaz|ing,** *n.* —*v.t.* **1** to put glass in; cover with glass. Pieces of glass cut to the right size are used to glaze windows and picture frames. **2** to make a smooth, glassy surface or glossy coating: *to glaze china, to glaze a ham.* **3** to cover (a painted surface) with a thin layer of transparent color to modify the tone.
—*v.i.* to become smooth, glassy, or glossy: *The man's eyes glazed with pain.*
—*n.* **1** a smooth, glassy surface or glossy coating: *the glaze on a china cup. A glaze of ice on the walk is dangerous.* **2** a substance used to make such a surface or coating on things. **3** *Cooking.* **a** a glossy covering on a food, such as one of sugar syrup. **b** stock cooked down to a thick paste, for coating meats. **4** *U.S.* a glassy coating of ice formed by rain that freezes upon striking the ground or some other surface. **5** a thin layer of transparent color spread over a painted surface to modify the tone.
[Middle English *glasen* < *glas* glass] —**glaz′er,** *n.*

gla|zier (glā′zhər), *n.* a person whose work is putting glass in windows, picture frames, mirrors, and the like. [Middle English *glasier* < *glas* glass]

gla|zier|y (glā′zhər ē), *n.* the work of a glazier; glazing; glass fitting.

glaz|ing (glā′zing), *n.* **1** the work of a glazier. **2** glass set or to be set in frames. **3** a substance used to make a smooth, glassy surface or glossy coating on things. **4** such a surface or coating. **5** the act of applying a glaze.

glaz|y (glā′zē), *adj.* resembling glaze; glossy; glasslike: *a glazy surface.* —**glaz′i|ness,** *n.*

GLCM (no periods), ground-launched cruise missile.

Gld., guilder or guilders.

gleam (glēm), *n., v.* —*n.* **1** a flash or beam of light: *We saw the gleam of headlights through the fog.* **2** a short or faint light: *the gleam of shining metal.* **3** *Figurative.* a short appearance; faint show: *After one gleam of hope, all was discouraging and dark.*
—*v.i.* **1** to send forth a gleam; flash or beam with light: *A candle gleamed in the dark.* **2** to shine with a short or faint light: *gleaming jewelry.* **3** *Figurative.* to appear suddenly; be shown briefly.
—*v.t.* to send forth in gleams: *Dying eyes gleamed forth their ashy lights* (Shakespeare).
[Old English *glǣm*] —**gleam′ing|ly,** *adv.*
—*Syn. n.* **2 Gleam, glimmer** mean an unsteady or not bright light. **Gleam** applies to a light that comes out of the darkness and goes again soon, or is softened or toned down as if by a curtain in front of it: *At the end of the passage they saw a gleam of light.* **Glimmer** applies to a light that is fainter or more wavering than a gleam: *We saw the glimmer of a distant light through the trees.*

gleam|er (glē′mər), *n.* a cosmetic for making the skin of the face gleam.

gleam|y (glē′mē), *adj.* gleaming; flashing.

glean (glēn), *v.t.* **1** to gather (stalks of grain, ears of corn, or the like) left on a field by reapers: *They gleaned enough potatoes from the field after harvest to fill a large sack.* **2** to strip (a field) of grain, corn, or the like left by the reapers. **3** *Figurative.* to gather little by little or slowly: *The spy gleaned information by listening to the soldiers' talk.* —*v.i.* **1** to gather grain, corn, or the like left on a field by the reapers: *I pray you, let me glean and gather after the reapers* (Ruth 2:7). **2** *Figurative.* to gather anything little by little or slowly.
[< Old French *glener* < Late Latin *glennāre* make a collection < a Celtic word] —**glean′er,** *n.*

glean|ing (glē′ning), *n.* **1** the act of one that gleans. **2** that which is gleaned.
gleanings, anything that is gleaned.

gle|ba (glē′bə), *n., pl.* **-bae** (-bē). the fleshy part of certain fungi in which the spores are borne.
[< New Latin *gleba* < Latin *glēba* lump, clod]

glebe (glēb), *n.* **1** a portion of land assigned to a parish church clergyman. **2** *Archaic.* the soil; earth; field; land. [< Latin *glēba* lump of soil]

glede (glēd), *n.* **1** the common European kite. **2** any related bird, such as the osprey. [Middle English *glede,* Old English *glida.* See related etym. at **glide,** verb.]

gledge (glej), *v.,* **gledged, gledg|ing,** *n. Scottish.*
—*v.i.* to look stealthily or slyly.
—*n.* a side glance; sly look.
[origin uncertain]

glee[1] (glē), *n.* **1** lively joy; great delight; mirth; merriment: *The children laughed with glee at the clown's antics.* SYN: gaiety, jollity. **2** a song for three or more voices singing different parts, usually without instrumental accompaniment. [Old English *glēo* or *glīw*]

glee[2] (glē), *v., n. Scottish.* —*v.i.* to squint; look sideways. —*n.* a squint; side glance. Also, **gley.**
[origin uncertain]

glee club, a group, often of men only, organized for singing part songs, ballads, and glees.

gleed (glēd), *n. British Dialect.* a burning coal; ember. [Old English *glēd*]

glee|ful (glē′fəl), *adj.* filled with glee; merry; joyous. —**glee′ful|ly,** *adv.* —**glee′ful|ness,** *n.*

gleek (glēk), *v., n. Obsolete.* —*v.i.* to scoff; jeer: *I have seen you gleeking and galling at this gentleman* (Shakespeare).
—*v.t.* **1** to trick. **2** to ridicule; jibe; jest.
—*n.* a trick; taunt; jeer.
[perhaps diminutive form of *glee*[1]]

glee|man (glē′mən), *n., pl.* **-men.** *Archaic.* a singer; minstrel.

glee|some (glē′səm), *adj.* = gleeful. —**glee′some|ly,** *adv.* —**glee′some|ness,** *n.*

gleet (glēt), *n.* **1** *Medicine.* **a** an infected discharge from the urethra, usually due to gonorrhea. **b** a thin, infected discharge from a wound, ulcer, etc. **2** *Veterinary Medicine.* a chronic nasal discharge in horses and other animals. **3** *Scottish.* slimy matter. [< Old French *glete,* or *glette* slime, jelly]

gleg[1] (gleg), *adj. Scottish and Northern English.* **1** quick in perception; sharp-sighted; quick-witted. **2** quick in action. **3** lively; cheerful: *Dr. Dinwiddie was a gleg man, of a jocose nature* (John Galt). **4** sharp, as a knife. [< Scandinavian (as in Old Icelandic *gleggr*)] —**gleg′ly,** *adv.* —**gleg′ness,** *n.*

Pronunciation Key: hat, āge, cãre, fär; let, ēqual, tėrm; it, īce; hot, ōpen, ôrder; oil, out; cup, pu̇t, rüle; child; long; thin; ᴛʜen; zh, measure;
ə represents **a** in about, **e** in taken, **i** in pencil, **o** in lemon, **u** in circus.

Gleich|schal|tung (glīн′shäl′tùng), *n.* political and cultural conformity on all levels of society. The Nazis enforced a policy of Gleichschaltung. [< German *Gleichschaltung* (literally) coordination]
glei|za|tion (glā zā′shən), *n.* the process of forming gley. [< *gley*[2] + *-ization*]
glen (glen), *n.* a small, narrow valley: *Wales' green valleys [are] strangely unlike Scotland's glens or the dales of Derbyshire* (New Yorker). See picture under **valley**. [< Scottish Gaelic *gleann*]
***glen|gar|ry** (glen gar′ē), *n., pl.* **-ries**. a Scottish cap with straight sides and a creased top, often having short ribbons at the back. [< *Glengarry,* a valley in Scotland]

***glengarry**

gle|noid (glē′noid), *n., adj. Anatomy.* **—*n.*** a slightly cupped cavity on a bone in which the end of another bone rests, forming a joint.
—*adj.* of or designating such a cavity: *the glenoid cavity of the scapula.*
[< Greek *glēnoeidēs* < *glēnē* shallow joint socket + *eîdos* form]
glen plaid, a plaid cloth or design having a subdued pattern of narrow and very narrow crisscross stripes of colors not strongly contrasting. [short for *Glenurquhart plaid* < *Glenurquhart,* a valley in Scotland]
glent (glent), *v., n. British Dialect.* **—*v.i.*** **1** to glide or dart off. **2** to look quickly; glance. **3** to gleam.
—*n.* **1** a darting movement. **2** a glance; glimpse. **3** a gleam; flash.
[Middle English *glenten;* see etym. under **glint**]
gley[1] (glī, glē), *v.i., n. Scottish.* glee[2].
gley[2] (glā), *n.* a sticky, clayey soil developed under the influence of excessive moistening. [< Russian *glei*]
gli|a (glī′ə), *n.* = neuroglia.
gli|a|din (glī′ə din), *n.* a protein found in the gluten of wheat, rye, or other grain. [< French *gliadine* < Late Greek *gliā* glue]
gli|al (glī′əl), *adj.* having to do with the neuroglia.
glib (glib), *adj.,* **glib|ber, glib|best. 1** speaking or spoken smoothly and easily: *A glib salesman sold her a set of dishes that she did not want.* **SYN:** voluble, smooth-tongued. See syn. under **fluent. 2** speaking or spoken too smoothly and easily to be sincere: *No one believed his glib excuses.* **3** *Dialect.* **a** smooth and slippery: *glib ice.* **b** easy; unimpeded: *a glib movement.* [origin uncertain. Compare East Frisian *glibberig* slippery.] **—glib′ly,** *adv.* **—glib′ness,** *n.*
glide (glīd), *v.,* **glid|ed, glid|ing,** *n.* **—*v.i.*** **1** to move along smoothly, evenly, and easily: *Birds, ships, dancers, and skaters glide.* **SYN:** See syn. under **slide. 2** to pass gradually, quietly, or without being noticed: *The years glided past.* **3** to come down slowly at a slant without using a motor. Under favorable circumstances, an airplane can glide about a mile for every thousand feet that it is above the ground. **4** *Music.* to pass from one tone to another without a break; slur. **5** *Phonetics.* to produce a glide in passing from one speech sound to the next.
—*v.t.* to cause to glide.
—*n.* **1** a smooth, even, easy movement: *To hear the dip of Indian oars, The glide of birch canoes* (John Greenleaf Whittier). **2** the act or process of coming down in an airplane slowly at a slant without using a motor. **3** *Music.* = slur. **4** *Phonetics.* **a** a transition sound; a sound made in passing from one speech sound to another, such as the *p* often produced between the *m* and *th* in *warmth.* **b** a semivowel, such as the *r* in *rest,* the *w* in *west,* and the *y* in *yes.* **5** *Dancing.* **a** a step made by sliding rather than raising the foot. **b** a waltz or other dance using such steps. **6** a metal or plastic attachment under a piece of furniture to make it easy to move. **7** a smoothly flowing expanse of shallow water.
glide into, to pass by gradual or imperceptible change into a state or from one thing into another: *I suffer one moment to glide into another* (Edward G. E. L. Bulwer-Lytton).
[Old English *glīdan*]
glide bomb, a bomb fitted with airfoils to provide lift. When released, it glides toward its target.
glide bombing, bombing a target by descending upon it at an angle of less than 65 degrees.
glide path, the path followed by an aircraft or spacecraft as it descends for a landing, especially the path indicated by a radio beam in an instrument landing system.

***glid|er** (glī′dər), *n.* **1** an airplane without a motor. Rising air currents keep a glider up in the air. **2** a person or thing that glides. **3** a swinging seat suspended on a frame. Gliders are usually placed on porches or outdoors.

***glider**
definition 1

glider bomb, = glide bomb.
glide slope, = glide path.
glide vehicle, a winged missile that reenters the atmosphere at an angle flatter than that of a ballistic course and glides.
glid|ing (glī′ding), *adj.* that glides. **—glid′ing|ly,** *adv.*
gliding machine, = glider (def. 1).
glim (glim), *n., v.,* **glimmed, glim|ming. —*n.*** **1** *Slang.* a light; lamp; candle: *Sure enough they left their glim here* (Robert Louis Stevenson). **2** *Slang.* an eye. **3** *Scottish.* a little bit; scrap.
—*v.t. Slang.* to look at: *Millions of fans glim her on ... TV* (Esquire).
[apparently related to **gleam, glimmer**]
glim|mer (glim′ər), *n., v.* **—*n.*** **1** a faint, unsteady light: *The white glimmer in the distance is the lighthouse.* **SYN:** See syn. under **gleam. 2** *Figurative.* a vague idea; dim notion; faint glimpse: *The doctor's report gave us only a glimmer of hope.*
—*v.i.* **1** to shine with a faint, unsteady light: *The candle glimmered and went out.* **SYN:** twinkle, flicker. **2** to fail gradually and perceptibly. **3** to appear faintly or dimly: (*Figurative.*) *The voice came glimmering and bubbling up a flight of stone steps* (Hawthorne). (*Figurative.*) *The idea of ever recovering happiness never glimmered in her mind for a moment* (George Eliot).
[Middle English *glemeren.* See related etym. at **gleam.**]
glim|mer|ing (glim′ər ing, glim′ring), *n., adj.* **—*n.*** **1** a faint, unsteady light; glimmer. **2** a vague idea; dim notion; faint glimpse: *A few glimmerings of hope appeared in the gloom* (Newsweek).
—*adj.* that glimmers.
go glimmering, to fail gradually; flicker out: *Hopes for a good crop went glimmering in the drought.*
—glim′mer|ing|ly, *adv.*
glimpse (glimps), *n., v.,* **glimpsed, glimps|ing.**
—*n.* **1** a very brief view; short look: *I caught a glimpse of the falls as our train went by.* **SYN:** See syn. under **glance. 2** a short, faint appearance or show: *There were glimpses of truth in what he said. With looks ... wherein appear'd Obscure some glimpse of joy* (Milton). **3** *Archaic.* a flash of light; gleam: *the glimpses of the moon* (Shakespeare). **4** *Obsolete.* a slight touch; trace.
—*v.t.* to catch a brief view of: *I glimpsed the falls as our train went by.*
—*v.i.* **1** to look quickly; glance: *Father glimpsed at the picture I drew and said it was good.* **2** to shine faintly or unsteadily; glimmer: *Yet sometimes glimpses on my sight, Through present wrong, the eternal right* (John Greenleaf Whittier).
[Middle English *glimsen.* See related etym. at **glim, glimmer.**] **—glimps′er,** *n.*
glint (glint), *n., v.* **—*n.*** **1** a gleam; flash: *There was a glint in her eye that showed she was angry.* **2** a short or momentary appearance. **3** brightness; shine. **4** *Scottish.* a glance; glimpse.
—*v.i.* **1** to gleam; flash: *Under a blue sky and a glinting sun* (New York Times). **2** to move quickly. **3** to glance aside. **4** *Scottish.* to glance; look.
—*v.t.* to cause to gleam.
[Middle English *glynten, glenten,* probably < Scandinavian (compare dialectal Swedish *glänta* shine)]
gli|o|ma (glī ō′mə), *n., pl.* **-ma|ta** (-mə tə), **-mas.** a tumor arising from and consisting largely of neuroglia, usually of the brain and spinal cord. [< New Latin *glioma* < *glia* glial (connecting) cells of the central nervous system (< Late Greek *gliā* glue) + *-oma* tumor]
gli|o|ma|tous (glī ō′mə təs, -om′ə-), *adj.* of or having to do with a glioma.
glisk (glisk), *n. Scottish.* a slight look; glimpse. [perhaps < root of Old English *glisian* shine]
gliss (glis), *n. Informal.* glissando.
glis|sade (gli säd′, -sād′), *n., v.,* **-sad|ed, -sad|ing. —*n.*** **1** a slide over snow or ice in descending a mountain slope. **2** a slide down any surface: *The figure ... descended ... with the glissade of a waterdrop down a bud* (Thomas Hardy). **3** *Ballet.* a gliding or sliding step, often combined with a leap.
—*v.i.* to make a glissade; slide.
[< French *glissade* < *glisser* to slide]
glis|san|do** (gli sän′dō), *adj., n., pl.* **-di** (-dē), **-dos.** *Music.* **—*adj. performed with a gliding effect. A pianist plays a glissando passage by running one finger rapidly over the piano keys.
—*n.* a part performed with a gliding effect; glissando passage. [Italianization of French *glissant,* present participle of *glisser* to slide]

***glissando**

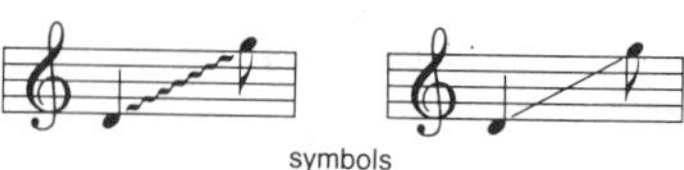
symbols

glis|ten (glis′ən), *v., n.* **—*v.i.*** to shine with a sparkling light or luster, as snow, dew, satin, or the eyes do; glitter; sparkle: *The stars glistened in the sky.* **SYN:** scintillate.
—*n.* a glitter; sparkle: *Their footsteps made no sound on the soft carpet in the deserted building in whose gloomy interior there was a soft glisten from the polished pews* (Leonard Holton).
[Old English *glisnian*] **—glis′ten|ing|ly,** *adv.*
glis|ter (glis′tər), *v., n.* **—*v.i.*** to glisten; glitter; sparkle: *All that glisters is not gold* (Shakespeare). **—*n.*** a glistening; glitter: *Still, the glister was not quite so golden* (New Yorker). [origin uncertain. Compare Middle Dutch *glisteren.*]
glitch (glich), *n., v. Slang.* **—*n.*** **1** a minor but irritating difficulty or obstacle; small foul-up: *Goofs and glitches always creep into the early blueprints for any new aircraft* (Time). **2** a sudden irregularity, such as a change in rotation, shown by a celestial body: *Some of these glitches were traced to terrestrial interference sources such as aircraft, while others remain a mystery* (New Scientist).
—*v.i.* to show or undergo a glitch: *Several times ... the Crab and Vela pulsars were observed to begin suddenly to pulse faster, or "glitch"* (Kenneth Brecher). [perhaps < Yiddish *glitsh* a slipping, *glitshen* to slip]
glit|ter (glit′ər), *v., n.* **—*v.i.*** **1** to shine with bright, sparkling light; gleam; sparkle: *The jewels and new coins glittered.* **2** to be bright and showy.
—*n.* **1** a bright, sparkling light: *There was a cold glitter in the cruel man's eyes.* **SYN:** See syn. under **flash. 2** brightness; showiness: (*Figurative.*) *Beneath all the glitter, [he] is regarded by friends as essentially still the small-town boy* (Time). **SYN:** brilliance, splendor, luster.
[perhaps < Scandinavian (compare Old Icelandic *glitra*)] **—glit′ter|er,** *n.* **—glit′ter|ing|ly,** *adv.*
glit|ter|a|ti (glit′ərä′tē, -rā′tī), *n. pl. U.S. Slang.* fashionable people, especially those who conspicuously attend to cultural endeavors and social events. [patterned on *literati*]
glit|ter|y (glit′ər ē), *adj.* glittering; sparkling.
glitz (glits), *n. Informal.* glitzy condition or appearance; showy display: *Helping [them] recreate the glitz and glitter of Paris gone-by are Richard Adams as Chevalier* (Maclean's). [back formation < *glitzy*]
glitz|y (glit′sē), *adj.,* **glitz|i|er, glitz|i|est.** *Informal.* glittering; flasy; showy: *glitzy costumes. For him, decadence is glitzy camp* (Pauline Kael). [< German *glitz(ern)* to glitter + English *-y*[1]] **—glitz′i|ness,** *n.*
gloam (glōm), *n., v.* **—*n.*** = gloaming.
—*v.i.* to grow dark. [back formation < *gloaming*]
gloam|ing (glō′ming), *n.* evening twilight; dusk. [Old English *glōmung* < *glōm* twilight]
gloat (glōt), *v., n.* **—*v.i.*** to gaze or think about intently and with satisfaction; ponder with pleasure: *His enemies gloated over his defeat.*
—*n.* an act of gloating; a look, feeling, or expression of self-satisfaction: *In a front-page gloat over its circulation figures the Sunday Express frankly describes itself as one of the three quality Sunday papers* (Punch). [origin uncertain]
—gloat′er, *n.* **—gloat′ing|ly,** *adv.*
glob (glob), *n.* a shapeless mass; lump; blob. [perhaps imitative]
glob|al (glō′bəl), *adj.* **1** spread throughout the world; of the earth as a whole; world-wide: *the threat of global war.* **2** shaped like a globe; spherical: *a global map.* **—glob′al|ly,** *adv.*
glob|al|ism (glō′bə liz əm), *n.* **1** the principle of the interdependence of the entire world and its peoples. **2** concern for the rest of the world at the expense of national self-development and self-interest.
glob|al|ist (glō′bə list), *n.* supporter of globalism.
glob|al|ize (glō′bə līz), *v.t.,* **-ized, -iz|ing.** to make global; extend, enlarge, or spread on a global scale: *We must globalize our universities* (Saturday Review). **—glob′al|i|za′tion,** *n.* **—glob′al|iz′er,** *n.*
global tectonics, = plate tectonics.

global village, the world, especially of the late 1900's, thought of as a village, a condition arising from shrinking distance by instantaneous world-wide electronic communication. [coined by Marshall McLuhan; see etym. under **McLuhanism**]

glo|bate (glō′bāt), *adj.* shaped like a globe. [< Latin *globātus*, past participle of *globāre* form into a mass < *globus* globe]

glo|bat|ed (glō′bā tid), *adj.* = globate.

globe (glōb), *n., v.,* **globed, glob|ing.** —*n.* **1** the earth; world: *The astronauts in an earth space station circle the globe many times a day.* SYN: See syn. under **earth. 2a** anything completely round like a ball; sphere: *The sun is an immense globe. Bright golden globes of fruit.* (Shelley). **b** anything rounded like a globe, such as an electric light bulb, some fishbowls, the eyeball, or the orb carried with a scepter as a sign of power in a government ceremony. **3** a sphere with a map of the earth or sky on it.
—*v.t.* **1** to gather or form into a globe. **2** to provide with a globe.
—*v.i.* to take the form of a globe.
[< Middle French *globe*, learned borrowing from Latin *globus*]

globe amaranth, a plant with round heads of purple, pink, and white flowers, very durable after being gathered.

globe artichoke, = artichoke (def. 1).

globe candytuft, an annual variety of candytuft that grows about 16 inches high and bears lavender, pink, or red blossoms. It is especially popular as a garden plant.

globe|fish (glōb′fish′), *n., pl.* **-fish|es** or (*collectively*) **-fish.** any one of a family of spiny, warm-water fishes that can make themselves nearly ball-shaped by drawing in air when they are disturbed; balloon fish; puffer.

globe|flow|er (glōb′flou′ər), *n.* a European plant of the crowfoot family with globe-shaped, yellow flowers.

globe-trot (glōb′trot′), *v.i.,* **-trot|ted, -trot|ting.** to travel widely over the world, usually for sightseeing: *The more I globe-trot, the more aware I am of the richness and variety of . . . lives and temperaments* (London Times). [back formation < *globe-trotter*]

globe-trot|ter (glōb′trot′ər), *n.* a person who travels widely over the world, usually for sightseeing.

globe tulip, = mariposa lily.

globe valve, a valve enclosed in a roundish chamber having two sections. A tap is screwed up or down to open or close a hole between the sections.

glo|big|er|i|na (glō bij′ə rī′nə), *n., pl.* **-nae** (-nē). any one of various one-celled sea animals whose shells form chalky beds of mud on the ocean floor. [< New Latin *Globigerina* the genus name < Latin *globus* globe + *gerere* to carry]

glo|bin (glō′bin), *n.* a protein substance formed in the decomposition of hemoglobin. [< Latin *globus* + English *-in*]

glo|boid (glō′boid), *adj., n.* —*adj.* approximately globular; globe-shaped.
—*n.* a globoid figure or body.

glo|bose (glō′bōs, glō bōs′), *adj.* completely or nearly spherical; globular. [< Latin *globōsus* < *globus* globe] —**glo′bose|ly,** *adv.*

glo|bos|i|ty (glō bos′ə tē), *n.* globose quality or condition.

glob|u|lar (glob′yə lər), *adj.* **1** shaped like a globe or globule; round; spherical. **2** made up of globules. —**glob′u|lar|ly,** *adv.*

globular cluster, *Astronomy.* a distant, compact, spherical cluster of stars or galaxies.

glob|u|lar|i|ty (glob′yə lar′ə tē), *n.* the property or state of being globular.

globular projection, a map projection used commonly for mapping hemispheres, in which the equator, the central meridian, and the peripheral circle are divided into even lengths.

glob|ule (glob′yül), *n.* a very small sphere or ball; tiny drop: *Globules of sweat stood out on the worker's forehead.* [< French *globule*, learned borrowing from Latin *globulus* (diminutive) < *globus* globe]

glob|u|li|cide (glob′yə lə sīd), *n.* a substance that destroys blood cells. [< *globule* + *-cide*[1]]

glob|u|lif|er|ous (glob′yə lif′ər əs), *adj.* bearing or producing globules.

glob|u|lin (glob′yə lin), *n.* any one of a group of proteins, found in plant and animal tissue, which are insoluble in pure water but soluble in dilute salt solutions and in weak acids and alkalis. Globulin is a protein component of blood plasma.

glob|u|lite (glob′yə līt), *n.* one of the tiny, rounded particles seen especially in glasslike igneous rocks when examined under the microscope. They are believed to be an early stage in crystallization.

glob|u|lit|ic (glob′yə lit′ik), *adj.* belonging to or containing globulites.

glo|chid|i|ate (glō kid′ē āt), *adj. Botany, Zoology.* barbed at the tip, as a hair or bristle. [< New Latin *glochidium* barbed hair of a plant (diminutive) < Greek *glōchís* point of an arrow + English *-ate*[1]]

glo|chid|i|um (glō kid′ē əm), *n., pl.* **-i|a** (-ē ə). a tiny, bivalve larva of certain freshwater mussels that lives as a parasite on fish in its early stages. [< New Latin *glochidium;* see etym. under **glochidiate** (because it is barbed at the tip)]

***glock|en|spiel** (glok′ən spēl′, -shpēl′), *n.* **1** a musical percussion instrument made up of a series of small, tuned bells, bars, or tubes mounted in a frame and played by striking with two little hammers. **2** a similar instrument, with a keyboard instead of hammers. [< German *Glockenspiel* chimes < *Glocke* bell + *Spiel* play]

***glockenspiel**
definition 1

glogg or **glögg** (glug, glüg), *n.* a sweet, hot punch of Sweden, made with alcoholic liquors, flavoring, and, sometimes, nuts and other ingredients. [< Swedish *glögg*]

glom[1] (glom), *v.t.,* **glommed, glom|ming.** *Slang.* to steal; take.
glom on to, *Slang.* **a** to get hold of; latch on to: *Two itinerant American writers . . . glommed on to an expatriate Greek royalist* (Maclean's). **b** to steal: *"I died when I saw you glom onto those books. . . . Augie, a crook!"* (Saul Bellow).
[variant of dialectal *glaum*]

glom[2] (glom), *n., v.,* **glommed, glom|ming.** *Slang.*
—*n.* a look; glimpse.
—*v.t.* to look at; watch: *Passers-by congregate on the sidewalk to glom the Bunnies* (Playboy).
[origin unknown]

glom|er|ate (glom′ər it), *adj.* clustered together; collected into a rounded mass. [< Latin *glomerātus*, past participle of *glomerāre* < *glomus, -eris* ball]

glom|er|a|tion (glom′ə rā′shən), *n.* **1** glomerate condition. **2** a glomerate mass.

glo|mer|u|lar (glə mer′ů lər, -yů-), *adj.* of or like a glomerule.

glom|er|ule (glom′ə rül), *n.* **1** any compact cluster. **2** *Botany.* a cyme condensed into a headlike cluster, such as that of flowering dogwood. [< New Latin *glomerulus;* see etym. under **glomerulus**]

glo|mer|u|lo|ne|phri|tis (glə mer′ə lō ni frī′tis, -yů-), *n.* a disease, sometimes fatal, of the glomeruli of the kidneys, associated with streptococcic infection elsewhere in the body.

glo|mer|u|lus (glə mer′ů ləs, -yů-), *n., pl.* **-li** (-lī). *Anatomy.* a tuft of capillaries in the tubules of the kidney, contained within a Bowman's capsule and serving to filter out waste products from the blood: *The filtering units of the kidneys are called glomeruli* (Science News Letter). [< New Latin *glomerulus* (diminutive) < Latin *glomus, -eris* ball]

glon|o|in (glon′ō in), *n.* nitroglycerin, especially as used in medicine. [< *gl*(ycerine) + *o*(xygen) + *n*(itrogen) + *o*(xygen) + *-in*]

gloom (glüm), *n., v.* —*n.* **1** deep shadow; darkness; dim light: *a gloom unbroken, except by a lamp burning feebly* (George Eliot). SYN: dimness, obscurity, shade. **2** a dark or deeply shaded place. **3** *Figurative.* dark thoughts and feelings; low spirits; sadness: *a fit of the glooms* (Mary Lamb). SYN: despondency, dejection, depression, melancholy. **4** a dejected or sad look. **5** *Scottish.* a frown; scowl. [perhaps back formation < *gloomy*]
—*v.i.* **1** to be or become dark, dim, or dismal: *The tower gloomed in the dark.* **2** *Figurative.* to be in low spirits; feel sad: *During production she worries and glooms to the point of nausea* (Time). **3** *Figurative.* to look sad or dismal. **4** *Figurative.* to frown; scowl.
—*v.t.* **1** to make dark, dim, or dismal. **2** to express gloomily.
[Middle English *gloumen* look sullen, to lower[2]]

gloom|ing (glü′ming), *n.* **1** a frown; scowl. **2** *Poetic.* twilight or early dawn.

gloom|y (glü′mē), *adj.,* **gloom|i|er, gloom|i|est. 1** full of gloom; dark; dim; obscure: *a gloomy winter day.* SYN: shadowy, somber. **2** in low spirits; sad; melancholy: *a gloomy mood.* SYN: dejected, downhearted. **3** causing low spirits; discouraging; dismal: *gloomy predictions, a gloomy scene of poverty. His views about the future are gloomy.* SYN: disheartening. [< *gloom*, verb] —**gloom′i|ly,** *adv.* —**gloom′i|ness,** *n.*

glop (glop), *n. Slang.* **1** anything disagreeably sloppy or gluey. **2** *Figurative: You cannot convey the quality of life . . . through Rachel's perspective without losing proportion in melodrama and glop* (Renata Adler). [probably imitative]

glo|ri|a (glôr′ē ə, glōr′-), *n.* **1a** a song of praise to God. **b** the music for it. **2** a halo; aureole. **3** an ornament in imitation of this. **4** a fabric made of silk and some other material, used especially for umbrellas. [< Latin *glōria* glory]

Glo|ri|a (glôr′ē ə, glōr′-), *n.* one of three songs of praise to God, beginning "Glory be to God on high," "Glory be to the Father," and "Glory be to Thee, O Lord." They form part of the Communion service or Mass.

Gloria in Ex|cel|sis (in ek sel′sis), the hymn "Glory be to God on High," forming part of the Communion service or Mass. [< Latin *glōria in excelsīs*]

Gloria Pa|tri (pat′rī, pä′trē), the doxology beginning "Glory be to the Father," that follows the recitation of the Psalms and certain canticles, and occurs in other places in the Communion service or Mass. [< Latin *glōria patrī*]

Gloria Tib|i (tib′ē), the response "Glory be to Thee, O Lord," that follows the announcement of the gospel in the Communion service or Mass. [< Latin *glōria tibi*]

glo|ri|e|ta (glôr′ē ā′tä, glōr′-), *n., pl.* **-tas.** a landscaped circle at a street intersection, such as those in Mexico City. [< Spanish *glorieta* arbor, bower]

glo|ri|ette (glôr′ē et′, glōr′-), *n.* a pavilion; summerhouse. [< French *gloriette*]

glo|ri|fi|ca|tion (glôr′ə fə kā′shən, glōr′-), *n.* **1** the act of glorifying. **2** the state of being glorified. **3** a celebration; festivity. **4** a glorified form of something.

glo|ri|fied (glôr′ə fīd, glōr′-), *adj.* **1** made glorious. **2** given a glory, magnificence, or dignity not naturally belonging: *The "lake" was merely a glorified mud hole.*

glo|ri|fy (glôr′ə fī, glōr′-), *v.t.,* **-fied, -fy|ing. 1** to give glory to; make glorious: *to glorify a hero or a saint.* **2** to praise; honor; worship: *We sing hymns to glorify God.* SYN: extol, laud. **3** to make more beautiful or splendid than it is: *Sunset glorified the valley.* **4** to throw a glorious light upon; give radiance to: *The bright sun glorifies the sky* (Shakespeare). **5** to exalt to the glory of heaven. [< Old French *glorifier*, learned borrowing from Latin *glōrificāre* < *glōria* glory + *facere* make]
—**glo′ri|fi′a|ble,** *adj.* —**glo′ri|fi′er,** *n.*

glo|ri|ole (glôr′ē ōl, glōr′-), *n.* = halo. [< French *gloriole*, learned borrowing from Latin *glōriola* (diminutive) < *glōria* glory]

glo|ri|o|sa (glôr′ē ō′sə, glōr′-), *n.* any one of a group of tuberous, vinelike lilies with showy red or yellow flowers. It is native to tropical Africa and Asia, and may climb to a height of five feet or more. [< New Latin *Gloriosa* the genus name < Latin *glōriōsus* glorious]

gloriosa daisy, = African daisy. [probably < Spanish *gloriosa* glorious]

glo|ri|ous (glôr′ē əs, glōr′-), *adj.* **1a** giving glory: *Our team won a glorious victory.* **b** having or deserving glory; illustrious: *The glorious knight slew the wretched dragon.* SYN: famous, renowned. **2** magnificent; splendid: *a glorious day. . . . the glorious planet Sol* (Shakespeare). SYN: brilliant. **3** admirable; delightful; fine: *The children had a glorious time at the fair.* **4** *Obsolete.* boastful. [< Anglo-French *glorious*, learned borrowing from Latin *glōriōsus* < *glōria* glory] —**glo′ri|ous|ly,** *adv.* —**glo′ri|ous|ness,** *n.*

glo|ry (glôr′ē, glōr′-), *n., pl.* **-ries,** *v.,* **-ried, -ry|ing.** —*n.* **1** great praise and honor given to a person or thing by others; fame; renown: *His heroic act won him glory. The paths of glory lead but to the grave* (Thomas Gray). SYN: distinction. **2** something that brings praise and honor; source of pride and joy: *America's great men and women are her glory.* **3** adoring praise and thanksgiving: *Fear God, and give glory to him* (Revelation 14:7). **4** radiant beauty; brightness; magnificence; splendor: *the glory of the royal palace. What will be the morning glory, when at dusk thus gleams the lake?* (Robert Browning). **5** a thing of radiant beauty or magnificence. **6** a condition of magnificence, splendor, or greatest prosperity: *Rome reached its greatest glory when it ruled the world at the time of Christ.* **7** the splendor and bliss of heaven; heaven: *the saints in glory.* **8** a halo, especially as represented in art. **9a** = anthelion. **b** = fogbow.

Pronunciation Key: hat, āge, cãre, fär; let, ēqual, tėrm; it, īce; hot, ōpen, ôrder; oil, out; cup, půt, rüle; child; long; thin; ᴛʜen; zh, measure; ə represents **a** in about, **e** in taken, **i** in pencil, **o** in lemon, **u** in circus.

— *v.i.* to be proud; rejoice (in): *to glory in success. The parents gloried in their children's achievements. The United States has traditionally gloried in its revolutionary heritage* (Saturday Review).

go to glory, to die: *Tell her you found me going to glory* (Harriet Beecher Stowe).

in one's glory, in a state of greatest satisfaction or enjoyment: *He's in his glory when he can sing before an audience.*

[< Old French *glorie,* learned borrowing from Latin *glōria*]

glory hole, 1 (in certain sailing ships) a space aft between decks, used as a storeroom. **2** sleeping quarters on a ship, especially those of the stewards and stokers: *Sailors slept in the glory hole, a long open dormitory ...* (Atlantic). **3** an opening in a small furnace used to reheat glass when shaping it by hand. **4** *Dialect.* a drawer, closet, or other place, where things are untidily dumped.

glo|ry|ing|ly (glôr′ē ing lē, glōr′-), *adv.* in a glorying manner: *No posterity of his would point them out gloryingly* (George Meredith).

glo|ry-pea (glôr′ē pē′, glōr′-), *n.* a grayish-green clianthus with scarlet flowers.

Glos. or **Gloss.,** Gloucester; Gloucestershire.

gloss[1] (glôs, glos), *n., v.* —*n.* **1** a smooth, shiny surface on anything; luster: *Polished furniture has a gloss.* **SYN:** sheen, polish. **2** *Figurative.* an outward appearance or surface that covers wrong underneath. **3** *British Dialect.* the glow of a fire.

— *v.t.* to put a smooth, shiny surface on; glaze: *The hot sun had glossed the surface of the snow.*

gloss over, to smooth over; make (something) seem right even though it is really wrong: *We all make mistakes, but sometimes we exaggerate them and at other times we gloss over them* (Listener). *The People's Action Party had proved their guilt in glossing over certain facts* (London Times).

[origin uncertain. Compare Old Icelandic *glossi* to gleam.] —**gloss′less,** *adj.*

gloss[2] (glôs, glos), *n., v.* —*n.* **1** a word inserted between the lines or in the margin of a text to explain or give the equivalent of a foreign or difficult word. **2** *Figurative.* **a** a comment; explanation; interpretation: *In the margins of library books earnest freshmen inscribed such helpful glosses as "Description of nature," "Irony," and "How true!"* (New Yorker). **b** an artfully misleading or false interpretation. **3** = glossary. **4** an interpretation or definition of a word or phrase given in a glossary or dictionary. **5** a translation inserted between the lines of a text printed in a foreign language. **6** a series of verbal interpretations of a text.

— *v.t.* **1** to insert glosses or comments on; explain. **SYN:** interpret, annotate. **2** to explain away; read a different sense into; misinterpret.

— *v.i.* to make glosses; comment.

[< Latin *glōssa* < Greek *glôssa* obsolete or foreign word that needs explaining; (literally) tongue. See etym. of doublet **gloze**[1].]

gloss., glossary.

glos|sa (glos′ə), *n., pl.* **glos|sae** (glos′ē). the center of the end of the labium of certain insects. [< New Latin *glossa* < Greek *glôssa* tongue]

glos|sal (glôs′əl, glos′-), *adj.* of or having to do with the tongue.

glos|sar|i|al (glo sãr′ē əl, glô-), *adj.* **1** having to do with a glossary. **2** like a glossary.

glos|sa|rist (glos′ər ist, glôs′-), *n.* **1** a writer of glosses; commentator. **2** a compiler of a glossary.

glos|sa|ry (glos′ər ē, glôs′-), *n., pl.* **-ries. 1** a list of special, technical, or hard words, usually in alphabetical order, with explanations or comments; collection of glosses: *a glossary to Shakespeare's plays. Some textbooks have glossaries at the end.* **SYN:** gloss, key. **2** a vocabulary or dictionary of limited scope: *a glossary of Scottish words, a glossary of the mining and mineral industry.* [< Latin *glōssārium* < *glōssa;* see etym. under **gloss**[2]]

glos|sa|tor (glo sā′tər, glô-), *n.* a writer of glosses; commentator.

glos|sec|to|my (glo sek′tə mē, glô-), *n., pl.* **-mies.** the surgical removal of all or a part of the tongue. [< Greek *glôssa* tongue + *ektomē* a cutting out]

glos|se|mat|ics (glos′ə mat′iks), *n.* the study of glossemes.

gloss|eme (glos′ēm), *n. Linguistics.* the smallest element that signals or conveys meaning in a language. [< Greek *glôssa* tongue + English *-eme,* as in *phoneme*]

gloss|er[1] (glôs′ər, glos′-), *n.* a person who puts a gloss or luster on something.
[< *gloss*[1] + *-er*[1]]

gloss|er[2] (glôs′ər, glos′-), *n.* = glossarist. [< *gloss*[2] + *-er*[1]]

glos|si|tis (glo sī′tis, glô-), *n. Medicine.* inflammation of the tongue.

gloss|me|ter (glôs′mē′tər, glos′-), *n.* a photoelectric device that measures the reflection of glossy surfaces, such as those of papers, paints, or fabrics.

glos|sog|ra|pher (glo sog′rə fər, glô-), *n.* a writer of glosses or commentaries.

glos|sog|ra|phy (glo sog′rə fē, glô-), *n.* the writing of glosses.

glos|so|la|li|a (glos′ə lā′lē ə, glôs′-), *n.* **1a** the gift of tongues; the power to speak in strange, foreign languages (in the Bible, Acts 2:4). **b** speech without meaning, uttered in a state of ecstasy (in the Bible, I Corinthians 14:2-14). **2** (at a revival meeting) the sudden ecstatic seizure of a participant during which he utters a succession of unrecognizable sounds. [< Greek *glôssa* tongue + *laliá* speech]

glos|so|log|i|cal (glos′ə loj′ə kəl, glôs′-), *adj.* = linguistic.

glos|sol|o|gist (glo sol′ə jist, glô-), *n.* **1** a person who writes glosses. **2** a person who compiles glossaries. **3** = linguist.

glos|sol|o|gy (glo sol′ə jē, glô-), *n., pl.* **-gies.** the science of language; linguistics. [< Greek *glôssa* tongue + English *-logy*]

glos|soph|a|gine (glo sof′ə jin, -jīn; glô-), *adj.* having to do with or characteristic of a group of large South American bats with long, extensible tongues. [< New Latin *Glossophaga* the genus name < Greek *glôssa* tongue + *phageîn* eat]

glos|so|pha|ryn|ge|al (glos′ō fə rin′jē əl, glôs′-), *adj., n.* —*adj.* having to do with the rear part of the tongue and of the pharynx: *Polio patients are learning to breathe through the glossopharyngeal method of taking breaths.*

—*n.* the glossopharyngeal nerve or muscle.

glos|sot|o|my (glo sot′ə mē, glô-), *n., pl.* **-mies.** surgical incision or dissection of the tongue. [< Greek *glôssa* tongue + *-tomíā* a cutting]

gloss|y (glôs′ē, glos′-), *adj.,* **gloss|i|er, gloss|i-est,** *n., pl.* **gloss|ies.** —*adj.* **1** smooth and shiny; highly polished; lustrous: *The beautiful, glossy coat of the cat shone as it lay in the sunlight.* **SYN:** sleek. **2** *Figurative.* having a specious appearance or smooth outward show; superficially or deceptively attractive; slick: *a glossy show, glossy advertisements, glossy duplicity.*

—*n.* **1** *Informal.* a photograph printed on glossy paper. **2** *British Informal.* a magazine printed on glossy paper; slick: *The editors of the two leading glossies ... make Paris cower* (Punch). **3** something superficially attractive and showy, especially a slick motion picture. —**gloss′i|ly,** *adv.* —**gloss′i|ness,** *n.*

glossy ibis, a long-legged wading bird with a decurved bill, and chestnut plumage of a glossy purplish or greenish hue, found in tropical areas of the Old World and the southern United States.

glost (glôst, glost), *n., adj.* —*n.* the glaze used for pottery, china, and the like.

—*adj.* having to do with glaze or glazing: *a glost firing.*

[dialectal alteration of *gloss*[1]]

glot|tal (glot′əl), *adj.* **1** of or having to do with the glottis. **2** *Phonetics.* produced in the glottis. *H* in *hope* is a glottal sound.

glot|tal|ize (glot′ə līz), *v.t.,* **-ized, -iz|ing.** *Phonetics.* to pronounce (a sound) with simultaneous glottal closure: *Glottalized stops are most commonly very fortis* (Henry A. Gleason, Jr.). —**glot′-tal|i|za′tion,** *n.*

glottal stop, *Phonetics.* a stop articulated by checking the breath stream in the glottis, often heard in English before an initial stressed vowel, or as a variant of the *t*-sound in *bottle.* In many languages it occurs as a phoneme.

glot|tic (glot′ik), *adj.* **1** of or having to do with language; linguistic. **2** = glottal.

glot|tis (glot′is), *n., pl.* **glot|tis|es, glot|ti|des** (glot′ə dēz). an opening at the upper part of the windpipe between the vocal cords. [< New Latin *glottis* < Greek *glōttís* < *glôtta,* variant of *glôssa* tongue]

glot|to|chron|o|log|i|cal (glot′ō kron′ə loj′ə kəl), *adj.* of or having to do with glottochronology.

glot|to|chro|nol|o|gy (glot′ō krə nol′ə jē), *n. Linguistics.* a method of dating a language in a particular stage, or the separation of related languages, based on the theory that over a considerable period linguistic changes take place at a fairly constant rate; lexicostatistics: *Glottochronology ... rests on the finding that in general a basic segment of any language changes at the fairly constant rate of about 19 per cent in each 1,000 years* (Scientific American). [< Greek *glôtta* tongue + English *chronology*]

glot|to|log|ic (glot′ə loj′ik), *adj.* = linguistic.

glot|to|log|i|cal (glot′ə loj′ə kəl), *adj.* = linguistic.

glot|tol|o|gist (glo tol′ə jist), *n.* = linguist.

glot|tol|o|gy (glo tol′ə jē), *n.* the science of language; linguistics. [< Greek *glôtta* tongue, speech + English *-logy*]

glove (gluv), *n., v.,* **gloved, glov|ing.** —*n.* **1** a covering for the hand, usually with separate places for each of the four fingers and the thumb. Gloves are worn to keep the hands warm, clean, or safe, and also sometimes as part of a dress or uniform. **2** = boxing glove. **3** a padded leather glove worn by baseball players in the field; mitt.

— *v.t.* **1** to cover with a glove; provide with gloves: *They glove their hands in the finest leather.* **2** to serve as a glove for. **3** (in sports) to catch with a glove: *The shortstop neatly gloved a towering pop fly.*

fit like a glove, to fit perfectly or tightly; suit perfectly: *The boots fitted me like a glove* (Tobias Smollett).

take off the gloves, to stop being soft; become aggressive; get tough: *Even before the Sino-Soviet ideological meeting had reached its predestined failure, both sides had taken off the gloves and were slugging it out* (New York Times).

[Old English *glōf*] —**glove′less,** *adj.* —**glove′-less|ness,** *n.*

***glove box, 1** a plastic box or similar enclosure containing a controlled environment, with rubber gloves fastened around holes in the side of the box through which a person can manipulate things in the box without introducing outside contamination; isolator. **2** *British.* a glove compartment.

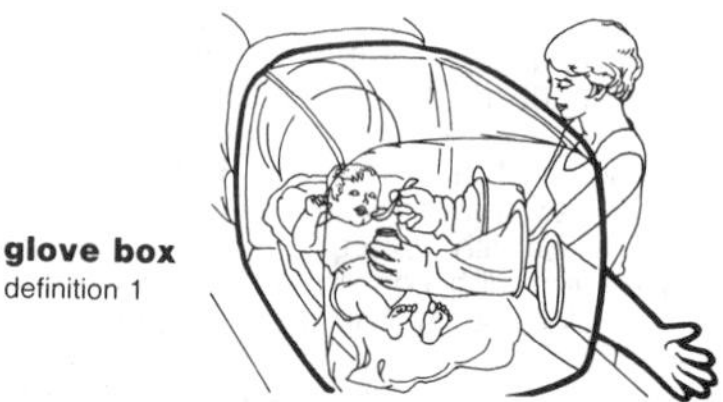

***glove box**
definition 1

glove compartment, a compartment recessed in an automobile's dashboard, that usually has a door and can be locked, intended to hold gloves, papers, etc.

glove|mak|er (gluv′mā′kər), *n.* a person who makes gloves: *Shakespeare's father was a glovemaker* (William H. Dooley).

glove|mak|ing (gluv′ma′king), *n.* the making of gloves: *American glovemaking is centered in New York.*

glove|man (gluv′man′, -mən), *n., pl.* **-men.** *Sports.* a fielder.

glove puppet, a puppet that fits over the hand and is manipulated with the fingers.

glov|er (gluv′ər), *n.* a person who makes or sells gloves.

gloves-off (gluvz′ôf′, -of′), *adj. Informal.* with or as if with bare knuckles; harsh.

glow (glō), *v., n.* —*v.i.* **1** to shine because of heat; be red-hot or white-hot: *a glowing ember.* **2** to give off light without heat; shine as if red-hot or white-hot: *Some clocks glow in the dark.* **3** to show a warm color; look warm; be red or bright: *Her cheeks glowed as she danced.* **4** *Figurative.* to be eager; look eager: *Her eyes glowed at the thought of a trip. He glowed with enthusiasm.* **5** *Figurative.* to burn with emotion or passion: *to glow with resentment.* **6** to be hot; be on fire; burn: *The torrid zone Glows with the passing and repassing sun* (John Dryden). **7** to burn with bodily heat.

— *v.t. Obsolete.* to make hot.

—*n.* **1** the shine from something that is red-hot or white-hot: *the glow of embers in the fireplace.* **2** a similar shine often without heat: *the glow of gold. Drifting sand-heaps feed my stock In summer's scorching glow* (Emerson). **3** a bright, warm color; brightness: *the glow of health on his cheeks, the glow of sunset.* **4** a warm feeling or color of the body; state of bodily heat: *a pleasant glow after swimming in cold water.* **5** *Figurative.* an eager look on the face: *a glow of interest or excitement.* **6** *Figurative.* warmth of feeling or passion; ardor: *He was filled with the glow of faith in God.*

[Old English *glōwan*]

glow discharge, a luminous electrical discharge in a tube containing gas at low pressure: *The type of discharge in a neon sign and a fluorescent lamp is called a glow discharge* (Sears and Zemansky).

glow|er[1] (glō′ər), *n.* **1** a person or thing that glows. **2** the light-giving rod in a Nernst lamp. [< *glow* + *-er*[1]]

glow|er[2] (glou′ər), *v., n.* —*v.i.* **1** to stare angrily or crossly; scowl fiercely: *The fighters glowered at each other. The sullen boy glowered at the stranger.* **2** *Scottish.* to stare or gaze intently.

—*n.* **1** an angry stare; fierce scowl. **2** *Scottish.* the act of glowering; an open-eyed gaze or stare.

[Middle English *gloren.* Perhaps related to obsolete *glow* to stare.]

glow·er·ing (glou′ər ing), *adj.* that glowers: *a glowering sky.* **—glow′er·ing·ly,** *adv.*

glow·fly (glō′flī′), *n., pl.* **-flies.** = firefly.

glow·ing (glō′ing), *adj.* **1** shining from something that is red-hot or white-hot. SYN: incandescent, luminous. **2** bright: *glowing colors.* **3** rich and warm in coloring: *glowing cheeks. Twelve days in the sun had given him a glowing tan* (Newsweek). **4** *Figurative.* eager; animated: *a glowing description.* **—glow′ing·ly,** *adv.*

glow lamp, an incandescent electric lamp.

glow plug, an electrical plug used to automatically reignite the flame of a gas turbine.

glow·worm (glō′wėrm′), *n.* **1** any one of various wormlike insects or insect larvae that glow in the dark. Fireflies develop from glowworms. **2** any one of several European beetles whose wingless females and larvae can produce light.

glox·in·i·a (glok sin′ē ə), *n.* a tropical American plant of the same family as the African violet, cultivated, especially as a house plant, for its large white, red, or purple, bell-shaped flowers. [< New Latin *Gloxinia* < Benjamin P. *Gloxin,* a German botanist of the 1700's]

gloze¹ (glōz), *v.,* **glozed, gloz·ing,** *n.* **—*v.t.*** **1** to smooth (over); explain away: *His friends glozed over his faults.* SYN: extenuate, palliate. **2** *Obsolete.* to make glozes or glosses upon; interpret. SYN: expound.
—*v.i.* **1** to talk speciously or flatteringly. **2** to make glosses; comment.
—*n.* **1a** flattery; deceit. **b** an instance of this; a flattering speech, etc. **2** a pretense; false show; specious appearance. **3** a disguise. **4** *Archaic.* gloss.
[< Old French *gloser* < *glose,* learned borrowing from Late Latin *glōsa,* variant of Latin *glōssa.* See etym. of doublet **gloss²**.]

gloze² (glōz), *v.,* **glozed, gloz·ing,** *n. Scottish.*
—*v.i.* **1** to shine brightly; blaze. **2** to gleam.
—*v.t.* to cause to shine.
—*n.* the blaze or clear flame of a fire.
[compare etym. under **gloss¹**]

glu·ca·gon (glü′kə gon), *n.* a hormone secreted by the pancreas that raises the blood sugar level by stimulating the breakdown of glycogen to glucose, used medically in the treatment of diabetes and tumors. [< *glucose*]

glu·case (glü′kās), *n. Chemistry.* an enzyme capable of converting maltose into glucose; maltase. [< *gluc*(ose) + *-ase*]

glu·cin·ic (glü sin′ik), *adj.* **1** of glucinum. **2** like glucinum.

glu·cin·i·um (glü sin′ē əm), *n.* = glucinum.

glu·ci·num (glü sī′nəm), *n.* = beryllium. [< New Latin *glucinum* < French *glucine* < Greek *glykýs* sweet (from the sweet taste of some of its salts)]

glu·co·cor·ti·coid (glü′kō kôr′tə koid), *n.* any one of a group of steroid hormones, such as cortisone, produced by the adrenal cortex and affecting glucose metabolism. They are used in the treatment of arthritis, asthma, etc. [< Greek *glykýs* sweet + English *corticoid*]

glu·co·nate (glü′kə nāt), *n.* a salt of gluconic acid.

glu·co·ne·o·gen·e·sis (glü′kō nē′ə jen′ə sis), *n.* the conversion of noncarbohydrate substances such as protein into glucose. [< Greek *glykýs* sweet + English *neo-* + *genesis*]

glu·co·ne·o·gen·ic (glü′kō nē′ə jen′ik), *adj.* having to do with gluconeogenesis.

glu·con·ic acid (glü kon′ik), an acid derived by oxidation of glucose, used in jellies, baking powder, and in cleaning metals. *Formula:* $C_6H_{12}O_7$

glu·co·pro·tein (glü′kō prō′tēn, -tē in), *n.* = glycoprotein.

glu·co·sa·mine (glü′kōs ə mēn′, -am′in), *n.* an amino sugar found in crustacean shells and body sugars that is added to antibiotics to increase their entry into the blood. *Formula:* $C_6H_{13}NO_5$ [< *glucos*(e) + *amine*]

glu·cose (glü′kōs), *n.* **1** a kind of sugar occurring in plant and animal tissues. Carbohydrate is present in the blood mainly in the form of glucose. Glucose is not as sweet as cane sugar. It is found in various optically different forms, especially as dextrose. *Glucose is used by the plant as a source of energy for the various metabolic activities, and as the basic material from which a great number of chemical compounds are formed* (Harbaugh and Goodrich). *Formula:* $C_6H_{12}O_6$ **2** a thick syrup made from starch by the action of hydrochloric acid. [< French *glucose,* earlier *glycose* < Greek *glykýs* sweet]

glu·co·sid (glü′kə sid), *n.* = glucoside.

glu·co·si·dase (glü′kō sə dās), *n.* an animal or plant enzyme that hydrolyzes glucosides.

glu·co·side (glü′kə sīd), *n.* a glycoside, especially one containing glucose. [< *glucos*(e) + *-ide*]

glu·co·su·ri·a (glü′kō sùr′ē ə), *n.* = glycosuria.

glu·cu·ron·ic acid (glü′kyù ron′ik), an acid derived from glucose and present in many animals and plants. It aids in the removal of toxic substances from the body and is used in the treatment of arthritis. *Formula:* $C_6H_{10}O_7$ [< *gluc*(oside) + *uronic acid*]

glu·cu·ro·nide (glü kyùr′ə nīd), *n.* any compound formed by the interaction of glucuronic acid with a phenol, an alcohol, or certain acids.

glue (glü), *n., v.,* **glued, glu·ing.** **—*n.*** **1** a substance used to stick things together. Glue is often made by boiling hide and other scraps, bones, and hoofs of animals in water to form a jelly. SYN: mucilage. **2** any similar sticky substance, especially one made of casein, rubber, or cement; adhesive. Glues are stronger than pastes.
—*v.t.* **1** to stick together with glue: *He glued the model boat together with plastic cement.* **2** *Figurative.* to fasten tightly or fix closely: *His hands were glued to the steering wheel as he drove down the dangerous mountain road.*
glue off, to apply a thin coat of glue to (the backbone of a book): *A machine glues off books to keep the threads from unraveling and to hold the signatures together.*
[< Old French *glu, glus* < Late Latin *glūs, glūtis,* related to Latin *glūten;* see etym. under **gluten**]
—glu′er, *n.* **—glue′like′,** *adj.*

glue·pot (glü′pot′), *n.* **1** a pot in which glue is melted by the heat of water in an outer vessel. **2** an expanse of wet or muddy ground in Australia.

glue sniffer, a person who sniffs glue for the intoxicating effect of the toluene used in it.

glue-sniff·ing (glü′snif′ing), *n.* the habit or practice of a glue sniffer.

glue·y (glü′ē), *adj.,* **glu·i·er, glu·i·est.** **1** like glue; sticky; viscid. **2** full of glue; smeared with glue.

glug (glug), *n., v.,* **glugged, glug·ging.** *Informal.*
—*n.* a sound of flowing liquid; gurgle.
—*v.i.* to make this sound. [imitative]

glu·i·no (glü ē′nō), *n., pl.* **-nos.** a hypothetical nuclear particle that is a weakly interacting form of the gluon: *A scenario with supersymmetry: gluinos from within a proton and an antiproton collide, and make supersymmetric gluinos, each of which decays into two quarks and one photino* (Discovery).

glum (glum), *adj.,* **glum·mer, glum·mest.** gloomy; dismal; sullen: *a glum look. He felt very glum when his friend moved away. Why should folk be glum . . . When Nature herself is glad?* (John Greenleaf Whittier). *Glummer tidings are ahead for most basic crops* (Wall Street Journal). SYN: dejected, frowning, dark. See syn. under **sullen.** [compare Low German *glum* turbid, muddy. See related etym. at **gloom.**] **—glum′ly,** *adv.* **—glum′ness,** *n.*

glu·ma·ceous (glü mā′shəs), *adj. Botany.* glumelike; like a glume; consisting of or having glumes.

glume (glüm), *n.* a chaffy bract at the base of the spikelet of grasses, sedges, and some other plants. [< Latin *glūma* hull or husk of grain]
—glume′like′, *adj.*

glume blotch, a fungous disease, especially of wheat, causing dark spots on the glumes.

glump·ish (glum′pish), *adj.* = glum.

glump·y (glum′pē), *adj.,* **glump·i·er, glump·i·est.** glum; sullen; sulky. [origin uncertain] **—glump′i·ly,** *adv.*

glunch (glùnsh, glunsh), *v., n., adj. Scottish.* **—*v.i.*** to look sour or glum.
—*n.* a sour look.
—*adj.* sulky.
[origin uncertain]

glu·on (glü′on), *n.* a hypothetical neutral component of elementary particles that holds together subnucleons such as partons and quarks: *The mass of the gluon can be estimated . . . as 10 billion or possibly tens of billions of electron volts* (Science News). [< *glue* + *-on*]

glut¹ (glut), *v.,* **glut·ted, glut·ting,** *n.* **—*v.t.*** **1** to fill too full; supply more than there is demand for: *The boys glutted themselves with cake. The prices for wheat dropped when the market was glutted with it.* SYN: gorge. **2** *Figurative.* to fill full; feed or satisfy fully: *A year of working aboard ship glutted his appetite for adventure.*
—*v.i.* to eat to satiety.
—*n.* **1** a full supply; great quantity. **2** *Figurative.* too great a supply; surfeit: *Pork glut is getting worse despite a government buying program* (Time). SYN: superfluity. **3** the act of glutting. **4** the condition of being glutted.
[probably < obsolete *glut* glutton¹ < Old French *glout* < Latin *gluttō, -ōnis*]

glut² (glut), *v.t.,* **glut·ted, glut·ting.** to swallow greedily; gulp down. [< Old French *gloutir* gulp down < Latin *gluttīre*]

glu·ta·mate (glü′tə māt), *n.* a salt or ester of glutamic acid: *Monosodium glutamate is used as a flavoring agent.*

glu·tam·ic acid (glü tam′ik), a white, crystalline amino acid found in plant and animal proteins, especially in seeds and beets. *Formula:* $C_5H_9NO_4$ [< *glut*(en) + *am*(ide) + *-ic*]

glu·ta·mine (glü′tə mēn, -min), *n.* a crystalline amino acid found in many plants and animals. *Formula:* $C_5H_{10}N_2O_3$ [< *glutam*(ic acid) + *-ine²*]

glu·tar·ic acid (glü tär′ik), a colorless, crystalline acid, a constituent of beets and crude wool, used in organic synthesis. *Formula:* $C_5H_8O_4$ [< *glut*(en) + (tart)*aric acid*]

glu·ta·thi·one (glü′tə thī′ōn, -thī ōn′), *n.* a polypeptide present in plant and animal tissues, important in physiological oxidations. *Formula:* $C_{10}H_{17}N_3O_6S$ [< *gluta*(mic) + Greek *theîon* brimstone (sulfur) + English *-one*]

glu·te·al (glü tē′əl, glü′tē-), *adj.* of or having to do with the buttock muscles or the buttocks. [< *glute*(us) + *-al¹*]

glu·te·lin (glü′tə lin), *n.* any one of a group of simple proteins found in corn, wheat, and other grains.

glu·ten (glü′tən), *n.* **1** the nitrogenous, tough, sticky substance that remains in flour when the starch is taken out. **2** glue, or some gluey substance. [< Latin *glūten* glue]

gluten bread, bread made from gluten flour.

gluten flour, wheat flour rich in gluten because a high proportion of its starch has been removed.

glu·te·nin (glü′tə nin), *n.* one of the proteins in wheat flour.

glu·te·nous (glü′tə nəs), *adj.* **1** like gluten. **2** containing much gluten.

glu·teth·i·mide (glü teth′ə mīd), *n.* a drug that depresses the central nervous system, used to induce sleep; Doriden. *Formula:* $C_{13}H_{15}NO_2$

glu·te·us (glü tē′əs), *n., pl.* **-te·i** (-tē′ī). any of the three large muscles of the buttocks. [< New Latin *gluteus* < Greek *gloutós* buttock, rump]

glu·ti·nant (glü′tə nənt), *n.* a kind of nematocyst that produces a sticky secretion: *Any small aquatic animal swimming within touch of a tentacle is at once . . . affixed by glutinants* (Hegner and Stiles).

glu·ti·nous (glü′tə nəs), *adj.* like glue; sticky; viscid. [< Latin *glūtinōsus* < *glūten, -inis* glue]
—glu′ti·nous·ly, *adv.* **—glu′ti·nous·ness,** *n.*

glut·ton¹ (glut′ən), *n.* **1** a greedy eater; person who eats too much: *Sometimes he gets very hungry and eats like a glutton.* SYN: gormandizer. **2** *Figurative.* a person who never seems to have enough of something: *The Germans were sun gluttons, and they could be seen all over the hills, stripped to the waist, sitting on rocks* (Saturday Evening Post). [< Old French *glouton* < Latin *gluttō, -ōnis*]

glut·ton² (glut′ən), *n.* the wolverine, especially the European variety. [translation of German *Vielfrass* gluttonous animal, by popular etymology < Scandinavian (compare dialectal Norwegian *fjeldfross,* Swedish *fjällfräs* (literally) mountain cat)]

glut·ton·ize (glut′ə nīz), *v.i., v.t.,* **-ized, -iz·ing.** to eat like a glutton.

glut·ton·ous (glut′ə nəs), *adj.* **1** greedy about food; having the habit of eating too much. SYN: voracious. **2** *Figurative.* greedy; insatiable. **—glut′ton·ous·ly,** *adv.* **—glut′ton·ous·ness,** *n.*

glut·ton·y (glut′ə nē), *n., pl.* **-ton·ies.** excess in eating; voracity.

glyc·er·al·de·hyde (glis′ə ral′də hīd), *n.* a colorless, crystalline solid produced by oxidizing glycerol. *Formula:* $C_3H_6O_3$ [< *glycer*(ol) + *aldehyde*]

gly·cer·ic (gli ser′ik, glis′ər), *adj.* **1** of or derived from glycerol. **2** relating to glycerol.

glyceric acid, a colorless, syruplike acid obtained by the partial oxidation of glycerol, and also formed during alcoholic fermentation. *Formula:* $C_3H_6O_4$

glyc·er·ide (glis′ə rīd, -ər id), *n.* an ester of glycerol.

glyc·er·in (glis′ər in), *n.* = glycerol. [< French *glycérine* < Greek *glykerós* sweet < *glykýs* sweet]
►Although still widely used, especially commercially, the term **glycerin** has been generally replaced by **glycerol** in chemistry.

gly·cer·in·ate (glis′ər ə nāt), *v.t.,* **-at·ed, -at·ing.** to mix or treat with glycerol.

glyc·er·ine (glis′ər in, -ə rēn), *n.* = glycerin.

glyc·er·ite (glis′ə rīt), *n. Pharmacy.* any of a class of preparations consisting of a medicinal substance dissolved or suspended in glycerol. [< *glycer*(in) + *-ite¹*]

glyc·er·ol (glis′ə rōl, -rol), *n.* a colorless, sweet, syrupy liquid obtained from animal and vegetable oils and fats; glycerin. Glycerol is used as a solvent, in lotions and ointments, explosives, and antifreezes. *Formula:* $C_3H_8O_3$ [< *glycer*(in) + *-ol¹*]
►See **glycerin** for usage note.

Pronunciation Key: hat, āge, cãre, fär; let, ēqual, tėrm; it, īce; hot, ōpen, ôrder; oil, out; cup, pùt, rüle; child; long; thin; ᴛʜen; zh, measure; ə represents **a** in about, **e** in taken, **i** in pencil, **o** in lemon, **u** in circus.

glyc|er|o|lize (glī′sər ə līz), *v.t.*, **-lized, -liz|ing.** to treat with glycerol.

glyc|er|yl (glis′ər əl), *n., adj. Chemistry.* —*n.* the hypothetical trivalent radical occurring in glycerol and the glycerides. *Formula:* C_3H_5
—*adj.* of or having to do with this radical.
[< *glycer*(ol) + *-yl*]

gly|cine (glī′sēn, glī sēn′), *n.* a colorless, sweet-tasting, crystalline amino acid formed when gelatin or various other animal substances are boiled in the presence of alkalis. *Formula:* $C_2H_5NO_2$ [< French *glycine* < Greek *glykýs* sweet]

gly|co|gen (glī′kə jən), *n.* a starchlike carbohydrate stored in the liver and other animal tissues. It is changed into glucose when the body needs energy. *Glycogen ... represents chemical energy in a stored form* (Harbaugh and Goodrich). *Formula:* $(C_6H_{10}O_5)_n$ [< French *glycogène* < Greek *glykýs* sweet + French *-gène* -gen]

gly|co|gen|e|sis (glī′kə jen′ə sis), *n.* the production or formation of glucose, especially in the animal body.

gly|co|gen|ic (glī′kə jen′ik), *adj.* of or having to do with the formation of sugar in animal tissue.

gly|co|gen|o|sis (glī′kō jə nō′sis), *n.* a condition affecting metabolism in young children, in which excess glycogen accumulates in one or more organs such as the liver or kidneys, making them expand greatly.

gly|col (glī′kōl, -kol), *n. Chemistry.* **1** a colorless, sweet-tasting alcohol; ethylene glycol. Glycol is obtained from various ethylene compounds and is used as an antifreeze for automobiles, as a solvent, and in making printing inks and lacquers. *Formula:* $C_2H_6O_2$ **2** any one of a class of similar alcohols containing two hydroxyl groups; diol. [< *glyc*(erin) + *-ol*[1]]

gly|co|late (glī′kə lāt), *n. Chemistry.* a salt or ester of glycolic acid.

gly|col|ic (glī kol′ik), *adj.* **1** of or containing glycol. **2** derived from glycol.

glycolic acid, a colorless, crystalline acid found in unripe grapes, and also made synthetically, used in dyeing and as a catalyst. *Formula:* $C_2H_4O_3$

gly|co|lip|id (glī′kə lip′id, -lī′pid), *n.* any one of a class of lipids that yield a sugar and a fatty acid upon hydrolysis. Cerebrosides are glycolipids.

gly|col|y|sis (glī kol′ə sis), *n.* the process by which a carbohydrate, such as glucose, is broken down to an acid.

gly|co|lyt|ic (glī′kə lit′ik), *adj.* having to do with glycolysis.

gly|co|pep|tide (glī′kə pep′tīd), *n.* = glycoprotein.

gly|co|pro|te|id (glī′kə prō′tē id), *n.* = glycoprotein.

gly|co|pro|tein (glī′kə prō′tēn, -tē in), *n.* a protein, such as mucin, containing a carbohydrate radical and a simple protein; glucoprotein.

gly|co|side (glī′kə sīd, -sid), *n. Chemistry.* any one of a large group of organic compounds which yield a sugar, often glucose, and another substance on hydrolysis in the presence of various ferments or enzymes or a dilute acid, such as amygdalin or salicin; glucoside.

gly|co|sid|ic (glī′kə sid′ik), *adj.* having to do with a glycoside. —**gly′co|sid′i|cal|ly**, *adv.*

gly|co|su|ri|a (glī′kə sůr′ē ə), *n.* a condition in which glucose is present in the urine, as in diabetes; glucosuria. [< Greek *glykýs* sweet + English *-uria*]

gly|co|su|ric (glī′kə sůr′ik), *adj.* **1** relating to glycosuria. **2** having glycosuria.

gly|cyr|rhi|zin (glī′sə rī′zin), *n.* an extract from the root of the licorice plant, used medicinally and as a flavoring. [< Latin *glycyrrhīza* licorice + English *-in*]

gly|ox|a|line (glī ok′sə lēn, -lin), *n.* = imidazole. [< *gly*(col) + *oxal*(ic) + *-ine*[2]]

glyph (glif), *n.* **1** an ornamental groove or channel, usually vertical, as in a Doric frieze. **2** a hieroglyph or similar symbol, especially one carved in relief. **3** any symbol used instead of a name: *... the glyphs, the pictorial symbols that international organisations, companies, and airports use in thousands* (Manchester Guardian Weekly). [< Greek *glyphḗ* carving, carved work < *glýphein* carve, cut out]

glyph|ic (glif′ik), *adj.* **1** of or having to do with carving or modeling. **2** like carving or modeling; sculptured; sculptural.

gly|phog|ra|phy (gli fog′rə fē), *n.* an electrotype process by which a plate with a raised surface suitable for printing is made from an engraved plate. [< Greek *glyphḗ* carving + English *-graphy*]

glyp|tic (glip′tik), *adj.* of or having to do with carving or engraving, especially on precious stones: *Most glyptic designs are still based on traditional forms—cuts that bear alluring names like "strawberry diamond" or "jewel star"* (London Times). [< Greek *glyptikós* < *glýphein* carve]

glyp|tics (glip′tiks), *n.* the art of carving or engraving, especially on precious stones.

glyp|to|dont (glip′tə dont), *n.* any one of an extinct genus of large American mammals related to the armadillo. [< New Latin *Glyptodon* the genus name < Greek *glyptós* carved + *odoús, odontós* tooth]

glyp|to|graph (glip′tə graf, -gräf), *n.* an engraving on a precious stone. [< Greek *glyptós* carved + English *-graph*]

glyp|tog|ra|pher (glip tog′rə fər), *n.* an engraver on precious stones.

glyp|to|graph|ic (glip′tə graf′ik), *adj.* of or having to do with glyptography.

glyp|tog|ra|phy (glip tog′rə fē), *n.* **1** the description or study of engraved gems. **2** the art or process of engraving on gems or the like; glyptics. [< Greek *glyptós* carved + English *-graphy*]

gm., gram or grams.

GM (no periods), **1** guided missile. **2** gunner's mate.

G.M., an abbreviation for the following:
1 general manager.
2 (in Great Britain) George Medal.
3 grand marshal.
4 (in Freemasonry) Grand Master.

G-man (jē′man′), *n., pl.* **-men.** *Informal.* a member of the police and detective staff of the Federal government; special agent of the United States Department of Justice; agent of the FBI. [American English abbreviation for *Government man*]

GMAT (no periods) or **G.m.a.t.**, Greenwich mean astronomical time.

Gmc., Germanic.

G-M counter, Geiger counter.

GMT (no periods), **G.M.T.**, or **G.m.t.**, Greenwich Mean Time.

GMV (no periods), gram-molecular volume.

GMW (no periods), gram-molecular weight.

gn., guinea.

gnar or **gnarr** (när), *v.i.*, **gnarred, gnar|ring.** to snarl; growl. [imitative]

gnarl[1] (närl), *n., v.* —*n.* a knot in wood; hard, rough lump: *Wood with gnarls is hard to cut.*
—*v.t.* to make knotted and rugged like an old tree; contort; twist. [back formation < *gnarled*]

gnarl[2] (närl), *v.i. Obsolete.* to snarl. [frequentative form of *gnar*]

gnarled (närld), *adj.* covered with gnarls; knotted; twisted; rugged: *A gnarled branch served as his walking stick. The farmer's gnarled hands grasped the plow firmly.* [probably variant of *knurled*]

gnarl|y (när′lē), *adj.* = gnarled.

gnash (nash), *v., n.* —*v.t.* **1** to strike or grind (the teeth) together, especially from rage or anguish; grind together: *The angry animals gnashed their teeth.* **2** to bite by gnashing the teeth; bite upon: *I strove ... To rend and gnash my bonds in twain* (Byron).
—*v.i.* to strike together or grind the teeth, especially from rage or anguish.
—*n.* the act of gnashing the teeth: *With a gnash of the teeth he slammed the door.*
[variant of Middle English *gnasten.* Compare Old Icelandic *gnastan* gnashing.]

gnat (nat), *n.* **1** any one of various small, two-winged insects or flies. Most gnats are blood-sucking and make bites that itch. **2** *British.* a mosquito.
strain at a gnat, to object to some small or very trifling thing: *Ye blind guides, which strain at a gnat, and swallow a camel* (Matthew 23:24).
[Old English *gnætt*]

gnat|catch|er (nat′kach′ər), *n.* any one of various small, insect-eating American birds.

gnath|ic (nath′ik), *adj.* of or having to do with the jaw. [< Greek *gnáthos* jaw + English *-ic*]

gnathic index, a measure of the projection of the upper jaw, expressed by multiplying the distance from basion to the alveolar point (middle point of the anterior surface of the upper jaw) by 100 and dividing by the distance from basion to nasion.

gna|thi|on (nā′thē on, nath′ē-), *n.* the lowest point in the middle of the anterior edge of the lower jaw. [< New Latin *gnathion* < Greek *gnáthos* jaw]

gna|thite (nā′thīt, nath′īt), *n.* one of the appendages of the mouth of an arthropod. [< Greek *gnáthos* jaw + English *-ite*[1]]

gna|thon|ic (na thon′ik), *adj.* parasitical; toadying. [< Latin *Gnathō, -ōnis,* a parasitical character in the *Eunuchus* of Terence (< Greek *Gnáthōn* a name, also, a parasite; (literally) full-mouth < *gnáthos* jaw) + English *-ic*]

gnat|like (nat′līk′), *adj.* like a gnat, especially in size; very small.

gnat|ty (nat′ē), *adj.*, **-ti|er, -ti|est.** **1** infested with gnats: *They can venture into the gnattiest woods without suffering any assault* (Amateur Photographer). **2** resembling a gnat.

gnaw (nô), *v.*, **gnawed, gnawed** or **gnawn, gnaw|ing.** —*v.t.* **1** to bite at and wear away: *A mouse has gnawed the cover of this box.* **2** to make by biting: *A rat can gnaw a hole through wood.* **3** *Figurative.* to wear away; consume; corrode: *When eating Time shall gnaw the proudest towers* (Phineas Fletcher). **4** *Figurative.* to trouble; harass; torment: *All that bitterness and defeat would not die. It would gnaw the souls of men* (James T. Farrell).
—*v.i.* **1** to bite: *to gnaw at a bone. A mouse has gnawed right through the cover of this book.* **2** to cause corrosion. **3** *Figurative.* to torment as if by biting; trouble; harass: *The feeling of guilt gnawed at my conscience day and night.*
[Old English *gnagan*] —**gnaw′er**, *n.*

gnaw|ing (nô′ing), *n., adj.* —*n.* **1** the act of one that gnaws. **2** *Figurative.* pain, as in the stomach, bowels, or conscience.
—*adj.* that gnaws.
gnawings, pangs: *gnawings of conscience, gnawings of hunger.*
—**gnaw′ing|ly**, *adv.*

gnawn (nôn), *v.* gnawed; a past participle of **gnaw**.

gneiss (nīs), *n.* a very dense rock which occurs in layers and is composed of quartz, feldspar, and mica or hornblende. It is distinguished from granite by its layered structure. *The hills were formed of gneiss and other crystalline rocks strongly resistant to erosion* (New Yorker). [< German *Gneis*]

gneiss|ic (nī′sik), *adj.* **1** like gneiss. **2** of or having to do with gneiss: *gneissic rocks.*

gneiss|oid (nī′soid), *adj.* resembling gneiss, especially in structure.

gneiss|ose (nī′sōs), *adj.* = gneissic.

gnoc|chi (nyôk′kē), *n.pl. Italian.* dumplings.

gnome[1] (nōm), *n.* **1** a dwarf in Norse folklore, supposed to live in the earth and guard treasures of precious metals and stones. SYN: troll. **2** an odd-looking, dwarfish person: *a little gnome of a man.* **3** *Informal.* a banker, especially a foreign or international banker: *the gnomes of Zurich.* [< French *gnome* < New Latin *gnomus* (coined by Paracelsus)]

gnome[2] (nōm, nō′mē), *n.* a short, pithy statement of a general truth; proverb. SYN: maxim. [< Greek *gnṓmē* judgment, opinion < *gignṓskein* know]

gnome owl, = pygmy owl.

gno|mic (nō′mik, nom′ik), *adj.* **1** full of maxims or instructive sayings; aphoristic; sententious: *Landor is gnomic rather than dramatic* (Sunday Times). SYN: epigrammatic. **2** of or having to do with certain older Greek poets who wrote aphorisms. [< Greek *gnōmikós* < *gnṓmē* gnome[2]]

gno|mi|cal (nō′mə kəl, nom′ə-), *adj.* = gnomic.
—**gno′mi|cal|ly**, *adv.*

gnom|ish (nō′mish), *adj.* resembling or suggesting a gnome.

gno|mist (nō′mist), *n.* a writer of gnomes.

gno|mol|o|gy (nō mol′ə jē), *n., pl.* **-gies.** **1** sententious writing. **2** a collection of maxims. [< Greek *gnōmologiā* < *gnṓmē* gnome[2] + *-logiā* discourse]

gno|mon (nō′mon), *n.* **1** a rod, pointer, or triangular piece on a sundial or similar device, that shows the time of day by casting its shadow on a marked surface. **2** *Geometry.* what is left of a parallelogram after a similar parallelogram has been taken away at one corner. [< Greek *gnṓmōn* indicator, (literally) one who knows < *gignṓskein* know]

gno|mon|ic (nō mon′ik), *adj.* **1** having to do with a gnomon or sundial. **2** having to do with measuring, especially of time, by a sundial.

gno|sis (nō′sis), *n.* **1** knowledge. **2** a special knowledge of spiritual things. [< New Latin *gnosis* < Greek *gnôsis* investigation < *gignṓskein* know]

Gnos|tic (nos′tik), *adj., n.* —*adj.* of or having to do with Gnosticism or the Gnostics.
—*n.* a believer in Gnosticism. [< Late Latin *Gnōsticus* < Greek *gnostikós* knowing < *gnōstós* < *gignṓskein*] —**Gnos′ti|cal|ly**, *adv.*

gnos|tic (nos′tik), *adj.* **1** relating to knowledge. **2** possessing knowledge, especially of spiritual things. [< *Gnostic*] —**gnos′ti|cal|ly**, *adv.*

gnos|ti|cal (nos′tə kəl), *adj.* = gnostic.

Gnos|ti|cal (nos′tə kəl), *adj.* = Gnostic.

Gnos|ti|cism (nos′tə siz əm), *n.* a mystical religious and philosophical doctrine of early Christian times. Gnostics claimed that spiritual knowledge, rather than faith, was essential to salvation.

gno|thi se|au|ton (gnō′thē se′ou ton′), *Greek.* know thyself.

gno|to|bi|ol|o|gy (nō′tō bī ol′ə jē), *n.* the branch of biology dealing with gnotobiotes and gnotobiotics: *A highly specialized segment of the ultraclean technology is gnotobiology, the raising of germfree animals, largely for research purposes* (Science Journal).

gno|to|bi|ote (nō′tō bī′ōt), *n.* a germfree animal infected with one or more known microorganisms for the purpose of studying the behavior of the known microorganisms in a controlled situation. [< Greek *gnōtós* known + *biotē* life]

gno|to|bi|ot|ic (nō′tō bī ot′ik), *adj.* **1** of or having to do with gnotobiotes or gnotobiotics. **2** free of germs or associated only with known germs.

gno|to|bi|ot|ics (nō′tō bī ot′iks), *n.* the study of organisms or conditions that are either free of germs or associated only with known germs: *Gnotobiotics includes the study of both "germ-free" animals and animals whose microbial flora can be completely specified.* (New Scientist).

GNP (no periods), gross national product.

gns., guineas.

***gnu** (nü, nyü), *n., pl.* **gnus** or (*collectively*) **gnu**. any one of various large African antelopes with an oxlike head, curved horns, high shoulders, and a long tail; wildebeest. [< Kaffir *i-nqu* black hartebeest or white-tailed gnu]

***gnu**

go¹ (gō), *v.,* **went, gone, go|ing,** *n., pl.* **goes,** *adj.* —*v.i.* **1** to move along: *Cars go on the road. Go straight home at once.* **2** to move away; leave: *Don't go yet. It is time for us to go.* **3** to be in motion; act; work; run: *Make the washing machine go. Does your watch go well?* **4** to get to be; become: *to go mad.* **5** to be habitually; be: *to go hungry for a week.* **6** to proceed; advance: *to go to New York.* **7** to be current: *A rumor went through the town.* **8** to be known: *She went under a false name.* **9** to put oneself: *Don't go to any trouble for me.* **10** to extend; reach: *His memory does not go back that far.* **11** to pass: *Summer had gone. Vacation goes quickly.* SYN: elapse. **12** to be given: *First prize goes to you.* **13** to be sold: *The painting goes to the highest bidder.* **14** to tend; lead: *This goes to show that you must work harder.* **15** to turn out; have a certain result: *How did the game go?* **16** to have its place; belong: *This book goes on the top shelf.* **17** to make a certain sound: *The cork goes pop.* **18** to have certain words; be said: *How does that song go?* **19** to refer; appeal: *to go to court.* **20** to carry an action to a given point: *to go as high as $50.* **21** to contribute to as a result: *the items which go to make up the total.* **22** to die: *My grandmother went peacefully in the night.* **23** to break down; give way; fail: *His eyesight is going. The engine in the old car finally went.* **24** to linger; wait: *another hour to go.* **25** to be permitted or accepted: *Anything goes.* **26** *Informal.* to say: *I asked him why he was late and he goes, "I overslept."*

—*v.t.* **1** to make a bid or bet of; stake; wager: *I'll go another five dollars.* SYN: risk, adventure. **2** to carry on as far as; go to the point of; cope with: *I really can't go another mouthful.* **3** *Informal.* to put up with; stand: *I can't go modern art.* SYN: endure, abide, tolerate. **4** to take on (an opponent).

—*n.* **1** the act of going: *The boat rolled gently with the come and go of small waves.* **2** *Informal.* an attempt at something; try; chance: *Let's have another go at this problem.* SYN: turn, spell. **3** *Informal.* something successful; a success: *He made a go of the new store. More than 100 farmers scattered across Georgia are convinced they can make a go of sheep raising* (Wall Street Journal). **4** *Informal.* spirit; energy; vigor: *A car so charged with verve and drive and "go" there's nothing in your experience so joyously alive* (Newsweek). SYN: dash, animation. **5** *Informal.* a state of affairs; the way things are: *This is a pretty go!* **6** *Informal.* the fashion; style; rage: *a thing which is all the go.* **7** *Informal.* a bargain; anything agreed on: *It's a go.* **8** *Informal.* the normal quantity of liquor, etc., consumed at one time: *He could estimate precisely the number of goes left in a bottle.* **9** the preliminary or final examination at Cambridge University for the degree of B.A.: *His little go and great go he creditably passed* (Thackeray). **10** *U.S. Informal.* a signal or permission to proceed; go-ahead: *On this statewise pass astronauts John Young and Bob Crippen were given a go to stay in orbit* (New York Times).

—*adj. U.S. Informal.* in perfect order and ready to proceed: *She was suddenly in a go condition with all the assurance of a woman on familiar ground* (Punch).

as they (people or things) **go**, considering how others are: *They call it fortified, and so it is, as fortifications go* (Daniel Defoe).

from the word go. See under **word**.

go about, **a** to be busy at; work on: *She went about her work with energy.* **b** to move from place to place: *It is great pity that such a ... gentleman should undervalue himself so, as to go about with these soldier fellows* (Henry Fielding). **c** to turn around; change direction: *If you will just go about, you will find the store we passed.* **d** to circulate; have currency: *A report went about that Henry had murdered him* (Charlotte M. Yonge).

go along, to cooperate: *You can buy your house, if the bank is willing to go along.*

go along with, to cooperate with; agree with: *The club members decided to go along with the president's recommendation.*

go around, **a** to satisfy everyone; be enough to give some for all: *There were enough apples and nuts to go around. When it* [*the turkey*] *was carved, there was not enough of it to go around* (P. T. Barnum). **b** to move from place to place: *I spent a day or two ... going around and seeing the other colleges* (Thomas Hughes).

go at, **a** to attack: *He went at the dog with a stick.* **b** *Figurative.* to take in hand with energy; work at: *Let's go at this problem in a different way.*

go back of, to investigate: *The public ... ought not to be compelled to go back of academic titles to find out what they mean* (Science).

go back on, *Informal.* **a** not to be faithful or loyal to; betray: *Some member of the secret organization has gone back on his comrades* (Liverpool Daily Post). **b** to fail to keep (one's word, etc.); withdraw from: *She went back on her promise. How could I strike my colours, go back on my basic principles?* (London Times).

go begging. See under **beg¹**.

go behind, to investigate the real or hidden reasons for: *I do not desire to go behind these proofs* (Congressional Globe).

go by, **a** to pass: *He let the insult go by. We went by that store often. Time goes by quickly.* **b** to be guided by; follow: *Go by what he says. I would go by the rules if I were you.* **c** to be known by: *He goes by the name of Smith.* **d** to do without; dispense with: *if he apologises ... or thinks, of his dollar, or cannot go by food* (Emerson).

go by the board. See under **board**.

go down, **a** to descend; slope downward; decline; sink: *His temperature is going down. The wrecked ship went down.* **b** *Figurative.* to be defeated; lose: *Their team went down before our superior playing.* **c** to be entered in an account, etc.: *All this ... went down on the account ... and was debited against them* (B. Farjeon). **d** to lose violence; subside: *The wind goes down before the waves.* **e** to be accepted by: *His motion did not go down with the assembly.* **f** (in contract bridge) to fail to fulfill one's contract: *If I pass and he doubles, you are bound to go down.* **g** *British.* to leave a residential university: *Some students go down at the end of term, but others go down permanently.*

go down the drain. See under **drain**.

go far, **a** to last long: *Mother's apple pie will not go very far.* **b** to tend very much: *This high duty ... went far to enable the distillers to fix the price of spirits* (John R. McCullough). **c** to get ahead: *If you are diligent and industrious, you will go far.*

go for, **a** to try to get: *He went for the big prize. Each dog selected his bird, and went for it steadily* (Scribner's Magazine). **b** *Figurative.* to favor; support: *The public goes for his ideas.* **c** *Informal.* to attack: *That dog goes for anyone who gets near him.* **d** *Figurative.* to be taken or considered as: *All his efforts went for nothing.* **e** *Informal.* to be attracted to: *She goes for his type.*

go for broke. See under **broke¹**.

go great guns. See under **great gun**.

go in for, *Informal.* to try to do; take part in; spend time and energy at: *He intends to go in for football.*

go into, **a** to enter into a condition or activity: *to go into many expenses. He went into a rage. The book is going into its third edition. He went into politics.* **b** to be contained in: *How many pints go into a gallon?* **c** to investigate: *The police have gone into the case and made some arrests. It is not easy to believe that any tribunal would have gone into such a question* (Macaulay).

go in with, to join; share with: *to go in a partnership with another. Are you going in with that unfortunate Masterton and men like that?* (Mrs. Campbell Praed).

go it, *Informal.* to go fast: *That's going it rather strong* (Frederick Marryat). *I say, young Copperfield, you're going it!* (Dickens).

go it alone, to act without assistance; act independently or solely: *A great increase in our own military establishment ... is the first essential if we intend to go it alone* (Newsweek).

go off, **a** to leave; set out; depart: *My brother has gone off to college. His daughter had ... gone off with a neighboring young clergyman* (Henry Fielding). **b** to explode; be fired: *The pistol went off unexpectedly.* **c** to take place; happen: *The picnic went off as planned.* **d** to stop using; discontinue: *America went off the gold standard after the Great Depression.* **e** to die: *The doctors told me that he might go off any day* (H. Rider Haggard). **f** to lose quality; deteriorate: *His style had then gone off* (Macaulay).

go on, **a** to go ahead; go forward; continue: *After a pause he went on reading. If you teach, you're expected to go on teaching whatever happens* (Eudora Welty). **b** to happen: *What goes on here?* **c** to behave: *He is foolish to go on in this manner.* **d** to manage: *For the first two days he went on very well.*

go one better. See under **better¹**.

go out, **a** to go to a party, show, or other entertainment: *He had a very good time when he went out Saturday night. We often go out to dinner.* **b** to leave (a place); go from one's house: *I am going out for a while.* **c** to stop burning: *Don't let the candle go out. His cigar had gone out.* **d** to give sympathy: *The love of a nation goes out to its great men.* **e** to go on strike: *The Penn Central switchmen went out.* **f** to retire from office: *The Government is likely to go out.* **g** to cease to be fashionable: *Has tolerance gone out with astrology?* **h** to come to an end: *March went out like a lion.* **i** *British.* to happen; take place; come off: *We were warned there might be an interruption to the programme but tonight it went out as scheduled* (London Times). **j** *Golf.* to play the first nine holes: *He went out with a score of 35.* **k** to collapse: *Water swept down the valley when the dam went out.*

go over, **a** to look at carefully: *to go over a problem. I really believe we shall have the whole business of civil government to go over* (E. Rutledge). **b** to do again; repeat: *He went over the explanation several times.* **c** to read again: *Go over the poem till you memorize it.* **d** *Informal.* to succeed: *The play went over on Broadway and became a big hit.*

go places. See under **place**.

go public. See under **public**.

go steady. See under **steady**.

go the distance. See under **distance**.

go through, **a** to go to the end of; do all of: *Let's go through the rehearsal without any interruptions. It would take far too long to go through all the propositions* (Lewis Carroll). **b** to undergo; experience: *He went through a serious operation.* **c** to search: *He went through his pockets looking for the missing key.* **d** to be accepted or approved: *The new schedule did not go through.* **e** to exhaust, as a fortune: *He went through his savings in just a few months and had to look for work again.*

go through with, to complete; carry out to the end: *The contractor went through with his bargain to build the house in three months in spite of the rainy weather. It's apparent this impact will grow, whether or not he goes through with his promised dismantling of* [*the*] *bases* (Wall Street Journal).

go to, *Archaic.* (in imperative only) an expression of disapproval, reproach, incredulity, etc.; come, come!; nonsense: *Go to! you are a wag* (Byron).

go to bat for. See under **bat¹**.

go together, **a** to harmonize; match: *These colors go together.* **b** to keep steady company as sweethearts: *They have been going together since high school.*

go to one's head. See under **head**.

go to pieces. See under **piece**.

go to town. See under **town**.

go under, **a** to be ruined; fail: *Poor management caused the business to go under. You have to adjust to change or go under* (Atlantic). **b** to sink in water; be overwhelmed: *Many warships went under when the Armada was defeated.*

go up, **a** to rise; ascend: *The thermometer is going up.* **b** to increase: *The price of milk has gone up.* **c** to be built; be raised: *New houses are going up quickly. The curtain goes up at 7 P.M.* **d** *U.S. Informal.* to become bankrupt: *The firm has now gone up.*

go with, **a** to go steadily with; accompany; attend: *The girls he had gone with were now married.* **b** to belong with; go well with: *Cheese goes with salad.*

go without, to do without; not have: *You can eat what is on the table or go without.*

here goes! *Informal.* now (I am, he is, we are,

Pronunciation Key: hat, āge, cãre, fär; let, ēqual, tėrm; it, īce; hot, ōpen, ôrder; oil, out; cup, pu̇t, rüle; child; long; thin; ᴛʜen; zh, measure; ə represents **a** in about, **e** in taken, **i** in pencil, **o** in lemon, **u** in circus.

etc.) going to do it: *"Here goes!" the paratrooper exclaimed as he jumped.*

let go, a to allow to escape: *Let me go.* **b** to give up one's hold: *Let go of my shirt.* **c** to give up; cease to control or attend to: *Do only what is necessary and let the rest go.* **d** to fail to keep in good condition: *The owners let the house go and now the paint is peeling off the sides.*

let oneself go, a to give way to one's feelings or desires: *He is too shy to let himself go.* **b** to fail to keep oneself in good condition: *The coach warned the boys on the team not to let themselves go during vacation.*

no go, *Informal.* not to be done or had; hopeless; useless; worthless: *I knew that the idea would be no go from the start.*

on the go, *Informal.* busily occupied; active or restless; on the move: *She is always on the go.*

to go, *Informal.* (of food) to be eaten outside a restaurant, cafeteria, or lunch counter: *two sandwiches to go.*

[Old English *gān*] – **go′er,** *n.*

– ***Syn.*** *v.i.* **2 Go, leave** mean to move away from a point or place. **Go,** the opposite of *come,* emphasizes the movement involved: *She comes and goes as she pleases.* **Leave** emphasizes the departure from the place where one is (or has been): *He has left home. The boat left yesterday.*

► In informal speech **go and** is often redundantly used before another verb: *Go and try it yourself. She went and bought herself a new hat.*

go² or **Go** (gō), *n.* a Japanese game which is probably as old as chess. It is played by placing black and white stones on a board marked with intersecting lines, the object being to surround and thus capture territory or the opponent's men. [< Japanese *go*]

G.O., general orders.

go|a (gō′ə), *n.* a gazelle of Tibet, having a black tail. [< Tibetan *dgoba*]

goad (gōd), *n., v.* – ***n.*** **1** a stick or rod for driving cattle that has a point on the end; gad. **2** something that pricks or wounds like such a stick. **3** *Figurative.* anything that drives or urges one on; spur; stimulus: *Perhaps we owe the goad of totalitarianism some wry thanks for teaching that artists can rush in where statesmen fear to tread* (Saturday Review).

– ***v.t.*** **1** to prick with a goad or other pointed instrument: *The cowboys goaded some of the slower cows with sticks.* **2** *Figurative.* to drive or urge on; act as a goad to; incite: *Hunger goaded him to steal a loaf of bread.* **SYN:** stimulate, spur, impel.

[Old English *gād*]

goaf (gōf), *n., pl.* **goaves** (gōvz), **goafs.** *Mining.* **1** a space from which coal has been worked away: *He could do an accurate gas analysis crouched up in the goaf of a colliery in a dim light* (New Scientist). **2** the refuse left in old workings. Also, **gob.** [origin uncertain]

go-a|head (gō′ə hed′), *n., adj. Informal.* – ***n.*** **1** permission to go ahead or begin; signal or authority to proceed: *United Gas Pipe Line Co., Shreveport, got the go-ahead to construct $2,653,210 of facilities in Terrebonne Parish* (Wall Street Journal). **2** the action of going forward; ambition; spirit: *a student with go-ahead.* **SYN:** zeal.

– ***adj.*** **1** disposed to push ahead; enterprising: *Now for a really go-ahead store that keeps the temperature down to zero in its overcoat department* (Punch). **SYN:** pushing, energetic, progressive. **2** proceeding straight forward without pause; forthright.

go-a|head|ism (gō′ə hed′iz əm), *n. Informal.* enterprise; initiative.

goal (gōl), *n.* **1** the place where a race ends: *The boy who reached the goal first was the winner.* **2** the place to which players try to advance a ball or puck in certain games in order to make a score: *We couldn't keep the ball out of the goal, and the other team scored a point.* **3** the act of advancing or carrying a ball or puck to this place. **4** an object marking the place of a goal. **5** a score or number of points won by reaching this place: *The other team beat us by six goals to two.* **6** = goalkeeper. **7** *Figurative.* a thing for which an effort is made; something desired: *The goal of his ambition was to be a great doctor. Our goal in Asia is similar to our goal in Europe—to maintain U.S. diplomatic and economic participation* (New York Times). **SYN:** aim, end. [Middle English *gol;* origin uncertain]

goal crease, *Lacrosse.* = crease (def. 3b).

goal-di|rect|ed (gōl′də rek′tid, -dī-), *adj.* directed toward a specific and achievable goal; not haphazard.

goal|er (gō′lər), *n. Canadian.* a goalkeeper.

goal|ie (gō′lē), *n.* = goalkeeper.

goal|keep|er (gōl′kē′pər), *n.* a player who tries to prevent the ball or puck from crossing or reaching the goal in certain games; goalie; goaltender.

goal kick, *Soccer.* a penalty kick given to the defending team when a member of the offensive team kicks the ball over the end line but not into the goal.

goal|less (gōl′lis), *adj.* without a goal.

goal line, a line marking the position of a goal in a game.

goal|mouth (gōl′mouth′), *n.* the space immediately in front of the goal in soccer or hockey; the entrance to a goal.

goal post, one of a pair of posts with a bar across them, forming a goal in football and soccer.

goal|tend|er (gōl′ten′dər), *n.* = goalkeeper.

goal|wor|thy (gōl′wėr′ᴛʜē), *adj.,* **-thi|er, -thi|est.** *Sports.* sufficient to be rewarded by a goal: *Though he did make one goalworthy effort,* [*he*] *was below his best form.*

Go|an (gō′ən), *adj., n.* – ***adj.*** of or having to do with Goa.

– ***n.*** a person born or living in Goa.

Go|an|ese (gō′ə nēz′, -nēs′), *adj.* of or having to do with Goa; Goan.

***go|an|na** (gō an′ə), *n.* any one of a group of large Australian monitor lizards, especially a species of eastern Australia that attains a length of about six feet. [probably alteration of *iguana*]

***goanna**

Go|a powder (gō′ə), = araroba. [< *Goa,* former Portuguese enclave, now part of India (the powder was exported from Brazil to Goa)]

go-a|round (gō′ə round′), *n.* **1a** a movement around a circular course, as of an aircraft returning to make a second approach to a landing. **b** a journey about a circuit and back to the starting point. **2** one complete performance, operation of a process, etc.

***goat** (gōt), *n., pl.* **goats** or (*collectively*) **goat.** **1** any one of various lively, cud-chewing mammals with hollow horns and usually a beard. Goats are closely related to sheep but are stronger, less timid, and more active than sheep. They are raised in all parts of the world for their milk, flesh, hair, and hides. **2** any one of certain related mammals, such as the mountain goat. **3** *Informal.* a person made to take the blame or suffer for the mistakes of others; scapegoat. **4** *Figurative.* a licentious man.

get one's goat, *Informal.* to make one angry or annoyed; tease a person: *Julian got his goat with his opinions on art, which were totally uninformed* (Philip Roth).

[Old English *gāt* she-goat, later, male goat] – **goat′like′,** *adj.*

***goat**
definition 1

***goatee**

Goat (gōt), *n.* a constellation and the tenth sign of the zodiac; Capricorn. [< *goat*]

goat antelope, any one of several goatlike antelopes, such as the chamois, goral, serow, and Rocky Mountain goat.

***goat|ee** (gō tē′), *n.* a pointed, trimmed beard on a man's chin. It looks like the beard of a he-goat. [American English < *goat*]

goat|eed (gō tēd′), *adj.* having a goatee.

goat|fish (gōt′fish′), *n., pl.* **-fish|es** or (*collectively*) **-fish.** any one of various mullets of the West Indies, with barbels at the chin.

goat god, the god Pan.

goat grass, a wild grass that often grows around the edges of wheat fields in the Mediterranean region. It has become introduced in the United States as a troublesome weed.

goat|herd (gōt′hėrd′), *n.* a person who tends goats.

goat|ish (gō′tish), *adj.* = lustful. – **goat′ish|ly,** *adv.* – **goat′ish|ness,** *n.*

goat moth, = carpenter moth.

goat or **goat's pepper,** the chili plant.

goats|beard (gōts′bird′), *n.* **1** = salsify. **2** a kind of spirea bearing long spikes of small, white flowers.

goat|skin (gōt′skin′), *n.* **1** the skin of a goat. **2** leather made from it. **3** a container made from this leather, used especially for holding wine.

goat's-rue (gōts′rü′), *n.* either of two herbs of the pea family, a European plant or an American plant, formerly used in medicine.

goat|suck|er (gōt′suk′ər), *n.* any one of a family of birds having large, flat heads, wide mouths fringed with stiff bristles, and long wings; nightjar. Whippoorwills and nighthawks are goatsuckers. Goatsuckers fly at dusk or at night and feed on flying insects.

goat|weed (gōt′wēd′), *n.* = St.-John's-wort.

goaves (gōvz), *n.* a plural of **goaf.**

go-a|way bird (gō′ə wā′), a gray South African crested touraco with a raucous call; go-way bird. [< its call, that scares off game]

gob¹ (gob), *n. Slang.* a sailor of enlisted rank in the United States Navy. [American English; origin uncertain]

gob² (gob), *n., v.,* **gobbed, gob|bing.** *Informal.* – ***n.*** a mass or lump.

– ***v.t.*** to throw a gob or mass of: *The politician, equipped with a trowel and the Fixed Smile, gobs mortar on a cornerstone, or noshes his way along the campaign trail* (Time).

gobs, *Informal.* a great deal; lots: *There were gobs of colourful oratory ...* (Alistair Cooke).

[apparently < Old French *gobe* mouth(ful), lump]

gob³ (gob), *n. Slang.* the mouth. [origin uncertain]

gob⁴ (gob), *n.* = goaf.

go|bang (gō bang′), *n.* a Japanese game played by two players on a board marked with intersecting lines and using black and white stones, each player trying to get five of his stones in a row before his opponent does. [< Japanese *goban*]

gob|bet (gob′it), *n.* **1** a lump; mass. **2** a portion or piece, such as one of raw meat or fat. **3** *Figurative.* a morsel or tidbit of anything: *Your reporters have been working round the clock to winkle out every succulent gobbet of news for the furtherance of truth* (Punch). [< Old French *gobet* < *gobe* gob²]

gob|ble¹ (gob′əl), *v.,* **-bled, -bling.** – ***v.t.*** **1** to eat fast and greedily; swallow hurriedly in large mouthfuls; gulp: *He gobbled the ice cream so fast he got a headache.* **SYN:** bolt. **2** *U.S. Slang.* to seize upon graspingly or greedily; lay hold of; collar.

– ***v.i.*** to eat fast and greedily.

gobble up, a *U.S. Informal.* to seize upon eagerly: *To sell it ... not to have it gobbled up by speculators* (Thomas Jefferson). **b** to devour; eat away: *While gobbling up huge quantities of new steel, the auto industry also is turning out growing amounts of a key ingredient of metal—steel scrap* (Wall Street Journal).

gob|ble² (gob′əl), *v.,* **-bled, -bling,** *n.* – ***v.i.*** to make the characteristic throaty sound of a male turkey or a sound like it: *Regiments of turkeys were gobbling through the farm-yard* (Washington Irving).

– ***n.*** the throaty sound that a male turkey makes. [imitative, perhaps variant of *gabble*]

gob|ble|dy|gook or **gob|ble|de|gook** (gob′əl dē-gu̇k), *n. Informal.* speech or writing that is hard to understand because it is full of long, involved sentences and big words: *I will not go into the many forms of gobbledygook—legal, medical, business, sociological—that plague us* (Atlantic). [(apparently coined by Maury Maverick, a U.S. government official) imitative of a turkey's call]

gob|bler¹ (gob′lər), *n.* a male turkey.

gob|bler² (gob′lər), *n.* a person or thing that gobbles food, land, or anything else.

Gob|e|lin (gob′ə lin; *French* gō blaɴ′), *adj., n.* – ***adj.*** **1** of or made at the factory and dye works of the Gobelins in Paris: *Gobelin tapestry or upholstery.* **2** resembling such tapestry or upholstery.

– ***n.*** a Gobelin tapestry.

go-be|tween (gō′bi twēn′), *n.* a person who goes back and forth between others, with messages, proposals, or suggestions; intermediary: *A prophet ... is the go-between of gods and men* (Lord Dunsany). **SYN:** middleman.

gob feeder, a machine that drops a measured amount of molten glass into a mold at regular intervals.

go|bi|oid (gō′bē oid), *adj., n.* – ***adj.*** resembling the goby.

– ***n.*** a fish like a goby. [< New Latin *Gobioides* the goby family < Latin *gōbius* goby]

gob|let (gob′lit), *n.* **1** a drinking glass that stands high above its base on a stem, and has no handle. **2** *Archaic.* **a** a hollow drinking bowl without a handle. **b** a wine cup. [< Old French *gobelet* (diminutive) < *gobel* cup, probably < *gober* to drink]

goblet cell, an epithelial cell, shaped roughly like a goblet, that produces mucus.

gob|lin (gob′lən), *n., adj.* – ***n.*** a mischievous sprite or elf in folklore, in the form of an ugly-looking dwarf. **SYN:** hobgoblin, bogy.

—*adj.* **1** of or having to do with goblins. **2** suitable for goblins.
[compare Old French *gobelin*]

goblin Robin, a hobgoblin; Robin Goodfellow.

go|bo (gō′bō), *n., pl.* **-bos.** *Especially U.S.* in motion pictures or television: **1** a dark strip used to keep lights from interfering with a camera lens, or to mold lighting effects, in pictures of the face. **2** a device used to prevent undesirable sounds from entering a microphone. [origin unknown]

go|boon (go bün′), *n. Slang.* a spittoon.

gobs (gobz), *n.pl.* See under **gob**[2].

gob|stop|per (gob′stop′ər), *n. British.* a large, round piece of very hard candy; jawbreaker. [< *gob*[3] + *stopper*]

go|by (gō′bē), *n., pl.* **-bies** or (*collectively*) **-by.** **1** any one of a family of bony, spiny-rayed fishes living near seacoasts. The ventral fins of gobies are united to form a suction cup by which they cling to rocks. **2** any one of various related fishes having disjoined pelvic fins. [< Latin *gōbius, cōbius* a kind of fish < Greek *kōbiós*]

go-by (gō′bī′), *n. Informal.* a going by or casting off; intentional neglect; slight: *He had ... tried to get a date with her, and for the third time since the dance she had given him the go-by* (James T. Farrell).

G.O.C., *British.* general officer commanding.

go-cart or **go|cart** (gō′kärt′), *n.* **1** a low seat on wheels for a small child to ride on; stroller. **2** a small framework moving on casters in which children may learn to walk; walker. **3** a kind of light open carriage.

gock (gok), *n. Slang.* some foul, nasty substance. [variant of *guck*]

god (god), *n., v.,* **god|ded, god|ding.** —*n.* **1a** a being that is thought to have greater powers than any man and considered worthy of worship: *Cupid is considered to be the god of love.* **SYN:** deity. **b** a male god. **c** a likeness or image of a god; idol: *Early Christians raided many Roman temples, smashing their gods and other statues.* **2** *Figurative.* a person or thing greatly admired and respected: *Sir Aylmer Aylmer, that almighty man, the county god* (Tennyson).
—*v.t.* to make into a god; deify; worship as a god.
gods, *Especially British.* the topmost gallery of a theater: *A robust and uninhibited live audience ... was resolved to get value for money and to boo from the gods if it did not* (London Times).
[Old English *god*]

God (god), *n.* **1** the maker and ruler of the world; the one Supreme Being who loves and helps man: *Jews and Christians worship God.* **2** the Supreme Being considered with reference to a particular attribute: *the God of justice, the God of mercy.*
please God, if it is God's will: *We will see you tomorrow at church, please God.*
so help me God!, a solemn oath that I am telling the truth: *I ... do swear that I will be faithful and bear true allegiance to Her Majesty ... according to law. So help me God!* (Tennyson).
[Old English *god*]

Go|dard|i|an (gô där′dē ən), *adj.* having to do with or characteristic of Jean-Luc Godard, born 1930, a French motion-picture director noted for his cinematic innovations: *"Partner" is a Godardian exercise of repetition, monologues, slogans, alienation effects, cheeky political symbolism* (Listener).

god-aw|ful (god′ô′fəl), *adj. Informal.* dreadful; terrible.

god|child (god′chīld′), *n., pl.* **-chil|dren.** a child whom a grown-up person sponsors at its baptism.

god|daugh|ter (god′dô′tər), *n.* a female godchild.

god|den (god′den′), *n., interj. Dialect.* good evening.

god|dess (god′is), *n.* **1** a female god: *Jupiter was a god and Juno was his goddess.* **2** a woman whom one worships or devotedly admires. **3** *Figurative.* a very beautiful or charming woman: *The beautiful young movie star was a goddess to the public.*

god|dess|hood (god′is hůd), *n.* the state or dignity of a goddess.

god|dess-ship (god′is ship), *n.* the rank, state, condition, or attributes of a goddess.

go|det (gō dā′), *n.* **1** a triangular insert of fabric used primarily on a skirt to give it fullness or decoration. **2** a wheel or roller of plastic or glass, used in spinning rayon yarn. [< French *godet*]

go|de|tia (gō dē′shə), *n.* any one of a group of American annual plants of the evening-primrose family commonly grown for their showy lilac, pink, or white flowers. [< New Latin *Godetia* < C. H. *Godet,* a Swiss botanist of the 1800's]

go-dev|il (gō′dev′əl), *n.* **1** a rough sled for holding one end of a log while it is being dragged. **2** *U.S.* a device used for exploding a dynamite cartridge in an oil well. **3** a device used to clean out oil pipelines. **4** a handcar.

god|fa|ther (god′fä′ᴛʜər), *n., v.* —*n.* **1** a man who sponsors a child when it is baptized. The godfather promises to help the child to be a good Christian. **2** *U.S. Slang.* the head of one of the units or families of the Mafia or Cosa Nostra.
—*v.t.* to act as godfather to; be sponsor for.

God-fear|ing (god′fir′ing), *adj.* having a reverential fear of God; religious.

God|for|sak|en (god′fər sā′kən), *adj.* **1** forsaken, or seemingly forsaken, by God. **2** abandoned to evil and its penalties: *a band of Godforsaken robbers.* **3** *Figurative.* Also, **godforsaken.** forlorn, desolate, or miserable: ... *the Sahara gave the impression of being a huge, godforsaken waste* (Atlantic).

God-giv|en (god′giv′ən), *adj.* **1** given by God: ... *mankind's God-given capacity to build* (Bulletin of Atomic Scientists). **2** *Figurative.* very welcome and suitable. **SYN:** beneficial.

god|head (god′hed), *n.* **1** divine nature; divinity; deity. **2** a deity or divinity.
the Godhead, God in all His attributes and relations: *'Tis true I am alone; So was the Godhead, ere he made the world* (John Dryden).
[< *god* + Middle English *hede* head]

god|hood (god′hůd), *n.* divine character; divinity.

God|hood (god′hůd), *n.* = Godhead.

Go|di|va (gə dī′və), *n.* **Lady**, the wife of an English nobleman who lived during the 1000's. According to legend, she rode naked through the town of Coventry to get her husband to grant relief to the people from a burdensome tax.

god-king (god′king′), *n.* a temporal ruler regarded as a god or as having divine powers: *The young Dalai Lama, ... as a reincarnation of a manifestation of the Buddha, is a god-king* (Newsweek).

god|less (god′lis), *adj.* **1** not believing in God; without a god; not religious. **SYN:** irreligious, ungodly, impious. **2** ungodly; wicked; evil: *a godless life of crime.* —**god′less|ly**, *adv.* —**god′less-ness**, *n.*

god|like (god′līk′), *adj.* **1** like God or a god; divine: *The seeds of godlike power are in us still; Gods are we, bards, saints, heroes, if we will* (Matthew Arnold). **2** suitable for God or a god.
—**god′like′ness**, *n.*

god|ling (god′ling), *n.* a little god; a minor or petty deity: *We are well along in an age in which our heroes and godlings are not Captains of Industry* (Harper's).

god|ly (god′lē), *adj.,* **-li|er, -li|est,** *adv.* —*adj.* **1** obeying, loving, and fearing God; devout; religious; pious: *Saint Francis led a godly life.* **SYN:** righteous. **2** *Archaic.* of or from God; divine; spiritual. —*adv.* in a godly manner. —**god′li|ly,** *adv.* —**god′li|ness**, *n.*

god|moth|er (god′muᴛʜ′ər), *n.* a woman who sponsors a child when it is baptized. The godmother promises to help the child to be a good Christian.

Go|dol|phin Barb (gə dol′fən), one of the three stallions from which all English thoroughbred horses are descended. The other two were the Byerly Turk and the Darley Arabian. [< the Earl of *Godolphin,* in Cambridgeshire, England, who acquired it in the mid-1700's]

go|down (gō doun′), *n.* a warehouse in India and Eastern Asia. [< Malay *gĕdong* or *gudong* warehouse]

god|par|ent (god′pãr′ənt), *n.* a godfather or godmother; sponsor.

go|droon (gə drün′), *n.* = gadroon.

go|drooned (gə dründ′), *adj.* = gadrooned.

go|droon|ing (gə drü′ning), *n.* = gadrooning.

gods (godz), *n.pl.* See under **god.**

God's acre, a churchyard with graves in it; burial ground; cemetery.

god|send (god′send′), *n.* something unexpected and very welcome, as if sent from God; sudden piece of good luck: *The chance to go to a warm climate was a godsend to the sick man.* **SYN:** boon, windfall. [alteration (influenced by *send,* verb) of *God's send,* Middle English *Godes sonde,* Old English *sond* message]

god|sent (god′sent′), *adj.* very welcome, as if sent from God: *godsent relief. I give you two godsent models of ... intellectuality and smooth education running rampant without talent* (J. D. Salinger).

god|ship (god′ship), *n.* **1** the character of a god; divinity. **2** a title for a god.

god|son (god′sun′), *n.* a male godchild.

God|speed (god′spēd′), *n.* a parting wish of success to a person starting on a journey or undertaking.

God|ward (god′wərd), *adv., adj.* **1** toward God. **2** in relation to God.

God|wards (god′wərdz), *adv.* = Godward.

God|win|i|an (god′win′ē ən), *adj.* having to do with or characteristic of the English philosopher William Godwin, or his views on politics and society.

god|wit (god′wit), *n.* any one of a genus of wading birds somewhat like a snipe, having long, upward curving bills and slender legs.

goe|duck (gwē′duk), *n.* a large edible clam of the northwest coast of the United States; gweduc. [alteration of *gweduc*]

goes (gōz), *v.* the third person singular present tense of **go**: *He goes to school.*

Goe|the|an (gœ′tē ən), *adj.* of or characteristic of Johann W. von Goethe, or his books, plays, or philosophy.

goe|thite (gō′thīt, gœ′tīt), *n.* a mineral consisting of a hydrous oxide of iron; göthite. [< Johann W. von *Goethe,* 1749-1832, a German writer and philosopher (because of his studies in mineralogy) + *-ite*[1]]

go|fer (gō′fər), *n. U.S. Slang.* an office worker who runs errands for the staff: *She* [*was*] *working as a "gofer" at a Minneapolis TV station* (Time). [alteration of *go for,* as in "go for coffee"]

gof|fer (gof′ər, gôf′-), *v., n.* —*v.t.* **1** to flute (as a frill) with a hot iron; crimp. **2** to impress (book edges) with an ornamental pattern.
—*n.* **1** an ornamental fluting formerly used especially for the borders of women's caps. **2** a tool used to goffer. Also, **gauffer.**
[< French *gaufrer,* or *gauffer* stamp with a figure or pattern < *gaufre* small cake, waffle, also earlier Old North French *walfre* < Dutch *wafel* waffle]

goff-ham|mer (gof′ham′ər), *n.* a machine that forges cast steel into such items as table knives. [*goff,* probably < *goffer*]

Gog (gog), *n.* **1** a prince of Magog who led the barbarian hordes of the north in an assault on Israel (in the Bible, Ezekiel 38-39). **2** one of the two nations (**Gog and Magog**) that make war against the kingdom of God at Armageddon after being deceived by Satan (in the Bible, Revelation 20:8).

go-get|ter (gō′get′ər), *n. Informal.* an energetic person who tries hard for and usually gets what he is after.

go-get|ting (gō′get′ing), *adj. Informal.* full of spirit; aggressive and enterprising: *The greatest two-fisted go-getting sales organization ...* (Wall Street Journal).

gog|ga (gog′ə), *n. Afrikaans.* **1** any type of insect. **2** anything that creeps or crawls; vermin. [< Hottentot *xoxon*]

gog|gle (gog′əl), *v.,* **-gled, -gling,** *adj., n.* —*v.i.* **1** to roll one's eyes; stare with bulging eyes; be goggle-eyed with surprise, wonder, or disbelief: ... *left them goggling at the Cremonese treasures that he dug up out of his sack* (London Times). **2** to roll; bulge: *The children's eyes goggled as the magician pulled a rabbit out of the empty hat.* **3** to turn the eyes to one side or the other; look obliquely; squint. **4** to turn to one side.
—*v.t.* to turn (one's eyes) from side to side with an unsteady motion, or to one side.
—*adj.* rolling; bulging: *A frog has goggle eyes.* **SYN:** protuberant, prominent.
—*n.* **1** a rolling of the eyes; a stare with bulging eyes: *the goggle of an owl.* **2** *British Slang.* = goggle-box.
goggles, large, close-fitting eyeglasses to protect the eyes from light, dust, or foreign objects: *The motorcycle rider wore goggles.*
[Middle English *gogelen;* origin uncertain]

gog|gle-box (gog′əl boks′), *n. British Slang.* a television set: ... *the drugged hours we spend in front of the goggle-box* (London Times).

gog|gled (gog′əld), *adj.* wearing or equipped with protective goggles: *a goggled frogman.*

gog|gle-eyed (gog′əl īd′), *adj.* having rolling, bulging, or staring eyes.

gog|gles (gog′əlz), *n.pl.* See under **goggle**.

gog|let (gog′lit), *n.* (in India) a long-necked earthenware water cooler. Also, **gurglet**. [Anglo-Indian < Portuguese *gorgoletto* narrow-necked jar, perhaps < Late Latin *gurga* gullet, for Latin *gurges*]

go-go (gō′gō), *adj., n.* —*adj.* **1a** of or having to do with the lively dancing and music performed at discothèques or similar night clubs: *Besides skiing, most of the areas offer go-go bands, bars and terraces for sun bathing* (New York Times). **b** performing in discothèques: *go-go girls.* **2** *Informal.* **a** lively; energetic; enterprising: *He's a go-go young intellectual and dresses like it* (William Granger). **b** fashionable; stylish; chic: *He was dressed for action, in a white polo shirt, red cardigan sweater* (*very go-go, being double-*

Pronunciation Key: hat, āge, cãre, fär; let, ēqual, tėrm; it, īce; hot, ōpen, ôrder; **oil**, **out**; cup, pu̇t, rüle; **ch**ild; lo**ng**; **th**in; **ᴛʜ**en; zh, measure; **ə** represents **a** in about, **e** in taken, **i** in pencil, **o** in lemon, **u** in circus.

breasted) and tan slacks (Maclean's). **3** of or having to do with go-go funds: *a go-go mutual fund.*
—*n.* **1** discothèque dancing: *It's golf and go-go, saunas and sunsets; paisleyed walls and chairs of patent leather* (New Yorker). **2** = go-go fund. [< earlier *a-go-go,* adjective, < French *à-gogo* aplenty, influenced by the reduplication of the English verb *go*]

go-go fund, an investment company that engages in speculative operations on the stock market.

Goi|del (goi′ŦHəl, gaŦH′əl; goi′dəl), *n.* **1** a member of a Goidelic people. **2** = Gael. [< Old Irish *Góidhel*]

Goi|del|ic (goi′ŦHə lik, gaŦH′ə-; goi del′ik), *adj., n.* —*adj.* of or having to do with the Gaels or their languages.
—*n.* one of the two large divisions of the Celtic languages (the other being Brythonic); the Gaelic branch of Celtic, including Irish, Scottish Gaelic, and Manx.

go|ing (gō′ing), *n., adj.* —*n.* **1** a going away; leaving: *His going was very sudden. There was already a great coming and going of secret agents between London and Paris* (Atlantic). SYN: departure. **2** the condition of the ground for walking, driving, or riding: *The going is bad on this muddy road.* **3** a course of action; condition of progress: *A ... request for higher postal rates will face rough going in an election-minded Congress* (Wall Street Journal). **4** *Obsolete.* a manner or style of going; gait.
—*adj.* **1** moving; in action; working; running: *Set the clock going.* **2** that goes; that can or will go; operating with success: *His business is a going concern.* **3** in existence; existing; to be had; current or prevalent: *the going price for gold.*
be going to, will; be about to: *It is going to rain. I am going to call you up from Boston.*
get going, *Informal.* to make a start; begin: *Better get going on that report if you want to finish it today.*
going away, *U.S.* **a** (in horse racing) gaining ground rapidly. **b** *Informal.* by a wide margin: *[He] recuperated from the body punches in a few seconds and went out gay for the seventh, which ... he won going away* (New Yorker).
going on, almost; nearly: *It is going on four o'clock.*
goings, proceeding or course: *For his eyes are upon the ways of man, and he seeth all his goings* (Job 34:21).

go-ing concern, *U.S.* a company, store, or any other enterprise or undertaking, that is doing good business.

go|ing-o|ver (gō′ing ō′vər), *n.* **1** a close, searching inspection; critical examination: *During the International Geophysical Year ... 10,000 scientists ... will give the earth a long, complex, intent going-over* (Time). **2** *U.S.* **a** a talking to; scolding: *I got a good going-over in the morning from Old Miss Watson on account of my clothes* (Mark Twain). **b** *Slang.* rough handling; severe beating.

go|ings (gō′ingz), *n.pl.* See under **going**.

go|ings-on (gō′ingz on′), *n.pl.* or **goings on**, actions or events; proceedings; behavior; conduct, especially such as is regarded with disfavor: *the goings-on at the convention.*

go-it-a|lone (gō′it ə lōn′), *adj. Informal.* independent; self-sufficient.

goi|ter or **goi|tre** (goi′tər), *n.* an enlargement of the thyroid gland which is often seen as a large swelling in the front of the neck; struma. It is usually caused by a diet with too little iodine. [< French *goitre,* ultimately < Latin *guttur* throat]

goi|tered or **goi|tred** (goi′tərd), *adj.* **1** having goiter. **2** having a swelling that looks like goiter.

goi|tro|gen (goi′trə jən), *n.* a substance that produces goiter.

goi|tro|gen|ic (goi′trə jen′ik), *adj.* = goitrogenous.

goi|trog|e|nous (goi troj′ə nəs), *adj.* producing goiter.

goi|trous (goi′trəs), *adj.* **1** having goiter. **2** of or like goiter. **3** marked by many cases of goiter.

***go-kart**

***go-kart** (gō′kärt′), *n.* a small, open, four-wheeled racing car for one person; kart. [< *Go-Kart,* a trademark for such a racing car]

go-kart|ing (gō′kärt′ting), *n.* the sport of driving or racing a go-kart; karting.

Gol|con|da (gol kon′də), *n.* a mine or other source of great wealth. [< *Golconda,* ancient city in southern India, once a famous center of diamond trade]

***gold** (gōld), *n., adj.* —*n.* **1** a shiny, bright-yellow, precious metal. Gold is a heavy chemical element which resists rust and other chemical changes and can easily be drawn out into fine wire or hammered into fine sheets. It is used chiefly in making coins and jewelry, and its relative purity is expressed in carats. **2** coins made of gold. **3** *Figurative.* money in large sums; wealth; riches: *The powerful king's treasury was overflowing with gold.* **4** *Figurative.* a bright, beautiful, or precious thing or material: *a heart of gold.* **5** the color of gold; a bright yellow.
—*adj.* **1** made of gold; consisting of gold: *The father bought his son a gold watch.* **2** like gold. **3** bright-yellow; golden. **4** that is to be paid in gold. **5a** (in the United States) of or designating a phonograph recording with sales of one million records or one million dollars: *a gold single, a gold album.* **b** (in Canada) of or designating a phonograph recording with sales of 50,000 to 100,000 records.
[Old English *gold.* See related etym. at **yellow**.]

***gold**
definition 1

symbol	atomic number	atomic weight	oxidation state
Au	79	196.967	3, 1

gold basis, the basing of monetary values on a gold standard.

gold-bear|ing (gōld′bãr′ing), *adj.* containing or yielding gold.

gold|beat|er (gōld′bē′tər), *n.* a person whose work is beating out gold metal into thin plates or gold leaf.

goldbeater's skin, the prepared outside membrane of the large intestine of the ox, used by goldbeaters to lay between the sheets of gold metal which they beat.

gold beetle, a beetle with a golden luster, especially the small beetle which feeds on the sweet potato and allied plants.

gold brick, *Informal.* anything that looks good at first but turns out to be worthless.

gold|brick (gōld′brik′), *v., n. Informal.* —*v.i.* **1** to avoid duties by any evasion or excuse, such as pretended illness: *The medics found that the airmen, far from goldbricking, had a baffling variety of symptoms* (Time). **2** to swindle, as by means of a gold brick: *He would endanger his chance for advancement if he were suspected of goldbricking because of his resentment over his taxes or for any reason* (J. K. Galbraith).
—*v.t.* to swindle; cheat.
—*n.* **1** a person, especially in the army or navy, who avoids duty or shirks work. **2** = gold brick: *Is the peaceful atom, then a goldbrick, a fiasco, a flop?* (David E. Lilienthal).
[American English < *gold* + *brick*] —**gold′brick′er**, *n.*

gold|bug (gōld′bug′), *n.* **1** = gold beetle. **2** *Informal.* a person who hoards gold, especially as a hedge against inflation.

gold certificate, a note formerly issued by the U.S. Treasury certifying that its value in gold is deposited in the Treasury and will be paid on presentation of the note.

gold|crest (gōld′krest′), *n.* a European kinglet with a yellow crest.

gold|cup (gōld′kup′), *n.* a crowfoot or buttercup.

gold cure, a treatment for alcoholism in which the chief remedy is chloride of gold.

gold digger, **1** a person who digs for or mines gold. **2** *U.S. Slang.* a woman who schemes to get money from men: *Our own Becky Sharp is an innocent compared with the gold digger, who is now a stock character of American fiction* (Observer).

gold digging, **1** the act or occupation of digging for or mining gold. **2** *U.S. Slang.* the act or process of getting money from men.
gold diggings, a place where gold is mined: *holes scooped out at the gold diggings.*

gold-dig|ging (gold′dig′ing), *adj. U.S. Slang.* scheming to get money from men.

gold dust, very tiny bits of gold; gold in a fine powder.

gold|en (gōl′dən), *adj., v.* —*adj.* **1** made of gold; consisting of gold: *a golden medal, golden dishes. Every door is barr'd with gold, and opens but to golden keys* (Tennyson). **2** containing or yielding gold: *a golden region or country.* **3** of gold coin or money. **4** shining like gold; bright-yellow: *golden hair, the golden sun.* **5** *Figurative.* resembling gold in value; very good; excellent; extremely favorable, valuable, or important: *golden deeds, a golden opportunity.* **6** *Figurative.* very happy and prosperous; flourishing; joyous: *golden years.* **7** having to do with the fiftieth year or event in a series.
—*v.t.* to make golden. —*v.i.* to become golden. —**gold′en|ly**, *adv.* —**gold′en|ness**, *n.*

Golden Age or **golden age**, **1** *Greek and Roman Mythology.* the first and best age of the world, in which Saturn ruled and mankind lived in a state of idyllic peace, prosperity, and happiness. **2** the period in which a nation or society is at its highest state of prosperity, or in which some human art or activity is at its most excellent: *Burghley directed England's foreign and domestic affairs during the reign of Elizabeth I, often called England's Golden Age* (Lacey Baldwin Smith).

golden age club, *U.S.* any one of various social or recreational organizations for elderly people.

golden ag|er (ā′jər), *U.S. Informal.* an elderly or old person, especially one who is retired: *There are no euphemisms in Dutch for being old—no "senior citizen," no "golden ager"* (New Yorker).

golden aster, a North American aster with yellow rays.

golden bell, = forsythia.

golden buck, Welsh rabbit (rarebit) with a poached egg on top.

golden calf, **1** an idol made of gold, set up by the Israelites in the wilderness (a popular usage, the passage in the Bible, Exodus 32:4, speaking of a "molten calf"). **2** wealth thought of much too highly.

golden calla, a calla lily having golden-yellow spathes.

golden carp, = goldfish.

golden chain, the common laburnum.

golden club, an aquatic plant of the arum family bearing a yellow, club-shaped spadix. It is found along the Atlantic coast from Florida to southern New England.

gold|en-crowned kinglet (gōl′dən kround′), a North American kinglet with a yellow or orange crown.

golden currant, a currant of the western United States having round, black berries and fragrant, yellow flowers; Missouri flowering currant. It is popular as a garden plant.

Golden Delicious, a golden-yellow, oval-shaped apple having a milder flavor than the Delicious apple.

golden eagle, a large, fierce eagle of the Northern Hemisphere with golden-brown feathers on the top of the head and back of the neck; mountain eagle; ring-tailed eagle.

gold|en|eye (gōl′dən ī′), *n., pl.* **-eyes** or (*collectively*) **-eye**. any one of certain diving ducks with black and white feathers, bright-yellow eyes, and white cheek patches, living in northern areas; whistler; garrot.

Golden Fleece, *Greek Legend.* a fleece of gold taken from a ram. It was guarded by a dragon until Jason and the Argonauts carried it away with the help of Medea, the daughter of Aeëtes, King of Colchis, who owned the ram.

gold|en-front|ed woodpecker (gōl′dən fran′tid), a black and white woodpecker with yellow on the forehead and abdomen, found from Texas to Costa Rica.

Golden Gloves, *U.S.* an annual amateur boxing tournament founded in 1926.

golden glow, a tall garden plant with showy, globe-shaped, double yellow flowers and a yellow center (disk). It is a variety of rudbeckia and belongs to the composite family.

golden goose, a legendary goose that laid a golden egg every day but was killed by its greedy owner in hope of getting all the gold at once.

golden hamster, a small hamster with short, golden-brown fur, native to Asia Minor and the Balkan peninsula; Syrian hamster. Most hamsters used as laboratory animals and kept as pets are of this species.

golden handshake, *British.* a large or generous severance pay: *Premature retirement even with a golden handshake can well lead to extensive frustration and waste of scarce human resources* (London Times).

Golden Horde, **1** the section of Russia and central Asia under the control of the Mongols from about 1240 to 1480. **2** the tribe of Mongols who ruled the Golden Horde. [translation of Russian *zolotaya orda,* in reference to the golden tent of Batu, a Mongol prince, who led troops into Russia in 1237]

golden jubilee, the 50th anniversary of the founding of an organization or similar event.

golden loosestrife, any one of a common species of loosestrife, native to Europe and Asia, having sword-shaped leaves and yellow flowers.

golden mean, the avoidance of extremes; safe, sensible way of doing things; moderation. [translation of Latin (Horace) *aurea mediocritās*]

golden nematode, an Old World nematode worm which eats the roots of plants, especially of potatoes, now a serious pest in North America.

golden number, the number of any year in the

Metonic cycle of 19 years, important in calculating the date of Easter.

golden oak, **1** oak stained a very light color and varnished. **2** a plant with yellow leaves resembling oak leaves.

golden parachute, an employment contract guaranteeing continued salary and benefits when control of a company is transferred to new owners: *Martin Marietta also disclosed that it had given so-called golden parachutes . . . to 29 key executives five days after it received the takeover bid from Bendix* (Raleigh News and Observer). [probably patterned after *golden handshake*]

golden pe|zi|za (pə zī′zə), any one of a group of edible mushrooms, having an orange-red, cuplike apothecium. [< New Latin *Peziza* genus name]

golden pheasant, any one of various brightly colored pheasants, native to parts of China and Tibet.

golden plover, either of two plovers having yellowish mottling, one of Europe and one of America. They are noted for their long migrations, the American species nesting in the Arctic and wintering in Hawaii and Central and South America.

golden rain, a small Oriental tree of the soapberry family introduced in other areas for its panicles of golden flowers.

golden retriever, a medium-sized dog with a golden, water-resistant coat, used in hunting to retrieve game, especially waterfowl.

golden robin, = Baltimore oriole.

gold|en|rod (gōl′dən rod′), *n.* any one of a group of plants with tall stalks of small yellow flowers. It blooms in late summer or early autumn. Goldenrod belongs to the composite family. The blossom of various species is the state flower of Kentucky and Nebraska.

golden rose, a rose made of pure gold, blessed by the Pope on the fourth Sunday of Lent, and occasionally sent as a mark of special honor to some Catholic sovereign or other notable person, or to some church, city, or other civic unit.

golden rule, the rule of conduct which states that a person should treat others as he would expect them to treat him. It was set forth by Jesus in the Sermon on the Mount: "All things whatsoever ye would that men should do to you, do ye even so to them" (in the Bible, Matthew 7:12, Luke 6:31).

gold|en|seal (gōl′dən sēl′), *n.* **1** a North American plant of the crowfoot family, whose thick, yellow rootstock (rhizome) is used in medicine; orangeroot. **2** the rootstock and roots.

golden section, the geometric proportion that results when a straight line is divided in such a way that the shorter part is to the longer part as the longer part is to the whole. The golden section was first formulated by Euclid and has been used widely in art and architecture to produce harmonious geometric figures.

golden shiner, a large, freshwater minnow, commonly found in eastern North America, having silver scales that reflect a gold color.

Golden State, a nickname of California.

golden warbler, = yellow warbler.

golden wattle, any one of various Australian acacias having yellow flowers, especially a species whose blossom is, unofficially, the floral emblem of Australia.

golden wedding, the fiftieth anniversary of a wedding.

golden-winged woodpecker, the yellow-shafted flicker.

gold-ex|change standard (gōld′eks chānj′), a monetary system in which the government promises to redeem its money at an established rate of exchange with money of some other country on the gold standard.

gold|eye (gōld′ī′), *n., pl.* **-eyes** or (*collectively*) **-eye.** a freshwater game fish of North America, resembling the herring. It is an important food fish in parts of Canada.

gold fern, any one of several ferns in which the undersurface of the frond is covered with bright yellow powder, giving a golden color.

gold field, a district or region in which gold is found.

gold-filled (gōld′fild′), *adj.* made of a cheap metal covered with a layer of gold.

gold|finch (gōld′finch′), *n.* **1** a small American songbird the male of which is yellow with black patches; yellowbird. It belongs to the same family as the sparrows. **2** a European songbird of the same family with a patch of yellow on its wings; redcap. [Old English *goldfinc*]

gold|fin|ny (gōld′fin′ē), *n., pl.* **-nies.** **1** a bright-colored cunner. **2** a bright-colored wrasse.

gold|fish (gōld′fish′), *n., pl.* **-fish|es** or (*collectively*) **-fish.** **1** a small fish, usually of a reddish or golden color; golden carp. Goldfish are often kept in garden pools or in glass bowls indoors. They belong to the same family as the carp. **2** *Slang.* canned salmon.

goldfish bowl, a small, round, glass bowl in which goldfish and other small fish are kept as pets.

in a goldfish bowl, openly; publicly: *It is impossible to negotiate . . . in a goldfish bowl* (Wall Street Journal).

gold|flow|er (gōld′flou′ər), *n.* any one of several plants or herbs having yellow or golden-yellow flowers, especially a hybrid of St.-John's-wort.

gold foil, gold beaten into a thin sheet. It is thicker than gold leaf.

gold|i|locks (gōl′dē loks′), *n.* **1** a person with golden hair. **2a** a European composite herb, whose small heads of yellow flowers resemble those of the goldenrod. **b** a buttercup of Europe. Also, **goldylocks.** [alteration of earlier *goldylocks*]

gold lace, ornamental cord or braid, as on uniforms, formerly made of gold wire, now of coated thread.

gold leaf, **1** a minute quantity of gold, alloyed with copper or silver and beaten out into a very thin sheet, averaging from 3 to 3½ inches square: *Gold leaf is made by beating the gold by hand* (W. R. Jones). **2** gold in this form used in gilding.

gold mine, **1** a mine where ore yielding gold is obtained. **2** *Informal, Figurative.* a source of something of great value: *a gold mine of ideas.*

gold mohur, = mohur.

gold note, *U.S.* a bank note redeemable in gold.

gold-of-pleas|ure (gōld′əv plezh′ər), *n.* a plant of the mustard family with small, yellowish flowers, naturalized in North America from Europe; wild flax; madwort; white flax.

gold plate, gold or gold-plated tableware.

gold-plate (gōld′plāt′), *v.t.,* **-plat|ed, -plat|ing.** to plate with gold. **—gold′-plat′er,** *n.*

gold points, the upper and lower limits in the variations of foreign-exchange rates at which it is as expensive to export or import gold as to buy or sell bills of exchange.

gold pool, a consortium of six European nations and the United States whose members contribute gold to a common reserve from which it is drawn to stabilize the price of gold.

gold reserve, the quantity or supply of gold kept by a nation or bank to redeem its notes.

gold rush, **1** a sudden rush of people to a place where gold has just been found. **2** a rush to buy gold, especially as a hedge against inflation.

gold salt, any one of various salts containing gold used in photography, in coloring glass, and in medicine.

Gold|schmidt process (gōld′shmit′), = aluminothermy. [< Hans *Goldschmidt,* 1861-1923, German chemist, who discovered it]

gold|smith (gōld′smith′), *n.* a person who makes or sells articles of gold. Until 1700, these tradesmen acted as bankers. [Old English *goldsmith* < *gold* gold + *smith* smith]

goldsmith beetle, a large, yellow beetle of North America.

gold|smith|ing (gōld′smith′ing), *n.* the work or art of a goldsmith: *Cellini studied the art of goldsmithing in Florence* (M. C. Ross).

gold standard, the use of gold as the standard of value for the money of a country. A nation's unit of money value is declared by the government to be equal to and exchangeable for a certain amount of gold. A modification of this is the gold bullion standard, in which there is no coinage of gold, and domestic currency can be redeemed with gold bullion only when demanded in large amounts.

gold star mother, a member of an American organization of women whose sons died in a war.

gold star wife, a member of an American organization of widows of servicemen who died in service or from service-connected disabilities.

gold stick, in England: **1** a gilded rod carried on state occasions by certain members of the royal household. **2** the person who carries it.

gold|stone (gōld′stōn′), *n.* = aventurine.

gold|thread (gōld′thred′), *n.* **1** an evergreen, white-flowered North American herb of the crowfoot family, having fibrous, yellow roots. **2** its root, used in medicine. **3** = dodder.

gold|tit (gōld′tit′), *n.* = verdin.

gold|y|locks (gōl′dē loks′), *n.* = goldilocks.

go|lem (gō′lem), *n.* (in Jewish legend) an artificially constructed human being, given life by magic rites. [< Hebrew *gōlem* shapeless mass; embryo]

golf (golf, gôlf), *n., v.* **—*n.*** a game played on an outdoor course with a small, hard ball and a set of long-handled clubs with wooden or metal heads. The player tries to hit the ball into each of a series of holes with as few strokes as possible. The clubs are designed for the various kinds of shots needed in hitting the ball from a series of tees into holes situated at the ends of fairways of varying shapes and distances, avoiding hazards and obstacles.

—*v.i.* to play this game.

[origin uncertain. Compare Dutch *kolf* club, *kolven* golf.]

Golf (golf, gôlf), *n. U.S.* a code name for the letter *g,* used in transmitting radio messages.

golf|ball (golf′bôl′, gôlf′-), *n.* **1** a small, hard ball with a dimpled surface, used in golf. **2** a ball-shaped, movable metal device on which the characters are located in certain electric typewriters.

golf cart, **1** a small, self-propelled vehicle used to carry one or more golfers and their equipment around a golf course. **2** a cart used to wheel golfing equipment around a golf course.

***golf club**, **1** any one of the set of long-handled clubs with wooden or metal heads used in playing golf. **2** a group of people joined together for the purpose of playing golf. **3** the buildings and land used by such a group.

***golf club**
definition 1

***golf course** or **links**, a parklike area where golf is played, containing tees, greens, and fairways.

***golf course**

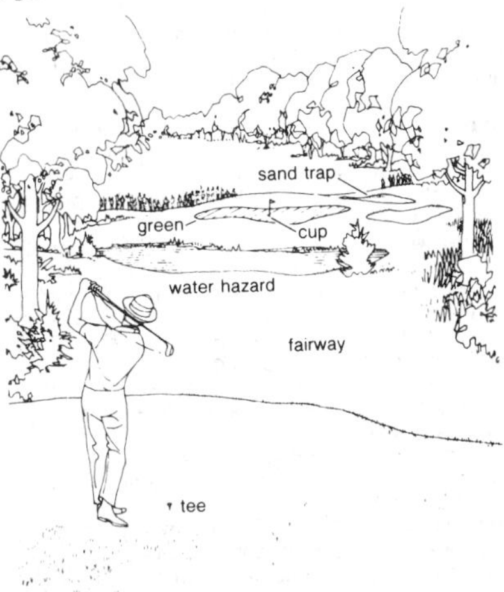

golf|dom (golf′dəm, gôlf′-), *n.* golf players and organizations concerned with the game of golf.

golf|er (gol′fər, gôl′-), *n.* a person who plays the game of golf.

golf widow, *Slang.* a woman often left alone while her husband goes to play golf.

Gol|gi apparatus (gol′jē), a network of vesicles in the cytoplasm of many cells, functioning in the manufacture of proteins and carbohydrates. See picture under **cell.** [< Camillo *Golgi,* 1844-1926 an Italian anatomist]

Golgi body, a unit or particle of the Golgi apparatus revealed by staining; dictyosome.

Golgi complex, = Golgi apparatus.

Gol|go|tha (gol′gə thə), *n.* **1** the place of Christ's Crucifixion; Calvary (in the Bible, Matthew 27:33). **2** a place of burial. **3** *Figurative.* a place or condition of great suffering: *The torture and socially —if not commercially—destroying force of all this—every hour of it a Golgotha!* (Theodore Dreiser). [< Late Latin *golgotha* < Greek *golgothá* < Aramaic *gulgaltā* skull]

gol|iard (gōl′yərd), *n.* one of the class of wandering students noted for their rioting and intemperance, and as authors of satirical Latin verse, who flourished chiefly in the 1100's and 1200's in Germany, France, and England. [< Old French *goliard* (originally) glutton < *gole* glutton; mouth

---

Pronunciation Key: hat, āge, cãre, fär; let, ēqual, tėrm; it, īce; hot, ōpen, ôrder; oil, out; cup, pu̇t, rüle; child; long; thin; ŦHen; zh, measure; ə represents **a** in about, **e** in taken, **i** in pencil, **o** in lemon, **u** in circus.

< Latin *gula* glutton; gullet]

gol|iar|der|y (gōl yär′dər ē), *n.* the practices or compositions of the goliards.

gol|ar|dic (gōl yär′dik), *adj.* having to do with the goliards or goliardery.

Go|li|ath (gə lī′əth), *n.* **1** giant whom David killed with a stone from a sling (in the Bible, I Samuel 17:4-51). **2** any huge, extremely strong man.

go|li|ath (gə lī′əth), *n.* **1** a person or thing of unusual size, importance, power, or accomplishment; giant: *The bill would benefit only a few goliaths in the coal industry* (Wall Street Journal). **2** = goliath beetle.

goliath beetle, any one of a group of white-striped African lamellicorn beetles, including the world's largest species, measuring four inches in length and more than two inches in width.

goliath frog, the largest known frog; giant frog. It lives in western Africa and attains a length of ten to twelve inches.

gol|li|wog or **gol|ly|wog** (gol′ē wog), *n.* a grotesque black (male) doll, fantastically dressed, with staring eyes and a shock of fuzzy black hair. [a coined word, perhaps after *polliwog*]

gol|ly (gol′ē), *interj.* an exclamation of wonder, pleasure, joy, or the like, used as a mild substitute for "God."

go|losh (gə losh′), *n.* = galosh.

go|lup|tious (gə lup′shəs), *adj. Slang.* delicious; delightful. [a coined word]

GOM (no periods) or **G.O.M.**, Grand Old Man (used in describing an old and venerable person or thing): *Thomas Hardy ... was eventually elevated to the position of GOM of letters* (Listener).

go|mas|io (gō mäs′yō), *n.* parched and salted sesame seeds. [< Japanese *gomashio*]

gom|been (gom bēn′), *n. British and Irish.* usury. [< Irish *gaimbin*]

gom|bo[1] (gum′bō), *n., pl.* **-bos.** = gumbo[1].

gom|bo[2] or **Gom|bo** (gum′bō), *n.* = gumbo[2].

gom|broon (gom brün′), *n.* a variety of Persian pottery or an imitation of it. [apparently < *Gambroon*, older name of a town on the Persian gulf]

gom|du|ra (gom dü′rə), *n.* a long dress worn over loose-fitting trousers by women in Saudia Arabia. [< a native name]

go|mer (gō′mər), *n. U.S. Slang.* an obnoxious undesirable person (used in an unfriendly way): *In hospital parlance, a "gomer" is a disgusting, filthy old man* (St. Louis Post-Dispatch). [perhaps < *gomerel*]

gom|er|el, gom|er|il, or **gom|er|al** (gom′ər əl), *n. Scottish.* a fool; simpleton; blockhead.

Go|mor|rah or **Go|mor|rha** (gə môr′ə, -mor′-), *n.* **1** a wicked city destroyed, together with Sodom, by fire from heaven (in the Bible, Genesis 18-19). **2** any extremely wicked place.

gom|pho|sis (gom fō′sis), *n., pl.* **-ses** (sēz). n immovable articulation in which one bone or part is received in a cavity in another, as a tooth in its socket. [< New Latin *gomphosis* < Greek *gómphōsis* < *gomphoûn* bolt together < *gómphos* bolt]

go|mu|ti (gə mü′tē), *n.* **1** Also, **gomuti palm.** a sago palm of the East Indies. **2** a black horsehairlike fiber obtained from it, used in cordage, etc. [< Malay *gomuti*]

go|nad (gon′ad, gō′nad), *n.* an organ in which reproductive cells develop in the male or female; sex glands. Ovaries and testicles are gonads. [< New Latin *gonad* < Greek *gonē* seed < *gígnesthai* be produced]

go|nad|al (gon′ad əl), *adj.* of or having to do with gonads.

go|na|di|al (gə nā′dē əl), *adj.* = gonadal.

go|nad|ic (gə nad′ik), *adj.* = gonadal.

gon|a|do|troph|ic (gon′ə də trof′ik, gə nad′ə-), *adj.* = gonadotropic.

gon|a|do|troph|in (gon′ə də trof′in, gə nad′ə-), *n.* = gonadotropin.

gon|a|do|trop|ic (gon′ə də trop′ik, gə nad′ə-), *adj.* affecting or stimulating the growth or activity of the gonads.

gon|a|do|trop|in (gon′ə də trop′in, gə nad′ə-), *n.* a gonadotropic hormone: *Gonadotropins helped quail lay eggs regularly up to ten days, if periods of extended darkness were provided* (Science News Letter).

go|nan|gi|al (gō nan′jē əl), *adj.* of or having to do with a gonangium.

go|nan|gi|um (gō nan′jē əm), *n., pl.* **-gi|a** (-jē ə), **-gi|ums.** **1** one of the reproductive polyps of a colonial hydrozoan; a capsule with a chitinous covering producing gonophores. **2** = gonotheca. [< Greek *gónos* seed + *angeîon* vessel]

Gond (gōnd), *n.* **1** a member of a Dravidian people, many of them jungle dwellers, of central India. **2** = Gondi.

Gon|di (gon′dē), *n.* the Dravidian language of the Gonds.

gon|dite (gon′dīt), *n.* an Indian rock composed of manganiferous garnet and quartz.

***gon|do|la** (gon′də lə, gon dō′-), *n.* **1** a long, narrow boat, with a high peak at each end, used on the canals of Venice. It is rowed or poled by a single oar near the stern. **2a** a car that hangs under an airship and holds the motors, passengers, and instruments. **b** a similar car or container that hangs from a balloon: *Auguste Piccard ascended to a height of about 53,000 feet in 1932 in the airtight aluminum gondola attached to his balloon* (Carl T. Chase). **3** an enclosed car that hangs from a cable, by which it is pulled to take skiers or sightseers to the top of a mountain: *Grouse [Mountain] is the one with the two 50-passenger gondolas* (Maclean's). **4** *U.S.* = gondola car. **5** *U.S.* a large, flat-bottomed riverboat with pointed ends, also used as a gunboat. [< Italian (Venice) *gondola* < *gondolar* to rock < *dondolare* rock, dandle]

***gondola**
definition 1

gondola car, *U.S.* a railroad freight car with low sides and no top, such as one for carrying scrap.

gon|do|lier (gon′də lir′), *n.* a person who rows or poles a gondola. [< French *gondolier* < Italian *gondoliere* < *gondola*; see etym. under **gondola**]

Gond|wa|na (gond wä′nə), *n.* **1** a great system of Indian rocks, chiefly sandstone and shale. **2** a hypothetical land mass including India, Australia, Antarctica, Africa, and South America, and that began to break up into the present continents at the end of the Mesozoic era. [< *Gondwana*, district in India inhabited by the Gond people]

Gond|wa|na|land (gond wä′nə land′), *n.* = Gondwana (def. 2).

gone (gôn, gon), *adj., v.* **—adj. 1** moved away; left: *The students are gone on their vacation.* **2** lost: *a gone case. We had given you up for gone.* **3** dead: *He is gone now.* **4** used up; consumed: *Is all the candy gone?* **5** failed; ruined: *The bankrupt was a gone man.* **6** weak; faint: *a gone feeling.* **7** *U.S. Slang.* **a** very good; great: *the gone blues sung by Bessie Smith.* **b** that carries strong feeling; transported; inspired: *a gone look on his face, gone music.* **8** *Slang.* pregnant: *eight months gone.*

—v. the past participle of **go**[1]. *He has gone far away.*

be gone, leave! get out!: *Be gone! The goddess cries with stern disdain* (Joseph Addison).

far gone, much advanced; deeply involved: *The business was far gone in debt and could not be saved.*

gone on, *Informal.* in love with: *They ought to get married; they are really gone on each other.*

real gone, *U.S. Slang.* good; fine: *Joe Sullivan plays (real gone) interlude piano* (New Yorker).

gone goose, *Slang.* a goner: *The man was suffering from iron-poor blood. He was a gone goose* (S. J. Perelman).

gone|ness (gôn′nis, gon′-), *n.* a sensation of faintness or exhaustion.

gon|er (gôn′ər, gon′-), *n. Informal.* a person or thing that is dead, ruined, or past help: *"Tom, we're goners! Can you pray?"* (Mark Twain).

Gon|er|il (gon′ər əl), *n.* the wicked eldest daughter in Shakespeare's play *King Lear.*

gon|fa|lon (gon′fə lən), *n.* a flag or banner hung from a crossbar instead of a pole, often having several streamers. Gonfalons were used especially by medieval Italian republics. [< French or Italian *gonfalone*, alteration of *gonfanone* < Old High German *gundfano* (literally) war banner]

gon|fa|lon|ier (gon′fə lə nir′), *n.* **1** the bearer of a gonfalon; standardbearer. **2** a high official in several medieval Italian republics. [< French *gonfalonier* < *gonfalon*; see etym. under **gonfalon**]

gong (gông, gong), *n.* **1** a large piece of metal shaped like a bowl or a saucer which makes a loud, resonant sound when struck. A gong is a kind of bell. *A gong sounded the hour of dinner.* **2** *Music.* a metal disk with a turned-up rim, which makes a loud noise when struck. **3** *British Slang.* a medal or decoration: *He had fought his war and won his gongs* (Listener). [< Malay or Javanese *gong*; perhaps imitative] **—gong′like′,** *adj.*

gon|go|rism (gong′gə riz əm), *n.* a type of mannered and ingeniously figurative diction and style in Spanish literature developed from culteranismo in the early 1600's by the poet Luis de Góngora y Argote. [< Spanish *gongorismo* < Luis de *Góngora* y Argote, 1561-1627 + *-ismo* -ism]

go|nid|i|al (gō nid′ē əl), *adj.* having to do with or containing a gonidium.

go|nid|i|um (gō nid′ē əm), *n., pl.* **-i|a** (-ē ə). *Botany.* **1** a reproductive cell produced asexually in algae, as a tetraspore or zoospore. **2** one of the algal cells filled with chlorophyll that are formed in the thallus (plant body) of lichens. [< New Latin *gonidium* (diminutive) < Greek *gónos* child, what is produced < *gígnesthai* be produced]

gon|if or **gon|iff** (gon′əf), *n.* = ganef.

go|ni|om|e|ter (gō′nē om′ə tər), *n.* **1** an instrument for measuring solid angles, as of crystals. **2** a direction finder, especially one for aircraft; radiogoniometer. [< Greek *gōniā* angle]

go|ni|o|met|ric (gō′nē ə met′rik), *adj.* of or having to do with goniometry.

go|ni|o|met|ri|cal (gō′nē ə met′rə kəl), *adj.* = goniometric.

go|ni|om|e|try (gō′nē om′ə trē), *n.* the measurement of solid angles.

go|ni|on (gō′nē on), *n., pl.* **-ni|a** (-nē ə). the point on either side of the lower jaw where the lower and posterior sections meet at a sharp angle. [< New Latin *gonion* < Greek *gōniā* angle]

go|ni|um (gō′nē əm), *n., pl.* **-ni|a** (-nē ə). *Biology.* a parent cell; germ cell before differentiation by mitosis; an oogonium or spermatogonium. [< New Latin *gonium* < Greek *goneíā* generation < *gígnesthai* be produced]

gon|na (gôn′ə, gon′-; gōn′-), *Especially U.S. Informal.* going to.

gon|o|coc|cal (gon′ə kok′əl), *adj.* having to do with or caused by gonococci.

gon|o|coc|cus (gon′ə kok′əs), *n., pl.* **-coc|ci** (-kok′sī). the bacterium that causes gonorrhea. [< Greek *gónos* seed + English *coccus*]

gon|o|cyte (gon′ə sīt), *n. Biology.* a germ cell; an oocyte or spermatocyte. [< Greek *gónos* seed]

gon|of (gon′əf), *n.* = ganef.

go-no-go (gō′nō′gō′), *adj.* requiring an instant decision about the continuation of a space flight: *the go-no-go point.*

gon|oph (gon′əf), *n.* = ganef.

gon|o|phore (gon′ə fôr, -fōr), *n.* **1** *Botany.* a prolongation of the axis of a flower above the perianth, and bearing the stamens and pistil. **2** *Zoology.* one of the generative buds in hydrozoans. [< Greek *gónos* seed + *-phore*]

gon|o|pod (gon′ə pod), *n.* an abdominal appendage in male myriapods and other anthropods, modified to serve as an organ of reproduction. [< Greek *gónos* seed + *poús, podós foot*]

gon|o|po|di|um (gon′ə pō′dē əm), *n., pl.* **-di|a** (-dē ə). an anal fin in the male of certain fishes, modified to serve as an organ of reproduction. [< New Latin *gonopodium* < Greek *gónos* seed + New Latin *podium* podium]

gon|o|pore (gon′ə pôr, -pōr), *n.* the reproductive opening or orifice of the female of certain worms. [< Greek *gónos* seed + *póros* passage]

gon|or|rhe|a or **gon|or|rhoe|a** (gon′ə rē′ə), *n.* a contagious venereal disease that causes inflammation of the mucous membrane of the genital and urinary organs, and also of certain other organs and tissues, especially the eyes. It is caused by a bacterium, the gonococcus. [< Late Latin *gonorrhoea* < Greek *gonórrhoia* < *gónos* seed + *rhoiā* flow < *rheîn* to flow (from the earlier idea that the discharge contained semen)]

gon|or|rhe|al or **gon|or|rhoe|al** (gon′ə rē′əl), *adj.* **1** having to do with or of the nature of gonorrhea. **2** having gonorrhea.

gon|o|the|ca (gon′ō thē′kə), *n., pl.* **-cae** (-sē). the chitinous covering of a gonangium. [< Greek *gónos* seed + *thēkē* case]

gon|o|the|cal (gon′ō thē′kəl), *adj.* of or having to do with gonotheca.

gon|zo (gon′zō), *adj. U.S. Slang.* mad or crazy; eccentric: *Gonzo Journalism supplements the techniques of the novelist with the technique of the lunatic* (Atlantic). [< Italian *gonzo* fool, perhaps short for *Borgonzone* a Burgundian]

goo (gü), *n. Slang.* **1** thick, sticky matter: *You woke me ... to make me drink that goo?* (Edna Ferber). **2** *Figurative: It is a remarkable job ... with hardly a trace of the sentimental goo* (Eliot Fremont-Smith). [probably imitative]

goo|ber (gü′bər), *n.*, or **goober pea,** *Southern U.S., Informal.* the peanut. [American English, probably < Kongo *nguba* peanut]

Goober State, a nickname for Georgia.

good (gůd), *adj.,* **bet|ter, best,** *n., interj., adv.* **—adj. 1** having high quality; excellent; superior: *a good piece of work, a good book, a good game. A craftsman insists on good tools.* SYN: admirable. **2a** as it ought to be; right; proper: *Do what seems good to you.* **b** such as should be desired or approved; satisfactory; desirable: *good health, good weather, good spirits. This is a good book for children.* **3** in good condition: *his good leg, a good motor.* **4** behaving well; that does what is right: *a good boy.* SYN: polite. **5** kind; friendly: *It is good of you to give me a ride home. Say a good word for me.* **6** honorable; worthy: *my good friend, a good reputation.* **7a** doing right; just: *a good king, to lead a good life.* **b** pious; devout: *He is a good member of the Church.* **8** reliable; dependable: *good judgment, good bonds.* **9** real; genuine: *It is hard to tell counterfeit money from* good money. **10** agreeable; pleasant: *good news. Have a good time at the party.* **11** beneficial; advantageous; useful: *A warm meal is good when you feel chilly.* **12** satisfying; enough; full: *a good meal.* **13** skillful; clever: *a good manager, to be good at arithmetic.* **14** fairly great; more than a little: *to work a good while.* **15** effective in communication; acceptable: *good English.* **16** valid; sound: *good reasons, a good contract.* SYN: effectual. **17** actual; serious: *in good earnest.* **18** (of meat, especially beef and veal) being a grade between choice and standard.

—n. **1** benefit; advantage; use: *What good will it do? Work for the common good.* **2** that which is good: *to find the good in people.* **3** a good thing. **4** good people. **5** *Philosophy.* something that is considered as belonging to the world's moral order.

—interj. that is good!

—adv. Informal. well: *"I bet he likes the snow real good," the hitchhiker said* (New Yorker).

as good as, a almost the same as; almost: *You are a married man—or as good as a married man* (Charlotte Brontë). **b** to all intents and purposes; practically: *a battle as good as won.*

feel good, *Informal.* to feel well or elated: *I feel good today.*

for good or **for good and all,** forever; finally; permanently: *They have moved out for good. Childhood is the fiery furnace in which we are melted down to essentials and that essential shaped for good* (Katherine Anne Porter).

good and, to a considerable extent; very: *Get the water good and hot.*

good for, a able to do, live, or last: *Our car is good for another year.* **b** able to pay or contribute: *He is good for about $10.* **c** useful; beneficial: *This medicine is good for a toothache.*

in good with, in good relations with; in favor with: *Says one: "There I am, standing at the President's elbow, obviously in good with him and his people"* (Wall Street Journal).

make good, a to make up for; give or do in place of; pay for: *Any deficiency in repayment shall be made good* (Manchester Examiner). **b** to carry out; fulfill: *Will you make good your promise?* (Scott). **c** to succeed in doing: *The rebels managed to make good their retreat* (Earl Dunmore). **d** to succeed: *Ability and talent make good as always* (Gertrude Atherton). **e** to prove: *Can you make good your charge against him?*

no good, *Informal.* good-for-nothing; useless: *His work is no good. It's no good arguing with them.*

to the good, on the side of profit or advantage; in one's favor: *By winning the second game our team is now two games to the good in the championship.*

[Old English *gōd*]

▶**good, well.** *Good* is an adjective; *well* is either an adjective or an adverb: *I feel good* and *I feel well* (adjectives) are both used, but have different connotations (*good* implying actual bodily sensation, *well* referring merely to a state, not ill). In nonstandard English *good* is often used adverbially in place of *well: The engine's running pretty good now.*

good afternoon, a form of greeting or farewell in the afternoon; hello or good-by.

Good Book, the Bible.

good-by or **good|by** (gu̇d′bī′), *interj., n., pl.* **-bys.** farewell: *We said "Good-by" and went home.*

kiss good-by, *Slang.* to give up; accept as a loss; consider as gone or ruined: *If you lend him money, you can kiss it good-by.*

[contraction of *God be with ye*]

good-bye or **good|bye** (gu̇d′bī′), *interj., n., pl.* **-byes.** = good-by.

good cheer, 1 feasting and merrymaking. **2** good food. **3** courage.

Good Conduct Medal, *U.S.* a medal awarded to military personnel for honorably serving for a length of time, usually one year in wartime or three years in peacetime.

good cop, bad cop, 1 a technique of interrogating suspects by a team of two police officers in which one officer is friendly and easygoing and the other is combative and easily angered. **2** any partnership where one person is friendly and relaxed and the other tense and difficult: *"There are many partnerships in Hollywood where it's 'good cop, bad cop,'" says one studio executive* (Spy Magazine).

good-cop, bad-cop (gu̇d′kop bad′kop), *adj.* having both good and bad qualities or characteristics; opposite: *It's a good-cop, bad-cop story of psychological subtlety* (Time).

good day, a form of greeting or farewell said in the daytime; hello or good-by.

good deal, 1 much; many. **2** *Slang.* very good.

good|den (gu̇d′den′), *n., interj. Dialect.* good evening.

good egg, *Slang.* a good fellow: *[He] has always seemed to be fundamentally a nice guy, no Sunday-school teacher, but a basically good egg* (Manchester Guardian Weekly).

good English, English that is effective for a particular communication, that is appropriate to the subject and situation, to the listener or reader, and to the speaker or writer.

good evening, a form of greeting or farewell in the evening; hello or good-by.

good faith, honesty; sincerity: *In all good faith, I wrote to you a few days ago commending this person on her helpfulness, etc. I was deceived* (Punch).

in good faith, honestly; sincerely: *It is admitted that the magistrates . . . acted in good faith* (J. Hannen).

good fellow, a companionable person.

good-fel|low|hood (gu̇d′fel′ō hu̇d), *n.* = good-fellowship.

good-fel|low|ship (gu̇d′fel′ō ship), *n.* **1** pleasant companionship. **2** friendly fellowship.

good-for-noth|ing (gu̇d′fər nuth′ing), *adj., n.*

—adj. worthless; useless.

—n. a person who is worthless or useless.

—good′-for-noth′ing|ness, *n.*

Good Friday, the Friday before Easter. It is a holy day of the Christian Church, observed as the anniversary of the Crucifixion of Christ.

good-heart|ed (gu̇d′här′tid), *adj.* kind and generous. **—good′-heart′ed|ly,** *adv.* **—good′-heart′ed|ness,** *n.*

good humor, a cheerful, pleasant disposition or mood. SYN: geniality.

good-hu|mored (gu̇d′hyü′mərd, -yü′-), *adj.* having good humor; cheerful; pleasant; amiable: *It is a good-humored book, full of energy, and ending in contentment for everybody* (New Yorker). SYN: genial. **—good′-hu′mored|ly,** *adv.* **—good′-hu′mored|ness,** *n.*

good-hu|moured (gu̇d′hyü′mərd, -yü′-), *adj. Especially British.* good-humored.

good|ie (gu̇d′ē), *n. Informal.* **1** a hero or one of his companions in a motion picture, etc.; goody. **2** = goody-goody.

good|ish (gu̇d′ish), *adj.* **1** rather good. **2** *Especially British.* fairly great; considerable: *It's a goodish distance to walk.*

good Joe, *U.S. Slang.* a good fellow.

good|li|ness (gu̇d′lē nis), *n.* **1** handsomeness. **2** excellence.

good-look|er (gu̇d′lu̇k′ər), *n. Informal.* a person who has good looks.

good-look|ing (gu̇d′lu̇k′ing), *adj.* having a pleasing appearance; handsome or pretty. SYN: comely.

good looks, handsome or pleasing personal appearance; handsomeness.

good luck, 1 the possession of wealth, position, health, or the like; luckiness; success. **2** a saying or wishing of "good luck."

good|ly (gu̇d′lē), *adj.,* **-li|er, -li|est. 1** of good quality; pleasant; excellent; fine: *a goodly land.* SYN: admirable, splendid. **2** good-looking: *a goodly youth.* SYN: comely, fair, handsome. **3** considerable; rather large; fairly great: *a goodly quantity.*

good|man (gu̇d′mən), *n., pl.* **-men.** *Archaic.* **1** the master of a household; husband. **2** a title of respect for a man ranking below a gentleman, especially a yeoman or farmer: *Goodman Brown.*

good morning, a form of greeting or farewell in the morning; hello or good-by.

good-morn|ing-spring (gu̇d′mōr′ning spring′), *n.* = spring beauty.

good morrow, *Archaic.* good morning.

good nature, a pleasant or kindly disposition; cheerfulness; agreeableness. SYN: amiability.

good-na|tured (gu̇d′nā′chərd), *adj.* having a pleasant disposition; kindly; cheerful; obliging; agreeable: *He overlooked the criticism with a good-natured smile.* SYN: good-humored, pleasant. **—good′-na′tured|ly,** *adv.* **—good′-na′tured|ness,** *n.*

good-neigh|bor|li|ness (gu̇d′nā′bər lē nis), *n.* the disposition and behavior characteristic of a good neighbor; friendly feeling and relation: *Trade-hungry Japan hoped such evidence of good-neighborliness would dispel Filipino suspicions and open the way to extended trade with the Philippines and all Southeast Asia* (Newsweek).

good-neigh|bor|ly (gu̇d′nā′bər lē), *adj.* characterized by good-neighborliness.

Good Neighbor Policy, a diplomatic policy, first sponsored by the United States in 1933, to encourage friendly relations and mutual defense among the nations of the Western Hemisphere.

good|ness (gu̇d′nis), *n., interj.* *—n.* **1** the quality or state of being good: *The drama of men is that their goodness creates, and their wickedness shatters, the goodness of others; so that pity holds us ever in leash* (Freya Madeleine Stark). **2** excellence; virtue. **3** kindness; friendliness. **4** valuable quality; best part.

—interj. an exclamation of surprise or alarm: *My goodness! Goodness me! "Goodness, have you been expelled?"* (New Yorker).

—Syn. n. **2 Goodness, virtue** mean excellence in character. **Goodness** applies to moral excellence that seems inborn: *Her goodness is shown by the many good deeds she does.* **Virtue** applies to moral excellence that is acquired by consciously developing particular qualities of character or by consciously following high moral principles: *He is a man of the highest virtue.*

Good News Bible, a revision of the Bible, published in the United States in 1976. It is a translation in modern English vernacular.

good night, a form of farewell said at parting in the night or at going to bed.

good offices, the services of a mediator in a dispute: *He has offered his "good offices" to the parties and already has been in touch with both sides* (Wall Street Journal).

good-oh or **good-o** (gu̇d′ō′), *interj. Australian Slang.* fine! excellent!

goods (gu̇dz), *n.pl.* **1a** personal property; belongings: *He gave half of his goods to the poor.* SYN: See syn. under **property. b** *Law.* property, especially movable or personal property. SYN: See syn. under **property. 2** a thing or things for sale; wares. **3** *U.S.* material for clothing; cloth. **4** *U.S. Slang.* what is needed to do something. **5** *Especially British.* freight.

catch with the goods, to catch in the act of committing a crime: *Detective Craddock informed Thubway Tham that sooner or later he was going to catch him with the goods* (Detective Story Magazine).

deliver the goods, to do what is expected or wanted: *There are men in the North who walk around . . . saying, "See me, . . . I will take you to victory." They cannot deliver the goods* (Congressional Record).

get (or **have) the goods on,** to find out or know something bad about: *They had the goods on us. We were going to hang—every one of us* (W. M. Raine).

Good Samaritan, 1 a traveler who aided another traveler who had been beaten and robbed by thieves (in the Bible, Luke 10:30-37). **2** a person who is unselfish in helping others.

good sense, sound judgment; common sense.

Good Shepherd, Jesus Christ (in the Bible, John 10:11-14).

good show, *British.* well done! bravo! bully!

good-sized (gu̇d′sīzd′), *adj.* somewhat large.

good speed, a farewell expressing a wish for success or good luck.

goods train, *British.* a freight train.

goods van, *British.* a boxcar.

goods yard, *British.* a freight yard.

good-tem|pered (gu̇d′tem′pərd), *adj.* easy to get along with; cheerful; agreeable: *A dog needs a good-tempered trainer.* SYN: easygoing. **—good′-tem′pered|ly,** *adv.*

Good Templar, a member of an organization founded in New York in 1851 for the promotion of temperance, peace, and brotherhood.

good-time Char|lie or **Char|ley** (gu̇d′tīm′ chär′lē), *Slang.* a sociable, fun-loving person.

good turn, a kind or friendly act; favor.

good use, ways of speaking and writing accepted as standard.

good|wife (gu̇d′wīf′), *n., pl.* **-wives.** *Archaic.* **1** the mistress of a household. **2** a title of respect for a woman ranking below a lady: *Goodwife Brown.*

good will, 1 kindly or friendly feeling; kindness; friendliness: *Our cast of principal characters is composed almost . . . entirely of men of good will* (Forum). SYN: See syn. under **favor. 2** cheerful consent; willingness. **3** the good reputation that a business has with its customers: *The tax law provides that any payments for a going business in excess of its assessed value are generally for "good will," a capital asset, not a deductible expense* (Wall Street Journal).

good-will (gu̇d′wil′), *adj.* of or intended to arouse good will: *a good-will tour, a good-will ambassador.*

good|will|y (gu̇d′wil′ē), *adj. Scottish.* **1** liberal (of). **2** cordial.

good|y[1] (gu̇d′ē), *n., pl.* **good|ies,** *interj., adj. Informal.* *—n.* **1** Often, **goodies.** something very good to eat; piece of candy or cake. **2** a hero or one of his companions, especially in a motion picture or television show.

—interj. an exclamation of pleasure: *Are we going? Oh, goody!*

—adj. making too much of being good; good in a weak way.

[< *good* + *-y*[1]]

Pronunciation Key: hat, āge, cãre, fär; let, ēqual, tėrm; it, īce; hot, ōpen, ôrder; oil, out; cup, pu̇t, rüle; child; long; thin; ᴛʜen; zh, measure; ə represents **a** in about, **e** in taken, **i** in pencil, **o** in lemon, **u** in circus.

good|y[2] (gu̇d′ē), *n., pl.* **good|ies**. *Archaic.* **1** an old woman of humble station. **2** a term of address for such a woman: *Old Goody Blake was old and poor* (Wordsworth). [contracted variant of *goodwife*]

good|y-good|y (gu̇d′ē gu̇d′ē), *adj., n., pl.* **-good|ies**. —*adj.* making too much of being good; good in an affected or artificial way.
—*n.* a person who makes too much of being good.

goo|ey (gü′ē), *adj.,* **goo|i|er, goo|i|est.** *Slang.* **1** like goo; sticky; viscid: *gooey asphalt, gooey frosting.* **2** *Figurative: Tomorrow I want you to try talking to babies, but there's no need to get gooey over it* (Punch).

goof (güf), *v., n. Slang.* —*v.i.* to make a stupid blunder or mistake; blunder; err: *All I need to do is goof once—just once—and I lose my chance to make Corporal* (Harper's).
—*v.t.* to mess up completely; fumble; do all wrong.
—*n.* **1** a mistake; blunder: *"Between you and me," he said, "it's a goof. They were so busy fixing up everything else, they forgot about putting in a clock"* (New Yorker). **2** a simpleton; fool.
goof off, *Slang.* to waste time, idle; loaf: *Those who goof off must face the weekly embarrassment of the conference* (Harper's).
[apparently < dialectal variant of earlier *goff* dunce]

goof|ball (güf′bôl′), *n. U.S. Slang.* **1** a barbiturate or tranquilizer used as a narcotic. **2** a crazy or eccentric person.

goof|i|ly (gü′fə lē), *adv. Slang.* in a goofy manner: *He is drilling, with the aid of a goofily willing adolescent, for oil* (London Times).

goof|i|ness (gü′fē nis), *n. Slang.* the state or quality of being goofy.

goof-off (güf′ôf′, -of′), *n. Slang.* an idler: *All the other kids knew that he was a lazy goof-off, and he never had a chance* (New Yorker).

goof|y (gü′fē), *adj.,* **goof|i|er, goof|i|est.** *Slang.* silly: *a goofy look.*

goog (güg, gu̇g), *n. Australian Slang.* **1** an egg. **2** a fool; simpleton.

goo|gle (gü′gəl), *v.i.,* **-gled, -gling.** in cricket: **1** (of the ball) to have a googly break and swerve. **2** (of the bowler) to bowl a googly or googlies.

goo|gly (gü′glē), *n., pl.* **-glies.** *Cricket.* a ball swerving one way and breaking in the other as it is bowled. [origin unknown]

goo|gol (gü′gol), *n.* the number 1 followed by a hundred zeros, or 10^{100}. [a coined word]

goo|gol|plex (gü′gol pleks), *n.* the number 10 multiplied by itself googol times, or $10^{10^{100}}$. [< *googol* + *-plex,* patterned on *duplex, triplex,* and the like]

goo|golth (gü′golth), *adj.* expressing the ordinal equivalent of a googol: ... *"ten to the tenth to the tenth"... is ten raised to the googolth power, i.e., a googolplex. A googol is ten to the tenth to the second power* (Science News).

goo-goo[1] (gü′gü), *adj. Slang.* **1** amorous (used of eyes or looks). **2** gaga: *I just go all goo-goo when I stand in front of it. It is one of the finest pictures in the world* (Time).

goo-goo[2] (gü′gü), *n. U.S.* a person or organization that advocates political reform: ... *a host of individuals that* [*Mayor James*] *Curley would simply have called goo-goos* (*after the old Boston Good Government Association*)*—persons more interested in municipal improvement and abstract political morality than in personal friendships and power* (Saturday Review).

gook (gu̇k, gük), *n. U.S. Slang.* **1** a foreigner, especially an Asian (used in an unfriendly way). **2** a freak in a circus or carnival troupe. **3** a sticky mess or mixture; goo. [origin uncertain]

goom|bay (güm′bā), *n.* the Bahamian form of calypso, accompanied by a bongo drum. [< a Bantu word]

goon (gün), *n. U.S. Slang.* **1** a thug hired to disrupt labor disputes. **2** a stupid person. [American English; originally the name of semihuman characters in a comic strip of the 1930's]

goon|da (gu̇n′də), *n.* a thug in India. [< Hindi *guṇḍā*]

goon squad, a gang of terrorists.

goon|y or **goon|ey** (gü′nē), *n., pl.* **goon|ies.** a goony bird; albatross.

goony or **gooney bird,** = albatross.

goop[1] (güp), *n. U.S. Slang.* a person who has bad manners; boor; stupid person. [< *Goop* an imaginary person invented by Gelett Burgess to be a warning to children against bad manners]

goop[2] (güp), *n. U.S. Slang.* anything oily or sticky. [probably alteration of *goo*]

goo|ral (gu̇r′əl), *n.* = goral.

goo|ra nut (gü′rə), = kola nut. [*goora,* apparently < Malinke *guro*]

Goor|kha (gu̇r′kə), *n.* = Gurkha.

goos|an|der (gü san′dər), *n.* = merganser. [apparently < *goose*]

***goose** (güs), *n., pl.* **geese** *for defs. 1-4,* **goos|es** *for def. 5, v.,* **goosed, goos|ing.** —*n.* **1** any one of numerous wild or tame birds like a duck, but larger and with a longer neck. A goose has webbed feet and has toothlike ridges just inside its bill. Geese and ducks belong to the same family. **2** a female goose. A male is called a gander. **3** the flesh of a goose used for food. **4** *Figurative.* a silly or foolish person: *Myers was a goose, but he was also brilliant, insightful and high-minded* (Scientific American). **SYN:** fool, nincompoop, simpleton. **5** a tailor's smoothing iron with a curved handle like a goose's neck. **6** *Obsolete.* a board game in which players follow a track of squares, according to the throw of dice, some squares permitting further advance on the same throw, some bearing penalties.
—*v.t. Slang.* to prod or poke in the buttocks so as to startle or surprise: (*Figurative.*) *Canned laughter is used by television to goose a laugh from the comatose home viewer* (Russell Baker).
cook one's goose, *Informal.* to ruin one's reputation, plan, chances, etc.: *The team's goose was cooked when it failed to win a single game the whole season.*
the goose hangs high, all is well; prospects are good: *The real reactions of the past have often developed when the goose hung the highest* (Wall Street Journal).
[Old English *gōs*] —**goose′like′,** *adj.*

***goose**
definition 1

goose

duck

goose barnacle, a barnacle that attaches itself to seaweed or the bottoms of ships by means of long stalks: *Goose barnacles* [*are*] *so called because barnacle geese were once supposed to hatch from them* (Hegner and Stiles). See picture under **barnacle**[1].

goose|ber|ry (güs′ber′ē, -bər-; güz′-), *n., pl.* **-ries.** **1** a small, sour berry somewhat like a currant but larger. Gooseberries are used to make pies, tarts, or jam. **2** the thorny bush that it grows on. The gooseberry belongs to the saxifrage family and to the same genus as the currant. **3** *Informal.* a third person accompanying a couple. [origin uncertain; probably < *goose* + *berry*]
► The traditional pronunciation (güz′bər i) is still almost universal in England but less common in the United States.

goose|bumps (güs′bumps′), *n.pl. Informal.* goose flesh: *I'm goosebumps all over* ... (New Yorker).

goose egg, **1** the egg of a goose. **2** *Slang.* (in athletic and other contests) a zero, indicating a miss or a failure to score.

goose-egg (güs′eg′), *v.t. U.S. Slang.* to cause to fail or lose.

goose|fish (güs′fish′), *n., pl.* **-fish|es** or (*collectively*) **-fish.** = angler (def. 3).

goose flesh, or **goose|flesh** (güs′flesh′), *n.* a rough condition of the skin, like that of a plucked goose, caused by cold or fear; goose pimples.

goose|foot (güs′fu̇t′), *n., pl.* **-foots.** any one of various weedy herbs with clusters of small, greenish flowers (so called from the shape of the leaves); pigweed.

***goosefoot family,** a group of dicotyledonous herbs and shrubs especially common in alkaline regions, having coarse leaves, clusters of very small flowers, and dry, seedlike fruits (utricles). The family includes the beet, spinach, pigweed, saltwort, and Russian thistle.

***goosefoot family**

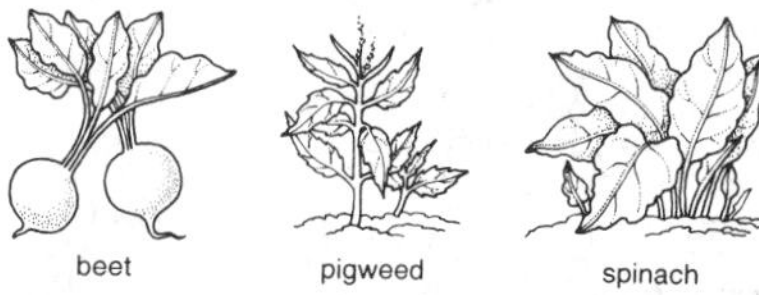
beet pigweed spinach

goose|girl (güs′gėrl′), *n.* a girl employed to take care of geese.

goose|gog (güz′gog′), *n. British Dialect.* gooseberry.

goose grass, = cleavers.

goose grease, the melted fat or grease of the goose, used as a salve and in cooking.

goose|herd (güs′hėrd′), *n.* a person who tends geese.

goose|neck (güs′nek′), *n.* something long and curved like a goose's neck, such as an iron hook, a movable support for a lamp, or a curved connecting pipe.

goose|necked (güs′nekt′), *adj.* shaped like the neck of a goose.

goose pimples or **skin,** = goose flesh.

goose quill, **1** one of the large feathers or quills of a goose. **2** a pen made from such a feather: *Many wearing rapiers are afraid of goose quills* (Shakespeare).

goose step, **1** a marching step in which the leg is swung high with a straight, stiff knee. It is used especially by the German and Russian armies. **2** an exercise in which first one foot and then the other is swung forward and back while standing on the other foot.

goose-step (güs′step′), *v.i.,* **-stepped, -step|ping.** to march with a goose step.

goose-step|per (güs′step′ər), *n.* a person who practices the goose step: *the most timorous, sniveling, poltroonish, ignominious mob of serfs and goose-steppers ever gathered under one flag* (H. L. Mencken).

goos|y or **goos|ey** (gü′sē), *adj.,* **goos|i|er, goos|i|est.** **1** of or like a goose, especially in intelligence; silly. **2** *Slang.* jumpy or ticklish: *a goosy sensation.*

G.O.P. or **GOP** (no periods), Grand Old Party (the Republican Party in the United States).

go|pak (gō′pak, hō′-), *n.* a very fast dance of the Ukraine. [< Russian *gopak*]

go|pher (gō′fər), *n.* **1** Also, **pocket gopher.** any one of various ratlike rodents of North and Central America, with large cheek pouches, long teeth, long claws, especially on the front feet, and small eyes and ears; pouched rat. Gophers dig holes in the ground and are herbivorous. **2** a striped ground squirrel of the western plains of the United States. **3** a land tortoise of the southern United States that burrows in the ground. **4** = gopher snake. [American English < French *gaufre* (literally) honeycomb (because of their burrowing habits)]

Go|pher (gō′fər), *n.* a nickname for a person born or living in Minnesota.

gopher ball, *U.S. Slang.* a baseball pitch that is hit for a home run.

gopher snake, **1** a harmless, burrowing bull snake of the southern United States. **2** = indigo snake.

Gopher State, a nickname for Minnesota.

go|pher|wood (gō′fər wu̇d′), *n.* **1** an unidentified wood used in the construction of Noah's Ark (in the Bible, Genesis 6:14). **2** yellowwood. [translation of Hebrew *'ӕṣe gofer*]

go|pu|ra (gō′pu̇r ə), *n.* a temple gateway in southern India, surmounted by a massive pyramidal tower arranged in stories. [< Sanskrit *gopura*]

go|ral (gôr′əl, gōr′-), *n.* a goatlike antelope of the mountains of central Asia. [< a native name in the Himalayas]

gor|bel|ly (gôr′bel′ē), *n., pl.* **-lies.** *Dialect.* **1** a prominent belly. **2** a person having one. [perhaps < *gore*[1] + *belly*]

gor|blim|ey (gôr blī′mē), *interj. British Cockney Slang.* blimey.

gor|cock (gôr′kok′), *n.* the male red grouse; moor cock. [origin uncertain]

gor|crow (gôr′krō′), *n.* = carrion crow.

Gor|di|an (gôr′dē ən), *adj.* **1** having to do with Gordius, an ancient king of Phrygia. **2** *Figurative.* intricate; involved.

Gordian knot, **1** an intricate knot tied by Gordius, legendary king of Phrygia, to be undone only by the person who should rule Asia. Alexander the Great cut it through with his sword. **2** *Figurative.* an intricate or baffling problem or great difficulty that needs solving: *We have come to the Gordian knot of the speculations on the build-up of the elements* (Scientific American).
cut the Gordian knot, to find and use a quick, easy way out of a difficulty: [*He*] *would have cut the Gordian knot of hereditary right* (Henry Bolingbroke).

Gor|don setter (gôr′dən), any one of a breed of hunting dogs having a black coat with tan markings and standing 23 to 27 inches high. [< the fourth Duke of *Gordon,* died 1827, who maintained hunting kennels]

gore[1] (gôr, gōr), *n.* blood that is spilled; thick blood; clotted blood: *The battlefield was covered with gore.* [Old English *gor* dirt, dung]

gore[2] (gôr, gōr), *v.t.,* **gored, gor|ing.** **1** to wound with a horn or tusk: *The angry bull gored the farmer in the leg.* **2** *Obsolete.* to pierce or stab deeply. [Middle English *goren;* origin uncertain]

gore[3] (gôr, gōr), *n., v.,* **gored, gor|ing.** —*n.* **1** a long, three-sided piece of cloth or other material put in a sail, skirt, coat, glove, or other article fitted to a special use, to give greater width or change the shape: *The skirt is all large gores below the hip yoke, which dips low in back* (New Yorker). **2** any one of a series of tapering strips

of paper or plastic, each containing a part of a printed map, that are pasted on a globe. **3** a local, minor civil division in Maine and Vermont. **4** *Dialect.* a wedge-shaped strip of land on the side of an irregular field.
—*v.t.* to put or make a gore in.
[Old English *gāra* angular point, related to *gār* spearhead (because of its shape)]

-gored, *combining form.* having a ______ gore or gores: *Five-gored = having five gores.*

gorge (gôrj), *n., v.,* **gorged, gorg|ing.** —*n.* **1** a deep, narrow valley, usually steep and rocky, especially one with a stream: *Through the gorge of this glen they found access to a blackbog* (Scott). See picture under **valley**. **2** a gorging; gluttonous meal. **3** the contents of a stomach. **4** *Figurative.* a feeling of disgust, indignation, resentment, or the like: *Cruelty to animals makes one's gorge rise.* **5** a narrow rear entrance from a fort into an outwork or outer part. **6** *U.S.* a mass stopping up a narrow passage: *An ice gorge blocked the river.* **7** the groove in a pulley. **8** *Archaic.* the throat; gullet.
—*v.i.* to eat greedily until full; stuff with food: *They ... Gorge from a stranger's hand and rend their master* (Shelley).
—*v.t.* **1** to swallow or devour greedily: *Though they see the hook and the string ... they gorge the bait nevertheless* (Thackeray). **2** to stuff with food: *He gorged himself with cake at the party.* **3** to fill full. SYN: glut, satiate.
[< Old French *gorge* throat < Late Latin *gurga,* for *gurges* gullet, throat, jaws < Latin, abyss, whirlpool] —**gorg'er**, *n.*

gorged (gôrjd), *adj.* **1** having a gorge or throat. **2** *Heraldry.* having the neck encircled with a collar, coronet, or the like.

gor|geous (gôr'jəs), *adj.* **1** richly colored; showy; magnificent: *The peacock spread his gorgeous tail. The gorgeous sunset thrilled us all.* SYN: dazzling. **2** splendid: *I am taxed on my income! This is perfectly gorgeous! I never felt so important in my life before* (Mark Twain). [< Old French *gorgias* fashionable, probably < *gorge* throat; see etym. under **gorge** (being suitable for adorning the neck)] —**gor'geous|ly**, *adv.* —**gor'geous-ness**, *n.*

gor|ger|in (gôr'jər in), *n. Architecture.* the necklike portion of a capital of a column, or a feature forming the junction between a shaft and its capital. [< French *gorgerin* < Old French *gorge;* see etym. under **gorge**]

gor|get (gôr'jit), *n.* **1** a piece of armor for the throat: *Unfix the gorget's iron clasp, And give him room for life to gasp* (Scott). **2** = collar. **3** = necklace. **4** a covering for the neck and breast, formerly worn by women; a wimple. **5** a patch of color on the throat of an animal or bird: *the golden-winged woodpecker, with ... his broad black gorget* (Washington Irving). **6** a grooved surgical instrument used in operations for removing stones, as from the bladder. [< Old French *gorgete* (diminutive) < *gorge;* see etym. under **gorge**]

gor|gi|o (gôr'jē ō, -jō), *n., pl.* **-gi|os**, *adj.* —*n.* the Romany name for anyone not of the Gypsy people. —*adj.* of or having to do with gorgios. [< Romany *gorjio*]

Gor|gon (gôr'gən), *n. Greek Legend.* any one of three sisters (Stheno, Euryale, and Medusa), having snakes for hair and faces so horrible that anyone who looked at them turned to stone. [< Latin *Gorgō, -ōnis* < Greek *Gorgṓ* < *gorgós* terrible]

gor|gon (gôr'gən), *n., adj.* —*n.* **1** a very ugly or terrible person, especially a repulsive woman. **2** anything fearful or unpleasant.
—*adj.* like a gorgon or gorgon's: *Your gorgon looks turn me to stone* (Phillip Massinger). [< *Gorgon*]

gor|go|nei|on (gôr'gə nē'on), *n., pl.* **-nei|a** (-nē'ə). a representation of a Gorgon's head. [< Greek *gorgóneion,* neuter of *gorgóneios* having to do with a Gorgon]

gor|go|ni|a (gôr gō'nē ə), *n.* = sea fan. [< New Latin *Gorgonia* the genus name < Latin *Gorgō, -ōnis;* see etym. under **Gorgon**]

gor|go|ni|an (gôr gō'nē ən), *adj., n.* —*adj.* of or having to do with the gorgonias.
—*n.* = sea fan.

Gor|go|ni|an (gôr gō'nē ən), *adj.* of or resembling a Gorgon; terrible; petrifying.

gorgonian coral, = sea fan.

gor|go|nin (gôr gō'nin), *n.* the horny substance making up the shell of the gorgonian coral (sea fan). [< *gorgon*(ian) + *-in*]

gor|gon|ize (gôr'gə nīz), *v.t.,* **-ized, -iz|ing.** **1** to petrify; make hard or stony. **2** to stare at with a Gorgon's look: *Next look, and she might have gorgonized me* (Punch).

Gor|gon|zo|la (gôr'gən zō'lə), *n.,* or **Gorgonzola cheese**, a strong, white, blue-veined Italian cheese made from milk, that looks and tastes somewhat like Roquefort cheese. [< *Gorgonzola,* a town in Italy, near Milan]

gor|hen (gôr'hen'), *n.* the female red grouse. [origin uncertain]

go|ril|la (gə ril'ə), *n.* **1** the largest and most powerful ape. The lowland gorilla is found in the forests of western Africa and the mountain gorilla lives in central Africa. It is mainly vegetarian in diet, social in habit, and very dangerous if irritated, wounded, or cornered, because of its strength. See picture under **ape**. **2** *Slang.* **a** a strong and brutal man. **b** a gangster. [American English < New Latin *Gorilla* the genus name < Greek *gorillas,* plural, probably < an African word]

go|ril|line (gə ril'īn, -in), *adj.* resembling the gorilla, especially in the skull and face: *Rhodesian man ... is far more primitive—more apelike, more gorilline—than any of modern man's variants, living or extinct* (A. Keith).

go|ril|loid (gə ril'oid), *adj.* like or having the characteristics of a gorilla: *gorilloid beasts with huge canine teeth* (Scientific American).

gor|ing (gôr'ing, gōr'-), *n.* a gore or gores.

gork (gôrk), *n. Medical Slang.* a person who has lost brain function through disease or age: *Like many other physicians, I have cared for hopelessly brain-dead people (referred to by the less genteel as "vegetables" or "gorks") who ... have been maintained by machines and nutritious solutions* (Mary E. Costanza). [origin unknown]

gor|mand (gôr'mənd), *n.* = gourmand.

gor|mand|ize (gôr'mən dīz), *v.i., v.t.,* **-ized, -iz|ing.** to stuff oneself with food; eat very greedily; gorge. SYN: cram, glut. [(originally) noun, gluttony < Middle French *gourmandise* < *gourmand;* see etym. under **gourmand**] —**gor'mand|iz'er**, *n.*

gorm|less (gôrm'lis), *adj. Especially British.* brainless; inept. [apparently variant of *gaumless* < *gaum, gome* heed, care < Scandinavian (compare Old Icelandic *gaumr*) + *-less*] —**gorm'less|ly**, *adv.* —**gorm'less|ness**, *n.*

go|rod|ki (gə rod'kē; *Russian* gə rot'kē'), *n.* a combination of shuffleboard and ninepins, formerly a favorite national game in Russia. [< Russian *gorodki*]

go-round (gō'round'), *n. U.S. Informal.* **1** a round of conflict; a stormy session: *the committee's first go-round.* **2** a performance; turn: *the last go-round of an actor.* **3** a tour.

gorp (gôrp), *n. U.S.* a mixture of nuts, sweets, and the like, eaten as a snack: *I took a ration of gorp—soybeans, sunflower seeds, oats, pretzels, Wheat Chex, raisins, and kelp—and poured another ration into Carol's hands* (John McPhee). [perhaps < earlier U.S. Slang *gorp,* verb, to eat greedily]

gorse (gôrs), *n.* = furze. [Old English *gorst*]

Gor|sedd (gôr'seŧh), *n.* a meeting of Welsh bards and druids, especially the assembly meeting daily as a preliminary to the eisteddfod. [< Welsh *gorsedd*]

gors|y (gôr'sē), *adj.* overgrown with gorse.

gor|y (gôr'ē, gōr'-), *adj.,* **gor|i|er, gor|i|est.** **1** covered with gore; stained with blood; bloody: *Everyone in the car accident was a gory mess.* **2** with much bloodshed; involving or concerned with bloodshed: *a gory murder or accident, a gory tale.* —**gor'i|ly**, *adv.* —**gor'i|ness**, *n.*

Gos|bank (gos'bangk'), *n.* the state bank of the Soviet Union. [< Russian *Gosbank* < *gos*(*udarstvennyj*) *bank* state bank]

gosh (gosh), *interj.* an exclamation or mild oath: *Gosh, it's cold out today.* [altered pronunciation of *God*]

gos|hawk (gos'hôk'), *n.* a large, powerful, short-winged hawk, formerly much used in falconry. [Old English *gōshafoc* < *gōs* goose + *hafoc* hawk]

Go|shen (gō'shən), *n.* **1** a fertile part of Egypt, east of the Nile delta, where the Israelites were permitted to live before the Exodus (in the Bible, Genesis 45: 10; Exodus 8: 20-22). **2** any land of plenty and comfort.

Go|si|ute (gō'sē yüt), *n., pl.* **-ute** or **-utes.** **1** a member of a small tribe of Indians of Shoshone stock in northwestern Utah. **2** their Shoshonean language.

gos|let (goz'lit), *n.* any one of several species of very small geese found in India, Africa, and Australia. [< *goose* + *-let;* perhaps patterned on *gosling*]

gos|ling (goz'ling), *n.* **1** a young goose. **2** *Figurative.* a foolish, inexperienced person. [Old English *gōs* goose + *-ling* - ling]

go-slow[1] (gō'slō'), *n. Informal.* **1** movement, progress, change, etc., at a deliberate or more deliberate pace: *a go-slow on tax reduction.* **2** a policy of deliberate action or change; gradualism.

go|slow strike, or **go-slow**[2] (gō'slō'), *n. Especially British.* slowdown.

gos|pel (gos'pəl), *n., adj., v.,* **-peled, -pel|ing** or (*especially British*) **-pelled, -pel|ling.** —*n.* **1a** the teaching of Jesus and the Apostles: *The old minister had preached the gospel for 40 years.* **b** glad tidings, especially concerning the coming of the promised Messiah in the person of Christ, of salvation through the Atonement, and of the kingdom of God. **2** anything earnestly believed or taken as a guide for action: *Drink plenty of water; that is my gospel. The law of the land is his gospel* (Sir Richard Steele). *Christianity has given the world the moral gospel; now France must preach the social gospel* (Edmund Wilson). **3** *Figurative.* the absolute truth: *She takes the doctor's words for gospel.* **4** = gospel music.
—*adj.* **1** of or like the gospel. **2** in agreement with the gospel; evangelical. **3** characterized by evangelical fervor; spreading the gospel: *gospel music, gospel hymns.* **4** of or having to do with gospel music or gospel songs: *a gospel singer, gospel shouts.*
—*v.t., v.i.* to evangelize.
[Old English *gōdspell* good tidings < *gōd* good + *spel* spell[2], a translation of Latin *bona adnūntiātiō,* a translation of Greek *evangélion* evangel]

Gos|pel (gos'pəl), *n.* **1** the story of Christ's life and teachings. **2a** any one of the first four books of the New Testament by Matthew, Mark, Luke, and John. They tell about the life and teachings of Christ. **b** a part of one of these books read during a religious service.

gos|pel|er (gos'pə lər), *n.* **1** the person who reads or sings the Gospel in the Eucharistic service. **2** a person who claims for his sect or party the exclusive possession of the true gospel or Christian doctrine. **3** a person who zealously professes faith in the gospel. **4** a singer of gospel songs.

gos|pel|ize (gos'pə līz), *v.t.,* **-ized, -iz|ing.** to instruct in the gospel; evangelize.

gos|pel|ler (gos'pə lər), *n. Especially British.* gospeler.

gospel music, music based on gospel songs, with elements of modern blues and jazz.

gospel oath, an oath sworn upon the Gospels; an oath of inviolable nature.

gospel shop, a Methodist chapel (used in an unfriendly way).

gospel side, the north side of the altar, at which the Gospel is read.

gospel song, *U.S.* a Negro church song similar to a spiritual but influenced by currently popular music, originally composed or improvised by a church singer and often popularized by jazz performers.

gospel truth, **1** the truth or truths contained in the gospel. **2** something absolutely true; something as true as the gospel.

Gos|plan (gos'plän'), *n.* the official Soviet planning agency in charge of programs for economic and industrial development, as for the five-year plans. [< Russian *Gosplan* < *gos* (*udarstvennaja*) *plan*(*ovaja*) *komissija* state planning commission]

gos|po|dar (gos'pə där), *n.* = hospodar.

gos|po|din (gos'pə dēn'), *n. Russian.* Mr.; mister.

gos|port (gos'pôrt, -pōrt), *n.* a rubber speaking tube by which a flight instructor formerly talked to a student pilot while in flight. [< *Gosport,* a town in England]

gos|sa|mer (gos'ə mər), *n., adj.* —*n.* **1** a film or thread of cobweb spun by small spiders, which is seen floating in the air in calm weather, especially in autumn, or spread on trees and bushes, or over a grassy surface: *Walking between two trees, she felt gossamer catch on her face.* **2** a very thin, light cloth or substance: *a summer dress of lightest gossamer.* **3** *U.S.* a thin, light, waterproof cloth or coat.
—*adj.* like gossamer; very light and thin; filmy: (*Figurative.*) *For if her reputation is tarnished ... the value of her gossamer illusion of innocence, falls correspondingly* (Harper's). SYN: delicate.
[Middle English *gossomer* goose summer, name for "Indian summer," as the season of goose and cobwebs]

gossamer spider, a small spider that weaves very slender threads often seen floating in the air.

gos|sa|mer|y (gos'ə mər ē), *adj.* like gossamer; very light and thin; filmy; flimsy.

gos|san (gos'ən, goz'-), *n. Mining.* decomposed rock of a reddish or rusty color, due to oxidized iron pyrites, that often forms a large part of the outcrop of a metal-bearing vein. Also, **gozzan**. [< a Cornish dialectal word]

gos|sip (gos'ip), *n., v.,* **-siped, -sip|ing.** —*n.* **1** idle talk, not always true, about other people and their affairs: *He heard nothing but neighborhood gossip from her without a single fact.* SYN:

Pronunciation Key: hat, āge, cãre, fär; let, ēqual, tėrm; it, īce; hot, ōpen, ôrder; oil, out; cup, pu̇t, rüle; child; long; thin; ŧhen; zh, measure; ə represents **a** in about, **e** in taken, **i** in pencil, **o** in lemon, **u** in circus.

tattle. **2** light, familiar talk or writing: *Somewhere past Sirius, shade called to shade, "Well, any gossip?..." "Not much. They say that solar god has made some quite amusing things out of his dust"* (J. B. Priestley). **3** a person who gossips a great deal: *a set of malicious, prating, prudent gossips, both male and female, who murder characters to kill time* (Richard Brinsley Sheridan). **4** *Archaic or Dialect.* a friend. **5** *Archaic or Dialect.* a godparent.
—***v.i.*** to repeat what one knows or hears about other people and their affairs: *The old ladies like to sit and gossip about the new neighbors.*
—***v.t.*** **1** to repeat like a gossip: *to gossip scandal.* **2** *Obsolete.* to stand godparent to.
[Old English *godsibb* (originally) godparent < *god* God + *sibb* relative] —**gos′sip|er**, *n.* —**gos′sip|ing|ly**, *adv.*

gossip column, a newspaper column devoted to gossip about celebrities, usually written in a light, chatty style.

gossip columnist, the writer of a gossip column.

gos|sip|ist (gos′ə pist), *n.* = gossip columnist.

gos|sip|mon|ger (gos′ip mung′gər, -mong′-), *n.* a person who spreads gossip or idle rumors about others.

gos|sip|red (gos′ip rid), *n.* **1** small talk; gossip. **2** the relationship or affinity between a godparent and godchild. [< *gossip* + Old English *rǣden* condition]

gos|sip|ry (gos′ip rē), *n.* small talk; gossip.

gos|sip|y (gos′ə pē), *adj.* **1** fond of gossip: *He was curious, meddlesome, gossipy* (Atlantic). **2** full of gossip: *a gossipy letter.* —**gos′sip|i|ness**, *n.*

gos|soon (go sün′), *n. Anglo-Irish.* **1** a boy. **2** a male servant. [alteration of French *garçon*]

gos|syp|lure (gos′əp lür′), *n.* a synthetic form of the sex attractant of the female pink bollworm. *The most promising way to use gossyplure is to saturate the field with the synthetic scent, overpowering the natural odor emitted by females. This confuses the males so that they cannot find the females, which then lay sterile eggs* (Frederick C. Price). [< New Latin (Pectiniphora) *gossyp* (iella) the pink bollworm + English *lure*]

gos|sy|pol (gos′ə pōl, -pol), *n.* a poisonous, yellow pigment in cottonseed which makes cottonseed meal unsuitable as a hog or poultry feed. *Formula:* $C_{30}H_{30}O_8$ [< Latin *gossypion* the cotton tree + English *-ol*[1]]

go-stop (gō′stop′), *n. British.* = stop-go.

got (got), *v.* a past tense and a past participle of **get:** *We got the letter yesterday. We had got tired of waiting for it.*

got up, artificially produced, elaborated, or adorned for effect or to deceive: *It's hard for us to imagine strontium 90—the name has a got-up sound, like something out of science fiction* (New Yorker).

▶**Have got** or **has got** is sometimes used for *have* or *has* otherwise used alone, as in showing obligation: *I've got to study now.* or with the meaning of "own, possess": *Have you got a pencil?* In speech, *got* was added because *have* almost disappears when unstressed. But in writing, where one can see each word, *got* is often avoided as unnecessary.

Go|ta|ma (gō′tə ma), *n.* = Gautama (Buddha).

Goth (goth), *n.* **1** a member of a Germanic people who invaded the Roman Empire from about 200 to 400 A.D. The Goths settled mainly in southern and eastern Europe. *Till Goths and Vandals, a rude Northern race, Did all the matchless monuments deface* (John Dryden). **2** *Figurative.* a person without culture or taste; an uncivilized person: *He must be a Goth and a barbarian if he did not enter into the spirit of such a happy... contrivance* (Tobias Smollett). [Old English *Gotan,* plural < Late Latin *Gothī,* probably < Greek *Góthos,* ultimately < Germanic (compare Gothic *Gut-thiuda* Gothic folk)]

Goth., Gothic.

Go|tha (gō′thə, -tä), *n.* **Al|ma|nach de** (äl′mä näɴ də), an annual register of the genealogy of the principal royal and aristocratic families of Europe. [< *Gotha,* a city in East Germany, where it was published]

Goth|am (goth′əm, gō′thəm), *n.* a nickname for New York City.

wise man of Gotham, a fool; simpleton: *The wise men of Gotham are risen again* (Alois Brandl).
[so called by Washington Irving, in "Salmagundi," after the English village of *Gotham* (pronounced got′əm), near Nottingham, proverbial for the foolishness of its inhabitants]

Goth|am|ite (goth′ə mīt, gō′thə-; got′ə mīt *for 2*), *n.* **1** a resident of New York City; a New Yorker. **2** a person who takes after the men of Gotham, England; blunderer; simpleton.

Goth|ic** (goth′ik), *n., adj.* —n.*** **1** a style of architecture using pointed arches, flying buttresses, and high, steep roofs. It was developed in western Europe during the Middle Ages from about 1150 to 1550. **2** the East Germanic language of the Goths. It is known chiefly from the translations of the Bible by Bishop Ulfilas in the 300's. **3** *Printing.* **a** Often, **gothic**. *U.S.* a square-cut style of type without serifs or hairlines. **b** *British.* black letter.
—***adj.*** **1a** of or having to do with Gothic architecture: *a Gothic cathedral.* **b** of or having to do with the period during which Gothic architecture flourished: *Gothic art, a Gothic manuscript.* **2** of the Goths or their language. **3** *Figurative.* uncivilized; crude; barbarous: *O! more than Gothic ignorance* (Henry Fielding). **4** having to do with or characteristic of a style of fiction using grotesque and supernatural elements and often medieval settings or details to produce horror and romance: *a Gothic story. The Grecian splendor of the old novels and the Gothic horror of the new ones are products of the same psychology* (Saturday Review). **5** *Obsolete.* Germanic.
[< Late Latin *Gothicus* < *Gothī;* see etym. under **Goth**] —**Goth′i|cal|ly**, *adv.*

***Gothic**
definitions 1, 3a

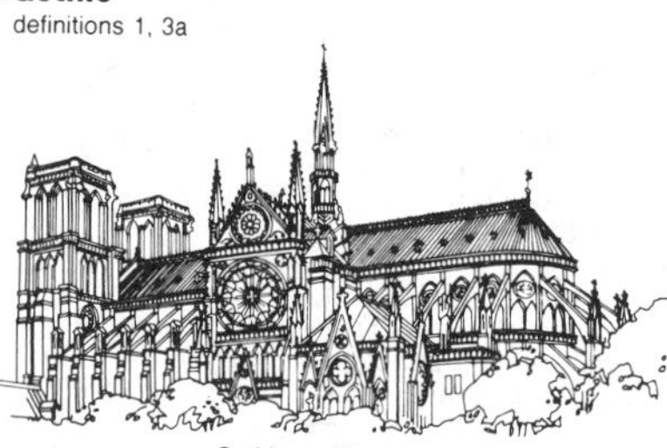

Gothic architecture

The World Book Dictionary
Gothic type

Gothic arch, a pointed arch.

Goth|i|cism (goth′ə siz əm), *n.* **1** conformity or adherence to the Gothic style of architecture, Gothic ideas, and the like: **2** *Figurative.* Also, **gothicism**. rudeness; barbarism. **3** a Gothic idiom.

Goth|i|cize (goth′ə sīz), *v.t.,* **-cized, -ciz|ing.** to make Gothic; make medieval: *Horace Walpole began to Gothicize the little house he had bought* (New York Times Book Review).

Goth|ick (goth′ik), *adj. British.* **1** in the sham Gothic style of the 1800's: *And for scenery what more fitting than the Gothick of the period?* (E. Croft-Murray). **2** Also, **gothick**. in the style of Gothic literature; grotesque; gruesome: *The tales... are full of Gothick horrors, ghosts, demons, hanged men who rise at night* (Punch). [archaic spelling of *Gothic*]

Goth|ic|ness (goth′ək nis), *n.* **1** the quality or condition of being Gothic. **2** a piece of Gothic ornamentation.

Gothic Revival, an architectural style of the 1700's and 1800's, consciously imitating.

gö|thite (gō′thīt, gœ′tīt), *n.* a mineral consisting of a hydrous oxide of iron, of reddish or dark brown color, occurring massive or in orthorhombic crystals. *Formula:* FeO (OH) Also, **goethite**. [see etym. under **goethite**]

got|ra (got′rə), *n.* the large, folded cloth of the Arab headdress or kaffiyeh. It is held in place by a band of twisted cord wrapped around the head. [< Arabic *guṭra*]

got|ten (got′ən), *v., adj.* —***v.*** a past participle of **get:** *It has gotten to be quite late.*
—***adj.*** obtained; acquired; won: *ill-gotten wealth.*
▶In Great Britain, **gotten** has been largely replaced by **got**, but in America *gotten* remains generally current. In American usage, *got* rather than *gotten* is used with *have* to show obligation or to mean "own, possess": *We have got* (not *gotten*) *to go tomorrow. We have got* (not *gotten*) *lots of time.* (In both examples *have* would usually replace *have got* in writing, though not in speech.) Otherwise, *got* and *gotten* are used freely, the choice depending mainly on rhythm or emphasis: *He could have gotten* (or *got*) *here by now. In the past I have gotten* (or *got*) *a good meal here.*

Göt|ter|däm|mer|ung (gœt′ər dem′ər ùng), *n.* **1** *Germanic Mythology.* the day of the great battle between the gods and the forces of evil, signaling the end of the world. **2** *Figurative.* total destruction; holocaust: *the Nazi Götterdämmerung.* **3** an opera (1876) by Richard Wagner, the last of his tetralogy of *The Ring of the Nibelung.* [< German *Götterdämmerung* (literally) twilight of the gods]

Gott mit uns (gôt mit′ùns), *German.* God with us (the motto of the former Prussian rulers of Germany).

gouache (gwäsh), *n.* **1** a method of painting with opaque water colors, prepared by mixing pigments with water and gum. **2** a color made in this way. **3** a painting made by this method: *The trustees have bought a gouache by the contemporary Italian artist Afro* (London Times). [< French *gouache* < Italian *guazzo* water colors; mire; earlier, watering place < Latin *aquātiō* < *aquārī* bring water < *aqua* water]

Gou|da (gou′də, gü′-), *n.,* or **Gouda cheese**, a flat, round, mild cheese made from whole milk. [< *Gouda,* a city in the Netherlands, where it was first made]

Gou|dy (gou′dē), *n.* any of various styles of printing type designed by Frederic William Goudy, 1865-1947, an American designer of printing types.

gouge** (gouj), *n., v.,* **gouged, goug|ing.** —n.*** **1** a chisel with a curved blade. Gouges are used for cutting round grooves or holes in wood. **2** a cutting with or as if with a gouge. **3** a groove or hole made by gouging: *Clumsy movers made several gouges in the table by forcing it through the doorway.* **4** *U.S. Informal.* **a** a trick; cheat; swindle. **b** a swindler; impostor.
—***v.t.*** **1** to cut with a gouge or as if with a gouge: *The cabinetmaker gouged fine curving lines in the molding about the door.* **2** to dig out; tear out; force out: *to gouge an eye.* **3** *Informal.* to trick; cheat; swindle.
[< Old French *gouge* < Late Latin *gulbia, gubia* hollow (beveled) chisel, perhaps < Gaulish (compare Old Irish *gulban* needle)]

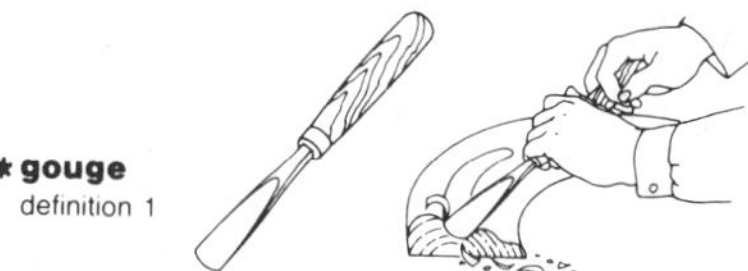

***gouge**
definition 1

goug|er (gou′jər), *n.* a person who gouges.

gou|lash (gü′läsh), *n.* **1** a stew made of beef or veal and vegetables, usually highly seasoned. **2** a redeal in contract bridge intended to produce freak hands, before which each player arranges his cards by suits and order of value. The cards are dealt without shuffling in blocks of five, five, and three. **3** *Figurative.* a hodgepodge: *What we get is a goulash of Gilbert and Sullivan, the Princeton Triangle Club, a girls' choir, and some genuine romantic melody* (Wall Street Journal). [< Hungarian *gulyás* (originally) herdsman]

goum (güm), *n.* **1** an Arab tribal contingent in the French military service. **2** a member of the Moroccan native militia. [< French *goum* < Arabic]

gou|mier (gü myā′), *n. French.* a goum.

gou|pen (gou′pən, gō′-), *n.* = gowpen.

gou|ra (gür′ə, gou′rə), *n.* any one of a group of large pigeons of New Guinea, with immense, erect, umbrellalike crests. [< a native name]

gou|ra|mi (gür′ə mē), *n., pl.* **-mis.** **1** a large freshwater Asiatic fish. **2** any one of various related but much smaller fish, bred for tropical-fish hobbyists. [< Malay *gurāmī*]

gourd (gôrd, gōrd, gùrd), *n.* **1** the fruit of certain vines, with hard rinds and many flat seeds. It belongs to the gourd family. One kind, the bottle gourd, is dried and hollowed out and used for cups, bowls, bottles, and other utensils. **2** the vine that it grows on. **3** a cup, bowl, bottle, or other utensil, made from the dried shell of a gourd: *a pebble rattled in a dry gourd* (Robinson Jeffers). **4** any plant of the gourd family. **5** *U.S. Slang.* the head; mind: *"Why would anyone want to jump out of a perfectly good airplane? You must be out of your gourd!" he exclaimed seven or eight times* (New Yorker). [< Old French *gourde,* alteration of *cohourde* < Latin *cucurbita*] —**gourd′like′**, *adj.*

gourde (gùrd), *n.* **1** the unit of money of Haiti, a coin equal to 100 centimes. **2** (formerly in Louisiana, Cuba, and Haiti) a dollar. [< French *gourde,* feminine of *gourd* heavy, numb < Latin *gurdus* dull; a numskull]

***gourd family**, a group of dicotyledonous, climbing herbs with hairy or prickly, branched tendrils and fruits which usually have rinds and spongy, seedy interiors. The family includes the cucumber, squash, melon, pumpkin, and bryony. See picture opposite on next page.

gourd|ful (gôrd′fůl, gōrd′-, gùrd′-), *n., pl.* **-fuls.** as much as a gourd can hold.

gourd-shaped (gôrd′shāpt′, gōrd′-, gùrd′-), *adj.* having the shape of a gourd; having a globular body and a long, slender neck: *a gourd-shaped bottle.*

gour|mand (gùr′mənd), *n.* **1** a person who is

fond of good eating. A gourmand is not so particular as an epicure nor so greedy as a glutton gourmand (Lord Chesterfield). **2** a person who eats to excess; glutton. Also, **gormand**. [< French *gourmand* gluttonous]

gour|mand|ise¹ (gůr′mən dīz, gůr′mən dēz′), *n.* the tastes or practices of a gourmand: *For the culinary expatriate there is no end of books on global gourmandise* (Atlantic). [< Middle French *gourmandise;* see etym. under **gormandize**]

gour|mand|ise² (gůr′mən dīz), *v.i., v.t.,* **-ised, -is|ing**. *Especially British.* gourmandize. **—gour′mand|is′er**, *n.*

gour|mand|ism (gůr′mən diz′əm), *n.* the tastes or practices of a gourmand; love of good eating.

gour|mand|ize (gůr′mən dīz), *v.i., v.t.,* **-ized, -iz|ing**. **1** to eat like a gourmand: *The Vintners' annual swan banquet, when dignity demands that they gourmandize on their own birds . . .* (Newsweek). **2** to indulge in good eating. **3** = gormandize. **—gour′mand|iz′er**, *n.*

gour|met (gůr′mā), *n., adj.* **—*n.*** a person who is expert in judging and choosing fine foods or wines; epicure.
—*adj.* by or for a gourmet; epicurean: *America's famous basic cookbook teaches gourmet cooking, too—with hundreds of gourmet recipes* (New Yorker).
[< Middle French *gourmet* < Old French *gourmet, gromet* wine tester, wine merchant's servant; origin uncertain]

gous|ty (gous′tē), *adj. Scottish.* large and empty; dreary; desolate. [origin uncertain]

gout (gout), *n.* **1** a painful disease of the joints, especially of the big toe. It is characterized by inflammation of the joints, an excess of uric acid in the blood, and the deposit of uric acid salts in and around the joints. *For that old enemy the gout Had taken him in toe* (Thomas Hood). **2** a drop, splash, or clot: *There are gouts of blood on the dagger.* **3** a disease in wheat and barley characterized by swelling of the joints of the stems, caused by the larva of the gout fly. **4** *British Slang.* a bunch; bundle: *a gout of money, gouts of hair.* [< Old French *goute* < Latin *gutta* a drop (in Medieval Latin, also gout) (thought to be caused by drops of viscous "humors")]

goût (gü), *n. French.* taste.

goû|ter (gü tā′), *n. French.* a snack, especially one eaten in the afternoon: *children trudging home at five o'clock for a quick goûter and a long evening of history and mathematics* (Atlantic).

gout fly, the small fly whose larva causes gout in wheat.

gout|y¹ (gou′tē), *adj.,* **gout|i|er, gout|i|est**. **1** diseased or swollen with gout. **2** of gout; caused by gout: *gouty arthritis.* **3** causing gout. **4** *Figurative.* swollen. **—gout′i|ly**, *adv.* **—gout′i|ness**, *n.*

gout|y² (gou′tē), *n., pl.* **gout|ies**. *British.* a kind of overshoe or arctic for wearing in snow: *For curling, or walking on the rinks, it is necessary to wear rubber snow-shoes, or gouties, and these are very handy to slip on over house-shoes* (Nation). [apparently < *gouty¹* (because of the swollen appearance of the feet when worn)]

gouty stem tree, **1** any one of a variety of baobab that grows in Australia. **2** any one of a variety of bottle tree that is grown especially as a shade tree in Queensland, Australia.

gou|ver|nante (gü ver näɴt′), *n. French.* **1** a housekeeper. **2** a governess. **3** a chaperon.

gov., **1** government. **2** governor.

Gov., governor.

gov|ern (guv′ərn), *v.t.* **1** to rule; control; manage: *The election determined which party would govern the United States for four years. Who, or rather, what new coalition shall next govern France?* (Time). **SYN:** direct, conduct. See syn. under **rule**. **2** to exercise a directing or restraining influence over; determine or guide: *What were the motives governing the king's decision to give up his throne?* **3** to hold back; restrain; check: *Govern your temper.* **4** to be a rule or law for: *the principles governing a case.* **5** *Grammar.* to require (a word) to be in a certain case or mood; require (a certain case or mood). **6** to control automatically the speed of (a machine). **—*v.i.*** **1** to exercise the function of government; rule: *And no President has ever governed over a more contented electorate—or a more united one* (Newsweek). **2** to have a predominating or decisive influence; prevail. [< Old French *governer* < Latin *gubernāre* (originally) to steer < Greek *kybernân*] **—gov′ern|a|ble**, *adj.*

gov|ern|ance (guv′ər nəns), *n.* government; rule; control.

gov|ern|ess (guv′ər nis), *n.* **1** a woman who teaches or trains children in their homes. **2** *Obsolete.* a female governor or ruler. **3** the wife of a governor (a humorous use).

***governess car** or **cart**, a light, two-wheeled vehicle with seats at the sides, on which passengers sit face to face.

***governess car**

gov|ern|ess|y (guv′ər nə sē), *adj.* like a governess; fussy; spinsterish; prim.

gov|ern|ment (guv′ərn mənt, -ər-), *n.* **1** the ruling of a country, state, district, or other area; direction of the affairs of state: *federal government, municipal government. All government is difficult. It is certain that the most natural and human government is that of consent, for that binds freely . . . when men hold their liberty by true obedience to rules of their own making* (Newsweek). **2** Sometimes, **Government**. a person or persons ruling a country, state, district or other area at a time; administration or ministry: *The government of the United States consists of the President and his cabinet, the Congress, and the Supreme Court. In Great Britain, "the government" may mean the cabinet.* **3** a system of ruling: *civil government. The United States has a democratic form of government.* **SYN:** regime. **4** the country, state, district, or other area, ruled: *Most governments are represented in the United Nations.* **5** = political science. **6** rule, control, or management: *the government of one's conduct.* **SYN:** regulation. **7** *Grammar.* the influence of one word in determining the case or mood of another.
governments, government bonds: *Buyers bid governments back up from ⅛ to ⅜ of a point* (Newsweek).
—gov′ern|ment|less, *adj.*
▶**Government** (def. 2). As a collective noun, *Government* is singular in the United States, plural or singular in Great Britain: *The Government is ready to present the budget to Congress* (U.S.). *The Government have* (or *has*) *issued a White Paper on the subject of education* (Great Britain).

gov|ern|men|tal (guv′ərn men′təl, -ər-), *adj.* of or having to do with government or a government. [American English < *government* + *-al¹*] **—gov′ern|men′tal|ly**, *adv.*

gov|ern|men|tal|ism (guv′ərn men′tə liz′əm, -ər-), *n.* the tendency to enlarge or extend the sphere of activity or power of a government.

gov|ern|men|tal|ist (guv′ərn men′tə list, -ər-), *n.* an advocate or follower of governmentalism.

government bond, a bond issued by a national government.

gov|ern|ment|ese (guv′ərn men tēz′, -tēs′; -ər-), *n.* federalese; the jargon of officialdom.

government house, the official residence of a governor or governor general, as in a British colony or dependency, or in some countries of the Commonwealth of Nations.

gov|ern|ment-in-ex|ile (guv′ərn mənt in eg′zīl, -ər-; -ek′sīl), *n., pl.* **gov|ern|ments-in-ex|ile**. an ousted government set up in a neutral or friendly foreign country in order to maintain its official status: *The Polish government-in-exile was in Great Britain during World War II.*

gov|ern|ments (guv′ərn mənts, -ər-), *n.pl.* See under **government**.

gov|er|nor (guv′ər nər, guv′nər), *n.* **1** the official elected as the executive head of a state of the United States. The governor of a state carries out the laws made by a state legislature. *Abbr:* Gov. **2** an official appointed to govern a province, colony, city, or fort: *History is full, down to this day, of the imbecility of kings and governors* (Emerson). **SYN:** ruler. **3** a person who manages or directs the affairs of a club, society, institution, or, sometimes, a business. A club often has a board of governors. **SYN:** manager, director, overseer. **4** an automatic device to keep a machine going at an even speed by controlling the supply of fuel or power: *Most steam engines are equipped with governors to regulate their speed.* **5** *Especially British Slang.* one's father, employer, or other superior (used as a familiar term of address). **6** *British Slang.* a prison warden. **7** *Obsolete.* a tutor. [< Old French *governeor* < Latin *gubernātor* (originally) steersman < *gubernāre;* see etym. under **govern**]

gov|er|nor|ate (guv′ər nə rāt, guv′nə-), *n.* a province or portion of country ruled by a governor, especially each of the administrative divisions of Egypt.

governor general, *pl.* **governors general** or **governor generals**. a governor who has subordinate or deputy governors under him, as in some countries of the Commonwealth of Nations.

gov|er|nor-gen|er|al|ship (guv′ər nər jen′ər əl ship, guv′nər jen′rəl-), *n.* the position, function, or term of office of a governor general.

gov|er|nor|ship (guv′ər nər ship, guv′nər-), *n.* the position, term of office, or duties of a governor: *He ought to have expected and had the governorship upon the death or removal of the former governor* (Samuel Pepys).

Gov.-Gen., governor-general (used as a title).

govt. or **Govt.**, government.

gow|an (gou′ən), *n. Scottish.* any one of various yellow or white field flowers, especially the English daisy. [apparently variant of Middle English *golland* any of various yellow wild flowers, related to *gold* marigold]

gow|aned (gou′ənd), *adj. Scottish.* full of gowans; covered with gowans.

gow|an|y (gou′ə nē), *adj. Scottish.* gowaned.

go-way bird (gō′wā′), = go-away bird.

gowd (goud), *n. Scottish.* gold.

gowk (gouk, gōk), *n. Especially Scottish.* **1** a cuckoo. **2** a fool; simpleton. [Middle English *goke* < Scandinavian (compare Old Icelandic *gaukr*)]

gown (goun), *n., v.,* **—*n.*** **1** a woman's dress, especially a formal or evening dress: *Her wedding dress was a long gown of beautiful white lace.* **2a** a loose outer garment worn by judges, lawyers, clergymen, members of a university, students graduating from a college, and others to show their position, profession, etc. **b** the members of a university: *arguments between town and gown.* **3** a nightgown or dressing gown: *I came down . . . in my gown and slippers* (Daniel Defoe). **4** a flowing outer garment worn by the ancients, especially the Roman toga. **5** *Archaic.* the dress of peace: *He Mars depos'd, and arms to gowns made yield* (John Dryden).
—*v.t., v.i.* to put a gown on; dress in a gown.
[< Old French *goune* or *gon* < Late Latin *gunna* leather garment, skin, hide] **—gown′less**, *adj.*

gowns|man (gounz′mən), *n., pl.* **-men**. **1** a person who wears a gown to show his position, profession, or station; judge, lawyer, clergyman, or member of a university. **2** a civilian, as distinguished from a soldier.

gow|pen (gou′pən, gō′-), *n. Scottish.* **1** the two hands held together in the form of a bowl. **2** as much as can be held thus; a double handful. **3** a great quantity. [< Scandinavian (compare Old Icelandic *gaupn*)]

GOX or **gox** (no periods), gaseous oxygen.

goy (goi), *n., pl.* **goy|im** or **goys**. *Slang.* **1** a non-Jew; gentile. **2** an unobservant or irreligious Jew. [< Yiddish *goy* < Hebrew *gōy* nation]

Go|ya|esque (goi′yə esk′), *adj.* of or having to do with the Spanish painter Francisco de Goya (1746-1828) or his style of art.

Go|ya|nás (gō′yə näz′), *n.pl.* a group of Indians formerly occupying the Brazilian coast between Angra dos Reis and Cananea and, inland, the country about São Paulo.

Go|ya|ta|cás (gō′yə tə käz′), *n.pl.* a tribe of Bra-

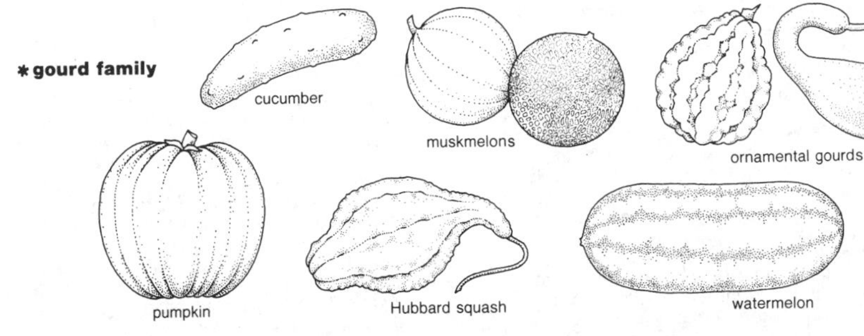

***gourd family**

Pronunciation Key: hat, āge, cãre, fär; let, ēqual, tėrm; it, īce; hot, ōpen, ôrder; oil, out; cup, pu̇t, rüle; child; long; thin; ᴛʜen; zh, measure; ə represents a in about, e in taken, i in pencil, o in lemon, u in circus.

zilian Indians that at the time of the conquest, occupied the region near the coast of the modern state of Rio de Janeiro.

goy|im (goi′im), *n.* a plural of **goy**.

goy|ish (goi′ish), *adj. Slang.* of or like a goy; gentile.

Go|zi|tan or **Go|zo|tan** (gō′zə tən), *adj., n.* —*adj.* of or having to do with Gozo, an island of the Malta group in the Mediterranean, south of Sicily, or its natives: *Gozitan women are noted for their beautiful lace* (London Times).
—*n.* a native of Gozo.

goz|zan (goz′ən), *n.* = gossan.

gp., group.

g.p., **1** general practice. **2** general practitioner. **3** great primer (18-point type).

Gp., group.

GP (no periods), **1** General-Parents (a symbol used in the United States for motion pictures recommended to the general audiences, with parental guidance advised). **2** general practitioner. **3** geographic position.

G.P., an abbreviation for the following:
1 Gallup poll.
2 general purpose.
3 glory be to the Father (Latin, *Gloria Patri*).
4 Graduate in Pharmacy.
5 Grand Prix.

GPA (no periods), grade-point average.

G.P.A., general passenger agent.

g.p.d., gallons per day.

g.p.h., gallons per hour.

g.p.m., gallons per minute.

GPM (no periods), graduated payment mortgage.

G.P.M., Grand Past Master.

GPO (no periods) or **G.P.O.**, **1** General Post Office. **2** Government Printing Office (of the U.S.).

g.p.s., gallons per second.

GPT (no periods), *Psychology.* group projective test.

GPU (no periods) or **G.P.U.**, a predecessor during the 1920's of the MVD as the official secret police of the Soviet Union; Gay-Pay-Oo. It followed the Cheka and was itself followed by the Ogpu.

G.Q., General Quarters.

gr., an abbreviation for the following:
1 grade.
2 grain or grains.
3 gram or grams.
4 grammar.
5 grand.
6 great.
7 gross (144 articles).

Gr., an abbreviation for the following:
1 grade.
2a Grecian. **b** Greece. **c** Greek.
3 gross (144 articles).
4 *British.* gunner.

Graaf|i|an follicle or **vesicle** (grä′fē ən), one of the small, fluid-filled sacs or cavities in an ovary that contains an ovum. [< Regnier de *Graaf,* 1641-1673, a Dutch physician]

Graal (gräl), *n.* = Grail.

grab[1] (grab), *v.,* **grabbed, grab|bing,** *n.* —*v.t.* **1** to grasp or seize suddenly; snatch: *The dog grabbed the meat and ran.* SYN: clutch. **2** to take possession of in an unscrupulous manner: *to grab land.* **3** to capture; arrest: *The police grabbed the robbers after a long chase.* **4** to get or take in a hurry: *to grab a sandwich, grab a shower. I planned to grab a bus in case I couldn't grab a taxicab* (New Yorker). **5** *Slang.* to cause (a person) to react; make an impression on: *The Women's Liberation Front . . . is charging the Cormorants with discrimination in hiring practices. How does that grab you?* (Roger Angell).
—*v.i.* to make a grab or snatch; snatch (at). SYN: clutch.
—*n.* **1** a snatching; a sudden seizing: *He made a grab at the butterfly.* **2** something that is grabbed. **3** a mechanical device for firmly holding something that is to be lifted or raised: *Cranes and mechanical grabs heave up loads of what the council call "reluctant London clay"* (London Times). **4** a person or thing that grabs. **5** *British.* a children's card game.
have the grab on, *British Slang.* to have great advantage of: *Burglars always have the grab on the police because burglars know where and when the act will take place.*
up for grabs, *U.S. Slang.* ready for the taking or seizing; available: *21 GOP seats are up for grabs [in the House of Representatives]* (Newsweek).
[compare Middle Dutch, Middle Low German *grabben*] —**grab′ba|ble,** *adj.* —**grab′ber,** *n.*

grab[2] (grab), *n.* a sailing ship with a long, sharp bow and usually two masts with lateen sails, drawing little water, used along the Malabar Coast of India. [Anglo-Indian < Arabic *ghurāb*]

grab bag, 1 a bag containing various unseen and unknown objects from which a person can take out one: *The other goodies in this tasteful grab bag are equally magical* (Atlantic). **2** *Figurative, Informal.* a miscellaneous collection; variety; mixture: *a grab bag of celebrities at the play's opening night.*

grab bar, a bar or rail attached to the side of a bathtub or shower for a person to take hold of so as not to slip or lose balance.

grab|ble (grab′əl), *v.,* **-bled, -bling.** —*v.i.* **1** to feel or search with the hands; grope. **2** to sprawl or scramble. —*v.t.* to catch hold of; clutch: *The speaker slowly rose, grabbling the face of the rock* (George Washington Cable).
[perhaps frequentative of *grab*]

grab|by (grab′ē), *adj.,* **-bi|er, -bi|est.** inclined to grab; grabbing; grasping.

gra|ben (grä′bən), *n., pl.* **-ben.** = rift valley. [< German *Graben* ditch]

grab line, *Nautical.* any one of certain lines or ropes on a ship for taking hold of if necessary, such as one for boatmen to hold on to when coming alongside.

grab rail, a rail inside an automobile, bus, or other vehicle for passengers to hold on to while riding.

grab rope, = grab line.

grab sample, = random sample.

grace (grās), *n., v.,* **graced, grac|ing.** —*n.* **1** beauty of form, movement, or manner: *The ballet dancer danced with much grace. Grace, indeed, is beauty in action* (Benjamin Disraeli). SYN: charm, ease, elegance. **2** a pleasing or agreeable quality or feature: *Possess'd of ev'ry manly grace* (Tobias Smollett). **3a** good will; favor: *The marks of grace which Elizabeth showed to young Raleigh* (Scott). SYN: kindness. **b** an instance or manifestation of favor: *Do me this grace, my child, to have my shield In keeping till I come* (Tennyson). SYN: kindness. **4** mercy; clemency; pardon; forgiveness. **5a** the favor and love of God; influence of God operating in man to improve and strengthen: *But where sin abounded, grace did much more abound* (Romans 5:20). **b** the condition of being influenced and favored by God: *Grace, in a sense, is that which conforms us to God—the Creator* (Time). **6** a short prayer of thanks before or after a meal: *A youth . . . pronounced the ancient form of grace before meals* (Emerson). **7** favor shown by granting a delay in the performance of an action, or the discharge of an obligation, or immunity from penalty during a specified period: *You may have a day's grace to decide. Stay a little! One golden minute's grace!* (Tennyson). **8** a legal allowance of time for the payment of a bill or the like, after the expiration of the term for which it is drawn: *Most firms allow a ten days' grace after a bill is due.* **9** virtue; merit; excellence: *He blushes again, which is a sign of grace* (Scott). **10** behavior put on to seem attractive: *My sister came back from boarding school with little airs and graces.* **11** Often, **Grace.** a title used in speaking to or of a duke, duchess, or archbishop (preceded by a possessive adjective): *May I assist Your Grace?* **12** = grace note. **13** *Obsolete.* one's fate, lot, or destiny.
—*v.t.* **1** to give or add grace to; set off with grace: *A vase of flowers graced the room. Still cheaper chicken may grace menus soon* (Wall Street Journal). SYN: adorn, decorate, embellish. **2** to give grace or honor to: *The queen graced the ball with her presence.* SYN: honor. **3** *Music.* to add grace notes to.
fall from grace, a *Informal.* to lose favor: *She fell from grace with her teacher when she persisted in coming late to class.* **b** to revert to sin or evildoing; backslide: *Calvinism denies the possibility of falling from grace.*
have the grace, to show a sense of what is right or proper: *In the church . . . will be represented a Miracle Play; and I hope you will all have the grace to attend* (Longfellow).
in one's bad graces or **in the bad graces of,** disfavored or disliked by: *That rude boy is always in the teacher's bad graces.*
in one's good graces or **in the good graces of,** favored or liked by: *I wonder if I am in the good graces of the teacher?*
take heart of grace. See under **heart.**
with bad grace, unpleasantly unwillingly: *The apology was made with bad grace.*
with good grace, pleasantly; willingly: *He obeyed the order with good grace.*
[< Old French *grace* < Latin *grātia* favor, thanks < *grātus* pleasing]

grace-and-fa|vour (grās′ən fā′vər), *adj. British.* **1** (of a house, pension, etc.) granted by the Crown, free of rent, rates, etc., to retired civil servants and the like. **2** of or having to do with a grace-and-favour house, pension, etc.: *grace-and-favour residents, a grace-and-favour tenant.*

grace cup, 1 a cup of wine formerly passed around the table, after the saying of grace at the end of a meal, from which a final toast was drunk. **2** a drink taken from it.

grace|ful (grās′fəl), *adj.* having or showing grace; beautiful in form, movement, or manner; pleasing; agreeable: *A good dancer must be graceful. She thanked him with a graceful speech.* —**grace′ful|ly,** *adv.* —**grace′ful|ness,** *n.*

grace|less (grās′lis), *adj.* **1** ugly in form, movement, or manner; without grace: *awkward, graceless movements.* **2** without any sense of what is right or proper; impolite: *That boy is a graceless rascal. She knows very well what graceless dogs sailors are* (Herman Melville). **3** lacking spiritual grace; unregenerate. —**grace′less|ly,** *adv.* —**grace′less|ness,** *n.*

grace note, *Music.* a note or group of notes not essential to the harmony or melody but added for ornament, such as an appoggiatura. Grace notes are printed in smaller type than the regular notes.

grace period, a delay granted in the performance of an action or the discharge of an obligation.

Grac|es (grā′siz), *n.pl. Greek and Roman Mythology.* three sister goddesses who give beauty, charm, and joy to people and nature. They are usually described as attendants of Aphrodite and as women of great beauty. They are Aglaia (brilliance), Euphrosyne (joy), and Thalia (bloom).

grace stroke, a finishing stroke; coup de grâce.

Grace's warbler, a warbler of the southwestern United States and Mexico with gray upper parts and yellow throat and chest. [< *Grace* Cones, sister of Elliott Cones, 1842-1899, an American naturalist]

grac|ile (gras′əl), *adj.* **1** slender; thin; lean. **2** gracefully slender. [< Latin *gracilis*] —**grac′ile|ness,** *n.*

grac|i|lis (gras′ə lis), *n., pl.* **-les** (-lēz). a muscle on the inner surface of the thigh that pulls the thigh in and flexes the leg. [< New Latin *gracilis* < Latin *gracilis* slender]

gra|cil|i|ty (grə sil′ə tē), *n.* slenderness.

gra|ci|os|i|ty (grā′shē os′ə tē), *n.* graciousness.

gra|ci|o|so (grā′shē ō′sō; *Spanish* grä thyō′ sō), *n., pl.* **-sos. 1** the buffoon of Spanish traditional comedy. **2** *Obsolete.* a court favorite. [< Spanish *gracioso* a favorite, clown; (literally) pleasing, amusing < Latin *grātiōsus.* See etym. of doublet **gracious.**]

gra|cious (grā′shəs) *adj., interj.* —*adj.* **1** pleasant and kindly; courteous: *She received her guests in a gracious manner that made them feel at ease.* SYN: See syn. under **kind**[1]. **2** pleasant, kindly, and courteous to people of lower social position: *The queen greeted the crowd with a gracious smile.* SYN: See syn. under **kind**[1]. **3** merciful; kindly; compassionate: *Thou art a God ready to pardon, gracious and merciful* (Nehemiah 9:17). **4** *Archaic.* pleasing; attractive; graceful. **5** *Obsolete.* enjoying grace or favor; fortunate; happy.
—*interj.* an exclamation of surprise.
[< Old French *gracious* < Latin *grātiōsus* < *grātia;* see etym. under **grace.** See etym. of doublet **gracioso.**] —**gra′cious|ly,** *adv.* —**gra′cious|ness,** *n.*

grack|le (grak′əl), *n.* **1** any one of several large American blackbirds related to the orioles, such as the purple grackle. **2** any one of various other birds with shiny black or dark feathers, such as the European myna and the starling. [< New Latin *Gracula* the genus name < Latin *grāculus* jackdaw]

grad[1] (grad), *n. Informal.* a graduate, especially of a college.

grad[2] (grad), *n. Navigation.* a unit for measuring angles or calculating a position on the earth's surface. A grad equals 9/10 of a degree.

grad., **1** graduate. **2** graduated.

gra|da|ble (grā′də bəl), *adj.* that can be graded: *cattle gradable according to weight.*

gra|date (grā′dāt), *v.,* **-dat|ed, -dat|ing.** —*v.i.* to pass by imperceptible degrees, as one color into another.
—*v.t.* **1** to cause to gradate. **2** to arrange in steps or grades.
[probably back formation < *gradation*]

gra|da|tim (grə dā′tim), *adv. Latin.* step by step; by degrees; gradually.

gra|da|tion (grā dā′shən), *n.* **1a** a change by steps or stages; gradual change: *Our acts show gradation between right and wrong. She sometimes contemplated a little sorrowfully the gradation from her former simplicity to her present sophistication.* **b** the fact or condition of including or being arranged in a series of degrees: *a variety of forms exhibiting gradation.* **2** Often, **gradations.** one of the steps, stages, or degrees in a series: *There are many gradations between poverty and wealth. The rainbow shows gradations of color besides the six main colors.* **3** the act or process of grading. **4** = ablaut. **5** *Geology.* the process by which the surface of the earth is leveled off, or the bed of a stream is brought to equilibrium, through the action of wind, ice, water, etc. **6** *Obsolete.* an advancing, step by step; gradual progress. [< Latin *gradātiō, -ōnis* <

gradus, -ūs step, degree; see etym. under **grade**]

gra|da|tion|al (grā dā′shə nəl), *adj.* **1** having to do with or exhibiting gradation. **2** *Geology.* the process of affecting or state of being affected by gradation. —**gra|da′tion|al|ly**, *adv.*

gra|da|tive (grā dā′tiv), *adj.* proceeding step by step, or by degrees or grades.

grad|a|to|ry (grad′ə tôr′ē, -tōr′-; grā′də-), *adj.* = gradative.

grade (grād), *n., v.,* **grad|ed, grad|ing.** —*n.* **1a** any one division of an elementary or high school, arranged according to the pupils' progress and covering a year's work: *the fifth grade.* **b** the group of pupils in any one of these divisions: *The whole fourth grade stayed after school to finish the work for their play.* **2** a step or stage in a course or process. **3** a degree or position in rank, quality, or value: *Grade A milk is the best milk. Motor routes leading to Paris were reported thick with family cars of all grades* (New Yorker). **4** a group of persons or things having the same rank, quality, or value; class: *All the rough grade of lumber should be stacked over here.* **5** *U.S.* a number or letter that shows how well one has done; mark: *Her grade in English is B.* **6a** the slope of a road or railroad track: *a steep grade, an up grade.* **b** the amount of slope of a road or railroad track. **c** the rate of ascent or descent. **7** a hybrid animal, especially a cross between native stock and a superior breed. **8** *Linguistics.* the position occupied in an ablaut series. **9** *Zoology.* a group in the genetic classification of animals whose members are presumed to have branched from the common stem at about the same point of its development.

—*v.t.* **1** to place in classes; arrange in grades; sort: *These apples are graded by size. With many hundreds of cheeses grading is very difficult* (J. A. Barnett). **2a** to give a mark or grade to: *The teacher graded the papers.* **b** to place in a grade (def. 1); separate into grades: *to grade new pupils, a graded school.* **3** to make more nearly level: *The road up the steep hill was graded.* **4** to color with shades or tints that pass one into another. **5** to improve (a breed) by crossing with a better one.

—*v.i.* **1** to change gradually; go through a series of steps, stages, or degrees: *Red and yellow grade into orange.* **2** to be of a particular grade or quality. **3** *Linguistics.* to be altered by gradation or ablaut.

at grade, *U.S.* **a** on the same level: *Does not the junction road ... cross the streets ... at grade?* (Congressional Globe). **b** having a stable pattern of erosion and deposition: *Steams, or parts of streams, that are thus balanced between erosion and deposition are said to be ... flowing at grade* (Robert M. Garrels).

make the grade, *Informal.* to overcome difficulties; be successful: *It took him a lot of hard work to make the grade in business.*

the grades, *U.S.* an elementary school; grade school: *Are you in high school or are you still in the grades?*

[< Middle French *grade,* learned borrowing from Latin *gradus, -ūs* step, degree, related to *gradī* to walk, go]

grade-A or **Grade-A** (grād′ā′), *adj. U.S.* of the highest grade; first-class.

grade creep, *U.S.* a steady increase in the classification level of civil-service jobs, resulting in automatic promotions.

grade crossing, a place where a railroad crosses a highway, street, or other railroad on the same level; level crossing.

grad|ed school (grā′did), = grade school.

grade labeling, the giving of information about the quality of goods on a label on the container in which the goods are sold.

grade|less (grād′lis), *adj.* without a grade or grades.

grade|ly (grād′lē), *adj., adv. Scottish.* —*adj.* **1** orderly, decent, or respectable; proper; good: *It may not have been great Rugby football at Clarence Field, Kirkstall, on Saturday, but it was a gradely performance* (London Times). **2** handsome, comely, or fine. **3** great; thorough.

—*adv.* **1** decently; properly; well. **2** thoroughly; very.

[Middle English *greithlic* < Scandinavian (compare Old Icelandic *greithligr* < *greithe* graith)]

grade point, *U.S. Education.* a unit of credit for a course or semester's work, varying with the grade or grades achieved during the semester.

grade-point average (grād′point′), *U.S. Education.* a measure of scholastic achievement obtained by dividing all the grade points earned by the number of hours of the course or courses taken: *Abbr:* GPA (no periods).

grad|er (grā′dər), *n.* **1** a person or thing that grades. **2** a student who is in a certain grade at school: *a sixth grader.* **3** a machine on large wheels that levels uneven or bumpy ground.

grades (grādz), *n.pl.* See under **grade.**

grade school, *U.S.* an elementary school or grammar school; graded school.

grade separation, an intersection of highways, streets, or railroads on different levels, with ramps from one level to another, so that traffic going in one direction crosses over or under traffic going in a cross direction.

gra|di|ent (grā′dē ənt), *n., adj.* —*n.* **1** the rate at which a road, railroad track, river channel, or other slope goes upward or downward. **2** the sloping part of a road, railroad track, river channel, or other grade. **SYN:** incline, slope, inclination. **3a** the rate at which a variable quantity, such as temperature or pressure, changes in value. **b** the curve that represents this rate.

—*adj.* **1** going up or down gradually. **SYN:** sloping, slant. **2a** progressing by taking steps with the feet, as an animal does; walking; ambulant. **b** modified for walking or running, as the feet of various birds are; gressorial.

[< Latin *gradiēns, -entis,* present participle of *gradī* walk, go, related to *gradus, -ūs* step]

gra|di|ent|er (grā′dē ən tər), *n.* a surveyor's instrument for fixing grades, consisting essentially of a telescope, a spirit level, and a graduated vertical arc, mounted on a tripod.

gra|din (grā′din; *French* grȧ daɴ′), *n.* **1** one of a series of low steps or seats raised one above the other. **2** a shelf or one of a series of shelves behind and above an altar. [< French *gradin* < Italian *gradino* (diminutive) < *grado* < Latin *gradus, -ūs* step]

gra|dine (grə dēn′), *n.* = gradin.

gra|di|om|e|ter (grā′dē om′ə tər), *n.* an instrument for measuring the gradient of the earth's gravitational or magnetic field.

grad|u|al (graj′ů əl), *adj., n.* —*adj.* by degrees too small to be separately noticed; little by little: *This low hill has a gradual slope. A child's growth into an adult is gradual. Isabel By gradual decay from beauty fell* (Keats).

—*n.* Also, **Gradual. 1** an antiphon sung between the Epistle and the Gospel of the Communion service. **2** a liturgical book with all the music and words to be sung by the choir during the Communion service.

[< Medieval Latin *gradualis* < Latin *gradus, -ūs* step, grade] —**grad′u|al|ly,** *adv.* —**grad′u|al|ness,** *n.*

grad|u|al|ism (graj′ů ə liz′əm), *n.* the principle or method of gradual, as opposed to immediate, change: *Yet gradualism is rejected by extremists on both sides* (Harper's).

grad|u|al|ist (graj′ů ə list), *n., adj.* —*n.* an advocate of gradualism: *Warren is a gradualist because "history, like nature, knows no jumps"* (Harper's). —*adj.* of gradualism or gradualists: *a gradualist approach.*

grad|u|and (graj′ů and), *n.* a student who is to be graduated. [< Medieval Latin *graduandus,* gerundive of *graduari;* see etym. under **graduate**]

grad|u|ate (*v.* graj′ů āt; *n., adj.* graj′ů it), *v.,* **-at|ed, -at|ing,** *n., adj.* —*v.i.* **1** to finish a course of study at a school, college, or university and receive a diploma or paper saying so: *Her brother graduated from the university last year.* **2** to change gradually.

—*v.t.* **1** to give a diploma or other document to (a student) for finishing a course of study: *He was graduated with honors. $228,000 [was] spent on a nurses' school that had graduated only forty-three nurses in seven years* (Harper's). **2a** to mark out in equal spaces for measuring: *My ruler is graduated in inches. A thermometer is graduated in degrees.* **b** to arrange in regular steps, stages, or degrees: *The federal income tax is graduated so that people who make more money pay a higher rate of taxes.*

—*n.* **1** a person who has finished a course of study and has his diploma: *The professor was a graduate of several schools.* **SYN:** alumnus. **2a** a container marked with degrees or quantities for measuring. **b** the quantity held in such a container.

—*adj.* **1** that has graduated, especially from a college or university; holding a bachelor's degree: *a graduate student.* **2** of or for graduates: *a graduate course, graduate study.*

[< Medieval Latin *graduari* (with English *-ate*) to take a degree, graduate < Latin *gradus, -ūs* step, grade]

▶**graduate.** Except in formal writing, the passive form *to be graduated from* is now usually replaced by the active form: *She graduated from Smith in 1961.*

grad|u|at|ed (graj′ů ā′tid), *adj.* **1** marked so as to indicate degrees or quantities: *a graduated flask.* **2** arranged in grades or gradations, as in size or in amount: *a string of graduated pearls.*

graduated payment mortgage, *U.S.* a mortgage on which monthly payments are low in the early years after purchase of a house, rising gradually thereafter.

graduate nurse, a person who has graduated from a school offering professional training for nurses.

graduate school, a division of a university, offering a curriculum leading to the master's and doctor's degrees.

grad|u|ate|ship (graj′ů it ship), *n.* the period or condition of being a graduate.

grad|u|a|tion (graj′ů ā′shən), *n.* **1** the act or process of graduating from a school, college, or university: *His graduation will never take place if he doesn't get to work.* **2** the condition of being graduated: *Graduation means he can go on to college.* **3** the ceremony of graduating; graduating exercises; commencement: *Graduation was held in the gym because of rain.* **4** division into equal spaces for measuring. **5** a mark or set of marks to show degrees for measuring. **6** arrangement in regular steps, stages, or degrees.

graduations, lines used to indicate degrees of latitude and longitude, quantity, or other measurement: *Sometimes the stopper is hollow, forms a cup, and has graduations for doses of certain amounts* (Edward H. Knight).

grad|u|a|tor (graj′ů ā′tər), *n.* a person or thing that graduates.

gra|dus (grā′dəs), *n.* **1** a dictionary of prosody for aid in writing Latin or Greek verses. **2** *Music.* a work consisting of exercises of gradually increasing difficulty. [short for *Gradus ad Parnassum* (literally) step to Parnassus, Latin title of a poetical dictionary of the 1600's]

Grae|ae (grē′ē), *n.pl. Greek Legend.* three aged sisters, with one eye and one tooth among them, who warned the Gorgons when anyone approached. Also, **Graiae.**

Grae|cism (grē′siz əm), *n.* = Grecism.

Grae|cize (grē′sīz), *v.t., v.i.,* **-cized, -ciz|ing.** = Grecize.

Graeco-, *combining form.* a variant form of **Greco-.**

Grae|co|phile (grē′kō fīl, -fil), *n.* = Grecophile.

Graf (gräf), *n., pl.* **Gra|fen** (grä′fən). a German, Austrian, or Swedish nobleman equivalent in rank to an English earl; count.

graff (graf, gräf), *v.t., v.i., n.* = graft.

graf|fi|ti (grə fē′tē), *n.* plural of **graffito.**

graffiti art, paintings or inscriptions on public walls or other surfaces, usually spray-painted in a flamboyant style. Graffiti art seems impromptu but is complex in its design and often carries a social message. *Crash does "installations"—graffiti art sprayed to order on the walls of museums, homes, and businesses* (Money). —**graffiti artist.**

graf|fi|tic (grə fē′tik), *adj.* of graffiti; in the form or style of graffiti: *graffitic inscriptions.*

graf|fi|tist (grə fē′tist), *n.* a person who draws graffiti.

graf|fi|to (grə fē′tō), *n., pl.* **-ti. 1** a crude drawing or inscription on a wall, fence, or other surface: *... that inexplicably evocative bit of graffito, "Kilroy was Here"* (Manchester Guardian Weekly). **2** *Archaeology.* an ancient drawing or writing scratched on a wall or other surface, such as those at Pompeii and Rome. **3** (in art) a method of decoration in which designs are scratched through an overlying layer of plaster, glaze, or other medium, showing a ground of a different color beneath; sgraffito. [< Italian *graffito* scribbling < *graffio* a scratch, scribble < *graffiare* to scribble, ultimately < Greek *gráphein* draw, write]

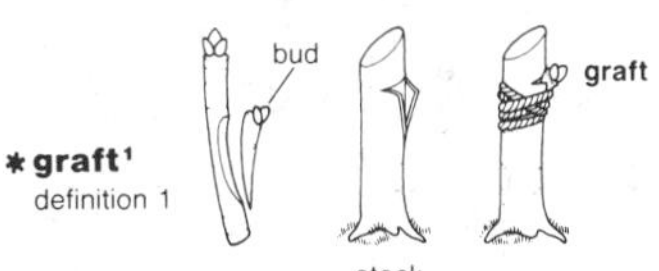

***graft** definition 1

***graft** (graft, gräft), *v., n.* —*v.t.* **1** to put (a shoot or bud from one tree or plant) into a slit in another tree or plant, so that it will grow there as a part of it; engraft. **2** to produce or improve (a fruit, flower, grain, or other plant product) by grafting. **3** to do grafting on (a plant or tree): *No one has been able to graft together trees belonging to quite distinct families* (Charles Darwin). **4** to transfer (a piece of skin or bone) from one part of the body to another, or to a new body, so that it will grow there permanently. **5** *Figurative.* to insert or fix as if by grafting: *to graft a pagan custom upon Christian institutions. No Art can be*

grafted with success on another art (Sir Joshua Reynolds).
—*v.i.* **1** to insert a graft or grafts. **2** to become grafted. [< earlier *graffen* < noun]
—*n.* **1** a shoot or bud used in grafting. A graft from a fine apple tree may be put on a worthless one to improve it. **2** the place on a tree or plant where the shoot or bud is inserted. **3** a tree or plant that has had a shoot or bud grafted on it. **4** the act or process of grafting. **5** a piece of skin, bone, etc., transferred from one place to another in grafting.
[alteration of *graff* < Old French *grafe* scion, stylus < Latin *graphium* stylus < Greek *grapheîon* < *gráphein* write (from the similarity of shape)]
—**graft′er**, *n.*

graft[2] (graft, gräft), *n., v.* —*n.* **1** the taking of money dishonestly in connection with city or government business; political dishonesty, corruption, and the like: *The crooked building inspector was guilty of accepting bribes and other forms of graft.* **2** a method of getting money dishonestly. **3** money dishonestly taken.
—*v.i., v.t.* to make or get money dishonestly through one's job, especially in political positions. [American English; origin uncertain] —**graft′er**, *n.*

graft[3] (graft, gräft), *n.* **1** the depth of earth that can be thrown up at one time with a spade. **2** a kind of spade, used in digging drains. [perhaps < Scandinavian (compare Old Icelandic *groftr* action of digging)]

graft|age (graf′tij, gräf′-), *n.* **1** the act or process of grafting on trees and plants. **2** the fact of being grafted.

graft hybrid, a graft having certain characteristics of both the scion and the stock.

graf|ton|ite (graf′tə nīt, gräf′-), *n.* a rare, pinkish, phosphate mineral occurring in pegmatites. [< *Grafton,* a town and county in New Hampshire, where it is found + *-ite*[1]]

gra|ham (grā′əm), *adj.* made from whole-wheat flour that has not been sifted: *graham crackers.* [American English < Sylvester *Graham,* 1794-1851, an American dietetic reformer]

graham cracker, a cracker made with graham flour.

graham flour, wheat flour that has not been sifted (bolted); flour made from whole-wheat kernels.

gra|ham|ite (grā′ə mīt), *n.* a black, lustrous ore occurring in veins, used in the making of asphalt. [American English < J. A. and J. L. *Graham,* owners of a mine where it was found + *-ite*[1]]

Graham's law, the rates of diffusion of two gases at the same pressure and temperature are inversely proportional to the square roots of their densities. [< Thomas *Graham,* 1805-1869, a Scottish chemist, who formulated it]

Gra|iae (grā′ē, grī′-), *n.pl.* = Graeae.

grail[1] (grāl), *n.* = gradual. [< Old French *grael* < Medieval Latin *gradale,* variant of *graduale,* neuter of *gradualis;* see etym. under **gradual**]

grail[2] (grāl), *n.* = gravel. [origin unknown]

grail[3] (grāl), *n.* a combmaker's file. [< French *grêle* < *grêler* make slender]

Grail (grāl), *n.* **1** the cup or dish supposed to have been used by Christ at the Last Supper, and by one of his followers to catch the last drops of blood from Christ's body on the cross; Holy Grail. In Arthurian legend the knights of the Round Table vowed to search for the Grail. **2** Often, **grail.** something greatly desired or sought; a goal: *Better craftsmanship + lower costs = nothing less than the well-known economic grail of Productivity* (Punch). [< Old French *graal* < Medieval Latin *gradalis* bowl, cup, perhaps ultimately < Latin *crātēr* cup < Greek *krātēr*]

grain[1] (grān), *n., v.* —*n.* **1** a seed or seedlike fruit of wheat, corn, oats, rye, and similar cereal grasses. In botanical usage a grain is not a seed but a fruit. SYN: kernel. **2** the seeds or seedlike fruits of such plants in the mass: *to grind grain.* **3** the plants that these seeds or seedlike fruits grow on: *a field of grain.* In British usage, grain is called *corn.* **4** one of the tiny bits of which sand, sugar, or salt are made up. SYN: granule. **5** the smallest United States and British unit of weight. It is equal to .0648 gram. One pound avoirdupois weight equals 7,000 grains; one pound troy weight or apothecaries' weight equals 5,760 grains. The grain was originally determined by the weight of a grain of wheat. *Abbr.:* gr. or g. **6** the unit of weight for pearls, equivalent to ¼ of a carat. **7** *Figurative.* the smallest possible amount; tiniest bit: *There isn't a grain of truth in his charge.* SYN: atom, molecule. **8** the arrangement, direction, or pattern of fibers in wood or layers in stone. Wood and stone split along the grain. **9** the little lines and markings in wood, marble, or some like substance: *That mahogany table has a fine grain.* **10** the quality of a substance due to the size, character, or arrangement of its constituent particles; texture: *a stone or salt of coarse grain.* **11** *Figurative.* natural character; disposition: *Hatred of innocent human obstacles was a form of moral stupidity not in Deronda's grain* (George Eliot). SYN: temper. **12a** the rough surface of leather. It is on the side of the skin from which the hair has been removed. **b** a similar surface produced artificially. **13** a roughness of surface, giving the appearance of small, roundish bodies side by side. **14a** the plane of cleavage in coal, stone, or the like; lamination. **b** the directions in which cleavage occurs in diamond polishing. **15** the fibers or threads of a fabric, as distinguished from the fabric itself. **16** a crystallized state. **17a** = kermes. **b** = cochineal. **c** the red dye made from either of these; any red-colored dye. **18a** dye or color in general, especially when fast. **b** color; hue: *a robe of darkest grain* (Milton). **19** *Photography.* any one of the small, separate particles of light-sensitive material emulsified and deposited on photographic film. The size of the particle limits the possible enlargement of the image and affects the speed of exposure. **20** a piece of solid fuel, often three or more feet long, used in a missile: *A vigorous controversy raged around the best type of grain for rocket power. The reader must not think of these grains in terms of a grain of sand, but rather of a three-foot length of rubber hose or cast-iron pipe* (James P. Baxter).
—*v.t.* **1** to paint to look like the grain of some solid, such as wood or marble. **2** to form into grains; granulate: *to grain sugar.* **3** to remove the hair from (a skin or skins). **4** to soften and raise the grain of (leather). **5** to give a granular surface to. **6** to dye in grain. **7** *U.S.* to feed with grain: *When our horses are not doing any kind of work, we do not grain them, but merely give them hay* (A. E. Boyd).
—*v.i.* to form grains; crystallize into grains, as sugar does.
go against the (or **one's**) **grain**, to be contrary to one's inclination, desire, or feeling: *Laziness went against his grain. The use of detention rooms also seems to go against the grain for most headmasters* (Manchester Guardian Weekly).
grains, refuse grain left after brewing or distilling: *grains in the cask.*
in grain, **a** dyed with the red dye obtained from kermes or cochineal: *How the red roses flush up in her cheeks ... like crimson ... in grain* (Edmund Spenser). **b** dyed in any fast color; dyed in the fiber or thoroughly: *'Tis in grain, sir; 'twill endure wind and weather* (Shakespeare). **c** *Figurative.* by nature; downright; genuine; thorough: *Being palpably a Turk in grain, his intents are wicked* (Thomas Carlyle).
with a grain of salt. See under **salt**.
[< Old French *grain* < Latin *grānum* grain, seed]
—**grain′er**, *n.* —**grain′less**, *adj.* —**grain′like′**, *adj.*

grain[2] (grān), *n. Dialect.* **1** a bough or branch. **2** one of the prongs of a fork.
grains, an iron instrument with barbed prongs, for spearing or harpooning fish: *For this purpose we procured a pair of grains, with a long staff like a harpoon* (Richard Henry Dana, Jr.).
[< Scandinavian (compare Old Icelandic *grein* division, distinction)]

grain alcohol, ordinary alcohol or ethyl alcohol, often made by the fermentation of grain.

grain beetle, any one of various beetles that breed in stored grain.

grained (grānd), *adj.* **1** having little lines and markings, as wood does. **2** painted to look like the grain in wood or marble. **3** of leather: **a** with the hair removed. **b** roughened on the surface to bring out the grain. **4** formed or divided into grains or small particles.

***grain elevator**, **1** a building for storing grain, often with machinery for loading and unloading, cleaning, and mixing the grain. **2** a machine that lifts grain from a train or ship to the storage bins.

***grain elevator**
definition 1

grain|field (grān′fēld′), *n.* a field in which grain grows.

grain|ing (grā′ning), *n.* **1** the grain in wood or marble: *Now I'll show you to your room—I want you to notice especially the graining of the highboy* (New Yorker). **2** painting in imitation of the grain in wood or marble. **3** the artificial markings on the surface of a skin to imitate morocco and other varieties of leather.

grain leather, leather dressed with the grain side outward.

grain moth, any one of various moths whose larvae feed on stored grain.

grains (grānz), *n. pl.* See under **grain**[1] and **grain**[2].

grain side, the side of a skin on which the hair grew.

grains of paradise, **1** cardamom seeds. **2** the seeds of an African plant of the ginger family; guinea grains. They are used as a flavoring in cordials, foods, and pharmaceuticals.

grain sorghum, a variety of sorghum, such as durra, kaoliang, or kaffir corn, used as food for people and livestock.

grain weevil, any one of various small beetles that feed on stored grain.

grain worm, the larva of a grain moth that infests stored grain.

grain|y (grā′nē), *adj.,* **grain|i|er, grain|i|est.** **1** like the grain of wood or marble. **2** grainlike; granular: *a grainy surface.* **3** full of grains or grain: *grainy wood.* —**grain′i|ness**, *n.*

graith (grāth), *n., v.* —*n.* **1** *Scottish and British Dialect.* readiness; order; preparation. **2** equipment; harness; apparatus. **3** possessions. **4** material; stuff.
—*v.t.* to make ready; prepare; equip.
[< Scandinavian (compare Old Icelandic *greithe*)]

graith|ly (grāth′lē), *adj.,* **-li|er, -li|est.** *British Dialect.* tidy; trim; decent; good.

gral|la|to|ri|al (gral′ə tôr′ē əl, -tōr′-), *adj.* of or having to do with long-legged wading birds, such as the storks and herons. [< Latin *grallātor, -ōris* one who walks on stilts (< *grallae* stilts) + English *-ial*]

gram[1] (gram), *n.* a unit of weight or mass in the metric system, equal to 15.432 grains avoirdupois. 28 grams weigh about 1 ounce avoirdupois. 1,000 grams equal 1 kilogram. In mass, a gram is approximately equal to the mass of one cubic centimeter of water at 39.2 degrees Fahrenheit or 4 degrees centigrade (Celsius). *Abbr.:* gm. Also, *British,* **gramme.** [< French *gramme* < Late Latin *gramma* small weight < Greek *grámma* division, letter as a division mark (for example, group *A*); (originally) letter < *gráphein* write]

gram[2] (gram), *n.* any one of several plants grown in the East Indies for food for people or animals, such as the chickpea and certain beans. [< Portuguese *grão,* earlier *gram* < Latin *grānum* grain]

-gram[1], *combining form.* **1** something drawn or written; a message: *Cablegram = a cable message. Telegram = a telegraph message.* **2** something recorded; record; tracing: *Cardiogram = a record or tracing of the heart's movements.*
[< Greek *-gramma* < *grámma;* see etym. under **gram**[1]]

-gram[2], *combining form.* **1** ____ grams: *Kilogram = a thousand grams.* **2** ____ of a gram: *Centigram = one hundredth of a gram.*
[< Greek *grámma;* see etym. under **gram**[1]]

gram., **1** grammar. **2** grammarian. **3** grammatical.

gra|ma (grä′mə), *n.,* or **grama grass**, any one of a genus of low pasture grasses abundant in the western and southwestern United States, especially blue grama, the most common variety. [American English < Spanish *grama* (kind of) grass < Latin *grāmen* grass, an herb]

gra|ma|dan (grä′mä dän′), *n.* = gramdan.

gram|a|rye, **gram|a|rie**, or **gram|a|ry** (gram′ər ē), *n. Archaic.* occult learning; magic: *dark words of gramarye* (Scott). [< Old French variant of *gramaire;* see etym. under **grammar**]

gram atom, *Chemistry.* the mass of an element in grams that equals numerically the element's atomic weight: *A gram atom of oxygen is 16 grams.*

gram-a|tom|ic weight (gram′ə tom′ik), = gram atom.

gram calorie, = small calorie: *One gram calorie is the quantity of heat which must be supplied to one gram of water to raise its temperature through one centigrade degree* (Sears and Zemansky).

gram centimeter, a unit equivalent to the work done in raising a mass of one gram vertically one centimeter.

gram|dan (gräm dän′), *n.* a village or other land unit in India, given voluntarily by the owners to the people who live on it as part of a program of social reform advocated by followers of Gandhi. Also, **gramadan.** [< Hindustani *grāmdān, grāmadān,* < *grāma* village + *dān* gift]

gram equivalent, *Chemistry.* that quantity of an element or compound whose weight in grams is numerically equal to its equivalent weight.

gra|mer|cy (grə mėr′sē), *interj. Archaic.* **1** many

thanks; thank you. **2** an exclamation of surprise or sudden feeling; mercy on us. [< Old French *grant merci* (literally) great reward; see etym. under **grand, mercy**]
gram|i|ci|din (gram′ə sī′din, gra mis′ə-), *n.* an antibiotic obtained from soil bacteria which is too toxic for introduction into the bloodstream but is used locally for certain infections of the skin or throat. [< *Gram* (see etym. under **Gram's method**) + *-cide*[1] + *-in*]
gra|min|e|ous (grə min′ē əs), *adj.* **1** of or having to do with grass; resembling grass. **2** of or belonging to the grass family; poaceous. [< Latin *grāmineus* (with English *-ous*) < *grāmen, -inis* grass]
gram|i|niv|o|rous (gram′ə niv′ər əs), *adj.* eating or feeding on grasses, grain, or seeds. [< Latin *grāmen, -inis* grass + *vorāre* devour + English *-ous*]
gram|ma grass (grä′mə), = grama.
gram|ma|logue (gram′ə lôg, -log), *n.* **1** a word represented by a single sign in shorthand. **2** = logogram. [< Greek *grámma* (see etym. under **gram**[1]) + *lógos* word]
gram|mar (gram′ər), *n.* **1** the study of the forms and uses of words in sentences of a particular language: *English grammar. Abbr:* gram. **2** the systematic study comparing the forms and constructions of two or more languages; comparative grammar. **3** the systematic study comparing present with past forms and usage of a language; historical grammar. **4** a treatise or book on grammar. **5** the system of sounds, forms, and structure employed in a language. **6** rules about the use of words in a language. **7** the use of words according to these rules: *The foreign boy's English grammar was full of mistakes.* **8a** the elements of any subject: *the grammar of painting.* **b** a book presenting these in methodical form (formerly common in the titles of books). [< Old French *grammaire* (Latin) learning, philology, learned borrowing from Latin *grammatica* < Greek *grammatikḗ* (*technḗ*) (art) of letters < *grámma;* see etym. under **gram**[1]]
gram|mar|i|an (grə mãr′ē ən), *n.* **1** an expert in grammar. **2** a user of grammar.
gram|mar|less (gram′ər lis), *adj.* **1** lacking grammar or grammatical forms. **2** not conforming to grammatical rules: *grammarless speech.* **3** ignorant of grammar: *a grammarless person.*
grammar school, **1** *U.S.* an elementary public school or the upper four grades of an elementary school, between primary school and high school. **2** *Especially British.* a secondary school that prepares students for a university. Originally it was a school intended to teach Latin, hence grammar.
gram|mat|ic (grə mat′ik), *adj.* = grammatical.
gram|mat|i|ca (grə mat′i kə), *n. Latin.* the study of literature, including grammar; the classical philology.
gram|mat|i|cal (grə mat′ə kəl), *adj.* **1** according to the correct use of words: *Our French teacher speaks grammatical English, but has a French accent.* **2** of grammar: *"He ain't," "you was," and "Between you and I" are three very common grammatical mistakes.*
gram|mat|i|cal|i|ty (grə mat′ə kal′ə tē), *n.* **1** = grammaticalness. **2** *Linguistics.* the quality of being grammatically acceptable to a native speaker or speakers: *If Chomsky established grammaticality as an effective criterion, as against occurrence in a corpus, the next step in linguistics would appear to be to establish appropriateness and acceptability* (Dell Hymes).
gram|mat|i|cal|i|za|tion (grə mat′ə kə lə zā′shən), *n.* the process of making grammatical; reducing to grammatical rules: *Absence of stress in general indicates grammaticalization of a morphemic element* (*as in ... Fitz-gérald*) (H. Marchand).
gram|mat|i|cal|ly (grə mat′ə klē), *adv.* according to the rules of grammar; as regards grammar.
grammatical meaning, the meaning that a form has in addition to its lexical meaning.
gram|mat|i|cal|ness (grə mat′ə kəl nis), *n.* the quality or condition of being grammatical.
gram|mat|i|cise (grə mat′ə sīz), *v.t., v.i.,* **-cised, -cis|ing.** *Especially British.* grammaticize: *I always said Shakespeare had Latin enough to grammaticise his English* (Samuel Johnson).
gram|mat|i|cism (grə mat′ə siz əm), *n.* a point or principle of grammar.
gram|ma|ti|cize (grə mat′ə sīz), *v.,* **-cized, -ciz|ing.** — ***v.t.*** to make grammatical; reduce to grammatical rules.
— ***v.i.*** **1** to display ones knowledge of grammar. **2** to discuss grammatical points.
gram|ma|tist (gram′ə tist), *n.* = grammarian.
gramme (gram), *n. British.* gram (unit of weight).
gram meter, a unit equivalent to the work done in raising a mass of one gram vertically one meter in height.
gram-mo|lec|u|lar (gram′mə lek′yə lər), *adj.* of or having to do with a gram molecule.
gram-molecular weight, = gram molecule.
gram molecule, *Chemistry.* the mass of an element or compound in grams that equals numerically the element's or compound's molecular weight; mol; mole: *A gram molecule of oxygen gas is 32 grams.*
Gram|my (gram′ē), *n., pl.* **-mys** or **-mies**. *U.S.* a gold-plated replica of a phonograph record awarded annually by the National Academy of Recording Arts and Sciences for outstanding achievement in phonograph recording. [< *gram-* (ophone) + *-y* (diminutive suffix)]
Gram-neg|a|tive or **gram-neg|a|tive bacteria** (gram′neg′ə tiv), bacteria that do not stain when treated with Gram's solution. Gram-negative bacteria appear pink and include those that cause urinary tract infections, typhoid fever, and various other diseases. [see etym. under **Gram's method**]
gram|o|phile (gram′ə fīl, -fil), *n.* a lover of phonograph records, especially one who likes to collect them.
gram|o|phone (gram′ə fōn), *n. Especially British.* a phonograph. [originally American English, apparently inversion of *phonogram,* in early sense of "phonograph." It is a trademark in the U.S.]
gram|o|phon|ic (gram′ə fon′ik), *adj.* of or like a gramophone.
gram|o|phon|i|cal|ly (gram′ə fon′ə klē), *adv.* in a gramophonic manner; by or on a gramophone.
Gram-pos|i|tive or **gram-pos|i|tive bacteria** (gram′poz′ə tiv), bacteria that stain when treated with Gram's solution. Gram-positive bacteria appear blue and include those that cause lobar pneumonia, scarlet fever, and staphylococcal infections. [see etym. under **Gram's method**]
gramps (gramps), *n. Informal.* grandfather; grandpa. [shortened and altered < *grandpa*]
gram|pus (gram′pəs), *n.* **1** a large marine mammal with a blunt nose, inhabiting oceans and seas through most of the world. It belongs to the same family as the dolphin. **2** = killer whale. **3** *Informal.* a person who breathes loudly. [earlier *graundepose,* alteration (influenced by *grand*) of Old French *graspeis* < Medieval Latin *crassus piscis* fat fish]
gram|ra|di|o (gram′rā′dē ō), *n.* (in South Africa) a radio phonograph.
Gram's method (gramz), a method of classifying bacteria by first staining them with gentian violet, treating them with Gram's solution, and washing them with alcohol. Gram-positive bacteria retain the violet dye; Gram-negative species lose it. [< Hans C. J. *Gram,* 1853-1938, a Danish bacteriologist, who discovered it]
Gram's solution, a solution of iodine and potassium iodide in distilled water, used in Gram's method to stain bacteria.
Gram stain or **Gram's stain**, = Gram's solution.
gran (gran), *n. Especially British Informal.* grandmother; grandma. [shortened < *granny*]
gra|na (grā′nə), *n.* plural of **granum**.
gra|na|de|ro (grä′nä ᴛʜā′rō), *n., pl.* **-ros**. a member of a special military force in Mexico, used especially to quell riots. [< Spanish *granadero* grenadier]
gran|a|dil|la (gran′ə dil′ə), *n.* **1** the edible fruit of various passionflowers, especially a tropical American kind used as a dessert fruit. **2** any one of the vines that produce this fruit. [< Spanish *granadilla* the passionflower (diminutive) < *granada* pomegranate; see etym. under **grenade**]
gran|a|ry (gran′ər ē, grā′nər-), *n., pl.* **-ries**. **1** a place or building where grain is stored: *His granary holds 4,000 bushels of corn and the same amount of oats* (Newsweek). **2** a region producing much grain. [< Latin *grānārium* < *grānum* grain]
granary weevil, = grain weevil.
grand (grand), *adj., n.* — ***adj.*** **1** large and of fine appearance: *grand mountains.* SYN: great, lofty. **2** of very high or noble quality; dignified; stately; splendid: *a very grand palace, grand music, a grand old man. In what used to be called the grand style, at once noble and natural* (James Russell Lowell). **3** highest or very high in rank; chief: *a grand jury, grand duke, grand marshal.* **4** great; important; main: *the grand staircase. Sin and Death, the two grand foes* (Milton). *No grand idea was ever born in a conference, but a lot of foolish ideas have died there* (F. Scott Fitzgerald). **5** complete; comprehensive: *a grand total.* **6** *Informal.* very satisfactory; very pleasing: *to have a grand time, grand weather.* **7** (in names of relationship) in the second degree of ascent or descent: *a grandmother, grandson.* **8** *Music.* **a** for a full orchestra or a large vocal ensemble. **b** (of a composition) large or extensive in form: *a grand sonata.*
— ***n.*** **1** *Slang.* a thousand dollars: *D'you think I'd pay a hundred grand for protection if it wasn't worth it?* (Eric Linklater). **2** = grand piano.
[< Old French *grant,* or *grand* < Latin *grandis* big] — **grand′ly**, *adv.* — **grand′ness**, *n.*
— ***Syn.*** *adj.* **2 Grand, stately, noble** mean great, dignified, and impressive. **Grand** implies imposing magnitude and splendor: *Milton's grand style.* **Stately** emphasizes dignity and impressiveness: *a stately Spanish galleon, the stately rhythm of processional music.* **Noble** emphasizes lofty grandeur: *The Statue of Liberty is a noble sight.*
gran|dad (gran′dad′), *n. Informal.* granddad; grandfather.
gran|dam (gran′dam), *n. Archaic.* **1** a grandmother. **2** an old woman; gossip. [< Anglo-French *graund dame* grandmother; see etym. under **grand, dame**]
gran|dame (gran′dām), *n.* = grandam.
Grand Army of the Republic, an organization of men who served in the Union Army or Navy during the Civil War, founded in 1866 and disbanded in 1956, after its last member died. *Abbr:* G.A.R.
grand|aunt (grand′ant′, -änt′), *n.* the aunt of one's father or mother; great-aunt.
grand|ba|by (gran′bā′bē), *n., pl.* **-bies**. *U.S. Informal.* a baby grandchild.
Grand Canyon State, a nickname for Arizona.
grand|child (grand′chīld′), *n., pl.* **-chil|dren**. the child of one's son or daughter.
grand climacteric, the sixty-third year of a person's life.
grand|dad (gran′dad′), *n. Informal.* a grandfather.
grand|dad|dy (gran′dad′ē), *n., pl.* **-dies**. *Informal.* **1** a grandfather. **2** *Figurative.* a person or thing that is the oldest, first, or foremost of its kind: *Woody Guthrie, the granddaddy of the American song of protest ...* (Atlantic). *The granddaddy of all sporting sharks is the great white shark, the world's biggest and most dangerous game fish* (Time).
grand|daugh|ter (gran′dô′tər), *n.* the daughter of one's son or daughter.
granddaughter clock, a small-sized grandfather clock: *There are even a few granddaughter clocks around—they stand about four and a half feet* (New York Times).
Grand Design, **1** a plan for European peace developed by King Henry IV of France in the early 1600's, proposing an international European council, supported by troops of member states, which would enforce peace. **2** any modern governmental policy involving international cooperation: *... President Kennedy's "Grand Design" for an Atlantic partnership of Western nations* (Wall Street Journal). [translation of French *le Grand Dessein*]
grand dragon, *U.S.* the head of a State organization of the present Ku Klux Klan.
grand-du|cal (grand′dü′kəl, -dyü′-), *adj.* of or having to do with a grand duke or duchess.
grand duchess, **1** the wife or widow of a grand duke. **2** a lady equal in rank to a grand duke. **3** a princess of the ruling house of Russia before the revolution in November, 1917.
grand duchy, a territory under the rule of a grand duke or grand duchess.
grand duke, **1** a prince, ranking just below a king, who rules a small state or country called a *grand duchy.* **2** a prince of the ruling house of Russia before the revolution in 1917. **3** the European great horned owl.
grande ar|mée (gräɴd år mā′), *French.* great or grand army (applied especially to the army organized by Napoleon in 1804, and to that assembled for his campaign of 1812).
grande dame (gräɴd dåm′), *pl.* **grandes dames** (gräɴd dåm′). *French.* a great lady, usually of a certain age and dignity: *The field glass alternates with the lorgnette still wielded by some grandes dames* (Holiday).
gran|dee (gran dē′), *n.* **1** a Spanish or Portuguese nobleman of the highest rank. **2** a person of high rank or great importance. [< Spanish and Portuguese *grande,* noun use of adjective < Latin *grandis* grand]
grande pas|sion (gräɴd på syôɴ′), *French.* great passion; love affair of great importance.
gran|deur (gran′jər, -jůr), *n.* **1** greatness; majesty; nobility: *The grandeur of Niagara Falls is famous.* **2** magnificence or splendor of appearance or style of living: *The English go to their estates for grandeur. The French live at court and exile themselves to their estates for economy* (Emerson). SYN: stateliness, dignity. **3** greatness of power or rank; eminence. [< Old French *gran-*

Pronunciation Key: hat, āge, cãre, fär; let, ēqual, tėrm, it, īce; hot, ōpen, ôrder; oil, out; cup, pu̇t, rüle; child; long; thin; ᴛʜen; zh, measure; ə represents **a** in about, **e** in taken, **i** in pencil, **o** in lemon, **u** in circus.

deur < *grand* grand]

grand|fa|ther (grand′fä′ᴛʜər), *n., adj., v.* —*n.* **1** the father of one's father or mother. See diagram under **family tree**. **2** any forefather. **3** *Figurative.* forerunner; predecessor.
—*adj.* *U.S.* having to do with or based on a grandfather clause: *a grandfather exemption from a new law.*
—*v.t.* *U.S.* to exempt under a grandfather clause: *As a subdivision that had been filed before the new laws went into effect, Chambers Point was exempt from their requirements—what real estate people call "grandfathered"* (New Yorker).

grandfather clause, *U.S.* **1** a clause or provision that exempts anyone who enjoyed rights or privileges prohibited by a new law or regulation: *Most of the state laws have "grandfather clauses" which automatically license almost anyone currently in business* (Harper's). **2** (originally) a clause in the constitutions of seven Southern states that restricted the voting rights of Negroes to those whose fathers or grandfathers voted before the Civil War. The clause was declared void in 1915 by the United States Supreme Court.

***grandfather** or **grandfather's clock**, a clock in a tall, wooden case, which stands on the floor.

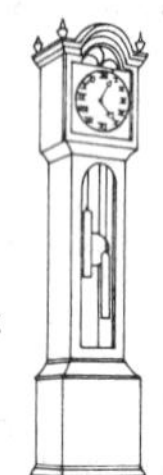

***grandfather clock**

grand|fa|ther|ly (grand′fä′ᴛʜər lē), *adj.* of, like, or characteristic of a grandfather.

grand fir, = lowland fir.

Grand Gui|gnol (gräɴ gē nyôl′), **1** a small theater in Paris which was famous for its horror plays. **2** Also, **grand guignol**. something designed to shock and horrify.

Grand-Gui|gnol (gräɴ gē nyôl′), *adj.* horrifying; morbid; shocking.

grand homme (gräɴ dôm′), *pl.* **grands hommes** (gräɴ dôm′). *French.* a great man.

gran|di|flo|ra (gran′də flôr′ə, -flōr′-), *n., adj.* —*n.* **1** any one of a group of tall, erect rosebushes that bear clusters of large blooms. **2** any kind of plant developed to bear large, showy flowers.
—*adj.* large-flowered. [< New Latin *Grandiflora* < Latin *grandis* grand + *flōs, flōris* flower]

gran|dil|o|quence (gran dil′ə kwəns), *n.* the use of lofty or pompous words, style, manner, or quality.

gran|dil|o|quent (gran dil′ə kwənt), *adj.* using lofty or pompous words, style, manner, or quality: *an orator's grandiloquent gesticulation.* [< Latin *grandiloquus* < *grandis* grand, big + *loquī* speak; apparently influenced by English *eloquent*] —**gran|dil′o|quent|ly**, *adv.*

gran|di|ose (gran′dē ōs), *adj.* **1** grand in an imposing or impressive way; magnificent: *Always the Americans had been fond of looking ahead to a grandiose future* (Atlantic). **syn:** stately. **2** grand in a showy or pompous way; not really magnificent, but trying to seem so: *a grandiose aping of Caesar, Alexander and Charlemagne* (H. G. Wells). [< French *grandiose* < Italian *grandioso* < Latin *grandis* grand, large] —**gran′di|ose|ly**, *adv.*

gran|di|os|i|ty (gran′dē os′ə tē), *n.* **1** the state or quality of being grandiose: *These visitors ... are awesomely impressed by Moscow, by the gilt and the grandiosity* (Time). **2** a pompous or affected style or manner.

gran|dio|so (grän dyō′sō), *adj. Music.* grand and noble in style (a direction). [< Italian *grandioso* < Latin *grandis* grand, large]

grand je|té (gräɴ zhə tā′), *French.* (in ballet) a large forward leap, passing from one foot to the other.

grand juror, a member of a grand jury.

grand jury, a jury chosen to investigate accusations of crime and decide whether there is enough evidence for a trial in court. If it finds enough evidence, a grand jury brings an indictment against the accused. A grand jury usually consists of more than 12 and up to 23 persons.

Grand Lama, = Dalai Lama.

grand larceny, theft in which the value of the property taken equals or is more than a certain amount, in most states between $25 and $50.

grand lodge, the headquarters of a society of Freemasons.

grand|ma (grand′mä′, gram′-; gram′ə), *n. Informal.* a grandmother.

grand mal (gräɴ mál′), an attack of epilepsy characterized by severe convulsions and loss of consciousness. [< French *grand mal* (literally) great sickness]

grand|mam|ma (grand′mə mä′), *n. Informal.* a grandmother.

grand march, a ceremony at a ball in which the guests march around the ballroom in couples.

grand master, **1** an honorary title given to a chess player who has distinguished himself in tournament play. **2** a person who has distinguished himself in any field: [*He*] *was one of the great creative intellects of our era ... a grand master of science* (Scientific American).

Grand Master, the head of an order of knighthood, a lodge, or a council.

grand monde (gräɴ môɴd′), *French.* **1** high society: *London grand monde in the era of Edwardian splendor* (Atlantic). **2** (literally) great world.

grand|moth|er (grand′muᴛʜ′ər), *n., v.* —*n.* **1** the mother of one's father or mother. See diagram under **family tree**. **2** any ancestress.
—*v.t.* *Informal.* to coddle.

grandmother clock, a clock resembling a grandfather clock, but with a smaller case.

grand|moth|er|ly (grand′muᴛʜ′ər lē), *adj.* **1** of, like, or characteristic of a grandmother. **2** *Figurative.* overly minute in detail; fussy.

Grand Mufti, the chief expounder and interpreter of religious law in Moslem countries.

grand|neph|ew (grand′nef′yü; *especially British* grand′nev′yü), *n.* the son of one's nephew or niece; great-nephew. See diagram under **family tree**.

grand|niece (grand′nēs′), *n.* the daughter of one's nephew or niece; great-niece.

Grand Old Party, the Republican Party in the United States. *Abbr:* G.O.P.

grand opera, a musical drama, having a serious and often tragic theme, in which all the speeches are sung or recited to the accompaniment of an orchestra.

grand|pa (grand′pä′, gram′-; gram′pə), *n. Informal.* a grandfather.

grand|pa|pa (grand′pə pä′), *n. Informal.* a grandfather.

grand|pap|py (grand′pap′ē, gram′-), *n., pl.* **-pies**. *Dialect or Informal.* a grandfather.

grand|par|ent (grand′pär′ənt), *n.* a grandfather or grandmother.

grand|pa|ren|tal (grand′pə ren′təl), *adj.* of or having to do with a grandparent or grandparents.

grand-père (gräɴ per′), *n. French.* a grandfather.

grand piano, a large piano mounted on legs and having horizontal strings in a harp-shaped wooden case.

grand prix (gräɴ prē′), *French.* a great prize; the first or highest prize.

Grand Prix (gräɴ prē′), **1** any one of a number of international sports-car races of speed and endurance, such as the 24-hour race held in France and the American 12-hour race held annually in Florida. **2** a famous French horse race for three-year-olds at Longchamp, established by Napoleon III.

grand sachem, the head of a body of twelve high officials in the Tammany Society of New York.

grand-scale (grand′skāl′), *adj.* large-scale; extensive: *Although the book contains no grand-scale revelations, it is full of fascinating tidbits* (Newsweek).

grand sei|gneur (gräɴ se nyœr′), *French.* a great lord; nobleman; aristocrat.

grand siè|cle (gräɴ sye′klə), *French.* **1** the reign of Louis XIV; the classical age of literature in France. **2** (literally) the great century. **3** *Figurative.* lavish; expensive.

grand|sir (grand′sėr′), *n. Archaic.* = grandsire (defs. 1, 2, 3).

grand|sire (grand′sīr′), *n., v.,* **-sired, -sir|ing.** —*n.* **1** *Archaic.* a grandfather. **2** *Archaic.* a forefather. **3** *Archaic.* an old man. **4** the sire of a sire of an animal. **5** a method of ringing the changes in bell ringing.
—*v.t.* to become the grandsire of: *I'm not unaware of the irony of a birth control proponent grandsiring a tribe such as this* (Life).

grand slam, **1** a winning all the tricks in a hand of bridge. **2** the winning of all the chief tournaments of a particular sport in succession. **3** *Baseball.* a grand-slam home run. —**grand-slam′**, *adj.*

grand-slam home run (grand′slam′), *Baseball.* a home run with the bases filled.

grand-slam|mer (grand′slam′ər), *n. Baseball.* a grand-slam home run.

grand|son (grand′sun′), *n.* the son of one's son or daughter. See diagram under **family tree**.

grand|stand (grand′stand′), *n., v.,* **-stand|ed, -stand|ing.** —*n.* the main seating place for people at an athletic field, race track, parade, or other event: *Grandstand fans anxious to be close to the scene of scuffle ...* (Atlantic).
—*v.i.* *Informal.* to show off; make a grandstand play: *He is usually grandstanding when he appears to be arguing fiercely with an umpire.* —**grand′stand′er**, *n.*

grandstand play, *U.S. Informal.* **1** a way of playing a game with an eye to the applause of the grandstand. **2** an act done for effect or to win applause: *It was a characteristically Rubinsteinian feat ... part grandstand play, part musical passion* (Time).

grand style, a style fitted to the expression of lofty ideas and great subjects.

grand total, the sum of the sums of several groups of numbers.

grand tour, an extended tour of continental Europe, formerly considered part of the education of young men of the British aristocracy.
make the grand tour of, to make the circuit of; go around: *The guests made the grand tour of our new house.*

grand tourer or **grand touring car**, = gran turismo.

grand|un|cle (grand′ung′kəl), *n.* the uncle of one's father or mother; great-uncle.

grand unified theory, = unified field theory.

grand vizier, the chief minister of state of a Moslem ruler, especially of the former sultan of the Ottoman Empire.

grange (grānj), *n.* **1** a farm with its barns and other buildings. **2** (formerly) an outlying farmhouse with barns and other buildings belonging to a feudal manor or a religious establishment: *a grange of the monks of Abingdon* (John R. Green). **3** *Archaic.* a granary; barn. [< Old French *grange* < Gallo-Romance *grānica* < Latin *grānum* grain]

Grange (grānj), *n.* **1** an association (the "Patrons of Husbandry") of farmers for the improvement of their welfare, founded in 1867. **2** a local branch of this association. [< *grange*]

grang|er (grān′jər), *n.* **1** a person who is in charge of a grange; farm bailiff. **2** = farmer.

Grang|er (grān′jər), *n. U.S.* a member of the Grange.

Grang|er|ism (grān′jə riz əm), *n.* the principles of the association of Grangers in the United States.

grang|er|ism (grān′jə riz əm), *n.* the practice of grangerizing books.

grang|er|ite (grān′jə rīt), *n.* a person who illustrates a book with pictures, engravings, etc., from other books.

grang|er|ize (grān′jə rīz), *v.t.,* **-ized, -iz|ing.** **1** to illustrate (a book) with pictures or diagrams from other books. **2** to cut pictures from (other books) for this purpose. [< Rev. James *Granger,* 1723-1776, who published in 1769 a "Biographical History of England" designed for such illustration] —**grang′er|i|za′tion**, *n.* —**grang′er|iz|er**, *n.*

gra|nif|er|ous (grə nif′ər əs), *adj.* producing or bearing grain, or seeds like grain. [< Latin *grānum* grain + English *-ferous*]

gran|i|form (gran′ə fôrm), *adj.* formed like a grain or as if composed of grains. [< Latin *grānum* grain + English *-form*]

gran|ite (gran′it), *n.* **1** a very hard, igneous rock, made up chiefly of the minerals quartz and feldspar, usually with mica and hornblende. Granite is usually gray and is much used for buildings and monuments. **2** *Figurative.* hardness, as of mind or heart; stoniness: *granite-faced, granite-jawed, a heart of granite.* [< Italian *granito* grained, past participle of *granire* yield grain < *grano* grain < Latin *grānum*] —**gran′ite|like′**, *adj.*

granite paper, a paper with a mottled, colored surface.

granite porphyry, a coarse porphyry composed mainly of quartz and feldspar.

Granite State, a nickname of New Hampshire.

gran|ite|ware (gran′it wãr′), *n.* **1** ironware covered with gray enamel. **2a** pottery with a speckled coloring imitating that of granite. **b** a fine, hard, white pottery.

gra|nit|ic (grə nit′ik), *adj.* **1** of or like granite: *granitic rocks.* **2** *Figurative.* hard; rigid; unimpressionable. —**gra|nit′i|cal|ly**, *adv.*

gra|nit|i|form (grə nit′ə fôrm), *adj.* having the form of granite.

gran|it|ite (gran′ə tīt), *n.* a variety of granite containing biotite.

gran|it|i|za|tion (gran′ə tə zā′shən), *n.* the act or process of granitizing.

gran|it|ize (gran′ə tīz), *v.t.,* **-ized, -iz|ing.** **1** to impregnate (a rock) with granitic material or minerals. **2** to change into granite; convert to granite.

gran|it|oid (gran′ə toid), *adj., n.* —*adj.* like granite. —*n.* a granitoid rock.

gran|i|vore (gran′ə vôr, -vōr), *n.* an animal that feeds on grain or seeds. [< Latin *grānum* grain + *vorāre* devour]

gra|niv|o|rous (grə niv′ər əs), *adj.* eating or feeding on grain or seeds.

Gran|jon (gran′jən), *n.* style of printing type based on that of Robert Granjon, French type designer.

gran|nie (gran′ē), *n.* = granny.
gran|ny (gran′ē), *n., pl.* **-nies**, *adj.* —*n. Informal.* **1** a grandmother. **2** an old woman. **3** *U.S. Dialect.* a nurse or midwife. **4** *Figurative.* a fussy person. **5** = granny knot. —*adj.* of, for, or in the style of granny dresses: *a granny shawl.*
***granny dress**, a loose dress reaching from the neck to the ankles, similar to those formerly worn by elderly women or "grandmothers".

***granny dress**

granny flat, *British.* an addition to a house, permitting an elderly relative to live independently: *A granny flat is a self-contained, single-story dwelling of about 378 feet; it's designed for easy installation in an average backyard* (Modern Maturity).
***granny glasses**, gold- or steel-rimmed eyeglasses, similar to those often worn formerly by elderly women.

***granny glasses**

granny knot, a knot differing from a square knot in having the ends crossed the wrong way; lubber's knot. It is easily jammed, yet often fails to hold under strain. See picture under **knot**[1].
granny woman, *U.S. Dialect.* granny (a nurse or midwife).
gran|o|di|o|rite (gran′ə dī′ə rīt), *n.* a granular, igneous rock intermediate between granite and quartz-diorite. [< Latin *grānum* grain + English *diorite*]
gra|no|la (grə nō′lə), *n.* a mixture of natural cereals, often sold as a health food: *Rows of unfamiliar foodstuffs are appearing in middle-class cupboards: brown rice by the bucketful, as well as packages of adsuki, granola, gomasio, ginseng and miso* (Time). [American English, probably < Italian *grano* grain + augmentative suffix *-ola*]
gran|o|lith|ic (gran′ə lith′ik), *adj.* (of buildings) made of a particular kind of concrete, consisting of cement and fine granite chips. [< Latin *grānum* grain + Greek *líthos* stone + English *-ic*]
gran|o|phyre (gran′ə fīr), *n.* a porphyritic rock in which the groundmass is a microscopic crystalline intergrowth of the component minerals. [< German *Granophyr* < *Granit* granite + (*Por*)*phyr* porphyry]
gran|o|phy|ric (gran′ə fī′rik), *adj.* composed of granophyre.
gran|sir (gran′sər), *n. Dialect.* grandsire.
grant (grant, gränt), *v., n.* —*v.t.* **1** to give (what is asked); allow: *to grant a request, to grant permission.* **2** to admit; accept without proof; concede: *I grant that you are right so far.* **3** to give or confer (as a right or ownership) by formal act or by writing: *They granted charters to the towns and privileges to the inhabitants* (Henry Buckle).
—*v.i.* to agree or consent: *The soldiers should have toss'd me on their pikes Before I would have granted to that act* (Shakespeare).
—*n.* **1** a gift, especially land or rights given by a government, or a gift of money. SYN: appropriation. **2** the act of granting. **3** a local, minor civil division in Maine, New Hampshire, and Vermont.
take for granted, a to assume to be true; regard as proved or agreed to: *We take for granted the existence of atoms.* **b** to accept as probable: *We took for granted that the sailor could swim.* **c** to fail to appreciate sufficiently: *You don't commit the idiotic mistake of doing every blessed thing that'll make him take you for granted, and then complain bitterly if indeed he does take you for granted* (Punch).
[< Anglo-French *graunter,* Old French *granter,* or *craanter,* variants of *creanter* promise, authorize, ultimately < Latin *crēdēns,* present participle of *crēdere* trust] —**grant′a|ble**, *adj.* —**grant′er**, *n.*
grant-aid (grant′ād′, gränt′-), *v.t. British.* to support (a school or educational program) from public funds, especially by paying a part of the maintenance costs. [back formation < *grant-aided* (*school*)]
grant-aid|ed school (grant′ā′did, gränt′-), *British.* a primary or secondary parochial school that receives half the cost of its maintenance from the Ministry of Education.
grant|ee (gran′tē′, grän′-), *n.* a person to whom a grant is made.
Granth (grunt), *n.* the sacred scriptures of the Sikhs. [< Hindustani *granth* book < Sanskrit *grantha*]
grant-in-aid (grant′in ād′, gränt′-), *n., pl.* **grants-in-aid**. **1** a grant of money by one unit of government to another to help it carry out some public service or program: *Grants-in-aid from the federal government rank as the largest single source of state income* (David Fellman). **2** a grant of money to a person or institution, especially a school, to help defray the cost of a particular project.
grant|or (gran′tər, grän′-; gran′tôr′, grän′-), *n.* a person who makes a grant.
Grant's caribou, a caribou living in the Alaskan Peninsula and Unimak Island.
Grant's gazelle, a large, white and fawn gazelle found in East Africa. The male weighs up to 150 pounds and has lyre-shaped horns 30 inches long. See picture under **antelope**. [< James A. *Grant,* 1827-1892, a Scottish explorer]
grants|man (grants′mən, gränts′-), *n., pl.* **-men**. an expert or specialist in grantsmanship. [back formation < *grantsmanship*]
grants|man|ship (grants′mən ship, gränts′-), *n.* the art of obtaining grants of money for research and other projects from various foundations or donors.
gran tu|ris|mo (grän′tü rēz′mō), a type of distinctively styled European sports car, originally designed for long-distance travel at high speeds; grand tourer. *Abbr:* GT (no periods). [< Italian *gran turismo* great touring]
gran|u|lar (gran′yə lər), *adj.* **1** consisting of or containing grains or granules; grainy: *granular sandstone.* **2** like grains or granules. **3** (of a diseased organ) having a granulated surface or structure. —**gran′u|lar|ly**, *adv.*
gran|u|lar|i|ty (gran′yə lar′ə tē), *n.* granular condition or quality.
gran|u|late (gran′yə lāt), *v.,* **-lat|ed, -lat|ing.** —*v.t.* **1** to make into grains or granules: *to granulate sugar.* **2** to roughen the surface of. —*v.i.* **1** to form grains or granules; become granular. **2** to develop granulations. Wounds granulate in healing. —**gran′u|la′tor**, *n.*
gran|u|lat|ed (gran′yə lā′tid), *adj.* **1** formed into grains or granules: *granulated sugar.* **2** roughened on the surface: *granulated leather.* **3** having granulations; mottled.
gran|u|la|tion (gran′yə lā′shən), *n.* **1** formation into grains or granules. **2** a roughening on the surface. **3** one of the grains on a roughened surface. **4** the formation of small, grainlike bodies, especially in the process of healing. **5** a small, grainlike body or elevation, especially one of those that form on the surface of wounds during healing. **6** *Astronomy.* one of the mottlings on the surface of the sun.
granulation tissue, a layer of pink-colored blood vessels having no nerve endings, that form over a wound and aid in the body's process of healing.
gran|u|la|tive (gran′yə lā′tiv), *adj.* characterized by granulation: *granulative growths.*
gran|ule (gran′yül), *n.* **1** a small grain. **2** a small bit or spot like a grain. **3** = corpuscle. **4** any one of the small patches of gas that make up the photosphere of the sun. [< Late Latin *grānulum* (diminutive) < Latin *grānum* grain]
gran|u|li|form (gran′yə lə fôrm), *adj.* having a granular structure.
gran|u|lite (gran′yə līt), *n.* a fine-grained gneiss or granite consisting chiefly of feldspar and quartz.
gran|u|lit|ic (gran′yə lit′ik), *adj.* of or having to do with granulite: *granulitic rock.*
gran|u|lit|ize (gran′yə lə tīz), *v.,* **-ized, -iz|ing.** *Geology.* —*v.t.* to make granulitic. —*v.i.* to become granulitic. —**gran′u|lit′i|za′tion**, *n.*
gran|u|lo|cyte (gran′yə lə sīt), *n.* any one of several types of white blood cells whose cytoplasm contains granules and which play an important part in the destruction of harmful bacteria. [< Late Latin *grānulum* granule + English *-cyte*]
gran|u|lo|cyt|ic leukemia (gran′yə lə sit′ik), a usually fatal form of leukemia in which an excessive number of granulocytes are produced in the bone marrow.
gran|u|lo|ma (gran′yə lō′mə), *n., pl.* **-mas, -ma|ta** (-mə tə). a small area of granulated tissue associated with certain infections.
granuloma in|gui|na|le (ing′wə nä′lē), a chronic venereal disease, common in the tropics, characterized by deep ulceration of the area around the groin. [< New Latin *granuloma inguinale* inguinal granuloma]
gran|u|lo|ma|to|sis (gran′yə lō′mə tō′sis), *n.* any one of several diseases characterized by the presence of multiple granulomas.
gran|u|lom|a|tous (gran′yə lom′ə təs, -lō′mə-), *adj.* like or having to do with granuloma: *granulomatous lesions.*
gran|u|lo|met|ric (gran′yə lə met′rik), *adj.* having to do with measurement of the different sizes of grains of sand.
gran|u|lo|pe|ni|a (gran′yə lə pē′nē ə), *n.* agranulocytosis. [< Late Latin *grānulum* granule + Greek *peniā* poverty]
gran|u|lo|sa cell (gran′yə lō′sə), any one of the epithelial cells lining the Graafian follicle. [< New Latin *granulosa* granular < Latin *grānulum* granule]
gran|u|lose[1] (gran′yə lōs), *n.* = amylose.
gran|u|lose[2] (gran′yə lōs), *adj.* = granular.
gran|u|lo|sis (gran′yə lō′sis), *n.* **1** the formation of granulomas. **2** a disease of the larvae of certain insects, characterized by the formation of tiny granules in the cells: *A granulosis virus causes the most mortality among the codling moth larvae* (Science News).
gran|u|lous (gran′yə ləs), *adj.* = granular.
gra|num (grā′nəm), *n., pl.* **-na**. one of the very small, disk-shaped granules within the chloroplasts of plant cells. They contain chlorophyll and are believed to act as photosensitive semiconductors in photosynthesis. [< New Latin *granum* < Latin *grānum* grain]
Gran|ville wilt (gran′vil), a common bacterial disease of tobacco that causes the plant to wilt and die. [< *Granville,* a county in North Carolina]
grape (grāp), *n.* **1** a small, round fruit like a berry, red, purple, or pale-green, that grows in bunches on the woody vines of certain plants of the grape family. Grapes are eaten raw or made into raisins, jelly, juice, or wine. Most grapes have one to four seeds. **2** = grapevine. **3** a dark purplish-red color. **4** the fermented juice of the grape; wine: *Bottles of the grape were put on the table.* **5** = grapeshot.
grapes, a diseased growth resembling a bunch of grapes on the skin of the pastern of a horse or mule: *Grapes upon the heels, of long standing and dry, are incurable* (Sporting Magazine).
[< Old French *grape* bunch of grapes < *graper* pick grapes < *grape* hook; see etym. under **grapnel**] —**grape′like′**, *adj.*
grape-ber|ry moth (grāp′ber′ē), any one of a variety of moths that lay their eggs in June on the berries of grapevines, which soon become discolored from the boring of the larvae inside.
grape brandy, brandy distilled from grapes or wine without any other ingredient.
grape family, a group of dicotyledonous shrubs, usually climbing by means of tendrils, bearing clusters of small, greenish flowers and having a berry as the fruit. The family includes the grape, Virginia creeper, and Japanese ivy.
grape|fruit (grāp′früt′), *n.* **1** a pale-yellow, roundish citrus fruit like an orange, but larger and sourer; pomelo. It grows in clusters. **2** the tropical or semitropical tree it grows on. It belongs to the rue family and is cultivated chiefly in the U.S.
grape hyacinth, any one of a group of plants of the lily family with spikes of round, blue flowers resembling tiny grapes.
grape ivy, an evergreen, tendril-bearing climber of the grape family.
grape rootworm, the larva of a small brown beetle of the eastern United States that feeds on grapevines.
grap|er|y (grā′pər ē), *n., pl.* **-er|ies**. **1** a hothouse for grapes. **2** a plantation of grapevines.
grapes (grāps), *n.pl.* See under **grape**.
grape|shot (grāp′shot′), *n.* a cluster of small iron balls, formerly used as a charge for cannon.
grapes of wrath, the sources of ferment or agitation; the seeds of rage and violence: *He is trampling out the vintage where the grapes of wrath are stored* (Julia Ward Howe). [in allusion to Revelation 14:19]
grape|stone (grāp′stōn′), *n.* the seed of a grape.
grape sugar, dextrose or glucose.
grape tree, a West Indian tree, so called from its grapelike berry.
grape|vine (grāp′vīn′), *n.* **1** a vine that grapes grow on. **2** *Informal.* **a** Also, **grapevine telegraph**. a way in which news or rumors are mysteriously spread: *Others say that intelligent guessing, plus the workings of the grapevine, left very few uninformed* (Bulletin of the Atomic Scientists). **b** a baseless rumor. **3** a figure in ice skating.

Pronunciation Key: hat, āge, cãre, fär; let, ēqual, tėrm; it, īce; hot, ōpen, ôrder; oil, out; cup, pu̇t, rüle; child; long; thin; ᴛʜen; zh, measure; ə represents **a** in about, **e** in taken, **i** in pencil, **o** in lemon, **u** in circus.

grapevine moth, a noctuid moth of Australia whose caterpillars damage grapevines.

graph**[1] (graf, gräf), *n., v.* **—*n. **1** a line or diagram showing how one quantity depends on or changes with another: *Draw a graph to show how your weight has changed each year with your change in age.* See diagram below. **2** *Mathematics.* a curve or other line representing relations of the elements in an equation or function.
—*v.t.* to make a graph of: **a** to draw a line or diagram representing (some change). **b** to draw a line representing (some equation or function).
[short for *graphic formula;* see etym. under **graphic**]

graph[2] (graf, gräf), *n., v.* **—*n.*** an apparatus using the principle of the hectograph for making copies, as of writing or drawings.
—*v.t.* to reproduce in a number of copies by means of a graph. [short for *hectograph*]

graph[3] (graf, gräf), *n. Linguistics.* any written sign or symbol representing a phoneme, morpheme, or similar unit. The form *ps* in *psyche* is a graph. The letter *e* in *ate* is a silent graph. [< Greek *graphḗ* writing]

-graph, *combining form.* **1** an instrument that writes, draws, describes, or records: *Seismograph = an instrument that records earthquake data.* **2** something written, drawn, described, or recorded: *Autograph = something written by one or oneself.* **3** to write, draw, describe, or record: *Lithograph = to record on stone.* **4** drawn, written, or recorded: *Holograph = written entirely in one's own hand.* [< Latin *-graphus* < Greek *-graphos* < *gráphein* draw, write]

graph|al|loy (graf′ə loi′), *n.* graphite mixed or impregnated with a metal, as bronze or babbitt, used to make bearings, bushings, and electrical brushes.

graph|eme (graf′ēm), *n. Linguistics.* the smallest distinctive unit of the written language; any form of a letter or combination of letters that represents a speech sound: *A writing system consists of a set of graphemes plus certain characteristic features of their use* (Henry A. Gleason, Jr.). [< *graph*[3] + *-eme,* as in *phoneme*]

gra|phe|mic (gra fē′mik), *adj.* of or having to do with graphemes or graphemics: *graphemic symbols.* **—gra|phe′mi|cal|ly**, *adv.*

gra|phe|mics (gra fē′miks), *n.* the study of graphemes.

graph|ic (graf′ik), *adj., n.* **—*adj.*** **1** producing by words the effect of a picture; lifelike; vivid: *The returned soldier gave a graphic account of a battle.* **2** of or about diagrams and their use; working by means of graphs rather than calculations.
3 shown by a graph: *The principal kept a graphic record of school attendance for a month.* **4** of or about drawing, painting, engraving, or etching: *graphic art.* **5** of or used in handwriting. The letters of the alphabet are graphic symbols. **6** written; inscribed. **7** presenting an appearance like writing or printing: *graphic ore.* **8** *Obsolete.* **a** drawn with a pencil or pen. **b** clearly traced.
—*n.* any work of graphics or the graphic arts, such as an etching, drawing, lithograph, or engraving.
[< Latin *graphicus* < Greek *graphikós* < *graphḗ* writing, drawing < *gráphein* write] **—graph′i|cal|ly, graph′ic|ly**, *adv.* **—graph′ic|ness**, *n.*

graphic accent, a written or printed mark, especially an acute accent, used to indicate stress.

graph|i|ca|cy (graf′ə kə sē), *n.* skill in the graphic arts.

graph|i|cal (graf′ə kəl), *adj.* = graphic.

graphic arts, drawing, painting, engraving, etching, and the like, involving representation or expression by means of lines on flat surfaces, especially as applied to making prints and to the art of designing books.

graph|i|cate (graf′ə kit), *adj.* skilled in the graphic arts.

graphic granite, a type of rock composed of quartz and feldspar that shows irregular crystals resembling Hebrew or Arabic characters.

graph|ics (graf′iks), *n.* **1** the art or science of drawing, especially by mathematical principles, as in mechanical drawing. **2** the science of calculating by means of graphs, diagrams, and the like. **3** the diagrams, charts, maps or other illustrative material included in printed material or on a computer. **4** the type design and layout of printed material or a computer program. **5** = graphic arts.

graph|ite (graf′īt), *n., v.,* **-it|ed, -it|ing.** **—*n.*** a soft, black form of carbon with a metallic luster, used for lead in pencils and for lubricating machinery; black lead; plumbago: *Graphite is a good conductor and has a metallic sheen when polished* (J. Crowther).
—*v.t.* to coat, mix, or lubricate with graphite.
[< German *Graphit* < Greek *gráphein* write + German *-it* -ite[1]]

graphite moderator, a pure form of graphite, used in nuclear reactors to slow down the action of neutrons to the required range.

gra|phit|ic (grə fit′ik), *adj.* having to do with or of the nature of graphite.

graph|i|tize (graf′ə tīz), *v.t.,* **-tized, -tiz|ing.** **1** to convert (carbon) into graphite. **2** to cover (the surface of an object) with graphite. **—graph′i|ti|za′tion**, *n.*

graph|i|toid (graf′ə toid), *adj.* resembling graphite.

graph|i|toi|dal (graf′ə toi′dəl), *adj.* = graphitoid.

graph|i|ure (graf′ē u̇r), *n.* a South African rodent with a tail ending in a pencil of hairs. [< New Latin *Graphiurus* the genus name < Greek *grapheîon* pencil + *ourá* tail]

graph|o|a|nal|y|sis (graf′ō ə nal′ə sis), *n.* the analysis of handwriting to discover a person's character, aptitudes, attitudes, and the like.

graph|o|log|i|cal (graf′ə loj′ə kəl), *adj.* of or having to do with graphology: *graphological analysis.*

graph|ol|o|gist (gra fol′ə jist), *n.* an expert in graphology.

graph|ol|o|gy (gra fol′ə jē), *n.* the study of handwriting, especially as a means of analyzing the writer's character, aptitudes, and attitudes.

graph|o|ma|ni|a (graf′ə mā′nē ə), *n.* an obsessive desire to write.

graph|o|ma|ni|ac (graf′ə mā′nē ak), *n.* a person obsessed with a desire to write.

graph|o|mo|tor (graf′ə mō′tər), *adj. Physiology.* having to do with or influencing the movements made in writing.

Graph|o|phone (graf′ə fōn), *n. Trademark.* a machine for recording and reproducing sound, and its records. It is a type of phonograph.

graph|o|scope (graf′ə skōp), *n.* a computer display unit on which the data can be modified by the use of a light pen or similar device.

graph|o|spasm (graf′ə spaz əm), *n.* writer's cramp.

graph|o|ther|a|py (graf′ə ther′ə pē), *n.* the diagnosis and treatment of mental or emotional problems through handwriting; the manipulation or alteration of handwriting as a form of therapy.

graph|o|type (graf′ə tīp), *n.* **1** a process of making blocks for use in surface printing. **2** the block or plate so produced.

graph paper, paper ruled in squares for making graphs and diagrams; plotting paper.

-graphy, *combining form.* **1** the process of writing, describing, or recording: *Cryptography = the process of writing in code. Radiography = the process of recording with X rays.*
2 such writing, description, or record: *Biography = a writing about someone's life. Filmography = a description or record of motion-picture films.*
3 a descriptive science: *Geography = descriptive science of the earth ('s surface).*
[< Greek *-graphiā* < *gráphein* write]

***grap|nel** (grap′nəl), *n.* **1** an instrument with one or more hooks for seizing and holding something; grapple; grappling iron. Grapnels thrown by ropes were once used for catching onto an enemy's ship. **2** a small anchor with three or more hooks. **3** any one of various other implements for grasping or clutching. [Middle English *grapenel* (diminutive) < Old French *grapin* and *grapil* hook. < Old Provençal < *grape* hook < unrecorded Frankish *krappo* (compare Old High German *chrapfo*)]

***grapnel** definition 2

grap|pa (gräp′pä), *n. Italian.* a brandy made of the dregs or mash left in a wine press.

grap|ple (grap′əl), *v.,* **-pled, -pling,** *n.* **—*v.t.*** **1** to seize and hold fast; grip or hold firmly: *The dog grappled the thief's leg in his jaws, pulling the thief to the ground.* SYN: grasp, clinch. **2** to fasten with a grapple; attach firmly: (*Figurative.*) *Those friends thou hast, and their adoption tried, Grapple them to thy soul with hoops of steel* (Shakespeare). **3** to come to close quarters with.
—*v.i.* **1** to struggle; fight: *The wrestlers grappled in the center of the ring.* SYN: wrestle. **2** *Figurative.* to try to overcome, solve, or deal with; contend (with): *He grappled with the problem for an hour before he solved it. In particular, they have been reluctant to grapple with two essential elements of the disarmament program* (New York Times). SYN: wrestle. **3** to search with a grapnel or grappling hook.
—*n.* **1** the act of seizing and holding fast; firm grip or hold: *The dog's grapple held the bone fast between his teeth.* **2** an iron bar with hooks at one end for seizing and holding fast an object; grappling hook; grapnel. **3** the act of grappling; struggle: (*Figurative.*) *His life ... has been a grope for, and grapple with, the English language* (Saturday Evening Post).
[< Old French *grapil* hook; see etym. under **grapnel**]

grap|pler (grap′lər), *n.* **1** a person who grapples. **2** = grapnel. **3** = wrestler.

grap|pling (grap′ling), *n.* = grapnel.

grappling hook or **iron**, an iron bar with hooks at one end for seizing and holding; grapnel.

grap|to|lite (grap′tə līt), *n.* any one of a group of small, extinct, invertebrate animals which lived in various forms of colonies, especially abundant during the Ordovician period. The presence of its fossil is a common means of dating rocks and rock formations. [< New Latin *Graptolites* the genus name < Greek *graptós* marked, painted + *líthos*]

grap|to|lit|ic (grap′tə lit′ik), *adj.* of or having to do with graptolites; produced by or containing graptolites: *graptolitic markings, graptolitic slate.*

grap|y (grā′pē), *adj.,* **grap|i|er, grap|i|est.** **1** of or having to do with grapes. **2** smelling of or tasting like grapes.

GRAS (gras), *n.* Generally Recognized as Safe (used by the U.S. Food and Drug Administration as a label for food ingredients not considered harmful or dangerous): *The list of GRAS food additives ... included table salt, chemical preservatives, vinegar, and baking powder* (William Spector).

gra|ser (grā′zər), *n.* a device that emits a beam of single-wavelength gamma rays like that of a laser. It consists of a rod of fissionable material on which pulses from a laser act to stimulate the emission of gamma rays from the rod's nuclei. *Packing the wallop of a miniature A-bomb and able to penetrate a wall several feet thick, the ... graser could create a revolution in scientific research and development* (Science News). [< *g* (amma-) *ra* (y) (la)*ser*]

grasp (grasp, gräsp), *v., n.* **—*v.t.*** **1** to seize and hold fast by closing the fingers or claws around: *The drowning man grasped the rope. If you grasp a nettle firmly it doesn't sting.* SYN: grip, clutch, grab, snatch. See syn. under **seize**. **2** to hold firmly, as with the hand; grip. **3** *Figurative.* to clutch at; seize greedily: *to grasp an opportunity.* **4** *Figurative.* to understand; lay hold of with the mind: *She grasped my meaning at once. The lips repeated bitterly the word "home" as if that were the only word she grasped* (Graham Greene). SYN: comprehend.
—*n.* **1** the act of seizing and holding tightly; clasp of the hand: *His firm grasp held the rope from slipping.* **2** the power of seizing and holding; reach: *That rope is within his grasp.* (*Figurative.*) *Success is within her grasp.* **3** *Figurative.* control; possession: *The people regained power from the grasp of the dictator.* SYN: mastery. **4** *Figurative.* understanding: *She has a good grasp of arithmetic. The mature Michelet is a strange phenomenon ... He had the novelist's social interest and grasp of character, the poet's imagination and passion* (Edmund Wilson).

grasp at, **a** to try to grasp, try to take hold of: *Old Yew, which graspest at the stones That*

bar graph:

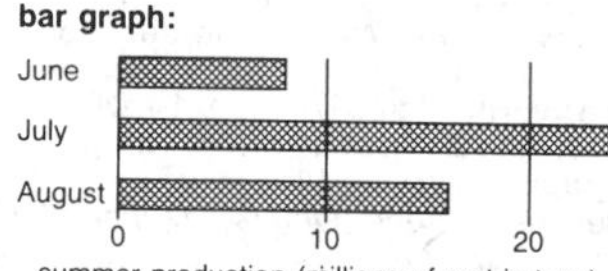

line graph:

May June July August
30 20 10 0
summer production (millions of metric tons)

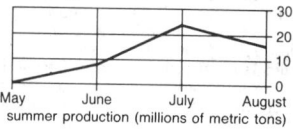

pictograph:

***graph**[1] definition 1

circle graph:

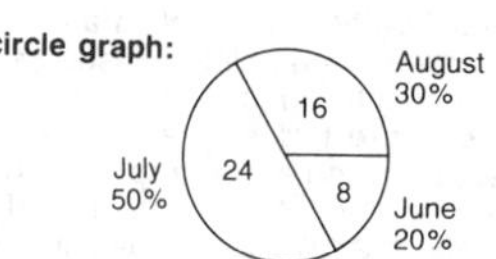

name the underlying dead (Tennyson). **b** to accept eagerly: *She grasped at the opportunity. I readily grasped at his proposal* (Washington Irving).
[Middle English *graspen.* See related etym. at **grip, gripe, grope.**] —**grasp'er,** *n.*

grasp|a|ble (gras'pə bəl, gräs'-), *adj.* that can be grasped: (*Figurative.*) *This still fairly young man is capable of turning his attention to almost any topic, mastering it in short order, and putting it ... in readily graspable form* (New Yorker).

grasp|ing (gras'ping, gräs'-), *adj.* **1** that grasps. SYN: tenacious. **2** *Figurative.* eager to get all that one can; greedy: *Stelling is moderate in his terms—he's not a grasping man* (George Eliot). SYN: avaricious. —**grasp'ing|ly,** *adv.* —**grasp'ing-ness,** *n.*

grasp|less (grasp'lis, gräsp'-), *adj.* **1** without grasp or grip; incapable of grasping. **2** not to be grasped.

grass[1] (gras, gräs), *n., v.* —*n.* **1** the plants with green blades that cover fields, lawns, and pastures. Horses, cows, and sheep eat grass. SYN: herbage. **2** *Botany.* any one of a group of plants that have jointed stems and long, narrow leaves; a plant of the grass family. Wheat, corn, sugar cane, and bamboo are grasses. Grasses usually have a small, dry, one-seeded fruit. **3** land covered with grass; pasture: *Half of the farm is grass.* **4** the season of the new growth of grass: *a horse five years old next grass.* **5** *Slang.* marijuana.
—*v.t.* **1** to cover with grass: *Asked about complaints that Central Park is not so naturally lovely or so well grassed as it used to be ...* (New York Times). **2** to feed (cattle) with grass. **3** to lay out (flax) on grass for the purpose of bleaching. **4** *Informal.* to knock, throw, or bring to the grass or ground.
—*v.i.* **1** to feed on growing grass; graze: *The horses had been left grassing at a short remove* (Charles Cornwallis). **2** to produce grass; become covered with grass.
at grass, a out to pasture: *Lost at grass ... a bay gelding* (London Gazette). **b** out of work; at leisure: *When I have been at grass in the summer and am new come up* [*to town*] *again* (John Dryden).
go to grass, a to graze; go to pasture: *The sturdy steed now goes to grass, and up they hang his saddle* (Beaumont and Fletcher).
b *Slang.* to go into retirement; resticate (often used contemptuously in the imperative): *Get out! Go to grass!*
let the grass grow under one's feet, to waste time; lose chances: [*He*] *was not a man who ever let the grass grow under his feet* (Edna Lyall).
put (send, or **turn out) to grass, a** to turn (an animal) out to pasture: *Our guides unharnessed our elks and turn'd them to grass* (P.M. de la Martiniere). **b** *Informal.* to dismiss (a person) from a position; force out: *If the worst comes to the worst—I'll turn my wife to grass* (William Congreve).
[Old English *græs*] —**grass'like',** *adj.*

grass[2] (gras, gräs), *v.i. British Slang.* to inform against someone; turn informer. [< *grass,* noun, British slang term for a police informer, shortened from *grasshopper* policeman, rhyming slang for *copper*]

grass bass, = calico bass.

grass|box (gras'boks', gräs'-), *n.* a removable container for the cut grass in a lawn mower.

grass carp, a carp of the South China Sea and adjacent waters, noted for its ability to eat large quantities of aquatic weeds and imported for this purpose to various western countries.

grass cloth, a thin, light fabric woven from the fiber of various plants, especially the ramie.

grass court, a grass-covered, outdoor tennis court.

grass cutter, 1 a person or thing that cuts grass. **2** *Baseball.* a fast grounder that travels across the field almost without a bounce: *Nagle ... belted a grass cutter that caromed off another woman's ankle* (Time). **3** *U.S. Slang.* a hedge-hopping airplane.

grass|er (gras'ər, gräs'-), *n.* a steer or other beef animal taken from grazing and sent to market without being fattened by special feeding.

***grass family,** a large group of plants that have jointed stems and long, narrow leaves, flower spikelets, and fruit often consisting of seedlike grain. It is the most important plant in its usefulness to man, including the cereal grains, sugar cane, bamboo, many forage crops, and many ornamental varieties. See picture below.

grass-feed (gras'fēd', gräs'-), *v.t., v.i.,* **-fed** (-fed'), **-feed|ing.** to feed chiefly on grass; pasture: *Grass-fed cattle ... furnish lower beef grades* (Wall Street Journal).

grass finch, 1 = vesper sparrow. **2** any one of certain weaverbirds of Australia.

grass flower, 1 = blue-eyed grass. **2** = spring beauty.

grass frog, any one of various common, green frogs of Europe or North America, such as the pickerel frog and leopard frog.

grass-green (gras'grēn', gräs'-), *adj.* **1** green as grass, especially somewhat yellowish green. **2** green with grass.

grass-grown (gras'grōn', gräs'-), *adj.* overgrown with grass.

grass hockey, (in Canada) field hockey.

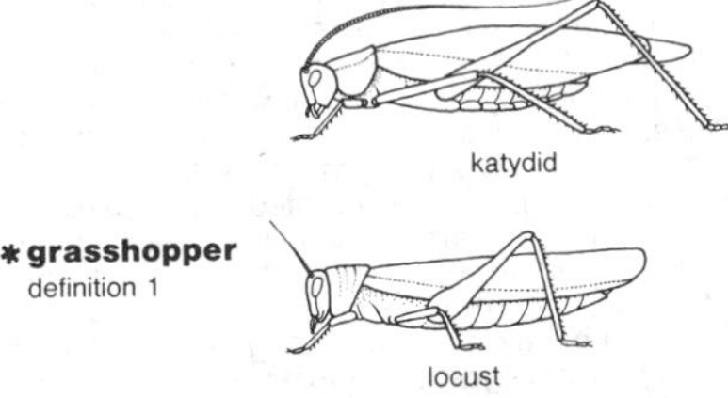

***grasshopper** definition 1

***grass|hop|per** (gras'hop'ər, gräs'-), *n.* **1** an insect with long and very strong hind legs for jumping, many also with wings. Grasshoppers often damage crops severely. They belong to two families, the long-horned grasshoppers which include the katydids, and the short-horned grasshoppers which include the locusts. **2** any small, low-flying airplane. **3** a small automatic device for recording and reporting weather conditions, designed to be dropped by parachute from an aircraft.
knee-high to a grasshopper, very short and often very young: *He started riding a horse when he was just knee-high to a grasshopper.*

grasshopper mouse, any one of several varieties of mice of western North America, related to the deer mouse, and having a short tail tipped with white.

grasshopper sparrow, a short-tailed North American sparrow of fields and pastures, so called because of its long buzzing song.

grasshopper warbler, a small European warbler with a chirping note.

grass|land (gras'land', gräs'-), *n.* **1** land with grass on it, used for pasture: *It is too often the case that grassland is left to take care of itself, and that no steps are taken for its improvement* (Nature). **2** a region with mostly grass and few trees: *In the great expanses of the grasslands hundreds of miles wide east of the Rockies, the early settlers of a century ago found hardly a shrub* (Fred W. Emerson).

grass|less (gras'lis, gräs'-), *adj.* without grass: *Paddocks next to stables often become grassless ...* (Sunset).

grass-of-Par|nas|sus (gras'əv pär nas'əs, gräs'-), *n.* any one of a group of perennial bog herbs of the saxifrage family, native to arctic and temperate areas, having entire leaves and solitary, white to pale-yellow flowers.

grass oil, any one of several fragrant oils obtained from Indian grasses.

grass|plot (gras'plot', gräs'-), *n.* a plot of grass or turf; lawn.

grass porgy, a porgy found off the coast of Florida, named for its habit of living among grasslike seaweed.

grass|quit (gras'kwit, gräs'-), *n.* any one of certain small Cuban finches.

grass-root (gras'rüt', gräs'-; -rủt'), *adj.* = grass-roots.

grass roots, 1 the rural areas of a country: *The grass roots is still the place to arouse people's interest in saving money on taxes* (Wall Street Journal). **2** the ordinary citizens of a region or state taken all together: *The senator is sure he will get support from the grass roots.* **3** the foundation; source: *the grass roots of international cooperation* (New York Times).

grass-roots (gras'rüts', gräs'-; -rủts'), *adj.* **1** of or having to do with the common people: *Most of them also contend that the grass-roots popularity of the Democrats was unimpaired by the inflation ...* (Atlantic). **2** of or having to do with rural areas: *The Senate subcommittee will hold up action until grass-roots farmers have been heard from.*

grass skiing, the sport of racing down grassy or straw-covered slopes on specially designed skates: *A new form of skiing called grass skiing uses what looks like a cross between a roller skate and a tractor belt* (Norris D. McWhirter).

grass skirt, a skirt made of long grasses or leaves and tied to a waistband or cord, worn by women in certain islands of Oceania.

grass snake, any one of certain small, harmless, grayish-green snakes living in meadows.

grass snipe, = pectoral sandpiper.

grass spider, any one of various spiders that spin funnel-shaped webs on grass, often seen covered with dew in the morning in meadows.

grass sponge, a large, brown, coarse sponge of some commercial value, found especially on the coast of Florida, Cuba, and Honduras.

grass staggers, staggers occurring in cattle in early spring as a result of grazing on forage deficient in magnesium.

grass tetany, a nutritional disease of ruminants, characterized by spastic convulsions and associated with a deficiency of magnesium in the diet.

grass tree, 1 any one of various Australian plants of the lily family, having a stout, trunklike stem bearing a tuft of long, grasslike, wiry foliage and a tall flower stalk with a dense cylindrical spike of small flowers. Some species yield acaroid gum. **2** any one of various similar Australasian plants.

grass widow, a woman divorced or separated from her husband.

grass-wid|owed (gras'wid'ōd, gräs'-), *adj.* living apart from one's husband.

grass widower, a man divorced or separated

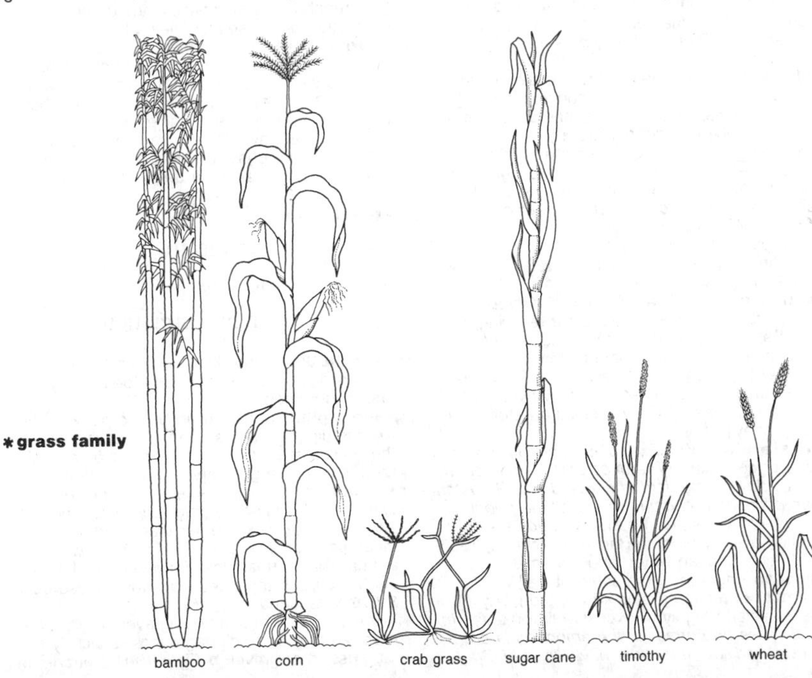

***grass family**

Pronunciation Key: hat, āge, cãre, fär; let, ēqual, tėrm, it, īce; hot, ōpen, ôrder; oil, out; cup, pủt, rüle; child; long; thin; ᴛʜen; zh, measure; ə represents **a** in about, **e** in taken, **i** in pencil, **o** in lemon, **u** in circus.

from his wife.

grass|worm (gras′wėrm′, gräs′-), *n.* the larva of a night-flying moth that occurs in great numbers, damaging cereal crops and pastures.

grass|y (gras′ē, gräs′-), *adj.*, **grass|i|er, grass|i-est. 1** covered with grass; having much grass: *the grassy carpet of the meadow.* **2** of or consisting of grass: *The pheasant builds a grassy nest.* **3** like grass: *the grassy appearance of the spruce and other long pine needles.* SYN: verdant. **4** = grass-green. **—grass′i|ness,** *n.*

grassy buttercup, a buttercup with long, grass-like leaves and bright yellow flowers that grows between six and twelve inches high.

grass|y-green (gras′ē grēn′, gräs′-), *adj.* = grass-green.

grassy sorghum, a variety of sorghum, such as Sudan grass and Johnson grass, used especially as cattle feed or hay.

grat., gratis.

*__grate__[1] (grāt), *n., v.,* **grat|ed, grat|ing.** **—*n.* 1** a framework of iron bars to hold burning fuel in a furnace or fireplace: *Many of the small hot coals fell through the grate.* **2** = fireplace. **3** a framework of bars over a window or opening; grating: *Each basement window of the store had a grate over it to protect the glass.* **4** *Mining.* a screen used for separating or grading ore. **5** *Obsolete.* a cage for animals or human beings; prison.

—*v.t.* to furnish with iron bars: *The windows were strongly grated.*

[< Medieval Latin *grata* lattice < Italian < Late Latin *crātis* grill < Latin, hurdle, wickerwork, related to *crassus* thick, dense. See etym. of doublet **crate.**] **—grate′like′,** *adj.*

***grate**[1]
definition 1

grate[2] (grāt), *v.,* **grat|ed, grat|ing,** *n.* **—*v.i.* 1** to have an annoying or unpleasant effect: *His rude manners and loud voice grate on me.* **2** to make a harsh, jarring noise by rubbing; sound harshly: *The door grated on its old, rusty hinges.*

—*v.t.* 1 to wear down or grind off in small pieces: *The cook grated the cheese before melting it.* **2** to rub harshly together: *to grate the teeth.* **3** to make a grinding sound against; sound harshly against: *A boat grates the shore.* **4** *Figurative.* to fret; annoy; irritate: *Grating so harshly all his days of quiet With turbulent and dangerous lunacy* (Shakespeare). SYN: nettle. **5** to produce by rough friction: *Open fly ... The infernal doors, and on their hinges grate Harsh thunder* (Milton). **6** *Obsolete.* to scrape, file, or abrade.

—*n.* a harsh, grinding noise: *the grate of old, rusty hinges.*

[< Old French *grater* < Germanic (compare Old High German *chrazzōn* to scratch)] **—grat′er,** *n.*

grate|ful (grāt′fəl), *adj.* **1** feeling kindly because of a favor received; wanting to do a favor in return; thankful: *I am grateful for your help.* **2** pleasing; welcome: *A breeze is grateful on a hot day, a fire on a cold one.* [< obsolete *grate* agreeable (< Latin *grātus* pleasing) + *-ful*] **—grate′ful|ly,** *adv.* **—grate′ful|ness,** *n.*

—*Syn.* 1 Grateful, thankful mean feeling or expressing gratitude. **Grateful** emphasizes recognizing and gladly acknowledging favors or kindness shown to one by others: *I am grateful to the friends who have helped me.* **Thankful** emphasizes giving thanks to some higher being or power, fate, or some force of nature, for one's good fortune: *We are thankful for this bountiful harvest. He was thankful that his son had not been harmed. I am thankful that I have good friends.*

gra|tic|u|late (grə tik′yə lāt), *v.t.,* **-lat|ed, -lat|ing.** to divide (a plan or design) into squares in order to make an accurate enlargement or reduction.

grat|i|cule (grat′ə kyül), *n.* **1a** a design or plan divided into squares to facilitate copying. **b** the network of lines or curves representing meridians and parallels on a map or chart. **2a** a measuring scale in the eyepiece of a telescope, microscope, or other optical instrument, for the location of objects in the field of view. **b** the glass disk or plate bearing this scale. [< French *graticule* < Medieval Latin *graticula, craticula* (diminutive) < Latin *crātis;* see etym. under **grate**[1]]

grat|i|fi|ca|tion (grat′ə fə kā′shən), *n.* **1** the act or process of gratifying; satisfaction: *The gratification of every wish of every person is not possible.* **2** the condition of being gratified: *In youth one's body is the perfect valet—obedient, unobtrusive, instantly responsive, a perpetual source of gratification* (S. N. Behrman). **3** something that pleases or satisfies: *His success was a great gratification to his parents.* SYN: pleasure, delight. **4** *Archaic.* a reward; fee.

grat|i|fy (grat′ə fī), *v.t.,* **-fied, -fy|ing. 1** to give pleasure to; please: *Praise gratifies most people.* SYN: delight. **2** to give satisfaction to; satisfy; indulge: *to gratify one's hunger with a large meal. A drunkard gratifies his craving for liquor.* SYN: See syn. under **humor. 3** *Archaic.* to give a fee to: *to gratify his noble service* (Shakespeare). [< Middle French *gratifier,* learned borrowing from Latin *grātificārī* < *grātus* pleasing + *facere* make, do] **—grat′i|fi′er,** *n.* **—grat′i|fy′ing|ly,** *adv.*

gra|tin (grä′tən; *French* grȧ taN′), *n.* **1** the topping of crumbs, grated cheese, or both, or a thick cream sauce, on a dish cooked *au gratin.* **2** a dish cooked with this topping. [< French *gratin* < Old French *gratter,* earlier *grater* to grate]

grat|i|nate (grat′ə nāt), *v.t.,* **-nat|ed, -nat|ing.** to cook (a dish) with a topping of crumbs, grated cheese, or thick cream sauce.

grat|ing[1] (grā′ting), *n.* **1** a framework of bars over a window or opening; grate. Windows in a prison, bank, or ticket office usually having gratings over them. SYN: grille. **2** *Physics.* = diffraction grating. [< *grate*[1]]

grat|ing[2] (grā′ting), *adj.* **1** irritating; unpleasant; annoying: *a grating manner.* **2** harsh or jarring in sound: *the grating sound of garbage cans being dragged across the sidewalk.* [< *grate*[2]] **—grat′-ing|ly,** *adv.*

grat|is (grat′is, grā′tis), *adv., adj.* for nothing; free of charge: *The club provided the service gratis* (adv.). *The service was gratis to club members* (adj.). [< Latin *grātīs,* contraction of *grātiīs,* ablative plural of *grātia* (literally) out of favor or kindness; without recompense, free]

grat|i|tude (grat′ə tüd, -tyüd), *n.* a kindly feeling because of a favor received; desire to do a favor in return; thankfulness: *Gratitude for God's forgiveness is empty save as accompanied by sympathy, understanding, and patience in all one's dealings with others* (London Times). [< Late Latin *grātitūdō* < *grātus* thankful, pleasing]

gra|tu|i|tous (grə tü′ə təs, -tyü′-), *adj.* **1** freely given or obtained; free: *a gratuitous gift. We ... mistake the gratuitous blessings of Heaven for the fruits of our own industry* (Roger L'Estrange). SYN: voluntary, spontaneous. **2** without reason or cause; unnecessary; uncalled-for: *a gratuitous insult. He has indulged in gratuitous suppositions* (Henry James). SYN: unwarranted, unjustifiable. **3** *Law.* (of a contract, deed, or other obligation) made or granted without any value being given in return. **4** *Economics.* freely given by nature, not produced by man: *a gratuitous good.* **—gra|tu′i-tous|ly,** *adv.* **—gra|tu′i|tous|ness,** *n.*

gratuitous act, = acte gratuit.

gra|tu|i|ty (grə tü′ə tē, -tyü′-), *n., pl.* **-ties. 1** a present of money in return for services; tip. Gratuities are given to waiters, porters, or servants. *[He] dismissed the postboys with a handsome gratuity* (Frederick Marryat). SYN: fee. **2** a present; gift: *I had a small gratuity above my wages* (Samuel Johnson). SYN: bounty. **3** *Especially British.* a payment given to soldiers on reenlistment, discharge, or retirement. [< Medieval Latin *gratuitas* < Latin *grātus* pleasing, thankful]

grat|u|lant (grach′ə lənt), *adj. Archaic.* expressing pleasure, joy, or satisfaction; congratulatory. [< Latin *gratulāns, -antis,* present participle of *grātulārī;* see etym. under **gratulate**]

grat|u|late (grach′ə lāt), *v.,* **-lat|ed, -lat|ing,** *adj. Archaic.* **—*v.t.* 1** to express joy at; congratulate: *I gratulate the news* (Ben Jonson). **2** to welcome; hail; greet; salute: *to gratulate the sweet return of morn* (Milton).

—*adj.* pleasing; gratifying.

[< Latin *grātulārī* (with English *-ate*[1]) (diminutive) < *grātus* pleasing, thankful]

grat|u|la|tion (grach′ə lā′shən), *n. Archaic.* **1** congratulation. SYN: felicitation. **2** rejoicing; joy.

grat|u|la|to|ry (grach′ə lə tôr′ē, -tōr′-), *adj. Archaic.* expressing joy; congratulatory.

grau|pel (grou′pəl), *n. Meteorology.* = snow pellets. [< German *Graupel-(wetter)* sleety (weather) < *graupeln* to sleet < *Graupe* small hailstone, groat, pearl barley]

Grau|stark (grou′stärk, grô′-), *n.* a very romantic place or condition: *[The director] has managed to provide an amalgam of Harvard and Graustark —an enchanted campus where all the people look like movie stars* (Time). [< *Graustark,* a romantic novel by George Barr McCutcheon, 1866-1928, an American writer, about a small European kingdom of the same name]

Grau|stark|i|an (grou stär′kē ən, grô-), *adj.* of or like Graustark; highly or excessively romantic: *In the Strauss operettas ... the emphasis is on romance, tradition, the never-never land of Graustarkian nostalgia* (Harper's).

gra|va|men (grə vā′mən), *n., pl.* **-vam|i|na** (-vam′ə nə). **1** a grievance. **2** *Law.* the burden or essential part of a charge or complaint. [< Late Latin *gravāmen* < Latin *gravāre* to load, burden < *gravis* heavy, weighty]

grave[1] (grāv), *n.* **1** a hole dug in the ground where a dead body is to be buried: *We buried the bird that the cat killed in a little grave dug in the backyard.* **2** the mound or monument over it; tomb. **3** any place of burial: *a watery grave.* **4** *Figurative.* death: *O grave, where is thy victory?* (I Corinthians 15:55).

as secret as the grave, very secret: *The correspondence I kept as secret as the grave* (Leigh Hunt).

dig one's own grave, to cause one's own downfall or ruin: *It [a regime] is, in fact, already corrupted by its own power and is probably digging its own grave as a result* (London Times).

(make one) turn in his grave, (to cause a dead person) to be disturbed by an action that was abhorrent to him in his lifetime: *Those abstract paintings would make Rembrandt turn in his grave. Jefferson might turn in his grave if he knew of such an attempt to introduce European distinctions of rank into his democracy* (James Bryce).

one foot in the grave. See under **foot.**

[Old English *græf.* See related etym. at **grave**[3].]

grave[2] (grāv), *adj.,* **grav|er, grav|est,** *n.* **—*adj.* 1** earnest; thoughtful; serious: *a grave situation, symptoms, or news. People are grave in church.* SYN: formidable. **2** dignified; solemn; not gay: *grave music, a grave face, a grave ceremony.* **3** important; weighty; momentous: *grave cares, a grave decision.* **4** somber: *grave colors.* **5** *Phonetics.* **a** low in pitch; not acute. **b** having a grave accent: *The first "a" in the French phrase "à la mode" has a grave accent over it.* **6** *Obsolete, Music.* low in pitch.

—*n.* = grave accent.

[< Old French *grave,* learned borrowing from Latin *gravis* weighty, serious, heavy] **—grave′ly,** *adv.* **—grave′ness,** *n.*

—*Syn.* *adj.* 2 Grave, serious, sober mean solemn in mood, looks, or behavior. **Grave** suggests the weighty dignity of one who has much on his mind: *His expression was grave.* **Serious** suggests thoughtfulness and solemnity of disposition: *He became serious when he spoke of finding a job.* **Sober** suggests a settled or self-restrained seriousness or gravity, especially in looks or speech: *His words were sober and wise.*

grave[3] (grāv), *v.t.,* **graved, graved** or **grav|en, grav|ing. 1** to engrave; carve; sculpture: *This be the verse you grave for me Here he lies where he longed to be* (Robert Louis Stevenson). **2** *Figurative.* to impress deeply; fix firmly. **3** *Archaic or Dialect.* to dig. **4** *Archaic.* to bury. [Old English *grafan.* Compare etym. under **grave**[1], **gravure, groove.**]

grave[4] (grāv), *v.t.,* **graved, grav|ing.** to clean (a ship's bottom) and cover it with pitch. [origin uncertain; perhaps < Old French *grave* shore]

gra|ve[5] (grä′vā), *adj., adv. Music.* **—*adj.*** slow and solemn in tempo.

—*adv.* slowly and solemnly.

[< French or Italian *grave,* learned borrowing from Latin *gravis* serious, heavy]

*__grave accent__ (grāv), a mark placed over a vowel letter of some languages to show the quality of its sound, as in French *père,* to show secondary stress, as in *àdvertìsement,* or to show a low or falling tone, as in ancient Greek. In English poetry a grave accent may be used to indicate that a word is pronounced with one more syllable than usual, as in *belovèd.*

***grave accent**

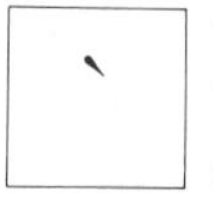

grave|clothes (grāv′klōz′, -klōᴛʜz′), *n.pl.* the clothes or wrappings in which a dead body is buried; cerements.

grave|dig|ger (grāv′dig′ər), *n.* **1** a person whose work is digging graves. **2** an insect which buries the bodies of other insects or small animals as food for its emerging larvae; burying beetle.

grav|el (grav′əl), *n., v.,* **-eled, -el|ing** or (*especially British*) **-elled, -el|ling,** *adj.* **—*n.* 1** pebbles and pieces of rock coarser than sand. Gravel is much used for roads and walks. **2** *Medicine.* **a** small, hard substances formed in the bladder and kidneys. **b** the disease in which these occur. **3** *Obsolete.* sand.

—*v.t.* 1 to lay or cover with gravel: *to gravel a road.* **2a** to run (a ship) aground, especially on rough sand or gravel. **b** *Figurative.* to puzzle; per-

plex: *The wisest doctor is gravelled by the inquisitiveness of a child* (Emerson). SYN: bewilder. **3** *U.S. Informal.* to be a cause of irritation to. —*adj.* rough; harsh; gravelly: [*He*] *strode straight to the rostrum. "Double-cross!" he bellowed, in his gravel baritone* (Time).
[< Old French *gravele* (diminutive) < *grave* sand]

grav|el-blind (grav′əl blīnd′), *adj.* almost totally blind.

grave|less (grāv′lis), *adj.* without a grave; unburied.

grav|el|ly (grav′ə lē), *adj.* **1** having much gravel. **2** of or like gravel: *The sediments nearest the shore are gravelly; those farther out are sandy; those still farther out are muddy* (Scientific American). **3** rough; rasping; grating: *a gravelly voice.*

grave marker, a sign that marks a grave, often bearing an inscription: *a bronze grave marker.*

gra|ve|men|te (grä vā men′tā), *adv. Music.* in a serious manner; gravely (as a direction). [< Italian *gravemente* < *grave;* see etym. at **grave**[5]]

grav|en (grā′vən), *adj., v.* —*adj.* **1** engraved; carved; sculptured: *graven images.* **2** deeply impressed; firmly fixed.
—*v.* graved; a past participle of **grave**[3]: *Figures had been graven in the rock.*

graven image, **1** a statue. **2a** an idol. **b** a false god.

Gra|ven|stein (grav′ən stēn, grä′vən stīn), *n.* a large, yellow apple with red stripes. [< *Gravenstein*, the German name of a town in Holstein, Denmark]

gra|ve|o|lent (grə vē′ə lənt), *adj.* having a strong, unpleasant smell; rank; fetid. [< Latin *graveolēns, -entis* < *grave*, adverb of *gravis* heavy + *olēns, olentis*, present participle of *olēre* to smell]

grav|er (grā′vər), *n.* **1** any one of various tools for cutting and engraving, such as a burin: *The artist uses tools called gravers to cut out his design on a solid block of wood* (Antonio Frasconi). **2** = engraver.

grave robber, a person who robs graves.

graves (grāvz), *n.pl.* = greaves.

Graves (grävz; *French* gräv), *n.pl.* red or white wine made in the Graves district of Bordeaux, France.

Graves' disease (grāvz), exophthalmic goiter. [< Robert J. *Graves*, 1796-1853, an Irish physician, who described it]

grave|side (grāv′sīd′), *n.* the space beside or immediately around a grave.

grave|stone (grāv′stōn′), *n.* a stone that marks a grave; headstone.

gra|vette (grä vet′), *n.*, or **gravette point**, a long, narrow, knife-shaped flint of prehistoric times: *The gravette point ... is a flake having one edge treated with secondary chipping and the other left sharp and untouched* (R. A. S. Macalister). [< (La) *Gravette;* see etym. under **Gravettian**]

Gra|vet|ti|an (grä vet′ē ən), *adj.* of or having to do with the upper part of the paleolithic, characterized by well-developed and delicately worked flint tools. [< (La) *Gravette*, Dordogne, France, where relics were found + *-ian*]

grave|ward (grāv′wərd), *adv., adj.* toward the grave.

grave|yard (grāv′yärd′), *n.* **1** a place for burying the dead; cemetery; burial ground. **2** *Figurative.* a lot, yard, or the like, in which old or useless objects are discarded.

graveyard shift, *Informal.* the working hours between midnight and the morning shift.

grav|id (grav′ĕd), *adj.* **1** = pregnant. **2** *Figurative.* filled; expanded: *The prim, serious young Queen, already gravid with middle-class virtue* (New Yorker). [< obsolete French *gravide* < Latin *gravidus* pregnant, laden, filled < *gravis* heavy] —**grav′id|ly**, *adv.* —**grav′id|ness**, *n.*

gra|vid|i|ty (grə vid′ə tē), *n.* = pregnancy.

gra|vied (grā′vēd), *adj.* served in or with gravy.

gra|vif|ic (grə vif′ik), *adj.* making heavy; producing weight.

grav|i|grade (grav′ə grād), *adj., n.* —*adj.* **1** walking with heavy steps. **2** of or having to do with a group of extinct edentate animals, including the megathere and the mylodon. —*n.* a gravigrade animal. [< New Latin *Gravigrada* the group name < Latin *gravis* heavy + *gradī* to walk]

gra|vim|e|ter (grə vim′ə tər), *n.* **1** any one of several devices for measuring gravity at the earth's surface; gravity meter. **2** a device for measuring specific gravity. [< French *gravimètre* < Latin *gravis* heavy + French *mètre* measure]

grav|i|met|ric (grav′ə met′rik), *adj.* **1** of or having to do with a gravimeter. **2** *Chemistry.* of or having to do with measurement by weight. **3** of or having to do with a method of calculating distances and drawing maps by using gravity measurements. —**grav′i|met′ri|cal|ly**, *adv.*

grav|i|met|ri|cal (grav′ə met′rə kəl), *adj.* = gravimetric.

gra|vim|e|try (grə vim′ə trē), *n.* the measurement of weight; determination of specific gravities.

grav|ing dock (grā′ving), a dry dock used in graving or cleaning the bottoms of ships.

grav|i|sphere (grav′ə sfir′), *n.* the sphere of gravity around a celestial body. [< *gravi*(ty) + *sphere*]

grav|i|tas (grav′ə tas), *n. Latin.* gravity; solemnity: *Like most of the statesmen of yore, he has about him a certain gravitas, expressed in ... a taste for old-fashioned circumlocutions* (Harper's).

grav|i|tate (grav′ə tāt), *v.*, **-tat|ed**, **-tat|ing.** —*v.i.* **1** to move or tend to move toward a body by the force of gravity: *The planets gravitate toward the sun.* **2** to settle down; sink; fall: *The sand and dirt in the water gravitated to the bottom of the bottle.* (*Figurative.*) *The market price ... is continually gravitating* (Adam Smith). **3** *Figurative.* to tend to go; be strongly attracted: *The attention of the audience gravitated to the stage as the lights dimmed.*
—*v.t.* to cause to move downward by the force of gravity. [< New Latin *gravitare* (with English *-ate*[1]), ultimately < Latin *gravis* heavy] —**grav′i|tat′er**, *n.*

grav|i|ta|tion (grav′ə tā′shən), *n.* **1a** the fact that the earth pulls any object toward it and that the sun, moon, stars, and other such bodies in the universe do the same; the force or pull that makes bodies in the universe tend to move toward one another. The fall of bodies to the earth is an instance of gravitation. **b** a moving or tendency to move caused by this force. SYN: attraction, pull. **2** a settling down; sinking; falling. **3** *Figurative.* a natural tendency toward some point or object of influence: *The gravitation of people to the cities leaves many farms vacant.*

grav|i|ta|tion|al (grav′ə tā′shə nəl), *adj.* of or having to do with gravitation: *Newton described the course of gravitational action, but expressly refrained from speculating on its cause* (Observer). —**grav′i|ta′tion|al|ly**, *adv.*

gravitational field, the area about a planet or other heavenly body in which gravitation exerts a force on any object: *It is the Sun's enormous gravitational field that holds all the planets, near and far, circling in their orbits* (Arthur C. Clarke).

gravitational lens, *Astronomy.* a lenslike effect produced by the strong gravitational field of a massive object, such as a galaxy, causing light reflected from a quasar or other very distant object to bend or intensify as it passes through the field: *The twin quasars go beyond this phenomenon in showing that a massive body can act as a gravitational lens, creating multiple images of an object as an optical lens does* (Scientific American).

gravitational pull, the attractive force exerted by a planet or other heavenly body on another object: *The problem of return from a small satellite would be much simpler than return from Mars, because the satellite's gravitational pull is negligible* (Atlantic).

gravitational water, = free water.

gravitational wave, an energy-carrying wave involving gravitational forces; gravity wave.

grav|i|ta|tive (grav′ə tā′tiv), *adj.* **1** of or having to do with gravitation. **2** tending or causing to gravitate.

grav|i|ti|no (grav′ə tē′nō), *n.* a hypothetical elementary particle with a spin of 3/2, postulated in the theory of supergravity: *... the supposedly "basic" building blocks of matter ... gluons that bind them inseparably, leptons, bosons and in one formulation that includes gravity, "gravitinos"* (New York Times). [< *gravit*(on) + *-ino* (as in *neutrino*)]

grav|i|tom|e|ter (grav′ə tom′ə tər), *n.* an instrument for measuring specific gravities.

grav|i|ton (grav′ə ton), *n.* a hypothetical particle constituting a unit of gravitational force: *Other candidates for dark matter include theoretical particles, such as axions, ... gravitons, and quarks* (Stephen S. Murray). [< *gravit*(y) + *-on*]

grav|i|ty (grav′ə tē), *n., pl.* **-ties.** **1a** the natural force that causes objects to move or tend to move toward the center of the earth. Gravity causes objects to have weight. **b** the natural force that makes objects move or tend to move toward each other; gravitation. *Abbr:* g. SYN: attraction, pull. **2** heaviness; weight: *He balanced the long pole at its center of gravity.* **3** *Figurative.* seriousness; solemnity; earnestness: *The gravity of the child playing nurse was amusing in one so small.* SYN: soberness. **4** *Figurative.* serious or critical character; importance: *The gravity of the situation was greatly increased by threats of war.* SYN: significance. **5** lowness of pitch. **6** a measure of the weight of oil at a given temperature. [< Latin *gravitās* < *gravis* heavy]

gravity cell, a kind of electric cell in which the two electrolytes form in layers and do not mingle on account of their different specific gravities. Horizontal electrodes are used.

gravity dam, a dam usually made of concrete or of cut-stone blocks that depends for stability primarily on the weight of materials used in its construction.

grav|i|ty-fed (grav′ə tē fed′), *adj.* supplied by the action of gravity: *a gravity-fed spring or well.*

gravity feed, the act or process of supplying by gravity.

gravity meter, an instrument that measures gravity at the earth's surface, used to locate oil, and in mapping; gravimeter.

gravity railroad, a railroad in which gravity moves cars down an incline.

gravity wave, **1** a wave between air and water or between layers of air, generated by the force of gravity: *The remarkably strong wind fields in the ionosphere ... were probably due largely to the effects of gravity waves, generated in the lower atmosphere, that propagate upwards* (William W. Kellogg). **2** = gravitational wave.

gravity wind, a wind produced by the downward motion of the air; katabatic wind.

gra|vure (grə vyůr′, grā′vyůr), *n.* **1** photogravure or rotogravure. **2** a plate or print produced by either of these processes. [shortened form of *photogravure*]

gra|vy (grā′vē), *n., pl.* **-vies.** **1** the juice that comes out of meat in cooking: *The gravy and fat filled the pan as the meat roasted.* **2** a sauce for meat, potatoes, or other food, made from this juice, usually by thickening it with flour: *When we dumped the flour in, the meat juice turned to lumpy gravy.* **3** *Slang.* easy gain or profit: *Some businesses fail while others get all the gravy.*
[Middle English *grave*, apparently a misreading of Old French *grane* sauce, (originally) properly grained (that is, seasoned) < Latin *grānum* grain, seed]

gravy boat, a small, boat-shaped dish for serving gravy or sauce.

gravy train, *Slang.* something that yields great or easy profits, such as a business boon: *Everybody seems bent on picking up "easy money," getting on the gravy train, getting theirs while the getting is good* (Wall Street Journal).

gray (grā), *n., adj., v.* —*n.* **1** a color made by mixing black and white. **2** a gray pigment or dye. **3** gray cloth or clothing. **4** a gray horse. **5** gray or subdued light: *In the gray of the daybreak* (Longfellow). **6** something gray. **7** person wearing gray. **8** an international unit for measuring absorbed doses of radiation, equal to 1 joule per kilogram. It is intended to replace the rad. *Among the SI's derived units with special names are those for ... absorbed dose of radiation* (*the gray, or joules per kilogram*) (Scientific American).
—*adj.* **1** having a color between black and white: *Ashes, lead, and hair getting white with age are gray.* **2** having gray hair. SYN: grizzled. **3** *Figurative.* old; ancient. SYN: hoary. **4** *Figurative.* dark; gloomy; dismal: *a gray day, a gray existence.* SYN: leaden. **5** *Figurative.* **a** not clearly defined or identified: *a gray area.* **b** less extreme but not fully acceptable or legal: *the gray market.* **6** wearing gray, as the Cistercian monks, and others do.
—*v.t., v.i.* to make gray; become gray: *The decrease in the blood delivered to his head causes first a "graying" of his vision, then total blackness* (Scientific American). Also, *especially British,* **grey**.
[Old English *grǣg*] —**gray′ness**, *n.*

gray area, an area between opposites, neither one thing nor the other, as a question of principle which can be categorized as neither wholly right nor wrong: *Flying saucers are still in the gray area of space phenomena.*

gray|back (grā′bak′), *n.* **1** any one of various animals, such as the gray whale of the northern Pacific, or various birds, such as the knot and the hooded crow. **2** *U.S. Informal.* a Confederate soldier in the Civil War. **3** = body louse.

gray|beard (grā′bird′), *n.* an old man.

gray birch, a birch tree of eastern North America, often reaching a height of 40 feet, having triangular leaves and grayish-white bark. Its wood is used for firewood and in the manufacture of spools, shoe pegs, and wood pulp.

gray body, a body that radiates at every wave length an amount of energy bearing a constant ratio to the amount radiated by a black body at the same temperature.

gray cast iron, = gray iron.

gray-cheeked thrush (grā′chēkt′), a grayish-brown thrush of eastern and northern North America, very similar to the olive-backed thrush but having grayish cheeks and no eye ring.

gray cloth, = gray goods.

Pronunciation Key: hat, āge, cãre, fär; let, ēqual, tėrm; it, īce; hot, ōpen, ôrder; **oi**l, **ou**t; cup, půt, rüle; **ch**ild; lo**ng**; **th**in; **ᴛʜ**en; **zh**, measure; ə represents **a** in about, **e** in taken, **i** in pencil, **o** in lemon, **u** in circus.

gray-col|lar (grā′kol′ər), *adj. U.S.* of or having to do with workers who perform technical services of repair or maintenance. [patterned on *blue-collar* and *white-collar*]

gray duck, any one of certain ducks whose young or females have grayish feathers, such as the gadwalls and pintails.

gray eminence, a person who wields power or exerts influence privately or secretly; powerful person behind the scenes; éminence grise.

gray-faced (grā′fāst′), *adj.* having or showing a pale, wearied face or facial expression.

gray|fish (grā′fish′), *n., pl.* **-fish|es** or (*collectively*) **-fish**. = dogfish.

gray-flan|nel (grā′flan′əl), *adj. U.S. Informal.* of or having to do with the world of company executives; belonging to or characteristic of organization men: *He is impatient with the ... orthodoxy and gray-flannel conformity that stifle so much originality in ... thinking* (Atlanta Constitution). [suggested by *The Man in the Gray Flannel Suit* (1955), a novel by Sloan Wilson]

gray-flan|neled (grā′flan′əld), *adj.* gray-flannel: *gray-flanneled success in the office cells of New York* (Sports Illustrated).

gray fox, a fox of North and Central America with grayish upper parts and reddish brown and white under parts.

Gray Friar or **gray friar**, a member of the Friars Minor; Franciscan friar.

gray ghost, = Weimaraner. [so called from its color and its silent movements when hunting]

gray goods, unbleached, undyed, and generally unfinished fabrics; greige.

gray goose, = graylag.

gray gum, any one of several varieties of eucalyptus.

gray-head|ed (grā′hed′id), *adj.* having gray hair.

gray-headed junco, a dark gray junco with a white belly, found in the higher mountains of Nevada, Utah, and Colorado.

gray hen, the female of the black grouse.

gray|hound (grā′hound′), *n.* = greyhound.

gray iron, a slightly malleable, grayish cast iron used in such manufacture as automobiles and radiators: *Gray iron is by far the leading variety of cast metal* (Wall Street Journal).

gray|ish (grā′ish), *adj.* somewhat gray.

Gray Lady, *pl.* **Gray Ladies**. a woman Red Cross volunteer in a hospital.

gray|lag (grā′lag′), *n.* a wild gray goose that is common in Europe. [< *gray* + *lag* the last (because they migrate south very late)]

gray|ling (grā′ling), *n.* **1** a freshwater fish of northern regions, related to the trout but having a longer and higher dorsal fin; umber. It is much valued as a food and game fish. **2** a gray-and-brown butterfly.

gray list, a list of persons, firms, or groups that are considered undesirable, but less undesirable than those on a blacklist.

gray|ly (grā′lē), *adv.* with a gray hue or tinge.

gray|mail (grā′māl′), *n. U.S.* a threat of possible public exposure of government secrets during prosecution in a trial: *Secret proceedings would not eliminate graymail. But the procedure would let all parties know where they stand and reduce the number of cases that cannot be prosecuted* (New York Times). [< *gray* + (black)*mail*]

gray manganese oxide, = manganite.

gray market, **1** the buying and selling of scarce products, usually secretly, but without explicit violation of law, at prices considered exorbitant: *The continued squeeze on metal supplies is keeping alive a gray market in steel obtained from various sources outside normal supply channels at prices that occasionally triple mill quotes* (Wall Street Journal). **2a** a source of supply for, or the scene of, such transactions. **b** the goods themselves.

gray marketeer, a person who transacts business on the gray market.

gray matter, **1** the grayish nerve tissue in the brain and spinal cord that contains nerve cells and some nerve fibers. **2** *Informal, Figurative.* intelligence; brains.

gray mullet, any one of a family of bluish-silver food fishes found in salt and fresh water.

gray nurse, an Australian shark about 15 feet long, with sharp teeth, thought to attack people.

gray|out (grā′out′), *n. Aeronautics.* a temporary condition of dim or hazy vision caused by a deficiency of oxygen.

Gray Panther, *U.S.* a member of an organization for promoting the interests of elderly people: *the Gray Panthers worked to influence local and state governments, social agencies, and business concerns* (Robert J. Havighurst).

gray shark, any one of certain sharks inhabiting warm coastal waters; ground shark.

Gray's Inn (grāz), one of four legal societies (Inns of Court) that determine who may practice law in English courts.

gray squirrel, a large, gray squirrel of the forests of the United States. See the picture under **squirrel**.

gray trout, = lake trout.

gray|wacke (grā′wak′, -wak′ə), *n. Geology.* a conglomerate of rounded pebbles and sand, derived chiefly from basic igneous rocks. [< German *Grauwacke* < *grau* gray + *Wacke* kind of rock; (originally) gravel]

gray|wat|er (grā′wôt′ər, -wot′-), *n.* wastewater, such as that from a sink, bathtub, or washing machine, that does not drain from a toilet or other heavily contaminating source of pollution: *In most countries, graywater simply goes into the backyard. Open ditches direct the water to trees or crops that need watering* (Peter Warshall).

gray whale, a grayish-black baleen whale of medium size found off the Pacific Coast of North America.

gray wolf, a large, gray, black, or white wolf of northern regions reaching a weight of over 180 pounds; timber wolf. It is rare over most of its former range, and in the United States is found only in several isolated areas.

graze[1] (grāz), *v.,* **grazed, graz|ing**, *n.* **—*v.i.*** **1** to feed on growing grass and other herbage. Cattle, sheep, and horses graze. *Cattle were grazing in the field. The ... horses were turned out to graze* (Washington Irving). **2** to pasture cattle, sheep, or other farm animals.

—*v.t.* **1** to put (cattle, sheep, or other farm animals) to feed on growing grass or a pasture: *The farmer grazed his sheep. Participating farmers would be forbidden even to graze cattle on any land put in the "acreage reserve"* (Newsweek). **2** to tend or look after (cattle, sheep, or other farm animals) while they are grazing: *When Jacob grazed his Uncle Laban's sheep* (Shakespeare). **3** to put cattle to feed on (grass or land): *You may graze the ground, when the trees are grown up* (Samuel Johnson). **4** *Archaic.* to feed on or eat (growing grass or herbage): *Flocks Grazing the tender herb* (Milton).

—*n.* the act of grazing or feeding on grass.

[Old English *grasian* < unrecorded *gras;* later *græs* grass] **—graz′a|ble, graze′a|ble**, *adj.* **—graz′er**, *n.*

graze[2] (grāz), *v.,* **grazed, graz|ing**, *n.* **—*v.t.*** **1** to touch lightly in passing; rub lightly: *The car grazed the garage door.* **SYN:** brush. **2** to scrape the skin from: *The bullet grazed his shoulder.* **SYN:** abrade. **—*v.i.*** to touch or rub something lightly in passing.

—*n.* **1** the act of grazing. **2** a slight wound made by grazing.

[origin uncertain] **—graz′er**, *n.* **—graz′ing|ly**, *adv.*

gra|zie (grä′tsyä), *interj. Italian.* thank you.

gra|zier (grā′zhər), *n.* a person who grazes or feeds cattle to sell them.

graz|ing (grā′zing), *n.* growing grass that cattle, sheep, or other animals feed on; pasture.

grazing land, land suitable for the grazing of livestock.

gra|zio|so (grä tsyō′sō), *adj. Music.* graceful (as a direction). [< Italian *grazioso* < Latin *grātiōsus;* see etym. under **gracious**]

Gr. Br. or **Gr. Brit.**, Great Britain.

grease (*n.* grēs; *v.* grēs, grēz), *n., v.,* **greased, greas|ing**. **—*n.*** **1** soft animal fat, melted or rendered: *bear's grease, goose grease.* **2** any thick, oily substance, used as a lubricant: *He spread thick grease over the axle of the wagon wheel after repairing it.* **3a** shorn, uncleaned wool. **b** the oily matter in wool. **4** (in hunting) the fat or fatness of game, with reference to the best time or season for killing. **5** *Slang.* a bribe or tip: *The garbage could not be carted without paying grease* (New York Post). **6** = grease-heels.

—*v.t.* **1a** to smear with grease; rub grease on: *to grease a turkey for roasting. The teacher explained that many Indians greased their bodies.* **b** to soil with grease. **2** to put grease in or on; cause to run smoothly by greasing; lubricate: *Please grease my car.* **3** *Slang, Figurative.* to give money to as a bribe or tip: *"It's an interesting gangster movie, only in real life, a gangster would grease a dick a little instead of letting himself be run out of town"* (James T. Farrell). **4** to cause (a horse) to become affected with grease-heels.

grease the palm of. See under **palm**[1].

in grease, fat and fit for killing: *boar and hare in grease.*

in the grease, that has not been cleansed after shearing: *Merino wools in the grease.*

[< Old French *graisse* < Vulgar Latin *crassia* < Latin *crassus* fat, crass] **—grease′less**, *adj.*

grease|ball (grēs′bôl′), *n. U.S. Slang.* a foreigner or foreign-looking person, especially one with swarthy skin (used in an unfriendly way).

grease|bush (grēs′bu̇sh′), *n.* = greasewood.

grease cup, a small cup, usually with a screw top, fastened on machinery to supply grease to parts that need it, usually placed just above a bearing. A turn or two of the top forces grease down.

grease gun, a tubelike device with a handle and piston, used to force grease into bearings on automobiles, machinery, etc.

grease-heels (grēs′hēlz′), *n.* an inflammation of a horse's skin on or below the fetlocks, accompanied by an oily secretion.

grease monkey, *Slang.* an automobile or airplane mechanic.

grease paint, **1** a mixture of tallow or hard grease and a pigment, used by actors in painting their faces. **2** any makeup used by actors.

grease pencil, a drawing pencil having a core of grease and pigment enclosed in paper: *She outlined her eyes with black grease pencil* (Harper's).

grease|proof (grēs′prüf′), *adj.* that will not absorb grease.

greas|er (grē′sər, -zər), *n.* **1** a person or thing that greases. **2** *Informal.* a cackling goose. **3** *U.S. Slang.* **a** a foreigner; greaseball (used in an unfriendly way). **b** a hot-rodder. **4** *Slang.* an obnoxious person. **5** *British.* a ship's engineer.

grease table, a set of three sloping aluminum steps covered with grease for sifting out mined diamonds from other stones. A concentrate of stones is washed down the steps by a stream of water and the diamonds adhere to the grease.

grease|wood (grēs′wu̇d′), *n.* **1** a stiff, prickly shrub of the goosefoot family with narrow leaves, growing in alkaline regions in the western United States and Canada; chico. It is valuable cattle and sheep food, and also contains some oil and is used for fuel. **2** any one of various similar shrubs.

greas|y (grē′sē, -zē), *adj.,* **greas|i|er, greas|i|est**. **1** having grease on it; smeared, covered, or soiled with grease: *The automobile mechanic took off his greasy coveralls.* **2** containing much grease or fat: *Greasy food is hard to digest.* **3** like grease; smooth and slippery: *Some coins have a greasy feel to them.* **4** *Figurative.* disagreeably unctuous; oily. **5** (of a horse) having grease-heels. **—greas′i|ly**, *adv.* **—greas′i|ness**, *n.*

greasy spoon, *Especially U.S. Slang.* a cheap, unsanitary restaurant: *Julie, working at Barona's dingy little greasy spoon ... dishing up chow for small-town customers* (Canadian Forum).

great (grāt), *adj., adv., n.* **—*adj.*** **1** big; large in extent, amount, size, or number: *a great house, a great crowd.* **2** more than usual; much: *great pain, great kindness, great ignorance, a great rise in temperature.* **3** loud: *a great noise.* **4** important; high in rank; remarkable; famous: *a great singer, a great event, a great picture, a great achievement.* **SYN:** renowned, eminent, distinguished. **5** most important; main; chief: *the great seal, the great attraction.* **6** noble; generous: *a great heart, great deeds.* **SYN:** magnanimous. **7** much in use; favorite: *His great sport was fishing. That is a great habit of his.* **8** very much of a: *a great talker.* **9** *Informal.* very good; fine: *We had a great time at the party.* **SYN:** first-rate, excellent. **10** *Informal.* skillful; expert: *to be great at mathematics. She is great at skiing.* **11** (in names of relationship) of the next generation before or after: *a great-grandmother, great-grandson.* **12** that is distinguished by its large size from other plants or animals of the same genus. **13** *Archaic or Dialect.* pregnant.

—*adv.* *Informal.* very well: *You're doing great. Things are going great with her. I'm feeling great.*

—*n.* *Informal.* a great person; person who is famous or important: *... England's Peter Radford, another great who shares the official world record for the 220 yards* (Maclean's).

by the great, *Dialect.* (of work done) at a fixed price for the whole amount; by the piece: *A merchant ... sells commodities of good cheer by the great* (Thomas Nashe).

greats, *British Informal.* at Oxford University: **a** the course in the classics or humanities. **b** Also, formerly, **great go**. the final examination for the degree of Bachelor of Arts, now especially, for honors in the classics or humanities.

the greats (or **great**), great or distinguished people; celebrities: *All the greats of show business have appeared at the Palace. He belongs among the great of his generation.*

[Old English *grēat*]

—*Syn.* *adj.* **1, 2 Great, large, big** mean above average in size or measure. **Great** applies particularly to size and degree: *We saw the great redwoods* (size). *They are trees of great age* (degree). **Large** applies particularly to size and quantity but not to degree: *We saw many large trees.* **Big** applies particularly to size and weight: *A redwood is a big tree, very heavy and thick.*

great anteater, = ant bear.

great ape, any anthropoid ape: *The living great apes* (*the gorilla, chimpanzee, and orangutan*) *are assigned, with their ancestors, to the family*

Pongidae (Ian Tattersall).

great auk, a large, black-and-white, flightless sea bird formerly of North Atlantic shores, now extinct; garefowl.

great-aunt (grāt′ant′, -änt′), *n.* an aunt of a person's father or mother; grandaunt. See diagram under **family tree**.

Great Awakening, a series of religious revivals among Protestants in the American Colonies, especially in New England during the 1700's, that had a strong influence on American religious life.

great barracuda, a large barracuda found mainly in the West Indies and off the coasts of the southeastern United States and Brazil.

Great Bear, the northern constellation Ursa Major, containing the seven bright stars forming the Big Dipper.

great bird of paradise, a bird of paradise about the size of a crow. The male has an emerald-green forehead and throat, a golden-yellow head, maroon wings and tail, and a dense mass of plumes about two feet long that springs from under the wings.

great black-backed gull, a very large gull with black wings and back, found along the Atlantic Coast.

great blue heron, a large, slate-colored American heron, standing about four feet tall, and found as far north as Canada.

great calorie, = large calorie.

★great circle, **1** any circle on the surface of a sphere having its plane passing through the center of the sphere. The equator is one of the great circles of the earth. **2** an arc of such a circle; the line of shortest distance between two points on the earth's surface.

★great circle
definitions 1, 2

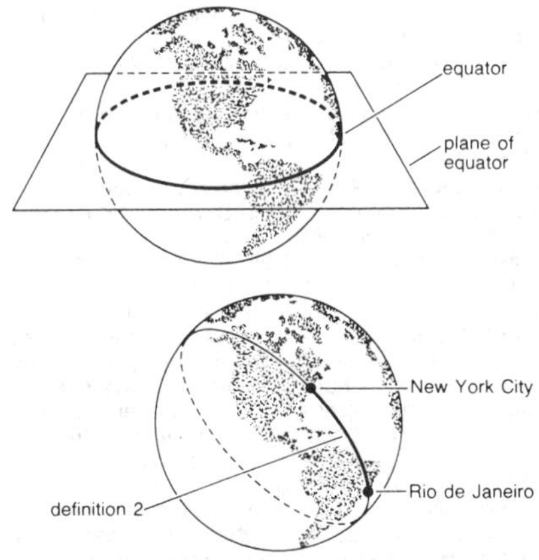

great-cir|cle route (grāt′sėr′kəl), the shortest, most direct route between two points on the earth's surface, by traveling along a great circle of the earth.

great-circle sailing, sailing on a course along a great circle of the earth, the shortest route.

great|coat (grāt′kōt′), *n.* a heavy overcoat.

great commoner, a nickname applied to various British and American political leaders for their championship of the rights of the common man, including the first William Pitt, William E. Gladstone, William Jennings Bryan, and Thaddeus Stevens.

great council, **1** in English history: **a** an assembly under the Norman kings of chief tenants and prelates, out of which the House of Lords evolved. **b** a general assembly of the barons or peers of later times. **2** a national assembly of certain countries, such as the Cortes of Spain or Portugal. **3** *U.S.* a deliberative body composed of Indian chiefs or leaders.

great crested flycatcher, the crested flycatcher of North and Central America.

great crested grebe, an old-world grebe with a dark crown, pink bill, and conspicuous black tufts on the sides of the head. It is the largest grebe.

Great Dane, any one of a breed of very large, powerful, short-haired dogs.

Great Dipper, = Big Dipper.

Great Divide, **1** the great ridge of the Rocky Mountains in North America; the Continental Divide. **2** Often, **great divide**. **a** any divide; watershed. **b** *Figurative.* a main dividing line: *On Great Heron, the great divide is not between rich and poor; there are no poor* (Time).

cross the Great Divide, *U.S. Informal.* to die: *I am still residing in Portland, Oregon, ... where I hope to remain until I cross the Great Divide* (Harry Young).

Great Dog, = Canis Major.

great|en (grā′tən), *Archaic.* —*v.t.* to make great or greater; increase; enlarge: *everything concurred to greaten the fire* (Samuel Pepys).
—*v.i.* to become great or greater: *Life greatens in these later years* (John Greenleaf Whittier).

Great English Vowel Shift, = Great Vowel Shift.

Great Ennead, a family of nine gods of ancient Egypt, consisting of Atum, Geb, Isis, Nephthys, Nut, Osiris, Set, Shu, and Tefnut.

great|er (grā′tər), *adj.* constituting the city and its immediate surrounding areas; metropolitan: *Motorists living in the Greater London area were on the roads early in the morning bound for the seaside or the country* (London Times).

greater Bairam, a Moslem festival lasting four days, celebrated 70 days after the lesser Bairam with animal sacrifices and the distribution of the meat to the poor; Great Festival.

greater orders, = holy orders.

greater prairie chicken, a variety of grouse about 18 inches long, with yellowish-brown and white feathers above, crossed with black bars, and white-and-brown barred feathers below. It lives from Michigan and Indiana westward to the Great Plains.

greater scaup duck, a freshwater diving duck of North America, about 20 inches long. The males have glossy black foreparts that give off a greenish luster, and the remaining parts are white marked with black.

greater shearwater, a dark-brown shearwater that lives in the Atlantic Ocean from near the Arctic Circle to southern South America and South Africa.

greater yellowlegs, the larger one of the two North American species of yellowlegs, having a length of about 15 inches.

great|est common divisor (grā′tist), the largest number or quantity that will divide two or more others without a remainder: *The greatest common divisor of 24 and 30 is 6. Abbr:* G.C.D.

Great Festival, = greater Bairam.

great go, *British.* greats (def. b.) See under **great**.

great-grand|child (grāt′grand′chīld′), *n., pl.* **-chil|dren.** a child of one's grandchild; grandchild of one's son or daughter.

great-grand|daugh|ter (grāt′gran′dô′tər), *n.* a daughter of one's grandchild; granddaughter of one's son or daughter.

great-grand|fa|ther (grāt′grand′fä′ᴛʜər), *n.* a father of one's grandparent; grandfather of one's father or mother. See diagram under **family tree**.

great-grand|moth|er (grāt′grand′muᴛʜ′ər), *n.* a mother of a grandparent; grandmother of one's father or mother. See diagram under **family tree**.

great-grand|par|ent (grāt′grand′pãr′ənt), *n.* a great-grandfather or great-grandmother; grandfather or grandmother of one's mother or father.

great-grand|son (grāt′grand′sun′), *n.* a son of one's grandson or granddaughter; grandson of one's son or daughter.

great gray owl, a very large, grayish-brown owl of northern North America, measuring 30 inches in length.

great grey kangaroo, = giant kangaroo.

great gross, twelve gross; 144 dozen; 1,728.

great gun, *U.S. Slang.* an important person; big gun.

go great guns, to move vigorously ahead; advance at full speed: *We're going great guns now and would be well ahead of a year ago except for ... a later Labor Day* (Wall Street Journal).

great-heart|ed (grāt′här′tid), *adj.* **1** noble; generous; magnanimous. **2** brave; fearless. SYN: courageous. **3** *Obsolete.* high-spirited; proud. —**great′-heart′ed|ly**, *adv.* —**great′-heart′ed|ness**, *n.*

great horned owl, a large North American owl that has two hornlike tufts of feathers on its head. See picture under **owl**.

Great Hunter, the constellation Orion.

Great Interglacial, the period between the second (Mindel) and third (Riss) glaciations of the Pleistocene in Europe. It lasted about 90,000 years.

great kangaroo, any one of the largest variety of kangaroo, having a yellowish brown body, darker above and lighter below, sometimes reaching a height of seven feet and weighing 200 pounds.

great laurel, = great rhododendron.

Great Leap Forward, a large-scale economic program of rural collectivization and rapid industrialization instituted in China by Mao Tsetung between 1958 and 1961.

great lobelia, a strong, weedlike perennial of the lobelia family, found from Maine to Louisiana, growing to a height of about two feet and having deep-blue or purplish flowers.

great|ly (grāt′lē), *adv.* **1** in a great manner: *Solomon ruled greatly and wisely.* **2** much: *greatly feared. He greatly desired to be rich.*

great mogul, **1** the ruler of a former empire in India with its capital at Delhi. **2** a great or important person.

great-neph|ew (grāt′nef′yü; *especially British* grāt′nev′yü), *n.* a son of one's nephew or niece; grandnephew.

great|ness (grāt′nis), *n.* **1** the condition or quality of being great; bigness. **2** high place or power. **3** great mind or character.

great nettle, = stinging nettle.

great-niece (grāt′nēs′), *n.* a daughter of one's nephew or niece; grandniece.

great northern diver, the common loon; embergoose.

great omentum, a double fold of peritoneum which extends from the stomach to the small intestines and then back to the transverse colon, serving to support the intestines; epiploon.

great organ, **1** the section of a pipe organ that has the largest pipes. **2** the manual for this section.

great pompano, = permit².

Great Power or **great power**, a nation that has the strength to play a decisive role in any conflict for power among the nations with which it is involved. The United States and the Soviet Union are considered Great Powers.

great primer, a size of type (18 point).

great purple hairstreak, a variety of hairstreak having blue-green wings, each ending in two, small, taillike appendages.

Great Pyr|e|nees (pir′ə nēz), a large, white sheep dog developed in the Pyrenees Mountains that stands 27 to 32 inches high and weighs up to 125 pounds.

great ragweed, = giant ragweed.

Great Rebellion, (in English history) the civil war of 1642-1649.

great rhododendron, a tall rhododendron of the eastern United States, with white or rose-colored flowers; the great laurel. It is the state flower of West Virginia.

great room, *U.S.* a large living area in a house that serves as a living room, dining room, family room, sitting room, and sometimes as a kitchen: *for making downsized homes seem larger ... eliminate the walls ... to form what many architects and builders call a "great room"* (New York Times).

Great Russian, **1** a member of a group of Slavic people living in the central part of the Soviet Union in Europe. **2** the Russian language. **3** of or having to do with Great Russians or their language.

greats (grāts), *n.pl.* See under **great**.

Great Sanhedrin, Sanhedrin (def. 1).

great seal, the most important seal of a country or state, stamped on official documents as proof of their approval by the government.

Great Seal, *Obsolete.* (in Great Britain) the Keeper of the Great Seal, now combined with the office of Lord Chancellor.

great skua, a large, rapacious skua found chiefly in the Southern Hemisphere.

Great Society, **1** the domestic policies and programs advocated by President Lyndon B. Johnson. **2** the administration of Lyndon B. Johnson.

Great Spirit, the chief god worshiped by certain tribes or groups of North American Indians.

great spotted woodpecker, a common woodpecker of Europe and Asia Minor, having plumage similar to the hairy woodpecker of North America.

great tit, a large Eurasian and African titmouse with a black head and chest, white cheeks, and yellow underparts.

great-un|cle (grāt′ung′kəl), *n.* an uncle of one's father or mother; granduncle.

Great Vowel Shift, a series of sound changes which occurred in Middle English vowels, resulting in the vowel system of Modern English. The Middle English long vowels ā, ō, and ä shifted upwards and became ē, ü, and ā; the two highest Middle English vowels, ē and ü, became diphthongized to ī and ou.

Great Wall of China, a huge stone wall about 2150 miles long near the boundary between China and Mongolia; Chinese Wall. It was begun in the 200's B.C. for the defense of China against attack by nomads from the north.

Great War, first World War, from 1914 to 1918.

Great Week, Holy Week; the week before Easter (the name used in the Greek Church).

Great White Father, *U.S. Informal.* **1** the President of the United States. **2** any person who occupies an important or commanding position.

great white heron, **1** a large white heron with yellowish legs, found in southern Florida. **2** a

Pronunciation Key: **h**a**t**, **ā**ge, **c**ã**re**, **f**ä**r**; **l**e**t**, **ē**qual, **t**ė**rm**; **i**t, **ī**ce; **h**o**t**, **ō**pen, **ô**rder; **oi**l, **ou**t; **c**u**p**, **p**u̇**t**, **r**ü**le**; **ch**ild; lo**ng**; **th**in; **ᴛʜ**en; **zh**, measure;
ə represents **a** in about, **e** in taken, **i** in pencil, **o** in lemon, **u** in circus.

cosmopolitan egret of tropical regions.

great white shark, = carcharodon.

great white trillium, a perennial trillium of eastern and central North America; large-flowered trillium. Its flowers have white petals which turn pale pink or rose.

Great White Way, the brightly lighted theater district along Broadway, in the Times Square area of New York City.

great willow herb, = willow herb.

great year, *Astronomy.* the period of a revolution of the equinoctial points, about 25,800 years; Platonic year.

greave (grēv), *n.* Often, **greaves**. armor for the leg below the knee; jambeau. See picture under **armor**. [< Old French *greves,* plural, perhaps < a Germanic word]

greaves (grēvz), *n.pl.* the fibrous matter of skin found in animal fat, that forms a sediment on melting and is pressed into cakes to serve especially as meat for dogs or hogs and as fish bait; refuse of tallow; cracklings. [apparently < Low German *greven,* plural; compare Old English *-grēofa* residue of an oily substance, as in *elegrē ofa* tinder made of olive pressings]

grebe (grēb), *n.* any one of the ducklike diving birds comprising a family related to the loons, having a short, flattened body, feet not completely webbed, a pointed bill, and short wings and tail, such as the eared grebe and the piedbilled grebe of America, and the little grebe of Europe. Its breast feathers are used to trim millinery. [< French *grèbe*]

Gre|cian (grē′shən), *adj., n.* **—*adj.*** = Greek. **—*n.*** **1** = Greek. **2** a person who is thoroughly familiar with the Greek language or literature; Hellenist.

Gre|cian|ize (grē′shə nīz), *v.t.,* **-ized, -iz|ing.** to make Grecian; Grecize.

***Grecian nose**, a straight nose; nose that does not curve inward at the forehead.

***Grecian nose**

Grecian stock, a small, branching, annual plant of southern Europe, bearing fragrant purple flowers which open at evening; evening stock.

Gre|cism (grē′siz əm), *n.* **1a** the spirit or style characteristic of Greek thought and art. **b** adoption or imitation of these. **c** an instance of this. **2** an idiom or peculiarity of the Greek language. Also, **Graecism**.

Gre|cize (grē′sīz), *v.,* **-cized, -ciz|ing.** **—*v.t.*** **1** to give Greek characteristics to. **2** to translate into Greek.
—*v.i.* to conform to what is Greek; adopt Greek speech, idioms, and customs. Also **Graecize**.
[< Greek *graikízein* (literally) speak Greek < *Graikós* Greek]

Greco-, *combining form.* **1** Greece; Greek things: *Grecophile = a lover of Greece or Greek things.* **2** Greek and ____: *Greco-Roman = Greek and Roman.* [< Latin *Graeco-* < Greek *Graikós* a Greek]

Gre|co|ma|ni|a (grē′kə mā′nē ə), *n.* an unusual fondness for Greek things.

Gre|co|ma|ni|ac (grē′kə mā′nē ak), *n.* a person who has an unusual fondness for Greek things.

Gre|co|phil (grē′kə fil), *n.* = Grecophile.

Gre|co|phile (grē′kō fīl, -fil), *n.* a lover of Greece or Greek things.

Gre|co-Ro|man (grē′kō rō′mən), *adj., n.* **—*adj.*** **1** Greek and Roman, especially in style or influence: *Greco-Roman monuments, Greco-Roman art.* **2** of or having to do with a style of wrestling in which a wrestler may not grasp an opponent's legs or use any hold below the waist and may use the legs only for support and not to hook, trip, or lift an opponent.

gree[1] (grē), *n.* **1** *Scottish.* **a** a preeminence; superiority; mastery; victory in battle. **b** the prize for a victory. **2** = degree. [< Old French *gre* < Latin *gradus, -ūs* pace, step]

gree[2] (grē), *n. Obsolete.* **1** favor or good will: **2** satisfaction, as for an injury done. [< Old French *gre,* earlier *gret* < Latin *grātum,* neuter of *grātus* pleasing, thankful]

gree[3] (grē), *v.i., v.t.,* **greed, gree|ing.** *Dialect.* to agree.

greed (grēd), *n.* the quality of wanting more than one's share; greedy behavior; greedy desire: *a miser's greed for money.* SYN: avidity, avarice, cupidity, covetousness. [back formation < *greedy*]

greed|y (grē′dē), *adj.,* **greed|i|er, greed|i|est.** **1** wanting to get more than one's share; eager for gain or wealth. SYN: avaricious, covetous, rapacious. **2** having a very great desire to possess something. **3** wanting to get a great deal. **4** wanting to eat or drink a great deal in a hurry; piggish: *I am not hungry; but thank goodness I'm greedy* (Punch). SYN: ravenous, voracious, gluttonous. [Old English *grǣdig*] **—greed′i|ly,** *adv.* **—greed′i|ness,** *n.*

gree|gree (grē′grē), *n.* an African charm, amulet, or fetish. Also, **grigri, gris-gris**. [alteration of Louisiana French *gris-gris* < a native name in western Africa]

Greek (grēk), *adj., n.* **—*adj.*** **1** of Greece, its people, or their language. **2** of or having to do with the Greek Church.
[< noun]
—*n.* **1a** a person born or living in Greece. **b** any person who used the ancient Greek language. **2a** the language of Greece, or a particular dialect or form of it. Greek is one of the oldest Indo-European languages spoken today. Classical Greek was the language until about 200 A.D.; Modern Greek is the language that began to take shape about 1500. **b** the group of dialects that constitute, with Greek, the Hellenic branch of Indo-European. **3** a member of the Greek Church. **4** a member of a school or college fraternity, identified by its Greek letters. **5** *Archaic.* a merry fellow; boon companion. **6** a cunning or wily person; swindler (used in an unfriendly way).
it's Greek to me, I can't understand it: *I have trouble with algebra; it's Greek to me.*
[< Latin *Graecus* < Greek *Graikós* a Greek]
—Greek′ness, *n.*

Greek Catholic, **1** a member of the Greek Orthodox Church. **2** a Byzantine or Greek acknowledging papal supremacy and adhering to Roman Catholic faith and doctrine, but differing especially in rites and ceremonies; Uniat.

Greek Church, = Greek Orthodox Church.

Greek cross, a cross whose four arms are of the same length and form right angles. See the diagram under **cross**.

Greek fire, a substance easily set on fire whose flames could not be put out by water; wildfire. It was used in warfare in ancient and medieval times.

Greek|ish (grē′kish), *adj.* **1** like what is Greek; after the Greek type. **2** *Archaic.* Greek or Grecian.

Greek Orthodox, of or having to do with the Greek Orthodox Church.

Greek Orthodox Church, **1** the Christian church of the countries in communion or doctrinal agreement with the patriarchs of Constantinople (Istanbul), Alexandria, Antioch, and Jerusalem; Eastern Church. **2** the part of this church forming the established church in Greece.

Greek Revival, a style of architecture and furnishings widespread during the first half of the 1800's, imitating classical Greek style and motifs.

Greek rite, the Eucharist, Mass, or other ceremony, as used in the Greek Orthodox Church or the Uniat churches.

Greek tortoise, a land turtle of the Old World.

green (grēn), *n., adj., v.* **—*n.*** **1** the color of most growing plants, grass, and the leaves of trees in summer; color in the spectrum between yellow and blue. It is one of the psychological primary colors. **2** green pigment or dye. **3** green cloth or clothing. **4** ground covered with grass; grassy land. **5** a piece of grassy land in a village or town, belonging to the community; village common. **6a** a putting green on a golf course. See picture under **golf course**. **b** a golf course. **7** Usually, **Green**. a politician or group dedicated to preserving the environment: *The Greens had pledged "to launch an all-out attack on the ongoing devastation of the environment"* (Kenneth Brown).
—*adj.* **1** having the color green: *green paint. Emerald is green.* **2** covered with growing plants, grass, or leaves: *green fields.* SYN: verdant. **3** characterized by growing grass; mild; temperate: *a green winter. A green Christmas is neither handsome nor healthful* (Thomas Fuller). **4a** not ripe; not fully grown: *Most green fruit is not good to eat.* SYN: immature, unripe. **b** consisting of leafy parts that have been exposed to sunlight as vegetables. **5** not dried, cured, seasoned, or otherwise prepared for use: *green tobacco, green lumber, green bacon or ham.* **6** *Figurative.* not trained or experienced; not mature in age or judgment: *a green crew on a ship. He was green compared with the other, more experienced, apprentices in the business.* SYN: inexperienced, untrained, unsophisticated, callow. **7** *Figurative.* easily fooled; easy to trick or cheat. SYN: naive, simple, gullible. **8** *Figurative.* full of life and strength: *green old age.* SYN: flourishing. **9** *Figurative.* recent; fresh; new: *a green wound.* **10** *Figurative.* having a pale, sickly color because of fear, jealousy, or sickness: *to turn green with envy.* **11a** (of meat) raw or underdone. **b** (of clay, bricks, pottery, and the like) not dried or fired. **12** concerned with the environment; promoting conservation of the environment: *[Prime Minister] Thatcher has turned "green" this year, as she sensed growing public concern over the [environmental] issue* (Washington Post).
—*v.i., v.t.* to make or become green: *Spring came again greening the hawthorn buds* (John Masefield).
greens, a freshly cut green leaves and branches used for decoration: *A triumphal arch, adorned with greens and flowers* (London Gazette). **b** the leaves and stems of plants used for food: *beet greens, dandelion greens, salad greens.*
the Green, the national color of the Irish Republic: *the wearing of the Green.*
[Old English *grēne*] **—green′ness,** *n.*

green algae, a class of bright grass-green algae living mainly in fresh water. Green algae have definite nuclei and chloroplasts.

green almond, = pistachio.

green|back (grēn′bak′), *n.* **1** a piece of United States paper money, especially a legal-tender note, having the back printed in green. Greenbacks were originally issued in 1861 without any gold or silver reserve behind them. *Since most dealers haven't enough greenbacks to shell out for big shipments of cars, they have to get temporary loans* (Wall Street Journal). **2** any one of various animals, such as the American golden plover, or a European garfish.

Green|back|er (grēn′bak′ər), *n. U.S.* a member of the Greenback Party.

Green|back|ism (grēn′bak′iz əm), *n.* the policies advocated by the Greenback Party.

Greenback Party, a former political party in the United States that wanted to make greenbacks the only paper currency.

green bean, the edible green pod of some kidney beans.

green|belt (grēn′belt′), *n.* a section partially or completely surrounding a town or a city with trees, parks, and the like, in which building is restricted or prohibited: *The family lives in a good-looking modern apartment in the outer greenbelt of the city* (Atlantic). **1** = green belt.

green belt, trees and shrubs planted around an area of little rainfall to protect it from becoming desert land.

green beret or **Green Beret**, **1** a member of the Special Forces of the U.S. Army. **2** the beret worn by members of the Special Forces.

green|bot|tle (grēn′bot′əl), *n.,* or **greenbottle fly**, **1** a blowfly having a lustrous green body. **2** any one of various allied or similar flies.

green|bri|er (grēn′brī′ər), *n.* **1** any one of a large genus of woody vines of the lily family with prickly stems, umbrella-shaped clusters of flowers, and blackish or red berries; smilax; cat brier; horse brier. **2** a climbing vine of this genus with thick green leaves and small greenish flowers, grown in the eastern United States.

green|bug (grēn′bug), *n.* a small, green aphid that is very destructive to wheat and other grains.

green card, **1** *U.S.* a green-colored permit which allows Mexican and other foreign workers to cross the Mexican border into the United States to work: **2** *British.* a green-colored insurance document covering motorists against accidents in foreign countries.

green-card|er (grēn′kär′dər), *n. U.S.* a Mexican or other foreign worker who holds a permit to work in the United States.

green chain, a conveyor belt in a lumber mill that moves boards from the trimmer to a shed where workmen can grade them.

green cod, = cultus (cod).

green consuming, the use of products that do not damage the environment: *Although "green consuming" in the supermarket has largely been a matter of what to avoid rather than what to buy this is changing* (Philadelphia Inquirer). **—green consumer.**

green corn, Indian corn, especially the ears in the tender, milky stage; sweet corn; roasting ears. It is eaten as a vegetable.

green crab, a greenish-yellow crab of Europe and the Atlantic Coast of America; shore crab.

green currency, any of various artificial rates of exchange, such as the green pound, created to protect the European Economic Community's common agricultural prices from the fluctuations in exchange value of the currencies of its member nations.

green dragon, a North American herb of the arum family, closely related to and somewhat like the jack-in-the-pulpit.

green earth, = greensand (def. 1).

green|er (grē′nər), *n. British Slang.* a green or inexperienced workman, especially a foreigner.

green|er|y (grē′nər ē, grēn′rē), *n., pl.* **-er|ies.** **1** green plants, grass, or leaves; verdure: *No glint of greenery on any storm-hit Key relieved this depressing desert expanse* (New Yorker). **2** green branches or leaves used for decoration. **3** = greenhouse.

green eye, a green light on a railroad signal.

green-eyed (grēn′īd′), *adj.* **1** having green eyes. **2** *Figurative.* jealous.

green-eyed monster, = jealousy.

green fee, the fee for the use of a golf course, usually charged at a golf club to persons who are not members.

green·field (grēn′fēld′), *adj. British.* of, having to do with, or built in an underdeveloped area. ▶**Greenfield** also often suggests an area that is free of labor strife.

green·finch (grēn′finch′), *n.* **1** a European finch of green and gold plumage. **2** = Texas sparrow.

green fingers, *British.* a green thumb.

green·fish (grēn′fish′), *n., pl.* **-fish·es** or (*collectively*) **-fish.** = opaleye.

green flash, a flash of vivid green light seen when the sun is just below the horizon. It is caused by atmospheric dispersion of sunlight.

green·fly (grēn′flī′), *n., pl.* **-flies.** = aphid.

green frog, **1** a frog having a length of two to four inches, common in the central and eastern United States and adjacent parts of Canada; spring frog. **2** = pickerel frog.

green·gage (grēn′gāj′), *n.* any one of several varieties of large plums having a light-green skin and pulp and a fine flavor. [< Sir William *Gage,* who introduced it into England from France]

green gland, one of a pair of excretory organs located in the head of certain crustaceans, such as the lobster.

green gold, **1** vegetation as a valuable natural resource, as in producing alcohol from cellulose or fodder. **2** an alloy of gold and silver.

green·gro·cer (grēn′grō′sər), *n. British.* a person who sells fresh vegetables and fruit.

green·gro·cer·y (grēn′grō′sər ē, -grōs′rē), *n., pl.* **-cer·ies.** *British.* a store that sells fresh vegetables and fruit.

green groceries, fresh vegetables and fruit.

green gum, = eucalyptus.

green·head (grēn′hed′), *n.* a male mallard duck.

green·heart (grēn′härt′), *n.* **1** a large South American tree of the laurel family, whose hard, durable timber is used especially in shipbuilding and whose bark yields bebeerine; bebeeru. **2** any one of various other tropical American timber trees. **3** the greenish, hard, and durable wood of any one of these trees.

green heron, a small, dark, short-legged North American heron, the most common heron of the eastern United States; fly-up-the-creek.

green·horn (grēn′hôrn′), *n. Informal.* **1** a person without training or experience: *mere greenhorns, men unused to Indian life* (Washington Irving). **2** a person easy to trick or cheat. **3** a person who has recently arrived in a country or other locale. [said originally of animals, perhaps of the immature, "green" horns of young oxen]

green·house (grēn′hous′), *n., adj.* —*n.* **1** a building with a glass roof and glass sides, kept warm for growing plants; hothouse; greenery. SYN: conservatory. **2** *Slang.* a glassed-in enclosure in an aircraft, such as a bombardier's compartment. —*adj.* of or having to do with the greenhouse effect: *There is still major uncertainty about the magnitude of greenhouse warming* (Science News).

greenhouse effect, the absorption and retention of the sun's radiation in the earth's atmosphere, resulting in an increase in the temperature of the earth's surface. The greenhouse effect acts much as the glass of a greenhouse that traps air underneath it that is heated by the sun.

greenhouse gas, a gas that warms the atmosphere by trapping heat of the long-wave solar radiation reflected from the earth's surface: *Carbon dioxide and other radiatively active gases such as methane, ozone, fluorocarbons and oxides of nitrogen . . . are the greenhouse gases* (Scientific American).

green·ing (grē′ning), *n.* **1** any one of various apples with a yellowish-green skin when ripe. **2** *Figurative.* a renewal of youthful freshness; rejuvenation; rebirth: *The extraordinary thing about this new consciousness is that it . . . seems a veritable greening of America* (Charles A. Reich).

green·ish (grē′nish), *adj.* somewhat green. —**green′ish·ly**, *adv.* —**green′ish·ness**, *n.*

green·keep·er (grēn′kē′pər), *n.* = greenskeeper.

Green·land·er (grēn′lən dər), *n.* a person born or living in Greenland.

Green·land halibut (grēn′lənd), a flatfish found in the cold waters of the Atlantic, often weighing about 20 pounds and colored on both sides.

Green·land·ic (grēn lan′dik), *adj., n.* —*adj.* of or having to do with Greenland, its inhabitants, or their language.
—*n.* the Eskimo language of Greenland.

Greenland whale, a large, black baleen whale of polar regions; arctic right whale.

green lead ore, = pyromorphite.

green·let (grēn′lit), *n.* = vireo.

green light, **1** a green traffic signal which indicates that vehicles or pedestrians may proceed. **2** *Informal, Figurative.* permission to proceed: *the Mississippi legislature gave the green light to the state to take over and develop any seaport in the state* (Wall Street Journal).

green·ling (grēn′ling), *n.* any one of a group of large fishes found around rocks and kelp in the northern Pacific, used for food. They are carnivorous.

green lung, *British Informal.* a park.

green·ly (grēn′lē), *adv.* **1** with a green color or tinge. **2** *Figurative.* with vigorous growth or life. **3** *Figurative.* in an awkward manner.

green·mail (grēn′māl′), *n., v. U.S.* —*n.* **1** the practice of buying a large block of a company's shares of stocks as if to threaten a takeover so that the company will purchase its stocks at a higher price. **2** the profit made by a speculator using greenmail. —*v.t.* to subject to greenmail. [<*green* (back) + (black)*mail*]

green malt, malt at the sprouting stage, before it is dried in a kiln.

green manure, **1** green leafy plants, such as clover or alfalfa, plowed under to enrich the soil. **2** manure that has not decayed.

green-ma·nure (grēn′mə nůr′, -nyůr′), *v.t.,* **-nured, -nur·ing.** to fertilize using green manure.

green mold, a greenish mold, usually of the same genus as that which yields penicillin. Green molds occur on cheese.

green monkey, a West African monkey having a greenish-gray back, a white ruff, and a long, yellow tail.

green monkey disease, = Marburg disease.

Green Mountain Boys, a group of men in Vermont organized about 1770 to roust settlers from New York from their land claims in Vermont. Later many of these men formed a group of soldiers from Vermont that fought in the American Revolution under Ethan Allen.

Green Mountain State, nickname of Vermont.

green·ock·ite (grē′nə kīt), *n.* a rare mineral consisting of cadmium sulfide, found in yellow incrustations of crystals. *Formula:* CdS [< Lord *Greenock,* 1783-1859, who discovered it + *-ite*[1]]

green onion, = scallion.

Green Paper, *British.* a government document in which a proposal or idea is put up for discussion, usually printed on green paper to distinguish it from a white paper, which presents fixed policy.

Green Party, a European political movement that represents environmental interests: *These organizations, often known as Green Parties, have had a growing influence on environmental policies in Western Europe* (Alan McGowan).

green peafowl, any one of a variety of peacocks having a golden-green neck and breast, found in Burma, Malaysia, and Java.

green pepper, **1** the unripe fruit of the sweet pepper plant. It is used as a vegetable. **2** the mild fruit of any variety of the common garden pepper, used as a vegetable before it is ripe.

green plover, = lapwing.

green pound, the rate of exchange at which agricultural transactions are conducted within the European Economic Community.

green power, the power of money.

green revolution, the large-scale development of inexpensive and high-yield varieties of wheat, rice, and other grains, especially to improve the economy of underdeveloped countries.

green·room (grēn′rüm′, -rům′), *n.* a room in a theater for the use of the performers when they are not on stage.

green Rus·su·la (rus′yə lə), any one of a large group of edible mushrooms, having a gray-green, trumpet-shaped cap. [< New Latin *Russula* the genus name < Late Latin *russulus* reddish]

greens (grēnz), *n.pl.* See under **green**.

green·sand (grēn′sand′), *n.* **1** a variety of sandstone containing a silicate of iron and potassium (glauconite) that gives it a greenish color. It is used as a water softener. **2** a mixture of sand, clay, water, and a binder to hold the sand grains together, used in casting metals.

greensand marl, a variety of marl having a low content of calcium carbonate and high amounts of potash and phosphorus, used as a fertilizer and as a water softener, especially in states of the Atlantic coast, where it is plentiful.

green sapphire, a green corundum.

green·schist (grēn′shist′), *n.* a kind of laminated metamorphic rock containing chlorite.

green·shank (grēn′shangk′), *n.* a European sandpiper with olive-colored legs.

green shell bean, **1** a variety of kidney bean that is picked when full grown, but before the edible seeds have ripened and turned hard. **2** the plant on which it grows.

green·sick (grēn′sik′), *adj.* sick with chlorosis.

green·sick·ness (grēn′sik′nis), *n.* = chlorosis (def. 2).

greens·keep·er (grēnz′kē′pər), *n.* a person whose job is the care of a golf course.

green snake, either of two harmless, green-colored snakes of North America that feed mainly on insects.

green soap, a soft soap used in treating skin diseases, cleansing wounds, and for other medicinal purposes.

green·stick fracture (grēn′stik′), a fracture in which the bone is bent and only partly broken. See picture under **fracture**.

green·stone (grēn′stōn′), *n.* **1** any one of various greenish igneous rocks, such as diorite or melaphyre. **2** nephrite, a variety of jade.

green·stuff (grēn′stuf′), *n. U.S. Informal.* green vegetables.

green-stuffs (grēn′stufs′), *n.pl. British Informal.* greenstuff.

green·sward (grēn′swôrd′), *n.* green grass; turf.

green·sward·ed (grēn′swôr′did), *adj.* covered with greensward.

green tea, tea whose leaves have been put immediately into firing machines without fermentation, to keep some of the original green color.

greenth (grēnth), *n.* = verdure.

green thumb, **1** an unusual ability to grow flowers, vegetables, and other plants: *A beautiful garden bespeaks a green thumb.* **2** interest in growing or caring for plants.

green thumber (thum′ər), *U.S. Informal.* a person who has a green thumb.

green turtle, a large sea turtle with a green shell, whose meat is used for food.

green vegetables, leafy vegetables, such as lettuce, chard, and kale.

green vitriol, a green sulfate of iron; copperas; ferrous sulfate. *Formula:* $FeSO_4 \cdot 7H_2O$

green wave, (in surfing) a long, uninterrupted wave.

Green·wich Time, Greenwich Civil Time, or **Greenwich Mean Time** (gren′ij, grin′-; -ich), the standard time used in Great Britain and formerly the basis for setting standard time elsewhere. It is determined by setting noon as the time at which the sun is directly overhead at the meridian passing through Greenwich, England.

green-winged teal (grēn′winged′), a small North American duck, the male having a green iridescence on its wings and the side of its head.

green·wood (grēn′wůd′), *n.* a forest when the trees are green with leaves.

green woodpecker, a European woodpecker about 12 inches long with a green back, red cap, and yellow rump; hickwall; popinjay.

green·y (grē′nē), *adj., n., pl.* **green·ies.** —*adj.* greenish: *a pale greeny yellow.* —*n. Slang.* a greenhorn, such as a freshman at college.

greet[1] (grēt), *v.t.* **1** to speak or write to in a friendly, polite way; address in welcome: *She greeted us with a friendly "Hello."* SYN: welcome. **2** to address; salute: *She greeted him with a nod.* SYN: hail, accost. **3** to respond to: *His speech was greeted with cheers.* **4** to present itself to; meet: *When she opened the door, a strange sight greeted her eyes.* —*v.i.* to offer a greeting: *None greets, for none the greeting will return* (John Dryden). [Old English *grētan*] —**greet′er**, *n.*

greet[2] (grēt), *v.i. Archaic or Scottish.* to weep; cry; lament; grieve. [Old English *grētan* and *grēotan,* meaning "to cry out, lament, weep (for)"]

greet·ing (grē′ting), *n.* the act or words of a person who greets somebody; welcome; salutation. **greetings**, friendly wishes on a special occasion: *Season's greetings, Christmas greetings.*

greeting card, a card that contains a printed message for a particular occasion, such as a birthday or anniversary, often with a picture.

greg·a·rine (greg′ə rīn, -ər in), *n., adj.* —*n.* one of a group of protozoans that are parasitic in the intestines of insects, worms, and other invertebrates. —*adj.* of or having to do with a gregarine. [< New Latin *Gregarina* the genus name < Latin *gregārius;* see etym. under **gregarious**]

gre·gar·i·ous (grə gãr′ē əs), *adj.* **1** living in flocks, herds, or other groups: *Sheep and cattle are gregarious; raccoons are not.* **2** fond of being with others: *Hermits are not gregarious; socialites are. A gregarious man, he enjoyed the companionship of a large number of convivial friends* (New Yorker). SYN: sociable. **3** of or having to do with a flock or crowd. [< Latin *gregārius* (with English *-ous*) <*grex, gregis* flock] —**gre·gar′i·ous·ly**, *adv.* —**gre·gar′i·ous·ness**, *n.*

grège (grāzh), *n.* a color between beige and grey. [< French *grège;* see etym. under **greige**]

Gregg (greg), *n.* a cultivated variety of dewberry, grown in North America.

gre·go (grē′gō, grā′-), *n., pl.* **-gos. 1** a coarse

Pronunciation Key: hat, āge, cãre, fär; let, ēqual, tėrm; it, īce; hot, ōpen, ôrder; oil, out; cup, půt, rüle; child; long; thin; ᴛʜen; zh, measure; ə represents a in about, e in taken, i in pencil, o in lemon, u in circus.

jacket with a hood, worn in the Levant. **2** *Obsolete Slang.* a rough greatcoat. [< some Romance form of Latin *Graecus* a Greek. Compare Portuguese *grego.*]

Gre|go|ri|an (grə gôr′ē ən, -gōr′-), *adj.* **1** of Pope Gregory I: *Gregorian music.* **2** of Pope Gregory XIII: *the Gregorian epoch.*

Gregorian calendar, the calendar now in use in the United States and most other countries, having 12 months and 365 days (366 in leap year). It was introduced by Pope Gregory XIII and first adopted in France in 1582, and adopted in Great Britain and its colonies in 1752. The Gregorian calendar corrected the Julian calendar by eliminating those centenary years not divisible by 400 as leap years and advanced the date to correct previous error. It is called *New Style* in contrast to the Julian calendar or *Old Style.*

***Gregorian chant**, vocal music having free rhythm and a limited scale, introduced by Pope Gregory I and still sometimes used in the Roman Catholic Church. It is usually sung without accompaniment.

***Gregorian chant**

Gregorian telescope, the earliest form of the reflecting telescope, resembling the Cassegrainian telescope, invented by James Gregory, 1638-1675, a Scottish mathematician.

Gregorian tone or **mode**, any one of the eight Gregorian scales used in singing the Psalms.

greige (grā, grāzh), *n., adj.* —*n.* = gray goods. —*adj.* (of fabrics) gray; undyed.
[alteration (influenced by *beige*) of French *grège* (*soie*) raw (silk)]

grei|sen (grī′zən), *n.* a modification of granite, a rock with crystalline, granular texture, consisting chiefly of quartz and mica. [< German *Greisen*]

gre|mi|al (grē′mē əl), *adj., n.* —*adj. Archaic.* **1a** of or having to do with the lap or bosom. **b** intimate. **2** of or having to do with a corporation or society. —*n.* a cloth placed on a bishop's lap to protect his vestments.
[earlier, a resident member < Latin *gremiālis* < *gremium* the lap, bosom]

grem|lin (grem′lən), *n.* **1** an imaginary creature that causes trouble in an aircraft or its engines or parts. **2** a cause of trouble: *Our biggest gremlin was rust* (New York Times). **3** *Slang.* = gremmie.
[origin uncertain]

grem|mie (grem′ē), *n., pl.* **-mies.** a person who is new to surfing or poor at the sport. [diminutive of *gremlin*]

gre|nade (grə nād′), *n.* **1** a small bomb, usually thrown by hand; hand grenade: *The soldiers threw grenades into the enemy's trenches.* **2** a round glass bottle filled with chemicals that scatter as the glass breaks. Fire grenades are thrown on fires to put them out. Illuminating grenades are used at night to light up land areas. [< Middle French *grenade* < Old French (*pume*) *grenate,* or (*pomme*) *grenade* pomegranate < Spanish *granada* < Latin (*malum*) *grānātum* (apple) having grains < *grānum* grain]

grenade launcher, = launcher (def. 2a).

gren|a|dier (gren′ə dir′), *n.* **1** (originally) a soldier who threw grenades. Soldiers of long service and acknowledged bravery were selected as grenadiers. **2** (later) a member of a specially chosen unit of foot soldiers, especially a member of a company composed of the tallest and best soldiers in a regiment. **3** (now) a member of a special regiment or other group in certain armies, especially a member of a special regiment of guards in the British army. They are attached to the royal household. **4** any one of a group of soft-finned, deep-sea fishes. **5** a South African weaverbird with vivid red and black feathers. [< French *grenadier* < Middle French *grenade* < Old French; see etym. under **grenade**] —**gren′a|dier′ly**, *adv.*

gren|a|dil|la (gren′ə dil′ə), *n.* = granadilla.

gren|a|dine[1] (gren′ə dēn, gren′ə dēn′), *n.* a thin, openwork fabric of wool, silk, cotton, or rayon, used for women's dresses. [< French *grenadine,* perhaps < *Granada,* Spain]

gren|a|dine[2] (gren′ə dēn, gren′ə dēn′), *n.* a syrup made from the juice of pomegranates or red currants, used especially to flavor or color cocktails. [< French (*sirop de*) *grenadine* < Middle French *grenade* pomegranate; see etym. under **grenade**]

Gren|del (gren′dəl), *n.* a monster slain by Beowulf.

Gre|po (grī′pō), *n.* a member of the East German border police: . . . *Communist Grepos guarding the* [*Berlin*] *Wall* (Time). [< German *Gre*(*nz*)-*po*(*lizei*) border police]

Gresh|am's law (gresh′əmz), the theory that bad money will drive out good. Thus, if two coins or notes are equal as legal tender, but differ in intrinsic value, the more valuable one is either hoarded or exported. [< Sir Thomas *Gresham,* 1519?-1579, an English economist, who propounded the theory in 1558]

gres|so|ri|al (gre sôr′ē əl, -sōr′-), *adj.* adapted for walking, as the feet of certain birds and insects. [< New Latin *gressorius* (< *gressor* one who walks < Latin *gradī* walk) + English *-al*[1]]

gres|so|ri|ous (gre sôr′ē əs, -sōr′-), *adj.* = gressorial.

Gret|na Green (gret′nə), any place to which eloping couples go to be married. [< *Gretna Green,* a village in Scotland, where until 1856 runaway couples were married without parental consent]

grew (grü), *v.* past tense of **grow**: *It grew colder as the sun went down.*

grew|some (grü′səm), *adj.* = gruesome. —**grew′some|ness**, *n.*

grey (grā), *n., adj., v.t., v.i.* = gray. —**grey′-ness**, *n.*

grey area, *British.* a geographical area showing low employment but not poor enough to qualify for special government assistance: *Towns in the Lancashire coal and cotton belt* [*are*] *frequently referred to as grey areas* (London Times).

Grey Cup, **1** a Canadian football trophy awarded annually to the champion team of the two Canadian Football League conferences. **2** the game played to choose the champion team. [< Earl *Grey,* 1851-1917, a Canadian governor general, who first presented the cup in 1909]

grey|hound (grā′hound′), *n.* **1** one of a breed of tall, slender hunting dogs with long noses. Greyhounds have a smooth coat and very good eyesight. Dog races often feature greyhounds, the fastest of all dogs. See picture under **hound[1]**. **2** a fast steamship, especially an ocean liner. Also, **grayhound.**
[probably alteration of Old English *grīghund* by influence of Old Icelandic *greyhundr* < *grey* greyhound + *hundr* dog]

greys (grāz), *n.pl. Especially British.* persons wearing gray military uniforms, such as the Scots Greys, a regiment of dragoons.

grib|ble (grib′əl), *n.* **1** a small, marine crustacean with seven pairs of legs, that bores into submerged timbers. **2** any one of certain related sea animals. [perhaps related to **grub**, noun]

grid (grid), *n.* **1** a framework of parallel iron bars with spaces between them; grating; gridiron. **2** the lead plate in a storage battery. **3** the electrode in a vacuum tube that controls the flow of electrons between the cathode and the anode. It usually consists of parallel wires, a screen, or a spiral of wire. **4** a network of electric lines and connections: *the national power grid.* **5** an arrangement of vertical and horizontal lines to determine the coordinates of given points or to locate points for which the coordinates are known. **6** the numbered squares drawn on maps and used for map references. **7** a football field. **8** a gridiron in a theater. [short for *gridiron*]

grid circuit, the part of the circuit in a vacuum tube that includes the grid and cathode.

grid condenser, a condenser in a vacuum tube connected in series with the grid circuit.

grid current, the current flowing in a vacuum tube between the grid and the cathode.

grid|ded (grid′id), *adj.* consisting of a grid.

grid|der (grid′ər), *n. U.S. Informal.* a football player.

grid|dle (grid′əl), *n., v.,* **-dled, -dling.** —*n.* a heavy, flat plate of metal or soapstone, on which to cook pancakes, bacon, hamburgers, and similar foods.
—*v.t.* to cook on a griddle.
on the griddle, *Informal.* in a position to be grilled or interrogated; submitting to inquiry: *We had Orbuthnot on the griddle when we heard Mrs. Ives call him "Jamie"* (Punch).
[< Old North French *gredil,* Old French *grail, greil* < Late Latin *crāticulum,* for Latin *crāticula* small griddle, gridiron. See etym. of doublet **grill[1]**.]

grid|dle|cake (grid′əl kāk′), *n.* a thin, flat cake of batter cooked on a griddle; pancake.
►See usage note under **pancake**.

gride (grīd), *v.,* **grid|ed, grid|ing,** *n. Archaic.* —*v.t., v.i.* **1** to grate or scrape harshly. **2** to pierce or cut: *Through his thigh the mortal steel did gride* (Edmund Spenser).
—*n.* a griding or grating sound: *The gride of hatchets fiercely thrown on wigwam-log and tree and stone* (John Greenleaf Whittier).
[perhaps alteration of *gird[2]* in its earlier sense, "strike at"]

grid|i|ron (grid′ī′ərn), *n., v.* —*n.* **1** a framework of parallel iron bars or wires for broiling, usually with a handle. **2** any frame or structure like this, such as a frame for supporting a ship that is being repaired. **3** a football field. **4** a structure above the stage of a theater, from which scenery is manipulated; grid. **5** a network of pipes, lines, etc.
—*v.t.* to mark with parallel bars or lines like those of a gridiron.
[Middle English alteration (influenced by *iron*) of *gredire* griddle, variant of *gredile*]

grid leak, a device of very high resistance used in a vacuum tube to permit excess current to escape from the grid.

grid line, any one of the meridians and parallels marked on a map.

grid|lock (grid′lok), *n., v.* —*n.* **1** a complete stoppage of all vehicular traffic on crossing streets in a given area of a city. **2** any complete stoppage of activity due to overcrowding: *jammed in telephone gridlock with everyone on the phone and no one getting through* (New Yorker).
—*v.t.* to subject to a gridlock: *The phones were also gridlocked at Stanford, in Palo Alto* (Rolling Stone). —**grid′locked**, *adj.*

grief (grēf), *n.* **1** great sadness caused by trouble or loss; heavy sorrow. SYN: anguish, heartache. See syn. under **sorrow**. **2** a cause or subject of sadness or sorrow: *A foolish son is a grief to his father* (Proverbs 17:25). **3** *Obsolete.* hardship, suffering, injury, or a cause of these.
come to grief, to have trouble; fail: *Since the book is a comedy, nobody comes to grief* (New Yorker).
good grief, an exclamation of alarm or surprise (now often used for humorous effect): *Good grief, it's nothing like that . . .* (Punch).
[< Old French *grief, gref* < *grever;* see etym. under **grieve**] —**grief′less**, *adj.*

grief-strick|en (grēf′strik′ən), *adj.* stricken with grief or sorrow.

grief-worn (grēf′wôrn′), *adj.* exhausted or worn by grief.

grie|shoch (grē′shəʜ), *n. Scottish.* hot embers, especially of peat. [< Scottish Gaelic *griosach* < *grios* heat]

griev|ance (grē′vəns), *n.* **1** a real or imagined wrong; reason for being annoyed or angry; cause for complaint: *The captain told his men to report any grievance to him.* SYN: injustice, injury. **2** *Obsolete.* suffering, distress, or trouble, or a cause of these.

grievance committee, a committee composed of union or both union and management representatives to discuss and remedy grievances.

grieve (grēv), *v.,* **grieved, griev|ing.** —*v.i.* to feel grief; be very sad; sorrow deeply: *The little girl grieved over her kitten's death.* —*v.t.* **1** to cause to feel grief; make very sad; afflict: *His bad behavior grieved his parents.* **2** *Archaic.* to do wrong, hurt, or harm to: *He doth not afflict willingly nor grieve the children of men* (Lamentations 3:33). [< Old French *grever* < Latin *gravāre* to burden, cause grief < *gravis* heavy, weighty] —**griev′er**, *n.* —**griev′ing|ly**, *adv.*

griev|ous (grē′vəs), *adj.* **1** hard to bear; causing great pain or suffering; severe: *grievous cruelty.* SYN: distressing. **2** very evil or offensive; outrageous; flagrant; atrocious: *Murder is a grievous crime in most societies. Wasting food when people were starving was a grievous wrong. It was a grievous fault And grievously hath Caesar answered it* (Shakespeare). SYN: heinous. **3** causing grief: *a grievous loss.* **4** full of grief; showing grief: *a grievous cry.* —**griev′ous|ly**, *adv.* —**griev′ous|ness**, *n.*

griff[1] (grif), *n.* = claw. [see etym. under **griffe[2]**]

griff[2] (grif), *n.* = griffe[1].

griff[3] (grif), *n.* a frame composed of horizontal bars, used in weaving patterns. Also, **griffe.** [origin unknown]

griff[4] (grif), *n.* = griffin[2].

griffe[1] (grif), *n. U.S. Dialect.* **1** the offspring of a Black and a mulatto. **2** a mulatto. **3** a person of mixed Black and American Indian parentage. Also, **griff, griffin.** [American English < Louisiana French *griffe,* also *griffone,* apparently < American Spanish *grifo* < Spanish, kinky, curled (because of the hair)]

griffe[2] (grif), *n.* a medieval architectural ornament used on the base of a column to connect each angle of the plinth with the torus. [< French *griffe* (literally) a claw < Old French *grif,* ultimately < Old High German *grīfan* seize]

griffe[3] (grif), *n.* = griff[3].

***grif|fin[1]** (grif′ən), *n. Greek Mythology.* a creature with the head, wings, and forelegs of an eagle, and the body, hind legs, and tail of a lion. Also, **griffon, gryphon.** [< Old French *grifon* < *grif,* learned borrowing from Latin *grȳphus,* variant of *grȳps, grȳphis* < Greek *gryps, grȳpós*]

✱griffin[1]

grif|fin[2] (grif′ən), *n.* a white person new to India or the East; newcomer; greenhorn. Also, **griff.** [Anglo-Indian; origin uncertain]
grif|fin[3] (grif′ən), *n. U.S. Dialect.* a griffe[1].
grif|fin|age (grif′ə nij), *n.* the state of being a griffin, or newcomer to India.
grif|fin|hood (grif′ən hu̇d), *n.* = griffinage.
grif|fon[1] (grif′ən), *n.* **1** = griffin[1]. **2** Also, **griffon vulture.** a very large vulture of Asia, southern Europe and Africa. [perhaps < Old French *griffon* a bird of prey, earlier, *griffin;* see **griffin[1]**]
grif|fon[2] (grif′ən), *n.* **1** any one of a breed of small, sturdy, rough or smooth-coated dogs developed in Belgium and weighing 8 to 10 pounds. **2** the wire-haired, pointing griffon, a medium-sized hunting dog with a rough coat. [< French *griffon* an English breed of dogs < Old French *grifon;* see etym. under **griffin[1]**]
grift (grift), *n., v. Slang.* = swindle. [perhaps variant of *graft[2]*]
grift|er (grif′tər), *n. Slang.* **1** a person who operates a wheel of chance or similar device, as at a fair, amusement park, or circus. **2** = swindler.
grig (grig), *n. Dialect.* **1** a cricket or young eel. **2** = cricket. **3** = grasshopper. **4** a cheerful, lively person. [Middle English *grege* a dwarf; origin uncertain; perhaps < Scandinavian (compare dialectal Swedish *krik* little animal)]
Gri|gnard reagent (grē nyär′), any one of a class of reagents derived from the union of magnesium with an organic radical and a halogen, important in organic synthesis. [< Victor *Grignard,* 1871-1935, a French chemist]
gri|gri[1] (grē′grē), *n.* = greegree.
gri|gri[2] (grē′grē), *n.* = grugru.
Gri|ha|stha (grē′hə stə), *n.* a Brahman in the second stage of his religious life.
grike (grīk), *n.* **1** a crevice; chink. **2** a ravine on the side of a hill.
grill[1] (gril), *n., v.* —*n.* **1** a framework of parallel iron bars for broiling; gridiron. It is used to hold meat or fish. **2** a dish of broiled meat or fish: *We ate a mixed grill of bacon, lamb chop, and sausage.* **3** a dining room in a hotel or restaurant that specializes in serving broiled meat or fish; grillroom: *We went to the member's grill for lunch.* **4** the act of grilling.
—*v.t.* **1** to cook by holding near the fire; broil: *The campers grilled hamburgers for dinner.* **2** *Figurative.* to torment with heat. **3** *Figurative.* to question severely and persistently: *The detectives grilled the prisoner until he confessed.*
—*v.i.* **1** to be broiled. **2** to be tortured by heat.
[< French *gril* < Old French *greil,* earlier *grail* < Late Latin *crātīculum,* for Latin *crātīcula* gridiron, small griddle (diminutive) < *crātis* latticework, grill. See etym. of doublet **griddle.**]
grill[2] (gril), *n., v.t.* = grille.
gril|lade (gri läd′; *French* grē yȧd′), *n.* steak or other piece of meat broiled or grilled. [< French *grillade* < *gril;* see etym. under **grill[1]**]
gril|lage (gril′ij), *n.* a heavy framework of crossed timbers or steel beams, used for foundations in soft, treacherous soils, swamps, and the like. [< French *grillage* < *grille;* see etym. under **grille**]

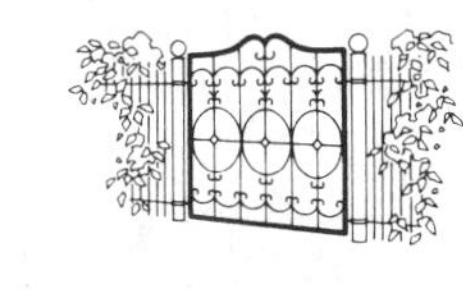

✱grille
definition 1

✱grille (gril), *n., v.,* **grilled, grill|ing.** —*n.* **1** an open, metal structure or screen, used as a gate, door, or window or to cover the opening in front of the radiator of an automobile; grating. **2** (in court tennis) a square-shaped opening in the corner of the back wall on the hazard side of the court, one of the three winning openings. **3** a card with holes in it, used to place over a sheet of paper and write a secret message in the holes, then filling in the rest of the paper to look like an ordinary letter. **4** a rectangular pattern of small dots on some issues of postage stamps.
—*v.t.* **1** to fit with a grille or grating. **2** to impress (postage stamps) with a grille.
[< French *grille* < Old French; variant of *gril, greil;* see etym. under **grill[1]**]
grilled[1] (grild), *adj.* broiled: *grilled steak.*
grilled[2] (grild), *adj.* furnished with a grille.
grill|er (gril′ər), *n.* a person or thing that grills; broiler.
grille|work (gril′wėrk′), *n.* = grillwork.
grill|room (gril′rüm′, -ru̇m′), *n.* a restaurant or dining room that specializes in serving broiled meat or fish; grill.
grill|work (gril′wėrk′), *n.* a grille or a pattern of grilles: *The rear ends of new cars are fancier than the grillwork in front* (Wall Street Journal).
grilse (grils), *n., pl.* **grilse.** a young salmon that has returned from the sea to the river for the first time. [origin uncertain. Compare Old French *grisle* gray.]
grim (grim), *adj.,* **grim|mer, grim|mest. 1** without mercy; stern, harsh, or fierce: *grim, stormy weather.* SYN: cruel, merciless. **2** not yielding; not relenting: *The losing team fought on with grim resolve.* SYN: relentless, unyielding. **3** looking stern, fierce, or harsh: *Father was grim when he heard about the six broken windows.* SYN: hard, forbidding, severe. **4** horrible; frightful; ghastly: *. . . grim jokes about graves, worms and epitaphs* (Thomas Love Peacock). [Old English *grimm* fierce]
—**grim′ly,** *adv.* —**grim′ness,** *n.*
gri|mace (grim′is, grə mās′), *n., v.,* **-maced, -mac|ing.** —*n.* a twisting of the face; ugly or funny smile: *a grimace caused by pain.*
—*v.i.* to make faces: *The clown grimaced at the children.*
[< Middle French *grimace* < *grimache* < Old French *grimuche,* perhaps < Germanic (compare Old High German *grimmiza* grimness, hostility)]
gri|mac|er (grə mā′sər, grim′ə sər), *n.* a person who makes grimaces or distorts his face.
gri|mal|kin (grə mal′kən, -môl′-), *n.* **1** a cat. **2** an old female cat: *A strange grimalkin . . . clambered hastily over the fence and vanished* (Hawthorne). **3** a spiteful old woman. [probably < *gray* + *Malkin* (diminutive) < *Maud,* a proper name]
grime (grīm), *n., v.,* **grimed, grim|ing.** —*n.* dirt rubbed deeply and firmly into a surface: *Soap and water removed only a little of the grime on the coal miner's hands.*
—*v.t.* to make very dirty; cover with grime: *Ceilings and walls were grimed with smoke* (Woman's Day). SYN: blacken, befoul.
[compare Flemish *grijmen* begrime]
Grimes Golden (grīmz), a yellow autumn eating apple. [American English < Thomas P. *Grimes,* who developed it]
Grimm alfalfa, a winter-hardy variety of alfalfa, grown extensively in the northern United States. [< Wendelin *Grimm,* a German settler, who introduced the variety in Minnesota in 1857]
grim|mish (grim′ish), *adj.* somewhat grim.
Grimm's law (grimz), *Linguistics.* a statement of the systematic changes in certain Indo-European consonants that took place in the Germanic languages and were carried still further in High German, as seen in the correspondences between the Germanic consonants and those in the other Indo-European languages in cognate words. For example, where Latin has *p,* English has *f:* Latin *pater,* English *father;* where Latin has *d,* English has *t* and High German has *ts* (spelled *z*) initially: Latin *decem,* English *ten,* High German *zehn.* Most of the changes were noted by Rasmus Rask in 1818 and a full statement of them was made by Jacob Grimm in 1822.
grimp (grimp), *v.i.* = climb. [< French *grimper*]
grim reaper, death personified, usually as a man holding a scythe: *Out of a company of thirty, seven of our brother argonauts were taken by the grim reaper* (New Yorker).
grim|y (grī′mē), *adj.,* **grim|i|er, grim|i|est.** covered with grime; very dirty: *grimy hands.* SYN: begrimed, black. —**grim′i|ly,** *adv.* —**grim′i|ness,** *n.*
grin[1] (grin), *v.,* **grinned, grin|ning,** *n.* —*v.i.* **1** to smile broadly: *He soon breaks training by thrusting a cigar into his toothy and perpetually grinning mouth* (Wall Street Journal). **2** to draw back the lips and show the teeth in anger, pain, or scorn: *The wolf grinned in an ugly way. A snarling dog grins.* —*v.t.* to show, make, or express by smiling broadly: *She grinned approval.*
—*n.* **1** a broad smile: *The happy new father wore a grin from ear to ear.* **2** an act of showing the teeth in anger, pain, or scorn. [Old English *grennian*] —**grin′ner,** *n.* —**grin′ning|ly,** *adv.*
grin[2] (grin), *n. Dialect.* a snare for catching birds or animals, made of cord, hair, wire, or the like, with a running noose. [Old English *grin*]
Grinch or **grinch** (grinch), *n. U.S. Informal.* a person or thing that spoils the enjoyment or plans of others; spoilsport; killjoy: *No print-medium Grinch is arguing that humor aimed at the young doesn't have a place in the video spectrum* (Newsweek). [< the name of the character in *How the Grinch Stole Christmas* (1957), a children's story by Dr. Seuss (Theodor Seuss Geisel), an American writer and illustrator]
grind (grīnd), *v.,* **ground** or (*Rare*) **grind|ed, grind|ing,** *n.* —*v.t.* **1** to crush into bits or powder: *That mill grinds corn into meal and wheat into flour. Your back teeth grind food.* SYN: pulverize. **2** *Figurative.* to crush by harsh rule or cruelty: *The slaves were ground down by their masters. They were an ill-famed lot, notorious for grinding the poor and trafficking in opium* (Atlantic). SYN: oppress. **3** to sharpen, smooth, or wear by rubbing on something rough: *He ground the ax on a grindstone.* **4** to make a harsh sound by rubbing; grate: *to grind one's teeth in anger.* SYN: grit. **5** to force by rubbing or pressing: *to grind one's heel in the dirt.* **6** to work by turning a handle; produce by turning a crank: *to grind a coffee mill. A man grinds a hand organ to grind out music.* **7** *Informal, Figurative.* **a** to teach (a subject) in a steady, laborious manner: *to get their living . . . by grinding Latin and Greek* (Thackeray). **b** to prepare (a pupil) in a subject.
—*v.i.* **1** to perform the act or operation of grinding something: *The . . . policeman at the wheel started his engine and began to grind into gear before releasing the clutch* (Graham Greene). (*Figurative*) *Though the mills of God grind slowly, yet they grind exceeding small* (Longfellow). **2** to be or become ground. **3** to rub harshly; grate. **4** *Informal, Figurative.* to work or study long and hard.
—*n.* **1** the act of grinding. **2** something made by grinding: *a fine grind of coffee.* **3** a grinding sound. **4** *Informal, Figurative.* **a** a long, hard work or study: *To some of the students, mathematics was a grind.* **b** a dull and laborious task: *No other auto race in the U.S. quite compares to the Sebring grind* (Time). **5** *Informal, Figurative.* a person who works long and hard at his studies. **6** *Slang.* a suggestive movement of the hips, as done in certain dances. [Old English *grindan*]
grin|de|li|a (grin dē′lē ə), *n.* **1** any one of a group of yellow-flowered, American herbs of the composite family. **2** the dried leaves and flowers of various species, used medicinally. [American English < New Latin *Grindelia* < D. H. *Grindel,* 1776-1836, a professor of botany at Riga, Latvia]
grind|er (grīn′dər), *n.* **1** a person or thing that grinds. **2** a person or machine that sharpens tools. **3** a back tooth for grinding food; molar. **4** *Slang.* = hero sandwich.
grinders, *Informal.* teeth: *He put his grinders to work on a juicy apple.*
grind|er|y (grīn′dər ē, -drē), *n., pl.* **-er|ies. 1** a place for grinding tools, weapons, etc. **2** *British.* the materials or tools used by leather workers.
grind house, *U.S. Slang.* a motion-picture theater where there are no intermissions between showings.
grind|ing (grīn′ding), *adj.* **1** grating or strident, as sounds. **2** burdensome or oppressive, as toil. **3** excruciating or racking: *grinding pain.* —**grind′ing|ly,** *adv.*
grinding belt, a rotating belt of abrasive material, used for grinding or polishing metals, glass, ceramics, and the like.
grinding wheel, a wheel or disk of abrasive material, used for grinding or polishing.
grind|stone (grīnd′stōn′), *n.* **1** a flat, round stone set in a frame and turned by hand, foot, or motor. It is used to sharpen tools, such as axes and knives, or to smooth and polish things. **2** *Obsolete.* a millstone.
have (keep, or **put) one's nose to the grindstone.** See under **nose.**
grin|ga (gring′gə), *n.* (among Spanish Americans) a woman gringo. [< Mexican Spanish *gringa,* feminine of *gringo;* see etym. under **gringo**]
grin|go (gring′gō), *n., pl.* **-gos.** a foreigner, especially an American or Englishman (used in an unfriendly way in Spain and Latin America): *Any European, except a Spaniard, was regarded as a gringo* (Willa Cather). [American English < Mexican Spanish *gringo* < Spanish, gibberish, perhaps < *griego* Greek]
gri|ot (grē ō′), *n.* a traditional roving poet, musician, and storyteller of western Africa. [< French *griot*]
grip (grip), *n., v.,* **gripped** or **gript, grip|ping.** —*n.*

Pronunciation Key: hat, āge, cãre, fär; let, ēqual, tėrm; it, īce; hot, ōpen, ôrder; oil, out; cup, pu̇t, rüle; child; long; thin; ᴛʜen; zh, measure;
ə represents **a** in about, **e** in taken, **i** in pencil, **o** in lemon, **u** in circus.

1 a seizing and holding tight; tight grasp; firm hold: *McGinnis's grip on the throttle loosened* (Newsweek). **2** the power of gripping: *the grip of a bear.* **3** a thing for gripping something, such as one by which a cable car is attached to or released from its cable. **4** a part to take hold of; handle: *The policeman put his hand on the grip of his pistol.* **5** a certain way of gripping the hand as a sign of belonging to some secret society: *He gave me the grip as a sign that he belonged to the club too.* **6** a small suitcase or handbag (formerly short for *gripsack*) : *As he left, he threw his grip in the back seat of his car.* **7** *Figurative.* firm control; hold: *to be in the grip of poverty.* **8** *Figurative.* understanding; mental grasp: *He has a grip of the subject.* **9** a sudden, sharp pain. **10** = grippe; influenza. **11** *Theater, U.S. Slang.* a stagehand, especially one who shifts scenery: *Around us, grips and prop men talked in hushed tones* (New Yorker).
—*v.t.* to seize and hold firmly; take a firm hold on: *The dog gripped the stick.* **2** *Figurative.* to get and keep the interest and attention of: *An exciting story grips you.* **3** to attach, as with a grip or grappling iron.
—*v.i.* to take firm hold; make a grasp; get a grip.
come to grips, to fight hand to hand; struggle close together: *I saw we were come to grips at last* (Robert Louis Stevenson).
come (or **get**) **to grips with**, to work hard and seriously on; struggle with; attempt to cope with: *So far the trustees have not come to grips with their most serious problem* (Maclean's).
lose one's grip, to lose control: *He was losing his grip on Das Kapital, the first volume of which had failed to bring him the public recognition he had expected* (Edmund Wilson).
[Old English *gripe,* related to *grīpan* grasp]
—grip′less, *adj.* **—grip′per**, *n.*

grip car, = cable car.

gripe[1] (grīp), *v.,* **griped, grip|ing**, *n.* **—*v.t.*** **1** to clutch or grasp tightly; pinch. **2** to oppress; distress. **3** *Informal, Figurative.* to irk; annoy; irritate: *It gripes me to see a man of that type move in and take over the fruits of our labor* (Harper's). **4** to cause pain in the bowels of: *Too much unripe fruit can gripe a person.* **5** *Archaic.* **a** to lay hold of; seize; catch; grasp. **b** to get into one's power or possession. **6** *Obsolete.* to grieve; afflict.
—*v.i.* **1a** to have pain in the bowels. **b** to cause such pain. **2** *Informal, Figurative.* to complain: *He was always griping about something. The Men of Protest are a disgruntled collection of snobs, grouches, and expatriates, grumbling and griping* (New York Review of Books). **3** *Nautical.* to tend to come up into the wind and lose headway. **4** *Obsolete.* to make a grasp or clutch; seek to get a hold: *Upon whose heart may all the Furies gripe* (Christopher Marlowe).
—*n.* **1** a fast hold; gripping; clutch. **2** grasp; control: *The empire held small nations in its gripe.* **3** the clutch or pinch of something painful. **4** *Informal, Figurative.* a complaint: *Bus driver and motorists ... made their gripes loud and clear* (Maclean's). **5** something that gripes or clutches. **6** something that is gripped or grasped, such as the handle of an implement.
gripes, a pain in the bowels; colic (not now in medical use): *Swift has said ... That he who daily smokes two pipes, the toothache never has—nor gripes* (William Combe). **b** iron bars or canvas strips passed over a boat to secure it on the deck or on chocks: *The boats ... are ... with fastening gripes secured* (William Falconer).
[Old English *grīpan* grasp, lay hold] **—grip′er**, *n.*

gripe[2] (grīp), *n. Obsolete.* **1** a griffin[1]. **2** a vulture. [< Latin *grȳps* griffin[1]]

grip|man (grip′mən), *n., pl.* **-men**. the man who works the grip on a cable car.

grippe (grip), *n.* a contagious disease like a very severe cold with fever; influenza. Also, **grip**. [< French *grippe* (originally) seizure < *gripper* to grasp, hook, perhaps reenforced by Russian *khrip* hoarseness]

grip|ping (grip′ing), *adj.* that grips, especially that catches and holds the attention or interest: *It is ... as gripping a musical drama as I have ever heard* (New Yorker). **—grip′ping|ly**, *adv.*

grip|ple (grip′əl), *adj. Dialect.* griping; grasping; avaricious: *While gripple owners still refuse to others what they cannot use* (Scott). [Old English *gripul,* related to *grīpan* grasp]

grip|py (grip′ē), *adj.,* **-pi|er, -pi|est**. *Informal.* having the grippe; characterized by the grippe.

grip|sack (grip′sak′), *n. U.S. Informal.* a traveling bag; valise.

gript (gript), *v.* gripped; a past tense and past participle of **grip**.

Gri|qua (grē′kwə, grik′wə), *n.* a South African of mixed African and European parentage. [< *Grigriqua,* a group of settlers of mixed blood who relocated in South Africa in the early 1800's]

gri|saille (grə zāl′; *French* grē zä′yə), *n.* **1** a method of decorative painting in monochrome in various shades of gray, to represent objects in relief, often used on glass or enamel. **2** a work, such as a stained-glass window, executed according to this method: *The younger Tiepolo also did ... grisailles of masked figures and clowns* (New Yorker). [< French *grisaille* < *gris* gray < Old French; see etym. under **grizzle**[1]]

Gri|sel|da (grə zel′də), *n.* **1** the heroine of Chaucer's "Clerk's Tale" and of several medieval romances, famed for her meekness and patience when cruelly ill-treated by her husband. **2** a very meek, patient woman.

gris|e|o|ful|vin (gris′ē ō ful′vin), *n.* an antibiotic used against fungous infections of the skin, and to destroy molds and mildew on plants. *Formula:* $C_{17}H_{17}ClO_6$ [< New Latin *griseofulvum* a species of penicillin mold, that is its source + English *-in*]

gris|e|ous (gris′ē əs, griz′-), *adj.* gray verging on blue; pearl-gray. [< Medieval Latin *griseus* (with English *-ous*) gray < Old High German *grīs* gray]

gri|sette (gri zet′), *n.* a French working girl, especially one employed as a shop assistant or a seamstress. [< French *grisette* < *gris* gray (because of the usual color of their dresses)]

gris-gris (grē′grē), *n., pl.* **gris-gris**. = greegree.

gris|kin (gris′kin), *n. British.* a loin of pork. [< *grice* pig + *-kin*]

gris|ly[1] (griz′lē), *adj.,* **-li|er, -li|est**. causing horror; frightful; horrible; ghastly: *the grisly symptoms of radiation sickness* (New York Times). SYN: See syn. under **ghastly**. [Old English *grislic*] **—gris′li|ness**, *n.*

gris|ly[2] (griz′lē), *adj. Obsolete.* **1** gristly. **2** grizzly.

gri|son (grī′sən, griz′ən), *n.* a weasellike, carnivorous mammal of South and Central America, with light upper parts and dark lower parts. [< French *grison* < *gris* gray]

grist (grist), *n.* **1a** grain to be ground: *The farmer took his grist to the mill.* **b** a batch of such grain. **2** grain that has been ground; meal or flour. **3** *U.S.* a lot, number, or quantity (of).
grist to (or **for**) **one's mill**, a source of profit or advantage to one: *All in all the companies overseas are in good heart and health and should bring grist to the mill in increasing measure as the years mature* (London Times).
[Old English *grīst,* related to *grindan* grind]

gris|tle (gris′əl), *n.* **1** a tough, elastic tissue, such as is sometimes found in meat; cartilage: *Babies have gristle instead of bone in some parts of the skull.* **2** a structure or formation consisting of cartilage; gristly part. [Old English *gristle*]

gris|tly (gris′lē), *adj.,* **-tli|er, -tli|est**. of or like gristle; cartilaginous. **—gris′tli|ness**, *n.*

grist mill, a mill for grinding grain.

grit (grit), *n., v.,* **grit|ted, grit|ting**. **—*n.*** **1** very fine bits of gravel or sand: *As the wind blew, grit seeped in around the cracks in the window.* **2** a coarse sandstone, especially of the kinds used for millstones and grindstones; gritstone. **3** the grain or texture of a stone, especially with respect to fineness or coarseness. **4** the abrasive quality of a sanding disk, cloth, or paper: *... many shops use three different grits to prepare the surface for painting* (Automotive Encyclopedia). **5** *Figurative.* courage; pluck; endurance: *For years and years most of the men and women of grit had gone away or been driven away* (J. W. R. Scott). SYN: fortitude.
—*v.t.* **1** to make a grating sound by holding closed and rubbing; grate; grind: *She gritted her teeth and plunged into the cold water.* **2** to put grit into or over. **—*v.i.*** **1** to give forth a grating sound. **2** to use grit as a covering or fill.
[Old English *grēot.* See related etym. at **grits, groats, grout.**]

Grit (grit), *n.* a member of the Liberal Party of Canada [< *grit*]

grit chamber, a tank in a sewage system, in which heavy inorganic matter settles to the bottom.

grith (grith), *n. Archaic or Historical.* **1** a place of protection; sanctuary; asylum. **2** guaranteed security; protection; defense; safe conduct. [Old English *grith*]

grits (grits), *n.pl.* **1** corn, oats, wheat, or other grain with the husks removed and coarsely ground. Grits are eaten boiled. **2** *U.S.* coarsely ground corn or hominy cooked as a cereal. [Middle English *gryttes* bran, chaff, alteration of Old English *gryttan,* plural of *grytte.* See related etym. at **grit, groats, grout.**]

grit|stone (grit′stōn′), *n.* a coarse sandstone, of the kind used for millstones and grindstones.

grit|ty (grit′ē), *adj.,* **-ti|er, -ti|est**. **1** of or containing grit; like grit; sandy. **2** *Informal, Figurative.* courageous; plucky: *The gritty, grinning captain of paratroopers had fought for almost a decade in jungle and mountains* (Time). SYN: resolute. **—grit′ti|ly**, *adv.* **—grit′ti|ness**, *n.*

griv|et (griv′it), *n.* a small African monkey with a greenish-gray back and long tail, closely related to the green monkey.

griz|zle[1] (griz′əl), *n., adj., v.,* **-zled, -zling**. **—*n.*** **1a** gray hair. **b** a gray wig. **2** the color gray. **3** a gray animal, especially a horse or dog.
—*adj.* gray; grizzled.
—*v.t.* to make gray. **—*v.i.*** to become gray.
[< Old French *grisel* (diminutive) < *gris* gray < Germanic (compare Old High German *chrīsil, grīs*)]

griz|zle[2] (griz′əl), *v.,* **-zled, -zling**, *n. British Dialect or Informal.* **—*v.i.*** **1** to show the teeth; grin or laugh, especially mockingly. **2** to fret; sulk; whine; whimper: *A man, grizzling about life in general, was being cheered up by one of his friends* (Cape Times).
—*n.* a whining; whimpering; complaining. [origin uncertain]

griz|zled (griz′əld), *adj.* **1** grayish; gray: *a grizzled beard.* **2** gray-haired.

griz|zler (griz′lər), *n. British Dialect or Informal.* a person who frets or grumbles.

griz|zly (griz′lē), *adj.,* **-zli|er, -zli|est**, *n., pl.* **-zlies**.
—*adj.* **1** grayish; gray. **2** grayhaired.
—*n.* = grizzly bear.

grizzly bear, a large, fierce, gray or brownish-gray bear of the mountains of western North America. Its fur is white at the tips, making it look grizzled. The grizzly bear is becoming rare. See picture under **bear**[1].

gro., gross (12 dozen).

groan (grōn), *n., v.* **—*n.*** a sound made down in the throat that expresses grief, pain, or disapproval; deep, short moan: *We heard the groans of the man who had fallen off the cliff.* [< verb]
—*v.i.* **1** to give a groan or groans: *The tired horse groaned under the heavy load. She groaned in wordless grief.* **2** *Figurative.* to be loaded or burdened so as to sound or seem to groan: *The table groaned with food. The press groans with productions* (Thomas Jefferson). **3** to call painfully or urgently: *He groaned for water.*
—*v.t.* **1** to express by groaning: *He groaned his disapproval.* **2** to utter with groans: *He groaned out an answer.*
[Old English *grānian*] **—groan′ing|ly**, *adv.*
— *Syn.* *n.* **Groan, moan** mean a low sound expressing painful feelings. **Groan** applies to a brief sound, sometimes sudden and violent, sometimes repeated irregularly, expressing pain or suffering or, sometimes, disapproval: *We heard the groans of the sick man.* **Moan** applies to a long drawn-out or continuous sound expressing grief or great suffering: *A moan rose from the watching crowd when the burning roof fell in.*

groan|er (grō′nər), *n.* **1** a person or thing that groans. **2** *U.S. Slang.* a singer of popular songs, especially a crooner. **3** *U.S. Slang.* a professional wrestler.

groat (grōt), *n.* **1** an old English silver coin, worth fourpence. **2** *Figurative.* a very small sum: *I do not care a groat what it is* (Lord Chesterfield). [< Middle Dutch *groot* (literally) thick (coin), ultimately < Late Latin *grossus* thick, gross]

groats (grōts), *n.pl.* **1** hulled grain; hulled and crushed grain, such as wheat or oats. **2** the parts of oat kernels that can be eaten. Also, **grouts**. [alteration of Old English *grotan,* plural. See related etym. at **grit, grits, grout.**]

gro|cer (grō′sər), *n.* a person who sells food and household supplies. [< Old French *grossier* wholesaler < Medieval Latin *grossarius* grocer < Late Latin *grossus* coarse (of food, spirit) < Latin, thick, gross]

gro|cer|y (grō′sər ē, grōs′rē), *n., pl.* **-cer|ies**. **1** a store that sells food and household supplies. **2** the business or trade of a grocer. **3** *U.S. Slang.* a bar; saloon: *I must a took a little too much at Welch's grocery* (Edward Eggleston).
groceries, articles of food and household supplies sold by a grocer: *We had at last the satisfaction of seeing him mounted upon the colt, with a ... box before him to carry groceries in* (Oliver Goldsmith).

gro|cer|y|man (grō′sər ē mən, grōs′rē-), *n., pl.* **-men**. *U.S.* a grocer.

grocery store, *U.S.* a grocery.

gro|ce|te|ri|a (grō′sə tir′ē ə), *n. U.S.* a grocery where people wait on themselves. [American English < *groce*(ry) + *-teria*]

gro|dy (grō′dē), *adj. U.S. Slang.* disgusting; gross: *Mom, like that's ... grody to the max, just gruesome* (New York Times). [perhaps alteration of *grotesque.* Compare **grotty**.]

grog (grog), *n.* **1** a drink made of rum and water or whiskey and water. **2** any strong alcoholic drink. [earlier *grogg,* supposedly short for *grogram,* nickname of Edward Vernon, 1684-1757, a British admiral, who ordered his seamen to dilute their rum, so called from his *grogram* cloak]

grog|ger|y (grog′ər ē), *n., pl.* **-ger|ies**. *Especially British.* a saloon; grogshop.

grog|gy (grog′ē), *adj.,* **-gi|er, -gi|est**. *Informal.* **1** not steady; shaky: *A blow on the head made* *me groggy.* **2** drunk; intoxicated. **—grog′gi|ly,** *adv.* **—grog′gi|ness,** *n.*

gro|gnard (grō nyär′), *n. French.* **1a** a soldier of the first French Empire. **b** an old soldier. **2** a grumbler; growler.

grog|ram (grog′rəm), *n.* a coarse cloth made of silk, of wool, or of combinations of these with mohair, often stiffened with gum. [< French *gros grain* coarse grain]

grog|shop (grog′shop′), *n. Especially British.* a bar; saloon; dramshop; public house; groggery.

groin** (groin), *n., v.* **—*n. **1** the hollow on either side of the body where the thigh joins the abdomen, or the surrounding region. **2** the curved edge where two vaults of a roof intersect. **3** Also, **groyne.** a structure of timber, masonry, or other material built out into the sea from a beach or shore, for the purpose of retaining the sand washed up by the tide and raising up a barrier against the waves.
—*v.t.* **1** to form into or build with groins: *He groined his arches and matched his beams* (James Russell Lowell). **2** Also, **groyne.** to furnish with groins, as a beach.
[Middle English *grynde,* perhaps Old English *grynde* abyss]

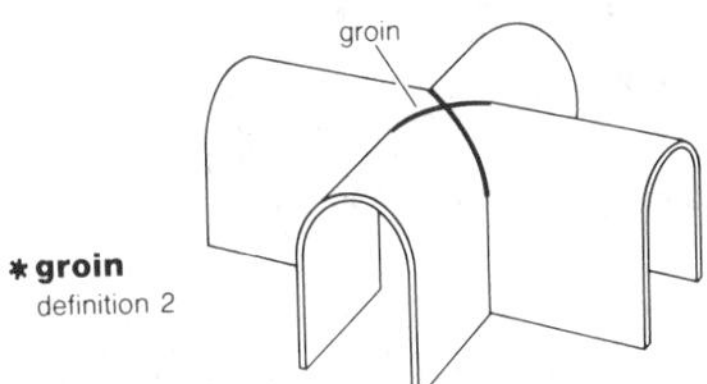

***groin**
definition 2

grok (grok), *v.i.,* **grokked, grok|king.** *U.S. Slang.* to communicate meaningfully or sympathetically. [< power of communication possessed by the hero of *Stranger in a Strange Land*]

Gro|li|er (grō′lē ər; *French* grô lyā′), *adj.* of or having to do with a style of decoration in bookbinding, consisting of bold lines of gold curiously interlaced in geometrical forms and intermixed with delicate leaves and sprays. [< Jean *Grolier* de Servières, 1479-1565, a French bibliophile]

grom|met (grom′it), *n.* **1** a metal eyelet, especially one in a piece of cloth. **2** a ring of rope, used as an oarlock or to hold a sail on its stays; becket. Also, **grummet.** [< Old French *gromette* or *gourmette* curb or bridle < *gourmer* to curb < *gourme* < Germanic (compare English *worm*)]

grom|well (grom′wəl), *n.* any one of a group of herbs of the borage family, with white, yellow, greenish-yellow, or blue flowers and hard, stony seeds formerly much used in medicine. [alteration of Middle English *gromel* < Old French; origin uncertain]

groom (grüm), *n., v.* **—*n.*** **1** a man just married or about to be married; bridegroom: *The lanky groom, decked out in brown suede shoes and a brown tail coat with a yellow carnation* (Newsweek). **2** a man or boy whose work is taking care of horses. **3** any of several officers of the English royal household. **4** *Archaic.* a manservant.
—*v.t.* **1** to feed, rub down, brush, and generally take care of (a horse or dog): *A dog with long hair needs grooming often.* **2** to take care of the appearance of; make neat and tidy: *He was grooming himself for the party.* **3** to prepare (a person) to run for political or other office: *The lawyer was being groomed as a candidate for mayor. Yet the Chancellor's fixed purpose seems to be not to groom a successor while he is himself still in office* (Manchester Guardian).
[Middle English *grome* boy; origin uncertain]
—groom′er, *n.*

grooms|man (grümz′mən), *n., pl.* **-men.** a man who attends the bridegroom at a wedding.

groove (grüv), *n., v.,* **grooved, groov|ing.** **—*n.*** **1** a long, narrow channel or furrow, especially one cut by a tool: *My desk has a groove for pencils. The plate rests in a groove on the rack.* **2** any similar channel; rut: *Wheels leave grooves in a dirt road.* **3** a channel or furrow of natural formation. **4** *Figurative.* a fixed way of doing things: *It is hard for him to get out of a groove.* **5** *Printing.* a channel on the base of a piece of type, between the feet. **6** *Slang.* something groovy or first-rate: *The show was a groove.*
—*v.t.* **1** to make a groove or grooves in: *The counter of the sink is grooved so that the water will run off.* **2** *Slang.* to record on (a phonograph record): *The disc . . . is grooved by the Harry Simeone Chorale and it is a winner* (Cape Times). **3** *Baseball.* to pitch (a ball) over the plate so as to make it easy for the batter to hit. **4** *Slang.* to give pleasure; entertain: *What better way to groove my contemporaries on earth than to decorate their material life with mind-expanding design?* (Peter Max).
—*v.i. Slang.* **1** to enjoy oneself; have fun: *The women really groove on his music* (New Yorker). **2** to be enjoyable; be fun: *"Life as it is . . . really grooves"* (John Updike).
groove it, *Slang.* to enjoy oneself: *"The first time I drove into Eastport I really grooved it"* (Saturday Review).
groove with, *Slang.* to like; appreciate: *Most [vendors] are under 30, grow their hair long, and groove with arts and crafts* (New York Times).
in the groove, *Slang.* **a** showing great skill; first-rate: *Those players are really in the groove.* **b** fashionable; up-to-date: *"They are in the groove here [in Germany] all right," Hampton explained. "Jazz is something new in music which hits them all"* (Newsweek).
[probably < Middle Dutch *groeve* furrow, ditch]
—groov′er, *n.*

groove-billed ani (grüv′bild′), a gregarious black tickbird found from northern South America to the southern United States. It is about 14 inches long and has an upper bill marked with parallel grooves and ridges.

groov|y (grü′vē), *adj.,* **groov|i|er, groov|i|est,** *for 3.* **1** of or resembling a groove. **2** *Dialect.* having a tendency to a fixed way of doing things. **3** *Slang.* in the groove; first-rate; excellent; perfect: *You want fresh ideas, groovy stuff?* (New Yorker). **—groov′i|ly,** *adv.* **—groov′i|ness,** *n.*

grope (grōp), *v.,* **groped, grop|ing,** *n.* **—*v.i.*** **1** to feel about with the hands: *I groped for a flashlight when the lights went out.* **2** *Figurative.* to search blindly and uncertainly: *The detectives groped for some clue to the mysterious crime.*
—*v.t.* to find by feeling about with the hands; feel (one's way) slowly: *The blind man groped his way to the door.*
—*n.* the action or an act of groping.
[Old English *grāpian.* See related etym. at **grasp, grip, gripe.**] **—grop′er,** *n.* **—grop′ing|ly,** *adv.*

grop|er (grō′pər), *n. Australian.* = grouper[1].

gros|beak (grōs′bēk′), *n.* any one of various colorful finches with a large, stout, cone-shaped bill, such as the rose-breasted grosbeak. [< French *grosbec* < *gros* large + *bec* beak]

gro|schen (grō′shən), *n., pl.* **-schen.** **1** a unit of money in Austria, a bronze coin worth 1/100 of an Austrian schilling. **2a** a small silver coin varying in value, formerly used in Germany. **b** *Informal.* a small nickel coin used in Germany, worth 10 pfennigs. [< German *Groschen,* ultimately < Latin *grossus* gross (in Late Latin, thick, coarse)]

gros de Lon|dres (grō′də lôɴ′drə), a heavy silk fabric having ribs of alternating color or texture, used for dresses. [< French *gros,* adjective, gross; *de Londres* of London]

gros|grain (grō′grān′), *n., adj.* **—*n.*** a closely woven silk or rayon cloth with heavy cross threads and a dull finish, used especially for ribbons and accessories. **—*adj.*** having heavy cross threads and dull finish. [< French *gros grain* coarse grain]

Gros Mi|chel (grō′mə shel′), the common, commercial banana grown in the Caribbean area; Martinique. [< French *gros Michel* big Michael]

gros point (grōs′point′; *French* grō pwaɴ′), a raised stitch used especially in certain kinds of embroidery for upholstery and in sewing on or with canvas. [< French *gros point* large stitch]

gross (grōs), *adj., n., pl.* **gross|es** *for 1,* **gross** *for 2, v.* **—*adj.*** **1** with nothing taken out; total; entire; whole. Gross receipts are all the money taken in before costs are deducted. **SYN:** aggregate. **2** very bad; easy to see; glaring; flagrant: *gross misconduct, gross superstition. She makes gross errors in adding.* **SYN:** outrageous. **3** *Figurative.* coarse; vulgar: *Her manners are too gross for a lady.* **SYN:** broad, indecent, low. **4** too big and fat; overfed: *One of them is well-known . . . a gross fat man* (Shakespeare). **5** thick; heavy; dense: *the gross growth of a jungle.* **SYN:** rank. **6** *Figurative.* lacking in culture or discrimination; without education or refinement: *gross taste in literature. . . . men now gross of ear, of vision dim* (John Greenleaf Whittier). **7** concerned with large masses or outlines; general. **8** *Obsolete.* striking; evident; obvious. **9** *Obsolete.* wanting in fineness or delicacy of texture, granulation, or outline.
—*n.* **1a** the whole sum; total amount: *The gross amount of his bill included the tax too.* **b** *Obsolete.* the greater part; majority; bulk. **2a** a unit consisting of twelve dozen; 144. *Abbr:* gr. or gro. **b** = great gross.
—*v.t.* **1** to make a gross profit of; earn a total of: *to gross $20,000 per year.* **2** *U.S. Slang.* Usually, **gross out.** to shock or disgust: *They [horror movies] offer dangling limbs, effusing guts, and gruesome decapitations—and audiences are lining up in droves to be "grossed out"* (New York Post).
in the gross, a in a general way; in the main; on the whole: *You cannot refuse in the gross what you have so often acknowledged in detail* (Edmund Burke). **b** in bulk; on a large scale; wholesale: *Department stores buy merchandise in the gross.*
[< Old French *gros* < Late Latin *grossus* thick, coarse < Latin, stout, fat] **—gross′ly,** *adv.* **—gross′ness,** *n.*

gross domestic product, *Economics.* the gross national product minus the net payments on foreign investments. *Abbr:* GDP (no periods).

gross|er (grō′sər), *n.* a person or thing that grosses; earner.

gross income, the total income from all sources before deductions have been made.

gross loss, the total loss before the expenses of doing business have been deducted.

gross national product, *Economics.* the total monetary value of all the goods and services produced in a nation during a certain period of time. It is a measure of the market value of the goods and services without deductions for depreciation or other business expenses. *Abbr:* GNP (no periods).

gross profit, the difference between cost of goods and the selling price; profit before the expenses of doing business have been deducted.

gross receipts, receipts before any deductions for expenses have been made.

gross social product, *Economics.* the total monetary value of all goods produced in a nation during a certain period of time; gross national product minus the value of services: *Investments . . . in Yugoslavia amounted to some 43 per cent of the gross social product (GSP) of the country* (Financial Times). *Abbr:* GSP (no periods).

gross ton, 1 a long ton; 2,240 pounds. **2** *Nautical.* a measure of volume; 100 cubic feet.

gros|su|lar|ite (gros′yə lə rīt), *n. Mineralogy.* a garnet of various colors composed of calcium and aluminum. [< New Latin *Grossularia* the gooseberry genus + English *-ite*[1]]

gross weight, weight including the container, waste, packing, and the like. *Abbr:* gr. wt.

Gros Ven|tre (grō′vän′trə), *pl.* **Gros Ven|tre** or **Gros Ven|tres** (grō′vän′trə). a name applied either to the Atsina or the Hidatsa tribes. [< French *gros ventre* big belly]

grosz (grôsh), *n., pl.* **gro|szy** (grô′shē). **1** a Polish unit of money, worth 1/100 of a zloty. **2** a bronze coin having this value. [< Polish *grosz*]

grot (grot), *n. Archaic.* a grotto. [< Middle French *grotte* < Italian *grotta,* variant of *grotto;* see etym. under **grotto**]

gro|tesque (grō tesk′), *adj., n.* **—*adj.*** **1** odd or unnatural in shape, appearance, or manner; fantastic; queer: *The book had pictures of hideous dragons and other grotesque monsters.* **SYN:** bizarre, strange. **2** ridiculous; absurd: *The monkey's grotesque antics made the children laugh.* **3** (of painting or sculpture) in or resembling the grotesque: *'Tis grotesque painting; the fine woman ends in a fish's tail* (John Dryden).
—*n.* **1** painting or sculpture combining designs, ornaments, or figures of persons or animals in a fantastic or unnatural way, much used in the Renaissance. **2** a grotesque person or thing: *It makes grotesques out of the actors* (London Times). **3** *Printing.* Also, **Grotesque. a** an ornate or fanciful style of type face. **b** = sans-serif. **c** *British.* Gothic.
[< French *grotesque* < Italian *grottesco* < *grotta;* see etym. under **grotto**] **—gro|tesque′ly,** *adv.* **—gro|tesque′ness,** *n.*

gro|tes|que|rie or **gro|tes|que|ry** (grō tes′kə rē), *n., pl.* **-ries.** **1** grotesque work. **2** grotesque character. **3** something grotesque.

grot|to (grot′ō), *n., pl.* **-toes** or **-tos.** **1** a cave or cavern, especially one that is picturesque or that forms an agreeable retreat. **2** an artificial cave made for coolness and pleasure. [< Italian *grotta,* earlier *grotto* < Latin *crypta* < Greek *kryptē* vault < *kryptós* hidden. See etym. of doublet **crypt.**]

grot|ty (grot′ē), *adj.,* **-ti|er, -ti|est.** *British Slang.* dreary; dull: *They live in bed-sitters . . . and their rooms are so grotty they just can't bear to stay in* (Manchester Guardian Weekly). [alteration of *grotesque,* perhaps influenced by *grotto*]

grouch (grouch), *n., v. Informal.* **—*n.*** **1** a fit of grumbling or complaining; a surly, ill-tempered mood. **2** a sulky person; a surly, ill-tempered person; grumbler. **3** a complaint or grumble: *Here he airs his latest enthusiasms and his pet grouches* (New Yorker).
—*v.i.* to be sulky; grumble or complain in a surly, ill-tempered way.
[American English, variant of *grutch* < Old French *groucher* murmur, grumble. See etym. of doublet **grudge.**]

Pronunciation Key: hat, āge, cãre, fär; let, ēqual, tėrm; it, īce; hot, ōpen, ôrder; oil, out; cup, pu̇t, rüle; child; long; thin; ŦHen; zh, measure; ə represents **a** in about, **e** in taken, **i** in pencil, **o** in lemon, **u** in circus.

grouch|y (grou′chē), *adj.*, **grouch|i|er, grouch|i|est.** *Informal.* tending to grumble or complain; surly; ill-tempered. —**grouch′i|ly,** *adv.* —**grouch′i|ness,** *n.*

ground¹ (ground), *n., adj., v.* —*n.* **1** the solid part of the earth's surface: *A blanket of snow covered the ground. He looked on the ground while he answered her* (Scott). **2** soil; earth; dirt: *And here the maiden, sleeping sound, On the dank and dirty ground* (Shakespeare). **SYN:** loam, mold. **3** a particular piece of land: *low ground, rising ground.* **4** Often, **grounds.** any piece of land or region used for some purpose: *fishing grounds, picnic grounds. The West was his favorite hunting ground.* **5** Often **grounds.** *Figurative.* the foundation for what is said, thought, claimed, or done; basis; reason: *There is no ground for complaining of his conduct. On what grounds do you say that is true?* **SYN:** premise, motive. **6a** any material surface for working upon, such as a layer of gesso on a panel or canvas for painting, a coating of wax on a metal plate for etching, or the meshes on which the pattern is worked in lacemaking. **b** background: *The cloth has a blue pattern on a white ground.* **7** the solid bottom underlying a body of water: *to strike ground in taking soundings.* **8** the connection of an electrical conductor with the earth, so that the electricity passes off into it. **9** a connection in a radio or television set for the conductor that leads to the earth. **10** the pit of a theater.
—*adj.* **1** of the ground; on the ground: *the ground floor.* **2** basic; fundamental. **3** living or growing in, on, or close to the ground.
—*v.t.* **1** to put on the ground; cause to touch the ground: *to ground arms.* **2** *Figurative.* **a** to fix firmly; establish: *His beliefs are grounded on facts.* **b** to instruct in the first principles or elements: *The class is well grounded in arithmetic.* **3** to furnish with a background for painting, decorating, or the like. **4** to connect (an electric wire or other conductor) with the earth, so that the electricity passes off into it: *When the charged body is grounded ... it and the whole earth become a single conductor* (Shortley and Williams). **5** to cause (a ship or boat) to run ashore or aground. **6** to keep (a pilot or an aircraft) from flying: *The pilot was grounded by injury. Trucks and trains can operate in storms that may ground airplanes* (Ernest W. Williams, Jr.). **7** *U.S. Informal.* to keep (a boy or girl) from going out socially, especially as a punishment.
—*v.i.* **1** to run aground; hit the bottom or shore: *The boat grounded in shallow water.* **2** *Baseball.* to hit a bouncing or rolling ball.

above (the) ground, alive: *While I remain above the ground, you shall hear from me still* (Shakespeare).

break ground, a to turn up soil with a plow, shovel, etc.; dig; plow: *to break ground for a new school.* **b** to begin building. **c** *Figurative.* to execute a plan or venture: *He showed no inclination to break new ground* (New York Times).

cover ground, a to go over a certain distance or area; travel: *Did you cover much ground on the hike?* **b** *Figurative.* to do a certain amount of work: *We covered considerable ground in our history class today.*

cut the ground from under one (or **under one's feet**), to spoil one's defense or argument by meeting it in advance: *A witness with evidence to the contrary cut the ground from under the defense attorney's argument.*

fall to the ground, (of schemes) to fail; be given up: *It fell to the ground with the rest of the King's plans and attempts* (Horace Walpole).

from the ground up, completely; entirely; thoroughly: *We conducted our research from the ground up.*

gain ground, a to go forward; advance; progress: *The fresh troops gained much ground against the exhausted enemy.* **b** *Figurative.* to become more common or widespread: *His ideas are gaining ground.*

get off the ground, to make a start; go forward; advance: *The magazine never got off the ground* (Time).

give ground, to retreat; yield: *They come, no man give ground ... Be Englishmen and beard them to their faces* (Thomas Dekker).

ground out, *Baseball.* to be put out on hitting a grounder: *The youngster ... calmly threw home to start a run-nipping double play, and then got* [*the outfielder*] *to ground out* (Time).

grounds, a land, lawns, and gardens around a house or other building: *the grounds of an estate.* **b** small bits that sink to the bottom of a drink such as coffee or tea; dregs; sediment: *Pour the grounds down the drain.*

hold one's ground, to keep one's position; not retreat or yield: *He could not hold his ground in the face of relentless opposition.*

lose ground, a to go backward; retreat; yield: *We lost ground because of the storm.* **b** *Figurative.* to become less common or widespread: *Superstition and illiteracy are losing ground as people become more educated.* **c** *Figurative.* to lose advantage: *To deal plainly with you, you have lost some ground at Court by it* (James Howell).

run into the ground, *Informal.* to carry to an extreme; overdo: *You have a good idea, but I hope you won't run it into the ground.*

shift one's ground, to change one's position; use a different defense or argument: *A friend, as willing to shift his ground as I, gave me an overture which I accepted* (Richard Ligon).

stand one's ground, to keep one's position; refuse to retreat or yield: *The Deserters ... stood their ground, and ... fired on 'em* (London Gazette).

take ground, to take up, or move into, a certain position: *Take ground to the right* (*or left*) *in fours* (F. A. Griffiths).

[Old English *grund* bottom]

ground² (ground), *v., adj.* —*v.* a past tense and past participle of **grind:** *The miller ground the corn into meal. The wheat was ground to make flour.*
—*adj.* **1** reduced to fine particles by grinding or crushing: *ground black pepper.* **2** subjected to the action or process of grinding: *a finely ground edge on a tool.*

ground|age (groun′dij), *n. Especially British, Commerce.* a charge levied on ships entering a port, or lying offshore.

ground alert, 1 a state of readiness in which aircraft and crews are ready for immediate take-off in defense against enemy aircraft. **2** the signal to take stations for such defense.

ground bait, bait thrown to the bottom of the water to attract fish.

ground ball, *Baseball.* a grounder.

ground-based (ground′bāst′), *adj.* based or located on the ground.

ground bass (bās), *Music.* a melodic figure constantly repeated in the bass while the remainder of the texture is developed freely.

ground beetle, any one of a family of mostly predacious, terrestrial beetles.

ground blackberry, = dewberry.

ground|break|er (ground′brā′kər), *n.* a person who begins or helps the beginning of something; pioneer; innovator.

ground|break|ing (ground′brā′king), *n.* the act of breaking ground to begin building.

ground|burst (ground′bėrst′), *n.* the explosion of a bomb at the surface, as contrasted with an airburst.

ground cherry, any one of a group of American plants of the nightshade family, such as one bearing edible, yellow berries, and the strawberry tomato; husk tomato.

ground cloth, = groundsheet.

ground connection, the electric wire or other conductor used to produce a ground.

ground control, the supervision and control of aircraft operations by a station or system of stations on the ground.

ground controlled approach, an approach and landing by an aircraft under ground control, due to poor visibility. *Abbr:* GCA (no periods).

ground controller, a man in charge of controlling flight operations from a station on the ground.

ground cover, low plants or shrubbery planted for ornament or to enrich the soil and prevent the topsoil from eroding or blowing away.

ground crew, the mechanics and other nonflying personnel responsible for the conditioning and maintenance of aircraft.

ground cuckoo, = road runner.

ground cushion, *Aeronautics.* a buoyant cushion of air set up by the air driven downward by an airplane or a helicopter hovering or flying close to the ground.

ground dove, a small grayish dove, only 6½ inches long, found from the southern United States to Brazil.

ground|ed|ly (groun′did lē), *adv.* in a well-grounded manner; with good reason.

ground effect machine, = air cushion vehicle. [so called because of the effect of the ground in trapping the air to form a cushion] *Abbr:* GEM (no periods).

ground|er (groun′dər), *n.* **1** a baseball hit so as to bounce or roll along the ground; ground ball. **2** a person or thing that founds, establishes, causes, etc. **3** a person who does the grounding in the manufacture of wallpaper, or in other arts of design.

ground fir, any one of several species of club moss or ground pine.

ground fire, a forest fire that spreads over the deposits of leaves, branches, and the like on the ground.

ground|fire (ground′fīr′), *n.* antiaircraft fire from the ground.

ground|fish (ground′fish′), *n., pl.* **-fish|es** or (*collectively*) **-fish.** any one of various fishes, such as the cod, haddock, hake, pollack, cusk, and ocean perch, that swim close to the bottom of the sea.

ground floor, 1 the floor in a building that is more or less on a level with the ground outside. **2** *U.S., Figurative.* the beginning of a venture: *He got in on the ground floor and made a fortune.* **3** *U.S., Figurative.* the most advantageous position in relation to a business deal or other venture.

ground fog, a low fog, usually below 100 feet, that occurs early in the morning as a result of the cooling of the earth's surface and the lower air at night.

ground force, the part of the armed forces of a nation that operates on the ground.

ground glass, 1 glass with the surface roughened so that it is not transparent. **2** glass that has been ground to powder.

ground hemlock, any one of several low, straggling yews that grow to a height of about six feet, found from Newfoundland to Virginia and west to Iowa; American yew.

ground hog or **ground|hog** (ground′hog′, -hôg′), *n.* **1** = woodchuck. **2** = sandhog.

ground-hog day (ground′hog′, -hôg′), February 2, the day when the woodchuck (ground hog) is believed to come out of his hole. If the sun is shining and he sees his shadow, the ground hog goes back in his hole and winter continues for six more weeks.

ground ice, ice formed at the bottom of a river or other body of water, supposed to be due to excessive radiation of heat from the bottom on cold, clear nights.

ground|ing (groun′ding), *n.* basic instruction or knowledge; fundamentals: *The training ... included the standard grounding in the current sociological and psychological theories* (New York Times).

ground itch, an irritation and itching of the skin where the larvae of hookworms have penetrated.

ground ivy, a common trailing herb of the mint family, having roundish leaves and small, purple or blue flowers; gill; hen-and-chickens; gill-over-the-ground.

ground|keep|er (ground′kē′pər), *n.* = groundskeeper.

ground-launched (ground′lôncht′, -läncht′), *adj.* set into motion from a position on the ground: *Air Force's Snark, ground-launched against ground targets, is a subsonic missile with ranges exceeding 5,000 miles* (Time).

ground laurel, = arbutus (def. 1).

ground lease, a lease of land for building.

ground|less (ground′lis), *adj.* without foundation, basis, or reason; unfounded: *a groundless rumor. A groundless fiction that cannot be proved* (Richard Baxter). **SYN:** baseless. —**ground′less|ly,** *adv.* —**ground′less|ness,** *n.*

ground|ling (ground′ling), *n.* **1** a plant or animal that lives close to the ground. **2** a fish that lives at the bottom of the water. **3** a person living or working on the ground, as opposed to a pilot or seaman: *To the groundling, the skies seem unlimited, but the traffic problem in the nation's air lanes is almost as bad as on the highways* (Time). **4** *Figurative.* a spectator or reader who has poor critical taste. **5** *Obsolete.* a person who sat in the pit of a theater, often on the ground.

ground log, a device for measuring a ship's speed in shallow water, consisting of a heavy weight on the end of a line. After the weight sinks to the bottom, the speed of the ship is determined by the amount of line paid out over a specific length of time.

ground loop, an uncontrolled, abrupt turn made by an aircraft while moving along the ground.

ground|mass (ground′mas′), *n.* the crystalline, granular, or glassy base of a porphyry, in which the more prominent crystals are embedded.

ground meristem, *Botany.* a group of cells in a stem that gives rise to the cortex, pericycle, and pith.

ground mine, a mine that rests on the ocean floor, used in naval warfare.

ground moraine, *Geology.* a mass of stones, broken rock, or other debris formed beneath a glacier, found in low and protected areas. See picture under **glacier.**

ground|nut (ground′nut′), *n.* **1** any one of several plants having underground parts which are used for food, such as the peanut and a North American plant of the pea family, with small, tuberous roots; groundpea. **2** its tuber, pod, or the like, which is good to eat.

ground observer, a person who observes and reports aircraft activity from the ground, especially in wartime.

ground|out (ground′out′), *n. Baseball.* a putout

on hitting a grounder: *Johnson . . . got Brock on a groundout as the sixth run crossed the plate* (New York Times).

ground owl, = burrowing owl.

ground parakeet, a parakeet of Australia and Tasmania that makes its home in bushes rather than in trees.

ground|pea (ground′pē′), *n.* **1** = peanut. **2** = groundnut (def. 1).

ground pearl, a bronze-colored shell that forms around certain scale insects living on the roots of plants, such as a variety found in the Bahamas. Ground pearl is used as beading for jewelry.

ground pig, 1 = aardvark. **2** = ground rat.

ground pine, 1 any one of various species of club moss, especially two creeping evergreens and an erect evergreen, used for Christmas decoration and the like. **2** a European herb of the mint family with a resinous smell.

ground pink, = moss pink.

ground plan, 1 the plan of a floor of a building. **2** *Figurative.* the first or fundamental plan upon which any work is constructed or composed.

ground plate, 1 a metal plate sunk in the ground and connecting an electric circuit with the earth. **2** = groundsill. **3** plate under a railroad tie.

ground plum, 1 a plant of the pea family, a milk vetch, growing in the American prairie regions. **2** its edible fruit, that resembles a plum in size and shape. **3** any one of various allied plants or their fruit.

ground rat, any one of several large African rodents; ground pig.

ground rent, *Especially British.* the rent paid for land leased for building purposes.

ground robin, = towhee.

ground row, a low piece of theatrical scenery with a shaped edge that gives the appearance of distant hills or rows of buildings.

ground rule, 1 *Sports.* one of a set of rules in effect at a certain playing field or stadium that regulates decisions relating to conditions of play. **2** one of a basic set of rules regulating the conduct of any activity: *Even in a cold war there are certain "ground rules" of international behaviour which are essential to keep the war cold* (Manchester Guardian Weekly).

grounds (groundz), *n.pl.* See under **ground**[1].

ground sea, a heavy sea or swell on the ocean, occurring without apparent cause but thought to be due to distant gales.

ground|sel[1] (ground′səl), *n.* any one of a large genus of plants of the composite family with yellow flower heads. The seeds of some kinds are used for bird food. Various species are called *ragwort.* [Old English *grundeswelge* < *grund* ground, or < *gund* pus + *swelgan* swallow[1] (either from its rapidity of growth or its use to reduce swellings)]

ground|sel[2] (ground′səl), *n.* = groundsill.

ground shark, any one of various sharks inhabiting warm coastal waters.

ground|sheet (ground′shēt′), *n.* a waterproof sheet spread on the ground as a protection against damp; ground cloth.

ground|sill (ground′sil′), *n.* a horizontal timber used as a foundation; lowest part of a wooden framework; sill; ground plate. [Middle English *gronsel* < Old English *grund* ground + *sylle* sill (influenced by English *ground* and *sill*)]

grounds|keep|er (groundz′kē′pər), *n.* a man whose work is to keep an athletic field in good repair. Also, **groundkeeper**.

ground sloth, any one of various toothless, extinct, American mammals related to the megathere and the present-day sloths. They did not climb trees and often grew to a length of 20 feet.

grounds|man (groundz′mən), *n., pl.* **-men.** *British.* a groundskeeper.

ground speed, the speed of an aircraft relative to the ground it passes over.

ground squirrel, any one of a group of burrowing rodents related to the squirrels, with short rounded ears, short legs, and short or medium-sized tails. In North America they occur only in the western part of the continent. Prairie dogs, marmots, and chipmunks are ground squirrels. See picture under **squirrel**.

ground state, *Physics.* that state of energy of an atom in which the electrons are as near to the nucleus as possible; state of lowest energy. For hydrogen, the electron is at an average distance of $.5 \times 10^{-10}$ meters from the proton.

ground stroke, (in tennis) a stroke made on a ball that has bounced from the ground.

ground substance, *Biology.* **1** the intercellular substance of tissue; matrix. **2** = hyaloplasm.

ground support equipment, the equipment required to keep a guided missile in constant preparedness for firing.

ground swell, 1 a broad, deep wave or swell of the ocean caused by a distant storm or earthquake. **2** a great rise or increase in the amount, degree, or force of anything: *there was a ground swell of opinion that something had better be done* (New Scientist).

ground tackle, cables, anchors, and other equipment, for securing a vessel at anchor.

ground-test (ground′test′), *v.t.* to test (a rocket, missile, or airplane) on the ground under simulated flying conditions.

ground-to-air (ground′tü ãr′), *adj.* directed from a position on the ground to a target in the air.

ground-to-ground (ground′tü ground′), *adj., n.* —***adj.*** directed from a position on the ground against a target at a distance on the ground. —***n.*** a ground-to-ground rocket or missile.

ground truth, information about the earth obtained by direct examination of features on the ground, especially to supplement or verify data obtained by remote sensing: *Scientists involved in these experiments, some of whom are skeptical about the accuracy of data from an orbiting spacecraft, will be scattered around the world to get what they call "ground truth"* (New Yorker).

ground water, water held beneath the earth's surface, especially water that flows or seeps downward and saturates the soil. The upper level of this saturated zone is called the water table. Ground water supplies springs and wells.

ground wave, a radio wave that travels along, or near, the ground.

ground wire, a wire connecting electric wiring, a radio or other appliance, or a lightning arrester, with the ground.

ground|wood (ground′wu̇d′), *n.* wood pulp made by grinding wood, used for making paper.

ground woodpecker, a woodpecker of South Africa, about ten inches long, having olive-brown feathers. It hunts insects on the ground or in the clay along riverbanks where it tunnels out its nests.

ground|work (ground′wėrk′), *n.* foundation; basis.

ground zero, the exact point where a bomb strikes the ground or, in a nuclear explosion, the area directly above or below the center of radiation. Ground zero is considered as the area of greatest destruction.

group (grüp), *n., v.* —***n.* 1** a number of persons, animals, or things together; cluster: *A group of children were playing tag. Since man does not live alone, the group is an important factor in his life. It helps to shape his personality and his conduct by bringing pressure to bear upon him to conform to the established patterns, rewarding approved behavior and punishing behavior that is not sanctioned* (William F. Ogburn). **SYN:** aggregation, assemblage. **2** a number of persons, animals, or things belonging or classed together: *Dutch, English, German, and Swedish belong to one language group, the Germanic group.* **3** a number of persons or things that act as a unit: *Man can only make progress in co-operative groups* (Walter Bagehot). **4** a number of figures arranged together in a work of art: *The statue will be a group of three figures.* **5** a military unit made up of two or more battalions of supporting personnel, usually commanded by a colonel. **6** a U.S. Air Force unit smaller than a wing and composed of two or more squadrons. It corresponds to an infantry regiment. **7** *Chemistry.* **a** = radical. **b** a number of elements having similar properties and forming one of the vertical columns of the periodic table: *Lithium, sodium and potassium belong to the alkali metal group.* **8** *Mathematics.* a set of elements with a binary operation under the associative law in which the product is a member of the set, the set has an identity element, and there is an inverse for every member of the set. **9** *Geology, U.S.* a division of rocks, including two or more formations, usually deposited during one period. **10** *British.* a combination of corporations acting together through joint ownership, management, or interest.
—***v.t.* 1** to form into a group: *The children grouped themselves in front of the steps for a picture.* **2** to put in a group; arrange in groups: *Group the numbers to form three columns.*
—***v.i.*** to form a group; be part of a group.
[< French *groupe* < Italian *gruppo* < a Germanic word]

group|age (grü′pij), *n.* arrangement in a group or groups; grouping.

group annuity, a plan which provides annuities at retirement to a group of persons, usually employees of a company.

group banking, a banking organization in which control of several banks is held by a holding company formed to acquire the stock of the banks.

group captain, an officer in the Royal Air Force and other Commonwealth air forces equivalent to a colonel in the U.S. Air Force.

group dynamics, 1 the interplay of personalities in a group of people: *Leadership is basically an expression of group dynamics* (Emory S. Bogardus). **2** the study of methods by which a group or its actions can be influenced.

groupe|ment (grüp′mənt), *n.* a military unit of approximately 12,000-13,000 men, roughly equivalent to a division, as in the armies of the European Defense Community. [< French *groupement* < *groupe;* see etym. under **group**]

group|er[1] (grü′pər), *n., pl.* **-ers** or (*collectively*) **-er.** any one of various ocean fishes with large mouths that live in warm and temperate seas, mostly around rocky shores and coral reefs. They resemble in color the corals and algae among which they live. [< Portuguese *garupa,* perhaps < a Tupi word]

group|er[2] (grü′pər), *n. U.S.* a member of a group, such as an encounter group: *When, for instance, the spirits of some grouper noticeably sag, he may be rocked tenderly in the air on the hands of the others* (Time).

group|ie (grü′pē), *n. Slang.* **1** a teen-age girl who is a fan of rock 'n' roll singing groups and follows them where they perform. **2** a teen-age fan who follows any celebrity where he appears. **3** any fan or devotee; aficionado: *a radical-chic restaurant where Toronto artists, entrepreneurs and culture groupies hang out* (Macleans's). *Court groupies and Hearst case buffs arrived from all over the country* (Time). **4** a group of associated companies designated by the term *Group: Groupies included the Medallion Group, the American Recreation Group, . . . the Energy Reserves Group* (New York Times).

group|i|ness (grü′pē nis), *n.* the tendency to think and act as part of a group rather than as an individual.

group|ing (grü′ping), *n.* **1** a placing or manner of being placed in a group or groups. **2** the persons or things forming a group.

group insurance, a type of low-cost insurance covering a group of people, rather than an individual.

group|ism (grü′piz əm), *n.* conformity with the group; groupiness.

group|ist (grü′pist), *n.* a person who practices groupism.

group libel, *U.S. Law.* the publication or dissemination of any statement which holds up to contempt or ridicule a particular group of citizens, for example a group of some single race or creed.

group marriage, a rare or postulated system of matrimony in which several brothers or members of the same kinship group all marry several sisters or women of another kinship group.

group mind, 1 the collective mind of a group, class, or society. **2** the beliefs, attitudes, and the like, common to the members of such a group.

Group of 77, an informal grouping of developing countries: *The wording of the compromise fell short of the demands of the Group of 77, the organization of poor countries that now numbers 112* (New York Times).

group practice, *U.S.* medical practice by a number of physicians working in association with each other through a central administration.

group psychotherapy, = group therapy.

group representation, a method of selecting members of a governmental body to represent interests rather than geographical units.

group theory, 1 a branch of mathematics dealing with the properties of groups. **2** *Nuclear Physics.* any theory that arranges nuclear particles in groups to explain their properties and predict the existence of new ones.

group therapy, *Psychiatry.* a technique in which patients are treated together, the group itself often contributing to the therapy.

group|think (grüp′thingk′), *n.* the handling of any problem by a group, such as a commission, a board of directors, or a research team.

group|us|cule (grü′pə skyül), *n.* a very small or minor group. [< French *groupuscule* (diminutive) < *groupe* group]

group work, social work performed with groups and communities rather than individuals, as in planning and carrying out youth and adult educational and recreational programs.

group|y (grü′pē), *adj.,* **group|i|er, group|i|est.** tending toward groupiness; not individualistic: *It is not altogether clear just why suburbanites want to be groupy* (Atlantic).

grouse[1] (grous), *n., pl.* **grouse,** *v.,* **groused, grous|ing.** —***n.*** a reddish-brown game bird with feathered legs. The prairie chicken, sage grouse, and ruffed grouse of the United States are different kinds of grouse. —***v.i.*** to hunt or shoot grouse. [origin uncertain]

grouse[2] (grous), *v.,* **groused, grous|ing,** *n. Informal.* —***v.i.*** to grumble; complain: *They didn't*

Pronunciation Key: hat, āge, cãre, fär; let, ēqual, tėrm; it, īce; hot, ōpen, ôrder; oil, out; cup, pu̇t, rüle; child; long; thin; ᴛʜen; zh, measure; ə represents **a** in about, **e** in taken, **i** in pencil, **o** in lemon, **u** in circus.

grouse an' shirk at an hour's extry work (Rudyard Kipling).
—*n.* a complaint.
[originally British Army slang, perhaps < Old French *groucer,* variant of *groucher* grumble] —**grous′er**, *n.*

grout (grout), *n., v.* —*n.* **1** a thin mortar used to fill cracks, especially around tile. **2** a similar type of plaster for finishing walls and ceilings. **3** sediment; dregs; grounds. **4** coarse meal. **5** coarse porridge.
—*v.t.* **1** to fill up or finish with grout. **2** to use as grout.
grouts, = groats: *The grouts and pieces of the corn remaining ... they boil three or four hours with water* (Captain John Smith).
[Old English *grūt* coarse meal, malt infusion. See related etym. at **grit, grits, groats.**] —**grout′er**, *n.*

grout|y[1] (grou′tē), *adj.,* **grout|i|er, grout|i|est.** *U.S.* sulky; cross. [< obsolete *grout* to grumble, sulk]

grout|y[2] (grou′tē), *adj.,* **grout|i|er, grout|i|est.** *British Dialect.* **1** muddy; dirty. **2** threatening: *grouty weather.* [< *grout* + *-y*[1]]

grove (grōv), *n.* **1** a group of trees standing together; small wood. An orange grove is an orchard of orange trees. **2** *Figurative.* a dense mass; thicket: *a grove of bayonets, groves of words.*
the groves of academe, the world of scholars; the academic sphere (in allusion to the grove near Athens where Plato taught): *The hero's talks with Lady Gregory and Yeats ... are literate but lifeless conversations in the groves of academe* (Bosley Crowther).
[Old English *grāf*]

grov|el (gruv′əl, grov′-), *v.i.,* **-eled, -el|ing** or (*especially British*) **-elled, -el|ling. 1** to lie face downward; crawl at someone's feet; cringe: *The dog groveled before his master when he saw the whip.* **SYN**: fawn. **2** *Figurative.* to humble oneself; remain in a degrading state: *A man apologizes when he's wrong, but he will grovel before no one.* **SYN**: fawn. **3** to enjoy low, mean, or contemptible things. [back formation < Middle English *groveling,* (originally) adverb < phrase *on grufe* prone < Scandinavian (compare Old Icelandic *ā grūfu*)] —**grov′el|er**, *especially British,* **grov′el|ler**, *n.*

grov|el|ing|ly (gruv′əl ing lē, grov′-), *adv.* in a groveling manner.

grow (grō), *v.,* **grew, grown, grow|ing.** —*v.i.* **1** to become bigger by taking in food, as plants and animals do; develop toward full size or age: *Plants grow from seeds.* **2** to live and become big; exist; thrive; flourish: *Few trees grow in a desert.* **3** *Figurative.* to become bigger; increase: *His fame grew. His business has grown fast.* **SYN**: expand, develop. **4** *Figurative.* to sprout; spring; arise: *How grew your quarrel?* (Shakespeare). **5** to come to be; become: *to grow rich. It grew cold. The population of the United States has begun to grow younger* (Atlantic). **6** to become gradually attached or united by growth: *The vine has grown fast to the wall.*
—*v.t.* **1** to cause to grow; produce; raise: *We grow cotton in the southern part of the United States.* **SYN**: cultivate. **2** to allow to grow: *to grow a beard.* **3** to cover with a growth: *a field grown with corn.* **4** to develop: *Specks of lime, deposited by dripping water, had grown these marvelous stalactites and stalagmites through the centuries.* **5** to make or increase the size of (a crystal, as of sugar, copper, or silver): *Suppose we start with our spherical crystal and grow it into a larger crystal by depositing more atoms on it* (Science News Letter).
grow on (or **upon**), **a** to have an increasing effect or influence on: *The habit grew on me.* **b** to become more liked or admired by: *Miss Bennet's pleasing manners grew on ... Mrs. Hurst* (Jane Austen).
grow out of, a to grow too large for; outgrow: *to grow out of childish habits. When I grew out of my jacket, I gave it to my little brother.* **b** to result from; develop from: *The American Revolution grew out of the colonists' dissatisfaction with British rule. Several ideas grew out of the discussion.*
grow up, a to become full-grown; become an adult: *What will you be when you grow up? His sons grow up that bear his name* (Tennyson). **b** to come into being; be produced; develop: *a hostile feeling grew up in the community.*
[Old English *grōwan*] —**grow′a|ble**, *adj.*

grow|er (grō′ər), *n.* **1** a person who grows something: *a fruit grower.* **2** a plant that grows in a certain way: *a quick grower.*

grow|ing (grō′ing), *adj.* characterized by growth, as of plants: *a growing season.*

grow|ing|ly (grō′ing lē), *adv.* increasingly.

growing pains, 1 pains in the limbs or joints during childhood and youth, formerly supposed to be caused by growing or rheumatic disorders. They are now considered as nonspecific pains of the muscles and joints. **2** *Figurative.* troubles when something new is just developing: [*Shortages*] *all go back to the fact that America has a severe case of growing pains* (New York Times).

growl (groul), *v., n.* —*v.i.* **1** to make a deep, low, angry sound: *The dog growled at the stranger.* **2** to complain angrily; grumble: *The sailors growled about the poor food.* **3** to rumble: *Thunder growled in the distance.*
—*v.t.* to express by growling: *The dog growled its suspicions of the stranger.*
—*n.* **1** a deep, low, angry sound; deep, warning snarl: *He answered the impertinent question with a growl.* **2** an angry complaint; grumble. **3** a rumble.
[probably imitative]

growl|er (grou′lər), *n.* **1** a person or animal that growls. **2** a fish that makes a grunting sound when taken from the water, such as the grunt. **3** a piece of floating ice, considerably smaller than an iceberg, that has broken off from a glacier or iceberg. **4** an electromagnetic device used for finding short circuits and for magnetizing and demagnetizing. The presence of a short circuit is indicated by a growling noise. **5** *U.S. Slang.* a pail or pitcher to get beer in. **6** *British Slang.* a four-wheeled, horse-drawn cab.

growl|ing|ly (grou′ling lē), *adv.* in a growling manner; with a growl.

growl|y (grou′lē), *adj.,* **growl|i|er, growl|i|est. 1** resembling a growl. **2** growling.

grown (grōn), *adj., v.* —*adj.* **1** arrived at full growth. A grown man is an adult. **SYN**: mature. **2** covered with a growth.
—*v.* the past participle of **grow**: *The corn has grown very tall.*

grown-up (grōn′up′), *adj., n.* —*adj.* **1** arrived at full growth; adult: *a grown-up person.* **2** characteristic of or suitable for adults: *grown-up manners.*
—*n.* an adult: *The boy eats like a grown-up.* —**grown′-up′ness**, *n.*

growth (grōth), *n.* **1** the process of growing; development. **2** the amount grown; increase; progress: *one year's growth.* **SYN**: expansion, enlargement. **3** what has grown or is growing: *A thick growth of bushes covered the ground.* **4** an abnormal mass of tissue formed in or on the body. A tumor is a growth. *Cancer causes a growth.* **5** origin; source: *a plant of foreign growth, a story of English growth.*

growth center, a center or institute providing sensitivity training, Gestalt therapy, or some form of group therapy for the development of people's potentials.

growth curve, 1 a mathematical expression of the growth of a living thing or a population in relation to time. **2** = learning curve.

growth factor, *Biology.* **1** any substance which affects the growth of an organism. **2** = growth hormone.

growth|ful (grōth′fəl), *adj.* growing vigorously.

growth fund, a mutual-fund investment company whose stated goal is growth or appreciation in capital value.

growth hormone, 1 a hormone, secreted by the anterior lobe of the pituitary gland, which controls the growth of the body; somatotropin. Oversecretion causes gigantism; undersecretion, dwarfism. **2** any hormone which regulates plant growth, such as an auxin; growth substance.

growth industry, an industry whose rate of development or expansion is higher than the rate of growth of the entire economic system.

growth|less (grōth′lis), *adj.* lacking in growth.

growth|man|ship (grōth′mən ship), *n.* emphasis on economic growth, especially as a national policy: *The nation is no longer being asked to cry for ... immediate 4 per cent growth. But neither has growthmanship been thrown out of the window by the Government* (London Times).

growth ring, = annual ring: *Growth rings are the layers of wood laid down by the cambium in successive periods* (Fred W. Emerson).

growth stock, (in finance) stock of a company that is expected to grow.

growth substance, = growth hormone (def. 2).

growth|y (grō′thē), *adj.* growing well or fast.

groyne (groin), *n., v.,* **groyned, groyn|ing.** —*n.* a low wall built out into the water from a riverbank or ocean shore to prevent erosion by current or tide; groin.
—*v.t.* to furnish with groynes; groin.
[variant of *groin*]

GR-S (jē′är′es′), *n.* a rubber produced by the copolymerization of butadiene and styrene. [< *g*(overnment) *r*(ubber), *s*(tyrene)]

grub (grub), *n., v.,* **grubbed, grub|bing.** —*n.* **1** a wormlike form or larva of an insect. A grub is usually the soft, smooth, thick larva of a beetle. **2** a dull, hard-working person; drudge: *this poor grub of literature* (Thomas De Quincey). **3** *Slang.* food: *How you'll relish your grub* (Frederick Marryat). [probably < verb]
—*v.i.* **1** to dig: *Pigs grub for roots.* **2** to lead a life of hard work; toil; drudge: *For years, Galileo grubbed away in underpaid mathematical teaching posts without losing his love of learning or his abiding contempt of the ossified scholars of his time* (Time). **3** *Figurative.* to search (for) or rummage about. **4** *Slang.* to eat.
—*v.t.* **1** to root out of the ground; dig up: *It took the farmer weeks to grub the stumps on his land.* **SYN**: uproot. **2** to rid (ground) of roots, stumps, rocks, or other debris: *Grubbing and removal of top soil began on both toll road sites last week* (Wall Street Journal). **SYN**: clear. **3** *Slang.* to provide with food.
[Middle English *grubben* dig, root up]

grub|ber (grub′ər), *n.* **1** a person who grubs. **2** an implement for breaking up ground, etc. **3** *Slang.* an eater; feeder.

grub|by (grub′ē), *adj.,* **-bi|er, -bi|est. 1** dirty; grimy; slovenly: *a grubby lot Of sooty sweeps* (Thomas Hood). *She was an exceptionally grubby girl—fat, sloppily dressed, and, like Willard, uncommunicative* (New Yorker). **2** *Western U.S.* infested with grubs, especially the botfly: *grubby cattle, grubby sheep.* **3** like a grub. **4** *Dialect.* stunted; small: *grubby trees.* —**grub′bi|ly**, *adv.* —**grub′bi|ness**, *n.*

grub|stake (grub′stāk′), *n., v.,* **-staked, -stak|ing.** *Informal.* —*n.* food, equipment, and money supplied to a prospector on the condition of sharing in whatever he finds.
—*v.t.* to supply with a grubstake.
[American English < *grub* provide with food + *stake*[2]]

grub|stak|er (grub′stā′kər), *n. U.S. Informal.* **1** a prospector who is supplied with a grubstake. **2** a person who supplies a grubstake.

Grub Street, 1 a former street in London, where struggling writers lived (now called Milton Street). **2** writers who write merely to earn money; hack writers: *He* [*Balzac*] *served a long apprenticeship in the labyrinth of Grub Street* (Listener).

grub-street (grub′strēt′), *adj.* having to do with or like hack writers or their work.

grub|worm (grub′wėrm′), *n.* the wormlike form or larva of an insect; grub.

grudge (gruj), *n., v.,* **grudged, grudg|ing.** —*n.* ill will; sullen feeling (against); dislike of long standing: *She has had a grudge against me ever since I disagreed with her. The Arians ... bore Athanasius a grudge* (Thomas North). *All over the country there is a grudge against La Paz, which could be construed as a grudge against the inadequacy and corruption of central government* (Manchester Guardian Weekly). **SYN**: resentment. See syn. under **spite**.
—*v.t.* **1** to feel anger or dislike toward (a person) because of (something); envy the possession of: *He grudged me my little prize, even though he had won a bigger one.* **SYN**: envy, begrudge. **2** to give or let have unwillingly: *The mean man grudged his horse the food that it ate.*
—*v.i. Obsolete.* to grumble; complain.
[earlier, grumble, complain (against); variant of *grutch* < Old French *groucher* murmur, grumble. See etym. of doublet **grouch.**] —**grudg′er**, *n.*

grudg|ing (gruj′ing), *adj.* unwilling; reluctant: *His industry earned the grudging praise of his enemies* (John R. Green). —**grudg′ing|ly**, *adv.*

grue (grü), *n., v.,* **grued, gru|ing.** —*n.* a shiver; shudder.
—*v.i. Scottish.* to feel horror; shudder; shiver.
[Middle English *gruen*]

gru|el (grü′əl), *n., v.,* **-eled, -el|ing** or (*especially British*) **-elled, -el|ling.** —*n.* **1** a nearly liquid food made by boiling oatmeal or other cereal in water or milk. Gruel is often given to those who are sick and old. **2** any similar substance. **3** *Informal.* punishment; defeat: *to get one's gruel. What have we to hope for? We may just as well take our gruel* (Arthur Conan Doyle).
—*v.t.* to tire out completely; exhaust.
[< Old French *gruel,* ultimately < a Germanic word] —**gru′el|er**, *especially British,* **gru′el|ler**, *n.*

gru|el|ing (grü′ə ling), *adj., n.* —*adj.* very tiring; exhausting: *The marathon is a grueling contest.*
—*n.* an exhausting or very tiring experience.
—**gru′el|ing|ly**, *adv.*

gru|el|ling (grü′ə ling), *adj., n. Especially British.* grueling. —**gru′el|ling|ly**, *adv.*

grue|some (grü′səm), *adj.* **1** causing fear or horror; horrible; frightful; revolting: *The dim, mysterious half-light of the cellar falling in a gruesome way upon the misshapen bulk of a Chinese deity* (Bret Harte). **SYN**: grisly. **2** *Scottish.* ugly; hideous. Also, **grewsome.** [probably < *grue* to shudder + *-some*[1]. Compare Middle Dutch *grusaem,* Dutch *gruwzaam,* German *grausam.*] —**grue′some|ly**, *adv.* —**grue′some|ness**, *n.*

gruff (gruf), *adj., v.* —*adj.* **1** deep and harsh;

hoarse: *a gruff voice.* SYN: guttural. **2** rough, rude, unfriendly, or bad-tempered: *a gruff manner.* SYN: grumpy, brusque, impolite, surly. **3** containing coarse particles.
—*v.i., v.t.* to act, speak, or say in a gruff manner: *Tough, burly Johnson gruffed: "This is the first time I've ever been called a handmaiden"* (Time). [< Middle Dutch or Middle Low German *grof*]
—gruff′ly, *adv.* **—gruff′ness,** *n.*

gruff|y (gruf′ē), *adj.,* **gruff|i|er, gruff|i|est.** gruff. **—gruff′i|ly,** *adv.* **—gruff′i|ness,** *n.*

gru|gru (grü′grü), *n.* **1** Also, **grugru palm.** a spiny palm of the West Indies. Its wood is very heavy and durable. **2** Also, **grugru worm.** the edible larva of a large weevil of tropical America, that lives in the wood of palm trees. Also, **grigri.** [< Spanish *grugrú* < a native name]

gru|i|form (grü′ə fôrm), *adj.* resembling the crane. [< Latin *grūs, gruis* crane + English *-form*]

Gru|is (grü′is), *n.* genitive of **Grus.**

grum (grum), *adj.,* **grum|mer, grum|mest.** glum; sullen; surly. [compare Danish *grum* cruel]

grum|ble (grum′bəl), *v.,* **-bled, -bling,** *n.* **—*v.i.*** **1** to complain in a rather sullen way; mutter in discontent; find fault: *He was always grumbling about his food* (Anthony Trollope). SYN: See syn. under **complain. 2** to make dull, inarticulate sounds; growl; mumble. SYN: murmur. **3** to make a low, heavy sound like far-off thunder; rumble.
—*v.t.* **1** to express by grumbling. **2** *Obsolete.* to cause to grumble or rumble.
—*n.* **1** a mutter of discontent; bad-tempered complaint. **2** a low growl. **3** a rumble.
grumbles, a grumbling, discontented mood: *Before we reach Njole I recognize my crew have got the grumbles, and at once inquire into the reason* (Mary Kingsley).
[perhaps < Middle Dutch *grommelen*] **—grum′bler,** *n.*

grum|bling|ly (grum′bling lē), *adv.* with grumbling or discontent.

grum|bly (grum′blē), *adj.* **-bli|er, -bli|est.** like a grumble; inclined to grumble.

grume (grüm), *n.* **1** any thick, sticky fluid. **2** a blood clot. [< *grūmus* little pile, hillock]

grum|met (grum′it), *n.* = grommet.

gru|mous (grü′məs), *adj.* **1** containing or like a grume; clotted; thick. **2** *Botany.* formed of clustered grains, as various roots; granulated.

grump (grump), *v., n.* **—*v.i.*** to sulk; grumble: *His decrepit old manservant grumps and bemoans the good old days* (Time).
—*v.t.* to say in a grumpy manner: *"I don't generally approve of these oddballs she goes out with," grumps brother Kell* (Time).
—*n.* *Informal.* a grumpy person: *Grandfather . . . was always very kind to me. They used to say he was a grump of a man but I couldn't say it* (Emily Woolcock).
grumps, the sulks; a fit of ill humor: *She had the grumps after staying up too late the night before.* [imitative]

grumph|ie or **grumph|y** (grum′fē, grům′pē), *n., pl.* **grumph|ies.** *Scottish.* a pig.

grump|ish (grum′pish), *adj.* = grumpy.

grump|y (grum′pē), *adj.,* **grump|i|er, grump|i|est,** *n., pl.* **grump|ies. —*adj.*** surly; ill-tempered; gruff: *The grumpy old man found fault with everything.* SYN: cantankerous, crabbed. **—*n.*** a grumpy person. **—grump′i|ly,** *adv.* **—grump′i|ness,** *n.*

grund|sko|la (gründ′skō′lə), *n.* a school in Sweden for children 7 to 16 years old: *The Swedes call it a grundskola, literally a "basic" or "foundation" school, although the last three years of it can be considered a kind of lower secondary school* (Saturday Review). [< Swedish *grundskola*]

Grun|dy (grun′dē), *n., pl.* **-dies.** Usually, **Mrs. Grundy.** a person who censors or supervises the manners and morals of others; social censorship personified: *And many are afraid of God—And more of Mrs. Grundy* (Frederick Locker-Lampson). *Only the Mrs. Grundies are seeking moral bogies* (Punch). [< name of a personage referred to in Thomas Morton's play *Speed the Plough,* 1798, chiefly in the question: "What will Mrs. Grundy say?"]

Grun|dy|ism (grun′dē iz əm), *n.* the principles of Mrs. Grundy; conventionalism.

grunge (grunj), *n. U.S. Slang.* something bad, inferior, or ugly: *Your average American rock-and-roll fan can stand the Dolls' brand of high-strung urban grunge only if it comes from somewhere besides New York—preferably England* (New Yorker). [origin uncertain]

grun|gy (grun′jē), *adj.,* **-gi|er, -gi|est.** *U.S. Slang.* bad, inferior, or ugly: *a grungy actor, a grungy place.* [origin uncertain]

grun|ion (grun′yən), *n.* a small fish having silver stripes on its sides, found along the coast of southern California; silversides. [American English, apparently < American Spanish *gruñón,* probably short for *pez gruñón* grunting fish < *gruñir* to grunt < Latin *grunnīre*]

grunt (grunt), *n., v.* **—*n.*** **1** the deep, hoarse sound that a hog makes. **2** a sound like this: *This fat boy stood up with a grunt.* **3** any one of a family of edible sea fishes that grunt when taken out of the water; porkfish. **4** *Slang.* a soldier or marine who fights at the front; infantryman: *The new warrant officer-pilots avoid both the "hassling" that the grunt endures and the responsibilities that an officer carries* (Time). [< verb]
—*v.i.* **1** to make the deep, hoarse sound of a hog. **2** to make a sound like this; grumble: *He grunted in discontent.* **3** *Obsolete.* to groan. **—*v.t.*** to say with a grunt: *The sullen boy grunted his apology.* [Old English *grunnettan* < *grunian* to grunt]

grunt|er (grun′tər), *n.* **1** a person or animal that grunts, especially a hog. **2** = grunt (def. 3).

grunt|ing|ly (grun′ting lē), *adv.* with grunting.

grunt|ing ox (grun′ting), the common, domestic yak.

grun|tle (grun′təl), *v.i.,* **-tled, -tling.** to utter a low grunt; murmur; grumble: *The dissatisfied customers kept gruntling about the poor service in the restaurant.* [< *grunt* + *-le* (frequentative)]

grun|tled (grun′təld), *adj.* pleased; contented: *The happy sound of gruntled ballet fans filled the Metropolitan Opera house* (Clive Barnes). [back formation < *disgruntled*]

grunt|work (grunt′wėrk′), *n. U.S. and Canadian Informal.* low, menial work: *. . . the dirty, tedious gruntwork needed to make a campaign successful* (New York Times).

grup|pet|to (grü pet′ō), *n., pl.* **-pet|ti** (-pet′ē). *Music.* turn: *The slow movement of Brahams' sonata would have flowed more easily had he not . . . reduced his trills to precise, five-note gruppetti* (London Times). [< Italian *gruppetto* (literally) small group < *gruppo* group]

Grus (grus), *n., genitive* **Gru|is.** a southern constellation near Capricorn. [< Latin *grūs* a crane]

grush|ie (grush′ē, grü′shē), *adj. Scottish.* healthy; thriving. [origin unknown]

grutch (gruch, grůch), *v., n. British Dialect.* **—*v.i.*** to grumble; complain.
—*v.t.* to give or let have unwillingly; begrudge.
—*n.* dislike of long standing; ill will.
[probably < Old French *grocher* grumble]

Gru|yère (gri yãr′, grü-), *n.,* or **Gruyère cheese,** a variety of firm, light-yellow cheese made from whole milk. [< *(La) Gruyère,* a district in Switzerland, where it is made]

gr. wt., gross weight.

gryph|on (grif′ən), *n.* = griffin[1].

grys|bok (grīs′bok), *n.* a small, reddish-brown South African antelope. [< Afrikaans *grysbok* < Dutch *grijsbok* < *grijs* gray + *bok* buck[1]]

g.s., ground speed (of an aircraft).

GS (no periods) or **G.S.,** **1** Bureau of General Services of the United Nations Secretariat. **2** general staff. **3** Girl Scouts.

GSA (no periods) or **G.S.A.,** *U.S.* General Services Administration.

G.S.A. or **GSA** (no periods), Girl Scouts of America.

GSE (no periods), ground support equipment.

GSP (no periods), gross social product.

GSR (no periods), galvanic skin response.

G string, 1 a strip of cloth passing between the legs and held up by a cord around the waist. **2** the string of a musical instrument tuned to G. **3** a single-wire method of television transmission.

*** G-suit** (jē′süt′), *n.* a suit containing automatically inflated air bladders, worn by a pilot or astronaut to counteract the effects of gravity and prevent blackout. [< *g*(ravity) *suit*]

*** G-suit**

GT (no periods), gran turismo.

gt., 1 great. **2** gutta (drop).

GT. Br. or **Brit.,** Great Britain.

g.t.c., 1 good till canceled. **2** good till countermanded.

G.T.C. or **GTC** (no periods), good till canceled.

gtd., guaranteed.

G tolerance, resistance to blackout when one is subjected to high gravitational forces.

G-2 (jē′tü′), *n.* the section of a general staff in the U.S. Army responsible for military intelligence.

GU (no periods), **1** genitourinary. **2** Guam (with postal Zip Code).

gua|ca|mo|le (gwä′kə mō′lā), *n.* a spread made of mashed avocado, minced onion, lemon juice, tomatoes, and seasonings. [< American Spanish *guacamole* < Nahuatl]

gua|cha|ro (gwä′chä rō), *n., pl.* **-ros.** a nocturnal, fruit-eating bird of South America and Trinidad; oilbird. Its fat is greatly valued and is used as a substitute for butter. [< Spanish *guácharo,* probably < Araucanian (Chile) name]

gua|co (gwä′kō), *n., pl.* **-cos. 1** a climbing tropical American composite plant. **2** its leaves, or a substance obtained from them, used in treating snakebites. **3** a climbing tropical American plant of the birthwort family also used as an antidote for snakebites. [< American Spanish *quaco* apparently < American Indian name]

Gua|da|lupe Day (gwä′də lüp′), December 12, observed in Mexico as the feast of Our Lady of Guadalupe, commemorating the day in 1531 when the Virgin Mary is believed to have appeared to a poor Indian on the way to Mexico City. Our Lady of Guadalupe became the patron saint of Mexico.

Guadalupe fur seal, a dark brown fur seal of the Pacific coast of southern California and Mexico, now near extinction. [< *Guadalupe* Island, off the Pacific coast of Mexico]

guai|ac (gwī′ak), *n.* the wood or resin of the guaiacum tree.

guai|ac|ic (gwī as′ik), *adj.* having to do with or obtained from guaiacum.

guai|a|col (gwī′ə kōl, -kol), *n.* a colorless, oily liquid or solid obtained from creosote or guaiacum resin, or made synthetically. Formerly used in treating bronchitis and tuberculosis, it is now used chiefly as an expectorant and anesthetic. *Formula:* $C_7H_8O_2$

guai|a|cum or **guai|o|cum** (gwī′ə kəm), *n.* **1** any one of various tropical trees and shrubs, having blue or purple flowers, a capsular fruit, and very hard wood; lignum vitae. **2** the brownish-green wood of any of these trees. **3** a greenish-brown resin obtained from this wood, formerly used in treating gout, rheumatism, and various skin diseases. [< New Latin *Guaiacum* the genus name < Spanish *guayacán* < Arawak (West Indies) *guayacan*]

guai|ol (gwī′ōl, -ol), *n.* an alcohol obtained from the wood of the champac tree and from a variety of guaiacum, used in perfumes and soaps; champacol. *Formula:* $C_{15}H_{26}O$

gua|ji|ro (gwä hē′rō), *n., pl.* **-ros.** (-rōs). *Spanish.* a peasant in Cuba.

Gua|ma|ni|an (gwä mā′nē ən), *adj., n.* **—*adj.*** of or having to do with Guam.
—*n.* a person born or living in Guam.

guan (gwän), *n.* any one of various South American game birds with greenish-black and white-and-brown feathers. Most species have crests on the head. [perhaps < Carib (South America) *kuano* a land eagle]

gua|na|co (gwä nä′kō), *n., pl.* **-cos.** a wild South American mammal, of the same family as the camel, which is similar in size and appearance to the llama. The guanaco has no hump and is valued for its fur. Domesticated llamas and alpacas are thought to have developed from guanacos. [< Spanish *guanaco* < Quechua (Peru) *huanacu*]

gua|nase (gwä′nās), *n.* an enzyme capable of breaking down guanine.

gua|nay (gwä nī′), *n.* a cormorant of South America, mainly greenish black above and white below, one of the chief sources of guano. [< American Spanish *guanay*]

Guan|che (gwän′chā), *n., pl.* **-ches** or **-che. 1** one of the aboriginal inhabitants of the Canary Islands, who were absorbed by the Spanish on their conquest of the islands in the 1400's. **2** a Berber language spoken in the Canary Islands until the 1700's.

gua|neth|i|dine (gwä neth′ə din, -dēn), *n.* a drug used in its sulfate form to treat hypertension. [< *guanidine* + inserted *eth*(yl)]

guan|i|din (gwan′ə din, gwä′nə-), *n.* = guanidine.

guan|i|dine (gwan′ə dēn, -din; gwä′nə-), *n.* a strongly alkaline, crystalline compound formed by the oxidation of guanine. Guanidine is used in organic synthesis. *Formula:* CH_5N_3

gua|nin (gwä′nin), *n.* = guanine.

gua|nine (gwä′nēn, -nin), *n.* a substance present in nucleic acids in all cells, and also found in guano. It is one of the purine bases in both DNA and RNA. *Formula:* $C_5H_5N_5O$ *Abbr:* G (no period). [< *guan*(o) + *-ine*[2]]

gua|no (gwä′nō), *n., pl.* **-nos. 1** the waste matter of sea birds and bats, used as a fertilizer. It is found especially on islands near Peru. **2** any comparable fertilizer, such as one made from

Pronunciation Key: hat, āge, cãre, fär; let, ēqual, tėrm; it, īce; hot, ōpen, ôrder; oil, out; cup, pu̇t, rüle; child; long; thin; ᴛʜen; zh, measure; ə represents **a** in about, **e** in taken, **i** in pencil, **o** in lemon, **u** in circus.

fish. [< Spanish *guano* dung, (originally) especially of sea fowl < Quechua (Peru) *huanu* dung]

gua|no|phore (gwä′nə fôr, -fōr), *n.* an iridescent chromatophore that contains guanine; iridocyte. It is found, for example, in the skin of certain fish. [< *guan*(ine) + *-phore*]

gua|no|sine (gwä′nə sin, -sēn), *n.* a substance composed of guanine and ribose, present in ribonucleic acid. Guanosine is a nucleoside. *Formula:* $C_{10}H_{13}N_5O_5$ [< German *Guanosin* < *Guanin* guanine]

guar (gwär), *n.* **1** a legume extensively grown for soil enrichment, livestock feed, and for a gum obtained from its seed: *Guar, described as one of the oldest crops known to man, is another "new" crop with countless industrial applications* (Scientific American). **2** the gum obtained from its seeds, used in various industrial products; guar gum. [< Hindustani *guār*]

guar., guaranteed.

gua|ra|cha (gwä rä′chä), *n.* **1** a fast Cuban song and dance. **2** a fast Spanish dance in two parts. [< Spanish *guaracha*]

gua|ra|na (gwä′rä nä′), *n.* **1** a South American shrub of the soapberry family. **2** an extract of its seeds containing caffein, used in certain alcoholic beverages and soft drinks. [< Spanish *guaraná* < Tupi]

gua|ra|ni (gwä′rä nē′), *n., pl.* **-ni, -nis,** or **-nies.** the unit of money of Paraguay, a note equal to 100 centimos. [apparently < *Guarani*]

Gua|ra|ni or **Gua|ra|ní** (gwä′rä nē′), *n., pl.* **-ni** or **-nis. 1** a member of a group of Tupian Indian tribes of central South America. **2** their Tupi-Guarani language.

guar|an|tee (gar′ən tē′), *n., v.,* **-teed, -tee|ing.** —*n.* **1** a promise or pledge to pay or do something if another fails to do it; pledge to replace goods or return the price paid if they are not as represented; backing: *We have a one-year guarantee on our new car. Bernard Docker and his repudiation of guarantees which he had signed* (London Times). SYN: warrant, security, surety. **2** something given or taken as security; guaranty. **3** a person who gives a guarantee; guarantor. **4** a person to whom a guarantee is given. **5** something having the force or effect of a guaranty: *Wealth and a multitude of possessions are no guarantee of happiness.*
—*v.t.* **1** to stand back of; give a guarantee for; assure genuineness or permanence of; answer for fulfillment of (a contract or other agreement): *This company guarantees its clocks for a year. The father guaranteed his son's future behavior.* **2** to undertake to secure for another: *The landlord will guarantee us possession of the house by May.* **3** to make secure (against or from); protect: *His insurance guaranteed him against money loss in case of fire.* **4** to pledge (to do something): *I will guarantee to prove every statement I made.* **5** to promise that (something) has been or will be: *Wealth does not guarantee happiness. The advance payment of money guarantees the good faith of the purchaser.*
[probably variant of *guaranty*]

guar|an|teed annual income (gar′ən tēd′), an annual compensation provided by the government to those citizens whose incomes fall below a specified level; negative income tax: *The unemployed in the United States have begun to demand not just the right to work but a guaranteed annual income whether they work or not* (Lewis Mumford).

guaranteed annual wage, a labor agreement providing for compensation during unemployment if a worker's yearly earnings fall below a specified amount. *Abbr:* G.A.W.

guaranteed income, = guaranteed annual income.

guar|an|tor (gar′ən tôr, -tər), *n.* a person who makes or gives a guarantee or guaranty.

guar|an|ty (gar′ən tē), *n., pl.* **-ties,** *v.,* **-tied, -ty|ing.** —*n.* **1** a pledge or promise by which a person gives security for the payment of a debt or the performance of an obligation by another person; guarantee. SYN: warranty. **2** property, money, or goods given or taken as security. **3** the act or fact of giving security. **4** something guaranteeing that a thing has been or will be: *The treaty was a guaranty of peace.* **5** = guarantor.
—*v.t.* = guarantee. SYN: insure.
[< Anglo-French *guarantie* < *guarantir* to warrant < Old French *guarant* a warrant < a Germanic word. See etym. of doublet **warranty.**]

guard (gärd), *v., n.* —*v.t.* **1** to keep safe; watch over carefully; defend; protect: *The dog guarded the child day and night. Mercy guard me* (Milton). **2** to keep from escaping; check; hold back: *Guard the prisoners. Guard your temper.* **3** to try to keep (an opponent) from scoring. **4** to provide with a protective covering: *to guard the body with armor.* **5** *Archaic.* to escort. **6** *Archaic.* to trim: *a long motley coat guarded with yellow* (Shakespeare). —*v.i.* **1** to take precautions (against): *to guard against errors.* SYN: safeguard, preserve. **2** to keep guard or watch. **3** to give protection: *Disorder wounds Where it should guard* (Shakespeare). [< Old French *guarder,* or perhaps < the noun]
—*n.* **1** a person or group that guards. A soldier or group of soldiers guarding a person or place is a guard. SYN: defender, protector, sentry, sentinel. **2** anything that gives protection; arrangement to give safety: *a trigger guard, a guard on a circular saw. A fender is a guard against mud.* **3** a careful watch: *A soldier kept guard over the prisoners. Keep a guard over your tongue.* **4** = guard duty. **5** defense; protection: *I was dispatched for their defence and guard* (Milton). SYN: bulwark, shield. **6** a position of defense in boxing, fencing, or cricket: *to beat down a person's guard.* **7** the arms or weapons held in a position of defense. **8** a person who opens and closes the doors or gates on a train; brakeman. **9** *British.* a conductor of a railroad train, streetcar, etc. **10** an offensive player at either side of the center in football. **11** *Basketball.* either of two players defending the goal in basketball. **12** *Obsolete.* caution; precaution. **13** *Obsolete.* guardianship.
guards, certain groups of soldiers in the British Army, especially those attached to the royal household: *Cholmondely, then in the guards, ran away at the battle of Dettingen* (Joseph Jekyll).
off (one's) guard, unprepared to meet a sudden attack; unwary: *Temerity puts a man off his guard* (Roger L'Estrange).
on (one's) guard, ready to defend or protect; watchful: *A sentry's job is to be on guard at his post. In like manner should the Reason be perpetually on its guard against the Passions* (Alexander Pope).
[< Old French *garde* < *garder,* earlier *guarder* < Germanic (compare Old Saxon *wardon*). See etym. of doublet **ward.**] —**guard′a|ble,** *adj.* —**guard′er,** *n.*
—*Syn. v.t.* **1 Guard, defend, protect** mean to keep safe. **Guard** implies watching over carefully: *A soldier guarded the prisoners.* **Defend** implies resisting danger or attack: *She defended her little brother against the bully.* **Protect** implies warding off danger or harm: *Proper food protects a person's health.*

guard|ant (gär′dənt), *adj., n.* —*adj.* guarding; protecting.
—*n. Obsolete.* a guard; guardian.

guard cell, *Botany.* one of the two specialized kidney-shaped cells of the plant epidermis that control the size of the stomata by expanding and contracting.

guard dog, = watchdog.

guard duty, military duties involving the watching over prisoners, equipment, or a particular area.

guard|ed (gär′did), *adj.* **1** kept safe; carefully watched over; defended; protected. SYN: watched. **2** careful; prudent; cautious: *"Maybe" was his guarded answer to my question.* SYN: circumspect. —**guard′ed|ly,** *adv.* —**guard′ed|ness,** *n.*

guard|ee (gär′dē), *n. British.* a member of the guards; guardsman. [< *guard* + *-ee*]

guard hair, the long, coarse hair in the fur of an animal.

guard|house (gärd′hous′), *n.* **1** a building used by soldiers on guard. **2** a building used as a jail for soldiers.

guard|i|an (gär′dē ən), *n., adj.* —*n.* **1** a person who takes care of another or of some special thing; defender: *A minister or priest is considered a guardian of the faith.* SYN: protector. **2** a person appointed by law to take care of the affairs of someone who is young or cannot take care of them himself: *Their uncle was declared guardian to the orphans.* SYN: trustee, warden, keeper, guard.
—*adj.* protecting: *My guardian spirit must have looked after me then.* SYN: guarding.
[< Anglo-French *gardein,* Old French *guarden,* earlier *guardenc* < *guarde* guard < a Germanic word. See etym. of doublet **warden.**]

guardian ad litem, *Law.* a person appointed in a particular lawsuit to take charge of the interests of an infant or other person who is legally incapacitated.

guardian angel, **1** an angel thought of as watching over a particular person or place. **2** a person in the same role.

guardian by nature, *Law.* either natural parent of a minor.

guard|i|an|ship (gär′dē ən ship), *n.* the position or care of a guardian.

guard|less (gärd′lis), *adj.* = unguarded.

guard of honor, = honor guard.

guard|rail (gärd′rāl′), *n.* a rail or railing for protection, such as one at the side of a highway or stairway.

guard ring, a narrow finger ring worn to keep another ring from slipping off.

guard|room (gärd′rüm′, -rum′), *n.* **1** a room used by soldiers on guard. **2** a room used as a jail for soldiers.

guards (gärdz), *n.pl.* See under **guard.**

guards|man (gärdz′mən), *n., pl.* **-men. 1** = guard. **2** a soldier who belongs to the National Guard. **3** *British.* a member of a regiment of the Foot Guards attached to the royal household.

guard's van, *British.* the railroad car or compartment occupied by the conductor.

guar gum, the gum obtained from the seeds of the guar, used as a thickening or stabilizing agent in foods and cosmetics, in sizings for textiles and paper, and in the manufacture of paper.

Guar|ne|ri|us (gwär nãr′ē əs), *n.* a violin made in the 1600's and 1700's by Giuseppe Guarneri or a member of his family.

guar|ri (gwä′rē), *n.* **1** any one of several South African trees or shrubs of the ebony family, whose fruit and leaves are much valued by natives. **2** the fruit of these trees or shrubs. [< Kaffir (um)*gwali*]

Gua|te|ma|lan (gwä′tə mä′lən), *adj., n.* —*adj.* of or having to do with Guatemala or its inhabitants.
—*n.* a person born or living in Guatemala.

Gua|te|mal|tec|an (gwä′tə mäl tek′ən), *n., adj.* = Guatemalan.

gua|te|mal|te|co (gwä′tā mäl tā′kō), *n., pl.* **-cos.** *Spanish.* a Guatemalan.

gua|va (gwä′və), *n.* **1** a tropical American tree or shrub with a yellow or red, round or pear-shaped fruit. It belongs to the myrtle family. **2** its fruit, used especially for jelly and jam. [< Spanish *guayaba* < Arawak (West Indies) *guayabo, guava*]

***gua|ya|be|ra** (gwä′yä bā′rä), *n. Spanish.* a loose-fitting shirt, worn especially by Cuban men: *The top suggests a Cuban guayabera, or workman's shirt* (New Yorker).

***guayabera**

gua|ya|can (gwä′yä kän′), *n.* any one of various trees of tropical America; guaiacum.

gua|yu|le (gwä yü′lā), *n.* **1** a small shrub of the composite family, growing in the Mexican desert and cultivated in California, Texas, and Arizona. Rubber is obtained from its juice. **2** Also, **guayule rubber.** this rubber. [American English < Mexican Spanish *guayule* < Nahuatl *cuauh-uli*]

gub|bins (gub′ənz), *n. pl. British Informal.* **1** mechanical devices or contrivances; gadgets: *A relatively cheap aeroplane ... it will carry all the electronic gubbins used in an F-104G fighter* (New Scientist). **2** worthless fragments or parings; refuse. [variant of obsolete *gobbons* portions, gobbets, perhaps < Old French *gobe* lump]

gu|ber|na|to|ri|al (gü′bər nə tôr′ē əl, -tōr′-; gyü′-), *adj.* of a governor; having to do with a governor: *The first gubernatorial primary will be held on May 8* (Wall Street Journal). [American English < Latin *gubernātor* (originally) pilot (< *gubernāre* govern) + English *-al*[1]]

gu|ber|ni|ya (gü ber′nē yə), *n.* **1** (in the Soviet Union) an administrative subdivision of a district or province. **2** a territorial subdivision or province in Russia before 1917. [< Russian *gubernija,* ultimately < Latin *gubernāre* govern]

guck (guk), *n. Slang.* **1** a slimy substance; oozy, sticky dirt; gunk: *to clean the guck out of the gutters.* **2** anything unpleasant, especially something unappetizing. **3** something left over and useless; waste: *The astronauts released the guck into outer space.* [variant of *gunk*]

guck|y (guk′ē), *adj.,* **guck|i|er, guck|i|est.** *Slang.* like guck; oozy; slushy.

gud|dle (gud′əl), *v.,* **-dled, -dling.** —*v.i.* **1** to grope for fish under the banks of a stream. **2** *Figurative:* ... *guddling in vain for a word, none are at a loss for an answer* (W. H. Auden).
—*v.t.* to catch (fish) by guddling: *Take a firm hold and pull it out. It is just like guddling a trout* (New Yorker). [origin uncertain]

gude (gyd), *adj., n., interj., adv. Scottish.* good.

gudg|eon[1] (guj′ən), *n., v.* —*n.* **1** a small European freshwater fish that is easy to catch and is often used for bait. It is related to the carp. **2** any one of several other small fishes; minnow. **3** *Figurative.* a person easily fooled or cheated. **4** a bait. —*v.t.* to cheat; dupe.
[< Old French *goujon* < Latin *gōbiō, -ōnis,* alteration of *gōbius* a kind of fish < Greek *kōbiós*]

gudg|eon[2] (guj′ən), *n.* **1** the metal pin or axle on which a wheel turns. **2** a socket or eye for a metal pin or axle. **3** a metal pin used to join two blocks of stone. [< Old French *goujon*]

Gud|run (gůd′rün), *n. Norse Mythology.* the

daughter of the king of the Nibelungs and wife of Sigurd (Siegfried).

Gue|ber or **Gue|bre** (gā'bər, gē'-), *n.* = Gheber.

guel|der-rose (gel'dər rōz'), *n.* a cultivated cranberry tree having round clusters of white flowers; snowball. [earlier *gelders rose,* or *gelderland rose* < *Guelders,* a town, now in Germany, or *Guelderland,* a province in Holland]

Guelph or **Guelf** (gwelf), *n., adj.* —*n.* **1** a member of a political party that supported the popes in their struggle with the emperors of the Holy Roman Empire in medieval Italy. The Guelphs opposed the Ghibellines. **2** a member of a German family of princes, ancestors of the present British royal family. —*adj.* = Guelphic.
[< Italian *Guelfo* < Middle High German *Welf,* name of the founder and several members of a German princely family]

Guelph|ic or **Guelf|ic** (gwel'fik), *adj.* of or having to do with the Guelphs.

gue|mal (gwā'məl), *n.* either of two species of medium-sized, South American deer that have two-pronged antlers. Also, **guemul**, **huemul**. [< American Spanish *güemul* < Araucan *huemul*]

gue|mul (gwā'mül), *n.* = guemal.

gue|non (gə nôɴ'), *n.* any one of various long-tailed monkeys, including the grivet and green monkey. [< French *guenon;* origin uncertain]

guerche (gersh), *n.* = girsh.

guer|don (gėr'dən), *n., v. Poetic.* —*n.* a reward: *Verse, like the laurel, its immortal meed, Should be the guerdon of a noble deed* (William Cowper).
—*v.t.* to reward; recompense.
[< Old French *guerdon,* variant of *werdon* < Medieval Latin *widerdonum,* half-translation of Old High German *widarlōn* repayment, with Latin *dōnum* gift] —**guer'don|er**, *n.*

guer|e|za (ger'ə zə), *n.* **1** a large Abyssinian monkey having long, white hair on the end of the tail and on the sides of the otherwise black body. **2** any one of several related species. [perhaps < a native name]

gué|ri|don or **gue|ri|don** (ger'ə don; *French* gā rē dôɴ'), *n.* a round table supported by a central column, branching into three feet. [< French *guéridon*]

gue|ril|la (gə ril'ə), *n., adj.* = guerrilla.

gue|ril|le|ro (ger'əl yā'rō), *n., pl.* **-ros**. = guerrillero.

guern|sey (gėrn'zē), *n., pl.* **-seys**. **1** a close-fitting knitted woolen shirt or sweater worn by sailors. **2** *Australian.* a jersey worn by football players.
[< *Guernsey,* one of the Channel Islands, where they were first made]

Guern|sey (gėrn'zē), *n., pl.* **-seys**. any one of a breed of tan-and-white dairy cattle resembling the Jersey, but somewhat larger. Guernseys give rich, cream-colored milk. [< *Guernsey,* one of the Channel Islands where the breed originated]

guerre à ou|trance (ger' à ü träɴs'), *French.* struggle to the bitter end.

guer|ril|la (gə ril'ə), *n., adj.* —*n.* **1** a member of a band of fighters who harass the enemy by sudden raids, ambushes, the plundering of supply trains, and the like. Guerrillas are not part of a regular army. **2** *Now rare.* warfare carried on by such fighters; guerrilla warfare.
—*adj.* of or by guerrillas: *a guerrilla attack.* Also, **guerilla**.
[< Spanish *guerrilla* (diminutive) < *guerra* war < Germanic (compare Old High German *werra*)]

guer|ril|la|ism (gə ril'ə iz əm), *n.* the principles and practices of guerrilla warfare.

guerrilla theater, a type of dramatic presentation of short antiwar or antiestablishment plays, usually in pantomime and in any public place where an audience will gather; street theater.

guerrilla warfare, warfare conducted by or using the tactics of guerrillas, characterized by short, sharp engagements, sudden raids on enemy supply and communications lines, and similar small-scale actions designed to harass and demoralize the enemy.

guer|ril|le|ro (ger'əl yā'rō), *n., pl.* **-ros**. a guerrilla, especially in a Latin-American country. Also, **guerillero**. [< Spanish *guerrillero* < *guerrilla*]

guess (ges), *v., n.* —*v.t.* **1** to form an opinion of without really knowing; conjecture; estimate: *to guess the height of a tree, guess what will happen next.* **2** to get right by guessing: *Can you guess the answer to that riddle?* **3** to think, believe, or suppose: *I guess she is really sick after all.*
—*v.i.* **1** to form an opinion when one does not know exactly; estimate: *Do you know this or are you just guessing? We guessed at her weight. Our present strength, I guess, is about seven hundred* (George Washington). **2** to get something right by guessing. **3** to think, believe, or suppose.
—*n.* **1** an opinion formed without really knowing: *My guess is that it will rain tomorrow.* **SYN**: supposition, surmise, conjecture. **2** a guessing.
[Middle English *gessen,* probably < Scandinavian (compare Middle Danish *getse*)] —**guess'er**, *n.*
—*Syn. v.t.* **1 Guess, conjecture, surmise** mean to form an opinion without knowing enough. **Guess**, the least formal word, suggests forming an opinion on the basis of what one thinks likely, without really knowing for certain: *I guessed the distance to the nearest town.* **Conjecture** suggests having some evidence, but not enough for proof: *The scholars conjectured that the poem had once existed in a longer form.* **Surmise** suggests having little or no evidence beyond what one merely suspects: *Were you able to surmise her thoughts?*

guess|a|ble (ges'ə bəl), *adj.* that can be guessed.

guess|a|bly (ges'ə blē), *adv.* in a guessable manner.

guess|ing game (ges'ing), **1** a game in which the players must guess the right answer, as to a riddle or question. **2** *Figurative.* something resembling this game, especially the attempt of opposing factions to keep one another guessing as to their moves or motives.

guess|ing|ly (ges'ing lē), *adv.* by guesswork.

guess-rope (ges'rōp'), *n.* = guest rope.

guess|ti|mate (*n.* ges'tə mit, -māt; *v.* ges'tə māt), *n., v.,* **-mat|ed**, **-mat|ing**. *U.S. Informal.* —*n.* an estimate based on conjecture: *The tool industry is made up of so many segments that only guesstimates can be made of its total sales* (Wall Street Journal).
—*v.i.* to make a guesstimate.
—*v.t.* to estimate by conjecture. Also, **guestimate**.
[blend of *guess* and *estimate*]

guess|work (ges'wėrk'), *n.* work, action, or results based on guessing; guessing.

guest (gest), *n., adj., v.* —*n.* **1** a person who is received and entertained at another's home, club, or table; person who is not a regular member; visitor: *My brother asked his friend over as a guest for the weekend.* **SYN**: See syn. under **visitor**. **2** a person who is staying at a hotel, motel, or boarding house: *The firemen got all of the guests out of the hotel when it was ablaze.* **3** a person brought in to appear on a regular program, series of concerts or lectures, or the like, as a substitute for a regular performer or as a special attraction. **4** *Zoology.* an animal, especially an insect, that lives in the nests of other animals; inquiline. **5** *Obsolete.* a stranger.
—*adj.* **1** of or for guests: *a guest list, a guest room, guest towels.* **2** being a guest: *a guest conductor, a guest lecturer.*
—*v.t.* to entertain as a guest.
—*v.i.* to be a guest: to guest on a TV show. *Laugh and be merry together like brothers akin Guesting awhile in the rooms of a beautiful inn* (John Masefield).
[Old English *giest;* influenced by Scandinavian (compare Old Icelandic *gestr*)]

guest|cham|ber (gest'chām'bər), *n.* a room for the lodging or entertainment of guests.

guest-con|duct (gest'kən dukt'), *v.t.* to conduct (an orchestra, chorus, or other musical group) as a guest: *Joseph Krips guest-conducted a concert with a doctors' orchestra* (St. Louis Post Dispatch). —*v.i.* to be or act as a guest conductor: *He spread himself around, guest-conducting in almost every city that had a good orchestra* (Time).

guest|house (gest'hous'), *n.* **1** a house or cottage all or part of which is rented out to tourists or vacationers on a temporary basis. **2** a house reserved for the use of visiting dignitaries. **3** a small house for guests on a large estate.

gues|ti|mate (*n.* ges'tə mit, -māt; *v.* ges'tə māt), *n., v.i., v.t.,* **-mat|ed**, **-mat|ing**. *U.S. Slang.* guesstimate.

guest|less (gest'lis), *adj.* without guests.

guest|ly (gest'lē), *adj.* of guests; suitable for guests: *guestly behavior, guestly courtesy.*

guest|mas|ter (gest'mas'tər, -mäs'-), *n.* a monk who supervises the lodging and entertainment of guests at a monastery.

guest rope, **1** a line over the side of a ship for boatmen in small boats to grab when coming alongside; grab rope. **2** a second line used to steady a boat being towed.

guest|ship (gest'ship), *n.* the position or relation of a guest.

guest-star (gest'stär'), *v.,* **-starred**, **-star|ring**.
—*v.i.* to be a guest star; perform a leading part as a guest: *Anne B. Davis ... will guest-star on the first two shows* (TV Guide).
—*v.t.* to present in a leading part as a guest: *He turns down most offers to guest-star his ventriloquist act on other television programs* (Time).

guest worker, = Gastarbeiter.

Gue|var|ist (gā vä'rist), *n.* a follower or supporter of Ernesto (Ché) Guevara (1928-1967) or of his ideas of implementing revolution through terrorist guerrilla tactics.

gu|fa (gü'fə), *n.* = kufa.

guff (guf), *n. Slang.* **1** empty talk; nonsense: *a paragraph of irrelevant guff. However, it's not much better than the sort of guff that television films have accustomed us to* (New Yorker). **2** back talk; lip: *Don't give me any more of your guff.* [imitative]

guf|faw (gu fô'), *n., v.* —*n.* a burst of loud, coarse laughter: *Young Buttons burst out into a guffaw* (Thackeray).
—*v.i.* to laugh loudly and coarsely: *For his monomaniacal follies, he is everywhere guffawed at* (Time).
[originally Scottish; probably imitative]

Gug|gen|heim (gü'gən hīm), *n. Informal.* a Guggenheim fellowship.

Guggenheim fellowship, a fellowship offered to scholars in all fields of knowledge and the arts by the Guggenheim Memorial Foundation. [< John Simon *Guggenheim,* son of Simon Guggenheim, 1867-1941, an American industrialist]

gug|gle (gug'əl), *v.,* **-gled**, **-gling**, *n.* —*v.i.* to make a gurgling sound; gurgle.
—*n.* a guggling sound.
[imitative. Compare etym. under **gurgle**.]

Gui|a|nan (gē ä'nən, -an'ən), *adj., n.* —*adj.* of or having to do with Guiana.
—*n.* a person born or living in Guiana.

Gui|a|nese (gē'ə nēz', -nēs'), *adj., n., pl.* **-nese**. = Guianan.

guib (gwib, gēb), *n.* = harnessed antelope. [< a native name in western Africa]

guiche (gēsh), *n.* a curl or lock of hair in front of the ear. [< French *guiche*]

gui|chet (gē shā'), *n.* a wicket, grating, or hatch, especially one through which tickets are issued. [< French *guichet*]

guid (gyd), *adj., n., interj., adv. Scottish.* good.

guid|a|ble (gī'də bəl), *adj.* that can be guided.

guid|ance (gī'dəns), *n., adj.* —*n.* **1** the action of guiding; direction; leadership: *Under her mother's guidance, she learned how to swim.* **2** a thing that guides: *Common sense is usually our best guidance in difficult situations.* **3** *Education.* studies and counseling given to students to help them solve their problems, plan their education, and choose careers. **4** *Aeronautics.* the regulating of the path of an unmanned aircraft, rocket, or other missile in flight by means of radar, computers, radio signals, and other communication controls.
—*adj.* **1** *Education.* of or having to do with guidance counseling: *a guidance program, a guidance counselor.* **2** *Aeronautics.* of or having to do with the directional control of an unmanned aircraft, rocket, or missile in flight: *guidance gear.*

guidance system, *Aeronautics.* any system of controls which regulates the path of an unmanned aircraft, rocket, or other missile in its flight, in air or in space.

guide (gīd), *v.,* **guid|ed**, **guid|ing**, *n.* —*v.t.* **1** to show the way; lead; direct; conduct: *The Indian scout guided the explorers through the mountain pass. The President skillfully guided the country through a difficult period.* **2** to direct the movement or course of: *to guide a ship through a storm.* **3** to direct in any course of action: *Good advice guided him in the choice of a career.* **4** to manage; control; regulate. **SYN**: govern.
—*v.i.* to act as one who guides.
—*n.* **1** a person or thing that shows the way, leads, conducts, or directs: *Tourists and hunters sometimes hire guides. The amount of money you have is a guide to how much you can spend. Your feelings are often poor guides for actions and beliefs.* **SYN**: leader, conductor, director, pilot. **2** a part of a machine or device for directing or regulating motion or action. **3** = guidebook. **4** = guidepost. **5** something which marks a position or serves to guide the eye. **6** a soldier posted at the right or left front of a column when marching, with whom all other members of a unit align. **7 Guide**, a member of the Girl Guides between the ages of eleven and fourteen.
[< Middle French *guiden,* alteration of Old French *guier,* ultimately < Germanic (compare Gothic *witan* observe, watch)] —**guide'less**, *adj.*
—*Syn. v.t.* **1 Guide, lead, conduct** mean to show the way. **Guide** implies being familiar with the way and all the points of interest or danger along it, and means to go along to point these out: *The Indian guided the hunters on their expedition into the wilderness.* **Lead** means to go ahead to show the way: *The dog led his master to the injured man.* **Conduct** means to go with

Pronunciation Key: hat, āge, cãre, fär; let, ēqual, tėrm, it, īce; hot, ōpen, ôrder; **oi**l, **ou**t; cup, pu̇t, rüle; **ch**ild; lo**ng**; **th**in; **ᴛʜ**en; **zh**, measure; ə represents **a** in about, **e** in taken, **i** in pencil, **o** in lemon, **u** in circus.

as guide and assistant: *He conducted a party of tourists to Europe.*

guide|board (gīd′bôrd′, -bōrd′), *n.* a board or sign with directions for travelers, often attached to a guidepost.

guide|book (gīd′bu̇k′), *n.* a book of directions and information, especially one for travelers or tourists.

guid|ed missile (gī′did), a missile that can be guided in flight to its target by means of radio signals from the ground or by automatic devices inside the missile which direct its course. Correction or alteration of the course of a missile in the atmosphere can be made aerodynamically. A missile operating outside the earth's atmosphere is guided only during the period of thrust and thereafter follows a ballistic trajectory unless thrust is resumed.

guid|ed-mis|sile (gī′did mis′əl), *adj.* **1** of or having to do with a guided missile or guided missiles: *a guided-missile base.* **2** able to carry and launch a guided missile or guided missiles: *a guided-missile submarine.*

guide dog, = seeing eye dog.

guide field, *Physics.* a field, usually a separate magnetic field, in a particle accelerator, that causes the particles to follow a desired path.

guide fossil, = index fossil.

guide|line (gīd′līn′), *n.* **1** Usually, **guidelines.** a guide, principle, or policy for determining a future course of action: *to adopt new guidelines for the national defense.* **2** a rope or other object serving as a guide.

guide|post (gīd′pōst′), *n.* **1** a post with signs and directions on it. A guidepost where roads meet tells travelers to what places each road goes and how far it is to each place. **2** *Figurative.* anything that serves as a guide; guideline: *... the Administration's anti-inflation guideposts* (New York Times).

guid|er (gī′dər), *n.* **1** a person or thing that guides; guide; leader. **2 Guider**, an adult leader associated with the Girl Guides.

guide rail, a track or rail designed to keep a train, sliding door, or moving part from becoming dislodged.

guide rope, **1** a rope used to guide and steady an object that is being hoisted. **2** a long rope hung from a balloon so as to trail along the ground, for regulating automatically the altitude of the balloon.

guide|way (gīd′wā′), *n. Machinery.* a track, channel, or runner on or in which a part slides or moves.

guide word, a word put at the top of a page as a guide to the contents of the page; catchword. The guide words for these two pages are *guideboard* and *gun.*

guid|ing light (gī′ding), a person or thing set forth as a guide; model: *His guiding light was Franklin Roosevelt, for whom he worked as an aide in the Navy Department* (Time).

guiding telescope, a telescope attached to a phototelescope that allows a person to observe the star being photographed and so regulate the position of the phototelescope.

gui|don (gī′dən, -don), *n.* **1** a small flag or streamer carried as a guide by soldiers, or used for signaling. **2** *U.S.* a flag, streamer, or pennant of a company, regiment or other group. **3** the soldier who carries the guidon. [< Middle French *guidon* < Italian *guidone* battle standard < *guidare* to direct, show]

gui|gnol (gē nyôl′), *n.* = Grand Guignol.

guild (gild), *n.* **1** an association of people for mutual aid or for some common purpose: *the Ladies' Guild of a church.* **2** a union of the men in one trade or craft or of merchants in the Middle Ages to keep standards high and to look out for the interests of their trade: *The handicraftsmen banded together for protection into guilds, the forerunners of the trade unions of today* (Ogburn and Nimkoff). **3** *Botany.* any one of four groups of plants, such as the parasites, in an ecological classification no longer current, each group having a characteristic manner of growth and nutrition. Also, **gild.** [Old English *gield,* influenced by Scandinavian (compare Old Icelandic *gildi*)]

guil|der (gil′dər), *n.* **1** a silver coin or unit of money of the Netherlands, equal to 100 Netherlands cents. **2** a gold or silver coin formerly used in the Netherlands, Germany, or Austria. Also, **gulden.** [earlier *gilders,* alteration of Middle English *gildren* or *guldren,* probably mispronunciation of Middle Dutch *gulden*]

guild|hall (gild′hôl′), *n.* **1** the hall in which a guild meets. **2** *British.* a town hall or city hall.

guild|ship (gild′ship), *n.* membership in a guild.

guilds|man (gildz′mən), *n., pl.* **-men.** a member of a guild.

guild socialism, an English form of socialism that is in favor of industries being owned by the nation but managed by guilds of workers.

guild socialist, a person who favors guild socialism.

guild-so|cial|is|tic (gild′sō′shə lis′tik), *adj.* of or having to do with guild socialism.

guile (gīl), *n., v.,* **guiled, guil|ing.** —*n.* **1** crafty deceit; cunning; crafty behavior; sly tricks; craftiness: *By guile the fox got the cheese from the crow. A swindler used guile; a robber uses force.* **SYN:** wiliness, trickery. See syn. under **deceit.** **2** *Obsolete.* a trick.
—*v.t. Archaic.* to beguile; deceive: *Ornament is but the guiled shore To a most dangerous sea* (Shakespeare).
[< Old French *guile,* apparently < a Germanic word]

guile|ful (gīl′fəl), *adj.* crafty and deceitful; sly and tricky. **SYN:** cunning, wily, artful. —**guile′ful|ly,** *adv.* —**guile′ful|ness,** *n.*

guile|less (gīl′lis), *adj.* without guile; honest; frank; straightforward; sincere. **SYN:** artless, candid. —**guile′less|ly,** *adv.* —**guile′less|ness,** *n.*

guil|le|mot (gil′ə mot), *n.* any one of a genus of arctic diving birds of the same family as the auk, with narrow, pointed bills. [< French *guillemot* (diminutive) < *Guillaume* William]

guil|loche (gi lōsh′), *n.* an ornament composed of interlacing curved bands. [< French *guillochis,* or *guilloche* the tool for making it]

***guil|lo|tine** (*n.* gil′ə tēn; *v. also* gil′ə tēn′), *n., v.,* **-tined, -tin|ing.** —*n.* **1** a machine for cutting off people's heads by means of a heavy blade that slides down in grooves made in two posts. The guillotine was used during the French Revolution. **2** an instrument for cutting out the tonsils. **3** a machine for cutting, such as one for cutting paper. **4** *British.* the official imposing of a time limit on a governmental debate; cloture.
—*v.t.* **1** to cut off the head of (someone) with a guillotine. **2** to cut (as paper) with a guillotine. **3** *British.* to end debate on (a bill, amendment, or other measure) by guillotine; apply cloture to.
[< French *guillotine* < Joseph I. *Guillotin,* 1738-1814, French physician and advocate of its use]

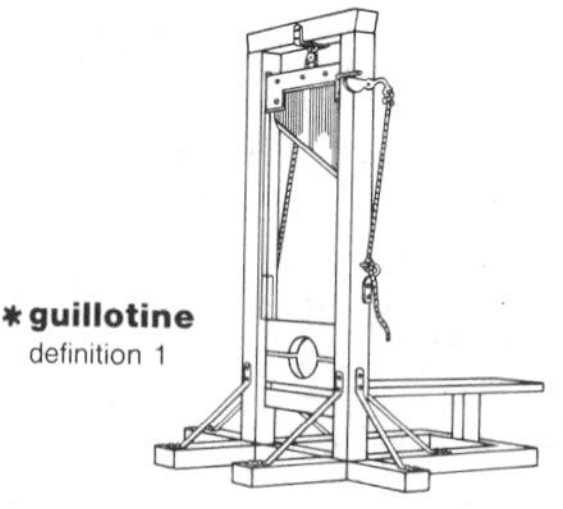
***guillotine**
definition 1

guilt (gilt), *n.* **1** the fact or state of having done wrong; being guilty; being to blame: *The evidence proved the accused thief's guilt.* **SYN:** guiltiness, culpability, criminality. **2** a guilty action or conduct; crime; offense; wrongdoing: *The guilt of blood is at your door* (Tennyson). **3** a feeling of having done wrong or being to blame. [Old English *gylt* offense]

guilt by association, guilt attached to a person by reason of his being associated with others who have been found guilty.

guilt|less (gilt′lis), *adj.* **1** free from guilt; not guilty; innocent: *Some Cromwell, guiltless of his country's blood* (Thomas Gray). **SYN:** See syn. under **innocent.** **2** having no knowledge or experience: *Heifers guiltless of the yoke* (Alexander Pope). —**guilt′less|ly,** *adv.* —**guilt′less|ness,** *n.*

guilt|y (gil′tē), *adj.,* **guilt|i|er, guilt|i|est.** **1** having done wrong; deserving to be blamed and punished: *The jury pronounced the prisoner guilty of murder.* **SYN:** culpable, sinful, criminal. **2** knowing or showing that one has done wrong: *The boy who hit the cat had a guilty conscience and a guilty look.* **3** *Obsolete.* deserving: *He is guilty of death* (Matthew 26:66). [Old English *gyltig*]
—**guilt′i|ly,** *adv.* —**guilt′i|ness,** *n.*

guimpe (gimp, gamp), *n.* a blouse worn under a dress or jumper and showing at the neck or at the neck and arms. A guimpe is usually worn with a low-necked dress. Also, **gimp.** [< French *guimpe,* Old French *guimple* < a Germanic word]

guin|ea (gin′ē), *n.* **1** a British gold coin worth 21 shillings. It has not been made since 1813. **2** an amount equal to 21 shillings, formerly used in Great Britain in stating prices, fees, etc.: *This hat is worth two guineas.* **3** = guinea fowl. [< *Guinea,* a region along the coast of West Africa (the coins were minted for the Guinea trade and were made of gold from Guinea)]

Guin|ea (gin′ē), *n.* = ginney.

Guinea corn, = durra.

guinea fowl, a plump domestic fowl somewhat like a pheasant, having dark-gray feathers with small, white spots. The guinea fowl belongs to a family native to Africa. Its flesh and its eggs are used as food. [< *Guinea* (from where they were imported)]

guinea grains, the seeds of an African plant of the ginger family used as a flavoring in cordials, foods, and pharmaceuticals; grains of paradise.

guinea grass, a coarse tropical grass of Africa, grown in many warm countries and extensively cultivated in the West Indies for pasturage.

guinea hen, **1** = guinea fowl. **2** a female guinea fowl.

Guin|e|an (gin′ē ən), *adj., n.* —*adj.* of or having to do with Guinea or its inhabitants.
—*n.* a person born or living in Guinea.

Guinea pepper, **1** the fruit of a pepper plant from which cayenne is obtained. **2** the aromatic fruit of an African tree of the custard-apple family, used as a stimulant. **3** the tree itself.

guinea pig, **1** a short-eared, tailless rodent kept as a pet and for experiments; cavy. It is like a big, fat, harmless rat. **2** *Figurative.* any person or thing serving as a subject for experiment or observation. [uncertain allusion to *Guinea*]

guin|ea-pig (gin′ē pig′), *v.,* **-pigged, -pig|ging.** —*v.t.* to use as a guinea pig: *They were guinea-pigged ... in disorientation machines that whirled them around till they became physically sick* (Time). —*v.i.* to act as a guinea pig: *I've been guinea-pigging through one psychoanalysis after another* (Kevin Wallace).

Guinea worm, a long, threadlike worm that is a parasite in man and animals. It is common on the Guinea Coast and in other warm regions.

Guin|e|vere (gwin′ə vir), *n.* King Arthur's queen in Arthurian legends, who was loved by Lancelot.

gui|pure (gi pyu̇r′; *French* gē pyr′), *n.* **1** a heavy kind of lace having patterns connected by large, coarse stitches. **2** heavy trimming made of cords, often with wire running through it. [< Middle French *guipure* < *guiper* cover with silk < Middle Dutch *wippen* to turn]

gui|ro or **güi|ro** (gwē′rō), *n., pl.* **-ros.** a notched gourd used as a musical instrument in Latin America. [< Spanish *güiro* (literally) gourd]

gui|sarme (gi zärm′), *n.* = gisarme.

guise (gīz), *n., v.,* **guised, guis|ing.** —*n.* **1** style of dress; garb: *The spy went in the guise of a monk and was not recognized by the enemy.* **SYN:** costume, attire. **2** outward appearance; aspect; semblance: (*Figurative.*) *His theory is nothing but an old idea in a new guise.* **3** *Figurative.* pretended appearance; pretense: *Under the guise of friendship, he plotted treachery.* **4** *Obsolete.* custom: *It never was our guise to slight the poor* (Alexander Pope). **5** *Obsolete.* a disguise.
—*v.t.* **1** *Archaic.* to attire; dress; garb. **2** *Obsolete.* to disguise. —*v.i. Especially Scottish.* to go in disguise; masquerade.
[< Old French *guise* < Germanic (compare Old High German *wīsa* manner, wise)]

***gui|tar** (gə tär′), *n.* a musical instrument usually having six strings, played with the fingers or with a pick. It belongs to the same class as the lute. [< French *guitare* < Spanish *guitarra* < Greek *kithára* cithara. See etym. of doublets **cithara, zither.**] —**gui|tar′like′,** *adj.*

***guitar**

gui|tar|fish (gə tär′fish′), *n., pl.* **-fish|es** or (*collectively*) **-fish.** any one of certain rays resembling a shark.

gui|tar|ist (gə tär′ist), *n.* a player on the guitar.

guit-guit (gwit′gwit′), *n.* a small, brilliantly colored tropical American bird; honey creeper. [imitative]

Gu|ja|ra|ti (gu̇j′ə rä′tē), *n.* **1** the Indic language of Gujarat and adjoining parts of western India. **2** a native of Gujarat.

Gu|je|ra|ti (gu̇j′ə rä′tē), *n.* = Gujarati.

Gu|lag (gü läg′, gü′läg), *n.* a concentration camp for political prisoners in a totalitarian country; labor camp. [< Russian *Gulag,* acronym for *G*(lavnoye) *U*(pravleniye) *Lag*(erei) Chief Administration of Camps]

gu|lar (gyü′lər), *adj., n.* —*adj.* of or situated on the throat. —*n.* a plate beneath the throat of a snake or fish. [< Latin *gula* throat + English *-ar*]

gu|lash (gü′läsh), *n.* = goulash.

gulch (gulch), *n.* a very deep, narrow ravine with steep sides, especially one marking the course of a stream or torrent; a small gorge. **SYN:** gully. [American English, perhaps < dialectal English *gulch* or *gulsh* (of land) to sink in, (of water) gush through a narrow passage]

gul|den (gůl′dən), *n., pl.* **-dens** or **-den.** = guilder. [< Dutch and German *Gulden* (literally) golden (coin)]

gules (gyülz), *n., adj. Heraldry.* **—*n.*** the color red, represented in engravings by parallel vertical lines.
—*adj.* red. [< Old French *gueules,* earlier *goules* red fur neckpiece, (originally) pieces cut from neck fur) < *goule* throat < Latin *gula*]

gulf (gulf), *n., adj., v.* **—*n.*** **1** a large bay; arm of an ocean or sea extending into the land: *The Gulf of Mexico is between Florida and Mexico.* See picture under **bay**[1]. **2** a very deep break or cut in the earth; chasm: *The earthquake made a gulf in the earth. A gulf in Vermont is a deep ravine between steep hills.* SYN: abyss. **3** *Figurative.* any wide separation: *The quarrel left a gulf between the old friends.* **4** something that swallows up; whirlpool.
—*adj.* of or having to do with a gulf, especially the Gulf of Mexico.
—*v.t.* to swallow; engulf: *Cast himself down, And gulfed his griefs in inmost sleep* (Tennyson).
[< Old French *golfe* < Italian *golfo,* ultimately < Greek *kólpos* (originally) bosom] **—gulf′like′,** *adj.*

gulf fritillary, a butterfly of the southern United States, Mexico, and West Indies, having reddish-brown wings marked with silvery dots near the head.

Gulf Stream, a strong, warm current that flows out of the Gulf of Mexico, north along the coast of the United States and Newfoundland, and northeast across the Atlantic toward the British Isles. It is 50 miles wide.

gulf|weed (gulf′wēd′), *n.* **1** an olive-brown seaweed having many berrylike sacs that keep it afloat; sargassum. It is found in the Gulf Stream and the Sargasso Sea. **2** any of various related species.

gull[1] (gul), *n.* any one of a group of graceful, usually gray-and-white birds, living on or near large bodies of water. A gull has long wings, webbed feet, and a thick, strong beak. [Middle English *gull,* perhaps < Celtic (compare Cornish *guilan*)]

gull[2] (gul), *v., n.* **—*v.t.*** to deceive; cheat; dupe: *Nothing is so easy as to gull the public* (Washington Irving). *Brighton had sought powers to deal with mock auctions, places where talkative salesmen gull people into buying rubbish* (London Times). SYN: trick.
—*n.* **1** a person who is easily deceived or cheated; dupe. SYN: simpleton, fool. **2** *Obsolete.* a trick; fraud.
[origin uncertain; perhaps special use of *gull*[1]]

gull[3] (gul), *n. British Dialect.* a young bird not having full-grown feathers, especially a young goose. [probably < obsolete *gull* pale, yellow < Scandinavian (compare Old Icelandic *gulr*)]

Gul|lah (gul′ə), *n.* **1** any one of a group of Negroes living along the coast of South Carolina and Georgia, and on the islands off the coast. **2** the dialect of English spoken by the Gullahs. [American English; apparently < an African tribal name]

gull-billed tern (gul′bild′), a tern found along the Atlantic and Gulf coasts, having a stout, black bill.

gull|er|y (gul′ər ē), *n., pl.* **-er|ies.** a haunt or breeding place for gulls.

gul|let (gul′it), *n.* **1** the passage for food from the pharynx to the stomach; esophagus: *I am going to cool my gullet at the blessed well* (John Synge). **2** = throat. **3** a narrow trench dug in beginning excavations. **4** *Figurative.* a gully; ravine. [< Old French *goulet* (diminutive) < *goule* or *gole* throat, neck < Latin *gula* throat]

gul|li|bil|i|ty (gul′ə bil′ə tē), *n.* the quality of being gullible; tendency to be easily deceived or cheated.

gul|li|ble (gul′ə bəl), *adj.* easily deceived or cheated. SYN: credulous. [earlier *gullable* < *gull*[2] + *-able*] **—gul′li|bly,** *adv.*

Gul|li|ver (gul′ə vər), *n.* **Lem|u|el** (lem′yů əl), the shipwrecked Englishman in Swift's satire, *Gulliver's Travels,* who visits four imaginary countries.

gull-winged (gul′wingd′), *adj.* (of an aircraft) having wings shaped like a gull's, sloping upward for a short distance from the root, then becoming horizontal, or nearly so, to the tip.

gul|ly[1] (gul′ē), *n., pl.* **-lies,** *v.,* **-lied, -ly|ing.** **—*n.*** **1** a narrow gorge; little steep valley; ditch made by heavy rains or running water. **2** *Cricket.* **a** the part of the playing field in back of the slips. **b** a fielder stationed in the gully.
—*v.t.* to make or wear gullies in.
[probably variant of *gullet*]

gul|ly[2] (gul′ē, gůl′-), *n., pl.* **-lies.** *Scottish.* a large household knife. [origin uncertain]

gul|ly|wash|er (gul′ē wosh′ər, -wôsh′-), *n. U.S. Dialect or Informal.* a sudden, heavy rainfall; downpour.

gu|los|i|ty (gyü los′ə tē), *n.* greediness. [< Late Latin *gulōsitās* < *gulōsus* gluttonous < *gula* gullet]

gulp (gulp), *v., n.* **—*v.t.*** **1** to swallow eagerly or greedily: *The hungry boy gulped down the bowl of soup.* **2** *Figurative.* to keep in; choke back; repress: *The disappointed boy gulped down a sob and tried to smile.*
—*v.i.* to gasp or choke: *The spray of cold water made me gulp.*
—*n.* **1** the act of swallowing: *He ate the cookie in one gulp.* **2** the amount swallowed at one time; mouthful: *She took a gulp of the wine.*
[probably imitative. Compare Middle Dutch *golpen,* verb, Flemish *gulpe,* noun.]

gulp|er (gul′pər), *n.* **1** a person or thing that gulps. **2** a large-mouthed, long-tailed, deep-sea fish.

gul|pin (gul′pin), *n. British Slang.* a person who would believe anything told him; a credulous person; simpleton or fool. [perhaps < the phrase *gulp in*]

gulp|ing|ly (gul′ping lē), *adv.* with a gulp.

gum[1] (gum), *n., v.,* **gummed, gum|ming.** **—*n.*** **1** the sticky juice of certain trees and plants, that hardens in the air and dissolves in water. Gum is used for sticking paper and other things together. It is also used to make candy and drugs. **2** any similar secretion, such as resin, gum resin, or balsam. **3** a preparation of such a substance for use in industry or the arts. **4a** a tree that yields gum; gum tree, such as the eucalyptus, tupelo, or sweet gum. **b** = gumwood. **5** = chewing gum. **6** the sticky substance on the back of a stamp, the flap of an envelope, or other piece of paper to affix it to another paper; mucilage; glue. **7** = rubber. **8** *U.S.* a hollowed-out log, cut from a gum tree, and used as a water trough or the like.
—*v.t.* **1** to smear, stick together, or stiffen with gum: *Gummed tape will hold the box together.* **2** to make sticky; clog with something sticky: *My pocket was all gummed with candy.*
—*v.i.* **1** to give off gum; form gum: *Pine trees gum in the spring.* **2** to become sticky; become clogged with something sticky: *My fingers gummed together as the sticky candy melted in my hand.*
gums, *U.S.* rubber overshoes: [*She*] *is outside cleaning her gums on the mat* (Richard White).
gum up, *U.S. Slang.* to mess up; put out of order: *When computers first came along, all they did was to speed up the flow of information within departments. Sometimes, by generating too many new reports, they actually gummed up the works* (Time).
[< Old French *gomme,* learned borrowing from Late Latin *gumma,* for Latin *gummi* < Greek *kómmi*] **—gum′like′,** *adj.*

gum[2] (gum), *n., v.,* **gummed, gum|ming.** **—*n.*** **1** Often, **gums.** the firm flesh around the teeth. **2** the portion of this attached to a single tooth.
—*v.t.* **1** to chew with the gums: *The old man smiled and resumed eating, looking like . . . Popeye as he cradled the food in his jaws and gummed it* (Hoyt W. Fuller). **2** to utter with a toothless mouth: *. . . a dyspeptic old man, gumming insults* (Atlantic). **3** *U.S.* to enlarge the spaces between the teeth of (a worn saw).
[Old English *gōma* palate]

gum[3] (gum), *interj.* **by gum,** an exclamation or mild oath: *Newmarket Heath may make you shiver, but, by gum! it gives you an appetite* (Hawley Smart). [altered pronunciation of *God*]

GUM (no periods) or **G.U.M.,** a state-operated department store in the Soviet Union: *G.U.M. is Moscow's answer to Macy's, Gimbel's, Sears Roebuck, Woolworth, and A. & P., all rolled into one* (Time). [< Russian *G*(lavnyj) *U*(niversal'nyj) *M*(agazin) Main Department Store]

gum acacia, = gum arabic.

gum ammoniac, a natural mixture of gum and resin used in medicine and as a cement for porcelain; ammoniac.

gum arabic, a gum obtained from acacia trees, used in making candy, medicine, and mucilage.

gum|bah (güm bä′), *n. U.S. Slang.* a close friend; chum: *The cops had collared a big gumbah of Frank Costello's and made a deal with him* (Marion K. Sanders). [alteration of Italian *compare* (literally) godfather; the spelling was influenced by the pronunciation]

gum|ball (gum′bôl′), *n. U.S.* chewing gum or bubble gum in the form of a candy-coated ball.

gum benzoin, = benzoin (def. 1).

gum|bo[1] (gum′bō), *n., pl.* **-bos.** **1** a soup usually made of chicken and rice and thickened with okra pods. **2** the okra plant. **3** its sticky pods. **4** a kind of soil that contains much silt and becomes very sticky when wet; gumbo mud. It is found in the southern and western parts of the United States. Also, **gombo.** [American English < a Central Bantu dialect (compare Mbundu *ki-ngombo* okra)]

gum|bo[2] or **Gum|bo** (gum′bo), *n.* a dialect spoken by Negroes and Creoles of the French West Indies and Louisiana. Also, **gombo.** [apparently < a native name]

gum|boil (gum′boil′), *n.* a small abscess on the gums.

gum|bo-lim|bo (gum′bō lim′bō), *n.* a tall, tropical American tree that yields a sweet, aromatic resin used in making varnishes; gum elemi. [< an African (Bantu) word]

gumbo mud, = gumbo[1] (def. 4).

gum|boot (gum′büt′), *n.* a rubber boot.

gum|bo|til (gum′bō til), *n.* a very sticky gray- or dark-colored clay, formed by the weathering of glacial till. [< *gumbo* + *til*(*l*)[4]]

gum copal, a lustrous resin from various tropical trees; copal: *. . . fossil insects embedded in gum copal* (Scientific American).

gum dammar, = dammar.

gum|drop (gum′drop′), *n.* a stiff, jellylike piece of candy made of gum arabic or gelatin, sweetened and flavored.

gum elastic, = rubber.

gum elemi, **1** = elemi. **2** = gumbo-limbo.

gum|ma (gum′ə), *n., pl.* **gum|mas, gum|ma|ta** (gum′ə tə). a tumor with gumlike contents, produced by syphilis. [< New Latin *gumma* < Latin *gummi* gum[1]]

gum|ma|tous (gum′ə təs), *adj.* of or like a gumma.

gum|mif|er|ous (gu mif′ər əs), *adj.* producing gum. [< Latin *gummi* gum[1] + English *-ferous*]

gum|mite (gum′īt), *n. Mineralogy.* a reddish-yellow hydrate of uranium, resembling gum. [< Latin *gummi* gum[1] + English *-ite*[1]]

gum|mose (gum′ōs), *adj.* = gummous.

gum|mo|sis (gu mō′sis), *n.* the abnormal formation of gum that oozes through the bark in certain trees such as the cherry or plum.

gum|mous (gum′əs), *adj.* of or like gum; gummy.

gum|my[1] (gum′ē), *adj.,* **-mi|er, -mi|est.** **1** sticky like gum; viscid. SYN: viscous, mucilaginous. **2** covered with gum. **3** giving off gum: *the gummy bark of a fir or pine.* **4** swollen, as if by gumlike matter: *gummy ankles.* **—gum′mi|ness,** *n.*

gum|my[2] (gum′ē), *adj.* = gummatous.

gum|my[3] (gum′ē), *n. pl.* **-mies.** any one of several small sharks found in Australian waters. Some species are edible. [< *gum*[2] + *-y*[2]]

Gum Nebula (gum), a very large and faintly glowing galactic nebula in the southern sky, discovered in 1952: *The Gum Nebula's radius of 360 parsecs makes it the largest nebula known in our galaxy* (Scientific American). [< Colin S. *Gum,* an Australian astronomer, who discovered it]

gump (gump), *n. Informal or Dialect.* a foolish person; dolt. [origin uncertain]

gum plant, any one of various composite plants whose leaves are covered with a sticky secretion.

gump|tion (gump′shən), *n. Informal.* **1** initiative; energy; resourcefulness. **2** common sense; good judgment. [originally Scottish; origin uncertain]

gum resin, a natural mixture of gum and resin, obtained from or given off by certain plants. Ammoniac, asafetida, gamboge, myrrh, and scammony are gum resins.

gums (gumz), *n.pl.* See under **gum**[1] and **gum**[2], *n.* (def. 1).

gum|shoe (gum′shü′), *n., adj., v.,* **-shoed, -shoe·ing.** **—*n.*** **1** *Slang.* a detective. **2** a rubber overshoe. **3** = sneaker (def. 1).
—*adj.* *U.S. Slang.* **1** done secretly or stealthily: *gumshoe work.* **2** used in investigating; detective: *gumshoe methods.* **3** of or dealing with detectives: *a gumshoe story.*
—*v.i.* *U.S. Slang.* to go quietly and secretly.
[American English < *gum*[1] + *shoe*]

gum silk, silk from which the natural gum has not been removed.

gum thus (thus), **1** = turpentine (def. 2). **2** = frankincense. [< *gum*[1] and Latin *thūs* incense; see etym. under **thurible**]

gum tragacanth, = tragacanth (def. 1).

gum tree, **1** any one of various trees that produce gum. The most common is the sapodilla, which produces a gum called chicle. North American gum trees include the sweet gum, tupelo, and black tupelo. Some Australian eucalyptus trees are also known as gum trees. **2** = eucalyptus.

gum|wood (gum′wůd′), *n.* the wood of a gum tree.

gun**[1] (gun), *n., v.,* **gunned, gun|ning.** **—*n. **1a** any weapon with a long metal tube for shooting bul-

Pronunciation Key: hat, āge, cãre, fär; let, ēqual, tėrm; it, īce; hot, ōpen, ôrder; oil, out; cup, pu̇t, rüle; child; long; thin; ᴛʜen; zh, measure; ə represents **a** in about, **e** in taken, **i** in pencil, **o** in lemon, **u** in circus.

lets or shot. A rifle or cannon is a gun. Pistols and revolvers are called guns in ordinary speech. **b** a long cannon that shoots a shell at a faster speed and at a lower angle than either a howitzer or a mortar. **2** anything resembling a gun in use or shape: *a spray gun.* **3** the shooting of a gun as a signal or salute: *The President gets twenty-one guns as a salute.* **4** the throttle of an aircraft, automobile, or other engine-driven device or vehicle. **5** *British.* a member of a hunting party. **6** *Slang.* a thief; pickpocket. **7** *U.S. Informal.* an expert in using a gun.
—***v.i.*** **1** to shoot with a gun; hunt with a gun: *He went gunning for rabbits.* **2** to speed; accelerate: *The driver gunned away home. The motorcycle gunned through the streets.*
—***v.t.*** **1** *U.S. Informal.* to shoot at with a gun; kill or wound with a gun. **2** *Slang.* to put at high speed; accelerate: *The pilot of the airplane gunned his engine for a sharp climb.*
beat the gun, to begin before the signal to start: *Anyone who tries to beat the gun will be eliminated from the race.*
give it the gun, *Informal.* to speed up; go faster: *Give it the gun or we'll miss the train.*
go great guns, *Informal.* to move vigorously or successfully ahead; advance at full speed: *The team was going great guns in the second half of the game.*
gun down, a to shoot down: *In the past cold-war decade, Soviet or Red Chinese combat planes have attacked and gunned down half a dozen U.S. patrol planes* (Time). **b** to do away with, by or as if by shooting; kill: *Initiatives to achieve European union . . . have systematically been gunned down* (Philip Shabecoff).
gun for, a to start a campaign for or against something: *Textile men have been gunning for quotas . . .* (Wall Street Journal). **b** to seek; try to get: *The champion was gunning for a third straight win.* **c** to shoot: *He is out gunning for ducks.* **d** to seek out to attack: *That bull Mick Shreedy is gunning for me just at present* (W. K. Post).
jump the gun, a to start too soon; start before the signal to do so: *I think we're both jumping the gun in predicting his career* (Harper's). **b** to get a head start on one's opposition: *The store jumped the gun and set up its Christmas decorations before others had taken down the ones for Halloween.*
spike one's guns, to make one powerless; frustrate one's plans: *The young contender's fast footwork and ability to dodge succeeded in spiking the champion's guns until the last round.*
stick to one's guns, to keep one's position; refuse to retreat or yield: *So far, . . . [he] has stuck to his guns, regardless of the pressure put on him* (New York Times).
[special use of Scandinavian *Gunna,* short for *Gunnhildr,* a woman's name]

***gun[1]**
definition 1

handgun

field gun

gun[2] (gun), *v. Archaic.* the past participle of **gin**[4].
gun., gunnery.
gun barrel, the metal tube of a gun.
gun·bear·er (gun′bãr′ər), *n.* a person who carries a gun or guns.
gun·boat (gun′bōt′), *n.* **1** a small warship that can be used in shallow water. **2** any small vessel armed with guns.
gunboat diplomacy, the ready use by a country of its military power to maintain or enforce diplomatic agreements with other countries: *In Macao they [Chinese Communist leaders] have displayed a savage skill for waging "gunboat diplomacy" against the miniscule Portuguese enclave, with as much finesse as the Western imperialists themselves ever played the ruthless game* (Atlantic).
gunboat diplomatist, a supporter or advocate of gunboat diplomacy.
gun camera, 1 a camera synchronized with a gun to photograph the results of firing. **2** a camera used in gunnery training to record the image of the target aimed at.
gun carriage, the structure on which a gun is mounted or moved and on which it is fired.
gun·cot·ton (gun′kot′ən), *n.* an explosive made by treating cotton or other cellulose fibers with a mixture of nitric and sulfuric acids.
gun crew, a section of a ship's company in charge of handling the ship's guns.
gun·di (gun′dē), *n., pl.* **-dis.** = ctenodactyl. [< Arabic *gundi*]
gun·dog (gun′dôg′, -dog′), *n.* a dog, such as a pointer or setter, trained to accompany a hunter in the field.
gun·fight (gun′fīt′), *n.* a fight in which the participants use guns.
gun·fight·er (gun′fī′tər), *n.* **1** a person who fights with a gun: *The story of Wyatt Earp, greatest gunfighter of them all* (New York Times). **2** *U.S. Informal.* a western badman or desperado.
gun·fight·ing (gun′fī′ting), *n.* **1** the act of fighting with guns. **2** the methods or technique of fighting with guns.
gun·fire (gun′fīr′), *n.* **1** the shooting of a gun or guns: *The Near East crackles with intermittent gunfire* (Newsweek). **2** the time at which the morning or evening gun is fired on a military post, etc. **3** *Military.* the use of weapons that shoot, such as artillery, machine guns, and rifles, in military engagement, distinguished from other forms of fighting, such as close fighting with bayonets or grenades: *The enemy was driven out of the village by gunfire.*
gun·flint (gun′flint′), *n.* the piece of flint used to produce the spark in a flintlock.
gunge (gunj), *n. British Slang.* a soft, sticky mass; goo; gunk: *They call this solid material tholin (after the Greek word for muddy), but it seems likely that chemists will continue to call this rather familiar material "gunge"* (New Scientist). [probably alteration of *gunk*]
gung ho (gung′hō′), *Informal.* **1** Also, **gung-ho,** *adj.* eager; enthusiastic; zealous: *Sometimes civic leadership and gung ho spirit revive a dying place* (Time). *If you're really gung ho and prefer stickshift, you can switch to manual operation* (Scientific American). **2** eagerness; enthusiasm: *When the Corps was born, there was . . . much gung ho about reforming the world* (New Yorker). **3** to work enthusiastically or zealously: *His son intended to gung ho for the Peace Corps* (Esquire).
[< *Gung Ho!,* a slogan used in World War II by certain units of the U.S. Marines < Chinese *kung ho* work together]
gun·ite (gun′īt), *n.* a concrete made of cement, sand, and water, applied through a hose under pressure, used for walls, swimming pools, and repairing structures.
gunk (gungk), *n. U.S. Slang.* an unpleasantly sticky mess or gooey substance. SYN: glop, goo. [apparently imitative]
gunk hole, a shallow, sheltered cove filled with growths and rocks.
gun·less (gun′lis), *adj.* having no gun.
gun·lock (gun′lok′), *n.* the part of a gun which controls the hammer and fires the charge.
gun·mak·er (gun′mā′kər), *n.* a person who makes or manufactures guns.
gun·mak·ing (gun′mā′king), *n.* the manufacture of guns.
gun·man (gun′mən), *n., pl.* **-men. 1** a man who uses a gun to rob or kill. **2** a man who is armed with a gun; an expert with a gun. **3** = gunsmith. [American English < *gun*[1] + *man*]
gun metal, 1 a dark-gray alloy used for chains, buckles, handles, etc.: *Gun metal, with 90% copper and 10% tin, is resistant to corrosion* (W. R. Jones). **2** a dark gray. **3** a kind of bronze formerly used for making guns. —**gun′-met′al,** *adj.*
gun moll, *Slang.* **1** a woman companion of a gunman or gangster. **2** a woman robber.
Gunn (gun), *adj.* of or based upon the Gunn effect.
Gun·nar (gůn′är), *n. Norse Mythology.* the brother-in-law of Sigurd (Siegfried). Sigurd won Brunhild for Gunnar (Gunther).
gunned (gund), *adj.* furnished with guns, as a ship.
Gunn effect, an electronic effect in which a semiconductor, such as gallium arsenide, becomes a source of electrical oscillations in the microwave frequencies when it is subjected to electrical voltage at a certain critical level: *Devices using the Gunn effect are expected to cause a miniaturization revolution in radar and other microwave systems* (Science News). [< Ian Gunn, who discovered the effect in 1963]
gun·nel[1] (gun′əl), *n.* = gunwale.
gun·nel[2] (gun′əl), *n.* any one of a genus of small, eel-shaped fishes somewhat resembling a perch, especially a species found in the North Atlantic. [origin uncertain]
gun·ner (gun′ər), *n.* **1** a man trained to fire artillery; soldier who handles and fires cannon: *The gunner fired the cannon in a salute as the flag was raised.* **2** a naval warrant officer in charge of a ship's guns. **3** the member of a gun crew in the artillery who sets the elevation and direction of fire. **4** *British.* a member of an artillery unit. **5** a member of the crew of certain military aircraft who has charge of a gun. **6** a person who hunts with a gun.
gun·ner·y (gun′ər ē), *n.* **1** the construction and management of big guns. **2** the use of guns; shooting of guns. **3** guns collectively.
gunnery sergeant, a noncommissioned officer in the Marine Corps, ranking above a staff sergeant and below a first sergeant.
gun·ning (gun′ing), *n.* the act, process, or skill of shooting with a gun; hunting with a gun.
gun·ny (gun′ē), *n., pl.* **-nies. 1** a strong, coarse fabric made of jute, used especially for sacks and bags. SYN: burlap. **2** = gunnysack. [Anglo-Indian < Hindi *gōnī* < Sanskrit *gonī* sack]
gun·ny·sack (gun′ē sak′), *n.* a sack or bag made of gunny.
gun·pa·per (gun′pā′pər), *n.* paper treated with nitric acid to make it explosive.
gun pit, an excavation where artillery is placed.
gun·play (gun′plā′), *n. U.S.* **1** a fight in which shooting takes place. **2** skill in shooting.
gun·point (gun′point′), *n.* the end of a gun barrel.
at gunpoint, with a gun pointed at one; threatened by a gun.
gun·port (gun′pôrt′, -pōrt′), *n.* a porthole for a gun.
gun·pow·der (gun′pou′dər), *n.* **1** a powder that goes off with noise and force when touched with fire. Gunpowder is used in guns, fireworks, and blasting. Modern gunpowder is made of saltpeter, sulfur, and charcoal. **2** = gunpowder tea.
gunpowder tea, a fine kind of green tea, whose leaves are rolled into little balls.
gun·pow·er (gun′pou′ər), *n.* the number and strength of guns available.
gun·rack (gun′rak′), *n.* a rack on a wall for small firearms.
gun room, 1 a room where guns are kept. **2** a room for junior officers on a British warship. It was originally occupied by the gunner and his mates.
gun·run·ner (gun′run′ər), *n.* a person who brings guns and ammunition into a country illegally.
gun·run·ning (gun′run′ing), *n.* the bringing of guns and ammunition into a country illegally.
guns and butter, a policy of putting equal emphasis on both military and domestic economic programs: *While it may be true technically and from a monetary point of view that you can have guns and butter, it is a fact of life that where your heart is there your money will go* (Martin Luther King, Jr.).
gun·sel[1] (gun′səl), *n. U.S. Slang.* a criminal; gunman. [irregular < *gun*[1]; probably influenced by *gunsel*[2] and *gunslinger*]
gun·sel[2] (gun′səl), *n. U.S. Slang.* **1** a foolish youth; simpleton. **2** a catamite. [probably < Yiddish *genzel* gosling < Middle High German *gensel*]
gun·ship (gun′ship′), *n.* a helicopter carrying heavy machine guns and rockets for support of ground troops.
gun·shot (gun′shot′), *n., adj.* —***n.*** **1** shot fired from a gun: *We heard the hunter's gunshot as it whistled over our heads.* **2** the shooting of a gun: *We heard gunshots.* **3** the distance that a gun will shoot: *The deer was within gunshot.*
—***adj.*** made by the shot from a gun.
gun-shy (gun′shī′), *adj.* **1** afraid of the sound of a gun. **2** afraid of loud noise. **3** suspicious; wary.
gun·sight (gun′sīt′), *n.* the sight of a gun; a device on a gun to assist in taking aim.
gun·sling·er (gun′sling′ər), *n. U.S. Informal.* **1** a man who wears and fights with a gun. **2** a badman, as in westerns.
gun·sling·ing (gun′sling′ing), *adj., n. Informal.*
—***adj.*** wearing a gun: *. . . the gunslinging marshal of the frontier town* (Time). —***n.*** a shooting or fighting with guns: *gang-style gunslinging.*
gun·smith (gun′smith′), *n.* a person whose work is making or repairing small guns.
gun·smith·ing (gun′smith′ing), *n.* the practice or business of a gunsmith.
gun·stock (gun′stok′), *n.* the wooden support or handle to which the barrel of a gun is fastened.
gun·ter (gun′tər), *n.,* or **gunter rig,** *Nautical.* a rig in which the topmast slides up and down the lower mast on rings or hoops. [< Edmund *Gunter,* 1581-1626, an English mathematician, who invented a mathematical instrument that this rig resembled]
Gunter's chain, a chain used by surveyors as a measuring instrument; surveyor's chain. It consists of 100 links, each 7.92 inches long. [< Edmund *Gunter* who invented it]
Gunter's scale, a plane rule containing scales of sines, tangents, and other functions on one side, and corresponding scales of logarithms on the other. It is used for solving problems me-

chanically, especially in trigonometry and navigation. [< Edmund *Gunter,* who invented it]

Gun|ther (gůn′tər), *n.* (in the *Nibelungenlied*) the king of Burgundy and husband of Brunhild.

gun-tot|ing (gun′tō′ting), *adj. U.S. Informal.* carrying a gun or pistol: *gun-toting guards.*

gun|wale (gun′əl), *n.* **1** the upper edge of a ship's or boat's side. **2** the highest planking on the hull of a ship. Also, **gunnel.** [< *gun*¹ + *wale* a plank (because it was formerly used to support the guns)]

gun|yah (gun′yə), *n.* a native Australian hut. [< a native name]

Günz (gints; *German* gʏnts), *n. Geology.* the first glaciation of the Pleistocene in Europe. [< *Günz,* river which flows through this area of glaciation]

gup|py (gup′ē), *n., pl.* **-pies.** a very small, brightly colored fish of tropical fresh water, often kept in aquariums. The female bears young instead of producing eggs. [< Robert J. L. *Guppy,* a British scientist of the 1800's from Trinidad, who supplied the first specimens for public viewing]

Gup|ta (gup′tə), *n.* a member of a Hindu dynasty that ruled India from the 300's to the 500's A.D. The reign of the Guptas is sometimes called the golden age of Hindu culture.

gur (gůr), *n.* a coarse sugar of southeastern Asia; jaggery. [< Hindustani *gur*]

Gur (gůr), *n.* a large group of West African languages; Voltaic. It is a branch of the Niger-Congo language family.

Gu|ra|ghe (gü′rä gā), *n.* a Semitic language spoken in the south of Ethiopia.

gur|dwa|ra (gůr dwär′ə), *n.* a Sikh temple. [< Panjabi *gurudūārā*]

gurge (gėrj), *v.,* **gurged, gurg|ing,** *n.* —*v.i.* to make a whirlpool; swirl. —*n.* a whirlpool. [< Latin *gurges* whirlpool]

gur|gi|ta|tion (gėr′jə tā′shən), *n.* a surging or whirling up and down; bubbling motion. [< Medieval Latin *gurgitatus* gorged, past participle of Late Latin *gurgitāre* engulf, steep in (< Latin *gurges* whirlpool) + English *-ion*]

gur|gle (gėr′gəl), *v.,* **-gled, -gling,** *n.* —*v.i.* **1** to flow or run with a bubbling sound: *Water gurgles when it is poured out of a bottle or flows over stones.* **2** to make a bubbling sound: *The baby gurgled happily.* —*v.t.* to express with a gurgle: *The baby gurgled its satisfaction with life.*
—*n.* the act or noise of gurgling; gurgling sound: *a gurgle of innumerable emptying bumpers* (Thomas Carlyle).
[perhaps imitative. Compare Italian *gorgogliare.*]

gur|glet (gėr′glit), *n.* = goglet.

gur|gling|ly (gėr′gling lē), *adv.* with a gurgle.

gur|goyle (gėr′goil), *n.* = gargoyle.

gur|jun (gėr′jən), *n.* **1** a large tree of the East Indies, valued for its balsam and wood. **2** the balsam of this tree and of certain other species of the same genus, used as a medicine and varnish. **3** the wood. [< a native name]

Gur|kha (gůr′kə), *n.* a member of a Nepalese Hindu people especially famous as warriors.

Gur|kha|li (gůr kä′lē), *n.* = Nepali (language).

gur|nard (gėr′nərd), *n., pl.* **-nards** or (*collectively*) **-nard.** **1** a sea fish with spiny fins, bony plates on the head, and three fingerlike feelers on the pectoral fins. **2** any one of various similar fishes. See also **flying gurnard.** [< Old French *gornart,* variant of *grognard* grunter < *grogner,* earlier *gronir* < Latin *grunnīre* grunt]

gur|net (gėr′nit), *n.* = gurnard.

***gur|ney** (gėr′nē), *n., pl.* **-neys.** **1** a four-wheeled stretcher for transporting hospital patients from place to place. **2** a wheeled cart or wagon with canvas sides, used in post offices to route mail. [origin uncertain]

***gurney**
definition 1

gu|ru (gü′rü, gů rü′), *n.* **1** a religious teacher or guide in India, especially in Hinduism: *Indians through the ages have gone to wise men, or gurus, to learn how to achieve inner tranquility* (Joseph Lelyveld). **2** any spiritual leader or guide. **3** any leader, as in the political, literary, or musical field: *Once the great guru of contemporary poets, Eliot has joined the "poets unfashionable" like A. E. Housman and Rupert Brooke* (Time). ... *one of the gurus of the current fashion scene* (Maclean's). **4** an expert or authority: *TV ratings gurus* ... (Time). **5** a long, loose outer garment similar to the ones worn by Indian holy men: *A handsome young man with long blonde hair and beard, wearing a silver lamé guru, arrives in a Mediterranean city* (London Times). [< Hindustani *gurū* < Sanskrit *guru* revered]

Gu|run|si (gə rün′sē), *n., pl.* **-si, -sis,** or **-sies.** **1** a member of a Voltaic people of Upper Volta. **2** the Gur language of this people.

gu|ru nut (gü′rü), = kola nut. [variant of *goora nut*]

gush (gush), *v., n.* —*v.i.* **1** to rush out suddenly; pour out: *Oil gushed from the new well.* (*Figurative.*) *In the great ballroom, the long speeches of welcome began to gush afresh* (Edmund Wilson). SYN: spurt, spout. See syn. under **flow.** **2** *Informal, Figurative.* to talk in a way that shows too much silly feeling: *All the girls gushed about the new movie star.* **3** *Figurative.* to have an abundant flow of blood, tears, or other liquid.
—*v.t.* to give forth suddenly or very freely: *The wound gushed blood.*
—*n.* **1** a rush of water or other liquid from an enclosed place: *a gush of tears. If you get a deep cut, there is usually a gush of blood.* **2** *Figurative.* a sudden and violent outbreak; burst: *a gush of anger.* **3** *Informal, Figurative.* talk that shows too much silly feeling.
[probably imitative. Perhaps related to **gust**¹.]

gush|er (gush′ər), *n.* **1** an oil well that gives oil in great quantities without pumping. **2** *Informal, Figurative.* a gushy person.

gush|ing (gush′ing), *adj.* **1** that gushes: *gushing fountains* (Washington Irving). **2** *Figurative.* gushy; effusive: *She was indeed a gushing thing, was the youngest Miss Pecksniff* (Dickens). —**gush′ing|ly,** *adv.* —**gush′ing|ness,** *n.*

gush|y (gush′ē), *adj.,* **gush|i|er, gush|i|est.** showing too much silly feeling; effusive; sentimental. —**gush′i|ly,** *adv.* —**gush′i|ness,** *n.*

gus|la (güs′lə), *n.* a Serbian musical instrument of the viol family, having one horsehair string stretched over a parchment sounding board: *And Slavic guslas will, forsooth, Lull both of us to sleep* (John Updike). [< Serbo-Croatian *gusle*]

***gus|set** (gus′it), *n., v.,* **-set|ed, -set|ing.** —*n.* **1** a triangular piece of material inserted in a garment to give greater strength or more room. **2** a bracket or plate used to reinforce the joints of a structure. **3** a flexible piece of mail, used to protect the armpit in a suit of armor.
—*v.t.* to furnish with a gusset.
[< Old French *gousset,* perhaps diminutive < *gousse* husk; origin uncertain]

***gusset**
definitions 1,2

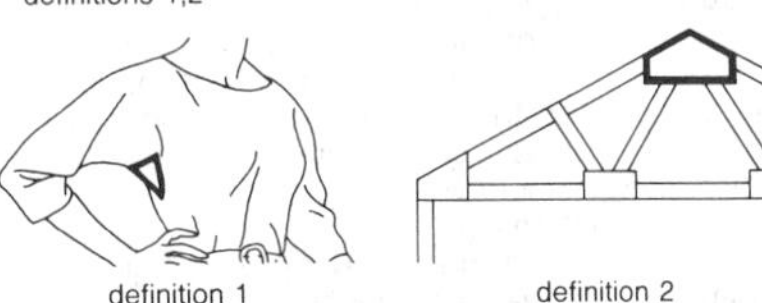
definition 1 definition 2

gus|sy (gus′ē), *v.t., v.i.,* **-sied, -sy|ing.** *U.S. Slang.* Usually, **gussy up,** to dress up attractively or showily; decorate: *Marguerite, who had a distinct flair for decoration ... helped Perle gussy up the legation at Luxembourg* (San Francisco Chronicle). [origin unknown]

gust¹ (gust), *n., v.* —*n.* **1** a sudden, violent rush of wind: *A gust upset the small sailboat.* SYN: squall. **2** a sudden burst of rain, smoke, or sound, usually carried by the wind. **3** *Figurative.* an outburst of anger or other feeling: *Gusts of laughter greeted the clown.*
—*v.i.* to blow in gusts: *With the northwesterly wind gusting up to 25 m.p.h., yesterday's race ... had to be shortened* (London Times).
[apparently < Scandinavian (compare Old Icelandic *gustr*)]

gust² (gust), *n., v. Archaic.* —*n.* **1** taste or liking: *I had no gust to antiquities* (Daniel Defoe). **2** a pleasing flavor: *The whole vegetable tribe have lost their gust with me* (Charles Lamb). **3** keen enjoyment; zest: *He drinks his simple beverage with a gust* (William Cowper).
—*v.t.* to taste; relish.
[< Latin *gustus, -ūs*] —**gust′a|ble,** *adj.*

gus|ta|tion (gus tā′shən), *n.* **1** the act of tasting. **2** the ability to taste.

gus|ta|tive (gus′tə tiv), *adj.* = gustatory. —**gus′ta|tive|ness,** *n.*

gus|ta|to|ri|al (gus′tə tôr′ē əl, -tōr′-), *adj.* = gustatory.

gus|ta|to|ry (gus′tə tôr′ē, -tōr′-), *adj.* of the sense of taste; having to do with tasting: *Eating fine foods gives gustatory pleasure.* [< Latin *gustātus,* past participle of *gustāre* to taste (< *gustus, -ūs* taste) + English *-ory*]

gustatory bud or **corpuscle,** any of the small, flask-shaped bodies in the epithelium of the tongue, believed to be organs of taste.

gust|ful¹ (gust′fəl), *adj.* gusty; windy: *on a gustful April morn* (Tennyson).

gust|ful² (gust′fəl), *adj.* **1** pleasant to the taste; tasty. **2** *Figurative.* agreeable to the mind or feelings. —**gust′ful|ly,** *adv.*

gus|to (gus′tō), *n., pl.* **-tos.** **1** hearty enjoyment; keen relish; zest: *The hungry boy ate his dinner with gusto. He read me, though with too much gusto, some little poems of his own* (Samuel Pepys). **2** liking or taste. **3** *Archaic.* artistic style. [< Italian *gusto* taste < Latin *gustus, -ūs*]

gust tunnel, a crude wind tunnel with a large cross section for testing the effects of gusts upon the flight of aircraft.

gust|y (gus′tē), *adj.,* **gust|i|er, gust|i|est.** **1** coming in gusts; windy; stormy. **2** *Figurative.* marked by outbursts: *gusty laughter.* —**gust′i|ly,** *adv.* —**gust′i|ness,** *n.*

gut (gut), *n., v.,* **gut|ted, gut|ting,** *adj.* —*n.* **1** the whole alimentary canal or one of its parts, such as the intestines or stomach. **2** a tough string made from the dried and twisted intestines of sheep and other animals; catgut. Gut is used mainly for the strings of musical instruments and tennis rackets, and sewing up wounds. **3** the silk fiber taken from a silkworm before it spins its cocoon. It is used in making snells for fishhooks. **4** a narrow channel or gully.
—*v.t.* **1** to remove the entrails of; disembowel. SYN: eviscerate. **2a** to destroy the inside of: *Fire gutted the building and left only the brick walls standing.* **b** *Figurative: The Supreme Court gutted this law in a 1951 opinion* (New York Times). *Dodge protected the Bureau against those who wanted to gut its staff* (Harper's).
—*adj. U.S. Informal.* **1** vital, basic, or elemental: *a gut feeling. The gut issue is the demand for higher wages and pensions* (Time). *There is little, as they would phrase it, "gut reaction" in favour of trade unionism among American workers* (Manchester Guardian Weekly). **2** = gutsy.
guts, a (1) the entrails; bowels: *A solution of this substance* [*was*] *injected into the ... guts of a dog* (John Thomson). (2) *Informal, Figurative.* the vital or essential part: *The old rule was that the guts of the story should be in the first paragraph* (Punch). **b** *Slang, Figurative.* pluck; courage; endurance: *I expect I haven't the guts to keep on and keep it up* (J. B. Priestley).
one's guts, *Slang.* a person (used as an intensifier): *"I hate him, Mother! I can't stand his guts!"* (Philip Roth). *The brass hate his guts because he isn't afraid of them* (Maclean's).
[Old English *guttas,* plural]

GUT (no periods), grand unified theory: *Several physicists have pointed out how GUTs can bring about an imbalance between matter and antimatter in the primeval cosmos* (P.C.W. Davies).

gut|buck|et (gut′buk′it), *n. U.S. Jazz Slang.* barrelhouse.

gut course, *U.S. Slang.* an easy college or university course: *Your pointed remarks about the gut courses surviving in American universities evoked feelings of nostalgic guilt* (Time).

gut|fight|er (gut′fī′tər), *n. U.S.* a hard-hitting, tough adversary: *President Nixon came to office convinced that he could govern only if he overcame his old reputation as a gutfighter and followed the politics of reconciliation* (James Reston).

Guth|run (gůᴛʜ′rün), *n.* = Gudrun.

gut|less (gut′lis), *adj. Informal.* **1** lacking courage; cowardly. **2** without vigor or vitality; spiritless: *Colleges are supposedly more gutless than ever* (Time). —**gut′less|ness,** *n.*

Gut|nic (güt′nik), *n.* the Swedish dialect of the island of Gotland. Also, **Gutnish.**

Gut|nish (güt′nish), *n.* = Gutnic.

guts (guts), *n.pl.* See under **gut.**

guts|y (gut′sē), *adj.,* **guts|i|er, guts|i|est.** *Slang.* **1** full of guts: (*Figurative.*) *a gutsy fighter.* **2** *Figurative.* full of vitality; lusty: *a gutsy singer.* —**guts′i|ly,** *adv.* —**guts′i|ness,** *n.*

gut|ta (gut′ə), *n., pl.* **gut|tae** (gut′ē). **1** a small, droplike ornament in the shape of the frustum of a cone. It is attached to the under side of the mutules, etc., of the Doric entablature. **2** a drop-shaped marking, as on an insect's wing. **3** *Pharmacy.* a drop of liquid medicine. [< Latin *gutta* a drop]

gut|ta-per|cha (gut′ə pėr′chə), *n.* a substance like rubber, made from the thick, milky juice of certain tropical trees of the same family as the sapodilla. It is used especially in dentistry and in insulating electric wires. [< Malay *gĕtah* gum + *pĕrcha* the tree producing it]

gut|tate (gut′āt), *adj.* **1** in the form of drops. **2** containing drops. **3** spotted as if by drops. [< Latin *guttātus* < *gutta* a drop]

gut|tat|ed (gut′ā tid), *adj.* = guttate.

Pronunciation Key: hat, āge, cãre, fär; let, ēqual, tėrm; it, īce; hot, ōpen, ôrder; oil, out; cup, pu̇t, rüle; child; long; thin; ᴛʜen; zh, measure; ə represents **a** in about, **e** in taken, **i** in pencil, **o** in lemon, **u** in circus.

gut|ta|tion (gu tā′shən), *n.* loss of water by a plant in the form of droplets, usually from the leaf.

***gut|ter**[1] (gut′ər), *n., adj., v.* —*n.* **1** a channel or ditch along the side of a street or road to carry off water; low part of a street beside the sidewalk. SYN: conduit, duct. **2** a channel or trough along or under the lower edge of a roof to carry off rain water: *The gutters could not take the water from the temporary roof.* **3** a furrow or track made by running water. **4** a channel; groove: *the gutters on either side of a bowling alley.* **5** *Figurative.* a low, poor, or wretched place: *a child of the gutter.* **6** *Printing.* the white space formed by the inner margins of two facing pages of a book. **7** *Philately.* the blank spaces between the stamps on a sheet where they are separated or perforated.
—*adj. Informal.* **1** of the lowest type or character; base or vulgar: *gutter language. Such gutter tactics are bound to backfire* (New York Times). SYN: vile. **2** of low value; cheap; sensational; lurid: *gutter journalism. The "gutter press" were dubbed in America as "yellow press"* (London Times).
—*v.t.* **1** to form gutters in; furnish with gutters. **2** to extinguish: *... the sternness of her command to buckle seat belts and gutter cigarettes* (Harper's). **3** to curb: *Gutter your dog* (New Yorker).
—*v.i.* **1a** to flow or melt in streams: *The candle guttered when the melted wax ran down its sides. Water guttered down the side of the hill.* **b** *Figurative: His screen career, for all practical purposes, had guttered out* (Harper's). **2** to become channeled. **3** to form gutters.
[< Old French *goutiere* < *goute,* earlier *gote* drop < Latin *gutta*]

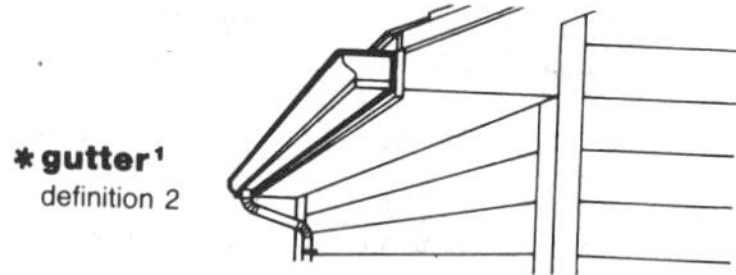
***gutter**[1]
definition 2

gut|ter[2] (gut′ər), *n.* a person or thing that guts: *The fish gutters refuse to be photographed* (Sunday Times). [< *gut* + *-er*[1]]

gut|ter|snipe (gut′ər snīp′), *n.* **1** *Informal.* an urchin who lives in the streets; street gamin. **2** any ill-bred person. **3** a gatherer of rags, paper, and other salvageable waste from street gutters. [originally, the snipe (from its feeding habits)]

gut|ter|y (gut′ər ē), *adj.* **1** grooved; channeled. **2** *Figurative.* miry; muddy.

gut|ti (gut′ī), *n.* plural of **guttus.**

gut|ti|fer (gut′ə fər), *n.* a plant that yields gum or resin. [< New Latin *guttifera* < Latin *gutta* a drop + *ferre* to bear]

gut|tif|er|ous (gu tif′ər əs), *adj.* yielding gum or resin.

gut|tle (gut′əl), *v.i., v.t.,* **-tled, -tling.** to eat or swallow greedily. [perhaps < *gut,* patterned on *guzzle*] —**gut′tler,** *n.*

gut|tu|la (gut′yə lə), *n., pl.* **-lae** (-lē). *Botany, Zoology.* a small droplike spot, as of color. [< Latin *guttula* (diminutive) < *gutta* a drop]

gut|tu|late (gut′yə lāt, -lit), *adj. Botany, Zoology.* having small, droplike spots.

gut|tur|al (gut′ər əl), *adj., n.* —*adj.* **1** of the throat. **2** formed in the throat; harsh: *The visitor from Germany spoke in a deep, guttural voice.* **3** formed between the back of the tongue and the soft palate; velar. The *g* in *go* is a guttural sound.
—*n.* a sound formed between the back of the tongue and the soft palate. The sound of the letter *c* is a guttural in the word *cool.*
[< New Latin *gutturalis* < Latin *guttur* throat]
—**gut′tur|al|ly,** *adv.* —**gut′tur|al|ness,** *n.*

gut|tur|al|i|ty (gut′ə ral′ə tē), *n.* the quality of being guttural.

gut|tur|al|ize (gut′ər ə līz), *v.t.,* **-ized, -iz|ing.** **1** to pronounce or utter gutturally. **2** *Phonetics.* to velarize. —**gut′tur|al|i|za′tion,** *n.*

gut|tus (gut′əs), *n., pl.* **gut|ti.** *Archaeology.* a narrow-necked cruet or oil flask.

gut|ty[1] (gut′ē), *adj.,* **-ti|er, -ti|est.** *Slang.* **1** spirited; courageous: *... a pretty gutty guy* (Newsweek). **2** with depth of feeling, as if dragged up from deep inside a person. —**gut′ti|ly,** *adv.* —**gut′ti|ness,** *n.*

gut|ty[2] (gut′ē), *adj., n., pl.* **-ties.** —*adj.* **1** *Music.* like gut strings being plucked. **2** made of gutta-percha: *a gutty ball.*
—*n.* a gutta-percha golf ball.
[< *gutt*(a percha) + *-y*[1]]

guv (guv), *n. British Slang.* governor (as a familiar term of address for one's father, employer, or other superior): *"Come off it, guv," he said. "I seen you on the telly"* (Sunday Times).

guy[1] (gī), *n., v.,* **guyed, guy|ing.** —*n.* a rope, chain, or wire attached to something to steady or secure it.
—*v.t.* to guide, steady, or secure with a guy or guys: *The mast was guyed by four ropes.*
[< Old French *guie* < *guier* to guide]

guy[2] (gī), *n., v.,* **guyed, guy|ing.** —*n.* **1** *Informal.* a man or boy; fellow; chap: *You guys must think I'm a quitter* (George Ade). **2** a queer-looking person. **3** an effigy of Guy Fawkes, carried about and burned on Guy Fawkes Day.
—*v.t. Informal.* to make fun of; tease; ridicule.
[originally, an effigy of *Guy* Fawkes, 1570-1606, an Englishman who was executed for his part in the Gunpowder Plot]

Guy|an|an (gī an′ən), *adj., n.* = Guyanese.

Guy|a|nese (gī′ə nēz′, -nēs′), *adj., n., pl.* **-nese.** —*adj.* of or having to do with Guyana (the former British Guiana, in northern South America) or its people. —*n.* a person born or living in Guyana.

Guy Fawkes Day (gī′fôks′), *British.* November 5, the anniversary of the Gunpowder Plot (a plot to blow up the Houses of Parliament in 1605). [see etym. under **guy**[2]]

guy|ot (gī′ət), *n.* a mountain, often an extinct volcano, rising from the ocean floor and having a flattened top; seamount. [< Arnold *Guyot,* 1807-1884, Swiss-American geologist, meteorologist]

guz|zle[1] (guz′əl), *v.t., v.i.,* **-zled, -zling.** to drink greedily; drink too much: *He's always guzzling soda. Drink slowly; don't guzzle.* [probably < Old French *gosiller* chatter, vomit, compare Old French *gosier* throat; influenced by Latin *gurges* or *guttur* throat] —**guz′zler,** *n.*

guz|zle[2] (guz′əl), *n.* **1** drink; liquor. **2** a drinking bout; debauch. **3** *Dialect.* the throat. **4** *Dialect.* a gutter; drain. [perhaps < *guzzle*[1]]

GVH disease, a condition in which grafted or transplanted tissue, especially of the bone marrow, attacks the tissues of the recipient's body, instead of the more common phenomenon in which the recipient's body rejects the graft. [*GVH,* abbreviation of *Graft Versus Host*]

GW or **gw** (no periods), gigawatt or gigawatts.

gwe|duc (gwē′duk), *n.* a large, edible clam of the northwest coast of the United States. With the siphons extended, it is sometimes 3 feet or more in length. Also, **goeduck.** [< a native American Indian name]

gy|as|cu|tus (jī′ə skyü′təs), *n.* an imaginary four-legged animal supposed to be of tremendous size, to have the legs on one side of the body much shorter than those on the other, and thus to be able to keep its balance in feeding on the side of a steep mountain. [American English; a humorous formation]

gybe (jīb), *v.i., v.t.,* **gybed, gyb|ing,** *n.* = jibe[1].

gym (jim), *n. Informal.* a gymnasium.

gym|kha|na or **gym|ka|na** (jim kä′nə), *n.* **1** a sports contest, meet, or gathering. **2** a building or grounds for athletic contests. [alteration (influenced by *gymnastic*) of Hindustani *gend-khāna* racket court, ball house; *khāna* < Persian]

gym|na|si|a (jim nā′zē ə), *n.* a plural of **gymnasium.**

gym|na|si|al (jim nā′zē əl), *adj.* **1** having to do with the Gymnasiums of continental Europe, or similar schools elsewhere. **2** classical as opposed to technical.

gym|na|si|arch (jim nā′zē ärk), *n.* **1** an official in ancient Athens in charge of the athletic schools and certain public games. **2** a leader among athletes. **3** a head instructor in a school or college. [< Latin *gymnasiarchus* < Greek *gymnasíarchos* < *gymnásion* gymnasium + *archós* ruler]

gym|na|si|ast (jim nā′zē ast), *n.* **1** a student in a Gymnasium or classical school in Europe. **2** = gymnast.

gym|na|si|um (jim nā′zē əm), *n., pl.* **-si|ums** or **-si|a.** **1** a room or building fitted up for physical exercise or training and for indoor athletic sports. **2** a school for gymnastics. **3** a place where athletic exercises were practiced in ancient Greece. [< Latin *gymnasium* < Greek *gymnásion* < *gymnázein* to exercise (naked) < *gymnós* naked]

Gym|na|si|um (jim nā′zē əm; *German* gim nä′zē ùm), *n.* a secondary school in Germany and certain other European countries that prepares students for the universities. [< German *Gymnasium* < Latin; see etym. under **gymnasium**]

gym|nast (jim′nast), *n.* an expert in gymnastics. [< Greek *gymnastḗs* < *gymnázein* to exercise; see etym. under **gymnasium**]

gym|nas|tic (jim nas′tik), *adj.* having to do with physical exercise or activities. —**gym|nas′ti|cal|ly,** *adv.*

gym|nas|ti|cal (jim nas′tə kəl), *adj.* = gymnastic.

gym|nas|tics (jim nas′tiks), *n.pl.* **1** exercises for developing the muscles and improving physical fitness and health, such as are done in a gymnasium: *Gymnastics have become one of the institutions of the country* (James Grant). **2** *Figurative.* feats like those of a gymnast; acrobatics: *All who prefer singing to musical gymnastics* (Richard A. Proctor). **3** (*singular in use*) the act or skill of performing physical exercises.

gym|no|car|pous (jim′nō kär′pəs), *adj. Botany.* having a naked fruit. [< Greek *gymnós* naked + *karpós* fruit + English *-ous*]

gym|nog|e|nous (jim noj′ə nəs), *adj.* = gymnospermous.

gym|nog|y|nous (jim noj′ə nəs), *adj. Botany.* having a naked ovary. [< Greek *gymnós* naked + English *-gynous*]

gym|nos|o|phist (jim nos′ə fist), *n.* one of a sect of ancient Hindu philosophers who wore little or no clothing, ate no meat, and devoted themselves to mystical contemplation. [< Latin *gymnosophistae,* plural < Greek *gymnosophistaí* < *gymnós* naked + *sophistḗs* sophist]

gym|nos|o|phy (jim nos′ə fē), *n.* the beliefs and practices of gymnosophists.

***gym|no|sperm** (jim′nə spėrm), *n.* any one of a large group of plants having the seeds exposed, not enclosed in ovaries or fruit. The pine, fir, and spruce are gymnosperms. They bear seeds on the surface of cone scales instead of in pods. The gymnosperms are a subdivision of the spermatophyte division of plants. [< New Latin *Gymnospermae* < Greek *gymnóspermos* < *gymnós* naked + *spérma* seed < *speírein* to sow]

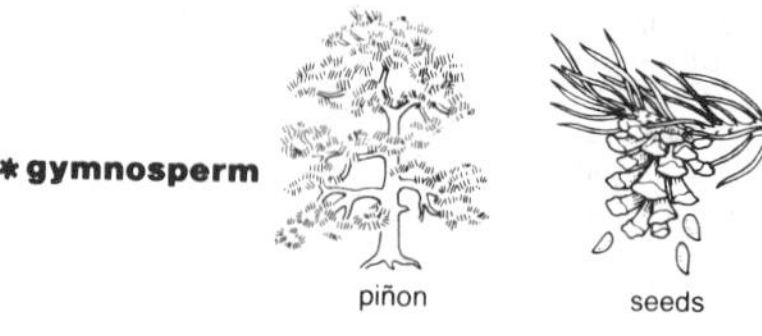

***gymnosperm**

gym|no|sper|mous (jim′nə spėr′məs), *adj.* belonging to the gymnosperms; having the seeds exposed.

gym|pie (gim′pē), *n.* (in Australia) a nettle tree. [< a native word]

gym shoe, a light canvas shoe with a soft rubber sole for use in gymnasiums.

gyn|ae|coc|ra|cy (jin′ə kok′rə sē, jī′nə-), *n., pl.* **-cies.** = gynecocracy.

gy|nae|col|o|gy (gī′nə kol′ə jē, jī′-; jin′ə-), *n.* = gynecology.

gyn|ae|co|mor|phous (jin′ə kə môr′fəs, jī′nə-), *adj.* = gynecomorphous.

gyn|ae|ol|a|try (jin′ē ol′ə trē, jī′nē-), *n.* = gyneolatry.

gy|nan|dro|morph (ji nan′drə môrf, jī-), *n. Zoology.* an organism in which one part or side of the body has male characteristics and the other female characteristics. [< Greek *gýnandros* (see etym. under **gynandrous**) + *morphḗ* form]

gy|nan|drous (ji nan′drəs, jī-), *adj.* having the stamens and pistil united in one column, as in orchids. [< Greek *gýnandros* (with English *-ous*) of doubtful sex < *gynḗ, -aikós* woman + *anḗr, ándros* man]

gy|nan|dry (ji nan′drē, jī-), *n.* = hermaphroditism.

gyn|ar|chic (ji när′kik, jī-), *adj.* of or having to do with gynarchy.

gyn|ar|chy (jin′ər kē, jī′nər kē), *n., pl.* **-ar|chies.** government by a woman or women. [< Greek *gynḗ* woman + *árchein* rule]

gy|ne|ci|um (jī nē′sē əm, ji-), *n., pl.* **-ci|a** (-sē ə). = gynoecium.

gyn|e|coc|ra|cy (jin′ə kok′rə sē, jī′nə-), *n., pl.* **-cies.** government by a woman or women. Also, **gynaecocracy.** [< Greek *gynaikokratía* < *gynḗ, -aikós* woman + *-kratía* rule]

gy|ne|co|crat (ji nē′kə krat, jī-), *n.* a supporter of gynecocracy.

gyn|e|co|crat|ic (jin′ə kə krat′ik, jī′nə-), *adj.* having to do with gynecocracy.

gy|ne|co|log|ic (gī′nə kə loj′ik, jī′-; jin′ə-), *adj.* of or having to do with gynecology.

gy|ne|co|log|i|cal (gī′nə kə loj′ə kəl, jī′-; jin′ə-), *adj.* = gynecologic.

gy|ne|col|o|gist (gī′nə kol′ə jist, jī′-; jin′ə-), *n.* an expert in gynecology.

gy|ne|col|o|gy (gī′nə kol′ə jē, jī′-; jin′ə-), *n.* the branch of medicine that deals with the functions and diseases specific to women, especially those of the reproductive system. Also, **gynaecology.** [< Greek *gynḗ, -aikós* woman + English *-logy*]

gyn|e|co|mor|phous (jin′ə kə môr′fəs, jī′nə-), *adj. Biology.* having the form, appearance, or characters of a female. Also, **gynaecomorphous.** [< Greek *gynaikómorphos* in female shape < *gynḗ, -aikós* woman + *morphḗ* form]

gyn|e|oc|ra|cy (jin′ē ok′rə sē, jī′nē-), *n., pl.* **-cies.** = gynecocracy.

gyn|e|ol|a|try (jin′ē ol′ə trē, jī′nē-), *n.* the extravagant worship of woman. [< Greek *gynḗ* woman *latreía* worship]

gy|ne|pho|bi|a (jī′nə fō′bē ə, jin′ə-), *n.* abnormal fear of women. [< Greek *gynḗ* woman + English *-phobia*]

gyn|i|at|rics (jin′ē at′riks, jī′nē-), *n.* the treatment of the diseases of women. [< Greek *gynê* woman + *iatreíā* a healing + English *-ics*]

gyn|o|base (jin′ə bās, jī′nə-), *n. Botany.* the short, conical or flat base of the receptacle of a flower, bearing the pistils. [< Greek *gynê* woman + English *base*[1]]

gy|noe|cious (jī nē′shəs, ji-), *adj.* of, like, or containing gynoecia; having female organs.

gy|noe|ci|um (jī nē′sē əm, ji-), *n., pl.* **-ci|a** (-sē ə). *Botany.* the pistil or pistils of a flower. Also, **gynecium.** [alteration of *gynaeceum,* by taking as if < Greek *gynê* woman + *oikíon* house]

gyn|o|phore (jin′ə fôr, -fōr; jī′nə-), *n.* an elongation of the receptacle of a flower, situated between the stamens and pistil, and bearing the pistil. [< Greek *gynê* woman + English *-phore*]

gyn|o|phor|ic (jin′ə fôr′ik, -for′-; jī′nə-), *adj.* having to do with or of the nature of a gynophore.

-gynous, *combining form.* **1** woman; female: *Misogynous = hating women.*
2 having female organs (pistils): *Monogynous = having a single pistil.*
[< Greek *-gynos* (with English *-ous*) < *gynê* woman]

gyp[1] (jip), *v.,* **gypped, gyp|ping,** *n. Slang.* **—*v.t., v.i.*** to cheat; swindle.
—*n.* **1** a cheating; fraud; swindle. **2** a person who cheats; swindler. Also, **gip.** [short for *gypsy*]

gyp[2] (jip), *n. British.* a male college servant as at Cambridge. [perhaps short for *gypsy*]

gyp|lure (jip′lůr′), *n.* a synthetic form of the sex attractant of the female gypsy moth. [< *gyp* (sy moth) + *lure*]

gyp|per (jip′ər), *n. Slang.* a cheat; swindler.

gyp|per|y (jip′ər ē), *n., pl.* **-per|ies.** the act of cheating or swindling; gyp.

gyp|po (jip′ō), *n., pl.* **-pos.** *U.S. Slang.* a migratory workman usually employed on a temporary or piecework basis. [probably alteration of *gypsy*]

gyp|se|ous (jip′sē əs), *adj.* like or containing gypsum. [< Late Latin *gypseus* (with English *-ous*) < Latin *gypsum* gypsum]

gyp|sif|er|ous (jip sif′ər əs), *adj.* containing or yielding gypsum.

gyp|soph|i|la (jip sof′ə lə), *n.* any one of a genus of plants of the pink family with many small, fragrant, white or pink flowers on delicate, branching stalks with few leaves, such as babies'-breath. [< New Latin *Gypsophila* the genus name < Latin *gypsum* gypsum (< Greek *gýpsos*) + Greek *philos* fond of < *phileîn* to love]

gyp|sum (jip′səm), *n., v.* **—*n.*** a mineral used to make fertilizer and plaster of Paris; hydrous calcium sulfate. Alabaster is one form of gypsum. *Formula:* $CaSO_4 \cdot 2H_2O$
—*v.t.* to dress (land or a crop) with gypsum.
[< Latin *gypsum* < Greek *gýpsos*]

Gyp|sy (jip′sē), *n., pl.* **-sies. 1** Also, **gypsy.** a person belonging to a group of people whose ancestors lived in India and began to migrate westward through the Middle East about A.D. 1000, arriving in Western Europe in the early 1400's. Gypsies now live in almost every part of the world. **2** the language of the Gypsies; Romany. Also, *especially British,* **Gipsy.** [ultimately < *Egyptian* (from the belief that they came from Egypt)]

gyp|sy (jip′sē), *n., pl.* **-sies,** *adj., v.,* **-sied, -sy|ing.**
—*n.* **1** = Gypsy. **2** a person who looks or lives like a Gypsy.
—*adj.* **1** of the Gypsies: *a gypsy girl, gypsy music.* **2** resembling a Gypsy or gypsy. **3** *Informal.* working independently or illegally: *gypsy truckers, a gypsy cab.*
—*v.i.* **1** to live or act like Gypsies. **2** to picnic: *There is to be a village picnic . . . a gypsying they call it . . . at East Egdon* (Thomas Hardy). Also, *especially British,* **gipsy.**
[< *Gypsy*]

gypsy cab, *U.S.* a taxicab that may be hired by a passenger at its place of business but is not licensed to cruise the streets seeking passengers.

Gyp|sy|dom (jip′sē dəm), *n.* **1** Gypsies as a group. **2** the life or habits of Gypsies.

Gyp|sy|hood (jip′sē hůd), *n.* = Gypsydom.

gyp|sy|ish (jip′sē ish), *adj.* **1** of a gypsy. **2** like a gypsy.

gypsy moth, a brownish or white moth whose larvae damage trees by eating the leaves. Gypsy moths were introduced to America from Europe. Also, **gipsy moth.**

gy|ral (jī′rəl), *adj., n.* **—*adj.*** **1** moving in a circle or spiral. **2** *Anatomy.* having to do with a cerebral gyrus.
—*n.* the enormous eddy in which the waters of each ocean circle.

gy|rase (jī′rās), *n.* an enzyme which changes double-helical DNA into superhelical DNA.

gy|rate (jī′rāt, jī rāt′), *v.,* **-rat|ed, -rat|ing,** *adj.*
—*v.i.* to go in a circle or spiral; whirl; rotate: *A spinning top gyrates.* (*Figurative.*) *Trading volume hit new highs, and prices gyrated wildly* (Newsweek). SYN: revolve.
—*adj.* **1** *Botany.* = circinate. **2** *Zoology.* having convolutions.
[< Late Latin *gȳrāre* (with English *-ate*[1]) < Latin *gȳrus* circle < Greek *gŷros*] **—gy|ra′tion,** *n.*
—gy′ra|tor, *n.*

gy|ra|to|ry (jī′rə tôr′ē, -tōr′-), *adj.* moving in a circle or spiral; gyrating.

gyre (jīr), *n., v.,* **gyred, gyr|ing.** **—*n.*** **1** *Poetic.* **a** a circular or spiral turn: *The lark Shot up and shrilled in flickering gyres* (Tennyson). **b** a ring or circle: *She rushing through . . . Perforce disparted their compacted gyre* (Edmund Spenser). **c** a vortex. **2** *Anatomy.* a gyrus.
—*v.t., v.i.* to turn round; revolve; wheel.
[< Latin *gȳrus* circle < Greek *gŷros*]

gy|rene (jī′rēn, jī rēn′), *n. U.S. Slang.* a United States marine. [altered spelling of *G.I.* (ma)*rine*]

gyr|fal|con (jėr′fôl′kən, -fal′-, -fô′-), *n.* any one of various large falcons of the Arctic. Gyrfalcons appear in any one of several color phases. Also, **gerfalcon.** [< Old French *gerfaucon* < Germanic]

gy|ri (jī′rī), *n.* plural of **gyrus.**

gy|ro (jī′rō), *n., pl.* **-ros.** *Informal.* **1** a gyroscope. **2** a gyrocompass.

gyro-, *combining form.* circle; spiral, as in *gyroscope.* [< Greek *gŷros* circle]

gy|ro|bus (jī′rō bus′), *n.* a bus powered by a rotating flywheel that generates electricity to run motors located at the wheels.

gy|ro|car (jī′rō kär′), *n.* a motorcar running on a monorail, and kept upright by means of a gyroscope or gyroscopes.

gy|ro|com|pass (jī′rō kum′pəs), *n.* a compass using a gyroscope instead of a magnetic needle. It is driven by a motor, points to the geographic North Pole instead of to the magnetic pole, and is not affected by nearby objects of iron and steel.

gy|ro|cop|ter (jī′rə kop′tər), *n.* = gyroplane.

gy|ro|fre|quen|cy (jī′rō frē′kwən sē), *n., pl.* **-cies.** *Physics.* the natural frequency of gyration of an electron or other charged particle in a constant magnetic field.

gyro horizon, a gyroscopic instrument used to indicate the attitude of an aircraft in relation to the horizon; artificial horizon.

gy|roi|dal (jī roi′dəl), *adj.* spiral in arrangement or movement. **—gy|roi′dal|ly,** *adv.*

gy|ro|mag|net|ic (jī′rō mag net′ik), *adj. Physics.* of or having to do with the magnetic properties of electrified particles in rotation, especially of electrons revolving around the nucleus of an atom.

gyromagnetic ratio, = g-factor.

gy|ro|pi|lot (jī′rō pī′lət), *n.* = automatic pilot. [< *gyro*(scope) + *pilot*]

gy|ro|plane (jī′rə plān), *n.* a type of aircraft, such as an autogiro, in which support and balance are provided by blades (horizontal or nearly so) rotating around a vertical axis.

***gy|ro|scope** (jī′rə skōp), *n.* an instrument consisting of a heavy wheel so mounted that its axis can turn freely in one or more directions. A spinning gyroscope tends to resist change in the direction of its axis, no matter which way its base is turned. Gyroscopes are used to keep ships, airplanes, and guided missiles steady. [< French *gyroscope* < Greek *gŷros* gyre + *skopós* watcher < *skeptésthai* look at, examine]

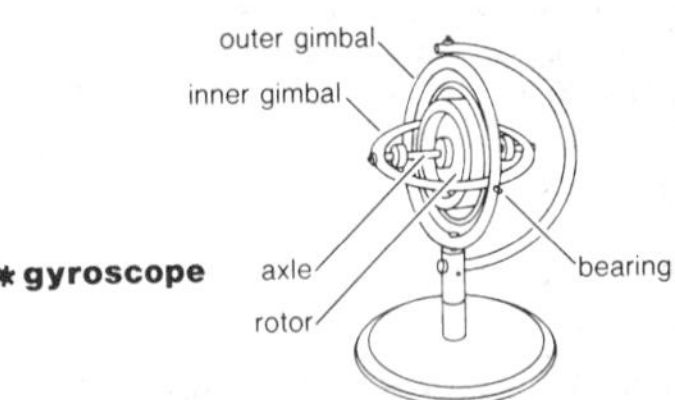

***gyroscope**

gy|ro|scop|ic (jī′rə skop′ik), *adj.* having to do with a gyroscope. **—gy′ro|scop′i|cal|ly,** *adv.*

gyroscopic inertia, the ability of the spinning axle of a gyroscope always to point in the same direction, no matter how the support of the gyroscope is moved.

gy|ro|scop|ics (jī′rə skop′iks), *n.* the principles of the operation of the gyroscope.

gy|rose (jī′rōs), *adj. Botany.* folded and waved; marked with wavy lines. [< *gyr*(e) + *-ose*[1]]

gy|ro|sta|bi|lize (jī′rō stā′bə līz), *v.t.,* **-lized, -liz|ing.** to stabilize by the use of a gyroscope.

gy|ro|sta|bi|liz|er (jī′rō stā′bə lī′zər), *n.* a device that uses a heavy gyroscope for stabilizing a ship or aircraft by counteracting its rolling motion.

gy|ro|stat (jī′rə stat), *n.* a gyroscope in a rigid case, used to illustrate the dynamics of rotating bodies. [< *gyro*(scope) + *-stat*]

gy|ro|stat|ic (jī′rə stat′ik), *adj.* having to do with a gyrostat or gyrostatics.

gy|ro|stat|i|cal|ly (jī′rə stat′ə klē), *adv.* **1** by or with a gyrostat. **2** according to gyrostatics.

gyrostatic compass, = gyrocompass.

gy|ro|stat|ics (jī′rə stat′iks), *n.* the part of physical science dealing with the rotation of solid bodies.

gy|rus (jī′rəs), *n., pl.* **-ri.** *Anatomy.* a convolution, especially of the brain: *a frontal gyrus of the cerebral cortex.* [< Latin *gȳrus* < Greek *gŷros* gyre]

gyte (gīt), *adj. Scottish.* crazy; mad.

gyve (jīv), *n., v.,* **gyved, gyv|ing.** *Archaic.* **—*n.*** a shackle, especially for the leg; fetter.
—*v.t.* to fetter; shackle.
[Middle English *give, gyfe;* origin uncertain]

***H**[1] or **h** (āch), *n., pl.* **H's** or **Hs, h's** or **hs. 1** the eighth letter of the English alphabet. There are two *h*'s in *high.* **2** any sound represented by this letter. **3** (used as a symbol for) the eighth (of an actual or possible series): *row H in a theater.*
4 *Slang.* heroin.
▶A nonstandard pronunciation (hāch) sometimes occurs.

H[2] (āch), *n., pl.* **H's.** anything shaped like a capital H: *I had a wound here that was like a T, But now 'tis like an H* (Shakespeare).

h (no period), an abbreviation or symbol for the following: **1** henry (unit of electrical inductance). **2** hydrocortisone. **3** Planck's constant.

h., an abbreviation for the following:
1 *Mineralogy.* **a** hard. **b** hardness.
2 *Physics, Chemistry.* head (unit of pressure).
3 height.
4 heir.
5 heller[1].
6 high.
7 *Baseball.* hit or hits.
8 hour or hours.
9 husband.

H (no period), an abbreviation or symbol for the following:
1 of a lead pencil: **a** hard. **b** hardness.
2 henry (unit of electrical inductance).
3 histocompatibility.
4 hydrogen (chemical element).
5 *Physics.* **a** intensity of magnetic field. **b** the earth's horizontal component of magnetic field.

H^1 (no period), protium (an isotope of hydrogen).

H^2 (no period), heavy hydrogen; deuterium (an isotope of hydrogen).

H^3 (no period), tritium (an isotope of hydrogen).

H^+ (no period), hydrogen ion.

H., an abbreviation for the following:
1 harbor.
2 hard.
3 high.
4 hour.
5 (of a periodical publication) number; part (German, *Heft*).

ha (hä), *interj.* **1** an exclamation of surprise, suspicion, joy, triumph, or other emotion: *Ha! I've caught you!" cried the giant to Jack.* **2** the sound of a laugh or laughter: *Ha! ha! ha!" laughed the boys.* Also, **hah.** [imitative]

ha. or **ha** (no period), hectare or hectares.

h.a., in this year (Latin, *hoc anno*).

Hab., Habakkuk (book of the Old Testament).

Ha|bab (hä bäb′), *n., pl.* **Ha|bab. 1** a member of a nomadic African people of the region of the Red Sea. **2** the language of the Habab.

Hab|a|cuc (hab′ə kuk, hə bak′ək), *n.* (in the Douay Bible) Habakkuk.

Hab|ak|kuk (hab′ə kuk, hə bek′ək), *n.* **1** a Hebrew prophet and poet, perhaps of the late 600's B.C. **2** a prophetic book of the Old Testament attributed to him, placed among the Minor Prophets. *Abbr:* Hab.

ha|ba|ne|ra (ä′bä nā′rä), *n.* **1** a slow Cuban dance in duple time, of African origin. **2** the music for it. [< Spanish *habanera* (literally) of *Habana* Havana]

hab|da|lah (häv də lä′, häv dô′lə), *n.* a ceremony performed by Jews at the conclusion of the Sabbath or a festival, at which blessings are recited over a candle, spices, and wine or spirits. [< Hebrew *habhdālāh* (literally) division]

ha|be|as cor|pus (hā′bē əs kôr′pəs), a writ or order requiring that a prisoner be brought before a judge or into court to decide whether he is being held lawfully: *In common law the writ of habeas corpus is intended to obtain the liberation of a person imprisoned without just cause* (New York Times). [< Latin *habeās corpus* you shall have the body]

Ha|ber-Bosch process (hä′bər bôsh′), a commercial method of manufacturing ammonia gas from gaseous hydrogen and nitrogen. [< Fritz *Haber*, 1868-1934, and Carl *Bosch*, 1874-1940, German chemists]

hab|er|dash|er (hab′ər dash′ər), *n.* **1** a dealer in the things men wear, such as hats, ties, shirts, and socks: *[His] sartorial habits would be the despair of any Ivy League haberdasher* (Saturday Review). **2** a dealer in small articles, such as buttons, needles, or trimmings. **3** *Obsolete.* a dealer in hats and caps. [perhaps < Anglo-French *hapertas* a kind of cloth; origin unknown]

hab|er|dash|er|y (hab′ər dash′ər ē, -dash′rē), *n., pl.* **-er|ies. 1** the store of a haberdasher. **2** the articles sold by a haberdasher. **3** *British.* a notions counter in a store.

hab|er|geon (hab′ər jən), *n.* **1** a short coat of mail without sleeves; haubergeon. **2** = hauberk. [< Old French *haubergeon* (diminutive) < *hauberc* hauberk]

Ha|ber process (hä′bər), = Haber-Bosch process.

ha|bil|a|to|ry (hə bil′ə tôr′ē, -tōr′-), *adj.* having to do with dressing or clothing: *habilatory art.* [< French *habiller* to dress + English *-ate*[1] + *-ory*]

hab|ile (hab′əl), *adj.* skillful; ready; handy; deft. SYN: adroit, dexterous. [< Middle French *habile*, learned borrowing from Latin *habilis* suitable, fit, proper < *habēre* have]

ha|bil|i|ment (hə bil′ə mənt), *n.* dress; attire. SYN: raiment, vesture, apparel.
habiliments, articles of clothing; garments; accouterments: *plated in habiliments of war* (Shakespeare).
[< Old French *habillement*, or *abillement* < *abiller* prepare, fit out; (originally) reduce (a tree) to a trunk by stripping off the branches < *a-* to (< Latin *ad-*) + *bille* long stick, billet; meaning influenced by English *habit* clothing]

ha|bil|i|ment|ed (hə bil′ə men′tid), *adj.* dressed; attired.

ha|bil|i|tate (hə bil′ə tāt), *v.,* **-tat|ed, -tat|ing.**
—*v.t.* 1 *Western U.S.* to furnish money or means to work (a mine). **2** to clothe; dress.
—*v.i.* to qualify as a teacher in a German university.
[< Medieval Latin *habilitare* (with English *-ate*[1]) < Latin *habilis* fit, suitable < *habēre* have]

ha|bil|i|ta|tion (hə bil′ə tā′shən), *n.* **1** *Western U.S.* the furnishing of money or means to work a mine. **2** Often, **Habilitation.** an academic qualification or degree for teaching at a German university.

ha|bil|i|ta|tor (hə bil′ə tā′tər), *n.* a person who advances money or property for working a mine, under contract with its owners.

Ha|bi|ru (hä bē′rü), *n.pl.* a group of nomadic Semites mentioned in Mesopotamian tablets who are thought by some scholars to have been the ancient Hebrews or their closest ancestors. [< Babylonian *khabiru*]

***hab|it** (hab′it), *n., v.* **—*n.* 1** a tendency to act in a certain way; usual way of acting; custom; practice. Doing a thing over and over again makes it a habit. *How use doth breed a habit in a man!* (Shakespeare). *Such deference [to gentlemen] was both political and social, and was supported by habit and custom* (New York Review of Books). SYN: usage, wont, use, habitude, consuetude, routine, rule. See syn. under **custom. 2** a particular practice, custom, or usage: *the habit of brushing your teeth twice a day, the habit of smoking, to fall into a habit of faultfinding. Old habits are always the most difficult to abolish* (New Yorker). **3** physical dependence on a drug; addiction: *Synanon ... uses ex-addicts to give junkies the support and understanding they need to kick the habit and stay clean* (Time). **4a** the dress or costume of persons belonging to a religious order. Monks and nuns sometimes wear habits. **b** a woman's costume for horseback riding: *At the horse show, the lady on the white horse wore a black habit.* **c** *Archaic.* dress; clothing, especially of persons of rank or distinction: *apparell'd in more precious habit.* (Shakespeare). *So honour peereth in the meanest habit* (Shakespeare). **5** condition of body or mind: *The runner was of lean habit.* **6** the usual way that an animal or plant grows: *The honeysuckle and the woodbine have a twining habit.* **7** the characteristic formation of a crystal.
—*v.t.* 1 to put a habit or garment on; dress: *A few minutes later, divested of silks and ornaments and habited in a plain wide-sleeved tunic of rough serge, she knelt once more* (Atlantic). *I discerned Jack Waller, habited in a very accurate black frock and dark trousers* (Charles J. Lever). SYN: clothe, attire. **2** *Archaic.* to live in; inhabit: *They had habited different parts of the globe* (Henry S. Merriman).
take the habit, to become a monk or nun: *Odeleric ... founded a monastery in Shrewsbury himself and took the habit there in old age* (Listener).
[< Old French *habit*, learned borrowing from Latin *habitus, -ūs* condition of life < *habēre* hold, live in, stay]

***habit**
definition 4b

hab|it|a|bil|i|ty (hab′ə tə bil′ə tē), *n.* the condition of being habitable; habitableness.

hab|it|a|ble (hab′ə tə bəl), *adj.* fit to live in; able to be inhabited: *Many repairs were needed to make the old, abandoned house habitable. Look round the habitable world* (John Dryden). **—hab′it|a|ble|ness,** *n.* **—hab′it|a|bly,** *adv.*

hab|it|an (á bē tän′), *n.* = habitant.

hab|it|ant (*n. 1,* hab′ə tənt; *n. 2, 3 and adj.,* á bē-tän′), *n., adj.* **—*n.* 1** = inhabitant. **2** Also, **habitan.** a farmer of French descent in Canada or Louisiana: *... calèches and long-bodied French carts are filled with habitants* (Harper's). **3** (formerly, in Canada) a peasant who farmed a section of land owned by seigneurs in return for a small rent, military service when needed, and work for the seigneur without pay for three to six days a year.
—*adj.* of, by, or having to do with the habitants of French descent: *excellent habitant pea soup* (Atlantic).
[< Old French *habitant*, learned borrowing from Latin *habitāns, -antis*, present participle of *habitāre* live in (frequentative) < *habēre* possess, have]

hab|i|tat (hab′ə tat), *n.* **1** the place where an animal or plant naturally lives or grows: *The jungle is the habitat of monkeys.* **2** a place of living; dwelling place; habitation: *They have 20 radio stations to distribute descriptions and likely habitats of crooks* (New York Times). **3** a watertight vessel consisting of a laboratory and living quarters for researchers or scientists conducting underwater studies of the ocean over an extended period of time: *Four scientists from the U.S. Department of the Interior spent two months in a four-room habitat, Tektite I, nearly 50 feet below the surface of the sea ...* (Myrl Hendershott).
4 an exhibit at a museum or fair showing reproductions of animals or plants in their natural surroundings: *Dr. Frank M. Chapman ... was the father of the habitat type of exhibition, which has been widely copied in museums all over* (New Yorker). [< Latin *habitat* it inhabits]

hab|i|ta|tion (hab′ə tā′shən), *n.* **1** a place or building to live in: *Early French settlers built habitations enclosed in stockades.* SYN: home, dwelling, residence, abode, domicile, quarters. **2** the act of living in; inhabiting: *A barn is not fit for human habitation.*

hab|it|ed (hab′ə tid), *adj.* clothed; dressed.

hab|it-form|ing (hab′it fôr′ming), *adj.* causing the user to crave it and depend on it: *The compound has sleep-producing qualities and National Drug said is less likely to be habit-forming than are barbiturates* (Wall Street Journal).

hab|it|mak|er (hab′it mā′kər), *n.* a tailor who makes women's riding habits.

ha|bit|u|al (hə bich′ù əl), *adj.* **1** done by habit; caused by habit: *a habitual smile. Habitual courtesy is always being polite to others. Habitual diffidence and awkwardness of address* (Washington Irving). **2** being or doing something by habit; regular; steady: *A habitual reader reads a great deal.* SYN: chronic, inveterate, confirmed.
3 often done, seen, or used; usual; customary:

***H**[1]
definition 1

Script letters look like examples of fine penmanship. They appear in many formal uses, such as invitations to social functions.

Hh *Hh*

Handwritten letters, both manuscript or printed (left) and cursive (right), are easy for children to read and to write.

Hh *Hh*

Roman letters have *serifs* (finishing strokes) adapted from the way Roman stonecutters carved their letters. This is *Times Roman* type.

Hh *Hh*

Sans-serif letters are often called *gothic.* They have lines of even width and no serifs. This type face is called *Helvetica.*

Hh *Hh*

Between roman and gothic, some letters have thick and thin lines with slight flares that suggest serifs. This type face is *Optima.*

H

Computer letters can be sensed by machines either from their shapes or from the magnetic ink with which they are printed.

Ice and snow are a habitual sight in arctic regions. SYN: accustomed, wonted, ordinary, everyday. —**ha·bit′u·al·ly,** *adv.* —**ha·bit′u·al·ness,** *n.*

ha·bit·u·ate (hə bich′ü āt), *v.,* **-at·ed, -at·ing.** —*v.t.* **1** to make used (to); accustom: *The average doctor has between three and five patients habituated to amphetamine* (Manchester Guardian Weekly). SYN: familiarize, acclimate, naturalize, harden, inure. **2** *U.S.* to frequent (a place).
—*v.i.* to become habitual: *The reflex also habituated more rapidly with weak rather than strong stimuli* (Scientific American).
[< Late Latin *habituāre* (with English *-ate*[1]) bring into a condition of body < Latin *habitus, -ūs* (see etym. under **habit**); meaning influenced by English *habit*]

ha·bit·u·a·tion (hə bich′ü ā′shən), *n.* **1** the act of habituating. **2** the state of being habituated: *Habituation, sometimes considered the most elementary form of learning, . . . occurs when an initially novel stimulus is presented repeatedly* (Eric R. Kandel).

hab·i·tude (hab′ə tüd, -tyüd), *n.* **1** characteristic condition of body or mind: *His real habitude gave life and grace To appertainings and to ornament* (Shakespeare). SYN: disposition. **2** habit; custom: *The wilderness required . . . habitudes of which they were totally deficient* (Washington Irving). SYN: usage, wont. [< Old French *habitude,* learned borrowing from Latin *habitūdo* < *habēre* have, possess]

ha·bit·u·é (hə bich′ü ā′), *n.* a person who has the habit of going to any place frequently: *a habitué of the theater.* SYN: frequenter. [< French *habitué,* past participle of *habituer* accustom, learned borrowing from Late Latin *habituāre* habituate]

hab·i·tus (hab′i təs), *n.* **1** *Medicine.* a characteristic state or condition: *. . . the consumptive habitus* (Science). **2** *Biology.* habit (def. 6): *The sheathbill . . . is a shore bird in heritage but a sea bird in habitus* (Scientific American). [< Latin *habitus, -ūs;* see etym. under **habit**]

ha·boob (hə büb′), *n.* a violent and oppressive wind of northern Africa. [< Arabic *habūb* blowing furiously]

hab·ro·come (hab′rə kōm), *n.* a South American rodent with fine, soft fur and large, rounded ears like those of the chinchilla. [< New Latin *Habrocoma* the genus < Greek *habrós* delicate + *kómē* hair]

ha·bu (hä′bü), *n.* a poisonous pit viper related to the rattlesnake, found in the Ryukyu Islands. [< Japanese *habu*]

hab·u·tai (hab′ü tī), *n.* a soft, plain-woven Japanese silk of even texture. [< Japanese *habutae*]

ha·cen·da·do (hä′sen dä′dō), *n., pl.* **-dos.** = haciendado. [< Spanish *hacendado* < *hacienda*]

ha·chure (ha shür′, hash′ür), *n., v.,* **-chured, -chur·ing.** —*n.* = hatch³.
—*v.t.* to shade (a map or drawing) with hachures to represent relief.
hachures, short lines used as shading to represent the slopes of mountains and hills on maps.
[< French *hachure* < Old French *hacher* to hatch³ < *hache* axe]

ha·ci·en·da (hä′sē en′də; *Spanish* ä syen′dä), *n.* in Spanish America: **1** a large ranch or landed estate. **2** a country house or the main dwelling on such a ranch or estate. **3** a farming, stockraising, mining, or manufacturing establishment in the country. [American English < Spanish *hacienda*]

ha·ci·en·da·do (hä′sē en dä′dō), *n., pl.* **-dos.** the owner of a hacienda. [alteration of Spanish *hacendado*]

hack[1] (hak), *v., n.* —*v.t.* **1** to cut roughly or unevenly; deal cutting blows to: *He hacked the meat into jagged, irregular pieces instead of slicing it evenly. "Our mechanic . . . hacked his way through the roof to save a paralyzed woman"* (Newsweek). SYN: See syn. under **cut. 2a** to break up the surface of (the ground). **b** to plant (seed), as with a hoe. **c** to cut up by the roots. **3a** *Basketball.* to hit the arm of (an opponent who has the ball). **b** *Rugby Football.* to kick (an opponent) in the shins. **4** *U.S. Informal.* **a** to deal with (anything); handle well: *As in most flying, instruments are crucial, the senses simply can't hack it* (Harper's). **b** to manipulate (computer programs), especially with skill: *For solitary entertainment, these young adults spend long hours hacking—inconsequentially toying with complex programs—at the terminals of university computers* (Charles M. Cegielski).
—*v.i.* **1** to make rough or uneven cuts; deal cutting blows. SYN: See syn. under **cut. 2** to give short, dry coughs. **3a** *Basketball.* to hit the arm of an opponent who has the ball. **b** *Rugby Football.* to kick an opponent's shin.
—*n.* **1a** a rough cut: *The tree stump was full of hacks from chopping wood.* **b** *U.S.* a cut or notch made in a tree to indicate a particular spot or to mark a path in a forest; blaze. **2** a tool or instrument for hacking or cutting, such as an ax, pick, or hoe. **3** a short, dry cough. **4** hesitation in speech. **5a** *Basketball.* a personal foul committed by striking the arm of a player who has the ball. **b** *Rugby Football.* an intentional kick in the shins, or a gash produced by such a kick. **6** *Curling.* a foothold 126 feet from the center of the house (target) at the opposite end of the ice.
hack around, *U.S. Slang.* to fool around; have fun; pass time idly: *a real great guy, always hacking around and cutting up* (Harper's).
[Middle English *hacken,* Old English *-haccian,* in *tohaccian* hack to pieces]

hack[2] (hak), *n., adj., v.* —*n.* **1a** a carriage for hire: *We rode around the park in a hack.* **b** *Informal.* a taxi: *Hacks were waiting at the airport.* **2** a horse for hire. **3** an old or worn-out horse; jade. **4** a horse for ordinary riding. **5** *Figurative.* a person hired to do routine work; drudge: *The papier mache proletarian novelists went on to become Hollywood hacks* (Saturday Review). **6** *Figurative.* a plodding, faithful, but undistinguished worker in an organization, such as a political party: *The party hacks got out the vote on election day.*
—*adj.* **1a** working just for the money; hired; drudging: *a hack writer.* **b** done just for the money; of a hired sort: *a hack job.* **2** much in use; hackneyed; trite; commonplace: *When the old world grows dull, And we are sick of its hack sounds and sights* (Byron).
—*v.i.* **1** to ride on horseback over roads, distinguished from cross-country or military riding. **2a** *Informal.* to drive a taxi: *the cabby readily confessed, "I used to hate hacking"* (New Yorker). **b** to drive around.
—*v.t.* **1** to make a hack of; put to indiscriminate use. **2** to make trite or stale by frequent use; hackney. **3** *Figurative.* to write as a hack: *He hacked out articles for cheap magazines.*
[short for *hackney*] —**hack′er,** *n.*

hack[3] (hak), *n.* a frame or rack, as for holding fodder for cattle, or for drying fish, cheese, or bricks. [alteration of *hatch*]

hack·a·more (hak′ə môr, -mōr), *n. U.S.* a bridle without a bit. It is used to guide a horse by pressure on the muzzle. [American English, perhaps < altered form of Spanish *jáquima*]

hack·ber·ry (hak′ber′ē, -bər-), *n., pl.* **-ries. 1** any one of a genus of North American trees of the elm family that have small, edible, cherrylike fruit; sugarberry. **2** the fruit. **3** the wood of any one of these trees. Also, **hagberry.** [American English; variant of *hagberry*]

hack·but (hak′but), *n.* an early type of harquebus. Also, **hagbut.** [< Middle French *haquebute,* alteration of *harquebusche* harquebus]

hack·er (hak′ər), *n.* **1** a person who hacks, especially a person who fools around to pass time. **2** *U.S. Informal.* a computer operator, especially one skilled in manipulation of computer programs: *Then came the movie War Games and a rash of long-distance, electronic break-ins by a group of computer-literate teenagers, or "hackers," from Milwaukee* (Inc.). [< *hack*[1] + *-er*[1]]

hack·ham·mer (hak′ham′ər), *n.,* or **hack hammer,** a tool shaped like an adz, used for dressing stone.

hack·ie (hak′ē), *n. Informal.* a taxicab driver.

hack·ing (hak′ing), *adj.* of or for horseback riding: *a hacking outfit.*

hacking jacket or **coat,** a jacket with side vents and slanted flap pockets, used for horseback riding.

hack·le[1] (hak′əl), *n., v.,* **-led, -ling.** —*n.* **1a** one of the long slender feathers on the necks of certain male birds, such as the domestic rooster, peacock, or pigeon. **b** the neck plumage of any one of these birds. **2** Also, **hatchel, heckle.** a comb used in splitting and combing out the fibers of flax, hemp, or the like. **3** the part of a fishing fly corresponding to the legs of an insect, made from feathers from the neck of a rooster.
—*v.t.* **1** Also, **hatchel, heckle.** to comb (flax, hemp, or the like) with a hackle. **2** to tie a hackle on (a fishing fly).
hackles, the hairs on the back of a dog's neck that can become erect: *Not a single hound with his hackles up* (Pall Mall Gazette).
raise (the) hackles, *Informal.* to arouse anger or suspicion; make mad: *He will also have raised some hackles in Labour Party circles by his disparaging remarks* (Manchester Guardian Weekly).
[Middle English *hakell.* See related etym. at **heckle.**] —**hack′ler,** *n.*

hack·le[2] (hak′əl), *v.,* **-led, -ling.** —*v.t.* to cut roughly; hack; mangle.
—*v.i. Obsolete.* to make a hacking; make rough cuts.
[< *hack*[1] + *-le* (frequentative)]

hack·le·back (hak′əl bak′), *n.* = shovel-nosed sturgeon.

hack line, a line drawn across a curling rink at a distance of twelve feet from the tee line. A player begins delivery between the back line and the hack line.

hack·ly (hak′lē), *adj.,* **-li·er, -li·est.** rough or jagged as if hacked.

hack·man (hak′mən), *n., pl.* **-men.** *U.S.* the driver of a hack or carriage for hire.

hack·ma·tack (hak′mə tak), *n.* **1a** a North American larch; tamarack. **b** its wood. **2** a variety of poplar; balsam poplar. [American English < an Algonkian word]

hack·ney (hak′nē), *n., pl.* **-neys,** *adj., v.,* **-neyed, -ney·ing.** —*n.* **1** a horse for ordinary riding or (later) driving: *He rode a strong hackney for the road to save his gallant warhorse* (Scott). **2** Also, **hackney carriage.** a carriage for hire. **3** *Obsolete.* a hired drudge.
—*adj.* **1** let out, employed, or done for hire; hired: *some starved hackney sonneteer* (Alexander Pope). **2** = hackneyed.
—*v.t.* **1** to use too often; make commonplace. **2** to use (a horse) as a hack (now usually in past participle).
[Middle English *hakeney,* apparently < *Hackney,* a town near London, supposedly famous for its horses]

Hack·ney (hak′nē), *n., pl.* **-neys.** any one of an English breed of sturdy, high-stepping horses. [see *hackney*]

hackney coach, a four-wheeled carriage for hire, pulled by two horses and having seats for six persons.

hack·neyed (hak′nēd), *adj.* **1** used too often; commonplace: *"White as snow" is a hackneyed comparison. Our language is too worn . . . Jaded and over-spurred, The hackneyed roadster every bagman mounts* (John Davidson). SYN: trite, stale, threadbare, banal. See syn. under **commonplace. 2** habituated; experienced: *His foreign accent . . . showed him not to be a hackneyed inhabitant of Paris* (Washington Irving).

Hackney pony, an English pony from 12 to 14½ hands high and weighing from 600 to 850 pounds.

hack·saw (hak′sô′), *n., v.* —*n.* a saw for cutting metal, consisting of a narrow, fine-toothed blade fixed in a frame.
—*v.t.* to cut with a hacksaw.

hack·work (hak′wėrk′), *n.* commonplace work suitable for, or done by, a hack.

had (had; *unstressed* həd, əd), *v.* the past tense and past participle of **have:** *She had a party. A fine time was had by all who came.*
be had, *Informal.* to be tricked or taken in; be deceived; be used for someone else's purposes: *We've been had by that butcher shop; the meat is tough.*
have had it. See under **have.**
►**had better, had rather.** *Had better* is the usual idiom for giving advice or making an indirect command: *You had better take cover when she sees you.* (Informally a shorter form without *had* is common: *If he asks you to do it, you better do it*). To express preference, *had rather* and *would rather* (more formal) are both used: *I had rather dance than eat. I would rather dance than eat.*

had·al (hā′dəl), *adj.* of or inhabiting the parts of the ocean below abyssal depths: *nearly 300 "hadal" animal species have now been dragged up from the deepest trenches in the ocean floor* (New Scientist). [< *Hades* + *-al*[1]]

ha·da·rim (ʜə dä rim′), *n.* a plural of **heder.**

Ha·das·sah (hə dä′sə, hä-), *n.* **1** *U.S.* a Jewish women's Zionist organization founded in 1912. **2** the Hebrew name of Queen Esther (in the Bible, Esther 2:7).

had·die (had′ē), *n. Scottish.* haddock.

had·dock (had′ək), *n., pl.* **-docks** or (*collectively*) **-dock. 1** a food fish of the northern Atlantic, related to the cod, but smaller. The haddock has a black stripe from head to tail. **2** = rosefish. [Middle English *haddok;* origin uncertain]

hade (hād), *n., v.,* **-had·ed, -had·ing.** *Mining, Geology.* —*n.* the inclination of a vein or fault from a vertical position.
—*v.i.* (of a shaft, vein, or fault) to incline or slope from a vertical position.
[perhaps < a dialectal pronunciation of *head*]

Ha·de·an (hā′dē ən, hā dē′ən), *adj.* of or belonging to Hades.

Ha·des (hā′dēz), *n.* **1** *Greek Mythology.* **a** the home of the dead, a gloomy place below the earth. **b** the ruler of the lower world, identified with the Roman god Pluto. **2** the home or state of the dead, sometimes construed as *purgatory,* sometimes as *hell* (used in the English Revised Version New Testament).

ha·des (hā′dēz), *n. Informal.* hell: *What the hades are you waiting there for?* (Arnold Bennett). [< *Hades*]

Pronunciation Key: hat, āge, cãre, fär; let, ēqual, tėrm; it, īce; hot, ōpen, ôrder; oil, out; cup, pu̇t, rüle; child; long; thin; ᴛʜen; zh, measure; ə represents **a** in about, **e** in taken, **i** in pencil, **o** in lemon, **u** in circus.

Ha|dith (hə dēth′), *n., pl.* **Ha|dith** or **Ha|diths**. the body of traditions relating to Mohammed, which now form a supplement to the Koran: *Many of the Hadith, already cited, will have shown the good sense, amiability, and liberality of the prophet* (Alfred Guillaume). [< Arabic *hadith*]

hadj (haj), *n.* = hajj.

hadj|i (haj′ē), *n., pl.* **hadj|is**. = hajji.

had|n't (had′ənt), had not.

Ha|dri|an's Wall (hā′drē ənz), an ancient wall built for defense by Hadrian, a Roman emperor, across the northern part of the Roman province of Britain between Solway Firth and the mouth of the Tyne.

had|ro|cen|tric (had′rō sen′trik), *adj.* having the xylem surrounded by the phloem.

had|ron (had′ron), *n.* any particle of a class of strongly interacting elementary particles that includes the pi-meson and all heavier elementary nuclear particles: *Now more than 200 kinds of particles have been observed, mostly of the strong interacting kinds called hadrons* (David Park). [< Greek *hadrós* thick, stout + English *-on*]

had|ron|ic (had ron′ik), *adj.* of or having to do with a hadron or hadrons.

had|ro|saur (had′rə sôr), *n.* an extinct dinosaurian reptile of gigantic size; duckbilled dinosaur. [< New Latin *Hadrosaurus* the genus name < Greek *hadrós* thick, stout + *saûros* lizard]

hadst (hadst), *v. Archaic.* had; 2nd person singular past tense of **have** (used only with *thou*). "Thou hadst" means "you had."

hae (hā, ha), *v.t. Scottish.* to have.

haem (hem), *n.* = hematin.

haem- *combining form.* the form of **haema-** before vowels, as in *haemal*.

haema- *combining form.* a form of **hema-**, as in *haemachrome*.

hae|ma|chrome (hē′mə krōm, hem′ə-), *n.* = hemachrome.

hae|mal (hē′məl), *adj.* = hemal.

hae|mo|glo|bin (hē′mə glō′bən; hē′mə glō′bən, hem′ə-), *n.* = hemoglobin.

haem|or|rhage (hem′ə rij, hem′rij), *n., v.i.,* **-rhaged, -rhag|ing.** = hemorrhage.

ha|e|re|ma|i (hä′ā rā mä′ē), *interj.* a word of kindly greeting or welcome in New Zealand and Australia. [< Maori *haeremai* (literally) come here]

hae|res (hir′ēz), *n., pl.* **hae|re|des** (hə rē′dēz). = heres.

haf|fet or **haf|fit** (haf′it, häf′-), *n. Scottish.* the side of the head above and in front of the ear; temple; cheek. [earlier *halfet, halfhed,* Old English *healfhēafod* forepart of the head]

haf|fir (ha fir′), *n.* (in northern Africa) a temporary pond built to store rain water and conserve the water table: *Adding to the number of points at which livestock can secure water helps to widen the area of grazing. This can be achieved by boring new wells and by constructing haffirs or artificial ponds in which seasonal rain water may be stored* (New Scientist). [< Arabic *hafīr*]

ha|fiz (hä′fiz), *n., pl.* **-fiz**. a Moslem who has memorized the Koran (a title of honor). [< Arabic *hafiz*]

Haf|ling|er (häf′ling gər), *n.* any one of a sturdy breed of small reddish horses of the western Alps: *This year, though, the British ponies have been temporarily knocked into second place as an attraction by a splendid display of Austrian Haflinger* (Manchester Guardian Weekly). [< *Hafling,* a village in the Austrian Tyrol]

***haf|ni|um** (haf′nē əm), *n.* a silvery, metallic chemical element somewhat like zirconium and occurring mainly in zirconium ores. It is used to make filaments for incandescent lamps. [< New Latin *hafnium* < Medieval Latin *Hafnia* Copenhagen, where it was discovered]

***hafnium**

symbol	atomic number	atomic weight	oxidation state
Hf	72	178.49	4

haft (haft, häft), *n., v.* **—*n.*** a handle of a knife, sword, dagger, sickle, or some other cutting or piercing instrument.
—*v.t.* to furnish with a handle or hilt; set in a haft: *The Indian farmers broke the ground and killed the weeds with flat limestone hoes hafted to short sticks* (Scientific American).
[Old English *hæft*]

haf|ta|rah (häf tôr′ə, -tōr′-; häf′tä rä′), *n.* = haphtarah.

haf|to|rah (häf tôr′ə, -tōr′-; häf′tä rä′), *n.* = haphtarah.

hag[1] (hag), *n.* **1** a very ugly old woman, especially one who is vicious or malicious: *The old hag made a face to chase the children from her yard.* **SYN:** beldam. **2** a witch: *the hags that ride on Halloween.* **3** *Archaic.* a female evil spirit, demon, goblin, or ghost. **4** = hagfish. [Middle English *hagge,* apparently contraction of Old English *hægtesse,* also *hegtes* witch, fury] **—hag′like′,** *adj.*

hag[2] (hag), *n. Scottish.* **1** a piece of soft bog, especially in a moor or morass. **2** one of the turfy or heathery spots of firmer ground that rise out of a peat bog: *A small and shaggy nag, That through a bog, from hag to hag, Could bound* (Scott). [perhaps < Scandinavian (compare Old Icelandic *högg* (originally) a cutting < *höggva* to cut, hack)]

hag[3] (hag), *n.* = hagden.

Hag., Haggai (a book of the Old Testament).

Ha|ga|nah (hä gä nä′), *n.* an underground Jewish military organization in Palestine founded in 1920 and active until 1948: *The Haganah ... later formed the nucleus of the Israeli Army* (Hannah Arendt). [< Hebrew *hăgănāh* (literally) defense]

Ha|gar (hā′gər, -gär), *n.* an Egyptian slave of Abraham's wife Sarah. She and her son Ishmael were driven into the desert because of Sarah's jealousy (in the Bible, Genesis 16, 21:1-21).

hag|ber|ry (hag′ber′ē, -bər-), *n., pl.* **-ries**. = hackberry. [probably < Scandinavian (compare Danish *hægge-bær; hægge* bird cherry)]

hag|bush (hag′bůsh′), *n.* = chinaberry tree.

hag|but (hag′but), *n.* = hackbut.

hag|den or **hag|don** (hag′dən), *n.* = greater shearwater. [origin unknown]

Ha|gen (hä′gən), *n.* **1** (in the *Nibelungenlied*) the murderer of Siegfried. **2** (in Richard Wagner's *Ring of the Nibelungs*) the one who tries to steal Siegfried's ring.

hag|fish (hag′fish′), *n., pl.* **-fish|es** or (*collectively*) **-fish**. any one of certain eel-shaped marine vertebrates related to the lampreys, with degenerate eyes and circular mouths surrounded by eight tentacles. The hagfish bores into fish and eats their flesh. [< *hag*[1] + *fish*]

Hag|ga|dah or **Hag|ga|da** (hə gä′də), *n., pl.* **-doth** (-dōth). **1a** a story or legend in the Talmud that explains or interprets the law. **b** the legendary, nonlegal part of the Talmud. **2a** the text of the Seder service read at the meal the first and second nights of Passover. It contains rabbinical exegesis of the Biblical story of the Exodus, prayers, psalms, and other matter, in ritual order. **b** a book with this text. **3a** the free exposition or illustration, chiefly homiletic, of the Scripture. **b** this literature collectively, with the Halakah constituting the Talmudic lore; Midrash. [< Hebrew *haggādāh*]

hag|gad|ic (hə gad′ik, -gä′dik), *adj.* of or like the Haggadah. **—hag|gad′i|cal|ly,** *adv.*

hag|gad|i|cal (hə gad′ə kəl, -gä′də-), *adj.* = haggadic.

hag|ga|dist (hə gä′dist), *n.* **1** a writer of haggadic legends, parables, and like matter. **2** a student of the Haggadah. **—hag′ga|dis′tic,** *adj.*

Hag|ga|i (hag′ē ī, hag′ī), *n.* **1** a Hebrew prophet who wrote about 520 B.C. and who urged, with Zechariah, the rebuilding of the temple. **2** a book of the Old Testament attributed to him, placed among the Minor Prophets. *Abbr:* Hag.

hag|gard (hag′ərd), *adj., n.* **—*adj.*** **1** looking worn from pain, fatigue, worry, or hunger; worn by care; gaunt: *The haggard faces of the rescued miners showed suffering.* **SYN:** lean, thin, wasted, emaciated, hollow-eyed. **2** of a hawk: **a** caught after having assumed the adult plumage. **b** wild; untamed.
—*n.* a haggard hawk.
[perhaps < Old French *hagard,* probably < a Germanic word] **—hag′gard|ly,** *adv.* **—hag′gard|ness,** *n.*

hagged (hagd, hag′id), *adj.* **1** *British Dialect.* haggard. **2** haglike.

hag|gis (hag′is), *n.* a pudding eaten especially in Scotland, made from the heart, lungs, and liver of a sheep or calf, chopped up and mixed with suet, oatmeal, onions, and seasonings, and boiled in the stomach of the animal. [perhaps < *hag* chop, hack + obsolete *es,* Old English *æs* food, meat]

hag|gish (hag′ish), *adj.* of or like a hag: *On us both did haggish age steal on* (Shakespeare). **—hag′gish|ness,** *n.*

hag|gle (hag′əl), *v.,* **-gled, -gling,** *n.* **—*v.i.*** to dispute, especially about a price or the terms of a bargain; stickle: *He went marketing ... to haggle with tradesmen over fish ... tapioca and so on* (Rudyard Kipling). *The Big Four Foreign Ministers wasted fifteen sessions haggling over an Austrian state treaty* (Newsweek). **SYN:** bargain, higgle.
—*v.t.* **1** to mangle in cutting; hack. **2** to harass with wrangling or haggling.
—*n.* the act of haggling; wrangle or dispute about terms.
[apparently frequentative of *hag* chop, hack] **—hag′gler,** *n.*

hag|i|ar|chy (hag′ē är′kē, hā′jē-), *n., pl.* **-chies**. **1** government by saints or priests. **2** the order of saints. [< Greek *hágios* holy + *archê* rule]

hag|i|oc|ra|cy (hag′ē ok′rə sē, hā′jē-), *n., pl.* **-cies**. government by a group considered holy; sacred or sacerdotal government. [< Greek *hágios* holy + *-kratíā* power, rule]

Hag|i|og|ra|pha (hag′ē og′rə fə, hā′jē-), *n.pl.* the third and last division of the Biblical canon recognized by the Jews, usually comprising Psalms, Proverbs, Job, the Song of Solomon, Ruth, Lamentations, Ecclesiastes, Esther, Daniel, Ezra, Nehemiah, and 1 and 2 Chronicles; Kethubim. [< Late Latin *hagiographa* < Late Greek *hagiógrapha,* plural of *hagiógraphos* inspired writing < Greek *hágios* holy + *gráphos* thing written < *graphê* writing]

hag|i|og|ra|pher (hag′ē og′rə fər, hā′jē-), *n.* **1** a writer of lives of the saints or on sacred subjects. **2** one of the writers of the Hagiographa.

hag|i|o|graph|ic (hag′ē ə graf′ik, hā′jē-), *adj.* of or having to do with hagiography. **—hag′i|o|graf′i|cal,** *adj.*

hag|i|og|ra|phy (hag′ē og′rə fē, hā′jē-), *n., pl.* **-phies**. **1** the writing of saints' lives. **2** a book about saints' lives. **3** *Figurative.* a biography that adulates or idolizes its subject: *"Proconsul in Politics" is not yet another full-scale life but an argumentative attack on the official hagiography* (Manchester Guardian).

hag|i|o|log|ic (hag′ē ə loj′ik, hā′jē-), *adj.* of or having to do with hagiology. **—hag′i|o|log′i|cal,** *adj.*

hag|i|ol|o|gy (hag′ē ol′ə jē, hā′jē-), *n., pl.* **-gies**. **1** the branch of literature that deals with the lives and legends of saints. **2** a book on this subject. **3** a list of saints. [< Greek *hágios* holy + English *-logy*]

hag|i|o|scope (hag′ē ə skōp, hā′jē-), *n.* a small opening, cut through a chancel arch or wall, to give a view of the main altar to worshipers in an aisle or side chapel. [< Greek *hágios* holy + English *-scope*]

hag moth, a North American moth whose larva has curious hairy appendages somewhat suggesting disheveled locks of hair. It feeds on a great variety of trees and plants. [< *hag*[1] + *moth*]

hag|rid|den (hag′rid′ən), *adj.* **1** worried or tormented as if by witches; harassed. **2** afflicted by a nightmare.

hag|ride (hag′rīd′), *v.t.,* **-rode, -rid|den, -rid|ing.** to oppress with or as if with nightmare. [< *hag*[1] + *ride*]

hag-seed (hag′sēd′), *n.* the child or descendant of a hag: *Hag-seed, hence!* (Shakespeare).

hag|ta|per (hag′tā′pər), *n.* the common mullein, a weed. [origin uncertain]

hah (hä), *interj.* = ha.

ha-ha[1] (hä′hä′), *n.* a barrier consisting of a trench or ditch; sunk fence. [< French *haha,* said to be < *ha,* an exclamation of surprise at coming upon it]

ha-ha[2] (hä′hä′), *interj.* an expression of laughter or derision: *Of course there was no market, so I had, ha-ha, to feed them* (Renata Adler).

Hah|ne|mann|i|an (hä′nə man′ē ən), *adj.* having to do with S. C. F. Hahnemann, 1755-1843, a German physician, founder of homeopathy.

Hah|ne|mann|ism (hä′nə mə niz′əm), *n.* the medical theories of S. C. F. Hahnemann, especially homeopathy.

hahn|i|um (hä′nē əm), *n.* the American name for element 105. [< New Latin *Hahnium* < Otto *Hahn,* 1879-1968, a German radiochemist]

hai (hī), *adv., n. Japanese.* yes.

hai|ak (hī′ək), *n.* = haik.

Hai|da (hī′də), *n., pl.* **-da** or **-das**. **1** a member of an Indian tribe of northern British Columbia and Alaska. **2** their Na-Dene language.

Hai|duk (hī′důk), *n. Historical.* **1** a former mercenary foot soldier of Magyar stock in Hungary. **2** Also, **haiduk**. (in Poland) one of the liveried personal followers or attendants of the nobles. **3** (in Balkan countries) a robber; marauder; brigand. Also, **Heiduc, Heiduk, Heyduc, Heyduck, Heyduke.**
[< German *Haiduck* < Hungarian *hajdúk,* plural of *hajdú* foot soldier]

haik (hīk, hāk), *n.* an oblong piece of cloth wrapped around the head and body and worn as an outer garment by Arab men and women, especially in northern Africa. Also, **hayk.** [< Arabic *hā′ik* wove]

hai|kai (hī′kī), *n., pl.* **-kai**. **1** a long Japanese poem, often humorous, with stanzas whose lines alternate between 17 and 14 syllables. Usually a small group of poets took turns composing the poem's stanzas. **2** = haiku. [< Japanese *haikai*]

hai|kal (hī′käl, hā′-), *n.* the central chapel of three altars, forming the sanctuary of a Coptic church.

haikal screen, a screen, often elaborately carved or decorated, which separates the haikal from the body of the church.

hai|ku (hī′kü), *n., pl.* **-ku** or **-kus**. a poem or verse form consisting of three unrhymed lines of five, seven, and five syllables respectively. *Example:*

Snail, my little man,
Slowly—ah, very slowly—
Climb up Mount Fuji!

Also, **hokku.** [< Japanese *haiku*]

hai|kwan tael (hī′kwän′), **1** the former official Chinese tael used by customs, equal to 1.20666 ounces of fine silver troy weight. **2** the former Chinese monetary unit or tael used by customs, superseded in 1935 by the yuan. [< Chinese (Mandarin) *haikuan* maritime customs < *hai* sea + *kuan* customs barrier]

hail[1] (hāl), *v., n., interj.* —***v.t.*** **1** to shout in welcome to; greet; cheer: *The crowd hailed the winner.* SYN: address, salute. **2** to greet as; call: *They hailed him leader.* **3** to call loudly to; shout to: *After our car stalled, we hailed passing cars to beg a ride. The captain hailed the passing ship.*
—***v.i.*** to call out in order to attract attention.
—***n.*** **1** a shout of welcome; greeting; cheer. **2** a loud call; shout: *The ship moved out without heeding our hails.*
—***interj.*** greetings! welcome!: *Hail to the winner!*
drink hail, a salutation in reply to the pledge of wassail: *The cup was offered with the salutation, "Wassail," to which the knight replied, "drink hail!"*
hail fellow well met. See under **fellow**.
hail from, to come from: *The ship hails from Boston.*
within hail, near enough to hear a call or shout: *When the President came within hail of us, we cheered. When we came within hail, we found that they were English* (William Dampier).
[originally, adjective, in *be hail!* < Scandinavian (compare Old Icelandic *heill* healthy)] —**hail′er**, *n.*

hail[2] (hāl), *n., v.* —***n.*** **1** small, roundish pieces of ice or frozen vapor coming down from the clouds in a shower; frozen rain; hailstones: *Hail fell with such violence that it broke windows.* **2a** a shower or storm of hail. **b** *Figurative: A hail of bullets met the soldiers.*
—***v.i.*** to fall in hail: *Sometimes it hails during a summer thunderstorm.*
—***v.t.*** *Figurative.* to pour down in a shower like hail: *The angry mob hailed blows on the thief.*
[Old English *hægel*]

hail[3] (hāl), *adj. Obsolete.* hale; whole.

Hail Columbia, *U.S. Slang.* **1** a bawling out; sharp reproof: *I got Hail Columbia from Father for that escapade* (New Yorker). **2** disturbance; uproar: *to raise Hail Columbia.* [< *Hail Columbia,* a patriotic song written in 1798 by Joseph Hopkinson, used as a euphemism for *hell*]

hail-fel|low (hāl′fel′ō), *adj., adv., n.* = hail fellow well met. See under **fellow**.

Hail Mary, an Ave Maria in the Roman Catholic Church.

hail|stone (hāl′stōn′), *n.* a ball or pellet of hail. Hailstones are usually very small, but sometimes they are as big as marbles.

hail|storm (hāl′stôrm′), *n.* a storm with hail.

hail|y (hā′lē), *adj.* consisting of or characterized by hail.

∗**hair** (hãr), *n., adj., v.* —***n.*** **1a** a fine, threadlike growth from the skin of people and animals. Hairs contain pigment. See picture above in next column. **b** any similar outgrowth from the body of insects and other invertebrates. **2** a mass of such growths: *The little girl's hair was yellow and silky.* **3** a fine, threadlike growth from the outer layer of plants. It consists of an elongated cell, or a row of cells, usually soft and flexible like the hair of animals. **4** a cloth, mat, or other fabric of hair, such as haircloth. **5** a very narrow space. **6** something very small; least degree; hair's-breadth: *The ball missed his head by a hair.*
—***adj.*** **1** of, having to do with, or connected with hair or a hair. **2** made of or with hair.
—***v.i.*** **1** to produce or grow hair. **2** to form hairlike fibers.
—***v.t.*** to free from hair.
by a hair's breadth, by the narrowest margin imaginable: *The car suddenly swerved and missed hitting the tree by a hair's breadth.*
get in one's hair, *Informal.* to bother one; be a nuisance to one: *The insistent salesman got so in her hair that she slammed the door in his face.*
hair of the dog (that bit one), a a drink of liquor taken to steady the nerves or alleviate the effects of drunkenness: *Drink again. Another hair of the dog that bit you, Captain* (Dickens). **b** *Figurative.* more of anything that has caused an ill or trouble, used as a remedy or means of relief: *At the first signs of an economic hangover from past inflation, the hair of the dog will be urged on the present Administration* (Wall Street Journal).
let one's hair down, *Slang.* **a** to be carefree or relaxed: *The older folks decided to let their hair down and join in the square dance.* **b** to be frank or candid: *The only person with whom she let her hair down and spoke freely was her older sister.*
make one's hair stand on end, to fill one with great fear; frighten or alarm one: *The horror picture made my hair stand on end.*
split hairs, to make too fine distinctions: *He splits hairs with such surprising versatility* (Leslie Stephen).
tear one's hair, to be frenzied with grief or rage: *Sir Ralph the Rover tore his hair And curst himself in his despair* (Robert Southey).
to a hair, exactly; just right: *Three or four single men, who suit my temper to a hair* (William Cowper).
turn a hair, to show signs of being disturbed or embarrassed: *Cletus never turned a hair. His nonchalance was remarkable* (Jessamyn West).
[Old English *hær*] —**hair′less**, *adj.*—**hair′like′**, *adj.*

∗**hair**
definition 1a

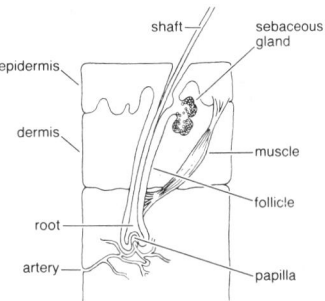

shaft
sebaceous gland
epidermis
dermis
muscle
follicle
root
artery
papilla

hair|ball (hãr′bôl′), *n.* a pellet or mass of hair accumulated in an animal's stomach.

hair|bell (hãr′bel′), *n.* = harebell.

hair|brained (hãr′brānd′), *adj.* = harebrained.

hair|breadth (hãr′bredth′, -bretth′), *adj., n.* —***adj.*** very narrow; extremely close; hair's-breadth: *When the tree fell, we had a hair-breadth escape.*
—***n.*** = hair's-breadth.

hair|brush (hãr′brush), *n.* a stiff brush for smoothing and dressing the hair.

hair|cap moss (hãr′kap′), any one of a group of mosses bearing fine hairs on the calyptra.

hair cell, a cell having very fine hairlike processes, in the organ of Corti in the inner ear.

hair|cloth (hãr′klôth′, -kloth′), *n.* a scratchy fabric made of cotton and horsehair or camel's hair. It is used especially to cover furniture and stiffen garments.

hair|comb (hãr′kōm′), *n.* **1** a style of combing the hair. **2** = comb (def. 1a.).

hair|curl|ing (hãr′kėr′ling), *adj. Informal.* terrifying; hair-raising: *Passengers have haircurling stories about many of the little lines, including engine failures, landings with the landing gear retracted, and even running out of gas* (Time).

hair|cut (hãr′kut′), *n.* the act or manner of cutting the hair.

hair|cut|ter (hãr′kut′ər), *n.* a person or thing that cuts hair.

hair|do (hãr′dü′), *n., pl.* **-dos.** a way of arranging the hair, especially women's hair. SYN: coiffure.

hair|dress (hãr′dres′), *n., v.* —***n.*** = hairdo.
—***v.i.*** to arrange the hair.

hair|dress|er (hãr′dres′ər), *n.* a person whose work is cutting and arranging people's hair, especially women's hair.

hair|dress|ing (hãr′dres′ing), *n., adj.* —***n.*** **1** the act or process, or occupation of cutting and arranging the hair. **2** the occupation or business of a hairdresser. **3** a preparation for dressing the hair, such as a hair oil: *A bottle of this popular British hairdressing had arrived* (Time).
—***adj.*** of or for the dressing of hair.

hair|dry|er or **hair|dri|er** (hãr′drī′ər), *n.* a blower or similar device for drying hair.

haired (hãrd), *adj.* having hair; covered with hair.

hair follicle, the cavity in the skin from which a hair grows.

hair hygrometer, a hygrometer activated by the lengthening and shortening in a parcel of hair strands, caused respectively by an increase or decrease in the relative humidity.

hair implant or **implantation**, the surgical sewing into the scalp of specially treated wire loops to which a hairpiece or tufts of hair are attached. See also **hair transplant**.

∗**hair|line** (hãr′līn′), *n., adj.* —***n.*** **1** a very thin line. **2** the irregular outline where hair growth ends on the head or forehead: *I think you'd look better with the ears covered, and then the hair brought forward over the face here, and here, you see, to hide the uneven hairline* (Punch). **3** a cloth woven with a very fine stripe. **4** *Printing.* a very fine line, especially a stroke or part of a letter thinner than other parts.
—***adj.*** very narrow or close: *a hairline decision.*

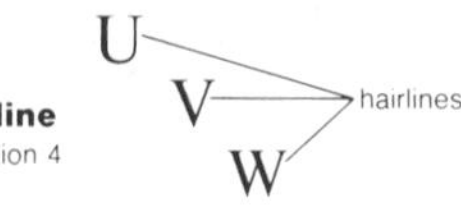

∗**hairline**
definition 4

hair net, a net worn to keep one's hair in place.

hair oil, an oil or oily preparation for dressing the hair.

hair|piece (hãr′pēs′), *n.* **1** = toupee. **2** a small wig worn by women as a hair accessory.

hair|pin (hãr′pin′), *n., adj., v.,* **-pinned, -pin|ning.** —***n.*** **1** a pin, usually a U-shaped piece of wire, shell, or plastic, used by women and girls to keep their hair in place. **2** a sharp bend in a road, river, or other course, likened to a hairpin.
—***adj.*** shaped like a hairpin: *a hairpin turn.*
—***v.t.*** **1** to make a hairpin turn. **2** *Western U.S.* to mount a horse. **3** to pick a lock of with a hairpin.

hair-rais|er (hãr′rā′zər), *n. Informal.* a hair-raising thing; something that causes fear or terror.

hair-rais|ing (hãr′rā′zing), *adj. Informal.* making the hair stand on end from fright; terrifying: *a hair-raising ghost story.* —**hair′-rais′ing|ly,** *adv.*

hair's-breadth or **hairs|breadth** (hãrz′bredth′, -bretth′), *adj., n.* —***adj.*** = hairbreadth.
—***n.*** a very small space or distance: *Our team was within a hair's-breadth of winning.*

hair seal, any one of the earless seals, having coarse hair with no soft underlying fur, and little hunted for their pelts.

hair shirt, **1** a rough shirt or girdle made of horsehair, worn as a penance. **2** *Figurative.* an imposing of penance, austerity, or self-sacrifice: *If low real interest rates and falling inflation are so important . . . then the hair shirt is the only answer* (Financial Times). **3** *Figurative.* a person who advocates austere and self-sacrificing remedies: *Although Orwell was certainly a bit of a hair shirt himself, he seemed to have a hair shirt's impatience with other hair shirts* (Christian Science Monitor).

hair-slide (hãr′slīd′), *n. British.* a barrette.

hair snake, = hairworm.

hair space, *Printing.* the thinnest space used in typesetting to separate letters.

hair|split|ter (hãr′split′ər), *n.* a person who makes too fine distinctions.

hair|split|ting (hãr′split′ing), *n., adj.* making too fine distinctions.

hair spray, a spray used on hair to keep the setting dry and in place.

hair|spring (hãr′spring′), *n.* a fine, hairlike spring that regulates the motion of the balance wheel in a watch or clock.

hair|streak (hãr′strēk′), *n.* any one of various small butterflies with hairlike markings on the wings.

hair stroke, a very thin stroke or line in writing or printing.

hair|style (hãr′stīl′), *n.* a style of wearing the hair: *an Afro hairstyle.*

hair|styl|ist (hãr′stī′list), *n.* = hairdresser.

hair|tail (hãr′tāl′), *n.* a marine fish with a silvery, bandlike body ending in a hairlike tail, common in tropical and subtropical Atlantic waters.

hair transplant or **transplantation**, the surgical procedure of removing plugs of hair follicles from the sides and back of a person's head and grafting them into bald or sparse spots on top of the head. See also **hair implant**.

hair trigger, a trigger that operates by very slight pressure.

hair-trig|ger (hãr′trig′ər), *adj.* **1** having a hair trigger. **2** *Figurative.* set off by the slightest stimulus.

hair weaver, a person who does hair weaving.

hair weaving, the sewing of a hairpiece or toupee into a person's remaining hair.

hair|worm (hãr′wėrm′), *n.* any one of various slender roundworms, parasitic in insects when young, free-swimming when adult, often found in ponds and rivers.

hair|y (hãr′ē), *adj.,* **hair|i|er, hair|i|est,** *n., pl.* **hair|ies.** —***adj.*** **1** covered with hair; having much hair: *hairy hands, a hairy ape.* **2** of or like hair: *the hairy feel of a stuffed teddy bear.* **3** characterized by hairlike growths, as a plant. **4** *Slang.* hair-raising; frightening: *a hairy nightmare, hairy adventures.*

Pronunciation Key: hat, āge, cãre, fär; let, ēqual, tėrm; it, īce; hot, ōpen, ôrder; oil, out; cup, pu̇t, rüle; child; long; thin; ᴛʜen; zh, measure; ə represents **a** in about, **e** in taken, **i** in pencil, **o** in lemon, **u** in circus.

—*n. Slang.* a man who wears his hair long. —**hair′i|ly**, *adv.* —**hair′i|ness**, *n.*

hairy mammoth, = woolly mammoth.

hairy vetch, a vetch that can withstand very cold winters, grown widely in the United States and in Europe to produce green manure.

hairy woodpecker, a common North American woodpecker with white markings on a black back, identical to the downy woodpecker except larger.

Hai|ti|an (hā′tē ən, hā′shən), *adj., n.* —*adj.* of or having to do with Haiti, its people, or their language.

—*n.* **1** a native or inhabitant of Haiti. **2** = Haitian Creole.

Haitian Creole, the native language of Haiti, a dialect of French; Haitian.

hajj or **haj** (haj), *n.* a pilgrimage to Mecca, required of every Moslem at least once in his life. Also, **hadj**. [< Arabic *ḥajj*]

haj|ji (haj′ē), *n., pl.* **-jis**. **1a** a Moslem who has made his pilgrimage to Mecca. **b** Often, **Hajji**. the title given to such a one. **2** a Greek or Armenian who has visited the Holy Sepulcher at Jerusalem. Also, **hadji**. [< Arabic *ḥājjī*, variant (especially in Persian and Turkish) of *ḥajj* pilgrimage]

ha|ka (hä′kä), *n.* a native dance performed in New Zealand with traditional actions or poses, often accompanied by song. [< Maori *haka*]

hake (hāk), *n., pl.* **hakes** or (*collectively*) **hake**. **1** any one of a group of fishes related to and resembling the cod, but much smaller, such as the silver hake, a food fish of New England. **2** any one of various related marine fishes, such as the white hake, and the squirrel hake of New England; codling. [perhaps < Scandinavian (compare Norwegian *hakefisk* (literally) hook fish, from the hooklike growth under the jaw)]

hak|er (hā′kər), *n.* a fisherman or fishing boat engaged in catching hake.

ha|kham (hä Hām′), *n.* a wise man (an official designation among Sephardic Jews, synonymous with *rabbi*). [< Hebrew *khakham*]

ha|kim¹ (hä kēm′), *n.* in Arabia, India, and other Moslem countries: **1** a wise or learned man. **2** a doctor. [< Arabic *ḥakīm* < *ḥakuma* he was wise]

ha|kim² (hä′kim), *n.* (formerly in Arabia, India, and other Moslem countries) a ruler; judge; governor. [< Arabic *hākim* < *hakama* he decided, gave judgment]

Hak|ka (hak′ə), *n., pl.* **-ka** or **-kas**. **1** a Chinese people living principally in southeastern China, especially in Kwangtung province, thought to be descendants of migrants from northern China in the 1200's. **2** one of this people. **3** the Chinese dialect spoken by this people.

Hal., **1** Halifax. **2** *Chemistry.* halogen.

ha|la|cha or **ha|la|chah** (hä′lä Hä′, hä lä′Hä), *n., pl.* **ha|la|chas, ha|la|choth** (hä′lä Hōth′, hä lä′Hōth). = halakah.

ha|la|chic (hə lā′kik, hä-; -kik), *adj.* of or having to do with halakah.

ha|la|chist (hä′lə kist, hə lä′-), *n.* = halakist.

ha|la|kah (hä′lä Hä′, hä lä′Hä), *n., pl.* **ha|la|koth** (hä′lä Hōth′, hä lä′Hōth). *Judaism.* **1a** (in rabbinical literature) usage; tradition. **b** Often, **Halakah**. the body of traditional or oral laws of the Jews, having the force of legal custom and supplementing or interpreting the law of the Scripture, with Haggadah constituting the Talmudic and Judaic lore. The Mishnah is the basic collection of the Halakah. **2** a single tradition or law. **3** an explanation or decision by a rabbi on a matter not specifically covered by Mosaic or Talmudic law but deduced from them. [< Hebrew *hălākhāh* the practice, rule; (originally) usual path, way of acting]

ha|la|kha (hä′lä Hä′, hä lä′Hä), *n., pl.* **ha|la|khoth** (hä′lä Hōth′, hä lä′Hōth). = halakah.

ha|la|kist (hä′lə kist, hə lä′-), *n.* a person who is an authority on, or renders, halakoth.

ha|lal (hə läl′), *v.,* **-lalled, -lal|ling**, *n.* —*v.t.* to slaughter (animals) for food in the manner prescribed by Moslem law.

—*n.* (in Moslem law) lawful food. [< Arabic *ḥalāl* lawful]

ha|la|tion (hā lā′shən, ha-), *n. Photography.* the spreading of light beyond its proper boundaries in a negative, such as the spreading around a white object photographed in sunlight, caused by reflection from the supporting layer under the emulsion of the film.

hal|a|zone (hal′ə zōn), *n.* a white powder containing chlorine, used in tablet form to disinfect drinking water. *Formula:* $C_7H_5Cl_2NO_4S$ [< *hal*(ogen) + *az*(o) + *-one*]

***hal|berd** (hal′bərd), *n.* a weapon that is both a spear and a battle-ax, used in warfare in the 1400's and 1500's. [< Middle French *hallebarde* < Old French *alabarde* < Italian *alabarda* < Middle High German *halmbarte* or *helmbarte* handle axe, or helmet axe]

hal|berd|ier (hal′bər dir′), *n.* a soldier armed with a halberd.

hal|bert (hal′bərt), *n.* = halberd.

hal|cy|on (hal′sē ən), *adj., n.* —*adj.* **1** calm; peaceful; happy: *The old man remembered the halcyon days of his youth. My heart is like a rainbow shell That paddles in a halcyon sea* (Christina Rossetti). SYN: serene, tranquil. **2** of or having to do with the halcyon, fabled as a bird supposed to breed in a nest on the sea. [< noun]

—*n.* **1** *Archaic.* a fabled bird supposed to breed at the winter solstice in a nest on the sea and calm the water, identifed with a kingfisher: *There came the halcyon whom the sea obeys When she her nest upon the water lays* (William Shenstone). **2** = kingfisher.

[< Latin *halcyon* < Greek *halkyṓn*, variant by association with *háls* (salt) sea of *alkyṓn* kingfisher]

halcyon days, **1** fourteen days of calm weather, anciently believed to occur about the winter solstice when the halcyon or kingfisher was nesting: *Expect St. Martin's summer, halcyon days* (Shakespeare). **2** *Figurative.* days of tranquility or peace; quiet, happy period.

hale¹ (hāl), *adj.,* **hal|er, hal|est**. **1** strong and well; healthy: *His grandfather was still hale and hearty at eighty.* SYN: robust, vigorous, hearty. **2** *Scottish.* **a** free from injury; unhurt; sound. **b** whole; complete; entire. [Old English *hāl*. See etym. of doublet **whole**. See related etym. at **heal**.] —**hale′ness**, *n.*

hale² (hāl), *v.,* **haled, hal|ing**. —*v.t.* **1** to force to go: *When he refused to obey the policeman, the man was haled into court.* SYN: summon. **2** to draw or pull by force; drag; tug: *Galling his kingly hands haling ropes* (Shakespeare).

—*v.i. Archaic.* to haul, pull, or tug: *A yoke of ... stolid oxen were patiently haling at the plough* (Robert Louis Stevenson). [< Old French *haler* < Germanic (compare Old High German *halōn*). See etym of doublet **haul**.]

ha|ler¹ (hä′lər), *n., pl.* **-lers, -le|ru** (-lə rü′). a copper coin of Czechoslovakia, worth 1/100 of a koruna; heller. [< Czech *haler* < Middle High German *haller;* see etym. under **heller¹**]

hal|er² (hā′lər), *n. Archaic.* a person who hales or hauls.

half (haf, häf), *n., pl.* **halves**, *adj., adv.* —*n.* **1** one of two equal parts into which a thing is or may be divided: *A half of 4 is 2. Two halves make a whole.* **2** one of two nearly equal parts: *Which is the bigger half?* **3** one of the two equal periods of active play in certain games. **4** *Golf.* a score equal to that of one's opponent, on any hole or on a round. **5** *Football.* = halfback.

—*adj.* **1** making half of; needing as much more to make a whole: *a half pound, a half barrel.* **2** not complete; being only part of: *A half truth is often no better than a lie.* SYN: partial, imperfect, incomplete. **3** *Bookbinding.* having only the back and corners bound in the material specified: *half morocco.*

—*adv.* **1** to a half of the full amount or degree: *half cooked, a glass half full of milk. This government cannot endure ... half slave and half free* (Abraham Lincoln). **2** not completely; partly: *She spoke half aloud.* **3** almost; nearly: *The beggar was half dead from hunger.*

by half, by a great deal; by far: *He is the better player by half.*

by halves. See under **halves**.

half past (or **after**), (in stating the time of day) half an hour past the hour named: *The train arrives at half past seven.*

not half, **a** a slight extent; a long way from: *I am not half done with the housework. They were not half well provided to go away upon the spur* (Thomas Stocker). **b** not at all; the reverse of: *not half bad.* **c** *British Informal.* quite a lot; very much: *"Did you like the show?" "Not half!"*

[Old English *healf*] —**half′ness**, *n.*

▶ **half**. The article may either follow or precede the adjective *half: half a mile* or *a half mile* (but not usually *a half a mile*); *half the amount* (or *half of the amount*).

hal|fa (hal′fə), *n.* = alfa.

half-and-half (haf′ən haf′, häf′ən häf′), *adj., adv., n.* —*adj.* **1** half one thing and half another.

***halberd**

2 not clearly one thing or the other. SYN: indefinite.

—*adv.* in two equal parts; in equal proportions.

—*n.* **1** something that is half one thing and half another. **2** *U.S.* a mixture of milk and cream. **3** *British.* a mixed drink of two alcoholic liquors, especially ale and porter.

half|back (haf′bak′, häf′-), *n.* **1** *Football.* either of two players in the backfield who stand farther back than, and to the right and left of, the quarterback. **2** (in Rugby, soccer, and football) a player who is stationed behind the forward line or scrum and in front of the fullback or fullbacks.

half-baked (haf′bākt′, häf′-), *adj.* **1** not cooked enough. **2** *Informal, Figurative.* **a** not fully worked out; incomplete: *The rebels' half-baked plans resulted in the failure of the revolt.* SYN: undeveloped. **b** not experienced; showing poor judgment: *half-baked theorists.* **3** *Dialect.* silly; half-witted.

half binding, a style of bookbinding in which one material, especially leather, is used for the back and the corners and another is used for the sides.

half blood, the relationship between persons who are related through one parent only.

half-blood (haf′blud′, häf′-), *n.* **1** = half-breed. **2** a person related to another through one parent only.

half-blood|ed (haf′blud′id, häf′-), *adj.* **1** having parents of different races. **2** related through one parent only. **3** (of animals) born of one parent of blooded stock and one of poor stock.

half boot, a boot reaching about halfway to the knee.

half-bound (haf′bound′, häf′-), *adj.* (of a book) bound in half binding.

half-bred (haf′bred′, häf′-), *adj.* of mixed breed; mongrel.

half-breed (haf′brēd′, häf′-), *n., adj.* —*n.* a person whose parents are of different races, as the child of an American Indian and a white person; half-blood; half-caste.

—*adj.* = half-blooded.

half brother, a brother related through one parent only.

half-camp (haf′kamp′, häf′-), *n.* a lean-to, used as a temporary shelter by pioneers in America.

half-caste (haf′kast′, häf′käst′), *n., adj.* —*n.* a person whose parents are of different races, especially one of European and Asian parentage; Eurasian: *The child of an English father and a Hindu mother is a half-caste.*

—*adj.* of or of the status of such a person or persons.

half cock, a position of the hammer of a gun when it is pulled back halfway. At half cock, the trigger is locked and the gun cannot be fired.

go off at half cock, *Informal.* to speak or act prematurely: *Don't go off at half cock and accept an offer you'll regret later.*

half|cock (haf′kok′, häf′-), *v., adj.* —*v.t.* to set (a gun) at half cock.

—*adj. Informal.* half-cocked.

half-cocked (haf′kokt′, häf′-), *adj.* **1** (of a gun) at the position of half cock. **2** *Informal, Figurative.* done or spoken without sufficient thought or preparation; fatuous or absurd: *... the half-cocked proud logic of the uncertain—the language of people who use words as clumsy tools* (Gareth L. Evans). **3** *Slang.* half drunk.

go off half-cocked, *U.S. Informal.* to speak or act without sufficient thought or preparation: *We aren't going off half-cocked and start shipping oil until we know what the whole picture is* (Wall Street Journal).

half-court (haf′kôrt′, häf′-; -kōrt′), *n.* half the court divided in various ball games by a line parallel with the side lines.

half crown, a former British coin, worth two shillings and sixpence, an eighth of a pound. It was of silver and later of nickel and copper.

half dime, a former silver coin of the United States, worth five cents. It was issued from 1794 until 1873.

half dollar, **1** a coin of the United States and Canada, worth 50 cents. It was formerly of silver and now is of nickel and copper. **2** the value of this coin.

half dozen, a group of six. —**half′-doz′en**, *adj.*

half eagle, a former gold coin of the United States worth $5.00.

half gainer, a dive in which the diver springs off the board facing forward, does a half somersault backwards, and enters the water headfirst, facing the board.

half-heart|ed (haf′här′tid, häf′-), *adj.* lacking courage, interest, or enthusiasm; not earnest. SYN: indifferent, perfunctory, lukewarm, faint. —**half′-heart′ed|ly**, *adv.* —**half′-heart′ed|ness**, *n.*

half hitch, a knot formed by passing the end of a rope under and over its standing part and then inside the loop.

half hose, stockings reaching about halfway to the knee; socks.

half-hour (haf′our′, häf′-), *n., adj.* —*n.* **1** 30 minutes. **2** the halfway point in an hour.

—*adj.* of a half-hour; lasting a half-hour: *a half-hour trip.*
half-hour|ly (haf′our′lē, häf′-), *adj., adv.* —*adj.* lasting half an hour. —*adv.* every half-hour.
half hunter, a timepiece similar to a hunting watch but with the central portion of the case cut away so that the hands are always visible.
half leather, a style of binding for a book, using leather for the back and corners.
half-length (haf′length′, häf′-), *n., adj.* —*n.* a portrait representing the upper half of the person.
—*adj.* of half the full length: *a half-length portrait.*
half-life (haf′līf′, häf′-), *n., pl.* **-lives**. the length of time it takes for half the atoms of a particular radioactive substance to break down or decay. The half-life of a particular radioactive substance is always the same and is the principal characteristic used to distinguish one radioactive substance from another, and to measure radioactivity.
half-light (haf′līt′, häf′-), *n.* **1** a light of half the full intensity. **2** a dim light: *Even in the half-light he could see her blue eyes shining like fragments of glass* (Punch).
half-line (haf′līn′, häf′-), *n. Geometry.* the part of a line on one side of a fixed point; ray. The point itself is usually not considered part of the half-line.
half-mar|a|thon (haf′mar′ə thon, häf′-), *n.* a foot race of 13.2 miles, approximately one half the length of a marathon.
half-mast (haf′mast′, häf′mäst′), *n., v.* —*n.* a position halfway or part way down from the top of a mast or staff; half-staff. A flag is lowered to half-mast as a mark of respect for someone who has died, or as a signal of distress.
—*v.t.* to hang at half-mast: *to half-mast a flag.*
half measure, an inadequate measure.
half-mil|er (haf′mī′lər, häf′-), *n.* a person who runs a distance of half a mile in a race.
half moon, **1** the moon when only half of its surface appears bright. **2** something shaped like a half moon or crescent. —**half′-moon′**, *adj.*
half mourning, **1** the period after full mourning. **2** the style of dress worn in this period.
half nelson, a hold used in wrestling. It is done by hooking one arm under an opponent's armpit, usually from behind, and putting a hand against the back of his neck.
***half note**, *Music.* a note played for one half as long a time as a whole note; minim.

***half note**
***half rest**

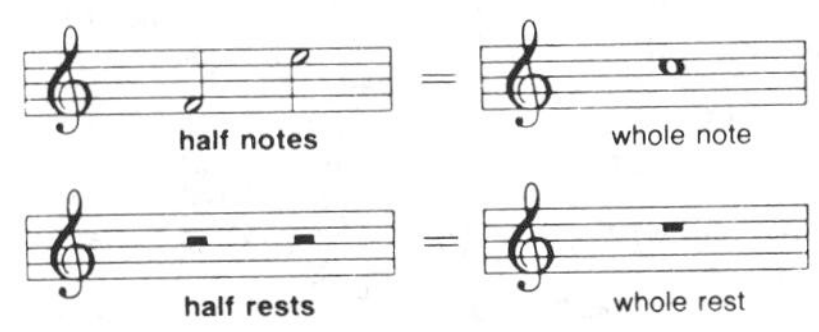

half|pace (haf′pās′, häf′-), *n.* = footpace (def. 2).
half pay, **1** half the usual or full wages or salary. **2** a payment made to a retired or inactive officer of the army or navy that is a prescribed percentage of his active pay. —**half′-pay′**, *adj.*
half|pence (hā′pəns), *n.* halfpennies.
half|pen|ny (hā′pə nē, hāp′nē), *n., pl.* **half|pen-nies, half|pence**, *adj.* —*n.* **1** a British coin worth half a penny. **2** the value of this coin.
—*adj.* **1** worth a halfpenny. **2** having little value; trifling. Also, **ha′penny**.
half|pen|ny|worth (hā′pə nē wėrth′, hāp′nē-), *adj.* as much as a halfpenny will buy; a very small quantity.
half-pint (haf′pīnt′, häf′-), *n., adj.* —*n.* **1** half of a pint. **2** *Slang.* a very small or unimportant person. —*adj. Slang.* very small: *half-pint foreign cars* (Time).
half-plane (haf′plān′, häf′-), *n. Geometry.* the part of a plane on one side of a straight line drawn in the plane. The line itself is usually not considered part of the half-plane.
half relief, = mezzo-relievo.
***half rest**, *Music.* a rest as long as a half note.
half-seas over (haf′sēz′, häf′-), **1a** halfway across the sea. **b** *Figurative: I am half-seas over to death* (John Dryden). **2** *Slang.* half drunk.
half shell, one shell of a bivalve: *oysters on the half shell.*
half-shot (*n.* haf′shot′, häf′-; *adj.* haf′shot′, häf′-), *n., adj.* —*n.* a stroke in golf made with half a swing, intended to carry less than the full shot. —*adj. U.S. Slang.* nearly drunk.
half sister, a sister related through one parent only.
half-slip (haf′slip′, häf′-), *n.* a woman's slip that hangs from the waist by an elastic band.
half snipe, = jacksnipe.
half sole, the sole of a shoe or boot from the toe to the instep.
half-sole (haf′sōl′, häf′-), *v.t.,* **-soled, -sol|ing.** to put a new half sole or half soles on (shoes or boots).
half sovereign, a former British gold coin, worth ten shillings or half a pound.
half-staff (haf′staf′, häf′stäf′), *n.* = half-mast.
half step, **1** *Music.* the difference in pitch between two keys next to each other on a piano; semitone. It is the smallest interval in pitch used in ordinary scales. **2** *U.S. Army.* a short step prescribed in marching, 15 inches long in quick time or 18 inches in double time.
half swing, *Sports.* a swing of half the usual distance.
half tide, the state or time of the tide halfway between flood and ebb.
half-tim|bered (haf′tim′bərd, häf′-), *adj.* having the walls of wooden framework with the spaces filled by plaster, stone, or brick.
half-time (haf′tīm′, häf′-), *n., adj.* —*n.* Also, **half time**. **1** the end of half of the total period of play in football, basketball, or other timed game, usually marked by an intermission: *East led by 14-7 at half-time.* **2** half of the available time; half of the usual working time: *He spent only half-time on it.*
—*adj.* half of the normal time: *schools on half-time sessions.*
half-tint (haf′tint′, häf′-), *n.* a half-tone in painting.
half title, **1** the title of a book printed on a full page by itself just before or after the title page; bastard title. **2** the title of any part of a book, or of the whole book, printed on a page preceding or including the text to which it applies.
half-tone or **half|tone** (haf′tōn′, häf′-), *n., adj.* —*n.* **1a** a process in photoengraving in which gradations of tone in the original painting, drawing, or photograph are reproduced by means of a series of very small dots between fine intersecting blank lines produced by a screen placed in the camera a short distance in front of the sensitized film. **b** an illustration made by this process. **c** the metal plate made by this process. **2** *Fine Arts, Photography.* a tone intermediate between the extreme lights and extreme shades.
—*adj.* of or used in the process of making half-tone engravings.
half tone, **1** = half step; semitone. **2** = half-tone.
***half-track** or **half|track** (haf′trak′, häf′-), *n.* **1** a type of motor vehicle having wheels in the front for steering, and caterpillar tracks at the rear for driving power, used especially in the armed forces for mounting heavy weapons and carrying troops. **2** the track at the rear of such a vehicle. **3** *Electronics.* a method of recording on magnetic tape, using two half-width tracks on a single tape and thus doubling its capacity.

***half-track**
definition 1

half-truth (haf′trüth′, häf′-), *n.* a statement, proposition, or measure, that contains some truth but is only half or partly true: *That air pollution control measures forced on landlords will result in further rent increase for tenants is the type of half-truths often used to becloud the facts and confuse the public* (New York Times).
half volley, a ball returned by hitting or kicking it the instant after it bounces, as in tennis, soccer, and cricket.
half-vol|ley (haf′vol′ē, häf′-), *v.t., v.i.,* **-leyed, -ley|ing.** to make a return of (a ball) the instant after it bounces; make a half volley.
half wave, half of a complete wave of electricity, light, or sound.
half-wave rectifier (haf′wāv′, häf′-), a circuit, vacuum tube, or other electrical device that uses one alternation of an alternating current to produce a pulsating direct current.
half|way (haf′wā′, häf′-), *adv., adj.* —*adv.* **1** half the way: *The rope reached only halfway around the tree.* **2** one half; to half the full extent: *The morning is halfway over. The lesson is halfway finished.*
—*adj.* **1** midway: *a halfway house between two towns.* **2** *Figurative.* not going far enough; insufficient; incomplete: *Fires can not be prevented by halfway measures.*
go (or **meet**) **halfway**, to do one's share to agree or be friendly with: *What the game needs now is for Dexter and Worrell to meet each other halfway in launching the series on a vibrant note* (London Times).
halfway house, **1** a place operated in connection with a hospital providing an intermediate stage between full hospital care and complete release. **2** *U.S.* a place where young offenders who have nearly completed terms of imprisonment are rehabilitated before discharge or parole. **3** *Figurative.* a middle ground; compromise: *Between these two concepts there is no middle ground, no halfway house* (Wall Street Journal). **4** *Figurative.* a midway point in a journey or toward a goal: *For him there was never a halfway house between beginning a business and succeeding in it.*
half-wit (haf′wit′, häf′-), *n.* **1** a feeble-minded person. **2** a stupid, foolish person. **SYN:** simpleton, nincompoop.
half-wit|ted (haf′wit′id, häf′-), *adj.* **1** = feeble-minded. **2** very stupid; foolish. —**half′-wit′ted|ly**, *adv.* —**half′-wit′ted|ness**, *n.*
half-world (haf′wėrld′, häf′-), *n.* **1** a hemisphere: *Oskar . . . flees . . . after the war is over, thus spanning both half-worlds* (Canadian Forum). **2** the demimonde: *much too nice a girl, at times, for the half-world* (London Times).
half-year (haf′yir′, häf′-), *n.* **1** half of a year; period or term of six months. **2** half of a school year or other year, whatever its length. —**half′-year′ly**, *adj., adv.*
hal|i|but (hal′ə bət, hol′-), *n., pl.* **-buts** or (*collectively*) **-but**. **1** a large flatfish much used for food, found in northern waters. Halibut sometimes weigh several hundred pounds. **2** any one of certain other flatfishes. Also, **holibut**. [Middle English *halybutte* < *haly* holy + *butte* flatfish (because it is eaten on holy days)]
hal|i|but-liv|er oil (hal′ə bət liv′ər, hol′-), *n.* an oil extracted from the liver of the halibut. It is the richest in vitamin A of all commercial oils.
hal|ide (hal′īd, -id; hā′līd, -lid), *n., adj.* —*n.* any compound of a halogen with another element or radical. Sodium chloride is a halide.
—*adj.* = haloid.
[< *hal*(ogen) + *-ide*]
hal|i|dom (hal′ə dəm), *n.* **1** *Archaic.* a holy place; sanctuary: *The men of the Halidom, as it was called, of St. Mary's* (Scott). **2** *Archaic.* anything regarded as holy; holy relic: *As help me God and halidom* (Sir Thomas More). **3** *Obsolete.* holiness; sanctity. [Old English *hāligdōm* < *hālig* holy + *-dōm* position, condition]
hal|i|dome (hal′ə dōm), *n.* = halidom.
hal|i|eu|tic (hal′ē yü′tik), *adj.* of or having to do with fishing. [< Latin *halieuticus* < Greek *halieutikós* < *halieýein* to fish < *háls* sea]
Hal|i|go|ni|an (hal′ə gō′nē ən), *adj., n.* —*adj.* of or having to do with Halifax, Nova Scotia or Halifax, England.
—*n.* a native or inhabitant of Halifax.
[< Medieval Latin *Haligonia* Halifax + English *-an*]
hal|ite (hal′īt, hā′līt), *n.* native sodium chloride; rock salt. [< New Latin *halites* < Greek *háls* salt]
hal|i|to|sis (hal′ə tō′sis), *n.* bad or offensive breath. [< New Latin *halitosis* < Latin *hālitus, -ūs* breath, related to *hālāre* to breathe + New Latin *-osis* -osis]
hal|i|tus (hal′ə təs), *n.* **1** the breath. **2** an exhalation; vapor. [< Latin *hālitus;* see etym. under **halitosis**]
Hal|i|ver (hal′i vər, hol′-), *n. Trademark.* = halibut-liver oil.
hall (hôl), *n.* **1** a way for going through a building; passageway: *A hall ran the length of the upper floor of the house.* **SYN:** corridor, hallway. **2** a passage or room at the entrance of a building; vestibule: *Leave your umbrella in the hall.* **SYN:** foyer. **3** a large room for holding meetings, parties, or banquets: *No hall in town was large enough for the crowd gathered to hear the famous singer.* **SYN:** auditorium. **4** a main room for common use, especially in a castle, palace, or other large dwelling. **5** a building for public business or assemblies: *The mayor's office is in the town hall where the town's business is conducted by its officials.* **6** a building of a school, college, or university in which students live or classes are held. **7** *British.* **a** a large dining room in a college or university. **b** dinner served or eaten there. **8** the house of an English lord, squire, or owner of a big estate. [Old English *heall*]
hal|lah (hä′lə, ʜä′lə), *n., pl.* **hal|lahs** or **hal|loth** (ʜä lōt′). a loaf of rich white bread, usually shaped like a braid, eaten by Jews on the Sabbath, holidays, or ceremonial occasions. Also, **challah**. [< Hebrew *ḥallāh*]
Hall effect, the deflection, within its conductor, of an electric current passing through a magnetic field. [< Edwin H. *Hall*, 1855-1938, an American physicist, who discovered it]

Pronunciation Key: hat, āge, cãre, fär; let, ēqual, tėrm; it, īce; hot, ōpen, ôrder; oil, out; cup, pu̇t, rüle; child; long; thin; ᴛʜen; zh, measure; ə represents **a** in about, **e** in taken, **i** in pencil, **o** in lemon, **u** in circus.

hal|lel (hə lāl′, hal′el), *n.* a Jewish ritual hymn of praise, consisting of Psalms 113 to 118, sung at Rosh Hodesh, Passover, Pentecost, Tabernacles, and Hanukkah. [< Hebrew *hăllēl* he praised]

hal|le|lu|iah (hal′ə lü′yə), *interj., n.* = hallelujah.

hal|le|lu|jah (hal′ə lü′yə), *interj., n.* **—*interj.*** praise ye the Lord! It occurs in many psalms and anthems. **—*n.*** **1** an exclamation of "hallelujah." **2** a song of praise to God. Also, **alleluia.** [< Hebrew *hălləlū-yāh* praise ye Jehovah]

Hal|ley's comet (hal′ēz, hāl′), the comet that Halley predicted could be seen about every 77 years. Its last return was in 1910. [< Edmond or Edmund *Halley,* 1656-1742, an English astronomer]

hal|liard (hal′yərd), *n.* = halyard.

hall|ing (hal′ing), *n.* **1** a Norwegian country dance in triple rhythm. **2** the music for such a dance. [< Norwegian *halling,* perhaps < *Hallingdal,* a district in Norway]

hall|mark (hôl′märk′), *n., v.* **—*n.*** **1** an official mark indicating standard of purity, put on gold or silver articles. **2** such a mark on any manufactured article. **3** *Figurative.* any mark or sign of genuineness or good quality: *Courtesy and self-control are hallmarks of a gentleman.* **4** any distinctive mark or characteristic: *The bowler was their hallmark and they used it as their main prop* (New York Times). *When measles virus attacks tissues such as the lungs, it leaves "hallmarks"* (Science News Letter).
—*v.t.* to put a hallmark on.
[< Goldsmiths' *Hall* in London, the seat of the Goldsmiths' Company, by whom the stamping was legally regulated + *mark*[1]]

hal|lo (hə lō′), *interj., n., pl.* **-los,** *v.,* **-loed, -lo|ing.** **—*interj., n.*** **1** a call or shout to attract attention: 102 *"Hallo!" she called from across the street* (interj.). *Her hallo stopped me in the middle of the street* (n.). **2** a call of greeting or surprise: *Hallo! What's that noise?* (interj.). *She uttered a frightened hallo when she heard the floorboards creak* (n.). **3** a shout; call.
—*v.i.* to shout; exlaim "hallo"; call.
[late variant of *hollo.* Compare etym. under **hello.**]

hal|loa (hə lō′), *interj., n., pl.* **-loas,** *v.i.,* **-loaed, -loa|ing.** = hallo.

Hall of Fame, 1 a colonnade in New York City containing tablets and busts in honor of famous Americans. **2** any of a number of shrines or museums honoring persons who have attained fame in particular fields: *the Baseball Hall of Fame.* **3** Also, **hall of fame.** any group of famous or immortal people: *He will someday be at the front of music's hall of fame.*

Hall of Fam|er (fā′mər), *U.S.* a person belonging to a Hall of Fame; famous person: *One impressive facet of that day was the astonishing number of Hall of Famers who participated* (New York Times).

hall of justice, = courthouse.

hal|loo (hə lü′), *interj., n., pl.* **-loos,** *v.,* **-looed, -loo|ing.** **—*interj., n.*** **1** a shout to make hounds run faster. **2** a call or shout to attract attention. **3** a shout; call.
—*v.i., v.t.* **1** to shout; call. **2** to shout "halloo" to hounds to make them run faster.
[probably variant of *hallow*[2]]

hal|low[1] (hal′ō), *v.t.* **1** to make holy or sacred: *a place hallowed by memories.* SYN: sanctify. **2** to honor as holy or sacred: *Our Father which art in heaven, Hallowed be thy name* (Matthew 6:9). **3** *Archaic.* to declare holy; consecrate; bless: *Sword, I will hallow thee for this thy deed* (Shakespeare). [Old English *hālgian,* related to *hālig* holy]

hal|low[2] (hə lō′), *interj., n., v.i., v.t.* = halloo. [probably < Old French *halloer* to shout (in pursuit)]

hal|lowed (hal′ōd; *in worship, often* hal′ō id), *adj.* **1** made holy; sacred; consecrated: *A churchyard is hallowed ground.* SYN: sanctified. **2** honored or observed as holy.

Hal|low|een or **Hal|low|e'en** (hal′ō ēn′; hol′-), *n.* the evening of October 31, before Allhallows or All Saints' Day. It is observed especially by children, who masquerade, beg for treats, or play pranks. [Scottish for *Allhallow-even,* earlier *All hallow eve*]

Hal|low|mas (hal′ō məs, -mas), *n.* the former name of the church feast of Allhallows or All Saints' Day, observed on November 1.

hal|loy|site (ha loi′zīt), *n.* a claylike, earthy mineral, an amorphous, hydrated aluminum silicate, similar to kaolin, used in oil refining. [< J. d'*Halloy,* 1783-1875, a Belgian geologist + *-'s*[1] + *-ite*[1]]

Hall or **Hall's scale,** a species of scale insect that attacks the bark of the peach tree and other stone-fruit trees. [< Maurice C. *Hall,* an American zoologist of the 1900's]

Hall|statt (hôl′stat; *German* häl′shtät), *adj. Archaeology.* denoting a period of transition from bronze to iron, and the type of civilization of that period.
[< *Hallstatt,* a village in Austria, where relics were found]

Hall|stat|ti|an (hôl′stat ē ən), *adj.* = Hallstatt.

hal|lu|ces (hal′yə sēz), *n.* plural of **hallux.**

hal|lu|ci|nant (hə lü′sə nənt), *n.* something that produces hallucinations.

hal|lu|ci|nate (hə lü′sə nāt), *v.,* **-nat|ed, -nat|ing.** **—*v.t.*** **1** to affect with hallucinations. **2** to view or represent in the form of a hallucination: *No longer content with hallucinating his life story, he has to crack open his fantasies to see what is inside* (New York Times).
—*v.i.* to be affected with hallucinations. [< Latin *hālūcinārī* (with English *-ate*[1]) wander (in the mind); dream, probably < Greek *alúein* be distraught]

hal|lu|ci|na|tion (hə lü′sə nā′shən), *n.* **1** the condition of seeing, hearing, tasting, smelling, or feeling things that exist only in a person's imagination. A person alone in a perfectly quiet room suffers from hallucination if he sees people around him or hears voices. Hallucinations may occur as a result of certain mental illnesses or fever, acute alcoholism, the taking of certain drugs, or other causes. **2** a thing seen, heard, or otherwise sensed when it exists only in a person's imagination.

hal|lu|ci|na|to|ry (hə lü′sə nə tôr′ē, -tōr′-), *adj.* **1** having to do with or like hallucination. **2** characterized by hallucination. **3** = hallucinogenic. **—hal|lu′ci|na|to′ri|ly,** *adv.*

hal|lu|cin|o|gen (hə lü′sə nə jen), *n.* a drug, such as LSD or mescaline, or other substance that produces or tends to produce hallucinations.

hal|lu|cin|o|gen|ic (hə lü′sə nə jen′ik), *adj., n.* **—*adj.*** producing or tending to produce hallucinations: *hallucinogenic drugs. The native Mexicans eat certain mushrooms because of their "miraculous" hallucinogenic effects* (Science News Letter).
—*n.* a drug that produces hallucinations; hallucinogen: *Known medically as hallucinogenics or psychotogenics, these drugs* [*LSD, mescaline, and psilocybin*] *are still subject to intense research* (Time). **—hal|lu′cin|o|gen′i|cal|ly,** *adv.*

hal|lu|ci|no|sis (hə lü′sə nō′sis), *n.* the condition of having or being subject to hallucinations.

hal|lux (hal′əks), *n., pl.* **-lu|ces. 1** the big toe of man. **2** the hind toe of birds. [< New Latin *hallux* < Latin *allex* the great toe]

Hall voltage, the voltage of the deflection in the Hall effect, which is different in different materials. Because of this difference the Hall voltage can be used to describe the electrical properties of materials.

hall|way (hôl′wā′), *n.* **1** a hall; passage in a building; passageway; corridor: *We walked down the hallway past several doctor's offices.*

halm (hôm), *n.* = haulm.

hal|ma (hal′mə), *n.* a game played by two or four persons with 19 or 13 pieces on a special checkered board. It resembles Chinese checkers. [< Greek *hálma* a leap < *hállesthai* to leap]

ha|lo (hā′lō), *n., pl.* **-los** or **-loes,** *v.,* **-loed, -lo|ing** **—*n.*** **1** a ring of light around the sun, moon, or other shining body. It is caused by the refraction of light through ice crystals suspended in the air. **2** a golden circle or disk of light represented about the head of a saint or angel, especially in pictures or statues; nimbus; aureole. **3** *Figurative.* the glory or glamour that surrounds a person or thing: *A halo of romantic adventure surrounds King Arthur and his knights. My head was in the clouds. I . . . fancied it already encircled by a halo of literary glory* (Washington Irving). SYN: aura.
—*v.t.* to surround with a halo.
—*v.i.* to form a halo.
[< Latin *halōs* < Greek *hálōs* a halo, disk; (originally) threshing floor (from the circular path of the oxen)] **—ha′lo|like′,** *adj.*

hal|o|bi|ont (hal′ō bī′ont), *n.* a halobiotic plant or animal.

hal|o|bi|ot|ic (hal′ō bī ot′ik), *adj.* living in a salty habitat, as the sea or seashore. [< Greek *háls, halós* salt + English *biotic*]

halo blight, 1 a bacterial disease that attacks the leaves, stems, and pods of beans, causing water-soaked spots surrounded by halolike areas of yellowish or reddish tissue. **2** a similar bacterial disease that attacks oats and certain other grasses.

hal|o|car|bon (hal′ō kär′bən), *n.* any compound of carbon and a halogen, used especially as a refrigerant and as a propellant.

hal|o|cline (hal′ə klīn), *n.* a sharp discontinuity in the salinity of seawater, usually at a depth of about 180 feet. [< Greek *háls, halós* salt + *klīnein* to lean, incline]

hal|o|gen (hal′ə jən), *n.* any one of the chemical elements fluorine, chlorine, bromine, iodine, and astatine. A halogen can combine directly with a metal to form a salt. They are the most active elements and are nonmetallic and electronegative. [< Greek *háls, halós* salt + English *-gen* (because it forms a salt with a metal)]

hal|o|gen|ate (hal′ə jə nāt), *v.t.,* **-at|ed, -at|ing.** to combine with a halogen. **—hal′o|gen|a′tion,** *n.*

hal|o|gen|ide (hal′ə jə nīd, hə loj′ə-), *n.* = halide. [< *halogen* + *-ide*]

ha|log|e|nous (hə loj′ə nəs), *adj.* of or like a halogen.

ha|log|e|ton (hə loj′ə ton), *n.* a toxic herb of the goosefoot family, native to Asia and the Mediterranean region. It is a common weed on the ranges of the western United States, where it kills a considerable number of livestock. [< New Latin *Halogeton* the genus name]

hal|oid (hal′oid, hā′loid), *adj., n.* **—*adj.*** **1** of or like a salt. **2** formed from a halogen.
—*n.* = halide. [< Greek *háls, halós* salt + English *-oid*]

hal|o|lim|nic (hal′ō lim′nik), *adj.* living in fresh water but having an affinity with saltwater forms. [< Greek *háls, halós* salt + *límnē* lake, marsh + English *-ic*]

hal|o|per|i|dol (hal′ō per′ə dōl, -dôl), *n.* a strong sedative drug, used especially in the treatment of chronic psychoses. *Formula:* $C_{21}H_{23}ClFNO_2$ [< *halo*(gen) + (pi)*perid*(ine) + *-ol*[1]]

hal|o|phile (hal′ə fīl), *n.* a halophilous plant or animal.

hal|o|phil|ic (hal′ə fil′ik), *adj.* = halophilous.

ha|loph|i|lous (hə lof′ə ləs), *adj.* **1** salt-loving. **2** *Biology.* growing in or living in marshes or regions that are rich in salt. [< Greek *háls, halós* salt + *philos* loving (with English *-ous*)]

hal|o|phyte (hal′ə fīt), *n.* a plant that grows naturally in salty soil, as on the seashore. Asparagus, saltwort, and mangrove are halophytes. [< Greek *háls, halós* salt + *phytón* plant]

hal|o|phyt|ic (hal′ə fit′ik), *adj.* **1** of or like a halophyte. **2** adapted to the growth of halophytes.

hal|o|plank|ton (hal′ə plank′tən), *n.* plankton of a salty, especially marine, environment. [< Greek. *háls, halós* salt + English *plankton*]

hal|o|thane (hal′ə thān), *n.* a sweetish, nonexplosive gas, widely used as a general anesthetic. *Formula:* $C_2HBrClF_3$ [< *halo*(gen) + (e)*thane*]

halt[1] (hôlt), *v., n.* **—*v.i.*** to stop for a time: *The soldiers halted and rested from their march.*
—*v.t.* to cause to halt; stop: *The policeman halted the speeding car. The company halted operations during the strike.* [< noun]
—*n.* a stop for a time: *When there is a strike all work comes to a halt.*
call a halt, to order a stop: *a simple matter of calling a halt and declaring that membership in the nuclear club is now closed* (Listener).
grind to a halt, to come to a complete stop: *It might usefully be asked why traffic has not already ground to a halt* (London Times). *Other East-West talks leading toward a détente are grinding to a halt* (New York Times).
[< French *halte* < German *Halt* < *halten* stop]

halt[2] (hôlt), *v., adj., n.* **—*v.i.*** **1** to be in doubt; hesitate; waver: *Shyness made her halt as she talked. How long halt ye between two opinions?* (I Kings 18:21). SYN: falter. **2** to be faulty or imperfect: *A poor argument halts. A poem with weak rhymes halts.* **3** *Archaic.* to be lame or crippled; limp.
—*adj.* lame; crippled; limping.
—*n.* *Archaic.* a lameness; crippled condition; limping walk.
the halt, persons who halt, limp, or hesitate: *He would spend hours daily . . . handing out money to widows, orphans, old soldiers, the halt* (Time). [Old English *halt,* adjective; *haltian,* verb]

***halter**[1]
definition 4

hal|ter**[1] (hôl′tər), *n., v.* **—*n. **1** a rope or strap with a noose or headstall, for leading or tying an animal. **2** a rope for hanging a person; noose. **3** death by hanging: *The criminal was sentenced to the halter.* **4** a woman's brief blouse that fastens behind the neck and across the back. It is used for sportswear, sunbathing, etc.
—*v.t.* **1** to put a halter on; tie with a halter. **2** to catch with a noose or lasso. **3** *Figurative.* to restrain; check. **4** to hang (a person).
[Old English *hælftre*]

hal|tere or **hal|ter**[2] (hal′tər), *n., pl.,* **hal|te|res** (hal tir′ēz). either of two club-shaped organs in dipterous insects that take the place of a pair of posterior wings and help in balancing the body. [< Greek *haltêres* dumbbell-like weights for balance in leaping < *hállesthai* to leap]

halt|ing (hôl′ting), *adj.* **1** that halts; limping; lame. **2** *Figurative.* **a** hesitating; wavering: *Shyness made the boy speak in a halting manner.* **b** feeble; ineffective; faulty: *halting verse.* **—halt′ing|ly,** *adv.* **—halt′ing|ness,** *n.*

ha|lutz (ʜä lüts′), *n., pl.* **ha|lu|tzim** (ʜä′lü tsēm′). a pioneer in a farm colony in Palestine or Israel, especially one who immigrated from Europe before World War II to help build up the Jewish national home. Also, **chalutz.** [< Hebrew *haluṭṣ*]

hal|vah or **hal|va** (häl vä′), *n.* a pasty, very sweet confection that originated in the Levant, made from ground sesame seeds and honey. [< Arabic *halwā*]

halve (hav, häv), *v.t.,* **halved, halv|ing. 1** to divide into two equal parts; share equally: *He and I decided to halve expenses on our trip. The knight halved his bread with the beggar.* **2** to reduce to half: *The new machine will easily halve the time and cost of doing the work by hand.* **3** to join (two pieces of wood) by cutting out half the thickness of each at the point of joining. **4** *Golf.* to complete (a hole, round, or match) with the same score as an opponent. [Middle English *halven, halfen* < *half*]

halves (havz, hävz), *n.* more than one half; plural of **half.** Two halves make one whole.
by halves, a not completely; partly: *The poor farmer was forced to pay his bills by halves.* **b** *Figurative.* imperfectly; in a half-hearted way: *Nadir, who did nothing by halves, was determined to pull off the mask* (Jonas Hanway).
go halves, to share equally: *Those that save themselves, and fly, go halves, at least, in the Victory* (Samuel Butler).

hal|yard (hal′yərd), *n.* a rope or tackle used on a ship to raise or lower something, such as a sail, yard, or flag. Also, **halliard.** See picture under **flag**[1]. [Middle English *halier, hallyer* < *hale*[2]; later influenced by *yard*[2]]

ham (ham), *n., v.,* **hammed, ham|ming.** **—*n.*** **1** meat from the upper part of a hog's hind leg, usually salted and smoked. **2** the upper part of an animal's hind leg, used for food. **3** the back of the hock or the hock itself. **4** the part of the leg back of the knee. **5** *Slang.* **a** an actor or performer who plays poorly and in an exaggerated manner. **b** poor or exaggerated acting. **6** *Informal.* an amateur radio operator.
—*v.i., v.t.* *Slang.* to act (a part) poorly or in an exaggerated manner; overplay.
ham it up, *Slang.* to overact; overplay; ham: *He continued . . . unhesitating, his face set sternly against the increasingly frenzied appeals to ham it up a bit* (Punch).
hams, the back of the thigh; thigh and buttock: *Squatting on their hams at respectful distance . . .* (Lippincott's Magazine).
[Old English *hamm*]

Ham (ham), *n.* a son of Noah, probably the second son, regarded as the legendary ancestor of African races (in the Bible, Genesis 5:32, 9:24).

ha|ma|da (hä mä′də), *n.* a rocky desert surface or region in northern Africa. [< Arabic *hammādah*]

ham|a|dry|ad (ham′ə drī′əd, -ad), *n., pl.* **-ads, -a|des** (-ə dēz). **1** *Greek Mythology.* a wood nymph supposed to live and die with the tree she dwelt in; dryad. **2** = hamadryas baboon. **3** the king cobra. [< Latin *Hamādryas* < Greek *Hamādryás, -ádos* < *háma* together (with) + *Dryás, -ádos* tree dryad < *drys, dryós* tree]

ham|a|dry|as baboon (ham′ə drī′əs), a large baboon of Ethiopia, having a mane of long, gray hair on its head and shoulders; sacred baboon. [< Latin *Hamādryas* hamadryad]

ha|mal (hə mäl′, -môl′), *n.* a Turkish or Oriental porter. Also, **hamaul, hammal, hummaul.** [< Arabic *hammāl* (partly through Turkish *hamal*)]

ham|a|me|lin (ham′ə mel′in), *n.* = witch hazel (def 2). [< *hamamelis* + *-in*]

ham|a|me|lis (ham′ə mē′lis), *n.* any one of a group of shrubs or small trees with yellow flowers which appear after the leaves are gone; witch hazel. [< New Latin *Hamamelis* the genus name < Greek *hamamēlís* a type of medlar < *háma* together + *mêlon* fruit, apple]

Ha|man (hā′mən), *n.* the prime minister of the Persian king Ahasuerus, who plotted to kill all the Jews of the Persian Empire but was stopped by Queen Esther and was himself hanged on a gallows about 75 feet high (in the Bible, Esther 3-7).

ha|mar|ti|a (hä′mär tē′ə), *n.* the error of judgment or tragic flaw in the character of the hero of an ancient Greek tragedy. [< Greek *hamartia* error, flaw]

ha|mate (hā′māt), *adj., n.* **—*adj.*** **1** of or having to do with a bone of the human carpus or wrist, closest to the ulna in the distal row. **2a** shaped like a hook. **b** having a hooklike part.
—*n.* the hamate bone; unciform.
[< Latin *hāmātus* having a hook; hook-shaped < *hāmus* hook]

ha|maul (hə mäl′, -môl′), *n.* = hamal.

Ham|ble|to|ni|an (ham′bəl tō′nē ən), *n., adj.* **—*n.*** **1** a breed of American trotting or harness horses. **2** the main American trotting race, held annually at Du Quoin, Illinois.
—*adj.* of or having to do with a Hambletonian.
[< *Hambletonian,* 1849-1876, a famous American stallion]

ham|burg (ham′bėrg), *n.* = hamburger.

Ham|burg (ham′bėrg, *German* häm′bůrk), *n.* **1** a black variety of grape, of German origin, widely grown in hothouses. **2** any chicken of an old domestic breed of white-skinned poultry, with a rose comb and spangled, penciled, or solid black or white plumage. **3** machine-made cotton embroidery. [< *Hamburg,* a city and state in West Germany]

ham|burg|er (ham′bėr gər), *n.* **1** ground beef, usually shaped into round, flat cakes and fried, grilled, or broiled. **2** a sandwich made with hamburger, usually in a roll or bun: *a hamburger dripping with catchup.* [American English < *hamburger steak* < German *Hamburger* having to do with *Hamburg,* a city in West Germany]

Hamburg or **hamburg steak,** = hamburger (def. 1).

hame[1] (hām), *n.* either of the two curved pieces on either side of the collar in a horse's harness. The traces are fastened to the hames. [Middle English *hame.* Compare Middle Dutch *hame* or *haem.*]

hame[2] (hām), *n. Scottish.* home.

ham|el (ham′əl), *n.* (in South Africa) a wether. [< Afrikaans *hamel* < Dutch]

ham-fist|ed (ham′fis′tid), *adj.* **1** having very big fists: *a ham-fisted heavyweight.* **2** *Figurative.* heavy-handed; clumsy; crude. **—ham′-fist′ed|ly,** *adv.* **—ham′-fist′ed|ness,** *n.*

ham-hand|ed (ham′han′did), *adj.* = ham-fisted. **—ham′-hand′ed|ly,** *adv.* **—ham′-hand′ed|ness,** *n.*

Ham|il|to|ni|an (ham′əl tō′nē ən), *adj., n.* **—*adj.*** **1** of or having to do with Alexander Hamilton (1757-1804), American statesman, or his political or financial principles. **2** of or having to do with Sir William Rowan Hamilton (1805-1865), a British mathematician, or his theories: *Hamiltonian mechanics.*
—*n.* **1** a follower of Alexander Hamilton. **2** *Mathematics, Physics.* a function defining the energy of a dynamic system in terms of generalized momenta, derived from certain equations formulated by Sir William Rowan Hamilton.

Ham|il|to|ni|an|ism (ham′əl tō′nē ə niz′əm), *n.* **1** the political doctrines and economic theories of Alexander Hamilton, who emphasized the need for a strong federal government and defended the doctrine of implied powers in the Constitution. **2** adherence to the doctrines or theories of Alexander Hamilton.

Ham|ite (ham′īt), *n.* **1** a descendant of Ham (in the Bible, Genesis 10:6-20). **2** a member of various ethnic groups in northern and eastern Africa, including the Berbers and the ancient Egyptians.

Ham|it|ic (ha mit′ik, hə-), *adj., n.* **—*adj.*** **1** of or having to do with the Hamites. **2** of or having to do with a family of languages in northern and eastern Africa, including ancient Egyptian, Berber, Coptic, Ethiopian, and others.
—*n.* **1** the Hamitic family of languages. **2** a Hamitic language.

Ham|i|ti|cize (ha mit′ə sīz), *v.t.,* **-cized, -ciz|ing.** *Anthropology.* to cause to acquire the character-stics of Hamites. **—Ham′i|ti|ci|za′tion,** *n.*

Ham|it|oid (ham′ə toid), *adj. Anthropology.* of or resembling the Hamites.

Ham|i|to-Se|mit|ic (ham′ə tō′sə mit′ik), *adj.* = Afro-Asiatic.

ham|let[1] (ham′lit), *n.* **1** a small village; little group of houses in the country. **2** *British.* a village without a church of its own, but belonging to the parish of another village or town. [< Old French *hamelete* (diminutive) < *hamel* village < a Germanic word. Compare etym. under **home.**]

ham|let[2] (ham′lit), *n.* a grouper (fish) of the eastern coast of tropical America.

Ham|let (ham′lit), *n.* **1** a tragedy by Shakespeare, first printed in 1603. **2** the principal character in this play, a prince of Denmark, who avenges his father's murder. **—Ham′let|like′,** *adj.*

ham|mal (hə mäl′, -môl′), *n.* = hamal.

ham|mer** (ham′ər), *n., v.* **—*n. **1** a tool with a metal head set crosswise on a handle, used to drive nails and beat metal into shape. **2** a machine in which a heavy block of metal is used for beating or striking: *a steam hammer, trip hammer.* **3** a small mallet used by auctioneers to indicate by a rap the sale of an article. **4** one of the padded mallets for striking the strings of a piano. **5** a lever with a hard head for striking a bell, such as one in a clock. **6** the part of the firing mechanism of a gun that is released by the trigger so that it strikes the percussion cap of a cartridge or pushes the firing pin and explodes the charge. **7** = malleus. **8** a metal ball attached to a length of wire with a handle on the other end. It is thrown for distance by athletes, who twist with it in a circle and let it go.
—*v.t.* **1** to drive, hit, or work with a hammer: *to hammer a nail into a board.* **2** to beat into shape with a hammer: *The silver was hammered into a bowl.* **3** to fasten by using a hammer: *to use nails to hammer a board in place.* **4** to hit again and again: *The messenger hammered the door until he got an answer.* **5** *Figurative.* to force by many efforts: *Arithmetic has to be hammered into that boy's head.* **6** *Figurative.* to work out with much effort.
—*v.i.* **1** to strike blows with or as if with a hammer: *The visitor hammered against the door with his fists.* **2** *Figurative.* to work out something with much effort.
come (or **go**) **under the hammer,** to be sold at auction: *His collection of rare books will come under the hammer in March.*
hammer (away) at, a to work hard at; keep working at: *He liked . . . to hammer away at his poems in a study where chaos reigned supreme* (Leslie Stephen). **b** to put repeated emphasis on; urge insistently: *On all sides, voices kept hammering at him to run . . . for re-election as President* (Newsweek). **c** to attack repeatedly: *The Russians hammered away at the hungry, half-frozen German troops* (William A. Jenks).
hammer out, a to form or forge with a hammer; shape by beating: *to hammer out the bolts.* **b** *Figurative.* to work out with much effort; contrive; devise: *Two centuries ago men from 13 colonies in North America, most of them with a deep attachment to what we would today call provincial rights, met in Philadelphia and hammered out a federal constitution* (Canada Month).
[Old English *hamor*] **—ham′mer|er,** *n.* **—ham′mer|like′,** *adj.*

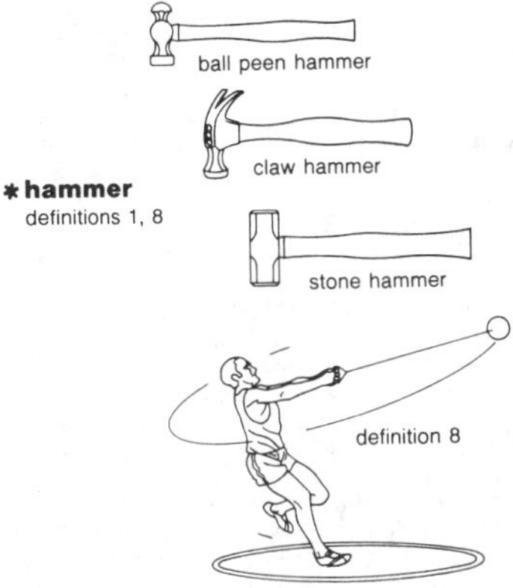

***hammer** definitions 1, 8

hammer and sickle, the symbol of a hammer and sickle crossed, used on the flag of the Soviet Union since 1923. The two elements represent the laborer and the farmer.

hammer and tongs, with all one's force and strength: *Mr. Peter Thorneycroft and Mr. George Brown were at it hammer and tongs over Polaris* (Listener).

ham|mer|blow (ham′ər blō′), *n.* **1** the blow or impact of a hammer. **2a** something resembling this, as the impact of an unbalanced wheel in a locomotive. **b** *Figurative:* [*He*] *dodged the well-aimed hammerblows of a Senate investigating committee* (Time).

ham|mer|cloth (ham′ər klôth′, -kloth′), *n.* a cloth covering the driver's box in a coach.

ham|mered (ham′ərd), *adj.* beaten out or shaped with a hammer: *hammered silver.*

ham|mer|head (ham′ər hed′), *n.* **1** Also, **hammerhead shark.** a fierce shark whose wide head looks somewhat like a double-headed hammer. **2** a variety of sucker with a broad, concave head, found in cool streams of eastern North America.

ham|mer|ing (ham′ər ing), *n.* **1** the action of striking or beating with or as with a hammer: (*Figurative.*) *He stood the hammering of his an-*

Pronunciation Key: hat, āge, cãre, fär; let, ēqual, tėrm; it, īce; hot, ōpen, ôrder; oil, out; cup, pu̇t, rüle; child; long; thin; ᴛʜen; zh, measure; ə represents **a** in about, **e** in taken, **i** in pencil, **o** in lemon, **u** in circus.

tagonist ... with uncommon firmness (Sporting Magazine). **2** a design produced, as on silverware, by a hammer. **3** *British Slang.* the action of declaring a member of the Stock Exchange to be a defaulter.

ham|mer|kop (ham′ər kop), *n. Afrikaans.* an African wading bird related to the herons; umbrette.

ham|mer|less (ham′ər lis), *adj.* having no hammer or no visible hammer. A hammerless pistol has its hammer covered.

hammer lock, or **ham|mer|lock** (ham′ər lok′), *n.* a hold used in wrestling, in which an opponent's arm is twisted and held behind his back.

ham|mer|mill (ham′ər mil′), *n.* a machine in which grain, animal feed, or minerals are ground up by the action of metal hammers revolving within a drum.

ham|mer|smith (ham′ər smith′), *n.* a person who works metal with a hammer.

ham|mer|stone (ham′ər stōn′), *n.* a prehistoric stone implement resembling, or used as, a hammer.

hammer throw, a track-and-field event in which a 16-pound hammer is swung in a circle and thrown.

ham|mer|toe (ham′ər tō′), *n.* **1** a deformity of the toe, especially the second toe, in which the first joint is longer than usual and is extended while the others are flexed, so that the toe bends upward at an angle. **2** a toe thus deformed.

***ham|mock[1]** (ham′ək), *n.* a hanging bed or couch made of canvas or netted cord. It has cords or ropes at each end for hanging it between uprights, such as two trees or posts. [earlier *hamaca* < Spanish < Arawak (West Indies) *hamaka,* meaning uncertain]

***hammock[1]**

ham|mock[2] (ham′ək), *n. U.S.* an elevated tract in a plain or swamp, often densely covered with hardwood trees, common in Florida and southeastern states. [variant of *hummock*]

hammock chair, a folding reclining chair with canvas support for the body, for use in a lounge or garden.

hammock moth, a South American moth whose larva constructs a portable habitation from its own excrement.

ham|my (ham′ē), *adj.,* **-mi|er, -mi|est.** *Slang.* acting like a ham; exaggerated; overacted: *When one of the dancers gave an especially hammy flourish, the crowd was delighted* (New Yorker). —**ham′mi|ly,** *adv.* —**ham′mi|ness,** *n.*

ha|mose (hā′mōs), *adj. Botany.* hooked. [< Latin *hāmus* a hook + English *-ose[1]*]

ha|mous (hā′məs), *adj.* = hamose.

ham|per[1] (ham′pər), *v., n.* —*v.t.* to get in the way of; hold back; hinder: *Clothing hampers a swimmer. Poor health and lack of money hampered his efforts to get a college education.* **SYN:** obstruct, restrain, restrict, entangle.
—*n. Nautical.* articles that are a necessary part of a ship's equipment, but sometimes get in the way.
[Middle English *hampren;* origin uncertain]

ham|per[2] (ham′pər), *n.* a large basket, often a wicker basket, usually with a cover: *a picnic hamper, a laundry hamper for dirty clothes.* [variant of *hanaper* < Old French *hanap* cup]

Hamp|shire (hamp′shir, -shər), *n.* **1** Also, **Hampshire Down.** any one of an English breed of hornless sheep that grow rapidly. **2** any one of a breed of black hogs having a white band around the shoulders and front legs. [< *Hampshire,* a county in South England]

hams (hamz), *n.pl.* See under **ham.**

ham|shack|le (ham′shak′əl), *v.t.,* **-led, -ling. 1** to shackle (as a horse) by means of a rope or strap connecting the head with one foreleg. **2** to curb or restrain.

ham|sin (ham′sin, ham sēn′), *n.* = khamsin.

ham|ster (ham′stər), *n.* **1** a rodent somewhat like a mouse but larger. Hamsters have a short tail and large cheek pouches. They are often kept as pets or used in scientific work and are native to Europe and Asia. See picture under **rodent. 2** its fur. [< German *Hamster*]

ham|string (ham′string′), *n., v.,* **-strung** or **-stringed, -string|ing.** —*n.* **1** either one of the two tendons at the back of the knee in human beings. **2** the great tendon at the back of the hock of a four-footed animal.
—*v.t.* **1** to cripple by cutting the hamstring or hamstrings. **2** *Figurative.* to destroy the activity or efficiency of; cripple; disable: *If this continues, it could seriously hamstring efforts to step up the development of U.S. scientists* (Newsweek). **SYN:** incapacitate.

ham|strung (ham′strung′), *v.* a past tense and a past participle of **hamstring:** (*Figurative.*) *Our building plans have been hamstrung by the bad weather.*

ham|u|late (ham′yə lāt, -lit), *adj.* **1** *Zoology.* hooked. **2** *Botany.* **a** hooked at the tip. **b** covered with little hooks. [< Latin *hāmulus* hamulus + English *-ate[1]*]

ham|u|lus (ham′yə ləs), *n., pl.* **-li** (-lī). a small hook or hooklike part, as in certain bones or in feathers. [< Latin *hāmulus* (diminutive) < *hāmus* hook]

***ham|za** (häm′zä), *n.* the mark or sign for the Arabic glottal stop. In English transliteration the hamza is usually an apostrophe. [< Arabic *hamzah*]

***hamza**

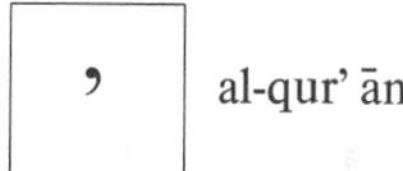

Han (hän), *n.* a Chinese dynasty (202 B.C.-A.D. 220) marked by the introduction of Buddhism, the extension of Chinese rule over Mongolia, the revival of letters, the invention of paper, and increase of wealth and culture.

han|cock|ite (han′kok īt), *n.* a silicate containing strontium and lead: *Hancockite ... occurs as brownish-red, cellular masses of minute, lath-shaped crystals which are monoclinic* (Journal Chemistry Society). [< E. P. *Hancock,* an American mineralogist of the 1800's + English *-ite*]

***hand**
definitions 1, 3b

bones of the hand:

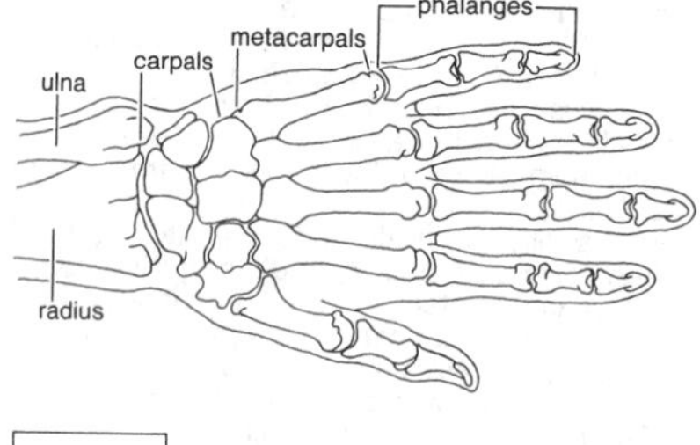

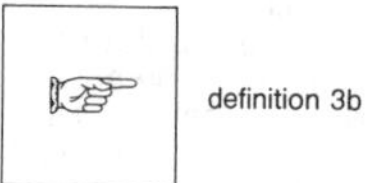
definition 3b

for departure at 11:00
☞ Members must board the bus...

***hand** (hand), *n., v., adj.* —*n.* **1** the end part of the arm, which takes and holds objects. Each hand of a person has four fingers, a thumb, and a wrist which is usually not considered part of the hand. *His hand was steady then* (Oliver Wendell Holmes). *I will not raise a hand against thee* (Edgar Allan Poe). **2** the end of any limb that grasps, holds, or clings. We call the hind foot of a monkey, the chela of a crustacean, or the foot of a hawk a hand. *The spider taketh hold with her hands* (Proverbs 30:28). **3a** something like a hand in shape, appearance, use, or function: *The hands of a clock or watch show the time.* **b** a sign, such as a fist with a pointing finger, drawing attention to something. **4a** a hired worker who uses his hands: *a factory hand, a farm hand.* **b** a member of a ship's crew; sailor: *There was a hand less at the halliards* (John Masefield). **5** *Figurative.* **a** a part or share in doing something: *He had no hand in the matter. The whole group took a hand in the discussion.* **b** means: *He died by his own hand.* **6** side: *At her left hand stood two men.* **7** a style of handwriting: *He writes in a clear hand.* **8** a person's signature: *They sent their agents ... to get hands to this petition* (John Winthrop). **9** *Figurative.* **a** skill; ability: *This painting shows the hand of a master.* **b** execution; touch: *the fine hand of a true craftsman.* **10** a person with reference to action, skill, or ability: *She is a great hand at thinking up new games.* **11** a round of applause or clapping: *The crowd gave the winner a big hand.* **12** a promise of marriage: *I gave him my hand within this hour* (Richard Brinsley Sheridan). **13** the breadth of a hand; four inches: *This horse is 18 hands high.* **14a** the cards held by a player in one round of a card game. **b** a single round of a card game. **c** a player in a card game. **15** *Commerce.* **a** a cluster of bananas. **b** a bundle of tobacco leaves. **c** a shoulder of pork. **16** (in Roman law) the control of a husband over his wife; manus. **17** the quality of touch or suppleness (of textiles or leather); handle: *Hand means tactile beauty, as distinguished from visual beauty* (Scientific American). *The fabric has a cashmere-like hand* (New Yorker).
—*v.t.* **1** to give with the hand; pass; pass along: *Please hand me a spoon.* **2** to help with the hand; assist: *He handed the ladies into the carriage with the air of a French marquis* (Oliver Wendell Holmes). **3** *Nautical.* to furl (a sail).
—*adj.* of, for, or by the hand: *a hand mirror, a hand signal, a hand mower.*

all hands, a all the sailors of a ship's crew: *All hands on deck.* **b** *Informal.* all the members of a group: *If all hands had been got together, they would not have more than half filled the room* (Dickens).

at first hand, from direct knowledge or experience: *Both had had experience at first hand of the worst aspects of that industrial-commercial system* (Edmund Wilson).

at hand, a within reach; near; close: *Satan was now at hand* (Milton). **b** at one's disposal; ready; available: *The evidence at hand suggests that they are exercising the franchise in steadily increasing numbers* (Reporter). **c** under consideration: *His question was not related to the matter at hand.*

at second hand, from the knowledge or experience of another; not directly: *She heard the story at second hand.*

at the hand (or **hands**) **of,** through the act or deed of: *We have received many favors at his hands.*

bear a hand, to help: *Get him to bear a hand.*

bind hand and foot, a to tie up completely: *The burglar bound his victim hand and foot before he made his getaway.* **b** *Figurative.* to constrain so as to deny freedom of choice or action: *The terms of the contract bound me hand and foot.*

bite the hand that feeds one, to knowingly hurt or wrong one's benefactor; pay back benevolence with malice: *He has used his newly-acquired status and prestige to bite the hand that fed him* (Punch).

by hand, a by using the hands, not machinery: *embroidered by hand.* **b** by special messenger: *delivery by hand.*

change hands, to pass from one person to another: *That building changed hands many times.*

clean hands. See under **clean hands.**

come to hand, to turn up; be obtained or received: *The enclosed letter ... came to hand yesterday* (Thomas Jefferson).

eat out of one's hand, to follow another's ideas, leadership, etc.; submit to another's authority: *At first he resisted, but now they've got him eating out of their hands.*

force one's hand, to make a person act prematurely or do something he dislikes: *The potato famine in Ireland precipitated a crisis, forced Peel's hand, and compelled him to open the ports* (Stephen Dowell).

free hand. See under **free hand.**

from hand to hand, from one person to another: *the paper money that passes from hand to hand* (Oliver Wendell Holmes).

(from) hand to mouth, without providing for the future: *Many poor people are forced to live from hand to mouth. Since he lost his job he has been living hand to mouth.*

give a hand, to assist; help: *Please give me a hand with this trunk.*

give one's hand, to hold out the hand to be clasped or shaken: *Give me your hands, God send you joy, Petruchio, 'tis a match* (Shakespeare).

hand and foot, a sparing no pain; diligently: *We'll wait on you hand and foot. Pamper you to death* (New Yorker). **b** completely; thoroughly: *Piasecki, who was tied hand and foot to the official Party machinery, made an almost fatal tactical error* (Atlantic).

hand and glove, in close relations; intimate: *He not only knows the mayor; he's hand and glove with him.*

hand down, a to pass along: *The story was handed down from father to son.* **b** to announce (a legal decision or opinion): *began a week of listening to arguments after which it* [*the Supreme Court*] *will meet to hand down more decisions next Monday* (Wall Street Journal).

hand in, to give; deliver: *Hand in your homework on time.*

hand in glove, in close relations; intimate: *The partners work as a team, hand in glove.*

hand in hand, a holding hands: *They hand in hand, with wandering steps and slow, Through*

Eden took their solitary way (Milton). **b** *Figurative.* together: *The two processes go forward hand in hand.*
hand it to, *Informal.* to give credit or praise to: *You've got to hand it to him; he's quite a salesman.*
hand off, *Football.* to transfer the ball at close range with the hands, rather than throwing it: *It's easier to hand off in freezing weather and wind than it is to pass* (Y. A. Tittle).
hand on, to pass along: *He handed on the family tradition to his sons.*
hand out, to give out; distribute: *The circus clown handed out balloons to the children.*
hand over, **a** to give to another; deliver: *Yet his sentence was again commuted, and he was now handed over to Russia* (Edmund Wilson). **b** *British.* to relinquish authority or a position: *While he might well have carried on as Prime Minister for some months yet, by next year's conference he would most probably have handed over* (Manchester Guardian Weekly).
hand over fist, **a** rapidly: *A heavy squall was coming up hand over fist along with the wind* (W. C. Russell). **b** substantially; considerably: *It pays hand over fist always to take the secondary roads that run along the "wrong" sides of rivers in preference to the main roads that run along their "right" sides* (London Times).
hand over hand, **a** *Nautical.* passing one hand over the other alternately, as in climbing up or down a rope: *Up went Martin, hand over hand* (Thomas Hughes). **b** *Figurative.* steadily: *Strange, brilliantly focussed, tumbledown situations ... carry the reader, hand over hand, through the book* (New Yorker).
hands, possession; control: *The property is no longer in my hands. Important evidence fell into the hands of the defense attorney.*
hands down, easily: *He won the contest hands down.*
hands off! let it alone! do not interfere! *"Hands off!" cried Silver leaping back a yard* (Robert Louis Stevenson).
hand's turn, *Informal.* a stroke of work: *He never does a hand's turn.*
hands up! to hold up both hands: **a** to signify yielding: *Hands up—every soul of you* (Julian Hawthorne). **b** to indicate approval, assent, or readiness to answer a question: *Hands up, those who have the right answer!*
hand to hand (or **fist**), close together; at close quarters: *The soldiers fought hand to hand.*
hand up, *U.S.* to deliver (an indictment): *An indictment is an accusation handed up to a high bench where a judge sits, for further adjudication* (William Safire). *Both men pleaded not guilty to the charges, which were handed up by a special grand jury* (New York Times).
have one's hands full, to be very busy; be able to do no more; have all one can do: *She would like to help on the charity drive, but what with her children and her housework she has her hands full.*
in hand, **a** held in the hand: *The waiter stood pad and pencil in hand, ready to take our order.* **b** under control: *He kept his feelings well in hand.* **c** in one's possession; ready: *cash in hand.* **d** going along; being done or to be done: *... having much business in hand* (Daniel Defoe).
in one's hand (or **hands**), in one's care: *In her hand their destinies* (Edgar Allan Poe).
join hands, **a** to become partners: *The two friends joined hands in a business venture.* **b** to marry: *The Vicar joined their hands* (Samuel Taylor Coleridge).
keep one's hand in, to keep up one's skill; keep in practice: *He plays just enough to keep his hand in.*
last hand, the finishing touch: *The compiler did not put his last hand to the work* (Matthew Arnold).
lay hands on, **a** to get hold of; seize; take; get: *There was no great ship on the Sea that the Frenchmen could lay their hands upon* (Richard Grafton). **b** to arrest: *Sooner or later the law will lay hands on him.* **c** to attack; harm: *Don't you lay hands on that kitten, you bad dog!* **d** to bless by touching with the hands: *O ye mitred heads ... lay not careless hands on skulls that cannot teach, and will not learn* (William Cowper).
lend a hand, to help: *He asked his brother to lend a hand with the chores. This box is too heavy for two persons—please lend us a hand.*
near at hand, **a** within easy reach; near: *The phone was near at hand in case of emergency.* **b** coming soon: *Summer is near at hand.*
off one's hands, out of one's care or charge: *A friend of the lady's will take the child off her hands* (Samuel Foote).
on hand, **a** within reach; near; close: *Try to be on hand when I need you.* **b** ready: *to have cash on hand.* **c** present: *I will be on hand again tomorrow.* **d** to be engaged in; be occupied with: *The builder had three contracts on hand.* **e** in one's possession: *We have large stocks on hand.*
on one's hands, **a** in one's care or charge: *I have got him on my hands.* **b** at one's disposal: *They find plenty of time on their hands* (Maclean's).
on the one hand, from this point of view: *On the one hand I want to buy this new car, but I feel that it costs too much money.*
on the other hand, from the opposite point of view: *On the other hand, it costs too much money.*
out of hand, **a** out of control: *His temper was getting out of hand.* **b** at once; without delay: *She will marry you out of hand* (Francis Marion Crawford). **c** without thought or consideration: *It would be sheer folly to dismiss Winters's neo-classicism out of hand* (Listener). **d** into a finished state; into a condition of being done: *Do what you have to do at once, and put it out of hand* (Samuel Taylor Coleridge).
play into the hands of, to act so as to give the advantage to: *If we delay the attack, we will play into the hands of the enemy.*
put one's hand to, to exert oneself; use one's energies; do: *Whatever he put his hand to, he did it "with all his might"* (M. J. Guest).
set one's hand to, to begin working on: *to set one's hand to a new job.*
shake by the hand, to shake hands with: *The visitor shook me by the hand and patted my little sister on the head.*
shake hands, to clasp each other's hand, usually the right one, with or without a shaking movement: *People shake hands in greeting and leave-taking, in token of friendship, in concluding an agreement, in offering congratulations, etc.*
show one's hand, to reveal one's real intentions: [*The chairman*] *of the Senate Banking Committee began showing his hand in the committee's broadening investigation of the stock market* (Wall Street Journal).
sit on one's hands, *U.S. Informal.* **a** to applaud feebly; show little enthusiasm for a play, performance, etc.: *The show closed after the people attending the première sat on their hands.* **b** to do nothing: *Most of them now will sit on their hands for a year or maybe two before they resume buying* (Wall Street Journal).
strike hands, to signify the conclusion of an agreement by clasping right hands: *A man void of understanding striketh hands, and becometh surety in the presence of his friend* (Proverbs 17:18).
take a hand, to join, participate, or assume a place: *Cawder allows himself to take a hand in the lives of Diamond and his frowzy mistress* (New York Times).
take hands, to grasp each other by the hand: *Come unto these yellow sands and then take hands* (Shakespeare).
take in hand. **a** to take charge of; bring under control: *Very obedient to me she was when a little child, before you took her in hand* (Henry Fielding). **b** to consider; deal with: *The matter will be taken in hand and a decision will soon be reached.* **c** to attempt; undertake: *Forasmuch as many have taken in hand to set forth in order a declaration of those things which are most surely believed among us* (Luke 1:1).
throw in one's hand, to give up a contest or struggle: *A large percentage ... have to throw in their hands after a few years of hopeless struggle* (London Daily Express).
throw up one's hands, to give up in exasperation; admit failure: *Our observer then has to make a judgment as to who fired first—an almost impossible job. Very often we throw up our hands and say they both violated the agreement* (New York Times).
tie one's hands, to make one unable to do something: *I'm sorry I can't help you; my hands are tied.*
tip one's hand, to let something slip, such as a plan or information, especially prematurely: *I am ... drafting a minimum wage bill to introduce next session, and I'm going to bring up another one that's even more touchy, but I don't want to tip my hand on that one* (Wall Street Journal).
to hand, **a** within reach; near; close: *By this, the dreadful Beast drew nigh to hand* (Edmund Spenser). **b** in one's possession; under control: *He ... brought the hawk to hand* (Tristram Risdon).
try one's hand, to try to do; test one's ability: *He determined to try his hand at negotiation* (Washington Irving).
turn one's hand (or **hands**) **to**, to work at: *She would not turn her hand to dry a single dish; so we did them alone.*
under one's hands, in one's care: *He that smiteth his servant ... that he die under his hands* (Miles Coverdale).
wash one's hands of, to have no more to do with; refuse to be responsible for: *I washed my hands of those schemers when I discovered what they were up to.*
wring one's hands, to bewail a circumstance or one's fate; despair: *The newspapers were also wringing their hands over the predicament of Japanese seamen working on board American military transport ships* (London Times).
[Old English *hand*] —**hand′like′**, *adj.*

hand ax or **axe**, a prehistoric tool shaped for holding in the hand and used especially for cutting and scraping.
hand|bag (hand′bag′), *n.* **1** a woman's small bag for money, keys, and cosmetics; purse. **2** a small traveling bag; valise.
hand|ball (hand′bôl′), *n.* **1** a game played by hitting a small, hard ball with the hand against a single wall or the four walls of a court. It is played by two opponents or sides. **2** the ball.
hand|bar|row (hand′bar′ō), *n.* **1** a frame with two handles at each end by which it is carried. **2** = handcart. **3** = wheelbarrow.
hand|bell (hand′bel′), *n.* a bell attached to a handle and held in the hand when rung.
hand|bill (hand′bil′), *n.* a notice or advertisement, usually printed on a single page, that is to be handed out to people. SYN: handout, dodger.
hand-blown (hand′blōn′), *adj.* shaped and expanded by means of a blowpipe manipulated by hand: *hand-blown glass.*
hand|book (hand′bu̇k′), *n.* **1** a small book of directions or reference, especially in some field of study; manual: *a handbook on birds. Abbr:* hdbk. **2** a guidebook for tourists. **3** a small book for recording bets. **4** a place where bets are taken.
hand brake, a brake operated by a lever worked by hand. On an automobile it is also called the emergency brake.
hand|breadth (hand′bredth′, -bretth′), *n.* the breadth of a hand, used as a measure. It varies from 2½ to 4 inches. Also, **hand's-breadth**.
***hand|car** (hand′kär′), *n.* a light, open car moved along railroad tracks by pumping a handle, used by workmen who maintain the tracks.

***handcar**

hand|cart (hand′kärt′), *n.* a small cart pulled or pushed by hand; barrow.
hand|clap (hand′klap′), *n.* the striking together of a person's hands, especially as applause, a signal or interruption, or a marking of rhythm.
hand|clasp (hand′klasp′, -kläsp′), *n.* the grasp of a person's hand as in agreement or greeting.
hand|craft (hand′kraft′, -kräft′), *n., v.* —*n.* = handicraft. —*v.t.* to make or work by hand: *Master cabinet makers are faithfully handcrafting Early American furniture in the old traditional manner* (Saturday Review). —**hand′craft′er**, *n.*
hand|crafts|man (hand′krafts′mən, -kräfts′-), *n.* = handicraftsman. —**hand′crafts′man|ship**, *n.*
hand|cuff (hand′kuf′), *n., v.* —*n.* Usually, **handcuffs**. **1** a device to keep a person from using his hands, usually one of two steel bracelets joined by a short chain and fastened around the wrists. **2** *Figurative.* a restraint: *One section of the bill ... is designed to undo what proponents call the handcuffs placed on the police by Supreme Court decisions* (New York Times).
—*v.t.* **1** to put handcuffs on: *to handcuff a prisoner.* **2** *Figurative.* to restrain: *The German generals ... were strategically handcuffed and limited to minor tactical decisions* (New Yorker).
hand drill, a drill held and worked by hand. Its gear is cranked with one hand while the other holds and puts pressure on the tool.
-handed, *combining form.* **1** using the ____hand: *Right-handed = using the right hand.*
2 having or involving ____hands: *Empty-handed = having empty hands. Two-handed* (*stroke*) = (*a stroke*) *involving two hands.*
3 having or involving ____ persons or players: *Short-handed = having fewer persons than necessary. Four-handed* (*cribbage*) = (*a game of cribbage*) *involving four players.*
hand|ed|ness (han′did nis), *n.* **1** *Psychology.* the preferential use of one hand instead of the other:

Pronunciation Key: hat, āge, cãre, fär; let, ēqual, tėrm; it, īce; hot, ōpen, ôrder; oil, out; cup, pu̇t, rüle; child; long; thin; ᴛʜen; zh, measure; ə represents **a** in about, **e** in taken, **i** in pencil, **o** in lemon, **u** in circus.

Students of handedness concentrate chiefly on left-handedness as their object of study. **2** *Physics.* a twisting or turning in one direction, as with a meson particle.

hand·fast (hand′fast′, -fäst′), *n. Archaic.* **1** a contract, especially of a betrothal or marriage. **2** the joining of hands as in making a bargain. **3** a firm hold or grip; custody: *If that shepherd be not in handfast, let him fly* (Shakespeare).

hand·fast·ing (hand′fas′ting, -fäs′-), *n. Archaic.* **1** a betrothal. **2** a kind of trial marriage, not recognized by the church.

hand-feed (hand′fēd′), *v.t.,* **-fed, -feed·ing.** **1** to feed by hand: *to hand-feed a pet.* **2** *Agriculture.* to feed (animals) by providing them with a standard portion of food at regular intervals.

hand·ful (hand′fu̇l), *n., pl.* **-fuls.** **1** as much or many as the hand can hold: *a handful of candy.* **2** *Figurative.* a small number or quantity: *A handful of men could defend this mountain pass against hundreds.* **3** *Figurative.* **a** as much as one can manage. **b** *Informal.* a person or thing that is hard to manage: *The mischievous boy is quite a handful.*

hand glass, 1 a small mirror with a handle. **2** a magnifying glass held in the hand in reading. **3** a framework of glass for protecting plants.

hand grenade, 1 a small bomb to be thrown by hand, usually set with a time fuze. **2** any similar thing thrown by hand, such as a bottle or other container with chemicals.

hand·grip (hand′grip′), *n.* **1** the act of grasping with the hand; grip of the hand, as in greeting. **2** a handle by which a thing is gripped.

come to handgrips, to come to close combat: *In the chase he almost came to handgrips with his attacker.*

hand·gun (hand′gun′), *n.* a gun that can be held and fired with one hand; pistol. See picture under **gun**[1].

hand·held (hand′held′), *adj.* able to be held in hand; portable: *a handheld television camera.*

hand·hold (hand′hōld′), *n.* a place to put the hands for holding on or in climbing: (*Figurative.*) *They saw they had lost their handhold on the civilian ladder of status* (Harper's).

hand horn, a musical instrument intermediate in development between the hunting horn and the French horn.

hand·i·cap (han′dē kap), *n., v.,* **-capped, -cap·ping.** —*n.* **1** something that puts a person at a disadvantage; hindrance: *A sore throat is a handicap to a singer.* SYN: impediment. **2** a race, contest, or game in which the poorer contestants are given special advantages and the better ones are given special disadvantages, so that all have an equal chance to win. **3** the disadvantage or advantage given in such a race, contest, or game.
—*v.t.* **1** to put at a disadvantage; hinder: *A lame arm handicapped the baseball player.* SYN: encumber. **2** to give a handicap to.
[< *hand in cap* (apparently referring to an old wagering game)]

hand·i·capped (han′dē kapt), *adj.* crippled; disabled; having a physical or mental handicap: *The physical, mental, social, and emotional needs of the handicapped person are no different from those of other people* (Joseph P. Anderson).

hand·i·cap·per (han′dē kap′ər), *n.* **1** a person who handicaps. **2** a person who determines the amount of handicap in a race or other contest.

hand·i·craft (han′dē kraft′, -kräft′), *n.* **1** skill with the hands. **2** a trade or art requiring skill with the hands: *Weaving baskets from rushes is a handicraft.* **3** a thing made with the hands. **4** *Obsolete.* a handicraftsman. Also, **handcraft.** [alteration of Old English *handcraft,* on analogy of *handiwork*]

hand·i·craft·er (han′dē kraf′tər, -kräf′-), *n.* = handicraftsman.

hand·i·crafts·man (han′dē krafts′mən, -kräfts′-), *n., pl.* **-men.** a person skilled with his hands in a trade or art; craftsman. SYN: artisan. —**hand′i·crafts′man·ship,** *n.*

hand·ie-talk·ie (han′dē tô′kē), *n.* **1** a very light portable radio for transmitting and receiving at short distances, as used by soldiers or firemen. **2 Handie-Talkie.** *Trademark.* such a radio.

hand·i·ly (han′də lē), *adv.* **1** in a skillful manner; expertly: *She plays the guitar handily.* **2** easily: *He finished the gallop handily, as the clockers put it* (New Yorker). **3** conveniently: *The telephone, clock, and radio were handily located by the patient's bedside.*

hand-in (hand′in′), *n.* (in badminton, squash, and other net games) the person or side serving.

hand·i·ness (han′dē nis), *n.* skill with the hands; the quality of being handy.

hand·i·work (han′dē wėrk′), *n.* **1** work done by a person's hands. SYN: handwork. **2** work that a person has done by himself, or work that another agent has done by itself: *A tree is the handiwork of nature.* **3** the result of a person's action: *This trouble is his handiwork.* [Old English *handgeweorc* handwork < *hand* hand + *geweorc* work]

hand·ker·chief (hang′kər chif), *n.* **1** a soft, usually square piece of cloth used for wiping the nose, face, hands, or eyes. *Abbr:* hdkf. **2** a piece of cloth worn over the head or around the neck; kerchief. SYN: scarf. [< *hand* + *kerchief*]

hand-knit (hand′nit′), *v.t.,* **-knit·ted** or **-knit, -knit·ting.** to knit by hand.

han·dle (han′dəl), *n., v.,* **-dled, -dling.** —*n.* **1** the part of a thing made to be held or grasped by the hand. Spoons, pitchers, hammers, and pails have handles. **2** something like a handle. **3** *Figurative.* a chance; opportunity; occasion: *Don't let your conduct give any handle for gossip.* **4** *Slang.* a name or title. **5** the feel, softness, or texture of a fabric or yarn; hand: *The handle of many artificial silk articles ... compares favourably with that of most of the corresponding textures in the other branches of the textile industry* (T. Woodhouse). **6** *Informal.* the total of betting on a race or on a series of races at a track.
—*v.t.* **1** to touch, feel, or use with the hands: *Don't handle that book until you wash your hands. The carpenter handles tools with ease and skill.* **2** to manage; direct; control: *He has lived with dogs all his life. He has bred them, handled them professionally* (New York Times). **3** to deal with; treat: *The teacher handled problems of discipline with ease without disturbing the class.* **4** to deal with in speech or writing: *A good writer handles dialogue easily.* **5** to deal in; trade in: *That store handles meat and groceries.*
—*v.i.* to behave or act when handled: *This car handles easily.*
fly off the handle, *Slang.* to get angry or excited; lose one's temper or self-control: *He flies right off the handle for nothing* (Thomas C. Haliburton).
get or **have a handle on,** to grasp or understand, especially so that one can direct or guide efforts to control or study: *If we could only get a better handle on the arms-building phenomenon, we could do something about it* (Washington Post). [*His*] *State of the Union speech failed to convince foreign moneymen that the Administration has a handle on the economy's problems* (Time).
[Old English *handle* < *hand* hand] —**han′dle·a·ble,** *adj.*

hand lead (led), a small lead used for sounding in rivers, harbors, or shoal waters.

handle bar, or **han·dle·bar** (han′dəl bär′), *n.* Often, **handle bars** or **handlebars.** the bar, usually curved, on a bicycle or motorcycle that the rider holds and steers by.

han·dle-bar or **han·dle·bar mustache** (han′dəl bär′), *Informal.* a wide, full, curved mustache, generally shaped like the handle bars on a bicycle.

han·dled (han′dəld), *adj.* furnished with or having a handle: *The bones were so huge that the Stone Age Man who split them had to use a stone axe or some other sharp, handled stone* (Science News Letter).

-handled, *combining form.* having a ___ handle or handles: *A long-handled spoon = a spoon having a long handle.*

han·dle·less (han′dəl lis), *adj.* without a handle.

han·dler (han′dlər), *n.* **1** a person or thing that handles. **2** a person who helps to train or manage a boxer, or who acts as his second during a boxing match. **3** a person who prepares a dog or cat for a show. The handler of a dog also directs him in the show. **4** *U.S. and Canadian.* a publicity agent or advance man, especially of a politician. **5** = rocker (a tanning liquor).

hand·less (hand′lis), *adj.* **1** without a hand or hands. **2** *Figurative.* awkward; inefficient.

hand·line (hand′līn′), *n.* a fishing line cast or dropped by hand.

han·dling (han′dling), *n.* **1** the act of a person who handles: *Handling was only one part of his job.* **2** the act of touching, grasping, or using with the hands: *Handling delicate instruments requires deftness.* **3** *Figurative.* manipulation; management; treatment: *The older teacher was very good at handling discipline in a quite firm way.*

hand·list (hand′list′), *n.* a list of the works of an artist, writer, or the like, for handy reference.

hand·loom (hand′lüm′), *n.* a weaver's loom worked by hand.

hand·loomed (hand′lümd′), *adj.* woven on a handloom: *handloomed skirts.*

hand·made (hand′mād′), *adj.* made by hand, not by machine: *handmade Indian pottery.*

hand·maid (hand′mād′), *n.* **1** a woman servant or attendant. **2** a person or thing that serves; servant: (*Figurative.*) *The confident theorist can become the ... handmaid to the drudgery of fact* (Manchester Guardian Weekly).

hand·maid·en (hand′mā′dən), *n.* a handmaid; servant: (*Figurative.*) *Production is the handmaiden of consumption* (Sunday Times).

hand-me-down (hand′mē doun′), *n., adj.* —*n.* **1** something handed down from one person to another, such as an heirloom or a used garment: *The younger children were outfitted in hand-me-downs from the family attic.* **2** a ready-made garment. —*adj.* having been handed down or passed on; second-hand.

hand·off (hand′ôf′, -of′), *n.* **1** the handing of a football from one offensive back to another: *He fumbled the handoff from the quarterback.* **2** the condition or period in which control of an aircraft is transferred from one airport's control tower to another: *On handoff from Los Angeles' FAA air-route traffic center to San Diego's FAA Approach Control Facility, he* [*the pilot*] *reported Lindbergh Field in sight* (Science).

hand organ, a large, portable music box that plays tunes by turning a crank; barrel organ.

hand·out (hand′out′), *n. Informal.* **1** a portion of food, clothing, or money given out: *The beggar asked for a handout.* SYN: dole. **2** a news story or piece of publicity issued to the press by a business organization, government agency, etc.: *The news, when it came, tumbled forth in a rash of handouts and briefing statements* (New York Times). SYN: release. **3** any printed material handed out to provide information: *handouts of papers read at a conference.* **4** = handbill. [American English < *hand,* verb + *out*]

hand-out (hand′out′), *n.* (in badminton, squash, and other net games) the person or side receiving the serve.

hand·o·ver (hand′ō′vər), *n.* a transfer of responsibilities, management, or other function from one to another, as from one firm to another.

hand-pick (hand′pik′), *v.t.* **1** to pick by hand. **2** select carefully: *A shrewd and involved teacher can hand-pick a talented or hard-driving student who will succeed despite low mental test scores* (Thomas Sowell). **3** to select for ulterior purposes, as a candidate for office.

hand-picked (hand′pikt′), *adj.* **1** picked by hand. **2** carefully selected. **3** personally or unfairly selected: *The hand-picked investigating committee was expected to whitewash the city administration.*

hand·press (hand′pres′), *n.* a printing press worked by hand.

hand·print (hand′print′), *n.* a mark or impression made by a hand: *The cave ... had Indian writings on the wall, and among them were thirteen handprints in red clay* (Atlantic).

hand puppet, any puppet that fits over the hand and resembles either a doll with a hollow head and cloth arms to insert the fingers or a mitten in which the fingers make various movements to imitate facial expressions, talking, and the like.

hand·rail (hand′rāl′), *n.* a rail or railing used as a guard or support to the hand on a stairway or platform.

hand·read·ing (hand′rē′ding), *n.* = palmistry.

hand-ride (hand′rīd′), *v.t., v.i.,* **-rode, -rid·den, -rid·ing.** to ride (a race horse) by maneuvering it with the hands.

hand-run·ning (hand′run′ing), *adv. Informal.* in unbroken succession; consecutively: *... fed their families chicken and apricot jam for two days hand-running* (New Yorker).

hands (handz), *n.pl.* See under **hand.**

hand·saw (hand′sô′), *n.* a saw used with one hand.

hand's-breadth (handz′bredth′, -bretth′), *n.* = handbreadth.

hand·sel (han′səl), *n., v.,* **-seled, -sel·ing** or (*especially British*), **-selled, -sel·ling.** —*n.* **1a** a gift made as a token of good wishes at New Year's or to one entering something new such as a job or house. **b** *Obsolete.* a gift or present given on any occasion; reward. **2a** a first payment or installment. **b** the first money taken by a dealer in the morning, or on opening a new store. **3** *Figurative.* the first experience of anything; foretaste.
—*v.t.* **1** to give handsel to (a person). **2** to inaugurate. **3** to be the first, as to use, try, or taste: *He carries his grief on a shoulder that handselled them long before* (A. E. Housman). Also, **hansel.**
[Old English *handselen* transfer of ownership < Scandinavian (compare Old Icelandic *handsal* transference by shaking hands)]

hand·set (hand′set′), *n.* a telephone that has the receiver and mouthpiece on the same handle.

hand-set (hand′set′), *v.t.,* **-set, -set·ting.** **1** to typeset (printed matter) by hand: *The designs, prints and typography are a joy; many of the books are hand-set* (Manchester Guardian Weekly). **2** to set (type) by hand.

hand·shake (hand′shāk′), *n., v.,* **-shook, -shak·en, -shak·ing.** —*n.* the act of clasping and shaking each other's hands in friendship, greeting, leave-taking, agreement, or congratulation: *His opening clue that he was being accepted came through handshakes* (Newsweek).
—*v.i.* to shake hands.
—*v.t.* to move up, on, or along with the shaking

of hands: *Ministers and imams . . . handshook their way right up to the polling boxes* (Time).
—**hand′shak′er**, *n.*

hands-off (handz′ôf′, -of′), *adj.* of or having to do with noninterference or nonintervention: *However, diplomats said that Spain's hands-off attitude toward French Morocco had not altered her policy of "friendly understanding" in Spanish Morocco* (New York Times).

hand|some (han′səm), *adj., adv.,* **-som|er, -som-est.** —*adj.* **1** pleasing in appearance; good-looking. We usually say that a man is handsome, but that a woman is pretty or beautiful. **SYN:** See syn. under **beautiful. 2** fairly large; considerable: *A thousand dollars is a handsome sum of money.* **3** generous; liberal: *Each year the employer gave each of his workers a handsome gift of one hundred dollars.* **4** gracious; proper: *He wrote a letter . . . to congratulate her and a very proper, handsome letter it was* (Jane Austen). **5** *Informal.* clever; graceful; fine: *a handsome performance.* **6** *Archaic.* appropriate; to the purpose; apt: *an honest method . . . and by very much more handsome than fine* (Shakespeare).
—*adv. Dialect.* handsomely: *Do you suppose highwaymen don't dress handsomer than that?* (Dickens).
handsome is as handsome does, actions, not appearances, are what really count: *But handsome is as handsome does, and nobody could have grudged the winners the sparkling reward of a spirited if tantalizingly late comeback* (London Times).
[Middle English *handsom* easy to handle, ready at hand < *hand* + *-some*[1]] —**hand′some|ly,** *adv.* —**hand′some|ness,** *n.*

hands-on (handz′on′, -ôn′), *adj.* designed for personal participation or encouraging involvement: *Skyline is a "magnet" school . . . that combines fast-paced academic work with hands-on training for real jobs* (Saturday Review).

hand|spike (hand′spīk′), *n.* a bar used as a lever, especially on a ship. [perhaps alteration (influenced by English *spike*[1] or *pike*) of earlier Dutch *handspaecke* < *hand* hand + Middle Dutch *spake* spoke, pole]

hand|spray (hand′sprā′), *n.* a spray of flowers to be held in the hand.

hand|spring (hand′spring′), *n.* a spring or leap in which a person turns his heels over his head while balancing on one or both hands.

hand|stand (hand′stand′), *n.* a balancing on one's hands with one's feet in the air.

hand-thrown (hand′thrōn′), *adj.* (of pottery and ceramics) shaped with the hands on a revolving wheel or platform.

hand-to-hand (hand′tə hand′), *adj.* close together; at close quarters: *It was a hand-to-hand bayonet fight* (Time).

hand-to-mouth (hand′tə mouth′), *adj.* not providing for the future; having nothing to spare; not thrifty: *a hand-to-mouth existence.*

hand|truck (hand′truk′), *n.* a cart pulled or pushed by hand.

hand|weave (hand′wēv′), *v.,* **-wo|ven, -weav|ing,** *n.* —*v.t., v.i.,* to weave by means of a handloom: *to handweave tapestries.*
—*n.* a handwoven fabric: *Among the domestic handweaves [is] a large and handsome assortment of upholstery and drapery goods* (New Yorker). —**hand′weav′er,** *n.*

hand|wheel (hand′hwēl′), *n.* a wheel worked with the hand, not by a machine.

hand|work (hand′wėrk′), *n.* work done by hand, not by machinery.

hand|work|er (hand′wėr′kər), *n.* a person who produces handwork: *Skilled handworkers in India had made fine cotton cloth long before Columbus's day* (Colby and Foster).

hand|wo|ven (hand′wō′vən), *v., adj.* —*v.* past participle of **handweave.**
—*adj.* woven or produced by means of a loom worked by hand.

hand|wring|er (hand′ring′ər), *n.* **1** a person who wrings his hands in or as if in despair. **2** a person who shows exaggerated and highly emotional concern over a situation: *Such handwringers failed to realize the bad impression they were creating.* **3** a hand-operated clothes wringer.

hand|wring|ing (hand′ring′ing), *n., adj.* —*n.* an emotional display of grief or despair over a situation. —*adj.* despairing; hopeless: *The field day of the handwringing pessimist is about over* (Christian Science Monitor).

hand|write (hand′rīt′), *v.t.,* **-wrote, -writ|ten, -writ|ing.** *Archaic.* to write with one's own hand.

hand|writ|ing (hand′rī′ting), *n.* **1** writing by hand; writing with pen or pencil. **SYN:** penmanship, calligraphy. **2** a manner or style of writing: *He recognized his mother's handwriting on the envelope.* **3** *Archaic.* a thing written by hand; document, manuscript.
handwriting on the wall, a a cryptic handwriting seen by Belshazzar, king of Babylon, on the wall of his palace, which Daniel interpreted as a prophecy of the division and decline of Babylon (in the Bible, Daniel 5:5-29). **b** a portent of change or of doom: *Within a half hour of the time when news tickers clicked out word of the judicial handwriting on the wall, a case had been filed in Georgia to challenge the county unit system of voting* (Atlantic).
see (or **read**) **the handwriting on the wall,** to perceive that an institution, order, way of life, or tradition is coming to its end: *. . . certain old buffalo hunters and wolfers who had seen the handwriting on the wall and settled down* (Atlantic).

handwriting expert, = graphologist.

hand|writ|ten (hand′rit′ən), *v., adj.* —*v. Archaic.* past participle of **handwrite.**
—*adj.* written by hand: *handwritten letters.*

hand|wrought (hand′rôt′), *adj.* made or shaped by hand: *handwrought silver jewelry.*

hand|y (han′dē), *adj.,* **hand|i|er, hand|i|est. 1** easy to reach or use; saving work; useful; convenient: *a handy device. There were handy shelves near the kitchen sink.* **2** skillful with the hands; dexterous: *He is handy with tools.* **3** easy to handle or manage. **4** (of a ship) easily brought to tack; steering and maneuvering easily. **5** *Obsolete.* done by the hand; manual.

hand|y-dan|dy (han′dē dan′dē), *n., adv.* —*n.* a children's game in which one guesses in which hand another holds some small object, as a pebble or a coin.
—*adv.* an expression used in offering the alternative for guessing in this game, and hence in general any alternative of choice.
[rhyming reduplication of *hand* + *-y*[2]]

hand|y|man (han′dē man′), *n., pl.* **-men.** a man who does many kinds of odd jobs.

hang (hang), *v.,* **hung** or (*especially for execution or suicide*) **hanged, hang|ing,** *n.* —*v.t.* **1** to fasten to something above; suspend: *Hang your cap on the hook.* **2** to fasten so as to leave swinging freely: *to hang a door on its hinges.* **3** to put to death by hanging with a rope around the neck: *sentenced to be hanged by the neck until dead. And he [Judas] cast down the pieces of silver in the temple, and departed, and went and hanged himself* (Matthew 27:5). **4** to bend down or forward; droop: *He hung his head in shame.* **5** to cover or decorate with things that are fastened to something above: *to hang a window with curtains. The walls were hung with pictures.* **6** to attach (paper) to walls. **7** to fasten in the proper position or angle: *to hang the blade of a scythe.* **8** to keep (a jury) from making a decision or reaching a verdict. One member can hang a jury by refusing to agree with the others when everyone must agree to a verdict.
—*v.i.* **1** to be fastened to something above; dangle: *The swing hangs from a tree. The folds of her evening gown hang gracefully.* **2** to be fastened so as to swing or turn freely: *The door hangs badly.* **3** to die by hanging, especially as a form of capital punishment. **4** to bend downward or forward; lean: *Heavily hangs the broad sunflower Over its grave i' the earth so chilly* (Tennyson). **5** *Figurative.* to depend: *My whole future hangs on your decision. Thereby hangs a tale* (Shakespeare). **6** to hold fast for support; cling. **7** *Figurative.* to be or remain in suspense; be doubtful or undecided; hesitate; waver: *He has been hanging betwixt life and death* (Jane Welsh Carlyle). **8** to fail to agree, as a jury. **9** to loiter; linger: *to hang about a place.*
—*n.* **1** the way that a thing hangs: *She changed the hang of her skirt.* **2** *Informal.* the way of using or doing: *Riding a bicycle is easy after you get the hang of it.* **3** *Figurative. Informal.* idea; meaning: *After studying an hour, I finally got the hang of the lesson.* **4** *Informal.* a trifle: *to not care a hang.* **5** a slackening or suspension of motion.
hang around (with), *Informal.* to keep company (with): *A mutual friend suggested I meet and hang around with him* (Bruce Jay Friedman).
hang back, to be unwilling to go forward; be backward: *There were definite signs that industry was hanging back, waiting for the legislation that would pump Government money into training schemes* (London Times).
hang in there, *Informal.* to hold on; be unwilling to let go, stop, or leave: *He has a long history of . . . confronting adversities, and it would be in his nature to hang in there and fight* (Atlantic).
hang it! an expression of annoyance: *Hang it! I forgot my keys.*
hang on, a (1) to hold tightly (to): *Hang on to my hand when we go down these steep stairs.* (2) *Figurative. The injured man hung on to life and recovered.* **b** *Figurative.* to consider or listen very carefully: *The audience hung on every word he spoke.*
hang one on, *Slang.* **a** to land a punch; hit hard: *He had finally lost his temper and hung one on the sergeant's chin* (New York Times). **b** to get excessively drunk: *I wish she would let me alone for at least an hour in the morning until I pull myself together if I hung one on the night before* (New Yorker).
hang out, a to show by hanging outside: *to hang out a flag.* **b** to lean out: *to hang out of a window.* **c** *Informal.* to keep company: *"I've done told him time and time again to stop hanging out with those Ebony Earls"* (Louise Meriwether). **d** *Slang.* to live or stay: *This is the house where I hang out.*
hang over, a to be about to happen to; threaten: *The prospect of defeat hangs over that political party.* **b** *Informal.* to remain from an earlier time or condition: *Isolationism still hangs over parts of the country.* **c** to attach to; remain with: *Infamous conduct—the phrase hangs over everybody who comes off the register for infringements of the code of professional discipline, whether their offence is serious or not* (London Times).
hang together, a to stick together; support each other: *We must all hang together, or assuredly we shall all hang separately* (attributed to Benjamin Franklin). **b** *Figurative.* to be coherent or consistent: *The story does not hang together.*
hang up, a to put on a hook, peg, or other fixture: *What heathen would have dar'd to strip Jove's statue of his oaken wreath, And hang it up in honour of a man?* (William Cowper). **b** to put a telephone receiver back in place: *He'd hung up, I guess. Anyway he didn't answer* (F. N. Hart). **c** to hold back; delay; detain: *Others . . . find . . . their logs "hung up" for want of water to float them* (Lumberman's Gazette). **d** *Slang.* to obsess; trouble: *We decided that we should not get hung up on artificial values* (Maclean's).
let it all hang out, *U.S. Slang.* **a** to be or become carefree; let one's hair down: *One area where the annual urge to let it all hang out is as strong as ever is the Rhineland with its century-old tradition of blowing off steam* (Time). **b** to be or become frank or candid; disclose everything; hold back nothing: *The accused man's lawyer advised him to let it all hang out and reveal publicly his part in the plot.*
[fusion of Old English *hōn* (past tense, *hēng*) suspend, and *hangian* be suspended; probably influenced by Scandinavian *hengja* suspend and *hanga* be suspended, hang] —**hang′a|ble,** *adj.*
▶**hanged, hung.** In formal English, the principal parts of *hang* when referring to the death penalty are *hang, hanged, hanged;* in other senses they are *hang, hung, hung: They hanged the renegade from the ship's yardarm. They hung the rifle over the fireplace mantel.* Informal usage does not keep this distinction.

han|ga (häng′gä′), *n.* an inexpensive Japanese block print. [< Japanese *hanga*]

hang|ar (hang′ər, -gər), *n., v.* —*n.* **1** a shed or garage for airplanes or airships. **2** a shed.
—*v.t.* to put or keep in a hangar.
[< French *hangar* < Middle French *hanghart,* perhaps < Medieval Latin *angarium* place for shoeing horses, perhaps < Germanic *hangen* hang, in the sense of "place to tie up horses for shoeing"]

hang|bird (hang′bėrd′), *n.* a bird that builds a hanging nest, such as the Baltimore oriole. [American English]

hang|dog (hang′dôg′, -dog′), *adj., n.* —*adj.* ashamed or sneaking; degraded: *the hangdog look of a boy caught stealing.* —*n.* a degraded fellow fit only to hang dogs or to be hanged like a dog.

hang|er (hang′ər), *n.* **1** a thing on which something else is hung. **2** a shaped piece of wood, wire, or plastic with a hook at the top, on which a coat, dress, skirt, or other garment is hung. **3** a loop or ring attached to something to hang it up by, such as the loop at the neck in a coat. **4** a person who hangs things: *A paper hanger put on that wallpaper.* **5** a tool or machine that hangs things. **6** a short, light sword formerly worn by sailors on their belts. **7** a part that serves to hold the spring shackle of an automobile to the chassis. **8** a person who puts another to death by hanging, or causes him to be hanged. **9** *Obsolete.* a loop or strap (often richly ornamented) on a sword belt, from which the sword was hung.

hang|er-on (hang′ər on′, -ôn′), *n., pl.* **hang|ers-on. 1** a follower or dependent. **SYN:** henchman. **2** an undesirable follower. **SYN:** parasite. **3** a person who frequents a place seeking favors there.

hang-fire (hang′fīr′), *n.* a delay in the explosion of the charge of a gun or the like.

hang five, *Surfing.* to curl the toes of one foot over the edge of a surfboard.

Pronunciation Key: hat, āge, cãre, fär; let, ēqual, tėrm; it, īce; hot, ōpen, ôrder; oil, out; cup, pu̇t, rüle; child; long; thin; ᴛʜen; zh, measure; ə represents **a** in about, **e** in taken, **i** in pencil, **o** in lemon, **u** in circus.

hang glider, **1** a device like a large kite or wing, beneath which a person hangs prone in a harness, used for gliding or soaring as a sport; Rogallo: *The most common type of hang glider is an A-shaped kite about 20 feet wide and weighing about 40 pounds* (New York Sunday News). **2** a person who rides such a device; Rogallist.

hang gliding, the sport of riding a hang glider.

han|gi (hang′gē), *n.* an earthen oven in which food is placed on heated stones and covered with soil and sticks, used by Maoris. [< Maori *hangi*]

hang|ing (hang′ing), *n., adj.* —*n.* **1** death by hanging with a rope around the neck. **2** Often, **hangings**. something that hangs from a wall or bed. Curtains and draperies are hangings. **3** the act or fact of being suspended; suspension.
—***adj.*** **1** that hangs; fastened to something above; suspended: *a hanging basket of flowers.* **2** leaning over or down; overhanging. **3** located on a height or steep slope: *a hanging wood, hanging gardens.* **4** deserving to be punished by hanging: *a hanging offense.* **5** likely to inflict death by hanging: *a hanging judge.* **6** able to support something that hangs. **7** gloomy-looking.

hanging bridge, = suspension bridge.

hanging indention, the indention of each line of a paragraph except the first, as in this dictionary.

hanging valley, an adjoining valley at a higher level than the main valley. See picture at **valley**.

hanging wall, *Mining.* the wall or side of rock that lies above a vein or lode.

hang|man (hang′mən), *n., pl.* **-men**. a person who puts condemned criminals to death by hanging them; public executioner.

hang|nail (hang′nāl′), *n.* a small piece of skin that hangs by one end at the side or base of a nail, especially a fingernail; agnail. [alteration (influenced by *hang*) of *agnail*]

hang|out (hang′out′), *n. Slang.* **1** a place one lives in or goes to often. **2** a rendezvous, especially for gangsters and other criminals: *an underworld hangout.*

hang|o|ver (hang′ō′vər), *n.* **1** *Informal.* something that remains from an earlier time or condition: *His thrift was a hangover from his poverty-stricken childhood.* **2** a condition of headache, nausea, or other symptoms of distress, resulting from drinking too much alcoholic liquor, often occurring in the morning: *to have a hangover the day after a late party.* (*Figurative.*) *The spiritual hangover of the Lost Generation has gone on for a quarter of a century* (Time).

hangs|man (hangz′mən), *n., pl.* **-men**. *British.* hangman.

hang|tag (hang′tag′), *n.* a tag on a garment that identifies the fabric and how it should be treated: *Be sure you launder any wash-and-wear shirts as the hangtag directs* (Good Housekeeping).

hang ten, *Surfing.* to curl the toes of both feet over the edge of a surfboard.

han|gul^1 (häng′gul), *n.* a deer of Kashmir related to and perhaps a variety of the red deer. [< Kashmiri *hāngul*]

han|gul^2 (häng′gül), *n.* the Korean alphabet, consisting of 24 phonetic symbols which are combined into syllabic units. [< Korean *hangul*]

hang-up (hang′up′), *n. U.S. Slang.* a problem, anxiety, worry, or other difficulty that a person cannot get rid of: *I very much want to stop analyzing my own hang-ups long enough to do what little I can for people who have real problems* (New York Times).

ha|ni|wa (hä′ni wä′), *n.* pottery with carvings of figures, placed outside ancient burial mounds, especially in Japan. [< Japanese *haniwa*]

hank (hangk), *n.* **1** a circular coil or loop of anything flexible: *a hank of hair.* **2** = skein (def. 1). **3** a skein of yarn containing a definite number of yards. There are 840 yards in a hank of cotton yarn, and 560 yards in a hank of worsted yarn. **4** *Nautical.* a ring of rope, iron, or wood around a stay, by which a fore-and-aft sail is attached. [apparently < Scandinavian (compare Old Icelandic *hönk;* also *hanki* hasp, clasp)]

han|ker (hang′kər), *v., n.* —***v.i.*** to have a longing or craving; wish; yearn: *The lonely child hankered for friends. She hankers after things she cannot afford. What business had he to be hankering after this girl at all!* (John Galsworthy).
—***n.*** = hankering. [origin uncertain; perhaps < Flemish *hankeren*] —**han′ker|er**, *n.*

han|ker|ing (hang′kər ing), *n.* a longing; craving. **SYN:** yearning, hunger.

han|kie (hang′kē), *n. Informal.* a handkerchief.

han|ky-pan|ky (hang′kē pang′kē), *n. Informal.* **1** trickery; underhand dealing. **2** jugglery; legerdemain. [probably alteration of *hocus-pocus*]

Han|ni|bal|i|an (han′ə bal′ē ən), *adj.* of, having to do with, or characteristic of the Carthaginian general, Hannibal.

Han|ni|bal|ic (han′ə bal′ik), *adj.* = Hannibalian.

Han|o|ver (han′ō vər), *n.* the English royal house from 1714 to 1901, to which the first four Georges and William IV belonged.

Han|o|ve|ri|an (han′ō vir′ē ən), *adj., n.*
—***adj.*** **1** of or having to do with the English royal house of Hanover. **2** of or having to do with Hanover, Germany.
—***n.*** **1** a supporter or member of the house of Hanover. **2** a native or inhabitant of Hanover.

Han|sard (han′sərd), *n. British.* the official verbatim reports of proceedings and debates in Parliament. [< *Hansard,* the name of a family that compiled them]

hanse (hans), *n.* in the Middle Ages: **1** the merchant guild of a town. **2** a fee paid to such a guild. [< Old French *hanse* < Middle High German *hanse* merchants' guild < Old High German *hansa* band]

Han|se|at|ic (han′sē at′ik), *adj.* of or having to do with a medieval league (**Hanseatic League**) of North German cities for the promotion and protection of commerce.

han|sel (han′səl), *n., v.t.,* **-seled**, **-sel|ing** or (*especially British*) **-selled**, **-sel|ling**. = handsel.

Han|sen's bacillus (han′sənz), the rod-shaped bacterium which causes leprosy. [< Gerhard A. *Hansen,* 1841-1912, a Norwegian physician, who discovered the bacillus in 1874]

Hansen's disease, = leprosy.

***han|som** (han′səm), *n.,* or **hansom cab**, a two-wheeled cab for two passengers, drawn by one horse. The driver sits on a seat high up behind the cab, and the reins pass over the roof. *He hailed a cruising hansom ... "'Tis the gondola of London," said Lothair* (Benjamin Disraeli). [< Joseph A. *Hansom,* 1803-82, a British architect and early designer of such cabs]

***hansom**

han|tle (han′təl, hän′-), *n. Scottish.* a considerable number or quantity; great deal.

Ha|nuk|kah or **Ha|nuk|ka** (hä′nu kä, ʜä′-), *n.* the yearly Jewish celebration of the rededication of the temple at Jerusalem after the victory in 165 B.C. of the Jews over the Syrians who had defiled it; Feast of Dedication; Feast of Lights. Candles are lighted on each of the eight days of Hanukkah. It falls in Kislev (approximately December). Also, **Chanukah**. [< Hebrew *hănukkāh* dedication]

hao|le (hou′lā, hou′lē), *n.* (in Hawaii) a foreigner, especially a Caucasian. [< Hawaiian *haole*]

***ha|o|ri** (hä′ō rē), *n.* a loose jacket worn in Japan: *Women under their umbrellas wore the graceful short overcoat they call haori, and tottered over the wet ground on high wooden pattens* (John La Farge). [< Japanese *haori*]

***haori**

hap^1 (hap), *n., v.,* **happed**, **hap|ping**. *Archaic.*
—***n.*** **1** chance; luck: *As hap would have it, I went there also.* **2** an occurrence; accident; happening: *to narrate the haps and mishaps of the day.*
—***v.i.*** to come about by chance; happen: *Make yourself ready ... for the mischance of the hour, if it so hap* (Shakespeare).
[< Scandinavian (compare Old Icelandic *happ*)]

hap^2 (hap, häp), *n., v.,* **happed**, **hap|ping**. *Scottish.* —***n.*** a covering of any kind. —***v.t.*** to cover up or over. [origin uncertain]

ha|pax le|go|me|non (hā′paks lə gom′ə non), *pl.* **ha|pax le|go|me|na** (hā′paks lə gom′ə nə). *Greek.* once said (used of a word or phrase of which there is only one recorded use): *The OED followed a policy of total literary inclusiveness for previous centuries, including hapax legomena of such authors as Chaucer, Gower and Shakespeare* (Philip Howard).

hap|chance (hap′chans, -chäns), *n.* a chance occurrence; happenstance: *Hapchance or hazard in no way diminish the glow of creation* (Sid Chaplin). [< *hap^1* + *chance*]

ha'pen|ny (hā′pə nē, hāp′nē), *n., pl.* **ha'pen|nies**, **ha'pence** (hā′pəns). = halfpenny.

hap|haz|ard (*adj., adv.* hap′haz′ərd; *n.* hap′haz′ərd), *adj., adv., n.* —***adj.*** not planned; random: *Haphazard answers are usually wrong.* **SYN:** See syn. under **random**.
—***adv.*** by chance; at random: *He took a card haphazard from the deck.*
—***n.*** chance: *Events seemed to happen at haphazard.*
[< *hap^1* + *hazard*] —**hap′haz′ard|ly**, *adv.* —**hap′haz′ard|ness**, *n.*

haph|ta|rah (häf tôr′ə, -tōr′-; häf′tä rä′), *n., pl.* **haph|ta|roth** (häf′tä rôt′, -rōs′). a portion of the Prophets read after the parashah or section of the Torah or Law in the Jewish synagogue on Sabbaths and festivals. Also, **haftarah**, **haftorah**. [< Hebrew *hafṭārāh* (literally) conclusion]

Ha|pi (hä′pē), *n. Egyptian Mythology.* the Nile as a deity; the god Nilus.

hap|less (hap′lis), *adj.* unlucky; unfortunate: *a hapless love affair.* **SYN:** inauspicious. —**hap′less|ly**, *adv.* —**hap′less|ness**, *n.*

hap|lite (hap′līt), *n.* = aplite.

hap|lit|ic (hap lit′ik), *adj.* = aplitic.

hap|loid (hap′loid), *adj., n. Biology.* —***adj.*** **1** having the gametic number of sets of chromosomes, or half as many as in the somatic cells of the species, such as a germ cell. **2** = monoploid.
—***n.*** **1** a haploid organism or cell. **2** = monoploid.
[< Greek *haploûs* single + English *-oid*]

hap|loi|dy (hap′loi dē), *n.* the condition of being haploid.

hap|lol|o|gy (hap lol′ə jē), *n.* the omission of one of two similar adjacent syllables or sounds, resulting in the contraction of a word, as in *symbolatry* for *symbololatry.* [< Greek *haploûs* single + English *-logy*]

hap|lont (hap′lont), *n.* a haploid organism or cell: *Success in producing a haplont—a plant with half the usual number of chromosomes—eluded researchers until ... Indian scientists grew a haplont morning-glory* (Science News).

hap|lo|phase (hap′lō fāz′), *n.* the haploid phase of an organism.

hap|lo|sis (hap lō′sis), *n. Biology.* the reduction of the number of chromosomes, forming two haploid sets of chromosomes, occurring during meiosis. [< Greek *haploûs* single + *-ōsis* condition]

hap|ly (hap′lē), *adv. Archaic.* by chance; perhaps.

hap|pen (hap′ən), *v.i.* **1** to come about; take place; occur: *Nothing interesting happens here; this is a very dull place.* **2** to be or take place by chance: *Accidents will happen.* **3** to have the fortune; chance: *I happened to sit by her at the party.* **4** to be done (to): *Something has happened to this lock; the key won't turn.*
happen on, **a** to meet: *The two friends happened on each other by chance.* **b** to find; discover: *She happened on a dime while looking for her ball. I deny not but that these men ... may some time happen on something that is good and great* (Ben Jonson).
[Middle English *happenen* < *hap^1*]
— *Syn.* **1 Happen, chance, occur** mean to take place or come about. **Happen**, the general word, suggests coming about either by chance or according to design: *The accident happened suddenly. What has happened lately?* **Chance** emphasizes happening without apparent reason: *There chanced to be someone there I knew.* **Occur** is often used interchangeably with *happen,* but applies particularly when definite or specific events are spoken of: *The accident occurred at the intersection. Important elections occur this fall.*

hap|pen|ing (hap′ə ning, hap′ning), *n.* **1** something that happens; event; occurrence: *The evening newscast reviewed the happenings of the day.* **2** Often, **Happening**. a spontaneous or improvised public performance, display, spectacle, or the like, often involving the audience or spectators: *The program was the fourth event in a series of dance concerts and Happenings staged by the First New York Theater Rally* (New York Times). *What was happening was a Happening—a combination of artists' ball, carnival, charade, and a Dadaesque version of the games some people play* (Time).

hap|pen|stance (hap′ən stans), *n., adj.* —***n.*** a chance occurrence; accident: *France took on this unpromising territory largely by happenstance* (Time).
—***adj.*** chance; accidental: *a happenstance event or witness.*
[< *happen* + (circum)*stance*]

hap|pi|ly (hap′ə lē), *adv.* **1** in a happy manner; with pleasure, joy, and gladness: *She lives happily with her family.* **2** by luck; with good fortune; fortunately: *Happily, I saved you from falling.* **SYN:** luckily. **3** aptly; appropriately: *His letter of congratulation was happily phrased.* **SYN:** successfully, fitly, felicitously.

hap|pi|ness (hap′ē nis), *n.* **1** the condition of being happy; gladness: *Life is one long search for happiness.* **2** good luck; good fortune. **3** aptness; appropriateness: *The happiness of the compari-*

son caught our attention. SYN: fitness, suitability.
—*Syn.* **1 Happiness, felicity, bliss** mean a feeling of satisfaction and pleasure. **Happiness** is the common and general word: *His promotion brought him happiness.* **Felicity** means great or joyous happiness: *I wish you felicity in marriage.* **Bliss** implies the highest degree of happiness: *They are in a state of bliss now that they are engaged.*

hap·py (hap′ē), *adj.,* **-pi·er, -pi·est. 1** feeling as a person does when he is well and having a good time; glad; contented: *She is happy in her new home.* SYN: joyous, joyful, gay, cheerful, elated, rapturous, exultant, delighted, gratified. See syn. under **glad**. **2** showing that one is glad; showing pleasure and joy: *a happy smile, a happy look.* SYN: joyous, joyful, gay, cheerful, elated, rapturous, exultant, delighted, gratified. See syn. under **glad**. **3** pleased: *I am happy to accept your invitation.* **4** lucky; fortunate: *By a happy chance, I found my lost book.* SYN: favorable, propitious, auspicious. **5** clever and fitting; successful and suitable; apt: *The writer has a happy way of expressing his ideas.* SYN: appropriate, felicitous. [Middle English *happy* <*hap*[1]]

happy camper, someone who is well-behaved and contented with his or her situation: *"She's a happy camper. She's a doll." Tamba . . . threw her trunk above her head like a lady flinging open a parasol* (New Yorker).

hap·py-go-luck·y (hap′ē gō luk′ē), *adj., adv.*
—*adj.* taking things easily as they come; trusting to luck: *Those people are certainly happy-go-lucky.*
—*adv.* as luck may have it; haphazard.

happy hunting ground or **grounds**, **1** the paradise of the American Indian. **2** any paradise: *The happy hunting ground for speculators also has booby traps* (Newsweek).

hap·ten (hap′ten), *n. Medicine.* a substance that can unite with a protein on injection to form an antigen. [<Greek *háptein* to fasten, join]

hap·ter·on (hap′tər on), *n., pl.* **-ter·a** (-tər ə). an organ of attachment by which many aquatic plants or marine algae fasten to rocks. [<New Latin *hapteron* <Greek *háptein* to fasten]

hap·tic (hap′tik), *adj.* of or having to do with the sense of touch. [<Greek *haptikós* able to touch <*háptein* to touch, fasten]

haptic lens, a contact lens which covers the white of the eye.

hap·to·glo·bin (hap′tə glō bin), *n.* one of a class of proteins in blood plasma, used in blood analysis. [<Greek *háptein* to touch, seize]

har., harbor.

har·a-kar·i (har′ə kar′ē, hä′rə kä′rē), *n.* = harakiri.

har·a-ki·ri (har′ə kir′ē, hä′rə-), *n.* **1** suicide by ripping open the abdomen with a knife according to a prescribed ritual. It is the ancient form of honorable suicide among the samurai or warrior class in Japan. **2** *Figurative: We must continue to help them when we can, providing we are not expected to commit intellectual harakiri* (London Times). Also, **hara-kari, hari-kari.** [<Japanese *harakiri* <*hara* belly + *kiri* cutting]

ha·ram·bee (hä räm′bā′), *interj., n. Swahili.* pull together (used especially in Kenya as a rallying call for the people to work together for national betterment).

ha·rangue (hə rang′), *n., v.,* **-rangued, -rangu·ing.** —*n.* **1** a noisy speech: *We had to listen to a long harangue about our own shortcomings.* SYN: tirade. **2** a long, pompous, formal speech. SYN: oration. **3** a speech addressed to an assembly.
—*v.t.* to address (someone) in a harangue.
—*v.i.* to deliver a harangue: *There is no subject, which men in general like better to harangue on than politics* (Coleridge). SYN: rant, rail.
[<Middle French *harangue,* earlier *arenge,* ultimately <Germanic (compare Old High German *hring*)] —**ha·rangu′er**, *n.*

Ha·rap·pa (hə rap′ə), *adj.* = Harappan.

Ha·rap·pan (hə rap′ən), *adj.* of or having to do with an ancient urban civilization that flourished from about 2500 to 1700 B.C. in the Indus river valley. [<*Harappa,* a village in Pakistan, where remains of this civilization were found]

har·ass (hə ras′, har′əs), *v.t.* **1a** to trouble by repeated attacks; harry: *Pirates harassed the villages along the coast.* **b** to worry or unnerve (an enemy) by continuous small attacks. **2** to disturb; worry; torment; distress with annoying labor, care, or misfortune: *The heat and the flies harassed us on the journey. He harassed them and embarrassed them with absolute ruthlessness* (Atlantic). SYN: plague, bother. See syn. under **worry**. **3** *Obsolete.* to lay waste; devastate; plunder.
[<French *harasser* <Old French *harer* set a dog on <*hare* a shout to excite dogs to attack] —**har′ass·er**, *n.* —**har′ass·ing·ly**, *adv.* —**har′ass·ment**, *n.*

har·ass·ing agent (hə ras′ing, har′əs-), *Military.* any temporary incapacitating substance, such as tear gas.

har·bin·ger (här′bin jər), *n., v.* —*n.* **1** one that goes ahead to announce another's coming; forerunner: *The robin is a harbinger of spring. The boding cry of the tree-toad, that harbinger of storm* (Washington Irving). **2** *Archaic or Historical.* a person sent on before to secure lodgings for an army, a royal train, or other group.
—*v.t.* to announce beforehand; foretell: *to harbinger his learned name* (George Daniel).
[Middle English *herbengar,* alteration of earlier *herbergere* provider of shelter (hence, one who goes ahead to seek lodging) <Old French *herbergeor* <*herbergier* provide lodging <*herberge* lodging <Germanic (compare Old High German *heriberga*)]

har·bor (här′bər), *n., v.* —*n.* **1** an area of deep water protected from wind and currents, forming a place of shelter for ships. A harbor may have loading and unloading facilities for passengers and cargo. *Great ocean liners dock in the harbor of New York.* See picture under **bay**[1]. **2** *Figurative.* any place of shelter: *The child fled to the harbor of her father's arms. Where lies the final harbor, whence we unmoor no more?* (Herman Melville). SYN: refuge.
—*v.t.* **1** to give shelter to; give a place to hide: *The dog's shaggy hair harbors fleas.* **2** *Figurative.* to have and keep in the mind: *He harbored plans for revenge on his enemies. Don't harbor unkind thoughts.* SYN: See syn. under **cherish**. **3** *Obsolete.* to lodge.
—*v.i.* **1** to take shelter or refuge. **2** (of an animal) to have its retreat. Also, *especially British,* **harbour**.
[Middle English *herebeorg* <Old English *here* army + *beorg* shelter] —**har′bor·er**, *n.* —**har′bor·less**, *adj.*
—*Syn. n.* **1 Harbor, port** mean place of shelter for ships. **Harbor** emphasizes shelter, and applies to a protected body of water on a coast, where land or breakwaters shield against wind and heavy waves: *Many yachts are in the harbor.* **Port** applies particularly to a harbor where commercial ships dock for loading and unloading: *The ship arrived in port.*

har·bor·age (här′bər ij, här′brij), *n.* **1** shelter for ships: *The ship rests in a quiet harborage.* **2** *Figurative.* any shelter.

harbor master, an officer who has charge of a harbor or port and enforces rules respecting it.

harbor seal, a common, spotted hair seal of northern coasts; sea dog; sea calf. See picture under **seal**[2].

har·bour (här′bər), *n., v.t., v.i. Especially British.* harbor. —**har′bour·er**, *n.*

hard (härd), *adj., adv.* —*adj.* **1** like steel, glass, and rock; not soft; not yielding to touch: *a hard nut, hard wood.* SYN: rigid. **2** firm; solid; tight: *a hard knot.* **3** needing much ability, effort, or time; difficult or troublesome: *a hard job, a hard language to learn, a hard man to get on with.* **4** acting or done with energy or persistence: *a hard worker.* SYN: industrious, persistent. **5** vigorous or violent: *a hard storm, a hard run.* SYN: strenuous. **6** *Figurative.* hardy; tough: *Men, a hard laborious kind* (John Dryden). **7** causing much pain, trouble, or care; bad; severe: *a hard illness. We had a hard winter last year.* **8** *Figurative.* not pleasant; harsh; ugly: *a hard laugh. That man has a hard face.* **9** *Figurative.* **a** not yielding to influence; stern; unfeeling: *a hard heart. He was a hard master.* SYN: strict, rigorous, exacting. **b** not visionary; practical: *We Americans have got hard heads* (R. B. Peake). **c** real and significant: *hard facts, hard news.* **10** without concession; strict in terms: *to drive a hard bargain.* **11** stingy: *Many wondered that a man could be so hard and niggardly in all pecuniary dealings* (Macaulay). **12** *Informal.* wicked; bad; disreputable: *a hard character.* **13** containing mineral salts that interfere with the action of soap: *hard water.* **14** containing much alcohol: *hard liquor.* **15** *Figurative.* harsh in style, outline, or execution: *His diction is hard, his figures too bold* (John Dryden). SYN: stiff, unnatural. **16a** in coin or specie rather than paper currency: *hard money.* **b** in coin, bills, or actual money as distinguished from other property: *hard cash.* **c** (of money) backed by gold or silver, not merely government credit. **17** *Phonetics.* pronounced as a stop, not as a fricative or an affricate. The *c* and *g* in *corn* and *get* are "hard"; in *city* and *gem* they are "soft." **18** *Physics.* (of X rays) having great penetrating power. **19** capable of being magnetized only in strong magnetic fields. Steel, iron, nickel, and cobalt are magnetically hard substances. **20** (of a missile site or missile) situated underground so as to be practically safe from enemy aerial attack.
—*adv.* **1** so as to be hard, solid, or firm: *The river is frozen hard.* **2** firmly; solidly; tightly: *He took me by the hand and held me hard.* **3** with difficulty: *to breathe hard.* **4** with steady effort or energy; strenuously: *Try hard to lift this log.* **5** with vigor or violence; fiercely: *to hit hard. It is raining hard.* **6** so as to cause trouble, pain, or care; severely; badly; harshly: *taxes that bear hard upon the poor.* **7** earnestly; intently: *to look hard at a person.* **8** close; near: *The house stands hard by the bridge.* **9** *Nautical.* to the extreme limit; fully: *The ship turned hard aport.*
hard and fast, that cannot be changed or broken; strict: *hard and fast rules of behavior.*
hard of hearing, **a** somewhat deaf: *You will have to speak up; that old man is very hard of hearing.* **b** persons who are somewhat deaf: *The hard of hearing who hate to admit it can just wear glasses [equipped with a hearing aid]* (Wall Street Journal).
hard put, having much difficulty or trouble: *Others are hard put to keep their drilling programs up to schedule* (New York Times).
hard put to it, in much difficulty or trouble: *He is hard put to it to conceal his irritation* (New Statesman).
hard up, *Informal.* needing money or anything else very badly; hard-pressed: *The party is not so hard up that it can't find somebody who stuck by his own family* (Time).
[Old English *heard*]
—*Syn. adj.* **3 Hard, difficult** mean needing much effort or ability. **Hard** is the general word meaning not easy to do, understand, handle, etc.: *We have a hard lesson to learn.* **Difficult** emphasizes needing special ability or skill, shrewdness, or good judgment in order to accomplish, understand, handle, or deal with something hard: *Studies in college are more difficult than those in high school.*

hard·back (härd′bak′), *n.* a hard-cover book.

hard·ball (härd′bôl′), *n., adj. U.S.* —*n.* = baseball.
—*adj. Informal, Figurative.* tough; hardboiled: *hardball politics. "They're absolutely ruthless . . . Our people just aren't used to this uncompromising hardball stuff"* (Time).

hard-bit·ten (härd′bit′ən), *adj.* **1** stubborn; unyielding; dogged: *Among them were two of the party's most hard-bitten and uncompromising revolutionaries* (Newsweek). SYN: obdurate. **2** given to biting hard, as a horse or dog.

hard·board (härd′bôrd′, -bōrd′), *n.* a strong, dense wallboard made of ground wood fibers bonded by heat and pressure. It is used for panels, cabinet doors, and dashboards.

hard-boil (härd′boil′), *v.t.* to boil (an egg or eggs) until the yolk and white are firm.

hard-boiled (härd′boild′), *adj.* **1** boiled until the yolk and white are firm: *hard-boiled eggs.* **2** *Informal, Figurative.* not easily moved by the feelings; tough; rough: *a hard-boiled veteran of two wars.* SYN: hardened, callous, hard-headed, shrewd. **3** *Informal, Figurative.* practical: *For TV, summer is a time of hard-boiled stocktaking* (Time). **4** *U.S. Slang.* hard or stiff: *a hard-boiled hat or shirt.*

hard bop, a jazz style similar to bebop but faster and more intense in delivery.

hard-bound or **hard·bound** (härd′bound′), *adj.* (of books) bound in cloth, boards, or leather, rather than in flexible paper.

hard-burned (härd′bėrnd′), *adj.* (of brick) made hard by intensified firing.

hard candy, a mixture of sugar, flavoring, water, and sometimes corn syrup, boiled and cooled usually without crystallizing.

hard-case (härd′kās′), *adj. Informal.* tough; hard-boiled: *a hard-case marine sergeant, hard-case dialogue.*

hard cash, **1** metal coins. **2** = cash.

hard cheese, *Especially British Slang.* hard luck.

hard cider, fermented cider, containing alcohol.

hard clam, = quahog.

hard coal, = anthracite.

hard copy, copy produced by or for a computer which can be read, as distinguished from punched cards or tape, coded data, and the like.

hard·core (härd′kôr′, -kōr′), *n. Especially British.* broken pieces of stone, brick, or other hard material, used for filling foundations and roads.

hard-core (härd′kôr′, -kōr′), *adj.* **1** of or belonging to the hard core: *a hard-core Communist.* **2** of or having to do with consistent or chronic economic deprivation or poverty: *hard-core unemployment.* **3** explicit; unequivocal: *hard-core pornography.* **4** physically addictive: *hard-core drugs.*

hard core, the firm, unyielding, central part, resistant to exterior pressures or change, of a movement or group of partisans; heart; core.

hard court, a tennis court paved with asphalt or concrete.

Pronunciation Key: hat, āge, cãre, fär; let, ēqual, tėrm; it, īce; hot, ōpen, ôrder; oil, out; cup, pu̇t, rüle; child; long; thin; ᴛʜen; zh, measure;
ə represents **a** in about, **e** in taken, **i** in pencil, **o** in lemon, **u** in circus.

hard-cov|er (härd′kuv′ər), *adj.* **1** (of books) bound in cloth, boards, or leather, as distinguished from paperback. **2** of or having to do with hard-cover books: *hard-cover sales.*

hard currency, = hard money.

hard detergent, a detergent that cannot be decomposed by bacteria in sewage.

hard disk, a rigid disk to store data in a computer, larger in capacity than a floppy disk.

hard dock, a joining of orbiting spacecraft by mechanical coupling: *Finally, they . . .* [*carried*] *out a dramatic series of maneuvers—and achieved a hard dock* (Newsweek).

hard-dock (härd′dok′), *v.i.* to join orbiting spacecraft with a mechanical coupling, as by a lock or other mechanism: *The crew finally hard-docked late the first night by hot-wiring the retract mechanism of the docking probe* (Science News).

hard-driv|ing (härd′drī′ving), *adj.* **1** demanding: *a hard-driving program.* **2** strongly aggressive; thrusting: *hard-driving ambition.*

hard drug, any drug that is physically and psychologically addictive, such as heroin and morphine.

hard-edge (härd′ej′), *adj., n.* —*adj.* of or belonging to a form of abstract painting characterized by sharply defined geometric forms, often set off by strong colors.
—*n.* a painting or paintings in the hard-edge style.

hard-edg|er (hard′ej′ər), *n.* a painter of hard-edges.

hard|en (här′dən), *v.t.* **1** to make hard: *Frost hardened the water of the puddles into ice.* SYN: solidify. **2** to make capable of endurance. SYN: accustom. **3** *Figurative.* to make unfeeling or pitiless: *The miser hardened his heart against the pleas of the beggar.* **4** to make (a missile site or missile) practically safe from enemy aerial attack by placing underground. **5** to temper or make (metals and alloys, especially steel) hard by raising to a high temperature and then cooling in oil, water, or air. —*v.i.* **1** to become hard: *When the candy cooled, it hardened.* SYN: solidify. **2** to become capable of endurance: *When he returned from a summer at camp, he had hardened and become fit.* SYN: accustom. **3** *Figurative.* to become hard in feeling or emotion: *His sympathies had hardened in the furnace of his early struggles.* **4** to become higher; rise: *Industrial shares were hardening at the close* (New York Times).

harden off, to inure (plants) to cold by gradually reducing the temperature of a hotbed or by increasing the time of exposure to wind and sunlight. —**hard′en|a|ble,** *adj.* —**hard′en|er,** *n.*

hard|ened (har′dənd), *adj.* **1** made hard or hardy; indurated. **2** *Figurative.* made unfeeling or callous; hard-hearted. SYN: inured, obdurate.

hard|en|ing (här′də ning), *n.* something that hardens, such as chromium or vanadium used as an alloy to harden steel.

hardening of the arteries, = arteriosclerosis.

hard-eyed (härd′īd′), *adj.* ruthlessly determined; coldly resolute: *the policemen's union, looked on the dark side, describing the attacks as "part of a coldly logical, hard-eyed, revolutionary strategy"* (New Yorker).

hard-face (härd′fās′), *v.t.,* **-faced, -fac|ing.** to apply a treatment or coating to (a metallic surface) to make it harder or more wear-resistant.

hard-fa|vored (härd′fā′vərd), *adj.* having a hard or unpleasing appearance or look. —**hard′-fa′vored|ness,** *n.*

hard-fea|tured (härd′fē′chərd), *adj.* having harsh or coarse features: *hard-featured women, weather-beaten brown* (John Masefield). —**hard′-fea′tured|ness,** *n.*

hard-fist|ed (härd′fis′tid), *adj.* stingy; niggardly. —**hard′-fist′ed|ness,** *n.*

hard goods, durable merchandise, especially not consumed by the purchaser, such as machinery, aircraft, furniture, appliances, or automobiles; durable goods.

hard|hack (härd′hak′), *n. U.S.* a low shrub of the rose family, common in New England, having dense terminal clusters of small, pink, purple, or white flowers, woolly leaves and branches, and an astringent root; steeplebush.

hard-hand|ed (härd′han′did), *adj.* **1** having hands hardened from manual labor. **2** *Figurative.* ruling with a firm or strong hand; severe.

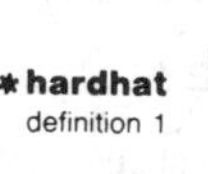

★hardhat
definition 1

★hard|hat (härd′hat′), *n.,* or **hard hat, 1** a rigid hat or helmet worn especially by construction workers as protection against falling objects. **2** *U.S.* a construction worker. **3** *U.S.,* an outspoken conservative or reactionary, especially one who believes in suppressing opposing opinions. **4** a bowler or derby.

hard|hat|tism (härd′hat′iz əm), *n. U.S.* the beliefs and practices of hardhats; militant conservatism or reactionary opposition to opposing opinions.

hard|head (härd′hed′), *n.* **1** a person who is not easily moved by sentiment; shrewd, practical person. **2** any one of various fishes, such as the gurnard and menhaden. **3** any one of various tough sponges, important commercially.

hard-head|ed (härd′hed′id), *adj.* **1** not easily excited or deceived; practical; shrewd: *a good hard-headed businessman.* **2** stubborn; obstinate: *He is very hard-headed and will not accept new ideas easily.* —**hard′-head′ed|ly,** *adv.* —**hard′-head′ed|ness,** *n.*

hard-heart|ed (härd′här′tid), *adj.* without pity; cruel; unfeeling: *a hard-hearted man who was cruel to most animals.* SYN: merciless. —**hard′-heart′ed|ly,** *adv.* —**hard′-heart′ed|ness,** *n.*

hard-hit (härd′hit′), *adj.* severely stricken by misfortune, grief, or disaster.

hard-hit|ting (härd′hit′ing), *adj. Informal.* striking or capable of striking with powerful impact; forceful; vigorous; aggressive; powerful.

har|di|hood (här′dē hůd), *n.* **1** boldness; daring: *With dauntless hardihood, And brandish'd blade, rush on him* (Milton). SYN: pluck. **2** audacity; effrontery. SYN: impudence. **3** sturdiness or robustness of body.

har|di|ly (här′də lē), *adv.* in a hardy manner; with hardihood; boldly; courageously.

har|di|ment (här′dē mənt), *n.* **1** *Archaic.* boldness; courage; daring; hardihood: *Vanguard of liberty, ye men of Kent . . . Now is the time to prove your hardiment!* (Wordsworth). **2** *Obsolete.* a bold exploit. [< Old French *hardiment* < *hardi* hardy]

har|di|ness (här′dē nis), *n.* **1** endurance; strength: *We all respect the hardiness of the pioneers.* **2** = hardihood.

hard labor, heavy work imposed on certain criminals in addition to imprisonment.

hard-land (härd′land′), *v.t., v.i.* to crashland a spacecraft, instruments, or other apparatus, on a body in outer space: *. . . to hard-land a well-padded seismograph for detecting Moon tremors* (New Scientist). —**hard′-land′er,** *n.*

hard landing, the landing of a spacecraft, instruments, or other apparatus, on a body in outer space, without first reducing speed by firing retrorockets; crash landing.

hard lens, a contact lens made of firm plastic that adheres to the eye by suction: *Hard lenses are advisable for those with severe astigmatism or cataracts* (Alexandra Penney).

hard line, firm or rigid adherence to an attitude or policy, especially in politics: *French diplomacy encouraged the Biafrans to adopt a hard line and refuse a compromise* (C. L. Sulzberger).

hard-line (härd′līn′), *adj.* favoring firm action or rigid adherence to a policy; inflexible; uncompromising: *hard-line feminism* (Harper's).

hard-lin|er (härd′lī′nər), *n.* a person who advocates taking an uncompromising attitude: *The mild wording of the communiqué . . . was attributed . . . to Egyptian reluctance to risk a split between Arab "moderates" and "hard-liners"* (New York Times).

hard-lin|ing (härd′līn′ing), *adj.* taking a hard line.

hard|ly (härd′lē), *adv.* **1** only just; barely: *We hardly had time to eat breakfast.* **2** not quite: *His story is hardly true. He is hardly strong enough to lift that trunk.* **3** probably not: *They will hardly come in all this rain.* **4** with trouble or effort: *a hardly fought game, money hardly earned.* **5** in a hard manner; harshly; severely: *to deal hardly with a person.*

—*Syn.* **1 Hardly, barely, scarcely** mean only just, or almost not, what is named or stated. **Hardly** means near or close to the minimum limit, with little to spare: *I had hardly reached there when it began to rain.* **Barely** means just enough, with nothing to spare: *He eats barely enough.* **Scarcely** means almost not at all, not quite enough: *He has scarcely anything to eat.*

▶**hardly. a** a double negative involving *hardly* (or *scarcely*) occurs with such frequency in speech that it often goes unnoticed but is frequently not regarded as standard in writing: *He couldn't hardly run* (for *could hardly*). *He won hardly nothing* (for *hardly anything*). *He won without hardly trying* (for *without really trying*). **b** English has two approximately equivalent idioms exemplified by *Hardly* (*scarcely*) *had he mailed the letter when he began to regret writing it* and *No sooner had he mailed the letter than he began to regret writing it.* If the *than* of the second construction replaces the *when* of the first, the substitution is not regarded as standard.

hard maple, *U.S.* the sugar maple.

hard money, 1 currency exchangeable for gold or other precious metal. **2** money maintained at a fixed value in foreign exchange as by means of balance of payments or shipments of gold. **3** money under a banking policy of restricted credit, high interest rates, and other limitations on speculative investment or unnecessary spending. —**hard′-mon′ey,** *adj.*

hard-mouthed (härd′mouᴛʜd′, -moutht′), *adj.* **1** having a hard mouth; not easily controlled by the bit or rein: *a hard-mouthed horse.* **2** *Figurative.* self-willed; obstinate.

hard|ness (härd′nis), *n.* **1** the quality or condition of being hard. **2** the quality of water holding mineral salts in solution that make it unfit for washing purposes. **3** the comparative capacity of one mineral to scratch, or be scratched by, another mineral. The degree of hardness of a mineral is expressed with reference to the Mohs scale, ranging from 1 (talc) to 10 (diamond). **4** the ability of a missile site or missile to withstand enemy aerial attack.

hard-nosed (härd′nōzd′), *adj. Informal.* stubborn; dogged: *I was on fine terms with the . . . union delegate, when he saw I didn't intend to be hard-nosed and difficult about the company's interests* (Saul Bellow).

hard pad, a severe viral disease of dogs similar to distemper and characterized by a hardening of the skin of the pads.

hard palate, the bony front part of the roof of the mouth.

hard|pan (härd′pan′), *n.* **1** a hard, firm layer of subsoil through which roots cannot grow; pan. It is made up of clayey, sandy, or gravelly detritus. **2** hard, unbroken ground. **3** *Figurative.* a solid foundation; hard, underlying reality; bedrock: *to get down to hardpan.* **4** *Figurative.* the lowest level: *Prices have reached hardpan.*

hard-paste porcelain (härd′pāst′), a translucent, glasslike porcelain requiring firing at a high temperature, made from kaolin and petuntse.

hard-pressed (härd′prest′), *adj.* experiencing difficulties or hardship; under pressure; troubled; harassed: *a hard-pressed company.*

hard rays, radiation of relatively short wave length and power, such as hard X rays.

hard rock, hard-driving rock'n'roll, played with a regular beat, often on electronically amplified instruments.

hard-rock (härd′rok′), *n., adj.* —*n.* dense rock that must be drilled and blasted to be removed.
—*adj.* skilled in or employed at the removal of hard-rock: *a hard-rock miner.*

hard rubber, a hard, black substance made by heating rubber with a large quantity of sulfur; ebonite; vulcanite.

hard sauce, butter and sugar, usually powdered, creamed together and flavored, used as a sauce for fruit cakes, steamed puddings, and the like.

hard|scape (härd′skāp), *n.* the man-made objects in a designed landscape, such as paving stones, benches, and fountains: *Landscape architect Ben Gary says* [*about*] *the material of hardscape: "It's wonderful stuff—you don't have to cut or water it"* (Mike Kenney).

hard science, any one of the natural or physical sciences, such as physics, chemistry, biology, geology, and astronomy.

hard scientist, a person trained or skilled in one of the hard sciences.

hard|scrab|ble (härd′skrab′əl), *adj. U.S.* marked by poverty and hardship; very poor: *a hardscrabble farm.*

hard sell, *Informal.* **1** forceful and aggressive sales techniques; high-pressure salesmanship: *A company chairman . . . startled a conference of big businessmen with a warning against overusing the hard sell* (Observer). **2** a difficult task of persuasion.

hard-sell (härd′sel′), *v.,* **-sold, -sell|ing,** *adj. Informal.* —*v.t.* to sell with forceful and aggressive techniques.
—*adj.* forceful and aggressive. —**hard′-sell′er,** *n.*

hard-set (härd′set′), *adj.* **1** in a hard or difficult position; beset by difficulty or trouble: *It's hard-set I am to know what would be right* (John M. Synge). **2** firmly or rigidly set. **3** determined; obstinate.

hard-shell (härd′shel′), *adj.* **1** having a hard shell: *hard-shell almond trees, hard-shell clamcatchers.* **2** *Informal, Figurative.* rigid and uncompromising, especially in religious orthodoxy; strict.

hard-shell clam, = quahog.

hard-shell or **hard-shelled crab,** any crab, especially the edible blue crab, having a hard shell between molting periods.

hard-shelled (härd′sheld′), *adj.* = hard-shell.

hard|ship (härd′ship), *n.* something hard to bear; hard condition of living: *Hunger, cold, and sickness were among the hardships of pioneer life.* SYN: trial, affliction, privation.

hard site, a missile-launching site built underground so as to be practically safe from enemy aerial attack.

hard-spun (härd′spun′), *adj.* tightly twisted in spinning: *hard-spun yarn.*

hard·stand (härd′stand′), *n.* hard-surfaced ground on which a vehicle or airplane is parked or equipment stored.

hard steel, steel containing a comparatively high percentage of carbon.

hard·stuff (härd′stuf′), *n. U.S. Slang.* hard drugs.

hard-sur·face (härd′sėr′fis), *v.t.*, **-faced, -fac·ing. 1** to render the surface of (something) hard or smooth: *to hard-surface a highway.* **2** = hard-face.

hard·tack (härd′tak′), *n.* a very hard, dry biscuit, eaten especially by sailors, and sometimes by soldiers; ship biscuit; pilot biscuit; sea biscuit; sea bread. Hardtack resists spoiling.

hard·top or **hard-top** (härd′top′), *n.* **1** an automobile with a rigid metal or plastic top but with window space comparable to that of a convertible. **2** an indoor motion-picture house, as contrasted with an outdoor drive-in.

hard·ware (härd′wãr′), *n.* **1** articles made from metal. Locks, hinges, nails, screws, knives, and tools are hardware. **2** military weapons or equipment such as tanks, guns, and airplanes. **3** any complete machine or component, such as one for a missile or an aircraft, actually manufactured, in contrast to its equivalent in the design stage. **4** the mechanical, electrical, or structural components of an electronic computer, teaching machine, or other automatic machine: *The basic computer consists of a standard box with wiring and power supplies . . . to which is added the right hardware and firmware for the particular job* (New Scientist). **5** the physical equipment or facilities of any complex system: *The Federal government . . . will provide only 50 per cent of the costs of "hardware"—that is, new correctional centers, crime laboratories and police academies* (New York Times).

hardware disease, a diseased condition of the abdominal organs in cattle, caused by ingesting metal objects and other indigestible matter.

hard wheat, wheat having a hard kernel, used especially for making macaroni, spaghetti, and bread. Durum wheat is a variety of hard wheat. Hard wheat has a high gluten content.

hard-wired (härd′wīrd′), *adj.* **1** wired directly to a computer. **2** *Figurative:* *The facial expressions of human beings really appear to be hard-wired . . . comparable to those found in the chimpanzee* (New York Times).

hard·wood (härd′wu̇d′), *n., adj.* —*n.* **1** any hard, compact wood. **2** any tree that has broad leaves or does not have needles. Oak, cherry, maple, ebony, and mahogany are hardwoods; pine and fir are softwoods. **3** the wood of such a tree.
—*adj.* **1** having such wood. **2** made of such wood: *a hardwood floor.*

hard-work·ing (härd′wėr′king), *adj.* working hard; showing steady effort: *a hard-working businessman.* SYN: diligent, industrious. —**hard′-work′ing·ly**, *adv.*

hard X ray, a highly penetrating X ray, produced by the higher voltages.

har·dy¹ (här′dē), *adj.*, **-di·er, -di·est**, *n., pl.* **-dies.** —*adj.* **1** able to bear hard treatment; strong; robust: *hardy frontier settlers.* SYN: hale, hearty, vigorous. **2** able to withstand the cold of winter in the open air: *Cold weather does not kill hardy plants.* **3** bold; daring: *a hardy knight.* SYN: courageous, intrepid. **4** too bold; rash: *Be not so hardy, scullion, as to slay One nobler than thyself* (Tennyson). **5** *Obsolete.* strong; enduring; tough.
—*n.* **1** a strong or robust person: *Most of the hardies operating the rides were boys who were adventuring, or sturdy knock-about hoboes* (Harper's). **2** a plant able to withstand the cold of winter in the open air.
[< Old French *hardi,* past participle of *hardir* to harden < a Germanic word]

har·dy² (här′dē), *n., pl.* **-dies.** a chisel or fuller with a square shank for insertion into a square hole (hardy hole) in a blacksmith's anvil. [probably < *hard*]

Har·dy·esque (här′dē esk′), *adj.* of or having to do with Thomas Hardy, 1840-1928, English novelist and poet, or his writings: *Cash saw a Hardyesque pathos in his early life* (Harper's).

hardy hole, a square hole in a blacksmith's anvil in which to insert a hardy.

Har·dy-Wein·berg (här′dē wīn′bėrg), *adj. Genetics.* of, having to do with, or derived from the principle that the relative frequency of genes and genotypes in a population remains constant as long as breeding is random and the environment stable from one generation to the next.
[< G.H. *Hardy,* an English mathematician, and W. *Weinberg,* a German biologist, who demonstrated this principle independently in 1908]

hare (hãr), *n., pl.* **hares** or (*collectively*) **hare**, *v.*, **hared, har·ing.** —*n.* **1** a gnawing mammal that has long ears, long hind legs, a short tail, a divided upper lip, and does not burrow. The hare is very much like a rabbit but larger. The jack rabbit is a hare; the cottontail is a rabbit. **2** one of the quarry in the game of hare and hounds.
—*v.i.* to move with great speed; run: *I seized my binoculars and hared off in pursuit* (Maclean's).
mad as a March hare, completely crazy: *. . . mad not as a March hare but as a mad dog* (Sir Thomas More).
start a hare, *British.* to start a controversy, especially as a diversionary tactic: *A flavour of rather crude political opportunism has marked* [*their*] *conduct. . . . They have been adept at scoring cheap points and starting hares* (Manchester Guardian Weekly).
[Old English *hara*] —**hare′like′**, *adj.*

Hare (hãr), *n.* the southern constellation Lepus.

hare and hounds, an outdoor sport in which one or more players, the hares, leaving a trail of bits of paper, attempt to utilize a few minutes' start to reach home, at some considerable distance, before their pursuers, the hounds, can catch them by following the trail.

hare·bell (hãr′bel′), *n.* a slender plant with drooping, blue, bell-shaped flowers; hairbell. It is a low herb belonging to the bellflower family. It is also called the bluebell of Scotland.

hare·brain (hãr′brān′), *adj.* = harebrained.

hare·brained (hãr′brānd′), *adj.* giddy, heedless, or reckless: *a harebrained scheme.*

Ha·re Krish·na (hä′rə krish′nə), **1** a member of the International Society for Krishna Consciousness, a sect founded in New York City in 1966 and practicing a form of Hinduism devoted to the god Krishna. **2** the title of a mantra, meaning "Lord Krishna," chanted by this sect.

hare·lip (hãr′lip′), *n.* **1** a deformity existing from birth in which parts of the upper lip fail to grow together. It resembles the lip of a hare. **2** a lip, usually the upper one, thus deformed.

hare·lipped (hãr′lipt′), *adj.* having a harelip.

har·em (hãr′əm), *n.* **1** the part of a Moslem house where the women live; seraglio. **2** its occupants; wives, female relatives, and female servants of a Moslem household. **3** a Moslem sacred place, prohibited to any but the faithful, such as Mecca and Medina, the holy cities. **4** the group of female animals controlled by one male. [< Arabic *harīm* women's quarters; (literally) something forbidden]

✱**harem pants**, loose and billowy informal trousers for women, usually in bright colors and drawn tight with a band at the ankle.

✱**harem pants**

hare's-tail (hãrz′tāl′), *n.* a species of cotton grass bearing a white cottonlike tuft.

hare's-tail grass, a species of grass with dense, oblong, woolly pannicles, common in the Mediterranean region and the Canary Islands.

Hare system, a system of proportional representation in which the voter numbers the candidates in order of choice, with a minimum number of votes needed for election, the votes above the quota being distributed among the candidates chosen second by the voters. [< Thomas *Hare,* 1806-1891, an English lawyer]

hare·wood (hãr′wu̇d′), *n.* stained sycamore wood, used by cabinetmakers.

Har·grave kite (här′grāv), = box kite. [< Lawrence *Hargrave,* of Australia, who invented it]

har·i·cot¹ (har′ə kō), *n.* **1** the common kidney bean or string bean. **2** the edible seed or green pod of one of these. [< French *haricot*]

har·i·cot² (har′ə kō), *n.* a ragout of meat and vegetables. [< French *haricot* < Middle French *herocoq,* probably < Old French *harigoter* cut in pieces]

Har·i·jan (har′ə jan), *n.* (in India) a member of the Scheduled Caste; an untouchable: *Harijans have now got full equality in every way before the law* (Santha Rama Rau). [< Hindi *Harijan* (literally) Vishnu's creature, a name given by Gandhi]

har·i-kar·i (har′ē kar′ē, hä′rē kä′rē), *n.* = hara-kiri.

hark (härk), *v., n.* —*v.i.* to listen; hearken: *Hark! Hark! the lark at heaven's gate sings* (Shakespeare). —*v.t. Archaic.* to listen to; hear: *Hark the clock within* (Tennyson).
—*n.* a cry to the hounds in hunting.
hark back, **a** to go back; turn back; revert: *His ideas hark back twenty years.* **b** to call back; recall: *There is but one that harks me back* (Henry Taylor).
[Middle English *herkien;* origin uncertain]

har·ka (här′kə), *n.* a body of Moroccan irregular troops. [< Arabic *harka*]

hark·en (här′kən), *v.i., v.t.* = hearken.

Har·ki (år kē′), *n.* a member of a former local military unit that supplemented the French army in its colonies in North Africa. [< French *harki*]

harl¹ (härl), *n.* **1** a fiber of flax or hemp. **2** a barb or barbs of a feather, much used for anglers' flies; herl. [compare Low German *harl*]

harl² (härl), *v.t. Scottish.* to roughcast.
—*v.i. British.* to troll: *. . . those sedentary fishermen who enjoy harling from motor boats* (London Times). [Middle English *harlen* to drag]

Har·lan's hawk (här′lənz), a blackish, broad-winged hawk of western North America, having a white tail with a black band.

Har·lem·ite (här′lə mīt), *n.* a resident of Harlem, part of New York City where many blacks live.

✱**har·le·quin** (här′lə kin, -kwin), *n., adj.*
—*n.* **1** Often, **Harlequin.** a stock character in comedy and pantomime, the lover of Columbine. He is usually masked, wears a costume of varied colors, and carries a wooden sword. **2** a mischievous person; buffoon.
—*adj.* **1** varied in color; many-colored: *a harlequin pattern.* **2** burlesque; ludicrous.
[< French *Harlequin* < Old French, variant of *Herlequin* < Middle English *Herle King* King Herla (a mythical figure); modern meaning in French is from Italian *arlechino* < Old French *Harlequin*]

✱**harlequin**
definition 1

har·le·quin·ade (här′lə ki nād′, -kwi-), *n.* **1** a pantomime, or that part of a pantomime, in which the Harlequin and clown play the principal parts. **2** fantastic procedure; buffoonery. [< French *arlequinade* < *harlequin;* see etym. at **harlequin**]

harlequin bug, a red-and-black stinkbug that damages cabbage; cabbage bug.

harlequin Dane, a Great Dane having a black and white coat.

harlequin duck, a northern sea duck, with bright patches of color on its plumage.

har·le·quin·esque (här′lə kwi nesk′, -ki-), *adj.* in the style or manner of a harlequin; harlequinlike.

harlequin snake, = coral snake.

har·lot (här′lət), *n., adj.* —*n.* **1** = prostitute. **2** *Obsolete.* **a** a rogue or knave. **b** a buffoon.
—*adj.* of or having to do with a harlot.
[< Old French *harlot* vagabond, tramp]

har·lot·ry (här′lə trē), *n., pl.* **-ries. 1** = prostitution. **2** = harlot.

harm (härm), *n., v.* —*n.* **1** something that causes pain or loss; injury; hurt; damage: *He slipped and fell down but suffered no harm.* **2** an evil; wrong: *It was an accident; she meant no harm.*
—*v.t.* to do harm to; damage; injure or hurt: *Do not pick or harm the flowers in the park. An unkind and untrue story harmed his reputation.*
[Old English *hearm*]
—*Syn. v.t.* **Harm, damage** mean to hurt or injure a person or thing. **Harm** means causing pain, loss, or suffering of any kind: *Unfounded and malicious rumors harmed his career.* **Damage** suggests lessening the value, usefulness, or appearance of a person or thing: *The fire damaged the furniture.*

har·ma·line (här′mə lēn), *n.* a stimulant and hallucinogenic drug obtained from the seeds of an African plant or from the bark of several malpighiaceous climbing plants. [< New Latin (Peganum) *harmala* the name of the African plant]

har·mat·tan (här′mə tan′), *n.* a very dry, dust-laden wind over the Sahara that blows west or southwest to the African coast. [apparently < a native name in West Africa]

harm·er (här′mər), *n.* a person or thing that harms.

Pronunciation Key: hat, āge, cãre, fär; let, ēqual, tėrm; it, īce; hot, ōpen, ôrder; oil, out; cup, pu̇t, rüle; child; long; thin; ᴛʜen; zh, measure; ə represents **a** in about, **e** in taken, **i** in pencil, **o** in lemon, **u** in circus.

harm|ful (härm′fəl), *adj.* causing harm; injurious; hurtful: *harmful slander. Irrationally held truths may be more harmful than reasoned errors* (T. H. Huxley). SYN: detrimental, deleterious, pernicious. —**harm′ful|ly**, *adv.* —**harm′ful|ness**, *n.*

har|mine (här′mēn), *n.* a drug similar to harmaline and obtained from the same source. *Formula:* $C_{13}H_{12}N_2O$

harm|less (härm′lis), *adj.* **1** causing no harm; not harmful; that would not harm anyone or anything: *harmless gossip, harmless as doves.* SYN: inoffensive, innocuous. **2** free from liability or loss, as by an agreement. **3** free from harm or injury; unharmed. —**harm′less|ly**, *adv.* —**harm′less|ness**, *n.*

har|mo|lod|ic (här′mə lod′ik), *adj., n.* —*adj.* combining harmonies, melodies, and rhythms in new, unconventional ways: *The "harmolodic" system ... broke down traditional harmonies and rhythms* (New York Times). —*n.* a harmolodic style or composition. [< *harmo*(ny) + (me)*lodic*]

Har|mo|ni|a (här mō′nē ə), *n. Greek Legend.* the daughter of Ares and Aphrodite, who was presented, on marrying Cadmus, with a robe and necklace fatal to all their successive possessors. [< Greek *Harmoniā* < *harmoniā* harmony]

har|mon|ic (här mon′ik), *adj., n.* —*adj.* **1** *Music.* **a** having to do with harmony, as distinguished from melody and rhythm. **b** having to do with fainter and higher tones heard along with the main tones. **c** musical. **d** relating to harmonics on stringed instruments. **2** in harmony; concordant; consonant. **3** *Physics.* of or designating any of the frequencies making up a wave or alternating current, that are integral multiples of the fundamental frequency. **4** *Mathematics.* having relations similar in some way to those of musical concords: *1, ½, ⅓, ¼, and so on, are in harmonic progression.*
—*n.* **1** *Music.* **a** a fainter and higher tone heard along with the main tone; overtone. **b** a flutelike tone produced on a stringed instrument by pressing the string lightly at a nodal point; flageolet. **2** *Physics.* a harmonic frequency.
[< Latin *harmonicus* < Greek *harmonikós* harmonic, musical < *harmoniā*; see etym. under **harmony**]

***har|mon|i|ca** (här mon′ə kə), *n.* **1** a small musical instrument with metal reeds, played by exhaling and inhaling through a set of openings; mouth organ. **2a** a kind of glockenspiel having glass plates, metal bars, or the like. **b** a musical instrument consisting of a set of glasses played by the application of the finger to the moistened rims; glass harmonica. [American English (coined by Benjamin Franklin) < Latin *harmonica*, feminine of *harmonicus*; see etym. under **harmonic**]

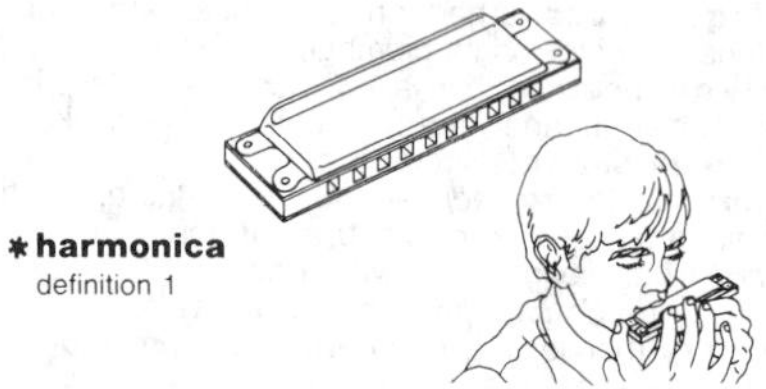

***harmonica**
definition 1

har|mon|i|cal (här mon′ə kəl), *adj.* = harmonic. —**har|mon′i|cal|ly**, *adv.*

harmonic analysis, **1** = Fourier analysis. **2** the study of Fourier series.

harmonic interval, the difference of pitch between two notes or tones that are played simultaneously.

harmonic mean, *Mathematics.* the reciprocal of the arithmetic mean of the reciprocals of a series of values.

harmonic minor, *Music.* a version of the minor scale having a semitone below the tonic (raised seventh step or leading tone). The interval between the sixth and seventh steps is one and a half steps. See picture under **minor scale**.

harmonic motion, *Physics.* a vibration, as of a violin string, in which the acceleration is directly proportional to but directed away from the displacement of the body from the mean position.

harmonic progression, *Mathematics.* a series of numbers whose reciprocals form an arithmetical progression. *Example:* ½, ¼, ⅙, ⅛.

har|mon|ics (här mon′iks), *n.* **1** the science of musical sounds. **2** the complete set of sounds produced by a musical note.

harmonic series, **1** = overtone series. **2** *Mathematics.* **a** = harmonic progression. **b** an infinite series of terms in harmonic progression.

harmonic tone, = overtone.

har|mo|ni|ous (här mō′nē əs), *adj.* **1** agreeing in feelings, ideas, or actions; getting along well together: *The children played together in a harmonious group.* SYN: peaceable, amicable, consentient, unanimous. **2** arranged so that the parts are orderly or pleasing; going well together: *A beautiful picture has harmonious colors.* SYN: congruous, consonant, consistent, concordant. **3** sweet-sounding; musical: *the harmonious sounds of a choir singing Christmas carols.* SYN: melodious. —**har|mo′ni|ous|ly**, *adv.* —**har|mo′ni|ous|ness**, *n.*

har|mo|nist (här′mə nist), *n.* **1** an expert in musical harmony; musician; composer. **2** a person who harmonizes the Gospels or different passages in the Bible. **3** a person who reduces something to harmony, agreement, or concord; harmonizer.

har|mo|nis|tic (här′mə nis′tik), *adj.* **1** having to do with the collation and harmonizing of parallel passages, especially of the Gospels. **2** *Obsolete.* having to do with musical harmony.

har|mo|nis|ti|cal|ly (här′mə nis′tə klē), *adv.* **1** in the manner of a harmonist. **2** in relation to a harmonization of writings.

Har|mo|nists (här′mə nists), *n.pl.* a religious group founded by George Rapp in Germany and brought by him to Pennsylvania in 1804.

har|mo|ni|um (här mō′nē əm), *n.* a reed organ played by means of a keyboard and powered by bellows and treadles. [< French *harmonium* < *harmonie;* see etym. under **harmony**]

har|mo|nize (här′mə nīz), *v.,* **-nized, -niz|ing.** —*v.t.* **1** to bring into harmony, agreement, or accord; make harmonious: *He harmonized the two plans by using parts from each one.* **2** to add tones to (a melody) to make chords: *The musicians harmonized the old song for part singing.* —*v.i.* **1** to be in harmony or agreement: *The colors in the room harmonized to give a pleasing effect.* **2** to sing or play in harmony. —**har′mo|ni|za′tion**, *n.* —**har′mo|niz′er**, *n.*

har|mon|o|gram (här mon′ə gram), *n.* a figure or curve traced by a harmonograph.

har|mon|o|graph (här mon′ə graf, -gräf), *n.* an instrument for tracing curves representing sonorous vibrations, consisting of two pendulums that vibrate at right angles to each other.

har|mo|ny (här′mə nē), *n., pl.* **-nies.** **1** agreement of feeling, ideas, or actions; getting along well together: *There was perfect harmony between the two brothers.* SYN: unity, friendship. **2** an orderly or pleasing arrangement of parts; quality or condition of going well together: *Her plans are in harmony with mine. In a beautiful landscape there is harmony of the different colors.* SYN: congruity. **3a** the sounding together of two or more musical tones in a chord. **b** the structure of a piece of music in relation to the chords of which it consists, as distinguished from melody and rhythm. **c** a study of chords in music and of relating them to successive chords. **4** a sweet or musical sound; music: *As the sun rose the harmony of the birds floated in my window.* **5** a grouping of passages on the same subject from different stories or accounts, showing their points of agreement: *a harmony of the Gospels.* [< Old French *harmonie*, learned borrowing from Latin *harmonia* < Greek *harmoniā* concord (of sounds), agreement; a joining < *harmós* joint, fastening]

har|most (här′most), *n.* (in ancient Greece) a military governor of a colony or province. [< Greek *harmostês* < *harmózein* to settle]

har|mo|tome (här′mə tōm), *n. Mineralogy.* a hydrous silicate of aluminum, barium, and potassium, occurring in brittle, vitreous, usually white form. [< French *harmotome* < Greek *harmós* joint + *-tomos* a cutting]

***har|ness** (här′nis), *n., v.* —*n.* **1** the leather straps, bands, and other pieces for a horse or other draft animal which connect it to a carriage, wagon, or plow, or are used in riding. Reins, collar, and bridle are parts of a horse's harness. **2** any similar arrangement of straps and bands, such as: **a** a combination of straps by which a parachute is attached to a person. **b** a combination of straps attached to an infant or young child to prevent his falling out of a crib or carriage or to control him in walking. **3** the heddles and connected parts in a loom, by which the sets of warp threads are shifted alternately. **4** the mechanism by which a large bell is suspended and rung. **5** an assembly of conducting wires in the service module of a spacecraft, held together by adhesive-coated strings, molded rubber, or plastic tubing. **6** *Archaic.* armor for a knight, warrior, or horse: *Arm, arm, and out! ... At least we'll die with harness on our back* (Shakespeare).
—*v.t.* **1** to put harness on: *Harness that horse.* **2** to use or control so as to produce power or some desired effect. Water in a stream is harnessed by building a dam and putting in turbines for the water to turn. **3** *Figurative.* to control; curb; restrain: *Karl Marx ... had tried to harness the primitive German Will* (Edmund Wilson). *Efforts were continued to harness science to education* (Leonard R. Buckley). **4** *Archaic.* to put armor on: *Harness yourselves for the war* (John Bunyan).
in harness, in or at one's regular work: *I got back in harness after my vacation.*
[Middle English *harneis* tackle, gear < Old French] —**har′ness|er**, *n.*

***harness**
definitions 1, 2a, 2b

parts of a horse's harness:

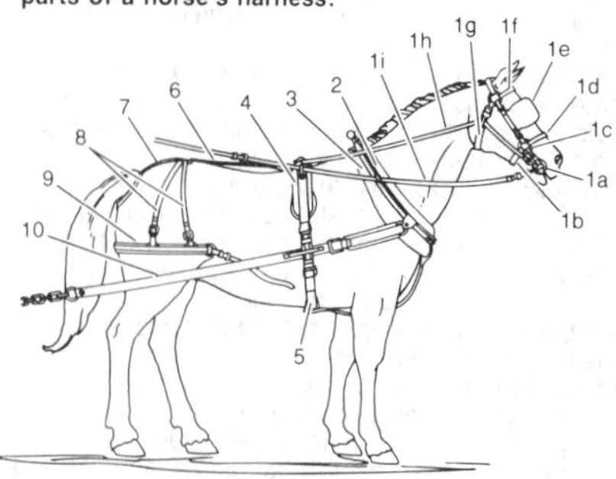

1. bridle	2. hame
1a. bit	3. collar
1b. chin strap	4. saddle
1c. cheek strap	5. girth
1d. noseband	6. backstrap
1e. blinder	7. crupper
1f. browband	8. hip straps
1g. throatlatch	9. breeching
1h. checkrein	10. trace or tug
1i. reins	

definition 2a

definition 2b

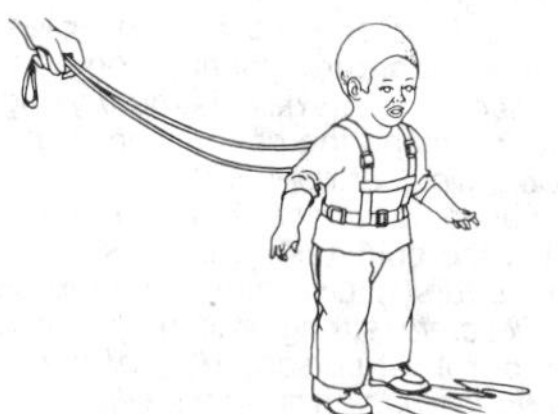

har|nessed (här′nist), *adj.* **1** equipped with or being in harness. **2** marked with streaks of color, as if wearing a harness.

harnessed antelope, any of a group of antelopes marked with streaks of color; guib.

harness hitch, a knot used especially in securing a pole, hook, or the like.

harness horse, **1** a horse used in harness racing. **2** a horse used to do farm work or to pull coaches, wagons, or artillery.

harness maker, person who makes harnesses.

harness race, a trotting or pacing race in which horses pull light sulkies and their drivers.

harness racing, the sport of racing horses harnessed to light sulkies; sulky racing. The race may be in a trotting or pacing style.

***harp** (härp), *n., v.* —*n.* **1** a large, stringed musical instrument played by plucking the strings with the fingers. The strings of a harp are set in a triangular frame. See picture above on opposite page. **2** *Scottish.* any one of various mechanical contrivances, such as a screen or sieve used in sifting and cleansing grain from weed seeds.
—*v.t.* **1** to play (music) on a harp. **2** to bring or put by playing on a harp: *to harp one to sleep.*

3 *Archaic.* to give voice to; guess: *Thou hast harp'd my fear aright* (Shakespeare).
—*v.i.* **1** to play the harp. **2** to make a sound like that of the harp.
harp on (or **upon**), to talk about very much or too much: *The Socialists could not deny the prosperity but harped on the high cost of living* (New York Times).
[Old English *hearpe*] —**harp′er**, *n.* —**harp′like′**, *adj.*

★harp definition 1

Harp (härp), *n.* the northern constellation Lyra.
harp|ings (här′pingz), *n.pl. Nautical.* the heavy planks of the hull of a ship near the bow. [perhaps < *harp*]
harp|ins (har′pinz), *n.pl. Nautical.* = harpings.
harp|ist (här′pist), *n.* a person who plays the harp; harper.
★har|poon (här pün′), *n., v.* —*n.* a barbed spear with a rope tied to it. It is used for catching whales and other sea animals. It is either thrown by the hand or fired from a gun.
—*v.t.* to strike, catch, or kill with a harpoon.
[< Middle French *harpon* < *harper* to grip, perhaps < a Germanic word] —**har|poon′er**, *n.*

★harpoon
★harpoon gun

har|poon|eer (här′pü nēr′), *n.* = harpooner.
★harpoon gun, a gun for shooting a harpoon, used especially in whaling.
harp seal, = saddleback seal.
★harp|si|chord (härp′sə kôrd), *n.* a stringed musical instrument like a piano, used especially from about 1550 to 1750 and again played extensively at present. It has a weak and tinkling sound because the strings are plucked by leather or quill points instead of being struck by hammers. [alteration of obsolete French *harpechorde* < *harpe* (see etym. under **harp**) + *chorde* string of a musical instrument] —**harp′si|chord′ist**, *n.*

★harpsichord

Har|py (här′pē), *n., pl.* **-pies**. *Greek and Roman Mythology.* any one of various filthy, greedy monsters, part woman and part bird. The Harpies served as ministers of divine vengeance, seizing the souls of the dead, and defiling everything they touched. [< Latin *harpȳia* < Greek *Hárpȳia*, probably related to *eréptesthai* feed on, with initial *ha-* after *harpázein* to snatch]
har|py (här′pē), *n., pl.* **-pies**. **1** a cruel, greedy person; person who preys upon others: *Those harpies, . . . for the mere sake of filthy lucre, were resolved to deliver me over into the hands of my father* (Washington Irving). **2** = harpy eagle. [< *Harpy*]
harpy eagle, a large, powerful eagle of South America and Central America, with a crested head and a long, fan-shaped tail.
har|que|bus or **har|que|buse** (här′kwə bəs), *n., pl.* **-bus|es**. an old form of portable gun, used before muskets were invented. It was provided at first with a matchlock, afterwards with a wheel lock. Also, **arquebus**. [< Middle French *harquebuse* < Italian *archibuso*, earlier *arcubuso* < Middle Dutch *hakebus* (literally) hook gun]
har|que|bus|ier (här′kwə bə sir′), *n.* a soldier armed with a harquebus.
har|que|buss (här′kwə bəs), *n., pl.* **-buss|es**. = harquebus.
har|ri|dan (har′ə dən), *n.* a bad-tempered, disreputable old woman. SYN: hag. [probably alteration of French *haridelle* a worn-out horse, perhaps < a Germanic word]
har|ri|er[1] (har′ē ər), *n.* **1** any one of a breed of hounds, very similar to the English foxhound but smaller, used to hunt hares. **2** a member of a hare and hounds team. **3** a cross-country runner. [apparently < *hare* + *-ier*]
har|ri|er[2] (har′ē ər), *n.* **1** a person who harries. **2** any one of a genus of slender hawks that feed on small animals, such as the hen harrier, marsh harrier, or marsh hawk. [< *harry* + *-er*[1]]
Har|ris poll (har′is), *U.S.* a poll of public opinion developed by Louis Harris, born 1921, an American journalist and public opinion analyst: *The factor of heavy Republican cross-over voting in the Wisconsin Democratic contest . . . is not reflected in Harris polls, since only Democratic and independent voters are tabulated* (Time).
Har|ris's hawk (har′ə siz), a brownish-black, broad-winged hawk with chestnut thighs and white tail, found in the southwestern United States, Central America, and South America. [< Edward *Harris*, an American naturalist of the 1800's]
Harris's sparrow, a large North American sparrow with a black crown, face, and throat that nests near Hudson Bay.
Harris tweed, **1** an especially fine quality of handwoven tweed cloth originating on the island of Harris and authentically woven only in the Hebrides. **2 Harris Tweed**, a trademark for this cloth.
Har|ro|vi|an (ha rō′vē ən), *adj., n.* —*adj.* of or having to do with Harrow, an English school for boys.
—*n.* a student or graduate of Harrow: *All the correspondents agreed that the King was conducting himself well—like a good Harrovian, the British said* (New Yorker).
har|row[1] (har′ō), *n., v.* —*n.* a heavy frame with iron teeth or upright disks. Harrows are used by farmers to break up plowed ground into finer pieces or to cover seed with earth. *The toad beneath the harrow knows Exactly where each tooth-point goes* (Rudyard Kipling).
—*v.t.* **1** to draw a harrow over (land): *to harrow a field after planting.* **2** to hurt; wound: *Thorns harrowed the flanks of the horse.* SYN: lacerate. **3** *Figurative.* to arouse uncomfortable feelings in; distress; torment: *He harrowed us with a tale of ghosts. He was harrowed with grief and anxiety when he saw that his house was on fire.* SYN: vex.
—*v.i.* (of land) to be gone over with a harrow.
[Middle English *harwe*. Compare Old Icelandic *herfi*.] —**har′row|er**, *n.*
har|row[2] (har′ō), *v.t. Archaic.* to harry. [variant of *harry*]
Har|row (har′ō), *n.* an old and famous boarding school for boys in Harrow, England, a borough of London, founded in 1571.
har|row|ing (har′ō ing), *adj.* that harrows; very painful or distressing: *The shipwreck was a harrowing experience.*
har|rumph (hə rumf′), *v., n.* —*v.i.* to snort; clear one's throat: *One or two professorial alumni good-naturedly harrumphed* (Atlantic).
—*v.t.* to express or say along with clearings of the throat or snorts: *Mr. Churchill harrumphed agreement* (New York Times).
—*n.* a snort; clearing of the throat: *He worked up a presidential harrumph of notable resonance* (Saturday Evening Post). Also, **harumph**.
har|ry (har′ē), *v.,* **-ried, -ry|ing**, *n., pl.* **-ries**.
—*v.t.* **1** to raid and rob with violence; lay waste: *The pirates harried the towns along the coast, burning what they could not carry off.* SYN: sack, pillage, spoil, ravage, devastate, despoil, plunder. **2** to keep troubling; worry; torment: *Fear of losing his job harried the clerk.* SYN: goad, harass, persecute. **3** *Scottish.* to carry off, as in a raid.
—*v.i.* to make predatory raids.
—*n.* the act of harrying; worry; vexation.
[Old English *hergian* < *here* army]
harsh (härsh), *adj.* **1** unpleasantly rough to the touch: *a harsh towel, fruit with a harsh rind.* SYN: rugged. **2** unpleasantly rough to the taste; astringent: *a harsh flavor.* SYN: acrid, sour, sharp. **3** unpleasing to the eye: *harsh outlines, colors, or features, a harsh painting.* **4** disagreeably rough to the ear: *a harsh voice.* SYN: jarring, grating, rasping, discordant, strident, raucous, inharmonious. **5** without pity; cruel; unfeeling: *a harsh man.* SYN: unkind. **6** rugged; bleak; severe: *a harsh coast, a harsh climate.* **7** stern; grim; forbidding: *a harsh expression.* SYN: strict, rigorous. [earlier *harrish* bitter, astringent, Middle English *harsk*, perhaps < Scandinavian (compare Danish *harsk* rancid, rank)] —**harsh′ly**, *adv.* —**harsh′ness**, *n.*
harsh|en (här′shən), *v.t.* to make harsh. —*v.i.* to become harsh: *Her voice never weakened, never harshened* (Eudora Welty).
hart (härt), *n., pl.* **harts** or (*collectively*) **hart**. a male deer, especially the male European red deer after its fifth year; stag. [Old English *heorot*]
har|tal (här täl′), *n.* (in India) a complete suspension of work and business: *A hartal was observed throughout the capital to-day as a mark of respect for the dead satyagrahis and in protest against Portuguese violence* (London Times). [< Hindi *harāl* for *haṭtāl* < Sanskrit *haṭta* market + *tāla* a lock, bolt]
har|te|beest (här′tə bēst′, härt′bēst′), *n., pl.* **-beests** or (*collectively*) **-beest**. **1** either one of two kinds of large, swift African antelopes of the same genus, with ringed, curved horns bent backward at the tips. See picture under **antelope**. **2** any one of several related antelopes. [< Afrikaans *hartebeest* hart beast]
harts|horn (härts′hôrn′), *n.* **1a** the form of ammonia used as smelling salts; sal volatile. **b** spirits of hartshorn; ammonia dissolved in water. **2** the horn or antler of a hart, formerly much used as a source of ammonia. [Old English *heorotes horn* hart's horn]
ha|rumph (hə rumf′), *v.i., v.t., n.* = harrumph.
har|um-scar|um (hãr′əm skãr′əm), *adj., adv., n.* —*adj.* too hasty; reckless; rash: *A dissolute, harum-scarum fellow . . . always in debt* (Edward G. Bulwer-Lytton).
—*adv.* recklessly; rashly; heedlessly; wildly: *He rushed harum-scarum down the main street.*
—*n.* **1** a reckless person. **2** reckless action or behavior.
[apparently < earlier *hare* frighten + *scare*, perhaps + *'em*, short for *them*]
ha|rus|pex (hə rus′peks, har′ə speks), *n., pl.* **ha-rus|pi|ces** (hə rus′pə sēz, har′ə spə-). a member of a class of minor priests or soothsayers in ancient Rome who predicted the future by looking at the entrails of animals killed in sacrifice, and by observing lightning and other phenomena. [< Latin *haruspex* < *haru-* (perhaps entrails; origin uncertain) + *-spex* < *specere* inspect]
har|vest (här′vist), *n., v.* —*n.* **1** a reaping and gathering in of grain and other food crops: *A field of Ceres, ripe for harvest* (Milton). **2a** the time or season of the harvest, usually in the late summer or early autumn. **b** *Dialect.* autumn. **3** one season's yield of any natural product; crop: *The oyster harvest was small this year.* SYN: yield, produce, fruit. See syn. under **crop**. **4** *Figurative.* result; consequences: *He is reaping the harvest of his mistakes. She is reaping the harvest of her years of study.*
—*v.t.* **1** to gather in and bring home for use: *to harvest wheat.* **2** to gather the crop from: *And, side by side . . . Harvest the fields wherein they fought* (John Greenleaf Whittier). **3** *Figurative.* to win or undergo as a result or consequence. **4** to cull out periodically (inferior individuals) from various species of protected wildlife so as to prevent overcrowding and improve the breed.
—*v.i.* to gather in crops.
[Old English *hærfest*] —**har′vest|a|ble**, *adj.* —**har′vest|er**, *n.* —**har′vest|less**, *adj.*
harvest bug, **1** = harvest mite. **2** = harvest fly.
harvester ant, any ant that gathers grain and grass seeds to store them underground, especially a long-legged, red or black, stinging ant common in the southwestern United States.
harvest fish, = lafayette.
harvest fly, any one of certain cicadas, such as the dog-day cicada, noted for its sharp trill.
harvest home, **1** the end of harvesting. **2** a festival to celebrate the end of the harvest. **3** a harvest song.
har|vest|man (här′vist mən), *n., pl.* **-men**. **1** = daddy longlegs. **2** a man who harvests. SYN: reaper, harvester.
harvest mite, a tiny red mite common in late summer or autumn, that creeps into the skin pores and hair follicles of man and animals and causes rash and itching; chigger.
harvest moon, the full moon at harvesttime or nearest to the autumnal equinox, about September 23. In the Southern Hemisphere, the harvest moon occurs in March, at the vernal equinox.
harvest mouse, **1** a very small European field mouse that nests on the stalks of growing grain. **2** any one of a group of American mice with brown fur, long tails, and grooved front teeth.
har|vest|time (här′vist tīm′), *n.* the part of the year when a certain crop or most crops are harvested.

Pronunciation Key: hat, āge, cãre, fär; let, ēqual, tėrm; it, īce; hot, ōpen, ôrder; oil, out; cup, pu̇t, rüle; child; long; thin; ᴛʜen; zh, measure; ə represents a in about, e in taken, i in pencil, o in lemon, u in circus.

Har|vey|ize (här′vē īz), *v.t.* **-ized, -iz|ing.** *U.S.* to harden the surface of (steel or armor plate) by a process involving cementation and chilling. [< H. A. *Harvey,* 1824-1893, an American steelmaker, who patented the process + *-ize*]

Har|vey Smith (här′vē smith′), *British Slang.* a V-sign made with the palm of the hand inwards, regarded as a gesture of contempt. [< the name of a show jumper who popularized it]

has (haz; *unstressed* həz, əz), *v.* the third person singular present indicative of **have**: *Who has my book? He has been sick.*

has-been (haz′bin′), *n. Informal.* a person or thing whose best days are past: *He is dismissed as a has-been in his profession* (New Yorker).

ha|sen|pfef|fer (hä′zən fef′ər, -pfef′-), *n.* a stew of rabbit marinated in vinegar or wine. [< German *Hasenpfeffer* < *Hase* hare + *Pfeffer* pepper]

hash[1] (hash), *n., v.* **—*n.*** **1** a mixture of cooked meat, potatoes, and other vegetables, chopped into small pieces and fried or baked: *corned-beef hash.* **2** *Figurative.* a mixture that is a jumble or a mess; muddle: *The clumsy workman made such a hash of the job that it had to be done over.* **3** *Figurative.* any presentation of old material worked over. **4** *Scottish.* a stupid or silly person.
—*v.t.* **1** to chop into small pieces; make into a hash. **2** *Figurative.* to make a mess or muddle of.
hash out, *U.S. Informal.* to discuss or argue in detail: *More and more of the Federation's member unions are hashing out long-standing disputes* (Wall Street Journal).
hash over, *Informal.* to discuss or review; reminisce about: *hashing over the old days.*
settle one's hash, *Informal.* to subdue or silence one completely; put an end to one: *You've to settle yet Gibson's hash* (Robert Browning).
[< French *hacher* to hack, hatch[3], chop < *hache* ax, hatchet < Germanic (compare Old High German *happa* hooked knife)]

hash[2] (hash), *n. Informal.* **1** = hashish. **2** = marijuana.

hash|eesh (hash′ēsh), *n.* = hashish.

Hash|em|ite (hash′ə mīt), *adj., n.* **—*adj.*** of or having to do with the royal dynasty of the kingdom of Jordan and the former kingdom of Iraq.
—*n.* a member of this dynasty, claiming descent from Mohammed. Also, **Hashimite.**

hash|er (hash′ər), *n. U.S. Slang.* a waiter or waitress, especially in a hash house.

hash|head (hash′hed′), *n. Slang.* a person who is addicted to hashish or marijuana.

hash house, *U.S. Slang.* a cheap restaurant.

hash|ish (hash′ēsh), *n.* **1** the dried flowers, top leaves, and tender parts of Indian hemp prepared for use as a narcotic. In the Orient especially, hashish is smoked or chewed, or used in a drink, for its intoxicating effect. **2** any one of certain other preparations made from this plant. **3** = marijuana. Also, **hasheesh.** [< Arabic *hashīsh* powdered hemp]

hash mark, *U.S. Military Slang.* a service stripe.

hash marks, *U.S.* two rows of broken lines on a football field running parallel to the sidelines and crossing the yard lines.

hash oil or **hashish oil,** the active ingredient of marijuana and hashish; tetrahydrocannabinol: *Hash oil is hard to detect; it can be mixed with coffee or wine, and because it has no distinctive odor, it is often dabbed onto ordinary cigarettes and smoked in public with impunity* (Newsweek). [because of its resemblance to motor oil]

hash|sling|er (hash′sling′ər), *n. U.S. Slang.* a hasher.

hash-up (hash′up′), *n. British Slang.* any old material reworked to make it look new; a rehash: . . . *a style perilously close to certain Colour Supplement hash-ups and clearly aligned for Overground consumption* (London Times).

Ha|sid|ic (hə sid′ik), *adj.* of or having to do with the Hasidim or with Hasidism. Also, **Chassidic, Hassidic.**

Has|i|dim (has′i dim, hä′si-; ʜä sē′-), *n., pl.* of **Has|id** (has′id, hä′sid; ʜä sēd′). **1** the members of a Jewish sect founded in the 1700's in Poland. The Hasidim believe in mysticism and emphasize religious piety and devotion over formal learning. **2** the members of a Jewish sect founded near the time of Judas Maccabaeus in the 200's B.C., Also, **Chassidim.**
[< Hebrew *hasidim* pious ones]

Has|i|dism (has′i diz əm, hä′si-), *n.* the movement, philosophy, or rituals of the Hasidim.

has|let (has′lit, hās′-, häz′-), *n.* the heart, liver, and other entrails of a hog, sheep, or the like, used for food. [< Old French *hastelet* roast meat; (probably diminutive) < *haste* piece of roast meat, a spit, learned borrowing from Latin *hasta* spear, pike[1]]

Has|mo|ne|an (haz′mə nē′ən), *n., adj.* **—*n.*** a member of a Jewish dynasty or family to which the Maccabees belonged.
—*adj.* of or having to do with this dynasty.

has|n't (haz′ənt), has not.

hasp (hasp, häsp), *n., v.* **—*n.*** a clasp or fastening, for a door, window, trunk, or box, especially a hinged metal clasp that fits over a staple or into a hole and is fastened by a peg or padlock.
—*v.t.* to fasten with, or as if with, a hasp.
[Middle English *haspe,* alteration of Old English *hæpse*]

Has|sid|ic (hə sid′ik), *adj.* = Hasidic.

has|sle (has′əl), *n., v.,* **-sled, -sling.** *Informal.* **—*n.*** a struggle or contest: *The legal hassle over his deportation is likely to stretch out for years* (Newsweek).
—*v.i.* to struggle; tussle: *The Senate Rules Committee hassled behind closed doors with the controversial problem* (San Francisco Chronicle).
—*v.t.* to annoy persistently; harass: *He [Jesus Christ] wore long hair and a beard, and when they hassled him, he taught more love* (Time).
[American English, apparently < Southern United States dialectal *hassle* pant, breathe noisily]

has|sock (has′ək), *n.* **1** a thick cushion or a cushioned footstool to rest the feet on, sit on, or kneel on. **2** a tuft or bunch of coarse grass or sedge, such as is found on boggy ground; tussock. [Old English *hassuc* clump of grass, coarse grass]

hast (hast), *v. Archaic.* a second person singular present indicative of **have.** "Thou hast" means "you have."

has|ta lue|go (äs′tälwā′g ō), *Spanish.* **1** until we meet again soon. **2** (literally) until soon.

has|tate (has′tāt), *adj.* **1** spearlike, as weapons. **2** shaped like the head of a spear. **3** (of a leaf) triangular, with two spreading lobes at the base. [< Latin *hastātus* < *hasta* spear] **—has′tate|ly,** *adv.*

haste (hāst), *n., v.,* **hast|ed, hast|ing.** **—*n.*** **1** a trying to be quick; hurrying: *All his haste was of no use; he missed the bus. The king's business required haste* (I Samuel 21:8). **SYN:** celerity, swiftness, speed, expedition. See syn. under **hurry.** **2** quickness without thought or care; rashness: *Haste makes waste.* **SYN:** precipitancy, impetuosity. **3** the condition of being obliged to act quickly on account of having little time: *to be breathless with haste.*
—*v.t., v.i.* = hasten.
in haste, a in a hurry; quickly: *Bring the doctor in haste.* **b** without careful thought; rashly: *Replying in haste, he gave the wrong answer.*
make haste, to hurry; be quick: *to make haste to reply. Make haste or you will miss your train.*
[< Old French *haste* < a Germanic word] **—haste′less,** *adj.*

haste|ful (hāst′fəl), *adj.* full of haste; hurrying.

has|ten (hā′sən), *v.t.* **1** to cause to be quick; speed; hurry: *to hasten everyone off to bed.* **SYN:** press, urge. **2** to cause to go faster; accelerate: *to hasten a process. Sunshine and rest hastened his recovery from illness.* **SYN:** quicken, expedite. **—*v.i.*** to be quick; go fast: *She hastened to explain that she had not meant to be rude. I saw the . . . Good steadily hastening towards immortality* (Walt Whitman). **—has′ten|er,** *n.*

hast|i|ly (hās′tə lē), *adv.* **1** in a hasty manner; quickly. **2** rashly; precipitately: *She had married hastily,* and as hastily grown weary of her choice (James A. Froude). **3** in a quick-tempered way: *He said he was sorry for speaking so hastily.*

hast|i|ness (hās′tē nis), *n.* **1** quickness of motion; promptitude. **2** rashness. **3** quick temper.

hast|y (hās′tē), *adj.,* **hast|i|er, hast|i|est.** **1** hurried; quick; done or made in a hurry: *a hasty visit. He gave his watch a hasty glance and ran for the train.* **SYN:** speedy, rapid, swift. **2** not well thought out; rash: *His hasty decisions caused many mistakes.* **SYN:** precipitate, foolhardy, reckless, impetuous, cursory, desultory. **3** easily angered; quick-tempered: *a hasty old gentleman.* **SYN:** irascible, irritable. **4** done or uttered in sudden anger or irritation: *He was sorry for his hasty words.* **5** *Obsolete.* eager; impatient: *where now the throng that . . . hasty to depart, Look'd to the sea for safety?* (William Cowper).
[< Old French *hasti,* for *hastif* < *haste;* see etym. under **haste**]

hasty pudding, **1** *U.S.* mush made of corn meal. **2** *British.* mush made of flour or oatmeal.

hat (hat), *n., v.,* **hat|ted, hat|ting.** **—*n.*** **1** a cover for the head. A hat usually has a crown and a brim and is usually worn outdoors. **2a** a red head covering worn by a cardinal of the Roman Catholic Church: *Wiseman continues to Rome to get his hat* (Richard Moncton Milnes). **b** the dignity or office of a cardinal.
—*v.t.* to provide with a hat; put a hat on: *The lady was beautifully gowned and hatted.*
hang one's hat on, *Informal.* to depend upon; count on: *"We're basically followers, not leaders. We had nothing to hang our hat on and so we did nothing"* (New York Times).
hat in hand, submissively; in a servile manner: *Coming late with hat in hand, Britain is in poor position to do much bargaining with the Common Market* (Time).
hold on to your hat, *Informal.* to get ready for a surprise or shock: *The woman on the dais said, "Hold on to your hats. Here's the final count"* (New Yorker).
pass the hat, to ask for contributions; take up a collection: *Lamartine, after passing round the hat in Europe and America, takes to his bed from wounded pride when the French Senate votes him a subsidy, and sheds tears of humiliation* (James Russell Lowell).
pull out of a hat, to produce easily and at will, as if by magic: *Crises cannot be pulled out of a hat to maintain the morale of soldiers* (London Times).
take off one's hat to, to remove or doff the hat, as a salute or sign of respect; honor; hail: *We should take off our hats to them and wish them godspeed* (Harper's).
talk through one's hat, to talk without knowing what one is talking about; talk foolishly: *People take care to find out whether they may be . . . talking through their hats* (New Scientist).
throw one's hat into the ring, *Informal.* to enter a contest, especially for election to a public office: *Meanwhile, insiders report that [he] may throw his hat into the ring* (Newsweek).
under one's hat, *Informal.* as a secret; to oneself: *She kept it under her hat. She meant to spring it on me later on, she said* (P. G. Wodehouse).
wear two hats, to have two jobs, responsibilities, or the like; play a dual role: *[He] wears two hats as president of the fair and chairman of the Triborough Authority* (New York Times).
[Old English *hætt*] **—hat′like′,** *adj.*

hat|band (hat′band′), *n.* **1** a band or narrow rib around the crown of a hat, just above the brim. **2** such a band of black, worn as a sign of mourning.

hat|box (hat′boks′), *n.* a box for holding a hat or hats.

hatch[1] (hach), *v., n.* **—*v.t.*** **1** to bring forth (young) from an egg or eggs: *A hen hatches chickens.* **2** to keep (an egg or eggs) warm until the young come out: *The heat of the sun hatches turtles' eggs.* **3** *Figurative.* **a** to arrange; plan: *We hatched all the arrangements for the dance.* **b** to plan secretly; plot: *The spies hatched a scheme to steal state secrets.* **SYN:** scheme, contrive.
—*v.i.* **1** to come out from the egg: *Three of the chickens hatched today.* **2** to develop to be young animals; bring forth young: *Not all eggs hatch properly.*
—*n.* **1a** the act of hatching; incubation. **b** the brood hatched: *There are twelve chickens in this hatch.* **2** anything that is hatched: *Such things become the hatch and brood of time* (Shakespeare).
[Middle English *hacchen;* origin uncertain]

hatch[2] (hach), *n., v.* **—*n.*** **1a** an opening in a ship's deck. A ship's cargo is loaded through the hatch. **b** a wood or metal cover for such an opening. **2a** an opening in a floor, roof of a building, etc. The escape hatch in an airplane permits passengers to get out in an emergency. **b** a trap door covering such an opening. **3** the lower half of a divided door. **4** a floodgate or sluice. **5** a frame in a river for catching fish.
—*v.t.* to close with or as if with a hatch.
[Old English *hæcc* a gate, wicket]

hatch[3] (hach), *v., n.* **—*v.t.*** **1** to draw, cut, or engrave fine parallel lines on. **2** to inlay with narrow strips or lines of a different material.
—*n.* a line or stroke for shading; hachure.
[< Old French *hacher* chop, hatch < *hache* ax; see etym. under **hash,** verb]

hatch|a|bil|i|ty (hach′ə bil′ə tē), *n.* the quality or condition of hatching or of being hatched: *The concentration of chemicals found . . . reduce the hatchability of eggs* (New Scientist).

hatch|a|ble (hach′ə bəl), *adj.* that can hatch or be hatched.

Hatch Acts, *U.S.* two acts of Congress, in 1939 and 1940, prohibiting federal and certain state employees from campaigning or contributing money in elections. [< Carl A. *Hatch,* 1889-1963, former United States Senator from New Mexico]

hatch|back (hach′bak′), *adj. U.S.* having a hatch on the sloping back of an automobile.

hat|check girl (hat′chek′), a girl or woman in charge of a checkroom, as in a restaurant or club.

hatch|el (hach′əl), *n., v.,* **-eled, -el|ing** or (*especially British*) **-elled, -el|ling.** **—*n.*** a comb used in cleaning flax or hemp.
—*v.t.* **1** to comb (flax or hemp) with a hatchel. **2** *Figurative.* to annoy; torment. Also, **hackle, heckle.**
[Middle English *hechill,* variant of *hackle*[1]] **—hatch′el|er,** *especially British* **hatch′el|ler,** *n.*

hatch|er (hach′ər), *n.* **1** an animal or thing that hatches, such as a bird or an incubator. **2** *Figurative.* a contriver; plotter.

hatch|er|y (hach′ər ē, hach′rē), *n., pl.* **-er|ies.** a

place for hatching eggs, as for fish or hens.
hatch|et (hach′it), *n.* **1** a small ax with a handle about a foot long and a hammerlike side opposite the blade, for use with one hand. See picture under **ax. 2** = tomahawk.
bury the hatchet, to stop quarreling or fighting; make peace: *Buried was the bloody hatchet, . . . There was peace among the nations* (Longfellow).
dig (or **take**) **up the hatchet**, to make war: *Shingis, sachem of the Delawares, . . . took up the hatchet at various times against the English* (Washington Irving).
[<Old French *hachette* (diminutive) <*hache* ax, hatchet, probably <Germanic (compare Middle High German *hacke*)] —**hatch′et|like′**, *adj.*
hatchet face, a sharp, narrow face.
hatch|et-faced (hach′it fāst′), *adj.* having a sharp, narrow face.
hatchet job, *Informal.* a merciless treatment or attack: *This book is not a hatchet job, although it criticizes the prime minister.*
hatchet man, *Informal.* a person employed or used to destroy the character and standing of opponents of a party or group, or, in some countries, the opponents themselves.
hatch|ett|in (hach′ə tin), *n.* = mineral tallow. [<Charles *Hatchett,* about 1765-1847, English chemist]
hatch|et|y (hach′ə tē), *adj.* **1** like a hatchet. **2** thin and sharp: *a hatchety face.*
hatch|ing[1] (hach′ing), *n.* **1** fine parallel lines drawn, cut, or engraved close together to produce the effect of shading. **2** one of the lines made. [<*hatch*[3] + *-ing*[1]]
hatch|ing[2] (hach′ing), *n.* a hatch, as of chickens; brood. [<*hatch*[1] + *-ing*[1]]
hatch|ling (hach′ling), *n.* a very young fish or bird, usually artificially hatched and not old enough to take care of itself.
hatch|ment (hach′mənt), *n.* a square tablet bearing the coat of arms of a dead person. [earlier *atchaement, achement,* reduction of *achievement*]
hatch|way (hach′wā′), *n.* **1** an opening in the deck of a ship to the hold or lower deck; hatch. **2** a similar opening in a floor, roof, or wall of a building.
***hatch|work** (hach′wėrk′), *n.* a pattern of fine parallel or crisscrossed lines. [<*hatch*[3] + *work*]

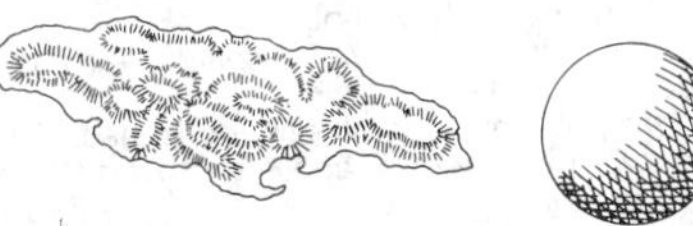
***hatchwork**

hate (hāt), *v.,* **hat|ed, hat|ing,** *n., adj.* —*v.t.* **1** to dislike very much; detest: *Cats usually hate dogs. Love your enemies, do good to them which hate you* (Luke 6:27). **2** to be very averse or unwilling; dislike: *I hate to travel alone. The easy-going who hate being bothered* (Thomas Hardy).
—*v.i.* to feel hatred: *She hated easily; she hated heartily; and she hated implacably* (Macaulay).
—*n.* **1** a very strong dislike; detestation: *He felt hate toward his enemies.* **2** an object of hatred: *Snakes are her special hate.*
—*adj.* **1** characterized by or showing hate: *Bigots . . . have been writing me hate letters because of my pronouncements* (New York Times). **2** arousing hatred, especially against certain races and nationalities: *hate literature.* **3** inspired by racial, ethnic, or sexual prejudice: *[The] Alabama-based Southern Poverty Law Center specializes in suing hate groups* (Time).
[Old English *hatian*] —**hate′a|ble**, *adj.* —**hate′less**, *adj.*
—***Syn.*** *v.t.* **1 Hate, detest, abhor** mean to dislike someone or something very much. **Hate**, the general word, implies very strong dislike and hostility, and often the desire to hurt or harm: *The prisoners hated the cruel guards.* **Detest** suggests strong or deep, fixed dislike mixed with scorn: *I detest a coward.* **Abhor** suggests a profound dislike that makes one shudder or shrink away from someone or something: *I abhor filth of any kind.*
hate crime, a crime usually committed by a group against an individual and motivated by prejudice: *Human-rights activists say San Diego's racial attacks are a microcosm of hate crimes flaring nationally* (Time).
hate|ful (hāt′fəl), *adj.* **1** causing hate; to be hated: *hateful behavior.* **2** feeling hate; showing hate: *a hateful comment.* **SYN:** malevolent. —**hate′ful|ly**, *adv.* —**hate′ful|ness**, *n.*
—***Syn.* 1 Hateful, odious, obnoxious** mean causing strong dislike or hate. **Hateful** applies to what is actually hated: *A bully does hateful things.* **Odious** applies to what excites strong displeasure or offense: *Conditions in the slums are odious.* **Obnoxious** means being so disagreeable or annoying to a person that he cannot stand the sight or thought of what is described: *His disgusting table manners made him obnoxious to us.*
hate|mon|ger (hāt′mung′gər, -mong′-), *n.* a person who stirs up hatred especially against certain groups or conditions.
hat|er (hā′tər), *n.* a person who hates.
hate|wor|thy (hāt′wėr′ᴛʜē), *adj.* = hateful.
hat|ful (hat′fu̇l), *n., pl.* **-fuls. 1** as much as a hat can hold. **2** a considerable quantity.
hath (hath), *v. Archaic.* a third person singular present indicative of **have**. "He hath" means "he has."
Hath|or (hath′ôr), *n.* the ancient Egyptian goddess of heaven, and also of love, joy, and music, represented with a cow's head. Also, **Athor**.
Ha|thor|ic (hə thôr′ik, -thor′-), *adj.* **1** of or having to do with Hathor. **2** *Architecture.* decorated with the head of Hathor, as the capital of a column.
hat|less (hat′lis), *adj.* having no hat; not wearing a hat. —**hat′less|ness**, *n.*
hat|mak|er (hat′mā′kər), *n.* a person who makes hats.
hat|pin (hat′pin′), *n.* a long pin used by women to fasten a hat to the hair.
hat|rack (hat′rak′), *n.* a rack, shelf, or arrangement of hooks or pegs to put hats on.
ha|tred (hā′trid), *n.* a very strong dislike; hate: *a healthy hatred of scoundrels* (Thomas Carlyle). **SYN:** loathing, aversion, animosity, detestation, ill will, malice, spite. [Middle English *hatrede, hatereden* <*haten* to hate + *-reden,* Old English *rǣden* condition, state]
hat|ter (hat′ər), *n.* a person who makes, cleans, or sells hats: *Poisoned by mercury vapor, almost one U.S. hatter in ten developed shakes and mental disturbances. The resulting cliché, mad as a hatter, survives* (Time).
mad as a hatter, completely crazy: *He was a very good fellow, but . . . mad as a hatter* (Thomas Hughes).
hat|ter's shakes (hat′ərz), mercury poisoning; Mad Hatter's disease.
hat|ter|y (hat′ər ē), *n., pl.* **-ter|ies. 1** the goods of a hatter. **2** the factory or the store of a hatter.
***hat tree**, a stand with projecting arms for hats and coats.

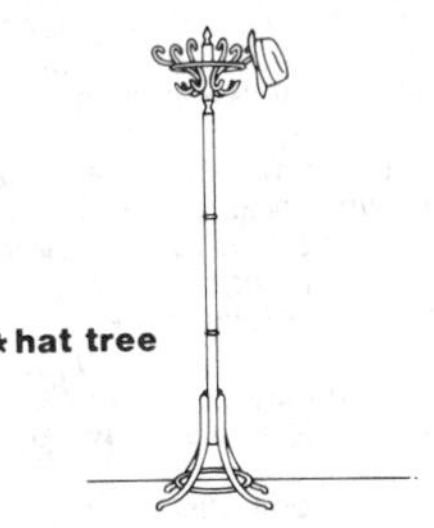
***hat tree**

hat-trick (hat′trik′), *n.* **1** *Cricket.* the knocking down of three wickets by the bowler with three successive deliveries of the ball. **2** three goals scored by a single player in a single game of hockey or soccer. **3** *Especially British.* any noteworthy feat characterized by three or more successive triumphs. [a *hat* is the prize for this feat in cricket]
hau|ber|geon (hô′bər jən), *n.* = habergeon.
hau|berk (hô′bėrk), *n.* **1** a long coat of mail worn in the 1100's and 1200's; haubergeon. **2** (originally) a piece of armor for protecting the neck and shoulders. [<Old French *hauberc,* earlier *halberc* <Germanic (as in Old High German *halsbërc*)]
haud (hôd), *v.t., v.i., n. Scottish.* hold[1].
haugh (häʜ, häf), *n. Scottish.* a piece of low-lying, flat ground by the side of a river. [Old English *healh* corner, nook]
haught (hôt), *adj. Archaic.* **1** high. **2** exalted; lofty; noble. **3** haughty. [Middle English *haught;* see etym. under **haughty**]
haugh|ty (hô′tē), *adj.,* **-ti|er, -ti|est. 1** too proud of oneself and too scornful of others: *A haughty person is often unpopular.* **2** showing too great pride of oneself and scorn for others: *a haughty smile, a haughty glance, haughty words.* **3** *Archaic.* of exalted character, style, or rank: *No haughty feat of arms I tell* (Scott). [Middle English *haute* <*haut* or *haught* (influenced by English *caught*) <Old French *haut* <Latin *altus* high] —**haugh′ti|ly**, *adv.* —**haugh′ti|ness**, *n.*
—***Syn.* 1 Haughty, arrogant** mean offensively proud. **Haughty** means feeling oneself superior to others and showing it by treating them with cold indifference and scorn: *A haughty girl is always unpopular at school.* **Arrogant** means thinking oneself more important than one is and showing it by treating others in a domineering and insulting way: *the arrogant manner of a dictator. He was so arrogant he lost his job.*
haul (hôl), *v., n.* —*v.t.* **1a** to pull or drag with force: *The logs were loaded on wagons and hauled to the mill by horses.* **SYN:** See syn. under **draw. b** to transport; carry: *Trucks, trains, and ships haul freight.* **SYN:** See syn. under **draw. 2** to change the course of (a ship), especially so as to sail closer to the wind.
—*v.i.* **1** to pull or tug: *The crew hauled at the heavy sail.* **2** to change; shift: *The wind hauled around to the east.* **3** to change or turn a ship's course; sail in a certain course. **4** to change one's course of action.
—*n.* **1** the act of hauling; hard pull. **2** the load hauled: *Powerful trucks are used for heavy hauls.* **3** the distance, or the route over which, a load is hauled: *Long hauls cost more than short ones.* **4a** the amount won or taken at one time; catch: *The fishing boats made a good haul and came back fully loaded.* **b** *Informal, Figurative: That [silver] . . . would ha' been a haul for Congress, if they could ha' got hold on't in war-time* (Harriet Beecher Stowe).
for (**over**) **the long haul**. See under **long haul**.
haul off, a *Informal.* to draw back one's arm to give a blow: *He hauled off and socked him in the nose.* **b** to turn a ship away from an object: *I told the Chief Officer to haul her off four points* (Merchant Marine Magazine). **c** to withdraw; change one's course of action: *He took it in mortal offense, and from that moment has been hauling off to his former enemies* (Thomas Jefferson).
haul up, a to change a ship's course; turn a ship nearer to the direction of the wind: *The enemy . . . hauled up on the Terpsichore's weather beam* (Archibald Duncan). **b** to bring oneself to a position of rest by hauling or drawing: *The boat hauled up at the pier.* **c** *Informal.* to bring up for a reprimand; call to account: *The first native . . . refused to sell his fowls at the Government prices [and] was hauled up before the irate commandant* (David Livingstone).
[<Old French *haler.* See etym. of doublet **hale**[2].] —**haul′er**, *n.*
haul|a|bout (hôl′ə bout′), *n. U.S.* a vessel resembling a barge, used for coaling ships.
haul|age (hô′lij), *n.* **1** the act or process of hauling. **2** the force used in hauling. **3** a charge made for hauling, especially that made by a railroad for cars or goods hauled. **4** a charge made by a railroad for the use of a line of track.
haul|age|way (hô′lij wā′), *n.* a passage in a coal mine used for hauling coal.
haul|ier (hôl′yər), *n. Especially British.* one that hauls; hauler.
haul|ing ground (hô′ling), a place where young male seals congregate, as contrasted with the rookery occupied by breeding seals.
haulm (hôm), *n.* **1** *British.* the stems or stalks of various cultivated plants, such as peas, beans, hops, or potatoes, especially as left after gathering the pods or ears and used for litter or thatching. **2** a stem or stalk of a bean, potato, grass, or the like. Also, **halm**.
[Old English *healm*]
haul|yard (hôl′yərd), *n.* = halyard.
haunch (hônch, hänch), *n.* **1** Usually, **haunches**. the hindquarter of an animal: *A dog sits on its haunches.* **2** the leg and loin of a deer, sheep, or other animal, used for food. **3** the part of the body around the hips; hip. **4** *Architecture.* either side of an arch, from the vertex or crown to the spring or impost.
[<Old French *hanche* <Germanic (compare Old High German *ancha*)]
haunch bone, 1 = hipbone. **2** = ilium.
haunt (hônt, hänt; *for n. 4 also* hant), *v., n.* —*v.t.* **1** to go to often; visit frequently: *I haunt the pine-dark solitudes* (James Russell Lowell). **2** *Figurative.* to be often with; come often to: *Memories of his youth haunted the old man.* **3** to frequent the company of: *to haunt the rich.* **4** to visit frequently and habitually, with manifestations of influence and presence: *People say ghosts haunt that old house.*
—*v.i.* **1** to stay or remain usually (in a place): *I have charged thee not to haunt about my doors* (Shakespeare). **2** to associate, as with a person.
—*n.* **1** Often, **haunts**. a place visited often: *The swimming pool was the children's favorite haunt on hot summer days. The bygone haunt of ancient revelry* (Walter de la Mare). **2** the usual feeding place of deer, game, or wild fowl. **3** a place frequented by criminals. **4** *Dialect.* a ghost. **5** *Archaic.* a habit, custom, or usage; habitual practice: *Of clothmaking she had such an haunt, She passed them of Ypres and of Gaunt* (Chaucer).

Pronunciation Key: hat, āge, cãre, fär; let, ēqual, tėrm; it, īce; hot, ōpen, ôrder; oil, out; cup, pu̇t, rüle; child; long; thin; ᴛʜen; zh, measure; **ə** represents **a** in about, **e** in taken, **i** in pencil, **o** in lemon, **u** in circus.

[< Old French *hanter,* perhaps < a Germanic word] —**haunt′er**, *n.* —**haunt′ing|ly**, *adv.*

haunt|ed (hôn′tid, hän′-), *adj.* **1** visited by ghosts: *a haunted house, a haunted man.* **2** *Figurative.* harried or harassed, as if by ghosts; troubled; worried: *Staring at the white Benita and at her haunted eyes* (H. Rider Haggard).

hau|pi|a (hou pē′ə), *n. Hawaiian.* a coconut pudding.

Hau|sa (hou′sä), *n., pl.* **-sa** or **-sas**. **1** a member of a widespread and numerous Negroid people of northern Nigeria and the Sudan. **2** the Chad language of this people.

hau|sen (hô′zən; *German* hou′zən), *n.* the largest sturgeon of the Black and Caspian seas and their rivers; beluga. [< German *Hausen*]

Haus|frau (hous′frou′), *n., pl.* **-fraus** (-frouz′), *German* **-frau|en** (-frou′ən). a housewife: *We're really Hausfraus, and we can cook and press our own dresses and keep house* (Time). [< German *Hausfrau*]

haus|mann|ite (hous′mə nīt), *n.* a native oxide of manganese found in Germany, Sweden, Brazil, and Arkansas. *Formula:* Mn_3O_4 [< J. F. L. *Hausmann,* 1782-1859, a German mineralogist]

Hauss|mann|ize (hous′mə nīz), *v.t.,* **-ized, -iz|ing.** to remodel (a city or its streets) after the manner of Baron Haussmann (1809-1891) in Paris, as by providing broad, straight thoroughfares and fine architectural effects. —**Hauss′mann|i|za′tion**, *n.*

haus|tel|late (hôs′tə lit), *adj.* fitted for sucking, as an insect.

haus|tel|lum (hô stel′əm), *n., pl.* **-la** (-lə). the sucking organ or proboscis of many insects. [< New Latin *haustellum* (diminutive) < Latin *haustrum* water hoist < *haurīre* to draw (water)]

haus|to|ri|al (hô stôr′ē əl, -stōr′-), *adj.* of or having to do with a haustorium or haustoria.

haus|to|ri|um (hô stôr′ē əm, -stōr′-), *n., pl.* **haus|to|ri|a** (hô stôr′ē ə, -stōr′-). *Botany.* **1** one of the small roots of parasitic plants that attach themselves to and penetrate the tissues of the host and absorb nourishment; sucker. **2** a specialized branch or organ of the mycelium of a fungus, whereby it attaches itself to its host. [< New Latin *haustorium* < Latin *haustor* a drainer < *haurīre* to draw (water)]

haus|tral (hôs′trəl), *adj.* of or having to do with the haustra.

haus|trum (hôs′trəm), *n., pl.* **-tra** (trə). *Anatomy.* each of the small folds, resembling sacs, in the terminal division of the colon. [< New Latin *haustrum* < Latin, bucket, scoop < *haurīre* to draw (water)]

haut (ō), *adj. French.* **1** high-class: ... *Fauchon, the epicures' haut grocery of Paris* (Time). **2** (literally) high.

haut|bois (hō′boi, ō′-), *n., pl.* **-bois**. = hautboy.

haut|boy (hō′boi, ō′-), *n.* = oboe. [< Middle French *hautbois* < *haut* high (see etym. under **haughty**) + *bois* wood (because of its high notes and wooden material)]

haute cou|ture (ōt kü tyr′), *French.* **1** the most notable fashion designers and dressmaking establishments of the world, such as those of Paris: *The unique flair of Parisian haute couture ... is now turning to revolutionize American men's wear* (New York Times). **2** the products of these designers and establishments. —**haute′-cou|ture′**, *adj.*

haute cui|sine (ōt kwē zēn′), *French.* **1** the art of preparing and cooking fine foods, especially as practiced by distinguished chefs in leading restaurants and hotels; cooking as a fine art: *Such a corn has long been among the specialties of that seat of American haute cuisine* (New Yorker). **2** the food thus prepared: *He loves fine wines and good food—from haute cuisine to chitlins* (Newsweek). —**haute′-cui|sine′**, *adj.*

haute é|cole (ōt ā kôl′), *French.* the more difficult feats of horsemanship. —**haute′-é|cole′**, *adj.*

hau|teur (hō tėr′, ō-), *n.* the quality of being proud and overbearing; haughty manner or spirit; haughtiness. [< Old French *hauteur* < *haut* high; see etym. under **haughty**]

haut goût (ō gü′), *French.* strong flavor.

haut monde (ō mônd′), *French.* **1** high society. **2** (literally) high world.

haut ton (ō tôn′), *French.* **1** high tone or style. **2** the usage or manners of high society.

ha|uyne (hä′win), *n.* = hauynite.

ha|uy|nite (hä′wə nīt), *n.* silicate and sulfate mineral containing aluminum, calcium, and sodium, usually having a bluish or greenish color. It is found embedded in igneous rocks. [< *hauyne* < French *haüyne* < René J. Haüy, 1743-1822, a French mineralogist]

Ha|van|a (hə van′ə), *n., adj.* —*n.* **1** a kind of cigar made from Cuban tobacco. **2** the tobacco from which these cigars are made.
—*adj.* of or having to do with this cigar, its tobacco, or its color.

have (hav; *unstressed* həv, əv), *v., pres. 1st person* **have**, *2nd person* **have** or (*Archaic*) **hast**, *3rd person* **has** or (*Archaic*) **hath**, *pl.* **have**; *pt. and pp.* **had**, *ppr.* **hav|ing**; *n.* —*v.t.* **1** to hold in one's keeping or in one's possession; possess: **a** to hold in one's hand or hands, or as if in one's hand or hands (something taken or received): *I have a stick in my hand. The pitcher throws the ball to the player who has the bat. She has no news of her brother.* **b** to possess as property; own: *We have a big house and farm.* **c** to possess or contain as a part or parts: *A house has windows. True flies have two wings. The year has twelve months.* **d** to possess as an attribute, quality, or right: *to have a dark complexion, to have a cheerful disposition, to have special privileges.* **2** to be forced; be compelled; be obliged: *All animals have to sleep. He will have to go now because his work begins.* **3** to cause (somebody to do something or something to be done): *Please have the boy bring my mail. She will have the car washed for me.* **4** to take; get: *Have a seat. You need to have a rest.* SYN: obtain. **5** to experience: *to have a pain, to have a fever, to have fear. Have a pleasant time. They had trouble with this engine.* **6** to allow; permit: *She won't have any noise while she is reading.* **7** to hold in the mind; keep in the mind; know; understand: *to have the directions in mind, to have doubts. He has no Latin. She has your idea.* **8** to engage in; carry on; perform: *Have a talk with him.* **9** to show by action: *to have the courage of one's convictions.* **10** to maintain; assert: *They will have it so. Rumor has it so.* **11** to be in a certain relation to: *to have friends. She has three brothers.* **12** to become the father or mother of: *to have a baby.* **13** *Informal, Figurative.* to hold an advantage over: *You have him there.* **14** *Slang.* to outwit or cheat. **15** *Archaic.* to bring, take, or put. **16** *Have* is used with words like *asked, been, broken, done,* or *called* to express completed action: *They have eaten. She had gone before. I have called her. They will have seen her by Sunday. He would have been late.*
—*n.* a person, group, or country that has much property or wealth: *People here say communism in Hungary made haves of a very small group of have nots* (Birmingham News).
have at, a to attack; hit: *Individuals ... having at each other with large round rocks* (Punch). **b** to criticize; assault verbally: *In this revue, ... a quartet of English comedians have at everything from The Establishment to modern tongue-tied philosophers* (New Yorker).
have done (with), to be through; stop: *Let's have done with this quarreling and start working again.*
have had it, *Slang.* **a** to become disgusted; become fed up: *After eating peanut butter sandwiches all week, I've had it.* **b** to reach an end; lose something that one has had: *By twenty they had begun to fade, by twenty-five they have had it* (New Yorker). *The B-47 is so much faster that if it starts flying you, you've had it* (Harper's).
have it, a to will; make happen: *As luck would have it, we missed the train.* **b** to receive a thrashing or punishment: *If he catches you, he'll let you have it.* **c** to discover or hit upon an answer, solution, etc.: *Eureka! I have it!* **d** *Informal.* to find oneself in certain (good or bad) circumstances: *You'll never have it so good.* **e** to gain a victory or advantage: *As many as are of that opinion, say Aye,—contrary, No—the Ayes have it* (Dickens).
have it in for, *Informal.* to have a grudge against; try to get revenge on: *I always wondered why he had it in for me. He seemed to have a special ... enmity for me* (S. E. White). *George Bernard Shaw had it in for the rich, one way or another* (Wall Street Journal).
have it out, to fight or argue until a question is settled: *We have had it out and now we are fast friends once more.*
have nothing on, to have no advantage of or superiority over: *Kerensky thought Napoleon had nothing on him* (London Daily Express). *The antique hussies of history ... had nothing on her* (Publisher's Weekly).
have on, a to be wearing: *What a nice hat you have on!* **b** *British Slang.* mislead; fool; deceive: *Many of the things I read about China these days leave me with the uncomfortable feeling that they are simply having us on* (New Scientist).
have oneself to thank, to be to blame; be solely responsible: *If he has lost his savings in a gamble, he has only himself to thank.*
have to do with, a to be connected with; be related to; deal with: *Botany has to do with the study of plants. What has a woman to do with politics, Mrs. Dangle?* (Richard Brinsley Sheridan). **b** to be a companion, partner, or friend of; associate with: *I refuse to have anything whatsoever to do with that cheating scoundrel.*
have up, *British Slang.* to cause to appear or answer in court: *The landlady had him up for failing to pay his rent.*
to have and to hold, to keep and possess: *to have and to hold till death do us part.*
[Old English *habban*]
—*Syn. v.t.* **1a, b Have, hold, own**, mean to possess or be in possession of something. **Have** is the general word: *She has a new suit.* **Hold** emphasizes having control over or keeping: *He holds the office of treasurer. He cannot hold a friend long.* **Own** suggests having a right, especially a legal right, to hold a thing as property: *He owns a big store. In the United States, a person cannot own another person.*
▶ **have**. In all forms of spoken English, standard and nonstandard, *have* and *of* frequently become identical in unstressed position, both being pronounced (əv). This phonetic identity frequently causes use of *of* when the required form is *have: I could of done it.*

✱have|lock (hav′lok), *n.* a white cloth covering for a cap. It falls over the back of the neck and gives protection against the sun. [American English < General Henry *Havelock,* a British officer, distinguished in the Sepoy Mutiny of 1857]

✱havelock

ha|ven (hā′vən), *n., v.* —*n.* **1** a place of shelter and safety: *To the weary hunters the cabin was a welcome haven.* SYN: retreat, refuge, asylum. **2** a harbor or port.
—*v.t.* **1** to put (a ship) into a haven or port. **2** *Figurative.* to shelter as in a haven: *Blissfully havened both from joy and pain* (Keats).
[Old English *hæfen*] —**ha′ven|less**, *adj.*

have-not (hav′not′), *n. Informal.* a person, group, or country that has very little or no property or wealth: *In the future atomic energy might act as a kind of equalizer between the haves and the have-nots in the world* (London Times).

have|n't (hav′ənt), have not.

ha|ver[1] (hā′vər), *v., n., interj. Scottish.* —*v.i.* to talk foolishly; prate.
—*n., interj.* **havers**, foolish talk; nonsense: *The havers the two of ye talk about auld Tam* (Samuel R. Crockett).
[origin unknown]

hav|er[2] (hav′ər), *n.* a person who has; possessor: *Valour is the chiefest virtue, and Most dignifies the haver* (Shakespeare). [< *hav*(e) + *-er*[1]]

ha|ver|el (hāv′rəl), *n. Scottish.* a foolish talker; silly chatterer; fool. [< *haver*[1]]

hav|er|sack (hav′ər sak), *n.* a bag or pouch used by soldiers and hikers for carrying food, utensils, and other things when on a march or hike. It is usually carried at the side by a shoulder strap. *We bore two days' rations in our haversacks* (Arthur Conan Doyle). [< French *havresac* < German *Habersack* (literally) sack for oats]

Ha|ver|sian (hə vėr′shən), *adj.* having to do with or discovered by Clopton Havers, 1650-1702, an English anatomist.

Haversian canal, a tiny, cylindrical hollow in a bone, through which blood vessels, lymphatics, connective tissues, and nerves run.

Haversian system, the layers of tissue surrounding the Haversian canals, which together with the canals make up the structure of compact bone.

hav|il|dar (hav′il där), *n.* (in British India) a native or sepoy sergeant. [< Persian *ḥawāl-dār* < Arabic *ḥawālah* charge, command + Persian *dār* a holder]

hav|ing (hav′ing), *n.* **1** possession. **2** what a person possesses; belonging: *Look to my house and havings; keep all safe* (Richard Brome). **3** Often, **havings**. *Scottish.* behavior or manners.

hav|ior or **hav|iour** (hāv′yər), *n. Archaic or Dialect.* behavior; deportment. [Middle English *havour* (influenced by *have*) < Old French *avoir* to have]

hav|oc (hav′ək), *n., v.,* **-ocked, -ock|ing.** —*n.* **1** very great destruction or injury: *Tornadoes, severe earthquakes, and plagues create widespread havoc.* SYN: devastation, ruin. **2** *Archaic.* the call used in medieval warfare signaling troops to begin to pillage.
—*v.t., v.i.* to make havoc (of); devastate.
cry havoc, to give warning of imminent danger; express alarm: *To cry havoc at what is happening in Prague might risk pushing the Czechoslovaks away from the socialist camp altogether* (London Times).

play (wreak, or **make) havoc with,** to injure severely, ruin, or destroy: *Today's hectic schedules can play havoc with your family's eating habits* (Atlantic).
[< Anglo French *havok,* alteration of Old French *havot* plundering, devastation] **—hav'ock|er,** *n.*

ha|vu|rah (hä vü'rä), *n., pl.* **ha|vu|rot** (hä vü rōt'). any one of a number of small groups of American Jews that meet informally for prayer sessions, meals, and classes or discussions on Judaism: *While havurah members do not necessarily live together or pool their finances, they share an intense commitment to making religion part of everyday living* (Time). [< Hebrew *hăbhurāh* fellowship < *hābhēr* friend, comrade]

haw¹ (hô), *n.* **1** the red berry of the hawthorn; thorn apple. **2** the fruit of other shrubs or trees of the same group as the hawthorn. **3** = hawthorn. [Old English *haga,* apparently same word as *haga* hedge]

haw² (ho), *interj., n., v.* **—*interj., n.*** a stammering sound between words: *"I am, haw, hum, very happy to be here," the speaker began* (interj.). *His speech was interrupted with haws* (n.).
—*v.i.* to make this sound; stammer: *Decisions come rapidly, with no hemming and hawing* (Newsweek).
[imitative]

haw³ (hô), *interj., n., v.* **—*interj., n.*** a call to direct horses, oxen, or other draft animals to turn to the left, especially without the use of reins: *"Get along! Haw!" the mule driver yelled at the team* (interj.). *You have to make your haws loud enough for the mule to hear* (n.).
—*v.i.* to turn to the left. **—*v.t.*** *U.S.* to direct (a horse or other draft animal) to turn to the left.
[origin uncertain]

haw⁴ (hô), *n.* **1** the vestigial nictitating membrane of the eye, especially of a horse or dog. **2** this membrane when inflamed or infected. [origin uncertain; perhaps < *haw¹* (resembling the membrane when swollen)]

Ha|wai|ian (hə wī'yən, -ən; -wä'yən, -wô'-), *adj., n.* **—*adj.*** of or having to do with Hawaii, its people, or their language.
—*n.* **1** a person born or living in Hawaii. **2** the native Polynesian language of Hawaii.

Hawaiian goose, = nene.

Hawaiian guitar, a specially tuned guitar in which the length and pitch of the strings are altered by sliding a metal bar over them.

Ha|wai|i Standard Time (hə wī'ē, -yə; -wä'yə, -wô'-), the standard time in Hawaii, two hours behind Pacific Standard Time. *Abbr:* HST (no periods).
▶ See **Alaska Standard Time** for usage note.

haw|finch (hô'finch'), *n.* the European grosbeak.

haw-haw (hô'hô'), *interj., n., v.* **—*interj.*** a word representing the sound of a loud, boisterous laugh.
—*n.* a loud, boisterous laugh; guffaw.
—*v.i.* to laugh loudly and boisterously; guffaw.

***hawk¹** definition 1

marsh hawk

hawk¹** (hôk), *n., v.* **—*n. **1** a bird of prey with a strong, hooked beak and long, curved claws. Hawks hunt in the daytime using their keen sight, often circling in flight for a long time on their broad wings. The hawk family includes the buzzard hawks, the kites, the harriers, the Old World vultures, and especially the accipiters. Some hawks are trained to hunt and kill other birds and small animals. **2** any one of the falcons, such as the duck hawk, or peregrine. **3** any one of certain other birds, such as the goatsucker. **4** *Figurative.* a person who preys on others. **5** *Informal.* a person who advocates a warlike or military solution in a conflict: *In our opinion, the general run of Americans—whether hawks or doves, or neither —are deeply preoccupied with the war* (New Yorker). SYN: warhawk.
—*v.i.* **1** to hunt with trained hawks. **2** to hunt on the wing as a hawk does. **3** to be or act as a hawk; be hawkish. **—*v.t.*** to pursue or attack on the wing as a hawk does.
hawk at, a to fly at or attack on the wing as a hawk does: *Accustomed to be welcomed with smiles, and even hawked at by young ladies on promotion* (Hawley Smart). **b** (of a person) to fly a hawk at: *But who does hawk at eagles with a dove?* (George Herbert).
know a hawk from a hernshaw, to know one thing from another: *The clever Elliot, who knew a hawk from a hernshaw, never floundered into that platitude* (Thomas Carlyle).
[Old English *heafoc*] **—hawk'like',** *adj.*

hawk² (hôk), *v.t.* **1** to carry (goods) about and offer them for sale by shouting: *Peddlers hawked their wares in the street. On TV the mixer will be hawked on the network programs* (Wall Street Journal). . . . *attempt to sell scientific theories as they hawk canned goods, automobiles and cigarettes* (Scientific American). **2** to spread (a report) around. **—*v.i.*** to practice the trade of a hawker. [back formation < *hawker¹*]

hawk³ (hôk), *v., n.* **—*v.i.*** to clear the throat noisily. **—*v.t.*** to raise (phlegm or other matter) with a strong effort of clearing the throat.
—*n.* **1** a noisy clearing of the throat. **2** the noise made in such an effort.
[probably imitative]

hawk⁴ (hôk), *n.* a small, flat board, with a handle underneath, used by plasterers to hold mortar. [origin uncertain]

hawk|bill (hôk'bil'), *n.* = hawksbill turtle.

hawk-billed (hôk'bild'), *adj.* having a mouth like a hawk's beak.

hawk cuckoo, a brown and white East Indian cuckoo, with a banded tail, resembling a hawk in appearance.

hawk|er¹ (hô'kər), *n.* a person who carries his wares around and offers them for sale by shouting or as if by shouting; peddler. [probably < Middle Low German *haker.* Compare etym. under **huckster.**]

hawk|er² (hô'kər), *n.* a person who hunts with trained hawks; falconer. [probably < *hawk¹* + *-er¹.* Compare Old English *hafocere.*]

Hawk|eye (hôk'ī'), *n.* a nickname for a native or inhabitant of Iowa.

hawk-eyed (hôk'īd'), *adj.* having sharp eyes like a hawk; keen-sighted.

hawk|ing (hô'king), *n.* hunting with trained hawks; falconry.

hawk|ish (hô'kish), *adj.* **1** like a hawk. **2** *Informal.* advocating a warlike or military solution in a conflict: *Some of his hawkish advisers . . . pressed him to bomb and invade the island* (Harper's).
—hawk'ish|ly, *adv.* **—hawk'ish|ness,** *n.*

hawk|ism (hô'kiz əm), *n.* hawkish tendency or attitude.

hawk moth, any one of various large, swift moths having narrow wings and long, stout bodies, which fly mostly at twilight and feed on the nectar of flowers; hummingbird moth; sphinx moth.

hawk-nosed (hôk'nōzd'), *adj.* having a nose curved like the beak of a hawk.

hawk owl, 1 a barred, brownish owl of northern North America that hunts by day and resembles a hawk in its habits; day owl. **2** = short-eared owl.

hawk parrot, a South American short-tailed parrot, with a large crest at the back of the neck that can be set upright.

hawk's-beard (hôks'bird'), *n.* any one of a group of yellow or orange-flowered herbs of the composite family, having a conspicuous, bristly, white pappus.

hawk's-bill or **hawks|bill** (hôks'bil'), *n.* = hawksbill turtle.

hawksbill turtle, a sea turtle having a beak shaped like that of a hawk. Tortoise shell is made from the overlapping horny plates covering its shell.

hawk's-eye (hôks'ī'), *n.* a variety of quartz similar to the tiger's-eye but blue or green.

Hawk|shaw or **hawk|shaw** (hôk'shô), *n.* a detective. [< *Hawkshaw,* the clever detective in *The Ticket-of-Leave Man,* by Tom Taylor, an English writer, 1817-1880]

hawk|weed (hôk'wēd'), *n.* **1** any one of a genus of weedy plants of the composite family, somewhat like chicory, with small, yellow, orange, or red flowers blossoming in summer and autumn. **2** any one of several related plants.

hawse (hôz, hôs), *n.* **1** the part of a ship's bow having holes for hawsers or cables to pass through. **2** one of these holes; hawsehole. **3** the space between the bow of a ship at anchor and her anchors. **4** the situation of the anchor cables of a ship moored with both bow anchors: *a foul hawse.* [earlier *halse, haulse,* probably < Scandinavian (compare Old Icelandic *hāls* neck)]

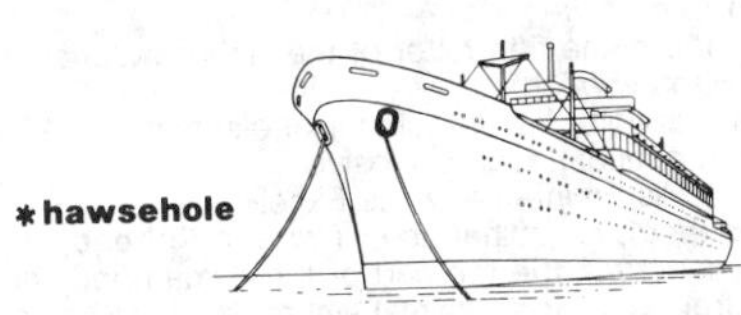
***hawsehole**

***hawse|hole** (hôz'hōl', hôs'-), *n.* a hole in the bow of a ship for a hawser or cable to pass through.

hawse|pipe (hôz'pīp', hôs'-), *n.* a metal pipe fitted into the hawse of a ship through which the anchor chain is drawn.

haw|ser (hô'zər, -sər), *n.* a large, stout rope or thin steel cable, used for mooring or towing ships. [< Anglo-French *hauceour,* Old French *haucier,* earlier *haulsier* to hoist, tug < Vulgar Latin *altiāre* < *altus* high; influenced by Frankish *hoh* high. Compare etym. under **haughty.**]

hawser bend, = sheet bend.

haw|ser-laid (hô'zər lād', -sər-), *adj.* = cable-laid.

haw|thorn (hô'thôrn), *n.* any one of a group of shrubs or small trees with many thorns and clusters of fragrant white, red, or pink flowers and small red berries called haws; haw; thorn apple. The hawthorn belongs to the rose family and is often grown in hedges. [Old English *haguthorn* < *haga* haw¹ + *thorn*]

Haw|thorne effect (hô'thôrn), an improvement in the performance of workers, students, or other subjects, resulting from the attention of researchers seeking means to achieve such an improvement. [< the Western Electric Company's *Hawthorne* Works in Chicago, where experiments during the 1920's to improve working performance yielded this effect]

hay¹ (hā), *n., v.* **—*n.*** **1** grass, clover, or alfalfa, cut and partially dried for use as food for cattle, horses, or other animals: *When cattle are comfortable, and have hay before them all the time, they eat more* (Newsweek). **2** grass ready for mowing.
—*v.i.* to cut and partially dry grass, clover, or alfalfa, for hay: *The men are haying in the east field.*
—*v.t.* to supply with hay.
hit the hay, *Slang.* to go to bed: *The workers hit the hay early.*
make hay, a to cut and dry grass, clover, or alfalfa for use as food for cattle, horses, or other animals: *The farmers hurried to make hay before the rains came.* **b** *Figurative.* to gain from or seize by opportunities; lose no time: *He's made loads of political hay with organization politicians in the past three years* (Wall Street Journal).
make hay of, a to thrash soundly; beat up: *The champ has made hay of every opponent he has faced.* **b** to throw into confusion; upset: *Oh! father, how you are making hay of my things!* (Maria Edgeworth).
make hay while the sun shines, to gain or seize the opportunity: *Resolved to make hay while the sun shone, she applied for both the scholarship and the fellowship.*
raise hay, *U.S. Slang.* to cause a disturbance; make trouble: *"We're not like a group of citizens trying to raise hay over on the campus"* (Harper's).
[Old English *hēg.* See related etym. at **hew.**]

hay² (hā), *n. Archaic.* a hedge or fence. [Old English *hege*]

hay|box (hā'boks'), *n.* a box filled with hay in which food brought to the boiling point in a saucepan is placed to finish cooking.

hay|burn|er (hā'bėr'nər), *n. U.S. Slang.* a horse: *Smitty bought his first horse in 1947 with $700—a no-good hayburner . . .* (Time).

hay|cock (hā'kok'), *n.* a small, cone-shaped pile of hay in a field.

hay fever, an allergy caused by the pollen of ragweed and certain other plants, characterized by sneezing, a running nose, and itching of the nose, throat, and eyes; pollinosis.

hay|field (hā'fēld'), *n.* a field where grass, alfalfa, or clover is grown for hay: *From the sun-burnt hayfield homeward creeps The loaded wain* (William Cowper).

hay|fork (hā'fôrk'), *n.* **1** = pitchfork. **2** a mechanical device equipped with hooks for moving hay into or out of a hayloft.

hay|ing (hā'ing), *n.* the act or process of mowing, bundling, and storing hay.

hayk (hīk, hāk), *n.* = haik.

hay|lage (hā'lij), *n.* half-dry hay stored in a silo; silage consisting of fifty per cent dry matter. [< *hay* + (si)*lage*]

hay|loft (hā'lôft', -loft'), *n.* a place in a barn or stable where hay is stored; haymow.

hay|mak|er (hā'mā'kər), *n.* **1** a person who lifts, tosses, and spreads the hay to dry after it is cut. **2** an apparatus for shaking up and drying hay. **3** *Slang.* a hard, swinging, upward blow with the fist in or as if in boxing: *Those twin punches set Sweden—still officially neutral—to looking to its*

Pronunciation Key: hat, āge, cãre, fär; let, ēqual, tėrm; it, īce; hot, ōpen, ôrder; oil, out; cup, pu̇t, rüle; child; long; thin; ᴛʜen; zh, measure; ə represents **a** in about, **e** in taken, **i** in pencil, **o** in lemon, **u** in circus.

defenses against whatever haymaker drives might come some day from the Communists (Newsweek).

hay|mak|ing (hā′mā′king), *n.* **1** = haying. **2** *Figurative.* the act of gaining from opportunities; a making hay: *the haymaking of the profiteer after the war* (W. R. Inge).

hay|mow (hā′mou′), *n.* **1** = hayloft. **2** a pile of hay, especially one stored in a barn.

hay press, *U.S.* a press for baling hay.

hay|rack (hā′rak′), *n.* **1** a rack or frame for holding hay to be eaten by cattle, horses, or other animals. **2** a framework on a wagon used in hauling hay or straw. **3** a wagon having such a framework.

hay|rake (hā′rāk′), *n.* **1** a rake for gathering hay. **2** an apparatus for raking hay, drawn by a horse or a tractor.

hay|rick (hā′rik′), *n.* = haystack.

hay|ride (hā′rīd′), *n.* an outing in a wagon or sleigh partly filled with hay.

hay|seed (hā′sēd′), *n.* **1** the grass seed shaken out of hay. **2** small pieces of chaff which drop from hay. **3** *U.S. Slang.* a person from the country; bumpkin; yokel. SYN: farmer, countryman, rustic.

hay|sel (hā′səl), *n. British Dialect.* the hay season: *Haysel is now well under way, mostly by baling* (London Times). [< *hay*[1] + Middle English *sele* season]

hay|shock (hā′shok′), *n. U.S. Dialect.* haycock.

hay|stack (hā′stak′), *n.* a large pile of hay outdoors.

hay tedder, a machine for spreading newly mown hay so as to expose it to the sun and air.

Hay|ti|an (hā′tē ən, -shən), *adj., n.* = Haitian.

hay|ward (hā′wôrd′), *n.* an officer of a manor, township, or parish having charge of fences, especially to keep cattle from breaking through, and to impound strays. [Middle English *heiward* < *hey* hay[1] + *ward* warden[1]]

hay|wire (hā′wīr′), *n., adj.* **—*n.*** wire used to tie up bales of hay.
—*adj.* *Slang.* **1** out of order; wrong: *Some of the rhythm is going haywire* (New Statesman). **2** out of control. **3** confused or crazy; insane: *to go haywire.*

ha|zan (ʜä′zən, ʜä zän′), *n.* = chazan.

haz|ard (haz′ərd), *n., v.* **—*n.*** **1** a chance of loss or harm; risk; danger; peril: *Mountain climbing is full of hazards.* SYN: jeopardy. **2** chance; venture: *to take a hazard, games of hazard.* **3** any obstruction on a golf course which can trap a ball, such as a pond, ditch, bunker, or bush. **4** any one of three places on the side of the court into which the ball is served in court tennis; the grille, the winning gallery, or the tambour; hazard side. **5** a stroke in pocket billiards or pool by which the player sends the object ball or his own ball (after it hits another) into a pocket. **6** an old and complicated dice game from which craps developed. **7** *Obsolete.* something risked or staked.
—*v.t.* **1** to take a chance with; risk; venture: *to hazard a battle. I would hazard my life on his honesty.* **2** to expose to hazard or risk: *to hazard a prize by clutching it too soon* (Edward A. Freeman).
at all hazards, whatever the risks; in spite of every danger or peril: *It was resolved at all hazards, to go* (George Shelvocke).
[< Old French *hasard* a game of dice < Arabic *az-zahr* the die[2]] **—haz′ard|a|ble,** *adj.* **—haz′ard|er,** *n.* **—haz′ard|less,** *adj.*

hazard light, a device to make both parking lights flash in the front and rear of an automobile or truck to warn that it has become a traffic hazard.

haz|ard|ous (haz′ər dəs), *adj.* **1** dangerous; risky; perilous: *Flying across the ocean in a small plane was a hazardous undertaking.* SYN: precarious. **2** dependent on chance; casual; fortuitous. **—haz′ard|ous|ly,** *adv.* **—haz′ard|ous|ness,** *n.*

hazardous waste, any waste material perilous to health, especially so as to have permanent damaging effects: *Congress has defined hazardous wastes as any solid waste which . . . may cause . . . a substantial present or potential hazard to human health or the environment* (Science News).

hazard side, = hazard (*n.* def. 4).

haze[1] (hāz), *n., v.,* **hazed, haz|ing.** **—*n.*** **1** a small amount of mist, smoke, or dust in the air. Haze makes distant objects indistinct. *A thin haze veiled the distant hills.* **2** *Figurative.* a vague condition of the mind; slight confusion: *After he was hit on the head, his mind was in a haze. The events of the old man's youth were veiled by the haze in his memory. In the fog and haze of confusion all is enlarged* (Edmund Burke).
—*v.i.* *British Dialect.* **1** to drizzle. **2** to be foggy.
—*v.t.* to obscure with haze. [origin uncertain]

haze[2] (hāz), *v.t.,* **hazed, haz|ing.** **1** to force (lower-class students or new members of a group) to do humiliating or ridiculous tasks: *The freshmen resented being hazed by the sophomores.* **2** *Especially Nautical.* to punish in a harassing or bullying manner by forcing unpleasant or unnecessary duties upon. **3** *Western U.S.* to drive (cattle or other herded animals) especially while on horseback. [probably special use of earlier *haze, hawze* terrify, punish, scold < Middle French *haser* irritate, annoy]

ha|zel** (hā′zəl), *n., adj.* **—*n. **1** any one of a group of shrubs or small trees whose light-brown nuts are good to eat. It belongs to the birch family. **2** the wood of any of these trees. **3** a stick or rod of this wood. **4** a hazelnut or filbert. **5** a light-brown color, like that of a hazelnut.
—*adj.* **1** of or having to do with hazel. **2** made of the wood of the hazel. **3** light-brown: *her . . . eye of hazel hue* (Scott).
[Old English *hæsel*]

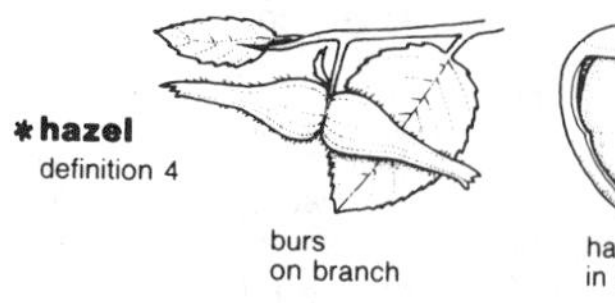

***hazel**
definition 4

hazel grouse or **hen,** a game bird of the woods of Europe and Asia, belonging to the same family as the ruffed grouse of North America; gelinotte.

ha|zel|ly (hā′zə lē), *adj.* **1** having many hazels. **2** having a hazel color.

ha|zel|nut (hā′zəl nut′), *n.* **1** the nut of the hazel; filbert. **2** the hazel plant.

haz|er (hā′zər), *n.* **1** a person who hazes, as on a ship or in a school. **2** *Western U.S.* a person who drives cattle or other herded animals.

haz|ing (hā′zing), *n.* **1** *U.S.* (among students) the forcing of humiliating or ridiculous tasks on freshmen by upperclassmen. **2** *Especially Nautical.* punishment by unpleasant or unnecessary duties; continual overwork. **3** the period of being hazed.

ha|zy (hā′zē), *adj.,* **-zi|er, -zi|est.** **1** full of haze; misty; smoky; dim: *a hazy sky.* SYN: indistinct. **2** *Figurative.* rather confused; vague; not distinct; obscure: *The injured man had only a hazy idea of what had happened.* SYN: uncertain. **—ha′zi|ly,** *adv.* **—ha′zi|ness,** *n.*

haz|zan (ʜä′zən, ʜä zän′), *n.* = chazan.

Hb (no period), hemoglobin.

HB (no periods), halfback.

H.B.M., His (or Her) Britannic Majesty.

HBO, Home Box Office (a commercial cable television service in the United States): *HBO is available only to cable TV subscribers and people who live in selected apartment buildings* (Time).

H-bomb (āch′bom′), *n., v.* **—*n.*** = hydrogen bomb. **—*v.t.*** to bomb with a hydrogen bomb.

H-bone (āch′bōn′), *n.* = aitchbone.

hbr., harbor.

H.C., **1** Heralds' College. **2** High Church. **3** High Commissioner. **4** House of Commons.

H.C.F., h.c.f., or **hcf** (no periods), highest common factor.

HCG (no periods), human chorionic gonadotropin.

H.C.J., High Court of Justice.

h.c.l., high cost of living.

HCl (no periods), hydrochloric acid.

hd., *pl.* **hds.** **1** hand. **2** head.

hdbk., handbook.

hdkf., *pl.* **hdkfs.** handkerchief.

HDL (no periods), high density lipoprotein: *High blood levels of HDL are . . . associated with a reduced risk of atherosclerosis* (New Scientist).

H. Doc., House of Representatives Document (always used with a number).

hdqrs., headquarters.

hdw., hardware.

hdwd., hardwood (lumber).

he[1] (hē; *unstressed* ē, i), *pron., nom.,* **he;** *poss.,* **his;** *obj.,* **him;** *pl. nom.,* **they;** *poss.,* **theirs, their;** *obj.,* **them;** *n., pl.* **hes.** **—*pron.*** **1** the boy, man, or male animal spoken about or mentioned before; male in question: *He works hard, but his work pays him well. The skipper he stood beside the helm* (Longfellow). **2** anyone; any person; one: *He who hesitates is lost.*
—*n.* a boy, man, or male animal; male: *Is your dog a he or a she?*
[Old English *hē*]

he[2] (hā), *n.* the fifth letter of the Hebrew alphabet. [< Hebrew *hē′*]

He (no period), helium (chemical element).

HE (no periods), high explosive.

H.E., **1** His Eminence. **2** His Excellency.

head (hed), *n., pl.* **heads** or (*for def. 5*) **head,** *adj., v.* **—*n.*** **1** the top part of the human body or the front part of an animal where the eyes, nose, ears, and mouth are. Your brain is in your head. *He'd leave his head behind him, if it was loose* (George Eliot). **2** the top part of anything: *the head of a pin, the head of a page, the head of a staircase, the head of a bed, the head of the table.* **3a** the front part or end of anything: *the head of a parade, the head of a comet, the head of a street, soldiers at the head of the column.* **b** the forward part of a ship, including the bow. **4** *Figurative.* **a** the chief person; leader; commander; director: *the head of a school. The chief is the head of an Indian tribe. He thought of himself habitually as the head of a great underground organization* (Edmund Wilson). SYN: ruler. **b** = headmaster. **c** the position of head; chief authority; leadership; command: *at the head of the administration.* **5** one or ones; individual or individuals; person or persons. Ten cows are ten head of cattle. *Kings and queens are crowned heads. Old heads are elders. The places are two-pence a head* (Horace Walpole). **6a** anything rounded like a head: *a head of lettuce, a head of cabbage, the head of a cane. The head of a violin is shaped like a scroll.* **b** *Botany.* a cluster of flowers in which the flowers or florets do not have individual stems, but grow close together from the main stem; flower head: *a head of clover. Botanists speak of such a flower cluster as a "head." This head is typical of the large group of flowering plants called the composites, including the daisies, sunflowers, ragweed and hundreds of others* (Science News Letter). **7** the part of a boil, pimple, or abscess where pus is about to break through the skin. **8a** the striking or cutting part of a tool or implement: *You hit the nail with the head of a hammer. You hit the ball with the head of a golf club.* **b** a chuck on a drill or lathe. **9a** an end or extremity of a thing, or either of two like ends: *As that great host, with measured tread . . . Rolled slowly toward the bridge's head* (Macaulay). **b** the piece of skin, cloth, or the like, stretched tightly over the end of a drum or tambourine; drumhead. **c** either end of a barrel or cask. **10** *Figurative.* the mind; understanding; intelligence; intellect: *He has a good head for figures. He's sudden if a thing comes to his head* (Shakespeare). **11** *Figurative.* **a** a main division; topic; subject: *He arranged his speech under four main heads.* SYN: heading, point. **b** the line or lines at the top of a newspaper article or at the top of a page as to indicate a section or contents: *Under a two-column head, the Times put his story in the coveted front-page turn (column eight) position* (Time). **12** *Figurative.* a decisive point; crisis or conclusion: *His sudden refusal brought matters to a head.* SYN: height, culmination. **13a** the pressure of water, gas, or other confined substance: *a full head of steam.* **b** *Figurative.* strength or force gained little by little: *As more people joined, the movement gathered head.* **c** *Obsolete.* a body or force gathered in opposition, as for war or revolt: *To save our heads, by raising of a head* (Shakespeare). **14a** the upper limit, as of a slope or body of water; source of a river or stream: *the head of a brook.* **b** a body of water kept at a height, as for supplying a mill. **c** the height of such a body of water or the force of its fall: *The energy in water power comes both from the weight of the water and from the head upon it. The head of the water is measured by the vertical distance through which the water falls in performing work* (Hope Holway). **d** *Geology.* a standard pressure of water used in determining the permeability of different rocks and rock formations. **15a** a figure, image, or representation of a head: *Coins often bear the head of a famous ruler.* **b** Often, **heads.** the top side of a coin; principal or obverse side, usually having a representation of a head. **16a** land that juts out into the sea; headland; cape; promontory: *Beachy Head is a promontory on the English Channel.* **b** a projecting part of a rock, mass of ice, sandbank, etc. **17a** the foam or froth on the top of beer or other liquor: *Many people prefer beer that has a good head.* **b** the cream on milk. **18** the upper edge or corner of a sail. **19** a lavatory, especially on a ship or boat. **20** *Grammar.* the modified member in a structure of a modification; a word which has the same grammatical function as the word group in which it occurs. In *very fresh milk* the head is *milk.* **21** *Electronics.* = magnetic head. **22** *Mining.* = heading. **23** the antlers of a deer. **24a** *Slang.* a drug user or addict, such as an acidhead or pothead: *"Most of the real heads were completely freaked out before they ever saw dope; that bag is just their outlet"* (New York Times). **b** a fan or devotee; freak: *a film head, a motorcycle head.* **25** the hair of the head: *I curled and combed his comely head* (Tennyson).
—*adj.* **1** at the head, front, or top: *the head group of a parade, the head section of a platoon.* **2** coming from in front; opposing: *a head wind, a head sea, head tides.* **3** *Figurative.* chief; leading; commanding; directing: *the head clerk in a store. Which is the head Lady?* (Shakespeare). **4** of or for the head; designed for the head; worn on the head: *head nets, head wrappings.*

—*v.t.* **1a** to be or go at the head, front, or top of; form the head of: *to head a parade. There are enough of them to make a large list in my private catalogue—headed, possibly, by Nino Perizi, whose "Morning by the River" has a lovely suggestion of sun-flecked blue water* (New Yorker). SYN: precede. **b** *Figurative.* to surpass; outdo; excel: *He heads all the records.* **2a** to cause to move or face in a certain direction: *to head a boat toward shore, to head a ship south. It's getting late, we'd better head our horses for home.* **b** to advance directly against or in opposition to the course of: *to head the driving snow.* **c** to get in front, often so as to cause to turn back or aside: *Priamos* [*a horse*] *took over from the early leaders fairly far along in the race and was never headed* (New Yorker). **3** *Figurative.* to be the head or chief of; lead; command; direct: *to head a business. Who will head the team? I in person will my people head* (Alexander Pope). SYN: rule. **4** to put a head on; furnish or fit with a head: *to cut and head nails, to head a letter with the date, to head a newspaper article with a title.* **5** to take the head off of; behead: *to head and gut fish.* **6** to lop the top branches off (a tree); poll: *Certain trees should be headed every few years.* **7** to go around the head of (a stream, lake, or the like): *The explorer headed the lake instead of crossing it.* **8** to collect (water) so as to form a head. **9** *Soccer.* to hit (the ball) with the head: *Good players can head the ball long distances* (George E. Fishwick).
—*v.i.* **1** to move or go toward or in a certain direction; face toward: *Our ship headed south. We headed for the hills.* **2** to move toward a specified state or plight: *They are heading for disaster.* **3** to grow to a head; form a head: *All my early wheat ... was headed or heading* (George Washington). **4** to have its head or source in a specified place, as a river or stream.

beat one's head against the wall, to attack or tackle something or someone without any hope of success; persist in a futile action or endeavor: *Nottingham Forest attacked and attacked, hit posts, missed chances, and generally beat their heads in frustration against* [*the*] *wall* (London Times).

bite off one's head, to speak to one in a sharp, rude, or curt manner: *Seldom have we seen* [*him*] *in a more snappy or irritable mood. Conservative peers could scarcely waggle their little fingers at him without having their heads bitten off* (London Times).

bury (or **hide**) **one's head in the sand**, to fail to face facts; hide from reality: *No use hiding your heads in the sand, folks. You can't turn back the clock* (S. J. Perelman).

by the head, **a** (of a ship) lower in the water at the bow than at the stern: *The vessel is too much by the head* (William Falconer). **b** *Slang.* slightly intoxicated: *He said he was a little by the head, but not drunk.*

come to a head, **a** (of a boil or other infection) to fill with pus; suppurate: *The medication should be applied before the infection comes to a head.* **b** *Figurative.* to come to a crisis, issue, culmination, maturity, or other result: *The trouble came to a head with the murder of an Opposition journalist* (Observer).

down by the head, to lower in the water at the bow; by the head: *As a result of the collision she is down by the head, but not in danger of sinking.*

eat one's head off, **a** to eat very much: *We ate our heads off at the clambake.* **b** to snap one's head off; speak to rudely or harshly: *If you argue with her she'll eat your head off.*

give one his head, to let someone do as he pleases: [*He*] *was given his head in choosing the programme* (Punch).

go to one's head, **a** to affect one's mind: *The poor man's troubles have gone to his head.* **b** to make one dizzy, excited, or intoxicated: *The whiskey has gone to his head.* **c** to make one conceited: *I'm afraid all this praise will go to my head.*

hang one's head, to show that one is ashamed: *He hung down his head, and ... withdrew quite abashed* (Charles Johnston).

head and shoulders, **a** by the amount of head and shoulders; considerably; very much: *He stood head and shoulders above his contemporaries ... as an orator* (Manchester Guardian). **b** bodily; irrelevantly; violently: *I must drag the mention of the fact in head and shoulders here, or else I shall forget it* (Anthony Trollope).

head first (or **foremost**), **a** with the head first or foremost: *She thrust him ... head foremost, into an oven* (James Hart). **b** *Figurative.* hastily; hurriedly: *The ... Dean plunged head foremost into the controversy* (Pall Mall Gazette).

head off, **a** to get in front of and turn back or aside; check: *The cowboys tried to head off the stampeding herd.* **b** to prevent; forestall: *He tried to head off possible trouble by extreme care in what he did.*

head over heels, **a** in a somersault: *He tripped and fell head over heels down the stairs.* **b** *Figurative.* hastily; rashly: *Away he went head over heels like a shot rabbit* (H. Rider Haggard). **c** *Figurative.* completely; thoroughly: *She is head over heels in love with him.*

heads (**would**, **will**, **are likely to**, etc.) **roll**, to punish people severely as by dismissal, suspension, or public disgrace: [*He*] *said that after his conviction heads would roll* (London Times).

head up, to serve or act as the head of; direct: *He heads up a staff of 50 lawyers.*

hide one's head, to show that one is ashamed: *He ought to hide his head after the way he mistreated that poor animal.*

keep one's head, to stay calm; not to get excited: *If only the man in the post of responsibility ... can ... keep his head* (George O. Trevelyan).

keep one's head above water, to avoid failure, loss, defeat, depression, or death: *Farmer Dobson, were I to marry him, has promised to keep our heads above water* (Tennyson).

keep one's head down, to make oneself inconspicuous; keep out of trouble: *The militant shop stewards have been keeping their heads down for months, both in London and Hull, under the impression that the Industrial Relations Act would be used to attack them if they became too prominent* (Sunday Times).

lay heads together, **a** to plan or plot together: *They will lay their heads together and conspire against the ... public* (Ralph Robinson). **b** to confer: *... and there lay their heads together and consult of matters* (John Bunyan).

light in the head, **a** dizzy: *The ride on the roller coaster made him feel light in the head.* **b** silly; foolish: *She blushed, giggled, and became light in the head in the company of boys.* **c** crazy; out of one's head: *Everybody thought that the old prospector still searching for gold was a little light in the head.*

lose one's head, to get excited; lose one's self-control: *The Embassy had been told ..., in explanation of the attack, that "a few people lost their heads"* (London Times).

make head, to move forward; make progress; advance: *They made head against the winds as best they could* (Dickens).

make head or tail of, to make any sense out of; understand: *His handwriting is so poor that I can't make head or tail of his letter.*

off (or **out**) **of one's head**, *Informal.* crazy; insane: *He transferred an inspector from one plant after Mr. Rubin had complained that the man "was off his head"* (New York Times).

on (or **upon**) **one's head**, **a** on one's responsibility: *The children's safety was on the teacher's head.* **b** falling, descending, or resting on a person: *The ... threats of vengeance on his head* (Alexander Pope).

out of one's own head, by one's own efforts; without borrowing ideas from others: *It came from you, and not out of my own head* (Daniel Defoe).

over head and ears, **a** completely immersed: *The poor lad plumped over head and ears into the water* (Henry Fielding). **b** *Figurative.* deeply involved, as in love or debt: *You are over head and ears in debt* (Anthony Trollope).

over one's head, **a** too hard for one to understand: *Einstein's theory is way over my head.* **b** to a person higher in authority: *Since her immediate superior didn't want to listen to her suggestion, she went over his head.* **c** passing over a person without giving him a chance to act, especially a person who has a senior status, a prior claim, or a better right: *An outsider has now been promoted over their heads.* **d** deeply involved: *He is over his head in gambling debts.*

put heads together, **a** to confer; consult: *We'll put heads together and consider what is to be done* (Sabine Baring-Gould). **b** to plan or plot together; conspire: *The rebels put heads together to plan the overthrow of the government.*

put one's head in the lion's mouth, to put oneself in a dangerous position: *He was warned not to put his head in the lion's mouth by going into the unexplored part of the cave.*

rear an (or **one's**) **ugly head**, to make an unwelcome appearance: *One of the old bogies of golf, the claiming of a hole for a putt not conceded, reared its ugly head again* (London Times).

set on one's head, to upset, confuse, or destroy the normal condition of: *Yorkshire gloried in the return of Boycott as captain—and he and they immediately set cricket on its head with a magnificent victory over Warwickshire* (Manchester Guardian Weekly).

shake one's head, to turn one's head from side to side in expressing denial, disapproval, dissent, doubt, scorn, sorrow, or other negative attitude: *"No, I shan't!" said Molly, shaking her head* (Elizabeth C. Gaskell).

snap one's head off, to speak to one in a sharply rude or harsh manner: *He had snapped Mr. Harold Wilson's head off the previous day, but ... was in command of himself when he ended the debate* (Manchester Guardian).

take it into one's head, **a** to get the idea: *The balance is lost if a rear-seat passenger takes it into his head to move from one side to the other* (New Scientist). **b** to plan; intend: *I took it into my head to walk up and down the gallery* (Benjamin Disraeli).

talk one's head off, to talk endlessly: *Don't get her started; she'll talk your head off!*

turn one's head, **a** to make one conceited: *Winning the contest turned his head so that he is now insufferable.* **b** to affect the mind: *The bad news must have turned his head, else he wouldn't act so queerly.* **c** to make one dizzy: *The dancing had turned her head, so that she had to lean on him to keep her balance.*

[Old English *hēafod*] —**head'like'**, *adj.*

head|ache (hed'āk'), *n.* **1** a pain in the head. **2** *Informal, Figurative:* *Packing everything to move to a new house is a headache.*

headache band, an ornamental band worn across the forehead. It was popular among flappers of the 1920's.

head|ach|y (hed'ā'kē), *adj. Informal.* **1** of or like a headache. **2** having somewhat of a headache; inclined to a headache.

head|band (hed'band'), *n.* **1** a band worn around the head; fillet. **2** *U.S.* a printed strip of decoration at the head of a chapter or page. **3** a decorative band attached to the top and bottom of the spine of a bound book. **4** the band connecting a pair of receivers or earphones.

head|board (hed'bôrd', -bōrd'), *n.* a board at the head or upper end of anything, such as a bedstead or a grave.

head|bor|ough (hed'bėr'ō), *n.* in England: **1** (formerly) the head of a frankpledge or tithing. **2** a parish officer having the functions of a petty constable. **3** a similar official elsewhere.

head|cheese (hed'chēz'), *n. U.S.* a jellied loaf formed of edible parts of the head and feet of hogs or other animals, cut up, cooked, and seasoned. [American English < *head* + *cheese*. Compare Dutch *hoofdkaas*.]

head cold, a cold affecting parts of the head, such as the nasal passages, ears, and eyes; coryza.

head count, *Informal.* **1** a count of individuals; census: *population head count.* **2** survey; poll.

head counter, *Informal.* **1** a census taker. **2** a pollster.

head|dress (hed'dres'), *n.* **1** a covering or decoration for the head: *the feathers and beads of an Indian headdress.* **2** a way of wearing or arranging the hair.

head|ed (hed'id), *adj.* **1** having a head. **2** having a heading. **3** grown or shaped into a head, as a plant or boil.

-headed, *combining form.* **1** having a ___ head: *Round-headed = having a round head.* **2** having ___ heads: *Three-headed = having three heads.*

head|er (hed'ər), *n.* **1** a person, tool, or machine that puts on or takes off heads, such as those of barrels, pins, or nails. **2** a harvesting machine that cuts off the heads of grain and puts them in a storage box or a wagon. **3** *Informal.* a plunge, dive, or fall headfirst: *He slipped and took a header over the pool's edge.* **4** a beam forming part of a framework around an opening of a floor or roof, placed so as to fit between two long beams and support the ends of the short ones. **5** a brick or stone laid with its length across the thickness of a wall. **6** the act of hitting the ball with the head in soccer: *He scored the second goal with a perfect header* (London Times). **7** *Nautical.* = head wind.

head|first (hed'fėrst'), *adv., adj.* —*adv.* **1** with the head first: *He caught the rail, pulled himself over it headfirst, and then went clawing up the deck* (Atlantic). **2** *Figurative.* hastily; rashly: *He made several mistakes, because he dove headfirst into the project without thinking about what he was doing.* SYN: headlong, precipitately.
—*adj.* done or going with the head first.

head|fish (hed'fish'), *n., pl.* **-fishes** or (*collectively*) **-fish.** = ocean sunfish.

head|fore|most (hed'fôr'mōst, -fōr'-), *adv.* = headfirst.

Pronunciation Key: hat, āge, cãre, fär; let, ēqual, tėrm; it, īce; hot, ōpen, ôrder; oil, out; cup, pu̇t, rüle; child; long; thin; ᴛʜen; zh, measure; ə represents a in about, e in taken, i in pencil, o in lemon, u in circus.

head|form (hed′fôrm′), *n.* the form of the head, especially in reference to the ratio of its breadth to its length: *The cephalic indices or headforms of great numbers of individuals over the earth are computed and plotted on a world map* (White and Renner).

head|frame (hed′frām), *n.* a framelike structure over the entrance to a mine, used to support the hoisting equipment.

head|ful (hed′fu̇l), *n., pl.* **-fuls.** as much as the head can hold.

head gate, **1** an upstream gate of a lock in a canal or river. **2** a floodgate of a race, sluice, irrigation ditch, or the like.

head|gear (hed′gir′), *n.* **1** a covering for the head; hat, cap, bonnet, helmet, or headdress of any kind. **2** the parts of a harness which fit around an animal's head. **3** = headguard.

head gland, one of several glands of a bee which produce the chemicals that bees add to nectar to make honey.

head|guard (hed′gärd′), *n.* a padded helmet worn to protect the head, as of boxers.

head|house (hed′hous′), *n.* an area in the top of a grain elevator where weighing and cleaning takes place; cupola.

head|hunt (hed′hunt′), *v., n. Informal.* **—*v.i., v.t.*** to recruit executives for a business: *Arch was headhunting ... to fill vacancies in a firm* (London Times). **—*n.*** an instance of headhunting.

head|hunt|er (hed′hun′tər), *n.* **1** a person who practices headhunting. **2** *Informal.* a person who recruits executives for business: *Corporate headhunters have been descending on campuses with uncommon force and flair* (Time).

head|hunt|ing (hed′hun′ting), *n., adj.* **—*n.*** the practice, among certain primitive tribes, of trying to get the heads of enemies, especially as a sign of victory or manhood.
—*adj.* of or having to do with headhunters.

head|ing (hed′ing), *n.* **1** something used as a head, front, or top. The pieces of wood for the heads of casks and barrels are headings. **2** something written or printed at the top of a page. A letterhead is a heading. **3** the title of a page, chapter, or topic. **4** a subject of discourse; topic. **5** the direction toward which an aircraft or ship is moving. **6** a passage driven through coal or sometimes rock, for working a mine, or for draining or ventilating; drift. **7** the end of a drift or gallery.

head|ker|chief (hed′kėr′chif), *n.* a kerchief worn on the head.

head|lamp (hed′lamp′), *n.* **1** a headlight on an automobile, locomotive, or other vehicle: *The headlamps of a police van lit an open door, and figures moved to and fro carrying packages* (Graham Greene). **2** a small lamp worn on the forehead or the front of a cap, as by miners, cave explorers, or night fishermen.

head|land (hed′lənd, -land′), *n.* **1** a point of land jutting out into water; cape; promontory. See picture under **peninsula. 2** a strip of land in a plowed field, left for turning the plow at the ends of furrows or near a border, fence, or wall.

head|less (hed′lis), *adj.* **1** having no head: *a broken, headless doll.* **2** *Figurative.* without a leader: *Headless, the Hittite civilization survived for another 500 years ... in several Asia Minor city states* (Newsweek). **3** without brains; foolish; stupid: *a headless simpleton.* [Old English *hēafodlēas* < *hēafod* head + *-lēas* -less]

head|light (hed′līt′), *n.* **1** a bright light on the front of an automobile, train, or other vehicle. **2** a light at a masthead.

head|line (hed′līn′), *n., v.,* **-lined, -lin|ing.** **—*n.*** **1** words printed in heavy type at the top of a newspaper article telling what it is about: *The headline across the top of the newspaper declared the war was over.* **2** a line printed at the top of a page giving the running title, page number, alphabetical span, and other information of content; running head.
—*v.t.* **1** to furnish with a headline: *to headline a news story.* **2** to give publicity to: *The newspapers headlined the story of the astronauts' trip to the moon.* **3** to list, or be listed in, as the main attraction: *The last show headlined another performer.* **—*v.i.*** to be the main attraction: *She is headlining in the new play.*
headlines, publicity: *His invention made the headlines of the day.*
make headlines, to receive publicity: *The International Geophysical Year made extensive headlines throughout the world.*

head|lin|er (hed′lī′nər), *n.* **1** *Informal.* an actor or performer whose name is given prominence in advertisements or on the program. **2** a person who writes newspaper headlines.

head|lin|ing (hed′lī′ning), *n.* the lining that covers the ceiling of an automobile.

head|load (hed′lōd′), *n.* **1** a way of carrying loads by balancing them on the head. **2** a load carried this way.

head|lock (hed′lok′), *n.* a wrestling hold in which an opponent's head is gripped and held between the body and arm of the wrestler applying the hold.

head|long (hed′lông, -long), *adv., adj.* **—*adv.*** **1** with the head first: *to plunge headlong into the sea.* **2** *Figurative.* with great haste and force: *to rush headlong into the crowd.* **3** *Figurative.* in too great a rush; without stopping to think; hurriedly or rashly: *The boy ran headlong across the busy street. One should not rush headlong into buying stocks.* SYN: precipitately.
—*adj.* **1** done or going headfirst: *a headlong plunge or dive.* **2** *Figurative.* done, caused by, or characterized by great haste and force: *a headlong course, headlong flight.* **3** *Figurative.* violently or suddenly rash; reckless: *headlong haste or folly.* SYN: precipitate. **4** descending steeply; precipitous: *a headlong slope. ... headlong leaps of water* (Elizabeth Barrett Browning).
[Middle English *hedlong,* alteration of earlier *hedlyng* < *hed* head + *-ling* -ling] **—head′long|ness,** *n.*

✱head louse, a species of louse that infests the human scalp.

✱head louse 

head|man (hed′man′, -mən), *n., pl.* **-men. 1** a chief; leader: *The headman greets you with a handshake and speaks to you in English, and the women, huddled over their untidy fires, smile at you* (Manchester Guardian Weekly). **2** *Obsolete.* a headsman; executioner. [Old English *hēafodman* < *hēafod* head + *man* man]

head|mas|ter (hed′mas′tər, -mäs′-), *n.* the man in charge of a school, especially a private school; principal. **—head′mas′ter|ly,** *adj.* **—head′mas′ter|ship,** *n.*

head metal, the head of metal at the upper end of a cylindrical casting.

head|mis|tress (hed′mis′tris), *n.* the woman in charge of a school, especially a private school; principal. **—head′mis′tress|ship,** *n.*

head money, **1** a tax or fee of so much per person. **2** a sum paid for each prisoner taken at sea, for each slave recovered, or for each enemy or criminal captured or killed.

head|most (hed′mōst), *adj.* most advanced; first; foremost.

head noises, *Medicine.* subjective sounds due to defective hearing or deafness, or to wax in the ears.

head|note (hed′nōt′), *n.* an explanatory note placed before an article, report, chapter, or the like.

head-on (hed′on′, -ôn′), *adj., adv.* **1** with the head or front first: *His car was involved in a head-on collision* (adj.). *It collided head-on with a truck* (adv.). **2** in a direct manner; headlong: *Some lawmakers currently are meeting conservative opposition head-on* (Wall Street Journal).

head|phone (hed′fōn′), *n.* a telephone or radio receiver or earphone for listening to recordings, held against the ear by a band over the head.
headphones, a pair of these: *Many people working in a TV or radio studio wear headphones.*

head|piece (hed′pēs′), *n.* **1** a piece of armor for the head; helmet worn with a suit of armor. **2** any covering for the head. **3** = headphone. **4** the head, especially as the seat of the intellect; brain; mind: *We are the stuffed men Leaning together Headpiece filled with straw* (T. S. Eliot). **5** *Printing.* a decoration at the head of a page, chapter, document, or other printed matter.

head pin, or **head|pin** (hed′pin′), *n.* the front pin of the triangle of pins in bowling; kingpin.

head|quar|ter (hed′kwôr′tər), *v.i.* to have or set up headquarters (in): *Will headquarter in N.Y.C. and travel abroad as required* (Wall Street Journal).

head|quar|ters (hed′kwôr′terz), *n.pl. or sing.* **1a** the place from which the chief or commanding officer of an army or police force sends out orders: *on the way to report himself at headquarters* (Washington Irving). **b** the part of a military unit or police force which controls the unit and consists of the person in command and his assistants. **2** the place from which any organization or activity is controlled and directed; main office; center of operations or of authority: *The headquarters of the American Red Cross is in Washington, D.C. Abbr:* hdqrs.

head|race (hed′rās′), *n.* the race, flume, or channel that brings water to a mill wheel.

head resistance, the resistance of air against the fuselage of an airplane.

head|rest (hed′rest′), *n.* **1** something against which to rest the head, such as the attachment on a dentist's or barber's chair. **2** a padded attachment on the back of an automobile seat, to keep the head from snapping backward in a collision; head-restraint.

head-re|straint (hed′ri strānt′), *n.* = headrest.

head|rig (hed′rig′), *n.* the sawing machinery of a sawmill.

head|right (hed′rīt′), *n., v.* **—*n.*** **1** the inheritable right to a tract of the public land of the state, formerly granted by Texas, Georgia, and other states, upon certain conditions, to heads of families, resident or immigrant. **2** a tract of land so granted.
—*v.t.* **1** to grant (land) by headright. **2** to acquire (land) by headright.

head|room (hed′rüm′, -ru̇m′), *n.* clear space overhead, such as that in a doorway, under an arch, or in an automobile; headway: *You get more headroom, leg room and more visibility* (Wall Street Journal).

head|sail (hed′sāl′; *Nautical* hed′səl), *n.* any triangular fore-and-aft sail attached to a stay in front of the foremast, such as a jib, flying jib, or forestay sail.

head|scarf (hed′skärf′), *n., pl.* **-scarves** (-skärvz). *British.* a woman's scarf worn around the head.

head|set (hed′set′), *n.* a pair of headphones used by telephone and radio operators or others.

head|shake (hed′shāk′), *n.* the act of turning the head from side to side to express denial, disapproval, dissent, doubt, scorn, or sorrow.

head|shak|ing (hed′shā′king), *n.* **1** the act of shaking one's head; headshake: *My only means of communication were paper and pen and pencil, and such weak natural adjuncts as nods [and] headshakings* (New Yorker). **2** an expression of doubt, disbelief, pessimism, or other negative feeling: *Macaulay is neither the first nor will he be the last to indulge in headshaking about democracy as a political system* (Wall Street Journal).

head|ship (hed′ship), *n.* **1** the position or office of head; chief authority; leadership. SYN: chiefship, primacy, supremacy. **2** *Especially British.* the position or office of a headmaster.

head shop, a store selling psychedelic wares, such as glowing posters, sticks for burning incense, and paraphernalia used in drug taking.

head|shrink|er (hed′shring′kər), *n.* **1** (among primitive peoples) a person who shrinks the cut-off heads of his enemies as trophies. **2** *Slang.* a psychiatrist.

heads|man (hedz′mən), *n., pl.* **-men.** a man who cuts off the heads of people condemned to death; public executioner.

head|space (hed′spās′), *n.* the space left at the top of a filled can or other container before it is sealed: *... analysis of the headspace ... in tins of coffee for the detection of unwanted oxygen* (New Scientist).

head spin, a move in wrestling, consisting of throwing the feet in the air and turning the head and body, used to escape a half nelson.

head|spring (hed′spring′), *n.* **1** the fountainhead or main source of a stream. **2** *Figurative.* the chief source of anything; place where anything originates.

head|square (hed′skwãr′), *n. British.* a headscarf.

head|stall (hed′stôl′), *n.* the part of a bridle or halter that fits around the head of a horse or other animal.

head|stand (hed′stand′), *n.* the act of balancing upon the head, with the hands placed in front of the head on the mat or ground.

head start, **1** an advantage or lead allowed someone at the beginning of a race. **2** an advantage gained by beginning something before somebody else; being ahead; lead: *The candidate who can convince voters he knows best ... will have a head start toward election* (Wall Street Journal).

Head Start, *U.S.* an educational project of the Federal antipoverty program established in the 1960's, consisting of classroom training for preschool children in order to give them a head start or prepare them for entry into the regular school system on a level comparable to that of children who got such training in their homes.

head|stock (hed′stok′), *n.* **1** a part of a machine, especially a bearing or housing, that contains the revolving or working parts. **2** the part of a lathe that holds the live spindle.

head|stone (hed′stōn′), *n.* **1** a stone marker set at the head of a grave; gravestone; tombstone. **2** the cornerstone of a building.

head|stream (hed′strēm′), *n.* a stream that is the source of a larger stream.

head|strong (hed′strông′, -strong′), *adj.* **1** rashly or foolishly determined to have one's own way; hard to control or manage; obstinate: *a headstrong horse, a headstrong child. The headstrong* *monarch was enraged by the very suggestion of foreign mediation in a domestic quarrel with his colonies* (Atlantic). SYN: willful. **2** showing rash or foolish determination to have one's way: *head-strong actions. I'll curb her mad and headstrong humour* (Shakespeare). **—head′strong′ness,** *n.*

heads-up (hedz′up′), *adj. Informal.* alert; resourceful. [< *heads up!*, an exclamation used by ballplayers to call attention to a falling ball]

head tax, a tax of so much per person; poll tax.

head|teach|er (hed′tē′chər), *n. British.* a person in charge of a school; headmaster.

head|tire (hed′tīr′), *n. Archaic.* a headdress.

head-to-head (hed′tə hed′), *adj., n.* **—*adj.*** (of a contest) very close; almost even.
—*n.* a contest or fight at very close quarters.

head tone, 1 a tone produced in the second or third register of the voice. **2** a tone in singing that causes vibration in the cavities of the head.

head|torch (hed′tôrch′), *n. British.* a lamp that can be worn on the forehead; headlamp.

head-to-toe (hed′tə tō′), *adj. Informal.* thorough; complete; from top to bottom: *a head-to-toe overhaul of the whole system.*

head|wait|er (hed′wā′tər), *n.* a man in charge of the waiters in a restaurant, hotel, or dining car.

head|ward (hed′wərd), *adv., adj.* toward the head.

head|wards (hed′wərdz), *adv.* = headward.

head|wa|ters (hed′wô′tərz, -wot′ərz), *n.pl.* the sources or upper parts of a river: *the headwaters of the Mississippi.*

head|way (hed′wā′), *n.* **1** motion forward or ahead; progress: *The ship could make no headway against the strong wind and tide.* **2** *Figurative.* progress with work or other activity; advance: *Science has made much headway in fighting disease.* **3** a clear space overhead, such as that in a doorway or under a bridge or arch; clearance: *The stairs should have seven feet headway.* **4** the interval of time between two trains, buses, aircraft, or ships, going in the same direction over the same route.

head|wear (hed′wãr′), *n.* a covering for the head; headgear.

head wind, a wind blowing from the direction in which a ship or aircraft is moving: *Against a head wind you make very little headway* (Harper's).

head word, or **head|word** (hed′wėrd′), *n.* **1** a word serving as a heading or title, as of a paragraph, article, or dictionary entry. **2** *Grammar.* a word around which clusters of modifiers are built. In *the small boy, very glad, is running fast,* the words *boy, glad,* and *running* are head words.

head|work (hed′wėrk′), *n.* **1** mental work; effort with the mind; brainwork; thought. **2** the use of the head to propel the ball in soccer.

head|work|er (hed′wėr′kər), *n.* a person who works with his head; one engaged in mental work.

head|y (hed′ē), *adj.,* **head|i|er, head|i|est. 1** hasty; rash; impetuous: *this heady, imaginative young enthusiast* (H. G. Wells). SYN: precipitate, headstrong, violent. **2** apt to affect the head and make one dizzy; intoxicating: *a heady wine. He would sit on a heady scaffold* (Atlantic). **3** *Informal.* intelligent. [contraction of Middle English *hevedi* (originally) headlong; (later) affecting the head] **—head′i|ly,** *adv.* **—head′iness,** *n.*

heal (hēl), *v.t.* **1** to make whole, sound, or well; bring back to health; cure: *The medicine and rest will soon heal your wound. Physician, heal thyself* (Luke 4:23). SYN: See syn. under **cure. 2** *Figurative.* to free from anything bad; save; cleanse: *So the waters were healed* (II Kings 2:22). **3** *Figurative.* to get rid of (anything bad): *Silence, like a poultice, comes To heal the blows of sound* (Oliver Wendell Holmes).
—*v.i.* to become whole or sound; grow well; become well; return to health; be cured: *His cut finger healed in a few days.*
[Old English *hǣlan*, related to *hāl* whole] **—heal′a|ble,** *adj.*

heal-all (hēl′ôl′), *n.* **1** a cure-all; panacea. **2** any one of various plants that supposedly have healing properties.

heald (hēld), *n. British.* heddle. [Old English *hefeld* thrum, looped end of a warp thread]

heal|er (hē′lər), *n.* **1** a person or thing that heals: *Time is the great healer of sorrow.* **2** a person who practices healing by Christian Science or some form of faith cure.

heal|ing (hē′ling), *adj., n.* **—*adj.* 1** that heals or cures; curative: *a healing salve.* (*Figurative.*) *The prospect of a Democratic bloodletting was eminently pleasing to Republicans. ... They reckoned, however, without the healing hand of Majority Leader Lyndon Johnson* (Time). SYN: curing, salutary. **2** growing sound; getting well: *The healing process was hastened by the new drugs.*
—*n.* the act of a person or thing that heals: *For of the most High cometh healing* (Ecclesiasticus 38:2). **—heal′ing|ly,** *adv.*

health (helth), *n.* **1** the condition of being well or not sick; freedom from illness of any kind: *Rest, sleep, exercise, and cleanliness are important to your health. Health alone is victory* (Thomas Carlyle). **2** the general condition of body or mind: *She is in poor health. He is in excellent health.* **3** sound condition; well-being; welfare: *the safety and health of the whole state.* **4** a drink in honor of a person with a wish that he may be healthy and happy: *We all drank a health to the bride.* **5** spiritual, moral, or mental soundness; salvation.
for one's health, without compensation or similar benefit; for nothing: *Naturally, I don't expect insurance companies to be in the business for their health, but, surely, it is also their function to provide a public service* (New York Times).
[Old English *hǣlth*, related to *hāl* whole]

health club, a club with equipment and facilities and a program of exercises and dieting for the improvement of health.

health food, any one of certain foods to which special therapeutic properties are ascribed, especially by food faddists: *The AMA warns ... that the term "health food" is a misnomer because it implies curative properties* (Maclean's).

health|ful (helth′fəl), *adj.* **1** giving health; good for the health; wholesome: *a healthful diet, healthful exercise.* SYN: salubrious. **2** helping to bring about moral or spiritual welfare or prosperity; saving: *a healthful spirit of cooperation.* SYN: salutary. **3** having intellectual or moral soundness: *healthful studies.* **4** having good health; healthy. **—health′ful|ly,** *adv.* **—health′-ful|ness,** *n.*
▶**healthful, healthy.** Though these words are often used interchangeably, some writers and speakers distinguish between them by using *healthful* to mean "giving health" and *healthy* to mean "having good health." Places and food are *healthful;* persons and animals are *healthy.*

health insurance, insurance that covers doctor's bills, medical expenses, loss of income due to illness, and other expenses associated with illness.

health maintenance organization, an organization that provides subscribers with comprehensive health care for a fixed fee: *Health maintenance organizations can be a third option for the Medicare recipient. An HMO is a one-stop shopping center that offers a broad range of health services—including hospitalization, preventive care, diagnosis, and nursing—for a fixed monthly or yearly premium* (Consumer Reports).

health officer, an officer charged with the administration of the laws regulating sanitary conditions and inspection.

health physics, the field of study that deals with the effects of radioactive radiation on health, including protection against radiation and treatment of those exposed to it. **—health physicist.**

health resort, a resort for improvement of health, often with baths, mineral springs, and sports facilities.

health|wise (helth′wīz′), *adv. Informal.* from the standpoint of (good) health.

health|y (hel′thē), *adj.,* **health|i|er, health|i|est. 1** having good health; sound; well: *a healthy baby.* **2** characteristic of good health or sound condition; showing good health: *a healthy appearance, a healthy appetite, healthy lung tissue.* **3** giving health; good for the health; healthful: *healthy exercise.* SYN: nourishing, salutary. **—health′i|ly,** *adv.* **—health′i|ness,** *n.*
—*Syn.* 1, 2 Healthy, wholesome mean having or showing health. **Healthy** suggests the strength and vigor that come of good health, the normal condition of someone who feels well: *a healthy body. He has a healthy appearance even though he is actually not well.* **Wholesome** suggests physical, mental, and moral soundness: *wholesome food, wholesome advice, wholesome appearance. The new baby sitter is a wholesome-looking girl. Our uncle gave us wholesome advice.*
▶See **healthful** for usage note.

HEAO (no periods), high-energy astronomy observatory (any of a series of unmanned earth satellites that gather data on X-ray stars, gamma-ray bursts, and other astronomical phenomena): *HEAO-1, at 7,000 pounds (3,175 kg) the heaviest unmanned earth orbiting satellite ever launched, carried a new generation of experiments that dwarfed earlier rocket and satellite experiments* (Pitt G. Thome).

heap (hēp), *n., v.* **—*n.* 1** a pile of many things thrown or lying together: *a heap of stones, a sand heap.* SYN: mass, stack, accumulation. **2** *Informal.* a large amount; a lot; multitude: *a heap of trouble. It did me a heap of good to see my old friends.*
—*v.t.* 1 to form into a heap; gather in heaps; amass; accumulate: *She heaped the dirty clothes next to the washing machine.* **2** to give generously or in large amounts: *The man heaped praise on his friends.* **3** to fill full or more than full; load: *to heap a plate with food.*
—*v.i.* to become heaped or piled; rise in a heap or heaps: *Snow heaped against the fence.*
[Old English *hēap* heap, chiefly of persons (troop, multitude, company)] **—heap′er,** *n.*

heap|stead (hēp′sted′), *n.* the entire plant above ground at the shaft of a coal mine.

heap|y (hē′pē), *adj.,* **heap|i|er, heap|i|est.** forming a heap or heaps: *White heapy clouds, looking like balls ... bring no rain* (New Yorker).

hear (hir), *v.,* **heard** (hėrd), **hear|ing,** *interj.* **—*v.t.* 1** to take in a sound or sounds through the ear: *to hear voices, to hear a bell. Can you hear my watch tick?* **2** to listen to; give ear to; hearken to: *You must hear what he has to say. I will not retreat a single inch; and I will be heard!* (William Lloyd Garrison). **3** to listen to with favor; accede to; grant: *Lord, hear my prayer.* **4a** to give a chance to be heard; give a formal hearing to, as a king, a judge, a teacher, or an assembly does: *to hear a complaint.* **b** to attend and listen to (a lecture, musical performance, or other entertainment or address); be among the audience at: *Did you go to hear Dylan Thomas?* **5** to find out by hearing; be told; be informed of: *to hear news.* **6** *U.S. Informal.* to understand: *They say "I hear you," meaning "I understand what you're saying"* (Harper's).
—*v.i.* 1 to be able to take in a sound or sounds through the ear: *He cannot hear well. Can fishes hear?* **2** to listen; give ear; hearken: *The town crier shouted, "Hear ye!"* **3** to be told; receive news or information: *What did you hear at the club meeting?*
—*interj.* hear! hear! *Especially British.* shouts of approval; cheering: *One Noble Lord or Honorable Member asking a question ... amid cries of hear! hear!* (James Russell Lowell).
hear from, a to receive news or information from: *Have you heard from your brother in Los Angeles?* **b** to receive a reprimand from: *If those louts up at the castle neglected to have dinner ready ... they would hear from him* (Munsey's Magazine).
hear out, to listen to till the end: *There was an agreement between us that you should hear me out* (Benjamin Jowett).
let's hear it for, *U.S. Informal.* let's cheer or applaud: *The leader ... is on his toes, up and down, flinging himself about and saying, "Let's hear it for President George Meany"* (Harper's).
not hear of, not listen to, think of, agree to, or allow: *The landlord would not hear of reducing the tenant's rent.*
[Old English *hēran*] **—hear′a|ble,** *adj.* **—hear′er,** *n.*
—*Syn.* *v.t.* **1, 2 Hear, listen** mean to perceive by the ear. **Hear** applies to the physical act of receiving sound through the ear: *Do you hear a noise?* **Listen** means to pay attention to a sound and try to hear or understand it: *I heard you talking but did not listen to what you said.*

heard (hėrd), *v.* past tense and past participle of **hear:** *I heard the noise. The gun was heard a mile away.*

hear|ing (hir′ing), *n.* **1** the power to hear; sense by which sound is perceived: *The old man's hearing is poor.* **2** the act or process of perceiving sound, of listening, or of receiving information: *Hearing the good news made her happy.* SYN: audition. **3** a formal or official listening, especially to evidence and arguments in court, as in a trial before a judge and without a jury: *The judge gave both sides a hearing in court.* **4** a chance to be heard; audience: *Give us a hearing.* **5** the distance that a sound can be heard; earshot: *to talk freely in the hearing of others.*
hard of hearing. See under **hard.**

***hearing aid,** a small battery-powered, electronic device which amplifies sounds, worn by people who cannot hear well. **—hear′ing-aid′,** *adj.*

***hearing aid**

hearing examiner, *U.S.* a person appointed by a government agency to conduct a hearing or to act as a fact-finder in a case under investigation

Pronunciation Key: hat, āge, cãre, fär; let, ēqual, tėrm; it, īce; hot, ōpen, ôrder; oil, out; cup, pu̇t, rüle; child; long; thin; ᴛʜen; zh, measure; ə represents **a** in about, **e** in taken, **i** in pencil, **o** in lemon, **u** in circus.

or consideration by the agency.

hearing room, a room in which hearings are held, especially court hearings.

hark|en (här′kən), *v.i.* to pay attention to what is said; listen attentively; listen: *If a ruler hearken to lies, all his servants are wicked* (Proverbs 29:12). **—*v.t.*** **1** to hear with attention; listen to; heed. **2** to understand or learn by hearing; perceive by the ear. Also, **harken**. [perhaps Old English *heorcnian*]

hear|say (hir′sā′), *n.* common talk; gossip or rumor: *All this is mere hearsay.* SYN: report.

hearsay evidence, *Law.* evidence at second hand, consisting of testimony based on information that a witness has obtained from another person, not from first-hand personal knowledge. Hearsay evidence is usually inadmissible, but is sometimes made to show reputation, relate dying declarations, or introduce into the record otherwise unobtainable information.

hearse (hėrs), *n., v.,* **hearsed** (hėrst), **hears|ing.** **—*n.*** **1** an automobile, carriage, boat, or other vehicle, for carrying a coffin to the cemetery. **2** a triangular frame with prickets or prongs for candles, used at the Holy Week Tenebrae service. **3** *Historical.* a structure over a royal or noble tomb or coffin, decorated with candles, heraldic devices, poems, and other paraphernalia. **4** *Archaic.* **a** a bier; coffin. **b** a tomb; grave: *And daffadillies fill their cups with tears, To strew the laureat hearse where Lycid lies* (Milton).
—*v.t.* **1** to carry to the grave in a hearse. **2** *Archaic.* to bury with funeral rites and ceremonies; place on a bier or in a coffin or tomb: *Tell Why thy canonized bones, hearsed in death, Have burst their cerements* (Shakespeare). **3** to enclose or contain as if in a bier or tomb; entomb: *I only see ... The hilltop hearsed with pines* (Longfellow).
[Middle English *herse* framework over a bier for candles < Old French *herce* < Latin *hirpex* harrow]

hears|y (hėr′sē), *adj.* resembling or characteristic of a hearse; funeral: *Full-clothed in black, with nodding hearsy plumes* (Thomas Hardy).

***heart**
definitions 1a, 8

parts of the heart:

exterior

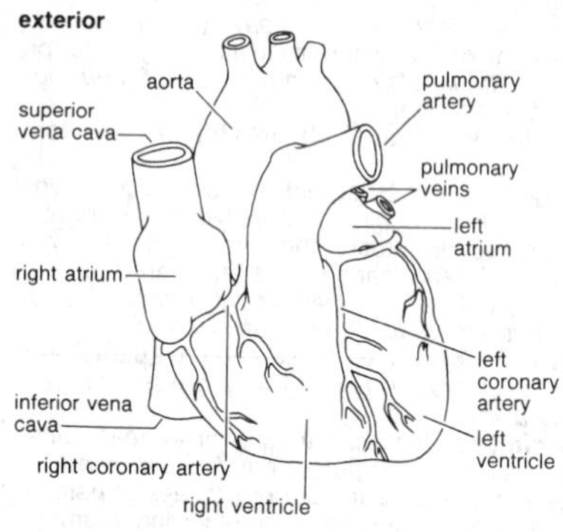

interior

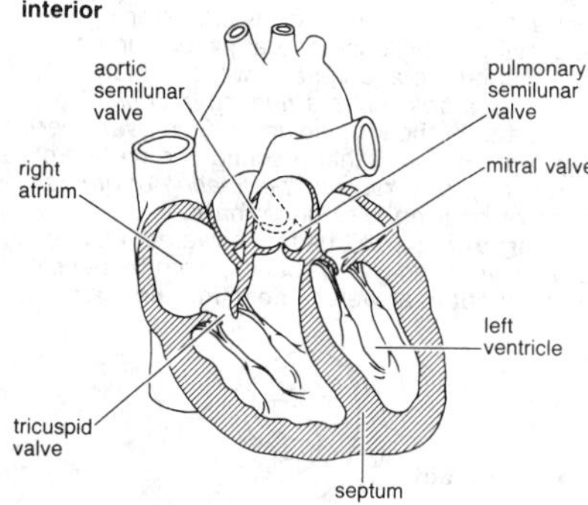

definition 8

heart** (härt), *n., v.* **—*n. **1a** the hollow, muscular organ of the body that pumps the blood by contracting and expanding. **b** the region of the heart; breast; bosom. **2** *Figurative.* the part that feels, loves, hates, and desires; seat of one's inmost thoughts and secret feelings; soul; mind: *a heavy heart. She has a kind heart. He knew in his heart that he was wrong.* **3** *Figurative.* love or affection; devotion: *to give one's heart to someone.* **4** a person, especially one who is loved or praised: *a group of stout hearts.* **5** *Figurative.* kindness; sympathy: *Have you no heart?* SYN: compassion. **6** *Figurative.* spirit; courage; enthusiasm; determination: *to lose heart. The losing team still had plenty of heart. Faint heart never won fair lady* (William S. Gilbert). SYN: resolution, fortitude. **7a** the innermost part; middle; center: *in the heart of the forest, the heart of a cabbage.* **b** *Figurative.* the main part; most important part; essence: *the very heart of the matter.* SYN: crux. **8** a figure shaped somewhat like the picture on the playing card: *The valentine was covered with hearts.* **9** a playing card marked with one or more red, heart-shaped figures: *He discarded a heart.* **10** *Botany.* the solid central part of a tree without sap or alburnum. See **heartwood**. **11** the power of producing; fertility (of land, etc.). **12** *Obsolete.* disposition; temperament; character.
—*v.t.* **1** *Archaic.* to hearten; inspire with confidence; encourage. **2** *Obsolete.* to fix in the heart: *I hate the Moor; my cause is hearted* (Shakespeare).
—*v.i.* to form a heart, core, or compact central portion, as cabbages or lettuce.
after one's own heart, just as one likes it; pleasing one perfectly: *Now that's a meal after my own heart!*
at heart, in one's deepest thoughts or feelings; really: *He is kind at heart, though he appears to be gruff.*
break one's heart, to crush with sorrow or grief: *Your disdain has broken my heart* (Joseph Addison).
by heart, a by memory: *We learned the poem by heart. We associate a name with a face, a word with its meaning, and so it goes with much of the "by-heart" learning that attends daily life* (Scientific American). **b** from memory: *He can recite the whole poem by heart.*
cross one's heart, to make the sign of the cross over one's heart when swearing that something is true: *The little girl crossed her heart and said she hoped to die if she was lying about what happened.*
cry one's heart out, to cry violently; shed many tears: *That baby is crying its heart out while the mother is chatting on the phone.*
eat one's heart out, to feel great sorrow, grief, or worry: *I'm just sitting here eating my heart out, thinking of my lost youth* (John O'Hara).
from one's heart, with deepest feeling; sincerely: *They wished us well from their hearts.*
get to the heart of, to find out the secret or hidden meaning of: *The judge decided to get to the heart of the matter by questioning the witnesses himself.*
have one's heart in one's mouth (or **boots**), to be very frightened: *His heart was in his mouth as he approached each high jump* (London Times).
have one's heart in the right place, to mean well; have good intentions: *Your heart is in the right place; if only you had the right words on your tongue* (Julius Stinde).
have the heart, a to be courageous or spirited enough (to do something): *The Turks being discouraged, [they] had not the heart to defend themselves* (Sir Thomas North). **b** (in negative sentences) to be hard-hearted enough: *Have you the heart to say this of your own son, unnatural mother!* (Dickens).
heart and soul, with all one's affections and energies: *He threw himself, heart and soul, into every requirement of his time* (John W. Burgon).
hearts, a a suit of playing cards marked with red, heart-shaped figures: *Clubs, diamonds, hearts, in wild disorder seen* (Alexander Pope). **b** (*sing. in use*) a card game in which a player is penalized one point for every heart he captures and the opposition is penalized if a player captures all the hearts, and the queen or jack of spades: *to play hearts.*
in good heart, *British.* **a** in good spirits: *The Times, this year, has found most industrialists in surprisingly good heart* (London Times). **b** in good condition: *My garden, lying over solid chalk, needs constant organic enrichment to keep it in good heart* (Manchester Guardian Weekly).
in one's heart of hearts, in one's deepest thoughts or feelings; really: *Yet in my heart of hearts I feel your might* (Wordsworth).
lay to heart, a to keep in mind; remember: *It contains ... a lesson which I should do wisely and well at this present time to lay to heart* (Richard Trench). **b** to think seriously about: *Lay it to thy heart, and farewell* (Shakespeare).
lose one's heart (to), to fall in love (with): *Surprisingly, Britain's Fleet Street seems to have lost its newspaper heart to the new President* (Time).
near (to), one's heart, of great value or interest to one: *... important for the cause which was nearest to his heart* (John W. Burgon).
take heart, to be encouraged: *Take heart, take heart. We'll find them* (Dickens).
take heart of grace, to take courage from favor or privilege given: *Take heart of grace, Thy steps retrace, Be not afraid* (William S. Gilbert).
take to heart, a to think seriously about: *If he would take the business to heart, and deal in it effectually, it would succeed well* (Sir Francis Bacon). **b** to be deeply affected by; grieve over: *Though I did not cry and take it to heart as some do ... yet I missed him all day long* (Charles Lamb).
to one's heart's content, as much as one wants: *There old Mrs. Louis ... petted her to her heart's content* (Lytton Strachey).
wear one's heart on (or **upon**) **one's sleeve**, to show one's feelings plainly: *A ... ready-tongued man, wearing his heart upon his sleeve* (George A. Sala).
with all one's heart, a sincerely: *He said that he loved her with all his heart.* **b** gladly: *That I will promise you, with all my heart* (Mayne Reid).
[Old English *heorte*]

heart|ache (härt′āk′), *n.* great sorrow or grief; deep pain. SYN: anguish, woe.

heart attack, a sudden failure of the heart to function properly, sometimes resulting in death. It can be caused by coronary thrombosis, arteriosclerosis, high blood pressure, or other bodily malfunction.

heart|beat (härt′bēt′), *n.* **1** a pulsation of the heart, including one complete contraction and expansion. **2** *Figurative.* the main source of activity: *Southern California was "the heartbeat of entertainment productions"* (New York Times).

heart|block (härt′blok′), *n.,* or **heart block**, an abnormal condition of the heart, caused by a blocking of the nervous tissue that conducts the contracting impulse from the auricle to the ventricle so that they act independently.

heart|break (härt′brāk′), *n.* a crushing sorrow.

heart|break|er (härt′brā′kər), *n.* **1** a person or thing that breaks the heart. **2** a curl or lovelock (humorous use).

heart|break|ing (härt′brā′king), *adj.* crushing with sorrow or grief; extremely distressing: *heartbreaking news.* **—heart′break′ing|ly**, *adv.*

heart|bro|ken (härt′brō′kən), *adj.* crushed by sorrow or grief; broken-hearted. **—heart′bro′ken|ly**, *adv.* **—heart′brok′en|ness**, *n.*

heart|burn (härt′bėrn′), *n.* **1** a burning feeling in the chest and throat; cardialgia. It is caused by a rising up of acid from the stomach. **2** envy; jealousy.

heart|burn|ing (härt′bėr′ning), *n.* rankling discontent, especially from a hidden feeling of envy or jealousy.

heart catheterization, the insertion of a tube into a chamber of the heart by way of an arm vein to diagnose heart conditions.

heart cherry, a sweet cherry, having heart-shaped fruit with soft flesh.

heart-cry (härt′krī′), *n., pl.* **-cries**. *British.* a heartfelt cry; an emotional appeal.

heart disease, any impaired condition of the heart.

-hearted, *combining form.* having a ____heart: *Kind-hearted = having a kind heart.*

heart|en (här′tən), *v.t.* to cheer; cheer up; encourage: *This good news will hearten you.* SYN: inspirit. **—heart′en|er**, *n.*

heart|en|ing (här′tə ning, härt′ning), *adj.* encouraging: *The economy ... seldom had been more sound. The picture in steel was particularly heartening* (Wall Street Journal). **—heart′en|ing|ly**, *adv.*

heart failure, stoppage or interference in the normal action of the heart so that the amount of blood flowing from the heart becomes inadequate: *Heart failure is not a disease in itself but is rather a common end point of all organic heart diseases* (Harry L. Jaffe).

heart|felt (härt′felt′), *adj.* very deeply felt; sincere; genuine: *heartfelt sympathy.* SYN: earnest.

heart-free (härt′frē′), *adj.* not in love: *Rose is still heart-free* (William S. Gilbert).

heart|ful (härt′fəl), *adj.* **1** hearty; cordial. **2** earnest; sincere. **—heart′ful|ly**, *adv.* **—heart′ful|ness**, *n.*

hearth (härth), *n.* **1** the stone or brick floor of a fireplace, often extending out into the room. **2** *Figurative.* the fireside; home: *The soldiers longed for their own hearths. Sweet household talk, and phrases of the hearth* (Tennyson). **3a** the lowest part of a blast furnace, where the molten metal and slag collect; crucible. **b** the floor of an open hearth, reverberatory furnace, or other furnace, on which the ore or iron is exposed to the flame to be smelted or heated. **c** = bloomery. **d** the fireplace of a forge. **4** the bottom or bed for the fire, as in a furnace or stove. **5** a portable brazier used in soldering. [Old English *heorth*]

hearth money or **tax**, **1** a tax upon hearths or chimneys. **2** an annual tax of two shillings on each hearth, imposed in England from 1662 to 1689.

hearth|rug (härth′rug′), *n., adj.* — ***n.*** a rug laid before a fireplace to protect the carpet or floor.
— ***adj.*** **1** fireside; domestic: *The sparrow is far too 'fly' a bird for the hearthrug-bred cat* (London Daily Chronicle). **2** resembling a hearthrug: *The inelegant, cumbrous, and shaggy hearthrug coats* (Westminster Gazette).

hearth|side (härth′sīd′), *n.* **1** the side of a hearth. **2** *Figurative.* home: *Memories of his boyhood hearthside flooded his mind.*

hearth|stone (härth′stōn′), *n.* **1** the stone forming a hearth: *How can I turn from any fire On any man's hearthstone?* (Rudyard Kipling). **2** *Figurative.* the fireside; home: *Around these hearthstones speak no evil word of any creature* (James Lane Allen). **3** a soft stone, or a preparation of powdered stone and pipe clay, used to scour hearths, doorsteps, and the like.

heart|i|ly (här′tə lē), *adv.* **1** with sincere feeling; in a warm, friendly way; genuinely: *She welcomed her cousins heartily.* **SYN**: sincerely. **2** with courage, spirit, or enthusiasm; with good will; vigorously: *to set to work heartily.* **SYN**: zealously. **3** with a good appetite: *to eat heartily.* **4** very; completely; thoroughly: *My mother was heartily tired of so much housework.* **SYN**: abundantly, exceedingly.

heart|i|ness (här′tē nis), *n.* **1** sincere feeling: *The duke with a seeming heartiness gave his consent* (Gilbert Burnet). **2** vigor.

heart|land (härt′land′), *n.* **1** any area or region that is the center of, or vital to, a country, institution, or industry: *an agricultural heartland, a Republican heartland. Strategic bombardment of vital elements of an enemy's heartland ... was conceived by forward-looking airmen* (United States Air Force Report on the Ballistic Missile). **2** an economically and militarily self-sufficient land mass, located centrally in and controlling the world island (the continents of Europe, Asia, and Africa), and relatively invulnerable to attack from the sea: *It is evident that the heartland is as real a physical fact within the world island as is the world island itself within the ocean ...* (Sir Halford J. Mackinder). *But from this Eurasian heartland came Aryans to populate the West, and across its pink sands marched generations of world conquerors* (Time).

heart|less (härt′lis), *adj.* **1** without kindness or sympathy; unfeeling; cruel; callous: *heartless words, a heartless coquette.* **SYN**: hard, pitiless. **2** without courage, spirit, or enthusiasm: *a heartless mood Of solitude* (Wordsworth). **SYN**: apathetic, spiritless. — **heart′less|ly**, *adv.* — **heart′less|ness**, *n.*

heart-lung machine (härt′lung′), a machine that pumps oxygenated blood through the body, while the heart is drained of blood during certain operations.

heart murmur, an abnormal sound due to a leaky valve in the heart. A functional heart murmur may appear after a person exercises strenuously.

heart point, = fess point.

heart|quake (härt′kwāk′), *n.* **1** palpitation of the heart. **2** *Figurative.* a sudden tremor of emotion: *How a lip's mere tremble, Look's half hesitation ... effect a heartquake* (Robert Browning).

heart-rend|ing (härt′ren′ding), *adj.* causing mental anguish; very distressing: *To lose one's parents in an airplane crash is a heart-rending experience.* — **heart′-rend′ing|ly**, *adv.*

heart|rot (härt′rot′), *n.* **1** a disease which causes decay in the heart of a tree. **2** a fungous disease of the roots of beets.

hearts (härts). *n.pl.* See under **heart**.

hearts and flowers, *U.S. Slang.* sentimentality: *Transplanted from stage to screen, Enid Bagnold's witty, pitiless ... high comedy yields only a withered bouquet of hearts and flowers* (Time).

heart-search|ing (härt′sėr′ching), *n., adj.* — ***n.*** an inquiry into one's deeper or deepest feelings and emotions.
— ***adj.*** that searches or rigorously examines the deepest feelings: *Few books in a dozen years have provoked such heart-searching reviews* (Time).

hearts|ease or **heart's-ease** (härts′ēz′), *n.* **1** peace of mind; tranquillity. **2** the pansy, especially the wild pansy. **3** some other kind of the same group as the pansy. **4** *U.S. Dialect.* the common persicary. [Middle English *hertes ese* (literally) heart's ease]

heart-shaped (härt′shāpt′), *adj.* having the shape of a heart; cordate.

heart|sick (härt′sik′), *adj.* sick at heart; very depressed; very unhappy: *Chatham, heartsick of his country's shame* (William Cowper). **SYN**: despondent. — **heart′sick′ness**, *n.*

heart|some (härt′səm), *adj. Especially Scottish.* **1** that gives heart or cheer; that rejoices the heart; animating: *Overhead the heartsome stars were set in the face of the night* (Robert Louis Stevenson). **SYN**: inspiring, exhilarating. **2** full of cheer or gladness; merry; joyous. **SYN**: cheerful, blithe. — **heart′some|ly**, *adv.*

heart|sore (härt′sôr′, -sōr′), *adj.* feeling or showing grief; grieved: *heartsore sighs* (Shakespeare).

heart-strick|en (härt′strik′ən), *adj.* struck to the heart with grief; shocked with fear; dismayed.

heart|strings (härt′stringz′), *n.pl.* **1** the deepest feelings; strongest affections: *The poor beggar's story tugged at our heartstrings.* **2** the tendons or nerves formerly thought to support the heart.

heart|throb (härt′throb′), *n.* **1** a throb or pulsation of the heart; heartbeat. **2** passionate or sentimental emotion. **3** *Slang.* a sweetheart.

heart-to-heart (härt′tə härt′), *adj.* without reserve; frank; sincere: *a heart-to-heart talk.*

heart urchin, any one of a group of generally heart-shaped sea urchins; spatangus: *Heart urchins have become modified by evolution to possess a partly bilateral symmetry that fits better with their mode of movement* (New Scientist).

heart-warm|ing (härt′wôr′ming), *adj.* tending to arouse warm and sympathetic feelings; sentimental; endearing: *the antique, the picturesque, and the unabashedly heart-warming* (New Yorker).

heart|wa|ter (härt′wô′tər, -wot′ər), *n.* a serious, infectious, rickettsial disease of sheep, goats, and cattle in South Africa, transmitted through the bont tick.

heart-whole (härt′hōl′), *adj.* **1** not in love; having the affections free: *Cupid hath clapped him o' the shoulder, but I'll warrant him heart-whole* (Shakespeare). **2** hearty; sincere: *heart-whole congratulations.* — **heart′whole′ness**, *n.*

heart|wood (härt′wu̇d′), *n.* the hard, central wood of a tree; duramen. Heartwood is nonliving wood, harder and more solid than the newer sapwood that surrounds it.

heart|worm (härt′wėrm′), *n.* a nematode worm that infests the hearts and arteries of dogs.

heart|y (här′tē), *adj.,* **heart|i|er, heart|i|est**, *n., pl.* **heart|ies.** — ***adj.*** **1** warm and friendly; full of feeling; genuine; sincere: *hearty wishes for a happy birthday. We gave our old friends a hearty welcome.* **SYN**: heartfelt, cordial, genial, cheery. **2** strong and well; vigorous: *The old man was still hale and hearty at ninety.* **SYN**: hale, healthy, robust. **3** full of energy and enthusiasm; not restrained: *He burst out a loud, hearty laugh.* **4a** with plenty to eat; satisfying to the appetite; abundant: *A hearty meal satisfied his hunger.* **SYN**: ample, full. **b** nourishing; strengthening: *hearty food.* **SYN**: invigorating. **5** requiring or using much food; having good appetite: *People who work outdoors are usually hearty eaters.* **6** fertile: *hearty farmland.*
— ***n.*** **1** a fellow sailor; brave and good comrade: *Monsoon, my hearty, how goes it?* (Charles Lever). **2** = backslapper.

heat (hēt), *n., v.* — ***n.*** **1a** the condition of being hot; high temperature; hotness; warmth: *the heat of fire.* **b** *Physics.* a form of energy caused by the motion of molecules. Friction, electricity, the sun, and your body all produce heat. The rate at which the molecules move determines the temperature. Heat is capable of being transmitted from one body to another by conduction, convection, or radiation. The effects of absorbed heat on a body are increase of temperature, expansion of volume, and possible change of state, as of a solid to a liquid, or of a liquid to a gas. **c** degree of hotness; temperature: *red heat, white heat, blood heat, animal heat.* **d** the sensation or perception of hotness or warmth, such as is experienced from nearness to fire. **e** a heated bodily condition: *He got into a heat by running.* **2** hot weather or a hot season. *the heat of summer.* **3** *Figurative.* warmth or intensity of feeling; anger, vehemence, violence, excitement, or ardor: *The heat of his spirit struck warm through all lands* (Rudyard Kipling). **SYN**: rage, fervor, animation. **4** the hottest or most intense point; most violent or active stage; excitement: *In the heat of the argument he lost his temper.* **SYN**: height, stress. **5** *Slang.* **a** pressure or coercion: *Rousting the teen-agers who now throng the Sunset Strip may take the political heat off the department* (Atlantic). **b** intense police pressure or activity: *But the heat was on and Antony took it on the lam* (Punch). **c** the police: *Out the door comes this great big porcine member of the heat, all belts and bullets and pistols and keys and flashlights and clubs and helmets* (New Yorker). **6** *Figurative.* a single intense effort or bout of action; one continuous operation; a stroke: *to do a thing at a heat.* **7a** one trial in a race; a section of a race, consisting of a complete running of the course: *He won the first heat, but lost the final race.* **b** any contest to eliminate competition: *The New Hampshire primary* [*is*] *the first of a series of Presidential trial heats* (New York Times). **8a** one complete operation of heating in a furnace or a forge. **b** the quantity of metal thus heated. **9a** a periodically recurring condition of sexual excitement in female animals; estrus. **b** the period of time that this excitement lasts, during which the female will mate with the male. **10** *Psychology.* a sensation with a stinging character when warm and cold receptors on the skin are stimulated simultaneously. **11** a hot place; fire.
— ***v.t.*** **1** to make hot or warm: *The stove heats the room.* **2** *Figurative.* to fill with strong feeling; excite; inflame: *His stirring speech heated the audience's imagination.*
— ***v.i.*** **1** to become hot or warm: *The soup is heating slowly.* **2** *Figurative.* to be filled with strong feeling; become excited.

heat up, to make or become hot, excited, more intense, or increased: *Steel price probe heats up as New York grand jury calls executives to testify* (Wall Street Journal).

put (or **turn**) **the heat on**, *Slang.* to apply pressure; intensify an effort, pursuit, etc.: *Tax progress lags. ... The Administration plans to turn the heat on* (Wall Street Journal).

[Old English *hǣtu.* See related etym. at **hot.**]
— **heat′a|ble**, *adj.* — **heat′less**, *adj.*

heat barrier, the point of speed beyond which the wings and fuselage of a plane are made dangerously hot by friction with the atmosphere; thermal barrier.

heat centers, *Physiology.* areas in the central nervous system which are concerned with the production and dissipation of heat.

heat cramp, muscle cramp accompanied by pain and nausea, caused by loss of salt and water through excessive perspiration.

heat|ed (hē′tid), *adj.* **1** angry, excited, or violent; vehement: *a heated argument.* **2** hot; inflamed.
— **heat′ed|ly**, *adv.*

heat energy, the form of energy that is manifested in heat.

heat engine, an engine that changes heat into motive power, especially a steam or internal-combustion engine.

heat equator, an imaginary line drawn near the earth's equator, through the middle of the belt which represents the hottest areas of the earth, with average annual temperatures of about 80°F or about 26°C; thermal equator.

heat|er (hē′tər), *n.* **1** a thing that gives heat or warmth, such as a stove, furnace, or radiator. **2** a container in which something is placed to be heated. **3** an element in a vacuum tube that indirectly heats the cathode. **4** a person who heats something. **5** *Slang.* a gun.

heat exchange, = heat transfer.

heat exchanger, a device for the transfer of heat from one medium to another so it may be utilized, as in an atomic power plant, or dispersed, as in the gas refrigerator. The radiator is a common heat exchanger.

heat exhaustion, a condition caused by excessive exposure to heat and characterized by a cold, clammy skin and general symptoms of shock; heat prostration.

heath (hēth), *n.* **1** *British.* open wasteland with heather or low bushes growing on it; moor. A heath has few or no trees. **2** any one of various plants and low bushes growing on such land. Heather is one kind of heath. **3** any one of a group of low, evergreen shrubs with needlelike leaves. Species of heath are widely distributed throughout Europe and the Mediterranean region, but are most abundant in South Africa, where they constitute one of the principal forms of vegetation. **4** any plant of the heath family. **5** any one of several shrubs resembling plants of the genus to which the heath belongs, but of a different family, such as the sea heath.

one's native heath, the place where one was born or brought up: *My foot is on my native heath* (Scott).

[Old English *hǣth* the plant; a tract of wasteland] — **heath′like′**, *adj.*

heath aster, a wild aster common in the eastern United States, having small, white flowers; dog fennel.

heath bell, the bell-shaped flower of the heath.

heath|ber|ry (hēth′ber′ē, -bər-), *n., pl.* **-ries.** any one of various berries growing on heaths, such as the crowberry and bilberry.

heath|bird (hēth′bėrd′), *n.* = black grouse.

heath cock, a male black grouse; blackcock.

hea|then (hē′ᴛʜən), *n., pl.* **-thens** or **-then**, *adj.*
— ***n.*** **1** a person who does not believe in the God

Pronunciation Key: hat, āge, cãre, fär; let, ēqual, tėrm; it, īce; hot, ōpen, ôrder; oil, out; cup, pu̇t, rüle; child; long; thin; ᴛʜen; zh, measure; ə represents **a** in about, **e** in taken, **i** in pencil, **o** in lemon, **u** in circus.

of the Bible or the Koran; person who is not a Christian, Jew, or Moslem; pagan: *I was sorry to find more mercy in an heathen than in a brother Christian* (Jonathan Swift). **2** people who are heathens: *The heathen invaded the country destroying all that lay before them.* **3** (in the Old Testament) the gentiles, or people who did not worship Jehovah, the God of the Jews. **4** a person who has no religion or culture; unenlightened person.
—***adj.*** **1** of or having to do with heathens; not Christian, Jewish, or Moslem; pagan: *Christian love among the Churches looked the twin of heathen hate* (Tennyson). **2** not religious or cultured; unenlightened.
[Old English *hǣthen* (probably originally) heath dweller < *hǣth* heath]
—***Syn.*** *n.* **1 Heathen, pagan** mean someone whose religion is not Christian and, usually, neither Jewish nor Moslem. **Heathen,** still often used in its earlier meaning of someone not converted to Christianity, and usually expressing an emotional attitude, applies particularly to those whose religions are regarded as primitive and unenlightened: *The heathens worshiped idols. Missionaries go to convert heathens.* **Pagan** expresses a more objective attitude, and is used especially of the religions of Greece, Rome, and other nations of antiquity: *The pagans believed in many gods. Julius Caesar was a pagan.*

hea|then|dom (hē′ᴛʜən dəm), *n.* **1** heathen worship or ways. **2** heathen lands or people.

hea|then|ish (hē′ᴛʜə nish), *adj.* **1** having to do with heathens. **2** *Figurative.* like heathens; uncivilized; barbarous. —**hea′then|ish|ly,** *adv.* —**hea′then|ish|ness,** *n.*

hea|then|ism (hē′ᴛʜə niz əm), *n.* **1** the religious or moral system of heathens; heathen worship or ways; paganism. **SYN:** idolatry. **2** lack of religion or culture; barbarism.

hea|then|ize (hē′ᴛʜə nīz), *v.,* **-ized, -iz|ing.** —***v.t.*** to make heathen or heathenish.
—***v.i.*** to practice heathenism; become heathen or heathenish.

hea|then|ry (hē′ᴛʜən rē), *n., pl.* **-ries. 1** = heathenism. **2** heathen people; the heathen.

heath|er (heᴛʜ′ər), *n.* **1** a low evergreen shrub with stalks of small, purple or pink, bell-shaped flowers, covering many heaths of Scotland and northern England; ling; heath. Heather belongs to the heath family. **2** any one of various heaths common in Devonshire, Cornwall, and other parts of England, Scotland, and Ireland. [Middle English *haddyr,* earlier *hathir.* Spelling perhaps influenced by *heath.*]

heather bell, = heath bell.

heath|er|y (heᴛʜ′ər ē), *adj.* **1** of or like heather. **2** covered with or full of heather.

***heath family,** a widely distributed group of shrubs or subshrubs, often having evergreen leaves. The family includes the heath, azalea, rhododendron, huckleberry, blueberry, wintergreen, and arbutus.

***heath family**

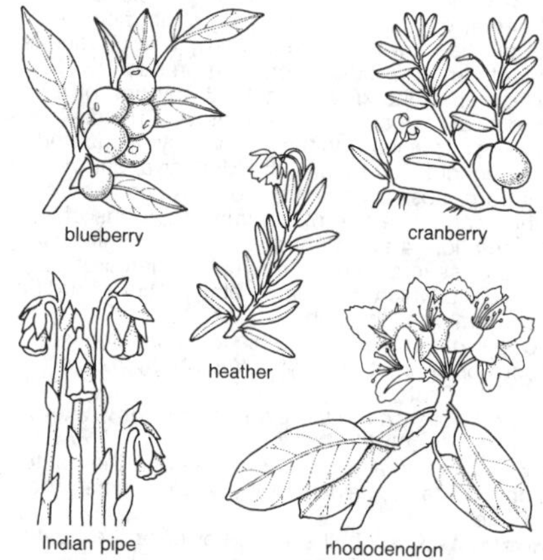

heath hen, 1 an extinct North American grouse closely related to the prairie chicken. **2** a female black grouse.

heath|land (hēth′land′), *n. British.* land covered with heath; heath; moor.

heath|y (hē′thē), *adj.,* **heath|i|er, heath|i|est. 1** of or having to do with a heath. **2** like a heath. **3** covered with or full of heath: *They walked for a couple of miles over heathy pasture land, for the most part in silence* (New Yorker). **4** = heathery.

heat|ing element (hē′ting), the part of an electrical device that provides heat, such as the set of exposed wires in a toaster.

heating pad, a pad heated on the same principle as an electric blanket, suitable for warming one part of the body.

heat lightning, flashes of lightning without any thunder, seen near the horizon, especially on hot summer evenings. The flashes are so distant that the thunder cannot be heard.

heat pipe, a pipe containing fluid to transfer heat from one end to the other by a difference in pressures without external pumping or supporting mechanisms: *Heat pipes—first developed for space applications ... can transfer heat from a component such as a high power transistor or valve to an external heat sink with fantastic efficiency* (New Scientist).

heat pollution, = thermal pollution.

heat prostration, = heat exhaustion.

heat pump, an electrically operated device that extracts heat from air, earth, or water.

heat rash, a red, itching rash on the skin; prickly heat.

heat-re|sist|ant (hēt′ri zis′tənt), *adj.* capable of withstanding high temperatures: *heat-resistant stainless steel or ceramic materials* (Wall Street Journal).

hea|tron|ic (hē tron′ik), *adj.* of or having to do with a molding process in which high-frequency radio waves are used to heat plastic material before or during the molding process. [< *heat* + (elect)*ronic*]

heat shield, a device that protects something from heat, especially the coating or covering of special material on the nose cone of a missile or spacecraft which absorbs or diffuses the heat induced by friction when it reenters the earth's atmosphere.

heat sink, any one of various devices or materials that absorb heat, such as heat exchangers or metallic elements: *In order to develop further the thermal conditions surrounding the spacecraft, these chambers are invariably equipped with shrouds of heat sinks* (Karl A. Geiger).

heat|stroke (hēt′strōk′), *n.* collapse or sudden illness with fever and dry skin, caused by overexposure to excessive heat, as from the infrared rays of the sun.

heat tone, the sum of heat produced in a chemical action and of the external work performed expressed in heat units.

heat transfer, the flow of heat from warmer bodies to colder bodies; the transfer of heat between solids, liquids, or gases, by conduction, convection, or radiation.

heat-treat (hēt′trēt′), *v.t.* **1** to treat by the application of heat: *to heat-treat strawberry plants, to heat-treat fabrics.* **2** to subject to heat treatment.

heat treatment, a process by which certain kinds of metal are improved by being heated to a high temperature, rapidly cooled, and then reheated to a lower temperature.

heat unit, the amount of heat required to raise the temperature of a unit weight, as a pound or gram, of water one degree: *The British thermal unit and the calorie are heat units.*

heat wave, a period of very hot weather: *Hundreds of tons of pineapples rendered unfit for consumption during the heat wave in December were being dumped or buried on farms in the East London area* (Cape Times).

heave (hēv), *v.,* **heaved** or (*especially Nautical*) **hove, heav|ing,** *n., interj.* —***v.t.*** **1** to lift with force or effort; hoist: *He heaved the heavy box into the wagon. I saw the angels heave up Sir Lancelot into heaven, and the gates of heaven opened against him* (Thomas Malory). **2** to lift and throw; cast; fling: *to heave a stone. The sailors heaved the anchor overboard.* **SYN:** hurl. **3** to give (a sigh or groan) with a deep, heavy breath or with effort: *to heave a sigh.* **4** to cause to rise and fall in repeated efforts: *When pity is heaving his bosom with emotion* (William S. Gilbert). **5** to cause to swell up or bulge out: *tho' the Giant Ages heave the hill* (Tennyson). **6** *Nautical.* to haul or pull on; draw, as with a rope or cable: *Sailors hove up the cable with windlass or capstan* (New Scientist). **7** *Geology.* to thrust (a vein, etc.) out of place.
—***v.i.*** **1a** to pull with force or effort; haul: *They heaved on the rope.* **b** to move a ship in a certain direction or way by such means. **2** to rise and fall alternately: *Waves heave in a storm.* **3** to breathe hard; pant; gasp. **4** to vomit or try to vomit; retch. **5** (of a ship) to move or turn in a certain direction or way. **6** to rise; swell; bulge; be raised, thrown, or forced up: *The ground heaved from the earthquake.*
—***n.*** **1** an act or fact of heaving; throw: *With a mighty heave, we pushed the boat into the water.* **2** the act of swelling or rising up; rhythmical rising (and falling), as of waves: *Scobie never succeeded in sleeping properly again: his head began to ache from the heave of the van* (Graham Greene). **3** *Geology.* a horizontal displacement or dislocation of a vein or stratum at a fault.
—***interj.*** **heave ho!** a cry of sailors when pulling up the anchor or doing other strenuous work as a group.
heave in (or **into**) **sight,** to come into view: *As the clock struck two the old car could be heard chugging down the next street and hove into sight just a minute or two later.*
heave to, a to stop (a ship) especially by bringing its head into the wind and trimming the sails so that they act against one another: *"Shorten sail ... and heave the ship to," said the Captain* (Michael Scott). **b** to stop in this manner: *The two vessels alternately sailed and dropped explosives, one being hove to and acting as receiving ship, while the other sailed* (New York Times).
[Old English *hebban*]

heave gate, *British.* a gate which is opened by being lifted out of the sockets or mortises.

heave-ho (hēv′hō′), *n., v.,* **-hoed** or **-ho'd, -ho|ing.** *Informal.* —***n.*** *Informal.* an ejection, rejection, or dismissal: *insubordinate and peevish types who ... give the old heave-ho to visiting American Senators* (Harper's).
—***v.i.*** **1** to cry "heave ho!" **2** to pull with great force: *The women ... are constantly hauling and heave-hoing on this packing case of merchandise* (Manchester Guardian Weekly).
—***v.t.*** to pull with great force.

heav|en (hev′ən), *n.* **1a** (in Christian and some other religious use) the place where God and the angels live and where the blessed go after death. **b** any one of various other celestial realms: *the seven heavens of the Talmud or of the Koran.* **2** *Figurative.* a place or condition of greatest happiness: *a heaven on earth* (Milton). **3** (in Christian Science) the atmosphere of Soul.
for heaven's sake! or **good heavens!** an exclamation of surprise, protest, or demand: *Hold on, for heaven's sake! Good heavens! What a place to stop at!*
heaven knows, a who knows: *It was skunk, rotten eggs, sulphur, and heaven knows what else, all rolled into one* (New Yorker). **b** certainly: *Heaven knows I should be used to it by now* (Maclean's).
heavens or **Heavens, a** the upper air in which clouds float, winds blow, and birds fly and in which the sun, moon, and stars seem to be set; sky: *Millions of stars were shining in the heavens. The heavens declare the glory of God* (Psalms 19:1). **b** a particular kind or region of sky, as of clearness, cloudiness, or climate. **c** heavenly beings; God and His angels as ruling over mankind: *Heavens keep him from these beasts* (Shakespeare).
in heaven's name! = for heaven's sake.
move heaven and earth, to do everything possible: *The mayor should be moving heaven and earth to enact this income tax immediately* (New York Times).
to high heaven, a very highly; to the skies: *... praising the Chinese Communist Party to high heaven* (Harper's). **b** too much; inordinately: *The air ... stinks to high heaven* (J. D. Salinger).
[Old English *heofon*]

Heav|en (hev′ən), *n.* God; Providence: *It was the will of Heaven. Heaven will protect the Working Girl* (Edgar Smith).

heav|en|ly (hev′ən lē), *adj.,* **-li|er, -li|est. 1** of or in heaven; divine: *God is our heavenly Father. ... from heavenly harmony This universal frame began* (John Dryden). **SYN:** celestial, holy. **2** *Figurative.* like heaven; suitable for heaven; very happy, beautiful, or excellent: *a heavenly spot, heavenly peace.* **SYN:** blissful. **3** of or in the heavens; in the sky or upper air: *The sun, moon, stars, planets, and comets are heavenly bodies.* —**heav′en|li|ness,** *n.*

heaven of heavens, (in Biblical use) the highest heaven; the abode of God: *Behold, the heaven and the heaven of heavens is the Lord's thy God* (Deuteronomy 10:14).

heav|ens (hev′ənz), *n.pl.* See under **heaven.**

heav|en-sent (hev′ən sent′), *adj.* very welcome or timely, as if sent from heaven; godsent: *We were ... extremely short of coal miners, and this sudden influx of fit, mostly unattached young men in search of employment seemed heaven-sent* (Elspeth Huxley).

heav|en|ward (hev′ən wərd), *adv., adj.* toward heaven: *The rocket soared heavenward* (adv.). *She cast a heavenward glance* (adj.).

heav|en|wards (hev′ən wərdz), *adv.* = heavenward.

heave offering, (in the Jewish priestly law) an offering which was lifted up (heaved) by the priest when presented, and which became the portion of the priests and their families.

heav|er (hē′vər), *n.* **1** a person or thing that heaves. **2** *Nautical.* a bar or staff used for twisting or tightening a rope or strap.

heaves (hēvz), *n.* a disease of horses, characterized by difficult breathing, coughing, and heaving of the flanks; broken wind; emphysema: *Heaves may be an allergic condition that results in faulty action of the air cells* (Raymond R. Birch).
▶**Heaves,** the disease of horses, is plural in form and singular in use.

heav|i|er-than-air (hev′ē ər ᴛʜən ãr′), *adj.* **1** (of an aircraft) having greater weight than the air it displaces. **2** of or having to do with aircraft of such weight.

Heav|i|side layer (hev′ē sīd), the layer of the ionosphere that reflects low-frequency radio waves such as those produced in short-wave broadcasting; Kennelly-Heaviside layer; E layer. [< Oliver *Heaviside,* 1850-1925, a British physicist]

heav|y[1] (hev′ē), *adj.,* **heav|i|er, heav|i|est,** *adv., n., pl.* **heav|ies.** —*adj.* **1** hard to lift or carry; having much weight: *a heavy load.* **2** having much weight for its size; of high specific gravity: *Iron is heavy and feathers are light. Osmium is the heaviest metal.* **3** of more than usual weight for its kind: *heavy silk, heavy bread, a heavy quality of webbing.* **4** greater than usual; of great amount, force, or intensity; large: *a heavy rain, a heavy crop, a heavy meal, a heavy vote, a heavy sea, a heavy sleep, a sweet, heavy odor, a heavy frost, a heavy fog, a heavy silence.* **SYN:** abundant.
5 doing or being such in an unusual degree: *a heavy buyer, a heavy smoker.* **6** *Figurative.* hard to bear or endure; harsh; oppressive: *heavy taxes. Her troubles became heavier and heavier.* **7** *Figurative.* hard to deal with or manage; trying or difficult in any way; laborious: *a heavy task or undertaking. A heavy road is muddy and sandy, so that a load is hard to draw. A heavy slope is a steep one. Heavy food is hard to digest. Heavy soil is hard to work. He could hear the heavy uneven breathing of the child* (Graham Greene).
8 weighted down; laden: *air heavy with moisture, eyes heavy with sleep.* **9** *Figurative.* **a** sorrowful; sad: *a heavy countenance. His heavy heart was full of sorrow.* **b** causing sorrow; distressing; gloomy: *heavy news.* **10** *Figurative.* grave; serious; sober; somber: *a heavy part in a play, heavy business. Trust him not in matter of heavy consequence* (Shakespeare). **11** cloudy; overcast; lowering: *a heavy sky.* **12** broad; thick; coarse: *a heavy line, heavy features,* a heavy scar.
13 clumsy; sluggish; slow: *a heavy walk.* **SYN:** lumbering. **14** uninteresting; dull; ponderous: *heavy reading.* **15** loud and deep: *the heavy roar of cannon.* **16** *Military.* **a** heavily armed or equipped: *heavy tanks.* **b** of large size: *heavy artillery.*
17 not risen enough: *heavy bread.* **18** *Chemistry.* **a** indicating an isotope possessing a greater atomic weight than another of the same element: *Heavy hydrogen.* **b** indicating a compound containing such an isotope: *heavy water.* **19** having much body: *heavy liquor.* **20** pregnant: *heavy with child.*
—*adv.* in a heavy manner; heavily.
—*n.* **1** a heavy person or thing. **2** a heavy animal, such as a hog, especially when ready to be slaughtered and sold to a butcher. **3** *Informal.* **a** the villain's part in a play. **b** an actor who plays such parts. **4** *Military.* a gun of large size, weight, or caliber. **5** a heavy tank. **6** *Especially British Informal.* = heavyweight (def. 2). **7** *Slang.* a burglar or armed robber. **8** *Slang.* a very large wave.
hang heavy, to pass slowly and uninterestingly: *Time hung heavy on his hands.*
[Old English *hefig,* related to *hebban* heave]
—**heav′i|ly,** *adv.* —**heav′i|ness,** *n.*
—*Syn. adj.* **1 Heavy, weighty, burdensome** mean of great weight. **Heavy,** when used figuratively, suggests something pressing down on or weighing down the mind or feelings: *The President has heavy responsibilities.* **Weighty** is used chiefly figuratively, applying to something of great importance: *He made a weighty announcement.* **Burdensome** refers chiefly to something that is difficult to do or puts a strain on the person or thing doing it: *The extra work was burdensome.*

heav|y[2] (hē′vē), *adj.* (of a horse) suffering from heaves.

heavy chain, any one of the pair of very long polypeptide chains in an antibody molecule. Each such molecule contains two heavy chains and two light chains.

heavy cream, cream having 30 per cent or more butterfat, and therefore capable of being whipped.

heav|y-du|ty (hev′ē dü′tē, -dyü′-), *adj.* **1** durably built to withstand hard use, strain, or exposure: *heavy-duty tires. . . . heavy-duty corrugated boxes are sealed with a fiber-reinforced paper tape* (Newsweek). **2** highly taxed by a tariff.

heavy earth, = baryta (def. 1).

heavy-fist|ed (hev′ē fis′tid), *adj.* harsh; oppressive: *heavy-fisted destinies* (Leonard Bacon).

heav|y-foot|ed (hev′ē fu̇t′id), *adj.* **1** stepping heavily; clumsy. **2** with tired feet. **3** *Figurative.* ponderous; unwieldy: *. . . and he composed touching, if sometimes heavy-footed, sonnets in her honor* (Atlantic). —**heav′y-foot′ed|ness,** *n.*

heav|y-hand|ed (hev′ē han′did), *adj.* **1** clumsy of hand or touch; rude; awkward: *heavy-handed humor. Nature's heavy-handed pruning shears slashed and tore* (New York Times). **2** *Figurative.* treating others harshly; oppressive; cumbersome: *. . . religious prints of a singular heavy-handed and literal period* (New Yorker). **3** having the hands heavy, as from weariness or weakness. **4** having the hands heavily laden. —**heav′y-hand′ed|ly,** *adv.* —**heav′y-hand′ed|ness,** *n.*

heav|y-head|ed (hev′ē hed′id), *adj.* **1** drowsy; sleepy: *With a heavy-headed glance he went back to sleep.* **2** dull; stupid. **3** having the head heavy, as with weight.

heav|y-heart|ed (hev′ē här′tid), *adj.* in low spirits; sad; gloomy. **SYN:** grieved, melancholy, sorrowful. —**heav′y-heart′ed|ly,** *adv.* —**heav′y-heart′ed|ness,** *n.*

heavy hydrogen, **1** = deuterium. **2** = tritium.

heavy industry, industry that manufactures products, such as machinery or steel, for use by other industries.

heav|y|ish (hev′ē ish), *adj.* somewhat heavy; tending to heaviness.

heavy meson, a meson having a rest mass or weight about 967 times that of an electron, and decaying in various ways to produce light mesons; K-meson; K-particle.

heavy metal, **1** *Especially U.S.* rock music that has a heavy beat and harsh, amplified instrumental effects: *beating up punks and heavy metal rock fans, whom they despise* (Manchester Guardian Weekly). **2** a metal such as lead, copper, or cadmium that has a specific gravity higher than 5.0: *Because of pollution from . . . heavy metals, the waters . . . have been pronounced biologically dead* (Rolling Stone).

heav|y-met|al (hev′ē met′əl), *adj.* **1** *Especially U.S.* of or having to do with rock music characterized by a heavy beat and sometimes amplified instrumental effects. **2** of or having to do with heavy metal (def. 2): *The award-winning film, . . . discusses heavy-metal contamination as well as the effects of acid rain and snow* (Christian Science Monitor).

heavy mineral, a mineral, such as gold, platinum, or iron, having a specific gravity of more than 2.9, and occurring in small quantities in sediments.

heavy oil, a product of the distillation of coal tar that is heavier than water.

heavy rail, of or belonging to a system of trains running as part of a conventional railroad system: *Transit specialists generally consider heavy rail transit, such as the subways . . . to be the best and most efficient way to move large numbers of people* (Ernest Holsendolph).

heav|y-set or **heav|y|set** (hev′ē set′), *adj.* built heavily; broad; stocky: *a middle-aged, heavy-set man.*

heavy spar, = barite.

heavy water, water formed of oxygen and deuterium (heavy hydrogen). Heavy water is much like ordinary water, but about 1.1 times as heavy and has a higher freezing point. It occurs in very small amounts in ordinary water. *Formula:* D_2O

heavy weather, problems; obstacles; difficulty: *The Geneva conference ran into heavy weather* (London Times).
make heavy weather of, *British.* to experience great difficulty with: *The feckless and muddle-headed, making heavy weather of the simplest tasks* (Ian Hay).

heav|y|weight (hev′ē wāt′), *n., adj.* —*n.* **1** a person or thing of more than average weight. **2** a boxer or wrestler who weighs 175 pounds or more (the heaviest weight class). **3** *Informal, Figurative.* a person who has much intelligence or importance: *The heavyweights on the program were a famous scholar and a noted politician.*
—*adj.* particularly heavy of its kind: *heavyweight cotton.*

Heb., **1** Hebrew (language). **2** Hebrews (book of the New Testament).

heb|do|mad (heb′də mad), *n.* **1** a week. **2** the number seven. **3** a group of seven. [< Latin *hebdomas, -adis* < Greek *hebdomás, -ádos* (a group of) seven < *hébdomos* seventh < *heptá* seven]

heb|dom|a|dal (heb dom′ə dəl), *adj.* weekly.

He|be (hē′bē), *n. Greek Mythology.* the goddess of youth and spring, daughter of Zeus and Hera. Hebe was the cupbearer of the gods before Ganymede was given the duty. [< Latin *Hēbē* < Greek *Hḗbē* < *hḗbē* youth, puberty]

he|be|phre|ni|a (hē′bə frē′nē ə), *n.* a form of schizophrenia often occurring at or near puberty, characterized primarily by a regression to extreme childishness. [< New Latin *hebephrenia* < Greek *hḗbē* puberty, youth + *phrḗn* mind]

he|be|phren|ic (hē′bə fren′ik), *adj., n.* —*adj.* **1** of or having to do with hebephrenia. **2** like hebephrenia. **3** having hebephrenia: *Reserpine is most successful in helping hebephrenic patients (those whose speech is unintelligible)* (Scientific American).
—*n.* a person affected with hebephrenia: *Hebephrenics may fly into a rage over trifles or laugh uproariously at moments of pathos* (Sunday Times).

heb|e|tate (heb′ə tāt), *v.,* **-tat|ed, -tat|ing,** *adj.*
—*v.t., v.i.* to make or become dull; blunt.
—*adj. Botany.* having a blunt, soft point, as awns or spines.
[< Latin *hebetāre* (with English *-ate*[1]) < *hebes, -etis* blunt, dull] —**heb′e|ta′tion,** *n.*

he|bet|ic (hi bet′ik), *adj.* **1** of or having to do with puberty. **2** occurring at the time of puberty. [< Greek *hēbētikós* youthful < *hḗbē* youth, puberty]

heb|e|tude (heb′ə tüd, -tyüd), *n.* the condition or state of being blunt or dull; obtuseness; lethargy. [< Latin *hebetūdō* < *hebes, -etis* dull]

heb|e|tu|di|nous (heb′ə tü′də nəs, -tyü′-), *adj.* characterized by hebetude: *His person was heavy and hebetudinous* (William H. Ainsworth).

Hebr., **1** Hebrews (book of the New Testament). **2** Hebrides.

He|bra|ic (hi brā′ik), *adj.* of or having to do with the Hebrews, their language, or their culture; Hebrew. **SYN:** Judaic. [< Late Latin *Hebraicus* < Greek *Hebraïkós* < stem *Hebrai-,* as in *Hebraîos* Hebrew]

He|bra|i|cal|ly (hi brā′ə klē), *adv.* after the manner of the Hebrews or the Hebrew language, especially with reference to the fact that Hebrew is written from right to left.

He|bra|i|cist (hi brā′ə sist), *n.* = Hebraist.

He|bra|i|cize (hi brā′ə sīz), *v.t.,* **-cized, -ciz|ing.** to change into Hebrew; make Hebrew in character; Hebraize: *His family name was Shkolnik, but he Hebraicized it to Eshkol after Israel became independent* (New York Times).

He|bra|ism (hē′brā iz əm), *n.* **1** a Hebrew usage or idiom. **2a** Hebrew character, spirit, thought, or practice. **b** = Judaism.

He|bra|ist (hē′brā ist), *n., adj.* —*n.* **1** a scholar skilled in the Hebrew language and literature. **2** a person imbued with the Hebraic spirit; person who has the qualities of the Hebrew people.
—*adj.* Hebraistic; Hebraic: *Shaw, in spirit, is Hebraist; Murray is Hellenist* (Atlantic).

He|bra|is|tic (hē′brā is′tik), *adj.* = Hebraic.

He|bra|is|ti|cal (hē′brā is′tə kəl), *adj.* = Hebraistic.

He|bra|ize (hē′brā īz), *v.,* **-ized, -iz|ing.** —*v.t.* to make Hebrew; give a Hebrew character to.
—*v.i.* **1** to use a Hebrew idiom or manner of speech. **2** to follow Hebraism as an ideal of thought and conduct. [< Greek *Hebraïzein* < stem of *Hebraïkós* Hebraic]

He|brew (hē′brü), *n., adj.* —*n.* **1** a descendant of one of the desert tribes led by Moses that settled in Palestine; person belonging to the Semitic tribe or nation descended from Abraham, Isaac, and Jacob; Israelite; Jew. **2** the ancient Semitic language of the Jews, in which most of the Old Testament was recorded. **3** the present-day language of Israel, a modern form of Hebrew.
—*adj.* **1** = Jewish. **2** of or having to do with ancient or modern Hebrew.
[< Old French *Ebreu,* learned borrowing from Latin *Hebraeus* < Greek *Hebraîos* < Aramaic *'Ebrai* < Hebrew *'ibri* (literally) one from beyond (the river) < *'eber* beyond]

Hebrew calendar, = Jewish calendar.

He|brews (hē′brüz), *n.* a book of the New Testament, supposedly written by the Apostle Paul to Christians of Hebrew ancestry at Rome. Its full title is *The Epistle of Paul the Apostle to the Hebrews. Abbr:* Heb.

Hebrew school, a school for the religious education of Jewish children from 6 to 13 years old, conducted by a synagogue or community after public school hours; Talmud Torah.

Heb|ri|de|an (heb′rə dē′ən), *adj., n.* —*adj.* of or having to do with the Hebrides, a group of Scottish islands off northwestern Scotland.
—*n.* a native or inhabitant of the Hebrides.

Hec|a|te (hek′ə tē), *n.* the Greek goddess of the moon, earth, and infernal regions, later associated with magic and witchcraft. Also, **Hekate.**

hec|a|tomb (hek′ə tōm, -tüm, -tom), *n.* **1** a great public sacrifice in ancient Greece and Rome of 100 oxen at one time. **2** *Figurative.* any great slaughter. **3** *Figurative.* a great number. [< Latin *hecatombē* < Greek *hekatómbē* sacrifice of 100 oxen; any huge sacrifice < *hekatón* hundred + *boûs* ox]

Pronunciation Key: hat, āge, cãre, fär; let, ēqual, tėrm; it, īce; hot, ōpen, ôrder; oil, out; cup, pu̇t, rüle; child; long; thin; ᴛʜen; zh, measure; ə represents **a** in about, **e** in taken, **i** in pencil, **o** in lemon, **u** in circus.

hech|i|ma (hech ē′mə), *n.* = loofah. [< Japanese *hechima*]

heck (hek), *n., interj.* hell (used mainly as a mild curse): *Our philosophy was "make a quick buck now and to heck with next year"* (Sports Illustrated).

heck|le (hek′əl), *v.,* **-led, -ling,** *n.* **—*v.t.*** **1** to interrupt and annoy (as a speaker or performer) by asking bothersome questions, jeering, or making loud remarks: *[The] M.P. for the Exchange division of Liverpool . . . after being rejected, was heckled when she addressed a May Day demonstration* (London Times). **SYN:** badger. **2** = hackle (comb flax). Also, **hatchel.**
[< noun]
—*n.* = hackle (comb for dressing flax).
[Middle English *hekele.* See related etym. at **hackle**[1].] **—heck′ler,** *n.*

hec|o|gen|in (hek′ə jen′in), *n.* a sugar compound obtained from certain plants such as the sisal, used as a source of cortisone. *Formula:* $C_{27}H_{42}O_4$
[apparently < New Latin *Hechtia* genus name of one of the source plants + English *-gen* + *-in*]

hect-, *combining form.* the form of **hecto-** before vowels, as in *hectare.*

***hec|tare** (hek′tãr), *n.* a unit of square measure in the metric system, equal to 100 ares, 10,000 square meters, or 2.471 acres. *Abbr:* ha.
[< French *hectare*]

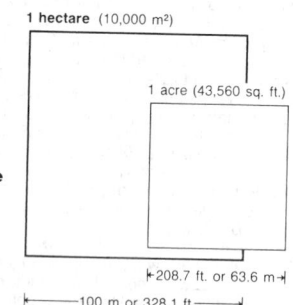

1 hectare (10,000 m²)
1 acre (43,560 sq. ft.)
***hectare**
208.7 ft. or 63.6 m
100 m or 328.1 ft.

hec|tic (hek′tik), *adj., n.* **—*adj.*** **1** very exciting; characterized by great excitement, activity, or confusion: *hectic pleasures, a hectic romance, a man with a hectic past. The children had a hectic time getting to school the morning after the big snowstorm.* **2** much excited: *Hectic citizens crowd through ecclesiastical doors to a club called Gold Street* (Esquire). **3** flushed: *leaves . . . pale and hectic red* (Shelley). **4** feverish. **5** showing the signs of a wasted condition of the body, as caused by tuberculosis or the like; consumptive.
—*n.* **1** any flush or fever: *A hectic of a moment pass'd across his cheek* (Laurence Sterne). **2a** a flush. **b** a fever. **c** a person having a hectic fever; a consumptive person.
[< Late Latin *hecticus* < Greek *hektikós* habitual, consumptive (of a disease) < *héxis* habit < *échein* have, hold] **—hec′ti|cal|ly,** *adv.*

hectic fever, a fever often accompanying tuberculosis or other wasting diseases, characterized by flushed cheeks and hot, dry skin.

hecto-, *combining form.* **1** a hundred: *Hectogram = a hundred grams.* **2** many: *Hectograph = a machine that makes many copies.* Also, **hect-** before vowels. [< French *hecto-,* alteration of Greek *hekatón* a hundred]

hec|to|cot|y|lus (hek′tə kot′ə ləs), *n., pl.* **-li** (-lī). an arm of the male of certain cephalopods modified to transfer sperm to the mantle cavity of the female. [< New Latin *Hectocotylus* a supposed worm genus < *hecto-* hecto- + Greek *kotýlē* small cup]

hec|to|gram (hek′tə gram), *n.* a unit of weight in the metric system, equal to 100 grams or 3.527 ounces. *Abbr:* hg. [< French *hectogramme*]

hec|to|gramme (hek′tə gram), *n. Especially British.* hectogram.

hec|to|graph (hek′tə graf, -gräf), *n., v.* **—*n.*** **1** a machine for making many copies of a page of writing or a drawing. The original writing is transferred to a surface coated with gelatin, and the copies are made from this. **2** the process of making copies with such a machine.
—*v.t.* to make copies of with a hectograph. Also, **hektograph.**
[< *hecto-* + *-graph*]

hec|to|graph|ic (hek′tə graf′ik), *adj.* **1** having to do with the hectograph. **2** produced by a hectograph.

hec|to|li|ter (hek′tə lē′tər), *n.* a unit of capacity in the metric system, equal to 100 liters, 2.8378 bushels, U.S. dry measure, or 26.4 gallons, U.S. liquid measure. *Abbr:* hl. Also, **hektoliter.**
[< French *hectolitre*]

hec|to|li|tre (hek′tə lē′tər), *n. Especially British.* hectoliter.

hec|to|me|ter (hek′tə mē′tər), *n.* a unit of linear measure in the metric system, equal to 100 meters, 0.1 kilometer, or 328.08 feet. *Abbr:* hm.
[< French *hectomètre*]

hec|to|me|tre (hek′tə mē′tər), *n. Especially British.* hectometer.

Hec|tor (hek′tər), *n. Greek Legend.* the bravest of the Trojan warriors, the son of Priam and Hecuba and husband of Andromache. Hector killed Patroclus and was killed by Achilles.

hec|tor (hek′tər), *n., v.* **—*n.*** a bragging, bullying fellow; swashbuckler.
—*v.t.* **1** to bluster at; bully: *He hectors his children, bewilders his friends* (New York Times). **SYN:** intimidate, threaten. **2** to tease.
—*v.i.* **1** to act in a blustering, domineering way. **2** to tease: *She does now and then hector a little.*
[< *Hector*] **—hec′tor|ing|ly,** *adv.*

hec|to|stere (hek′tə stir), *n.* a unit of cubic measure in the metric system, equal to 100 steres, 100 cubic meters, or 130.8 cubic yards. [< French *hectostère*]

Hec|u|ba (hek′yů bə), *n. Greek Legend.* the wife of Priam and the mother of Hector, Paris, and Cassandra.

he'd (hēd; *unstressed* ēd, id, *or* hid), **1** he had. **2** he would.

hed|dle (hed′əl), *n.* one of the two sets of small cords or wires in the harness of a loom to guide and separate the warp threads. See picture under **loom**[1]. [apparently alteration of *heald*]

he|der (ʜā′dər, ʜed′ər), *n., pl.* **ha|da|rim** or **heders.** an old type of Hebrew school which emphasized prayer and the study of the Bible and Talmud in Hebrew and Yiddish. Also, **cheder.**
[< Yiddish *kheder* < Hebrew *hedher* room]

hedge (hej), *n., v.,* **hedged, hedg|ing,** *adj.* **—*n.*** **1** a thick row of bushes or small trees, planted as a fence or boundary: *The rabbit ran under the hedge into the neighbor's yard.* **2** *Figurative.* any barrier, limit, or boundary: *The Administration officials put two hedges on these rosy forecasts* (Wall Street Journal). **3** *Figurative.* a means of protection or defense: *The optimist buys because he figures business is expanding; the pessimist buys as a hedge against inflation* (Newsweek). **4** the act of hedging.
—*v.t.* **1** to put a hedge around: *to hedge a garden.* **2** to enclose or separate with a hedge or fence: *There was a certain householder, which planted a vineyard, and hedged it round about* (Matthew 21:33). **3** *Figurative.* to obstruct with a hedge or any barrier: *I will hedge up thy way with thorns* (Hosea 2:6). **4** to reduce one's possible losses on (a bet, risk, or speculation) by betting or speculating on both sides. **5** to avoid answering (a question) directly; evade (something): *The President hedged the question of tax relief.*
—*v.i.* **1** to avoid giving a direct answer or taking a definite stand; evade questions or problems: *Prophesy as much as you like, but always hedge* (Oliver Wendell Holmes). **SYN:** shift, dodge, trim, shuffle. **2** to bet on both sides in order to reduce one's possible losses. **3** to turn aside or swerve: *If you . . . hedge aside from the direct forthright . . . they all rush by and leave you hindmost* (Shakespeare). **4** to hide as if in a hedge; skulk.
—*adj.* **1** of or for a hedge: *hedge plants, hedge clippers.* **2** *Figurative.* as though born, brought up, sheltered by, or working under hedges, or by the roadside (a contemptuous use): *a hedge lawyer, a hedge parson.* **3** *Figurative.* done, produced, or worked under a hedge, or secretly: *a hedge marriage.* **4** of such kind as is met with by the wayside; of inferior or common quality: *I was forced to go to a little hedge place for my dinner* (Jonathan Swift). **5** of, for, or having to do with a speculative hedge: *A let-up in hedge sales helped the cotton futures market* (Wall Street Journal).
hedge in, a to hem in; surround on all sides: *The town was hedged in by mountains and a dense forest.* **b** *Figurative.* to keep from getting away or moving freely: *to be hedged in by difficulties.*
[Old English *hecg.* See related etym. at **haw**[1].]
—hedge′less, *adj.*

hedge apple, *U.S. Dialect.* = Osage orange.

hedge bindweed, a perennial vine growing in the temperate regions of Europe, America, and Asia along roads, on beaches, and in thickets and fields; wild morning-glory.

hedge fund, *U.S.* an investment fund set up as a limited partnership for investing private capital speculatively: *The hedge funds, so-called, have been operating on borrowed money in order to concentrate the capital gains of their customers* (Harper's).

hedge|hog (hej′hog′, -hôg′), *n., adj.* **—*n.*** **1** any one of a group of small insect-eating mammals of Europe, Asia, and Africa, with spines on the back. Hedgehogs are active at night. When attacked, a hedgehog rolls up into a bristling ball. **2** the porcupine of America. **3** *Military.* **a** an X-shaped portable obstacle, usually laced with barbed wire. **b** an area defended by pillboxes, mines, and lanes for machine-gun fire.
—*adj.* strongly defended; difficult to break through.

hedge-hop or **hedge|hop** (hej′hop′), *v.t., v.i.,* **-hopped, -hop|ping.** to fly (an airplane) very low over the ground, especially in short, repeated flights, as for dusting crops or bombing: *He gunned the left engine and hedgehopped over land for half a mile* (New York Times). **—hedge′-hop′per, hedge′hop′per,** *n.*

hedge hyssop, 1 any one of a group of low herbs of the figwort family, especially a European species formerly used widely as a medicine. **2** any one of various similar British plants, such as a species of skullcap.

hedge|pig (hej′pig′), *n.* = hedgehog.

hedg|er (hej′ər), *n.* **1** a person who makes, repairs, or trims hedges. **2** a person who shifts or evades; shuffler. **3** a person who hedges in betting, taking a risk, or speculating.

hedge|row (hej′rō′), *n.* a thick row of bushes or small trees forming a hedge.

hedge sparrow, a small European warbler that frequents hedges; dunnock.

hedg|y (hej′ē), *adj.,* **hedg|i|er, hedg|i|est.** full of hedges.

he|don|ic (hē don′ik), *adj.* **1** of or having to do with pleasure. **2** having to do with hedonism or hedonics. **3** *Economics.* concerned with maximizing benefits or profits; utilitarian: *hedonic pricing of goods.*
[< Greek *hēdonikós* pleasurable < *hēdonē* pleasure < *hēdesthai* enjoy oneself] **—he|don′i|cal|ly,** *adv.*

hedonic calculus, = felicific calculus.

he|don|ics (hē don′iks), *n.* **1** the branch of psychology dealing with the pleasant and unpleasant states of consciousness. **2** the branch of ethics dealing with pleasure.

he|don|ism (hē′də niz əm), *n.* **1** the doctrine that pleasure or happiness is the highest good, or the proper end of action. **2** belief in or practice of living only for pleasure.
[< Greek *hēdonē* pleasure + English *-ism*]
—he′don|ist, *n.*

he|do|nis|tic (hē′də nis′tik), *adj.* of or having to do with hedonists or hedonism. **—he′do|nis′ti|cal|ly,** *adv.*

hee|bie-jee|bies (hē′bē jē′bēz), *n. pl. Slang.* the jitters; fidgets: *In spring you can get the heebie-jeebies Untangling chickadees from phoebes* (E. B. White). [a humorous coinage]

heed (hēd), *v., n.* **—*v.t.*** to give careful attention to; take notice of; mind: *Now heed what I say. They pass, and heed each other not* (William Cullen Bryant). **SYN:** note, consider, regard.
—*v.i.* to pay careful attention; notice.
—*n.* careful attention; notice; regard: *She pays heed to her clothes. Full slowly pacing o'er the stones, with caution and good heed* (William Cowper).
[Old English *hēdan*] **—heed′er,** *n.*

heed|ful (hed′fəl), *adj.* careful; attentive: *heedful of advice.* **SYN:** mindful, watchful. **—heed′ful|ly,** *adv.* **—heed′ful|ness,** *n.*

heed|less (hēd′lis), *adj.* careless; thoughtless: *Hobbling downstairs with heedless haste, I set my foot full in a pail of water* (Sir Richard Steele). **SYN:** mindless, inconsiderate. **—heed′less|ly,** *adv.* **—heed′less|ness,** *n.*

hee|haw (hē′hô′), *n., v.* **—*n.*** **1** the braying sound made by a donkey: *asinine heehaws* (Robert Browning). **2** a loud, coarse laugh.
—*v.i.* **1** to make the braying sound of a donkey. **2** to laugh loudly and coarsely.
[imitative]

heel[1] (hēl), *n., v.* **—*n.*** **1** the back part of a person's foot, below the ankle: *I have a blister on my heel from shoes that are too small.* **2** the part of a stocking or shoe that covers the heel: *I walked so much in my stocking feet that I have a hole in my heel.* **3** the part of a shoe or boot that is under the heel or raises the heel: *Mother's shoes have high heels.* **4a** the part of the hind leg of an animal that corresponds to a person's heel: *The horse kicked up his heels trying to throw the rider.* **b** the foot as a whole: *Fauns with cloven heel* (Milton). **5** anything shaped, used, or placed at an end like a heel, such as: **a** the crust at the end of a loaf of bread: *I couldn't eat that stale heel.* **b** the rind of a cheese or piece of cheese: *We shredded the heel to make toasted cheese sandwiches.* **c** (1) the lower end of a rudder, mast, or piece of timber. (2) the rear end of a ship's keel. **d** the part of a knife blade, sword, or tool next to the handle. **e** the small projecting part at the back of the bowl of a spoon. **f** *Golf.* the crook in the head of a club, below the shaft. **g** *Horticulture.* a projecting bit of older wood taken off with a cutting. **6** the latter part or end of a meeting or speech.
—*v.t.* **1** to follow closely; run at the heels of. **2** to put a heel or heels on: *to heel a pair of shoes.*

3 to perform (a dance) with the heels. **4** *Golf.* to strike (the ball) with the heel of the club. **5a** to arm (a gamecock) with a gaff or spur. **b** *U.S. Informal.* to furnish or arm (a person) with something, especially with a weapon.
—*v.i.* **1** to follow closely at a person's heels: *A well-trained dog heels at the command of his master.* **2** to touch the ground or floor with the heel.
at heel, near the heels; close behind: *Ruksh, his horse, followed him like a faithful hound at heel* (Matthew Arnold).
at one's heels, close behind one: *The Hollanders are at our heels, in the race of naval power* (Sir William Petty).
cool one's heels, *Informal.* to be kept waiting a long time: *passengers ... cooling their heels between delayed flights* (Wall Street Journal).
dig in one's heels, to resist anything, especially change or pressure, by assuming a hard and fast attitude or policy: *The American delegation has dug in its heels. ... It won't budge* (New York Times).
down at the heel (or **heels**), **a** with the heel of the shoes worn down: *Her shoes went down at the heel* (Richard Barham). **b** *Figurative.* shabby; slovenly: *Thus the unhappy notary ran gradually down at the heel* (Longfellow).
drag one's heels, to act or move sluggishly or hesitantly; drag one's feet: *The agency dragged its heels during the 1940's in enforcing an anti-trust ... decree against major oil companies* (Wall Street Journal).
heel in, to cover the roots of (a plant) temporarily with soil: *To preserve the young plants during the winter they may be simply heeled in ... in the cellar* (J. A. Warder).
kick one's heels, **a** to be kept waiting for a very long time: *... to let your uncle kick his heels in your hall* (Samuel Foote). **b** to wait impatiently: *I'll trouble him not to leave me here kicking my heels* (Frederick Marryat).
kick up one's heels, to have a good time; celebrate: *Kick up your heels in the nightclubs that spill irresistible ... music into the velvet darkness of every evening* (New Yorker).
lay by the heels, to put in prison or in stocks: *The lord chief justice ... will lay the undersheriff by the heels* (Narcissus Luttrell).
on (or **upon**) **one's heels**, close behind: *Thus grief still treads upon the heels of pleasure* (William Congreve).
out at (**the**) **heels**, **a** with the heel of the stocking or shoe worn through: *Some rich* [*men*]*... go with their hose out at heels* (Thomas Wilson). **b** *Figurative.* worn down; shabby; down at the heel: *... my present situation being, as I may say, a little out at heels* (William Horsley).
show a clean pair of heels, to run; run away: *The thief showed a clean pair of heels.*
take to one's heels, to run away: *The rabble incontinently took to their heels* (Washington Irving).
to heel, **a** near the heels; close behind: *... the dogs, a spaniel and a retriever, keeping to heel* (George Davies). **b** *Figurative.* under control: *The cadets at Polytechnique have been brought to heel with a sharp reimposition of military discipline* (London Times).
turn on one's heel, to turn around quickly; turn away: *The insult made him so mad he turned on his heel and walked out.*
under the heel (or **heels**) **of**, under the control of; in subjection to: *Nations must not perish under the heel or by the hand of those who refuse to honor their own agreements* (Lyndon B. Johnson).
[Old English *hēla*] —**heel′less**, *adj.* —**heel′like′**, *adj.*

heel[2] (hēl), *v., n.* —*v.i., v.t.* to lean over to one side; tilt; tip: *The sailboat heeled as it turned.* SYN: cant, careen, list. —*n.* the act of heeling: *The sudden heel of the boat jerked him overboard.* [alteration of obsolete *hield,* or *heild,* Old English *hieldan* < *heald* inclined]

heel[3] (hēl), *n. Informal.* a hateful person. [special use of *heel*[1]]

heel-and-toe (hēl′ən tō′), *adj.* (of a pace used in walking contests) touching the ground with the heel of the forward foot before the toe of the rear foot leaves the ground.

heel·ball (hēl′bôl′), *n.* **1** a mixture of wax and lampblack used especially by shoemakers for polishing the edges of soles and the like and in taking rubbings of brass surfaces. **2** the ball or underpart of the heel.

heel-drag·ging (hēl′drag′ing), *n.* the action of holding back; slowing up; reluctance; procrastination: *The new policy is a result of the heel-dragging of our allies* (Wall Street Journal).

heeled (hēld), *adj.* **1** *U.S. Informal.* provided with money (usually preceded by a modifier): *This Northern group, backed by wealthy Frederick Flick and others, is perhaps even better heeled than the southern one* (Wall Street Journal). **2** having a heel or heellike projection. **3** with a revolver or other weapon.

heel·er[1] (hē′lər), *n.* **1** a person who puts heels on shoes. **2** *U.S. Informal.* a follower or hanger-on of a political boss: *a ward heeler.* **3** a person who follows at the heels.

heel·er[2] (hēl′ər), *n.* **1** a lurch to one side. **2** a boat that tends to lurch.

heel fly, a botfly whose larva is parasitic in animals such as cattle, goats, and deer; cattle warble. The grub burrows through the skin, causing great damage to the hide.

heel·piece (hēl′pēs′), *n.* **1** the piece forming or covering the heel of a shoe. **2** a piece added to the heel of a shoe. **3** armor for the heel. **4** the iron bar connecting the soft iron cores in an electromagnet. **5** *Figurative.* an end piece or part.

heel·plate (hēl′plāt′), *n.,* or **heel plate**. **1** a protective metal plate on the heel of a shoe, boot, or ski. **2** a metal plate on the heel of a shoe to which a skate can be attached.

heel·post (hēl′pōst′), *n.* **1** the post to which a door or gate is fastened. **2** the post which supports a propeller shaft at the outer end, nearest the screw in a ship.

heel·tap (hēl′tap′), *n.* a layer of leather in the heel of a shoe. **2** a small amount of liquor left in a glass after drinking: *Toss it off, don't leave any heeltap* (Dickens).

heeze (hēz), *v.t.,* **heezed, heez·ing.** *Scottish.* to hoist; raise. [earlier *hoise, hyse,* apparently < Low German *heisen*]

heft (heft), *n., v.* —*n. Informal.* **1a** weight; heaviness: *He tested the heft of the stone before he threw it.* **b** *Figurative.* ponderousness; significance. **2** *U.S.* the greater part; bulk. **3** *Obsolete.* a heaving effort; a heave; strain.
—*v.t.* **1** to lift; heave: *Workers hefted sandbags.* **2** to judge the weight of by lifting.
[< *heave;* patterned on *weft* < *weave*]

heft·y (hef′tē), *adj.,* **heft·i·er, heft·i·est,** *adv. Informal.* —*adj.* **1** weighty; heavy: *a hefty load. This baby is a hefty armful.* **2** *Figurative.* substantial; considerable: *Rail officials expect some hefty returns on the millions they're spending on new classification yards* (Wall Street Journal). **3** big and strong. **4** violent. —*adv.* powerfully; exceedingly: *It's hefty damp in here* (Rudyard Kipling).
—**heft′i·ly,** *adv.* —**heft′i·ness,** *n.*

he·gar·i (hi gär′ē, heg′ər-), *n.* an African grain sorghum grown, in an early-maturing variety, in the southwestern United States. [< Arabic *hegarī,* variant of *hajarī* stony]

He·ge·li·an (hā gā′lē ən, hi jē′-), *adj., n.* —*adj.* of or having to do with the German philosopher Georg Hegel (1770-1831) or his philosophy. —*n.* a person who believes in the philosophical system of Hegel.

He·ge·li·an·ism (hā gā′lē ə niz′əm, hi jē′-), *n.* the philosophy of Hegel, especially his view of reality as a dynamic process determined by the dialectics of thesis, antithesis, and synthesis.

heg·e·mon (hej′ə mon), *n.* a leading or paramount power. [< Greek *hēgémōn* leader]

heg·e·mon·ic (hej′ə mon′ik, hē′jə-), *adj.* ruling; supreme.

he·gem·o·nism (hi jem′ə niz əm), *n.* = hegemony.

he·gem·o·nist (hi jem′ə nist), *n.* a person who favors hegemony.

he·gem·o·nis·tic (hi jem′ə nis′tik, hej′ə mō-), *adj.* of or characterized by hegemony: *... a hegemonistic policy of territorial claims* (London Times).

he·gem·o·ny (hi jem′ə nē, hej′ə mō′-), *n., pl.* **-nies.** political domination, especially the leadership or domination of one state over others in a group; leadership; predominance: *The headship, or hegemony, was in the hands of Athens* (George Grote). [< Greek *hēgemoniā* < *hēgémōn* leader < *hēgeîsthai* to lead]

He·gi·ra (hi jī′rə, hej′ər ə), *n.* **1** the flight of Mohammed from Mecca to Medina in A.D. 622. The Moslems use a calendar reckoned from this date. The abbreviation A.H. following a date signifies "after the Hegira." **2** the Moslem era. Also, **Hejira.** [< Medieval Latin *hegira* < Arabic *hijra* flight, departure]

he·gi·ra (hi jī′rə, hej′ər ə), *n.* departure; flight: *the summer hegira from the cities to the coast and lakes. Completely contrary to the famous trip of the salmon, which crowds the rivers and creeks in spring with fish eager to spawn, the hegira of the eel is toward the sea* (Science News Letter). Also, **hejira.** [< *Hegira*]

he-goat (hē′gōt′), *n.* a male goat.

Hei·an or **Hei′an** (hā′än′), *adj.* of or having to do with a culture that flourished in Japan between the 800's and 1100's: *The Heian world was devoted to the arts* (New Yorker). [< *Heian-* kyo, former name of Kyoto, the historic capital of Japan and center of this culture]

hei·au (hā′ou), *n.* an ancient place of worship, usually a terrace or a platform of stone; temple. [< Hawaiian]

Hei·del·berg man (hī′dəl bėrg), a prehistoric man of the Pleistocene epoch, who lived during the period of the great glaciers, reconstructed from a human lower jawbone found in 1907 near Heidelberg, Germany.

Hei·duc or **Hei·duk** (hī′dủk), *n.* = Haiduk.

heif·er (hef′ər), *n.* **1** a young cow that has not had a calf. **2** *Slang.* a girl or young lady. [Old English *hēahfore*]

heigh (hī, hā), *interj.* a sound used to attract attention, give encouragement, or express surprise [perhaps imitative.]

heigh-ho (hī′hō′, hā′-), *interj.* a sound made to express surprise, joy, sadness, weariness, or boredom. [< *heigh* + *ho*[2]]

height (hīt), *n.* **1** how tall a person is; how high anything is; how far up a thing goes: *the height of a mountain. Seven feet is an unusual height for a man.* **2** a fairly great distance up: *rising at a height above the valley.* **3** a high point or place; hill: *on the mountain heights.* **4** the highest part; top; summit: *When we reached the height we rested.* (*Figurative.*) *He* [*Tennyson*] *could not think up to the height of his own towering style* (G. K. Chesterton). **5** *Figurative.* the highest point; greatest degree; extremity: *the height of fashion. Fast driving on icy roads is the height of folly.* SYN: summit, zenith, acme. **6** *Figurative.* high rank; high degree. **7** *Archaic.* loftiness of mind. [Old English *hīehthu,* related to *hēah* high]
—*Syn.* **1 Height, altitude** mean extent or distance above a level. **Height** is the general term for any such distance, great or small: *What is the height of the Empire State Building?* **Altitude** applies chiefly to height above a given level, especially sea level or the earth's surface: *The plane quickly lost altitude.*

height·en (hī′tən), *v.t.* **1** to make higher; elevate: *The builder heightened the doorway to accommodate the tall owner.* **2** *Figurative.* to make stronger or greater; increase: *The clowns and the band heightened the children's pleasure. Wax applied to a floor heightens the shine.* SYN: raise, augment, intensify. **3** to make (a color) more luminous. **4** *Obsolete.* to elate; excite: *Satiate at length, and hight'nd as with wine* (Milton). —*v.i.* **1** to become higher; increase in height; rise: *Day by day the structure heightened.* **2** *Figurative.* to become stronger or greater; increase: *Their industry always heightened at the boss's approach.*
—**height′en·er,** *n.*

height-to-pa·per (hīt′tủ pā′pər), *n.* the standard and customary distance from the feet to the face of modern printing type (in the United States, 0.9186 inch; in Great Britain, 0.918 inch).

heil (hīl), *interj., v. German.* —*interj.* hail!
—*v.t.* to hail; greet.

Heim·dall (hām′däl), *n. Norse Mythology.* a god of light, guardian of Asgard, city of the gods.

hei·min (hā′min), *n.* (in Japan) the common people; the working class. [< Japanese *heimin* < *hei* common + *min* people]

hei·mish (hā′mish), *adj. Especially U.S. Slang.* cozy; friendly; informal: *The restaurant attracts this crowd not only because of its heimish cuisine but because of its five-man team of countermen, a couple of whom mainly provide counter-talk entertainment and a couple of whom mainly provide food* (New Yorker). [< Yiddish *heimish* (literally) homelike]

Heim·lich maneuver (hīm′lik), a procedure to prevent choking on something lodged in the windpipe by grasping the victim from behind and locking one's hands in a fist over the victim's upper abdomen and with a quick squeeze forcing the fist up under the diaphragm to expel air through the windpipe. [< Henry J. *Heimlich,* an American surgeon who devised it]

Hei·ne (hī′nē), *n.* = Heinie.

Hei·nie (hī′nē), *n. Slang.* a German (used in an unfriendly way). [< German *Heinrich* Henry]

hei·nous (hā′nəs), *adj.* very wicked; extremely offensive; hateful: *The gangster was punished for his heinous crimes by a long prison sentence.* SYN: odious, infamous, atrocious. [< Old French *haïnos* (with English *-ous*) < *haïne* hatred < *haïr* to hate < Germanic (compare Old Saxon *hatōn*)]
—**hei′nous·ly,** *adv.* —**hei′nous·ness,** *n.*

heintz·ite (hīn′tsīt), *n.* a colorless or white hydrous borate of magnesium and potassium found in monoclinic crystals. [< German *Heintzit* < William H. *Heintze,* a German chemist + *-it* - ite[1]]

heir (ãr), *n., v.* —*n.* **1** a person who has the right to someone's property or title after the death of its owner; person who inherits property: *The rich man adopted the boy and made him his heir.*

Pronunciation Key: hat, āge, cãre, fär; let, ēqual, tėrm; it, īce; hot, ōpen, ôrder; oil, out; cup, pủt, rüle; child; long; thin; ᴛʜen; zh, measure; ə represents a in about, e in taken, i in pencil, o in lemon, u in circus.

2a *Figurative.* a person who inherits anything; person who receives or has something from someone before him: *We are truly heirs of all the ages* (John Tyndall). **b** (in civil law) a person who succeeds to the property, real and personal, and to the rights and obligations of a deceased person. **3** *Obsolete.* offspring; product.
—***v.t.*** to inherit: *When falls a mate in battle broil, His comrade heirs his portion'd spoil* (Scott).
fall heir to, to inherit: *He fell heir to a small fortune. The new government fell heir to the problems of the old one.*
[< Old French *heir* < Latin *hērēs, -ēdis* heir. See etym. of doublet **heres.**] —**heir′less,** *adj.* —**heir′ship,** *n.*
▶Technically, an **heir** is a person who receives money or property left by someone who died without disposing of his estate in his will. **Legatee** is the legal term for the beneficiary of a will. However, the word *heir* is commonly used for any person who is awarded an estate, whether or not the deceased person left a will.

heir apparent, *pl.* **heirs apparent. 1** a person who will be heir if he lives longer than the one holding the property or title: *The king's oldest son is heir apparent to the throne.* **2** *Figurative.* a person who seems certain to succeed another: *Young Saint-Laurent ... had been Christian Dior's heir apparent* (Time).

heir at law, a person who receives, or is legally entitled to receive, the real property of an intestate person at his death.

heir|dom (ãr′dəm), *n.* heirship; inheritance.

heir|ess (ãr′is), *n.* **1** an heir who is a woman or girl: *His daughter was named in the will as his heiress.* **2** a woman or girl inheriting great wealth: *an heiress to a great fortune.*

heir|loom (ãr′lüm′), *n.* **1** a possession handed down from generation to generation: *This old grandfather clock is a family heirloom.* **2** *Law.* a personal chattel that is passed on with an inheritance to the heir. [< *heir* + *loom*[1] (originally) implement]

heir presumptive, *pl.* **heirs presumptive.** a person who will be heir unless someone with a stronger claim is born.

Hei|sen|berg effect (hī′zən bėrg), a change in a subject under investigation due to the effect of the investigative process: *No one does or can do—the same things on stage that he does unobserved. It's the popularized Heisenberg effect: The act of observing inevitably changes the process under observation* (Richard Reeves). [< *Heisenberg* uncertainty principle]

Heisenberg uncertainty principle = uncertainty principle. [< Werner K. *Heisenberg,* 1901-1976, a German physicist]

heist (hīst), *v., n. Slang.* —***v.t., v.i.*** to rob or steal: *He'd heist a round of his master's ... whiskey and disguise the drainage* (New Yorker).
—***n.*** a robbery or theft: *a payroll heist.* [alteration of *hoist*] —**heist′er,** *n.*

hei-ti|ki (hā′tē′kē), *n.* a greenstone ornament worn by the Maoris, representing the first man. [< Maori *hei-tiki* < *hei* ornament + *tiki* maker of man]

he|ji|ra (hi jī′rə, hej′ər ə), *n.* = hegira.

He|ji|ra (hi jī′rə, hej′ər ə), *n.* = Hegira.

Hek|a|te (hek′ə tē), *n.* = Hecate.

he|kis|to|therm (he kis′tə thėrm), *n. Botany.* a plant which needs very little heat, as the arctic and antarctic lichens and mosses. [< Greek *hḗkistos* smallest + *thérmē* heat]

he|kis|to|ther|mic (he kis′tə thėr′mik), *adj.* of or having to do with hekistotherms.

hek|te (hek′tē), *n.* an ancient Greek silver coin equal to a sixth of a stater. [< Greek *héktē,* feminine of *héktos* a sixth]

hek|to|graph (hek′tə graf, -gräf), *n., v.t.* = hectograph.

hek|to|li|ter (hek′tə lē′tər), *n.* = hectoliter.

Hel (hel), *n. Norse Mythology.* **1** the goddess of death and of the lower world, daughter of Loki. **2** the lower world, inhabited by those who died of disease or old age. [< Old Icelandic *Hel.* Compare etym. under **hell.**]

Hel|a (hel′ä), *n.* = Hel.

He|La cell (hē′lə), a cancerous cell originally obtained from the human uterus. It is raised in cultures for use in studying certain diseases, such as poliomyelitis. [< *He*(nrietta) *La*(cks), a cancer patient in Baltimore from whose cells the first cultures were grown in 1951]

hé|las (ā läs′), *interj. French.* alas.

held (held), *v., adj.* —***v.*** the past tense and past participle of **hold**[1]: *Mother held the new baby. The swing is held by strong ropes.* —***adj.*** kept in; restrained; detained: *a held suspect.*

hel|den|ten|or (hel′dən ten′ər; *German* hel′dən te nōr′), *n.* a tenor with a voice suited to heroic roles, especially in Wagnerian operas. [< German *Heldentenor* < *Held* hero + *Tenor* tenor]

hel|e|nine (hel′ə nin), *n.* a drug obtained from a penicillium mold, used to treat certain virus diseases.

he|le|ni|um (hi lē′nē əm), *n.* = sneezeweed. [< New Latin *Helenium* the genus name < Greek *helenion* a plant (perhaps elecampane), probably < *Helenē* Helen]

Hel|en of Troy (hel′ən), *Greek Legend.* a very beautiful Greek woman, the daughter of Zeus and Leda, and the wife of King Menelaus of Sparta. Her kidnaping by Paris caused the Trojan War.

hel|gra|mite (hel′grə mīt), *n.* = hellgrammite.

heli-, *combining form.* the form of **helio-** before vowels, as in *helianthus.*

he|li|ac (hē′lē ak), *adj.* = heliacal.

he|li|a|cal (hi lī′ə kəl), *adj. Astronomy.* having to do with or occurring near the sun, as the risings and settings of stars that are most nearly coincident with those of the sun while yet being visible. [< Latin *hēliacus* (< Greek *hēliakós* < *hḗlios* the sun) + English *-al*[1]] —**he|li′a|cal|ly,** *adv.*

he|li|an|thus (hē′lē an′thəs), *n.* = sunflower. [< New Latin *Helianthus* the genus name < Greek *hḗlios* sun + *ánthos* flower]

he|li|arc welding (hē′lē ärk′), a type of electric arc welding in which helium is used to prevent burning or corroding.

hel|i|borne (hel′ə bôrn′, -bōrn′; hē′lə-), *adj.* carried or done by helicopter.

hel|i|cal (hel′ə kəl), *adj.* having to do with, or having the form of, a helix; spiral: *At the end of a minute a dull splashing reverberated from the bottom of the well; the helical twist he had imparted to the rope had reached the grapnel below* (Thomas Hardy) —**hel′i|cal|ly,** *adv.*

helical gear, a gearwheel whose teeth run at an angle to the shaft; spiral gear.

hel|i|car (hel′ə kär′, hē′lə-), *n.* a vehicle that is both a helicopter and an automobile. [< *heli*(copter) + *car*]

he|liced (hē′list, hel′ist), *adj.* having helices; decorated with helices: *... a foliated and heliced acroterium* (Lewis and Street).

hel|i|ces (hel′ə sēz), *n.* a plural of **helix.**

hel|i|chry|sum (hel′i krī′səm), *n.* = strawflower. [< New Latin *Helichrysum* the genus name < Greek *hélix* spiral + *chrȳsós* gold]

he|lic|i|ty (hē lis′ə tē), *n. Nuclear Physics.* the direction of the spin of an elementary particle. [< *helic-* (for *helik-,* stem of Greek *hélix* spiral) + *-ity*]

hel|i|coid (hel′ə koid), *n., adj. Geometry.* —***n.*** a surface in the form of a coil or screw; a warped surface generated by a straight line moving so that it always passes through or touches a fixed helix and is parallel to a fixed plane. —***adj.*** like a helix; curved spirally, as certain univalve shells are; spiral. [< Greek *helikoeidḗs* spiral < *hélix, -ikos* spiral + *eîdos* form] —**hel′i|coi′dal|ly,** *adv.*

hel|i|coi|dal (hel′ə koi′dəl), *adj.* = helicoid.

Hel|i|con (hel′ə kon, -kən), *n.* poetry and poetic inspiration, regarded in legend as flowing from two fountains on the side of Mount Helicon in southern Greece.

hel|i|con (hel′ə kon, -kən), *n.* a large bass tuba, circular in form. [< *Helicon;* meaning influenced by *helix*]

Hel|i|co|ni|an (hel′ə kō′nē ən), *adj.* having to do with or obtained from Helicon.

hel|i|copt (hel′ə kopt, hē′lə-), *v.i., v.t.* = helicopter.

hel|i|cop|ter** (hel′ə kop′tər, hē′lə-), *n., v.* —n.*** an aircraft that is lifted from the ground and kept in the air by horizontal propellers or rotors. Helicopters have no wings.
—***v.i.*** to travel by helicopter: *A Democratic Representative ... helicoptered over Tennessee* (Harper's). —***v.t.*** to send or carry by helicopter. [< French *hélicoptère* < Greek *hélix, -ikos* spiral + *pterón* wing, related to *pétesthai* to fly]

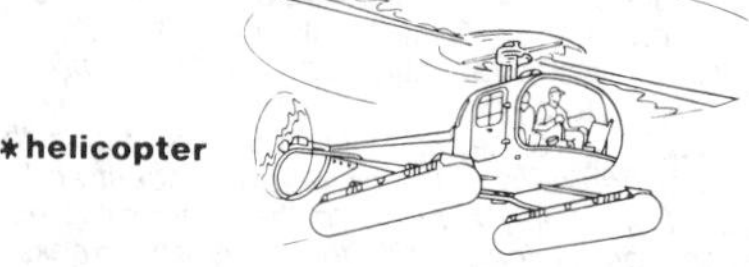

***helicopter**

hel|i|cop|ter|ist (hel′ə kop′tər ist, hē′lə-), *n.* the pilot of a helicopter.

he|lic|tis (hi lik′tis), *n.* any one of a group of small carnivorous animals of southern and eastern Asia belonging to the family that includes the weasels, badgers, and martens. [< New Latin *Helictis* the genus name, probably < Greek *hélos* marsh + *iktis* a kind of weasel]

he|lic|tite (hi lik′tīt), *n.* a twig-shaped formation of lime on the wall of a cave. [< Greek *heliktós* twisted + English *-ite*[1]]

hel|i|lift (hel′ə lift′, hē′lə-), *v.t.* to transport by helicopter, especially in an emergency.

he|li|o (hē′lē ō), *n., pl.* **-li|os.** *Informal.* a heliograph or heliogram.

helio-, *combining form.* the sun: *Helioscope = a device for looking at the sun.* Also, **heli-** before vowels. [< Greek *hēlio-* < *hḗlios* sun]

he|li|o|cen|tric (hē′lē ō sen′trik), *adj.* **1** viewed or measured from the center of the sun: *heliocentric latitude.* **2** having or representing the sun as a center: *Both the ancient Egyptians and ancient Greeks preceded Galileo in postulating a heliocentric universe.* —**he′li|o|cen′tri|cal|ly,** *adv.*

he|li|o|cen|tric|i|ty (hē′lē ō sen tris′ə tē), *n.* = heliocentrism.

heliocentric parallax, = annual parallax.

he|li|o|cen|trism (hē′lē ō sen′triz əm), *n.* the theory that the sun is the center of the solar system, with the earth and the other eight planets revolving about it.

he|li|o|chrome (hē′lē ə krōm), *n.* a photograph of an object in its natural colors.

he|li|o|chro|mic (hē′lē ə krō′mik), *adj.* of or like a heliochrome; by means of heliochromy.

he|li|o|chro|my (hē′lē ə krō′mē), *n.* photography in natural colors.

he|li|o|cul|ture (hē′lē ə kul′chər), *n.* heliolithic culture.

he|li|o|don (hē′lē ə don), *n.* a device for taking sunlight and shadow measurements artificially for a proposed building or buildings on any place on the earth's surface at any time of the day or year. It consists of a projector that casts simulated sunlight upon a platform containing a model of the proposed building or buildings. [< Greek *hḗlios* sun + *hodós* way]

he|li|o|dor (hē′lē ə dôr), *n.* a golden variety of beryl, used as a semiprecious stone in jewelry. [< *helio-* + French *doré* gilded]

he|li|o|gram (hē′lē ə gram), *n.* a message sent by a heliograph. [< *helio*(graph) + (tele)*gram*]

he|li|o|graph (hē′lē ə graf, -gräf), *n., v.* —***n.*** **1** a device for signaling by means of a movable mirror that flashes beams of sunlight to a distance. The flashes of the mirror represent the dots and dashes of the Morse code. **2** an apparatus for taking photographs of the sun. **3** a printing image obtained by a process in which a specially sensitized plate is acted on chemically by exposure to light.
—***v.t., v.i.*** to signal or communicate by heliograph: *They are heliographing the message to the ship.* —**he′li|og′ra|pher,** *n.*

he|li|o|graph|ic (hē′lē ə graf′ik), *adj.* of a heliograph or heliography.

he|li|og|ra|phy (hē′lē og′rə fē), *n.* the system of signaling with the heliograph.

he|li|o|gra|vure (hē′lē ō grə vyůr′, -grāv′yər), *n.* **1** = photogravure. **2** a photogravure plate or print.

he|li|o|la|ter (hē′lē ol′ə tər), *n.* a sun worshiper.

he|li|o|la|trous (hē′lē ol′ə trəs), *adj.* worshiping the sun.

he|li|o|la|try (hē′lē ol′ə trē), *n.* = sun worship. [< *helio-* + Greek *latreíā* worship]

he|li|o|lith|ic (hē′lē ə lith′ik), *adj.* of or having to do with a culture characterized by megaliths and sun worship.

he|li|ol|o|gy (hē′lē ol′ə jē), *n.* the science of the sun. [< *helio-* + *-logy*] —**he′li|ol′o|gist,** *n.*

he|li|om|e|ter (hē′lē om′ə tər), *n.* an astronomical instrument, originally for measuring the sun's diameter, but now used especially in determining the angular distance between two stars.

he|li|o|met|ric (hē′lē ə met′rik), *adj.* having to do with a heliometer or heliometry. —**he′li|o|met′ri|cal|ly,** *adv.*

he|li|om|e|try (hē′lē om′ə trē), *n.* the technique of making measurements with the heliometer.

he|li|o|phile (hē′lē ə fīl), *n.* a heliophilous person or organism.

he|li|oph|i|lous (hē′lē of′ə ləs), *adj.* attracted by sunlight; sun-loving. [< *helio-* + Greek *philos* (with English *-ous*) loving]

he|li|o|po|lar (hē′lē ō pō′lər), *adj.* of or having to do with the pole or poles of the sun.

he|li|o|port (hē′lē ə pôrt′, -pōrt′), *n.* = heliport.

He|li|os (hē′lē os), *n. Greek Mythology.* the god of the sun, son of Hyperion. Helios is pictured driving a chariot drawn by four horses through the heavens. He was later identified with Apollo. The Romans called him Sol. [< Greek *Hḗlios* < *hḗlios* sun]

he|li|o|scope (hē′lē ə skōp), *n.* **1** a device for looking at the sun without injury to the eye. **2** a telescope having such a device. [< French *hélioscope* < Greek *hḗlios* sun + *skópos* viewer]

he|li|o|sphere (hē′lē ə sfir), *n.* the region in space over which the sun's gases and magnetic field extend: *It [a spacecraft] may even be able to detect the unknown limits of the heliosphere ... and chart the fringes of interstellar space* (Time).

he|li|o|stat (hē′lē ə stat), *n.* an apparatus consisting of a mirror turned by clockwork for reflecting the light of the sun in a fixed direction. [< New

Latin *heliostata* < Greek *hêlios* sun + *statós* stopping, standing]

he|li|o|tac|tic (hē′lē ə tak′tik), *adj.* having the property of heliotaxis.

he|li|o|tax|is (hē′lē ə tak′sis), *n. Biology.* movement in response to sunlight. [< *helio-* + Greek *táxis* arrangement]

he|li|o|trope (hē′lē ə trōp, hēl′yə-), *n., adj.* —*n.* **1** any one of a group of herbs or shrubs with clusters of small, sweet-smelling, purple or white flowers; turnsole. It belongs to the borage family. **2** the common valerian. **3** any plant whose flowers turn to follow the sun (formerly applied to the sunflower, marigold, and the like). **4** a pinkish purple. **5** = bloodstone. **6** *Surveying.* an instrument for reflecting the sun's rays to a distant point.
—*adj.* pinkish-purple.
[< Latin *hēliotropium* < Greek *hēliotrópion* heliotropic plant; bloodstone < *hêlios* sun + *-tropos* turning < *trépein* to turn]

he|li|o|trop|ic (hē′lē ə trop′ik, -trō′pik), *adj. Botany.* turning or bending in response to sunlight. —**he′li|o|trop′i|cal|ly**, *adv.*

he|li|o|tro|pin (hē′lē ə trō′pin, hē′lē ot′rə pin), *n.* = piperonal. [< *heliotrope* + *-in*]

he|li|ot|ro|pism (hē′lē ot′rə piz əm), *n.* the tendency of plants to turn toward sunlight. Heliotropism is a type of phototropism. [< *helio-* + *tropism*]

he|li|o|zo|an (hē′lē ə zō′ən), *n., adj.* —*n.* any one of a group of chiefly freshwater protozoans having a globular body with raylike pseudopods.
—*adj.* of or belonging to the heliozoans.
[< New Latin *Heliozoa* the order name (< Greek *hêlios* sun + *zôion* animal) + English *-an*]

he|li|o|zo|ic (hē′lē ə zō′ik), *adj.* = heliozoan.

hel|i|pad (hel′ə pad′, hē′lə-), *n.* a small area for helicopters to take off or land on. [< *heli-*(copter) + *pad*]

hel|i|port (hel′ə pôrt′, -pōrt′; hē′lə-), *n.* an airport for helicopters. Heliports may be built on the tops of buildings or in other small areas in large cities. [< *heli*(copter) + (air)*port*]

hel|i|spher|i|cal (hel′ə sfer′ə kəl), *adj.* winding spirally on a sphere: *a helispherical line.*

***he|li|um** (hē′lē əm), *n.* a very light, colorless, odorless gas that will not burn, much used in balloons and airships. Helium is an inert chemical element which occurs in small amounts in the air, in natural gas, in certain minerals, and as a product of many radioactive substances and processes. Helium, in the liquid state, is used as a refrigerant. It is also used in place of flammable gases in electric welding. [< New Latin *helium* < Greek *hêlios* sun (because its existence in the sun's atmosphere was inferred from the sun's spectrum)]

***helium**

symbol	atomic number	atomic weight
He	2	4.0026

helium speech, an unnatural, squeaky quality in the voice of undersea explorers or divers due to the higher frequency of sound in the helium gas contained in the pressurized mixture of gases breathed undersea: *There is an urgent requirement for speech converters to unscramble the extraordinary 'Donald Duck' noises of helium speech* (Science Journal).

***he|lix** (hē′liks), *n., pl.* **hel|i|ces, he|lix|es. 1** anything having a spiral, coiled form. A screw thread, a watch spring, or a snail shell is a helix. **2** *Architecture.* **a** a spiral ornament. **b** a volute, especially one of the small ones just below the abacus of a Corinthian capital. **3** *Anatomy.* the rim of the outer ear. **4** *Geometry.* the curve traced by a straight line on a plane that is wrapped around a cylinder, like the thread of a screw. [< Latin *helix* < Greek *hélix,* related to *eileîn* to turn, roll]

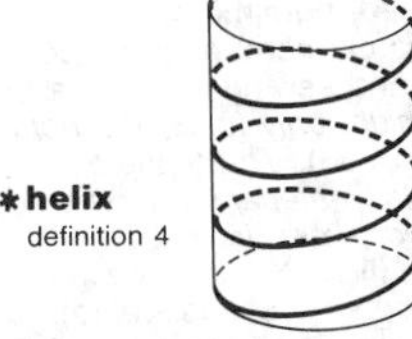

***helix**
definition 4

he|lix|in (hə lik′sin), *n.* an antibiotic derived from an actinomycete, used in the treatment of fungous diseases of plants. [< *helix* + *-in* (because of the shape of the fungus)]

hell (hel), *n., interj.* —*n.* **1** (in Christian and some other religious use) the place where wicked persons are punished after death; the abode of devils and damned spirits: *Hell is a city much like London—a populous and smoky city* (Shelley). **2** the powers of evil: *The compact ... is an agreement with hell* (William Lloyd Garrison). **3** the persons in hell: *All hell broke loose* (Milton). **4** the home of the dead; the lower world regarded as a place of existence after death; Hades; Sheol: *She that had no need of me, Is a little lonely child Lost in Hell* (Edna St. Vincent Millay). **SYN:** Avernus, Tartarus. **5** *Figurative.* **a** any very bad or wicked place or condition, or one of torment or misery. **b** something very difficult or unpleasant: *The third part was hell, even though I won it* (Atlantic). **c** *Slang.* a scolding: *to get or catch hell.* **6** = gambling house. **7** a place under a tailor's board, in which shreds or pieces of cloth are thrown. **8** *Printing.* = hellbox. **9** *Obsolete.* a part of a building, etc., which for its darkness or discomfort, or for a similar reason, was compared to hell. **10** *Obsolete.* a place of confinement for debtors.
—*interj.* a mild curse or exclamation of anger, annoyance, or surprise; heck.
come hell or high water, no matter what might happen: *She allowed herself six weeks ... and announced that "come hell or high water" the deadline would be kept* (London Times).
for the hell of it, *Slang.* for the pleasure derived from it; for kicks: *The guy who runs the gadget ... sent everything into motion just for the hell of it* (Arthur Daley).
hell of a, *Slang.* **a** very bad; rotten: *Business is in one hell of a mess* (John Tebbel). **b** very good; exceptional: *His partner ... describes Watts as "one hell of a man"* (Ian Adams). **c** very; exceptionally: *What a hell of a quiet dog* (Graham Greene).
play hell with, *Slang.* play havoc with; ruin: *A ten percent alteration in the specifications of a transistor will play hell with the circuit* (Esquire).
raise hell, *Slang.* to make a disturbance; raise the devil: *Parents ... raise hell if their child is expected to study under miserable conditions* (Brian Jackson).
to hell and gone, *Slang.* to an extreme distance or degree: *I'd lost a lot of weight while Dick and me were out on the road riding all to hell and gone* (New Yorker).
[Old English *hell*]

he'll (hēl; *unstressed* hil), **1** he will. **2** he shall.

Hel|lad|ic (he lad′ik), *adj.* of, from, or having to do with the ancient pre-Hellenic civilization in Greece from about 2500 to 1100 B.C.: *vases from the Helladic period.* [< Greek *Helladikós* < *Hellás, -ádos* Greece]

hel|land|ite (hel′ən dīt), *n.* a mineral, a silicate of calcium and the rare earths, found in pegmatite veins.

hell|bend|er (hel′ben′dər), *n.* **1** a large salamander common especially in the Ohio River and its tributaries. **2** *Slang.* a long and reckless debauch or drunken frolic. [American English < *hell* + *bender* that which bends]

hell|bent or **hell-bent** (hel′bent′), *adj., adv. Informal.* —*adj.* strongly bent (on); firmly determined: *Washington is hellbent on strangling industry with regulations* (New Yorker). —*adv.* resolutely; with no holds barred; recklessly: *driving his Ford pickup hellbent through the creek* (Dan Cushman).
hellbent for leather. See under **leather**.

hell|box (hel′boks′), *n. Printing.* a waste box for damaged or broken type.

hell|broth (hel′brôth′, -broth′), *n.* a magic broth prepared for an infernal purpose.

hell|cat (hel′kat′), *n.* **1** an evil, spiteful, or ill-tempered woman; vixen: *She went on in such a listless tone that I could no longer believe her reputation as a very hellcat of pugnacity* (Maclean's). **2** a witch.

hell-div|er or **hell|div|er** (hel′dī′vər), *n.* a small grebe, especially a pied-billed grebe.

Hel|le (hel′ē), *n. Greek Legend.* a maiden drowned in the Hellespont while fleeing with her brother on the ram with the golden fleece.

hel|le|bore (hel′ə bôr, -bōr), *n.* **1** any one of various perennial European herbs of the crowfoot family, with showy yellow, green, or purple flowers that bloom on erect stems before spring, especially the black hellebore and the bear's-foot. **2** the root of any one of these plants, which is dried and used in medicine. **3** any one of various tall herbs of the lily family, with clusters of purple, green, or white flowers that bloom on erect stems, especially the American hellebore and the white hellebore, both of which have roots with medicinal and poisonous properties; false hellebore. **4** an insecticide made from the dried roots of the American hellebore. **5** a cardiac medicine made from the roots of the American hellebore. [Middle English *elebre* < Latin *elleborus* < Greek *helléboros*]

hel|leb|o|rin (he leb′ər in, hel′ə bər-), *n.* a poisonous, crystalline glucoside, a narcotic, found in hellebore. *Formula:* $C_{28}H_{36}O_6$

Hel|len (hel′ən), *n.* a king of Thessaly, legendary ancestor of the Hellenes.

Hel|lene (hel′ēn), *n.* = Greek. [< Greek *Héllēnes* a Thessalian tribe, plural of *Héllēn* Hellen]

Hel|len|ic (he len′ik, -lē′nik), *adj., n.* —*adj.* **1** = Greek. **2** of Greek history, language, or culture from 776 B.C. to the death of Alexander the Great in 323 B.C.
—*n.* **1** the Greek language. **2** the branch of the Indo-European family of languages that includes the various dialects of Greek.

Hel|len|ism (hel′ə niz əm), *n.* **1** ancient Greek culture or ideals; the national character or spirit of the ancient Greeks. **2** the adoption or imitation of Greek speech, ideals, or customs. **3** an idiom or expression peculiar to the Greek language. [< Greek *Hellēnismós* imitation of the Greeks < *Hellēnízein* to make Greek < *Héllēn* Hellen]

Hel|len|ist (hel′ə nist), *n., adj.* —*n.* **1** a scholar skilled in the ancient Greek language, literature, and culture. **2** a person who uses or imitates Greek language, ideals, or customs, especially a Jew who after the conquests of Alexander the Great in the 300's B.C. came under Greek influence. **3** one of the Byzantine Greeks who contributed to the revival of classical learning in Europe during the Renaissance.
—*adj.* = Hellenistic.
[< Greek *Hellēnistês* one who imitates the Hellenes]

Hel|len|is|tic (hel′ə nis′tik), *adj.* **1** of or having to do with Greek history, language, and culture after the death of Alexander the Great in 323 B.C., when foreign elements modified ancient Greek characteristics. **2** of or having to do with the Hellenists. **3** using the Greek language and following Greek customs. —**Hel′len|is′ti|cal**, *adj.* —**Hel′len|is′ti|cal|ly**, *adv.*

Hel|len|ize (hel′ə nīz), *v.,* **-ized, -iz|ing.** —*v.t.* to make Greek in form or character: *The priests of the Temple ... had become Hellenized and thus completely alienated from the ordinary people* (Hans Küng).
—*v.i.* to use or imitate the Greek language, ideals, or customs.
[< Greek *Hellēnízein* < *Héllēn* Hellen] —**Hel′len|i|za′tion**, *n.* —**Hel′len|iz′er**, *n.*

Hel|le|no|phil (hel′ə nō fil), *n.* = Hellenophile.

Hel|le|no|phile (hel′ə nō fīl, -fil), *n.* a lover of Greece or Greek things. **SYN:** Grecophile.

hel|ler[1] (hel′ər), *n., pl.* **-ler. 1** a former German coin, worth ½ of a pfennig. **2** a former Austrian copper coin, worth 1/100 of a krone. **3** = haler[1]. [earlier *haller* < Middle High German *haller,* or *häller,* supposedly < (*Schwäbisch-*) *Hall,* the city where first coined]

hell|er[2] (hel′ər), *n. Slang.* a person who creates mischief and excitement: *His father was a lazy farmer, a local heller who loved his booze* (Time).

hell|fire (hel′fīr′), *n., adj.* —*n.* the fire of hell; punishment in hell.
—*adj.* promising damnation and punishment; raising visions of fire and brimstone: *children terrorised by a hellfire puritanism* (Manchester Guardian).
[Old English *helle fyr* fire of hell]

hell-for-leath|er (hel′fər leᴛʜ′ər), *adj., adv. Slang.* at breakneck speed; hellbent: *a hell-for-leather race.* (adj.) *It was written hell-for-leather* (Robert Frost). (adv.)

hell|gram|mite (hel′grə mīt), *n.* the large, black, aquatic larva of the dobson fly, often used for fish bait; dobson. Also, **helgramite**. [American English; origin unknown]

hell|hole (hel′hōl′), *n.* a very unpleasant place; den; dive.

hell|hound (hel′hound′), *n.* **1** a hound or dog of hell. **2** *Greek and Roman Mythology.* Cerberus, the watchdog of Hades. **3** a fiend or fiendish person. [Old English *helle hund* dog of hell; (originally) Cerberus]

hel|lion (hel′yən), *n. U.S. Informal.* a mischievous, troublesome person: *A gang of young hellions roamed the streets at night.*

hell|ish (hel′ish), *adj.* **1** fit to have come from hell; devilish; fiendish: *hellish shrieks, a hellish thing to do.* **SYN:** diabolical, wicked. **2** of hell; infernal: *diabolical and hellish magic* (Daniel Defoe). —**hell′ish|ly**, *adv.* —**hell′ish|ness**, *n.*

hel|lo (he lō′, hə-), *interj., n., pl.* **-los,** *v.,* **-loed, -lo|ing.** —*interj.* **1** an exclamation to express greeting or attract attention. We usually say "hello" when we call or answer a call on the telephone. *"Hello, Mother!" the boy said.* **2** an

Pronunciation Key: hat, āge, cãre, fär; let, ēqual, tėrm; it, īce; hot, ōpen, ôrder; oil, out; cup, pu̇t, rüle; **child**; long; **thin**; ᴛʜen; **zh**, measure; **ə** represents **a** in about, **e** in taken, **i** in pencil, **o** in lemon, **u** in circus.

exclamation of surprise.
—*n.* **1** a call of greeting or surprise. **2** a call to attract attention: *The girl gave a loud hello to let us know where she was.*
—*v.i.* to say or call "hello"; shout; call: *He asked us to hello until somebody came.* Also, **hullo.**
[variant of *hallo,* or *hollo*]

hel|lo-girl (he lō′gėrl′, hə-), *n. Slang.* a telephone operator.

hell raiser, *U.S. Informal.* a person who stirs up trouble or mischief.

Hell's Kitchen, an area of Manhattan's lower west side at one time notorious for its lawlessness.

hel|lu|o li|bro|rum (hel′yů ō lī brôr′əm, -brōr′-), *Latin.* **1** a bookworm. **2** (literally) devourer of books.

hell|u|va (hel′ə və), *adj., adv. Especially U.S. Slang.* —*adj.* **1** very bad; rotten: *We'll have a helluva time in the last six months matching the first half* (Wall Street Journal). **2** very good; exceptional: *Ideally, Yale . . . could have a helluva football team* (San Francisco Chronicle). **3** great in extent; considerable: *"Money isn't everything, but it's a helluva way ahead of whatever comes in second place"* (Manchester Guardian Weekly).
—*adv.* very; exceptionally: *Jim wrote a helluva good story* (Newsweek).
[altered spelling of *hell of a*]

helm¹ (helm), *n., v.* —*n.* **1a** the handle or wheel by which a ship is steered: *The helm spun out of the sailor's grip in the storm.* **b** the steering apparatus of a ship, including the wheel, rudder, and connecting parts. **c** a movement of the helm of a ship. **2** *Figurative.* a position of control or guidance: *Upon the President's death, the Vice-President took the nation's helm.* SYN: command.
—*v.t.* to guide with a helm; steer: (*Figurative.*) *The business he hath helmed, must . . . give him a better proclamation* (Shakespeare).
luff the helm, (of a ship) to head into the wind: *Luff, luff cried the Quartermaster . . . keep her full, luff the helm* (Peter A. Motteux).
[Old English *helma*] —**helm′less,** *adj.*

helm² (helm), *n., v. Archaic.* —*n.* a helmet.
—*v.t.* to cover or provide with a helmet.
[Old English *helm*]

***hel|met** (hel′mit), *n.* **1** a covering to protect the head. Soldiers wear steel helmets; firemen wear leather helmets; football players wear plastic helmets. **2** a piece of armor for the head. Knights wore helmets as part of their armor. **3** anything that resembles a helmet in shape, appearance, or position: *With his head held high under its heavy black helmet of hair . . .* (Edmund Wilson). *A fetching helmet of navy net, which hides every strand of hair on the head* (New Yorker). **4** = pith helmet. **5** a mask of reinforced wire mesh worn over the head to protect the face in fencing and some other sports. **6** *Biology.* a galea. [< Old French *helmet* (diminutive) < *helme* helm² < Germanic (compare Old Saxon *helm*)] —**hel′met-like′,** *adj.*

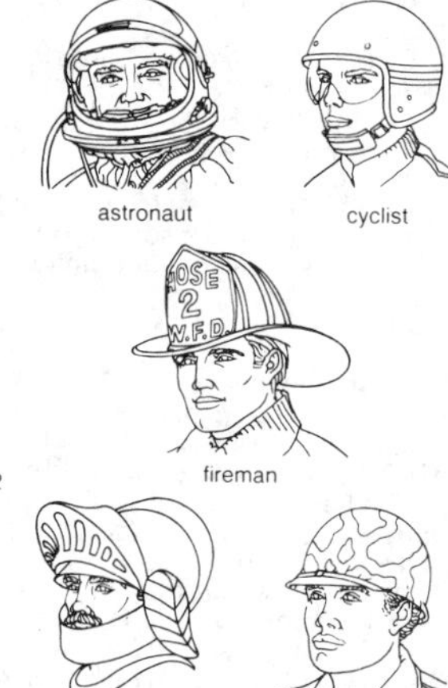

***helmet**
definitions 1, 2

helmet diver, a person engaged in helmet diving as his work or as a sport.

helmet diving, underwater diving in which the diver wears a waterproof suit, weighted shoes, and a copper helmet to which an air hose is attached.

hel|met|ed (hel′mə tid), *adj.* wearing a helmet.

hel|minth (hel′minth), *n.* a worm, especially an intestinal worm, such as the tapeworm or the roundworm. [< Greek *hélmins -inthos,* related to *eileîn* to turn, roll]

hel|min|thi|a|sis (hel′min thī′ə sis), *n.* a disease characterized by the presence of parasitic worms in the body. [< New Latin *helminthiasis* < Greek *helminthiân* suffer from worms < *hélmins, -inthos* helminth]

hel|min|thic (hel min′thik), *adj.* **1** having to do with a helminth or intestinal worm. **2** expelling worms.

hel|min|thol|o|gy (hel′min thol′ə jē), *n.* the science of helminths or worms, especially of parasitic worms. —**hel′min|thol′o|gist,** *n.*

helms|man (helmz′mən), *n., pl.* **-men.** a man who steers a ship; steersman. —**helms′man-ship,** *n.*

he|lo|derm (hē′lə dėrm), *n.* the Gila monster or a related Mexican lizard. [< New Latin *Heloderma* the genus name < Greek *hêlos* nail + *dérma* skin]

Hel|ot (hel′ət, hē′lət), *n.* a member of a class of slaves or serfs in ancient Sparta. [< Latin *Helōtēs,* plural < Greek *Heilōs,* associated with *Hēlos,* a Laconian town whose inhabitants were enslaved by Sparta, but probably related to *halís kesthai* be captured]

hel|ot (hel′ət, hē′lət), *n.* a slave; serf; bondsman. [< *Helot*]

hel|ot|ism (hel′ə tiz əm, hē′lə-), *n.* **1** serfdom like that of ancient Sparta. **2** *Biology.* symbiosis in which one organism is dominant over the other, such as that existing in a lichen in which the fungus mycelium is dominant.

hel|ot|ry (hel′ə trē, hē′lə-), *n.* **1** helots or slaves, as a class. **2** serfdom; slavery.

help (help), *v.,* **helped** or (*Archaic*) **holp, helped** or (*Archaic*) **hol|pen, help|ing,** *n.* —*v.t.* **1a** to give or do what is needed or useful: *to help a hospital with one's money. To help who want, to forward who excel* (Alexander Pope). **b** to relieve (a person) in want, trouble, or distress; succor; save: *Help us from famine and plague and strife!* (Tennyson). **2** to aid; assist: **a** to provide (a person) with one's efforts or labors: *My father helped me with my homework. Mother helps us. Help me put my coat on.* **b** to make (an action, process, or condition) more effectual; assist in bringing about; further; promote: *remedies that help digestion.* **c** to be of service or advantage to: *Her knowledge of French helped her in Quebec.* **d** to assist to attain or obtain something specified: *Help me to a candle, and pen, ink and paper* (Shakespeare). **3** to make better; relieve or cure: *This medicine will help your cough.* SYN: remedy, heal. **4** to prevent; stop: *It can't be helped.* **5** to avoid; keep from: *He cannot help falling asleep. Notwithstanding his vices, one can't help feeling for him* (Richard Brinsley Sheridan). **6** to give food to; serve with food: *Help her to some cake.*
—*v.i.* **1** to give aid or assistance: *We could finish the job faster if he would help.* **2** to serve food at a meal.
—*n.* **1** a thing done or given in helping: *Your advice is a great help.* **2** the act of helping or the condition of being helped; aid; assistance; succor: *I need some help with my work. The dying woman was beyond help.* **3** a person or thing that helps; source or means of assistance; aid; helper: *A sewing machine is a help in making clothes.* **4** a hired helper or group of hired helpers, such as a domestic servant or a group of laborers on a farm: *The storekeeper treats his help well. The maid was known as the hired help. The help all refused to return to the haunted house.* **5** a means of making better; remedy: *The medicine was a help.* SYN: relief, cure. **6** a means of preventing, avoiding, or stopping something: *The thing is done, and there is no help for it.* **7** a portion of food; helping.
help but, to avoid; fail to: *I can't help but admire her endurance.*
help oneself, a to put forth needed effort in one's own behalf; do by oneself what is needed: *The Lord helps him who helps himself.* **b** to control a habit or impulse: *She tried to be serious, but she couldn't help herself and burst out laughing.* **c** to take what one wants: *The dinner guests were told to help themselves.*
help oneself to, a to take what is needed or what one wants: *Help yourself to milk and sugar.* **b** to appropriate; steal: *My roommate helped herself to my best nylons.*
help out, to help in doing or getting; be helpful; assist: *There was only a young girl to help out in the kitchen.*
so help me, I am telling the truth; upon my word: *I haven't had a wink of sleep all night, so help me!*
so help me God. See under **God.**
[Old English *helpan*] —**help′a|ble,** *adj.* —**help′er,** *n.* —**help′ing|ly,** *adv.*
—*Syn.* *v.t.* **1, 2 Help, aid, assist** mean to give support to someone or something by providing something needed or useful. **Help** emphasizes actively providing whatever support another needs: *She helps her mother at home.* **Aid** suggests helping in a less active and less personal way but implies that the support is needed: *She aids the children's hospital. These scholarships are designed to aid students who cannot pay the full tuition.* **Assist** suggests standing by and being ready to serve in any way needed, especially in a subordinate capacity: *She assisted the hostess at the tea. Several nurses and an anesthesiologist assisted the surgeon during the operation.*
►See **can't** for usage note.

helper T cell, a T cell that bolsters the activity of B cells: *Helper T cells, which normally make up 40 to 60 per cent of all T cells in the blood, boost immune activity* (Paul Katz).

help|ful (help′fəl), *adj.* giving help; useful; serviceable. SYN: beneficial, profitable. —**help′ful|ly,** *adv.* —**help′ful|ness,** *n.*

help|ing (hel′ping), *n.* **1** a portion of food served to a person at one time. **2** a portion (of something): *Standard symphonic fare predominates, but the helpings of ballet, opera, . . . and popular music are growing* (New York Times).

helping hand, a measure of support; certain amount of assistance: *The Defense Department is said to look with favor on the idea and will lend a helping hand* (New York Times).

helping profession, *U.S.* any profession, such as vocational guidance or occupational therapy, whose purpose is to help people improve their lives and cope with everyday problems.

helping verb, = auxiliary verb.

help|less (help′lis), *adj.* **1** not able to help oneself; weak: *a helpless cripple. A little baby is helpless.* SYN: dependent. **2** without help or protection; having no assistance from others: *Though he was alone and helpless, he managed to keep the boat from sinking until help arrived.* SYN: defenseless. **3** affording no help; unavailing: *All her efforts to comfort him were helpless.*
—**help′less|ly,** *adv.* —**help′less|ness,** *n.*

help|mate (help′māt′), *n.* a companion and helper; wife or husband. [perhaps alteration of *helpmeet*]

help|meet (help′mēt′), *n.* = helpmate. [< "an *help meet* for him," Genesis 2:18, 20 (King James Version); *meet* = suitable]

Hel|sing|fors (hel′sing fôrz, -fôrs), *adj.* of, from, or having to do with Helsinki, Finland. [< Swedish *Helsingfors* Helsinki]

hel|ter-skel|ter (hel′tər skel′tər), *adv., adj., n.* —*adv.* with headlong, disorderly haste; pell-mell: *The children ran helter-skelter when the dog rushed at them.*
—*adj.* carelessly hurried; disorderly; confused: *This helter-skelter way of doing business is costly to the Government and burdensome to the tax payer* (Wall Street Journal). SYN: precipitate.
—*n.* **1** noisy and disorderly haste, confusion, etc. **2** a helter-skelter action or deed: *such a helter-skelter of prayers and sins* (Longfellow). **3** *Especially British.* a kind of spiral slide at an amusement park or fairground.
[perhaps imitative rhyme]

helve (helv), *n., v.,* **helved, helv|ing.** —*n.* a handle of a tool or weapon, such as an ax or hammer. —*v.t.* to fit with a helve.
throw (fling or **toss) the helve after the hatchet,** to take further risk in a losing venture: *Rather throw the helve after the hatchet, and leave your ruins to be repaired by your prince* (Raphael Holinshed).
[Old English *helfe*]

helv|er (hel′vər), *n. Especially British.* a person or thing that helves.

Hel|ve|tian (hel vē′shən), *adj., n.* —*adj.* **1** having to do with the ancient Helvetii. **2** = Swiss.
—*n.* **1** one of the ancient Helvetii. **2** a Swiss.
[< Latin *Helvētius* of the *Helvētiī,* plural, the tribe; or < *Helvētia* (*terra*) Helvetia]

Hel|vet|ic (hel vet′ik), *n., adj.* —*n.* a Swiss Protestant; Zwinglian. —*adj.* Helvetian; Swiss.

Hel|vet|i|ca (hel vet′ə kə), *n.* a style of sans-serif printing face.

Hel|ve|ti|i (hel vē′shē ī), *n.pl.* (in the time of Julius Caesar) the inhabitants of what is now western Switzerland.

hem¹ (hem), *n., v.,* **hemmed, hem|ming.** —*n.* **1** the border or edge on a garment; edge made by folding over the cloth and sewing it down: *and besought him that they might only touch the hem of his garment* (Matthew 14:36). *The triangle flare skirt is fully lined with [material] in pastel colors to give it a majestic sweep from a tiny waist to the billowed hem* (New Yorker). **2** *Figurative: The very hem o' the sea* (Shakespeare).
—*v.t.* **1** to fold over and sew down the edge of (cloth): *She hemmed six napkins.* **2** to edge or border (a garment or a piece of cloth): *All the skirt about Was hemmed with golden fringe* (Edmund Spenser).
hem in (around or **about), a** to surround on all sides: *Even the fence that hems them in by the river is a relic—a hand-me-down from the*

World's Fair (New York Times). **b** *Figurative: The angelic squadron . . . began to hem him round With ported spears* (Milton).
[Old English *hemm*] —**hem′less**, *adj.*

hem² (hem), *interj., n., v.,* **hemmed, hem|ming.** —***interj., n.*** a sound like clearing the throat, used to attract attention or show doubt or hesitation: *Hem! I would like to say something* (interj.). *We ignored his hems since we didn't want to hear him speak* (n.).
—***v.i.*** **1** to make a sound like clearing the throat: *If anyone is about, come to the foot of the stairs and hem* (Charlotte Brontë). **2** to hesitate in speaking.
hem and haw, a to hesitate in speaking: *He hemmed and hawed a lot in his poorly prepared speech.* **b** to stall or put off; hedge: *But ask the experts, "Who'll win?" and they'll hem and haw and say, "Well, on the one hand . . ."* (Newsweek).
[imitative]

hem-, *combining form.* the form of **hema-** before vowels, as in *hemangioma.*

hema-, *combining form.* blood: *Hemachrome = coloring matter of the blood.* [< Greek *haîma* blood]

he|ma|chrome (hē′mə krōm, hem′ə-), *n.* the red coloring matter of the blood; hemoglobin. Also, **haemachrome.** [< *hema-* + Greek *chrôma* color]

he|ma|cy|tom|e|ter (hē′mə sī tom′ə tər, hem′ə-), *n.* = hemocytometer.

hem|ad|sorp|tion (hem′ad sôrp′shən, -zôrp′-), *n.* a laboratory method of identifying viruses by means of a test in which tissue cells containing the virus adsorb red blood cells. [< *hem-* + *adsorption*]

hemadsorption virus, any virus identifiable by hemadsorption.

he|mag|glu|ti|nate (hē′mə glü′tə nāt, hem′ə-), *v.t., v.i.,* **-nat|ed, -nat|ing.** to cause hemagglutination.

he|mag|glu|ti|na|tion (hē′mə glü′tə nā′shən, hem′ə-), *n.* the clumping of red blood cells by hemagglutinin, used to determine the presence of various diseases such as arthritis.

he|mag|glu|ti|nin (hē′mə glü′tə nin, hem′ə-), *n.* an antibody produced in the blood that causes red blood cells to clump together.

he|mal (hē′məl), *adj.* **1** of or having to do with the blood or blood vessels. **2** having to do with or on the side of the body containing the heart and great blood vessels; ventral. Also, **haemal.** [< *hem-* + *-al*¹]

he-man (hē′man′), *n., pl.* **-men,** *adj. Informal.* —***n.*** a virile, rugged man: *The Maya field, to his mind, was an exclusive, he-men's club for a select group who could fight their way through tangled forests and bottomless mud* (New Yorker).
—***adj.*** rugged; tough; masculine: *written in the hard-hitting, he-man manner you'd expect from this ex-Marine and ex-pro footballer* (New Yorker).

he|man|gi|o|ma (hi man′jē ō′mə), *n., pl.* **-mas, -ma|ta** (-mə tə). a small benign tumor containing blood vessels. It may occur internally, as in the liver, but it appears most commonly on the skin as a birthmark.

he|ma|phe|re|sis (hē′mə fə rē′sis), *n.* a process for separating and removing part of the blood, while returning the remainder to the bloodstream. Hemapheresis is used in blood banks and in therapy. [< *hem-* + Greek *aphaíresis* a taking away]

hemat-, *combining form.* the form of **hemato-** before vowels, as in *hematal.*

he|ma|tal (hē′mə təl, hem′ə-), *adj.* having to do with the blood or blood vessels.

he|ma|te|in (hē′mə tē′in, hem′ə-), *n.* a reddish-brown, crystalline powder obtained from the coloring matter of logwood. *Formula:* $C_{16}H_{12}O_6$

he|ma|tem|e|sis (hē′mə tem′ə sis, hem′ə-), *n.* the vomiting of blood. [< *hemat-* + Greek *émesis* a vomiting]

he|ma|te|met|ic (hē′mə tə met′ik, hem′ə-), *adj.* **1** having to do with hematemesis. **2** suffering from hematemesis.

he|ma|ther|mal (hē′mə thėr′məl, hem′ə-), *adj.* = hematothermal.

he|mat|ic (hē mat′ik), *n., adj.* —***n.*** medicine that acts on the blood. —***adj.*** **1** of, having to do with, or containing blood; of the color of blood. **2** acting on the blood: *a hematic remedy.* [< Greek *haimatikós* < *haîma, -atos* blood]

he|ma|tim|e|ter (hē′mə tim′ə tər), *n.* a device for counting blood corpuscles in a given amount of blood, consisting of a microscope slide having a cell that contains a known amount of blood.

hem|a|tin (hem′ə tin, hē′mə-), *n.* **1** a bluish-black pigment containing iron, formed in the decomposition of hemoglobin. *Formula:* $C_{34}H_{32}N_4O_4 \cdot FeOH$ **2** = heme.

hem|a|tin|ic (hem′ə tin′ik, hē′mə-), *n., adj.* —***n.*** a medicine, such as a compound of iron, that increases the number of red blood cells in the blood. —***adj.*** of or obtained from hematin.

hem|a|ti|nom|e|ter (hem′ə tə nom′ə tər, hē′mə-), *n.* a device for determining the amount of hemoglobin in the blood.

hem|a|tite (hem′ə tīt, hē′mə-), *n.* an important iron ore that is usually reddish-brown when powdered; bloodstone. It is a widely distributed mineral, occurring in crystalline, massive, or granular form. *Formula:* Fe_2O_3 [< Latin *haematītēs* < Greek *haimatī́tēs* (literally) bloodlike < *haîma, -atos* blood]

hem|a|tit|ic (hem′ə tit′ik, hē′mə-), *adj.* of or having to do with hematite; like hematite.

hemato-, *combining form.* blood: *Hematology = study of blood.* Also, **hemat-** before vowels. [< Greek *haîma, -atos*]

hem|a|to|blast (hem′ə tō blast, hē′mə-), *n.* a cell, as in bone marrow, from which a red corpuscle may develop. [< *hemato-* + Greek *blastós* sprout, germ]

hem|a|to|blas|tic (hem′ə tō blas′tik, hē′mə-), *adj.* of or having to do with hematoblasts.

hem|a|to|cele (hem′ə tō sēl, hē′mə-), *n.* a tumor containing blood. [< *hemato-* + Greek *kḗlē* tumor]

hem|a|to|crit (hem′ə tō krit, hē′mə-), *n.* a centrifuge used to determine the relative volume of plasma and blood cells in a given amount of blood. [< *hemato-* + Greek *kritḗs* a judge < *krínein* to judge]

hem|a|toc|ry|al (hem′ə tok′rē əl, -tō krī′-; hē′mə-), *adj.* cold-blooded, as reptiles, fishes, and amphibians; poikilothermal. [< *hemato-* + Greek *krýos* cold, frost + English *-al*¹]

hem|a|to|gen (hem′ə tō jen, hē′mə-), *n.* **1** a compound containing iron obtained from the yolk of hens' eggs. It is supposed to be concerned in the production of hemoglobin. **2** any one of various preparations used especially in the treatment of anemia.

hem|a|to|gen|e|sis (hem′ə tō jen′ə sis, hē′mə-), *n.* the formation of blood; hematopoiesis.

hem|a|tog|e|nous (hem′ə toj′ə nəs, hē′mə-), *adj.* **1** having its origin in the blood. **2** producing blood.

he|ma|toid (hē′mə toid, hem′ə-), *adj.* like blood. [< Greek *haimatoeidḗs* < *haîma, -atos* blood + *eîdos* form]

hem|a|to|log|ic (hem′ə tə loj′ik, hē′mə-), *adj.* = hematological.

hem|a|to|log|i|cal (hem′ə tə loj′ə kəl, hē′mə-), *adj.* having to do with hematology.

hem|a|tol|o|gy (hem′ə tol′ə jē, hē′mə-), *n.* the branch of physiology that deals with the structure, functions, and diseases of the blood, and studies the body tissues and organs that produce constituents of the blood. —**hem′a|tol′o|gist,** *n.*

he|ma|to|ma (hē′mə tō′mə, hem′ə-), *n., pl.* **-mas, -ma|ta** (-mə tə). a tumor or swelling composed of blood. Hematoma sometimes occurs as a black and blue swelling in the skin. [< *hemat-* + *-oma*]

hem|a|tom|e|ter (hem′ə tom′ə tər, hē′mə-), *n.* any one of various blood-testing devices for determining the amount of hemoglobin in the blood, estimating the number of blood corpuscles present, or measuring the blood pressure.

he|ma|toph|a|gous (hē′mə tof′ə gəs, hem′ə), *adj.* feeding on blood. [< *hemato-* + Greek *phageîn* eat + English *-ous*]

hem|a|to|poi|e|sis (hem′ə tō poi ē′sis, hē′mə-), *n.* the formation of blood. [< *hemato-* + Greek *poíēsis* a making < *poieîn* make]

hem|a|to|poi|et|ic (hem′ə tō poi et′ik, hē′mə-), *adj.* having to do with hematopoiesis.

hem|a|to|por|phy|rin (hem′ə tō pôr′fər in, hē′mə-), *n.* a dark-red crystalline substance obtained from hemin, formerly used in the treatment of psychoses and now used to detect cancerous tissue. *Formula:* $C_{34}H_{38}N_4O_6$

hem|a|tose (hem′ə tōs, hē′mə-), *adj.* full of blood.

he|ma|to|sis (hē′mə tō′sis, hem′ə-), *n.* **1** the formation of blood. **2** the aeration of venous blood in the lungs. [< Greek *haimátōsis* < *haimatoûn* make into blood < *haîma, -atos* blood]

hem|a|to|ther|mal (hem′ə tō thėr′məl, hē′mə-), *adj.* warm-blooded, as mammals and birds; having a constant temperature; homeothermal.

he|ma|tox|y|lin (hē′mə tok′sə lin, hem′ə-), *n.* **1** any one of a group of trees of the pea family, of Central America and the West Indies, especially the logwood. **2** the wood obtained from logwood. **3** a crystalline substance obtained from logwood, colorless when pure, but making fine red, blue, and purple dyes by the action of alkalis and oxygen. Its aqueous solution also yields a fluid used for staining vegetable tissues. *Formula:* $C_{16}H_{14}O_6 \cdot 3H_2O$ [< New Latin *haematoxylon* (< Greek *haîma, -atos* blood + *xýlon* wood) + English *-in*]

hem|a|to|zo|ic (hem′ə tō zō′ik, hē′mə-), *adj.* living in the blood as a parasite.

hem|a|to|zo|on (hem′ə tō zō′on, hē′mə-), *n., pl.* **-zo|a** (-zō′ə). an animal parasite living in the blood. [< *hemato-* + Greek *zôion* animal]

he|ma|tu|ri|a (hē′mə tůr′ē ə, hem′ə-; -tyůr′-), *n. Medicine.* the presence of blood in the urine. [< *hemat-* + *-uria*]

hem|bar (hem′bär), *n.* a hybrid variety of barley developed in 1969 by the U.S. Department of Agriculture. [coined by Dr. Robert T. Ramage, research scientist of the U.S. Department of Agriculture < arbitrary prefix *hem-* + *bar* (ley)]

heme (hēm), *n.* an iron compound, the non-protein part of the hemoglobin molecule. *Formula:* $C_{34}H_{32}N_4O_4Fe$

hem|el|y|tral (he mel′ə trəl), *adj.* having to do with or like a hemelytron. Also, **hemielytral.**

hem|el|y|tron (he mel′ə tron), *n., pl.* **-tra** (-trə). the forewing of an insect that is leathery at the base and membranous at the tip. Certain hemipters, such as chinch bugs, have hemelytrons. Also, **hemielytron, hemielytrum.** [< New Latin *hemielytrum* < Greek *hēmi-* half + *élytron* sheath]

hem|el|y|trum (he mel′ə trəm), *n., pl.* **-tra** (-trə). = hemelytron.

hem|er|a|lo|pi|a (hem′ər ə lō′pē ə), *n.* a condition of the eyes in which good vision is possible only at night or in dim light; day blindness. [< New Latin *hemeralopia* < Greek *hēméra* day + *alaós* blind + *ōps* eye]

hem|er|a|lop|ic (hem′ər ə lop′ik), *adj.* of or affected by hemeralopia.

hem|er|o|cal|lis (hem′ər ō kal′is), *n.* = day lily. [< Greek *hēmerokallés* day lily < *hēméra* day + *kállos* beauty]

hemi-, *prefix.* half: *Hemisphere = a half sphere.* [< Greek *hēmi-*]

hem|i|al|gi|a (hem′ē al′jē ə), *n.* a pain affecting only one side of the body or head. [< *hemi-* + Greek *-algíā* < *álgos* pain]

he|mic (hē′mik, hem′ik), *adj.* having to do with the blood: *hemic asthma.*

hem|i|cel|lu|lose (hem′ē sel′yə lōs), *n.* any one of a group of gummy polysaccharide carbohydrates less complex than cellulose, and readily hydrolyzed to simple sugars.

hem|i|chor|date (hem′ē kôr′dāt), *n., adj.* —***n.*** any one of a group of small, wormlike marine chordates having three body regions and a notochord limited to the front part of the body.
—***adj.*** of or having to do with the hemichordates.

hem|i|clas|tic (hem′ē klas′tik), *adj.* of volcanic origin: *hemiclastic rocks.*

hem|i|cra|ni|a (hem′ē krā′nē ə), *n.* a pain affecting only one side of the head. [< Latin *hēmicrānia* < Greek *hēmikrāníā* < *hēmi-* half + *krāníon* skull]

hem|i|cy|cle (hem′ē sī′kəl), *n.* **1** a half circle; semicircle. **2** a semicircular structure. [< French *hémicycle,* learned borrowing from Latin *hēmicyclium* < Greek *hēmikýklion* < *hēmi-* half + *-kyklos* circle]

hem|i|cy|clic (hem′ē sī′klik, -sik′lik), *adj.* having some of its parts arranged spirally and others in whorls: *a hemicyclic flower.*

hem|i|cy|lin|dri|cal (hem′ē sə lin′drə kəl), *adj.* having the form of half of a cylinder divided in the direction of its axis.

hem|i|dem|i|sem|i|qua|ver (hem′ē dem′ ē sem′-ē kwā′vər), *n. Music, especially British.* a sixty-fourth note or the symbol for it.

hem|i|el|y|tral (hem′ē el′ə trəl), *adj.* = hemelytral.

hem|i|el|y|tron (hem′ē el′ə tron), *n., pl.* **-tra** (-trə). = hemelytron.

hem|i|el|y|trum (hem′ē el′ə trəm), *n., pl.* **-tra** (-trə). = hemelytron.

hem|i|he|dral (hem′ē hē′drəl), *adj.* having only half the planes required by the highest degree of symmetry: *a hemihedral crystal.* [< *hemi-* + Greek *hédra* base¹ + English *-al*¹] —**hem′i|he′dral|ly,** *adv.*

hem|i|he|drism (hem′ē hē′driz əm), *n.* the property of being hemihedral.

hem|i|he|dron (hem′ē hē′drən), *n., pl.* **-drons, -dra** (-drə). a hemihedral crystal or form.

hem|i|hy|drate (hem′ē hī′drāt), *n. Chemistry.* a hydrate containing half as many molecules of water as the number of molecules of the compound forming the hydrate.

hem|i|met|a|bol|ic (hem′ē met′ə bol′ik), *adj.* having to do with or characterized by hemimetabolism.

hem|i|me|tab|o|lism (hem′ē mə tab′ə liz əm), *n.* a form of insect metamorphosis in which the pupal stage is lacking, as in cockroaches, crickets, and grasshoppers.

hem|i|me|tab|o|lous (hem′ē mə tab′ə ləs), *adj.* = hemimetabolic.

hem|i|mor|phic (hem′ē môr′fik), *adj.* having un-

Pronunciation Key: hat, āge, cãre, fär; let, ēqual, tėrm; it, īce; hot, ōpen, ôrder; oil, out; cup, pu̇t, rüle; child; long; thin; ᴛʜen; zh, measure; ə represents **a** in about, **e** in taken, **i** in pencil, **o** in lemon, **u** in circus.

like planes or modifications at the ends of the same axis: *a hemimorphic crystal.* [< *hemi-* + Greek *morphē* form + English *-ic*]

hem|i|mor|phism (hem′ē môr′fiz əm), *n.* the state of being hemimorphic.

hem|i|mor|phite (hem′ē môr′fīt), *n.* a mineral, a silicate of zinc, occurring in orthorhombic crystals. *Formula:* $Zn_4(Si_2O_7)(OH)_2 \cdot H_2O$ [< *hemimorph* (ic) + *-ite*[1]]

he|min (hē′min), *n.* very small, reddish crystals obtained when blood is heated with hydrochloric acid or glacial acetic acid and sodium chloride. The appearance of the crystals indicates the presence of blood in stains, or fibers or other material. *Formula:* $C_{34}H_{32}N_4O_4 \cdot FeCl$ [< *hem-* + *-in*]

hem|i|par|a|site (hem′ē par′ə sīt), *n.* a partially parasitic plant.

hem|i|par|a|sit|ic (hem′ē par′ə sit′ik), *adj.* partially parasitic.

hem|i|ple|gi|a (hem′ē plē′jē ə), *n.* paralysis of only one side of the body. [< Greek *hēmiplēgiā* < *hēmi-* half + *plēgē*, for *plēxē* stroke]

hem|i|pleg|ic (hem′ē plej′ik, -plē′jik), *adj., n.* —***adj.*** **1** having to do with hemiplegia. **2** suffering from hemiplegia.
—***n.*** a person suffering from hemiplegia.

he|mip|ter (hi mip′tər), *n.* any one of a large order of hemipterous insects. Their forewings are thick and leathery at the base and membranous at the tip. Bedbugs, chinch bugs, plant lice, and stinkbugs belong to this group. [< New Latin *Hemiptera* the order name < Greek *hēmi-* half + *pterón* wing]

he|mip|ter|al (hi mip′tər əl), *adj.* = hemipterous.

he|mip|ter|an (hi mip′tər ən), *n., adj.* —***n.*** = hemipter.
—***adj.*** of or belonging to the order of hemipters.

he|mip|ter|oid (hi mip′tər oid), *adj.* of or like the hemipters.

he|mip|ter|ous (hi mip′tər əs), *adj.* **1** belonging to a large order of insects that have pointed beaks for piercing and sucking, usually two pairs of wings, and young that differ little from adults. **2** having forewings that are thick and leathery at the base and membranous at the tip.

hem|i|sect (hem′ē sekt), *v.t.* to cut into halves; bisect, especially longitudinally or into equal right and left parts: *to hemisect an animal body.* [< *hemi-* + Latin *sectus,* past participle of *secāre* to cut]

hem|i|sec|tion (hem′ē sek′shən), *n.* one of two equal parts.

***hemisphere**
definition 2a

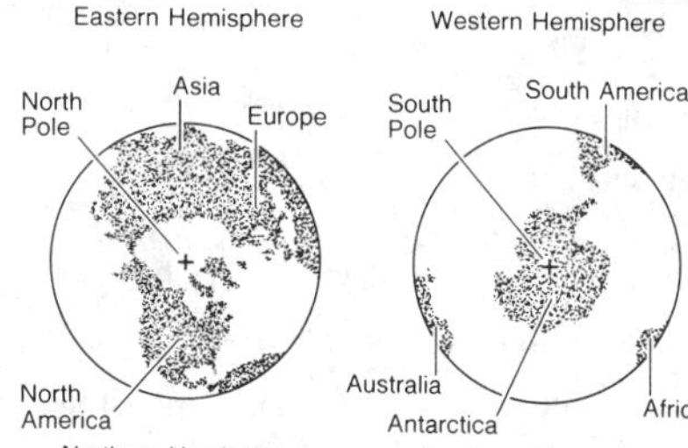

Eastern Hemisphere | Western Hemisphere
Northern Hemisphere | Southern Hemisphere

***hem|i|sphere** (hem′ə sfir), *n.* **1** a half sphere or globe, formed by a plane passing through the center. **2a** half of the earth's surface. North America and South America are in the Western Hemisphere; Europe, Asia, Africa, and Australia are in the Eastern Hemisphere. All countries north of the equator are in the Northern Hemisphere; those south of the equator are in the Southern Hemisphere. **b** half of the earth, based on a division into a land hemisphere and a water hemisphere. The land hemisphere includes half of the earth with the most land. Its center lies near London, England. The other half of the earth, mostly water, makes up the water hemisphere. Its center lies near New Zealand. **3** half of the celestial sphere, as divided by the celestial equator, the ecliptic, or the horizon. **4** a map or model of half the terrestrial or celestial globe. **5** *Figurative.* an area of action, life, or thought; sphere; circle. **6** *Anatomy.* either of the two parts that together form most of the cerebrum; cerebral hemisphere. [< Old French *hemisphere,* learned borrowing from Latin *hēmisphaerium* < Greek *hēmisphaírion* < *hēmi-* half + *sphaîra* sphere]

hem|i|spher|ic (hem′ə sfer′ik), *adj.* = hemispherical.

hem|i|spher|i|cal (hem′ə sfer′ə kəl), *adj.* **1** shaped like a hemisphere. **2** of a hemisphere. —**hem′i|spher′i|cal|ly,** *adv.*

hem|i|sphe|roid (hem′ə sfir′oid), *n.* half of a spheroid. —**hem′i|sphe|roi′dal,** *adj.*

hem|i|stich (hem′ə stik), *n.* **1** half a line of verse, especially the part of a verse preceding or following the main caesura. **2** an incomplete line, or a line of verse having less than the usual length. [< Latin *hēmistichium* < Greek *hēmistíchion* < *hēmi-* half + *stíchos* line, row < *steíchein* walk, march]

he|mis|ti|chal (hi mis′tə kəl, hem′ə stik′əl), *adj.* having to do with a hemistich; making up a hemistich.

hem|i|sys|to|le (hem′ē sis′tə lē), *n.* a contraction of only one ventricle of the heart.

hem|i|ter|pene (hem′ē tėr′pēn), *n. Chemistry.* any one of a series of isomeric hydrocarbons related to the terpenes. *Formula:* C_5H_8

hem|i|trope (hem′ē trōp), *adj., n.* —***adj.*** having two similar parts or halves, one of which is turned half way round upon the other, as of a compound or twin crystal.
—***n.*** a hemitrope crystal.
[< French *hémitrope* < *hémi-* hemi- + Greek *trópos* turning]

hem|i|trop|ic (hem′ē trop′ik), *adj.* = hemitrope.

hem|i|zy|gote (hem′ē zī′gōt, -zig′ōt), *n. Genetics.* an animal or plant whose chromosomes have only one of a pair of genes.

hem|i|zy|gous (hem′ē zī′gəs), *adj.* of or having to do with a hemizygote.

hem|line (hem′līn′), *n.* the border of a garment; hem.

hem|lock (hem′lok), *n.* **1** a poisonous plant with spotted stems, finely divided leaves, and small, white flowers; poison hemlock. It belongs to the parsley family and was formerly used in medicine as a powerful sedative. **2** a poison made from it: *A drowsy numbness pains My sense, as though of hemlock I had drunk* (Keats). **3** any one of a group of evergreen trees of the pine family. Hemlocks have short blunt needles, small cones, drooping branches, and reddish bark. Bark from hemlocks is used in tanning. **4** its wood. [Old English *hymlic*]

hemlock looper, a kind of measuring worm that is a pest in some North American forests.

hemlock spruce, = hemlock (def. 3).

hem|mer (hem′ər), *n.* **1** a person or thing that hems. **2** an attachment to a sewing machine for hemming.

hem|ming machine (hem′ing), **1** a machine for hemming cloth. **2** a machine that bends over the edges of sheet metal. —**hemming machinist.**

hemo-, *combining form.* blood: *Hemorrhage = a discharge of blood.* [< Greek *haîma* blood]

he|mo|chro|ma|to|sis (hē′mə krō′mə tō′sis, hem′ə-), *n.* a disease characterized by a bronzing of the skin, cirrhosis, and often diabetes, caused by the absorption of an excessive amount of iron by the bloodstream and the deposition of a hematogenous pigment, usually hemosiderin, in the liver and in other organs and tissues; bronze diabetes. [< *hemo-* + *chromat-* + *-osis*]

he|mo|chro|mo|gen (hē′mə krō′mə jən, hem′ə-), *n.* a protein compound in the blood, related to hemoglobin.

he|mo|coele (hē′mə sēl, hem′ə-), *n.* a cavity or space between the organs of arthropods and mollusks through which the blood circulates. [< *hemo-* + Greek *koîlos* hollow]

he|mo|cy|a|nin (hē′mə sī′ə nin, hem′ə-), *n.* a respiratory pigment found in the blood of certain crustaceans, mollusks, and arachnids that corresponds to hemoglobin in higher animals. It contains copper and becomes blue when combined with oxygen. [< *hemo-* + Greek *kýanos* blue substance + English *-in*]

he|mo|cyte (hē′mə sīt, hem′ə-), *n.* a blood cell.

he|mo|cy|tom|e|ter (hē′mō sī tom′ə tər, hem′ō-), *n.* an instrument for counting the number of blood cells in a sample of blood. [< *hemo-* + English *-cyte* + *-meter*]

he|mo|di|al|y|sis (hē′mō dī al′ə sis, hem′ō-), *n., pl.* **-ses** (-sēz). dialysis of the blood performed by a hemodialyzer. [< *hemo-* + *dialysis*]

he|mo|di|a|lyz|er (hē′mō dī′ə lī zər, hem′ō-), *n.* a machine that separates waste matter from the blood, used in place of the kidney; a blood dialyzer or artificial kidney.

he|mo|dy|nam|ic (hē′mə dī nam′ik, hem′ə-), *adj.* of or having to do with hemodynamics: *the hemodynamic effects of drugs in the bloodstream.* —**he′mo|dy|nam′i|cal|ly,** *adv.*

he|mo|dy|nam|ics (hē′mə dī nam′iks, hem′ə-), *n.* hydrodynamics of the bloodstream; the study of blood pressure and flow.

he|mo|flag|el|late (hē′mə flaj′ə lāt, -lit; hem′ə-), *n.* a one-celled animal with a whiplike tail that lives as a parasite in the blood, such as a trypanosome.

he|mo|gas|tric (hē′mə gas′trik, hem′ə-), *adj.* characterized by the pouring out of blood into the stomach: *hemogastric fever.*

he|mo|glo|bin (hē′mə glō′bən; hē′mə glō′bən, hem′ə-), *n.* a substance in the red corpuscles of the blood made up of iron and protein. It carries oxygen from the lungs to the tissues and some of the carbon dioxide from the tissues to the lungs. *Hemoglobin is the chemical that gives the red color to blood* (Science News Letter). Also, **haemoglobin.** [alteration of earlier *hematoglobulin* < *hemato-* blood + *globulin*]

he|mo|glo|bi|nu|ri|a (hē′mə glō′bə nůr′ē ə, -nyůr′-; hem′ə-), *n.* the presence of hemoglobin in the urine.

he|mo|glo|bi|nu|ric (hē′mə glō′bə nůr′ik, -nyůr′-; hem′ə-), *adj.* characterized by the presence of hemoglobin in the urine.

he|mo|gram (hē′mə gram, hem′ə-), *n.* a graph or tabulation showing the results of a count and analysis of leucocytes in a blood sample. [< *hemo-* + *-gram*[1]]

he|moid (hē′moid), *adj.* like blood.

he|mol (hē′mol), *n.* a compound containing iron obtained from hemoglobin. It is used as a hematinic. [< *hem-* + *-ol*[1]]

he|mo|leu|co|cyte (hē′mə lü′kə sīt, hem′ə-), *n.* a white blood cell that circulates in the blood. [< *hemo-* + *leucocyte*]

he|mo|leu|co|cyt|ic (hē′mə lü′kə sit′ik, hem′ə-), *adj.* having to do with hemoleucocytes.

he|mo|lymph (hē′mə limf, hem′ə-), *n.* a nutritive fluid, analogous to blood or lymph, found in the body cavity of certain invertebrates: *The fluid hemolymph in the insect's body cavity contains no respiratory pigment* (Scientific American). [< *hemo-* + *lymph*]

he|mo|ly|sin (hē′mə lī′sin, hem′ə-; hi mol′ə sin), *n.* a substance in the blood that destroys red blood cells and frees hemoglobin. Hemolysins may be antibodies, or they may be contained in bacterial toxins or snake venoms. [< *hemo-* + *lys* (is) + *-in*]

he|mol|y|sis (hi mol′ə sis), *n.* a process of dissolution of the red blood cells, with the liberation of hemoglobin.

he|mo|lyt|ic (hē′mə lit′ik, hem′ə-), *adj.* tending to dissolve the red blood cells: *hemolytic anemia.*

he|mo|lyze (hē′mə līz, hem′ə-), *v.,* **-lyzed, -lyz|ing.** —***v.i.*** to undergo hemolysis.
—***v.t.*** to destroy (red blood cells) by hemolysis.

he|mo|phile (hē′mə fīl, -fil; hem′ə-), *n., adj.* —***n.*** **1** = hemophiliac. **2** a hemophilic bacterium.
—***adj.*** = hemophilic.

he|mo|phil|i|a (hē′mə fil′ē ə, hem′ə-), *n.* an inherited disorder of the blood in males in which clotting does not occur normally: *People afflicted with hemophilia have a very slow coagulation and bleed a long time from minor wounds* (A. Franklin Shull). [< New Latin *haemophilia* < Greek *haîma* blood + *philiā* affection; (medically) a tendency < *phileîn* to love]

he|mo|phil|i|ac (hē′mə fil′ē ak, hem′ə-), *n., adj.* —***n.*** a person who has hemophilia; bleeder.
—***adj.*** = hemophilic.

he|mo|phil|ic (hē′mə fil′ik, hem′ə-), *adj.* **1** of or having hemophilia. **2** flourishing in blood or a medium containing blood: *hemophilic bacteria.*

he|mo|poi|e|sis (hē′mə poi ē′sis, hem′ə-), *n.* = hematopoiesis.

he|mo|poi|et|ic (hē′mə poi et′ik, hem′ə-), *adj.* = hematopoietic.

he|mo|pro|tein (hē′mə prō′tēn, hem′ə-; -tē in), *n. Biochemistry.* any one of a group of protein substances, including hemoglobin, cytochromes, peroxidase, and catalase, which absorb oxygen and are pigments important in the spectral analysis of cells.

he|mop|ty|sis (hi mop′tə sis, hē mop′-), *n.* the coughing up of blood or bloody mucus, usually from the lungs or bronchi. [< *hemo-* + Greek *ptýsis* spitting < *ptýein* to spit]

hem|or|rhage (hem′ə rij, hem′rij), *n., v.,* **-rhaged, -rhag|ing.** —***n.*** **1** a bleeding, either within the body or from the body surface; discharge of blood, especially a heavy discharge from a damaged blood vessel. A nosebleed is a mild hemorrhage. **2** *Figurative: The Union has since lost 240,000 members. The hemorrhage is not yet over* (Financial Times).
—***v.i.*** to have a hemorrhage; lose much blood.
have a hemorrhage, to get overly excited: *He had a hemorrhage when things didn't go right.*
[< Latin *haemorrhagia* < Greek *haimorrhagiā,* ultimately < *haîma* blood + *rhēgnýnai* to break]

hem|or|rhag|ic (hem′ə raj′ik), *adj.* of or having to do with hemorrhage.

hemorrhagic septicemia, an acute blood infection in animals, caused by a bacterium.
hem|or|rhoid (hem′ə roid), *n.* Usually, **hemorrhoids.** a painful swelling formed by the dilation of blood vessels near the anus; piles. [< Latin *haemorrhoida,* plural < Greek *haimorrhoís, -rhoidos,* < *haîma* blood + *rheîn* to flow]
hem|or|rhoi|dal (hem′ə roi′dəl), *adj.* **1** having to do with or caused by hemorrhoids. **2** suffering from hemorrhoids.
hem|or|rhoi|dec|to|my (hem′ə roi dek′tə mē), *n., pl.* **-mies.** the surgical removal of hemorrhoids.
he|mo|sid|er|in (hē′mə sid′ər in, hem′ə-), *n.* a dark pigment containing iron, produced when hemoglobin decomposes. [< *hemo-* + Greek *sídēs* iron]
he|mo|sid|er|o|sis (hē′mə sid′ə rō′sis), *n.* an abnormal condition in which hemosiderin is deposited in tissues or organs. [< *hemosider(in)* + *-osis*]
he|mo|spa|sia (hē′mə spā′zhə, hem′ə-), *n.* the drawing of blood to a part of the body by a cupping glass or other device. [< New Latin *hemospasia* < Greek *haîma* blood + *spásis* suction]
he|mo|spas|tic (hē′mə spas′tik, hem′ə-), *adj.* having to do with hemospasia.
he|mo|sta|sia (hē′mə stā′zhə, hem′ə-), *n.* **1** the stopping of blood in a part of the body. **2** the stopping of a hemorrhage, as by tying an artery. [< New Latin *hemostasia* < Greek *haîma* blood + *stásis* a standing]
he|mos|ta|sis (hi mos′tə sis), *n.* = hemostasia.
he|mo|stat (hē′mə stat, hem′ə-), *n.* a clamp that compresses the ends of small blood vessels, used to stop hemorrhage.
he|mo|stat|ic (hē′mə stat′ik, hem′ə-), *adj., n.* —*adj.* **1** stopping hemorrhage; styptic. **2** having to do with the stopping of bleeding. —*n.* = hemostat. [< *hemo-* + Greek *statikós* causing to stand]
he|mo|tho|rax (hē′mə thôr′aks, hem′ə-; -thōr′-), *n.* the presence of blood in a pleural cavity.
he|mo|tox|ic (hē′mə tok′sik, hem′ə-), *adj.* toxic to blood cells, especially red blood cells; causing blood poisoning.
he|mo|tox|in (hē′mə tok′sən, hem′ə-), *n.* a cytotoxin or other substance injurious to blood cells, especially red blood cells.
hemp (hemp), *n.* **1** a tall plant of Asia whose tough fibers are made into heavy string, rope, and coarse cloth; cannabis. Hemp is an annual plant of the mulberry family. It is also raised in Europe and North America. **2** the tough fibers obtained from the bark of this plant. **3** hashish, marijuana, or other narcotic drug made from the female hemp plant. **4** any one of various other plants resembling hemp. **5** any one of various fibers resembling hemp: *Manila hemp.* **6** *Informal.* a hangman's rope: *"The hemp that shall hang me is not grown!"* (Stephen Vincent Benét). [Old English *henep*]
hemp agrimony, 1 a European composite plant having dull reddish or purplish flowers. **2** any one of various plants like this.
hemp|en (hem′pən), *adj.* **1** made of hemp. **2** of or like hemp.
hemp hook, a knife for cutting hemp.
hemp nettle, a coarse weed of the mint family that looks like hemp and has bristles like nettles.
hemp palm, 1 a palm of the Mediterranean region, yielding a fiber of commercial value. **2** a palm of China and Japan, valued for its fiber.
hemp|seed (hemp′sēd′), *n.* **1** the seed of hemp, used as food for pet birds. **2** *Slang.* a person who should be hanged; rogue.
hemp tree, = chaste tree.
hemp|weed (hemp′wēd′), *n.* = hemp agrimony.
***hem|stitch** (hem′stich′), *v., n.* —*v.t., v.i.* to hem along a line from which threads have been drawn out, gathering the cross threads into a series of little groups.
—*n.* **1** the stitch used. **2** ornamental needlework made by hemstitching. —**hem′stitch′er,** *n.*

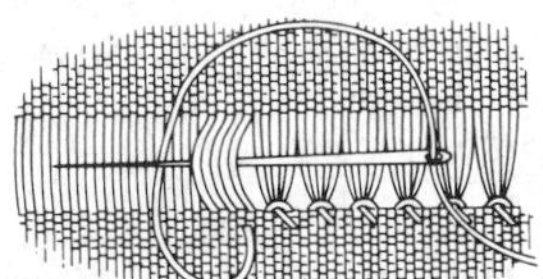
***hemstitch**

hen (hen), *n.* **1** the female of the common domestic bird kept for its eggs and meat; female chicken: *a hen and her chicks.* **2** the female of other birds: *a hen sparrow.* **3** a female fish or shellfish, such as a lobster. **4** *Slang, Figurative.* a woman.
scarce (or **rare**) **as hens' teeth,** very scarce or rare: *Domestic cleaners, now rarer than hens' teeth in London, may earn more per hour than some junior civil servants* (Maclean's).
[Old English *henn*] —**hen′like′,** *adj.*
hen-and-chick|ens (hen′ən chik′ənz), *n.,* or **hen and chickens,** any one of various plants that spread rapidly, as by means of offshoots, such as European houseleek or, in some localities, ground ivy.
hen|bane (hen′bān′), *n.* a coarse, bad-smelling plant of the nightshade family, with sticky, hairy leaves and clusters of greenish-yellow, purple-veined flowers; black henbane. It is poisonous, especially to fowls. [Middle English *henne bane* hen's bane]
hen|bit (hen′bit′), *n.* a purple-flowered weed of the mint family, whose leaves resemble those of the nettle but lack stinging hairs. [< *hen* + *bit*[2] (because of the indentations on the leaves)]
hence (hens), *adv., interj.* —*adv.* **1** as a result of this; therefore: *It is very late; hence you must go to bed. He was penniless; hence he had to accept the first offer.* **2** from now; from this time onward: *Come back a week hence. Years hence he was to remember his father's advice.* **3** from this source or origin: *The sun's orb ... great palace now of light ... hence the morning planet gilds her horns* (Milton). **4** from here; from this place: *"Go hence, I pray thee."* **5** from this world: *before I go hence, and be no more* (Psalms 39:13).
—*interj.* go away; depart: *"Hence, foul fiend!"*
hence with, go away with; take away: *Hence with your tempting offers! I shall not yield.*
[Middle English *hennes* < Old English *heonan* + adverbial genitive *-s*]
▶**Hence** is a more formal term than *consequently, therefore,* and *so that: They performed a series of experiments, all successful; hence their theory is well supported.*
hence|forth (hens′fôrth′, -fōrth′), *adv.* from this time on; from now on: *The fate of every object which had undergone this process was henceforth irrevocably sealed* (Lytton Strachey). **SYN:** hereafter.
hence|for|ward (hens′fôr′wərd), *adv.* = henceforth.
hench|man (hench′mən), *n., pl.* **-men. 1** a trusted attendant or follower. **2** an obedient, unscrupulous follower: *You will become a catspaw of corrupt functionaries and the henchman of ambitious humbugs* (George Bernard Shaw). **3** *Obsolete.* a squire; page: *I do but beg a little changeling boy, To by my henchman* (Shakespeare). [Middle English *henxstman* (originally) a groom < Old English *hengest* horse + *man* man]
hen|coop (hen′küp′, -kůp′), *n.* a coop for hens.
***hen|dec|a|gon** (hen dek′ə gon), *n.* a plane figure having eleven angles and eleven sides. [< Greek *héndeka* eleven (< *hén* one + *déka* ten) + *-gōnon* < *gōniā* angle] —**hen′de|cag′o|nal,** *adj.*

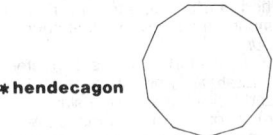

***hendecagon**

hen|dec|a|syl|lab|ic (hen′dek ə sə lab′ik), *adj.* containing eleven syllables.
hen|dec|a|syl|la|ble (hen′dek ə sil′ə bəl), *n.* a metrical line of eleven syllables. [< Latin *hendecasyllabus* < Greek *hendekasyllabos;* influenced by English *syllable*]
hen|di|a|dys (hen dī′ə dis), *n.* a figure of speech in which a single complex idea is expressed by two words connected by a conjunction, as in "to pour from cups and gold" instead of "from golden cups." [< Medieval Greek *endíadys* < Greek *hèn diàdyoîn* one through two]
hen|e|quen or **hen|e|quin** (hen′ə kin), *n.* **1** a yellow fiber from the leaves of an agave of Yucatán, used for making twine, ropes, and coarse fabrics. **2** the plant that yields this fiber. [< Spanish *jeniquén* < the Maya (Yucatán) native name]
henge (henj), *n.* a circular structure of stone or wood surrounded by an earth wall, used in prehistoric England for certain sacred rites. Stonehenge is the best preserved example.
hen harrier, a hawk that preys on small animals.
hen hawk, = chicken hawk.
hen|house (hen′hous′), *n.* a house for poultry: *When you start a chicken farm, you don't get the chickens before you get the henhouse, the feed and the fencing* (Wall Street Journal).
Hen|le's loop (hen′lēz), a U-shaped loop formed by a tubule conveying urine when it enters the inner layer of the kidney and then turns around to pass up again into the outer layer of the kidney; loop of Henle. [< F. G. J. *Henle,* 1809-1885, a German anatomist]
hen|na (hen′ə), *n., adj., v.,* **-naed, -na|ing.**
—*n.* **1** a dark reddish-brown dye used especially on the hair. **2** a small, thorny tree of tropical Asia and Africa from whose leaves this dye is made. Henna belongs to the loosestrife family. It bears small, fragrant white flowers and is much used as a hedge in India. **3** a reddish brown.
—*adj.* reddish-brown.
—*v.t.* to dye or color with henna: *... young Japanese women with hennaed hair and painted fingernails* (New Yorker).
[< Arabic *hinnā* the henna (plant)]
hen|ner|y (hen′ər ē), *n., pl.* **-ner|ies.** a farm, building, or yard where poultry is kept or raised.
***hen|nin** (hen′ən), *n.* a high, cone-shaped headdress with a veil hanging from it, worn by French women in the 1400's. [< obsolete French *hennin;* origin unknown]

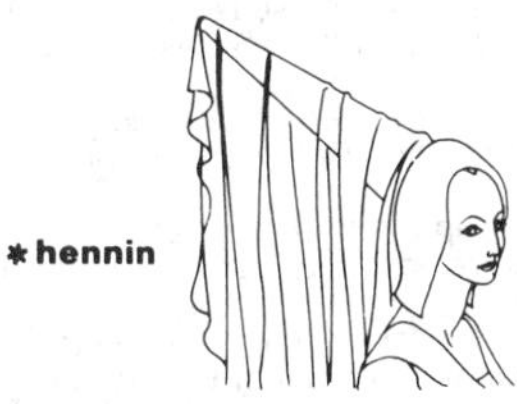
***hennin**

hen|o|the|ism (hen′ə thē′iz əm), *n.* the belief in one god as the deity of a race, tribe, or other group, without claiming he is the only god. [< Greek *heîs, henós* one + *theós* god + English *-ism*]
hen|o|the|ist (hen′ə thē′ist), *n.* a person who believes in one god without claiming he is the only god.
hen|o|the|is|tic (hen′ə thē is′tik), *adj.* having to do with henotheism; characterized by henotheism.
he|not|ic (he not′ik), *adj.* tending to make one; unifying; harmonizing. [< Greek *henōtikós* < *hénōsis* unification < *hén* one]
hen party, *Informal.* a party or gathering attended only by women.
hen|peck (hen′pek′), *v.t.* to domineer over or rule (one's husband): *He was henpecked by his wife. Ye lords of ladies intellectual, Inform us truly, have they not henpeck'd you all?* (Byron). **SYN:** browbeat.
Hen|ri|cian (hen rish′ən), *adj., n.* —*adj.* **1** of or having to do with Henry VIII of England or his reign. **2** supporting the religious movement or laws of Henry VIII of England.
—*n.* a person who supports the religious movement or policy of Henry VIII.
[< Medieval Latin *Henricianus* < *Henricus* Henry]
hen|ri|et|ta (hen′rē et′ə), *n.,* or **Henrietta cloth,** a soft, lustrous, woolen cloth having a silk warp. It has a twilled face and resembles a fine cashmere. [< *Henrietta,* a proper name]
hen|roost (hen′rüst′), *n.* a place where poultry roost at night.
hen|ry (hen′rē), *n., pl.* **-ries** or **-rys.** the unit of electrical inductance. When a current varying at the rate of one ampere per second induces an electromotive force of one volt, the circuit has an inductance of one henry. *Abbr:* h (no period). [< Joseph *Henry,* 1797-1878, an American physicist]
hent (hent), *v.,* **hent, hent|ing,** *n.* —*v.t. Archaic.* to seize; grasp: *What hellish fury hath ... thee hent?* (Shakespeare).
—*n. Obsolete.* **1** a seizing; grasping. **2** a purpose; intention: *Up, sword; and know thou a more horrid hent* (Shakespeare). [Old English *hentan*]
Hen|te|ni|an (hen tē′nē ən), *adj.* of or having to do with John Henten or the editions of the Vulgate Bible prepared by him and used for a time by the Roman Catholic Church. [< John *Henten,* 1499-1566, a French theologian + *-ian*]
hen tracks, *U.S. Slang.* illegible marks or figures in handwriting.
hen|tri|a|con|tane (hen′trī ə kon′tān), *n.* a solid hydrocarbon of the methane series, occurring in petroleum and beeswax. *Formula:* $C_{31}H_{64}$ [< Greek *heîs, henós* one + *triakonta* thirty + English *-ane*]
he|or|to|log|i|cal (hē′ôr tə loj′ə kəl), *adj.* of or having to do with heortology.
he|or|tol|o|gy (hē′ôr tol′ə jē), *n.* the study of the origin, meaning, growth, and history of the religious feasts and seasons of the Christian year. [< Greek *heortḗ* feast + English *-logy*] —**he′or|tol′o|gist,** *n.*
hep[1] (hep), *adj. U.S. Slang.* having intimate knowledge; informed; hip: *They are hep to all the passing fads of the teen-age cult. To restore his confidence, I infused a contemporary note into my reply. "I assure you, Commissioner, when it*

Pronunciation Key: hat, āge, cãre, fär; let, ēqual, tėrm; it, īce; hot, ōpen, ôrder; oil, out; cup, pu̇t, rüle; child; long; thin; ᴛʜen; zh, measure; ə represents a in about, e in taken, i in pencil, o in lemon, u in circus.

comes to poisons I am hep" (New Yorker). [American English; origin uncertain]

hep² (hep, hup, hut), *interj.* a military command used to mark cadence in marching, as in "hep, two, three, four!" Also, **hup, hut.** [origin uncertain]

he|par (hē′pär), *n.* **1** a reddish-brown or liver-colored compound containing sulfur and a metal formerly used as medicine. **2** (in homeopathy) calcium sulfide. [< Medieval Latin *hepar* < Greek *hêpar* the liver]

hep|a|rin (hep′ər in), *n.* a glucoside present in the liver and other animal tissues, that prevents the blood from clotting. Heparin is used in the treatment of thrombosis and other diseases. [American English < Greek *hêpar, hêpatos* the liver + English *-in*]

hep|a|rin|ize (hep′ər ə nīz), *v.t.,* **-ized, -iz|ing.** to treat or infuse with heparin: *heparinized blood samples.*

hep|a|tec|to|mize (hep′ə tek′tə mīz), *v.t.,* **-mized, -miz|ing.** to remove the liver of; perform a hepatectomy upon.

hep|a|tec|to|my (hep′ə tek′tə mē), *n., pl.* **-mies.** the surgical removal of part or all of the liver. [< Greek *hêpar, hêpatos*the liver + *ektomê* a cutting out]

he|pat|ic (hi pat′ik), *adj., n.* —*adj.* **1** of or having to do with the liver: *the hepatic artery.* **2** acting on the liver as a medicine. **3** liver-colored; dark reddish-brown. **4** *Botany.* of or belonging to the liverworts.
—*n.* **1** a medicine that acts on the liver. **2** *Botany.* a liverwort.
[< Latin *hēpaticus* < Greek *hēpatikós* < *hêpar, hêpatos* liver]

he|pat|i|ca (hi pat′ə kə), *n.* any one of a small group of low plants with three-lobed leaves and delicate purple, pink, or white flowers that bloom early in the spring; liverleaf; liverwort. It belongs to the crowfoot family. [< New Latin *hepatica* (*herba*), feminine of Latin *hēpaticus* (see etym. under **hepatic**) (because of its liver-shaped leaves)]

hepatic duct, the duct of the liver that carries the bile into the gall bladder.

he|pat|i|co|gas|tros|to|my (hi pat′ə kō gas tros′tə mē), *n., pl.* **-mies.** a connection made by surgery between the hepatic duct and the stomach.

he|pat|i|co|len|tic|u|lar degeneration (hi pat′ə kō len tik′yə lər), = Wilson's disease.

he|pat|i|cot|o|my (hi pat′ə kot′ə mē), *n., pl.* **-mies.** a surgical incision into the hepatic duct.

hepatic tanager, a small, reddish-brown songbird of tropical America, related to the finches.

hep|a|ti|tis (hep′ə tī′tis), *n.* **1** inflammation of the liver. **2** a contagious virus disease characterized by inflammation of the liver, fever, and usually jaundice. [< Greek *hêpar, hêpatos* liver]

hepatitis A, = infectious hepatitis.

hepatitis B, = serum hepatitis.

hep|a|ti|za|tion (hep′ə tə zā′shən), *n.* the conversion of any tissue, especially lung tissue, into a liverlike material.

hep|a|tize (hep′ə tīz), *v.t.,* **-tized, -tiz|ing.** to affect the lungs or other organ by hepatization. [< Greek *hêpar, hêpatos* liver + English *-ize*]

hep|a|to|cel|lu|lar jaundice (hep′ə tō sel′yə lər), jaundice resulting from damage to the liver cells so that they do not produce enough bile. [< Greek *hêpar, hêpatos* liver + English *cellular*]

hep|a|to|cir|rho|sis (hep′ə tō sə rō′sis), *n.* cirrhosis of the liver. [< Greek *hêpar, hêpatos* the liver + English *cirrhosis*]

hep|a|to|gen|ic (hep′ə tə jen′ik), *adj.* produced in or arising from the liver.

hep|a|to|ma (hep′ə tō′mə), *n., pl.* **-mas, -ma|ta** (-mə tə). a tumor of the liver, especially a malignant tumor.

hep|a|to|pex|i|a (hep′ə tə pek′sē ə), *n.* the surgical fixation of a floating liver. [< New Latin *hepatopexia* < Greek *hêpar, hêpatos* liver + *pêxis* a fixing]

hep|a|tot|o|my (hep′ə tot′ə mē), *n., pl.* **-mies.** a surgical incision into the liver.

hep|a|to|tox|ic (hep′ə tō tok′sik), *adj.* toxic to the liver: *hepatotoxic compounds.*

hep|a|to|tox|in (hep′ə tō tok′sən), *n.* a substance poisonous to the liver. [< Greek *hepâr, hêpatos* liver + English *toxin*]

hep|cat (hep′kat′), *n. Slang.* **1** an informed admirer of swing or jazz music: *This is not cool chatter between some young hepcats in a smoke-filled jazz joint, . . .* (Science News Letter). **2** a performer in a swing or jazz band.

He|phaes|te|um (hi fes′tē əm), *n.* = Theseum (def. 2).

He|phaes|tus (hi fes′təs), *n. Greek Mythology.* the god of fire and metalworking, son of Zeus and Hera, identified by the Romans with Vulcan.

hepped-up (hept′up′), *adj. Slang.* = hopped-up.

***Hep|ple|white** (hep′əl hwīt), *n., adj.* —*n.* a style of furniture made from the designs of George Hepplewhite, an English cabinetmaker in the 1700's, and characterized by lightness, delicacy, and graceful curves.
—*adj.* of or like this style of furniture.

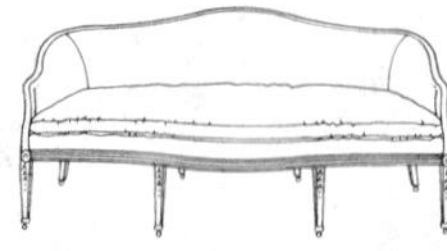

***Hepplewhite**

hept-, *combining form.* the form of **hepta-** before vowels, as in *heptarchy.*

hepta-, *combining form.* **1** seven, as in *heptagon, heptameter.* **2** having seven atoms of a specified element: *Heptane = a hydrocarbon having seven atoms of carbon.* Also, **hept-** before vowels. [< Greek *heptá* seven]

hep|ta|chlor (hep′tə klôr, -klōr), *n.* a very toxic hydrocarbon used to kill insect pests of vegetables, fruit, and grain. *Formula:* $C_{10}H_7Cl_7$ [< *hepta-* + *chlor*(ine)]

hep|ta|cron (hep′tə kron), *n.* a solid figure having seven verticles. [< *hept-* + Greek *ákron* vertex]

hep|tad (hep′tad), *n.* **1** the number seven. **2** a group of seven. **3** *Chemistry.* an element, atom, or radical with a valence of seven. [< Greek *heptás, -ados* (group of) seven < *heptá* seven]

***hep|ta|gon** (hep′tə gon), *n.* a plane figure having seven angles and seven sides. [< Greek *heptágōnon* < *heptá* seven + *gōniā* angle]

***heptagon**
***heptahedron**

heptagon heptahedron

hep|tag|o|nal (hep tag′ə nəl), *adj.* having the form of a heptagon.

hep|ta|he|dral (hep′tə hē′drəl), *adj.* having seven sides.

***hep|ta|he|dron** (hep′tə hē′drən), *n., pl.* **-drons, -dra** (-drə). a solid figure having seven surfaces. [< New Latin *heptahedron* < Greek *heptá* seven + *hédra* base]

hep|ta|hy|drat|ed (hep′tə hī′drā tid), *adj. Chemistry.* containing seven molecules of water.

hep|ta|hy|dric (hep′tə hī′drik), *adj. Chemistry.* containing seven hydroxyl groups.

hep|tam|er|ous (hep tam′ər əs), *adj.* (of a flower) having seven members in each whorl. It is generally written *7-merous.*

hep|tam|e|ter (hep tam′ə tər), *n.* a line of poetry having seven feet. *Example:* And thrice/he rout/ed all/his foes,/ and thrice/he slew/the slain./

hep|tane (hep′tān), *n.* one of nine isomeric hydrocarbons of the methane series, used especially as solvents and for the octane rating of gasolines. *Formula:* C_7H_{16}

hep|tan|gu|lar (hep tang′gyə lər), *adj.* having seven angles.

hep|tar|chic (hep tär′kik), *adj.* having to do with a heptarchy.

Hep|tar|chy (hep′tär kē), *n.* the seven principal Anglo-Saxon kingdoms between about 600 A.D. and A.D. 829. [< New Latin *heptarchia* < Greek *hêpta* seven + *-archiā* empire < *árchein* rule]

hep|tar|chy (hep′tär kē), *n., pl.* **-chies. 1** a government by seven persons. **2** a group of seven districts or states, each under its own ruler.

hep|ta|stich (hep′tə stik), *n.* a stanza, strophe, or poem of seven lines. [< *hepta-* + Greek *stíchos* line (of poetry) < *steíchein* walk]

hep|ta|style (hep′tə stīl), *n. Architecture.* a form of columniation having seven columns in the end row. [< *hepta-* + Greek *stylos* column, pillar]

Hep|ta|teuch (hep′tə tük, -tyük), *n.* the first seven books of the Old Testament. [< Greek *heptáteuchos* < *heptá* seven + *teûchos* book]

hep|tath|lon (hep tath′lon), *n.* a two-day competition for women in the Olympic Games, consisting of seven events that include the 100-meter hurdles, high jump, shot-put, and 200-meter run on the first day, and the long jump, javelin throw, and 800-meter run on the second day. [< Greek *heptá* seven + *âthlon* exercise of skill; patterned on *pentathlon*]

hep|ta|ton|ic (hep′tə ton′ik), *adj. Music.* having seven tones: *a heptatonic scale.*

hep|ta|va|lent (hep′tə vā′lənt, hep tav′ə-), *adj. Chemistry.* having a valence of seven.

hep|tose (hep′tōs), *n.* a monosaccharide with seven atoms of carbon in each molecule.

her (hėr; *unstressed* hər, ər), *pron., adj.* —*pron. Objective case of* **she.** *She* and *her* mean the girl or woman or female animal spoken about: *She is not here. Find her. It belongs to her.*
—*adj. Possessive form of* **she.** of her; belonging to her; done by her: *She has left her book. The cat won't let you touch her kittens.*
[Old English *hire*]

her., **1** heraldic. **2** heraldry.

He|ra (hir′ə), *n. Greek Mythology.* a goddess who was the wife of Zeus and queen of the gods and men and the goddess of women and marriage. The Romans called her Juno. Also, **Here.**

Her|a|cles (her′ə klēz), *n.* = Hercules.

He|ra|cli|te|an (her′ə klī tē′ən), *adj.* of or having to do with the ancient Greek philosopher Heraclitus, or with his philosophy.

Her|a|kles (her′ə klēz), *n.* = Hercules.

her|ald (her′əld), *n., v.* —*n.* **1** (formerly) an officer who carried messages, made announcements, arranged and supervised tourneys and other public ceremonies, and regulated the use of armorial bearings: *The king sent two heralds to the duke.* **2** a person who carries messages and makes announcements; messenger: *A herald is arrived from Caesar's camp* (Joseph Addison). *"Herald" is often used as the name of a newspaper.* SYN: envoy. **3** *Figurative.* one that goes before or is sent before and shows something more is coming; forerunner; harbinger: *It was the lark, the herald of the morn* (Shakespeare). SYN: precursor. **4** an official in Great Britain who has authority over coats of arms and keeps a record of families that have them. He is a member of the Queen's Household and of the Heralds' College.
—*v.t.* **1** to bring news of; announce: *The newspapers heralded the arrival of the army.* **2** to go before and announce the coming of.
[Middle English *herauld* < Old French *herault,* or *heralt,* perhaps ultimately < a Germanic word]

he|ral|dic (he ral′dik), *adj.* of or having to do with heraldry or heralds; resembling the devices on coats of arms: *We saw, heraldic in the heat, A scorpion on a stone* (William Plomer). —**he|ral′di|cal|ly,** *adv.*

her|ald|ist (her′əl dist), *n.* a person who studies heraldry.

***her|ald|ry** (her′əl drē), *n., pl.* **-ries. 1** the science or art of dealing with coats of arms. Heraldry determines a person's right to use a coat of arms, traces family descent, and designs coats of arms for new countries. **2** a heraldic device, or a collection of such devices. **3** = coat of arms. SYN: blazonry. **4** the ceremony or pomp connected with the life of noble families: *He would proclaim it far and wide, With trump and solemn heraldry* (Samuel Taylor Coleridge).

***heraldry**
definition 1

terms of heraldry

shield divisions:

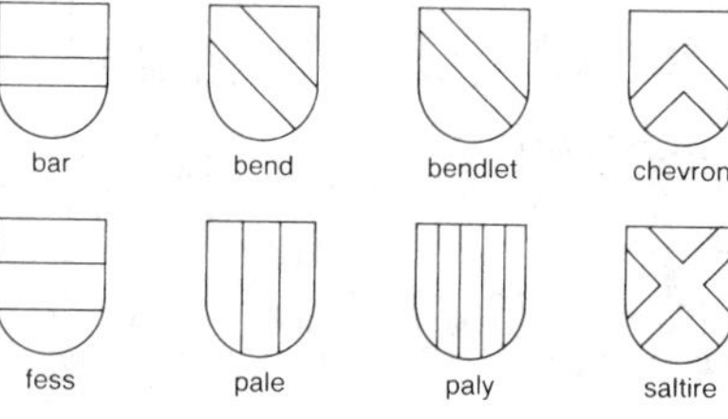

line divisions:

dovetailed
nowy
embattled
potent
escartelé
raguly
invecked
rayonné
nebulé
ondé

Heralds' College, a royal corporation in England, founded in 1484, in charge of granting armorial bearings and coats of arms, recording genealogies, and the like; College of Arms.

herb (ėrb, hėrb), *n.* **1** a plant whose leaves or stems are used for medicine, seasoning, food, or perfume. Sage, mint, caraway, and lavender are herbs. **2** a flowering plant whose stems live only one season. Herbs do not usually form woody tissue as shrubs and trees do, though their roots may live many years. Peonies, buttercups, corn, wheat, cabbage, and lettuce are herbs. Herbs can be annuals, such as corn, or biennials, such as the onion, but most are perennials, such as the rose. **3** = herbage: *Underfoot the herb was dry*

(Tennyson). [< Old French *herbe* < Latin *herba*] —**herb′less**, *adj.* —**herb′like′**, *adj.*

her·ba·ceous (hėr bā′shəs, ėr-), *adj.* **1** of an herb; like an herb; having stems that are usually soft and not woody. **2** having the texture, color, etc., of an ordinary leaf; green: *a herbaceous flower.* [< Latin *herbāceus* (with English *-ous*) < *herba* herb]

herb·age (ėr′bij, hėr′-), *n.* **1** herbs or grass; low-growing plants covering a large extent of ground. Cows graze on herbage in a pasture. *Chalk hills covered with a scanty herbage* (Sir Benjamin Brodie). **2** the green leaves and soft stems of plants. [< Old French *herbage* < Medieval Latin *herbaticum* < Latin *herba* herb]

herb·al (hėr′bəl, ėr′-), *adj., n.* —*adj.* of, having to do with, or made from herbs. —*n.* **1** a book about herbs or plants, giving their kinds, qualities, uses, and the like. **2** = herbarium.

herb·al·ism (hėr′bə liz əm, ėr′-), *n.* the study or use of herbs, especially medicinal herbs.

herb·al·ist (hėr′bə list, ėr′-), *n.* **1** a person who gathers or deals in herbs, especially medicinal herbs. **2** (formerly) a person who studies herbs or plants; botanist.

her·bar·i·um (hėr bãr′ē əm), *n., pl.* **-i·ums, -i·a** (-ē ə). **1** a collection of dried plants systematically arranged. **2** a room or building where such a collection is kept. [< Late Latin *herbārium,* neuter of Latin *herbārius* < *herba* herb. See etym. of doublet **arbor**[1].]

herb bennet, a common European plant of the rose family, with yellow flowers and an aromatic root.

herb doctor, a person who treats illnesses with herbs.

herbed (ėrbd, hėrbd), *adj.* seasoned with herbs: *herbed potato salad.*

her·bes·cent (hėr bes′ənt), *adj.* growing like an herb; herbaceous. [< Latin *herba* herb + English *-escent*]

her·bi·cid·al (hėr′bə sī′dəl, ėr′-), *adj.* having to do with herbicides: *Herbicidal compounds are used in weed control* (Wall Street Journal). —**her′bi·cid′al·ly**, *adv.*

her·bi·cide (hėr′bə sīd, ėr′-), *n.* a toxic chemical used especially to kill weeds, such as 2,4-D; weedkiller. [< *herb* + *-cide*[1]]

her·bif·er·ous (hėr bif′ər əs), *adj.* bearing or producing herbs. [< Latin *herbifer* bearing grass (< *herba* herb, plant + *ferre* to bear) + English *-ous*]

her·bi·vore (hėr′bə vôr, -vōr), *n.* any one of a large group of animals that feed on grass or other plants. The ungulates are herbivores. *From infancy on, we humans delight in tales in which nice little herbivores escape from the clutches of big bad carnivores* (Science News Letter). [< French *herbivore* < New Latin *herbivorus* herb-eating < Latin *herba* herb, plant + *vorāre* devour]

her·biv·o·rous (hėr biv′ər əs), *adj.* **1** feeding on grass or other plants. Cattle are herbivorous animals. **2** of or belonging to the herbivores. —**her·biv′o·rous·ly**, *adv.*

her·bo·rize (hėr′bə rīz), *v.i.,* **-rized, -riz·ing.** to gather herbs for study. [< French *herboriser* (with English *-ize*) < *herbe* herb < Latin *herba*] —**her′bo·ri·za′tion**, *n.* —**her′bo·riz′er**, *n.*

herb Paris, a European herb of the lily family, bearing a single greenish flower; truelove. Its roots and berries are considered poisonous. [< Medieval Latin *herba paris;* origin uncertain]

herb Robert, a plant of the geranium family having dissected leaves and small, reddish-purple flowers; red robin. [< Medieval Latin *herba Roberti,* perhaps < *Robert,* a duke of Normandy]

herb·y (ėr′bē, hėr′bē), *adj.,* **herb·i·er, herb·i·est.** **1** having many herbs; grassy. **2** of or like herbs.

her·cu·le·an (hėr kyü′lē ən, hėr′kyə lē′-), *adj.* **1** of great strength, courage, or size; very powerful: *a herculean warrior.* SYN: colossal. **2** requiring great strength, courage, or size; very hard to do: *a herculean task.* [< Latin *Hercules* (see etym. under **Hercules**) + English *-an*]

Her·cu·le·an (hėr kyü′lē ən, hėr′kyə lē′-), *adj.* of or having to do with Hercules.

Her·cu·les (hėr′kyə lēz), *n., genitive* (def. 3) **Her·cu·lis.** **1** *Greek and Roman Mythology.* a hero, son of Zeus and Alcmene, famous for his great strength that made him able to perform twelve extraordinary labors imposed on him by the King of Argos, as a result of Hera's hatred of him; Alcides. **2** Also, **hercules.** a person of great strength, courage, or size. **3** a northern constellation near Lyra. Also, **Heracles, Herakles.** [< Latin *Hercules* < Greek *Hēraklês,* contraction of *Hēraklées* (literally) the glory of Hera < *Hêra* Hera + *kléos* glory]

Hercules beetle, a large, strong tropical American beetle with two long curved horns, one above the other, in the male. It sometimes grows to a length of 6 inches.

Her·cu·les′-club (hėr′kyə lēz klub′), *n.* **1** a small, prickly tree of the rue family, whose bark and seeds are used in medicine. **2** a small, prickly tree of the ginseng family, whose bark, root, and berries are used in medicine; angelica tree. **3** a gourd whose dried fruit is used as an ornament.

Hercules moth, a very large, boldly patterned moth with a wingspread of about ten inches and tails on its hind wings, found in New Guinea and Australia.

Her·cu·lis (hėr′kyə lis), *n.* genitive of **Hercules** (def. 3).

Her·cyn·i·an (hėr sin′ē ən), *adj. Geology.* of or having to do with a series of mountain-building fractures and folds of the late Paleozoic, especially in southern Europe and northern Africa. [< *Hercynian* Forest, a mountain range in ancient geography identified with various European ranges < Latin *Hercynia* Silva]

herd[1] (hėrd), *n., v.* —*n.* **1** a group of animals of one kind, especially large animals, keeping, feeding, or moving together: *a herd of cattle, a herd of elephants, a herd of whales. The lowing herd winds slowly o'er the lea* (Thomas Gray). SYN: drove. **2** *Figurative.* **a** a large number of people; crowd; multitude: *a herd of ragged children.* **b** the common people; rabble: *Who o'er the herd would wish to reign, Fantastic, fickle, fierce, and vain* (Scott). SYN: populace.
—*v.i., v.t.* **1** to join together; flock together; associate: *Several people herded under an awning to get out of the shower.* **2** to form into a flock, herd, or group; place in or among a herd: *The farmer herded the cows over to the barn door.*
ride herd on, a to guard (cattle or other animals) by riding on the outer edge of a herd: *Several cowboys were riding herd on a drove heading south.* **b** *Figurative.* to keep within bounds; control carefully and strictly: *Congressmen now are vowing to make the President pay for his words by riding herd on his new budget* (Newsweek).
[Old English *heord*] —**herd′like′**, *adj.*

herd[2] (hėrd), *v.t.* to tend, drive, or take care of (cattle, sheep, or other animals). [Old English *hierde;* see etym. under **-herd**]

-herd, *combining form.* a keeper of a herd of _____: *Cowherd = a keeper of a herd of cows.* [Old English *hierde,* related to *heord* flock, herd[1]]

herd·boy (hėrd′boi′), *n.* a boy or man in charge of a herd: *They kept a herdboy herding [the camels] up and down the forest* (New Yorker).

herd·er (hėr′dər), *n.* = herdsman.

her·dic (hėr′dik), *n. U.S.* a low-hung carriage having two or four wheels, the entrance at the back, and the seats along the sides. [American English < Peter *Herdic,* 1824-1888, an American inventor]

herd immunity, immunity acquired by unvaccinated individuals through exposure to the weakened virus spread by recently vaccinated individuals: *Herd immunity is a great public health benefit, since even in the United States large numbers of individuals remain unvaccinated* (Rick Weiss).

herd instinct, *Psychology.* the tendency to think and act as one of a crowd.

herd's-grass (hėrdz′gras′, -gräs′), *n.* any one of various grasses, grown for hay or pasture, such as timothy and redtop.

herds·man (hėrdz′mən), *n., pl.* **-men.** a man in charge of a herd, especially of cattle or goats.

Herds·man (hėrdz′mən), *n.* = Boötes.

herds·wom·an (hėrdz′wum′ən), *n., pl.* **-wom·en.** a woman in charge of a herd.

here (hir), *adv., n., interj.* —*adv.* **1** in this place; at this place: *We will live here in the summer. Place it here. We will stop here.* **2** to this place; hither: *Come here. Bring the children here for their lesson.* **3** at this time; now: *Here the speaker paused.* **4** in this life. **5** in this case: *Here can then be no injustice, where no one is injured* (Sir Richard Steele). **6** who or which is here (used to call attention to some person or thing): *My friend here can help you.*
—*n.* **1** this place: *Where do we go from here?* **2** this life; the present: *Full of all the tender pathos Of the Here and the Hereafter* (Longfellow).
—*interj.* **1** an answer showing that one is present when the roll is called. **2** an exclamation used to call attention to some person or thing, or to introduce a command: *John! here! quick! Here, take away the dishes.*
here and there, a in this place and that; at intervals: *. . . able to understand but here and there a word of what they said* (Joseph Addison). **b** hither and thither: *Be attentive, turning not thine eyes here and there* (Francis Hawkins).
here below, on earth; in this life: *Man wants but little here below, Nor wants that little long* (Oliver Goldsmith).
here (we, you) are, here is what (we, you) want: *Here you are; this jacket is your size. Now let's see, here we are—the G-i-a-o-u-r—that's a nice word to talk about* (Francis Smedley).
here's to (you). See under **here's**.
neither here nor there, not to the point; off the subject; unimportant: *True it is that our so doing is neither here nor there . . . in respect of God* (Arthur Golding).
the here and now, the immediate present: *Christians should be more interested in heaven and hell rather than in just living the here and now* (New York Times). *In the here and now, my strongest bias is not . . . economic at all, but simply in favor of political liberty* (Listener).
up to here, *Informal.* **a** to the full; to capacity: *[He] spent years since World War II immersed up to here in documents* (Charles Poore). **b** surfeited; fed up: *It weighs all of 8 pounds, so when you're up to here with TV, you can pull it [the set] out of sight* (New Yorker).
[Old English *hēr*]
►**Here** is often placed after a noun or noun phrase to emphasize or call attention to someone or something: *Bob here is a lawyer. This house here is for sale.* When placed between a demonstrative adjective and a noun, *here* is considered nonstandard: *This here building is the oldest in town.*

He·re (hir′ē), *n.* = Hera.

here·a·bout (hir′ə bout′), *adv.* = hereabouts.

here·a·bouts (hir′ə bouts′), *adv.* about this place; around here; near here: *The farm population hereabouts is getting smaller and smaller, so the farmers want bigger tractors to be able to do more work* (Wall Street Journal).

here·af·ter (hir af′tər, -äf′-), *adv., n.* —*adv.* **1** after this; after now; in the future: *Do not bring that question up hereafter.* **2** in life after death.
—*n.* **1** the future. **2** the life or time after death: *The minister committed his soul to the hereafter.*

here·at (hir at′), *adv.* **1** when this happened; at this time. **2** because of this.

here·a·way (hir′ə wā′), *adv.* **1** in this neighborhood: *They told us below, we should find settlers something thinnish, hereaway* (James Fenimore Cooper). **2** *Slang.* hither.

here·by (hir bī′), *adv.* **1** by this; by this means; in this way: *The license said: "You are hereby given the right to hunt and fish in Dover County."* **2** *Obsolete.* nearby.

he·re·des (hə rē′dēz), *n.* plural of **heres.**

he·red·i·ta·bil·i·ty (hə red′ə tə bil′ə tē), *n.* = heritability.

he·red·i·ta·ble (hə red′ə tə bəl), *adj.* that can be inherited. —**he·red′i·ta·bly**, *adv.*

her·e·dit·a·ment (her′ə dit′ə mənt), *n. Law.* any thing that can be inherited: *all the landed possessions, houses, mills . . . and other hereditaments which formed the royal patrimony* (Washington Irving). [< Medieval Latin *hereditamentum* < Late Latin *hērēditāre* inherit < Latin *hērēs, -ēdis* heir]

he·red·i·tar·i·an (hə red′ə ter′ē ən), *n., adj.* —*n.* a person who maintains that individual traits are acquired chiefly by genetic transmission or heredity. —*adj.* maintaining that individual traits are determined chiefly by heredity: *Current studies do not support either an "environmentalist" or a "hereditarian" interpretation of differences in intelligence* (Saturday Review).

he·red·i·tar·y (hə red′ə ter′ē), *adj.* **1** coming by inheritance: *"Prince" is a hereditary title.* **2** holding a position by inheritance: *The Queen of England is a hereditary ruler.* **3** caused or transmitted by heredity: *Color blindness is hereditary.* SYN: inherited. **4** coming from one's parents or ancestors: *a hereditary belief, a hereditary custom.* **5** having to do with inheritance or heredity: *hereditary descent.* [< Latin *hērēditārius* < *hērēditās* heredity] —**he·red′i·tar′i·ly**, *adv.* —**he·red′i·tar′i·ness**, *n.*

he·red·i·tist (hə red′ə tist), *n.* a person who believes that all individuality is determined by inheritance.

he·red·i·ty (hə red′ə tē), *n., pl.* **-ties.** **1** the fact that one generation of plants and animals produces the next. **2** the passing of physical or mental characteristics from one generation of plants or animals to the next: *It has long been known that heredity is determined by the chromosomes, the threadlike bodies in the nucleus of the cell, and by their subunits the genes* (Scientific American). **3** the qualities of body and mind that have come to a child from its parents: *His father was a very gentle man and so it was not in the son's heredity to resort to outbursts of temper.* SYN: heritage. **4** the tendency of offspring to be like the parents: *Variation, then, is quite as universal a fact in life as is heredity, and both are significant in understanding man* (Beals and Hoijer). [< Latin *hērēditās* heirship < *hērēs, -ēdis* heir]

Here|ford (hėr′fərd, her′ə-), *n.* **1** one of a breed of beef cattle having a reddish-brown body, white face, and white markings under the body. **2** any one of an American breed of red hog with white markings. [< *Hereford*(shire), a county in England]

here|from (hir from′, -frum′), *adv.* **1** from this place. **2** from this fact or statement.

here|in (hir in′), *adv.* **1** in here; in this place; in this passage or book. **2** in this matter; in this way.

here|in|a|bove (hir′in ə buv′), *adv.* above in this document, statement, or the like: *The factual record of the Mandatory's conduct, as hereinabove more particularly set forth, has a ... remarkable consistency* (E. J. Kahn, Jr.).

here|in|af|ter (hir′in af′tər, -äf′-), *adv.* afterward in this document, statement, or the like.

here|in|be|fore (hir in′bi fôr′, -fōr′), *adv.* before in this document, statement, or the like.

here|in|to (hir in′tü), *adv.* **1** into this place. **2** into this matter.

here|of (hir ov′, -uv′), *adv.* of this; about this.

here|on (hir on′, -ôn′), *adv.* **1** on this. **2** immediately after this.

He|re|ro (hə rer′ō), *n., pl.* **-ros. 1** a member of a Bantu tribe living in central South-West Africa. **2** their language.

he|res (hir′ēz), *n., pl.* **he|re|des**. *Law.* an heir. Also, **haeres**. [< Latin *hērēs, -ēdis.* See etym. of doublet **heir**.]

here's (hirz), here is.
here's to, a wish of health, happiness, or success to: *Here's to you! Here's to the maiden of bashful fifteen; Here's to the widow of fifty; Here's to the flaunting extravagant quean, And here's to the housewife that's thrifty!* (Richard Brinsley Sheridan).

he|re|si|arch (hə rē′sē ärk, her′ə-), *n.* a leader or founder of a heresy: *Kandinsky was the last great heresiarch of painting, the last master who could be wrong* (Art News). [< Late Latin *haeresiarcha* < Greek *hairesiárchēs* leader of a sect < *hairesis* a choosing (see etym. under **heresy**) + *-archēs* leader < *árchein* to lead]

her|e|si|ol|o|gy (her′ə sē ol′ə jē), *n., pl.* **-gies. 1** the study of heresies. **2** a book about heresies. [< Greek *haíresis* heresy + English *-logy*] — **her′e|si|ol′o|gist,** *n.*

her|e|sy (her′ə sē), *n., pl.* **-sies. 1** a belief different from the accepted belief of a church, school, profession, or other group: *It is the customary fate of new truths to begin as heresies* (Thomas Huxley). SYN: heterodoxy. **2** the holding of such a belief: *to fall into heresy.* [< Old French *heresie,* alteration of Latin *haeresis* < Greek *hairesis* a choosing; heresy < *haireîn* choose]

her|e|tic (her′ə tik), *n., adj.* — ***n.*** a person who holds a belief that is different from the accepted belief of his church, school, profession, or other group: *Many young poets regard themselves as heretics in their art. Pelagius's ideas were officially condemned, and he himself was excommunicated as a heretic* (Atlantic). SYN: dissenter.
— ***adj.*** holding such a belief; heretical.
[< Old French *heretique,* learned borrowing from Late Latin *haereticus* < Greek *hairetikós* able to choose < *haireîn* choose]

he|ret|i|cal (hə ret′ə kəl), *adj.* **1** of or having to do with heresy or heretics: *Galileo's theory that the earth goes round the sun was regarded as a heretical opinion.* **2** containing heresy; characterized by heresy. — **he|ret′i|cal|ly,** *adv.*

here|to (hir tü′), *adv.* **1** to this place, thing, document, etc. **2** *Obsolete.* hitherto.

here|to|fore (hir′tə fôr′, -fōr′), *adv., adj., n.* — ***adv.*** before this time; until now: *Heretofore, doctors have tried low fat diets ... to reduce the cholesterol in the blood* (Science News Letter). SYN: hitherto.
— ***adj.*** former: *Considering the heretofore reluctance of our film folk to move into this realm ... this coincidental emergence of two films ... is something to hum about* (New York Times).
— ***n.*** time past.

here|un|der (hir un′dər), *adv.* **1** under this. **2** under authority of this.

here|un|to (hir′un tü′), *adv.* to this place, thing, document, etc.; hereto.

here|up|on (hir′ə pon′, -pôn′), *adv.* **1** upon this thing, point, subject, or matter: *Hereupon we disagree.* **2** immediately after this: *We had an argument; hereupon she left.*

here|with (hir wiᴛʜ′, -with′), *adv.* **1** with this: *I am sending ten cents in stamps herewith.* **2** by this means; in this way.

her|i|ot (her′ē ət), *n.* (in English law) a feudal payment due a lord at the death of a tenant. [Old English *heregeatwa* military equipment (especially that restored to a lord on a tenant's death) < *here* army + *geatwa* gear; spelling influenced by Anglo-French *heriet*]

her|it|a|bil|i|ty (her′ə tə bil′ə tē), *n.* heritable quality or condition.

her|it|a|ble (her′ə tə bəl), *adj., n.* — ***adj.*** **1** that can be inherited; inheritable: *heritable diseases, heritable tendencies. In Mendel's experiments one could discern the constant heritable characters which might disappear for a time in hybrids only to reappear again unchanged* (Atlantic). **2** capable of inheriting.
— ***n.*** (in Scottish law) a possession or right that can be inherited.
[< Old French *heritable* < *heriter;* see etym. under **heritage**]

her|it|a|bly (her′ə tə blē), *adv.* by way of inheritance.

her|it|age (her′ə tij), *n.* **1a** what is or may be handed on to a person from his ancestors, such as land, a trait, beliefs, or customs; inheritance: *a great cultural heritage. The heritage of freedom is precious to Americans. It was ... part of my heritage, which my dead father did bequeath to me* (Shakespeare). **b** *Figurative.* what comes to a person from the circumstances of his birth: *Poverty was his heritage.* **c** *Figurative.* inherited portion; lot; fate: *Let us hope that the heritage of old age is not despair* (Benjamin Disraeli). **2** the Israelites, God's chosen people (in the Bible, Joel 3:2). **3** the Christian church (in the Bible, I Peter 5:3).
[< Old French *heritage* < *heriter* inherit < Late Latin *hērēditāre,* ultimately < Latin *hērēs, -ēdis* heir]

her|it|ance (her′ə təns), *n.* = inheritance. [< Old French *heritance* < *heriter;* see etym. under **heritage**]

her|i|tor (her′ə tər), *n.* **1** an inheritor: *He resembled a squatter rather than an heritor* (James Purdy). **2** (in Scottish law) the owner of heritable, taxable property in a parish. [< Anglo-French *heriter,* Old French *heritier* < Latin *hērēditārius* hereditary]

her|i|tress (her′ə tris), *n.* = heiress.

herl (hėrl), *n.* **1** a fiber or barb of a feather, especially of a peacock, used in trimming artificial fishing flies. **2** a fishing fly trimmed with herls. [Middle English *herle.* Compare Middle Low German *herle, harle.*]

herm (hėrm), *n.* = herma.

her|ma (hėr′mə), *n., pl.* **-mae** (-mē), **-mai** (-mī). an ancient Greek monument, consisting of a head of Hermes placed on top of a square pillar. It was used especially as a boundary mark or milepost. Also, **hermes**. [< Latin *Herma, Hermes* the god Hermes < Greek *Hermês*]

her|ma|ic (hėr mā′ik), *adj.* having to do with a herma.

Her|ma|ic (hėr mā′ik), *adj.* **1** having to do with Hermes or Mercury. **2** having to do with Hermes Trismegistus or the writings and beliefs attributed to him. [< Greek *Hermaïkós* < *Hermês* Hermes]

her|maph|ro|dite (hėr maf′rə dīt), *n., adj.*
— ***n.*** **1a** an animal or plant having both male and female reproductive organs. **b** *Figurative.* a person or thing having two opposite qualities. **2** = hermaphrodite brig.
— ***adj.*** of or like a hermaphrodite.
[< Latin *hermaphroditus* < Greek *Hermaphródītos* Hermaphroditus]

hermaphrodite brig, a ship with two masts, square-rigged forward and schooner-rigged aft; brigantine.

her|maph|ro|dit|ic (hėr maf′rə dit′ik), *adj.* of or like a hermaphrodite; bisexual. — **her|maph′ro|dit′i|cal|ly,** *adv.*

her|maph|ro|dit|i|cal (hėr maf′rə dit′ə kəl), *adj.* = hermaphroditic.

her|maph|ro|dit|ism (hėr maf′rə dī tiz′əm), *n. Biology.* the condition of a hermaphrodite; union of the two sexes in the same individual.

Her|maph|ro|di|tus (hėr maf′rə dī′təs), *n. Greek Mythology.* the son of Hermes and Aphrodite, who became united in body with the nymph Salmacis.

her|ma|typ|ic (hėr′mə tip′ik), *adj.* that build reefs: *hermatypic corals.* [< Greek *herma* reef + *týptein* to strike, beat + English *-ic*]

her|me|neu|tic (hėr′mə nü′tik, -nyü′-), *adj.* of or concerned with interpretation; interpretive; explanatory. [< Greek *hermēneutikós* < *hermēneutḗs* interpreter < *hermēneúein* to interpret, perhaps related to *eírein* speak; associated with *Hermês* Hermes, as the patron deity of speech] — **her′me|neu′ti|cal|ly,** *adv.*

her|me|neu|ti|cal (hėr′mə nü′tə kəl, -nyü′-), *adj.* = hermeneutic.

her|me|neu|tics (hėr′mə nü′tiks, -nyü′-), *n.* the science of interpretation, especially the branch of theology that deals with the principles of Scriptural interpretation.

Her|mes (hėr′mēz), *n.* **1** *Greek Mythology.* a god who was the messenger of Zeus and the other gods. He was portrayed wearing winged cap and shoes and carrying a caduceus. He was the god of boundaries, roads, and commerce; of science and invention; of eloquence, luck, and cunning; and the patron of thieves and gamblers. The Romans called him Mercury. **2** a small asteroid that at times approaches closer to the earth than any other heavenly body does.

her|mes (hėr′mēz), *n.* = herma.

Hermes Tris|me|gis|tus (tris′mə jis′təs), the Greek name given to the Egyptian god Thoth. He was more or less identified with the Greek god Hermes, and regarded as the author of all mystical, astrological, and alchemical doctrines. [< Greek *Hermês tris mégistos* Hermes thrice greatest]

her|met|ic (hėr met′ik), *adj.* **1a** closed tightly so that air cannot get in or out; airtight: *The bottle has a hermetic seal.* **b** *Figurative.* tightly sealed; confined: *None of man's works are so hermetic that a little of truth does not seep out* (Manchester Guardian Weekly). **2a** magical; alchemical. **b** *Figurative.* abstruse; obscure: *His two volumes are not hermetic, but they are not easy, either* (Joseph Alsop). [< Medieval Latin *hermeticus* < Greek *Hermês* (*tris mégistos*) Hermes Trismegistus (because he knew the secrets of alchemy)] — **her|met′i|cal|ly,** *adv.*

Her|met|ic (hėr met′ik), *adj.* of or having to do with Hermes Trismegistus or the writings and beliefs attributed to him: *The Hermetic philosopher Robert Fludd ... aimed, like Giulio Camillo, at a universal memory* (New Yorker).

her|met|i|cal (hėr met′ə kəl), *adj.* = hermetic.

Her|met|i|cism (hėr met′ə siz′əm), *n.* hermetic quality or condition.

hermetic school, a group of Italian poets of the 1930's who wrote in an obscure, personal style that seemed sealed off from everyday life.

Her|met|ism (hėr′mə tiz əm), *n.* Hermetic teaching or philosophy.

Her|met|o|log|ist (hėr′mə tol′ə jist), *n.* a Hermetic philosopher.

Her|mi|o|ne (hėr mī′ə nē), *n. Greek Legend.* the daughter of Menelaus and Helen of Troy.

her|mit (hėr′mit), *n.* **1** a person who goes away from other people, and lives by himself; recluse. A hermit often lives a religious life. *Hermit hoar in solemn cell* (Samuel Johnson). SYN: eremite, anchorite. **2** any one of various animals of solitary habits, such as the hermit crab. **3** a spiced, brown sugar, drop cookie, usually containing raisins and nuts. **4** *Obsolete.* a beadsman. [< Old French *hermite* < Late Latin *erēmīta* < Greek *erēmī́tēs* < *erêmos* uninhabited. See etym. of doublet **eremite**.] — **her′mit|like′,** *adj.*

her|mit|age (hėr′mə tij), *n.* **1** the home of a hermit: *The peaceful hermitage, The hairy gown and mossy cell* (Milton). **2** a solitary and secluded dwelling place: *Stone walls do not a prison make Nor iron bars a cage; Minds innocent and quiet take that for an hermitage* (Richard Lovelace).

Her|mit|age (hėr′mə tij; *French* er mi tázh′), *n.* a French table wine made on the left bank of the Rhone, near Tain. The greater part of it is red wine, but some is white. [< French (*Vin de*) *l'Hermitage* (Wine of) the Hermitage < a ruin, a supposed hermit's cell, near Valence, where it was made]

hermit crab, a crab with a soft body that lives in the empty shells of snails, whelks, and like animals, as a means of protection.

Her|mi|tian (hər mē′shən, -mish′-; er mē′-), *adj.* of or having to do with the theories of the French mathematician Charles Hermite, 1822-1901, especially his theories of algebraic forms and elliptic functions.

her|mit|ic (hėr mit′ik), *adj.* = hermitical.

her|mit|i|cal (hėr mit′ə kəl), *adj.* of or having to do with a hermit. — **her|mit′i|cal|ly,** *adv.*

Hermit Kingdom, a name applied to Korea from 1637 to 1876 because it refused any contact with foreigners except the Chinese.

her|mit|ry (hėr′mə trē), *n.* a hermit's condition or way of life: *[He] lives in near hermitry* (Time).

hermit thrush, a brown thrush of North America with spotted breast and reddish tail. It is noted for its song.

hern or **herne** (hėrn), *n. Dialect.* heron.

her|ni|a (hėr′nē ə), *n., pl.* **-ni|as, -ni|ae** (-nē ē). the protrusion of some tissue or organ of the body, especially a part of the intestine, through the wall of the cavity which should hold it in; rupture. [< Latin *hernia*]

her|ni|al (hėr′nē əl), *adj.* of or having to do with hernia.

her|ni|ate (hėr′nē āt), *v.i.,* **-at|ed, -at|ing.** (of a body organ or part) to rupture: *A gap has occurred in the diaphragm muscle around the esophagus, and a small portion of the stomach has herniated* (Newsweek). — **her′ni|a′tion,** *n.*

Her|ni|ci (hėr′ni sī), *n.pl.* an ancient Italian people of the Apennines, subdued by the Romans in 486 B.C.

Her|ni|cians (hėr nish′ənz), *n.pl.* = Hernici.

her|ni|ot|o|my (hėr′nē ot′ə mē), *n., pl.* **-mies.** surgical cutting for relief of hernia.

hern|shaw (hėrn′shô), *n. Archaic.* heronsew.

he|ro (hir′ō), *n., pl.* **-roes. 1** a man or boy admired for his bravery, great deeds, or noble qualities: *George Washington is one of our great heroes. Any father can be a hero to his son.* **2** a person admired for contribution to a particular field: *heroes of science.* **3** the most important male person in a story, play, or poem: *Vanity Fair: A novel without a hero* (Thackeray). *I want a hero . . . I'll therefore take our ancient friend Don Juan* (Byron). **4** *Greek Legend.* a man of more than human strength, courage, or ability, especially a warrior favored by the gods. Hercules and Achilles were heroes. **5** *U.S.* hero sandwich. [ultimately < Latin *hērōs* < Greek *hērōs*]

He|ro (hir′ō), *n. Greek Legend.* a priestess of Aphrodite at Sestos. Her lover, Leander, swam the Hellespont from Abydos nightly to visit her, and was drowned. Hero killed herself because of his death.

He|ro|di|an (hə rō′dē ən), *adj.* of or having to do with Herod, especially Herod the Great, or the political party in ancient Palestine supporting his family.

He|ro|di|as (hə rō′dē əs), *n.* the second wife of Herod Antipas. She and her daughter Salome brought about the death of John the Baptist. (in the Bible, Matthew 14:3-11).

He|rod|o|te|an (hə rod′ə tē′ən), *adj.* of or having to do with Herodotus, 484?-424? B.C., Greek historian.

he|ro|ic (hi rō′ik), *adj., n.* —*adj.* **1** like a hero, his deeds, or his qualities; very brave; great; noble: *the heroic deeds of our firemen.* **2a** of or about heroes and their deeds; epic: *The "Iliad" and the "Odyssey" are heroic poems.* **b** resembling the language or style of heroic poetry: *heroic prose.* **3** unusually daring or bold; using extreme means to get a necessary result: *Only heroic measures could save the town from the flood.* **4** unusually large; larger than life size: *a heroic statue.*
—*n.* a heroic poem.
heroics, a words, feelings, or actions that seem grand or noble but are only for effect: *He stopped his heroics only when he saw that they were laughing at him.* **b** high-sounding language: *Women, it is said, . . . cannot write moderately. They are always in hysterics or heroics* (John Skelton). **c** = heroic verse: *When he was but . . . a freshman in Cambridge he . . . sent his accounts to his father in . . . heroics* (Thomas Nashe).
—**he|ro′i|cal|ly,** *adv.* —**he|ro′i|cal|ness,** *n.* —**he-ro′ic|ness,** *n.*

heroic age, the time when the famous heroes of a nation or folk are supposed to have lived: *the heroic age of Greece.*

he|ro|i|cal (hi rō′ə kəl), *adj.* = heroic.

heroic couplet, two successive lines of poetry in iambic pentameter that rhyme together.

heroic drama, a type of English drama of the late 1600's, heavily written in heroic couplets.

heroic tenor, = dramatic tenor.

heroic tragedy, = heroic drama.

heroic verse, a poetic form used in heroic and other long poems. In English, German, and Italian, it is iambic pentameter. In French it is the Alexandrine. In Greek and Latin it is dactylic hexameter. *Example in English:* "Why on those shores are we with joy surveyed, Admired as heroes, and as gods obeyed."

her|o|in (her′ō in), *n.* a very dangerous, habit-forming drug, made from morphine: *The U.S. government forbids the manufacture, importation, and use of heroin, but many people obtain it illegally* (Donald J. Wolk). *Formula:* $C_{21}H_{23}NO_5$ [< German *Heroin,* a trademark for heroin, said to be < Greek *hērōs* (because of the inflated feeling it produces)]

her|o|ine (her′ō in), *n.* **1** a girl or woman admired for her bravery, great deeds, or noble qualities; female hero: *Boadicea, a queen of ancient Britain, was a heroine when she led a revolt against the Romans. Florence Nightingale was a heroine during the Crimean War when she nursed the wounded.* **2** the most important female person in a story, play, or poem: *Take Lilia, then, for heroine . . . And make her some great princess* (Tennyson). **3** *Greek Legend.* a girl or woman of more than human qualities, favored by the gods. [< Latin *hērōīnē* < Greek *hērōīnē,* feminine of *hērōs* hero] —**her′o|ine|ship,** *n.*

her|o|in|ism (her′ō ə niz′əm), *n.* the condition or position of a heroine.

her|o|ism (her′ō iz əm), *n.* **1** the actions and qualities of a hero or heroine; great bravery; daring; courage: *Heroism feels and never reasons and therefore is always right* (Emerson). **SYN:** valor, gallantry, intrepidity. **2** a very brave act or quality; doing something noble at great cost to oneself: *His heroism in saving the drowning boy from the river was greatly praised in the newspapers.*

he|ro|ize (hir′ō īz), *v.t.,* **-ized, -iz|ing.** to make a hero of; treat as a hero. —**he′ro|i|za′tion,** *n.*

her|on (her′ən), *n.* a wading bird like a crane with a long neck, a long bill, long legs, and a short tail. Herons feed on fish, frogs, etc. Egrets and bitterns are herons. [< Old French *hairon* < Germanic (compare Old High German *heiger,* variant of *hreigir* heron)]

her|on|ry (her′ən rē), *n., pl.* **-ries.** a place where herons come annually in large numbers and build their nests.

her|on's-bill (her′ənz bil′), *n.* any one of a group of low herbs of the geranium family, growing in temperate regions, and cultivated in flower gardens or for forage, such as the alfilaria.

her|on|sew or **her|on|sewe** (her′ən sō, -syü), *n. Archaic or Dialect.* a heron, especially a small or young one. Also, **hernshaw.** [< Old French *heronceau* (diminutive) < *hairon* heron]

hero sandwich, *U.S.* a whole loaf of Italian or French bread sliced in half and filled with meat, cheese, or other filling.

hero worship, 1 the idolizing of individuals or their memory, especially of persons accepted as heroes: *Most cases of hero worship . . . have a positive value in the development of the rapidly changing boy or girl* (Sidonie M. Gruenberg).
2 the worship of deified heroes in ancient Greece and Rome.

he|ro-wor|ship (hir′ō wėr′ship), *v.t.,* **-shiped, -ship|ing** or (*especially British*) **shipped, -shipping.** to worship as a hero; idolize: *In his twilight years he is beguiled by an aggressive young lady who hero-worships him* (New York Times). —**he′-ro-wor′ship|er,** *n.*

her|pan|gi|na (hėr′pən jī′nə), *n.* a virus disease of children characterized by a sore, ulcerated throat. [< New Latin *herpangina* < Latin *herpes* herpes + *angīna* angina]

her|pes (hėr′pēz), *n.* any one of various virus diseases causing spreading blisterlike blotches on the skin or mucous membrane, such as shingles and cold sores. [< Latin *herpes* < Greek *hérpēs* the disease shingles < *hérpein* to creep]

herpes fa|ci|a|lis (fā′shē ā′lis), cold sores on the face. [< New Latin *herpes facialis*]

herpes la|bi|a|lis (lā′bē ā′lis), cold sores on the lips. [< New Latin *herpes labialis*]

herpes sim|plex (sim′pleks), cold sores on the body, face, or lips. [< New Latin *herpes simplex*]

her|pes|vi|rus (hėr′pēz vī′rəs), *n.* any one of a group of viruses which contain DNA and are sensitive to ether, including the viruses causing herpes and chicken pox.

herpes zos|ter (zos′tər), = shingles.

her|pe|tar|i|um (her′pə tãr′ē əm), *n., pl.* **-i|ums, -i|a** (-ē ə). an enclosure, building, or facility for the keeping and display of reptiles or amphibians. [< Greek *herpetón* reptile + Latin *-ārium* place for]

her|pet|ic (hėr pet′ik), *adj.* having to do with or like herpes.

her|pe|toid (hėr′pə toid), *adj.* having the form of a reptile; reptilelike. [< Greek *herpetón* reptile + English *-oid*]

her|pe|to|log|ic (hėr′pə tə loj′ik), *adj.* = herpetological.

her|pe|to|log|i|cal (hėr′pə tə loj′ə kəl), *adj.* of or having to do with herpetology. —**her′pe|to|log′i-cal|ly,** *adv.*

her|pe|tol|o|gy (hėr′pə tol′ə jē), *n.* the branch of zoology dealing with reptiles and amphibians. [< Greek *herpetón* reptile (< *hérpein* creep) + English *-logy*] —**her′pe|tol′o|gist,** *n.*

Herr (her), *n., pl.* **Her|ren** (her′ən). *German.* **1** Mr.; Sir. **2** a gentleman.

her|ren|grun|dite (her′ən grun′dīt), *n.* a basic hydrous sulfate of calcium and copper, occurring in green tabular crystals. [< German *Herrengrundit* < *Herrengrund,* Germany, where it is found + English *-ite*[1]]

Her|ren|volk (her′ən fôlk′), *n. German.* the master race; (in Nazi Germany) the Germans.

her|ring (her′ing), *n., pl.* **-rings** or (*collectively*) **-ring. 1** any one of various small food fishes of the North Atlantic and North Pacific. Herring are bony fish that have spineless fins, the ventral fins back of the pectorals, no fleshy fin back of the dorsal fin, and no scales on the head. The grown fish are eaten fresh, salted, or smoked, and the young are canned as sardines or sold in tins as whitebait. **2** any fish of the clupeid family, including the herring, sardine, and shad. [Old English *hēring, hæring*]

★her|ring|bone (her′ing bōn′), *adj., n., v.,* **-boned, -bon|ing.** —*adj.* having a zigzag pattern or arrangement like the spine of a herring.
—*n.* **1a** a zigzag pattern, arrangement, or stitch. **b** a fabric having such a pattern, especially a fabric with a twill weave. **2** the spine of a herring. **3** *Skiing.* a type of ascent made by walking with the skis at an angle to each other and the outer edges turned up. The tracks form a herringbone pattern.
—*v.t., v.i.* **1** to embroider or sew with a herringbone stitch; make a herringbone pattern: *In sheets assembled from narrow widths of linen and among pillows, too, one may note traces of elaborate herringboning* (London Times). **2** *Skiing.* to ascend by use of a herringbone.

★herringbone
definitions 1,2,3

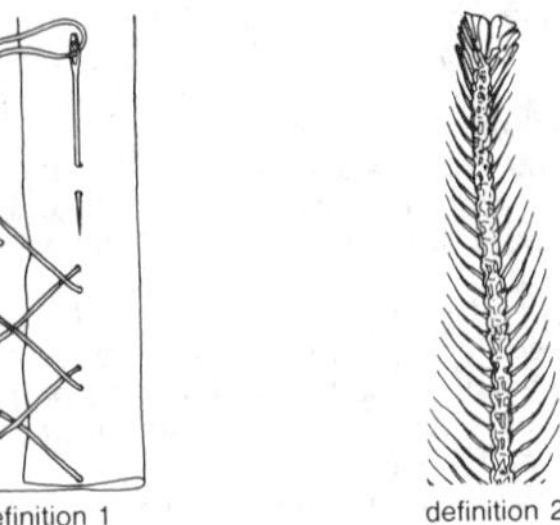
definition 1 definition 2

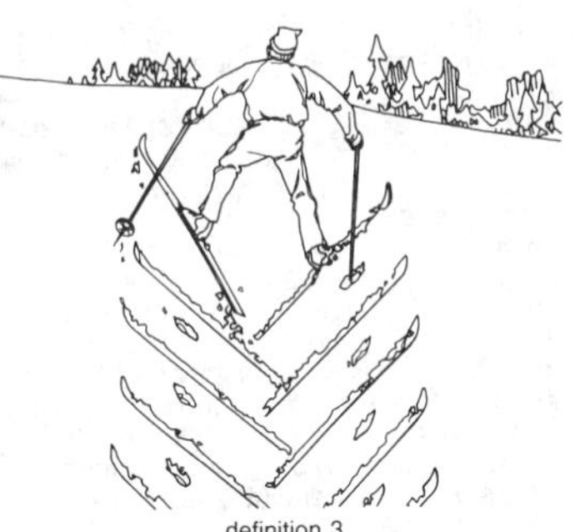
definition 3

herringbone stitch, an embroidery stitch consisting of crosses in a herringbone design. It is used also to fasten down the hems on thick material.

herring gull, a large, gray-and-white gull of northern regions, common around Atlantic and Pacific ports, and sometimes seen on inland waters.

herring pond, the sea; ocean (a humorous use).

herring rake, a long pole with a jagged point, used by American Indians of the Northwest to catch herring.

her|ry (her′ē), *v.t., v.i.,* **-ried, -ry|ing.** *Scottish.* harry.

hers (hėrz), *pron. Possessive form of* **she.** the one or ones belonging to her: *This money is hers. Your answers are wrong; hers are right.*
of hers, belonging to her: *A friend of hers called and left a message.*

herse (hėrs), *n.* **1** *Obsolete.* a troop formation used in battle. **2** *Heraldry.* a bearing showing a portcullis or a harrow. [< Old French *herse* harrow < Latin *hirpex* large rake, harrow. Compare etym. under **hearse.**]

her|self (hėr self′), *pron.* **1** the form of **she** or **her,** used to make a statement stronger; emphatic form of **she** or **her:** *She herself did it. She herself brought the book.* **2** her self; the reflexive form of **her:** *She hurt herself. She did it by herself.* **3** her real or true self: *In those fits she is not herself.*

hertz (hėrts), *n., pl.* **hertz** or **hertz|es.** *Physics.* a unit of frequency in the centimeter-gram-second system, equivalent to one cycle per second. *Abbr:* Hz (no period). [< Heinrich R. *Hertz,* 1857-1894, a German physicist]

hertz|i|an (hert′sē ən, hėrt′-), *adj.* of or having to do with Heinrich R. Hertz, the apparatus used or invented by him, or the phenomena discovered by him.

hertzian telegraphy, = radiotelegraphy.

hertzian waves or **Hertzian waves,** electromagnetic radiation, such as the now-familiar waves used in communicating by radio. Hertzian waves are produced by irregular fluctuations of electricity in a conductor.

Hertz|sprung-Rus|sell diagram (hert′sprung-rus′əl), = Russell diagram. [< Ejnar *Hertzsprung,* 1873-1967, a Danish astronomer, and Henry N. *Russell,* 1877-1957, an American astronomer]

Her|ze|go|vin|i|an (her′tsə gō vin′ē ən), *adj., n.* —*adj.* of or having to do with Herzegovina, a re-

gion in the Balkan peninsula.
—*n.* a native or inhabitant of Herzegovina.

Her|zog (her′tsōk), *n., pl.* **-zo|ge** (-tsō gə). a prince who rules over a small state, or a member of the highest rank of nobility; duke. [< German *Herzog* duke]

he's (hēz; *unstressed* ēz, iz, hiz), **1** he is. **2** he has.

he/she (hē′shē′), *pron.* he or she (used to replace the standard "he" when the antecedent may be either male or female): *Unless a young poet is extraordinarily gifted or lucky or has an influential patron, he/she is hard put to it to find an audience* (Kenneth Lamott).

Hesh|van or **Hesh|wan** (hesh′van), *n.* the eighth month of the ecclesiastical year and the second month of the civil year in the Jewish calendar, corresponding to parts of October and November. Also, **Hesvan**. [< Hebrew *heshwān*]

hes|i|fla|tion (hez′ə flā′shən), *n.* a condition in which continuous inflation is combined with a wavering rate of business and industrial growth. [blend of *hesitation* and *inflation*]

He|si|od|i|an (hē′sē od′ē ən, hes′ē-), *adj.* = Hesiodic.

He|si|od|ic (hē′sē od′ik, hes′ē-), *adj.* of or like the style of Hesiod, a Greek poet who lived in the 700's B.C.

He|si|o|ne (hi sī′ə nē), *n. Greek Legend.* a daughter of Laomedon of Troy, sacrificed to a sea monster but rescued by Hercules, who later made her a slave.

hes|i|tance (hez′ə təns), *n.* = hesitancy.

hes|i|tan|cy (hez′ə tən sē), *n., pl.* **-cies. 1** hesitation; tendency to hesitate; doubt; indecision; vacillation: *Children have no hesitancy in speaking unwelcome truths.* **2** an instance of this.

hes|i|tant (hez′ə tənt), *adj.* **1** tending to hesitate; hesitating; doubtful; undecided: *She was hesitant about accepting the invitation.* **2** stammering: *hesitant speech.* SYN: irresolute, vacillating.
—hes′i|tant|ly, *adv.*

hes|i|tate (hez′ə tāt), *v.,* **-tat|ed, -tat|ing. —*v.i.* 1** to hold back; feel doubtful; be undecided; show that one has not yet made up one's mind: *I hesitated about taking his side until I knew the whole story. But it is clear enough that he has not hesitated to seize the opportunity presented by the settlers' rising and the generals' mutiny* (Observer). **2** to feel that perhaps one should not; be unwilling; not wish (to): *She hesitated to hurt the child's feelings. I hesitated to ask you; you were so busy.* **3** to stop for an instant; pause: *He hesitated before asking the question.* **4** to speak with short stops or pauses; stammer. SYN: stutter.
—*v.t.* to express with indecision or unwillingness: *Willing to wound, and yet afraid to strike, Just hint a fault, and hesitate dislike* (Alexander Pope). [< Latin *haesitāre* (with English *-ate*[1]) < *haerēre* stick fast] **—hes′i|tat′er, hes′i|ta′tor**, *n.*
—*Syn.* *v.i.* **1 Hesitate, falter, waver** mean to fail to act promptly and resolutely. **Hesitate** emphasizes holding back because of doubt or indecision: *I hesitated about taking the new job.* **Falter** suggests losing courage and hesitating or giving way after starting to act: *He went to apologize, but faltered at the door.* **Waver** suggests not holding firmly to a decision or course of action: *I said I would help but wavered when I saw how much there was to do.*

hes|i|tat|ing (hez′ə tā′ting), *adj.* that hesitates.
—hes′i|tat′ing|ly, *adv.*

hes|i|ta|tion (hez′ə tā′shən), *n.* **1** the act of hesitating; doubt; indecision; unwillingness; delay: *We have no hesitation in deciding what is right and what is wrong.* SYN: hesitancy. **2** a speaking with short stops or pauses; stammering: *a hesitation in one's speech.*

hesitation waltz, a waltz in which the dancers perform a rocking or gliding movement at intervals.

hes|i|ta|tive (hez′ə tā′tiv), *adj.* characterized by hesitation; hesitating: *a hesitative manner of speaking.* **—hes′i|ta′tive|ly**, *adv.*

hes|i|ta|to|ry (hez′ə tə tôr′ē, -tōr′-; *especially British* hez′ə tā′tər ē), *adj.* = hesitative.

hes|ped (hes′ped), *n., pl.* **hes|peds, hes|pe|dim** (hes pā′dim). a funeral oration given at a Jewish memorial service. [< Hebrew *hespēdh*]

Hes|per (hes′pər), *n.* = Hesperus.

Hes|pe|ri|a (hes pir′ē ə), *n.* the land of the west, a name given by Greek poets to Italy, and by Roman poets to Spain or regions beyond. [< Latin *Hesperia* < Greek *Hesperiā* < *Hésperos* Hesperus]

Hes|pe|ri|an (hes pir′ē ən), *adj.* **1** of or having to do with the land of the west or where the sun sets; western. **2** of or having to do with the Hesperides: *Happy isles, Like those Hesperian gardens, famed of old* (Milton). [< Greek *Hésperos* Hesperus, originally adjective, of the evening, western]

Hes|per|id (hes′pər id), *n.* one of the Hesperides.

Hes|per|i|des (hes per′ə dēz), *n.pl. Greek Mythology.* **1** the nymphs who guarded the golden apples of Hera. **2** the garden at the western extremity of the earth where these apples were kept. [< Latin *Hesperides* < Greek *Hesperídes*, plural, daughters of *Hésperos* Hesperus]

Hes|per|id|i|an (hes′pə rid′ē ən), *adj.* of or having to do with the Hesperides or their garden.

hes|per|i|din (hes per′ə din), *n. Chemistry.* a glucoside, occurring in most citrus fruits when unripe. *Formula:* $C_{28}H_{34}O_{13}$ [< New Latin *Hesperides* (in early use) the orange family < Latin (see etym. under **Hesperides**) + English *-in*]

hes|per|id|i|um (hes′pə rid′ē əm), *n., pl.* **-i|a** (-ē ə). Botany. the fruit of the orange, lemon, grapefruit, and some other members of the rue family, a berry having a fleshy interior covered by a leathery, separable rind. [< New Latin *Hesperidium* < Latin *Hesperides;* see etym. under **Hesperides**]

Hes|per|or|nis (hes′pə rôr′nis), *n.* a very large, extinct diving bird with long, conical teeth and rudimentary wings, known through its fossil remains found in the Cretaceous soils of Kansas, other parts of the United States, and also in England. [< Greek *hésperos* western + *órnis* bird (because it was discovered in the Western Hemisphere)]

Hes|per|us (hes′pər əs), *n.* Venus when it appears as the evening star; the evening star: *Some shed a mild and silver beam Like Hesperus o'er the western Sea* (Shelley). [< Latin *Hesperus* < Greek *Hésperos* having to do with evening, western]

Hes|sian** (hesh′ən), *adj., n.* **—*adj. of Hesse or its people.
—*n.* 1 a person born or living in Hesse. **2a** a German soldier hired by England to fight against the Americans during the American Revolution. **b** a military or political hireling; mercenary. [< *Hesse*, a state in West Germany + *-ian*]

***Hessian**
definition 2a

hes|sian (hesh′ən), *n.* = burlap (def. 1).

Hessian boots, high boots with tassels, reaching a little below the knee. They were introduced by the Hessians, and were popular in England during the 1800's.

Hessian fly, a small, two-winged insect whose larvae are very destructive to wheat.

hess|ite (hes′īt), *n.* telluride of silver, a rare mineral, usually occurring in gray, sectile masses. One variety also contains some gold. *Formula:* Ag_2Te [< G. H. *Hess*, 1802-1850, a Swiss chemist + English *-ite*[1]]

hes|so|nite (hes′ə nīt), *n.* a yellowish or brownish variety of garnet, found especially in Ceylon, (Sri Lanka), and sometimes used in jewelry; essonite. [variant of *essonite*]

hest (hest), *n.* **1** *Archaic.* behest; command; bidding. **2** *Obsolete.* a vow.
[alteration of Old English *hǣs*]

hes|ter|nal (hes tėr′nəl), *adj.* of or having to do with yesterday: *enervating slumbers, from the hesternal dissipation or debauch* (Edward G. Bulwer-Lytton). [< Latin *hesternus* of yesterday + English *-al*[1]]

Hes|ti|a (hes′tē ə), *n. Greek Mythology.* the goddess of the hearth, identified by the Romans with Vesta.

Hes|van (hes′van), *n.* = Heshvan.

het (het), *v.t., v.i. Dialect.* heated; a past tense and a past participle of **heat**.
het up, *Dialect.* heated up; excited; riled: *She said she had taken a sedative from the medicine chest because she felt het up* (Punch).

he|tae|ra (hi tir′ə), *n., pl.* **-tae|rae** (-tir′ē). **1** a courtesan or concubine in ancient Greece. **2** any courtesan or concubine. [< Greek *hetaírā* courtesan, mistress, companion]

he|tae|ri|o (hi tir′ē ō), *n., pl.* **-ri|os**. a fruit consisting of a number of distinct, indehiscent carpels produced by a single flower, such as the raspberry or strawberry. [< New Latin *hetaerio* < Greek *hetaîros* an associate]

he|tae|rism (hi tir′iz əm), *n.* **1** the practice of concubinage. **2** a primitive type of society characterized by communal marriage. [< Greek *hetairismós*, ultimately < *hetaírā* hetaera]

he|tae|ro|lite (hi tir′ə līt), *n.* a metallic oxide containing zinc and manganese. [< Greek *hetaîros* an associate + English *-lite* (because it is found in association with another mineral)]

he|tai|ra (hi tī′rə), *n., pl.* **-rai** (-rī). = hetaera.

he|tai|rism (hi tī′riz əm), *n.* = hetaerism.

heter-, *combining form.* the form of **hetero-** before vowels, as in *heteroecious.*

het|er|o (het′ər ō), *adj., n., pl.* **-er|os**. *Informal.* heterosexual.

hetero-, *combining form.* of different kinds; other than the usual kind; other; different: *Heterogeneous = different in kind. Heterogamete = different or other gamete.* Also, **heter-** before vowels. [< Greek *hetero-* < *héteros* different, another]

het|er|o|at|om (het′ər ō at′əm), *n.* an atom which substitutes for one of the atoms in a hydrocarbon aromatic structure.

het|er|o|aux|in (het′ər ō ôk′sin), *n.* = indoleacetic acid.

het|er|o|blas|tic (het′ər ə blas′tik), *adj.* having a marked difference between the immature and adult forms of a plant. **—het′er|o|blas′ti|cal|ly**, *adv.*

het|er|o|cer|cal (het′ər ə sėr′kəl), *adj.* **1** having a tail in which the upper lobe is larger than the lower, and which contains the end of the spinal column: *a heterocercal fish.* **2** of or having to do with this form of tail. [< *hetero-* + Greek *kérkos* tail + English *-al*[1]]

het|er|o|chro|mat|ic (het′ər ə krō mat′ik), *adj.* **1** having a complex pattern of more than one color. **2** of or having more than one color. **3** of or having to do with heterochromatin.

het|er|o|chro|ma|tin (het′ər ə krō′mə tin), *n. Biology.* the chromatin of a chromosome that stains intensely. It is thought to regulate partially the metabolism of the cell nucleus. A sex chromosome may have large areas of heterochromatin.

het|er|o|chrome (het′ər ə krōm), *adj.* = heterochromatic.

het|er|o|chro|mo|some (het′ər ə krō′mə sōm), *n.* = allosome.

het|er|o|chro|mous (het′ər ə krō′məs), *adj.* **1** of different colors. **2** *Botany.* having the florets of the center different in color from those of the margin, as in the daisy or aster. [< *hetero-* + Greek *chrôma* color + English *-ous*]

het|er|och|thon (het′ə rok′thən), *n.* one of the animals of a region which have evidently been derived by immigration from another region. [< *hetero-* + Greek *chthōn* earth, country]

het|er|och|tho|nous (het′ə rok′thə nəs), *adj.* not native; naturalized.

het|er|o|clite (het′ər ə klīt), *adj., n.* **—*adj.* 1** deviating from the ordinary rule; exceptional; abnormal: *His world, too, is made up of the most heteroclite materials, which his insatiable intellectual thirst has driven him to test and explore* (Atlantic). SYN: irregular, anomalous, eccentric. **2** *Grammar.* irregular in declension or inflection.
—*n.* 1 a thing or person that deviates from the ordinary rule. SYN: anomaly. **2** *Grammar.* a word, especially a noun, irregularly inflected.
[< Middle French *hétéroclite*, learned borrowing from Latin *heteroclitus* < Greek *heteróclitos* < *héteros* different + *klínein* bend; inflect]

het|er|o|cy|cle (het′ər ə sī′kəl), *n. Chemistry.* a heterocyclic compound.

het|er|o|cy|clic (het′ər ə sī′klik, -sik′lik), *adj., n. Chemistry.* **—*adj.*** of or containing a ring made up of several carbon atoms and one of another kind. **—*n.*** = heterocycle.

het|er|o|cyst (het′ər ə sist), *n.* a large, colorless cell found irregularly along a filament in certain species of algae.

het|er|o|cy|to|tox|in (het′ər ə sī′tə tok′sin), *n.* a poisonous substance destructive to the cells of an animal, obtained from an animal of another species.

het|er|o|dont (het′ər ə dont), *adj.* differentiated for various uses, as into the canines, incisors, and molars of man: *heterodont teeth.* [< *heter-* + Greek *odoús, odóntos* tooth]

het|er|o|dox (het′ər ə doks), *adj.* **1** rejecting generally accepted beliefs or doctrines, especially in a religion; differing from an acknowledged standard; not orthodox: *Some of the heterodox opinions which he avows ... particularly his Arianism* (Macaulay). **2** holding opinions not in accord with some acknowledged standard: *Small Cars, like Little Magazines, offer satisfaction to individual and heterodox tastes* (Harper's). [< Late Latin *heterodoxos* < Greek *heteródoxos* < *héteros* another + *dóxa* opinion < *dokeîn* seem] **—het′er|o|dox′ly**, *adv.*

het|er|o|dox|y (het′ər ə dok′sē), *n., pl.* **-dox|ies**. **1** the rejection of generally accepted beliefs or doctrines, especially in a religion; departure from an acknowledged standard; opposite of orthodoxy: *Orthodoxy is my doxy; heterodoxy is another man's doxy* (Bishop William Warburton). *We need to persuade them to minimize the dangers of heterodoxy and be ready, as Jefferson* was, to take a calculated risk* (Atlantic). **2** a belief, doctrine, or opinion not in agreement with what is generally accepted: *Communism and fascism are heterodoxies in the Free World.*

het|er|od|ro|mous (het′ə rod′rə məs), *adj.* having the spiral arrangement of the leaves on the stem in one direction and of those on the branches in the opposite direction. [< New Latin *heterodromus* (with English *-ous*) < Greek *héteros* other + *drómos* a running]

het|er|o|dy|na|mous (het′ər ə dī′nə məs), *adj. Biology.* having to do with the dominance of certain characteristics in inheritance. [< Greek *heterodýnamos* (with English *-ous*) of different power < *héteros* different + *dýnamis* power]

het|er|o|dyne (het′ər ə dīn), *adj., v.,* **-dyned, -dyn|ing.** **—*adj.*** receiving radio waves by combining the signal-carrying current with a current of different frequency generated in the receiving set, in such a way that audible beats are produced. A component of the resulting output of the circuit has a frequency equivalent to the difference between the frequencies of the original oscillations, and may be amplified and the like more easily.
—*v.i.* to produce sounds by a heterodyne system.

het|er|oe|cious (het′ə rē′shəs), *adj.* going through different stages of growth on different hosts, as certain parasitic fungi. [< *heter-* + Greek *oikíā* house + English *-ous*]

het|er|oe|cism (het′ə rē′siz əm), *n.* the condition of being heteroecious.

het|er|o|ga|mete (het′ər ō gə mēt′), *n.* either of two gametes, differing in character or behavior, which can unite with the other to form a zygote. A large, nonmotile egg and a small, motile sperm are heterogametes.

het|er|o|ga|met|ic (het′ər ō gə met′ik), *adj.* of or having to do with heterogametes.

het|er|og|a|mous (het′ə rog′ə məs), *adj.* **1** reproducing by the union of unlike gametes. **2** characterized by the alternation of two types of sexual reproduction in the successive generations. **3** having flowers or florets of two sexually different kinds.

het|er|og|a|my (het′ə rog′ə mē), *n.* **1** heterogamous condition. **2** = alteration of generations.

het|er|o|ge|ne|i|ty (het′ər ə jə nē′ə tē), *n., pl.* **-ties. 1** heterogeneous quality or condition; wide dissimilarity: *The variety of his books demonstrated the heterogeneity of his interests. It is heterogeneity rather than homogeneity that describes the society of a large state* (William F. Ogburn). **2** a heterogeneous element or part.

het|er|o|ge|ne|ous (het′ər ə jē′nē əs, -jēn′yəs), *adj.* **1** different in kind; not at all similar; unlike; varied: *She invited a heterogeneous group of people to her party. The heterogeneous qualities of the human race are the raw material of history. I had indulged myself with an evening of reading as heterogeneous as the page of a dictionary* (J. W. R. Scott). SYN: incongruous. **2** made up of unlike elements or parts; miscellaneous: *Tin cans, old shoes, and papers made a heterogeneous mass of rubbish in the yard. This world is a heterogeneous aggregate, no doubt, but its parts are bound together by various economic or cultural interactions* (Bulletin of the Atomic Scientists). **3** *Mathematics.* of different kinds and having no common integral divisor except 1. **4** of different degrees or dimensions. [< Medieval Latin *heterogeneus* (with English *-ous*) , ultimately < Greek *héteros* another + *génos* kind, race, stock] **—het′er|o|ge′ne|ous|ly,** *adv.* **—het′er|o|ge′ne|ous|ness,** *n.*

het|er|o|gen|e|sis (het′ər ə jen′ə sis), *n.* = alternation of generations.

het|er|o|ge|net|ic (het′ər ə jə net′ik), *adj.* of or like heterogenesis.

het|er|og|e|nous (het′ə roj′ə nəs), *adj.* coming from without; not arising within the body.

het|er|og|e|ny (het′ə roj′ə nē), *n.* = heterogenesis.

het|er|og|o|nism (het′ə rog′ə niz əm), *n.* heterogonous condition; heterogony.

het|er|og|o|nous (het′ə rog′ə nəs), *adj.* **1** *Botany.* of or denoting monoclinous flowers occurring in two or more forms, in which cross-fertilization is accomplished by the forms differing in the relative length of stamens and pistils. **2** *Biology.* characterized by heterogony.

het|er|og|o|ny (het′ə rog′ə nē), *n.* **1** *Biology.* alternation of generations in which a parthenogenetic generation alternates with a sexual generation. **2** *Botany.* the condition of being heterogonous. [< *hetero-* + Greek *-goniā* < *gónos* birth]

het|er|o|graft (het′ər ə graft, -gräft), *n.* tissue from an individual grafted on a member of another species (distinguished from *homograft*); xenograft. See also **autograft.**

het|er|o|graph|ic (het′ər ə graf′ik), *adj.* of or like heterography.

het|er|og|ra|phy (het′ə rog′rə fē), *n.* **1** spelling different from that in current use. **2** spelling in which the same letter is used to represent different sounds. *Example: c* in *call* and *city.*

het|er|og|y|nal (het′ə roj′ə nəl), *adj.* = heterogynous.

het|er|og|y|nous (het′ə roj′ə nəs), *adj. Zoology.* having females of different kinds, one sexual and the other neuter: *Ants and bees are heterogynous.* [< *hetero-* + Greek *gynē* woman + English *-ous*]

het|er|o|junc|tion (het′ər ə jungk′shən), *n.* **1** a junction made between different semiconducting materials, as distinguished from a junction between different conductivity types (p-n junction). **2** = heterostructure.

het|er|o|kar|y|on (het′ər ō kar′ē on), *n.* a cell having several genetically different nuclei: *Protoplasts of potato and tomato are fused to give a heterokaryon, which regenerates its cell wall and divides* (New Scientist). [< *hetero-* + Greek *káryon* nut, kernel]

het|er|o|kar|y|o|sis (het′ər ō kar′ē ō′səs), *n.* the condition of having or forming heterokaryons.

het|er|o|kar|y|ot|ic (het′ər ō kar′ē ot′ik), *adj.* of or having to do with heterokaryons.

het|er|o|log|i|cal (het′ər ə loj′ə kəl), *adj.* = heterologous.

het|er|ol|o|gous (het′ə rol′ə gəs), *adj.* **1** having a different relation; not corresponding. **2** (of cells and antiserums) immunologically related but not identical. **3** *Medicine.* having abnormal tissue, as a tumor. [< *hetero-* + Greek *lógos* ratio, relation + English *-ous*]

het|er|ol|o|gy (het′ə rol′ə jē), *n.* **1** *Biology.* lack of correspondence between parts, resulting from unlike origins or different compositions of the parts. **2** *Medicine.* abnormality, especially of structure or development.

het|er|ol|y|sis (het′ə rol′ə sis), *n.* **1** *Biology.* the destruction of cells by enzymes or lysins from another organism. **2** *Chemistry.* the breaking of a bond in an unsymmetrical manner, so that the bonding pair of electrons remains attached to one of the bonded atoms.

het|er|o|lyt|ic (het′ər ə lit′ik), *adj.* of or having to do with heterolysis.

het|er|om|er|ous (het′ə rom′ər əs), *adj.* **1** having the flower parts of one or more whorls differing in number from those of the others. **2** *Chemistry.* unrelated in chemical composition. [< *hetero-* + Greek *méros* part + English *-ous*]

het|er|o|mor|phic (het′ər ə môr′fik), *adj.* **1** of different form or size; deviating from the normal structure or type; abnormal. **2** *Zoology.* undergoing metamorphosis, as those insects which have different forms at different stages of growth. **3** *Botany.* occurring in forms that differ in the relative length of the stamens and pistils. [< *hetero-* + Greek *morphē* form + English *-ic*]

het|er|o|mor|phism (het′ər ə môr′fiz əm), *n.* the condition or property of being heteromorphic.

het|er|o|mor|pho|sis (het′ər ə môr fō′sis), *n., pl.* **-ses** (-sēz). *Zoology.* the replacement or substitution of one organ or lost part by another organ or new part that is different from the part that has been removed or is in an abnormal position.

het|er|o|mor|phous (het′ər ə môr′fəs), *adj.* = heteromorphic.

het|er|o|mor|phy (het′ər ə môr′fē), *n.* = heteromorphism.

het|er|on|o|mous (het′ə ron′ə məs), *adj.* **1** subject to or involving different laws. **2** subject to the law or will of another. **3** *Biology.* having different laws or modes of growth, as parts or organs. [< *hetero-* + Greek *nómos* law + English *-ous*]

het|er|on|o|my (het′ə ron′ə mē), *n.* heteronomous quality or condition.

het|er|o|nu|cle|ar (het′ər ə nü′klē ər, -nyü′-), *adj.* consisting of different atoms or groups of atoms: *CO is a heteronuclear molecule.*

het|er|o|nym (het′ər ə nim), *n.* a word spelled the same as another but having a different sound and meaning. *Example: lead,* to conduct, and *lead,* a metal. [probably back formation < *heteronymous*]

het|er|on|y|mous (het′ə ron′ə məs), *adj.* **1** of or like a heteronym. **2** having different names, as a pair of correlatives: *"Husband" and "wife" are heteronymous.* **3** *Optics.* of or having to do with a kind of double vision in which the image seen by the right eye is on the left side and that seen by the left eye is on the right. [< Greek *heterṓnymos* (with English *-ous*) (literally) having different names < *héteros* another + *ónyma* name] **—het′er|on′y|mous|ly,** *adv.*

het|er|on|y|my (het′ə ron′ə mē), *n.* heteronymous character or condition.

Het|er|o|ou|si|an (het′ər ō ü′sē ən, -ou′sē-), *n., adj. Theology.* **—*n.*** a person who believes that the Father and the Son are different in essence or substance; Arian.
—*adj.* of different essence or substance. [< Greek *heterooúsios* (< *héteros* different + *ousíā* essence, substance) + English *-an*]

het|er|o|pel|mous (het′ər ə pel′məs), *adj.* having one of the two deep flexor tendons of the toes dividing and going to the first and second digits, and the other dividing and going to the third and fourth digits: *a bird with heteropelmous feet.* [< *hetero-* + Greek *pélma* sole of the foot]

het|er|o|pho|bi|a (het′ər ə fō′bē ə), *n.* sexual aversion to or fear of the opposite sex.

het|er|o|phon|ic (het′ər ə fon′ik), *adj. Music.* of or using heterophony. **—het′er|o|phon′i|cal|ly,** *adv.*

het|er|oph|o|ny (het′ə rof′ə nē), *n. Music.* limited polyphony in which the two or more parts differ only slightly. [< *hetero-* + Greek *phōnē* sound]

het|er|o|pho|ri|a (het′ər ə fôr′ē ə, -fōr′-), *n.* a tendency of the eye to squint or move from its normal position, due to improper muscle function. [< New Latin *heterophoria* < Greek *héteros* different + *phórein* to bear]

het|er|o|phyl|lous (het′ər ə fil′əs), *adj.* bearing different kinds of leaves on the same plant. [< *hetero-* + Greek *phýllon* leaf + English *-ous*]

het|er|o|phyl|ly (het′ər ə fil′ē), *n.* the condition of being heterophyllous.

het|er|o|pla|sia (het′ər ə plā′zhə), *n.* the formation of tissue different from the normal tissue.

het|er|o|plas|ty (het′ər ə plas′tē), *n.* **1** the surgical repairing of wounds or diseased parts with tissue taken from another individual. **2** = heteroplasia. [< *hetero-* + Greek *plastós* something molded]

het|er|o|ploid (het′ər ə ploid), *adj.* having a chromosome number that is not the exact multiple of the haploid number of chromosomes of the species.

het|er|o|po|lar (het′ər ə pō′lər), *adj. Chemistry.* having a distribution of charge which is unequal, as in a semipolar bond.

het|er|op|ter|an (het′ə rop′tər ən), *adj., n.* **—*adj.*** = heteropterous. **—*n.*** a heteropterous insect. [< *hetero-* + Greek *pterón* wing + English *-an*]

het|er|op|ter|ous (het′ə rop′tər əs), *adj.* **1** of or having to do with the order of hemipterous insects that comprises the true bugs. **2** having wings composed of distinct parts; hemipterous.

het|er|o|sce|das|tic (het′ər ə si das′tik), *adj. Statistics.* showing unequal variability; not showing the same standard deviation: *a heteroscedastic distribution.* [< *hetero-* + Greek *skédastikós* that can be scattered]

het|er|o|sex|ism (het′ər ə sek′siz əm), *n. U.S.* discrimination against homosexuals. [blend of *heterosexual* and *sexism*]

het|er|o|sex|u|al (het′ər ə sek′shü əl), *adj., n.* **—*adj.*** **1** *Biology.* of or having to do with the different sexes. **2** having to do with or manifesting sexual feeling for a person of the opposite sex. **—*n.*** a heterosexual person. **—het′er|o|sex′u|al|ly,** *adv.*

het|er|o|sex|u|al|i|ty (het′ər ə sek′shü al′ə tē), *n.* **1** sexual feeling for a person of the opposite sex. **2** sexual behavior toward a person of the opposite sex.

het|er|o|sis (het′ə rō′sis), *n. Genetics.* an increase in vigor of growth, fertility, size, or other characteristics, resulting from crossbreeding; hybrid vigor. [< New Latin *heterosis* < Greek *heterōsis* alteration < *héteros* another, different]

het|er|o|sphere (het′ər ə sfēr′), *n.* the part of the atmosphere, beginning at a height of about 50 miles and extending indefinitely, that is made up of several layers, each differing markedly in chemical composition from the others.

het|er|os|po|rous (het′ə ros′pər əs; -ər ə spôr′-, -spōr′-), *adj. Botany.* having more than one kind of asexual spores.

het|er|os|po|ry (het′ə ros′pər ē), *n. Botany.* the production of more than one kind of spores.

het|er|o|struc|ture (het′ər ə struk′chər), *n.* a semiconducting device made up of several different types of semiconductors, used in lasers; heterojunction: *Minute sandwich-like "heterostructures" composed of two or more different semiconducting materials show great promise as cheap, efficient carrier-wave generators for use in mass communications* (Scientific American).

het|er|o|tac|tic (het′ər ə tak′tik), *adj.* characterized by or exhibiting heterotaxis.

het|er|o|tax|i|a (het′ər ə tak′sē ə), *n.* = heterotaxis.

het|er|o|tax|ic (het′ər ə tak′sik), *adj.* = heterotactic.

het|er|o|tax|is (het′ər ə tak′sis), *n.* abnormal or irregular arrangement of parts, as of the body or

---

Pronunciation Key: hat, āge, cãre, fär; let, ēqual, tėrm; it, īce; hot, ōpen, ôrder; oil, out; cup, pu̇t, rüle; child; long; thin; ᴛʜen; zh, measure; ə represents **a** in about, **e** in taken, **i** in pencil, **o** in lemon, **u** in circus.

of geological strata. [< *hetero-* + Greek *táxis* arrangement]

het|er|o|tax|y (het′ər ə tak′sē), *n.* = heterotaxis.

het|er|o|thal|lic (het′ər ə thal′ik), *adj. Botany.* having two distinct kinds of mycelium, which act as male and female. [< *hetero-* + Greek *thallós* young shoot (< *thállein* to bloom) + English *-ic*]

het|er|o|thal|lism (het′ər ə thal′iz əm), *n.* the condition of being heterothallic.

het|er|o|thal|ly (het′ər ə thal′ē), *n.* = heterothallism.

het|er|o|therm (het′ər ə thėrm), *n.* = poikilotherm.

het|er|o|ther|mal (het′ər ə thėr′məl), *adj.* poikilothermal; cold-blooded.

het|er|ot|ic (het′ə rot′ik), *adj.* of or characterized by heterosis.

het|er|o|to|pi|a (het′ər ə tō′pē ə), *n. Medicine.* displacement in position of an organ or part. [< New Latin *heterotopia* < Greek *héteros* different + *tópos* place]

het|er|o|top|ic (het′ər ə top′ik), *adj.* characterized by or exhibiting heterotopia.

het|er|ot|o|pism (het′ə rot′ə piz əm), *n.* = heterotopia.

het|er|ot|o|pous (het′ə rot′ə pəs), *adj.* = heterotopic.

het|er|ot|o|py (het′ə rot′ə pē), *n.* = heterotopia.

het|er|o|troph (het′ər ə trof), *n.* an organism that cannot manufacture its own food, but is dependent upon complex organic substances for nutrition. Animals and some plants, such as fungi, are heterotrophs.

het|er|o|troph|ic (het′ər ə trof′ik), *adj.* of or having to do with a heterotroph. Heterotrophic plants live as parasites on other plants or on decaying organic matter. [< *hetero-* + Greek *trophḗ* nourishment + English *-ic*]

het|er|o|typ|ic (het′ər ə tip′ik), *adj. Biology.* of the first stages of meiosis in a cell, during which the chromosomes appear to be reduced from the diploid to the haploid number.

het|er|o|zy|go|sis (het′ər ə zī gō′sis), *n.* = heterozygosity.

het|er|o|zy|gos|i|ty (het′ər ə zī gos′ə tē), *n.* the condition of having developed from a heterozygote; development from a heterozygote.

het|er|o|zy|gote (het′ər ə zī′gōt, -zig′ōt), *n. Genetics.* an animal or plant whose chromosomes contain both genes of an opposed pair and which, therefore, does not always breed true to type.

het|er|o|zy|gous (het′ər ə zī′gəs), *adj.* of or having to do with a heterozygote.

heth (ʜet, ʜeth, ʜes), *n.* the eighth letter of the Hebrew alphabet. Also, **cheth**. [< Hebrew *heth*]

het|man (het′mən), *n., pl.* **-mans**. a Cossack leader or chief. [< Polish *hetman* < Middle High German *heuptman* captain]

heu|land|ite (hyü′lən dīt), *n.* a hydrated silicate of aluminum and calcium, found in crystals of various colors with pearly luster. *Formula:* $CaO \cdot Al_2O_3 \cdot 6SiO_2 \cdot 5H_2O$ [< Henry *Heuland,* an English mineralogist of the 1800's + *ite*[1]]

he|u|mite (hā′ü mīt), *n.* a dark, aphanitic, igneous rock resembling nephelinite. [< *Heum,* a place in Norway where it is found + *-ite*[1]]

Heu|ri|gen (hoi′ri gən), *n. German.* an Austrian wine garden or tavern.

Heu|ri|ger (hoi′ri gər), *n. German.* **1** Austrian wine of the current year. **2** a place where such wine is sold; Heurigen. **3** (literally) this year's.

heu|rism (hyůr′iz əm), *n.* the principles of heuristic teaching.

heu|ris|tic (hyů ris′tik), *adj.* serving to find out or discover; leading to or stimulating investigation or research: *heuristic teaching. What methods will lead students to become more inquisitive, flexible, heuristic, which, in turn, would lead to scientific creativity?* (New York Times). [< Greek *heur-*, root of *heurískein* to find + English *-ist* + *-ic*] **—heu|ris′ti|cal|ly,** *adv.*

heu|ris|tics (hyů ris′tiks), *n.* **1** the study or use of discovery procedures in science. **2** a heuristic approach or procedure: *The rules are not necessarily rules of logic; various strategies, or heuristics, may be available for different types of problems* (Scientific American).

he|ve|a (hē′vē ə), *n.* a tropical tree of the spurge family, the source of natural rubber; rubber tree. [< New Latin *Hevea* the genus name < a native word in Ecuador]

hew (hyü), *v.,* **hewed, hewed** or **hewn, hew|ing.** —*v.t.* **1** to cut with an ax, sword, or the like; fell by cutting; chop: *He hewed down the tree.* **2** to cut into shape; form by cutting with an ax, hammer and chisel, or other tool: *to hew stone for building. They hewed the logs into beams.* **3** to make or produce with cutting blows: *The knight hewed his way through the enemy.*
—*v.i.* to make cutting blows with an ax, sword, or the like.

hew to, to hold firmly to; stick fast or cling to: *to hew to the rules.*
[Old English *hēawan*] **—hew′er,** *n.*

HEW (no periods), Health, Education, and Welfare (a former department of the U.S. government).

hewn (hyün), *v.* hewed; a past participle of **hew**.

hex (heks), *v., n. U.S.* —*v.t.* to practice witchcraft on; bewitch.
—*n.* **1** a witch. **2** a magic spell: *Maybe there's a hex on the number five, because Big Pete rang up that many firsts before he ran second to Mr. Brick . . . at Monmouth last month* (Audax Minor). [American English < Pennsylvania Dutch *hex* < German *Hexe* witch]

hex-, *combining form.* the form of **hexa-** before vowels, as in *hexose.*

hexa-, *combining form.* **1** six: *Hexagon = a polygon having six sides.*
2 having six atoms of a specified substance: *Hexose = a simple sugar having six atoms of carbon.* [< Greek *hexa-* < *héx* six]

hex|a|ba|sic (hek′sə bā′sik), *adj. Chemistry.* **1** having six hydrogen atoms that can be replaced by basic atoms or radicals: *a hexabasic acid.* **2** having six atoms or radicals of a univalent metal.

hex|a|chlo|ro|ben|zene (hek′sə klôr′ə ben′zēn, -klōr′-), *n.* a compound combining a hydrocarbon with a chloride, used especially in organic synthesis and in the treatment of grain seeds. *Formula:* C_6Cl_6 [< *hexa-* + *chlor*(ine) + *benzene*]

hex|a|chlo|ro|eth|ane (hek′sə klôr′ə eth′ān, -klōr′-), *n.* a highly toxic, colorless, crystalline compound, used in smoke devices and explosives, in organic synthesis, and as a retarding agent and solvent. *Formula:* C_2Cl_6

hex|a|chlo|ro|phene (hek′sə klôr′ə fēn, -klōr′-), *n.* a germicide used in soap. *Formula:* $C_{13}H_6Cl_6O_2$ [< *hexa-* + *chlor*(ine) + *phen*(yl)]

hex|a|chord (hek′sə kôrd), *n. Music.* **1** a diatonic series of six tones which, in medieval music, had an interval of a half step between the third and fourth and of whole steps between the others. **2** an instrument having six strings. [< Late Greek *hexáchordos* < *hexa-* (< *héx* six) + *chordḗ* string, chord[1]]

hex|act (hek′sakt), *adj., n.* —*adj.* having six rays. —*n.* a sponge spicule having six rays. [< *hex-* + Greek *aktís* ray]

hex|ad (hek′sad), *n.* **1** a series of six; a group of six. **2** *Chemistry.* an element, atom, or radical with a valence of six. [< Greek *hexás, -ádos* (a group of) six, the number six < *héx* six]

hex|a|dec|a|drol (hek′sə dek′ə drōl, -drol), *n.* a steroid drug similar to cortisone, used to treat arthritis. *Formula:* $C_{22}H_{29}FO_5$

hex|a|de|ca|nol (heks′ə dē′kə nōl, -nol), *n.* = cetyl alcohol.

hex|a|dec|i|mal (hek′sə des′ə məl), *adj.* using the decimal number 16 or its equivalent as a base, especially in computer arithmetic systems: *The hexadecimal numeral system . . . as contrasted with the base 10 of the decimal system and base 2 of the binary system* (R. Clay Sprowl). [< *hexa-* + *decimal*]

hex|ad|ic (hek sad′ik), *adj.* of or having to do with the number six as a base in counting; increasing by sixes.

hex|a|em|er|ic (hek′sə em′ər ik), *adj.* having to do with the six days of Creation. Also, **hexahemeric.**

hex|a|em|er|on (hek′sə em′ər on), *n.* **1** the six days of the Creation of the world. **2** a history of the period, such as the one in Genesis. **3** a treatise on the Biblical account of Creation. Also, **hexahemeron.** [< Late Latin *hexaēmeron* < Greek *hexaḗmeron,* neuter of *hexaḗmeros* of six days < *héx* six + *hēméra* day]

***hex|a|gon** (hek′sə gon), *n.* a plane figure having six angles and six sides. [< Latin *hexagōnum* < Greek *hexágōnon,* neuter of *hexágōnos* hexagonal, ultimately < *héx* six + *gōníā* angle]

***hexagon**
***hexagram**
definition 1
***hexahedron**

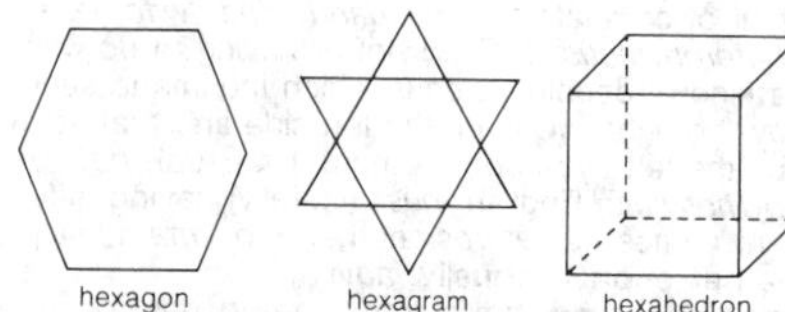

hex|ag|o|nal (hek sag′ə nəl), *adj.* **1** having the form of a hexagon. **2** having a hexagon as base or cross section: *a hexagonal pyramid.* **3** of a hexagon. **4** divided into hexagons: *a hexagonal surface.* **5** *Crystallography.* of or belonging to the hexagonal system. **—hex|ag′o|nal|ly,** *adv.*

hexagonal system, *Crystallography.* a system of crystallization with lateral axes, normally inclined to each other at 60 degrees, and a vertical axis at right angles to these and differing from them in length.

***hex|a|gram** (hek′sə gram), *n.* **1** a six-pointed star formed of two equilateral triangles. **2** *Geometry.* a figure formed by six intersecting lines. **3** a figure of six parallel lines used in various combinations in Chinese divination. [< *hexa-* + Greek *grámma* line]

hex|a|he|dral (hek′sə hē′drəl), *adj.* having six sides; like a hexahedron.

***hex|a|he|dron** (hek′sə hē′drən), *n., pl.* **-drons, -dra** (-drə). a solid figure having six faces. [< Greek *hexáedron,* neuter of *hexáedros* < *hexa-* (< *héx* six) + *hédrā* base, surface]

hex|a|hem|er|ic (hek′sə hem′ər ik), *adj.* = hexaemeric.

hex|a|hem|er|on (hek′sə hem′ər on), *n.* = hexaemeron.

hex|a|hy|drate (hek′sə hī′drāt), *n.* a compound having six molecules of water.

hex|a|hy|dric (hek′sə hī′drik), *adj. Chemistry.* having six hydroxyl (—OH) radicals.

hex|am|er|ism (hek sam′ə riz əm), *n.* hexamerous condition.

hex|am|er|ous (hek sam′ər əs), *adj.* **1** *Zoology.* having the radiating parts or organs numbering six or a multiple of six. **2** (of a flower) having six members in each whorl (usually written *6-merous*). [< *hexa-* + Greek *méros* part]

hex|am|e|ter (hek sam′ə tər), *n., adj.* —*n.* **1** a line of poetry consisting of six feet or measures. *Example:* "This' is the/ for'est pri/ me'val. The/ mur'muring/ pines' and the/ hem'locks." **2** (in Greek and Latin epic poetry) a line of six feet, of which the first four may be dactyls or spondees, the fifth is a dactyl, and the sixth is a spondee or trochee. A line in this form is dactylic hexameter.
—*adj.* consisting of six feet or measures to a line of poetry. [< Latin *hexameter* < Greek *hexámetros* < *hexa-* (< *héx* six) + *métron* measure]

hex|a|me|tho|ni|um (hek′sə me thō′nē əm), *n.* a ganglionic blocking agent used to treat high blood pressure. [< *hexa-* + *meth*(yl) + (amm)*onium*]

hex|a|meth|yl|ene|te|tram|in (hek′sə meth′ə lēn te tram′in), *n.* = hexamethylenetetramine.

hex|a|meth|yl|ene|tet|ra|mine (hek′sə meth′ə lēn tet′rə mēn′), *n.* a white or colorless, crystalline compound, used in medicine as a urinary antiseptic, as an absorbent of phosgene in gas masks, in vulcanizing rubber, and in making synthetic resins. *Formula:* $C_6H_{12}N_4$

hex|am|e|tral (hek sam′ə trəl), *adj.* = hexametric.

hex|a|met|ric (hek′sə met′rik), *adj.* consisting of hexameters. **—hex′a|met′ri|cal,** *adj.*

hex|am|i|ti|a|sis (hek sam′ə tī′ə sis), *n.* a highly fatal disease of young domestic fowl, caused by a protozoan parasite. [< New Latin *Hexamita* the parasite genus name + English *-iasis*]

hex|ane (hek′sān, hek sān′), *n.* any one of five colorless, volatile, liquid isomeric hydrocarbons of the methane series, derived from petroleum and used as solvents. *Formula:* C_6H_{14} [< *hex-* + *-ane*]

hex|an|gu|lar (hek sang′gyə lər), *adj.* having six angles.

hex|a|ploid (hek′sə ploid), *adj. Genetics.* having six times the haploid set of chromosomes in the somatic cells.

hex|a|pod (hek′sə pod), *n., adj.* —*n.* a true insect; an arthropod having six feet.
—*adj.* having six feet.
[< Greek *hexápous, -podos* < *hexa-* (< *héx* six) + *poús, podós* foot]

hex|ap|o|dous (hek sap′ə dəs), *adj.* having six feet; having to do with a hexapod.

hex|ap|o|dy (hek sap′ə dē), *n., pl.* **-dies**. a line or verse consisting of six metrical feet.

hex|a|ra|di|al (hek′sə rā′dē əl), *adj.* having six radii.

hex|arch (hek′särk), *adj., n. Botany.* —*adj.* having six strands. —*n.* a stele having six strands. [< *hex-* + Greek *archḗ* a beginning]

hex|ar|chy (hek′sär kē), *n., pl.* **-chies**. a group of six states, each under its own ruler. [< *hex-* + Greek *-archíā* empire < *árchein* to rule]

hex|a|stich (hek′sə stik), *n.* a group of six lines or verses forming a stanza, strophe, or poem. [< New Latin *hexastichon* < Greek *hexástichon,* neuter of *hexástichos* of six verses < *hexa-* (< *héx* six) + *stíchos* row (of verse)]

hex|a|stich|ic (hek′sə stik′ik), *adj.* of six metrical lines.

hex|as|ti|chon (hek sas′tə kon), *n., pl.* **-cha** (-kə). = hexastich.

hex|a|style (hek′sə stīl), *adj., n.* —*adj.* having six columns in front, as a temple or a portico.
—*n.* a hexastyle structure.
[< Greek *hexástȳlos* < *hexa-* (< *héx* six) + *stylos* pillar]

Hex|a|teuch (hek′sə tük, -tyük), *n.* the first six books of the Old Testament, consisting of Genesis, Exodus, Leviticus, Numbers, Deuteronomy, and Joshua. [< German *Hexateuch* < Greek *hexa-* (< *héx* six) + *teûchos* book, instrument; patterned on *Pentateuch*]

hex|a|tom|ic (hek′sə tom′ik), *adj. Chemistry.* **1** having six atoms in the molecule. **2** containing six replaceable atoms or groups.

hex|a|va|lent (hek′sə vā′lənt, hek sav′ə-), *adj. Chemistry.* having a valence of six.

hex|en|be|sen (hek′sən bā′zən), *n.* = witches'-broom. [< German *Hexenbesen* < *Hexe* witch + *Besen* broom, besom]

hex|ite (hek′sīt), *n.* an alcohol containing six hydroxyl groups. [< *hex-* + *-ite*[1]]

hex|o|bar|bi|tal (hek′sō bär′bə tôl, -tal), *n.* a white, crystalline sedative and hypnotic drug, used also in the form of the sodium derivative as an anesthetic in surgery. *Formula:* $C_{12}H_{16}N_2O_3$

hex|oc|ta|he|dral (hek sok′tə hē′drəl), *adj.* having 48 equal triangular sides; like a hexoctahedron.

hex|oc|ta|he|dron (hek sok′tə hē′drən), *n., pl.* **-drons, -dra** (-drə). an isometric crystal with 48 equal triangular sides.

hex|ode (hek′sōd), *adj.* of or having to do with a system of telegraphy in which six messages can be sent simultaneously over the same wire. [< *hex-* + Greek *hodós* way]

hex|o|gen (hek′sə jən), *n.* = RDX.

hex|o|ki|nase (hek′sō kī′nās, -kin′ās), *n.* an enzyme which catalyzes the formation of adenosine diphosphate from adenosine triphosphate: *The first step in the metabolism of glucose in animal tissues . . . involves the interaction between glucose and ATP under the influence of the enzyme hexokinase* (New Scientist).

hex|one (hek′sōn), *n.* any one of a group of organic bases that contain six carbon atoms in the molecule. [< *hex-* + *-one*]

hex|os|a|min|i|dase (hek′sō min′ə dās), *n.* either one of a pair of enzymes, a deficiency of which causes various degenerative diseases of the central nervous system, including Tay-Sachs disease.

hex|o|san (hek′sə san), *n.* any one of several hemicelluloses that yield hexoses on hydrolysis.

hex|ose (hek′sōs), *n.* any one of a class of simple sugars that contain six carbon atoms in the molecule, such as glucose and fructose.

hex|o|side (hek′sə sīd), *n.* a glycoside derived from a hexose.

hex sign, a sign or mark, usually triangular, put by the Pennsylvania Dutch on barns or other buildings as a protection against evil spells.

hex|yl (hek′səl), *n.* a univalent hydrocarbon radical (C_6H_{13}) derived from hexane.

hex|yl|res|or|cin|ol (hek′səl re zôr′sə nōl, -nol), *n.* a pale-yellow, crystalline compound, used to treat infections by intestinal worms, such as the tapeworm and hookworm. *Formula:* $C_{12}H_{18}O_2$

hey (hā), *interj.* a sound made to attract attention, to express surprise or other feeling, or to ask a question: *Hey! Stop! Hey! what did you say?* [Middle English *hei;* perhaps imitative]

hey|day (hā′dā′), *n., interj.* **—*n.*** the period of greatest strength, vigor, spirits, prosperity, or other quality or condition: *After years of emptiness and dullness and suppression, she* [*Queen Victoria*] *had come suddenly, in the heyday of youth, into freedom and power* (Lytton Strachey).
—*interj.* exclamation of cheerfulness or wonder. [origin uncertain]

Hey|duc or **Hey|duck** or **Hey|duke** (hī′du̇k), *n.* = Haiduk.

He|ze|ki|ah (hez′ə kī′ə), *n.* a king of Judah (in the Bible, II Kings 18-19 and Isaiah 36-37).

hf., half.

h.f., **1** high fidelity. **2** high-frequency.

Hf (no period), hafnium (chemical element).

Hf (no periods) or **H.F.**, **1** high fidelity. **2** high-frequency.

hg., hectogram.

Hg (no period), mercury (chemical element). [abbreviation or symbol for *hydrargyrum*]

HG (no periods), High German.

H.G., **1** Her Grace. **2** His Grace. **3** Home Guard.

HGH (no periods) or **H.G.H.**, human growth hormone.

hgt., height.

H.H., **1** Her Highness. **2** His Highness. **3** His Holiness.

hhd., hogshead.

HHFA (no periods), or **H.H.F.A.**, Housing and Home Finance Agency.

H-hour (āch′our′), *n.* the prearranged time for beginning an attack; zero hour: *They synchronized their watches and headed for the store, took their positions, and waited impatiently for H-hour* (Time). [< *H,* the first letter of *hour.* Compare etym. under **D-day.**]

HHS (no periods), Health and Human Services (a department of the U.S. Government).

hi (hī), *interj., n.* a call of greeting; hello. [Middle English *hy,* variant of *hei* hey]

HI (no periods), **1** Hawaiian Islands (with postal Zip Code). **2** hospital insurance.

H.I., Hawaiian Islands.

hi|a|tal (hī ā′təl), *adj.* of or having to do with a hiatus or opening.

hiatal hernia, hiatus hernia.

hi|a|tus (hī ā′təs), *n., pl.* **-tus|es** or **-tus. 1** an empty space; space that needs to be filled; gap. A lost or erased part of a manuscript is a hiatus. *After the accident there was a hiatus of several hours in his memory of that day's events. There was a long hiatus in the talk filled in with private thoughts* (New Yorker). **2** *Grammar, Prosody.* a slight pause between two vowels that come together in successive syllables or words, such as between the *e's* in *preeminent.* **3** *Anatomy.* an opening: *the hiatus of the facial canal.* [< Latin *hĭātus, -ūs* gap < *hiāre* gape]

hiatus hernia, a hernia, usually of part of the stomach, protruding through an opening in the diaphragm into the esophagus.

Hi|a|wath|a (hī′ə woth′ə, hē′-), *n.* the young Indian brave who is the hero of Henry W. Longfellow's poem *The Song of Hiawatha.*

***hi|ba|chi** (hi bä′chē), *n., pl.* **-chi** or **-chis.** a small, portable, potlike container, covered by a grill, used for burning charcoal for cooking or heating; brazier. [< Japanese *hibachi* < *hi* fire + *bachi* bowl, pot]

***hibachi**

Japanese

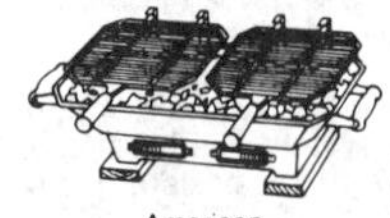

American

hi|ba|ku|sha (hi bä′kü shə), *n. sing. or pl.* a survivor or survivors of the atomic explosions that destroyed Hiroshima and Nagasaki in 1945. [< Japanese *hibakusha*]

hi|ber|nac|le (hī′bər nak′əl), *n.* = hibernaculum (def. 2a.).

hi|ber|nac|u|lum (hī′bər nak′yə ləm), *n., pl.* **-la** (-lə). **1** *Botany.* a bud or bulb that protects a plant embryo during the winter. **2** *Zoology.* **a** a place where an animal hibernates during the winter. **b** an encysted winter bud of a bryozoan that germinates in the following spring. [< Latin *hībernāculum* winter quarters (diminutive) < *hīberna* winter quarters, neuter plural of *hībernus* wintry < *hiems, hiemis* winter]

hi|ber|nal (hī bėr′nəl), *adj.* of or having to do with winter; wintry. [< Latin *hībernālis* < *hībernus* wintry < *hiems, hiemis* winter]

hi|ber|nate (hī′bər nāt), *v.i.,* **-nat|ed, -nat|ing. 1** *Zoology.* to spend a period, either during a whole season or during periods of severe weather, in a state of deep sleep, especially one marked by a distinct lowering of metabolism and body temperature, as bears, woodchucks, and some other wild animals do: *During long, severe winters some animals, such as badgers, ground squirrels, and some insects, hibernate* (Harbaugh and Goodrich). **2a** to spend the winter; winter: *to hibernate in the warm South.* **b** to spend any period in a sleeplike state: *Some bats hibernate every day and become active again every night* (A. R. Dawe). **3** *Figurative.* to be or remain inactive: *Inclination would lead me to hibernate during half the year* (Robert Southey). *Latin hasn't died or even extensively hibernated* (Harper's). [< Latin *hībernāre* (with English *-ate*[1]) < *hībernus* wintry < *hiems, hiemis* winter]

hi|ber|na|tion (hī′bər nā′shən), *n.* the act or state of hibernating: *True hibernation, such as is found in ground squirrels and marmots, is a state of death-like sleep, wherein the animal's breath and pulse almost stop and its temperature drops to a point very little above that of its environment* (Science News Letter). (*Figurative.*) *The politicos come straggling back from their summer hibernation* (Punch).

hi|ber|na|tor (hī′bər nā′tər), *n.* an animal that hibernates, such as the woodchuck.

Hi|ber|ni|a (hī bėr′nē ə), *n.* Ireland. [< Latin *Hibernia,* alteration of *Iverna, Iuverna* < Celtic (compare Old Irish *Erinn,* accusative of *Eriu* Erin)]

Hi|ber|ni|an (hī bėr′nē ən), *adj., n.* **—*adj.*** Irish.
—*n.* a native of Ireland; an Irishman.

Hi|ber|ni|an|ism (hī bėr′nē ə niz′əm), *n.* **1** Irish nationality or character. **2** an Irish characteristic, trait, or idiom.

Hi|ber|ni|cism (hī bėr′nə siz əm), *n.* **1** an Irish characteristic, idiom, or turn of speech. **2** the condition or quality of being Irish; Irish nationality.

hi|bis|cus (hə bis′kəs, hī-), *n., pl.* **-cus** or **-cus|es.** any one of a group of plants, shrubs, or trees with large, red, pink, or white, bell-shaped flowers; rose mallow. Hibiscus belongs to the mallow family. The blossom of one kind is the state flower of Hawaii. *In southern gardens hibiscus are planted as hedges which grow four to six feet tall and are covered with bloom, or as specimen shrubs as much as twenty feet high* (New York Times). [< Latin *hibiscus* < Greek *ibiskos*]

hic (hik), *interj.* the sound of a hiccup, written especially to mark such an interruption in the speech of a drunken person.

hic|cough (hik′up, -əp), *n., v.i., v.t.* = hiccup.

hic|cup (hik′up, -əp), *n., v.,* **-cuped, -cup|ing** or **-cupped, -cup|ping. —*n.* 1** an involuntary catching of the breath. A hiccup occurs when the glottis suddenly closes, accompanied by a sharp, clicklike sound, caused by a muscular spasm of the diaphragm. **2** *Figurative.* a short-lived decline or disruption: *The managers took advantage of the recent hiccup in the market to buy the dividend units at a lower price* (London Times).
—*v.i.* 1 to have the hiccups. **2** to make the sound of a hiccup: *His face revealing an alcoholic stupor, Lonigan hiccupped* (James T. Farrell).
—*v.t.* to utter or bring out with hiccups: (*Figurative.*) *The ubiquitous car . . . hiccups its way through crowded cobbled streets* (Punch).
hiccups, the condition of having one hiccup after another: *She tried to stop her hiccups by breathing into a paper bag.*
[earlier *hicket, hickock;* probably imitative]

hic ja|cet (hik jā′sit), **1** *Latin.* here lies. **2** an epitaph: *the cold hic jacets of the dead* (Tennyson).

hick (hik) *n., adj. Informal.* **—*n.* 1** a person who lives in the country, in a small town, or in a backward community; unsophisticated person: *I come from a small town and that makes me a hick. My opinions aren't worth much.* (H. L. Wilson). **2** a farmer; countryman.
—*adj.* of, like, or full of hicks: *"The city," he said then, "can't remain a hick town forever"* (Maclean's).
[< *Hick,* a nickname for *Richard,* a man's name]

hick|ey (hik′ē), *n., pl.* **-eys. 1** *Informal.* a dingus; gadget. **2** a fitting for attaching an electric fixture to an outlet box. **3** a T-shaped instrument used to bend a conduit. **4** *Informal.* a pimple or other red mark on the skin. [American English; origin uncertain]

***hick|o|ry** (hik′ər ē, hik′rē), *n., pl.* **-ries,** *adj.* **—*n.* 1** any one of a group of North American trees bearing a hard nut that is good to eat. The hickory belongs to the walnut family. **2** its tough, hard wood. **3** a switch, stick, or rod made of this wood.
—*adj.* made of hickory.
[American English alteration of Algonkian (perhaps Powhatan) *pohickery* and other similar Algonkian words for a species of walnut]

***hickory** definition 1

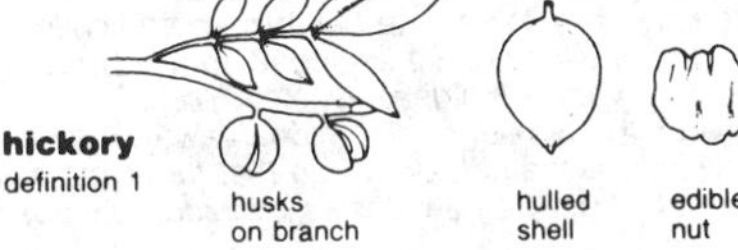

hickory nut, the nut of the hickory.

hickory pine, bristlecone pine.

Hicks|ite (hik′sīt), *n.* a member of a group of American Quakers, founded by Elias Hicks (1748-1830), that held Socinian doctrines: *The Hicksites broke away from the Orthodox Quakers, taking their stand for a personal questing approach to the Bible* (Saturday Review).

hick|wall (hik′wôl′), *n.* = green woodpecker. [probably imitative of its cry]

hick|y (hik′ē), *n., pl.* **hick|ies.** = hickey.

hid (hid), *v.* a past tense and a past participle of **hide**[1]: *The dog hid his bone. The money was hid in a safe place.*

hi|dal|go (hi dal′gō), *n., pl.* **-gos.** a Spanish nobleman ranking below a grandee. [< Spanish *hidalgo* < Old Spanish *hijo de algo* son of something (that is, someone important)]

Hi|dat|sa (hi dät′sä), *n., pl.* **-sa** or **-sas. 1** a member of a Siouan tribe of American Indians that practiced agriculture, located in the Missouri Valley and often associated with the Arikara; Minitari. **2** the language of this tribe.

hid|den (hid′ən), *adj., v.* **—*adj.*** put or kept out of sight; not clear; concealed; secret; mysterious; obscure: *The story is about hidden treasure.* SYN: covert, clandestine, occult, esoteric, latent.
—*v.* a past participle of **hide**[1]: *The moon was hidden behind a dark cloud.*

Pronunciation Key: **hat, āge, cãre, fär; let, ēqual, tėrm; it, īce; hot, ōpen, ôrder; oil, out; cup, pu̇t, rüle; child; long; thin; ᴛʜen; zh,** measure; **ə** represents **a** in about, **e** in taken, **i** in pencil, **o** in lemon, **u** in circus.

hidden hunger, an unfelt deficiency in nutrition caused by consumption of an inadequate diet over a long period of time.

hid|den|ite (hid′ə nīt), *n.* a transparent, emerald-green variety of spodumene, sometimes used as a gem. [American English < William E. *Hidden,* 1832-1918, an American mineralogist, who discovered it + *-ite*¹]

hidden tax, an indirect tax; a tax paid by a person in a form other than conventional taxes.

hide¹ (hīd), *v.,* **hid, hid|den** or **hid, hid|ing,** *n.* **—*v.t.*** **1** to put or keep out of sight; conceal: *Hide it where no one else will know of it or know where it is.* **2** to cover up; shut off from sight; be in front of: *Clouds hide the sun. . . . a huge town, continuous and compact, Hiding the face of earth for leagues* (Wordsworth). **3** to keep secret: *She hid her disappointment.* **4** to turn away: *Hide not thine ear at my breathing, at my cry* (Lamentations 3:56).
—*v.i.* to hide oneself; lie concealed: *I'll hide, and you find me.*
—*n.* *British.* a hiding place used in hunting game or in bird watching.
[Old English *hȳdan*]
—*Syn.* *v.t.* **1 Hide, conceal** mean to put or keep out of sight. **Hide** is the general word: *I hid the present under my bed.* **Conceal** is more formal and usually suggests conscious purpose: *She concealed the note in her dress.*

hide² (hīd), *n., v.,* **hid|ed, hid|ing.** **—*n.*** **1** the skin of an animal, either raw or tanned. Leather is made from the hides of cattle. SYN: See syn. under **skin. 2** *Informal.* **a** a person's skin: *He tried to save his own hide by putting the blame on us. He was lucky to emerge from the fight with a whole hide.* **b** life: *The bachelor may risk 'is 'ide To 'elp you when you're downed; But the married man will wait beside Till the ambulance comes round* (Rudyard Kipling).
—*v.t.* **1** to remove the hide from. **2** *Informal.* to beat; thrash. SYN: flog.
neither hide nor hair, nothing at all; nothing whatever: *He gambled until there was left neither hide nor hair of his former wealth.*
[Old English *hȳd*]

hide³ (hīd), *n.* an old English measure of land, usually about 120 acres. [Old English *hīd,* or *hīgid*]

hide-and-go-seek (hīd′ən gō sēk′), *n.* = hide-and-seek.

hide-and-seek (hīd′ən sēk′), *n.* a children's game in which all but one hide and the one tries to find them: *The ragged boys . . . played . . . hide-and-seek among the tombstones* (Dickens).

hide|a|way (hīd′ə wā′), *n., adj.* **—*n.*** **1** a place in which to hide; a place of concealment: *Many an early settler's home had a hideaway built around the chimney to secrete the women and children of the household.* **2** a secluded spot; retreat: *a private vacation hideaway* (New Yorker).
—*adj.* **1** that is or can be hidden away: *a hideaway valley, a hideaway bed that turns into a couch.* **2** used as a hideaway: *a hideaway apartment.*

hide|bound (hīd′bound′), *adj.* **1** narrow-minded and stubborn: *He was too hidebound to accept new ideas even when they were good. The hidebound humor which he calls his judgement* (Milton). SYN: bigoted. **2** having the skin sticking close to the back and ribs. **3** (of a tree) having the bark so close or unyielding as to hinder growth.

hid|e|os|i|ty (hid′ē os′ə tē), *n., pl.* **-ties. 1** a hideous thing: *There were paintings of ugliness, of contrived hideosities . . .* (New Yorker). **2** = hideousness.

hid|e|ous (hid′ē əs), *adj.* **1** very ugly; frightful; horrible: *a hideous monster.* **2** terrible; revolting; abominable: *a hideous crime.* SYN: repulsive. [< Anglo-French *hidous,* Old French *hideus, hidos* < *hide, hisde* horror, fear, perhaps < a Germanic word]—**hid′e|ous|ly,** *adv.* —**hid′e|ous|ness,** *n.*

hide|out or **hide-out** (hīd′out′), *n.* a place for hiding or being alone: *"For security reasons," they moved $380,000 to another hideout the same night but did not divide the loot until weeks later* (Newsweek).

hid|er (hī′dər), *n.* a person who hides.

hide|y-hole (hī′dē hōl′), *n. Informal.* a hiding place; hideout: *A desperate man will seek refuge in the flimsiest hidey-hole* (Leslie March).

hid|ing¹ (hī′ding), *n.* **1** the state of being hidden; concealment: *The fox remained in hiding.* **2** a place to hide.

hid|ing² (hī′ding), *n. Informal.* a beating; thrashing.

hi|dro|sis (hi drō′sis), *n.* **1** sweating, especially excessive sweating. **2** a skin disease characterized by excessive sweating. [probably < New Latin *hidrosis* < Greek *hidrōsis* < *hidrôn* to sweat < *hidrôs* sweat]

hi|drot|ic (hi drot′ik), *adj., n.* **—*adj.*** of, having to do with, or causing sweat or perspiration.
—*n.* a hidrotic agent or medicine.
[< Medieval Latin *hidroticus* < Greek *hidrōtikós* < *hidrôs* sweat]

hid|y-hole (hī′dē hōl′), *n.* = hidey-hole.

hie (hī), *v.,* **hied, hie|ing** or **hy|ing.** **—*v.i.*** to go quickly; hasten; hurry; speed.
—*v.t.* to cause to hasten: *to hie oneself to work. This reviewer suggests that the beginner hie herself to a good teacher before she gets in real trouble* (Saturday Review).
[Old English *hīgian* strive, pant]

hi|e|mal (hī′ə məl), *adj.* of or belonging to winter; occurring in winter: *the hiemal solstice.* [< Latin *hiemālis* < *hiems, hiemis* winter]

hi|er|arch (hī′ə rärk), *n.* a chief priest or church official; person who has rule or authority in sacred things. [< Medieval Latin *hierarcha* < Greek *hierárchēs* leader of sacred rites < *hierós* sacred + *árchein* to lead]

hi|er|ar|chal (hī′ə rär′kəl), *adj.* of or having to do with a hierarch.

hi|er|ar|chi|al (hī′ə rär′kē əl), *adj.* = hierarchal.

hi|er|ar|chic (hī′ə rär′kik), *adj.* = hierarchical.

hi|er|ar|chi|cal (hī′ə rär′kə kəl), *adj.* of a hierarchy; having to do with or belonging to a hierarchy: *It simply means that our goal has always been the classless society. We aren't there yet, but are closer than anybody else has ever come; and at this late date we are hardly going to swerve back toward the hierarchical patterns of European culture* (Harper's). —**hi′er|ar′chi|cal|ly,** *adv.*

hi|er|ar|chism (hī′ə rär′kiz əm), *n.* the principles, practices, or system of a hierarchy.

hi|er|ar|chist (hī′ə rär′kist), *n.* a supporter of a hierarchy.

hi|er|ar|chize (hī′ə rär′kīz), *v.t.,* **-chized, -chiz|ing.** to organize or build up into a hierarchy.

hi|er|ar|chy (hī′ə rär′kē), *n., pl.* **-chies. 1** an organization of persons or things arranged into higher and lower ranks, classes, or grades: *O latest born . . . Of all Olympus' faded hierarchy* (Keats). **2** government by priests or church officials. **3** a group of church officials of different ranks. The church hierarchy is composed of archbishops, bishops, priests, and deacons. **4** *Theology.* **a** one of the divisions of the angels, each made up of three orders, and each ranked according to its duties and nearness to God. **b** the angels. [< Medieval Latin *hierarchia* < Greek *hierarchíā* < *hierarchíein* be high priest < *hierárchēs;* see etym. under **hierarch**]

hi|er|at|ic (hī′ə rat′ik), *adj.* **1** of or having to do with the priestly class; used by the priestly class; priestly. SYN: sacerdotal. **2** of or having to do with a form of Egyptian writing used by the early priests in their records. Hieratic writing is a simplified form of hieroglyphics. **3** of or having to do with certain styles in art, such as the Egyptian or Greek, in which earlier types or methods, fixed by religious tradition, are conventionally followed. [< Latin *hierāticus* < Greek *hierātikós,* ultimately < *hierós* sacred] —**hi′er|at′i|cal|ly,** *adv.*

hi|er|at|i|cal (hī′ə rat′ə kəl), *adj.* = hieratic.

hi|er|oc|ra|cy (hī′ə rok′rə sē), *n., pl.* **-cies. 1** government by priests or clergymen. **2** = hierarchy. [< Greek *hierós* sacred + *krátos* rule]

hi|er|o|crat|ic (hī′ər ə krat′ik), *adj.* of or having to do with a hierocracy. —**hi′er|o|crat′i|cal,** *adj.*

hi|er|o|dule (hī′ər ə dül, -dyül), *n.* a slave living in an ancient Greek temple and dedicated to the service of a god. [< Late Latin *hierodūlus* < Greek *hieródoulos* < *hierón* temple, noun use of neuter of *hierós* sacred + *doûlos* slave]

hi|er|o|du|lic (hī′ər ə dü′lik, -dyü′-), *adj.* of or belonging to a hierodule.

hi|er|o|glyph (hī′ər ə glif), *n., v.* **—*n.*** = hieroglyphic. **—*v.t.*** to represent by or inscribe with hieroglyphics: *hieroglyphed limestone tablets* (Amelia B. Edwards). [back formation < *hieroglyphic*]

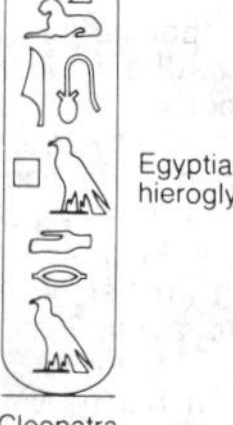

***hieroglyphic** definition 1

hi|er|o|glyph|ic** (hī′ər ə glif′ik), *n., adj.* **—*n. **1** a picture, character, or symbol standing for a word, idea, or sound; hieroglyph. The ancient Egyptians used hieroglyphics instead of an alphabet like ours. **2** *Figurative.* a letter or word that is hard to read. **3** *Figurative.* a secret symbol; emblem. **—*adj.*** **1** of or written in hieroglyphics. **2** *Figurative.* hard to read. **3** *Figurative.* having a hidden meaning; symbolical. SYN: emblematic.
hieroglyphics, a any writing that uses hieroglyphics like that of the ancient Egyptians: *Between the figures is a cartouche, containing a name in hieroglyphics* (Austen Layard). **b** *Figurative.* writing that is hard to read: *I can't make out his hieroglyphics in this memo.*
[< Late Latin *hieroglyphicus* < Greek *hieroglyphikós* < *hierós* sacred + *glyphé* carving < *glýphein* carve]—**hi′er|o|glyph′i|cal|ly,** *adv.*

hi|er|o|glyph|i|cal (hī′ər ə glif′ə kəl), *adj.* = hieroglyphic.

hi|er|og|ly|phism (hī′ə rog′lə fiz əm), *n.* the use of hieroglyphics.

hi|er|og|ly|phist (hī′ə rog′lə fist), *n.* **1** a writer of hieroglyphics. **2** one who studies hieroglyphics.

hi|er|o|gram (hī′ər ə gram), *n.* = hierograph. [< Greek *hierós* sacred + English *-gram*¹]

hi|er|o|graph (hī′ər ə graf, -gräf), *n.* a sacred inscription or symbol; hieroglyph. [< Greek *hierós* sacred + English *-graph*]—**hi′er|o|graph′ic,** *adj.*

hi|er|ol|a|try (hī′ə rol′ə trē), *n.* the worship of saints or holy beings; hagiolatry. [< Greek *hierós* sacred + *latreiā* worship]

hi|er|ol|o|gy (hī′ə rol′ə jē), *n., pl.* **-gies. 1** sacred literature or learning: *The Old Testament is part of both the Christian and Jewish hierology.* **2** = hagiology. **3** the history of religions, as a branch of study. [< Greek *hierós* sacred + English *-logy*]

Hi|er|o|nym|i|an (hī′ər ə nim′ē ən), *adj.* = Hieronymic.

Hi|er|o|nym|ic (hī′ər ə nim′ik), *adj.* of or having to do with Saint Jerome, who made the Latin Vulgate translation of the Bible. [< Latin *Hieronymus* Jerome (< Greek *Hierônymos* (originally) having a sacred name < *hierós* sacred + *ónyma* name) + English *-ic*]

Hi|er|on|y|mite (hī′ə ron′ə mīt), *n.* a hermit belonging to any one of several orders named for Saint Jerome.

hi|er|o|phant (hī′ər ə fant, hī er′-), *n.* **1** an interpreter of sacred mysteries or religious knowledge: *Poets are the hierophants of an unapprehended inspiration* (Shelley). **2** (in ancient Greece) an official interpreter of sacred mysteries or religious ceremonies, especially the chief priest of the Eleusinian mysteries. [< Latin *hierophantēs* < Greek *hierophántēs* < *hierós* sacred + *phaínein* to show] —**hi′er|o|phan′tic,** *adj.*

hi|fa|lu|tin (hī′fə lü′tən), *adj., n.* = highfalutin.

hi-fi (hī′fī′), *n., adj., v. Informal.* **—*n.*** **1** high-fidelity reproduction of music. **2** equipment for high fidelity. **—*adj.*** of or for high fidelity.
—*v.i.* to listen to high-fidelity recordings or record-playing equipment.

hig|gle (hig′əl), *v.i.,* **-gled, -gling. 1** to dispute about terms in a petty way; haggle. SYN: chaffer, stickle. **2** to go about with small wares, etc., for sale; peddle. [apparently related to **haggle**]

hig|gle|dy-pig|gle|dy (hig′əl dē pig′əl dē), *adv., adj., n.* **—*adv.*** in jumbled confusion; in a disorderly manner. **—*adj.*** jumbled; confused: *. . . narrow uneven alleys leading to higgledy-piggledy workshops and kilns* (Arnold Bennett).
—*n.* a jumble; confusion. [origin uncertain; often associated with disorganized flocking of pigs]

hig|gler (hig′lər), *n.* a person who higgles.

Higgs boson (higz), *Nuclear Physics.* a hypothetical particle with a spin of O, thought to be the carrier of a force that generates the masses of all the fundamental particles: *The fact that in the standard model the Higgs boson is responsible for all observed masses implies that, even if in the end there is no such thing as a Higgs boson, there is at least a common source for all masses* (Scientific American). [< Peter W. Higgs, a British physicist of the 1900's, who proposed it]

high (hī), *adj., adv., n.* **—*adj.*** **1** having height; rising up; tall: *a high building, high country. The mountain is 20,000 feet high.* **2** up above or far above the ground or some other base; at a height or from a height: *an airplane high in the air, a high dive.* **3** *Figurative.* above others: *a high official. Washington was a man of high character. "Human law," he* [St. Thomas Aquinas] *wrote, "does not bind a man in conscience, and if it conflicts with the higher law, human law should not be obeyed"* (Time). SYN: eminent, elevated, exalted, noble. **4a** greater, stronger, or better than others; great: *a high wind, a high price, high speed. Two hundred is a high number; two is a low one.* **b** far from the equator and given a high number: *a high latitude.* **5** *Figurative.* most important; chief; main: *high finance, the high altar of a church.* **6** *Figurative.* **a** extreme of its kind; serious; grave: *Murder and kidnaping are high crimes. A high Tory has extremely conservative political opinions.* **b** most advanced; latest; newest: *high fashion, to dress in high style.* **7** expensive; costly: *Strawberries are high in winter.* **8a** not low in pitch; shrill; sharp: *a high note, a*

high voice. **b** produced by rapid vibrations: *high sounds.* **9** *Figurative.* advanced to its peak: *high summer.* **10** *Figurative.* **a** lofty; noble: *Plain living and high thinking are no more* (Wordsworth). **b** haughty; arrogant: *a high manner. Some of those bankers are as high and mighty as the oldest families* (Thackeray). **11** slightly tainted: *Game is often eaten after it has become high.* **12** *Figurative.* happily excited: *high glee.* **13** *Informal, Figurative.* **a** somewhat drunk. **b** exhilarated or dazed under the influence of a narcotic drug: *No one was surprised if a student came to class "high" on drugs* (New York Times). **14** designating an arrangement of gears that gives the highest speed: *the high gear of an automobile.* **15** *Biology.* highly developed; more advanced, especially in structure or intelligence: *the higher algae, the higher apes.* **16** *Figurative.* more difficult or advanced: *an institution of higher learning.* **17** *Phonetics.* said with a part of the tongue raised high in the mouth. The *i* in *pit* and the *u* in *put* are high vowels.
—***adv.*** at or to a high point, place, rank, amount, degree, price, or pitch: *The eagle flies high. Gamblers play high. Strawberries come high in winter. Can you sing high?* (*Figurative.*) *Sports stand high in popular attention.* (*Figurative.*) *Passions run high in an election.*
—***n.*** **1** a high point, level, or position: *Food prices reached a new high last month.* **2** an arrangement of gears to give the greatest speed; high gear: *This car can't climb the hills in high.* **3** *Meteorology.* an area of relatively high barometric pressure; anticyclone: *The weatherman reports a high moving in.* **4** *U.S. Informal.* high school. **5** a high card in card games, such as a king or a high trump. **6** *Slang, Figurative.* exhilaration or stupor caused by a narcotic drug: *Methadone does not produce the "high," or euphoria, brought on by heroin* (Scientific American).
be high on, *Informal.* to be excited about; be especially fond of: *Almond goes for obsessions and fatalities and an elliptical style—he's very high on portents* (New Yorker).
fly high, to have big ideas, plans, hopes, or ambitions: *In his youth he saw himself flying high.*
from (on) high, a from a high place or position: *From high in the sky, an eagle slowly winged its way to earth.* **b** from heaven: *We, whose souls are lighted With wisdom from on high* (Reginald Heber).
high and dry, a up out of water: *The boat came ashore, high and dry.* **b** *Figurative.* all alone; without help; stranded: *The depression left his business high and dry.*
high and low, everywhere: *He searched high and low for his pen.*
on high, a high above; up in the air: *On high, clouds were gathering.* **b** in heaven: *When he ascended up on high, he led captivity captive, and gave gifts unto men* (Ephesians 4:8).
run high, a to become heated; reach a high pitch: *Tempers run high at election time.* **b** to be strong or rough: *The tide runs high.*
[Old English *hēh, hēah*]
—***Syn.*** *adj.* **1 High, lofty, tall** mean of more than usual height. **High** applies to things, not people: *High hills surround the valley.* **Lofty,** a more literary term, also applies to things, and suggests an impressive height: *We saw the lofty Mount Shasta, snow-capped and rising over 14,000 feet.* **Tall** applies to both people and things, and suggests slenderness or narrowness as well as height: *He is a tall man. The corn is tall for this time of year.*

high-al|ti|tude (hī′al′tə tüd, -tyüd), *adj.* **1** having to do with or occurring at a great distance above the level surface of the earth: *high-altitude phenomena, high-altitude research.* **2** aimed at or reaching such a distance: *high-altitude rockets.*

high-and-might|y (hī′ən mī′tē, -ənd-), *adj., n.* —***adj.*** arrogant; overbearing: *a high-and-mighty attitude.*
—***n.*** *Informal.* persons of great power or high position: *seduced by the friendship of the political high-and-mighty in Washington* (Hanson W. Baldwin). —**high′-and-might′i|ness,** *n.*

high|ball¹ (hī′bôl′), *n.,* or **high ball,** *U.S.* whiskey, brandy, or other alcoholic liquor, mixed with soda water, ginger ale, or other light liquid, and served with ice in a tall glass. [American English; origin uncertain]

high|ball² (hī′bôl′), *n., v. U.S.* —***n.*** **1** a signal for a railroad train to proceed or to increase its speed. **2** *Slang.* a clear way; straight course.
—***v.i.*** *Informal.* to move, travel, or drive ahead rapidly: *Highballing along behind the second bus was a trailer-tanker truck* (Time).
[American English, apparently <the *high* position of the *ball* on early semaphore signals]

high beam, the stronger of the two beams in automobile headlights.

high|bind|er (hī′bīn′dər), *n. U.S.* **1** a rowdy; ruffian. **2** a swindler: *The art world has its highbinders just as the stock world once had its Jim Fisks* (Wall Street Journal). **3** a member of a former Chinese society that committed crimes for hire. [American English; origin uncertain]

high|bind|ing (hī′bīn′ding), *n., adj.* —***n.*** *U.S.* dishonest behavior; fraud: *Many of the techniques of larceny and highbinding that one encounters in our own great civilization were developed and refined over the centuries* (New Yorker).
—***adj.*** *U.S.* dishonest; fraudulent: *In his usual highbinding style, Nikita tried to turn a defensive outburst into a strident success story* (Time).

high blood pressure, = hypertension.

high-blown (hī′blōn′), *adj.* inflated; conceited: *My high-blown pride At length broke under me* (Shakespeare).

high|born (hī′bôrn′), *adj.* of noble birth. SYN: aristocratic, patrician.

∗high|boy (hī′boi′), *n.* a tall chest of drawers on legs. [American English <*high* + *boy*]

∗highboy

high brass, **1** = yellow brass. **2** *U.S. Slang.* top brass.

high|bred (hī′bred′), *adj.* **1** of superior breeding or stock. **2** well-mannered; very refined.

high|brow (hī′brou′), *n., adj. Informal.* —***n.*** a person who cares, or claims to care, a great deal about knowledge and culture: *There was the theatre* (*so much better than the highbrows asserted*) (Hugh Walpole). —***adj.*** of or fit for a highbrow; characteristic of a highbrow: *To all who think vaguely of ballet as a highbrow affair of classical serenity* (Punch). [American English <*high* + *brow*] —**high′brow′ism,** *n.*

high-browed (hī′broud′), *adj.* **1** having a high forehead. **2** *Informal, Figurative.* highbrow: *If artistic, earnest, and high-browed women only knew how to dress!* (Arnold Bennett).

high|bush blueberry (hī′bu̇sh′), **1** any one of several eastern North American bushy shrubs with small white or pinkish flowers in dense clusters and a sweet, dark-blue berry. **2** its berry.

highbush cranberry, = cranberry tree.

high chair, or **high|chair** (hī′chãr′), *n.* a chair with a high seat and a tray for feeding babies.

High Church, a party in the Anglican Communion that lays great stress on church and priestly authority, ceremonial observances, the apostolic succession, and the Catholicism of the church.

High-Church (hī′chėrch′), *adj.* of or having to do with the High Church; laying great stress on church and priestly authority, ceremonial observances, and the Catholicism of the church.

High Churchman, a person who belongs to or supports the principles of the High Church.

high-class (hī′klas′, -kläs′), *adj.* of or for a class or category regarded as superior: *The most interesting, entertaining, and illuminating novel about high-class, old-fashioned Germans* (New Yorker).

high-col|ored (hī′kul′ərd), *adj.* **1** having a high color; deep in color. **2** florid; red. **3** *Figurative.* exaggerated; forced: *He gave a high-colored account of his adventure.*

high comedy, comedy dealing with polite society and depending more on witty dialogue and well-drawn characters than on comic situations.

high command, 1 the highest headquarters of a military force, or the supreme commanders of the armed forces of a nation or of allied nations: *President Eisenhower's reshuffle of the high command in the Pentagon* (Newsweek). **2** the top leadership of any organization: *The decision of the A.F.L.-C.I.O. high command not to support the International Brotherhood of Longshoremen . . . may seem only a defeat for the forces of good in their battle against evil* (New York Times).

High Commissioner or **high commissioner, 1** a representative or ambassador of a member nation of the Commonwealth at the capital of another: *In Pakistan, my function was diplomatic; our High Commissioners in the Commonwealth countries are really ambassadors* (New Yorker). **2** the head of any special commission of one country to another, such as a commission sent to govern temporarily an occupied territory.

High Court, = Supreme Court.

High Court of Justice, the chief criminal and civil court in England.

high day, a solemn or festal day; festival.

high-domed (hī′dōmd′), *adj. Informal.* **1** having a high forehead or receding hairline: *a thin, high-domed fellow who wore horn-rimmed glasses* (Time). **2** *Figurative.* highbrow.

High Dutch, the Dutch language as spoken in the Netherlands: *. . . that South African Dutch which has overridden High Dutch and is called Afrikaans* (Sarah G. Millin).

high-end (hī′end′), *adj.* **1** including or comprising the high-income consumers;upscale: *the high-end segment of the housing market.* **2** most advanced or expensive of its kind: *Some systems available on the PC [personal computer] could go up as far in resolution as you can get on a high-end workstation today* (Microage Quarterly).

high-en|er|gy (hī′en′ər jē), *adj.* **1** of or having to do with the high speeds imparted by particle accelerators: *high-energy collisions.* **2** of or having to do with high-energy physics.

high-energy fuel, a fuel for aircraft or missiles yielding greater energy per unit of weight than the conventional petroleum derivatives, as a boron compound.

high-energy particle, a nuclear particle that has been accelerated to very high speeds in a particle accelerator: *High-energy particles are necessary in order to probe deeply into the interior of the nucleus* (New Yorker).

high-energy physics, a branch of physics dealing with nuclear particles moving at very high speeds and their interaction: *Accelerators are the chief instruments of high-energy physics* (Scientific American).

high|er criticism (hī′ər), scientific investigation of a literary work, especially the Bible, with regard to text, authorship, sources, and date against its historical and cultural background.

higher education, education at a level beyond the secondary schools, especially college education.

higher mathematics, advanced mathematics, beyond those branches commonly taught in the secondary schools.

high|er-up (hī′ər up′), *n. U.S. Informal.* a person occupying a superior position.

high|est (hī′ist), *adj., n., adv.* —***adj.*** superlative of **high**: *The highest mountain in the world is Everest.*
—***n.*** that which is highest: *We needs must love the highest when we see it* (Tennyson).
—***adv.*** to the most high point, place, rank, amount, degree, price, or pitch: *Of all the archers, he shot highest.*

high explosive, an explosive compound, such as nitroglycerin and TNT, that forms gas rapidly when detonated and shatters its container with great force. High explosives that are especially sensitive to heat are used in making detonators. —**high′-ex|plo′sive,** *adj.*

high|fa|lu|tin or **high|fa|lu|ting** (hī′fə lü′tən), *adj., n. Informal.* —***adj.*** high-sounding; pompous; bombastic. —***n.*** pompous speech or writing; bombast. [American English, possibly variant of *high-flown,* or *highflying*] —**high′fa|lu′tin|ly,** *adv.*

high-fash|ion (hī′fash′ən), *adj.,* of or having to do with the fashions taken up by the leaders in fashionable dress and living; of the most exclusive style: *the high-price, high-fashion field gets itself reorganized every six months by peregrinating waistlines and hemlines* (New Yorker).

high fidelity, the reproduction of sound by a radio, phonograph, or tape recorder with as little distortion of the original sound as possible. —**high′-fi|del′i|ty,** *adj.*

high-field (hī′fēld′), *adj.* of or having to do with a very strong electric or magnetic field: *a high-field electromagnet.*

high five, *U.S.* an informal gesture of greeting or congratulation in which two people each slap a raised hand with the other, usually overhead.

high|fli|er (hī′flī′ər), *n.* **1** a person or thing that flies high. **2** *Figurative.* a person who is extravagant or has pretentious ideas or ambitions. **3** *Slang.* a pretentious or fashionable strumpet. **4** an extremist in Tory politics or in High-Church doctrines in England in the 1700's.

high-flown (hī′flōn′), *adj.* **1** aspiring or extravagant: *high-flown ideas.* **2** attempting to be elegant or eloquent: *high-flown compliments.* SYN: fustian.

high|fly|er (hī′flī′ər), *n.* = highflier.

high|fly|ing (hī′flī′ing), *adj.* **1** that flies high: *a highflying bird.* **2** *Figurative.* extravagant or pretentious.

high forest, *U.S.* a forest of trees raised from seed.

high-fre|quen|cy (hī′frē′kwən sē), *adj.* of or having to do with a frequency ranging from 3 to 30 megahertz: *high-frequency radio receivers, high-frequency sound waves.*

Pronunciation Key: hat, āge, cãre, fär; let, ēqual, tėrm; it, īce; hot, ōpen, ôrder; oil, out; cup, pu̇t, rüle; child; long; thin; ᴛʜen; zh, measure; ə represents **a** in about, **e** in taken, **i** in pencil, **o** in lemon, **u** in circus.

high gear, the gear ratio in a common automotive transmission used for normal driving, by which the driving wheels are turned fastest in relation to engine speed.
in (or **into**) **high gear**, at full speed: *The automobile industry is in high gear* (Wall Street Journal).
High German, the literary and official language of Germany and Austria and one of the official languages of Switzerland. It developed from the dialects of central and southern Germany.
high-grade (hī′grād′), *adj., v.,* **-grad|ed, -grad|ing.** —*adj.* **1** of fine quality; superior: *high-grade oil, high-grade securities.* **2** rich in metal value: *high-grade ore.*
—*v.i., v.t.* to steal high-grade ore.
high-hand|ed (hī′han′did), *adj.* acting or done in a bold, arbitrary way; domineering; overbearing: *high-handed methods.* SYN: tyrannical, autocratic. —**high′-hand′ed|ly,** *adv.* —**high′-hand′ed|ness,** *n.*
high-hat (hī′hat′), *v.,* **-hat|ted, -hat|ting,** *adj., n. U.S. Slang.* —*v.t.* to treat as inferior; snub.
—*adj.* **1** snobbish: *Christmas Cove's a nice place; not so high-hat as Bar Harbor* (P. Marks). **2** stylish or grand.
—*n.* a snobbish person.
high hat, a tall, black, silk hat; top hat.
high-head|ed (hī′hed′id), *adj.* proud; arrogant.
high-heeled (hī′hēld′), *adj.* having high heels: *high-heeled shoes.*
high-hold|er (hī′hōl′dər), *n. U.S.* = flicker[2].
high|hole (hī′hōl′), *n.* = high-holder.
High Holidays or **High Holy Days**, the Jewish holidays of Rosh Hashanah and Yom Kippur.
high horse, an arrogant or condescending attitude or disposition: *Relax and enjoy it, without getting up on a high horse* (Harper's).
high hurdles, a race in which the runners jump over hurdles 3½ or 3¼ feet high over a distance of 120 yards. See picture under **hurdle**.
high iron, a main line of a railroad.
high|ish (hī′ish), *adj.* somewhat high: . . . *a skirt gathered at the highish waistline* (New Yorker).
high|jack (hī′jak′), *v.t., n.* = hijack. —**high′jack′er,** *n.*
high jinks, *Informal.* lively or boisterous behavior; unrestrained merrymaking: *a milling crowd of undergraduates bent on a spree of spring high jinks* (New York Times).
***high jump**, **1** an athletic contest or event to determine how high each contestant can jump over a raised crossbar. **2** the jump itself.

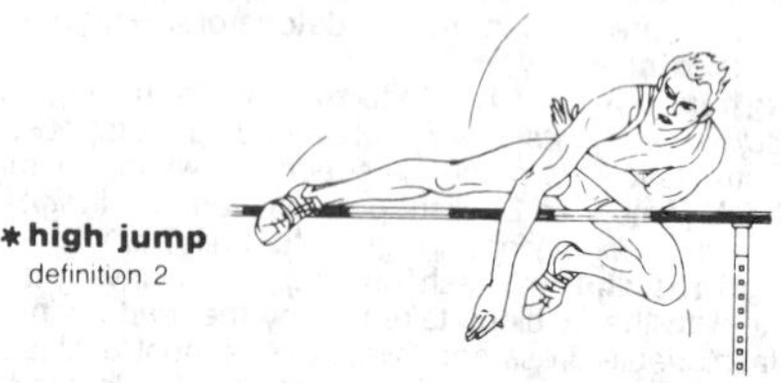
***high jump**
definition 2

high-jump (hī′jump′), *v.i.* to do a high jump or jumps. —*v.t.* to get across (a certain height or obstacle) by a high jump. —**high′-jump′er,** *n.*
high-keyed (hī′kēd′), *adj.* **1** easily excited; high-strung; keyed-up: *When one of his high-keyed and difficult friends needs help, Joe can always be relied on to appear* (Newsweek). **2** overstated; played up: *high-keyed comedy.* (Newsweek).
high|land (hī′lənd), *n., adj.* —*n.* Often, **highlands.** a country or region that is higher or hillier than the neighboring country; land high above sea level; elevated region; plateau.
—*adj.* of or in such country.
High|land (hī′lənd), *adj.* of or having to do with the Scottish Highlands: *Highland scenery.*
high|land|er (hī′lən dər), *n.* a person born or living in a highland.
High|land|er (hī′lən dər), *n.* **1** a person born or living in the Highlands of Scotland. **2** a soldier of a regiment from the Highlands of Scotland.
Highland fling, a lively dance of the Highlands of Scotland.
Highland pony, one of a breed of ponies originating in the Highlands of Scotland.
high-lead logging (hī′lēd′), a method of pulling logs up inclines or across ravines by using a system of pulleys and cables.
high-lev|el (hī′lev′əl), *adj.* **1** of or having to do with persons of high rank or occupying positions of leadership: *high-level talks.* **2** having or reaching a great height: *a high-level dam.* **3** occurring high up in the atmosphere: *high-level turbulence.* **4** intensely radioactive: *to store high-level waste in geological formations* (New Scientist).
high-level language, a computer programming language which employs terms and grammar often found in the vocabulary of the user: *COBOL and FORTRAN are examples of high-level languages which aim to be independent of the machine, oriented to specific applications, and relatively simple to understand, as they use English words like "open" and "assign"* (New Scientist).
high|life (hī′līf′), *n.* **1a** life in high or fashionable society: *In his youth he was fatally beglamoured by Edwardian highlife* (Punch). **b** persons in such society. **2a** jazz of the West Coast of Africa, characterized by a fast calypso beat. **b** a song in this jazz style.
high|light (hī′līt′), *v.,* **-light|ed, -light|ing,** *n.* —*v.t.* **1** to cast a bright light on. **2** to emphasize (parts, as of a painting or photograph) with lighting, the use of certain light colors, or other devices that give the effect of using bright light. **3** *Figurative.* to make prominent; focus on: *Now I would like to highlight some of the main features of the past year* (New Scientist).
—*n.* **1** an effect or representation of bright light. **2** a part, as of a painting or photograph, in which light is represented as falling with greatest intensity. **3** *Figurative.* the most prominent or interesting part, as of an event or scene: *The highlights of the circus were the daredevil jumps and the dancing clowns.*
high|light|er (hī′lī′tər), *n.* a cosmetic used to highlight or emphasize facial features.
high|line (hī′līn′), *n., adj.* —*n.* **1** a line or cable used in transferring stores at sea or between sea and shore. **2** an electric line or cable carrying a high voltage. **3** *U.S. and Canada.* a highliner.
—*adj.* **1** sent or carried by a highline: *highline power.* **2** *U.S. and Canada.* taking the most fish with his or its line; being a highliner.
highline chair, a metal chair attached to a cable used to rescue a person from a ship, especially by transferring him to another ship or to a helicopter.
high|lin|er (hī′lī′nər), *n. U.S. and Canada.* **1** the fishing boat making the largest catch within a given time. **2** the captain of such a boat.
high liver, a person who lives on a rich scale; high-living person: *the uneasy high livers of the postwar period* (Paul West).
high-liv|ing (hī′liv′ing), *adj.* eating or living on a rich, expensive scale: *some high-living, free-spending Pennsylvania oil millionaires* (Harper's).
high-low (hī′lō′), *n.* a boot reaching up over the ankle.
high-low-jack (hī′lō′jak′), *n.* the card game of seven-up, or one like it.
high|ly (hī′lē), *adv.* **1** in a high degree; to a high degree; very much; very: *highly amusing, highly recommended.* SYN: greatly, extremely. **2** with great praise or honor; with much approval; very favorably: *to speak highly of your best friend.* SYN: laudably. **3** at a high rate or price: *highly paid.* SYN: dearly. **4** in or to a high position or rank: *a highly placed government official.*
High Mass, a complete ritual of Mass with music, the burning of incense, and other ceremonies. The choir sings responses. At High Mass, the priest chants the service, assisted by a deacon and subdeacon.
high-met|tled (hī′met′əld), *adj.* high-spirited; courageous.
high milling, a process of making flour by grinding it many times.
high-mind|ed (hī′mīn′did), *adj.* **1** having or showing high principles and feelings: *well-bred and high-minded youths* (Washington Irving). SYN: honorable. **2** *Archaic.* proud; arrogant: *Lord, I am not high-minded: I have no proud looks* (Book of Common Prayer, Psalms 131:1). —**high′-mind′ed|ly,** *adv.* —**high′-mind′ed|ness,** *n.*
high-muck|y-muck or **high-muck-a-muck** (hī′muk′ə muk′), *n. U.S. Slang.* an important or powerful person: . . . *the high-mucky-mucks and panjandrums of the Republican Party in the age of Mark Hanna* (Louis Kronenberger). [< Chinook jargon *hiu muckamuck* plenty to eat]
high-necked (hī′nekt′), *adj.* (of a garment) high at the neck; covering the shoulders and neck.
high|ness (hī′nis), *n.* the state of being high; height; loftiness.
High|ness (hī′nis), *n.* a title of honor given to members of royal families: *The Prince of Wales is addressed as "Your Highness" and spoken of as "His Royal Highness."*
high noon, midday; exactly twelve o'clock in the daytime.
high-oc|tane (hī′ok′tān), *adj.* **1** (of gasoline) having a high octane number, or percentage of octane. **2** *Figurative.* powerful; inspiriting; enriching: *Schools which often do get high-octane thought out of future professional men* (Punch).
high old time, *Informal.* high time.
high-pitched (hī′picht′), *adj.* **1** of high tone or sound; shrill: *a high-pitched voice.* SYN: piercing. **2** having a steep slope; steep: *a high-pitched roof.*
high place, (in the Bible) a place of worship or sacrifice on a hill or high ground.
high pole, *U.S.* a tree from 8 to 12 inches in diameter and about 4 to 5 feet high.
high polymer, or **high-pol|y|mer** (hī′pol′ē mər), *n.* a very large molecule in which atoms or groups are bonded to form chains or networks in two or three dimensions, such as nylon.
high-pow|er (hī′pou′ər), *adj.* = high-powered.
high-pow|ered (hī′pou′ərd), *adj.* **1** having much power: *a high-powered car, a high-powered rifle.* **2** *Figurative.* using strong, vigorous methods; high-pressure: *high-powered salesmanship.*
high-pre|ci|sion (hī′pri sizh′ən), *adj.* very precise.
high-pres|sure (hī′presh′ər), *adj., v.,* **-sured, -sur|ing.** —*adj.* **1** having, using, or resisting more than the usual pressure: *a high-pressure boiler.* **2** having high barometric pressure: *Air generally moves from a high-pressure area into a low-pressure area* (James E. Miller). **3** *Figurative.* using strong, vigorous methods: *high-pressure selling.*
—*v.t. Figurative.* to use strong, vigorous methods on, in selling: *to high-pressure a customer.* [American English < *high* + *pressure*]
high-priced (hī′prīst′), *adj.* expensive; costly.
high priest, **1** a chief priest. **2** the head of the ancient Jewish priesthood. **3** *Figurative.* an outstanding leader or authority: *Louis Aragon is the high priest of the Communist writers in France* (Manchester Guardian).
high priestess, **1** a chief priestess. **2** *Figurative.* a preeminent woman leader or authority: . . . *Wanda Landowska, the harpsichord's high priestess* (Time).
high-pri|or|i|ty (hī′prī ôr′ə tē, -or′-), *adj.* having, giving, or taking precedence over other items, policies, or persons.
high profile, **1** an attitude or position that is direct, open, and emphatic; a conspicuously clear-cut stance. **2** a person who attracts attention or notoriety: *Such high profiles as Mariel Hemingway . . . and Sigourney Weaver were flashed by paparazzi* (Vanity Fair).
high-pro|file (hī′prō′fīl), *adj.* attracting much notice; conspicuous: *Progress on nuclear-arms reduction . . . could yield a high-profile political victory* (Atlantic).
high-proof (hī′prüf′), *adj.* containing a high percentage of alcohol; strongly alcoholic: *high-proof whiskey.*
high-rank|ing (hī′rang′king), *adj.* of high rank or position; prominent: *A high-ranking Democrat on the House Appropriations Committee predicted the House would approve the request* (Wall Street Journal).
high relief, carving or sculpture in which the figures project well out from the background; alto-relievo.
high-rid|ing (hī′rī′ding), *adj.* proceeding prosperously and confidently; favorably placed: *high-riding organized labor, a high-riding senator.*
high-rise (hī′rīz′), *adj., n.* —*adj.* **1** having many stories; very tall; multistory: *Corbusier proposed to stack people vertically in high-rise towers so that the surrounding land could be freed for parks and playgrounds* (Time). **2a** having very long handle bars: *a high-rise bike.* **b** of bicycles or motorcycles with such handle bars: *high-rise riders.*
—*n.* a high-rise building: *the twenty-fifth story of a new high-rise* (New Yorker).
high|road (hī′rōd′), *n.* **1** a main road; highway: *the highroad to England* (Samuel Johnson). **2** *Figurative.* a direct and easy way: *the highroad to success.*
high roller, *U.S. Slang.* a big spender.
high school, a school attended after the elementary school or junior high school. High school consists of grades 9 or 10 through 12. See also **junior high school.** —**high′-school′,** *adj.*
►**High school** is capitalized only when it refers to a particular school: *I graduated from high school at seventeen. I graduated from Lincoln High School last year.*
high-school|er (hī′skü′lər), *n. U.S.* a high-school student.
high seas, the open ocean. The high seas are outside the authority of any country.
high-sound|ing (hī′soun′ding), *adj.* **1** having an imposing or pretentious sound. SYN: grandiloquent. **2** high or loud in sound.
high-speed (hī′spēd′), *adj.* designed for, operated or moving at, or characterized by very fast speeds: *high-speed computers.*
high-speed steel, an alloy steel of extreme toughness and hardness that can be made into tools cutting so rapidly as to become red-hot.
high-spir|it|ed (hī′spir′ə tid), *adj.* **1** proud. **2** courageous. **3** spirited; fiery: *a high-spirited horse.* —**high′-spir′it|ed|ly,** *adv.* —**high′-spir′it|ed|ness,** *n.*
high spirits, happiness; cheerfulness; gaiety: *The team was in high spirits after winning the game.* SYN: elation.
high spot, **1** the main feature; noteworthy part: *In a book where nearly every chapter is excellent, it is difficult to single out the high spots*

(Science). **2** a place of interest; attraction: *New York's high spots.*
high steel, steel with a high percentage of carbon.
high-step|per (hī′step′ər), *n.* a horse with a high-stepping gait.
high-step|ping (hī′step′ing), *adj. Informal.* **1** lifting the feet high in walking, trotting, or marching: *a high-stepping marcher.* **2** *Figurative.* quick-moving; fast: *the high-stepping U.S. economy.* **3** *Figurative.* proud; haughty. **4** *Figurative.* showy; fast: *a high-stepping blonde.*
high|stick (hī′stik′), *Ice Hockey.* **—*v.i.*** **1** to carry or raise one's stick illegally, above shoulder height. **2** to check, hinder, or strike an opponent by highsticking.
—*v.t.* to check, hinder, or strike (an opponent) illegally with the stick raised above shoulder height.
high street, *British.* the main street, usually the business section, of a town or city.
high-strung (hī′strung′), *adj.* **1** easily excited; very sensitive; very nervous: *All the members of her family were high-strung artists.* **2** strung to a high tension or pitch: *a high-strung guitar.*
high-style (hī′stīl′), *adj.* in or displaying the most advanced and polished style or fashion.
hight¹ (hīt), *adj., v., past tense and past participle* **hight.** *Archaic.* **—*adj.*** named; called.
—*v.t., v.i.* to name or be named; call: *a little pest, hight Tommy Moore* (Washington Irving).
[fusion of Old English *hātte* call oneself and of *heht,* past tense of *hātan* be called]
hight² (hīt), *n. Obsolete.* height.
high table, (in a British college) the table in the dining hall reserved for dons and traditionally served with wines and superior food.
eat (or **dine**) **at high table**, *British.* to eat in style; eat well: *At the Duke's, one eats at high table.*
high-tail (hī′tāl′), *v.i. Informal.* to run quickly; hurry: *high-tailing home.*
high-tail it, to run fast; hurry: *the really vast majority high-tailed it from the danger zones in plenty of time* (New York Herald Tribune).
high tea, *British.* a tea at which meat is served, usually later than the ordinary tea.
high-tech (hī′tek′), *n., adj.* **—*n.*** a style of design or interior decoration that uses or imitates objects normally found in factories, warehouses, restaurant kitchens, etc.: *High-tech . . . uses utilitarian industrial equipment and materials, out of context, as home furnishings* (New York Daily News).
—*adj.* *Informal.* = high-technology: *high-tech industries.*
high-tech|nol|o|gy (hī′tek nol′ə jē), *adj.* of or having to do with advanced, highly specialized, and sophisticated technology: *High-technology goods such as computers* (Newsweek).
high-tem|per|a|ture superconductor (hī′tem′pərə chər, -chůr; -prə-), any one of a class of ceramic compounds conducting electric current with no resistance at temperatures above 77 degrees Kelvin (the boiling point of liquid nitrogen): *The new high-temperature superconductors . . . may revolutionize various technologies by allowing electricity to flow without losses and without much cooling—making magnetically levitated trains feasible, for example* (Science News).
high-ten|sion (hī′ten′shən), *adj.* having or using a high voltage: *high-tension wires.*
high-test (hī′test′), *adj.* **1** that passes some test; of good quality. **2** having a very low boiling point. High-test gasoline, used in some automobiles, quickly forms a vapor in the engine.
highth (hītth, hīth), *n. Dialect.* height.
high tide, **1** the highest level of the tide. **2** the time when the ocean comes up highest on the shore. **3** *Figurative.* the highest point.
high time, **1** time just before it is too late: *It is high time he began to study harder.* **2** *Informal.* a gay, jolly time, as at a party; high old time.
high-toned (hī′tōnd′), *adj.* **1** having a high character or high principles. **2a** pretentiously stylish and exclusive: *a high-toned gathering.* **b** excellent; superior. **3** high in tone or pitch: *a high-toned voice.*
high treason, treason against one's ruler, state, or government.
high-up (hī′up′), *n., adj.* **—*n.*** an official near the top in power or importance in an organization.
—*adj.* *Informal.* important; occupying a position of importance.
high-warp (hī′wôrp′), *adj.* having a vertically strung warp: *a tapestry with a high-warp weave.*
high water, **1** the highest level of water. **2** = high tide.
high-wa|ter mark (hī′wôt′ər, -wot′-), **1** the highest level reached by the tide or by a flooded river or lake. **2** the mark or line left by the water after it has receded. **3** *Figurative.* any highest point: *Elizabethan drama reached its high-water mark in Shakespeare's tragedies.*
high|way (hī′wā′), *n.* **1** a public road; highroad. **2** a main road or route: *The Platte has become a highway for the fur traders* (Washington Irving). **3** *Figurative.* a direct line or way to some end: *the highway to promotion.*
highway hypnosis, a dazed condition in automobile drivers similar to a hypnotic trance, induced by monotonous driving.
high|way|man (hī′wā′mən), *n., pl.* **-men.** a man who, in former times, robbed travelers on a public road. **SYN:** bandit, brigand.
highway robbery, **1** robbery committed on a public road. **2** *Informal.* an exorbitant price or charge: *$100 a tooth! That's highway robbery* (Goodman Ace).
high wheeler, = ordinary (def. 6).
high wind, *Meteorology.* a wind having a velocity of 32-38 miles per hour.
high wine, wine of high percentage of alcohol.
high wire, a tightwire raised very high above the ground: *He crosses his theatrical high wire with a sure tread* (London Times).
high-wrought (hī′rôt′), *adj.* **1** wrought with great skill; highly finished. **2** very agitated or excited; high-strung.
high yellow, *U.S. Slang.* a light-skinned black (often used in an unfriendly way). **—high′-yel′-low,** *adj.*
high-yield (hī′yēld′), *adj.* **1** producing or giving a comparatively large amount of a product or derivative, as a soil, a plant, or a process. **2** (of nuclear or atomic devices) putting a large amount of radioactive substances into the atmosphere.
hi|jack (hī′jak′), *v., n.* **—*v.t.*** to rob or take by force (goods in transit or an airplane or other vehicle): *The insurgents Tuesday turned over 31 people seized in two hijacked Cuban airliners* (Wall Street Journal). **—*n.*** the act or crime of stealing or taking over by force a vehicle in transit, especially an airplane. Also, **highjack.**
[American English, probably back formation < *hijacker*]
hi|jack|er (hī′jak′ər), *n. Informal.* **1** a person who robs or takes a vehicle or goods in transit by force. **2** (formerly) one who robbed bootleggers of liquor in transit. Also, **highjacker.** [American English; origin uncertain]
hi|jinks (hī′jinks′), *n.pl.* = high jinks.
Hij|ra or **Hij|rah** (hij′rə), *n.* = Hegira.
hike (hīk), *v.,* **hiked, hik|ing,** *n.* **—*v.i.*** **1** to take a long walk; tramp or march: *At first all of us city boys hiked on very sore feet.* **2** *Informal.* to draw or pull (up): *Her tight skirt hikes up when she sits down.* **—*v.t.*** **1** *Informal.* to move, draw, or raise with a jerk; hitch; pull (up): *Hike up your socks, they are falling down.* **2** *U.S. Informal.* to raise; increase: *to hike wages. While there is no general hotel rate increase in Italy, you'll probably find Rome hotels hiking prices about 5 per cent* (Rosellen Callahan).
—*n.* **1** a long walk; tramp or march: *It was a four-mile hike to the camp.* **2** *Informal.* an increase or rise: *a hike in prices. U.S. Steel, similarly, has signed a new contract . . . with the 40-cent pay hikes* (Wall Street Journal).
[apparently variant of earlier *hoicks,* variant of *yoicks.* Perhaps related to **hitch.**] **—hik′er,** *n.*
hi|ki (hē′kē), *n.* (formerly, in Japan) a person who pulled a jinrikisha. [< Japanese *hiki* pull]
hi|la (hī′lə), *n.* plural of **hilum.** [< Latin *hīla,* plural of *hīlum* hilum]
HILAC (hī′lak), *n.* Heavy Ion Linear Accelerator.
hi|lar (hī′lər), *adj.* of or having to do with a hilum.
hi|lar|i|ous (hə lãr′ē əs, hī-), *adj.* very merry; noisily gay; mirthful: *a hilarious tale, a hilarious party.* **SYN:** rollicking. [< Latin *hilaris* (with English *-ous*); see etym. under **hilarity**] **—hi|lar′i|ous|ly,** *adv.* **—hi|lar′i|ous|ness,** *n.*
hi|lar|i|ty (hə lãr′ə tē, hī-), *n.* great merriment; noisy gaiety: *The party grew in wild hilarity. Fan the sinking flame of hilarity with the wing of friendship; and pass the rosy wine* (Dickens). **SYN:** jollity. [< Latin *hilaritās* < *hilaris* or *hilarus* gay < Greek *hilarós* < *hīlaos* happy]
Hil|bert space (hil′bert), *Mathematics, Physics.* a generalization of vectors in ordinary space to a space with an infinite number of dimensions. [< David *Hilbert,* 1862-1943, a German mathematician]
hil|ding (hil′ding), *n., adj. Archaic.* **—*n.*** a mean, worthless person. **—*adj.*** worthless; base: *He was some hilding fellow that had stolen the horse he rode on* (Shakespeare).
[perhaps < obsolete *hield* to bend down + *-ing*¹]
hill (hil), *n., v.* **—*n.*** **1** a raised part of the earth's surface, smaller than a mountain: *The hills, Rock-ribbed and ancient as the sun* (William Cullen Bryant). **2** a little heap or pile: *Ants and moles make hills.* **3** a small heap of soil put over and around the seeds or roots of a plant or cluster of plants: *The farmer made a hill for each three squash seeds.* **4** a plant with a small heap of soil put over its roots: *a hill of corn.*
—*v.t.* **1** to put a little heap of soil over and around. **2** to form into a little heap.
over the hill, a past the prime; on the downgrade: *Some people rudely suggested that Arnie, at 34, was over the hill* (Time). **b** *Army Slang.* absent without leave: *Some rookies have gone temporarily over the hill, but none deserted.*
take to the hills, *Informal.* to run away; decamp: *Nothing that these [political] leaders did last Friday dispels the public distrust that they are, once more, taking to the hills* (New York Times).
the Hill, Capitol Hill: *The liberals complain that . . . they never saw the bill until it was released by the White House on being sent to the Hill* (New York Times).
[Old English *hyll*]
hill|bil|ly (hil′bil′ē), *n., pl.* **-lies,** *adj. Informal.* **—*n.*** a person who lives in the backwoods or a mountain region, especially in the South.
—*adj.* of or characteristic of hillbillies: *hillbilly music, a hillbilly politician, hillbilly TV shows.*
[American English < *hill* + *Billy,* nickname]
hill climb, the act of climbing hills, especially as a contest or race for automobiles or motorcycles.
hill country, an area of hills or high ground.
-hilled, *combining form.* having a hill or hills: *A seven-hilled city = a city having seven hills.*
hill|er (hil′ər), *n.* **1** a person or thing that hills. **2** a device or attachment for hilling plants.
hill|man (hil′mən), *n., pl.* **-men.** a person who lives in hilly country or who likes to climb: *So, and no otherwise—hillmen desire their Hills* (Rudyard Kipling).
hill myna or **mynah**, an Asiatic bird related to the starling family, which is easily taught to speak.
hil|lo (hil′ō, hi lō′), *interj., n., pl.* **-los,** *v.i., v.t.* **-loed, -lo|ing.** = hollo.
hil|loa (hil′ō, hi lō′), *interj., n., pl.* **-loas,** *v.i., v.t.* = hollo.
hill|ock (hil′ək), *n.* a little hill: *hillocks green and soft, Raised by the mole, the miner of the soil* (Cowper). **SYN:** hummock. [Middle English *hillok* < *hill* + *-ok* -ock]
hill|ock|y (hil′ə kē), *adj.* full of hillocks.
hill of beans, *Informal.* something of little consequence or importance: *The removal of a few minor missiles, . . . would not have amounted to a hill of beans* (Wall Street Journal).
hill|side (hil′sīd′), *n.* the side or slope of a hill.
hills|man (hilz′mən), *n., pl.* **-men.** = hillman.
hill station, a post in the hills or foothills where troops, government officials, or others are stationed, especially in southeast Asian countries such as India and Burma, as a refuge from summer heat.
hill|top (hil′top′), *n.* the top of a hill.
hill|town (hil′toun′), *n.* a town that occupies a hill or high ground.
hill|y (hil′ē), *adj.,* **hill|i|er, hill|i|est.** **1** having many hills: *hilly country.* **2** like a hill; steep: *a hilly slope.* **—hill′i|ness,** *n.*
hi|lo grass (hē′lō), a large, coarse, and fast-spreading Hawaiian grass. [< Hawaiian *hilo*]
hilt (hilt), *n., v.* **—*n.*** the handle of a sword, dagger, or tool.
—*v.t.* to furnish with a hilt.
(up) to the hilt, thoroughly; completely: *He was involved in politics to the hilt.*
[Old English *hilt*]
hi|lum (hī′ləm), *n., pl.* **-la** (-lə). **1a** the mark or scar on a seed at the point of attachment to the plant. The eye of a bean is a hilum. **b** the central point of a grain of starch. **2** *Anatomy.* an opening in an organ where nerves or blood vessels enter. [< Latin *hīlum* a trifle]
him (him; *unstressed* im), *pron. Objective case of* **he:** *Don't hit him hard. Give him a drink. Go to him.* [Old English *him,* dative of *hē* he]
Him|a|la|yan (him′ə lā′ən, hə mäl′yən), *adj.* of or having to do with the Himalaya.
Himalayan bear, = black bear (def. 2).
Himalayan raccoon, = lesser panda.
hi|mat|i|on (hi mat′ē on), *n., pl.* **-i|a** (-ē ə). a rectangular piece of cloth draped over the left shoulder and wrapped about the body, worn as a garment in ancient Greece. [< Greek *himátion*]
him|self (him self′ *or, except when following a pause,* im self′), *pron.* **1** the form of **he** or **him** used to make a statement stronger: *He himself did it. Did you see John himself?* **2** the reflexive form of **him:** *He cut himself. He asked himself what he really wanted. He kept the toy for himself. He cared more for himself than for anything else.* **3** his real or true self: *He feels like himself again.* **4** *Archaic or Irish Dialect.* a form that takes the place of the subject: *The dagger which himself Gave Edith* (Tennyson).
Him|yar|ite (him′yə rīt), *n., adj.* **—*n.*** **1** a member of an ancient group of people that lived in south-

---

Pronunciation Key: hat, āge, cãre, fär; let, ēqual, tėrm; it, īce; hot, ōpen, ôrder; oil, out; cup, půt, rüle; child; long; thin; ᴛʜen; zh, measure; ə represents **a** in about, **e** in taken, **i** in pencil, **o** in lemon, **u** in circus.

ern Arabia. **2** an Arab descended from this group. **—*adj.*** Himyaritic. [< Arabic *Himyar,* a legendary king in Yemen + English *-ite*[1]]

Him|yar|it|ic (him′yə rit′ik), *adj., n.* **—*adj.*** of or having to do with the Himyarites, their language, and their culture.

—*n.* the language of the ancient Himyarites, an Arabic dialect related to Ethiopic.

hin (hin), *n.* a Hebrew unit of liquid measure, containing a little more than one gallon. [< Hebrew *hīn*]

hi|na|u (hē′nä ü, -nou), *n.* **1** an evergreen tree of New Zealand: *Hinau, a small tree about fifty feet high and eighteen inches thick in stem, with brown bark which yields a permanent blue-black dye, used for tanning* (J. Hector). **2** the wood of this tree. [< Maori *hinau*]

Hi|na|ya|na (hē′nə yä′nə), *n.* the traditional form of Buddhism, observed chiefly in Burma, Kampuchea, Ceylon (Sri Lanka), Laos, Thailand, and Vietnam, that reveres Buddha as a great human teacher but not a divinity; Theravada. [< Sanskrit *Hīnayāna* (literally) small vehicle]

Hi|na|ya|nist (hē′nə yä′nist), *adj., n.* **—*adj.*** of or having to do with Hinayana.

—*n.* a believer in Hinayana.

hinc|ty (hingk′tē), *adj.,* **-ti|er, -ti|est.** *U.S. Slang.* snobbish; conceited. [origin unknown]

hind[1] (hīnd), *adj.,* **hind|er, hind|most** or **hind|er-most.** back; rear; posterior: *hind legs. The hind wings of some aphids are shorter than the forewings.* [Middle English *hind,* perhaps back formation < *hinder* hinder[2]]

hind[2] (hīnd), *n., pl.* **hinds** or (*collectively*) **hind.** **1** a female deer, especially a female red deer in and after its third year. **SYN:** doe. **2** any one of various food fishes of the Caribbean, such as certain groupers, sea bass, the red hind, and the rock hind. [Old English *hind*]

hind[3] (hīnd), *n. Archaic.* **1** a farm worker or servant: *Laborious hinds That had survived the father, served the son* (William Cowper). **2** a peasant; rustic. [variant of Middle English *hine,* Old English *hīne,* plural, contraction of *hīwna* or *hīgna,* genitive plural of *hīwa, hīga* member of a household]

Hind., **1** Hindu. **2** Hindustan. **3** Hindustani.

hind|brain (hīnd′brān′), *n. Embryology.* the back part of the brain, composed of the metencephalon and the myelencephalon; rhombencephalon. It includes the cerebellum and the medulla oblongata.

hind|cast (hīnd′kast′, -käst′), *v.i.,* **-cast** or **-cast|ed, -cast|ing.** to provide weather information based on the record of past atmospheric conditions.

hin|der[1] (hin′dər), *v.t.* to keep back; hold back; get in the way of; make hard to do; stop; prevent: *Deep mud hindered travel. My tears must stop, for every drop Hinders needle and thread* (Thomas Hood). **SYN:** impede, encumber, retard, hamper. See syn. under **prevent.** **—*v.i.*** to get in the way; be a hindrance: *Help out; don't hinder. It is not the dark place that hinders, but the dim eye* (Thomas Carlyle). [Old English *hindrian.* See related etym. at **hind**[1].]

hind|er[2] (hīn′dər), *adj.* hind; back; rear: *They divided the deer's carcass, the hunter taking the hinder parts.* **SYN:** posterior. [Middle English *hinder.* Compare Old English *hinder* and *hindan* in back, behind.]

hind|er|most (hīn′dər mōst), *adj.* = hindmost.

hind|gut (hīnd′gut′), *n.* **1** *Embryology.* the back section of the embryonic alimentary canal, from which the posterior part of the digestive tract develops. **2** *Zoology.* the posterior part of the digestive tract of an insect.

Hin|di (hin′dē), *n., adj.* **—*n.*** **1** an Indo-European vernacular language of northern India, comprising various dialects. **2** the official language of India. It is a Sanskritized form of Hindustani used by educated Hindus. **3** a native of India.

—*adj.* of or having to do with Hindi: *a Hindi dialect, Hindi writing.*

[< Hindustani *Hindī* < *Hind* India < Persian. Compare etym. under **Hindu.**]

hind leg, rear leg of an animal or insect.

get (or **stand**) **up on one's hind legs,** to act firmly or independently: [*He*] *urged U.S. automakers to "get up on their hind legs" to voice their criticism when the plan was made known* (Wall Street Journal).

talk the hind leg (or **legs**) **off a donkey** (or **dog, horse**), *U.S. Informal.* to talk to a wearying extent.

hind|limb (hīnd′lim′), *n.* = hind leg.

hind|most (hīnd′mōst), *adj.* farthest back; nearest the rear; last.

Hin|doo (hin′dü), *n., pl.* **-doos,** *adj.* = Hindu.

Hin|doo|ism (hin′dü iz əm), *n.* = Hinduism.

Hin|doo|ize (hin′dü īz), *v.t.,* **-ized, -iz|ing.** = Hinduize.

Hin|doo|sta|ni (hin′dù stä′nē, -stan′ē), *adj., n.* = Hindustani.

Hin|do|sta|ni (hin′də stä′nē, -stan′ē), *adj., n.* = Hindustani.

hind|quar|ter (hīnd′kwôr′tər), *n.* the rear half of a side of meat, especially of beef, veal, lamb, or pork, including the leg, loin, and one or more ribs.

hindquarters, the rear part of an animal's body, including the lower back, buttocks, and thighs; haunches.

hin|drance (hin′drəns), *n.* **1** a person or thing that hinders; obstacle; obstruction: *Heavy clothes are a hindrance to swimming. An attachment that would be a hindrance to him in any honourable career* (Thomas Hardy). **SYN:** See syn under **obstacle.** **2** the act of hindering.

hind shank, a cut of meat from the upper part of the hind leg.

hind|sight (hīnd′sīt′), *n.* **1** the ability to see, after the event is over, what should have been done: *With the invaluable aid of hindsight, it is possible to see that throughout all the early months the stage was being set for the final disaster* (Harper's). **2** the rear sight of a firearm. [American English, formed as opposite of *foresight*]

hind|sight|ed (hīnd′sī′tid), *adj.* having or showing hindsight.

Hin|du (hin′dü), *n., pl.* **-dus,** *adj.* **—*n.*** **1** a member of a native race of India or Hindustan, especially one speaking an Indo-European language. **2** a person who believes in Hinduism.

—*adj.* of or having to do with Hindus, their language, or their religion; Indian.

[< Persian *Hindū* < *Hind* India < Old Persian *Hindu*]

Hindu., Hindustani.

Hin|du-Ar|a|bic numerals (hin′dü ar′ə bik), = Arabic numerals.

Hindu calendar, the calendar used by the Hindus, which divides the year into 12 months of 30 or 31 days. The modern form of the calendar, officially introduced in India in 1957, counts the years from A.D. 78.

Hin|du|ism (hin′dü iz əm), *n.* the religious and social system of the Hindus, a development of ancient Brahmanism. The caste system and the worship of many gods are parts of Hinduism.

Hin|du|ize (hin′dü īz), *v.t.,* **-ized, -iz|ing.** to make Hindu in character, customs, or religion. **—Hin′du|i|za′tion,** *n.*

Hin|du|sta|ni (hin′dù stä′nē, -stan′ē), *adj., n.* **—*adj.*** of or having to do with India, its people, or their languages.

—*n.* the commonest language of northern India. A form of it called Hindi is the official language of India. A Persian-Arabic form, Urdu, is one of the major languages of Pakistan.

[< Hindustani, Persian *Hindūstānī* Indian < Persian *Hindūstān* India < *Hindū* Hindu + *stān* place, country]

hind|ward (hīnd′wərd), *adv., adj.* backward; rearward.

hinge** (hinj), *n., v.,* **hinged, hing|ing.** **—*n. **1** a joint on which a door, gate, cover, or lid moves back and forth. **2** a natural joint doing similar work: *the hinge of the knee, the hinge of a clam.* **3** *Figurative.* that on which something else turns or depends; central principle; critical point: *We usually call reward and punishment the two hinges upon which all government turns* (Jonathan Swift). **4** a small piece of gummed paper with a slot, by which stamps can be mounted in an album without gluing them to the pages. **5** *Obsolete.* **a** the axis of the earth. **b** one of the four cardinal points: *Nor slept the winds Within their stony caves, but rush'd abroad From the four hinges of the world* (Milton).

—*v.t.* to furnish with hinges; attach by hinges: *The ailerons on an airplane are hinged to the wing.*

—*v.i.* **1** to hang and turn on a hinge. **2** *Figurative.* to depend: *The success of the picnic hinges on the kind of weather we will have.*

[Middle English *heng* axis, hinge. See related etym. at **hang.**]**—hing′er,** *n.*

***hinge**
definition 1

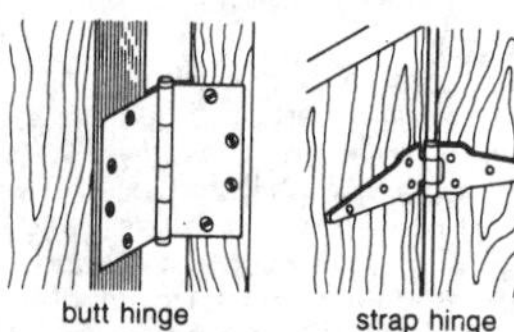

hinged (hinjd), *adj.* having hinges.

hinge joint, *Anatomy.* a joint, such as the elbow, in which a convex part of one bone fits into a concave part of another, allowing motion in only one plane; ginglymus.

hinge teeth, the small, sharp projections of the shell near the hinge in bivalves.

Hing|lish (hing′glish), *n., adj.* a blend of Hindi and English spoken in India: *Hinglish . . . uses English parts of speech for more complicated functions, as in this Hinglish sentence: "Dekho great democratic institutions kaise India main develop ho rahi hain," which in English is "See how the great democratic institutions are developing here in India"* (Ved Mehta). [blend of *hindi* and *English*]

hin|ny (hin′ē), *n., pl.* **-nies.** a hybrid animal that is the offspring of a male horse and female ass. A hinny resembles a mule. [< Latin *Hinnus* < Greek *ínnos*]

hint (hint), *n., v.* **—*n.*** **1** a slight sign; indirect suggestion: *A small black cloud gave a hint of a coming storm.* **SYN:** intimation, allusion, inkling, innuendo, insinuation. See syn. under **suggestion.** **2** a very slight amount. **3** *Obsolete.* an occasion; opportunity.

—*v.t.* to give a slight sign of; suggest indirectly: *She hinted that she wanted to go to bed by saying, "Do you often stay up this late?" Just hint a fault* (Alexander Pope).

hint at, to give a hint of; suggest: *The spectator's imagination completes what the artist merely hints at* (Hawthorne).

[apparently < *hent*] **—hint′er,** *n.*

—*Syn.* *v.t.* **Hint, intimate, insinuate** mean to suggest indirectly. **Hint** means to convey an idea in a roundabout way: *The bellboy hinted that a tip would be acceptable, by saying, "Is everything all right, sir?"* **Intimate** means to suggest something in a delicate way, touching it lightly and cleverly so that others understand without being told outright: *He intimated that he will accept if he is invited.* **Insinuate** means to suggest or hint something unkind or nasty in a sly or underhand way: *Are you insinuating that I am a liar?*

hin|ter|land (hin′tər land′), *n.* **1** the land or district behind a coast. **2** a region far from towns and cities, that is rural and thinly settled; back country. **3** *Figurative.* the remote parts; background.

[< German *Hinterland* < *hinter-* behind (compare English **hinder**[2]) + *Land* land]

hint|ing|ly (hin′ting lē), *adv.* in a hinting manner; suggestively: *He kept talking about gum hintingly, finally suggesting I get some.*

hip[1] (hip), *n., v.,* **hipped, hip|ping.** **—*n.*** **1a** the part that sticks out on each side of the body below a person's waist where the leg joins the body; haunch. **b** the ball-and-socket joint formed by the upper thighbone and the pelvis; hip joint. **2** a similar part in animals where the hind leg joins the body, such as the coxa in arthropods. **3** *Architecture.* the projecting angle formed by the meeting of two sloping sides of a roof. See also **hip roof.**

—*v.t.* **1** *Architecture.* to form (a roof) with a hip or hips. **2** to dislocate or injure the hip of. **3** *U.S.* to carry on the hip.

hip and thigh, with overwhelming blows; unsparingly: *He smote them hip and thigh with a great slaughter* (Judges 15:8).

on (or **upon**) **the hip,** at a disadvantage (originally applied to wrestling): *I'll have our Michael Cassio on the hip* (Shakespeare).

shoot from the hip, *Slang.* to speak or act in an impulsive and reckless manner: *Shooting from the hip is no substitute for careful analysis* (Wall Street Journal).

[Old English *hype*] **—hip′less,** *adj.* **—hip′like′,** *adj.*

hip[2] (hip), *n.* the seedcase containing the ripe seed of a rosebush: *The oaks bear mast, the briers scarlet hips* (Shakespeare). [Old English *hēope*]

hip[3] (hip), *interj.* an exclamation used in cheering or calling for a cheer: *Hip, hip, hurrah!* [origin unknown]

hip[4] (hip), *adj., n., v.,* **hipped, hip|ping.** *U.S. Slang.* **—*adj.*** **1** informed; up-to-date; hep. **2** of or having to do with hipsters or their style, language, or other characteristics.

—*n.* **1** = hipster. **2** the condition of being smart and stylish: *Grooviness* [*at the discothèque*] *merges with aplomb, and hip attains a state akin to quiet well-being* (New Yorker).

—*v.t.* to keep informed; alert; wise up: *to be hipped on a plan.*

[variant of *hep*] **—hip′ly,** *adv.* **—hip′ness,** *n.*

hip[5] (hip), *n., v.,* **hipped, hip|ping.** *Informal.* **—*n.*** low spirits; the blues.

—*v.t.* to make sad or depressed. [short for *hypochondria*]

HIP (no periods), Health Insurance Plan (of Greater New York).

hip bath, = sitz bath.

hip|bone (hip′bōn′), *n.* **1** either of the two, wide irregular bones which, with the lower backbone, form the pelvis in man and other mammals, each consisting of three consolidated bones (the ilium, ischium, and pubis); innominate bone. **2** the upper part of the femur.

hip boot, a rubber boot extending to the hip, usually used by fishermen.

hip disease, any disease, such as a form of tuberculosis, that affects the hip joint.

hip flask, a flask for alcoholic liquor usually curved to carry in a hip pocket.

hip-hop *(hip′hop′), adj. U.S. Slang* of, having to do with, or characteristic of music intended for dancing, with a rap or Latin beat: *the hip-hop scene.*

hip-hug|ger (hip′hug′ər), *adj.* clinging closely to the hips: *hip-hugger pants.*

hip-hug|gers (hip′hug′ərz), *n.pl.* trousers that start about an inch and a half below the waistline and cling closely to the hips.

hip-hug|ging (hip′hug′ing), *adj.* clinging closely to the hips; hip-riding.

hip joint, the joint formed by the upper thighbone and the hipbone.

hip knob, *Architecture.* a knob or other ornament placed on the top of the hip of a roof, or on the apex of a gable.

hip-length (hip′lengkth′, -length′), *adj.* reaching down to the hips: *a hip-length jacket.*

hip|line (hip′līn′), *n.* **1** the line around the body at the widest part of the hips. **2** the part of a woman's dress covering this line.

hipped[1] (hipt), *adj. Architecture.* formed with hips: *a hipped roof.*

hipped[2] (hipt), *adj.* **1** *U.S. Slang.* having the mind full of a certain subject; obsessed: *He's all hipped on building his own radio.* **2** *Informal.* depressed; melancholy. **3** offended; vexed.

-hipped, *combining form.* having _____hips: *small-hipped = having small hips.*

hip|pe|ty-hop (hip′ə tē hop′), *adv., adj., v.,* **-hopped, -hop|ping.** *Informal.* **—*adv., adj.*** with a hopping or springing motion: *to go hippety-hop down the street* (adv.); *a hippety-hop stride* (adj.). **—*v.i.*** to go hippety-hop: *I noticed great activity at Aqueduct, so I hippety-hopped out there the other morning* (New Yorker). [jingling combination of dialectal *hip* to hop + *hop*[1]]

hip|pe|ty-hop|pe|ty (hip′ə tē hop′ə tē), *adv., adj.* = hippety-hop.

hip|pic (hip′ik), *adj.* of or having to do with horses or horse racing. [< Greek *hippikós* < *híppos* horse]

hip|pie (hip′ē), *n., adj.* **—*n.*** a person who breaks away from conventional society, believing in complete freedom of expression, shown typically by wearing unconventional clothes and letting the hair go ungroomed, and often living in communes engaging in free love and the free use of narcotic drugs.
—*adj.* of, having to do with, or characteristic of hippies: *Almost every newspaper account emphasized the hippie dress and hair* (Atlantic). Also, **hippy.**
[originally (1950's) "a person who is very or overly hip" (i.e., excessively eager to be ahead in the latest styles, extremely unconventional) < *hip*[4] alert, informed, up-to-date + *-ie*]

hip|pie|dom (hip′ē dəm), *n.* the realm or world of hippies; hippies as a group.

hip|pi|ness or **hip|pie|ness** (hip′ē nis), *n.* the quality or condition of being a hippie.

hip|pish (hip′ish), *adj. Informal.* somewhat depressed or sad: *To divert my thoughts a little space, Because I'm rather hippish* (Byron). [< *hip*[5] + *-ish*]

hip|po (hip′ō), *n., pl.* **-pos.** *Informal.* a hippopotamus.

hip|po|cam|pal (hip′ə kam′pəl), *adj.* of or having to do with the hippocampus in the brain.

hip|po|cam|pus (hip′ə kam′pəs), *n., pl.* **-pi** (-pī). **1** any one of a group of small fishes having a horse-shaped head; sea horse. **2** *Anatomy.* a ridge along the extension of each lateral ventricle of the brain. [< Latin *hippocampus* < Greek *hippókampos* sea horse (of Neptune); the fish < *híppos* horse + *kámpos* sea monster]

hip|po|cras (hip′ə kras), *n.* a liqueur made of wine and spices, formerly used as a medicine. [< Middle French *ipocras* < Medieval Latin (*vinum*) *Hippocraticum* (wine) of Hippocrates (apparently named after the filter ("Hippocrates' sleeve") through which it was run)]

Hip|po|crat|ic (hip′ə krat′ik), *adj.* of or having to do with Hippocrates.

Hippocratic oath, a famous oath, attributed to Hippocrates, describing the duties and obligations of a physician. It is usually taken by those about to become physicians.

Hip|po|crene (hip′ə krēn, hip′ə krē′nē), *n. Greek Mythology.* **1** a fountain on Mount Helicon, sacred to the Muses and regarded as a source of poetic inspiration. It was supposed to have been produced by a stroke of Pegasus' hoof. **2** the waters of the fountain: *O for a beaker full of the warm South, Full of the true, the blushful Hippocrene* (Keats). [< Latin *Hippocrēnē* < Greek *Hippokrēnē* < *híppos* horse + *krēnē* fountain]

hip|po|drome (hip′ə drōm), *n.* **1** an arena or building with an arena as for a circus or rodeo. **2** (in ancient Greece and Rome) an oval track for horse races and chariot races, surrounded by tiers of seats for spectators. [< Latin *hippodromos* < Greek *hippódromos* < *híppos* horse + *drómos* course]

hip|po|griff or **hip|po|gryph** (hip′ə grif), *n.* a fabulous winged creature resembling a griffin, but having the body and hind parts of a horse. [< French *hippogriffe* < Italian *ippogrifo* < Greek *híppos* horse + Italian *grifo* griffon]

hip|pol|o|gist (hi pol′ə jist), *n.* an expert in hippology.

hip|pol|o|gy (hi pol′ə jē), *n.* the study of horses. [< Greek *híppos* horse + English *-logy*]

Hip|pol|y|ta (hi pol′ə tə), *n. Greek Legend.* a queen of the Amazons, slain by Hercules in carrying out his ninth labor, which was to bring back her girdle.

Hip|pol|y|te (hi pol′ə tē), *n.* = Hippolyta.

Hip|pol|y|tus (hi pol′ə təs), *n. Greek Legend.* the son of Theseus, who rejected the love of his stepmother Phaedra. Falsely accused by Phaedra of ravishing her, he was cursed by Theseus, and killed when Poseidon caused his chariot to overturn.

Hip|pom|e|don (hi pom′ə don), *n. Greek Legend.* one of the Seven against Thebes.

Hip|pom|e|nes (hi pom′ə nēz), *n. Greek Legend.* the youth who defeated Atalanta in a race.

hip|po|phile (hip′ə fīl), *n.* a lover of horses. [< Greek *híppos* horse + *phílos* loving]

***hip|po|pot|a|mus** (hip′ə pot′ə məs), *n., pl.* **-mus|es, -mi** (-mī). **1** a huge animal with almost no hair, found in and near the rivers and swamps of Africa; river horse. It often weighs as much as four tons and has short legs and a large body covered with thick skin. Hippopotamuses feed on plants and can stay under water for a long time. They are even-toed ungulates, related to swine. **2** a smaller, similar mammal of the same family. [< Latin *hippopotamus* < Greek *hippopótamos* < *híppos* horse + *potamós* river]

***hippopotamus**
definition 1

hip|pus (hip′əs), *n., pl.* **-pus|es.** a tremor of the iris of the eye, characterized by rapid contraction and dilation of the pupil.

hip|py[1] (hip′ē), *adj.,* **-pi|er, -pi|est.** having wide hips: *. . . the curvy, hippy type that publicists like to call the "all-American girl"* (Wall Street Journal).

hip|py[2] (hip′ē), *n., pl.* **-pies,** *adj.* = hippie.

hip-rid|er (hip′rī′dər), *n.* a hip-riding garment.

hip-rid|ing (hip′rī′ding), *adj.* riding on the hipbone; worn below the waistline and clinging closely to the hips; hip-hugging.

***hip roof**, a roof with sloping ends and sides.

***hip roof**

hip-roofed (hip′rüft′, -rüft′), *adj.* having a hip roof.

hip|shot (hip′shot′), *adj.* **1** having a dislocated hip; hipped. **2** having one hip lower than the other. **3** *Figurative.* lame; awkward; clumsy: *this hipshot grammarian* (Milton). [< *hip*[1] + *shot*[2]]

hip|ster (hip′stər), *n. U.S. Slang.* **1** a person who keeps up with new and usually unconventional ideas, styles, and attitudes; person who is or is considered hip: *Broadway goes to Oriental culture in the same spirit that hipsters go to Zen Buddhism* (Harper's). **2** a jazz fan. [< *hip*[4] + *-ster*]

hip|ster|ism (hip′stər iz əm), *n.* the beliefs and practices of hipsters: *Mailer makes it clear that the appeal of hipsterism for him lies in its undiscriminating rejection of all the values of contemporary society* (Saturday Review).

hi|ra|ga|na (hir′ə gä′nə), *n.* one of the two styles of writing the Japanese syllabary of 46 or (formerly) 48 letters (the other being katakana) consisting of rounded characters joined together. [< Japanese *hiragana* < *hira* plain + *kana* kana]

hir|cine (hėr′sīn, -sən), *adj.* **1** of or having to do with goats; resembling a goat, especially in odor. **2** = lustful. [< Latin *hircīnus* < *hircus* he-goat]

hire (hīr), *v.,* **hired, hir|ing.** **—*v.t.*** **1** to pay for the use of (a thing) or the work or services of (a person): *He hired a car and a man to drive it. The storekeeper hired a boy to deliver groceries.* **SYN:** lease, rent. See syn. under **employ. 2** to give the use of (a thing) or the work or services of (a person) in return for payment: *He hired himself to work in the fields for one summer. They hired the money, didn't they?* (Calvin Coolidge).
[Old English *hȳrian* < noun]
—*n.* **1** payment for use of a thing or the work or services of a person: *Do you perform in plays for hire or just for pleasure? The labourer is worthy of his hire* (Luke 10:7). **2** the act of hiring or fact of being hired.
for (or **on**) **hire**, for use or work in return for payment: *To keep one's conscience, too, on hire, as . . . Isham down there at the livery stable does a horse* (W. M. Baker). *Owners of* [*knitting*] *frames . . . let frames out on hire* (English Guilds).
hire out, to give one's work in return for payment: *Poor white girls never hired out to do servants' work* (Frederick L. Olmsted).
[Old English *hȳr*] **—hire′a|ble, hir′a|ble,** *adj.*

hired hand, **1** a hired laborer. **2** = farm hand.

hire|ling (hīr′ling), *n., adj.* **—*n.*** **1** a person who works only for money, without interest or pride in the work. **2** a person hired to do whatever another orders him to do: *He had no authority; he was merely a hireling.*
—*adj.* to be had for hire; mercenary.

hire-pur|chase (hīr′pėr′chəs), *n., adj.* **—*n.*** *British.* **1** a purchase made on the installment plan. **2** the installment plan: *I see that hire-purchase is now available to the citizens of Moscow and that there is a "brisk sale for wireless sets and radiograms"* (Punch).
—*adj.* of or having to do with hire-purchase. *Abbr:* H.P.

hir|er (hīr′ər), *n.* a person who employs others or rents something.

hir|ing hall (hīr′ing), a large room in which a foreman selects and hires longshoremen: *The law has established 13 state-run hiring halls in the port to replace the shape-up* (Wall Street Journal).

hi-rise (hī′rīz′), *n. U.S. Informal.* high-rise.

hir|mo|lo|gi|on (hėr′mə lō′jē ən), *n., pl.* **-gi|a** (-jē ə). a book containing Eucharistic prayers and hirmoi of the Eastern Church. [< Medieval Greek *heirmologion* < Greek *heirmós* series, connection + *légein* say, read]

hir|mos (hėr′məs), *n., pl.* **-moi** (-moi). a model stanza in the hymnology of the Eastern Church, forming a pattern for other stanzas. [< New Latin *hirmos, hirmus* < Greek *heirmós* series, connection]

hir|ple (hėr′pəl, hir′-), *v.,* **-pled, -pling,** *n. Scottish.* **—*v.i.*** to move lamely or with difficulty; hobble.
—*n.* hobble.

hir|sute (hėr′süt), *adj.* **1** covered with hairs; hairy; shaggy; rough. **2** *Biology.* covered with long, stiff hairs. [< Latin *hirsūtus*] **—hir′sute|ly,** *adv.* **—hir′sute|ness,** *n.*

hir|sut|ism (hėr′sü tiz əm), *n.* the inordinate growth of hairs on the body.

hir|u|din (hir′yü din), *n.* a substance obtained from an active principle extracted from leeches, used to slow down or prevent coagulation of the blood. [< Latin *hirūdō* leech + English *-in*]

his (hiz; *unstressed* iz), *adj., pron.* **—*adj.*** **1** of him; belonging to him: *His name is Bill. This is his book.* **2** of things that one does not own but has a share or interest in or has to deal with: *He always gets his man. He finally won his letter as a senior.*
—*pron.* *Possessive form of* **he.** the one or ones belonging to him: *My books are new; his are old. The others are not his.*
[Old English *his,* genitive of *hē* he]

his-and-hers (hiz′ən hėrz′), *adj.* designed as a matching pair for wear or use by a married couple: *his-and-hers towels.*

his heels, *Cribbage.* a jack played as a turnup.

his nobs, *Cribbage.* a jack of the same suit as the turnup.

His|pa|ni|a (his pā′nē ə, -pän′yə), *n.* **1** the Latin name for Spain and Portugal. **2** a literary name for Spain. [< Latin *Hispānia*]

His|pan|ic (his pan′ik), *adj., n.* **—*adj.*** **1** = Spanish. **2** = Latin-American.
—*n.* *U.S.* a person living in the United States who is of Spanish or Latin-American descent: *The*

Pronunciation Key: hat, **ā**ge, c**ã**re, f**ä**r; let, **ē**qual, t**ė**rm; it, **ī**ce; h**o**t, **ō**pen, **ô**rder; **oi**l, **ou**t; cup, p**u̇**t, r**ü**le; **ch**ild; lo**ng**; **th**in; **ᴛʜ**en; **zh**, measure;
ə represents **a** in about, **e** in taken, **i** in pencil, **o** in lemon, **u** in circus.

68-person unit includes twelve blacks, twelve Hispanics, and two women (Newsweek).

His·pan·i·cism (his pan′ə siz əm), *n.* a Spanish idiom or expression.

His·pan·i·cist (his pan′ə sist), *n.* a student of the Spanish language and culture.

His·pan·i·cize (his pan′ə sīz), *v.t.,* **-cized, -ciz·ing.** to make Spanish; give a Spanish character or accent to.

his·pa·ni·dad (ēs pä′nē ŧʜäŧʜ′), *n. Spanish.* a movement in Latin America advocating the spiritual and, sometimes, political unity of Spanish-speaking lands.

His·pa·nism (his′pə niz əm), *n.* **1** a movement affirming the cultural unity of Spanish-speaking peoples. **2** pride in Spanish culture. **3** = Hispanicism.

His·pa·nist (his′pə nist), *n.* = Hispanicist.

His·pa·no (his pan′ō), *n., pl.* **-nos.** *U.S.* **1** a person living in the southwestern United States who is of Spanish or Mexican descent. **2** a Spanish-speaking person living in the United States: *The combined newspapers are using El Diario's slogan of "Champion of the Puerto Ricans and Hispanos"* (New York Times). [< *Hispano-*]

Hispano-, *combining form.* Spanish: *Hispano-American = Spanish-American.* [< Spanish *hispano* Spanish < Latin *Hispānus* < *Hispānia* Spain]

his·pid (his′pid), *adj. Biology.* rough with stiff hairs, bristles, or spines. [< Latin *hispidus,* related to *hircus* he-goat]

his·pid·i·ty (his pid′ə tē), *n.* hispid quality or state.

hiss (his), *v., n.* —*v.i.* **1** to make a sound like *ss: Air or steam rushing out of a small opening hisses. Geese and snakes hiss.* **2** to show disapproval or scorn by hissing: *Thou art disgraced and hissed at* (Jeremy Taylor). —*v.t.* **1** to show disapproval or scorn for by hissing: *The audience cheered the hero and hissed the villain.* **2** to force or drive by hissing: *They hissed the actors off the stage.* **3** to say or show by hissing.
—*n.* **1** a sound like *ss: the hiss of escaping steam.* SYN: sibilance. **2** a hissing sound as an expression of disapproval or scorn: *Hisses were heard from many who disliked what the speaker was saying.*
[imitative] —**hiss′er,** *n.*

hiss·a·ble (his′ə bəl), *adj.* deserving to be hissed; detestable: *[He] is marvelously hissable as a swarthy outlaw costumed in traditional black* (Time).

his·self (hi self′, hiz-), *pron. Substandard or Dialect.* himself: *She wasn't but sixteen; he wasn't but nineteen hisself* (Truman Capote).

hiss·ing (his′ing), *n., adj.* —*n.* something to be hissed; a scornful thing: *Their reputations had . . . been blasted and their names made a hissing* (London Times).
—*adj.* of or like a hiss: *a hissing sound.* —**hiss′ing·ly,** *adv.*

hist (hist), *interj., v.* —*interj.* be still! listen!: *The guide said: "Hist! You can hear the deer coming."* SYN: hush.
—*v.t. Archaic.* to urge on by saying "hist": *And the mute silence hist along* (Milton).
[imitative]

hist-, *combining form.* the form of **histo-** before vowels, as in *histoid.*

hist., 1 histology. **2a** historian. **b** history.

his·tam·i·nase (his tam′ə nās), *n.* an enzyme that can make a histamine inactive.

his·ta·mine (his′tə min, -mēn), *n.* an amine released by the body in allergic reactions that lowers the blood pressure, used to treat or diagnose various allergies, Ménière's disease, and other disorders. *Formula:* $C_5H_9N_3$ [< *hist*(idine) + *amine*]

his·ta·min·ic (his′tə min′ik), *adj.* of or induced by histamine: *a histaminic headache.*

his·ti·dine (his′tə dēn, -din), *n.* a basic amino acid present in many simple proteins and yielded by hydrolysis. It is important in diet, and sometimes used to treat ulcers and arteriosclerosis. *Formula:* $C_6H_9N_3O_2$ [< German *Histidin* < Greek *histíon* tissue, web]

hist·ing (his′ting), *n.* the raising of a player's hand from the ground when shooting marbles. [origin unknown]

his·ti·o·cyte (his′tē ə sīt), *n.* a highly phagocytic cell of the connective tissue. [< Greek *histíon* tissue + English *-cyte*]

his·ti·o·cyt·ic (his′tē ə sit′ik), *adj.* composed of histiocytes: *a histiocytic tumor.*

histo-, *combining form.* tissue: *Histochemistry = the chemistry of (organic) tissues.* Also, **hist-** before vowels. [< Greek *histós* web, related to *histánai* to stand]

his·to·blast (his′tə blast), *n.* a cell that is forming tissue; primary element or unit of an organic tissue. [< *histo-* + Greek *blastós* cell]

his·to·chem·i·cal (his′tō kem′ə kəl), *adj.* of or having to do with histochemistry. —**his′to·chem′i·cal·ly,** *adv.*

his·to·chem·is·try (his′tō kem′ə strē), *n.* the chemistry of organic tissues.

his·to·clas·tic (his′tə klas′tik), *adj. Medicine.* destroying or breaking down tissue.

his·to·com·pat·i·bil·i·ty (his′tō kəm pat′ə bil′ə tē), *n.* the condition in which grafted or transplanted tissue is accepted by surrounding tissue; compatibility of graft tissue: *Organ transplantation has brought urgency to the problem of the genetics of histocompatibility* (Victor A. McKusick).

his·to·com·pat·i·ble (his′tō kəm pat′ə bəl), *adj.* exhibiting histocompatibility: *histocompatible guinea pigs.*

his·to·gen (his′tə jen), *n.* one of the areas of a plant in which tissues become differentiated.

his·to·gen·e·sis (his′tə jen′ə sis), *n.* the development of tissues from embryonic germ layers.

his·to·ge·net·ic (his′tə jə net′ik), *adj.* of or having to do with histogenesis: *histogenetic studies of flowers.*

his·tog·e·nous (his toj′ə nəs), *adj.* formed by the tissues: *the histogenous cells which originate locally as the result of local tissue proliferation* (Practitioner).

his·tog·e·ny (his toj′ə nē), *n.* = histogenesis.

his·to·gram (his′tə gram), *n. Statistics.* a graph of a frequency distribution in which vertical rectangles or columns are constructed with the width of each rectangle being a class interval and the height a distance corresponding to the frequency in that class interval. [< *histo-* + *-gram*[1]]

his·tog·ra·phy (his tog′rə fē), *n.* the description of organic tissues.

his·toid (his′toid), *adj.* of or like tissue, especially normal or connective tissue: *a histoid tumor.* [< *hist-* + *-oid*]

his·to·in·com·pat·i·bil·i·ty (his′tō in′kəm pat′ə bil′ə tē), *n.* incompatibility of graft tissue; graft rejection: *These animals have virtually no immunological reactivity, so we felt confident that our test would not be complicated in any important way by histoincompatibility reactions between cells and hosts* (New Scientist and Science Journal).

his·to·in·com·pat·i·ble (his′tō in′kəm pat′ə bəl), *adj.* exhibiting histoincompatibility.

his·to·log·i·cal (his′tə log′ə kəl), *adj.* of or having to do with histology. —**his′to·log′i·cal·ly,** *adv.*

his·tol·o·gy (his tol′ə jē), *n.* **1** the branch of biology that deals with the structure, especially the microscopic structure, of the tissues of animals and plants; the science of organic tissues. *Abbr:* hist. **2** the tissue structure of an animal or plant. —**his·tol′o·gist,** *n.*

his·tol·y·sis (his tol′ə sis), *n.* the disintegration or dissolution of organic tissue.

his·to·lyt·ic (his′tə lit′ik), *adj.* of or having to do with histolysis.

his·ton (his′ton), *n.* = histone.

his·tone (his′tōn), *n. Biochemistry.* any one of a class of proteins, such as globin, that are basic in reaction and are soluble in water. They often occur in combination with nucleic acid. [< German *Histon* < Greek *histánai* to stay, stand + German *-on* -one (apparently because it halts coagulation)]

his·to·path·o·log·ic (his′tō path′ə loj′ik), *adj.* = histopathological.

his·to·path·o·log·i·cal (his′tō path′ə loj′ə kəl), *adj.* of or having to do with diseased tissue: *histopathological changes.*

his·to·pa·thol·o·gy (his′tō pa thol′ə jē), *n.* the study of diseased tissues.

his·to·phys·i·ol·o·gy (his′tō fiz′ē ol′ə jē), *n.* the physiology of the tissues.

his·to·plas·min (his′tə plaz′min), *n.* a sterile culture of the fungus causing histoplasmosis, used as a skin test for the presence of the active fungus.

his·to·plas·mo·sis (his′tə plaz mō′sis), *n.* a serious fungous disease that attacks especially the lungs, throat, spleen, liver, and lymph nodes. It is most common in the eastern and central United States. [< New Latin *Histoplasma* the genus name of the fungus + English *-osis*]

his·to·ri·an (his tôr′ē ən, -tōr′-), *n.* **1** a person who writes about history. **2** an expert in history. *Abbr:* hist.

his·tor·ic (his tôr′ik, -tor′-), *adj.* **1** famous or important in history: *Plymouth Rock and Bunker Hill are historic spots. The entry of the free people of Germany into the Atlantic association of nations is an event of historic significance* (New York Times). SYN: celebrated, noted, renowned. **2** = historical.

his·tor·i·cal (his tôr′ə kəl, -tor′-), *adj.* **1** of or having to do with history: *historical documents.* **2** according to history; based on history: *a historical novel.* **3** known to be real or true; in history, not in legend: *It is a historical fact that George Washington was the first President of the United States.* **4** famous in history; historic: *a historical town. This historical and gallant little ship [the Mayflower]* (Longfellow). **5** (of words) obsolete except in historical accounts or as a historical term. [< Latin *historicus* (< Greek *historikós* < *historíā* history) + English *-al*[1]] —**his·tor′i·cal·ly,** *adv.* —**his·tor′i·cal·ness,** *n.*

historical grammar, the systematic study comparing present with past forms and usage of a language.

historical linguistics, the systematic study of the history and historical relationship of languages and linguistic forms.

historical materialism, the theory that all historic processes are fundamentally economic, all other social changes deriving from economic factors. Historical materialism is a part of the Marxist theory of dialectical materialism.

historical method, a method of investigation in which the history of a subject is studied to determine principles governing its origin, behavior, and other features.

historical present, *Grammar.* the present tense used in describing past events to make them seem more vivid.

historical school, 1 a group of economists, first prominent in Germany in the 1800's, who advocate (in opposition to the classical economists) the historical method, or the deduction of economic principles from a study of the past. **2** the school of jurisprudence which affirms that law is the outgrowth of usage based upon the instinctive sense of right, instead of being created by rules.

his·tor·i·cism (his tôr′ə siz əm, -tor′-), *n.* the excessive use or influence of earlier ideas that substitute or smother original achievement, especially in architectural design: *Far from leading to useful criticism, accusations of historicism merely divert attention from the real merits or defects of a building under discussion* (Peter Collins). —**his·tor′i·cist,** *n., adj.*

his·to·ric·i·ty (his′tə ris′ə tē), *n.* the quality of being true as history; real existence or occurrence.

his·tor·i·cize (his tôr′ə sīz, -tor′-), *v.t.,* **-cized, -ciz·ing.** to make historical; record or represent as history.

historico-, *combining form.* historical and _____, as in *historico-cultural, historico-legal.* [< *historical*]

his·tor·i·co-le·gal (his tôr′ə kō lē′gəl, -tor′-), *adj.* based on both history and law; historical and legal: . . . *historico-legal arguments about the unequivocal cession of Gibraltar* (London Times).

his·to·ried (his′tər ēd, -trēd), *adj.* **1** having a history: *some great-historied land* (Matthew Arnold). **2** recorded or celebrated in history; historic.

his·to·ri·ette (his tôr′ē et′, -tōr′-), *n.* a short history or story; anecdote. [< French *historiette* < *histoire,* learned borrowing from Latin *historia* (see etym. under **history**) + *-ette* -ette]

his·tor·i·fy (his tôr′ə fī, -tor′-), *v.t.,* **-fied, -fy·ing.** to deal with in history; record in history.

his·to·ri·og·ra·pher (his tôr′ē og′rə fər, -tōr′-), *n.* **1** = historian. **2** the official historian of a court, public institution, society, or other group. [< Late Latin *historiographus* (< Greek *historiográphos* < *historíā* history + *gráphein* write) + English *-er*[1]]

his·to·ri·o·graph·i·cal (his tôr′ē ə graf′ə kəl), *adj.* of or having to do with historiography.

his·to·ri·og·ra·phy (his tôr′ē og′rə fē, -tōr′-), *n., pl.* **-phies. 1** the study of the writing of history; examination of the methods of historians and the development of history as a branch of knowledge. **2a** the writing of history. **b** written history.

his·to·ry (his′tər ē, -trē), *n., pl.* **-ries. 1** a story or record of important events that happened to a person or nation, usually with an explanation of causes and effects: *the history of the United States. The oldest and most venerable of the social sciences is history, which is the record, as the historian Ranke said, of "what has actually happened"* (George Simpson). **2** a known past: *This ship has a history. Life histories were used . . . in the study of the adjustment made by Polish peasants who had emigrated to America* (Science News Letter). **3** all past events considered together; course of human affairs: *the lessons of history. To the Christian much of history is a fulfillment of God's will and of His judgment* (New York Times). *Human history is in essence a history of ideas* (H. G. Wells). *How can there be a true History when we see no man living is able to write truly the History of the last week?* (Thomas Shadwell). **4** a recording and explaining of past events. **5** the branch of knowledge or study that deals with past events: *a class in history. The study of history is useful to the historian by teaching him his ignorance of women* (Henry Adams). **6** a statement of what has happened; account: *In me appears The history of a hundred years* (Thomas Hardy). **7** a statement or record of all the facts or events having to do with a person being treated by a doctor, social worker, etc.; a case history. **8** a historical play: *The History of Henry the Fourth by Shakespeare.*

9 *Obsolete.* a narrative; tale; story: *The History of the Adventures of Joseph Andrews by Henry Fielding.*
make history, a to influence or guide the course of history: *The average man is of the Center; and history in the long run is made by the average man* (Edinburgh Review). **b** to do something spectacular or worthy of remembrance: *We shall have a chance of making history over this, old man* (Ian Hay).
[< Latin *historia* < Greek *historíā* history, record, inquiry < *historeîn* inquire < *hístōr* learned. See etym. of doublet **story**[1].]
his|to|tox|ic (his′tō tok′sik), *adj.* poisonous to tissues.
histotoxic anoxia, a condition caused by poisons, such as cyanide, in which body tissue is incapable of using the oxygen supply of the blood.
his|tri|on (his′trē on), *n. Archaic.* a stage player; actor. [< Latin *histriō, -ōnis* actor]
his|tri|on|ic (his′trē on′ik), *adj., n.* **—*adj.*** of or having to do with actors or acting; dramatic: *histrionic talents.* (*Figurative.*) *The spoiled child gave a superb histrionic performance.*
—*n.* an actor.
[< Latin *histriōnicus* < *histriō, -ōnis,* actor] **—his′tri|on′i|cal|ly,** *adv.*
his|tri|on|i|cism (his′trē on′ə siz əm), *n.* histrionic action; acting.
his|tri|on|ics (his′tr ē on′iks), *n. sing. or pl.* **1** dramatic representation; theatricals; dramatics. **2** a theatrical manner or expression: (*Figurative.*) *There is no sign that these histrionics have cowed the hooting populations of Arabia* (Harper's).
hit (hit), *v.,* **hit, hit|ting,** *n.* **—*v.t.*** **1** to come against with force; give a blow to; strike; knock: *He hit the ball with a bat. She hit her head against the shelf. When boys fight they hit each other.* **SYN:** See syn. under **beat. 2** to get to (what is aimed at): *His second arrow hit the bullseye.* **3** *Figurative.* to come on; meet with; get to; reach or find: *We hit the right road in the dark.* **4** *Figurative.* to have a painful effect on; influence in a bad way; affect severely: *The store's owner was hard hit by the failure of his business.* **5** *Figurative.* to attack or criticize sharply: *The reviews hit the new play.*
6 to agree with; suit exactly; please: *This hits my fancy.* **7** *Informal.* to come to mind; occur to: *It hit me all of a sudden that I'd made a mistake.* **8** *Figurative.* to reach or touch directly and effectively: *Dear Countess! you have charms all hearts to hit* (Alexander Pope). **9** *Informal.* to appear in: *The story hit the front page.* **10** *Slang.* to go at vigorously; attack: *to hit the books before a test.*
11 *Slang.* to demand from: *"Joe comes here every few days and hits me for a handout"* (New Yorker). **12** *U.S. Slang.* to kill. **13** *Slang.* to give an injection of narcotics; shoot up.
—*v.i.* **1** to give a blow or blows: *The man hit out at the thieves who attacked him. When I become angry my first impulse is to hit.* **2** to knock or strike with force: *The ball hit against the window.*
3 to ignite the mixture in a cylinder of an internal-combustion engine: *to hit on all cylinders.* **4** *Baseball.* to make a base hit: *He hit safely in 16 straight games.* **5** *Slang.* to give oneself an injection of narcotics; shoot up.
—*n.* **1** a blow; stroke: *The hit on his head knocked him out.* **2** a getting to what is aimed at: *a hit, a very palpable hit* (Shakespeare). **3** *Figurative.* a sharp attack or criticism. **4** *Figurative.* a successful attempt, performance, or production: *The new play is the hit of the season.* **5** a successful hitting of the baseball by a batter so that he gets at least to first base; base hit. **6** *Figurative.* a stroke of luck or chance: *What late he call'd a blessing, now was wit, And God's good providence, a lucky hit* (Alexander Pope). **7** a game in backgammon won by a player after his opponent has thrown off one or more men from the board. **8** the knocking of a marble out of the ring on a shot. **9** *Slang.* an injection of a narcotic drug, especially heroin: *None of them will admit to an outsider that they are addicted but boast of the occasional sniff or "hit" as their elder brothers boasted of getting drunk—as a virility symbol* (London Times). **10** *U.S. Slang.* a killing, especially by a hired killer.
hit at, to criticize; make fun of; ridicule: *He hit at several political figures.*
hit it off, to get along well together (with); agree: *The two friends hit it off from the start. How did you hit it off with her?*
hit off, a to produce or imitate on the spur of the moment: *We hit off a little wit now and then, but no animosity* (William Congreve). **b** to represent or describe cleverly: *He has very well hit off the sense* (Daniel Waterland).
hit on (or **upon**), **a** to come on; meet with; get to: *The boys hit upon a plan for making money.* **b** to find, especially by accident; guess correctly: *He finally hit upon a solution to his problem.*
hit or miss, with no plan; regardless of results; by chance; haphazardly; at random: *He stacked the books hit or miss, and they fell to the floor.*
hit out, a to deal blows at random: *When other children . . . irritated him, he hit out* (Maclean's).
b *Figurative.* to proceed vigorously; strike out: *Give credit to the plucky producer . . . for hitting out in the right direction* (New York Times).
hit the ceiling. See under **ceiling.**
hit the hay. See under **hay**[1].
hit the jackpot. See under **jackpot.**
hit the nail on the head. See under **nail.**
hit the spot. See under **spot.**
[Old English *hittan* come upon < Scandinavian (compare Old Icelandic *hitta*)] **—hit′less,** *adj.*
hit-and-miss (hit′ən mis′), *adj.* = hit-or-miss.
hit-and-run (hit′ən run′), *adj., n.* **—*adj.*** **1** of, by, or having to do with hitting a person or vehicle and driving away without stopping to see what happened: *a hit-and-run accident.* **2** characterized by the tactic of carrying out a series of military actions suddenly and disappearing as quickly: *a mobile hit-and-run attack styled for atomic warfare* (New York Times).
—*n.* = hit-and-run play.
hit-and-run driver, a driver who hits another vehicle or a pedestrian and drives away without helping the victim or reporting the accident.
hit-and-run play, *Baseball.* a play in which a player on a base starts to run to the next base as the pitch is being thrown to the batter, and the batter tries to hit the ball to advance or protect the runner.
hitch** (hich), *v., n.* **—*v.t. **1** to fasten with a hook, ring, rope, or strap: *He hitched his horse to a post. Now that is the wisdom of a man . . . to hitch his wagon to a star* (Emerson). **SYN:** attach, tie, hook, tether. **2** to harness to a wagon, carriage, plow, or other implement or vehicle: *The farmer hitched up his team and drove to town.*
3 to move or pull with a jerk: *He hitched his chair nearer to the fire.* **4** *Informal.* to get (a ride) by hitchhiking: *We hitched rides toward Chicago and spent a night on the beach* (Saul Bellow).
—*v.i.* **1** to become fastened or caught; fasten; catch: *A knot made the rope hitch. The lariat hitched on one of his ears* (Washington Irving).
2 *U.S. Informal.* to get on well together; agree.
3 to move with a jerk; move jerkily: *He hitched along, with one shoulder higher than the other.*
4 to limp; hobble. **5** *Informal.* to hitchhike.
—*n.* **1a** a fastening; catch: *The hitch joining the plow to the tractor is broken.* **b** any one of various types of knots used for temporary fastening, such as the clove hitch or the diamond hitch: *He put a hitch in the rope to keep it tight.* **2** a short, sudden pull or jerk; jerky movement: *The sailor gave his trousers a hitch.* **3** a limp; hobble. **4** *Figurative.* an obstacle; stopping; hindrance; obstruction: *A hitch in their plans made them miss the train.* **5** *U.S. Informal, Figurative.* period of time, especially a period of service in the armed forces.
6 *Informal.* a free ride from a passing automobile.
hitch up, a to harness an animal or team to a vehicle or implement: *The farmer hitched up and set out for the fair.* **b** to ride up: *The co-ed . . . was wearing a navy-blue miniskirt that hitched up when she sat down* (Maclean's).
without a hitch, smoothly; successfully: *The plans were carried out without a hitch.*
[Middle English *hychen;* origin uncertain]

***hitch**
definition 1b

kinds of hitches:

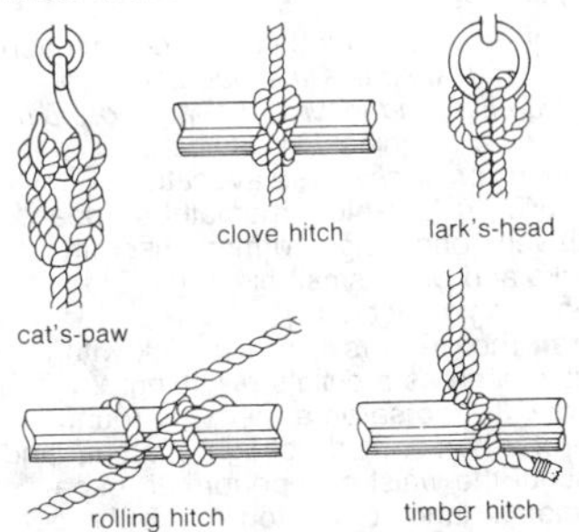

Hitch|cock chair (hich′kok), a side chair with turned legs, slatted back, and painted or stenciled decoration. [< Lambert *Hitchcock,* 1795-1852, an American chair manufacturer]
hitch|er (hich′ər), *n.* **1** a person or thing that hitches. **2** *U.S. Informal.* a hitchhiker.
hitch|hike or **hitch-hike** (hich′hīk′), *v.,* **-hiked, -hik|ing.** **—*v.i.*** to travel by walking and getting free rides from passing automobiles or trucks. **—*v.t.*** to get (a ride) by hitchhiking. [American English < *hitch* (a ride), idiom, get a free lift]
hitch|hik|er (hich′hī′kər), *n.* a person who hitchhikes.
hitch|ing post (hich′ing), a post to which to hitch horses, or other animals.
hith|er (hiᴛʜ′ər), *adv., adj.* **—*adv.*** to this place; toward this place; here: *Come hither, child!*
—*adj.* on this side; toward this side; nearer.
hither and thither, here and there: *A Power . . . that moves us hither and thither through the ordinary courses of our lives* (Richard H. Hutton).
hither and yon, here and there: *There is a commotion caused by people screaming and racing hither and yon* (Howard Taubman).
[Old English *hider.* See related etym. at **here.**]
hith|er|most (hiᴛʜ′ər mōst), *adj.* nearest.
hith|er|to (hiᴛʜ′ər tü′), *adv.* **1** up to this time; until now: *a fact hitherto unknown.* **2** *Archaic.* to this place or point: *Hitherto shalt thou come, but no further* (Job 38:11).
hith|er|ward (hiᴛʜ′ər wərd), *adv.* toward this place; in this direction; hither.
Hit|ler|i|an (hit lir′ē ən), *adj.* of or characteristic of Adolf Hitler.
Hit|ler|ism (hit′lə riz əm), *n.* **1** the program and policies of Adolf Hitler and the German Nazi Party, which he led; Nazism. **2** the use or support of totalitarian, dictatorial methods.
Hit|ler|ist (hit′lə rist), *n.* = Hitlerite.
Hit|ler|ite (hit′lə rīt), *n., adj.* **—*n.*** a supporter of Hitler.
—*adj.* of or characteristic of Adolf Hitler.
hit list, *U.S. Slang.* **1** a list of persons slated to be killed: *His immediate superior had been on the "hit list" of the Symbionese Liberation Army* (New York Times). **2** *Figurative: A particular sore point was Carter's original "hit list" of 32 water projects* (Time).
hit man, *U.S. Slang.* a hired killer.
hit-or-miss (hit′ər mis′), *adj.* not planned; random; haphazard: *In hit-or-miss fashion, man has been fighting corrosion ever since he first rubbed a little grease on the blade of his hunting knife* (Wall Street Journal).
hit parade, a list of currently successful songs or recordings: *Mayer rushed out another record which was climbing the hit parade very steadily* (Atlantic).
hit|ter (hit′ər), *n.* **1** a person or thing that hits. **2** a batter in baseball: *a weak hitter.*
Hit|tite (hit′īt), *n., adj.* **—*n.*** **1** a member of an ancient people in Asia Minor and Syria. Their civilization existed from about 1900 B.C. until about 1200 B.C. They were conquered by the Assyrians. **2** the Indo-European language of the Hittites, preserved in both cuneiform and hieroglyphic writing.
—*adj.* of or having to do with the Hittites or their language.
[< Hebrew *hittim* the Hittites + English *-ite*[1]]
HIV (no periods), the retrovirus that causes AIDS by invading and destroying the helper T cells of the body: *Researchers hope that their experimental vaccine will stimulate the body to produce vast numbers of killer T cells that would be able to recognize and destroy any of the variant forms of HIV* (Paul Katz). [< *H*(uman) *I*(mmunodeficiency) *V*(irus)]
hive (hīv), *n., v.,* **hived, hiv|ing.** **—*n.*** **1** a house or box for bees to live in; beehive. **2** a large number of bees living in such a place: *The whole hive was busy.* **3** *Figurative.* a busy place full of people or animals: *a hive of industry. This great Hive, the City* (Abraham Cowley). **4** *Figurative.* a swarming or teeming crowd.
—*v.t.* **1** to put (bees) in a hive. **2** to store up (honey) in a hive. **3** *Figurative.* to lay up for future use: *hiving wisdom with each studious year* (Byron). **SYN:** hoard.
—*v.i.* **1** to live close together as bees do. **2** to enter a hive.
hive off, *Especially British.* to break away or isolate: *I believe it is wrong to hive off institutions such as the Post Office into a limbo* (Manchester Guardian Weekly).
[Old English *hȳf*]
hive nest, a large nest, or group of nests, in which many pairs of birds live as a colony.
hiv|er (hī′vər), *n.* a person who puts bees in a hive.
hives (hīvz), *n.* a condition in which the skin itches and shows raised patches of red; urticaria. It is caused by an allergy to some food or drug, or a reaction as to heat or light. [origin uncertain]
Hi|zen (hē zen′), *adj.* of or having to do with a class of Japanese porcelains of rich decoration, delicate coloring, and fine workmanship. [< *Hizen,* a province in Japan]
H.J., here lies (Latin, *hic jacet*).

H.J.Res., House (of Representatives) Joint Resolution (always with a number).
hl., hectoliter or hectoliters.
H.L., House of Lords.
HLA or **HL-A** (āch′el′ā′), *adj.* of or having to do with a system of tissue typing based on the presence in the body of certain antigens: *Studies of the many HLA types found in the population have also shown that some of them are associated with specific diseases: for example, a high proportion of all patients with some form of arthritis are found to have HLA B27 antigens* (London Times). [< *h*(uman) *l*(eucocyte) *a*(ntigen)]
HLBB (no periods), Home Loan Bank Board.
h'm (həm), *interj.* hem; hum.
hm., hectometer or hectometers.
H.M., **1** Her Majesty. **2** His Majesty.
H.M.A.S., **1** Her Majesty's Australian Ship. **2** His Majesty's Australian Ship.
H.M.C.S., **1** Her Majesty's Canadian Ship. **2** His Majesty's Canadian Ship.
HMD (no periods), hyaline membrane disease.
HMO (no periods), health maintenance organization (an organization providing medical care to subscribers for fixed periodic payments).
H.M.S., **1a** Her Majesty's Service. **b** His Majesty's Service. **2a** Her Majesty's Ship. **b** His Majesty's Ship.
H.M.S.O. or **HMSO** (no periods), **1** Her Majesty's Stationery Office. **2** His Majesty's Stationery Office.
ho[1] (hō), *interj.* a call to an animal to stop or stand still. [probably < Old French *ho* halt! stop!]
ho[2] (hō), *interj.* **1** an exclamation of surprise, joy, or scornful laughter. **2** an exclamation to get attention: *The captain said, "Ho, men! Listen."* **3** a word used with another word that tells the destination: *There lies your way, due west. Then westward-ho!* (Shakespeare). [Middle English *ho*]
ho., house.
Ho (no period), holmium (chemical element).
ho|ac|tzin (hō ak′tsin), *n.* = hoatzin.
hoa|gy or **hoa|gie** (hō′gē)), *n., pl.* **-gies.** *U.S.* = hero sandwich. [origin unknown]
hoar (hôr, hōr), *adj., n.* **—*adj.*** **1** white or grayish-white. **2** white or gray with age. **3** old; ancient. **4** *Obsolete or Dialect.* white or gray with mold; moldy; musty. **—*n.*** **1** = hoarfrost. **2** = hoariness. [Old English *hār*]
hoard (hôrd, hōrd), *v., n.* **—*v.t.*** to save and store away: *The squirrel hoarded nuts for the winter. The miser hoarded his money.* SYN: treasure, amass, accumulate. **—*v.i.*** to save and store away money, goods, etc. **—*n.*** what is saved and stored away; things stored: *The squirrel kept his hoard in a tree.* SYN: stock, store.
[Old English *hord*] **—hoard′er,** *n.*
hoard|ing[1] (hôr′ding, hōr′-), *n.* **1** the act of one who hoards. **2** something hoarded.
hoard|ing[2] (hôr′ding, hōr′-), *n. British.* **1** a temporary board fence around a building that is being put up, repaired, or torn down. **2** a billboard. [< earlier *hoard* fence, apparently < Anglo-French *hurdis,* ultimately < Germanic (compare Old High German *hurdī,* plural) + *-ing*[1]]
hoar|frost (hôr′frôst′, -frost′; hōr′-), *n.* the white, feathery crystals of ice formed when dew freezes; white frost; rime.
hoar|hound (hôr′hound′, hōr′-), *n.* = horehound.
hoar|i|ness (hôr′ē nis, hōr′-), *n.* hoary quality or condition.
hoarse (hôrs, hōrs), *adj.,* **hoars|er, hoars|est.** **1** sounding rough and deep: *the hoarse croak of the bullfrog.* SYN: raucous. **2** having a rough voice: *A bad cold has made me hoarse. Warwick is hoarse with calling thee to arms* (Shakespeare). [Middle English *hors.* Compare Old English *hās.*] **—hoarse′ly,** *adv.* **—hoarse′ness,** *n.*
hoars|en (hôr′sən, hōr′-), *v.t., v.i.* to make or become hoarse.
hoar|y (hôr′ē, hōr′-), *adj.,* **hoar|i|er, hoar|i|est.** **1** old; ancient: *the hoary ruins of a castle. According to the hoary rules of American politics, any strong presidential candidate can pick his running mate* (Atlantic). **2** white or grayish-white. **3** white or gray with age: *hoary hair.*
hoary bat, a large, migratory bat of North America with white-tipped hairs.
hoar|y-head|ed (hôr′ē hed′id, hōr′-), *adj.* having white or gray hair.
ho|at|zin (hō at′sin), *n.* a crested, brightly colored South American bird, somewhat smaller than a pheasant. Also, **hoactzin.** [< Mexican Spanish *uatzin,* probably < the native Nahuatl name]
hoax (hōks), *n., v.* **—*n.*** a mischievous trick, especially a made-up story passed off as true: *The report of an attack on the earth from Mars was a hoax.* SYN: imposture.
—*v.t.* to play a mischievous trick on; deceive in fun or to injure. SYN: bamboozle, hoodwink.
[probably alteration of *hocus*] **—hoax′er,** *n.*
hob[1] (hob), *n., v.,* **hobbed, hob|bing.** **—*n.*** **1** a shelf at the back or side of a fireplace, on which to keep food warm. **2a** a round, slender peg used as a target in quoits and similar games. **b** any game using such a target. **3** = hobnail. **4** a hard metal tool with a spiral thread, used especially for cutting gears and tools.
—*v.t.* to cut or thread (a gear or tool) with a hob.
[origin uncertain. Compare etym. under **hub.**]
hob[2] (hob), *n.* **1** a hobgoblin; elf; sprite. **2** a countryman; rustic.
play (or **raise**) **hob,** *Informal.* to cause trouble: *Rain played hob with our plans for a picnic.*
[Middle English *hob,* alteration of *Rob,* a nickname for *Robert* or *Robin*]
hob|ber (hob′ər), *n.* **1** a person employed to drive hobnails into boots. **2** = leaner (def. 2).
Hobbes|i|an (hob′zē ən), *adj.* of or having to do with the English philosopher Thomas Hobbes, 1588-1679, or with Hobbism.
Hob|bism (hob′iz əm), *n.* the philosophy of Thomas Hobbes; theory that without an absolute government, anarchy will prevail.
Hob|bist (hob′ist), *n.* an advocate of Hobbism.
hob|bit (hob′it), *n.* any one of an imaginary race of genial, elflike creatures who love peace, pleasure, and beauty, created by the British writer J. R. R. Tolkien (1892-1973).
hob|ble (hob′əl), *v.,* **-bled, -bling,** *n.* **—*v.i.*** **1** to walk awkwardly; limp: *The wounded man hobbled away.* **2** to move unsteadily; wobble: (*Figurative.*) *She hobbles in alternate verse* (Matthew Prior). **—*v.t.*** **1** to cause to walk awkwardly or limp. **2** to tie the legs of (a horse, camel, or other large animal) together: *He hobbled his horse at night so that it would not wander away.* **3** = hinder.
—*n.* **1** an awkward walk; limp. **2** a rope or strap used to hobble a horse or other large animal. **3** *Informal, Figurative.* an awkward or difficult situation: *Pray get out of this hobble as fast as you can* (Byron).
[Middle English *hobelen.* Compare Dutch *hobbelen* to rock.]
hob|ble|bush (hob′əl bůsh′), *n.* a shrub of the honeysuckle family found in eastern North America, having clusters of white flowers and a purple, berrylike fruit.
hob|ble|de|hoy (hob′əl dē hoi′), *n.* **1** an awkward, clumsy boy. **2** a youth between boyhood and manhood. [origin uncertain]
hob|bler (hob′lər), *n.* one that hobbles.
*** hobble skirt,** a woman's skirt that is very narrow below the knees, usually tapering to the bottom.

*** hobble skirt**

hob|bling (hob′ling), *adj.* that hobbles; wobbling; limping. **—hob′bling|ly,** *adv.*
hob|by[1] (hob′ē), *n., pl.* **-bies.** **1** something a person especially likes to work at or study which is not his main business; any favorite pastime or topic of conversation: *Growing roses is our doctor's hobby. No man is really happy or safe without a hobby* (Sir William Osler). SYN: avocation. **2** = hobbyhorse. **3** *British Dialect.* a small or medium-sized horse.
ride a hobby, to give too much time or attention to one's hobby: *Transgress the boundaries of scientific evidence, and incur the charge of riding a hobby too hard* (Archibald H. Sayce).
[probably short for *hobbyhorse* avocation]
hob|by[2] (hob′ē), *n., pl.* **-bies.** a small European falcon, with very long wings, formerly used in hawking larks and other small birds. [< Old French *hobe;* origin uncertain]
hob|by|horse (hob′ē hôrs′), *n.* **1** a stick with a horse's head, used as a child's plaything. **2** = rocking horse. **3** a horse on a merry-go-round. **4a** a figure of a horse, made of light material and fastened about the waist of a performer, especially in a morris dance or pantomime. **b** the performer himself. **5** a hobby; favorite pastime or topic of conversation: *This was the band of propagandists whose hobbyhorse had long been fighting the United Nations* (Atlantic). **6** English bicycle of the early 1800's. **7** *Obsolete.* **a** a foolish fellow; buffoon. **b** a lewd person. [Middle English *hobby,* earlier *hobyn* small horse + *horse*]
hob|by|ist (hob′ē ist), *n.* a person who is much interested in his hobby or hobbies.
hob|gob|lin (hob′gob′lən), *n.* **1** a goblin; elf. SYN: sprite. **2** *Figurative.* a bogy; bugbear: *A foolish consistency is the hobgoblin of little minds* (Emerson). **3** an alarming or terrifying ghost or phantom. [< *hob*[2] + *goblin*]
hob|nail (hob′nāl′), *n.* **1** a short nail with a large head to protect the soles of heavy shoes and boots. **2** a rustic; clodhopper; buffoon. [< *hob*[1] + *nail*]
hob|nailed (hob′nāld′), *adj.* **1** furnished with hobnails: *hobnailed boots.* **2** rustic or cloddish.
hobnail glass, pressed glassware with a pattern of small, raised bumps, made during the 1800's.
hob|nob (hob′nob′), *v.,* **-nobbed, -nob|bing,** *n., adv.* **—*v.i.*** **1** to be on familiar terms; associate intimately: *He hobnobs with some important people.* **2** to drink together.
—*n.* **1** a familiar association or conversation. **2** a drinking together.
—*adv.* *British Dialect.* haphazard.
[apparently < drinking phrase *hob or nob* give or take, probably ultimately < Old English *hæbbe* have + *næbbe* not have] **—hob′nob′ber,** *n.*
ho|bo (hō′bō), *n., pl.* **-bos** or **-boes,** *v.,* **-boed, -bo|ing.** *U.S.* **—*n.*** **1** a person who wanders about and lives by begging or doing odd jobs; tramp. **2** a migratory workman.
—*v.i.* to live as a hobo. **—*v.t.*** to make (one's way) in the manner of a hobo: *At eighteen he hoboed his way to the Kansas wheat fields* (Atlantic).
[American English; origin uncertain]
ho|bo|dom (hō′bō dəm), *n.* the world of the hobo or hobos.
Hob|son's choice (hob′sənz), the choice of taking the thing offered or nothing: *The exercise of this clause resulted in a Hobson's choice for the player—he could either renew his contract or quit organized baseball* (Richard E. Day). [< Thomas *Hobson,* died 1631, a stablekeeper in Cambridge, England, who rented the horse nearest his stable door or none]
Hoch|deutsch (hōʜ′doich′), *n.* = High-German. [< German *Hochdeutsch*]
Hoch|hei|mer (hok′hī′mər; *German* hōʜ′hī′mər), *n.* a Rhine wine made at Hochheim, Germany. [< German *Hochheimer*]
hock[1] (hok), *n., v.* **—*n.*** **1** the joint in the hind leg of a horse, cow, or other four-legged animal, above the fetlock joint, corresponding to the ankle of man but raised from the ground and protruding backward when bent. **2** the corresponding joint in the leg of a fowl.
—*v.t.* to cripple by cutting the tendons of the hock; hamstring. Also, **hough.**
[variant of *hough,* Old English *hōh*]
hock[2] (hok), *n. Especially British.* **1** = Hochheimer. **2** any white Rhine wine. [short for *Hockamore,* alteration of German *Hochheimer* Hochheimer]
hock[3] (hok), *v., n. Slang.* **—*v.t., v.i.*** to pawn.
—*n.* pawn; debt.
in hock, a in another's possession as security; in pawn: *Among rare types of Americans are those who at this time of year place their winter clothing, including furs, in hock* (Wall Street Journal). **b** in debt: *He is in hock because he spends more then he earns.*
out of hock, a no longer in another's possession as security: *He paid the pawnshop and got his watch out of hock.* **b** no longer in debt: *After one more payment on the car, we will be out of hock.*
[American English < phrase *in hock,* in earlier sense "a losing position at cards." Compare Dutch *hok* jail, pen, doghouse.]
hock|et (hok′it), *n., v. Music.* **—*n.*** **1** an interruption of a voice part by rests to produce a broken, spasmodic effect. **2** a composition in which this effect is used. **—*v.i.*** to interrupt vocal parts for expressive purposes: *the three hocketing horns in the second movement* (London Times). [< Old French *hocquet* hiccup, sudden interruption]

*** hockey**
definition 1

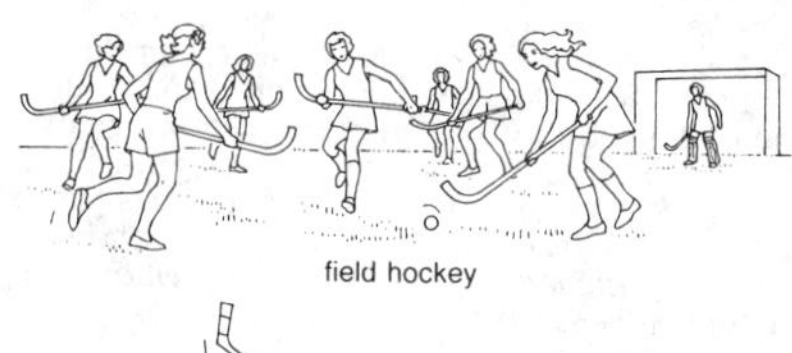
field hockey

ice hockey

*** hock|ey** (hok′ē), *n., pl.* **-eys.** **1** a game played by two teams on ice or on a field. The players hit a rubber disk or a ball with curved sticks to drive it into or across a goal. The game played on ice is ice hockey, with six on a team; the game played on a field is field hockey, with eleven on a team. **2** = hockey stick. [perhaps < Old French *hoquet* (shepherd's) crook]

hockey skate, an ice skate with a straight, heavy blade and a strong, heavy shoe, for playing hockey.
hockey stick, a stick that is curved at the bottom, used in playing hockey.
hock shop, *U.S.* a pawnshop.
ho|cus (hō′kəs), *v.t.*, **-cused**, **-cus|ing** or (*especially British*) **-cussed**, **-cus|sing**. **1** to play a trick upon; hoax; cheat. **2** to stupefy with drugs. **3** to put drugs in (alcoholic drink). [short for *hocus-pocus*]
ho|cus-po|cus (hō′kəs pō′kəs), *n.*, *v.*, **-cused**, **-cus|ing** or (*especially British*) **-cussed**, **-cus|sing**. **—*n.*** **1** a meaningless form of words used in performing magic tricks. **2** sleight of hand; magic. **3** trickery; deception: *If Mr. Mahoney is to be faulted at all it is because of a tendency to resort to some old vaudeville hocus-pocus* (New York Times). **4** *Obsolete.* a conjurer; juggler.
—*v.i.* to play tricks; practice deception.
—*v.t.* to play tricks on or with. Also, **hokey-pokey**.
[perhaps Latinization used by jugglers; origin uncertain]
***hod** (hod), *n.* **1** a trough or tray with a long, straight handle, used by builders for carrying bricks or mortar on the shoulder. **2** = coal scuttle. [alteration of Middle English *hott* pannier < Old French *hotte*, apparently < Germanic (compare Middle Dutch *hodde*)]

***hod**
definition 1

ho-dad (hō′dad), *n. Surfing.* a person who doesn't surf or who surfs poorly.
hod carrier, a laborer employed to carry bricks, mortar, and the like in a hod.
hod|den (hod′ən), *n. Scottish.* a coarse cloth of undyed wool sometimes called hodden gray. [perhaps dialectal variant of *holden*, archaic past participle of *hold*[1]]
hodge|podge (hoj′poj′), *n.* **1** a disorderly mixture; mess; jumble: *Her room was a hodgepodge of things strewn all over the floor. The result has been a hodgepodge of misinformation* (Bulletin of Atomic Scientists). *So now they have made our English tongue a . . . hodgepodge of all other speeches* (Edmund Spenser). **SYN:** mishmash, medley, farrago. **2** a stew containing a variety of ingredients. Also, **hotchpotch**. [variant of Middle English *hotchpotch*, variant of *hotchpot* < Old French *hochepot* ragout < *hocher* shake (< a Germanic word) + *pot* pot]
Hodg|kin's disease (hoj′kinz), an often fatal, cancerous disease of the lymphatic tissue, characterized by enlargement of the spleen and lymph nodes; lymphogranulomatosis. [< Thomas *Hodgkin*, 1798-1866, an English physician, who described it]
ho|di|er|nal (hō′dē ėr′nəl), *adj.* of or having to do with the present day: *The rule and hodiernal life of a good man is benefaction* (Emerson). [< Latin *hodiernus* (< *hodiē* today) + English *-al*[1]]
hod|man (hod′mən), *n., pl.* **-men**. = hod carrier.
ho|dom|e|ter (hō dom′ə tər), *n.* **1a** a device attached to a wheeled vehicle for recording the number of revolutions of a wheel and thus indicating the distance traveled. **b** a similar instrument for measuring distances in surveying. **2** = pedometer. [< Greek *hodós* way + English *-meter*]
hod|o|scope (hod′ə skōp), *n.* an instrument for tracing the paths of charged particles, composed of a series of radiation detectors, each with its own neon light. The flashing of light indicates the path of a particle passing through. [< Greek *hodós* way + English *-scope*]
hoe (hō), *n.*, *v.*, **hoed**, **hoe|ing**. **—*n.*** a tool with a thin blade set across the end of a long handle, used for loosening soil or cutting weeds.
—*v.t.* to loosen, dig, or cut with a hoe: *to hoe a garden.*
—*v.i.* to use a hoe.
[< Old French *houe* < Germanic (compare Old High German *houwa*)] **—hoe′like′**, *adj.*
hoe|cake (hō′kāk′), *n. U.S.* a kind of bread made of corn meal, originally baked on a hoe in the fireplace.
hoe|down (hō′doun′), *n. U.S.* **1** a noisy, riotous dance, especially a square dance. **2** a piece of music to which this is danced: *a medley of old-time hoedowns and jig music* (T. K. Holmes).
ho|er (hō′ər), *n.* a person who hoes.
hog (hog, hôg), *n.*, *v.*, **hogged**, **hog|ging**. **—*n.*** **1** a pig: *a barnyard full of grunting hogs wallowing in mud.* **2** a full-grown pig, raised for food, usually weighing more than 120 pounds. **3** any animal of the same family as the pig, such as the wild boar. **4** *Informal, Figurative.* a selfish, greedy, or dirty person. **5** (in Scotland and England) a young sheep, no longer a lamb, but not yet shorn. **6** a coarse broom for scrubbing the bottom of a ship under water. **7** *Railroad Slang.* a locomotive.
—*v.t.* **1** *Slang.* to take more than one's share of: *Army planners claimed the Air Force is trying to hog the defense budget* (Wall Street Journal). **2** to arch (the back) upward like that of a hog. **3** to cause (a ship or a plank) to sag at both ends. **4** to clean (a ship's bottom) with a hog. **5** to cut (a horse's mane) short, so that it stands up like the bristles of a hog.
—*v.i.* (of a ship) to sag at the bow and stern.
go the whole hog, *Informal.* to go to the limit; do something thoroughly: *I believe in federation and I am prepared to go the whole hog to maintain it* (Wall Street Journal).
high on the hog, *Informal.* in a lavish manner; luxuriously: *The heroine is an aging international gadabout . . . who is living high on the hog in Italy* (New Yorker).
low on the hog, *Informal.* in a thrifty manner; without excessive or lavish spending: *Compared to a Congressman, an M.P. lives lower on the hog, campaigns more quietly and takes fewer lavish junkets* (London Times).
[Old English *hogg* young pig]
ho|gan (hō′gôn), *n.* a dwelling used by the Navaho Indians of North America. Hogans are built with logs and covered with earth, and have an opening at the top through which smoke from the fire can escape. [American English < Athapaskan (Navaho) *hōghan* dwelling, house]
hog|back (hog′bak′, hôg′-), *n.* **1** *Geology.* a low, sharp ridge with steep sides, often caused by an outcrop of a resistant stratum. **2** an arching back like that of a hog.
hog cholera, an infectious, often fatal viral disease of hogs, characterized by weakness, fever, and diarrhea.
hog|fish (hog′fish′, hôg′-), *n., pl.* **-fish|es** or (*collectively*) **-fish**. any one of various food fishes that somewhat resemble a hog, such as a wrasse of the Florida and West Indian seas, an American darter, or a grunt.
hog|ger|y (hog′ər ē, hôg′-), *n., pl.* **-ger|ies**. **1** the act of taking more than one's share, hoggishness. **2** a place where hogs are kept or raised.
hog|get (hog′it, hôg′-), *n.* **1** *British.* a yearling sheep. **2** wool from lambs 12 to 14 months old.
hog|gish (hog′ish, hôg′-), *adj.* **1** like a hog; greedy; very selfish. **SYN:** piggish, swinish. **2** dirty; filthy. **SYN:** piggish, swinish. **—hog′gish|ly**, *adv.* **—hog′gish|ness**, *n.*
hog|line, a line drawn across a curling rink at a distance of 7 yards from each tee. A curling stone that does not cross this line is removed from the ice.
hog|ly (hog′lē, hôg′-), *adj.*, **-li|er**, **-li|est**. = hoggish. **—hog′li|ness**, *n.*
hog|ma|nay (hog′mə nā′), *n.* (in Scotland and northern England) the last day of the year, when children call at friends' houses and ask for oatmeal cakes and presents. [apparently ultimately < Old French *aguillanneuf*; origin uncertain]
hog|nose (hog′nōz′, hôg′-), *n.*, or **hognose snake**, a harmless North American snake with an upturned snout like that of a hog; adder. Hognose snakes hiss, while dilating and flattening the head, when alarmed.
hog-nosed (hog′nōzd′, hôg′-), *adj.* having a snout like that of a hog.
hog-nosed skunk, a large skunk of the southwestern United States and Central and South America, with a white back and tail and a long snout used for rooting in the ground; conepatl.
hog|nut (hog′nut′, hôg′-), *n.* **1** *U.S.* **a** the pignut. **b** the hickory tree on which it grows. **2** a European earthnut.
hog peanut, an American vine of the pea family, whose pear-shaped pods ripen in or on the ground like peanuts; earthpea.
hog|pen (hog′pen′, hôg′-), *n.* **1** a place where hogs are kept; hoggery. **2** *Figurative.* a filthy place.
hog score, = hog line.
hogs|head (hogz′hed, hôgz′-), *n.* **1** a large barrel or cask. In the United States, a hogshead contains from 63 to 140 gallons; in Great Britain it contains from 50 to 100 gallons. **2** a liquid measure equal to 63 gallons.
hog|skin (hog′skin′, hôg′-), *n.* **1** the skin of a hog. **2** leather made from this. **3** the skin of a hog used as a bottle.
hog-tie (hog′tī′, hôg′-), *v.*, *n.* **—*v.t.***, **-tied**, **-ty|ing**. *U.S.* **1** to tie, as a hog is tied, with all four feet together, or with feet and hands together: *And unless he was almost literally hog-tied and gagged, he would babble on until the bell* (New Yorker). **2** *Figurative.* to hinder; hold back.
—*n.* a secure hold: *They sure do hate to turn loose a gringo when they have got the hog-tie on him* (W. M. Raine).
hog|wash (hog′wosh′, -wôsh′; hôg′-), *n.* **1** refuse used to feed hogs; swill. **2** *Slang.* worthless stuff; nonsense.
hog|weed (hog′wēd′, hôg′-), *n.* any one of various plants thought to be fit only for hogs, such as the ragweed, knotweed, and sow thistle.
hog-wild (hog′wīld′, hôg′-), *adj. U.S. Slang.* very wild; crazy; berserk.
Hoh|en|zol|lern (hō′ən zol′ərn; *German* hō′ən-tsôl′ərn), *n.*, *adj.* **—*n.*** a member of a German princely family, prominent since the Middle Ages, which ruled Prussia from 1701 to 1918, and Germany from 1871 to 1918.
—*adj.* of this family: *the Hohenzollern dynasty.*
Hoh|mann ellipse (hō′män′), *Aerospace.* the elliptical trajectory of a Hohmann orbit.
Hohmann orbit, *Aerospace.* a spacecraft trajectory between two planets that requires the least expenditure of energy. It consists of an elliptical path that is tangent to the orbits of both the departure planet and the target planet. [< Walter *Hohmann*, 1880-1945, a German aerospace engineer]
ho-hum (hō′hum′), *interj.*, *adj.* **—*interj.*** a sound made to express boredom or indifference.
—*adj.* *Slang.* **1** boring. **2** bored; indifferent: *a ho-hum attitude.*
[imitative of yawning]
hoick[1] (hoik), *v.*, *n. Especially British Informal.*
—*v.t.* to pull suddenly; jerk: *He was hoicked full out of his seat* (New Yorker).
—*v.i.* to draw or pull up.
—*n.* a sudden pull; jerk.
[see related etym. at **hike**]
hoick[2] (hoik), *interj.*, *n.*, *v.t.*, *v.i.* = hoicks.
hoicks (hoiks), *interj.*, *n.*, *v.* **—*interj.*** a shout to make hounds run faster.
—*n.* a shout of "hoicks."
—*v.t.*, *v.i.* to shout to make (hounds) run faster.
[earlier *hoika*, apparently earlier variant of *hike* move! Compare etym. under **yoicks**.]
hoi|den (hoi′dən), *n.*, *adj.*, *v.i.* = hoyden.
hoi|den|ish (hoi′də nish), *adj.* = hoydenish. **—hoi′den|ish|ness**, *n.*
hoi pol|loi (hoi′pə loi′), ordinary people; the masses: *These were not aristocrats, but hoi polloi with a thin veneer of polish* (Atlantic). **SYN:** populace. [< Greek *hoipolloí*, plural, the many (people)]
hoise (hoiz), *v.t.*, **hoised** or **hoist**, **hois|ing**. raise on high; hoist: *Then the boat had been hoist inboard again and the ship had departed* (Ian Fleming). [earlier *hysse* < Dutch *hijschen*]
hoist (hoist), *v.*, *n.* **—*v.t.*** to raise on high; lift up, often with ropes and pulleys: *to hoist a flag, to hoist sails, to hoist blocks of stone in building.*
—*n.* **1** the act of hoisting; lift; boost: *He gave me a hoist up the wall.* **2** an elevator or other apparatus for hoisting heavy loads. **3** *Nautical.* the perpendicular height of a sail or flag. See picture under **flag**[1]. **4** a signal or message sent by means of flags hoisted on a ship.
[variant of *hoise*] **—hoist′er**, *n.*
hoi|ty-toi|ty (hoi′tētoi′tē), *interj.*, *adj.*, *n.* **—*interj.*** an exclamation expressing surprise and some contempt: *Hoity-toity! . . . madam is in her airs, I protest* (Henry Fielding).
—*adj.* **1** giddy; flighty. **2** inclined to put on airs; haughty. **3** petulant; huffy.
—*n.* **1** giddy behavior; flightiness. **2** a fuss; disturbance. **3** = haughtiness.
[varied reduplication of earlier *hoit* act wantonly]
ho|ja blan|ca (ō′häbläng′kä), a serious disease of rice that causes stunted growth and white stripes on the leaf. It was first found in Cuba and Venezuela and is believed to be a virus disease transmitted by insects. [< Spanish *hoja blanca* white leaf]
Ho|kan (hō′kən), *n.* a grouping of North American Indian languages of the Western United States usually including the Yuman and various other linguistic groups.
hoke (hōk), *v.t.*, **hoked**, **hok|ing**.
hoke up, *Slang.* to seek to make (a story, drama, or the like) emotionally moving or comic by the use of hokum; fill with hokum: *Certain kinds of emotional situations recur and are, shall we say, hoked up* (Punch).
[apparently short for *hokum*]
hoked-up (hōkt′up′), *adj. Slang.* hokey.

Pronunciation Key: hat, āge, cãre, fär; let, ēqual, tėrm; it, īce; hot, ōpen, ôrder; oil, out; cup, pu̇t, rüle; child; long; thin; ᴛʜen; zh, measure; ə represents **a** in about, **e** in taken, **i** in pencil, **o** in lemon, **u** in circus.

hok|ey (hō′kē), *adj. Slang.* filled with hokum; contrived: *Modern wrestling is interesting entertainment for its devotees but, generally, it is a hokey spectacle* (Maclean's).

ho|key-po|key or **ho|ky-po|ky** (hō′kē pō′kē), *n., pl.* **-kies. 1** trickery; deception; hocus-pocus. **2** a cheap kind of ice cream sold by street vendors.

hok|ku (hok′kü) *n., pl.* **-ku. 1** = haiku. **2** the first stanza in a Japanese verse form in which the stanzas are composed alternately by various poets. [< Japanese *hokku*]

ho|kum (hō′kəm), *n. Slang.* **1** outworn melodramatic material or crude humor introduced into a play or the like for emotional effect or the laughs it may bring: *This may be groundling comedy, but it is not pure hokum* (New York Times). *Hokum—they lap it up* (Carl Sandburg). **2** humbug; nonsense; bunk: *It is pure hokum to suggest that all authors are always interesting* (Publishers' Weekly). [perhaps < *hocus;* influenced by *bunkum*]

hol (hol), *n. British Informal.* holiday.

hol-, *combining form.* the form of **holo-** before vowels, as in *holistic.*

hol|a|ble (hō′lə bəl), *adj.* = holeable.

Hol|arc|tic (hol ärk′tik), *adj.* belonging to a zoogeographical division consisting of the Nearctic division of the New World and the Palearctic division of the Old World.

Hol|boell's grebe (hōl′bůlz), a large, grayish grebe of North America and northern Europe and Asia, with a reddish-brown neck and whitish cheeks in the breeding plumage; red-necked grebe. [< Carl *Holboell,* a Danish naturalist of the 1800's]

∗**hold**[1] (hōld), *v.,* **held, held** or (*Archaic*) **hold|en, hold|ing,** *n.* —*v.t.* **1** to grasp and keep; take in the hands or arms and keep: *Please hold my hat. Hold my watch while I play this game. The boy was left awkwardly holding the baby. The man held his head in his hands.* **SYN:** support, bear, sustain. **2a** to keep in some place, position, or condition; cause to stay: *Hold the dish level. He will hold the paper steady while you draw.* **b** to oblige (a person) to adhere to a promise or agreement: *They held him to his promise. It is impossible to hold all children to the same high standards of academic achievement* (Saturday Review). **3a** to keep from acting; hold back; restrain: *Hold your breath. . . . the only restraining motive which may hold the hand of a tyrant* (Thomas Jefferson). *I wish you'd hold your noise* (Dickens). **SYN:** check. **b** to keep back; detain, delay, or retain: *to hold newspaper copy for further use, to hold a letter for additional postage. This package will be held until called for.* **4** to keep; defend: *The soldiers held the fort against the enemy.* **5a** to contain; have room for: *How much water will this cup hold? This theater holds 500 people. These canisters hold sugar and flour.* **SYN:** See syn. under **contain. b** to drink (liquor) without showing its effect: *A man must hold his liquor badly if he isn't still sober after the first glass.* **6** to have: **a** to carry on together: *to hold a celebration, hold a conversation. Shall we hold a meeting of the club?* **SYN:** convene, convoke. **b** to have and keep; possess or occupy: *He holds much property in the city. That man has held the office of mayor for eight years. That was a play that long held the boards.* **SYN:** See syn. under **have. c** to keep or have in the mind: *She holds a good opinion of you.* **d** to observe or preserve (silence): *If these should hold their peace, the stones would immediately cry out* (Luke 19:40). **7a** to think; believe or consider: *People once held that the world was flat. For their absence the king was held responsible* (Macaulay). **SYN:** regard, deem. **b** to think a certain way about; feel toward: *Wise men are held in honor.* **8** to bear or carry in a certain position or attitude: *to hold oneself erect. She held her head as proudly as ever.* **9** to satisfy; suffice: *This meal should hold you until tomorrow.* **10** to decide legally: *The court held that the accused men were innocent.* **11** *Law.* to bind (to or in bail): *The prisoner was held in $2,500 bail.* **12** *Music.* to keep on singing or playing (a note). —*v.i.* **1** to remain fast or firm; not break, loosen, or give way: *The dike held during the flood. Will your anchor hold?* **2** to remain in a specified state; continue in a course; last; persist: *The frost still holds.* **3** to maintain one's grasp on anything; cling: *The wind was so strong I had to hold onto the rail.* **4** to maintain one's position against opposition or attack; hold out: *Our force by land hath nobly held* (Shakespeare). **5** to be faithful or firm; adhere; abide: *She held to her promise.* **6** to be true; be in force or effect; apply: *The rule holds in all cases.* **7** to keep the same; continue; proceed: *The weather held warm. Fair held the breeze behind us* (Rudyard Kipling). **8** to restrain oneself; refrain; stop; cease (usually imperative): *Lay on, Macduff, And damned be him, that first cries "Hold, enough!"* (Shakespeare). **9a** to hold property by some tenure: *a tenant holding under a long lease.* **b** to derive title to something: *I am the Woman of Shamlegh, and I hold from the Rajah* (Rudyard Kipling).

—*n.* **1a** the act or manner of grasping and holding; grasp or grip: *to release one's hold. You must take a better hold if you are to pull your weight.* **b** a way of holding an opponent in wrestling. **2a** a thing to hold by: *The face of the cliff had enough holds for a good climber.* **b** a thing to hold something else with. **3** *Figurative.* a controlling force or influence; power; sway: *A habit has a hold on you. The idea has a strong hold on your imagination.* **4a** a holding back; delay: *a hold in the launching of a missile.* **b** an order to delay or temporarily halt something. **5** a sign for a pause in music; symbol above or below a note or rest indicating that it is to be held for a longer time. **SYN:** fermata. **6** an abode, place of shelter, or lurking place of a human being, fish, or other animal: *His hold is usually under the roots of trees.* **7a** a prison cell: *You were put into a species of condemned hold at the back* (Dickens). **b** *Archaic.* imprisonment; confinement: *They laid hands on them, and put them in hold unto the next day* (Acts 4:3). **8** *Archaic.* a fort; stronghold. **9** *Obsolete.* a having in charge; possession.

get hold of, to get; obtain: *I must get hold of some money before the banks close today.*

hold a candle to. See under **candle.**

hold back, a to keep back; keep from acting; restrain: *Some divinity holds back mine arm* (John Dryden). **b** to avoid disclosing: *to hold back the truth. He is holding something back.*

hold down, a to keep down; keep under control; repress: *The more they were held down, the more they flourished.* **b** *Informal, Figurative.* to have and keep: *to hold down a job.*

hold forth, a to talk or preach; harangue (often used disparagingly): *He is able to hold forth upon canes longer than upon any one subject in the world* (Sir Richard Steele). **b** to offer: *A chapel . . . where Mass was publicly held forth every day* (Thomas Lediard).

hold good, to continue valid; apply: *It will hold good in nineteen out of twenty instances* (John R. McCulloch).

hold in, a to keep in; keep back; restrain; check: *He held in the dogs until the fox was seen.* **b** to restrain oneself; keep silence: *I could hardly hold myself in when he kicked my dog.*

hold off, a to keep off or at a distance; keep from attacking: *to hold off the enemy. Hold off your hand* (Shakespeare). **b** to keep from acting; keep away or aloof: *The storm may hold off. If you love me, hold not off* (Shakespeare).

hold on, a to keep one's hold: *He found himself holding on to a piece of plank.* **b** *Figurative.* to keep on; continue: *He held on until there was no chance of winning.* **c** *Informal.* stop! wait a minute!: *Hold on! Wait until I get my coat.*

hold one's own. See under **own.**

hold out, a to keep up; continue; last: *The food will only hold out two more days. No way to fly, nor strength to hold out flight* (Shakespeare). **b** *Figurative.* to keep resisting; not give in; endure: *Her constitution could not long hold out.* **c** to offer; present: *Hopes were held out to him that his life would be spared* (Macaulay). **d** *U.S. Informal.* to keep back (something expected or due): *to hold out on a promise.* **e** to stretch forth; extend: *Hold out your hand.*

hold over, a to keep for further action or consideration; postpone: *The bill has been held over until next year.* **b** to stay in office beyond the regular term: *He held over until his successor was appointed.* **c** *Music.* to hold (a tone) from one bar to the next: *She held over the high note into the next measure.*

hold the bag. See under **bag.**

hold the fort. See under **fort.**

hold the line. See under **line**[1].

hold up, a to keep from falling; support: *The roof is held up by pillars.* **b** *Figurative.* to maintain; keep up: *Prices have been holding up pretty well.* **c** to show, display: *He held up the sign so we could all see it.* **d** to continue; last; endure: *If this wind holds up, we can go sailing.* **e** to keep back; withhold; stop: *We will hold up our answer to your proposal until we know the cost.* **f** *Informal.* to stop by force and rob: *He was held up in the alley.* **g** to subject (to); make the target of: *Bacon has been held up to criticism.*

hold water. See under **water.**

hold with, a to side with: *Some there were, that held with both sides* (Meredith Hanmer). **b** to agree with: *I don't hold with him buying flowers when his children haven't got enough to eat* (Cornhill Magazine). **c** to approve of: *My grandmother does not hold with newfangled ways.*

lay (or **take) hold of** (or **on**), **a** to seize; grasp: *They took hold of each other's hands. The officers . . . were laid hold on* (Daniel Defoe). **b** *Figurative.* to get control or possession of: *His declaration . . . failed to dispel the malaise taking hold of the capital* (New York Times).

no hold (or **holds) barred,** no rules or restraints; complete freedom of action or expression: *There were no holds barred when the enemies met in combat.*

on hold, *U.S. and Canadian.* **a** on a telephone connection held open automatically until someone is available to take the call: *Phone calls sometimes come in from Florida, Nova Scotia, and Missouri; the callers may be put on hold for an hour or more* (New Yorker). **b** *Figurative.* in a suspended state; put off; delayed: *"A massive reorganization of our elevator operation, based on a two-year engineering study, has been 'on hold' for over a year . . ." Mr. Christian said* (New York Times).

take hold, to become attached: *It is hard for him to take hold in the new place, to build himself a new career there* (Edmund Wilson).

[< Old English *haldan, healdan*] —**hold′a|ble,** *adj.*

∗**hold**[1]
n., definition 5

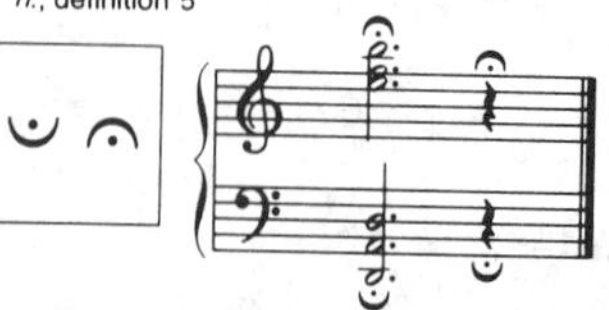

hold[2] (hōld), *n.* the part inside a ship or airplane where the cargo is carried. A ship's hold is below the deck. [variant of *hole;* or perhaps < Dutch *hol;* perhaps influenced by *hold*[1]]

hold|all (hōld′ôl′), *n.* **1** a portable traveling case for holding clothes and miscellaneous articles. **2** a potpourri: *In a sense Proust's masterpiece is just such a holdall, in which the writer permits himself long digressions on all sorts of subjects* (Manchester Guardian).

hold|back (hōld′bak′), *n., adj.* —*n.* **1** a thing that holds back; restraint; hindrance. **2** the act of restraining or preventing action. **3** an iron or strap on the shaft of a wagon or carriage to which the harness is attached, enabling a horse to hold back or to back the wagon or carriage. **4** something withheld, especially money or wages: *The holdback also includes $90 million for the new solid-fueled Minuteman missile* (Wall Street Journal). **5** a person who does not commit himself. —*adj.* = unprogressive.

hold|down (hōld′doun′), *n. U.S.* the prevention of rises or increases so far as possible or convenient; repression: *a holddown on all spending.*

hold|en (hōl′dən), *v. Archaic.* held; a past participle of **hold**[1].

hold|er (hōl′dər), *n.* **1** a person or thing that holds something: *The holder must remember to hold the saw in a tight grip.* **2** a person who owns, possesses, or occupies property, such as an owner, possessor, or tenant: *Holders of leases pay rent.* **3a** a thing to hold something else with: *a cigarette holder, a napkin holder.* **b** a pad of cloth for lifting hot dishes: *Mother picked up the hot vegetable dish with two holders.* **4** a person who is legally entitled to receive payment on, or negotiate, a note, bill, or check.

holder up, a worker who holds the rivet in place while the riveter closes its open end.

hold|fast (hōld′fast′, -fäst′), *n.* **1** a thing used to hold something else in place, such as a hook or clamp. **2** the act or fact of holding fast; firm or sure grasp. **3** a branched or disk-shaped basal portion by which a sessile organism, such as a barnacle, attaches itself to a rock or other object.

hold|ing (hōl′ding), *n.* **1** land; a piece of land: *The government has vast holdings in the West that are used as national parks.* **2a** *Football.* an illegal use of the hands and arms to seize or obstruct an opposing player: *Navy was called for holding and penalized 15 yards* (New York Times). **b** a similar foul in basketball or soccer.

holdings, property in stocks or bonds: *He has large holdings in our vicinity.*

holding company, a company that owns stocks or bonds of other companies and controls them.

holding pattern, a circular pattern flown by an aircraft above or near an airport while it waits to be cleared for landing.

holding tank, *U.S.* a tank on a boat for holding sewage to be pumped out at a dockside station.

hold|out (hōld′out′), *n. Informal.* **1** a person, group, or organization that refuses to accept terms, submit, or comply as with a trend or order: *Despite their reputation as long-time holdouts against Government handouts, the nervous beef raisers are asking the U.S. Tariff Commission to step in* (Wall Street Journal). **2** continued resistance; refusal to accept terms, submit, or

comply: *The buyer threatened a holdout when the contract was ready to be signed.* 3 a stronghold.
hold|o|ver (hōld′ō′vər), *n.* **1a** a person who continues to hold an office after his term has expired: *He was a holdover from the Cabinet that quit on Monday* (New York Times). **b** a person or thing that remains behind from a former period: *the little village of Washington in Connecticut, one of the most charming holdovers of the past that state possesses* (Atlantic). **2** *U.S.* something left over; remainder: *doing the best it could on crackers and cheese and holdovers* (Los Angeles Express). **3** *U.S.* a student who repeats a course, grade, or program. **4** a tree left standing after others have been cut down.
hold time, a delay in the countdown or launching operations of a rocket or missile.
hold|up (hōld′up′), *n.* **1** *Informal.* the act of stopping by force and robbing. **2** the act or process of stopping; stoppage: *So far we have not had a single holdup of job activity due to any lack of steel supply* (Wall Street Journal). **3** *Informal.* **a** asking too high a price. **b** something priced too high. **4** a catch for holding the rear door of a truck or station wagon. **5** *Bridge.* the retaining of a card in one's hand instead of using it at the first opportunity to take a trick.
hole (hōl), *n., v.,* **holed, hol|ing.** —*n.* **1** an open place; opening; gap: *a hole in a sock.* **2** a hollow place in something solid: *a hole in the road. Swiss cheese has holes in it.* **3a** a hollow place in the earth in which an animal lives; burrow: *Rabbits dig holes in the ground to live in. The foxes have holes, and the birds of the air have nests* (Matthew 8:20). **b** a deep place, such as in a stream or pond: *The boys went to the swimming hole after school.* **4** *Figurative.* **a** a small, dark, dirty place: *This apartment is a hole.* **b** a prison cell or dungeon. **5** *Informal, Figurative.* a flaw; defect: *There's a hole in your argument.* **6** *Informal, Figurative.* a position hard to get out of; embarrassing position; predicament: *He found himself in a hole.* SYN: fix, scrape, mess. **7a** a small, round, hollow place on a green, into which a golf ball is hit. **b** one of the divisions of a golf course leading from a tee to such a place. A regular golf course consists of 18 holes. *We played only ten holes.* **8** *U.S.* a cove or small harbor. **9** *Physics.* a vacant spot in certain semiconductors in which there is no electron.
—*v.t.* **1** to make a hole or holes in; perforate. **2** to make (a hole); sink (a shaft); bore (a tunnel). **3** to hit or drive (a golf ball) into a hole: *Pattinson missed only one putt that looked holeable and holed a good number that were missable* (London Times).
—*v.i.* **1** to make a hole or holes. **2** to go into a hole.
blow a hole in, to damage, weaken, or ruin: *The provision blows a hole in the entire fabric that the Supreme Court has woven to deter official lawlessness* (Time).
burn a hole in one's pocket, (of money) to make a person want very much to spend it: *The dollar burned a hole in the boy's pocket until he bought candy and ice cream with it.*
hole out, to hit a golf ball into a hole: *An uppish stroke off the last ball of Goodwin's opening saw him hole out* (London Times).
hole up, **a** to go or put into a hole: *In November the badgers all hole up for the winter.* **b** *Figurative:* *The robbers holed up in an old cabin.*
in the hole, **a** in debt or financial difficulties: *Fort Wayne's symphony was $22,000 in the hole, but contributions pulled it out* (Wall Street Journal). **b** (of a card in stud poker) not showing; face down: *He was as calmly exasperating as a strange poker player with a pair of tens showing who goes on betting into a pair of jacks; either he is silly or he has the third ten in the hole* (New Yorker).
make a hole in, *Informal.* to use up a large amount of: *An average daily consumption of four glasses . . . makes a hole in the income of the working class* (Spectator).
pick holes in, to find fault with; criticize: *We do not go to visit a neighbour, in order to pick holes in him and his establishment* (Dinah M. Mulock).
shoot full of holes, to criticize; show the fault with: *His harebrained scheme was shot full of holes by the older boys.*
[Old English *hol*] —**hole′less**, *adj.*
—***Syn.*** *n.* **1, 2, 3 Hole, cavity** mean an open or hollow place in something. **Hole** is the common word applying to an opening in or through anything, or to a hollow space in something solid: *Fire burned a hole in the roof. He bored a hole in the tree.* **Cavity** is chiefly scientific or technical, and applies only to a hollow space inside a solid mass or body, often with an opening at the surface: *The dentist filled several cavities in my teeth.*
hole|a|ble (hō′lə bəl), *adj. Golf.* (of a putt) that can be holed (in a certain number of strokes): *four holeable putts which he missed* (Westminster Gazette).
hole card, **1** a card dealt face down in stud poker. **2** a concealed advantage.
hole in one, *Golf.* a shot from the tee which goes into the hole; ace.
hole-in-the-wall (hōl′in ᴛʜə wôl′), *adj.* small; grubby; miserable: *I went into a hole-in-the-wall bakery where the proprietor recognized me after ten years* (Atlantic).
hole|proof (hōl′prüf′), *adj.* **1** made to protect against holes: *a holeproof jacket.* **2** *Figurative.* made so as to close or prevent loopholes: *a holeproof legal document.* **3** *Figurative.* without a flaw or defect: *Quite a jolly trick-solution tale. . . . Far from holeproof, but easy reading* (Peter Dickinson).
hole|y (hō′lē), *adj.* full of holes.
Ho|li (hō′lē), *n.* the Hindu festival of spring. [< Hindi *holī*]
hol|i|but (hol′ə bət), *n.* = halibut.
-holic, *combining form.* a person who is obsessed with or has a strong craving for something; a ______addict: *Chocoholic = a person who has a strong craving for chocolate.*
[variant of *-aholic*]
hol|i|day (hol′ə dā), *n., adj., v.* —*n.* **1** a day when one does not work; day for pleasure and enjoyment: *New Year's is a holiday for everyone.* **2** a day fixed by law on which ordinary business is suspended, usually in honor of a famous event or person: *The Fourth of July is a holiday in the United States.* **3** Often, **holidays.** a vacation; period of rest or recreation: *He is spending his holidays camping.* **4** a holy day; religious festival.
—***adj.*** of or suited to a holiday: *holiday clothes.*
—***v.i.*** to spend a holiday or vacation: *We holidayed in Great Britain last summer.*
[Old English *hāligdæg* holy day] —**hol′i|day′er**, *n.*
hol|i|day-mak|er or **hol|i|day|mak|er** (hol′ə dā mā′kər), *n. British.* a vacationer.
ho|li|er-than-thou (hō′lē ər ᴛʜən ᴛʜou′), *adj., n.* —***adj.*** self-righteous; pharisaic: *a holier-than-thou attitude.* —*n.* a self-righteous person; pharisee.
ho|li|ly (hō′lə lē), *adv.* in a holy manner; piously or devoutly; sacredly.
ho|li|ness (hō′lē nis), *n.* the condition or quality of being holy.
[Old English *hālignes*]
Ho|li|ness (hō′lē nis), *n.* a title used in speaking to or of the Pope: *The Pope is addressed as "Your Holiness."*
Holiness church, one of a group of American Protestant sects deriving from the early Methodist church, that emphasize the doctrine of Christian perfection in faith and works.
ho|lism (hō′liz əm), *n.* a theory that the tendency in nature is to produce whole organisms from small units or structures. [(coined by J. C. Smuts) < Greek *hólos* whole + English *-ism*]
ho|lis|tic (hō lis′tik), *adj.* **1** taking in the whole of something; overall; inclusive: *a holistic approach.* **2** based on the theory that a whole culture or organism is a more fruitful field of study than its parts or symptoms. [< *hol-* + *-ist* + *-ic*] —**ho|lis′ti|cal|ly**, *adv.*
hol|la (hə lä′, hol′ə), *interj., n., v.i., v.t.* = hollo.
hol|land or **Hol|land** (hol′ənd), *n.* a linen, or linen and cotton, cloth, used especially for window shades and upholstery. It is usually light-brown and sometimes glazed. [< *Holland,* formerly a province of the Netherlands, where it was first made]
hol|lan|daise sauce, or **hol|lan|daise** (hol′ən dāz), *n.* a creamy yellow sauce made from egg yolks, butter, lemon juice, and seasoning.
[< French *sauce hollandaise,* feminine of *hollandais* Dutch < *Hollande* Holland]
Hol|land|er (hol′ən dər), *n.* a person born or living in Holland or the Netherlands; Dutchman.
Holland gin, = Hollands.
Hol|lands or **hol|lands** (hol′əndz), *n.* **1** a strong gin made in Holland; geneva; schnapps. **2** = holland (cloth). [< Dutch *hollandsch* (*genever*) Hollands (gin)]
hol|ler[1] (hol′ər), *v., n. Informal.* —*v.i., v.t.* to cry or shout loudly; hollo.
—*n.* **1** a loud cry or shout: *I put up a holler right at the jump* (George Ade). **2** *U.S.* a work song of Negro slaves and laborers: *These field hollers, which employed the pentatonic scale now common to African and American Negro music . . . were the foundation of the blues* (Saturday Review).
[American English, variant pronunciation of *hollo, holla*] —**hol′ler|er**, *n.*
hol|ler[2] (hol′ər), *n. U.S. Dialect.* hollow (valley): *It was a long way from the backwoods hollers of West Virginia* (Time). [American English; variant of *hollow*]
hol|lo (hə lō′, hol′ō), *interj., n., pl.* **-los,** *v.,* **-loed, -lo|ing.** —***interj.*** ho there! hello! an exclamation to someone at a distance, in order to call attention, or to answer who hails.
—*n.* **1** a shout of greeting or surprise. **2** a loud shout; a shout of "hollo," especially as a cry to the hounds in hunting.
—***v.i.*** to call out loudly; shout.
—***v.t.*** to urge or call by shouting. Also, **holla, hullo.**
[earlier *hollow,* apparently variant of *hallow*[2]]
hol|loa (hə lō′, hol′ō), *interj., n., v.i., v.t.* = hollo.
hol|low (hol′ō), *adj., n., v., adv.* —***adj.*** **1** having nothing, or only air, inside; with a hole inside; not solid; empty: *A tube or pipe is hollow. Most rubber balls are hollow.* SYN: void, unfilled. **2** shaped like a bowl or cup: *a hollow dish for soup. Through hollow lands and hilly lands* (William Butler Yeats). **3** as if coming from something hollow; deep and dull: *a hollow voice, hollow groans, the hollow boom of a foghorn.* **4** deep and sunken: *A starving person has hollow eyes and cheeks.* **5** *Figurative.* not real or sincere; false; worthless; empty: *hollow promises, hollow joys.* SYN: idle, vain, insincere. **6** hungry: *By twelve o'clock we felt rather hollow.*
—*n.* **1** a hollow place; hole: *a hollow in the road.* **2** low land between hills; valley; basin: *The Legend of Sleepy Hollow* (Washington Irving).
—***v.t.*** **1** to make by hollowing; bend or dig out to a hollow shape: *He hollowed a whistle out of a piece of wood.* **2** to make hollow: *The old man hollowed one hand against his ear to hear better.*
—***v.i.*** to become hollow: *His cheeks hollowed as he sucked the drink through the straw.*
—***adv.*** **1** in a hollow manner: *His voice rang hollow in the empty hall.* **2** *Informal.* thoroughly.
beat (all) hollow, *Informal.* to beat thoroughly: *The professional team beat the local competition all hollow.*
hollow out, to form by hollowing: *to hollow out a tunnel or a trench.*
[Middle English *holwe* < Old English *holh,* noun] —**hol′low|ly**, *adv.* —**hol′low|ness**, *n.*
hol|low-eyed (hol′ō īd′), *adj.* having sunken eyes.
hol|low-horned (hol′ō hôrnd′), *adj.* having hollow horns formed upon a solid core of true bone that do not shed.
hol|low|ware (hol′ō wãr′), *n.* bowl-shaped or tube-shaped dishes, such as cups and tureens, usually of silver, as contrasted with flatware, such as knives and forks.
hol|lus|chick (hol′əs chik′), *n., pl.* **-chick|ie** (-chik′ē). a young bachelor fur seal: *The holluschickie are the champion swimmers of all the seal-tribe* (H. W. Elliott). [< Russian *goloshchok* (perhaps, literally) bare cheek < *gol* naked + *shcheka* cheek]
***hol|ly** (hol′ē), *n., pl.* **-lies.** **1** a tree or shrub with glossy, sharp-pointed green leaves and clusters of bright-red berries; ilex. Hollies are evergreens. **2** its leaves and berries, often used as Christmas decorations. **3** = holm oak. [Old English *holegn,* or *holen*]

***holly** definition 2

hol|ly|hock (hol′ē hok), *n.* **1** a tall plant with clusters of large, showy flowers of various colors and fuzzy, heart-shaped leaves that grow along a tall stem. It belongs to the mallow family. **2** its flower. [Middle English *holihoc* < *holi* holy (Old English *hālig*) + *hoc* mallow, Old English *hocc*]
holly oak, = holm oak.
Hol|ly|wood (hol′ē wu̇d), *n.* the American motion-picture industry. [< *Hollywood,* a section of Los Angeles, center of the United States motion-picture industry]
Hollywood bed, a bed consisting of a mattress on a box spring resting on short legs, and sometimes a headboard.
Hol|ly|wood|ish (hol′ē wu̇d′ish), *adj.* characteristic of the American motion-picture industry; gaudy and spectacular.
Hollywood kitchen, *U.S.* a kitchen with built-in cabinets, oven, stove, and sink, often as one complete unit.
holm[1] (hōm), *n.* **1** low, flat land by a river or stream: *O Derwent! winding among grassy holms* (Wordsworth). **2** a small island in a river or lake near a large island or near the mainland. [Old

Pronunciation Key: hat, āge, cãre, fär; let, ēqual, tėrm; it, īce; hot, ōpen, ôrder; oil, out; cup, pu̇t, rüle; child; long; thin; ᴛʜen; zh, measure; ə represents **a** in about, **e** in taken, **i** in pencil, **o** in lemon, **u** in circus.

English *holm*, probably influenced by Scandinavian (compare Old Icelandic *holmr*)]

holm² (hōm), *n.* **1** = holm oak. **2** *Dialect.* the holly. [alteration of Middle English *holn*, Old English *holen* or *holegn* holly]

Holmes·i·an (hōm′zē ən), *adj.* **1** characteristic of Sherlock Holmes, the fictional detective created by Sir Arthur Conan Doyle (1859-1930): *He has a Holmesian power of analysis and deduction, too* (Punch). **2** of or having to do with the works of Sir Arthur Conan Doyle that feature Sherlock Holmes.

***hol·mi·um** (hōl′mē əm), *n.* a highly magnetic, metallic chemical element, one of the rare-earth elements, which occurs in combination with certain minerals, such as gadolinite. [< New Latin *holmium* < *Holmia*, Latinization of *Stockholm*, Sweden, near where it was first found]

***holmium**

symbol	atomic number	atomic weight	oxidation state
Ho	67	164.930	3

holm oak, **1** an evergreen oak of southern Europe with leaves like those of holly. It is also called the *holm, holly oak,* and *ilex.* **2** its hard wood. [< *holm²* + *oak*]

holo-, *combining form.* whole; entire; wholly: *Holocaust = entire or complete destruction. Holocryptic = wholly hidden.* Also, **hol-** before vowels. [< Greek *hólos*]

hol·o·ben·thic (hol′ə ben′thik), *adj. Biology.* living at or near the bottom of the sea during all stages of life.

hol·o·blast (hol′ə blast, hō′lə-), *n. Embryology.* an ovum consisting entirely or mostly of formative or germinal matter. [< *holo-* + Greek *blastós* germ]

hol·o·blas·tic (hol′ə blas′tik, hō′lə-), *adj. Embryology.* (of an ovum) consisting entirely or mostly of germinal matter and therefore undergoing complete segmentation: *holoblastic cleavage.*

Hol·o·caine hydrochloride, (hol′ə kān, hō′lə-), *Trademark.* phenacaine hydrochloride, a local anesthetic. [< *holo-* + (co)*caine*]

hol·o·caust (hol′ə kôst), *n.* **1** complete destruction by fire, especially of animals or human beings. **2** great or wholesale destruction: *nuclear holocaust.* **3** a sacrificial offering which is completely burned; burnt offering.
the Holocaust, the mass destruction or extermination of European Jews by the Nazis during World War II.
[< Latin *holocaustum* < Greek *holókauston*, neuter of *holókaustos* < *hólos* whole + *kaustós* burned < *kaíein* to burn]

hol·o·caus·tic (hol′ə kôs′tik), *adj.* belonging to or like a holocaust.

Hol·o·cene (hol′ə sēn), *adj., n.* —*adj.* of or having to do with the Recent geological epoch.
—*n.* this epoch; Recent. [< *holo-* + Greek *kainós* recent]

hol·o·clas·tic (hol′ə klas′tik), *adj.* of or having to do with clastic rocks of aqueous origin as contrasted with those of volcanic origin.

hol·o·crine (hol′ə krin, -krīn), *adj.* **1** that produces a secretion consisting of cells which have disintegrated: *a holocrine gland.* **2** of or produced by such a gland. [< *holo-* + Greek *krínein* to separate]

hol·o·en·zyme (hol′ō en′zīm), *n.* an enzymatically active complex composed of a protein component and a coenzyme.

Hol·o·fer·nes (hol′ə fėr′nēz), *n.* (in the book of Judith) an Assyrian general, beheaded by Judith.

hol·o·gram (hol′ə gram), *n.* a record or reproduction of an image produced on a photographic plate or film by holography: *Lasers alone can produce coherent beams strong enough to make holograms* (Science News). [< *holo-* + *-gram¹*]

hol·o·graph¹ (hol′ə graf, -gräf), *adj., n.* —*adj.* wholly written in the handwriting of the person in whose name it appears: *a holograph manuscript.*
—*n.* a holograph manuscript, letter, or document; autograph.
[< Late Latin *holographus* < Greek *hológraphos* < *hólos* whole + *gráphein* to write]

hol·o·graph² (hol′ə graf, -gräf), *v.t.* to make a hologram of; produce by holography: *A hologram stores a faithful three-dimensional record of the object being 'holographed', and the reconstructed image can be matched against the object itself* (Science Journal). [back formation < *holography*] —**ho·log′ra·pher,** *n.*

hol·o·graph·ic¹ (hol′ə graf′ik), *adj. Law.* written, dated, and signed entirely in the handwriting of the testator, and therefore sometimes accepted as valid without the signature of witnesses: *a holographic will.*

hol·o·graph·ic² (hol′ə graf′ik), *adj.* of, having to do with, or made by holography: *a holographic image. Holographic studies may eventually lead to the development of three-dimensional television* (Irwin Stambler). —**hol′o·graph′i·cal·ly,** *adv.*

hol·o·graph·i·cal (hol′ə graf′ə kəl), *adj.* = holographic.

***ho·log·ra·phy** (ho lôg′rə fē, -log′-), *n., pl.* **-phies,** *v.,* **-phied, -phy·ing.** —*n.* a method of photography without the use of lenses in which a three-dimensional image is recorded on a photographic plate or film by means of laser light. The laser light is split into two beams that interfere with each other to form a pattern which depends on the shape of the photographed object. When the pattern on the plate or film is then exposed to visible light, a three-dimensional image of the object is formed. *Holography differs from photography in that it uses the coherent properties of laser light to record all the information in an arrangement of light rays on a piece of photographic film* (New Scientist).
—*v.t.* to produce a hologram; photograph by holography.
[< *holo-* + *-graphy*]

laser
object beam
beam-splitting mirror
reference beam
hologram
object

***holography**

hol·o·he·dral (hol′ə hē′drəl, hō′lə-), *adj.* having the full number of planes required by the maximum symmetry: *a holohedral crystal.* [< *holo-* + Greek *hédra* base + English *-al¹*]

hol·o·he·drism (hol′ə hē′driz əm, hō′lə-), *n.* the property of having all parts similarly modified or of having the full number of planes that are crystallographically possible.

hol·o·he·dron (hol′ə hē′drən, hō′lə-), *n., pl.* **-drons, -dra** (-drə). a holohedral crystal or form.

***ho·lo·ku** (hō lō kü′, hō lō′kü), *n.* a long, fitted dress with a train, worn by Hawaiian women on formal occasions. [< Hawaiian *holokū*]

***holoku**

hol·o·me·tab·o·lism (hol′ə mə tab′ə liz əm), *n. Biology.* = complete metamorphosis.

hol·o·me·tab·o·lous (hol′ə mə tab′ə ləs), *adj.* of or having to do with complete metamorphosis: *... the larval-pupal transformation of holometabolous insects* (Science).

hol·o·mi·cros·co·py (hol′ə mī kros′kə pē), *n.* the taking of three-dimensional pictures of microscopic objects; three-dimensional microscopy.

hol·o·mor·phic (hol′ə môr′fik, hō′lə-), *adj.* holohedral, especially as distinguished from hemimorphic. [< *holo-* + Greek *morphḗ* form + English *-ic*]

hol·o·mor·phism (hol′ə môr′fiz əm, hō′lə-), *n.* the property of being holomorphic.

ho·lo·muu (hō′lō mü), *n. Hawaiian.* a fitted version of the muumuu.

hol·o·phone (hol′ə fōn), *n.* a device for recording an acoustical hologram: *A holophone records patterns in time in a manner analogous to the way an optical hologram records patterns in space* (New Scientist and Science Journal).

hol·o·phrase (hol′ə frāz′), *n.* a holophrastic word: *The first word comes at about twelve months, when the child utters what the linguists call holophrases ("Mum ... dad ... see") or very short phrases used as one word ("gimme ... allgone")* (Sunday Times).

ho·loph·ra·sis (hə lof′rə sis), *n.* the expression of a whole phrase or sentence in a single word. [< *holo-* + Greek *phrásis* speech]

hol·o·phras·tic (hol′ə fras′tik), *adj.* expressing a whole phrase or sentence by a single word: *"Forget-me-not" and "good-bye" are holophrastic words.* [< *holo-* + Greek *phrastikós* having to do with speech < *phrázein* tell, express]

hol·o·phyte (hol′ə fīt), *n. Botany.* a plant that manufactures its own food. [< *holo-* + Greek *phytón* plant]

hol·o·phyt·ic (hol′ə fit′ik), *adj.* of or like a holophyte.

hol·o·plank·ton (hol′ə plangk′tən), *n. Biology.* organisms that live as plankton through all the stages of their life cycle.

hol·o·scope (hol′ə skōp), *n.* an optical instrument for producing holographic images: *A suggestion to combine the optical non-linear effects with holography has led to a proposal that can in principle yield a "holoscope," a true three-dimensional microscope that could be used in much the same way as a normal two-dimensional one* (New Scientist).

hol·o·scop·ic (hol′ə skop′ik), *adj.* of or based upon complete or overall observation; comprising everything in sight: *a holoscopic view of society.*

hol·o·ste·an (hol′ə stē′ən, hō′lə-), *adj., n.* —*adj.* of or having to do with a group of largely extinct bony fishes that were the ancestors of the teleosts. The gar is a living example.
—*n.* a holostean fish. [< *hol-* + Greek *osteón* bone + English *-an*]

hol·o·sym·met·ri·cal (hol′ə si met′rə kəl, hō′lə-), *adj.* = holohedral.

hol·o·thu·ri·an (hol′ə thůr′ē ən, hō′lə-), *n.* any one of a class of echinoderms, having an elongated, leathery body covered with very small calcareous plates; sea cucumber. [< New Latin *Holothuria* the sea cucumber genus (< Latin *holothuria*, neuter plural < Greek *holothoúrion* a kind of sea polyp) + English *-an*]

hol·o·thu·rin (hol′ə thůr′in, hō′lə-), *n.* a poisonous substance that is a complex mixture of steroid glycosides, extracted from a species of sea cucumber and used experimentally in medicine to destroy bacteria and suppress the growth of tumors: *In addition to their hemolytic activities, holothurins cause irreversible inhibition of nerve conduction* (J. W. Daly). [< *holothur*(ian) + *-in*]

hol·o·trich (hol′ə trik), *n.* any one of a group of protozoans uniformly covered with cilia: *The paramecium is a holotrich.* [< *holo-* + Greek *thríx, trichós* hair]

ho·lot·ri·chous (hə lot′rə kəs), *adj. Zoology.* uniformly covered with cilia.

hol·o·type (hol′ə tīp), *n. Biology.* a single specimen on which the description of a species, variety, or other lesser taxonomic group, is based.

hol·o·typ·ic (hol′ə tip′ik), *adj.* of or based upon a holotype.

hol·o·zo·ic (hol′ə zō′ik), *adj. Zoology.* obtaining its food through the ingestion of solid material. [< *holo-* + Greek *zôion* animal + English *-ic*]

holp (hōlp), *v. Archaic.* helped; a past tense of **help.**

hol·pen (hōl′pən), *v. Archaic.* helped; a past participle of **help.**

hols (holz), *n.pl. British Informal.* holidays; vacation. [short for *holidays*]

Hol·stein (hōl′stīn, -stēn), *n., adj.* —*n.* any one of a breed of large black-and-white dairy cattle, originally of Holland and Friesland. —*adj.* of or having to do with any animal of this breed. [< *Holstein*, a region in North Germany]

Hol·stein-Frie·sian (hōl′stīn frē′zhən, -stēn-), *n., adj.* = Holstein.

hol·ster (hōl′stər), *n., v.* —*n.* a case for a pistol, usually made of leather and attached to a person's belt or a horseman's saddle: *In the holsters, at his saddle-bow, Two aged pistols he did stow* (Samuel Butler).
—*v.t.* to put into the holster. [origin uncertain; perhaps < Swedish *hölster* (< Old Icelandic *hulstr* sheath); perhaps related to Old English *heolster* concealment]

hol·stered (hōl′stərd), *adj.* **1** bearing holsters. **2** in a holster.

holt (hōlt), *n.* **1** *Poetic and Dialect.* a wood; grove: *She sent her voice thro' all the holt* (Tennyson). **2** a wooded hill. [Old English *holt*]

ho·lus-bo·lus (hō′ləs bō′ləs), *adv.* all in a lump; all at once: *The seal swallowed the fish holus-bolus.* [humorous Latinization of English *whole bolus*]

ho·ly (hō′lē), *adj.,* **-li·er, -li·est,** *n., pl.* **-lies.** —*adj.* **1** given or belonging to God; set apart for God's service; coming from God; sacred: *the Holy Bible, Holy Communion.* **2** declared sacred by religious use and authority; consecrated: *a holy day. Holy oil is used by some churches in baptism and other rites.* **3** dedicated or devoted to the service of God, the church, or religion: *a holy life.* **4** like a saint; spiritually perfect; very good; pure in heart: *a holy man. As He died to make men holy ...* (*Julia Ward Howe*). **SYN:** devout, pious, pure, saintly, sinless. **5** *Figurative.* worthy of reverence: *The grave of the unknown soldier is a holy place.* **6** *Informal, Figurative.* awesome; awful; terrible: *Those children are holy terrors.*
—*n.* **1** a holy place; sanctuary. **2** a holy thing. **3** a holy person. [Old English *hālig*]
—*Syn. adj.* **1, 2 Holy, sacred** mean set apart for worship or reverence. **Holy** implies an inherent quality that makes someone or something worthy of worship: *God is holy. Jerusalem and Mecca are Holy Cities.* **Sacred** implies a quality given by dedicating or consecrating something to religious

uses, making it worthy of reverence: *Churches are sacred. The Bible, Talmud, and Koran are sacred writings.*
Holy Bible, = Bible.
Holy City, **1** a city considered sacred by the adherents of any religion. Jerusalem, Rome, and Mecca are Holy Cities. **2** heaven.
Holy Communion, **1** a sharing in the Lord's Supper as a part of church worship; receiving of the Eucharist. **2** the celebration of the Lord's Supper.
holy cow, *U.S. Informal.* an exclamation of surprise or astonishment: *"Holy cow!" he said. "That was expensive"* (Time).
Holy Cross, the cross on which Christ died.
holy day, or **ho\|ly\|day** (hō′lē dā′), *n.* a religious festival, especially one not occurring on Sunday. Ash Wednesday and Good Friday are holy days.
holy day of obligation, **1** any one of certain days on which Roman Catholics are required to abstain from servile work and to attend Mass. **2** a day on which members of the Episcopal Church are required to take Communion.
Holy Family, the name given in art to pictures of the Virgin Mary, the baby Jesus, and Joseph or others with them.
Holy Father, a title of the Pope.
Holy Ghost, the Spirit of God; third person of the Trinity; Holy Spirit.
Holy Grail, the Grail, the cup or dish supposed to have been used by Christ at the Last Supper and the great object of search by the knights of the Round Table.
Holy Innocents' Day, **1** a Christian church festival in commemoration of the murder of the children of Bethlehem by Herod's order; Childermas. Matthew 2:16. **2** December 28, the day this is celebrated.
Holy Joe, *U.S. Slang.* **1** a chaplain in the armed forces. **2** any clergyman. **3** an excessively pious or self-righteous person.
Holy Land, Palestine.
holy mackerel, *U.S. Informal.* an exclamation of surprise or astonishment: *Holy mackerel, I couldn't recognize the landscape anymore* (Curtis Cate).
holy man, a saint or mystic, especially in one of the religions of the Far East.
Holy Office, **1** the Papal congregation which has charge of protecting Catholic faith and morals. **2** the Inquisition.
holy of holies, **1** the most sacred place. **2** Also, **Holy of Holies.** the inner shrine in the Jewish tabernacle and temple, containing the Ark of the Covenant; sanctum sanctorum.
holy orders, **1** the rite or sacrament of ordination. **2** the rank or position of an ordained Christian minister or priest. **3** the three higher ranks or positions in the Roman Catholic and Anglican churches. Bishops, priests, and deacons are members of holy orders.
take holy orders, to become ordained as a Christian minister or priest.
Holy Roller, *U.S.* (often used in an unfriendly way) a member of any one of various small religious sects whose revival meetings are often marked by the ecstatic seizure of participants.
Holy Roman Empire, an empire in western and central Europe regarded both as the continuation of the Roman Empire and as the temporal aspect of a universal dominion whose spiritual head was the Pope. It began in A.D. 962 with the coronation of Otto I, or, according to some, in A.D. 800 with the coronation of Charlemagne, and ended in 1806, when Francis II renounced the imperial crown.
Holy Rood, **1** the cross on which Jesus died. **2** Also, **holy rood.** a representation of it.
Holy Saturday, the Saturday before Easter.
Holy Scripture, = Bible.
Holy See, **1** the office or jurisdiction of the Pope; Apostolic See. **2** the Pope's court.
Holy Sepulcher, the tomb at Jerusalem where the body of Christ is believed to have lain between His burial and the Resurrection.
Holy Spirit, = Holy Ghost.
ho\|ly\|stone (hō′lē stōn′), *n., v.,* **-stoned, -stoning.** *—n.* a piece of soft sandstone used for scrubbing the wooden decks of ships.
—v.t., v.i. to scrub or clean with a holystone. [origin uncertain]
Holy Synod, the church council that governs an Orthodox church.
Holy Thursday, **1** (in the Roman Catholic Church) the Thursday before Easter; Maundy Thursday. **2** (in the Anglican Church) the fortieth day after Easter; Ascension Day.
ho\|ly\|tide (hō′lē tīd′), *n.* a holy season.
Holy Trinity, = Trinity.
holy war, **1** a war fought for an allegedly holy purpose: *The Crusaders waged a holy war against the Moslems in the Middle Ages.* **2** = jihad.
holy water, water blessed by a priest.
Holy Week, the week before Easter.
Holy Writ, the Bible; Scriptures.
Holy Year, a year decreed by the pope for special religious observances, beginning and ending on Christmas Eve.
hom-, *combining form.* the form of **homo-** before vowels, as in *homorganic.*
hom\|age (hom′ij, om′-), *n.* **1** respect; reverence; honor: *Everyone paid homage to the great leader.* **SYN:** deference. See syn. under **honor**. **2** in the Middle Ages: **a** a formal acknowledgment by a vassal that he owed loyalty and service to his lord. **b** a thing done or given to show such acknowledgment. **c** the relation established between a vassal and his lord by such an acknowledgment. [< Old French *homage* < Medieval Latin *hominaticum* state of being a vassal < Latin *homō, -inis* man]
hom\|ag\|er (hom′ə jər, om′-), *n.* a person who owes homage.
hom\|a\|lo\|graph\|ic (hom′ə lə graf′ik), *adj.* = homolographic.
hom\|bre¹ (om′bər), *n.* = omber.
hom\|bre² (ôm′brā, um′brē), *n.* **1** *Southwestern U.S.* man. **2** *U.S. Slang.* a robust fellow; he-man, especially a character in a Western. [< Spanish *hombre* man]
***Hom\|burg** or **hom\|burg** (hom′bėrg), *n.* a man's soft felt hat with a slightly rolled brim, and the crown dented lengthwise. [< *Homburg,* a health resort in former Prussia, where it was first worn]

*Homburg

home (hōm), *n., adj., adv., v.,* **homed, hom\|ing.** *—n.* **1** the place where a person or family lives; one's own house or dwelling place: *a beautiful home. Her home is at 25 South Street. Home is the place where, when you have to go there, They have to take you in* (Robert Frost). *Ancient homes of lord and lady, Built for pleasure and for state* (Tennyson). *Stanford University is the home of the Hoover Institution on War, Revolution, and Peace* (Peter C. Allen). **SYN:** residence, dwelling, abode. **2a** a family or other group living together: *a happy home.* **b** a seat of domestic life and interest: *O happy day, When a new household finds its place Among the myriad homes of earth* (Longfellow). **3** the place where a person was born or brought up; one's own town or country: *to be far from home, to long for home. His home is Virginia. The land of the free and the home of the brave* (Francis Scott Key). **4** the place where a thing is specially common; native habitat: *Alaska is the home of fur seals.* **5** *Figurative.* a place where one can rest and be safe; an asylum: *We come From God, who is our home* (Wordsworth). **6** a place where people who are homeless, poor, old, sick, or blind may live: *a nursing home, a home for the aged.* **7** *Figurative.* the place where a person lives after death; the grave: *Wiser men become As they draw to their eternal home* (Edmund Waller). **8** *Figurative.* a place of existence: *a heavenly home.* **9** a goal in many games. **10** = home plate.
—adj. **1** having to do with one's own home or country; domestic: *Write me all the home events.* **2** of, for, or belonging in a home: *home cooking, home remedies, a home loan.* **3** belonging to or occurring in one's own home grounds: *the home team, a home game.* **4** *Figurative.* reaching its goal; to the point; effective: *a home thrust in argument.* **5** of or belonging to headquarters; principal: *the home office of a company.* **6** in various games: **a** having to do with, or situated at or near, home: *a home position.* **b** reaching, or enabling a player to reach, home: *a home hit.*
—adv. **1** at or to one's home or country: *I want to go home. I lugged the money home* (Daniel Defoe). **2** *Figurative.* to the place where it belongs; to the thing aimed at: *The criticism struck home. Time is precious . . . strike quick and home* (Horatio Nelson). **3** *Figurative.* to the heart or center; deep in: *to drive a nail home. One who cannot get closely home to his sorrow* (Hawthorne). **4** *Figurative.* directly and effectively: *to speak home.* **5** *Nautical.* **a** toward or into the ship: *to bring the anchor home.* **b** into or toward shore. **c** to the full extent; as far as possible: *to sheet home.*
—v.i. **1a** to go home. **b** (of birds) to return home. **2** to have a home; dwell.
—v.t. **1** to bring, carry, or send home. **2** to provide with a home.
at home, **a** at or in one's own home or country: *to find a person at home, affairs at home and abroad.* **b** in a friendly place or familiar condition; at ease; comfortable: *to make oneself at home in a friend's house, to be at home in society.* **c** ready to receive visitors: *The ladies of the family were at home on Wednesdays.*
bring home, See under **bring**.
home free, ahead by a safe margin and certain of success: *to be home free in a national election.*
home in on, **a** (of a guided missile) to locate and move in a straight line toward (the target) by means of a self-contained guidance system: *Others might home in on their targets via a reflected radar beam* (Keith Saunders). **b** (of an aircraft or pilot) to fly toward a directing radio signal: *The plane homed in on the beam of the radio.*
home on, to home in on: *The beacon is installed in a rendezvous airplane and craft wishing to refuel home on the system* (Wall Street Journal). [Old English *hām*]
▶**home, house.** In general usage, *home* refers to any place that is the center of one's family affections; *house* refers only to a building. In real-estate advertising and the like, *home* is frequently used in place of *house* because of its favorable connotations.
home-and-home (hōm′ən hōm′), *adj.* (of an athletic contest) played alternately at the home of each opposing team.
home base, **1** = home plate. **2** = headquarters.
home\|bod\|y (hōm′bod′ē), *n., pl.* **-bod\|ies.** a person who prefers the pleasures of his home and family to outside attractions; a domestic person.
home-born (hōm′bôrn′), *adj.* born or originating at home; native; domestic.
home\|bound or **home-bound** (hōm′bound′), *adj.* **1** homeward-bound. **2** confined to one's home; housebound.
home\|boy (hōm′boi′), *n. U.S.* a boy or man from one's own hometown, region, or community: *"I don't know how to read or write 'cause I was always out with the homeboys"* (People Weekly).
home\|bred (hōm′bred′), *adj.* **1** bred or reared at home; native; indigenous; domestic: *foreign invaders or homebred rebels* (Edward A. Freeman). **2** not polished or refined; crude; unsophisticated: *homebred humor.*
home-brew (hōm′brü′), *n.* beer or other alcoholic liquor made at home.
home\|brewed (hōm′brüd′), *adj.* brewed at home, especially for home consumption.
home\|build\|ing (hōm′bil′ding), *n.* the designing or building of homes.
home\|com\|ing (hōm′kum′ing), *n., adj.* *—n.* **1** the act of coming or returning home. **2a** a return to one's school, college, camp, or other place where one formerly lived or stayed. A yearly reunion of college or university alumni is often called a homecoming. **b** a time set aside for this.
—adj. of or having to do with a homecoming.
home computer, a microcomputer for home use, usually consisting of a magnetic disk that transfers data and programs to the microprocessor, a keyboard, and a video screen that displays information.
home confinement, *U.S.* a term of imprisonment served in one's home and carried out by monitoring signals from an electronic transmitter attached to the prisoner to determine his or her whereabouts.
home\|craft (hōm′kraft′, -kräft′), *n.* special skills that deal with homemaking.
home economics, **1** the science and art that deals with the management of a household; domestic science; domestic art. Home economics includes housekeeping, budgeting of finances, preparation of food, and child care. **2** instruction or practice in this.
home economist, a person skilled in home economics.
home\|folk (hōm′fōk′), *n.pl.* = homefolks.
home\|folks (hōm′fōks′), *n.pl.* the people at one's home or in one's hometown; relatives; neighbors; friends.
home fries, boiled potatoes cut and fried in butter or shortening.
home front, civilian activity in support of the armed forces; home.
home-grown (hōm′grōn′), *adj.* grown or made at home: *home-grown vegetables.* (*Figurative.*) *Many nations will have power reactors, home-grown or imported* (New Scientist).
home guard, *U.S.* a member of a local volunteer force.
Home Guard, = Territorial Army.
home help, *British.* a woman who is hired to do housework.
home-keep\|ing (hōm′kē′ping), *adj., n.* *—adj.*

Pronunciation Key: hat, āge, cãre, fär; let, ēqual, tėrm; it, īce; hot, ōpen, ôrder; **oi**l, **ou**t; cup, pu̇t, rüle; **ch**ild; lo**ng**; **th**in; **ᴛʜ**en; **zh**, measure; **ə** represents **a** in about, **e** in taken, **i** in pencil, **o** in lemon, **u** in circus.

staying at home: *Home-keeping youth have ever homely wits* (Shakespeare).
—*n.* the act of staying at home.

home|land (hōm′land′), *n.* **1** the country that is one's home; one's native land. **2** one of the Bantu tribal regions set aside by the South African government as separate states; Bantustan.

home|less (hōm′lis), *adj., n.* **—*adj.*** without a home; having no home: *a stray, homeless dog.*
—*n.* the homeless, persons having no home: *Send these, the homeless, tempest-tost to me* (Emma Lazarus). **—home′less|ness,** *n.*

home|like (hōm′līk′), *adj.* like home; friendly; familiar; comfortable. **—home′like′ness,** *n.*

home|li|ness (hōm′lē nis), *n.* **1** the condition of being homely; plain looks. **2** familiarity or comfort.

home|ly (hōm′lē), *adj.,* **-li|er, -li|est. 1** not good-looking; ugly; plain: *Cinderella's sisters were very homely. Let time, that makes you homely, make you sage* (Thomas Parnell). **SYN:** uncomely. See syn. under **ugly. 2** suited to home life; simple; everyday: *homely pleasures, homely food. The excellent and homely type of house architecture that still prevails in Philadelphia* (H. G. Wells). **SYN:** plain, unadorned, commonplace, unpolished, rough, rude. **3** of plain manners; unsophisticated; unpretending: *a simple, homely man.* **SYN:** simple, unpretentious. **4** *Archaic.* **a** familiar; intimate; at home (with). **b** friendly; kindly.

home|made or **home-made** (hōm′mād′), *adj.* made at home; of domestic manufacture: *homemade bread.*

home|mak|er (hōm′mā′kər), *n.* a person who manages a home and its affairs, especially a housewife: *The mother is a sensible, hardworking homemaker, warmhearted but hard-pressed to make ends meet* (Time).

home|mak|ing or **home-mak|ing** (hōm′mā′king), *n.* the managing of a home and its affairs; work of a homemaker.

Home Office, the British government department in charge of internal affairs.

ho|me|o|mor|phic (hō′mē ə môr′fik, hom′ē-), *adj.* **1** = homeomorphous. **2** = homomorphic.

ho|me|o|mor|phism (hō′mē ə môr′fiz əm, hom′ē-), *n.* similarity in crystalline form between substances of unlike chemical composition.

ho|me|o|mor|phous (hō′mē ə môr′fəs, hom′ē-), *adj.* crystallizing in the same or a related form (used especially of substances not having an analogous chemical composition). [< Greek *homoiomorphós* (with English *-ous*) < *hómoios* of the same kind (< *homós* the same) + *morphḗ* form]

ho|me|o|path (hō′mē ə path, hom′ē-), *n.* a person who practices or advocates homeopathy.

ho|me|o|path|ic (hō′mē ə path′ik, hom′ē-), *adj.* **1** of or like homeopathy. **2** practicing or advocating homeopathy. **—ho′me|o|path′i|cal|ly,** *adv.*

homeopathic magic, = sympathetic magic.

ho|me|op|a|thy (hō′mē op′ə thē, hom′ē-), *n.* the method of treating diseases by very small doses of drugs, which in large doses would produce in a healthy person symptoms similar to those of the disease. [< German *Homöopathie* < Greek *hómoios* like + *páthos* suffering]

ho|me|o|sta|sis (hō′mē ə stā′sis, hom′ē-), *n. Physiology.* the tendency of an organism to maintain internal equilibrium, as of temperature and fluid content, by the regulation of its bodily processes. [< Greek *hómoios* like + *stásis* position]

ho|me|o|stat|ic (hō′mē ə stat′ik, hom′ē-), *adj.* **1** of or having to do with homeostasis. **2** (of an organism) maintaining internal equilibrium, as of temperature and fluid content, by the regulation of bodily processes. **3** like homeostasis. **—ho′me|o|stat′i|cal|ly,** *adv.*

ho|me|o|therm (hō′m ē ə thėrm′, hom′ē-), *n. Physiology.* an organism that maintains a constant internal temperature: *Man, like other mammals, is a homeotherm—his temperature varying little with alterations of the temperature of his surroundings* (Eric Neil). Also, **homoiotherm.**

ho|me|o|ther|mal (hō′mē ə thėr′məl, hom′ē-), *adj. Physiology.* maintaining a constant internal temperature. Also, **homoiothermal.** [< Greek *hómoios* like + English *thermal*]

ho|me|o|ther|mic (hō′mē ə thėr′mik, hom′ē-), *adj.* = homeothermal. Also, **homoiothermic.**

ho|me|o|typ|ic (hō′mē ə tip′ik, hom′ē-), *adj. Biology.* of the second stage of meiosis, during which the chromosomes divide equally. [< Greek *hómoios* like, similar + English *typ(e)* + *-ic*]

ho|me|o|typ|i|cal (hō′mē ə tip′ə kəl, hom′ē-), *adj.* = homeotypic.

home|own|er (hōm′ō′nər), *n.* a person who owns his own home.

home permanent, 1 a permanent wave that a woman can put in her hair at home. **2** the equipment necessary to give oneself a permanent wave at home.

home|place (hōm′plās ′), *n.* the place where a person or family lives, or had lived originally.

home plate, the block or slab beside which a player stands to bat the ball in baseball, and to which he must return, after getting on base, in order to score; home base.

home|port (hōm′pôrt′, -pōrt′), *n.* the port from which a ship originally sets out and to which it usually returns.

hom|er[1] (hō′mər), *n.* = homing pigeon.

hom|er[2] (hō′mər), *n., v. Informal.* **—*n.*** = home run. **—*v.i.*** to hit a home run. [American English, apparently < *home,* or *home run*]

ho|mer[3] (hō′mər), *n.* **1** a Hebrew unit of dry measure, equal to 10 ephahs; kor. **2** a Hebrew unit of liquid measure, equal to 10 baths; kor. [< Hebrew *homer*]

home range, a definite area over which an animal roams.

Ho|mer|ic (hō mer′ik), *adj.* **1** by the ancient Greek poet Homer. The *Iliad* and the *Odyssey* are Homeric poems. **2** of or having to do with Homer, his style, or his poems. **3** in the style of Homer; having some characteristics of Homer's poems. **4** of or having to do with the age in Greek life from about 1200 B.C. to about 800 B.C. **—Ho|mer′i|cal|ly,** *adv.*

Homeric laughter, loud, hearty laughter.

home|room (hōm′rüm′, -rům′), *n. U.S.* **1** a classroom where members of a class meet, especially to answer roll call and hear announcements. **2** the period during which this class meets: *Miss Fritz was reading to them during homeroom* (John Updike).

home rule, management of the affairs of a country, district, or city by its own people; local self-government.

home run, a hit in baseball which allows the batter to round the bases without a stop and reach home plate to score a run, without aid from fielding errors.

home|school|ing (hōm′skü′ling), *n.* the teaching of children by their parents, especially as an alternative to sending them to school: *This survey of homeschoolers in Australia ... offers useful explanations for those who are curious or skeptical about homeschooling* (John Holt). **—home′school′er,** *n.*

Home Secretary, the head of the Home Office.

home|sick (hōm′sik′), *adj.* overcome by sadness because home is far away; ill with longing for home: *I long to see my master's face again, For I turn homesick* (Yeats). **—home′sick′ness,** *n.*

home|site (hōm′sīt′), *n.* a plot of ground where a house can be built.

home|spun (hōm′spun′), *adj., n.* **—*adj.* 1** spun or made at home: *homespun yarn.* **2** made of homespun cloth. **3** *Figurative.* not polished; plain; simple: *homespun manners.* **SYN:** unsophisticated, unvarnished, homely, unpolished, rude.
—*n.* 1 cloth made of yarn spun at home. **2** a coarse, loosely woven cloth similar to it. **3** a person who wears homespun; a rustic.

home|stead (hōm′sted), *n., v.* **—*n.* 1** a house with its land and other buildings; farm with its buildings: *There are many old homesteads in New England.* **2** *U.S.* the public land granted to a settler under certain conditions by the United States government. **3** the place of one's dwelling or home: *To make the West ... The homestead of the free* (John Greenleaf Whittier). **4** *U.S.* a lot and the buildings on it, which the owner and his family occupy as a home and which is legally exempted from seizure or forced sale for debt.
—*v.t.* to take up and occupy as a homestead: *My grandfather homesteaded 160 acres of land.*
—*v.i. U.S.* to settle on a homestead.
[Old English *hāmstede*]

home|stead|er (hōm′sted ər), *n.* **1** a person who has a homestead. **2** a settler granted a homestead by the United States government.

homestead law, *U.S.* **1** a law protecting a homestead from seizure or forced sale for debt. **2** any one of several laws passed by Congress, especially the Homestead Act of 1862, granting each settler 160 acres of public land under certain specified conditions.

home stretch, 1 the straight part of a race track between the last turn and the finish line. **2** the last part of a race. **3** the last part of anything.

home-stud|y (hōm′stud′ē), *adj.* having to do with a correspondence school or a course of study offered by one.

home table, *Backgammon.* the half of the inner table nearest to the player.

home|town (hōm′toun′), *n., adj.* **—*n.*** the town in which one's home is, or was originally.
—*adj.* of or having to do with a hometown: *hometown pressures on Congress for tariff protection* (Wall Street Journal).

home unit, *Australian.* an apartment.

home|ward (hōm′wərd), *adv., adj.* **—*adv.*** toward home: *homeward bound.* **—*adj.*** being in the direction of home: *The ship is on a homeward course.*

home|wards (hōm′wərdz), *adv.* = homeward.

home|work (hōm′wėrk′), *n.* **1** work done at home. **2** a lesson to be studied or prepared outside the classroom.
do one's homework, *Informal.* to study a subject or situation; be well versed in something: *The Soviet Communist leaders have done their homework in history ...* (Wall Street Journal).

home|y (hō′mē), *adj.,* **hom|i|er, hom|i|est.** like home; cozy and comfortable; homelike: *Homey, fireside qualities that endear him to his family and friends* (Saturday Review). Also, **homy.**

home|y|ness (hō′mē nis), *n.* homey quality or condition. Also, **hominess.**

hom|i|cid|al (hom′ə sī′dəl, hō′mə-), *adj.* **1** of or having to do with homicide. **2** = murderous.
—hom′i|cid′al|ly, *adv.*

hom|i|cide[1] (hom′ə sīd, hō′mə-), *n.* a killing of one human being by another. Intentional homicide is murder. [< Old French *homicide,* learned borrowing from Latin *homicīdium* < *homō, -inis* man + *-cīdium* -cide[2]]

hom|i|cide[2] (hom′ə sīd, hō′mə-), *n.* a person who kills another human being. [< Old French *homicide,* learned borrowing from Latin *homicīda* < *homō, -inis* man + *-cīda* -cide[1]]

hom|i|let|ic (hom′ə let′ik), *adj., n.* **—*adj.* 1** of or having to do with sermons or the art of preaching. **2** like or characteristic of a homily.
—*n.* a sermon; homily: *The Cardinal's letter is an unadorned homiletic* (William F. Buckley, Jr.).
[< Late Latin *homileticus* < Greek *homīlētikós* affable < *hómīlos* a throng] **—hom′i|let′i|cal|ly,** *adv.*

hom|i|let|ics (hom′ə let′iks), *n.* the art of composing and preaching sermons.

hom|i|list (hom′ə list), *n.* a person who writes or delivers homilies.

hom|i|ly (hom′ə lē), *n., pl.* **-lies. 1** a sermon, usually on some part of the Bible. **2** a serious moral talk or writing that warns, urges, or advises, especially one that is tedious. [< Old French *omelie,* learned borrowing from Late Latin *homīlia* < Greek *homīlíā* < *hómīlos* a throng]

hom|i|nes (hom′ə nēz), *n.* plural of **homo**[1].

hom|i|ness (hō′mē nis), *n.* = homeyness.

hom|ing (hō′ming), *n., adj.* **—*n.* 1** the action of a missile or torpedo which directs itself to or toward a target in response to signals or radiation emanating from or reflected by the target. **2** the system which receives the signals or radiation and directs the course of the missile or torpedo.
—*adj.* returning home.

homing pigeon, any one of a special breed of pigeons trained to fly home from great distances and used in racing or to carry messages; carrier pigeon.

hom|i|nid (hom′ə nid), *adj., n.* **—*adj.*** resembling or having to do with any one of a family of primates that includes man. Man is the only hominid extant.
—*n.* a hominid animal: *The orangs ... disported themselves with that mixture of economy, play and pleasure, which should be the birthright of all hominids* (The Observer).
[< New Latin *Hominidae;* see etym. under **hominoid**]

hom|i|ni|za|tion (hom′ə nə zā′shən), *n.* the act or process of making manlike in character or nature: *Dehumanization of the living worker was complemented, paradoxically, by the progressive hominization of the machine—hominization in the sense of giving the automation some of the mechanical equivalents of lifelike motion and purpose* (New York Times).

hom|i|nize (hom′ə nīz), *v.t.,* **-nized, -niz|ing.** to make manlike: *hominized primates.*

hom|i|noid (hom′ə noid), *adj., n.* **—*adj.*** of the form of or resembling man.
—*n.* a hominoid animal.
[< New Latin *Hominidae* the family name (< Latin *homō, -inis* man) + English *-oid*]

hom|i|ny (hom′ə nē), *n.* hulled corn, often crushed or coarsely ground, or soaked whole in a weak solution of lye. Hominy is eaten boiled. [American English, probably short for earlier *rockahominy* < Algonkian (Powhatan) *rokēhamēn* parched corn]

hominy grits, coarsely ground hulled corn meal.

homme (ôm), *n.* the French word for "man," used in English in various French compounds, as in the entries below.

homme d'af|faires (ôm′ də fãr′), *French.* a businessman; man of affairs.

homme de con|fiance (ôm də kôN fyäNs′), *French.* a man of trust; a right-hand man.

homme d'es|prit (ôm′ des prē′), *French.* a man of wit or spirit.

homme du monde (ôm′ dY môNd′), *French.* a man of the world.

ho|mo[1] (hō′mō), *n., pl.* **hom|i|nes.** the Latin word for "man," used in various Latin compounds to describe some essential characteristic or quality, as in *homo ludens* and *homo faber.* [< *Homo*]

ho|mo[2] (hō′mō), *n., pl.* **-mos.** *Slang.* a homosexual.

Ho|mo (hō′mō), *n. Zoology.* the genus of primate mammals comprising man, including one extant species, *Homo sapiens,* and various extinct species known from fossil remains. [< New Latin *Homo* < Latin *homō, -inis* man]

homo-, *combining form.* the same; equal: *Homogeneous = of the same kind.* Also, **hom-** before vowels. [< Greek *homo-* < *homós* same]

ho|mo|cen|tric (hō′mə sen′trik, hom′ə-), *adj.* = concentric.

ho|mo|cer|cal (hō′mə sėr′kəl, hom′ə-), *adj.* **1** having a tail in which the upper and lower lobes are symmetrical or almost symmetrical, the end of the spinal column coinciding with the base of the tail fin: *a homocercal fish.* **2** of or having to do with this form of tail. [< *homo-* + Greek *kérkos* tail + English *-al*[1]]

ho|mo|chro|mat|ic (hō′mə krō mat′ik, hom′ə-), *adj.* relating to or possessing one color or hue; homochromous.

ho|mo|chro|ma|tism (hō′mə krō′mə tiz əm, hom′ə-), *n.* the condition of being homochromatic.

ho|mo|chro|mous (hō′mə krō′məs, hom′ə-), *adj.* **1** of the same color. **2** *Botany.* having all the florets of the same color, as a composite flower or flower head. [< *homo-* + Greek *chrôma* color + English *-ous*]

ho|mo|cy|clic (hō′mə sik′lik, -sī′k′-), *adj., n. Chemistry.* — ***adj.*** having a ring structure in which the ring is composed of carbon atoms only.
— ***n.*** a homocyclic compound.

ho|mo|cys|te|ine (hō′mə sis′tē ēn, -in), *n.* a crystalline amino acid that is an intermediate in the metabolic conversion of methionine to cysteine. *Formula:* $C_4H_9NO_2S$

ho|mo|cys|tine (hō′mə sis′tēn, -tin), *n.* the oxidized, disulfide form of homocysteine. *Formula:* $C_8H_{16}N_2O_4S_2$

ho|mo|cys|ti|nu|ri|a (hō′mə sis′tə nu̇r′ē ə), *n.* a genetic disorder, inherited recessively, characterized by the presence of abnormal amounts of homocystine in the urine: *In homocystinuria ... patients may be mentally retarded and suffer from osteoporosis and dislocation of the lenses of the eyes* (Science News).

ho|mod|ro|mous (hō mod′rə məs), *adj. Botany.* having the spiral arrangement of the leaves on the stem and of those on the branches in the same direction. [< *homo-* + Greek *drómos* a running + English *-ous*]

ho|moe|o|mor|phous (hō′mē ə môr′fəs, hom′ē-), *adj.* = homeomorphous.

ho|moe|op|a|thy (hō′mē op′ə thē, hom′ē-), *n.* = homeopathy.

Ho|mo e|rec|tus (hō′mō i rek′təs), a species of man, including Java man, Peking man, and Chellean man, regarded by some scholars as the ancestor of Homo sapiens, into which it evolved at several different stages. [< New Latin *homō ērēctus* erect man]

ho|mo|e|rot|ic (hō′mō i rot′ik, hom′ō-), *adj.* = homosexual.

ho|mo|er|o|tism (hō′mō er′ə tiz əm, hom′ō-), *n.* = homosexuality.

ho|mo fa|ber (hō′mō fā′bər, fā′bər), man as a worker or artisan: *Homo faber we all know: the shaping of a stone ax is no less a technique than the engineering of a chemical plant* (Scientific American). [< New Latin *homō faber* worker man]

ho|mog|a|mous (hō mog′ə məs), *adj. Botany.* **1** having flowers or florets that do not differ sexually. **2** having the stamens and pistils maturing at the same time, as a monoclinous flower.

ho|mog|a|my (hō mog′ə mē), *n.* **1** *Botany.* homogamous condition, especially the condition of having the stamens and pistils of a monoclinous flower mature at the same time. **2** the mating of individuals of the same species or of similar characteristics; inbreeding.

ho|mog|e|nate (hə moj′ə nāt), *n.* a homogenized substance, especially tissue that has been homogenized for study or analysis.

ho|mo|ge|ne|i|ty (hō′mə jə nē′ə tē, hom′ə-), *n.* the quality or condition of being homogeneous. **SYN:** uniformity.

ho|mo|ge|ne|ous (hō′mə jē′nē əs, -jēn′yəs hom′ə-), *adj.* **1** of the same kind, nature, or character; similar: *a dull city of homogeneous buildings.* **SYN:** alike, congruous. **2** made up of similar elements or parts; of uniform nature or character throughout: *Africa is not a homogeneous place but a collection of territories that vary enormously in their qualities and their problems* (New York Times). **3** *Mathematics.* **a** of the same degree or dimensions. **b** of the same kind and commensurable. **4** *Biology.* homogenous. [< Medieval Latin *homogeneus* (with English *-ous*) < Greek *homogenḗs* of the same kind < *homós* same + *génos* kind] — **ho′mo|ge′ne|ous|ly**, *adv.* — **ho′mo|ge′ne|ous|ness**, *n.*

homogeneous catalysis, catalysis that occurs when the reacting chemicals, their products, and the catalyst are all liquids or all gases.

homogeneous function, *Mathematics.* a polynomial in two or more variables, all the terms being of the same degree.

ho|mo|gen|e|sis (hō′mə jen′ə sis, hom′ə-), *n. Biology.* the ordinary course of generation in which the offspring is like the parent and goes through the same cycle of development.

hom|o|ge|net|ic (hō′mə jə net′ik, hom′ə-), *adj. Biology.* **1** having to do with homogenesis. **2** having a common origin; derived from the same structure, however modified.

ho|mog|e|nize (hə moj′ə nīz), *v.t.,* **-nized, -nizing.** **1** to break up the particles in (an emulsion) so that they are small enough not to separate. In homogenizing milk or cream, the fat globules are forced through narrow openings at high pressure, thus breaking the large globules into small ones, which are distributed evenly throughout. **2** to make homogeneous; make similar or uniform: *Newspapers, the big magazines, radio, television, and films have homogenized us. By reaching people in vast numbers with powerful effect, ... they show us a world that we all seem to share* (Saturday Review). — **ho|mog′e|ni|za′tion**, *n.* — **ho|mog′e|niz′er**, *n.*

homogenized milk, milk so processed that the fat is distributed evenly throughout and does not rise to the top in the form of cream.

ho|mog|e|nous (hō moj′ə nəs), *adj. Biology.* corresponding in structure because of a common origin: *homogenous organs.* [< *homo-* + *-gen* + *-ous*]

ho|mo|gen|tis|ic acid (hō′mə jen tis′ik), a crystalline substance found in the urine, as in alkaptonuria. It causes the urine to turn dark on standing. *Formula:* $C_8H_8O_4$ [< *homo-* + *gentisic acid*]

ho|mog|e|ny (hō moj′ə nē), *n.* homogenous condition. [< Greek *homogéneia* community of origin < *homogenḗs* homogeneous]

hom|o|graft (hom′ə graft, -gräft; hō′mə-), *n.* tissue from one individual grafted on another individual of the same species; allograft.

hom|o|graph (hom′ə graf, -gräf; hō′mə-), *n.* a word of the same spelling as another, but a different origin and meaning. *Bass* (bas) meaning "a kind of fish," and *bass* (bās) meaning "a male singing voice," are homographs. All homonyms (def. 1) are also homographs. [< Greek *homógraphos* < *homós* same + *graphḗ* writing < *gráphein* write]

hom|o|graph|ic (hom′ə graf′ik), *adj.* **1** having to do with homographs. **2** having to do with homography.

ho|mog|ra|phy (hō mog′rə fē), *n. Geometry.* the relation between two figures (as two representations of the same thing in different perspective) such that for every point, line, or angle in one there is a corresponding point, line, or angle in the other.

Ho|mo hab|i|lis (hō′mō hab′ə ləs), an extinct species of man believed to have been the earliest toolmaker, whose fossil fragments were discovered in the early 1960's at the Olduvai Gorge in northern Tanzania. [< Latin *homō habilis* skillful man]

ho|moi|o|therm (hō moi′ə thėrm), *n.* = homeotherm.

ho|moi|o|ther|mal (hō moi′ə thėr′məl), *adj.* = homeothermal.

ho|moi|o|ther|mic (hō moi′ə thėr′mik), *adj.* = homeothermal.

Ho|moi|ou|si|an (hō′moi ü′sē ən, -ou′-), *adj., n. Theology.* — ***adj.*** relating to or maintaining likeness of substance between the Father and the Son.
— ***n.*** a member of a church party of the 300's that maintained that the essence of the Son is similar to, but not identical with, that of the Father.
[< Greek *homoioúsios* of like essence (< *hómoios* like + *ousíā* essence) + English *-an*]

ho|mo|lec|i|thal (hō′mə les′ə thəl), *adj. Embryology.* having a small amount of yolk evenly distributed throughout the egg. [< *homo-* + Greek *lékithos* yolk + English *-al*[1]]

hom|o|log (hom′ə lôg, -log), *n.* **1** *Chemistry.* a member of a series of organic compounds showing similar chemical properties but different physical properties. **2** = homologue.

ho|mol|o|gate (hō mol′ə gāt), *v.,* **-gat|ed, -gat|ing.** — ***v.t.*** to express approval of or agreement with; confirm; ratify.
— ***v.i.*** to express agreement or consent.
[< Medieval Latin *homologare* (with English *-ate*[1]) < Greek *homologeîn* confess, acknowledge, agree with < *homólogos;* see etym. under **homologous**] — **ho|mol′o|ga′tion**, *n.*

ho|mo|log|ic (hō′mə loj′ik, hom′ə-), *adj.* = homologous. — **ho′mo|log′i|cal|ly**, *adv.*

ho|mol|o|gize (hō mol′ə jīz), *v.,* **-gized, -giz|ing.**
— ***v.t.*** to make homologous; show the correspondence of.
— ***v.i.*** to be homologous; correspond.

ho|mol|o|gous (hō mol′ə gəs), *adj.* **1** corresponding in position, proportion, value, structure, or other property. **2** *Biology.* corresponding in type of structure and in origin but not necessarily in function or appearance. The foreleg of a horse, the arm of a man, and the wing of a bird are homologous. See picture under **analogy.** **3** *Chemistry.* belonging to a series where successive members differ regularly in formula, especially a series of organic compounds differing by multiples of $-CH_2$, such as the alcohols and aldehydes. **4** (of cells or antiserums) immunologically identical. [< Greek *homólogos* (with English *-ous*) agreeing < *homós* same + *lógos* relation, ratio, related to *légein* reckon]

homologous chromosomes, *Biology.* pairs of like chromosomes in a diploid organism, one derived from the egg and the other from the sperm, that pair during the early stage of meiosis, and are again separated into different germ cells.

hom|o|lo|graph|ic (hom′ə lə graf′ik), *adj.* representing in equal proportions, as in a map projection in which equal areas of the earth's surface are represented by equal areas on a map or chart. [< Greek *homalós* even, level + English *graphic*]

hom|o|logue (hom′ə lôg, -log), *n.* a homologous thing, organ, or part. Also, **homolog.**

ho|mol|o|gy (hō mol′ə jē), *n.* **1** correspondence in position, proportion, value, structure, or the like. **2** *Biology.* correspondence in type of structure and in origin. **3** *Chemistry.* the relation of the compounds forming a homologous series. [< Greek *homologiā* agreement < *homólogos;* see etym. under **homologous**] — **ho|mol′o|gist**, *n.*

ho|mol|o|sine (hō mol′ə sin, -sīn), *adj.* having to do with a kind of map projection (homolosine projection) made by combining a sinusoidal projection with a homolographic projection. [< Greek *homalós* even + English *sine*[1]]

homo lu|dens (hō′mō lü′denz), *Latin.* playful or sportive man: *The Cyprus problem ... embraces almost every aspect of the diplomatic game and homo ludens cannot fail to have an entertaining time delving into its subtleties on the spot* (Listener).

ho|mol|y|sis (hō mol′ə sis), *n.* the breaking of a chemical bond in a symmetrical manner, so that the bonding pair of electrons are separated and two free radicals are produced.

ho|mo|lyt|ic (hō′mə lit′ik), *adj.* of or having to do with homolysis.

ho|mo|mor|phic (hō′mə môr′fik, hom′ə-), *adj.* **1** of the same or similar form. **2** *Biology.* similar in external appearance, but not related in structure or origin. [< *homo-* + Greek *morphḗ* form + English *-ic*]

ho|mo|mor|phism (hō′mə môr′fiz əm, hom′ə-), *n.* **1** the condition of being homomorphic. **2** *Zoology.* resemblance of form between the immature and adult stages of an animal.

ho|mon|o|mous (hō mon′ə məs), *adj.* **1** subject to the same or a constant law. **2** *Biology.* having the same law or mode of growth, as parts or organs. [< *homo-* + Greek *nómos* law + English *-ous*]

ho|mo|nu|cle|ar (hō′mə nü′klē ər, -nyü′-), *adj.* consisting of identical atoms or groups of atoms: *O_2 is a homonuclear molecule.*

hom|o|nym (hom′ə nim, hō′mə-), *n.* **1** a word having the same pronunciation and spelling as another word, but different in meaning and origin. *Mail,* meaning "letters," and *mail,* meaning "armor," are homonyms. **2** = homograph. **3** = homophone. **4** *Biology.* a name that has been applied previously to a different species or genus, and therefore cannot be used for a new species or genus, on the basis of the law of priority. **5** a person or thing having the same name as another; namesake. [< Latin *homōnymum* < Greek *homṓnymon,* neuter of *homṓnymos;* see etym. under **homonymous**]

ho|mo|nym|ic (hō′mə nim′ik, hom′ə-), *adj.* of or having to do with homonyms or homonymy.

ho|mon|y|mous (hō mon′ə məs), *adj.* **1** alike in sound or spelling but not in meaning; of the nature of homonyms. **2** having or called by the same name. **3** *Optics.* of or having to do with the two images of one object seen in looking at a point nearer than the object, when the right image is that seen by the right eye and the left by the left. [< Latin *homōnymus* (with English *-ous*) < Greek *homṓnymos* < *homós* same + dialectal *ónyma* name]

Pronunciation Key: hat, **ā**ge, c**ã**re, f**ä**r; l**e**t, **ē**qual, t**ė**rm; **i**t, **ī**ce; h**o**t, **ō**pen, **ô**rder; **oi**l, **ou**t; c**u**p, p**u̇**t, r**ü**le; **ch**ild; lo**ng**; **th**in; **ᴛʜ**en; **zh**, measure; **ə** represents **a** in about, **e** in taken, **i** in pencil, **o** in lemon, **u** in circus.

ho|mon|y|my (hō mon′ə mē), *n.* homonymous condition.

Ho|mo|ou|si|an (hō′mō ü′sē ən, -ou′-), *adj., n. Theology.* —*adj.* relating to or maintaining the consubstantiality of Father and Son.
—*n.* a member of a church party of the 300's that maintained that the essence or substance of the Father and the Son is the same.
[< Greek *homooúsios* of the same essence (< *homós* same + *ousíā* essence) + English *-an*]

ho|mo|phile (hō′mə fīl), *n., adj.* —*n.* **1** a person attracted to members of his own sex; homosexual. **2** a person who opposes laws that discriminate against homosexuals.
—*adj.* concerned with the rights or the welfare of homophiles.

ho|mo|phobe (hō′mə fōb), *n.* person who fears, dislikes, or hates homosexuals. —**ho′mo|pho′bic,** *adj.*

ho|mo|pho|bi|a (hō′mə fō′bē ə), *n.* fear, dislike, or hatred of homosexuals.

hom|o|phone (hom′ə fōn, hō′mə-), *n.* **1** a word having the same pronunciation as another, but a different meaning and origin. *Ate* and *eight* are homophones. All homonyms (def. 1) are also homophones. **2** a letter or symbol representing the same sound as another. The letters *c* and *k* are homophones in *cork.* [< Greek *homóphōnos* < *homós* same + *phōnḗ* sound]

hom|o|phon|ic (hom′ə fon′ik, hō′mə-), *adj.* **1** having the same sound. **2** *Music.* **a** in unison. **b** having one part or melody predominating.

ho|moph|o|nous (hō mof′ə nəs), *adj.* = homophonic.

ho|moph|o|ny (hō mof′ə nē, hom′ə fō′-), *n.* **1** sameness of sound. **2** homophonic music.

ho|mo|plas|tic (hō′mə plas′tik, hom′ə-), *adj. Biology.* similar but of different origin: *homoplastic organs.* [< *homo-* + Greek *plastós* something molded + English *-ic*] —**ho′mo|plas′ti|cal|ly,** *adv.*

ho|mop|la|sy (hō mop′lə sē; hō′mə plas′ē, hom′ə-), *n.* homoplastic condition. [< *homo-* + Greek *plásis* a molding]

ho|mo|po|lar (hō′mə pō′lər, hom′ə-), *adj. Physical Chemistry.* of or characterized by a symmetrical distribution of positive and negative electric charges between two atoms, as in the common covalent bond.

ho|mo|pol|y|mer (hō′mə pol′i mər), *n.* a polymer of two or more molecules of the same kind.

ho|mo|pol|y|mer|ize (hō′mə pol′i mə rīz), *v.t., v.i.,* **-ized, -iz|ing.** *Chemistry.* to change or be changed by a reaction in which two or more molecules of the same kind polymerize to form a complex molecule, as in the manufacture of polystyrene. —**ho′mo|pol′y|mer|i|za′tion,** *n.*

ho|mop|ter (hō mop′tər), *n.* = homopteran.

ho|mop|ter|an (hō mop′tər ən), *n., adj.* —*n.* any one of an order of insects that have mouthparts adapted for piercing and sucking and wings, when present, of the same thickness and texture throughout. Cicadas, aphids, and scale insects belong to this order.
—*adj.* of or belonging to this order. [< New Latin *Homoptera* the suborder name (< Greek *homós* same + *pterón* wing) + English *-an*]

ho|mop|ter|ous (hō mop′tər əs), *adj.* of or belonging to the homopterans.

Ho|mo sa|pi|ens (hō′mō sā′pē ənz), the species including all existing races of mankind; human beings; man. [< Latin *homō sapiēns* (literally) man (that is, human being) having wisdom; *sapiēns,* present participle of *sapīre* be wise]

ho|mo|sce|das|tic (hō′mə si das′tik), *adj. Statistics.* showing equal variability; showing the same standard deviation: *homoscedastic arrays or values.* [< *homo-* + Greek *skédastikós* that can be scattered]

ho|mo|sex|u|al (hō′mə sek′shů əl), *adj., n.* —*adj.* having to do with or manifesting sexual feelings for one of the same sex; homoerotic.
—*n.* a homosexual person.

ho|mo|sex|u|al|i|ty (hō′mə sek′shů al′ə tē), *n.* **1** sexual feelings for one of the same sex. **2** sexual activity with a person of the same sex.

ho|mos|po|rous (hō mos′pər əs; hō′mə spôr′-, -spōr′-), *adj. Botany.* having only one kind of asexually produced spores.

ho|mos|po|ry (hō mos′pər ē), *n. Botany.* the production of only one kind of asexual spores.

ho|mo|tax|i|al (hō′mə tak′sē əl, hom′ə-), *adj.* = homotaxic. —**ho′mo|tax′i|al|ly,** *adv.*

ho|mo|tax|ic (hō′mə tak′sik, hom′ə-), *adj.* of or having to do with homotaxis.

ho|mo|tax|is (hō′mə tak′sis, hom′ə-), *n.* similarity of arrangement, such as of geological strata that have the same relative position in a series, or of the fossiliferous deposits found in them. [< *homo-* + Greek *táxis* arrangement]

ho|mo|thal|lic (hō′mə thal′ik, hom′ə-), *adj.* having only one kind of mycelium, producing self-fertile cells which can mate with one another: *a homothallic fungus.* [< *homo-* + Greek *thállos* young shoot + English *-ic*]

ho|mo|trans|plant (hō′mō trans′plant, -plänt; hom′ə-), *n.* = homograft.

ho|mo|trans|plan|ta|tion (hō′mō trans′plan tā′shən, -plän-; hom′ə-), *n.* = homograft.

ho|mo|zy|go|sis (hō′mə zī gō′sis, -zi-; hom′ə-), *n. Genetics.* the condition of being homozygous at many genetic loci. [< *homo-* + Greek *zýgōsis* an equating]

ho|mo|zy|gote (hō′mə zī′gōt, -zig′ōt; hom′ə-), *n. Genetics.* an animal or plant whose chromosomes contain an identical pair of genes and which, therefore, always breeds true to type.

ho|mo|zy|gous (hō′mə zī′gəs, hom′ə-), *adj.* of or having to do with a homozygote. —**ho′mo|zy′gous|ly,** *adv.*

ho|mun|cu|lus (hō mung′kyə ləs), *n., pl.* **-li** (-lī). **1** a little man; dwarf. SYN: pygmy. **2** a small model of a man used especially for demonstrating anatomy. **3** the human fetus. [< Latin *homunculus* (diminutive) < *homō, -inis* man, human being]

hom|y (hō′mē), *adj.,* **hom|i|er, hom|i|est.** = homey.

hon (hun), *n. Informal.* darling; dear: *Come sit by me, hon* (Jesse Hill Ford). [short for *honey* (def. 5)]

hon., **1a** honorable. **b** honorably. **2** honorary.

Hon., **1** Honorable. **2** honorary.

hon|cho (hon′chō), *n., pl.* **-chos.** *U.S. Slang.* chief; headman; boss. [originally U.S. Army use in Asia < Japanese *hanchō* group leader]

Hond., Honduras.

hon|da knot (hon′də), a fixed loop at the end of a rope through which the other end of the rope can be passed so that the rope can be pulled tight or slacked off. See picture under **knot**[1].
[< Spanish *honda* sling]

Hon|du|ran (hon důr′ən, -dyůr′-), *adj., n.* —*adj.* of or having to do with Honduras.
—*n.* a native or inhabitant of Honduras.

hone[1] (hōn), *n., v.,* **honed, hon|ing.** —*n.* a fine-grained whetstone on which to give a fine finish to the edge of cutting tools, especially razors.
—*v.t.* to sharpen on a hone: (*Figurative.*) *We regret the delays, but it gives a chance to hone our capabilities* (John Glenn).
[Old English *hān* a stone] —**hon′er,** *n.*

hone[2] (hōn), *v.i.,* **honed, hon|ing.** *Dialect.* **1** to grumble; whine; moan: *He lies . . . honing and moaning to himself* (Charles Lamb). **2** to yearn or pine. [< Old French *hogner* to mutter, grumble]

hon|est (on′ist), *adj., adv.* —*adj.* **1** not lying, cheating, or stealing; fair and upright; truthful: *He was an honest man. He lived an honest life.* SYN: just, incorruptible. **2** obtained by fair means; without lying, cheating, or stealing: *honest profits.* **3** not hiding one's real nature; frank; open: *She has an honest face.* SYN: sincere, candid, ingenuous. **4** not mixed with something of less value; genuine; pure: *Stores should sell honest goods.* **5** bringing honor; creditable; commendable: *Provide things honest in the sight of all men* (Romans 12:17). **6** = respectable. **7** *Archaic.* chaste; virtuous: *Wives may be merry, and yet honest too* (Shakespeare).
—*adv.* **1** *Informal.* truly; really: *"Tell me, Joe—honest now, old feller—did I do it?"* (Mark Twain). **2** *Archaic.* in an honest manner; honestly: *As I have ever found thee honest true* (Shakespeare).
[< Old French *honeste,* learned borrowing from Latin *honestus* honorable, decent, respected < *honōs, -ōris* honor]

honest broker, **1** an impartial go-between; mediator: *He offered the good offices of the Soviet Union . . . for a summit meeting and himself as an honest broker* (New York Times). **2** (originally) a nickname for Prince Bismarck.

honest Injun, *U.S. Informal.* truly; honestly.

hon|est|ly (on′ist lē), *adv.* **1** in an honest way; with honesty: *The salesman dealt honestly with his customers.* **2** indeed; really: *Honestly! I never saw such rudeness.*

hon|est-to-God (on′is tů god′), *adj. Informal.* honest-to-goodness: *It is obvious that your reporters never got within a country mile of an honest-to-God farmer with manure and dirt on his boots* (Herb Karner).

hon|est-to-good|ness (on′is tů gůd′nis), *adj. Informal.* genuine.

hon|es|ty (on′ə stē), *n.* **1** honest behavior; honest nature; honest quality: *To make your children capable of honesty is the beginning of education* (John Ruskin). SYN: truthfulness. **2** freedom from deceit or fraud; straightforwardness. **3** a European garden herb of the mustard family, with large, purple flowers and flat, round, semitransparent, satiny pods; moonwort; satinpod or satinflower. **4** *Archaic.* chastity. **5** *Obsolete.* honor.
—*Syn.* **1, 2 Honesty, integrity** mean the quality of being honorable and upright in character and actions. **Honesty** emphasizes fairness and uprightness in relations with others, and refusal to steal, lie, cheat, or misrepresent: *He shows honesty in all his business affairs.* **Integrity** applies more directly to character than to actions, and means soundness of character and possession of very high standards of right and wrong: *A man of integrity can be trusted.*

hone|wort (hōn′wėrt′), *n.* the stone parsley or any one of various other plants of the parsley family. [< obsolete *hone* a swelling + *wort* (because it is a reputed cure for swellings)]

hon|ey (hun′ē), *n., pl.* **hon|eys,** *adj., v.,* **hon|eyed** or **hon|ied, hon|ey|ing.** —*n.* **1** a thick, sweet, yellow or golden liquid, good to eat, that bees make out of the nectar they collect from flowers. **2** any one of various similar substances produced by insects or in other ways. **3** the drop of liquid found in many flowers that draws bees to them. **4** *Figurative.* something sweet like honey; sweetness: *the honey of flattery. Death hath sucked the honey of thy breath* (Shakespeare). **5** darling; dear. **6** a color like that of honey.
—*adj.* **1** of or like honey; sweet; honeyed. **2** lovable; dear.
—*v.t.* **1** to sweeten with or as if with honey. **2** to talk sweetly to; flatter.
—*v.i.* **1** to talk sweetly; use endearments. **2** *Figurative.* to become sweet or agreeable: *his tutor, rough to common men, But honeying at the whisper of a lord* (Tennyson). [Old English *hunig*]
—**hon′ey|less,** *adj.* —**hon′ey|like′,** *adj.*

honey badger, = ratel.

honey bear, **1** = sloth bear. **2** = kinkajou.

hon|ey|bee (hun′ē bē′), *n.* any one of various bees that make honey, especially the domestic bee. See picture under **bee**[1].

honey bird, = honey guide.

***hon|ey|comb** (hun′ē kōm′), *n., adj., v.* —*n.* **1** a structure of wax containing rows of six-sided cells formed by bees, in which to store honey, pollen, and their eggs; comb. **2** anything like this, such as a type of automobile radiator, or a type of architectural construction having a regular cellular pattern. **3** the second stomach of a ruminant animal; reticulum. **4** a bath sponge of commercial value found in the Mediterranean Sea.
—*adj.* like a honeycomb; arranged in the form of a honeycomb: *a honeycomb weave of cloth, a honeycomb pattern in knitting.*
—*v.t.* **1** to pierce with many holes; make like a honeycomb: *The old castle was honeycombed with passages.* **2** *Figurative.* to weaken or harm by spreading through; undermine: *That city is honeycombed with crime. His theory is honeycombed with errors of fact.* —*v.i.* to become like a honeycomb. [Old English *hunigcamb*]

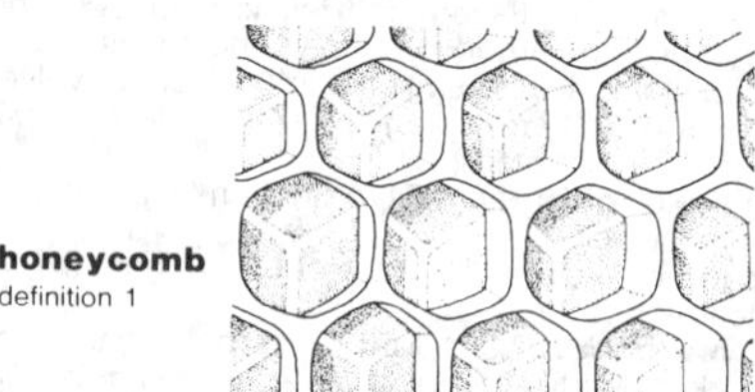

***honeycomb**
definition 1

honeycomb tripe, tripe prepared from the second stomach of a ruminant.

honey creeper, or **hon|ey|creep|er** (hun′ē krē′pər), *n.* **1** any of various small, brightly colored birds of tropical America; guit-guit. **2** any of a group of similar birds in Hawaii.

hon|ey|dew (hun′ē dü′, -dyü′), *n.* **1a** the sweet substance that oozes from the leaves of certain plants in hot weather: *For he on honeydew hath fed And drunk the milk of Paradise* (Samuel Taylor Coleridge). **b** a sweet substance on leaves and stems, secreted by aphids, leaf hoppers, or other tiny insects, or by a fungus. **2** = honeydew melon.

honeydew melon, a variety of melon with sweet, green flesh and a smooth, pale greenish skin. It is good to eat.

honey eater or **hon|ey|eat|er** (hun′ē ē′tər), *n.* any one of a large family of Australasian oscine birds, including the wattlebirds and the friarbirds, with a bill and tongue adapted for feeding on honey and the nectar of flowers.

hon|eyed (hun′ēd), *adj., v.* —*adj.* **1** sweetened with honey: *honeyed drinks.* **2** laden with honey. **3** *Figurative.* sweet as honey; sweet-sounding: *honeyed tones, honeyed words.* **a** past tense and past participle of **honey.** Also **honied.**

honey guide, any one of various small birds of Africa, Asia, and the East Indies, related to the woodpecker, that are supposed to guide men and animals to places where honey may be found; honey bird.

honey locust, any one of a group of thorny, ornamental trees of the pea family, with long, divided leaves and large, flat pods containing sweet pulp. Most honey locusts are native to Asia, Africa, and South America.

hon|ey|moon (hun′ē mün′), *n., v.* —*n.* **1** a holiday spent together by a newly married couple. **2** the first month of marriage. **3** *Figurative.* a period of good feeling or good relations: *the beginning of the end of the decade-long honeymoon between India and China* (London Times).
—*v.i.* to spend or have a honeymoon. —**hon′ey·moon′er**, *n.*
hon|ey|mouthed (hun′ē moutht′, -mouᴛʜd′), *adj.* sweet-talking; sweet-sounding; glib.
honey plant, the cleome or any other plant that furnishes much nectar to bees.
hon|ey|pot (hun′ē pot′), *n.* **1** a pot in which honey is stored. **2** a receptacle, of wax or other substance, in which wild bees store their honey.
honey sac, the enlargement of the alimentary canal in which the bee produces and carries its honey.
honey stomach, = honey sac.
hon|ey|suck|le (hun′ē suk′əl), *n.* **1** any one of various upright or climbing shrubs or vines with white, yellow, pink, scarlet, red, or purple, often fragrant, tubular flowers, that are succeeded by sweetish red, purple, yellow, white, black, or blue berries, such as the woodbine and trumpet honeysuckle. Honeysuckle is native to the temperate parts of both hemispheres. It belongs to the honeysuckle family. **2** any one of various similar shrubs or plants. **3** *Obsolete or Dialect.* clover. [Middle English *hunisuccle* privet, also clover (diminutive) < Old English *hunigsūge* privet, (literally) honey-suck < *hunig* honey + *sūcan* suck]
hon|ey|suck|led (hun′ē suk′əld), *adj.* abounding in or fragrant with honeysuckle.
honeysuckle family, a group of dicotyledonous shrubs and, occasionally, herbs, found chiefly in northern temperate regions, having opposite leaves, bisexual, sometimes showy flowers, and bearing a berry or capsule as the fruit. The family includes the viburnum, honeysuckle, elder, snowberry, and coralberry.
honeysuckle ornament, flowers or leaves arranged in a flat, radiating cluster, as in architectural decoration.
hong (hong, hông), *n.* formerly in China: **1** a series of rooms or buildings used as a warehouse or factory, especially: **a** one of the foreign factories maintained at Canton. **b** any foreign trading establishment in China or Japan. **2** a corporation of Chinese merchants at Canton who had the exclusive privilege of trading with the Europeans.
[< Chinese (Pekin) *hang,* (Canton) *hong* series of rooms, warehouse]
Hong Kong dollar (hong′kong′, hông′kông′), the monetary unit of Hong Kong; British dollar.
Hong Kong flu, a variety of Asian flu, caused by a virus first identified in Hong Kong; Mao flu.
hon|ied (hun′ēd), *v., adj.* —*v.* honeyed; a past tense and a past participle of **honey**.
—*adj.* = honeyed.
ho|ni soit qui mal y pense (ô nē swá′ kē màl ē-päɴs′), *French.* shame on him who thinks evil of it. This is the motto of the Order of the Garter.
honk (hongk, hôngk), *n., v.* —*n.* **1** the cry of the wild goose. **2** a sound like the cry of a wild goose: *the honk of an automobile horn.*
—*v.i.* **1** to make the cry of the wild goose or a similar sound. **2** to make the sound of an automobile horn: *We honked as we drove by our friend's house. Outside traffic honked, belching smoke around us* (Manchester Guardian).
—*v.t.* to cause to make a honking sound: *Stop honking that horn!*
[American English; imitative]
honk|er (hong′kər, hông′-), *n.* a person or thing that honks, especially the common wild goose of North America: *More than a hundred of the big grey honkers had wintered in the cove . . . but each day a V of 30 or 40 birds took off, circled, and disappeared* (Time).
hon|ky-tonk (hong′kē tongk′, hông′kē tôngk′), *n., adj. U.S. Slang.* —*n.* **1** a cheap, low-class night club or dance hall. **2** a drinking saloon; gin mill.
—*adj.* having to do with or characteristic of the music or entertainment in a cheap night club or dance hall: *a honky-tonk jazz tempo, honky-tonk dancers.*
[American English; perhaps imitative of the typical music or noise in such a place]
hon|or (on′ər), *n., v.* —*n.* **1** glory; fame; renown: *Alexander Graham Bell won honor and wealth for inventing the telephone.* ꜱʏɴ: reputation. **2** good name; credit for acting well: *It was greatly to her honor that she refused the reward. To their honor, the patriot nobles did not take thought for themselves alone* (Edith Thompson). **3** a source of credit; person or thing that reflects honor: *to be an honor to one's family, school, or country. It is an honor to be chosen class president.* **4** a sense of what is right and proper; nobility of mind: *A man of honor always keeps his promises. Honor is sometimes found among thieves* (Scott). ꜱʏɴ: integrity, uprightness, honesty. **5** great respect; high regard: *George Washington is held in honor. True wealth I hold in great honor* (John Ruskin). **6** an act that shows respect or high regard; something given or done to show honor: *military honors. The queen was received with honor.* **7** high rank or position; dignity; distinction: *Knighthood is an honor. Papists were admitted in crowds to offices and honors* (Macaulay). ꜱʏɴ: eminence. **8** a special privilege or favor: *to have the honor of being presented at court.* **9** chastity; virtue. **10** *Golf.* the privilege of teeing off first, awarded to the player or side winning the previous hole. **11** *Archaic.* a decoration or adornment: *Geranium boasts Her crimson honors* (William Cowper).
—*v.t.* **1** to respect highly; think highly of: *Everyone honors justice.* **2** to show respect to; treat with honor: *We honor our country's dead soldiers every year on Memorial Day.* **3** to give an honor to; favor: *to be honored by a royal visit.* **4** to adore or worship: *Honor the Lord with thy substance, and with the first fruits of all thine increase* (Proverbs 3:9). **5** to accept and pay (a bill, draft, or note) when due: *His credit was good because he always honored his bills as soon as he received them.*
do honor to, a to show honor to; treat with great respect: *He did me the honour to say that this was precisely true* (E. E. Hale). **b** to do credit to; bring honor to: *She does honor to her upbringing.*
do the honors, to act as host or hostess: *The mayor called this morning to do the honours of the town* (Dickens).
honor bright, *Informal.* truly; honestly: *I finished all my homework, honor bright.*
honors, a special favors or courtesies: *Others . . . came, and were healed: who also honoured us with many honours* (Acts 28:9, 10). **b** special mention, grade, or credit given to a student by a school, college, or university for having done work much above the average: *I very early in the Sophomore year gave up all thoughts of obtaining high honors* (C. A. Bristed). **c** a course of study or series of examinations given in many universities of a higher or more specialized character than is required for a pass or ordinary degree: *He studied law, took honors in classics and history, and became president of the university debating society* (Time). **d** (in bridge) the ace, king, queen, jack, and ten of trumps, or the four aces in no-trump: *Having all the honors in clubs, he made a grand slam.* **e** (in whist) the ace, king, queen, and jack of trumps: *We cast in, and . . . I had all four honours the first time* (Samuel Richardson).
on one's honor, pledged to speak the truth and to do what is right: *to put students on their honor not to cheat in examinations.*
[< Anglo-French *honour,* Old French *honor,* learned borrowings from Latin *honōs, -ōris*]
—**hon′or|er**, *n.* —**hon′or|less**, *adj.*
—*Syn. n.* **5 Honor, deference, homage** mean respect shown to someone. **Honor** means respect felt or shown in acknowledgment or appreciation of a person's high character, position, or achievement: *We pay honor to heroes.* **Deference** means respect shown a person by putting his wishes or opinions before one's own: *In deference to his parents' wishes, he agreed to stop smoking.*
Homage implies honor paid with reverence and deference: *He bowed in homage to the Unknown Soldier.*
Hon|or (on′ər), *n.* a title of respect used in speaking to a judge, mayor, governor, senator, or similar public official: *His Honor the Judge.*
hon|or|a|bil|i|ty (on′ər ə bil′ə tē), *n.* honesty; uprightness.
hon|or|a|ble (on′ər ə bəl), *adj., n.* —*adj.* **1** having or showing a sense of what is right and proper; honest; upright: *It is not honorable to cheat.*
2 causing honor; bringing honor or honors to somebody: *honorable wounds.* **3** accompanied by honor or honors: *an honorable discharge.* **4** worthy of honor; to be respected; noble: *an honorable name, to perform honorable deeds. Brutus is an honorable man* (Shakespeare). **5** showing honor or respect: *honorable burial.* **6** having a title, rank, or position of honor: *of honorable rank.* **7** *Obsolete.* respectable in quality or amount; considerable; decent.
—*n.* a member of a nobility, especially one given the title of Honorable: *She . . . claims descent from a back-country tribe rather than from one of Liberia's elite founding "honorables"* (Time).
—**hon′or|a|ble|ness**, *n.* —**hon′or|a|bly**, *adv.*
Hon|or|a|ble (on′ər ə bəl), *adj.* a title of respect or distinction used before the names of certain officials and (in England) the children of certain nobles: *The Honorable* (or *Hon.*) *Earl Warren.*
honorable mention, an honorary award or distinction, generally next below those that win prizes.
hon|or|and (on′ər ənd), *n.* = honoree.
hon|o|rar|i|um (on′ə rãr′ē əm), *n., pl.* **-i|ums, -i|a** (-ē ə). a fee for professional services on which no fixed price is set; honorary payment: *Being paid by the lecture, he was anxious to run up a sizable honorarium* (Harper's). [< Latin *honō rārium* (originally), neuter of *honōrārius;* see etym. under **honorary**]
hon|or|ar|y (on′ə rer′ē), *adj., n., pl.* **-ar|ies.** —*adj.* **1** given or done as an honor: *The university will award honorary degrees to three prominent scientists. The simple crown of olive, an honorary reward* (George Grote). **2** as an honor only; without pay or regular duties; titulary: *That association has an honorary secretary as well as a regular paid secretary who does the actual work.* **3** (of an obligation) depending on one's honor for fulfillment, but not enforceable otherwise.
—*n.* **1** an honorary title, degree, or award. **2** = honorarium. *Abbr:* hon.
[< Latin *honōrārius* < *honōs, -ōris* honor] —**hon′or|ar′i|ly**, *adv.*
hon|or-bound (on′ər bound′), *adj.* required as an obligation of honor: *an affront he was honor-bound to avenge* (Harper's).
honor box, *U.S.* a newspaper vending machine which opens trusting the customer to take a single copy: *The blue-and-white newspaper-vending machines that have been multiplying on city streets as newsstands approach extinction . . . are called "honor boxes"* (New Yorker).
honor code, an honor system, especially at a military academy.
hon|or|ee (on′ə rē′), *n.* a person who has been given an honor. [< *honor* + *-ee*]
honor guard, a special group, generally military, designated as part of an official welcoming committee, or to accompany the coffin at a military funeral; guard of honor.
hon|or|if|ic (on′ə rif′ik), *adj., n.* —*adj.* **1** doing or giving honor; imparting honor or respect. **2** showing respect or deference: *The [Arabic] epithet Abu, father, is honorific* (Maurice B. Keatinge).
—*n.* an honorific phrase or word: *But among his followers Hadji Sahib is enough, even though "Sahib" is merely a general honorific in these parts* (New Yorker).
[< Latin *honōrificus* < *honōs, -ōris* honor + *facere* make] —**hon′or|if′i|cal|ly**, *adv.*
ho|no|ris cau|sa (ho nôr′is kô′zə, -nōr′-), *Latin.* for the sake of honor; as a mark of honor; honorary: *all of whom were made Doctor of Laws honoris causa* (London Times).
honor man, a person who has received or is studying for honors from a school, college, or university.
honor roll, **1** a list of students who have achieved the highest grades during the school term or year. **2** a commemorative list of local citizens who served in the armed forces.
hon|ors (on′ərz), *n.pl.* See under **honor**.
honor score, (in bridge) points scored above the line but not counting toward game, by holding certain honors, taking more tricks than were bid, bidding and making a slam, or setting an opponent.
honors list, **1** a list of persons designated as receiving or to receive special honors. **2** Also, *especially British,* **Honours List**. a list of persons honored each year on New Year's Day and on the sovereign's official birthday with titles of nobility or of chivalrous orders.
honor society, a society which honors men and women who have done outstanding academic or professional work.
honor system, a system of trusting people, especially in schools and other institutions, to obey the rules and do their work without being watched or forced.
hon|our (on′ər), *n., v.t. Especially British.* honor.
—**hon′our|er**, *n.*
Hons. or **hons.**, *British.* honours: *Candidates should have a good Hons. degree in physics or mathematics* (London Times).
hoo (hü), *interj.* **1** an exclamation used to express excitement, delight, contempt, or approval. **2** an imitation of an owl's cry, the wind, or some similar sound. [imitative]
hooch[1] (hüch), *n. U.S. Slang.* alcoholic liquor, especially that which is made or bought illegally. Also, **hootch**.
[American English, apparently short for *hoochinoo* a distilled liquor made by the Hutsnuwa, a tribe of Alaskan Indians]
hooch[2] (hüch), *n.* = hootch[2].
hooch|ie-cooch|ie (hü′chē kü′chē), *n., adj.* = hootchy-kootchy.
hood[1] (hùd), *n., v.* —*n.* **1a** a soft covering for the head and neck, either separate or as part of a

Pronunciation Key: hat, āge, cãre, fär; let, ēqual, tėrm; it, īce; hot, ōpen, ôrder; oil, out; cup, pu̇t, rüle; child; long; thin; ᴛʜen; zh, measure;
ə represents **a** in about, **e** in taken, **i** in pencil, **o** in lemon, **u** in circus.

coat or cape: *My raincoat has a hood.* **b** a monk's cowl. **2** anything like a hood in shape or use, such as a covering for machinery: *The hood over the street light shielded the apartments above from the glare of the light.* **3** a movable metal covering over an engine, especially of an automobile: *At the gas station they raised the hood of our car to put oil in the engine.* **4** *British.* the cover of the passenger compartment of an automobile, the top of a baby carriage, or the like. **5a** a rounded protective covering over the top of a chimney, ventilator, or the like. **b** a raised cover over a stove, often connected with a ventilator, to protect the ceiling and draw off smoke. **6a** a fold of cloth, banded with distinguishing colors to show what degrees are held and the wearer's department of learning, that hangs down over the gown worn by graduates of universities and colleges. **b** a similar garment worn as a mark of official or professional dignity, as by ecclesiastics. **7** a crest or other part on a bird's or animal's head that suggests a hood in shape or color. **8** any hoodlike part in plants serving as a covering, especially the arched upper part of the corolla or calyx in some flowers. **9** that part of a horse blanket that covers the animal's head and neck. **10** *Falconry.* a covering for the head of a hawk, used to blind the hawk when not pursuing game.
—***v.t.*** to cover with or as if with a hood; furnish with a hood.
[Old English *hōd*] —**hood′less**, *adj.* —**hood′like′**, *adj.*

hood² (hu̇d), *n. U.S. Slang.* a hoodlum; gangster; gunman: *He finds himself tangling with a big-time racketeer and his hoods* (Charles J. Rolo). [apparently short for *hoodlum*]

-hood, *suffix added to nouns and adjectives to form other nouns.*
1 the state or condition of being: *Boyhood* = *the state of being a boy. Likelihood* = *the condition of being likely.*
2 the character or nature of: *Sainthood* = *the character of a saint.*
3 a group of; the body of: *Priesthood* = *the body or group of priests.*
4 a concrete instance of: *Falsehood* = *a concrete instance of falsity.*
[Middle English *-hode, -hade,* Old English *-hād* < *hād* condition, position]

hood|ed (hu̇d′id), *adj.* **1** having a hood; wearing or covered with a hood: *a hooded cape.* **2** shaped like a hood, especially: **a** (of a corolla or other part) cucullate; cowled. **b** (of a flower or plant) having a corolla, calyx, or other part, shaped like a hood. **3a** (of birds and animals) having a crest or other structure or arrangement of colors on the head resembling or suggesting a hood: *the hooded crow.* **b** having elastic skin at the neck that, when distended, resembles a hood, as a cobra.

hooded crow, a European crow with a gray body and black head.

hooded seal, a large seal of the North Atlantic; bladdernose. On the front of its head, the male has a large hoodlike sac that it can inflate when threatened.

hooded violet, = meadow violet.

hood|lum (hüd′ləm), *n. Informal.* **1** a criminal or gangster. **2** a young rowdy; street ruffian; tough. [American English, perhaps < German (Bavarian dialect) *hodalum, huddellump*]

hood|lum|ism (hüd′lə miz əm), *n. U.S. Informal.* the acts and practices of hoodlums.

hood|man (hu̇d′mən), *n., pl.* **-men.** *Archaic.* the blindfolded player in hoodman-blind.

hood|man-blind (hu̇d′mən blīnd′), *n. Archaic.* blindman's buff.

hoo|doo (hü′dü), *n., pl.* **-doos**, *v.,* **-dooed, -doo-ing**, *adj.* —*n.* **1** *Informal.* **a** a person or thing that brings bad luck: *From the moment the overture struck up, in fact, it was evident that a hoodoo was pursuing the show* (New Yorker). **b** bad luck. **2** = voodoo. **3** a fantastic column of rock formed by erosion or other natural cause, occurring in the western United States.
—***v.t.*** *Informal.* to bring or cause bad luck to; bewitch: *Mumbo-Jumbo will hoodoo you* (Vachel Lindsay).
—***adj.*** **1** of or having to do with hoodoo: *hoodoo magic.* **2** bringing bad luck; unlucky: *He's the hoodoo planet of the heavens* (O. Henry).
[American English, apparently variant of *voodoo*]

hoo|doo|ism (hü′dü iz əm), *n.* the practice of hoodoo rites.

hood|wink (hu̇d′wingk), *v.t.* **1** to mislead by a trick; deceive: *So perhaps the West has succeeded in hoodwinking the Russians after all into wasting their money on weapons of war?* (Manchester Guardian). **2** to blindfold: *We'll have no Cupid hoodwinked with a scarf* (Shakespeare). **3** to cover or hide: *The prize I'll bring thee to shall hoodwink this mischance* (Shakespeare). [< *hood* + *wink*] —**hood′wink|er**, *n.*

hoo|ey (hü′ē), *n., interj. U.S. Slang.* nonsense.

hoof (hu̇f, hüf), *n., pl.* **hoofs** or **hooves**, *v.* —*n.* **1** the hard, horny covering on the feet of horses, cattle, sheep, pigs, and some other animals: *The horses' hoofs clattered over the pavement.* **2** the whole foot of such animals: *The dogs nipped the hoofs of the sheep to drive them into the pen.* **3** *Figurative.* a hoofed animal: *Our cattle also shall go with us; there shall not an hoof be left behind* (Exodus 10:26). **4** *Slang.* the human foot. **5** *Geometry.* = ungula.
—***v.i.*** *Informal.* **1** to go on foot; walk. **2** to dance.
—***v.t.*** **1** to strike with the hoof. **2** *Especially British.* to dismiss; expel.
hoof it, *Informal.* to go on foot; walk: *Back by the shore, men in bulky "thermo clothes" and fur hoods hoofed it gingerly on snowshoes or skis across snow-roofed crevasses* (Newsweek).
on the hoof, not killed and butchered; alive: *He is majoring on live stock as a money crop, selling milk, hogs on the hoof* (Baltimore Sun).
pad the hoof, *Slang.* to go on foot; walk along on one's way: *Charley Bates expressed his opinion that it was time to pad the hoof* (Dickens).
[Old English *hōf*] —**hoof′less**, —**hoof′like′**, *adj.*

hoof-and-mouth disease (hu̇f′ən mouth′, hüf′-), = foot-and-mouth disease.

hoof|beat (hu̇f′bēt′, hüf′-), *n.* the sound made by an animal's hoof.

hoof|bound (hu̇f′bound′, hüf′-), *adj.* having a painful contraction of the hoof, usually from disease, that causes lameness.

hoofed (hu̇ft, hüft), *adj.* having hoofs; ungulate.

hoof|er (hu̇f′ər, hü′fər), *n. Slang.* **1** a professional dancer, especially a tap-dancer. **2** a habitual walker.

hoof|let (hu̇f′lit, hüf′-), *n.* a small hoof, such as one of the pair behind and above the regular hoofs of the deer or pig.

hoof|print (hu̇f′print′, hüf′-), *n.* the mark made by an animal's hoof.

hoo-ha (hü′hä), *n. Slang.* excitement; fuss: *all the rest of the hoo-ha with which they can so effectively smother any fresh, original notion* (Punch).
hoo-ha's, the jitters; heebie-jeebies: *When you're alone in the middle of the night and you wake . . . you've got the hoo-ha's coming to you* (Time).

hook (hu̇k), *n., v.* —*n.* **1** a piece of metal, wood, or other stiff material, curved or having a sharp angle for catching hold of something or for hanging things on: *Several people hung their coats on the hook fastened to the wall.* **2** a curved piece of wire, usually with a barb at the end, for catching fish; fishhook: *Beauty without grace is the hook without the bait* (Emerson). **3** *Figurative.* a snare; trap. **4** a bent metal appliance for fastening together two parts of an article of clothing. See also **hook and eye**. **5** anything curved or bent like a hook: *I carried the umbrella by putting the hook of the handle over my arm.* **6** a large, curved knife for cutting down grass or grain; sickle. **7** a sharp bend: *a hook in the river.* **8** a curved point of land: *the Hook of Holland.* See picture under **peninsula**. **9** a recurved and pointed organ or appendage of an animal or plant. **10** the act of hooking. **11** a curving throw or hit in baseball. **12** a golf ball's path of flight curving to the left away from a right-handed player. **13** the act of pulling the ball in cricket. **14** *Bowling.* a throw where the ball rolls down the alley, then turns sharply toward the pins. **15** *Boxing.* a swinging, usually short blow with the elbow bent and rigid. **16** *Surfing.* the crest of a wave. **17** *Ice Hockey.* an act or instance of hooking. **18** a line at the end of the stem of certain musical notes; flag. The eighth note has one.
—***v.t.*** **1** to fasten or attach with or as if with a hook or hooks: *Will you hook my dress for me?* **2** to catch or take hold of with a hook: *The farmer hooked each blade of hay and threw it on the wagon.* **3** to join or fit like a hook. **4** to catch (fish) with a hook: *We hooked a trout and had it for breakfast.* **5** *Figurative.* to catch by a trick, as a husband: *The first woman who fishes for him, hooks him* (Thackeray). **6** *Informal.* to steal; pilfer: *to hook the money and hide it* (Mark Twain). **7** to give the form of a hook to. **8** to throw or hit (a baseball) so that it curves. **9** to hit (a golf ball) so that it curves widely to the left. **10** to pull (the ball) in cricket. **11** *Rugby.* to push (the ball) back with the foot to a teammate out of the center of scrummage. **12** *Boxing.* to hit (an opponent) with a short, swinging blow. **13** *U.S.* to make (a rug, pillow cover, or other article) by pulling loops of yarn or strips of cloth through canvas, burlap, or other loosely woven material, with a hook. **14** to catch on the horns; attack with the horns, as a cow or bull does. **15** *Ice Hockey.* to hinder illegally the advance of (a puck carrier) by catching at his body from the side or rear with one's stick.
—***v.i.*** **1** to be fastened with or as if with a hook: *The gate hooked shut with a click as he left the garden.* **2** to be curved or bent like a hook. **3** to bend or curve like a hook: *At this point the river hooks around to the north.* **4** to move suddenly: *always hooking about on mysterious voyages* (Washington Irving).
by hook or (by) crook, in any way at all; by fair means or foul: *The question of the refugees must be settled, by hook or by crook,* [*since*] *they present a grave security risk, besides an economic problem* (London Times).
get the hook, *Slang.* to be dismissed; lose one's job: *If he is late once more, he will get the hook.*
hook it, *Slang.* to run away: *Here come the cops—you'd better hook it!*
hook, line, and sinker, *Slang.* wholly; entirely: *I swallowed the story hook, line, and sinker* (New Yorker).
hook up, a to attach or fasten with a hook or hooks: *They saw a horse hooked up to the post of the inn* (W. S. Hayward). **b** to arrange and connect the parts of (a radio set, telephone, or other device): *They decided to hook up another radio in the house.* **c** *Informal.* to fasten a garment with hooks on: *Please hook me up.*
off the hook, *Informal.* free of responsibility; out of a predicament: *The administration was searching for a way to get off the hook on Quemoy* (New Yorker).
on one's own hook, *Informal.* independently: *There is a non-personal entity called "History" which accomplishes things on its own hook* (Edmund Wilson).
[Old English *hōc*] —**hook′a|ble**, *adj.* —**hook′less**, *adj.* —**hook′like′**, *adj.*

***hook|ah** or **hook|a** (hu̇k′ə), *n.* a tobacco pipe with a long tube by which the smoke is drawn through water in a vase and cooled. Hookahs are used in the Orient. [< Arabic *huqqah*]

***hookah**

***hook and eye**, a small hook and loop, usually of metal, used as a fastener on clothing.

***hook and eye**

hook-and-lad|der truck (hu̇k′ən lad′ər), a fire truck equipped with ladders, hooked instruments, axes, and other fire-fighting tools.

hooked (hu̇kt), *adj.* **1** curved or bent like a hook. **2** having a hook or hooks. **3** made with a hook or by hooking. See also **hooked rug**. **4** *Informal.* caught as if by a hook; slavishly dependent; addicted: *public clinics where people hooked on narcotics could receive care* (Harper's). *He also got hooked on jazz* (Time). **5** *U.S. Slang.* married.

hooked rug, a rug made by pulling loops of yarn or strips of cloth through a piece of canvas, burlap, or other loosely woven cloth, with a hook.

hook|er¹ (hu̇k′ər), *n.* **1** a person or thing that hooks. **2** *Informal.* a pilferer or thief. **3** *Informal.* a prostitute. **4** *Slang.* **a** a hidden difficulty; catch: *Canada can be trusted by nearly everyone. But—and this is the hooker—Canadian statesmen will only be effective if they speak softly* (Maclean's). **b** something to catch the imagination or attract attention: *The structure of a television program . . . should have a hooker, a teaser and a conclusion* (New York Times). [< *hook* + *-er¹*]

hook|er² (hu̇k′ər), *n.* **1** a small fishing boat. **2** an old-fashioned or clumsy ship: *A long pull, a strong pull, and warp the hooker out* (John Masefield). [apparently < Dutch *hoeker, hoeckerschip* < *hoeck* hook; allusion uncertain]

hook|ey (hu̇k′ē), *n.* = hooky².

hook ladder, a ladder with hooks at one end by which it can be suspended.

hook|let (hu̇k′lit), *n.* a small hook.

hook-mon|ey (hu̇k′mun′ē), *n.* money consisting of pieces of silver in the form of fishhooks, formerly used especially in Ceylon (Sri Lanka), Iran, and the Maldive islands.

hook-nose (hu̇k′nōz′), *n.* an aquiline nose.

hook-nosed (hu̇k′nōzd′), *adj.* having a hook-nose.

hook shot, *Basketball.* a shot in which a player, with his back to the basket, throws the ball over his head in a wide, sideward motion.

hook|up (hu̇k′up′), *n.* **1** the arrangement and connection of the parts of a radio set, telephone, radio-broadcasting facilities, or other electrical or electronic equipment: *He gave ... a speech before 10,000 people in Cleveland, which was broadcast over a nationwide radio and television hookup* (New York Times). **2** a diagram showing this. **3** *Informal.* a connection or combination: *The specific idea of a deep-water hookup with the Atlantic via the St. Lawrence River was born about a century ago* (Newsweek).

hook|worm (hu̇k′wėrm′), *n.* **1** any one of several roundworms which have strong cutting plates or teeth. Hookworms enter the body through the skin and suck blood from the intestinal walls of people and animals, causing hookworm disease. **2** = hookworm disease. [American English < *hook* + *worm*]

hookworm disease, a disease caused by hookworms sucking blood from the small intestine, characterized by severe anemia, weakness, and apparent laziness; ancylostomiasis; uncinariasis.

hook|y[1] (hu̇k′ē), *adj.* **1** full of hooks. **2** hook-shaped. [< *hook* + *-y*[1]]

hook|y[2] (hu̇k′ē), *n.* **play hooky**, *Informal.* **a** to stay away from school without permission; play truant: *The boys played hooky to go to see the parade.* **b** to stay away from work or other duty without a valid reason or justification: *A physician, playing hooky from his office ...* (Newsweek). [American English, apparently < *hook it* to run away]

hoo|li|gan (hü′lə gən), *n., adj.* —*n.* a young street tough; a member of a street gang; hoodlum.
—*adj.* having to do with or characteristic of hooligans: *hooligan performances. What we should call nowadays a hooligan class ... ready to turn out to fight and loot on either side* (H. G. Wells).
[perhaps < an Irish surname]

hoo|li|gan|ism (hü′lə gə niz′əm), *n.* rough, noisy, or lawless behavior; horseplay: *Russia has a growing crime rate, and a special conference on juvenile delinquency and hooliganism was held this winter in Moscow* (Friends Journal).

ho|o|ma|li|ma|li (hō′ō mä′lē mä′lē), *n. Hawaiian.* flattery.

hoop[1] (hu̇p, hüp), *n., v.* —*n.* **1** a ring or flat band in the form of a circle: *a hoop for holding the staves of a barrel.* **2** a large ring of wood, metal, or plastic used as a toy, especially for rolling along the ground by a child. **3** a circular frame formerly used to hold out a woman's skirt: *But from the hoop's bewitching round, Her very shoe has power to wound* (Edward Moore). *The petticoat ... stiff with hoops and arm'd with ribs of whale* (Alexander Pope). **4** = hoop skirt. **5** an arch of iron or wire shaped like a U upside down, through which the ball is hit in croquet; wicket. **6** anything shaped like a hoop; circle; ring; arc: *Those friends thou hast ... Grapple them to thy soul with hoops of steel* (Shakespeare). **7** a ring for the finger.
—*v.t.* **1** to bind or fasten together with a hoop or hoops; confine with hoops: *The smith was hooping a cartwheel.* **2** *Figurative.* to encircle; embrace.
go (or **jump**) **through hoops**, *Informal.* to undergo trials and difficulties: *The Treasury is now a large-scale user of consultants, and makes them jump through a long series of hoops to win their assignments* (London Times).
[Old English *hōp*] —**hoop′like′**, *adj.*

hoop[2] (hüp), *n., v.i., v.t., interj.* = whoop.

hoop dance, a dance performed as a religious ceremony with a hoop by North American Indians living west of the Mississippi.

hooped (hu̇pt, hüpt), *adj.* **1** having a hoop or hoops. **2** held out with hoops, as a woman's skirt. **3** wearing a hoop skirt.

hoop|er (hu̇p′ər, hü′pər), *n.* a craftsman who fits the hoops on casks, barrels, and other containers; cooper.

hoop|ing cough (hü′ping), whooping cough.

hoop|la (hüp′lä), *n. Informal.* **1** excitement; hullabaloo: *Most of our present hoopla about space is certainly in this category* (New Scientist). **2** sensational publicity; ballyhoo. Also, **whoopla**. [probably < French *houp-là* upsy-daisy]

hoo|poe (hü′pü), *n.* any one of a group of bright-colored birds of the Old World having long, sharp bills and fanlike crests on their heads. The call of the hoopoe sounds like its name. [earlier *hoopoop*, and *hoop* < Old French *huppe* < Latin *upupa* < Greek *épops, épopos* hoopoe]

hoop pine, an araucaria tree of Australia that grows as high as 200 feet, valuable as a source of lumber.

***hoop skirt**, **1** a frame of flexible hoops to hold out or expand a woman's skirt; crinoline. **2** a skirt worn over such a frame.

hoop snake, a harmless North American snake, formerly thought to roll like a hoop with its tail in its mouth.

hoo|ray (hu̇ rā′), *interj., n., v.i., v.t.* = hurrah.

hoose|gow or **hoos|gow** (hüs′gou), *n. U.S. Slang.* a jail; lockup. [American English < Spanish (as pronounced in Mexican Spanish) *juzgado* court, tribunal, past participle of *juzgar* to judge < Latin *jūdicāre* < *jūdex* a judge]

Hoo|sier (hü′zhər), *n., adj. U.S.* —*n.* a nickname for a native or inhabitant of Indiana.
—*adj.* of or having to do with Indiana. [American English, apparently special use of dialectal *hoozer* anything unusually large]

Hoosier State, a nickname for Indiana.

hoot[1] (hüt), *n., v.* —*n.* **1** the sound that an owl makes: *We could hear the distant hoot of an owl in the woods.* **2** a shout to show disapproval or scorn: *The hoot of the audience drowned out the politician's campaign promises.* **3** a loud shout; outcry. **4** *Informal.* the smallest thought; trifle: *We don't give a hoot to know just what it's all about* (New Yorker). **5** a toot with a horn: *Every time you gave him a hoot he accelerated and pulled into the middle of the road* (Punch). **6** *Slang.* something hilariously amusing or funny: *'The Projector' [a play] was a marvellous hoot, it was a very elaborate parody but everybody thought it was the real thing* (Manchester Guardian Weekly).
—*v.i.* **1** to make the sound that an owl makes or one like it: *the owlet Atheism ... hooting at the glorious sun in heaven* (Samuel Taylor Coleridge). **2** to shout to show disapproval or scorn: *The crowd hooted at the soapbox orator.* **3** to shout; call out. **4** to make any of various sounds mechanically produced, especially that of a steam whistle, used as a signal to workmen for beginning or stopping work. **5** to toot with a horn.
—*v.t.* **1** to show disapproval of, or scorn for, by hooting: *The audience hooted the speaker's plan.* **2** to force or drive by hooting: *What he said was so foolish that they hooted him off the platform.* **3** to say or show by hooting.
[perhaps imitative]

hoot[2] (hüt), *interj. Scottish.* an exclamation of dissatisfaction, impatience, etc. [probably imitative. Perhaps related to **hoot**[1].]

hootch[1] (hüch), *n.* = hooch[1].

hootch[2] (hüch), *n. U.S. Slang.* **1** a thatched hut in which natives of southeastern Asia live. **2** any house or dwelling: *The term "hootches" ... is used universally here in Vietnam to describe any dwelling, including our own, and that there is nothing "jocular" or malicious or belittling about the word at all* (Saturday Review). Also, **hooch**. [< Japanese *uchi* house; the form was probably influenced by *hutch*]

hootch|y-kootch|y (hü′chē kü′chē), *n., adj.* —*n. U.S. Slang.* a seductive dance consisting primarily of bodily contortions by a scantily-clad female performer, featured especially at carnival side shows.
—*adj.* of or characteristic of a hootchy-kootchy: *a hootchy-kootchy performer.* Also, **hoochie-coochie**.
[origin uncertain]

hoot|e|nan|ny (hü′tə nan′ē, hüt′nan′-), *n., pl.* **-nies**. *U.S. Slang.* an informal gathering featuring folk singers, especially one in which the audience participates: *A hootenanny is to folk singing what a jam session is to jazz* (Time). [origin uncertain]

hoot|er (hü′tər), *n.* **1** a person or thing that hoots. **2** an owl. **3** *Especially British.* a steam whistle or siren. **4** *Especially British.* an automobile horn. **5** *British Slang.* a nose.

hoot owl, any owl that hoots, such as the barred owl.

hoots (hüts), *interj. Scottish.* hoot[2].

hoo|ver (hü′vər), *n., v. British.* —*n.* a vacuum cleaner.
—*v.t., v.i.* to clean with a vacuum cleaner. [< *Hoover,* a trademark for a vacuum cleaner]

Hoo|ver|ism (hü′və riz əm), *n.* the practice of being economical in the use of food or other commodities. [< Herbert *Hoover,* from 1917 to 1919 head of the United States Food Administration, where he reduced domestic consumption of scarce foods + *-ism*]

Hoo|ver|ize (hü′və rīz), *v.,* **-ized, -iz|ing**. *Informal.*
—*v.t.* to use economically, as food; economize.
—*v.i.* to be economical or sparing in the use of food or other commodities; practice economy.

***hoop skirt**
definition 1

Hoo|ver|ville (hü′vər vil), *n. U.S.* a group of makeshift dwellings where unemployed workers lived during the depression of the 1930's. [Herbert *Hoover* + *-ville* (as in *Nashville,* etc.)]

hooves (hu̇vz, hüvz), *n.* hoofs; a plural of **hoof**.

hop[1] (hop), *v.,* **hopped, hop|ping**, *n.* —*v.i.* **1** to spring, or move by springing, on one foot: *How far can you hop on your right foot?* **2** to spring, or move by springing, with both or all feet at once: *A kangaroo hops. Robins hop, but grackles primly walk.* **3** *Informal.* to fly in an airplane. **4** *Informal.* to dance. **5** to limp: *the limping smith ... hopping here and there* (John Dryden). **6** Also, **hop it**. *Slang.* to depart; go off.
—*v.t.* **1** to hop or jump over: *to hop a ditch.* **2** *Informal.* to fly across in an airplane: *to hop the Atlantic.* **3** *Informal.* to jump on (a moving train, car, etc.). **4** to obtain (a ride) in this way: *That morning he was able to hop a ride to work.* **5** to hop about (a place).
—*n.* **1** the act of hopping; spring: *He cleared the puddle in one large hop.* **2** *Informal.* a flight in an airplane. **3** *Informal.* **a** a dancing party, especially an informal one. **b** a dance. **4** a short trip.
caught on the hop, *British Slang.* to catch unawares in the act: *No wonder the nation's motorists were "caught on the hop," as one report put in on the Monday morning* (Basil Boothroyd).
hop and jump, *U.S. Informal.* a short distance: *The house was just a hop and jump from the road.*
hop off, *Informal.* to take off in an airplane: *They hop off from La Guardia Field this afternoon for Cincinnati* (New York Times).
[Old English *hoppian*]

hop[2] (hop), *n., v.,* **hopped, hop|ping**. —*n.* **1** a vine having flower clusters that look like small, yellow pine cones. The hop belongs to the mulberry family. It is native to Europe but much cultivated elsewhere. **2** *Slang.* a narcotic drug, especially opium.
—*v.i.* to pick hops; gather hops.
—*v.t.* to flavor with hops.
hops, the dried ripe flower clusters of the hop vine, used to flavor beer and other malt drinks, and as a tonic and soporific: *Brewers use about one-half pound of hops per barrel of beer* (Wall Street Journal).
[< Middle Dutch *hoppe*]

hop|bine (hop′bīn′), *n.* the twining stem of the hop.

hop clover, any one of the yellow clovers whose withered flowers resemble the flower clusters of the hop.

hope[1] (hōp), *n., v.,* **hoped, hop|ing**. —*n.* **1** a feeling that what one desires will happen: *His promise gave me hope. Hope springs eternal in the human breast* (Alexander Pope). SYN: expectation, anticipation, optimism. **2** the thing hoped for: *Her great hope is a bicycle for Christmas.* **3** a cause of hope; person or thing that gives hope to others or that others have hope in: *He is the hope of the family.* **4** the ground for expecting something desired; promise: *There is no hope for his recovery.* **5** *Archaic.* trust; reliance: *Happy is he ... whose hope is in the Lord his God* (Psalms 146:5).
—*v.t.* **1** to wish and expect: *You hope to do well in school this year. You hoped we were both broken-hearted* (Algernon Charles Swinburne). **2** to desire very much: *Fondly do we hope, fervently do we pray that this mighty scourge of war may speedily pass away* (Abraham Lincoln). **3** to trust: *I hope I know what I'm talking about.*
—*v.i.* **1** to look with expectation: *Love can hope where reason would despair* (George, Lord Lyttleton). **2** *Archaic.* to trust; rely: *Hope thou in God* (Psalms 42:5).
hope against hope, to keep on hoping even though there is no good reason to have hope: *They hoped against hope that the stolen money would be returned.*
[Old English *hopa*]

hope[2] (hōp), *n. Scottish.* **1** a small enclosed valley. **2** a small bay or inlet. [Old English *-hop*]

hope chest, *U.S.* a chest in which a young woman collects articles, such as linens or tableware, that will be useful in furnishing a home of her own after she marries.

hope|ful (hōp′fəl), *adj., n.* —*adj.* **1** feeling or showing hope; expecting to receive what one wants: *a hopeful attitude.* **2** causing hope; giving hope; likely to succeed. SYN: promising.
—*n.* **1** a boy or girl thought likely to succeed: *a young hopeful.* **2** a person who hopes to obtain or achieve something. —**hope′ful|ness**, *n.*

hope|ful|ly (hōp′fə lē), *adv.* in a hopeful manner or with a feeling of hope or ground for expectation: *He left all his female kindred ... either*

Pronunciation Key: hat, āge, cãre, fär; let, ēqual, tėrm; it, īce; hot, ōpen, ôrder; **oi**l, **ou**t; cup, pu̇t, rüle; **ch**ild; lo**ng**; **th**in; **ᴛʜ**en; **zh**, measure; **ə** represents **a** in about, **e** in taken, **i** in pencil, **o** in lemon, **u** in circus.

matched with peers of the realm actually, or hopefully with earls' sons and heirs (Henry Wotton). *Some day soon, we hope, he will combine the three books. And, "hopefully," as current jabberwocky has it, make the reader's task just a trifle easier* (New York Times).
▶**Hopefully** in the usage "it is to be hoped that" has been avoided by some writers who were perhaps unaware of this long-established pattern of adverbial use in English as in *doubtlessly, surely,* and *absolutely.*

hope|less (hōp′lis), *adj.* **1** feeling no hope; without hope: *He was disappointed so often that he became hopeless. Alas for him ... Who, hopeless, lays his dead away* (John Greenleaf Whittier). **2** giving no hope; desperate: *hopeless illness.* —**hope′less|ly,** *adv.* —**hope′less|ness,** *n.*
—*Syn.* **1 Hopeless, desperate, despairing** mean without hope. **Hopeless** implies being passively willing to endure whatever may come: *After trying every means of escape and finding them all blocked, I sat in hopeless apathy.* **Desperate** implies being rashly willing to run any risk to improve the situation: *People were so desperate they jumped from the burning building.* **Despairing** implies being utterly dejected and unable to think of anything else to do or anywhere else to look for help: *Despairing of saving his debt-ridden business, the desperate man declared bankruptcy.*

Hope|well (hōp′wel′), *adj.* of or having to do with a culture of the North American Indian from about 500 B.C. to 500 A.D., characterized by the surviving burial mounds and art objects found in southern Ohio and the Illinois Valley. [< M. C. *Hopewell,* a farmer on whose land remains of the culture were found]

Hope|well|i|an (hōp′wel′ē ən), *adj.* = Hopewell.

hop|head (hop′hed′), *n. U.S. Slang.* a drug addict. [< *hop*² + *head* person]

Ho|pi (hō′pē), *n., pl.* **-pi** or **-pis.** **1** a member of a tribe of Pueblo Indians living largely in adobe-built villages in northern Arizona. **2** their Shoshonean language. [American English, contraction of Shoshonean (Hopi) *hópitu* peaceful ones, or *hópitu shinumu* "peaceful all people" the native Hopi tribal name]

hop|lite (hop′līt), *n.* a heavily armed foot soldier of ancient Greece. [< Greek *hoplī́tēs* < *hópla* arms, plural < *hóplon* tool, instrument]

hop-off (hop′ôf′, -of′), *n. Slang.* the taking-off of an aircraft.

hop-o'-my-thumb (hop′ə mī thum′, -mi-), *n.* a dwarf; pygmy. [earlier *hop on my thombe* < *hop*¹]

hopped-up (hopt′up′), *adj. U.S. Slang.* **1** stimulated; excited; spirited: *a hopped-up team eager to win.* **2** souped up: *a hopped-up hot rod, a hopped-up rocket.* **3** stimulated with drugs; high: *a hopped-up dope addict.*

hop|per¹ (hop′ər), *n.* **1** a person or thing that hops: *Frogs are good hoppers.* **2** a grasshopper or other hopping insect: *In some fields, the 'hoppers have eaten more than 20 bales of grass to the acre* (Wall Street Journal). **3** a container to hold something and feed it to another part. A hopper is usually larger at the top than at the bottom. **4** something shaped like such a container, such as a car for carrying coal. **5** *U.S.* a receptacle into which members of a lawmaking body drop bills proposed for enactment. **6** a part that raises the hammer of a piano key.

hop|per² (hop′ər), *n.* a hop picker.

***hopper car,** *U.S.* a freight car with high sides, no top, and a mechanism for dumping, used especially to carry coal, gravel, sand, grain, or cement.

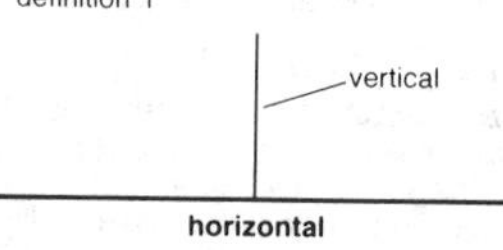

***hopper car**

hop|per|doz|er (hop′ər dō′zər), *n. U.S.* a device for catching and killing locusts, consisting of a large, shallow pan of oil or kerosene mounted upon runners and pulled by a tractor across a field, so that the jumping insects fall into the pan. [< *hopper*¹ + (bull)*dozer*]

hop|ping (hop′ing), *adj.* extremely active; busy: *In the hopping days of late August and September, ... the hounds go cubbing over their country near the woods* (Manchester Guardian Weekly).

hopping mad, very mad: *GOP members of the Labor Committee were hopping mad at the outcome* (Wall Street Journal).

Hopping John, *U.S.* a stew of bacon with rice and peas.

hop|ple (hop′əl), *v.i., v.t.,* **-pled, -pling,** *n.* = hobble.

hops (hops), *n.pl.* See under **hop²**.

hop-sack|ing (hop′sak′ing), *n.* **1** a coarse sacking, used for hops. **2** a woolen, loose-textured cloth, woven of heavy thread, used for clothing.

***hop|scotch** (hop′skoch′), *n., v.* —*n.* a children's game in which the players hop over the lines of a figure drawn on the ground and pick up an object thrown or kicked into one of the numbered squares of the figure.
—*v.i.* to hop, go, or travel here and there: *He hopscotched about the town looking for odd jobs.* [< *hop*¹ + *scotch* a scratch, line]

***hopscotch**

hop, skip, and jump, 1 a contest or sport in which the contestants try to cover as much distance as possible by successively hopping, taking one stride, and jumping. **2** *Informal.* a short distance: *After that it will be only a hop, skip, and jump to a nice round million-dollar super-spectacular* (New Yorker).

hop, step, and jump, = hop, skip, and jump (def. 1).

hop|toad (hop′tōd′), *n. Informal.* a toad.

hop tree, any one of a group of North American shrubs or small trees of the rue family, with trifoliate leaves, small, greenish-white flowers, and a bitter fruit sometimes used as a substitute for hops. See picture under **rue family.**

hop trefoil, 1 = hop clover. **2** = black medic.

hop|vine (hop′vīn′), *n.* **1** the trailing stem of the hop. **2** the hop plant.

hor., 1 horizon. **2** horizontal. **3** horology.

ho|ra (hôr′ə, hōr′ə), *n., pl.* **-ras.** a lively Israeli and Romanian folk dance performed by moving around to the left or right in a circle. [< Hebrew *hōrāh* < Romanian *horă*]

Ho|rae (hôr′ē, hōr′-), *n.pl. Greek and Roman Mythology.* the goddesses of the seasons and hours, and also of order and justice; the Hours. [< Latin *Hōrae,* plural of *hōra* hour]

ho|ral (hôr′əl, hōr′-), *adj.* of or having to do with an hour or hours; hourly. [< Late Latin *hōrālis* < Latin *hōra* hour]

ho|ra|ry (hôr′ər ē, hōr′-), *adj.* **1** of or having to do with an hour or hours. **2** indicating the hours. **3** occurring every hour; hourly. **4** *Astrology.* having to do with horary questions: *a horary prediction.* [< Medieval Latin *horarius* < Latin *hōra* hour]

horary question, *Astrology.* a question, the answer to which is obtained by erecting a figure of the heavens for the moment at which it is propounded.

Ho|ra|tian (hə rā′shən), *adj.* of or like the Roman poet and satirist Horace (65-8 B.C.) or his poetry.

Horatian ode, a lyric poem having an undetermined number of short stanzas, all alike in form.

Ho|ra|tio Al|ger (hə rā′shō al′jər), characteristic of a success story; having to do with rising from rags to riches through one's own efforts: *By working harder ... with Horatio Alger celerity they acquired property and transformed themselves into bankers* (Atlantic). ... *the American Dream, with its Horatio Alger belief in self-improvement* (Manchester Guardian Weekly). [< *Horatio Alger,* 1832-1899, an American author of a series of books for boys]

Ho|ra|tius (hə rā′shəs), *n. Roman Legend.* a Roman hero who held back the Etruscan army until a bridge behind him over the Tiber was destroyed by the Romans.

hor|cha|ta (ôr chä′tä), *n.* a white, sweet soft drink of Spain and Latin America, made from an emulsion of ground melon or pumpkin seeds and sometimes almonds, mixed with sugar. [< Spanish *horchata,* ultimately < Latin *hordeum* barley]

horde (hôrd, hōrd), *n., v.,* **hord|ed, hord|ing.** —*n.* **1** a crowd; swarm; multitude: *hordes of grasshoppers. Society is now one polished horde, Formed of two mighty tribes, the Bores and Bored* (Byron). SYN: troop, gang, crew. **2** a wandering tribe or troop: *Hordes of Mongols and Turks invaded Europe in the Middle Ages.*
—*v.i.* to gather in a horde; live in a horde: *My fathers' house shall never be a cave For wolves to horde and howl in* (Byron).
[probably < French *horde* < German *Horde,* earlier *Horda,* perhaps < Polish *horda* < Turkic (compare Tatar *urda* horde). Compare etym. under **Urdu.**]

Ho|reb (hôr′eb, hōr′-), *n.* Mount Sinai, where God gave Moses the Ten Commandments (in the Bible, Deuteronomy 4:15).

hore|hound (hôr′hound′, hōr′-), *n.* **1** a plant with woolly, whitish leaves, and clusters of small, whitish flowers. It belongs to the mint family. **2** a bitter extract made from the leaves of this plant. **3** a candy or cough medicine flavored with it. Also, **hoarhound.** [Old English *hārhūne* < *hār* hoar + *hūne,* the name of a plant]

Ho|rite (hōr′īt), *n.* a member of an ancient people that were living in Palestine when the Israelites arrived there. Many scholars believe that the Horites were Hurrians.

***ho|ri|zon** (hə rī′zən), *n.* **1** the line where the earth and sky seem to meet. You cannot see beyond the horizon. *Lord of the far horizons, Give us the eyes to see Over the verge of the sundown The beauty that is to be* (Bliss Carman). **2** *Figurative.* the limit of one's thinking, experience, interest, or outlook: *The horizon should be vivid with splendor and hope* (Walter Lippmann). **3** *Astronomy.* **a** the plane at right angles to the direction of gravity that passes through the eye of the observer at a given place; sensible horizon. **b** the great circle of the celestial sphere that has a plane parallel to the sensible horizon and passes through the center of the earth, or the plane of this great circle. It is called astronomical, celestial, true, or rational horizon. **c** a level reflecting surface, usually of mercury, used in measuring altitudes; artificial or false horizon. **4** *Geology.* a stratum or series of strata having fossils, etc., that differ from the deposits above or below. **5** one of the layers in a vertical cross section of a series of soils and subsoils. **6** the actual or imaginary horizontal line in perspective drawing toward which receding parallel lines converge. It represents the eye level of the observer. [< Old French *orizonte,* learned borrowing from Latin *horīzōn, -ontis* < Greek *horízōn* (*kýklos*) bounding (circle), ultimately < *hóros* limit] —**ho|ri′zon-less,** *adj.*

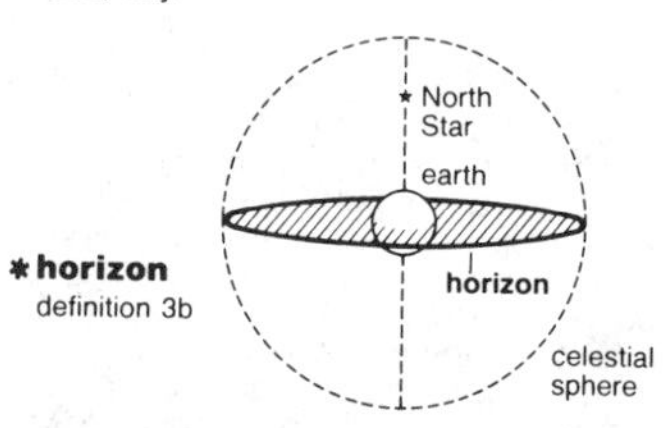

***horizon**
definition 3b

horizon blue, a light grayish blue.

horizon glass, the fixed mirror of a sextant, in which the horizon is reflected.

***hor|i|zon|tal** (hôr′ə zon′təl, hor′-), *adj., n.* —*adj.* **1** parallel to the horizon; at right angles to a vertical line: *The ground was horizontal to the flagpole.* **2** flat; level: *the vast horizontal prairie of America.* **3** measured in a line parallel to the horizon: *a horizontal distance.* **4** placed, acting, or working wholly or mainly in a horizontal direction: *a horizontal boiler.* **5** of or having to do with the horizon; on or near the horizon. **6** so organized as to include only one stage in production or one group of people or crafts: *horizontal trusts. Carpenters and plumbers belong to horizontal unions.* **7** of or having to do with the series of sounds which form a melody, especially in a contrapuntal composition.
—*n.* a horizontal line, plane, direction, or position. —**hor′i|zon′tal|ly,** *adv.* —**hor′i|zon′tal|ness,** *n.*

***horizontal**
definition 1

vertical

horizontal

horizontal bar, an elevated bar for gymnastic exercises such as chinning or swinging.

horizontal integration, = horizontal merger.

hor|i|zon|tal|i|ty (hôr′ə zon tal′ə tē, hor′-), *n.* the condition of being horizontal.

hor|i|zon|tal|ize (hôr′ə zon′tə līz), *v.t.,* **-ized, -izing.** to make horizontal.

horizontal merger, a merger of companies that produce the same products or otherwise compete directly with each other: *Unlike ... the horizontal merger (the combination of firms producing similar products), the conglomerate merger involves unrelated business* (Joel Segall).

horizontal stabilizer, *U.S.* a fixed horizontal airfoil on each side of the fuselage or boom at an aircraft's tail to keep it from unwanted up-and-down motion. See picture under **airplane.**

horizontal union, = craft union.

hor|mic (hôr′mik), *adj. Psychology.* of or characterized by a vital or purposeful energy transcending the purely physical or chemical functioning of the body. [< Greek *hormē* impulse + English *-ic*]

hor|mo|nal (hôr mō′nəl), *adj.* of, having to do with, or like a hormone. —**hor|mo′nal|ly**, *adv.*

hor|mone (hôr′mōn), *n.* **1** a substance formed in the endocrine glands, which enters the bloodstream and affects or controls the activity of some organ, or of cells or tissues. Adrenalin and insulin are hormones. **2** a substance carried in the protoplasm of plants that acts similarly. Auxins are hormones.
[< Greek *hormôn* setting in motion, present participle of *hormân* impel < *hormē* impulse] —**hor′mone-like′**, *adj.*

hor|mon|ic (hôr mon′ik), *adj.* = hormonal.

hor|mon|ize (hôr′mō nīz), *v.t.*, **-ized, -iz|ing.** to furnish or treat with hormones: *Each chick is vigorously hormonized, vitaminized (A,B,D,E,K) and debeaked* (Time).

hor|mo|nol|o|gy (hôr′mō nol′ə jē), *n.* the scientific study of hormones.

hor|mo|no|poi|et|ic (hôr mō′nə poi et′ik), *adj. Physiology.* **1** producing hormones, as certain organs. **2** having to do with the production of hormones.
[< *hormone* + Greek *poiētikós* productive < *poieîn* to make]

***horn** (hôrn), *n., adj., v.* —*n.* **1** a hard, hollow growth, usually curved and pointed and in pairs, on the heads of cattle, sheep, goats, and some other animals. The horns of these animals are permanent. **2** one of a pair of solid, branching growths on the head of a deer, elk, or related animal, that fall off and grow back each year; antler. **3** anything that sticks up on the head of an animal: *a snail's horns, an insect's horns.* **4** the substance or material of horns, principally keratin. Horn is hard, durable, and partly transparent. **5** any similar material, such as that of hoofs, nails, the beaks of birds, and tortoise shells. **6** a thing made, or formerly made, of horn, such as a thimble or shoehorn. **7** a container made by hollowing out a horn. It was used to drink out of or to carry gunpowder. **8** a drink in such a container. **9** the horn of plenty; cornucopia: *No richer gift has Autumn poured From out her lavish horn* (John Greenleaf Whittier). **10** a musical instrument sounded by blowing into the smaller end. It was once made of horn, but now it is made of brass and other metal. A French horn and a hunting horn are different types of horns: **a** any brass wind instrument, especially a trumpet. **b** a musician who plays a trumpet or other brass wind instrument. **11** a device sounded as a warning signal: *an automobile horn.* **12** anything that sticks out like a horn or is shaped like a horn: *a saddle horn, the horn of a bay.* **13** either pointed tip of a new or old moon, or of a crescent: *The moon Wears a wan circle round her blunted horns* (James Thomson). **14** the point of an anvil.
15a any one of the short levers attached to a control surface of an aircraft to which the operating cable or rod is fastened. **b** the small part of a control surface forward of the main hinge.
16 *Radio.* a tube used in certain loudspeakers to couple the diaphragm with the outer air. **17** a symbol of strength, power, or glory in the Bible.
18 a horn, like that of an animal, attributed to a deity or demon: *the devil's horn.*
—*adj.* made of horn.
—*v.t.* **1** to hit or wound with horns; gore. **2** to furnish with horns. **3** to make horn-shaped. **4** *Obsolete.* to cuckold.
blow one's own horn, to boast: *Three minutes is more than enough time to blow one's own horn* (New Yorker).
draw (or **pull**) **in one's horns**, **a** to restrain oneself: *So I began to pull in my horns, as they say* (Samuel Richardson). **b** to back down; withdraw: *They are imploring the Council to draw in its horns* (Saturday Review).
horn in, *U.S. Slang.* to meddle or intrude: *Tickets for the Notre Dame-Oklahoma football game were sold out as far back as last May, but that didn't keep numerous persons from making rather remarkable efforts to horn in on the show at Oklahoma's Owen Field* (Newsweek).
horns of a dilemma, **a** two unpleasant choices, one of which must be taken: *The current situation finds those states on the horns of a dilemma. . . . If they allow oil to flow unchecked, they say, they risk market chaos in the industry on which they are so reliant. . . . If, on the other hand, they cut allowable production, they slash their own revenues* (Wall Street Journal). **b** *Logic.* the alternatives of a dilemma: *In disputation, the adversary who is refuted by a dilemma is said to be "fixed on the horns of a dilemma"* (Thomas Fowler).
lock horns, to engage in combat; quarrel; fight: *The engineer union . . . has locked horns with the Curran men on ship contracts with other ship lines* (New York Times).
the horn, *U.S. Slang.* the telephone: *This morning, I got on the horn to Secretary Finch, just on a hunch, and asked him* (New Yorker).
[Old English *horn*] —**horn′like′**, *adj.*

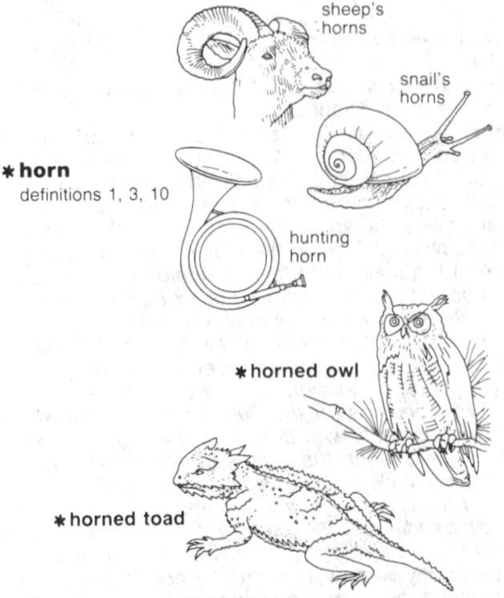

***horn** definitions 1, 3, 10
***horned owl**
***horned toad**

horn antenna, a microwave antenna that is wider at the open end and radiates radio waves into space.

horn|beam (hôrn′bēm′), *n.* any one of a genus of trees of the birch family, with very hard, heavy, white wood and hanging clusters of nuts.

horn|bill (hôrn′bil′), *n.* any one of a family of large birds having a very large down-turned bill with a horn or horny lump on it.

horn|blende (hôrn′blend′), *n.* any one of a group of common black, dark-green, or brown silicate minerals containing aluminum and varying proportions of several other elements. Hornblende is a variety of amphibole which is found in granite and many other igneous and metamorphic rocks.
[< German *Hornblende* < *Horn* horn + *Blende* blende]

hornblende schist, a metamorphic rock consisting essentially of hornblende.

horn|blen|dic (hôrn blen′dik), *adj.* **1** containing hornblende. **2** like hornblende.

***horn|book** (hôrn′bu̇k′), *n.* **1** a page with the alphabet or figures on it, covered with a sheet of transparent horn, and fastened in a frame with a handle, formerly used in teaching children to read, figure, and spell. **2** a first book in reading; primer.

***hornbook** definition 1

horned (hôrnd), *adj.* **1** having a horn, horns, or hornlike growths: *the young horned moon.* **2** having or wearing a hornlike ornament, etc.

horned dace, = creek chub.

horned lark, a brownish bird with black ear tufts, yellow throat, and black, white, or yellow face markings.

horned lizard, = moloch.

***horned owl**, any one of various owls with hornlike tufts of feathers on the head, such as the great horned owl. See picture under **horn**.

***horned toad**, a small, harmless lizard with a broad, flat body, short tail, and many spines. It is common in the arid regions of western North America. See picture under **horn**.

horned viper, a poisonous snake of Africa and Asia, having a horny growth above each eye.

horn|er (hôr′nər), *n.* **1** a person who works or deals in horn. **2** a person who blows or plays a horn.

hor|net (hôr′nit), *n.* a large wasp that can give a very painful sting. The hornet is one of the social wasps. Hornets usually live in paperlike nests.
stir up a hornets' nest, to stir up trouble: *Had Knowland stirred up a hornets' nest of organized-labor opposition?* (Time).
[Old English *hyrnetu;* perhaps influenced by English *horn*]

horn|fels (hôrn′fels), *n.* a compact rock composed of quartz, feldspar, mica, or the like, formed by the action of intrusive rock upon shale or other sedimentary rock. [< German *Hornfels* < *Horn* horn + *Fels* rock]

horn fly, a small fly that attacks cattle, causing loss of weight and lowered milk production.

Horn|ie (hôr′nē), *n.* **Auld**, *Scottish.* the Devil.

horn|i|ness (hôr′nē nis), *n.* the condition of being horny.

horn|ing (hôr′ning), *n.* **1** the act of a person or thing that horns. **2** *U.S.* a mock serenade with tin horns and other discordant instruments; charivari.

horn|ist (hôr′nist), *n.* a person who plays a horn, especially the French horn.

horn|less (hôrn′lis), *adj.* without horns; having no horns, as some cattle: *Aberdeen Angus is a breed of hornless beef cattle.* —**horn′less|ness**, *n.*

horn-mad (hôrn′mad′), *adj. Archaic.* **1** enraged enough to gore, as a bull: *Sure, my master is horn-mad* (Shakespeare). **2** raging mad; furious. —**horn′-mad′ness**, *n.*

horn of plenty, **1** a horn-shaped container overflowing with fruits, vegetables, and flowers. **2** a horn-shaped container or ornament; cornucopia.

***horn|pipe** (hôrn′pīp′), *n.* **1** a lively dance done by one person. It was formerly popular among sailors. **2** the music for this dance. **3** a musical wind instrument of former times, consisting of a wooden pipe with a bell-shaped end made of horn.

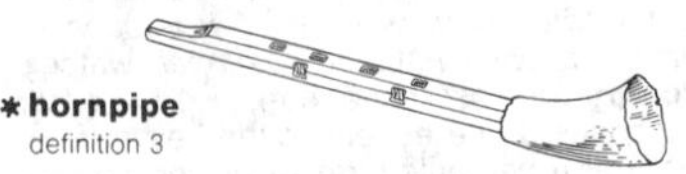
***hornpipe** definition 3

horn|pout (hôrn′pout′), *n.* the common bullhead, a catfish with a broad head.

horn-rimmed (hôrn′rimd′), *adj.* having rims made of horn or plastic colored to look like horn: *horn-rimmed glasses.*

horn silver, = cerargyrite.

horn|stone (hôrn′stōn′), *n.* a variety of quartz resembling flint. [translation of German *Hornstein* < *Horn* horn + *Stein* stone (because of its appearance)]

horn|swog|gle (hôrn′swog′əl), *v.t.*, **-gled, -gling.** *U.S. Slang.* to get the better of; cheat; hoodwink: *The ad's chief function is to hornswoggle the consumer* (Boston Herald). [probably a coined word]

horn|tail (hôrn′tāl′), *n.* any one of certain hymenopterous insects related to the sawflies and wasps whose larvae develop in the wood of trees and shrubs. The female has a projecting ovipositor.

horn|worm (hôrn′wėrm′), *n.* the larva of certain sphingid moths, such as the tobacco worm, having a hornlike growth on the end of the tail.

horn|wort (hôrn′wėrt′), *n.* any one of a group of aquatic plants, having dense whorls of finely divided leaves. They are common in ponds and slow streams in most parts of the world.

horn|y (hôr′nē), *adj.*, **horn|i|er, horn|i|est.** **1** made of horn or a substance like it: *the horny shell of a lobster.* **2** hard like a horn; calloused: *A farmer's hands are horny from work.* **3** translucent like horn; semiopaque. **4** having a horn or horns; horned. **5** *Slang.* feeling lust; lascivious.

horny coral, = sea fan.

horn|y-hand|ed (hôr′nē han′did), *adj.* having the hands hardened by hard work: *Though a working lad, Tony is no horny-handed proletarian* (Time).

horny sponge, a sponge having a skeleton consisting of spongin rather than spicules, such as the elephant-ear sponge.

ho|rog|ra|phy (hô rog′rə fē, hō-), *n.* the art of constructing instruments for marking the hours.
[< French *horographie* < Greek *hôra* time, season + *-graphíā* writing]

horol., horology.

hor|o|loge (hôr′ə lōj, -loj; hor′-), *n.* any device that indicates the time, such as a clock, sundial, or hourglass; timepiece: *On the left stands the slender octagon tower of the horologe* (Longfellow).
[< Old French *horloge,* learned borrowing from Latin *hōrologium* < Greek *hōrológion* < *hôra* time + *-logos* telling]

ho|rol|o|ger (hô rol′ə jər, hō-), *n.* a person who studies horology.

hor|o|log|ic (hôr′ə loj′ik, hor′-), *adj.* of or having to do with a horologe or horology. —**hor′o|log′i|cal**, *adj.*

Hor|o|lo|gi|i (hôr′ə lō′jē ī, hor′-), *n.* genitive of **Horologium.**

Hor|o|lo|gi|um (hôr′ə lō′jē əm, hor′-), *n., genitive* **Hor|o|lo|gi|i.** a southern constellation.

ho|rol|o|gy (hô rol′ə jē, hō-), *n.* **1** the science of measuring time. **2** the art of designing or making

Pronunciation Key: ha**t, ā**ge**, cã**re**, fä**r**; l**e**t, ē**qual**, tė**rm**; i**t**, ī**ce**; h**o**t, ō**pen**, ô**rder**; oi**l**, ou**t**; c**u**p, pu̇**t**, rü**le**; ch**ild**; lo**ng**; th**in**; ᴛʜ**en**; zh**, measure;
ə represents **a** in about, **e** in taken, **i** in pencil, **o** in lemon, **u** in circus.

timepieces. [< Greek *hōra* time + English *-logy*] —**ho|rol′o|gist**, *n.*

ho|rop|ter (hô rop′tər, hō-), *n. Optics.* **1** the line or surface containing all the points in space that in any position of the eyes are projected on corresponding points of the two retinas. **2** the aggregate of points that are seen single while the position of the two eyes remains unchanged. [< Greek *hóros* limit + *optēr* one who looks]

hor|op|ter|ic (hôr′op ter′ik, hor′-), *adj.* of or having to do with the horopter.

hor|o|scope (hôr′ə skōp, hor′-), *n.* **1** the relative position of the planets at a particular time, especially at the hour of a person's birth, regarded as influencing his life. **2** a diagram of the twelve signs of the zodiac, showing the arrangement of the heavens at a particular time. A horoscope is used in telling fortunes by the planets and the stars. **3** a fortune told by this means.

cast a horoscope, to discover the influence that the stars and planets are supposed to have upon a person's life: *The court astrologers, according to custom, cast the horoscope of the infant* (Washington Irving).

[< Middle French *horoscope*, learned borrowing from Latin *hōroscopus* < Greek *hōroskópos* < *hōra* time + *skopós* watcher < *skopeîn* watch]

ho|ros|co|py (hô ros′kə pē, hō-), *n.* **1** the casting of horoscopes. **2** the aspect of the heavens, especially at a person's birth. —**ho|ros′co|pist**, *n.*

hor|ren|dous (hô ren′dəs, ho-), *adj.* causing horror; horrible; terrible; frightful: *The only important deterrent to another world war today seems ... to be the horrendous potentialities of nuclear war* (Bulletin of Atomic Scientists). [< Latin *horrendus* (with English *-ous*), gerundive of *horrēre* bristle with fear, shudder] —**hor|ren′dous|ly**, *adv.*

hor|rent (hôr′ənt, hor′-), *adj. Archaic.* **1** standing up like bristles; bristling: *Him round A globe of fiery seraphim inclosed, With ... horrent arms* (Milton). **2** horrified; shuddering. [< Latin *horrēns, -entis*, present participle of *horrēre* bristle with fear]

hor|ri|ble (hôr′ə bəl, hor′-), *adj., n.* —***adj.*** **1** causing horror; terrible; dreadful; frightful; shocking: *a horrible crime, a horrible disease.* **SYN:** hideous, grim, horrid. See syn. under **ghastly**. **2** *Informal.* extremely unpleasant or amazing: *a horrible smell, a horrible noise.* **SYN:** excessive, immoderate, extreme.

—***n.*** a horrible person or thing: *Author Grant makes Lucia's life a masochistic nightmare of Halloween horribles* (Time).

[< Old French *horrible*, learned borrowing from Latin *horribilis* < *horrēre* bristle with fear] —**hor′ri|ble|ness**, *n.* —**hor′ri|bly**, *adv.*

hor|rid (hôr′id, hor′-), *adj.* **1** causing great fear; terrible; dreadful; frightful: *Moloch, horrid King, besmeared with blood Of human sacrifice* (Milton). **SYN:** abominable, detestable. **2** *Informal.* very unpleasant; disagreeable: *a horrid little boy, a horrid day. My life is one demd horrid grind* (Dickens). **SYN:** offensive. **3** *Archaic.* bristling; shaggy; rough: *The forest ... horrid with fern, and intricate with thorn* (John Dryden). [< Latin *horridus* rough, shaggy, bristling < *horrēre* bristle with fear] —**hor′rid|ly**, *adv.* —**hor′rid|ness**, *n.*

hor|rif|ic (hô rif′ik, ho-), *adj.* causing horror; horrifying. —**hor|rif′i|cal|ly**, *adv.*

hor|ri|fi|ca|tion (hôr′ə fə kā′shən, hor′-), *n.* **1** the act of horrifying. **2** a thing that causes horror.

hor|ri|fy (hôr′ə fī, hor′-), *v.t.,* **-fied, -fy|ing.** **1** to cause to feel horror: *the horrifying cry of the tiger at night.* **2** *Informal.* to shock very much: *We were horrified by the wreck.* [< Latin *horrificāre* < *horrificus* causing horror < *horrēre* bristle with fear + *facere* make] —**hor′ri|fy′ing|ly**, *adv.*

hor|rip|i|la|tion (hô rip′ə lā′shən, ho-), *n.* the act or process of the hair bristling on the skin as from cold or fear; goose flesh. [< Late Latin *horripilātiō, -ōnis* < *horripilāre* (of the hackles) to rise, bristle with fear < Latin *horrēre* bristle + *pilus* hair]

hor|ror (hôr′ər, hor′-), *n., adj.* —***n.*** **1** a shivering, shaking fear and dislike; terror and disgust caused by something frightful or shocking: *The crime aroused universal horror.* **SYN:** dread. **2** a very strong dislike; very great disgust: *That little girl has a horror of snakes and spiders.* **SYN:** loathing, abhorrence, aversion. **3** the quality of causing horror. **4** a thing that causes great fear: *I have supp'd full with horrors* (Shakespeare). **5** *Informal.* something very bad, unpleasant, or unattractive: *There is a man in a yellow house, a little man with a lean horror of a wife* (Edmund Wilson). **6** a shuddering or shivering, especially as a symptom of disease. **7** *Poetic.* roughness; ruggedness.

—***adj.*** causing horror: *a horror story, horror films.*

the horrors, *Informal.* **a** a fit of horror, as in delirium tremens: *He does take a drop too much at times, and then he has the horrors* (Anthony Trollope). **b** extreme depression; the blues: *As you promise our stay shall be short, if I don't die of the horrors, I shall certainly try to make [it] agreeable* (Susan E. Ferrier).

[< Latin *horror* < *horrēre* bristle with fear]

hor|ror-struck (hôr′ər struk′, hor′-), *adj.* horrified.

hors de com|bat (ôr′də kôɴ bá′), *French.* out of the fight; disabled.

hors d'oeu|vre (ôr′dėrv′; French ôr′dœ′vrə), *pl.* **d'oeu|vres** (dėrvz′). **1** a relish, light food, or dainty sandwich, served as an appetizer before the regular courses of a meal. Olives, celery, cheese, nuts, and anchovies are used as hors d'oeuvres. **2** outside the major concern; apart from the main undertaking: *Adolpho ... was an important boutiquier when other custom milliners ventured no farther hors d'oeuvre than an occasional scarf or handbag* (New Yorker). **3** something beyond the main concern; something peripheral: *Restraints on free speech are usually hors d'oeuvres for the Supreme Court, but when Congress outlawed draft card burning to squelch antiwar dissent, the Justices backed the law, 7 to 1* (New York Times). *Dictionaries ... of space and medical terms, and a number of other little compendia that look substantial in a table of contents but are essentially mere hors d'oeuvres* (Saturday Review). [< French *hors d'oeuvre* (literally) apart from the main work]

▶In French **hors d'oeuvre** is usually hyphenated and does not take a plural *-s*.

horse** (hôrs), *n., pl.* **hors|es** or (*collectively*) **horse**, *v.,* **horsed, hors|ing,** *adj.* —n.*** **1** a large, four-legged animal with a flowing mane and tail of long, coarse hair. Horses have been used from very early times to pull loads and carry riders. They have solid hoofs and are herbivorous mammals. **2** a full-grown male horse; stallion or gelding. **3** any animal of the same family as the horse, including asses and zebras. **4** any one of various extinct animal species thought to be ancestors of the present horse, such as the eohippus. **5** soldiers on horses; cavalry: *a thousand horse, a troop of horse.* **6** anything on which one rides, sits astride, or is carried, as if on horseback: *a rocking horse.* **7** a piece of gymnasium apparatus to jump or vault over. **8** a frame with legs to support something: *Five boards laid on two horses made our picnic table.* **9** = sawhorse. **10** = clotheshorse. **11** *Figurative.* a man (used contemptuously or playfully): *If I tell thee a lie, spit in my face, call me horse* (Shakespeare). **12** *U.S. Slang.* a translation or other aid for illicit use in schoolwork; pony. **13** *Mining.* a mass of rock or earthy matter enclosed within a lode or vein. **14** *Chess, Informal.* a knight. **15** *U.S. Slang.* heroin or other narcotics.

—***v.t.*** **1** to provide with a horse or horses. **2** to put on horseback. **3a** to set or carry on a person's back. **b** to carry on one's own back. **4** to set on a person's back or on a wooden horse or other place of punishment, in order to be flogged: *The biggest boy ... horsed me ... and I was flogged* (Thackeray). **5** to flog. **6** *Informal.* to make fun; play jokes on. **7** *Slang.* to drive or urge (a person) at work, especially unfairly or tyrannically: *to horse a ship's crew.* **8** *Slang.* to perform boisterously, as a part or a scene in a play.

—***v.i.*** to mount or go on horseback.

—***adj.*** **1** of or having to do with a horse or horses: *a horse collar, a horse show.* **2** on a horse or horses: *The horse grenadiers were mounted infantry.* **3** large or coarse for its kind: *a horse mackerel.*

back the wrong horse, *Informal.* to support a losing candidate, cause, or other enterprise: *[He] is doubtless well aware that his lack of experience in African politics may mean he will often back the wrong horse* (Atlantic).

beat (or **flog**) **a dead horse**. See under **dead horse**.

from the horse's mouth, from the original source; from a well-informed source; from the person in charge: *The prophecies were direct relays from the horse's mouth* (New York Times).

hold one's horses, *Informal.* to slow down, pause, or be patient: *Just hold your horses, boys—he'll come out directly* (J. S. Robb).

horse around, *Slang.* to fool around; get into mischief: *She never let us horse around and so none of us ever got very clubby with each other* (New Yorker).

horse of a different (or **another**) **color**, something different: *Many lay people believe that if we*

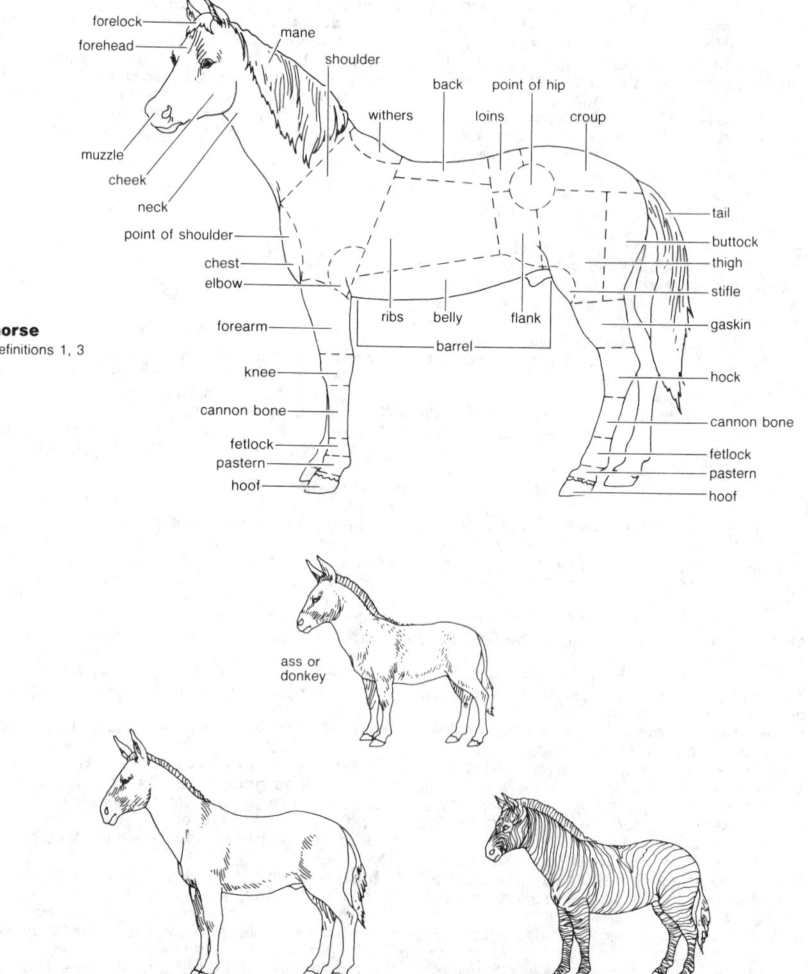

***horse**
definitions 1, 3

can put a man on the moon, we can also conquer cancer. Space probes are scientific instruments. Cancer is a horse of a different color (Science).
look a gift horse in the mouth. See under **gift horse**.
to horse! mount horses! get on horseback!: *"To horse!" Said Ida, "home! to horse!"* (Tennyson). [Old English *hors*] **—horse'like'**, *adj.*

horse-and-bug|gy (hôrs'ən bug'ē), *adj.* **1** of or having to do with the period when horses and buggies were used for traveling; characteristic of the 1800's: *. . . rusty hitching weights from the horse-and-buggy era* (Atlantic). **2** old-fashioned; out-of-date: *horse-and-buggy approaches to modern problems. The City of New York is not a horse-and-buggy town* (New York Times).

horse|back (hôrs'bak'), *adv., adj., n.* **—*adv.*** on the back of a horse: *to ride horseback.*
—*adj.* *U.S. Informal.* given or reached offhand without full consideration: *a horseback opinion.*
—*n.* **1** the back of a horse. **2** *U.S.* a low, somewhat sharp ridge of gravel, sand, or rock; hogback.

horse bean, = broad bean.

horse block, a small platform for convenience in mounting a horse.

horse botfly, any one of several kinds of botflies whose larvae live in the stomachs of horses. The females lay their eggs on the hair of the horse's legs, his throat, and mouth.

horse|box (hôrs'boks'), *n.* a trailer or railroad car used for transporting horses.

horse|break|er (hôrs'brā'kər), *n.* a person employed to break or train horses.

horse brier, = greenbrier.

horse|car (hôrs'kär'), *n. U.S.* **1** a streetcar or a railroad car pulled by a horse or horses. **2** a car used for transporting horses. [American English]

horse chestnut, **1** a large shade tree with spreading branches, large leaves, clusters of showy, white flowers, and glossy, brown nuts resembling chestnuts. See also **buckeye**. **2** its nut. See picture under **chestnut**. **3** any tree or shrub of the same family as the horse chestnut.

horse|cloth (hôrs'klôth', -kloth'), *n.* a rug or cloth used to cover a horse or as part of its trappings.

horse-col|lar (hôrs'kol'ər), *v.t. Baseball Slang.* to prevent from scoring; keep scoreless.

horse crab, **1** = horseshoe crab. **2** either one of two types of crab having a rough surface, found on the Pacific coast of North America; bristly crab.

horse doctor, *Informal.* a veterinarian.

horse|feath|ers (hôrs'feᴛʜ'ərz), *n., interj. U.S. Slang.* nonsense.

horse|flesh (hôrs'flesh'), *n.* **1** horses for riding, driving, or racing. **2** meat from horses.

horse|fly (hôrs'flī'), *n., pl.* **-flies. 1** any one of a group of large flies with two wings, the females of which bite animals, especially horses; gadfly. **2** any one of certain other flies which are troublesome to horses.

horse|foot (hôrs'fůt'), *n., pl.* **-foots.** = horseshoe crab.

horse gentian, any one of a group of perennial herbs of the honeysuckle family, especially the feverroot.

horse godmother, *British Dialect.* a big, coarse, masculine woman.

horse|hair (hôrs'hãr'), *n., adj.* **—*n.*** **1** hair, or a hair, from the mane or tail of a horse: *Much of our furniture was once stuffed with horsehair.* **2** a stiff fabric made of this hair; haircloth. **3** a similar fabric made of rayon or other synthetic.
—*adj.* made of or stuffed with horsehair: *a horsehair cushion.*

horsehair snake or **worm**, = hairworm.

horse|heal (hôrs'hēl'), *n.* = elecampane.

horse|hide (hôrs'hīd'), *n.* **1** the hide of a horse. **2** leather made from the hide of a horse. **3** *Slang.* a baseball.

horse|jock|ey (hôrs'jok'ē), *n., pl.* **-eys.** = jockey.

horse latitudes, either of two regions where the winds are usually calm or very light. They extend around the earth at about 30 degrees north and 30 degrees south of the equator. The name is also used for regions of very light rainfall, about 25 degrees north and 30 degrees south of the equator. [said to be from a former Spanish nautical phrase *el golfo de las yeguas* the mares' sea (because of the unsettled wind conditions there)]

horse|laugh (hôrs'laf', -läf'), *n.* a loud, boisterous laugh.

horse|leech (hôrs'lēch'), *n.* a large European leech, supposed to attack the mouths and noses of horses as they drink.

horse|less (hôrs'lis), *adj.* **1** without a horse. **2** not requiring a horse; self-propelled: *Automobiles used to be called horseless carriages.*

horse mackerel, **1** = tuna[1] (def. 1). **2** any one of certain other fishes, such as the carangoid and bluefish.

horse|man (hôrs'mən), *n., pl.* **-men. 1** a person who rides on horseback; a rider: *The horseman dismounted and asked for lodgings.* **2** a person who is skilled in riding or managing horses: *That horseman won first prize in the jumping contest.* **3** a person who takes care of horses. **4** *Obsolete.* a cavalryman.

horse|mane oats (hôrs'mān'), = side oats.

horse|man|ship (hôrs'mən ship), *n.* the art of riding on horseback; skill in riding or managing horses: *She is proud of her horsemanship.*

horse marine, **1** a humorous reference to a member of an imaginary corps of marines mounted on horseback. **2** a marine or sailor performing shore duty on horseback, or a cavalryman performing duty on a ship. **3** *Figurative.* a person out of his natural surroundings.

horse|meat (hôrs'mēt'), *n.* the flesh of a horse, especially as an article of food; horseflesh.

horse|mint (hôrs'mint'), *n.* **1** any one of a group of mints that includes the Oswego tea and the wild bergamot; monarda. **2** *U.S.* any one of various other aromatic plants of the mint family, especially varieties bearing white or yellow flowers.

horse nettle, a prickly North American weed of the nightshade family, bearing white flowers and yellow berries.

horse opera, *Slang.* a motion picture about horses and cowboys; western: *This editorial approach is reducing U.S. television to a bland gruel of horse opera, soap opera and Walt Disney* (Maclean's).

horse parlor, *Slang.* a bookmaker's establishment for making bets on horse races.

horse pistol, a type of large pistol that used to be carried by horsemen.

horse|play (hôrs'plā'), *n.* rough, boisterous fun: *The girls of our community, which was mainly agricultural, were accustomed to all kinds of horseplay and usually gave as good as they got* (Atlantic).

horse|play|er (hôrs'plā'ər), *n.* a person who bets on horse races.

horse|play|ing (hôrs'plā'ing), *n.* the act or practice of betting on horse races.

horse|pow|er (hôrs'pou'ər), *n.* **1** a unit for measuring the power of an engine or motor. One horsepower is the power to lift 550 pounds one foot in one second. It is equivalent to 746 watts. *Abbr:* h.p. **2** the power of a horse or horses as employed in driving a machine, as an early threshing machine.

horse|pow|er-hour (hôrs'pou'ər our'), *n.* a unit representing the work performed or energy consumed in working at the rate of one horsepower for one hour.

horse|pox (hôrs'poks'), *n.* = equine variola.

horse race, **1** a race between horses on a race track. A harness race is a type of horse race. **2** *Figurative.* any contest, especially a particularly close or strenuous one.

horse racing, the sport of racing between horses.

horse|rad|ish (hôrs'rad'ish), *n.* **1** a tall plant with white flowers and broad, rough leaves, grown for its white, hot-tasting root. Horseradish belongs to the mustard family. **2** its root, which is ground up and used as a relish with meat, fish, salads, and other food. **3** a relish made of this root.

horse room, *Slang.* horse parlor.

horse sense, *Informal.* plain, practical good sense; common sense; shrewdness: *Besides an evaluation of the engineers' estimates, we're going to rely more on what our horse sense tells us* (Wall Street Journal).

***horseshoe**
definition 1

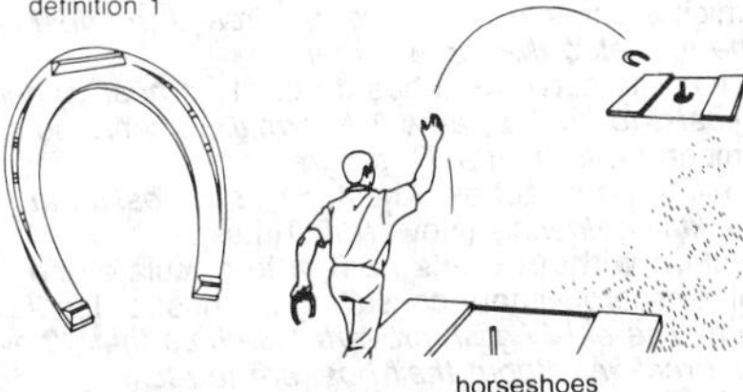

horseshoes

horse|shoe** (hôrs'shü', hôrsh'-), *n., v.,* **-shoed, -shoe|ing. —*n. **1** a metal plate shaped like a U, nailed to a horse's hoof to protect it. **2** a horseshoe regarded as a good luck omen: *Happy art thou, as if every day thou hadst picked up a horseshoe* (Longfellow). **3a** a thing shaped like a horseshoe: *The river making a kind of a double horseshoe* (Daniel Defoe). **b** a piece of iron shaped like a U, weighing no more than 2½ pounds, used in the game of horseshoes. **4** = horseshoe crab.
—*v.t.* to put a horseshoe or horseshoes on.
horseshoes, a game in which players try to throw horseshoes or similar objects around or nearest a stake 40 feet away: *The men are in the park playing horseshoes.*
►**Horseshoes**, meaning the game, is plural in form and singular in use: *Horseshoes is often played by men.*

horseshoe arch, an arch that is greater than a semicircle, narrower at the springing line than above.

horseshoe crab, a crablike sea animal related to the spiders and scorpions, with a shell shaped like a horseshoe and a long, spiny tail; king crab; horsefoot; horse crab.

horseshoe magnet, a magnet in the shape of a horseshoe. See picture under **magnet**.

horse|sho|er (hôrs'shü'ər, hôrsh'-), *n.* a person who makes horseshoes, or puts horseshoes on horses. SYN: blacksmith.

horse sickness, = African horse sickness.

horse sponge, any one of several large, coarse sponges, some of important commercial value, found in the warm waters off Florida and the West Indies, such as the sheepswool, or the honeycomb, found in the Mediterranean Sea; grass sponge; yellow sponge; velvet sponge.

horse stinger, = dragonfly.

horse|tail (hôrs'tāl'), *n.* **1** the tail of a horse. **2** any one of various plants with hollow, jointed stems, and scalelike leaves at each joint; equisetum; scouring rush. **3** = mare's-tail (def. 2). **4** a horse's tail formerly used as a Turkish military standard or to show the rank of a pasha, the higher ranks being distinguished by additional horsetails. **5** = ponytail.

horsetail tree, = casuarina.

horse trade, **1** a selling or buying of horses. **2** *U.S. Informal.* a political bargain; a shrewd compromise: *There's a lingering resentment, too, over what the British call America's attempted horse trade with the Germans* (Newsweek).

horse-trade (hôrs'trād'), *v.i., v.t.,* **-trad|ed, -trad|ing.** *Informal.* to trade or barter shrewdly: *The delegates . . . should now be able to get down to the real horse-trading—including the swapping and balancing of concessions on manufactures and products* (London Times).

horse trader, **1** a person who sells or buys horses. **2** a person who trades or barters shrewdly.

horse|way (hôrs'wā'), *n.* a way or passage for horses.

horse|weed (hôrs'wēd'), *n.* **1** a North American composite plant that is a troublesome weed; Canada fleabane. **2** any one of several other weeds, such as the wild lettuce.

horse|whip (hôrs'hwip'), *n., v.,* **-whipped, -whip|ping. —*n.*** a whip for driving or controlling a horse.
—*v.t.* to beat with a horsewhip: *Slaves were sometimes horsewhipped.*

horse|wom|an (hôrs'wům'ən), *n., pl.* **-wom|en. 1** a woman who rides on horseback. **2** a woman skilled in riding or managing horses.

horse wrangler, *U.S.* a ranch hand or cowboy who rounds up or has charge of a herd of horses or cow ponies.

hors|ey (hôr'sē), *adj.,* **hors|i|er, hors|i|est.** = horsy.

horst (hôrst), *n. Geology.* **1** any part of the earth's surface that has resisted lateral thrust and against which surrounding areas have been pressed and dislocated. **2** an area which has become raised above surrounding areas that have been depressed by faulting. See diagram under **fault**. [< German *Horst* heap, mass, sandbank]

hors texte (ôr'tekst'), *French.* outside the text; printed on a separate leaf of a book, not with the text: *James A. Michener's text for Facing East, printed on Arches paper, with nine original in-text woodcuts by Levine, plus one hors texte original woodcut* (New Yorker).

hors|y (hôr'sē), *adj.,* **hors|i|er, hors|i|est. 1** like a horse or horses. **2** having to do with horses. **3** fond of horses or horse racing: *The horsy set of the town of Much Wenlock . . . where much of the movie was filmed, was uncooperative during the shooting because of the novel's anti-fox hunting message* (Time). **4** dressing or talking like people who spend much time with horses. **5** *Slang.* large and awkward in appearance. **—hors'i|ly**, *adv.* **—hors'i|ness**, *n.*

hort., **1** horticultural. **2** horticulture.

hor|ta|tive (hôr'tə tiv), *adj., n.* **—*adj.*** characterized by exhortation; serving or tending to exhort.
—*n.* an exhortation.

Pronunciation Key: hat, āge, cãre, fär; let, ēqual, tėrm; it, īce; hot, ōpen, ôrder; oil, out; cup, půt, rüle; child; long; thin; ᴛʜen; zh, measure; ə represents **a** in about, **e** in taken, **i** in pencil, **o** in lemon, **u** in circus.

[< Latin *hortātīvus* < *hortārī* exhort, encourage] —**hor'ta|tive|ly**, *adv.*

hor|ta|tor (hôr tā'tər), *n.* a person who exhorts. [< Latin *hortātor* < *hortārī* exhort]

hor|ta|to|ry (hôr'tə tôr'ē, -tōr'-), *adj.* serving to urge or encourage; giving advice; exhorting: *the maddening hortatory speeches of smug age to eager youth. Their elders had a few reservations which they expressed unstintingly last week in hundreds of hortatory speeches* (Newsweek). SYN: hortative, exhortatory.

hor|ti|cul|tur|al (hôr'tə kul'chər əl), *adj.* having to do with the growing of flowers, fruits, vegetables, and plants: *Florists sometimes give a horticultural exhibit in the spring.* —**hor'ti|cul'tur|al|ly**, *adv.*

hor|ti|cul|ture (hôr'tə kul'chər), *n.* **1** the art or science of growing flowers, fruits, vegetables, and plants. **2** the cultivation of a garden. [< Latin *hortus* garden + *cultūra* culture; probably patterned on *agriculture*]

hor|ti|cul|tur|ist (hôr'tə kul'chər ist), *n.* a person who studies horticulture.

Ho|rus (hôr'əs, hōr'-), *n.* a sun god of ancient Egypt, son of Osiris and Isis. Horus was usually represented as having the head of a hawk.

Hor|wat (hôr'wot), *n. U.S.* a Croat. [< Serbo-Croatian *Hrvat.* Compare etym. under **cravat.**]

Hos., Hosea (book of the Old Testament).

ho|sa (hō'zə), *n.pl.* long, tight stockings worn by noblemen in the Middle Ages. [< Medieval Latin *hosa* < Germanic (compare Old English *hosa* hose)]

ho|san|na (hō zan'ə), *interj., n., pl.* **-nas**, *v.,* **-naed**, **-na|ing.** —*interj.* a shout of praise to God: *And the multitudes . . . cried, saying, Hosanna to the son of David . . . Hosanna in the highest* (Matthew 21:9). SYN: hallelujah.

—*n.* **1** a cry of "hosanna." **2** a shout of praise or adoration; acclamation: *In the face of Democratic hosannas over the contract's imminent death, President Eisenhower again defended it as "a good, fair agreement"* (New York Times).

—*v.t.* to praise or acclaim with shouts of "hosanna": *This James Naylor suffered himself to be hosannaed into Bristol as Christ was into Jerusalem* (Charles Leslie).

—*v.i.* to cry or shout "hosanna."

[< Late Latin *hōsanna* < Greek *hōsanná* < Hebrew *hōshā'-nå*, short for *hōshī 'āh-nnå* save, we pray]

hose (hōz), *n., pl.* **hose** or (*Archaic*) **ho|sen** (hō'zən) *for 2-4,* **hos|es** *for 1, 5, 6, v.,* **hosed**, **hos|ing.** —*n.* **1** a tube of rubber, canvas, or other material that will bend, used to carry water and other liquids for short distances: *a garden hose, a fire hose. A hose is used in pumping gasoline into automobiles.* **2** stockings. **3** a covering for the legs, sometimes reaching only to the ankle, such as a legging or gaiter, now especially a covering for the foot also, such as a sock. **4a** long, tight breeches worn by men in olden times. **b** an article of clothing for the legs and loins; breeches; drawers (especially in the phrase "doublet and hose," as the typical male apparel): *O fine villain! A silken doublet! a velvet hose!* (Shakespeare). **5** a sheath or sheathing part, especially the sheath enclosing an ear of corn. **6** a socket, especially one receiving the shaft or handle of a tool, golf club, or the like.

—*v.t.* **1** to put water or other liquid on with a hose: *to hose a garden.* **2** to wash or drench with water or other liquid from a hose: *to hose the walls of a building clean.* [Old English *hosa*]

Ho|se|a (hō zē'ə, -zā'-), *n.* **1** a prophetic book of the Old Testament, placed among the Minor Prophets. *Abbr:* Hos. **2** its author, a Hebrew prophet who lived in the 700's B.C.

hose|pipe (hōz'pīp'), *n.* a flexible tube for carrying water or other liquids; hose.

Ho|she|a (hō shē'ə), *n.* (in Biblical history) the last king of Israel (700's B.C.), whose revolt against Assyria was crushed.

ho|sier (hō'zhər), *n.* a person who makes or sells hosiery or goods similarly knitted or woven.

ho|sier|y (hō'zhər ē, hōzh'rē), *n.* **1** hose; stockings; any goods in which a hosier deals. **2** the business of a hosier.

hosp., hospital.

hos|pice (hos'pis), *n.* **1** a house where travelers can stop and rest, especially one belonging to a religious order, such as those of the monks of St. Bernard and St. Gotthard in the Alps. **2** a home for the destitute or the sick. **3** an institution devoted to the care of the terminally ill: *The hospice aims . . . to make dying as pleasant as possible. The accent is on sun, fresh flowers, and open visiting hours even for young children and pets* (James Hassett). [< French, Old French *hospice*, learned borrowing from Latin *hospitium* guest house; hospitality < *hospes, -itis* guest, host[1]. See etym. of doublet **hospitium.**]

hos|pi|ta|ble (hos'pi tə bəl, hos pit'ə-), *adj.* **1** giving or liking to give a welcome, food and shelter, and friendly treatment to guests or strangers: *a hospitable family.* **2** inclined to, or characterized by, hospitality: *a hospitable disposition, a hospitable reception.* **3** *Figurative.* willing and ready to entertain; favorably receptive or open: *People who want progress are hospitable to new ideas.* [< Middle French *hospitable* < Latin *hospitārī* stay as a guest < *hospes, -itis* guest, host[1]] —**hos'pi|ta|ble|ness**, *n.* —**hos'pi|ta|bly**, *adv.*

hos|pi|tal (hos'pi təl), *n.* **1** a place where sick or injured people or others who need medical treatment are cared for: *The doctor removed my tonsils at the hospital.* **2** a similar place for animals. **3** a repair shop usually for small items, such as dolls and fountain pens. **4** a charitable institution for the shelter and care of the poor, sick, or aged, or for the education of needy children (now only in English legal use and in proper names like Greenwich Hospital, originally a home for retired seamen). **5** *Obsolete.* a hospice. [< Old French *hospital* hostel, learned borrowing from Medieval Latin *hospitale* inn, singular of Latin *hospitālia* guest rooms, ultimately < *hospes, -itis* guest, host[1]. See etym. of doublets **hostel, hotel, spital.**]

Hos|pi|tal|er or **Hos|pi|tal|ler** (hos'pi tə lər), *n.* a member of an order of military monks, the Knights Hospitalers, or the Knights (of the Hospital) of St. John of Jerusalem. The organization was founded during the first Crusade from a hospital at Jerusalem. [< Old French *hospitalier* < *hospital;* see etym. under **hospital**]

hos|pi|tal|er or **hos|pi|tal|ler** (hos'pi tə lər), *n.* **1** a member of any one of various religious orders formed for charitable purposes, especially for the care of the sick or needy. **2** the chief resident official of some London hospitals, which were originally religious foundations. **3** a hospital chaplain. **4** an inmate of a hospital.

hos|pi|tal|i|sa|tion (hos'pi tə lə zā'shən), *n. Especially British.* hospitalization.

hos|pi|tal|i|ty (hos'pə tal'ə tē), *n., pl.* **-ties.** friendly reception; generous treatment of guests or strangers.

hospitalities, hospitable courtesies: *Women are always more cautious in their casual hospitalities than men* (Hawthorne).

[< Latin *hospitālitās* < *hospes, -itis* host[1]]

hos|pi|tal|i|za|tion (hos'pi tə lə zā'shən), *n.* **1** the act of putting someone in a hospital for treatment: *The doctor advised hospitalization for the child.* **2** the state of being put in a hospital for treatment. **3** the period of being hospitalized: *His long hospitalization left him weak and destitute.* **4** a form of insurance that pays or helps pay hospital expenses.

hos|pi|tal|ize (hos'pi tə līz), *v.t.,* **-ized**, **-iz|ing.** **1** to put in a hospital for treatment: *So frail that he had to be hospitalized, he took his cure in his own hands* (Newsweek). **2** to accustom to hospital treatment.

hos|pi|tal|man (hos'pi təl man'), *n., pl.* **-men.** a corpsman of the United States Navy.

hospital ship, a vessel fitted up as a hospital, such as one accompanying a fleet of warships.

hos|pi|ti|um (hos pish'ē əm), *n., pl.* **-pi|ti|a** (-pish'ē ə). = hospice. [< Latin *hospitium* guest house; hospitality. See etym. of doublet **hospice.**]

hos|po|dar (hos'pə där), *n.* a title formerly given to the governors or princes of Walachia and Moldavia (now included in Romania). [< Rumanian *hospodár* < Ukrainian *hospodar* (literally) master]

host[1] (hōst), *n., v.* —*n.* **1** a person who receives another person at his house or elsewhere as his guest: *the host of a house party.* **2** the keeper of an inn or hotel. **3** a living plant or animal in or on which a parasite lives: *The oak tree is the host of the mistletoe that grows on it.*

—*v.t.* **1** to serve as a host to or at: *to host dinner guests, to host a party.* **2** *Informal.* to serve as an emcee of: *to host a TV program.*

—*v.i.* to be or act as a host: *Higgs is hosting at a cocktail gathering* (New York Times).

reckon without one's host, **a** to calculate one's bill or score without consulting the host or landlord: *The old English proverb telleth us that "they that reckon without their host are to reckon twice"* (Peter Heylin). **b** *Figurative.* to overlook the chances of one's plans going wrong: *He reckoned strangely in this matter, without the murderous host into whose clutches he had fallen* (John Addington Symonds).

[< Old French *hoste* < Latin *hospes, -itis* guest, host[1]]

host[2] (hōst), *n.* **1** a great company; a large number; multitude: *As it grew dark, a few stars appeared, then a host of them. Tagore produced a host of short fiction* (The Reporter). **2** an army: *Nebuchadnezzar king of Babylon came, he, and all his host, against Jerusalem, and pitched against it* (II Kings 25:1). **3** the sun, moon, and stars, or heavenly bodies: *Hesperus, that led the starry host, rode brightest* (Milton). **4** the angels of heaven: *Praise Him above, ye heavenly host!* (Bishop Thomas Ken). [< Old French *host* < Late Latin *hostis* army < Latin, enemy; (originally) stranger]

Host (hōst), *n.* Often, **host**. the bread or wafer regarded as the body of Christ in the Mass of the Roman Catholic Church and at Holy Communion in some other churches. [< Old French *hoiste* < Latin *hostia* sacrifice, the animal sacrificed; spelling influenced by *host*[1]]

hos|tage (hos'tij), *n.* **1a** a person seized by an enemy, political group, or criminal and held to obtain a demand, such as safe passage, a large sum of money, or the surrender of armed resistance: *Militants seized the U.S. embassy in Teheran and announced that the occupants would be held hostage until the shah was returned* (Keith S. McLachlan). *54 political prisoners will . . . fly to Syria for the start of their exchange for the hostages . . . held on board the hijacked Pakistani airliner for 12 days* (London Times). **b** a person seized and punished in retaliation for some act. **c** a person given up to another or held by an enemy as a pledge that certain promises or agreements will be carried out: *In early times, countries commonly exchanged hostages to guarantee that a treaty would be carried out* (Payson S. Wild). **2** the standing, state, or condition of the person thus handed over. **3** *Figurative.* a pledge or security.

give hostages to fortune, to have persons or things that one may lose: *He that hath wife and children hath given hostages to fortune* (Francis Bacon).

[< Old French *hostage, ostage* (originally) lodging, probably fusion of Medieval Latin *hostaticus* (ultimately < Latin *hospes* guest, host[1]), with Vulgar Latin *obsidāticus* condition or state of a hostage, ultimately < *ob-* against + *sedēre* to sit]

hos|tage|ship (hos'tij ship), *n.* the condition of a hostage.

host cell, an animal or plant cell in which a parasitic or commensal organism, as a virus, lives.

hos|tel (hos'təl), *n., v.,* **-teled**, **-tel|ing.** —*n.* **1** a lodging place, especially a supervised lodging place for young people on bicycle trips, hikes, or other outings; inn; hotel. **2** a residence hall in a British university, especially one for students at a nonresident college. **3** *Obsolete.* a house where one lodges.

—*v.i.* **1** to maintain a hostel. **2** to stop at a hostel in the course of a trip.

[< Old French *hostel* < Medieval Latin *hospitale* inn. See etym. of doublets **hospital, hotel, spital.**]

hos|tel|er (hos'tə lər), *n.* **1** a guest at a hostel: *Sometimes the hostelers lend a helping hand—painting a barn or bringing in hay* (Sidonie M. Gruenberg). **2** *Archaic.* an innkeeper.

hos|tel|ry (hos'təl rē), *n., pl.* **-ries.** an inn or hotel. [< Old French *hostellerie* < *hostel;* see etym. under **hostel**]

host|ess (hōs'tis), *n., adj., v.* —*n.* **1** a woman who receives another person as her guest: *Katherine went up to her hostess and dropped a curtsy. "It was nice of you to ask me to your party, Mrs. Howells," she said, without mumbling* (New Yorker). **2** a woman who keeps an inn or hotel, or who helps her husband to do so: *my hostess of the tavern* (Shakespeare). **3** a woman hired to greet and attend to guests in a hotel, restaurant, or other establishment. **4** a woman paid to entertain or dance with guests or travelers. **5** = airline hostess. **6** a woman who welcomes and entertains at a military canteen.

—*adj.* of or for a hostess; designed to be worn by a woman for informal entertaining at home: *a hostess gown, hostess pants.*

—*v.t.* to serve as a hostess to or at: *to hostess a party.*

—*v.i.* to be a hostess; act as hostess.

[< Old French *hostesse*, feminine of *hoste* host[1]]

hos|tile (hos'təl; *sometimes* hos'tīl), *adj., n.* —*adj.* **1** of or having to do with an enemy or enemies: *the hostile army, hostile ground or positions. The hooked chariot stood Unstain'd with hostile blood* (Milton). **2** *Figurative.* like an enemy; opposed; unfriendly; unfavorable: *a hostile look, a hostile reception.* **3** carried on by an enemy: *hostile operations.*

—*n.* **1** a hostile person; enemy. **2** *U.S. History.* a North American Indian unfriendly to the whites.

[< Latin *hostīlis* < *hostis* enemy] —**hos'tile|ly**, *adv.*

—*Syn. adj.* **2 Hostile, unfriendly, inimical** mean not friendly or favorable. **Hostile** suggests whatever is characteristic of an enemy: *Their hostile looks showed that he was unwelcome.* **Unfriendly** suggests not being agreeable, kindly, helpful, or encouraging in any way: *A cold, damp climate is unfriendly to people who suffer from arthritis.* **Inimical**, a formal word, particularly suggests the harmful effects resulting from a hostile disposition: *Censorship is inimical to freedom of the press.*

hos·til·i·ty (hos til′ə tē), *n., pl.* **-ties.** **1** the feeling that an enemy has; being an enemy; unfriendliness; opposition: *The guard dog showed signs of hostility toward the intruders.* **SYN:** enmity, antagonism. **2** the state of being at war: *The enemy admitted that a state of active hostility existed.* **3** *Figurative.* opposition; resistance: *They carry on mad hostility against all established institutions* (Daniel Webster). **4** a hostile act: *The hostility was close to an act of war.*
hostilities, acts of war; warfare; fighting.

host·ing (hōs′ting), *n.* **1** an assembling of a host or armed multitude. **2** a hostile expedition or encounter: *Strange to us it seem'd . . . that angel should with angel war, And in fierce hosting meet* (Milton).

hos·tler (os′lər, hos′-), *n.* **1** a person who takes care of horses at an inn or stable; stableman; groom. **2** a person who moves locomotives around a railroad yard or shop. **3** *Obsolete.* an innkeeper. Also, **ostler.** [Middle English *hostiler* innkeeper, head of a hospice < Old French *hostelier* < *hostel* hostel]

host of heaven, 1 the sun, moon, and stars, or heavenly bodies: *the sun, or moon, or any of the host of heaven* (Deuteronomy 17:3). **2** the angels of heaven: *I saw the Lord sitting on his throne, and all the host of heaven standing by him* (I Kings 22:19). [translation of Hebrew *tsəbā hāshāmāyim*]

host-spe·cif·ic (hōst′spi sif′ik), *adj.* living on or in a particular species of host: *The plague bacterium is transferred from rat to rat by a particular flea which like all other fleas is host-specific; ordinarily it will feed on the blood of rats and rats alone* (London Times).

hot (hot), *adj.,* **hot·ter, hot·test,** *adv., v.,* **hot·ted, hot·ting.** *—adj.* **1** much warmer than the body; having or giving off much heat: *That fire is hot. The sun is hot today.* **SYN:** scorching, scalding. **2** having a relatively high temperature: *The food is too hot to eat.* **3** having the feeling of high bodily heat: *That long run has made me hot. Lords, I am hot with haste, in seeking you* (Shakespeare). **4** having a sharp, burning taste; pungent; biting: *Pepper and mustard are hot.* **SYN:** peppery, acrid. **5** *Figurative.* **a** full of strong feeling; fervent; passionate; ardent; *a hot argument. Prophetic Lips hot with the bloodbeats of song* (Algernon Charles Swinburne). **SYN:** fervid. **b** full of great interest or enthusiasm; very eager: *The boys were hot after the treasure.* **c** fiery; violent; angry; wrathful: *a hot temper, hot words, hot with rage.* **d** lustful. **6** intense; violent: *a hot fight. Set ye Uriah in the forefront of the hottest battle* (II Samuel 11:15). **7** dangerous: *a hot situation.* **8a** strong or fresh; new: *news hot from the press, a hot scent, a hot trail.* **b** *Slang.* fashionable because exciting or novel: *The new dances are hot stuff. But even the sleekest, hottest automobiles, as the proudest new car owner will ruefully admit, are not ends in themselves, but only means—means to roll free of the city* (Time). **c** *Slang.* good; satisfactory: *For president he's not so hot. Business won't support him* (Blue Valley Farmer). **9** following closely: *The sheriff was hot on the heels of the bandits.* **10** very near or approaching an object or answer one is searching for. **11** charged with radioactivity; dangerously radioactive: *the hot debris left by an atomic explosion.* **12** electrically charged. **13** kept open or ready for use: *a hot telephone line between the White House and the Pentagon.* **14a** (of swing music or jazz) played with exciting variations from the score: *One of Shawn's few relaxations is occasional hot piano playing* (Newsweek). **b** (of a musician) playing with such variations: *a hot saxophone player.* **c** (of music) stirring, or able to stir, great enthusiasm and admiration. **15** *Slang.* **a** obtained illegally; stolen: *hot diamonds.* **b** contraband. **16** *Slang.* likely to win or succeed; difficult to beat, stop, or hinder: *a hot team.* **17** *Slang.* wanted by the police. **18** *Slang.* unbelievable.
—adv. in a hot manner; with much heat; hotly: *The sun beats hot upon the sand.*
—v.t. British Informal. to heat.
blow hot and cold. See under **blow**[2].
hot and bothered, *Informal.* excited: *So why should we become hot and bothered about our own country, which has an excellent record of . . . guarding its interests?* (London Times).
hot and hot, served hot from the fire to the table, without delay, as food: *The crisp slices came off the gridiron hot and hot* (Dickens).
hot it up, *Slang.* to have a good time; make things hot: *Next evening, Jimmy McPartland's gang, with George Wettling on drums, will start hotting it up* (New Yorker).
hot under the collar. See under **collar.**
hot up, *Informal.* **a** to make or become livelier or more intense, active, or enthusiastic: *as the situation hots up. The economic cold war in Rhodesia is to be abruptly hotted up* (New Yorker). **b** to heat up; make hot: *He will try to hot up the cauldron* (Economist).
make it hot for, *Informal.* to make trouble for; make things unpleasant or uncomfortable for: *His opponents soon made the town too hot for him.*
[Old English *hāt*] **—hot′ly,** *adv.* **—hot′ness,** *n.*

hot air, *Slang.* empty, boastful, or showy talk or writing: *They strolled under the Maples, and he talked what is technically known as Hot Air* (George Ade).

hot·bed (hot′bed′), *n.* **1** a bed of earth covered with glass and kept warm for growing plants. Fermenting manure is often used to provide the heat. **2** *Figurative.* a place or atmosphere that favors the rapid growth or development of any condition, especially something evil: *Dirty, crowded cities are hotbeds of disease and crime. The German army, furthermore, was never a particular hotbed of Nazism* (Atlantic).

hot-blast drying (hot′blast′), a method of drying vegetables by forcing hot air over them.

hot-blood·ed (hot′blud′id), *adj.* **1** easily excited or angered. **SYN:** ardent, excitable. **2** rash; reckless: *hot-blooded youth.* **SYN:** impetuous. **3** passionate. **4** *U.S.* (of horses) containing blood of the thoroughbred breed. **—hot′-blood′ed·ness,** *n.*

hot·box (hot′boks′), *n.* an overheated bearing on a shaft or axle, especially in the journal box of a railroad car, caused by friction: *It seemed as if the train would never reach Baltimore . . . A hotbox had to be cooled at Wilmington* (Mark Twain). [American English < *hot* + (journal) *box*]

hot-brained (hot′brānd′), *adj.* = hot-headed.

hot button, a matter of immediate interest or concern: *Graphics and bright colors highlight stories on baby-boomer "hot buttons," such as the environment, divorce, personal finance, etc.* (Wall Street Journal).

hot cake, a pancake or griddlecake.
sell (or **go**) **like hot cakes,** to sell well; sell rapidly; be much in demand: *Here he sells lampshades, which he runs up himself in his spare time, and they are going like hot cakes* (Punch).

hot cargo, 1 the freight or other shipments of a company having a labor-management disagreement. **2** having a clause in a labor contract permitting a union to refuse to handle goods or cross picket lines of a company the union has labeled unfair to labor.

hotch (hoch), *v.t., v.i. Scottish.* to jog; fidget; hitch. [origin uncertain. Compare Dutch *hotsen* to jog, jolt.]

hotch·pot (hoch′pot′), *n.* **1** *Law.* the uniting in a common lot of properties for the purpose of dividing them equally, as in distributing the estate of an intestate parent. **2** = hotchpotch (def 2). [< Anglo-French *hochepot* < Old French *hocher* shake + *pot* pot]

hotch·potch (hoch′poch′), *n.* **1** = hodgepodge. **2** a dish containing a mixture of many ingredients, especially a mutton broth thickened with young vegetables of all sorts stewed together. **3** *Law* = hotchpot. [variant of *hotchpot.* Compare etym. under **hodgepodge.**]

hot corner, *Baseball Slang.* third base.

hot cross bun, a special bun marked with a cross, usually eaten during Lent.

hot dish, anything to eat served hot, especially as a main course to a meal.

hot dog, 1 *Informal.* **a** = frankfurter. **b** a sandwich made of a hot frankfurter enclosed in a roll or bun and often served with mustard or relish. **2** *Slang.* an exclamation of pleasure, admiration, or enthusiasm: *Hot dog! We won!* **3** *Slang.* **a** a very skillful athlete or sportsman, especially one able to perform stunts, such as an expert surfer. **b** a show-off in sports.

hot-dog (hot′dôg′, -dog′), *v.i.,* **-dogged, -dog·ging.** *Slang.* (of an athlete, especially a skier or surfboarder) to perform acrobatics or stunts.

hot dogger, *Slang.* = hot dog (def. 3).

ho·tel (hō tel′), *n.* **1** a house or large building that supplies rooms and food for pay to travelers and others; inn: *The great advantage of a hotel is that it's a refuge from home life* (George Bernard Shaw). **2** in French use: **a** a large private residence; town mansion. **b** a public official residence.
[< French *hôtel* < Old French *hostel* < Medieval Latin *hospitale* inn. See etym. of doublets **hospital, hostel, spital.**]

Ho·tel (hō tel′), *n. U.S.* a code name for the letter *h,* used in transmitting radio messages.

hô·tel de ville (ō tel′ də vēl′), *French.* a city hall; town hall.

hô·tel Dieu (ō tel dyœ′), *French.* the hospital of a French town.

hô·te·lier (ō tə lyā′), *n. French.* hotelier.

ho·tel·ier (hō′tə lir′), *n.* a hotelkeeper or hotelman. [< French *hôtelier*]

ho·tel·keep·er (hō tel′kē′pər), *n.* a person who manages, and often owns, a hotel.

ho·tel·man (hō tel′man′, -mən), *n., pl.* **-men.** *U.S.* a person who owns or manages a hotel or chain of hotels.

hot-eyed (hot′īd′), *adj.* fervent; ardent; intense: *hot-eyed fervor, a hot-eyed fanatic.*

hot flash, a sudden, temporary sensation of heat spreading over the body, felt especially by women undergoing menopause.

hot·foot (hot′fu̇t′), *v., adv., n., pl.* **-foots.** *Informal.* *—v.i.* Also, **hotfoot it.** to go in great haste; hurry: *Seven elephants had been secured, and the other seven were hotfooting through the hills* (Maclean's).
—adv. in great haste: *The Prime Minister had come to the House of Commons hotfoot from his meeting* (Manchester Guardian).
—n. **1** a prank in which a match is inserted in the welt of an unsuspecting person's shoe and then lighted. **2** *Figurative.* a mental jolt; an awakening: *He has tickled his reader's funny bone while slipping him a cultural hotfoot* (Time).

hot-gos·pel (hot′gos′pəl), *v.t., v.i.,* **-peled, -pel·ing.** to evangelize by stirring up religious feeling; preach or gospelize in the manner of a revivalist: *hot-gospeling his message of personal martyrdom* (Canada Month). **—hot′gos′pel·er,** *n.*

Hoth (hoth), *n. Norse Mythology.* the blind son of Odin who unwittingly killed his brother Balder with a mistletoe dart given to him by Loki.

hot·head (hot′hed′), *n.* a hot-headed person: *Rebel students and their leaders were no left-wing hotheads preparing the great anti-France revolution* (Atlantic).

hot-head·ed or **hot·head·ed** (hot′hed′id), *adj.* **1** having a fiery temper; easily angered: *We're both a little hot-headed, I guess, and do things we're sorry for* (Winston Churchill). **SYN:** hot-tempered. **2** impetuous; headstrong; rash. **SYN:** reckless, precipitate. **—hot′-head′ed·ly, hot′head′ed·ly,** *adv.* **—hot′-head′ed·ness, hot′head′ed·ness,** *n.*

hot·house (*n., adj.* hot′hous′; *v.* -houz′), *n.,* **-hous·es** (-hou′ziz), *adj., v.,* **-housed, -hous·ing.** *—n.* **1** a building with a glass roof and walls, kept warm for growing plants, especially plants belonging naturally to warmer climates; greenhouse. **SYN:** conservatory. **2** *Figurative.* a place or atmosphere favoring rapid growth or development; hotbed: *a hothouse of culture.* **3** *Obsolete.* a bathing house with hot baths, steam baths, etc.
—adj. **1** from or of a hothouse: *hothouse flowers.* **2** *Figurative.* characteristic of a hothouse: *a hothouse climate.*
—v.t. Education. to begin teaching (children) at a very early age in order to stimulate or advance their mental development: *As the debate over the "superbaby" phenomenon intensifies, researchers have coined a verb form to describe it: "hothousing"* (New York Times).

hothouse effect, = greenhouse effect.

hothouse lamb, *U.S.* a lamb born during autumn or winter and raised indoors.

hot issue, *U.S.* a glamour stock or other speculative stock that rises rapidly in price after the initial public offering.

hot laboratory or **lab,** a laboratory exposed to radiations of more than one curie.

hot lick, *Slang.* a special flourish or improvisation in jazz, generally upon a trumpet or clarinet.

hot line, 1 a direct telephone or teletype line providing instantaneous communication in a crisis or emergency: *Since the hot-line link between Washington and Moscow was first put into operation on Aug. 30, 1963 it had conveyed nothing more dramatic than New Year's greetings and hourly testing messages* (Time). **2** *U.S. and Canada.* a radio or television program which broadcasts conversations with people who telephone the studio with questions or problems. [originally (early 1950's) a U.S. Air Force term for a direct telephone circuit between distant bases]

hot money, 1 short-term capital moved from one investment to another, usually in a different country to obtain quick profits from high interest rates: *There has been no sudden surge of hot money from France into the mortgage market, for the French government is keeping a stern eye on bank balances* (Economist). **2** *Slang.* stolen money.

hot moon·er (mü′nər), a scientist who believes there is thermal or volcanic activity in the moon's core and that this activity, rather than the impact of meteorites, produced the lunar craters.

hot pack, a heavy towel, blanket, or the like, dipped in hot water, wrung out, and put on some part of the body.

hot-pack (hot′pak′), *v.t.* to can (vegetables, meats, or preserves) by hot packing.

hot packing, a method of canning in which vegetables, meats, or preserves are first heated to the boiling point, and then processed in boiling water or a pressure cooker to insure sterilization.

hot pants, very short, close-fitting pants worn by women and girls.

hot pepper, any one of several very pungent green or red peppers, often elongated and having thin walls, used as a spice.

hot plate, **1** a small, portable electric stove with one or two burners, for heating or cooking food or beverages. **2** a plate with a cover for keeping food hot. **3** a heated flat surface on a stove for cooking or keeping dishes or food warm. **4** a plate of hot food.

hot pot, a stew of mutton or beef, potatoes and other vegetables, cooked in a covered pot.

hot potato, *Slang.* something difficult to handle; something too complicated or controversial to deal with: *Such a diplomatic hot potato was the 900 page FTC report that President Truman ordered it impounded* (Newsweek).

hot|press (hot′pres′), *n., v.* **—*n.*** a machine in which heat and pressure are applied together, as in giving paper or cloth a smooth, glossy surface.
—*v.t.* to subject to pressure in a hotpress. **—hot′press′er**, *n.*

hot pursuit, following closely, usually with speed or intensity and often disregarding the consequences or jurisdictional boundaries.

hot rod, *U.S. Slang.* **1a** an automobile with a rebuilt motor for faster starts and higher speeds. **b** a car specially rebuilt to meet certain racing standards. **2** = hot-rodder. **—hot′-rod′**, *adj.*

hot-rod|der (hot′rod′ər), *n. U.S. Slang.* **1** a driver of a hot rod. **2** a reckless driver or pilot. **3a** a speed racer. **b** a member of an organization that promotes the racing of hot rods.

hot-rod|ding (hot′rod′ing), *n. Slang.* **1** hot-rod driving or racing. **2** reckless driving.

hot-roll (hot′rōl′), *v.t.* to roll (metal or metal parts) by applying heat: *to hot-roll steel.*

hot room, a room heated to a high temperature, especially for inducing sweating, as in a bathing establishment.

hot seat, **1** *Informal.* an uncomfortable situation or position; an unpleasant or difficult duty, office, or the like: *If something is wrong, then I'll sit on the hot seat and take the responsibility* (Wall Street Journal). **2** *U.S. Slang.* the electric chair.

hot-short (hot′shôrt′), *adj.* (of iron) brittle at a forging temperature.

hot-shot or **hot|shot** (hot′shot′), *n., adj. U.S. Slang.* **—*n.*** **1** a person having more than ordinary skill at something and often showing some conceit: *making one-day stands in small towns against local hot-shots* (Time). **2** a person expert at something; highly skilled person. **3** *Railroading.* a fast freight train.
—*adj.* **1** expert; skillful: *a gathering place for the topnotch hot-shot musicians* (New Yorker). **2** flashy; showy: *a hot-shot salesman.* **3** fast; express: *a hotshot freight train.*

hot spot, **1** *Informal.* a troublesome locality; a dangerous place: *Uneasy peace settled over Central America's hot spots* (Wall Street Journal). **2** *U.S. Slang.* **a** a place offering entertainment, dancing, food, and alcoholic beverages, such as a night club or cafe patronized by celebrities: *Downtown, once a noisy New York hot spot, was closed for nonpayment of taxes* (Newsweek). **b** a place offering cheap entertainment and illegal activities, as a gambling house or speakeasy. **c** the general areas in which these establishments are located. **3** *Geology.* a source of extreme heat lying deep in the lower crust or upper mantle of the earth: *Hot spots are associated with chains of volcanic activity.*

hot spring, a natural spring from which heated water issues; thermal spring: *The hot springs and geysers of Yellowstone National Park produce enough heat to melt three tons of ice every second* (Edmund B. Rogers).

hot|spur (hot′spėr′), *n.* an impetuous or reckless person. **SYN:** madcap. [< *Hotspur,* the nickname of Sir Henry Percy, who fell in the rebellion against Henry IV, in 1403]

hot stuff, *Slang.* a person or thing of exceptional quality.

hot|sy-tot|sy (hot′sē tot′sē), *adj. Slang.* perfect; hunky-dory: *Prosperity might now really be around the corner, it would all turn out hotsy-totsy* (James T. Farrell). [American English; apparently coined in the 1920's by Billie De Beck, an American cartoonist]

hot-tem|pered (hot′tem′pərd), *adj.* having a quick temper; easily angered: *Hot-tempered students and war veterans ordered a general protest strike* (Time).

Hot|ten|tot (hot′ən tot), *n., adj.* **—*n.*** **1** a member of a people who live mainly in southwestern Africa, having a pale reddish-yellow complexion. The Hottentots are related to the Bushmen. **2** their language, related to Bushman. **3** a small, black-backed, flat South African fish found around the Cape of Good Hope Peninsula.
—*adj.* of the Hottentots or their language.
[< Afrikaans *Hottentot,* Dutch, (originally) one who stammers; perhaps imitative of their clicking sounds in speech]

hot|tish (hot′ish), *adj.* somewhat hot: *Another hottish subject—the brain drain—was debated in the House of Commons* (Manchester Guardian).

hot tray, an electrical tray to keep foods hot.

hot tub, a large tub or vat of hot water, for bathing as recreation or physical therapy, often in a group.

hot war, a war involving actual fighting.

hot water, *Informal.* a scrape; trouble; difficulty: *His lies got him into hot water.*

hot-wa|ter bottle (hot′wô′tər, -wot′ər), a container for holding hot water, usually made of rubber. It is used in the treatment of certain ailments, chiefly to relieve pain.

hot water pollution, = thermal pollution.

hot-wire (hot′wīr′), *v.t.* **-wired, -wir|ing.** *Slang.* to start the motor of (an automobile, airplane, etc.) by short-circuiting the ignition switch: *16-year-olds hustle pool-players for money, hot-wire cars, get shot at, flunk chemistry exams* (London Sunday Times).

hou|dah (hou′də), *n.* = howdah.

Hou|dan (hü′dan), *n.* any one of a French breed of chicken characterized by a large crest, a full, well-developed beard, five toes, and white skin. The two varieties are mottled and white.
[< French *Houdan* (originally) a town in France, where the breed was developed]

Hou|di|ni (hü dē′nē), *n.* a magician: *Haley, the fiscal Houdini, who arrived at the B.B.C. in 1943, quickly put it back on its feet* (New Yorker).
[< Harry *Houdini,* 1874-1926, American magician]

hough (hok), *n., v.t.* = hock[1].

***hound[1]**
definition 1

several kinds of hounds:

hound[1]** (hound), *n., v.* **—*n. **1** a dog of any one of certain breeds which hunt by scent or sight and have large, drooping ears and short hair. Many hounds are named for the game they were originally trained to hunt, such as the deerhound, foxhound, staghound, and wolfhound. **2** any dog (a humorous or contemptuous use). **3** a contemptible person: *Take that, you hound, and that! and that! and that!* (Sir Arthur Conan Doyle). **4** one of the pursuers in the game of hare and hounds. **5** *Slang.* a person who is very fond of something: *a bridge hound, a candy hound.*
—*v.t.* **1** to hunt or chase with hounds or as a hound does. **2** *Figurative.* to keep on chasing or driving: *The police hounded the thief until they caught him.* **3** *Figurative.* to urge on; incite: *The lazy boy's parents hounded him to do his homework. In addition, the retired scientist is hounded to take chairmanships of various government and civic committee activities* (Science News Letter).
ride to (or **follow the**) **hounds**, to go hunting on horseback with a pack of hounds: *He would like to have a good-looking wife . . . to go riding to hounds with him* (William A. Black).
[Old English *hund*] **—hound′er**, *n.*

hound[2] (hound), *n.* one of two or more wooden bars in a wagon, carriage, or the like, that serve as supports or connections to the fifth wheel, and to bear the force of the pull.
hounds, projections or shoulders on a masthead which support the trestletrees and thereby support the upper rigging: *The ice . . . in the tops and round the hounds of the lower masts* (Richard Henry Dana).
[Middle English *hune,* apparently < Scandinavian (compare Old Icelandic *hūnn* knob)]

hound dog, *Southern U.S.* a hound.

hound|fish (hound′fish′), *n., pl.* **-fish|es** or (*collectively*) **-fish.** any one of various fishes, such as certain small sharks and certain large voracious fishes.

hound's-tongue (houndz′tung′), *n.* a weed of the borage family, having prickly nutlets, tongue-shaped leaves, and dark-red flowers; dog's-tongue.
[Old English *hundes tunge,* translation of Latin *cynoglōssos* < Greek *kynóglōsson* dog's tongue < *kýōn, kynós* dog + *glōssa* tongue]

***hound's-tooth** or **hounds|tooth** (houndz′tüth′), *adj.* having a broken check pattern: *About these go wrap-around skirts of tennis length, in a giant hound's-tooth tweed* (New Yorker).

***hound's-tooth**

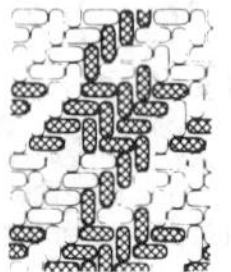

hour (our), *n.* **1** one of the 12 equal periods of time between noon and midnight, or between midnight and noon. 60 minutes make an hour. 24 hours make a day. *Abbr:* hr. **2** one of the 12 points that measure time from midnight to noon and from noon to midnight: *Trains leave every hour on the hour.* **3** the time of day: *Some clocks strike the hours and the half-hours. What is the hour?* **4** the time of anything: *Our breakfast hour is at seven o'clock. Mine hour is not yet come* (John 2:4). **5** a short or limited space of time: *After his hour of glory, he was soon forgotten.* **6** the distance which can be traveled in an hour: *The concert hall is only an hour away.* **7** in schools and colleges: **a** the period for which a class meets, often less than a full hour: *What hour does your German class meet?* **b** a unit of credit, usually received for satisfactory work and attendance at one period per week of a particular course: *The football hero received only seven hours' credit for the semester.* **8** the present time: *The hour calls for immediate action.* **9** *Astronomy, Geography.* 15 degrees of right ascension of longitude.
hours, a a time for work or study: *What are the hours in this office? Our school hours are 9 to 12 and 1 to 4.* **b** the usual time for getting up and going to bed: *regular hours, early hours, late hours.* **c** seven special times of the day set aside for prayer and worship in religious orders: *During each of the hours, candles were lighted in the chapel.* **d** the prayers and services for these times: *A nun saying her hours . . .* (Sabine Baring-Gould). See also **canonical hours.**
in an evil (or **ill**) **hour**, at a bad or unlucky time; unhappily; unfortunately: *In an ill hour . . . I went on board a ship bound for London* (Daniel Defoe).
of the hour, of the present hour; of the very time that is now with us: *the question of the hour, the man of the hour.*
[< Old French *hore, ure* < Latin *hōra* < Greek *hṓra* hour, time, season]
►In consecutive writing, especially if it is formal, **hours** are written in words: *four o'clock:* In much informal writing, figures are used, especially if they occur several times or if several figures are used close together: *at 4 p.m., just after 9 a.m., from 10 to 12.*

hour|age (our′ij), *n.* time spent, measured in hours.

hour angle, *Astronomy.* the angular distance or arc of the celestial equator between the meridian and the hour circle of a heavenly body, measured westward, used in determining solar time or, sometimes, in designating the position of a celestial body.

hour circle, *Astronomy.* any great circle on the celestial sphere which passes through its poles, equivalent in the celestial system of coordination to a meridian of the earth, and, like it, used in measuring longitude.

***hour|glass** (our′glas′, -gläs′), *n., adj.* —*n.* **1** a device for measuring time. It takes just an hour for its contents (sand or mercury) to go from a glass bulb on top through a narrow opening into one on the bottom. **2** any similar sand glass, though the time taken for sifting may not necessarily be one hour.
—*adj.* shaped like an hourglass, with a very narrow central section swelling outward at each end: *Handsomely sheathed in a low-cut hourglass gown* ... (Time).

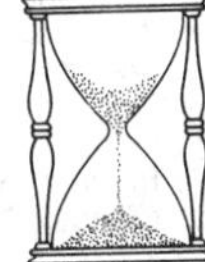

***hourglass**
definition 1

hour hand, the hand on a clock or watch which indicates the hours. It moves around the whole dial once in twelve hours.

hou|ri (hu̇r′ē, hou′rē), *n., pl.* **-ris**. one of the young, eternally beautiful girls of the Mohammedan paradise. [< French *houri* < Persian *ḥūrī* < Arabic *ḥūr,* plural of *ḥawrā,* feminine of *'ahwar* bright-eyed]

hour|long (our′lông′, -long′), *adj.* lasting an hour: *an hourlong conference.*

hour|ly (our′lē), *adj., adv.* —*adj.* **1** done, happening, or counted every hour: *to give hourly doses of medicine. hourly weather reports on the radio.* **2** coming very often; frequent: *hourly messages.* **3** paid by the hour: *an hourly employee.*
—*adv.* **1** every hour; hour by hour: *Give two doses of medicine hourly.* **2** very often; frequently: *Messages were coming from the front hourly.*

hours (ourz), *n.pl.* See under **hour**.

Hours (ourz), *n.pl. Greek and Roman Mythology.* = Horae.

house¹ (*n.* hous; *v.* houz), *n., pl.* **hous|es** (hou′ziz), *v.,* **housed, hous|ing.** —*n.* **1** a building in which people live, especially a building that is the ordinary dwelling place of a family: *Our house has six rooms and is next door to the drugstore.* **2** the place in which an animal lives or into which it retires, such as the nest of a bird or the den of a bear: *The snail ... Carrying his own house* (John Donne). **3** the people living in a house; household: *Bid her hasten all the house to bed* (Shakespeare). **4** Often, **House.** a family with its ancestors, descendants, and kindred, especially a noble or royal family: *the house of Hanover. He was a prince of the house of David.* **5** a building for any purpose: *an engine house, a house of worship.* **6** *Figurative.* a place of abode, rest, deposit, or the like: *the peaceful house of death* (Scott). **7** a place of business or a business firm or establishment: *a publishing house.* **8** Often, **House. a** an assembly for making laws and considering questions of government; lawmaking body; legislature. In the United States, the House of Representatives is the lower house of Congress; the Senate is the upper house. **b** the building or room in which such an assembly meets. **c** a quorum of such an assembly: *to make a house.* **9** a place of entertainment; theater: *The house was jammed for the first night's performance.* **10** the audience or attendance at a theater: *The singer sang to a large house. We had a good house.* **11** a residence hall in a school or the students living in it. **12** *Especially British.* a college in a university or its students. **13** the residence of a religious order. **14** a religious order. **15** any one of various ecclesiastical or collegiate deliberative assemblies. **16** *Astrology.* **a** a twelfth part of the heavens as divided by great circles through the north and south points of the horizon. **b** a sign of the zodiac considered as the seat of the greatest influence of a particular planet. **17** the target in curling. It is three circles, the outer or largest having a six-foot radius. The tee is in the center of the smallest circle.
—*v.t.* **1** to take or put into a house; provide with a house; shelter: *Where can we house all these children? A big influx of workers is expected and they will have to be housed, educated, protected* (Newsweek). **2** to keep or store in a house or building: *The campers housed their surplus provisions in a makeshift shed.* **3** *Figurative.* to give shelter to; harbor; lodge: *caves that house the cold-crowned snake* (Tennyson). **4** *Nautical.* to place in a secure or protected position, especially to lower a topmast and secure it to the fore part of the lower mast, with its gear: *A large ship with her top-gallant-masts housed* (Richard Henry Dana). **5** *Carpentry.* to fix in a socket, mortise, or other space cut out.
—*v.i.* to dwell or take shelter: *He wends unfollow'd, he must house alone* (Matthew Arnold).
bring down the house, *Informal.* to be loudly applauded: *One can see that this programme might deservedly have brought down the house in a college hall, but it is not well enough organised to justify transplantation* (Punch).
clean house, a to clean a house or apartment and its furnishings: *She cleaned house in the early morning.* **b** *Figurative.* to get rid of bad conditions in an institution, organization, or business, by putting it in order and freeing it of undesirable persons or practices: *By dismissing the two culprits, the manager felt he had cleaned house completely.*
keep house, to manage a home and its affairs; do housework: *In this the children play'd at keeping house* (Tennyson).
on the house, paid for by the owner of the business; free: *What d'ya mean treat them? You mean on the house?* (New Yorker).
put (or **set**) **one's house in order**, to arrange one's affairs in good order: *The Prussians, after the disaster of Jena in 1807, had set to work to put their house in order* (H. G. Wells).
the House, a the House of Representatives. **b** the House of Commons. **c** the House of Lords.
[Old English *hūs*] —**house′like′**, *adj.*
▶ See usage note under **home**.

house² (*n.* hous; *v.* houz), *n., v.,* **housed, hous|ing.** *Archaic.* —*n.* = housing².
—*v.t.* to equip (a horse, etc.) with a housing².
[< Old French *houce* < Medieval Latin *hucia;* origin uncertain]

house agent, *Especially British.* a real-estate agent.

house arrest, a form of arrest in which a person is confined under guard in his own house: *Authorities insisted no one had been jailed but said some strikers were under house arrest* (Tuscaloosa News).

house|boat (hous′bōt′), *n.* a boat that can be used as a place to live in, especially one having a flat bottom and a houselike structure built on the deck.

house|bod|y (hous′bod′ē), *n., pl.* **-bod|ies.** *U.S.* = homebody.

house|bound (hous′bound′), *adj.* confined to one's house, especially by illness or a physical handicap; shut-in: *The suitor's mother is not housebound by palsy, as his family pretends, but is insane* (New Yorker).

house|boy (hous′boi′), *n.* a boy or man employed as a servant in a house, usually a native of Asia or Africa.

house|break (hous′brāk′), *v.t.,* **-broke, -bro|ken, -break|ing.** to train (a dog, cat, or other pet) where to urinate and defecate and thus to live indoors; make housebroken: *If you have to have a pig, by all means have a pig, but you're not going to housebreak it* (New York Times).

house|break|er (hous′brā′kər), *n.* a person who breaks into a house to steal or commit some other crime.

house|break|ing (hous′brā′king), *n.* the act of breaking into a house to steal or commit some other crime.

house|bro|ken (hous′brō′kən), *adj.* **1** (of a dog, cat, or other pet) trained to have clean habits for living indoors. **2** *Figurative.* socially acceptable; tame: *The housebroken, whitewashed tunes she sang were designed to tweak the white conscience ever so slightly* (Atlantic).

house|build|er (hous′bil′dər), *n.* a person whose business is the building of houses.

house|build|ing (hous′bil′ding), *n.* the business or occupation of building houses.

house call, **1** a visit by a doctor, nurse, or therapist to the home of a patient to make an examination or administer treatment. **2** a visit by a repairman or salesperson to the house of a customer.

house|carl (hous′kärl′), *n.* a member of the bodyguard or household troops of a Danish or early English king or noble. [Old English *hūscarl* < Scandinavian (compare Old Icelandic *hūskarl* manservant < *hūs* house + *karl* man, carl)]

house|clean (hous′klēn′), *v.i.* to do a housecleaning: *When we all pitch in we can houseclean in about an hour* (Maclean's). —*v.t.* to subject to a housecleaning: *I ... tucked it in my flat middle desk drawer, the one that never gets housecleaned* (Harper's). [back formation < *housecleaning*]

house|clean|er (hous′klē′nər), *n.* a person whose work is cleaning houses or apartments.

house|clean|ing (hous′klē′ning), *n.* **1** the cleaning of a house and its furnishings: *The only fault she had to find with Mrs. Hearn was that she didn't do any spring housecleaning* (New Yorker). **2** *Figurative.* the act or process of getting rid of bad conditions: *Many observers believed that there would be a great housecleaning in the Army* (New York Times).

house|coat (hous′kōt′), *n.* **1** a loose, flowing garment, originally long but now of any length, worn indoors by women and girls instead of a dress. **2** a bathrobe or dressing gown.

house cricket, a European cricket that frequents houses, especially in the neighborhood of fireplaces.

house detective, a detective employed by a hotel, store, or other business establishment to keep out thieves, loiterers, and the like.

house|dress (hous′dres′), *n.* a dress, usually of an inexpensive cotton fabric, worn by women, especially for housework.

house|fa|ther (hous′fä′ᴛʜər), *n.* **1** the father of a household or family. **2** the male head of a community or number of persons living together as a family. **3** a man who supervises a group, such as a group of children in a private institution, living together like a family.

house finch, a brownish, streaked finch of Mexico and the western United States, with red cheeks, throat, and rump in the male. It is especially common about houses.

house flag, a flag flown by a merchant ship which identifies the company that owns or operates the ship.

house|fly (hous′flī′), *n., pl.* **-flies.** a common two-winged fly that lives around and in houses in all parts of the world, feeding on food, garbage, and filth. Houseflies carry disease germs. Housefly larvae or maggots develop in decaying organic matter.

house|front (hous′frunt′), *n.* the front or facade of a house.

house|ful (hous′fu̇l), *n., pl.* **-fuls.** as much or as many as a house will hold: [*Her*] *best-seller was a plotless package of anecdotes about her parental ordeal in raising a houseful of Lovable Brats* (Maclean's).

house girl, = housemaid.

house|guest (hous′gest′), *n.* a guest who stays at one's house overnight or longer: *They had no trouble getting ... invitations to be houseguests for the night* (New York Times).

house|hold (hous′hōld), *n., adj.* —*n.* **1** all the people living in a house; family; family and servants; domestic establishment: *Persons living in institutions, hotels, and large rooming houses are not counted as households* (Wall Street Journal). **2** a home and its affairs: *The orphan had little trouble making a place for himself in the friendly household.* **3** a royal or imperial household: *He had two good places, one in the Treasury, the other in the household* (Macaulay).
—*adj.* **1** of a household; having to do with a household; domestic: *household expenses, household cares.* **2** *Figurative.* familiar or common; intimate; homely: *good, plain household judgment* (Laurence Sterne). *His enterprise and spirit caught the popular imagination and for years he was something of a household name* (London Times).

household arts, the teaching or study of the management of a household and family life.

house|hold|er (hous′hōl′dər), *n.* **1** a person who owns or lives in a house. **2** the head of a family.

household god, **1** one of the lares and penates of the ancient Romans. **2** any person or thing greatly cherished or revered in a home or household: *The Motor God is a household god that has to be washed and polished and propitiated with accessories* (Anthony W. Benn).

house|hold|ing (hous′hōl′ding), *adj., n.* —*adj.* **1** that occupies a house. **2** that manages a house.
—*n. Obsolete.* **1** the management of a household; housekeeping. **2** the occupation of a house.

household troops, troops assigned to guard or otherwise serve a royal household.

household word, a very familiar word or phrase: *William A. Shea ... is celebrated mostly for the stadium which bears his name and which the Mets and Jets have made a household word* (New York Times).

house|hus|band (hous′huz′bənd), *n.* a married man who manages a household (correlative of *housewife*): *I Am a Househusband But Call Me Mister* (Redbook).

house|keep (hous′kēp′), *v.i.,* **-kept, -keep|ing.** to

Pronunciation Key: hat, **ā**ge, c**ã**re, f**ä**r; let, **ē**qual, t**ė**rm; it, **ī**ce; hot, **ō**pen, **ô**rder; **oi**l, **ou**t; cup, p**u̇**t, r**ü**le; **ch**ild; lo**ng**; **th**in; **ᴛʜ**en; **zh**, measure; **ə** represents **a** in about, **e** in taken, **i** in pencil, **o** in lemon, **u** in circus.

manage a home and its affairs; keep house: *She housekeeps in London for a visiting American playwright* (Manchester Guardian Weekly). [back formation < *housekeeper*]

house|keep|er (hous′kē′pər), *n.* **1** a woman who manages a home and its affairs and does the housework: *"And I'm going to have a home for the boys," he added. "I'll find a housekeeper."* (Newsweek). **2** a woman who directs the servants that do the housework in a home, hotel, hospital, school, or other institution.

house|keep|ing (hous′kē′ping), *n.* **1** management of a home and its affairs; doing the housework. **2** a directing of the servants that do the housework. **3** management of a business or other concern.

hou|sel (hou′zəl), *n., v.,* **-seled, -sel|ing** or (*especially British*) **-selled, -sel|ling.** *Archaic.* —*n.* **1** the Eucharist. **2** the administration or reception of the Eucharist.
—*v.t.* to administer the Eucharist to. [Old English *hūsel* a sacrifice, offering, consecrated thing]

house|leek (hous′lēk′), *n.* **1** a plant of the same family as the sedum, with thick, juicy stems and leaves, and pink flowers; hen-and-chickens. It commonly grows on the walls and roofs of houses. **2** any other plant of the same genus as the houseleek.

house|less (hous′lis), *adj.* **1** without a house or shelter; homeless. **2** (of a place) destitute of houses: *the houseless ocean's heaving field* (Tennyson). —**house′less|ness,** *n.*

house|lights (hous′līts′), *n.pl.* the lights used to illuminate a theater before and after a performance: *The houselights dimmed on opening night* (New York Times).

house|line (hous′līn′), *n. Nautical.* a small line, especially for seizings, made of three strands woven left-handed.

house magazine, = house organ.

house|maid (hous′mād′), *n.* a woman servant who does housework.

house|maid|ing (hous′mā′ding), *n.* the work or occupation of a housemaid.

housemaid's knee, *Informal.* an inflammation on the kneecap or near the knee, usually caused by kneeling; bursitis of the knee.

house|man (hous′mən), *n., pl.* **-men.** a manservant employed to do general work about a house, hotel, or sometimes, other institutional buildings.

house martin, 1 the common European martin, or swallow. **2** = purple martin.

house|mas|ter (hous′mas′tər, -mäs′-), *n.* a teacher supervising a residence hall in a school where students board.

house|mate (hous′māt′), *n.* a person who lives in the same house with another; fellow member of a household.

house|mis|tress (hous′mis′tris), *n.* **1** the mistress of a house. **2** a woman housemaster.

house|moth|er (hous′muᴛʜ′ər), *n.* a woman who supervises and takes care of a group of young people living together like a family, as in a college dormitory or fraternity.

house mouse, a small, destructive, grayish-brown mouse living about buildings throughout the world.

House of Assembly, 1 the lower house of the Republic of South Africa legislature. **2** Also, **house of assembly.** the legislature of some governments in the Commonwealth: *the Newfoundland House of Assembly.*

House of Burgesses, the lower house of the colonial legislature in Virginia or Maryland.

house of cards, anything that can be easily knocked down; a flimsy structure: *and the whole structure of her existence crumbled into nothingness like a house of cards* (Lytton Strachey).

House of Commons, the lower house of the Parliament of Great Britain and Northern Ireland, or of Canada, composed of elected representatives; the Commons. *Abbr:* H.C.

house of correction, a place of confinement and reform for persons convicted of minor offenses and not regarded as confirmed criminals.

House of Delegates, the lower house of the legislature in Maryland, Virginia, and West Virginia.

house of detention, 1 a special building for the temporary housing of persons detained to answer criminal charges or to appear as witnesses before a trial. **2** = detention home.

house of God, a place of worship; church; temple.

house of ill fame, = brothel.

House of Keys, the body of 24 representatives which constitutes the lower house of the legislature of the Isle of Man.

House of Lords, the upper house of the Parliament of Great Britain and Northern Ireland, composed of nobles and clergymen of high rank; the Lords. *Abbr.:* H. L.

House of Peers, the former upper house of the legislature (Diet) in Japan.

House of Representatives, 1 the lower house of Congress of the United States. **2** the lower house of the legislature of certain states in the United States. **3** the lower house of the Parliament of Australia, Japan, etc. **4** the Parliament of New Zealand. *Abbr:* H. R.

house of tolerance, a licensed brothel. [translation of French *maison de tolérance*]

house organ, a magazine or newspaper published by a business concern for circulation among its employees or patrons.

house painter, a person whose business is to paint and decorate houses.

house|par|ent (hous′pãr′ənt), *n.* a housemother or a housefather.

house party, 1 an entertainment of guests in a home or at a college for a few days. **2** the guests staying in a house.

house|per|son (hous′pėr′sən), *n,* a person who manages a household; housewife or househusband: *That evening, on TV, she looked a winner: her* sang froid *hairdo, and clarity of diction perfect, but her well-known persona of a chilly suburban houseperson infused with a new warmth, real or assumed* (New Statesman).

house physician, a resident physician of a hotel, hospital, or other public institution.

house plant, a plant in a pot or box, kept inside the house. Ferns are often used as house plants.

house-pride (hous′prīd′), *n.* the quality of being house-proud.

house-proud (hous′proud′), *adj.* taking pride in one's house and the way it is maintained.

house-rais|ing (hous′rā′zing), *n. U.S.* a gathering of neighbors in a rural region to help a person raise the frame of his house.

house|room (hous′rüm′, -rům′), *n.* room or space in a house; lodging.

house shoe, = slipper (def. 1).

house-sit (hous′sit′), *v.i. Especially U.S.* to live in and take care of a house while the regular occupants are away: *If you want to house-sit in a remote vacation home for a year or so, contact local real estate agents who may know of these homes* (Robert Coram). —**house′-sit′ter,** *n.*

house|smith (hous′smith′), *n.* a mechanic who works upon the ironwork or steelwork of houses or other buildings.

house snake, = milk snake.

house sparrow, = English sparrow.

house spider, a spider, commonly found in houses, that spins an irregular, loosely-woven web of dry silk with strands extending in many directions.

house surgeon, resident surgeon in a hospital.

house-to-house (hous′tə hous′), *adj.* going from one house, apartment, or building, to the next and so on: *Believing he was in the vicinity ... detectives surrounded the block and began a house-to-house check* (New York Times).

house|top (hous′top′), *n.* the top or roof of a house; roof.
from the housetops, publicly: *That is a question which not only needs to be asked, but needs to be answered ... and from the housetops* (Sunday Times).

house trailer, a trailer designed and furnished to serve as a dwelling.

house|train (hous′trān′), *v.t. Especially British.* housebreak.

house|wares (hous′wãrz′), *n.pl.* articles made and sold for use in the home, mainly in the kitchen or bathroom, such as can openers, pots and pans, or soap dishes.

house|warm|ing (hous′wôr′ming), *n.* a party given when a family moves into a house for the first time.

house|wife (hous′wīf′; huz′if *especially for n. 3*), *n., pl.* **-wives,** *v.,* **-wifed, -wif|ing.** —*n.* **1** a woman who manages a home and its affairs. A housewife plans the housework and usually does the buying for the family. *Housewives demonstrated against the sharply rising prices* (Newsweek). **2** a woman who is the head of a household. **3** Also, **hussy.** a small case for needles, thread, pins, scissors, and other sewing equipment. **4** *Obsolete.* a hussy (defs. 1,2).
—*v.i.* Also, **housewife it.** to manage a household with skill and thrift; economize: *With such a small income, she housewifed it well.*
—*v.t.* to manage as a good housewife does; manage with skill and thrift: *I must housewife the money* (Daniel Defoe).
[Middle English *huswif* < Old English *hūs* house + *wīf* wife. Compare etym. under **hussy.**]

house|wife|ly (house′wīf′lē), *adj., adv.* —*adj.* of or like a housewife; skillful and thrifty in the management of household affairs.
—*adv. Obsolete.* in a manner befitting a housewife. —**house′wife′li|ness,** *n.*

house|wif|er|y (hous′wī′fər ē, -wīf′rē), *n.* the work of a housewife; housekeeping.

house|wive (hous′wīv′), *v.i., v.t.,* **-wived, -wiving.** to housewife.

house|work (hous′wėrk′), *n.* the work to be done in housekeeping, such as washing, ironing, cleaning, and cooking.

house|work|er (hous′wėr′kər), *n.* a person who does housework.

house wrecker, a person whose business it is to demolish houses or other buildings.

house wren, a plain greyish-brown wren of eastern North America that nests in birdhouses, or almost any protected place; brown wren.

hous|ey-hous|ey (hou′sē hou′sē), *n. British.* bingo. [< *housey-housey!,* a cry to summon players to *house,* a slang term meaning "bingo"]

hous|ing[1] (hou′zing), *n.* **1** the act of sheltering; providing shelter: *The housing of some plants will allow keeping them through the winter.* **2** a putting or enclosing in a house. **3** a dwelling or lodging in a house. **4** houses or buildings collectively: *There is not enough housing in that city for the number of people living there.* **5** shelter; covering; lodging. **6** a frame, plate, or the like, to hold part of a machine in place. **7** *Carpentry.* the space, surface, or groove made in one piece of wood for the attachment of another. **8** *Nautical.* **a** the end of a bowsprit enclosed in the hull. **b** the part of a mast enclosed below the deck. **c** a roofing for a vessel laid up in dock. **9** *Obsolete.* a niche for a statue. [< *hous*(e)[1] + *-ing*[1]]

hous|ing[2] (hou′zing), *n.* **1** an ornamental covering on an animal's back, especially the back of a horse; caparison; trappings: *Under the saddle was a housing of red velvet.* **2** Also, **housings.** a covering, especially of cloth or the like. [< *hous*(e)[2] a covering + *-ing*[1]]

housing development, = housing project.

housing estate, *British.* = housing project.

housing project, a group of residential buildings, especially apartment buildings, built and run as a unit: *The six-block Manhattan housing project under study by the union is called Penn Station South* (Wall Street Journal).

hous|to|ni|a (hyüs tō′nē ə), *n.* any one of a group of North American herbs of the madder family, such as the common bluet or innocence, a small, delicate plant with bluish or white flowers. [American English < New Latin *Houstonia* the genus name < William *Houston,* about 1695-1733, an English botanist]

Hous|to|ni|an (hyüs tō′nē ən), *n.* a native or inhabitant of Houston, Texas.

Ho|va (hō′və), *n., pl.* **-va** or **-vas. 1** a member of one of the principal native peoples of Madagascar. **2** the language of this people.

hove (hōv), *v.* heaved; a past tense and past participle of **heave**: *The ship hove to in the lee of the island.*

hov|el (huv′əl, hov′-), *n., v.,* **-eled, -el|ing** or (*especially British*) **-elled, -el|ling** —*n.* **1** a house that is small, crude, and unpleasant to live in: *The poor old man lived in a hovel down by the railroad tracks.* **syn:** shanty. **2** an open shed for sheltering cattle, grain, tools, or machinery.
—*v.t.* to shelter as in a hovel or shed: *to hovel thee with swine* (Shakespeare).
[Middle English *hovel;* origin uncertain]

hov|er (huv′ər, hov′-), *v., n.* —*v.i.* **1** to stay in or near one place in the air; hang fluttering or suspended in air: *The helicopter hovered over the spot where the lost men had been seen.* **2** to stay in or near one place; wait nearby: *The dogs hovered around the kitchen door at mealtime.* (*Figurative.*) *Pestilence was hovering in the track of famine* (George Eliot). **syn:** linger. **3** *Figurative.* to be in an uncertain condition; waver: *The sick man hovered between life and death.*
—*v.t.* **1** to brood over; cover with wings and body: *a hen with more chickens than she can hover.* **2** to hang over or about: *The President would hover her typewriter ... demanding to know the reason for the delay* (New York Times).
—*n.* **1** an act of hovering. **2** the state of hovering.
[Middle English *hoveren* (frequentative) < *hoven* hover] —**hov′er|er,** *n.* —**hov′er|ing|ly,** *adv.*

★hovercraft

★hov|er|craft or **Hov|er|craft** (huv′ər kraft′, hov′-; -kräft′), *n., pl.* **-craft.** *Especially British.* a vehicle that travels a few feet above the surface of land or water on a cushion of air provided by jets or fans blowing downward.

hov|er|fer|ry (huv′ər fer′ē, hov′-), *n., pl.* **-ries.**

British. a hovercraft used as a ferry.

hover fly, = syrphus fly.

hov|er|pad (huv′ər pad′, hov′-), *n. British.* a metal plate forming the base of a hovercraft or hovertrain.

hov|er|port (huv′ər pôrt′, hov′-; -pōrt′), *n.* a port or terminal for hovercraft: *The new car ferry and hoverport at Dover will further enhance what is already, . . . the world's leading port for international passenger traffic by sea* (London Times).

hov|er|train (huv′ər trān′, hov′-), *n.* a train supported on an air cushion while running over a special concrete track.

how (hou), *adv., conj., n.* **—adv. 1** in what way or manner; by what means: *Tell her how to do it. How did it happen?* **2** to what degree or amount: *How tall are you? How much shall I bring you? How do you like the dress? How hot is it?* **3** at what rate or price: *How long will it take you to do this? How do you sell these apples?* **4** in what state or condition: *How is your health? How do I look?* **5** for what reason; why: *How is it you are late?* **6a** to what effect; with what meaning: *How do you mean?* **b** by what name: *How do you call yourself?* **7** *Obsolete.* how is it that; how comes it that; why: *"How," cried I, "is that all you are to have for your two shillings?"* (Oliver Goldsmith).
—conj. 1 in what way; by what means: *I don't know how I overlooked that detail. I wonder how you go there.* **2** to what degree, amount, or extent: *Please tell us how far it is to Atlanta.* **3** in what state or condition: *Let me know how she is.*
—n. the way or manner: *She considered all the hows and wherefores. Must we in all things look for the how, and the why, and the wherefore?* (Longfellow).
and how, *Informal.* certainly: *Do you like ice cream? And how!*
any old how, *Informal.* carelessly: *She did the job just any old how paying little attention.*
how about, *Informal.* what do you say to; would you consider: *How about coming over tonight?*
how come. See under **come.**
how far, how much; to what distance, point, or degree: *I have no idea how far they will carry their grievances.*
how now (or **then**), what does this mean? (often used interjectionally): *How now? My Duke's crown wrecked?* (Robert Browning).
how so, why is it so?: *How so sir, did she change her determination?* (Shakespeare).
[Old English *hū*]

How., Howard (United States Supreme Court Reports).

how|adj|i (hou aj′ē), *n., pl.* **-adj|is.** in the East: **1** a merchant. **2** a rich man. **3** a gentleman. **4** (in respectful address) sir. [< Arabic *khawāja*]

how|be|it (hou bē′it), *adv., conj.* **—adv.** *Archaic.* however it may be; nevertheless; however.
—conj. *Obsolete.* though; although. [< *how be it* how(ever) it may be]

***how|dah** (hou′də), *n.* a seat for persons riding on the back of an elephant or camel. It is usually fitted with a railing or canopy. . . . *gorgeous state processions of elephants bearing royalty in their howdahs* (London Times). Also, **houdah.** [< Hindustani *hawdah* < Arabic *haudaj* a litter]

***howdah**

how-de-do (hou′dē dü′), *n. Informal.* a troublesome situation: *Here's a pretty how-de-do* (William S. Gilbert). [spelling for variant pronunciation of *how do you do*]

how|die or **how|dy**[1] (hou′dē, hō′-), *n., pl.* **-dies.** *Scottish.* a midwife. [origin unknown]

how do you do, a form of greeting used by a person on being introduced to another.

how-do-you-do (hou′də yə dü′), *n. Informal.* a troublesome situation; how-de-do: *"Bill, isn't this a fine how-do-you-do on Christmas morning?" the father said accusingly* (James T. Farrell).

how|dy[2] (hou′dē), *interj., n., pl.* **-dies.** *Dialect.* how do you do.

howe (hou), *n. Scottish.* a hollow place or depression; basin; valley. [Middle English *holl,* Old English *hol*]

how|e'er (hou ãr′), *conj., adv.* = however.

how|ev|er (hou ev′ər), *conj., adv.* **—conj. 1** nevertheless; yet; in spite of all that: *It is his; however, you may borrow it. We were very late for dinner; however, there was plenty left for us.* SYN: See syn. under **but. 2** *Archaic.* however much; notwithstanding that; although.
—adv. 1 in whatever way; by whatever means: *However did you get so dirty? However you do it, the effect will be the same.* **2** to whatever extent or degree; no matter how: *I'll come, however busy I am.*

howff or **howf** (houf, hōf), *n., v. Scottish.* **—n.** a place of resort; haunt.
—v.i. to have one's haunt.
[apparently < *Howff,* a burial ground at Dundee, Scotland, and a meeting place for tradesmen]

how|itz|er (hou′it sər), *n.* a short cannon for firing shells in a high curve, capable of striking hidden targets. [earlier *howitz, hauwitzer* < Dutch *houwitser,* or German *Haubitze* < Czech *houfnice* catapult < *houf* heap]

howl (houl), *v., n.* **—v.i. 1** to give a long, loud, mournful cry: *Our dog often howls at night. The winter winds howled around our cabin.* **2** to give a long, loud cry of pain, scorn, or rage: *He still howls about the expense of printing* (Scott). **3** to yell or shout: *It was so funny that we howled with laughter.* **—v.t. 1** to force or drive by howling: *The angry crowd howled the speaker off the platform.* **2** to utter with howling.
—n. 1 a long, loud, mournful cry: *the howl of a wolf.* **2** a loud cry of pain or rage. **3** a yell of scorn or amusement. **4** a yell or shout: *We heard howls of laughter.*
howl down, to drown out the words of by howling: *When Winston Churchill finally attempted in the House of Commons to obtain a delay which would benefit the King's case, he was, in effect, howled down* (Atlantic).
[Middle English *houlen;* probably imitative]

howl|er (hou′lər), *n.* **1** a person or thing that howls. **2** an animal that howls. **3** = howling monkey. **4** *Informal.* a ridiculous mistake; stupid blunder. **5** *Dialect.* a person hired to wail at a funeral or the bedside of the dying. **6** *Surfing.* a large wave that only an expert surfer can ride; zipper.

howler monkey, = howling monkey.

howl|et (hou′lit), *n. Archaic.* an owl. [< Middle French *hulote*]

howl|ing (hou′ling), *adj., adv.* **—adj. 1** that howls. **2** characterized by howling. **3** dreary: *the waste howling wilderness* (Deuteronomy 32:10). **4** *Slang, Figurative.* very great: *a howling success.* **—adv.** in the highest degree.

howling monkey, any one of the large, arboreal, gregarious, prehensile-tailed monkeys of Central and South America the males of which make extraordinary, loud howling noises; howler.

how|so|ev|er (hou′sō ev′ər), *adv., conj.* **—adv. 1** to whatever extent, degree, or amount: *No man, howsoever strong of limb, Had dared across that swollen stream to go* (William Morris). **2** in whatever way; by whatever means.
—conj. nevertheless; yet; however.

how-to (hou′tü′), *adj. U.S. Informal.* explaining how to do something: *Do-it-yourself fad sparks boom in "how-to" magazines and books* (Wall Street Journal).

hoy[1] (hoi), *n.* a former type of small ship with fore-and-aft sails, used along a coast. [apparently < Middle Dutch *hoei;* origin unknown]

hoy[2] (hoi), *interj., n.* **—interj.** a cry used to call attention. **—n.** a call of "hoy!": *I see your young man . . . and I give him a Hoy!* (Dickens). [imitative]

hoy|a (hoi′ə), *n.* = waxplant. [New Latin *Hoya* the genus name < Thomas *Hoy,* an English gardener of the 1800's]

hoy|den (hoi′dən), *n., adj., v.* **—n. 1** a boisterous, romping girl; tomboy: *a fine, fresh hoyden just from boarding school* (Washington Irving). SYN: romp. **2** a rude or ill-bred girl or woman.
—adj. of the character of or resembling a hoyden; inelegant in behavior; roistering; hoydenish.
—v.i. to play the hoyden. Also, **hoiden.**
[earlier, rude clown, boor; origin uncertain]

hoy|den|ish (hoi′də nish), *adj.* of or like a hoyden; boisterous; romping. **—hoy′den|ish|ness,** *n.*

Hoyle (hoil), *n.* a book of rules (and often instructions) for games, especially card games.
according to Hoyle, a according to the rules (of whist) laid down by Edmond Hoyle: *They always played the game according to Hoyle.* **b** *Figurative.* according to the accepted rules or customs; in a fair or correct manner: *I was willing to take the word of the many technically competent persons involved that the grinding of the machinery by which these numbers obtained had been according to Hoyle* (Science).

hp. or **hp** (no period), **1** half pay. **2** high pressure. **3** horsepower.

h.p., **1** half pay. **2** high pressure. **3** hire-purchase. **4** horsepower.

H.P. or **HP** (no periods), an abbreviation for:
1 high power.
2 high pressure.
3 hire-purchase.
4 horsepower.
5 House of Parliament.

HQ (no periods), headquarters.

hr., hour or hours.

Hr., Herr.

H.R. or **HR** (no periods), an abbreviation for:
1 Home Rule.
2 home run.
3 House of Representatives.
4 House (of Representatives) bill (always with a number).

H.R.A., Human Resources Administration.

H-ras (āch′ras′), *n.* a human gene of the ras group: . . . *yeast cells contain two genes that are similar to a human cancer gene known as H-ras* (Maynard V. Olson). [< *H*(uman) + *ras*]

H-R diagram, = Hertzsprung-Russell diagram.

H. Rept., House (of Representatives) report (always with a number).

H. Res., House (of Representatives) resolution (always with a number).

H.R.H. or **HRH** (no periods), His (or Her) Royal Highness.

hrs., hours.

H.S., high school.

hsien (shyen), *n.* a district or county of a Chinese province: *Each hsien has been given the target of becoming self-sufficient in food and light industrial products* (New York Times). [< Chinese *hsien*]

H.S.S., Fellow of the Royal Historical Society.

HST (no periods), **1** Also, **H.S.T.** Hawaii Standard Time. **2** hypersonic transport.

H-sub|stance (āch′sub′stəns), *n.* any one of the substances causing allergic reactions as a result of the interaction of allergens and antibodies. Histamine is the chief H-substance causing allergy in man. [< *H*(istamine)]

ht., **1** heat. **2** height.

HT (no periods), high tension.

H.T., Hawaiian Territory (the former name of the state of Hawaii).

htee (tē), *n.* tee; an umbrella-shaped decoration atop a pagoda. [< Burmese *h'ti* umbrella]

HTGR (no periods), high temperature gas-cooled reactor.

HTLV-III or **HTLV-3** (no periods), the retrovirus that causes AIDS by invading and destroying the helper T cells of the body; HIV: *Unlike many viruses, which have only a few strains, HTLV-III comprises a great many variants that form a continuum of related strains* (Robert C. Gallo). [< *H*(uman) *T-l*(ymphotrophic) *v*(irus) (Type) *III*]

HTR (no periods), high temperature reactor (a nuclear power plant using steam generators in which steam reaches a temperature of 1000° F).

HUAC (no periods) or **H.U.A.C.,** House Un-American Activities Committee (former name of the Committee on Internal Security, a standing committee of the United States House of Representatives from 1945 to 1975, charged largely with investigating subversion and anti-American propaganda, and making recommendations to Congress and to executive agencies for action).

hua|ca (wä′kä, hwä′-), *n.* **1a** spirits supposed by the Peruvian Indians to be throughout the world. **b** any object supposed to be the dwelling place of such a spirit. **2** a prehistoric Peruvian tomb or temple, usually a pyramid of stone. [< Spanish *huaca, guaca* < Quechua]

hua|chi|nan|go (wä′chē näng′gō), *n.* a Mexican soup made from red snapper or other fish. [< Mexican Spanish *huachinango*]

hua|pan|go (wä päng′gō), *n., pl.* **-gos.** a very fast Mexican dance performed by couples. [< *Huapango,* a town in Veracruz, Mexico]

***hua|ra|ches** (hə rä′chiz; *Spanish* wä rä′chās), *n.pl.* heavy leather sandals with flat soles, common in Mexico. [American English < Mexican Spanish *huaraches*]

***huaraches**

hua|so (wä′sō), *n., pl.* **-sos.** a Chilean cowboy or farm hand. [< American Spanish *guaso, huaso* peasant < Quechua *huasu*]

hub (hub), *n.* **1** the central part of a wheel, which rotates on or with the axle: *The wagon tipped over as the axle slipped out of the hub of the wheel.* **2** *Figurative.* any center of interest, importance, or activity. *London is the hub of English life. Boston State-House is the hub of the solar system* (Oliver Wendell Holmes). SYN: pivot, heart, core. **3** = hob[1] (def. 2). **4** a cylindrical piece of steel on which the design for a coin is engraved in relief. After hardening, it is used to make the dies employed in coining. [variant of *hob*[1] (of a fireplace)] —**hub′like′**, *adj.*

hub-and-spoke (hub′ənd spōk′), *adj.* of or having to do with a system of transportation, especially of small airlines, by which passengers or freight are carried on branch routes to a central city to make connections for transportation to a large metropolitan area: *Another post-deregulation trend . . . was hub-and-spoke operations [that] depend largely on feeder traffic* (Grant M. Davis). *Hub-and-spoke systems make for many shorter, better-filled and hence more profitable flights than nonstops* (New York Times Magazine).

hub·ba-hub·ba (hub′ə hub′ə), *interj. U.S. Slang.* an exclamation of pleasure and approval. [supposedly < Chinese *hao, pu hao* (literally) good, not good]

Hub·bard squash (hub′ərd), *U.S.* a winter squash with yellowish flesh and a smooth or warted skin of a dark greenish color. See picture under **gourd family**.

hub·ble (hub′əl), *n.* a small hump. [perhaps back formation < earlier *hubbly* rough, variant of dialectal English *hobbly* < *hobble* move unsteadily up and down]

hub·ble-bub·ble (hub′əl bub′əl), *n.* **1** = hookah. **2** a bubbling sound. **3** confused talk. [imitative formation < *bubble*]

Hub·ble's constant (hub′əlz), an astronomical measure used in calculating the velocity at which galaxies recede according to Hubble's law. [< Edwin P. *Hubble,* 1889-1953, an American astronomer, who formulated the law]

Hubble's law, the astronomical observation that the velocity of the recession of galaxies is proportional to their distance from our own galaxy, as shown by the systematic shift of lines in the spectra of the galaxies toward the red in linear proportion to their distance from us.

hub·bub (hub′ub), *n.* a loud, confused noise; uproar: *The crowd of boys was in a hubbub.*

hub·by (hub′ē), *n., pl.* **-bies.** *Informal.* husband. [< *hub,* short for *husband* + *-y*[2]]

hub·cap (hub′kap′), *n.* a removable, dish-shaped piece of metal that covers the center of the outer side of a wheel.

hub·less (hub′lis), *adj.* without a hub.

hu·bris (hyü′bris), *n.* insolent pride; arrogance. Also, **hybris**. [< Greek *hýbris*]

hu·bris·tic (hyü bris′tik), *adj.* arrogant: *It is hubristic to think that we have the ability to inflict a "pax Americana" on the world, or that we could make it stick . . . by threat of . . . military superiority* (Bulletin of Atomic Scientists). [< Greek *hýbristikos* < *hýbris* hubris]

hub·shi or **hub·shee** (hub′shē), *n. sing. or pl.* **1** an Ethiopian. **2** (in India) any African Negro. [< Persian *habshī* < Arabic *habashi* of or belonging to *Habash* (Abyssinia)]

huch·en (huk′ən, hük′-), *n.* a long, slender, salmonlike game fish of the Danube, with a flat snout and large teeth. [< German *huchen*]

huck[1] (huk), *n.* = huckaback.

huck[2] (huk), *n. Dialect.* the hip or haunch. [perhaps < Scandinavian (compare Old Icelandic *hūka* to crouch, squat)]

huck·a·back (huk′ə bak), *n.* a heavy, coarse linen or cotton fabric with a rough surface, used especially for towels. [origin uncertain]

huck·le (huk′əl), *n.* the hip or haunch. [< *huck*[2] + *-le*]

huck·le·ber·ry (huk′əl ber′ē), *n., pl.* **-ries.** **1** a small berry like a blueberry but darker in color and with larger seeds. **2** any one of the shrubs that it grows on. The huckleberry belongs to the heath family. **3** = blueberry (def. 1). [American English; apparently alteration of *hurtleberry* < unrecorded *hurtle* (diminutive of dialectal English *hurt,* Old English *hortan* whortleberries) + *berry*]

huck·le·bone (huk′əl bōn′), *n.* **1** = hipbone. **2** = anklebone. [< *huckle* + *bone*]

huck·ster (huk′stər), *n., v.* —*n.* **1** a peddler; hawker. **2** a person who sells small articles. **3** *Figurative.* a person willing to profit in a small, mean way. **4** *Slang.* a person in the advertising business.

—*v.i., v.t.* to peddle or sell, especially in a petty way or in small quantities.

[Middle English *hokester.* Compare Middle Dutch *hokester,* and Middle English *hukken* to haggle, bargain.] —**huck′ster·er**, *n.*

huck·ster·ism (huk′stə riz əm), *n. Especially U.S.* high-pressure selling and advertising.

HUD (hud), *n.* Housing and Urban Development (full name, Department of Housing and Urban Development, a department of the U.S. government created in 1965).

hud·dle (hud′əl), *v.,* **-dled, -dling,** *n.* —*v.i.* **1** to crowd close: *The sheep huddled together in a corner. Your huddled masses yearning to be free* (Emma Lazarus). **2** to nestle in a heap: *She huddled close to the fire on the hearth.* **3** (of football players) to group together behind the line of scrimmage to receive signals or call a play. **4** *Informal.* to confer secretly: *House Democrats will huddle this week-end for a final decision on immediate tax legislation* (Wall Street Journal).

—*v.t.* **1** to put close together; crowd: *She huddled all four boys into one bed. The animals huddled themselves in the lee of the hill out of the wind.* **2** to nestle in a heap; coil up: *The cat huddled itself on the cushion and went to sleep.* **3** to prepare, finish, compile, or organize in haste and without proper care; throw together hastily: *The English ministry hastened to huddle up a peace with France and Holland at Breda* (Macaulay). **4** *Obsolete.* to drive or push hurriedly and without order or ceremony; hurry (a person or thing).

—*n.* **1** a confused heap, mass, or crowd; conglomeration: *The soldiers were crowded together in a huddle* (Benjamin Franklin). **2** disorderly or indecent haste; hurry; bustle; confusion. **3** a grouping of football players behind the line of scrimmage to receive signals, plan the next play, etc. **4** *Informal.* a secret consultation: *a lawyer in a huddle with his client.*

go into a huddle, *Informal.* to confer secretly: *During the crisis, the President and the Cabinet went into a huddle.*

huddle on, to put on (clothes) hurriedly and carelessly: *I got up and huddled on my clothes* (Tobias Smollett).

[(originally) to conceal; origin uncertain. Compare Middle English *hodren.*] —**hud′dler**, *n.*

Hu·di·bras·tic (hyü′də bras′tik), *adj.* of or in the style of Samuel Butler's *Hudibras,* a mock-heroic, satirical poem directed against the Puritans, published 1663-1678.

Hud·so·ni·an (hud sō′nē ən), *adj.* of or having to do with Hudson Bay in central Canada or with the fauna or flora of that region. [< Henry *Hudson* (the English navigator and explorer in America for whom Hudson Bay was named)]

Hudsonian chickadee, a brown chickadee with black, white, and red underparts, found in Canada and Alaska.

Hudsonian curlew, an arctic bird about 18 inches long with a whitish striped crown; whimbrel. It is a kind of curlew.

Hudsonian godwit, a large shore bird with a long, up-curved bill and a white patch at the base of the tail. It breeds in the Arctic and lives in southern South America in the winter.

Hud·son River School (hud′sən), a group of American artists of the 1800's who painted romantic landscapes, especially in the region of the Hudson River.

Hudson seal, a muskrat fur that is dyed and plucked to look like seal.

hue[1] (hyü), *n.* **1** that property of color by which it can be distinguished from gray of equal brightness as red, yellow, blue, and other regions of the spectrum; color: *silks of many hues. The girls' dresses showed most of the hues of the rainbow.* SYN: See syn. under **color**. **2** a variety of a color; shade or tint: *She finally found silk of the particular pinkish hue that she sought.* **3** *Figurative.* aspect or type: *politicians of every hue.* **4** *Archaic.* color of the skin; complexion: *the ashen hue of age* (Scott). **5** *Obsolete.* form; appearance: *the native hue of resolution* (Shakespeare). [Old English *hīw*] —**hue′less**, *adj.*

hue[2] (hyü), *n.* a shouting; outcry. SYN: clamor.

hue and cry, a shouts of alarm or protest; outcry: *The fashionable, the cautious, the Protectionists, the pious, all joined in the hue and cry* (Lytton Strachey). **b** an outcry or alarm formerly raised to call people to pursue a criminal, in which they were obliged by law to join: *To dare offend . . . now is for a thief to leave the covert, and meet a strong hue and cry* (John Donne). **c** the pursuit of a criminal in this way: *The hue and cry ended in the capture of the thief.*

[< Old French *hu* a hunting cry < *huer* to shout]

hue-and-cri·er (hyü′ən krī′ər), *n.* a person who raises a hue and cry about some condition in protest or alarm.

hueb·ner·ite (hēb′nə rīt, hyüb′-), *n.* wolframite containing more manganese than iron. [< German *Hübnerit* < A. *Hübner,* a German metallurgist of the 1800's + *-it* -ite[1]]

hued (hyüd), *adj.* having a hue; colored.

huel·ga (wel′gä), *n. Spanish.* a labor strike.

hue·mul (wā mül′), *n.* = guemal. [< American Spanish *huemul* < Araucan]

hue·vos ran·che·ros (hwā′vōs rän chär′ōs), a Mexican dish of fried or poached eggs with tomato sauce. [< Spanish *huevos rancheros* (literally) ranch eggs]

huff (huf), *n., v.* —*n.* a fit of anger or peevishness: *He had a great dispute with the congressmen about politics, and left the place in a huff* (Washington Irving).

—*v.t.* **1** to make angry; offend. **2** to treat with arrogance or contempt. **3** (in checkers) to remove (a piece from the board which one's opponent could have jumped but did not). **4** *Obsolete.* to puff up; swell.

—*v.i.* **1** to puff; blow: *I'll huff and I'll puff till I blow your house down!* (Nursery Tale: The Three Little Pigs). **2** *Obsolete.* to swell with pride or arrogance; swagger; bluster.

huff and puff, to bluster; storm; rant: *Both sides will huff and puff down to the end, orating from their grandstands at the start, then making a hurry-up effort to talk to each other* (Time).

[probably imitative]

huff-duff (huf′duf′), *n.* a device for indicating the direction from which high-frequency radio signals come. [apparently < *h*(igh) *f*(requency) *d*(irection) *f*(inding)]

huff·er·y-puff·er·y (huf′ər ē puf′ər ē), *n., pl.* **-er·ies.** inflated or pompous speech or writing.

huff·ish (huf′ish), *adj.* = huffy. —**huff′ish·ly**, *adv.* —**huff′ish·ness**, *n.*

huff·y (huf′ē), *adj.,* **huff·i·er, huff·i·est.** **1** in a huff; offended: *You're not huffy with myself* (John Millington Synge). SYN: affronted. **2** easily offended; touchy. SYN: petulant. **3** arrogant; blustering: *After several weeks of blank silence the rather huffy reply came back* (Listener). —**huff′i·ly**, *adv.* —**huff′i·ness**, *n.*

hug (hug), *v.,* **hugged, hug·ging,** *n.* —*v.t.* **1** to put the arms around and hold close, especially to show love or friendship; embrace: *The girl hugs her big doll. She hugg'd the offender, and forgave the offence* (John Dryden). **2** to squeeze tightly with the arms, as a bear does. **3** *Figurative.* to cling firmly or fondly to: *to hug an opinion. From the beginning the Public Health Service has hugged its procedures as if they were deadly secrets that should not be revealed* (New York Times). *But Faith . . . once wedded fast To some dear falsehood, hugs it to the last* (Thomas Moore). **4** *Figurative.* to keep close to: *The little boat hugged the shore. [He] sat himself down at a table which like the chairs hugged the wall* (Graham Greene).

—*v.i.* to cling together; lie close: *to hug with swine* (Shakespeare).

—*n.* **1** a tight clasp with the arms; warm embrace: *Give Mother a hug. A kiss and hug expressed her unspoken thanks for her father's understanding.* **2** a tight squeeze with the arms; grip in wrestling.

[earlier *hugge.* Compare Old Icelandic *hugga* to comfort.]

huge (hyüj), *adj.,* **hug·er, hug·est.** **1** very, very large; unusually large in size, bulk, or dimensions: *Whales and elephants are huge animals.* **2** extremely large in quantity or number: *He won a huge sum of money in the lottery.* **3** unusually great in extent, scope, degree, or capacity: *a huge undertaking. Your mynheers are huge sleepers* (Washington Irving). [Middle English *huge,* apparently short for Old French *ahuge*] —**huge′ly**, *adv.* —**huge′ness**, *n.*

—*Syn.* **1 Huge, enormous, immense** mean unusually large. **Huge** suggests massiveness or bulkiness: *A St. Bernard is a huge dog.* **Enormous** means abnormally or excessively large: *I have an enormous appetite.* **Immense** means so large or great in any way as to be impossible to measure by ordinary standards of measurement: *The national debt is immense.*

huge·ous (hyü′jəs), *adj. Archaic.* huge: *My master is close by . . . beside the hugeous oak* (Scott).

hug·ga·ble (hug′ə bəl), *adj.* such as invites hugging: *The teddy bear is such a huggable creature* (London Daily Chronicle).

hug·ger (hug′ər), *n.* a person who hugs.

hug·ger-mug·ger (hug′ər mug′ər), *n., adj., adv., v.* —*n.* **1** confusion; disorder; muddle: *In the hugger-mugger of their hasty departure they had forgotten the dog.* **2** *Archaic.* secrecy; concealment: *We have done but greenly, In hugger-mugger to inter him* (Shakespeare).

—*adj.* **1** confused; disorderly. SYN: slovenly. **2** secret; clandestine.

—*adv.* in a confused, disorderly manner.

—*v.i.* **1** to do anything in a confused or disorderly manner. **2** to act in a secret manner.

—*v.t.* to keep secret or concealed.

[origin uncertain]

hug-me-tight (hug′mē tīt′), *n.* a tight-fitting, short, usually knitted jacket, with or without sleeves.

Hu·gue·not (hyü′gə not), *n., adj.* —*n.* a French Protestant of the 1500's and 1600's, belonging to the Calvinistic or Reformed communion.

—*adj.* of or belonging to the Huguenots: *Protestantism in France, however, is not confined to the low-income brackets. Some of the wealthiest families are Huguenot* (New York Times).

[< French *huguenot,* earlier *eigenot* (originally

used of Genevans who were partisans against the Duke of Savoy) perhaps <Swiss German *Eidgenoss* confederate; subsequently influenced by the name of Besançon *Hugues,* a party leader]

Hu|gue|not|ism (hyü′gə not′iz əm), *n.* beliefs and practices of Huguenots; French Protestantism.

huh (hu), *interj.* a sound made to express surprise or contempt, or to ask a question. [imitative]

hu|i (hü′ē), *n. Hawaiian.* **1** a club; an association. **2** a corporation.

hu|ia (hü′yä), *n.,* or **huia bird,** a New Zealand bird having black tail feathers tipped with white, used for ornament by the Maoris. [<Maori *huia*]

***hui|pil** (wē pēl′), *n.* a square-necked overblouse slipped over the head, worn by women in Mexico. [<Mexican Spanish *huipil* <Nahuatl *huipilli*]

***huipil**
***huipil grande**

huipil

huipil grande

***huipil gran|de** (grän′dā), a wide lacy headdress, worn on holidays by Indian women on the Isthmus of Tehuantepec in southern Mexico.

Hui|tzi|lo|poch|tli (wē′tsē lō pōch′tlē), *n. Aztec Mythology.* the god of war and the sun, often represented as wearing snakes and feathers.

Huk (huk), *n.* a member of a communist guerrilla movement in the Philippines, operating chiefly in the rural areas of central Luzon. [shortened <the Tagalog name *Hukbalahap*]

Huk|ba|la|hap (huk bä′lä häp), *n.* = Huk.

hu|ki|lau (hü′ki′lou), *n.* a Hawaiian fishing festival. [<Hawaiian *hukilau* (literally) net pulling]

hu|la (hü′lə), *n., pl.* **-las,** *v.,* **-laed, -la|ing.** —*n.* a native Hawaiian dance that tells a story in pantomime. —*v.i.* to dance the hula: *Graceful girls hulaed on the dock* (San Francisco Chronicle). [<Hawaiian *hula*]

hula hoop, a plastic hoop that is easily rotated around the body by swinging the hips.

hulk (hulk), *n., v.* —*n.* **1** the body of an old or worn-out ship: *Several hulks of old fishing boats lay rotting on the beach.* **2** Often, **hulks.** a ship used for storage or as a prison: *Many prisoners died in the British hulks anchored in New York during the Revolutionary War.* **3** a big, clumsy ship: *Many tugboats clustered about the huge oil tanker, pushing the hulk into her berth.* **4** *Figurative.* a big, clumsy person or thing: *That hulk of a boy is still at the awkward age.*
—*v.i.* **1** to be bulky or unwieldy; loom bulkily: *His huge pursuer suddenly hulked in the dimly lighted doorway.* **2** to lounge or slouch clumsily.
[Old English *hulc,* perhaps <Medieval Latin *hulcus* <Greek *holkás* merchant ship <*hélkein* drag, draw]

hulk|ing (hul′king), *adj.* big and clumsy; ungainly: *a large, hulking boy.* SYN: bulky, unwieldy.

hulk|y (hul′kē), *adj.,* **-ki|er, -ki|est.** = hulking.

hull¹ (hul), *n., v.* —*n.* **1** the outer covering of a seed or fruit: *The hull of wheat is removed to make white flour.* **2** the calyx of some fruits. The green leaves at the stem of a strawberry are its hull. **3** any outer covering; envelope.
—*v.t.* to remove the hull or hulls from.
[Old English *hulu*] —**hull′er,** *n.*

hull² (hul), *n., v.* —*n.* **1** the body or frame of a ship. The masts, yards, sails, and rigging are not part of the hull. **2a** the main body or frame of an airship. **b** the boatlike fuselage of a flying boat that makes it buoyant.
—*v.t.* to strike or pierce the hull of (a ship) with a shell, torpedo, or other weapon.
hull down, so far away that the hull is below the horizon: *They were hull down . . . and we but hailed their topsails on the line* (Stevenson).
[origin uncertain. Compare Middle English *hoole,* or *holle* hull, English *hold²,* Dutch *hol* ship's hold.]

hul|la|ba|loo or **hul|la|bal|loo** (hul′ə bə lü′), *n.* a loud noise or disturbance; uproar; clamor. SYN: racket, tumult. [apparently <*hullo*]

hull|borne (hul′bôrn′, -bōrn′), *adj., adv.* —*adj.* (of a boat equipped with hydrofoils) supported by or using its hull rather than operating with the use of hydrofoils: *hullborne speeds.*
—*adv.* on its hull: *operated hullborne.*

hulled¹ (huld), *adj.* **1** having a hull or husk. **2** with the hull removed: *hulled grain.* [<*hull¹* + *-ed²*]

hulled² (huld), *adj.* having a hull or body. [<*hull²* + *-ed²*]

hul|lo (hə lō′), *interj., n., pl.* **-los,** *v.i., v.t.* **-loed, -lo|ing. 1** = hollo. **2** = hello.

hul|ly gul|ly (hul′ē gul′ē), a dance consisting of the twist performed as a square dance.

hum (hum), *v.,* **hummed, hum|ming,** *n., interj.* —*v.i.* **1** to make a continuous murmuring sound like that of a bee or of a spinning top or wheel: *The sewing machine hums busily.* SYN: drone, buzz, murmur. **2** to make a low sound like *mm* or *hm,* as in hesitation, embarrassment, or dissatisfaction: *Don't stand humming and hawing, but speak out* (Henry Fielding). **3** to sing with closed lips, not sounding words. **4** to give forth an indistinct sound of mingled voices or noises; buzz: *The theater audience hummed with excitement.* **5** *Informal.* to be busy and active: *The new coach made things hum when he took charge of the team.* —*v.t.* **1** to sing with closed lips, not sounding words: *She was humming a little tune.* **2** to put or bring by humming: *hum to sleep.*
—*n.* **1** a continuous, murmuring sound: *the hum of the bees, the hum of the mill.* **2** an indistinct sound of mingled voices or noises: *the hum of a city street.* **3** a singing with closed lips, not sounding words.
—*interj.* a low sound like *mm* or *hm,* as made in hesitation, embarrassment, or disagreement: *Hum, I don't know what to do.*
[probably imitative. Compare German *hummen.*]

hu|ma|lin (hyü′mə lin), *n.* insulin made for humans through genetic engineering: *The Food and Drug Administration approved the marketing of "humalin"—human insulin made artificially from gene-splicing techniques* (Carol Bellamy). [<*huma*(n) + (insu)*lin*]

hu|man (hyü′mən), *adj., n.* —*adj.* **1** of persons; that people have: *Kindness is a human trait. To know what will happen in the future is beyond human power. No life that breathes with human breath Has ever truly longed for death* (Tennyson). **2** being a person or persons; having the form or qualities of people: *Men, women, and children are human beings. Those monkeys look almost human.* **3** having or showing qualities (good and bad) natural to people: *Their offer of help to the stranded motorist was a very human reaction. Yet do I fear your nature; It is too full o' the milk of human kindness* (Shakespeare). **4** having to do with people; belonging to mankind: *human affairs, human interest.*
—*n.* a human being; person; man: *Unfortunately many people believe that the problems of national survival are too big for humans to handle* (Saturday Evening Post).
[<Old French *humain,* learned borrowing from Latin *hūmānus,* related to *homō, -inis* man] —**hu′man|like′,** *adj.* —**hu′man|ness,** *n.*
—*Syn. adj.* **3 Human, humane** mean having or showing qualities belonging to man. **Human** describes or suggests any quality, good or bad, belonging to man as apart from animals or God, but particularly suggests his feelings or faults: *He is a very human person, warm and understanding, and not too perfect.* **Humane** chiefly suggests man's tender and compassionate feelings and actions toward people or animals that are helpless, troubled, or suffering: *We believe in humane treatment of prisoners.*
▶**human, human being.** In informal and technical writing, *human* is common but the standard form is *human being.*

hu|mane (hyü mān′), *adj.* **1** kind; merciful; not cruel or brutal: *Humane people are considerate of animals.* SYN: tender, compassionate. See syn. under **human. 2** tending to humanize and refine: *humane studies.* [variant of *human*] —**hu|mane′ly,** *adv.* —**hu|mane′ness,** *n.*

human engineering, 1 the manipulation of human beings and their actions. **2** the application of scientific knowledge of human behavior to designing machines and equipment, such as office equipment and farm and industrial machines, in order to create a better working environment: *. . . human engineering, is a new departure in the application of psychological principles to industry* (Scientific American).

humane society, a group of persons organized to protect children or animals from cruelty.

human geography, = anthropogeography.

human growth hormone, a synthetic form of the pituitary hormone somatotropin, which regulates growth of the human body.

hu|man|ics (hyü man′iks), *n.* the scientific study of human nature: *the impact of genetic engineering on humanics, which includes the possible modification of human nature toward previously unattainable ideals* (Joshua Lederberg).

hu|man|ise (hyü′mə nīz), *v.t., v.i.,* **-ised, -is|ing.** *Especially British.* humanize.

hu|man|ism (hyü′mə niz əm), *n.* **1** any system of thought or action principally or exclusively concerned with human interests and values. **2** the study of the humanities; literary culture. Humanism spread throughout Europe in the Middle Ages when scholars began to study Latin and Greek culture. As a result, there was the great revival of art and learning called the Renaissance. **3** the character or quality of being human.

hu|man|ist (hyü′mə nist), *n., adj.* —*n.* **1** a student of human nature or affairs; follower of humanism. **2** a student of the humanities or of Latin or Greek culture: *Milton was born a humanist, but the Puritan temper mastered him* (Matthew Arnold). **3** *Archaic.* a classical scholar.
—*adj.* = humanistic.

hu|man|is|tic (hyü′mə nis′tik), *adj.* of humanism or humanists. —**hu′man|is′ti|cal|ly,** *adv.*

hu|man|i|tar|i|an (hyü man′ə tãr′ē ən), *adj., n.* —*adj.* **1** helpful to humanity; philanthropic. **2** of or having to do with humanitarianism, especially in theology.
—*n.* **1** a person who is devoted to the welfare of all human beings. SYN: philanthropist. **2** a believer in theological or ethical humanitarianism.
[<*humanity;* patterned on *unitarian*]

hu|man|i|tar|i|an|ism (hyü man′ə tãr′ē ə niz′əm), *n.* **1** humanitarian principles or practices. **2** *Theology.* the doctrine that Jesus Christ was human, not divine. **3** the ethical doctrine that man's obligations are concerned wholly with human relations and the welfare of the human race.

hu|man|i|ty (hyü man′ə tē), *n., pl.* **-ties. 1** human beings taken as a group; people; mankind: *Advances in science help all humanity. After all there is but one race—humanity* (George Moore). **2** a being human; human nature, character, or quality: *Humanity is a mixture of good and bad qualities.* SYN: humanism. **3** a being humane; humane treatment; kindness; mercy: *Treat animals with humanity.* SYN: benevolence.
the humanities, a the Latin and Greek languages and literatures: *the teaching of the humanities and of the Hebrew* (James Russell Lowell). **b** cultural studies as opposed to the sciences, including language, literature, philosophy, and art: *An Eton captain . . . learned in all the humanities* (Emerson). **c** the branches of learning concerned with man: *. . . the fair humanities of old religion* (Samuel Taylor Coleridge).
[<Old French *humanite,* learned borrowing from Latin *hūmānitās* <*hūmānus* human]

hu|man|ize (hyü′mə nīz), *v.,* **-ized, -iz|ing.** —*v.t.* **1** to make human; give a human character or quality to: *humanizing what is brute* (William Cowper). **2** to make humane; cause to be kind or merciful; civilize; refine.
—*v.i.* to become human or humane. —**hu′man|i|za′tion,** *n.* —**hu′man|iz′er,** *n.*

hu|man|kind (hyü′mən kīnd′), *n.* human beings; people; human race; mankind.

hu|man|ly (hyü′mən lē), *adv.* **1** by human means: *The doctor did all that is humanly possible to save the dying man.* **2** according to the feelings, knowledge, or experience of human beings: *Humanly speaking, what he is asking is impossible to achieve.* **3** in a human manner: *Even a judge is humanly liable to make a mistake.*

human nature, the qualities and characteristics shared by all human beings: *Men everywhere possess common attributes called human nature: "those sentiments and impulses that are human . . . in the sense that they belong to mankind at large, and not to any particular race or time"* (Hinkle and Hinkle).

hu|man|oid (hyü′mə noid), *adj., n. Anthropology.* —*adj.* of human form; having human characteristics (as distinguished from a lower stage of development); manlike: *Certain traits manifest the characteristics of modern man earlier than others. The teeth, for example, became humanoid long before the jaw* (Melville J. Herskovits).
—*n.* a humanoid being: *The Neanderthal man and Cro-Magnon man were humanoids.* Also, **hominoid.** [<*human* + *-oid*]

human potentials movement, a social movement to improve the self-respect of individuals and their relationships with others, chiefly in group sessions in which various techniques are utilized to make people aware of their own feelings and sensitive to the feelings of others.

hu|man-pow|ered (hyü′mən pou′ərd), *adj.* powered by a person or persons, not by an engine or other machine; powered by human energy: *The "Gossamer Albatross" [was] the first human-powered aircraft to cross the English Channel* (David G. Wilson).

human relations, 1 the study of group behavior in order to achieve desired goals with a minimum of effort and conflict between individuals: *Beyond "market psychology" another new field of psychology has arisen, based on the wish to under-*

Pronunciation Key: hat, āge, cãre, fär; let, ēqual, tėrm; it, īce; hot, ōpen, ôrder; **oil, out;** cup, pu̇t, rüle; **ch**ild; lo**ng**; **th**in; **ᴛʜ**en; **zh,** measure; **ə** represents **a** in about, **e** in taken, **i** in pencil, **o** in lemon, **u** in circus.

stand and manipulate the employe. This is called "human relations" (Erich Fromm). **2** relations of people with one another: *Miss Davis, too, avows that "today's secretary has to be a connoisseur of human relations"* (Wall Street Journal).

human rights, the rights of all human beings to fair treatment and justice and to basic needs, such as food, shelter, and education.

human services, *U.S.* **1** aid provided to improve social conditions, such as that given by child welfare bureaus and public health clinics or free medical care for the elderly. **2** = social work.

human shield, **1** any person or group of people who acts as a shield against some danger. **2** a person or group of people, including civilians, prisoners of war, or other noncombatants held hostage at a location of strategic military importance to protect it from enemy attack: *If, by vowing to deploy the POWs as human shields, . . . Saddam aimed to curtail the allied aerial campaign, the plan backfired* (Time). —**hu'man-shield**, *adj.*

hu|ma|num est er|ra|re (hyü mā'nəm est e rär'ē), *Latin.* to err is human.

hu|mate (hyü'māt), *n.* salt or ester of humic acid.

hum|ble (hum'bəl, um'-), *adj.*, **-bler, -blest**, *v.*, **-bled, -bling.** —*adj.* **1** low in position or condition; not important; not grand: *He has a humble job with very low wages. Lincoln was born in a humble log cabin; he was of humble origin.* SYN: unpretentious, common, poor. **2** modest in spirit; not proud: *Defeat and failure make people humble.* **3** deeply or courteously respectful: *in my humble opinion.*
—*v.t.* **1** to make humble or meek; lower the pride of; humiliate. **2** to make lower in position, condition, or importance: *The mighty man shall be humbled* (Isaiah 5:15).
[< Old French *humble,* earlier *humele,* learned borrowing from Latin *humilis* (physically) low (in Late Latin, humble) < *humus* earth] —**hum'ble|ness**, *n.* —**hum'bler**, *n.* —**hum'bly**, *adv.*
—*Syn. adj.* **2 Humble, lowly, meek** mean not proud in spirit or behavior. **Humble** in its good sense means modest, without wrongful pride in oneself or one's accomplishments, but now usually suggests feeling inferior and belittling oneself: *The vastness of the universe makes a person feel humble.* **Lowly**, though interchangeable with *humble,* is more literary and is seldom used to describe people: *The saint had a lowly heart.* **Meek** means patient and mild in disposition, often suggests being without pride or spirit, submitting tamely to abuse: *The boy was meek when the older boys made fun of him.*

hum|ble|bee (hum'bəl bē'), *n.* = bumblebee. [Middle English *humbylbee*]

humble pie, an inferior pie made of the inward parts of an animal, formerly served to the huntsmen and servants after a hunt.
eat humble pie, to be forced to do something very disagreeable and humiliating; admit one's mistakes and say that one is sorry: *The British Prime Minister . . . had to eat humble pie and could not even exert an independent, diplomatic initiative* (London Times).
[spelling variant of *umble pie* < *umbles,* variant of *numbles* edible inward parts of deer]

hum|bling (hum'bling, um'-), *adj.* that humbles; humiliating. —**hum'bling|ly**, *adv.*

Hum|boldt Current (hum'bōlt), = Peru Current.

hum|boldt|ite (hum'bōlt īt), *n.* a silicate of boron and calcium; datolite. [< Alexander von *Humboldt,* 1769-1859, a German naturalist + *-ite*[1]]

hum|bug (hum'bug'), *n., v.,* **-bugged, -bug|ging.** —*n.* **1** a person who pretends to be what he is not; fraud; impostor: *What a humbug that woman is* (Thackeray). SYN: charlatan. **2** a cheat. SYN: swindler. **3** nonsense or pretense; sham: *There is no humbug about him; he speaks his mind straight out.* SYN: deception.
—*v.t.* to deceive with a sham; cheat: *I won't be humbugged into buying something I don't want.*
—*v.i.* to practice humbug.
[origin unknown] —**hum'bug'ger**, *n.*

hum|bug|ger|y (hum'bug'ər ē), *n., pl.* **-ger|ies.** false pretense; humbugging.

hum|ding|er (hum ding'ər), *n. Slang.* a person or thing remarkable for its kind: *A gay blade of an uncle . . . plans to give her a humdinger of a wedding* (Wall Street Journal). [probably a coined word]

hum|drum (hum'drum'), *adj., n., v.,* **-drummed, -drum|ming.** —*adj.* without variety; commonplace; dull: *a humdrum existence.* SYN: boring, monotonous.
—*n.* **1** humdrum routine; monotony. **2** monotonous or tiresome talk. **3** a commonplace, dull person.
—*v.i.* to proceed in a humdrum way.
[varied reduplication of *hum,* verb] —**hum'drum'ness**, *n.*

hu|mec|tant (hyü mek'tənt), *n.* a moistening agent used especially in tobacco, cosmetics, and textiles: *Humectants help replace the natural youthful moisture that's lost with the years* (New Yorker).
[< Latin *hūmectāns, -antis,* present participle of *hūmectāre* to moisten]

hu|mer|al (hyü'mər əl), *adj.* **1** of or near the humerus. **2** of or near the shoulder.

hu|mer|us (hyü'mər əs), *n., pl.* **-mer|i** (-mə rī). **1** the long bone in the upper part of the arm or forelimb, from the shoulder to the elbow. See picture under **arm**[1]. **2** the upper part of the arm or forelimb.
[< Latin *umerus* shoulder]

hu|mic (hyü'mik), *adj.* of or having to do with humus; derived from humus. [< Latin *humus* humus, soil, mold[3] + *-ic*]

humic acid, any acid derived from humus.

hu|mid (hyü'mid), *adj.* slightly wet; moist; damp: *The air is very humid near the sea.* SYN: See syn. under **damp.** [< Latin *hūmidus,* variant of *ūmidus* < *ūmēre* be moist] —**hu'mid|ly**, *adv.* —**hu'mid|ness**, *n.*

hu|mid|i|fi|ca|tion (hyü mid'ə fə kā'shən), *n.* the process of humidifying.

hu|mid|i|fi|er (hyü mid'ə fī'ər), *n.* a device for keeping air moist.

hu|mid|i|fy (hyü mid'ə fī), *v.t.,* **-fied, -fy|ing.** to make moist or damp; make humid.

hu|mid|i|stat (hyü mid'ə stat'), *n.* an instrument for regulating the degree of humidity.

hu|mid|i|ty (hyü mid'ə tē), *n.* **1** the state of being humid; moistness; dampness: *The humidity of soil helps plants to grow.* **2** the amount of moisture in the air. The relative humidity is the ratio between the amount of water vapor present in the air and the greatest amount the air could contain at the same temperature. *On a hot, sultry day the humidity is high. The humidity today is 90 per cent.* [< Middle French *humidité,* learned borrowing from Latin *hūmiditās* < *hūmidus* humid]

hu|mi|dor (hyü'mə dôr), *n.* **1** a box, jar, or other container fitted with the means for keeping tobacco properly moist. **2** any similar device. [< *humid;* perhaps patterned on *cuspidor*]

hu|mi|fi|ca|tion (hyü'mə fə kā'shən), *n.* the process by which organic substances are changed into humus.

hu|mil|i|ate (hyü mil'ē āt), *v.t.,* **-at|ed, -at|ing.** to lower the pride, dignity, or self-respect of; make ashamed; mortify: *We felt humiliated by our failure. In 1303 King Philip IV of France humiliated Pope Boniface VIII by having him arrested* (Lewis W. Spitz). SYN: humble, chagrin, disgrace, shame. [< Latin *humiliāre* (with English *-ate*[1]) < *humilis;* see etym. under **humble**]

hu|mil|i|at|ed (hyü mil'ē ā'tid), *adj.* made to feel ashamed. SYN: See syn. under **ashamed.**

hu|mil|i|at|ing (hyü mil'ē ā'ting), *adj.* that humiliates; mortifying. —**hu|mil'i|at'ing|ly**, *adv.*

hu|mil|i|a|tion (hyü mil'ē ā'shən), *n.* **1** the act or process of lowering pride, dignity, or self-respect: *His humiliation of his enemy brought him only false satisfaction.* SYN: abasement. **2** the state or the feeling of being humiliated: *I nursed my humiliation for a couple of days* (Atlantic). SYN: mortification.

hu|mil|i|a|tor (hyü mil'ē ā'tər), *n.* a person who humiliates.

hu|mil|i|a|to|ry (hyü mil'ē ə tôr'ē, -tōr'-), *adj.* that tends to humiliate; humiliating.

hu|mil|i|ty (hyü mil'ə tē), *n., pl.* **-ties.** humbleness of mind; lack of pride; meekness: *Humility before God is vain save as it expresses itself in the acceptance of every man as a brother* (London Times). SYN: lowliness, modesty.
humilities, acts showing a humble spirit: *With these humilities they satisfied the young king* (John Davies).
[< Old French *humilite,* learned borrowing from Latin *humilitās* < *humilis;* see etym. under **humble**]

hum|ma|ble (hum'ə bəl), *adj.* easy to hum; likely to be hummed: *a hummable tune.*

hum|maul (hə môl'), *n.* = hamal.

hum|mel (hum'əl), *adj.* **1** (of grain) awnless. **2** (of cattle) hornless. [origin uncertain. Compare Low German *hummel* hornless beast.]

hum|mer (hum'ər), *n.* a person or thing that hums.

hum|ming (hum'ing), *adj.* **1** that hums; buzzing. **2** *Informal.* brisk; vigorous; energetic. **3** *Informal.* foaming, strong, or heady. —**hum'ming|ly**, *adv.*

***hummingbird**

***hum|ming|bird** (hum'ing bėrd'), *n.* any one of a large group of very small, brightly colored American birds with a long, narrow bill and narrow wings that move so rapidly they make a humming sound in the air.

hummingbird hawk moth, *Especially British.* a hawk moth.

hummingbird moth, *U.S.* a hawk moth.

hum|mock (hum'ək), *n.* **1** a very small, rounded hill; knoll; hillock: *The highway mounts into a group of hummocks covered with scrub and surrounded by a tangle of barbed wire* (Atlantic). **2** a bump or ridge in a field of ice: *This, too, had to be abandoned when a snowmobile, sent out for a trial run, hit hummocks "as high as houses and ten times as solid"* (Harper's). **3** a tract of thickly wooded land within a marshy area; hammock. [origin uncertain]

hum|mock|y (hum'ə kē), *adj.* **1** full of hummocks. **2** like a hummock.

hum|mus (hum'əs, hům'əs), *n.* a purée of chickpeas made with sesame oil, garlic, and parsley, eaten in the Middle East as an appetizer. [< Arabic *hummus*]

hu|mon|gous (hyü mung'gəs), *adj.* = humungous.

hu|mor (hyü'mər, yü'-), *n., v.* —*n.* **1** funny or amusing quality: *I see no humor in your tricks.* **2** the ability to see or show the funny or amusing side of things: *Mark Twain was famous for his humor.* SYN: See syn. under **wit.** **3** speech, writing, etc., showing this ability: *His chief output is humor.* **4** state of mind; mood; disposition; temper: *Is the teacher in a good humor this morning? I feel in the humor for working.* SYN: See syn. under **mood.** **5** fancy; whim: *There is no crossing him in 's humour* (Shakespeare). **6** any one of four body fluids formerly supposed to determine a person's health and disposition. The four humors, or the cardinal humors, were blood, phlegm, choler (yellow bile), and melancholy (black bile). **7** any animal or plant fluid, whether natural or diseased, such as the blood or lymph. **8** a chronic skin disease caused by an unhealthy blood condition. **9** *Obsolete.* moisture; vapor.
—*v.t.* **1** to give in to the fancies or whims of (a person); indulge: *That sick child has to be humored.* **2** *Figurative.* to adapt oneself to; act so as to agree with: *He humored every turn of the conversation toward his future wife.* Also, *especially British,* **humour.**
humors, whimsical or odd traits, ways, or actions: *And so well could paint The village-folk, with all their humors quaint* (John Greenleaf Whittier).
out of humor, angry or displeased; cross; in a bad mood: *Out of humour with myself, and at every thing about me* (Joseph Addison).
[< Anglo-French *humour,* Old French *humor,* learned borrowing from Latin *ūmor* fluid, (medical) humor < *ūmēre* to be wet, moist]
—*Syn. v.t.* **1 Humor, indulge, gratify** mean to give someone what he wants. **Humor** means to give in to whims, changing moods, unreasonable demands, or purely imaginary desires, in order to quiet or comfort: *to humor a sick child. Unless the little boy is humored, he has tantrums.* **Indulge** means to give way, often too easily, to someone's wishes, especially wishes that should not be granted, in order to please: *Many parents indulge their children by giving them too much candy and ice cream.* **Gratify** means to make happy by satisfying longings or likings: *Praise gratifies most people.*

hu|mor|al (hyü'mər əl, yü'-), *adj.* having to do with or caused by the bodily humors.

-humored, *combining form.* having a ______ humor: *Good-humored = having a good humor.*

hu|mor|esque (hyü'mə resk'), *n.* a light, playful, or humorous piece of music; caprice. [< German *Humoreske* < Latin *hūmor* humor; English spelling patterned on *arabesque*]

hu|mor|ist (hyü'mər ist, yü'-), *n.* **1** a humorous talker or actor; person who tells or writes jokes and funny stories. **2** a person with a strong sense of humor: *The irrepressible humorist is seldom popular.* **3** *Obsolete.* a person subject to humors or whims.

hu|mor|is|tic (hyü'mə ris'tik, yü'-), *adj.* belonging to or characteristic of a humorist.

hu|mor|less (hyü'mər lis, yü'-), *adj.* without humor. —**hu'mor|less|ly**, *adv.* —**hu'mor|less|ness**, *n.*

hu|mor|ous (hyü'mər əs, yü'-), *adj.* **1** full of humor; funny; amusing: *Mark Twain wrote humorous stories.* SYN: jocose. **2** *Archaic.* full of or characterized by humors or whims: *a vain, giddy, shallow, humorous youth* (Shakespeare). **3** *Obsolete.* having to do with or caused by bodily humors. **4** *Obsolete.* moist; humid; damp. —**hu'mor|ous|ly**, *adv.* —**hu'mor|ous|ness**, *n.*

hu|mors (hyü'mərz, yü'-), *n. pl.* See **humor.**

hu|mour (hyü'mər, yü'-), *n., v.t. Especially British.* humor.

hu|mous (hyü'məs), *adj.* having to do with, containing, or derived from humus.

hump (hump), *n., v.* —*n.* **1** a rounded lump that sticks out. A hump on the back of a person is

formed by a crooked spine. *Some camels have two humps on their backs; others have only one.* SYN: protuberance. **2** a rounded mound of earth or rock; hummock. **3** a long, gradual hill in a railroad yard where cars are uncoupled and allowed to roll down into the classification yard, where switches sort them onto different tracks. **4** a mountain or mountain range over which airplanes frequently fly, such as the eastern range of the Himalayas over which air transport missions between China and India or Burma were flown in World War II: *He flew the hump sixteen times.* **5** *Slang.* a fit of ill humor or gloomy dissatisfaction. **6** *Australian Slang.* a walk or tramp with a load on one's back.
—*v.t.* **1** to raise or bend up into a hump: *The cat humped her back when she saw the dog.* **2** *U.S. Slang.* to exert (oneself) in great effort: *You'd better hump yourself if you expect to catch that train.* **3** *Australian Slang.* to hoist or carry (a bundle) upon the back. **4** to hove (a railroad car) over the hump for sorting in a classification yard.
—*v.i.* **1** to rise in a hump. **2** *U.S. Slang.* to exert oneself; make an effort.
over the hump, *Informal.* past a difficult period or crucial test: *With an increase in salary, he was over the hump for the moment.*
[origin uncertain. Compare Dutch *homp* lump, Norwegian *hump* knoll.] —**hump′less,** *adj.* —**hump′like′,** *adj.*

hump|back (hump′bak′), *n.* **1** = hunchback. **2** a back having a hump on it. **3** a whalebone whale that has a thick body with a humplike roll of fat on the back and very large flippers. **4** = humpback salmon.

hump|backed (hump′bakt′), *adj.* **1** = hunchbacked.

humpbacked salmon, = humpback salmon.

humpback salmon, the smallest and most numerous kind of salmon, weighing between three and seven pounds, found in Pacific waters from Asia to North America; pink salmon. The male has a dorsal hump especially noticeable in the spawning season.

humpback whale, = humpback (def. 3).

humped (humpt), *adj.* having a hump or humps.

humph (humpf), *interj., n., v.* —*interj., n.* an exclamation expressing doubt, dissatisfaction, disgust, contempt, or dislike.
—*v.t.* to say or express with a humph: *He humphed his mistrust.*
—*v.i.* to say "humph."
[imitative]

Hump|ty-Dump|ty (hump′tē dump′tē), *n.* **1** an egg-shaped figure in an old nursery rhyme that falls down and breaks. **2** *Figurative.* anything that is shattered beyond repair.

hump|y[1] (hum′pē), *adj.,* **hump|i|er, hump|i|est.** **1** full of humps. **2** like a hump.

hump|y[2] (hum′pē), *n., pl.* **hump|ies.** *Australian Slang.* a roughly built hut; shack.

hu|mung|ous (hyü mung′gəs), *adj.* unusually large or great in any way; impossible to measure by ordinary standards; colossal; gigantic.

hu|mus (hyü′məs), *n.* a dark-brown or black part of soil formed from decayed leaves and other vegetable matter, containing valuable plant foods. [<Latin *humus* earth, soil]

Hun (hun), *n.* **1** a member of a warlike Asian people who invaded Europe in the 300's and 400's A.D. under the leadership of Attila. **2** *Figurative.* a barbarous, destructive person. **3** a German (a contemptuous term, used especially during World War I).
[probably <Late Latin *Hunne,* apparently <the native name of the tribe. Compare Old English *Hūne,* Chinese *Han.*]

Hun., Hungary.

hunch (hunch), *n., v.* —*n.* **1** a hump: *a hunch in the shoulders.* **2** *Informal.* a feeling or suspicion that you don't know the reason for: *Having had a hunch that it would rain, he took along an umbrella. I have a hunch that a certain horse will win that race.* SYN: premonition. **3** a thick slice or piece; chunk.
—*v.t.* **1** to hump: *to hunch one's shoulders.* **2** to draw, bend, or form into a hump: *He sat hunched up with his chin on his knees.* **3** *Informal.* to have a vague feeling; suspect: *They hunched that he would win the election.* **4** *Dialect.* to move, push, or shove by jerks.
—*v.i.* **1** to move, push, or shove by jerks. **2** to move with the shoulders or back hunched: *He hunched along in the rain.* **3** to draw, bend, or form oneself into a hump: *We hunched over the table.* **4** to move the hand forward across the ring line or from the spot where the shooter stopped inside the ring in the game of marbles.
[origin unknown]

hunch|back (hunch′bak′), *n., adj.* —*n.* **1** a person with a hump on his back; humpback: *The hunchback was a dwarf about 30 years old.* **2** a back having a hump on it.
—*adj.* = hunchbacked.

hunch|backed (hunch′bakt′), *adj.* having a hump on the back; humpbacked.

hun|dred (hun′drəd), *n., pl.* **-dreds** or (*as after a numeral*) **-dred,** *adj.* —*n.* **1** ten times ten; 100. There are one hundred cents in a dollar. **2** a large number: *hundreds of uses.* **3** a division of an English county. **4** a similar division in Delaware.
—*adj.* being ten times ten.
[Old English *hundred* <*hund* 100 + *-red* reckoning]

hun|dred|al (hun′drə dəl), *adj.* of or having to do with a hundred (county division).

hun|dred|er or **hun|dred|or** (hun′drə dər), *n.* **1** the chief officer, or bailiff, of a hundred. **2** an inhabitant of a hundred, especially one liable to service on a jury.

hun|dred|fold (hun′drəd fōld′), *adj., adv., n.* a hundred times as much or as many.

hun|dred-per|cent|er (hun′drəd pər sen′tər), *n. U.S. Slang.* **1** an extreme nationalist; a jingo or chauvinist. **2** a businessman who will go to any length to make profit.

hun|dredth (hun′drədth), *adj., n.* **1** next after the 99th; last in a series of 100: *After they had counted out the hundredth penny, they asked for a dollar bill.* **2** one, or being one, of 100 equal parts: *With a hundredth part gone, a dollar becomes 99 cents.*

hun|dred|weight (hun′drəd wāt′), *n., pl.* **-weights** or (*as after a numeral*) **-weight.** **1** a measure of weight, equal to 100 pounds (short hundredweight) in the United States and Canada or 45.3592 kilograms. **2** a measure of weight, equal to 112 pounds (long hundredweight) in Great Britain or 50.80 kilograms. **3** a measure of weight, equal to 50 kilograms in countries that use the metric system. *Abbr:* cwt.

Hundred Years' War, a series of wars between England and France from 1337 to 1453.

hung (hung), *v.* a past tense and a past participle of **hang:** *He hung up his cap. Your dress has hung here all day.*
hung up, *Slang.* **a** in a difficulty or predicament; stymied: *Durrell now wants to do a comic novel, but is hung up* (Newsweek). **b** anxious, troubled, or upset: *She admits her songs are not yet very commercial. "I usually write them when I am very emotionally disturbed, really hung up," she explains* (London Times).
hung up on, *Slang.* **a** preoccupied or obsessed with: *Each is hung up on his syndrome* (*which often takes the form of atavistic racial fears*), *unable to live without it* (New York Times). **b** emotionally attached to; infatuated with: *Most of the bishops seem to be sincerely hung up on the word "change" and agree that it is needed here and now* (Manchester Guardian Weekly).
►See **hang** for usage note.

Hung., **1** Hungarian. **2** Hungary.

Hun|gar|i|an (hung gãr′ē ən), *adj., n.* —*adj.* of Hungary, a country in central Europe, its people, or their language.
—*n.* **1** a person born or living in Hungary; Magyar. **2** the Finno-Ugric language of Hungary; Magyar.

Hungarian millet, a type of foxtail millet having a small brown or purple flower head, grown chiefly in Kansas, Missouri, Texas, and neighboring states for hay.

Hungarian partridge, a grayish Eurasian partridge with a reddish-brown tail, introduced into areas of North America.

Hungarian pointer, = Vizsla.

hun|ger (hung′gər), *n., v.* —*n.* **1** pains or an uncomfortable feeling in the stomach caused by having had nothing to eat. Sometimes hunger makes a person feel weak. **2** a desire or need for food: *The little boy who ran away from home soon felt hunger.* SYN: appetite. **3** *Figurative.* a strong desire or craving: *The badly treated boy had a hunger for kindness and affection.* SYN: longing, yearning.
—*v.i.* **1** to feel hunger; be hungry. **2** *Figurative.* to have a strong desire: *The lonely girl hungered for friends.* SYN: long.
—*v.t.* to subject to hunger; starve.
[Old English *hungor*] —**hun′ger|er,** *n.*

hun|ger|ing|ly (hung′gər ing lē), *adv.* hungrily; longingly.

hun|ger|ly (hung′gər lē), *adj. Archaic.* having a hungry or starved look.

hunger strike, a refusal to eat, especially on the part of a prisoner, until certain demands are granted or as a protest against certain conditions.

hunger striker, a person who goes on a hunger strike.

hung jury, a jury that cannot come to a unanimous verdict and is therefore dismissed: *A previous trial on the same charges ended with a hung jury* (Wall Street Journal).

hung|o|ver (hung′ō′vər), *adj. Slang.* **1** suffering from a hangover: *Hungover we might be, from our long . . . spree, but with moderation we expect to greet the future with clear eyes and strong legs* (Wall Street Journal). **2** characteristic of a hangover; miserable; wretched.

hun|gry (hung′grē), *adj.,* **-gri|er, -gri|est.** **1** feeling a desire or need for food: *Mother says the boys in our family always seem hungry. I came home, hungry as a hunter* (Charles Lamb). **2** showing hunger: *The cook saw a hungry look on the beggar's face. Cassius has a lean and hungry look* (Shakespeare). **3** causing hunger; that leaves one hungry: *hungry fare.* **4** *Figurative.* having a strong desire or craving; eager: *hungry for books. A person who longs to read and study is hungry for knowledge.* **5** not rich or fertile: *hungry soil.* [Old English *hungrig*] —**hun′gri|ly,** *adv.* —**hun′gri|ness,** *n.*
—*Syn.* **1 Hungry, famished** mean needing food. **Hungry** is the general word: *Boys are always hungry.* **Famished** means brought to a serious condition of physical exhaustion, sometimes even to the point of dying, by lack of food: *We try to feed and save famished war orphans.* But in informal use, it often means no more than very hungry.

hung-up (hung′up′), *adj.* = hung up. See at **hung.**

hunk[1] (hungk), *n.* **1** *Informal.* a big lump or piece: *a hunk of cheese.* SYN: chunk. **2** a man with a strong, very masculine build or appearance. [origin uncertain. Compare dialectal Flemish *hunke* a hunk.]

hunk[2] (hungk), *n. U.S.* the goal, base, or home in children's games.
on hunk, *U.S.* in a safe or satisfactory position or condition: *They had reached the secret meeting place without interception, so they were now on hunk.*
[American English <Dutch *honk*]

hunk|er[1] (hung′kər), *n.* a person who opposes innovation or change; fogy. [<*Hunker,* a conservative in the New York Democratic Party of the 1840's]

hunk|er[2] (hung′kər), *v., n.* —*v.i.* to squat on one's haunches, or with the haunches brought near the heels: *to hunker down in front of the TV. So there he was one day, . . . hunkered on his moccasins* (Dan Cushman).
—*n.* = haunch.
on one's hunkers, in a squatting position, on one's haunches: *They argued squatting on their hunkers in the dust and emphasizing their words by frequent banging of rifle butts on the ground* (London Times).
[origin uncertain]

hunks (hungks), *n.* **1** a crabbed, disagreeable person: *some old hunks of a sea captain* (Herman Melville). **2** a stingy person; miser: *They all think me a close old hunks* (John Boyle Orrery). [origin unknown]

hunk|y (hung′kē), *adj. U.S. Slang.* in good condition; safe and sound; all right: *North . . . ventured to ask how the child was doing . . . 'She's all hunky, and has an appetite'* (Bret Harte). [American English <*hunk[2]* + *-y[1]*]

hunk|y-do|ry (hung′kē dôr′ē, -dōr′-), *adj. U.S. Slang.* safe and sound; hunky; O.K.: *It would be odd for any Congressional committee to run a full-scale probe and decide everything is hunky-dory* (Wall Street Journal). [apparently varied reduplication of *hunky*]

Hun|nish (hun′ish), *adj.* of, having to do with, or like the Huns. —**Hun′nish|ness,** *n.*

hunt (hunt), *v., n.* —*v.t.* **1** to chase (game or other wild animals) to catch or kill them for food or sport: *Man used to hunt animals to eat; now his table has meat from animals he raises to eat.* **2a** to search through (a region) in pursuit of game: *He has hunted all our local woods.* **b** *Figurative: She hunted the house over for her lost ring.* SYN: ransack, rummage. **3** to use (horses or dogs) in the chase. **4** to drive; chase: *We hunted the neighbor's chickens out of our yard.* **5** *Figurative.* to pursue; harry; persecute: *Evil shall hunt the violent man to overthrow him* (Psalms 140:11). **6** to try to find; search for; seek: *to hunt a clue.* **7** (in change ringing) to alter the position of (a bell) in successive changes shifting it by degrees from first place to the last.
—*v.i.* **1** to chase or go out after wild animals or game: *Most men hunt only for sport today.* **2** *Figurative.* to look thoroughly; search carefully: *to hunt through drawers, to hunt for a lost book.* SYN: ransack, rummage. **3** (in change ringing) to hunt a bell.
—*n.* **1** the act of hunting: *The hunt drew many spectators.* **2** a group of persons hunting together: *The hunt met in the farthest village this time.* **3** *Figurative.* an attempt to find something; thorough look; careful search: *a treasure hunt.*

Pronunciation Key: hat, āge, cãre, fär; let, ēqual, tėrm; it, īce; hot, ōpen, ôrder; oil, out; cup, pu̇t, rüle; child; long; thin; ᴛʜen; zh, measure; ə represents a in about, e in taken, i in pencil, o in lemon, u in circus.

The hunt for the lost child continued until she was found. **4** the district hunted with dogs: *The hunt covers an area four by five miles.* **5** (in change ringing) the act of hunting a bell.

hunt down, a to hunt for until caught or killed: *We should single every criminal out of the herd, and hunt him down* (Joseph Addison). **b** *Figurative.* to look for until found: *Errors, popular or not, are lawful game, and free to everyone to hunt down* (Maurice Keatinge).

hunt up, a to look carefully for: *. . . hunting up earlier quotations for recent words* (J. A. H. Murray). **b** to find by search: *[He] employed his time in hunting up all the old students that he had known formerly* (Albert R. Smith).

[Old English *huntian*] —**hunt′a|ble,** *adj.*

hunt and peck, **1** a manner of typewriting by looking at the keyboard to find the keys before striking them. **2** to typewrite in this manner: *She used to hunt and peck, but she has learned to touch-type.*

hunt|er (hun′tər), *n.* **1** a person who hunts wild animals, game birds, or other game; huntsman. **2** a horse or dog trained for hunting. **3** *Figurative.* a person who searches eagerly for something; seeker: *a fortune hunter.* **4** = hunting watch.

hunt|er-kill|er (hun′tər kil′ər), *adj.* grouped or designed for finding and destroying enemy submarines: *hunter-killer ships.*

hunter-killer satellite, an artificial earth satellite that destroys orbiting enemy satellites; killer satellite: *The Soviet Union and the United States have developed hunter-killer satellites armed with laser beams which can search out and destroy each other's reconnaissance satellites in the vast reaches of space* (New Yorker).

hunter's moon, the full moon next after the harvest moon.

hunt|ing (hun′ting), *n., adj.* —*n.* **1** the act of chasing game. **2** (in a synchronous machine) a variation, occurring periodically, from a true synchronous speed.
—*adj.* of or for hunting.

hunting box, a small house for use during the hunting season.

hunting case, a watchcase with a hinged cover to protect the crystal.

hunting dog, **1** a dog used in hunting. **2** any one of various doglike animals that hunt their prey in packs, such as the dhole.

Hunting Dogs, = Canes Venatici.

hunting ground, a place or region for hunting.

hunting gull, = jaeger (def. 1).

hunting horn, **1** a horn used to give signals in a hunt; bugle. **2** the earliest type of musical horn, consisting of a coiled tube, a flaring end, and a mouthpiece like that of a trumpet. See picture under **horn**.

hunting knife, a large, strong, sharp knife, used to skin and cut up game, or sometimes to kill it. See picture under **knife**.

hunting leopard, = cheetah.

hunting lodge, a lodge for the accommodation of hunters.

Hun|ting|ton's chorea or **disease** (hun′ting tənz), an inherited disorder of the central nervous system, characterized by involuntary twitching of the muscles, distorted speech, and progressive degeneration of the brain. [< George *Huntington,* 1851-1916, an American physician, who first described it]

hunting wasp, a wasp found in the Southwestern United States and in parts of Europe and Africa. The female feeds her young on fresh meat by capturing and storing up small caterpillars, crickets, and the like, before laying eggs.

hunting watch, a watch with a hunting case.

hunt|ress (hun′tris), *n.* **1** a woman who hunts. **2** a mare used in hunting.

hunts|man (hunts′mən), *n., pl.* **-men.** *Especially British.* **1** a hunter. **2** the manager of a hunt.

Hunts|man (hunts′mən), *n.* = Boötes.

hunts|man's-cup (hunts′mənz kup′), *n.* a North American pitcher plant that grows in swamps, so called from its pitcher-shaped leaves.

huntsman spider, a large, tan crab spider of the Southern United States.

hunt's-up (hunts′up′), *n.* **1** a song sung or tune played to arouse huntsmen in the morning. **2** any similar song or tune.

Hu|on pine (hyü′on), a large, evergreen, coniferous timber tree of Tasmania. Its wood is used especially for boats and carving. [< the river *Huon* in Tasmania, where it was first found]

hup (hup), *interj.* = hep² (military command).

Hu|pa (hü′pə), *n., pl.* **-pa** or **-pas.** **1** a member of a North American Indian tribe of northwestern California. **2** the Athapascan language of this tribe.

hup|pa (hůp′ə, hü pä′), *n., pl.* **hup|pas, hup|poth** (hůp′ōt, hü pōt′). = chuppah.

hup|pah (hůp′ə, hü pä′), *n., pl.* **hup|pahs, hup|poth** (hůp′ōt, hü pōt′). = chuppah.

hur|dies (hėr′dēz), *n.pl. Scottish.* the buttocks or hips. [origin unknown]

***hur|dle** (hėr′dəl), *n., v.,* **-dled, -dling.** —*n.* **1** a barrier for people or horses to jump over in a race. **2** *Figurative.* an obstacle or difficulty: *The poor boy overcame the many hurdles in his way to become a doctor.* **3** a frame made of sticks, used as a temporary fence. **4** a sledlike frame on which traitors used to be dragged to execution.
—*v.t.* **1** to jump over: *The horse hurdled both the fence and the ditch.* **2** *Figurative.* to overcome (an obstacle or difficulty): *He hurdled the great odds of poor health to be President.* **3** to enclose with hurdles or fences.
—*v.i.* to jump over a hurdle or other barrier.

hurdles, a race in which the runners jump over hurdles: *He figures to . . . train for the 400-meter hurdles* (Time).

[Old English *hyrdel*] —**hur′dler,** *n.*

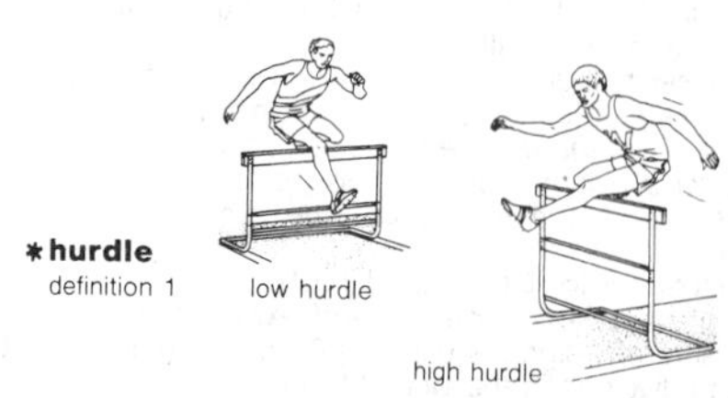

***hurdle** definition 1

hur|dling (hėr′dling), *n.* a foot race in which the runners jump over obstacles called hurdles.

***hur|dy-gur|dy** (hėr′dē gėr′dē), *n., pl.* **-dies.** **1** a hand organ or street piano played by turning a handle: *a hurdy-gurdy's whine* (Stephen Vincent Benét). **2** an obsolete instrument shaped like a guitar, played by turning a wheel. [probably imitative of the sound produced]

***hurdy-gurdy** definition 1

hurl (hėrl), *v., n.* —*v.t.* **1** to throw with much force; cast; fling: *The man hurled his spear at one bear, and the dogs hurled themselves at the other.* **2** *Figurative.* to throw forth (words, cries, or shouts) violently; utter with vehemence: *He hurled insults at me. . . . hurling defiance toward the vault of heaven* (Milton). **3** to throw down; overthrow: *Lucifer was hurled from heaven.*
—*v.i.* **1** to throw; cast; fling. **2** *Baseball.* to pitch. **3** *Archaic.* to rush impetuously: *The very streams . . . impatient seem To hurl into the covert of the grove* (James Thomson).
—*n.* a forcible or violent throw; fling.
[Middle English *hurlen* move violently. Compare Low German *hurreln.*] —**hurl′er,** *n.*

hurl|ey (hėr′lē), *n., pl.* **-eys.** **1** = hurling. **2** the stick or club used in hurling. [< *hurl*]

hurl|ing (hėr′ling), *n.* a game similar to field hockey, played in Ireland.

hurl|y¹ (hėr′lē), *n., pl.* **hurl|ies.** commotion; hurly-burly: *with the hurly, death itself awakes* (Shakespeare). [< *hurl*]

hurl|y² (hėr′lē), *n., pl.* **hurl|ies.** = hurley.

hurl|y-burl|y (hėr′lē bėr′lē), *n., pl.* **-burl|ies,** *adj.* —*n.* disorder and noise; tumult; confusion: *One can get used to anything in life—even to the hurly-burly of New York* (Atlantic). SYN: hubbub, commotion.
—*adj.* disorderly and noisy; tumultuous.
[earlier *hurling and burling,* varied reduplication of *hurling* in obsolete sense, "commotion" < *hurl*]

Hu|ron (hyůr′ən), *n.* **1** a member of a group of Iroquoian Indian tribes formerly living between Lake Huron and Lake Ontario. **2** the language of this group. [American English < French *huron* unkempt person, ruffian < Old North French *hure* disheveled head of hair (the name was applied to the Indians about 1600)]

Hu|ro|ni|an (hyů rō′nē ən), *adj., n. Geology.* —*adj.* of or having to do with a system of rocks discovered north of Lake Huron or with the geological period in which these rocks originated.
—*n.* **1** this system. **2** the geological period in which it originated, a subdivision of the Proterozoic Era.

hur|rah (hə rä′, -rô′), *interj., n., v.* —*interj. n.* a shout of joy or approval: *"Hurrah!" they shouted as the team scored again* (interj.). *Give a hurrah for the hero!* (noun).
—*v.i.* to shout hurrahs; cheer: *We hurrahed as the astronauts rode by in the parade.*
—*v.t.* to receive or encourage with shouts; cheer. Also, **hooray, hurray.**
[probably variant of *huzzah*]

hur|ray (hə rā′), *interj., n., v.i., v.t.* = hurrah.

Hur|ri|an (hůr′ē ən), *n., adj.* —*n.* **1** a member of an ancient, non-Semitic people who were scattered over most of the Middle East from about 2000 to 1200 B.C. Many scholars identify them with the Horites. **2** the language of this people, discovered on clay tablets and written in the alphabet of the Canaanites.
—*adj.* of or having to do with the Hurrians or their language.

hur|ri|cane (hėr′ə kān), *n.* **1a** *Meteorology.* a wind having a velocity of 74 or more miles per hour (on the Beaufort scale, force 12). **b** a tropical cyclone originating usually in the West Indies, often accompanied by violent thunderstorms. **2** a storm with a violent wind and, usually, very heavy rain. **3** *Figurative.* a sudden, violent outburst: *a hurricane of cheers.* [< Spanish *huracán* < Arawak (West Indies) *hurakán*]

hurricane deck, the upper deck on some steamers, such as a riverboat.

hurricane hunter, a pilot or an aircraft of the U.S. Air Force or Navy that flies into hurricanes with instruments to record their size, strength, and other characteristics, and to plot their positions.

***hurricane lamp** or **lantern,** a lamp in which the source of light, usually a candle or a wick drawing kerosene, is protected by a chimney.

***hurricane lamp**

hurricane warning, two square red flags with black centers displayed during the day or a white light between two vertical red lights displayed at night along a seacoast or lakeshore to warn of an approaching hurricane.

hur|ri|coon (hėr′ə kün), *n.* a balloon equipped with a camera and other instruments which is sent into a hurricane to record information about it. [< *hurric*(ane) (ball)*oon*]

hur|ried (hėr′id), *adj.* **1** done or made in a hurry; hasty: *a hurried escape, a hurried reply.* SYN: cursory. **2** forced to hurry. —**hur′ried|ly,** *adv.* —**hur′ried|ness,** *n.*

hur|ri|er (hėr′ē ər), *n.* a person who hurries.

hur|ry (hėr′ē), *v.,* **-ried, -ry|ing,** *n., pl.* **-ries.** —*v.t.* **1** to move, drive, carry, or send quickly or with more than a natural or easy speed: *They hurried the sick child to the doctor. He hurried his book out of sight when the teacher appeared.* **2** to urge to act soon or too soon: *to be hurried into an imprudent action or decision. The salesman hurried the customer to make a choice.* SYN: quicken, accelerate, expedite. **3** to urge to great speed or to too great speed: *Don't hurry the driver. A second fear . . . madly hurries her she knows not whither* (Shakespeare). **4** to make go on or occur more quickly; hasten: *Please hurry dinner.*
—*v.i.* to move or act with more than an easy or natural speed: *If you hurry, your work may be poor. He hurried to get the doctor.*
—*n.* **1** a hurried movement or action: *In her hurry, she dropped the eggs.* **2** eagerness to have quickly or do quickly; rush: *She was in a hurry to see her father.* **3** need of haste: *There is no hurry for this.*

hurry up! make haste; increase your speed: *Hurry up! We'll miss the train if you don't.*

[origin uncertain. Compare Swedish *hurra* to whirl, Danish *hurre* to whir.] —**hur′ry|ing|ly,** *adv.*

—*Syn. n.* **1 Hurry, haste, speed** mean swiftness or quickness in action or movement. **Hurry** suggests urgency, rushing, or bustling: *The boy knocked his little brother down in his hurry.* **Haste** suggests eager or necessary swiftness, but without really effective results: *All this haste was of no use.* **Speed** suggests calm and effective swiftness: *They did the work with speed.*

hurry call, a call for immediate help in an emergency.

hur|ry-scur|ry or **hur|ry-skur|ry** (hėr′ē skėr′ē), *n., pl.* **-ries,** *adj., adv., v.,* **-ried, -ry|ing.** *Informal.* —*n.* hurry and confusion.
—*adj.* hurried and confused: *stand out bold against this humdrum, hurry-scurry world* (New Yorker).
—*adv.* with hurry and confusion: *We fled hurry-scurry before the storm.*
—*v.i.* to move or rush in confused and undignified haste.
—*v.t.* to cause to move in a hurry.

hur|ry-up (hėr′ē up′), *adj. U.S. Informal.* used for, involving, or requiring hurry.

hurst (hėrst), *n. Dialect.* **1** a grove or small wood.

2 a wooded eminence; knoll; hill; bank.
3 a sandbank. [Old English *hyrst*]

hurt (hėrt), *v.,* **hurt, hurt|ing,** *n.* —*v.i.* **1** to suffer injury or pain; be painful: *My hand hurts.* **2** to cause pain, harm, or damage: (*Figurative.*) *His friend's sudden coldness really hurt.*
—*v.t.* **1** to cause pain or injury to; wound; injure: *The stone hurt his foot badly.* **SYN**: See syn. under **injure**. **2** to have a bad effect on; do damage or harm to: *Will it hurt this hat if I get it wet?* **SYN**: See syn. under **injure**. **3** *Figurative.* to give mental pain to; grieve; distress: *He hurt his mother's feelings.* **SYN**: vex, offend.
—*n.* **1** a cut, bruise, or the breaking of a bone; any wound or injury: *A scratch is not a serious hurt.* **SYN**: lesion. **2** a bad effect; harm; wrong; damage: *It would do no hurt to get the house painted this summer.* **SYN**: detriment. **3** *Obsolete.* a knock, blow, or stroke causing a wound or damage.
[apparently < Old French *hurter* push, strike, collide, perhaps < a Germanic word]

hurt|a|ble (hėr′tə bəl), *adj.* capable of being hurt or damaged.

hurt|er (hėr′tər), *n.* **1** a person or thing that hurts. **2** the shoulder of an axle, or a strengthening piece on the shoulder, against which the hub of the wheel strikes. **3** the part of a gun carriage which prevents it from rolling when put in firing position. [Middle English *hurtour,* perhaps < Old French *hurtouoir* knocker, bumper < *hurter;* see etym. under **hurt**]

hurt|ful (hėrt′fəl), *adj.* causing hurt, harm, or damage; injurious: (*Figurative.*) *a mean and hurtful remark.* **SYN**: detrimental, prejudicial, pernicious, noxious, harmful. —**hurt′ful|ly,** *adv.* —**hurt′ful|ness,** *n.*

hur|tle (hėr′təl), *v.,* **-tled, -tling,** *n.* —*v.i.* **1** to dash or drive violently; rush suddenly; come with a crash: *The car hurtled across the road into a fence.* **SYN**: dart, shoot. **2** to move with clattering or clashing; rush noisily or violently: *The express train hurtled past.* **3** to come into collision; dash; clash: *Spears hurtled against shields.* **4** to resound as in collision or rapid motion: *The clash of their onslaught hurtled across the field.*
—*v.t.* **1** to dash or drive violently; fling: *The impact of the crash hurtled the driver against the windshield of the car.* **2** to strike or dash against; collide with.
—*n.* act or fact of hurtling; clash; clatter. **SYN**: collision, conflict.
[Middle English *hurtelen* < *hurten* hurt, in early sense "knock or dash against"]

hur|tle|ber|ry (hėr′təl ber′ē), *n., pl.* **-ries. 1** the whortleberry or bilberry. **2** the huckleberry. [see etym. under **huckleberry**]

hurt|less (hėrt′lis), *adj.* **1** harmless. **2** free from hurt; unhurt.

hus|band (huz′bənd), *n., v.* —*n.* **1** a man who has a wife; married man. **2** *Archaic.* the manager of a household or establishment; steward.
—*v.t.* **1** to manage carefully; be saving of; make the most of: *to husband one's resources. That man must husband his strength while he is ill.* **SYN**: economize. **2** to marry. **3** *Figurative.* to have or espouse an opinion: *to husband a doctrine on this or any other palpably unprovable proposition* (George Bancroft). **4** to provide or match with a husband; mate: *Being so father'd and so husbanded* (Shakespeare). **5** *Archaic.* to till (soil); cultivate or tend (plants).
[Old English *hūsbōnda* (< *hūs* house + *bōnda* head of a family), perhaps < Scandinavian (compare Old Icelandic *hūsbōndi* master, husband, ultimately < *hūs* house + *bōndi* freeholder)] —**hus′band|less,** *adj.*

hus|band|ly (huz′bənd lē), *adj.* of or befitting a husband; marital: *Ellis skipped most of his husbandly duties on the plea that his work came first* (Time).

hus|band|man (huz′bənd mən), *n., pl.* **-men.** = farmer.

hus|band|ry (huz′bən drē), *n.* **1** farming; agriculture. **2** the management of one's affairs or resources: *To let a roof leak is bad husbandry.* **3** careful management; thrift; frugality: *Borrowing dulls the edge of husbandry* (Shakespeare). **SYN**: economy.

hush (hush), *v., n., interj., adj.* —*v.i.* to stop making a noise; become silent or quiet: *The wind has hushed.*
—*v.t.* **1** to make silent or quiet: *Hush your dog. Hush your tongue.* **2** *Figurative.* to soothe; calm: *All her fears were hush'd together* (William Cowper). **SYN**: allay, lull, pacify, tranquilize.
—*n.* a stopping of noise; silence; quiet: *There we subsided in a cool hush* (New Yorker). **SYN**: stillness.
—*interj.* stop the noise! be silent! keep quiet!
—*adj. Archaic.* silent; still; quiet; hushed.
hush up, a to stop talk, mention, or discussion of; keep from being told: *The facts were hushed up to keep them secret. The thing was hushed up, and never known at court* (Jonathan Swift). **b** *Informal.* to be silent; hush: *We passed out, Greene following us with loud words, ... when I told him to hush up, or I would take him prisoner* (William T. Sherman).
[Middle English *hussht* silent; (originally) interjection, silence; perhaps imitative]

hush|ful (hush′fəl), *adj.* silent; still. —**hush′ful|ly,** *adv.*

hush-hush (hush′hush′), *adj. Informal.* having to do with any object, process, plan, policy, or undertaking, the details or existence of which are kept secret: *a hush-hush meeting. The project is so very hush-hush that even some military agencies working on parts of it don't know the overall purpose* (Newsweek).

hush money, money paid to keep a person from telling something: *Hush money encourages blackmail.*

hush-pup|py (hush′pup′ē), *n., pl.* **-pies,** *adj.* —*n. Southern U.S.* a small ball of corn meal fried in deep fat.
—*adj. Slang.* of or characteristic of the South, especially the rural areas of the South: *hush-puppy country, a hush-puppy accent.*
[supposedly < the fact that they were given to puppies to quiet them]

hush ship, one of a class of light cruisers of very high speed, provided with long-range guns, built by the British during World War I, so called because of the secrecy in regard to their construction.

husk[1] (husk), *n., v.* —*n.* **1** the dry outer covering of certain seeds and fruits: **a** *U.S.* the outer covering of an ear of corn. Corn husks are still green when the corn is ready to eat. **b** carob pods (in the parable of the prodigal son, Luke 15:16). **2** *Figurative.* the dry or worthless outer covering of anything: *His spirit was gone; only the husk of a man remained.*
—*v.t.* to remove the husk from: *Husk the corn before cooking it.*
[Middle English *huske;* origin uncertain. Compare earlier Dutch *huysken.*] —**husk′er,** *n.*

husk[2] (husk), *n.* a husky quality or state, as of the voice. [apparently back formation < *husky*[1]]

husk[3] (husk), *n.* a disease of cattle, characterized by a hacking cough, due to roundworms in the bronchial tubes. [origin uncertain. Compare etym. under **husky**[1].]

husk|ing (hus′king), *n. U.S.* **1** the removal of the husk from corn. **2** = husking bee.

husking bee, *U.S.* a gathering of neighbors and friends to husk corn.

husk tomato, = ground cherry.

husk|y[1] (hus′kē), *adj.,* **husk|i|er, husk|i|est,** *n., pl.* **husk|ies.** —*adj.* **1** dry in the throat; rough of voice; hoarse: *a husky tone. A cold sometimes causes a husky cough.* **2** of or having husks. **3** like a husk: *a husky covering.* **4** big and strong; vigorous: *a husky young man.* **SYN**: burly.
—*n. Informal.* a big, strong person.
[< *husk*[1] + *-y*[1]] —**husk′i|ly,** *adv.* —**husk′i|ness,** *n.*

husk|y[2] (hus′kē), *n., pl.* **husk|ies. 1** = Siberian husky: *starving huskies ... from some Indian village* (Jack London). **2** = Eskimo dog. **3** an Eskimo. [American English; origin uncertain; perhaps alteration of *Eskimo*]

Husk|y (hus′kē), *n., pl.* **Husk|ies. 1** = husky[2]. **2** the Eskimo language.

hus|sar (hu̇ zär′), *n.* **1** a light-armed cavalry soldier in various European armies. **2** one of a body of light cavalry organized in Hungary during the 15th century. [< Hungarian *huszár* < Old Serbian *husar,* apparently < Greek (Byzantium) *chosarios* scout, spy]

Huss|ite (hus′īt), *n., adj.* —*n.* a follower of John Huss, a Bohemian religious reformer, executed in 1415.
—*adj.* of or having to do with Huss or his teachings.

Huss|it|ism (hus′ī tiz əm), *n.* the doctrines of John Huss or his followers.

hus|sy (huz′ē, hus′-), *n., pl.* **-sies. 1** a bad-mannered or pert girl; minx: *The hussy dared to talk back to me! Alice may only turn out a story-telling little hussy after all* (William de Morgan). **2** a worthless woman; woman who flaunts her immorality; jade. **3** *Obsolete.* a housewife (def. 3). Also, **huzzy.** [alteration of Middle English *huswif;* see etym. under **housewife**]

hus|tings (hus′tingz), *n.pl. or sing.* **1** the platform or place from which speeches are made in a political campaign: *There seems to be a reluctance on the part of many Republicans to take to the hustings; or perhaps it is just inertia* (Wall Street Journal). **2** the platform from which candidates for the British Parliament were formerly nominated and from which they addressed the voters. **3** *Especially British.* the proceedings at an election. **4** Also, **hustings court.** a local court in certain cities of Virginia. **5** *Historical.* a local court of justice, once common in English boroughs. [< Scandinavian (compare Old Icelandic *hūsthing* council < *hūs* house + *thing* assembly)]

hus|tle (hus′əl), *v.,* **-tled, -tling,** *n.* —*v.t.* **1** to carry, send, or move quickly; hurry; bustle: *Mother hustled the baby to bed.* **2** to push or shove roughly; jostle rudely: *The other boys hustled him along the street.* **3** to force hurriedly or roughly: *The police hustled the tramp out of town.* **4** *Informal.* **a** to sell or hawk: *I ... visited the stand at which I once hustled potatoes and tomatoes* (Atlantic). **b** to get or sell in a hurried, rough, or illegal manner: *to hustle used cars, to hustle stolen goods.* —*v.i.* **1** to hurry; bustle. **2** to rush roughly; push one's way: *to hustle along through the crowd.* **3** *Informal.* to go or work with tireless energy: *He had to hustle to make enough money to support his large family.* **4** *Informal.* to get money, business, or other activity, in a hurried, rough, or illegal manner: *to hustle on the streets to pay for drugs.* **5** = Hustle.
—*n.* **1** a hurry; bustle: *It was a hustle to get the dishes washed by seven o'clock.* **2** *Informal.* tireless energy; energetic or pushing activity; push: *It was done with much hustle and bustle.* **3** rough pushing or shoving; rude jostling. **4** *Informal.* a business or activity, often an illegal one: *His hustle is bookmaking.* **5** *Informal.* a sale, often an illegal one: *arrested for a hustle of narcotics.* **6** = Hustle.
[< Dutch *hutselen,* or *husseln* shake]

Hus|tle (hus′əl), *n., v.,* **-tled, -tling.** —*n.* **1** a lively, syncopated ballroom dance with various steps, figures, and patterns performed by couples in close contact: *The Hustle is a dance of posture, rigor, and coordination ... that demands little floor space* (New York Times). **2** music for this dance. —*v.i.* to dance the Hustle: *Hustling is done to specially written dance music* (New York Sunday News). [< *hustle*]

hus|tler (hus′lər), *n.* **1** a person who hustles. **2** *U.S. Informal.* a very energetic or pushing person. **3a** *U.S. Slang.* a petty criminal. **b** a prostitute.

hus|tling (hus′ling), *adj. Informal.* **1** that hustles; energetic. **2** strenuous.

hut[1] (hut), *n., v.,* **hut|ted, hut|ting.** —*n.* **1** a small, roughly made cabin: *The boys built a hut in the woods.* **SYN**: shack. **2** a temporary wooden or metal structure for quartering troops. See also **Nissen hut, Quonset hut. 3** a stockman's cottage in Australia.
—*v.t.* **1** to place in a hut or huts; furnish with a hut or huts. **2** to place (troops or other men) in huts, especially for winter quarters. —*v.i.* **1** to lodge or take shelter in a hut or huts. **2** to go into winter quarters.
[< Middle French *hutte* < Middle High German *hütte*] —**hut′like′,** *adj.*

hut[2] (hut), *interj.* = hep[2] (military command).

hutch (huch), *n., v.* —*n.* **1** a box or pen for small animals. Rabbits are kept in hutches. **2** a hut or cabin. **3** a box, chest, or bin. **4** a cupboard with open shelves on the upper part, especially for holding dishes.
—*v.t.* to put in a hutch; lay up, as in a chest.
[< Old French *huche* < Medieval Latin *hutica* chest, perhaps < Germanic (compare Old High German *hutta* hut)]

Hutch|ins' goose (huch′ənz), a Canada goose breeding in the Canadian Arctic and flying south to the Gulf Coast of Mexico; Richardson's goose. [< Thomas *Hutchins,* an English diplomat]

hu|ti|a (hü tē′ə), *n.* any one of a group of large ratlike rodents, native to South America and the larger islands of the West Indies. It is closely related to the coypu. [< Spanish *hutía* < the Arawakan name]

hut|ment (hut′mənt), *n.* **1** a hut, especially for troops: *Less than a mile and a half from the port is Jordan territory, with the British garrison's hutments at Akaba plainly visible* (London Times). **2** accommodation in huts. **3** a camp of huts.

Huts|nu|wa (huts′nə wə), *n., pl.* **-wa** or **-was.** a member of a small tribe of American Indians living on the western and southern coasts of the Admiralty Island, Alaska.

Hut|ter|i|an (hut ir′ē ən), *adj.* of or having to do with the Hutterities.

Hut|ter|ite (hut′ə rīt), *n., adj.* —*n.* a member of a religious sect dwelling in parts of Canada, Montana, and South Dakota, made up chiefly of communal farmers: *He said the basic principles of the Hutterites are community of goods and nonresistance; they refuse to fight, to hold public office, or to vote* (Listener).
—*adj.* of or belonging to the Hutterites: *In school Hutterite children start off with instruction in Ger-*

Pronunciation Key: hat, āge, cãre, fär; let, ēqual, tėrm; it, īce; hot, ōpen, ôrder; oil, out; cup, pu̇t, rüle; child; long; thin; ᴛʜen; zh, measure; ə represents **a** in about, **e** in taken, **i** in pencil, **o** in lemon, **u** in circus.

man, the sect's basic language, and religious training (Canada Month).
[< Jacob *Hutter,* a Moravian religious reformer, who led the sect in the 1530's + *-ite*[1]]

Hut|to|ni|an (hə tō′nē ən), *adj.* of or having to do with the geological theories of James Hutton (1726-1797), a Scottish physician, who formulated the theory of uniformitarianism and held that the earth's crust was continually changing due to natural agents.

Hu|tu (hü′tü), *n.* = Bahutu.

hutz|pah or **hutz|pa** (hůts′pə), *n.* = chutzpah.

Hux|ley|an or **Hux|lei|an** (huks′lē ən), *adj.* **1** of or characteristic of the English biologist Thomas Henry Huxley, 1825-1895, or his works: *Huxleyan evolutionism.* **2** of or characteristic of the English novelist Aldous Huxley, 1894-1963, or his works: *a Huxleyan brave new world.*

huz|za (hə zä′), *interj., n., pl.* **-zas**, *v.,* **-zaed**, **-za|ing**. **—*interj.*** a loud shout of joy, encouragement, or applause; hurrah.
—*n.* the shout of "huzza"; hurrah.
—*v.i.* to shout "huzza"; cheer. **—*v.t.*** to acclaim with huzzas: *Consider, for example, the much huzzaed British newspapers* (Harper's).
[earlier *hussa,* noun, perhaps variant of Middle English *hissa* a sailor's cry]

huz|zah (hə zä′), *n.* = huzza.

huz|zy (huz′ē), *n., pl.* **-zies**. = hussy.

HV (no periods), **H.V.**, or **h.v.**, high voltage.

hvid gje|tost (vid′gā′tost, yā′-) a type of goat's milk cheese, made in Norway. [< Norwegian *hvid gjetost* white gjetost]

hwan (hwän), *n., pl.* **hwan**. a former unit of money of South Korea used from 1953 to 1962, replaced by the won. [< Korean *hwan*]

hwy., highway.

hwyl (hü′əl), *n., adj.* **—*n.*** great emotional fervor or eloquence, especially as a characteristic ascribed to the Welsh people: *Then, after a dramatic entrance, Richard Burton complete with hwyl . . . read a short poem by Dylan Thomas* (London Times).
—*adj.* filled with or characterized by hwyl.
[< Welsh *hwyl* the peroration of Welsh preachers, typically intoned in a singsong fashion that rises to a high pitch of eloquence]

hy|a|cinth (hī′ə sinth), *n.* **1** any one of various spring plants that grow from bulbs and have spikes of small, fragrant, bell-shaped flowers. Hyacinths belong to the lily family. **2** a flower or bulb of any of these plants. **3** *Greek Mythology.* a plant said to have sprung from the blood of the slain youth Hyacinthus, variously identified by different authors as the Turk's-cap lily, the iris, gladiolus, or larkspur. **4** a brownish or reddish-orange variety of zircon, used as a gem; jacinth. **5** (in ancient times) a precious stone of a blue color, probably the sapphire. **6** a purplish blue. [< Latin *hyacinthus* < Greek *hyákinthos* a kind of flower. See etym. of doublet **jacinth**.]

hyacinth bean, = lablab.

hy|a|cin|thine (hī′ə sin′thən, -thīn), *adj.* **1** of or made of hyacinths. **2** like hyacinths. **3** adorned with hyacinths. **4** having some resemblance to Hyacinthus: *hyacinthine locks.*

Hy|a|cin|thus (hī′ə sin′thəs), *n. Greek Mythology.* a handsome youth, killed accidentally by Apollo because of the jealousy of Zephyrus, and from whose blood Apollo caused a flower to grow.

Hy|a|des (hī′ə dēz), *n.pl.* **1** a group of stars in the shape of a V in the head of the constellation Taurus. When they rose with the sun, they were supposed by the ancients to be a sign of rain. **2** *Greek Mythology.* the daughters of Atlas, nymphs who supplied the earth with moisture and who were placed in the sky by Zeus.

Hy|ads (hī′adz), *n.pl.* = Hyades.

hy|ae|na (hī ē′nə), *n.* = hyena.

hy|a|lin (hī′ə lin), *n.* **1** a horny, nitrogenous substance resembling and closely related to chitin, present in the walls of hydatid cysts. **2** an almost transparent, homogeneous, glassy substance normally found in the matrix of cartilage, in the vitreous body, and elsewhere, and pathologically in the breakdown of connective tissue. [< Greek *hýalos* glass + English *-in*]

hy|a|line (hī′ə lin, -līn), *adj., n.* **—*adj.*** glassy or transparent: *fresh from the hyaline streams* (Thomas H. Chivers). **—*n.*** **1** something glassy or transparent: *the clear hyaline, the glassy sea* (Milton). **2** = hyalin. [< Late Latin *hyalinus* < Greek *hyálinos* < *hýalos* glass]

hyaline cartilage, a translucent bluish cartilage which forms most of the fetal skeleton and is present especially in joints, the nose, and the trachea in adults.

hyaline membrane disease, a respiratory disease of newborn babies, especially when born prematurely, characterized by the formation of glassy film over the air sacs of the lungs; respiratory distress syndrome.

hy|a|lite (hī′ə līt), *n. Mineralogy.* a colorless variety of opal, sometimes transparent like glass and sometimes whitish and translucent. [probably < German *Hyalit* < Greek *hýalos* glass + German *-it* -ite[1]]

hy|al|o|gen (hī al′ə jen), *n.* any one of certain insoluble substances, usually translucent, occurring in cartilage and the vitreous body. [< *hyal*(in) + *-gen*]

hy|a|loid (hī′ə loid), *adj., n.* **—*adj.*** glassy or transparent; crystalline.
—*n.* the hyaloid membrane of the eye.
[< Latin *hyaloīdes* < Greek *hyaloeidēs* glassy]

hyaloid membrane, the thin, transparent membrane around the vitreous humor of the eye, forming the suspensory ligament.

hy|a|lo|plasm (hī′ə lə plaz′əm), *n.* the clear, fluid portion of the protoplasm of a cell, as distinguished from the granular and reticular portions. [< Greek *hýalos* glass + *plásma* something molded]

hy|a|lo|plas|mic (hī′ə lə plaz′mik), *adj.* having to do with or like hyaloplasm.

hy|a|lu|ron|ic acid (hī′ə lů ron′ik), a sticky, sugarlike, organic substance that is a constituent of connective tissues and serves to cement together certain cells in tissues. [< Greek *hýalos* glass + English *uronic acid*]

hy|a|lu|ron|i|dase (hī′ə lů ron′ə dās), *n.* an enzyme present in snake venom, sperm, and some germs, having the power to break down or disperse hyaluronic acid. It increases tissue permeability and has been used to prevent or check the formation of kidney stones and break up scar tissue. [< *hyaluron*(ic acid) + *-id*(e) + *-ase*]

Hy|blae|an (hī blē′ən), *adj.* **1** of or having to do with the town of Hybla in ancient Sicily, famous for its honey. **2** honeyed; mellifluous.

hy|brid (hī′brid), *n., adj.* **—*n.*** **1** the offspring of two animals or plants of different races, varieties, or species. The loganberry is a hybrid because it is a cross between a raspberry and blackberry. The mule is a hybrid of a female horse and a male donkey. **2** *Genetics.* the offspring of two individuals that differ in at least one gene. **3** *Figurative.* anything of mixed origin. A word formed of parts from different languages is a hybrid.
—*adj.* **1** bred from two different races, varieties, or species: *a hybrid rose. A mule is a hybrid animal.* **2** *Figurative.* of mixed origin. **3** (of a word) formed of parts from different languages.
[< Latin *hybrida,* variant of *ibrida* mongrel, hybrid]

hybrid computer, a computer that combines the features of both a digital and analog computer.

hy|brid|ise (hī′brə dīz), *v.t., v.i.,* **-ised**, **-is|ing**. *Especially British.* hybridize.

hy|brid|ism (hī′brə diz əm), *n.* **1** the production of hybrids; crossbreeding. **2** hybrid character, nature, or condition.

hy|brid|ist (hī′brə dist), *n.* a person who produces hybrids by crossing different species; hybridizer.

hy|brid|i|ty (hī brid′ə tē), *n.* hybrid character, nature, or condition.

hy|brid|ize (hī′brə dīz), *v.,* **-ized**, **-iz|ing**. **—*v.t.*** **1** to cause to produce hybrids: *Botanists hybridize different kinds of plants in order to get new varieties.* **2** to form in a hybrid manner: *to hybridize words.*
—*v.i.* to produce a hybrid or hybrids; cross; interbreed. **—hy′brid|i|za′tion**, *n.* **—hy′brid|iz′er**, *n.*

hy|brid|o|ma (hī brə dō′mə), *n.* a cell formed by the fusion of two different cells: *Tissue typing . . . is the labour to which immunologists foresaw the end when they made the first antibody-secreting hybridoma: a hybrid between an ordinary mouse antibody-secreting cell, which has only a limited lifespan, and an immortal tumour cell from a mouse myeloma* (New Scientist).

hybrid vigor, = heterosis.

hy|bris (hī′bris), *n.* = hubris.

hyd., **1** hydraulics. **2** hydrographic. **3** hydrostatics.

hy|dan|to|in (hī dan′tō in), *n.* a white, crystalline compound, found in molasses, used in making pharmaceuticals and resins. *Formula:* $C_3H_4N_2O_2$ [< Greek *hýdōr* water + English (all)*antoin*]

hy|da|thode (hī′də thōd), *n.* a specialized layer of cells on the tips and margins of certain leaves, from which water is secreted. [< Greek *hýdōr, -atos* water + *hodós* way]

hy|da|tid (hī′də tid), *n., adj.* **—*n.*** **1** a cyst containing a clear, watery fluid, produced in man and animals by a tapeworm in its larval state. **2** the larva of a tapeworm in its encysted state.
—*adj.* of, belonging to, or like a hydatid.
[< Greek *hydatís, -idos* watery vesicle; (originally) a drop of water < *hýdōr, -atos* water]

Hyde (hīd), *n.* **Mr.**, the evil side of Dr. Jekyll's personality in Robert Louis Stevenson's story, *The Strange Case of Dr. Jekyll and Mr. Hyde.*

hyd|no|car|pate (hid′nō kär′pāt), *n.* a salt or ester of hydnocarpic acid.

hyd|no|car|pic acid (hid′nō kär′pik), an acid derived from chaulmoogra oil, used in treating leprosy. *Formula:* $C_{16}H_{28}O_2$ [< New Latin *Hydnocarpus*the genus name of a plant that yields the oil (< Greek *hýdnon* truffle + *karpós* fruit) + English *-ic*]

hydr-, *combining form.* the form of **hydro-** before vowels, as in *hydrant.*

Hy|dra (hī′drə), *n., genitive* (def. 2) **Hy|drae**. **1** *Greek Mythology.* a monstrous serpent having nine snakelike heads. When one head was cut off, two heads grew in its place. Hercules finally killed it. **2** a southern constellation that stretches nearly one third of the way around the southern sky, seen by ancient astronomers as having the rough outline of a serpent and called the Water Snake. [< Latin *hydra* < Greek *hýdra* water serpent < *hýdōr, -atos* water]

***hy|dra** (hī′drə), *n., pl.* **-dras**, **-drae** (-drē). **1** a kind of freshwater polyp or coelenterate with a tubelike body and stinging tentacles. When the tubelike body is cut into pieces, each piece forms a new individual. **2** *Figurative.* any persistent evil; evil that is hard to overcome: *Traffic in narcotics is a modern hydra.* [< *Hydra*]

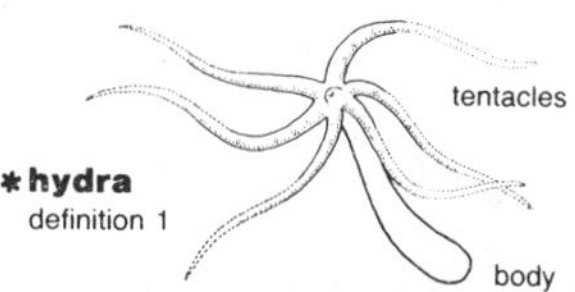

***hydra**
definition 1

hy|drac|id (hī dras′id), *n.* an acid that contains no oxygen, such as hydrochloric acid, which is composed of hydrogen and chlorine.

Hy|drae (hī′drē), *n.* genitive of **Hydra** (def. 2).

hy|dra-head|ed (hī′drə hed′id), *adj.* **1** having many heads, like the Hydra. **2** self-renewing, like the Hydra. **3** *Figurative.* difficult to destroy: *the hydra-headed corruption of bureaucracy.*

hy|dral|a|zine (hī dral′ə zēn, -zin), *n.* a drug sometimes used in the treatment of high blood pressure, though often accompanied by side effects. *Formula:* $C_8H_8N_4$ [< *hydr*(azino-phth) *alazine,* the chemical name]

Hy|dra-Mat|ic (hī′drə mat′ik), *adj. Trademark.* utilizing a fluid coupling to transmit power from the engine to the drive shaft: *Hydra-Matic transmission.*

hy|dran|gea (hī drān′jə), *n.* **1** any one of a group of shrubs with opposite leaves and large, showy clusters of small, white, pink, or blue flowers. It belongs to the saxifrage family. **2** its flower. [< New Latin *Hydrangea* < Greek *hýdōr, -atos* water + *angeîon* vessel, capsule < *ángos* vessel (because of its vessel-shaped seed capsule)]

hy|dran|ge|a|ceous (hī dran′jē ā′shəs), *adj.* characteristic of the hydrangeas.

hy|drant (hī′drənt), *n.* a large upright pipe with a valve for drawing water directly from a water main; a hose connection; fire hydrant; fire plug. Hydrants are used to get water to put out fires and to wash the streets.
hook the hydrant, to attach a fire hose to a hydrant: *As the fire truck passed by, a fireman threw off the end of the hose and another man hooked the hydrant.*
[American English < Greek *hýdōr, -atos* water + English *-ant*]

hy|dranth (hī′dranth), *n.* the flower-shaped structure at the top of the stalk of a hydroid polyp, containing the digestive cavity and a terminal mouth, usually surrounded by tentacles. [< *hydra* polyp + Greek *ánthos* flower]

hy|drar|gy|ri|a|sis (hī′drär jə rī′ə sis), *n.* mercurial poisoning. [< *hydrargyr*(um) + *-iasis*]

hy|drar|gyr|ic (hī′drär jir′ik), *adj.* of or having to do with mercury; mercurial.

hy|drar|gy|rism (hī drär′jə riz əm), *n.* mercurial poisoning.

hy|drar|gy|rol (hī drär′jə rol), *n.* an organic salt of mercury, occurring in brownish-red scales, used as an antiseptic.

hy|drar|gy|rum (hī drär′jər əm), *n.* = mercury. *Abbr:* Hg (no period). [< New Latin *hydrargyrum* < Latin *hydrargyrus* < Greek *hydrárgyros* < *hýdōr* water + *árgyros* silver]

hy|drase (hī′drās), *n.* an enzyme that catalyzes the addition of water to a substrate without hydrolyzing it. [< *hydr-* + *-ase*]

hy|dras|tin (hī dras′tin), *n.* = hydrastine.

hy|dras|tine (hī dras′tēn, -tin), *n.* a crystalline alkaloid found in the rootstock of the goldenseal, formerly used in medicine. *Formula:* $C_{21}H_{21}NO_6$ [< New Latin *Hydrastis* the goldenseal genus name + English *-ine*[2]]

hy|dras|ti|nine (hī dras′tə nin, -nēn), *n.* a colorless, crystalline compound formed by the oxidation of hydrastine, used in medicine. *Formula:* $C_{11}H_{13}NO_3$

hy|dras|tis (hī dras′tis), *n.* = goldenseal. [< New

Latin *Hydrastis* the genus name]

hy|drate (hī′drāt), *n., v.,* **-drat|ed, -drat|ing.** —*n.* any chemical compound made when certain substances unite chemically with water in a definite weight ratio, represented in formulas as containing molecules of water. Washing soda ($Na_2CO_3 \cdot 10H_2O$) is a hydrate.
—*v.i., v.t.* to become or cause to become a hydrate; combine with water to form a hydrate. Washing soda is hydrated sodium carbonate.
[< *hydr-* + *-ate*²] —**hy|dra′tion,** *n.*

hy|dra|tor (hī′drā tər), *n.* a thing that hydrates.

hydraul., hydraulics.

hy|drau|lic (hī drô′lik), *adj.* **1** having to do with water or other liquids at rest or in motion. **2** operated by the pressure of water or other liquids in motion, especially when forced through an opening or openings: *a hydraulic crane, a hydraulic press.* **3** hardening under water: *hydraulic cement.* **4** having to do with hydraulics: *hydraulic engineering, hydraulic mining.* [< Latin *hydraulicus* < Greek *hydraulikón,* neuter < *hýdōr, -atos* water + *aúlos* pipe] —**hy|drau′li|cal|ly,** *adv.*

hydraulic brake, a brake in which fluid under pressure operates the mechanical parts.

hydraulic clutch, = fluid coupling.

hydraulic gradient, the rate of fall of pressure head along a conduit filled with flowing liquid.

hy|drau|lic|i|ty (hī′drô lis′ə tē), *n.* the quality or property of being hydraulic: *the hydraulicity of cement.*

hydraulic jump, an abrupt, turbulent rise in the level of a flowing liquid caused by an obstruction or a change in the slope of its path: *At low discharges a hydraulic jump . . . is formed upstream of the weir which marks the transition from shallow, fast flow to deeper, slower flow* (New Scientist).

hy|drau|lick|ing (hī drô′lə king), *n.* a form of placer mining using a powerful stream of water shooting through a large nozzle to move mineral-bearing gravel or sand directly from a deposit into a riffle.

hydraulic press, a machine in which the pressure exerted by a small piston is communicated through a confined liquid to a large piston, the force being multiplied as many times as the area of the smaller piston must be multiplied to equal that of the larger.

hydraulic ram, a device by which the energy of descending water is used to raise a part of the water to a height greater than that of the source.

hy|drau|lics (hī drô′liks), *n.* the science dealing with water and other liquids at rest or in motion, their uses in engineering, and the laws of their actions. Hydraulics deals with both hydrodynamics and hydrostatics.

hydraulic torque converter, = fluid drive.

hy|dra|zide (hī′drə zīd), *n.* = isoniazid.

hy|dra|zin (hī′drə zin), *n.* = hydrazine.

hy|dra|zine (hī′drə zēn, -zin), *n.* **1** a colorless, fuming, highly corrosive liquid used in organic synthesis and as a fuel for rockets. *Formula:* N_2H_4 **2** any one of a group of compounds derived from this liquid by replacement of one or more hydrogen atoms with an organic radical.

hy|dra|zo|ate (hī′drə zō′āt), *n.* a salt of hydrazoic acid, especially one of silver or mercury.

hy|dra|zo|ic (hī′drə zō′ik), *adj.* of or having to do with hydrazoic acid; triazoic.

hydrazoic acid, a colorless, poisonous, volatile acid with a penetrating odor, obtained by treating hydrazine with nitrous acid and in various other ways; triazoic acid. Hydrazoic acid and most of its salts (hydrazoates) are highly explosive. *Formula:* HN_3

hy|dra|zone (hī′drə zōn), *n.* any one of a class of organic compounds formed by the action of a hydrazine on a compound containing a carbonyl group, water being eliminated.

hy|dre|mi|a (hī drē′mē ə), *n.* an excess of water in the blood. [< *hydr-* + *-emia*]

Hy|dri (hī′drī), *n.* genitive of **Hydrus.**

hy|dri|a (hī′drē ə), *n., pl.* **-dri|ae** (-drē ē). an ancient Greek vase for carrying water, with a large body, narrow mouth, a large handle at the back, and a small one at each side. [< Latin *hydria* < Greek *hydríā* < *hýdōr* water]

hy|dric (hī′drik), *adj.* of or containing hydrogen, especially hydrogen gas.

hy|drics (hī′driks), *n.* the branch of physics that deals with the properties of water.

hy|drid (hī′drid), *n.* = hydride.

hy|dride (hī′drīd, -drid), *n.* a compound of hydrogen with another element or a radical.

hy|dri|od|ic (hī′drē od′ik), *adj.* containing hydrogen and iodine.

hydriodic acid, a colorless, corrosive solution of hydrogen iodide in water, used as a disinfectant and reducing agent. *Formula:* HI

hy|dro¹ (hī′drō), *adj., n., pl.* **-dros.** *Especially Canadian.* —*adj.* that produces electricity through the use of water power; hydroelectric: *a hydro plant.*
—*n.* **1** hydroelectric power: *The three most common sources of energy* [*are*] *hydro, coal, or oil* (New Scientist). **2** electricity: *It was dark on the farm. There is no hydro* (Maclean's).

hy|dro² (hī′drō), *n., pl.* **-dros.** *British.* a sanitarium, hotel, or other place where water cures are given; hydropathic establishment: *She is here to refresh herself at a new health hydro* (London Times). [short for *hydropathic*]

hy|dro³ (hī′drō), *n., pl.* **-dros.** = hydroplane.

hydro-, *combining form.* **1** of or having to do with water: *Hydrodynamic = having to do with the force of water.*
2 containing hydrogen: *Hydrochloric = containing hydrogen and chlorine.* Also, **hydr-** before vowels.
[< Greek *hydro-* < *hýdōr, -atos* water]

hy|dro|a|cous|tic (hī′drō ə küs′tik, -kous′-), *adj.* of or having to do with underwater sound: *hydroacoustic sound detection.*

hy|dro|air|plane (hī′drō ãr′plān), *n.* a floatplane or flying boat; seaplane.

hy|dro|ar|thro|sis (hī′drō är thrō′sis), *n.* the condition of having water present in the joints, as in the knee.

hy|dro|bi|ol|o|gy (hī′drō bī ol′ə jē), *n.* the study of bodies of water with reference to their biological features. —**hy′dro|bi|ol′o|gist,** *n.*

hy|dro|bomb (hī′drō bom′), *n.* an aerial torpedo.

hy|dro|bro|mic (hī′drō brō′mik), *adj.* containing hydrogen and bromine.

hydrobromic acid, a colorless, corrosive solution of hydrogen bromide in water, used in making organic compounds. *Formula:* HBr

hy|dro|car|bon (hī′drō kär′bən), *n.* any one of a class of chemical compounds containing only hydrogen and carbon. Methane, benzene, and acetylene are hydrocarbons. Gasoline is a mixture of hydrocarbons.

hy|dro|cele (hī′drō sēl), *n.* a collection of serous fluid, especially in the scrotum. [< Middle French *hydrocèle,* learned borrowing from Latin *hydrocēlē* < Greek *hydrokḗlē* < *hýdōr* water + *kḗlē* tumor]

hy|dro|cel|lu|lose (hī′drō sel′yə lōs), *n.* a colloidal substance obtained from cellulose by combination with water, as by the action of acids. It is used in making paper and fibers. *Formula:* $C_{12}H_{22}O_{11}$

hy|dro|ce|phal|ic (hī′drō sə fal′ik), *adj.* having to do with or affected with hydrocephalus.

hy|dro|ceph|a|lus (hī′drō sef′ə ləs), *n.* an accumulation of cerebrospinal fluid within the cranium, especially in infancy, often causing great enlargement of the head. [< New Latin *hydrocephalus* < Greek *hydroképhalon* < *hýdōr* water + *kephalḗ* head]

hy|dro|chlo|ric (hī′drə klôr′ik, -klōr′-), *adj.* containing hydrogen and chlorine.

hydrochloric acid, a clear, colorless liquid with a strong, sharp odor and strongly acid taste; muriatic acid. It is obtained by treating common salt with sulfuric acid, by the direct combination of hydrogen and chlorine, and by other methods. Hydrochloric acid is highly corrosive and is used to clean metals, in food processing, in dyeing, as a reagent in organic analysis, and in many industrial processes. *Formula:* HCl

hy|dro|chlo|ride (hī′drə klôr′īd, -id; -klōr′-), *n.* a compound of hydrochloric acid with an organic base.

hy|dro|chlo|ro|thi|a|zide (hī′drə klôr′ə thī′ə zīd, -klōr′-), *n.* a drug taken orally, effective as a diuretic and in reducing high blood pressure. *Formula:* $C_7H_8ClN_3O_4S_2$

hy|dro|col|loid (hī′drə kol′oid), *n.* any substance that forms a gel with the addition of water, such as natural gums and marine algae products.

hy|dro|cor|ti|sone (hī′drō kôr′tə zōn), *n.* an adrenal hormone derived from cortisone, used in treating arthritis and other inflammations; cortisol. *Formula:* $C_{21}H_{30}O_5$

hy|dro|crack|er (hī′drō krak′ər), *n.* the apparatus used in hydrocracking: *The last of the four units in the complex . . . is a 30,000-barrel-a-day hydrocracker* (New York Times).

hy|dro|crack|ing (hī′drō krak′ing), *n.* a method of cracking hydrocarbons utilizing hydrogen and catalysts under high pressure.

hy|dro|cy|an|ic (hī′drō sī an′ik), *adj.* containing hydrogen and cyanogen.

hydrocyanic acid, a colorless, volatile, extremely poisonous liquid that smells like bitter almonds, used in making plastics and dyes; prussic acid. *Formula:* HCN

hy|dro|dy|nam|ic (hī′drō dī nam′ik, -di-), *adj.* having to do with the force or motion of water or other liquids, or with hydrodynamics. —**hy′dro|dy|nam′i|cal|ly,** *adv.*

hy|dro|dy|nam|i|cal (hī′drō dī nam′ə kəl, -di-), *adj.* = hydrodynamic.

hy|dro|dy|nam|i|cist (hī′drō dī nam′ə sist, -di-), *n.* an expert in hydrodynamics.

hy|dro|dy|nam|ics (hī′drō dī nam′iks, -di-), *n.* the branch of physics dealing with the forces that water and other liquids in motion exert.

hy|dro|e|lec|tric (hī′drō i lek′trik), *adj.* developing electricity from water power. —**hy′dro|e|lec′tri|cal|ly,** *adv.*

hy|dro|e|lec|tric|i|ty (hī′drō i lek′tris′ə tē, -ē′lek-), *n.* electricity produced from water power.

hy|dro|fin|er (hī′drō fī′nər), *n.* the apparatus used in hydrofining.

hy|dro|fin|ing (hī′drō fī′ning), *n.* a method of refining petroleum by freeing it from sulfur through partial hydrogenation and the use of catalysts.

hy|dro|flu|or|ic (hī′drō flü ôr′ik, -or′-), *adj.* containing hydrogen and fluorine.

hydrofluoric acid, a colorless, corrosive, volatile, fuming solution of hydrogen fluoride in water, with an irritating, suffocating odor. It is used for etching glass and as a cleaning agent. *Formula:* HF

* **hy|dro|foil** (hī′drō foil), *n.* **1** a fin just below the water line of a boat that raises the hull out of the water at high speeds, decreasing friction and increasing the speed of the boat. **2** a boat with hydrofoils: *Next time you're in Manila take the hydrofoil out to Corregidor* (New Yorker).

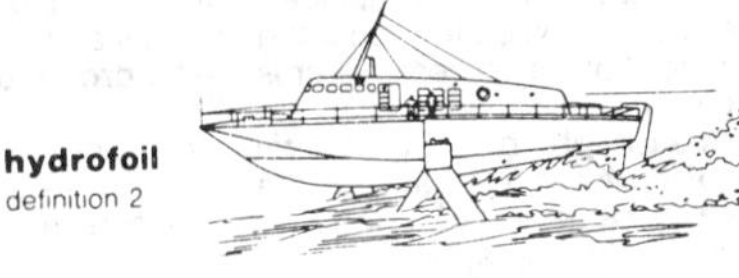

* **hydrofoil**
definition 2

hy|dro|form|er (hī′drō fôr′mər), *n.* the apparatus used in hydroforming.

hy|dro|form|ing (hī′drō fôr′ming), *n.* a method for converting petroleum hydrocarbons to molecular structures that yield high-octane gasoline by utilizing hydrogen and catalysts under high temperatures and pressure.

hy|dro|gas|i|fi|ca|tion (hī′drō gas′ə fə kā′shən), *n.* the conversion of coal into gas by interacting it with hydrogen at high pressures to yield methane.

hy|dro|gas|i|fi|er (hī′drō gas′ə fī′ər), *n.* an apparatus used in hydrogasification.

hy|dro|gel (hī′drō jel), *n. Physical Chemistry.* a gel in which the gelatinous particles are surrounded by water.

* **hy|dro|gen** (hī′drə jən), *n.* a colorless, odorless gas that burns easily. Hydrogen weighs less than any other known element. Hydrogen combines chemically with oxygen to form water and is present in most organic compounds. [< French *hydrogène* < Greek *hýdōr, -atos* water + French *-gène* -gen]

* **hydrogen**

symbol	atomic number	atomic weight	oxidation state
H	1	1.00797	±1

hy|dro|gen|ase (hī′drə jə nās), *n.* an enzyme found in various bacteria that can move molecular hydrogen in and out of organic compounds.

hy|dro|gen|ate (hī′drə jə nāt, hī droj′ə-), *v.t.,* **-at|ed, -at|ing.** to combine with hydrogen; treat with hydrogen. When vegetable oils are hydrogenated, they become solid fats. —**hy′dro|gen|a′tion,** *n.*

hy|dro|gen|a|tor (hī′drə jə nā′tər, hī droj′ə nā-tər), *n.* a device used to combine or treat substances with hydrogen: *The hydrogenator carries out the necessary adjustment of the hydrogen carbon ratio . . . by adding hydrogen to the fuel* (London Times).

hydrogen bomb, a bomb that uses the fusion of atoms to cause an explosion of tremendous force; fusion bomb; superatomic bomb. It is many times more powerful than the atomic bomb. *On Mar. 1, 1954 the United States exploded a hydrogen bomb estimated in strength at between 15 and 17 megatons—or the equivalent of 15 to 17 million tons of TNT* (Newsweek). Also, **H-bomb.**

hydrogen bond, a chemical bond in which the hydrogen atom of one molecule is attracted to the electronegative atom of another molecule, as in compounds containing nitrogen, oxygen, or fluorine: *Hydrogen bonds hold life's molecules in shape, and play a vital role in enzyme catalysis, the action of drugs and anaesthetics, and taste* (New Scientist).

hydrogen cyanide, = hydrocyanic acid.

Pronunciation Key: hat, āge, cãre, fär; let, ēqual, tėrm; it, īce; hot, ōpen, ôrder; oil, out; cup, pu̇t, rüle; child; long; thin; ᴛʜen; **zh,** measure; **ə** represents **a** in about, **e** in taken, **i** in pencil, **o** in lemon, **u** in circus.

hydrogen dioxide, = hydrogen peroxide.

hydrogen fluoride, a colorless, corrosive, poisonous gas which can cause severe burns. *Formula:* HF

hydrogen ion, a positively charged ion of hydrogen found in all acids in the hydrated form.

hy|dro|gen|ize (hī′drə jə nīz, hī droj′ə-), *v.t.,* **-ized, -iz|ing.** = hydrogenate.

hy|dro|gen|ol|y|sis (hī′drə jə nol′ə sis), *n., pl.* **-ses** (-sēz). chemical decomposition in which a compound is broken down and changed into other compounds by interaction with hydrogen.

hy|drog|e|nous (hī droj′ə nəs), *adj.* of or containing hydrogen.

hydrogen peroxide, a colorless liquid compound of hydrogen and oxygen; hydrogen dioxide; peroxide. It is used in water solution as an antiseptic, to bleach hair, and as a rocket propellant. *Formula:* H_2O_2

hydrogen sulfide, an inflammable, poisonous gas with an odor like that of rotten eggs, often found in mineral waters. *Formula:* H_2S

hy|dro|ge|o|log|i|cal (hī′drō jē ə loj′ə kəl), *adj.* of or having to do with hydrogeology.

hy|dro|ge|ol|o|gy (hī′drō jē ol′ə jē), *n.* a branch of geology that deals with surface and subterranean water, its geographical distribution, and the ways in which it affects the features and composition of the earth's crust. **—hy′dro|ge|ol′o|gist,** *n.*

hy|dro|graph (hī′drə graf, -gräf), *n.* a hydrographic record, diagram, or chart.

hy|drog|ra|pher (hī drog′rə fər), *n.* a person skilled in hydrography.

hy|dro|graph|ic (hī′drə graf′ik), *adj.* of or having to do with hydrography: *a hydrographic survey.* **—hy′dro|graph′i|cal|ly,** *adv.*

hy|drog|ra|phy (hī drog′rə fē), *n.* the science of measuring, describing, and charting seas, lakes, rivers, and other bodies of water, with special reference to their use for navigation and commerce. [< *hydro-* + *-graphy*]

hy|droid (hī′droid), *n., adj.* **—*n.*** **1** the polyp form of a coelenterate as distinguished from a jellyfish. Hydroids grow in branching colonies by budding. **2** any sessile hydrozoan.
—*adj.* of or like the hydrozoans.
[American English]

hy|dro|ki|net|ic (hī′drō ki net′ik, -kī-), *adj.* having to do with the motion of fluids, or with hydrokinetics.

hy|dro|ki|net|ics (hī′drō ki net′iks, -kī-), *n.* the kinetics of fluids; branch of physics dealing with the motion of fluids. See also **hydraulics.**

hy|dro|lase (hī′drə lās), *n.* an enzyme that catalyzes the removal of water from a substrate. [< *hydrol*(ysis) + *-ase*]

hy|dro|lite (hī′drə līt), *n.* a type of red geode found in Uruguay that contains quartz crystals left when water that once contained silica evaporated; water stone. [< *hydro-* + *-lite*]

hy|dro|log|ic (hī′drə loj′ik), *adj.* of or having to do with hydrology. **—hy′dro|log′i|cal|ly,** *adv.*

hy|dro|log|i|cal (hī′drə loj′ə kəl), *adj.* = hydrologic.

hydrologic cycle, = water cycle.

hy|drol|o|gy (hī drol′ə jē), *n.* the science that deals with water, with special reference to its properties, laws, and geographical distribution. [< New Latin *hydrologia* < Greek *hýdōr, -atos* water + *-logiā* -logy] **—hy|drol′o|gist,** *n.*

hy|dro|lyse (hī′drə līz), *v.t., v.i.,* **-lysed, -lys|ing.** *Especially British.* hydrolyze.

hy|drol|y|sis (hī drol′ə sis), *n., pl.* **-ses** (-sēz). a chemical process in which a compound is broken down and changed into other compounds by taking up the elements of water. [< *hydro-* + *lysis*]

hy|dro|lyte (hī′drə līt), *n.* a compound that undergoes hydrolysis.

hy|dro|lyt|ic (hī′drə lit′ik), *adj.* of or producing hydrolysis. **—hy′dro|lyt′i|cal|ly,** *adv.*

hy|drol|y|zate (hī′drol′ə zāt), *n.* a product of hydrolysis.

hy|dro|lyze (hī′drə līz), *v.t., v.i.,* **-lyzed, -lyz|ing.** to decompose by hydrolysis: *When a peptide or protein is hydrolyzed ... it breaks down into amino acids* (Scientific American). **—hy′dro|lyz′a|ble,** *adj.* **—hy′dro|ly|za′tion,** *n.*

hy|dro|mag|net|ic (hī′drō mag net′ik), *adj.* of or having to do with hydromagnetics. **—hy′dro|mag|net′i|cal|ly,** *adv.*

hy|dro|mag|net|ics (hī′drō mag net′iks), *n.* a branch of physics that deals with the principles of hydrodynamics applied to electrically conducting fluids, such as plasma, and that studies the relationship of such fluids with a magnetic field.

hy|dro|man|cy (hī′drə man′sē), *n.* divination by means of water. [< Middle French *hydromancie,* learned borrowing from Late Latin *hydromantīa* < Greek *hýdōr, -atos* water + *manteiā* divination] **—hy′dro|manc′er,** *n.*

hy|dro|man|tic (hī′drə man′tik), *adj.* of or having to do with hydromancy.

hy|dro|me|chan|i|cal (hī′drō mə kan′ə kəl), *adj.* **1** of or having to do with hydromechanics. **2** of or having to do with the use of water in mechanical devices.

hy|dro|me|chan|ics (hī′drō mə kan′iks), *n.* the science of the mechanics of fluids or of their laws of equilibrium and motion.

hy|dro|me|du|sa (hī′drō mə dü′sə, -dyü′-), *n., pl.* **-sae** (-sē). a free-swimming jellyfish produced asexually by a hydroid. [< *hydro-* + *medusa*]

hy|dro|me|du|san (hī′drō mə dü′sən, -dyü′-), *adj., n.* **—*adj.*** of or having to do with the hydromedusae.
—*n.* = hydromedusa.

hy|dro|mel (hī′drə mel), *n.* a liquor consisting of honey and water. Hydromel when fermented is called mead. [< Latin *hydromel* < Greek *hydrómeli* < *hýdōr, -atos* water + *méli* honey]

hy|dro|met|al|lur|gi|cal (hī′drō met′ə lėr′jə kəl), *adj.* of or having to do with hydrometallurgy.

hy|dro|met|al|lur|gy (hī′drō met′ə lėr′jē), *n.* the treatment of minerals and ores by wet processes, especially the dissolving of metals in aqueous solutions of acids, bases, or salts, and related operations in connection with extracting the metals.

hy|dro|me|te|or (hī′drō mē′tē ər), *n.* a meteorological phenomenon involving the vapor of water, as rain, snow, or hail.

hy|dro|me|te|or|o|log|i|cal (hī′drō mē′tē ər ə loj′ə kəl), *adj.* of or having to do with hydrometeorology.

hy|dro|me|te|or|ol|o|gy (hī′drō mē′tē ə rol′ə jē), *n.* the branch of meteorology dealing with atmospheric phenomena depending on water vapor. **—hy′dro|me′te|or|ol′o|gist,** *n.*

hy|drom|e|ter (hī drom′ə tər), *n.* a graduated instrument for finding the specific gravity of liquids. A hydrometer is used to test the battery of an automobile. The amount that the weighted inner glass tube sinks in the liquid indicates the concentration of acid in the battery.

hy|dro|met|ric (hī′drə met′rik), *adj.* of or having to do with hydrometry or a hydrometer.

hy|dro|met|ri|cal (hī′drə met′rə kəl), *adj.* = hydrometric.

hy|drom|e|try (hī drom′ə trē), *n.* the determination of specific gravity by means of a hydrometer.

hy|dro|naut (hī′drə nôt), *n.* a member of the United States Navy trained to work in undersea vessels engaged in search and rescue missions and in research projects. [< *hydro-* + *-naut,* as in *astronaut*]

hy|dron|ic (hī dron′ik), *adj.* of or having to do with hydronics: *hydronic heating.*

hy|dron|ics (hī dron′iks), *n.pl.* the methods or operations involved in the cooling or heating by electrically regulated circulation of fluids. [< *hydr-* + (electr)*onics*]

hy|dro|ni|um (hī drō′nē əm), *n.* a hydrogen ion combined with a molecule of water.

hy|dro|path (hī′drə path), *n.* = hydropathist.

hy|dro|path|ic (hī′drə path′ik), *adj., n.* **—*adj.*** of or using hydropathy.
—*n.* a sanitarium that specializes in hydropathy.

hy|drop|a|thist (hī drop′ə thist), *n.* a person who practices or favors hydropathy.

hy|drop|a|thy (hī drop′ə thē), *n.* the treatment of disease by using quantities of water externally and internally; water cure. [< German *Hydropathie* < Greek *hýdōr, -atos* water + German *-pathie* -pathy; meaning influenced by English *homeopathy*]

hy|dro|per|ox|ide (hī′drō pə rok′sīd), *n.* any one of a class of compounds containing the group OOH-. Hydrogen peroxide is the simplest hydroperoxide.

hy|dro|phane (hī′drə fān), *n.* a partly translucent variety of opal which becomes more translucent when immersed in water. [< *hydro-* + Greek *phaínein* to show]

hy|droph|a|nous (hī drof′ə nəs), *adj.* having to do with or like hydrophane; becoming transparent when immersed in water.

hy|dro|phil|ic (hī′drə fil′ik), *adj.* **1** that can readily absorb or dissolve in water, as a gelatin does. **2** = hydrophilous. [< *hydro-* + *-phil* + *-ic*]

hy|droph|i|lous (hī drof′ə ləs), *adj.* pollinated by the action of water: *hydrophilous plants.* [< *hydro-* + Greek *phílos* loving (with English *-ous*)]

hy|dro|pho|bi|a (hī′drə fō′bē ə), *n.* **1** = rabies. **2** an unhealthy dread of water. [< Late Latin *hydrophobia* < Greek *hydrophobiā* < *hýdōr, -atos* water + *phóbos* dread, fear]

hy|dro|pho|bic (hī′drə fō′bik), *adj.* **1** of or having to do with hydrophobia. **2** suffering from hydrophobia. **3** of or having to do with a substance that has little or no ability to combine with or dissolve in water, such as wax.

hy|dro|phone (hī′drə fōn), *n.* **1** an instrument used to detect sound under water and to determine its source and position. **2** an instrument used to detect the flow of water through a pipe. It is used in finding leaks. **3** *Medicine.* an instrument used in auscultation, whereby sounds are carried through a column of water.

hy|dro|phyl|la|ceous (hī′drō fə lā′shəs), *adj.* belonging to the waterleaf family of herbs and plants. [< *hydro-* + Greek *phýllon* leaf + English *-aceous*]

hy|dro|phyte (hī′drə fīt), *n.* any plant that can grow only in water or very wet soil. Most algae are hydrophytes. [< *hydro-* + Greek *phytón* plant]

hy|dro|phyt|ic (hī′drə fit′ik), *adj.* of or like a hydrophyte.

hy|drop|ic (hī drop′ik), *adj.* = dropsical. [< Latin *hydrōpicus* < Greek *hydrōpikós* < *hýdrōps, hydrōpis* dropsy]

hy|dro|plane** (hī′drə plān), *n., v.,* **-planed, -plan|ing.** **—*n. **1** a light, fast motorboat that glides on the surface of water: *A flat-bottomed inboard motorboat called a hydroplane has a light hull and a powerful motor designed especially for racing* (William W. Robinson). **2** an airplane provided with floats or with a boatlike underpart that can land or take off on water; seaplane. **3** a structure on an airplane that enables it to float on water. **4** a horizontal rudder on a submarine that enables it to surface or submerge.
—*v.i.* **1** to glide on the surface of water. **2** to use or ride in a hydroplane. **3** (of a vehicle) to undergo hydroplaning.

***hydroplane** definition 1

hy|dro|plan|ing (hī′drə plā′ning), *n.* the action of tires on a vehicle floating or sliding on wet pavement, caused by the build-up of water between the moving tires and the pavement to a point where the tires lose contact with the road: *Film ["Grooving for Safety"] illustrates a new technique currently being employed to prevent tire hydroplaning, by putting narrow grooves in highways to provide an escape route for the water and improving tire traction* (Science News).

hy|dro|pneu|mat|ic (hī′drō nü mat′ik, -nyü-), *adj.* having to do with or produced by the action or use of both water and air or water and gas.

hy|dro|pon|ic (hī′drə pon′ik), *adj.* of hydroponics; produced or grown by hydroponics: *Hydroponic farming ... is a potential source of increased crop yield* (William C. Baggs). **—hy′dro|pon′i|cal|ly,** *adv.*

hy|dro|pon|ics (hī′drə pon′iks), *n.* the growing of plants without soil, by the use of water containing the necessary mineral nutrients; chemical culture; nutriculture.

hy|drop|o|nist (hī drop′ə nist), *n.* a person skilled in hydroponics.

hy|dro|pow|er (hī′drō pou′ər), *n.* electricity generated by means of water power.

hy|drops (hī′drops), *n.* = dropsy. [< Latin *hydrōps* < Greek *hýdrōps*]

hy|drop|sy (hī′drop sē), *n.* = dropsy.

hy|dro|psy|cho|ther|a|py (hī′drō sī′kō ther′ə pē), *n.* the treatment of mental or emotional disorders by techniques involving the use of baths or pools.

hy|dro|quin|ol (hī′drō kwin′ōl, -ol), *n.* = hydroquinone.

hy|dro|qui|none (hī′drō kwi nōn′, -kwin′ōn), *n.* a white, sweetish, crystalline compound formed by the reduction of quinone, used in photographic developers and other chemical products, and in medicine. *Formula:* $C_6H_6O_2$

hydros., hydrostatics.

hy|dro|scope (hī′drə skōp), *n.* **1** an optical apparatus that enables the observer to view objects below the surface of the sea. **2** an ancient device that measured the lapse of time by the sinking of water in a graduated tube perforated at the bottom.

hy|dro|scop|ic (hī′drə skop′ik), *adj.* having to do with or made with a hydroscope.

hy|dro|ski (hī′drō skē), *n., pl.* **-skis** or **-ski.** a retractable device on an airplane permitting it to take off and land on any smooth surface, as land, water, or snow.

hy|dro|skim|mer (hī′drō skim′ər), *n.* a hovercraft for traveling over water, with a fin along each side that pierces the water's surface: *Using a "cushion of air," the hydroskimmer has no upper limit on the speed at which it can "fly" nor on the weight which it can carry* (Science News Letter).

hy|dro|sol (hī′drə sol, -sōl), *n.* a colloidal solution in water. [< *hydro-* + *sol*[4]]

hy|dro|sole (hī′drə sōl), *n.* = hydrosol.

hy|dro|so|ma (hī′drə sō′mə), *n.* = hydrosome.

hy|dro|some (hī′drə sōm), *n.* the entire body of a compound hydrozoan; hydroid. [< New Latin *hy-*

drosoma < *hydra* hydra + Greek *sôma* body]
hy|dro|space (hī′drə spās), *n.* **1** the unexplored, underwater regions of the earth; inner space: *Other categories of plot include a growing preoccupation with "inner space" or "hydrospace" . . . the opening up of the watery four-fifths of our own planet* (New Scientist). **2** the field of science, technology, and industry dealing with these regions and their exploration.
hy|dro|sphere (hī′drə sfir), *n.* **1** the water on the surface of the globe; the water portion of the earth as opposed to the lithosphere and the atmosphere. **2** the water vapor in the atmosphere.
hy|dro|stat (hī′drə stat), *n.* **1** any one of various devices for preventing injury to a steam boiler from low water. **2** an electrical device for detecting the presence of water from overflow, leakage, etc.
hy|dro|stat|ic (hī′drə stat′ik), *adj.* of or having to do with hydrostatics. —**hy′dro|stat′i|cal|ly**, *adv.*
hy|dro|stat|i|cal (hī′drə stat′ə kəl), *adj.* = hydrostatic.
hydrostatic press, = hydraulic press.
hy|dro|stat|ics (hī′drə stat′iks), *n.* the branch of physics that deals with the laws of liquids at rest and of liquids and gases under pressure; the statics of liquids.
hy|dro|sul|fate (hī′drə sul′fāt), *n.* a compound of sulfuric acid with an organic base.
hy|dro|sul|fid (hī′drə sul′fid), *n.* = hydrosulfide.
hy|dro|sul|fide (hī′drə sul′fīd, -fid), *n.* a compound formed by the replacement of one of the hydrogen atoms of hydrogen sulfide (H_2S) with another element or radical, as NaHS.
hy|dro|sul|fite (hī′drə sul′fīt), *n.* a salt of hydrosulfurous acid, especially sodium hyposulfite ($Na_2S_2O_4$) used as a bleaching agent.
hy|dro|sul|fu|ric (hī′drō sul fyu̇r′ik), *adj.* containing hydrogen and sulfur: *hydrosulfuric acid.*
hy|dro|sul|fur|ous (hī′drə sul′fər əs, -fyər-; -sul-fyu̇r′əs), *adj.* = hyposulfurous.
hydrosulfurous acid, = hyposulfurous acid.
hy|dro|sul|phate (hī′drə sul′fāt), *n.* = hydrosulfate.
hy|dro|sul|phide (hī′drə sul′fīd, -fid), *n.* = hydrosulfide.
hy|dro|tac|tic (hī′drə tak′tik), *adj.* of or having to do with hydrotaxis.
hy|dro|tax|is (hī′drə tak′sis), *n.* a movement toward or away from water, as of plasmodia or other organisms. [< *hydro-* + Greek *táxis* arrangement]
hy|dro|tech|ny (hī′drə tek′nē), *n.* hydraulic engineering with special reference to the storage and distribution of water; the technics of water supply. [< *hydro-* + Greek *téchnē* skill]
hy|dro|ther|a|peu|tic (hī′drō ther′ə pyü′tik), *adj.* of or having to do with hydrotherapy.
hy|dro|ther|a|peu|tics (hī′drō ther′ə pyü′tiks), *n.* = hydrotherapy.
hy|dro|ther|a|py (hī′drō ther′ə pē), *n.* the treatment of disease by means of water; hydropathy. —**hy′dro|ther′a|pist**, *n.*
hy|dro|ther|mal (hī′drə thėr′məl), *adj.* of or having to do with heated water, especially with the action of heated waters in producing geological changes by dissolving and redepositing minerals. —**hy′dro|ther′mal|ly**, *adv.*
hy|dro|tho|rac|ic (hī′drō thə ras′ik), *adj.* of or having to do with hydrothorax.
hy|dro|tho|rax (hī′drə thôr′aks, -thōr′-), *n.* a disease characterized by the presence of serous fluid in one or both of the pleural cavities. [< *hydro-* + *thorax*]
hy|dro|trop|ic (hī′drə trop′ik), *adj.* bending or turning in response to moisture. [< *hydro-* + Greek *trópos* a turning]
hy|drot|ro|pism (hī drot′rə piz əm), *n.* a tendency of plants to bend or turn in response to moisture. Hydrotropism causes roots to grow toward water.
hy|drous (hī′drəs), *adj.* **1** containing water; watery. **2** containing water, usually in combination: *A hydrous salt is a crystalline compound.*
hydrous lanolin, = lanolin (def. 1).
hy|drox|id (hī drok′sid), *n.* = hydroxide.
hy|drox|ide (hī drok′sīd, -sid), *n.* any compound consisting of an element or radical combined with one or more hydroxyl radicals. Calcium hydroxide is slaked lime. Hydroxides of metals are bases; those of nonmetals are acids.
hydroxide ion, a negatively charged ion found in most basic solutions.
hy|drox|y acid (hī drok′sē), **1** an organic compound having both a carboxyl (-COOH) and a hydroxyl (-OH) radical. **2** any organic acid of a group which have a hydroxyl (-OH) radical and which exhibit both alcoholic and acidic characteristics.
hy|drox|y|ap|a|tite (hī drok′sē ap′ə tīt), *n.* a crystalline substance, containing calcium and phosphorus, found in certain rocks. It is the basic constituent of bone.
hy|drox|y|bu|tyr|ic acid (hī drok′sē byü tir′ik), a chemical intermediate that is present in acetone bodies. *Formula:* $C_4H_8O_3$
hy|drox|yl (hī drok′səl), *n.* a univalent radical, -OH. It is in all hydroxides. [< *hydr*(ogen) + *ox*(ygen) + *-yl*]
hy|drox|yl|am|in (hī drok′sə lam′in), *n.* = hydroxylamine.
hy|drox|yl|a|mine (hī drok′sə lə mēn′, -lam′in), *n.* a colorless, crystalline base, similar to ammonia in chemical properties but less basic, used as a reducing agent. *Formula:* NH_2OH
hy|drox|yl|ase (hī drok′sə lās), *n.* an enzyme that catalyzes hydroxylation.
hy|drox|yl|ate (hī drok′sə lāt), *v.t.,* **-at|ed, -at|ing.** to introduce one or more hydroxyls into (a compound). —**hy|drox′yl|a′tion**, *n.*
hy|drox|yl|ic (hī′drok sil′ik), *adj.* of or having to do with hydroxyls.
hydroxyl ion, = hydroxide ion.
hy|drox|y|pro|line (hī drok′sē prō′lēn, -lin), *n.* a colorless, crystalline amino acid derived by hydroxylation of proline, used in biochemical research. *Formula:* $C_5H_9NO_3$
hy|drox|y|tol|u|ene (hī drok′sē tol′yu̇ ēn), *n.* = cresol.
hy|drox|y|tryp|ta|mine (hī drok′sē trip′tə mēn), *n.* = serotonin.
hy|drox|y|u|re|a (hī drok′sē yu̇ rē′ə, -yu̇r′ē ə), *n.* a drug used in the treatment of certain cancers, especially malignant melanoma and lymphocytic leukemia. *Formula:* $CH_4N_2O_2$
hy|drox|y|zine (hī drok′sə zin, -zēn), *n.* a white odorless powder used as a tranquilizer and antihistamine. *Formula:* $C_{21}H_{27}ClN_2O_2$ [< *hydroxy*(l) + (pipera)*zine*]
hy|dro|zo|an (hī′drə zō′ən), *n., adj.* —*n.* any marine coelenterate of a class including hydras, polyps, and Portuguese men-of-war.
—*adj.* of or belonging to this class.
[< New Latin *Hydrozoa* the class name < Greek *hýdōr, -atos* water + *zôion* animal]
Hy|drus (hī′drəs), *n., genitive* **Hy|dri.** a southern constellation near Argo. [< Latin *hydrus* < Greek *hýdros* water snake < *hýdōr* water]
hy|e|na (hī ē′nə), *n.* a wild animal of Africa and Asia much like a large dog in shape and size. Hyenas feed on flesh at night, usually on carrion. Most hyenas are cowardly, but utter terrifying yells. Also, **hyaena**. See picture under **dog**. [< Latin *hyaena* < Greek *hýaina* < *hys, hyós* pig]
hyena dog, a large, spotted wild hunting dog of Africa, with ears like those of the hyena.
hy|e|to|graph (hī′ə tə graf, -gräf), *n.* a chart showing rainfall.
hy|e|to|graph|ic (hī′ə tə graf′ik), *adj.* of or having to do with hyetography. —**hy′e|to|graph′i|cal|ly**, *adv.*
hy|e|tog|ra|phy (hī′ə tog′rə fē), *n.* the branch of meteorology that deals with the distribution of rainfall. [< Greek *hyetós* rain + English *-graphy*]
hy|e|to|log|i|cal (hī′ə tə loj′ə kəl), *adj.* of or having to do with hyetology.
hy|e|tol|o|gy (hī′ə tol′ə jē), *n.* the branch of meteorology that deals with rain, snow, and other precipitation. [< Greek *hyetós* rain + English *-logy*]
Hy|fil (hī′fil), *n. Trademark.* a plastic or resin strengthened with carbon fiber.
Hy|ge|ia (hī jē′ə), *n. Greek Mythology.* the goddess of health, daughter of Asclepius. [< Greek *Hygeiā*, earlier *Hygíeiā* goddess of health < *hygiês* healthy]
hy|ge|ist or **hy|gie|ist** (hī′jē ist), *n.* = hygienist.
hy|giene (hī′jēn, -jē ēn), *n.* the science of keeping well; rules of health. [< French *hygiène*, learned borrowing from New Latin (*ars*) *hygieina* the healthful art, translation of Greek *hygieinê* (*téchnē*) < *hygiês* healthy]
hy|gi|en|ic (hī′jē en′ik, hī jē′nik), *adj.* **1** favorable to health; healthful; sanitary. **2** having to do with health or hygiene. —**hy′gi|en′i|cal|ly**, *adv.*
hy|gi|en|ics (hī′jē en′iks, hī jē′niks), *n.* = hygiene.
hy|gien|ist (hī′jē nist, -jē ə nist), *n.* an expert in hygiene, especially an expert in oral hygiene who performs routine examinations for a dentist.
hy|grine (hī′grēn), *n.* a clear liquid alkaloid obtained from dried coca leaves, used in medicine. *Formula:* $C_8H_{15}NO$ [< German *Hygrin* < Greek *hygrós* wet + *-in* -ine]
hygro-, *combining form.* wet; moist; moisture: *Hygrograph = an instrument that records humidity. Hygrometer = an instrument for measuring moisture.* [< Greek *hygrós* wet]
hy|gro|graph (hī′grə graf, -gräf), *n.* an instrument for recording the amount of moisture in the air.
hy|gro|ma (hī grō′mə), *n., pl.* **-mas, -ma|ta** (-mə tə). a swelling of the knee or hock of cattle due to repeated brusing from pressure on a hard surface. [< New Latin *hygroma* < Greek *hygrós* wet + *-ōma* growth]
hy|grom|e|ter (hī grom′ə tər), *n.* an instrument for measuring the amount of moisture or humidity in the air.
hy|gro|met|ric (hī′grə met′rik), *adj.* **1** of or having to do with the measurement of moisture in the air. **2** absorbing moisture readily; sensitive to moisture.
hy|grom|e|try (hī grom′ə trē), *n.* the branch of physics that deals with the measurement of moisture in the air.
hy|groph|i|lous (hī grof′ə ləs), *adj.* growing in water or moist places.
hy|gro|phyte (hī′grə fīt), *n.* a plant that grows in moist places; hydrophyte. [< *hygro-* + Greek *phytón* a plant]
hy|gro|scope (hī′grə skōp), *n.* an instrument that shows the variations in the amount of moisture or humidity in the air.
hy|gro|scop|ic (hī′grə skop′ik), *adj.* **1** having to do with or perceptible by the hygroscope. **2** absorbing or attracting moisture from the air. —**hy′gro|scop′i|cal|ly**, *adv.*
hy|ing (hī′ing), *v.* hieing; a present participle of hie.
Hyk|sos (hik′sos, -sōs), *n.pl.* a succession of six foreign rulers of Egypt between the 13th and 18th dynasties, from about 1730 B.C. to about 1570 B.C.; Shepherd Kings.
hy|la (hī′lə), *n.* = tree frog. [< New Latin *Hýla* the genus name < Greek *hylē* (originally) wood, forest]
hy|lic (hī′lik), *adj.* of or having to do with matter; material. [< Medieval Latin *hylicus* < Greek *hylikós* < *hýlē* substance]
hy|loph|a|gous (hī lof′ə gəs), *adj.* eating wood: *hylophagous beetles.* [< Greek *hýlē* wood + *phageîn* eat + English *-ous*]
hy|lo|the|ism (hī′lə thē′iz əm), *n.* the doctrine that matter or the material universe is God. [< Greek *hýlē* matter, substance + English *theism*]
hy|lo|zo|ic (hī′lə zō′ik), *adj.* having to do with or characterized by hylozoism.
hy|lo|zo|ism (hī′lə zō′iz əm), *n.* the theory that all matter is endowed with life, or that life is a property of matter. [< Greek *hýlē* matter + *zōē* life + English *-ism*] —**hy′lo|zo′ist**, *n.*
hy|lo|zo|is|tic (hī′lə zō is′tik), *adj.* of or having to do with hylozoists or hylozoism. —**hy′lo|zo|is′ti|cal|ly**, *adv.*
Hy|men (hī′mən), *n.* the Greek god of marriage, represented as a young man carrying a torch and veil. [< Latin *Hymen* < Greek *Hymēn* < *hymēn* membrane]
hy|men[1] (hī′mən), *n.* a fold of mucous membrane extending partly across the opening into the vagina. The hymen is often ruptured by exercise or by sexual intercourse. [< New Latin *hymen* < Late Latin *hymēn* < Greek *hymēn, -énos* thin skin or membrane]
hy|men[2] (hī′mən), *n.* **1** marriage; wedlock. **2** a wedding song. [< *Hymen*]
hy|men|al (hī′mə nəl), *adj.* of or having to do with the hymen of the vagina.
hy|me|ne|al (hī′mə nē′əl), *adj.* of or having to do with marriage. —**hy′me|ne′al|ly**, *adv.*
hy|me|ne|als (hī′mə nē′əlz), *n.pl.* wedding songs.
hy|me|ne|an (hī′mə nē′ən), *adj.* = hymeneal.
hy|me|ni|al (hī mē′nē əl), *adj.* of or having to do with the hymenia of fungi.
hy|me|ni|um (hī mē′nē əm), *n., pl.* **-ni|a** (-nē ə). the spore-bearing surface of fungi, composed of numerous asci or basidia. In the common mushroom the hymenium covers the gills. [< New Latin *hymenium* < Greek *hymēn* membrane]
hy|me|nop|ter (hī′mə nop′tər), *n., pl.* **-ter|a** (-tər ə). a hymenopterous insect.
hy|me|nop|ter|an (hī′mə nop′tər ən), *n., adj.* —*n.* a hymenopterous insect.
—*adj.* of or having to do with hymenopterans.
hy|me|nop|ter|ist (hī′mə nop′tər ist), *n.* a person who studies or collects hymenopterous insects.
hy|me|nop|ter|on (hī′mə nop′tə ron), *n., pl.* **-ter|a** (-tər ə). = hymenopteran.
hy|me|nop|ter|ous (hī′mə nop′tər əs), *adj.* of or belonging to an order of insects, including ants, bees, wasps, and sawflies, almost all having four transparent membranous wings, and the ovipositor of the female modified to form a stinger. The order includes all the social insects except the termites. Most kinds live in communities of complex organization and have a caste system within each group. [< Greek *hymenópteros* (with English *-ous*) < *hymēn, -énos* membrane + *pterón* wing]
hymn (him), *n., v.* —*n.* **1** a song in praise or honor of God: *Jonah prays and sings his canticles and hymns* (Aldous Huxley). **2** any song of praise, such as one in honor of a country: *What hymns are sung, what praises said For home-*

Pronunciation Key: hat, āge, cãre, fär; let, ēqual, tėrm; it, īce; hot, ōpen, ôrder; oil, out; cup, pu̇t, rüle; child; long; thin; ᴛʜen; zh, measure; ə represents **a** in about, **e** in taken, **i** in pencil, **o** in lemon, **u** in circus.

made miracles of bread? (Louis Untermeyer).
— ***v.t.*** **1** to praise or honor in a hymn or song: *As sons of one great Sire, Hymning the Eternal Father* (Milton). **2** to sing or express in a hymn. **3** to praise or extol: *to hymn a newly elected administration.* — ***v.i.*** to sing hymns.
[< Latin *hymnus* < Greek *hýmnos*] — **hymn′like′**, *adj.*

hym|nal (him′nəl), *n., adj.* — ***n.*** a book of hymns; hymnbook. — ***adj.*** of or having to do with hymns.

hym|nar|y (him′nər ē), *n., pl.* **-nar|ies.** = hymnal.

hymn|book (him′bu̇k′), *n.* a book containing a collection of hymns, for use in divine worship; hymnal.

hym|nist (him′nist), *n.* a composer of hymns.

hym|no|dy (him′nə dē), *n.* **1** the singing of hymns. **2** the composition of hymns. **3** hymns collectively. [< Medieval Latin *hymnodium* < Greek *hymnōidiā* singing of hymns < *hýmnos* hymn + *aeídein* sing, related to *ōidē* song, ode]

hym|nog|ra|pher (him nog′rə fər), *n.* a writer or composer of hymns.

hym|nog|ra|phy (him nog′rə fē), *n.* the writing or composition of hymns.

hym|no|log|ic (him′nə loj′ik), *adj.* of or having to do with hymnology.

hym|nol|o|gy (him nol′ə jē), *n.* **1** the study of hymns, their history, classification, and use. **2** hymns collectively. **3** the composition of hymns. — **hym|nol′o|gist,** *n.*

hy|oid (hī′oid), *n., adj.* — ***n.*** **1** the U-shaped bone at the root of the tongue in human beings. **2** a corresponding bone or series of bones in animals.
— ***adj.*** denoting or having to do with this bone.
[< French *hyoïde* < New Latin *hyoides* < Greek *hyoeidēs* U-shaped < υ (upsilon) + *eîdos* form]

hy|os|cine (hī′ə sēn, -sin), *n.* = scopolamine. [< *hyosc*(yamine) + *-ine*²]

hy|os|cy|a|min (hī′ə sī′ə min), *n.* = hyoscyamine.

hy|os|cy|a|mine (hī′ə sī′ə mēn, -min), *n.* an extremely poisonous alkaloid obtained from the seeds of henbane and other plants of the nightshade family, used in medicine as a hypnotic, as a sedative, and to dilate the pupils of the eyes. *Formula:* $C_{17}H_{23}NO_3$ [< New Latin *Hyoscyamus* the henbane genus < Greek *hyoskýamos* (< *hûs, hyós* pig + *kýamos* bean) + English *-ine*²]

hyp (hip), *n. Archaic.* low spirits; depression: *Belmont was a melancholy place, and I was dying there of hyp!* (R. P. Ward). [short for *hypochondria*]

hyp-, *prefix.* the form of **hypo-** before vowels, as in *hypesthesia.*

hyp., **1** hypotenuse. **2** hypothesis.

hyp|a|byss|al (hip′ə bis′əl), *adj. Geology.* of or having to do with rocks partly crystalline in texture, intermediate between abyssal or plutonic forms and extrusive lavas. — **hyp′a|byss′al|ly,** *adv.*

hy|pae|thral (hi pē′thrəl, hī-), *adj.* open to the sky; having no roof, as a building. Also, **hypethral.** [< Latin *hypaethrus* (< Greek *hýpaithros* < *hypo-* under + *aithḗr* air, ether) + English *-al*¹]

hy|pal|la|ge (hi pal′ə jē, hī-), *n.* a figure of speech in which word order is inverted. *Example:* "to give the winds to the fleets," instead of "to give the fleets to the winds" (Virgil). [< Latin *hypallagē* < Greek *hypallagḗ* exchange < *hypo-* under + *allássein* to exchange]

hy|pan|thi|al (hi pan′thē əl, hī-), *adj.* belonging to or like a hypanthium.

hy|pan|thi|um (hi pan′thē əm, hī-), *n., pl.* **-thi|a** (-thē ə). an enlargement of the receptacle of a flower below the calyx. [< New Latin *hypanthium* < *hypo-* beneath + Greek *ánthos* flower]

hype (hīp), *v.,* **hyped, hyp|ing,** *n. Slang.* — ***v.t.*** Often, **hype up. 1** to stimulate artificially; promote, especially with tricks or stunts: *They're so lacking in confidence in the attraction of the games they televise that they feel they have to hype them up with some hysterical commentator in order to get anyone to watch them* (Peter Gzowski). **2** to stir up in feeling; excite: *Sandy ... is so hyped up about the Boston opening Sept. 4 that some fear she may blow all the fuses* (Time). **3** to trick or deceive: *Are you trying to hype me?*
— ***n.*** **1** something that artificially stimulates sales or interest, such as advertising or promotion: *Detached from hype and trend, almost entirely dependent upon their fine heads and solid musicianship, there are few groups and a few individual performers in the new music who endure* (Time). **2** any trick or stunt to attract attention: *The talk, the publicity, the putting on, the 'hype' worked* (Listener). **3** a person or thing publicized or promoted through hype: *The performer who is written off as a hype becomes no longer the darling of the underground in-crowd, whatever his sincerity or intrinsic merit* (London Times). **4** a drug addict.
[alteration of *hypo*²] — **hyp′er,** *n.*

hyper-, *prefix.* over; above; exceedingly; more than normal; excessive: *Hypersensitive = exceedingly sensitive.* [< Greek *hyper-*, related to *hypér* beyond, over, overly]

hy|per|ac|id (hī′pər as′id), *adj.* excessively acid.

hy|per|a|cid|i|ty (hī′pər ə sid′ə tē), *n.* excessive acidity, as of the gastric juice.

hy|per|ac|tive (hī′pər ak′tiv), *adj.* overactive; abnormally active: *hyperactive children.*

hy|per|ac|tiv|i|ty (hī′pər ak tiv′ə tē), *n.* = overactivity.

hy|per|a|cu|sia (hī′pər ə kyü′zhə), *n.* extraordinary acuteness of hearing. [< New Latin *hyperacusia* < Greek *hyper-* hyper- + *ákousis* hearing]

hy|per|a|cu|sis (hī′pər ə kyü′sis), *n.* = hyperacusia.

hy|per|ag|gres|sive (hī′pər ə gres′iv), *adj.* excessively aggressive: *The actively "normal" parents, for instance, have created a hyperaggressive daughter who wants to "mold" men* (Atlantic).

hy|per|al|ge|si|a (hī′pər al jē′zē ə, -sē-), *n.* excessive sensitiveness to pain. [< New Latin *hyperalgesia* < Greek *hyperalgeîn* be pained exceedingly < *hyper-* over + *álgos* pain]

hy|per|al|ge|sic (hī′pər al jē′zik, -sik), *adj.* having to do with or affected with hyperalgesia.

hy|per|al|ge|sis (hī′pər al jē′sis), *n.* = hyperalgesia.

hy|per|al|i|men|ta|tion (hī′pər al′ə men tā′shən), *n.* the use of intravenous feeding to provide all the calories, vitamins, minerals, and other nutrients required by individual patients: *Surgeons in hospitals around the world now use hyperalimentation in the treatment of various types of intestinal ulcers, cancers and blockages* (Science News).

hy|per|bar (hī′pər bär), *n. Meteorology.* a ridge of high barometric pressure. [< *hyper-* + Greek *báros* weight, pressure]

hy|per|bar|ic (hī′pər bar′ik), *adj.* of, at, or utilizing pressures greater than normal atmospheric pressure, especially in medical operations and experimentation: *hyperbaric oxygen treatment.* [< *hyper-* + Greek *báros* weight, pressure]

hyperbaric chamber, an airtight compartment in which oxygen under high pressure is forced into the tissues of a person undergoing open-heart surgery, or treatment for poisoning, acute infections, or hyaline membrane disease or other respiratory ailment.

hy|per|ba|ton (hī pėr′bə ton), *n., pl.* **-ta** (-tə). inversion of the natural or logical order of words for emphasis. *Example:* "Great is Diana of the Ephesians" (Acts 19:28). [< Latin *hyperbaton* < Greek *hypérbaton* < *hyper-* over + *baínein* step]

***hy|per|bo|la** (hī pėr′bə lə), *n., pl.* **-las.** *Geometry.* a plane curve formed when a right circular cone is cut by a plane making a larger angle with the base than the side of the cone makes. [< New Latin *hyperbola* < Greek *hyperbolḗ* extravagance < *hyper-* beyond + *bállein* to throw]

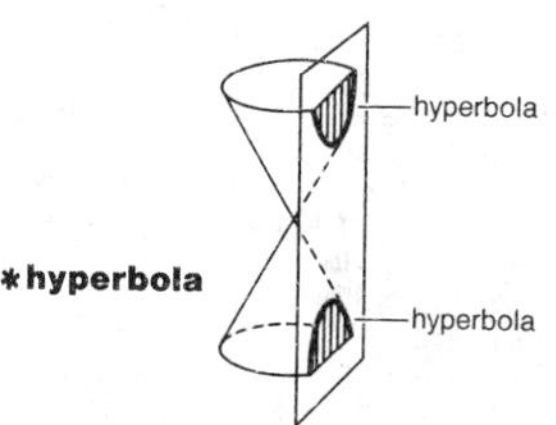

***hyperbola**

hy|per|bo|le (hī pėr′bə lē), *n.* **1** an exaggerated statement used for effect and not meant to be taken literally. *Example:* Waves high as mountains broke over the reef. *Taffeta phrases, silken terms precise, Thrice-piled hyperboles* (Shakespeare). **2** the use of such exaggeration: *Speaking in a perpetual hyperbole is comely in nothing but love* (Francis Bacon). [< Latin *hyperbolē* < Greek *hyperbolḗ;* see etym. under **hyperbola**]

hy|per|bol|ic (hī′pər bol′ik), *adj.* **1** like hyperbole; using hyperbole; exaggerated; exaggerating. **2** of or having to do with hyperbolas: *a hyperbolic curve, hyperbolic conoids.* — **hy′per|bol′i|cal|ly,** *adv.*

hy|per|bol|i|cal (hī′pər bol′ə kəl), *adj.* = hyperbolic.

hyperbolic function, *Mathematics.* a function having a relation to a rectangular hyperbola similar to that of the ordinary trigonometric functions to a circle; a hyperbolic sine, cosine, tangent, or other function.

hyperbolic geometry, a system of geometry in which two or more lines can be drawn through any point in a plane and not intersect a given line in the plane (contrasted with *elliptic geometry*).

hyperbolic paraboloid, a curved surface of which every plane section is either a parabola or a hyperbola, the curvature being concave in one direction and convex in another.

hy|per|bo|lism (hī pėr′bə liz əm), *n.* the use of hyperbole.

hy|per|bo|list (hī pėr′bə list), *n.* a person who uses hyperbole.

hy|per|bo|lize (hī pėr′bə līz), *v.,* **-lized, -liz|ing.** — ***v.i.*** to use hyperbole; exaggerate.
— ***v.t.*** to express or represent with exaggeration.

hy|per|bo|loid (hī pėr′bə loid), *n. Mathematics.* a quadric surface having a center not at infinity, and some of its plane sections hyperbolas.

hy|per|bo|loi|dal (hī pėr′bə loi′dəl), *adj.* of or having to do with a hyperboloid.

hy|per|bo|re|an (hī′pər bôr′ē ən; -bōr′-), *n., adj.* — ***n.*** an inhabitant of the far north.
— ***adj.*** of the far north; arctic; frigid. [< Late Latin *Hyperboreanus* < Latin *Hyperboreus* < Greek *Hyperbóreos* beyond the north < *hyper-* beyond + *bóreios* northern < *bóreās* the north wind]

Hy|per|bo|re|an (hī′pər bôr′ē ən, -bōr′-), *n., adj.* — ***n.*** *Greek Legend.* one of a group of people described as living in a land of perpetual sunshine and plenty beyond the north wind.
— ***adj.*** of or having to do with the Hyperboreans.

hy|per|cal|ce|mi|a (hī′pər kal sē′mē ə), *n.* an excessive amount of calcium in the blood.

hy|per|cal|ce|mic (hī′pər kal sē′mik), *adj.* of or having to do with hypercalcemia.

hy|per|cap|ni|a (hī′pər kap′nē ə), *n. Medicine.* an excessive amount of carbon dioxide in the blood. [< *hyper-* + Greek *kapnós* smoke]

hy|per|cat|a|lec|tic (hī′pər kat′ə lek′tik), *adj.* having one or two additional syllables after the last complete measure in a line of poetry.

hy|per|cau|tious (hī′pər kô′shəs), *adj.* excessively cautious: *... the hypercautious instincts of the politically insecure youths who now occupy the upper reaches of the Administration* (Manchester Guardian Weekly).

hy|per|charge (hī′pər chärj′), *v.,* **-charged, -charg|ing,** *n.* — ***v.t.*** to charge to excess; supercharge: *The atmosphere in Rhodesia was hypercharged with fear* (Manchester Guardian Weekly).
— ***n.*** *Nuclear Physics.* a quantum number which is equal to twice the average electric charge in a group of strongly interacting particles: *Each eightfold way multiplet consists of several subgroups of particles having the same mass, hypercharge and isotopic spin* (Science News Letter).

hy|per|cho|les|ter|e|mi|a (hī′pər kə les′tə rē′mē ə), *n.* = hypercholesterolemia.

hy|per|cho|les|ter|ol|e|mi|a (hī′pər kə les′tə rō lē′mē ə), *n. Medicine.* an excessive amount of cholesterol in the blood. [< New Latin *hypercholesterolemia* < *hyper-* + *cholesterol* + *-emia*]

hy|per|com|plex number (hī′pər kom′pleks), = quaternion.

hy|per|crit|ic (hī′pər krit′ik), *n.* a person who is too critical.

hy|per|crit|i|cal (hī′pər krit′ə kəl), *adj.* too critical: *I take the official oath today with no mental reservations, and with no purpose to construe the Constitution or laws by any hypercritical rules* (Abraham Lincoln, in his first inaugural address, March 4, 1861). — **hy′per|crit′i|cal|ly,** *adv.*

hy|per|crit|i|cism (hī′pər krit′ə siz əm), *n.* very petty or severe criticism; excessive criticism.

hy|per|du|li|a (hī′pər dyü lī′ə, -du̇-), *n.* (in the Roman Catholic Church) the veneration offered to the Virgin Mary as the most exalted of mere creatures. [< Medieval Latin *hyperdulia* < Greek *hyper-* higher, over + *douleíā* servitude]

hy|per|e|mi|a (hī′pər ē′mē ə), *n.* an excessive accumulation of blood in a part of the body; congestion. [< New Latin *hyperemia* < Greek *hyperaimeîn* have too much blood < *hyper-* over + *haîma* blood]

hy|per|e|mic (hī′pər ē′mik), *adj.* affected with hyperemia.

hy|per|es|the|sia (hī′pər es thē′zhə), *n.* excessive sensitivity of the skin or of any sense organ. [< New Latin *hyperesthesia* < Greek *hyper-* over + *aísthēsis* perception]

hy|per|es|thet|ic (hī′pər es thet′ik), *adj.* affected with hyperesthesia; extremely sensitive.

hy|per|eu|tec|tic (hī′pər yü tek′tik), *adj.* having more carbon or other minor constituent than the corresponding eutectic alloy.

hy|per|ex|cit|a|bil|i|ty (hī′pər ek sī′tə bil′ə tē), *n.* excessive or abnormal excitability.

hy|per|ex|cit|a|ble (hī′pər ek sī′tə bəl), *adj.* excessively or abnormally excitable: *The animals became hyperexcitable and leaped into the air squealing pathetically when shocked on the tail* (G. Luce and E. Peper).

hy|per|ex|ten|sion (hī′pər ik sten′shən), *n. Medicine.* the drawing of a limb or other part beyond the plane of the body, as in correcting a deformity or aligning fractured bones.

hy|per|fine (hī′pər fīn′), *adj.* excessively fine: *Electric and magnetic effects of atomic nuclei will cause a so-called hyperfine splitting of the light ... emitted by the atoms* (Science News).

hy|per|fo|cal (hī′pər fō′kəl), *adj. Photography.* designating the nearest distance from a lens at and beyond which all objects are in acceptable focus when the lens is focused on infinity.

hy|per|func|tion (hī′pər fungk′shən), *n.* excessive functioning of a bodily organ: *Pituitary hyperfunction may cause . . . enlargement of face and nose* (Alfred L. Kroeber).

hy|per|ga|mous (hī pėr′gə məs), *adj.* of or having to do with hypergamy.

hy|per|ga|my (hī pėr′gə mē), *n.* a Hindu custom which compels a woman to marry into a caste of equal or superior rank.

hy|per|ge|o|met|ric distribution (hī′pər jē′ə-met′rik), *Statistics.* a distribution showing the probable frequency of each of two kinds of elements in a sample chosen at random from a population consisting of specified quantities of the two kinds of elements.

hy|per|gly|ce|mi|a (hī′pər gli sē′mē ə), *n.* an abnormally high amount of sugar in the blood. [< *hyper-* + Greek *glykýs* sweet + English *-emia*]

hy|per|gly|ce|mic (hī′pər gli sē′mik), *adj.* having to do with or causing hyperglycemia.

hy|per|gol (hī′pər gol), *n.* a hypergolic fuel or propellant. [< German *Hypergol* < Greek *hyp*(er)- hyper- + *érgon* work + German *-ol* -ol²]

hy|per|gol|ic (hī′pər gol′ik), *adj.* (of a rocket fuel) igniting spontaneously on contact with its oxidizer.

hy|per|i|cum (hī per′ə kəm), *n.* = St.-John's-wort. [< New Latin *Hypericum* the genus name < Latin *hyperīcum* < Greek *hyper-* over + *ereíkē* heath]

hy|per|in|fla|tion (hī′pər in flā′shən), *n.* excessive inflation: *uncontrolled inflation with its inherent danger of hyperinflation* (New York Times).

hy|per|in|su|lin|ism (hī′pər in′sə lin iz′əm), *n.* the condition of having an excessive amount of insulin in the body, as in cases of obesity, or from an overdose of the substance.

Hy|pe|ri|on (hī pir′ē ən), *n. Greek Mythology.* **1** a Titan, son of Uranus and Gaea and father of the sun god Helios. **2** = Helios. **3** = Apollo.

hy|per|ir|ri|ta|bil|i|ty (hī′pər ir′ə tə bil′ə tē), *n.* excessive or abnormal irritability.

hy|per|ir|ri|ta|ble (hī′pər ir′ə tə bəl), *adj.* excessively or abnormally irritable: *There have been studies where cats have been deprived of REM sleep for excessively long intervals. Such animals become hyperirritable* (Anthony Kales).

hy|per|ker|a|to|sis (hī′pər ker′ə tō′sis), *n.* **1** a chronic poisoning of cattle, characterized by hardening and scaliness of the skin, caused by ingestion of or contact with various toxic substances present in certain lubricants, wood preservatives, and feeds. **2** rough, dry skin caused by a deficiency of vitamin A in the diet. [< *hyper-* + Greek *kéras, -atos* horn + *-osis*]

hy|per|ki|ne|sia (hī′pər ki nē′zhə, -kī-), *n.* excessive muscular movement; spasm. [< New Latin *hyperkinesia* < Greek *hyper-* excessive + *kínēsis* movement < *kīneîn* put in motion; move]

hy|per|ki|ne|sis (hī′pər ki nē′sis, -kī-), *n.* = hyperkinesia.

hy|per|ki|net|ic (hī′pər ki net′ik, -kī-), *adj.* having to do with or affected with hyperkinesia.

hy|per|li|pe|mi|a (hī′pər li pē′mē ə), *n.* = lipemia.

hy|per|lip|id|e|mi|a (hī′pər lip′ə dē′mē ə), *n.* = lipemia.

hy|per|ma|ni|a (hī′pər mā′nē ə), *n. Psychiatry.* intense mania, with delirium, incoherent speech, and frenzied activity.

hy|per|mar|ket (hī′pər mär′kit), *n. British.* a very large ground-floor store, usually built in the suburbs: *Hypermarkets—monster out-of-town shops, perhaps up to 10 times bigger than a big supermarket—are the latest challenge to traditional shopping* (Sunday Times).

hy|per|me|ter (hī pėr′mə tər), *n.* a hypermetric line of poetry. [< Greek *hypérmetros* beyond measure < *hyper-* over, beyond + *métron* measure, meter]

hy|per|met|ric (hī′pər met′rik), *adj.* having one or more syllables beyond those normal to the meter of a line of poetry; having an extra syllable.

hy|per|met|ri|cal (hī′pər met′rə kəl), *adj.* = hypermetric.

hy|per|met|rope (hī′pər met′rōp), *n.* a person affected with hyperopia.

***hypermetropia**

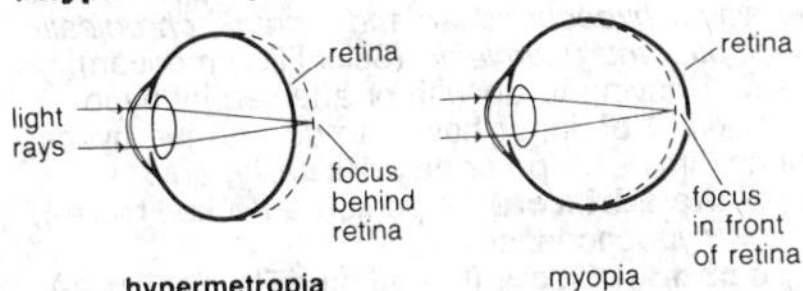

***hy|per|me|tro|pi|a** (hī′pər mə trō′pē ə), *n.* an abnormal condition of the eye in which distant objects produce images more distinct than near ones because parallel rays of light reach the retina before they are focused; far-sightedness [< New Latin *hypermetropia* < Greek *hypérmetros* beyond measure (see etym. under **hypermeter**) + *ōps, ōpós* eye]

hy|per|me|trop|ic (hī′pər mə trop′ik), *adj.* = having to do with or affected by hypermetropia; far-sighted. —**hy′per|me|trop′i|cal|ly**, *adv.*

hy|per|met|ro|py (hī′pər met′rə pē), *n.* = hypermetropia.

hy|perm|ne|sia (hī′pərm nē′zhə), *n.* unusual power of recollection. [< New Latin *hypermnesia* < *hyper-* over + Greek *mnêsis* a recollecting]

hy|perm|ne|sis (hī′pərm nē′sis), *n.* = hypermnesia.

Hy|perm|nes|tra (hī′pərm nes′trə), *n. Greek Legend.* one of the Danaides, the one who disobeyed their father's command to kill their husbands.

hy|per|na|tre|mi|a (hī′pər nə trē′mē ə, -nā-), *n.* an excessive amount of sodium in the blood. [< New Latin *hypernatremia* < *hyper-* + *natrium* + *-emia*]

hy|per|nu|cle|ar (hī′pər nü′klē ər, -nyü′-), *adj.* of or having to do with hypernuclei; containing a hypernucleus: *a hypernuclear atom.*

hy|per|nu|cle|us (hī′pər nü′klē əs, -nyü′-), *n., pl.* **-cle|i** (-klē ī). an atomic nucleus bound to or containing a hyperon: *Hypernuclei . . . are usually produced by the breaking up or fragmentation of a larger nucleus after interaction with a suitable high-energy particle* (London Times). [< *hyper*(on) + *nucleus*]

hy|per|on (hī′pə ron), *n.* a highly unstable atomic particle having a mass greater than the proton. [< *hyper-* + *-on*, as in *proton*]

hy|per|o|pi|a (hī′pər ō′pē ə), *n.* = hypermetropia.

hy|per|op|ic (hī′pər op′ik), *adj.* = hypermetropic. —**hy′per|op′i|cal|ly**, *adv.*

hy|per|os|mi|a (hī′pər oz′mē ə, -os′-), *n.* an abnormally acute sense of smell. [< New Latin *hyperosmia* < *hyper-* hyper- + Greek *osmê* smell]

hy|per|os|mic (hī′pər oz′mik, -os′-), *adj.* having an abnormally acute sense of smell. [< *hyper-* + Greek *osmê* smell + *-ic*]

hy|per|os|to|sis (hī′pər os tō′sis), *n., pl.* **-ses** (-sēz). **1** an abnormal outgrowth of bone from a bone. **2** a normal increase or outgrowth of bony tissue. [< *hyper-* + Greek *ostéon* bone + English *-osis*]

hy|per|os|tot|ic (hī′pər os tot′ik), *adj.* having to do with or affected with hyperostosis.

hy|per|ox|ide (hī′pər ok′sīd), *n.* = peroxide.

hy|per|par|a|site (hī′pər par′ə sīt), *n. Biology.* an organism parasitic upon a parasite: *Insect hyperparasites have also been hopefully cultured but not, it seems, with much success. Mistletoe continues to spread* (New Scientist).

hy|per|par|a|sit|ic (hī′pər par′ə sit′ik), *adj.* parasitic on or in a parasite.

hy|per|par|a|sit|ism (hī′pər par′ə sī′tiz əm), *n.* the condition of being a hyperparasite.

hy|per|par|a|thy|roid|ism (hī′pər par′ə thī′roid-iz əm), *n.* excessive activity of the parathyroid glands, involving either a loss of calcium or an imbalance of calcium and phosphorus in the body and resulting in softening of the bones and kidney damage.

hy|per|pha|gi|a (hī′pər fā′jē ə), *n.* an insatiable craving for food; bulimia. [< New Latin *hyperphagia* < *hyper-* + Greek *phágein* to eat]

hy|per|phag|ic (hī′pər faj′ik), *adj.* voracious; bulimic.

hy|per|phys|i|cal (hī′pər fiz′ə kəl), *adj.* above or beyond what is physical; supernatural.

hy|per|pi|e|sia (hī′pər pī ē′zhə), *n.* abnormally high blood pressure. [< New Latin *hyperpiesia* < Greek *hyper-* over, excessive + *píesis* pressure < *piézein* press]

hy|per|pi|e|sis (hī′pər pī ē′sis), *n.* = hyperpiesia.

hy|per|pi|tu|i|ta|rism (hī′pər pə tü′ə tə riz′əm, -tyü′-), *n.* **1** excessive activity of the anterior pituitary gland. **2** a condition resulting from this, such as acromegaly.

hy|per|plane (hī′pər plān′), *n. Mathematics.* a plane in a space of more than three dimensions.

hy|per|pla|sia (hī′pər plā′zhə), *n. Medicine, Biology.* **1** an abnormal multiplication of cells or structural elements of a part or organ. It is a form of hypertrophy. **2** the resulting increase in size of the part or organ. [< German *Hyperplasie* < Greek *hyper-* over + *plásis* formation]

hy|per|plas|ic (hī′pər plas′ik), *adj.* = hyperplastic.

hy|per|plas|tic (hī′pər plas′tik), *adj.* having to do with or affected with hyperplasia.

hy|per|ploid (hī′pər ploid), *adj., n. Biology.* —*adj.* having or denoting a chromosome number greater than, but not a multiple of, the diploid number for the species.
—*n.* a hyperploid number of chromosomes. [< *hyper-* + (di)*ploid*]

hy|per|ploid|y (hī′pər ploi′dē), *n.* hyperploid quality or state.

hy|perp|ne|a (hī′pərp nē′ə, -pər nē′-), *n.* excessively deep or labored breathing. [< New Latin *hyperpnea* < Greek *hyper-* over + *pnoiê* breathing < *pneîn* breathe]

hy|per|po|lar|ize (hī′pər pō′lə rīz), *v.t.,* **-ized, -iz|ing.** to increase the polarity or polarization of: *Neurons react to an electrical current in fundamentally different ways depending on their location in the brain. Some are depolarized or excited; others are hyperpolarized or blocked* (Science News). —**hy′per|po′lar|i|za′tion**, *n.*

hy|per|py|ret|ic (hī′pər pī ret′ik), *adj.* having to do with or affected with hyperpyrexia.

hy|per|py|rex|i|a (hī′pər pī rek′sē ə), *n.* a very high fever.

hy|per|py|rex|i|al (hī′pər pī rek′sē əl), *adj.* = hyperpyretic.

hy|per|sen|si|tive (hī′pər sen′sə tiv), *adj.* **1** extremely sensitive: *She was hypersensitive to the slightest criticism.* **2** having a high degree of sensitivity: *hypersensitive film, hypersensitive dye.* —**hy′per|sen′si|tive|ly**, *adv.* —**hy′per|sen′si|tive|ness**, *n.*

hy|per|sen|si|tiv|i|ty (hī′pər sen′sə tiv′ə tē), *n.* extreme sensitiveness.

hy|per|sen|si|tize (hī′pər sen′sə tīz), *v.t.,* **-tized, -tiz|ing.** to treat (a substance) so as to make it hypersensitive: *to hypersensitize film.* —**hy′per-sen′si|ti|za′tion**, *n.*

hy|per|sex|u|al (hī′pər sek′shü əl), *adj.* sexually overactive: *hypersexual behavior.*

hy|per|sex|u|al|i|ty (hī′pər sek′shü al′ə tē), *n.* the condition of being hypersexual.

hy|per|slow (hī′pər slō′), *adj.* excessively slow.

hy|per|son|ic (hī′pər son′ik), *adj.* **1** denoting any speed which is five or more times faster than the speed of sound in a given medium. In air, hypersonic speed is at least 5,435 feet per second. **2** that moves or is able to move at this speed: *a hypersonic aircraft, a hypersonic missile.* —**hy′per|son′i|cal|ly**, *adv.*

hy|per|son|ics (hī′pər son′iks), *n.* the branch of aerodynamics that deals with the effects of hypersonic speeds.

hy|per|space (hī′pər spās′), *n. Mathematics.* space consisting of four or more dimensions; multidimensional space: *Although it is not possible to represent such a "hyperspace" pictorially, the computation of distances within it is still quite simple* (Scientific American).

hy|per|spe|cial|i|za|tion (hī′pər spesh′ə lə zā′-shən), *n.* = overspecialization.

hy|per|sthene (hī′pər sthēn), *n. Mineralogy.* a grayish, greenish-black, or brown silicate of iron and magnesium, an orthorhombic pyroxene. [< French *hypersténe* < Greek *hyper-* excessive + *sthénos* strength (because it is stronger than hornblende)]

hy|per|sthen|ic (hī′pər sthen′ik), *adj.* containing or resembling hypersthene.

hy|per|sur|face (hī′pər sėr′fis), *n. Mathematics.* a surface in a space of more than three dimensions: *Albert Einstein . . . tried to abolish the endless regress of distance by bending three-dimensional space around to form the hypersurface of a four-dimensional sphere* (Martin Gardner).

hy|per|sus|cep|ti|bil|i|ty (hī′pər sə sep′tə bil′ə tē), *n.* **1** abnormal susceptibility. **2** *Medicine.* anaphylaxis.

hy|per|sus|pi|cious (hī′pər sə spish′əs), *adj.* excessively suspicious.

hy|per|tense (hī′pər tens′), *adj.* excessively tense: *a hypertense baby that cries a lot* (Maclean's).

hy|per|ten|sin (hī′pər ten′sin), *n.* = angiotensin. [< *hyper-* + *tens*(ion) + *-in*]

hy|per|ten|sin|o|gen (hī′pər ten sin′ə jən), *n.* a constituent of blood plasma and serum produced by the liver and converted by renin into hypertensin.

hy|per|ten|sion (hī′pər ten′shən), *n.* **1** an abnormally high blood pressure. **2** a disease, especially of the arteries, resulting from or characterized by abnormally high blood pressure.

hy|per|ten|sive (hī′pər ten′siv), *adj., n.* —*adj.* having to do with, characterized by, or affected with high blood pressure.
—*n.* a person who has high blood pressure.

hy|per|ther|mi|a (hī′pər thėr′mē ə), *n. Medicine.* **1** very high temperature induced artificially as therapy, especially to destroy malignant cells. **2** hyper pyrexia. [< New Latin *hyperthermia* < *hyper* + Greek *thérmē* heat]
—**hy′per|ther′mic**, *adj.*

hy|per|thy|roid (hī′pər thī′roid), *n., adj.* —*n.*

Pronunciation Key: hat, āge, cãre, fär; let, ēqual, tėrm; it, īce; hot, ōpen, ôrder; oil, out; cup, pu̇t, rüle; child; long; thin; ᴛʜen; zh, measure; ə represents **a** in about, **e** in taken, **i** in pencil, **o** in lemon, **u** in circus.

1 an excessively active thyroid gland. 2 a person having such a gland.
—***adj.*** having to do with hyperthyroidism.

hy|per|thy|roid|ism (hī′pər thī′roi diz əm), *n.* 1 excessive activity of the thyroid gland. 2 the abnormal condition resulting from this, characterized by a high metabolic rate, nervousness, and often an enlargement of the thyroid gland.

hy|per|ton|ic (hī′pər ton′ik), *adj.* 1 having excessive muscular tone or tension in response to stimuli. 2 (of a solution) having a higher osmotic pressure than an isotonic solution.

hy|per|to|nic|i|ty (hī′pər tō nis′ə tē), *n.* hypertonic condition.

hy|per|troph|ic (hī′pər trof′ik), *adj.* 1 producing or affected with hypertrophy. 2 characterized by hypertrophy.

hy|per|troph|i|cal (hī′pər trof′ə kəl), *adj.* = hypertrophic.

hy|per|tro|phy (hī pėr′trə fē), *n., pl.* **-phies**, *v.,* **-phied, -phy|ing.** —***n.*** an enlargement of a part or organ due to a diseased condition or overuse of the organ.
—***v.t., v.i.*** to grow too big; affect or be affected with hypertrophy.
[< *hyper-* over + Greek *trophē* nourishment]

hy|per|var|i|a|ble mini|sat|el|lite (hī′pər vãr′ē ə bəl min′ē sat′ə līt), any of a class of short segments of satellite DNA, containing repeating sequences of base pairs whose number varies from individual to individual: *Since hypervariable minisatellites are completely specific to an individual, they provide a powerful tool for paternity testing.*

hy|per|ve|loc|i|ty (hī′pər və los′ə tē), *n., pl.* **-ties.** extremely high velocity, such as that of spacecraft or of nuclear particles.

hy|per|ven|ti|late (hī′pər ven′tə lāt), *v.,* **-lat|ed, -lat|ing.** —***v.i.*** to breathe deeply or excessively: *Preparing for a dive, the ama hyperventilates for five to 10 seconds, takes a final deep breath and then makes the plunge* (Scientific American).
—***v.t.*** to increase the amount of oxygen in (the lungs) by excessive or forced respiration.

hy|per|ven|ti|la|tion (hī′pər ven′tə lā′shən), *n.* excessive or forced respiration, causing a lowering of the normal amount of carbon dioxide in the blood.

hy|per|ver|bal (hī′pər vėr′bəl), *adj.* excessively verbal: *He is hyperverbal and is given to self-lacerating bitter tirades* (Pauline Kael).

hy|per|vi|ta|mi|no|sis (hī′pər vī′tə mə nō′sis), *n.* a condition caused by an excess of vitamins.

hyp|es|the|sia (hip′es thē′zhə), *n.* diminished capacity for sensation; dulled sensitiveness. [< New Latin *hypesthesia* < Greek *hypo-* less, low + *aísthēsis* sensation, sensitivity]

hyp|es|the|sic (hip′es thē′zik), *adj.* of or characterized by hypesthesia.

hy|pe|thral (hi pē′thrəl, hī-), *adj.* = hypaethral.

hy|pha (hī′fə), *n., pl.* **-phae** (-fē). *Botany.* the structural element of the plant body of fungi, consisting of long, slender, branched filaments, usually having dividing membranes, and together constituting the mycelium. [< New Latin *hypha* < Greek *hyphē* web]

hy|phal (hī′fəl), *adj.* of or having to do with the hypha of a fungus.

hy|phen** (hī′fən), *n., v.* —n.*** a mark used to connect the parts of a compound word, or the parts of a word divided at the end of a line. The hyphen comes in the middle of the line between the top and the bottom of an m or other letter like it.
—***v.t.*** = hyphenate.
[< Late Latin *hyphen* < Greek *hyphén* hyphen; in one < *hypo-* under + *hén* one]

***hyphen**

– . . . a well-written report on the subject . . .

hy|phen|ate (hī′fə nāt), *v.,* **-at|ed, -at|ing,** *adj., n.* —***v.t.*** to join by a hyphen; write or print with a hyphen.
—***adj.*** = hyphenated.
—***n.*** *U.S.* 1 a hyphenated citizen. 2 *Informal.* a person who has more than one job or fills more than one position, especially in the creative arts: *He [Robert Redford] is the most recent and successful example of a burgeoning new Hollywood hyphenate, the actor-producer* (Mel Gussow).

hy|phen|at|ed (hī′fə nā′tid), *adj. U.S.* of or having to do with persons, or their activities, whose national origin is indicated by a hyphenated form, such as Anglo-American or Irish-American.

hy|phen|a|tion (hī′fə nā′shən), *n.* the act of joining by a hyphen; writing or printing with a hyphen.

hy|phen|ism (hī′fə niz əm), *n. U.S.* the spirit or practices of hyphenates.

hy|phen|i|za|tion (hī′fə nə zā′shən), *n.* = hyphenation.

hy|phen|ize (hī′fə nīz), *v.t.,* **-ized, -iz|ing.** = hyphenate.

hy|phen|less (hī′fən lis), *adj.* without a hyphen.

hypn-, *combining form.* the form of **hypno-** before vowels, as in *hypnosis.*

hyp|na|gog|ic (hip′nə goj′ik), *adj.* 1 inducing sleep; hypnic. 2 *Psychology.* happening while falling asleep; having to do with drowsiness or the coming on of sleep, when the brain has difficulty separating reality from subconscious images: *a hypnagogic illusion or hallucination.* Also, **hypnogogic.** [< French *hypnagogique* < Greek *hýpnos* sleep + *ágein* to lead]

hyp|na|gogue (hip′nə gôg, -gog), *n.* something that induces sleep; a hypnotic.

hyp|nic (hip′nik), *adj.* = hypnagogic. [< Greek *hypnikós* < *hýpnos* sleep]

hypno-, *combining form.* 1 sleep: *Hypnology = the science of sleep.* 2 hypnosis or hypnotic effect: *Hypnogenous = producing hypnosis.* Also, **hypn-** before vowels. [< Greek *hypno-* < *hýpnos* sleep]

hyp|no|a|nal|y|sis (hip′nō ə nal′ə sis), *n.* the treatment of mental disorder by using hypnosis to obtain analytical data from the subject.

hyp|no|dra|ma (hip′nə drä′mə, -dram′ə), *n.* a form of psychodrama in which a situation experienced under hypnosis is acted out.

hyp|no|gen|e|sis (hip′nə jen′ə sis), *n.* induction of the hypnotic state.

hyp|no|ge|net|ic (hip′nō jə net′ik), *adj.* = hypnogenous.

hyp|no|gen|ic (hip′nə jen′ik), *adj.* = hypnogenous.

hyp|nog|e|nous (hip noj′ə nəs), *adj.* producing the hypnotic state.

hyp|nog|e|ny (hip noj′ə nē), *n.* = hypnogenesis.

hyp|no|gog|ic (hip′nə goj′ik), *adj.* = hypnagogic.

hyp|noid (hip′noid), *adj.* resembling hypnosis.

hyp|noi|dal (hip noi′dəl), *adj.* 1 = hypnoid. 2 *Psychology.* designating a state similar to that of mild hypnosis.

hyp|no|log|ic (hip′nə loj′ik), *adj.* of or having to do with hypnology.

hyp|no|log|i|cal (hip′nə loj′ə kəl), *adj.* = hypnologic.

hyp|nol|o|gy (hip nol′ə jē), *n.* science dealing with phenomena of sleep. —**hyp|nol′ogist**, *n.*

hyp|no|pe|di|a (hip′nə pē′dē ə), *n.* the act or process of teaching oneself or someone else while asleep, usually by means of a record or tape recording; sleep-learning. Repetition of a lesson is supposed to implant information in the sleeper's subconscious. *The Soviets are quick to emphasize that hypnopedia is not a teaching method in itself, but only an important supplementary aid* (New Scientist). [< Greek *hýpnos* sleep + *paideíā* education < *paîs, paidós* child]

hyp|no|pe|dic (hip′nə pē′dik), *adj.* of or having to do with hypnopedia. —**hyp′no|pe′di|cal|ly**, *adv.*

hyp|no|pho|bi|a (hip′nə fō′bē ə), *n.* an abnormal fear of falling asleep.

hyp|no|pom|pic (hip′nō pom′pik), *adj. Psychology.* happening while waking up; having to do with the state or moment of coming out of sleep, when a subconscious image or dream persists: *a hypnopompic illusion or hallucination.* [< *hypno-* + Greek *pompē* procession, parade; (literally) a sending + English *-ic*]

Hyp|nos (hip′nos), *n.* the Greek god of sleep.

hyp|no|sis (hip nō′sis), *n., pl.* **-ses** (-sēz). 1 a condition somewhat resembling deep sleep, but more active, in which a person has little will of his own, and acts according to the suggestions of the person who brought about the condition. 2 = hypnotism (def. 3). [< Greek *hýpnos* sleep + English *-osis*]

hyp|nos|o|phy (hip nos′ə fē), *n.* knowledge or the science of the phenomena of sleep. [< *hypno-* + Greek *sophíā* wisdom] —**hyp|nos′o|phist**, *n.*

hyp|no|ther|a|py (hip′nə ther′ə pē), *n.* the treatment of physical or mental disorders by means of hypnotism, or the use of hypnotism as a substitute for anesthetics. —**hyp′no|ther′a|pist**, *n.*

hyp|not|ic (hip not′ik), *adj., n.* —***adj.*** 1 having to do with hypnosis or hypnotism. 2 easily hypnotized. 3 in a hypnotized state. 4 causing or tending to cause hypnosis: *a hypnotic stare.*
—***n.*** 1 a drug or other means of causing sleep; sedative; soporific. 2 a person who is hypnotized or who is easily hypnotized.
[< Late Latin *hypnōticus* < Greek *hypnōtikós* putting to sleep; sleepy < *hypnoûin* put to sleep < *hýpnos* sleep] —**hyp|not′i|cal|ly**, *adv.*

hyp|no|tise (hip′nə tīz), *v.t.,* **-tised, -tis|ing.** *Especially British.* hypnotize.

hyp|no|tism (hip′nə tiz əm), *n.* 1 the act or process of putting into a sleeplike state; hypnotizing. 2 the science dealing with hypnosis. 3 a hypnotic condition.

hyp|no|tist (hip′nə tist), *n.* a person who hypnotizes.

hyp|no|tiz|a|ble (hip′nə tī′zə bəl), *adj.* that can be hypnotized.

hyp|no|ti|za|tion (hip′nə tə zā′shən), *n.* 1 the act of hypnotizing. 2 the state of being hypnotized.

hyp|no|tize (hip′nə tīz), *v.t.,* **-tized, -tiz|ing.** 1 to put into a state somewhat like deep sleep, but more active, in which a person has little will of his own and little feeling. A hypnotized person acts according to the suggestions of the person who has hypnotized him. 2 *Figurative.* to dominate or control by suggestion; cast a spell over: *The candidate's eloquence so hypnotized his audience that even his opponents cheered what he said.* —**hyp′no|tiz′er**, *n.*

hy|po[1] (hī′pō), *n.* a colorless or white crystalline salt used to treat photographic negatives and prints to keep them from fading; sodium thiosulfate; fixer; fixing bath. *Formula:* $Na_2S_2O_3$ [short for *hyposulfite*]

hy|po[2] (hī′pō), *n., pl.* **-pos**, *v. Informal.* —***n.*** 1 = hypodermic. 2 *Figurative.* a stimulus: *Easier credit could provide a major hypo for retail sales in the months just ahead* (Wall Street Journal).
—***v.t.*** 1 to inject (a drug) by hypodermic syringe. 2 *Figurative.* to stimulate, often artificially; increase or promote: *to hypo the sales of foreign cars in the United States. Shopkeepers in one city dragged out old depression remedies to hypo trade* (Newsweek).

hy|po[3] (hī′pō), *n., pl.* **-pos.** 1 *Slang.* a hypochondriac. 2 *Obsolete.* hypochondria.

hypo-, *prefix.* 1 under; beneath; below: *Hypodermic = under the skin.* 2 to a lesser degree: *Hypothyroid = a deficient thyroid gland.* 3 *Chemistry.* indicating a compound which is less oxidized than the corresponding compound without the prefix: *Hypochlorous acid = acid less oxidized than chlorous acid.*
[< Greek *hypo-*, related to *hypó* under]

hy|po|a|cid|i|ty (hī′pō ə sid′ə tē), *n.* acidity that is less than usual or normal.

hy|po|al|ler|gen|ic (hī′pō al′ər jen′ik, hip′ō-), *adj.* free of or having reduced allergy-producing ingredients.

hy|po|ben|thos (hī′pə ben′thōs), *n.* life in the ocean below 3,000 feet.

hy|po|blast (hī′pə blast, hip′ə-), *n. Embryology.* the inner layer of a blastoderm or embryo; the endoderm or endoblast. [< *hypo-* + Greek *blastós* germ, sprout]

hy|po|blas|tic (hī′pə blas′tik, hip′ə-), *adj.* of or belonging to the hypoblast.

hy|po|bran|chi|al (hī′pə brang′kē əl, hip′ə-), *adj. Zoology.* situated under the branchiae or gills.

hy|po|cal|ce|mi|a (hī′pə kal sē′mē ə), *n.* a deficient amount of calcium in the blood.

hy|po|cal|ce|mic (hī′pə kal sē′mik), *adj.* of or having to do with hypocalcemia.

hyp|o|caust (hip′ə kôst, hī′pə-), *n.* a hollow space or flue in the floor or wall of a building through which heat from the furnace is received and distributed.
[< Late Latin *hypocauston* < Greek *hypókauston* room heated from below < *hypo-* under + *kaíein* to burn]

hy|po|cen|ter (hī′pə sen′tər), *n.* 1 the area immediately below the explosion of an atomic bomb. 2 the area or region where an earthquake is initiated: *Seismic waves travel in all directions from hypocenter of an earthquake and cause the earth to tremble and crack* (Frank Press).

hy|po|cen|tral (hī′pə sen′trəl), *adj.* of or in the hypocenter.

hy|po|chlo|rite (hī′pə klôr′īt, -klōr′-; hip′ə-), *n.* a salt or ester of hypochlorous acid.

hy|po|chlo|rous acid (hī′pə klôr′əs, -klōr′-; hip′ə-), an unstable, weak acid existing as a yellow solution with an irritating odor, used as a bleach, disinfectant, etc. *Formula:* HClO

hy|po|chon|dri|a (hī′pə kon′drē ə, hip′ə-), *n.* 1 an abnormal anxiety over one's health, often involving imaginary illnesses accompanied by actual pains. 2 low spirits without any real reason. 3 plural of **hypochondrium.**
[< Late Latin *hypochondria* the abdomen < Greek *hypóchondria,* neuter plural < *hypo-* under + *chóndros* cartilage (of the breastbone) (because it was the supposed seat of melancholy, considered a disease)]

hy|po|chon|dri|ac (hī′pə kon′drē ak, hip′ə-), *n., adj.* —***n.*** a person who imagines that he is ill when he is not; person affected by hypochondria: *He was a hypochondriac and a crank, chronically dyspeptic and unamiable* (Scientific American).
—***adj.*** 1 having to do with or affected by hypochondria. 2 of, in, or having to do with the hypochondrium. —**hy′po|chon|dri′a|cal|ly**, *adv.*

hy|po|chon|dri|a|cal (hī′pə kon drī′ə kəl, hip′ə-), *adj.* = hypochondriac.

hy|po|chon|dri|a|sis (hī′pə kon drī′ə sis, hip′ə-), *n.* the condition of suffering from hypochondria.

hy|po|chon|dri|um (hī′pə kon′drē əm, hip′ə-), *n., pl.* **-dri|a.** the upper region of the abdomen on either side.

hy|po|chro|mic anemia (hī′pə krō′mik, hip′ə-), anemia due to a deficiency of hemoglobin, characterized by abnormally small and pale red blood cells. [< *hypo-* + Greek *chrôma* color + English *-ic*]

hy|poc|o|rism (hi pok′ə riz əm, hī-), *n.* a pet name.

hyp|o|co|ris|tic (hip′ə kə ris′tik, hī′pə-), *adj.* endearing, as a pet name; diminutive. [< Greek *hypokoristikós* like an endearment < *hypokorismón ónoma* pet name < *hypokorizesthai* use pet names; (literally) act like a child < *hypo-* less, slightly + *kóros* child] —**hyp′o|co|ris′ti|cal|ly,** *adv.*

hyp|o|co|ris|ti|cal (hip′ə kə ris′tə kəl, hī′pə-), *adj.* = hypocoristic.

hy|po|cot|yl (hī′pə kot′əl, hip′ə-), *n.* the part of a plant embryo below the cotyledons, between the stem and the roots. See picture under **embryo.**

hy|po|cot|y|le|don|ar|y (hī′pə kot′ə lē′də ner′ē, hip′ə-), *adj.* below the cotyledons.

hy|po|cot|y|lous (hī′pə kot′ə ləs, hip′ə-), *adj.* of or having to do with the hypocotyl.

hy|po|cra|ter|i|form (hī′pə krə ter′ə fôrm, hip′ə-), *adj.* = salverform.

hy|poc|ri|sy (hi pok′rə sē), *n., pl.* **-sies. 1** the act or fact of pretending to be very good or religious: *Hypocrisy, the only evil that walks Invisible, except to God alone* (Milton). **2** the act or fact of pretending to be what one is not; pretense; sham. [< Old French *ypocrisie,* learned borrowing from Late Latin *hypocrisis* < Greek *hypókrisis* acting, dissimulation < *hypo-* under + *krísis* judgment < *krīnein* to judge]

hyp|o|crite (hip′ə krit), *n.* **1** a person who pretends to be very good or religious: *Woe be to those ... who play the hypocrites, and deny necessaries to the needy* (Koran: Translation by Sale). *Mr. Pecksniff was a hypocrite, even to himself* (Dickens). **2** a person who pretends to be what he is not; pretender: *Her cousins, seeing her with red eyes, set her down as a hypocrite* (Jane Austen). [< Old French *ypocrite,* learned borrowing from Latin *hypocrita* < Greek *hypokritês* actor < *hypo-* under + *kritês* a judge < *krīnein* to judge]

hyp|o|crit|i|cal (hip′ə krit′ə kəl), *adj.* of or like a hypocrite; insincere. —**hyp′o|crit′i|cal|ly,** *adv.*

hy|po|cy|cloid (hī′pə sī′kloid, hip′ə-), *n. Geometry.* a curve traced by a point moving on the circumference of a circle which rolls upon the concave side of another circle.

hy|po|cy|cloi|dal (hī′pə sī kloi′dəl, hip′ə-), *adj.* having the form of a hypocycloid.

hy|po|derm (hī′pə dėrm, hip′ə-), *n. Zoology.* the soft cellular layer under the shell of an arthropod. [< New Latin *hypoderma* < Greek *hypo-* under + *dérma* skin]

hy|po|der|ma (hī′pə dėr′mə, hip′ə-), *n.* **1** *Botany.* a tissue or layer of cells beneath the epidermis. **2** *Zoology.* the hypodermis.

hy|po|der|mal (hī′pə dėr′məl, hip′ə-), *adj.* **1** *Botany.* **a** of or having to do with the hypoderma. **b** situated under the epidermis. **2** *Zoology.* hypodermic.

hy|po|der|mic (hī′pə dėr′mik), *adj., n.* —*adj.* **1** under the skin: *hypodermic cells.* **2** injected or used to inject under the skin: *a hypodermic injection.* **3** *Zoology.* having to do with the hypodermis.

—*n.* **1** a dose of medicine injected under the skin: *The doctor gave her a hypodermic to make her sleep.* **2** = hypodermic syringe. —**hy′po|der′mi|cal|ly,** *adv.*

***hypodermic needle,** a hollow needle used to inject medicine under the skin.

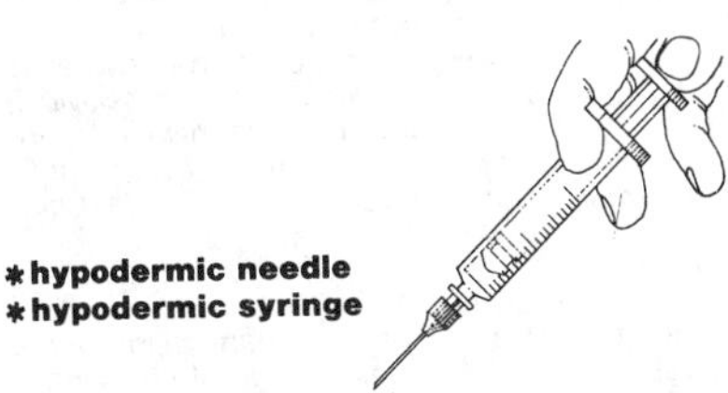

***hypodermic needle**
***hypodermic syringe**

***hypodermic syringe,** a small syringe fitted with a hollow needle, used to inject a dose of medicine under the skin.

hy|po|der|mis (hī′pə dėr′mis, hip′ə-), *n.* **1** *Zoology.* a layer of tissue lying under and secreting the integument of certain insects, crustaceans, and worms. **2** *Botany.* the layer of cells just beneath the epidermis. **3** a loose layer of connective tissue beneath the dermis, in many regions consisting of subcutaneous fatty tissue. [< *hypo-* + (epi)*dermis*]

hy|po|eu|tec|tic (hī′pō yü tek′tik, hip′ō-), *adj.* having less carbon or other minor constituent than the corresponding eutectic alloy.

hy|po|gas|tric (hī′pə gas′trik, hip′ə-), *adj.* of or having to do with the lower middle region of the abdomen: *hypogastric diseases.*

hy|po|gas|tri|um (hī′pə gas′trē əm, hip′ə-), *n., pl.* **-tri|a** (-trē ə). the lower part of the human abdomen, especially the part between the right and left iliac regions. [< New Latin *hypogastrium* < Greek *hypogástrion* < *hypo-* under, lower + *gastêr, -trós* belly]

hy|po|ge|al (hī′pə jē′əl, hip′ə-), *adj.* **1** underground; subterranean. **2** *Botany.* hypogeous. [< Latin *hypogēus* < Greek *hypógeios* (see etym. under **hypogeum**) + English *-al*[1]]

hy|po|ge|an (hī′pə jē′ən, hip′ə-), *adj.* = hypogeal.

hyp|o|gene (hip′ə jēn, hī′pə-), *adj. Geology.* formed beneath the surface of the earth (contrasted with *epigene*): *Granite is a hypogene rock.*

hy|po|gen|e|sis (hī′pə jen′ə sis), *n. Biology.* reproduction in which the alternation of generations is suppressed or absent.

hy|pog|e|nous (hī poj′ə nəs, hi-), *adj. Botany.* growing beneath or on the under surface of a part, as fungi on leaves.

hy|po|ge|ous (hī′pə jē′əs, hip′ə-), *adj.* **1** underground; subterranean. **2** *Botany.* growing or remaining underground. [< Latin *hypogēus* (with English *-ous*) < Greek *hypógeios;* see etym. under **hypogeum**]

hyp|o|ge|um (hip′ə jē′əm, hī′pə-), *n., pl.* **-ge|a** (-jē′ə). an underground chamber or vault. [< Latin *hypogēum* < Greek *hypógeion,* neuter singular of *hypógeios* underground < *hypo-* under + *gê* earth]

hy|po|glos|sal (hī′pə glos′əl, hip′ə-), *adj., n.* —*adj.* **1** situated under the tongue wholly or in part. **2** designating either of the pair of cranial nerves which control the movements of the tongue.

—*n.* a hypoglossal nerve.

[< New Latin *hypoglossus* (< Greek *hypo-* under + *glôssa* tongue) + English *-al*[1]]

hy|po|gly|ce|mi|a (hī′pō gli sē′mē ə, hip′ō-), *n.* an abnormally low amount of sugar in the blood, often caused by an overdose of insulin or malfunction of the liver. [< *hypo-* + Greek *glykýs* sweet + English *-emia*]

hy|po|gly|ce|mic (hī′pō gli sē′mik, hip′ō-), *adj.* causing or caused by a reduction of sugar content in the blood: *a hypoglycemic agent, hypoglycemic shock.*

hy|pog|y|nous (hī poj′ə nəs, hi-), *adj. Botany.* **1** situated on the receptacle below the ovary, as sepals, petals, and stamens. **2** having its parts so arranged, as the magnolia blossom.

hy|pog|y|ny (hī poj′ə nē, hi-), *n.* the state of being hypogynous.

hy|poid gear (hī′poid), a bevel gear in which the axis of the pinion is not on the same plane, but is at a right angle to the gear. The slippage provided is used to advantage in an automobile differential.

hy|po|ka|le|mi|a (hī′pō kə lē′mē ə, hip′ō-), *n.* a condition caused by an acute deficiency of potassium in the blood and body tissues. [< New Latin *hypokalemia* < *hypo-* less + *kalium* potassium, kalium + Greek *haîma* blood]

hy|po|lim|ni|on (hī′pə lim′nē ən), *n., pl.* **-ni|a** (-nē ə). the cold, lower layer of water in a lake. [< *hypo-* + Greek *límnion,* diminutive of *límnē* marsh, lake]

hy|po|mag|ne|se|mi|a (hī′pō mag′nə sē′mē ə), *n.* a condition of cattle or sheep caused by an acute deficiency of magnesium in the blood; grass staggers or grass tetany. [< *hypo-* + *magnes*(ium) + *-emia*]

hy|po|ma|ni|a (hī′pə mā′nē ə, hip′ə-), *n. Psychiatry.* a mental state of abnormal excitement, less intense than mania.

hy|po|ma|nic (hī′pə mā′nik, -man′ik; hip′ə-), *adj.* of or characterized by hypomania.

hy|po|met|a|bol|ic (hī′pō met′ə bol′ik, hip′ō-), *adj.* producing hypometabolism.

hy|po|me|tab|o|lism (hī′pō mə tab′ə liz əm, hip′ō-), *n.* metabolism that is lower than normal.

hy|po|nas|tic (hī′pə nas′tik, hip′ə-), *adj.* of or having to do with hyponasty; like hyponasty.

hy|po|nas|ty (hī′pə nas′tē, hip′ə-), *n. Botany.* increased growth along the lower surface of an organ or part, causing the part to bend upward. [< *hypo-* + Greek *nastós* pressed + English *-y*[3]]

hy|po|ni|trite (hī′pə nī′trīt), *n.* a salt of hyponitrous acid.

hy|po|ni|trous acid (hī′pə nī′trəs), an unstable acid, explosive in solid form, used as a reducing and oxidizing agent. *Formula:* $H_2N_2O_2$

hy|po|par|a|thy|roid|ism (hī′pō par′ə thī′roid iz əm), *n.* abnormally decreased activity of the parathyroid glands, resulting in a loss of calcium in the blood and sometimes leading to tetany.

hy|po|phar|ynx (hī′pə far′ingks, hip′ə-), *n., pl.* **-phar|ynx|es, -pha|ryn|ges** (-fə rin′jēz). a median projection from the internal surface of the lower lip in most insects.

hy|po|phos|phate (hī′pə fos′fāt), *n.* a salt of hypophosphoric acid.

hy|po|phos|phite (hī′pə fos′fīt), *n.* a salt of hypophosphorous acid, used in medicine as a tonic.

hy|po|phos|phor|ic acid (hī′pō fos fôr′ik, -for′-), a crystalline acid produced by the slow oxidation of phosphorus in moist air. *Formula:* $H_4P_2O_6$

hy|po|phos|pho|rous acid (hī′pə fos′fər əs), an acid of phosphorus produced by the action of phosphorus on an alkaline solution, used as a reducing agent, and formerly as a nerve tonic. *Formula:* H_3PO_2

hy|poph|y|ge (hī pof′ə jē, hi-), *n. Architecture.* a depression of curved profile, as a hollow molding beneath some Doric capitals. [< Greek *hypophygê* a recess; refuge < *hypopheúgein* flee; retire < *hypo-* under + *pheúgein* flee]

hy|poph|y|sec|to|mize (hī prof′ə sek′tə mīz, hi-), *v.t.,* **-mized, -miz|ing.** to remove the pituitary gland of: *hypophysectomized rats.*

hy|poph|y|sec|to|my (hī pof′ə sek′tə mē, hi-), *n., pl.* **-mies.** the removal of the pituitary gland by surgery.

hy|po|phys|i|al (hī′pə fiz′ē əl, hip′ə-), *adj.* of or having to do with the hypophysis.

hy|poph|y|sis (hī pof′ə sis, hi-), *n., pl.* **-ses** (-sēz). = pituitary gland. [< Greek *hypóphysis* outgrowth < *hypo-* under + *phýsis* a growing < *phýein* cause to grow]

hy|po|pi|tu|i|ta|rism (hī′pō pə tü′ə tə riz′əm, -tyü′-; hip′ō-), *n.* **1** abnormally decreased activity of the anterior pituitary gland. **2** the condition resulting from this, such as obesity or loss of sexual power.

hy|po|pi|tu|i|tar|y (hī′pō pə tü′ə ter′ē, -tyü′-; hip′ō-), *adj.* having a deficiency in the secretion of the pituitary gland.

hy|po|pla|sia (hī′pə plā′zhə, hip′ə-), *n.* the defective or incomplete growth of an organ or tissue. [< New Latin *hypoplasia* < *hypo-* hypo- + Greek *plásis* formation]

hy|po|plas|tic (hī′pə plas′tik, hip′ə-), *adj.* of or characterized by hypoplasia.

hy|po|ploid (hī′pə ploid, hip′ə-), *adj., n. Biology.* —*adj.* having or denoting a chromosome number less than the usual diploid number for the species.

—*n.* a hypoploid number of chromosomes.

[< *hypo-* + (di)*ploid*]

hy|po|ploid|y (hī′pə ploi′dē, hip′ə-), *n.* hypoploid quality or state.

hy|po|po|di|um (hī′pə pō′dē əm, hip′ə-), *n., pl.* **-di|a** (-dē ə). *Botany.* the base of a leaf, including the petiole. [< New Latin *hypopodium* < *hypo-* under + Greek *poús, podós* foot]

hy|po|py|on (hī pō′pē on, hi-), *n.* an accumulation of pus in the anterior chamber of the eye. [< New Latin *hypopyon* < Greek *hypópyon* an ulcer; neuter of *hypópyos* tending to suppurate, or form pus < *hypo-* underneath + *pýon* pus]

hy|po|sen|si|ti|za|tion (hī′pō sen′sə tə zā′shən, hip′ō-), *n.* a lowering of body sensitivity to allergy-producing agents.

hy|po|sen|si|tize (hī′pə sen′sə tīz, hip′ō-), *v.t.,* **-tized, -tiz|ing.** = desensitize.

***hy|po|spray** (hī′pō sprā′), *n.* an instrument which injects drugs painlessly by spraying them through the skin.

***hypospray**

hy|pos|ta|sis (hī pos′tə sis, hi-), *n., pl.* **-ses** (-sēz). **1** *Philosophy.* the essential part of anything; substance; essence. **2** *Theology.* **a** the essential nature of God, the divine essence, possessed also by the persons of the Trinity. **b** one of the persons of the Trinity, partaking of or possessing this nature and essence. **c** the one entire personality or nature of Christ as distinguished from his two natures, human and divine: *That two natures could be concentred into one hypostasis or person* (Jeremy Taylor). **3** *Medicine.* **a** the settling of blood or fluid in the dependent organs of the body. **b** a sediment or deposit, especially in the urine. [< Late Latin *hypostasis* < Greek *hypóstasis* essence, groundwork < *hypo-* underneath + *stásis* a standing, position < *histánai* to stand]

Pronunciation Key: hat, āge, cãre, fär; let, ēqual, tėrm; it, īce; hot, ōpen, ôrder; oil, out; cup, pu̇t, rüle; child; long; thin; ᴛʜen; zh, measure; ə represents **a** in about, **e** in taken, **i** in pencil, **o** in lemon, **u** in circus.

hy|pos|ta|size (hī pos′tə sīz, hi-), *v.t.,* **-sized, -siz|ing.** = hypostatize.

hy|po|stat|ic (hī′pə stat′ik, hip′ə-), *adj.* **1** *Metaphysics.* of or having to do with substance or essence; essential. **2** *Theology.* having to do with divine personality or nature. **3** *Medicine.* caused by or like hypostasis. **4** masked by another gene which is not an allele. —**hy′po|stat′i|cal|ly,** *adv.*

hy|po|stat|i|cal (hī′pə stat′ə kəl, hip′ə-), *adj.* = hypostatic (def. 2).

hy|pos|ta|tize (hī pos′tə tīz, hi-), *v.t.,* **-tized, -tiz|ing.** to treat or regard as a distinct substance or reality; attribute substantial existence to. —**hy|pos′ta|ti|za′tion,** *n.*

hy|po|stome (hī′pə stōm), *n.* a part or organ of the mouth of arthropods and some other animals. [< New Latin *hypostoma* < *hypo-* + *stoma* stoma]

hyp|o|style (hip′ə stīl, hī′pə-), *adj., n. Architecture.* —*adj.* having the roof supported by pillars.
—*n.* a building whose roof is supported by pillars. [< Greek *hypóstylos* < *hypo-* under + *stylos* pillar]

hy|po|sul|fite (hī′pə sul′fīt), *n.* **1** a salt of hyposulfurous acid; dithionite. **2** = sodium thiosulfate.

hy|po|sul|fur|ous (hī′pə sul′fər əs, -fyůr′-; -sul-fyůr′əs), *adj.* of or having to do with hyposulfurous acid.

hyposulfurous acid, an acid found only in solution or as salts, used as a reducing and bleaching agent; hydrosulfurous acid. *Formula:* $H_2S_2O_4$

hy|po|tac|tic (hī′pə tak′tik, hip′ə-), *adj. Grammar.* dependent; subordinate.

hy|po|tax|is (hī′pə tak′sis, hip′ə-), *n. Grammar.* dependent relation or construction; subordination. [< Greek *hypótaxis* < *hypo-* beneath + *tássein* to place]

hy|po|ten|sion (hī′pə ten′shən, hip′ə-), *n.* **1** an abnormally low blood pressure. **2** a condition resulting from or characterized by low blood pressure.

hy|po|ten|sive (hī′pə ten′siv), *adj., n.* —*adj.* **1** having to do with, characterized by, or affected with hypotension. **2** causing hypotension.
—*n.* **1** a person who has hypotension. **2** a drug that lowers blood pressure.

***hy|pot|e|nuse** (hī pot′ə nüs, -nyüs; hi-), *n.* the side of a right triangle opposite the right angle. Also, **hypothenuse.** [< Late Latin *hypotēnūsa* < Greek *hypoteínousa* stretching under, subtending, feminine present participle of *hypoteínein* < *hypo-* under + *teínein* stretch]

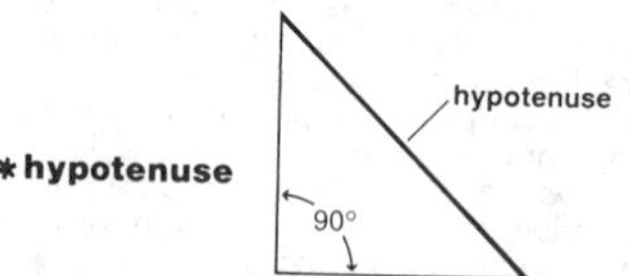

***hypotenuse**

hypoth., **1** hypothenuse. **2** hypothesis.

hy|po|tha|lam|ic (hī′pə thə lam′ik, hip′ə-), *adj.* of or having to do with the hypothalamus.

hy|po|thal|a|mus (hī′pə thal′ə məs, hip′ə-), *n., pl.* **-mi** (-mī). the part of the brain under the thalamus, controlling temperature, hunger, thirst, and the pituitary gland.

hy|poth|ec (hī poth′ik, hi-), *n.* (in Roman and civil law) a lien on property given by contract to a creditor as security, without giving possession of the property.
the whole hypothec, *Scottish Informal.* the whole stock or lot; the whole business: *And at last ... saddle and all, the whole hypothec turned and grovelled in the dust below the donkey's belly* (Robert Louis Stevenson).
[< Late Latin *hypothēca* < Greek *hypothḗkē* a pledge, mortgage < *hypotithénai* deposit as a pledge < *hypo-* down + *tithénai* put]

hy|poth|e|car|y (hī poth′ə ker′ē, hi-), *adj.* of or secured by a hypothec.

hy|poth|e|cate[1] (hī poth′ə kāt, hi-), *v.t.,* **-cat|ed, -cat|ing. 1** to pledge (as property or stock) to a creditor as security for a loan or debt without delivering over; mortgage: *He had no power to hypothecate any part of the public revenue* (Macaulay). **2** to deliver (as stocks or bonds) as security for a loan. [< Medieval Latin *hypothecare* (with English *-ate*[1]) < Latin *hypothēca;* see etym. under **hypothec**] —**hy|poth′e|ca′tion,** *n.*

hy|poth|e|cate[2] (hī poth′ə kāt, hi-), *v.t.,* **-cat|ed, -cat|ing.** = hypothesize.

hy|poth|e|ca|tor (hī poth′ə kā′tər, hi-), *n.* a person who pledges something as security.

hy|poth|e|nuse (hī poth′ə nüs, -nyüs; hi-), *n.* = hypotenuse.

hy|po|ther|mal (hī′pə thėr′məl, hip′ə-), *adj.* **1** having to do with the reduction of the heat of the body, especially to subnormal temperature. **2** = tepid.

hy|po|ther|mi|a (hī′pə thėr′mē ə, hip′ə-), *n.* a condition of reduced temperature, especially subnormal body temperature caused by exposure to cold or as artificially induced to slow the flow of blood in the body in performing operations on the heart, brain, or other organs controlling vital functions. [< New Latin *hypothermia* < *hypo-* under + Greek *thérmē heat*]

hy|po|ther|mic (hī′pə thėr′mik, hip′ə-), *adj.* = hypothermal.

hy|poth|e|ses (hī poth′ə sēz, hi-), *n.* plural of **hypothesis.**

hy|poth|e|sis (hī poth′ə sis, hi-), *n., pl.* **-ses. 1** something assumed because it seems likely to be a true explanation; theory: *Let us act on the hypothesis that he is honest.* **SYN:** See syn. under **theory. 2** a proposition assumed as a basis for reasoning; supposition. A theorem in geometry is made up of a hypothesis and a conclusion. **3** a mere assumption; guess: *Your reasoning ... seems plausible, but still it is only hypothesis* (Scott). [< New Latin *hypothesis* < Greek *hypóthesis* < *hypo-* under + *thésis* a placing < *tithénai* to place]

hy|poth|e|size (hī poth′ə sīz, hi-), *v.,* **-sized, -siz|ing.** —*v.i.* to make a hypothesis.
—*v.t.* to assume; suppose.

hy|po|thet|ic (hī′pə thet′ik, hip′ə-), *adj.* = hypothetical.

hy|po|thet|i|cal (hī′pə thet′ə kəl, hip′ə-), *adj.* **1** of a hypothesis; based on or like a hypothesis; assumed; supposed: *a hypothetical case.* **2** *Logic.* **a** involving a hypothesis or condition in a proposition; conditional. **b** having a hypothetical proposition for one of the premises of a syllogism. **3** fond of making hypotheses. —**hy′po|thet′i|cal|ly,** *adv.*

hy|po|thy|roid (hī′pə thī′roid), *n., adj.* —*n.* **1** an insufficiently active thyroid gland. **2** a person having such a gland.
—*adj.* having or having to do with hypothyroidism.

hy|po|thy|roid|ism (hī′pə thī′roi diz əm), *n.* **1** abnormally decreased activity of the thyroid gland. **2** the abnormal condition resulting from this, characterized by a low metabolic rate and sluggishness, and sometimes producing cretinism in childhood.

hy|po|ton|ic (hī′pə ton′ik, hip′ə-), *adj.* **1** possessing less than the normal muscular tone or tension in response to stimuli. **2** possessing an osmotic pressure below that of an isotonic solution.

hy|po|to|nic|i|ty (hī′pə tō nis′ə tē, hip′ə-), *n.* hypotonic condition.

hy|po|tra|che|li|um (hī′pə trə kē′lē əm, hip′ə-), *n., pl.* **-li|a** (-lē ə). *Architecture.* **1** the neck of a column, between the echinus and the shaft. **2** (in the Doric order) the junction of this member with the shaft, marked by a bevel or cut. [< Latin *hypotrachēlium* < Greek *hypotrachḗlion* lower part of the neck < *hypo-* below + *tráchēlos* neck]

hy|po|tro|choid (hī′pə trō′koid, hip′ə-), *n. Geometry.* a curve which can be traced by a point rigidly connected with a circle which rolls upon the interior of another circle.

hy|po|vi|ta|mi|no|sis (hī′pō vī′tə mə nō′sis), *n.* a condition caused by a lack of one or more essential vitamins in the diet.

hy|po|xan|thic (hī′pə zan′thik), *adj.* derived from or like hypoxanthine.

hy|po|xan|thin (hī′pə zan′thin), *n.* = hypoxanthine.

hy|po|xan|thine (hī′pə zan′thēn, -thin), *n.* a crystalline, nitrogenous compound, related to xanthine, and found in the muscles, liver, and spleen, as well as in various plant tissues. *Formula:* $C_5H_4N_4O$

hyp|ox|e|mi|a (hī′pok sē′mē ə, hip′ok-), *n.* a low or deficient oxygen level in the blood: *The collapse of alveoli may be the commonest cause of arterial hypoxemia ... in surgical patients* (Scientific American). [< *hypo-* + *ox*(ygen) + *-emia*]

hy|pox|i|a (hī pok′sē ə, hi-), *n.* lack of oxygen, especially resulting from an inability of body tissue to absorb oxygen under decreasing pressure at high altitudes.

hy|pox|ic (hī pok′sik, hi-), *adj.* **1** of hypoxia. **2** suffering from hypoxia.

hyps (hips), *n.pl.* = hypochondria.

hyp|si|ce|phal|ic (hip′sē sə fal′ik), *adj.* characterized by a high skull. [< Greek *hýpsi* on high + *kephalḗ* head + English *-ic*]

hyp|so|graph|ic (hip′sə graf′ik), *adj.* = hypsographical.

hyp|so|graph|i|cal (hip′sə graf′ə kəl), *adj.* of or having to do with hypsography.

hyp|sog|ra|phy (hip sog′rə fē), *n.* **1** the branch of geography that deals with the configuration of the earth's surface with respect to differences of elevation. **2** the matter dealt with by this science; topographic relief. **3** the parts of a map that show topographic relief. **4** = hypsometry. [< Greek *hýpsos* height + English *-graphy*]

hyp|som|e|ter (hip som′ə tər), *n.* an instrument for measuring altitudes of points on the earth's surface by determining atmospheric pressure from the boiling points of liquids at a given height; thermobarometer.

hyp|so|met|ric (hip′sə met′rik), *adj.* of or having to do with hypsometry. —**hyp′so|met′ri|cal|ly,** *adv.*

hyp|so|met|ri|cal (hip′sə met′rə kəl), *adj.* = hypsometric.

hyp|som|e|try (hip som′ə trē), *n.* the measuring of altitudes, especially above sea level.

hy|ra|coid (hī′rə koid), *adj.* **1** like the hyrax. **2** belonging to the group of mammals represented by the hyrax.

hy|ra|coi|de|an (hī′rə koi′dē ən), *adj., n.* —*adj.* = hyracoid.
—*n.* a hyracoid animal.

hy|rax (hī′raks), *n., pl.* **-rax|es, -ra|ces** (-rə sēz). any one of an order of small, timid, rabbitlike mammals of Africa and Asia, related to the hoofed mammals, such as the daman. The cony of the Bible was a hyrax. [< Greek *hýrax, -akos* the shrew]

hy|son (hī′sən), *n.* a Chinese green tea. [< Cantonese *hi-ch'un* (literally) bright spring]

hys|sop (his′əp), *n.* **1** a fragrant, bushy plant used especially for medicine and flavoring. It belongs to the mint family. **2** a plant whose twigs were used for sprinkling water in certain religious ceremonies, mentioned in the Bible; aspergillus: *Purge me with hyssop, and I shall be clean* (Psalms 51:7). [< Latin *hyssōpus* < Greek *hýssōpos* < Hebrew *'ezob* an aromatic plant]

hys|ter|ec|to|mize (his′tə rek′tə mīz), *v.t.,* **-mized, -miz|ing.** to remove the uterus of surgically; perform a hysterectomy on.

hys|ter|ec|to|my (his′tə rek′tə mē), *n., pl.* **-mies.** surgical removal of the uterus. [< Greek *hystérā* uterus + *ektomḗ* a cutting out]

hys|ter|e|sis (his′tə rē′sis), *n. Physics.* **1** a lagging of an effect behind its cause, as when a magnetic body is subjected to a varying force, or when a body is subjected to stress, or when an electric substance is subjected to a changing intensity. **2** the persistence of such an effect after the cause has been removed. [< Late Greek *hystérēsis* lack, deficiency < Greek *hystereîn* lag, come late < *hýsteros* late]

hysteresis constant, *Physics.* hysteresis loss expressed in ergs per cubic centimeter per cycle.

hysteresis loop, *Electricity.* a closed curve showing, for a ferromagnetic material, the magnetic intensity and the resulting magnetic induction when the magnetization is carried through a complete cycle.

hysteresis loss, *Physics.* a loss of energy in electromagnetic devices as a result of hysteresis.

hys|ter|et|ic (his′tə ret′ik), *adj.* of or having to do with hysteresis. —**hys′ter|et′i|cal|ly,** *adv.*

hys|te|ri|a (his tir′ē ə, -ter′-), *n.* **1** a nervous disorder that causes fits of laughing and crying, imaginary illnesses as well as real physical disability, such as paralysis, blindness, or digestive upsets, and general lack of self-control. Hysteria results from anxiety. **2** *Figurative.* senseless excitement; unrestrained emotion: *mob hysteria.* [< New Latin *hysteria* < Greek *hystérā* uterus (because originally women were thought to be the only ones so affected)]

hys|ter|ic (his ter′ik), *adj., n.* —*adj.* = hysterical: *She often broke into a little, nervous, hysteric laugh* (Hawthorne).
—*n.* a person who is subject to hysteria.

hys|ter|i|cal (his ter′ə kəl), *adj.* **1** unnaturally excited or emotional; resembling or suggesting hysteria: *hysterical weeping.* **2** showing an extreme lack of control; unable to stop laughing, crying, or other emotional display; suffering from hysteria: *This hysterical girl was unable to stop her violent laughing and crying.* **3** of hysteria; having to do with or characteristic of hysteria: *a hysterical fit.* **4** *Informal, Figurative.* very funny: *Isn't that picture hysterical!* —**hys|ter′i|cal|ly,** *adv.*

hys|ter|ics (his ter′iks), *n.pl.* a fit of hysterical laughing and crying.

hys|ter|i|tis (his′tə rī′tis), *n.* inflammation of the uterus; metritis. [< Greek *hystérā* uterus + English *-itis*]

hys|ter|o|cat|a|lep|sy (his′tər ō kat′ə lep′sē), *n.* hysteria accompanied by catalepsy.

hys|ter|o|ep|i|lep|sy (his′tər ō ep′ə lep′sē), *n.* a form of hysteria with epileptiform attacks.

hys|ter|o|ep|i|lep|tic (his′tər ō ep′ə lep′tik), *adj., n.* —*adj.* characterized by hysteria and epilepsy.
—*n.* a person affected with hysteria and epilepsy.

hys|ter|o|gen|ic (his′tər ə jen′ik), *adj.* producing hysteria; having to do with the production of hysteria.

hys|ter|oid (his′tə roid), *adj.* resembling hysteria or some of its symptoms.

hys|ter|oi|dal (his′tə roi′dəl), *adj.* = hysteroid.

hys|ter|om|e|ter (his′tə rom′ə tər), *n.* an instrument for measuring the uterus.

hys|ter|o|neu|ras|the|ni|a (his′tər ō nůr′əs thē′-nē ə, -nyůr′-), *n.* hysteria and neurasthenia together.

hys|ter|on prot|er|on (his′tə ron prot′ə ron), **1** the position or arrangement of things in the reverse of their natural or rational order. **2** a figure of speech in which the word, phrase, or clause that logically should come last is put first. *Example:* Let us die and rush into the midst of the fray. **3** inversion of the natural or logical order, as by placing the conclusion before the premises. [< Greek *h₄steron próteron* the latter thing (put instead of) the former]

hys|ter|o|pex|i|a (his′tər ə pek′sē ə), *n.* the fixation of the uterus by suturing it to the anterior wall of the abdomen. [< New Latin *hysteropexia* < Greek *hystérā* uterus + *pêxis* a fixing]

hys|ter|o|pex|y (his′tər ə pek′sē), *n.* = hysteropexia.

hys|ter|op|to|sis (his′tər op tō′sis), *n.* a downward displacement of the uterus; falling of the womb. [< Greek *hystérā* uterus + *ptôsis* a falling]

hys|ter|or|rha|phy (his′tə ror′ə fē), *n., pl.* **-phies.** **1** the closing of a wound in the uterus by sutures. **2** = hysteropexia. [< Greek *hystérā* uterus + *rhaphḗ* a sewing]

hys|ter|o|scope (his′tər ə skōp), *n.* an instrument for examining the uterus.

hys|ter|ot|o|my (his′tə rot′ə mē), *n., pl.* **-mies.** **1** = Caesarean section. **2** surgical incision into the uterus.

hys|tri|co|mor|phic (his′tri kə môr′fik), *adj.* of or belonging to a group of rodents that includes porcupines, cavies, chinchillas, agoutis, guinea pigs, etc. [< New Latin *Hystricomorpha* a division of rodents (< Latin *hystrix, -icis* porcupine < Greek *h₄strix, -ichos)* + Greek *morphḗ* form]

hy|zone (hī′zōn), *n.* = tritium. *Formula:* H^3[< *hy*(drogen); patterned on *ozone*]

Hz (no period), hertz: *frequencies vary to 40 Hz.*

I i

***I**[1] or **i** (ī), *n., pl.* **I's** or **Is, i's** or **is. 1** the ninth letter of the English alphabet. There are two *i*'s in *India.* **2** any sound represented by this letter.
3 (used as a symbol for) the ninth (of an actual or possible series): *row I in a theater.* **4** the Roman numeral for 1: *The foreword begins on page vii.*
I[2] (ī), *pron., nom.* **I**, *poss.* **my** or **mine**, *obj.* **me**; *pl. nom.* **we**, *poss.* **our** or **ours**, *obj.* **us**; *n., pl.* **I's**.
—*pron.* the person who is speaking or writing: *John said, "I am ten years old." I like my dog, and he likes me.*
—*n.* **1** the pronoun regarded as a word. **2** *Metaphysics.* the ego.
[Old English *ic*]
►The pronoun *I* is written with a capital simply because in the old handwritten manuscripts a small *i* was likely to be lost or to get attached to a neighboring word, and a capital helped keep it a distinct word.
I[3] (ī), *n., pl.* **I's**. anything shaped like the letter I.
i-, *prefix.* the form of **in-**[1] before *gn,* as in *ignore, ignoble.*
i (no period), **1** inclination (angle of a planet's orbit). **2** *Mathematics.* the imaginary unit $\sqrt{-1}$, square root of minus one.
i., **1** interest. **2** intransitive. **3** island.
I (no period), an abbreviation or symbol for the following:
1 iodine (chemical element).
2 international.
3 interstate.
4 *Physics.* electric current.
I., an abbreviation for the following:
1a Emperor (Latin, *Imperator*). **b** Empress (Latin, *Imperatrix*).
2 independent (in politics).
3 *Biochemistry.* inosine.
4a island or islands. **b** isle or isles.
5 *Nuclear Physics.* isotopic spin.
6a Israel. **b** Israeli.
i.a., in absentia.
Ia., Iowa.
IA (no periods), Iowa (with postal Zip Code).
IAA (no periods), indoleacetic acid.
IAAF (no periods) or **I.A.A.F.**, International Amateur Athletic Federation.
IADB (no periods), **1** Inter-American Defense Board. **2** Inter-American Development Bank.
IAEA (no periods), International Atomic Energy Agency
IAF (no periods) or **I.A.F.**, International Astronautical Federation.
I|a|go (ē ä′gō), *n.* the villain in Shakespeare's play *Othello,* who deludes Othello into killing his innocent wife.
-ial, *suffix.* a form of **-al**[1], as in *adverbial, facial.*
i|amb (ī′amb), *n.* an iambic foot or measure: *First and foremost among the purveyors of Shakespeare's inspired iambs was the Memorial Theater in Stratford, England* (Newsweek). [< Middle French *ïambe,* learned borrowing from Latin *iambus* < Greek *íambos*]
i|am|bic (ī am′bik), *n., adj.* —*n.* **1** a foot or measure in poetry consisting of two syllables, an unaccented followed by an accented. *Example:*
"The sún that brief De cém ber dáy
Rose chéer less ó ver hílls of gráy."
2 a foot in Greek and Latin poetry consisting of two syllables, a short followed by a long. *Example:* ămō. **3** a piece of satire in iambic verse.
—*adj.* of or consisting of iambic measures. Much English poetry is iambic.
iambics, a verse of iambics: *Thy genius calls thee not to purchase fame in keen iambics, but mild anagram* (John Dryden).
—**i|am′bi|cal|ly**, *adv.*
iambic pentameter, a basic measure of English poetry, five iambic feet in each line. Blank verse is in unrhymed iambic pentameter. Heroic verse is in rhymed or unrhymed iambic pentameter.

i|am|bus (ī am′bəs), *n., pl.* **-bi** (-bī), **-bus|es**. = iamb.
[< Latin *iambus* < Greek *íambos*]
-ian, *suffix.* a form of **-an**, as in *Bostonian, Episcopalian, Proustian, tragedian, amphibian, Italian.*
-iana, *suffix.* a form of **-ana**, as in *Lincolniana.*
I|ap|e|tus (ī ap′ə təs), *n.* **1** *Greek Mythology.* one of the Titans, father of Atlas and Prometheus.
2 *Astronomy.* one of the ten satellites of the planet Saturn.
IAPF (no periods), Inter-American Peacekeeping Force.
iar|o|vize (yär′ə vīz), *v.t.,* **-vized, -viz|ing.** = jarovize.
IARU (no periods), International Amateur Radio Union.
IAS (no periods), **1** indicated air speed (of an aircraft). **2** Institute for Advanced Study.
-iasis, *suffix.* **1** a process: *Odontiasis = the process of cutting teeth; teething.* **2** a diseased condition: *Amebiasis = a diseased condition caused by amebas.*
[< New Latin *-iasis* < Greek *-íāsis,* a noun suffix]
I.A.T.A. or **IATA** (no periods), International Air Transport Association.
i|at|ric (ī at′rik), *adj.* of or having to do with a physician or medicine; medical; medicinal: *a tour de force of iatric intuition* (Time). [< Greek *iātrikós* medicinal < *iātrós* physician < *iâsthai* to heal]
i|at|ri|cal (ī at′rə kəl), *adj.* = iatric.
i|at|ro|chem|is|try (ī at′rō kem′ə strē), *n.* **1** the application of chemistry to medicine and therapeutics. **2** a school of medicine in the 1500's and the first half of the 1600's that substituted remedies prepared by artificial chemical processes for the roots and herbs of earlier medicine and believed that diseases could be explained entirely in terms of chemistry.
[< Greek *iātrós* physician + English *chemistry*]
—**i|at′ro|chem′ist**, *n.*
i|at|ro|gen|ic (ī at′rō jen′ik), *adj.* (of a symptom or disease) induced by a physician, as in physical conditions caused by worry over a physician's diagnosis: *iatrogenic heart trouble.* —**i|at′ro|gen′i|cal|ly**, *adv.*
i|at|ro|phys|ics (ī at′rō fiz′iks), *n.* **1** the use of physical or mechanical measures in the treatment of diseases. **2** a school of medicine in the 1600's that used the laws of physics and mechanics in explaining the functions of the body and in applying remedies.
IAU (no periods) or **I.A.U.**, International Astronomical Union.
ib., ibidem (in the same place).
IB (no periods), International Baccalaureate: *The IB is already a recognised qualification for university entrance in 20 countries* (New Scientist).
I.B.A. or **IBA** (no periods), Independent Broadcasting Authority (regulating commercial radio and television in Great Britain).
I|ba|dite (i bä′dīt), *n.* a member of a very strict Moslem sect, found mainly in Oman, Zanzibar, and northern Africa.
[< Abdull'ah ibn *Ibad,* a Moslem leader of the 600's + English *-ite*[1]]
I|ban (ē′bän, ē bän′), *n., adj.* —*n.* a member of a tribe of Dyaks living along the seacoast and rivers of Borneo; Sea Dyak.
—*adj.* of or having to do with this tribe.
I-bar (ī′bär′), *n.* = I-beam.
I.B.E., **1** International Bureau of Education. **2** International Bureau of Exhibitions.
***I-beam** (ī′bēm′), *n.* a metal beam having a cross section like the letter capital I (with serifs I): *Standard structural beams are known as I-beams* (Wall Street Journal).

***I-beam**

IBEC (no periods), International Bank for Economic Cooperation.
I|be|ri|an (ī bir′ē ən), *adj., n.* —*adj.* **1** of or having to do with Iberia, peninsula in southwestern Europe, or its people: *Better be first, he [Julius Caesar] said, in a little Iberian village, Than be second in Rome* (Longfellow). **2** having to do with the Iberian language. **3** of or having to do with ancient Iberia (south of the Caucasus in Asia) or its people.
—*n.* **1** a native or inhabitant of Iberia. The Basques are supposed to be descended from the ancient Iberians. **2** the language of ancient Iberia.
3 a member of a dark, long-headed race once inhabiting a great part of southern Europe and parts of northern Africa.
***i|bex** (ī′beks), *n., pl.* **i|bex|es, ib|i|ces** (ib′ə sēz, ī′bə-), or (*collectively*) **i|bex**. a wild goat of mountainous regions of Europe, Asia, and North Africa. The male has very large horns which curve backward, up to 50 to 60 inches long. [< Latin *ibex*]

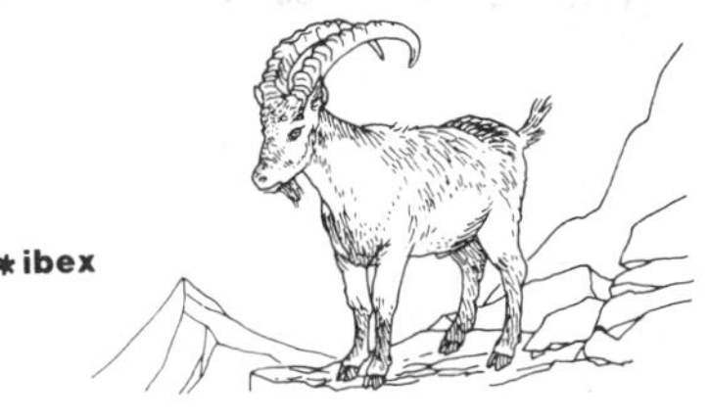
***ibex**

I|bi|bi|o (i′bə bē′ō), *n., pl.* **-bi|o** or **-bi|os. 1** a member of a tribe living in the eastern region of Nigeria. **2** the Bantu language of this tribe.
ibid., ibidem.
►**Ibid.** is used in a footnote to refer to the work mentioned in the immediately preceding footnote.
i|bi|dem (i bī′dem), *adv. Latin.* in the same place; in the same book, chapter, page, passage, or other source. *Abbr:* ibid. or ib.
i|bi|dine (ī′bə dīn, -din), *adj.* of or having to do with the ibis.
[< Greek *îbis, íbidos* ibis]
i|bis (ī′bis), *n., pl.* **i|bis|es** or (*collectively*) **i|bis**. a large, long-legged wading bird of warm regions, related to the heron, having black, white, or scarlet plumage and a long, downward-curving bill. The ancient Egyptians regarded the ibis as sacred.
[< Latin *ībis* < Greek *îbis, íbidos* < an Egyptian word]
I|bi|zan hound (ē bē′zən), any one of a rare breed of dogs that originated on Ibiza, an island off the eastern coast of Spain. The Ibizan hound resembles the greyhound.
-ible, *suffix added to verbs to form adjectives.* that can be _____ed; able to be _____ed: *Divisible = that can be divided. Perfectible = that can be perfected. Reducible = that can be reduced.*
[< Latin *-ibilis, -ībilis,* a suffix forming adjectives from verbs with infinitives in *-ēre, -ere, -īre,* being one form of the suffix *-bilis*]
►See **-able** for usage note.
Ib|lis (ib′lis), *n.* = Eblis.
IBM (no periods) or **I.B.M.**, **1** intercontinental ballistic missile; ICBM. **2** International Business Machines.
ibn-, *combining form. Arabic.* son; son of: *Abdul ibn-Saud, a king of Saudi Arabia.*
I|bo (ē′bō), *n., pl.* **-bo** or **-bos. 1** a member of a West African people forming a large part of the population of Nigeria. **2** the Kwa language of this people. Also, **Igbo**.
ibp (no periods), initial boiling point.
IBP (no periods), International Biological Program (scientific study of ways to control animal and plant life for man's welfare).
IBRD (no periods), International Bank for Reconstruction and Development.
Ib|sen|i|an (ib sen′ē ən), *adj.* = Ibsenite.
Ib|sen|ism (ib′sə niz əm), *n.* the aims, ideas, and dramatic method characteristic of the Norwegian dramatist and poet Henrik Ibsen, 1828-1906, and his followers.
Ib|sen|ist (ib′sə nist), *n., adj.* = Ibsenite.
Ib|sen|ite (ib′sə nīt), *n., adj.* —*n.* a follower of Ibsen.
—*adj.* of or having to do with Ibsen or Ibsenism.
-ic, *suffix added to nouns to form adjectives.* **1** of or having to do with _____: *Atmospheric = of or having to do with the atmosphere. Icelandic = of Iceland.*
2 having the nature of _____: *Heroic = having the nature of a hero.*
3 constituting or being _____: *Bombastic = constituting or being bombast.*
4 containing _____; made up of _____: *Alcoholic = containing alcohol.*

***I**[1]
definition 1

Script letters look like examples of fine penmanship. They appear in many formal uses, such as invitations to social functions.

Handwritten letters, both manuscript or printed (left) and cursive (right), are easy for children to read and to write.

Ii *Ii*
Roman letters have *serifs* (finishing strokes) adapted from the way Roman stonecutters carved their letters. This is *Times Roman* type.

Ii *Ii*
Sans-serif letters are often called *gothic.* They have lines of even width and no serifs. This type face is called *Helvetica.*

Ii *Ii*
Between roman and gothic, some letters have thick and thin lines with slight flares that suggest serifs. This type face is *Optima.*

Computer letters can be sensed by machines either from their shapes or from the magnetic ink with which they are printed.

5 made by___; caused by___: *Volcanic = made by a volcano.*
6 like___; like that of___; characteristic of___: *Meteoric = like a meteor.*
7 an art or system of thought, as in *stoic, logic, music.*
8 *Chemistry.* indicating the presence of an element in a compound or ion that is of a higher valence than indicated by the suffix *-ous,* as in *boric, chloric, ferric, sulfuric.*
[< French *-ique* < Latin *-icus* < Greek *-ikós*]
▶Many words ending in *-ic* have two or more of meanings 1 to 6.
i/c (no periods), in charge (of): *officer i/c distribution.*
IC (no periods), **1** immediate constituent. **2** integrated circuit: *An IC is a circuit consisting of up to 20 transistors and diodes on a microscopic chip of silicon* (Robert E. Stoffels). **3** internal combustion.
I.C., Jesus Christ (*Latin,* Iesus Christus).
ICA (no periods) or **I.C.A.**, **1** International Cooperation Administration. **2** International Cooperative Alliance.
-ical, *suffix.* **1** *-ic,* as in *geometrical, parasitical, hysterical.*
2 *-ic,* but specialized or differentiated in meaning, as in *economical.*
3 *-ic* + *-al* or *-ics* + *-al,* as in *critical, musical, ethical, statistical.*
[< Late Latin *-icālis* < *-icus* - ic + *-ālis* - al[1]]
-ically, *suffix. -ic* + *-ly.* Instead of *artistic-ly* we write *artistically;* instead of *alphabetic-ly* we write *alphabetically.* In speaking, the suffix *-ically* is ordinarily pronounced in two syllables (-ə klē).
ICAO (no periods) or **I.C.A.O.**, International Civil Aviation Organization.
I|car|i|an (i kãr′ē ən, ī-), *adj.* **1** rash; carelessly bold: *an Icarian undertaking.* **2** of or characteristic of Icarus.
Ic|a|rus (ik′ər əs, ī′kər-), *n.* **1** *Greek Legend.* the son of Daedalus. Icarus and his father escaped from Crete by using wings that Daedalus had made. Icarus flew so high that the sun melted the wax by which his wings were attached, and he drowned in the sea. *The envy of birds is very old in human history; the faith of Daedalus and Icarus has come down to us from a classical antiquity* (Atlantic). **2** a planetoid whose orbit approaches closer to the sun than any other planetary body does.
ICBM (no periods) or **I.C.B.M.**, intercontinental ballistic missile, a ballistic missile with a range of over 5,000 miles.
ICC (no periods) or **I.C.C.**, an abbreviation for the following:
1 Interstate Commerce Commission: *ICC has ordered the truckers to boost rates* (Time).
2 International Chamber of Commerce.
3 International Control Commission.
4 International Copyright Convention.
ice (īs), *n., adj., v.,* **iced, ic|ing.** *—n.* **1** water made solid by cold; frozen water: *Snowflakes, frost, and glaciers are all ice* (H. T. McDermott). **2** a layer or surface of ice, as on a body of water: *the Arctic ice.* **3** a frozen surface for ice-skating, curling, and the like; rink. **4** something that looks or feels like ice: *camphor ice.* **5** *U.S.* a frozen dessert, usually made of sweetened fruit juice: *raspberry ice.* **6** a sugary covering for a cake; frosting; icing. **7** *Slang,* diamonds. **8** *British.* ice cream. **9** *U.S. Slang.* **a** money given as bribe, especially to the police. **b** under-the-counter money given to a theater employee for choice or extra tickets to a performance: *The take on 'ice' in one recent musical was over a million dollars a year* (San Francisco Chronicle).
—adj. of ice; having to do with ice: *an ice crystal.*
—v.t. **1a** to make cool with ice; put ice in or around: *to ice a drink.* **b** *Figurative.* to make cold as if with ice; deprive of warmth of feeling. **2** to cover with ice. **3** to turn to ice; freeze. SYN: congeal. **4** to cover (cake) with icing: *The baker iced the cake with fancy decorations of sugar.* **5** *Ice Hockey.* to shoot (the puck) across the rink past the goal line: *Such emergencies were met only for desperate checking and icing of the puck* (Andy O'Brien). **6** *U.S. Slang.* to kill.
—v.i. to freeze.
break the ice, a to make a beginning; start something dangerous or difficult: *... to be the first to break the ice of the enterprise* (Thomas North). **b** to overcome first difficulties in talking or getting acquainted: *A trade unionist, he breaks the ice by displaying his membership card* (London Times).
cut (much, any, or **no) ice,** *Informal.* to have (much, any, or no) effect; make (much, any, or no) difference: *Present power cuts more ice in diplomatic relations than past virtue* (Manchester Guardian Weekly). *The big expensive car cuts no ice with the repairman* (Maclean's).
ice out, to ignore or exclude socially: *It [Washington] is not a big city, and when a lady is down and out and getting herself dumped from someone's guest list there, it is not the same as getting herself iced out in New York or Chicago* (Harper's).
ice up, to fill up with ice; take on a coating of ice: *Ice formed on the windshield and most of the instruments iced up, and a heavy hailstorm buffeted the plane* (London Times).
on ice, a in reserve; out of sight, consideration, or activity: *The French rejection of the treaty caused it to be laid on ice* (London Times).
b safely assured: *The home team had the game on ice.*
on thin ice, in a dangerous, vulnerable, or difficult position: *on the thin ice of debt* (Ouïda). *This statement ... is also on very thin ice historically* (New York Times).
[Old English *īs*] *—***ice′like′,** *adj.* *—***ic′er,** *n.*
Ice., **1** Iceland. **2** Icelandic.
ICE (no periods), internal-combustion engine.
ice age, 1 any of the times when the earth was covered with glaciers, as in the late pre-Cambrian (about 700 million years ago), in the early Cambrian (about 600 million years ago), and in the Permian (about 230 million years ago); glacial epoch: *In ice age times apparently there were also land bridges across the mid-Mediterranean* (Scientific American). **2** Usually, **Ice Age.** the most recent such time, when most of the Northern Hemisphere was covered with glaciers; Pleistocene: *The Hungarian site of Vértesszöllös, which dates from the last Ice Age (200,000* B.C.*), has yielded many stone tools* (Henri V. Vallois).
ice apron, a pointed structure for protecting a bridge pier from ice carried down by the stream.
ice avalanche, a mass of ice that thaws and detaches from high glaciers during warm weather; summer avalanche.
***ice ax,** a small ax, used in mountain climbing, with a slender wooden handle and a head combining a blade and a pick: *He and another officer chopped an 18-in. hole in the snow with an alpine ice ax* (Time).

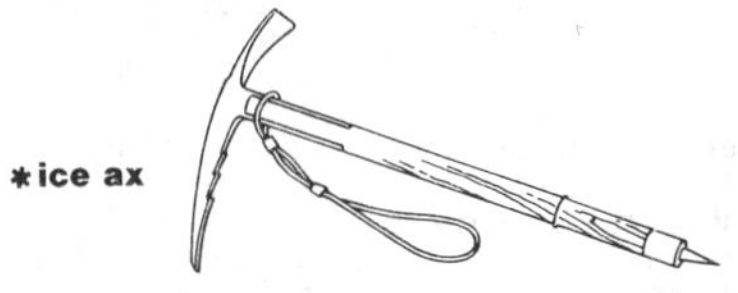
***ice ax**

ice bag, a waterproof bag to be filled with ice and applied to some part of the body.
***ice|berg** (īs′bėrg′), *n.* **1** a large mass of ice floating in the sea; a detached portion of a glacier carried out to sea; berg. About 90 per cent of its mass is below the surface of the water. *icebergs and field ice in the treacherous fog-laden Grand Banks* (Science News Letter). **2** *Figurative.* a cold, unemotional person. **3** *Figurative.* anything that is only partly visible or known: *Information which had been missed earlier remained to be discovered, though we cannot measure this "iceberg"* (New Scientist).
the tip of the iceberg, a small or superficial part of something; that which appears only on the surface: *The news article reported only the tip of the iceberg. Hidden is a serious situation for engineers in the United States and Great Britain* (Manchester Guardian Weekly).
[< Dutch *ijsberg* (literally) ice mountain]

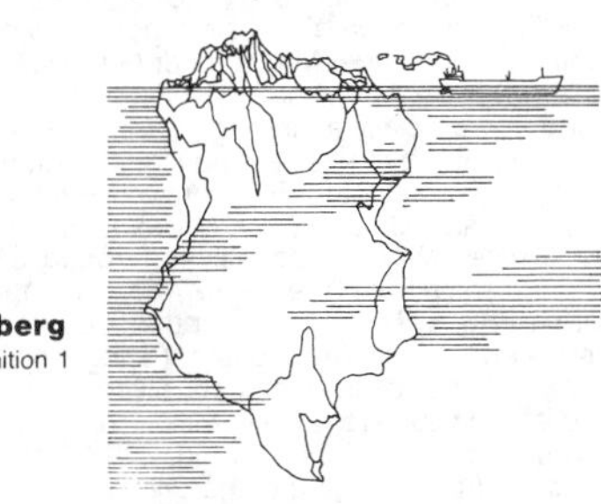
***iceberg**
definition 1

iceberg lettuce, a crisp kind of lettuce growing in tight, round heads. See picture at **lettuce.**
ice|blink (īs′blingk′), *n.* a luminous appearance near the horizon, caused by the reflection of light from ice; blink.
***ice|boat** (īs′bōt′), *n.* **1** a triangular frame on runners, fitted with sails or an engine for sailing on ice at great speed. One runner, for steering, is attached to the front or rear of the body, and the other two are at the ends of a crosspiece. **2** = icebreaker (def. 1).

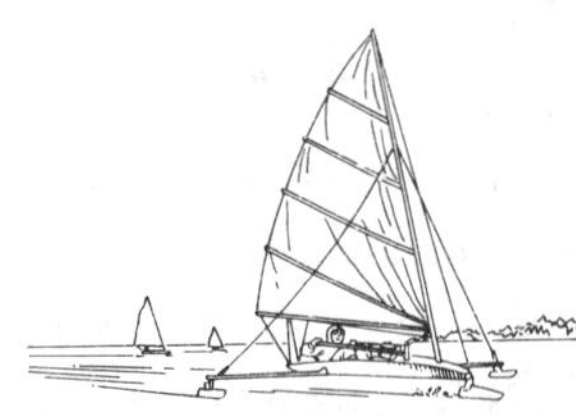
***iceboat**
definition 1

ice|boat|er (īs′bō′tər), *n.* a person who engages in iceboating.
ice|boat|ing (īs′bōt′ing), *n.* the sport of racing or sailing an iceboat: *Iceboating is the fastest of all winter sports* (Time).
ice|bound (īs′bound′), *adj.* **1** held fast by ice; frozen in: *The whole expedition was icebound* (Atlantic). **2** shut in or obstructed by ice: *The ship could not make its way into the icebound harbor.*
ice|box (īs′boks′), *n.* **1** = refrigerator. **2** an insulated box in which to keep food cooled with ice: *Put the meat and salad in the icebox* (New Yorker). [American English < *ice* + *box*[1]]
ice|break|er (īs′brā′kər), *n.* **1** a strong boat used to break a channel through ice; iceboat: *An atomic-powered icebreaker [makes] possible much broader explorations of polar regions* (Wall Street Journal). **2** a structure for protection against moving ice, such as an ice apron: *The supporting columns ... had to be designed to work as icebreakers* (Wall Street Journal). **3** a tool or machine for breaking ice into small pieces. **4** *Figurative.* something that breaks the ice; anything that serves to stimulate or enliven conversation, a social gathering, or other meeting or discussion: *Salesmen use an icebreaker in the form of a large lapel button* (Wall Street Journal). [American English < *ice* + *breaker*[1]. Compare Dutch *ijsbreker.*]
ice-break|ing (īs′brā′king), *n., adj. Figurative.* *—n.* the practice of stimulating or enlivening conversation, a social gathering, or other meeting or discussion between persons or groups.
—adj. that serves to stimulate or enliven conversation, a social gathering, or other meeting or discussion: *that ice-breaking first hello.*
ice|cap (īs′kap′), *n.* **1** a permanent covering of ice and snow over an area, sloping down on all sides from a high center: *And reports ... show that the Antarctic icecap is up to 10,000 feet thick* (Scientific American). **2** a glacier, usually one covering a large area, that flows in all directions from its center. **3** an ice bag for the head.
ice-ca|pades (īs′kə pādz), *n.pl.* = ice show. [< *Ice Capades,* a popular American ice show first produced in the 1940's]
ice cave, a cave that has an accumulation of ice inside it throughout the year. The ice forms when the temperature drops, freezing any water that seeps into the cave.
ice chest, = icebox.
ice-cold (īs′kōld′), *adj.* cold as ice: (*Figurative.*) *in the ice-cold criminal line* (New York Times).
ice cream, a frozen dessert made of cream or custard, sweetened and flavored.
ice-cream (īs′krēm′), *adj.* **1** containing ice cream: *ice-cream cake.* **2** of a light, creamy color; yellowish white: *ice-cream pants.*
ice-cream cone, 1 a wafer shaped into a cone to hold a portion of ice cream. **2** the cone with ice cream in it.
ice-cream parlor, a shop which specializes in serving ice cream.
ice-cream sandwich, a layer of ice cream sandwiched between two wafers.
ice crystal, = ice needle.
ice cube, a small, square piece of ice made in an ice tray or ice machine and used for keeping drinks cool.
iced (īst), *adj.* **1** cooled with ice: *iced tea.* **2** covered with ice: *an iced stream.* **3** covered with icing: *an iced cake.*
ice dancing, the act or art of dancing on ice skates, which combines the movements of ice skating with ballet: *A gesture or a pause became as important as the most spectacular jumps and spins. No, you've never seen anything like ice dancing before* (Saturday Review). *—***ice dancer.**
ice fall, a mass of glacial ice occurring on a steep grade: *Foot over foot ... the rugged*

Pronunciation Key: hat, āge, cãre, fär; let, ēqual, tėrm; it, īce; hot, ōpen, ôrder; oil, out; cup, pu̇t, rüle; child; long; thin; ᴛʜen; zh, measure; ə represents **a** in about, **e** in taken, **i** in pencil, **o** in lemon, **u** in circus.

Himalayan porters . . . drive up a jagged ice fall of 3,000 feet (Time).

ice field, **1** a large sheet of ice floating in the sea. **2** a large sheet of ice on land.

ice|fish (īs′fish′), *n., pl.* **-fish|es** or (*collectively*) **-fish**. **1** any one of a group of translucent fishes of the South Atlantic: *One curious family of this order, the icefishes, includes species that have no circulating red blood* (Scientific American). **2** a small translucent fish of the rivers of Japan and China. **3** = capelin.

ice fisherman, a person who engages in ice fishing.

ice fishing, fishing in winter through holes made in the ice.

ice floe, a large sheet of floating ice.

ice|flow (īs′flō′), *n.* the flow of ice within a glacier: *boreholes deformed by iceflow* (Science News Letter).

ice-fog (īs′fog′, -fôg′), *n.* a fog of ice crystals formed during extremely low temperatures, especially in the Arctic.

ice foot, a belt or wall of ice extending along the coast in arctic regions.

ice hockey, the game of hockey played on ice, composed of six players on a side who try to drive the rubber puck into the opposing team's goal. See picture under **hockey**.

ice|house (īs′hous′), *n.* a building where ice is stored and kept from melting.

ice house, = ice shanty.

ice island, any one of a group of very large, irregular bodies of ice floating in the Arctic Ocean, sometimes up to 200 square miles in area and 200 feet in thickness, that have broken off from shelf ice during seasons of relatively warm weather.

ice jam, **1a** a mass of broken ice obstructing a river: *A cofferdam collapsed under the weight of an ice jam* (Wall Street Journal). **b** a mass of broken ice piled onto the shore of a lake by the wind. **2** *Figurative.* anything that feels like a mass of ice: *The ice jam within him breaks, and he begins to uncontrollably mourn* (New Yorker).

Icel., Icelandic.

Ice|land disease (īs′lənd), an epidemic disease first identified in Akureyri, Iceland, in 1948, marked by inflammation of the tissues of the central nervous system, muscular weakness, and partial paralysis. It is thought to be caused by a virus.

Ice|land|er (īs′lan′dər, -lən-), *n.* a person born or living in Iceland, a large island republic in the North Atlantic.

Ice|lan|dic (īs lan′dik), *adj., n.* **—*adj.*** of or having to do with Iceland, its people, or their language.
—*n.* the Scandinavian language of Iceland.

Iceland moss, a lichen of north temperate and arctic regions, used to make a jelly or powder which is added to bread and other foods. It is also used as a laxative and for other medicinal purposes, and in dyeing and papermaking.

Iceland poppy, a poppy native to northern regions of the globe, of which several cultivated varieties exist; arctic poppy.

Iceland spar, a mineral, a transparent variety of calcite, used extensively for optical purposes.

ice|less (īs′lis), *adj.* **1** free from ice. **2** requiring no ice.

ice-lol|ly (īs′lol′ē), *n., pl.* **-lol|lies**. *British.* a molded fruit-flavored ice on a stick.

ice machine, a machine for making ice, usually automatically and in the form of small cubes.

ice|man (īs′man′, -mən), *n., pl.* **-men**. **1** a man who sells, delivers, or handles ice. **2** a man skilled in traveling over ice. **3** a man in charge of the ice on a rink.

ice milk, a frozen dessert resembling ice cream, but with less butterfat content and of a softer consistency.

ice-mi|nus (īs′mī′nəs), *adj.* of or designating a strain of bacteria developed by genetic engineering to resist the effect of ice formation on plants: *The researchers believe that spraying this ice-minus bacteria on plants . . . will prevent the growth of the normal bacteria which do catalyze frost formation, and thereby minimize frost damage to crops* (Thomas H. Maugh II).

ice needle, a slender bit of ice floating in the air in cold weather; ice crystal.

I|ce|ni (ī sē′nī), *n.pl.* an ancient British tribe of eastern England. Their queen, Boadicea, led a revolt against the Romans in A.D. 61.

I|ce|ni|an (ī sē′nē ən), *adj.* of or having to do with Iceni.

I|ce|nic (ī sē′nik), *adj.* = Icenian.

ice-out (īs′out′), *n.* the melting of the ice on the surface of a body of water.

ice pack, **1** a large area of floating ice, consisting of separate masses more or less packed together: *The Atka saw very little of the drifting ice pack that surrounds the continent* (Scientific American). **2** a bag containing ice for application to the body.

ice pan, a small sheet or slab of floating ice: *For five months this little group survived the most harrowing hardships on the drifting ice pans* (Maclean's).

ice pick, a sharp-pointed hand tool for breaking up ice.

ice plant, **1** a low, spreading plant of the carpetweed family, native to the Mediterranean region, South Africa, and southern California, having leaves covered with glistening watery spots. **2** a place where artificial ice is made.

ice point, the temperature at which water and ice are in equilibrium at atmospheric pressure; freezing point.

ice|quake (īs′kwāk′), *n.* the rending and crashing preceding or accompanying the breaking up of great masses of ice.

ice rain, **1** half-frozen rain. **2** rain that freezes on the ground after it falls.

ice|scape (īs′skāp), *n.* a landscape consisting of ice, especially the polar landscape: *The whole icescape was awash with light* (Sunday Times).

ice-scour|ing (īs′skour′ing), *n.* the action of glacial ice on rock.

ice shanty, a hut that can be towed out onto the ice of a lake or bay and used by ice fishermen; ice house.

ice sheet, a broad, thick sheet of ice covering a very large area for a long time.

ice shelf, = shelf ice.

ice show, a musical revue or extravaganza performed on ice by skaters: *In 1940 the first ice show was installed* (New Yorker).

***ice skate**, **1** a metal runner attached to a shoe for skating on ice. **2** the shoe and runner together.

***ice skate**
definition 2

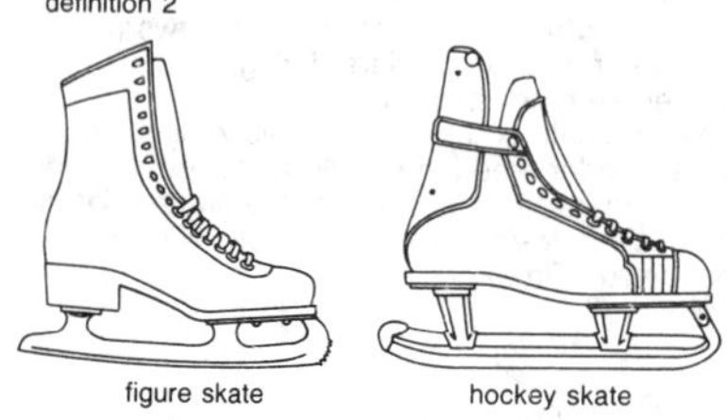

figure skate — hockey skate

ice-skate (īs′skāt′), *v.i.,* **-skat|ed, -skat|ing.** to skate on ice.

ice skater, a person who ice-skates.

ice storm, a fall of freezing rain, forming a coating of ice on the objects or surfaces that it strikes. It is often heavy enough to break trees and bring down electrical wires.

ice tray, a metal or plastic tray for freezing ice cubes in a refrigerator or freezer.

ice-up (īs′up′), *n.* the freezing over of snow or water: *In southern France snow had stopped falling in most areas, but the low temperatures were bringing about an ice-up* (London Times).

ice water, **1** water cooled with ice: *a glass of ice water.* **2** water from melted ice: *Ice water was all over the top of the melting lake.*

ice yacht, = iceboat (def. 1).

ice yachting, = iceboating.

ICFTU (no periods) or **I.C.F.T.U.**, International Confederation of Free Trade Unions.

ich dien (iн dēn′), *German.* I serve (the motto of the Prince of Wales).

I Ching (ī′ching′, ē′jing′), **1** a Chinese classical book of the Confucian age, consisting of a system of symbols and texts for use in fortunetelling. **2** the system of this book: *The . . . I Ching is, for Cage as for the Chinese sages, a divinatory or intuitive technique* (Manchester Guardian Weekly).

ich|neu|mon (ik nü′mən, -nyü′-), *n.* **1** a mongoose, especially a large, gray, African variety that looks like a weasel. The ichneumon was formerly revered by the Egyptians. **2** = ichneumon fly. [< Latin *ichneumōn* < Greek *ichneúmōn* (literally) searcher (supposedly for crocodile's eggs) < *ichneúein* hunt after, track < *íchnos* a track]

ichneumon fly, a four-winged insect, related to bees and wasps, that does not sting. Its larvae live as parasites in or on caterpillars, other insects, and spiders, usually killing them.

ich|neu|mon|id (ik nü′mə nid, -nyü′-), *adj., n.* **—*adj.*** of or belonging to the group of insects that includes the ichneumon fly.
—*n.* an ichneumonid insect.

ich|no|graph|ic (ik′nə graf′ik), *adj.* having to do with ichnography.

ich|nog|ra|phy (ik nog′rə fē), *n.* **1** the drawing of ground plans of a building. **2** a ground plan; map. [< Middle French *ichnographie,* learned borrowing from Latin *ichnographia* < Greek *ichnographíā* a ground plan, tracing out < *íchnos* track + *gráphein* draw, write out]

ich|no|lite (ik′nə līt), *n.* a footprint preserved in rock; fossil footprint. [< Greek *íchnos* footprint + English *-lite*]

ich|nol|o|gy (ik nol′ə jē), *n.* the branch of paleontology that deals with fossil footprints. [< Greek *íchnos* track, footprint + English *-logy*]

i|chor¹ (ī′kôr, -kər), *n. Greek Mythology.* the fluid supposed to flow like blood in the veins of the gods: *The ichor conducive to the contemplation of art was there, too* (New Yorker). [< Greek *ichṓr*]

i|chor² (ī′kôr, -kər), *n. Medicine.* an acrid watery discharge, especially from ulcers and wounds. [< New Latin *ichor* < Greek *ichṓr* ichor¹]

i|chor|ous (ī′kər əs), *adj. Medicine.* like ichor; containing or discharging ichor.

ichth., ichthyology.

ich|thy|ic (ik′thē ik), *adj.* of or characteristic of fishes; piscine. [< Greek *ichthyikós* fishy < *ichthys, -ýos* fish]

ich|thy|og|ra|phy (ik′thē og′rə fē), *n.* the description of fishes. [< Greek *ichthys, -ýos* fish + English *-graphy*]

ich|thy|oid (ik′thē oid), *n., adj.* **—*n.*** a fishlike animal.
—*adj.* like a fish. [< Greek *ichthys* fish + English *-oid*]

ich|thy|o|log|ic (ik′thē ə loj′ik), *adj.* of or having to do with ichthyology.

ich|thy|ol|o|gy (ik′thē ol′ə jē), *n.* **1** the branch of zoology dealing with fishes. **2** a book about fishes. [< Greek *ichthys, -ýos* fish + English *-logy*] **—ich′thy|ol′o|gist**, *n.*

ich|thy|oph|a|gi (ik′thē of′ə jī), *n.pl.* people who eat or live on fish: *They are still ichthyophagi, existing without any other subsistence but what the sea affords* (Richard F. Burton).

ich|thy|oph|a|gous (ik′thē of′ə gəs), *adj.* feeding on fish; fish-eating. [< Greek *ichthyophágos* (with English *-ous*) < *ichthys, -ýos* fish + *phageîn* eat]

ich|thy|o|plank|ton (ik′thē ō plangk′tən), *n.* the small fish that float or drift in water.

ich|thy|or|nis (ik′thē ôr′nis), *n., pl.* **-or|ni|thes** (-ôr′nə thēz). any bird of an extinct genus with vertebrae resembling those of fishes. Their fossils have been found in Texas and Kansas. *Ichthyornis was a smaller flying type somewhat resembling modern birds* (Tracy I. Storer). [< New Latin *Ichthyornis* the genus name < Greek *ichthys* fish + *órnīs* bird]

***ich|thy|o|saur** (ik′thē ə sôr), *n.* any extinct fishlike marine reptile of an order with a long beak, four paddlelike flippers, a tapering body resembling a dolphin or small whale, and a tail with a large fin: *On the land were the dinosaurs, in the sea the ichthyosaurs (looking like porpoises or sharks)* (A. Franklin Shull). [< New Latin *Ichthyosaurus* the genus name < Greek *ichthys, -ýos* fish + *saûros* lizard]

***ichthyosaur**

ich|thy|o|sau|ri|an (ik′thē ə sôr′ē ən), *adj., n.* **—*adj.*** of or belonging to the group of extinct fishlike reptiles that include the ichthyosaur.
—*n.* an ichthyosaurian reptile.

ich|thy|o|sau|rus (ik′thē ə sôr′əs), *n., pl.* **-sau|ri** (-sôr′ī). = ichthyosaur.

ich|thy|o|sis (ik′thē ō′sis), *n., pl.* **-ses** (-sēz). any one of several diseases in which the skin becomes dry, rough, and scaly; fishskin disease: *Common to all the ichthyoses . . . is increased production of epidermal cells* (J. T. Kalivas and T. B. Fitzpatrick). [< New Latin *ichthyosis* < Greek *ichthys, -ýos* fish + *-ōsis* condition]

ich|thy|o|ste|gal|i|an (ik′thē ə stə gal′ē ən), *adj., n.* **—*adj.*** of or having to do with a group of extinct vertebrates that are the most primitive amphibians known, having tails supported by fin rays and feet instead of fins. **—*n.*** an ichthyostegalian vertebrate. [< New Latin *Ichthyostegalia* the order name (< Greek *ichthys, -ýos* fish + New Latin *Steg(oceph) alia* the stegocephalians) + English *-an*]

ICI (no periods) or **I.C.I.**, *British.* Imperial Chemical Industries.

i|ci|cle (ī′si kəl), *n.* **1** a pointed, hanging stick of ice formed by the freezing of dripping water: *In winter icicles hung from the edge of the roof as the sun melted the snow.* **2** anything resembling this, such as tinsel for trimming a Christmas tree. **3** *Informal.* a cold or unemotional person. [Middle English *isykle* < Old English *īs* ice + *gicel* icicle]

i|ci|cled (ī′si kəld), *adj.* hung with icicles.

i|ci|ly (ī′sə lē), *adv.* in an icy manner; coldly: *The wind blew icily against our backs.*

i·ci·ness (ī′sē nis), *n.* the quality of being icy; extreme coldness: (*Figurative.*) *The iciness of his tone made everyone think he was unfriendly.*

ic·ing (ī′sing), *n.* a mixture of sugar and some liquid, with white of egg or other ingredients, used to cover cakes; frosting.

i·ci on parle fran·çais (ē sē′ôɴ pärl fräɴ sā′), *French.* French is spoken here.

ick·er (ik′ər), *n. Scottish.* an ear of corn. [probably < variant of Old Northumbrian *æhher* ear of grain. See related etym. at **ear**².]

ick·y (ik′ē), *adj.*, **ick·i·er, ick·i·est.** *U.S. Slang.* **1** unpleasantly sticky; messy. **2** unpleasant; obnoxious: *icky grownups who have long conversations . . . about free will, duty, and syllogisms* (Harper's). **3** *Figurative.* oversentimental; cloying: *icky lyrics.* [< children's pronunciation of *sticky*] —**ick′i·ly,** *adv.* —**ick′i·ness,** *n.*

ick·y-poo (ik′ē pü′), *adj. Slang.* icky.

ICN (no periods), International Council of Nurses.

***i·con** (ī′kon), *n., pl.* **i·cons, i·co·nes** (ī′kə nēz). **1** a picture or image of Christ, the Virgin Mary, or a saint, venerated as sacred in the Eastern Orthodox Church. Icons are usually painted on wood or ivory. **2** a picture; image; figure; statue. **3** a picture or drawing representing a command to a computer, as for example the picture of a garbage can representing the command to erase a file: *When the user inserts a program disk into the computer, [there] appears on the computer's display screen . . . an icon, or sketch, of each program on the disk* (Howard Bierman). Also, **ikon, eikon.** [< Latin *īcōn* < Greek *eikṓn*]

***icon**
definition 1

i·con·ic (ī kon′ik), *adj.* **1** of or having to do with an icon; like an icon. **2** following a conventional style in art. [< Latin *īconicus* < Greek *eikonikós* < *eikṓn* image] —**i·con′i·cal·ly,** *adv.*

i·con·i·cal (ī kon′ə kəl), *adj.* = iconic.

i·con·ize (ī′kə nīz), *v.t.*, **-ized, -iz·ing.** to make an idol of; venerate uncritically: *In the land of his birth Lenin has been iconized and transmogrified into a sugary shibboleth* (New Scientist).

i·con·o·clasm (ī kon′ə klaz əm), *n.* **1** the attacking of cherished beliefs or traditional institutions regarded as based on error or superstition. **2** the doctrine or act of breaking or destroying images.

i·con·o·clast (ī kon′ə klast), *n.* **1** a person who attacks cherished beliefs or institutions which he thinks are wrong or foolish: *I have become a reformer, and, like all reformers, an iconoclast . . . I shatter creeds and demolish idols* (George Bernard Shaw). **2** a person opposed to worshiping images or who breaks or destroys them. **3a** a Protestant who practiced or approved of the destruction of church images in the 1500's and 1600's, especially a Protestant in the Netherlands. **b** one of a sect in the Greek Orthodox Church of the 700's and 800's opposed to the use and worship of images. [< Medieval Latin *ikonoklastes* < Medieval Greek *eikonoklastes* < Greek *eikṓn* image + *klas-*, stem of *klân* to break]

i·con·o·clas·tic (ī kon′ə klas′tik), *adj.* of or having to do with iconoclasts or iconoclasm: *Even the most iconoclastic young scholar hesitates to say anything unfavorable about a large foundation* (New Yorker). —**i·con′o·clas′ti·cal·ly,** *adv.*

i·con·o·graph (ī kon′ə graf, -gräf), *n.* a drawing, engraving, or other picture for illustrating a book or other publication.

i·con·o·graph·ic (ī kon′ə graf′ik), *adj.* of iconography having to do with symbolic representation: *Let me give an example of iconographic triumph and disaster from one painter in one place: Titian in Venice* (Harper's). —**i·con′o·graph′i·cal·ly,** *adv.*

i·con·o·graph·i·cal (ī kon′ə graf′ə kəl), *adj.* = iconographic.

i·co·nog·ra·phy (ī′kə nog′rə fē), *n., pl.* **-phies.** **1** the illustration of a subject by means of drawings or figures. **2** a book or work in which this is done. **3** the art of representing persons ideas, or objects by pictures, images, or the like: *In Christian iconography, the dove represents the Holy Ghost* (New Yorker). [< Medieval Latin *ikonographia* < Greek *eikonographiā* sketch, description < *eikṓn* image + *gráphein* draw, describe] —**i′co·nog′ra·pher,** *n.*

i·co·nol·a·try (ī′kə nol′ə trē), *n.* the worship of images. [< Greek *eikṓn, -ónos* icon + *latreiā* worship]

i·con·o·log·i·cal (ī kon′ə loj′ə kəl), *adj.* of or having to do with iconology.

i·co·nol·o·gy (ī′kə nol′ə jē), *n.* **1** the branch of knowledge concerned with pictorial or sculptural representations. **2** icons collectively. **3** symbolical representation; symbolism. —**i′co·nol′o·gist,** *n.*

i·con·o·phile (ī kon′ə fīl), *n.* a lover or connoisseur of pictures, engravings, or the like. [< Greek *eikṓn, -ónos* image + English *-phile*]

i·co·noph·i·lism (ī′kə nof′ə liz əm), *n.* a liking for pictures, engravings, or the like.

i·con·o·scope (ī kon′ə skōp), *n.* an early kind of cathode-ray tube used in television cameras, which made television transmission possible. It consists of a vacuum tube enclosing a photosensitive screen on which the optical image is focused for scanning by a cathode-ray beam. [< Greek *eikṓn, -ónos* image + *-scope*]

i·co·nos·ta·sis (ī′kə nos′tə sis), *n., pl.* **-ses** (-sēz). a screen or partition in the Eastern Orthodox Church on which icons are placed, separating the sanctuary from the main part of the church. [< New Latin *iconostasis* < New Greek *eikonóstasis* < Greek *eikṓn* image + *stásis* a standing, position < *histánai* to stand]

i·co·sa·he·dral (ī′kō sə hē′drəl), *adj.* having twenty faces. —**i′co·sa·he′dral·ly,** *adv.*

***i·co·sa·he·dron** (ī′kō sə hē′drən), *n., pl.* **-drons, -dra** (-drə). *Geometry.* a solid having twenty faces. [< Greek *eikosáedron,* (originally) neuter of *eikosáedros* < *eíkosi* twenty + *hédrā* seat, base]

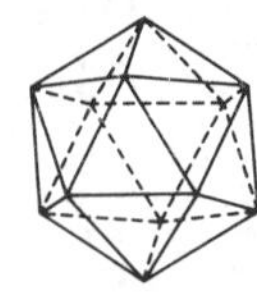

***icosahedron**

ICRC (no periods) or **I.C.R.C.**, International Committee of the Red Cross.

-ics, *suffix.* **1** a body of facts or principles; a system of thought; a science or field of study, as in *optics, aesthetics, metaphysics, genetics.* **2** a system or a method of action; art or practice, as in *tactics, gymnastics, geodetics, ceramics.* [originally plural of *-ic* < Latin *-ica* < Greek *-iká,* neuter plural, matters having to do with]

I.C.S., **1** *British.* Indian Civil Service. **2** *U.S.* International Correspondence School.

ICSH (no periods), interstitial cell stimulating hormone.

ICSU (no periods) or **I.C.S.U.**, International Council of Scientific Unions.

ICSW (no periods), International Council of Social Welfare.

ic·ter·ic (ik ter′ik), *n., adj.* —*n.* **1** a remedy for jaundice. **2** a person affected with jaundice.
—***adj.*** **1** having to do with or affected with jaundice; jaundiced: *The liver was enlarged and icteric and showed typical changes of mechanical jaundice* (Beaumont and Dodds). **2** used for curing jaundice.
[< Latin *ictericus* < Greek *ikterikós* jaundiced < *íkteros* jaundice, icterus]

ic·ter·id (ik′tə rid), *adj., n.* —***adj.*** of or having to do with a large group of American passerine birds, having sharp cone-shaped bills.
—***n.*** an icterid bird.
[< New Latin *Icteridae* the family name < Latin *icterus* a yellow bird; see etym. under **icterus**]

ic·ter·ine (ik′tər ēn), *n.,* or **icterine warbler,** a European warbler with an olive back and lemon-colored breast. [< Latin *icterus* a yellow bird + English *-ine*¹]

ic·ter·us (ik′tər əs), *n.* **1** = jaundice. **2** a yellowing of grain and certain other plants when exposed to excess moisture and cold. [< Latin *icterus* a yellow bird, which supposedly cured jaundice < Greek *íkteros*]

ic·tus (ik′təs), *n., pl.* **-tus·es** or **-tus.** **1** *Prosody.* rhythmical or metrical stress or accent. **2** *Medicine.* a fit; stroke. [< Latin *ictus, -ūs* < *īcere* to hit, beat]

i·cy (ī′sē), *adj.*, **i·ci·er, i·ci·est.** **1** like ice; very cold or slippery: *the icy blasts of winter wind.* SYN: frosty, frigid. **2** having much ice; covered with ice: *an icy sidewalk.* **3** of ice: *an icy cover on the frozen pond.* **4** *Figurative.* without warm feeling; cold and unfriendly: *an icy tone of voice.* [< *ic*(e) + *-y*¹. Compare Old English *īsig.*]

id (id), *n. Psychoanalysis.* the source of energy of the unconscious, associated with primitive, instinctual drives for pleasure and gratification. The name was invented by Sigmund Freud. *The ego . . . has the difficult assignment of forcing back the id's uncivilized urges or of disguising them in such a way as to make them socially acceptable* (Alfred B. Heilbrun, Jr.).
[< Latin *id* it, as a translation of German *es* (literally) it]

I'd (īd), **1** I should. **2** I would. **3** I had.

-id¹, *suffix.* **1** structure; body, as in *capsid, plasmid.* **2** (one) belonging to a group, as in *ichneumonid.* [< Latin or Greek *-id-, -is,* a patronymic suffix]

-id², *suffix.* a variant of **-ide.**

id., idem.

i.d., inside diameter; internal diameter.

Id., Idaho.

ID (no periods), **1** Idaho (with postal Zip Code). **2** Iraqi dinar.

I.D., an abbreviation for the following:
1 identification: *Owners of rifles and shotguns must be 18, and need only the basic I.D.* (Time).
2 *British.* Intelligence Department.
3 *U.S.* Intelligence Division (of the U.S. Army).

Ida., Idaho.

IDA (no periods), International Development Association (an agency to provide low-cost loans to underdeveloped countries).

I·da·ho·an (ī′də hō′ən), *n., adj.* —***n.*** a native or inhabitant of Idaho.
—***adj.*** of or having to do with Idaho.

IDB (no periods) or **I.D.B.**, **1** (in South Africa) illicit diamond buyer. **2** Inter-American Development Bank.

I.D. bracelet (ī′dē′), a bracelet marked with a person's identification: *She was wearing . . . an I.D. bracelet I gave her last January for her sixteenth birthday—with her name on one side and mine on the other* (Truman Capote).

I.D. card, = identity card.

IDDM (no periods), insulin-dependent diabetes mellitus.

ide¹ (īd), *n.* an edible freshwater fish of northern Europe that resembles the chub.
[< Scandinavian (compare Swedish and Norwegian *id*)]

ide² (īd), *n.* singular of **ides.**

-ide, *suffix.* compound of, as in *oxide, chloride, sulfide.* Also, **-id.** [< (ox)*ide,* the first compound classified in this way]

i·de·a (ī dē′ə), *n.* **1a** a picture or notion of anything in the mind; mental image: *to have an idea about how a thing should look. Eating candy and playing with toys are that little child's idea of happiness. What space does the idea of a pyramid occupy more than the idea of a grain of corn?* (Samuel Johnson). **b** any result of mental activity or understanding; a thought, fancy, or opinion; view; belief: *old-fashioned ideas. The new boy had no idea that work at school was so easy. I had an idea that the man might be a spy.* **2a** an understanding of what is to be aimed at or what is desirable or ought to be; a governing principle; point or purpose: *The idea of a vacation is to get a rest. The statue has been restored and . . . because the idea is perfect and indestructible, all these injuries do not . . . impair the effect* (Hawthorne). SYN: conception, concept. **b** a notion of something to be done; plan of action; intention: *the idea of an election by ballot* (Edmund Burke). *It's a good idea, if you can carry it out.* SYN: conception, concept. **3** *Music.* a theme, phrase, or figure. **4a** (in Platonic philosophy) one of the patterns of which things are imperfect copies and from which they derive their existence. **b** the immediate object of thought or mental perception according to René Descartes and John Locke. **5** *Obsolete.* a person or thing regarded as perfect of its kind. **6** *Obsolete.* the mental image or picture of something previously seen or known: *Though I despaired of possessing you . . . I doated still on your charming idea* (Henry Fielding). **7** *Obsolete.* a figure; representation; likeness.
[< Latin *idea* < Greek *idéā* < *ideîn* to see]
—**i·de′a·less,** *adj.*
—***Syn.*** **1a, b Idea, notion, thought** mean something understood or formed in the mind. **Idea** is the general word applying to something existing in the mind as the result of understanding, thinking, reasoning, imagination, etc.: *Learn to express your ideas clearly.* **Notion** applies to an idea not fully, clearly, plainly, or completely formed or understood: *I have only a notion of what you mean.* **Thought** applies to an idea formed by reflection or reasoning, rather than by the imagination: *Tell me your thoughts on this proposal.*
▶**idea.** With a dependent verb, the idiom is *idea of* plus a gerund: *They got the happy idea of climbing Sugarloaf Hill.* Not: *They got the happy idea to climb Sugarloaf Hill.*

i·de·al (ī dē′əl), *n., adj.* —***n.*** **1** a perfect type; model to be imitated; what one would wish to be: *Her mother is her ideal.* SYN: example, pattern. **2** an ideal end; goal: *Religion holds up high ideals for us to follow. The severest challenge*

facing American society ... is to make the practice of American life and the processes of American institutions conform reasonably to those ideals of liberty and equality and justice so often and so ringingly proclaimed (Tom Wicker).
—*adj.* **1** just as one would wish; perfect: *A warm, sunny day is ideal for a picnic.* **2** existing only in thought; imaginary: *A point without length, breadth, or thickness is an ideal object.* **3** not practical; visionary. **SYN:** unreal, fanciful. **4** having to do with ideas; representing an idea. **5** *Philosophy.* regarding ideas as the only reality.
[< Late Latin *ideālis* < Latin *idea* idea] —**i|de'al-ness,** *n.*

i|de|al|ise (ī dē'ə līz), *v.t., v.i.,* **-ised, -is|ing.** *Especially British.* idealize.

i|de|al|ism (ī dē'ə liz əm), *n.* **1** the action or process of acting according to one's ideals of what ought to be regardless of what happens or of what people may think; cherishing of fine ideals. **2** the act of neglecting practical matters in following ideals; not being practical. **3** *Philosophy.* the belief that reality is made up of ideas only and not of material objects. Idealism, as opposed to materialism, holds that objects do not really exist apart from our ideas. **4** the representation in art or literature of imagined types rather than exact likenesses of people, instances, or situations. Idealism is opposed to realism. **5** an ideal representation.

i|de|al|ist (ī dē'ə list), *n., adj.* —*n.* **1** a person who has high ideals and acts according to them: *There is need for both the pragmatist who would harness in the public service man's drive for worldly goods and the idealist who would lift man's drive to more lofty goals* (Charles L. Schultze). **2** a person who neglects practical matters in following ideals. **SYN:** visionary. **3** an adherent of idealism in art, literature, or philosophy.
—*adj.* = idealistic.

i|de|al|is|tic (ī dē'ə lis'tik), *adj.* **1** having high ideals and acting according to them: *America is the only idealistic nation* (Woodrow Wilson). *The Japanese are an extremely idealistic people, for all their pragmatism* (Shigeru Yoshida). **2** forgetting or neglecting practical matters in trying to follow one's ideals; not practical. **SYN:** impractical, visionary. **3** of idealism or idealists. —**i|de'al|is'ti-cal|ly,** *adv.*

i|de|al|i|ty (ī'dē al'ə tē), *n., pl.* **-ties. 1** ideal quality or character. **2** the ability to idealize. **3** something ideal or imaginary.

i|de|al|ize (ī dē'ə līz), *v.,* **-ized, -iz|ing.** —*v.t.* to make ideal; think of or represent as perfect rather than as is actually true: *She idealized her older sister and thought that everything she did was right.*
—*v.i.* **1** to imagine or form an ideal or ideals. **2** to represent something in an ideal form. —**i|de'al|i-za'tion,** *n.* —**i|de'al|iz'er,** *n.*

i|de|al|less (ī dē'əl lis), *adj.* without an ideal.

i|de|al|ly (ī dē'ə lē), *adv.* **1** according to an ideal; perfectly. **2** only as an idea or theory; not really.

i|de|a|logue (ī dē'ə lôg, -log), *n.* = ideologue.

ideal point, *Mathematics.* a point at infinity; the point at which parallel lines intersect.

idea man, one who is fertile or adept in conceiving new ideas that can be put into practice: *The hand of the artist has no part in the evolution of the work but is the mere executor of the idea man's command* (New Yorker).

ideas man, *British.* = idea man.

i|de|ate (*v.* ī dē'āt; *n.* ī dē'it, -āt), *v.,* **-at|ed, -at-ing,** *n.* —*v.t.* to form the idea of; imagine; conceive: *a state which Plato ideated* (John Donne).
—*v.i.* to form ideas; think.
—*n.* the external object of which an idea is formed.
[< *ide*(a) + *-ate*[1]]

i|de|a|tion (ī'dē ā'shən), *n.* the formation of ideas.

i|de|a|tion|al (ī'dē ā'shə nəl), *adj.* of or having to do with the formation of ideas: *By hewing to the fine line between the reportage of the living facts and their desiccated ideational background he provides a very lively account* (Saturday Review). —**i'de|a'tion|al|ly,** *adv.*

i|dée fixe (ē dā'fēks'), *pl.* **i|dées fixes** (ē dā' fēks'). *French.* a fixed idea; obsession: *After the Anschluss the gambler* [*Hitler*] *with the idée fixe sat at the driver's wheel* (Manchester Guardian Weekly). *He was right away her absorption and idée fixe* (Saul Bellow).

i|dée re|çue (ē dā'rə sʏ'), *pl.* **i|dées re|çues** (ē dā'rə sʏ'). *French.* **1** a prevailing or conventional idea, opinion, or outlook: [*He*]*repeats a number of idées reçues which do not stand up to closer examination* (Manchester Guardian Weekly). *Children ... may be less articulate than adults, but they ... are often, having accepted fewer idées reçues, more perceptive* (New Yorker). **2** (literally) received idea.

i|dem (ī'dem, id'em), *pron., adj. Latin.* the same as previously given or mentioned. *Abbr:* id.

i|dem|po|ten|cy (ī dem'pə tən sē), *n. Mathematics.* the property of remaining unchanged under multiplication by itself: *Idempotency ... corresponds to reflexiveness and occurs if an operation produces no change in the number or set on which it operates* (New Scientist). [< Latin *idem* the same + English *potency*]

i|dem|po|tent (ī dem'pə tənt), *adj. Mathematics.* having or characterized by idempotency: *Logical multiplication is said to be idempotent, signifying that all "powers" of a set are the same, and hence there is no need for the exponential symbolism of common algebra* (Edna E. Kramer).

i|den|tic (ī den'tik), *adj.* **1** = identical. **2** denoting identical language or action in diplomacy agreed on by two or more governments dealing simultaneously with a third: *an identic note.*

i|den|ti|cal (ī den'tə kəl), *adj.* **1** the same: *Both events happened on the identical day.* **SYN:** See syn. under **same. 2** exactly alike: *The two new pennies were identical. 6 feet 2 inches and 74 inches are identical amounts.* **3** *Logic.* expressing identity of terms, as in the proposition "Man is a human being." An identical proposition is one whose subject and predicate mean the same thing. [< Medieval Latin *identicus,* related to Late Latin *identitās* identity + English *-al*[1]] —**i|den'ti-cal|ly,** *adv.* —**i|den'ti|cal|ness,** *n.*

identical equation, = identity.

identical twins, twins of the same sex and physical appearance coming from a single fertilized egg cell rather than from two egg cells as fraternal twins do: *The occurrence of human identical twins has been known for a long time, and their potential usefulness in genetic research has been widely recognized* (J. Hancock).

i|den|ti|fi|a|ble (ī den'tə fī'ə bəl), *adj.* that can be identified.

i|den|ti|fi|a|bly (ī den'tə fī'ə blē), *adv.* in an identifiable manner: *Dr. Suzuki leads a life that is identifiably but by no means self-consciously Japanese* (New Yorker).

i|den|ti|fi|ca|tion (ī den'tə fə kā'shən), *n.* **1** the act or process of identifying: *Pasteur's identification of rabies virus has saved many lives.* **2** the fact or state of being identified: *A positive means of prompt baby identification brings peace of mind to parents and hospital administrators alike* (Newsweek). **3** something used to identify a person or thing: *He offered his driver's license as identification.* **4** *Psychology.* **a** the act or process of forming, consciously or unconsciously, an emotional tie with another and patterning one's actions or behavior after that person. **b** reaction to a person in ways that are appropriate to another, as to a teacher as if she were the mother.

identification card, = identity card.

i|den|ti|fi|er (ī den'tə fī'ər), *n.* **1** one that identifies. **2** one who recognizes and proves the identity of others, especially of criminals.

i|den|ti|fy (ī den'tə fī), *v.,* **-fied, -fy|ing.**
—*v.t.* **1a** to recognize as being a particular person or thing; prove to be the same: *He identified the wallet as his by telling what it contained. The Roman god Jupiter may be identified with the Greek god Zeus.* **b** *Biology.* to refer (an organism) to its proper species. **2** to make the same; treat as the same: *The good king identified the well-being of his people with his own.* **3** to connect closely; link; associate: *He identified himself with the movement for peace. I tried to identify my mind with the old fellow's, and take his view of the world* (Hawthorne). *Hundreds of people identified themselves with the conductor, standing ... with rulers and pencils in their hands and giving the beat and tempo* (Time).
—*v.i.* **1** to feel a close connection with; have a sense of oneness; sympathize: *He is probably the only big businessman in the country with whom the average voter can identify* (Harper's). *Despite the exotic locale ..., a great many people will presumably identify with the author, sympathize and laugh with her* (Newsweek).
2 *Psychology.* to make, show, or engage in identification.

I|den|ti-kit (ī den'tə kit), *n. British, Trademark.* an apparatus containing cutouts of different facial features, used by police to make composite portraits of wanted criminals: *Scotland Yard on Monday night issued an Identi-kit picture of one of the four gunmen who got away with £400* (London Times). [< *identi*(fication) *kit*]

i|den|ti|ty (ī den'tə tē), *n., pl.* **-ties. 1** who a person is; what a thing is; individuality: *The writer concealed his identity by signing his stories with a false name.* **2a** an exact likeness; sameness; oneness: *The identity of the two crimes led the police to think that the same person committed them. Poets would sometimes note the identity of the Sun with Apollo ..., with the Egyptian Ra, or the Persian Mithras* (Harold Mattingly). **b** an instance of likeness or sameness: *to note the identities in the two cases.* **3** the state or fact of being the same one: *to establish the identity of a person seen today with one seen yesterday. The museum established the identity of the painting with one described in an old document.* **4** = identity element. **5** *Algebra.* an equation that is satisfied by any number that replaces the letter for which the equation is defined; identical equation. [< Late Latin *identitās,* ultimately < Latin *idem* same]

identity card, a card issued to a person to prove his identity.

identity crisis, a time of disturbance and anxiety when a person is in a self-conscious stage of personality development or adjustment, occurring especially during adolescence: *In the course of analyzing* [*George Bernard*] *Shaw's essay, Erikson refers to Shaw's "identity crisis," and calls the long period of lonely, introspective writing a "moratorium"—an "interval between youth and adulthood" when one tries to achieve an inner and outer coherence* (New Yorker).

identity element, *Mathematics.* an element that does not change any other element on which it operates; identity. The identity element for addition is 0. The identity element for multiplication is 1. *Example:* $28 \times 1 = 28$.

ideo-, *combining form.* idea: *Ideograph = a character that represents an idea.* [< Greek *idéā* idea]

id|e|o|gram (id'ē ə gram, ī'dē-), *n.* = ideograph.

***id|e|o|graph** (id'ē ə graf, -gräf; ī'dē-), *n.* a character or graphic symbol that represents a thing or an idea directly, without representing the sounds of the word for the thing or idea, such as +, −, or α. Some Chinese characters and most Egyptian hieroglyphics are ideographs.

Chinese characters:

***ideograph** 

Egyptian hieroglyphics:

id|e|o|graph|ic (id'ē ə graf'ik, ī'dē-), *adj.* **1** of the nature of an ideograph. **2** like an ideograph.
3 having to do with ideographs or ideography.
4 consisting of or containing ideographs: *Chinese is the typical example of a writing system which is alleged to be ideographic* (Henry A. Gleason, Jr.). —**id'e|o|graph'i|cal|ly,** *adv.*

id|e|og|ra|phy (id'ē og'rə fē, ī'dē-), *n.* a system of writing that uses ideographs: *In ideography, each picture conveyed an idea, and anyone could understand it, even if he did not know the language of the man who drew it* (I. J. Gelb).

i|de|o|log|ic (ī'dē ə loj'ik, id'ē-), *adj.* = ideological.

i|de|o|log|i|cal (ī'dē ə loj'ə kəl, id'ē-), *adj.* **1** having to do with ideology. **2** dealing with ideas rather than facts. **3** visionary; speculative. —**i'de-o|log'i|cal|ly,** *adv.*

i|de|ol|o|gism (ī'dē ol'ə jiz əm), *n.* strict conformity or adherence to an ideology.

i|de|ol|o|gist (ī'dē ol'ə jist, id'ē-), *n.* **1** a person who studies ideology or ideologies. **2** a person occupied with ideas. **3** visionary; theorist.

i|de|o|logue (ī dē'ə lôg, -log), *n.* a person occupied with ideas, especially of an impractical nature; ideologist: *He defends it against the ideologue, the mugwump, the party fanatic* (Punch). Also, **idealogue.**

i|de|ol|o|gy (ī'dē ol'ə jē, id'ē-), *n., pl.* **-gies. 1** a set of doctrines or body of opinions that people have: *The majority of teachers and professors do not teach any ideology* (Bulletin of Atomic Scientists). **2** the combined doctrines, assertions, and intentions of a social or political movement: *communist ideology.* **3** abstract speculation, especially theorizing or speculation of a visionary or impractical nature. **4** the science of the origin and nature of ideas. **5** a system of philosophy that derives all ideas exclusively from sensations.

id|e|o|mo|tor (id'ē ə mō'tər, ī'dē-), *adj.* of or denoting automatic muscular movements arising from complete occupation of the mind by an idea, or the cerebral centers controlling such movements: *Propaganda operates on the principle of the ideomotor suggestibility of persons* (Ogburn and Nimkoff)

ides (īdz), *n.pl.* the 15th day of March, May, July, and October, and the 13th day of the other months in the ancient Roman calendar. [< Old French *Ides* < Latin *Īdūs*]

id est (id est'), *Latin.* that is; that is to say. *Abbr:* i.e.

id|i|o|blast (id'ē ə blast), *n.* **1** *Botany.* a cell that differs greatly in form, content, size, or in other characteristic from the neighboring cells. **2** *Biology.* a hypothetical structural unit of living protoplasm. [< Greek *ídios* one's own, distinct + *blastós* germ, sprout]

id|i|o|cy (id′ē ə sē), *n., pl.* **-cies. 1** the state of being an idiot: *Only because of an earlier naive reliance on tests of intelligence did we get the idea that idiocy and imbecility were deficiencies merely of an intellectual sort* (Stone and Taylor). **2** great stupidity or folly: *the bottomless idiocy of the world* (Henry James). SYN: fatuity. **3** an action like that of an idiot; something very stupid or foolish: *Leaving a loaded gun within the reach of a child is an idiocy.* [apparently < *idiot* + *-cy,* as in *prophecy.* Compare Greek *idiōteíā* uncouthness.]

id|i|o|graph (id′ē ə graf, -gräf), *n.* a private mark or signature; trademark (as contrasted with *ideograph*). [< Greek *idiógraphon* < *ídios* private + *gráphein* write]

id|i|o|graph|ic (id′ē ə graf′ik), *adj. Psychology.* having to do with the study of individual cases or instances.

id|i|o|lect (id′ē ə lekt), *n. Linguistics.* the way any individual speaks his native language; the form of speech of a single person: *There are just as many idiolects, or just as many varieties of a living language, as there are speakers of that language* (Simeon Potter). [< Greek *ídios* one's own + English (dia)*lect*]

id|i|om (id′ē əm), *n.* **1** a phrase or expression whose meaning cannot be understood from the ordinary meanings of the words in it. "Give in" is an English idiom meaning "yield." **2** the language or dialect of a particular area or group: *the idiom of the French Canadians. He spoke in the idiom of the New England countryside.* SYN: See syn. under **language. 3** a people's way of expressing themselves: *It is often hard to translate English into the French idiom. The French idiom can say "of a rapidity" for "rapid."* SYN: See syn. under **language. 4** an individual manner of expression in music, art, or other form: *Igor Stravinsky's post-Webern musical idiom* (Allen Hughes). [< Late Latin *idiōma* < Greek *idíōma, -atos,* ultimately < *ídios* one's own]

id|i|o|mat|ic (id′ē ə mat′ik), *adj.* **1** containing an idiom; having or using idioms. **2** of idioms; concerning idioms. **3** showing the individual character of a language; characteristic of a particular language: *The American spoke excellent idiomatic French.* **—id′i|o|mat′i|cal|ly,** *adv.* **—id′i|o|mat′i|cal|ness,** *n.*

id|i|o|mor|phic (id′ē ə môr′fik), *adj.* **1** having its own characteristic form. **2** of or denoting a mineral constituent of a rock that has its own characteristic crystalline form, and not one forced upon it by the other constituents of the rock. [< Greek *ídios* one's own + *morphē* form + English *-ic*] **—id′i|o|mor′phi|cal|ly,** *adv.*

id|i|o|path|ic (id′ē ə path′ik), *adj.* of or having to do with idiopathy.

id|i|op|a|thy (id′ē op′ə thē), *n., pl.* **-thies.** a disease not caused or preceded by any other; primary disease. [< New Latin *idiopathia* < Greek *idiopátheia* < *ídios* peculiar to, individual + *páthos* a suffering, disease]

id|i|o|plasm (id′ē ə plaz′əm), *n. Biology.* that kind of protoplasm which is regarded as the physical basis of inheritance; germ plasm. [< Greek *ídios* one's own + English *plasm*]

id|i|o|plas|mic (id′ē ə plaz′mik), *adj.* of or having to do with idioplasm.

id|i|or|rhyth|mic (id′ē ə riᴛʜ′mik), *adj.* **1** (of a Greek Orthodox monastery or convent) consisting of self-governing members; having each member regulate his own manner of life. **2** belonging to such a monastery or convent. [< Late Greek *idiórrhythmós* < Greek *ídios* one's own + *rhythmós* measure, rhythm]

id|i|o|stat|ic (id′ē ə stat′ik), *adj. Electricity.* denoting or having to do with the measurement of potential by electrostatic methods in which no auxiliary electrification is employed.

id|i|o|syn|cra|sy (id′ē ə sing′krə sē, -sin′-), *n., pl.* **-sies. 1** a personal peculiarity as of taste, behavior, or opinion: *One of his idiosyncrasies was eating a hamburger for breakfast.* **2** *Medicine.* a constitutional peculiarity that causes an unusual reaction to a drug, treatment, or the like.
[< Greek *idiosynkrāsíā* < *ídios* one's own + *sýnkrāsis* temperament < *sýn* together + *krâsis* a mixing < *kras-,* stem of *kerannýnai* to mix]

id|i|o|syn|crat|ic (id′ē ə sin krat′ik), *adj.* having to do with, like, or caused by idiosyncrasy: *The section devoted to the individualistic and idiosyncratic genius of Frank Lloyd Wright is warm with an intelligently critical understanding* (Wall Street Journal). **—id′i|o|syn|crat′i|cal|ly,** *adv.*

id|i|ot (id′ē ət), *n., adj.* **—*n.* 1** a person born with such a weak mind that he can never learn to read or count; person who does not develop beyond the mental age of three. **2** a very stupid or foolish person: *What an idiot I was to forget my pocketbook! You idiot; do you know what peril you stand in?* (Dickens). SYN: See syn. under **fool. 3** *Obsolete.* a professional jester: *The head of an idiot dressed in a cap and bells* (Joseph Addison).
—*adj.* very stupid; idiotic: *On jukebox and radio, all we seemed to hear was the idiot blare of "Lay That Pistol Down"* (David Boroff). *How, with this setup, does Russia manage to find men idiot enough to accept leadership?* (Punch).
[< Latin *idiōta* < Greek *idiṓtēs* ignoramus, layman; (originally) private person, individual (as opposed to the state) < *ídios* one's own]

idiot box, *Slang.* a television set: *about the dangers of easy education [and] free, endless idiot box entertainment* (New York Times).

idiot card or **board,** *Slang.* a cue card, used especially in television performances: *The . . . producer . . . was yelling over the intercom to the floor director . . . to hold up the idiot card saying "Smile!"* (Maclean's).

id|i|ot|ic (id′ē ot′ik), *adj.* of or like an idiot; very stupid or foolish: *His idiotic ideas sometimes made people wonder whether he was smart or not.* [< Late Latin *idiōticus* uneducated, plebeian < Greek *idiōtikós* < *idiṓtēs* idiot]

id|i|ot|i|cal|ly (id′ē ot′ə klē), *adv.* in an idiotic manner; very foolishly.

id|i|ot|ism (id′ē ə tiz′əm), *n.* **1** = idiocy. **2** *Obsolete.* idiom.

id|i|ot sa|vant (id′ē ət sə vänt′; *French* ē dyō′ sȧ väɴ′), *pl.* **id|i|ot sa|vants** or **id|i|ots sa|vants.** *Psychiatry.* a mentally retarded person who has a remarkable special skill: *Exceptional retentiveness is the chief explanation of the feats performed by idiots savants* (New Scientist). [< French *idiot savant* (literally) scholarly idiot]

id|i|o|type (id′ē ō tīp), *n.* the molecular structure of an antibody that determines the specific antigen with which the antibody will react: *All of the cells of a B lymphocyte clone are specialized in making antibody of precisely the same idiotype as the antibody produced by the original lymphocyte* (Michael Shodell). [< Greek *ídios* one's own + English *type*]

IDL (no periods), International Date Line.

i|dle (ī′dəl), *adj.,* **i|dler, i|dlest,** *v.,* **i|dled, i|dling.** **—*adj.* 1** doing nothing; not busy; not working; unoccupied; unemployed: *idle hands, idle machines, idle hours of a holiday. Give me some help; don't just stand there idle.* **2** not willing to do things; fond of doing nothing; lazy: *The idle boy would not study.* **3** having no real worth, use, or significance; useless; worthless: *to waste time in idle pleasure. It is idle for a girl to wish to be a boy.* SYN: ineffective, vain, frivolous. **4** without any good reason, cause, or foundation: *idle fears. Stop worrying about idle rumors.*
—*v.i.* 1 to be idle; do nothing: *Are you going to spend your whole vacation just idling?* **2** to move or saunter idly: *Presently a vagrant poodle came idling along . . . lazy with the summer softness* (Mark Twain). **3** to run slowly without transmitting power. A motor idles when it is out of gear and running slowly.
—*v.t.* 1 to spend or waste (time): *She idled away many hours lying in the hammock.* **2** to cause (a person or thing) to be idle; take out of work or use: *Day shift workers refused to cross the picket lines, idling some 2,200* (Wall Street Journal).
[Old English *īdel*] **—i′dle|ness,** *n.*
—*Syn.* *adj.* **1, 2 Idle, lazy, indolent** mean not active or working. **Idle** means not busy or working at the moment, and often implies no blame: *They like to be idle on Sundays. The long drought made many farmworkers idle.* **Lazy** regularly implies blame, for it means not liking to work, and not industrious when at work: *Lazy people are seldom successful.* **Indolent** means by nature or habit fond of ease and opposed to work or activity: *Too much idleness sometimes makes one indolent.*

idle pulley, a pulley running loosely on a shaft to take up the slack on a belt or to disengage the pulley drive from its load.

i|dler (ī′dlər), *n.* **1** a lazy person: *Every man is, or hopes to be, an idler* (Samuel Johnson). SYN: loafer, sluggard. **2** a device allowing a motor to idle. **3** *U.S.* an idle pulley or idle wheel. **4** *U.S.* an empty railroad car placed between other cars to carry extra long objects. **5** a member of a ship's crew who is subject to constant day duty and not required to keep night watch.

idler gear, an extra gear placed between two others: *To back up the car, it is necessary to change the direction in which the propeller shaft revolves. This is done by adding an . . . idler gear to the combination* (Franklin M. Reck).

i|dlesse (ī′dlis), *n. Archaic.* idleness: *The tables were drawn, it was idlesse all* (Scott). [a coined variant of *idleness*]

idle time, working time unavoidably lost: *[The] fee . . . is designed to compensate for idle time between service calls* (Time).

idle wheel, 1 a gearwheel placed between two others to transfer motion from one axis to another without change in direction or speed. **2** a pulley for taking up slack in a belt; idle pulley.

i|dly (ī′dlē), *adv.* in an idle manner; doing nothing; vainly; uselessly; lazily: *Mother idly looked through a magazine while waiting for us to come out of the doctor's office.*

i|do|crase (ī′də krās, id′ə-), *n.* = vesuvianite.
[< French *idocrase* < Greek *eîdos* form, shape + *krâsis* a mixing < *kras-,* stem of *kerannýnai* to mix]

i|dol (ī′dəl), *n.* **1** an image or other object that is worshiped as a god. **2** a false god: *All the gods of the nations are idols* (Psalms 96:5). **3** *Figurative.* a person or thing loved very much; object of extreme devotion: *The baby boy was the idol of his family.* **4** a phantom, reflection, or any mere image or semblance, visible but without substance, such as an image in a mirror. **5** a false idea or concept; fallacy. **6** *Obsolete.* an image; effigy.
[< Old French *idole,* learned borrowing from Latin *īdōlum* < Greek *eídōlon* image < *eîdos* form. See etym. of doublet **idolum.**]

i|dol|a|ter (ī dol′ə tər), *n.* **1** a person who worships idols or images. **2** *Figurative.* an admirer; adorer; devotee.
[< Old French *idolatre,* learned borrowing from Latin *īdōlolatres* < Greek *eidōlolátrēs* < *eídōlon* idol + *-latrēs* worshiper]

i|dol|a|trous (ī dol′ə trəs), *adj.* **1** worshiping idols. **2** having to do with idolatry. **3** *Figurative.* blindly adoring. **—i|dol′a|trous|ly,** *adv.* **—i|dol′a|trous|ness,** *n.*

i|dol|a|try (ī dol′ə trē), *n., pl.* **-tries. 1a** the worship of idols. **b** the paying or offering of divine honors to any created object. **2** *Figurative.* the worship of a person or thing; great love or admiration; extreme devotion: *The queen was adored to the point of idolatry. I loved the man [Shakespeare] and do honour his memory, on this side idolatry, as much as any* (Ben Jonson). [< Old French *idolatrie,* ultimately < Latin *īdōlolatrīa* < Greek *eidōlolatreíā* + *eídōlon* idol + *latreíā* service, worship]

i|dol|ize (ī′də līz), *v.,* **-ized, -iz|ing.** **—*v.t.* 1** to worship as an idol; make an idol of: *They [my soldiers] do not idolize me, but look upon the Cause they fight for* (Oliver Cromwell). **2** *Figurative.* to love or admire very much; be extremely devoted to: *The little boy idolized his father.*
—*v.i.* to worship idols: *The Israelites refused to idolize after the manner of the pagans.* **—i′dol|i|za′tion,** *n.* **—i′dol|iz′er,** *n.*

i|do|lum (ī dō′ləm), *n., pl.* **-la** (-lə). **1** an image; phantom. **2** a false idea; fallacy. [< Latin *īdōlum.* See etym. of doublet **idol.**]

I|dom|e|neus (ī dom′ə nüs, -nyüs), *n. Greek Legend.* a king of Crete who fought with the Greeks against Troy in the Trojan War.

i|do|ne|ous (ī dō′nē əs), *adj.* apt; fit; suitable.
[< Latin *idōneus* (with English *-ous*)]

I.D.P., 1 integrated data processing. **2** international driving permit.

i|dyl or **i|dyll** (ī′dəl), *n.* **1** a short description in poetry or prose of a simple and charming scene or event, especially one connected with country or domestic life. The poetic form was invented by Theocritus of Sicily in the 200's B.C. **2** a simple and charming scene, event, or experience, suitable for such a description: *The love affair begins with the traditional boy-meets-girl idyll* (Pierre Han). **3** a short musical composition, in a pastoral or sentimental mood.
[< Latin *īdyllium* < Greek *eidýllion* (diminutive) < *eîdos* form]

i|dyl|ist or **i|dyl|list** (ī′də list), *n.* a writer of idyls; idyllic poet.

i|dyl|li|an (ī dil′ē ən), *adj.* = idyllic.

i|dyl|lic (ī dil′ik), *adj.* **1** suitable for an idyl; simple and charming; rustic: *idyllic simplicity. The beach is idyllic* (New Yorker). **2** of or like an idyl: *an idyllic description.* **—i|dyl′li|cal|ly,** *adv.*

-ie, *suffix.* **1** little: *Dearie = little dear. Birdie = little bird.*
2 used to show kind feeling or intimacy, as in *auntie, Annie.* [variant of *-y*[2]]

i.e., that is; that is to say; namely: *31 per cent of all married women were in the labor force (i.e., actually working or looking for a job)* (Daniel J. Boorstin).
►**i.e.** is the abbreviation for Latin *id est,* meaning "that is." It is commonly written out *that is,* except in reference works.

IE (no periods), **I.E.,** or **IE.,** Indo-European.

I.E.E., *British.* Institute of Electrical Engineering.

Pronunciation Key: hat, āge, cãre, fär; let, ēqual, tėrm; it, īce; hot, ōpen, ôrder; oil, out; cup, pu̇t, rüle; child; long; thin; ᴛʜen; zh, measure; ə represents **a** in about, **e** in taken, **i** in pencil, **o** in lemon, **u** in circus.

IEEE (no periods), Institute of Electrical and Electronics Engineers.

-ier, *suffix.* person occupied or concerned with ___: *Financier = a person concerned with finance.* [< French *-ier* < Latin *-ārius*]

if (if), *conj., n.* —*conj.* **1** supposing that; on condition that; in case that: *Come if you can. If you are going, leave now. If it rains tomorrow, we shall stay at home.* **2** whether: *I wonder if he will go. I do not know if he is rich or poor.* **3** although; even though; granted that: *It was a welcome if unexpected holiday. If he is little, he is strong.*
—*n.* a condition; supposition: *The ifs of history are not very profitable* (C. P. Snow).
as if. See under **as**[1].
[Old English *gif*]
▶**if, whether.** In formal usage, *if* is used to express conditions: *If the gasoline holds out, he will reach Cleveland before dawn. If* is not used with *or. Whether,* usually with *or,* is used, though not consistently, in: **a** conditions of two parts: *Whether it rains or not, they are determined to go.* **b** indirect questions: *He asked whether they should go or stay.* **c** expressions of doubt: *They wondered whether their decision had been wise.* In informal usage, *if* would commonly take the place of *whether* in sentences **b** and **c** above.

IF (no periods), **1** interferon. **2** intermediate frequency.

i-f (no periods), or **I.F.**, intermediate frequency.

IFALPA (no periods) or **I.F.A.L.P.A.**, International Federation of Air Line Pilots' Association.

IFC (no periods) or **I.F.C.**, International Finance Corporation.

I|fe (ē'fē), *adj.* of or belonging to an ancient center of African culture in what is now western Nigeria, noted especially for its fine sculptures of bronze and terra cotta: *Ife antiques.*

IFF (no periods), identification, friend or foe (in military radar).

if|fi|ly (if'ə lē), *adv. Informal.* in an iffy manner.

if|fi|ness (if'ē nis), *n. Informal.* doubtfulness; uncertainty.

if|fy (if'ē), *adj.,* **-fi|er, -fi|est.** *Informal.* conditional; questionable; doubtful: *There is no guesswork and can be no fuzzy or iffy allowances* (Science News Letter). [< *if* + *-y*[1]]

IFIP (no periods) or **I.F.I.P.**, International Federation for Information Processing.

IFJ (no periods) or **I.F.J.**, International Federation of Journalists.

IFLA (no periods) or **I.F.L.A.**, International Federation of Library Associations.

I.F.L.W.U., International Fur and Leather Workers' Union.

IFO (no periods), identified flying object: *Instead of considering UFOs, the symposium panel would debate IFOs* (Saturday Review).

I-for|ma|tion (ī'fôr mā'shən), *n.* an offensive formation in football in which the backs line up behind one another and behind the center, in the general shape of an I.

IFR (no periods), instrument flight rules.

I.F.S., Irish Free State.

Ig (no period), immunoglobulin.

I.G. or **IG** (no periods), **1** Indo-Germanic. **2** Inspector General. **3** combination; trust (German, *Interessengemeinschaft*).

IgA (no periods), immunoglobulin A: *The immunoglobulin known as IgA ... is found only in external secretions* (*saliva, tears, sweat ...*) (Lee Edson).

Ig|bo (ig'bō), *n., pl.* **-bo** or **-bos.** = Ibo.

IGC (no periods) or **I.G.C.**, intellectually gifted children: *My daughter has been in the IGC program since fourth grade* (Harper's).

Ig|dra|sil or **Igg|dra|sil** (ig'drə sil), *n. Norse Mythology.* Yggdrasil.

***ig|loo** (ig'lü), *n., pl.* **-loos.** **1** an Eskimo hut that is shaped like a dome, often built of blocks of hard snow. **2** a building or structure like this in shape: *Designs exist for movable plastic "igloos" capable of covering concentrated crops of wide varieties of foodstuffs* (London Times). **3** a cavity made in the snow by a seal over its breathing hole. [American English < common Eskimo word for "house, dwelling" (compare Greenland dialect *igdlo*)]

***igloo**
definition 1

ign., **1** ignition. **2** unknown (Latin, *ignotus*).

ig|ne|ous (ig'nē əs), *adj.* **1** *Geology.* produced by fire, great heat, or the action of a volcano; solidified from a molten state. Igneous rock is formed by the cooling and solidification of magma. Granite is an igneous rock. *There are three main kinds of rocks: igneous, sedimentary, and metamorphic* (Frederick H. Pough). *An igneous intrusion ... forms the crests of most of the highest ridges* (C. J. Schuberth). **2** of fire; having to do with fire; fiery. [< Latin *igneus* (with English *-ous*) < *ignis* fire]

ig|nes|cent (ig nes'ənt), *adj., n.* —*adj.* **1** bursting into flame; kindling. **2** giving off sparks of fire, as certain stones when struck with steel.
—*n.* an ignescent substance. [< Latin *ignēscēns, -entis,* present participle of *ignēscere* take fire, ultimately < *ignis* fire]

ig|nif|er|ous (ig nif'ər əs), *adj.* bringing or producing fire. [< Latin *ignis* fire + English *-ferous*]

ig|nip|o|tent (ig nip'ə tənt), *adj.* ruling over fire: *the ignipotent Vulcan.* [< Latin *ignipotēns, -entis* having power over fire < *ignis* fire + *potēns* powerful]

ig|nis fat|u|us (ig'nis fach'ů əs), *pl.* **ig|nes fat|u|i** (ig'nēz fach'ů ī). **1** a flitting phosphorescent light seen at night chiefly over marshy ground; will-o'-the-wisp. It is supposed to be caused by the spontaneous combustion of gas from decaying organic matter. *An ignis fatuus that bewitches And leads men into pools and ditches* (Samuel Butler). **2** *Figurative.* something deluding or misleading: *Reason, an ignis fatuus of the mind* (John Wilmot, Earl of Rochester). [< New Latin *ignis fatuus* (literally) foolish fire]

ig|nit|a|ble (ig nī'tə bəl), *adj.* = ignitible.

ig|nite (ig nīt'), *v.,* **-nit|ed, -nit|ing.** —*v.t.* **1a** to set on fire; kindle: *He ignited the match by scratching it on the box.* SYN: See syn. under **kindle. b** *Figurative.* to stir up; spark: *A seizure of independence ... could ignite racial war in Central Africa* (New York Times). **2** to make intensely hot; cause to glow with heat. **3** *Chemistry.* to heat to the point of combustion or chemical change. —*v.i.* to take fire; begin to burn: *Gasoline ignites easily.*
[< Latin *ignītus,* past participle of *ignīre* to set afire < *ignis* fire]

ig|nit|er (ig nī'tər), *n.* **1** a person or thing that ignites. **2** a device for producing an electric spark that ignites the charge of gas or vapor in the cylinder of an internal-combustion engine. **3** the part of a jet engine that ignites the fuel in starting the engine. See picture under **rocket**[1].

ig|nit|i|bil|i|ty (ig nī'tə bil'ə tē), *n.* the quality of being ignitible.

ig|nit|i|ble (ig nī'tə bəl), *adj.* that can be ignited.

ig|ni|tion (ig nish'ən), *n.* **1a** the switch and apparatus controlling the sparks that set the fuel mixture on fire in the cylinders of an internal-combustion engine. Spark plugs are part of the ignition of most cars and trucks. **b** any chemical or mechanical device used to ignite a rocket propellant or a fuel mixture in a jet engine. **2** the act of setting on fire: *The ignition of the forest was caused by lightning.* **3** the fact or process of catching fire: *By rubbing briskly a match is brought to the point of ignition.* SYN: combustion. **4** a means of igniting or setting on fire. **5** an electrode, such as a rod of Carborundum or graphite, used to start conduction in an ignitron.

ignition coil, a spark coil used in an ignition system to increase the voltage of electric current; transformer.

***ignition system**, the system which serves to ignite the fuel mixture in an internal-combustion engine. Its main parts are usually a battery or magneto, an ignition coil, a distributor, and spark plugs. In diesel engines the compression of the fuel produces enough heat to cause ignition.

ig|ni|tor (ig nī'tər), *n.* = igniter.

ig|ni|tron (ig'nə tron), *n.* a rectifier tube having a cathode consisting of a pool of mercury and, immersed in this pool, an igniter that is energized by an auxiliary circuit at the start of each cycle. [< *igni*(te) + *-tron,* as in *electron*]

ig|no|bil|i|ty (ig'nō bil'ə tē), *n.* the fact or state of being ignoble.

ig|no|ble (ig nō'bəl), *adj.* **1** without honor; disgraceful; mean; base; sordid: *To betray a friend is ignoble. Love of comfort may be ignoble, but one may trust it to be accommodating* (Bulletin of Atomic Scientists). SYN: degraded, dishonorable, contemptible. **2** not of noble birth or position: *Some very great men have come from ignoble families.* **3** of low grade or quality; inferior. **4** *Falconry.* denoting the short-winged hawks, such as the sparrow hawk, that chase or rake after their prey. [< Middle French *ignoble,* learned borrowing from Latin *īgnōbilis* < *in-* not + *nōbilis* noble] —**ig|no'ble|ness**, *n.* —**ig|no'bly**, *adv.*

ig|no|min|i|ous (ig'nə min'ē əs), *adj.* **1** shameful; disgraceful; discreditable; dishonorable; humiliating: *After an ignominious defeat the army surrendered. ... a precipitate and ignominious retreat* (Edward Gibbon). **2** deserving ignominy; infamous; contemptible. [< Latin *īgnōminiōsus* < *īgnōminia* ignominy] —**ig'no|min'i|ous|ly**, *adv.* —**ig'no|min'i|ous|ness**, *n.*

ig|no|min|y (ig'nə min'ē), *n., pl.* **-min|ies.** **1** loss of one's good name; public shame and disgrace; dishonor: *So I had the ignominy of being canned and was read the riot act in the kitchen* (Saul Bellow). SYN: infamy. See syn. under **disgrace.** **2** shameful action or conduct: *He then repays by ingratitude the benefits which he has purchased by ignominy* (Macaulay). [< Latin *īgnōminia* < *in-* not + *nōmen, -inis* name]

ig|no|ra|mus (ig'nə rā'məs, -ram'əs), *n., pl.* **-mus|es.** an ignorant person: *I am quite an ignoramus. I know nothing—nothing in the world* (Charlotte Brontë). [< Latin *ignōrāmus* we do not know, 1st person plural of *īgnōrāre* not know; see etym. under **ignore**]

ig|no|rance (ig'nər əns), *n.* lack of knowledge; quality or condition of being ignorant: *Ignorance has never been either an effective or a desirable safeguard for freedom* (Wall Street Journal). SYN: nescience.

ig|no|rant (ig'nər ənt), *adj.* **1** knowing little or nothing; without knowledge. A person who has not had much chance to learn may be ignorant but not stupid. *People who live in the city are often ignorant of farm life.* **2** caused by lack of knowledge; showing lack of knowledge: *Saying that the earth is flat is an ignorant remark.* SYN: unknowing. **3** uninformed; unaware. *He was ignorant of the fact that it had snowed while he was away.*
[< Latin *īgnōrāns, -antis,* present participle of *īgnōrāre* not know; see etym. under **ignore**]
—**ig'no|rant|ly**, *adv.*
—*Syn.* **1 Ignorant, illiterate, uneducated** mean without knowledge. **Ignorant** means without general knowledge, or without knowledge of some subject: *People who live in the wealthy part of town are often ignorant of street life.* **Illiterate** means unable to read and write: *There are many illiterate people in some underdeveloped countries.* **Uneducated** means without systematic training or learning, in schools or from books: *He was an uneducated but intelligent man.*

ig|no|ran|ti|a ju|ris ne|mi|nem ex|cu|sat (ig'nō ran'shē əjůr'is nem'i nem eks kyü'sat), *Latin.* ignorance of the law is no excuse.

ig|no|ra|ti|o e|len|chi (ig'nō rā'shē ōē leng'kī), *Latin.* **1** a logical fallacy that consists of proving or disproving the wrong point. **2** any irrelevant argument.

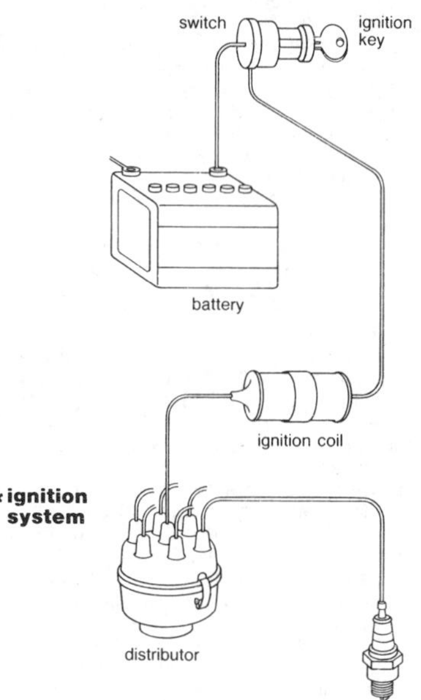

***ignition system**

ig|nore (ig nôr', -nōr'), *v.t.,* **-nored, -nor|ing.** **1** to pay no attention to; disregard: *The driver ignored the policeman's warning and got into trouble. When you scratch your knee, it is better to ignore the pain than to cry.* SYN: overlook, neglect. **2** (of a grand jury) to reject (a bill of indictment) for insufficient evidence. [< Latin *īgnōrāre* not know < *īgnārus* unaware < *in-* not + *gnārus* aware, acquainted with] —**ig|nor'a|ble**, *adj.* —**ig|nor'er**, *n.*

Ig|o|rot (ig'ə rōt'), *n., pl.* **-rot** or **-rots.** **1** a member of a Malay people of the Philippines. **2** the Indonesian language of these people. [< Spanish *Igorrote*]

I|graine (i grān'), *n.* the mother of King Arthur. Also, **Ygerne.**

IGS (no periods), imperial general staff.

IGU (no periods), International Geographic Union.

i|gua|na (i gwä′nə), *n.* **1** a large, climbing lizard found in tropical America. It has a crest of scales like a fringe along the back. **2** any one of several similar lizards. [< Spanish *iguana* < Arawak (West Indies)]

★iguana
definition 1

i|gua|ni|an (i gwä′nē ən), *adj., n.* **—*adj.*** **1** of or having to do with an iguana. **2** like an iguana.
—*n.* = iguana.

i|guan|o|don (i gwan′ə don), *n.* any huge reptile of an extinct genus, 25 to 30 feet long, that walked on the hind legs and had teeth like the iguana's. Their fossils have been found in Europe. [< *iguan*(a) + Greek *odoús, odóntos* tooth]

i|guan|o|dont (i gwan′ə dont), *adj, n.* **—*adj.*** **1** having teeth like the iguana's. **2** belonging to a fossil family of animals similar to the iguanodon.
—*n.* an iguanodont reptile.

IGY (no periods) or **I.G.Y.**, International Geophysical Year.

IH. or **I.H.**, Indo-Hittite.

IHD (no periods), International Hydrological Decade (a program to study the world's water resources during the decade 1965-1975).

★I-head engine (ī′hed′), an internal-combustion engine having cylinders with both intake and exhaust valves side by side in the cylinder head.

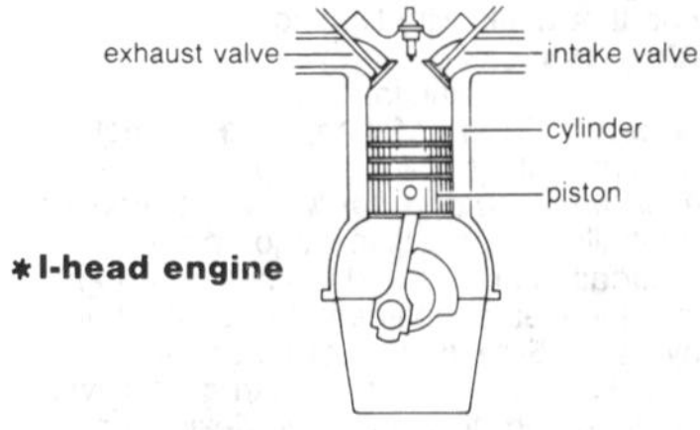

★I-head engine

I.H.N., in His name.

i.hp. or **i.h.p.**, indicated horsepower.

★ih|ram (i räm′), *n.* **1** the dress worn by Moslem pilgrims to Mecca, consisting of a cotton cloth worn around the waist and another thrown over the left shoulder and knotted at the right. **2** the consecrated state of a pilgrim while wearing this dress. **3** the rules he must observe during this time. [< Arabic *iḥrām* (literally) interdiction, a state considered sacred]

★ihram
definition 1

IHS (no periods), three letters of the name of Jesus, a Latin rendering of the Greek. It is used as a decorative symbol and as the emblem of the Jesuit order.

I.H.S., **1** in this (cross) is salvation (Latin, *In Hoc* (*Cruce*) *Salus*). **2** in this sign (thou shalt conquer) (Latin, *In Hoc Signo* (*Vinces*)). **3** Jesus the Saviour of men (Latin, *Iesus Hominum Salvator*).

IIE (no periods) or **I.I.E.**, Institute of International Education.

i|i|wi (ē ē′wē), *n.* a scarlet honey creeper of Hawaii. Its feathers were once widely used to make hats. [< Hawaiian *'i'iwi*]

i|ke|ba|na (ē′ke bä′nä), *n.* the Japanese art of arranging flowers for decoration in a vase or as models for still-life paintings. [< Japanese *ikebana* < *ikeru* arrange + *hana* flower]

I-Kir|i|ba|ti (ē′kir′ē bä′tē), *n.pl.* the Micronesian people of Kiribati (an island country in the southwestern Pacific).

i|kon (ī′kon), *n., pl.* **i|kons, i|ko|nes** (ī′kə nēz). = icon: *But he is no "rebel," no smasher of ikons* (St. Louis Post-Dispatch).

il-[1], *prefix.* the form of **in-[1]** before *l*, as in *illegal.*

il-[2], *prefix.* the form of **in-[2]** before *l*, as in *illuminate.*

Il (no period), illinium (chemical element).

IL (no periods), Illinois (with postal Zip Code).

ILA (no periods) or **I.L.A.**, International Longshoremen's Association.

i|lang-i|lang (ē′läng ē′läng), *n.* = ylang-ylang. [< Tagalog *ilang-ilang*]

Il Du|ce (ēl dü′chā), the title of Benito Mussolini as head of the Fascists of Italy. It means "the Leader."

il|e|ac (il′ē ak), *adj.* of or having to do with the ileum. Also, **iliac**.

il|e|al (il′ē əl), *adj.* = ileac.

il|e|i|tis (il′ē ī′tis), *n.* an inflammation of the ileum, caused by infection, a tumor, or other condition, and involving partial or complete blocking of the passage of food through the small intestine. [< Medieval Latin *ileum* + English *-itis*]

il|e|o|ce|cal (il′ē ō sē′kəl), *adj.* of or having to do with both the ileum and the cecum: *... the ileocecal valve, where the small bowel joins the large* (Time).

il|e|o|co|los|to|my (il′ē ō kə los′tə mē), *n., pl.* **-mies**. a surgical operation to form an opening between the ileum and colon. [< *ileum* + *colostomy*]

il|e|os|to|my (il′ē os′tə mē), *n., pl.* **-mies**. the making of an artificial opening into the ileum by surgery. [< *ileum* + Greek *stóma* mouth + *English -y[3]*]

il|e|um (il′ē əm), *n.* **1** the lowest part of the small intestine, from the jejunum to the large intestine. See picture under **digestion**. **2** the portion of the alimentary canal of an insect immediately behind the midgut. [< Medieval Latin *ileum*, alteration of Latin *īlia*, feminine plural, the loins, entrails]

il|e|us (il′ē əs), *n.* a painful intestinal condition, usually caused by obstruction and often accompanied by the absence of peristalsis, producing a protrusion of the abdomen. [< Latin *īleus* < Greek *eileós* < *eilein* to twist]

i|lex (ī′leks), *n., pl.* **i|lex|es**. **1** any species of holly. **2** = holm oak. [< Latin *īlex, īlicis*]

ILGWU (no periods) or **I.L.G.W.U.**, International Ladies' Garment Workers' Union.

il|i|a (il′ē ə), *n.* the plural of **ilium**.

il|i|ac (il′ē ak), *adj.* **1** of or having to do with the ilium; near the ilium. **2** of or having to do with the ileum; ileac. [< Late Latin *īliacus* < *īleus* ileus; influenced by Latin *īlia* the flanks, loins, and by Medieval Latin *ilium* hipbone, ilium]

Il|i|ad (il′ē əd), *n.* **1** a long Greek epic poem about the siege of Ilium, or Troy, by the Greeks. Homer is supposed to be its author. **2** any similar poem. **3** a long story or account. **4** *Figurative.* a long series of disasters or the like. [< Latin *Īlias, -iadis* < Greek *Īliás, -iádos* < *Ī́lion* Ilium (Troy)]

Il|i|ad|ic (il′ē ad′ik), *adj.* of or having to do with the Iliad.

Il|i|an (il′ē ən), *adj., n.* **—*adj.*** of or having to do with ancient Troy, or the Greco-Roman city of New Ilium in the Trojan Plain.
—*n.* an inhabitant of New Ilium.

il|i|ca|ceous (il′ə kā′shəs), *adj.* belonging to the family of plants typified by the holly. [< Latin *īlex, īlicis* holly + English *-aceous*]

i|lic|ic (i lis′ik), *adj.* having to do with or derived from holly: *ilicic acid.* [< Latin *īlex, īlicis* holly + English *-ic*]

il|i|o|fem|o|ral (il′ē ō fem′ər əl), *adj.* having to do with or connecting the ilium and the femur: *the iliofemoral ligament.*

Il|i|on (il′ē ən), *n.* ancient Troy.

il|i|o|sa|cral (il′ē ō sā′krəl), *adj.* having to do with the ilium and the sacrum.

il|i|um (il′ē əm), *n., pl.* **-i|a**. *Anatomy.* the broad upper portion of the hipbone. [< New Latin *ilium* < Medieval Latin *ilium*, singular < Latin *īlia* loins, entrails]

Il|i|um (il′ē əm), *n.* ancient Troy.

ilk[1] (ilk), *n., adj.* **—*n.*** class; kind; sort: [*He*] *begged Hollywood to stop putting stogies in the mouths of Edward G. Robinson and his ilk* (Harper's).
—*adj.* *Archaic.* same; identical.
of that ilk, *Informal.* **a** of the same place or name: *... a canon and two choristers sent from St. George's to the hospital of that ilk* (Thomas P. Thompson). **b** of that kind or sort: *He kept away from gamblers and other men of that ilk.*
[Old English *ilca* same]

ilk[2] (ilk), *adj. Scottish.* each; every. [Middle English *ilke*, Old English *ǣlc*]

il|ka (il′kə), *adj. Scottish.* ilk; each; every. [Middle English *ilk* each + *a*, the indefinite article]

ill (il), *adj.,* **worse, worst**, *n., adv.* **—*adj.*** **1** having some disease; not well; sick; indisposed: *to be ill with a fever, ill with smallpox.* **SYN:** ailing. **2a** evil; bad; wicked: *an ill deed.* **b** injurious; harmful: *an ill effect.* **3** unfavorable; unfortunate; unlucky; unpropitious: *an ill omen.* **SYN:** adverse. **4** unkind; harsh; cruel: *Ill tongues shall wound me* (Shelley). **5** not good; defective; imperfect; faulty: *ill manners.* **6** unskillful; inefficient.
—*n.* **1** a sickness; disease: *All the ills she has had this year have left her very weak. Peter now grew old, and had An ill no doctor could unravel* (Shelley). **SYN:** illness. **2** an evil; harm; misfortune; trouble: *Poverty is an ill.* **3** something unfavorable or unkind: *I can think no ill of her.*
—*adv.* **1** badly; harmfully: *His strength was ill used in bullying other children.* **2** unfavorably; unfortunately: *to fare ill.* **3** in an unkind manner; harshly; cruelly: *He speaks ill of his former friend.* **4** with trouble or difficulty; scarcely: *You can ill afford to waste your money.* **5** improperly; unskillfully: *The bridges are ill built.*
ill at ease. See under **ease**.
take ill, to take offense at; be offended by: *Look, when I serve him so, he takes it ill* (Shakespeare).
[< Scandinavian (compare Old Icelandic *illr*)]
▶See **sick** for usage note.

I'll (īl), **1** I shall. **2** I will.

ill., **1** illustrated. **2** illustration. **3** most distinguished (Latin, *illustrissimus*).

Ill., Illinois.

ill-ad|vised (il′əd vīzd′), *adj.* acting or done without enough thought; unwise. **SYN:** imprudent, injudicious.

ill-ad|vis|ed|ly (il′əd vī′zid lē), *adv.* in an ill-advised manner; unwisely.

ill-as|sort|ed (il′ə sôr′tid), *adj.* = ill-sorted.

il|la|tion (i lā′shən), *n.* **1** the act of inferring. **2** an inference; conclusion. [< Late Latin *illātiō, -ōnis* < Latin *inferre* bring in, infer]

il|la|tive (il′ə tiv, i lā′-), *adj. Grammar.* **1** introducing or expressing an inference. *Thus* and *therefore* are illative conjunctions. **2** (in Finnish and Hungarian) a case that expresses direction or motion. [< Late Latin *illātīvus* < Latin *inferre* bring in, infer]

il|la|tive|ly (il′ə tiv lē, i lā′-), *adv.* by illation or inference.

il|laud|a|ble (i lô′də bəl), *adj.* not laudable; unworthy of praise; blameworthy: *sentiments which were not in themselves illaudable* (Jane Austen).

ill-be|got|ten (il′bi got′ən), *adj.* brought into life or existence in an untimely or unpropitious way; ill-fated at birth.

ill-be|ing (il′bē′ing), *n.* illness, unhappiness, or poverty; not being or doing well.

ill-bod|ing (il′bō′ding), *adj.* that bodes evil; ominous; unfavorable: *O malignant and ill-boding stars* (Shakespeare).

ill-bred (il′bred′), *adj.* badly brought up; impolite; rude; unmannerly. **SYN:** uncivil.

ill-con|ceived (il′kən sēvd′), *adj.* poorly planned or designed: *Buildings of steel and aluminum ... these ill-conceived structures vie with the automobile in making life in cities disagreeable, inefficient, and oppressive* (New Yorker).

ill-con|di|tioned (il′kən dish′ənd), *adj.* **1** having bad qualities. **2** in a bad condition: *Tired, ... my ill-conditioned critical reflexes already screaming in protest* (New Yorker).

ill-con|sid|ered (il′kən sid′ərd), *adj.* not well considered; unwise; unsuitable: *Ill-considered hasty attempts at integration, ... increase rather than alleviate racial tensions* (Atlantic).

ill-de|fined (il′di fīnd′), *adj.* not adequately explained; not well marked out; unclear: *The two nations share a vast and ill-defined border* (Harper's).

ill-dis|posed (il′dis pōzd′), *adj.* unfriendly; unfavorable.

il|le|gal (i lē′gəl), *adj., n.* **—*adj.*** **1** not lawful; against the law; forbidden by law: *Driving faster than the speed limit is illegal.* **SYN:** unlawful, illicit. **2** not according to official regulations.
—*n.* **1** a person who acts illegally. **2** a secret agent who adopts a fictitious identity to avoid detection. **—il|le′gal|ly**, *adv.* **—il|le′gal|ness**, *n.*

il|le|gal|i|ty (il′ē gal′ə tē), *n., pl.* **-ties**. **1** illegal condition or quality; unlawfulness. **2** an illegal act; act contrary to law.

il|le|gal|ize (i lē′gə līz), *v.t.,* **-ized, -iz|ing**. to make illegal.

il|leg|i|bil|i|ty (i lej′ə bil′ə tē), *n., pl.* **-ties**. illegible quality or condition.

il|leg|i|ble (i lej′ə bəl), *adj.* very hard or impossible to read; not plain enough to read; not legible: *The boy's handwriting was so bad that his letter to his mother was illegible. The ink had faded so that many words were illegible.* **SYN:** indecipherable. **—il|leg′i|ble|ness**, *n.* **—il|leg′i|bly**, *adv.*

il|le|git|i|ma|cy (il′ə jit′ə mə sē), *n.* the fact or condition of being illegitimate.

il|le|git|i|mate (il′ə jit′ə mit), *adj., v.,* **-mat|ed, -mat|ing**. **—*adj.*** **1** born of parents who are not married to each other; bastard. **SYN:** natural. **2** not according to the law or the rules; unauthorized; unwarranted. **3** not logical; not according to good usage; improper. **4** *Biology.* abnormal, as fertiliza-

Pronunciation Key: hat, āge, cãre, fär; let, ēqual, tėrm; it, īce; hot, ōpen, ôrder; oil, out; cup, pu̇t, rüle; child; long; thin; ᴛʜen; zh, measure;
ə represents **a** in about, **e** in taken, **i** in pencil, **o** in lemon, **u** in circus.

tion; produced by irregular or abnormal fertilization. **5** *Genetics.* not occurring through the regular mechanisms of transmission; irregular: *It has become increasingly apparent that there are various "illegitimate" recombinational processes, which can join together DNA segments having little or no nucleotide-sequence homology* (Scientific American).

—***v.t.*** to declare or pronounce illegitimate. —**il'le|git'i|mate|ly,** *adv.* —**il'le|git'i|mate|ness,** *n.* —**il'-le|git'i|ma'tion,** *n.*

ill-e|quipped (il'i kwipt'), *adj.* not provided with the necessary equipment or qualifications: *Judges are ill-equipped to determine whether or not a person is a "security risk"* (Canadian Forum).

ill-famed (il'fāmd'), *adj.* of bad reputation; notorious.

ill-fat|ed (il'fā'tid), *adj.* **1** sure to have a bad fate or end: *an ill-fated person.* **2** bringing bad luck; unlucky: *an ill-fated hour.*

ill-fa|vored (il'fā'vərd), *adj.* **1** not pleasant to look at; ugly: *a poor virgin, Sir, an ill-favored thing, sir, but mine own* (Shakespeare). SYN: uncomely. **2** unpleasant; offensive: *O, what a world of vile ill-favour'd faults* (Shakespeare). —**ill'-fa'vored-ly,** *adv.* —**ill'-fa'vored|ness,** *n.*

ill feeling, suspicious dislike; mistrust; animosity: *At midnight the dinner broke up, in an atmosphere of sullen ill feeling* (Time).

ill-fit|ted (il'fit'id), *adj.* unsuited: *An Eskimo is ill-fitted for living in the tropics.*

ill-found|ed (il'foun'did), *adj.* without a good reason or sound basis: *an ill-founded argument.*

ill-got|ten (il'got'ən), *adj.* acquired by evil or unfair means; dishonestly obtained: *ill-gotten gains.*

ill-hu|mored (il'hyü'mərd, -yü'-), *adj.* cross; unpleasant. SYN: sullen, petulant.

il|lib|er|al (i lib'ər əl, -lib'rəl), *adj.* **1** not liberal; narrow-minded; prejudiced: *Illiberal attitudes . . . do not sound the death knell of the Republic* (Scientific American). SYN: bigoted. **2** stingy; miserly: *an illiberal attitude toward charities.* **3** without liberal culture; unscholarly; ill-bred. —**il|lib'er|al-ly,** *adv.* —**il|lib'er|al|ness,** *n.*

il|lib|er|al|ism (i lib'ər ə liz'əm, -lib'rə-), *n.* illiberal principles.

il|lib|er|al|i|ty (i lib'ə ral'ə tē), *n.* the condition of being illiberal.

il|lic|it (i lis'it), *adj.* not permitted by law; forbidden; improper: *the illicit sale of liquor.* SYN: unlawful, illegal, illegitimate. [< Middle French *illicite,* learned borrowing from Latin *illicitus* < *in-* not + *licitus* licit, past participle of *licēre* be allowed] —**il|lic'it|ly,** *adv.* —**il|lic'it|ness,** *n.*

► See **elicit** for usage note.

il|lim|it|a|bil|i|ty (i lim'ə tə bil'ə tē), *n.* the condition of being illimitable.

il|lim|it|a|ble (i lim'ə tə bəl), *adj.* without limit; boundless; infinite: *a dark illimitable ocean without bound* (Milton). SYN: limitless. —**il|lim'it|a|ble-ness,** *n.* —**il|lim'it|a|bly,** *adv.*

ill-in|formed (il'in fôrmd'), *adj.* **1** lacking reliable or correct information: *ill-informed rumors.* **2** lacking knowledge or information; ignorant: *He was astonished that people so well respected should be so ill-informed* (Manchester Guardian Weekly).

il|lin|i|um (i lin'ē əm), *n.* the former name of promethium. [< New Latin *Illinium* < *Illinois,* the state (because it was discovered by chemists at the University of Illinois)]

Il|li|noi|an (il'ə noi'ən), *adj., n.* —***adj.*** **1** = Illinoisan. **2** of or having to do with the third period of glaciation in North America, beginning about 230,000 years ago, and lasting about 55,000 years.

—***n.*** = Illinoisan.

Il|li|nois (il'ə noi', -noiz'), *n., pl.* **-nois. 1** a member of a confederacy of North American Indians, formerly living between the Mississippi and Wabash rivers, and in parts of Iowa and Missouri. **2** the Algonkian language of this confederacy, with various dialects, such as Peoria and Miami. [American English < French *Illinois,* alteration of Algonkian *Iliniwek* men]

Il|li|nois|an (il'ə noi'zən), *adj, n.* —***adj.*** of or having to do with the Illinois.

—***n.*** **1** an Illinois Indian. **2** a native or inhabitant of Illinois.

ill-in|ten|tioned (il'in ten'shənd), *adj.* showing ill will; malicious: *ill-intentioned persons* (London Times). [*He*] *apologized for his ill-intentioned, one-sided, and destructive reports* (Newsweek).

il|liq|uid (i lik'wid), *adj.* **1** (of assets) not easily turned into cash. **2** (of a debt, claim, or title) not clear; not supported by a written obligation, court decree, or the like.

il|liq|uid|i|ty (i lik'wid'ə tē), *n.* the fact or character of being illiquid: *Gold producers . . . have for years held that an upward revaluation of gold is the proper cure for international illiquidity* (Wall Street Journal).

il|lite (il'īt), *n.* any one of various hydrous silicates resembling mica, found in clay. [< *Ill*(inois) + *-ite*[1]]

il|lit|er|a|cy (i lit'ər ə sē), *n., pl.* **-cies. 1** lack of knowledge of how to read and write. **2** a lack of education; lack of knowledge of books and literature; deficiency in cultural knowledge. **3** an error in speaking or writing, caused by a lack of education or knowledge.

il|lit|er|ate (i lit'ər it), *adj., n.* —***adj.*** **1** not knowing how to read and write: *People who have never gone to school are usually illiterate.* SYN: See syn. under **ignorant**. **2** showing a lack of education; not cultured: *He writes in a very illiterate way.* SYN: unpolished, unlearned.

—***n.*** **1** a person who does not know how to read and write. **2** an uneducated person; person who lacks culture: *a boorish illiterate.*

[< Latin *illiterātus* < *in-* not + *litterātus* literate, having a liberal education] —**il|lit'er|ate|ly,** *adv.* —**il|lit'er|ate|ness,** *n.*

ill-judged (il'jujd'), *adj.* unwise; rash: *The young lawyer launched an ill-judged attack upon the more experienced defense attorney's client.* SYN: injudicious.

ill-man|nered (il'man'ərd), *adj.* having or showing bad manners; impolite; rude. SYN: unmannerly, discourteous. —**ill'-man'nered|ly,** *adv.* —**ill'--man'nered|ness,** *n.*

ill-na|tured (il'nā'chərd), *adj.* having or showing ill nature; cross; disagreeable; spiteful; churlish: *The lonely, spiteful old lady was always retailing the latest ill-natured gossip.* SYN: surly, malevolent. —**ill'-na'tured|ly,** *adv.* —**ill'-na'tured|ness,** *n.*

ill|ness (il'nis), *n.* **1** an abnormal, unhealthy condition; poor health; sickness; disease: *Scarlet fever is a serious illness. He felt a certain illness creep over him whenever anyone mentioned spinach.* SYN: ailment, malady. **2** *Obsolete.* wickedness; badness: *Ambition . . . without the illness that should attend it* (Shakespeare).

il|lo|cal (i lō'kəl), *adj.* not existing in a locality or space: *His miraculous power is illocal and universal* (Patrick Fairbairn).

il|lo|cal|i|ty (il'ō kal'ə tē), *n.* the state of not existing in a locality or space.

il|log|ic (i loj'ik), *n.* the reverse of logic; illogical character; unreasonableness: *A dizzy new high in Communist illogic and a dismal new low in progress* (Newsweek).

il|log|i|cal (i loj'ə kəl), *adj.* **1** contrary to the principles of sound reasoning; not logical; fallacious; unsound: *an illogical reason. Her illogical behavior makes it hard to guess what she will do next.* **2** not reasonable; foolish: *Many children have an illogical fear of the dark.* —**il|log'i|cal|ly,** *adv.* —**il-log'i|cal|ness,** *n.*

il|log|i|cal|i|ty (i loj'ə kal'ə tē), *n., pl.* **-ties. 1** lack of logic; irrationality; unreasonableness: *Courteline's plays are about logical persons confronted with the illogicality of life* (London Times). **2** something illogical; an absurdity: *"Irishisms," those mild and repeatable illogicalities that used to amuse the ruling class in Ireland* (Punch).

ill-o|mened (il'ō'mənd), *adj.* having bad omens; ill-starred; inauspicious: *For Julius Caesar the ides of March were ill-omened.*

ill-sort|ed (il'sôr'tid), *adj.* badly assorted or arranged; poorly matched: *He and his wife were an ill-sorted pair* (Byron).

ill-spent (il'spent'), *adj.* spent badly; wasted; misspent: *Drunkenness and the ill-spent wage-packet are still hardly known* (Manchester Guardian Weekly).

ill-starred (il'stärd'), *adj.* unlucky; unfortunate; disastrous: *Romeo and Juliet were ill-starred lovers.*

ill-suit|ed (il'sü'tid), *adj.* poorly suited; unsuitable.

ill-tem|pered (il'tem'pərd), *adj.* having or showing a bad temper; often angry or annoyed; cross: *Ill-tempered and hasty remarks are always a source of bad feeling.* SYN: bad-tempered, crabbed, cantankerous. —**ill'-tem'pered|ly,** *adv.* —**ill'-tem'pered|ness,** *n.*

ill-timed (il'tīmd'), *adj.* at or coming at a bad time; not appropriate: *His ill-timed joke caused everybody embarrassment.* SYN: inappropriate.

ill-treat (il'trēt'), *v.t.* to treat badly; treat cruelly; do harm to; abuse. SYN: maltreat, ill-use.

ill treatment, or **ill-treat|ment** (il'trēt'mənt), *n.* bad or cruel treatment; harm; abuse: *. . . an assurance by Mr. Sandys that he could find nothing to support allegations of torture or any sort of ill treatment* (Norman Shrapnel). SYN: mistreatment, ill-usage.

ill turn, 1 an action that is unkind, unfriendly, or spiteful. **2** a change for the worse: *an ill turn of events.* SYN: deterioration.

il|lude (i lüd'), *v.t.,* **-lud|ed, -lud|ing.** to deceive; trick. [< Latin *illūdere* mock < *in-* at + *lūdere* to play < *lūdus* game]

il|lume (i lüm'), *v.t.,* **-lumed, -lum|ing.** = illuminate. [short for *illuminate*]

il|lu|mi|nance (i lü'mə nəns), *n.* = illumination (def. 2).

il|lu|mi|nant (i lü'mə nənt), *n., adj.* —***n.*** something that gives light. Gas and oil are illuminants.

—***adj.*** giving light; illuminating.

il|lu|mi|nate (*v.* i lü'mə nāt; *adj., n.* i lü'mə nit, -nāt), *v.,* **-nat|ed, -nat|ing,** *adj., n.* —***v.t.*** **1** to light up; make bright: *The room was illuminated by four large lamps. The big searchlight illuminates a spot a mile away.* **2** *Figurative.* to make clear; explain; elucidate: *Our interesting teacher could illuminate almost any subject we studied.* **3** to decorate with lights: *The streets were illuminated for the celebration.* **4** to decorate with gold, silver, colors, pictures, and designs. The letters and pages in some old books and manuscripts were illuminated. **5** *Figurative.* to enlighten; inform; instruct. **6** to make illustrious.

—***v.i.*** **1** to become illuminated. **2** to display lights.

—***adj.*** **1** *Archaic.* lighted up. **2** *Obsolete.* enlightened: *illuminate by learning* (Francis Bacon).

—***n.*** *Archaic.* a person who is or claims to be especially enlightened. [< Latin *illūmināre* (with English *-ate*[1]) < *in-* in + *lūmen, -inis* light]

il|lu|mi|nat|ed (i lü'mə nā'tid), *adj.* **1** lighted up; made luminous: *illuminated dials.* **2** *Figurative.* enlightened: *Every revelation . . . has many meanings, which it is given to the illuminated only to unfold* (George Eliot). —**il|lu'mi|nat'ed|ly,** *adv.*

il|lu|mi|na|ti (i lü'mə nä'tī, -nä'tē), *n.pl., sing.* **-to** (-tō). persons who have or claim to have superior knowledge or enlightenment. Various sects and societies have called themselves illuminati. *But, as is common with such illuminati, they prove too much* (Harper's). [< Latin *illūminātī,* plural of *illūminātus* enlightened (one), past participle of *illūmināre;* see etym. under **illuminate**]

il|lu|mi|nat|ing (i lü'mə nā'ting), *adj.* that illuminates. —**il|lu'mi|nat'ing|ly,** *adv.*

illuminating engineering, a branch of electrical engineering that deals with lighting.

illuminating gas, gas burned with air to give a yellow flame used for illumination.

***il|lu|mi|na|tion** (i lü'mə nā'shən), *n.* **1** the act or process of illuminating; a lighting up; a making bright: *the illumination of a bonfire.* **2** the amount of light; light; illuminance. Illumination per unit area of a surface is measured in lumens. **3** *Figurative.* a making clear; explanation. **4** decoration with many lights. **5** decoration of letters and pages in books and manuscripts with gold, silver, colors, pictures, and designs. **6** the designs, pictures, and the like, used in decoration. **7** *Figurative.* intellectual or spiritual enlightenment: *The sermon was an illumination of the text.*

illuminations, the lights used in decoration: *The illuminations on the streets during the festival were magnificent.*

***illumination**
definition 5

il|lu|mi|na|tive (i lü'mə nā'tiv), *adj.* tending to illuminate; illuminating.

il|lu|mi|na|tor (i lü'mə nā'tər), *n.* **1** a person or thing that illuminates. **2** any instrument for illuminating, such as a lens for concentrating light or a mirror for reflecting light. **3** a person who decorates manuscripts, books, or documents, with color, gold, or the like.

il|lu|mine (i lü'mən), *v.,* **-mined, -min|ing.** —***v.t.*** **1** to make bright; illuminate; light up: *Electric lights illumine our houses. A smile often illumines a homely face.* **2** *Figurative.* to enlighten; inspire.

—***v.i.*** to become bright; light up. [< Old French *illuminer,* learned borrowing from Latin *illūmināre;* see etym. under **illuminate**] —**il|lu'mi|na|ble,** *adj.*

il|lu|mi|nism or **Il|lu|mi|nism** (i lü'mə niz əm), *n.* **1** the doctrine or principles of illuminati. **2** a doctrine advocating enlightenment.

il|lu|mi|nist or **Il|lu|mi|nist** (i lü'mə nist), *n.* a person who holds the doctrine of illuminism.

il|lu|mi|nom|e|ter (i lü'mə nom'ə tər), *n.* a light meter for measuring lighting in such places as homes, schools, and offices.

illus., 1 illustrated. **2** illustration.

ill-us|age (il'yü'sij, -zij), *n.* bad, cruel, or unfair treatment: *The ill-usage of children is the blackest mark against the Industrial Revolution.*

ill-use (*v.* il'yüz'; *n.* il'yüs'), *v.,* **-used, -us|ing,** *n.* —***v.t.*** to treat badly, cruelly, or unfairly.

—*n.* bad, cruel, or unfair treatment.

∗**il|lu|sion** (i lü′zhən), *n.* **1** an appearance or feeling that misleads because it is not real; thing that deceives by giving a false idea; misleading appearance. The sides of a road give one an illusion of coming closer and closer together until they meet in the distance. *The old man's ruddy complexion gave an illusion of good health. He* [*Clemenceau*] *had one illusion—France* (Lord Keynes). **2** a false impression or perception: *That slender snow-covered bush at the gate produced an illusion of a woman waiting there.* **3** a false idea, notion, or belief; fancy: *Many people have the illusion that wealth is the chief cause of happiness.* **4** a delicate silk net or gauze, often used for veils and over wedding gowns: *Wedding veils of French illusion are twisted into coronets* (New Yorker). **5** *Archaic.* apparition; phantom: *Stay, illusion! If thou hast any sound or use of voice, Speak to me* (Shakespeare). [< Latin *illūsiō, -ōnis* a mocking < *illūdere* to mock; see etym. under **illude**]

—*Syn.* **1 Illusion, delusion** mean something mistakenly or falsely believed to be true or real. **Illusion** applies to something appearing to be real or true, but actually not existing or being quite different from what it seems: *Good motion pictures create an illusion of reality.* **Delusion** applies to a false and often harmful belief about something that does exist: *The old woman had the delusion that the butcher was always trying to cheat her.*

► **Illusion, allusion** are sometimes confused. An **illusion** is a misleading appearance: *an illusion of wealth.* An **allusion** is an indirect reference or slight mention: *He made allusions to recent events without recounting them.*

∗**illusion**
definition 1

optical illusions:

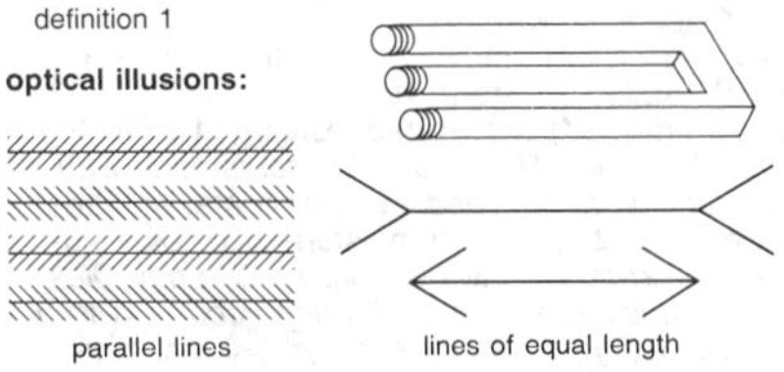

parallel lines — lines of equal length

il|lu|sion|al (i lü′zhə nəl), *adj.* having to do with, characterized by, or subject to illusions.

il|lu|sion|ar|y (i lü′zhə ner′ē), *adj.* like an illusion; characterized by illusion; illusory.

il|lu|sion|ism (i lü′zhə niz əm), *n.* **1** the theory or doctrine that the material world is an illusion. **2** the use of illusion in art to suggest reality: *He was able to give a satisfactory account of his subject on the flat surface of a canvas without resorting to illusionism of one sort or another* (London Times).

il|lu|sion|ist (i lü′zhə nist), *n., adj.* —*n.* **1** a person who produces illusions; conjurer: *not only straight actors, but also singers* [*and*] *illusionists* (Punch). **2** an artist who practices illusionism: *A favorite device of illusionists is illuminating the texture of newspapers, the torn sides or folded corners of old letters ...* (New Yorker). **3** a person who has illusions. **4** a believer in illusionism.

—*adj.* = visionary.

il|lu|sion|is|tic (i lü′zhə nis′tik), *adj.* **1** characterized by illusion or fantasy: *a highly illusionistic depiction of the United States seen in the round* (Atlantic). **2** of or having to do with illusionism: *illusionistic art.* —**il|lu′sion|is′ti|cal|ly,** *adv.*

il|lu|sive (i lü′siv), *adj.* due to illusion; unreal; misleading; deceptive; illusory. **SYN:** delusive. —**il|lu′sive|ly,** *adv.* —**il|lu′sive|ness,** *n.*

il|lu|so|ry (i lü′sər ē), *adj.* = illusive. —**il|lu′so|ri|ly,** *adv.* —**il|lu′so|ri|ness,** *n.*

illust., 1 illustrated. **2** illustration.

il|lus|trate (il′ə strāt, i lus′trāt), *v.,* **-trat|ed, -trat|ing.** —*v.t.* **1** to make clear or explain by stories, examples, or comparisons; elucidate: *The way that a pump works is used to illustrate how the heart sends blood around the body. These graphs illustrate the results of the experiment.* **SYN:** demonstrate, exemplify. **2** to provide with pictures, diagrams, or maps that explain or decorate: *This book is well illustrated.* **3** *Archaic, Figurative.* to enlighten. **4** *Archaic.* to illuminate; light. **5** *Obsolete.* to make illustrious. **6** *Obsolete.* to make bright; embellish. —*v.i.* to give an illustration: *To illustrate, the teacher compared the heart to a pump.* [< Latin *illūstrāre* (with English *-ate*[1]) light up < *in-* in + *lūstrāre* to light (as, a sacrificial fire) < *lūstrum* purification]

il|lus|trat|ed (il′ə strā′tid), *adj., n.* —*adj.* having pictorial illustrations: *illustrated articles, an illustrated book.*

—*n. Especially British.* an illustrated newspaper or magazine: *He is a photographer for one of the illustrateds.*

il|lus|tra|tion (il′ə strā′shən), *n.* **1** a picture, diagram, or map used to explain or decorate something, especially the written part of a printed work such as a book. *Abbr:* ill. **2** a story, example, or comparison used to make clear or explain something: *The teacher cut an apple into four equal pieces as an illustration of what ¼ means.* **3** the act or process of illustrating: *Illustration is used in teaching children.*

il|lus|tra|tion|al (il′ə strā′shə nəl), *adj.* of or having to do with illustrations; characterized by the use of illustrations: *A good deal of the work of Picasso has also illustrational interest* (Edmund Wilson).

il|lus|tra|tive (i lus′trə tiv, il′ə strā′-), *adj.* used to illustrate; helping to explain; illustrating: *A good teacher uses many illustrative examples to explain ideas that are hard to understand.* —**il|lus′tra|tive|ly,** *adv.*

il|lus|tra|tor (il′ə strā′tər), *n.* **1** an artist who makes pictures to be used as illustrations. **2** a person or thing that illustrates.

il|lus|tri|ous (i lus′trē əs), *adj.* **1** very famous; great; outstanding; renowned: *Washington and Lincoln are illustrious Americans.* **SYN:** distinguished, eminent. **2** bringing or conferring glory; glorious: *Illustrious acts high raptures do infuse* (Edmund Waller). **3** *Obsolete.* luminous; bright. [< Latin *illūstris* (with English *-ous*) lighted up, bright < *in-* in + *lūstrum* purification] —**il|lus′tri|ous|ly,** *adv.* —**il|lus′tri|ous|ness,** *n.*

il|lu|vi|al (i lü′vē əl), *adj.* having to do with or produced by illuviation.

il|lu|vi|a|tion (i lü′vē ā′shən), *n.* the addition to underlying levels of soil of material moving downward by chemical or mechanical processes, most common in humid regions. [< *il-*[2] into + (al)*luvi*(al) + *-ation*]

ill will, an unkind or unfriendly feeling; dislike; hate; spite: *He bears much ill will toward his old enemy. ... the mouthings of Russia's salesmen of ill will* (Newsweek). **SYN:** malevolence, malice, enmity.

ill-willed (il′wild′), *adj.* feeling ill will.

ill wind, misfortune; affliction; calamity: *A savage assortment of ill winds—communism, corruption, mass poverty and insane inflation—pound Brazil* (Wall Street Journal).

ill-wish|er (il′wish′ər), *n.* a person who wishes ill to another: *If he was left to his ill-wishers he would be a bloody corpse ere morn* (Scott).

il|ly (il′ē, il′lē), *adv.* badly; ill: *I can very illy spend the money* (George Washington).

Il|lyr|i|an (i lir′ē ən), *adj., n.* —*adj.* of or having to do with ancient Illyria.

—*n.* **1** a native or inhabitant of Illyria, an ancient territory extending eastward from the Adriatic. **2** the language of ancient Illyria. It is considered a branch of the Indo-European linguistic family that includes Albanian.

il|men|ite (il′mə nīt), *n.* a luminous black mineral composed of iron, titanium, and oxygen. *Formula:* $FeTiO_3$ [< the *Ilmen* mountain range, in the Urals, where it was discovered + *-ite*[1]]

il n'y a pas de quoi (ēl nyà pä də kwà′), *French.* it is nothing; don't mention it; you're welcome.

ILO (no periods) or **I.L.O.,** International Labor Organization.

Il|o|ka|no or **Il|o|ca|no** (ē′lō kä′nō), *n., pl.* **-no** or **-nos. 1** a member of a large civilized group of people inhabiting the northern part of Luzon in the Philippine Islands. **2** their Indonesian language. [< Spanish (Philippines) *Ilocano* < *Ilocos,* a place name, (literally) the rivermen < Tagalog *ilog* river]

I.L.P., *British.* Independent Labour Party.

ILS (no periods), instrument landing system (for aircraft).

ILTF (no periods) or **I.L.T.F.,** International Lawn Tennis Federation.

im-[1], *prefix.* the form of **in-**[1] before *b, m, p,* as in *imbalance, immoral, impossible, impatient.*

im-[2] *prefix.* the form of **in-**[2] before *b, m, p,* as in *imbibe, immure, impart.*

I'm (īm), I am.

IM (no periods), infectious mononucleosis.

I.M., Isle (of) Man.

im|age (im′ij), *n., v.,* **-aged, -ag|ing.** —*n.* **1** a likeness or copy: *You will see your image in this mirror. She is almost the image of her mother. God created man in his own image* (Genesis 1:27). **SYN:** resemblance, form, appearance. **2a** a likeness made of stone, wood, or some other material; statue: *The shelf was full of little images of all sorts of animals. The ancient Greeks and Romans worshiped images of their gods.* **b** a likeness painted, drawn, or carved on a surface: *an image of Caesar on a coin.* **3** a picture in the mind; idea: *I can shut my eyes and see images of things and persons.* **SYN:** conception. **4** a comparison, description, or figure of speech that helps the mind to form forceful or beautiful pictures. Poetry often contains images. **5** a symbol; representation; example: *This play is the image of a murder done in Vienna* (Shakespeare). *An awful image of calm power ... now thou sittest* (Shelley). **SYN:** embodiment. **6** the impression that a person, group, or organization presents to the public or a segment of it: *to create a new corporate image, to project a favorable image.* **7** the optical reproduction of an object, especially one produced by reflection in a mirror, or refraction through a lens or small hole. **8** a television picture. **9** *Psychology.* a sensory experience revived in whole or in part in the absence of the original stimulation. **10** *Archaic.* an illusion; apparition.

—*v.t.* **1** to make or form an image of; represent by an image; portray. **2** to reflect as a mirror does; mirror: *The clouds were imaged in the still waters of the lake.* **3** to picture in one's mind; imagine; conceive: *The soldier could image what his friends were doing at home.* **4** to describe with images: *The flight of Satan to the gates of hell is finely imaged* (Joseph Addison). **5** to symbolize; typify: *O stream! ... Thou imagest my life* (Shelley).

[< Old French *image,* learned borrowing from Latin *imāgō, -inis.* See etym. of doublet **imago.**]

—**im′age|less,** *adj.*

im|age-build|er (im′ij bil′dər), *n.* a person or thing devoted to image-building: *He warned of "the inherent danger of the broadcast operations' becoming a tool and image-builder for the corporate conglomerate"* (Saturday Review).

im|age-build|ing (im′ij bil′ding), *n.* the use of publicity and advertising to create or maintain a favorable impression before the public: *The program also gave a sympathetic hearing to policemen and showed ... some of the new techniques of image-building being employed to reach the communities they serve* (New York Times).

image converter, an electronic device with a photosensitive surface, used to reproduce on its fluorescent screen an image of a pattern of radiation; image tube. Image converters are used in television cameras, in high-speed photography, and in telescopes to increase their effective power. *An especially designed electronic tube called an "image converter" is the heart of the camera* (Science News Letter).

image dissector, a device used in early television cameras, similar to the iconoscope. Instead of a beam scanning the image, the image is focused through an aperture which breaks it up into a series of lines.

image intensifier, any one of various devices used with fluoroscopes, telescopes, and other instruments, to make optical images more intense: *A new image intensifier ... can be made to amplify light as much as a million and a half times* (Science News Letter). *The most highly developed of all image intensifiers is the signal-generating image orthicon used in commercial television* (W. C. Livingston).

im|age|mak|er (im′ij mā′kər), *n.* **1** a maker of painted, drawn, or carved images: *Man ... as an imagemaker, artist, and dreamer* (Harper's). **2** a person whose work is to alter or improve the public image of something, such as a company or public figure; image-builder: *Mr. Soames has been held back in the hierarchy because the party imagemakers believe him to look too much like the cartoonists' versions of the Tory squire* (Manchester Guardian Weekly).

image orthicon, a very sensitive cathode-ray tube used in television cameras to convert light images into electronic impulses. It consists of an orthicon, an electron gun, and an electron multiplier. *The standard tube in the United States for television cameras is the image orthicon* (Kenneth Harwood).

im|age|ry (im′ij rē, -i jər ē), *n., pl.* **-ries. 1** a picture formed in the mind; things imagined: *a dream's dim imagery* (Shelley). **2** comparisons, descriptions, and figures of speech that help the mind form forceful or beautiful pictures. Poetry often contains imagery. *Imagery is best defined as the total sensory suggestion of poetry* (John Ciardi). **3** images; statues.

image tube, = image converter.

i|mag|i|na|ble (i maj′ə nə bəl, -maj′nə-), *adj.* that can be imagined; possible: *We had the best time imaginable at the party. Cinderella was dressed with the greatest splendor imaginable. He ran into all the extravagancies imaginable* (Sir Richard Steele). **SYN:** conceivable, thinkable. —**i|mag′i|na|ble|ness,** *n.* —**i|mag′i|na|bly,** *adv.*

Pronunciation Key: hat, āge, cãre, fär; let, ēqual, tėrm; it, īce; hot, ōpen, ôrder; oil, out; cup, pu̇t, rüle; child; long; thin; ᴛʜen; zh, measure; ə represents **a** in about, **e** in taken, **i** in pencil, **o** in lemon, **u** in circus.

i|mag|i|nal (i maj′ə nəl), *adj.* **1** of or having to do with the imagination; using or involving the imagination: *imaginal education.* **2** *Entomology.* of or having to do with an imago.

i|mag|i|nar|i|ly (i maj′ə ner′ə lē), *adv.* in an imaginary way.

i|mag|i|nar|i|ness (i maj′ə ner′ē nis), *n.* the fact or state of being imaginary.

i|mag|i|nar|y (i maj′ə ner′ē), *adj., n.* **—*adj.*** **1** existing only in the imagination; not real: *Ghosts are imaginary. The equator is an imaginary circle around the earth.* SYN: illusory. **2** *Mathematics.* of or having to do with the even root of a negative number or any expression involving such a root. $\sqrt{-1}$, $3 + \sqrt{-15}$, $\sqrt{-4} = 2\sqrt{-1}$ are imaginary numbers or expressions. **3** *Obsolete.* imaginative: *My soul's imaginary sight Presents thy shadow to my sightless view* (Shakespeare).
—*n.* *Mathematics.* an imaginary number or expression.

i|mag|i|na|tion (i maj′ə nā′shən), *n.* **1** the action of imagining; power of forming pictures in the mind of things not present to the senses. Imagination leads people to think they see, hear, or feel things that are not there. *The child's imagination filled the woods with strange animals and fairies.* **2** the ability to create new things or ideas or to combine old ones in new forms: *Poets, artists, and inventors need imagination.* **3** a creation of the mind; mental image; fancy. **4** *Obsolete.* a scheming or planning; plot: *Thou hast seen all their vengeance and all their imaginations against me* (Lamentations 3:60) [< Old French *imagination,* learned borrowing from Latin *imāginātiō, -ōnis* < *imāginārī* imagine]
— *Syn.* **1, 2 Imagination, fancy** mean the power of forming pictures of things in the mind. **Imagination** applies to the ability to create believable or realistic pictures of things that never existed or happened: *His fascinating characters are the products of a fertile imagination.* **Fancy** applies to ability to make unbelievable or fantastic pictures, by inventing them or by putting together in unrealistic ways things from reality: *Many comic strips are products of fancy.*

i|mag|i|na|tion|al (i maj′ə nā′shə nəl), *adj.* of or having to do with imagination.

i|mag|i|na|tive (i maj′ə nə tiv, -nā′-), *adj.* **1** showing imagination: *Fairy tales are imaginative.* SYN: inventive, creative. **2** having a good imagination; able to imagine well; fond of imagining: *The imaginative child made up fairy stories.* SYN: inventive, creative. **3** of imagination: *The mind of the storyteller has great imaginative powers.*
—i|mag′i|na′tive|ly, *adv.* **—i|mag′i|na′tive|ness,** *n.*

i|mag|ine (i maj′ən), *v.,* **-ined, -in|ing.** **—*v.t.*** **1** to form a picture of in the mind; have an idea of: *The girl likes to imagine herself an actress. We can hardly imagine life without electricity.* **2** to suppose; guess; suspect: *I cannot imagine what you mean.* **3** to think; believe: *She imagined someone was watching her.* **4** *Archaic.* to plot; plan; scheme: *How long will ye imagine mischief against a man?* (Psalms 62:3).
—*v.i.* **1** to form mental images; have an idea. **2** to suppose; conjecture: *How he got such a silly answer I can't imagine.* **3** to think; fancy.
[< Old French *imaginer,* learned borrowing from Latin *imāginārī* < *imāgō, -inis* image]
— *Syn.* *v.t.* **1 Imagine, conceive** mean to form an idea of something in the mind. **Imagine** means to form a clear and definite picture of something: *I like to imagine myself flying a plane.* **Conceive** means to bring an idea into existence and give it an outline or pattern or shape in the mind: *The Wright brothers conceived the design of the first successful motor-powered plane.*

im|ag|ism (im′i jiz əm), *n.* **1** a theory in modern poetry, originating about 1909, that sought clarity of expression as opposed to the vague. It is characterized by the use of precise images, free verse, colloquial language, and varied rhythms rather than conventional metrical forms. **2** = field painting.

im|ag|ist (im′i jist), *n., adj.* **—*n.*** **1** a poet who practices imagism. Most imagists use free verse. **2** = field painter.
—*adj.* having to do with imagists or imagism.

im|ag|is|tic (im′i jis′tik), *adj.* of or having to do with imagism or imagists: *... the imagistic emphases of Keats' "Eve of St. Agnes"* (New York Times). **—im′ag|is′ti|cal|ly,** *adv.*

i|ma|go (i mā′gō), *n., pl.* **i|ma|gos, i|mag|i|nes** (i maj′ə nēz). **1** an insect in the final adult, especially winged, stage: *The embryonic life of insects continues until the formation of the perfect insect, or imago* (Scientific American). **2** *Psychoanalysis.* unconscious childhood concept of a parent or other person, carried over unchanged into adulthood. [< New Latin *imago,* special use of Latin *imāgō, -inis* image. See etym. of doublet **image.**]

i|mam (i mäm′), *n.* **1** a Moslem priest: *Clad in dignity and finery, the imam ascends the pulpit* (Time). **2** a Moslem leader or chief, such as the Caliph. Also, **imaum.** [< Arabic *'imām* leader]

i|mam|ate (i mä′māt), *n.* **1** the office or function of an imam. **2** the area governed by an imam.

i|mam|ic (i mä′mik), *adj.* of or having to do with an imam: *an imamic regime.*

i|ma|ret (i mä′ret), *n.* an inn for pilgrims and other travelers in Turkey. [< Turkish *imaret* charitable institution; kitchen for distributing food to the poor < Arabic *'imārat* a building]

I|ma|ri ware (i mä′rē), brightly colored and elaborately decorated Hizen porcelain. [< *Imari,* a port in Japan]

i|maum (i môm′), *n.* = imam.

im|bal|ance (im bal′əns), *n.* **1** lack of balance: *The trade imbalance and the drain of gold and hard currency reserves have lessened* (New York Times). **2** a lack of muscular or functional balance of the eyes or the endocrine glands.

im|bal|anced (im bal′ənst), *adj.* lacking balance: *School officials may assign pupils on the basis of neighborhood even though racially imbalanced classes result, the Court said* (Wall Street Journal).

im|balm (im bäm′), *v.t.* = embalm.

im|bark (im bärk′), *v.t., v.i.* = embark.

im|be|cile (im′bə səl), *n., adj.* **—*n.*** **1** a person born with such a weak mind that he can be trained to do only very simple tasks and will probably never learn to read; person who develops beyond the mental age of three but not beyond the mental age of eight. An imbecile is almost an idiot. **2** a very stupid or foolish person. SYN: See syn. under **fool.**
—*adj.* **1** very weak in mind; lacking normal intelligence. **2** very stupid or foolish. SYN: idiotic, fatuous. **3** weak; feeble: *His stunted nature and imbecile frame* (Shelley).
[< Middle French *imbécile,* learned borrowing from Latin *imbēcillus* weak < *in-* without + *bacillus* small staff (diminutive) < *baculum* staff, walking stick] **—im′be|cile|ly,** *adv.*

im|be|cil|ic (im′bə sil′ik), *adj.* **1** of, having to do with, or characterized by imbecility: *... imbecilic, senile and feeble-minded patients* (Maclean's). **2** very stupid or foolish; idiotic: *[They] consider the hobby imbecilic* (New York Times).

im|be|cil|i|ty (im′bə sil′ə tē), *n., pl.* **-ties.** **1** the condition of being an imbecile; feebleness of mind; mental weakness. **2** great stupidity or dullness: *He knew that the essence of war is violence, and that moderation in war is imbecility* (Macaulay). **3** something very stupid or foolish, such as an action or remark. **4** inability; incapacity.

im|bed (im bed′), *v.t.,* **-bed|ded, -bed|ding.** = embed.

im|bibe (im bīb′), *v.,* **-bibed, -bib|ing.** **—*v.t.*** **1** to drink in; drink: *He filled a quart flagon from a barrel ... Oliver ... imbibed the contents* (Scott). SYN: See syn. under **drink. 2** to absorb: *The roots of a plant imbibe moisture from the earth. If other conditions are suitable, the first step of germination is that the seed imbibes water* (Science News Letter). **3** *Figurative.* to take into one's mind: *A child often imbibes superstitions that last all his life. They had imbibed some notions of the Christian faith from Catholic missionaries* (Washington Irving). **4** *Obsolete.* to soak; saturate.
—*v.i.* **1** to drink. SYN: See syn. under **drink. 2** to absorb moisture. [< Latin *imbibere* < *in-* in + *bibere* to drink] **—im|bib′er,** *n.*

im|bi|bi|tion (im′bə bish′ən), *n.* the act of imbibing; absorption: *The water used by the more complex plants passes by imbibition from the soil into the cell walls of root hairs* (Harbaugh and Goodrich).

im|bit|ter (im bit′ər), *v.t.* = embitter.

im|bod|y (im bod′ē), *v.t.,* **-bod|ied, -bod|y|ing.** = embody.

im|bold|en (im bōl′dən), *v.t.* = embolden.

im|bos|om (im bu̇z′əm, -bü′zəm), *v.t.* = embosom.

im|bow|er (im bou′ər), *v.t., v.i.* = embower.

im|bri|cate (*v.* im′brə kāt; *adj.* im′brə kit, -kāt), *v.,* **-cat|ed, -cat|ing,** *adj.* **—*v.t., v.i.*** to overlap as tiles or shingles do.
—*adj.* **1** like the pattern of overlapping tiles. **2** like roof tiles in shape, composition, etc. **3** *Biology.* covered with or made of scales or scalelike parts overlapping like shingles, as fish scales or leaf buds do.
[< Latin *imbricāre* (with English *-ate*[1]) cover with tiles < *imbrex, -icis* hollow tile, gutter tile < *imber, -bris* rain] **—im′bri|cate|ly,** *adv.*

im|bri|cat|ed (im′brə kā′tid), *adj.* imbricate; overlapping.

***im|bri|ca|tion** (im′brə kā′shən), *n.* **1** the act or fact of overlapping like that of tiles or shingles. **2** a decorative pattern in imitation of this.

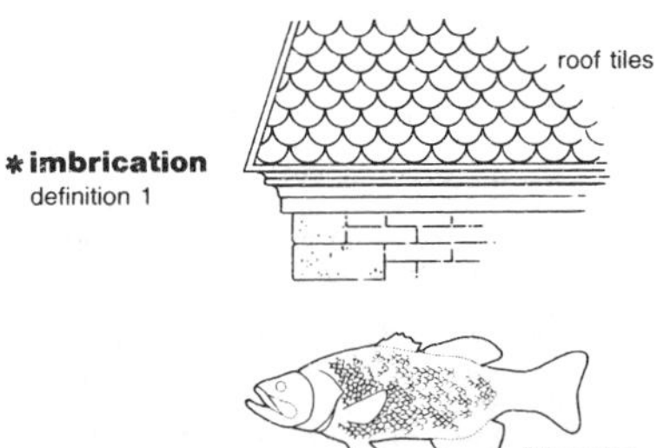

***imbrication** definition 1

im|bro|glio (im brōl′yō), *n., pl.* **-glios.** **1** a complicated or difficult situation: *Disturbing factors included the Suez imbroglio* (Wall Street Journal). **2** a complicated misunderstanding or disagreement. **3** a confused heap: *I keep my prints, an imbroglio, Fifty in one portfolio* (Robert Browning). Also, **embroglio.** [< Italian *imbroglio* < *imbrogliare* confuse, embroil < *im-* in + *brogliare,* probably < Old French *brouiller* to broil, be in disorder]

im|brown (im broun′), *v.t., v.i.* = embrown.

im|brue (im brü′), *v.t.,* **-brued, -bru|ing.** to wet; stain: *His sword was imbrued with blood.* [< Old French *embreuver,* earlier *embrever* give to drink < Vulgar Latin *imbiberāre* < Latin *in-* in + *bibere* to drink] **—im|brue′ment,** *n.*

im|brute (im brüt′), *v.,* **-brut|ed, -brut|ing.**
—*v.t.* to degrade to the level of a brute: *They have been ground down and debased and imbruted till human nature can bear no longer* (Harriet Beecher Stowe).
—*v.i.* to sink to the level of a brute. [< *im-*[2] + *brute*] **—im|brute′ment,** *n.*

im|bue (im byü′), *v.t.,* **-bued, -bu|ing.** **1** to fill the mind of; inspire: *He imbued his son's mind with the ambition to succeed.* SYN: permeate, pervade, impregnate. **2** to fill with moisture or color; saturate: *a skirt imbued with blood. Parting day Dies like the dolphin, whom each pang imbues With a new color* (Byron). SYN: dye, tinge. [< Latin *imbuere* moisten, stain, taint] **—im|bue′ment,** *n.*

im|bu|ia (im bü′yə), *n.* **1** a Brazilian tree whose wood is used for making furniture and cabinets. **2** the wood of the imbuia: *Most rooms are fitted with built-in imbuia cupboard sets* (Cape Times). Also, **embuia.** [< Portuguese *embuia* < a native word in Brazil]

im|burse (im bėrs′), *v.t.,* **-bursed, -burs|ing.** **1** to put into a purse; store up. **2** to pay; reimburse. [< Medieval Latin *imbursare* < Latin *in-* in + *bursa* purse] **—im|burse′ment,** *n.*

IMCO (no periods), Inter-Governmental Maritime Consultative Organization (of the United Nations that promotes cooperation in shipping).

IMF (no periods) or **I.M.F.,** International Monetary Fund.

im|id (im′id), *n.* = imide.

im|id|az|ol (im′id az′ōl, -ə zōl′), *n.* = imidazole.

im|id|az|ole (im′id az′ōl, -ə zōl′), *n. Chemistry.* an organic crystalline base; glyoxaline. *Formula:* $C_3H_4N_2$ [< *imid* (e) + *azole*]

im|ide (im′īd, -id), *n. Chemistry.* a compound containing the bivalent radical -NH in combination with a bivalent acid radical. [alteration of *amide*]

im|i|do (i mē′dō, im′i-) *adj.* of or having to do with an imide or imides.

i|mid|o|gen (i mid′ə jen), *n. Chemistry.* a bivalent radical occurring in imides. *Formula:* - NH

i|mine (i mēn′, im′in), *n. Chemistry.* a compound containing the -NH radical in combination with a bivalent nonacid radical. [alteration of *amine*]

i|mi|no (i mē′nō, im′-), *adj.* of or having to do with an imine or imines.

IMINT (im′ int), *n.* intelligence obtained through aerial photography: *The most solid evidence the U.S. has about events in Central America comes from IMINT* (Time). [< *im*(age) *int*(elligence)]

i|mip|ra|mine (i mip′rə mēn), *n.* a stimulant drug used in the treatment of severe depression. *Formula:* $C_{19}H_{24}N_2$ [< *imi*(ne) + *pr*(opyl) + *amine*]

imit., **1** imitation. **2** imitative.

im|i|ta|bil|i|ty (im′ə tə bil′ə tē), *n.* the character of being imitable.

im|i|ta|ble (im′ə tə bəl), *adj.* that can be imitated: *simple and imitable virtues, which are within every man's reach* (Washington Irving).

im|i|tate (im′ə tāt), *v.t.,* **-tat|ed, -tat|ing.** **1** to try to be or act like; follow the example of: *The little boy imitates his father.* **2** to make or do something like; copy: *A parrot imitates the sounds it hears* SYN: reproduce. See syn. under **copy. 3** to act like; make fun of by acting like: *He amused the class by imitating a baby, an old man, and a bear.* SYN: mimic, ape. **4** to be like; become like; look like; resemble: *Wood is sometimes painted* *to imitate stone.* SYN: simulate. [< Latin *imitārī* (with English *-ate*[1]), related to *imāgō* image]

im|i|ta|tion (im′ə tā′shən), *n., adj.* **—*n.*** **1** the action or practice of imitating: *We learn many things by imitation.* **2** a thing that imitates something else; likeness; copy; counterfeit: *Give as good an imitation as you can of a rooster crowing.* **3** *Music.* the repetition of a melodic phrase or theme at a different pitch or key from the original, or in a different voice part, or with modifications of rhythm or intervals that do not destroy the resemblance. **4** *Biology.* = mimicry. **5** *Psychology.* the performance of an act as a result of observing a similar act performed by another. **6** *Sociology.* the act of copying the behavior of other people, as in the process of acculturation.

—*adj.* made to look like something better; not real or genuine: *You can buy imitation pearls in many jewelry stores.*

in imitation of, in order to be like or look like; imitating: *Carved timber work, painted in imitation of old oak* (John Rutter).

im|i|ta|tive (im′ə tā′tiv), *adj.* **1** fond of imitating; likely or inclined to imitate others: *Monkeys are imitative.* **2** showing imitation; imitating: *"Bang" and "whiz" are imitative words.* **3** not real; counterfeit. SYN: simulative, fictitious. **4** *Biology.* closely resembling: *imitative coloration in animals.* **—im′i-ta′tive|ly,** *adv.* **—im′i|ta′tive|ness,** *n.*

im|i|ta|tor (im′ə tā′tər), *n.* a person or animal that imitates: *... and includes Aaron Copland, Walter Piston, Roy Harris, and their numerous imitators and pupils* (New Yorker).

im|mac|u|la|cy (i mak′yə lə sē), *n.* the state of being immaculate.

im|mac|u|late (i mak′yə lit), *adj.* **1** without a spot or stain; absolutely clean: *The newly washed shirts were immaculate. His gym shoes were immaculate in spite of the rain* (Graham Greene). SYN: spotless, undefiled. **2** *Figurative.* free from fault or errors. **3** *Figurative.* without sin; pure: *She was a woman ... of ... immaculate and inaccessible virtue* (Washington Irving). **4** *Biology.* without colored marks or spots; unspotted. [< Latin *immaculātus* < *in-* not + *macula* spot, blemish] **—im|mac′u|late|ly,** *adv.* **—im|mac′u|late-ness,** *n.*

Immaculate Conception, 1 a doctrine of the Roman Catholic Church that the Virgin Mary was conceived free of original sin. **2** a feast observed on December 8 commemorating this.

im|mal|le|a|ble (i mal′ē ə bəl), *adj.* not malleable.

im|mane (i mān′), *adj. Archaic.* **1** monstrous; huge; enormous. **2** inhumanly cruel or savage. [< Latin *immānis* < *im-* not + Old Latin *mānus* good, related to *Mānes* good spirits]

im|ma|nence (im′ə nəns), *n.* **1** the state of being immanent. **2** *Theology.* the pervading presence of God in His creation.

im|ma|nen|cy (im′ə nən sē), *n.* = immanence.

im|ma|nent (im′ə nənt), *adj.* **1** remaining within; inherent: *By the same process of fusion philosophers assume that one thing exists in another, in which case the former is said to be immanent in the latter* (Michael Polanyi). **2** in the mind; subjective. [< Latin *immanēns, -entis,* present participle of *immanēre* < *in-* in + *manēre* to stay, dwell] **—im′ma|nent|ly,** *adv.*

im|ma|nent|ism (im′ə nən tiz′əm), *n. Theology.* belief in the immanence of God.

im|ma|nent|ist (im′ə nən tist), *adj. Theology.* having to do with or characterized by immanentism.

Im|man|u|el (i man′yu̇ əl), *n.* Christ (in the Bible, Isaiah 7:14, Matthew 1:23). Also, **Emmanuel.** [< Hebrew *'immânu'el* (literally) God with us]

im|ma|te|ri|al (im′ə tir′ē əl), *adj.* **1** not important; insignificant: *The error is immaterial.* SYN: unimportant, unessential. **2** not material; spiritual rather than physical. **—im′ma|te′ri|al|ly,** *adv.* **—im′ma|te′ri|al|ness,** *n.*

im|ma|te|ri|al|ism (im′ə tir′ē ə liz′əm), *n.* **1** the doctrine that all things exist only in the mind. **2** = immateriality. **—im′ma|te′ri|al|ist,** *n.*

im|ma|te|ri|al|i|ty (im′ə tir′ē al′ə tē), *n., pl.* **-ties. 1** condition of being immaterial: *All the conclusions of reason enforce the immateriality of mind* (Samuel Johnson). **2** something immaterial. **3** = unimportance.

im|ma|te|ri|al|ize (im′ə tir′ē ə līz), *v.t.,* **-ized, -iz-ing.** to make immaterial.

im|ma|ture (im′ə chu̇r′, -tu̇r′, -tyu̇r′), *adj., n.* **—*adj.*** **1** not mature; not ripe; not full-grown; undeveloped. Immature apples are usually green. **2** *Physical Geography.* reduced to only a slight extent by erosion, etc. **3** *Archaic.* premature.

—*n.* an immature person or animal: *The number of immatures seems lower than it ought to be to maintain the species* (Atlantic).

[< Latin *immātūrus* untimely, unripe < *in-* not + *mātūrus* mature] **—im′ma|ture′ly,** *adv.* **—im′ma-ture′ness,** *n.*

im|ma|tu|ri|ty (im′ə chu̇r′ə tē, -tu̇r′-, -tyu̇r′-), *n.* immature condition or quality.

im|meas|ur|a|ble (i mezh′ər ə bəl, -mā′zhər-), *adj.* that cannot be measured; without limits; boundless: *immeasurable faith.* SYN: infinite, illimitable. **—im|meas′ur|a|ble|ness,** *n.*

im|meas|ur|a|bly (i mezh′ər ə blē, -mā′zhər-), *adv.* beyond measure; to an extent or degree too great to be measured.

im|me|di|a|cy (i mē′dē ə sē), *n., pl.* **-cies. 1** the quality or condition of being immediate: *The record companies settled on immediacy as a promotional gambit* (Newsweek). **2** *Philosophy.* the condition of being directly present to the consciousness as distinguished from what is known by inference.

immediacies, immediate needs: *The old things and the foul things, customs, delusions, habits ... base immediacies, triumph over us* (H. G. Wells).

im|me|di|ate (i mē′dē it), *adj.* **1** coming at once; done without delay: *Please send an immediate reply.* **2** with nothing between: *in immediate contact.* **3** direct: *the immediate result.* SYN: See syn. under **direct. 4** closest; nearest; next: *Your immediate neighbors live next door.* **5** close; near: *the immediate neighborhood. I expect an answer today, tomorrow, or in the immediate future.* **6** having to do with the present; current: *What are your immediate plans?* **7** *Philosophy.* (of knowledge) self-evident; intuitive, as distinguished from knowledge arrived at by means of demonstration or proof. [< Late Latin *immediātus* < Latin *in-* not + *medius* middle] **—im|me′di|ate-ness,** *n.*

immediate constituent, any of the two or three largest structural components of a sentence, phrase, or word. *Example:* the immediate constituents of *ungentlemanly* are *un-* and *gentlemanly* (not *ungentle* and *manly,* nor *ungentleman* and *-ly*). *Abbr:* IC (no periods).

im|me|di|ate|ly (i mē′dē it lē), *adv., conj.* **—*adv.*** **1** at once; without delay; instantly: *I answered his letter immediately.* **2** with nothing between: *The houses in the crowded neighborhood are immediately upon each other.* **3** next. **4** directly: *Immediately in the route of the travellers lay a high mountain* (Washington Irving).

—*conj.* as soon as.

—*Syn.* *adv.* **1 Immediately, instantly, presently** mean with little or no delay. **Immediately** implies little delay: *My biology class comes immediately after my English class.* **Instantly** implies no delay: *The driver was killed instantly.* **Presently** implies some delay: *I will do the dishes presently, but I want to finish this story first.*

im|med|i|ca|ble (i med′ə kə bəl), *adj.* that cannot be healed; incurable: *immedicable wrongs.*

***Im|mel|mann turn** (im′əl mən), a maneuver in which an aircraft changes direction and gains altitude by making a half loop and a half roll. [< Max *Immelmann,* 1890-1916, a German aviator, said to have invented it]

***Immelmann turn**

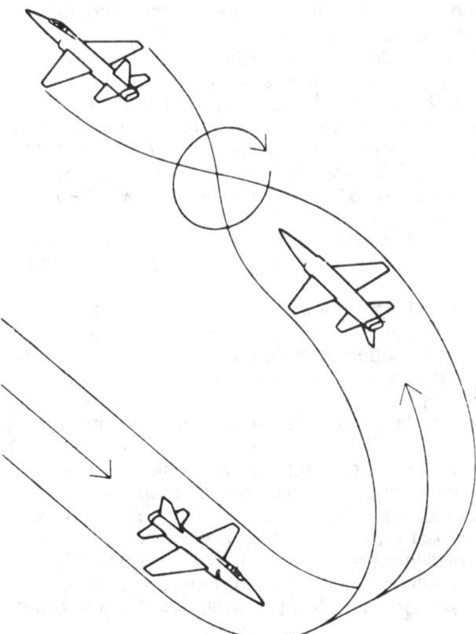

im|mem|o|ra|ble (i mem′ər ə bəl), *adj.* not memorable; not worth remembering: *The piece is grotesquely unfunny, acted with sledge-hammer clumsiness, and, with its immemorable music, it is an appalling bore* (Sunday Times).

im|me|mo|ri|al (im′ə môr′ē əl, -mōr′-), *adj.* extending back beyond the bounds of memory; very, very old; ancient beyond record or knowledge: *immemorial elms* (Tennyson). [< Medieval Latin *immemorialis* < Latin *in-* not + *memoriālis* memorial, in memory] **—im′me|mo′ri|al|ly,** *adv.*

im|mense (i mens′), *adj., n.* **—*adj.*** **1** very big; huge; vast: *An ocean is an immense body of water.* SYN: enormous. See syn. under **huge. 2** *Informal.* very good; fine; excellent. **—*n.*** a boundless expanse or quantity: *When ... the solid shores of sense Melt into the vague immense* (John Greenleaf Whittier). [< Latin *immēnsus* < *in-* not + *mēnsus,* past participle of *mētīrī* to measure] **—im|mense′ness,** *n.*

im|mense|ly (i mens′lē), *adv. Informal.* very greatly; hugely; *We enjoyed the party immensely.*

im|men|si|ty (i men′sə tē), *n., pl.* **-ties. 1** very great size; boundless extent; vastness: *the ocean's immensity.* **2** infinite space or existence; infinity. **3** something that is immense: a vast expanse; great quantity: *rough-looking desperadoes with ... an immensity of beard* (Hawthorne).

im|men|su|ra|ble (i men′shər ə bəl), *adj.* not mensurable; immeasurable. [< Late Latin *immēnsūrābilis* < Latin *in-* not + *mēnsūrābilis* mensurable]

im|merge (i mėrj′), *v.,* **-merged, -merg|ing. —*v.t.*** = immerse. **—*v.i.*** **1** to plunge or dip oneself in a liquid; sink. **2** to disappear (into, behind, or under something else): *The star immerged into the light of the sun.* [< Latin *immergere;* see etym. under **immerse**]

im|mer|gence (i mėr′jəns), *n.* the act of plunging or sinking into anything; immersion: *immergence in water.*

im|merse (i mėrs′), *v.t.,* **-mersed, -mers|ing. 1** to dip or lower into a liquid until covered by it; plunge into a liquid; soak thoroughly: *He immersed his aching feet in a bucket of hot water.* SYN: submerge, duck. See syn. under **dip. 2** to baptize by dipping (a person) completely under water. **3** *Figurative.* to involve deeply; absorb: *immersed in thought, immersed in debts. The ambitious man immersed himself in business affairs seven days a week.* SYN: engross, occupy. **4** to embed; bury. [< Latin *immersus,* past participle of *immergere* < *in-* in + *mergere* to plunge] **—im-mers′er,** *n.*

im|mersed (i mėrst′), *adj.* **1** covered by a liquid. **2** *Figurative.* deeply absorbed, as in thought or grief. **3** baptized by immersion. **4** *Biology.* mostly or wholly sunk in surrounding parts, as the eyes of some beetles. **5** *Botany.* growing wholly under water.

im|mer|si|ble (i mėr′sə bəl), *adj.* that can be immersed.

im|mer|sion (i mėr′zhən, -shən), *n.* **1** the act of immersing. **2** the condition of being immersed. **3** baptism by dipping a person completely under water. **4** *Astronomy.* the disappearance of the sun, moon, or other heavenly body in an eclipse.

immersion course, an intensive course of oral instruction in a foreign language: *an immersion course in French. In Winnipeg, a total of 1,123 students were enrolled in immersion courses this fall* (Maclean's).

immersion foot, a diseased condition of the lower limbs and feet, resembling frostbite, caused by prolonged exposure to wet, but not necessarily freezing, cold; trench foot.

immersion heater, an electric heater designed to be immersed in water that is to be heated.

im|mesh (im mesh′), *v.t.* = enmesh.

im|me|thod|i|cal (im′ə thod′ə kəl, im′mə-), *adj.* not methodical; having no method; irregular: *My reading has been lamentably desultory and immethodical* (Charles Lamb). **—im′me|thod′i|cal|ly,** *adv.*

im|met|ri|cal (i met′rə kəl), *adj.* not metrical. **—im|met′ri|cal|ly,** *adv.*

im|mie (im′ē), *n. U.S. Informal.* a colored playing marble; agate. [short for *imitation agate*]

im|mi|grant (im′ə grənt), *n., adj.* **—*n.*** a person who comes into a foreign country or region to live: *Canada has many immigrants from Europe. California has many immigrants from other states.* **—*adj.*** immigrating.

im|mi|grate (im′ə grāt), *v.,* **-grat|ed, -grat|ing. —*v.i.*** to come into a foreign country or region to live: *During the 1800's many thousands of poor from Europe immigrated into the United States to make a new home.* **—*v.t.*** to bring in or introduce as settlers. [< Latin *immigrāre* (with English *-ate*[1]) < *in-* into + *migrāre* to move, migrate] ►See **emigrate** for usage note.

im|mi|gra|tion (im′ə grā′shən), *n.* **1** the act of coming into a foreign country or region to live: *There has been immigration to America from all the countries of Europe.* **2** persons who immigrate; immigrants: *The immigration of 1956 included many people from Hungary.*

Pronunciation Key: hat, āge, cãre, fär; let, ēqual, tėrm; it, īce; hot, ōpen, ôrder; **oi**l, **ou**t; cup, pu̇t, rüle; **ch**ild; lo**ng**; **th**in; **ŧh**en; **zh**, measure; **ə** represents **a** in about, **e** in taken, **i** in pencil, **o** in lemon, **u** in circus.

im|mi|gra|tor (im′ə grā′tər), *n.* a person who immigrates.

im|mi|nence (im′ə nəns), *n.* **1** the state or fact of being imminent: *The very imminence of the emergency paralyzed his invention* (Mark Twain). **2** a thing that is imminent, especially some evil or danger about to occur.

im|mi|nent (im′ə nənt), *adj.* **1** likely to happen soon; about to occur: *The black clouds, thunder, and lightning show that a storm is imminent.* **2** projecting or leaning forward; overhanging: *Flake by flake, the beetling avalanches Build up their imminent crags of noiseless snow* (James Russell Lowell). [< Latin *imminēns, -entis,* present participle of *imminēre* to overhang, < *in-* in (over) + unrecorded *-minēre* hang, jut] —**im′mi|nent|ly,** *adv.*
—***Syn.*** **1 Imminent, impending** mean likely to happen soon. **Imminent** suggests being likely to happen any minute without further warning: *Swept along by the swift current, he was in imminent danger of going over the falls.* **Impending** suggests something hanging over one, often indefinitely, and keeping him in suspense: *For weeks I have had a feeling of impending disaster.*
►See **eminent** for usage note.

im|min|gle (im ming′gəl), *v.t., v.i.* **-gled, -gling.** to mix or mingle in; intermingle; blend: *Where . . . with the chestnut the oak trees immingle* (Arthur Hugh Clough).

im|mis|ci|bil|i|ty (i mis′ə bil′ə tē), *n.* the quality of being immiscible.

im|mis|ci|ble (i mis′ə bəl), *adj.* that cannot be mixed: *Water and oil are immiscible.* [< Late Latin *immiscibilis* < Latin *in-* not + *miscēre* to mix] —**im|mis′ci|bly,** *adv.*

im|mis|sion (im mish′ən), *n.* the act or process of sending or letting in; injection; introduction. [< Latin *immissiō, -ōnis* < *immittere;* see etym. under **immit**]

im|mit (im mit′), *v.t.,* **-mit|ted, -mit|ting.** to send or let in; inject; introduce. [< Latin *immittere* < *in-* in + *mittere* send]

im|mit|i|ga|ble (i mit′ə gə bəl), *adj.* that cannot be softened or mitigated; not mitigable: *the immitigable end* (William Ernest Henley). [< Latin *immītigābilis* < *in-* not + *mītigābilis* mitigable] —**im|mit′i|ga|ble|ness,** *n.*

im|mit|i|ga|bly (i mit′ə gə blē), *adv.* in an immitigable manner or degree.

im|mix (im miks′), *v.t., v.i.* to mix in; mix intimately; mingle: *amongst her teares immixing prayers meeke* (Edmund Spenser). [Middle English *immixten* < Latin *immiscēre* < *in-* in + *miscēre* to mix]

im|mix|ture (im miks′chər), *n.* the process of immixing or the fact of being mixed in.

im|mo|bile (i mō′bəl, -bēl), *adj.* **1** not movable; firmly fixed; stable. **2** not moving; not changing; motionless: *Although immobile once more, he . . . was suffering at last from a socially approved ailment: a broken hip* (Time). [< Old French *immobile,* learned borrowing from Latin *immōbilis* < *in-* not + *mōbilis* mobile]

im|mo|bi|lise (i mō′bə līz), *v.t.,* **-lised, -lis|ing.** *Especially British.* immobilize.

im|mo|bi|lism (i mō′bə liz əm), *n.* the absence of any decisive action or policy by a government or organization; political stagnation: *He set new standards of do-nothingness in a regime where immobilism had been raised to the level of a fine art* (Newsweek).

im|mo|bi|lisme (ēm mô bē lēz′mə), *n. French.* = immobilism.

im|mo|bi|list (i mō′bə list), *n., adj.* —*n.* a person who favors or advocates immobilism: *The immobilists are committed to the principle that the church has been stable for 2,000 years in spite of stress and storm and so stand pat in the traditional position* (New York Times).
—***adj.*** favoring or advocating immobilism: *Gorton . . . did try to lead the Liberals out of some immobilist attitudes* (Sunday Times).

im|mo|bil|i|ty (im′ō bil′ə tē), *n.* immobile quality or condition.

im|mo|bi|lize (i mō′bə līz), *v.t.,* **-lized, -liz|ing.** **1** to make immobile. **2** to withdraw (specie) from circulation, holding it as security against bank notes or other financial paper; change or transform (circulating capital) into fixed capital. **3** *Surgery.* to keep (a joint or limb) without motion, as by splints. —**im|mo′bi|li|za′tion,** *n.* —**im|mo′bi|liz|er,** *n.*

Im|mo|bi|lon (i mō′bə lon), *n. Trademark.* a drug used to immobilize wild animals: *A rhinoceros injected with new drug Immobilon* (London Times).

im|mod|er|a|cy (i mod′ər ə sē), *n., pl.* **-cies.** lack of moderation; excess: *Creatively, Marlowe matches his hero's immoderacies; he shows a like hunger and fever, a commensurate strut and rant* (Time).

im|mod|er|ate (i mod′ər it), *adj.* **1** not moderate; too much; going too far; extreme; more than is right or proper: *loud and immoderate laughter. A fanatic has immoderate ideas.* **syn:** excessive, intemperate, exorbitant, inordinate. **2** *Obsolete.* without limits; boundless. [< Latin *immoderātus* < *in-* not + *moderātus* restrained] —**im|mod′er|ate|ly,** *adv.* —**im|mod′er|ate|ness,** *n.*

im|mod|er|a|tion (i mod′ə rā′shən), *n.* lack of moderation; excess.

im|mod|est (i mod′ist), *adj.* **1** not modest; bold and rude. **syn:** forward, impudent. **2** indecent; improper; indelicate: *Immodest words admit of no defence For want of decency is want of sense* (Wentworth Dillon). **syn:** lewd, obscene. —**im|mod′est|ly,** *adv.*

im|mod|es|ty (i mod′ə stē), *n.* **1** lack of modesty; boldness and rudeness. **2** lack of decency; improper behavior.

im|mo|late (im′ə lāt), *v.t.,* **-lat|ed, -lat|ing.** **1** to kill as a sacrifice: *The women and children were immolated on funeral pyres* (Time). **2** *Figurative.* to offer in sacrifice; sacrifice. [< Latin *immolāre* (with English *-ate*[1]) to sacrifice; (originally) sprinkle with sacrificial meal < *in-* on + *mola* sacrificial meal]

im|mo|la|tion (im′ə lā′shən), *n.* **1** the act of immolating. **2** the state of being immolated. **3** *Figurative.* a sacrificial offering; sacrifice.

im|mo|la|tor (im′ə lā′tər), *n.* a person who offers in sacrifice.

im|mo|la|to|ry (im′ə lə tôr′ē, -tōr′-), *adj.* = sacrificial.

im|mor|al (i môr′əl, -mor′-), *adj.* **1** morally wrong; wicked: *Lying and stealing are immoral.* **2** lewd; unchaste. —**im|mor′al|ly,** *adv.*

im|mor|al|ist (i môr′ə list, -mor′-), *n.* **1** a person who advocates or accepts immorality; one who justifies evil in himself or others. **2** a person who is immoral.

im|mo|ral|i|ty (im′ə ral′ə tē), *n., pl.* **-ties.** **1** wickedness; wrongdoing; vice. **2** lewdness; lack of chastity. **syn:** unchastity. **3** an immoral act or practice.

im|mor|tal (i môr′təl), *adj., n.* —***adj.*** **1** living forever; never dying; everlasting: *Most churches believe that a man's body dies, but his soul is said to be immortal. The fame of Shakespeare should be immortal.* **syn:** eternal, endless, unfading, imperishable. **2** of or having to do with immortal beings or immortality; divine: *These be they that have put off the mortal clothing, and put on the immortal* (II Esdras 2:45). **3** remembered or famous forever: *the immortal power of Winston Churchill's wartime speeches. A great hero is immortal.*
—***n.*** **1** an immortal being. **2** a person remembered or famous forever: *Shakespeare is one of the immortals.* **3 Immortal,** one of the forty members of the French Academy: *Marguerite Yourcenar, a 76-year-old respected French classicist and novelist—had finally been elected an Immortal* (Maclean's).
immortals, the gods of ancient Greece and Rome: *Never, believe me, appear the immortals . . . alone* (Samuel Taylor Coleridge).
[< Latin *immortālis* < *in-* not + *mortālis* dying, mortal] —**im|mor′tal|ly,** *adv.*

im|mor|tal|i|ty (im′ôr tal′ə tē), *n.* **1** endless life; living forever: *The Greeks believed in the immortality of their gods; many believe in the immortality of the soul.* **2** fame that lasts forever: *the immortality of the great achievements of Newton and Einstein.*

im|mor|tal|i|za|tion (i môr′tə lə zā′shən), *n.* **1** the act of immortalizing. **2** the state of being immortalized.

im|mor|tal|ize (i môr′tə līz), *v.t.,* **-ized, -iz|ing.** **1** to make immortal. **2** to cause to be remembered or famous forever; give everlasting fame to: *Great authors are immortalized by their works.* —**im|mor′tal|iz′er,** *n.*

im|mor|tals (i môr′təlz), *n.pl.* See under **immortal.**

***im|mor|telle** (im′ôr tel′), *n.* any one of several composite plants whose flowers keep their shape and color after they have entirely dried, such as an annual with rose or purple flowers, native to the Mediterranean; everlasting. [< French *(fleur) immortelle* immortal (flower), feminine of *immortel,* learned borrowing from Latin *immortālis* immortal]

***immortelle**

im|mo|tile (im mō′təl), *adj.* not motile; incapable of movement.

im|mov|a|bil|i|ty (i mü′və bil′ə tē), *n.* the condition of being immovable.

im|mov|a|ble (i mü′və bəl), *adj., n.* —***adj.*** **1** that cannot be moved; firmly fixed: *immovable mountains.* **syn:** immobile. **2** not moving or changing; motionless: *In his [Newton's] eyes the sun stood immovable in the center of the universe* (Sir David Brewster). **3** *Figurative.* firm; steadfast; unyielding: *an immovable purpose. The ignorant man was immovable in his belief that the earth was flat.* **4** *Figurative.* unfeeling; impassive. **5** *Law.* not liable to be removed; fixed in place: *immovable property.* **6** falling on the same date each year: *All Saints' Day is an immovable feast.*
—***n.*** **immovables,** *Law.* land, buildings, and other property that cannot be carried from one place to another: *If he has property, it consists either in immovables or in movables* (Jeremy Bentham). —**im|mov′a|ble|ness,** *n.* —**im|mov′a|bly,** *adv.*

im|mune (i myün′), *adj., n.* —***adj.*** **1a** protected from disease or poison; not susceptible; having immunity: *Some persons are immune to poison ivy. Vaccination makes a person practically immune to polio.* **b** having to do with or producing immunity: *an immune reaction.* **2** free (from); exempt: *Nobody is immune from criticism.* **3** protected; shielded: *Among the graves, she felt immune from the world* (D. H. Lawrence).
—***n.*** an immune person or animal.
[< Latin *immūnis* (originally) free from obligation < *in-* not + *mūnis* obliging < *mūnia* duties]

immune body, an antibody present in blood and lymph that assists in the cytolysis of erythrocytes and other cells; amboceptor.

immune serum, a serum in which antibodies to a particular disease are present, especially in increased number as a result of stimulation by an antigen: *Injections of an immune serum (from the blood of a person who has recovered from the disease) and a vaccine provide limited resistance to attack* (Austin Edward Smith).

im|mu|ni|ty (i myü′nə tē), *n., pl.* **-ties.** **1** resistance to disease or poison: *One attack of measles usually gives a person immunity to that disease.* **2** freedom; protection: *The law gives schools and churches immunity from taxation. Ambassadors have diplomatic immunity in the countries in which they are stationed.* **syn:** See syn. under **exemption.** **3** exemption from natural liability or from anything evil. [< Latin *immūnitās* < *immūnis* immune]

im|mu|nize (im′yù nīz), *v.t.,* **-nized, -niz|ing.** to protect from disease or poison; give immunity to; make immune: *Vaccination immunizes one against smallpox.* —**im′mu|ni|za′tion,** *n.*

immuno-, *combining form.* immunity; immunization, as in *immunobiology, immunoreaction.*

im|mu|no|ad|sorb|ent (i myü′nō ad sôr′bənt, -zôr′-), *n.* a chemical substance that adsorbs antigens or antibodies: *The antigens cling to the antibodies and when the immunoadsorbent is removed the antigens come with it* (Science News).

im|mu|no|as|say (i myü′nō as′ā, -ə sā′), *n.* analysis of the characteristics of a bodily substance by testing its immunological or antibody-producing reactions.

im|mu|no|bi|ol|o|gy (i myü′nō bī ol′ə jē), *n.* the study of biological immunity or immunization.

im|mu|no|chem|i|cal (i myü′nō kem′ə kəl), *adj.* of or having to do with immunochemistry. —**im|mu′no|chem′i|cal|ly,** *adv.*

im|mu|no|chem|is|try (i myü′nō kem′ə strē), *n.* the science dealing with chemical relationships of immunology. —**im|mu′no|chem′ist,** *n.*

im|mu|no|com|pe|tence (i myü′nō kom′pə təns), *n.* the ability to produce immunity.

im|mu|no|com|pe|tent (i myü′nō kom′pə tənt), *adj.* capable of producing or developing immunity to disease: *The antibody-forming cells are frequently designated as immunocompetent cells* (Felix Haurowitz).

im|mu|no|com|pro|mised (i myü′nō kom′prə mīzd), *adj.* made vulnerable to a disease or opportunistic infection by a deficiency in the immune system: *The [Epstein-Barr] virus is a causative cofactor of some cancers . . . in patients who are profoundly immunocompromised, e.g. by AIDS* (Allen D. Allen).

im|mu|no|cyte (i myü′nə sīt), *n.* any cell, such as a lymphoid or plasma cell, that is a part of the mechanism of immunization: *The autoimmune process and the surveillance mechanism are both attributed to the same system of thymus-dependent immunocytes* (New Scientist).

im|mu|no|de|fi|cien|cy disease (i myü′nō di fish′ən sē), any disease caused by a deficiency in the immunity mechanism of the body.

im|mu|no|dif|fu|sion (i myü′nō di fyü′zhən), *n.* a process for separating the components of an antigen-antibody complex by the diffusion of antigen and antibody solutions through a gel.

im|mu|no|e|lec|tro|pho|re|sis (i myü′nō i lek′trō fə rē′sis), *n.* a process for analyzing complex proteins by separating the proteins according to their colloidal movement under the influence of an electric field and identifying each protein by its immune reaction.

im|mu|no|e|lec|tro|pho|ret|ic (i myü′nō i lek′trō fə ret′ik), *adj.* of or having to do with immunoelectrophoresis.

im|mu|no|flu|o|res|cence (i myü′nō flü′ə res′əns), *n.* the labeling of antibodies with a fluorescent dye to reveal antigens when viewed under ultraviolet light.

im|mu|no|flu|o|res|cent (i myü′nō flü′ə res′ənt), *adj.* of or having to do with immunofluorescence.

im|mu|no|gen (i myü′nə jən), *n.* **1** an antigenic substance; antigen. **2** an immunogenic substance.

im|mu|no|ge|net|ic (i myü′nō jə net′ik), *adj.* of or having to do with immunogenetics.

im|mu|no|ge|net|ics (i myü′nō jə net′iks), *n.* **1** the study of the relationship between genetic factors and immunity to disease. **2** the study of biological relationships by means of serums.

im|mu|no|gen|ic (i myü′nō jen′ik), *adj.* making immune to a certain disease.

im|mu|no|ge|nic|i|ty (i myü′nō jə nis′ə tē), *n.* the property of causing immunity to a disease.

im|mu|no|glob|u|lin (i myü′nō glob′yə lin), *n.* any globulin that acts as an antibody; a protein in blood plasma that confers immunity. *Abbr:* Ig

im|mu|no|hem|a|to|log|ic (i myü′nō hem′ə tə loj′ik, -hē′mə-), *adj.* of or having to do with immunohematology.

im|mu|no|hem|a|tol|o|gy (i myü′nō hem′ə tol′ə jē, -hē′mə-), *n.* the study of the immunological or antibody-producing properties of the blood.

im|mu|no|log|ic (i myü′nə loj′ik), *adj.* = immunological.

im|mu|no|log|i|cal (i myü′nə loj′ə kəl), *adj.* of or having to do with immunology: *If this proves to be a consistent point of immunological difference between normal and cancer cells, the way could be opened for development of a general cancer diagnostic test* (Science News Letter). **—im|mu′no|log′i|cal|ly,** *adv.*

immunological barrier, the rejection by the body of foreign transplanted tissue.

immunological privilege, a condition under which the body does not reject foreign transplanted tissue. Sites in the body and kinds of tissue may possess immunological privilege.

immunological rejection, = immunological barrier.

im|mu|nol|o|gy (im′yü nol′ə jē), *n.* the science dealing with the nature and causes of immunity from diseases. **—im′mu|nol′o|gist,** *n.*

im|mu|no|mod|u|la|tor (i myü′nō moj′ü lā′tər), *n.* a drug used to stimulate activity of the body's immune system: *The class of drugs ... is called immunomodulators, meaning drugs which can modify the body's own defense system* (Financial Times).

im|mu|no|pa|thol|o|gy (i myü′nō pə thol′ə jē), *n.* the study of the pathological aspects of immunity or immunization.

im|mu|no|re|ac|tion (i myü′nō rē ak′shən), *n.* a reaction between an antibody and the antigen of that antibody.

im|mu|no|stim|u|lant (i myü′nō stim′yə lənt), *n.* = immunomodulator.

im|mu|no|sup|pres|sant (i myü′nō sə pres′ənt), *n., adj.* **—*n.*** an immunosuppressive drug, used especially to suppress rejection of grafted or transplanted tissue. **—*adj.*** = immunosuppressive.

im|mu|no|sup|pres|sion (i myü′nō sə presh′ən), *n.* suppression, especially by the use of drugs or radiation, of the immunological reaction of the body to foreign substances, as to prevent the rejection of grafts or transplants by the recipient's body: *In order to coerce the body into accepting a donor's organ, full immunosuppression has been necessary ..., often leading, unfortunately, to fatal secondary infection* (New Scientist).

im|mu|no|sup|pres|sive (i myü′nō sə pres′iv), *adj., n.* **—*adj.*** suppressing immunity; causing immunosuppression: *immunosuppressive drugs given to ... suppress organ rejection foster the rise of cancer* (Science News). **—*n.*** an immunosuppressive agent or drug; immunosuppressant.

im|mu|no|ther|a|peu|ti|cal (i myü′nō ther′ə pyü′tə kəl), *adj.* of or having to do with immunotherapy.

im|mu|no|ther|a|py (i myü′nō ther′ə pē), *n.* the treatment of disease by either the stimulation or suppression of immunological reactions: *Immunotherapy has been demonstrated to be effective in allergy management* (Irwin J. Polk).

im|mure (i myůr′), *v.t.,* **-mured, -mur|ing. 1** to shut up or enclose within walls; put in prison. **2** *Figurative.* to shut in; confine closely: *love ... Lives not alone immured in the brain* (Shakespeare). **3** to build into or entomb in a wall. [< Medieval Latin *immurare* < Latin *in-* in + *mūrus* wall] **—im|mure′ment,** *n.*

im|mu|ta|bil|i|ty (i myü′tə bil′ə tē), *n.* the condition of being immutable: *Michelangelo shared this view of the immutability of art* (Atlantic).

im|mu|ta|ble (i myü′tə bəl), *adj.* never changing; not changeable: *nature's immutable laws. She was as immutable as the Hills* (Rudyard Kipling). SYN: unchangeable, unalterable, permanent. **—im|mu′ta|ble|ness,** *n.* **—im|mu′ta|bly,** *adv.*

imp (imp), *n., v.* **—*n.* 1** a young or small devil or demon; evil spirit. **2** a mischievous child: *The little imp fell asqualling, and scratching, and biting* (Jonathan Swift). **3** *Archaic.* an offspring; child: *My imps ... hard, bold and wild, As best befits the mountain child* (Scott). **4** *Obsolete.* a young shoot of a plant or tree; scion; offshoot.
—*v.t.* 1 in falconry: **a** to graft (feathers) in a bird's wing to improve its powers of flight. **b** to graft feathers into or on (a wing, etc.). **2** to fasten (wings) on; equip with wings: *Imp'd with wings, The grubs proceed to bees with pointed stings* (John Dryden). **3** to extend or enlarge; mend; repair. **4** *Obsolete.* to graft; implant.
[Old English *impa, impe* a shoot, graft, ultimately < Vulgar Latin *imputus* < Greek *émphytos* engrafted, implanted < *en-* in + *phytós* fruitful < *phýein* to produce, beget]

IMP (no periods), **1** International Match Point (a unit of scoring used in European contract bridge tournaments). **2** interplanetary monitoring platform.

imp., 1 imparted. **2** imperative. **3** imperfect. **4** imperial. **5** impersonal. **6a** import. **b** imported. **c** importer. **7a** imprimatur. **b** imprimis. **8** imprint.

Imp., 1 emperor (Latin, *imperator*). **2** empress (Latin, *imperatrix*).

im|pact (*n.* im′pakt; *v.* im pakt′), *n., v.* **—*n.* 1** a striking (of one thing against another); collision: *The impact of the heavy stone against the windowpane shattered the glass. The impact of the two swords broke both of them.* **2** *Physics.* the single instantaneous blow of a moving body when it meets another body. **3** *Figurative.* a forceful or dramatic effect: *We cannot afford to ignore the impact of a deteriorating prison system on human dignity* (A. S. Alexander, Jr.).
—*v.t.* 1 to drive or press closely or firmly into something; pack in. **2** to come upon; hit; reach: *The capsule impacted the moon the day after it was launched.* SYN: strike. **3** *Figurative.* to have a forceful or dramatic effect (on): *The Mayor noted that if the deep cuts have to be made they would "... impact heavily on the poor"* (New York Times).
—*v.i.* to strike against something with force; collide; crash: *"Think of that! I was examining material from a meteor that impacted on the moon!"* (New Yorker).
[< Latin *impactus* struck against, past participle of *impingere;* see etym. under **impinge**] **—im|pac′tion,** *n.* **—im|pac′tor,** *n.*

impact area, the area within which a bomb or missile lands.

impact crater, a crater produced by the impact of falling meteorites or of material ejected from volcanoes: *Evidently the maria are ... in many cases enormous impact craters ... that were filled with basaltic lava early in the history of the moon* (Scientific American).

im|pact|ed (im pak′tid), *adj.* **1** firmly wedged in place. **2** (of a tooth) wedged between the jawbone and another tooth. **3** closely packed; driven or pressed tightly together. **4** (of a fracture) driven together so that the parts of a broken bone become locked. **5** *U.S.* **a** financially burdened by the demand on public services, especially schools, caused by the sudden influx of many new residents into an area: *proposed that $1.5 billion in federal funds be made available to "racially impacted areas"* (Time). **b** designed to relieve an impacted area: *"impacted aid"—that is, Federal assistance to certain school districts to help them bear the impact of the children of Federal employees on their education costs* (New York Times).

im|pact|ite (im pak′tīt), *n.* a glassy kind of rock fragment formed as a result of the impact of a meteorite on the surface of the earth: *Impactites ... are usually discovered near huge craters* (New Scientist). [< *impact* + *ite*[1]]

impact statement, a review of the possible consequences of a proposed idea or project, especially one affecting the environment: *In the first draft of an impact statement on the transportation of radioactive materials near and through large, densely populated areas, the agency counted in ... New York City approximately 280,000 radioactive shipments* (New Yorker).

im|pair (im pãr′), *v.t.* to make worse; damage; harm; weaken: *Poor food impaired her health.* SYN: hurt. See syn. under **injure**. [< Old French *empeirer,* ultimately < Latin *in-* (intensive) + *pejor* worse] **—im|pair′er,** *n.*

im|pair|ment (im pãr′mənt), *n.* **1** the act of impairing. **2** the fact of being impaired. **3** injury; damage.

im|pa|la (im pä′lə), *n.* a swift, African antelope of medium size, usually yellow-brown in color. [< Zulu *i-mpālaj*]

im|pal|a|tion (im′pə lā′shən), *n.* the state of being impaled; impalement.

im|pale (im pāl′), *v.t.,* **-paled, -pal|ing. 1** to pierce through with anything pointed; fasten upon anything pointed: *The butterflies were impaled on small pins stuck in a sheet of cork.* SYN: transfix. **2** to torture or punish by thrusting upon a pointed stake. **3** *Figurative.* to enclose or surround with stakes; fence in. **4** *Figurative.* to make helpless as if by piercing: *The teacher impaled the noisy student with a stern look.* **5** *Heraldry.* to combine (two coats of arms) side by side on one shield. Also, **empale.** [probably < Middle French *empaler* < *en-* on, en-[1] + Old French *pal,* learned borrowing from Latin *pālus* stake] **—im|pal′er,** *n.*

im|pale|ment (im pāl′mənt), *n.* **1** the act of impaling or fact of being impaled. **2** an enclosure. **3** an enclosed space. **4** *Heraldry.* **a** the impaling of two coats of arms. **b** two coats of arms put side by side on one shield.

im|pal|pa|bil|i|ty (im pal′pə bil′ə tē), *n.* the quality or state of being impalpable.

im|pal|pa|ble (im pal′pə bəl), *adj.* **1** that cannot be felt by touching; intangible: *Color is impalpable. Sunlight and shadows are impalpable. A thread of a spider's web is so thin as to be almost impalpable.* **2** *Figurative.* very hard to understand: *The speaker's audience failed to perceive his impalpable distinctions.* **—im|pal′pa|bly,** *adv.*

im|pan|el (im pan′əl), *v.t.,* **-eled, -el|ing** or (*especially British*) **-elled, -el|ling. 1** to put on a list for duty on a jury. **2** to select (a jury) from such a list. Also, **empanel. —im|pan′el|ment,** *n.*

im|par|a|dise (im par′ə dīs), *v.t.,* **-dised, -dis|ing. 1** to put in or as if in paradise; make supremely happy. **2** to make a paradise of.

im|par|i|pin|nate (im par′ə pin′āt), *adj.* pinnate with an odd terminal leaflet; unevenly pinnate: *an imparipinnate leaf.* [< Latin *impar* uneven + English *pinnate*]

im|par|i|ty (im par′ə tē), *n.* lack of parity or equality; inequality.

im|park (im pärk′), *v.t.* **1** to shut up (animals) in a park, as for hunting. **2** to enclose (land) for a park; fence in. [< Old French *emparquer* < *en-*[1] + *parc* park]

im|part (im pärt′), *v.t.* **1** to give a share in; give: *The new furnishings imparted an air of newness to the old house.* SYN: bestow, convey. **2** to communicate; tell: *Impart the secret to me.* SYN: relate, reveal. See syn. under **communicate**. [< Middle French *impartir* to share, bestow, learned borrowing from Latin *impartīre* < *in-* in + *pars, partis* part] **—im|part′a|ble,** *adj.* **—im|part′er,** *n.*

im|par|ta|tion (im′pär tā′shən), *n.* the act of imparting; communication.

im|par|tial (im pär′shəl), *adj.* showing no more favor to one side than to the other; fair; just: *A judge should be impartial.* SYN: unbiased, unprejudiced, equitable. See syn. under **fair**[1]. **—im|par′tial|ly,** *adv.* **—im|par′tial|ness,** *n.*

im|par|ti|al|i|ty (im′pär shē al′ə tē), *n.* fairness; justice; not taking sides.

im|part|i|ble[1] (im pär′tə bəl), *adj.* that cannot be parted or divided; indivisible. [< Late Latin *impartībilis* < Latin *in-* not + *partībilis* partible]

im|part|i|ble[2] (im pär′tə bəl), *adj.* that can be imparted; communicable. [< *impart* + *-ible*]

im|part|i|bly (im pär′tə blē), *adv.* so as to be incapable of partition.

im|part|ment (im pärt′mənt), *n.* **1** the act of imparting. **2** something that is imparted; a communication; disclosure.

im|pass|a|bil|i|ty (im pas′ə bil′ə tē, -päs′-), *n.* the quality or condition of being impassable.

im|pass|a|ble (im pas′ə bəl, -päs′-), *adj.* not passable; so that one cannot go through, across, or along: *Snow and ice made the road impassable.* **—im|pass′a|ble|ness,** *n.* **—im|pass′a|bly,** *adv.*

im|passe (im pas′, im′pas), *n.* **1** a position from which there is no escape; deadlock: *The impasse was avoided by an agreement to divide the library* (London Times). **2** a road or way closed at one end; blind alley. [< French *impasse* < *in-* not, in- + Old French *passer* to pass]

im|pas|si|bil|i|ty (im pas′ə bil′ə tē), *n.* the quality or condition of being impassible.

im|pas|si|ble (im pas′ə bəl), *adj.* **1** unable to suffer or feel pain. **2** that cannot be harmed. **3** without feeling or emotion; impassive: *He was impassible before victory, before danger, before defeat* (Thackeray). SYN: indifferent, apathetic, passive. [< Old French *impassible,* learned borrowing from Latin *impassibilis* < *in-* not + *passibilis* passible, subject to suffering] **—im|pas′si|ble|ness,** *n.* **—im|pas′si|bly,** *adv.*

im|pas|sion (im pash′ən), *v.t.* to fill or affect

Pronunciation Key: hat, āge, cãre, fär; let, ēqual, tėrm; it, īce; hot, ōpen, ôrder; **oi**l, **ou**t; cup, pu̇t, rüle; **ch**ild; lo**ng**; **th**in; **ᴛʜ**en; **zh**, measure; **ə** represents **a** in about, **e** in taken, **i** in pencil, **o** in lemon, **u** in circus.

strongly with passion. [< Italian *impassionare* < *in-* in- + *passione* passion < Latin *passiō, -ōnis*]

im|pas|sioned (im pash′ənd), *adj.* full of strong feeling; stirring; rousing; ardent; emotional: *The general made an impassioned speech to his soldiers.* **SYN**: fervid. – **im|pas′sioned|ly,** *adv.* – **im-pas′sioned|ness,** *n.*

im|pas|sive (im pas′iv), *adj.* **1** without feeling or emotion; unmoved: *The Indians trained themselves to endure pain with impassive faces.* **SYN**: indifferent, apathetic, passive. **2** not feeling pain or injury; insensible: *The wounded soldier lay as impassive as if he were dead.* **3** incapable of being injured. – **im|pas′sive|ly,** *adv.* – **im|pas′sive-ness,** *n.*

im|pas|siv|i|ty (im′pa siv′ə tē), *n.* the quality or condition of being impassive; impassiveness.

im|paste (im pāst′), *v.t.,* **-past|ed, -past|ing. 1** to cover with or enclose in a paste or with something suggesting a paste. **2** to paint by laying on color thickly. **3** to make or form into a paste or crust. [< Italian *impastare* beplaster < *in-* in- + *pasta* paste, pastry < Late Latin *pasta*]

im|pas|to (im päs′tō), *n., pl.* **-tos,** *v.,* **-toed, -to-ing.** *Painting.* – *n.* **1** the laying on of paint thickly, often with a palette knife. **2** the paint so laid on. **3** a style or technique using impasto.
– ***v.t.*** to paint or decorate by laying on paint thickly; impaste: *Primitive in manner and thickly impastoed, Groom's paintings are nostalgic vignettes of ordinary life* (Time). [< Italian *impasto* < *impastare;* see etym. under **impaste**]

im|pa|tience (im pā′shəns), *n.* **1** lack of patience; being impatient: *Her impatience with the boy began to show in the teacher's voice.* **2** uneasiness and eagerness; restlessness: *In his impatience to start to school he forgot to take his homework.*

im|pa|ti|ens (im pā′shē enz), *n.* any plant of a genus of annuals or perennials, which includes the balsam, with pods that burst open and eject the seeds, and irregular flowers in which the calyx and corolla are colored alike; jewelweed; touch-me-not. [< New Latin *Impatiens* the genus name < Latin *impatiēns* impatient]

im|pa|tient (im pā′shənt), *adj.* **1** not patient; not willing to bear delay, opposition, pain, or bother: *He is impatient with his little sister.* **2** uneasy and eager; restless: *The horses were impatient to start in the race.* **3** showing lack of patience; cross: *an impatient answer.* **4** *Figurative.* characterized by, or attended with, impatience of delay: *the five or six impatient minutes before the dinner is quite ready* (Charles Lamb).
impatient of, unwilling to endure; not liking or wanting: *The most ignorant are ... most impatient of advice* (Sir Richard Steele).
[< Old French *impacient,* learned borrowing from Latin *impatiēns, -entis,* < *in-* not + *patiēns,* present participle of *patī* suffer, endure] – **im|pa′-tient|ly,** *adv.* – **im|pa′tient|ness,** *n.*

im|pav|id (im pav′id), *adj.* fearless; undaunted. [< Latin *impavidus* < *in-* not + *pavidus* fearful < *pavēre* be frightened] – **im|pav′id|ly,** *adv.*

im|pawn (im pôn′), *v.t.* to put in pawn; pledge as security.

im|peach (im pēch′), *v., n.* – ***v.t.*** **1** to accuse (a public officer) of wrong conduct during office before a competent tribunal: *The House of Representatives has the sole power to impeach an officer of the United States government* (Arthur E. Sutherland). *The only member of the Supreme Court to be impeached by the House was Samuel Chase, and he was acquitted by the Senate* (James Reston). **2** to charge with wrongdoing; accuse. **3** to cast doubt on; call in question: *to impeach a person's honor or accuracy.*
– ***n.*** impeachment: *It is war's prize to take all vantages; and ten to one is no impeach of valour* (Shakespeare).
[< Old French *empechier* to hinder < Late Latin *impedicāre* to fetter < Latin *in-* on + *pedica* shackle < *pēs, pedis* foot] – **im|peach′er,** *n.*

im|peach|a|bil|i|ty (im pē′chə bil′ə tē), *n.* the quality of being impeachable.

im|peach|a|ble (im pē′chə bəl), *adj.* **1** liable to be impeached. **2** likely to cause impeachment: *an impeachable offense.*

im|peach|ment (im pēch′mənt), *n.* **1** the act or process of impeaching: *Edmund G. Ross ... voted decisively against the impeachment of President Andrew Johnson* (Newsweek). **2** the condition of being impeached: *The verdict resulting from his impeachment destroyed his political career.*

im|pearl (im pėrl′), *v.t.* **1** to form into pearllike drops: *Dew-drops, which the sun Impearls on every leaf and every flower* (Milton). **2** to adorn with pearls or pearllike drops: *Proud be the rose, with rains and dews Her head impearling* (Wordsworth). **3** to make pearllike or pearly.

im|pec|ca|bil|i|ty (im pek′ə bil′ə tē), *n.* impeccable quality; faultlessness.

im|pec|ca|ble (im pek′ə bəl), *adj., n.* – ***adj.*** **1** faultless; irreproachable: *impeccable manners, an impeccable appearance. Sir John is impeccable, a paradigm of the gentleman-soldier* (Harper's). **2** not to be doubted; unimpeachable: *According to impeccable sources, the Naval Board met twenty-three times from January 1st to October 22nd* (Canadian Saturday Night). **3** not capable of or liable to sin; sinless.
– ***n.*** a person who is impeccable.
[< Latin *impeccābilis* < *in-* not + *peccāre* to sin] – **im|pec′ca|bly,** *adv.*

im|pec|cance (im pek′əns), *n.* the quality of being without or free from sin.

im|pec|cant (im pek′ənt), *adj.* not sinning; sinless; unerring.

im|pe|cu|ni|os|i|ty (im′pi kyü′nē os′ə tē), *n.* lack of money; poverty: *Impecuniosity was the caste mark of the demobilized soldier* (Samuel Hopkins Adams).

im|pe|cu|ni|ous (im′pi kyü′nē əs), *adj.* having little or no money; penniless; poor: *Certainly an impecunious Subaltern was not a catch* (Rudyard Kipling). **SYN**: indigent. [< *im-*[1] not + Latin *pecūniōsus* rich < *pecūnia* money, property < *pecū* head of cattle] – **im′pe|cu′ni|ous|ly,** *adv.* – **im′pe|cu′ni|ous|ness,** *n.*

im|ped|ance (im pē′dəns), *n.* **1** *Electricity.* **a** the apparent resistance in an alternating-current circuit, made up of two components, reactance and true or ohmic resistance. **b** the square root of the sum of the squares of the true resistance and the difference between the inductive reactance and the capacitive reactance. **2** *Physics.* the ratio of the pressure in a sound wave to the product of the particle velocity and the area of a cross section of the wave at a given point.

im|pede (im pēd′), *v.t.,* **-ped|ed, -ped|ing.** to stand in the way of; hinder; obstruct: *The deep snow impeded travel.* **SYN**: hamper, retard. See syn. under **prevent.** [< Latin *impedīre* < *in-* on + *pēs, pedis* foot] – **im|ped′er,** *n.*

im|pe|di|ent (im pē′dē ənt), *adj., n.* – ***adj.*** impeding; hindering.
– ***n.*** a thing that impedes or hinders.

im|ped|i|ment (im ped′ə mənt), *n.* **1** a hindrance; obstruction: *As an impediment to South American tourism, the expensiveness of getting to some places is being given serious study* (Newsweek). **2** some physical defect, especially a defect in speech: *Stuttering is a speech impediment. They bring unto him one that was deaf, and had an impediment in his speech* (Mark 7:32). **3** *Law.* a bar to the making of a valid marriage contract. [< Latin *impedīmentum* < *impedīre;* see etym. under **impede**]

im|ped|i|men|ta (im ped′ə men′tə), *n.pl.* **1** things that impede or encumber progress, such as baggage: *The impedimenta of modern science was rising about him everywhere he went* (New Scientist). **2** the military supplies carried along with an army. **3** *Law.* obstacles; hindrances. [< Latin *impedīmenta,* plural of *impedīmentum* impediment]

im|ped|i|men|tal (im ped′ə men′təl), *adj.* like an impediment; impeditive.

im|ped|i|men|ta|ry (im ped′ə men′tər ē), *adj.* = impedimental.

im|ped|i|tive (im ped′ə tiv), *adj.* tending to impede; obstructive; hindering.

im|pel (im pel′), *v.t.,* **-pelled, -pel|ling. 1** to drive or force; cause: *The cold impelled her to go indoors. Hunger impelled the lazy man to work. I cannot tell what impels me to speak thus boldly* (Scott). **SYN**: See syn. under **compel. 2** to cause to move; drive forward; push along: *The wind impelled the boat toward the shore. Projectiles continue in their motions, so far as they are not ... impelled downward by the force of gravity* (Science News Letter). *The wave behind impels the wave before* (John Dryden). [< Latin *impellere* < *in-* on + *pellere* to push]

im|pel|lent (im pel′ənt), *adj., n.* – ***adj.*** that impels; impelling.
– ***n.*** a thing that impels or urges; impelling force, agent, body, or action.

im|pel|ler (im pel′ər), *n.* **1** a person or thing that impels. **2** the rotating blades of a centrifugal pump or blower.

im|pend (im pend′), *v.i.* **1** to be likely to happen soon; be about to happen; be near: *Black clouds are signs that a storm impends. When war impends, wise men try to prevent it.* **2** to hang threateningly; hang: *Great boulders impended over the narrow mountain path.* (*Figurative.*) *Destruction sure o'er all your heads impends* (Alexander Pope). [< Latin *impendēre* < *in-* over, on + *pendēre* hang]

im|pend|ent (im pen′dənt), *adj.* = impending.

im|pend|ing (im pen′ding), *adj.* **1** likely to happen soon; threatening; about to occur: *an impending war. There were symptoms of an impending storm* (Washington Irving). **SYN**: See syn. under **imminent. 2** overhanging: *Above him were impending cliffs. Aquiline his nose, And overbuilt with most impending brows* (William Cowper).

im|pen|e|tra|bil|i|ty (im pen′ə trə bil′ə tē), *n.* **1** the quality or condition of being impenetrable: *Outside, the wind spiraled over an airfield that tapered to white impenetrability* (Philip Wylie). **2** *Physics.* the property of matter that prevents two bodies from occupying the same space at the same time.

im|pen|e|tra|ble (im pen′ə trə bəl), *adj.* **1** that cannot be entered, pierced, or passed: *The thorny branches made a thick, impenetrable hedge. A thick sheet of steel is impenetrable by an ordinary bullet. The lowlands presented early explorers with apparently impenetrable jungle* (Atlantic). **2** *Figurative.* that cannot be seen into or understood; impossible to explain or understand; inscrutable: *His sudden disappearance was hidden in an impenetrable mystery.* **3** *Figurative.* not open to ideas or influences: *an impenetrable mind.* **4** *Physics.* (of a body) excluding all other bodies from the space it occupies. – **im|pen′e-tra|ble|ness,** *n.* – **im|pen′e|tra|bly,** *adv.*

im|pen|e|trate (im pen′ə trāt), *v.t.,* **-trat|ed, -trat-|ing.** to penetrate within; permeate. – **im|pen′e-tra′tion,** *n.*

im|pen|i|tence (im pen′ə təns), *n.* lack of any sorrow or regret for doing wrong.

im|pen|i|tent (im pen′ə tənt), *adj., n.* – ***adj.*** not penitent; feeling no sorrow or regret for having done wrong: *Her anger was directed with almost equal vehemence against Mr. Reeve for his having published "such an abominable book." ... Mr. Reeve, however, was impenitent* (Lytton Strachey).
– ***n.*** an impenitent person. – **im|pen′i|tent|ly,** *adv.*

im|pen|nate (im pen′āt), *adj.* **1** featherless. **2** wingless. **3** having small wings covered with scalelike feathers, as the penguins.

imper., imperative.

im|per|a|tive (im per′ə tiv), *adj., n.* – ***adj.*** **1** not to be avoided; that must be done; urgent; necessary: *It is imperative that this very sick child stay in bed.* **2** expressing a command, request, or warning; commanding: *an imperative statement.* **3** *Grammar.* having to do with a verb form that expresses a command, request, or warning. "Go!" and "stop, look, listen!" are in the imperative mood.
– ***n.*** **1** something imperative; command: *The great imperative is "Love thy neighbor as thyself."* **2** *Grammar.* **a** the imperative mood. **b** a verb form that expresses a command, request, or warning. In "Try to be quiet" and "Make up your mind," *try* and *make* are imperatives. A verb in the imperative mood has the form of the infinitive.
[< Latin *imperātīvus* < *imperāre* to command < *in-* in + *parāre* make ready, prepare] – **im|per′a-tive|ly,** *adv.* – **im|per′a|tive|ness,** *n.*

im|pe|ra|tor (im′pə rā′tər), *n.* **1** an absolute or supreme ruler. **2** the Roman emperor. **3** the title given to a victorious Roman military commander. [< Latin *imperātor* < *imperāre.* Compare etym. under **emperor.**]

im|per|a|to|ri|al (im per′ə tôr′ē əl, -tōr′-), *adj.* imperial; commanding. – **im|per′a|to′ri|al|ly,** *adv.*

im|per|cep|ti|bil|i|ty (im′pər sep′tə bil′ə tē), *n.* the quality or state of being imperceptible.

im|per|cep|ti|ble (im′pər sep′tə bəl), *adj.* **1** very slight; gradual: *The road took an imperceptible rise over the low hill.* **2** that cannot be perceived or felt; subtle or indistinct: *There were imperceptible differences between the original painting and the copy. The process by which this result was reached had been so gradual as to be almost imperceptible* (Lytton Strachey). – **im′per-cep′ti|ble|ness,** *n.* – **im′per|cep′ti|bly,** *adv.*

im|per|cep|tive (im′pər sep′tiv), *adj.* not perceptive; lacking perception: *About the theatre he is equally unfair, or imperceptive* (New Statesman). – **im′per|cep′tive|ness,** *n.*

im|per|cep|tiv|i|ty (im′pər sep tiv′ə tē), *n.* the quality of being imperceptive.

im|per|cip|i|ence (im′pər sip′ē əns), *n.* lack of perception: *The committee men were persuaded to let Lew adjudicate the bass solo competition which he did with an impercipience that still inhibits a fair belt of singers* (Punch).

im|per|cip|i|ent (im′pər sip′ē ənt), *adj.* lacking perception; imperceptive: *He [Whistler] had been agitated by the strangely impercipient criticisms of his work in the London and Parisian press* (Harper's).

imperf., imperfect.

im|per|fect (im pėr′fikt), *adj., n.* – ***adj.*** **1** not perfect; having some defect or fault: *A crack in the cup made it imperfect.* **2** not complete; lacking some part: *The imperfect set of dominoes had lost several pieces over the years.* **3** *Grammar.* expressing incompleted, continued, or customary action. English has no imperfect tense, but some constructions, such as *was studying* and *used to study* are like the imperfect verbs of other lan-

guages. 4 *Law.* incomplete; unenforceable: *an imperfect law.* 5 *Music.* **a** denoting a major or minor third or sixth. **b** (of an interval) diminished.
—*n.* *Grammar.* the imperfect tense or verb form.
—im|per'fect|ly, *adv.* **—im|per'fect|ness,** *n.*

imperfect fungus, any fungus of a group that forms only asexual spores or conidia.

im|per|fect|i|bil|i|ty (im'pər fek'tə bil'ə tē), *n.* inability to become or be made perfect: *... the stubborn imperfectibility of human institutions* (Manchester Guardian Weekly).

im|per|fect|i|ble (im'pər fek'tə bəl), *adj.* that cannot reach perfection: *This theory of limits is part of the Christian residue in Cozzens' thought, i.e., that man is flawed and imperfectible* (Time).

im|per|fec|tion (im'pər fek'shən), *n.* **1** lack of perfection; imperfect condition or character: *The imperfection of language makes some ideas hard to express.* **2** a fault; defect: *There are many imperfections in the old painting where the paint has flaked off.*

im|per|fec|tive (im'pər fek'tiv), *adj., n. Grammar.* **—*adj.*** denoting an aspect of the verb, especially in Slavic languages, that expresses action not completed.
—*n.* **1** the imperfective aspect. **2** a verb form in this aspect.

im|per|fo|rate (im pėr'fər it, -fə rāt), *adj., n.* **—*adj.*** **1** not pierced through with holes. **2** (of stamps) not separated from other stamps by perforations; having the margins whole.
—*n.* an imperforate stamp.

im|pe|ri|al** (im pir'ē əl), *adj., n.* **—*adj. **1** of or having to do with an empire or its ruler: *Imperial Caesar dead and turned to clay* (Keith Preston). **2** of or having to do with the rule or authority of one country over other countries and colonies: *The imperial power of Great Britain in India ended after World War II.* **3** *Figurative.* having the rank of an emperor; supreme in authority: *the imperial power of the state over its citizens.* **4** *Figurative.* very fine or grand; supreme; majestic; magnificent: *The Lily's height bespoke command—A fair imperial flow'r* (William Cowper). **5** of larger size or better quality. **6** according to the former British standard of weights and measures: *The Hodgson committee reported that the metric system was clearly better than the imperial system* (New Scientist).
—*n.* **1** a very small beard growing beneath the lower lip. Napoleon III wore such a beard. **2** a size of paper, 23 by 31 inches (in England 22 by 30 inches). **3** an article of special size or quality, especially as a trade name. **4** a former Russian gold coin, worth 10 rubles. **5a** the roof of a closed carriage. **b** a case or trunk for luggage carried there: *The imperials were packed, and the post-chariot was at the door* (Thomas Love Peacock).
[< Old French *imperial,* learned borrowing from Latin *imperiālis* < *imperium* empire < *imperāre* to command; see etym. under **imperative**] **—im|pe'ri|al|ly,** *adv.* **—im|pe'ri|al|ness,** *n.*

***imperial**
n., definition 1

Im|pe|ri|al (im pir'ē əl), *n.* **1** a supporter of the emperor of the Holy Roman Empire. **2** one of his soldiers.

imperial bushel, the British bushel, equal to 2,219.36 cubic inches or 36.3659 liters.

imperial eagle, a large eagle of Spain and eastern Europe. The imperial eagle lives near plains and marshes and has some white feathers at the shoulders.

***imperial gallon,** the British gallon, equal to about 277.420 cubic inches or 4.546 liters.

***imperial gallon**

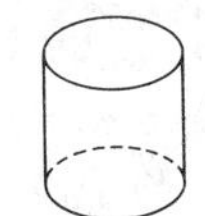

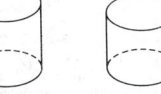

1 imperial gallon = 277.420 cu. in. 1 U.S. gallon = 231 cu. in. 1 liter = 61.02 cu. in.

im|pe|ri|al|ism (im pir'ē ə liz'əm), *n.* **1** the policy of extending the rule or authority of one country over other countries and colonies: *The active imperialism of today is communist* (Newsweek). **2** an imperial system of government. **3** the act or fact of dominating another nation's economic, political, and even military structure without actually taking governmental control. **4** support of imperial interests.

im|pe|ri|al|ist (im pir'ē ə list), *n., adj.* **—*n.*** a person who favors imperialism. **—*adj.*** = imperialistic.

im|pe|ri|al|is|tic (im pir'ē ə lis'tik), *adj.* **1** of imperialism or imperialists. **2** favoring imperialism. **—im|pe'ri|al|is'ti|cal|ly,** *adv.*

im|pe|ri|al|ize (im pir'ē ə līz), *v.t.,* **-ized, -iz|ing.** to make imperial; provide with imperial character or form. **—im|pe'ri|al|i|za'tion,** *n.*

imperial moth, a large, yellow American moth, with brown bands.

imperial presidency, the Presidency of the United States viewed as exceeding in power and authority the executive role provided by the Constitution: *One area in which the imperial presidency is as regal as ever is the matter of international airline routes: by law the President can bestow on any airline of his choice the right to fly between any American city and any foreign one and he need not bother to state a reason* (Time). [coined by Arthur M. Schlesinger, Jr., born 1917, American historian] **—imperial president.**

imperial quart, the British quart, one fourth of an imperial gallon.

im|per|il (im per'əl), *v.t.,* **-iled, -il|ing** or (*especially British*) **-illed, -il|ling.** to put in danger: *He imperiled their lives by standing up and rocking the rowboat.* **SYN:** endanger, jeopardize.

im|per|il|ment (im per'əl mənt), *n.* **1** the act of imperiling. **2** the state of being imperiled.

im|pe|ri|ous (im pir'ē əs), *adj.* **1** haughty or arrogant; domineering; overbearing: *The nobles treated the common people in an imperious way, looking down on them and ordering them around.* **SYN:** dictatorial. **2** not to be avoided; imperative; necessary; urgent: *They worked to satisfy the imperious demands of hunger.* **3** *Obsolete.* imperial: *imperious Caesar, dead and turn'd to clay* (Shakespeare). [< Latin *imperiōsus* commanding < *imperium* empire < *imperāre* to command; see etym. under **imperative**] **—im|pe'ri|ous|ly,** *adv.* **—im|pe'ri-ous|ness,** *n.*

im|per|ish|a|bil|i|ty (im per'i shə bil'ə tē), *n.* the condition of being imperishable; enduring quality.

im|per|ish|a|ble (im per'i shə bəl), *adj.* not perishable; unable to be destroyed; lasting forever; enduring; indestructible: *But in contentment I still feel the need of some imperishable bliss* (Wallace Stevens). **SYN:** immortal. **—im|per'ish|a|ble|ness,** *n.* **—im|per'ish|a|bly,** *adv.*

im|pe|ri|um (im pir'ē əm), *n., pl.* **-pe|ri|a** (-pir'ē ə). **1** command; supreme power; empire. **2** *Law.* the right to use the force of the state to enforce the law. [< Latin *imperium* empire < *imperāre* to command; see etym. under **imperative**]

im|per|ma|nence (im pėr'mə nəns), *n.* the fact or condition of being impermanent.

im|per|ma|nen|cy (im pėr'mə nən sē), *n.* = impermanence.

im|per|ma|nent (im pėr'mə nənt), *adj.* not lasting; temporary: *a policy entirely divorced from natural self-interest is equally unsound and impermanent* (Harper's). **—im|per'ma|nent|ly,** *adv.*

im|per|me|a|bil|i|ty (im pėr'mē ə bil'ə tē), *n.* impermeable quality or condition.

im|per|me|a|ble (im pėr'mē ə bəl), *adj.* **1** that cannot be permeated; impassable: *Charing Cross ... became absolutely impermeable* (Hawthorne). **2** not permitting the passage of water, gas, or other fluid, through the pores, interstices, or membranes: *Gas masks are impermeable only to certain kinds of gas.* **—im|per'me|a|ble|ness,** *n.* **—im|per'me|a|bly,** *adv.*

im|per|mis|si|bil|i|ty (im'pər mis'ə bil'ə tē), *n.* the condition of being impermissible: *the impermissibility of resorting to extreme measures* (Time).

im|per|mis|si|ble (im'pər mis'ə bəl), *adj.* not permissible *But there is that line between the permissible and the impermissible in demagoguery* (Harper's). **—im'per|mis'si|bly,** *adv.*

im|per|son|al (im pėr'sə nəl, -pėrs'nəl), *adj., n.* **—*adj.*** **1** referring to all or any persons, not to any special one: *The teacher's criticism of the class was impersonal. History is usually written from an impersonal point of view.* **2** having no existence as a person: *Electricity is an impersonal force.* **3** (of a verb) not requiring a subject or having indefinite *it* as subject. *Example: rained* in "It rained yesterday," or Latin *pluit,* "(it) rains." **—*n.*** **1** an impersonal thing. **2** *Grammar.* impersonal verb. [< Late Latin *impersōnālis* having no person as (grammatical) subject < Latin *in-* not + *persōnālis* personal] **—im|per'son|al|ly,** *adv.*

im|per|son|al|i|ty (im pėr'sə nal'ə tē), *n., pl.* **-ties.** **1** impersonal character; absence of personal quality: *the question of whether the modern state does not have a natural predilection for grim impersonality and dreary standardization* (Wall Street Journal). **2** an impersonal thing, force, etc.

im|per|son|al|i|za|tion (im pėr'sə nə lə zā'shən), *n.* **1** the act or process of making impersonal: *Dewey, the Vermont farm boy, had watched the same process of impersonalization take place with the industrialization and urbanization of the United States* (George Simpson). **2** an impersonalized condition or form.

im|per|son|al|ize (im pėr'sə nə līz), *v.t.,* **-ized, -iz|ing.** to make impersonal.

im|per|son|ate (im pėr'sə nāt), *v.,* **-at|ed, -at|ing,** *adj.* **—*v.t.*** **1** to play the part of: *He impersonated Long John Silver when we gave "Treasure Island" as a play.* **2** to pretend to be; mimic the voice, appearance, and manners of: *He impersonated well-known radio announcers to amuse us.* **3** to represent in personal form; personify; typify: *To many people, Daniel Boone impersonates the American pioneer spirit.*
—*adj.* embodied in a person; given a personality: *Love impersonate* (Keats).
[< *im-*[2] + *person* + *-ate*[1]]

im|per|son|a|tion (im pėr'sə nā'shən), *n.* **1** the act of impersonating: *The entertainer gave an impersonation of a famous movie actor.* **2** the fact or condition of being impersonated. **3** a representation; personification; type: *The face of a pretty, laughing girl ... the very impersonation of good-humour and blooming beauty* (Dickens).

im|per|son|a|tor (im pėr'sə nā'tər), *n.* **1** a person who pretends to be someone else. **2** an actor who impersonates particular types of persons.

im|per|ti|nence (im pėr'tə nəns), *n.* **1** impertinent quality; boldness and rudeness; impudence; insolence: *Older people are sometimes angered to see impertinence in the young.* **2** an impertinent act or speech: *The boy's bold impertinence embarrassed the class and his teacher.* **3** lack of pertinence; irrelevance.

im|per|ti|nen|cy (im pėr'tə nən sē), *n., pl.* **-cies.** = impertinence.

im|per|ti|nent (im pėr'tə nənt), *adj.* **1** rudely bold; saucy; impudent; insolent: *The girl made an impertinent reply that angered her mother.* **2** not pertinent; not to the point; out of place: *His impertinent remarks wasted valuable time.* **SYN:** inappropriate, incongruous, irrelevant. [< Latin *impertinēns, -entis* not belonging < *in-* not + *pertinēns* pertinent] **—im|per'ti|nent|ly,** *adv.*
—*Syn.* **1 Impertinent, impudent, saucy** mean showing lack of proper respect. **Impertinent** means showing lack of respect for others' privacy or rights, by taking too much interest in what is not one's business or too many liberties with those deserving respect: *Talking back to older people is impertinent.* **Impudent** adds the idea of shamelessness and defiance: *The impudent boy made faces at the teacher.* **Saucy** suggests a disrespectful attitude shown by light and flippant manner or speech: *The saucy girl laughed when her father scolded her.*

im|per|turb|a|bil|i|ty (im'pər tėr'bə bil'ə tē), *n.* the quality of being imperturbable; calmness: *An imperturbability which passed ... for courage* (Thomas Carlyle).

im|per|turb|a|ble (im'pər tėr'bə bəl), *adj.* not easily excited or disturbed; calm: *A man ... Cool, and quite English, imperturbable* (Byron). **—im'per|turb'a|ble|ness,** *n.* **—im'per|turb'a|bly,** *adv.*

im|per|vi|a|ble (im pėr'vē ə bəl), *adj.* impervious; impermeable.

im|per|vi|ous (im pėr'vē əs), *adj.* **1** having no way through; not letting things pass through; allowing no passage: *A raincoat made of rubber is impervious to rain.* **SYN:** impermeable. **2** *Figurative.* not open to argument, suggestions, etc.: *Because he was impervious to our hints, we finally told him it was time to go.* [< Latin *impervius* (with English *-ous*) < *in-* not + *pervius* pervious] **—im|per'vi|ous|ly,** *adv.* **—imper'vi|ous|ness,** *n.*

im|pe|tig|i|nous (im'pə tij'ə nəs), *adj.* of, having to do with, or like impetigo.

im|pe|ti|go (im'pə tī'gō), *n.* an infectious skin disease, characterized by pimples of pus, and often affecting children. [< Latin *impetīgō, -inis* < *impetere* to attack < *in-* at + *petere* aim for]

im|pe|trate (im'pə trāt), *v.t.,* **-trat|ed, -trat|ing.** **1** to request earnestly; entreat: *a slight testimonial, sir, which I thought fit to impetrate from that worthy nobleman* (Scott). **2** to obtain by request or entreaty; procure. [< Latin *impetrāre* (with English *-ate*[1]) obtain, procure < *in-* + *patrāre* achieve] **—im|pe|tra'tion,** *n.*

im|pet|u|os|i|ty (im pech'ů os'ə tē), *n., pl.* **-ties.** **1** sudden or rash energy; hastiness; ardor: *The impetuosity of his temper got him into many arguments.* **2** rushing force or violence: *The impetuosity of the flood swept all before it.* **3** an impetuous action: *The king's impetuosities almost caused a war.*

im|pet|u|ous (im pech'ů əs), *adj.* **1** acting hastily,

Pronunciation Key: hat, āge, cãre, fär; let, ēqual, tėrm; it, īce; hot, ōpen, ôrder; oil, out; cup, půt, rüle; child; long; thin; ᴛʜen; zh, measure; ə represents **a** in about, **e** in taken, **i** in pencil, **o** in lemon, **u** in circus.

rashly, or with sudden feeling; hasty: *Boys are more impetuous than men.* **SYN**: ardent. **2** moving with great force or speed: *The dam broke and an impetuous torrent of water swept away the town.* [< Late Latin *impetuōsus* < Latin *impetus, -ūs* an attack < *impetere* < *in-* in + *petere* attack, aim for] — **im|pet'u|ous|ly**, *adv.* — **im|pet'u|ous|ness**, *n.*

im|pe|tus (im'pə təs), *n., pl.* **-tus|es**. **1** the force with which a moving body tends to maintain its velocity and overcome resistance: *the impetus of a moving automobile. Anything that can stop easily has little impetus.* **SYN**: momentum. **2** a driving force; cause of action or effort; incentive: *His ambition was an impetus to work for success.* **SYN**: stimulus, impulse. [< Latin *impetus;* see etym. under **impetuous**]

im|pi (im'pē), *n., pl.* **-pies**. a group of Kaffir warriors: *We would advance on a colony in a semicircle like a Zulu impi* (V. Pohl). [< Zulu *impi*]

im|pic|ture (im pik'chər), *v.t.,* **-tured**, **-tur|ing**. to represent as if in a picture.

im|pi|e|ty (im pī'ə tē), *n., pl.* **-ties**. **1** lack of piety or reverence for God; wickedness. **2** lack of dutifulness or respect. **3** an impious act: *To reveal a desire for money is—Allah defend us!—an impiety* (Harper's).

im|pinge (im pinj'), *v.,* **-pinged**, **-ping|ing**. — ***v.i.*** **1** to hit; strike; dash: *Rays of light impinge on the eye.* **2** to encroach; infringe: *Heaven forbid that I should do aught that might ... impinge upon the right of my kinsman* (Scott).
— ***v.t.*** to encroach upon: *The hippies ... impinge the security of my new-found tower* (Leonard Baskin).
[< Latin *impingere* < *in-* on + *pangere* to strike] — **im|ping'er**, *n.* — **im|pinge'ment**, *n.*

im|pi|ous (im pī'əs, im'pē-), *adj.* not pious; not having or not showing reverence for God; wicked; profane. — **im|pi'ous|ly**, *adv.* — **im|pi'ous|ness**, *n.*

imp|ish (im'pish), *adj.* of an imp; like an imp; mischievous. — **imp'ish|ly**, *adv.* — **imp'ish|ness**, *n.*

im|pla|ca|bil|i|ty (im plā'kə bil'ə tē, -plak'ə-), *n.* the quality of being implacable.

im|pla|ca|ble (im plā'kə bəl, -plak'ə-), *adj.* unable to be appeased; refusing to be reconciled; unyielding: *an implacable hatred. He was constantly persecuted by his implacable enemies.* **SYN**: relentless, unforgiving, inexorable. — **im|pla'ca|ble|ness**, *n.* — **im|pla'ca|bly**, *adv.*

im|place (im plās'), *v.t.,* **-placed**, **-plac|ing**. = emplace.

im|pla|cen|tal (im'plə sen'təl), *adj., n.* — ***adj.*** (of lower mammals) having no placenta.
— ***n.*** an implacental animal.

im|plant (*v.* im plant', -plänt'; *n.* im'plant, -plänt), *v., n.* — ***v.t.*** **1** to instill; fix deeply: *A good teacher implants high ideals in children.* **2** to insert: *a steel tube implanted in a socket. Teeth are implanted in the jaw.* **3** to set in the ground; plant. **4** to graft or set (a piece of tissue, an organ, or any living or artificial substance) into the body: *Investigations of alloys implanted in the body for purposes of prosthesis ...* (Norbert D. Greene).
— ***v.i.*** to become implanted: *The graft failed to implant.*
— ***n.*** **1** a piece of tissue, an organ, or any living or artificial substance grafted into the body: *According to the patent, the plastics, called hydrogels, are suitable for body implants* (New York Times). **2** a small radioactive tube or needle inserted in the body, especially to treat cancer.
[< *im-*[2] in + *plant,* verb] — **im|plant'er**, *n.*

im|plant|a|ble (im plan'tə bəl, -plän'-), *adj.* that can be implanted: *Experiences indicate that total cardiac replacement with an artificial, implantable heart is possible* (Michael E. DeBakey).

im|plan|ta|tion (im'plan tā'shən), *n.* **1** the act or process of implanting. **2** the state of being implanted. **3** the introduction of tissue or an organ or any living or artificial substance into the body. **4** the passage of cells from one part of the body to another. **5** the process in which an embryo becomes attached for nourishment to the uterine wall in higher mammals, or to the yolk in other vertebrates.

im|plau|si|bil|i|ty (im plô'zə bil'ə tē), *n., pl.* **-ties**. **1** implausible quality: *The show relied too much on the elements of implausibility and coincidence* (New York Times). **2** an implausible thing: *Among other implausibilities: a psychedelic-balletic version of Alice in Wonderland* (Time).

im|plau|si|ble (im plô'zə bəl), *adj.* not plausible; not having the appearance of truth or reason. — **im|plau'si|bly**, *adv.*

im|pleach (im plēch'), *v.t. Poetic.* interweave.

im|plead (im plēd'), *v.t., v.i.* **1** to sue in a court of law. **2** to accuse; impeach. **3** to plead (a suit). [< Anglo-French *empleder* make a (legal) plea against, Old French *empleidier,* or *emplaidier* < *em-* in + *plaidier* to plead] — **im|plead'a|ble**, *adj.*

im|ple|ment (*n.* im'plə mənt; *v.* im'plə ment), *n., v.* — ***n.*** **1a** a useful piece of equipment; tool; instrument; utensil. Plows and threshing machines are farm implements. A pail, an ax, a shovel, and a broom are implements. **SYN**: See syn. under **tool**. **b** a person or agent considered as an instrument or tool: *This old man was a most useful implement to us everywhere* (Daniel Defoe). **2** *Scottish.* fulfillment, performance, or execution, as of a contract.
— ***v.t.*** **1** to provide with implements or other means. **2** to provide the power and authority necessary to accomplish or put (something) into effect: *to implement an order. It can implement bonds of friendship, and respect, by ties that transcend language and semantics* (Saturday Review). **3** to carry out; get done: *Do not undertake a project unless you can implement it.*
[< Late Latin *implēmentum* (literally) that which fills (a need) < Latin *implēre* to fill < *in-* in + *-plēre* to fill] — **im'ple|men|ta'tion**, *n.* — **im'ple|ment|er**, *n.*

im|ple|men|tal (im'plə men'təl), *adj.* acting or used as an implement; serving to implement.

im|ple|tion (im plē'shən), *n.* **1** the act of filling. **2** the state of being filled. [< Late Latin *implētiō, -ōnis* < *implēre;* see etym. under **implement**]

im|pli|cate (im'plə kāt), *v.t.,* **-cat|ed**, **-cat|ing**. **1** to show to have a part or to be connected; involve: *The thief's confession implicated the two other men who had helped him steal. The disease may implicate various organs.* **SYN**: See syn. under **involve**. **2** = imply. **3** to fold or twist together; entangle: *The meeting boughs and implicated leaves Wove twilight o'er the Poet's path* (Shelley). [< Latin *implicāre* (with English *-ate*[1]) < *in-* in + *plicāre* to fold. See etym. of doublets **employ**, **imply**.]

im|pli|ca|tion (im'plə kā'shən), *n.* **1** the act of implying or state of being implied. **2** something implied; indirect suggestion; hint: *She did not actually refuse, but the way she frowned was an implication of her unwillingness. There was no implication of dishonesty in his failure in business.* **3** an implicating or a being implicated.

im|pli|ca|tive (im'plə kā'tiv), *adj.* tending to implicate or imply; characterized by or involving implication. — **im'pli|ca'tive|ly**, *adv.*

im|plic|it (im plis'it), *adj.* **1** meant, but not clearly expressed or distinctly stated; implied: *He gave us implicit consent to take the apples, for he smiled when he saw us do it. Her silence gave implicit consent.* **SYN**: tacit. **2** without doubting, hesitating, or asking questions; absolute: *He has implicit confidence in his friends. A soldier must give implicit obedience to his officers.* **SYN**: unquestioning, unreserved. **3** involved as a necessary part or condition; contained (in): *The oak tree is implicit in the acorn.* **4** *Psychology.* involving activity that cannot easily be observed, such as a glandular or muscular reaction: *implicit behavior, an implicit response.* **5** *Obsolete.* entangled; entwined: *Th' humble shrub, And bush with frizzled hair implicit* (Milton). [< Latin *implicitus,* variant past participle of *implicāre;* see etym. under **implicate**] — **im|plic'it|ness**, *n.*

im|plic|it|ly (im plis'it lē), *adv.* **1** = unquestioningly. **2** by implication.

im|plied (im plīd'), *adj.* involved, indicated, suggested, or understood without express statement: *an implied rebuke.* — **im|pli'ed|ly**, *adv.*

im|plied-con|sent (im plīd'kən sent'), *n.* a legal principle that a person assumes responsibility or willingness to do something if he accepts a license, credit card, franchise, or other privilege. A person who accepts a driver's license gives implied-consent to take a chemical test for intoxication whenever asked to by proper authority.

implied warranty, a warranty not expressed in a contract, but resulting from the making of the contract, as in the sale of something in which the seller gives an implied warranty that he is the legal owner.

im|plode (im plōd'), *v.,* **-plod|ed**, **-plod|ing**. — ***v.i.*** to burst inward: *Scratched tubes may implode more easily* (Occupational Health Newsletter).
— ***v.t.*** *Phonetics.* to pronounce by implosion.
[< *im-*[2] in + *-plode,* as in *explode*]

im|plore (im plôr', -plōr'), *v.,* **-plored**, **-plor|ing**. — ***v.t.*** **1** to beg earnestly for: *The prisoner implored pardon.* **SYN**: beseech, entreat. See syn. under **beg**. **2** to beg (a person to do something): *She implored her mother to give permission for her to go on the trip.*
— ***v.i.*** to beg earnestly; make urgent supplication.
[< Latin *implōrāre* (originally) invoke with weeping < *in-* toward + *plōrāre* to cry] — **im'plo|ra'tion**, *n.* — **im|plor'er**, *n.*

im|plor|ing (im plôr'ing, -plōr'-), *adj.* that implores; beseeching; supplicatory. — **im|plor'ing|ly**, *adv.* — **im|plor'ing|ness**, *n.*

im|plo|sion (im plō'zhən), *n.* **1** the action of bursting inward: *the implosion of a vacuum tube from external pressure;* (*Figurative.*) *an implosion of anger, an implosion caused by the sudden convergence of many cultures.* **2** *Phonetics.* **a** the closure at the beginning of the articulation of a stop, as in *p, t, k.* **b** the inrush of air at the end of the articulation of a suction stop. [< *im-*[2] in + *-plosion,* as in *explosion*]

im|plo|sive (im plō'siv), *adj., n.* — ***adj.*** of or involving implosion: *An implosive technique ... holds promise that the attainment of usable million-gauss fields may be near* (Scientific American).
— ***n.*** an implosive articulation or sound. — **im|plo'sive|ly**, *adv.*

im|plu|vi|um (im plü'vē əm), *n., pl.* **-vi|a** (-vē ə). (in ancient Roman houses) a rectangular basin or tank in the middle of the atrium or hall, for receiving the rain water from an opening in the roof above. [< Latin *impluvium* < *impluere* rain into < *in-* into + *pluere* to rain]

im|ply (im plī'), *v.t.,* **-plied**, **-ply|ing**. **1** to mean (a thing) without saying it outright; express in an indirect way; suggest: *Silence often implies consent. Mother's smile implied that she had forgiven us.* **SYN**: insinuate. **2** to involve as a necessary part or condition: *Speech implies a speaker.* **3** to signify; mean. **4** *Obsolete.* to entangle; involve: *Striving to loose the knott ... Himself in streighter bandes too rash implyes* (Edmund Spenser). [< Old French *emplier* involve, put (in) < Latin *implicāre.* See etym. of doublets **employ**, **implicate**.]

► **Imply, infer.** Formerly it was held that a writer or speaker *implies* something in his words or manner; a reader or listener *infers* something from what he reads, sees, or hears: *She implied by the look in her eyes that she did not intend to keep the appointment. We inferred from the principal's announcement that he knew who had broken the window.* Now the distinction has broken down widely in speech and *infer* has been used so much with the meaning of *imply* that that is given as a secondary sense of the word in dictionaries, though many writers and commentators on language deplore this secondary sense.

im|po|lite (im'pə līt'), *adj.* not polite; having or showing bad manners; rude; discourteous. **SYN**: disrespectful. — **im'po|lite'ly**, *adv.* — **im'po|lite'ness**, *n.*

im|pol|i|tic (im pol'ə tik), *adj.* not politic; not expedient; not judicious; unwise: *It is impolitic to offend people who can help you. A provision as impolitic as it was barbarous* (William E. H. Lecky). — **im|pol'i|tic|ly**, *adv.* — **im|pol'i|tic|ness**, *n.*

im|pon|der|a|bil|i|a (im pon'dər ə bil'ē ə), *n.pl.* imponderables: *The matters learned by the delegates ... were mainly imponderabilia* (Bulletin of Atomic Scientists).

im|pon|der|a|bil|i|ty (im pon'dər ə bil'ə tē), *n., pl.* **-ties**. **1** the quality of being imponderable. **2** something imponderable.

im|pon|der|a|ble (im pon'dər ə bəl), *adj., n.* — ***adj.*** without weight that can be felt or measured: *Faith and love are imponderable forces.*
— ***n.*** something imponderable, such as that which cannot be explained or foreseen: *The rest lies among the imponderables of the future* (Wall Street Journal). *Ed says you have to have an instinct for the imponderables if you are going to manage a ball team* (New Yorker). — **im|pon'der|a|ble|ness**, *n.* — **im|pon'der|a|bly**, *adv.*

im|pone (im pōn'), *v.t.,* **-poned**, **-pon|ing**. *Obsolete.* to stake; wager. [< Latin *impōnere* < *in-* on + *pōnere* to place]

im|port (*v.* im pôrt', -pōrt', im'pôrt, -pōrt; *n.* im'pôrt, -pōrt), *v., n.* — ***v.t.*** **1** to bring in from a foreign country for sale or use (opposed to *export*): *The United States imports coffee from Brazil.* **2** *Figurative.* to bring in (persons, ideas, customs, or the like) from another country or outside source: *Buddhism ... was imported from India by way of China and Korea 1,400 years ago* (New York Times). *Others import yet nobler arts from France* (Alexander Pope). **3** to mean; make known; signify: *Tell me what your remark imports.* **4** to be of importance or consequence to: *It doth import him much to speak with me* (Shakespeare). *Yet first, let me say ... what it imports thee to know* (Scott).
— ***v.i.*** to be of importance or consequence.
— ***n.*** **1** an article brought into a country (opposed to *export*): *Rubber is a useful import.* **2** a person brought in from another country or outside source; importee: *He is the third new end and the 24th new import to be signed by the Saskatchewan Roughriders* (Edmonton Journal). **3** the act or fact of importing; importation: *The import of diseased animals was forbidden.* **4** meaning; implication; significance: *Explain the import of your remark.* **5** importance; consequence: *matters of great import.*
[< Latin *importāre* < *in-* in + *portāre* carry] — **im|port'a|ble**, *adj.*

im|port|a|bil|i|ty (im pôr'tə bil'ə tē, -pōr'-), *n.* the quality or condition of being importable.

im|por|tance (im pôr′təns), *n.* **1** the fact or quality of being important; consequence; value; significance: *You can't ignore the importance of a good digestion* (Joseph Conrad). **2** *Obsolete.* **a** an important matter. **b** import; meaning.
—*Syn.* **1 Importance, consequence** mean the quality of having much value, meaning, influence, or moment. **Importance** is the general word: *Anybody can see the importance of good health.* **Consequence** applies particularly to that which is important for its results or effects: *The discovery of insulin was an event of great consequence to diabetics.*

im|por|tant (im pôr′tənt), *adj.* **1** meaning much; worth noticing or considering; having value or significance: *important business, an important occasion. The great, the important day, big with the fate Of Cato and Rome* (Joseph Addison). SYN: significant, momentous, weighty. **2** having social position or influence: *Mr. Harris is an important man in our town.* **3** acting as if important; seeming to have influence: *An important busybody rushed around giving orders.* SYN: pretentious, grandiose, pompous. **4** *Obsolete.* importunate: *If the prince be too important, tell him there is measure in everything* (Shakespeare). [< Middle French *important,* learned borrowing from Medieval Latin *importans, -antis,* present participle of *importare* be significant in < Latin *importāre* bring in; see etym. under **import**] —**im|por′tant|ly,** *adv.*

im|por|ta|tion (im′pôr tā′shən, -pōr-), *n.* **1** the act of importing: *In 1774, Rhode Island became the first state to prohibit the importation of slaves* (Edgar Allan Toppin). **2** something brought in; import: *Her shawl is a recent importation from Mexico.*

im|port|ed (im pôr′tid, -pōr′-), *adj.* **1** brought in from a foreign country: *imported products.* **2** *Figurative.* brought in from outside; introduced: *imported ideas.*

im|port|ee (im′pôr tē′, -pōr-), *n.* a person imported from another country or region: *The new western and northern territories of Poland ... are neglected and thinly populated by reluctant importees* (London Times).

im|port|er (im pôr′tər, -pōr′-; im′pôr tər, -pōr-), *n.* a person or company whose business is importing goods.

im|por|tu|na|cy (im pôr′chə nə sē), *n., pl.* **-cies.** importunate quality; importunity.

im|por|tu|nate (im pôr′chə nit), *adj.* **1** asking repeatedly; annoyingly persistent; urgent: *Importunate hours ... Each clamorous with its own sharp need* (John Greenleaf Whittier). **2** *Obsolete.* troublesome. —**im|por′tu|nate|ly,** *adv.* —**im|por′tu-nate|ness,** *n.*

im|por|tune (im′pôr tün′, -tyün′; im pôr′chən), *v.,* **-tuned, -tun|ing,** *adj.* —*v.t.* **1** to ask urgently or repeatedly; annoy with pressing demands: *The boy importuned the teacher to raise his grade. Similarly, there is little real concern that ... she may importune him to betray his country* (Bulletin of Atomic Scientists). **2** to beg (for something) urgently or repeatedly: *The children importuned their mother for ice cream.* **3** *Obsolete.* to trouble; annoy: *... the last [Pope] who was importuned by the presence of a Roman emperor* (Edward Gibbon).
—*v.i.* to make urgent or repeated requests; be importunate: *Too poor for a bribe and too proud to importune* (Thomas Gray).
[< Middle French *importuner* < *importun;* see the adjective]
—*adj.* importunate; pertinacious.
[< Middle French *importun* persistent, learned borrowing from Latin *importūnus* inconvenient < *in-* not + *portus* harbor] —**im′por|tune′ly,** *adv.* —**im′por|tun′er,** *n.*

im|por|tu|ni|ty (im′pôr tü′nə tē, -tyü′-), *n., pl.* **-ties.** urgent or repeated asking; the act of demanding again and again.

im|pose (im pōz′), *v.,* **-posed, -pos|ing.** —*v.t.* **1** to put (a burden, tax, or punishment) on: *The judge imposed a fine of $500 on the guilty man. Thus the group that foments the revolution will not try to impose on the people any political organization from above* (Edmund Wilson). **2** to force or thrust (oneself or one's company) on another or others; obtrude; presume. **3** to palm off (a thing upon a person) to deceive. **4** *Ecclesiastical.* to lay on (hands) in confirmation or ordination. **5** *Printing.* to arrange (pages of type) for printing. **6** *Archaic.* to put or place on something or in a particular place.
—*v.i.* to force or thrust one's authority or influence on another or others.
impose on (or **upon**), **a** to take advantage of; use selfishly: *Do not let the children impose on you.* **b** to deceive; cheat; trick: *There are some so weak as to be imposed upon by fine things and false addresses* (Sir Richard Steele).
[< Middle French *imposer* < *in-* on + *poser* to put, place, pose¹] —**im|pos′a|ble,** *adj.* —**im-pos′er,** *n.*

im|pos|ing (im pō′zing), *adj.* impressive because of size, appearance, or dignity: *The Capitol at Washington, D.C., is an imposing building.* SYN: commanding, stately, majestic. —**im|pos′ing|ly,** *adv.* —**im|pos′ing|ness,** *n.*

im|po|si|tion (im′pə zish′ən), *n.* **1** the act or fact of putting a burden, tax, or punishment on: *A war requires the imposition of heavy taxes.* **2** something imposed; a burden, tax, or punishment. **3** an unfair burden, tax, or punishment. **4** the action of imposing upon a person by taking advantage of his good nature: *Would it be an imposition to ask you to mail this parcel?* **5** the act of passing off of something false or genuine or true; deception; fraud; trick. **6** *Ecclesiastical.* a ceremonial laying on of hands, as in confirmation. **7** *Printing.* the laying of pages of type or plates upon an imposing stone or the bed of a press, and securing them in a chase. **8** *Obsolete.* a charge; injunction.

im|pos|si|bil|i|ty (im pos′ə bil′ə tē, im′pos-), *n., pl.* **-ties.** **1** the quality of being impossible: *We all realize the impossibility of living long without food.* **2** something impossible: *The sergeant always demanded impossibilities of his men.*

im|pos|si|ble (im pos′ə bəl), *adj., n.* —*adj.* **1** that cannot be or happen: *an accident that had seemed impossible. It is impossible for two and two to make six.* **2** not possible to use; not to be done: *He proposed an impossible plan. Few things are impossible to diligence and skill* (Samuel Johnson). SYN: impracticable, unfeasible. **3** that cannot be true: *an impossible story.* **4** not possible to endure; very objectionable: *an impossible situation, an impossible person. A summer without swimming would be impossible.*
—*n.* **1** something that is or seems impossible: *The sergeant always demanded the impossible of his men.* **2** an impossibility: *His statement is in the nature of an impossible.*
[< Old French *impossible,* learned borrowing from Latin *impossibilis* < *in-* not + *possibilis* possible] —**im|pos′si|ble|ness,** *n.* —**im|pos′si|bly,** *adv.*

im|post¹ (im′pōst), *n., v.* —*n.* **1** a tax or duty, especially on goods brought into a country; customs duty: *There is an impost on wool imported from other countries.* **2** a tax; tribute. **3** (in racing) the weight that a horse must carry in a handicap, assigned on a basis of age.
—*v.t. U.S.* to classify (imported goods) according to a certain rate of duty.
[< Middle French *impost* < Latin *impōnere* place upon < *in-* on + *pōnere* to place, set] —**im′post-er,** *n.*

im|post² (im′pōst), *n. Architecture.* the uppermost part of a column on which the end of an arch rests. [< Middle French *imposte* < Italian *imposta* < Latin *impōnere;* see etym. under **impost¹**]

im|pos|tor or **im|pos|ter** (im pos′tər), *n.* **1** a person who pretends to be someone else in order to deceive or defraud others. **2** a deceiver; cheat. [< Latin *impositor* < *impōnere;* see etym. under **impost¹**]

im|pos|tume (im pos′chüm, -tyüm), *n. Archaic.* an abscess. [< Old French *empostume,* alteration of *aposteme,* ultimately < Greek *apóstēma*]

im|pos|ture (im pos′chər), *n.* deception; fraud. [< Late Latin *impostūra* < Latin *impōnere*]

im|pos|tur|ous (im pos′chər əs), *adj.* like an impostor or imposture; deceitful.

im|po|sure (im pō′zhər), *n.* the act of imposing; imposition.

im|po|ta|ble (im pō′tə bəl), *adj.* not drinkable; unfit for drinking.

im|po|tence (im′pə təns), *n.* a lack of strength or power; helplessness; quality or condition of being impotent: *The government was overthrown because of its impotence when the crisis arose.*

im|po|ten|cy (im′pə tən sē), *n.* = impotence.

im|po|tent (im′pə tənt), *adj., n.* —*adj.* **1** not having power; helpless: *The cripple fell back in an impotent rage. Without guns and ammunition the soldiers were impotent. We were impotent against the force of the tornado.* SYN: weak, feeble, infirm. **2** (of males) incapable of sexual intercourse. **3** *Obsolete.* without control or restraint.
—*n.* an impotent person. —**im′po|tent|ly,** *adv.* —**im′po|tent|ness,** *n.*

im|pound (im pound′), *v.t.* **1** to shut up in a pen or pound: *The town impounds stray animals.* **2** to enclose or confine within limits: *A dam impounds water. Outraged by this exploitation, the father ordered them all home, impounded their instruments* (New Yorker). **3a** to put in the custody of a law court: *The court impounded the documents to use as evidence.* **b** to seize or hold back, especially by legal means: *The Administration moved to impound the funds of discontinued government programs.* —**im|pound′a|ble,** *adj.* —**im|pound′er,** *n.*

im|pound|ment (im pound′mənt), *n.* **1** water that is impounded by a dam or other enclosure. **2** the act of impounding.

im|pov|er|ish (im pov′ər ish, -pov′rish), *v.t.* **1** to make very poor: *A long drought had impoverished the farmers whose crops had died.* **2** to exhaust the strength, richness, or resources of: *to impoverish the mind or the blood. Careless farming impoverishes the most fertile soil.* Also, **empoverish.** [< Old French *empoveriss-,* stem of *empoverir* < *em-* em-¹ + *povre* poor] —**im|pov′er-ish|er,** *n.* —**im|pov′er|ish|ment,** *n.*

im|pov|er|ished (im pov′ər isht, -pov′risht), *adj.* very poor: *Compared to research for the farmer, the science of getting food from the sea is an impoverished newcomer in the U.S.* (Newsweek). SYN: See syn. under **poor.**

im|pow|er (im pou′ər), *v.t.* = empower.

im|prac|ti|ca|bil|i|ty (im prak′tə kə bil′ə tē), *n., pl.* **-ties.** **1** the quality or condition of being impracticable. **2** something impracticable.

im|prac|ti|ca|ble (im prak′tə kə bəl), *adj.* **1** not working well in practice; not practicable: *impracticable suggestions.* **2** that cannot be used: *an impracticable road. Owing to a slight miscalculation, the invention proved to be impracticable* (Lytton Strachey). **3** very hard to manage or deal with; intractable: *an impracticable horse, an impracticable person. You are so utterly unreasonable and impracticable* (George Bernard Shaw). SYN: unmanageable. —**im|prac′ti|ca|ble|ness,** *n.*
► See **impractical** for usage note.

im|prac|ti|ca|bly (im prak′tə kə blē), *adv.* in an impracticable manner.

im|prac|ti|cal (im prak′tə kəl), *adj.* **1** not practical; not useful. **2** not having good sense. —**im|prac′ti-cal|ly,** *adv.* —**im|prac′ti|cal|ness,** *n.*
► **Impractical, impracticable.** *Impractical* is applied to things that are useless or to people who are unrealistic or show little judgment or common sense in what they do: *Buying useless things because they are on sale is impractical. Impracticable* describes things that have been proved unusable in actual practice or would be impossible to put into practice: *Most schemes to abolish poverty are impracticable.*

im|prac|ti|cal|i|ty (im prak′tə kal′ə tē), *n., pl.* **-ties.** **1** the quality of being impractical: *I very much resent comments on the impracticality of small cars* (New Yorker). **2** an impractical thing.

im|pre|cate (im′prə kāt), *v.,* **-cat|ed, -cat|ing.**
—*v.t.* to call down (evil, curses, or other calamity): *The prophet imprecated ruin on his enemies.*
—*v.i.* to curse.
[< Latin *imprecārī* (with English *-ate*¹) invoke, pray for < *in-* on + *prex, precis* prayer] —**im′pre-ca′tor,** *n.*

im|pre|ca|tion (im′prə kā′shən), *n.* **1** the act of calling down evil, curses, or calamity on a person: *Those gave way to torrents of the hatred, imprecation, and entreaty that have welled in Cyprus* (Harper's). **2** a curse: *The angry man shouted imprecations after the children who had broken his window.*

im|pre|ca|to|ry (im′prə kə tôr′ē, -tōr′-), *adj.* invoking evil; maledictory.

im|pre|cise (im′pri sīs′), *adj.* not precise; lacking precision; inaccurate: *Wisdom was imprecise, my hand's loose judgment dark* (New Yorker). SYN: inexact. —**im′pre|cise′ly,** *adv.* —**im′pre|cise′-ness,** *n.*

im|pre|ci|sion (im′pri sizh′ən), *n.* lack of precision; inexactness: *the general mess of imprecision of feeling* (T. S. Eliot).

im|preg|na|bil|i|ty (im preg′nə bil′ə tē), *n.* the quality of being impregnable.

im|preg|na|ble¹ (im preg′nə bəl), *adj.* that cannot be overthrown by force; able to resist attack: *an impregnable fortress.* (*Figurative.*) *The lawyer won his case with an impregnable argument. The terrible land of his exile loomed before him a frigid, an impregnable mass* (Lytton Strachey). SYN: invincible, unconquerable. [< Middle French *imprenable* < *in-* not, in- + *prenable* pregnable] —**im|preg′na|ble|ness,** *n.* —**im|preg′na|bly,** *adv.*

im|preg|na|ble² (im preg′nə bəl), *adj.* that can be impregnated, as an egg. [< Late Latin *impraegnāre* to impregnate + English *-able*]

im|preg|nant (im preg′nənt), *n.* a material or substance which has been impregnated into something else, especially as a preservative: *... a waffle-shaped network of lead holds the impregnant that keeps the battery alive* (New Scientist). [< Late Latin *impraegnāns, -antis,* present partici-

Pronunciation Key: hat, āge, cãre, fär; let, ēqual, tėrm; it, īce; hot, ōpen, ôrder; oil, out; cup, pu̇t, rüle; child; long; thin; ᴛʜen; zh, measure; ə represents **a** in about, **e** in taken, **i** in pencil, **o** in lemon, **u** in circus.

ple of *impraegnāre;* see etym. under **impregnate**]

im|preg|nate (im preg′nāt), *v.,* **-nat|ed, -nat|ing,** *adj.* — ***v.t.*** **1** to make pregnant; fertilize. **2a** to spread through the whole of; fill (with); saturate: *Seawater is impregnated with salt.* **b** to mix (with); interpenetrate: *rock impregnated with magnetite.* **3** *Figurative.* to fill the mind of; inspire; imbue: *The captain impregnated the soldiers with his own fearless courage. A great book impregnates the mind with new ideas.* **4** *Figurative.* to make fruitful or productive.
— ***adj.*** impregnated.
[< Late Latin *impraegnāre* (with English *-ate*[1]) make pregnant < *in-* (intensive) + *praegnāre* be pregnant]

im|preg|na|tion (im′preg nā′shən), *n.* **1** the act or process of impregnating. **2** the state of being impregnated. **3** a thing, influence, or element with which anything is impregnated.

im|preg|na|tor (im preg′nā tər), *n.* a person or thing that impregnates.

im|pre|sa (im prā′zə), *n. Heraldry, Obsolete.* an emblem or motto. [< Italian *impresa* device < Vulgar Latin *imprēnsa* < *imprēndere* undertake < Latin *in-* on + *prēndere,* earlier *prehendere* take]

im|pre|sa|ri|o (im′pre sä′rē ō), *n., pl.* **-sa|ri|os,** *Italian* **-sa|ri** (-sä′rē). **1** the organizer, director, or manager of a concert tour, an opera or ballet company, or other, especially musical, entertainment. **2** a showman: *a night club impresario.* **3** a producer: *... one of Broadway's top impresarios on the strength of his production of My Fair Lady* (Wall Street Journal). [< Italian *impresario* < *impresa* device, undertaking; see etym. under **impresa**]

im|pre|scrip|ti|ble (im′pri skrip′tə bəl), *adj.* existing independently of law or custom; not justly to be taken away or violated: *imprescriptible rights.* — **im′pre|scrip′ti|bly,** *adv.*

im|prese (im prēz′), *n. Obsolete.* impresa.

im|press[1] (*v.* im pres′; *n.* im′pres), *v.,* **-pressed** or (*Archaic*) **-prest, -press|ing,** *n.* — ***v.t.*** **1** to have a strong effect on the mind or feelings of; influence deeply: *A hero impresses us with his courage.* **2** *Figurative.* to fix in the mind: *She repeated the words to impress them in her memory.* **3** to make marks on by pressing or stamping: *We can impress wax with a seal.* **4** to produce by pressure; imprint; stamp: *The clerk impressed his signature on the documents with a rubber stamp.* **5** to apply with pressure: *But he ... his foot impress'd On the strong neck of that destructive beast* (John Dryden). **6** to produce or generate (an electromotive force or potential difference) in a conductor from some outside source, such as a battery or dynamo.
— ***v.i.*** to make an impression, especially a favorable one: (*Figurative.*) *He could hear his own voice cracking with the desire to impress* (Graham Greene).
— ***n.*** **1** an impression; mark; stamp: (*Figurative.*) *An author leaves the impress of his personality on what he writes.* **2** the act of impressing. **3** *Figurative.* an impression on the mind or feelings: *This kind of upbringing leaves an impress which some Texans are never able to outgrow* (Harper's).
[< Latin *impressus,* past participle of *imprimere* < *in-* in + *premere* to press] — **im|press′er,** *n.*

im|press[2] (im pres′), *v.,* **-pressed** or (*Archaic*) **-prest, -press|ing,** *n.* — ***v.t.*** **1** to seize by authority for public use: *The police impressed our car in order to pursue the escaping robbers.* **2** to force (men) to serve in the armed forces: *The captain ... obtained permission to send parties on shore to impress seamen* (Frederick Marryat). **3** to bring in and use; press (a thing) into service by argument, etc.
— ***n.*** = impressment.
[< *im-*[2] + *press*[2]]

im|press|i|bil|i|ty (im pres′ə bil′ə tē), *n.* the quality of being impressible; impressionability.

im|press|i|ble (im pres′ə bəl), *adj.* that can be impressed; impressionable. — **im|press′i|ble|ness,** *n.* — **im|press′i|bly,** *adv.*

im|pres|sion (im presh′ən), *n.* **1** *Figurative.* **a** an effect produced on a person: *Punishment seemed to make little impression on the child.* **b** an effect produced by any operation or activity: *The rain made little impression on the dry fields.* **2** *Figurative.* an idea; notion: *I have a vague impression that I left the house door unlocked.* **3** something made by pressure, such as a mark, stamp, or print: *The thief had left an impression of his foot in the garden.* **4** the act of impressing. **5** the state of being impressed. **6** *Dentistry.* a mold of the teeth and the surrounding gums. **7** *Printing.* **a** the total number of copies of a book made at one time. **b** a printed copy. **c** the process or result of printing paper from type, plates, etc. **8** *Psychology.* the immediate neural results of stimulation of the senses. **9** an imitation of a famous person; impersonation: *The comedian entertained us with his impressions of political figures.*

im|pres|sion|a|bil|i|ty (im presh′ə nə bil′ə tē, -presh′nə-), *n.* impressionable quality.

im|pres|sion|a|ble (im presh′ə nə bəl, -presh′nə-), *adj.* sensitive to impressions; easily impressed or influenced: (*Figurative.*) *Children are more impressionable than adults.* — **im|pres′sion|a|ble|ness,** *n.* — **im|pres′sion|a|bly,** *adv.*

im|pres|sion|al (im presh′ə nəl), *adj.* **1** of or having to do with an impression or impressions. **2** = impressionable.

im|pres|sion|ism (im presh′ə niz əm), *n.* **1** a style of painting that gives the impression made by the subject on the artist without much attention to details. Impressionism was developed by French painters of the late 1800's. **2** a style of literature characterized by the creation of general impressions and moods rather than realistic detail. **3** a style of music characterized by the use of unusual and rich harmonies, tonal qualities, and other effects, to suggest the composer's impressions, as of a scene or an emotion.

im|pres|sion|ist (im presh′ə nist), *n., adj.* — ***n.*** **1** an artist, writer, or composer who uses impressionism: *The main strength of the impressionists, both foreign and domestic, was color* (Time). **2** an entertainer who does impersonations: *She got her first job—as a nightclub singer and impressionist in Canada* (Time).
— ***adj.*** = impressionistic.

im|pres|sion|is|tic (im presh′ə nis′tik), *adj.* **1** of impressionism or impressionists. **2** giving only a general or hasty impression: *He is also a casual and somewhat impressionistic thinker* (Wall Street Journal). — **im|pres′sion|is′ti|cal|ly,** *adv.*

im|pres|sive (im pres′iv), *adj.* able to impress the mind, feelings, or conscience; able to excite deep feelings: *an impressive sermon, an impressive storm, an impressive ceremony.* **SYN:** imposing, commanding, striking. — **im|pres′sive|ly,** *adv.* — **im|pres′sive|ness,** *n.*

im|press|ment (im pres′mənt), *n.* the act or practice of impressing property for public use or men to serve in the armed forces.

im|pres|sure (im presh′ər), *n. Archaic.* impression.

im|prest[1] (im prest′), *v. Archaic.* a past tense and a past participle of **impress.**

im|prest[2] (im prest′), *n., adj.* — ***n.*** **1** an advance or loan of money, especially for use in carrying out some public business. **2** (in accounting) an advance or loan of money to be drawn upon as needed but allowed to build up during inactive periods, as in a petty cash account. **3** *British.* (formerly) an advance payment made to a soldier or sailor at enlistment.
— ***adj.*** lent; advanced.
[< *im-*[2] + obsolete *prest* loan, perhaps patterned on Italian *impresto* a loan < *imprestare* < *im-* in- + *prestare* < Latin *praestāre* act as surety for]

im|pri|ma|tur (im′pri mā′tər), *n.* **1** an official license to print or publish a book or other work, now usually used to refer to works sanctioned by the Roman Catholic Church. **2** *Figurative: Therefore, his calculations and conclusions bear no imprimatur of the Atomic Energy Commission* (Bulletin of Atomic Scientists). **SYN:** sanction, approval. [< New Latin *imprimatur* let it be printed]

im|pri|mis (im prī′mis), *adv. Latin.* in the first place; first.

im|print (*n.* im′print; *v.* im print′), *n., v.* — ***n.*** **1** a mark made by pressure; print: *Your foot made an imprint in the sand.* **2** an impression; mark: (*Figurative.*) *Suffering left its imprint on her face.* **3** the printer's or publisher's name, with the place and date of publication, on the title page or at the end of a book.
— ***v.t.*** **1** to mark by pressing or stamping; print: *to imprint a postmark on an envelope, to imprint a letter with a postmark.* **2** to put by pressing: *She imprinted a kiss on his lips.* **3** *Figurative.* to fix firmly in the mind: *His boyhood home was imprinted in his memory.* **4** *Obsolete.* to print (letters, words, or figures) from type. **5** *Biology, Psychology.* (of newborn animals) to fix the affections and interests upon (another animal, or object identified as, or in place of, the parent): *In many cases, animals that become imprinted toward animals of another species never learn to recognize members of their own species* (Wilbert J. McKeachie).
— ***v.i.*** *Biology, Psychology.* to be or become the object of the affections and interests of an animal: *Goats and sheep apparently imprint on their own young in the first few moments after birth* (George W. Barlow).
[< Old French *empreinter* < *empreindre* to print; assail, set on, ultimately < Latin *in-* on + *premere* press[1]] — **im|print′er,** *n.*

im|print|a|bil|i|ty (im prin′tə bil′ə tē), *n.* the quality of being imprintable: *... the imprintability of ducklings rapidly declines soon after they are 16 hours old* (Scientific American).

im|print|a|ble (im prin′tə bəl), *adj.* that can be imprinted, especially on the mind or memory.

im|pris|on (im priz′ən), *v.t.* **1** to put in prison; keep in prison: *to imprison a criminal in a cell for many months.* **2** *Figurative: He imprisoned his anger before the insults of the court.* **SYN:** confine, restrain.

im|pris|on|a|ble (im priz′ə nə bəl), *adj.* deserving or involving imprisonment: *an imprisonable offense.*

im|pris|on|ment (im priz′ən mənt), *n.* **1** a putting or keeping in prison: *The imprisonment of her son caused great sorrow.* **2** the fact or condition of being put or kept in prison: *At the start of his imprisonment he was just 20 years old.* **3** *Figurative.* close confinement; restraint.

im|prob|a|bil|i|ty (im′prob ə bil′ə tē, im prob′-), *n., pl.* **-ties. 1** the quality or condition of being improbable; unlikelihood. **2** something improbable.

im|prob|a|ble (im prob′ə bəl), *adj.* not probable; not likely to happen; not likely to be true; unlikely: *The boy told an improbable story of seeing a ghost in the haunted house. If this were played upon a stage now, I could condemn it as an improbable fiction* (Shakespeare). — **im|prob′a|ble|ness,** *n.* — **im|prob′a|bly,** *adv.*

im|pro|bi|ty (im prō′bə tē), *n.* lack of integrity; dishonesty; wickedness. [< Latin *improbitās* < *improbus* wicked, persistent < *in-* not + *probus* good]

im|promp|tu (im promp′tü, -tyü), *adv., adj., n.*
— ***adv.*** without previous thought or preparation; offhand: *a speech made impromptu.*
— ***adj.*** made or done without previous thought or preparation; improvised; makeshift: *an impromptu party. He had not expected to make a speech, but he gave an impromptu talk when he was asked to say a few words.*
— ***n.*** **1** something so made or done; improvisation. **2** *Music.* a composition, characteristic of the 1800's, that gives the impression of improvisation, but follows a set form and style.
[< French *impromptu* < Latin *in promptū* in readiness. Compare etym. under **prompt.**]

im|prop|er (im prop′ər), *adj.* **1** not in accordance with accepted standards; irregular; wrong; not correct: *He learned in school that "We ain't" is improper speech.* **SYN:** incorrect. **2** not suitable; inappropriate; ill-adapted: *That bright dress is improper for a funeral.* **3** not decent; unbecoming; unseemly: *I am too old to be improper* (Horace Walpole). **4** showing bad judgment. — **im|prop′er|ly,** *adv.* — **im|prop′er|ness,** *n.*
— ***Syn.*** **1, 3 Improper, indecent** mean not right or fitting according to accepted standards. **Improper** emphasizes bad judgment as to what is right or wrong: *It is an improper use of authority for a policeman to break one law to enforce another.* **Indecent** emphasizes bad taste as to what is acceptable or proper: *Leaving a dinner party without thanking one's host is indecent.*

improper fraction, a fraction equal to or greater than 1. *Examples:* 3/2, 4/3, 27/4, 8/5, 21/12, and 8/8.

im|pro|pri|ate (*adj.* im prō′prē it; *v.* im prō′prē āt), *adj., v.,* **-at|ed, -at|ing.** — ***adj.*** (of church property, tithes, or the like) placed in lay hands.
— ***v.t.*** **1** to put (church property, tithes, or the like) in lay hands. **2** *Obsolete.* to appropriate.
[< New Latin *impropriare* (with English *-ate*[1]) < Latin *in-* in + *proprius* one's own, private] — **im-pro′pri|a′tion,** *n.* — **im|pro′pri|a′tor,** *n.*

im|pro|pri|e|ty (im′prə prī′ə tē), *n., pl.* **-ties. 1** a lack of propriety; quality of being improper. **2** improper conduct. **3** an improper act, expression, etc.: *Using "learn" to mean "teach" is an impropriety. Every language has likewise its improprieties and absurdities* (Samuel Johnson).

im|prov|a|bil|i|ty (im prü′və bil′ə tē), *n.* the state or quality of being improvable: *I believe in man. Not his perfectibility, but at least his improvability* (Harper's).

im|prov|a|ble (im prü′və bəl), *adj.* that can be improved. — **im|prov′a|ble|ness,** *n.* — **im|prov′a|bly,** *adv.*

im|prove (im prüv′), *v.,* **-proved, -prov|ing.** — ***v.t.*** **1** to make better: *You could improve your handwriting if you tried.* **2** to increase the value of (land or property): *Land is improved by using it for a farm or putting up a building on it.* **SYN:** develop. **3** to use well; make good use of: *We had two hours to wait and improved the time by seeing the city.* **SYN:** utilize, employ.
— ***v.i.*** **1** to become better: *His health is improving.* **2** to make improvements.
improve on (or **upon**), to make better than; do better than: *to improve on one's earlier work.*
[< Anglo-French *emprover* < Old French *en-* in, en-[1] + *prou,* earlier *proz* profit < Vulgar Latin *pros, prodis* profit] — **im|prov′er,** *n.*
— ***Syn.*** *v.t.* **1 Improve, better** mean to raise to a higher or more satisfactory state or condition. **Im-**

prove, the more general word, emphasizes increasing in value, making more desirable or more satisfactory: *You must improve your grades.* **Better** emphasizes increasing in good qualities or raising to a higher level or position: *The pole vaulter bettered his last year's record.*

im|prove|ment (im prüv′mənt), *n.* **1** a making better or becoming better: *His schoolwork shows much improvement since last term.* SYN: betterment, amelioration. **2** an increase in value. **3** a change or addition that adds value: *An old house can be made modern by making improvements. The improvements in our house cost several thousand dollars.* **4** a better condition; thing that is better than another; gain; advance: *Electric lights are an improvement over candles.* **5** good use.

im|prov|i|dence (im prov′ə dəns), *n.* lack of foresight; failure to look ahead; carelessness in providing for the future; lack of thrift.

im|prov|i|dent (im prov′ə dənt), *adj.* lacking foresight; not looking ahead; not careful in providing for the future; not thrifty: *An improvident man spends his money freely as long as he has it. Improvident soldiers! had your watch been good, this sudden mischief never could have fallen* (Shakespeare). SYN: shiftless, imprudent, wasteful. —**im|prov′i|dent|ly**, *adv.*

im|prov|ing (im prü′ving), *adj.* **1** that improves or makes better; instructive; elevating: *a book of travels . . . very improving too* (Weir Mitchell). **2** making or becoming better. —**im|prov′ing|ly**, *adv.*

im|pro|vi|sa|tion (im′prə vī zā′shən, im′prov ə-), *n.* **1** the act or process of improvising: *When I play jazz, I'm in the new school, and improvisation is alive* (New Yorker). **2** something improvised.

im|pro|vi|sa|tion|al (im′prə vī zā′shə nəl, im′-prov ə-), *adj.* of or characterized by improvisation: *Many of the new jazz pianists bend all of their improvisational efforts toward either melody or rhythm* (New Yorker). —**im′pro|vi|sa′tion|al|ly**, *adv.*

im|pro|vi|sa|tor (im′prə vī zā′tər, im prov′ə-), *n.* a person who improvises; improviser.

im|pro|vi|sa|to|re (im prov′ə zə tôr′ē, -tōr′-), *n., pl.* **-to|ri** (-tôr′ē, -tōr′ē), **-to|res.** a person who improvises music or verse: *I have met many . . . improvisatori of our period and I must give the first place to Axel Munthe* (London Times). [< Italian *improvvisatore* < *improvvisare* improvise]

im|prov|i|sa|to|ri|al (im prov′ə zə tôr′ē əl, -tōr′-), *adj.* of or having to do with improvising or an improviser. —**im|prov′i|sa|to′ri|al|ly**, *adv.*

im|pro|vi|sa|to|ry (im′prə vī′zə tôr′ē, -tōr′-), *adj.* = improvisatorial.

im|pro|vise (im′prə vīz), *v.*, **-vised, -vis|ing.** —*v.t.* **1** to make up (something, such as music or poetry) on the spur of the moment; sing, recite, or speak without preparation: *He improvised a new stanza for the school song at the football game.* **2** to prepare or provide offhand; make for the occasion; extemporize: *The boys improvised a tent out of two blankets and some long poles.* —*v.i.* to compose, utter, or do anything without preparation or on the spur of the moment. [< French *improviser* < Italian *improvvisare* < *improvviso* unprepared, ultimately < Latin *in-* not + *prō* forth, ahead + *vidēre* to see, look] —**im′pro|vis′er**, *n.*

im|pru|dence (im prü′dəns), *n.* lack of prudence; imprudent behavior. SYN: indiscretion, rashness.

im|pru|dent (im prü′dənt), *adj.* not prudent; not discreet; rash; heedless; unwise: *It is imprudent to rush into something without thinking what may happen.* SYN: indiscreet, ill-advised, incautious. [< Latin *imprūdēns, -entis* < *in-* not + *prūdēns* prudent] —**im|pru′dent|ly**, *adv.* —**im|pru′dent|ness**, *n.*

im|pu|dence (im′pyə dəns), *n.* **1** lack of shame or modesty; rude boldness. SYN: insolence, presumption. **2** impudent conduct or language.

im|pu|den|cy (im′pyə dən sē), *n., pl.* **-cies.** = impudence.

im|pu|dent (im′pyə dənt), *adj.* without shame or modesty; rudely bold; insolent; forward: *The impudent boy made faces at the teacher.* SYN: presumptuous. See syn. under **impertinent.** [< Latin *impudēns, -entis*, ultimately < *in-* not + *pudēre* be modest, feel shame] —**im′pu|dent|ly**, *adv.* —**im′pu|dent|ness**, *n.*

im|pu|dic|i|ty (im′pyə dis′ə tē), *n.* shamelessness; immodesty. [< Old French *impudicite* < *impudique* shameless, learned borrowing from Latin *impudīcus* < *in-* not + *pudīcus* modest]

im|pugn (im pyün′), *v.t.* to call in question; attack by words or arguments; challenge, especially as false or worthless: *Do not impugn the umpire's fairness.* [< Old French *impugner* < Latin *impūgnāre* to assault, attack < *in-* against + *pūgnāre* to fight < *pūgna* a battle] —**im|pugn′a|ble**, *adj.* —**im|pugn′er**, *n.*

im|pu|is|sance (im pyü′ə səns; im′pyü is′əns, im-pwis′-), *n.* powerlessness; weakness. [< Middle French *impuissance* < *im-* not + *puissance* puissance]

im|pu|is|sant (im pyü′ə sənt; im′pyü is′ənt, im-pwis′-), *adj.* powerless; impotent; weak.

im|pulse (im′puls), *n.* **1** a sudden, driving force or influence; thrust; push: *the impulse of a wave, the impulse of curiosity. The impulse of hunger compelled the proud man to go begging for food.* SYN: impetus, drive. **2** the effect of a sudden, driving force or influence. **3** *Figurative.* a sudden inclination or tendency to act: *He quickly and clumsily, on an impulse, kissed her* (James T. Farrell). *Distrust all in whom the impulse to punish is powerful* (Friedrich Nietzsche). **4** *Figurative.* a suggestion; instigation: *He was not a man . . . to yield timidly to the impulses of others* (William Prescott). **5** *Figurative.* the stimulating force of desire or emotion: *An angry person is influenced more by impulse than by reason.* **6** a message or stimulus transmitted by nerve cells along nerve fibers, influencing action in the muscle, gland, or nerve cells that it reaches. **7** *Mechanics.* the product obtained by multiplying value of force by the time during which it acts. **8** a surge of electrical current in one direction: *These impulses were recorded previously from actual signals transmitted from the control machine* (Wall Street Journal). [< Latin *impulsus, -ūs* < *impellere* impel]

impulse buyer, a person who often buys without previous thought or planning, especially as to cost, quality, or utility.

impulse buying, the act of an impulse buyer; buying something without previous thought or planning: *There is a lot of impulse buying in discount stores* (Wall Street Journal).

impulse generator, a device for producing brief electrical surges of extremely high voltage.

impulse turbine, a turbine operated by a jet of water or other fluid. Impulse turbines are used especially at dams in the generation of electricity.

im|pul|sion (im pul′shən), *n.* **1** the action or fact of impelling; driving force: *The impulsion of hunger drove the man to steal.* **2** the condition of being impelled. **3** *Figurative.* a mental impulse. **4** = impetus. [< Latin *impulsiō, -ōnis* influence, instigation < *impellere* impel]

im|pul|sive (im pul′siv), *adj.* **1** acting upon impulse; easily moved: (*Figurative.*) *The impulsive child gave all his money to the beggar.* SYN: rash, hasty. **2** driving onward; impelling; pushing. **3** *Mechanics.* (of forces) not continuous. —**im|pul′sive|ly**, *adv.* —**im|pul′sive|ness**, *n.*

im|pu|ni|ty (im pyü′nə tē), *n.* freedom from punishment, injury, or other bad consequences: *If laws are not enforced, crimes are committed with impunity. Even militarily weak and small nations have defied U.N. decisions with impunity* (Wall Street Journal). [< Latin *impūnitās* < *impūnis* unpunished < *in-* not + *pūnīre* punish]

im|pure (im pyůr′), *adj.* **1** not pure; dirty; unclean: *The air in cities is often impure.* **2** mixed with something of lower value; adulterated: *The salt we use is slightly impure.* **3** *Figurative.* bad; corrupt: *to avoid impure talk, thought, acts, and people.* **4** not of one color, style, or other quality; mixed. **5** forbidden by religion as unclean. **6** containing foreign idioms or grammatical errors. [< Latin *impūrus* < *in-* not + *pūrus* pure] —**im|pure′ly**, *adv.* —**im|pure′ness**, *n.*

im|pu|ri|ty (im pyůr′ə tē), *n., pl.* **-ties. 1** a lack of purity; being impure. **2** an impure thing or element; thing that makes something else impure: *Filtering the water removed its impurities.*

im|put|a|bil|i|ty (im pyü′tə bil′ə tē), *n.* the quality of being imputable.

im|put|a|ble (im pyü′tə bəl), *adj.* that can be imputed; attributable. —**im|put′a|ble|ness**, *n.* —**im-put′a|bly**, *adv.*

im|pu|ta|tion (im′pyů tā′shən), *n.* **1** an imputing or being imputed: *But against the imputation of softness and vague Utopianism there have been one or two hints of steel* (Wall Street Journal). **2** a charge or hint of wrongdoing: *No imputation has ever been made against his good name.*

im|put|a|tive (im pyü′tə tiv), *adj.* **1** that imputes. **2** belonging or existing by imputation; imputed. —**im|put′a|tive|ly**, *adv.* —**im|put′a|tive|ness**, *n.*

im|pute (im pyüt′), *v.t.*, **-put|ed, -put|ing. 1** to consider as belonging; charge (a fault, error, or crime) to a person or a cause; attribute; blame: *I impute his failure to laziness.* **2** *Theology.* to attribute (righteousness or guilt) as coming from another: *Abraham believed God, and it was imputed unto him for righteousness* (James 2:23). [< Latin *imputāre* < *in-* in + *putāre* reckon, think] —**im|put′er**, *n.*

i|mu (ē′mü), *n. Hawaiian.* a shallow pit used for cooking.

Im|u|ran (im′yə rən, im yůr′ən), *n. Trademark.* an immunosuppressive drug given to patients receiving homografts or other transplanted tissue; azathioprine.

in (in), *prep., adv., adj., n., v.*, **inned, in|ning.** —*prep.* *In* expresses inclusion, situation, presence, existence, position, and action within limits of space, time, state, and circumstances. **1** within; not outside: *in the box, in the doorway. We live in the country during the summer.* **2** during; at; after: *in the present time. I'll be back in an hour.* **3** into: *Go in the house.* **4** with; having; by: *to cover a letter in an envelope.* **5** of; made of; using: *a dress in silk, a painting in oils.* **6** surrounded by; in the midst of: *in the dust, in hot water.* **7** from among; out of: *one in a hundred.* **8** because of; for: *to act in self-defense, weep in sorrow. The party is in honor of her birthday.* **9** about; concerning: *a book in American history.* **10** while; when: *in crossing the street.* **11** clothed with; wearing: *a lady in court dress, a man in slippers.*

—*adv.* **1** in or into some place, position, or condition; on the inside: *to come in, sailing close in by the shore. Lock the dog in. A sheepskin coat has the woolly side in.* **2** present, especially in one's home or office: *The doctor is not in today.*

—*adj.* **1** having power and influence: *The in party has won another election.* **2** coming or leading in: *The train is on the in track.* **3** *Informal.* in style; up-to-date; fashionable: *an in outfit, in boots. The subjects of the interviews are often "in" novelists like Joseph Heller and Norman Mailer* (Canadian Forum). **4** that is in; being in: *We sat on in seats of the row.*

—*n.* **1** a position of familiarity or influence: *to have an in with the company president. . . . Assembly Speaker Unruh's White House "in"* (Wall Street Journal). **2** access: *A magical charm was her protection, even giving her an "in" to the cool clique* (Punch).

—*v.t.* **1** *Dialect.* to include; enclose. **2** to harvest; gather.

have it in for. See under **have.**

in for, unable to avoid; sure to get or have: *We are in for a storm.*

in for it, *Slang.* in trouble: *"What is all that filth lying about all over the place? . . . You wait till the officer comes in. You'll be in for it"* (Peter Ustinov).

in on, *Informal.* **a** aware of: *Is he in on the secret?* **b** involved in: *I was in on the planning of the party from the start.*

ins, the people in office; political party in power: *The ins are all in favor of keeping the organization closed to outsiders.*

ins and outs, **a** turns and twists; nooks and corners: *He knew the ins and outs of the road because he had traveled it so often.* **b** different parts; details: *The manager knows the ins and outs of the business better than the owner. . . . keen appreciation of the ins and outs of legal method* (Richard H. Hutton).

in that, because: *The director was held responsible in that he managed the program.*

in with, **a** friendly with: *They knew that . . . against him they had been in with Diabolus* (John Bunyan). **b** partners with: *She was in with him in the robbery.*

[Old English *in*]

▶**in, into.** *In* generally shows location; *into* generally shows direction: *He was in the house. She came into the house. He was in a stupor. She fell into a deep sleep.*

▶See **at** for another usage note.

in-[1], *prefix.* not ——; lack of ——; the opposite of ——: *Incorrect = not correct. Injustice = the lack of justice. Inconvenient = the opposite of convenient.* Also, **i-** before *gn;* **il-** before *l;* **im-** before *b, m, p;* **ir-** before *r.* [< Latin *in-*]

▶**In-** or **un-** prefixed to many words gives them a negative meaning, as in *inconsiderate, incapable, uneven, unloved.* American and British usage differs in many words. If you are not sure whether a word takes *in-* or *un-* consult this dictionary.

in-[2], *prefix.* **1** in; into; on; upon: *Intrust = (give) in trust. Inscribe = write in or on.* **2** **In-** is also used to strengthen a meaning or change an intransitive verb to a transitive, usually altering the meaning very little, as in *inweave.* Also, **il-** before *l;* **im-** before *b, m, p;* **ir-** before *r.* [< Latin *in-*, related to *in*, preposition]

▶For a note on variant spellings, see **en-**[1].

in-[3], *prefix.* in; within; into; toward: *Indoors = within doors. Inland = toward land.* [Middle English *in-*, Old English, < *in*, adverb]

in-[4], *combining form.* within a ——, as in *in-company, in-country, in-house.*

Pronunciation Key: hat, āge, cãre, fär; let, ēqual, tėrm; it, īce; hot, ōpen, ôrder; oil, out; cup, pu̇t, rüle; child; long; thin; ᴛʜen; zh, measure; ə represents **a** in about, **e** in taken, **i** in pencil, **o** in lemon, **u** in circus.

▶ Such compounds are derived from a corresponding prepositional phrase: *in-depth interview* from *interview in depth.*

in-[5], *combining form.* exclusive, as in *in-group, in-crowd, in-joke.*

-in[1], *combining form.* **1** in public protest or demonstration, as in *sit-in, teach-in.*
2 gathering by a group, as for socializing, as in *be-in, love-in.*

-in[2], *suffix.* a variant of **-ine**[2], that usually denotes neutral substances such as fats, glycosides, and proteins, as in *olein, digitoxin, albumin, stearin.* Basic substances are usually indicated by *ine*[2]. [< New Latin *-ina* < Latin *-īna,* feminine suffix of abstract nouns]

in., inch or inches.

In (no period), indium (chemical element).

IN (no periods), Indiana (with postal Zip Code).

in|a|bil|i|ty (in'ə bil'ə tē), *n.* lack of ability, means, power, or capacity; being unable: *the inability to pay one's debts.*

in ab|sen|tia (in ab sen'shə), *Latin.* in one's absence; while absent: *Though the winner of the first prize was ill, he received his award in absentia.*

in|ac|ces|si|bil|i|ty (in'ək ses'ə bil'ə tē), *n.* lack of accessibility; being inaccessible.

in|ac|ces|si|ble (in'ək ses'ə bəl), *adj.* **1** hard to get at; hard to reach or enter: *The house on top of the steep hill is inaccessible.* **2** *Figurative.* not accessible; that cannot be reached or entered at all; unapproachable: *This savage hero was not inaccessible to pity* (Edward Gibbon). **3** that cannot be obtained; hard to obtain. **—in'ac|ces'si-ble|ness**, *n.* **—in'ac|ces'si|bly**, *adv.*

in|ac|cu|ra|cy (in ak'yər ə sē), *n., pl.* **-cies.** **1** lack of accuracy; a being inaccurate: *His inaccuracy in copying the numbers made the sum wrong.*
2 an error; mistake: *The inaccuracy was found in the first column.*

in|ac|cu|rate (in ak'yər it), *adj.* not accurate; not exact; containing mistakes; inexact: *Inaccurate measurement caused him to cut the board too short.* **SYN**: erroneous, faulty, incorrect. **—in|ac'cu-rate|ly**, *adv.* **—in|ac'cu|rate|ness**, *n.*

in|ac|tion (in ak'shən), *n.* absence of action; idleness; inactivity: *He soon grew impatient ... of the quiet and inaction of his mimic kingdom* (Washington Irving).

in|ac|ti|vate (in ak'tə vāt), *v.t.,* **-vat|ed, -vat|ing.**
1 to make inactive: *to inactivate a bomb.* **2** to destroy the activity of: *to inactivate a virus.* **—in'ac-ti|va'tion**, *n.*

in|ac|tive (in ak'tiv), *adj.* **1** not active: *Wall Street is sometimes inactive. There is also a listing of 2,000 inactive and defunct companies* (New York Times). **2** idle; slow; sluggish: *Bears are inactive during the winter. Inactive persons are rarely healthy.* **3** *Chemistry.* showing little tendency to combine with other elements, as rare gases.
4 *Physics.* showing no optical activity in polarized light. **5** *Military.* not on active duty. **—in|ac'tive|ly**, *adv.* **—in|ac'tive|ness**, *n.*
—*Syn.* 1, 2 Inactive, inert, dormant mean not in action or not showing activity. **Inactive** suggests inability or unwillingness to act: *He is an inactive member of the club.* **Inert** suggests being difficult or impossible to set in action or motion: *I dragged the inert, unconscious body from the water.* **Dormant** suggests a condition of sleep, sluggishness, or stupor: *Some animals and plants are dormant during the winter.*

in|ac|tiv|ism (in ak'tə viz əm), *n.* lack of activism: *inactivism in politics.*

in|ac|tiv|ist (in ak'tə vist), *n.* a person who is not an activist: *Having been an activist for a very long time, I am now a masterly inactivist* (Walter Lippmann).

in|ac|tiv|i|ty (in'ak tiv'ə tē), *n.* absence of activity; idleness; slowness; sluggishness.

in|a|dapt|a|bil|i|ty (in'ə dap'tə bil'ə tē), *n.* lack of adaptability.

in|a|dapt|a|ble (in'ə dap'tə bəl), *adj.* not adaptable; incapable of being adapted.

in|ad|e|qua|cy (in ad'ə kwə sē), *n., pl.* **-cies.**
1 the quality or condition of being inadequate; insufficiency: *He experienced feelings of inadequacy as a parent. This inadequacy of knowledge results from the lack of interest in the deep seas* (Science News Letter). **2** something that is inadequate.

in|ad|e|quate (in ad'ə kwit), *adj.* not adequate; not enough; not as much as required: *Inadequate preparation caused the boy to fail his final examination.* **—in|ad'e|quate|ly**, *adv.* **—in|ad'e|quate-ness**, *n.*

in|ad|mis|si|bil|i|ty (in'əd mis'ə bil'ə tē), *n.* the state of being inadmissible.

in|ad|mis|si|ble (in'əd mis'ə bəl), *adj.* **1** not to be permitted; not allowable. **2** not to be admitted or considered as evidence or proof: *Confessions taken in violation of these rights are inadmissible* (William D. Hawkland). **—in'ad|mis'si|bly**, *adv.*

in-a-door bed (in'ə dôr', -dōr'), = Murphy bed.

in|ad|vert|ence (in'əd vėr'təns), *n.* **1** lack of attention; carelessness. **2** an inadvertent act; oversight; mistake: *I am confident that this was no more than an inadvertence or a lapse of memory* (Time).

in|ad|vert|en|cy (in'əd vėr'tən sē), *n., pl.* **-cies.** = inadvertence.

in|ad|vert|ent (in'əd vėr'tənt), *adj.* **1** not attentive; careless; heedless; negligent. **SYN**: thoughtless, inattentive. **2** not done on purpose; caused by oversight: *His rudeness was inadvertent, and we forgave it.* **SYN**: unintentional, accidental.
3 characterized by inattention. **—in'ad|vert'ent|ly**, *adv.*

in|ad|vis|a|bil|i|ty (in'əd vī'zə bil'ə tē), *n.* the state of being inadvisable.

in|ad|vis|a|ble (in'əd vī'zə bəl), *adj.* not advisable; not prudent; unwise. **—in'ad|vis'a|bly**, *adv.*

in ae|ter|num (in ē tėr'nəm), *Latin.* forever.

in|al|ien|a|bil|i|ty (in āl'yə nə bil'ə tē, in ā'lē ə-), *n.* the condition of being inalienable.

in|al|ien|a|ble (in āl'yə nə bəl, -ā'lē ə-), *adj.* that cannot be given away or taken away: *Life, liberty, and the pursuit of happiness have been called the inalienable rights of man.* Also, **unalienable. —in|al'ien|a|bly**, *adv.*

in|al|ter|a|bil|i|ty (in ôl'tər ə bil'ə tē), *n.* unchangeableness.

in|al|ter|a|ble (in ôl'tər ə bəl), *adj.* not alterable; unchangeable. **SYN**: unalterable, immutable. **—in-al'ter|a|bly**, *adv.*

in|am|o|ra|ta (in am'ə rä'tə), *n., pl.* **-tas.** a girl or woman with whom one is in love; sweetheart: *I know not how the lover had behaved ... so as to decline in the favour of his inamorata* (Tobias G. Smollett). [< Italian *innamorata,* feminine of *innamorato* lover]

in|am|o|ra|to (in am'ə rä'tō), *n., pl.* **-tos.** a woman's lover: *Our girl wastes no time arranging to steal her inamorato's vehicle* (New Yorker). [< Italian *innamorato,* past participle of *innamorare* to fall in love, ultimately < Latin *in-* in + *amor* love]

in-and-in (in'ənd in'), *adv.,* **1** repeatedly within the same limits, as of family or strain: *to breed stock in-and-in.* **2** with constant interaction of any kind: *two minds forced in-and-in upon the matter in hand* (Robert Louis Stevenson).

in-and-out (in'ənd out'), *adj., adv.* **—*adj.*** **1** coming in and going out alternately; temporary: *in-and-out tourists.* **2** characterized by short-term buying and quick selling, especially for speculative gain on the stock market.
—*adv.* alternately in and out; now in, now out.

in-and-out|er (in'ənd out'ər), *n.* a person or thing that is temporarily engaged in something, especially to gain a profit.

in|ane (in ān'), *adj., n.* **—*adj.*** **1** without sense or ideas; silly or foolish; senseless: *It is inane to use the city universities as depositories for inferior students* (New York Times). **SYN**: empty-headed, frivolous, puerile, trifling. **2** empty; void: *the inane reaches of outer space.*
—*n.* **1** that which is without substance. **2** empty space; the void of infinite space.
[< Latin *inānis* empty] **—in|ane'ly**, *adv.* **—in-ane'ness**, *n.*

in|an|i|mate (in an'ə mit), *adj.* **1** not alive or animate; lifeless: *Stones are inanimate objects. He then fell, like an inanimate log, to the earth* (James Fenimore Cooper). **2** seeming to be lifeless; unconscious: *The lifeguard pulled the inanimate body out of the pool.* **3** *Figurative.* without liveliness or spirit; dull: *an inanimate face, an inanimate scene.* **SYN**: spiritless. [< Late Latin *inanimātus* lifeless < *in-* not + *animāre* to animate] **—in|an'i|mate|ly**, *adv.* **—in|an'i|mate|ness**, *n.*

in|a|ni|tion (in'ə nish'ən), *n.* **1** weakness from lack of food. **2** the condition of being empty; emptiness: *To escape inanition he sought to express himself in religion* (Harold Mattingly). [< Old French *inanition,* learned borrowing from Late Latin *inānītiō, -ōnis* < Latin *inānīre* to empty < *inānis* empty]

in|an|i|ty (in an'ə tē), *n., pl.* **-ties.** **1** lack of sense or ideas; silliness. **SYN**: frivolity, senselessness.
2 a silly or senseless act, practice, or remark: *The Mufti is a little man with a sweetly importuning face who imparts these inanities ... in the soft voice of the True Believer* (Harper's). **3** emptiness. **SYN**: vacuity, void.

in an|tis (in an'tis), *Latin.* between antae: *a portico in antis.*

in|ap|par|ent (in'ə par'ənt), *adj.* not apparent; not noticeable: *inapparent damage.*

in|ap|peas|a|ble (in'ə pēz'ə bəl), *adj.* not appeasable; not to be appeased: *inappeasable appetite or longing, inappeasable anger.*

in|ap|pel|la|bil|i|ty (in'ə pel'ə bil'ə tē), *n.* **1** incapability of being appealed from: *the inappellability of the councils.* **2** the condition of being without the possibility of appeal.

in|ap|pel|la|ble (in'ə pel'ə bəl), *adj.* not admitting of appeal: *inappellable authority.*

in|ap|pe|tence (in ap'ə təns), *n.* lack of or failure of appetite.

in|ap|pli|ca|bil|i|ty (in ap'lə kə bil'ə tē, in'ə-plik'ə-), *n.* the fact or condition of being inapplicable.

in|ap|pli|ca|ble (in ap'lə kə bəl, in'ə plik'ə-), *adj.* not applicable; not appropriate; not suitable: *The name Tiny is inapplicable to that big dog.* **SYN**: unbecoming, unfitting, inapposite, irrelevant. **—in-ap'pli|ca|ble|ness**, *n.* **—in|ap'pli|ca|bly**, *adv.*

in|ap|pli|ca|tion (in'ap lə kā'shən), *n.* **1** lack of application; negligence; inattention. **2** the quality of being inapplicable.

in|ap|po|site (in ap'ə zit), *adj.* not apposite; not pertinent; not suitable; inappropriate: *Past experience—the lawyer's "precedent"—may be useful ... or it may be wholly inapposite* (Nicholas deB. Katzenbach). **SYN**: inapplicable. **—in|ap'po-site|ly**, *adv.* **—in|ap'po|site|ness**, *n.*

in|ap|pre|ci|a|ble (in'ə prē'shē ə bəl, -shə-), *adj.* **1** too small to be noticed or felt; very slight. **SYN**: imperceptible, insignificant, intangible. **2** *Obsolete.* invaluable; priceless. **—in'ap|pre'ci|a|bly**, *adv.*

in|ap|pre|ci|a|tive (in'ə prē'shē ā'tiv, -shə tiv), *adj.* not appreciative; wanting in appreciation.
—in'ap|pre'ci|a'tive|ly, *adv.* **—in'ap|pre'ci|a'-tive|ness**, *n.*

in|ap|proach|a|ble (in'ə prō'chə bəl), *adj.* not approachable; inaccessible.

in|ap|pro|pri|ate (in'ə prō'prē it), *adj.* not appropriate; not suitable; not fitting; improper: *Jokes are inappropriate at a funeral.* **SYN**: unsuitable, unbecoming. **—in|ap|pro'pri|ate|ly**, *adv.* **—in|ap-pro'pri|ate|ness**, *n.*

in|apt (in apt'), *adj.* **1** not apt; not suitable; unfit. **SYN**: inappropriate, inapposite. **2** unskillful; awkward. **SYN**: unhandy. **—in|apt'ly**, *adv.* **—in|apt'-ness**, *n.*

in|ap|ti|tude (in ap'tə tüd, -tyüd), *n.* **1** unfitness; inappropriateness. **2** lack of skill: *He was acquiring a look of well-meaning but absolute inaptitude for arbitrating a difficult dispute of this kind* (J. D. Salinger). **SYN**: unskillfulness, unhandiness, awkwardness.

in|ar|bi|tra|ble (in är'bə trə bəl), *adj.* not subject to arbitration: *I ... challenge the view that all our values are ultimate values that are inarbitrable* (Sidney Hook).

in|arch (in ärch'), *v.t.* to graft by uniting a growing branch to a stock without separating the branch from its parent stock. [< *in-*[3] + *arch*[1], verb]

in|ar|gu|a|ble (in är'gyů ə bəl), *adj.* indisputable; unquestionable: *Its total and inarguable failure to produce a repeatable experiment ...* (New Scientist).

in|arm (in ärm'), *v.t.* to encircle with or as with the arms; embrace: *A flowing stream inarms a boulder in its passing.*

in|ar|tic|u|la|cy (in'är tik'yə lə sē), *n.* inarticulateness: *Inarticulacy ... makes a child incapable of communication in normal language* (London Times).

in|ar|tic|u|late (in'är tik'yə lit), *adj., n.* **—*adj.***
1 not distinct; not uttered in distinct syllables or words; not like regular speech: *When they called to him they heard only an inarticulate mutter. A baby makes inarticulate sounds.* **2** unable to speak in words; dumb: *Cats and dogs are inarticulate.* **SYN**: mute, speechless. **3** not able to put one's thoughts or feelings into words easily and clearly: *His grief made him inarticulate.* **4** *Zoology.* **a** not jointed or hinged; not composed of jointed segments: *A jellyfish's body is inarticulate.* **b** of or belonging to a division of brachiopods with nonarticulate valves.
—*n.* the quality of being inarticulate: *Each venture Is a new beginning, a raid on the inarticulate* (T. S. Eliot).
[< Latin *inarticulātus* < *in-* not + *articulāre* to articulate] **—in|ar|tic'u|late|ly**, *adv.* **—in|ar|tic'u-late|ness**, *n.*

in|ar|ti|fi|cial (in är'tə fish'əl), *adj.* **1** not artificial; natural. **2** artless; unaffected. **3** constructed without art or skill; clumsy; inartistic. **—in|ar'ti|fi'cial-ly**, *adv.*

in|ar|tis|tic (in'är tis'tik), *adj.* **1** not artistic; lacking good taste: *inartistic figures crowding the canvas of life without adequate effect* (George Eliot). **2** having no appreciation for or love of art; unskilled in art. **—in'ar|tis'ti|cal|ly**, *adv.*

in|as|much (in'əz much'), *adv.*
inasmuch as, a because; since: *Tim was given a head start in the race, inasmuch as he was smaller than the others.* **b** insofar as; to such a degree as: *God is only God inasmuch as He is the Moral Governor of a moral world* (William Hamilton).

in|as|sim|i|la|tion (in'ə sim'ə lā'shən), *n.* lack of assimilation.

in|as|suage|a|ble (in'ə swā'jə bəl), *adj.* that cannot be assuaged; unmitigable: [*She*] *was a melancholic, ... given to periods of inassuageable grief* (Rebecca West).

in|at|ten|tion (in′ə ten′shən), *n.* lack of attention; carelessness; negligence: *The boy lost his job through inattention to details. "The habit of inattention," Alexis de Tocqueville wrote of America ..."must be considered the greatest defect of the democratic character"* (Newsweek). **SYN**: disregard, heedlessness.

in|at|ten|tive (in′ə ten′tiv), *adj.* not attentive; careless; negligent. **SYN**: unmindful, preoccupied, absent-minded. —**in|at|ten′tive|ly**, *adv.* —**in|at|ten′tive|ness**, *n.*

in|au|di|bil|i|ty (in ô′də bil′ə tē), *n.* the state or quality of being inaudible: *If they clapped their palms, it would take perhaps two seconds for the sound to die to inaudibility* (Time).

in|au|di|ble (in ô′də bəl), *adj.* not audible; that cannot be heard: *the inaudible and noiseless foot of Time* (Shakespeare).

in|au|di|bly (in ô′də blē), *adv.* in an inaudible manner; so as not to be heard.

in|au|gu|ral (in ô′gyər əl), *adj., n.* —*adj.* **1** of or for an inauguration: *The President gave an inaugural address when he took office.* **2** beginning; first.
—*n.* **1** the address or speech made by a person when formally admitted to an office. **2** = inauguration.
[< French *inaugural* < *inaugurer* inaugurate, learned borrowing from Latin *inaugurāre*]

in|au|gu|rate (in ô′gyə rāt), *v.t.*, **-rat|ed, -rat|ing.** **1** to install in office with a ceremony: *A President of the United States is inaugurated every four years.* **SYN**: install, invest, induct. **2** to make a formal beginning of; begin: *The invention of the airplane inaugurated a new era in transportation.* **3** to open for public use with a ceremony or celebration: *The new city hall was inaugurated with a parade and speeches.* [< Latin *inaugurāre* (with English *-ate*[1]) consecrate by augury < *in-* for, on + *augurāre* to act as an augur, to predict < *augur* augur, soothsayer] —**in|au′gu|ra′tor**, *n.*

in|au|gu|ra|tion (in ô′gyə rā′shən), *n.* **1** the act or ceremony of installing a person in office. The inauguration of a President of the United States takes place on January 20. **2** a formal beginning; beginning. **3** an opening for public use with a ceremony or celebration.

Inauguration Day, *U.S.* the day upon which the President of the United States is inaugurated, now falling on January 20 of every year immediately following a year divisible by four. Before 1934 it fell on March 4.

in|aus|pi|cious (in′ô spish′əs), *adj.* with signs of failure, unfavorable; unlucky: *a tardy and inauspicious season* (Elisha K. Kane). *In spite of inauspicious economic conditions, the natural gas industry moved ahead* (Harper's). **SYN**: unpromising, unfortunate, unpropitious, untoward. —**in′aus|pi′cious|ly**, *adv.* —**in′aus|pi′cious|ness**, *n.*

in|au|then|tic (in′ô then′tik), *adj.* not authentic. —**in′au|then′ti|cal|ly**, *adv.*

in|au|then|tic|i|ty (in′ô then tis′ə tē), *n.* the condition of not being authentic.

in|au|thor|i|ta|tive (in′ə thôr′ə tā′tiv, -thor′-), *adj.* not authoritative. —**in′au|thor′i|ta′tive|ness**, *n.*

in|bark (in′bärk′), *n. Forestry.* a condition of wood in which portions of the external bark are included within the wood. It is often produced by the trunk and a branch growing together at the fork.

in-bas|ket (in′bas′kit, -bäs′-), *n.* a rectangular, shallow container with a low rim, used to hold incoming mail and memoranda and other current work; in-box or in-tray.

in-be|tween (in′bi twēn′), *adj., adv., n.* —*adj.* **1** that is in the middle; that comes in the space or time separating two places or persons: *Some patients need an in-between period after leaving the hospital and before going home* (Maclean's). **2** that is neither one kind nor the other; indifferent or uncommitted: *For ninety years the Secret Service has had hard jobs and easy jobs and jobs in-between* (New York Times).
—*adv.* = between.
—*n.* a person or thing that is in-between: *Some personality traits are common to all strongly opinionated persons, ... whether they are liberals, conservatives, or in-betweens* (Science News Letter). —**in′-be|tween′ness**, *n.*

in-be|tween|er (in′bi twē′nər), *n.* a person or thing that is in-between.

in|board (in′bôrd′, -bōrd′), *adv., adj., n.* —*adv., adj.* **1** inside the hull of a ship or boat: *an inboard motor.* **2** in or toward the middle of a ship or boat: *The cables were passed inboard through a block.* **3** in or toward the center of an aircraft or spacecraft close to the fuselage: *an inboard wing, an aerial mounted inboard.* **4** (in machinery) inside; interior.
—*n.* a boat containing an inboard motor.

in|board-out|board (in′bôrd out′bôrd, -bōrd-, -bōrd), *adj., n.* —*adj.* of or having to do with an inboard motorboat engine attached to an outboard drive shaft: *a boat with inboard-outboard power.*
—*n.* an inboard engine with an outboard drive unit; stern drive.

in|board-out|drive (in′bôrd out′drīv, -bōrd-), *adj., n.* = inboard-outboard.

in|born (in′bôrn′), *adj.* born in a person; instinctive; natural: *an inborn sense of rhythm. The artist had an inborn talent for drawing.* **SYN**: innate, inbred, inherent, ingrained, congenital, inherited.

in|bound (in′bound′), *adj.* inward bound: *an inbound vessel. The inbound flights were delayed by the storm.*

in|bounds (in′boundz′), *adj. Sports.* coming from out-of-bounds: *With three seconds remaining and the score 108-108, Baylor took an inbounds pass from Fred Crawford near midcourt* (New York Times).

inbounds lines, *U.S. Football.* = hash marks.

in-box (in′boks′), *n.* = in-basket.

in|break|ing (in′brā′king), *n., adj.* —*n.* the act of breaking in.
—*adj.* breaking in.

in|breath (in′breth′), *n.* an indrawn breath.

in|breathe (in brēŧʜ′), *v.t.*, **-breathed, -breath|ing.** **1** to breathe in. **2** to inspire.

in|bred (in′bred′, in bred′), *adj., v.* —*adj.* **1** inborn; natural: *The man, though poor, showed an inbred courtesy.* **SYN**: innate, native. **2** produced by breeding between closely related ancestors: *an inbred strain of horses.* **3** *Figurative.* exclusive; cliquish: *this inbred little writers' colony on Cape Cod* (New York Times).
—*v.* past tense and past participle of **inbreed**.

in|breed (in′brēd′, in brēd′), *v.t.*, **-bred, -breed|ing.** **1** to breed from closely related animals or plants. **2** to produce or develop within.

in|breed|ing (in′brē′ding), *n.* **1** breeding from closely related persons, animals, or plants, so as to preserve desired or eliminate undesired characteristics. **2** *Figurative.* exclusiveness; cliquishness: *There is less encouragement to political inbreeding than there was during the long generations when one party was completely dominant* (Harper's).

in|built (in′bilt′), *adj.* = built-in.

inc., an abbreviation for the following:
1 inclosure.
2a included. **b** including.
3 inclusive.
4 income.
5 increase.

Inc., Incorporated.

in|ca (ing′kə), *n.* a sea bird of the western coast of South America having dark plumage with a bundle of white plumes on each side of the head; inca tern. [< *Inca* (because it is found in Peru)]

In|ca (ing′kə), *n., pl.* **-cas** or **-ca.** **1** a member of the group of South American Indians who ruled a large empire in Peru and other parts of South America before the Spanish conquest in the 1500's. The Incas were highly civilized. **2** a ruler or a member of the royal family of this group. The Incas were Quechuans. [< Spanish *Inga*, or *Inca* < Quechua (Peru) *ynca* king; prince of the ruling family]

Inca dove, a small, grayish dove with feathers edged with black, found from Texas and Arizona south to Central America.

In|ca|ic (ing kā′ik), *adj.* = Incan.

in|cal|cu|la|bil|i|ty (in kal′kyə lə bil′ə tē), *n.* the quality of being incalculable.

in|cal|cu|la|ble (in kal′kyə lə bəl), *adj., n.* —*adj.* **1** too many to be counted; too great to be calculated; innumerable; beyond counting; numerous: *The sands of the sea are incalculable in number. In an instant, a treasure of incalculable value lay gleaming before us* (Edgar Allan Poe). **2** impossible to foretell or reckon beforehand: *A flood in the valley would cause incalculable losses.* **3** that cannot be relied on; uncertain: *He has an incalculable disposition.*
—*n.* something incalculable: *All the considerations are here, some resolved into formulae ... and some still too much hampered by incalculables* (New Scientist). —**in|cal′cu|la|ble|ness**, *n.*

in|cal|cu|la|bly (in kal′kyə lə blē), *adv.* in an incalculable manner; immeasurably.

in|ca|les|cent (in′kə les′ənt), *adj.* growing warm; increasing in heat. [< Latin *incalēscēns, -entis*, present participle of *incalēscere* < *in-* (intensive) + *calēscere* grow warm] —**in′ca|les′cence**, *n.*

in ca|me|ra (in kam′ər ə), *Latin.* **1** in private, or within closed doors; secret: *Legislative investigations can be successfully carried on in camera without hoopla* (New Yorker). **2** (literally) in a chamber.

In|can (ing′kən), *n., adj.* —*n.* an Inca.
—*adj.* of or having to do with the Incas.

in|can|desce (in′kən des′), *v.i., v.t.*, **-desced, -desc|ing.** to glow or cause to glow with heat. [< Latin *incandēscere* begin to glow < *in-* (intensive) + *candēscere* become white-hot]

in|can|des|cence (in′kən des′əns), *n.* the condition of a body which glows and gives off light when it is heated; red-hot or white-hot condition: *It was found that electrical energy could be converted into light by sending a current through a wire of high resistance, thereby heating it to incandescence.* (Hardy and Perrin).

in|can|des|cent (in′kən des′ənt), *adj.* **1** glowing with heat; red-hot or white-hot; heated to such a high temperature that it gives out light: *The embers of the fire were still incandescent even though the flames had disappeared. The light of an electric lamp comes from an incandescent filament.* **2** *Figurative.* intensely bright; brilliant; radiant: *the young man with the dark forelock dropping over his incandescent eyes* (Time). [*He*] *makes a first appearance of incandescent charm* (Manchester Guardian Weekly). **3** having to do with or containing a material that gives light by incandescence. [< Latin *incandēscēns, -entis*, present participle of *incandēscere;* see etym. under **incandesce**] —**in′can|des′cent|ly**, *adv.*

***incandescent lamp** or **bulb**, a lamp containing a material that gives light by incandescence, especially an electric lamp with a filament of very fine wire that becomes white-hot and gives off light when current flows through it; light bulb: *Mercury lamps provide a source of light two or three times as efficient as incandescent lamps* (Science News Letter).

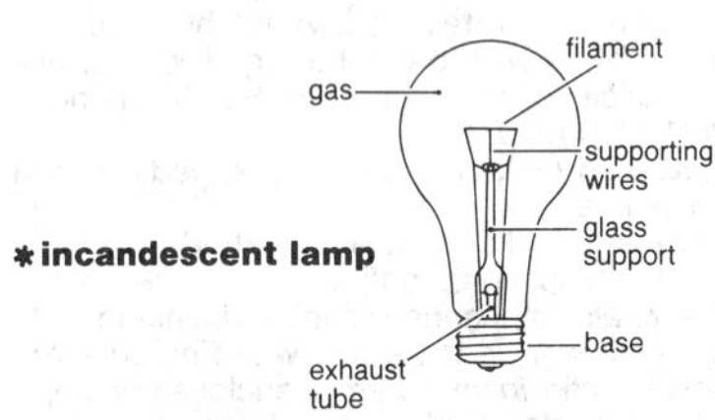

***incandescent lamp**

incandescent light, **1** the light produced from an incandescent object, lamp, or the like. **2** = incandescent lamp.

in|cant (in kant′), *v.t.* **1** to use (a set of words) as incantation. **2** *Obsolete.* to enchant; charm. —*v.i.* to use incantation or enchantment: *He recited, he incanted, and one way or another interposed himself between Yeats and* [*others*] (London Times). [< Latin *incantāre;* see etym. under **incantation**. See etym. of doublet **enchant**.] —**in′can|ta′tor**, *n.*

in|can|ta|tion (in′kan tā′shən), *n.* **1** a set of words spoken or chanted as a magic charm or to cast a magic spell. "Double, double, toil and trouble, Fire burn and caldron bubble," is an incantation. **2** the use of such words. **3** magical ceremonies; magic; sorcery. [< Latin *incantātiō, -ōnis* < *incantāre* chant a magic formula against < *in-* against + *cantāre* to chant]

in|can|ta|tion|al (in′kan tā′shə nəl), *adj.* = incantatory.

in|can|ta|to|ry (in kan′tə tôr′ē, -tōr′-), *adj.* of or like an incantation: *Malraux strives to convert us to an old faith, and his style, appropriately, is incantatory, intoxicant, and Wagnerian* (Harper's).

in|cap (in′kap), *n. Slang.* an incapacitant.

IN|CAP (in′kap), *n.* Institute of Nutrition for Central America and Panama.

in|ca|pa|bil|i|ty (in′kā pə bil′ə tē, in kā′-), *n.* a being incapable; incapacity; unfitness. **SYN**: inability, incompetence.

in|ca|pa|ble (in kā′pə bəl), *adj., n.* —*adj.* having very little ability; without ordinary ability; not capable; not efficient; not competent: *An employer cannot afford to hire incapable workers.* **SYN**: incompetent, inefficient, unable, unfit.
—*n.* a thoroughly incompetent person; person without capacity or ability: *No greater mistake can be made than, as journalists and politicians are apt to do, to treat the mass of members of a Trade Society as dupes, idlers, drunkards, or incapables* (Punch).
incapable of, a without the ability, power, or fitness for: *That weak boy is incapable of making the football team. His honesty made him incapable of lying.* **b** not legally qualified for: *A foreigner is incapable of becoming president of the United States.* **c** not open or ready for; not susceptible to: *incapable of exact measurement. Gold is almost incapable of rusting.* **d** *Archaic.* not capable

Pronunciation Key: hat, āge, cãre, fär; let, ēqual, tėrm; it, īce; hot, ōpen, ôrder; oil, out; cup, pu̇t, rüle; child; long; thin; ŧʜen; zh, measure; ə represents **a** in about, **e** in taken, **i** in pencil, **o** in lemon, **u** in circus.

of understanding or comprehending; insensible to: *She chanted snatches of old tunes, As one incapable of her own distress* (Shakespeare). [< Late Latin *incapābilis* < *in-* not + *capābilis* capable] —**in|ca′pa|ble|ness**, *n.* —**in|ca′pa|bly**, *adv.*

in|ca|pa|cious (in′kə pā′shəs), *adj.* **1** not capacious; lacking capacity; narrow; limited. **2** mentally incapable. [< Late Latin *incapāx, -ācis* (with English *-ous*) < *in-* not + Latin *capāx, -ācis* capacious] —**in′ca|pa′cious|ness**, *n.*

in|ca|pac|i|tant (in′kə pas′ə tənt), *n.* a chemical agent or drug temporarily inducing sleepiness, dizziness, disorientation, or paralysis.

in|ca|pac|i|tate (in′kə pas′ə tāt), *v.t.*, **-tat|ed, -tat|ing.** **1** to limit in ability, power, or fitness; disable: *The player's injury incapacitated him for playing football.* **2** to disqualify legally: *The people cannot incapacitate the King* (John Dryden).

in|ca|pac|i|ta|tion (in′kə pas′ə tā′shən), *n.* = incapacity.

in|ca|pac|i|ta|tor (in′kə pas′ə tā tər), *n.* any substance used, especially in warfare, to disable a person temporarily, as by inducing sleep or mental confusion; incapacitant.

in|ca|pac|i|ty (in′kə pas′ə tē), *n., pl.* **-ties. 1a** lack of ability, power, or fitness; disability: *a leaden incapacity of motion that seized him* (Charles Reade). **SYN:** unfitness, inability, incompetence. **b** an instance of this. **2** legal disqualification. [< Middle French *incapacité,* learned borrowing from Latin *incapācitās* < *incapāx* incapacious]

In|cap|a|ri|na (in′kap ə rē′nə), *n.* any one of several inexpensive, protein-rich, vegetable foods developed by INCAP to combat conditions of nutritional deficiency in Central and South America. [< *INCAP* + (f)*arina*]

in|cap|su|late (in kap′sə lāt), *v.t.*, **-lat|ed, -lat|ing.** = encapsulate.

in|car|cer|ate (in kär′sə rāt), *v.*, **-at|ed, -at|ing,** *adj.* —***v.t.*** to imprison; confine.
—***adj.*** *Archaic.* imprisoned; confined; shut in.
[< Medieval Latin *incarcerare* (with English *-ate*[1]) imprison < Latin *in-* in + *carcer* enclosed place, prison] —**in|car′cer|a′tion**, *n.* —**in|car′cer|a′tor**, *n.*

in|car|di|nate (in kär′də nāt), *v.t.*, **-nat|ed, -nat|ing. 1a** to institute or attach as chief presbyter, priest, or deacon, in a particular place, church, or diocese. **b** (in the Roman Catholic Church) to make formal observance of the accession of (a candidate to the priesthood or a priest to a diocesan post). **2** to institute as a cardinal. [< Late Latin *incardināre* (with English *-ate*[1]) < *in-* in + *cardināre* assign to a church < Latin *cardō, -inis* hinge, pivot] —**in|car′di|na′tion**, *n.*

in|car|na|dine (in kär′nə din, -dīn, -dēn), *adj., n., v.*, **-dined, -din|ing.** *Archaic.* —***adj.*** **1a** crimson or blood-red. **b** = bloodstained. **2** = flesh-colored.
—***n.*** **1** flesh color; blush color. **2** a crimson or blood-red color.
—***v.t.*** to make blood-red or flesh-colored.
[< French *incarnadin* < Italian *incarnadino,* variant of *incarnatino* < *incarnato* flesh-colored < Latin *incarnāre* to incarnate]

in|car|nate (*adj.* in kär′nit, -nāt; *v.* in kär′nāt), *adj., v.*, **-nat|ed, -nat|ing.** —***adj.*** **1** embodied in flesh, especially in human form: *the Devil incarnate. The villain was evil incarnate.* **2** personified or typified, as a quality or idea: *Liberty and independence itself seemed incarnate in his name* (John R. Green). **3** *Botany.* flesh-colored.
—***v.t.*** **1** to make incarnate; embody. **2** to put into an actual form; realize: *The sculptor incarnated his vision in a beautiful statue.* **3** to be the living embodiment of: *She incarnates all the virtues of womanhood. Lancelot incarnated the spirit of chivalry.* **SYN:** personify. [< Latin *incarnātus* < *in-* in + *carō, carnis* flesh]

In|car|na|tion (in′kär nā′shən), *n.* **1** the union of divine nature and human nature in the person of Jesus Christ; the assumption of human form by the Son of God; the hypostatic union. **2** the embodiment of God in the person of Jesus Christ. **3** *Obsolete.* the birth of Jesus.

in|car|na|tion (in′kär nā′shən), *n.* **1** the act or fact of taking on human form by a divine being: *the incarnation of an angel.* **2** a person or thing that represents some quality or idea; embodiment: *The miser was an incarnation of greed.* **3** the person or form in which a god or spirit is incarnated; avatar; personification: *Krishna is an incarnation of Vishnu. When shall my soul her incarnation quit?* (Edward Young). **4** a distinct period or stage of life: *There are still enough people around him [the Secretary of State] who knew him in his previous incarnation as the busy academic* (Manchester Guardian Weekly).

in|case (in kās′), *v.t.*, **-cased, -cas|ing.** = encase.

in|case|ment (in kās′mənt), *n.* = encasement.

inca tern, = inca.

in|cau|tion (in kô′shən), *n.* lack of caution; carelessness; heedlessness.

in|cau|tious (in kô′shəs), *adj.* not cautious; wanting in caution; heedless; reckless; rash: *In an incautious moment he revealed the secret he had sworn to keep.* **SYN:** imprudent, unwary, careless. [< *in-*[1] + *cautious*] —**in|cau′tious|ly**, *adv.* —**in-cau′tious|ness**, *n.*

in|cen|di|a|rism (in sen′dē ə riz′əm), *n.* **1** the crime of setting fire to property intentionally. **SYN:** arson. **2** *Figurative.* the deliberate sitrring up of strife, violence, or rebellion.

in|cen|di|a|rist (in sen′dē ə rist), *n.* = incendiary.

in|cen|di|ar|y (in sen′dē er′ē), *adj., n., pl.* **-ar|ies.**
—***adj.*** **1** having to do with the setting of property on fire intentionally: *an incendiary act.* **2** causing fire or containing chemicals that are used to start a fire: *The enemy town was set on fire with incendiary shells and bombs.* **3** *Figurative.* deliberately stirring up strife, violence, or rebellion: *The agitator was arrested for making incendiary speeches.*
—***n.*** **1** a person who intentionally sets fire to property. **SYN:** arsonist. **2** *Figurative.* a person who deliberately stirs up strife, violence, or rebellion: *The Jesuits had been the incendiaries of the late insurrection* (Horace Walpole). **SYN:** agitator. **3** a shell or bomb containing chemical agents that cause fire.
[< Latin *incendiārius* causing fire < *incendium* fire < *incendere* to set afire < *in-* (intensive) + *candēre* glow white]

in|cen|dive (in sen′div), *adj.* capable of setting fire; incendiary.

in|cense[1] (in′sens), *n., v.*, **-censed, -cens|ing.**
—***n.*** **1** a substance giving off a sweet smell when burned, such as an aromatic gum or other vegetable product, or a mixture of fragrant gums and spices. **2** the perfume or smoke from it, especially when burned in religious ceremonies. **3** something sweet like incense: *the incense of flowers,* (*Figurative.*) *the incense of flattery,* (*Figurative.*) *the incense of praise.* **4** *Figurative.* homage or praise.
—***v.t.*** **1** to burn or offer incense before, especially in connection with a religious ceremony; perfume with incense. **2** to perfume with any pleasant fragrance; scent.
—***v.i.*** to burn or offer incense.
[< Old French *encens,* learned borrowing from Late Latin *incēnsus, -ūs* burnt incense < Latin *incendere* to set afire < *in-* (intensive) + *candēre* glow white]

in|cense[2] (in sens′), *v.t.*, **-censed, -cens|ing.** **1** to make very angry; fill with rage: *Cruelty incenses kind people.* **SYN:** enrage, madden, provoke, exasperate. **2** *Obsolete.* to inflame, excite, or kindle (passion or ardent feeling): *Will God incense his ire For such a petty trespass?* (Milton). [< Latin *incēnsus,* past participle of *incendere* to set afire; enrage; see etym. under **incense**[1]] —**in|cense′ment**, *n.*

incense burner, a vessel or receptacle, often highly ornamental, for holding incense when burned; censer; thurible.

incense tree, any one of various trees that yield incense, or whose wood or foliage has a fragrance like that of incense.

in|cen|ter (in′sen′tər), *n. Mathematics.* the center of the inscribed circle in a triangle.

in|cen|tive (in sen′tiv), *n., adj.* —***n.*** a thing that urges a person on; a cause of action or effort; motive; stimulus: *The fun of playing the game was a greater incentive than the prize. This accentuated the world shortage, and added incentive to soaring prices for the metal* (Wall Street Journal). **SYN:** spur, incitement, provocation. See syn. under **motive**.
—***adj.*** arousing to feeling or action; inciting; encouraging. **SYN:** exciting, provocative.
[< Latin *incentīvum,* noun use of neuter adjective (in Late Latin, inciting) < *incinere* strike up; blow into (a flute) < *in-* in, into + *canere* to sing]

incentive pay or **bonus**, a payment or bonus to induce a worker, employee, or farmer to increase or improve production: *[The] management wanted some 250 workers to give up their present incentive pay, which would have cut their daily wages by about $5 a man* (Wall Street Journal).

incentive rate, a wage rate under which a worker may earn more by producing more; piece rate.

in|cept (in sept′), *v.i.* **1** to complete the taking of a degree of master or doctor (in certain English universities, now especially at Cambridge). **2** to enter upon one's career or office. —***v.t.*** **1** to take in (matter), as an organism or cell. **2** to begin; arouse: *... full of breathless satisfaction at having incepted progressive action in his commander* (Atlantic). [< Latin *inceptus, -ūs* a beginning < *incipere* begin, take in hand < *in-* on + *capere* take, seize]

in|cep|tion (in sep′shən), *n.* a beginning or originating; commencement: *the inception of a plan.* **SYN:** origin.

in|cep|tive (in sep′tiv), *adj., n.* —***adj.*** **1** beginning; initial. **SYN:** incipient. **2** *Grammar.* (of verbs, tense, or aspect) expressing the beginning of an action.
—***n.*** an inceptive verb. —**in|cep′tive|ly**, *adv.*

in|cep|tor (in sep′tər), *n.* **1** = beginner. **2** *British.* a person who incepts in a university.

in|cer|ti|tude (in sėr′tə tüd, -tyüd), *n.* **1** uncertainty; doubt; hesitation. **SYN:** dubiety. **2** uncertain or insecure condition; insecurity. [< Late Latin *incertitūdō* < Latin *incertus* < *in-* not + *certus* determined, certain]

in|ces|san|cy (in ses′ən sē), *n.* = ceaselessness.

in|ces|sant (in ses′ənt), *adj.* never stopping; continual: *The roar of Niagara Falls is incessant. The incessant noise from the factory kept me awake all night.* **SYN:** ceaseless, constant. [< Late Latin *incessāns, -antis* unceasing < Latin *in-* not + *cessāns,* present participle of *cessāre* cease, stand back] —**in|ces′sant|ly**, *adv.* —**in|ces′sant-ness**, *n.*

in|cest (in′sest), *n.* sexual intercourse between persons so closely related that their marriage is prohibited by law or by custom, as between brother and sister or parent and child. [< Latin *incestum,* noun < *incestus* unchaste, impure < *in-* not + *castus* pure]

in|ces|tu|ous (in ses′chu̇ əs), *adj.* **1** involving or of the nature of incest. **2** guilty of incest. —**in-ces′tu|ous|ly**, *adv.* —**in|ces′tu|ous|ness**, *n.*

inch**[1] (inch), *n., v.* —n.*** **1** a measure of length, equal to 1/12 of a foot or 1/36 of a yard or 2.54 centimeters. *Abbr:* in. **2** the amount of rainfall or snowfall that would cover a surface to the depth of one inch. **3** = water-inch. **4** *Figurative.* the smallest part, amount, degree, measure, or distance; very little bit: *Neither debater would yield an inch. [He] refused to give an inch in argument* (London Times). **5** the pressure corresponding to one inch of a vertical column of mercury, or some similar substance in a barometer.
—***v.i.*** to move slowly or little by little: *The worm inched along. The value of the stock inched up toward its all-time high.*
—***v.t.*** to move by inches or small degrees: *The defendant had been given a signal ... to come out, and as he was inching his way out the plaintiff, who had not seen the side road, collided with him* (London Times).
by inches, slowly; little by little; gradually: *The small town grew by inches.*
every inch, in every way; completely: *every inch a king* (Shakespeare).
inch by inch, slowly; little by little: *The idea developed inch by inch in his mind until he perfected it.*
within an inch of, very near; very close to: *He came within an inch of being caught in the sudden storm.*
within an inch of one's life, to the point of death: *He was beaten within an inch of his life.*
[Old English *ynce* < Latin *uncia* (originally) a twelfth part. See etym. of doublets **ounce**[1], **oka.**]

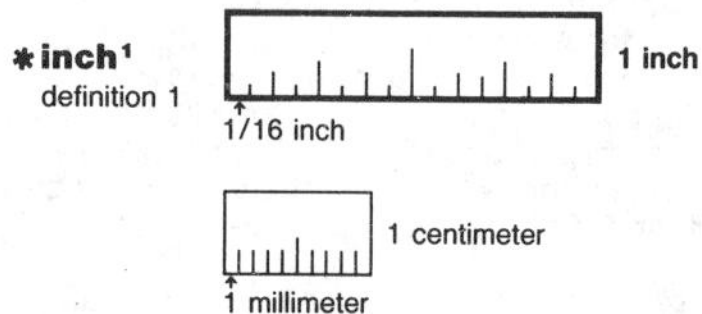

inch[2] (inch), *n.* a small island (frequent in the names of small islands belonging to Scotland). [< Gaelic *innis, innse,* genitive, island]

inch|age (in′chij), *n.* the length or distance of something in inches: *the maximum inchage of print* (Atlantic).

-incher, *combining form.* a person or thing of a specified length or height: *We took and released three other fish, keeping one fourteen-incher* (New York Times).

inch|meal (inch′mēl′), *adv., adj., n.* —***adv.*** little by little; slowly: *He saved up his money inchmeal.*
—***adj.*** very slow: *After an inchmeal start he made rapid progress at school.*
—***n.*** **by inchmeal**, little by little; slowly: *To lengthen our miserable lives a few hours, to die, as it were, by inchmeal* (John Flavel).
[< *inch*[1] + *-meal,* as in *piecemeal*]

in|cho|ate (*adj.* in kō′it; *v.* in′kō āt), *adj., v.*, **-at-ed, -at|ing.** —***adj.*** just begun; in an early stage; incomplete; undeveloped: *Yet he stood ... tensing with an inchoate sense of his conspicuousness* (Atlantic). *Each one of us has the prerogative of completing his inchoate and rudimental nature* (Cardinal Newman).
—***v.t., v.i.*** to begin; commence; start: *[He] grows in stature when you see his thought inchoated* (New Statesman).

[< Latin *inchoātus*, variant of *incohātus*, past participle of *incohāre* begin; (originally) harness < *in-* on + *cohum* yoke fastener] — **in|cho′ate|ly**, *adv.* — **in|cho′ate|ness**, *n.* — **in′cho|a′tion**, *n.*

in|cho|a|tive (in kō′ə tiv), *adj., n.* — ***adj.*** **1** = inchoate. **2** *Grammar.* = inceptive.
— ***n.*** an inceptive verb.

inch-pound (inch′pound′), *n.* one twelfth of a foot-pound, or the quantity of energy needed to raise a weight of one pound avoirdupois against gravity to a height of one inch. *Abbr:* in.-lb.

***inch|worm** (inch′wėrm′), *n.* a measuring worm; larva of a geometrid; cankerworm. [American English < *inch*[1] + *worm*]

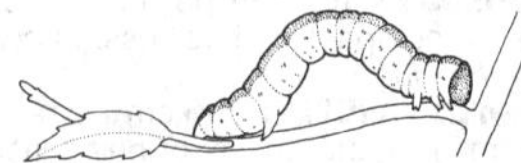
***inchworm**

in|ci|dence (in′sə dəns), *n.* **1** the way in which (something, such as a tax or disease) falls or distributes itself; range of occurrence or influence: *In an epidemic the incidence of a disease is widespread. The incidence of a tax is limited if only a few people must pay the tax.* **2** a falling on or affecting. **3a** the falling or striking of a projectile or ray of light or heat upon a surface: *In equal incidences there is considerable inequality of refraction* (Sir Isaac Newton). **b** the angle formed by this line or ray with a line perpendicular to the surface; angle of incidence. **4** *Geometry.* partial coincidence of figures, in which all of one figure forms part of another.

in|ci|dent (in′sə dənt), *n., adj.* — ***n.*** **1a** a happening or event, viewed as a separate circumstance: *So carefully has the incident been planned that all concerned ... feel themselves in the power of a machine* (London Times). **SYN**: occurrence, episode. See syn. under **event. b** a troublesome or disturbing happening: *In South Africa the official policy of apartheid continued to provoke incidents in the universities* (Leonard R. Buckley). **2** an event that happens in connection with something else more important: *She told all the main facts of her trip and a few of the amusing incidents.* **3** a distinct piece of action in a story, play, or poem, usually subordinate to the main action: *A tale should be judicious, clear, succinct; The language plain, and incidents well link'd* (William Cowper). **4** *Especially Law.* something connected with or dependent on something else (the principal). **5** (in feudal law) any of the provisions or conditions, such as homage and wardship, on which the agreement between lord and vassal depended.
— ***adj.*** **1** liable to happen; belonging: *Hardships are incident to the life of an explorer.* **SYN**: relating. **2** falling or striking (upon): *rays of light incident upon a mirror.* **3** *Especially Law.* connected with or dependent on something else. **4** *Rare or Obsolete.* casual; incidental.
[< Latin *incidēns, -entis*, present participle of *incidere* befall < *in-* on + *cadere* fall]

in|ci|den|tal (in′sə den′təl), *adj., n.* — ***adj.*** **1** happening or likely to happen in connection with something else, especially something else more important; of little importance: *Certain discomforts are incidental to the joys of camping out. The report was so full of incidental details that it was hard to understand what the main point was.* **SYN**: See syn. under **accidental. 2** occurring by chance: *an incidental meeting of an old friend on the street.* **SYN**: occasional, casual. **3** incurred casually and in addition to the main amount: *incidental expenses or charges.*
— ***n.*** **1** something incidental; an incidental circumstance or event. **2** *Music.* a tone not properly belonging to a chord, or a harmony foreign to a key.
incidentals, incidental items, especially of expense: *On our trip we spent $52 for meals, room, and railroad fare, and $1.50 for incidentals, such as candy and magazines.*

in|ci|den|tal|ly (in′sə den′tə lē, -dent′lē), *adv.* **1** as an incident along with something else; by the way: *He said, incidentally, that he had had no dinner.* **2** accidentally.

incidental music, music played during a motion picture, play, or display, to help bring about a desired emotional response from the audience; mood music.

in|ci|den|tals (in′sə den′təlz), *n.pl.* See under **incidental.**

in|cin|der|jell (in sin′dər jel′), *n.* jellied gasoline combined with napalm and used in flame throwers and fire bombs. [alteration of *incendiary gel*]

in|cin|er|ate (in sin′ə rāt), *v.,* **-at|ed, -at|ing.**
— ***v.t.*** to burn to ashes; cremate.
— ***v.i.*** to become reduced to ashes. [< Medieval Latin *incinerare* (with English *-ate*[1]) < Latin *in-* into + *cinis, -eris* ashes] — **in|cin′er|a′tion**, *n.*

in|cin|er|a|tor (in sin′ə rā′tər), *n.* a furnace or other arrangement for burning trash and other things to ashes; cremator.

in|cip|i|ence (in sip′ē əns), *n.* the very beginning; early stage. **SYN**: inchoateness, outset.

in|cip|i|en|cy (in sip′ē ən sē), *n., pl.* **-cies.** = incipience.

in|cip|i|ent (in sip′ē ənt), *adj.* just beginning; in an early stage; commencing: *The medicine stopped the boy's incipient cough from becoming worse.* **SYN**: initial. [< Latin *incipiēns, -entis*, present participle of *incipere* begin < *in-* on + *capere* take] — **in|cip′i|ent|ly**, *adv.*

in|ci|pit (in′si pit), *Latin.* **1** here begins (used by medieval scribes to mark the beginning of a selection in a manuscript). **2** the beginning words of such a selection.

in|cise (in sīz′), *v.t.,* **-cised, -cis|ing. 1** to cut into: *to incise wood with lettering.* **2** to carve; engrave: *to incise a figure or inscription.* (*Figurative.*) *The characters are broadly incised with plenty of Shakespearean humor* (New Yorker). [< Middle French *inciser* < Old French *enciser* < Latin *incīdere* < *in-* into + *caedere* to cut]

in|cised (in sīzd′), *adj.* **1** cut into. **2** produced by cutting; carved; engraved. **3** having notches around the edge: *an incised leaf.* **SYN**: serrated.

in|ci|sion (in sizh′ən), *n.* **1** a cut made in something; gash: *The doctor made a tiny incision to take out the splinter in my hand.* **2** a deep indentation or notch, such as one in the margin of a leaf or of an insect's wing. **3** the act of incising. **4** *Figurative.* incisive quality; incisiveness.

in|ci|sion|al (in sizh′ə nəl), *adj.* of or having to do with an incision: *an incisional scar.*

incisional hernia, a hernia resulting from a surgical or accidental incision.

in|ci|sive (in sī′siv), *adj.* **1** that cuts; sharp; penetrating; piercing; keen: *An incisive criticism goes directly to the point and uses plain words. Niebuhr's style is so incisive ... that one hesitates to challenge him* (Saturday Review). **SYN**: acute, cutting, trenchant. **2** incising; cutting. **3** of, having to do with, or in the region of the incisors. — **in|ci′sive|ly**, *adv.* — **in|ci′sive|ness**, *n.*

in|ci|sor (in sī′zər), *n.* a tooth having a sharp edge for cutting; one of the front teeth in mammals between the canine teeth in either jaw. Human beings have eight incisors in all. [< New Latin *incisor* < Latin *incīdere*; see etym. under **incise**]

in|ci|so|ry (in sī′sər ē), *adj.* adapted for cutting, as the incisor teeth.

in|cis|ur|al (in sizh′ər əl), *adj.* having an incisure.

in|cis|ure (in sizh′ər), *n.* an incision, cleft, or notch; a deep indentation.

in|cit|ant (in sī′tənt), *adj., n.* — ***adj.*** that incites: *an incitant force.*
— ***n.*** something that incites: *a disease incitant.*

in|ci|ta|tion (in′sī tā′shən, -sə-), *n.* **1** an inciting; moving into action. **2** *Obsolete.* a stimulus; incentive; incitement.

in|cite (in sīt′), *v.,* **-cit|ed, -cit|ing.** — ***v.t.*** to urge on; stir up; rouse; stimulate to action: *The captain's example incited the men to bravery. Agitators incited the men to strike. Each host now joins, and each a god inspires, These Mars incites, and those Minerva fires* (Alexander Pope).
— ***v.i.*** to cause or be an incitement; stir up others: *Criminal sanctions are still imposed on those who incite to crime and violence by words* (Philip B. Kurland).
[< Latin *incitāre* < *in-* on + *citāre* arouse (frequentative) < *ciēre* to set in motion] — **in|cit′er**, *n.*
— ***Syn.*** **Incite, instigate** mean to stir up or urge on to action. **Incite** means to stir up or stimulate to action, whether good or bad: *to incite men to fight bravely, to incite a riot.* **Instigate** chiefly means to stir up to do something bad, or, more often, to bring about something bad, such as a plot or rebellion, by inciting others to act: *to instigate a rebellion. Police never discovered who instigated the lynching.*

in|cite|ment (in sīt′mənt), *n.* **1** anything that urges on, stirs up, or rouses: *Abject poverty can be an incitement to steal. Interest is an incitement to study.* **SYN**: motive, incentive. **2** the act of urging on, stirring up, or rousing. **SYN**: stimulation.

in|cit|ing (in sī′ting), *adj.* that incites; stimulating; provoking. — **in|cit′ing|ly**, *adv.*

in|ci|vil|i|ty (in′sə vil′ə tē), *n., pl.* **-ties. 1** lack of courtesy; impoliteness; rudeness. **SYN**: discourtesy, disrespect. **2** a rude or impolite act: *No person offered me the least incivility* (John M. Ludlow).

in|ci|vism (in′sə viz əm), *n.* bad citizenship; neglect of civic duties: *Socrates is to be ... exculpated from the charge of incivism* (George Grote).

incl., **1** inclosure. **2** including. **3** inclusive.

in|clem|en|cy (in klem′ən sē), *n., pl.* **-cies.** inclement condition or quality; severity; harshness: *The inclemency of the weather kept us at home during the snowstorm.* **SYN**: rigor.

in|clem|ent (in klem′ənt), *adj.* **1** rough or stormy: *Inclement weather is common in winter.* **SYN**: rigorous. **2** not merciful or kindly; severe; harsh: *The dictator was an inclement ruler.* **SYN**: cruel, pitiless. [< Latin *inclēmēns, -entis* < *in-* not + *clēmēns* gentle, clement] — **in|clem′ent|ly**, *adv.*

in|clin|a|ble (in klī′nə bəl), *adj.* **1** inclined; disposed. **2** favorably disposed; favorable: *an inclinable mood, inclinable to a plan.*

in|cli|na|tion (in′klə nā′shən), *n.* **1** tendency; a tending toward a certain quality or condition; natural bent: *He has an inclination to become fat.* **SYN**: proneness, propensity. **2** preference; liking: *Most boys have an inclination for sports.* **SYN**: bias, predilection, affection. **3** a leaning, bending, or bowing: *A nod is an inclination of the head.* **4a** a slope; slant: *That high roof has a sharp inclination.* **SYN**: declivity. **b** the amount of slope or deviation from the horizontal position. **c** an inclined surface; incline. **5** *Geometry.* the difference of direction of two lines or planes, especially as measured by the angle between them. **6** *Astronomy.* **a** the angle between the plane of the orbit of a planet and the ecliptic. **b** the angle between the plane of the orbit of a satellite and the equatorial plane of the primary. [< Latin *inclīnātiō, -ōnis* < *inclīnāre;* see etym. under **incline**]

in|cli|na|tion|al (in′klə nā′shə nəl), *adj.* **1** relating to slope or inclination to the horizon. **2** of or having to do with mental inclination or disposition.

in|cline (*v.* in klīn′; *n.* in′klīn, in klīn′), *v.,* **-clined, -clin|ing,** *n.* — ***v.i.*** **1** to be favorable; be willing; tend: *Dogs incline to eat meat as a food. I incline toward your idea.* **2** to slope; slant. **3** to lean, bend, or bow.
— ***v.t.*** **1** to make favorable; make willing; influence: *Incline your hearts to obey God's laws.* **2** to lean, bend, or bow: *He inclined his head in prayer.* **3** to cause to slope or slant; tilt.
— ***n.*** **1** a slope; slant: *There is a slight incline to the counter.* **2** a sloping surface. The side of a hill is an incline.
[< Old French *encliner* < Latin *inclīnāre* < *in-* in + *clīnāre* to bend] — **in|clin′er**, *n.*

in|clined (in klīnd′), *adj.* **1** favorable; willing; tending: *I am inclined to agree with you.* **SYN**: disposed, minded. **2** sloping; slanting: *The planes of the orbits of these two satellites are considerably inclined* (Scientific American). **3** *Mathematics.* forming an angle with something else.

***inclined plane**, a plank or other plane surface put at an angle to a horizontal surface, one of the six simple machines. An inclined plane is used with relatively small force.

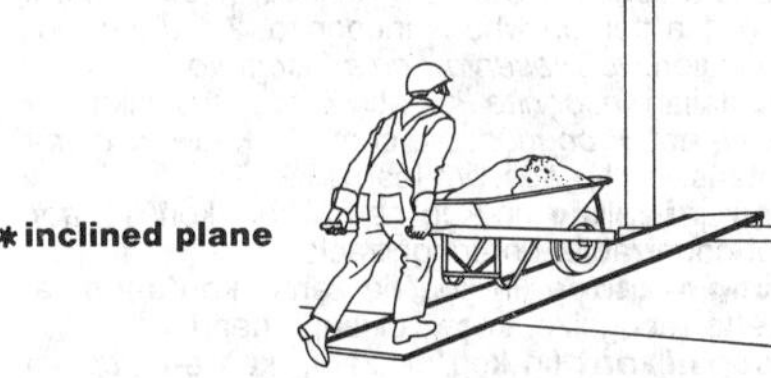
***inclined plane**

in|clin|ing (in klī′ning), *n.* **1** a tendency, propensity, or bent (physical or mental). **2** *Archaic.* party; following.

in|cli|nom|e|ter (in′klə nom′ə tər), *n.* **1** an instrument for measuring the angle that an aircraft makes with the horizontal plane. **2** an instrument for measuring the angle that the earth's magnetic force makes with the horizontal; dipping needle. **3** = clinometer. [< *incline*, noun + *-meter*]

in|clip (in klip′), *v.t.,* **clipped, -clip|ping.** to enclasp; engird.

in|close (in klōz′), *v.t.,* **-closed, -clos|ing.** = enclose.
▶ **Inclose** is more frequently used than **enclose** in legal and statutory language referring to land.

in|clo|sure (in klō′zhər), *n.* = enclosure.

in|clude (in klüd′), *v.t.,* **-clud|ed, -clud|ing. 1** to have within itself; contain; comprise: *The farm includes 160 acres.* **2** to put in a total, a class, or the like; reckon in a count: *The price includes the land, house, and furniture. All on board were lost, including the captain.* **3** to put, hold, or enclose within limits. **4** *Obsolete.* to shut up; confine. [< Latin *inclūdere* < *in-* in + *claudere* to shut] — **in|clud′a|ble, in|clud′i|ble**, *adj.*
— ***Syn.*** **1 Include, comprise, comprehend** mean to contain or take in as a part or parts. **Include**

Pronunciation Key: hat, āge, cãre, fär; let, ēqual, tėrm; it, īce; hot, ōpen, ôrder; oil, out; cup, pu̇t, rüle; child; long; thin; ᴛʜen; zh, measure; ə represents a in about, e in taken, i in pencil, o in lemon, u in circus.

implies taking in either all or only one or several parts of the whole: *The list includes my name.* **Comprise** implies taking in all the parts that make up the whole: *This list comprises the names of those who passed.* **Comprehend** implies that the parts are held or fall within the limits or scope of the whole: *The examination comprehended the whole course.*

in|clud|ed (in klü′did), *adj.* **1** enclosed; contained; comprised. **2** *Botany.* not protruding beyond the corolla, as a style or stamens.

in|clu|sion (in klü′zhən), *n.* **1** the act or fact of including: *The Dutch should have obliged themselves to make no peace without the inclusion of their Allies* (Sir William Temple). **2** the state of being included. **3** a thing included: **a** a body present in the cytoplasm of a cell, such as a starch grain or fat droplet. **b** a small solid body, or a gaseous or liquid substance, contained in a crystal or a mineral mass. [< Latin *inclūsiō, -ōnis* < *inclūdere;* see etym. under **include**]

inclusion body, a stainable body found in the cells of tissues infected with a filterable virus, as in rabies or smallpox.

in|clu|sive (in klü′siv), *adj.* **1** including; taking in; counting in; comprising: *"Read pages 10 to 20 inclusive" means "Begin with page 10 and read through to the very end of page 20." Abbr:* incl. **2** including much; including everything concerned: *Make an inclusive list of your expenses.* SYN: comprehensive.
inclusive of, including; taking in; counting: *Our company has a staff of 30 people, inclusive of the secretaries, typists, and the janitor.*
—**in|clu′sive|ly**, *adv.* —**in|clu′sive|ness**, *n.*

in|clu|siv|i|ty (in′klü siv′ə tē), *n.* the quality or state of being inclusive; inclusiveness.

in|co|er|ci|ble (in′kō ėr′sə bəl), *adj.* **1** not coercible. **2** *Physics.* incapable of being liquefied by pressure (formerly said of some gases).

incog., incognito.

in|cog|i|ta|ble (in koj′ə tə bəl), *adj.* unthinkable; inconceivable. [< Latin *incōgitābilis* < *in-* not + *cōgitābilis* thinkable < *cōgitāre* cogitate]

in|cog|i|tant (in koj′ə tənt), *adj.* **1** thoughtless; inconsiderate. **2** not having the faculty of thinking.

in|cog|ni|ta (in kog′nə tə), *adj., adv., n., pl.* **-tas.** the feminine form of **incognito**: *Miss Page ... arrives incognita at a Gulf Coast Hotel with her latest escort* (New York Times Magazine). [< Italian *incognita;* feminine of *incognito* incognito]

in|cog|ni|to (in kog′nə tō, in′kog nē′tō), *adj., adv., n., pl.* **-tos.** —***adj., adv.*** with one's name, character, rank, or other recognizable characteristics hidden: *The prince traveled incognito to avoid crowds and ceremonies. I myself ... had decided to go incognito, in an old raincoat* (New Yorker).
—***n.*** **1** a person who is incognito. **2** a disguised condition: *to preserve one's incognito.*
[< Italian *incognito* < Latin *incognitus* unknown < *in-* not + *cognōscere* come to know < *com-* (intensive) + *gnōscere* learn]

in|cog|ni|za|ble (in kog′nə zə bəl, -kon′ə-), *adj.* not cognizable; unrecognizable.

in|cog|ni|zance (in kog′nə zəns, -kon′ə-), *n.* failure to recognize, know, or apprehend.

in|cog|ni|zant (in kog′nə zənt, -kon′ə-), *adj.* not cognizant; unaware.

in|co|gno|scen|te (in′kō nyō shen′tā), *n., pl.* **-ti** (-tē). an uninformed person; uninitiate: *The other day it broadcast ... an act of worship by a chapter of the Society of Friends* (*Quakers, I had better perhaps say, for the benefit of any incognoscenti who might, by chance, read this*) (New Scientist). [< *in-*[1] + *cognoscente*]

in|co|her|ence (in′kō hir′əns), *n.* **1** disconnected thought or speech: *the incoherence of a frightened child.* **2** lack of logical connection. **3** failure to stick together; looseness.

in|co|her|ent (in′kō hir′ənt), *adj.* **1** having or showing no logical connection of ideas; not coherent; disconnected; confused. **2** not sticking together. SYN: loose. **3** *Physics.* having waves of irregular and random phases: *incoherent radiation. The light emitted by lasers ... is quite different from the incoherent light emitted by any other source of light—whether stars, candles, or electric lamps* (New Scientist). —**in′co|her′ent|ly**, *adv.*

in|co|he|sive (in′kō hē′siv), *adj.* not cohesive. —**in′co|he′sive|ness**, *n.*

in|com|bus|ti|bil|i|ty (in′kəm bus′tə bil′ə tē), *n.* the condition of being incombustible.

in|com|bus|ti|ble (in′kəm bus′tə bəl), *adj., n.* —***adj.*** that cannot be burned; fireproof.
—***n.*** an incombustible substance. —**in′com|bus′ti|ble|ness**, *n.* —**in′com|bus′ti|bly**, *adv.*

in|come (in′kum), *n.* **1a** what comes in from property, business, or work; money that comes in; receipts; returns: *A person's yearly income is all the money that he gets in a year. The grocer's store brings in an income of $5,000.* SYN: revenue, proceeds, profit, salary. **b** *Law.* any gain or profit derived from an estate or property. **2** a coming in. **3** something that comes in.

income account, an account of the money received and spent by a business.

income maintenance, government compensation or subsidy of those whose incomes fall below a specified level: *Some urged a form of income maintenance, such as ... a negative income tax that would put money in the hands of those without it* (New York Times).

in|com|er (in′kum′ər), *n.* a person who comes in.

incomes policy, a policy to combat inflation by various means without government controls on wages and prices: *An "incomes policy" ... might involve presidential persuasion to hold down wages and prices* (Norman Thompson).

income tax, a government tax on a person's or a corporation's income above a certain amount, usually with certain deductions and exemptions: *The triple income tax—Federal, state, and local—such as New Yorkers pay, is a relative rarity* (Richard E. Mooney).

in|com|ing (in′kum′ing), *adj., n.* —***adj.*** **1** coming in; succeeding: *the incoming tide. The incoming tenant will pay more rent.* **2** coming in as profit; accruing. **3** (of a period of time) about to begin; ensuing.
—***n.*** a coming in: *the incoming of the tide.* SYN: advent, entry.
incomings, money that comes in; revenue: *More followers than he can support by honest means, or by his own incomings* (Scott).

in|com|men|su|ra|bil|i|ty (in′kə men′shər ə bil′ə tē, -sər-), *n.* the condition of being incommensurable; absence of a common measure or standard of comparison.

in|com|men|su|ra|ble (in′kə men′shər ə bəl, -sər-), *adj., n.* —***adj.*** **1** that cannot be compared because not measurable in the same units or by the same scale: *Money and human life are incommensurable.* **2a** (of lengths or numbers) having no common measure or number of which all the given lengths or numbers are integral multiples. $\sqrt{2}$ and 3 are incommensurable numbers because there is no third number which divides both of them evenly. A foot and a meter are incommensurable since the ratio between them must be expressed as an irrational number. **b** = irrational.
—***n.*** **incommensurables**, incommensurable quantities, magnitudes, or things: *Puzzling enquiries concerning ... incommensurables* (Isaac Watts).
—**in′com|men′su|ra|ble|ness**, *n.* —**in′com|men′su|ra|bly**, *adv.*

in|com|men|su|rate (in′kə men′shər it, -sər-), *adj.* **1** not in proportion; not adequate: *His salary is incommensurate with the time he spends working.* **2** having no common measure; that cannot be compared; incommensurable. —**in′com|men′su|rate|ly**, *adv.* —**in′com|men′su|rate|ness**, *n.*

in|com|mode (in′kə mōd′), *v.t.,* **-mod|ed, -mod|ing.** to cause trouble, difficulty, discomfort, or embarrassment to; inconvenience: *Will it incommode you if we open the window?* SYN: trouble, disturb, annoy, discomfort. [< Latin *incommodāre* < *incommodus* inconvenient < *in-* not + *commodus* convenient < *com-* with + *modus* manner, mode]

in|com|mo|di|ous (in′kə mō′dē əs), *adj.* **1** not roomy enough. **2** inconvenient; uncomfortable. SYN: troublesome, annoying, disagreeable. —**in′com|mo′di|ous|ly**, *adv.* —**in′com|mo′di|ous|ness**, *n.*

in|com|mod|i|ty (in′kə mod′ə tē), *n., pl.* **-ties.** **1** inconvenience; disadvantage; discomfort. **2** something inconvenient or disadvantageous; discomfort; annoyance.

in|com|mu|ni|ca|bil|i|ty (in′kə myü′nə kə bil′ə tē), *n.* the quality of being incommunicable.

in|com|mu|ni|ca|ble (in′kə myü′nə kə bəl), *adj.* that cannot be communicated or told. —**in′com|mu′ni|ca|ble|ness**, *n.* —**in′com|mu′ni|ca|bly**, *adv.*

in|com|mu|ni|ca|do (in′kə myü′nə kä′dō), *adv., adj., n.* —***adv.*** so as not to communicate with others: *The prisoner could not reach his lawyer or friends because he was being held incommunicado. After the jury was sworn and the trial began the simple but effective safeguard ... was to hold the jury incommunicado until the delivery of the verdict* (Listener).
—***adj.*** without any way of communicating with others: *The way in which this idea of incommunicado ego, unable to communicate with others, influenced Eliot's early poetry is apparent at once* (New Yorker).
—***n.*** the state of being incommunicado; absence of communication: *He experienced, in the agonizing incommunicado of sudden death, the most public private moment of his life* (Jonathan Miller).
[American English < Spanish *incomunicado*]

in|com|mu|ni|ca|tive (in′kə myü′nə kā′tiv), *adj.* not communicative; uncommunicative; reserved. —**in′com|mu′ni|ca′tive|ly**, *adv.* —**in′com|mu′ni|ca′tive|ness**, *n.*

in|com|mut|a|bil|i|ty (in′kə myü′tə bil′ə tē), *n.* the condition or quality of being incommutable.

in|com|mut|a|ble (in′kə myü′tə bəl), *adj.* **1** unchangeable; immutable. **2** not commutable; not exchangeable. —**in′com|mut′a|bly**, *adv.*

in|com|mu|ta|tion (in′kom yə tā′shən), *n. U.S.* commutation from the city to work in the suburbs.

in|com|pact (in′kəm pakt′), *adj.* not compact; loose in structure or consistency. —**in′com|pact′ly**, *adv.* —**in′com|pact′ness**, *n.*

in-com|pa|ny (in′kum′pə nē), *adj.* carried on within a company or business: *in-company supervisor training.*

in|com|pa|ra|bil|i|ty (in′kom pə rə bil′ə tē, -prə-; in kom′-), *n.* the quality of being incomparable.

in|com|pa|ra|ble (in kom′pər ə bəl, -prə-), *adj., n.* —***adj.*** **1** without an equal; matchless: *Helen of Troy had incomparable beauty.* SYN: peerless, unequaled, transcendent. **2** not able to be compared; unsuitable for comparison.
—***n.*** an incomparable or matchless person or thing: *No one has a calculus with which to compare such incomparables* (New Scientist).
—**in|com′pa|ra|ble|ness**, *n.* —**in|com′pa|ra|bly**, *adv.*
▶The pronunciation (in′kəm pãr′ə bəl), stressed on the analogy of *compare,* is not standard.

in|com|pas|sion|ate (in′kəm pash′ə nit), *adj.* not compassionate; lacking pity or tenderness: *The umpires made their incompassionate decision and Leicestershire's batsmen their embarrassed exit* (London Times). —**in′com|pas′sion|ate|ly**, *adv.*

in|com|pat|i|bil|i|ty (in′kəm pat′ə bil′ə tē), *n., pl.* **-ties.** **1** the quality of being incompatible; lack of harmony. **2** an incompatible thing, quality, or characteristic.

in|com|pat|i|ble (in′kəm pat′ə bəl), *adj., n.* —***adj.*** **1** not able to live or act together peaceably; opposed in character: *My cats and dogs are incompatible. The Government had been swinging between two incompatible policies—that of non-interference and that of threats supported by force* (Lytton Strachey). SYN: uncongenial. **2** not able to exist together; inconsistent: *Bad eating habits are incompatible with good health.* SYN: irreconcilable. **3** designating drugs, blood types, or tissues that cannot be combined or used together because of undesirable chemical or physiological reactions. **4** (of benefices) incapable of being held together.
—***n.*** an incompatible person or thing: *In the inevitable jangle of these incompatibles the church had become dogmatic* (H. G. Wells).
incompatibles, drugs, blood types, or tissues that are incompatible: *Incompatibles cannot be used in blood transfusion.*
—**in′com|pat′i|ble|ness**, *n.* —**in′com|pat′i|bly**, *adv.*

in|com|pe|tence (in kom′pə təns), *n.* **1** lack of ability, power, or fitness: *The workman was discharged for incompetence.* SYN: inability, incapacity. **2** lack of legal qualification. SYN: disqualification.

in|com|pe|ten|cy (in kom′pə tən sē), *n.* = incompetence.

in|com|pe|tent (in kom′pə tənt), *adj., n.* —***adj.*** **1** not competent; without ability, power, fitness, or other qualifications: *A poor manager is incompetent to run a business.* SYN: incapable, unfit. **2** not legally qualified or acceptable: *incompetent evidence.* SYN: incapable, unfit. —***n.*** a person who is without ability; one who is incompetent: *Idiots and other incompetents need someone to look after them. Watching the barely seaworthy fleet ... officered by incompetents* (Time). [< Late Latin *incompetēns, -entis* unsuitable < *in-* not + *competēns* competent]
—**in|com′pe|tent|ly**, *adv.*

in|com|plete (in′kəm plēt′), *adj.* **1** not complete; lacking some part; unfinished: *The artist was working on several paintings which at his death remained incomplete.* SYN: imperfect, deficient, defective. **2** (of a flower) lacking one or more of the four kinds of floral organs, sepals, petals, stamens, and pistils. [< Late Latin *incomplētus* < Latin *in-* not + *complētus* complete] —**in′com|plete′ly**, *adv.* —**in′com|plete′ness**, *n.*

in|com|pli|ant (in′kəm plī′ənt), *adj.* not compliant; unaccommodating; unyielding. —**in′com|pli′ant|ly**, *adv.*

in|com|pre|hen|si|bil|i|ty (in′kom pri hen′sə bil′ə tē), *n.* the fact or quality of being incomprehensible: *the incomprehensibility of eternity. Incomprehensibility is the reader's fault ... the writer's reasoning ... cannot be responsible* (Atlantic).

in|com|pre|hen|si|ble (in′kom pri hen′sə bəl), *adj.* **1** impossible to understand: *She was perfectly incomprehensible to me* (Dickens). *Miss*

Lane's pronunciation, however, was incomprehensible to most of the critics (New York Times). **2** *Archaic.* illimitable; boundless: *The firmament . . . And all her number'd stars, that seem to roll Spaces incomprehensible* (Milton). —**in'com|pre|hen'si|ble|ness**, *n.* —**in'com|pre|hen'si|bly**, *adv.*

in|com|pre|hen|sion (in'kom pri hen'shən), *n.* lack of comprehension or understanding: *She screwed up her face into an urgent snarl of incomprehension* (New Yorker).

in|com|pre|hen|sive (in'kom pri hen'siv), *adj.* **1** not comprehensive; unduly limited or restricted. **2** lacking in understanding. —**in'com|pre|hen'sive|ly**, *adv.*

in|com|press|i|bil|i|ty (in'kəm pres'ə bil'ə tē), *n.* incompressible condition or quality.

in|com|press|i|ble (in'kəm pres'ə bəl), *adj.* not capable of being squeezed into a smaller size.

in|com|put|a|ble (in'kəm pyü'tə bəl), *adj.* that cannot be computed; incalculable.

in|con|ceiv|a|bil|i|ty (in'kən sē'və bil'ə tē), *n.* the state or quality of being inconceivable.

in|con|ceiv|a|ble (in'kən sē'və bəl), *adj.* **1** impossible to imagine; unthinkable: *A circle without a center is inconceivable.* SYN: unimaginable. **2** hard to believe; incredible: *It is inconceivable that two nations so friendly for centuries should now be at war.* —**in'con|ceiv'a|ble|ness**, *n.* —**in'con|ceiv'a|bly**, *adv.*

in|con|clu|sion (in'kən klü'zhən), *n.* **1** the quality of being inconclusive. **2** an inconclusive end or result: *On the frostbitten ridges of Korea, it became necessary to carry a stalemate to its logical inconclusion* (Time).

in|con|clu|sive (in'kən klü'siv), *adj.* not convincing; not settling or deciding something doubtful; not effective: *The jury found the evidence against the defendant inconclusive and acquitted him.* —**in'con|clu'sive|ly**, *adv.* —**in'con|clu'sive|ness**, *n.*

in|con|den|sa|ble or **in|con|den|si|ble** (in'kən den'sə bəl), *adj.* that cannot be condensed.

in|con|dite (in kon'dit, -dīt), *adj.* **1** badly constructed or composed (especially of literary or artistic works). **2** without delicacy of finish; unformed; crude: *[They] forgot themselves, kicked up their legs, shouted to the bystanders, and were altogether incondite* (Charles Kingsley). SYN: rude, unpolished, unrefined. [< Latin *inconditus* not connected, disordered, not put together < *in-* not + *condere* to put together]

in|con|du|cive (in'kən dü'siv, -dyü'-), *adj.* not conducive: *Habits are formed inconducive to good government* (Tait's Magazine).

In|co|nel (ing'kə nəl), *n. Trademark.* an alloy of nickel and about 16 percent chromium and 7 percent iron, highly resistant to heat and corrosion.

in|con|form|a|ble (in'kən fôr'mə bəl), *adj.* not conformable; unconformable: *There are scarcely any inconformable or troublesome ministers noted in this report* (W. S. Perry).

in|con|form|i|ty (in'kən fôr'mə tē), *n.* lack of conformity.

in|con|gru|ence (in kong'grü əns), *n.* lack of congruence or agreement; incongruity.

in|con|gru|ent (in kong'grü ənt), *adj.* not congruent; disagreeing; incongruous. —**in|con'gru|ent|ly**, *adv.*

in|con|gru|i|ty (in'kən grü'ə tē, -kon-, -kong-), *n., pl.* **-ties. 1** the condition of being out of place; unfitness; inappropriateness: *Without incongruity . . . we cannot speak of geometrical beauty* (Samuel Johnson). **2** lack of agreement or harmony; inconsistency: *the incongruity of the clerk's apparel* (Scott). **3** something that is incongruous: *He denounced the Administration's foreign policy for what he called its incongruities* (Newsweek).

in|con|gru|ous (in kong'grü əs), *adj.* **1** out of keeping; not appropriate; out of place: *Heavy walking shoes are incongruous with a party dress.* SYN: unsuited, inappropriate, absurd. **2** lacking in agreement or harmony; not consistent: *I have since often observed how incongruous and irrational the common temper of mankind is* (Daniel Defoe). SYN: inharmonious, inconsistent. [< Latin *incongruus* (with English *-ous*) inconsistent < *in-* not + *congruus* congruous] —**in|con'gru|ous|ly**, *adv.* —**in|con'gru|ous|ness**, *n.*

in|con|nu (in'kə nü', -nyü'), *n.* a large salmonoid food fish of the rivers of northwestern Canada and of Alaska: *One of the species found in the Mackenzie River is the distinctive "coney," or inconnu, so named by Alexander Mackenzie, because the fish was not known in other parts of Canada* (Donald F. Putnam). [< French *inconnu* unknown]

in|con|scient (in kon'shənt, -shē ənt), *adj.* **1** lacking consciousness; unconscious. **2** lacking intelligence or perception; imperceptive: *She fought jauntily a daily battle against . . . inefficient servants and inconscient boarders* (M. F. K. Fisher). [< French *inconscient* < *in-* not + *conscient* conscious] —**in|con'scient|ly**, *adv.*

in|con|sec|u|tive (in'kən sek'yə tiv), *adj.* not consecutive; disconnected: *His argument is altogether lame and inconsecutive* (G. S. Faber). —**in'con|sec'u|tive|ly**, *adv.* —**in'con|sec'u|tive|ness**, *n.*

in|con|se|quence (in kon'sə kwens, -kwəns), *n.* **1** lack of logic or logical sequence; being inconsequent; inconclusiveness; irrelevance: *That mingling of inconsequence which belongs to us all, and not unhappily* (George Eliot). **2** something that is inconsequent.

in|con|se|quent (in kon'sə kwent, -kwənt), *adj.* **1a** not logical; not logically connected: *an inconsequent argument.* **b** not in keeping with the general character or design: *inconsequent features of a work, inconsequent ornamentation.* **2** not to the point; off the subject; irrelevant: *an inconsequent remark.* **3** apt to think or talk without logical connection. [< Latin *incōnsequēns, -entis* < *in-* not + *cōnsequēns* following together, consequent] —**in|con'se|quent|ly**, *adv.* —**in-con'se|quent|ness**, *n.*

in|con|se|quen|tial (in'kon sə kwen'shəl), *adj.* **1** not important; trifling: *A half century ago, natural gas furnished only an inconsequential 3.3 per cent of the nation's mineral fuel energy* (Harper's). **2** = inconsequent. SYN: unimportant. —**in-con'se|quen'tial|ly**, *adv.*

in|con|se|quen|ti|al|i|ty (in kon'sə kwen'shē al'ə tē), *n., pl.* **-ties. 1** the state of being inconsequential. **2** something inconsequential.

in|con|sid|er|a|ble (in'kən sid'ər ə bəl), *adj.* not worth consideration; not important; insignificant: *I am an inconsiderable fellow, and know nothing* (Sir John Denham). *Many of these measures may place new and not inconsiderable burdens on the budget* (Bulletin of Atomic Scientists). SYN: unimportant, trifling, petty. —**in'con|sid'er|a|ble|ness**, *n.* —**in'con|sid'er|a|bly**, *adv.*

in|con|sid|er|ate (in'kən sid'ər it), *adj.* **1** not thoughtful of others and their rights and feelings. **2** thoughtless; heedless: *the inconsiderate multitude* (Milton). SYN: rash, unadvised, precipitate. —**in'con|sid'er|ate|ly**, *adv.* —**in'con|sid'er|ate|ness**, *n.*

in|con|sid|er|a|tion (in'kən sid'ə rā'shən), *n.* lack of consideration; inconsiderate action.

in|con|sist|ence (in kən sis'təns), *n.* = inconsistency.

in|con|sist|en|cy (in'kən sis'tən sē), *n., pl.* **-cies. 1** lack of agreement or harmony; variance: *There was a great inconsistency between what he said he would do and what he actually did.* **2** failure to keep to the same principles or habits; changeableness: *He was accused of inconsistency in upholding what he had previously condemned. Inconsistency—the only thing in which men are consistent* (Horace Smith). **3** a thing or act that is inconsistent: *Nor is there any inconsistency in wise and good fathers having foolish . . . sons* (Benjamin Jowett). *Like the British Constitution, she owes her success in practice to her inconsistencies in principle* (Thomas Hardy). SYN: discrepancy, incongruity.

in|con|sist|ent (in'kən sis'tənt), *adj.* **1** not consistent; not in agreement; lacking in agreement with itself or something else; at variance: *The policeman's failure to arrest the thief was inconsistent with his duty.* SYN: discrepant, incongruous. **2** failing to keep to the same principles or habits; changeable: *What an inconsistent person says or does today does not agree with what he said or did yesterday.* **3** lacking harmony between its different parts; not uniform. **4** *Mathematics.* having no common solution, as of two or more equations or inequalities. —**in'con|sist'ent|ly**, *adv.*

in|con|sol|a|bil|i|ty (in'kən sō'lə bil'ə tē), *n.* the state of being inconsolable.

in|con|sol|a|ble (in'kən sō'lə bəl), *adj.* not to be comforted; broken-hearted: *The girl was inconsolable at the loss of her kitten. The Duchess of Kent . . . remained in Buckingham Palace, a discarded figure, powerless and inconsolable* (Lytton Strachey). SYN: disconsolate. —**in'con|sol'a|ble-ness**, *n.*

in|con|sol|a|bly (in kən sō'lə blē), *adv.* in an inconsolable manner or degree: *Sometimes they laugh incessantly and sometimes lament inconsolably* (R. T. Smith).

in|con|so|nance (in kon'sə nəns), *n.* lack of harmony; disagreement; discordance.

in|con|so|nant (in kon'sə nənt), *adj.* not harmonious; not in agreement or accord. —**in|con'so-nant|ly**, *adv.*

in|con|spic|u|i|ty (in kon'spə kyü'ə tē), *n.* = inconspicuousness.

in|con|spic|u|ous (in'kən spik'yü əs), *adj.* not conspicuous; attracting little or no attention: *He was so inconspicuous that he could come and go, not specially noticed around hotel lobbies and service passages* (Saul Bellow). —**in'con-spic'u|ous|ly**, *adv.* —**in'con|spic'u|ous|ness**, *n.*

in|con|stan|cy (in kon'stən sē), *n.* lack of constancy; changeableness; fickleness.

in|con|stant (in kon'stənt), *adj., n.* —*adj.* not constant; changeable; variable: *an inconstant person, character, or action. O, swear not by the moon, the inconstant moon, that monthly changes in her circled orb* (Shakespeare). SYN: fickle, mutable, irregular.
—*n.* an inconstant person or thing. —**in|con'stant|ly**, *adv.*

in|con|sum|a|ble (in'kən sü'mə bəl), *adj.* **1** that cannot be consumed. **2** *Economics.* not designed or intended to be consumed in use, as machinery or coin.

in|con|test|a|bil|i|ty (in'kən tes'tə bil'ə tē), *n.* the character or quality of being incontestable.

in|con|test|a|ble (in'kən tes'tə bəl), *adj.* too clear or certain to be denied; beyond dispute or doubt; unquestionable: *The genius and daring of Bolingbroke were . . . incontestable* (William Lecky). SYN: indisputable, undeniable, certain, incontrovertible. —**in'con|test'a|bly**, *adv.*

in|con|ti|nence (in kon'tə nəns), *n.* **1** lack of self-control: *[They] do not waste themselves by incontinence of tongue* (Thomas Carlyle). **2** lack of chastity.

in|con|ti|nen|cy (in kon'tə nən sē), *n., pl.* **-cies.** the fact or condition of being incontinent; incontinence: *My own present incontinencies in the matter of milk do not stem from . . . not being properly "fed-up" as an infant* (Igor Stravinsky).

in|con|ti|nent[1] (in kon'tə nənt), *adj.* **1** not continent; without self-control: *Melantho with imperious mien Renew'd the attack, incontinent of spleen* (Alexander Pope). SYN: unrestrained. **2** not chaste; licentious. SYN: unchaste. **3** *Medicine.* unable to control natural evacuations. [< Latin *incontinēns, -entis* < *in-* not + *continēns* continent, temperate]

in|con|ti|nent[2] (in kon'tə nənt), *adv.* at once; immediately. [< Old French *incontinent,* learned borrowing from Late Latin *in continentī* (*tempore*) in continuous (time), without an interval; immediately]

in|con|ti|nent|ly[1] (in kon'tə nənt lē), *adv.* in an incontinent manner; without self-control or restraint.

in|con|ti|nent|ly[2] (in kon'tə nənt lē), *adv.* = incontinent[2].

in|con|trol|la|ble (in'kən trō'lə bəl), *adj.* = uncontrollable.

in|con|tro|vert|i|ble (in'kon trə vėr'tə bəl), *adj.* that cannot be disputed or denied; too clear or certain to be argued about; unquestionable. SYN: incontestable, indisputable, indubitable. —**in'con-tro|vert'i|ble|ness**, *n.* —**in'con|tro|vert'i|bly**, *adv.*

in|con|ven|ience (in'kən vēn'yəns), *n., v.,* **-ienced, -ienc|ing.** —*n.* **1** lack of convenience or ease; trouble; bother: *She could have spared him without the smallest inconvenience* (Dickens). SYN: discomfort, disadvantage, incommodity. **2** something inconvenient; cause of trouble, difficulty, or bother.
—*v.t.* to cause trouble, difficulty, or bother to: *Will it inconvenience you to carry this package to your mother?* SYN: incommode, trouble.

in|con|ven|ient (in'kən vēn'yənt), *adj.* **1** not convenient; causing bother, difficulty, or discomfort; troublesome: *Shelves that are too high to reach easily are inconvenient. We have a good choice of inconvenient lodgings in the town* (Dickens). SYN: awkward, incommodious, embarrassing, disadvantageous. **2** *Obsolete.* out of place; unsuitable; inappropriate. [< Latin *inconveniēns, -entis* < *in-* not + *conveniēns* agreeing, meeting with, convenient] —**in'con|ven'ient|ly**, *adv.*

in|con|vert|i|bil|i|ty (in'kən vėr'tə bil'ə tē), *n.* the quality of being inconvertible.

in|con|vert|i|ble (in'kən vėr'tə bəl), *adj.* not convertible; that cannot be converted or exchanged. Paper money is inconvertible when it cannot be exchanged for gold or silver. —**in'con|vert'i|ble-ness**, *n.* —**in'con|vert'i|bly**, *adv.*

in|con|vin|ci|ble (in'kən vin'sə bəl), *adj., n.* —*adj.* that cannot be convinced; not open to conviction. —*n.* an inconvincible person. —**in'con|vin'ci|bly**, *adv.*

in|con|y (in kun'ē), *adj. Obsolete.* rare; fine; pretty: *O, super-dainty Canon! Vicar incony!* (Ben Jonson). [origin uncertain]

incor. or **incorp.**, incorporated.

in|cor|po|ra|ble (in kôr'pər ə bəl), *adj.* that can be incorporated.

in|cor|po|rate[1] (*v.* in kôr'pə rāt; *adj.* in kôr'pər it),

Pronunciation Key: hat, āge, cãre, fär; let, ēqual, tėrm; it, īce; hot, ōpen, ôrder; **oi**l, **ou**t; cup, pu̇t, rüle; **ch**ild; lo**ng**; **th**in; ᴛʜen; **zh**, measure; **ə** represents **a** in about, **e** in taken, **i** in pencil, **o** in lemon, **u** in circus.

v., **-rat|ed**, **-rat|ing**, *adj.* **—*v.t.*** **1** to make (some thing) a part of something else; join or combine (something) with something else: *to incorporate fertilizer with soil. We will incorporate your suggestion in this new plan.* **2a** to form into a legal corporation: *When the business became large, the owners incorporated it.* **b** to admit (a person) as a member of an association or corporation. **3** to embody; give material form to: *to incorporate one's thoughts in an article.* **—*v.i.*** **1** to become a corporation. **2** to unite or combine so as to form one body; become blended; merge: *to mix ingredients until they incorporate.*
—*adj.* united; combined; incorporated.
[< Latin *incorporāre* (with English *-ate*[1]) < *in-* into + *corpus, corporis* body]

in|cor|po|rate[2] (in kôr′pər it), *adj.* incorporeal; unembodied. [< Late Latin *incorporātus* unembodied < Latin *in-* not + *corpus, corporis* body]

in|cor|po|rat|ed (in kôr′pə rā′tid), *adj.* **1** made into a corporation; chartered as a corporation. *Abbr:* inc. **2** combined into one body, mass, or substance.

in|cor|po|ra|tion (in kôr′pə rā′shən), *n.* **1** the act or process of incorporating: *The new design reflected the incorporation of many revisions. The incorporation of air bubbles in the glass spoiled it.* **2** the fact of being incorporated: *Incorporation gives a company power to act as one person.*

in|cor|po|ra|tive (in kôr′pə rā′tiv), *adj.* characterized by incorporation; tending to incorporate.

in|cor|po|ra|tor (in kôr′pə rā′tər), *n.* **1** a person who incorporates. **2** one of the original members of a corporation, named in the articles of incorporation or specified in a legislative act of incorporation.

in|cor|po|re|al (in′kôr pôr′ē əl, -pōr′-), *adj.* **1** not made of any material substance; spiritual: *two active incorporeal principles, heat and cold* (Henry Hallam). SYN: immaterial, disembodied. **2** *Law.* without material existence, as a franchise or right of way. **—in′cor|po′re|al|ly**, *adv.*

in|cor|po|re|al|i|ty (in′kôr pôr′ē al′ə tē, -pōr′-), *n., pl.* **-ties.** = incorporeity.

in|cor|po|re|i|ty (in kôr′pə rē′ə tē, in′kôr-), *n., pl.* **-ties.** **1** the condition of being incorporeal. **2** something incorporeal.

in|cor|rect (in′kə rekt′), *adj.* **1** not correct; containing errors or mistakes; wrong; faulty: *The newspaper gave an incorrect account of the accident.* SYN: erroneous, inaccurate. **2** not agreeing with a good standard of taste; improper: *an incorrect practice.* **—in′cor|rect′ly**, *adv.* **—in′cor-rect′ness**, *n.*

in|cor|ri|gi|bil|i|ty (in kôr′ə jə bil′ə tē, -kor′-), *n.* the quality of being incorrigible: *There is an incorrigibility in which when the reproof cannot lead the will it must draw blood* (John Donne).

in|cor|ri|gi|ble (in kôr′ə jə bəl, -kor′-), *adj., n.* **—*adj.*** **1** so firmly fixed (in bad ways, a bad habit, or the like) that reform or change cannot be expected: *An incorrigible liar will lie in spite of any punishment.* SYN: irredeemable. **2** so fixed that it cannot be changed or cured: *Nothing could break her of her incorrigible habit of giggling.*
—*n.* an incorrigible person or animal. **—in|cor′ri-gi|ble|ness**, *n.* **—in|cor′ri|gi|bly**, *adv.*

in|cor|rod|i|ble (in′kə rō′də bəl), *adj.* incapable of being corroded.

in|cor|rupt (in′kə rupt′), *adj.* **1** not corruptible; morally uncorrupted; pure in life; honest: *To say of a judge that he was incorrupt was hardly to eulogize him* (Archer Polson). **2** free from decay; not decayed or rotten; sound. **3** not marred by errors or alterations, as a text. **—in′cor|rupt′ly**, *adv.* **—in′cor|rupt′ness**, *n.*

in|cor|rupt|i|bil|i|ty (in′kə rup′tə bil′ə tē), *n.* the character or quality of being incorruptible.

in|cor|rupt|i|ble (in′kə rup′tə bəl), *adj., n.* **—*adj.*** **1** not to be corrupted; honest: *The incorruptible man could not be bribed.* SYN: scrupulous, upright. **2** not subject to decay; lasting forever: *Diamonds are incorruptible.*
—*n.* an incorruptible person or thing: *Our incorruptibles are our hold on sanity* (Atlantic). **—in′-cor|rupt′i|ble|ness**, *n.* **—in′cor|rupt′i|bly**, *adv.*

in|cor|rup|tion (in′kə rup′shən), *n.* freedom from corruption.

in-coun|try (in′kun′trē), *adj.* carried on within a country, as distinguished from its borders or neighbors.

incr., **1** increased. **2** increasing.

in|cras|sate (*adj.* in kras′it, -āt; *v.* in kras′āt), *adj., v.,* **-sat|ed**, **-sat|ing.** **—*adj.*** *Biology.* thickened; swollen. **—*v.t., v.i.*** to thicken.
[< Latin *incrassātus*, past participle of *incrassāre* < *in-* (intensive) + *crassāre* thicken < *crassus* thick, crass] **—in′cras|sa′tion**, *n.*

in|creas|a|ble (in krē′sə bəl), *adj.* that can be increased.

in|crease (*v.* in krēs′; *n.* in′krēs), *v.,* **-creased**, **-creas|ing**, *n.* **—*v.t.*** to make greater, more numerous, or more powerful; add to: *to increase taxes, increase one's possessions. The driver increased the speed of the car.*
—*v.i.* **1** to become greater; advance in quality, success, or power: *to increase in wisdom. His weight has increased by ten pounds. The danger increases.* **2** to grow in numbers, especially by propagation; become more numerous; multiply: *These flowers will increase every year.*
—*n.* **1** a gain in size or numbers; growth: *an increase in our family. There has been a great increase in student enrollment during the past year. Equally characteristic of this primary step of germination is the increase in volume of the seed* (A. M. Mayer). SYN: enlargement, extension. **2** multiplication by propagation. **3** the amount added; result of increasing; addition. SYN: enlargement, extension. **4** offspring: *All the increase of thine house shall die in the flower of their age* (I Samuel 2:33).
on the increase, becoming greater or more frequent; increasing: *The movement of people from the cities to the suburbs is on the increase.*
[< Anglo-French *encress-*, variant of Old French *encreiss-*, stem of *encreistre* < Latin *incrēscere* < *in-* in + *crēscere* grow] **—in|creas′er**, *n.*
—*Syn.* *v.t.* **Increase, enlarge, augment** mean to make greater. **Increase** means to make greater, as in amount, number, wealth, or power: *to increase sales.* **Enlarge** means to make larger, chiefly in size, extent, or capacity: *They enlarged the school auditorium.* **Augment**, more formal, means to increase by added amounts or sums: *Many teachers do outside work to augment their salaries.*

in|creas|ing (in krē′sing), *adj.* becoming greater or more numerous: *U.S. manufacturers ... feel increasing competition from such firms as Fiat* (Wall Street Journal). **—in|creas′ing|ly**, *adv.*

in|cre|ate (in′krē āt′, in′krē āt), *adj.* not created; existing without having been created: *Hail, holy Light! ... Bright effluence of bright essence increate* (Milton). [< Medieval Latin *increatus* < Latin *in-* not + *creāre* create]

in|cred|i|bil|i|ty (in kred′ə bil′ə tē), *n.* **1** the quality of being incredible. **2** something incredible.

in|cred|i|ble (in kred′ə bəl), *adj.* hard to believe; seeming too extraordinary to be possible; beyond belief; unbelievable: *The hero fought with incredible bravery. Some old superstitions seem incredible to educated people. How has it happened that in our efforts to renounce an incredible heaven we have constructed instead an incredible earth?* (Saturday Review). SYN: inconceivable. **—in|cred′i|ble|ness**, *n.* **—in|cred′i|bly**, *adv.*
▶**Incredible, incredulous** are not synonymous. *Incredible* means unbelievable; *incredulous* means unbelieving: *His story of having seen a ghost seemed incredible to his family. If they look incredulous, show them the evidence.*

in|cre|du|li|ty (in′krə dü′lə tē, -dyü′-), *n.* lack of belief; doubt: *Mr. Crisparkle looked in his face, with some incredulity* (Dickens). SYN: distrust.

in|cred|u|lous (in krej′ə ləs), *adj.* **1** not ready to believe; not credulous; doubting: *People nowadays are incredulous about ghosts and witches.* SYN: skeptical. **2** showing a lack of belief: *He listened to the neighbor's story with an incredulous smile.* **—in|cred′u|lous|ly**, *adv.* **—in|cred′u|lous-ness**, *n.* ▶See **incredible** for usage note.

in|cre|ment (in′krə mənt, ing′-), *n.* **1** an increasing or becoming greater; increase; growth: *The Service lost not only the professor's services but all the increments of knowledge bound up with his research* (Harper's). SYN: accretion, augmentation. **2** an amount by which something increases: *The wages are $80 a week with an increment of $10 for each year of service.* SYN: addition. **3** *Mathematics.* a positive or negative change, usually small, in the value of a variable. [< Latin *incrēmentum* < *incrē-*, stem of *incrēscere* increase]

in|cre|men|tal (in′krə men′təl, ing′-), *adj.* of or having to do with an increment; like an increment: *The annual incremental traffic growth at these three airports in recent years has been approximately 10 per cent* (Jacob K. Javits). **—in′-cre|men′tal|ly**, *adv.*

in|cre|men|tal|ism(in′krə men′tə liz′əm, ing′-), *n.* gradual change, especially in social behavior and attitudes or political policy, or government intervention: *In particular, the Bureau [of the Budget] had become central to the process of creeping government or incrementalism ... Under the incremental approach, small programs expanded year by year in reach and cost until they became major items* (Atlantic).

in|cre|men|ta|tion (in′krə mən tā′shən), *n.* the action of increasing; augmentation; increment.

in|cres|cent (in kres′ənt), *adj.* increasing or waxing: *The good Queen ... sent, Between the increscent and decrescent moon, Arms for her son* (Tennyson). [< Latin *incrēscēns, -entis,* present participle of *incrēscere* increase]

in|cre|tion (in krē′shən), *n.* **1** the process of internal secretion. **2** a hormone or other product of internal secretion. [probably < *in-*[3] + (se)*cretion*]

in|crim|i|nate (in krim′ə nāt), *v.t.,* **-nat|ed**, **-nat-ing.** to accuse of a crime; show to be guilty; involve in an accusation: *In his confession the thief incriminated two others who helped him steal.* SYN: inculpate. [< Late Latin *incrīmināre* (with English *-ate* [1]) < Latin *in-* against + *crīmen, -inis* a charge; crime] **—in|crim′i|na′tion**, *n.* **—in-crim′i|na′tor**, *n.*

in|crim|i|na|to|ry (in krim′ə nə tôr′ē, -tōr′-), *adj.* tending to incriminate. SYN: accusatory.

in-crowd (in′kroud′), *n.* an exclusive set or circle of acquaintances; group of insiders; clique: *The performer who is ... no longer the darling of the underground in-crowd, whatever his sincerity or instrinsic merit* (London Times).

in|croy|a|ble (aɴ krwä yä′blə), *n.* **1** a French fop or dandy of the period of the Directory. **2** any fop or dandy: *... the republican young man of fashion, the incroyable* (Westminster Review). [< French *incroyable* (literally) incredible < *in-* not + *croyable* credible]

in|crust (in krust′), *v.t.* = encrust.

in|crus|tate (in krus′tāt), *v.t.,* **-tat|ed**, **-tat|ing.** = encrust.

in|crus|ta|tion (in′krus tā′shən), *n.* = encrustation.

in|crust|ment (in krust′mənt), *n.* = encrustation.

in|cu|bate (in′kyə bāt, ing′-), *v.,* **-bat|ed**, **-bat|ing.**
—*v.t.* **1** to sit on (eggs) in order to hatch them; brood. **2** to keep (eggs, premature babies, cultures of microorganisms, or other living matter) warm, and supplied with moisture and oxygen, so that they will hatch or grow. **3** *Figurative.* to plan; develop; hatch: *A $100 million research centre ... near Toronto will soon be incubating ideas that may shape Canada's future* (Maclean's).
—*v.i.* **1** to sit on eggs; brood. **2** *Medicine.* (of a disease) to go through the process of incubation. **3** *Figurative.* to undergo development: *Then nothing until Sartre, though plenty was incubating* (Listener). [< Latin *incubāre* (with English *-ate*[1]) < *in-* on + *cubāre* lie[2]]

in|cu|ba|tion (in′kyə bā′shən, ing′-), *n.* **1** the action of incubating. **2** the state of being incubated. **3** the stage of a disease from the time of infection until the first symptoms appear.

in|cu|ba|tion|al (in′kyə bā′shə nəl, ing′-), *adj.* of or having to do with incubation; incubative.

in|cu|ba|tion|ar|y (in′kyə bā′shə ner′ē), *adj.* = incubational.

incubation period, = incubation (def. 3).

in|cu|ba|tive (in′kyə bā′tiv, ing′-), *adj.* of or having to do with incubation; incubational.

in|cu|ba|tor (in′kyə bā′tər, ing′-), *n.* **1** a box or chamber for keeping eggs warm, and properly supplied with moisture and oxygen, so that they will hatch. **2** any similar box or chamber. Very small babies and premature babies are sometimes kept for a time in incubators. **3** an apparatus in which cultures of microorganisms are developed. **4** *Figurative.* a place for developing or nurturing: *The California junior colleges are incubators for the big-time football universities of the Pacific Coast* (New York Times). [< New Latin *incubator* < Latin *incubātor* one who sleeps (in a temple) < *incubāre* incubate]

incubator bird, = megapode.

in|cu|ba|to|ry (in kyü′bə tôr′ē, -tōr′-), *adj.* = incubative.

in|cu|bus (in′kyə bəs, ing′-), *n., pl.* **-bi** (-bī), **-bus-es.** **1** an evil spirit supposed to descend upon sleeping persons. **2** = nightmare. **3** an oppressive or burdensome thing: *This debt will be an incubus until I have paid it. Everybody would benefit from ... shedding the incubus of inflation* (New York Times). [< Late Latin *incubus* nightmare (popularly considered a demon lying on the sleeper) < Latin *incubāre* to lie on < *in-* on + *cubāre* lie[2]]

in|cu|des (in kyü′dēz), *n.* plural of **incus.**

in|cul|cate (in kul′kāt, in′kul-), *v.t.,* **-cat|ed**, **-cat-ing.** to impress (ideas, opinions, or the like) on the mind of another by frequent repetition; teach persistently: *Week after week, she inculcated respect for knowledge in her pupils.* [< Latin *inculcāre* (with English *-ate* [1]) (originally) trample in < *in-* in + *calcāre* trample < *calx, calcis* heel] **—in′cul|ca′tion**, *n.* **—in|cul′ca|tor**, *n.*

in|cul|ca|to|ry (in kul′kə tôr′ē, -tōr′-), *adj.* serving to inculcate.

in|cul|pa|ble (in kul′pə bəl), *adj.* = blameless.

in|cul|pa|bly (in kul′pə blē), *adv.* blamelessly; innocently.

in|cul|pate (in kul′pāt, in′kul-), *v.t.,* **-pat|ed**, **-pat-ing.** **1** to involve in responsibility for wrongdoing; incriminate: *[He]confessed to a plot to murder the broker ... and inculpated the Count in the crime* (Washington Irving). **2** to blame; accuse: *The poor lady could have had no rational motive for inculpating herself* (Thomas De Quincey). [< Late Latin *inculpāre* (with English *-ate*[1]) < Latin *in-* in + *culpāre* to blame < *culpa* blame] — **in′cul|pa′tion**, *n.*

in|cul|pa|to|ry (in kul′pə tôr′ē, -tōr′-), *adj.* tending to blame or accuse; incriminating.

in|cult (in kult′), *adj.* = uncultivated. [< Latin *incultus* uncouth < *in-* not + *colere* to cultivate, cherish]

in|cum|ben|cy (in kum′bən sē), *n., pl.* **-cies. 1** a term of office: *During his incumbency as governor, the state prospered.* **2** the state of being incumbent; incumbent duty or obligation. **3** something that is incumbent; an incumbent weight or mass.

in|cum|bent (in kum′bənt), *adj., n.* — *adj.* **1** resting (on a person) as a duty: *She felt it incumbent upon her to answer the letter at once. I have come home with a deep sense of the duty incumbent upon me* (William Ewart Gladstone). SYN: binding, obligatory. **2** currently holding an office or position: *the incumbent governor, the incumbent Republican candidate.* **3** lying, leaning, or pressing on something. **4** *Botany.* **a** (of an anther) lying flat against the inner side of the filament. **b** (of cotyledons) having the back of one against the hypocotyl. **5** *Geology.* overlying; resting (upon): *an incumbent stratum.* **6** *Archaic.* overhanging.
— *n.* a person holding an office, position, or benefice: *An incumbent who has done a good job in office and has shown that he is progressive, intelligent, fearless, and alert ... should be returned to office* (New York Times).
[< Latin *incumbēns, -entis,* present participle of *incumbere* lie (down) on, lean on < *in-* on + *-cumbere* lay oneself, related to *cubāre* lie[2]] — **in|cum′bent|ly**, *adv.*

in|cum|ber (in kum′bər), *v.t.* = encumber.

in|cum|brance (in kum′brəns), *n.* = encumbrance.

in|cu|na|ble (in kyü′nə bəl), *n.* an incunabulum.

in|cu|nab|u|la (in′kyů nab′yə lə), *n.pl., sing.* (*for 2*) **-lum** (-ləm). **1** the earliest stages or first traces in the development of anything; beginnings. **2** books printed before 1501. [< Latin *incūnābula,* neuter plural, cradle; childhood, origin, beginning < *in-* in + *cūnābula* cradle; beginning < *cūnae* cradle]

in|cu|nab|u|lar (in′kyů nab′yə lər), *adj.* of or having to do with books printed before 1501.

in|cu|nab|u|lum (in′kyů nab′yə ləm), *n.* singular of **incunabula**.

in|cur (in kėr′), *v.t.,* **-curred, -cur|ring.** to run or fall into (something unpleasant); bring (blame, punishment, or danger) on oneself: *The explorers incurred great danger when they tried to cross the rapids. He incurred great debts by buying more than he could afford. They are in danger of incurring his royal displeasure* (Jonathan Swift). [< Latin *incurrere* < *in-* upon + *currere* to run]

in|cur|a|bil|i|ty (in kyůr′ə bil′ə tē), *n.* the quality or state of being incurable.

in|cur|a|ble (in kyůr′ə bəl), *adj., n.* — *adj.* that cannot be cured; that cannot be healed, remedied, or corrected: *an incurable invalid, an incurable disease, incurable ignorance.* SYN: irremediable.
— *n.* a person having an incurable disease: *That building is a home for incurables.* — **in|cur′a|ble|ness**, *n.*

in|cur|a|bly (in kyůr′ə blē), *adv.* in an incurable manner or condition; to an incurable degree: *He is incurably romantic.*

in|cu|ri|os|i|ty (in′kyůr ē os′ə tē), *n.* lack of curiosity; inattentiveness; indifference.

in|cu|ri|ous (in kyůr′ē əs), *adj.* **1** not curious; uninquiring; indifferent: *an incurious student. Listless and incurious eyes* (James Fenimore Cooper). *Like anyone of twenty, Jane was incurious about the past* (Saturday Review). SYN: inattentive, unobservant. **2** deficient in interest or novelty. — **in|cu′ri|ous|ly**, *adv.* — **in|cu′ri|ous|ness**, *n.*

in|cur|rence (in kėr′əns), *n.* the act or fact of incurring: *the incurrence of liabilities.*

in|cur|rent (in kėr′ənt), *adj.* running, flowing, or carrying inward: *an incurrent blood vessel.* [< Latin *incurrēns, -entis,* present participle of *incurrere* (literally) run in; see etym. under **incur**]

in|cur|sion (in kėr′zhən, -shən), *n.* **1** a sudden attack; invasion; raid: *The pirates made incursions along the coast.* SYN: foray. **2** a running or flowing in: *Dikes protected the lowland from incursions of the sea.* [< Latin *incursiō, -ōnis* < *incurrere;* see etym. under **incur**]

in|cur|sive (in kėr′siv), *adj.* making incursions; invading.

in|cur|vate (*adj.* in kėr′vit, -vāt; *v.* in kėr′vāt), *adj., v.,* **-vat|ed, -vat|ing.** — *adj.* curving inward.
— *v.t., v.i.* to turn from a straight line or course; curve or bend inward; curve.
[< Latin *incurvātus,* past participle of *incurvāre;* see etym. under **incurve**]

in|cur|va|tion (in′kėr vā′shən), *n.* **1** the act or process of curving inward. **2** the condition of being curved inward.

in|cur|va|ture (in kėr′və chər), *n.* a curving inward; inward curve or bend.

in|curve (*v.* in kėrv′; *n.* in′kėrv′), *v.,* **-curved, -curv|ing,** *n.* — *v.t., v.i.* to curve or bend inward.
— *n.* **1** an inward curve: *She will cross her legs and look down ... on the pleasing swell of calf, incurve of ankle* (Prudence Glynn). **2** an inward curve, such as a baseball pitch curving toward the batter.
[< Latin *incurvāre* to bend in, crook < *in-* in + *curvāre* to curve, bend]

in|cus (ing′kəs), *n., pl.* **in|cu|des.** the middle one of a chain of three small bones in the middle ear of man and some other animals. It is shaped somewhat like an anvil. See the diagram under **ear**[1]. [< Latin *incūs* anvil < *incūdere;* see etym. under **incuse**]

in|cuse (in kyüz′), *v.,* **-cused, -cus|ing,** *adj., n.*
— *v.t.* to impress by striking or stamping: *to incuse a coin.*
— *adj.* hammered or stamped in: *an incuse design on a coin.*
— *n.* an incuse figure or impression.
[< Latin *incūsus,* past participle of *incūdere* fabricate, forge < *in-* in, on + *cūdere* strike (with a hammer), forge]

Ind (ind), *n.* **1** *Archaic.* India: *this ... golden realm of Ind* (Byron). **2** *Obsolete.* the East or West Indies.

ind., an abbreviation for the following:
1 independent.
2 index.
3 indicative.
4 industrial.
5 industry.

Ind., an abbreviation for the following:
1 Independent.
2 India.
3 Indian.
4 Indiana.
5 Indies.

IND (no periods), investigational new drug (a drug tested on animals that is submitted to the Food and Drug Administration for approval or permission to use it in human tests).

I.N.D., in the name of God (Latin, *in nomine Dei*).

in|da|ba (in dä′bə), *n.* a conference between or with South African natives: *It was on the second occasion that the famous indaba took place between Rhodes and the Matabele chiefs* (Napier Davitt). [< Zulu *in-daba* subject, affair, business]

in|da|gate (in′də gāt), *v.t.,* **-gat|ed, -gat|ing.** to search out; investigate: *How from them should we indagate the time of his expulsion?* (Robert Cary). [< Latin *indāgāre* (with English *-ate*[1]) investigate] — **in′da|ga′tion**, *n.* — **in′da|ga′tor**, *n.*

In|da|lone (in′də lōn), *n. Trademark.* a chemical used as an insect repellent. *Formula:* $C_{12}H_{18}O_4$

in|da|mine (in′də mēn, -min), *n. Chemistry.* any one of a series of basic organic compounds that form unstable bluish and greenish salts, used in making dyes. [< *ind*(igo) + *amine*]

In|dan|threne (in dan′thrēn), *n. Trademark.* indanthrone.

in|dan|throne (in dan′thrōn), *n.* a coal-tar pigment related to anthracene and resembling natural indigo, used to dye cotton and other vegetable fibers. *Formula:* $C_{28}H_{14}O_4N_2$

in|debt (in det′), *v.t. Archaic.* to bring or involve in debt; make obligated. [perhaps back formation < *indebted*]

in|debt|ed (in det′id), *adj.* owing money or gratitude; in debt; obliged: *We are indebted to men of science for many of our comforts.* [alteration of Middle English *endetted* < Old French *endette,* past participle of *endetter* put in debt < *en-* en- + *dette* debt; spelling influenced by Latin *dēbitum* debt]

in|debt|ed|ness (in det′id nis), *n.* **1** the condition of being in debt. **2** an amount owed; debts: *The new notes constitute the company's entire indebtedness* (Wall Street Journal).

in|de|cen|cy (in dē′sən sē), *n., pl.* **-cies. 1** lack of decency; being indecent. **2** an indecent act or word.

in|de|cent (in dē′sənt), *adj.* **1** not decent; in very bad taste; unbecoming; improper: *He showed an indecent lack of gratitude to the man who saved his life. They left the party with indecent haste.* SYN: unsuitable, unseemly. See syn. under **improper. 2** not modest; morally bad; disgusting; obscene: *[They] have made numerous arrests for such crimes as ... indecent exposure* (New York Times). SYN: coarse. — **in|de′cent|ly**, *adv.*

indecent assault, *Law.* any sexual act against a person's will other than rape.

in|de|cid|u|ate (in′di sij′ů it, -āt), *adj. Zoology.* (of a placenta) not deciduate; having no decidua.

in|de|cid|u|ous (in′di sij′ů əs), *adj.* **1** not deciduous, as a leaf. **2** (of a tree or plant) not losing the leaves seasonally.

in|de|ci|pher|a|bil|i|ty (in′di sī′fər ə bil′ə tē), *n.* the quality or condition of being indecipherable.

in|de|ci|pher|a|ble (in′di sī′fər ə bəl), *adj.* that cannot be deciphered; illegible: *The coded message was indecipherable.* — **in′de|ci′pher|a|bly**, *adv.*

in|de|ci|sion (in′di sizh′ən), *n.* lack of decision; tendency to delay or to hesitate; tendency to put off deciding or to change one's mind: *the strange indecision of mind ... which we may observe in some people* (James Boswell). *And time yet for a hundred indecisions, ... Before the taking of a toast and tea* (T. S. Eliot). SYN: hesitation, uncertainty.

in|de|ci|sive (in′di sī′siv), *adj.* **1** having the habit of hesitating and putting off decisions: *an indecisive person.* **2** not deciding or settling the matter; without a clear result; inconclusive: *Neither side wins in an indecisive battle. "Maybe" is an indecisive answer.* — **in′de|ci′sive|ly**, *adv.* — **in′de|ci′sive|ness**, *n.*

indecl., indeclinable.

in|de|clin|a|ble (in′di klī′nə bəl), *adj.* having the same form in all grammatical constructions. *None* is an indeclinable pronoun. — **in′de|clin′a|bly**, *adv.*

in|de|com|pos|a|ble (in′dē kəm pō′zə bəl), *adj.* that cannot be decomposed.

in|dec|o|rous (in dek′ər əs; in′di kôr′-, -kōr′-), *adj.* not in accordance with proper behavior; in poor taste; not suitable; improper; unseemly; undignified: *Every young sculptor seems to think that he must give the world some specimen of indecorous womanhood and call it Eve* (Hawthorne). [< Late Latin *indecōrōsus* < Latin *indecōrus* < *in-* not + *decōrus* decorous] — **in|dec′o|rous|ly**, *adv.* — **in|dec′o|rous|ness**, *n.*

in|de|co|rum (in′di kôr′əm, -kōr′-), *n.* **1** lack of decorum; impropriety. **2** improper behavior, speech, dress, or other social manner. [< Latin *indecōrum,* (originally) neuter of *indecōrus* indecorous]

in|deed (in dēd′), *adv., interj.* — *adv.* **1** in fact; in truth; really; surely: *She is hungry; indeed, she is almost starving.* **2** without doubt; admittedly: *War is indeed terrible.*
— *interj.* an expression of surprise, doubt, or contempt: *Indeed! I never would have thought it.*
[Middle English *in dede*]

in|deed|y (in dē′dē), *interj. Informal.* indeed. *"Yes indeedy," Alfred said. "They are one of the truly good things in life"* (Punch).

indef., indefinite.

in|de|fat|i|ga|bil|i|ty (in′di fat′ə gə bil′ə tē), *n.* indefatigable quality or condition; tirelessness.

in|de|fat|i|ga|ble (in′di fat′ə gə bəl), *adj.* never getting tired or giving up; tireless: *An indefatigable worker keeps on working until his work is done. His diligence was indefatigable* (Edward Gibbon). SYN: untiring, persistent, unflagging. [< Latin *indēfatīgābilis* < *in-* not + *dēfatīgāre* tire out < *dē-* out, down + *fatīgāre* to tire] — **in′de|fat′i|ga|ble|ness**, *n.* — **in′de|fat′i|ga|bly**, *adv.*

in|de|fea|si|bil|i|ty (in′di fē′zə bil′ə tē), *n.* indefeasible quality or character: *the indefeasibility of a title.*

in|de|fea|si|ble (in′di fē′zə bəl), *adj.* not to be annulled, made void, or done away with: *Kings were once believed to have an indefeasible right to rule.* [< *in-*[1] not + *defeasible*] — **in′de|fea′si|bly**, *adv.*

in|de|fect|i|bil|i|ty (in′di fek′tə bil′ə tē), *n.* the quality of being indefectible.

in|de|fect|i|ble (in′di fek′tə bəl), *adj.* **1** not liable to defect, failure, or decay; unfailing. **2** without blemish or flaw; faultless. — **in′de|fect′i|bly**, *adv.*

in|de|fec|tive (in′di fek′tiv), *adj.* free from defect; faultless; flawless.

in|de|fen|si|bil|i|ty (in′di fen′sə bil′ə tē), *n.* the quality or state of being indefensible.

in|de|fen|si|ble (in′di fen′sə bəl), *adj.* **1** that cannot be defended: *an indefensible island.* **2** not justifiable; inexcusable: *an indefensible lie.* — **in′de|fen′si|ble|ness**, *n.* — **in′de|fen′si|bly**, *adv.*

in|de|fin|a|bil|i|ty (in′di fī′nə bil′ə tē), *n.* the condition of being indefinable.

in|de|fin|a|ble (in′di fī′nə bəl), *adj., n.* — *adj.* that cannot be defined or described exactly: *"Truth" and "beauty" are practically indefinable.*
— *n.* an indefinable person or thing: *His talk is a series of verbal conjuring tricks with indefinables* (London Times). — **in′de|fin′a|ble|ness**, *n.* — **in′de|fin′a|bly**, *adv.*

in|def|i|nite (in def′ə nit), *adj.* **1** not clearly defined; not precise; vague: *"Maybe" is a very indefinite answer.* SYN: obscure, ambiguous, equivocal, inexact. **2** not limited: *We have an in-*

Pronunciation Key: hat, āge, cãre, fär; let, ēqual, tėrm; it, īce; hot, ōpen, ôrder; oil, out; cup, půt, rüle; child; long; thin; ᴛʜen; zh, measure;
ə represents **a** in about, **e** in taken, **i** in pencil, **o** in lemon, **u** in circus.

definite time to finish this work. **3** *Grammar.* not specifying precisely. An indefinite adjective, pronoun, etc., does not refer to a specific person, thing, time, etc. *Some, many,* and *few* are often indefinite pronouns. *Abbr:* indef. **4** *Botany.* **a** very numerous; not easily counted: *indefinite stamens.* **b** (of an inflorescence) indeterminate. [< Latin *indēfīnītus* < *in-* not + *dēfīnīre* to limit. Compare etym. under **define.**] – **in|def′i|nite|ly,** *adv.* – **in|def′i|nite|ness,** *n.*

indefinite article, *a* or *an.* "A dog" or "an animal" means "any dog" or "any animal"; "the dog" means "a certain or particular dog."

in|de|fin|i|tive (in′di fin′ə tiv), *adj.* not definitive. – **in′de|fin′i|tive|ness,** *n.*

in|de|his|cence (in′di his′əns), *n.* the quality of being indehiscent.

in|de|his|cent (in′di his′ənt), *adj. Botany.* not splitting open at maturity, as certain seed pods do. Acorns are indehiscent fruits.

in|de|lib|er|ate (in′di lib′ər it), *adj.* without deliberation; unintentional; unpremeditated. – **in′de|lib′er|ate|ly,** *adv.* – **in′de|lib′er|ate|ness,** *n.*

in|del|i|bil|i|ty (in del′ə bil′ə tē), *n.* the quality of being indelible; permanence.

in|del|i|ble (in del′ə bəl), *adj.* **1** that cannot be erased or removed; permanent: *indelible ink, an indelible disgrace. Three years as a soldier left an indelible impression on his memory. Man, with all his noble qualities ... still bears in his bodily frame the indelible stamp of his lowly origin* (Charles Darwin). **SYN:** fixed, fast, ineffaceable. **2** making an indelible mark: *The papers were graded with an indelible pencil.* [< Latin *indēlēbilis* < *in-* not + *dēlēbilis* able to be destroyed < *dēlēre* delete, destroy; spelling apparently influenced by English *-ible*] – **in|del′i|ble|ness,** *n.*

in|del|i|bly (in del′ə blē), *adv.* in an indelible manner; so as to be indelible: *These premises are indelibly written in the minds of men by nature* (Edward Reynolds).

in|del|i|ca|cy (in del′ə kə sē), *n., pl.* **-cies. 1** lack of delicacy; a being indelicate. **2** an indelicate act, remark, or the like.

in|del|i|cate (in del′ə kit), *adj.* **1** not delicate; coarse; crude: *It is indelicate to boo in a theater.* **2** improper; immodest. **SYN:** vulgar, indecent. – **in-del′i|cate|ly,** *adv.* – **in|del′i|cate|ness,** *n.*

in|dem|ni|fi|ca|tion (in dem′nə fə kā′shən), *n.* **1** the act of indemnifying. **2** the fact of being indemnified. **3** compensation; recompense: *What indemnification is one great man for populations of pigmies!* (Emerson).

in|dem|ni|fi|ca|to|ry (in dem′nə fə kā′tər ē), *adj.* having to do with or tending to indemnification.

in|dem|ni|fi|er (in dem′nə fī′ər), *n.* a person or agency that indemnifies.

in|dem|ni|fy (in dem′nə fī), *v.t.,* **-fied, -fy|ing. 1** to compensate for damage, loss, or hardship; make good; repay: *The railroad indemnified him for his injuries. Here they found deer and other game in abundance, and indemnified themselves for past famine* (Washington Irving). **SYN:** recompense, reimburse. **2** to secure against damage or loss; insure: *The act indemnified the peace-officers ... if they killed any of the mob in endeavouring to suppress such riot* (William Blackstone). [< Latin *indemnis* unhurt (< *in-* not + *damnum* damage) + English *-fy*]

in|dem|ni|tee (in dem′nə tē′), *n.* a person to whom indemnity is given.

in|dem|ni|tor (in dem′nə tər), *n.* a person who gives indemnity.

in|dem|ni|ty (in dem′nə tē), *n., pl.* **-ties. 1** payment for damage, loss, or hardship. Money demanded by a victorious nation at the end of a war as a condition of peace is an indemnity. **2** security against damage or loss; insurance. **3** legal immunity from the penalties or liabilities resulting from an action, granted to public officials. [< Late Latin *indemnitās* < Latin *indemnis* unhurt < *in-* not + *damnum* damage]

in|dem|ni|za|tion (in dem′nə zā′shən), *n.* compensation; indemnification: *Indemnization to the owner of the expropriated property would have to be paid, but not necessarily in cash* (Robert L. Ross).

in|de|mon|stra|bil|i|ty (in′di mon′strə bil′ə tē), *n.* the quality or condition of being indemonstrable: *Kant was the first person, and perhaps the last, that ever undertook formally to demonstrate the indemonstrability of God* (Thomas De Quincey).

in|de|mon|stra|ble (in′di mon′strə bəl), *adj.* that cannot be demonstrated or proved. – **in′de-mon′stra|bly,** *adv.*

in|dene (in′dēn), *n.* a colorless, oily hydrocarbon obtained by the fractional distillation of coal tar. *Formula:* C_9H_8 [< *ind*(ole) + *-ene*]

in|dent[1] (*v.* in dent′; *n.* in′dent, in dent′), *v., n.* – *v.t.* **1** to make notches in (an edge, line, or border); notch: *The mountains indent the horizon.* **2** to form notches or deep bays in; penetrate: *an indented coast.* **3** to begin (a line) farther from the edge than the other lines: *The first line of a paragraph is usually indented.* **4a** to notch or groove (a board, stone slab, or the like) for joining to another. **b** to join by such notching. **5a** to cut an identical wavy line on (two copies of a document) for identification. **b** to draw up (a document) in two copies in this way. **6a** to order (goods) by an official requisition. **b** to draw an order upon (a source of supply). **7** = indenture.

– *v.i.* **1** to form a notch or recess; recede. **2a** to draw upon a person or thing for something: *For weeks I've been asking to have my transport repaired, but now they tell me I shall have to indent for it through proper channels* (Atlantic). **b** to make an order in duplicate. **3** to enter into an agreement by indenture.

– *n.* **1** a notch; indentation. **2** an official requisition for supplies. **3** an order for goods. **4** an indented agreement; indenture. **5** a certificate issued by the United States government at the close of the American Revolutionary War for the principal or interest of the public debt.

[< Old French *endenter* to notch, cut in < Late Latin *indentāre* to crunch on < Latin *in-* in + *dēns, dentis* tooth] – **in|dent′er,** *n.*

in|dent[2] (in dent′), *v., n.* – *v.t.* **1** to make a dent or dents in; mark with a dent: *sand indented by footprints. Deep in the neck his fangs indent their hold* (Alexander Pope). **2** to press in; stamp. **3** to form as a dent: *Deep scars were seen indented on his breast* (John Dryden).

– *n.* a dent; indentation.

[< *in-*[2] in + *dent*[1]; meanings largely associated with *indent*[1]]

in|den|ta|tion (in′den tā′shən), *n.* **1** the act of indenting or state of being indented. **2** a dent, notch, or cut. **3** = indention. [chiefly < *indent*[1] + *-ation;* with meanings from *indent*[2]]

in|dent|ed (in den′tid), *adj.* **1** having a notched edge or outline; having a zigzag direction or course. **2** bound by a contract to serve someone else; indentured: *I lead the life of an indented slave* (Tobias Smollett). **3** set in or back from the margin.

in|den|tion (in den′shən), *n.* **1** the action or fact of beginning a line farther from the margin than the other lines. **2** the blank space left by doing this. **3** = indentation.

in|den|tor (in den′tər), *n.* a person or thing that indents.

in|den|tur|age (in den′chər ij), *n.* the act or condition of being indentured.

in|den|ture (in den′chər), *n., v.,* **-tured, -tur|ing.** – *n.* **1** a written agreement, such as a contract or deed. **2** Also, **indentures.** a contract by which a person is bound to serve or work for someone else: *An apprentice has an indenture with the master from whom he is learning a trade.* **3** an official or formal list, inventory, certificate, or other document, authenticated for use as a voucher or requisition. **4** = indentation.

– *v.t.* **1** to bind by a contract to serve someone else: *Many persons came to the colonies indentured for several years.* **2** = indent.

[< Anglo-French *endenture,* Old French *endenteüre* indentation < *endenter;* see etym. under **indent**[1]]

in|den|ture|ship (in den′chər ship), *n.* the condition or time of being indentured.

in|de|pend|ence (in′di pen′dəns), *n.* **1** the condition of being independent; freedom from the control, influence, support, or help of others: *The American colonies won independence from England. Today, ardent nationalists demand independence* (Newsweek). **SYN:** See syn. under **freedom. 2** *Archaic.* enough to live on; competency: *In old-fashioned times, an "independence" was hardly ever made without a little miserliness as a condition* (George Eliot).

Independence Day, 1 the Fourth of July, a legal holiday in the United States celebrating the adoption of the Declaration of Independence on July 4, 1776. **2** a day set aside in any country to celebrate its independence: *Mexico celebrates September 16 as Independence Day.*

in|de|pend|en|cy (in′di pen′dən sē), *n., pl.* **-cies. 1** = independence. **2** an independent country, territory, or other self-governing unit.

in|de|pend|ent (in′di pen′dənt), *adj., n.* – *adj.* **1** needing, wishing, or getting no help from others: *independent work, independent thinking. With his horse and his rifle he is independent of the world* (Washington Irving). **2** acting, working, or especially, voting by one's own ideas, not as the crowd does: *An independent person votes as he pleases.* **3** guiding, ruling, or governing oneself; not under another's rule or control: *The United States is an independent country. An independent state university is as essential to the community as an independent judiciary* (Atlantic). **4a** not depending on others for one's support: *Since she inherited her father's fortune, she is completely independent.* **b** enough to live on without working: *an independent income.* **5** refusing to be under obligation to others: *He is too independent to accept a favor.* **6** not resulting from another thing; not controlled or influenced by something else; separate; distinct. **7** *Mathematics.* **a** of or having to do with an independent variable. **b** indicating an equation which, when compared to one or more other equations, does not have as a solution at least one solution that satisfies the other equations.

– *n.* **1** a person who is independent in thought or behavior: *those artists who are independents and do not follow any school of painting.* **2** a person who votes without regard to party: *So many independents voted for the candidate of their choice that the weaker party won.* **3** a business that operates without any outside management or control by another company or companies: *A crowd of oil explorers, mostly small independents* (Wall Street Journal).

independent of, apart from; without regard to: *Independent of his inheritance, he had a good income from his job. The town of St. Gaul is a Protestant republic, independent of the abbot* (Joseph Addison).

independent clause, *Grammar.* = main clause.

in|de|pend|ent|ist (in′di pen′dən tist), *n., adj.* – *n.* a member of any political party or group advocating independence, as in a colony or territory.

– *adj.* of or having to do with a party or group advocating independence.

in|de|pend|ent|ly (in′di pen′dənt lē), *adv.* in an independent manner; without depending on another: *The two firms are negotiating independently* (Wall Street Journal).

independently of, apart from; without regard to: *Independently of the strength of its works, it [Tarento] was rendered nearly inaccessible by its natural position* (William H. Prescott).

independent school, *British.* a school that does not receive any grant or aid either locally or from the Ministry of Education.

independent suspension, an automobile suspension system in which the wheels on either side, not being connected by an axle, are capable of independent vertical motion.

independent variable, *Mathematics and Statistics.* a variable whose value does not depend upon that of another or others.

in-depth (in depth′), *adj.* going deeply into a subject; very thorough; comprehensive: *He has spent hours reading Government cables, memoranda and classified files to brief himself for in-depth discussions* (New York Times). ... *an in-depth study of how the executive branch is running the nation's scientific effort* (Science News Letter).

in|de|scrib|a|bil|i|ty (in′di skrī′bə bil′ə tē), *n.* the quality or condition of being indescribable.

in|de|scrib|a|ble (in′di scrī′bə bəl), *adj., n.* – *adj.* that cannot be described; beyond description: *a scene of indescribable beauty.*

– *n.* an indescribable person or thing: *We've come across ... sweaters, jackets, shirts, and one or two delightful indescribables* (New Yorker). – **in′de|scrib′a|ble|ness,** *n.* – **in′de-scrib′a|bly,** *adv.*

in|de|struct|i|bil|i|ty (in′di struk′tə bil′ə tē), *n.* an indestructible quality or condition: *The remarkable thing about the gambling dollar is its apparent indestructibility* (Newsweek).

in|de|struct|i|ble (in′di struk′tə bəl), *adj., n.* – *adj.* that cannot be destroyed: *Even if all these orchids died to-night yet their beauty is an indestructible memory* (Lord Dunsany).

– *n.* an indestructible person or thing: *This old indestructible conceals an element of iron beneath his flexible charm* (London Times). – **in′de|struct′i|ble|ness,** *n.* – **in′de|struct′i|bly,** *adv.*

in|de|ter|mi|na|ble (in′di tėr′mə nə bəl), *adj., n.* – *adj.* **1** not capable of being settled or decided. **2** not capable of being found out exactly: ... *a light-skinned, thin-featured man whose age is indeterminable* (Esquire).

– *n.* an indeterminable point or problem.

in|de|ter|mi|na|bly (in′di tėr′mə nə blē), *adv.* in an indeterminable manner.

in|de|ter|mi|na|cy (in′di tėr′mə nə sē), *n.* the state or condition of being indeterminate: *The ordinary tensions in his life have gone slack and he hovers in indeterminacy* (Harper's).

indeterminacy principle, = uncertainty principle.

in|de|ter|mi|nate (in′di tėr′mə nit), *adj.* **1a** not determined; not fixed; indefinite; vague; uncertain: *an indeterminate future. He looked up the word because he had only an indeterminate idea of its meaning.* **b** not settled or decided; left doubtful: *an indeterminate contest.* **2** having flowers which arise from axillary buds so that the tip continues to grow forming new bracts and flowers; racemose. – **in′de|ter′mi|nate|ly,** *adv.* – **in′de|ter′mi|nate|ness,** *n.*

indeterminate sentence, a sentence in a criminal case which imposes not more than the maximum nor less than the minimum prescribed by law. The term served usually depends on the prisoner's behavior.

in|de|ter|mi|na|tion (in′di tėr′mə nā′shən), *n.* **1** lack of determination. **2** an unsettled state.

in|de|ter|min|ism (in′di tėr′mə niz əm), *n.* the doctrine that events and particularly human actions are not entirely governed by motives or conditions, but depend in part on the will of each individual.

in|de|ter|min|ist (in′di tėr′mə nist), *n.* a believer in indeterminism.

in|de|ter|min|is|tic (in′di tėr′mə nis′tik), *adj.* of or having to do with indeterminism.

in|de|vo|tion (in′di vō′shən), *n.* lack of devotion; impiety; irreligion.

in|de|vout (in′di vout′), *adj.* not devout; irreligious.

in|dex** (in′deks), *n., pl.* **-dex|es** or **-di|ces**, *v.* **—*n. **1a** a list of what is in a book, telling on what pages to find each thing. An index is usually put at the end of the book and arranged in alphabetical order. **b** = card index. **2** a thing that points out or shows; a sign, token, or indication: (*Figurative.*) *A person's face is often an index of his mood.* (*Figurative.*) *The State Constitutions . . . are . . . an index to the present tendencies of American democracy* (James Bryce). **3** = index finger. **4** a pointer. A dial or scale usually has an index. **5** *Printing.* a sign, especially a fist with a pointing finger, used to point out a particular note, paragraph, or other part of a text; fist; hand. **6a** a number or formula expressing some property, relationship, ratio, or other characteristic, in science. **b** a number that indicates the amount of business activity in relation to past levels of business activity: *the wholesale price index, the cost of living index. The weekly index is calculated as an estimated percentage change from the latest published monthly comprehensive index* (Wall Street Journal). **7** *Mathematics.* **a** the number indicating the root: *In* $\sqrt[3]{764}$ *the index is 3.* **b** = exponent. **8** *Obsolete.* **a** a table of contents; summary: *Even as an index to a book, So to his mind was young Leander's look* (Christopher Marlowe). **b** a preface; prologue.
—*v.t.* **1** to provide with an index; make an index of: *The author indexed his own book.* **2** to enter in an index. **3** to serve as an index of; indicate. **4** to adjust (income, rates of interest, or other economic indicators) to price changes in goods and services as reflected by the cost-of-living index: *to index . . . pensions so that cost of living rises are compensated for at least once a year* (London Guardian).
[< Latin *index, -dicis* forefinger, (originally) informer, anything which points out < *indicāre* point out, reveal < *in-* in, to + *dīcere* speak, say]
—in′dex|er, *n.*

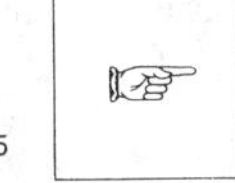

***index**
definition 5

for departure at 11:00
☞ Members must board the bus…

In|dex (in′deks), *n.* **1** = Index Expurgatorius. **2** = Index Librorum Prohibitorum.

in|dex|a|tion (in′dek sā′shən), *n.* **1** the use of an index or indexes. **2** the process of indexing. **3** *Economics.* the adjustment of income, interest rates, taxes, and other earnings to price changes in goods and services reflected in the cost-of-living index: *These obstacles to ending inflation can be substantially reduced through what has come to be called "indexation"—the widespread use of price-escalator clauses in private and governmental contracts* (Milton Friedman).

index crime or **Index Crime**, *U.S.* any one of the most serious types of crimes on which annual statistical reports are published by the FBI: *Of the seven index crimes in the Uniform Crime Reports, four are crimes of personal violence —murder, aggravated assault, rape, and robbery . . . The remaining three index crimes are burglary, larceny of $50 or more, and auto theft* (Norval Morris and Gordon Hawkins).

Index Ex|pur|ga|to|ri|us (ek spėr′gə tôr′ē əs, -tōr′-), a list of books that the Roman Catholic Church forbade its members to read until objectionable parts had been taken out or changed. After 1966 it no longer had the force of ecclesiastical law.

index finger, the finger next to the thumb; forefinger.

index fossil, any abundant and widely distributed fossil that is used to identify or date the rock or strata in which it is found.

index fund, *U.S.* an investment fund consisting of stocks listed in one or more of the major stock market indexes: *The one great advantage of the index fund is that once you have decided what "average" is . . . you can never again do worse* (*or better*) *than average* (Seattle Times).

index glass, the movable mirror of a sextant, which reflects the image of the sun or other object upon the horizon glass.

in|dex|i|cal (in dek′sə kəl), *adj.* having to do with an index; arranged like an index.

in|dex|ing (in′dek sing), *n.* = indexation (def. 3).

in|dex|less (in′deks lis), *adj.* having no index.

Index Li|bro|rum Pro|hib|i|to|rum (lī brôr′əm prō hib′ə tôr′əm; -brōr′-; -tōr′-), a list of books that the Roman Catholic Church forbade its members to read. After 1966 it no longer had the force of ecclesiastical law.

index number, *Statistics.* a number that shows relative changes, as in prices, sales, credit, or employment, at any given time with reference to the level of some predetermined time, or to a certain standard, the base level usually being equated to 100.

index of refraction, the ratio of the velocity of light in one medium, usually a vacuum or air, to its velocity in another of different density; refractive index.

index wheel, a wheel with notches, holes, and of various shapes, rotating at regular intervals to regulate other machinery.

In|di (in′dī), *n.* genitive of **Indus**.

In|di|a (in′dē ə), *n. U.S.* a former code name for the letter *i*, used in radio messages.

India ink, **1** a black pigment consisting of lampblack mixed with a binding material and molded into sticks or cakes. It was formerly made chiefly in China and Japan. **2** a black paint or ink prepared from this pigment.

In|di|a|man (in′dē ə mən), *n., pl.* **-men**. a ship formerly used in trade with India, especially a large one belonging to the East India Company.

In|di|an (in′dē ən), *n., adj.* **—*n.*** **1** one of the people living in America before the Europeans came; an American Indian: *When Columbus met the Indians from the West Indies, the Vikings had already seen the Indians from Newfoundland.* **2** any one of the languages of the American Indians. **3** a person born or living in India or the East Indies: *The Indians had already had a great civilization before the British conquered India.* **4** a European, especially an Englishman, who lives or has lived in India or the East Indies: *He appeared at Bath and at Cheltenham, where . . . there are many old Indians* (Thackeray). **5** the constellation Indus.
—*adj.* **1** of or having to do with American Indians: *an Indian camp, Indian blankets, an Indian language.* **2** made of Indian corn or maize: *Indian pudding.* **3** of or having to do with India or the East Indies: *Indian elephants, Indian temples.*

Indian agency, *U.S.* the office or headquarters of an Indian agent.

Indian agent, *U.S.* an official that represents the government in dealing with an Indian tribe.

In|di|an|an (in′dē an′ən), *adj., n.* = Indianian.

Indian bean, a catalpa native to the southeastern United States.

Indian bison, = gaur.

Indian bread, bread made of the meal of Indian corn.

Indian canna, a variety of canna found in tropical America, having bright red flowers tipped with orange; Indian shot. It is often kept as a garden plant in the United States.

***Indian club**, a bottle-shaped wooden club swung for exercise.

***Indian club**

Indian cobra, cobra of India; spectacled snake.

Indian corn, **1** a plant whose grains grow on large ears, a species of cereal grass first raised by the American Indians; maize. Various forms of Indian corn have been developed, such as sweet corn, popcorn, and flint corn. **2** the grain or ears of this plant. **3** any one of various types of flint corn having red, yellow, white, gray, or multicolored kernels, often used for decorative purposes.

Indian cucumber, a plant of the lily family that grows in damp woods in eastern North America, and has a fleshy rootstock that tastes like a cucumber; cucumber root.

Indian dipper, = pitcher plant.

Indian elephant, an elephant of the genus native to Asia, smaller than the African elephant.

Indian English, the dialect of English spoken by educated natives in the Republic of India, as distinguished from Anglo-Indian.

Indian fig, = prickly pear.

Indian file, = single file.

Indian giver, *U.S. Informal.* a person who takes back a gift after having bestowed it.

Indian giving, **1** the custom among certain American Indians of bestowing a gift with the expectation of its being returned or reciprocated: *Many tribes practised Indian giving* (Maclean's). **2** *U.S. Informal.* the practice of taking back a gift after having bestowed it: *The promised peerage was revoked—an act of Indian giving that has rarely, if ever, been equalled in Great Britain's history* (New Yorker).

Indian grass, any one of various perennial North American grasses, used especially for hay.

Indian Guides, an organization for fathers and sons sponsored by the Y.M.C.A., with a program of activities based on American Indian lore.

Indian hay, *U.S. Slang.* marijuana.

In|di|an-head (in′dē ən hed′), *adj. U.S.* bearing a representation of the head of an American Indian: *an Indian-head penny or nickel.*

Indian hemp, **1** a North American perennial plant of the dogbane family, whose tough, fibrous bark was used by the American Indians, especially for making nets. Its dried root is used in medicine as a heart stimulant. **2** a variety of hemp grown in India; bhang.

In|di|an|i|an (in′dē an′ē ən), *adj., n.* **—*adj.*** of or having to do with Indiana.
—*n.* a native or inhabitant of Indiana.

In|di|an|ism (in′dē ə niz′əm), *n.* **1** a word or phrase characteristic of Indians, especially American Indians: *Paiutes consider such literary Indianisms corny, and use them only for laughs* (New Yorker). **2** action or policy devoted to the interest of Indians, especially American Indians.

In|di|an|ist (in′dē ə nist), *n.* **1** a person skilled in the languages, history, and customs of Indians, especially American Indians. **2** a person who favors or advocates Indianism.

In|di|an|i|za|tion (in′dē ə nə zā′shən), *n.* the act or process of Indianizing.

In|di|an|ize (in′dē ə nīz), *v.t.,* **-ized, -iz|ing**. to make Indian in appearance, customs, or character: *Under the Indian Government's policy, the management of tea estates is being gradually Indianized but still most of the managers and assistant managers are British* (London Times).

Indian lamb, a fur from lambs of India, similar to Persian lamb.

Indian licorice, a tropical twining shrub of the pea family, native to India, whose seeds are used for beads, and whose root is used as a substitute for licorice; rosary pea.

Indian mallow, **1** a yellow-flowered, Asiatic plant of the mallow family, common as a weed in the eastern United States and on the Pacific coast; velvetleaf; stamp weed. **2** any one of various related plants.

Indian meal, meal made from Indian corn; corn meal.

Indian millet, **1** = durra. **2** = pearl millet.

Indian mound, an earthen mound in the central and eastern United States raised by the Mound Builders as burial places or fortifications.

In|di|an|ness (in′dē ən nis), *n.* **1** the fact of being an American Indian: *After mastering the meaning of Negritude and machismo they would have to grapple with the meaning of Indianness* (New Yorker). **2** a quality suggestive of India and its culture: *Gandhi always thought that a common thread of Indianness would somehow hold the two* [*India and Pakistan*] *together* (Time).

Indian nut, = pine nut.

Indian paintbrush, **1** any one of a genus of plants of the figwort family, especially a kind found in western North America with showy crimson, yellow, or pink bracts, whose blossom is the floral emblem of Wyoming; paintbrush; painted cup. **2** a hawkweed with reddish-orange flowers, that grows as a weed in much of North America.

Indian peacock or **peafowl**, the common peacock.

Indian physic, **1** either of two North American herbs of the rose family whose roots were used by the Indians as an emetic. **2** = Indian hemp (def. 1).

Indian pipe, a waxy white, leafless plant with a solitary bell-shaped flower that resembles a white clay pipe. It lives on dead organic matter in moist woods of North America and Asia.

Indian poke, = American hellebore.

Pronunciation Key: hat, āge, cãre, fär; let, ēqual, tėrm; it, īce; hot, ōpen, ôrder; oil, out; cup, pu̇t, rüle; child; long; thin; ᴛʜen; zh, measure; ə represents **a** in about, **e** in taken, **i** in pencil, **o** in lemon, **u** in circus.

Indian Power, = Red Power.

Indian pudding, a baked pudding made with corn meal (Indian meal), molasses, milk, and suet.

Indian python, a spotted python of southern Asia and Sri Lanka, about 20 feet long.

Indian red, a red pigment, originally a reddish earth from the East Indies, now made artificially.

Indian rice, an aquatic grass of North America; wild rice.

Indian root, **1** the spikenard of North America. **2** = Indian physic.

Indian runner, a very erect and slender breed of domestic duck having white or fawn-colored plumage. It is the most popular and prolific of the egg-laying varieties.

Indian shot, = Indian canna.

Indian sign, *U.S.* **1** a track or trace of the presence of Indians. **2** a signal or token used by Indians.

have (or **put**) **the Indian sign on**, *Informal.* to make helpless; defeat; overcome: *Paul put the Indian sign on them before he went away, and now they rarely bother anyone* (Stan Newton).

Indian snakeroot, a shrub of the dogbane family found in India and other areas of southeast Asia. An extract of its roots is used as a tranquilizer and in the treatment of high blood pressure.

Indian summer, **1** a time of mild, dry, hazy weather in late October or early November, after the first frosts of autumn; second summer: *Indian summer is a season which everyone looks forward to each year, but on whose exact arrival no two people usually agree* (New York Times). **2** *Figurative.* a time of happiness or success coming late in life or at the end of an age: *Welesz's reputation is rightly enjoying an Indian summer in critical esteem* (Listener).

Indian tobacco, a North American weed of the lobelia family having small blue flowers and swollen capsules, used in medicine as an emetic and expectorant.

Indian turmeric, = goldenseal.

Indian turnip, **1** = jack-in-the-pulpit. **2** its root.

Indian wild dog, = dhole.

Indian wolf, an Asiatic wolf, smaller than the gray wolf, found south of the Himalayas.

In|di|an-wres|tle (in′dē ən res′əl), *v.i.*, **-tled, -tling.** to take part in Indian wrestling: *He would Indian-wrestle with five men at the same time* (Gabriel García Márquez).

***Indian wrestling**, any one of various contests of strength between two people, especially one in which the contenders lock hands while resting their elbows on a table and each tries to force down the other's hand to the table.

***Indian wrestling**

India paper, **1** a thin, tough printing paper, used chiefly for Bibles, prayer books, and reference books. **2** a thin, soft, absorbent paper, made chiefly in China and Japan, used for the first and finest impressions of engravings.

India print, a cotton cloth with colorful block-print floral patterns, imported from India.

India proof, a proof or first impression of an engraving on India paper.

India rubber or **india rubber**, **1** a substance of great elasticity obtained from the coagulated, milky juice of various tropical plants; rubber. **2** *U.S.* a rubber; overshoe.

In|di|a-rub|ber (in′dē ə rub′ər), *adj.* **1** of or having to do with India rubber: *an India-rubber ball.* **2** like India rubber.

In|dic (in′dik), *adj., n.* —*adj.* **1** of or having to do with India; Indian. **2** denoting or having to do with the Indian division of the Indo-Iranian languages, which includes Hindi, Urdu, Sanskrit, and others.
—*n.* the Indian division of the Indo-Iranian languages.
[< Latin *Indicus* < Greek *Indikós* < *Indiā*]

indic., **1** indicating. **2** indicative.

in|di|ca (in′də kə), *n.* a fine-grained variety of Asian rice that is not sticky and is rich in amylose, used in developing new hybrid types of rice. [< New Latin *indica* < Latin *Indica,* feminine of *Indicus* Indian, Indic]

in|di|can (in′də kən), *n.* **1** a natural glucoside formed in plants yielding indigo, and which upon decomposition yields natural indigo. *Formula:* $C_{14}H_{17}NO_6$ **2** a substance found in the urine and other body fluids of animals. *Formula:* $C_8H_6NSO_4K$ [< *indico,* early variant of *indigo* + *-an,* variant of *-ane*]

in|di|cant (in′də kənt), *adj., n.* —*adj.* that indicates; indicative.
—*n.* something that indicates a suitable remedy or treatment: *A symptom is an indicant.*

in|di|cate (in′də kāt), *v.t.*, **-cat|ed, -cat|ing. 1** to point out; point to: *The arrow on the sign indicates the right way to go.* SYN: designate. **2** to show; make known: *A dog indicates his feelings by growling, barking, or wagging his tail. A thermometer indicates temperature. Viewing all she sees, As meant to indicate a God to man* (William Cowper). SYN: reveal, disclose. **3** to be a sign or hint of: *Fever indicates illness. The asterisk indicates a footnote. His hesitation indicates unwillingness.* **4** to give a sign or hint of: *to indicate one's views. People often indicate their feelings by facial expressions.* **5** *Medicine.* **a** to show to be needed as a remedy or treatment: *In this case surgery is indicated.* **b** to show the presence of (a disease). [< Latin *indicāre* (with English *-ate*[1]) < *in-* in + *dīcere* speak, say. Compare etym. under **index**.]

in|di|cat|ed horsepower (in′də kā′tid), the net horsepower of an engine, determined by average piston pressure, area, stroke, and number of cylinders.

in|di|ca|tion (in′də kā′shən), *n.* **1** the act of indicating: *We use different words for the indication of different meanings.* **2** a thing that indicates; sign: *There was no indication that the house was occupied. Modesty is the certain indication of a great spirit* (Sir Richard Steele). **3** the amount or degree indicated: *The speedometer indication was 45 miles.* **4** *Medicine.* a symptom that points out a suitable remedy or treatment or shows the presence of a disease.

in|dic|a|tive (in dik′ə tiv), *adj., n.* —*adj.* **1** pointing out; showing; being a sign (of): *A headache is sometimes indicative of eyestrain.* SYN: suggestive. **2** *Grammar.* having to do with a verb form which expresses or denotes a state, act, or happening as actual, or which asks a question of simple fact. In "I go" and "Did you win?" *go* and *did win* are in the indicative mood.
—*n.* *Grammar.* **1** the indicative mood. **2** a verb form in this mood. —**in|dic′a|tive|ly**, *adv.*

in|di|ca|tor (in′də kā′tər), *n.* **1** a person or thing that indicates. **2** a pointer on a dial that shows the amount of heat, pressure, speed, or other factor under measurement. **3** a measuring or recording instrument. **4** an index of business activity: *The stock market's most widely used indicator* [*is*] *the Dow-Jones average of the prices of 30 major industrial companies' shares* (Wall Street Journal). **5** a substance used to indicate chemical conditions or changes, usually by a change in color. Litmus paper is an indicator. **6** *Chemistry.* a tracer: *a radioactive indicator.* **7** *Ecology.* **a** a species of animal or plant whose existence in an area is indicative of specific environmental conditions. **b** an organism at or near the top of a food chain that reflects or indicates the lower levels in the chain by the food residues found in its body.

in|di|ca|to|ry (in′də kə tôr′ē, -tōr′-), *adj.* serving to indicate.

in|di|ces (in′də sēz), *n.* indexes; a plural of **index**.

in|di|ci|a (in dish′ē ə), *n.pl., sing.* **-di|ci|um** (-dish′ē əm). **1** indications; signs; tokens; symptoms: . . . *discovering this truth by means of the far and faint indicia which were within his reach* (G. C. Lewis). **2** markings printed on mail in bulk, instead of the usual stamps, cancellations, or postmarks. [< Latin *indicia,* plural of *indicium* sign < *indicāre;* see etym. under **indicate**]

in|di|cial (in dish′əl), *adj.* **1** of the nature of indicia; indicative. **2** of or like an index. **3** of or having to do with the index finger.

in|dic|o|lite (in dik′ə līt), *n.* a blue variety of tourmaline. [< Spanish *índico* (< Latin *indicum* indigo) + English *-lite*]

in|dict (in dīt′), *v.t.* **1** to charge with an offense or crime; accuse: *Let anyone who will, indict him on the charge of loving base gains* (Benjamin Jowett). **2** (of a grand jury) to find evidence against (an accused person) to be enough so that a trial is necessary: *The jury indicted all eleven men named by the FBI* (Newsweek). [alteration of Middle English *endyten* < Anglo-French *enditer* to charge, accuse, Old French, to indite, dictate < Latin *in-* in + *dictāre* declare, dictate, express in writing (frequentative) < *dīcere* say, speak]

in|dict|a|ble (in dī′tə bəl), *adj.* **1** (of a person) liable to be indicted. **2** making a person liable to be indicted: *an indictable offense.*

in|dict|er (in dī′tər), *n.* a person or group that indicts.

in|dic|tion (in dik′shən), *n.* **1a** a proclamation by a Roman emperor, made every 15 years, fixing the valuation of property as a basis for taxation. **b** a tax assessed on this basis. **2a** the fiscal period of 15 years adopted by the Emperor Constantine and long used to date ordinary events. **b** a specified year in this period, or the number indicating it. **3** a proclamation; declaration. [< Latin *indictiō, -ōnis* < *indīcere* announce < *in-* in + *dīcere* say, speak]

in|dict|ment (in dīt′mənt), *n.* **1** a formal written accusation, especially on the recommendation of a grand jury: *an indictment for murder. When an indictment does come down, the accused individuals will have an opportunity at trial to defend their innocence* (New York Times). *I do not know the method of drawing up an indictment against a whole people* (Edmund Burke). **2** an indicting or being indicted; accusation: *Mr. Bond has written . . . a perfectly stunning indictment of the welfare state* (New Yorker).

in|dict|or (in dī′tər), *n.* = indicter.

in|die (in′dē), *n. Informal.* **1** an independent producer, especially of motion pictures or phonograph records. **2** an independently produced motion picture or phonograph record. [short for *independent*]

In|di|enne (in′dē en′; *French* AN dyen′), *n., adj.*
—*n.* printed calico, especially one printed in bright colors with a rather small pattern.
—*adj.* seasoned in East Indian style: *rice salad Indienne.*
[< French *Indienne,* feminine of *Indien* Indian]

In|dies (in′dēz), *n.pl.* **1** the East Indies. **2** the West Indies. **3** the East Indies, India, and Indochina.

in|dif|fer|ence (in dif′ər əns, -dif′rəns), *n.* **1** lack of interest or attention; not caring: *The boy's indifference to his homework worried his parents.* **2** lack of importance: *It was a matter of indifference to him whether his hands were clean or dirty.* SYN: insignificance.
—*Syn.* **1 Indifference, unconcern, apathy** mean absence of feeling or lack of interest. **Indifference** suggests not caring one way or the other: *A lazy, careless person treats his work with indifference.* **Unconcern** suggests not caring enough to take a real interest, or being unaware of any need to do so: *The teacher does not understand the unconcern of the girl's parents.* **Apathy** suggests indifference to everything except one's own troubles, sorrow, or pain: *Her apathy since her husband's death worries her children.*

in|dif|fer|en|cy (in dif′ər ən sē, -dif′rən-), *n.* = indifference.

in|dif|fer|ent (in dif′ər ənt, -dif′rənt), *adj.* **1** not caring one way or the other; having or showing no interest: *indifferent to an admirer. I enjoyed the trip but she was indifferent.* SYN: apathetic, unconcerned. **2** impartial; neutral; without preference: *The Supreme Court makes indifferent decisions. These mighty cliffs . . . Indifferent to the sun or snow* (Scott). *He the indifferent judge of all* (Robert Southey). SYN: unbiased, disinterested, fair. **3** not mattering much; unimportant: *The time for starting is indifferent to me.* **4** neither good nor bad; just fair: *an indifferent ballplayer.* SYN: mediocre. **5** rather bad; poor: *Her indifferent state of health . . . prevents her being in town* (Jane Austen). **6** neutral in chemical, electrical, or magnetic quality. **7** *Biology.* undifferentiated; not specialized: *indifferent cells.* [< Latin *indifferēns, -entis* < *in-* not + *differēns* differing]

in|dif|fer|ent|ism (in dif′ər ən tiz′əm, -dif′rən-), *n.* **1** the spirit or practice of being indifferent: *Often . . . was I blamed . . . for my so-called Hardness . . . my Indifferentism towards men* (Thomas Carlyle). **2** the principle that differences of religious belief are basically of no importance: *They would be . . . encouraging the heresy of indifferentism, i.e., that as we are all going the same way it doesn't really matter how we get there* (London Times).

in|dif|fer|ent|ist (in dif′ər ən tist, -dif′rən-), *n.* a person who practices or advocates indifferentism.

in|dif|fer|ent|ly (in dif′ər ənt lē, -dif′rənt-), *adv.* **1** with indifference: *He looked indifferently upon subjects that did not interest him.* **2** without distinction; equally. **3** neither very well nor very badly; moderately; tolerably; passably: *He did do his work but indifferently.* **4** poorly; badly: *Montmorency . . . now took the command for which his rash and impetuous temper but indifferently qualified him* (William H. Prescott).

in|di|gen (in′də jən), *n.* = indigene.

in|di|gence (in′də jəns), *n.* **1** extreme need; poverty. **2** indigent people: *aiding helpless indigence* (William Cowper).

in|di|gene (in′də jēn), *n.* a person, animal, or plant native to a region; native. [< Middle French *indigène,* learned borrowing from Latin *indigena* a native; see etym. under **indigenous**]

in|dig|e|nist (in dij′ə nist), *n., adj.* —*n.* an advocate of policies or action devoted to the interest of the indigenous inhabitants of a Latin American country.
—*adj.* of or having to do with indigenists.

[< American Spanish *indigenista* < *indigena* a native < Latin *indigena;* see etym. under **indigenous**]

in|di|gen|i|ty (in′də jen′ə tē), *n.* indigenous quality; indigenousness.

in|dig|e|ni|za|tion (in dij′ə nə zā′shən), *n.* the process of indigenizing or of becoming indigenized: *The pope stressed the fact that Christianity is not a European thing, urging "indigenization"—the use of native clergy and adaptation to local culture* (C. J. McNaspy).

in|dig|e|nize (in dij′ə nīz), *v.t.,* **-nized, -niz|ing.** to make native; bring under the control of the natives of a country: *Not since the end of Nigeria's civil war has so much heat been generated by government policy as the decision to indigenize some aspects of the economy* (London Times).

in|dig|e|nous (in dij′ə nəs), *adj.* **1** originating in the region or country where found; native: *Lions are indigenous to Africa. Shinto is the indigenous or ethnic religion of Japan* (Atlantic). **2** *Figurative.* born in a person; innate; inherent. [< Latin *indigena* a native; native (ultimately < *in* in + *gen-,* root of *gignere* beget, bear; be born) + English *-ous*] — **in|dig′e|nous|ly,** *adv.* — **in|dig′e|nous|ness,** *n.*

in|di|gent (in′də jent), *adj., n.* — ***adj.*** **1** lacking the necessities of life; poor or needy: *He became a legendary hero ... to the indigent and the oppressed* (Atlantic). **2** *Archaic.* **a** wanting; deficient: *How low, how little are the proud, How indigent the great!* (Thomas Gray). **b** destitute; void (of).
— ***n.*** a poor or needy person: *House and Senate bills setting up a paid public defender system for indigents accused of Federal crimes haven't been sent to conference* (Wall Street Journal).
[< Old French *indigent,* learned borrowing from Latin *indigēns, -entis,* present participle of *indigēre* need < *indu* in (< *in*) + *egēre* be in need, be poor; want] — **in′di|gent|ly,** *adv.*

in|di|gest|ed (in′də jes′tid, -dī-), *adj.* **1** not digested; undigested. **2** without arrangement or order; unformed; shapeless: *Foul indigested lump, As crooked in thy manners as thy shape!* (Shakespeare). **3** not properly thought out; ill-considered.

in|di|gest|i|bil|i|ty (in′də jes′tə bil′ə tē, -dī-), *n.* indigestible nature or quality.

in|di|gest|i|ble (in′də jes′tə bəl, -dī-), *adj., n.*
— ***adj.*** that cannot be digested; hard to digest: *greasy indigestible food.*
— ***n.*** an indigestible substance: *We put up the original machines in 1941 to keep people from feeding indigestibles to the animals* (Harper's).
— **in′di|gest′i|ble|ness,** *n.* — **in′di|gest′i|bly,** *adv.*

in|di|ges|tion (in′də jes′chən, -dī-), *n.* an inability to digest food; difficulty in digesting food: *Indigestion can sometimes be prevented by avoiding rich, highly seasoned foods* (E. Clinton Texter). **SYN:** dyspepsia.

in|di|ges|tive (in′də jes′tiv, -dī-), *adj.* having or suffering from indigestion; dyspeptic.

in|dign (in dīn′), *adj. Archaic.* **1** unworthy; undeserving: *She her selfe was of his grace indigne* (Edmund Spenser). **2** undeserved. **3** unbecoming; disgraceful: *indign and base adversities* (Shakespeare). [< Middle French *indigne* < Old French *endigne,* learned borrowing from Latin *indignus* unworthy < *in-* not + *dignus* worthy]

in|dig|nant (in dig′nənt), *adj.* angry at something unworthy, unjust, unfair, or mean: *She was indignant at the man who beat his horse.* **SYN:** incensed, provoked, displeased. [< Latin *indignāns, -antis,* present participle of *indignārī* be indignant (at); regard as unworthy < *indignus* unworthy; see etym. under **indign**] — **in|dig′nant|ly,** *adv.*

in|dig|na|tion (in′dig nā′shən), *n.* anger at something unworthy, unjust, unfair, or mean; anger mixed with scorn; righteous anger: *Cruelty to animals aroused his indignation.* **SYN:** See syn. under **anger.**

indignation meeting, a meeting held for the purpose of expressing indignation, as at some public abuse: *While the other attorneys split up into little indignation meetings up and down the corridors* (New York Times).

in|dig|ni|ty (in dig′nə tē), *n., pl.* **-ties. 1** an injury to one's dignity; lack of respect or proper treatment; insult; slight: *He felt that his aunt's use of baby talk was an indignity.* **SYN:** See syn. under **insult. 2** *Obsolete.* **a** disgrace; a disgraceful act. **b** unworthiness. [< Latin *indignitās* < *indignus* unworthy; see etym. under **indign**]

in|di|go (in′də gō), *n., pl.* **-gos** or **-goes,** *adj.*
— ***n.*** **1** a blue dye that can be obtained from various plants. It is now usually made artificially, especially from aniline. *The source of the world's indigo until the end of the nineteenth century was India, where over a million acres were set aside for the dye-producing plant* (Atlantic). **2** a plant from which indigo was formerly obtained. Indigo belongs to the pea family. **3** a deep violet-blue color, one of the seven prismatic or primary colors. **4** = indigo blue (def. 2). Synthetic indigo is the same as indigotin, but natural indigo contains additional substances. — ***adj.*** deep violet-blue.
[< Spanish *índigo,* and *índico* < Latin *indicum* < Greek *indikón* the blue Indian dye]

indigo bird, = indigo bunting.

indigo blue, 1 the color indigo. **2** the blue coloring matter of indigo, an odorless, crystalline solid insoluble in water or alcohol; indigotin. *Formula:* $C_6H_{10}N_2O_2$ — **in′di|go-blue′,** *adj.*

indigo bunting, a small American finch, the male of which is a deep violet-blue with blackish wings and tail. The female is brown.

in|di|goid (in′də goid), *adj., n.* — ***adj.*** **1** of the same quality and color as indigo. **2** of or belonging to a group of vat dyes that produce a color resembling indigo. — ***n.*** an indigoid dye.

indigo snake, a harmless snake of tropical America and the southern United States, reaching a length of about eight feet and having a deep violet-blue color; gopher snake.

in|di|got|ic (in′də got′ik), *adj.* **1** having to do with or derived from indigo or indigotin. **2** deep-blue.

in|dig|o|tin (in dig′ə tin, in′də gō′-), *n.* = indigo blue (def. 2). [< *indigo* + inserted *-t-* + *-in*]

in|dig|o|tine (in dig′ə tin, -tēn; in′də gō′tin), *n.* = indigotin.

in|di|rect (in′də rekt′, -dī-), *adj.* **1** not going straight to the point: *She would not say yes or no, but gave an indirect answer to my question.* **SYN:** roundabout. **2** not directly connected; secondary: *Happiness is an indirect result of doing one's work well.* **SYN:** incidental. **3** not direct; not straight: *We walk to town by a road that is indirect, but very pleasant.* **SYN:** circuitous, roundabout. **4** not straightforward and honest; deceitful: *indirect methods.* **5** that repeats a speaker's words without directly quoting him. In the sentence *He said that I was right* the words "I was right" are an indirect quotation. — **in′direct′ly,** *adv.* — **in′di|rect′ness,** *n.*

indirect discourse, the repetition of the substance of a person's speech without directly quoting it. *Example:* "He said that he would come," instead of "He said, 'I will come.' "

indirect initiative, a procedure by which a statute or amendment may be proposed by a petition of the voters and must then go to the legislature before being put on the ballot. See also **initiative** (def. 4).

in|di|rec|tion (in′də rek′shən, -dī-), *n.* **1** a roundabout act, course, or method: *Thus do we ... By indirections find directions out* (Shakespeare). **2** deceitful or crooked dealing; dishonesty; deceit.

indirect lighting, artificial lighting that is diffused or reflected to illuminate without glare.

indirect object, a person or thing that is indirectly affected by the action of the verb. In modern English grammar the indirect object usually comes before the direct object and shows to whom or for whom something is done. *Example:* In "I gave John the book," *John* is the indirect object and *book* is the direct object.

indirect tax, a tax paid indirectly by the consumer and included in the price of the article.

in|dis|cern|i|ble (in′də zėr′nə bəl, -sėr′-), *adj., n.*
— ***adj.*** not discernible; imperceptible: *a rapid look, indiscernible by male eye* (Charles Reade).
— ***n.*** a thing that cannot be discerned: *Among the indiscernibles are absolute space, time and direction* (Scientific American). — **in′dis|cern′i|ble|ness,** *n.* — **in′dis|cern′i|bly,** *adv.*

in|dis|cerp|ti|bil|i|ty (in′də sėrp′tə bil′ə tē), *n.* the quality of being indiscerptible.

in|dis|cerp|ti|ble (in′də sėrp′tə bəl), *adj.* not to be destroyed by the dissolution of parts; indivisible. [< *in-*[1] not + *discerptible*]

in|dis|ci|pline (in dis′ə plin), *n.* lack of discipline; lack of systematic training or regulating control: *He was criticised for overproduction, for sentimentality ... and indiscipline* (Manchester Guardian).

in|dis|ci|plined (in dis′ə plind), *adj.* = undisciplined.

in|dis|cov|er|a|ble (in′dis kuv′ər ə bəl), *adj.* not discoverable; undiscoverable.

in|dis|creet (in′dis krēt′), *adj.* not discreet; not wise and judicious; imprudent: *The indiscreet girl often revealed secrets to strangers.* **SYN:** unwise, foolish, rash. [< *in-*[1] not + *discreet*] — **in′dis|creet′ly,** *adv.* — **in′dis|creet′ness,** *n.*

in|dis|crete (in′dis krēt′, in dis′krēt), *adj.* not discrete; not consisting of distinct parts. [< Latin *indiscrētus* < *in-* not + *discrētus* separated, discrete]

in|dis|cre|tion (in′dis kresh′ən), *n.* **1** the fact of being indiscreet; lack of good judgment; imprudence: *They were embarrassed at his indiscretion in talking about family matters in front of strangers.* **SYN:** unwiseness. **2** an indiscreet act: *a youth, guilty only of an indiscretion* (Macaulay). *We feel that this action turned a minor indiscretion into a serious breach of loyalty* (London Times). [< Old French *indiscretion,* learned borrowing from Late Latin *indiscrētiō, -ōnis* < *indiscrētus* undiscriminating; see etym. under **indiscrete**]

in|dis|cre|tion|ar|y (in′dis kresh′ə ner′ē), *adj.* = indiscreet.

in|dis|crim|i|nate (in′dis krim′ə nit), *adj.* **1** mixed up; confused: *He tipped everything out of his suitcase in an indiscriminate pile.* **2** not discriminating; not distinguishing carefully especially between persons, things, or feelings: *He is an indiscriminate reader; he shows no feeling for the differences between good books and bad ones.* **SYN:** See syn. under **miscellaneous.** — **in′dis|crim′i|nate|ly,** *adv.* — **in′dis|crim′i|nate|ness,** *n.*

in|dis|crim|i|nat|ing (in′dis krim′ə nā′ting), *adj.* not discriminating; undiscriminating. — **in′dis|crim′i|nat′ing|ly,** *adv.*

in|dis|crim|i|na|tion (in′dis krim′ə nā′shən), *n.* lack of discrimination.

in|dis|crim|i|na|tive (in′dis krim′ə nā′tiv), *adj.* making no distinctions; not discriminative: *That sweeping violence of indiscriminative depreciation* (Algernon Charles Swinburne).

in|dis|crim|i|na|to|ry (in′dis krim′ə nə tôr′ē, -tōr′-), *adj.* = indiscriminative.

in|dis|pen|sa|bil|i|ty (in′dis pen′sə bil′ə tē), *n.* indispensable quality or condition; absolute necessity.

in|dis|pen|sa|ble (in′dis pen′sə bəl), *adj., n.*
— ***adj.*** absolutely necessary: *Oxygen is indispensable to life. Knowledge then is the indispensable condition of expansion of mind* (Cardinal Newman). **SYN:** See syn. under **necessary.**
— ***n.*** a person or thing that is indispensable.
— **in′dis|pen′sa|ble|ness,** *n.* — **in′dis|pen′sa|bly,** *adv.*

in|dis|pose (in′dis pōz′), *v.t.,* **-posed, -pos|ing. 1** to make unwilling; make not inclined: *Hot weather indisposes a person to work hard.* **SYN:** disincline. **2** to make unfit or unable. **SYN:** disqualify. **3** to make slightly ill.

in|dis|posed (in′dis pōzd′), *adj.* **1** slightly ill; unwell: *I have been indisposed with a cold.* **2** unwilling; not inclined; averse.

in|dis|po|si|tion (in′dis pə zish′ən), *n.* **1** a disturbance of health; slight illness. **2** unwillingness; disinclination; aversion.

in|dis|put|a|bil|i|ty (in′dis pyü′tə bil′ə tē, in dis′pyə tə bil′-), *n.* the quality or state of being indisputable.

in|dis|put|a|ble (in′dis pyü′tə bəl, in dis′pyə-), *adj.* too evident to be disputed; undoubtedly true; certain; unquestionable: *It is an indisputable fact that George Washington was the first President of the United States.* **SYN:** undoubted, undeniable. — **in′dis|put′a|ble|ness,** *n.*

in|dis|put|a|bly (in′dis pyü′tə blē, in dis′pyə-), *adv.* in an indisputable manner; unquestionably: *If the bank's statement agrees with my bank balance, it does not follow indisputably that the balance is correct* (Scientific American).

in|dis|so|cia|ble (in′di sō′shə bəl), *adj.* not dissociable; that cannot be dissociated: *Moral action and religion, although not identical, are indissociable* (New York Times).

in|dis|sol|u|bil|i|ty (in′di sol′yə bil′ə tē), *n.* indissoluble quality or condition; stability.

in|dis|sol|u|ble (in′di sol′yə bəl), *adj.* that cannot be dissolved, undone, or destroyed; lasting; firm: *Let us make an indissoluble agreement. She had become an indissoluble part of their whole scheme of things* (Lytton Strachey). — **in′dis|sol′u|ble|ness,** *n.*

in|dis|sol|u|bly (in′di sol′yə blē), *adv.* in an indissoluble manner; so as not to be dissolved, undone, or destroyed: *The splitting of the atom indissolubly fused the world of man* (Bulletin of Atomic Scientists).

in|dis|tinct (in′dis tingkt′), *adj.* not distinct; not clear to the eye, ear, or mind; confused: *an indistinct picture, indistinct speech. He had an indistinct memory of the accident. We could hear an indistinct roar from the distant ocean.* **SYN:** undefined, vague, obscure, faint, dim. [< Latin *indistinctus* < *in-* not + *distinctus* distinguishable, distinct] — **in′dis|tinct′ly,** *adv.* — **in′dis|tinct′ness,** *n.*

in|dis|tinc|tion (in′dis tingk′shən), *n.* **1** lack of distinction or discrimination; failure to distinguish. **2** absence of distinction or difference; being indistinguishable. **3** absence of distinction or eminence.

in|dis|tinc|tive (in′dis tingk′tiv), *adj.* not distinctive; without distinctive features. — **in′dis|tinc′tive|ly,** *adv.* — **in′dis|tinc′tive|ness,** *n.*

Pronunciation Key: hat, āge, cãre, fär; let, ēqual, tėrm; it, īce; hot, ōpen, ôrder; oil, out; cup, pu̇t, rüle; child; long; thin; ᴛʜen; zh, measure; ə represents **a** in about, **e** in taken, **i** in pencil, **o** in lemon, **u** in circus.

in·dis·tin·guish·a·bil·i·ty (in′dis ting′gwi shə bil′ə tē), *n.* the quality or state of being indistinguishable.

in·dis·tin·guish·a·ble (in′dis ting′gwi shə bəl), *adj.* that cannot be distinguished; indiscernible; imperceptible. –**in′dis·tin′guish·a·ble·ness**, *n.*

in·dis·tin·guish·a·bly (in′dis ting′gwi shə blē), *adv.* so as not to be distinguishable: *Many Hindus ... would like to melt the Sikhs indistinguishably into the nation* (New Yorker).

in·dite (in dīt′), *v.t.*, **-dit·ed, -dit·ing.** **1** to put in words or writing; compose: *to indite a letter.* **2** *Archaic.* to deal with or describe in a literary composition: *Not sedulous by nature to indite Wars ...* (Milton). **3** *Obsolete.* to dictate; prescribe: *Hear how learn'd Greece her useful rules indites* (Alexander Pope). [< Old French *enditer;* see etym. under **indict**] –**in·dit′er**, *n.*

in·dite·ment (in dīt′mənt), *n.* the act of putting in words or writing; composition.

***in·di·um** (in′dē əm), *n.* a silvery metallic chemical element found only in combination with other elements, chiefly in sphalerite and lead mining. It is very soft but resistant to acids and abrasion and is used as a coating on metal parts. [< New Latin *indium* < Latin *indicum* indigo (because of the blue lines in its spectrum)]

***indium**

symbol	atomic number	atomic weight	oxidation state
In	49	114.82	3

indium antimonide, a crystalline compound of indium and antimony, used as a semiconducting device. *Formula:* InSb

in·di·vert·i·ble (in′də vėr′tə bəl, -dī-), *adj.* not divertible; not to be turned aside.

in·di·vert·i·bly (in′də vėr′tə blē, -dī-), *adv.* in a way that cannot be turned aside.

individ., individual.

in·di·vid·u·al (in′də vij′ù əl), *n., adj.* –*n.* **1** a person: *He is the tallest individual in his family.* **2** a single person, animal, or thing: *the conflict between the individual and the group. We saw a herd of giraffes containing 30 individuals.* **3** *Biology.* a single or simple organism that can exist independently; member of a compound organism or colony.
–*adj.* **1** single; particular; separate: *an individual question. To him the individual human being is at once a lonely entity and a mere part of a larger whole* (London Times). **2** for one only: *individual saltcellars, food served in individual portions. Washbowls are for general use; toothbrushes are for individual use. Benches are for several people; chairs are individual seats.* **3** of, having to do with, or peculiar to one person or thing: *individual tastes.* **4** marking off one person or thing specially: *She has an individual style of arranging her hair.* **5** *Obsolete.* indivisible.
[< Medieval Latin *individualis* < Latin *indīviduus* < *in-* not + *dīviduus* divisible < *dīvidere* to divide]
▶ See **person** for usage note.

in·di·vid·u·al·ise (in′də vij′ù ə līz), *v.t.*, **-ised, -is·ing.** *Especially British.* individualize.

in·di·vid·u·al·ism (in′də vij′ù ə liz′əm), *n.* **1** the belief that individual freedom is as important as the welfare of the community or group as a whole: *the American system of rugged individualism* (Herbert Hoover). *The Economist became Britain's firmest editorial defender of laissez-faire individualism* (Newsweek). **2** any ethical, economic, or political theory that emphasizes the importance of individuals. **3** absence of cooperation; wanting a separate existence for oneself; the pursuit of one's own ends or ideas as a mode or principle of life. **4** individual character; individuality.

in·di·vid·u·al·ist (in′də vij′ù ə list), *n., adj.* –*n.* **1** a person who lives his own life for himself and does not try to cooperate with or follow others. **2** a supporter of individualism.
–*adj.* = individualistic.

in·di·vid·u·al·is·tic (in′də vij′ù ə lis′tik), *adj.* of or having to do with individualism or individualists: *The French are too individualistic to take to bosom buddies* (Time). –**in′di·vid′u·al·is′ti·cal·ly**, *adv.*

in·di·vid·u·al·i·ty (in′də vij′ù al′ə tē), *n., pl.* **-ties.** **1** the character or qualities which distinguish one person or thing from another; individual character: *Each human being begins in infancy to build an individuality of his own. Individuality is the salt of common life* (Henry van Dyke). **SYN**: See syn. under **character**. **2** the state of being individual; existence as an individual. **3** an individual person or thing. **4** *Obsolete.* indivisibility; inseparability.

in·di·vid·u·al·i·za·tion (in′də vij′ù ə lə zā′shən), *n.* **1** the act or process of individualizing. **2** the state of being individualized.

in·di·vid·u·al·ize (in′də vij′ù ə līz), *v.t.*, **-ized, -iz·ing.** **1** to make different for each individual; give a distinctive character to: *This school individualizes its course of study. Carlyle's strong prose style individualizes his work.* **2** to consider as individuals; list one by one; specify. –**in′di·vid′u·al·iz′er**, *n.*

in·di·vid·u·al·ly (in′də vij′ù ə lē), *adv.* **1** personally; one at a time; as individuals: *Sometimes our teacher helps us individually.* **2** each from the others: *People differ individually.*

individual medley, a swimming contest or event in which a swimmer must use three or four different strokes, usually the butterfly stroke, backstroke, breaststroke, and crawl, for each third or fourth of the course.

in·di·vid·u·ate (in′də vij′ù āt), *v.*, **-at·ed, -at·ing.** –*v.t.* **1** to give distinctive character to; individualize. **2** to form into a distinct entity.
–*v.i.* **1** to assume an individual character; become individual: *It is consciousness of this deity within us that leaves us free to become truly human—to individuate* (New Yorker). [< Medieval Latin *individuare* (with English *-ate*[1]) < Latin *indīviduus* undivided, individual]

in·di·vid·u·a·tion (in′də vij′ù ā′shən), *n.* **1** the act of individuating. **2** the state of being individuated; individual existence. **3** distinctive form or condition. **4** *Philosophy.* the process leading to individual existence, as distinct from that of the species.

in·di·vis·i·bil·i·ty (in′də viz′ə bil′ə tē), *n.* indivisible condition or quality.

in·di·vis·i·ble (in′də viz′ə bəl), *adj., n.* –*adj.* **1** that cannot be divided: *"One nation under God, indivisible, with liberty and justice for all." Freedom is an indivisible word* (Wendell Willkie). *Supreme power is indivisible, insomuch as no man can serve two Masters* (Thomas Hobbes). **2** that cannot be divided without a remainder: *Any odd number is indivisible by 2.*
–*n.* something indivisible. –**in′di·vis′i·ble·ness**, *n.*

in·di·vis·i·bly (in′də viz′ə blē), *adv.* in an indivisible manner; so as to be indivisible.

Indo-, *combining form.* **1** Indian and: *Indo-European* = *Indian and European.*
2 Indian; of India or the East Indies: *Indo-Aryan* = *of or having to do with Aryans of India.*
3 Indian Ocean and: *Indo-Pacific.*
[< Greek *Indós* the Indus river]

In·do-Ar·y·an (in′dō ãr′ē ən, -ãr′yən), *adj., n.* –*adj.* of or having to do with Aryans of India, or the Indo-Iranian languages; Indic.
–*n.* a native of India of Aryan stock and speech.

In·do·chi·nese or **In·do-Chi·nese** (in′dō chī-nēz′, -nēs′), *adj., n., pl.* **-nese.** –*adj.* **1** of or having to do with Indochina, the Mongoloid peoples living there, or their languages. **2** of or having to do with the family group of languages comprising these languages and the Tibetan and Chinese groups of languages; Sino-Tibetan.
–*n.* a native or inhabitant of Indochina.

Indochinese forest ox, = kouprey.

in·do·chi·nite (in′dō chī′nīt), *n.* a kind of tektite found in Indochina.

in·doc·ile (in dos′əl), *adj.* not docile; not amenable to discipline or guidance; unteachable; intractable.

in·do·cil·i·ty (in′dō sil′ə tē), *n.* unteachableness; intractableness.

In·do·cin (in dō′sən), *n. Trademark.* = indomethacin.

in·doc·tri·nate (in dok′trə nāt), *v.t.*, **-nat·ed, -nat·ing.** **1** to teach a doctrine, belief, or principle to. **2** to teach fundamentals, especially of military customs and discipline: *The recruits were indoctrinated at Camp Blanding.* **3** to teach; instruct. **SYN**: inculcate. [probably < Medieval Latin *indoctrinare* (with English *-ate*[1]) < *in-* in + *doctrinare* teach < Latin *doctrīna* doctrine]

in·doc·tri·na·tion (in dok′trə nā′shən), *n.* **1** the act of indoctrinating. **2** the state of being indoctrinated: *His indoctrination in democracy was good training to become a Congressman.*

in·doc·tri·na·tor (in dok′trə nā′tər), *n.* a person who indoctrinates.

in·doc·tri·na·to·ry (in dok′trə nə tôr′ē, -tōr′-), *adj.* of or characterized by indoctrination: *We admit the possibility of a kind of moral education which is not wholly committed to a particular creed or code and which is not indoctrinatory* (London Times).

In·do-Eu·ro·pe·an (in′dō yůr′ə pē′ən), *adj., n.* –*adj.* **1** of India and Europe. **2** of or having to do with a group of related languages spoken in India, western Asia, and Europe; Aryan. English, German, Latin, Greek, Russian, Persian, and Sanskrit are some of the Indo-European languages.
–*n.* **1** this group of languages and the assumed prehistoric language from which they are derived. *Abbr:* IE (no periods). **2** a member of a people that speak an Indo-European language.

In·do-Eu·ro·pe·an·ist (in′dō yůr ə pē′ə nist), *n.* a student of the Indo-European languages; linguist who specializes in Indo-European.

In·do-Ger·man·ic (in′dō jėr man′ik), *adj., n.* –*adj.* = Indo-European (def. 2).
–*n.* = Indo-European.

In·do-Hit·tite (in′dō hit′īt), *n.* a linguistic family that includes Indo-European as one branch and Hittite as the other.

In·do-I·ra·ni·an (in′dō ī rā′nē ən), *adj., n.* –*adj.* of or having to do with a division of the Indo-European languages comprising the Indic and Iranian branches.
–*n.* this division.

in·dole or **in·dol** (in′dōl, -dol), *n.* **1** a white, crystalline chemical compound with an unpleasant odor, produced artificially by the reduction of indigo or by other forms of syntheses, and also formed within the intestines. It is used as a reagent and in making perfumes. *Psychotic behavior can be induced in the guppies by treating them with indole* (Newsweek). *Formula:* C_8H_7N **2** any one of various derivatives of this compound. [< *ind*(igo) + *-ole, -ol*[2]]

in·dole·a·ce·tic acid (in′dōl ə sē′tik, -set′ik), a plant hormone, the principal auxin, which regulates plant growth and development; heteroauxin. It is synthesized in the protoplasm of the young and active parts of plants. *Formula:* $C_{10}H_9O_2N$

in·dole·bu·tyr·ic acid (in′dōl byü tir′ik), a synthetic compound used to regulate plant growth and development: *A definite growth response was observed using as little as one part per billion of gibberellin or one part per million of indolebutyric acid* (Scientific American). *Formula:* $C_{12}H_{13}NO_2$

in·do·lence (in′də ləns), *n.* dislike of work; laziness, idleness: *He is one of the many, many hundreds in whom indolence has strangled genius* (Scott). **SYN**: sluggishness, slothfulness.

in·do·lent (in′də lənt), *adj.* **1** disliking work; lazy; idle: *I am naturally indolent and without application to any kind of business* (Horace Walpole). **SYN**: slothful, sluggish, listless, supine. See syn. under **idle**. **2** *Medicine.* progressing slowly; causing little or no pain: *an indolent tumor or ulcer.* [< Late Latin *indolēns, -entis* < Latin *in-* not + *dolēns,* present participle of *dolēre* be in pain]
–**in′do·lent·ly**, *adv.*

in·dol·ic (in dō′lik, -dol′-), *n.* having to do with, consisting of, or derived from an indole: *Melatonin is an indolic compound. Many hallucinogenic drugs are indolic.*

In·dol·o·gist (in dol′ə jist), *n.* a person who studies Indology.

In·dol·o·gy (in dol′ə jē), *n.* the study of the history, customs, institutions, languages, and literature of India.

in·do·meth·a·cin (in′dō meth′ə sən), *n.* an analgesic drug used in the treatment of rheumatoid arthritis; Indocin. *Formula:* $C_{19}H_{16}ClNO_4$ [< *in-do*(le) + *meth*(yl) + *ac*(etic acid) + *-in*]

in·dom·i·ta·bil·i·ty (in dom′ə tə bil′ə tē), *n.* the quality or state of being indomitable: *I must add, a trifle shamefacedly, that this indomitability has been at least partly justified* (New Yorker).

in·dom·i·ta·ble (in dom′ə tə bəl), *adj.* that cannot be conquered; bravely or stubbornly unyielding: *The soldiers showed indomitable courage against overwhelming odds. The indomitable freedom of the human spirit* (Newsweek). **SYN**: unconquerable. [< Late Latin *indomitābilis* < Latin *indomitus* untamed < *in-* not + *domāre* to tame]
–**in·dom′i·ta·ble·ness**, *n.*

in·dom·i·ta·bly (in dom′ə tə blē), *adv.* in an indomitable manner: *If the single man plant himself indomitably on his instincts, and there abide, the huge world will come round to him* (Emerson).

In·do·ne·sian (in′də nē′zhən, -shən), *adj., n.* –*adj.* **1** of or having to do with the Republic of Indonesia or its people. **2** of or having to do with the Malay Archipelago or its people. **3** of or having to do with the Indonesian language or division of languages.
–*n.* **1** a native or inhabitant of Indonesia. **2a** an inhabitant of the Malay Archipelago; Malay. **b** a member of a race with light-brown skin, supposed to have been dominant on the Malay Archipelago before the Malays. **3** a division of Austronesian languages, including Malay, Indonesian, and the languages of Madagascar, Formosa, and the Philippines. **4** the official language of the Republic of Indonesia. It is based chiefly on Malay, and contains elements from other related languages of the area. [< *Indo-* + Greek *nêsos* island + English *-ian*]

in·door (in′dôr′, -dōr′), *adj.* **1** done or used in a house or building: *indoor tennis.* **2** having to do with the interior of a house or other building. **3** of or belonging to a hospital, poorhouse, or similar institution: *indoor relief, the indoor poor.*

indoor baseball, a form of softball played indoors.

in·doors (in′dôrz′, -dōrz′), *adv.* in or into a house

or building; under cover: *Go indoors.*

in|door|sy (in′dôr′zē, -dōr′-), *adj.* characteristic of or suitable for inside the house; belonging indoors: *an indoorsy outfit, an indoorsy type of man.*

in|do|phe|nol (in′dō fē′nōl, -nol), *n.* any one of various synthetic blue or green dyes derived from quinonimine. [< *ind*(igo) + *phenol*]

in|dorse (in dôrs′), *v.t.*, **-dorsed, -dors|ing.** = endorse.

in|dox|yl (in dok′səl), *n.* a crystalline chemical compound obtained from aniline and converted by oxidation into indigo blue. *Formula:* C_8H_7NO [< *ind*(igo) + *-oxyl,* as in *hydroxyl*]

In|dra (in′drə), *n.* the chief god of the ancient Hindu religion.

in|draft or **in|draught** (in′draft′, -dräft′), *n.* **1** act of drawing in; inward attraction. **2** an inward flow, stream, or current, as of water or air: *There is sometimes a strong indraught setting up St. George's Channel, which deceives seamen* (Benjamin Franklin).

in|draw|al (in drô′əl), *n.* = indraft.

in|draw|ing (in′drô′ing), *adj.* drawing in.

in|drawn (in′drôn′), *adj.* **1** drawn in. **2** = introspective.

in|dri (in′drē), *n.* a large lemur of Madagascar which has a rudimentary tail. It is black, with white or red-brown undersides, about two feet in length, and usually walks upright, bearing a superficial resemblance to a human being. [< French *indri,* apparently < Malagasy *indry* lo! see! (which was mistaken for the animal's name)]

in|du|bi|ta|ble (in dü′bə tə bəl, -dyü′-), *adj.* too evident to be doubted; perfectly certain or evident; unquestionable: *Laziness and ignorance were the two indubitable causes of his failure. There is a core of indubitable knowledge in education* (Atlantic). — **in|du′bi|ta|ble|ness,** *n.*

in|du|bi|ta|bly (in dü′bə tə blē, -dyü′-), *adv.* in an indubitable manner; unquestionably; without doubt; evidently: *The way of the Eternal was most indubitably a way of peace and joy* (Matthew Arnold).

induc., induction.

in|duce (in düs′, -dyüs′), *v.t.*, **-duced, -duc|ing. 1** to lead on; influence; persuade: *Advertisements induce people to buy. Pray what could induce him to commit so rash an action?* (Oliver Goldsmith). **SYN:** incite, impel. **2** to bring about; cause: *The doctor says that his medicine will induce sleep. Harsh discipline induced discontent. Their purpose is not to induce thought but to prevent it* (John Kenneth Galbraith). **3a** to produce (an electric current, electric charge, or magnetic change) without direct contact. **b** to bring about (radioactivity) in an element artificially by bombardment with particles. **4** to infer by reasoning from particular facts to a general rule or principle or from the known to the unknown; derive as an induction. [< Latin *indūcere* introduce; imply, persuade < *in-* in + *dūcere* to lead]

in|duced drag (in düst′, -dyüst′), the drag on an airplane caused by the flow of air about the lifting surfaces, especially the wing tips.

in|duce|ment (in düs′mənt, -dyüs′-), *n.* **1** something that influences or persuades; incentive: *A new bicycle for the winner was an inducement to try hard to win the contest.* **2** the act of influencing or persuading. **3** *Law.* the introductory portion of a pleading, explaining the circumstances of the case.

in|duc|er (in dü′sər, -dyü′-), *n.* **1** a person or thing that induces. **2** *Genetics.* a component of the operon that helps to activate genes; derepressor: *The French scientists advanced the theory, now substantially verified, that genes are ... kept turned off by a "repressor" until another substance, an "inducer," comes along and disengages the repressor, thus allowing the gene to express itself* (Robert Reinhold).

in|duc|i|ble (in dü′sə bəl, -dyü′-), *adj.* that can be induced.

in|duct (in dukt′), *v.t.* **1** to put formally in possession (of an office); install: *He was inducted into the office of governor.* **2** to bring in; introduce (into a place, seat, or position). **3** to take into the armed forces. **4** to initiate; introduce in knowledge or experience: *the pleasures to which the footman inducted him* (Thackeray). **5** (in the Church of England) to install formally into possession of a benefice. [< Latin *inductus,* past participle of *indūcere;* see etym. under **induce**]

in|duct|ance (in duk′təns), *n.* **1a** the property of an electric circuit by which an electromotive force is induced in it or in a nearby circuit. The tuner of a radio varies the inductance of its coils. **b** a circuit or a device having this property. **2** the lag in an electric circuit when the current goes on or off. **3** a device or apparatus for providing inductance; inductor.

inductance coil, = choke coil.

in|duc|tee (in duk′tē′, -duk′tē), *n.* a person who has been or soon will be inducted, especially into the armed forces: *The average inductee was reading on the sixth grade level in World War I* (Atlantic).

in|duc|tile (in duk′təl), *adj.* not ductile; not pliable; unyielding: *A man of honour ... but inductile, unimaginative, hard* (F. W. Robinson).

in|duc|til|i|ty (in′duk til′ə tē), *n.* the quality of being inductile.

in|duc|tion (in duk′shən), *n.* **1a** the process by which an object having electrical or magnetic properties produces similar properties in a nearby object, usually without direct contact; inductance: *Induction can give a conductor a permanent charge ... until it leaks off or is otherwise dissipated* (Scientific American). **b** a tendency exhibited by currents of electricity to resist change. **2a** reasoning from particular facts to a general rule or principle. **b** a conclusion reached in this way: *Every induction is a speculation and it guesses at a unity which the facts present but do not strictly imply* (J. Bronowski). **3a** the act of inducting; act or ceremony of installing a person in office; installation. **b** *U.S.* enrollment in military service. **4** the act of bringing into existence or operation; producing; causing; inducing: *induction of a hypnotic state.* **5** the taking of the explosive mixture or air into the cylinder of an internal-combustion engine. **6** *Embryology.* the change in form or shape caused by the action of one tissue of an embryo on adjacent tissues or parts. **7** *Archaic.* an introductory statement in a literary work; a preface or prelude.

► See **deduction** for usage note.

induction center, a place where draftees are examined and processed: *Camp Dodge was an induction center in World Wars I and II.*

induction coil, a device in which an interrupted direct current of low voltage, in a coil consisting of a few turns of wire, induces an alternating current of high voltage in a surrounding coil consisting of a larger number of turns of wire.

induction furnace, = electric furnace.

induction heater, any device that uses induction heating, especially an electric furnace.

induction heating, the process of heating metals by causing, through electromagnetic induction, an electric current to flow through them.

***induction motor,** the commonest type of electric motor, in which alternating current supplied to a coil produces a rotating electromagnetic field inducing a similar field in the armature that causes it to rotate.

***induction motor**

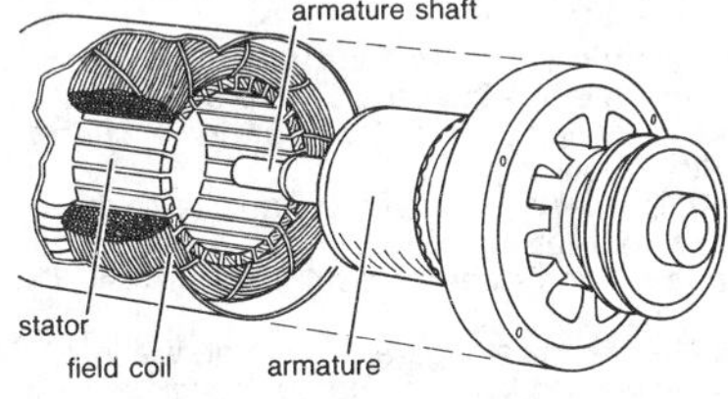

in|duc|tive (in duk′tiv), *adj.* **1** of or using induction; reasoning by induction: *The inductive process itself sometimes suggests the deductive proof* (Scientific American). **2** having to do with or caused by electric or magnetic induction. **3** leading on (to some action, etc.); inducing: *A brutish vice, Inductive mainly to the sin of Eve* (Milton). **4** *Physiology.* giving rise to an internal reaction. — **in|duc′tive|ly,** *adv.* — **in|duc′tive|ness,** *n.*

in|duc|tiv|i|ty (in′duk tiv′ə tē), *n., pl.* **-ties.** *Physics.* **1** the capacity for induction. **2** inductive property; inductance. **3** a measure or coefficient of induction, as of magnetic induction; inductive capacity.

in|duc|tor (in duk′tər), *n.* **1** a person who inducts another into office. **2a** any part of an electric apparatus that works or is worked by induction. An inductor is a tiny coil of wire which transfers current from one stage to another. **b** = choke coil. **3** *Biology.* an embryonic tissue capable of influencing the differentiation of another embryonic tissue; organizer.

in|duc|to|ri|um (in′duk tôr′ē əm, -tōr′-), *n., pl.* **-to|ri|ums, -to|ri|a** (-tôr′ē ə, -tōr′-). = induction coil. [< New Latin *inductorium,* neuter of Late Latin *inductōrius* leading on < Latin *indūcere;* see etym. under **induct**]

in|due (in dü′, -dyü′), *v.t.*, **-dued, -du|ing.** = endue. [< Latin *induere* to put on]

in|dulge (in dulj′), *v.*, **-dulged, -dulg|ing.** — *v.i.* to give way to one's pleasure (in); let oneself have, use, or do what one wants: *A smoker indulges in tobacco.*

— *v.t.* **1a** to give in to; let oneself have, use, or do: *She indulged her fondness for candy by eating a whole box of it. We do not indulge all our desires.* **b** to cherish; foster: *to indulge a vain hope.* **2** to give in to the wishes or whims of; humor: *We often indulge a sick person.* **SYN:** pamper, cocker, baby. See syn. under **humor. 3** to give free course to one's inclination or liking; gratify (oneself): *to indulge oneself in pleasing fancies.* **4** *Commerce.* **a** to allow (a person or company) an extension of time for payment of a bill. **b** to allow this on (a bill or other obligation). **5** *Ecclesiastical.* to grant an indulgence, privilege, or dispensation to. **6** to allow; concede: *In the utterance of great passions, something must be indulged to the extravagance of Nature* (James Russell Lowell).
[< Latin *indulgēre* yield; bestow (a favor)] — **in|dulg′er,** *n.* — **in|dulg′ing|ly,** *adv.*

in|dul|gence (in dul′jəns), *n., v.*, **-genced, -genc|ing.** — *n.* **1a** the act of indulging: *Each person needs some degree of indulgence from his friends.* **b** the condition of being indulgent. **2** something indulged in: *Luxuries are indulgences. ... to have a cup of tea, an indulgence which she rarely allowed herself* (George Eliot). **3** a favor; privilege: *He was forever seeking indulgence.* **4** in the Roman Catholic Church: **a** a freeing from all or part of the temporal punishment still due for sin after the guilt has been forgiven. **b** = dispensation. **5** the granting of certain illegal religious liberties to Protestant dissenters and Roman Catholics by Charles II and James II. **6** *Commerce.* an extension of time, given as a favor, for payment or performance.
— *v.t.* (in the Roman Catholic Church) to attach an indulgence to (an act or object).

in|dul|gent (in dul′jənt), *adj.* **1** giving in to another's wishes or whims; too kind or agreeable: *The indulgent mother bought her boy everything he wanted.* **2** making allowances; not critical; lenient: *Our indulgent teacher praised every poem we wrote.* [< Latin *indulgēns, -entis,* present participle of *indulgēre* indulge] — **in|dul′gent|ly,** *adv.*

in|du|lin (in′dyu̇ lin), *n.* = induline.

in|du|line (in′dyu̇ lēn, -lin), *n.* any one of a series of nitrogen compounds related to aniline dyes and producing blue or gray dyes. [< *ind*(igo) + *-ul,* a diminutive suffix + *-ine²*]

in|dult (in dult′), *n.* a license from the Pope granting some privilege not authorized by the common law of the Roman Catholic Church. [< Latin *indultum,* noun use of neuter past participle of *indulgēre* indulge]

in|dul|to (in dül′tō), *n., pl.* **-tos. 1** a special privilege granted by authority, such as an amnesty. **2** = indult. [< Spanish *indulto* exemption, privilege < Latin *indultum;* see etym. under **indult**]

in|du|men|tum (in′du̇ men′təm, -dyu̇-), *n. Botany.* a hairy or scaly covering, often very dense. [< New Latin *indumentum* < Latin *indūmentum* garment, clothing < *induere* to put on]

in|du|na (in dü′nə), *n.* an officer under the king or chief of the Zulus and other South African tribes: *Here the indunas from the neighboring kraals are wont to sit and drink beer when anything particular is on hand* (F. Oates). [< Zulu *in-duna*]

in|du|pli|cate (in dü′plə kit, -dyü′-), *adj. Botany.* having the edges bent or rolled inward: *an induplicate calyx or bud leaf.*

in|du|pli|ca|tion (in dü′plə kā′shən, -dyü′-), *n.* **1** the state of being induplicate. **2** something induplicate.

in|du|pli|ca|tive (in dü′plə kā′tiv, -dyü′-), *adj.* = induplicate.

in|du|rate (*v.* in′du̇ rāt, -dyu̇-; *adj.* in′du̇ rit, -dyu̇-), *v.*, **-rat|ed, -rat|ing,** *adj.* — *v.t.* **1** to make (a substance) hard; harden: *Surgeons ... Spend raptures upon perfect specimens Of indurated veins* (Elizabeth Barrett Browning). **2** to make hardy; inure. **3** to make callous or unfeeling; make stubborn or obstinate.
— *v.i.* **1** to become hard. **2** to become unfeeling.
— *adj.* **1** hardened. **2** unfeeling or stubborn. **SYN:** callous.
[< Latin *indūrāre* (with English *-ate¹*) < *in-* in + *dūrus* hard]

in|du|ra|tion (in′du̇ rā′shən, -dyu̇-), *n.* **1** the act or process of growing hard. **2** a hardened part or mass. **3** hardness of heart.

in|du|ra|tive (in′du̇ rā′tiv, -dyu̇-), *adj.* producing induration; hardening: *The habit of analysis and self-examination has also a great indurative effect* (Saturday Review).

In|dus (in′dəs), *n., genitive* **In|di.** a constellation in the southern sky; the Indian.

in|du|si|a (in dü′zē ə, -dyü′-; -zhē-), *n.* plural of **indusium.**

in|du|si|al (in dü′zē əl, -dyü′-; -zhē-), *adj.* **1** having to do with indusia. **2** composed of or containing indusia.

indusial limestone, a limestone found in France, supposed to be composed of the agglomerated indusia of the larvae of caddis flies.

in|du|si|ate (in dü′zē it, -dyü′-; -zhē-), *adj. Botany.* having an indusium.

in|du|si|um (in dü′zē əm, -dyü′-; -zhē-), *n., pl.* **-si|a.** **1** *Botany.* **a** the membranous shield or scale covering the cluster of spore cases (sorus) of a fern. **b** a cuplike collection of hairs enclosing the stigma in certain plants. **2** *Anatomy.* a covering layer or membrane, especially the amnion. **3** the covering of a larval insect. [< Latin *indūsium* tunic < *induere* to put on]

in|dus|tri|al (in dus′trē əl), *adj., n.* —*adj.* **1** of or resulting from industry or productive labor: *industrial products.* **2** having many industries: *industrial nations.* **3** engaged in or connected with industries, trades, or manufactures: *industrial activity, an industrial exhibition. Industrial workers work at trades or in factories. An industrial school teaches trades.* **4** of or having to do with the workers in industries: *industrial insurance.* **5** for use in industry: *industrial machines.* **6** much greater or much more than normally is needed or used: *Laurie . . . put a lock on the bedroom door: "an industrial-strength Segal lock," he says with amusement* (New York Magazine).
—*n.* **1** a worker in some industry. **2** an owner or a manager of an industrial enterprise. **3** a stock, bond, etc., of an industrial enterprise: *Dow-Jones industrials closed . . . with a spurt to the highest levels in history* (Wall Street Journal).
[earlier < Medieval Latin *industrialis* < Latin *industria* diligence, industry; later < French *industriel* < *industrie,* learned borrowing from Latin *industria*] —**in|dus′tri|al|ly,** *adv.*

industrial arts, 1 the practical arts employed in industry. **2** these arts as taught in schools.

industrial design, the profession of planning and developing industrial techniques and of designing equipment, especially equipment which is mass-produced.

industrial designer, a specialist in industrial design: *The industrial designer may . . . plan a cabinet of the best possible design for a new type of refrigerator motor* (Raymond Loewy).

industrial diamond, 1 any flawed or inferior diamond, such as bort or carbonado, used widely for industrial purposes: *Industrial diamonds are . . . the hardest substance known to man. Attach a cluster of little diamonds to a drill and you can bore through anything* (Wall Street Journal). **2** any similar material, made synthetically.

industrial disease, a disease that occurs as a result of working in a particular industry: *. . . measures to prevent this grave malady of the lungs from being added to the catalogue of industrial diseases* (Scientific American).

industrial engineer, a specialist in industrial engineering.

industrial engineering, the profession of planning techniques of working and the uses of machines in industry.

industrial insurance, a form of life insurance for industrial workers, with weekly premiums of low cost.

in|dus|tri|al|ise (in dus′trē ə līz), *v.t., v.i.,* **-ised, -is|ing.** *Especially British.* industrialize.

in|dus|tri|al|ism (in dus′trē ə liz′əm), *n.* a system of social and economic organization in which large industries are very important and industrial activities or interests prevail: *In 1765 Watt's steam engine was constructed, a very important date in the history of industrialism* (H. G. Wells).

in|dus|tri|al|ist (in dus′trē ə list), *n.* **1** a person who manages or owns an industrial enterprise: *The promise of high profits also saw a new type of industrialist rise to prominence* (Time). **2** an industrial worker.

in|dus|tri|al|i|za|tion (in dus′trē ə lə zā′shən), *n.* the development of large industries as an important feature in a country or economic system: *Productivity has become a major concern wherever men seek to raise the level of living by means of industrialization* (Scientific American).

in|dus|tri|al|ize (in dus′trē ə līz), *v.,* **-ized, -iz|ing.** —*v.t.* **1** to make industrial; develop large industries as an important feature in (a country or economic system): *Industrialized nations consume natural resources at several times the rate of agrarian countries* (Newsweek). **2** to organize as an industry. —*v.i.* to become industrial; develop large industries: *Communist China must increase its foreign trade to industrialize* (Harper's).
—**in|dus′tri|al|iz′er,** *n.*

industrial medicine, a branch of preventive medicine dealing with the sanitary and working conditions of factories.

industrial melanism, the natural selection of darker genetic forms of certain species of moths in industrial areas, caused by evolutionary adaptation to the sooty environment.

industrial park, a section or district removed from or outside a city, planned and built, especially for manufacturing plants, warehouses, and other industrial concerns: *The impressive . . . plant . . . covers 73,800 square feet on a donated site in a modern industrial park* (Wall Street Journal).

industrial psychologist, a specialist in industrial psychology: *Industrial psychologists try to understand how workers behave on the job, why they behave as they do, and how to make jobs more rewarding to workers, to industry, and to society* (Patricia C. Smith).

industrial psychology, the use of psychological methods in business and industry to improve the selection and performance of workers, the methods of supervising them, the quality of working conditions, the effectiveness of jobs, and to deal with other related matters.

industrial relations, relationship between labor and management.

Industrial Revolution, 1 the change from an agricultural to an industrial society and from home manufacturing to factory production, especially the one that took place in England from about 1750 to about 1850. **2** the period during which this change occurred: *A man who lived at the beginning of the Industrial Revolution was only dimly aware that science was changing his world* (Newsweek).

industrial school, 1 a school for teaching one or more branches of industry; trade school. **2** such a school for neglected or delinquent children.

industrial union, a labor union of all persons in the same industry without regard to the various crafts or jobs; vertical union.

in|dus|tri|ous (in dus′trē əs), *adj.* **1** working hard and steadily; diligent: *An industrious student usually has good grades.* SYN: assiduous, active. See syn. under **busy. 2** *Obsolete.* showing intelligent or skillful work. **3** *Obsolete.* zealous. [< Latin *industriōsus* < *industria* industry] —**in|dus′tri|ous|ly,** *adv.* —**in|dus′tri|ous|ness,** *n.*

in|dus|try (in′də strē, -dus′trē), *n., pl.* **-tries.**
1 any branch of business, trade, or manufacture: *The steel industry and the automobile industry employ hundreds of thousands of men.* **2** all such enterprises taken collectively: *Canadian industry is expanding.* **3** systematic work or labor; continual employment in some useful work. **4** steady effort; busy application: *Industry and thrift favor success.* SYN: diligence. **5** *Obsolete.* skill; cleverness; ingenuity. [< Latin *industria*]

in|dus|try|wide (in′də strē wīd′), *adj.* covering or embracing an entire industry: *On the other hand, he said, there has been industrywide price cutting* (Wall Street Journal).

in|dwell (in dwel′), *v.,* **-dwelt** or **-dwelled, -dwell|ing.** —*v.t.* to dwell in; inhabit.
—*v.i.* to have one's abode; dwell (in). —**in′dwell′er,** *n.*

in|dwell|ing (in′dwel′ing), *adj.* dwelling within: *. . . she explained and justified her mistakes . . . as well as she could to her indwelling enemy* (Katherine Anne Porter).

-ine[1], *suffix forming adjectives from nouns.* of; like; like that of: *Crystalline* = *of crystal. Elephantine* = *like an elephant.* [< Latin *-īnus,* sometimes < Greek *-inos*]

-ine[2], *suffix forming nouns. Chemistry.* denoting names of basic substances and the halogen elements, as in *aniline, chlorine, fluorine.* See **-in.** [< French *-ine* (< Latin *-īna*), or directly < Latin *-īna*]

in|earth (in ėrth′), *v.t.* to bury: *Refusing rest, Till I had seen in holy ground inearth'd My poor lost brother* (Robert Southey).

in|e|bri|ant (in ē′brē ənt), *adj., n.* —*adj.* intoxicating.
—*n.* an intoxicant.

in|e|bri|ate (*v.* in ē′brē āt; *n., adj.* in ē′brē it), *v.,* **-at|ed, -at|ing,** *n., adj.* —*v.t.* **1** to make drunk; intoxicate: *Sweet wines do not so much inebriate and overturn the brain as others* (Philemon Holland). **2** *Figurative.* to intoxicate mentally; excite beyond self-control; stupefy: *A sophistical rhetorician, inebriated with the exuberance of his own verbosity* (Benjamin Disraeli).
—*n.* a habitual drunken person.
—*adj.* intoxicated; drunk: (*Figurative.*) *Inebriate with the deep delight, Dim grew the Pilgrim's swimming sight* (Robert Southey).
[< Latin *inēbriāre* (with English *-ate*[1]) < *in-* (intensive) + *ēbriāre* intoxicate < *ēbrius* drunk]

in|e|bri|at|ed (in ē′brē ā′tid), *adj.* drunk or intoxicated.

in|e|bri|a|tion (in ē′brē ā′shən), *n.* drunkenness or intoxication.

in|e|bri|e|ty (in′i brī′ə tē), *n.* drunkenness, especially habitual drunkenness.

in|e|bri|ous (in ē′brē əs), *adj.* drunken or intoxicated.

in|ed|i|bil|i|ty (in′ed ə bil′ə tē, in ed′-), *n.* the quality or condition of being inedible.

in|ed|i|ble (in ed′ə bəl), *adj.* not fit to eat; not edible: *Poisonous mushrooms are inedible. Over carefully-preened fields the insatiable hounds once more pursue the inedible fox* (Saturday Review).

in|ed|it|ed (in ed′ə tid), *adj.* **1** not edited. **2** = unpublished.

in|ed|u|ca|bil|i|ty (in ej′ů kə bil′ə tē), *n.* the quality or condition of being ineducable.

in|ed|u|ca|ble (in ej′ů kə bəl), *adj.* not capable of being educated; uneducable: *If you hear your child called "ineducable," remember that it only means he is ineducable at school* (London Evening News).

in|ef|fa|bil|i|ty (in ef′ə bil′ə tē), *n.* ineffable condition or quality; unspeakableness.

in|ef|fa|ble (in ef′ə bəl), *adj.* **1** not to be expressed in words; too great to be described in words: *the ineffable beauty of a sunset.* **2a** that must not be spoken: *Jehovah was regarded by the Jews as an ineffable name too sacred for utterance and hence replaced in the reading of the Scriptures by Adonai or Elohim.* **b** *Obsolete.* not to be disclosed or made known. [< Latin *ineffābilis* < *in-* not + *effābilis* speakable < *ex-* out + *fārī* speak] —**in|ef′fa|ble|ness,** *n.*

in|ef|fa|bly (in ef′ə blē), *adv.* in an ineffable manner; unspeakably: *There is nothing intrinsically interesting about the old boy, and his life has been ineffably humdrum* (New Yorker).

in|ef|face|a|bil|i|ty (in′ə fā′sə bil′ə tē), *n.* ineffaceable quality or condition.

in|ef|face|a|ble (in′ə fā′sə bəl), *adj.* that cannot be rubbed out or wiped out; indelible. —**in′ef-face′a|bly,** *adv.*

in|ef|fec|tive (in′ə fek′tiv), *adj.* **1** not producing the desired effect; of little use: *ineffective efforts, ineffective blows. An ineffective medicine fails to cure a disease or relieve pain.* SYN: insufficient, ineffectual. **2** unfit for work; incapable: *The doctor said I would be ineffective in my job until after a convalescence of several weeks.* SYN: inefficient. **3** lacking in artistic effect. —**in′ef|fec′tive|ly,** *adv.* —**in′ef|fec′tive|ness,** *n.*

in|ef|fec|tu|al (in′ə fek′chů əl), *adj.* **1** without effect; useless: *The searchlights were ineffectual in the fog.* SYN: ineffective, futile, vain, fruitless, unavailing. See syn. under **useless. 2** not able to produce the effect wanted; powerless. —**in′ef|fec′tu|al|ly,** *adv.* —**in′ef|fec′tu|al|ness,** *n.*

in|ef|fec|tu|al|i|ty (in′ə fek′chů al′ə tē), *n., pl.* **-ties. 1** ineffectual quality. **2** something that fails to produce the desired effect.

in|ef|fi|ca|cious (in′ef ə kā′shəs), *adj.* not efficacious; not able to produce the effect wanted.
—**in′ef|fi|ca′cious|ly,** *adv.* —**in′ef|fi|ca′cious-ness,** *n.*

in|ef|fi|ca|cy (in ef′ə kə sē), *n.* lack of efficacy; inability to produce the effect wanted: *The prince . . . went away convinced of the emptiness of rhetorical sound, and the inefficacy of polished periods and studied sentences* (Samuel Johnson).

in|ef|fi|cien|cy (in′ə fish′ən sē), *n.* **1** lack of efficiency; wastefulness: *the natural inefficiency of big government.* **2** a being incapable; inability to get things done.

in|ef|fi|cient (in′ə fish′ənt), *adj., n.* —*adj.* **1** not efficient; not able to produce an effect without waste of time or energy: *A machine that uses too much fuel is inefficient.* SYN: wasteful, ineffective. **2** not able to get things done; incapable: *An inefficient housekeeper has an untidy house.* SYN: incompetent.
—*n.* an inefficient person. —**in′ef|fi′cient|ly,** *adv.*

in|e|gal|i|tar|i|an (in′i gal′ə tãr′ē ən), *adj., n.* —*adj.* not egalitarian; not democratic: *The credit card is just another privilege denied them* [*the poor*], *another move to promote inegalitarian distribution of the national income* (Punch).
—*n.* an inegalitarian person.

in|e|las|tic (in′i las′tik), *adj.* **1** not elastic; stiff; inflexible; unyielding. **2** *Economics.* that does not change greatly under altering conditions, as the demand for certain commodities that remains almost stationary whatever the price. —**in′e|las′ti-cal|ly,** *adv.*

inelastic collision, *Physics.* a collision between two particles in which part of their kinetic energy is transformed to another form of energy: *Inelastic collisions are constantly boosting the electrons to the higher energy states appropriate to the temperature* (Scientific American).

in|e|las|tic|i|ty (in′i las tis′ə tē), *n.* lack of elasticity.

inelastic scattering, *Physics.* the scattering of particles resulting from inelastic collision.

in|el|e|gance (in el′ə gəns), *n.* **1** lack of elegance; lack of good taste: *. . . no matter how cruelly its inelegance may shatter the spell of the day* (Atlantic). **2** something that is not elegant or graceful.

in|el|e|gan|cy (in el′ə gən sē), *n., pl.* **-cies.** = inelegance.

in|el|e|gant (in el′ə gənt), *adj.* not elegant; not in good taste; crude; vulgar: *It was thought inelegant among the Romans to entertain less than three or more than nine at their banquets* (Edward G. Bulwer-Lytton). **SYN**: rough, unrefined, coarse, unpolished. —**in|el′e|gant|ly**, *adv.*

in|el|i|gi|bil|i|ty (in el′ə jə bil′ə tē), *n.* lack of eligibility; being ineligible.

in|el|i|gi|ble (in el′ə jə bəl), *adj., n.* —*adj.* not eligible; not suitable or qualified; unfit to be chosen: *A foreign-born citizen of the United States is ineligible for the Presidency.*
—*n.* a person who is not suitable or not qualified. —**in|el′i|gi|bly**, *adv.*

in|el|o|quence (in el′ə kwəns), *n.* lack of eloquence: *We feel keenly the ineloquence of finite words to express our emotions* (London Daily News).

in|el|o|quent (in el′ə kwənt), *adj.* not eloquent; lacking eloquence: *Nor are thy lips, ungraceful, Sire of men, Nor tongue ineloquent* (Milton). —**in|el′o|quent|ly**, *adv.*

in|e|luc|ta|bil|i|ty (in′i luk′tə bil′ə tē), *n.* the state or quality of being ineluctable.

in|e|luc|ta|ble (in′i luk′tə bəl), *adj.* that cannot be escaped or avoided; inevitable: *the ineluctable grip of Time. All this is deeply imbedded in the ineluctable logic of scientific progress* (Bulletin of Atomic Scientists). [< Latin *inēluctābilis* < *in-* not + *ēluctābilis* escapable < *ēluctārī* to escape < *ex-* out + *luctārī* to struggle, wrestle]

in|e|luc|ta|bly (in′i luk′tə blē), *adv.* so that there is no escape; irresistibly: *His film coldly and intelligently surveys those faltering, reluctant steps that led ineluctably to Freud's basic premise* (Saturday Review).

in|e|lud|i|ble (in′i lü′də bəl), *adj.* that cannot be eluded; inescapable: *The criminal could not escape the ineludible pursuit of the law.*

in|e|nar|ra|ble (in′i nar′ə bəl), *adj. Obsolete.* that cannot be narrated, told, or declared. [< Old French *inenarrable,* learned borrowing from Latin *inēnarrābilis* < *in-* not + *ēnarrāre* to narrate]

in|ept (in ept′), *adj.* **1** not suitable; out of place: *Such a poor player would be an inept choice as captain.* **SYN**: inappropriate. **2** awkward; clumsy: *That was certainly an inept performance.* **3** absurd; foolish. **SYN**: silly. [< Latin *ineptus* absurd, unsuitable < *in-* not + *aptus* apt] —**in|ept′ly**, *adv.* —**in|ept′ness**, *n.*

in|ept|i|tude (in ep′tə tüd, -tyüd), *n.* **1** inept quality; unfitness; foolishness: *Unfortunately, a weakness in military logistics was equaled by his ineptitude for financial infighting* (Newsweek). **2** a silly or inappropriate act or remark: [*He*] *lived no day of his life without doing and saying more than one pretentious ineptitude* (Thomas Carlyle).

in|eq|ua|ble (in ek′wə bəl), *adj.* changeable; fitful: *an inequable temper.*

in|e|qual|i|tar|i|an (in′i kwol′ə tãr′ē ən), *adj., n.* —*adj.* not equalitarian; not democratic: [*In*] *the age of chivalry ... punishment was notably inequalitarian* (Punch).
—*n.* an inequalitarian person: *Gladstone never outlived the conservatism that had once led him to proclaim himself "an out-and-out inequalitarian"* (Atlantic).

***in|e|qual|i|ty** (in′i kwol′ə tē), *n., pl.* **-ties. 1** lack of equality; being unequal in amount, size, value, or rank: *There is a great inequality between the salaries of a bank president and an office boy.* **SYN**: disparity. **2** lack of evenness, regularity, or uniformity. **SYN**: unevenness, variableness. **3** an instance of this; an irregularity or variation: *There are many inequalities in the surface of this old road.* **4** lack of due proportion; uneven distribution. **5** a mathematical expression showing that two quantities are unequal. *Example:* a > b means a is greater than b; a < b means a is less than b; a ≠ b means a and b are unequal. **6** *Astronomy.* **a** any deviation from uniformity, such as in the motion of a planet or the rise of the tides. **b** the amount of such a deviation.

***inequality**
definition 5

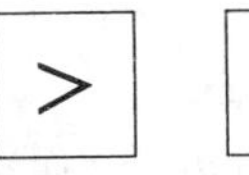

a > b
a is greater than b

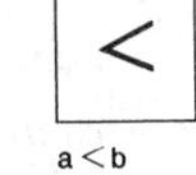

a < b
a is less than b

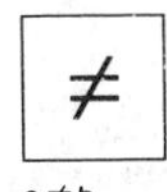

a ≠ b
a is not equal to b

in|e|qua|tion (in′i kwā′zhən, -shən), *n.* = inequality (def. 5).

in|e|qui|ax|i|al (in′ē kwē ak′sē əl), *adj.* having unequal axes.

in|e|qui|lat|er|al (in′ē kwə lat′ər əl), *adj.* not equilateral; having unequal sides. —**in′e|qui|lat′er|al|ly**, *adv.*

in|e|qui|lo|bate (in′ē kwə lō′bāt), *adj.* having unequal lobes.

in|e|qui|lobed (in ē′kwə lōbd′), *adj.* = inequilobate.

in|e|qui|po|ten|tial (in′ē kwə pə ten′shəl), *adj.* not equipotential.

in|eq|ui|ta|ble (in ek′wə tə bəl), *adj.* not equitable; unfair; unjust. —**in|eq′ui|ta|bly**, *adv.*

in|eq|ui|ty (in ek′wə tē), *n., pl.* **-ties. 1** lack of equity; unfairness; injustice. **SYN**: partiality. **2** an unfair or unjust matter or action.

in|e|qui|valve (in ē′kwə valv′), *adj.* having valves of unequal size, as a shell.

in|e|rad|i|ca|bil|i|ty (in′i rad′ə kə bil′ə tē), *n.* ineradicable quality or condition: *... the seeming ineradicability of poverty* (Time).

in|e|rad|i|ca|ble (in′i rad′ə kə bəl), *adj.* that cannot be rooted out or got rid of: *Misdemeanors and offenses ... were as ineradicable from her brain as the patrician wrinkle was between her eyes* (Saul Bellow). *Once convalescent, he is ordered to return again to ... his ineradicable malaise* (New Yorker). —**in′e|rad′i|ca|bly**, *adv.*

in|e|ras|a|ble (in′i rā′sə bəl), *adj.* not erasable; not to be erased or effaced. —**in′e|ras′a|bly**, *adv.*

in|er|ra|bil|i|ty (in er′ə bil′ə tē, -ėr′-), *n.* = infallibility.

in|er|ra|ble (in er′ə bəl, -ėr′-), *adj.* incapable of erring; infallible. [< Latin *inerrābilis* < *in-* not + *errāre* wander] —**in|er′ra|ble|ness**, *n.* —**in|er′ra|bly**, *adv.*

in|er|ran|cy (in er′ən sē, -ėr′-), *n.* freedom from error.

in|er|rant (in er′ənt, -ėr′-), *adj.* not erring; free from error.

in|er|rat|ic (in′i rat′ik), *adj.* not erratic or wandering; fixed.

in|ert (in ėrt′), *adj., n.* —*adj.* **1** having no power to move or act; lifeless: *A stone is an inert mass of matter.* **2** inactive; slow; sluggish: *A dull, lazy person is inert. The Honourable Mrs. Jamieson ... was fat and inert, and very much at the mercy of her old servants* (Elizabeth C. S. Gaskell). **SYN**: See syn. under **inactive**. **3** with few or no active chemical, physiological, or other properties: *the inert ingredients in a medicine. Helium and neon are inert gases.*
—*n.* an inert person, thing, or substance.
[< Latin *iners, inertis* idle, unskilled < *in-* without + *ars, artis* art, skill] —**in|ert′ly**, *adv.* —**in|ert′ness**, *n.*

inert gas, any gas of a group including helium, neon, argon, krypton, xenon, and radon, formerly considered chemically inactive; rare gas.

in|er|tia (in ėr′shə), *n.* **1** a tendency to remain in the state one is in, and not start changes: *Urgently needed reforms ... have bogged down in a morass of political confusion and inertia* (Newsweek). **2a** the tendency of all objects and matter in the universe to stay still if still, or, if moving, to go on moving in the same direction, unless acted on by some outside force. **b** a like property of electricity, magnetism, and various other physical forces. [< Latin *inertia* inactivity, unskillfulness < *iners;* see etym. under **inert**]

in|er|tial (in ėr′shəl), *adj.* having to do with or of the nature of inertia.

inertial guidance, a method of guiding a missile, aircraft, or ship along a given course by means of gyroscopes and electronic equipment that react to inertial force, automatically adjusting the course: *A missile aimed by inertial guidance carries "sensing" devices* (New York Times).

in|er|tial|ly (in ėr′shə lē), *adv.* by means of inertia: *There are gyroscopically and inertially stabilized camera mountings which aim ... at producing a truly vertical photograph* (London Times).

inertial navigation, = inertial guidance.

inertial navigator, the instruments used for inertial guidance: *Passengers ... will jet to transoceanic destinations from take-off to landing by a new inertial navigator* (New York Times).

inertia selling, *British.* the act of sending unsolicited goods to potential customers and charging for them if not returned: *If you are the victim of ... inertia selling and do not intend to use the system, make a point of returning the rejection card* (London Times).

inertia starter, a device for starting an aircraft engine, consisting of a small flywheel that is set spinning by hand or by an electric motor that is engaged with the engine crankshaft to turn the engine.

in|er|tion (in ėr′shən), *n.* the condition of being or remaining inert; inaction; sluggishness.

in|er|u|dite (in er′u̇ dīt, -yu̇-), *adj.* not erudite; unlearned. —**in|er′u|dite|ly**, *adv.*

in|es|cap|a|bil|i|ty (in′ə skā′pə bil′ə tē), *n.* inevitability: *The work of the judge involves the inescapability of choice* (Bulletin of Atomic Scientists).

in|es|cap|a|ble (in′ə skā′pə bəl), *adj.* that cannot be escaped or avoided; sure to happen; inevitable: *An inescapable aspect of U.S. economic prowess is the foreign-aid program* (Time).

in|es|cap|a|bly (in′ə skā′pə blē), *adv.* in an inescapable manner; inevitably: *Business and government are inescapably involved in each other's affairs* (Newsweek).

in|es|cu|lent (in es′kyə lənt), *adj.* = inedible.

in|es|cutch|eon (in′es kuch′ən), *n. Heraldry.* a small escutcheon borne as a charge upon a larger escutcheon. [< *in* + *escutcheon*]

in es|se (in es′ē), *Latin.* in being; actually existing.

in|es|sen|tial (in′ə sen′shəl), *adj., n.* —*adj.* **1** not essential; not necessary: *First of all he realized that it is inessential for the machine to be able to move around* (Scientific American). **2** without essence; unsubstantial; immaterial.
—*n.* something that is inessential.

in|es|sen|ti|al|i|ty (in′ə sen′shē al′ə tē), *n.* the state or condition of being inessential.

in|es|sive (in es′iv), *adj. Grammar.* indicating place; locative. [< Latin *inesse* to be at + English *-ive*]

in|es|ti|ma|ble (in es′tə mə bəl), *adj.* too great to be estimated; priceless; invaluable: *Freedom of speech is an inestimable privilege. Heaps of pearls, Inestimable stones, unvalued jewels* (Shakespeare). **SYN**: incalculable.

in|es|ti|ma|bly (in es′tə mə blē), *adv.* so as to be inestimable.

in|ev|i|ta|bil|i|ty (in ev′ə tə bil′ə tē), *n.* the fact or condition of being inevitable: *The inevitability that brought us together on this mountain of wet grass was greater than the total of all other considerations* (Saul Bellow).

in|ev|i|ta|ble (in ev′ə tə bəl), *adj., n.* —*adj.* not to be avoided; sure to happen; certain to come: *Death is inevitable; it comes to everyone.*
—*n.* that which is inevitable: *There is no use arguing with the inevitable* (James Russell Lowell).
[< Latin *inēvītābilis* < *in-* not + *ēvītābilis* avoidable < *ēvītāre* avoid < *ex-* from + *vītāre* avoid, shun] —**in|ev′i|ta|ble|ness**, *n.*

in|ev|i|ta|bly (in ev′ə tə blē), *adv.* in an inevitable manner; unavoidably.

in|ex|act (in′ig zakt′), *adj.* **1** not exact; with errors or mistakes; not accurate: *In quantum mechanics certain statements must in principle remain inexact* (Scientific American). **2** not strict or rigorous. —**in′ex|act′ly**, *adv.* —**in′ex|act′ness**, *n.*

in|ex|act|i|tude (in′ig zak′tə tüd, -tyüd), *n.* lack of accuracy or precision: *terminological inexactitude.* [< *in-*[1] not + *exactitude*]

in ex|cel|sis (in′ək sel′sis), *Latin.* beyond comparison; above all others; on the highest level: *He was the contact man in excelsis* (Atlantic).

in|ex|cus|a|bil|i|ty (in′ik skyü′zə bil′ə tē), *n.* the quality or state of being inexcusable or unjustifiable.

in|ex|cus|a|ble (in′ik skyü′zə bəl), *adj.* that ought not to be excused; that cannot be justified; unpardonable: *The insolent boy's rudeness to his parents was inexcusable. Her failure to thank her hostess when the party ended was inexcusable.* **SYN**: unjustifiable, indefensible, unwarrantable. —**in′ex|cus′a|ble|ness**, *n.*

in|ex|cus|a|bly (in′ik skyü′zə blē), *adv.* in an inexcusable manner; unpardonably.

in|ex|e|cut|a|ble (in ek′sə kyü′tə bəl, in′ig zek′yə-), *adj.* not executable; that cannot be executed.

in|ex|e|cu|tion (in ek′sə kyü′shən), *n.* lack or neglect of execution.

in|ex|er|tion (in′ig zėr′shən), *n.* absence of exertion; inaction.

in|ex|haust|ed (in′ig zôs′tid), *adj.* unexhausted; unfailing.

in|ex|haust|i|bil|i|ty (in′ig zôs′tə bil′ə tē), *n.* inexhaustible nature or quality: *the inexhaustibility of hope.*

in|ex|haust|i|ble (in′ig zôs′tə bəl), *adj.* **1** that cannot be exhausted; very abundant: *The wealth of our country seems inexhaustible to many people abroad. We feel that the potentialities of the human brain are inexhaustible* (Scientific American). **2** tireless; that cannot be wearied: *The new president is a man of inexhaustible energy.* —**in′ex|haust′i|ble|ness**, *n.*

in|ex|haust|i|bly (in′ig zôs′tə blē), *adv.* in an inexhaustible manner; to an inexhaustible degree.

in|ex|ist (in′ig zist′), *v.i.* to exist (in something else); inhere.

in|ex|ist|ence[1] (in′ig zis′təns), *n.* existence in something else; inherence. [< *in-*[2] in + *existence*]

in|ex|ist|ence[2] (in′ig zis′təns), *n.* absence of ex-

Pronunciation Key: hat, āge, cãre, fär; let, ēqual, tėrm; it, īce; hot, ōpen, ôrder; oil, out; cup, pu̇t, rüle; child; long; thin; ᴛʜen; zh, measure; ə represents **a** in about, **e** in taken, **i** in pencil, **o** in lemon, **u** in circus.

istence; nonexistence. [< *in-*¹ not + existence]

in·ex·ist·en·cy (in′ig zis′tən sē), *n.* = inexistence.

in·ex·ist·ent (in′ig zis′tənt), *adj.* not existing; having no existence.

in·ex·o·ra·bil·i·ty (in ek′sər ə bil′ə tē), *n.* inexorable nature or quality.

in·ex·o·ra·ble (in ek′sər ə bəl), *adj.* not influenced by prayers or entreaties; relentless; unyielding: *The forces of nature are inexorable.* SYN: unrelenting, implacable, immovable. See syn. under **inflexible.** [< Latin *inexōrābilis* < *in-* not + *exōrābilis* easily entreated or moved; exorable < *exōrāre* to prevail upon, pray earnestly < *ex-* out + *ōrāre* pray] —**in·ex′o·ra·ble·ness,** *n.*

in·ex·o·ra·bly (in ek′sər ə blē), *adv.* in an inexorable manner.

in·ex·pan·si·ble (in′ik span′sə bəl), *adj.* not expansible.

in·ex·pan·sive (in′ik span′siv), *adj.* not expansive.

in·ex·pect·an·cy (in′ik spek′tən sē), *n.* absence of expectancy.

in·ex·pect·ant (in′ik spek′tənt), *adj.* not expectant; without expectation.

in·ex·pe·di·ence (in′ik spē′dē əns), *n.* = inexpediency.

in·ex·pe·di·en·cy (in′ik spē′dē ən sē), *n.* lack of expediency; being inexpedient; inadvisability.

in·ex·pe·di·ent (in′ik spē′dē ənt), *adj.* not expedient; not practicable, suitable, or wise. SYN: inadvisable, unprofitable, impolitic. —**in′ex·pe′di·ent·ly,** *adv.*

in·ex·pen·sive (in′ik spen′siv), *adj.* not expensive; cheap; low-priced: *inexpensive shoes to do jobs in around the house.* SYN: See syn. under **cheap.** —**in′ex·pen′sive·ly,** *adv.* —**in′ex·pen′sive·ness,** *n.*

in·ex·pe·ri·ence (in′ik spir′ē əns), *n.* lack of experience; lack of practice; lack of skill or wisdom gained from experience: *Inexperience caused the young lawyer's mistake in judgment.*

in·ex·pe·ri·enced (in′ik spir′ē ənst), *adj.* not experienced; without practice; lacking the skill and wisdom gained by experience: *Inexperienced help caused an accident.* SYN: unpracticed, untrained, unskilled, raw, green.

in·ex·pert (in′ik spėrt′, in ek′spėrt), *adj., n.* —*adj.* not expert; unskilled.
—*n.* an inexpert or unskilled person. —**in′ex·pert′ly,** *adv.* —**in′ex·pert′ness,** *n.*

in·ex·per·tise (in eks′pėr tēz′), *n.* lack of or contempt for expert knowledge and opinion: *Inexpertise has conquered wider fields than these. In industry, for example, the philosophy of making do is a reason for not providing workmen with proper tools* (Manchester Guardian Weekly).

in·ex·pi·a·ble (in ek′spē ə bəl), *adj.* **1** that cannot be atoned for: *Murder is an inexpiable crime.* **2** that cannot be appeased by expiation; implacable; irreconcilable: *inexpiable hate.* [< Latin *inexpiābilis* < *in-* not + *expiābilis* reconcilable < *expiāre* expiate] —**in·ex′pi·a·ble·ness,** *n.*

in·ex·pi·a·bly (in ek′spē ə blē), *adv.* in an inexpiable manner; so as to admit of no atonement.

in·ex·plain·a·ble (in′ik splā′nə bəl), *adj.* that cannot be explained; inexplicable.

in·ex·pli·ca·bil·i·ty (in ek′splə kə bil′ə tē, in′ik-splik′ə-), *n.* unexplainable nature or quality: *Characteristically, the Basques remain utterly unperturbed by the mystery of their origins; on the contrary, they are delighted by their own inexplicability* (New Yorker).

in·ex·pli·ca·ble (in ek′splə kə bəl, in′ik splik′ə-), *adj.* that cannot be explained; that cannot be understood or accounted for; mysterious: *an inexplicable fire,* SYN: inscrutable, unintelligible, unaccountable. [< Latin *inexplicābilis* < *in-* not + *explicābilis* explicable < *explicāre* explicate] —**in·ex′pli·ca·ble·ness,** *n.*

in·ex·pli·ca·bly (in ek′splə kə blē, in′ik splik′ə-), *adv.* in an inexplicable manner; to a degree that cannot be explained: *We can see the ice skaters milling about on the rink, inexplicably avoiding collision with each other* (Atlantic).

in·ex·plic·it (in′ik splis′it), *adj.* not explicit; not clearly expressed. [< Latin *inexplicitus* unexplained, obscure < *in-* not + *explicitus* explicit] —**in′ex·plic′it·ly,** *adv.* —**in′ex·plic′it·ness,** *n.*

in·ex·plo·sive (in′ik splō′siv), *adj.* not liable to explode; not of an explosive nature: *To enjoy themselves in the mild, inexplosive fashion which seems to satisfy Italian nature* (William Dean Howells).

in·ex·press·i·bil·i·ty (in′ik spres′ə bil′ə tē), *n.* the quality of being inexpressible; inexpressibleness.

in·ex·press·i·ble (in′ik spres′ə bəl), *n.* —*adj.* that cannot be expressed in words; impossible to express in words; beyond expression; indescribable. SYN: unutterable, unspeakable.
—*n.* something inexpressible.

inexpressibles, *Informal.* breeches; trousers (used humorously): *A pair of old inexpressibles . . . contained seven thousand guineas!* (Helen Bedingfeld).
—**in′ex·press′i·ble·ness,** *n.*

in·ex·press·i·bly (in′ik spres′ə blē), *adv.* beyond expression; indescribably: *All appeared new, and strange at first, inexpressibly rare and delightful and beautiful* (Thomas Traherne).

in·ex·pres·sive (in′ik spres′iv), *adj.* **1** not expressive; lacking in expression. **2** *Archaic.* inexpressible. —**in′ex·pres′sive·ly,** *adv.* —**in′ex·pres′sive·ness,** *n.*

in·ex·pug·na·bil·i·ty (in′ik spug′nə bil′ə tē), *n.* the quality or condition of being inexpugnable.

in·ex·pug·na·ble (in′ik spug′nə bəl), *adj.* unconquerable; impregnable . . . the place the Florida Everglades, and the danger the almost inexpugnable Seminole Indians (Newsweek). [< Latin *inexpūgnābilis* < *in-* not + *expūgnābilis* conquerable < *expūgnāre* take by assault < *ex-* out + *pūgnāre* to assault < *pūgna* a fight] —**in′ex·pug′na·ble·ness,** *n.* —**in′ex·pug′na·bly,** *adv.*

in·ex·pung·i·ble (in′ik spun′jə bəl), *adj.* that cannot be rubbed out or obliterated.

in·ex·tend·ed (in′ik sten′did), *adj.* not extended; without extension.

in·ex·ten·si·bil·i·ty (in′ik sten′sə bil′ə tē), *n.* the quality of being inextensible.

in·ex·ten·si·ble (in′ik sten′sə bəl), *adj.* that cannot be extended; not extensible.

in·ex·ten·sion (in′ik sten′shən), *n.* lack of extension.

in·ex·ten·so (in ek sten′sō), *Latin.* at full length; in full.

in·ex·tin·guish·a·ble (in′ik sting′gwi shə bəl), *adj.* that cannot be put out or stopped: *An inextinguishable fire keeps on burning.* (*Figurative.*) *inextinguishable rage or laughter. The scholar had an inextinguishable passion for knowledge.* SYN: unquenchable, indestructible. —**in′ex·tin′guish·a·bly,** *adv.*

in·ex·tir·pa·ble (in′ik stėr′pə bəl), *adj.* that cannot be extirpated or entirely rooted out. —**in′ex·tir′pa·ble·ness,** *n.*

in ex·tre·mis (in ek strē′mis), *Latin.* **1** at the point of death: *No doubt such an alliance is a solution in extremis* (Atlantic). **2** (literally) amid the final things.

in·ex·tri·ca·bil·i·ty (in ek′strə kə bil′ə tē), *n.* the quality or state of being inextricable.

in·ex·tri·ca·ble (in ek′strə kə bəl), *adj.* **1** that one cannot get out of: *an inextricable maze.* (*Figurative.*) *inextricable difficulty.* **2** that cannot be disentangled, untied, or solved; hopelessly involved or perplexing: *inextricable confusion.* [< Latin *inextrīcābilis* < *in-* not + *extrīcāre* extricate] —**in·ex′tri·ca·ble·ness,** *n.*

in·ex·tri·ca·bly (in ek′strə kə blē), *adv.* in an inextricable manner; beyond extrication or disentanglement: . . . *the irritations and the depressions which were almost inextricably involved with membership in the Griffiths family* (Theodore Dreiser).

inf., **1** below (Latin, *infra*). **2** infantry. **3** infinitive. **4** information.

in f., finally; in short; to sum up (Latin, *in fine*).

Inf., infantry.

I.N.F. or **INF** (no periods), Intermediate-range Nuclear Forces (the European-based nuclear weapons of the United States and the Soviet Union): *The polls show that the public supports the I.N.F. treaty* (Alan Cranston).

in·fall (in′fôl′), *n., v.,* **-fell, -fall·en, -fall·ing.** —*n.* **1** the junction of one stream, road, etc., with another. **2** the place where water enters a reservoir, canal, pond, or lake. **3** an incursion or inroad. **4** the action of falling inward or toward the earth: . . . *the rate of infall of micrometeorites* (New Scientist).
—*v.i.* to fall inward: *What happens to the imploded core? When the infalling material exceeds a density of 100 tons per cubic inch . . . the core turns into a mass of neutrons while the collapse is in progress* (Scientific American).

in·fal·li·bi·lism (in fal′ə bə liz′əm), *n.* the principle of infallibility, especially of the infallibility of the pope.

in·fal·li·bi·list (in fal′ə bə list), *n.* a person who maintains the dogma of the infallibility of the pope.

in·fal·li·bil·i·ty (in fal′ə bil′ə tē), *n.* **1** absolute freedom from error; inability to be mistaken: *The infallibility of the pope when speaking officially on matters of faith and morals was proclaimed by the first Vatican Council in 1870.* **2** absolute reliability; sureness.

in·fal·li·ble (in fal′ə bəl), *adj., n.* —*adj.* **1** free from error; that cannot be mistaken: *an infallible rule.* **2** absolutely reliable; unfailing in operation; sure: *infallible obedience, an infallible remedy.* SYN: certain. **3** incapable of error in the exposition of doctrine on faith and morals (said of the pope as head of the Roman Catholic Church).
—*n.* a person or thing that is infallible.
[< Medieval Latin *infallibilis* < *in-* not + *fallibilis* fallible < Latin *fallere* deceive] —**in·fal′li·ble·ness,** *n.*

in·fal·li·bly (in fal′ə blē), *adv.* in an infallible manner; without failure or mistake; certainly; surely.

in·fam·a·to·ry (in fam′ə tôr′ē, -tōr′-), *adj.* = defamatory.

in·fa·mize (in′fə mīz), *v.t.,* **-mized, -miz·ing. 1** to make infamous. **2** = defame.

in·fa·mous (in′fə məs), *adj.* **1** so bad as to deserve public disgrace; shamefully bad; very wicked: *Benedict Arnold's treason was an infamous betrayal of his country.* SYN: disgraceful, scandalous, odious. **2** having a very bad reputation; in public disgrace: *A traitor's name is infamous.* SYN: notorious, disreputable. **3** *Law.* **a** having lost some or all of the rights of citizenship because of conviction for certain crimes. **b** (of a crime or punishment) entailing such a loss.
[< Medieval Latin *infamous* < Latin *in-* not + *fāmōsus* famous; influenced by Latin *īnfāmis;* see etym. under **infamy**] —**in′fa·mous·ly,** *adv.* —**in′fa·mous·ness,** *n.*

in·fa·my (in′fə mē), *n., pl.* **-mies. 1** a very bad reputation; public disgrace: *Traitors are held in infamy.* **2** shameful badness; extreme wickedness: *to reveal the infamy of a proceeding.* **3** an infamous or disgraceful act. **4** *Law.* the loss of honor and all or certain rights of citizenship incurred on conviction of any of certain crimes. [< Middle French *infamie,* learned borrowing from Latin *īnfāmia* < *īnfāmis* of ill fame < *in-* without + *fāma* fame, reputation]

in·fan·cy (in′fən sē), *n., pl.* **-cies. 1** the condition or time of being an infant; early childhood; babyhood: *The transition line between infancy and childhood is an arbitrary one* (Beals and Hoijer). **2** *Figurative: Space travel is still in its infancy. Latin America's long infancy in the capitalistic pattern . . . must soon come to an end* (Marion A. Czerniecki). **3** the condition of being under the legal age of responsibility (in common law, under 21; in certain states, under 18); minority. [< Latin *īnfantia* < *īnfāns, -fantis* infant, (literally) not speaking < *in-* not + *fārī* speak]

in·fant (in′fənt), *n., adj.* —*n.* **1** a very young child, usually from birth to ten months; baby: *The infant turned out to be a male and was christened Samuel Ellis* (New Yorker). **2** *Figurative.* a beginner. **3** a person under the legal age of responsibility; minor. **4** *Archaic.* a youth of noble or gentle birth.
—*adj.* **1** of or for an infant or infants: *infant food, infant baptism, an infant dress.* **2** *Figurative: an infant industry. We are still in our infant years and we still need halters* (Time). **3** that is an infant or like an infant: *an infant king.* SYN: childlike, childish, infantile. **4** of or having to do with legal infancy or minority.
[< Latin *īnfāns, -fantis;* see etym. under **infancy**]

in·fan·ta (in fan′tə), *n.* **1** a royal princess of Spain or Portugal. **2** the wife of an infante. [< Spanish and Portuguese *infanta,* feminine of *infante* (literally) child < Latin *īnfāns;* see etym. under **infancy**]

in·fan·te (in fan′tā), *n.* a royal prince of Spain or Portugal but not the heir to the throne. [< Spanish and Portuguese *infante* (literally) child < Latin *īnfāns;* see etym. under **infancy**]

in·fant·hood (in′fənt hu̇d), *n.* infancy or babyhood.

in·fan·ti·cid·al (in fan′tə sī′dəl), *adj.* having to do with infanticide.

in·fan·ti·cide¹ (in fan′tə sīd), *n.* the killing of a baby.
[< Latin *īnfanticīdium* < *īnfāns, -fantis* infant + *-cīdium* -cide²]

in·fan·ti·cide² (in fan′tə sīd), *n.* a person who kills a baby.
[< Latin *īnfanticīda* < *īnfāns, -fantis* infant + *-cīda* -cide¹]

in·fan·tile (in′tən tīl, -til), *adj.* **1** of an infant or infants; having to do with infants: *Measles and chicken pox are infantile diseases.* **2** like an infant; babyish; childish: *His father was annoyed at his infantile behavior.* **3a** *Figurative.* in an early stage; just beginning to develop. **b** (of physical geographical features) in an early stage of development. [< Latin *īnfantilis* < *īnfāns, -fantis* child, infant]

infantile paralysis, an acute infectious disease that destroys nervous tissue in the brain and spinal cord, causing fever, paralysis of various muscles, and sometimes death; poliomyelitis; polio. It is caused by a virus and attacks children especially, often leaving them crippled.

infantile scurvy, a disease of childhood, caused by improper diet, characterized by progressive anemia, mental apathy, spongy gums, and other symptoms of scurvy; Barlow's disease.

infantile sore mouth, = thrush² (def. 1).

in·fan·til·ism (in fan′tə liz əm), *n.* **1** an abnormal persistence or appearance of childish traits in adults, often characterized by mental retardation and physical underdevelopment, especially of the sexual organs. **2** the retention by an adult of characteristics of articulation and intonation normally found only in the speech of young children:

I persisted in asking to be taught adult French, and did get fewer infantilisms (New Yorker).

in|fan|til|i|ty (in′fən til′ə tē), *n.* infantile quality or condition.

in|fan|ti|lize (in fan′tə līz), *v.t.,* **-lized, -liz|ing.** to treat as an infant; make childish: *The boy has been made to feel infantilized if he is short and can't play basketball* (Science News). *The present system teaches in a highly structured, infantilizing setting which seems to devalue the need for the student making critical judgment* (Donald Weston and Michael McGarvey).

in|fan|tine (in′fən tīn, -tin), *adj.* infantile; babyish; childish: *an infantine flow of tears.*

in|fan|try (in′fən trē), *n., pl.* **-tries. 1** soldiers trained, equipped, and organized to fight on foot. Infantry commonly carry small arms, now especially rifles. **2** a branch of an army consisting of such troops. *Abbr:* Inf. [< French *infanterie* < Italian *infanteria* < *infante,* or *fante* foot soldier; (originally) a youth < Latin *īnfāns;* see etym. under **infancy**]

in|fan|try|man (in′fən trē mən), *n., pl.* **-men.** a soldier who fights on foot; foot soldier.

infant or **infants' school,** *British.* a school for young children, usually under seven years of age.

in|farct (in färkt′), *n.* **1** a portion of dying tissue, caused by obstruction of the blood supply, as by an embolus or thrombus. **2** the matter that fills such tissue. [< Medieval Latin *infarctus* < Latin *īnfarcīre* stop up < *in-* in + *farcīre* to stuff (like sausage)]

in|farct|ec|to|my (in färk tek′tə mē), *n., pl.* **-mies.** the surgical removal of an infarct.

in|farct|ed (in färk′tid), *adj.* characterized by or showing infarction.

in|farc|tion (in färk′shən), *n.* **1** the formation of an infarct. **2** = infarct.

in|fare (in′fãr′), *n. Scottish and U.S. Dialect.* a housewarming, especially upon the entrance of a bride into her new home. [Old English *infær* entrance < *inne* in + *fær* a going, journey]

in|fat|u|ate (*v.* in fach′u̇ āt; *adj., n.* in fach′u̇ it, -āt), *v.,* **-at|ed, -at|ing,** *adj., n.* **—*v.t.* 1** to inspire with a foolish, extreme, or unreasoning passion: *to be infatuated by a woman. Some to the fashion of a name Surrender judgment, hood-wink'd. Some the style* [*of a book*] *infatuates* (William Cowper). **2** to make foolish.
—*adj.* = infatuated. **—*n.*** an infatuated person: *Incensed by infatuates with facism, . . . she* [*Dame Rebecca West*] *eventually agreed to write . . . a series of papers* (Atlantic).
[< Latin *infatuāre* (with English *-ate*[1]) < *in-* in + *fatuus* foolish, (literally) garrulous < *fārī* speak]

in|fat|u|at|ed (in fach′u̇ ā′tid), *adj.* having an exaggerated fondness or passion; foolishly in love; adoring.

in|fat|u|a|tion (in fach′u̇ ā′shən), *n.* **1** exaggerated fondness or passion; foolish love. **2** the action of infatuating. **3** the state of being infatuated.

in|fau|na (in′fô′nə), *n., pl.* **-nas, -nae** (-nē). = epifauna.

in|fau|nal (in′fô′nəl), *adj.* = epifaunal.

in|faust (in fôst′), *adj.* unfavorable; inauspicious; unlucky.
[< Latin *infaustus* < *in-* not + *faustus* favorable < *favēre* be favorable]

in|fea|si|bil|i|ty (in fē′zə bil′ə tē), *n.* = impracticability.

in|fea|si|ble (in fē′zə bəl), *adj.* not feasible; impracticable.

in|fect (in fekt′), *v.t.* **1** to cause disease or an unhealthy condition in by introducing germs, such as bacteria or a virus: *Dirt infects an open cut. Anyone with a bad cold may infect the people around him.* **2** *Figurative.* to influence in a bad way: *One bad boy may infect a whole class.* SYN: pollute, contaminate, deprave. **3** *Figurative.* to influence by spreading from one to another: *The captain's courage infected his soldiers. Her enthusiasm infected everyone who worked with her. As the strike fever spread, even stockbrokers were infected and staged a walkout* (Newsweek). SYN: imbue, permeate. **4** to fill with something that affects quality, character, or condition, especially unfavorably: *to infect the air with noisome gases.* **5** *Law.* to taint with illegality; make liable to seizure, forfeiture, etc. **6** a computer virus into (a computer operating system or program): *Whenever the infected computer comes in contact with an uninfected piece of software, a fresh copy of the virus passes into the new program* (Time).
[< Latin *īnfectus,* past participle of *īnficere* to dye; (originally) put in < *in-* in + *facere* make]

in|fect|ant (in fek′tənt), *adj., n.* **—*adj.*** infecting. **—*n.*** an infectant agent.

in|fect|i|bil|i|ty (in fek′tə bil′ə tē), *n.* infectible quality or condition.

in|fect|i|ble (in fek′tə bəl), *adj.* that can be infected.

in|fec|tion (in fek′shən), *n.* **1** a causing of disease in people, animals, and plants by the introduction of germs, such as bacteria or a virus. Air, water, clothing, and insects are all means of infection. **2** a disease that can be spread from one person to another: *Measles is an infection.* **3** the agent by which an infectious disease is communicated or transmitted. **4** *Figurative.* an influence, feeling, or idea spreading from one to another: *While her tears deplored the godlike man, Through all her train the soft infection ran* (Alexander Pope). **5** the fact or condition of being infected. **6** (used humorously) affection; liking. **7** (in Celtic languages) the alteration of a sound under the influence of a neighboring sound.

in|fec|tious (in fek′shəs), *adj.* **1** (of a disease) spread by infection; caused by bacteria, virus, or other microorganisms that invade some part of the body: *Measles is an infectious disease.* SYN: catching. **2** causing infection. **3** *Figurative.* apt to spread from one to another: *He has a jolly, infectious laugh.* **4** *Law.* (of contraband, hijacked, or unlawfully possessed goods) tainting with illegality. **5** *Obsolete.* infected with disease. **—in|fec′tious|ly,** *adv.* **—in|fec′tious|ness,** *n.*

infectious bronchitis, an acute, highly contagious, viral, respiratory disease of poultry.

infectious hepatitis, a contagious, systemic virus disease of man and animals characterized by inflammation of the liver, fever, and usually jaundice; hepatitis A.

infectious mononucleosis, a disease characterized by fever, swelling of the lymph glands, and often an enlarged liver and spleen; glandular fever.

in|fec|tive (in fek′tiv), *adj.* causing infection; infectious: *It has been shown that pneumonic plague patients may be directly infective* (New Scientist).

in|fec|tiv|i|ty (in′fek tiv′ə tē), *n.* infectious quality or condition: *A group of St. Louis biochemists has taken apart and reassembled a virus without destroying its infectivity* (Scientific American).

in|fec|tor (in fek′tər), *n.* a person or thing that infects.

in|fe|cund (in fē′kənd, -fek′ənd), *adj.* not fecund; unfruitful; barren.

in|fe|cun|di|ty (in′fi kun′də tē), *n.* the state of being infecund; unfruitfulness; barrenness.

in|fe|lic|i|tous (in′fə lis′ə təs), *adj.* **1** not appropriate; unsuitable. **2** unfortunate; unhappy. **—in′felic′i|tous|ly,** *adv.*

in|fe|lic|i|ty (in′fə lis′ə tē), *n., pl.* **-ties. 1** unsuitability; inappropriateness. **2** something unsuitable, such as an inappropriate word or remark. **3** the state of being unhappy or unfortunate: . . . *that pure infelicity which accompanies some people in their walk through life* (Charles Lamb). **4** an unfortunate circumstance or event; misfortune.

in|felt (in′felt′), *adj.* felt within; heartfelt.

in|fer (in fėr′), *v.,* **-ferred, -fer|ring. —*v.t.* 1** to find out by reasoning; come to believe after thinking; conclude: *People inferred that so able a governor would make a good President.* SYN: gather, deduce. See syn. under **conclude. 2** to be a sign or hint of; suggest indirectly; indicate; imply: *Ragged clothing infers poverty.* **3** *Obsolete.* **a** to bring on; cause: *Who . . . fled fast away, afeard Of villainy to be to her inferred* (Edmund Spenser). **b** to adduce; allege: *Full well hath Clifford play'd the orator, Inferring arguments of mighty force* (Shakespeare).
—*v.i.* to draw inferences.
[< Latin *īnferre* introduce, inflict, bring in or on (in Late Latin, adduce) < *in-* in + *ferre* bring]
►See **imply** for usage note.

in|fer|a|ble (in fėr′ə bəl, in′fər-), *adj.* that can be inferred or drawn as a conclusion; deducible.

in|fer|a|bly (in fėr′ə blē, in′fər-), *adv.* so as to be inferred.

in|fer|ence (in′fər əns), *n.* **1** the act or process of inferring: *to form a judgment by inference from known facts. What happened is only a matter of inference; no one saw the accident.* SYN: deduction, illation, presumption, assumption, surmise. **2** that which is inferred; conclusion: *to make rash inferences. What inference do you draw from smelling smoke?* SYN: deduction, illation, presumption, assumption, surmise.

in|fer|en|tial (in′fə ren′shəl), *adj.* having to do with inference; depending on inference.

in|fer|en|tial|ly (in′fə ren′shə lē), *adv.* by inference.

in|fe|ri|or (in fir′ē ər), *adj., n.* **—*adj.* 1** low in quality; below average; below most others: *an inferior mind, an inferior grade of coffee.* **2** lower in quality; not so good; worse: *His grades are inferior this semester. This cloth is inferior compared to real silk.* **3** lower in position or rank: *A lieutenant is an inferior officer compared to a captain.* **4** *Botany.* **a** growing below some other part or organ: *an inferior calyx, an inferior ovary.* **b** belonging to the part of a flower that is farthest from the main stem. **5** (of animal organs) below or posterior to others of the same kind, or the usual or normal position: *the inferior vena cava.* **6** *Astronomy.* **a** between the earth and the sun: *an inferior conjunction of Mercury with the sun.* **b** below the horizon: *the inferior passage of a star.* **7** *Printing.* set below the main line of type, as letters or numerals are in chemical formulas: *In H_2O, the 2 is inferior.*
—*n.* 1 a person who is lower in rank or station; subordinate: *A good leader gets on well with inferiors.* **2** something that is below average; an inferior thing. **3** *Printing.* an inferior letter.
inferior to, a not so good or so great as; worse than: *This cloth is inferior to real silk.* **b** below; lower than; less than: *A lieutenant is inferior to a captain.*
[< Latin *īnferior,* comparative of *īnferus* situated below] **—in|fe′ri|or|ly,** *adv.*

in|fe|ri|or|i|ty (in fir′ē ôr′ə tē, -or′-), *n.* inferior nature or condition; quality of being inferior.

inferiority complex, an abnormal feeling of being inferior to other people, leading to a variety of symptoms and sometimes compensated for by overly aggressive behavior.

inferior vocal cords, the lower of two pairs of vocal cords, which upon vibration produces the sound of voice.

in|fer|nal (in fėr′nəl), *adj.* **1a** of the lower world; of hell. **b** of the lower world which the ancient Greeks and Romans thought was the abode of the dead. **2** fit to have come from hell; hellish; diabolical: *The heartless conqueror showed infernal cruelty.* SYN: fiendish, devilish. **3** *Informal.* abominable; outrageous: *If you go ashore, you will get into some infernal row* (Herman Melville). SYN: confounded, detestable, execrable. [< Late Latin *īnfernālis* < Latin *īnfernus* lower; the underground region (in Late Latin, hell) < *īnferus* situated below] **—in|fer′nal|ly,** *adv.*

in|fer|nal|i|ty (in′fər nal′ə tē), *n.* the quality of being infernal.

infernal machine, a disguised bomb or other explosive apparatus for maliciously destroying life and property.

in|fer|no (in fėr′nō), *n., pl.* **-nos. 1** = hell. **2** a place of torment like hell: *Firemen fought their way through a roaring inferno of flames.* [< Italian *inferno* < Late Latin *īnfernus* hell < Latin, the lower region; see etym. under **infernal**]

in|fe|ro|an|te|ri|or (in′fər ō an tir′ē ər), *adj.* situated below and in front. [< Latin *īnferus* situated below + English *anterior*]

in|fer|rer (in fėr′ər), *n.* a person who infers.

in|fer|ri|ble (in fėr′ə bəl), *adj.* = inferable.

in|fer|tile (in fėr′təl), *adj.* not fertile; not fruitful; sterile. SYN: unproductive, barren.

in|fer|til|i|ty (in′fėr til′ə tē), *n.* lack of fertility; being infertile.

in|fest (in fest′), *v.t.* **1** to swarm in or about so as to trouble or disturb, frequently or in large numbers: *Mosquitoes infest swamps. The mountains were infested with robbers.* **2** *Figurative.* to spread over; overrun: *The landscape was drab and infested with brick ovens* (Atlantic). [< Latin *īnfestāre* to attack < *īnfestus* hostile] **—in|fest′er,** *n.*

in|fes|ta|tion (in′fes tā′shən), *n.* **1** the action of infesting: *Ravenous grasshoppers descend on Southwestern rangelands in the worst infestation since World War II* (Wall Street Journal). **2** the state of being infested. **3** anything that infests.

in|feu|da|tion (in′fyü dā′shən), *n. English Law.* **1a** the conferring of an estate in fee. **b** the feudal relation which such a grant established. **2** the granting of tithes to laymen. [< Medieval Latin *infeudatio, -onis* < *infeudare* to enfeoff < *in-* in + *feudum* fee, feud]

in|fib|u|late (in fib′yə lāt), *v.t.,* **-lat|ed, -lat|ing.** to fasten or confine with or as if with a buckle, clasp, ring, or pin.
[< Latin *infībulatus,* past participle of *infībulare* < *in-* in-[2] + *fībula* clasp]

in|fib|u|la|tion (in fib′yə lā′shən), *n.* **1** the act of infibulating. **2** the fastening of the sexual organs with a fibula or clasp to prevent copulation.

in|fi|del (in′fə dəl, -del), *n., adj.* **—*n.* 1** a person who does not believe in religion in general; unbeliever; disbeliever. **2** a person who does not accept a particular religion. During the Crusades, Moslems called Christians infidels. **3** a person who does not accept Christianity: *Under the banner of Christianity, the Crusaders fought the Saracens and other infidels.* **4** a person who is not a supporter or follower of a cause, idea, or the like: [*They*] *carefully shun the board of education offices to avoid the thunderbolts that would, they believe, shortly strike the infidels* (Dan O'-Neil).

Pronunciation Key: hat, āge, cãre, fär; let, ēqual, tėrm; it, īce; hot, ōpen, ôrder; oil, out; cup, pu̇t, rüle; child; long; thin; ᴛʜen; zh, measure; ə represents a in about, e in taken, i in pencil, o in lemon, u in circus.

—*adj.* **1** not believing in religion. **2** not accepting a particular faith, especially the Christian or the Moslem faith. **3** rejecting the Christian religion. **4** of or like unbelievers or infidels.
[< Old French *infidele*, learned borrowing from Latin *īnfidēlis* unfaithful, unbelieving < *in-* not + *fidēlis* faithful < *fidēs* faith < *fīdere* to trust]

in|fi|del|ic (in′fə del′ik), *adj.* having to do with unbelievers or their views.

in|fi|del|i|ty (in′fə del′ə tē), *n., pl.* **-ties. 1** lack of religious faith. **2** unbelief in Christianity. **3** lack of faithfulness, especially to husband or wife; disloyalty. **4** an unfaithful or disloyal act.

in|field (in′fēld′), *n.* **1a** the part of a baseball field roughly bounded by the bases; diamond. **b** the first, second, and third basemen and shortstop of a baseball team. **2** the part of a cricket field closest to the wickets. **3** the inside or enclosed part of a race track or running track: *The shots of the saddling in the infield were good* (Audax Minor). **4a** the part of farm lands nearest the buildings. **b** land regularly cultivated.

in|field|er (in′fēl′dər), *n. Baseball.* the first, second, or third baseman, or the shortstop; a player of the infield.

in|fields|man (in′fēldz′mən), *n., pl.* **-men.** *Cricket.* a player who fields close to the wicket.

in|fight (in′fīt′), *v.i.* to engage in infighting: *The moments when they should have been infighting were simply pauses until the referee separated them* (New Yorker). [back formation < *infighting* and *infighter*]

in|fight|er (in′fī′tər), *n.* **1** a boxer who tends to fight at close quarters: *Before long Blackbeard had proved himself . . . a brutal infighter* (Cape Times). **2** *Informal, Figurative.* a person who is or becomes involved in conflict with his associates: *a tough political infighter.*

in|fight|ing (in′fī′ting), *n.* **1** *Boxing.* fighting at close quarters, where only short-range blows can be delivered. **2** *U.S. Informal, Figurative.* conflict or controversy among persons who are closely associated; internal dissension: *Well versed in the tough infighting of a university campus . . .* (Saturday Review).

in|fill (*v.* in fil′; *n.* in′fil), *v., n.* —*v.t.* to fill in; fill up. —*n.* an infilling: *. . . a steel frame, recessed windows, brick infills, and precast spandrel panels* (Architectural Forum).

in|fill|ing (in′fil′ing), *n.* something that serves to fill in or up.

in|fil|ter (in fil′tər), *v.t., v.i.* to filter in.

in|fil|trate (in fil′trāt; *also* in′fil trāt *for v.t. def. 1*), *v.,* **-trat|ed, -trat|ing,** *n.* —*v.t.* **1a** to pass into or through by filtering. **b** *Figurative.* to penetrate or slip through (an enemy's lines) individually or in small groups: *Enemy troops infiltrated the front lines.* **c** *Figurative.* to penetrate (an organization) for purposes of spying, sabotage, or the like. **2** to filter into or through; permeate. —*v.i.* **1** to pass through or into a substance by filtration. **2** *Figurative.* **a** to penetrate or slip through an enemy's lines individually or in small groups. **b** to penetrate an organization, such as a political party, for purposes of spying, sabotage, or the like.
—*n.* **1** something that infiltrates; infiltration. **2** cells or fluids that pass into the tissues of the body and form a diseased accumulation.
[< *in-*² + *filtrate,* verb]

in|fil|trat|er (in′fil trā′tər, in fil′trā-), *n.* = infiltrator.

in|fil|tra|tion (in′fil trā′shən), *n.* **1** the act or process of infiltrating. **2** the condition of being infiltrated. **3a** a thing that infiltrates. **b** an infiltrated deposit. **4** *Figurative.* **a** a method of attack in which small groups of men penetrate the enemy's lines at various weak points to fire on the enemy from the side or rear. **b** the action of a person infiltrating for purposes of spying, sabotage, or the like: *The . . . unit will be trained to detect and report infiltration attempts by saboteurs or subversive agents* (New York Times).

in|fil|tra|tive (in fil′trə tiv), *adj.* of the nature of or producing infiltration.

in|fil|tra|tor (in′fil trā′tər, in fil′trā-), *n.* a person who infiltrates: *If an infiltrator was lucky enough not to be shot, he was tried for "illegal" entry* (New York Times).

in|fil|tree (in′fil trē′), *n.* = infiltrator.

infin., infinitive.

in|fin|i|tate (in fin′ə tāt), *v.t.,* **-tat|ed, -tat|ing. 1** to make infinite. **2** *Logic.* to make indefinite by attaching a sign of negation to it, as a positive term. —**in|fin′i|ta′tion,** *n.*

in|fi|nite (in′fə nit), *adj., n.* —*adj.* **1** without limits or bounds; endless: *the infinite reaches of outer space, infinite time, the infinite wisdom of God. The interpretation also suggests how an infinite world could be represented by a geometry with finite lines* (Scientific American). SYN: boundless, unlimited. **2** very, very great: *Teaching little children takes infinite patience. He . . . told him that the treasury in Jerusalem was full of infinite sums of money* (II Maccabees 3:6). SYN: immeasurable, immense, vast. **3** *Mathematics.* **a** greater than any assignable quantity or magnitude of the sort in question. **b** (of an assemblage) equivalent, as in value or degree, to some proper part of itself. **c** (of a magnitude) beyond any finite magnitude. **4** *Grammar.* not finite; infinitive.
—*n.* **1** that which is infinite. **2** *Mathematics.* an infinite quantity or magnitude.
(the) Infinite, God: *No rival Infinite could share thy Throne, There no more Infinites can be but one* (Thomas Ken).
[< Latin *īnfīnītus* < *in-* not + *fīnīre* to limit, bound < *fīnis* a limit, border] —**in′fi|nite|ly,** *adv.* —**in′fi|nite|ness,** *n.*

in|fi|ni|tes|i|mal (in′fi nə tes′ə məl), *adj., n.* —*adj.* **1** so small as to be almost nothing; extremely minute or insignificant: *Germs are infinitesimal animals and plants. A millionth of an inch is an infinitesimal length.* **2** *Mathematics.* less than any assignable quantity or magnitude of the sort in question.
—*n.* **1** an extremely small quantity or amount. **2** *Mathematics.* a variable continually approaching zero as a limit.
[< New Latin *infinitesimus* the "nth" (< Latin *īnfīnītus* infinite + *-esimus,* an ordinal suffix) + English *-al*¹] —**in′fi|ni|tes′i|mal|ly,** *adv.*

infinitesimal calculus, differential calculus and integral calculus, collectively.

in|fin|i|ti|val (in′fi nə tī′vəl, in fin′ə-), *adj. Grammar.* of or having to do with the infinitive. —**in′fin|i|ti′val|ly,** *adv.*

in|fin|i|tive (in fin′ə tiv), *n., adj. Grammar.* —*n.* a form of a verb not inflected for person or number and commonly preceded by *to. Examples:* Let him *go.* We want *to go* now. *Abbr:* inf.
—*adj.* of the infinitive.
[< Late Latin *īnfīnītīvus* < Latin *īnfīnītus* unrestricted; see etym. under **infinite**]
►**infinitive.** The present infinitive is the simple form of the verb, with or without *to: I want* to buy *a hat. Let him* leave *if he wants* to leave. Infinitives are used as: **a** nouns: To swim *across the English channel is his ambition.* **b** adjectives: *They had money* to burn. **c** adverbs: *He went home* to get *his hat.* **d** part of verb phrases: *She* will do *most of the work.*
►See also usage notes under **split infinitive** and **dangling participle.**

in|fin|i|tive|ly (in fin′ə tiv lē), *adv.* as an infinitive.

in|fin|i|tize (in fin′ə tīz), *v.t.,* **-tized, -tiz|ing.** to make infinite: *to infinitize life.*

in|fin|i|tude (in fin′ə tüd, -tyüd), *n.* **1** the condition of being infinite. **2** an infinite extent, amount, or number.

***in|fin|i|ty** (in fin′ə tē), *n., pl.* **-ties. 1** the condition of being infinite. **2** an infinite distance, space, time, or quantity: *an infinity of rumors. As a young newspaper reporter I had to spend what seemed to be an infinity of dull, orderly afternoons in Canadian courts* (Maclean's). **3** an infinite extent, amount, or number: *the infinity of God's mercy.* **4a** *Mathematics.* an infinite quantity or magnitude. **b** *Geometry.* infinite distance, or the part of anything, such as a line or plane, infinitely removed from the part under consideration.
to infinity, without limits or bounds; endlessly: *You may delight yourselves in varying to infinity the fashion* (Edmund Burke).
[< Latin *īnfīnitās* < *in-* not, without + *fīnis* end, limit, boundary]

***infinity** definition 4a — symbol

infinity microphone or **transmitter,** an extremely sensitive and far-ranging listening device concealed in a telephone: *The CIA is believed to be making extensive use of the "infinity microphone" . . . Hitched to the victim's telephone, it can transmit either phone conversations or voices in the room; it uses telephone current for power, and can't be found with a radio detector* (Newsweek).

in|firm (in fėrm′), *adj., v.* —*adj.* **1** lacking strength or health; physically weak; feeble: *Great-grandmother was old and infirm. Here I stand . . . A poor, infirm, weak, and despised old man* (Shakespeare). SYN: shaky, decrepit, debilitated, sickly. **2** without a firm purpose; weak in will or character; not steadfast; faltering: *The boy was infirm in his ambitions.* SYN: irresolute. **3** not firm, solid, or strong; not stable: *Infirm the stalks, unsolid are the leaves* (John Dryden).
—*v.t.* to invalidate (a law, custom, privilege, etc.); declare invalid; call in question.
[< Latin *īnfirmus* weak, feeble < *in-* not + *firmus* firm, strong] —**in|firm′ly,** *adv.* —**in|firm′ness,** *n.*

in|fir|mar|i|an (in′fėr mãr′ē ən), *n.* a person in charge of an infirmary.

in|fir|ma|ry (in fėr′mər ē), *n., pl.* **-ries. 1** a place for the care of the infirm, sick, or injured, especially a hospital or dispensary in a school or institution. **2** any hospital. [< Medieval Latin *infirmaria* quarters for the sick < Latin *īnfirmus* infirm]

in|fir|ma|to|ry (in fėr′mə tôr′ē, -tōr′-), *adj.* tending to invalidate or weaken; making infirm or insubstantial: *journals critical of Dr. Eysenck's thinking or infirmatory of his demonstrations in the field of introversion-extraversion studies* (New Scientist).

in|fir|mi|ty (in fėr′mə tē), *n., pl.* **-ties. 1** the state of being infirm; weakness; feebleness: *His appearance in itself was enough to indicate the infirmity of his physical powers* (Lytton Strachey). SYN: debility. **2** a physical weakness or ailment; sickness; illness: *the infirmities of age.* **3** a weakness, flaw, or defect in a person's character: *Fame . . . That last infirmity of noble mind* (Milton). SYN: failing, foible.

in|fix (*v.* in fiks′; *n.* in′fiks), *v., n.* —*v.t.* **1** to fix or fasten (one thing) in (another); drive in; implant: *to infix a spear.* **2** *Figurative.* to fix (a fact or other matter) in the mind or memory; impress. **3** *Grammar.* to insert (a formative element) in the body of a word.
—*n. Grammar.* an element inserted in the body of a word, instead of being prefixed or suffixed to the stem: *Tagalog uses several infixes which are added before the first vowel of the underlying form: from* [′su:lat] *'a writing' are derived* [su′mu:lat] *'one who wrote,' with the infix* [-um-], *and* [si′nu: lat] *'that which was written,' with infix* [-in-] (Leonard Bloomfield).

in|fix|ion (in fik′shən), *n.* **1** the act of infixing. **2** the state of being infixed.

in fla|gran|te de|lic|to (in flə gran′tē di lik′tō), *Latin.* **1** in the very act of committing the crime; in the performance of the deed; red-handed: *She frequently surprised us in flagrante delicto gorging trifles and sausage rolls in the protective womb of the bedclothes* (Peter Thorogood). **2** (literally) in blazing crime.

in|flame (in flām′), *v.,* **-flamed, -flam|ing.** —*v.t.* **1** to make more violent; excite: *His stirring speech inflamed the crowd.* SYN: arouse, fire. **2** to make unnaturally hot, red, sore, or swollen: *The smoke had inflamed the fireman's eyes.* **3** to set ablaze; set on fire. —*v.i.* **1** to become excited with strong feeling. **2** to become red or hot from disease or irritation. **3** to burst into flame; catch fire: *Old wood inflam'd doth yield the bravest fire* (Philip Sidney). **4** to light or redden with or as if with flame: *The setting sun inflames the sky.*
[< Old French *enflamer,* learned borrowing from Latin *īnflammāre* < *in-* + *flamma* flame] —**in|flam′er,** *n.* —**in|flam′ing|ly,** *adv.*

in|flam|ma|bil|i|ty (in flam′ə bil′ə tē), *n.* **1** susceptibility of taking fire: *the inflammability of alcohol.* **2** *Figurative.* excitability; fieriness: *the inflammability of crusading oratory.*

in|flam|ma|ble (in flam′ə bəl), *adj., n.* —*adj.* **1** easily set on fire; flammable: *Paper is inflammable.* **2** *Figurative.* easily excited or aroused; excitable: *He had an inflammable temper.* —*n.* something inflammable. —**in|flam′ma|ble|ness,** *n.*
►See **flammable** for usage note.

in|flam|ma|bly (in flam′ə blē), *adv.* in an inflammable manner.

in|flam|ma|tion (in′flə mā′shən), *n.* **1a** a diseased condition of some part of the body, marked by heat, redness, swelling, and pain: *A boil is an inflammation of the skin.* **b** the condition of being inflamed. **2** the action of inflaming. **3** *Gunnery.* the propagation of ignition from grain to grain when a charge of powder is set off.

in|flam|ma|to|ri|ly (in flam′ə tôr′ə lē, -tōr′-), *adv.* in an inflammatory manner.

in|flam|ma|to|ry (in flam′ə tôr′ē, -tōr′-), *adj.* **1** tending to excite or arouse: *The leader of the mob made an inflammatory speech attacking the government.* **2** of or accompanied by inflammation: *an inflammatory condition of the tonsils.*

in|flat|a|ble (in flā′tə bəl), *adj., n.* —*adj.* that can be inflated.
—*n.* any object that can be inflated: *The most popular toys are the inflatables: an 8-foot-long sausage and a 10-foot-square air mattress that looks like an upside-down wading pool* (Time).

in|flate (in flāt′), *v.,* **-flat|ed, -flat|ing.** —*v.t.* **1** to force air or gas into (something, such as a balloon or ball) causing it to swell; blow out or swell with air or gas: *to inflate a tire.* SYN: distend, expand, enlarge. **2** *Figurative.* to puff up with pride, self-importance, or satisfaction; elate: *After his success he was inflated with self-importance.* **3** to increase (prices or currency) beyond the normal amount or beyond the limits of sound business practice, especially rapidly: *We inflate our paper currency* (Emerson).
—*v.i.* to swell or puff out: (*Figurative.*) *to inflate with pride.*
[< Latin *īnflāre* (with English *-ate*¹) < *in-* into + *flāre* to blow]

in|flat|ed (in flā′tid), *adj.* **1** distended with air or gas. **2** *Figurative.* turgid; bombastic: *Poems . . . so inflated with metaphor* (Oliver Goldsmith). **3** abnormally or unjustifiably increased: *inflated prices, inflated values.* **4** *Botany.* swollen; puffed up: *inflated petioles, inflated bladderwort.* **—in·flat′ed|ness,** *n.*

in|flat|er (in flā′tər), *n.* **1** a person or thing that inflates or puffs up. **2** an air pump for inflating pneumatic cushions, tires, air bags, or the like.

in|flat|tile (in flā′təl), *adj.* sounded by blowing, as a wind instrument.

in|fla|tion (in flā′shən), *n.* **1** the act of swelling (as with air, gas, pride, or satisfaction). **2** a swollen state; too great expansion. **3** an increase of the currency of a country by issuing much paper money. **4** a sharp and sudden rise in prices resulting from a too great expansion in paper money or bank credit: *Inflation spirals inexorably on* (Atlantic).

in|fla|tion|ar|y (in flā′shə ner′ē), *adj.* **1** of or having to do with inflation; tending to inflate: *the inflationary effect of government spending.* **2** *Astronomy.* of or having to do with a model of the big bang theory which postulates that in the first fraction of a second following the cosmic explosion in which it originated, the universe underwent an extremely rapid expansion: *the inflationary universe, the inflationary model. Even more "dark matter" is implied in the inflationary concept of the universe* (Walter Sullivan).

inflationary spiral, a continuous and expanding increase in the level of prices, wages, employment, and other economic indicators, in which each increase leads to further increases.

in|fla|tion|ism (in flā′shə niz əm), *n.* the policy or practice of inflating currency or credit.

in|fla|tion|ist (in flā′shə nist), *n., adj.* **—n.** a person who favors inflation, especially of currency. **—*adj.*** of or having to do with inflationism: *an inflationist policy.*

in|fla|tor (in flā′tər), *n.* = inflater.

in|fla|tus (in flā′təs), *n.* inspiration; afflatus: *He described himself as a victim of "the inflatus of oratory"* (Time). [< Latin *inflātus,* past participle of *inflāre* inflate; see etym. under **inflate**]

in|flect (in flekt′), *v.t.* **1** to change the tone or pitch of (the voice). **2** *Grammar.* to vary the form of (a word) to show case, number, gender, person, tense, mood, voice, or comparison. By inflecting *who* we have *whose* and *whom.* **SYN:** decline, conjugate. **3a** to bend; curve. **b** *Biology.* to bend or turn inward; bend into a curve or angle. **—*v.i.*** *Grammar.* to be subject to inflection. [< Latin *īnflectere* < *in-* in + *flectere* to bend]

in|flect|ed (in flek′tid), *adj.* inflectional: *an inflected language.*

inflected class, any class of words, such as nouns, pronouns, verbs, and adjectives, that can be inflected.

in|flect|ion (in flek′shən), *n.* **1** a change in the tone or pitch of the voice: *We usually end questions with a rising inflection.* **2** *Grammar.* **a** a variation in the form of a word to show case, number, gender, person, tense, mood, voice, or comparison. **b** an inflected form of a word. **c** a set or pattern of such forms. **d** a suffix or other ending used in inflecting: *-est and -ed are common inflections in English.* **3** the act of bending; curving. **4** a bend; curve. **5** *Mathematics.* **a** a change of curvature from convex to concave or from concave to convex. **b** a point at which this takes place.

in|flec|tion|al (in flek′shə nəl), *adj.* of, having to do with, or showing grammatical inflection. **—in·flec′tion|al|ly,** *adv.*

inflectional language, a language in which words change form in accordance with grammatical relationships, as Latin and Russian.

in|flec|tion|less (in flek′shən lis), *adj.* without inflection.

inflection point, *Mathematics.* a point on a curve at which inflection takes place.

in|flec|tive (in flek′tiv), *adj.* **1** *Grammar.* having to do with or characterized by inflection. **2** tending to bend.

in|flec|tor (in flek′tər), *n.* something that inflects or bends, as a muscle.

in|flexed (in flekst′), *adj.* turned or bent inward; incurved; twined inward; *an inflexed leaf.*

in|flex|i|bil|i|ty (in flek′sə bil′ə tē, in′flek-), *n.* lack of flexibility; being inflexible.

in|flex|i|ble (in flek′sə bəl), *adj.* **1** firm; unyielding; steadfast: *Neither threats nor promises could change the captain's inflexible determination.* **2** that cannot be changed; unalterable: *In religion that law is written, and inflexible, never to do evil* (Oliver Goldsmith). **3** not easily bent; stiff; rigid: *an inflexible rod.* **SYN:** unbending, firm. [< Latin *īnflexibilis* < *in-* not + *flexibilis* flexible] **—in|flex′i|ble|ness,** *n.*

—*Syn.* 1 Inflexible, inexorable, unrelenting mean unyielding in character or purpose. **Inflexible** emphasizes holding fast or doggedly to what one intends, thinks, or believes: *You waste time when you argue with a prejudiced person whose attitude is inflexible.* **Inexorable** emphasizes remaining coldly determined and unaffected by begging or pleading: *The conquerors made inexorable demands for tribute. The principal was inexorable in his decision to suspend the boy.* **Unrelenting** emphasizes not softening and showing pity, or lessening in force, harshness, or cruelty: *He was unrelenting in his hatred.*

in|flex|i|bly (in flek′sə blē), *adv.* in an inflexible manner; rigidly; inexorably.

in|flex|ion (in flek′shən), *n. Especially British.* inflection.

in|flex|ion|al (in flek′shə nəl), *adj. Especially British.* inflectional. **—in|flex′ion|al|ly,** *adv.*

in|flex|ion|less (in flek′shən lis), *adj. Especially British.* inflectionless.

in|flict (in flikt′), *v.t.* **1** to cause to have or suffer; give (a stroke, a blow, pain, or a wound): *A knife can inflict a bad wound on a person.* **2** to cause to be suffered or borne; impose (a burden, suffering, or something unwelcome): *to inflict a harsh sentence. Only cruel people like to inflict pain. The disagreeable woman inflicted herself on her relatives for a long visit.* [< Latin *īnflictus,* past participle of *īnflīgere* < *in-* on + *flīgere* to dash, strike] **—in|flict′er, in|flic′tor,** *n.*

in|flict|a|ble (in flik′tə bəl), *adj.* that can be inflicted.

in|flic|tion (in flik′shən), *n.* **1** the act of inflicting: *The cruel emperor delighted in the infliction of pain.* **2** something inflicted; pain, suffering, burden, or punishment: *The Bible tells how Job endured many inflictions with patience.*

in|flic|tive (in flik′tiv), *adj.* **1** tending to inflict. **2** having to do with infliction.

in-flight (in′flīt′), *adj.* during flight: *in-flight refueling.*

in|flood (in flud′), *v.i., v.t.* to flow in.

in|flo|res|cence (in′flô res′əns, -flō-), *n.* **1a** the way in which the flowers of a plant are arranged on the stem or axis and in relation to each other; the flowering system; anthotaxy. The two fundamental types of inflorescence are determinate and indeterminate. **b** a flower cluster. **c** the part of a plant bearing flowers. **d** one flower, if occurring on a plant bearing a single flower, such as the tulip. **2** a beginning to blossom; flowering stage. [< New Latin *inflorescentia* (coined by Linnaeus) < Latin *in-* in + *flōrēscere* begin to blossom < *flōrēre* to blossom < *flōs, flōris* a blossom, flower]

in|flo|res|cent (in′flô res′ənt, -flō-), *adj.* showing inflorenscence; flowering.

in|flow (in′flō′), *n.* **1** the act or fact of flowing in or into; influx: *The discovery of gold in Alaska caused an inflow of people.* **2** that which flows in: *The capital inflow in the first quarter . . . was $171 million* (Wall Street Journal).

in|flu|ence (in′flü əns), *n., v.,* **-enced, -enc|ing.** **—*n.*** **1** the power of persons or things to act on others, seen only in its effects: *the influence of the moon on the tides, the influence of example on the young.* **SYN:** See syn. under **authority.** **2** the power to produce an effect without using force: *Use your influence to persuade your friends to join our club. A person may have influence by his ability, personality, position, or wealth.* **3** a person or thing that has such power: *His thoughtfulness for others made the captain of our football team a good influence throughout the school.* **4** *Electricity.* induction, especially electrostatic induction. **5** *Astrology.* the power of the stars over the characters and destinies of men, originally considered to be an ethereal fluid streaming toward earth from the stars.

—*v.t.* **1** to have power or influence on; change the nature or behavior of: *to be influenced by a sense of duty. The moon influences the tides. What we read influences our thinking.* **SYN:** move, stir, sway. **2** to use influence on: *Dishonest people tried to influence the judge by offering him money.* **SYN:** persuade. **3** *U.S. Informal.* to add alcoholic liquor to (a drink); spike: *The old graduates . . . assembled for a ham and beef banquet, looking prosperous for their ages and, because of state liquor laws, influencing their Cokes from brown paper bags* (Time).

under the influence, *Informal.* drunk (from the phrase "under the influence of alcoholic liquor"): *A . . . stockman was fined $25 last week for riding a horse while under the influence* (Manchester Guardian Weekly).

[< Old French *influence* emanation from the stars, learned borrowing from Medieval Latin *influentia* (originally) a flowing in < Latin *in-* in + *fluere* to flow. See etym. of doublet **influenza.**] **—in′flu|enc|er,** *n.*

in|flu|ence|a|ble (in′flü ən sə bəl), *adj.* susceptible to influence.

influence mine, = magnetic mine.

influence peddler, *U.S.* a person who sells the use of his position and influence in government to businessmen or others who seek federal contracts, rate increases, and other favors.

influence peddling, *U.S.* the activities or practices of influence peddlers.

in|flu|ent (in′flü ənt), *adj., n.* **—*adj.*** flowing in. **—*n.*** a stream flowing into another stream.

in|flu|en|tial (in′flü en′shəl), *adj., n.* **—*adj.*** **1** having much influence; having influence: *Influential friends helped him to get a job.* **2** using influence; producing results.

—*n.* Also, **Influential.** *U.S.* a person who influences or molds the opinions of others: *You find Influentials in every walk of life, from Actors to Zoologists* (New Yorker).

[< Medieval Latin *influentia* (see etym. under **influence**) + English *-al*[1]] **—in′flu|en′tial|ly,** *adv.*

in|flu|en|za (in′flü en′zə), *n.* **1** an acute, contagious disease, caused by a virus, and like a very bad cold in its symptoms, but much more dangerous and exhausting; flu; grippe. Influenza. often spreads into an epidemic. **2** a contagious virus fever of horses, affecting the membranes of the nose and throat and causing shivers, weakness, and difficult breathing. [< Italian *influenza* (originally) visitation, influence (of the stars), learned borrowing from Medieval Latin *influentia.* See etym. of doublet **influence.**]

in|flu|en|zal (in′flü en′zəl), *adj.* of, having to do with, or characterized by influenza.

in|flux (in′fluks), *n.,* **1** the act or fact of flowing in; steady flow; inflow: *An influx of immigrants from Europe greatly increased the population of the United States.* **2** the point where a river or stream flows into another river, a lake, or the sea; mouth. [< *in-*[2] in + Latin *fluxus, -ūs* a flowing, flux < *fluere* to flow]

in|flux|ion (in fluk′shən), *n.* an influx or flowing in.

in|fo (in′fō), *n. Informal.* information.

in|fo|bit (in′fō bit′), *n.* an item of information in a databank. [< *info* + *bit*[4]]

in|fold (in fōld′), *v.t.* = enfold.

in|fold|ment (in fōld′mənt), *n.* = enfoldment.

in|form[1] (in fôrm′), *v.t.* **1** to supply with knowledge, facts, or news; tell: *Please inform your students of the changes in today's schedule. The witness informed the jury about the details.* **2** to inspire; animate: *God informed their hearts with pity.* **3** to endow or imbue with something that determines character: *The god of soldiers . . . inform Thy thoughts with nobleness* (Shakespeare). **4** *Obsolete.* **a** to form; shape; mold; fashion. **b** to train; instruct. **5** *Obsolete.* to make known; report: *Haply thou may'st inform Something to save thy life.* (Shakespeare). **6** *Obsolete.* to direct; guide: *Where else shall I inform my unacquainted feet In the blind mazes of this tangled wood?* (Milton).

—*v.i.* to tell tales; make a complaint; accuse: *The thief who was caught informed against the others who had helped him steal.* [< Latin *īnfōrmāre* < *in-* into + + *forma* form]

—*Syn. v.t.* 1 Inform, acquaint, notify mean to tell or let someone know something. **Inform** emphasizes telling or passing along directly to a person facts or knowledge of any kind: *Her letter informed us how and when she expected to arrive.* **Acquaint** emphasizes introducing someone to facts or knowledge that he has not known before: *He acquainted us with his plans.* **Notify** means to inform someone, by an official announcement or formal notice, of something he should or needs to know: *The college notified him that he was awarded a scholarship.*

in|form[2] (in fôrm′), *adj. Obsolete.* without form; formless. [< Middle French *informe,* learned borrowing from Latin *īnformis* < *in-* without + *forma* shape, form]

in|for|mal (in fôr′məl), *adj. n.* **—*adj.*** **1** not formal; not in the regular or prescribed manner: *informal proceedings.* **SYN:** irregular, unofficial. **2** done without ceremony; casual; comfortable; relaxed: *an informal party, informal clothes.* **SYN:** unceremonious, unconventional, easy. **3** used in everyday common talk but not used in formal speaking or writing; colloquial. Such an expression as *kids* for *children* is informal, as are *ad* for *advertisement, funny* for *strange,* and *fire* for *dismiss.*

—*n.* a dance at which formal dress is not required. **—in|for′mal|ly,** *adv.*

▶**Informal English** is the typical language used by an educated person in going about his everyday affairs. It is the level of usage between the uncultivated and the formal levels. It is used not only for personal affairs, but for most public affairs—in business and politics, for example, ex-

---

Pronunciation Key: hat, āge, cãre, fär; let, ēqual, tėrm; it, īce; hot, ōpen, ôrder; oil, out; cup, pu̇t, rüle; child; long; thin; ᴛʜen; zh, measure; ə represents a in about, e in taken, i in pencil, o in lemon, u in circus.

cept in strictly legal matters—for most newspaper and magazine articles, and for the bulk of fiction and drama.

in|for|mal|i|ty (in′fôr mal′ə tē), *n., pl.* **-ties. 1** the quality or fact of being informal; lack of ceremony. **2** an informal act or behavior.

informal vote, (in Australia and New Zealand) a vote that is not properly cast; a faulty or invalid vote.

in|form|ant (in fôr′mənt), *n.* **1** a person who gives information to another: *I found out what happened from my informant, who saw it happen. Those came who wished to gain information on a subject new to them, from informants whom they . . . regarded as authorities* (Cardinal Newman). **2** a native speaker of a language or dialect who repeats words, phrases, or other elements of a language, for linguistic analysis or for imitation in language learning.

in for|ma pau|pe|ris (in fôr′mə pô′pər is), *Latin.* as a pauper; having recourse to laws or relief for paupers.

in|for|mat|ics (in′fər mat′iks), *n.* = information science.

in|for|ma|tion (in′fər mā′shən), *n.* **1** knowledge given or received of some fact or circumstance; news: *We have just received information of the astronauts' safe landing. Knowledge is of two kinds. We know a subject ourselves, or we know where we can find information upon it* (Samuel Johnson). SYN: See syn. under **knowledge.** **2** things known; facts: *A dictionary contains much information about words.* SYN: data. **3** the act of telling or fact of being told something; an informing: *A guidebook is for the information of travelers.* **4** a person or office whose duty is to answer questions. **5** an accusation or complaint against a person, such as one sworn to before a magistrate or presented by a public official. **6** *Law.* a charge instituting criminal proceedings without a formal indictment. **7** any message or part of a message in coded form assembled by or fed to a computer.

in|for|ma|tion|al (in′fər mā′shə nəl), *adj.* having to do with or giving information; instructive: *A library's reference department provides informational services.*

information retrieval, the methods and procedures for recovering specific information from a central storage area.

information science, the study of the means by which information is collected, processed, classified, and transmitted, especially through computers and other automatic equipment: *Information science . . . is concerned with devising means for providing more efficient access to documents and improving the dissemination of information* (Harold Borko).

information technology, the application of computers and techniques of using computers to the handling of masses of data.

information theory, the branch of science that deals with the quality and characteristics of transmitted information, especially by studying or measuring the information content of messages and the factors that interfere with the transmission of information; communication theory. Information theory is used especially to improve the efficiency of communication systems such as telephone, telegraph, television, and radar.

in|form|a|tive (in fôr′mə tiv), *adj.* giving information; instructive: *This class trip to see how a newspaper is printed was very informative.* **—in|form′a|tive|ly,** *adv.* **in|form′a|tive|ness,** *n.*

in|form|a|to|ry (in fôr′mə tôr′ē, -tōr′-), *adj.* = instructive.

informatory double, a double in bridge intended to give information to one's partner, with further bidding indicated.

in|formed (in fôrmd′), *adj.* having knowledge or information; instructed; educated: *. . . known in the best informed circles in London* (Macaulay).

informed consent, consent given by a patient for an operation or medical experiment with an understanding of what is involved.

in|form|er (in fôr′mər), *n.* **1** a person who tells authorities of violations of the law; person who informs on another: *An informer told the police that the store was selling stolen goods.* **2** = informant.

in|for|mer|cial (in′fər mėr′shəl), *n. U.S.* a television commercial in the form of a program featuring demonstrations or discussions of various products or services.
[blend of *information* and *commercial*]

in|for|mi|da|ble (in fôr′mə də bəl), *adj.* not formidable; not to be dreaded.

in|for|tune (in fôr′chən), *n.* **1** *Astrology.* a planet or aspect of evil influence, especially Saturn or Mars. **2** *Obsolete.* misfortune. [< Middle French *infortune,* learned borrowing from Latin *īnfortūnium,* ultimately < *in-* not + *fortūna* fortune]

in|fo|tain|ment (in′fə tān′mənt), *n. U.S.* television or other entertainment based on or including factual information: *The airwaves are now flooded with syndicated "infotainment" shows that give TV viewers . . . peeks at the public and private lives of their favorite celebrities* (Newsweek). [< *info* + (enter)*tainment*]

in|fra (in′frə), *adv., prep. Latin.* below; beneath.

infra-, *prefix.* below; beneath; beyond, as in *infrahuman, infrasonic, infrared.* [< Medieval Latin *infra-* < Latin *īnfrā below, under*]

in|fra|cos|tal (in′frə kos′təl, -kôs′-), *adj.* located beneath the ribs: *infracostal muscles.*

in|fract (in frakt′), *v.t.* to break (a law or obligation); violate. [American English < Latin *īnfractus,* past participle of *īnfringere* infringe]**—in|frac′tor,** *n.*

in|frac|tion (in frak′shən), *n.* **1** the act of breaking a law or obligation; violation: *Reckless driving is an infraction of the law.* SYN: infringement. **2** a bone fracture in which parts remain in position.

in|fra|di|an (in frā′dē ən), *adj.* of or having to do with biological rhythms or cycles that recur less than once per day. [< *infra-* below + Latin *diēs* day + English *-an*]

in|fra dig (in′frə dig′), *Informal.* undignified: *Not only bad form—strictly infra dig* (New Yorker). [abbreviation of Latin *īnfrādignitātem* beneath (one's) dignity]

in|fra dig|ni|ta|tem (in′frə dig′nə tā′təm), *Latin.* beneath one's dignity.

in|fra|gla|cial (in′frə glā′shəl), *adj.* = subglacial.

in|fra|hu|man (in′frə hyü′mən), *adj., n.* **—*adj.*** **1** (of animals) beneath man in development. **2** = subhuman. **—*n.*** an infrahuman creature.

in|fra|la|bi|al (in′frə lā′bē əl), *adj., n.* **—*adj.*** below the lips. **—*n.*** one of the horny plates covering the lower lip in snakes and lizards.

in|fra|lap|sar|i|an (in′frə lap sãr′ē ən), *adj., n. Theology.* **—*adj.*** of or having to do with infralapsarianism or its followers. **—*n.*** a believer in the doctrine of infralapsarianism.

in|fra|lap|sar|i|an|ism (in′frə lap sãr′ē ə niz′əm), *n. Theology.* the doctrine that God decreed the division of mankind into the elect and the damned after the Fall and not from all eternity; sublapsarianism. [< *infra-* under + Latin *lapsus* (the) fall, lapse]

in|fra|me|di|an zone (in′frə mē′dē ən), those parts of the bottom of the ocean that are 300 to 600 feet below the surface.

in|fran|gi|bil|i|ty (in fran′jə bil′ə tē), *n.* the quality of being infrangible.

in|fran|gi|ble (in fran′jə bəl), *adj.* **1** that cannot be broken or separated into parts; unbreakable: *For centuries the atom was regarded as infrangible.* **2** that cannot be infringed; inviolable: *the infrangible laws of nature.* [< *in-*[1] not + *frangible*] **—in|fran′gi|ble|ness,** *n.* **—in|fran′gi|bly,** *adv.*

in|fra|or|bit|al (in′frə ôr′bə təl), *adj.* suborbital: *an infraorbital gland.*

in|fra|red (in′frə red′), *adj., n.* **—*adj.*** of the invisible part of the spectrum, whose rays have wave lengths longer than those of the red part of the visible spectrum and shorter than those of microwaves. Most of the heat from sunlight, incandescent lamps, carbon arcs, and resistance wires is from infrared rays.
—*n.* the infrared part of the spectrum.

infrared astronomy, the branch of astronomy that utilizes infrared rays to detect nebulae and stars otherwise invisible.

infrared detector, a device sensitive to infrared radiation, used in such varying applications as guided-missile tracking and navigation and high-altitude aerial mapping.

infrared radiation, electromagnetic radiation with wave lengths longer than those of the red part of the visible spectrum.

in|fra|scope (in′frə skōp), *n.* an instrunment for observing and measuring infrared radiation.

in|fra|son|ic (in′frə son′ik), *adj.* having a frequency below the audible range.

in|fra|son|ics (in′frə son′iks), *n.* the study of sound waves having a frequency below the audible range (less than 10 vibrations a second).

in|fra|sound (in′frə sound′), *n.* sound below the audible range.

in|fra|spe|cif|ic (in′frə spi sik′ik), *adj.* occurring within a species.

in|fra|struc|tur|al (in′frə struk′chər əl), *adj.* of, having to do with, or like an infrastructure.

in|fra|struc|ture (in′frə struk′chər), *n.* the essential elements forming the basis of a system or structure: *The infrastructure of the French ecomony—the transport system, for example—is now perhaps the best in Europe* (Listener).

in|fre|quence (in frē′kwəns), *n.* = infrequency.

in|fre|quen|cy (in frē′kwən sē), *n.* the fact or condition of being infrequent; uncommonness; scarcity; rarity.

in|fre|quent (in frē′kwənt), *adj.* not frequent; occurring seldom or far apart; scarce; rare: *words of infrequent occurrence, an infrequent visitor, a coast with infrequent lighthouses, a flowering plant which is infrequent in this region.* [< Latin *īnfrequēns, -entis* < *in-* not + *frequēns* frequent] **—in|fre′quent|ly,** *adv.*

in|fringe (in frinj′), *v.,* **-fringed, -fring|ing.** **—*v.t.*** **1** to act contrary to or violate (a law, obligation, or right); transgress; *A false label infringes the food and drug law. The inventor sued the company for infringing his patent.* SYN: break. **2** *Obsolete.* to break down; invalidate. **3** *Obsolete.* to frustrate. **—*v.i.*** to go beyond the proper or usual limits; trespass; encroach: *Do not infringe upon the rights of others.* SYN: intrude.
[< Latin *īnfringere* < *in-* in + *frangere* break] **—in|fring′er,** *n.*

in|fringe|ment (in frinj′mənt), *n.* **1** a violation: *Necessity is the plea for every infringement of human freedom. It is the argument of tyrants; it is the creed of slaves* (William Pitt). SYN: breach. **2** the act of trespassing. SYN: encroachment, intrusion.

in|fun|dib|u|lar (in′fən dib′yə lər), *adj.* funnel-shaped; infundibuliform.

in|fun|dib|u|late (in′fən dib′yə lāt, -lit), *adj* = infundibuliform.

in|fun|dib|u|li|form (in′fən dib′yə lə fôrm), *adj.* funnel-shaped: *an infundibuliform flower.*

in|fun|dib|u|lum (in′fən dib′yə ləm), *n., pl.* **-la** (-lə). *Biology.* a funnel-shaped part, organ, or structure, such as the prolongation of the third ventricle of the brain, connecting with the pituitary gland. [< Latin *īnfundibulum* (originally) a funnel < *īnfundere* pour in < *in-* in + *fundere pour*]

in|fu|ri|ate (in fyůr′ē āt), *v.,* **-at|ed, -at|ing,** *adj.* **—*v.t.*** to fill with wild, fierce anger; make furious; enrage: *Their insults infuriated him.*
—*adj.* excited to fury; full of fury; maddened; enraged: *Inflamed beyond the most infuriate wrath Of the worst monster that e'er roamed the waste* (James Thomson). SYN: raging, frantic.
[< Medieval Latin *infuriare* (with English *-ate*[1]) < Latin *in-* into + *furia* fury] **—in|fu′ri|ate|ly,** *adv.* **—in|fu′ri|at′ing|ly,** *adv.* **—in|fu′ri|a′tion,** *n.*

in|fus|cate (in fus′kāt), *adj.* clouded with brown; darkened. [< Latin *īnfuscātus,* past participle of *īnfuscāre* < *in-* in + *fuscāre* darken < *fuscus* dark brown]

in|fus|cat|ed (in fus′kā tid), *adj.* = infuscate.

in|fuse (in fyüz′), *v.t.,* **-fused, -fus|ing. 1** to put in; pour in; instill: *The captain infused his own courage into his soldiers.* SYN: implant. **2** to inspire: *The soldiers were infused with his courage.* SYN: imbue. **3** to steep or soak (a plant or leaves) in a liquid: *Tea leaves are infused in hot water to make tea.* **4** *Obsolete.* to pour (a liquid) into a place or vessel. [< Latin *īnfusus,* past participle of *īnfundere* pour in < *in-* in + *fundere* pour]

in|fus|er (in fyü′zər), *n.* **1** a person or thing that infuses. **2** a device for automatically injecting at preset intervals a dose of a drug into a person's vein. It is strapped to the arm and consists of a hypodermic syringe and a tiny battery-operated motor. *Patients with osteoporosis . . . could also be helped by using infusers to inject low doses of parathyroid hormones* (New York Post).

in|fu|si|bil|i|ty (in fyü′zə bil′ə tē), *n.* an incapability of being fused or dissolved.

in|fu|si|ble[1] (in fyü′zə bəl), *adj.* that cannot be fused or melted. [< *in-*[1] not + *fusible*] **—in|fu′si|ble|ness,** *n.*

in|fu|si|ble[2] (in fyü′zə bəl), *adj.* that can be infused. [< *infuse* + *ible*]

in|fu|sion (in fyü′zhən), *n.* **1** the act or process of infusing: *The plan was changed by the infusion of new ideas.* **2** a liquid extract obtained by steeping or soaking: *Tea is an infusion of tea leaves in hot water.* **3** something infused; something poured in or mingled; mixture: *He was a gentle man with a slight infusion of the footman* (Charles Lamb). SYN: tincture. **4** *Medicine.* the injection of a saline or other solution into a vein. **5** *Biology.* a liquid suspension of decaying organic matter used as a culture medium.

in|fu|sion|ism (in fyü′zhə niz əm), *n.* the doctrine that the soul has existed in a previous state and is infused into the body at conception or birth. **—in|fu′sion|ist,** *n.*

in|fu|sive (in fyü′siv), *adj.* having the quality or power of infusing.

in|fu|so|ri|a (in′fyů sôr′ē ə, -sōr′-), *n.pl.,* the infusorians.

in|fu|so|ri|al (in′fyů sôr′ē əl, -sōr′-), *adj.* having to do with or containing infusorians: *infusorial strata.*

in|fu|so|ri|an (in′fyů sôr′ē ən, -sōr′-), *n., adj.* **—*n.*** any one of a group of minute, usually microscopic, one-celled animals that move by vibrating filaments, such as the paramecium; ciliate. They occur in both free-living and parasitic forms.
—*adj.* of or belonging to this group.
[< New Latin *Infusoria* the genus name (< Latin *īnfundere*; see etym. under **infuse**) + English *-an*].

in fu|tu|ro (in fyü tyůr′ō, -tůr′ō), *Latin.* in the future.

-ing[1], *suffix forming nouns chiefly from verbs.* **1** the act of a person or thing that ____s: *Painting = the act of one that paints.* **2** the product or result of such an act, as in *a drawing, a painting.* **3** a thing that ____s: *Lining = a thing that lines.* **4** action, result, product, material, etc., of some other part of speech, as in *lobstering, offing, shirting, overcoating.* **5** of those who ____: *Smoking habit = the habit of a person who smokes. Printing trade = the trade of persons who print.*
[Middle English *-ing,* earlier *-ung,* Old English *-ing, -ung*]

-ing[2], **1** *suffix forming the present participle of verbs,* as in *going, talking, raining, staying.* **2** *suffix forming adjectives from verbs.* that ____s: *Lasting happiness = happiness that lasts. Growing child = a child that grows.*
[Middle English *-ing,* variant of *-ind, -end,* Old English *-ende*]
► The substitution of *-n* for *-ng* in the termination of the present participle and the gerund is very old. The frequency and the acceptability of this type of pronunciation in former centuries is attested by rhymes like *pursuing: ruin, willing: villain,* which may be found, even in serious poetry, from the time of Shakespeare to that of Wordsworth and Tennyson. In the 1800's the pronunciation came to be viewed with disfavor because it did not accord with the spelling, and since then has been steadily receding in the speech of the educated. Even today, however, it survives to some extent in cultivated conversational speech throughout the English-speaking world. In the United States it is particularly common in the South and New England.

in|ga (ing′gə), *n.* any one of a group of trees or shrubs of the pea family, native to South and Central America, having pinnate leaves and red or white flowers. [< New Latin *Inga* the genus name < Portuguese *inga* < Tupi]

in|gate (in′gāt′), *n.* **1** a way to go in; gate; entrance: *The speed of flow, particularly through the ingates, should be as low as possible* (New Scientist). **2** the hole in a mold through which a metal is poured in casting; geat.

in|gath|er (in′gaᴛʜ′ər), *v.t.* to gather in; collect; bring in, as a harvest. — **in′gath′er|er,** *n.*

in|gath|er|ing (in′gaᴛʜ′ər ing), *n., adj.* — *n.* **1** a gathering together; collecting: (*Figurative.*) *Zionists desire the ingathering of exiled Jewish people in modern Israel.* **2** that which is gathered in, such as a harvest; collection.
— ***adj.*** gathering in; gathering together: (*Figurative.*) *the ingathering harvest of time.*

in|gem|i|nate (in jem′ə nāt), *v.t.,* **-nat|ed, -nat|ing.** to repeat; reiterate. [< Latin *ingemināre* (with English *-ate*[1]) < *in-* on + *gemināre* to double, geminate] — **in|gem′i|na′tion,** *n.*

in|gen|er|ate[1] (*adj.* in jen′ər it; *v.* in gen′ə rāt), *adj., v.,* **-at|ed, -at|ing.** — ***adj.*** inborn; innate.
— ***v.t.*** to generate within; engender; produce: *The Spirit of God must ingenerate in us a true humility* (Jeremy Taylor).
[< Latin *ingenerātus* < *in-* in + *generāre* to generate] — **in|gen′er|a′tion,** *n.*

in|gen|er|ate[2] (in jen′ə rāt), *adj.* not generated; unbegotten; self-existent. [< Late Latin *ingenerātus* < *in-* not + *generātus* generated]

in|gen|er|os|i|ty (in jen′ə ros′ə tē), *n.* lack of generosity; ungenerous behavior.

in|gen|ious (in jēn′yəs), *adj.* **1** skillful in making; good at inventing; clever: *The ingenious boy made a radio set for himself.* **SYN**: inventive, resourceful. See syn. under **clever**. **2** cleverly planned and made: *This trap made of an old tin can and some wire is an ingenious device.* **3** *Obsolete.* possessed of genius; showing cleverness or talent. **4** *Obsolete.* ingenuous. [< Latin *ingeniōsus* < *ingenium* natural talent < *in-* in + unrecorded *gen-,* root of *gignere* beget, produce, be born] — **in|gen′ious|ly,** *adv.* — **in|gen′ious|ness,** *n.*
► **ingenious, ingenuous.** *Ingenious* means clever or skillful; *ingenuous* means frank, sincere, or simple: *My sister is so ingenious that she will think of a way to do this work more easily. The ingenuous child had never thought of being suspicious of what others told her.*

in|ge|nue or **in|gé|nue** (an′jə nü, än′-; -zhə-; *French* ᴀɴ zhā ɴʏ′), *n., pl.* **-nues,** *adj.* — ***n.*** **1** a simple, innocent girl or young woman, especially as represented on the stage. **2** an actress who plays the part of such a girl or young woman.
— ***adj.*** of or suitable for an ingenue; simple; unsophisticated: *There were some ankle-length styles and some ingenue dresses with tiny puffed sleeves that looked extraordinarily simple* (New York Times).
[< French *ingénue,* (originally) feminine adjective ingenuous, learned borrowing from Latin *ingenua*]

in|ge|nu|i|ty (in′jə nü′ə tē, -nyü′-), *n., pl.* **-ties.** **1** skill in planning or inventing; cleverness: *The boy showed ingenuity in making toys out of scraps of discarded wood.* **SYN**: inventiveness. **2** skillfulness of contrivance or design: *the ingenuity of a puzzle.* **3** an ingenious device or contrivance. **4** *Archaic.* candor; frankness. [< Latin *ingenuitās* frankness < *ingenuus* ingenuous; meaning influenced by *ingenious*]

in|gen|u|ous (in jen′yů əs), *adj.* **1** frank and open; free from restraint or reserve; sincere: *The boy gave an ingenuous account of his acts, concealing nothing.* **SYN**: candid, straightforward. **2** simple and natural; innocent: *an ingenuous country girl. Little children are ingenuous.* **SYN**: guileless, artless, naive. **3** *Archaic.* noble; generous; high-minded. [< Latin *ingenuus* (with English *-ous*) (originally) freeborn, native < *in-* in + unrecorded *gen-;* see etym. under **ingenious**] — **in|gen′u|ous|ly,** *adv.* — **in|gen′u|ous|ness,** *n.*
► See **ingenious** for usage note.

in|gest (in jest′), *v.t.* **1** to take (food or other substance) into the body for digestion: *Higher animals ingest by swallowing.* **2** *Figurative.* to take in; accommodate: *to ingest a new idea. Subways ingest thousands of commuters every workday.*
[< Latin *ingestus,* past participle of *ingerere* carry in < *in-* in + *gerere* carry] — **in|gest′i|ble,** *adj.*

in|ges|ta (in jes′tə), *n.pl.* substances ingested into the body, especially through the mouth. [< New Latin *ingesta* < Latin, neuter plural of *ingestus;* see etym. under **ingest**]

in|ges|tion (in jes′chən), *n.* the act of taking food or other substance into the body for digesting: *Ingestion is the first step in the digestive process.*

in|ges|tive (in jes′tiv), *adj.* of or having to do with ingestion.

in|gle (ing′gəl), *n.* **1** an open fireplace. **2** a fire burning upon the hearth. [perhaps < Scottish Gaelic *aingeal* fire]

in|gle|nook (ing′gəl nůk′), *n.* the nook or corner beside a fireplace: *Old Fyther Taft ... had some time ago gone back to his inglenook* (George Eliot).

in|gle|side (ing′gəl sīd′), *n.* a fireside.

in|glo|ri|ous (in glôr′ē əs, -glōr′-), *adj.* **1** bringing no glory; shameful; disgraceful: *The army suffered an inglorious defeat at the hands of a much weaker enemy. Calhoun was now approaching the inglorious twilight of his career* (Atlantic). **SYN**: ignominious, ignoble. **2** having no glory; not famous; obscure; humble: *Some mute inglorious Milton here may rest* (Thomas Gray).
— **in|glo′ri|ous|ly,** *adv.* — **in|glo′ri|ous|ness,** *n.*

In God We Trust, the official motto of the United States since 1956.

in|go|ing (in′gō′ing), *adj., n.* — ***adj.*** that goes in or inward; that enters.
— ***n.*** a going in; entrance.

✱in|got (ing′gət), *n., v.* — ***n.*** **1** a mass of metal, such as gold, silver, or steel, cast into a block or bar to be recast, rolled, or forged at a later time. **2** *Obsolete.* a mold in which metal is cast.
— ***v.t.*** to turn or shape into ingots.
[Middle English *ingot* ingot mold, perhaps < *in-* in + Old English *goten,* past participle of *gēotan* pour]

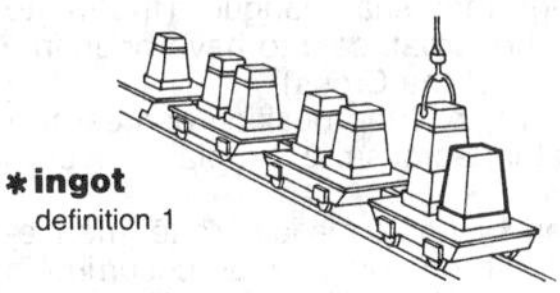

✱ingot
definition 1

ingot iron, a commercially pure form of malleable iron, containing too little carbon to be hardened or tempered, which has been poured into molds when molten.

in-grade (in′grād′), *adj.* coming within the same job level; given without an accompanying promotion to a higher position: *... in-grade bonus pay for tough jobs* (Time).

in|graft (in graft′, -gräft′), *v.t.* = engraft.

in|grain (*v.* in grān′; *adj.* in grān′, in′grān′; *n.* in′grān′), *v., adj., n.* — ***v.t.*** **1** to dye through the fiber or yarn before manufacture. **2** *Figurative.* to fix deeply and firmly: *A habit becomes ingrained in us.*
— ***adj.*** **1** dyed before manufacture. **2** made of yarn dyed before weaving, so that the pattern appears on both sides: *an ingrain rug.*
— ***n.*** **1** yarn, wool, or other fiber, dyed before manufacture. **2** *U.S.* an ingrain carpet or rug.
[variant of *engrain*]

in|grained (in grānd′, in′grānd′), *adj. Figurative.* deeply and firmly fixed in one's very nature or being: *ingrained honesty, an ingrained rebel. The American quality of his music is ... deeply ingrained in his art* (Saturday Review). **SYN**: inveterate. — **in|grain′ed|ly,** *adv.*

in|grate (in′grāt), *n., adj.* — ***n.*** an ungrateful person: *This is worse than your treachery and deceit, you base ingrate* (Richard Brinsley Sheridan).
— ***adj.*** *Archaic.* ungrateful.
[< Latin *ingrātus* < *in-* not + *grātus* thankful]

in|gra|ti|ate (in grā′shē āt), *v.t.,* **-at|ed, -at|ing.** to bring (oneself) into favor; make (oneself) acceptable: *He tried to ingratiate himself with the teacher by giving her presents.* [apparently < Italian *ingratiare,* or *ingraziare* (with English *-ate*[1]), ultimately < Latin *in grātiam* into favor < *grātus* pleasing, thankful] — **in|gra′ti|a′tion,** *n.*

in|gra|ti|at|ing (in grā′shē ā′ting), *adj.* agreeable; especially pleasing: *ingratiating manners.* — **in-gra′ti|at′ing|ly,** *adv.* — **in|gra′ti|at′ing|ness,** *n.*

in|gra|ti|a|to|ry (in grā′shē ə tôr′ē, -tōr′-), *adj.* serving or intended to ingratiate.

in|grat|i|tude (in grat′ə tüd, -tyüd), *n.* lack of thankfulness; being ungrateful: *Blow, blow, thou winter wind, Thou art not so unkind As man's ingratitude* (Shakespeare). **SYN**: thanklessness, ungratefulness, unthankfulness.

in|gra|ves|cence (in grə ves′əns), *n.* increase of gravity or severity.

in|gra|ves|cent (in′grə ves′ənt), *adj. Medicine.* increasing in severity; growing worse. [< Latin *ingravēscēns, -entis,* present participle of *ingravēscere* grow heavy < *in-* (intensive) + *gravis* heavy, grave[2]]

in|gre|di|ent (in grē′dē ənt), *n., adj.* — ***n.*** one of the parts of a mixture: *The ingredients of a cake usually include eggs, sugar, flour, and flavoring. Honesty is an important ingredient of character.* **SYN**: constituent, component, element. — ***adj.*** *Archaic.* that is a component part or element. [< Latin *ingrediēns, -entis,* present participle of *ingredī* enter < *in-* in + *gradī* go]

in|gress (in′gres), *n.* **1** the act of going in or entering: *A high fence prevented ingress to the field when the gate was locked. Our ingress into the world Was naked and bare* (Longfellow). **2** a way of going in; entrance: *A trap door in the floor was the only ingress to the secret room below.* **3** the right to go in: *All citizens have free ingress to the public library.* **SYN**: entrée. [< Latin *ingressus, -ūs* < *ingredī;* see etym. under **ingredient**]

in|gres|sion (in gresh′ən), *n.* the act of going in or entering; entrance.

in|gres|sive (in gres′iv), *adj.* **1** entering. **2** having to do with entrance. **3** *Grammar.* inceptive. — **in-gres′sive|ness,** *n.*

in-group (in′grüp′), *n.* a group of persons united by a common cause, interest, or goal and from which outsiders are often excluded: *A second characteristic of scientists as an exclusive in-group was their intense commitment to the ideals and pursuit of science* (Bulletin of Atomic Scientists).

in|grow|ing (in′grō′ing), *adj.* **1** growing within; growing inward. **2** growing into the flesh: *an ingrowing toenail.*

in|grown (in′grōn′), *adj.* **1** grown within; grown inward; natural; native: *A great artist has ingrown ability.* **2** grown into the flesh: *An ingrown toenail is often painful.*

in|growth (in′grōth′), *n.* **1** growth inward or within. **2** something that grows or has grown inward.

in|gui|nal (ing′gwə nəl), *adj.* of or in the region of the groin: *an inguinal gland, an inguinal hernia.* [< Latin *inguinālis* < *inguen, -inis* groin] — **in′gui-nal|ly,** *adv.*

in|gulf (in gulf′), *v.t.* = engulf.

in|gur|gi|tate (in gėr′jə tāt), *v.,* **-tat|ed, -tat|ing.**
— ***v.t.*** **1** to swallow greedily or immoderately. **2** *Figurative.* to engulf: *There is only ... a momentary eddy—very small, as compared with the apparent magnitude of the ingurgitated object* (Hawthorne).
— ***v.i.*** to eat or drink to excess; gormandize; guzzle. [< Latin *ingurgitāre* (with English *-ate*[1]) to gorge, flood in < *in-* + *gurges, -itis* whirlpool] — **in-gur′gi|ta′tion,** *n.*

In|gush (in′güsh), *n., pl.* **-gush, -gush|es, -gu|shi** (-gü shē). a member of a Moslem people occupying the mountainous region north of the Caucasus.

INH (no periods), isoniazid. [< *i*(so)*n*(icotinic acid) *h*(ydrazide)]

in|hab|it (in hab′it), *v.t.* **1** to live in (a place, region, house, cave, or tree): *Fish inhabit the sea.* (*Figurative.*) *Thoughts inhabit the mind.* **2** *Obsolete.* to establish in a place of abode; locate. **3** *Obsolete.* to occupy or people (a place). — ***v.i.*** to live; dwell. **SYN**: abide, lodge. [< Old French

Pronunciation Key: hat, āge, cãre, fär; let, ēqual, tėrm; it, īce; hot, ōpen, ôrder; oil, out; cup, půt, rüle; child; long; thin; ᴛʜen; zh, measure; ə represents **a** in about, **e** in taken, **i** in pencil, **o** in lemon, **u** in circus.

enhabiter, learned borrowing from Latin *inhabitāre* < *in-* in + *habitāre* dwell < *habēre* have, occupy] — **in|hab′it|a|ble,** *adj.* — **in|hab′i|ta′tion,** *n.* — **in|hab′it|er,** *n.*

in|hab|it|a|bil|i|ty (in hab′ə tə bil′ə tē), *n.* the quality of being inhabitable.

in|hab|it|an|cy (in hab′ə tən sē), *n., pl.* **-cies.** **1** residence as an inhabitant. **2** a place of habitation.

in|hab|it|ant (in hab′ə tənt), *n.* a person or animal that lives in a place; permanent resident; dweller: *Our town has ten thousand inhabitants.* SYN: denizen, occupant. [< Old French *inhabitant,* learned borrowing from Latin *inhabitāns, -antis,* present participle of *inhabitāre* inhabit]

in|hab|it|ed (in hab′ə tid), *adj.* lived in; having inhabitants: *an inhabited house.*

in|hab|i|tive|ness (in hab′ə tiv nis), *n.* a tendency to remain in one place of residence; fondness for home.

in|hal|ant (in hā′lənt), *n., adj.* —*n.* **1** a medicine to be inhaled. **2** an apparatus for inhaling it. —*adj.* used for inhaling.

in|ha|la|tion (in′hə lā′shən), *n.* **1** the act of inhaling or breathing in. **2** something inhaled or to be inhaled, such as a medicine.

in|ha|la|tion|al (in′hə lā′shə nəl), *adj.* of, characterized by, or promoting inhalation.

in|ha|la|tor (in′hə lā′tər), *n.* an apparatus for breathing in medicine, gas, or anesthetic; inhaler.

in|hale (*v.* in hāl′; *n.* in′hāl, in hāl′), *v.,* **-haled, -hal|ing,** *n.* —*v.t.* to draw into the lungs; breathe in (air, gas, fragrance, or smoke): *When he inhaled the strong fumes, he began to cough.*
—*v.i.* **1** to draw air, gas, fragrance, or smoke, into the lungs. **2** *Figurative: People inhale deeply of the past by ... looking at chairs inscribed with such names as Kit Carson, Zebulon Pike, Horace Tabor, and Horace Greeley* (New Yorker).
—*n.* an inhalation: *On colder mornings ... it was swell and invigorating taking inhales* (James T. Farrell).
[< Latin *inhālāre* breathe upon < *in-* upon, in + *hālāre* breathe; sense arises from taking verb as contrasting with *exhale*]

in|hale|ment (in hāl′mənt), *n.* = inhalation.

in|hal|er (in hā′lər), *n.* **1a** an apparatus for inhaling medicine, gas, or an anesthetic. **b** an apparatus for filtering dust, pollen, gases, or smoke from air. **c** a respirator to help a person breathe. **2** a person who inhales.

in|har|mon|ic (in′här mon′ik), *adj.* not harmonic; not in harmony; dissonant.

in|har|mo|ni|ous (in′här mō′nē əs), *adj.* not harmonious; disagreeing; conflicting; discordant. SYN: untuneful. —**in′har|mo′ni|ous|ly,** *adv.* —**in′har|mo′ni|ous|ness,** *n.*

in|har|mo|ny (in här′mə nē), *n.* lack of harmony; discord.

in|haul (in′hôl′), *n.* a rope used to haul in a sail or spar.

in|haul|er (in′hô′lər), *n.* = inhaul.

in|here (in hir′), *v.i.,* **-hered, -her|ing.** to belong as a quality or attribute; be inherent (in); exist: *The need to be loved inheres in human nature. Power to legislate laws for the United States inheres in Congress.* [< Latin *inhaerēre* < *in-* in + *haerēre* to stick]

in|her|ence (in hir′əns, -her′-), *n.* **1** the fact of being inherent. **2** *Philosophy.* the relation of a quality or attribute to its subject.

in|her|en|cy (in hir′ən sē, -her′-), *n., pl.* **-cies.** **1** = inherence. **2** something that is inherent: *an inherency of kindness.*

in|her|ent (in hir′ənt, -her′-), *adj.* belonging to a person or thing as a quality or attribute; essential: *inherent honesty. In spite of flattery, the pretty girl kept her inherent modesty. There is an inherent tendency in opinion to feed upon rumors excited by our own wishes and fears* (Atlantic). SYN: innate, inborn, inbred, intrinsic. [< Latin *inhaerēns, -entis,* present participle of *inhaerēre* inhere] —**in|her′ent|ly,** *adv.*

in|her|it (in her′it), *v.t.* **1a** to get or have after someone dies; receive as an heir: *After the farmer's death his wife and children will inherit the farm.* **b** to be heir to (a person): *Our sons inherit us* (Tennyson). **2a** to get (characteristics) from one's parents or ancestors: *She inherits her blue eyes from her father.* **b** to receive (anything) from one who came before: *I inherited this old pen from the person who used to have my desk.* (*Figurative.*) *The new government inherited a financial crisis.* **3** to come into possession of; receive as one's portion: *Good Master, what shall I do to inherit eternal life?* (Luke 18:18). **4** *Obsolete.* to make heir; put in possession; cause to inherit. —*v.i.* **1** to succeed as an heir to property, a right, title, privilege, or office. **2** to receive qualities, powers, duties, or position, as by inheritance (from). [< Old French *enheriter,* learned borrowing from Late Latin *inhērēditāre,* variant of *inhērēdāre* < Latin *in-* + *hērēs, -ēdis* heir]

in|her|it|a|bil|i|ty (in her′ə tə bil′ə tē), *n.* inheritable quality.

in|her|it|a|ble (in her′ə tə bəl), *adj.* **1** that can be inherited. **2** capable of inheriting; qualified to inherit. **3** *Obsolete.* entitled to possess or enjoy something as one's birthright. —**in|her′it|a|ble|ness,** *n.* —**in|her′it|a|bly,** *adv.*

in|her|it|ance (in her′ə təns), *n.* **1** the act of inheriting: *He received his house by inheritance from an aunt.* **2** the right of inheriting. **3** anything inherited: *The house was his inheritance. Good health is a fine inheritance from one's parents. Her frailness was a fact, a mixture of chance and inheritance* (New Yorker). SYN: heritage, legacy.

inheritance tax, *U.S.* a tax on inherited property.

in|her|it|ed (in her′ə tid), *adj.* received by or as an inheritance: *inherited property, inherited characters.* —**in|her′it|ed|ly,** *adv.*

in|her|i|tor (in her′ə tər), *n.* a person who inherits; heir.

in|her|i|tress (in her′ə tris), *n.* a female inheritor; heiress.

in|her|i|trix (in her′ə triks), *n., pl.* **in|her|i|trix|es, in|her|i|tri|ces** (in her′ə trī′sēz). = inheritress.

in|he|sion (in hē′zhən), *n.* the act or fact of inhering, especially as a quality or attribute; inherence. [< Late Latin *inhaesiō, -ōnis* < *inhaerēre* inhere]

in|hib|it (in hib′it), *v.t.* **1** to hold back; hinder or restrain; check: *The girl's honesty inhibited her impulse to keep the ring she found. Insistence on pontificating about national questions ... merely serves to inhibit discussion of the fundamentally important state questions* (James D. Griffin). SYN: prevent, stop, repress. **2** to forbid; prohibit: *A clause was ... inserted which inhibited the Bank from advancing money to the Crown without authority from Parliament* (Macaulay). SYN: interdict.
—*v.i.* to act or serve as an inhibitor: *Two more wires, one to "sense" and one to "inhibit," are separately threaded through all cores in each plane* (Scientific American). [< Latin *inhibitus,* past participle of *inhibēre* < *in-* in + *habēre* hold] —**in|hib′it|a|ble,** *adj.* —**in|hib′it|er,** *n.*

in|hi|bi|tion (in′ə bish′ən, in′hi-), *n.* **1** the act of holding back; restraint; checking: *Some drugs can cause the inhibition of normal bodily activity.* **2** an idea, emotion, attitude, habit, or other inner force holding back or checking one's impulses, desires, or the like. SYN: block. **3** prohibition; forbidding. **4** *Physiology.* a restraining or hindering of the function of a structure or organ by the action upon it of a chemical substance elaborated by another structure or organ.

in|hib|i|tive (in hib′ə tiv), *adj.* = inhibitory.

in|hib|i|tor (in hib′ə tər), *n.* **1** a person or thing that inhibits: *Many seeds have water-soluble germination inhibitors in their covering* (Scientific American). **2** *Physical Chemistry.* **a** any substance which slows down or hinders a chemical reaction. **b** a negative catalyst. **3** *Biochemistry.* a substance which inhibits the activity of an enzyme.

in|hib|i|to|ry (in hib′ə tôr′ē, -tōr′-), *adj.* inhibiting; tending to inhibit.

in hoc sig|no vin|ces (in hok sig′nō vin′sēz), *Latin.* by this sign thou shalt conquer (the motto of Constantine the Great, said to have been inspired by a vision of the Cross).

in-home (in′hōm′), *n.* **1** the position nearest the opponent's goal in lacrosse. **2** the player occupying this position.

in|ho|mo|ge|ne|i|ty (in′hō mə jə nē′ə tē, -hom ə-), *n., pl.* **-ties.** a difference or variation occurring in spatial matter, magnetic fields, and optical mediums: *The theory is that high-frequency radio waves are scattered by pockets of inhomogeneity produced by turbulence in the atmosphere* (Scientific American).

in|ho|mo|ge|ne|ous (in′hō mə jē′nē əs, -jēn′yəs; -hom ə-), *adj.* having the characteristic of inhomogeneity: *an inhomogeneous electric field.*

in|hos|pi|ta|ble (in hos′pi tə bəl, in′hos pit′ə-), *adj.* **1** not hospitable; not making visitors comfortable: *That inhospitable man never offers visitors any refreshments.* **2** providing no shelter or entertainment; barren: *The Pilgrims landed on a rocky, inhospitable shore.* SYN: cheerless, uninviting. —**in|hos′pi|ta|ble|ness,** *n.* —**in|hos′pi|ta|bly,** *adv.*

in|hos|pi|tal|i|ty (in hos′pə tal′ə tē), *n.* lack of hospitality; inhospitable behavior.

in-house (in′hous′), *adj., adv.* —*adj.* being within or done within a business firm, organization, or other group: *While a few companies ... employ their own in-house anthropometric specialists, most rely on outside consultants* (Time).
—*adv.* within a business firm, organization, or other group: *C4 [an explosive] is produced in-house by the Army and is not available commercially* (New York Times).

in|hu|man (in hyü′mən), *adj.* **1** without kindness, mercy, or tenderness; brutal; cruel; hard-hearted: *Only an inhuman mother would desert her child.* SYN: unfeeling, pitiless, merciless. **2** not having the qualities natural to a human being; not human: *The daring explorer seemed to have inhuman powers of endurance.* [spelling alteration (influenced by Latin *inhūmānus*) of Middle English *inhumayn* < Middle French *inhumain,* learned borrowing from Latin *inhūmānus* < *in-* not + *hūmānus* human] —**in|hu′man|ly,** *adv.* —**in|hu′man|ness,** *n.*

in|hu|mane (in′hyü mān′), *adj.* not humane; lacking in kindness, mercy, or tenderness. SYN: brutal, cruel. [partly variant of *inhuman,* partly < *in-*[1] not + *humane*] —**in′hu|mane′ly,** *adv.*

in|hu|man|i|ty (in′hyü man′ə tē), *n., pl.* **-ties.** **1** the quality or condition of being inhuman; lack of kindness, mercy, or tenderness; cruelty; brutality: *The worst sin towards our fellow creatures is not to hate them, but to be indifferent to them; that's the essence of inhumanity* (George Bernard Shaw). SYN: savagery. **2** an inhuman, cruel, or brutal act. SYN: outrage.

in|hu|ma|tion (in′hyü mā′shən), *n.* burial; interment.

in|hume (in hyüm′), *v.t.,* **-humed, -hum|ing.** to bury or inter (a corpse): *No hand his bones shall gather, or inhume* (Alexander Pope). [< Latin *inhumāre* < *in-* (intensive) + *humus* ground, earth]

in|i|al (in′ē əl), *adj.* of or belonging to the inion.

in|im|i|ca|ble (in im′ə kə bəl), *adj.* = inimical.

in|im|i|cal (in im′ə kəl), *adj.* **1** unfavorable; harmful: *Lack of ambition is inimical to success. To continue to prepare to fight such a war is to make the earth's atmosphere inimical to life* (New Yorker). SYN: injurious, adverse. **2** unfriendly; hostile: *The natives were inimical to all strangers.* SYN: antagonistic. See syn. under **hostile.** [< Late Latin *inimīcālis* < Latin *inimīcus* hostile; an enemy < *in-* not + *amīcus* friendly] —**in|im′i|cal|ly,** *adv.*

in|im|i|cal|i|ty (in im′ə kal′ə tē), *n.* **1** the quality or condition of being unfavorable or harmful. **2** hostility; unfriendliness.

in|im|i|ta|bil|i|ty (in im′ə tə bil′ə tē), *n.* the quality of being inimitable.

in|im|i|ta|ble (in im′ə tə bəl), *adj.* impossible to imitate or copy; matchless: *The inimitable beauties of the lilies of the field* (James Martineau). SYN: incomparable, peerless, unequaled. —**in|im′i|ta|ble|ness,** *n.* —**in|im′i|ta|bly,** *adv.*

in|i|on (in′ē ən), *n. Anatomy.* a point at the external occipital protuberance of the skull. [< New Latin *inion* < Greek *īníon* nape of the neck; muscles at the back of the neck < *īs, īnós* sinew; (originally) strength]

in|iq|ui|tous (i nik′wə təs), *adj.* very unjust; wicked: *iniquitous opinions.* SYN: nefarious, unrighteous. —**in|iq′ui|tous|ly,** *adv.* —**in|iq′ui|tous|ness,** *n.*

in|iq|ui|ty (i nik′wə tē), *n., pl.* **-ties.** **1** very great injustice; wickedness: *The iniquity of the transaction aroused general indignation.* SYN: unrighteousness. **2** a wicked or unjust act: *Taking children from their parents and selling them was one of the iniquities of slavery. If I have done iniquity, I will do no more* (Job 34:32). [< Old French *iniquite,* learned borrowing from Latin *inīquitās* < *inīquus* unjust < *in-* not + *aequus* just]

in|isle (in īl′), *v.t.,* **-isled, -isl|ing.** = enisle.

init., initial.

i|ni|tial (i nish′əl), *adj., n., v.,* **-tialed, -tial|ing** or (*especially British*) **-tialled, -tial|ling.** —*adj.* **1** occurring at the beginning; first; earliest: *the initial letter of a word. His initial effort at skating was a failure, but he succeeded the second time that he tried.* SYN: incipient, initiatory. **2** *Phonetics.* occurring at the beginning of an utterance or word: *an initial vowel.*
—*n.* **1** the first letter of a word, especially the first letter of a person's name or surname: *The initials U.S. stand for United States. When he bought the new suitcase, he had his initials printed on it in gold lettering.* **2** an extra large letter, often decorated, at the beginning of a chapter or other division of a book or illuminated manuscript. **3** *Phonetics.* an initial speech sound or cluster.
—*v.t.* **1** to mark or sign with initials; put one's initials upon: *John Allen Smith initialed the note J. A. S.* **2** to put one's initials on (a treaty) as a step before signing, so as to show the negotiators' satisfaction pending the consent of the signatory governments: *... to initial a treaty banning nuclear tests in the atmosphere* (Manchester Guardian Weekly).
[< Latin *initiālis* < *initium* a beginning < *inīre* begin < *in-* in + *īre* go] —**i|ni′tial|ly,** *adv.*

i|ni|tial|ism (i nish′ə liz əm), *n.* an abbreviation formed from the initial letters of a phrase, such as *IFC* (for International Finance Corporation) or *IFR* (for instrument flight rules).

▶ An **initialism** differs from an acronym in that it does not form a pronounceable word. Thus *NATO* and *radar* are acronyms, whereas *AAAS* and *vhf* are initialisms.

i|ni|tial|ize (i nish′ə līz), *v.t.*, **-ized, -iz|ing.** to set (an instruction, switch, or the like) to start or restart a computer program or routine. —**i|ni′tial|i-za′tion,** *n.*

initial side, *Trigonometry.* the line whose amount of rotation determines the size of an angle.

i|ni|ti|ate (*v.* i nish′ē āt; *n., adj.* i nish′ē it, -āt), *v.,* **-at|ed, -at|ing,** *n., adj.* —*v.t.* **1** to be the first one to start; set going; begin: *This year we shall initiate a series of free concerts.* SYN: originate, commence. **2** to admit (a person) by special forms or ceremonies into a group or society: *The old members initiated the new members.* SYN: install, induct. **3** to help to get a first understanding; introduce into the knowledge of some art or subject: *to initiate a person into business methods. The teacher initiated the class into the wonders of science by telling a few interesting things about the earth and stars.*

—*n.* a person who is or has been initiated.

—*adj.* **1** initiated. **2** *Obsolete.* having to do with one newly initiated.

[< Latin *initiāre* (with English *-ate*[1]) < *initium* a beginning; see etym. under **initial**] —**i|ni′ti|a′tor,** *n.*

i|ni|ti|a|tion (i nish′ē ā′shən), *n.* **1** the act or process of being the first one to start something; beginning; initiating. **2** the fact of being initiated. **3** formal admission into a group or society. **4** the ceremonies by which one is admitted to a group or society: *A great many members of the club showed up for the initiation.*

i|ni|ti|a|tive (i nish′ē ə tiv, -ē ā′tiv), *n., adj.* —*n.* **1** the active part in taking the first steps in any undertaking; lead: *She is shy and does not take the initiative in making acquaintances. No one suggested that he should take up painting; he did it entirely on his own initiative.* **2** readiness and ability to be the one to start something; enterprise: *A good leader must have initiative.* **3** the right to be the first to act, legislate, or otherwise begin legally. **4** the right of citizens outside the legislature to introduce or enact a new law by vote, especially by petition. This right exists in about 25 states and many cities of the United States, and in Switzerland. **5** the procedure for doing this.

—*adj.* serving to initiate; initiatory. —**i|ni′ti|a|tive-ly,** *adv.*

i|ni|ti|a|to|ry (i nish′ē ə tôr′ē, -tōr′-), *adj.* **1** beginning; introductory; opening; first. **2** of initiation; serving to initiate into some society or some special knowledge.

i|ni|ti|a|tress (i nish′ē ā′tris), *n.* a female initiator.

i|ni|ti|a|trix (i nish′ē ā′triks), *n., pl.* **i|ni|ti|a|trix|es, in|i|ti|a|tri|ces** (i nish′ē ā trī′sēz). = initiatress.

in|ject (in jekt′), *v.t.* **1** to force (liquid or medicine) into a cavity, passage, or tissue: *Drugs are often injected into the body. The biologist injected coloring matter into anatomical specimens for the study of the structure.* **2** to fill (a cavity, passage, or tissue) with liquid forced in: *The dentist injected the boy's gums with novocaine.* **3** *Figurative.* to throw in; insert: *While she and I were talking, he injected a remark into the conversation.* SYN: introduce, suggest. [< Latin *injectus,* past participle of *inicere* throw in < *in-* in + *jacere* throw]

in|ject|a|ble (in jek′tə bəl), *adj., n.* —*adj.* that can be injected.

—*n.* a drug or medicine that may be injected directly into the bloodstream.

in|jec|tion (in jek′shən), *n.* **1** the act or process of injecting: *Those drugs are given by injection as well as through the mouth.* **2** a liquid injected: *A drug is given as an injection.* **3** a bloodshot or hyperemic condition. **4** the act or process of placing a spacecraft into orbit.

injection laser, *Electronics.* a laser that generates radiant energy by the injection of charges into a p-n junction of gallium arsenide or other semiconductor; semiconductor laser.

injection molding, a method of producing thermoplastic materials by forcing the thick resin out of a heated cylinder into a mold.

in|jec|tor (in jek′tər), *n.* **1** a person or thing that injects. **2** a device for forcing water into a steam boiler. **3** a device for injecting fuel into a gasoline motor, diesel engine, or rocket motor.

in|je|ra (in′zhə rə), *n.* a slightly sour bread, somewhat like a pancake, eaten in Ethiopia. [< Amharic *injera*]

in-joke (in′jōk′), *n.* a joke that only members of an in-group can appreciate.

in|ju|di|cious (in′jü dish′əs), *adj.* showing bad judgment; unwise; not judicious: *An injudicious person says or does things without thinking what their results may be. The American public raised very little fuss about the injudicious odds* (Harper's). SYN: indiscreet, impractical, imprudent.

—**in′ju|di′cious|ly,** *adv.* —**in′ju|di′cious|ness,** *n.*

In|jun or **in|jun** (in′jən), *n. U.S. Informal or Dialect.* an American Indian.

in|junc|tion (in jungk′shən), *n.* **1** a command; order: *He obeyed his mother's injunction to hurry straight home. Injunctions of secrecy did not prevent the news from leaking out.* SYN: behest. **2** a formal order from a law court ordering a person or group to do, or not to do, something: *The owner got an injunction prohibiting people from lighting fires on the vacant lot next to his house. Sheriff's deputies arrived to enforce a court injunction against mass picketing* (Newsweek). **3** the act of commanding or authoritatively directing. [< Late Latin *injunctiō, -ōnis* < Latin *injungere* enjoin < *in-* in + *jungere* join]

in|junc|tive (in jungk′tiv), *adj.* serving to command.

in|jure (in′jər), *v.t.,* **-jured, -jur|ing.** **1** to do damage to; harm; hurt: *Do not break or injure the bushes in the park. The misunderstanding injured their friendship.* **2** to be unfair to; do wrong to: *Those that are not favoured will think themselves injured* (Samuel Johnson). [back formation < *injury*] —**in′jur|a|ble,** *adj.* —**in′jur|er,** *n.*

—*Syn.* **1 Injure, hurt, impair** mean to do harm or damage to someone or something. **Injure** implies any sort of damage, large or small: *Dishonesty injures a business.* **Hurt,** a less formal substitute for *injure,* particularly means to cause physical injury or bodily or mental pain to a person or animal: *He hurt my hand by twisting it.* **Impair** means to injure by weakening strength or value gradually in ways that cannot be remedied: *Poor eating habits impair health.*

in|ju|ri|ous (in jür′ē əs), *adj.* **1** causing injury; harmful: *Hail is injurious to crops.* SYN: hurtful, detrimental, deleterious, damaging. **2** unfair; unjust; wrongful: *Call him my king by whose injurious doom My elder brother ... Was done to death?* (Shakespeare). **3** *Obsolete.* willfully offensive in language; insulting. SYN: calumnious. [< Latin *injūriōsus* < *injūria;* see etym under **injury**] —**in|ju′ri|ous|ly,** *adv.* —**in|ju′ri|ous|ness,** *n.*

in|ju|ry (in′jər ē), *n., pl.* **-ries.** **1** hurt or loss caused to or endured by a person or thing; harm; damage: *He escaped from the train wreck without injury. The accident will be an injury to the reputation of the railroad.* **2** unfairness; wrong: *The saint never did injury to any man.* SYN: injustice. **3** *Law.* a wrong which furnishes grounds for a lawsuit. **4** *Obsolete.* intentionally offensive speech or words; insult. [< Latin *injūria,* (originally) feminine adjective < *in-* not + *jūs, jūris* right, law, justice]

in|jus|tice (in jus′tis), *n.* **1** lack of justice; being unjust: *Injustice is inevitable in war* (Atlantic). **2** an unjust act or circumstance; a wrong: *It is an injustice to send an innocent man to jail. A scientific man must expect his little disappointments and injustices* (Charles Kingsley).

ink (ingk), *n., v.* —*n.* **1** a colored or black liquid used for writing, printing, or drawing. **2** a dark liquid thrown out for protection especially by cuttlefish or squid.

—*v.t.* **1** to put ink on; mark or stain with ink: *A poor gentleman who inks the seams of his coat* (Herman Melville). **2** to cover (type, an engraving, or printing block) with ink to print with.

[< Old French *enque* < Late Latin *encaustum* < Greek *énkauston,* neuter adjective < stem of *enkaiein* burn in < *en-* in + *kaiein* to burn] —**ink′er,** *n.* —**ink′less,** *adj.* —**ink′like′,** *adj.*

ink|ber|ry (ingk′ber′ē), *n. pl.* **-ries.** **1** a holly of eastern North America, having shiny leathery evergreen leaves and small black berries. **2** its berry. **3** = pokeweed. **4** its berry.

ink|blot (ingk′blot′), *n.* **1** a spot or stain made with ink. **2** one of the designs or patterns used in the Rorschach test.

inkblot test, = Rorschach test.

ink|horn (ingk′hôrn′), *n., adj.* —*n.* a small container, often made of horn, formerly used to hold ink: *Pulling out an old inkhorn, he proceeded to fill out a bill of sale* (Harriet Beecher Stowe).

—*adj.* learned or bookish; pedantic.

inkhorn term, a learned or bookish term.

ink-jet (ingk′jet′), *adj.* of or having to do with a high-speed printing process using jets of ink broken up into electrically charged droplets that form letters and pictures on paper in a magnetic field regulated by a computer: *Ink-jet printers have to be used in conjunction with a computer* (New Scientist). *The ink-jet machines are appearing where high speed or automated typing is required* (Richard K. Pefley).

in|kle[1] (ing′kəl), *n.* **1** a narrow, colored linen tape. **2** the thread or yarn from which it is manufactured. [origin uncertain]

in|kle[2] (ing′kəl), *v.t., v.i.,* **-kled, -kling.** **1** to give a hint of; hint. **2** *Dialect.* to get an inkling or notion of. [Middle English *inclen* to whisper, hint < Old English *inca* suspicion]

ink|ling (ingk′ling), *n.* a vague notion; slight suspicion; hint: *to give a person an inkling of what is going on.* [< *inkl*(e)[2] + *-ing*[1]]

ink|sling|er (ingk′sling′ər), *n. Slang.* **1** a writer. **2** a clerk in a loggers' camp.

ink|stand (ingk′stand′), *n.* **1** a stand to hold ink and pens. **2** a container used to hold ink.

ink|well (ingk′wel′), *n.* a container used to hold ink on a desk or table.

ink|wood (ingk′wu̇d), *n.* a small tree of the soapberry family, found in the West Indies and southern Florida. It has hard, reddish-brown wood.

ink|y (ing′kē), *adj.,* **ink|i|er, ink|i|est.** **1** like ink; dark or black: *inky shadows.* **2** covered with ink; marked or stained with ink: *the inky hands of a printer.* **3** of ink; written with ink; using ink. **4** full of ink. —**ink′i|ly,** *adv.* —**ink′i|ness,** *n.*

inky cap, any one of a genus of mushrooms whose top disintegrates into a black liquid after the spores are discharged.

in|lace (in lās′), *v.t.,* **-laced, -lac|ing.** = enlace.

in|laid (in′lād′), *adj., v.* —*adj.* **1** set in the surface as a decoration or design: *The desk has an inlaid design of light wood in dark.* **2** decorated with a design or material set in the surface: *The wooden box has an inlaid top of silver.* —*v.* the past tense and past participle of **inlay:** *The workmen inlaid colored tiles in a design in the kitchen floor. The floor was inlaid with colored tiles.*

in|land (*adj.* in′lənd; *n., adv.* in′lənd, -land′), *adj., n., adv.* —*adj.* **1** away from the coast or the border; situated in the interior: *Illinois is an inland state. An inland waterway is a canal, river, or lake which may be used by boats or barges* (Edward J. Taaffe). **2** not foreign; domestic: *Commerce between the states of the United States is inland trade.*

—*n.* **1** the interior of a country; land away from the borders or the coast: *A wall sufficient to defend Our inland from the pilfering borderers* (Shakespeare). **2** *Obsolete.* the inlying districts near the capital and centers of population, as opposed to the remote or outlying wild parts.

—*adv.* in or toward the interior: *He traveled inland from New York to Chicago.*

in|land|er (in′lən dər), *n.* a person who lives in the interior of a country; inland inhabitant.

Inland Mails, *British.* domestic mails.

Inland Revenue, *British.* internal revenue.

in|law (in lô′), *v.t. Old English Law.* to clear of outlawry or attainder; restore to the protection of the law.

in-law (in′lô′), *n. Informal.* a person related by marriage: *The stories, which he has absorbed by listening to his wife and in-laws ...* (Atlantic).

in|law|ry (in′lô′rē), *n. Old English Law.* restoration to the protection of the law.

in|lay (in′lā′), *v.,* **-laid, -lay|ing,** *n., pl.* **-lays.** —*v.t.* **1** to set into the surface as a decoration or design: *The craftsman inlaid strips of gold in the top of the wooden box.* **2** to decorate with a design set in the surface: *to inlay a wooden box with gold.* **3** to insert (a page, picture, or notice) in a book in a heavy page which serves as a frame or mount. **4** to provide (a book) with such insertions. **5** *Horticulture.* to insert (a scion) into a slit in the bark of a stock.

—*n.* **1** an inlaid decoration, design, or material. **2** a shaped piece of gold or porcelain, cemented in a tooth as a filling. **3** an inlaid page, picture, or notice in a book. **4** *Horticulture.* a graft made by inlaying. —**in′lay′er,** *n.*

inlay graft, *Horticulture.* a graft made by inserting a scion into a slit in the bark of the stock.

in.-lb., inch-pound.

in|leak|age (in′lē′kij), *n.* **1** the act of leaking in: *... tightening up the system to avoid air inleakage* (C. Rogers McCullough). **2** something that leaks in. **3** the amount leaking in.

in|let (in′let), *n., v.,* **-let, -let|ting.** —*n.* **1** a narrow strip of water running from a larger body of water into the land or between islands: *The fishing village was on a small inlet of the sea.* SYN: arm. See picture under **bay**[1]. **2** a way of entering; entrance: *an inlet to a parking lot.* (*Figurative.*) *The bank was an inlet for a flood of paper money.* **3** a piece let in or inserted. **4** a letting in; admission.

—*v.t.* to let in; insert (one thing) in another.

in|li|er (in′lī′ər), *n. Geology.* a part of one formation completely surrounded by another formation of a later date.

in li|mi|ne (in lim′ə nē), *Latin.* **1** at the outset; at the start. **2** (literally) on the threshold.

in-line (in′līn′), *adj.* **1** operating on the same plane or from the same center, as parts of a gasoline engine, or a series of machines: *It is an in-line machine; that is, the frames are loaded at one end and leave, finished, at the other* (New Scientist). **2** *Electronics.* coaxial.

Pronunciation Key: hat, āge, cãre, fär; let, ēqual, tėrm; it, īce; hot, ōpen, ôrder; oil, out; cup, pu̇t, rüle; child; long; thin; ᴛʜen; zh, measure; ə represents **a** in about, **e** in taken, **i** in pencil, **o** in lemon, **u** in circus.

in loc. cit., in the place cited (Latin, *in loco citato*).

in lo|co (in lō′kō), *Latin.* in place; in the correct place.

in lo|co pa|ren|tis (in lō′kō pə ren′tis), *Latin.* in the place of a parent; as a parent: *At the heart of the matter is the colleges' role as guardians "in loco parentis," or substitute parents* (New York Times).

in|ly (in′lē), *adv., adj.* —*adv.* **1** inwardly; within: *What warm, poetic heart but inly bleeds, And execrates man's savage, ruthless deeds* (Robert Burns). **2** thoroughly; deeply. SYN: heartily, intimately, closely.
—*adj. Obsolete.* **1** inwardly felt; heartfelt: *the inly touch of love* (Shakespeare). **2** inward; interior; internal.
[Old English *inlīc,* adjective; *inlīce,* adverb]

in|mate (in′māt), *n.* **1** a person confined in a prison, asylum, or hospital. The inmates of a prison are confined for a declared period of time, while those of an asylum or hospital can leave whenever they are well. **2** a person who lives in the same building with another; occupant; inhabitant. [< *in-*[3] within + *mate*[1]]

in me|di|as res (in mē′dē əs rēz′; in me′dē äs räs′), *Latin.* in or into the midst of things; in the middle of the action, rather than at the beginning: *Having begun in medias res, with Yankee inventiveness as it was applied to beating the Redcoats in 1776, Mr. Fuller skips back to ... 1670* (Wall Street Journal).

in me|mo|ri|am (in mə môr′ē əm, -mōr′-) *Latin.* in memory (of); to the memory (of).

in|mesh (in mesh′), *v.t.* = enmesh.

in-mi|grant (in′mī′grənt), *n.* a person who moves to another community, county, state, or other area within the same country or territory.

in-mi|grate (in′mī′grāt), *v.i.,* **-grat|ed, -grat|ing.** to move into a new community, county, state, or other area within a country or territory. —**in′-mi·gra′tion,** *n.*

in|most (in′mōst), *adj.* **1** farthest in; deepest: *We went to the inmost depths of the mine.* **2** *Figurative.* most private; most secret: *one's inmost thoughts. Her inmost desire was to be an actress.* [alteration of Old English *innemest* < *inne* in + *-mest* -most]

inn (in), *n., v.* —*n.* **1** a place where travelers and others can get meals and a room to sleep in. Hotels have largely taken the place of the old inns. **2** a restaurant or tavern. **3** = Inn. **4** *Obsolete.* a place of sojourn, dwelling, or shelter of any kind.
—*v.t., v.i.* to lodge; put up (at an inn).
[Old English *inn* a lodging < *inne* in]

Inn (in), *n. Especially British.* **1** a place of residence for students (now retained only in names of buildings originally so used): *the Inns of Court.* **2** a legal society which owns such a building.

in|nards (in′ərdz), *n.pl. Informal.* **1** the internal parts of the body; inwards; viscera. **2** the internal parts of any complex mechanism or structure; workings: *With transistors instead of tubes in its innards ... the new machine will hum* (Harper's). [variant of *inwards*]

in|nate (i nāt′, in′āt), *adj.* **1** born in a person; natural: *A good artist has an innate talent for drawing. A good comedian has an innate wit.* SYN: native, inborn, inbred. **2** existing naturally in anything; inherent. **3** *Philosophy.* (of ideas or principles) present in the mind or soul as originally constituted or created; not learned or otherwise acquired. [< Latin *innātus* < *in-* in + *nāscī* be born] —**in|nate′ly,** *adv.* —**in|nate′ness,** *n.*

in|na|tive (i nā′tiv), *adj.* innate; native: *Some innative weakness there must be In him* (James Russell Lowell).

in|nav|i|ga|ble (i nav′ə gə bəl, in-), *adj.* not navigable: *th' innavigable lake* (John Dryden).

in|ner (in′ər), *adj., n.* —*adj.* **1** farther in; inside: *A closet is usually an inner room.* SYN: inward, internal, interior. **2** more intimate; more private; more secret. *She kept her inner thoughts to herself.* **3** of the mind or soul: *a person's inner life.* SYN: mental, spiritual.
—*n.* the inner or inside part of anything.
[Old English *innera,* comparative of *inne* within]
—**in′ner|ly,** *adv.* —**in′ner|ness,** *n.*

inner cabinet, *British.* a committee or other small group within an organization that performs unofficially the advisory function of a cabinet.

inner circle, a group of people who are closest to a center of power or influence or who have an intimate relationship to one another: *Most of [the President's] inner circle have been friends and confidants of the President's for years* (Hugh Sidey).

inner city, *Especially U.S.* **1** the central part of a large city or metropolitan area; the heart or core of a city. **2** this part characterized by congestion, poverty, dirt, and violence; the city slums: *The argument for building new colleges in the inner cities ... is that deprived youths who live there will otherwise have no chance to go to college* (Fred M. Hechinger).

in|ner-cit|y (in′ər sit′ē), *adj.* of or in an inner city: *An ambitious slum-clearance program ... held real hope of improving the lives of the inner-city poor* (Time).

inner core, the fourth layer and central portion of the earth; centrosphere. See picture under **core**[1].

in|ner-di|rect|ed (in′ər də rek′tid, -dī-), *adj.* guided in thought and action by one's own principles and values, apart from those of the community or one's associates: *The Brontës' genius was inner-directed* (Harper's). —**in′ner-di|rect′ed|ness,** *n.*

in|ner-di|rec|tion (in′ər də rek′shən, -dī-), *n.* the tendency to be inner-directed.

inner ear, the space in the bone behind the middle ear of man and other animals; labyrinth. It contains the organs of balance and the organs that change sound into nerve messages. The cochlea, vestibule, semicircular canals, and the sensory ends of the auditory nerve are the parts of the inner ear. See the diagram under **ear**[1].

Inner Light, 1 the light of Christ in the soul, acting as a spiritual guide (a Quaker use). **2** spiritual illumination.

inner liner, a band of soft rubber applied as an airtight seal on the casing of a pneumatic tire.

inner man, 1 the spiritual or mental side of man; the soul or mind: *This attracts the soul, Governs the inner man, the nobler part* (Milton). **2** *Informal.* a person's stomach; appetite.

in|ner|most (in′ər mōst), *adj., n.* —*adj.* farthest in; inmost: *the innermost parts of the machine.*
—*n.* the inmost part.
[Middle English *inner* + *-most,* Old English *innemest* inmost]

inner product, *Mathematics.* = dot product.

inner sanctum, *Informal.* a place of utmost privacy (usually used humorously).

in|ner|sole (in′ər sōl′), *n.* = insole.

inner space, 1 the space beneath the surface of the sea: *Like outer space, the inner space of the ocean is three-dimensional* (Newsweek). **2** the region of the mind beyond the surface; the subconscious. **3** the quality or suggestion of depth in an abstract painting.

in|ner|spring mattress (in′ər spring′), a mattress designed for greater elasticity, consisting of a framework of coiled wire springs, usually in addition to the hair or cotton stuffing.

inner table, the side of a backgammon board towards which each player's pieces are moved.

Inner Temple, 1 one of the four legal societies of London that constitute the Inns of Court. **2** the buildings belonging to it.

inner tube, a separate rubber tube inside the cover of a tire that is inflated with air.

in|ner|vate (i nėr′vāt, in′ər vāt), *v.t.,* **-vat|ed, -vat|ing. 1** to stimulate (an organ or muscle) through nerves: *The facial nerve innervates the muscles of expression.* **2** to supply (an organ or muscle) with nerves. [< *in-*[3] into + *nerv*(e) + *-ate*[1]]

in|ner|va|tion (in′ər vā′shən), *n.* **1** the stimulation of a muscle or organ by nerves. **2** the arrangement of nerves in a body or part of it.

in|ner|va|tion|al (in′ər vā′shə nəl), *adj.* **1** of or having to do with innervation. **2** characterized by innervation.

in|nerve (i nėrv′, in-), *v.t.,* **-nerved, -nerv|ing.** to supply with nervous energy; stimulate; invigorate. [< *in-*[3] into + *nerve*]

in|ness (in′nis), *n.* **1** the fact or condition of being in or inside; innerness. **2** *Informal.* the fact or condition of being up-to-date or fashionable: *How to get along with white hunters, barmen, muleteers, and where the best food and drink are to be found ... is our form of "inness"* (Harper's).

inn|hold|er (in′hōl′dər), *n.* = innkeeper.

In|nig|keit (in′iH kīt′), *n. German.* **1** depth of feeling. **2** (literally) intimacy.

in|ning (in′ing), *n.* **1** the time when each team is at bat in turn in baseball. **2** the turn of one side in a game; chance to play. **3** Usually, **innings.** *Figurative.* the time a person or party is in power; chance for action: *When our party lost the election, the other side had its innings.* **4** the act of taking in or enclosing, especially the reclaiming of marsh or flooded land. **5** the act of getting in, especially the gathering of crops; harvesting. [Old English *innung* a putting or getting in, ultimately < *in* in]

in|nings (in′ingz), *n.* **1** *British.* an inning in cricket. **2** lands taken in or reclaimed.

inn|keep|er (in′kē′pər), *n.* a person who owns, manages, or keeps an inn.

inn|keep|ing (in′kē′ping), *n.* the keeping of an inn; business of an innkeeper: *The secret of good innkeeping is to save money without letting the guests realize that any scrimping is going on* (Time).

in|no|cence (in′ə səns), *n.* **1** freedom from sin, wrong, or guilt: *The accused man proved his innocence of the crime.* SYN: guiltlessness. **2** lack of cunning; simplicity: *The saint had the innocence of a child.* SYN: naiveté, guilelessness, artlessness. **3** lack of sense; ignorance; silliness. **4** (of things) harmlessness; innocuousness. **5** an innocent person or thing. **6** = bluet. **7a** a small, slender annual herb of the figwort family, having a blue-and-white flower. **b** a closely related herb of California.

in|no|cen|cy (in′ə sən sē), *n., pl.* **-cies.** = innocence.

in|no|cent (in′ə sənt), *adj., n.* —*adj.* **1** doing no wrong or evil; free from sin or wrong; not guilty: *"I am not a thief!" the prisoner cried. "I am an innocent man!"* **2** without knowledge of evil: *A baby is innocent. The innocent brightness of a new-born day* (Wordsworth). **3** having or showing the simplicity and trusting nature of a child; guileless; naive: *For all she looks so innocent ... take my word for it she is no fool* (Sir Richard Steele). SYN: simple, artless, ingenuous. **4** doing no harm; harmless: *innocent amusements.* SYN: innocuous. **5** that does not transgress the law; lawful; not contraband: *innocent goods carried to a belligerent.* **6** spotless; stainless. **7** lacking in sense; silly; half-witted. **8** *Medicine.* not malignant: *an innocent tumor.*
—*n.* **1** an innocent person: *the souls of the poor innocents* (Jeremiah 2:34). **2** an idiot; fool; simpleton. **3a** a young child, not yet acquainted with evil. **b** a guileless, simple, or unsuspecting person: *He is more or less of a political innocent, a bystander* (Newsweek).
innocent of, lacking; devoid of; free from: *The sermon ... was quite innocent of meaning* (John Wesley).
innocents, *U.S.* the common bluet: *... filling his hat with wild violets, sorrel, and the frail, azure innocents* (Marion Harland).
[< Latin *innocēns, -entis* (literally) harmless < *in-* not + *nocēre* to harm < *necāre* kill] —**in′no·cent|ly,** *adv.*
—*Syn. adj.* **1 Innocent, blameless, guiltless** mean free from fault or wrong. **Innocent** implies having intended or consciously done no wrong, and therefore not deserving punishment for a particular offense: *The truck driver was proved innocent of manslaughter.* **Blameless** means neither at fault nor deserving blame, whether or not wrong has actually been done: *He was held blameless in the accident.* **Guiltless** is close in meaning to *innocent,* but emphasizes freedom from guilt or a feeling of guilt: *The other driver was not guiltless.*

in|noc|u|i|ty (i nok′yü ə tē), *n., pl.* **-ties. 1** innocuous quality; harmlessness: *Some vaccines have more innocuity and efficiency than others.* **2** a harmless, insignificant act or occupation: *The doctor said that smoking and eating too much are not the innocuities they seem to be.*

in|noc|u|ous (i nok′yü əs), *adj.* not hurtful or injurious; harmless: *She took my innocuous remark as an insult. ... wit ... like summer lightning, lambent but innocuous* (Edward M. Goulburn). SYN: inoffensive. [< Latin *innocuus* (with English *-ous*) < *in-* not + *nocuus* hurtful < *nocēre* to harm < *necāre* to kill] —**in|noc′u|ous|ly,** *adv.* —**in|noc′u|ous|ness,** *n.*

in|nom|i|nate (i nom′ə nit), *adj., n.* —*adj.* not named; unnamed; nameless; anonymous.
—*n.* an innominate bone, artery, or vein.
[< Late Latin *innōminātus* < Latin *in-* not + *nōmen, -inis* name]

innominate artery, an artery arising from the arch of the aorta. It divides into the right carotid and subclavian arteries.

innominate bone, either one of the two bones forming the sides of the pelvis in man and other mammals, each consisting of three consolidated bones (the ilium, ischium, and pubis); hipbone; coxa.

innominate vein, either one of the two veins formed by the junction of the subclavian and internal jugular veins. The innominate veins unite to form the superior vena cava.

in|no|vate (in′ə vāt), *v.,* **-vat|ed, -vat|ing.** —*v.i.* to make changes; bring in something new or new ways of doing things: *It is difficult to innovate when people prefer the old, familiar way of doing things. It were good ... that men in their innovations would follow the example of time itself, which indeed innovateth greatly, but quietly* (Francis Bacon).
—*v.t.* to introduce (something); bring in for the first time: *The scientist innovated new ways of research. Every moment alters what is done, And innovates some act till then unknown* (John Dryden).
[< Latin *innovāre* (with English *-ate*[1]) < *in-* (intensive) + *novus* new] —**in′no|va′tor,** *n.*

in|no|va|tion (in′ə vā′shən), *n.* **1** a change made in the established way of doing things: *The new* *principal made many innovations. The scheme of a Colony revenue by British authority appeared therefore to the Americans in the light of a great innovation* (Edmund Burke). SYN: novelty. **3** the act of making changes; bringing in new things or new ways of doing things: *Many people are opposed to innovation. Innovation is for showoffs and pioneers alike* (New Yorker).

in|no|va|tion|al (in′ə vā′shə nəl), *adj.* **1** of or having to do with innovation. **2** characterized by innovation.

in|no|va|tive (in′ə vā′tiv), *adj.* tending to innovate; characterized by innovation: *Inventors are innovative people.* —**in′no|va′tive|ness**, *n.*

in|no|va|to|ry (in′ə və tôr′ē, -tōr′), *adj.* characterized by innovation; innovative.

in|nox|ious (i nok′shəs, in-), *adj.* not noxious; harmless; innocuous. —**in|nox′ious|ly**, *adv.* —**in-nox′ious|ness**, *n.*

Inns of Court, **1** the four legal societies in London (Lincoln's Inn, the Inner Temple, the Middle Temple, and Gray's Inn) which have the exclusive privilege of calling students to the English bar, but instruction and examination for their students, formerly conducted by these societies, is now conducted by the Council of Legal Education. **2** the four buildings which belong to these societies.

in|nu|en|do (in′yü en′dō), *n., pl.* **-does**, *v.,* **-doed**, **-do|ing**. —*n.* **1** an indirect hint or reference. SYN: insinuation. **2** an indirect suggestion meant to discredit a person: *The gossipy old woman spread scandal by innuendoes. Their original meanings have been lost beneath layers of innuendo and insult* (Newsweek). **3** *Law.* **a** a parenthetical explanation or clarification of what certain expressions refer to, especially of allegedly defamatory words in a libel suit. **b** the expression so explained or clarified. **c** (originally) a formula used to introduce such an explanation or clarification, meaning "namely," "that is to say," etc.

—*v.i.* to make an innuendo or innuendoes: *There is a lot of gesturing, posturing, and innuendoing* (Wall Street Journal).

—*v.t.* to suggest by innuendo; hint at: [*He*] *would innuendo his own version of the story as dexterously as he could* (R. S. Surtees).

[< Latin *innuendō* (literally) by giving a nod to, ablative gerund of *innuere* nod to, signify < *in-* in + *-nuere* nod]

In|nu|it (in′yü it), *n., pl.* **-it** or **-its**. = Inuit.

in|nu|mer|a|ble (i nü′mər ə bəl, -nyü′-), *adj.* too many to count; very many; countless: *innumerable stars, innumerable troubles.* SYN: numberless, myriad. See syn. under **many**. —**in|nu′mer|a|ble-ness**, *n.* —**in|nu′mer|a|bly**, *adv.*

in|nu|mer|a|cy (i nü′mər ə sē, -nyü′-), *n.* the inability to understand or use mathematics. [patterned after *illiteracy*]

in|nu|mer|ate (i nü′mə rit, -nyü′-), *adj., n.* —*adj.* unable to understand or use mathematics: *Of course, there are brilliant teachers whose pupils do not end up innumerate* (New Scientist).

—*n.* an innumerate person: *We now have innumerates the way we used to have illiterates* (Norman Shrapnel).

[patterned after *illiterate*]

in|nu|mer|ous (i nü′mər əs, -nyü′-), *adj.* = innumerable.

in|nu|tri|tion (in′nü trish′ən, -nyü-), *n.* lack of nutrition; failure of nourishment.

in|nu|tri|tious (in′nü trish′əs, -nyü-), *adj.* supplying little or no nourishment; not nutritious.

inn|yard (in′yärd′), *n.* a yard around or next to an inn.

in|ob|serv|ance (in′əb zėr′vəns), *n.* **1** inattention; heedlessness. **2** neglect or failure to observe a law, custom, promise, or other obligation; nonobservance: *inobservance of the Sabbath.*

in|ob|serv|ant (in′əb zėr′vənt), *adj.* **1** = inattentive. **2** not observant; not quick to notice. SYN: unobserving.

in|ob|tru|sive (in′əb trü′siv), *adj.* not obtrusive; unobtrusive.

in|oc|cu|pa|tion (in′ok yə pā′shən), *n.* lack of occupation.

in|o|cer|a|mus (in′ə ser′ə məs, ī′nə-), *n.* any fossil bivalve mollusk of a group characteristic of the Cretaceous period. [< New Latin *Inoceramus* the genus name < Greek *îs, īnós* muscle + *kéramos* earthen vessel]

in|oc|u|la (i nok′yə lə), *n.* plural of **inoculum**.

in|oc|u|la|bil|i|ty (i nok′yə lə bil′ə tē), *n.* the quality of being inoculable.

in|oc|u|la|ble (i nok′yə lə bəl), *adj.* **1** that can be inoculated. **2** that can be infected or transmitted by inoculation.

in|oc|u|lant (i nok′yə lənt), *n.* a substance used in inoculating.

in|oc|u|late (i nok′yə lāt), *v.,* **-lat|ed**, **-lat|ing**. —*v.t.* **1** to give (to a person or animal) a preparation made from killed or weakened germs or viruses that causes a mild form of the disease. Thereafter the individual will not get that disease or will suffer only a very mild form of it. The preparation stimulates the body to produce antibodies to combat a germ, virus, or toxin. *You can take your child to the doctor to be inoculated against polio* (New York Herald Tribune). **2** to put bacteria, serums, or other agents, into. Farmers inoculate the soil with bacteria that will take nitrogen from the air and change it so it can be used by plants. **3** to introduce (microorganisms) into surroundings suited to their growth. **4** *Figurative.* to fill (a person's mind) with ideas, opinions, feelings, or habits: *His parents inoculated him with a desire for knowledge.* SYN: imbue. **5** *Obsolete.* to graft by budding.

—*v.i.* to use disease germs or a virus to prevent or cure diseases, usually by building up an immunity. Doctors inoculate against smallpox, diphtheria, typhoid fever, and other diseases.

[< Latin *inoculāre* (with English *-ate*[1]) engraft < *in-* in + *oculus* bud, eye]

in|oc|u|la|tion (i nok′yə lā′shən), *n.* **1** the act or process of inoculating, especially to prevent disease: *Inoculation has greatly reduced the number of deaths from diphtheria and typhoid fever.* **2** the bacteria, serums, or other agents, used in inoculating. **3** *Figurative.* a filling the mind with ideas, opinions, feelings, or habits: *a thorough inoculation with patriotism.*

in|oc|u|la|tive (i nok′yə lā′tiv), *adj.* of or having to do with inoculation.

in|oc|u|la|tor (i nok′yə lā′tər), *n.* a person or thing that inoculates.

in|oc|u|lum (i nok′yə ləm), *n., pl.* **-la**. the virus, bacteria, or other antigen used in inoculating: *Preparing an inoculum of penicillium spores . . . at an antibiotic plant at Ulverston, Lancashire* (London Times).

[< New Latin *inoculum* < Latin *inoculāre;* see etym. under **inoculate**]

in|o|dor|ous (in ō′dər əs), *adj.* not odorous; odorless. —**in|o′dor|ous|ness**, *n.*

in|of|fen|sive (in′ə fen′siv), *adj.* not offensive; not arousing objections; harmless: *an inoffensive animal, an inoffensive odor or taste, a mild, inoffensive man. "Please try to be quieter" is an inoffensive way of telling people to stop their noise.* SYN: innocuous, unobjectionable. —**in′of|fen′sive-ly**, *adv.* —**in′of|fen′sive|ness**, *n.*

in|of|fi|cial (in′ə fish′əl), *adj.* = unofficial.

in|of|fi|cious (in′ə fish′əs), *adj.* **1** *Law.* not in accordance with moral duty: *An inofficious testament or will is one which disposes of property contrary to the dictates of natural affection or to just expectations.* **2** without office or function. **3** not operative. **4** *Obsolete.* disobliging.

in om|ni|a pa|ra|tus (in om′nē ə pə rā′təs), *Latin.* prepared for all things; ready for anything.

in|op|er|a|bil|i|ty (in op′ər ə bil′ə tē), *n.* the condition of being inoperable.

in|op|er|a|ble (in op′ər ə bəl), *adj.* **1** unfit for a surgical operation, usually because of great extent of lesion or weakness of the patient; unable to be cured by surgery: *an inoperable tumor located deep in the brain.* **2** not operable; unworkable: *It has been cluttered up with so many restrictions and prohibitions that it is virtually inoperable* (Harper's).

in|op|er|a|tive (in op′ə rā′tiv, -op′rə-), *adj.* **1** not operative; not working; without effect: *The circuit whose operation depends upon the gate being opened remains inoperative until the correct stimulus is applied to the gate* (Science News Letter) SYN: ineffective. **2** *Law.* without practical force; invalid: *The resolutions . . . not having been so ratified, were inoperative* (Law Times). —**in|op′er-a′tive|ness**, *n.*

in|op|por|tune (in′op ər tün′, -tyün′; in op′-), *adj.* not opportune; coming at a bad time; unsuitable: *An inopportune telephone call delayed us just as we were about to begin our trip.* SYN: untimely, unseasonable, inappropriate, inconvenient. —**in|op′-por|tune′ly**, *adv.* —**in′op|por|tune′ness**, *n.*

in|op|por|tu|ni|ty (in′op ər tü′nə tē, -tyü′-; in op′-), *n.* the state of being inopportune.

in|orb (in ôrb′), *v.t. Poetic.* to encircle.

in|or|di|na|cy (in ôr′də nə sē), *n., pl.* **-cies**. **1** inordinate quality or condition. **2** an inordinate act.

in|or|di|nate (in ôr′də nit), *adj.* **1** much too great; not kept within proper limits; excessive: *He lost a fortune trying to satisfy his inordinate desire for gambling.* SYN: immoderate, intemperate, unrestrained. See syn. under **excessive**. **2** not properly regulated; irregular; disorderly: *Marcus Antonius . . . was indeed a voluptuous man, and inordinate* (Francis Bacon). [< Latin *inōrdinātus* < *in-* not + *ōrdō, -inis* row, order] —**in|or′di-nate|ly**, *adv.* —**in|or′di|nate|ness**, *n.*

inorg., inorganic.

in|or|gan|ic (in′ôr gan′ik), *adj., n.* —*adj.* **1** not organic; neither animal nor vegetable; not having the organized physical structure characteristic of animals and plants. Water and minerals are inorganic substances. **2** *Chemistry.* not containing organic matter. Chemical compounds without hydrocarbons are usually inorganic. **3** not characterized by the processes peculiar to living animals and plants. **4** not belonging to the constitution or structure of a thing; not fundamental; extraneous.

—*n.* an inorganic substance. —**in′or|gan′i|cal-ly**, *adv.*

inorganic chemistry, the branch of chemistry dealing with inorganic compounds and elements, primarily compounds not containing carbon.

in|or|gan|i|za|tion (in ôr′gə nə zā′shən), *n.* lack of organization.

in|or|gan|ized (in ôr′gə nīzd), *adj.* not organized.

in|or|nate (in′ôr nāt′), *adj.* not ornate; unadorned; plain: *inornate language.*

in|os|cu|late (in os′kyə lāt), *v.t., v.i.,* **-lat|ed**, **-lat-ing**. **1** to unite by openings: *to inosculate arteries with veins.* **2** to join or connect so as to become or make continuous; blend: *to inosculate fibers.* **3** to unite intimately. [< Latin *in-* in + Late Latin *osculāre* supply with a mouth (< *osculum* little mouth) + English *-ate*[1]] —**in|os′cu|la′tion**, *n.*

in|o|sine (in′ə sēn, -sin), *n.* a compound of hypoxanthine and ribose obtained from the deamination of adenosine. *Formula:* $C_{10}H_{12}N_4O_5$ [< Greek *îs, īnós* sinew, muscle + English *-ine*[2]]

in|o|site (in′ə sīt), *n.* = inositol.

in|o|si|tol (i nō′sə tōl, -tol), *n.* a white, crystalline alcohol found especially in certain muscle tissues and plants. It occurs in several isomeric forms and is one of the B-complex vitamins. *Formula:* $C_6H_{12}O_6 \cdot 2H_2O$ [< earlier *inosite* (< Greek *îs, īnós* sinew, muscle + English *-ite*) + *-ol*[1]]

in|o|trop|ic (in′ə trop′ik), *adj.* influencing or modifying the contractility of muscles: *an inotropic agent or compound.* [< Greek *îs, īnos* muscle + *trópos* turn, manner + English *-ic*]

in|ox|i|dize (in ok′sə dīz), *v.t.,* **-dized**, **-diz|ing**. to keep from oxidizing. —**in|ox′i|diz′a|ble**, *adj.*

in|paint (in pānt′), *v.t.* to repaint (a damaged part) in a painting: *The charred portions . . . would have to be filled with gesso and inpainted* (New Yorker).

in par|ti|bus in|fi|de|li|um (in pär′ti bus in fi dē′lē əm) or **in partibus**, *Latin.* in the regions of infidels; in countries inhabited by unbelievers: *bishops in partibus infidelium; . . . churchmen serving in partibus* (London Times).

in par|vo (in pär′vō), *Latin.* **1** in miniature: *Student governments often embody democracy in parvo.* **2** (literally) in little.

in|pa|tient (in′pā′shənt), *n.* a patient who is lodged and fed in a hospital while undergoing treatment: *A psychiatrist concluded that* [*she*] *needed more treatment than he could give her as an outpatient, but not enough to require admission to the full-time inpatient hospital* (Time).

in pec|to|re (in pek′tə rē, pek tôr′ā), *Latin.* **1** undisclosed; secret; in petto. **2** (literally) in the breast.

in per|pe|tu|um (in pər pet′yü əm, -pech′u̇ əm), *Latin.* **1** forever: *By "all of this" he meant the first-class funeral, the giant wreaths, the large plot they had purchased in perpetuum* (New Yorker). **2** as a perpetual possession.

in-per|son (in′pėr′sən), *adj.* done directly by a person; personal: *an in-person appearance.*

in per|so|nam (in pər sō′nam), *Latin.* against a specific person; against persons (used especially of a legal proceeding).

in pet|to (in pet′tō), *Italian.* **1** secret; not announced; undisclosed (used especially of cardinals appointed by the Pope but not named in consistory): *His very name had just become known in Rome, having been kept in petto by the dead Pontiff* (Time). **2** (literally) in the breast.

in|phase (in′fāz′), *adj.* of the same electric current phase.

in-pig (in pig′), *adj.* (of a pig) with young; pregnant.

in-plant (in′plant′), *adj.* within a factory or plant: *in-plant inspection.*

in pos|se (in pos′ē), *Latin.* in possibility; not yet actually existing; potentially.

in|pour (in′pôr′, -pōr′), *n., v.* —*n.* a pouring in; influx. SYN: inflow, inrush.

—*v.i., v.t.* to pour in.

in prae|sen|ti (in prē zen′tī), *Latin.* at the present time.

in-proc|ess (in′pros′es; *especially British* in′prō′-ses), *adj.* during or in the process of manufacturing: *to carry a greater proportion of in-process work inventory than formerly* (Wall Street Journal).

in pro|pri|a per|so|na (in prō′prē ə pər sō′nə),

Pronunciation Key: hat, āge, cãre, fär; let, ēqual, tėrm; it, īce; hot, ōpen, ôrder; oil, out; cup, pu̇t, rüle; child; long; thin; ᴛʜen; zh, measure; ə represents **a** in about, **e** in taken, **i** in pencil, **o** in lemon, **u** in circus.

Latin. in one's own person; in person; in one's own character.

in|put (in′pu̇t′), *n., v.,* **-put, -put|ting.** *—n.* **1** what is put in or taken in: *Get all the reluctant variables under control and measure the ... intellectual and emotional input* (Saturday Review). **2** the power supplied to a machine. **3** coded information put into a computer. **4** the point of putting in or taking in something such as information or power. **5** *Scottish.* a contribution.
—v.t., v.i. to put or be put into a computer or any system like that of a computer: *Part of the reason for the much faster rates at which data can be accepted by computers than by man is that data is carefully preprocessed before being input to a computer, whereas man has to extract information from the buzzing confusion of the real world* (Science Journal).

in|put-out|put analysis (in′pu̇t′out′pu̇t′), *Economics.* a method for studying the interdependence of all parts of the economy by analyzing the relationship between the total output of each industry and the size of its inputs, such as the raw materials and machinery used in production; interindustry analysis.

input-output coefficient, a coefficient used in input-output tables to measure the value of the purchases by one industry of another industry's products that are needed to produce $1000 worth of sales by the first industry.

input-output table, a numerical table which breaks down the economy into various industrial groups, used in input-output analysis.

in|quest (in′kwest), *n.* **1** a legal inquiry, especially before a jury: *An inquest was held to determine whether his death was the result of a crime.* **2** a jury appointed to hold such an inquiry. **3** the finding of a jury in such an inquiry. **4** an investigation: *The Republican Party held an inquest on the causes of its candidates' failure at the polls.* [< Old French *enqueste,* ultimately < Latin *inquīrere* inquire]

in|qui|e|tude (in kwī′ə tüd, -tyüd), *n.* uneasy feeling; restlessness. **SYN**: anxiety, uneasiness.

in|qui|line (in′kwə līn, -lin), *n., adj. Zoology. —n.* an animal that lives in the nest or shell of another, such as certain hymenopterous insects that inhabit the galls made by true gall insects; a commensal.
—adj. living in the nest or shell of another. [< Latin *inquilīnus* lodger < *in-* in + *colere* dwell]

in|qui|lin|i|ty (in′kwə lin′ə tē), *n.* the condition or the way of life of an inquiline.

in|qui|li|no (ēng′kē lē′nō), *n., pl.* **-nos.** a tenant farmer on a large estate in Chile. [< Spanish *inquilino* lodger < Latin *inquilīnus;* see etym. under **inquiline**]

in|qui|li|nous (in′kwə lī′nəs), *adj.* = inquiline.

in|quire (in kwīr′), *v.,* **-quired, -quir|ing.** *—v.t.* **1** to try to find out by questions; ask: *to inquire a person's name. The detective went from house to house, inquiring whether anyone had seen the lost boy.* **SYN**: See syn. under **ask. 2** *Obsolete.* to search for: *Well known to me the palace you inquire* (Alexander Pope). Also, **enquire.** *—v.i.* **1** to try to find out something by questions; ask: *If you lose your way, inquire at a service station.* **2** to make a search for information, knowledge, or truth: *The man read many old documents while inquiring into the history of the town.* **SYN**: search, seek.
inquire after, to ask how (a person) is; ask about one's welfare or health: *Everyone has been inquiring after you during your illness.*
[< Latin *inquīrere* < *in-* into + *quaerere* ask] **—in|quir′er,** *n.* **—in|quir′ing|ly,** *adv.*

in|quir|y (in kwīr′ē, in′kwər-), *n., pl.* **-quir|ies.** **1** the act of inquiring; asking: *Inquiry of the operator will get you the right telephone number.* **SYN**: interrogation. **2** a search for information, knowledge, or truth: *The research and inquiry into the whereabouts of the old treasure took years of work.* **SYN**: search, research, examination. See syn. under **investigation. 3** a question: *The guide answered all our inquiries.* Also, **enquiry.**

in|qui|si|tion (in′kwə zish′ən), *n.* **1** a thorough investigation; searching inquiry: *It is dangerous to institute an inquisition into the motives of individuals* (Edward Everett). **SYN**: examination, research. **2** an official investigation; judicial inquiry. **SYN**: inquest. **3** the finding in such an investigation. **4** the document recording such an investigation and its result. [< Latin *inquīsītiō, -ōnis* < *inquīrere* inquire]

In|qui|si|tion (in′kwə zish′ən), *n.* **1** a court appointed by the Roman Catholic Church about 1229-1231 to discover and suppress heresy, and to punish heretics. It was abolished in the 1800's. **2** the activities of this court.

in|qui|si|tion|al (in′kwə zish′ə nəl), *adj.* **1** = inquisitorial. **2** of or having to do with the Inquisition.

in|qui|si|tion|ist (in′kwə zish′ə nist), *n.* = inquisitor.

in|quis|i|tive (in kwiz′ə tiv), *adj., n. —adj.* **1** asking many questions; curious: *Children are usually inquisitive.* **SYN**: See syn. under **curious. 2** too curious; prying into other people's affairs: *The old lady was very inquisitive about what her neighbors were doing. The police are, I believe, proverbially inquisitive* (Lord Dunsany).
—n. an inquisitive person. **—in|quis′i|tive|ly,** *adv.* **—in|quis′i|tive|ness,** *n.*

in|quis|i|tor (in kwiz′ə tər), *n.* **1** a person who makes inquisition; official investigator. **2** an inquisitive person.

In|quis|i|tor (in kwiz′ə tər), *n.* a member of the Inquisition.

inquisitor general, a chief official of the court of Inquisition: *Tomás de Torquemada was appointed inquisitor general in 1483 and directed the Inquisition in most Spanish lands for 15 years.*

in|quis|i|to|ri|al (in kwiz′ə tôr′ē əl, -tōr′-), *adj.* **1** of an inquisitor or inquisition. **2** making searching inquiry; thorough. **3** unduly curious; prying. **4** *Law.* **a** having to do with a court proceeding in which the court is concerned with trying to discover if a fact is true. **b** having to do with a trial in which a person or group acts as both judge and prosecutor, or in which prosecution is conducted secretly. **—in|quis′i|to′ri|al|ly,** *adv.* **—in|quis′i|to′ri|al|ness,** *n.*

in re (in rē′, rā′), *Latin.* in the matter of; concerning.

in rem (in rem′), *Latin.* against a thing or person generally, as a right of property (used especially of a legal proceeding).

in re|rum na|tu|ra (in rir′əm nə tyu̇r′ə, -tu̇r′-), *Latin.* in the nature of things.

in-res|i|dence (in′rez′ə dəns), *adj.* residing in the place of duty or active work; resident: *an in-residence physician. Several* [*universities*] *now have professional schools staffed by in-residence acting companies* (Time).

in-res|i|den|cy (in′rez′ə dən sē), *n., pl.* **-cies.** the position of an in-residence professional or group of professionals: *... the many "in-residencies" on campuses by major American dance artists* (Saturday Review).

I.N.R.I. or **INRI** (no periods), Jesus of Nazareth, King of the Jews (Latin, *Iesus Nazarenus, Rex Iudaeorum*).

in|ro (in′rō), *n., pl.* **-ro.** a small ornamental nest of boxes, used to hold medicines, perfumes, and the like, and carried at the waist by Japanese. [< Japanese *inrō*]

in|road (in′rōd′), *n., v. —n.* **1** an attack or raid. **SYN**: incursion. **2** *Figurative.* encroachment by force: *The expenses of her illness made inroads upon the money that she had saved.*
—v.i. to make inroads.

in|run (in′run′), *n.* **1** the act or fact of running in; inrush. **2** *Skiing.* the incline leading to the take-off for a jump: *The hollow, rising hum of skies on the 130-foot-long wooden inrun ended ... as the jumper became airborne in the New Hampshire sky* (Newsweek).

in|rush (in′rush′), *n.* the act or fact of rushing in; inflow: *The inrush of water soon filled the pool. The Roman Imperial system dissolved under the barbarian inrush* (H. G. Wells).

in|rush|ing (in′rush′ing), *adj., n. —adj.* rushing in; entering with force or speed: *inrushing currents, an inrushing crowd.*
—n. = inrush.

ins (inz), *n.pl.* See under **in.**

ins., an abbreviation for the following:
1 inches.
2 inspector.
3a insulated. **b** insulation.
4 insurance.

in sae|cu|la sae|cu|lo|rum (in sek′yə lə sek′yə lôr′əm, -lōr′-), *Latin.* forever and ever; for ages and ages.

in|sal|i|vate (in sal′ə vāt), *v.t.,* **-vat|ed, -vat|ing.** to mix (food) with saliva in the chewing process. **—in|sal′i|va′tion,** *n.*

in|sa|lu|bri|ous (in′sə lü′brē əs), *adj.* unhealthful; unwholesome: *insalubrious living conditions.* **—in′sa|lu′bri|ous|ly,** *adv.*

in|sa|lu|bri|ty (in′sə lü′brə tē), *n.* unhealthfulness; unwholesomeness.

in|sal|u|tar|y (in sal′yə ter′ē), *adj.* not salutary; unwholesome; unfavorable.

in|sane (in sān′), *adj.* **1** not sane; mentally ill; crazy: *The judge declared the man insane and so not responsible for his actions.* **SYN**: demented, lunatic, mad. See syn. under **crazy. 2** for insane people: *Hospitals for people who are mentally ill are often called insane asylums.* **3** characteristic of one who is mentally ill: *an insane laugh.* **4** extremely foolish; completely lacking in common sense: *Nobody paid any attention to his insane plan for crossing the ocean in a canoe.* **SYN**: senseless, wild, irrational, idiotic. [< Latin *īnsānus* < *in-* not + *sānus* healthy, sound, sane] **—in|sane′ly,** *adv.* **—in|sane′ness,** *n.*

in|san|i|tar|y (in san′ə ter′ē), *adj.* not sanitary; not healthful. **SYN**: unhealthful. **—in|san′i|tar′i|ness,** *n.*

in|san|i|ta|tion (in san′ə tā′shən), *n.* lack of sanitation; insanitary condition.

in|san|i|ty (in san′ə tē), *n., pl.* **-ties. 1a** the condition of being insane; mental disorder; madness. **b** *Law.* any state of mental unsoundness, temporary or permanent, in which a person is not held responsible or considered competent: *The accused murderer insisted he had fired the shot during a fit of temporary insanity.* **2a** extreme folly; complete lack of common sense: *It is insanity to drive a car without any brakes.* **b** an instance of this.

in|sa|tia|bil|i|ty (in sā′shə bil′ə tē), *n.* insatiable quality.

in|sa|tia|ble (in sā′shə bəl), *adj.* that cannot be satisfied; extremely greedy; unquenchable: *The growing boy had an insatiable appetite.* **SYN**: unappeasable. **—in|sa′tia|ble|ness,** *n.* **—in|sa′tia|bly,** *adv.*

in|sa|ti|ate (in sā′shē it), *adj.* never satisfied: *A vain person has an insatiate desire for praise.* **SYN**: insatiable. **—in|sa′ti|ate|ly,** *adv.* **—in|sa′ti|ate|ness,** *n.*

in|scape (in′skāp′), *n.* an interior view or scene: *... the blank inscape of a man's mind* (Brendan Gill). [< *in* + *-scape*]

in|sce|na|tion (in′sē nā′shən), *n.* = mise en scène. [< *in-*³ + *scene* + *-ation*]

in|sci|ence (in′shē əns, -shəns), *n.* lack of knowledge; ignorance; nescience: *My narrative gradually progresses from inscience to awareness* (Sean O'Faolain). [< Latin *inscientia* < *īnsciēns;* see etym. under **inscient**]

in|sci|ent (in′shē ənt, -shənt), *adj.* not knowing; ignorant. [< Latin *īnsciēns, -entis* < *in-* not + *scīre* know]

in|scribe (in skrīb′), *v.t.,* **-scribed, -scrib|ing.** **1** to write, engrave, or mark (words, names, letters, or symbols) on stone, metal, paper, or other material: *Her name was inscribed on the ring. Please inscribe my initials on the watch.* **2** to mark or engrave (stone, metal, paper, or other material) with words, names, letters, or symbols: *How shall we inscribe the bracelet? His tombstone was inscribed with his name and the date of his death.* **3** to address or dedicate (a book, picture, or other work) informally to a person. **4** *Figurative.* to impress deeply: *My father's words are inscribed on my memory.* **5** to put in a list; enroll. **6** *Geometry.* to draw (one figure) within another figure so that the inner touches the outer at as many points as possible. **7** *British.* to register the names of the holders of (bonds, stocks, or other securities). [< Latin *īnscrībere* < *in-* on + *scrībere* write] **—in|scrib′a|ble,** *adj.* **—in|scrib′er,** *n.*

in|scrip|tion (in skrip′shən), *n.* **1** something inscribed; words, names, letters, or symbols, written or engraved on stone, metal, paper, or other material: *the inscription on a monument, the inscription on a coin, an inscription on an old temple.* **2** an informal dedication in a book, on a picture, or other work. **3** the act of writing upon or in something. **4** *British.* the registering of securities.
inscriptions, *British.* registered securities: *The inscriptions rose to forty.*
[< Latin *īnscrīptiō, -ōnis* < *īnscrībere* inscribe] **—in|scrip′tion|less,** *adj.*

in|scrip|tion|al (in skrip′shə nəl), *adj.* = inscriptive.

in|scrip|tive (in skrip′tiv), *adj.* of or having to do with inscription; used in inscriptions. **—in|scrip′tive|ly,** *adv.*

in|scroll (in skrōl′), *v.t.* to write on a scroll. Also, **enscroll.**

in|scru|ta|bil|i|ty (in skrü′tə bil′ə tē), *n., pl.* **-ties.** **1** the quality of being inscrutable. **2** something inscrutable.

in|scru|ta|ble (in skrü′tə bəl), *adj.* that cannot be understood; so mysterious or obscure that one cannot make out its meaning; incomprehensible: *... he faced the firing squad; erect and motionless, proud and disdainful ... inscrutable to the last* (James Thurber). *The historian undertook to make us intimately acquainted with a man singularly dark and inscrutable* (Macaulay). *A locust sang once or twice in some inscrutable seclusion of the tree* (Hawthorne). **SYN**: unfathomable, impenetrable, unintelligible. See syn. under **mysterious.** [< Late Latin *īnscrūtābilis* < Latin *in-* not + *scrūtārī* examine, search thoroughly < *scrūta,* plural, trash < Greek *grūtē* frippery, small wares] **—in|scru′ta|ble|ness,** *n.* **—in|scru′ta|bly,** *adv.*

in|sculp (in skulp′), *v.t.* to carve; engrave. [< Latin *īnsculpere* < *in-* on + *sculpere* carve, variant of *scalpere.* Compare etym. under **scalpel.**]

in|sculp|sit (in skulp′sit), *Latin.* (the person indicated) engraved it.

in·sculp·ture (in skulp′chər), *n., v.,* **-tured, -tur·ing.** *—n. Rare.* a carved or engraved figure or inscription.
—v.t. to carve; engrave.
[< obsolete French *insculpture,* ultimately < Latin *īnsculpere* < *in-* in + *sculpere* carve]

in·seam (in′sēm′), *n.* **1** the inner seam of a trouser leg from the bottom of the trouser to the crotch. **2** the forearm seam of a sleeve. **3** the inner seam of a shoe.

in-sea·son (in′sē′zən), *adj.* **1** in or for the period when something is in season; not off-season: *in-season travel, in-season hotel rates.* **2** (of a female animal) being in the estrus or heat period: *in-season vixen.*

***in·sect** (in′sekt), *n., adj. —n.* **1** any one of a group of small animals without a backbone and with the body divided into three parts (head, thorax, and abdomen). Insects have three pairs of legs, and usually two pairs of wings. Flies, mosquitoes, grasshoppers, gnats, bees, butterflies, and beetles are insects. Insects belong to the arthropods. **2** any similar small animal with its body divided into several parts, and with several pairs of legs, especially any one of the wingless forms having four pairs of legs. Spiders, centipedes, mites, and ticks are often called insects. **3** *Figurative.* an insignificant or despicable person.
—adj. **1** of or like an insect. **2** for insects: *an insect trap.*
[< Latin *(animal) īnsectum* (literally) divided (animal), neuter past participle of *īnsecāre* cut into < *in-* into + *secāre* cut (from the segmentation of its body)] **—in′sect·like′,** *adj.*

***insect**
definition 1

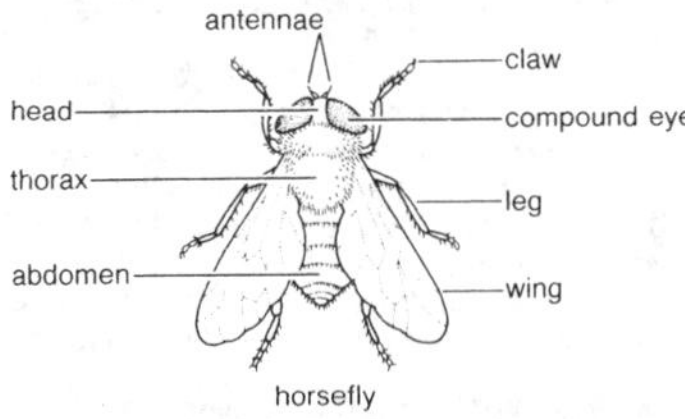

in·sec·tar·i·um (in′sek tãr′ē əm), *n., pl.* **-i·a** (-ē ə). a place for keeping, observing, and breeding insects. [< *insect* + *-arium,* perhaps patterned on *aquarium*]

in·sec·tar·y (in′sek ter′ē), *n., pl.* **-tar·ies.** = insectarium.

in·sec·ti·cid·al (in sek′tə sī′dəl), *adj.* having to do with the killing of insects.

in·sec·ti·cide (in sek′tə sīd), *n.* a substance for killing insects: *Insecticides have rescued millions of acres of forest from the gypsy moth and the spruce budworm* (Harper's). [< Latin *īnsectum* insect + English *-cide*¹]

in·sec·ti·fuge (in sek′tə fyüj), *n.* a substance or preparation for driving away insects. [< Latin *īnsectum* insect + *fugere* flee]

in·sec·tile (in sek′təl), *adj.* **1** of or like an insect. **2** consisting of insects.

in·sec·ti·val (in′sek tī′vəl, in sek′tə-), *adj.* of or having to do with an insect or insects.

in·sec·ti·vore (in sek′tə vôr, -vōr), *n.* **1** any animal or plant that feeds mainly on insects. Mantises are insectivores. **2** any one of an order of small mammals including moles, shrews, and hedgehogs that feed chiefly on insects at night. They are the least developed of the placental animals. [< French *insectivore,* learned borrowing from New Latin *insectivorus* insectivorous]

in·sec·tiv·o·rous (in′sek tiv′ər əs), *adj.* **1** insect-eating; feeding mainly on insects: *Flying insects . . . are eaten by such insectivorous birds of the treetops as warblers, vireos, orioles, and nuthatches* (Charles F. Wurster, Jr.). **2** of or belonging to the insectivores. [< New Latin *insectivorus* (with English *-ous*) < Latin *īnsectum* insect + *vorāre* devour; patterned on Latin *carnivorus* meat-eating]

in·sec·tol·o·gy (in′sek tol′ə jē), *n.* the scientific study of insects; entomology.

in·se·cure (in′si kyůr′), *adj.* **1** exposed as to danger, loss, or attack; not secure; unsafe: *a region where life is insecure.* SYN: See syn. under **uncertain. 2** liable to give way; not firm: *an insecure support, an insecure hold, an insecure lock.* **3** lacking confidence; not sure of oneself; fearful; timid: *an insecure person.* **—in′se·cure′ly,** *adv.* **—in′se·cure′ness,** *n.*

in·se·cu·ri·ty (in′si kyůr′ə tē), *n., pl.* **-ties. 1** lack of security; being insecure; unsafe condition. SYN: precariousness. **2** something insecure. SYN: hazard.

in·sel·berg (in′səl bėrg′), *n.* a stump or core of a mountain left rising above a surrounding plain primarily by the process of wind erosion. [< German *Inselberg* < *Insel* island + *Berg* mountain]

in·sem·i·nate (in sem′ə nāt), *v.t.,* **-nat·ed, -nat·ing. 1** to inject semen into; fertilize; impregnate. **2** to sow (seeds); implant. **3** *Figurative.* to fertilize; enrich: *Egyptian culture inseminated Crete and Greece* (Time). [< Latin *īnsēmināre* (with English *-ate*¹) < *in-* in + *sēmināre* to sow < *sēmen, -inis* seed] **—in·sem′i·na′tion,** *n.*

in·sem·i·na·tor (in sem′ə nā′tər), *n.* a person who or thing that inseminates, especially artificially in breeding animals.

in·sen·sate (in sen′sāt, -sit), *adj.* **1** without sensation; lifeless; inanimate: *insensate stones.* **2** unmoved; unfeeling; brutal: *insensate cruelty.* **3** senseless; stupid; foolish: *insensate folly. The insensate barbarous trade of war* (James Thomson). SYN: fatuous, asinine. **—in·sen′sate·ly,** *adv.* **—in·sen′sate·ness,** *n.*

in·sen·si·bil·i·ty (in sen′sə bil′ə tē), *n.* **1** lack of feeling; unawareness. SYN: apathy. **2** lack of consciousness; senselessness.

in·sen·si·ble (in sen′sə bəl), *adj.* **1a** not sensitive; not able to feel or notice: *insensible to cold. A blind man is insensible to colors.* **b** without emotion; unmoved; callous: *a cold, insensible man. A lifetime as a soldier had not made him insensible to the suffering and sorrow of war.* **2** not aware; indifferent: *The boys in the boat were insensible of the danger. Nothing disturbs the tranquillity of their souls, equally insensible to disasters and to prosperity* (Washington Irving). **3** not able to feel anything; unconscious; senseless: *The man hit by the truck was insensible for four hours.* **4** not easily felt; too slow to be noticed; imperceptible: *The room grew cold by insensible degrees as the sun went down.* **5** = nonmaterial. **6** *Obsolete.* unintelligible. **—in·sen′si·bly,** *adv.*

in·sen·si·tive (in sen′sə tiv), *adj.* **1** not sensitive; without feeling: *an insensitive area of the skin, insensitive to light.* **2** slow to feel or notice: *insensitive to the power of music.* **—in·sen′si·tive·ly,** *adv.* **—in·sen′si·tive·ness,** *n.*

in·sen·si·tiv·i·ty (in sen′sə tiv′ə tē), *n.* insensitive condition or quality.

in·sen·ti·ence (in sen′shē əns, -shəns), *n.* **1** lack of sensation. **2** = inanimateness.

in·sen·ti·en·cy (in sen′shē ən sē, -shən-), *n.* = insentience.

in·sen·ti·ent (in sen′shē ənt, -shənt), *adj.* unable to feel; inanimate; lifeless: *She had seen herself sunning on deck . . . insentient with ease* (New Yorker).

in·sep·a·ra·bil·i·ty (in sep′ər ə bil′ə tē, -sep′rə-), *n.* the state of being inseparable.

in·sep·a·ra·ble (in sep′ər ə bəl, -sep′rə-), *adj.* **1** that cannot be separated; not separable: *inseparable parts. Heat is inseparable from fire.* SYN: indivisible. **2** constantly together: *The two friends are inseparable companions.* **—in·sep′a·ra·ble·ness,** *n.* **—in·sep′a·ra·bly,** *adv.*

in·sep·a·ra·bles (in sep′ə rə bəls, -sep′rə-), *n.pl.* inseparable persons or things.

in·sert (*v.* in sėrt′; *n.* in′sėrt), *v., n. —v.t.* to put in; set in; introduce: *He inserted the key into the lock. He inserted a letter into the misspelled word.*
—n. **1** something set in or to be set in: *The book contained an insert of several pages of pictures.* **2** *Journalism.* material written for insertion in the body of a completed story.
[< Latin *īnsertus,* past participle of *īnserere* put in < *in-* in + *serere* entwine, join] **—in·sert′er,** *n.*

in·sert·ed (in sėr′tid), *adj.* **1** *Botany.* attached to or common with some part: *The calyx, corolla, and stamens of many flowers are inserted on the receptacle.* **2** *Anatomy.* joined at a specific point; attached, as a muscle.

in·ser·tion (in sėr′shən), *n.* **1** the act of inserting: *The insertion of one word can change the meaning of a whole sentence.* **2** something inserted. **3** a band of lace or embroidery to be sewed at each edge between parts of other material. **4** each printing of an advertisement, as in a newspaper. **5** *Biology.* the place or manner of attachment of an organ, part, or tissue. **6** *Anatomy.* the part of a muscle attached to the bone or some other part that it moves. **7** the act or process of placing a spacecraft into orbit; injection.

in-serv·ice (in′sėr′vis), *adj.* taking place or acquired on the job: *. . . an extensive in-service training program for men and women already employed* (New York Times).

in·ses·so·ri·al (in′se sôr′ē əl, -sōr′-), *adj.* **1** habitually perching, as certain birds do. **2** adapted for perching: *insessorial feet.* [< Latin *īnsessor, -ōris* occupant (< *īnsidēre* < *in-* on + *sedēre* sit) + English *-ial*]

***in·set** (*v.* in set′, in′set′; *n.* in′set′), *v.,* **-set, -set·ting,** *n. —v.t.* to set in; insert.
—n. **1** something inserted: **a** a smaller map, picture, or diagram inserted within the border of a larger one. **b** an extra leaf or leaves inserted in a folded sheet or a book before binding. **c** a piece of cloth inserted into a garment. **2** an inflow; influx.

***inset**
definition 1a

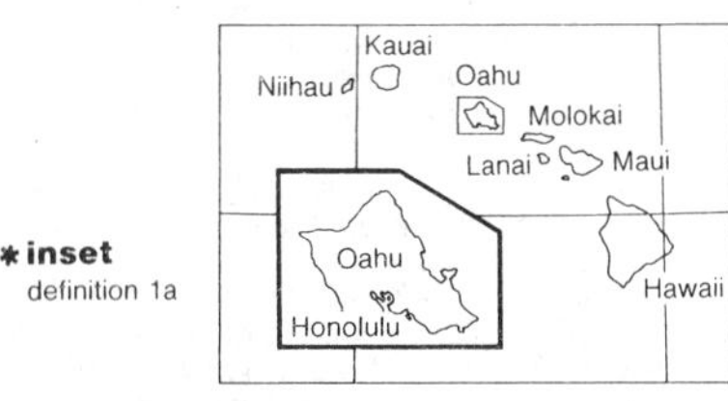

in·sev·er·a·ble (in sev′ər ə bəl), *adj.* that cannot be severed. **—in·sev′er·a·bly,** *adv.*

in·shal·lah (in′shä lä′), *interj. Arabic.* God willing.

in·sheathe (in shēᴛʜ′), *v.t.,* **-sheathed, -sheath·ing.** to cover with a sheath; ensheathe.

in·shoot (in′shüt′), *n. Baseball.* an incurve.

in·shore (in′shôr′, -shōr′), *adj., adv. —adj.* near the shore: *Inshore fishing is not allowed where people swim. —adv.* in toward the shore: *The boat was driven inshore by the winds.*

in·side (*n., adj.* in′sīd′; *adv., prep.* in′sīd′), *n., adj., adv., prep. —n.* **1a** the part within; inner surface: *the inside of a house. The inside of a sidewalk is the part farthest from the road. The inside of a seat or row of seats is the part away from the window or the aisle. The inside of the box was lined with colored paper.* **b** the contents: *The inside of the book was more interesting than the cover.* **c** *Figurative.* the members, employees, or officers who make up a government, or other organization: *If the movement had to be cleaned up it should be done from the inside* (London Times). **2** the inward nature or meaning. **3** *Informal, Figurative.* those who are in a position to know about something or who are in a position of authority. **4** *Printing.* the side of a sheet containing the second page.
—adj. **1** being on the inside: *an inside seat, inside layers.* SYN: internal. **2** of or used for the inside: *an inside paint.* SYN: interior. **3** *Figurative.* **a** done or known by those inside; secret; private: *inside information. The police thought that the theft was an inside job and suspected the maid.* **b** *Slang.* working within a group or company as an emissary or spy: *an inside man.* **4** barely within the utmost limit; smallest: *an inside chance of winning.* **5** working indoors; indoor. **6** that is nearer the center of a curve: *The left-hand wheels are the inside wheels in a turn to the left.* **7** *Baseball.* **a** (of a pitch) close to the batter and missing the strike zone. **b** (of a part of home plate) on the same side as the batter.
—adv. **1** on or to the inside; within; in the inner part: *Please step inside.* **2** = indoors.
—prep. inside of; within the limits of; in: *The nut is inside the shell.*
inside of, *Informal.* in; within the limits of: *They should be back inside of an hour.*
inside out, a so that what should be inside is outside; with the inside showing: *He turned his pocket inside out.* **b** completely; thoroughly: *He learned his lessons inside out. We know the D major and the "Emperor" inside out, backwards and forwards* (Harper's).
insides, *Informal.* the parts inside the body, especially the stomach and bowels: *My insides are out of order* (Frederick Marryat).
—in′side·ness, *n.*

in·sid·er (in′sī′dər), *n.* **1** a person who belongs to a certain club, society, organization, political party, or other group. **2** a major stockholder, director, or officer of a company. **3** a person who has private or secret information about something not known to most others: *Washington insiders.*

insider trading, the buying and selling of stock on the basis of information obtained from persons with secret knowledge of a company's action that is likely to change its stock price on the market. Insider trading is now illegal in the United States. **—insider trader**

in·sides (in′sīdz′), *n.pl.* See under **inside.**

inside skinny, *U.S. Slang.* secret or confidential information.

inside track, 1 the lane nearest the inside of the curve on a race track; the shorter side of the track. **2** *Informal, Figurative.* a position of advantage: *Experts figure American firms would have an inside track on "big orders" for the earthmoving gear and other equipment needed* (Wall Street Journal).

Pronunciation Key: hat, āge, cãre, fär; let, ēqual, tėrm; it, īce; hot, ōpen, ôrder; oil, out; cup, pu̇t, rüle; child; long; thin; ᴛʜen; zh, measure; ə represents **a** in about, **e** in taken, **i** in pencil, **o** in lemon, **u** in circus.

in|sid|i|ous (in sid′ē əs), *adj.* **1** seeking to entrap or ensnare; wily or sly; crafty; tricky; treacherous: *an insidious foe.* SYN: cunning, underhand. **2** working secretly or subtly; developing without attracting attention; more dangerous than is apparent: *He died of an insidious disease before the doctors realized he was sick.* [< Latin *īnsidiōsus* < *īnsidiae,* plural, ambush < *īnsidēre* sit in < *in-* in + *sedēre* sit] —**in|sid′i|ous|ly,** *adv.* —**in|sid′i|ous|ness,** *n.*

in|sight (in′sīt′), *n.* **1** a viewing of the inside or inner parts (of something) with understanding: *Take the machine apart and get an insight into how it works.* **2** wisdom and understanding in dealing with people or with facts: *We study science to gain insight into the world we live in.* **3** *Psychology.* **a** the relatively sudden awareness of a solution. **b** understanding of oneself. **4** *Psychiatry.* a patient's recognition and understanding of his condition. —**in′sight′less,** *adj.*

—*Syn.* **2 Insight, discernment, penetration** mean ability to understand people or things. **Insight** implies both the power to see deeply and sympathetic understanding: *Good teachers have insight into the problems of students.* **Discernment** emphasizes the power to make accurate judgments: *He shows discernment in selecting employees.* **Penetration** emphasizes the ability to go deeply into things and to see fine distinctions and relations: *The detective's solution of the mystery required many hours of thoughtful penetration.*

in|sight|ful (in′sīt′fəl), *adj.* having insight; penetrating; perceptive.

insight learning, *Psychology.* behavioral change involving the apparent sudden awareness of the solution to a problem, as distinguished from arrival at the solution by trial and error.

in|sig|ne (in sig′nē), *n.* singular of **insignia**: *The insigne on his sleeve reads "volunteer"* (New York Times).

►Although rarely used, the singular **insigne** is still occasionally referred to by those writers and speakers who regard *insignia* as a plural. See also the usage note under **insignia.**

in|sig|ne cum lau|de (in sig′nē kum lô′dē; in-sig′ne kům lou′de), *Latin.* with very high honor.

in|sig|ni|a (in sig′nē ə), *n., pl. of* **in|sig|ne,** also *pl.* **-as** (when *insignia* is considered singular). **1** the medals, emblems, badges, or other distinguishing marks of a position, some honor, or a military order: *The crown and scepter are the insignia of kings. White stripes on the cuff are the seamen's insignia of rating* (Thomas E. Griess). **2** *Figurative.* the marks or signs of anything: *Rags . . . are the Beggar's robes, and graceful insignia of his profession* (Charles Lamb). [< Latin *īnsignia,* neuter plural of *īnsigne* badge, mark < *in-* on + *signum* mark. See etym. of doublet **ensign.**]

►**Insignia,** although plural in form, is often used as a singular, with **insignias** as its plural: *His insignia is a cross. The PX sold all sorts of insignias.* Several outstanding authors of the 1800's have used *insignia* as a singular, but this has been regarded as erroneous by some writers and speakers who still tend to avoid such usage.

in|sig|nif|i|cance (in′sig nif′ə kəns), *n.* **1** unimportance; uselessness. SYN: triviality. **2** meaninglessness. SYN: senselessness.

in|sig|nif|i|can|cy (in′sig nif′ə kən sē), *n., pl.* **-cies.** **1** = insignificance. **2** an unimportant or contemptible thing or person.

in|sig|nif|i|cant (in′sig nif′ə kənt), *adj.* **1** having little importance or influence: *The ideas of an insignificant person have no influence.* **2** too small to be important; trivial: *an insignificant detail. A tenth of a cent is an insignificant amount of money.* SYN: petty, trifling, immaterial. **3** having little meaning; meaningless: *insignificant chatter, an insignificant gesture.* —**in′sig|nif′i|cant|ly,** *adv.*

in|sin|cere (in′sin sir′), *adj.* not sincere; not honest or candid; deceitful: *The insincere way he said he was sorry made me doubt that he really was sorry.* SYN: hypocritical, dissembling, false, disingenuous. —**in′sin|cere′ly,** *adv.*

in|sin|cer|i|ty (in′sin ser′ə tē), *n., pl.* **-ties.** **1** lack of sincerity; being insincere; hypocrisy. **2** an act or instance of hypocrisy; pretense: *He raised his voice unceasingly in condemnation of the fashionable insincerities of his day* (Austin Dobson).

in|sin|u|ate (in sin′yů āt), *v.,* **-at|ed, -at|ing.** —*v.t.* **1** to suggest in an indirect way; hint: *To say "That man can't do it; no coward can" is to insinuate that the man is a coward. Without making any direct charges, he insinuated that the mayor had accepted bribes.* SYN: imply. See syn. under **hint.** **2** to push in or get in by an indirect, twisting way: *The stray cat insinuated herself into our kitchen. The spy insinuated himself into the confidence of important army officers.*

—*v.i.* **1** to make hints or indirect suggestions. **2** *Obsolete.* **a** to ingratiate oneself. **b** to get in by an indirect or twisting way.

[< Latin *īnsinuāre* (with English *-ate*[1]) < *in-* in + *sinus, -ūs* a curve, winding] —**in|sin′u|at′ing|ly,** *adv.* —**in|sin′u|a′tor,** *n.*

in|sin|u|a|tion (in sin′yů ā′shən), *n.* **1** the act of insinuating: *the insinuation of oneself into the confidence of others.* **2** an indirect suggestion meant to discredit someone: *The student objected strongly to the insinuation of dishonesty.* **3** a hint; suggestion. SYN: implication. **4** an act or speech to gain favor in an indirect, subtle way.

in|sin|u|a|tive (in sin′yů ā′tiv), *adj.* **1** insinuating; ingratiating. **2** subtly suggesting or hinting.

in|sin|u|a|to|ry (in sin′yů ə tôr′ē, -tōr′-), *adj.* = insinuative.

in|sip|id (in sip′id), *adj.* **1** without any particular flavor; tasteless: *A mixture of milk and water is an insipid drink.* SYN: flat. **2** *Figurative.* lacking interest or spirit; dull; uninteresting, colorless, or weak: *His insipid conversation bored everyone. A faded beauty . . . Insipid as the queen upon a card* (Tennyson). SYN: stupid, vapid, lifeless. [< Late Latin *īnsipidus* < Latin *in-* not + *sapidus* tasty < *sapere* to taste] —**in|sip′id|ly,** *adv.* —**in|sip′id|ness,** *n.*

in|si|pid|i|ty (in′si pid′ə tē), *n., pl.* **-ties.** **1** lack of flavor; lack of interest. **2** something insipid.

in|sip|i|ence (in sip′ē əns), *n.* lack of wisdom; foolishness; folly. [< Latin *īnsipientia* < *īnsipiēns, -entis* < *in-* not + *sapere* have judgment]

in|sip|i|ent (in sip′ē ənt), *adj.* not wise; foolish.

in|sist (in sist′), *v.i.* **1** to keep firmly to some demand, some statement, or some position: *He insists on playing another game. The accused man insisted on his innocence.* SYN: urge, persist, press. **2** to dwell at length or with emphasis: *to insist on a point in a lecture.* **3** *Archaic.* to persevere. —*v.t.* to maintain or demand persistently: *He insists that he had a right to use his brother's tools. Mother insists that we wash our hands before eating.*

[< Latin *īnsistere* < *in-* on + *sistere* take a stand < *stāre* to stand] —**in|sist′er,** *n.* —**in|sist′ing|ly,** *adv.*

in|sist|ence (in sis′təns), *n.* **1** the act of insisting: *We remembered Mother's insistence that we wash before eating.* **2** the quality of being insistent. SYN: urgency, pertinacity.

in|sist|en|cy (in sis′tən sē), *n., pl.* **-cies.** = insistence.

in|sist|ent (in sis′tənt), *adj.* **1** continuing to make a strong, firm demand or statement; insisting: *In spite of the rain he was insistent on going out.* SYN: persistent. **2** compelling attention or notice; pressing; urgent: *We heard insistent calls of "Help! Help!" There was an insistent knocking on my door.* —**in|sist′ent|ly,** *adv.*

in|si|ti|tious (in′si tish′əs), *adj.* introduced from without; inserted: *insititious passages in a text.* [< Latin *īnsitīcius* (with English *-ous*) < *īnserere* to insert]

in si|tu (in sī′tü, -tyü), *Latin.* in its original place; in position: *Here and there, one can see Graeco-Roman-Buddhist remains in situ* (New Yorker).

in|snare (in snãr′), *v.t.,* **-snared, -snar|ing.** = ensnare. —**in|snare′ment,** *n.*

in|snar|er (in snãr′ər), *n.* = ensnarer.

in|so|bri|e|ty (in′sə brī′ə tē), *n.* intemperance; drunkenness.

in|so|cia|bil|i|ty (in sō′shə bil′ə tē), *n.* = unsociability.

in|so|cia|ble (in sō′shə bəl), *adj. Rare.* unsociable: *this austere insociable life* (Shakespeare). —**in|so′cia|bly,** *adv.*

in|so|cial (in sō′shəl), *adj.* = unsocial.

in|so|far (in′sō fär′), *adv.,* or **in so far,** to such an extent or degree (usually followed by *as*): *Insofar as I can tell, the weather should be pleasant tomorrow.*

insol., insoluble.

in|so|late (in′sō lāt), *v.t.,* **-lat|ed, -lat|ing.** to expose to the sun's rays for drying or bleaching. [< Latin *īnsōlāre* (with English *-ate*[1]) < *in-* in + *sōl, sōlis* sun]

in|so|la|tion (in′sō lā′shən), *n.* **1** exposure to the sun's rays for drying or bleaching. **2** *Meteorology.* the amount of solar radiation per unit of horizontal surface in a given time. **3** medical treatment by exposure to the sun's rays. **4** = sunstroke.

in|sole (in′sōl′), *n.* **1** the inner sole of a shoe or boot. **2** a layer of warm or waterproof material put on the sole inside a shoe or boot. Also, **inner-sole.**

in|so|lence (in′sə ləns), *n.* **1** bold rudeness; insulting behavior or speech; intentional disregard of the feelings of others. SYN: effrontery. **2** *Obsolete.* pride; arrogance.

in|so|lent (in′sə lənt), *adj., n.* —*adj.* **1** boldly rude; intentionally disregarding the feelings of others; insulting: *an insolent fellow, an insolent remark. "Shut up!" the insolent boy said to his father.* SYN: impudent. **2** *Obsolete.* arrogant; overbearing: *How insolent is upstart pride* (John Gay).

—*n.* an insolent person.

[< Latin *īnsolēns, -entis* (literally) unusual < *in-* not + *solēre* be accustomed] —**in′so|lent|ly,** *adv.*

in|sol|u|bil|i|ty (in′sol yə bil′ə tē, in sol′-), *n.* insoluble condition or quality.

in|sol|u|bil|ize (in sol′yə bə līz), *v.t.,* **-ized, -iz|ing.** *Chemistry.* to make (a substance) insoluble. —**in-sol′u|bil|i|za′tion,** *n.*

in|sol|u|ble (in sol′yə bəl), *adj.* **1** that cannot be dissolved; not soluble: *Diamonds are insoluble. Fats are insoluble in water.* **2** that cannot be solved; unsolvable: *The detective finally gave up, declaring the mystery insoluble.* **3** that cannot be undone or loosened. —**in|sol′u|ble|ness,** *n.* —**in-sol′u|bly,** *adv.*

in|solv|a|ble (in sol′və bəl), *adj.* that cannot be solved: *an insolvable problem.* —**in|solv′a-bly,** *adv.*

in|sol|ven|cy (in sol′vən sē), *n., pl.* **-cies.** the condition of not being able to pay one's debts; bankruptcy.

in|sol|vent (in sol′vənt), *adj., n.* —*adj.* **1** not able to pay one's debts; bankrupt: *an insolvent estate, an insolvent business. We see that most nations are insolvent, cannot satisfy their own wants* (Emerson). **2** of or having to do with bankrupt persons or bankruptcy.

—*n.* an insolvent person.

in|som|ni|a (in som′nē ə), *n.* inability to sleep; sleeplessness. [< Latin *īnsomnia* < *īnsomnis* sleepless < *in-* not + *somnus* sleep]

in|som|ni|ac (in som′nē ak), *n.* a person who has insomnia.

in|som|ni|ous (in som′nē əs), *adj.* having insomnia.

in|so|much (in′sō much′), *adv.* in such a way; to such an amount; so: *And he answered him to never a word; insomuch that the governor marvelled greatly* (Matthew 27:14).

insomuch as, **a** inasmuch as; seeing that; since: *The present law is inoperative, insomuch as the Universities . . . contain teachers who have never subscribed this famous confession* (Westminster Review). **b** to such an extent as; so as: *They attribute their fortune to . . . a lucky or unlucky place [etc.] . . . insomuch as to believe they have the power to turn a stone into bread* (Thomas Hobbes).

in|sou|ci|ance (in sü′sē əns), *n.* freedom from care or anxiety; carefree feeling: *The letter . . . suggests in its air of gay insouciance something of their mutual sympathy and complete understanding* (Atlantic). SYN: indifference, unconcern.

in|sou|ci|ant (in sü′sē ənt), *adj.* free from care or anxiety; carefree: *This insouciant, light-tempered, gay, and thoughtless disposition conducted René . . . to a hale and mirthful old age* (Scott). SYN: indifferent, unconcerned. [< French *insouciant* < *in-* not, in-[1] + *souciant,* present participle of Old French *soucier* to care, ultimately < Latin *sollicitus* solicitous] —**in|sou′ci|ant|ly,** *adv.*

in|soul (in sōl′), *v.t.* **1** to put in the soul. **2** to endow with a soul. Also, **ensoul.**

insp., inspector.

in|span (in span′), *v.t., v.i.,* **-spanned, -span|ning.** (in South Africa) to yoke (oxen) or harness (horses) to a wagon. [< Afrikaans *inspannen* < Dutch < *in-* in + *spannen* to span[2], bend]

in|spect (in spekt′), *v.t.* **1** to look over carefully; examine: *A dentist inspects my teeth twice a year.* SYN: scan, scrutinize. **2** to examine formally or officially: *Government officials inspect all factories and mines to make sure that they are safe for workers.* [< Latin *īnspectus,* past participle of *īnspicere* < *in-* upon + *specere* look] —**in|spect′-a|ble,** *adj.*

in|spec|tion (in spek′shən), *n.* **1** the act of inspecting; examination: *An inspection of the roof showed no leaks.* **2** a formal or official examination: *The soldiers lined up for their daily inspection by their officers.* **3** a district under an inspector.

in|spec|tion|al (in spek′shə nəl), *adj.* of or having to do with inspection.

in|spec|tive (in spek′tiv), *adj.* given to inspection; watchful; attentive.

in|spec|tor (in spek′tər), *n.* **1** a person who inspects: *The inspector discarded several defective watches on the production line.* **2** an officer appointed to inspect: *a government meat inspector.* **3** a police officer, usually ranking next below a superintendent.

[< Latin *īnspector, -ōris* < *īnspicere;* see etym. under **inspect**]

in|spec|tor|al (in spek′tər əl), *adj.* of or belonging to inspectors.

in|spec|tor|ate (in spek′tər it), *n.* **1** the office or function of an inspector. **2** a group of inspectors. **3** a district under an inspector. [< *inspector* + *-ate*[3]]

inspector general, **1** an officer charged with the supervision of some system of inspection. **2** *U.S.* an officer of the Army, Navy, or Air Force who inspects installations of his branch of the armed forces.

in|spec|tor|i|al (in′spek tôr′ē əl, -tōr′-), *adj.* **1** of or having to do with inspectors. **2** having the rank or position of an inspector.

in|spec|tor|ship (in spek′tər ship), *n.* the office of an inspector.

Insp. Gen., Inspector General.

in|sphere (in sfir′), *v.t.*, **-sphered, -spher|ing.** = ensphere.

in|spir|a|ble (in spīr′ə bəl), *adj.* that can be inspired.

in|spi|ra|tion (in′spə rā′shən), *n.* **1** the influence of thought and strong feelings on actions, especially on good actions: *Some people get inspiration from sermons, some from nature.* **2** any influence that arouses effort to do well: *The captain was an inspiration to his men.* **3** an idea that is inspired; sudden brilliant idea: *They had the happy inspiration of commissioning ... a friend ... to tackle the score and lyrics* (New Yorker). **4** a suggestion to another; act of causing something to be told or written by another. **5** God's influence on the mind or soul of man; divine influence. Inspiration helped men to write the Bible. **6** a breathing in; act of drawing air into the lungs; inhalation.

in|spi|ra|tion|al (in′spə rā′shə nəl), *adj.* **1** tending to inspire; inspiring: *The sermon was both instructive and inspirational.* **2** under the influence of inspiration; inspired. **3** of or having to do with inspiration. **—in′spi|ra′tion|al|ly,** *adv.*

in|spi|ra|tor (in′spə rā′tər), *n.* **1** a person or thing that inspires; inspirer. **2** an apparatus for drawing in or inhaling air or vapor.

in|spir|a|to|ry (in spīr′ə tôr′ē, -tōr′-), *adj.* of or having to do with inspiration or inhalation.

in|spire (in spīr′), *v.*, **-spired, -spir|ing.**
—*v.t.* **1a** to fill with a thought or feeling; influence; affect: *A chance to try again inspired him with hope. His sly ways inspire me with distrust.* **b** to cause; occasion: *Behold in Aetna's emblematic fires The mischiefs your ambitious pride inspires* (William Cowper). **2** to awaken or cause (thought or feeling): *The leader's courage inspired confidence in others. I have here given my own paraphrase of this document, which has inspired so much controversy* (Edmund Wilson). **3** to put thought, feeling, life, or force into: *The coach inspired the boys with a desire to win. The speaker inspired the crowd.* **4** to cause to be told or written; suggest: *His enemies inspired false stories about him.* **5** to fill with God's influence or divine force: *to inspire a prophet or an oracle.* **6** to breathe in; inhale: *All breathing animals inspire and expire.* **7** *Archaic.* **a** to breathe or blow upon or into. **b** to breathe (life, a soul, or existence) into: *That pure breath of life, the spirit of man Which God inspired* (Milton).
—*v.i.* **1** to breathe into the lungs. **2** to give inspiration.
[< Old French *inspirer,* learned borrowing from Latin *īnspīrāre* < *in-* in + *spīrāre* breathe]

in|spired (in spīrd′), *adj.* **1** guided by or as if by a divine or supernatural influence: *an inspired prophet, inspired poetry.* **2** breathed in; inhaled: *Oxygen streams into the blood from the inspired air* (London Times). **—in|spired′ly,** *adv.*

in|spir|er (in spīr′ər), *n.* a person or thing that inspires.

in|spir|ing (in spīr′ing), *adj.* that inspires; affecting; stimulating: *an inspiring story, an inspiring teacher.* **—in|spir′ing|ly,** *adv.*

in|spir|it (in spir′it), *v.t.* to put spirit into; encourage; hearten; cheer. **SYN:** animate, quicken.

in|spir|it|ing (in spir′ə ting), *adj.* that inspirits; animating; cheering; encouraging: *He played several inspiriting choruses* (New Yorker). **—in|spir′it|ing|ly,** *adv.*

in|spis|sate (in spis′āt), *v.t., v.i.*, **-sat|ed, -sat|ing.** to thicken, as by evaporation; condense. [< Late Latin *īnspissāre* (with English *-ate*[1]) < Latin *in-* + *spissus* thick] **—in′spis|sa′tion,** *n.* **—in′spis|sa′tor,** *n.*

in|spis|sat|ed (in spis′ā tid), *adj.* thickened or made dense: (*Figurative.*) *inspissated gloom.*

inst., **1** instant: *"The 10th inst." means "the tenth day of the present month."* **2** institute. **3** institution. **4** instrumental.
▶**inst.** Abbreviations such as *inst.* (of the current month) and *ult.* (of last month) are no longer considered good form in business correspondence.

Inst., **1** Institute. **2** Institution.

in|sta|bil|i|ty (in′stə bil′ə tē), *n., pl.* **-ties. 1** lack of firmness; liability to fall, give way, or change; being unstable; unsteadiness: *Lincoln dreaded the effects of another family death on his wife's neurotic instability* (Newsweek). **SYN:** unstableness. **2** an instance of this.

in|sta|ble (in stā′bəl), *adj.* = unstable.

in|stall or **in|stal** (in stôl′), *v.t.*, **-stalled, -stall|ing. 1** to place (a person) in office with ceremonies: *The new judge was installed without delay.* **SYN:** inaugurate. **2** to establish (in a place or condition); settle: *The cat installed itself in a chair near the fireplace.* **SYN:** ensconce. **3** to put in place for use: *The new owner of the house had a telephone installed.* [< Medieval Latin *installare* < *in-* in (< Latin) + *stallum* stall] **—in|stall′er,** *n.*

in|stal|la|tion (in′stə lā′shən), *n.* **1** the act or fact of installing: *the installation of a new mayor. The installation of more electric lights made the room brighter.* **2** the state of being installed: *I attended my mother's installation as president of the P.T.A.* **3** something installed, especially machinery, electrical equipment, telephones, etc., placed in position for use. **4** a military base or camp, including personnel, equipment, and buildings.

in|stall|ment[1] (in stôl′mənt), *n.* **1** a part of a sum of money or of a debt to be paid at stated times: *The furniture cost $100; we paid for it in installments of $10 a month for ten months.* **2** *Figurative.* one of several parts issued at different times: *This magazine has a serial story appearing in six installments.* [alteration of earlier *estallment* < *stall* agree to payment of (a debt) by installments (< Old French *estaler* to fix, place < *estal* position < a Germanic word)]

in|stall|ment[2] (in stôl′mənt), *n.* **1** the action of installing: *the installment of electric lights in a house.* **2** the fact of being installed: *our installment in our new home.* [< install + *-ment*]

installment plan, *U.S.* a system of paying for goods in installments: *The Kleins seemed to need a great many things and bought them all on the installment plan* (Saul Bellow).

in|stal|ment (in stôl′mənt), *n.* = installment.

in|stance (in′stəns), *n., v.*, **-stanced, -stanc|ing.**
—*n.* **1** a person or thing serving as an example; illustration; case: *Lincoln is an instance of a poor boy who became famous. Television is an instance of improved communication facilities.* **SYN:** See syn. under **case**[1]. **2** a stage or step in an action; occasion: *I went in the first instance because I was asked to go.* **3** a request; suggestion; urging: *He came at our instance. At the instance of the losing team we agreed to play them again next week.* **SYN:** instigation. **4** *Law.* a process or function in a court of law. **5** *Archaic.* urgent entreaty; persistence. **6** *Obsolete.* **a** an impelling motive: *Tell him his fears are shallow, wanting instance* (Shakespeare). **b** a sign; token: *I beg you to accept a guinea as a small instance of my gratitude* (Henry Fielding).
—*v.t.* **1** to give as an example; cite: *He instanced the fly as a dirty insect.* **2** to show by an instance; exemplify. **—*v.i.*** to cite an instance.
for instance, as an example; for example: *His many different hobbies include, for instance, skating and stamp collecting. The daily motion of the earth is very different in different parts—at the equator and at a pole, for instance* (J. Norman Lockyer).
[< Old French *instance,* learned borrowing < Latin *īnstantia* insistence < *īnstāns* insistent; see etym. under **instant**]

in|stan|cy (in′stən sē), *n.* the quality of being instant; pressing nature; urgency; pressure; immediateness.

in|stant (in′stənt), *n., adj., adv.* **—*n.*** **1** a particular moment: *Stop talking this instant!* **2** a moment of time: *He paused for an instant.* **SYN:** See syn. under **minute**[1].
—*adj.* **1** coming at once; without delay; immediate: *The medicine gave instant relief from pain.* **2** pressing; urgent: *When there is a fire, there is an instant need for action.* **SYN:** importunate. **3** prepared beforehand and requiring little or no cooking, mixing, or additional ingredients: *instant coffee, instant potatoes, instant pudding.* **4** of the present month; present. "The 10th instant" means "the tenth day of the present month." **5** close at hand; impending; imminent: *The evil which to me in other stations may seem far distant, to him is instant, and ever before his eyes* (Sir Richard Steele). **6** *Figurative.* designed to work quickly or produce quick results: *instant math. The Socialists favour the creation of "instant soldiers" with basic training limited to six months* (London Times).
—*adv.* *Archaic.* instantly; at once: *You, my sinews, grow not instant old, But bear me stiffly up* (Shakespeare).
on the instant, at once; forthwith; immediately: *He ran for the ball on the instant.*
the instant, just as soon as: *The instant he leaves you, you, all the world, are nothing to him* (Horace Walpole).
[< Latin *īnstāns, -antis,* present participle of *īnstāre* to insist, urge; stand near < *in-* in + *stāre* stand]

in|stan|ta|ne|i|ty (in′stən tə nē′ə tē, in stan′-), *n.* the quality or condition of being instantaneous.

in|stan|ta|ne|ous (in′stən tā′nē əs), *adj.* **1** coming or done in an instant: *A flash of lightning is instantaneous. When the speaker finished talking, the applause was instantaneous.* **2** existing at or having to do with a particular instant: *the instantaneous velocity of something.* **—in′stan|ta′ne|ous|ly,** *adv.* **—in′stan|ta′ne|ous|ness,** *n.*

instant camera, a camera that develops its pictures, ejecting each one soon after it is taken: *New instant cameras featured automatic focusing based on the subject's reflection of ultrasonic sound waves* (Kenneth Poli).

instant coffee, **1** a dehydrated, crystallized essence of coffee, requiring only the addition of water to prepare. **2** the drink made from the essence.

in|stan|ter (in stan′tər), *adv.* at once; immediately: *"I promised to lend you that book ... I will get it for you instanter"* (New Yorker). [< Latin *īnstanter* insistently (in Late Latin, presently) < *īnstāns;* see etym. under **instant**]

in|stan|ti|ate (in stan′shē āt), *v.t.*, **-at|ed, -at|ing.** to give an instance or instances of; substantiate with concrete examples.

in|stant|ize (in′stən tīz), *v.t.*, **-ized, -iz|ing.** to make instant; make available in instant (premixed, precooked, or otherwise prepared) form.

instant lottery, *U.S.* a type of lottery in which tickets are so marked, usually with matching numbers or symbols, that the players learn upon buying them whether they are winners without having to wait for a drawing.

in|stant|ly (in′stənt lē), *adv., conj.* **—*adv.*** **1** in an instant; at once; immediately. **2** *Archaic.* urgently; persistently: *When they came to Jesus, they besought him instantly* (Luke 7:4). **SYN:** See syn. under **immediately**.
—*conj.* the moment that; as soon as.

in|stant|on (in′stən ton), *n.* a hypothetical quantum unit for the interaction occurring between states of the lowest energy: *Instantons ... affect the interactions between quarks* (New Scientist). [< *instant* + *-on*]

instant replay, the instantaneous playback, often in slow motion, of a videotape or any part of it on television: *Don Drysdale, the Dodger starter, was out so fast that he could have watched himself on instant replay* (Time).

instant tea, **1** a dehydrated, crystallized essence of tea, requiring only the addition of water to prepare. **2** the drink made from the essence.

in|star[1] (in stär′), *v.t.*, **-starred, -star|ring. 1** to place in the sky as a star: *Jove instarred Castor and Pollux after Castor's death.* **2** to set with stars or with anything suggesting stars: *a bracelet instarred with diamonds.* [< *in-*[2] + *star*]

in|star[2] (in′stär), *n.* the particular stage of an insect or other arthropod between moltings. [< New Latin *instar* < Latin *īnstār* likeness, form]

in|state (in stāt′), *v.t.*, **-stat|ed, -stat|ing. 1** to put into a certain state, position, or office; install. **2** *Obsolete.* **a** to endow; invest. **b** to confer upon. **—in|state′ment,** *n.*

in sta|tu pu|pil|la|ri (in stā′tyü pyü′pə lär′ē, stach′ü), *Latin.* in a state of pupilage; subject to collegiate laws, discipline, and officers:

in sta|tu quo (in stā′tyü kwō′, stach′ü), *Latin.* in the same situation, condition, or state.

in|stau|ra|tion (in′stô rā′shən), *n.* restoration, renovation, renewal, or repair. [< Latin *īnstaurātiō, -ōnis* < *īnstaurāre* restore, renew, establish with ceremony]

in|stau|ra|tor (in′stô rā′tər), *n.* a restorer; renovator.

in|stead (in sted′), *adv.* in another's place; as a substitute: *She stayed home, and her sister went riding instead.*
instead of, rather than; in place of; as a substitute for: *Instead of studying, she watched TV.*

✱in|step (in′step), *n.* **1a** the upper surface of the human foot between the toes and the ankle. **b** the lower surface of this part. **2** the part of a shoe or stocking over the instep: *He scuffed his instep when he tripped on the curb.* **3** the front part of the hind leg of a horse between the hock and the pastern joint. [perhaps < *in-*[3] + *step*]

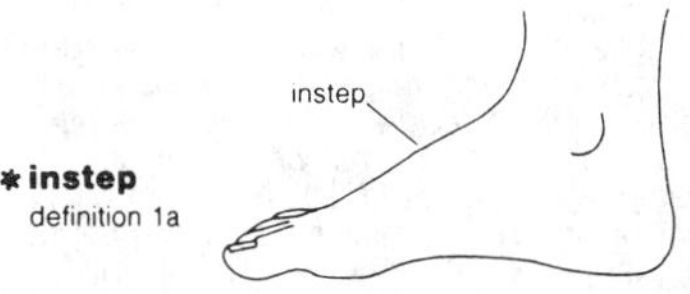

✱instep
definition 1a

in|sti|gate (in′stə gāt), *v.t.*, **-gat|ed, -gat|ing.** to urge on; stir up; bring about by inciting: *The older boy instigated a quarrel between his two younger brothers. Foreign agents instigated a rebellion.* **SYN:** provoke, foment. See syn. under **incite**. [< Latin *īnstīgāre* (with English *-ate*[1]) < *in-* in, on +

Pronunciation Key: hat, āge, cãre, fär; let, ēqual, tėrm; it, īce; hot, ōpen, ôrder; oil, out; cup, pu̇t, rüle; child; long; thin; ᴛʜen; zh, measure; ə represents **a** in about, **e** in taken, **i** in pencil, **o** in lemon, **u** in circus.

unrecorded *stīgāre* to prick, urge] —**in′sti|ga′tor**, *n.*

in|sti|ga|tion (in′stə gā′shən), *n.* **1** the act of instigating; urging on; stirring up; incitement. **2** an incentive; stimulus.

at the instigation of, instigated by: *Chunda Sahib ... was put to death, at the instigation probably of his competitor* (Macaulay).

in|sti|ga|tive (in′stə gā′tiv), *adj.* tending to instigate; stimulative.

in|still or **in|stil** (in stil′), *v.t.*, **-stilled, -still|ing.** **1** to put in little by little; cause to enter the mind, heart, or feelings, gradually: *Reading good books instills a love of really fine literature.* **2** to put in drop by drop. [< Latin *īnstīllāre* < *in-* in + *stīlla* a drop] —**in′stil|la′tion**, *n.* —**in|still′er**, *n.* —**in|still′ment, in|stil′ment**, *n.*

in|stinct[1] (in′stingkt), *n.* **1** a natural feeling, knowledge, or power, such as that which guides animals; inborn tendency to act in a certain way. An instinct is a chain of unlearned, coordinated acts characteristic of a particular species or group of animals. *Birds do not learn to build nests but build them by instinct. The very essence of an instinct is that it is followed independently of reason* (Charles Darwin). **2** a natural tendency or ability; talent: *Even as a child the artist had an instinct for drawing. He had ... neither the grander nor the meaner instincts of the born tyrant* (John R. Green). [< Latin *īnstinctus, -ūs* < *īnstinguere* impel < *in-* in, on + unrecorded root *sting-* urge]

in|stinct[2] (in stingkt′), *adj.* **1** charged or filled (with something): *The picture is instinct with life and beauty.* **2** *Obsolete.* impelled; excited. [< Latin *īnstinctus,* past participle of *īnstinguere* impel; see etym. under **instinct**[1]]

in|stinc|tive (in stingk′tiv), *adj.* of or having to do with instinct; caused or done by instinct; born in an animal or person; not learned: *Climbing is instinctive in monkeys. The spinning of webs is instinctive in spiders. An action ... when performed by many individuals in the same way, without their knowing for what purpose it is performed, is usually said to be instinctive* (Charles Darwin). **SYN**: intuitive, natural, innate. —**in|stinc′tive|ly**, *adv.*

in|stinc|tu|al (in stingk′chů əl), *adj.* of or having to do with the instincts: *instinctual drives.*

in|sti|tute (in′stə tüt, -tyüt), *n., v.,* **-tut|ed, -tut|ing.** —*n.* **1a** an organization or society for some special purpose. An art institute teaches or displays art. A technical school is often called an institute. *Abbr:* Inst. **b** the building used by such an organization or society: *We spent the afternoon in the Art Institute.* **2a** a short program of instruction for a particular group: *a teacher's institute.* **b** an elementary principle or element of instruction. **3** something instituted; an established principle, law, custom, organization, or society; institution. —*v.t.* **1** to set up; establish; begin; start: *The Pilgrims instituted Thanksgiving Day. After the accident the police instituted an inquiry into its causes.* **SYN**: found, organize, introduce, initiate. **2** *Ecclesiastical.* to assign to a spiritual charge; invest with the cure of souls. **3** *Roman Law.* to appoint as an heir or executor.

institutes, a digest of the elements of a subject, especially of law: *the Institutes of Justinian and Gaius, Quintilian's Institutes of Oratory.*

[< Latin *īnstitutus,* past participle of *īnstituere* < *in-* in + *statuere* establish < *status, -ūs* position, status]

in|sti|tut|er (in′stə tü′tər, -tyü′-), *n.* = institutor.

in|sti|tu|tion (in′stə tü′shən, -tyü′-), *n.* **1** a society, club, college, or any organization established for some public or social purpose. A church, school, university, hospital, asylum, or prison is an institution. *Abbr:* Inst. **2** the building used for the work of an institution: *The institution was under guard when the art exhibit was there.* **3** an established law or custom: *Giving presents at Christmas is an institution. Marriage is an institution among most peoples of the earth. Vast institutions, such as the church or industry or monogamy, are important* (New York Times). **4** the act or process of instituting; setting up; beginning, starting, establishing, or providing for: *We hope for the institution of hot lunches at school this winter. Wise men favor the institution of a savings bank in every large city.* **SYN**: foundation. **5** *Informal, Figurative.* a familiar person or thing. **6** *Ecclesiastical.* **a** the establishment of a sacrament of the Christian church by Christ. **b** the investment of a clergyman with a spiritual charge. **7** *Law.* a first principle of a subject, or a book of instruction containing first principles.

in|sti|tu|tion|al (in′stə tü′shə nəl, -tyü′-), *adj.* **1** of or like an institution: *About 80 per cent of the institutional vote customarily goes to management* (Newsweek). **2** promoting reputation and establishing good will for a business rather than aiming at immediate sales: *institutional advertising.* **3** *U.S.* (of a church) possessing organizations and societies of a charitable or educational nature in addition to the purely religious work. **4** of or having to do with the elements of a subject, such as those of law. —**in′sti|tu′tion|al|ly**, *adv.*

in|sti|tu|tion|al|ise (in′stə tü′shə nə līz, -tyü′-), *v.t.*, **-ised, -is|ing.** *Especially British.* institutionalize.

in|sti|tu|tion|al|ism (in′stə tü′shə nə liz′əm, -tyü′-), *n.* **1** a strong attachment to established institutions, such as of religion. **2** the system of institutions for public, charitable, or similar purposes.

in|sti|tu|tion|al|ist (in′stə tü′shə nə list, -tyü′-), *n., adj.* —*n.* a person who strongly supports or favors established institutions.

—*adj.* strongly attached to or demanding strong attachment to an institution or institutions: *Although he was one of the founders ... he later came to criticize the organization as "too institutionalist"* (Time).

in|sti|tu|tion|al|ize (in′stə tü′shə nə līz, -tyü′-), *v.t.*, **-ized, -iz|ing.** **1** to make into an institution: *There are other wrongs which seem to be becoming institutionalized, but perhaps the economic wrongs are an obvious starting point* (New York Times). **2** to put into an institution; subject (a person) to institutional life: *As a young girl [she] was institutionalized for schizophrenia* (Saturday Review). —**in′sti|tu′tion|al|i|za′tion**, *n.*

institutional revolution, = cultural revolution.

institutional revolutionary, = cultural revolutionary.

in|sti|tu|tion|ar|y (in′stə tü′shə ner′ē, -tyü′-), *adj.* **1** having to do with legal institutes or principles. **2** having to do with an ecclesiastical institution. **3** having to do with social or political institutions.

in|sti|tu|tive (in′stə tü′tiv, -tyü′-), *adj.* **1** tending to institute; having to do with institution. **2** instituted; established. —**in′sti|tu′tive|ly**, *adv.*

in|sti|tu|tor (in′stə tü′tər, -tyü′-), *n.* **1** a person who institutes or establishes; founder; organizer. **2** the bishop of the Protestant Episcopal Church or his deputy who institutes a clergyman into a parish or church.

instr., an abbreviation for the following:
1 instructions.
2 instructor.
3 instrument.
4 instrumental.

in|stream|ing (in′strē′ming), *n., adj.* —*n.* the act or fact of streaming in; influx; inflow.

—*adj.* streaming in.

in|struct (in strukt′), *v.t.* **1** to give knowledge to; show how to do; teach; train; educate: *We have one teacher who instructs us in reading, English, and history.* **SYN**: tutor, coach. See syn. under **teach.** **2** to give directions or orders to; direct; order: *The doctor instructed him to go to bed and rest. The owner of the house instructed his agent to sell it.* **SYN**: command. **3** to inform; tell: *My lawyer instructs me that the contract will be signed Monday.* **SYN**: apprise. **4** (of a judge) to give (the jury) a final explanation of the points of law in a case. **5** (of a solicitor) to engage the services of (a barrister) on behalf of his client. [< Latin *īnstructus,* past participle of *īnstruere* arrange, furnish with information, instruct < *in-* on + *struere* to pile]

in|struct|i|ble (in struk′tə bəl), *adj.* that can be instructed; teachable.

in|struc|tion (in struk′shən), *n.* **1** the act of instructing or teaching; communication of knowledge. **2** the knowledge or teaching given; lesson. **3** an item of such knowledge. **4** a charge by a judge to a jury at the close of a trial, instructing them as to the legal points in the case: *The judge's instruction bore hard upon the prisoner.* **5** a set of characters in machine language or computer language which specifies that the computer take a certain action.

instructions, directions or orders: *The teacher's instructions were clearly understood.*

in|struc|tion|al (in struk′shə nəl), *adj.* of or for instruction; educational.

instructional television, *U.S.* closed-circuit television programs designed as courses for instruction within the classroom. *Abbr:* ITV (no periods).

in|struc|tive (in struk′tiv), *adj.* useful for instruction; giving knowledge or information; instructing: *A trip around the world is an instructive experience.* —**in|struc′tive|ly**, *adv.* —**in|struc′tive|ness**, *n.*

in|struc|tor (in struk′tər), *n.* **1** a person who instructs; teacher: *The swimming instructor asked his class to jump into the pool.* **2** a teacher ranking below an assistant professor in American colleges and universities. [< Medieval Latin *instructor* teacher < Latin *īnstructor* preparer < *īnstruere;* see etym. under **instruct**]

in|struc|tor|ship (in struk′tər ship), *n.* the office or position of an instructor in American colleges and universities.

in|struc|tress (in struk′tris), *n.* a woman instructor or teacher.

in|stru|ment (*n.* in′strə mənt; *v.* -ment), *n., v.* —*n.* **1** a thing used to do something; tool or mechanical device: *A forceps and a drill are two instruments used by dentists.* **2** a device for producing musical sounds: *wind instruments, stringed instruments. A violin, cello, and piano were the instruments in the trio.* **3** a device for measuring, recording, or controlling. A thermometer is an instrument for measuring temperature. A compass and sextant are instruments of navigation. **4** *Figurative.* a thing with or by which something is done, or a person made use of by another; means: *The master criminal used many men and women as instruments in his crimes. The North Atlantic Pact was, he emphasized, not an instrument of aggression* (London Times). **5** a formal legal document, such as a contract, deed, or grant.

—*v.t.* to equip with instruments, especially for recording scientific data: *Rockets can be instrumented to record observations in geomagnetism, cosmic rays, and other phenomena of the universe.*

[< Latin *īnstrumentum* < *īnstruere;* see etym. under **instruct**]

in|stru|men|tal (in′strə men′təl), *adj., n.* —*adj.* **1** acting or serving as a means; useful; helpful: *My uncle was instrumental in getting me a job.* **2** played on or written for musical instruments: *An orchestra provided instrumental music to accompany the singing.* **3** of an instrument; made by a device or tool: *instrumental error.* **4** *Grammar.* **a** of or denoting a case that indicates the instrument or means by which something is done. English no longer has such a case. **b** of or denoting an affix or other form that indicates instrument or means.

—*n.* **1** *Grammar.* a the instrumental case. **b** a word in the instrumental case. **2** *Obsolete.* an instrument; means. —**in′stru|men′tal|ly**, *adv.*

instrumental conditioning, = instrumental learning.

in|stru|men|tal|ism (in′strə men′tə liz əm), *n.* *Philosophy.* the theory that thoughts and ideas are valuable according to their function as instruments in the control of the environment.

in|stru|men|tal|ist (in′strə men′tə list), *n., adj.* —*n.* **1** a person who plays on a musical instrument. **2** *Philosophy.* a follower of instrumentalism.

—*adj.* = instrumentalistic.

in|stru|men|tal|is|tic (in′strə men′tə lis′tik), *adj.* *Philosophy.* having to do with instrumentalists or instrumentalism.

in|stru|men|tal|i|ty (in′strə men tal′ə tē), *n., pl.* **-ties.** **1** the quality or condition of being instrumental; helpfulness; means; agency: *The permanent instrumentality of power in the Soviet Union is the Communist party* (Wall Street Journal). **2** an executive arm or branch: *The Export-Import Bank in Washington is an instrumentality of the government.*

instrumental learning, *Psychology.* a form of conditioning in which the subject learns to respond by reinforcement of his previous responses; operant conditioning: *In instrumental learning a conditioned stimulus is presented along with an opportunity to respond in various ways. The correct response is reinforced, or rewarded* (Scientific American).

instrumental riot, *Sociology.* a riot in which groups resort to violence because of discontent over specific issues (contrasted with *expressive riot*). Instrumental riots include labor, prison, and student riots.

in|stru|men|tar|i|um (in′strə men târ′ē əm), *n.* *Medicine.* the equipment or instruments required for any particular purpose.

in|stru|men|tate (in′strə men tāt), *v.t.*, **-tat|ed, -tat|ing.** *Music.* to instrument.

in|stru|men|ta|tion (in′strə men tā′shən), *n.* **1** the arrangement or composition of music for instruments. **2** the use of instruments; work done with instruments. **3** the mechanized use of instruments, especially for scientific or technical purposes: *... another significant forward step in the planned expansion into new fields of instrumentation and automation* (Wall Street Journal). **4** = instrumentality.

instrument board, = instrument panel.

in|stru|ment|ed (in′strə men′tid), *adj.* equipped with instruments for guidance: *a fully instrumented missile.*

instrument flight, a flight in which navigation is based on the readings from instruments within the aircraft, as at night.

instrument flying, the directing of an aircraft by instruments only.

instrument landing, an approach and landing made by an aircraft with the aid of a system of electronic devices in the aircraft that are coordinated with radio beacons, radar equipment, and transmitters on the ground: *The plane, attempting to make an instrument landing, came in short of the runway* (Wall Street Journal).

instrument panel, a panel containing dials, lights, and other devices that indicate how various instruments, machines, or other devices connected to them are functioning: *Airplanes and many complex electronic apparatus have instrument panels.*

in|sub|or|di|nate (in′sə bôr′də nit), *adj., n.* —*adj.* not submitting to authority; refusing to obey; disobedient; rebellious; unruly. SYN: mutinous.
—*n.* an insubordinate person. —**in′sub|or′di|nate|ly**, *adv.*

in|sub|or|di|na|tion (in′sə bôr′də nā′shən), *n.* resistance to authority; refusal to obey; disobedience; rebellion; unruly behavior: *In the Mexican War he got into trouble for insubordination and general swellheadedness* (Harper's).

in|sub|stan|tial (in′səb stan′shəl), *adj.* **1** frail; flimsy; weak: *A cobweb looks very insubstantial.* SYN: unsubstantial. **2** not actual; unreal; imaginary: *Dreams and ghosts are insubstantial.* SYN: illusive.
—**in′sub|stan′tial|ly**, *adv.*

in|sub|stan|ti|al|i|ty (in′səb stan′shē al′ə tē), *n.* insubstantial quality.

in|suf|fer|a|ble (in suf′ər ə bəl, -suf′rə-), *adj.* not sufferable; unbearable; intolerable: *His insufferable rudeness cost him many friends. A sense of insufferable gloom pervaded my spirit* (Edgar Allan Poe). SYN: insupportable. —**in|suf′fer|a|ble|ness**, *n.* —**in|suf′fer|a|bly**, *adv.*

in|suf|fi|cience (in′sə fish′əns), *n.* = insufficiency.

in|suf|fi|cien|cy (in′sə fish′ən sē), *n.* **1** too small an amount; lack; deficiency. SYN: inadequacy. **2** something deficient, inadequate, or unfit. **3** *Archaic.* unfitness; incompetence.

in|suf|fi|cient (in′sə fish′ənt), *adj.* **1** not enough; less than is needed; inadequate: *He was tired because he had had insufficient sleep. The scientist had insufficient evidence to prove his theory. Life is the art of drawing sufficient conclusions from insufficient premises* (Samuel Butler). **2** *Archaic.* unfit; incompetent. —**in′suf|fi′cient|ly**, *adv.*

in|suf|flate (in suf′lāt, in′sə flāt), *v.t.*, **-flat|ed, -flat|ing.** **1** to blow or breathe in or upon. **2** *Medicine.* **a** to blow (air or gas) into some opening of the body. **b** to treat by insufflation: *to insufflate the lungs of a newborn baby.* **3** to breathe upon (a person to be baptized or the water of baptism).
[< Latin *īnsufflāre* (with English *-ate*[1]) < *in-* on + *sufflāre* puff out] —**in′suf|fla′tion**, *n.* —**in′suf|fla′tor**, *n.*

in|su|la (in′sə lə), *n., pl.* **-lae** (-lē). **1** (in ancient Rome) a block of buildings composed of distinct apartments and surrounded by streets. **2** *Anatomy.* the central lobe of the cerebrum. [< Latin *īnsula* island]

in|su|lant (in′sə lənt), *n.* that which insulates; an insulating material.

in|su|lar (in′sə lər), *adj.* **1** of or having to do with islands or islanders. **2** living or situated on an island. **3** *Figurative.* standing alone like an island; isolated: *No nation can now keep an insular position in world affairs.* **4** *Figurative.* narrow-minded; prejudiced. **5** *Medicine.* characterized by isolated spots, patches, or pustules, as a rash. **6** *Anatomy.* of or having to do with the islets of Langerhans in the pancreas. [< Late Latin *īnsulāris* < Latin *īnsula* island] —**in′su|lar|ly**, *adv.*

Insular Celtic, the Celtic languages spoken in the British Isles.

in|su|lar|ism (in′sə lə riz′əm), *n.* narrowness of ideas or opinions.

in|su|lar|i|ty (in′sə lar′ə tē), *n.* **1** the condition of being an island: *the insularity of New Zealand.* **2** the condition of living on an island. **3** *Figurative.* narrow-mindedness; prejudice.

in|su|late (in′sə lāt), *v.t.*, **-lat|ed, -lat|ing.** **1** to keep from losing or transferring electricity, heat, or sound, especially by covering, packing, or surrounding with a material that does not conduct electricity, heat, or sound: *Telephone wires are often insulated by a covering of rubber.* **2** *Figurative.* to set apart; separate from others; isolate: *The English Channel insulates Great Britain from France and Belgium.* [< Latin *īnsula* island + *-ate*[1]]

in|su|la|tion (in′sə lā′shən), *n.* **1** the act or process of insulating: *The electrician checked the insulation of the wiring.* **2** the fact or condition of being insulated: *The insulation of the outer walls helps keep our house warm in the winter.* **3** something that insulates; material used in insulating: *Asbestos is often used as an insulation against heat and fire.*

in|su|la|tive (in′sə lā′tiv), *adj.* used as insulation; insulating: . . . *insulative products made of plastics* (Wall Street Journal).

***in|su|la|tor** (in′sə lā′tər), *n.* that which insulates; something that prevents the passage of electricity, heat, or sound; nonconductor: *Glass is an effective insulator.*

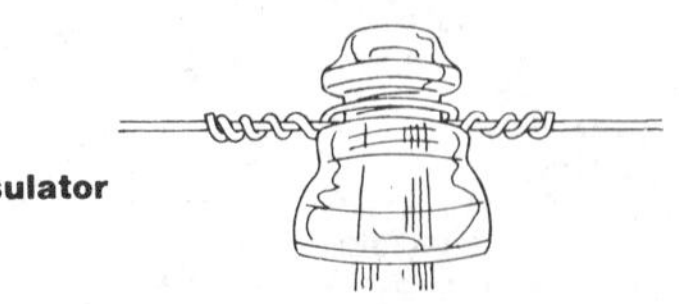
***insulator**

in|su|lin (in′sə lin), *n.* **1** a protein hormone secreted by the islets of Langerhans in the pancreas that enables the body to use sugar and other carbohydrates by regulating the sugar metabolism of the body. **2** a drug containing insulin, used in treating diabetes. Insulin is obtained from the pancreas of slaughtered animals. *Insulin, of course, is standard treatment for diabetics which keeps them alive and well* (Science News Letter).
[< Latin *īnsula* island + English *-in*]

in|su|lin|ase (in′sə lə nās), *n.* an enzyme secreted by the liver, which breaks down and destroys insulin. [< *insulin* + *-ase*]

in|su|lin-de|pend|ent diabetes mellitus (in′sə lin di pen′dənt), a form of diabetes usually occurring before the age of 20. It is caused by malfunction of the pancreas often after a general viral infection and may be affected by a hereditary condition: *Insulin-dependent diabetes mellitus defines a group of patients who are literally dependent on exogenous insulin to prevent . . . death* (Merck Manual).

in|su|lin|ize (in′sə lə nīz), *v.t.*, **-ized, -iz|ing.** to administer insulin to.

insulin shock or **coma**, **1** a condition of weakness or unconsciousness resulting from an overdose of insulin. **2** a method of shock therapy for treatment of forms of schizophrenia.

in|sult (*v.* in sult′; *n.* in′sult), *v., n.* —*v.t.* **1** to say or do something very scornful, rude, or harsh to: *The man insulted me by calling me a liar. The rebels insulted the flag by throwing mud on it.* **2** to attack; assail: *Harsh noises insulted our ears.* **3** *Military, Obsolete.* to attack suddenly.
—*v.i. Archaic.* to behave with scornful pride or insolence: *So he walks, insulting o'er his prey* (Shakespeare).
—*n.* **1** an insulting speech or action; affront; indignity: *To be called a coward is an insult. Ten shillings would have been an insult to the old fellow* (Lord Dunsany). **2** *Archaic.* an attack; assault: *Many a rude tower and rampart there Repell'd the insult of the air* (Scott).
add insult to injury, to make matters worse: *To add insult to injury, we are usually too busy to accept new patients* (Harper's).
[< Latin *īnsultāre* (frequentative) < *īnsilīre* leap upon < *in-* on, at + *salīre* leap] —**in|sult′er**, *n.*
—*Syn. n.* **1 Insult, affront, indignity** mean something said or done to offend someone or something. **Insult** applies to an insolent and contemptuous statement or act intended to humiliate or anger someone: *Stamping on the flag is an insult.* **Affront** applies to a deliberate and open show of disrespect: *Leaving during her song was an affront to my sister.* **Indignity** applies to an act or statement that hurts a person's feelings or dignity: *Spanking is an indignity to a teen-ager.*

in|sul|ta|tion (in′sul tā′shən), *n. Archaic.* the act of insulting; insult.

in|sult|ing (in sul′ting), *adj.* that insults; derogatory; abusive. —**in|sult′ing|ly**, *adv.*

in|su|per|a|bil|i|ty (in sü′pər ə bil′ə tē), *n.* insuperable quality.

in|su|per|a|ble (in sü′pər ə bəl), *adj.* that cannot be passed over or overcome; unconquerable: *The deep river was an insuperable barrier to those who could not swim.* (*Figurative.*) *An insuperable aversion to all kinds of profitable labor* (Washington Irving). SYN: insurmountable, impassable, invincible. —**in|su′per|a|ble|ness**, *n.* —**in|su′per|a|bly**, *adv.*

in|sup|port|a|ble (in′sə pôr′tə bəl, -pōr′-), *adj.* not endurable; unbearable; intolerable; insufferable: *Henry could be utterly insupportable; but he was always worth it* (Harper's). —**in′sup|port′a|ble|ness**, *n.* —**in′sup|port′a|bly**, *adv.*

in|sup|press|i|ble (in′sə pres′ə bəl), *adj.* that cannot be suppressed; irrepressible: *Local pride is always fierce and spontaneous, and often insuppressible among Georgians* (Harper's). —**in′sup|press′i|bly**, *adv.*

in|sur|a|bil|i|ty (in shůr′ə bil′ə tē), *n.* insurable quality.

in|sur|a|ble (in shůr′ə bəl), *adj.* that can be insured; fit to be insured.

in|sur|ance (in shůr′əns), *n.* **1** the act or process of insuring property, person, or life. Fire insurance, burglary insurance, accident insurance, life insurance, and health insurance are some of the many kinds. **2a** the business of insuring property, person, or life. **b** the contract made between an insurance company and a person or group as set forth in a policy. **3** the amount of money for which a person or thing is insured: *He has $10,000 life insurance, which his wife will receive if he dies first.* **4** the amount of money paid for insurance; premium: *His fire insurance is $300 a year.* **5** any means of making certain, insuring, or protecting: *A balanced diet is an insurance against malnutrition.* **6** *Sports.* a score that insures a team's lead for the rest of the game.

in|sur|ant (in shůr′ənt), *n.* a person who takes out insurance.

in|sure (in shůr′), *v.*, **-sured, -sur|ing.** —*v.t.* **1** to arrange for money payment in case of loss, accident, or death: *An insurance company will insure your house against fire.* **2** to make safe against loss by paying money to an insurance company: *He insured his car against accident, theft, and fire.* **3** to make sure or certain; guarantee; ensure: *Check your work to insure its accuracy.* **4** to make safe; protect; ensure: *More care will insure you against making so many mistakes.*
—*v.i.* to give or buy insurance.
[variant of *ensure* < Anglo-French *enseürer* < *en-* in + Old French *seür* sure < Latin *sēcūrus.* See related etym. at **sure.**]
►See **ensure** for usage note.

in|sured (in shůrd′), *n.* a person who carries insurance.

in|sur|er (in shůr′ər), *n.* **1** a person or company that insures; underwriter. **2** something that insures or protects. **3** a person who is insured. **4** a person who sells insurance.

in|sur|gence (in sėr′jəns), *n.* the act of rising in revolt; rebellion; uprising.

in|sur|gen|cy (in sėr′jən sē), *n., pl.* **-cies.** **1** = insurgence. **2** *International Law.* a minor revolt against a government, not recognized as belligerency.

in|sur|gent (in sėr′jənt), *n., adj.* —*n.* **1** a person who rises in revolt; rebel: *The insurgents captured the town.* **2** *U.S.* a rebel within a political party. **3** a stockholder who attempts to wrest control of a company: *It is not known how much stock the insurgents have under their control* (New York Times).
—*adj.* of or having to do with insurgents; rising in revolt; rebellious.
[< Latin *īnsurgēns, -entis,* present participle of *īnsurgere* rise up against < *in-* against + *surgere* rise]

in|sur|mount|a|bil|i|ty (in′sər moun′tə bil′ə tē), *n.* the state or quality of being insurmountable.

in|sur|mount|a|ble (in′sər mount′tə bəl), *adj.* that cannot be overcome: *There are no insurmountable difficulties in the manufacture, testing and administration of the Salk vaccine* (New York Times). —**in′sur|mount′a|bly**, *adv.*

in|sur|rec|tion (in′sə rek′shən), *n.* a rising against established authority; revolt; rebellion: *France combines an imperishable structure with the perpetual preachings of insurrection* (Newsweek). SYN: revolution, riot. See syn. under **revolt.**
[< Late Latin *īnsurrectiō, -ōnis* < Latin *īnsurgere;* see etym. under **insurgent**]

in|sur|rec|tion|al (in′sə rek′shə nəl), *adj.* of or having to do with insurrection. —**in′sur|rec′tion|al|ly**, *adv.*

in|sur|rec|tion|ar|y (in′sə rek′shə ner′ē), *adj., n., pl.* **-ar|ies.** —*adj.* **1** having a tendency to revolt. **2** having to do with revolt. —*n.* = insurrectionist.

in|sur|rec|tion|ism (in′sə rek′shə niz əm), *n.* the principle of revolt against established authority. —**in′sur|rec′tion|ist**, *n.*

in|sur|rec|to (in′sə rek′tō), *n., pl.* **-tos.** an insurgent; rebel. [< Spanish *insurrecto*]

in|sur|rec|to|ry (in′sə rek′tər ē), *adj.* = insurrectionary.

in|sus|cep|ti|bil|i|ty (in′sə sep′tə bil′ə tē), *n.* the fact or quality of being insusceptible.

in|sus|cep|ti|ble (in′sə sep′tə bəl), *adj.* not susceptible; not easily affected or influenced: *insusceptible to new ideas.* —**in′sus|cep′ti|bly**, *adv.*

in|swathe (in swāᴛʜ′), *v.t.*, **-swathed, -swath|ing.** = enswathe. —**in|swathe′ment**, *n.*

in|swept (in′swept′), *adj.* curving inward or tapering at the end or tip: *an inswept chassis, an inswept wing.*

in|swing|er (in′swing′ər), *n. Cricket.* an inward-hooking ball bowled to a batsman.

int., an abbreviation for the following: **1** interest. **2** interior. **3** internal. **4** international.

in|tact (in takt′), *adj.* with no part missing; as if untouched; uninjured; whole: *dishes left intact after being dropped. The money was returned intact by the boy who found it. At the session, an-*

other scientist discussed heroic new experiments on the intact human heart (New York Times). SYN: unblemished, unimpaired. [< Latin *intactus* < *in-* not + *tactus,* past participle of *tangere* to touch] —**in·tact′ness**, *n.*

in·tag·li·at·ed (in tal′yā tid), *adj.* carved on the surface; engraved in intaglio.

***in·tag·lio** (in tal′yō, -täl′-), *n., pl.* **-ios**, *v.,* **-ioed**, **-io·ing**. —*n.* **1** the process of engraving or carving by making cuts in the surface. **2** ornamentation by figures or designs sunk below the surface. **3** a figure or design engraved or carved in this way. **4** a gem ornamented in this way: *He had also a seal ring, a veritable antique intaglio* (Washington Irving). **5** a mold to be cast in relief, such as a countersunk die. **6** *Graphic Arts.* a method of printing in which paper is pressed into inked lines below the surface of the plate or cylinder. The ink is wiped off the surface but remains in the recesses, as in etching, photogravure, and similar processes.
—*v.t.* to carve or engrave in intaglio.
[< Italian *intaglio* < *intagliare* engrave < *in-* into + *tagliare* cut < Late Latin *tāliāre* to cut]

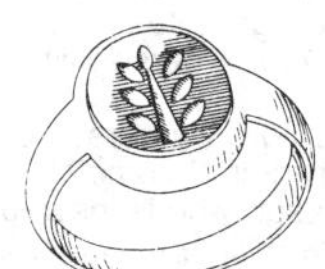

***intaglio**
definition 4

in·take (in′tāk′), *n.* **1** the place where water, air, or gas enters a channel, pipe, chamber, or other narrow opening: *The intake is clogged with dirt so that no air can be drawn in.* **2** the act or process of taking in: *The intake of gasoline was stopped by a clogged fuel line.* **3** the amount or thing taken in: *The intake through the pipe was 5,000 gallons a day. The intake of orders for the first four months is higher than ever before* (London Times). **4** *Physics.* the amount of energy taken in. **5** a narrowing or contraction in a tube, stocking, etc., or the point at which this begins.

intake manifold, pipe or pipes in an internal-combustion engine that conveys a mixture of fuel and air to the cylinders.

intake valve, a valve in an engine that opens to let the steam or fuel mixture enter the cylinders.

in·tan·gi·bil·i·ty (in tan′jə bil′ə tē), *n., pl.* **-ties**. **1** the state of being intangible. **2** = intangible.

in·tan·gi·ble (in tan′jə bəl), *adj., n.* —*adj.* **1** not capable of being touched or felt: *Sound and light are intangible.* SYN: insubstantial, impalpable. **2** *Figurative.* not easily grasped by the mind; vague: *She had that intangible something called charm.* —*n.* something intangible, such as good will. —**in·tan′gi·ble·ness**, *n.* —**in·tan′gi·bly**, *adv.*

in·tar·si·a (in tär′sē ə), *n.* **1** wood inlay: *a mahogany table decorated with satinwood intarsia.* **2** the art or process of inlaying wood. **3** a design or pattern in fabric in which colors look like tapestry. [< Italian *in tarsia, intarsio*]

in·te·ger (in′tə jər), *n.* **1a** a whole number: *1, 15, and 106 are integers* (*as distinct from fractions*). **b** any positive or negative whole number, or zero. **2** a thing complete in itself; something whole. [< Latin *integer* whole < *in-* not + unrecorded root *teg-* to touch. See etym. of doublet **entire**.]

in·te·ger vi·tae scel·e·ris·que pu·rus (in′tə jər vī′tē sel′ə ris kwē pyůr′əs), *Latin.* blameless in life and free from crime.

in·te·gra·bil·i·ty (in′tə grə bil′ə tē), *n.* integrable quality.

in·te·gra·ble (in′tə grə bəl), *adj. Mathematics.* that can be integrated, as a function or differential equation.

in·te·gral (in′tə grəl, in teg′rəl), *adj., n.* —*adj.* **1** necessary to make something complete; essential: *Steel is an integral part of a modern skyscraper.* **2** entire; complete. SYN: unbroken. **3** made up of parts that together constitute a whole. **4** *Mathematics.* **a** having to do with an integer or whole number; not fractional. **b** of or involving integrals.
—*n.* **1** a whole; a whole number. **2** *Mathematics.* **a** the result of an integration in calculus; the quantity of which a given function is the differential or differential coefficient. **b** an expression from which a given function, equation, or system of equations can be derived by differentiating.
[< Late Latin *integrālis* < Latin *integer;* see etym. under **integer**] —**in′te·gral·ly**, *adv.*

integral calculus, the branch of higher mathematics that investigates integrals, methods of finding integrals, and their applications in area, volume, or other functions.

integral domain, *Mathematics.* a set of elements subject to the operations of addition and multiplication, in which multiplication is commutative, which contains an identity element of multiplication, and in which at least one of a pair of elements is zero when the product of the pair equals zero.

in·te·gral·i·ty (in′tə gral′ə tē), *n.* integral state or character; entirety.

in·te·grand (in′tə grand), *n. Mathematics.* the expression to be integrated. [< Latin *integrandus,* gerundive of *integrāre* make whole, integrate]

in·te·grant (in′tə grənt), *adj., n.* —*adj.* making up or belonging as a part to a whole; constituent; component. —*n.* an integrant part; component. [< Latin *integrāns, -antis,* present participle of *integrāre* integrate]

in·te·grase (in′tə grās), *n.* a viral enzyme that promotes insertion of genetic material from a virus into genes of a bacterial cell: *Direct evidence for such viral enzymes . . . have shown that the enzyme product of a specific viral gene* (*dubbed integrase*) *is required for the insertion of viral DNA* (Scientific American). [< *intergr(ate)* + *-ase*]

in·te·grate (*v.* in′tə grāt; *adj.* in′tə grit), *v.,* **-grat·ed**, **-grat·ing**, *adj.* —*v.t.* **1** to make (schools, parks, and other facilities) available to people of all races on an equal basis; desegregate: *to integrate a neighborhood. They've integrated a school just a few blocks from the plant* (Wall Street Journal). *These politicians expect a few states to be completely integrated within the next five to ten years* (Newsweek). **2** to make into a whole; complete, as parts do: *to integrate the different circuits of a television set or computer.* **3** to put or bring together (parts) into a whole: *The committee will try to integrate the different ideas into one uniform plan.* **4** to find the mathematical integral of (a given function or equation). **5** to give the sum or mean value of.
—*v.i.* **1** to abolish racial segregation in schools, theaters, trains, or other facilities. **2** to become integrated. **3** to perform the operation of integration. **4** to find the function, equation, or set of equations whose derivative is an integrand.
—*adj.* **1** entire; complete. **2** = composite.
[< Latin *integrāre* (with English *-ate*[1]) < *integer* whole; see etym. under **integer**]

in·te·grat·ed (in′tə grā′tid), *adj.* **1** available to or serving people of all races on an equal basis: *an integrated school.* **2** having all its parts combined into a harmonious whole; coordinating diverse elements: *an integrated curriculum, an integrated system, an integrated corporation.*

integrated circuit, an electronic circuit produced on a single chip of semiconducting material, such as silicon, in which the components cannot be redistributed and still perform the same electronic function; monolithic circuit; microcircuit: *Integrated circuits . . . are already vital components in the computer industry: electronics for mass-produced cars, desk calculators, and further ahead, the household computer, are on a long list of areas the industry would like to penetrate* (Manchester Guardian Weekly). *Abbr:* IC

integrated circuitry, components or equipment consisting of integrated circuits; microcircuitry.

in·te·gra·tion (in′tə grā′shən), *n.* **1** the inclusion of people of all races on an equal basis in neighborhoods, schools, parks, or other facilities. **2** the act or process of integrating: *the integration of the activities of all the people who are working on a project.* **3** *Psychology.* **a** the arrangement of ideas, responses, and personality traits into a harmonious whole. **b** the coordination of the functions of the receptor, connector, and effector or motor cells.

in·te·gra·tion·ist (in′tə grā′shə nist), *n., adj.* —*n.* a person who believes in the integration of people of all races.
—*adj.* having to do with or favoring racial integration: *an integrationist policy of education.*

in·te·gra·tive (in′tə grā′tiv), *adj.* tending to integrate.

in·te·gra·tor (in′tə grā′tər), *n.* **1** a person or thing that integrates. **2** a machine for performing certain calculations involving integrals.

in·teg·ri·ty (in teg′rə tē), *n.* **1** honesty or sincerity; uprightness: *A man of integrity is respected.* SYN: See syn. under **honesty**. **2** undivided or unbroken condition; completeness; wholeness; entirety: *Soldiers defend the integrity of their country against those who want part of it. France regained its integrity in 1945.* **3** perfect condition; soundness: *the integrity of a text or a work of art. The integrity of my faculties* (Samuel Johnson). [< Latin *integritās* < *integer* whole; see etym. under **integer**]

in·te·gro·dif·fer·en·tial (in′tə grō dif′ə ren′shəl), *adj. Calculus.* containing or involving both integrals and differentials of a function: *integrodifferential equations.*

in·teg·u·ment (in teg′yů mənt), *n.* **1** a natural outer covering. The pod of a pea is its integument. *The skin or shell of an animal is its integument. He* [*a pig*] *must be roasted. I am not ignorant that our ancestors ate them seethed or boiled—but what a sacrifice of the exterior integument* (Charles Lamb). **2** the layer or layers of tissue surrounding an ovule. **3** *Figurative.* any covering or coating. [< Latin *integumentum* < *integere* to cover, enclose < *in-* on + *tegere* to cover]

in·teg·u·men·tal (in teg′yů men′təl), *adj.* of or belonging to an integument: *integumental covering.*

in·teg·u·men·ta·ry (in teg′yů men′tər ē), *adj.* of or like an integument: *integumentary membrane.*

in·tel·lect (in′tə lekt), *n.* **1** the power of knowing; understanding. A man's actions are influenced by his intellect, will, and feelings. SYN: See syn. under **mind**. **2** great intelligence; high mental ability: *Isaac Newton was a man of intellect.* **3** a person of high mental ability: *He was one of the great intellects of his time.* **4** a mind or minds: *the intellect of the time.* [< Latin *intellectus, -ūs* discernment; a perceiving < *intelligere* to understand, perceive; see etym. under **intelligent**]

in·tel·lec·tion (in′tə lek′shən), *n.* **1** the act or process of reasoning or understanding. **2** a particular act of the intellect: *The immortality of man is as legitimately preached from the intellections as from the moral volitions* (Emerson). **3** a conception, notion, or idea.

in·tel·lec·tive (in′tə lek′tiv), *adj.* **1** having the power to reason or understand; intelligent. **2** of or having to do with the intellect. —**in′tel·lec′tive·ly**, *adv.*

in·tel·lec·tu·al (in′tə lek′chů əl), *adj., n.* —*adj.* **1** needing or using intelligence: *Teaching is an intellectual occupation.* **2** of the intellect: *Thinking is an intellectual process.* **3** having or showing intelligence: *an intellectual person, an intellectual face.* **4** directed or inclined toward things that involve the intellect: *intellectual tastes, an intellectual book.*
—*n.* a person who is well-informed and intelligent, and interested in activities involving the intellect: *Most of the signatories of the Declaration of Independence were intellectuals* (Time).
intellectuals, a things having to do with the intellect: *Orthodoxy in the department of . . . intellectuals may be divorced from orthodoxy in life and conduct* (Philip Schaff). **b** *Archaic.* mental powers; wits: *those instructions . . . being too refined for the intellectuals of their workmen* (Jonathan Swift).
[< Latin *intellectuālis* < *intellectus, -ūs* perception, intellect] —**in′tel·lec′tu·al·ly**, *adv.* —**in′tel·lec′tu·al·ness**, *n.*

in·tel·lec·tu·al·ise (in′tə lek′chů ə līz), *v.t., v.i.,* **-ised**, **-is·ing**. *Especially British.* intellectualize.

in·tel·lec·tu·al·ism (in′tə lek′chů ə liz′əm), *n.* **1** the exercise of the intellect: *He is like those classical Japanese artists who . . . were indifferent to the intellectualism of Chinese painting* (Atlantic). **2** devotion to intellectual pursuits. **3** *Philosophy.* the doctrine that knowledge is wholly or chiefly derived from pure reason. —**in′tel·lec′tu·al·ist**, *n.*

in·tel·lec·tu·al·is·tic (in′tə lek′chů ə lis′tik), *adj.* of or having to do with intellectualism or the doctrine of intellectualism.

in·tel·lec·tu·al·i·ty (in′tə lek′chů al′ə tē), *n., pl.* **-ties**. **1** the state of being intellectual; intellectual nature or power. **2** an intellectual person.

in·tel·lec·tu·al·ize (in′tə lek′chů ə līz), *v.,* **-ized**, **-iz·ing**. —*v.t.* to make intellectual; give an intellectual quality to. —*v.i.* to become intellectual; reason; philosophize. —**in′tel·lec′tu·al·i·za′tion**, *n.*

in·tel·li·gence (in tel′ə jəns), *n.* **1a** the ability to learn and know; quickness of understanding; intellect; mind: *A dog has more intelligence than a worm.* **b** the level of this ability as measured on an intelligence test. **2** knowledge, news, or information: *intelligence of a person's whereabouts. The spy gave the general secret intelligence of the plans of the enemy.* **3** the getting or distributing of information, especially secret information. **4** a group or agency engaged in obtaining secret information; secret service: *Intelligence sent agents to infiltrate the enemy missile bases.*

In·tel·li·gence (in tel′ə jəns), *n.* an intelligent being or spirit: *The great Intelligences fair That range above our mortal state* (Tennyson).

intelligence agency, = intelligence department.

intelligence agent, a spy; undercover agent.

intelligence bureau, = intelligence department.

intelligence department, any one of the branches of the government that collect and study information that will help its armed forces or department of foreign affairs.

intelligence office, **1** an intelligence department or bureau. **2** *U.S. Obsolete.* an employment agency for domestic help.

intelligence officer, an officer in the service of an intelligence department or bureau.

intelligence quotient, a number that shows the rating of a person's intelligence. It is found by dividing the mental age, as shown in tests, by the actual age (16 is the top age used) and multiplying it by 100. *Abbr:* IQ (no periods).

in|tel|li|gen|cer (in tel′ə jən sər), *n.* **1** a person or thing that conveys intelligence or information. **2** a spy; informer.
intelligence service, = intelligence department.
intelligence test, any test used to measure mental development.
in|tel|li|gent (in tel′ə jənt), *adj.* **1** having or showing understanding; able to learn and know; quick at learning: *an intelligent student, an intelligent remark. Elephants are intelligent animals.* SYN: bright, clever, knowing, sensible, sagacious.
2 having understanding or knowledge: *The association of these masters with each other, and with men intelligent of their merits, is mutually agreeable and stimulating* (Emerson). **3a** capable of processing data by a built-in microprocessor: *Because of the falling costs of hardware, it is becoming economically feasible for students to have their own intelligent terminals* (New Scientist). **b** capable of making fine distinctions or performing certain logical operations: *The gadget . . . is so "intelligent" that it knows immediately if a piece of paper . . . is slid under the object in an attempt to remove it* (New York Times). [< Latin *intelligēns, -entis,* present participle of *intelligere* discern < *inter-* between + *legere* choose] **—in|tel′li|gent|ly,** *adv.*
in|tel|li|gen|tial (in tel′ə jen′shəl), *adj.* **1** of intelligence or understanding. **2** having intelligence: *an intelligential being.* **3** conveying intelligence or news.
in|tel|li|gent|si|a (in tel′ə jent′sē ə, -gent′-), *n., pl.* the persons representing, or claiming to represent, the educated class; the intellectuals of a country: *Each country has its own intelligentsia.* [< Russian *intelligencija,* ultimately < Latin *intelligentia* intelligence, understanding < *intelligēns* intelligent]
in|tel|li|gi|bil|i|ty (in tel′ə jə bil′ə tē), *n., pl.* **-ties.** **1** the fact or quality of being intelligible; capability of being understood. **2** an intelligible thing or action.
in|tel|li|gi|ble (in tel′ə jə bəl), *adj.* **1** that can be understood; clear; comprehensible: *I believe Shakespeare was not a whit more intelligible in his own day than he is now to an educated man, except for a few local allusions of no consequence* (Samuel Taylor Coleridge). SYN: understandable, plain. **2** *Philosophy.* that can be known only by the intellect, not by the senses. [< Latin *intelligibilis* < *intelligere;* see etym. under **intelligent**] **—in|tel′li|gi|ble|ness,** *n.* **—in|tel′li|gi|bly,** *adv.*
In|tel|sat (in′tel sat′), *n.* **1** International Telecommunications Satellite Consortium (organization of over 70 nations formed to control and promote work in global communications by means of satellites). **2** any one of several communications satellites launched under the auspices of Intelsat.
in|tem|er|ate (in tem′ər it), *adj.* inviolate, undefiled, unblemished, or pure. [< Latin *intemerātus* < *in-* not + *temeratus,* past participle of *temerāre* violate]
in|tem|per|ance (in tem′pər əns, -prəns), *n.* **1** lack of moderation or self-control; excess; immoderation: *His intemperance in eating caused him to become very fat.* **2** too much drinking of intoxicating liquor: *Intemperance caused him to become an alcoholic.*
in|tem|per|ate (in tem′pər it, -prit), *adj.* **1** not moderate; lacking self-control; excessive: *intemperate anger, an intemperate appetite. Use not thy mouth to intemperate swearing* (Ecclesiasticus 23:13). *He remained silent in the face of the intemperate attacks upon the Supreme Court of the United States* (New York Times). **2** drinking too much intoxicating liquor: *The intemperate man was arrested for drunkenness.* **3** not temperate; extreme in temperature; severe; inclement: *an intemperate climate.* **—in|tem′per|ate|ly,** *adv.* **—in|tem′per|ate|ness,** *n.*
in|tem|pes|tive (in′tem pes′tiv), *adj.* inopportune; untimely. [< Latin *intempestīvus* < *in-* not + *tempestīvus* seasonable < *tempus* time, season]
in|tend (in tend′), *v.t.* **1** to have in the mind as a purpose; plan; mean: *No insult was intended by his remarks. He intends that his sons shall go to college. We intend to go home soon.* **2** to mean for a particular purpose or use: *That gift was intended for you. He is intended for the ministry.* **3** *Archaic.* to direct: *Caesar through Syria intends his journey* (Shakespeare). **4** *Law.* to construe, interpret, or hold legally. **5** *Obsolete.* to devote one's attention to: *Herodicus, who did nothing all his life long but intend his health* (Francis Bacon).
—*v.i.* **1** to have a purpose or design: *He may intend otherwise.* **2** *Archaic.* to direct one's course: *to intend homeward.*
[< Latin *intendere* < *in-* toward + *tendere* stretch (the mind or thought)] **—in|tend′er,** *n.*
—***Syn.*** *v.t.* **1 Intend, mean** signify having in mind as a purpose. **Intend** implies having something firmly in mind as a definite purpose or plan: *I intend to finish this work before I go to bed.* **Mean** suggests less certainty about carrying it out: *I meant to get up early, but forgot to set the alarm.*
in|tend|ance (in ten′dəns), *n.* **1** the function of an intendant; superintendence; direction. **2** a department of the French public service, or the officials in charge of it. **3** the official quarters of an intendant.
in|tend|an|cy (in ten′dən sē), *n., pl.* **-cies.** **1** the position or work of an intendant. **2** intendants. **3** a district in Spanish America under an intendant.
in|tend|ant (in ten′dənt), *n.* **1** a person in charge; superintendent; manager; director. **2** the official who governs a district in Spanish America. **3** the administrative head of the colonial government in Canada during French rule. [< French *intendant,* learned borrowing from Latin *intendēns, -entis,* present participle of *intendere* attend to; see etym. under **intend**]
in|tend|ed (in ten′did), *adj., n.* —*adj.* **1** in the mind as a purpose; meant; planned; intentional: *an intended surprise. The medicine did not have the intended effect.* **2** going to be; future; prospective: *A woman's intended husband is the man she is going to marry.*
—*n. Informal.* an intended husband or wife: *The plot concerns an aging wolf who manages to marry his nephew's intended* (Time). **—in|tend′ed|ly,** *adv.* **—in|tend′ed|ness,** *n.*
in|tend|ing (in ten′ding), *adj.* that is (such) in intention; planning or aiming to be; prospective: *intending immigrants.*
in|tend|ment (in tend′mənt), *n.* **1** *Law.* the manner of understanding or viewing something: *intendment of the law.* **2** *Obsolete.* intention; design.
in|ten|er|ate (in ten′ə rāt), *v.t.,* **-at|ed, -at|ing.** to make tender; soften: *Thus she [nature] contrives to intenerate the granite and felspar* (Emerson). [< *in-*[2] in + Latin *tener* tender, soft + English *-ate*[1]] **—in|ten′er|a′tion,** *n.*
intens., intensive.
in|ten|sate (in ten′sāt), *v.t.,* **-sat|ed, -sat|ing.** to intensify. **—in′ten|sa′tion,** *n.*
in|tense (in tens′), *adj.* **1** very much; very great; very strong; extreme: *intense happiness, intense light. Intense heat melts iron. A bad burn causes intense pain. Deep, earnest thought is intense.* SYN: violent, vehement, excessive. **2** full of vigorous activity or strong feelings: *An intense life is crowded with action and interests.* **3** having or showing strong feeling; eager. An intense person is one who feels things very deeply and is likely to be extreme in action. SYN: earnest, ardent.
4 *Photography.* dense. [< Latin *intēnsus* tight, eager, forcible, past participle of *intendere* to strain; see etym. under **intend**] **—in|tense′ly,** *adv.* **—in|tense′ness,** *n.*
in|ten|si|fi|ca|tion (in ten′sə fə kā′shən), *n.* **1** the act or process of intensifying: *In recent years there has been an intensification of the struggle for political power in the United States* (Atlantic). **2** the condition of being intensified.
in|ten|si|fi|er (in ten′sə fī′ər), *n.* **1** *Grammar.* a word, prefix, or other element of language, that expresses intensity; an intensive. **2** a person or thing that intensifies. **3** *Photography.* a chemical used to make parts of a negative more dense or opaque.
▶See **adverb** for usage note.
in|ten|si|fy (in ten′sə fī), *v.,* **-fied, -fy|ing.** —*v.t.* **1** to make intense or more intense; strengthen; increase: *Blowing on a fire intensifies the heat. My first failure only intensified my desire to succeed. The nations are intensifying their struggle for peace* (New York Times). SYN: heighten.
2 *Photography.* to make (parts of a negative) more dense or opaque by treating with chemicals. —*v.i.* **1** to become intense or more intense; augment. **2** *Photography.* (of parts of a negative) to become more dense or opaque.
in|ten|sion (in ten′shən), *n.* **1** increase in degree; intensification. SYN: augmentation. **2** high degree; intensity. SYN: depth, strength, force. **3** exertion of the mind; attention; determination. SYN: intentness, resolution. **4** *Logic.* the sum of the attributes included in a given term or conception: *"Biped," "feathered," and so on, form the intension of "chicken."* **5** *Rare.* a stretching; straining. [< Latin *intēnsiō, -ōnis* < *intendere;* see etym. under **intend**]
in|ten|sion|al (in ten′shə nəl), *adj.* having to do with or characterized by intension. **—in|ten′sion|al|ly,** *adv.*
in|ten|si|ty (in ten′sə tē), *n., pl.* **-ties.** **1** the quality of being intense; great strength: *the intensity of sunlight. They feel they have reached an identical point of intensity* (New Yorker). **2** extreme degree; great vigor; violence: *intensity of thought, intensity of feeling, to look at someone with intensity.* **3** the amount or degree of strength of electricity, heat, light, or sound per unit of area or volume: *the intensity of gravitation.* **4** the strength of a color resulting from the degree to which it is lacking its complementary color. **5** *Speech.* the ability of the voice to carry effectively. **6** *Photography.* density of parts of a negative; opaqueness.
in|ten|sive (in ten′siv), *adj., n.* —*adj.* **1** having the quality or character of intensity; deep and thorough: *An intensive study of a few books is more valuable than much careless reading.* **2** having to do with a system of farming in which additional money and work are spent on a given area to produce larger crops. **3** *Grammar.* giving force or emphasis; expressing intensity. *Example:* In "He himself said it," *himself* is an intensive pronoun. **4** *Medicine.* **a** increasing progressively in intensity or strength: *an intensive series of inoculations.* **b** denoting treatment using large doses, strong remedies, and the like.
—*n.* **1** something that makes intense. **2** a word, prefix, or other language element that expresses intensity or gives force or emphasis. *Example:* In "It's terribly late," *terribly* is an intensive. **—in|ten′sive|ly,** *adv.* **—in|ten′sive|ness,** *n.*
intensive care unit, a medical unit equipped with lifesaving and monitoring devices providing constant hospital care for severely ill patients, or immediate field care in emergencies, especially for heart attacks.
in|tent[1] (in tent′), *n.* **1** a purpose; intention; that which is intended: *I'm sorry I hurt you; that wasn't my intent. The thief shot with intent to kill. This is called criminal intent. They contended that the commission is evading the intent of the law* (Wall Street Journal). **2** meaning; significance: *What is the intent of that remark?* SYN: import, purport. **3** the end or object intended; ultimate end; aim: *Jehu did it in subtilty, to the intent that he might destroy the worshippers of Baal* (II Kings 10:19). **4** *Obsolete.* a design; plan: *have no spur to prick the sides of my intent* (Shakespeare).
to all intents and purposes, in almost every way; almost; practically: *The materials are so hardened and knit together that to all intents and purposes they form one solid mass* (Ruskin).
[< fusion of Old French *entent,* and *entente,* learned borrowings from Latin *intentus, intenta,* masculine and feminine past participles of *intendere;* see etym. under **intend**]
in|tent[2] (in tent′), *adj.* **1** very attentive; having the eyes or thoughts earnestly fixed on something; earnest: *A stare is an intent look. He was intent on a task.* SYN: intense, keen. **2** earnestly engaged; much interested: *He is intent on making money. She is intent on doing her best.* SYN: eager, bent, resolved. [< Latin *intentus,* variant form of *intēnsus,* past participle of *intendere;* see etym. under **intend**] **—in|tent′ly,** *adv.* **—in|tent′ness,** *n.*
in|ten|tion (in ten′shən), *n.* **1** a purpose; design; plan: *Her intention to help was good, but she was only in our way.* **2** an intending or purposing: *The boy hurt his sister's feelings without intention.* **3** meaning; significance: *The intention of the poem was clear.* **4** the ultimate purpose; aim: *The chief intention of the builders was stability.* **5** *Logic.* a general concept. **6** *Medicine.* a manner or process of healing of a wound. Healing by first intention is healing by direct union of the wounded parts without granulations; healing by second intention is healing by the formation of granulated tissue in the wound cavity, after forming pus. **7** *Roman Catholic Church.* **a** the dedication of the priest or ministrant to the purpose of the Church in conferring one of the sacraments. **b** Often, **special** or **particular intention.** a special purpose for which Mass is celebrated, prayers are offered, or an act of devotion is made. **8** *Obsolete.* attention.
intentions, *Informal.* purposes with respect to marrying: *[He] had made it clear that he had no intentions at all, and . . . she did not mean to be unhappy about him* (Jane Austen).
—***Syn.* 1 Intention, purpose, design** indicate what a person means or plans to get or do. **Intention** often suggests lack of determination in carrying out the plan: *My intention was to arrive early.* **Purpose** suggests determination but not necessarily success in carrying it out: *My purpose was to avoid the crowd.* **Design** suggests careful preliminary planning or preparation: *I arrived early by design.*
in|ten|tion|al (in ten′shə nəl), *adj.* **1** done on purpose; meant; planned; intended: *His insult was intentional; he clearly wanted to hurt your feel-*

Pronunciation Key: hat, āge, cãre, fär; let, ēqual, tėrm; it, īce; hot, ōpen, ôrder; oil, out; cup, pu̇t, rüle; child; long; thin; ᴛʜen; zh, measure; ə represents **a** in about, **e** in taken, **i** in pencil, **o** in lemon, **u** in circus.

ings. **SYN:** See syn. under **deliberate. 2** of or having to do with intention or purpose. —**in|ten'tion|al|ly,** *adv.*

in|ten|tion|al|i|ty (in ten'shə nal'ə tē), *n.* the quality or fact of being intentional.

in|ter (in tėr'), *v.t.,* **-terred, -ter|ring.** to put (a dead body) into a grave or tomb; bury. [< Old French *enterrer,* learned borrowing from Medieval Latin *interrare* < Latin *in-* in + *terra* earth]

inter-, *prefix.* **1** one with the other; together: *intercommunicate = communicate with each other.* **2** between; among: *Interpose = put between.* **3** between or among (members of) a group: *International = between or among nations.* [< Latin *inter-* < *inter* among, between, during]

inter., interrogation.

in|ter|act[1] (in'tər akt'), *v.i.* to act upon each other: *There are still far too many variables and combinations of variables interacting in countless ways* (New Yorker).

in|ter|act[2] (in'tər akt'), *n. Especially British.* entr'acte.

in|ter|ac|tant (in'tər ak'tənt), *n.* something that interacts, such as a substance in a chemical reaction.

in|ter|ac|tion (in'tər ak'shən), *n.* action upon or influence on each other: *When two or more chemical reactions take place together, there is an interaction between them* (Science News).

in|ter|ac|tion|al (in'tər ak'shə nəl), *adj.* of or characterized by interaction.

in|ter|ac|tion|ism (in'tər ak'shə niz əm), *n. Philosophy.* the theory that the relation between the mind and the body is one of mutual influence of action. —**in'ter|ac'tion|ist,** *n.*

in|ter|ac|tive (in'tər ak'tiv), *adj.* **1** acting on each other. **2** of a computer, acting in response to directions from a computer user who then bases succeeding actions on the computer's responses: *"Interactive," . . . means that what you do influences what the computer does next* (New York Times).

interactive fiction, a computer or video game in which an adventure, mystery, or other story develops through the player's interaction with the story's characters: *Interactive fiction allows players to become heroes . . . by typing in commands on the computer's keyboard* (Shay Addams).

in|ter|ac|tiv|i|ty (in'tər ak tiv'ə tē), *n.* **1** the process of interacting. **2** the condition of being interactive.

in|ter|a|gen|cy (in'tər ā'jən sē), *n., pl.* **-cies,** *adj.* —*n.* an intermediate agency. —*adj.* between agencies, especially those of the Federal government: . . . *to iron out interagency disagreements on policy* (Time).

in|ter|a|gent (in'tər ā'jənt), *n.* an intermediate agent; intermediary.

in|ter a|li|a (in'tər ā'lē ə), *Latin.* among other things: *Geography and planning both deal, inter alia, with spatial distributions* (Listener).

in|ter a|li|os (in'tər ā'lē ōs), *Latin.* among other persons.

in|ter|al|lied (in'tər al'īd, -ə līd'), *adj.* between or among allied powers or nations.

in|ter-A|mer|i|can (in'tər ə mer'ə kən), *adj.* between or among the countries of North, Central, or South America.

in|ter|am|ni|an (in'tər am'nē ən), *adj.* lying or situated between rivers: *New York is an interamnian city lying between the North and the East Rivers.* [< Latin *interamnus* < *inter-* between + *amnis* river + English *-an*]

in|ter|a|tom|ic (in'tər ə tom'ik), *adj.* between atoms of the same molecule: *interatomic bonds.* —**in'ter|a|tom'i|cal|ly,** *adv.*

in|ter|au|thor|i|ty (in'tər ə thôr'ə tē, -thor'-), *adj.* between authorities: *Interauthority arrangements.*

in|ter|a|vail|a|bil|i|ty (in'tər ə vā'lə bil'ə tē), *n. British.* reciprocal availability, as of a service or facility: . . . *interavailability of return tickets whereby a passenger may make his outward journey on a train and use his return ticket on a bus* (London Times).

in|ter|band|ed (in'tər ban'did), *adj.* with bands or layers, usually alternating two different materials, colors, or the like.

***in|ter|bang** (in'tər bang'), *n.* a mark of punctuation with the exclamation point superimposed on a question mark, used for rhetorical questions. [< *inter* (rogation point) + *bang* printers slang for an exclamation point]

***interbang**

‽ you're kidding‽

in|ter|bank (in'tər bangk'), *adj.* between two or more banks: *interbank dealings.*

in|ter|bed (in'tər bed'), *v.t.,* **-bed|ded, -bed|ding.** = interstratify.

in|ter|blend (in'tər blend'), *v.t., v.i.,* **-blend|ed** or **-blent, -blend|ing.** to blend with each other.

in|ter|bor|ough (in'tər bėr'ō), *adj.* between boroughs: *interborough railway.*

in|ter|bra|chi|al (in'tər brā'kē əl, -brak'ē-), *adj. Zoology.* between the brachia or arms, as of a starfish.

in|ter|brain (in'tər brān'), *n.* = diencephalon.

in|ter|breed (in'tər brēd'), *v.t., v.i.,* **-bred, -breed|ing.** to breed by the mating of different kinds; breed by using different varieties or species of animals or plants. Many of our cultivated plants are hybrids developed by interbreeding various plants to combine their desirable qualities.

in|ter|ca|lar|y (in tėr'kə ler'ē), *adj.* **1** inserted in the calendar to make the calendar year agree with the solar year. February 29 is an intercalary day. **2** having an added day, month, or other period of time: *an intercalary year.* **3** put in between; interposed; intervening. [< Latin *intercalārius* < *intercalāre;* see etym. under **intercalate**]

in|ter|ca|late (in tėr'kə lāt), *v.t.,* **-lat|ed, -lat|ing. 1** to put (an additional day, month, or other period of time) into the calendar. **2** to put in between; interpolate. [< Latin *intercalāre* (with English *-ate*[1]) < *inter-* between + *calāre* proclaim] —**in|ter'ca|la'tion,** *n.*

in|ter|ca|la|tive (in tėr'kə lā'iv), *adj.* that intercalates.

in|ter|cal|i|bra|tion (in'tər kal'ə brā'shən), *n.* reciprocal calibration: *the intercalibration of oceanographic instruments.*

in|ter|car|di|nal points (in'tər kär'də nəl), the four directions of the compass lying midway between the cardinal points; northeast, southeast, southwest, and northwest.

in|ter|caste (in'tər kast', -käst'), *adj.* between castes: *intercaste marriage.*

in|ter|cede (in'tər sēd'), *v.i.,* **-ced|ed, -ced|ing. 1** to plead for another; ask a favor from one person for another: *He did not dare ask the teacher himself, so I interceded for him. Friends of the condemned man interceded with the governor for a pardon.* **2** to interfere in order to bring about an agreement; mediate: *The debate between the lawyers became so heated that the judge had to intercede.* **3** *Roman History.* (of officials, such as the tribunes) to interpose a veto. [< Latin *intercēdere* intervene (in Medieval Latin, act as intercessor for) < *inter-* between + *cēdere* go, come] —**in'ter|ced'er,** *n.*

in|ter|cel|lu|lar (in'tər sel'yə lər), *adj.* situated between or among cells: *Intercellular spaces are usually filled with gases or substances secreted by cells.*

in|ter|cen|sal (in'tər sen'səl), *adj.* between censuses: *the intercensal increase in population.*

in|ter|cen|tral (in'tər sen'trəl), *adj.* between centers.

in|ter|cept (in'tər sept'), *v., n.* —*v.t.* **1** to take or seize on the way from one place to another: *to intercept a letter before it is delivered, to intercept a mysterious foreign airplane, to intercept illicit drug shipments.* **2** to cut off (light, water, or gas). **3** to check; stop: *The police intercepted the flight of the escaped criminal and put him back in jail.* **4** to cut or mark off between two points or lines. —*n.* **1** an act of interception: *the intercept of a bomber by a missile, intercepts of secret messages.* **2** *Mathematics.* **a** an intercepted part. **b** the distance from the origin to the point where a line, curve, or surface intercepts a coordinate axis. [< Latin *interceptus,* past participle of *intercipere* < *inter-* between + *capere* to catch]

in|ter|cept|er (in'tər sep'tər), *n.* = interceptor.

in|ter|cep|tion (in'tər sep'shən), *n.* **1** the act of intercepting. **2** the state of being intercepted.

in|ter|cep|tive (in'tər sep'tiv), *adj.* that serves to intercept.

in|ter|cep|tor (in'tər sep'tər), *n.* **1** a person or thing that intercepts: *We flew interceptor missions over France* (New Yorker). **2** a fast fighter plane or missile having a high rate of climb, used for engaging and repelling attacking enemy bombers. **3** a large sewer that carries waste to a plant for treatment.

in|ter|ces|sion (in'tər sesh'ən), *n.* **1** the act or fact of interceding; pleading for another: *The girl's intercession for her brother won their parents' consent to his request. Only the President's intercession could save the spy's life.* **2** a prayer pleading for others. **3** *Roman History.* the interposing of a veto, as by a tribune. [< Medieval Latin *intercessio* mediation by prayer < Latin *intercessiō, -ōnis* act of interposing < *intercēdere* intercede]

in|ter|ces|sion|al (in'tər sesh'ə nəl), *adj.* of or containing intercession.

in|ter|ces|sor (in'tər ses'ər, in'tər ses'ər), *n.* **1** a person who intercedes. **2** a person who intercedes with God in behalf of men.

in|ter|ces|so|ry (in'tər ses'ər ē), *adj.* making or relating to intercession; interceding.

in|ter|change (*v.* in'tər chānj'; *n.* in'tər chānj'), *v.,* **-changed, -chang|ing,** *n.* —*v.t.* **1** to put each of (two or more persons or things) in the place of the other: *to interchange two drawers in a dresser. The two girls interchanged hats.* **2** to give and take; make an exchange of: *The friends interchanged things when one traded his kite for the other's ball.* **SYN:** See syn. under **exchange. 3** to cause to happen by turns; alternate: *to interchange severity with indulgence.* —*v.i.* **1** to occur by turns; alternate: *Fever interchanges with chills in this disease.* **2** to change places. —*n.* **1** a putting each of two or more persons or things in the other's place: *The word "team" may be turned into "meat" by the interchange of the end letters.* **2** the act or process of giving and taking; exchanging. **3** alternate succession; alternation: *an interchange of hard work with rest.* **4** the point at which a highway, especially an express highway, connects with another main traffic route. An interchange is designed so that none of the streams of traffic interfere with each other. *The permanent Thruway interchange at Suffern will open at 2 P.M. today* (New York Times). [alteration (influenced by Latin *inter-*) of Middle English *entrechangen* < Old French *entrechangier* < *entre-* (< Latin *inter-*) + *changier* < Latin *cambiāre* change, exchange] —**in'ter|chang'er,** *n.*

in|ter|change|a|bil|i|ty (in'tər chān'jə bil'ə tē), *n.* the condition of being interchangeable.

in|ter|change|a|ble (in'tər chān'jə bəl), *adj.* **1** capable of being used in the place of each other: *interchangeable parts. The sources of air, water, and land pollution are interrelated and often interchangeable* (New York Times). **2** able to change places with something else: *The word "concept" is often interchangeable with the word "idea."* —**in'ter|change'a|ble|ness,** *n.* —**in'ter|change'a|bly,** *adv.*

in|ter|church (in'tər chėrch'), *adj.* between or involving different churches; interdenominational.

in|ter|cit|y (in'tər sit'ē), *adj.* between cities: *intercity automobile traffic.*

in|ter|civ|ic (in'tər siv'ik), *adj.* between citizens of the same place.

in|ter|class (in'tər klas', -kläs'), *adj.* between classes: *interclass swimming meets.*

in|ter|clav|i|cle (in'tər klav'ə kəl), *n.* a bone located between the clavicles in fishes, amphibia, reptiles, and birds.

in|ter|cla|vic|u|lar (in'tər klə vik'yə lər), *adj.* situated between the clavicles.

in|ter|coast|al (in'tər kōs'təl), *adj.* between seacoasts; from coast to coast.

in|ter|col|le|giate (in'tər kə lē'jit, -jē it), *adj., n.* —*adj.* between colleges or universities: *intercollegiate football games.* —*n.* **intercollegiates,** sports events held between colleges, especially under the auspices of one of the associations regulating and supervising such contests.

in|ter|co|lo|ni|al (in'tər kə lō'nē əl), *adj.* between colonies. —**in'ter|co|lo'ni|al|ly,** *adv.*

in|ter|co|lum|nar (in'tər kə lum'nər), *adj.* between two columns.

in|ter|co|lum|ni|a|tion (in'tər kə lum'nē ā'shən), *n. Architecture.* **1** the space between two adjacent columns or pillars in a building. **2** the system of spacing between columns. [< Latin *intercolumnium*]

in|ter|com (in'tər kom'), *n.* any system or apparatus, usually using microphones and loudspeakers, with which members of an office staff or the crew of an airplane, tank, or ship can talk to each other; intercommunication system.

in|ter|com|mon (in'tər kom'ən), *v.i. English Law.* **1** to share in the use of the same common. **2** to use two commons jointly.

in|ter|com|mon|age (in'tər kom'ə nij), *n. English Law.* the privilege of sharing in the use of the same common.

in|ter|com|mu|nal (in'tər kə myü'nəl, -kom'yə-), *adj.* being between two or more communities or countries: *India and Pakistan should restore normal relations and intercommunal harmony in their two countries* (London Times).

in|ter|com|mu|ni|cate (in'tər kə myü'nə kāt), *v.t., v.i.,* **-cat|ed, -cat|ing.** to communicate with each other: *The ships of the convoy intercommunicated by radio.* (*Figurative.*) . . . *a labyrinth of intercommunicating guilts and anguishes* (Harper's).

in|ter|com|mu|ni|ca|tion (in'tər kə myü'nə kā'shən), *n.* the act of communicating with each other.

intercommunication system, = intercom.

in|ter|com|mu|ni|ca|tive (in'tər kə myü'nə kā'tiv), *adj.* characterized by, or adapted for, intercommunication.

in|ter|com|mun|ion or **in|ter-Com|mun|ion**

(in′tər kə myün′yən), *n.* a relationship or fellowship between churches of different denominations or communions; mutual communion.

in|ter|com|mu|ni|ty (in′tər kə myü′nə tē), *n., adj.* —*n.* the quality of being common to various parties; common ownership or use.
—*adj.* being between or serving two or more communities: *an intercommunity social center.*

in|ter|com|pa|ny (in′tər kum′pə nē), *adj.* between two or more companies: *These giant companies [were] setting prices and wages according to their own intercompany agreements* (Atlantic).

in|ter|com|pare (in′tər kəm pâr′), *v.t.,* **-pared, -par|ing.** to compare with each other. —**in′ter-com′pa|ra|ble,** *adj.*

in|ter|com|par|i|son (in′tər kəm par′ə sən), *n.* **1** the act or process of intercomparing. **2** the state of being intercompared.

in|ter|con|cep|tion|al (in′tər kən sep′shə nəl), *adj.* occurring between successive conceptions or pregnancies.

in|ter|con|nect (in′tər kə nekt′), *v.t.* **1** to connect with each other. **2** to connect (parts, as of machinery, electrical circuits, or computer modules) so that when any part functions the others also function. **3** to connect (several telephones) on the same line. —**in′ter|con|nec′tion,** *n.* —**in′ter-con|nec′tor,** *n.*

in|ter|con|nect|ed|ness (in′tər kə nek′tid nis), *n.* mutual connection; interrelation.

in|ter|con|ti|nen|tal (in′tər kon′tə nen′təl), *adj.* between continents; from one continent to another: *an intercontinental railroad, intercontinental warfare.* —**in′ter|con′ti|nen′tal|ly,** *adv.*

intercontinental ballistic missile, a ballistic missile with a range of over 5,000 miles. *Abbr:* ICBM

in|ter|con|ver|sion (in′tər kən vėr′zhən, -shən), *n.* reciprocal conversion.

in|ter|con|vert (in′tər kən vėrt′), *v.t.* to change from one to another; interchange.

in|ter|con|vert|i|bil|i|ty (in′tər kən vėr′tə bil′ə tē), *n.* the quality or state of being interconvertible.

in|ter|con|vert|i|ble (in′tər kən vėr′tə bəl), *adj.* that can be changed from one to another; interchangeable: *The concept that matter and energy are interconvertible strikes directly to the core of the universe* (Atlantic). —**in′ter|con|vert′i|bly,** *adv.*

in|ter|cool|er (in′tər kü′lər), *n.* an apparatus for cooling air between intervals of compression.

in|ter|cor|po|rate (in′tər kôr′pər it, -prit), *adj.* between or involving different corporations: *intercorporate funds.*

in|ter|cos|tal (in′tər kos′təl, -kôs′-), *adj., n.* —*adj.* **1** between the ribs: *an intercostal muscle, intercostal rheumatism. The spaces between the ribs, called intercostal spaces, contain arteries, veins, muscles, and nerves* (Marshall R. Urist). **2** *Botany.* situated between the veins of a leaf.
—*n.* a muscle or part situated between the ribs.
[< New Latin *intercostalis* < Latin *inter-* between + *costa* rib] —**in′ter|cos′tal|ly,** *adv.*

in|ter|course (in′tər kôrs, -kōrs), *n.* **1** dealings between people, businesses, schools, or governments, such as exchange of thoughts, services, or feelings; communication: *Airplanes, good roads, and telephones make intercourse with different parts of the country far easier than it was 50 years ago.* **2** = sexual intercourse. [alteration (influenced by Latin *inter-*) of Middle English *entercourse* < Old French *entrecours* < Latin *intercursus, -ūs* a running between < *intercurrere* run between < *inter-* between + *currere* run]

in|ter|creed|al (in′tər krē′dəl), *adj.* between or involving different creeds; interdenominational.

in|ter|crop (in′tər krop′), *v.,* **-cropped, -crop-ping,** *n.* —*v.t., v.i.* to plant (two or more crops) together, one between the rows of another.
—*n.* **1** the raising of two or more crops on the same land in alternate rows. **2** a crop so grown.

in|ter|cross (in′tər krôs′, -kros′), *v., n.* —*v.t.* **1a** to cross (each other). **b** to lay or place across each other. **2** = interbreed.
—*v.i.* **1** to cross each other. **2** = interbreed.
—*n.* an instance of intercrossing.

in|ter|crys|tal|line (in′tər kris′tə lin, -līn), *adj.* between crystals of a solid substance: *intercrystalline corrosion.*

in|ter|crys|tal|lize (in′tər kris′tə līz), *v.t., v.i.,* **-lized, -liz|ing.** to crystallize together (two or more substances). —**in′ter|crys|tal|li|za′tion,** *n.*

in|ter|cul|tur|al (in′tər kul′chər əl), *adj.* between different groups or cultures: *intercultural understanding.* —**in′ter|cul′tur|al|ly,** *adv.*

in|ter|cur|rent (in′tər kėr′ənt), *adj.* **1** that runs or comes between; intervening. **2** *Medicine.* (of a disease) occurring during another disease, and modifying it.

in|ter|cut (*v.* in′tər kut′; *n.* in′tər kut′), *v.,* **-cut, -cut|ting,** *n.* —*v.t.* to interpose (a camera shot or scene) in a motion-picture sequence: *The by now standard stuff of girls squealing as pop idols perform is ... intercut with documentary footage of the suffering and horror of war* (Pauline Kael).
—*v.i.* to be intercut: *[Her] collage technique calls for scenes to collide with one another, to intercut* (Dan Sullivan).
—*n.* **1** the act or fact of intercutting. **2** an intercut scene or shot.

in|ter|date (in′tər dāt′), *v.t., v.i.,* **-dat|ed, -dat|ing.** *U.S.* to go out on dates with members of a different religion or denomination: *Among the Catholic students 74 per cent interdated frequently and 66 per cent thought it likely they would marry non-Catholics* (New York Times).

in|ter|de|nom|i|na|tion|al (in′tər di nom′ə nā′shə nəl, -nāsh′nəl), *adj.* between or involving different religious denominations: *Television's religious note is more often interdenominational and inspirational* (Time).

in|ter|de|nom|i|na|tion|al|ism (in′tər di nom′ə-nā′shə nə liz′əm, -nāsh′nə-), *n.* belief in or support of fellowship between different religious denominations.

in|ter|den|tal (in′tər den′təl), *adj.* **1** situated or placed between teeth. **2** *Phonetics.* produced by placing the tip of the tongue between the upper and lower teeth.

in|ter|de|part|men|tal (in′tər di pärt′men′təl, -dē′-pärt-), *adj.* between departments: *an interdepartmental committee.* —**in′ter|de|part′men′tal|ly,** *adv.*

in|ter|de|pend (in′tər di pend′), *v.i.* to depend on each other; be interdependent.

in|ter|de|pend|ence (in′tər di pen′dəns), *n.* dependence on each other; mutual dependence: *There is an intimate interdependence of intellect and morals* (Emerson).

in|ter|de|pend|en|cy (in′tər di pen′dən sē), *n.* = interdependence.

in|ter|de|pend|ent (in′tər di pen′dənt), *adj.* dependent upon each other; mutually dependent.
—**in′ter|de|pend′ent|ly,** *adv.*

in|ter|dict (*v.* in′tər dikt′; *n.* in′tər dikt), *v., n.* —*v.t.* **1** to prohibit or forbid. **2** to restrain from the doing or use of something: *They are difficult to disseminate and control, but properly used could deny or interdict areas* (Bulletin of Atomic Scientists). **3** to hinder or check (the enemy) by gunfire or bombardment. **4** to cut off from certain privileges in the Roman Catholic Church.
—*n.* **1** a prohibition based on authority; formal order forbidding something: *At last the interdict will be raised, and people can go about their ordinary business* (Time). **2a** the act of cutting off from certain privileges in the Roman Catholic Church. **b** the authoritative sentence ordering this. **3** *Law.* a decree; order. **4** a provisional order in Roman law of the praetor in property disputes, usually prohibiting something.
[< Latin *interdictum,* neuter past participle of *interdīcere* prohibit < *inter-* between + *dīcere* speak] —**in′ter|dic′tion,** *n.* —**in′ter|dic′tor,** *n.*

in|ter|dic|tive (in′tər dik′tiv), *adj.* = interdictory.

in|ter|dic|to|ry (in′tər dik′tər ē), *adj.* that serves to interdict. **SYN**: prohibitory.

in|ter|dif|fuse (in′tər di fyüz′), *v.t., v.i.,* **-fused, -fus|ing.** to diffuse one with another. —**in′ter|dif-fu′sion,** *n.*

in|ter|dig|it|al (in′tər dij′ə təl), *adj.* between or joining fingers or toes: *The webbing of a duck's foot is interdigital.*

interdigital ringworm, = athlete's foot.

in|ter|dig|i|tate (in′tər dij′ə tāt), *v.i.,* **-tat|ed, -tat-ing.** to be inserted between each other like the fingers of both hands when clasped. [< *inter-* + Latin *digitus* finger] —**in′ter|dig′i|ta′tion,** *n.*

in|ter|dis|ci|pli|nar|y (in′tər dis′ə plə ner′ē), *adj.* between different fields of study: *interdisciplinary collaboration in research.*

in|ter|dit (äɴ ter dē′), *adj. French.* prohibited.

in|ter|est (in′tər ist, -trist), *n., v.* —*n.* **1** a feeling of wanting to know, see, do, own, share in, or take part in: *He has an interest in sports and he also has an interest in collecting stamps. Research indicates that fear and punishment are not as effective motivating forces as interest* (Atlantic). **2** the power of arousing such a feeling: *questions of great interest. A dull book lacks interest.* **3** a share in property and actions; right or claim: *He bought a half interest in that farm.* **4** a thing in which a person has a share or part. Any business, activity, or pastime can be an interest. **5** a group of people having the same business, activity, goal, principle, political party, or religion: *the business interests of the town.* **6** advantage; profit; benefit: *Mother and Father look after the interests of the family. One who has our interest at heart* (Edmund Burke). *Interest was the master-key of Madame's nature—the mainspring of her motives* (Charlotte Brontë). **7a** money paid for the use of money. If you borrow money from a bank, you must pay interest on the loan. **b** the rate per cent per unit of time of such a payment: *The interest on the loan was 5 per cent a year.* **8** *Figurative.* something extra given in return: *She returned our favor with interest.* **9** *Economics.* a payment for the use of capital goods in production.
—*v.t.* **1** to arouse a feeling of wanting to know, see, do, own, share in, or take part in; make curious and hold the attention of: *An exciting story interests us.* **SYN**: engage, occupy, entertain. **2** to cause (a person) to take a share or part in something; induce to participate in: *The agent tried to interest us in buying a car. Most of the businesses in town have been interested in the chamber of commerce for years.*
in the interest of, for; to help: *The Mayor thought the proposition was not in the interest of the city.*
[< Latin *interest* it is of importance; it makes a difference, third person singular present of *interesse* to be between < *inter-* between + *esse* be]

in|ter|est|ed (in′tər ə stid, -trə-; -tə res′-), *adj.* **1** feeling or showing interest, sympathy, or curiosity: *an interested spectator.* **2** having an interest or share; concerned. **3** influenced by personal considerations; prejudiced: *An interested person cannot make a fair decision.* —**in′-ter|est|ed|ly,** *adv.* —**in′ter|est|ed|ness,** *n.*
► **Interested** has two opposites: *uninterested,* which is its negative, and *disinterested,* which means free from selfish motives; impartial; fair: *He was uninterested in the outcome of the game. A disinterested spectator offered to referee.* See also **disinterested.**

interest group, any group organized to further the interest or concern of its members: *The genius of American politics has been its ability to compromise the conflicting needs and desires of the great variety of interest groups that make up so huge and diverse a nation* (Tom Wicker).

in|ter|est|ing (in′tər ə sting, -trə-; -tə res′-), *adj.* arousing interest; holding one's attention; of interest: *Stories about travel and adventure are interesting for children.* —**in′ter|est|ing|ly,** *adv.* —**in′-ter|est|ing|ness,** *n.*

interest test or **inventory,** a standardized list of questions about a person's interests, often given in conjunction with an aptitude test. It is used especially for guidance in schools.

in|ter|face (in′tər fās′), *n., v.,* **-faced, -fac|ing.** —*n.* **1** a surface lying between two bodies or spaces, and forming their common boundary. **2** a connection of two or more things brought together in an association, partnership, meeting, or other relationship: *"Interface" refers to anything that mediates between disparate items: machinery, people, thought. The equipment that makes the computer work visible to the user is often called an "interface," and the word is used highly metaphorically, as in "the interface between man and the computer, between the scientist and society"* (Atlantic). *Responsibilities include master scheduling, customer interface* (New York Times).
—*v.i., v.t.* to match, harmonize, or work together smoothly: *This was to be a full-dress affair, including inflated space suits, which have to "interface"—a space-age verb meaning, roughly, to coordinate—with equipment in the cabin* (New Yorker).

in|ter|fa|cial (in′tər fā′shəl), *adj.* **1** included between two faces of a solid: *An interfacial angle is formed by the meeting of two planes.* **2** of or having to do with an interface.

in|ter|fac|ing (in′tər fā′sing), *n.* a material inserted between the lining and outer cloth of a garment to help retain its shape.

in|ter|faith (in′tər fāth′), *adj.* **1** for more than one faith or religion: *an interfaith chapel.* **2** of different faiths or religions: *an interfaith conference.*

in|ter|fen|es|tra|tion (in′tər fen′ə strā′shən), *n.* the spacing between the windows of a building.

in|ter|fere (in′tər fir′), *v.i.,* **-fered, -fer|ing.** **1** to get in the way of each other; come into opposition; clash; conflict: *The two plans interfere; one must be changed. Come on Saturday if nothing interferes.* **SYN**: collide. **2** to mix in the affairs of others; meddle: *That woman is always interfering in other people's affairs.* **SYN**: See syn. under **meddle.** **3** to take part for a purpose; intervene: *The police interfered to stop the riot. Father interfered to stop the argument.* **4** *Sports.* to obstruct the action of an opposing player in a way barred by the rules. **5** *Physics.* to cause interference: *Light waves from these two sources do not interfere.* **6** (of a horse) to strike one foot or leg against the opposite foot or leg. **7** *Law.* to claim to have first made the same invention as another.

Pronunciation Key: hat, āge, cãre, fär; let, ēqual, tėrm; it, īce; hot, ōpen, ôrder; oil, out; cup, pu̇t, rüle; child; long; thin; ᴛʜen; zh, measure; ə represents **a** in about, **e** in taken, **i** in pencil, **o** in lemon, **u** in circus.

interfere with, to hinder: *Don't interfere with your brother when he's busy.*
[< Old French *entreferir* strike each other < *entre-* between, inter- + *ferir* strike < Latin *ferīre*] **—in′ter|fer′er,** *n.* **—in′ter|fer′ing|ly,** *adv.*

in|ter|fer|ence (in′tər fir′əns), *n.* **1** the act or fact of interfering: *Her interference spoiled our game.* **2** something that interferes. **3** *Physics.* the reciprocal action of waves by which they reinforce or diminish one another: *Interference is also evidence of waves. Its characteristic pattern is formed when rays interact* (Scientific American). *Interference cancels two waves if crest meets trough, but intensifies them if the crests meet* (S. Y. Lee). **4** *Radio and Television.* **a** the interruption or scrambling of a desired signal by other signals. **b** the signals thus interfering. **5** *Football.* **a** the protecting of the player who has the ball by blocking opposing players. **b** the players protecting or blocking for the player with the ball. **6** *Sports.* the obstruction of an opposing player in a way barred by the rules. **7** *Aerodynamics.* the disturbance of the airflow over a surface of an aircraft due to airflow over an adjoining surface.

interference drag, additional drag caused by the interaction of different airflows over the wings, fuselage, tail, and other aircraft components.

interference fringes, alternate light and dark or colored bands caused by the interference of light waves; fringes.

interference microscope, a microscope used to examine and measure the surface structure of reflecting or transparent specimens, such as a living cell.

interference microscopy, the use of an interference microscope.

in|ter|fe|ren|tial (in′tər fə ren′shəl), *adj. Physics.* of, having to do with, or working by means of interference.

in|ter|fer|o|gram (in′tər fir′ə gram), *n.* a recording, usually photographic, of the output of an interferometer: *Holographic interferograms have been used to trap successive instants in the lifetimes of such lightning-fast events as the flight of a rifle bullet and the warming of a light bulb* (Science News Letter).

in|ter|fer|om|e|ter (in′tər fə rom′ə tər), *n.* an instrument for measuring very small lengths, distances, and other changes in the dimensions, density, and other properties of substances by means of the interference of two rays of light: *A kind of spectroscope that is coupled with existing telescopes, the interferometer gives a 10-times improved view of the weak absorption lines of atoms and molecules in space* (Wade Tilleux).

in|ter|fer|o|met|ric (in′tər fir′ə met′rik), *adj.* of or having to do with the measurement of wave lengths and other small dimensions and structural differences by means of an interferometer or similar device. **—in′ter|fer′o|met′ri|cal|ly,** *adv.*

in|ter|fer|om|e|try (in′tər fə rom′ə trē), *n.* the technique of measuring wave lengths and other small dimensions and structural changes by an interferometer or similar device.

in|ter|fer|on (in′tər fir′on), *n.* a protein produced within cells infected by a virus to protect similar types of cells for several days from infection by the same or other viruses. [< *interfer*(e) + New Latin *-on*]

in|ter|fer|tile (in′tər fėr′təl), *adj.* able to interbreed: *interfertile plant species.*

in|ter|fin|ger (in′tər fing′gər), *v.i. Geology.* (of strata) to be inserted between and into one another laterally.

in|ter|flow (*v.* in′tər flō′; *n.* in′tər flō′), *v., n.* **—*v.i.*** **1** to flow between. **2** to flow into each other; intermingle. **—*n.*** the act of interflowing.

in|ter|flu|ent (in tėr′flü ənt), *adj.* **1** flowing between. **2** flowing into each other.

in|ter|fluve (in′tər flüv), *n.* the land that separates two adjacent river valleys. [< *inter-* + Latin *fluvius* river]

in|ter|fold (in′tər fōld′), *v.t.* to fold one within another; fold together.

in|ter|fo|li|ate (in′tər fō′lē āt), *v.t.,* **-at|ed, -at|ing.** = interleave. [< *inter-* + Latin *folium* leaf]

in|ter|fra|ter|ni|ty (in′tər frə tėr′nə tē), *adj.* between or involving two or more fraternities: *an interfraternity conference.*

in|ter|fuse (in′tər fyüz′), *v.,* **-fused, -fus|ing.** **—*v.t.*** **1** to spread through; be diffused through; permeate. **2** to intersperse with something: *floating vapors interfused with light* (Longfellow). **3** to fuse together; blend; mix. **4** to pour in; infuse. **—*v.i.*** to become blended or fused.
[< Latin *interfūsus,* past participle of *interfundere* < *inter-* + *fundere* pour] **—in′ter|fu′sion,** *n.*

in|ter|ga|lac|tic (in′tər gə lak′tik), *adj.* situated or taking place between galaxies: *intergalactic space.*

in|ter|gen|er|a|tion|al (in′tər jen′ə rā′shə nəl), *adj.* occurring or existing between two or more generations: *They [most parents] may give a child the name of a relative to strengthen feelings of kinship, to keep alive an intergenerational awareness, or possibly to make a legacy more likely* (Science Journal).

in|ter|ge|ner|ic (in′tər jə ner′ik), *adj.* between genera: *an intergeneric hybrid.*

in|ter|gla|cial (in′tər glā′shəl), *adj., n. Geology.* **—*adj.*** occurring or formed between two glacial periods: *The present sea level corresponds approximately to the last interglacial high level of the sea that occurred about 30,000 to 35,000 years ago* (Richard C. Vetter).
—*n.* the period between two glacial epochs: *. . . the larger mammalian and reptilian fauna present in Britain since the great interglacial about 170,000 years ago* (New Scientist).

In|ter|glos|sa (in′tər glos′ə, -glôs′-), *n.* an artificial language devised by Lancelot Hogben about 1943, consisting of Latin and Greek roots combined with a Chinese system of syntax.

in|ter|gov|ern|men|tal (in′tər guv′ərn men′təl, -ər-), *adj.* between governments.

in|ter|gra|da|tion (in′tər grā dā′shən), *n.* the process of intergrading.

in|ter|grade (*n.* in′tər grād′; *v.* in′tər grād′), *n., v.,* **-grad|ed, -grad|ing.** **—*n.*** an intermediate grade or stage.
—*v.i.* to become alike through a continuous series of intermediate forms: *One population of animals or plants may intergrade with another.*

in|ter|graft (in′tər graft′, -gräft′), *v.t., v.i.* to graft together, usually reciprocally: *The tomato and potato are easily intergrafted* (Henry T. Northen).

in|ter|group (in′tər grüp′), *adj.* between groups: *intergroup relations.*

in|ter|growth (in′tər grōth′), *n.* a growing of things into each other.

in|ter|hem|i|spher|ic (in′tər hem ə sfer′ik), *adj.* **1** between hemispheres. **2** *Anatomy.* between the cerebral hemispheres.

in|ter|hu|man (in′tər hyü′mən), *adj.* between human beings; interpersonal: *interhuman behavior.*

in|ter|im (in′tər im), *n., adj.* **—*n.*** **1** the time between; meantime. **2** a temporary arrangement.
—*adj.* for the meantime; provisional; temporary: *an interim report.*
[< Latin *interim* in the meantime < *inter* between]

in|ter|in|dus|try (in′tər in′də strē, -dus trē), *adj.* between industries: *interindustry relations, interindustry transactions.*

interindustry analysis, = input-output analysis.

in|ter|in|sti|tu|tion|al (in′tər in′stə tü′shə nəl, -tyü′-), *adj.* between institutions: *interinstitutional arrangements, interinstitutional rivalry.*

in|ter|i|on|ic (in′tər ī on′ik), *adj.* between ions: *interionic forces, interionic attraction.*

in|te|ri|or (in tir′ē ər), *n., adj.* **—*n.*** **1** the inner surface or part; inside: *The interior of the house was beautifully decorated.* **2** the part of a region or country away from the coast or border: *There are deserts in the interior of Asia. To this tangled equatorial wilderness the young missionaries flew last week from an outpost in the interior* (Newsweek). **3** the affairs within a country, regarded as separate from foreign affairs: *The United States has a Department of the Interior to deal with patents, public lands, Indian affairs, and other matters.* **4** a picture of the inside of a room, house, factory, ship, aircraft, automobile, or other enclosed area. **5** the inner nature or character of anything.
—*adj.* **1** on the inside; inner: *The interior walls of the house are thinner than the heavy exterior walls.* **2** away from the coast or border; inland: *interior waterways that lead to the coast.* **3** having to do with affairs within a country; domestic. **4** private; secret. **5** of or in the mind or soul; mental; spiritual.
[< Latin *interior* inner, comparative of *inter* within] **—in|te′ri|or|ly,** *adv.*

***interior angle, 1** any one of the four angles formed inside two lines intersected by a straight line. **2** an angle formed inside a polygon by two adjacent sides.

interior angle
exterior angle

***interior angle**
definition 1

interior decoration, 1 the planning and arranging of furnishings and decorations for homes, offices, or public buildings. **2** the art or profession of an interior decorator.

interior decorator, a person whose business is planning and arranging the furnishings and decoration of houses, offices, or public buildings.

interior design, = interior decoration.

interior designer, = interior decorator.

interior drainage, drainage in which the waters do not reach the sea, but evaporate or sink into the ground.

in|te|ri|or|i|ty (in tir′ē ôr′ə tē, -or′-), *n.* **1** the state of being interior. **2** inner character or nature.

in|te|ri|or|ize (in tir′ē ə rīz), *v.t.,* **-ized, -iz|ing.** **1** to make interior: *to interiorize a scene or setting.* **2** = internalize.

interior monologue, a monologue, inaudible to other characters, by which a fictional or dramatic character externalizes his stream of consciousness.

in|ter|is|land (in′tər ī′lənd), *adj.* operating or existing between islands.

interj., interjection.

in|ter|ja|cent (in′tər jā′sənt), *adj.* lying between; intervening. [< Latin *interjacēns, -entis,* present participle of *interjacēre* < *inter-* between + *jacēre* to recline]

in|ter|jac|u|late (in′tər jak′yə lāt), *v.t.,* **-lat|ed, -lat|ing.** to interject (a remark or exclamation). [< *inter* + Latin *jaculārī* (with English *-ate*[1]) to throw, dart]

in|ter|ject (in′tər jekt′), *v.t.* to throw in between other things; insert; interpose: *Every now and then the speaker interjected a joke or story to keep us interested.* **—*v.i.*** *Obsolete.* to come between. [< Latin *interjectus,* past participle of *interjicere* < *inter-* between + *jacere* throw]

in|ter|jec|tion (in′tər jek′shən), *n.* **1a** an exclamation showing emotion. *Oh! ah! alas!* and *hurrah!* are interjections. **b** a part of speech or form class consisting of such exclamations. **2** the act of interjecting; sudden throwing in; abrupt insertion: *His interjection of amusing stories into his speech made it more interesting.* **3** something interjected; remark thrown in; exclamation.

in|ter|jec|tion|al (in′tər jek′shə nəl), *adj.* **1** of an interjection; used as an interjection. **2** containing an interjection. **3** interjected. **—in′ter|jec′tion|al|ly,** *adv.*

in|ter|jec|tive (in′tər jek′tiv), *adj.* that interjects; interjectory: *[He] writes what might be called interjective prose—he frequently interrupts himself for digressions* (New Yorker).

in|ter|jec|tor (in′tər jek′tər), *n.* a person who interjects.

in|ter|jec|to|ry (in′tər jek′tər ē), *adj.* interjectional; interjected. **—in′ter|jec′to|ri|ly,** *adv.*

in|ter|knit (in′tər nit′), *v.t., v.i.,* **-knit|ted** or **-knit, -knit|ting.** to knit together; intertwine.

in|ter|knot (in′tər not′), *v.t.,* **-knot|ted, -knot|ting.** to knot together.

in|ter|lace (*v.* in′tər lās′; *n.* in′tər lās′), *v.,* **-laced, -lac|ing,** *n.* **—*v.t.*** **1** to arrange (threads, strips, or branches) so that they go over and under each other; weave together; intertwine: *Baskets are made by interlacing reeds or fibers.* **2** *Figurative.* to give variety to; intersperse: *meadows interlaced with streams.*
—*v.i.* to cross each other over and under; mingle together in an intricate manner: *The branches of the trees interlaced above the path. The pilot looked down on interlacing roads and streams.*
—*n.* an ornament of thread, ribbon, or the like, woven together in an intricate pattern.

in|ter|lace|ment (in′tər lās′mənt), *n.* **1** the process of interlacing. **2** the state of being interlaced. **3** the result of interlacing; something interlaced.

in|ter|lam|i|nate (in′tər lam′ə nāt), *v.t.,* **-nat|ed, -nat|ing.** **1** to put between layers. **2** to apply in alternate layers. [< *inter-* + Latin *lāmina* thin layer of a substance + English *ate*[1}] **—in′ter|lam′i|na′tion,** *n.*

in|ter|lan|guage (in′tər lang′gwij), *n.* an artificial auxiliary language intended for international use: *Esperanto is an interlanguage.*

in|ter|lap (in′tər lap′), *v.i.,* **-lapped, -lap|ping.** = overlap.

in|ter|lard (in′tər lärd′), *v.t.* **1** to give variety to; mix; intersperse: *The speaker interlarded his long speech with amusing stories to keep his listeners interested. There also is a heavy interlarding of music, choral and solo* (New York Times). **SYN:** mingle. **2** (of things) to be intermixed in. **3** to insert; interpose: *When a little trifle of new matter was interlarded [in the prayer], his ear detected it* (Mark Twain). **4** *Obsolete.* to insert fat into lean meat for cooking purposes; lard. [< Old French *entrelarder* < *entre-* between + *larder* to lard < *lard* lard, fat < Latin *lārdum*] **—in′ter|lard′ment,** *n.*

in|ter|lay (in′tər lā′), *v.t.,* **-laid, -lay|ing.** **1** to lay between; interpose. **2** to vary with something laid between or inserted.

in|ter|lay|er (in′tər lā′ər), *n.* a layer between two or more layers.

in|ter|leaf (in′tər lēf′), *n., pl.* **-leaves.** **1** a leaf of paper put between other leaves of a book, for notes or the like. **2** the matter written on it.

in|ter|leave (*v.* in′tər lēv′; *n.* in′tər lēv′), *v.,* **-leaved, -leav|ing,** *n.* **—*v.t.*** **1** to insert a leaf or leaves of paper between the pages of. **2** *Figurative.* to insert anything like a leaf between.

—*n.* the correlation, by means of successive numbers, of physically separate locations of storage units in a computer.

in|ter|leu|kin-1 (in′tər lü′kin wun′), *n.* a protein secreted by various cells that functions especially in stimulating the production of T cells: *Interleukin-1 . . . is a protein with a molecular weight of 17,000 daltons that is synthesized primarily by the phagocytic white blood cells called macrophages* (Scientific American). [< *inter-* + *leuk* (ocyte) + *-in*[2]]

in|ter|leu|kin-2 (in′tər lü′kin tü′), *n.* **1** a protein secreted by T cells activated by certain antigens, important as mediators of cellular immunity. **2** this protein produced by genetic engineering, used experimentally in the treatment of cancer: *Interleukin-2 transforms specialized white blood cells into natural killer cells which attack and destroy cancer cells* (J. E. Bishop).

in|ter|li|brar|y loan (in′tər lī′brer′ē, -brər-), **1** an arrangement whereby one library can borrow books or other materials from other libraries. **2** a book or other library item borrowed by this arrangement.

in|ter|line[1] (in′tər līn′), *v.t.*, **-lined, -lin|ing.** to insert an extra lining in (a garment) between the outer cloth and the ordinary lining. [< *inter-* + *line*[2]]

in|ter|line[2] (in′tər līn′), *v.*, **-lined, -lin|ing,** *n.* —*v.t., v.i.* **1** to insert words or symbols between the lines of: *to interline a document.* **2** to write, print, or mark between the lines: *The teacher interlined corrections on the students' themes.* —*n.* an intervening line. [< Medieval Latin *interlineare* < Latin *inter-* between + *līneāre* reduce to a line < *līnea* (linen) thread, line]

in|ter|lin|e|al (in′tər lin′ē əl), *adj.* **1** = interlinear. **2** arranged in alternate lines. —**in′ter|lin′e|al|ly,** *adv.*

in|ter|lin|e|ar (in′tər lin′ē ər), *adj.* **1** inserted between the lines: *interlinear notes.* **2** containing two different languages or versions in alternate lines: *an interlinear translation of Virgil.* —**in′ter|lin′e|ar|ly,** *adv.*

Gallia est omnis dīvīsa in partēs trēs
Gaul as a whole is divided into three parts
Interlinear translation of Caesar

in|ter|lin|e|ate (in′tər lin′ē āt), *v.i., v.i.*, **-at|ed, -at|ing.** = interline[2]. —**in′ter|lin′e|a′tion,** *n.*

in|ter|lin|gua (in′tər ling′gwə), *n.* an international language, devised by the International Auxiliary Language Association of New York City and published in 1951, based on English and Romance and having a simplified grammatical structure. [< *inter-* + Latin *lingua* tongue, language]

in|ter|lin|ing (in′tər lī′ning), *n.* **1** an extra lining inserted between the outer cloth and the ordinary lining of a garment. **2** a fabric for such a lining. [< *inter-* + *lining*]

in|ter|link (*v.* in′tər lingk′; *n.* in′tər lingk′), *v., n.* —*v.t., v.i.* to link together. —*n.* a connecting link.

in|ter|lo|cal (in′tər lō′kəl), *adj.* carried on between or connecting different localities: *interlocal traffic.*

in|ter|lock (*v.* in′tər lok′; *n.* in′tər lok′), *v., n., adj.* —*v.t.* **1** to lock or join with one another: *The two stags interlocked their horns while fighting.* **2** to connect (railroad signals, switches, and bridges) in such a way that they cannot operate independently. —*v.i.* **1** to lock or join with each other: *The different pieces of a jigsaw puzzle interlock. The bumpers of the cars interlocked.* **2** to be arranged and operated in conjunction with each other, as two or more railroad switches. —*n.* the state of being interlocked. —*adj.* knitted with a set of alternately arranged needles . . . *interlock cotton lisle mesh* (New Yorker). —**in′ter|lock′er,** *n.*

interlocker signal system, a system of interlocking signals.

in|ter|lock|ing directorate (in′tər lok′ing), the directorate of a company, some of whose members are also on the boards of directors of other companies, thus extending their control over several corporations.

interlocking signals, railroad signals connected by catches, bolts, and other apparatus, in such a way that their operation is dependent on other signals being activated first, as by a train passing through.

interlocking tower, a building or tower from which the switches and signals of a railroad yard or section of the line are controlled.

in|ter|lo|cu|tion (in′tər lō kyü′shən), *n.* **1** = conversation. **2** = dialogue. [< Latin *interlocūtiō, -ōnis* < *interloquī* converse < *inter-* between + *loquī* speak]

in|ter|loc|u|tor (in′tər lok′yə tər), *n.* **1** a person who takes part in a conversation or dialogue: *Our interlocutors were never arrogant or acrimonious, but earnestly inquiring* (Harper's). **2** the man in a minstrel show who asks the end man questions.

in|ter|loc|u|to|ry (in′tər lok′yə tôr′ē, -tōr′-), *adj.* **1** of or in conversation or dialogue. **2** *Law.* **a** made during a lawsuit or other action; not final: *an interlocutory decree.* **b** of or having to do with a decision so made. **3** interjected into the main course of speech.

in|ter|lope (in′tər lōp′), *v.i.*, **-loped, -lop|ing. 1** to thrust onself into the affairs of others. **2** to intrude into some region or field of trade without a proper license. [back formation < *interloper*, probably < *inter-* + *lope* to run, or Dutch *looper* runner] —**in′ter|lop′er,** *n.*

in|ter|lu|ca|tion (in′tər lü kā′shən), *n.* the thinning of a tree or a wood to let in light. [< Latin *interlūcātiō, -ōnis* < *interlūcāre* to thin a tree < *inter-* between + *lūx, lūcis* light]

in|ter|lude (in′tər lüd), *n., v.*, **-lud|ed, -lud|ing.** —*n.* **1** anything that is thought of as filling time between two things; interval: *There was an interlude of sunshine between the two showers. He would look on the affair as no more than an interlude in the main business of his life* (Hawthorne). **2** a piece of instrumental music played between the parts of a song, church service, or drama. **3** an entertainment between the acts of a play. **4** in early English and medieval drama: **a** a short, humorous play, commonly introduced between the parts of the long mystery plays or given as part of other entertainment. **b** a stage play of a popular nature; comedy; farce. —*v.i.* = intervene. —*v.t.* to interrupt, as with an interlude. [< Medieval Latin *interludium* < Latin *inter-* between + *lūdus* a play]

in|ter|lu|nar (in′tər lü′nər), *adj.* having to do with the time when the moon is not seen at night; being between the old moon and the new moon. [< *inter-* + Latin *lūnāris* lunar]

in|ter|lu|na|tion (in′tər lü nā′shən), *n.* **1** the period between the old and the new moon. **2** *Figurative.* any blank or dark interval.

in|ter|mar|riage (in′tər mar′ij), *n.* **1** marriage between members of different families, tribes, religions, or racial groups. **2** marriage between close blood relations within a family, clan, or other group.

in|ter|mar|ry (in′tər mar′ē), *v.i.*, **-ried, -ry|ing. 1** to become connected by marriage, as of families, tribes, or religious or racial groups: *The families of the old town have intermarried for generations.* **2** to marry within the family or with close relations.

in|ter|max|il|lar|y (in′tər mak′sə ler′ē), *adj., n., pl.* **-lar|ies.** —*adj.* situated between the maxillae. —*n. Anatomy.* the premaxilla.

in|ter|med|dle (in′tər med′əl), *v.*, **-dled, -dling.** —*v.i.* to meddle; interfere. —*v.t. Obsolete.* to intermingle; intermix. —**in′ter|med′dler,** *n.*

in|ter|me|di|a[1] (in′tər mē′dē ə), *n.* a plural of **intermedium.**

in|ter|me|di|a[2] (in′tər mē′dē ə), *n.* the combined use of many different artistic devices and techniques to produce a show, exhibition, or other entertainment; mixed media. [< *inter-* + *media*]

in|ter|me|di|a|cy (in′tər mē′dē ə sē), *n., pl.* **-cies.** intermediate position, relation, or agency.

in|ter|me|di|ar|y (in′tər mē′dē er′ē), *n., pl.* **-ar|ies,** *adj.* —*n.* **1** a person who acts between others to bring about an agreement; person who acts for one person with another; go-between: *The teacher acted as an intermediary for the students with the principal.* SYN: middleman, mediator. **2** a medium; means. **3** an intermediate form or stage. —*adj.* **1** acting between others; acting for another; mediating. **2** being between; intermediate: *A cocoon is an intermediary stage between caterpillar and butterfly.* [< Latin *intermedius* intermediate (< *inter-* between + *medius* in the middle) + English *-ary*]

in|ter|me|di|ate[1] (in′tər mē′dē it), *adj., n.* —*adj.* **1** being or occurring between; middle: *The intermediate department of the Sunday School is between the primary and the adult departments. Gray is intermediate between black and white.* SYN: interposed. **2** acting between others; intervening. —*n.* **1** something in between. **2** a person who acts between others to bring about an agreement; mediator. **3** a compound formed between the initial and final stages in a chemical process. **4** *U.S.* an automobile between the standard and the compact models in size. [< Medieval Latin *intermediatus* < Latin *intermedius*; see etym. under **intermediary**] —**in′ter|me′di|ate|ly,** *adv.* —**in′ter|me′di|ate|ness,** *n.*

in|ter|me|di|ate[2] (in′tər mē′dē āt), *v.i.*, **-at|ed, -at|ing. 1** to act between others; mediate. **2** *Obsolete.* to intervene. [< *inter-* + *mediate*, verb]

intermediate boson or **intermediate vector boson,** = W particle.

intermediate frequency, the middle frequency in a superheterodyne radio receiver, resulting from the change of the incoming signal by the heterodyne process.

intermediate host, the host of an adult parasite in which the parasite may reproduce only asexually.

in|ter|me|di|ate-range (in′tər mē′dē it rānj′), *adj.* **1** *Military.* able to operate effectively beyond a short range but not at long-range distances. **2** *Business, Commerce.* having or lying within an intermediate price range; neither very high nor very low in cost or yield.

intermediate range ballistic missile, a ballistic missile with a range of over 200 but less than 1,500 miles.

intermediate school, 1 in the United States: **a** a junior high school. **b** a school consisting of grades 4, 5, and 6. **c** any school intermediate between primary school and high school. *Abbr:* I.S. or IS (no periods). **2** (in Great Britain) a school for pupils from 12 to 14 years of age, between junior school and senior school.

in|ter|me|di|a|tion (in′tər mē′dē ā′shən), *n.* **1** the action of intermediating. **2** the state of being intermediate.

in|ter|me|di|a|tor (in′tər mē′dē ā′tər), *n.* a person or thing that intermediates.

in|ter|med|in (in′tər med′in), *n.* a hormone formed by the pituitary gland, that controls pigmentation, causing changes in body color. [< New Latin (*pars*) *intermedia* a section of the pituitary gland + English *-in*]

in|ter|me|di|um (in′tər mē′dē əm), *n., pl.* **-di|ums** or **-di|a. 1** an intervening agent or medium; intermediary. **2** a musical or dance interlude. **3** *Anatomy.* a bone of the wrist situated between the ulna and radius, or the corresponding bone of the ankle between the tibia and fibula. [< Latin *intermedium*, neuter of *intermedius*; see etym. under **intermediary**[1]]

in|ter|men|stru|al (in′tər men′strů əl), *adj.* occurring between the menstrual periods.

in|ter|ment (in′tėr′ment), *n.* the act of putting a dead body into a grave or tomb; burial. [< *inter* bury + *-ment*]

in|ter|mesh (in′tər mesh′), *v.i.* to mesh together: *The armadillo, his precision-made armor plate intermeshing fluidly, moseys along, oblivious of time* (Time).

in|ter|me|tal|lic (in′tər mə tal′ik), *adj., n.* —*adj.* formed by the union of two or more metallic elements. Intermetallic compounds are stronger and more heat-resistant than ordinary metals. —*n.* an intermetallic compound.

in|ter|mez|zo (in′tər met′sō, -med′zō), *n., pl.* **-mez|zos, -mez|zi** (-met′sē, -med′zē). **1** a short musical composition played between the main divisions of an opera, symphony, or other long musical work. **2** a short dramatic, musical, or other entertainment of light character between the acts of a drama. **3** an independent musical composition of similar character. **4** a short comic opera played in the intervals between the acts of a main opera in the 1600's and 1700's. [< Italian *intermezzo* < Latin *intermedius* intermediate]

in|ter|mi|gra|tion (in′tər mī grā′shən), *n.* reciprocal migration.

in|ter|mi|na|ble (in tėr′mə nə bəl), *adj.* **1** never stopping; unceasing; endless: *the interminable noise of city streets.* SYN: unending, limitless. **2** so long as to seem endless; very long and tiring: *interminable talk.* [< Late Latin *interminābilis* < Latin *in-* not + *termināre* to end < *terminus* end] —**in|ter′mi|na|ble|ness,** *n.* —**in|ter′mi|na|bly,** *adv.*

in|ter|min|gle (in′tər ming′gəl), *v.t., v.i.*, **-gled, -gling.** to mix together; mingle: *He was left alone with endless memories of intermingled farce and tragedy* (Lytton Strachey).

in|ter|min|is|te|ri|al (in′tər min′ə stir′ē əl), *adj.* between or involving different ministries: *an interministerial committee.*

in|ter|mis|sion (in′tər mish′ən), *n.* **1** a time between periods of activity; pause: *After the first act of the play, there was a 10-minute intermission.* SYN: interval. **2a** the act of stopping for a time; interruption: *The rain continued all day without intermission.* **b** *Rare.* temporary cessation, respite, relief, etc. (from something). [< Latin *intermissiō, -ōnis* < *intermittere* intermit]

in|ter|mis|sive (in′tər mis′iv), *adj.* = intermittent.

in|ter|mit (in′tər mit′), *v.t., v.i.*, **-mit|ted, -mit|ting.** to stop for a time; discontinue; suspend: *Let me know the exact time when your courts intermit* (Samuel Johnson). [< Latin *intermittere* < *inter-*

Pronunciation Key: hat, āge, cãre, fär; let, ēqual, tėrm; it, īce; hot, ōpen, ôrder; oil, out; cup, pu̇t, rüle; child; long; thin; ᴛʜen; zh, measure;
ə represents **a** in about, **e** in taken, **i** in pencil, **o** in lemon, **u** in circus.

between + *mittere* send] —**in′ter|mit′ter**, *n.*
in|ter|mit|tence (in′tər mit′əns), *n.* the state or condition of being intermittent: *the intermittence of a fever.*
in|ter|mit|ten|cy (in′tər mit′ən sē), *n.* = intermittence.
in|ter|mit|tent (in′tər mit′ənt), *adj.* stopping and beginning again; pausing at intervals: *The pilot watched for an intermittent red light, flashing on and off every 15 seconds.* —**in′ter|mit′tent|ly**, *adv.*
intermittent current, an electric current that is repeatedly interrupted.
intermittent fever, a fever that alternately ceases for a time and then begins again, as in malaria.
in|ter|mix (in′tər miks′), *v.*, **-mixed** or **-mixt**, **-mix·ing**. —*v.t.* to mix together; blend; intermingle.
—*v.i.* to be or become mixed together; mix, blend, or associate intimately: *Oil and water do not intermix.*
in|ter|mix|ture (in′tər miks′chər), *n.* **1** the act of mixing together; blending. **2** the state of being intermixed. **3** a mass of ingredients mixed together; mixture; blend. **4** something added by intermixing.
in|ter|mo|dal (in′tər mō′dəl), *adj.* **1** combining or integrating different modes of transportation: *Both vessels are part of an intermodal system in which United States Freight uses railroads to "piggyback" trailers and container vans to ports for delivery* (New York Times). **2** used in an integrated system of transportation: *intermodal containers.*
in|ter|mo|lec|u|lar (in′tər mə lek′yə lər), *adj.* being or occurring between molecules. —**in′ter|mo·lec′u|lar|ly**, *adv.*
in|ter|mon|tane (in′tər mon′tān), *adj.* located between mountains or neighboring mountain ranges: *the depth and ruggedness of intermontane valleys* (Science News). [< *inter-* + Latin *montānus* mountainous < *mōns, montis* mountain]
in|ter|moun|tain (in′tər moun′tən), *adj.* = intermontane.
in|ter|mun|dane (in′tər mun′dān), *adj.* occurring between worlds or between heavenly bodies. [< *inter-* + Latin *mundānus* mundane]
in|ter|mus|cu|lar (in′tər mus′kyə lər), *adj.* located between muscles or muscular fibers.
in|tern[1] (in tėrn′), *v., n.* —*v.t.* to confine within the limits of a country or place; force to stay in a certain place. Soldiers or ships who enter a neutral country or its ports in war are interned there until the war is over.
—*n.* a person who is interned, such as an enemy alien during wartime; internee.
[< French *interner* < Middle French *interne;* see etym. under **intern**[3]]
in|tern[2] (in′tėrn), *n., v.* —*n.* **1** a doctor acting as an assistant and undergoing training in a hospital. After a student graduates from medical school, he is usually an intern for a year before he starts his own practice. **2** a student in a professional field who receives in-service training under experienced supervision, such as a student teacher. **3** an inmate. Also, **interne**.
—*v.i.* to be an intern.
[American English < French *interne*, adjective < Middle French; see etym. under **intern**[3]]
in|tern[3] (in tėrn′), *adj. Archaic.* internal. [< Middle French *interne*, learned borrowing from Latin *internus* internal]
in|ter|nal (in tėr′nəl), *adj., n.* —*adj.* **1** on the inside; inner: *the internal organs of the body. An accident often causes internal injuries as well as cuts and bruises.* **2** to be taken inside the body: *Pills are internal remedies.* **3** entirely inside; coming from within; belonging to a thing or subject in itself; intrinsic: *Internal evidence of the date of a book is evidence obtained from the book itself.*
4 having to do with affairs within a country; domestic: *internal disturbances, internal politics.* See also **internal revenue**. **5** of or belonging to the inner nature or life; of the mind or soul; subjective: *Thoughts are internal.* **6** *British.* (of a student) having studied in the university where he is examined. **7** *Anatomy.* situated inward from the surface of the body, or nearer the median line (used in the names of vessels, nerves, and the like, correlated with others called *external*).
8 *Psychology.* coming from within the body of the individual, as a stimulus.
—*n.* an intrinsic or essential attribute or quality.
internals, the internal parts of the body; entrails: *We ... counted his teeth and compared his internals with those of the common species* (James Wilson).
[< Medieval Latin *internalis* < Latin *internus* within < *in* in] —**in|ter′nal|ly**, *adv.*
in|ter|nal-com|bus|tion (in tėr′nəl kəm bus′chən), *adj.* having to do with or relating to internal-combustion engines.

***internal-combustion engine**, **1** an engine in which power is produced by exploding a mixture of fuel and air inside the engine itself, usually inside cylinders. Gasoline engines and diesel engines are internal-combustion engines; steam engines are not. **2** a gas turbine installation in which combustion occurs within a continuously flowing system.

***internal-combustion engine**
definition 1

two-stroke cycle gasoline engine:

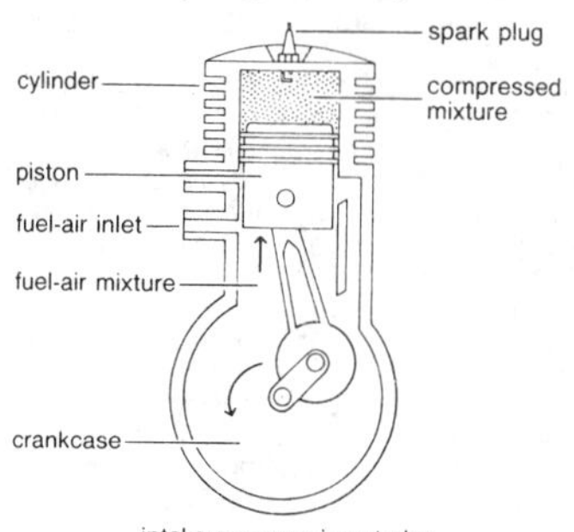

intake-compression stroke

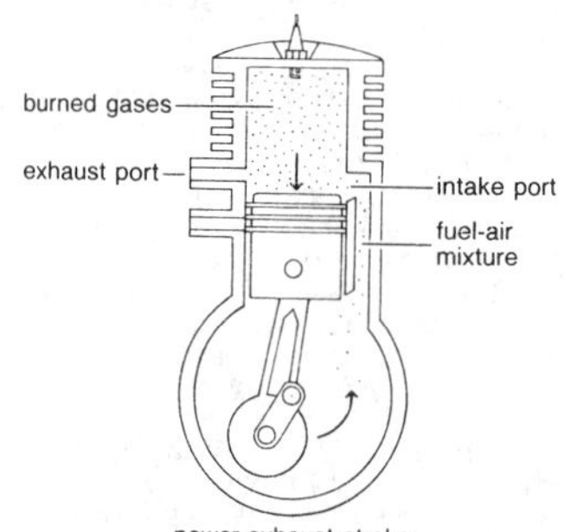

power-exhaust stroke

internal ear, = inner ear.
internal environment, *Biology.* the fluid in which the cells of the organs and tissues of the body exist. Too much or too little water or salt in the internal environment can damage or kill cells.
in|ter|nal|i|ty (in′tər nal′ə tē), *n., pl.* **-ties**. **1** state or quality of being internal. **2** something internal.
in|ter|nal|i|za|tion (in tėr′nə lə zā′shən), *n.* **1** *Psychology.* the act or process of internalizing. **2** *U.S. Finance.* a system of trading securities within brokerage offices rather than transmitting trading orders to the floor of an exchange: *For the public, moreover, internalization could lead to drastic changes in the way that securities are bought and sold* (Leonard Sloane).
in|ter|nal|ize (in tėr′nə līz), *v.t.*, **-ized**, **-iz|ing**. *Psychology.* **1** to adopt and assimilate (an idea, habit, custom, or mannerism) into the framework of one's personality. **2** to withdraw (an emotion, problem, or thought) into oneself; repress; suppress: *Compared with the adolescent who internalizes his distress ... the delinquent has received a disproportionate share of attention* (New York Times).
internal jugular vein, either of two large veins in the neck that collect blood from the brain, face, and neck and return it toward the heart.
internal medicine, the branch of medicine dealing with the internal organs and the diagnosis and treatment of their diseases.
internal pollution, harmful ingestion of synthetic substances in drugs and foods.
internal respiration, the exchange of oxygen and carbon dioxide between the blood cells and the tissue cells; tissue respiration.
internal revenue, the revenue derived from taxes on domestic goods and incomes. The Internal Revenue Service in the United States government deals with the collection of these taxes.
internal rhyme, the rhyming of a word within a line of verse with a word at the end of the line. *Example: that orbèd* maiden, *with white fire* laden (Shelley).
in|ter|nals (in tėr′nəlz), *n.pl.* See under **internal**.

***internal screw**
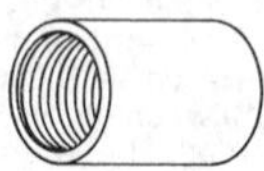

***internal screw**, a hollow cylindrical part with an interior spiral thread to receive the thread of the external screw; female screw.

internal secretion, a substance secreted by a gland, discharged within the body; hormone.
internal senses, the senses that are stimulated by changes taking place inside the body and regulate such feelings as hunger, fatigue, pain, and thirst; the interoceptive senses.
internal thread, = internal screw.
internat., international.
in|ter|na|tion|al (in′tər nash′ə nəl, -nash′nəl), *adj., n.* —*adj.* **1** between or among nations: *A treaty is an international agreement.* **2** having to do with the relations between nations.
—*n.* **1** a person belonging to two different nations, such as one who is native of one country and resident in another. **2** *British.* **a** an international tournament. **b** a person who takes part or has taken part in such a tournament. —**in′ter|na′·tion|al|ly**, *adv.*
In|ter|na|tion|al (in′tər nash′ə nəl, -nash′nəl), *n.* one of several international socialistic organizations.
international candle, = candle (def. 3b).
international code, continental code, a modified form of the Morse code.
***International Date Line**, an imaginary line agreed upon as the place where each new calendar day begins. It runs north and south through the Pacific, mostly along the 180th meridian. When it is Sunday east of the International Date Line it is Monday west of it.

***International Date Line**

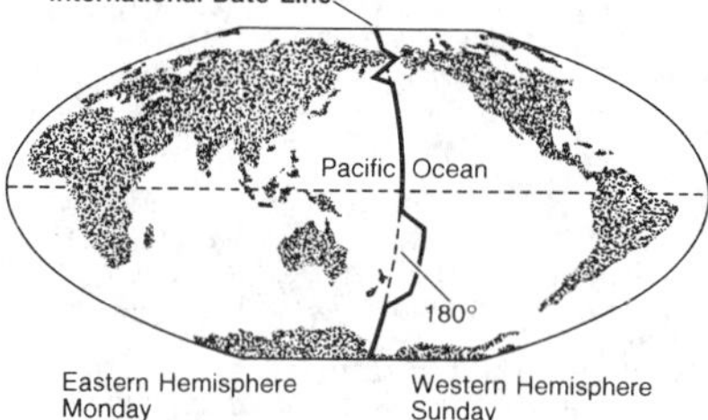

in|ter|na|tion|al|ise (in′tər nash′ə nə līz, -nash′nə-), *v.t., v.i.*, **-ised**, **-is|ing**. *Especially British.* internationalize.
in|ter|na|tion|al|ism (in′tər nash′ə nə liz′əm, -nash′nə liz-), *n.* the principle of international cooperation for the good of all nations.
in|ter|na|tion|al|ist (in′tər nash′ə nə list, -nash′nə-), *n., adj.* —*n.* **1** a person who favors internationalism. **2** an expert in international affairs or international law. —*adj.* favoring internationalism.
in|ter|na|tion|al|is|tic (in′tər nash′ə nə lis′tik, -nash′nə-), *adj.* = internationalist.
in|ter|na|tion|al|i|ty (in′tər nash′ə nal′ə tē), *n.* international quality, condition, or character.
in|ter|na|tion|al|ize (in′tər nash′ə nə līz, -nash′nə-), *v.*, **-ized**, **-iz|ing**. —*v.t.* **1** to make international: *to internationalize units of weights and measures.* **2** to bring (territory) under the control of several nations or of an international body.
—*v.i.* to become international: *They [the merchants] broke down the old local self-sufficiencies of the earlier middle ages; they internationalized* (Listener). —**in′ter|na′tion|al|i|za′tion**, *n.*
international law, the system of rules regarding peace, war, and neutrality which many nations consider binding in their relations with each other.
international mile, = international nautical mile.
international Morse code, = continental code.
international nautical mile, a unit of linear measure recommended for sea and air navigation and adopted by several countries, equal to 1,852 meters or 6,076.11549 feet.
International Phonetic Alphabet, an alphabet developed by the International Phonetic Association, with which the pronunciation of any language can be represented. *Abbr:* IPA (no periods).
international pitch, *Music.* a fixed standard of concert pitch that places A above middle C at 440 vibrations a second; Stuttgart pitch.
international relations, the official contacts between countries that have independent, national governments, carried on by the exchange of ambassadors or ministers.
International Style, a style of architecture that began in Europe between 1920 and 1930 as a revolt against traditional forms. It is characterized by an emphasis on functional design, large window and porch area, and strong base construction.
international unit, any one of various units used internationally to measure the potency of biological substances such as vitamins, hormones, and enzymes: *If the label gives the strength in international units ... instead of milligrams, divide by 20 to convert into milligrams* (Science News

Letter). *Abbr:* IU (no periods).

in|terne (in′tėrn), *n.* = intern[2].

in|ter|ne|cine (in′tər nē′sən, -sīn), *adj.* **1** destructive to both sides: *an internecine struggle for control of a party. Any international war will be internecine.* **2** deadly; destructive. SYN: murderous. [< Latin *internecīnus* < *internecāre* kill < *inter-* between (beyond) + *nex, necis* slaughter]

in|ter|nee (in′tėr nē′), *n.* a person who is interned, such as a prisoner of war or enemy alien.

in|terne|ship (in′tėrn ship), *n.* = internship.

in|ter|neu|ral (in′tər nůr′əl, -nyůr′-), *adj.* between nerves: *interneural transmission of hearing.*

in|ter|neu|ron (in′tər nůr′on, -nyůr′-), *n.* a nerve cell that connects afferent and efferent, or sensory and motor, nerve cells; internuncial neuron.

in|ter|neu|ron|al (in′tər nůr′ə nəl, -nyůr′-; -nů rō′-, -nyů-), *adj.* of or having to do with an interneuron or interneurons: *interneuronal communication.*

in|tern|ist (in tėr′nist), *n.* **1** a doctor who treats internal diseases, or those of the internal organs not curable by surgery. **2** a physician, as distinguished from a surgeon: *A man's brain, if he had a stroke, was in the province of the general internist* (Time). [< *intern*(al) + *-ist*]

in|tern|ment (in tėrn′mənt), *n.* **1** the act of interning. **2** the condition of being interned; confinement within the limits of a country or place.

internment camp, a camp in which enemy aliens, prisoners of war, or others considered dangerous to pursuing a war effort are confined during wartime.

in|ter|nod|al (in′tər nō′dəl), *adj.* **1** of or having to do with an internode. **2** situated between nodes. **3** constituting or including an internode.

in|ter|node (in′tər nōd′), *n.* **1** *Botany.* that part of a stem or branch between two of the nodes from which leaves arise. **2** *Anatomy, Zoology.* any part between two nodes or joints, such as a bone, a part of the neural cord of an arthropod, or the stem of a bryozoan.

in|ter nos (in′tər nōs′), *Latin.* between ourselves; confidentially.

in|tern|ship (in′tėrn ship), *n.* **1** position or service as an intern. **2** = apprenticeship.

in|ter|nun|cial (in′tər nun′shəl), *adj.* **1** *Anatomy.* serving to connect nerve fibers or their paths of transmission: *internuncial neurons.* **2** of or having to do with an internuncio. [< *inter-* + Latin *nuncius,* or *nuntius* messenger + English *-al*[1]] **—in′ter|nun′cial|ly,** *adv.*

in|ter|nun|ci|a|ture (in′tər nun′shē ə chər), *n.* **1** a nation, territory, or other region having an internuncio. **2** the office or function of an internuncio.

in|ter|nun|ci|o (in′tər nun′shē ō), *n., pl.* **-ci|os.** **1** an ambassador of the Pope ranking next below a nuncio. **2** a minister representing a government. [< Italian *internunzio* < Latin *internuntius* < *inter-* between + *nuncius,* or *nuntius* messenger, nuncio]

in|ter|nup|tial (in′tər nup′shəl), *adj.* **1** having to do with intermarriage. **2** occurring between two marriages of the same person.

in|ter|o|ce|an|ic (in′tər ō′shē an′ik), *adj.* between oceans: *an interoceanic canal.*

in|ter|o|cep|tive (in′tər ə sep′tiv), *adj.* having to do with or aroused by stimuli from inside or within the viscera of the body: *The interoceptive senses respond to changes in the organs and tissues.*

in|ter|o|cep|tor (in′tər ə sep′tər), *n.* a sense organ stimulated inside the body, as by some chemical change in the muscles, nerves, or blood. [< Latin *interus* inner + English (re)*ceptor*]

in|ter|oc|u|lar (in′tər ok′yə lər), *adj., n.* **—*adj.*** placed or occurring between the eyes, as a stereo camera.
—*n.* an interocular camera or adjustment device.

in|ter|of|fice (in′tər ôf′is, -of′-), *adj.* between offices of an organization: *an interoffice phone, an interoffice memo.*

in|ter|op|er|a|ble (in′tər op′ər ə bəl, -op′rə-), *adj.* capable of operating together or reciprocally: *The two nations' forces are working in parallel, and Skynet [The Royal Navy's satellite communications system] is compatible and interoperable with the US Defence Communications Satellite System* (Science Journal).

in|ter|os|cu|late (in′tər os′kyə lāt), *v.i.,* **-lat|ed, -lat|ing.** **1** to interpenetrate or inosculate with each other. **2** to have points of contact or resemblance. **3** to form a connecting link between objects, species, or the like.

in|ter|os|cu|la|tion (in′tər os′kyə lā′shən), *n.* interconnection by or as if by osculation.

in|ter|par|ty (in′tər pär′tē), *adj.* occurring between political parties: *interparty strife, interparty dispute.*

in|ter|pel|lant (in′tər pel′ənt), *n., adj.* **—*n.*** a person who interpellates.
—*adj.* that interpellates.

in|ter|pel|late (in′tər pel′āt, in tėr′pə lāt), *v.t.,* **-lat|ed, -lat|ing.** to ask formally in a legislature for an explanation of official action or of government policy. [< Latin *interpellāre* (with English *-ate*[1]) interrupt (in speaking) < *inter-* between + *pellere* push, drive]

in|ter|pel|la|tion (in′tər pə lā′shən, in tėr′-), *n.* a formal request made in a legislature for an explanation of official action or government policy.

in|ter|pel|la|tor (in′tər pə lā′tər, in tėr′pə lā′-), *n.* = interpellant.

in|ter|pen|e|trate (in′tər pen′ə trāt), *v.,* **-trat|ed, -trat|ing.** **—*v.t.*** to penetrate thoroughly or between the parts of; permeate; pervade.
—*v.i.* to penetrate each other; unite or mingle by mutual penetration. **—in′ter|pen′e|tra′tion,** *n.*

in|ter|pen|e|tra|tive (in′tər pen′ə trā′tiv), *adj.* intimately or mutually penetrative.

in|ter|per|son|al (in′tər pėr′sə nəl), *adj.* **1** between persons: *Aggressive behavior may be the response of a disordered brain to the demands of interpersonal dynamics* (Science News Letter). **2** requiring or seeking contact with other people: *Man is not only a biological animal but also an interpersonal, social, and cultural being.* **—in′ter|per′son|al|ly,** *adv.*

in|ter|phase (in′tər fāz′), *n. Biology.* the stage or condition of a cell when it is not dividing and activities other than cell division are paramount.

in|ter|phone (in′tər fōn′), *n.* a telephone system over which members of an office staff, the crew of an airplane, tank, or ship, or some other group of people can talk to each other; intercom.

in|ter|plane (in′tər plān′), *adj.* being between planes: *interplane struts of an airplane.*

in|ter|plan|e|tar|y (in′tər plan′ə ter′ē), *adj.* **1** situated or taking place between planets; in the region of the planets: *interplanetary gases. To achieve new living space for men will require an immense leap forward from interplanetary flight to interstellar flight* (Atlantic). **2** within the solar system, but outside the atmosphere of any planet or the sun.

in|ter|plant[1] (in′tər plant′), *v.t.* to plant between: *A few tulips interplanted amongst wallflowers* (Listener). [< *inter-* + *plant,* verb]

in|ter|plant[2] (in′tər plant′), *adj.* **1** between factories or plants: *interplant wage benefits.* **2** in more than one factory or plant: *an interplant truck driver.* [< *inter-* + *plant* factory]

in|ter|play (in′tər plā′), *n., v.* **—*n.*** action or influence on each other; reciprocal play: *the interplay of light and shadow. The interplay of events and characters makes a story interesting. No one of its parts is more essential than the interplay of every part with every other* (Harper's). SYN: interaction.
—*v.i.* to exert mutual action or influence.

in|ter|plead (in′tər plēd′), *v.i. Law.* to plead or go to trial with each other in order to determine which is the rightful claimant against a third party.

in|ter|plead|er (in′tər plē′dər), *n. Law.* **1** the process of interpleading. **2** a person who interpleads.

in|ter|point|ing (in′tər poin′ting), *n.* a method of printing in Braille so that the dots on one side of the page do not interfere with those printed on the other side.

In|ter|pol (in′tər pōl′, -pol′), *n.* the International Criminal Police Organization, organized to assist police of its member nations in international crime investigations: *In response to messages from Interpol, the police made inquiries in various parts of the country yesterday* (London Times). [< *inter*(national) *pol*(ice)]

in|ter|po|lar (in′tər pō′lər), *adj.* situated between or connecting the poles, as of a voltaic battery.

in|ter|po|late (in tėr′pə lāt), *v.,* **-lat|ed, -lat|ing.** **—*v.t.*** **1** to alter (a book, passage, music, or other written material) by putting in new words or groups of words, especially without authorization or deceptively: *So many writers had interpolated the old manuscript that it was hard to tell what parts were genuine.* **2** to put in (new words, passages, music, or other written material). **3** *Mathematics.* to find or insert (an unknown term) between two known terms in a series. **4** to insert or introduce (something additional or different) between other things, or in a series; interpose. SYN: intercalate, interject.
—*v.i.* to make insertions or interpolations. [< Latin *interpolāre* (with English *-ate*[1]) freshen up, alter < *inter-* (intensive) + *polīre* to smoothe, polish] **—in|ter′po|lat′er,** *n.* **—in|ter′po|la′tion,** *n.*

in|ter|po|la|tive (in tėr′pə lā′tiv), *adj.* having the effect of interpolation.

in|ter|po|la|tor (in tėr′pə lā′tər), *n.* a person who interpolates.

in|ter|pop|u|la|tion|al (in′tər pop′yə lā′shə nəl), *adj.* occurring or existing between populations.

in|ter|pos|al (in′tər pō′zəl), *n.* interposition; intervention.

in|ter|pose (in′tər pōz′), *v.,* **-posed, -pos|ing.** **—*v.t.*** **1** to put between; insert: *to interpose the hand between the eye and a light.* **2** to put forward; break in with: *She interposed an objection at this point.*
—*v.i.* **1** to come between other things; be between other things: *A cloud interposing hid the sun.* **2** to interrupt. **3** to interfere in order to help; intervene: *Mother interposed in the dispute between my brothers.* SYN: intercede, mediate. [< French *interposer* < *inter-* between, inter- + *poser* to place, pose[1]] **—in′ter|pos′er,** *n.* **—in′ter|pos′ing|ly,** *adv.*

in|ter|po|si|tion (in′tər pə zish′ən), *n.* **1** the act of interposing: *I resented his interposition of an objection before I finished speaking.* **2** something interposed: *A shelter, and a kind of shading cool Interposition, as a summer's cloud* (Milton).

in|ter|po|si|tion|ist (in′tər pə zish′ə nist), *n.* a person who advocates, or takes part in, interposition: *These interpositionists who stand on railroad tracks to block U.S. troop trains* (Time).

in|ter|pret (in tėr′prit), *v.t.* **1** to explain the meaning of: *to interpret a hard passage in a book, to interpret a dream. They shall call his name Emmanuel, which being interpreted is, God with us* (Matthew 1:23). SYN: expound, elucidate, unfold. See syn. under **explain.** **2** to bring out the meaning of (a dramatic work, a character, music, or other written material); render: *The actor interpreted the part of the soldier with wonderful skill.* **3** to understand or construe in a particular way: *We interpreted your silence as consent.* **4** *Archaic.* to express: indicate; reveal: *Arms hanging idly down, hands clasp'd below, Interpret to the marking eye distress* (William Cowper). **—*v.i.*** to serve as an interpreter; translate. [< Latin *terpretārī* < *interpres, -pretis* agent, interpreter]

in|ter|pret|a|bil|i|ty (in tėr′prə tə bil′ə tē), *n.* the quality of being interpretable.

in|ter|pret|a|ble (in tėr′prə tə bəl), *adj.* that can be interpreted; explicable: *New methods have been developed for digesting large numbers of accident reports into readily interpretable facts* (Science News Letter).

in|ter|pre|ta|tion (in tėr′prə tā′shən), *n.* **1** the act of interpreting or explaining; explanation; exposition: *People often give different interpretations of the same facts. What is your interpretation of his strange behavior?* SYN: elucidation. **2** the act or process of bringing out the meaning of a dramatic work, a character, music, or other written material: *The actor's interpretations were praised by most of the newspapers. A musician usually has his own interpretation of a piece of music.* **3** the work of an interpreter; translation.

in|ter|pre|ta|tion|al (in tėr′prə tā′shə nəl), *adj.* of or having to do with interpretation.

in|ter|pre|ta|tive (in tėr′prə tā′tiv), *adj.* used for interpreting; explanatory. **—in|ter′pre|ta′tive|ly,** *adv.*

in|ter|pret|er (in tėr′prə tər), *n.* **1** a person who interprets or explains: *The two greatest interpreters of Jesus in the New Testament are the author of the Fourth Gospel and ... Paul the Apostle* (Time). **2** a person whose business is translating, especially orally, from a foreign language.

in|ter|pret|er|ship (in tėr′prə tər ship), *n.* the office or position of an interpreter.

in|ter|pre|tive (in tėr′prə tiv), *adj.* = interpretative. **—in|ter′pre|tive|ly,** *adv.*

in|ter|pre|tress (in tėr′prə tris), *n.* a female interpreter.

in|ter|pro|fes|sion|al (in′tər prə fesh′ə nəl, -fesh′nəl), *adj.* between or involving different professions: *An interprofessional working party of women recently set up to study different aspects of women's careers ...* (London Times).

in|ter|pro|vin|cial (in′tər prə vin′shəl), *adj.* between provinces.

in|ter|punc|tion (in′tər pungk′shən), *n.* **1** = punctuation. **2** a mark of punctuation. [< Latin *interpunctiō, -ōnis,* ultimately < *inter-* between + *pungere* to prick]

in|ter|punc|tu|ate (in′tər pungk′chů āt), *v.t.,* **-at|ed, -at|ing.** = punctuate.

in|ter|pu|pil|lar|y (in′tər pyü′pə ler′ē), *adj.* between the pupils of the eyes: *Interpupillary distance adjustable* (Scientific American).

in|ter|ra|cial (in′tər rā′shəl), *adj.* between or involving different racial groups: *interracial housing developments. There is more interracial social equality in jazz than in any other area of American society* (Harper's). **—in′ter|ra′cial|ly,** *adv.*

in|ter|ra|cial|ism (in′tər rā′shə liz əm), *n.* a policy or doctrine of equality between the races: *At one*

Pronunciation Key: hat, āge, cãre, fär; let, ēqual, tėrm; it, īce; hot, ōpen, ôrder; oil, out; cup, pu̇t, rüle; child; long; thin; ᴛʜen; zh, measure; ə represents **a** in about, **e** in taken, **i** in pencil, **o** in lemon, **u** in circus.

extreme is the Malayan Communist Party, which, though it maintains a façade of interracialism, has always drawn most of its membership and all of its leaders from the Chinese (Atlantic).

in|ter|ra|di|al (in′tər rā′dē əl), *adj.* situated between radii or rays, as are parts of an echinoderm.

in|ter|re|act (in′tər rē akt′), *v.i.* to react on each other: *To enable his Church to keep march with mankind,* [*Pope*] *John developed three simple interreacting ideas* (Harper's).

in|ter|re|ges (in′tər rē′jēz), *n.* plural of **interrex.**

in|ter|re|gion|al (in′tər rē′jə nəl), *adj.* between or involving different regions: *Powerful coordinating authorities were needed at the centre of a great country with many interregional links* (London Times).

in|ter|reg|nal (in′tər reg′nəl), *adj.* **1** belonging to an interregnum. **2** like an interregnum.

in|ter|reg|num (in′tər reg′nəm), *n., pl.* **-nums, -na** (-nə). **1** a period of inactivity; pause. **2** the time between the end of one ruler's reign and the beginning of his successor's reign. **3** any time during which a nation is without its usual ruler. [< Latin *interrēgnum* < *inter-* between + *rēgnum* reign < *rēx, rēgis* king, ruler]

in|ter|re|late (in′tər ri lāt′), *v.t., v.i.,* **-lat|ed, -lat|ing.** to bring into relation to each other: *In Europe economic and political factors must be interrelated* (Atlantic).

in|ter|re|lat|ed (in′tər ri lā′tid), *adj.* closely connected with each other; mutually related. **—in′ter|re|lat′ed|ness,** *n.*

in|ter|re|la|tion (in′tər ri lā′shən), *n.* close connection with each other; mutual relationship.

in|ter|re|la|tion|ship (in′tər ri lā′shən ship), *n.* = interrelation.

in|ter|re|li|gious (in′tər ri lij′əs), *adj.* between or involving different religions: *interreligious affairs, interreligious understanding.*

in|ter|rex (in′tər reks), *n., pl.* **in|ter|re|ges.** a person who holds supreme authority in a state during an interregnum. [< Latin *interrēx, -rēgis* < *inter-* between + *rēx, rēgis* king]

in|ter|ro|bang (in ter′ə bang), *n.* = interbang.

interrog., 1 interrogation. **2** interrogative.

in|ter|ro|gate (in ter′ə gāt), *v.,* **-gat|ed, -gat|ing.**
—*v.t.* to ask questions of; examine or get information from by asking questions; question thoroughly: *The principal interrogated the boy about the work he had done in his former school. The lawyer took a long time to interrogate the witness fully.* SYN: See syn. under **question.**
—*v.i.* to ask a series of questions. SYN: See syn. under **question.**
[< Latin *interrogāre* (with English *-ate*[1]) < *inter-* between + *rogāre* ask] **—in|ter′ro|gat′ing|ly,** *adv.*

in|ter|ro|ga|tion (in ter′ə gā′shən), *n.* **1** the act or process of questioning. The formal examination of a witness by asking questions is an interrogation. **2** a question.

in|ter|ro|ga|tion|al (in ter′ə gā′shə nəl), *adj.* like an interrogation; interrogative.

interrogation mark or **point,** = question mark.

in|ter|rog|a|tive (in′tə rog′ə tiv), *adj., n.*
—*adj.* **1** asking a question; having the form or force of a question: *an interrogative sentence, an interrogative tone of voice, an interrogative look.* **2** *Grammar.* used in asking a question. *Where, when,* and *why* are interrogative adverbs. *Who* and *what* are interrogative pronouns.
—*n.* *Grammar.* a word or form used in asking a question. *Who, why,* and *what* are interrogatives. **—in′ter|rog′a|tive|ly,** *adv.*

in|ter|ro|ga|tor (in ter′ə gā′tər), *n.* **1** a person who interrogates; questioner: *The interrogator goes over the ... past with a mind magnetized to attract every particle of experience* (Time). **2** a radio or radar transmitter that emits signals or pulses to trigger a transponder for purposes of navigation or identification.

in|ter||rog|a|to|ri|ly (in′tə rog′ə tôr′ə lē, -tōr′-), *adv.* in an interrogatory manner; questioningly.

in|ter|rog|a|to|ry (in′tə rog′ə tôr′ē, -tōr′-), *adj., n., pl.* **-to|ries.** **—*adj.*** questioning; conveying or suggesting a question; interrogative: *an interrogatory manner.*
—*n.* **1** a formal question or set of questions. **2** any question or inquiry.

in|ter|ro|ga|trix (in ter′ə gā′triks), *n., pl.* **-ga|trix-es, -ga|tri|ces** (-gā trī′sēz). a female interrogator.

in|ter|ro|gee (in ter′ə gē′), *n.* a person who is interrogated: *Interrogees, when they eventually appear in court, tend to protest that their confessions have been extracted under duress* (London Times).

in ter|ro|rem clause (in te rôr′əm, -rōr′-), *Law.* a provision in a will stating that the recipient of a legacy shall lose it if he contests the will. [< Latin *in terrōrem* as a warning]

in|ter|rupt (in′tə rupt′), *v., n.* **—*v.t.*** **1** to break in upon (talk, work, rest, or a person speaking); hinder; stop: *A fire drill interrupted the lesson. I don't want to be interrupted in my business* (Joseph Conrad). **2** to make a break in; stand in the way of; obstruct: *A building interrupts the view from our window.*
—*v.i.* to cause a break; break in: *It is not polite to interrupt when someone is talking.*
—*n.* **1** a temporary stop; interruption: [*The computer*] *can deal with foreground real-time interrupts in 6 microseconds without losing control of any of its other jobs, yet every background user will get his answers faster than he needs them* (Scientific American). **2** any breach, separation, or gap: *Wide though the interrupt be that divides us ... we nod them as neighbors* (W. H. Auden).
[< Latin *interruptus,* past participle of *interrumpere* break apart < *inter-* between + *rumpere* break]

in|ter|rupt|ed (in′tə rup′tid), *adj.* **1** acting irregularly or unequally; broken; discontinuous: *All is silent, save the faint And interrupted murmur of the bee* (William Cullen Bryant). **2** *Botany.* having the principal leaflets or flower spikes divided by series of smaller ones. **3** *Zoology.* suddenly stopped; having a gap: *an interrupted stria.* **—in′ter|rupt′ed|ly,** *adv.*

***interrupted screw,** a screw with part of its thread cut away, especially a screw used to form the closure of a breechloading gun, with screw threads removed from alternate sectors.

***interrupted screw**

in|ter|rupt|er (in′tə rup′tər), *n.* **1** a person who interrupts. **2** a device used to make and break an electric circuit periodically and (usually) automatically.

in|ter|rupt|i|ble (in′tə rup′tə bəl), *adj.* that can be interrupted: *interruptible electric power.*

in|ter|rup|tion (in′tə rup′shən), *n.* **1** the act of interrupting; breaking in. **2** the state of being interrupted; break; stopping: *The rain continued without interruption all day.* **3** something that interrupts. **4** = intermission.

in|ter|rup|tive (in′tə rup′tiv), *adj.* tending to interrupt.

in|ter|rup|tor (in′tə rup′tər), *n.* = interrupter.

in|ter|scap|u|lar (in′tər skap′yə lər), *adj. Anatomy.* situated between the shoulder blades.

in|ter|scho|las|tic (in′tər skə las′tik), *adj.* between schools: *Our team won the interscholastic softball competition.*
▶See **intramural** for usage note.

in|ter|school (in′tər skül′), *adj.* = interscholastic.

in|ter se (in′tər sē′), *Latin.* between or among themselves.

in|ter|sect (in′tər sekt′), *v.t.* to cut or divide by passing through or crossing; cross: *A path intersects the field.* **—*v.i.*** **1** to cross or cut each other: *Streets usually intersect at right angles.* **2** *Geometry.* to pass through or across another line or surface so as to have one or more points in common: *The lines intersect at X and Y.* [< Latin *intersectus,* past participle of *intersecāre* < *inter-* between + *secāre* to cut]

***in|ter|sec|tion** (in′tər sek′shən), *n.* **1** the act of intersecting or crossing: *Bridges are used to avoid the intersection of a railroad and a highway.* **2** the point or line where one thing crosses another. In the diagram, there are two intersections where the line AB crosses the parallel lines. **3** *Mathematics.* the set in a group of two or more sets which contains those elements that belong to all the sets. *Example:* If set A = {1, 2, 3, 4} and set B = {3, 4, 5, 6}, then the intersection of the two sets is {3, 4}.

***intersection**
definitions 2, 3

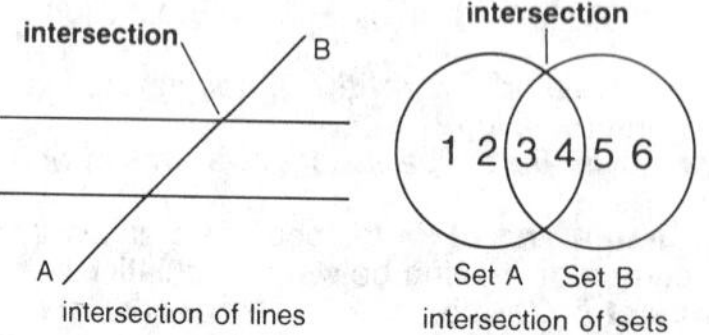

in|ter|sec|tion|al (in′tər sek′shə nəl), *adj.* **1** of or having to do with intersection. **2** characterized by intersection. **3** existing or prevailing between sections. **4** coming from different sections: *an intersectional mayor's conference.*

in|ter|sen|so|ry (in′tər sen′sər ē), *adj.* involving use of all or several senses at the same time.

in|ter|sep|tal (in′tər sep′təl), *adj.* situated between septa or partitions.

in|ter|serv|ice (in′tər sėr′vis), *adj.* between military services or members of different military services: *an interservice conference.*

in|ter|ses|sion (in′tər sesh′ən), *n. U.S.* the interval between two school sessions or semesters, especially at a college or university.

in|ter|ses|sion|al (in′tər sesh′ə nəl), *adj.* between sessions: *Two one-month plenaries with an intersessional working party active for most of the intervals makes this the longest ... international conference* (Science Journal).

in|ter|sex (in′tər seks′), *n.* **1** *Biology.* an intersexual organism. **2** = unisex.

in|ter|sex|u|al (in′tər sek′shü əl), *adj.* **1** existing between the sexes. **2** *Biology.* having sexual characteristics that are intermediate between, or combining, those of the typical female and the typical male.

in|ter|sex|u|al|i|ty (in′tər sek′shü al′ə tē), *n.* the state of being intersexual.

in|ter|si|de|re|al (in′tər sī dir′ē əl), *adj.* = interstellar. [< *inter-* + *sidereal*]

in|ter|space (*n.* in′tər spās′; *v.* in′tər spās′), *n., v.,* **-spaced, -spac|ing.** **—*n.*** a space between two things; interval: *The lucid interspace of world and world, Where never creeps a cloud* (Tennyson). **—*v.t.*** **1** to put a space between. **2** to occupy or fill the space between.

in|ter|spa|tial (in′tər spā′shəl), *adj.* of or having to do with an interspace. **—in′ter|spa′tial|ly,** *adv.*

in|ter|spe|cies (in′tər spē′shēz), *adj.* = interspecific.

in|ter|spe|cif|ic (in′tər spi sif′ik), *adj.* occurring or arising between species: *an interspecific hybrid.*

in|ter|sper|sal (in′tər spėr′səl), *n.* = interspersion.

in|ter|sperse (in′tər spėrs′), *v.t.,* **-spersed, -spers|ing.** **1** to vary with something put here and there; diversify with something at intervals: *He interspersed his narrative with many comments. The grass was interspersed with beds of flowers.* **2** to scatter among other things: *Bushes were interspersed among the trees.* [< Latin *interspersus* scattered < *inter-* + *spargere* scatter]

in|ter|spers|ed|ly (in′tər spėr′sid lē), *adv.* in an interspersed manner; here and there among other things.

in|ter|sper|sion (in′tər spėr′zhən, -shən), *n.* **1** the act of interspersing. **2** the state of being interspersed.

in|ter|sta|di|al (in′tər stā′dē əl), *n., adj.* **—*n.*** a period within a glacial epoch when the climate becomes temporarily warmer.
—*adj.* occurring or formed during this period. [< *inter-* + *stad*(ium) stage + *-ial*]

in|ter|stage (in′tər stāj′), *n.* a section that connects two stages of a rocket: *The 18-ft.-high interstage ... is jettisoned 32 seconds after second-stage ignition* (New York Times).

in|ter|state (in′tər stāt′, in′tər stāt′), *adj., adv., n.* **—*adj., adv.*** between persons or organizations in different states; between states: *an interstate highway* (adj.). *St. Johnsbury Trucking is a common carrier operating interstate* (Wall Street Journal) (adv.).
—*n.* *U.S.* an interstate highway: *The wildcat blockades ... began early in the week on interstates in the East and quickly spread to other parts of the country* (Newsweek).

in|ter|stel|lar (in′tər stel′ər), *adj.* situated or taking place between the stars; in the region of the stars: *interstellar space, interstellar travel.*

in|ter|stice (in tėr′stis), *n., pl.* **-sti|ces** (-stə siz). **1** a small or narrow space between things or parts; narrow crack or opening; chink: *the interstices of the larynx.* SYN: crevice. **2** an interval of time: *The book records the family's wanderings as it moved from place to place, trying to find, in the interstices between upheavals, somewhere to settle* (New Yorker). [< Late Latin *interstitium* < *intersistere* to pause < Latin *inter-* between + *stāre* stand]

in|ter|sti|tial (in′tər stish′əl), *adj.* **1** of or forming interstices. **2** *Anatomy.* occupying interstices of tissue: *interstitial cells.* **—in′ter|sti′tial|ly,** *adv.*

interstitial cell stimulating hormone, a pituitary hormone which acts on the interstitial cells of the testicles to produce testosterone; luteinizing hormone. *Abbr:* ICSH (no periods).

in|ter|stock (in′tər stok′), *n. Botany.* a stock grafted between the rootstock and the scion.

in|ter|strat|i|fi|ca|tion (in′tər strat′ə fə kā′shən), *n.* the condition or fact of being interstratified; an interposed formation or deposit.

in|ter|strat|i|fy (in′tər strat′ə fī), *v.,* **-fied, -fy|ing.**
—*v.i.* to lie as strata between other strata.
—*v.t.* to lay between other strata; arrange in alternate strata.

in|ter|sub|jec|tive (in′tər səb jek′tiv), *adj.* between different subjective states or points of view: *There can be wide intersubjective agreement about the values of certain subjective probabilities* (Science).

in|ter|sub|jec|tiv|i|ty (in′tər sub′jek tiv′ə tē), *n.* the quality or condition of being intersubjective.

in|ter|sys|tem (in′tər sis′təm), *adj.* of or between different systems: *Intersystem analysis and integration involving launch vehicle, tracking and data acquisition, spacecraft systems and space flight* (Scientific American).

in|ter|tan|gle (in′tər tang′gəl), *v.t., v.i.,* **-gled, -gling.** to tangle, one with another.

in|ter|tan|gle|ment (in′tər tang′gəl mənt), *n.* **1** intertangled state or condition. **2** something intertangled.

in|ter|ter|ri|to|ri|al (in′tər ter ə tôr′ē əl, -tōr′-), *adj.* carried on between or connecting different territories.

in|ter|tes|ta|men|tal (in′tər tes′tə men′təl), *adj.* written in or belonging to the period between the completion of the Old Testament and the writing of the New Testament: *The apocalyptic Book of Enoch is an intertestamental work* (Edmund Wilson).

in|ter|tex|ture (in′tər teks′chər), *n.* **1** the act of interweaving. **2** the condition of being interwoven. **3** something formed by interweaving: *Lanes ... skirted thick with intertexture firm Of thorny boughs* (William Cowper).

in|ter|tid|al (in′tər tī′dəl), *adj., n.* **—*adj.*** **1** living between the high-water mark and the low-water mark, as limpets do. **2** located between the watermarks: *intertidal rocks. But in all the intertidal area the pulse of life is adjusted to the rhythm of the tides* (New Yorker).
—*n.* the region between the high-water mark and the low-water mark.

in|ter|tie (in′tər tī′), *n. U.S.* a connecting or interlocking system or network.

in|ter|trib|al (in′tər trī′bəl), *adj.* between tribes: *intertribal war or commerce.*

in|ter|trop|i|cal (in′tər trop′ə kəl), *adj.* within the tropics; tropical.

in|ter|twine (in′tər twīn′), *v.t., v.i.,* **-twined, -twin|ing.** to twine, one with another: *She intertwined two ribbons to make a band for her hair. Two vines intertwined on the wall.* SYN: interlace. **—in′ter|twin′ing|ly,** *adv.*

in|ter|twine|ment (in′tər twīn′mənt), *n.* **1** the fact of intertwining. **2** intertwined state or condition. **3** an intertwined formation.

in|ter|twist (in′tər twist′), *v., n.* **—*v.t., v.i.*** to twist, one with another.
—*n.* **1** the act or process of intertwisting. **2** the state of being intertwisted. **3** an intertwisted formation; tangle; maze. **—in′ter|twist′ing|ly,** *adv.*

in|ter|un|ion (in′tər yün′yən), *adj., n.* **—*adj.*** between unions: *interunion disputes, interunion committees.*
—*n.* an interblending: *... interunion of human voices in a choir* (George Washington Cable).

in|ter|ur|ban (in′tər ėr′bən), *adj.* between cities or towns: *Interurban bus lines have replaced many interurban railways.*

***interval**
definition 4

intervals in the key of C:

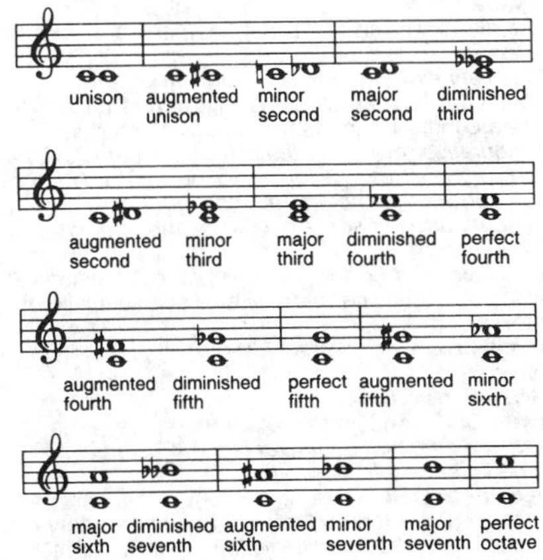

***in|ter|val** (in′tər vəl), *n.* **1** the time between: *In their school they have an interval of fifteen minutes for recess. She has intervals of freedom from worry. There is an interval of a week between Christmas and New Year's Day.* SYN: pause, break. **2** the space between things; intervening space: *an interval of ten feet between trees.* (*Figurative.*) *The interval was immense between discontent and rebellion* (Macaulay). (*Figurative.*) *There seems to be no interval between greatness and meanness* (Emerson). **3** *Especially British.* an intermission in the theater. **4** *Music.* the difference in pitch between two tones. **5** *Military.* the prescribed distance between men or lines of men in formation. **6** = intervale.

at intervals, a now and then: *There was a drizzling rain falling at intervals.* **b** here and there: *Villages are located at intervals along the river. There are trees at intervals of ten feet.*
[< Latin *intervallum* (originally) space between palisades or ramparts < *inter-* + *vallum* wall]

in|ter|vale (in′tər vāl), *n.* a low, level tract of land in North America along a river or between hills. [apparently American English use of variant form of *interval;* meaning influenced by *vale*[1]]

in|ter|val|ic or **in|ter|val|lic** (in′tər val′ik), *adj.* of or having to do with a musical interval or intervals: *I always compose as it were in syllables, not with words. You might say I am an intervalic composer* (Igor Stravinsky).

in|ter|val|om|e|ter (in′tər və lom′ə tər), *n.* a device in a photographic camera which can be preset to make exposures at regular intervals. It is used especially in aerial photography.

in|ter|vein (in′tər vān′), *v.t.* to intersect with or as with veins.

in|ter|vene (in′tər vēn′), *v.i.,* **-vened, -ven|ing. 1** to come between; be between: *A week intervenes between Christmas and New Year's Day.* **2** to come between persons or groups to help settle a dispute; act as intermediary: *The President was asked to intervene in the coal strike.* SYN: mediate, intercede. **3** *Law.* to enter as a third party into a lawsuit or other legal action. [< Latin *intervenīre* < *inter-* between + *venīre* come] **—in′ter|ven′er, in′ter|ve′nor,** *n.*

in|ter|ven|ient (in′tər vēn′yənt), *adj.* **1** intervening, as in place, time, order, or action. **2** = incidental.

intervening sequence, a segment of DNA that has no specific genetic code; intron: *The genes of higher plants and animals and their viruses contain "intervening sequences," segments that are snipped out of the intermediary between DNA and protein synthesis and thus are not represented in any protein product* (Julie Ann Miller).

in|ter|ven|tion (in′tər ven′shən), *n.* **1** an intervening or interfering in any affair, so as to affect its course or issue: *The strike was settled by the intervention of the President.* **2** interference by one nation in the affairs of another. **3** an intervening thing, event, or period of time. [< Late Latin *interventiō, -ōnis* < Latin *intervenīre;* see etym. under **intervene**]

in|ter|ven|tion|al (in′tər ven′shə nəl), *adj.* of or having to do with intervention.

in|ter|ven|tion|ism (in′tər ven′shə niz əm), *n.* the favoring of intervention, especially in international affairs.

in|ter|ven|tion|ist (in′tər ven′shə nist), *n., adj.* **—*n.*** **1** a person who favors intervention, especially in the affairs of another country. **2** *Medicine.* a person who favors medical intervention in the course of a disease rather than leaving the patient to nature.
—*adj.* **1** favoring intervention: *interventionist foreign policy.* **2** of or having to do with intervention or interventionists.

in|ter|ven|tor (in′tər ven′tər), *n.* **1** (in Latin America) a person appointed by a government to intervene in the affairs of a company, agency, or other organization, during a time of dispute: *The Castro regime appointed an "interventor" to run Cuban Telephone Co.* (Wall Street Journal). **2** a church official appointed to act as a mediator in ecclesiastical affairs. [< Latin *interventor* < *intervenīre; see etym. under* **intervene**]

in|ter|ven|tric|u|lar (in′tər ven trik′yə lər), *adj.* between the ventricles of the heart or brain.

in|ter|ver|te|bral (in′tər vėr′tə brəl), *adj.* between the vertebrae: *intervertebral cartilages, the intervertebral joint.* **—in′ter|ver′te|bral|ly,** *adv.*

intervertebral disk or **disc,** the mass of fibrous cartilage between the bodies of adjacent vertebrae. See picture under **disk.**

in|ter|view (in′tər vyü), *n., v.* **—*n.*** **1** a meeting, generally of persons face to face, to talk over something special: *Father had an interview with the teacher about my work. The interview, in its various forms, is a basic tool of social research* (Science News). **2** a meeting between a reporter and a person from whom information is sought for publication or broadcast. **3** a newspaper, magazine article, or broadcast containing the information given at such a meeting.
—*v.t.* to have an interview with; meet and talk with, especially to obtain information: *Reporters from the newspaper interviewed the returning explorers.*
[< Middle French *entrevue* < Old French *entrevoir* to glimpse < *entre-* between (< Latin *inter-*) + *voir* < Latin *vidēre* to see]

in|ter|view|a|ble (in′tər vyü′ə bəl), *adj.* that can be interviewed: *The interviewable people ... in the second floor press center were government information people* (Saturday Review).

in|ter|view|ee (in′tər vyü ē′), *n.* a person who is interviewed: *As has been the case in the Castro interviews, ... the interviewer decisively outtalked the interviewee* (John Lardner).

in|ter|view|er (in′tər vyü′ər), *n.* a person who interviews: *Interviewers using this technique are trained to ask the questions precisely ... and to express no attitudes or opinions themselves which might influence the reply of the respondent* (Science News).

in|ter|vis|it (in′tər viz′it), *v.i.* to exchange visits: *... the more public social habits of the countries whose peoples intervisit on so large a scale* (London Times).

in|ter|vis|it|a|tion (in′tər viz′ə tā′shən), *n.* the act of intervisiting; exchange of visits: *The rules and rights of intervisitation among prisoners.*

in|ter|vi|tal (in′tər vī′təl), *adj.* between two lives or stages of existence. [< *inter-* + Latin *vīta* life + English *-al*[1]]

in|ter vi|vos (in′tər vī′vōs), *Latin.* between living persons (used in law of gifts, donations, or gratuities from one living person to another).

in|ter|vo|cal|ic (in′tər vō kal′ik), *adj.* between vowels: *an intervocalic consonant.*

in|ter|volve (in′tər volv′), *v.t., v.i.,* **-volved, -volv|ing.** to roll, wind, or involve, one within another: *Mystical dance ... mazes intricate, Eccentric, intervolved* (Milton). [< *inter-* + Latin *volvere* to roll]

in|ter|war (in′tər wôr′), *adj.* between wars: *interwar history, the interwar years.*

in|ter|weave (in′tər wēv′), *v.t., v.i.,* **-wove** or **-weaved, -wo|ven** or **-wove** or **-weaved, -weav|ing. 1** to weave together; interlace; intertwine: *to interweave bamboo strips to make a basket. The branches interwove to form an unbroken hedge.* **2** to connect closely; mix together; blend; intermingle: *to interweave truth with fiction in a story. Different impressions of the city interwove in his memory.* **—in′ter|weav′er,** *n.*

in|ter|weave|ment (in′tər wēv′mənt), *n.* **1** the act or process of weaving together or intermingling intricately; intertexture. **2** an interwoven texture or structure.

in|ter|wind (in′tər wīnd′), *v.t., v.i.,* **-wound, -wind|ing.** to wind together, one with another; intertwine.

in|ter|work (in′tər wėrk′), *v.,* **-worked** or **-wrought, -work|ing. —*v.t.*** to work together or combine, one with another.
—*v.i.* **1** to work, one upon another; interact. **2** to work or operate intermediately.

in|ter|wound (in′tər wound′), *v.* past tense and past participle of **interwind.**

in|ter|wove (in′tər wōv′), *v.* a past tense and past participle of **interweave.**

in|ter|wo|ven (in′tər wō′vən), *adj., v.* **—*adj.*** **1** woven together: *the interwoven strands of yarn in a blanket.* **2** mixed together; blended; mingled: *Its lacework of interwoven light and shade* (Charles Kingsley).
—*v.* a past participle of **interweave:** *Various strands were interwoven to create a colorful pattern.*

in|ter|wreathe (in′tər rēᴛʜ′), *v.t.,* **-wreathed, -wreath|ing.** to wreathe together; intertwine.

in|ter|wrought (in′tər rôt′), *v.* interworked; a past tense and a past participle of **interwork.**

in|ter|zon|al (in′tər zō′nəl), *adj.* between zones: *interzonal trade, interzonal traffic.*

in|ter|zone (in′tər zōn′), *adj.* = interzonal.

in|tes|ta|ble (in tes′tə bəl), *adj.* legally incompetent to make a will. [< Late Latin *intestābilis* < *in-* not + *testārī* make a will]

in|tes|ta|cy (in tes′tə sē), *n.* the fact of being intestate at death.

in|tes|tate (in tes′tāt, -tit), *adj., n.* **—*adj.*** **1** having made no will: *to die intestate.* **2** not disposed of by a will.
—*n.* a person who has died without making a will.
[< Latin *intestātus* < *in-* not + *testārī* make a will]

in|tes|ti|nal (in tes′tə nəl), *adj.* **1** of or in the intestines: *intestinal worms.* **2** affecting the intestines. **—in|tes′ti|nal|ly,** *adv.*

intestinal fortitude, *U.S.* pluck; courage; tenacity.

in|tes|tine** (in tes′tən), *n., adj.* **—*n. **1** the lower part of the alimentary canal, that extends below the stomach; bowels. Food from the stomach passes into the intestine for further digestion and

Pronunciation Key: hat, āge, cãre, fär; let, ēqual, tėrm; it, īce; hot, ōpen, ôrder; oil, out; cup, pu̇t, rüle; child; long; thin; ᴛʜen; zh, measure; ə represents **a** in about, **e** in taken, **i** in pencil, **o** in lemon, **u** in circus.

for absorption. In adult humans the small intestine is about twenty feet long; the large intestine is about five feet long. SYN: entrails, guts. **2** *Biology.* the whole alimentary canal from the mouth downward in certain invertebrates; entrails; guts.
—*adj.* within a country; internal; domestic. Intestine strife is civil war. SYN: civil.
intestines, the intestine; bowels: *The contents of the stomach and intestines were of a similar nature* (British Medical Journal).
[< Latin *intestīna,* neuter plural of *intestīnus* internal < *intus* within < *in* in]

***intestine**
definition 1

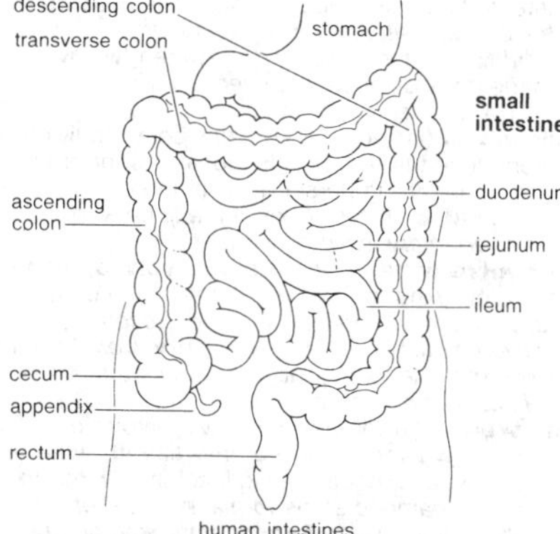

human intestines

in·thrall or **in·thral** (in thrôl′), *v.t.,* **-thralled, -thrall·ing.** *Obsolete.* enthrall.
in·thrall·ment or **in·thral·ment** (in thrôl′mənt), *n. Obsolete.* enthrallment.
in·throne (in thrōn′), *v.t.,* **-throned, -thron·ing.** *Obsolete.* enthrone.
in·ti·fa·da or **in·ti·fa·deh** (in′tə fä′də), *n.* a popular uprising of Palestinian Arabs against Israeli occupation of the West Bank and Gaza Strip, begun in 1988. [< Arabic *intifāda* uprising]
in·ti·ma (in′tə mə), *n., pl.* **-mae** (-mē). *Anatomy.* the innermost membrane, coat, or lining of some organ or part, especially of a blood or lymphatic vessel. [< New Latin (*tunica*) *intima* inmost (coat), feminine of Latin *intimus;* see etym. under **intimate**[1]]
in·ti·ma·cy (in′tə mə sē), *n., pl.* **-cies. 1** the fact or condition of being intimate; close acquaintance; closeness: *The intimacy with which the two friends talked showed how fond they were of one another.* **2** a familiar or intimate act; familiarity. **3** a euphemism for illicit sexual relations.
in·ti·mate[1] (in′tə mit), *adj., n.* —*adj.* **1** very familiar; known very well; closely acquainted: *Although the governor knew many people, he had few intimate friends. The English colonists at Rome perforce became intimate, and in many cases friendly* (Thackeray). SYN: See syn. under **familiar. 2** involving or resulting from close familiarity; close: *intimate knowledge of a matter. Winter . . . I crown thee King of intimate delights, Fireside enjoyments, home-born happiness* (William Cowper). **3** very personal; most private: *A diary is an intimate book.* **4** far within; deepest; inmost; most inward; deep-seated: *the most intimate recesses of the heart.* **5** essential; intrinsic: *the intimate structure of an organism.* **6** maintaining illicit sexual relations.
—*n.* a very close friend or associate: *The lawyer was an intimate of many in public office.*
[earlier *intime* < Middle French, learned borrowing from Latin *intimus* inmost; close friend, superlative of *in* in; later altered under the influence of Latin *intimātus,* past participle of *intimāre;* see etym. under **intimate**[2]] —**in′ti·mate·ly,** *adv.* —**in′ti·mate·ness,** *n.*
in·ti·mate[2] (in′tə māt), *v.t.,* **-mat·ed, -mat·ing. 1** to suggest indirectly; hint; imply: *Her smile intimated that she was pleased. He intimated that he was dissatisfied with his job.* SYN: See syn. under **hint. 2** to make known formally; announce; notify: *The miners posted a notice intimating a strike unless their demands for pay were met.* SYN: state.
[< Latin *intimāre* (with English *-ate*[1]) (originally) press in < Latin *intimus* inmost; see etym. under **intimate**[1]] —**in′ti·mat′er,** *n.*
in·ti·ma·tion (in′tə mā′shən), *n.* **1** an indirect suggestion; hint: *A frown is often an intimation of disapproval.* **2** an announcement; notice: *The official intimation of tax assessment was posted throughout the land.*
in·time (aɴ tēm′), *adj. French.* intimate: *. . . anything that seats less than a couple of hundred or so is considered terribly intime* (New York Times).
in·tim·i·date (in tim′ə dāt), *v.t.,* **-dat·ed, -dat·ing. 1** to frighten; make afraid; overawe: *to intimidate one's opponents with threats.* SYN: cow. **2** to influence or force by fear: *to intimidate workers during a strike. The mayor's enemies accused him of trying to use policemen to intimidate voters on election day.* [< Medieval Latin *intimidare* (with English *-ate*[1]) < Latin *in-* + *timidus* fearful] —**in·tim′i·dat′ing·ly,** *adv.*
in·tim·i·da·tion (in tim′ə dā′shən), *n.* **1** the act of intimidating; making afraid. **2** the state of being intimidated; being made afraid: *Witnesses were kept from testifying by intimidation.*
in·tim·i·da·tor (in tim′ə dā′tər), *n.* a person who intimidates.
in·tim·i·da·to·ry (in tim′ə dā′tər ē), *adj.* of intimidating nature or tendency: *Eighty-eight other longshoremen were reprimanded for alleged intimidatory conduct or violence* (New York Times).
in·ti·mism (in′tə miz əm), *n.* a style of painting that shows scenes from ordinary, domestic life, as seen in the work of painters like Edouard Vuillard and Pierre Bonnard.
in·ti·mist (in′tə mist), *n., adj.* —*n.* a painter who uses intimism.
—*adj.* having to do with intimism or intimists.
in·tim·i·ty (in tim′ə tē), *n.* **1** intimate character or quality; closely personal nature; privacy. **2** *Obsolete.* intimate association or intimacy.
in·tinc·tion (in tingk′shən), *n. Ecclesiastical.* the act of dipping the bread or wafer in the wine in order to administer both together. [< Latin *intinctiō, -ōnis* < *intinguere* dip (something) into < *in-* in + *tinguere* moisten, tinge]
in·tine (in′tin, -tīn), *n. Botany.* the inner membrane of a pollen grain. [< Latin *intus* within + English *-ine*[1]]
in·ti·tle (in tī′təl), *v.t.,* **-tled, -tling.** = entitle.
in·tit·u·la·tion (in tit′yů lā′shən), *n.* the giving of a title to; entitling.
in·tit·ule (in tit′yül), *v.t.,* **-uled, -ul·ing.** to give a title or designation to (now especially by an act of Parliament). [< Old French *intituler,* learned borrowing from Late Latin *intitulāre* dedicate, name after, entitle]
in·to (in′tü; *before consonants often* in′tə), *prep.* **1** to the inside of; toward and inside; within: *Come into the house. We drove into the city. I will look into the matter.* **2** to the condition of; to the form of: *to come into contact with someone. Divide the apple into three parts. Freezing weather turns water into ice. Dollar stocks were lowered sharply into line with Wall Street* (London Times). **3** *Mathematics.* by (implying or expressing division): *5 into 30 is 6.*
be into, *Slang.* **a** to be deeply involved or interested in: *"We've got five architects in Earth People's Park now, and they're really into inflatables,"* *Harry told us* (New Yorker). **b** to be in debt to: *He was a hi-fi nut who . . . was into us for several hundred dollars for some acoustical components* (Maclean's).
[Old English (originally, two words) *into* < *in,* adverb + *tō* to]
►See **in** for usage note.
in·toed (in′tōd′), *adj.* with toes turned in.
in·tol·er·a·bil·i·ty (in tol′ər ə bil′ə tē), *n.* intolerable quality or condition; unbearableness.
in·tol·er·a·ble (in tol′ər ə bəl), *adj.* too hard to be endured; unbearable: *The pain of the toothache was intolerable. Something that has oppressed us all has become intolerable and has to be ended* (H. G. Wells). SYN: unendurable, insufferable.
[< Latin *intolerābilis* < *in-* not + *tolerābilis* able to be borne, tolerable] —**in·tol′er·a·ble·ness,** *n.*
in·tol·er·a·bly (in tol′ər ə blē), *adv.* in an intolerable manner; unbearably: *intolerably weary, intolerably hot.*
in·tol·er·ance (in tol′ər əns), *n.* **1** unwillingness to let others do and think as they choose, especially in matters of religion: *The Pilgrims came to America because of intolerance and persecution.* SYN: bigotry. **2** inability to tolerate; lack of tolerance: *She developed an intolerance to penicillin.*
in·tol·er·ant (in tol′ər ənt), *adj., n.* —*adj.* not tolerant; not willing to let others do and think as they choose, especially in matters of religion: *Some of the Puritans were strict and intolerant. Intolerant, as is the way of youth unless itself be pleased* (Wordsworth). SYN: bigoted, narrow, dogmatic.
—*n.* an intolerant person.
intolerant of, not able to endure; unwilling to endure: *intolerant of cold. We are intolerant of everything that is not simple* (John Addington Symonds).
—**in·tol′er·ant·ly,** *adv.*
in·tol·er·a·tion (in tol′ə rā′shən), *n.* lack of toleration; intolerance.
in·tomb (in tüm′), *v.t.* = **entomb.**
in·tomb·ment (in tüm′mənt), *n.* = entombment.
in·to·nate (in′tō nāt), *v.t.,* **-nat·ed, -nat·ing. 1** to utter with a particular tone. **2** *Phonetics.* to voice. **3** to intone; chant.
[< Medieval Latin *intonare* (with English *-ate*[1]) intone]
in·to·na·tion (in′tō nā′shən, -tə-), *n.* **1** the act of intoning: *the intonation of a psalm.* **2** something intoned. **3** the manner of producing musical notes, especially with regard to pitch. **4** the manner of sounding words or speaking, especially with regard to the rise and fall in the pitch of the voice. **5** the opening phrase of a Gregorian chant, usually sung by the priest and the chorus.
in·to·na·tion·al (in′tō nā′shə nəl), *adj.* consisting of or having to do with intonation. —**in′to·na′tion·al·ly,** *adv.*
intonation pattern or **contour,** *Linguistics.* a distinctive speech pattern formed by differences in pitch, as for example the rising intonation pattern in questions (*Is he going?*) and the falling intonation pattern in declarative statements (*Yes, he is going*).
in·tone (in tōn′), *v.,* **-toned, -ton·ing.** —*v.t.* **1** to read or recite in a singing voice, especially in a monotone; chant: *to intone a psalm or a prayer. A cantor intones part of the service.* **2** to utter with a particular tone; intonate.
—*v.i.* to speak or recite in a singing voice, especially in monotone.
[< Medieval Latin *intonare,* ultimately < Latin *in-* in + *tonus* tone] —**in·ton′er,** *n.*
in·tor·sion (in tôr′shən), *n.* the act or fact of twisting or winding, as of the stem of a plant.
[< French *intorsion* < Latin *intortiō, -ōnis* < *intortus;* see etym. under **intort**]
in·tort (in tôrt′), *v.t.* to twist inward; curl in: *intorted horns* (Alexander Pope).
[< Latin *intortus,* past participle of *intorquēre* to twist, turn against, curl < *in-* on, in + *torquēre* to twist, wrench]
in·tor·tion (in tôr′shən), *n.* = intorsion.
in to·to (in tō′tō), *Latin.* as a whole; completely: *The boy already had transcribed Pope's "Essay on Man" in toto and knew long passages by heart* (Catherine Drinker Bowen).
In·tour·ist (in tůr′ist), *n., adj.* —*n.* the Soviet government agency which handles all arrangements for tourists visiting Russia.
—*adj.* provided or conducted by Intourist: *an Intourist hotel, Intourist guides.*
in-town (in′toun′), *adj.* located in the central or main section of a town or city: *an in-town motel.*
in·tox·i·cant (in tok′sə kənt), *n., adj.* —*n.* **1** an alcoholic liquor. **2** any drug that intoxicates.
—*adj.* = intoxicating.
in·tox·i·cate (in tok′sə kāt), *v.,* **-cat·ed, -cat·ing,** *adj.* —*v.t.* **1** to make drunk: *Too much wine intoxicates people.* SYN: inebriate. **2** *Figurative.* to excite greatly or beyond self-control; exhilarate: *The joy of victory so intoxicated the members of the team that they jumped and sang and behaved like crazy men.* **3** *Medicine.* to poison.
—*adj. Archaic.* intoxicated: (*Figurative.*) *intoxicate with joy and pride* (Robert Southey).
[< Medieval Latin *intoxicare* (with English *-ate*[1]) to poison < Latin *in-* in + *toxicum* poison < Greek *toxikón* (*phármakon*) (poison) for use on arrows < *tóxon* bow, weapon]
in·tox·i·cat·ed (in tok′sə kā′tid), *adj.* **1** drunk: *an intoxicated man.* SYN: inebriated. **2** *Figurative.* very much excited: *I grew intoxicated with my own eloquence* (Benjamin Disraeli). —**in·tox′i·cat′ed·ly,** *adv.*
in·tox·i·cat·ing (in tok′sə kā′ting), *adj.* **1** making drunk: *Whiskey is an intoxicating liquor.* **2** *Figurative.* very exciting. —**in·tox′i·cat′ing·ly,** *adv.*
in·tox·i·ca·tion (in tok′sə kā′shən), *n.* **1** an intoxicated condition; drunkenness. SYN: inebriation. **2** *Figurative.* great excitement: *the sweet intoxication of young love.* **3** *Medicine.* poisoning: *No one can consume immoderate amounts of aspirin . . . without suffering some degree of intoxication* (New Yorker).
in·tox·i·ca·tive (in tok′sə kā′tiv), *adj.* **1** tending to intoxicate. **2** having to do with or characteristic of intoxication.
in·tox·i·ca·tor (in tok′sə kā′tər), *n.* one that intoxicates.
intr., intransitive.
intra-, *prefix.* within; inside; on the inside, as in *intrastate, intramural, intravenous.* [< Late Latin *intrā-* < Latin *intrā* inside of]
in·tra-ar·te·ri·al (in′trə är tir′ē əl), *adj.* **1** within an artery or the arteries. **2** of, for, or into an artery or arteries: *an intra-arterial injection.* —**in′tra·ar·te′ri·al·ly,** *adv.*
in·tra-a·tom·ic (in′trə ə tom′ik), *adj.* within an atom: *intra-atomic energy.*
in·tra·car·di·ac (in′trə kär′dē ak), *adj.* within the heart.
[< *intra-* + *cardiac*]
in·tra·car·di·al (in′trə kär′dē əl), *adj.* = intracardiac.
in·tra·cel·lu·lar (in′trə sel′yə lər), *adj.* occurring within a cell or cells: *intracellular digestion or cir-*

culation. —**in'tra|cel'lu|lar|ly,** *adv.*

in|tra|cer|e|bral (in'trə ser'ə brəl, -sə rē'brəl), *adj.* within the brain of the cerebrum: *an intracerebral hemorrhage, an intracerebral injection.* —**in'tra|cer'e|bral|ly,** *adv.*

in|tra|cit|y (in'trə sit'ē), *adj.* within a city: *intracity housing, intracity traffic.*

in|tra|coast|al (in'trə kōs'təl), *adj., n.* —*adj.* **1** situated within a coastal area: *intracoastal waterways.* **2** of or having to do with intracoastal waterways: *intracoastal trade.*
—*n.* an intracoastal waterway.

in|tra|col|le|giate (in'trə kə lē'jit, -jē it), *adj.* within a college.

in|tra|com|pa|ny (in'trə kum'pə nē), *adj.* within a company: *An intracompany struggle for control . . . would run the price up* (Atlantic).

in|tra|con|ti|nen|tal (in'trə kon'tə nen'təl), *adj.* existing or operating within a continent; being in the interior of a continent: *There is room in the world aircraft market for both an intracontinental plane capable of flying at 1450 miles an hour and an intercontinental craft that could fly 2000 miles per hour* (Robert F. Six).

in|tra|cra|ni|al (in'trə krā'nē əl), *adj.* within the skull. —**in'tra|cra'ni|al|ly,** *adv.*

in|tra|crys|tal|line (in'trə kris'tə lin, -līn), *adj.* within a crystal: *intracrystalline cavities.*

in|trac|ta|bil|i|ty (in trak'tə bil'ə tē), *n.* the state or quality of being intractable; stubbornness.

in|trac|ta|ble (in trak'tə bəl), *adj.* **1** hard to handle or manage; stubborn: *an intractable mule. When pain becomes so severe that doctors call it "intractable," they mean that it cannot be controlled by any safe and simple dosage of drugs* (Time). SYN: unruly, perverse, uncontrollable, refractory. **2** not easily treated: *an intractable disease.* [< Latin *intractābilis* < *in-* not + *tractābilis* tractable] —**in|trac'ta|ble|ness,** *n.*

in|trac|ta|bly (in trak'tə blē), *adv.* in an intractable manner; unmanageably.

in|tra|cu|ta|ne|ous (in'trə kyü tā'nē əs), *adj.* within the layers of the skin; intradermal: *an intracutaneous injection.* [< *intra-* + *cutaneous*] —**in'tra|cu|ta'ne|ous|ly,** *adv.*

intracutaneous test, = scratch test.

in|tra|cy|to|plas|mic (in'trə sī'tə plaz'mik), *adj.* within the cytoplasm of a cell.

in|tra|der|mal (in'trə dėr'məl), *adj.* within the layers of the skin: *Injections were given to patients by various routes from intradermal to intravenous* (Science News). [< *intra-* + *dermal*] —**in'tra|der'mal|ly,** *adv.*

in|tra|dis|ci|pli|nar|y (in'trə dis'ə plə ner'ē), *adj.* within a particular field of study: *an intradisciplinary conference of political scientists.*

in|tra|dos (in trā'dos), *n., pl.* **-dos, -dos|es** (-dəs əz). the interior curve or surface of an arch or vault.
[< French *intrados* < Latin *intrā* within + French *dos* back < Latin *dorsum*]

in|tra|ep|i|the|li|al (in'trə ep'ə thē'lē əl), *adj.* within epithelial tissue: *intraepithelial cancer.*

in|tra|fa|mil|ial (in'trə fə mil'yəl), *adj.* within a family; between members of the same family: *Stature and intelligence . . . were studied by Galton, but, apart from proving that there were general intrafamilial likenesses, the results were rather difficult to interpret* (New Scientist).

in|tra|fam|i|ly (in'trə fam'ə lē, -fam'lē), *adj.* = intrafamilial.

in|tra|ga|lac|tic (in'trə gə lak'tik), *adj.* within a galaxy: *an intragalactic communication network, intragalactic travel.*

in|tra|gen|ic (in'trə jen'ik), *adj.* within a gene: *intragenic recombinants.*

in|tra|group (in'trə grüp'), *adj. Sociology.* existing or arising within a group: *intragroup conflicts, intragroup needs.*

in|tra|mam|ma|ry (in'trə mam'ə rē), *adj.* within a mammary gland: *Given by intramammary injection to cows, some of the chemical entered the milk* (Alfred Byrne).

in|tra|mar|gin|al (in'trə mär'jə nəl), *adj.* within the margin, as of a leaf.

in|tra|mar|i|tal (in'trə mar'ə təl), *adj.* within the bonds of marriage: . . . *the distinctions between intramarital and extramarital relations* (Listener).

in|tra|mo|lec|u|lar (in'trə mə lek'yə lər), *adj.* occurring or acting within a molecule or molecules: *An acceptable sunscreen must . . . not undergo any intramolecular changes that would affect its absorptive capacity* (New Scientist). —**in'tra|mo|lec'u|lar|ly,** *adv.*

in|tra|mun|dane (in'trə mun'dān), *adj.* within the world or the material universe.

in|tra|mu|ral (in'trə myůr'əl), *adj.* **1a** carried on by members of the same school, college, or organization: *Intramural games are played between the students of the same school. Following a stormy intramural debate, two of the League's members resigned.* **b** of or having to do with activities in the same school, college, or organization: *Our class basketball team has first place in intramural standing.* **2** within the walls or a wall, especially of an organ or cavity of the body.
[< *intra-* + Latin *mūrus* wall + English *-al*¹]
—**in'tra|mu'ral|ly,** *adv.*
►**Intramural** is written without a hyphen. It applies specifically to groups belonging to the same school as contrasted with *interscholastic,* which applies to groups belonging to different schools.

in|tra mu|ros (in'trə myůr'ōs), *Latin.* within the walls, usually of a college or city.

in|tra|mus|cu|lar (in'trə mus'kyə lər), *adj.* within or into a muscle: *an intramuscular injection.* —**in'tra|mus'cu|lar|ly,** *adv.*

in|tra|na|sal (in'trə nā'zəl), *adj.* within the nasal cavity: *intranasal surgery.*

in|tra|na|tion|al (in'trə nash'ə nəl, -nash'nəl), *adj.* within a nation.

intrans., intransitive.

in trans., in transitu.

in|tran|si|geance (aɴ trän zē zhäɴs'), *n. French.* intransigence.

in|tran|si|geant (aɴ trän zē zhäɴ'), *adj., n. French.* intransigent.

in|tran|si|gence (in tran'sə jəns), *n.* the quality of being intransigent; uncompromising hostility: *The intransigence of one great power can unsettle the whole world. His intransigence made further negotiation futile.*

in|tran|si|gen|cy (in tran'sə jən sē), *n.* = intransigence.

in|tran|si|gent (in tran'sə jənt), *adj., n.* —*adj.* unwilling to agree or compromise; uncompromising; irreconcilable: *The strong, intransigent spirit of the Puritans led them to emigrate from the Old World and found colonies in the New World.*
—*n.* a person who is unwilling to agree or compromise, especially in politics.
[< French *intransigeant* < Spanish (*los*) *intransigentes,* a name for various extreme political parties, ultimately < Latin *in-* not + *trānsigere* come to an agreement, transact < *trāns-* through + *agere* act, drive] —**in|tran'si|gent|ly,** *adv.*

in-trans|it (in'tran'sit, -zit), *adj.* in the process of being transported: *in-transit cargo.*

in|tran|sit|a|ble (in tran'sə tə bəl), *adj.* not permitting passage or transit; impassable: *A road along the coast would become lost in intransitable gorges of the coast range of mountains* (Geographical Journal).

in|tran|si|tive (in tran'sə tiv), *adj., n.* —*adj.* not taking a direct object. The verbs *belong, go,* and *seem* are intransitive. The verb *run* may be transitive or intransitive. In "I run to school" *run* is intransitive. In "I run the machine" *run* is transitive.
—*n.* an intransitive verb. —**in|tran'si|tive|ly,** *adv.*
—**in|tran'si|tive|ness,** *n.*
►See **verb** for usage note.

in|trant (in'trənt), *n.* a person who enters (a college, a society, holy orders, or other group); entrant.
[< Latin *intrāns, -antis,* present participle of *intrāre* enter < *intrā* inside]

in|tra|nu|cle|ar (in'trə nü'klē ər, -nyü'-), *adj.* within the nucleus of an atom or cell.

in|tra|oc|u|lar (in'trə ok'yə lər), *adj.* within the eye: *intraocular tumor.* [< *intra-* + *ocular*] —**in'tra|oc'u|lar|ly,** *adv.*

in|tra|par|ty (in'trə pär'tē), *adj.* occurring within a political party: *intraparty rivalries.*

in|tra|per|i|to|ne|al (in'trə per'ə tə nē'əl), *adj.* within the peritoneum: *The drug was given in large doses by intraperitoneal injection* (Science).
—**in'tra|per'i|to|ne'al|ly,** *adv.*

in|tra|pre|neur (in'trə prə nėr'), *n.* a corporation executive empowered to act as an entrepreneur in undertaking new ventures: *Intrapreneurs, the people who start new businesses inside established companies, will soon be as big a catchword as entrepreneurs* (Economist). [blend of *intra-* and *entrepreneur*] —**in'tra|pre|neur'ship,** *n.*

in|tra|psy|chic (in'trə sī'kik), *adj. Psychology.* developed or occurring within the mind of an individual. —**in'tra|psy'chi|cal|ly,** *adv.*

in|tra|re|gion|al (in'trə rē'jə nəl), *adj.* within a region: *intraregional trade.*

in|tra|spe|cies (in'trə spē'shēz), *adj.* within one species; among members of a species; intraspecific.

in|tra|spe|cif|ic (in'trə spi sif'ik), *adj.* within a species; involving members of the same species: *intraspecific competition for food.* —**in'tra|spe|cif'i|cal|ly,** *adv.*

in|tra|spi|nal (in'trə spī'nəl), *adj.* within the spinal column or spinal cord.

in|tra|state (in'trə stāt'), *adj.* within a state, especially within a state of the United States: *intrastate commerce.*

in|tra|tel|lu|ric (in'trə te lůr'ik), *adj.* **1** located or formed far beneath the earth's surface: *intratelluric rock.* **2** noting the period in the formation of eruptive rock just before its appearance on the earth's surface. [< German *intratellurisch* < *intra-* intra- + Latin *tellus, -ūris* earth + German *-isch* -ic]

in|tra|the|cal (in'trə thē'kəl), *adj.* contained or enclosed in the theca, as of a polyp.

in|tra|tho|rac|ic (in'trə thô ras'ik, -thō-), *adj.* situated, placed, or occurring within the thorax: *The heart and the lungs are intrathoracic organs.*

in|tra|u|ter|ine (in'trə yü'tər in, -tə rīn), *adj.* **1** within the uterus: *the intrauterine development of an embryo or fetus.* **2** having to do with life within the uterus: *the intrauterine period in an animal's life.*

intrauterine device, a loop, coil, ring, or the like, placed within the uterus as a physical barrier to implantation of a fertilized ovum. *Abbr:* IUD

in|trav|a|sa|tion (in trav'ə sā'shən), *n. Pathology.* the entrance into vessels of matters formed in the surrounding tissues. [< *intra-,* patterned on *extravasation*]

in|tra|vas|cu|lar (in'trə vas'kyə lər), *adj.* within a blood vessel or the blood vessels: *intravascular obstruction.* —**in'tra|vas'cu|lar|ly,** *adv.*

in|tra|ve|hic|u|lar (in'trə vi hik'yə lər), *adj.* of, having to do with, or used inside a space vehicle: *the intravehicular space suit.*

in|tra|ve|nous (in'trə vē'nəs), *adj., n.* —*adj.* **1** within a vein or the veins. **2** of, for, or into a vein or veins: *When a person is too ill to digest food, glucose is sometimes given by an intravenous injection.*
—*n.* an intravenous injection.
[< *intra-* + Latin *vēna* vein + English *-ous*]
—**in'tra|ve'nous|ly,** *adv.*

in|tra vi|res (in'trə vī'rēz), within the powers granted by authority or by law: *It was held that the regulation was intra vires* (Cape Times). [< New Latin *intra vires* (literally) within the power]

in|tra|vi|tal (in'trə vī'təl), *adj. Biology, Medicine.* occurring in or performed upon a living individual.

in|tra vi|tam (in'trə vī'təm), *Biology.* within a living cell, tissue, or organism: *the injection of a stain intra vitam.* [< New Latin *intra vitam* (literally) within life]

in-tray (in'trā'), *n. Especially British.* in-basket.

in|tra|zo|nal (in'trə zō'nəl), *adj.* within a zone or region: *intrazonal trade. An intrazonal type of soil is typical of a particular topographic area.*

in|treat (in trēt'), *v.t.* = entreat.

in|trench (in trench'), *v.t.* **1** = entrench. **2** to wrinkle; furrow: *His face Deep scars of thunder had intrench'd* (Milton). —**in|trench'er,** *n.*

in|trench|ing tool (in tren'ching), a tool, such as a shovel or pick, carried by a soldier in the field for the purpose of digging foxholes, breastworks, trenches, or other earthworks.

in|trench|ment (in trench'mənt), *n.* = entrenchment.

in|trep|id (in trep'id), *adj.* very brave; fearless; courageous; dauntless: *A fireman must be intrepid. The intrepid explorers scoffed at danger.* SYN: bold, daring. [< Latin *intrepidus* < *in-* not + *trepidus* alarmed] —**in|trep'id|ly,** *adv.* —**in|trep'id|ness,** *n.*

in|tre|pid|i|ty (in'trə pid'ə tē), *n.* great bravery; dauntless courage; fearlessness: *There is something about this naive intrepidity that compels admiration* (Harper's). SYN: valor, heroism, daring.

Int. Rev., Internal Revenue.

in|tri|ca|cy (in'trə kə sē), *n., pl.* **-cies. 1** intricate nature or condition; complexity: *The intricacy of the plan made it hard to understand.* **2** an intricate thing or event; complication: *the intricacies of political intrigue. The laws are full of intricacies.*

in|tri|cate (in'trə kit), *adj.* **1** with many twists and turns; perplexing, entangled, or complicated: *An intricate knot is very hard to tie or untie. A mystery story usually has an intricate plot.* SYN: involved, complex. **2** very hard to understand: *an intricate design, an intricate piece of machinery, intricate directions. The bearded Indian frowned over intricate calculations on the back of an envelope* (Graham Greene). SYN: obscure. [< Latin *intrīcātus,* past participle of *intrīcāre* entangle < *in-* in + *trīcārī* make difficulties < *trīcae* hindrances, tricks] —**in'tri|cate|ly,** *adv.* —**in'tri|cate|ness,** *n.*

in|tri|gant or **in|tri|guant** (in'trə gənt; *French* aɴ trē gäɴ'), *n., pl.* **-gants, -guants** (-gənts; *French* -gäɴ'). a person who habitually intrigues; intriguer. [< French *intrigant* < Italian *intrigante,* present participle of *intrigare* to intrigue < Latin *intrīcāre;* see etym. under **intricate**]

in|tri|gante or **in|tri|guante** (in'trə gant', -gänt'; *French* aɴ trē gänt'), *n., pl.* **-gantes, -guantes** (-gants', -gänts'; *French* -gäɴt'). a woman who habitually intrigues. [< French *intrigante,* feminine of *intrigant*]

Pronunciation Key: hat, āge, cãre, fär; let, ēqual, tėrm; it, īce; hot, ōpen, ôrder; oil, out; cup, pu̇t, rüle; child; long; thin; ᴛʜen; zh, measure; ə represents **a** in about, **e** in taken, **i** in pencil, **o** in lemon, **u** in circus.

in|trigue (*n.* in trēg′, in′trēg; *v.* in trēg′), *n., v.,* **-trigued, -tri|guing.** —*n.* **1** secret scheming and plotting; crafty dealing: *The royal palace was filled with intrigue.* SYN: conspiracy. **2** a crafty plot; secret scheme: *The king's younger brother took part in the intrigue to make himself king.* **3** a secret love affair: *the intrigue between a man and his mistress.* SYN: liaison. **4** the plot of a play, dramatic poem, or other literary piece, especially the development of a complex situation.
—*v.i.* **1** to form and carry out plots; plan in a secret or underhand way: *He pretended to be loyal while he intrigued against his employer. He will fight openly, but he is too honorable to intrigue against you.* **2** to have a secret love affair.
—*v.t.* **1** to excite the curiosity and interest of: *The book's unusual title intrigued me into reading it.* **2** to bring or get by intrigue: *to intrigue a person out of office.* **3** to puzzle; perplex. **4** *Archaic.* to trick; cheat.
[< French *intrigue* < Italian *intrigo* < *intrigare* < Latin *intrīcāre* to entangle; see etym. under **intricate**] —**in|tri′guer,** *n.*

in|tri|guing (in trē′ging), *adj.* exciting the curiosity and interest: *The book's intriguing title caught my attention. Astronomers may get their clearest look so far at the intriguing planet Mars* (Wall Street Journal). —**in|tri′guing|ly,** *adv.*

in|trin|sic (in trin′sik), *adj.* **1** belonging to a thing by its very nature; essential; inherent: *The intrinsic value of a dollar bill is the cost of the paper it's printed on.* SYN: innate, ingrained. **2** *Anatomy.* originating or being inside the part on which it acts: *the intrinsic muscles of the larynx.* [< Middle French *intrinsèque* < Old French, learned borrowing from Medieval Latin *intrinsecus* internal < Latin *intrīnsecus* inwardly] —**in|trin′si|cal|ly,** *adv.* —**in|trin′si|cal|ness,** *n.*

in|trin|si|cal (in trin′sə kəl), *adj.* = intrinsic.

intrinsic factor, a substance secreted in the stomach that is needed for the utilization of vitamin B_{12} by the body. Lack of it causes pernicious anemia.

in|tro (in′trō), *n., pl.* **-tros.** *Informal.* **1** a social introduction: *Thank you, headmaster, for that very, very kind intro* (Punch). **2** an introductory passage of music.

intro-, *prefix.* inwardly; within; into; inward, as in *introvert, introduce, introduction.* [< Latin *intrō-* < *intrō* within, inwardly]

intro. or **introd.,** **1** introduction. **2** introductory.

in|tro|duce (in′trə düs′, -dyüs′), *v.t.,* **-duced, -duc|ing.** **1** to bring in: *She introduced a story into the conversation.* **2** to put in; insert: *The doctor introduced a long tube into the sick man's throat so he could breathe.* **3** to bring into use, notice, or knowledge: *to introduce a new fashion, to introduce a new food, to introduce a reform. Television and space travel are introducing many new words into our language.* **4** to make known: *The principal introduced the speaker to the students.* **5** to bring (a person) to the knowledge or acquaintance of something: *I introduced my country cousin to the city by showing him the sights.* **6** to bring forward for consideration: *to introduce a question for debate, to introduce a bill to the legislature.* **7** to present formally: *The girl was introduced to society at her debut.* **8** to begin; start: *He introduced his speech by telling a joke. Relative pronouns introduce adjective clauses.* [< Latin *intrōdūcere* < *intrō-* in + *dūcere* to lead] —**in′tro|duc′er,** *n.* —**in′tro|duc′i|ble, in′tro|duce′a|ble,** *adj.*
—*Syn.* **4, 5 Introduce, present** mean to make someone known to another or others. **Introduce** is the less formal term and applies when the persons involved are more or less equals in status: *Mrs. Brown, may I introduce Mrs. Smith?* **Present** suggests some degree of ceremony and applies particularly when the persons are not of equal status: *Freshmen are presented to the president of a college.*

in|tro|duc|tion (in′trə duk′shən), *n.* **1** the act of introducing: *The introduction of steel as a building material made very tall buildings possible.* **2** the fact or state of being introduced: *She was shy at her introduction to the company.* **3** the beginning of a speech, piece of music, or a book, leading up to the main part. **4** a first book for beginners; book that explains the elementary principles of a subject: *an introduction to the study of botany.* **5** a thing made known; thing brought into use: *Television is a later introduction than radio.* **6** the formal presentation of one person to another or others: *The hostess made brief introductions as the guests arrived.* [< Latin *intrōductiō, -ōnis* < *intrōdūcere;* see etym. under **introduce**]
—*Syn.* **3 Introduction, preface, foreword** mean a section at the beginning of a book, etc. **Introduction** applies to an actual part of the book, article, play, or other, usually written, work, that leads into or gives what is necessary for understanding the main part: *The symbols used in the pronunciation key are explained in the introduction to this dictionary.* **Preface** applies to a preliminary statement, often signed by the author, explaining his purpose in writing, his obligation to others, etc. **Foreword** means a short, simple preface: *The foreword was no more than a statement thanking those who had helped the author with his book.*

in|tro|duc|tive (in′trə duk′tiv), *adj.* introductory: *Laws, when prudently framed, are by no means subversive but rather introductive of liberty* (William Blackstone).

in|tro|duc|to|ri|ly (in′trə duk′tər ə lē, -trə lē), *adv.* in an introductory manner; by way of introduction.

in|tro|duc|to|ry (in′trə duk′tər ē, -trē), *adj.* used to introduce; serving as an introduction; preliminary: *an introductory chapter. The speaker began his talk with a few introductory remarks about his subject.* SYN: prefatory, precursory.

in|tro|gres|sant (in′trə gres′ənt), *n.* a gene which is acquired by a species through introgression.

in|tro|gres|sion (in′trə gresh′ən), *n. Genetics.* the introduction, often by chance backcrossing, of the genes of one species into another species.

in|tro|gres|sive hybridization (in′trə gres′iv), = introgression.

in|tro|it (in trō′it), *n.* **1** Also, **Introit.** (in the Roman Catholic Church) a hymn or responsive anthem recited by the priest at the beginning of Mass or sung by the choir at High Mass. It consists of a verse or antiphon, a verse from the Psalms, the Gloria Patri, and the first verse again. **2** (in the Anglican Church) a psalm or anthem at the beginning of the Communion service. [< Latin *introitus, -ūs* a going in, entrance < *introīre* enter < *intrō-* in + *īre* to go]

in|tro|ject (in′trə jekt′), *v.t.* **1** *Psychology.* to take in and absorb into the unconscious (the attitudes of other persons or the characteristics of outside objects). **2** to incorporate (any idea, feeling, or belief): *We have introjected an even stronger dose of nostalgia into the Pax Britannica ... than when the* [*Forsyte*] *Saga appeared as a whole in 1922* (Cyril Connolly). [< *intro-* + (pro)*ject*]

in|tro|jec|tion (in′trə jek′shən), *n.* the act or process of introjecting.

in|tro|mis|sion (in′trə mish′ən), *n.* **1** introduction; admission. **2** = interference.

in|tro|mit (in′trə mit′), *v.t.,* **-mit|ted, -mit|ting.** **1** to send, put, or let in; admit; introduce. **2** to interfere; meddle. [< Latin *intrōmittere* < *intrō-* inside + *mittere* send]

in|tro|mit|tent (in′trə mit′ənt), *adj.* that intromits.

in|tro|mit|ter (in′trə mit′ər), *n.* a person or thing that intromits.

in|tron (in′tron), *n.* a segment of DNA that has no specific genetic code; intervening sequence: *One possibility is that some of the introns are promoters—regions of DNA where the enzyme RNA polymerase first binds to a gene before transcribing it. Introns may also play a role in control of gene expression* (Thomas H. Maugh II). [< *intro-* inward, inside + *-on*]

in|tro|pu|ni|tive (in′trə pyü′nə tiv), *adj.* inflicting punishment upon oneself, especially subconsciously; having feelings of guilt and self-blame: *an intropunitive criminal.* [< *intro-* + *punitive*] —**in′tro|pu′ni|tive|ness,** *n.*

***in|trorse** (in trôrs′), *adj. Botany.* turned or facing inward, toward the axis. A violet has introrse anthers. [< Latin *introrsus,* ultimately < *intrō-* inward + *vertere* turn] —**in|trorse′ly,** *adv.*

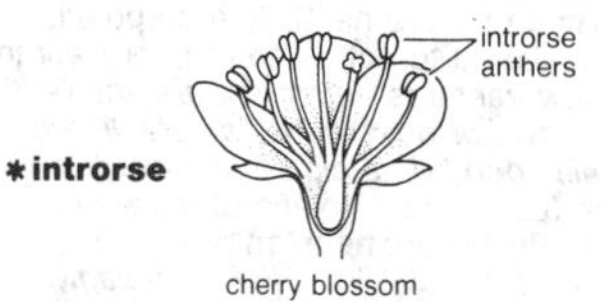

***introrse**

cherry blossom

in|tro|scope (in′trə skōp′), *n.* an instrument that allows a view of the interior of a tube or cavity by means of an adjustable objective lens and a system of mirrors to reflect light rays into the tube. [< *intro-* + *-scope*]

in|tro|spect (in′trə spekt′), *v.i.* to look within; be introspective. —*v.t.* to look into; examine. [< Latin *intrōspectus,* past participle of *intrōspicere* < *intrō-* into + *specere* to look]

in|tro|spec|tion (in′trə spek′shən), *n.* the examination of one's own thoughts and feelings: *Philosophical people are given to introspection. I was forced to make an introspection into mine own mind* (John Dryden).

in|tro|spec|tion|al (in′trə spek′shə nəl), *adj.* of or having to do with introspection.

in|tro|spec|tion|ism (in′trə spek′shə niz əm), *n.* the doctrine that introspection and the mental content of experience is the chief subject matter of psychological study. —**in′tro|spec′tion|ist,** *adj., n.*

in|tro|spec|tive (in′trə spek′tiv), *adj.* inclined to examine one's own thoughts and feelings; characterized by introspection: *an introspective essay.* —**in′tro|spec′tive|ly,** *adv.* —**in′tro|spec′tive|ness,** *n.*

in|tro|ver|sion (in′trə vėr′zhən, -shən), *n.* **1** a tendency to be more interested in one's own thoughts and feelings than in what is going on around one; tendency to think rather than act. **2** an inward turn or bent. [< *intro-,* patterned on *reversion*]

in|tro|ver|sive (in′trə vėr′siv), *adj.* of, characterized by, or inclined to introversion; introvertive. —**in′tro|ver′sive|ly,** *adv.*

in|tro|vert (*n., adj.* in′trə vėrt; *v.* in′trə vėrt′), *n., adj., v.* —*n.* a person more interested in his own thoughts and feelings than in what is going on around him; person tending to think rather than act and so having qualities attributed as shy and unsociable: *They grew up to be shy little introverts, heavily dependent on each other* (Newsweek). [< verb]
—*adj.* characterized by introversion.
—*v.t.* **1** to direct (one's thoughts or feelings) inward or upon oneself. **2** to turn or bend inward: *introverted toes.* **3** to turn (a tubular organ or part) back within itself; infold.
—*v.i.* to be or become an introvert.
[< *intro-* + Latin *vertere* to turn]

in|tro|vert|ed (in′trə vėr′tid), *adj.* characterized by introversion.

in|tro|ver|tive (in′trə vėr′tiv), *adj.* = introversive.

in|trude (in trüd′), *v.,* **-trud|ed, -trud|ing.** —*v.i.* to thrust oneself in; come unasked and unwanted: *If you are busy, I will not intrude. Do not intrude upon the privacy of your neighbors.*
—*v.t.* **1** to give (something) unasked and unwanted; force in: *Do not intrude your opinions upon others.* **2** *Geology.* to thrust in; force in: *rock melted by heat and intruded into fissures.* [< Latin *intrūdere* < *in-* in + *trūdere* to thrust, push] —**in|trud′er,** *n.* —**in|trud′ing|ly,** *adv.*
—*Syn. v.i.* **Intrude, trespass, encroach** mean to invade the rights or property of another. **Intrude** implies thrusting in where one is unwanted, uninvited, or has no right to go and often suggests rudeness and invasion of privacy: *I was unwilling to intrude upon them so late at night. He intrudes upon their hospitality.* **Trespass** means to intrude unlawfully or in an offensive manner: *The hunters trespassed upon the farmer's land. She often unthinkingly trespasses upon my time. He trespassed on my brother's paper route.* **Encroach** means to trespass upon the property or rights of another, usually secretly or gradually: *Our neighbor's irrigation system is encroaching on our land.*

in|tru|sion (in trü′zhən), *n.* **1** the act of intruding; coming unasked and unwanted: *Excuse my intrusion; I didn't know that you were busy. Why this intrusion? Were not my orders that I would be private?* (Joseph Addison). SYN: encroachment, infringement. **2** an unlawful entry or seizure of land or rights belonging to another. **3** *Geology.* **a** the forcing of molten rock into fissures or between strata. **b** the molten rock forced in and solidified in place. [< Medieval Latin *intrusio, -onis* < Latin *intrūdere* intrude]

in|tru|sive (in trü′siv), *adj., n.* —*adj.* **1** intruding; coming unasked and unwanted: *Let me shake off the intrusive cares of day* (James Thomson). SYN: obtrusive. **2** *Geology.* forced into fissures or between strata while molten. **3** *Phonetics.* inserted without any etymological or historical basis: *The "r" pronounced by some speakers in "the idear of it" is called an intrusive "r."*
—*n. Geology.* an intrusive rock or formation. —**in|tru′sive|ly,** *adv.* —**in|tru′sive|ness,** *n.*

in|trust (in trust′), *v.t.* = entrust.

in|tu|bate (in′tü bāt, -tyü-), *v.t.,* **-bat|ed, -bat|ing.** **1** to insert a tube into some body opening, especially as a treatment. **2** to treat by inserting a tube. [< *in-*[2] + Latin *tubus* pipe, tube + English *-ate*[1]] —**in′tu|ba′tion,** *n.*

in|tu|it (in tü′it, -tyü′-; in′tü-, -tyü-), *v.t., v.i.,* **-it|ed, -it|ing.** to know or receive knowledge by immediate perception; know by intuition: *Afterward, Dr. Schmeidler asked the agent and the percipient ... to tell her what each had intuited about the other* (New Yorker). [< Latin *intuitus,* past participle of *intuērī;* see etym. under **intuition**] —**in|tu′it|a|ble,** *adj.*

in|tu|i|tion (in′tü ish′ən, -tyü-), *n.* **1** the immediate perception or understanding of truths, facts, or events, without reasoning: *By experience with all kinds of people the doctor had developed great powers of intuition.* **2** an act of immediate perception: *to regard a happy guess as an intuition.* **3** a truth, fact, or event perceived or understood immediately and without reasoning. [< Late Latin *intuitiō, -ōnis* < Latin *intuērī* consider, look upon < *in-* at, on + *tuērī* to look]

in|tu|i|tion|al (in′tü ish′ə nəl, -tyü-), *adj.* of or characterized by intuition; based on intuition. —**in′tu|i′tion|al|ly,** *adv.*

in|tu|i|tion|al|ism (in′tü ish′ə nə liz′əm, -tyü-), *n.* = intuitionism.

in|tu|i|tion|al|ist (in′tü ish′ə nə list, -tyü-), *n.* = intuitionist.

in|tu|i|tion|ism (in′tü ish′ə niz əm, -tyü-), *n.* **1** the doctrine that truth and reality are intuitively recognized. **2** the doctrine that perceived objects are intuitively known to have actual existence. —**in′tu|i′tion|ist,** *n., adj.*

in|tu|i|tive (in tü′ə tiv, -tyü′-), *adj.* **1** perceiving or understanding immediately and without reasoning: *The lawyers had great respect for the judge's intuitive mind.* **2** acquired by intuition; instinctive; natural: *intuitive knowledge. The artist's understanding of color seems to have been intuitive. Basing his argument on wholly intuitive premises, he may develop it with impeccable logic* (Bulletin of Atomic Scientists). **3** of the nature of an intuition: *Her perception of right seemed almost intuitive.* —**in|tu′i|tive|ly,** *adv.* —**in|tu′i|tive|ness,** *n.*

in|tu|i|tiv|ism (in tü′ə tə viz′əm, -tyü′-), *n.* **1** the doctrine that the fundamental principles of ethics are reached by intuition. **2** intuitive perception; insight.

in|tu|i|tiv|ist (in tü′ə tə vist, -tyü′-), *n.* a follower of intuitivism in ethics.

in|tu|mesce (in′tü mes′, -tyü-), *v.i.,* **-mesced, -mesc|ing.** to swell up; bubble up; become tumid, as with heat. [< Latin *intumēscere* < *in-* + *tumēscere* swell up < *tumēre* to be swollen]

in|tu|mes|cence (in′tü mes′əns, -tyü-), *n.* **1** the act or process of swelling up or bubbling up. **2** swollen state. **3** a swollen mass or growth, such as a tumor.

in|tu|mes|cent (in′tü mes′ənt, -tyü-), *adj.* swelling up; becoming tumid.

in|turn (in′tėrn′), *n.* an inward turn.

in|turned (in′tėrnd′), *adj.* **1** turned inward: *inturned teeth.* **2** *Especially British.* self-centered; introverted.

in|tus|sus|cept (in′təs sə sept′), *v.t.* to take within, as in telescoping one part of the intestine into another part; invaginate. [< Latin *intus* within + *susceptus,* past participle of *suscipere* take up < *sub-* from under + *capere* take]

in|tus|sus|cep|tion (in′təs sə sep′shən), *n.* **1** the act or process of taking within, as of ideas; reception. **2** *Biology.* **a** the taking in of foreign matter, especially food, by a living organism and converting it into living tissue. **b** new materials or particles interpolated among old parts already in place. **3** the inversion of one part of the intestine and its slipping into an adjacent part, occurring especially in infants; invagination. **4** a serious intestinal obstruction of horses, characterized by an introverting of the bowel.

in|tus|sus|cep|tive (in′təs sə sep′tiv), *adj.* of or characterized by intussusception.

in|twine (in twīn′), *v.t., v.i.,* **-twined, -twin|ing.** = entwine.

in|twist (in twist′), *v.t.* = entwist.

In|u|it (in′yu it), *n., pl.* **-it** or **-its.** an Eskimo of North America. The Eskimos of Siberia are called Yuit. Also, **Innuit.**
[< Eskimo *innuit* the people, plural of *innuk* man]

in|u|lase (in′yə lās), *n.* an enzyme that converts inulin into fructose.

in|u|lin (in′yə lin), *n.* a white, starchlike substance obtained from the roots of various composite plants, especially elecampane and dahlia, used as a substitute for starch in foods for persons who have diabetes. *Formula:* $(C_6H_{10}O_5)_n$ [< New Latin *Inula* the elecampane genus (< Latin *inula* elecampane < Greek *helénion*) + English *-in*]

in|unc|tion (in ungk′shən), *n.* **1** the act of anointing, especially as a religious rite. **2** the rubbing in of oil or ointment. **3** an ointment or liniment.
[< Latin *inunctiō, -ōnis* < *inunguere* besmear, anoint < *in-* on + *unguere* to smear]

in|un|date (in′un dāt, in un′-), *v.t.,* **-dat|ed, -dat|ing.** **1** to overflow; overspread with a flow of water; flood: *Heavy rains caused the river to rise and inundate the valley.* **2** *Figurative:* *Requests for free tickets inundated the studio. A tidal wave of students has inundated the schools.* SYN: overwhelm.
[< Latin *inundāre* (with English *-ate*[1]) < *in-* onto + *undāre* to flow < *unda* wave]

in|un|da|tion (in′un dā′shən), *n.* the act or fact of overflowing; flood: *Heavy rains were causing inundations and much damage throughout the country.* SYN: See syn. under **flood.**

in|un|da|tor (in′un dā′tər, in un′dā-), *n.* a thing that inundates.

in|un|da|to|ry (in un′də tôr′ē, -tōr′-), *adj.* that inundates; inundating.

in|ur|bane (in′ėr bān′), *adj.* not urbane; impolite; discourteous.

in|ur|ban|i|ty (in′ėr ban′ə tē), *n.* lack of urbanity; discourtesy; impoliteness.

in|ure (in yůr′), *v.,* **-ured, -ur|ing.** —*v.t.* to toughen or harden; accustom; habituate: *Poverty had inured the beggar to hardship.* SYN: season.
—*v.i.* to have effect; be useful: *The agreement inures to the benefit of the employees.* Also, **enure.**
[< *in-*[2] in + obsolete *ure* use, noun < Anglo-French *ure* < Latin *opera* work < *opus, operis* work]

in|ure|ment (in yůr′mənt), *n.* the act of inuring or the state of being inured.

in|urn (in ėrn′), *v.t.* **1** to put (the ashes of a cremated body) in an urn. **2** to entomb; bury. —**in|urn′ment,** *n.*

in u|te|ro (in yü′tə rō), in the uterus; before being born: *Fraternal twins interchange blood-forming tissue during the time they spend in utero* (New Scientist).
[< Latin *in uterō* < *in* in; *uterus* womb]

in|u|tile (in yü′təl), *adj.* useless; unprofitable: *inutile speculation.* [< Middle French *inutile,* learned borrowing from Latin *inūtilis* < *in-* not + *ūtilis* useful] —**in|u′tile|ly,** *adv.*

in|u|til|i|ty (in′yü til′ə tē), *n., pl.* **-ties.** **1** the quality or state of being useless; uselessness. **2** a useless thing or person.

in u|trum|que pa|ra|tus (in yü trum′kwē pə rā′təs), *Latin.* prepared for either alternative.

in|ut|ter|a|ble (in ut′ər ə bəl), *adj.* unutterable; inexpressible.

inv., an abbreviation for the following:
1 invenit.
2a invented. **b** invention. **c** inventor.
3 inventory.
4 investment.
5 invoice.

in va|cu|o (in vak′yů ō), *Latin.* in a vacuum: *Liquids with a low boiling point can be made to distil at room temperature when radiated . . . in vacuo* (Science News). (*Figurative.*) *The present chart must not be studied in vacuo* (Harper's).

in|vade (in vād′), *v.,* **-vad|ed, -vad|ing.** —*v.t.* **1a** to enter with force or as an enemy; attack: *Soldiers invaded the country to conquer it. Grasshoppers invaded the fields and ate the crops. Diseases invade the body.* **b** (*Figurative.*) *Tourists invaded the city. Night invades the sky.* **2** to interfere with; break in on; violate: *The law punishes people who invade the rights of others.*
—*v.i.* to make an invasion.
[< Latin *invādere* < *in-* in + *vādere* go, walk] —**in|vad′er,** *n.*

in|vag|i|nate (in vaj′ə nāt), *v.,* **-nat|ed, -nat|ing,** *adj.* —*v.t.* **1** to fold or draw (a hollow structure) back within itself; introvert; intussuscept. **2** = sheathe.
—*v.i.* to become invaginated.
—*adj.* invaginated.
[< *in-*[2] in + Latin *vagīna* sheath + English *-ate*[1]]

in|vag|i|na|tion (in vaj′ə nā′shən), *n.* **1** the act or process of invaginating. **2** invaginated condition. **3** an invaginated part. **4** intussusception. **5** the drawing inward of a portion of the wall of a blastula in the formation of a gastrula.

in|va|lid[1] (in′və lid), *n., adj., v.* —*n.* **1** a sick or weak person not able to get about and do things: *I have invented an invaluable permanent invalid called Bunbury* (Oscar Wilde). **2** a soldier or sailor retired from active service because of sickness or injury.
—*adj.* **1** not well; weak and sick. **2** for the use of invalids: *an invalid chair, an invalid car.*
—*v.t.* **1** to make sick or weak; disable. **2** to remove from active service because of sickness or injury: *The wounded soldier was invalided and sent home.*
—*v.i.* **1** to become an invalid. **2** to retire from active service because of sickness or injury.
[< Latin *invalidus* not strong; influenced by Middle French *invalide,* learned borrowing from Latin *invalidus;* see etym. under **invalid**[2]]

in|val|id[2] (in val′id), *adj.* not valid; without force or effect; without value; worthless: *Unless a check is signed, it is invalid.* SYN: null, void. [< Latin *invalidus* < *in-* not + *validus* strong < *valēre* be strong] —**in|val′id|ly,** *adv.* —**in|val′id|ness,** *n.*

in|val|i|date (in val′ə dāt), *v.t.,* **-dat|ed, -dat|ing.** to make not valid; cause to be worthless or not good; deprive of force or effect: *A contract is invalidated if only one party signs it.* SYN: annul, nullify. —**in|val′i|da′tor,** *n.*

in|val|i|da|tion (in val′ə dā′shən), *n.* the act of invalidating or making invalid: *The invalidation of fair trade laws by court decision in several states . . . created increasing complexities for the effective enforcement of fair trade* (Wall Street Journal).

in|va|lid|ism (in′və lə diz′əm), *n.* the condition of being an invalid; prolonged ill health.

in|va|lid|i|ty (in′və lid′ə tē), *n.* **1** lack of validity, force, or effect; worthlessness: *the invalidity of a theory, of evidence, or of a passport.* **2** prolonged ill health; invalidism: *Countries provide benefits for permanent disability or invalidity through their social security programs* (Saturday Review).

in|val|u|a|ble (in val′yů ə bəl, -yə bəl), *adj.* valuable beyond measure; very precious; priceless: *Good health is an invaluable blessing. Honest and faithful friends are an invaluable jewel* (Abraham Fleming). SYN: inestimable. —**in|val′u|a|ble|ness,** *n.* —**in|val′u|a|bly,** *adv.*

In|var (in vär′), *n. Trademark.* an alloy of nickel, iron, and other metals, having a coefficient of expansion which is virtually zero, used especially for making scientific instruments. [< *invar*(iable) (because of its slight degree of expansion)]

in|var|i|a|bil|i|ty (in vãr′ē ə bil′ə tē), *n.* lack of variability; being invariable. SYN: immutability, unchangeableness, constancy, uniformity.

in|var|i|a|ble (in vãr′ē ə bəl), *adj., n.* —*adj.* always the same; not changing; unchangeable: *After dinner it was his invariable habit to take a nap.* SYN: uniform, constant.
—*n. Mathematics.* something invariable; a constant. —**in|var′i|a|ble|ness,** *n.*

in|var|i|a|bly (in vãr′ē ə blē), *adv.* in an invariable manner; without change; without exception: *Spring invariably follows winter. He invariably eats breakfast at 6:30* A.M.

in|var|i|ance (in vãr′ē əns), *n.* invariant condition or quality: *the invariance of time and space.*

in|var|i|ant (in vãr′ē ənt), *adj., n.* —*adj.* unvarying; invariable; constant.
—*n. Mathematics.* an invariable entity or quantity.

in|va|sion (in vā′zhən), *n.* **1a** the act or fact of invading; entering by force or as an enemy; attack: *We are waiting for the long-promised invasion. So are the fishes* (Sir Winston Churchill). SYN: incursion. **b** *Figurative: the invasion of disease, the invasion of cornfields by locusts.* **2** interference; encroachment; violation: *Wire tapping is an invasion of individual privacy.* **3** the growth of a large population of an animal or plant in a region not before inhabited by the species.
[< Late Latin *invāsiō, -ōnis* < *invādere;* see etym. under **invade**]

in|va|sive (in vā′siv), *adj.* **1** tending to invade; invading: *an invasive force.* **2** characterized by or involving invasion: *invasive action.* **3** aggressive; offensive; intrusive: *an invasive person.*

in|va|siv|i|ty (in′vā siv′ə tē), *n.* the tendency to invade; invasive quality or character: *the invasivity of a germ.*

in|vecked (in vekt′), *adj. Heraldry.* bordered by or formed of small convex or outward curves or slightly projecting rounded lobes. [< *inveck,* variant of obsolete *invect* draw in (< Latin *invehī;* see etym. under **inveigh**) + *-ed*[2]]

in|vect|ed (in vek′tid), *adj.* = invecked.

in|vec|tive (in vek′tiv), *n., adj.* —*n.* a violent attack in words; abusive speech: *His opponents were overcome by the fury of his invective. It does seem that they do not want to revert to their earlier reliance on threat and invective* (Time). SYN: vituperation.
—*adj.* inveighing; denouncing. SYN: vituperative, abusive.
[< Late Latin *invectīvus* abusive < Latin *invehī* attack with words; see etym. under **inveigh**] —**in|vec′tive|ly,** *adv.* —**in|vec′tive|ness,** *n.*

in|veigh (in vā′), *v.i.* to make a violent attack in words; rail: *The agitator inveighed against the government. The leadership passed to the popular orators, who rose to power by inveighing against property* (James A. Froude). [< Latin *invehī* launch an attack (with words), passive of *invehere* bring in, carry in < *in-* against + *vehere* carry] —**in|veigh′er,** *n.*

in|vei|gle (in vē′gəl, -vā′-), *v.t.,* **-gled, -gling.** **1** to lead astray by trickery; entice; lure: *The saleswoman inveigled the young girl into buying four hats.* SYN: allure, ensnare, beguile, dupe. **2** to obtain by trickery: *to inveigle a promise.* [apparently alteration of earlier unrecorded *aveglen* < Old French *aveugler* make blind, delude < *aveugle* blind < Vulgar Latin *aboculus* < Latin *ab-* without, away + *oculus* eye] —**in|vei′gler,** *n.* —**in|vei′gle|ment,** *n.*

in|ve|nit (in vē′nit), *Latin.* (he or she) invented, devised, or designed it.

in|vent (in vent′), *v.t.* **1** to make up for the first time; make or think out (something new): *Alexander Graham Bell invented the telephone.* SYN: See syn. under **discover.** **2** to make up; think up: *When she had no good reason for being late, she invented some excuse.* SYN: fabricate. **3** *Obsolete.* to come upon; find: *And vowed never to returne againe, Till him alive or dead she did invent* (Edmund Spenser). —*v.i.* to devise something new, as by thought or ingenuity; originate; create: *But when did woman ever yet invent?* (Tennyson).
[< Latin *inventus,* past participle of *invenīre* discover, find (out) < *in-* in, on + *venīre* come]

in|vent|er (in ven′tər), *n.* = inventor.

Pronunciation Key: hat, āge, cãre, fär; let, ēqual, tėrm; it, īce; hot, ōpen, ôrder; oil, out; cup, pu̇t, rüle; child; long; thin; ᴛʜen; zh, measure; ə represents **a** in about, **e** in taken, **i** in pencil, **o** in lemon, **u** in circus.

in|vent|i|ble (in ven′tə bəl), *adj.* that can be invented.

in|ven|tion (in ven′shən), *n.* **1** the act or process of inventing; the original making of something new: *the invention of gunpowder. For the last three centuries, Western civilization has dedicated a good part of its energies to the invention of machines* (New Yorker). **2** a thing invented: *Television is a modern invention.* **3** the power of inventing: *An author must have invention to think up new ideas for stories.* **4** a made-up story; false statement: *That rumor was the old gossip's own invention.* **5** *Music.* a short composition in which a single theme is developed in simple counterpoint: *Bach's piano Inventions.* **6** (in classical rhetoric) the selection of suitable topics or arguments. **7** *Archaic.* the act of finding, or finding out; discovery.

in|ven|tion|al (in ven′shə nəl), *adj.* of, having to do with, or like invention.

in|ven|tive (in ven′tiv), *adj.* **1** good at inventing; quick to invent things: *An inventive person thinks up ways to save time, money, and work.* **SYN:** imaginative, ingenious. **2** of invention. **3** showing power of inventing: *Great art . . . must be inventive, that is, be produced by the imagination* (John Ruskin). —**in|ven′tive|ly**, *adv.* —**in|ven′tive|ness**, *n.*

in|ven|tor (in ven′tər), *n.* a person who invents: *Edison was a great inventor.*

in|ven|to|ri|al (in′vən tôr′ē əl, -tōr′), *adj.* of or having to do with an inventory. —**in′ven|to′ri|al|ly**, *adv.*

in|ven|to|ry (in′vən tôr′ē, -tōr′-), *n., pl.* **-ries**, *v.,* **-ried**, **-ry|ing**. —*n.* **1** a complete and detailed list of articles. An inventory of property or goods tells how many there are of each article and what they are worth. **2** all the articles listed or to be listed; stock: *The storekeeper had a sale to reduce his inventory.* **3** any detailed account: *There are stores laid up in our human nature that our understanding can make no complete inventory of* (George Eliot).
—*v.t.* to make a detailed list of; enter in a list: *Some stores inventory their stock once a month.*
[< Medieval Latin *inventorium,* for Late Latin *inventārium* < *inventus;* see etym. under **invent**]

inventory control or **management**, the maintenance of inventories at a desired level; control of the level of normal or basic stock: *His company's campaign to improve inventory control has enabled it to handle growing sales . . . without increasing its stocks* (Wall Street Journal).

in|ven|tress (in ven′tris), *n.* a woman inventor.

in|ve|ra|cious (in′və rā′shəs), *adj.* not veracious; untruthful.

in|ve|rac|i|ty (in′və ras′ə tē), *n., pl.* **-ties**. **1** untruthfulness. **2** an untruth.

***in|ver|ness** (in′vər nes′, in′vər nes), *n.,* or **Inverness cape**, an overcoat with a removable cape. [< *Inverness,* a city and county in Scotland]

***inverness**

in|verse (in vėrs′, in′vėrs), *adj., n., v.,* **-versed**, **-vers|ing**. —*adj.* **1** exactly opposite; reversed in position, direction, or tendency; opposite in nature or effect: *DCBA is the inverse order of ABCD. The reigning taste was so bad, that the success of a writer was in inverse proportion to his labor, and to his desire of excellence* (Macaulay). **2** turned upside down; inverted: *I saw a tower builded on a lake, Mock'd by its inverse shadow* (Thomas Hood). **3** *Mathematics.* of or having to do with an inverse or an inverse function: *an inverse operation, inverse elements.*
—*n.* **1** something reversed: *The inverse of ¾ is 4/3.* **2** the direct opposite: *Evil is the inverse of good.* **3** *Mathematics.* **a** an operation which cancels what another operation does: *The inverse of addition is subtraction.* **b** = inverse function. **c** either one of two elements in a set that by combining in a binary operation yield the identity element of the set.
—*v.t.* to invert; reverse.
[< Latin *inversus,* past participle of *invertere;* see etym. under **invert**] —**in|verse′ly**, *adv.*

inverse coefficient, *Economics.* a coefficient used in input-output tables to show to what extent the demand for one industry's products affects the production requirements of another industry.

inverse function, *Mathematics.* **1** a function which is the inverse of another function. **2** a function which replaces another function's independent variable with a value of its dependent variable.

inverse square law, *Physics.* **1** a law stating that the intensity of light falling on a surface varies inversely with the square of the distance between the source and the surface. **2** this law applied to sound, electricity, and other forms of energy: *As everyone knows, it is an inverse square law force: the gravitational attraction between two masses varies inversely as the square of the distance between them* (Scientific American).

in|ver|sion (in vėr′zhən, -shən), *n.* **1** the act of inverting or condition of being inverted. **2** something inverted. **3** *Rhetoric.* reversal of the usual or natural order of words; anastrophe. *Example:* happy is the returning traveler; the house beautiful. **4** *Meteorology.* an increase of air temperature with elevation instead of the usual decrease. **5** *Mathematics.* the reversal of a ratio by interchanging the positions of the numerator and denominator. **6** *Medicine.* a turning inside out or inward; introversion. **7** *Chemistry.* the hydrolysis of certain carbohydrates, such as cane sugar into glucose and fructose, in which the optical rotation of the solution is reversed. **8** *Music.* the process or result of changing the relative position of the notes of an interval, chord, etc., by transposing the lowest note or the root of a chord to a higher octave. **9** = homosexuality. **10** *Phonetics.* articulation with the tip of the tongue raised and bent backward. **11** *Genetics.* the reversal of one segment of a chromosome. In chromosomal inversion, the linear order of a chromosome segment is turned around 180 degrees.

inversion layer, *Meteorology.* a layer of air that is warmer than the air below it: *The inversion layer thought characteristic of tornadoes may actually disappear gradually several hours before "twisters" are born* (Science News Letter).

in|ver|sive (in vėr′siv), *adj.* characterized by inversion.

in|vert (*v.* in vėrt′; *adj., n.* in′vėrt), *v., adj., n.* —*v.t.* **1** to turn upside down: *He inverted the glass and the water ran out.* **SYN:** See syn. under **reverse**. **2** to turn the other way; change to the opposite; reverse in position, direction, or order: *If you invert "I can," you have "Can I?"* (*Figurative.*) *Inflation in time of depression inverts all the old canons of economics.* **3** *Music.* to change by making the lower or lowest note an octave higher or the higher or highest note an octave lower. **4** *Medicine.* to turn outside in or inside out. **5** *Chemistry.* to decompose by inversion. **6** *Phonetics.* to pronounce with the tip of the tongue raised and bent backward.
—*adj.* *Chemistry.* inverted.
—*n.* **1** a person or thing that is inverted. **2** = homosexual. **3** a postage stamp printed with an inverted design.
[< Latin *invertere* < *in-* in, on + *vertere* to turn]

in|vert|ase (in vėr′tās), *n.* an enzyme which acts as a catalyst to convert sucrose into glucose and fructose; saccharase; sucrase. Invertase is found in plants, yeast, and the digestive juices of animals. [< *invert,* verb + *-ase*]

in|ver|te|bra|cy (in vėr′tə brə sē), *n.* invertebrate condition or quality; spinelessness.

in|ver|te|brate (in vėr′tə brit, -brāt), *adj., n.* —*adj.* **1** without a backbone: *invertebrate animals including the worm, the spider, and the beetle.* **2** of or having to do with invertebrates. **3** *Figurative.* lacking moral strength; without character, conviction, or purpose: *The book is invertebrate, with none of the dramatic structure that a long, detailed novel so much needs* (New Yorker).
—*n.* **1** any one of the large number of types of animals without a backbone. Worms and insects are invertebrates; fishes, amphibians, reptiles, birds, and mammals are vertebrates. **2** *Figurative.* a person without moral strength or character.
[< *in-*[1] not + *vertebrate*]

in|vert|ed (in vėr′tid), *adj.* turned upside down; in a reverse position, direction, or order: (*Figurative.*) *In a strange sort of inverted way he did well by his country there in the dock in Moscow* (Listener).

inverted arch, an arch set upside down, used especially in foundation construction.

inverted comma, **1** *British.* = quotation mark. **2** a comma turned upside down, used to denote a foreign vowel sound (as in Arabic *'iqāl* iqal) or to mark the beginning of a quotation within another quotation.

inverted mordent, *Music.* a pralltriller.

in|vert|er (in vėr′tər), *n.* **1** a person or thing that inverts. **2** *Electricity.* a device for transforming direct current into alternating current.

in|vert|i|ble in vėr′tə bəl), *adj.* that can be inverted.

in|ver|tor (in vėr′tər), *n.* = inverter.

invert soap, a soap in which the organic portion is positively charged, rather than negatively as in ordinary soap: *Invert soaps have strong disinfectant and acid-resistant qualities.*

invert sugar, a mixture of glucose and fructose occurring as a result of the inversion of cane sugar. Honey contains invert sugar.

in|vest (in vest′), *v.t.* **1a** to use (money) to buy something that will produce a profit, or an income, or both: *If I had any money, I would invest it in land. He invested his money in stocks and bonds.* **b** *Figurative.* to spend or devote (time, energy, or other nonmaterial resources) for later benefit: *"I have already invested several years of my life in Joe"* (Maclean's). **2** to clothe; cover; surround: *Darkness invests the earth at night. Spring invests the trees with leaves.* (*Figurative.*) *The castle was invested with mystery and romance.* **3** to give power, authority, or right to: *He invested his lawyer with complete power to act for him.* **4** to give a quality or characteristic to: *He invested his friend with every virtue.* **5** to put in office with a ceremony: *A king is invested by being crowned.* **6** to surround with soldiers or ships; besiege: *The enemy invested the city and cut it off from our army.* **7** to adorn: *The turban on his head was invested with jewels.* **8** *Obsolete.* to put on (clothes) *Cannot find one this girdle to invest* (Edmund Spenser). —*v.i.* to invest money; make an investment: *Learn to invest wisely.*
[< Latin *investīre* to clothe < *in-* in + *vestis* clothing] —**in|vest′a|ble**, *adj.*

in|ves|ti|ga|ble (in ves′tə gə bəl), *adj.* that can be investigated.

in|ves|ti|gate (in ves′tə gāt), *v.,* **-gat|ed**, **-gat|ing**. —*v.t.* to search into carefully; examine closely: *to investigate a complaint. Detectives investigate crimes to find out who did them. Scientists investigate nature to learn more about it.* **SYN:** explore, scrutinize. —*v.i.* to search; make investigation. [< Latin *investīgāre* (with English *-ate*[1]) < *in-* in, on + *vestīgāre* to track, trace < *vestīgium* footstep, vestige] —**in|ves′ti|gat′ing|ly**, *adv.*

in|ves|ti|ga|tion (in ves′tə gā′shən), *n.* a careful search; detailed or careful examination.
— ***Syn.* Investigation, examination, inquiry** mean a search for information or truth. **Investigation** emphasizes a careful and systematic search for facts, especially one carried out by officials: *An investigation of the accident by the police put the blame on the drivers of both cars.* **Examination** emphasizes a search for facts by inspection: *The doctor gave her a physical examination.* **Inquiry** especially suggests a search for facts made by asking questions: *Advertisers began an inquiry into the buying habits of consumers.*

in|ves|ti|ga|tion|al (in ves′tə gā′she nəl), *adj.* **1** = investigative. **2** under investigation; experimental: *The drug was given to many patients on an investigational basis* (Wall Street Journal).

in|ves|ti|ga|tive (in ves′tə gā′tiv), *adj.* **1** of or having to do with investigation: *investigative powers.* **2** inclined or tending toward investigation: *House leaders clamp down hard on the investigative urge* (Wall Street Journal).

investigative reporting, news gathering by investigation, as of crime or corruption, when official investigation is lagging.

in|ves|ti|ga|tor (in ves′tə gā′tər), *n.* a person who investigates.

in|ves|ti|ga|to|ry (in ves′tə gə tôr′ē, -tōr′-), *adj.* = investigative.

in|ves|ti|tive (in ves′tə tiv), *adj.* **1** serving to invest authority, power, right, office, or dignity. **2** of or having to do with investiture.

in|ves|ti|ture (in ves′tə chůr, -chər), *n.* **1** a formal investing of a person with authority, power, right, office, or dignity: *the investiture of bishops.* **SYN:** induction, installation. **2** clothing; covering. **SYN:** apparel. **3** (in feudal law) the act of delivering possession of a fief or benefice. [< Medieval Latin *investitura* < Latin *investīre* to clothe < *in-* in + *vestis* clothing]

in|vest|ment (in vest′mənt), *n.* **1** the act of investing; a laying out of money for something that is expected to produce a profit or benefit: *Getting an education is a wise investment of time and money.* **2** the amount of money invested: *His investments amounted to thousands of dollars.* **3** something bought that is expected to yield money as income or profit or both: *He has a good income from wise investments. I consider United States savings bonds a safe investment.* **4** the act of surrounding with soldiers or ships; siege. **5** = investiture. **6** *Biology.* an outer covering or coating of a plant or animal.

investment bank, a bank that specializes in buying securities from corporations and governments in large quantities and reselling them in smaller units to investors. —**investment banker** —**investment banking**

investment casting, any one of several casting processes in which molds are formed around patterns which are later melted away, such as cire-perdue casting.

investment club, a mutual fund run by private individuals forming a club.

investment company, an investment trust or mutual fund.

investment trust, a corporation or organization that invests in various securities, and pays dividends on its own stock from income received from the securities it owns.

in|ves|tor (in ves′tər), *n.* a person who invests money.

in|vet|er|a|cy (in vet′ər ə sē), *n., pl.* **-cies.** **1** settled, fixed condition; habitualness: *Their boldness has betrayed an inveteracy of criminal disposition* (Thomas Jefferson). **2** deep-rooted prejudice, hostility, or hatred; enmity of old standing: *I shall not fail to sow as much inveteracy against the French as is possible* (Horatio Nelson).

in|vet|er|ate (in vet′ər it), *adj.* **1** confirmed in habit, practice, or feeling; habitual: *It is hard for an inveterate smoker to give up tobacco. These savages are . . . the inveterate foe of the trappers* (Washington Irving). **SYN:** hardened, chronic. **2** long and firmly established; deeply rooted: *Cats have an inveterate dislike of dogs.* **SYN:** deep-rooted. [< Latin *inveterātus,* past participle of *inveterāscere* grow old < *in-* (intensive) + *veterāscere* grow old < *vetus, -eris* old] —**in|vet′er|ate|ly,** *adv.* —**in|vet′er|ate|ness,** *n.*

in|vi|a|bil|i|ty (in vī′ə bil′ə tē), *n.* inability to survive, especially because of a genetic defect: *prenatal or postnatal inviability.*

in|vi|a|ble (in vī′ə bəl), *adj.* unable to survive; not viable.

in|vid|i|ous (in vid′ē əs), *adj.* **1** likely to cause ill will or resentment; giving offense because unfair or unjust: *invidious comparisons or distinctions. Wise teachers avoid invidious rules. The highest court stated that districts cannot be apportioned arbitrarily, irrationally, or with "invidious discrimination"* (Look). **SYN:** hateful. **2** *Obsolete.* envious; grudging; jealous. [< Latin *invidiōsus* < *invidia* envy] —**in|vid′i|ous|ly,** *adv.* —**in|vid′i|ous|ness,** *n.*

in|vig|i|late (in vij′ə lāt), *v.,* **-lat|ed, -lat|ing.** —*v.i.* **1** keep watch. **2** *British.* to watch students at an examination.
—*v.t.* **1** to make watchful or aware. **2** *British.* to serve as proctor at (an examination).
[< Latin *invigilāre* (with English *-ate*[1]) < *in-* on, over + *vigilāre* keep watch < *vigil* alert] —**in|vig′i|la′tion,** *n.* —**in|vig′i|la′tor,** *n.*

in|vig|or|ant (in vig′ər ənt), *n.* something that invigorates, especially a tonic or medicine.

in|vig|or|ate (in vig′ə rāt), *v.t.,* **-at|ed, -at|ing.** to give vigor to; fill with life and energy; strengthen: *Exercise invigorates the body. A cool breeze invigorates you on a hot day.* **SYN:** brace, refresh, stimulate, animate. [< *in-*[2] in + *vigor* + *-ate*[1]] —**in|vig′or|at′ing|ly,** *adv.* —**in|vig′or|a′tion,** *n.* —**in|vig′or|a′tor,** *n.*

in|vig|or|a|tive (in vig′ə rā′tiv), *adj.* invigorating. —**in|vig′or|a′tive|ly,** *adv.*

in|vin|ci|bil|i|ty (in vin′sə bil′ə tē), *n.* invincible quality or condition.

in|vin|ci|ble (in vin′sə bəl), *adj.* not to be overcome; unconquerable; indomitable: *The champion wrestler seemed invincible.* (*Figurative.*) *invincible courage.* **SYN:** insuperable, insurmountable. [< Latin *invincībilis* < *in-* not + *vincībilis* conquerable < *vincere* conquer] —**in|vin′ci|ble|ness,** *n.* —**in|vin′ci|bly,** *adv.*

in vi|no ve|ri|tas (in vī′nō ver′ə tas), *Latin.* in wine (there is) truth; intoxication makes people speak their true thoughts.

in|vi|o|la|bil|i|ty (in vī′ə lə bil′ə tē), *n.* the quality of being inviolable.

in|vi|o|la|ble (in vī′ə lə bəl), *adj.* **1** that must not be violated or injured; sacred: *an inviolable vow, an inviolable sanctuary.* **SYN:** hallowed, sacrosanct. **2** that cannot be violated or injured: *The gods are inviolable.* —**in|vi′o|la|ble|ness,** *n.* —**in|vi′o|la|bly,** *adv.*

in|vi|o|la|cy (in vī′ə lə sē), *n.* the state of being inviolate: *The belief in the inviolacy of human personality and the freedom to worship will prevail over the forces of reaction* (New York Times).

in|vi|o|late (in vī′ə lit, -lāt), *adj.* not violated; uninjured; unbroken; not profaned: *the inviolate sanctity of a church. An inviolate promise is carried out.* —**in|vi′o|late|ly,** *adv.* —**in|vi′o|late|ness,** *n.*

in|vis|cid (in vis′id), *adj.* not viscid; lacking viscosity: *inviscid fluids.*

in|vis|i|bil|i|ty (in viz′ə bil′ə tē), *n.* invisible quality or condition.

in|vis|i|ble (in viz′ə bəl), *adj., n.* —*adj.* **1** not visible; not capable of being seen: *Thought is invisible.* **2** not in sight; not to be seen: *The queen kept herself invisible in the palace.* **3** too small to be perceived: *Germs are invisible to the naked eye.* **4** so dark as to be hardly distinguishable from black: *invisible indigo.* **5a** not listed in the regular financial statements: *an invisible asset.* **b** not appearing in returns of exports and imports, but from which payment is accepted or made to a foreign country.
—*n.* an invisible being or thing.
invisibles, invisible exports or imports: *Insurance, freight, royalties, and investment earnings are invisibles.*
the invisible, the unseen world: *I sent my soul through the invisible Some letter of that afterlife to spell* (Edward FitzGerald).
the Invisible, God: *The maintenance of faith in the Invisible . . . And by that I mean a living faith in a personal God* (William Edward Gladstone).
—**in|vis′i|ble|ness,** *n.* —**in|vis′i|bly,** *adv.*

invisible ink, a writing ink that remains invisible until it is treated with heat or chemicals; sympathetic ink. Milk, whey, sugar solutions, vegetable juice, and certain chemicals may be used as invisible ink. *His aide . . . was a graceful spy who regularly wrote information in invisible ink* (Newsweek).

invisible light, ultraviolet rays; black light.

in|vi|ta|tion (in′və tā′shən), *n.* **1** a polite request to come to some place or to do something. Formal invitations are written or printed. *The children received invitations to the party.* **2** the act of inviting: *The guests at his house come by invitation only.* **3** attraction; allurement: *She gives the leer of invitation* (Shakespeare). [< Latin *invītātiō, -ōnis* < *invītāre* invite]

in|vi|ta|tion|al (in′və tā′shə nəl), *adj., n.* —*adj.* restricted to invited guests or participants: *an invitational tennis match.* —*n.* an invitational event.

in|vi|ta|to|ry (in vī′tə tôr′ē, -tōr′-), *adj., n., pl.* **-ries.** —*adj.* inviting; containing an invitation.
—*n.* **1** an invitation. **2** an invitation to praise God in a church service, especially the Venite (Psalm 95) and the antiphon preceding it, or just the antiphon itself.

in|vite (*v.* in vīt′; *n.* in′vīt), *v.,* **-vit|ed, -vit|ing,** *n.* —*v.t.* **1** to ask (someone) politely to come to some place or to do something: *She invited her friends to a party. We invited her to join our club.* **SYN:** bid. See syn. under **call. 2** to make a polite request for: *She invited our opinion of her story.* **SYN:** request. **3** to give a chance for; tend to cause: *The letter invites some questions. Carelessness invites trouble.* **4** to attract; tempt: *The cool water invited us to swim. I saw nothing in this country that could invite me to a longer continuance* (Jonathan Swift). **SYN:** encourage.
—*n. Slang.* an invitation: *She had had a last-minute dinner invite from her boss* (Playboy).
[< Middle French *inviter,* learned borrowing from Latin *invītāre*] —**in|vit′er,** *n.*

in|vi|tee (in vī′tē, in′vī tē′), *n.* a person who is invited; guest: *The Soviet Premier will speak to a smaller and more select gathering of invitees* (Times of India).

in|vit|ing (in vī′ting), *adj.* attractive; tempting: *an inviting offer. The cool water looks inviting.* **SYN:** alluring. —**in|vit′ing|ly,** *adv.* —**in|vit′ing|ness,** *n.*

in vi|tro (in vī′trō, vit′rō), in an artificial environment, such as a test tube; not in the living animal or plant: *An enzyme which produces DNA in vitro has been known for some time* (B. S. Strauss). [< New Latin *in vitro* < Latin *in* in; *vitrum* glass]

in vitro fertilization, = external fertilization: *In vitro fertilization . . . was developed in England by Dr. Patrick Steptoe and physiologist Robert Edwards to help women who cannot conceive because their Fallopian tubes are blocked* (Reader's Digest).

in vi|vo (in vī′vō), in a living organism; inside a living animal or plant: *Inorganic compounds could be made in vitro: organic compounds could only be made 'in vivo'* (John Perret). [< New Latin *in vivo* < Latin *in* in + *vīvum* living thing]

in|vo|ca|ble (in vō′kə bəl, in′və-), *adj.* capable of being invoked: *[He] required all his business agents to submit undated resignations, invocable at his pleasure* (A. H. Raskin).

in|vo|cate (in′və kāt), *v.t., v.i.,* **-cat|ed, -cat|ing.** *Archaic.* to invoke. [Latin *invocāre;* see etym. under **invoke**] —**in′vo|ca′tor,** *n.*

in|vo|ca|tion (in′və kā′shən), *n.* **1** the act of calling upon in prayer; appealing for help or protection: *A church service often begins with an invocation to God.* **2** the form of words used in this. **3a** the act or process of calling forth spirits by magic words or charms: *The magician made an invocation to demons long gone.* **b** a set of magic words used to call forth spirits; incantation. **4** a formal appeal at or near the beginning of a long poem, in which the poet asks a Muse to give him inspiration. **5** *Law.* a call for evidence, papers, or the like, from another case.

in|vo|ca|tion|al (in′və kā′shə nəl), *adj.* = invocatory.

in|voc|a|tive (in vok′ə tiv, in′və kā′-), *adj.* that invokes; invocatory.

in|voc|a|to|ry (in vok′ə tôr′ē, -tōr′-), *adj.* of the nature of, characterized by, or used in invocation.

in|voice (in′vois), *n., v.,* **-voiced, -voic|ing.** —*n.* **1** a list of goods sent to a purchaser, often showing prices, amounts, and shipping charges. **2** a shipment of invoiced goods.
—*v.t.* to make an invoice of; enter on an invoice: *Shipments . . . will be invoiced at the old prices* (Wall Street Journal).
[earlier *invoyes,* plural of *invoy,* variant of *envoy*[2]]

in|voke (in vōk′), *v.t.,* **-voked, -vok|ing. 1a** to call on in prayer; appeal to for help or protection: *The Pilgrims invoked God's help in their undertaking.* **b** to appeal to for confirmation or judgment: *to invoke an authority.* **2** to ask earnestly for; beg for: *The condemned criminal invoked the judge's mercy.* **3** to call forth by magic; conjure: *Aladdin invoked the powerful genie of the magic lamp.* **4** to call or bring into effect; implement: *[He] rounded up the Republican votes necessary to invoke cloture* (Time). [< Middle French *invoquer,* learned borrowing from Latin *invocāre* < *in-* on + *vocāre* to call] —**in|vok′er,** *n.*

in|vol|a|tile (in vol′ə təl), *adj.* not volatile; incapable of being vaporized.

***in|vol|u|cel** (in vol′yů sel), *n. Botany.* a whorl of bracts surrounding a division of a compound umbel; partial or secondary involucre. [< New Latin *involucellum* (diminutive) < Latin *involūcrum;* see etym. under **involucre**]

***involucel**
***involucre**
definition 1

in|vol|u|cel|late (in vol′yů sel′āt), *adj. Botany.* having involucels.

in|vo|lu|cral (in′və lü′krəl), *adj. Botany.* of or having to do with an involucre.

in|vo|lu|crate (in′və lü′krit, -krāt), *adj. Botany.* having an involucre.

***in|vo|lu|cre** (in′və lü′kər, -lyü′-), *n.* **1** *Botany.* a circle of small leaves or bracts at the base of a flower or flower cluster. **2** *Anatomy.* a membranous covering, such as the pericardium. [< Middle French *involucre,* learned borrowing from Latin *involūcrum* a covering, wrapper < *involvere* involve]

in|vo|lu|cred (in′və lü′kərd), *adj. Botany.* having an involucre; involucrate.

in|vo|lu|crum (in′və lü′krəm), *n., pl.* **-cra** (-krə). = involucre.

in|vol|un|tar|y (in vol′ən ter′ē), *adj.* **1** not voluntary; not done of one's own free will; unwilling: *He was threatened until he gave involuntary consent to the plan.* **SYN:** compulsory, forced. **2** not intended; not done on purpose: *an involuntary injury. An accident is involuntary. The driver of the truck was indicted for involuntary manslaughter and reckless driving* (Time). **SYN:** unintentional, inadvertent. **3** not controlled by the will; under the control of some mechanism operating independently of the cerebral cortex: *Breathing is mainly involuntary.* **SYN:** instinctive. See syn. under **automatic.** [< Late Latin *involuntārius* < *in-* not + Latin *voluntārius* voluntary] —**in|vol′un|tar′i|ly,** *adv.* —**in|vol′un|tar′i|ness,** *n.*

involuntary muscle, = smooth muscle.

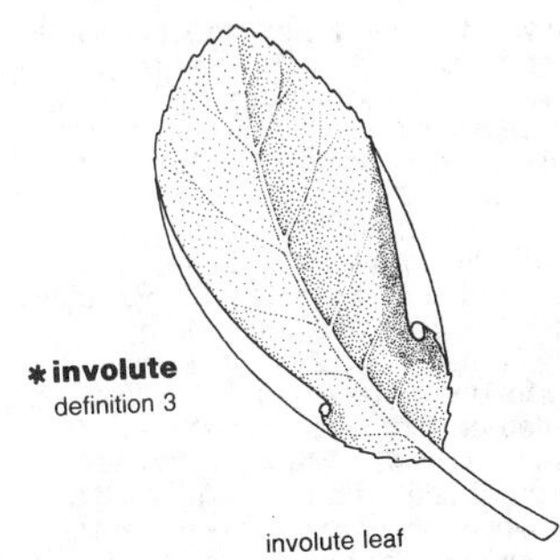

***involute**
definition 3

***in|vo|lute** (in′və lüt), *adj., n., v.,* **-lut|ed, -lut|ing.** —*adj.* **1** involved; intricate: *the possible moves [in chess] being not only manifold, but involute*

Pronunciation Key: hat, āge, cãre, fär; let, ēqual, tėrm; it, īce; hot, ōpen, ôrder; oil, out; cup, půt, rüle; child; long; thin; ᴛʜen; zh, measure; ə represents **a** in about, **e** in taken, **i** in pencil, **o** in lemon, **u** in circus.

(Edgar Allan Poe). **2** rolled up on itself; curved spirally. **3** *Botany.* rolled inward from the edge: *An apple leaf is involute with both edges rolled in toward the midrib on the upper side* (New York Times). **4** (of shells) having the whorls closely wound.
—*n.* **1** *Geometry.* the curve traced by any point of a flexible and inextensible string when the string is unwrapped from or wrapped onto a given curve under tension. **2** something involved or intricate.
—*v.i.* to become involuted.
[< Latin *involūtus,* past participle of *involvere* involve] —**in′vo|lute|ly,** *adv.* —**in′vo|lute|ness,** *n.*

in|vo|lut|ed (in′və lü′tid), *adj.* involute: *an involuted decoration on a column.* —**in′vo|lut′ed|ly,** *adv.*

in|vo|lu|tion (in′və lü′shən), *n.* **1** the act or process of involving. **2** the fact or state of being involved; entanglement; complexity. **3** something involved; complication. **4** *Mathematics.* the raising of a quantity to any power. **5** *Grammar.* a complicated or entangled construction in a sentence, such as a clause inserted between subject and predicate. **6** *Biology.* degeneration; retrograde change. **7** *Medicine.* **a** the return of an organ to its normal size or condition after enlargement, such as that of the uterus after childbirth. **b** a decline in bodily activity, especially sexual activity, in old age. **8** *Botany.* **a** a rolling inward from the edge. **b** a part thus formed.

in|vo|lu|tion|al (in′və lü′shə nəl), *adj.* of or having to do with involution.

involutional melancholia, a mental disorder characterized by great depression, occurring in persons between the ages of forty-five and sixty.

in|vo|lu|tion|ar|y (in′və lü′shə ner′ē), *adj.* characterized by involution.

in|volve (in volv′), *v.t.,* **-volved, -volv|ing. 1** to have as a necessary part, condition, or result; take in; include: *Housekeeping involves cooking, washing dishes, sweeping, and cleaning. Any man's death diminishes me, because I am involved in mankind* (John Donne). SYN: entail. **2** to have an effect on; affect: *These changes in the business involve the interest of all the owners.* **3** to bring (into difficulty or danger); cause to be unpleasantly concerned: *One foolish mistake can involve you in a good deal of trouble. When they fell, they involved armies and provinces in their fall* (Edward Gibbon). **4** *Figurative.* to entangle; complicate: *We must not further involve the statement; it is already too hard to understand.* **5** *Figurative.* to take up the attention of; occupy: *She was involved in working out a puzzle.* SYN: absorb. **6** *Figurative.* to wrap; enfold; envelop: *Clouds involved the mountain top. The outcome of the war was involved in doubt.* SYN: surround. **7** to wind spirally; coil: *The serpent involved his scaly folds.* **8** *Mathematics.* to raise to a given power. [< Old French *involver,* learned borrowing from Latin *involvere* < *in-* in + *volvere* to roll]
—**in|volv′er,** *n.*
—*Syn.* **3 Involve, implicate** mean to draw someone or something into a situation hard to get out of. **Involve** suggests entanglement in a situation that is unpleasantly embarrassing or hard to settle, but not necessarily a disgraceful one: *Buying an expensive car involved me in debt. Telling one lie usually involves a person in many more.* **Implicate** means to connect someone with something disgraceful or bad: *Having the stolen goods in his possession implicated him in the robbery.*

in|volved (in volvd′), *adj.* **1** intricate; complicated: *an involved sentence.* **2** = involute (def. 4). —**in-volv′ed|ly,** *adv.* —**in|volv′ed|ness,** *n.*

in|volve|ment (in volv′mənt), *n.* **1** the action of involving. **2** the state of being involved. **3** something that is involved.

invt. or **invty.,** inventory.

in|vul|ner|a|bil|i|ty (in vul′nər ə bil′ə tē), *n.* the quality or state of being invulnerable: (*Figurative.*) *The U.S. income tax remains a marvel of invulnerability* (Time).

in|vul|ner|a|ble (in vul′nər ə bəl), *adj.* **1** that cannot be wounded or hurt; safe from attack: *Achilles was invulnerable except for his heel.* **2** *Figurative.* proof against attack; not easily assailable: *an invulnerable argument.* SYN: tenable, impregnable. —**in|vul′ner|a|ble|ness,** *n.* —**in|vul′ner|a|bly,** *adv.*

in|wall (*v.* in wôl′; *n.* in′wôl′), *v., n.* —*v.t.* to enclose within a wall; wall in.
—*n.* an inner or inside wall.

in|ward (in′wərd), *adv., adj., n.* —*adv.* **1** toward the inside: *a passage leading inward.* **2** *Figurative.* into the mind or soul: *Turn your thoughts inward. Thou, celestial Light, Shine inward, and the mind through all her powers Irradiate* (Milton). **3** *Obsolete.* within; internally; inwardly.
—*adj.* **1** placed within; internal: *the inward parts of the body.* **2** directed toward the inside: *an inward slant of the eyes.* **3** *Figurative.* in mind or soul; mental or spiritual: *inward peace.* **4** inland; interior: *inward Australia.* **5** intrinsic; inherent; essential: *the inward nature of a thing.* **6** *Archaic.* internal; domestic: *inward war.* **7** *Obsolete.* intimate; private; secret: *What is inward between us, let it pass* (Shakespeare). *Friendly to all men, inward to few* (Francis Quarles).
—*n.* the inward or internal part; the inside.
[Old English *inweard,* adjective < *inne* in + *-weard* -ward]

in|ward|ly (in′wərd lē), *adv.* **1** on the inside; within: *He had bled inwardly.* **2** toward the inside: *The line curved inwardly.* **3** *Figurative.* **a** in the mind or soul: *to suffer inwardly.* **b** at heart; in reality. **4** not aloud or openly: *She laughed inwardly.* **5** *Obsolete.* intimately; closely.

in|ward|ness (in′wərd nis), *n.* **1** inner nature or meaning: *Sense cannot arrive to th' inwardness Of things* (Henry More). SYN: core, heart. **2** occupation with what concerns man's inner nature; spirituality. **3** *Figurative.* depth of thought or feeling; earnestness. **4** *Obsolete.* intimacy; familiarity: *In the ... inwardness of conjugal conference* (Sir Richard Steele).

in|wards (*adv., n. 2* in′wərdz; *n. 1 also* in′ərdz), *adv., n.* —*adv.* = inward.
—*n.pl. Informal.* **1** the parts inside the body, especially the stomach and intestines. SYN: innards. **2** *British.* imported articles or duties on them.

in|weave (in wēv′), *v.t.,* **-wove** or **-weaved, -woven** or **-wove** or **-weaved, -weav|ing.** to weave in; weave together; interweave.

in|wind (in wīnd′), *v.t.,* **-wound, -wind|ing.** = enwind.

in|wound (in wound′), *v.* a past tense and a past participle of **inwind.**

in|wove (in wōv′), *v.* a past tense and a past participle of **inweave.**

in|wo|ven (in wō′vən), *v., adj.* —*v.* a past participle of **inweave.**
—*adj.* woven in; interwoven.

in|wrap (in rap′), *v.t.,* **-wrapped, -wrap|ping.** = enwrap.

in|wreathe (in rēᴛʜ′), *v.t.,* **-wreathed, -wreath|ing.** = enwreathe.

in|wrought (in rôt′, in′rôt′), *adj.* **1** having a decoration worked in: *Shirt of doeskin ... All inwrought with beads of wampum* (Longfellow). **2** worked in. **3** *Figurative.* mixed together; closely blended.

in|ya|la (in yä′lə), *n.* a South African antelope; nyala. [< a native name]

In|yen|zi (in yen′zē), *n.* a terrorist organization of Watusi tribesmen trying to overthrow the ruling Bahutus in Rwanda and restore the Watusi monarchy.

I|o (ī′ō), *n.* **1** *Greek Mythology.* a maiden loved by Zeus. Zeus changed Io into a white heifer to conceal her from the jealous Hera, who in turn set Argus to watch her, and later sent a great gadfly to torment her continually. **2** the third largest satellite of Jupiter. **3** = Io moth.

Io (no period), ionium (isotope).

I-O (no periods), inboard-outboard.

I/O (no periods), input-output.

IOC (no periods), **1** Intergovernmental Oceanographic Commission. **2** initial operational capability.

I.O.C., International Olympic Committee.

IOCU (no periods), International Organization of Consumers Unions.

iod-, *combining form.* the form of **iodo-** before vowels, as in *iodate.*

i|o|date (ī′ə dāt), *n., v.,* **-dat|ed, -dat|ing.** —*n.* a salt of iodic acid.
—*v.t.* to combine, impregnate, or treat with iodine. —**i′o|da′tion,** *n.*

IODE (no periods) or **I.O.D.E.,** Imperial Order of the Daughters of the Empire (an organization of Canadian women founded in 1900, whose purpose is to stimulate patriotism and promote good citizenship).

i|od|ic (ī od′ik), *adj.* **1** of or containing iodine, especially with a valence of five. **2** caused by iodine. [< French *iodique* < *iode* iodine]

iodic acid, a white crystalline powder or colorless solid having strong oxidizing properties, used chiefly as a reagent. *Formula:* HIO_3

i|o|dide (ī′ə dīd, -did), *n.* a chemical compound of iodine with another element or radical; a salt of hydriodic acid. [< *iod-* + *-ide*]

i|o|dim|e|try (ī′ə dim′ə trē), *n.* = iodometry.

i|o|din (ī′ə din), *n.* = iodine.

i|o|di|nate (ī′ə də nāt), *v.t.,* **-nat|ed, -nat|ing.** = iodate. —**i′o|di|na′tion,** *n.*

✱i|o|dine (ī′ə dīn, -din; *Chemistry* ī′ə dēn), *n.* **1** a nonmetallic element in the form of bluish-black crystals that when heated give off dense, violet vapor with an irritating odor like that of chlorine. Iodine occurs naturally only in combination with other elements and is used in medicine as an antiseptic, in photography, and in making dyes. **2** a brown liquid containing iodine, put on wounds to kill germs and prevent infection; tincture of iodine. [< French *iode* iodine < Greek *ioeidēs* like the violet (< *ion* violet + *eîdos* form) + English *-ine*[2] (because the vapor of iodine is violet in color)]

✱iodine
definition 1

symbol	atomic number	atomic weight	oxidation state
I	53	126.9044	±1, +5, +7

iodine 131, a radioactive isotope of iodine having a mass number of 131, that is a product of the fission of uranium and is present in fallout; radioiodine. It causes cancer of the thyroid if absorbed in sufficient quantities.

i|o|dism (ī′ə diz əm), *n.* a diseased condition produced by the excessive use of iodine or its compounds.

i|o|dize (ī′ə dīz), *v.t.,* **-dized, -diz|ing.** to treat or impregnate with iodine or an iodide, as in photography and medicine. —**i′o|diz′er,** *n.*

i|o|dized salt (ī′ə dīzd), common table salt containing small quantities of an iodide as a supplement to the diet, especially of persons with an iodine deficiency.

iodo-, *combining form.* iodine; iodine compound: *Iodoform = an iodine compound.* Also, **iod-** before vowels. [< New Latin *iodum* iodine < French *iode*]

i|o|do|form (ī ō′də fôrm, -od′ə-), *n.* a yellowish, crystalline compound of iodine, used as an antiseptic, especially in surgical dressings. *Formula:* CHI_3 [< *iodo-* + *form*(yl)]

i|o|dol (ī′ə dōl, -dol), *n.* a crystalline compound containing iodine, used as a substitute for iodoform. *Formula:* C_4I_4NH

i|o|do|met|ric (ī′ə də met′rik, ī ō′-), *adj.* of or having to do with iodometry.

i|o|dom|e|try (ī′ə dom′ə trē), *n.* **1** determination of the amount of iodine in a mixture, usually by measuring the amount of sodium thiosulfate required to react with it. **2** quantitative analysis with iodine, by determining the amount of a substance (in a mixture) that will react with or liberate iodine; iodimetry.

i|o|do|phor (ī ō′də fôr, -od′ə-), *n.* an antiseptic which combines iodine, a detergent, and a solvent, and which slowly releases the iodine when it comes into contact with bacteria: *The ... reservoirs were emptied and disinfected with iodophor* (New Yorker). [< *iodo-* + Greek *-phóros* carrier]

i|o|dop|sin (ī ə dop′sin), *n.* a violet pigment that is sensitive to light, found in the cones of the retina of the eye. [< *iod-* + Greek *ōps, ōpós* eye + English *-in*]

i|o|dous (ī ō′dəs, ī od′əs), *adj.* **1** of or containing iodine, especially with a valence of three. **2** like iodine.

I.O.F., Independent Order of Foresters.

Iof|fe bar (yof ē′), one of a set of current-carrying bars used to increase the strength of a magnetic field in a nuclear fusion reaction: *By adding several ... Ioffe bars, around the plasma and parallel to the axis, a true magnetic well can be created* (Ernest P. Gray). [< M. S. *Ioffe,* a Russian physicist, who first used it in 1962]

i|o|lite (ī′ə līt), *n.* a blue to violet mineral consisting of a silicate of aluminum, iron, and magnesium, occurring in granular form or in short orthorhombic crystals; cordierite; dichroite. *Formula:* $Mg_2Al_4Si_5O_{18}$ [< German *Iolith* < Greek *ion* a violet + *líthos* stone, lite]

I|o or **i|o moth** (ī′ō), a large yellowish moth of North American forests with a bluish eyespot on each hind wing. Its caterpillar is a green silkworm with a red and white stripe down each side and poisonous bristles.

✱ion
definition 1

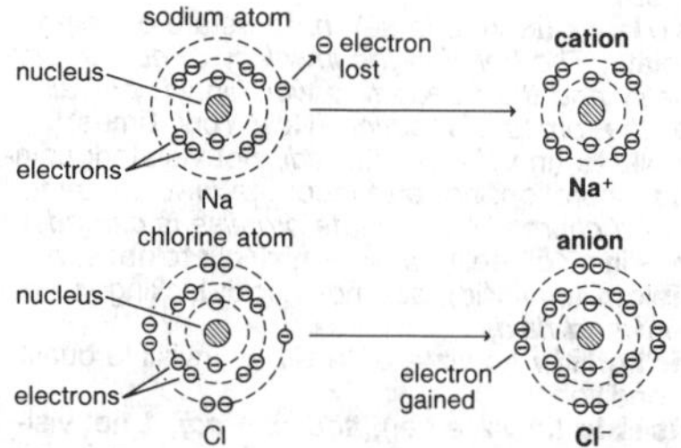

✱i|on (ī′ən, -on), *n.* **1** an atom or a group of atoms having a negative or positive electric charge as a result of having lost or gained one or more electrons. When an acid, base, or salt dissolves in water, some of its molecules separate into positive and negative ions. Each molecule forms two

or more ions whose electric charges neutralize each other when the ions are recombined into a molecule. Cations are positive ions formed by the loss of electrons and move toward the cathode; anions are negative ions formed by the gain of electrons and move toward the anode. The number of electrons lost or gained is denoted by a plus sign (for positive ions), as in Na^+ or Mg^{2+}, or a minus sign (for negative ions), as in Cl^- or S^{2-}. **2** an electrically charged particle formed in a gas, as by the action of X rays or an electric current.
[< Greek *ión,* neuter present participle of *iénai* to go]

-ion, *suffix added to verbs to form nouns.* **1** act or process of ___ing: *Attraction = act of attracting. Calculation = act of calculating.*
2 condition of being ___ed: *Adoption = condition of being adopted. Fascination = condition of being fascinated.*
3 result of ___ing; thing that was ___ed: *Abbreviation = result of abbreviating. Collection = result of collecting.*
4 thing or process that is ___ing: *Connection = thing that is connecting. Transmission = process that is transmitting.*
[< Old French *-ion* < Latin *-iō, -iōnis,* or directly < Latin]

Ion., Ionic.

ion chamber, = ionization chamber.

ion counter, any instrument that detects the emission of ions from radioactive material, such as the Geiger counter.

ion engine, a reaction engine employing ion propulsion: *U.S. scientists are working on more than one type of electric rocket engine. ... The most complex variety, the "ion engine," generates thrust by shooting a stream of positively charged atoms, or ions, of gas out the rocket's tail* (Wall Street Journal).

ion etching, a method of eroding materials such as metals, glass, polymers, and body tissue, atom by atom, by bombarding them with high-energy ions, in order to reveal their smallest structural features.

ion exchange, a process in which an insoluble substance, commonly a resin or zeolite, exchanges ions with the solution it is in, thereby removing a substance from the solution. It is widely used in water softeners, in the analysis and separation of chemicals, the extraction of minerals, and the desalting of water.

ion exchanger, any substance or device by means of which ion exchange is effected: *The new process ... uses a continuous ion exchanger to decontaminate milk* (Science News Letter).

ion exchange resin, a synthetic resin which has the ability to exchange ions with a solution, used in the ion exchange process.

I|o|ni|an (ī ō′nē ən), *adj., n.* — *adj.* **1** of or having to do with Ionia (ancient region on the west coast of Asia Minor) or its people. **2** having to do with one of the main branches of the ancient Greek people. The Athenians were of Ionian descent.
— *n.* a Greek of this branch.

Ionian mode, **1** one of the modes in ancient Greek music, characterized as soft and feminine. **2** a mode of medieval church music corresponding to the modern scale of C.

i|on|ic (ī on′ik), *adj.* of, having to do with, or present as ions or an ion: *Ionic speeds are quite small. Ions in ionic crystals are held together by the attraction between their opposite charges* (Ralph E. Lapp). [< *ion* + *-ic*]

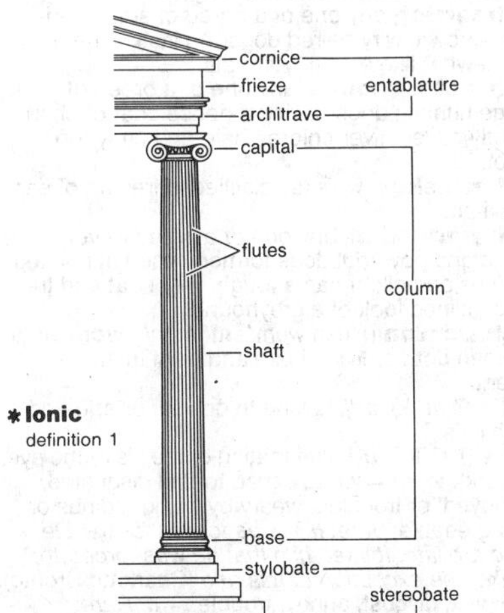

***Ionic**
definition 1

***I|on|ic** (ī on′ik), *adj., n.* — *adj.* **1** of or having to do with the order of Greek architecture having scrolls in the capitals of the columns. **2** of Ionia (ancient region on the west coast of Asia Minor) or its people. **3** having to do with or consisting of Ionics in Greek and Latin verse.
— *n.* **1** the dialect of ancient Greek spoken by the Ionians and including Homeric and Attic Greek. **2** in Greek and Latin verse: **a** a foot consisting of two long syllables followed by two short (the greater Ionic), or two short followed by two long (the lesser or smaller Ionic). **b** an Ionic line or meter. **3** *Printing.* a heavy-face type.
[< Latin *Iōnicus* < Greek *Iōnikós* < *Iōnia* Ionia]

ionic bond, *Chemistry.* a bond between two ions with opposite charges.

i|on|ic|i|ty (ī′ə nis′ə tē), *n.* capacity for ionization.

ionic lattice, a regular, repeating arrangement of positive and negative ions in a salt crystal. When the salt crystal dissolves in water, these ions are released and move about freely in the solution.

ion implantation, a process of making semiconducting devices by implanting the necessary impurities into silicon chips electronically instead of diffusing them.

i|on|ise (ī′ə nīz), *v.i., v.t.,* **-ised, -is|ing.** *Especially British.* ionize. — **i′on|is′er**, *n.*

i|o|ni|um (ī ō′nē əm), *n.* a radioactive isotope of thorium, formed from disintegrating uranium. [< *ion* + New Latin *-ium,* a suffix meaning "metal"]

ionization chamber, a closed, gas-filled chamber or tube containing a positive and a negative electrode. Cosmic rays or other forms of radiation passing through it are measured according to the degree of ionization they cause in the gas. The electroscope is a simple ionization chamber.

ionization potential, the potential energy required to free an electron from its atom, as measured by spectroscopic or other methods.

i|on|ize (ī′ə nīz), *v.,* **-ized, -iz|ing.** — *v.i.* to separate into ions. Acids, bases, and salts ionize in solution.
— *v.t.* to cause to separate or change into ions; produce ions in. The gas in a neon light must be ionized before it can conduct an electric current.
— **i′on|iz′a|ble**, *adj.* — **i′on|i|za′tion**, *n.* — **i′on|iz′er**, *n.*

i|on|iz|ing radiation (ī′ə nī′zing), high-energy radiation, such as an X ray, that causes the formation of ions in substances through which it passes, as in the treatment of cancer and sterilization of food.

ion microscope, = field-ion microscope.

i|on|o|gen (ī on′ə jən), *n.* a compound which produces ions when in solution; electrolyte. [< *ion* + *-gen*]

i|o|none (ī′ə nōn), *n.* one of two isomeric ketones with an odor like that of violets, used in making perfumes. *Formula:* $C_{13}H_{20}O$ [< Greek *íon* violet + English *-one*]

i|on|o|pho|re|sis (ī on′ə fə rē′sis), *n.* = electrophoresis.

i|on|o|pho|ret|ic (ī on′ə fə ret′ik), *adj.* = electrophoretic.

i|on|o|sonde (ī on′ə sond), *n.* an instrument for studying the ionosphere. [< *iono*(sphere) + (radio)*sonde*]

i|on|o|sphere (ī on′ə sfir), *n.* the region of the atmosphere between the stratosphere and the exosphere. It begins about 50 miles above the earth and ends at an altitude of about 300 miles. The ionosphere is composed of layers of air ionized by solar ultraviolet radiation that reflect certain radio waves, making transmission over long distances on earth possible. [< *ion* + *sphere*]

i|on|o|spher|ic (ī on′ə sfer′ik), *adj.* in or having to do with the ionosphere. — **i|on′o|spher′i|cal|ly**, *adv.*

ion propulsion, an experimental method of propelling space vehicles by the ejection of beams of ions. The propulsion system includes an energy source such as a nuclear reactor, a heat exchanger, or a generator, an ion source such as cesium, and an ejection device.

ion pump, a device for producing a vacuum by ionizing gas molecules and then collecting them with the aid of an electric field: *In spite of the many advantages of the diffusion pump, it is often replaced in small laboratory systems by the ion pump* (Scientific American).

ion rocket, a rocket propelled by ion propulsion.

i|on|to|pho|re|sis (ī on′tō fə rē′sis), *n.* a method of injecting ionized drugs or other substances by the use of a direct current and two electrodes attached to the body. [< Greek *ión, iontós* (see etym. under **ion**) + *phórēsis* being carried < *phérein* to carry]

i|on|to|pho|ret|ic (ī on′tō fə ret′ik), *adj.* of or having to do with iontophoresis.

I.O.O.F., Independent Order of Odd Fellows.

I.O.R.M., Improved Order of Red Men.

***i|o|ta** (ī ō′tə), *n.* **1** a very small part or quantity; bit; jot: *There is not an iota of truth in his story. I utter these words without the least iota of doubt in my own mind* (James T. Farrell). **SYN**: particle, whit, mite. **2** the ninth letter of the Greek alphabet. [< Latin *iota* < Greek *iôta.* See etym. of doublet **jot.**]

***iota**
definition 2

Ι	ι
capital letter	lower-case letter

i|o|ta|cism (ī ō′tə siz əm), *n.* **1** excessive use or repetition of the letter iota (or *I*) or of its sound. **2** the pronunciation of other Greek vowels like iota (as *I* in *machine*), as in modern Greek. [< Latin *iōtacismus* < Greek *iōtakysmós* a stressing, or repeating of *iôta* iota]

I.O.U. or **I O U** (no periods) (ī′ō′ū′), **1** I owe you. **2** an informal note showing a debt: *Write me an IOU for ten dollars and I'll give you ten dollars. Joe collected on more than 30 of the many I.O.U.s he holds* (Time).

I.O.W., Isle of Wight.

I|o|wa (ī′ə wə, -wā), *n., pl.* **-wa** or **-was.** **1** a member of a small Indian tribe of the Plains region of the United States. **2** the Siouan language of this tribe. [American English < French *Iowa* < Siouan (Dakota) *Ayuhwa* sleepy ones (applied to the Iowa Indians in ridicule)]

I|o|wan (ī′ə wən), *adj., n.* — *adj.* of or having to do with Iowa.
— *n.* a native or inhabitant of Iowa.

IPA (no periods) or **I.P.A.**, **1** International Phonetic Alphabet. **2** International Phonetic Association.

ip|e|cac (ip′ə kak), *n.* **1** a medicine made from the dried roots and rhizomes of a South American shrub, used chiefly as an emetic and expectorant. **2** the dried roots and rhizomes. **3** the shrub. It belongs to the madder family. [American English, short for *ipecacuanha* < Portuguese < Tupi (Brazil) *ipecacuana* a medicinal plant]

ip|e|cac|u|an|ha (ip′ə kak′yủ an′ə), *n.* = ipecac.

Iph|i|ge|ni|a (if′ə jə nī′ə), *n. Greek Legend.* the daughter of Agamemnon and Clytemnestra. Her father intended to sacrifice her to Artemis to obtain favorable winds for the Greek ships sailing to Troy, but Artemis put a hart in her place and carried Iphigenia off to Tauris to become her priestess.

ip|o|moe|a (ip′ə mē′ə, ī′pə-), *n.* **1** any one of a group of largely twining or creeping plants of the morning-glory family, including the sweet potato, morning-glory, and many tropical American varieties used medicinally as cathartics. **2** the dried root of one of these plants, from which a cathartic resin is obtained. [< New Latin *Ipomoea* the genus name (coined by Linnaeus) < Greek *íps, ipos* worm + *hómoios* like]

IPPF (no periods), International Planned Parenthood Federation.

i|pro|ni|a|zid (ī′prō nī′ə zid), *n.* a drug prepared from isoniazid, formerly used in the treatment of tuberculosis but now primarily used in the treatment of mental depression. *Formula:* $C_9H_{13}N_3O$ [< *i*(so)*pro*(pyl) + (iso)*niazid*]

ips or **IPS** (no periods), inches per second.

IPSA (no periods), International Political Science Association.

ip|se dix|it (ip′sē dik′sit), a dogmatic assertion; opinion based merely on someone's authority: *Mr. Moore assures us that he has given us all that any reasonable reader could require; but one cannot be satisfied with an editor's ipse dixit* (Listener). [< Latin *ipse dīxit* he himself said (it)]
▶ The Latin phrase, when used in English as a noun, takes the regular plural ending: *In language one should beware ipse dixits* (Paul Roberts).

ip|si|lat|er|al (ip′sə lat′ər əl), *adj.* that is on the same side: *The response ... was significantly larger for contralateral than for ipsilateral stimulation* (Stone and Taylor). [< Latin *ipse* self + English *lateral*] — **ip′si|lat′er|al|ly**, *adv.*

ip|sis|si|ma ver|ba (ip sis′ə mə vėr′bə), *Latin.* the very same words; word for word.

ip|so fac|to (ip′sō fak′tō), *Latin.* by that very fact; by the fact itself: *Any economic function that has persisted so long, ipso facto will surely continue far into the distant future* (Sales Management).

ip|so ju|re (ip′sō jůr′ē), *Latin.* by the law itself.

Ips|wich sparrow (ips′wich), a large, pale-brownish sparrow with a streaked breast, that nests on Sable Island, Nova Scotia.

IPTS (no periods), International Practical Temperature Scale (the temperature scale in common

Pronunciation Key: hat, āge, cãre, fär; let, ēqual, tėrm; it, īce; hot, ōpen, ôrder; oil, out; cup, pủt, rüle; child; long; thin; ᴛʜen; zh, measure; ə represents a in about, e in taken, i in pencil, o in lemon, u in circus.

scientific and industrial use, expressed in terms of the centigrade (Celsius) scale).

I.P.U. or **IPU** (no periods), Inter-Parliamentary Union (an organization of members of parliaments and other legislative bodies, formed in 1888 to promote the peaceful settlement of international disputes).

i.q., the same as (Latin, *idem quod*).

IQ (no periods) or **I.Q.**, intelligence quotient: *Overambitious parents frequently pressure their children beyond their IQ capacities in the effort to get them into prestige colleges* (Wall Street Journal).

i|qal (ē käl′), *n.* the thick band of twisted chord that keeps the Arab headdress or kaffiyeh in place. [< Arabic *'iqāl*]

IQSY (no periods) or **I.Q.S.Y.**, International Quiet Sun Year.

ir-[1], *prefix.* the form of **in-**[1] (not) before *r*, as in *irrational, irregular, irresistible.*

ir-[2], *prefix.* the form of **in-**[2] (in) before *r*, as in *irrigate.*

Ir (no period), iridium (chemical element).

Ir., **1** Ireland. **2** Irish.

IR (no periods), **1** information retrieval. **2** infrared.

I.R., **1** *British.* Inland Revenue. **2** Internal Revenue.

IRA[1] (no periods) or **I.R.A.**[1], Irish Republican Army (an association of Irish nationalists outlawed in 1931 that continues to operate, often by sabotage and other means, for a united Ireland to include the Irish Republic and Northern Ireland).

IRA[2] (no periods), International Reading Association.

IRA[3] (no periods) or **I.R.A.**[2] (ī′rə), Individual Retirement Account (a pension fund, into which a person deposits wages and defers paying tax on them or on the interest until withdrawals begin). IRA's are administered by banks, savings and loan associations, insurance companies, etc. The money in an IRA earns interest that is added to the account. *Keogh . . . retirement accounts . . . are in many ways similar to IRAs but are available only to the self-employed* (Chicago Tribune).

i|ra|cund (ī′rə kund), *adj.* easily made angry; irascible. [< Latin *īrācundus* < *īra* ire, anger]

i|ra|cun|di|ty (ī′rə kun′də tē), *n.* readiness to become angry; irascibility.

i|ra|de (ē rä′de), *n.* a decree of the former Sultan of Turkey or other Moslem ruler. [< Turkish *irade* < Arabic *'irāda* will, desire]

i|ra fu|ror bre|vis est (ī′rə fyü′rôr brē′vis est), *Latin.* anger is a brief insanity.

Iran., Iranian.

I|ra|ni (i rä′nē), *adj.* = Iranian.

I|ra|ni|an (i rä′nē ən, ī-), *adj., n.* —*adj.* of or having to do with Iran, its people, or their language; Persian. —*n.* **1** a person born or living in Iran, especially one speaking an Iranian language; Persian. **2** the language of Iran; Persian. **3** the branch of Indo-European languages that includes Old Persian and Avestan.

I|ran|ic (i ran′ik, ī-), —*adj.* Iranian. —*n.* Iranian (def. 3).

I|ra|nol|o|gist (i rə nol′ə jist, ī-), *n.* a person who studies the history, language, customs, and culture of Iran.

I|ra|qi (i rä′kē), *adj., n.* —*adj.* of or having to do with Iraq, its people, or their language. —*n.* **1** a person born or living in Iraq. **2** Arabic as spoken in Iraq.

I|ra|qi|an (i rä′kē ən), *adj.* = Iraqi.

i|ras|ci|bil|i|ty (i ras′ə bil′ə tē, ī-), *n.* quickness of temper; irritability.

i|ras|ci|ble (i ras′ə bəl, ī-), *adj.* **1** easily made angry; with a quick temper; irritable: *an irascible old man.* SYN: testy. See syn. under **irritable**. **2** showing anger: *an irascible reply.* [< Late Latin *īrāscibilis* < Latin *īrāscī* grow angry < *īra* anger, ire] —**i|ras′ci|ble|ness**, *n.* —**i|ras′ci|bly**, *adv.*

i|rate (ī′rāt, ī rāt′), *adj.* angry; enraged: *The irate colonel, with glaring eyes and purple face . . . stood . . . speechless before his young enemy* (Thackeray). SYN: incensed. [< Latin *īrātus*, past participle of *īrāscī* grow angry < *īra* anger] —**i′rate|ly**, *adv.* —**i′rate|ness**, *n.*

IRBM (no periods), intermediate range ballistic missile, (with a range of up to 1,500 miles).

IRC[1] (no periods), International Rescue Committee.

I.R.C. or **IRC**[2] (no periods), International Red Cross.

ire (īr), *n., v.,* **ired, ir|ing.** —*n.* anger; wrath. SYN: choler, fury. —*v.t.* to anger: *What ires Dutchmen is not Von Amsberg's pedigree but his war record* (Time). [< Old French *ire* < Latin *īra*] —**ire′less**, *adj.*

Ire., Ireland.

ire|ful (īr′fəl), *adj.* **1** angry; wrathful: *Many an ireful glance and frown . . . the angry visage of the Phantom wore.* (Richard H. Barham). **2** = irascible. —**ire′ful|ly**, *adv.* —**ire′ful|ness**, *n.*

I|re|ne (ī rē′nē), *n. Greek Mythology.* the goddess of peace, daughter of Themis and Zeus. [< Greek *Eirēnē* < *eirēnē* peace]

i|ren|ic (ī ren′ik, -rē′nik), *adj.* tending to promote peace, especially with respect to theological or ecclesiastical difference; peaceful; pacific. [< Greek *eirēnikós* < *eirēnē* peace] —**i|ren′i|cal|ly**, *adv.*

i|ren|i|cal (ī ren′ə kəl, -rē′nə-), *adj.* = irenic.

i|ren|i|cism (īren′ə siz əm, -rē′nə-), *n.* an irenic philosophy, policy, or condition.

i|ren|i|con (īren′ə kon, -rē′nə-), *n., pl.* **-ca** (-kə). a proposal for promoting peace, especially in the church. [< Greek *eirēnikón*, neuter of *eirēnikós*; see etym. under **irenic**]

i|ren|ics (īren′iks, -rē′niks), *n.* theology that tends to promote peace, especially by indicating the similarities in differing sects.

i|ren|ol|o|gy (ī′rə nol′ə jē), *n.* the study of peace, especially as part of international relations. [< Greek *eirēnē* peace + English *-logy*]

i|ri|da|ceous (ī′rə dā′shəs, ir′ə-), *adj.* of or belonging to the iris family of plants, including the crocus, gladiolus, and freesia. [< New Latin *Iridaceae* the order name (< Latin *īris, īridis* iris < Greek *îris, īridos*) + English *-ous*]

ir|i|dec|to|my (ir′ə dek′tə mē, ī′rə-), *n., pl.* **-mies.** the removal of part of the iris of the eye by surgery. [< Greek *îris, īridos* iris + *ektomē* a cutting out]

ir|i|des|cence (ir′ə des′əns), *n.* a display of changing colors; change of colors when moved or turned, like those of the rainbow: *the iridescence of soap bubbles.*

ir|i|des|cent (ir′ə des′ənt), *adj., n.* —*adj.* displaying changing colors like those of the rainbow; changing colors when moved: *Soap bubbles are iridescent.* SYN: prismatic, opalescent. —*n.* an iridescent garment, fabric, paint, or color. [< Latin *īris, īridis* rainbow (see etym. under **iris**) + English *-escent*] —**ir′i|des′cent|ly**, *adv.*

ir|id|ic (i rid′ik, ī-), *adj.* of or containing iridium, especially with a valence of four.

***i|rid|i|um** (i rid′ē əm, ī rid′-) *n.* a silver-white, hard, brittle metallic element which occurs in platinum ores and is used as an alloy with platinum for jewelry and the points of fountain pens. [< New Latin *iridium* < Latin *īris, īridis*; see etym. under **iris** (with reference to its iridescence)]

***iridium**

symbol	atomic number	atomic weight	oxidation state
Ir	77	192.2	3, 4

ir|i|dize (ir′ə dīz, ī′rə-), *v.t.,* **-dized, -diz|ing.** **1** to cover with iridium. **2** to make iridescent. —**ir′i|di|za′tion**, *n.*

ir|i|do|cy|cli|tis (ir′ə dō si klī′tis, ī′rə-; -sī-), *n.* inflammation of the iris of the eye and the ciliary muscle and process.

i|rid|o|cyte (i rid′ə sīt, ī-), *n.* = guanophore. [< Greek *îris, íridos* iris + English *-cyte*]

ir|i|dol|o|gy (ir′ə dol′ə jē), *n.* a method of examining the iris of the eye as an aid in medical diagnosis: *The basis for iridology is the neuro-optic reflex, an intimate marriage of the . . . nerve filaments of the iris with the cervical ganglia of the sympathetic nervous system* (Esquire). [< Greek *îris, íridos* iris + English *-logy*] —**ir′i|dol′o|gist**, *n.*

ir|i|dos|mine (ir′ə doz′min, -dos′-; ī′rə-), *n.* a natural alloy of the metals iridium and osmium, usually occurring in flattened grains with platinum, and used for the points of gold pens; osmiridium. [< German *Iridosmin* < New Latin *iridium* iridium + *osmium* osmium + German *-in*]

ir|i|dos|mi|um (ir′ə doz′mē əm, -dos′-; ī′rə-), *n.* = iridosmine.

ir|i|dous (ir′ə dəs, ī′rə-), *adj.* containing iridium, especially with a valence of three.

i|ris (ī′ris), *n.* **1** any one of a group of plants with leaves shaped like swords, and large, showy flowers most of which have three upright petals and three drooping sepals; fleur-de-lis; flag. The iris grows from a bulb or rhizome. See picture under **iris family**. **2** the flower of any of these plants. **3** the colored part of the eye around the pupil. It is a contractile disc between the cornea and the lens of the eye. The amount of light entering the eye is controlled by the iris. See diagram under **eye**. **4a** = rainbow. **b** anything like a rainbow; iridescence. **5** a variety of rock crystal that reflects the prismatic colors, used especially by French jewelers. [< Latin *īris, īridis*, iris, iris plant, rainbow < Greek îris, *īridos* (originally) the rainbow goddess]

I|ris (ī′ris), *n. Greek Mythology.* the goddess of the rainbow and messenger of the gods. [< Greek îris; see etym. under **iris**]

iris diaphragm, *Optics.* a diaphragm made of thin opaque plates, in which the size of the aperture can be varied by turning a ring attached to the plates. It is used to regulate the light admitted to a camera.

i|rised (ī′rist), *adj.* **1** rainbow-colored or iridescent: *Till dying sunset sheds his crimson stains Through the faint halos of the irised panes* (Oliver Wendell Holmes). **2** (of the eye) having a certain kind of iris.

***iris family**, a group of monocotyledonous perennial plants widely distributed in temperate and warm regions of the world. The family includes iris, blackberry lily, crocus, gladiolus, and freesia.

***iris family**

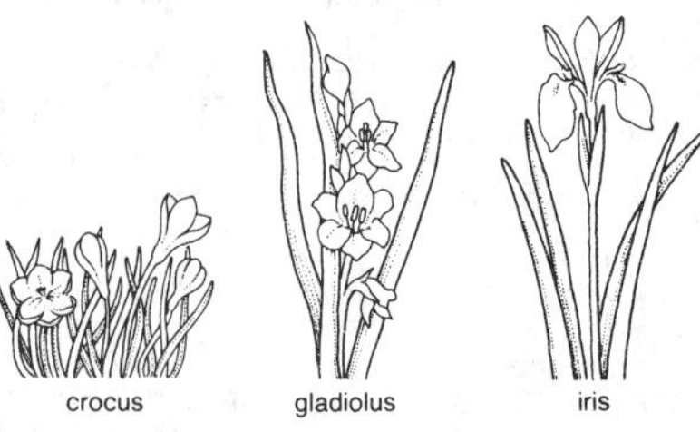

I|rish (ī′rish), *adj., n.* —*adj.* of or having to do with Ireland, its people, or their language. —*n.* **1** the people of Ireland or their descendants in other countries. **2** their Celtic language; Irish Gaelic. **3** English as spoken by the Irish. **4** *Informal.* temper: *to get one's Irish up.* [Middle English *Irisc* < stem of Old English *Irland* Ireland, and *Iras* the Irish people + *-isc* -ish[1]] —**I′rish|ness**, *n.*

Irish bull, an absurd and amusing mistake in language; bull.

Irish coffee, strong, hot coffee with Irish whiskey and a float of plain or whipped cream.

Irish daisy, the common dandelion.

Irish elk, an extinct species of deer whose remains have been found in Ireland and other areas of Europe. The development of huge, unwieldy antlers, measuring up to 11 feet from tip to tip, is believed to have brought about its extinction.

Irish Gaelic, the Celtic language of Ireland; Gaelic; Erse.

I|rish|ism (ī′ri shiz əm), *n.* an Irish characteristic, idiom, or turn of speech; Hibernicism.

Irish linen, a light, handwoven linen of very fine texture, used especially for handkerchiefs, collars, and trimmings.

***Irish mail**, a toy handcar.

***Irish mail**

I|rish|man (ī′rish mən), *n., pl.* **-men.** a man born or living in Ireland or of Irish descent.

Irish moss, = carrageen.

Irish potato, the common white potato.

I|rish|ry (ī′rish rē), *n., pl.* **-ries.** **1** the native Irish, as distinguished from the English settlers in Ireland. **2** Irish character; an Irish trait.

Irish setter, any one of a breed of large hunting dogs with long, silky, reddish-brown hair. See picture under **dog**.

Irish stew, a stew made of mutton or lamb, potatoes, onions, and other vegetables.

Irish terrier, any one of a breed of small, reddish-brown, wiry-haired dogs. An irish terrier is somewhat like a small Airedale.

Irish water spaniel, any one of a breed of large hunting dogs having a dense coat of short, tightly curled, liver-colored hair, and curly topknot.

Irish whiskey, whiskey distilled in Ireland of barley malt.

Irish wolfhound, any one of a breed of very large and powerful dogs formerly used in hunting wolves and elk. It has a rough, wiry coat and the streamlined look of a greyhound.

I|rish|wom|an (ī′rish wům′ən), *n., pl.* **-wom|en.** a woman born or living in Ireland or of Irish descent.

i|rit|ic (ī rit′ik), *adj.* having to do with or affected with iritis.

i|ri|tis (ī rī′tis), *n.* inflammation of the iris of the eye.

irk (ėrk), *v., n.* —*v.t.* to cause to feel disgusted, annoyed, or troubled; weary by being tedious or disagreeable; bore: *It irks us to wait for people who are late. It irked him that he was forced to make one exception to this rule* (Charlotte Brontë). SYN: vex, disgust, annoy, trouble. —*n. Rare.* tedium; irksomeness; annoyance. [Middle English *irken* be weary of, disgusted with; origin uncertain]

irk|some (ėrk′səm), *adj.* tiresome; tedious; annoying: *Washing dishes all day would be an irksome task. Company was irksome to me* (Mary W. Shelley). SYN: wearisome. —**irk′some|ly**, *adv.* —**irk′some|ness**, *n.*

IRO (no periods) or **I.R.O.**, International Refugee Organization.

I.R.O., *British.* Inland Revenue Office.

i|ro|ko (i rō′kō), *n.* **1** a timber tree of the mulberry family, found in tropical Africa. **2** its tough, fine-grained wood, used as a substitute for teak. [< Ibo *iroko*]

***i|ron** (ī′ərn), *n., adj., v.* —*n.* **1** the commonest and most useful metal, from which tools and machinery are made. It is a very hard, strongly magnetic, silver-white chemical element that becomes oxidized in moist air and is malleable especially when heated. Steel is made from iron. Iron occurs in the hemoglobin of the red blood cells where it serves to carry oxygen to all parts of the body. **2** something made of iron: *The mechanic used a long tire iron to pry the flat tire from the rim.* **3** *Figurative.* great hardness and strength; firmness: *men of iron. Muscles and sinews of iron* (Longfellow). **4** an implement with a flat surface for smoothing cloth or pressing clothes; flatiron. **5** a golf club with an iron or steel head. **6** *Slang.* a pistol; shooting iron. **7a** = branding iron. **b** = harpoon. **c** = soldering iron. **8** *Medicine.* a preparation of or containing iron, used as a tonic. **9** *Archaic.* a sword.

—*adj.* **1** made of iron: *an iron fence.* **2** having to do with iron. **3** *Figurative.* like iron; hard or strong; unyielding: *an iron will, an iron constitution.* **4** *Figurative.* harsh or cruel; merciless: *the iron hand of fate.* **5** of or having to do with the iron age.

—*v.t.* **1** to smooth or press (cloth or clothes) with a heated iron: *She ironed the shirt to get the wrinkles out.* **2** to fit, furnish, or cover with iron: *The gate that was iron'd within and without* (Samuel Taylor Coleridge). **3** to shackle with irons; put in irons. —*v.i.* to press cloth or clothes with a heated iron: *Mrs. Nubbles ironed away in silence* (Dickens).

have too many irons in the fire, to try to do too many things at once: *[He] had too many irons in the fire to find time for original research* (John Overton).

in irons, *Nautical.* sailing into the wind without enough speed to turn on either tack; unable to fill on either tack: *The yards would not swing round; . . . and the ship was in irons* (Frederick Marryat).

iron out, to smooth away or overcome (difficulties, differences, inconsistencies, or the like): *The dispute between the two players was ironed out by the coach.*

irons, a chains or bands of iron; handcuffs; shackles: *When the Earl reached the castle his legs were put in irons* (Macaulay). **b** (in horse racing and horseback riding) the stirrups: *He put his feet in the irons and rode off.*

pump iron, *Slang.* to lift weights: *Many body builders are asked by the uneducated: What would happen if you stopped pumping iron? Would you turn to fat, or what?* (Judy Klemesrud).

strike while the iron is hot, to act while conditions are favorable: *Striking while the iron was hot, the army scored a major victory.*

[Old English *īren*, earlier *īsern*, ultimately < Celtic (compare Old Irish *īarn*)] —**i′ron|a|ble**, *adj.* —**i′ron|like′**, adj.

***iron**
definition 1

symbol	atomic number	atomic weight	oxidation state
Fe	26	55.847	2, 3

Iron Age, **1** the period after the Bronze Age, when people used iron tools, weapons, and other implements (around 1000 B.C. to 100 A.D.). **2** Also, **iron age**. (in classical mythology) the last and worst age of the world, characterized by selfishness, wickedness, and oppression.

i|ron|bark (ī′ərn bärk′), *n.,* or **ironbark tree**, any eucalyptus tree with a hard, solid bark, valued for its wood.

iron blue, **1** any one of several artificial flies of steel-blue coloration used by fishermen. **2** a blue pigment prepared from ferrocyanides, such as Prussian blue. **3** = steel blue.

i|ron|bound (ī′ərn bound′), *adj.* **1** bound with iron. **2** *Figurative.* hard; firm; rigid; unyielding: *The French, though beyond question the best actors in the world, judge from ironbound standards* (The American). **3** = rocky. SYN: craggy.

i|ron|clad (ī′ərn klad′), *adj., n.* —*adj.* **1** protected with iron plates. **2** *Figurative.* very hard to change or get out of: *An ironclad agreement must be kept.*

—*n.* a warship protected with iron plates.

Iron Cross, a German medal awarded for services in war.

Iron Curtain or **iron curtain**, **1** an imaginary wall or dividing line, separating the Soviet Union and the nations under Soviet control or influence from the non-Communist nations after World War II. Strict censorship and secrecy are enforced behind it. *Correspondents . . . interviewed escapees from behind the Iron Curtain* (Newsweek). **2** *Figurative: An iron curtain had been dropped over events taking place in Alabama* (New York Times). [popularized through its use by Sir Winston Churchill in a speech delivered in 1946]

i|rone (ī rōn′, ī′rōn), *n.* a colorless terpene found in orrisroot, used in making perfumes. *Formula:* $C_{14}H_{22}O$ [< *ir*(is) + *-one*]

i|ron|er (ī′ər nər), *n.* **1** a person or thing that irons. **2** a machine used to iron clothes.

i|ron-fist|ed (ī′ərn fis′tid), *adj.* characterized by rigor and harshness; unbending; ruthless; dictatorial.

iron gray, a dark gray color like that of freshly broken cast iron. —**i′ron-gray′**, *adj.*

Iron Guard, a fascist party in Romania, abolished after World War II.

iron hand, a firm, strict manner: *Because of the secrecy of its research work, Oak Ridge remained . . . barred to tourists and visitors, and the Government ran the town with an iron hand* (Wall Street Journal).

i|ron-hand|ed (ī′ərn han′did), *adj.* firm and strict; severe; harsh; despotic: *iron-handed rule.* —**i′ron-hand′ed|ly**, *adv.* —**i′ron-hand′ed|ness**, *n.*

iron hat, **1** a helmet of iron or steel shaped like a hat, used during the Middle Ages and later. **2** = gossan.

i|ron-heart|ed (ī′ərn här′tid), *adj.* hard-hearted; unfeeling.

iron horse, *Informal.* **1** an early steam locomotive. **2** a bicycle or tricycle.

i|ron|ic (ī ron′ik), *adj.* = ironical.

i|ron|i|cal (ī ron′ə kəl), *adj.* **1** expressing one thing and meaning the opposite: *"Speedy" would be an ironical name for a turtle. His ironical laugh showed that he was not the least bit amused.* SYN: sarcastic. **2** contrary to what would naturally be expected: *It was ironical that the man was run over by his own automobile.* **3** using or given to using irony. [< Late Latin *īrōnicus* (< Greek *eirōnikós* feigning ignorance, insincere < *eirōneíā* irony) + English *-al*[1]] —**i|ron′i|cal|ly**, *adv.* —**i|ron′i|cal|ness**, *n.*

i|ron|ing (ī′ərn ing), *n.* **1** the smoothing or pressing of cloth, clothes, or linens with a heated iron: *This shirt needs a good ironing.* **2** a batch of clothes or linens ironed or to be ironed.

ironing board, a flat board, usually padded, and covered with a smooth cloth, on which clothes are ironed. Most ironing boards include folding legs.

i|ro|nist (ī′rə nist), *n.* a person, especially an author, who uses irony or has an ironical view of life or certain incidents.

i|ro|nize (ī′rə nīz), *v.,* **-nized, -niz|ing.** —*v.t.* to make ironical; bring irony into: *to ironize a sad situation.* —*v.i.* to use irony; speak ironically.

i|ron-jawed (ī′ərn jôd′), *adj.* **1** having a powerful jaw, as if made of iron: *an iron-jawed boxer.* **2** *Figurative.* doggedly stubborn or determined: *an iron-jawed drive to achieve power.*

i|ron|less (ī′ərn lis), *adj.* having no iron.

***iron lung**, a device which applies periodic pressure on the chest wall to force air in and out of the lungs. Iron lungs are used to enable people whose chest muscles are paralyzed to breathe.

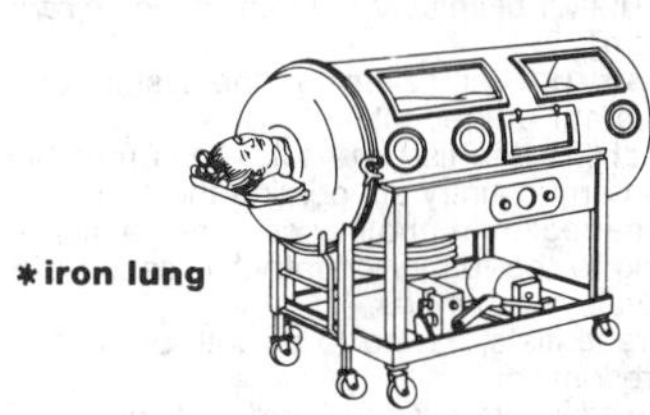

***iron lung**

***Iron Maiden**, a large metal casket in the shape of a woman, filled with spikes, and formerly used as an instrument of torture.

***Iron Maiden**

i|ron|mak|ing (ī′ərn mā′king), *adj., n.* —*adj.* designed or used to make iron: *an ironmaking blast furnace.*

—*n.* the process of producing iron: *Ironmaking was highly developed early in the industrial revolution.*

iron man, *U.S. Slang.* a dollar: *The savings banks and Uncle Sam are competing for my iron man* (Wall Street Journal).

i|ron|mas|ter (ī′ərn mas′tər, -mäs′-), *n. Especially British.* a manufacturer of iron.

iron mike, *Slang.* an automatic pilot.

iron mold, discoloration, especially in cloth and paper, caused by stains from rusted iron.

i|ron|mon|ger (ī′ərn mung′gər, -mong′-), *n. Especially British.* a dealer in ironware or hardware.

i|ron|mon|ger|y (ī′ərn mung′gə rē, -mong′-), *n., pl.* **-ger|ies**. *Especially British.* the goods, shop, or business of an ironmonger.

iron monoxide, = ferrous oxide.

iron oxide, a compound of iron and oxygen, used especially as a pigment; ferric oxide.

iron plant, = aspidistra.

iron pyrites, pyrite, a mineral that looks somewhat like gold.

iron ration, a ration issued to soldiers in the field; D ration.

iron rust, the rust of iron.

i|rons (ī′ərnz), *n.pl.* See under **iron**.

i|ron|sand (ī′ərn sand′), *n.* sand containing iron ore.

i|ron|shod (ī′ərn shod′), *adj.* shod, tipped, or lined with iron: *ironshod boots.*

i|ron|side (ī′ərn sīd′), *n.* = ironsides.

i|ron|sides (ī′ərn sīdz′), *n.* **1** an armor-clad warship. **2** Often, **Ironsides**. a name given in praise of strength: *He had won for himself the appellation of Ironsides as a testimony to the strength of his character and the resolution with which he pursued the British Fleet in those days of trouble between Great Britain and America* (Westminster Gazette). **3** a man of great strength or power of endurance.

► **Ironsides**, meaning warship, is singular in use: *An ironsides is protected with iron plates.*

i|ron|smith (ī′ərn smith′), *n.* a worker in iron; blacksmith.

i|ron|stone (ī′ərn stōn′), *n.* **1** any clay, silica, or other type of rock that contains iron; iron ore. **2** = ironstone china.

ironstone china or **ware**, a kind of hard, white, opaque pottery, used for dishes and bathroom fixtures; stone china.

iron sulfarsenide, = arsenopyrite.

i|ron|ware (ī′ərn wãr′), *n.* articles made of iron, such as pots, kettles, or tools; hardware.

i|ron|weed (ī′ərn wēd′), *n.* any one of various American plants of the composite family, with flat-topped clusters of small tubular purple, pink, or white flowers.

i|ron-willed (ī′ərn wild′), *adj.* having a firm will. SYN: unyielding, resolute, determined.

i|ron|wood (ī′ərn wu̇d′), *n.* **1** any one of various trees or shrubs with hard, heavy wood, especially the hornbeam. **2** the wood itself.

i|ron|work (ī′ərn wėrk′), *n.* things made of iron; work in iron.

i|ron|work|er (ī′ərn wėr′kər), *n.* **1** a person whose work is making iron or iron articles. **2** a person whose work is building the steel framework of bridges, skyscrapers, and other structures.

i|ron|work|ing (ī′ərn wėr′king), *n.* the act or process of using iron to make things.

i|ron|works (ī′ərn wėrks′), *n.pl. or sing.* a place where iron is made or worked into iron articles.

i|ro|ny[1] (ī′rə nē), *n., pl.* **-nies**. **1** a way of speaking or writing in which the ordinary meaning of the words is the opposite of the thought in the speaker's mind: *the boys called the very thin boy "Fatty" in irony. A drayman in a passion calls out, "You are a pretty fellow," without suspecting that he is uttering irony* (Macaulay). **2** *Figurative.* an event or outcome which is the opposite of what would naturally be expected: *By the irony of fate the farmers had rain when they needed sun, and sun when they needed rain.* **3** an ironical statement or expression; ironical quality: *There was staid irony in his tone* (Charles Kingsley). **4** pretending ignorance in a discussion in order to gain an advantage over one's opponent; Socratic irony. [< Latin *īrōnīa* < Greek *eirōneíā* dissimulation < *eírōn* dissembler < *eírein* speak]

► **Irony, sarcasm, satire** are humorous forms of expression. *Irony* consists in deliberately saying the opposite of what one means, relying on tone

Pronunciation Key: hat, āge, cãre, fär; let, ēqual, tėrm; it, īce; hot, ōpen, ôrder; oil, out; cup, pu̇t, rüle; child; long; thin; ᴛʜen; zh, measure; ə represents **a** in about, **e** in taken, **i** in pencil, **o** in lemon, **u** in circus.

of voice or on context to indicate one's real intent: *that noble and loyal patriot, Benedict Arnold.* In *sarcasm* the aim is to hurt someone's feelings and so, whether stated ironically or not, it is always cruel and biting: *When a boy refers to another boy as "mamma's little darling," he is using sarcasm.* In *satire* the aim is to expose and attack vice or folly, using irony, sarcasm, or other forms of humor to do so: *In "Gulliver's Travels" Jonathan Swift makes notable use of satire.*

i|ron|y[2] (ī′ər nē), *adj.* consisting of, containing, or like iron. [< *iron* + *-y*[1]]

Ir|o|quoi|an (ir′ə kwoi′ən), *adj., n.* —*adj.* **1** of or having to do with a family of North American Indian languages including Huron, Mohawk, Oneida, Onondaga, Cayuga, Seneca, Tuscarora, and Cherokee. **2** of or having to do with the Iroquois.
—*n.* **1** this language family. **2** an Indian belonging to an Iroquoian tribe; Iroquois.

Ir|o|quois (ir′ə kwoi, -kwoiz), *n., pl.* **-quois,** *adj.*
—*n.* a member of a powerful group of American Indian tribes called the Five Nations (later, the Six Nations), formerly living mostly in what is now Quebec, Ontario, and New York State.
—*adj.* of or having to do with these Indians.
[American English < French *Iroquois* < Algonkian (Algonkin) *Irinakoiw* adders, enemies]

ir|ra|di|ant (i rā′dē ənt), *adj.* irradiating; radiant; shining.

ir|ra|di|ate (*v.* i rā′dē āt; *adj.* i rā′dē it, -āt), *v.,* **-at|ed, -at|ing,** *adj.* —*v.t.* **1** to shine upon; light up; make bright; illuminate: *The midnight lightnings ... irradiate heaven* (Robert Southey). **2** *Figurative.* to throw light upon intellectually or brighten spiritually: *a sordid life ... irradiated by no sublime principles, no romantic visions* (George Eliot). **3** to radiate; give out (light or other radiant energy). **4a** to treat with some form of radiant energy, such as radiant heat from ultraviolet rays: *to irradiate fruit and vegetables to rid them of insects.* **b** to subject to the action of X rays or similar radiations.
—*v.i.* **1** to emit luminous rays; shine. **2** to become radiant; light up.
—*adj.* irradiated; bright.
[< Latin *irradiāre* (with English *-ate*[1]) < *in-* in, on + *radiāre* to shine < *radius* ray]

ir|ra|di|a|tion (i rā′dē ā′shən), *n.* **1** the act of irradiating or the state of being irradiated: *Irradiation involves bombarding food molecules with relatively high amounts of energy [that] causes changes to occur in molecular structure which show up as changes in odor, flavor, color, or texture* (Science News). **2** a ray of light; beam. **3** *Figurative.* intellectual or spiritual enlightenment. **4** *Optics.* the apparent enlargement or extension of a bright object when seen against a dark background. **5** the treatment of disease with ultraviolet rays, X rays, or other forms of radiant energy. **6** *Physics.* the intensity of the radiation falling upon a surface; the radiant energy falling per unit of time per unit area upon a surface at a specified point.

ir|ra|di|a|tive (i rā′dē ā′tiv), *adj.* serving to irradiate.

ir|ra|di|a|tor (i rā′dē ā′tər), *n.* a person or thing that irradiates.

ir|ra|tion|al (i rash′ə nəl, -rash′nəl), *adj., n.* —*adj.* **1** not rational; contrary to reason; unreasonable; illogical: *It is irrational to be afraid of the number 13. The irrational laws which bad critics have framed for the government of poets* (Macaulay). **2** unable to think and reason clearly: *to become irrational with rage.* **3** *Mathematics.* **a** (of an equation or expression) involving radicals or fractional exponents. **b** of or relating to an irrational number. **c** (of functions) that cannot be expressed as the ratio of two algebraic polynomials in its variables. **4** in Greek and Latin prosody: **a** designating a syllable that is long instead of short, as the conventional metrical pattern requires. **b** designating a metrical foot containing such a syllable.
—*n.* **1** that which is irrational or unreasonable. **2** an irrational number.
[< Latin *irratiōnālis* < *in-* not + *ratiōnālis* rational] —**ir|ra′tion|al|ly,** *adv.* —**ir|ra′tion|al|ness,** *n.*

ir|ra|tion|al|ism (i rash′ə nə liz′əm, -rash′nə-), *n.* irrationality in thought or action. —**ir|ra′tion|al|ist,** *adj., n.*

ir|ra|tion|al|i|ty (i rash′ə nal′ə tē), *n., pl.* **-ties.** **1** the quality of being irrational: *There is a great deal of talk these days about the irrationality of modern man* (Harper's). **2** something irrational; an absurdity: *the confused irrationalities into which you all allow yourselves to fall* (Charles Kingsley).

ir|ra|tion|al|ize (i rash′ə nə līz, -rash′nə-), *v.t.,* **-ized, -iz|ing.** to make irrational.

***irrational number**, any number that cannot be expressed as an integer or a ratio between two integers.

***irrational number**

$\sqrt{2} = 1.4142 \ldots$ | $\pi = 3.14159265 \ldots$

ir|re|al (i rē′əl), *adj.* not real; unreal.

ir|re|al|i|ty (ir ē al′ə tē), *n.* lack of reality; unreality.

ir|re|cip|ro|cal (ir′ə sip′rə kəl), *adj.* not reciprocal.

ir|rec|i|proc|i|ty (i res′ə pros′ə tē), *n.* lack of reciprocity.

ir|re|claim|a|bil|i|ty (ir′i klā′mə bil′ə tē), *n.* the quality or condition of being irreclaimable.

ir|re|claim|a|ble (ir′i klā′mə bəl), *adj.* that cannot be reclaimed or redeemed: *irreclaimable land, an irreclaimable drunkard.* **SYN:** irredeemable. —**ir′re|claim′a|ble|ness,** *n.*

ir|re|claim|a|bly (ir′i klā′mə blē), *adv.* so as to be irreclaimable.

ir|rec|on|cil|a|bil|i|ty (i rek′ən sī′lə bil′ə tē), *n.* the quality or condition of being irreconcilable.

ir|rec|on|cil|a|ble (i rek′ən sī′lə bəl, -rek′ən sī′-), *adj., n.* —*adj.* that cannot be reconciled; that cannot be made to agree; opposed: *irreconcilable enemies, irreconcilable statements. Good and evil are irreconcilable.*
—*n.* a person who persists in opposing. —**ir|rec′on|cil′a|ble|ness,** *n.* —**ir|rec′on|cil′a|bly,** *adv.*

ir|rec|on|cil|i|a|tion (i rek′ən sil′ē ā′shən), *n.* the fact or condition of being irreconcilable or unreconciled.

ir|re|cov|er|a|ble (ir′i kuv′ər ə bəl, -kuv′rə-), *adj.* **1** that cannot be got back or regained: *Wasted time is irrecoverable. If the path is ... once lost, it is irrecoverable* (Thomas Hardy). **SYN:** irretrievable. **2** *Figurative.* that cannot be remedied: *irrecoverable sorrow.* **SYN:** irremediable, irreclaimable. —**ir′re|cov′er|a|ble|ness,** *n.* —**ir′re|cov′er|a|bly,** *adv.*

ir|re|cu|sa|ble (ir′i kyü′zə bəl), *adj.* not to be objected to or rejected: *an irrecusable proposition.* [< Late Latin *irrecūsābilis* < Latin *in-* not + *recūsābilis* that can be refused < *recūsāre* to refuse] —**ir′re|cu′sa|bly,** *adv.*

ir|re|deem|a|ble (ir′i dē′mə bəl), *adj., n.* —*adj.* **1** that cannot be redeemed or bought back: *an irredeemable annuity.* **2** that cannot be exchanged for coin: *irredeemable paper money.* **3** *Figurative.* impossible to change; beyond remedy; hopeless: *irredeemable misery. The auditor's mistake was serious, but not irredeemable.* **4** beyond saving; irreclaimable: *an irredeemable scoundrel.*
—*n.* a bond that cannot be redeemed before maturity: *Yields are temptingly high whether you are a low taxpayer going for the latest high coupon stock or the irredeemables like War Loan and Treasury 3 per cent* (Sunday Times). —**ir′re|deem′a|bly,** *adv.*

ir|re|den|ta (ir′i den′tə), *n.* **1** any one of certain regions situated near Italy and having a considerable Italian population, whose union to Italy was advocated by an Italian political party that became important in 1878. **2** any region included politically in one country, but desired or claimed by another as properly belonging to it: *To date no nation has been willing to surrender an irredenta making up a third of its former territory* (New York Times). [< Italian (*Italia*) *irredenta* unredeemed (Italy), ultimately < Latin *in-* not + *redimere* redeem]

ir|re|den|tism (ir′i den′tiz əm), *n.* the system or political program of irredentists.

ir|re|den|tist (ir′i den′tist), *n., adj.* —*n.* a member of a party in any country advocating the taking over of some region in another country claimed as belonging to the former country by reason of racial, cultural, or other ties.
—*adj.* of irredentists; having to do with or advocating irredentism.
[< Italian *irredentista* < (*Italia*) *irredenta* unredeemed (Italy); see etym. under **irredenta**]

ir|re|duc|i|bil|i|ty (ir′i dü′sə bil′ə tē, -dyü′-), *n.* the quality or condition of being irreducible.

ir|re|duc|i|ble (ir′i dü′sə bəl, -dyü′-), *adj.* **1** impossible to make less, smaller, simpler, or less potent. **2** unable to be changed or brought into a wanted condition. **3** impossible to conquer or overcome. —**ir′re|duc′i|ble|ness,** *n.* —**ir′re|duc′i|bly,** *adv.*

ir|re|flec|tion (ir′i flek′shən), *n.* lack of reflection; thoughtlessness.

ir|re|flec|tive (ir′i flek′tiv), *adj.* not reflective; unthinking; thoughtless. —**ir′re|flec′tive|ly,** *adv.* —**ir′re|flec′tive|ness,** *n.*

ir|re|form|a|ble (ir′i fôr′mə bəl), *adj.* not reformable; that cannot be reformed.

ir|ref|ra|ga|bil|i|ty (i ref′rə gə bil′ə tē), *n.* the quality or condition of being irrefragable.

ir|ref|ra|ga|ble (i ref′rə gə bəl), *adj.* that cannot be refuted; unanswerable; undeniable: *irrefragable proofs that the account in the newspapers was correct* (Thomas Hardy). **SYN:** irrefutable, indisputable. [< Late Latin *irrefrāgābilis* < Latin *in-* not + *refrāgārī* oppose < *re-* back + *fragor* crash, noise] —**ir|ref′ra|ga|bly,** *adv.*

ir|re|fran|gi|ble (ir′i fran′jə bəl), *adj.* **1** not to be broken or violated; inviolable: *an irrefrangible contract, an irrefrangible code of conduct.* **2** not refrangible; that cannot be refracted. [< *ir-*[1] not + *refrangible*] —**ir′re|fran′gi|bly,** *adv.*

ir|ref|u|ta|bil|i|ty (i ref′yə tə bil′ə tē, ir′i fyü′-), *n.* the quality or condition of being irrefutable.

ir|ref|u|ta|ble (i ref′yə tə bəl, ir′i fyü′-), *adj.* that cannot be refuted or disproved; undeniable; unanswerable: *irrefutable arguments.* —**ir|ref′u|ta|bly,** *adv.*

irreg., **1** irregular. **2** irregularly.

ir|re|gard|less (ir′i gärd′lis), *adj. Informal.* regardless (not considered good usage).

ir|reg|u|lar (i reg′yə lər), *adj., n.* —*adj.* **1** not regular; not according to rule; out of the usual order or natural way: *irregular breathing. It would be quite irregular for a child of ten to drive a car.* **2** not according to law or morals: *irregular behavior. Now that to steal by law is grown an art ... And "slightly irregular" dilutes the shame Of what had once a somewhat blunter name* (James Russell Lowell). **SYN:** lawless. **3** not even; not smooth or straight; broken and rough; without symmetry: *an irregular pulse, irregular features, an irregular pattern. New England has a very irregular coastline.* **SYN:** uneven, variable. **4** not in the regular army: *irregular troops.* **5** *Grammar.* (of a word) not inflected in the usual way. *Be* is an irregular verb. **6** *Botany.* (of a flower) not having all the members of the same series alike, as in the bean and larkspur. They are bilaterally rather than radially symmetrical. **7** (of stocks or the stock market) not balanced or even, as when some prices fall while others rise: *Tea shares were quietly irregular* (London Times). *The market then steadied, but closed irregular* (New York Times).
—*n.* **1** a soldier not in the regular army. **2** any person or thing that is irregular: *The Baker Street irregulars* (Arthur Conan Doyle).
[< Old French *irreguler,* learned borrowing from Late Latin *irrēgulāris* < *in-* not + Latin *rēgulāris* regular] —**ir|reg′u|lar|ly,** *adv.*
—*Syn. adj.* **1 Irregular, abnormal** mean out of the usual or natural order or way. **Irregular** means not according to the accepted standard: *She has irregular habits.* **Abnormal** means above or below what is regarded as normal, average, or typical, and applies either to people or to things: *Seven feet is an abnormal height for a person.*

ir|reg|u|lar|i|ty (i reg′yə lar′ə tē), *n., pl.* **-ties.** **1** lack of regularity; a being irregular: *Judges cannot permit irregularity in carrying out justice.* **SYN:** unevenness. **2** something irregular: *State investigators ... have been collecting evidence of alleged irregularities in public construction projects* (New York Times). **SYN:** anomaly.

irregular variable, a star that varies in brightness or magnitude but not at regularly recurring periods.

ir|rel|a|tive (i rel′ə tiv), *adj.* **1** not relative; without relation; unrelated; unconnected. **2** = irrelevant. **3** *Music.* not having any notes in common: *irregular chords.* —**ir|rel′a|tive|ly,** *adv.* —**ir|rel′a|tive|ness,** *n.*

ir|rel|e|vance (i rel′ə vəns), *n.* **1** the state of being irrelevant. **2** something irrelevant.

ir|rel|e|van|cy (i rel′ə vən sē), *n., pl.* **-cies.** = irrelevance.

ir|rel|e|vant (i rel′ə vənt), *adj.* **1a** not to the point; off the subject: *A question about biology is irrelevant in a music lesson.* **SYN:** inapposite, inapplicable. **b** not important or meaningful: *A poor relation ... is the most irrelevant thing in nature* (Charles Lamb). *[He] chose not to join his father's "irrelevant" business* (Time). **2** *Law.* (of evidence) **a** not proving or disproving any point at issue. **b** not admissible. —**ir|rel′e|vant|ly,** *adv.*

ir|re|liev|a|ble (ir′i lē′və bəl), *adj.* that cannot be relieved.

ir|re|li|gion (ir′i lij′ən), *n.* **1** lack of religion. **2** hostility to religion; disregard of religion.

ir|re|li|gion|ist (ir′i lij′ə nist), *n.* a person who opposes religion.

ir|re|li|gious (ir′i lij′əs), *adj.* **1** not religious; indifferent to religion. **2** contrary to religious principles; impious. [< Latin *irreligiōsus* < *in-* not + *religiōsus* religious] —**ir′re|li′gious|ly,** *adv.* —**ir′re|li′gious|ness,** *n.*

ir|rem|e|a|ble (i rem′ē ə bəl, -rē′mē-), *adj. Archaic.* from, by, or through which there is no return: *My three brave brothers in one mournful day All trod the dark, irremeable way* (Alexander Pope). [< Latin *irremeābilis* < *in-* not + *remeābilis* returnable]

ir|re|me|di|a|ble (ir′i mē′dē ə bəl), *adj.* that cannot be corrected or remedied; incurable: *irremediable disease.* —**ir′re|me′di|a|ble|ness**, *n.* —**ir′re|me′di|a|bly**, *adv.*

ir|re|mis|si|bil|i|ty (ir′i mis′ə bil′ə tē), *n.* the quality or condition of being irremissible; unpardonableness.

ir|re|mis|si|ble (ir′i mis′ə bəl), *adj.* **1** not remissible; unpardonable: *an irremissible sin.* **2** that cannot be remitted: *an irremissible duty.* —**ir′re|mis′si|ble|ness**, *n.* —**ir′re|mis′si|bly**, *adv.*

ir|re|mov|a|bil|i|ty (ir′i mü′və bil′ə tē), *n.* the quality or condition of being irremovable.

ir|re|mov|a|ble (ir′i mü′və bəl), *adj.* that cannot be removed. —**ir′re|mov′a|bly**, *adv.*

ir|re|nun|ci|a|ble (ir′i nun′sē ə bəl), *adj.* that cannot be renounced: ... *essential and irrenunciable parts of the modern international monetary system* (New York Times).

ir|rep|a|ra|bil|i|ty (i rep′ər ə bil′ə tē), *n.* the quality or condition of being irreparable.

ir|rep|a|ra|ble (i rep′ər ə bəl), *adj.* that cannot be repaired, put right, or made good: *Losing a leg is an irreparable injury.* —**ir|rep′a|ra|ble|ness**, *n.* —**ir|rep′a|ra|bly**, *adv.*

ir|re|peal|a|bil|i|ty (ir′i pē′lə bil′ə tē), *n.* the quality or condition of being irrepealable.

ir|re|peal|a|ble (ir′i pē′lə bəl), *adj.* not repealable; irrevocable.

ir|re|place|a|bil|i|ty (ir′i plā′sə bil′ə tē), *n.* the quality or condition of being irreplaceable.

ir|re|place|a|ble (ir′i plā′sə bəl), *adj.* not replaceable; impossible to replace with another. —**ir′re|place′a|ble|ness**, *n.* —**ir′re|place′a|bly**, *adv.*

ir|re|plev|i|a|ble (ir′i plev′ē ə bəl), *adj.* = irreplevisable.

ir|re|plev|i|sa|ble (ir′i plev′ə sə bəl), *adj. Law.* that cannot be replevied or recovered. [< *ir-*[1] not + *replevisable*]

ir|re|press|i|bil|i|ty (ir′i pres′ə bil′ə tē), *n.* the condition of being irrepressible.

ir|re|press|i|ble (ir′i pres′ə bəl), *adj.* that cannot be repressed or restrained; uncontrollable: *irrepressible laughter, irrepressible wrath.* —**ir′re|press′i|ble|ness**, *n.* —**ir′re|press′i|bly**, *adv.*

ir|re|proach|a|bil|i|ty (ir′i prō′chə bil′ə tē), *n.* the quality or condition of being irreproachable.

ir|re|proach|a|ble (ir′i prō′chə bəl), *adj.* free from blame; faultless: *The Frenchman spoke excellent, irreproachable English.* —**ir′re|proach′a|ble|ness**, *n.* —**ir′re|proach′a|bly**, *adv.*

ir|re|pro|duc|i|ble (i rē′prə dü′sə bəl, -dyü′-), *adj.* incapable of being reproduced.

ir|re|sist|i|bil|i|ty (ir′i zis′tə bil′ə tē), *n.* the quality or condition of being irresistible.

ir|re|sist|i|ble (ir′i zis′tə bəl), *adj.* that cannot be resisted; too great to be withstood; overwhelming: *An irresistible desire to succeed drives a person on even after failure.* —**ir′re|sist′i|ble|ness**, *n.* —**ir′re|sist′i|bly**, *adv.*

ir|res|o|lu|ble (i rez′ə lyə bəl), *adj.* **1** that cannot be dissolved or liquefied; indissoluble: *Diamonds are irresoluble.* **2** that cannot be relieved. **3** that cannot be solved or explained; insoluble: *an irresoluble mystery.*

ir|res|o|lute (i rez′ə lüt), *adj.* not resolute; unable to make up one's mind; not sure of what one wants; hesitating: *Irresolute persons make poor leaders.* **SYN**: doubtful, vacillating. —**ir|res′o|lute′ly**, *adv.* —**ir|res′o|lute′ness**, *n.*

ir|res|o|lu|tion (i rez′ə lü′shən), *n.* lack of resolution; being irresolute; lack of firm decision; hesitation: *His countenance betrayed irresolution and reluctance* (Charles Brockden Brown). **SYN**: indecision, vacillation.

ir|re|solv|a|ble (ir′i zol′və bəl), *adj.* **1** that cannot be solved; insoluble. **2** that cannot be resolved into elements or parts.

ir|re|spec|tive (ir′i spek′tiv), *adj.* **1** without respect or regard to something else; regardless (of): *All pupils, irrespective of age, may join the club.* **2** not respecting or regarding particular persons, circumstances, or conditions: *an irrespective decree.* —**ir′re|spec′tive|ly**, *adv.*

ir|re|spon|si|bil|i|ty (ir′i spon′sə bil′ə tē), *n.* lack of responsibility; a being irresponsible.

ir|re|spon|si|ble (ir′i spon′sə bəl), *adj., n.* —*adj.* **1** not responsible; that cannot be called to account: *the hare-brained chatter of irresponsible frivolity* (Benjamin Disraeli). *A dictator is an irresponsible ruler.* **2** without a sense of responsibility; untrustworthy; unreliable.

—*n.* an irresponsible person: *Eight ... Committee irresponsibles voted for the major changes* (Time). —**ir′re|spon′si|ble|ness**, *n.* —**ir′re|spon′si|bly**, *adv.*

ir|re|spon|sive (ir′i spon′siv), *adj.* not responsive; not responding readily to speech, action, or feeling: *a dull, irresponsive nature.* —**ir′re|spon′sive|ness**, *n.*

ir|re|ten|tion (ir′i ten′shən), *n.* lack of retention; inability to retain.

ir|re|ten|tive (ir′i ten′tiv), *adj.* not retentive; lacking power to retain: *an irretentive memory.* —**ir′re|ten′tive|ness**, *n.*

ir|re|trace|a|ble (ir′i trā′sə bəl), *adj.* that cannot be retraced.

ir|re|triev|a|bil|i|ty (ir′i trē′və bil′ə tē), *n.* the state or quality of being irretrievable.

ir|re|triev|a|ble (ir′i trē′və bəl), *adj.* that cannot be retrieved or recovered; impossible to recall or restore to its former condition; irrecoverable; irreparable: *an irretrievable loss.* —**ir′re|triev′a|ble|ness**, *n.* —**ir′re|triev′a|bly**, *adv.*

ir|rev|er|ence (i rev′ər əns), *n.* **1** lack of reverence; disrespect. **2** an act showing irreverence. **3** the condition of not being held in reverence; dishonor.

ir|rev|er|en|cy (i rev′ər ən sē), *n., pl.* **-cies.** an instance of irreverence; an irreverent act or statement: ... *tongue-in-cheek irreverencies* (New York Times).

ir|rev|er|ent (i rev′ər ənt), *adj.* not reverent; disrespectful: *an irreverent reply.* [< Latin *irreverēns, -entis* < *in-* not + *reverēns* reverent] —**ir|rev′er|ent|ly**, *adv.*

ir|re|vers|i|bil|i|ty (ir′i vėr′sə bil′ə tē), *n.* the quality or condition of being irreversible.

ir|re|vers|i|ble (ir′i vėr′sə bəl), *adj.* **1** not capable of being turned the other way; that cannot be reversed. **2** unable to be changed or repealed; unalterable; irrevocable. —**ir′re|vers′i|ble|ness**, *n.* —**ir′re|vers′i|bly**, *adv.*

ir|rev|o|ca|bil|i|ty (i rev′ə kə bil′ə tē), *n.* the state of being irrevocable.

ir|rev|o|ca|ble (i rev′ə kə bəl), *adj.* **1** not to be revoked; final; unalterable; irreversible: *Nothing could change his irrevocable decision to leave. Firm and irrevocable is my doom Which I have pass'd upon her* (Shakespeare). **2** impossible to call or bring back: *Yesterday belongs to the irrevocable past.* —**ir|rev′o|ca|ble|ness**, *n.* —**ir|rev′o|ca|bly**, *adv.*

ir|ri|ga|ble (ir′ə gə bəl), *adj.* that can be irrigated.

ir|ri|gate (ir′ə gāt), *v.,* **-gat|ed, -gat|ing.** —*v.t.* **1** to supply (land) with water by using ditches, by flooding, or by sprinkling: *After a desert is irrigated, crops will grow there.* **2** to supply (a wound or a cavity in the body) with a continuous flow of some liquid: *The doctor showed her how to irrigate her nose and throat with hot water.* **3** *Figurative.* to refresh or make fruitful as if with a supply of moisture.

—*v.i.* to supply lands, wounds, or a cavity in the body, with water or other liquid: *Is it time for the farmer to irrigate?*

[< Latin *irrigāre* (with English *-ate*[1]) < *in-* into + *rigāre* moisten, conduct water] —**ir′ri|ga′tor**, *n.*

ir|ri|ga|tion (ir′ə gā′shən), *n.* **1** the act of irrigating: *Irrigation is needed to make crops grow in dry regions.* **2** the state of being irrigated.

ir|ri|ga|tion|al (ir′ə gā′shə nəl), *adj.* belonging to irrigation.

ir|ri|ga|tive (ir′ə gā′tiv), *adj.* serving for or having to do with irrigation.

ir|rig|u|ous (i rig′yü əs), *adj. Archaic.* **1** well-watered; moist; wet: *The flowery lap Of some irriguous valley* (Milton). **2** watering; irrigative. [< Latin *irriguus* (with English *-ous*) < *irrigāre*; see etym. under **irrigate**]

ir|ri|sor (i rī′sər), *n.* any one of a group of African birds with long curved bill, long tail, and glossy plumage; wood hoopoe. [< New Latin *Irrisor* the genus name < Latin *irrīsor* one who laughs < *irrīdēre* laugh at < *in-* (intensive) + *rīdēre* to laugh (because of its noisy call)]

ir|ri|ta|bil|i|ty (ir′ə tə bil′ə tē), *n., pl.* **-ties.** **1** the quality or state of being irritable; impatience: *The gloomy irritability of his [Johnson's] nature* (James Boswell). **2** a thing that irritates or annoys; irritation: *The exile's quest has dwindled into a contest with minor irritabilities* (Penelope Gilliatt). **3** *Medicine.* an unnatural sensitiveness of an organ or part of the body. **4** *Biology.* the property that a living plant or animal tissue has of responding to a stimulus: *Responsiveness of protoplasm to environmental stimuli is often called irritability.* [< Latin *irrītābilitās* < *irrītābilis*; see etym. under **irritable**]

ir|ri|ta|ble (ir′ə tə bəl), *adj.* **1** easily made angry; impatient: *When the rain spoiled her plans, she was irritable for the rest of the day.* **2** *Medicine.* (of an organ or part of the body) more sensitive than is natural or normal: *A baby's skin is often quite irritable.* **3** *Biology.* able to respond to stimuli. [< Latin *irrītābilis* < *irrītāre* excite, provoke, irritate] —**ir′ri|ta|ble|ness**, *n.* —**ir′ri|ta|bly**, *adv.*

—*Syn.* **1 Irritable, irascible** mean easily made angry. **Irritable** means easily annoyed, either because of one's disposition or because of some temporary condition: *Ill health made him irritable.* **Irascible** implies a quick temper and a tendency to become angry at trifles: *an irascible old tyrant. Irascible people should not have positions which require them to meet the public.*

ir|ri|tan|cy (ir′ə tən sē), *n.* irritating quality or character; irritation; annoyance.

ir|ri|tant (ir′ə tənt), *n., adj.* —*n.* a thing that irritates or causes irritation: *Chlorine in swimming pools can be an irritant to the eyes.*

—*adj.* causing irritation.

[< Latin *irrītāns, -antis,* present participle of *irrītāre* excite, provoke, irritate]

ir|ri|tate (ir′ə tāt), *v.t.,* **-tat|ed, -tat|ing.** **1** to make impatient or angry; annoy; provoke; vex: *The boy's foolish questions irritated his mother. Flies irritate horses.* **2** to make (a part of the body) more sensitive than is natural or normal: *Sunburn irritates the skin.* **3** *Biology.* to stimulate (as an organ, muscle, or tissue) to respond: *A muscle contracts when it is irritated by an electric shock.* [< Latin *irrītāre* (with English *-ate*[1]) excite, provoke] —**ir′ri|tat′ing|ly**, *adv.* —**ir′ri|ta′tor**, *n.*

—*Syn.* **1 Irritate, exasperate, provoke** mean to excite to impatience or anger. **Irritate** suggests annoying a person until he loses patience or flares up in anger: *Her untidiness irritates me.* **Exasperate** suggests annoying someone beyond endurance or self-control: *His constant cheating exasperates me.* **Provoke** suggests annoying someone into strong anger or disgust: *Their constant interruptions provoke me.*

ir|ri|ta|tion (ir′ə tā′shən), *n.* **1** the act or process of irritating: *The irritation of the pollen makes her sneeze.* **2** the condition of being irritated; vexation: *The irritation of her nose made her sneeze. He couldn't hide his irritation when the car wouldn't start.* **3** something that irritates; annoyance: *The day was filled with many minor irritations.*

ir|ri|ta|tive (ir′ə tā′tiv), *adj.* **1** serving or tending to irritate; annoying; irritating. **2** *Medicine.* characterized by or accompanied with irritation: *an irritative fever.* **3** *Biology.* stimulating to some characteristic action or function.

ir|ro|ta|tion|al (ir′ō tā′shə nəl), *adj.* not rotational; characterized by lack of rotation. —**ir′ro|ta′tion|al|ly**, *adv.*

ir|rupt (i rupt′), *v.i.* **1** to break or burst in violently. **2** (of animals) to increase suddenly in population. [< Latin *irruptus,* past participle of *irrumpere* < *in-* in + *rumpere* break]

ir|rup|tion (i rup′shən), *n.* a breaking or bursting in; violent invasion: *The irruption of barbarians was one cause of the downfall of the Roman Empire.* [< Latin *irruptiō, -ōnis* < *irruptus*; see etym. under **irrupt**]

ir|rup|tive (i rup′tiv), *adj.* **1** bursting in; rushing in or upon anything. **2** *Geology.* intrusive.

I.R.S. or **IRS** (no periods), Internal Revenue Service.

ir|tron (ėr′tron), *n.* a galactic source of strong infrared radiation: *Irtrons radiate fantastic amounts of energy, in some cases many times more than the total power emitted by all the stars in the largest galaxies* (Science News). [< *i*(nfra)*r*(ed) (spec)*tr*(um) + *-on*]

is (iz), *v.* the 3rd person singular, present indicative, of **be.** He is, she is, it is. *The earth is round. He is at school. The child is loved by its mother.*

as is, as it is now; in its present condition, without a guarantee of good or perfect quality: *If you buy the car as is, you may save a great deal of money.*

[Old English *is,* third person singular present indicative of *be*]

is-, *combining form.* the form of **iso-** before vowels, as in *isallobar.*

is., **1** island or islands. **2** isle or isles.

Is. or **Isa.**, Isaiah (book of the Old Testament).

IS (no periods) or **I.S.**, intermediate school.

I|saac (ī′zək), *n.* the son of Abraham and Sarah, and father of Jacob and Esau (in the Bible, Genesis 21:3).

is|a|bel|la (iz′ə bel′ə), *n.* a grayish-yellow color. [< *Isabella,* a proper name]

is|a|bel|line (iz′ə bel′in, -īn), *adj.* grayish-yellow. [< *isabell*(a) + *-ine*[1]]

is|ab|nor|mal (īs′ab nôr′məl), *adj., n.* —*adj.* denoting or having to do with an imaginary line on the earth's surface, or a corresponding line on a map, connecting places which have the same deviation of the observed from the normal temperature, pressure, or the like.

—*n.* an isabnormal line.

[< *is-* + *abnormal*]

is|a|cous|tic (īs′ə küs′tik, -kous′-), *adj.* of or having to do with equality or equal intensity of sound. [< *is-* + *acoustic*]

i|sa|go|ge (ī′sə gō′jē), *n.* an introduction, especially to a complex field of study. [< Latin *īsagōgē* < Greek *eisagōgê* < *eis* into + *agōgê* a leading < *ágein* to lead]

Pronunciation Key: hat, āge, cãre, fär; let, ēqual, tėrm; it, īce; hot, ōpen, ôrder; oil, out; cup, pu̇t, rüle; child; long; thin; ᴛʜen; zh, measure; ə represents **a** in about, **e** in taken, **i** in pencil, **o** in lemon, **u** in circus.

i|sa|gog|ic (ī′sə goj′ik), *adj.* introductory, especially to the interpretation of the Bible.

i|sa|gog|ics (ī′sə goj′iks), *n.pl.* **1** introductory studies. **2** the branch of theological study deals with the literary history of the books of the Bible as a preparation for interpretation.

I|sai|ah (ī zā′ə, -zī′-), *n.* **1** one of the greatest of the Hebrew prophets, who lived in Judah in the late 700's B.C. **2** a book of the Old Testament containing his prophecies, together with later material. *Abbr:* Isa.

I|sai|as (ī zā′əs, -zī′-), *n.* (in the Douay Bible) Isaiah.

is|al|lo|bar (ī sal′ə bär), *n.* a line on a weather map, or an imaginary line drawn in space, connecting points at which changes in atmospheric pressure are equal over a given period. [< *is-* + Greek *állos* other + *báros* weight]

is|al|lo|bar|ic (ī sal′ə bär′ik), *adj.* **1** of or containing isallobars. **2** having or indicating equal atmospheric pressure over a given period.

i|sa|tin (ī′sə tin), *n.* an orange-red crystalline compound obtained chiefly from indigo by oxidation, used as a dyestuff. *Formula:* $C_8H_5O_2N$ [< Latin *īsatis* a healing herb (< Greek *isátis*, a plant that produces a dark blue dye) + English *-in*]

is|ba (iz bä′, iz′bə), *n.* **1** a Russian peasant's log hut. **2** an entertainment of singing and dancing representing Russian peasant life. Also, **izba.** [< Russian *izba*]

ISBN (no periods), **1** International Standard Book Number (a system for numbering newly published books, widely adopted by publishers, especially to facilitate ordering and mailing). **2** a number in this system.

I.S.C., International Student Conference.

Is|car|i|ot (is kar′ē ət), *n.* **1** the surname of Judas, the disciple who betrayed Jesus for thirty pieces of silver (in the Bible, Matthew 26:14). **2** a traitor.

is|che|mi|a or **is|chae|mi|a** (is kē′mē ə), *n.* local anemia caused by an obstruction of the supply of arterial blood. [< New Latin *ischaemia* < Greek *ischaimos* that stops bleeding < *ischein* to hold, check (< *échein* to hold, have) + *haîma* blood]

is|che|mic or **is|chae|mic** (is kē′mik, -kem′ik), *adj.* having to do with or affected with ischemia.

is|chi|ad|ic (is′kē ad′ik), *adj.* having to do with the ischium; sciatic.

is|chi|al (is′kē əl), *adj.* = ischiadic.

is|chi|at|ic (is′kē at′ik), *adj.* = ischiadic.

is|chi|um (is′kē əm), *n., pl.* **-chi|a** (-kē ə), the lowest bone of the three bones forming either half of the pelvis: *Each hipbone develops embryonically from three separate bones, the ilium, the ischium, and the pubic, which fuse early in childhood* (Harbaugh and Goodrich). [< New Latin *ischium* < Greek *ischíon* ischium; earlier, hip socket or joint]

-ise, *suffix.* a variant of **-ize**, as in *supervise.* ▶See **-ize** for usage note.

is|en|trop|ic (īs′ən trop′ik), *adj.* of or having to do with a constant or equal entropy. [< *is-* + *entropy* + *-ic*]

I|seult (i sült′), *n. Medieval Legend.* **1** the daughter of the king of Ireland and the wife of King Mark of Cornwall, loved by Tristan (Tristram). **2** the daughter of the king of Brittany, whom Tristan married after his love for the Irish Iseult was discovered. Also, **Isolde, Isolt.**

-ish, *suffix forming adjectives from other adjectives and from nouns.* **1** somewhat ___: *Sweetish = somewhat sweet.*
2 like a ___: *Childish = like a child.*
3 like that of a ___: *Girlish = like that of a girl.*
4 of or having to do with ___: *English = of or having to do with England.*
5 tending to ___; inclined to be a ___: *Bookish = tending to books. Thievish = inclined to be a thief.*
6 near, but usually somewhat past ___: *Fortyish = near, but somewhat past, forty.*
[Middle English *-ish, -issh, -isch,* Old English *-isc*]

Ish|ma|el (ish′mē əl), *n.* **1** the son of Abraham and Hagar, driven into the desert because of the jealousy of Sarah (in the Bible, Genesis 16). **2** an outcast; one at war with society: *... men who were the very Ishmaels of the labour world* (Westminster Gazette).

Ish|ma|el|ite (ish′mē ə līt), *n.* **1** a descendant of Ishmael (in the Bible, Genesis 25:12-18). **2** an outcast.

Ish|ma|el|it|ish (ish′mē ə lī′tish), *adj.* of, having to do with, or like the Ishmaelites.

Ish|ma|el|it|ism (ish′mē ə lī′tiz əm), *n.* the character or action of an Ishmaelite or outcast: *social Ishmaelitism.*

Ish|tar (ish′tär), *n.* the chief goddess of the Babylonians and Assyrians. Ishtar was the goddess of love and fertility, sometimes of war, and is equivalent to the Canaanite-Phoenician goddess Astarte.

I|si|ac (ī′sē ak), *adj.* of or having to do with the Egyptian goddess Isis.

i|sid|i|um (ī sid′ē əm), *n., pl.* **-i|a** (-ē ə). *Botany.* a coral-like outgrowth of the thallus in certain lichens, having the function of a soredium. [< New Latin *isidium*]

i|sin|glass (ī′zing glas′, -gläs′; -zən-), *n.* **1a** a kind of gelatin obtained from the air bladders of sturgeon, hake, and similar fishes, used for making glue or clearing liquors. **b** any one of various similar substances made especially from hides or hoofs. **2** mica, especially in thin semitransparent layers. [earlier *Isom glas,* alteration of Middle Dutch *huysenblas* sturgeon bladder; perhaps influenced by *glass*]

I|sis (ī′sis), *n.* the chief goddess of ancient Egypt, sister and wife of Osiris. She represented fertility and was shown as wearing a cow's horns and solar disk on her head.

isl., **1** island or islands. **2** isle or isles.

Is|lam (is′ləm, iz′-; is läm′, iz-), *n.* **1** the Moslem religion, based on the teachings of Mohammed as they appear in the Koran. It holds that there is only one God, Allah, and Mohammed is his prophet, that the Koran is revealed literature containing a sufficient rule of life, and that salvation is achieved by the righteous. **2** Moslems as a group. **3** the countries under Moslem rule or inhabited by Moslems. [< Arabic *'Islām* submission (to the will of God). Compare etym. under **Moslem.**]

Is|lam|ic (is lam′ik, -lä′mik; iz-), *adj.* of Islam; Moslem.

Islamic calendar, calendar used by Moslems, having cycles of 30 years, 12 months in a year, and alternate months of 30 and 29 days, with a day added to the last month each second and third year. It counts the years from A.D. 622, the date of Mohammed's flight from Mecca to Medina.

Is|lam|ics (is lam′iks, iz-), *n.* the study of Islam.

Is|lam|ism (is′lə miz əm, iz′-; is lam′iz əm, iz-), *n.* the Moslem religion.

Is|lam|ist (is′lə mist, iz′-; is lam′ist, iz-), *n.* **1** an orthodox Moslem. **2** a student of Islam.

Is|lam|ite (is′lə mīt, iz′-), *n., adj.* = Moslem.

Is|lam|it|ic (is′lə mit′ik, iz′-), *adj.* = Islamic.

Is|lam|ize (is′lə mīz, iz′-), *v.t., v.i.,* **-ized, -iz|ing.** to make or become Moslem. **—Is′lam|i|za′tion,** *n.*

is|land (ī′lənd), *n., v.* **—*n.*** **1a** a body of land surrounded by water, smaller than a continent: *Cuba is a very large island. To reach the island you go on a boat or plane. Abbr:* I. **b** something that suggests a piece of land surrounded by water. Platforms in the middle of crowded busy streets are called safety islands. **c** *Figurative: No nation can be an industrial island* (Atlantic). **2** the superstructure, especially of a battleship or aircraft carrier. **3a** a piece of woodland surrounded by prairie. **b** an elevated piece of land surrounded by marshes, swamps, or the like. **4** *Anatomy.* a group of cells different in structure or function from those around it. **5** a local, minor civil division in Maine. **6** a large platform built over the ocean by means of caissons for use as a military base or scientific station.
—*v.t.* **1** to make into an island or something resembling an island; isolate: *A thousand streamlets ... With labyrinthine channels islanding A thousand rocks* (Robert Southey). **2** to dot with or as if with islands: *The waveless plain of Lombardy ... Islanded by cities fair* (Shelley).
[spelling alteration (influenced by *isle*) of Middle English *iland,* Old English *īgland* < *īg* island + *land* land] **—is′land|like′,** *adj.*

is|land|er (ī′lən dər), *n.* a person born or living on an island.

islands of Lang|er|hans (läng′ər häns), = islets of Langerhans.

Islands of the Blessed, *Greek and Roman Mythology.* the Elysian Fields; Elysium.

island universe, *Astronomy.* a galaxy.

island white bear, a white variety of American black bear that inhabits the coastal islands of British Columbia; Kermode's bear.

isle (īl), *n., v.,* **isled, isl|ing.** **—*n.*** **1** a small island: *The Statue of Liberty is on an isle by itself in New York harbor.* **2** an island.
—*v.t.* to make into or as if into an isle; place on or as if on an isle. **—*v.i.*** to live or remain on an isle. [< Old French *isle,* earlier *ile* < Latin *īnsula*]

Isle of Wight disease (wīt), an acariasis of bees. [< *Isle of Wight,* an island south of England, in the English Channel, where the disease broke out in the early 1900's]

isles|man (īlz′mən), *n., pl.* **-men.** = islander.

is|let (ī′lit), *n.* **1** a small island. **2** a small, isolated tract or area: *an islet of color.* **3** *Anatomy.* an island, as of the pancreas. [< Old French *islette* (diminutive) < *isle* isle]

islets of Lang|er|hans (läng′ər häns), the small scattered endocrine glands in the pancreas that secrete insulin. Also, **islands of Langerhans.** [< Paul *Langerhans,* 1847-1888, a German physician and anatomist]

isls., **1** islands. **2** isles.

ism (iz′əm), *n. Informal.* a distinctive doctrine, theory, system, or practice (usually unfriendly in use): *Communism and Fascism are well-known isms.* [< *-ism*]

-ism, *suffix forming nouns.* **1** (*added to verbs*) act or practice of ___: *Baptism = act or practice of baptizing.*
2 (*added to nouns or adjectives*) quality or condition of being a ___: *Heroism = quality of being a hero. Paganism = condition of being a pagan.*
3 (*added to nouns or adjectives*) illustration or instance of being ___: *Witticism = instance of being witty.*
4 (*added to nouns*) an unhealthy condition caused by ___: *Alcoholism = an unhealthy condition caused by alcohol.*
5 (*added to nouns or adjectives*) doctrine, theory, system, or practice of ___: *Darwinism = theory of Charles Darwin.*
[< Greek *-ismós* action of, or *-isma* act of (directly or through Latin *-ismus*)]

Is|ma|e|li|an (is′mā ē′lē ən), *n.* = Ismailian.

Is|ma|i|li or **Is|ma|i|′li** (is mä′ə lī), *n.* a present-day Ismailian.

Is|ma|il|i|an (is′mā il′ē ən), *n.* a member of a Moslem sect derived from the Shiites, having a body of secret doctrine revealed only to initiates [< *Ismail,* died 760, the disinherited son of one of the Shiite imams]

Is|ma|i|lite (is′mā ə līt), *n.* = Ismaili.

Is|mel|in (is mel′in), *n. Trademark.* = guanethidine.

is|n't (iz′ənt), is not.

iso-, *combining form.* equal; alike: *Isometric = metrically equal. Isosceles = having two sides equal. Isothermal = having to do with equal temperatures. Isotope = any of two or more elements having the same place (on the periodic table of elements).* Also, **is-** before vowels. [< Greek *iso-* < *ísos* equal]

ISO (no periods) or **I.S.O.**, International Standards Organization.

i|so|ab|nor|mal (ī′sō ab nôr′məl), *adj., n.* = isabnormal.

i|so|ag|glu|ti|na|tion (ī′sō ə glü′tə nā′shən), *n.* the agglutination of the red blood corpuscles of an animal by antibodies normally present in the serum of another animal of the same species.

i|so|ag|glu|ti|na|tive (ī′sō ə glü′tə nā′tiv), *adj.* having to do with or causing isoagglutination.

i|so|ag|glu|ti|nin (ī′sō ə glü′tə nin), *n.* an antibody normally present in serum that will agglutinate the red blood corpuscles of another animal of the same species.

i|so|an|ti|bod|y (ī′sō an′tē bod′ē), *n., pl.* **-bod|ies.** an antibody which acts against the antigen produced by another animal of the same species.

i|so|an|ti|gen (ī′sō an′tə jən), *n.* an antigen that stimulates the production of a specific antibody in another animal of the same species.

i|so|bar (ī′sə bär), *n.* **1** a line on a weather map connecting places having the same average barometric pressure (after allowance for height above sea level). Isobars show the distribution of atmospheric pressure at a particular time, and are used in making forecasts of the weather. See diagram at **isoline.** **2** *Chemistry, Physics.* one of two or more kinds of atoms that have the same atomic weight, but in most cases different atomic numbers. [< Greek *isobarēs* of equal weight < *ísos* equal + *báros* weight < *barýs* heavy]

i|so|bar|ic (ī′sə bar′ik), *adj.* **1** having or indicating equal atmospheric pressure. **2** of or containing isobars.

i|so|bar|ism (ī′sə bär′iz əm), *n.* equality or similarity of weight.

i|so|bath (ī′sə bath), *n.* a line on a map connecting points that have the same depth below the surface of a body of water. See diagram at **isoline.** [< *iso-* + Greek *báthos* depth]

i|so|bath|ic (ī′sə bath′ik), *adj.* of or having to do with an isobath.

i|so|bath|y|therm (ī′sə bath′ə thėrm), *n.* a line connecting points of equal temperature in a vertical section of a part of the ocean. [< *iso-* + Greek *báthos* depth + *thérmē* heat]

i|so|bath|y|ther|mal (ī′sə bath′ə thėr′məl), *adj.* of or having to do with an isobathytherm.

i|so|bath|y|ther|mic (ī′sə bath′ə thėr′mik), *adj.* = isobathythermal.

i|so|bu|tane (ī′sə byü′tān, -byü tān′), *n.* a hydrocarbon obtained from gas and gasoline, used as a refrigerant, a fuel, and in the synthesis of various chemical products. *Formula:* C_4H_{10}

i|so|bu|ty|lene (ī′sə byü′tə lēn), *n.* a colorless hydrocarbon obtained from isobutane, used in the production of high-octane gasoline and butyl rubber. *Formula:* $(CH_3)_2C{:}CH_2$

i|so|car|pic (ī′sə kär′pik), *adj.* (of a flower) having the same number of carpels as other floral parts. [< *iso-* + Greek *karpós* fruit + English *-ic*]

i|so|ce|phal|ic (ī′sə sə fal′ik), *adj.* of or having to do with isocephaly.

***i|so|ceph|a|ly** (ī′sə sef′ə lē), *n.* a convention of art in ancient Greece of representing the heads of the figures, whether seated or standing, at about the same level in a frieze, on a bowl, or other work. [< *iso-* + Greek *kephalē* head]

***isocephaly**

i|so|cheim or **i|so|chime** (ī′sə kīm), *n.* a line on a weather map connecting places that have the same mean winter temperature. [< *iso-* + Greek *cheîma* winter weather]

i|so|chei|mal (ī′sə kī′məl), *adj., n.* —***adj.*** (of lines on a map) indicating equal mean winter temperature.
—***n.*** an isocheimal line; isocheim.

i|so|chei|me|nal (ī′sə kī′mə nəl), *adj., n.* = isocheimal.

i|so|chor or **i|so|chore** (ī′sə kôr), *n. Physics.* a curve denoting the relations between two variables, such as temperature and pressure, of a gas or quantity having a constant volume. [< *iso-* + Greek *chṓrā* space]

i|so|chor|ic (ī′sə kôr′ik, -kor′-), *adj.* having to do with equal volume or density: *an isochoric curve.*

i|so|chro|mat|ic (ī′sə krō mat′ik), *adj.* **1** *Optics.* of the same color or tint, as two lines or curves in a figure formed when light waves going through a biaxial crystal interfere. **2** *Physics.* having to do with the variations involved when radiation is of constant wave length or frequency.

i|so|chron (ī′sə kron), *n.* = isochrone.

i|soch|ro|nal (ī sok′rə nəl), *adj.* **1** equal or uniform in time. **2** performed or happening in equal periods of time. **3** characterized by motions or vibrations of equal duration. [< New Latin *isochronus* (< Greek *isóchronos* < *isos* equal + *chrónos* time) + English *-al*[1]] —**i|soch′ro|nal|ly,** *adv.*

i|so|chrone (ī′sə krōn), *n.* a line connecting points on a map where the same event occurs or would occur simultaneously. [< *iso-* + Greek *chrónos* time]

i|soch|ro|nism (ī sok′rə niz əm), *n.* isochronal character, property, or action: *Galileo discovered the isochronism of the pendulum.*

i|soch|ro|nize (ī sok′rə nīz), *v.t.,* **-nized, -niz|ing.** to make isochronal.

i|soch|ro|nous (ī sok′rə nəs), *adj.* = isochronal. —**i|soch′ro|nous|ly,** *adv.*

i|soch|ro|ous (ī sok′rō əs), *adj.* being of the same color throughout. [< *iso-* + Greek *chróā* color + English *-ous*]

i|so|cit|ric acid (ī′sə sit′rik), a crystalline isomer of citric acid produced during the Krebs cycle.

i|so|cli|nal (ī′sə klī′nəl), *adj., n.* —***adj.*** **1** of, having to do with, or indicating equal magnetic inclination; inclining or dipping in the same direction. **2** denoting or having to do with a line on a map drawn through points on the earth's surface at which the magnetic dip is the same. **3** *Geology.* (of strata) of or like an isocline.
—***n.*** an isoclinal line.
[< *iso-* + Greek *klī́nein* to dip, incline + English *-al*[1]] —**i′so|cli′nal|ly,** *adv.*

i|so|cline (ī′sə klīn), *n. Geology.* a fold of strata so tightly compressed that the parts on each side of the axis dip in the same direction.

i|so|clin|ic (ī′sə klin′ik), *adj., n.* = isoclinal.

i|soc|ra|cy (ī sok′rə sē), *n., pl.* **-cies.** a government in which all possess equal political power. [< Greek *isokratíā* balance of power < *isos* equal + *krátos* strength, power]

i|so|crat|ic (ī′sə krat′ik), *adj.* of, having to do with, or advocating isocracy.

i|so|cry|mal (ī′sə krī′məl), *n., adj.* —***n.*** = isocryme.
—***adj.*** of, having to do with, or containing an isocryme.

i|so|cryme (ī′sə krīm), *n.* a line on a map connecting points at which the temperature is the same during some specified coldest portion of the year. [< *iso-* + Greek *krȳmós* cold]

i|so|cy|a|nate (ī′sə sī′ə nāt), *n.* any one of a group of compounds containing the -NCO radical, used especially in making foams and resins.

i|so|cy|a|nine (ī′sə sī′ə nēn, -nin), *n.* any one of a group of dyes used in photography as sensitizing agents. [< *iso-* + *cyanine*]

i|so|cy|clic (ī′sə sī′klik), *adj. Chemistry.* of or having to do with a ring in which all the atoms are of the same element: *Carbocyclic compounds are isocyclic.*

i|so|di|a|met|ric (ī′sə dī′ə met′rik), *adj.* **1** having equal diameters or axes. **2** *Botany.* having the diameter similar throughout: *an isodiametric cell.* **3** (of crystals) having equal lateral axes.

i|so|di|mor|phism (ī′sō dī môr′fiz əm), *n. Mineralogy.* isomorphism between the forms of two dimorphous substances.

i|so|di|mor|phous (ī′sō dī môr′fəs), *adj. Mineralogy.* having the quality of isodimorphism.

i|so|dose (ī′sə dōs′), *adj., n.* —***adj.*** of, having to do with, or representing surfaces or areas receiving equal doses of radiation: *The radiologist is aided in his calculations by an isodose chart superimposed over the patient's body-section diagram* (Saturday Review).
—***n.*** any one of several surfaces or areas on a chart or on irradiated tissue, showing equal doses or intensities of radiation.
[< *iso-* + *dose*]

i|so|dy|nam|ic (ī′sō dī nam′ik), *adj.* **1** of or having equality of force, intensity, value, etc. **2** connecting points at which the intensity of the magnetic force is the same: *isodynamic lines on a map.*

i|so|dy|nam|i|cal (ī′sō dī nam′ə kəl), *adj.* = isodynamic.

i|so|e|lec|tric (ī′sō i lek′trik), *adj.* having equal electric potential; alike in potential.

isoelectric point, *Chemistry.* **1** the point at which a compound, such as a protein, neither accepts nor yields protons, commonly expressed in terms of pH value. **2** the point at which a colloidal particle has no significant excess of positive or negative charges so that it does not move in either direction in an electrical field.

i|so|e|lec|tron|ic (ī′sō i lek′tron′ik), *adj.* having an equal number of electrons outside the nucleus. —**i′so|e|lec′tron′i|cal|ly,** *adv.*

i|so|en|zyme (ī′sō en′zīm), *n.* one of the forms of an enzyme, differing chemically but not functionally, found in a single species of an organism; isozyme: *Chymotrypsin-A and chymotrypsin-B [a pair of digestive enzymes] are the most closely related, their sequences differing only in about 20 per cent of the positions, and as their catalytic activities and specifications are practically identical they can correctly be considered as isoenzymes—"twins" in the family* (New Scientist).

i|so|ga|mete (ī′sō gə mēt′, -gam′ēt), *n. Biology.* either of two gametes, not differing in character or behavior, which can unite with the other to form a zygote. The gametes of certain algae are isogametes.

i|so|ga|met|ic (ī′sō gə mē′tik, -gam′ē-), *adj.* of or having to do with isogametes.

i|sog|a|mous (ī sog′ə məs), *adj. Biology.* having two similar gametes; reproducing by the fusion of two similar gametes.

i|sog|a|my (ī sog′ə mē), *n. Biology.* the fusion of two similar gametes, as in certain algae. [< *iso-* + *-gamy*]

i|so|gen|ic (ī′sə jen′ik), *adj.* of, having to do with, or possessing isogeny.

i|sog|e|nous (ī soj′ə nəs), *adj. Biology.* having the same or a similar origin, as organs or parts derived from the same or corresponding tissue of the embryo.

i|sog|e|ny (ī soj′ə nē), *n. Biology.* identity or similarity of origin; origination in or derivation from the same or corresponding tissues. [< *iso-* + *-gen* + *-y*[3]]

i|so|ge|o|therm (ī′sə jē′ə thėrm), *n.* an imaginary line or surface passing through points in the interior of the earth that have the same mean temperature. [< *iso-* + *geo-* + Greek *thérmē* heat]

i|so|ge|o|ther|mal (ī′sə jē′ə thėr′məl), *adj.* **1** of or having to do with an isogeotherm. **2** like an isogeotherm.

i|so|ge|o|ther|mic (ī′sə jē′ə thėr′mik), *adj.* = isogeothermal.

i|so|gloss (ī′sə glôs, -glos), *n.* a line on a map separating areas that differ in a given feature of language, such as pronunciation or syntax. [< *iso-* + Greek *glôssa* tongue, word]

i|so|glos|sal (ī′sə glôs′əl, -glos′-), *adj.* of or having to do with isoglosses.

i|so|gon (ī′sə gon), *n. Geometry.* a figure whose angles are equal. [< Greek *isogṓnios* having equal angles < *isos* equal + *gōniā* angle]

i|sog|o|nal (ī sog′ə nəl), *adj., n.* —***adj.*** having equal angles; equiangular.
—***n.*** an isogonic line.

i|so|gon|ic (ī′sə gon′ik), *adj., n.* —***adj.*** **1** having equal angles; having to do with equal angles. **2** of or having to do with an isogonic line. **3** having equal deviations of the magnetic needle from the true north.
—***n.*** = isogonic line.

isogonic line, a line on a map connecting points on the earth's surface where the magnetic declination is the same.

i|so|graft (ī′sə graft′), *n.* = homograft.

i|so|gram (ī′sə gram), *n.* = isoline.

i|so|graph (ī′sə graf, -gräf), *n.* a line on a map indicating the limit of a linguistic feature or features; isogloss.

i|so|hel (ī′sə hel), *n.* a line on a weather map or an imaginary line drawn in space, connecting points receiving equal amounts of sunshine. [< *iso-* + Greek *hḗlios* the sun]

i|so|hy|et (ī′sə hī′ət), *n.* a line on a weather map or an imaginary line drawn in space, connecting points at which rainfall is equal. See diagram at **isoline.** [< *iso-* + Greek *hyetós* rain < *hȳein* to rain]

i|so|hy|e|tal (ī′sə hī′ə təl), *adj.* having to do with or marking equality of rainfall.

i|so|la|ble (ī′sə lə bəl, is′ə-), *adj.* that can be isolated.

i|so|lat|a|ble (ī′sə lā′tə bəl, is′ə-), *adj.* = that can be isolated.

i|so|late (ī′sə lāt, is′ə-), *v.,* **-lat|ed, -lat|ing,** *n., adj.* —***v.t.*** **1** to place apart; separate from others; keep alone: *People with contagious diseases should be isolated. It became the maxim of Tory statesmen that England should ... isolate herself from continental embarrassments* (William E. H. Lecky). **SYN:** segregate, detach. **2** *Chemistry.* to obtain (a substance) in an uncombined or pure state: *A chemist can isolate the oxygen from the hydrogen in water.* **3** *Electricity.* = insulate. **4** *Bacteriology.* to separate (a species or strain) in pure culture.
—***n.*** **1** *Psychology.* **a** a person who avoids social contacts. **b** a feature or quality that is considered by itself. **2** *Genetics.* a group of people or animals living in a limited or isolated environment. As a consequence of inbreeding over several generations, such groups tend to develop recessive hereditary defects more often than the general population. **3** *Microbiology.* an isolated virus or microorganism.
—***adj.*** separate; isolated: *He has become the essential American soul that D. H. Lawrence once characterized as "harsh, isolate, stoic ..."* (Time).
[back formation < *isolated* < French *isolé* < Italian *isolare* < Latin *īnsulāre* < *īnsula* island. See etym. of doublet **insulate.**]

i|so|lat|ed camera (ī′sə lā tid), a television videotape camera that is focused on a single player or a single area of play during a game in order to record action that will permit instant replay of any segment.

i|so|lat|ing (ī′sə lā′ting, is′ə-), *adj.* designating languages in which each element is an independent word, with meaning determined mainly by word order.

isolating mechanism, *Biology.* any feature of morphology or behavior that prevents interbreeding between populations.

i|so|la|tion (ī′sə lā′shən, is′ə-), *n.* **1** the act of isolating: *His isolation of the dog in the garage only made it bark more.* **2** the fact or condition of being isolated: *The real problem of leisure is to find places where increasing multitudes of people can simultaneously give themselves the illusion of isolation* (New Scientist). **SYN:** See syn. under **solitude. 3** complete separation.

isolation booth, a soundproof booth in a television studio or language or scientific laboratory, furnished with sound transmission or reproduction equipment.

i|so|la|tion|ism (ī′sə lā′shə niz əm, is′ə-), *n.* the principles or practice of a person who objects to his country's participation in political and economic relations with other nations.

i|so|la|tion|ist (ī′sə lā′shə nist, is′ə-), *n., adj.* —***n.*** **1** a person who objects to his country's participation in political and economic relations with other nations. **2** a person who favored keeping the United States out of the first or second World War.
—***adj.*** of or having to do with isolationists or isolationism: *We ... have given up our own isolationist thinking* (Harper's).

i|so|la|tion|is|tic (ī′sə lā′shə nis′tik), *adj.* having to do with or characterized by isolationism.

i|so|la|tive (ī′sə lā′tiv, is′ə-), *adj. Phonetics.* (of sound change) taking place independently of neighboring sounds.

i|so|la|tor (ī′sə lā′tər, is′ə-), *n.* **1** a person, place, or thing that isolates. **2** = glove box.

I|sol|de (i sol′də, -sōld′, -zōl′də), *n.* = Iseult.

i|so|leu|cine (ī′sə lü′sēn, -sin), *n.* an amino acid present in casein and body tissue, that is essential to the diet of man and animals. *Formula:* $C_6H_{13}NO_2$ [< *iso-* + *leucine*]

Pronunciation Key: hat, āge, cãre, fär; let, ēqual, tėrm; it, īce; hot, ōpen, ôrder; oil, out; cup, pu̇t, rüle; child; long; thin; ᴛʜen; zh, measure; ə represents **a** in about, **e** in taken, **i** in pencil, **o** in lemon, **u** in circus.

***i|so|line** (ī′sə līn′), *n.* = a line on a diagram, chart, or map, indicating equality of some physical condition or quantity, as isotherms and isobars; isogram. [< *iso-* + *line*]

***isoline**

isobar:

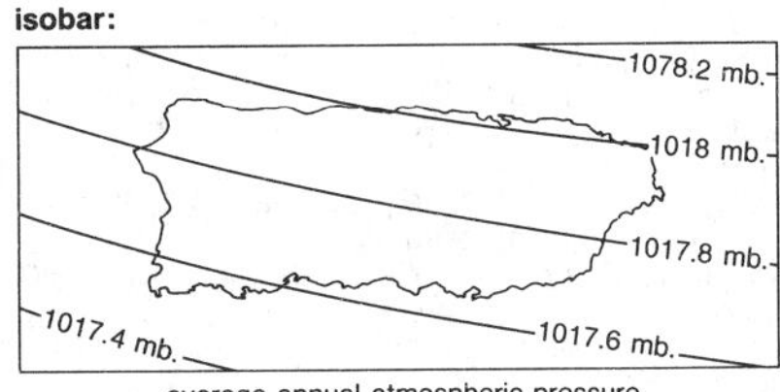

average annual atmospheric pressure

isobath:

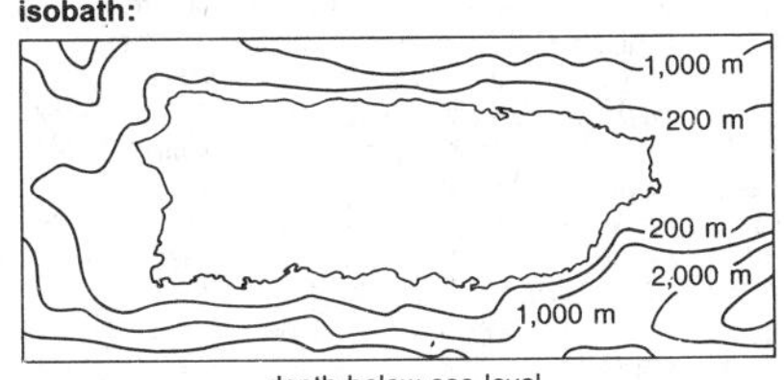

depth below sea level

isohyet:

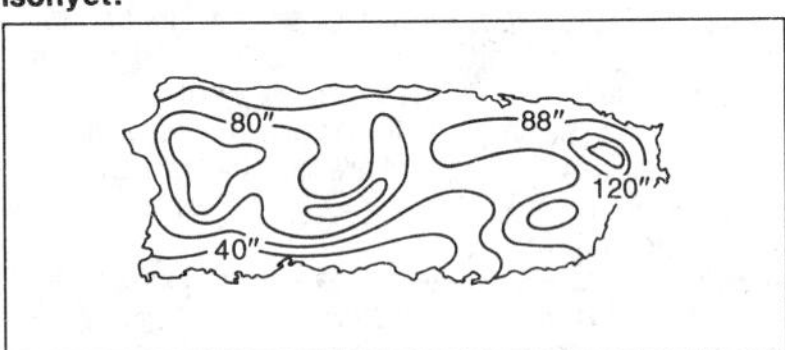

average annual rainfall

isotherm:

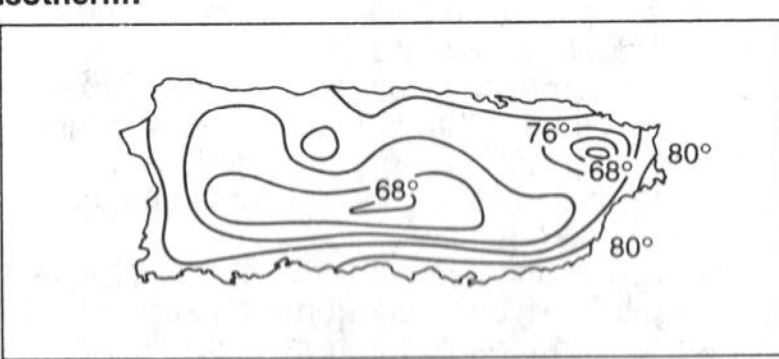

average annual temperature

i|sol|o|gous (ī sol′ə gəs), *adj. Chemistry.* having similar relations. In an isologous series of hydrocarbons, each member has two hydrogen atoms less than the one above it. [< *iso-* + Greek *lógos* word, relation + English *-ous*]

i|so|logue or **i|so|log** (ī′sə lôg, -log), *n. Chemistry.* an isologous compound.

I|solt (i sōlt′), *n.* = Iseult.

i|so|mag|net|ic (ī′sō mag net′ik), *adj., n.* — ***adj.*** **1** having or showing equality of magnetic force. **2** of or denoting a line on a map or chart connecting places that have the same magnetic properties. — ***n.*** an isomagnetic line.

i|so|mer (ī′sə mər), *n.* an isomeric compound, ion, atom, or nucleus. [< Greek *isomerḗs* sharing equally < *ísos* equal + *méros* part]

i|som|er|ase (ī som′ə rās), *n.* an enzyme that catalyzes the formation of an isomer or isomers.

i|so|mer|ic (ī′sə mer′ik), *adj.* **1** composed of the same chemical elements in the same proportions by weight, and (in the usual, restricted sense of the term) having the same molecular weight, but differing in at least one physical or chemical property because of the difference in arrangement of atoms. **2** (of the nuclei of atoms) differing in energy and behavior, but having the same atomic number and mass number.

i|som|er|ism (ī som′ə riz əm), *n.* the property or condition of being isomeric.

i|som|er|i|za|tion (ī som′ər ə zā′shən), *n.* the process by which a chemical is changed to an isomeric form.

i|som|er|ize (ī som′ə rīz), *v.t., v.i.,* **-ized, -iz|ing.** to change into an isomer.

i|som|er|ous (ī som′ər əs), *adj.* **1** having an equal number of parts, markings, etc. **2** *Botany.* (of a flower) having the same number of members in each whorl.

i|so|met|ric (ī′sə met′rik), *adj., n.* — ***adj.*** **1** having to do with equality of measure; having equality of measure. **2** having three equal axes at right angles to one another: *an isometric crystal.* See picture under **crystal. 3** *Physiology.* denoting lack of contraction of a muscle when under a constant tension. **4** having to do with or representing an isometric projection: *an isometric drawing.* **5** having to do with isometrics: *an isometric manual of physical fitness.* — ***n.*** *Physics.* isochor. [< Greek *isómetros* (< *ísos* equal + *métron* measure) + English *-ic*] — **i′so|met′ri|cal|ly,** *adv.*

i|so|met|ri|cal (ī′sə met′rə kəl), *adj.* = isometric.

isometric exercises, = isometrics.

***isometric projection,** the projection of an object upon a plane equally inclined to the object's three principal axes, so that dimensions parallel to these are represented in their true proportions.

***isometric projection**

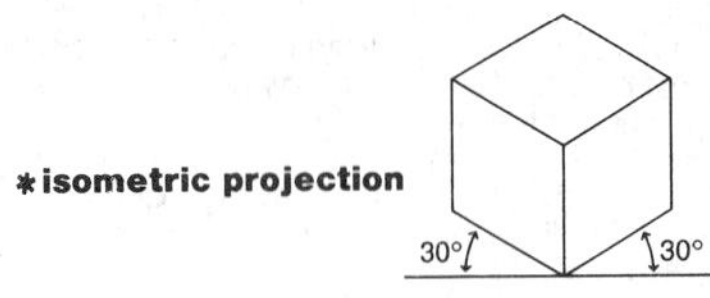

i|so|met|rics (ī′sə met′riks), *n.pl.* exercises which are intended to strengthen muscles by pressing one part of the body against another or against an immovable object, such as a wall.

i|so|me|tro|pi|a (ī′sō mə trō′pē ə), *n.* equal refraction in both eyes. [< *iso-* + Greek *métron* a measure + English *-opia* < Greek *ōps, ōpós* eye]

i|som|e|try (ī som′ə trē), *n.* equality of measure, especially of altitude.

i|so|morph (ī′sə môrf), *n.* **1** an isomorphous substance. **2** an organism isomorphic with another or others. [< *iso-* + Greek *morphḗ* form]

i|so|mor|phic (ī′sə môr′fik), *adj.* **1** *Biology.* having a similar appearance or structure, but belonging to different species or races. **2** = isomorphous. **3** in a one-to-one correspondence: *an isomorphic mathematical set.* — **i′so|mor′phi|cal|ly,** *adv.*

i|so|mor|phism (ī′sə môr′fiz əm), *n.* the property of being isomorphic or isomorphous.

i|so|mor|phous (ī′sə môr′fəs), *adj.* crystallizing in the same form or related forms (used especially of substances of analogous chemical compositions); isomorphic.

i|so|ni|a|zid (ī′sō nī′ə zid), *n.* a drug chemically related to an isomer of nicotinic acid, widely used in the treatment of tuberculosis. *Formula:* $C_6H_7N_3O$ [< *isoni*(cotinic acid) + (hydr)*azid*(e)]

i|so|nic|o|tin|ic acid (ī′sə nik′ə tin′ik), an acid synthesized from citric acid and other substances, that is the source of certain drugs used to treat tuberculosis. *Formula:* $C_6H_5NO_2$

i|so|nom|ic (ī′sə nom′ik), *adj.* of or having to do with isonomy; equal in law or rights.

i|son|o|my (ī son′ə mē), *n.* equality of laws, or of people before the law; equality of political rights. [< New Latin *isonomia* < Greek *isonomíā* possession of equal political rights < *ísos* equal + *nómos* law]

i|so|oc|tane (ī′sō ok′tān), *n.* an isomer of octane used in determining the octane number of gasoline. *Formula:* C_8H_{18}

i|so|pen|tane (ī′sə pen′tān), *n.* a flammable, liquid pentane with a boiling point near 80°F, derived from petroleum. It is used chiefly as a solvent. *Formula:* $(CH_3)_2CHCH_2CH_3$

i|so|pe|rim|e|ter (ī′sō pə rim′ə tər), *n. Geometry.* a figure equal in perimeter to another.

i|so|phot or **i|so|phote** (ī′sə fōt, -fot), *n.* a line drawn on a map or chart to connect points receiving equal light from a source, such as a star. [< *iso-* + Greek *phôs, phōtós* light]

i|soph|thal|ic acid (ī′sof thal′ik), an isomeric form of phthalic acid, used in the manufacture of paints and plastics. *Formula:* $C_8H_6O_4$

i|so|pi|es|tic (ī′sō pī es′tik), *adj., n.* — ***adj.*** of or denoting equal pressure; isobaric.
— ***n.*** a curve showing the relation between volume and temperature in a body or system whose pressure remains constant; isobar.
[< *iso-* + Greek *piestós* compressible (< *piézein* to squeeze, press) + English *-ic*]

i|so|pleth (ī′sə pleth), *n.* **1** a graph showing variations in occurrence or frequency of a phenomenon, especially in meteorology, with reference to two variables, such as time and space. **2** *Mathematics.* the straight line on a graph connecting the equal or corresponding values of the dependent and independent variables. [< Greek *isoplēthḗs* < *ísos* equal + *plêthos* number]

i|so|pod (ī′sə pod), *n., adj.* — ***n.*** a crustacean that has a flat, oval body, a short abdomen, and, usually, seven pairs of similar legs, such as the gribble or pill bug. The isopods constitute an order.
— ***adj.*** of or like an isopod.
[< New Latin *Isopoda* the order name < Greek *ísos* equal + *poús, podós* foot]

i|sop|o|dan (ī sop′ə dən), *n., adj.* = isopod.

i|sop|o|dous (ī sop′ə dəs), *adj.* = isopod.

i|so|po|lit|i|cal (ī′sō pə lit′ə kəl), *adj.* of or having to do with isopolity; involving mutual rights of citizenship.

i|so|pol|i|ty (ī′sə pol′ə tē), *n.* equality of rights of citizenship between different communities or states; mutual political rights. [< Greek *isopolīteíā* < *ísos* equal + *polī́tēs* citizen]

i|so|pren|a|line (ī′sə pren′ə lin, -lēn), *n.* = isoproterenol.

i|so|prene (ī′sə prēn), *n.* a colorless, volatile, liquid hydrocarbon of the terpene group, obtained chiefly as a distillation product of rubber and from turpentine. Isoprene is used in making synthetic rubber. *Formula:* C_5H_8 [< *iso-* + *pr*(opyl) + *-ene*]

i|so|pren|oid (ī′sə prē′noid), *adj., n.* — ***adj.*** having a chemical structure similar to that of isoprene.
— ***n.*** an isoprenoid compound: *Isoprenoids ... provide the architectural base for cholesterol and many other well known biological materials* (Science News Letter).

i|so|pro|pa|nol (ī′sə prō′pə nōl, -nol), *n.* a colorless, flammable liquid soluble in water, ether, and alcohol, used to make acetone, and as a solvent and rocket fuel; isopropyl alcohol. *Formula:* C_3H_8O

i|so|pro|pyl (ī′sə prō′pəl), *n.* a univalent radical, $(CH_3)_2CH$-. [< *iso-* + *propyl*]

isopropyl alcohol, = isopropanol.

isopropyl ether, a colorless liquid compound, used as a solvent. *Formula:* $C_6H_{14}O$

i|so|pro|te|re|nol (ī′sə prō′tə rē′nol), *n.* a compound related chemically to adrenalin, used to treat asthma and as a heart stimulant. *Formula:* $C_{11}H_{17}NO_3$

i|sop|ter|an (ī sop′tər ən), *n., adj.* — ***n.*** any one of the order of insects comprising the termites; termite.
— ***adj.*** of or belonging to this order.

i|sop|ter|ous (ī sop′tər əs), *adj.* having to do with or belonging to termites: *American isopterous insects have four wings that are all equal in size.* [< New Latin *Isoptera* the order name (< *iso-* equal + Greek *pterón* wing) + English *-ous*]

i|so|pyc|nic (ī′sə pik′nik), *adj.* of or having to do with equal density. [< *iso-* + Greek *pyknós* dense + English *-ic*]

i|so|pyre (ī′sə pīr), *n.* an impure variety of opal, sometimes used as a semiprecious stone, containing alumina, iron, and lime. [< *iso-* + Greek *pŷr* fire]

i|so|rhythm (ī′sə riᴛʜ′əm), *n. Music.* a technique characteristic of certain medieval motets, in which a rhythmic pattern is repeated over and over while the melody and other constituents of the music are free to vary: ... *the elaborate isorhythm of the fifteenth-century Burgundians* (Harper's).

i|so|rhyth|mic (ī′sə riᴛʜ′mik), *adj.* of or characterized by isorhythm: *This is an isorhythmic passacaglia, and a dazzling example of ... contrapuntal virtuosity and general technical mastery* (Listener).

***i|sos|ce|les** (ī sos′ə lēz), *adj.* (of a triangle or trapezoid) having two equal sides. [< Late Latin *isoscelēs* < Greek *isoskelḗs* with equal sides < *ísos* equal + *skélos* leg]

***isosceles**

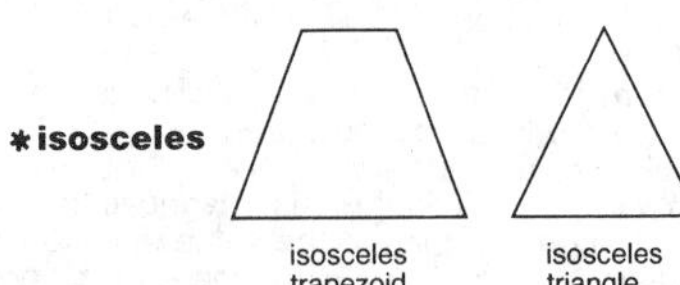
isosceles trapezoid — isosceles triangle

i|so|se|bac|ic acid (ī′sō sə bas′ik, -bā′sik), an acid produced from butadiene, used in the manufacture of plastics and lubricants.

i|so|seis|mal (ī′sə sīz′məl, -sīs′-), *adj., n.* — ***adj.*** **1** having to do with equal intensity of earthquake shock. **2** of or having to do with an imaginary line on the earth's surface connecting points characterized by such intensity.
— ***n.*** an isoseismal line.
[< *iso-* + Greek *seismós* earthquake + English *-al*[1]]

i|so|seis|mic (ī′sə sīz′mik, -sīs′-), *adj., n.* = isoseismal.

is|os|mot|ic (īs′os mot′ik), *adj.* of or containing equal osmotic pressure; isotonic: *an isosmotic medium.* [< *is-* + *osmotic*]

i|so|spin (ī′sō spin′), *n. Nuclear Physics.* a quantum number based on the theory that the neutron and proton are different states of the same particle: *Isospin is a number, with no simple physical meaning, that represents mathematically the difference between neutrons and protons* (Science News). [contraction of *isotopic spin*]

i|sos|ta|sy (ī sos′tə sē), *n.* **1** equilibrium of the earth's crust, believed to be due to the movement of rock material below the surface. **2** equilibrium or stability caused by equality of pressure; hydrostatic equilibrium. [< *iso-* + Greek *stásis* a stopping < *histánai* to stand]

i|so|stat|ic (ī′sə stat′ik), *adj.* having to do with or characterized by isostasy. — **i′so|stat′i|cal|ly,** *adv.*

i|so|ste|mo|nous (ī′sə stē′mə nəs, -stem′ə-), *adj.*

Botany. having the stamens equal in number to the sepals or petals. [< *iso-* + Greek *stēmōn* thread, but taken as equaling *stamen* (compare etym. under **pentstemon**) + English *-ous*]

i|so|tac|tic (ī′sō tak′tik), *adj.* of or having to do with a polymer which has its attached groups of atoms in a regular order on one side of the central chain of atoms.

i|so|ten|i|scope (ī′sə ten′ə skōp), *n.* an instrument for measuring the pressure at which a liquid and its vapor are at equilibrium at a given temperature. [< *iso-* + *ten-* (stem of Latin *tenēre* to hold) + *-scope*]

i|soth|er|al (ī soth′ər əl), *n., adj.* **—*n.*** = isothere. **—*adj.*** of, having to do with, or by means of isotheres: *an isotheral chart, isotheral lines.*

i|so|there (ī′sə thir), *n.* a line on a weather map or an imaginary line drawn in space connecting points that have the same mean summer temperature. See also **isocheim.** [< French *isothère* < *iso-* iso- + Greek *théros, -eos* summer]

i|so|therm (ī′sə thėrm), *n.* **1** a line on a weather map connecting places having the same average temperature. See diagram at **isoline. 2** = isothermal line. [< French *isotherme* < *iso-* iso- + Greek *thérmē* heat]

i|so|ther|mal (ī′sə thėr′məl), *adj., n.* **—*adj.* 1** having or indicating equal temperatures. **2** having to do with isotherms. **—*n.* 1** = isotherm. **2** = isothermal line. **—i′so|ther′mal|ly,** *adv.*

isothermal line or **curve, 1** a line or curve connecting points corresponding to pressure or volume changes, with the temperature of the substance constant. **2** = isotherm.

i|so|ther|mic (ī′sə thėr′mik), *adj.* = isothermal.

i|so|tone (ī′sə tōn), *n.* one of two or more atoms having an equal number of neutrons. [< *iso-* + Greek *tónos* tone, force, tension]

i|so|ton|ic (ī′sə ton′ik), *adj.* **1** *Chemistry, Physiology.* characterized by equal osmotic pressure; denoting or having to do with a solution containing just enough salt to prevent the destruction of the red blood corpuscles when added to the blood. A solvent isotonic with a solution will not pass through a semipermeable membrane and mix with the solution. **2** *Physiology.* denoting or having to do with a contraction of a muscle when under a constant tension. **3** *Music.* having to do with or characterized by equal tones. [< Greek *isótonos* of equal tension or tone (< *isos* equal + *tónos* tone) + English *-ic*] **—i′so|ton′i|cal|ly,** *adv.*

i|so|to|nic|i|ty (ī′sə tō nis′ə tē), *n.* isotonic quality or state.

i|so|tope (ī′sə tōp), *n.* any one of two or more forms of a chemical element that have the same chemical properties and the same atomic number, but different atomic weights and slightly different physical properties. Chlorine, whose atomic weight is 35.453, is a mixture of two isotopes, one having an atomic weight of 37, the other, 35. Hydrogen and heavy hydrogen are isotopes. Splitting of atoms can produce isotopes. [< *iso-* + Greek *tópos* place]

i|so|top|ic (ī′sə top′ik), *adj.* having to do with an isotope or isotopes; like an isotope. **—i′so|top′i|cal|ly,** *adv.*

isotopic spin, = isospin.

i|sot|o|py (ī sot′ə pē), *n.* the occurrence or existence of isotopes.

i|so|tron (ī′sə tron), *n.* a device that separates isotopes by the electrical sorting and collecting of ions. [< *iso* (tope) + *-tron*]

i|so|trop|ic (ī′sə trop′ik), *adj.* **1** *Physics.* having the same properties, such as elasticity or conduction, in all directions. **2** *Zoology.* without predetermined axes. [< *iso-* + Greek *trópos* turn, manner + English *-ic*] **—i′so|trop′i|cal|ly,** *adv.*

i|sot|ro|pous (ī sot′rə pəs), *adj.* = isotropic.

i|sot|ro|py (ī sot′rə pē), *n.* the state or property of being isotropic.

i|so|zyme (ī′sō zīm), *n.* = isoenzyme.

i|so|zy|mic (ī′sə zī′mik, -zim′ik), *adj.* of or having to do with isoenzymes.

Is|pa|han (is′pə hän), *n.* a handmade Persian rug, usually of deeply dyed wool decorated in natural motifs. [< *Ispahan,* a city in central Iran]

I-spy (ī′spī′), *n. Especially British.* hide-and-seek.

Isr., Israel.

ISR (no periods), intersecting storage rings (a type of particle accelerator consisting of two ring-shaped tracks in which nuclear particles are accelerated in opposite directions).

Is|ra|el (iz′rē əl), *n.* **1** a name given to Jacob after he had wrestled with the angel (in the Bible, Genesis 32:28). **2** a name given to his descendants; the Jews; the Hebrews. **3** *Figurative.* a people or group regarded as chosen by God; the elect. [< Hebrew *yisrā'ēl,* literally, "God strives," but later construed as meaning "he who wrestles with God"]

Is|rae|li (iz rā′lē), *n., pl.* **-lis,** *adj.* **—*n.*** a person born or living in modern Israel.

—*adj.* of or having to do with modern Israel.

Is|ra|el|ite (iz′rē ə līt), *n., adj.* **—*n.* 1** a Jew; a Hebrew; a descendant of Israel (Jacob).

2 *Figurative.* one of any group regarded as chosen by God.

—*adj.* of or having to do with Israel or the Jews; Hebrew; Jewish.

Is|ra|el|it|ic (iz′rē ə lit′ik), *adj.* = Israelitish.

Is|ra|el|it|ish (iz′rē ə lī′tish), *adj.* of the Israelites; Jewish; Hebrew.

Is|ra|fil (iz′rə fil, -fēl), *n.* the Moslem angel of music, who will blow the final trumpet on Judgment Day.

iss., issue.

Is|sa (is′ə), *n., pl.* **-sas** or **-sa.** a member of a Hamitic people in Djibouti (the former French Territory of Afars and Issas).

Is|sa|char (is′ə kär), *n.* **1** the ninth son of Jacob, by Leah (in the Bible, Genesis 30:18). **2** the Israelite tribe that claimed him as ancestor.

Is|sei (ēs′sā′), *n., pl.* **-sei.** a Japanese immigrant to the United States or Canada. [American English < Japanese *is-sei* first generation < *ichi* one + *sei* generation]

is|su|a|ble (ish′ü ə bəl), *adj.* **1** that can issue. **2** that can be issued; authorized to be issued, as bonds or currency. **3** *Law.* that can be made an issue. **—is′su|a|bly,** *adv.*

is|su|ance (ish′ü əns), *n.* the action of issuing; issue.

is|su|ant (ish′ü ənt), *adj.* **1** issuing; emerging. **2** *Heraldry.* showing only the upper half: *an issuant lion in a coat of arms.*

is|sue (ish′ü; *especially British* is′yü), *v.,* **-sued, -su|ing,** *n.* **—*v.t.* 1** to send out; put forth: *The government issues money and stamps.* **2** to put into public circulation; publish: *This magazine is issued every week. Warnings to jaywalkers were issued by the police. Many reprints of "Tom Sawyer" have been issued.* **SYN:** print. **3** to distribute to a person or persons: *Every student was issued a geography book on the first day of school. Each soldier was issued a rifle.* **4** to send forth; discharge; emit: *The chimney issues smoke from the fireplace.*

—*v.i.* 1 to come out; go out; proceed: *Smoke issues from the chimney. The vital spirit issued at the wound* (Alexander Pope). **2** to be published: *when the proclamation issued* (Thomas Jefferson). **3** to emerge. **4** to result or end (in): *The game issued in a tie.* **5** to result (from). **6** *Law.* to be born; be descended; be derived. **7** *Law.* to come as a yield or profit, as from land. [< noun]

—*n.* 1 something sent out; quantity (of bonds, stamps, copies of a magazine, or other publications) sent out at one time: *The last issue of our weekly paper consisted of 1,000 copies.* **2** the act of sending out; putting forth: *The government controls the issue of stamps.* **3a** the act of coming forth; flowing out; a discharge: *A nosebleed is an issue of blood from the nose.* **SYN:** outflow. **b** a cut to enable blood or pus to flow out. **4** a way out; outlet; exit. **5** something that comes out. **6** profit; production. **7** result; outcome: *The issue of the battle was in doubt.* **SYN:** conclusion, upshot. **8** a point to be debated; problem: *The voters had four issues to settle at the polls. Peace is one of the issues of this political campaign. Some awful moment to which Heaven has joined great issues, good or bad for human kind* (Wordsworth). **9** a child or children; offspring: *The old bachelor died without issue.*

at (or **in**) **issue, a** in question; to be considered or decided: *The matter really at issue was who was to be master.* **b** in disagreement: *The boys were at issue as to who would captain the team. Your views and mine ... are decisively at issue* (William Godwin).

face the issue, to admit the facts and do what must be done: *The strike can only be settled if both sides face the issue.*

join issue, a to take opposite sides in an argument: *We shall be very ready to join issue with them upon this very point* (Daniel Waterland). **b** to submit a disputed point jointly for legal decision: *Subject to the last preceding rule, the plaintiff by his reply may join issue upon the defence* (John J. S. Wharton).

make an issue (of), to provoke argument or discussion (of): *It doesn't pay to make an issue of such a trifle.*

take issue, to disagree: *I must take issue with you on that point.*

[< Old French *issue,* earlier *eissue,* (originally) feminine past participle < *issir,* earlier *eissir* go out < Latin *exīre* < *ex-* out + *īre* go] **—is′sue|less,** *adj.* **—is′su|er,** *n.*

—*Syn.* *v.i.* 1, 3 Issue, emerge, emanate mean to come out. **Issue** means to go or come out, usually through an opening, from a source or place where it has been confined, and often suggests flowing out in a moving mass like water: *Pus issued from the wound.* **Emerge** means to come into sight from a place where it has been hidden or covered up: *The train emerged from the tunnel.* **Emanate,** used only of things without physical body, means to flow out from a source: *Heat emanates from fire. The story emanated from the mayor's office.*

-ist, *suffix forming nouns chiefly from other nouns.* **1** a person who does or makes: *Tourist = a person who tours.*

2 an expert in an art or science: *Botanist = an expert in botany.*

3 a person who plays a musical instrument: *Organist* = a person who plays the organ.

4 a person engaged in or working with: *Journalist = a person engaged in journalism. Machinist = a person working with machines.*

5 a person who believes in: *Socialist = a person who believes in socialism.*

[< Greek (directly or through Latin *-ista*) *-istēs,* a noun suffix]

isth., isthmus.

isth|mi|an (is′mē ən), *adj., n.* **—*adj.*** of or having to do with an isthmus; situated in an isthmus; forming an isthmus: *an isthmian tour.* **—*n.*** a native or inhabitant of an isthmus.

Isth|mi|an (is′mē ən), *adj.* **1** of or having to do with the Isthmus of Panama. **2** of or having to do with the Isthmus of Corinth in Greece.

Isthmian games, a national festival of ancient Greece, celebrated every two years on the Isthmus of Corinth.

isth|mus (is′məs), *n., pl.* **-mus|es, -mi** (-mī). **1** a narrow strip of land with water on both sides of it, connecting two larger bodies of land: *The Isthmus of Panama connects North America and South America.* See picture under **peninsula.** **2** *Anatomy.* a narrow part of an organ connecting two larger parts or cavities. [< Latin *isthmus* < Greek *isthmós*]

is|tle (is′tlē), *n.* **1** a fiber obtained from the leaves of certain tropical American agaves, used in making bags, carpets, cordage, and nets. **2** a similar fiber, obtained chiefly from a wild pineapple. Also, **ixtle.** [earlier *ixtli* < Mexican Spanish *ixtle* < Nahuatl *ichtli*]

Is|tri|an (is′trē ən), *adj., n.* **—*adj.*** of or having to do with Istria, a peninsula in northwestern Yugoslavia extending into the Adriatic Sea.

—*n.* a native or inhabitant of Istria.

it (it), *pron., sing. nom.* **it,** *poss.* **its** or (*Obsolete or Dialect*) **it,** *obj.* **it;** *pl. nom.* **they,** *poss.* **their** or **theirs,** *obj.* **them,** *n.* **—*pron.* 1** the thing, part, animal, or person spoken about: *Here is your paper; read it. Look at it carefully. He said, "It is I."* **2** the subject of an impersonal verb: *It rains. It is cold. What is it you want? It snows in winter. It is now my turn.* **3** an apparent subject of a clause when the logical subject comes later: *It is hard to believe that he is dead.* **4** the antecedent to any relative pronoun when separated by the predicate: *It was a blue car that passed.* **5** an object without definite force or reference: *They lorded it over us. Confound it!*

—*n.* 1 the player who must catch, find, guess, or otherwise get something in certain games. **2** *Slang.* sex appeal.

[Old English *hit*]

It., 1 Italian. **2** Italy.

ITA¹ (no periods) or **i.t.a.,** Initial Teaching Alphabet (a code supposedly to give closer phonetic regularity than traditional spelling).

I.T.A. or **ITA²** (no periods), Independent Television Authority (Great Britain's commercial television network, replaced in 1971 by the Independent Broadcasting Authority, or I.B.A.).

it|a|col|u|mite (it′ə kol′yə mīt), *n.* a granular quartzite that is very flexible when found in thin slabs. [< *Itacolumi,* a mountain in Brazil]

it|a|con|ic acid (it′ə kon′ik), an organic acid produced by fermentation of glucose, used in paints, plastics, and other chemical products. *Formula:* $C_5H_6O_4$ [an anagram of *aconitic*]

i|tai-i|tai (ē′tī ē′tī), *n.* a bone and kidney disease caused by the ingestion of cadmium from contaminated fish and shellfish: *Another painful new disease called itai-itai* (*literally, ouch-ouch*) *derived from cadmium flowing ... from a mining and smelting factory* (Time). [< Japanese *itai-itai,* reduplication of *itai,* a cry of pain]

ital., 1 italic. **2** italics.

Ital., 1 Italian. **2** Italy.

I|ta|lia (*Italian* ē tä′lyä; *Latin* i tal′ē ə, -yə), *n.* the Latin and Italian name of Italy.

I|tal|ian (i tal′yən), *adj., n.* **—*adj.*** of Italy, its people, or their language.

—*n.* 1 a person born or living in Italy. **2** the Romance language of Italy. **—I|tal′ian|ness,** *n.*

Pronunciation Key: hat, āge, cãre, fär; let, ēqual, tėrm; it, īce; hot, ōpen, ôrder; oil, out; cup, pu̇t, rüle; child; long; thin; ᴛʜen; zh, measure; ə represents **a** in about, **e** in taken, **i** in pencil, **o** in lemon, **u** in circus.

▶ The pronunciation (ī tal′yən) is substandard.

I|tal|ian|ate (*adj.* i tal′yə nāt, -nit; *v.* i tal′yə nāt), *adj., v.,* **-at|ed, -at|ing.** —***adj.*** of Italian character, form, or aspect: *the house most commodiously built in the French fashion, or perhaps Italianate* (Robert Louis Stevenson).
—***v.t.*** to Italianize.

Italian broccoli, the variety of broccoli commonly grown in the United States, originally from southern Europe; sprouting broccoli.

Italian clover, = crimson clover.

Italian corn salad, a species of valerian with pink flowers, found in southern Europe and grown in North America as a potherb.

Italian greyhound, any small dog of a breed resembling miniature greyhounds, weighing from 6 to 10 pounds.

I|tal|ian|ism (i tal′yə niz əm), *n.* **1** an Italian practice, trait, or idiom. **2** Italian quality, spirit, or principles. **3** attachment to Italy or sympathy with Italian ideas, customs, or the like.

I|tal|ian|ize (i tal′yə nīz), *v.t., v.i.,* **-ized, -iz|ing.** to make or become Italian in habits, customs, or character. —**I|tal′ian|i|za′tion,** *n.*

Italian overture, *Music.* a type of baroque overture having three movements in a fast-slow-fast tempo.

Italian ryegrass, an annual, or short-lived, perennial grass, grown in Europe and North America for pasture and hay.

Italian sonnet, a type of sonnet established by Dante and Petrarch; Petrarchan sonnet. It has two parts, the first eight lines (octave) rhyming *abba abba* and the last six lines (sestet) rhyming in two's or three's, *cd cd cd, cde cde,* etc.

i|tal|ic** (i tal′ik, ī-), *adj., n.* —adj.*** of or in type whose letters slant to the right: *These words are in italic type.*
—***n.*** an italic type, letter, or number.
italics, type whose letters slant to the right. Italics are used to set off book titles, foreign words and expressions, and other matter from the main body of material.
[< *Italic* (because it was introduced by an Italian printer from Venice)]
▶ **italics.** In manuscript, both longhand and typewritten, italics are indicated by underlining.

***italic** *The World Book Dictionary*

I|tal|ic (i tal′ik), *adj., n.* —***adj.*** of ancient Italy, its people, or their languages.
—***n.*** a division of Indo-European languages including Latin and other ancient dialects of Italy, such as Oscan and Umbrian.
[< Latin *Italicus* < *Ītalia* Italy]

I|tal|i|cism (i tal′ə siz əm), *n.* = Italianism.

i|tal|i|ci|za|tion (i tal′ə sə zā′shən, ī-), *n.* the act of italicizing: *The italicization is mine; but comment I have none* (W. Sharp).

i|tal|i|cize (i tal′ə sīz, ī-), *v.,* **-cized, -ciz|ing.**
—***v.t.*** **1** to print in type in which the letters slant to the right. **2** to underline (written words) with a single line to indicate italics. We italicize expressions which we wish to distinguish or emphasize.
—***v.i.*** to use italics.

Italo-, *combining form.* **1** of Italy; of the Italians: *Italophile = friend of Italy or the Italians.*
2 Italian and ____: *Italo-American = Italian and American.*

I|tal|o-A|mer|i|can (i tal′ō ə mer′ə kən), *adj., n.*
—***adj.*** **1** Italian and American: *Italo-American relations, an Italo-American treaty.* **2** of or having to do with Americans of Italian descent: *the Italo-American community.*
—***n.*** an American of Italian descent.

I|tal|o|phile (i tal′ə fīl, -fil), *n., adj.* —***n.*** a friend or admirer of Italy or the Italians. —***adj.*** friendly to or admiring Italy, the Italians, or Italian culture.

itch (ich), *n., v.* —***n.*** **1** a prickling feeling in the skin that makes one want to scratch: *to have an itch from a mosquito bite.* **2** *Figurative.* a restless, uneasy feeling, longing, or desire for anything: *People often have an itch to explore.* [Old English *gicce*]
—***v.i.*** **1** to cause a prickling feeling in the skin: *Mosquito bites itch.* **2** to have a prickling feeling in the skin: *My nose itches.* **3** *Figurative.* to have an uneasy desire or craving: *He itched to find out our secret. Their hands had felt Queen Ino's gold, And itched for more* (William Morris).
—***v.t.*** to cause to itch: *This wool shirt itches my back.*
the itch, a contagious disease of the skin caused by a tiny mite, accompanied by a prickling feeling; scabies: *There really is a special parasite which gives rise to the itch* (Robert T. Hulme).
[Old English *giccan*]

itch|ing palm (ich′ing), a great desire for gain; greedy disposition.

itch mite, a parasitic mite that burrows under the skin of men and animals, causing a dermatitis.

itch|y (ich′ē), *adj.,* **itch|i|er, itch|i|est. 1** that itches; itching: *an itchy sore, itchy skin.* **2** *Figurative.* restless; impatient: *Buyers had money to spare and, like the ordinary investors, were getting itchy fingers* (Manchester Guardian Weekly). *He got itchy feet, quit school at 16 and ... sailed for Canada* (Maclean's). —**itch′i|ly,** *adv.* —**itch′i-ness,** *n.*

itch|y-fin|gered (ich′ē fing′gərd), *adj.* **1** having a restless trigger finger: *an itchy-fingered gunman.* **2** = light-fingered: *Some Macy stores install dummy cameras ... in plain sight to discourage itchy-fingered customers* (Wall Street Journal).

it'd (it′əd), **1** it had. **2** it would.

-ite[1], *suffix forming nouns.* **1** a native or inhabitant of ____: *Canaanite = a native or inhabitant of Canaan.*
2 a descendant of ____: *Israelite = a descendant of Israel.*
3 a follower or supporter of ____: *Trotskyite = a follower or supporter of Leon Trotsky.*
4 resembling, derived from, or having the property of ____: *Ebonite = resembling ebony.*
5 a mineral species, or a rock substance, as in *hematite, humboldtite.*
6 a fossil, as in *trilobite, lignite.*
7 a segment of a part of a body, as in *dendrite.*
8 a person associated with, as in *laborite.*
9 a substance of organic origin; an explosive; a commercial product, as in *dynamite, Bakelite.*
[< French *-ite* (< Latin *-īta, -ītēs*) or < Latin (< Greek *-ítēs*), or directly < Greek]

-ite[2], *suffix forming nouns.* ester or salt of an acid whose name ends in *-ous,* as in *phosphite, sulfite, nitrite.* [< French *-ite,* alteration of *-ate* -ate[2]]

i|tem (ī′təm), *n., adv., v.* —***n.*** **1** a separate thing or article: *The shopping list had twelve items on it, mostly groceries.* **2** a piece of news; bit of information: *There were several interesting items in yesterday's paper.* **3** *Obsolete.* **a** an admonition; warning: *He ... has need of an item, to caution him to take heed every moment of the day* (John Bunyan). **b** an intimation; hint.
—***adv.*** also; likewise (used in introducing each item of an enumeration).
—***v.t.*** to set down or enter as an item or by items.
[< Latin *item,* adverb, likewise < *ita* thus]
—***Syn.*** ***n.*** **1 Item, detail, particular** mean a separate thing that is part of a whole. **Item** applies to a separate thing included in a list, account, or total, or to an article listed: *An itemized accound should list every item.* **Detail** applies to a separate thing that is part of something put together or done: *His report gave all the details.* **Particular** applies to a detail or item that is very small or insignificant: *Nobody wants to hear all the particulars of your troubles.*

i|tem|ise (ī′tə mīz), *v.t.,* **-ised, -is|ing.** *Especially British.* itemize.

i|tem|ize (ī′tə mīz), *v.t.,* **-ized, -iz|ing.** to give each item of; list by items: *to itemize the cost of a house. The storekeeper itemized the bill to show the price of each article.* —**i′tem|i|za′tion,** *n.* —**i′tem|iz′er,** *n.*

item veto, *U.S.* a veto of only part of a bill passed by a legislature and not of the entire bill. In some states, the governor may use this veto, but the Constitution does not grant it to the President.

it|er|ance (it′ər əns), *n.* repetition; iteration.

it|er|ant (it′ər ənt), *adj.* repeating; iterating. [< Latin *iterāns, -antis,* present participle of *iterāre* iterate]

it|er|ate (it′ə rāt), *v.t.,* **-at|ed, -at|ing. 1** to say again or repeatedly; repeat: *iterating and speaking again that which thou hast heard* (Ecclesiasticus 41:23). **2** to do (something) over again; perform or present a second time: *the iterated nodes of a sea-shell* (Emerson). [< Latin *iterāre* (with English -ate[1]) < *iterum* again] —**it′er|a′tion,** *n.*

it|er|a|tive (it′ə rā′tiv, -ər ə tiv), *adj.* **1** repeating; full of repetitions. **2** *Grammar.* frequentative. —**it′er|a′tive|ly,** *adv.* —**it′er|a′tive|ness,** *n.*

ith|er (iᴛʜ′ər), *adj., pron., adv. Scottish.* other.

I|thunn or **I|thun** (ē′ᴛʜün), *n. Norse Mythology.* the goddess of spring and youth, wife of Bragi, and keeper of the gods' golden apples of youth.

ith|y|phal|lic (ith′ə fal′ik), *adj., n.* —***adj.*** **1** having to do with the phallus carried in processions at festivals of Bacchus. **2** grossly indecent; obscene. **3** (in ancient prosody) of or composed in one of the meters used in hymns sung at the festivals of Bacchus, especially in lines of three trochees.
—***n.*** **1** a poem in ithyphallic meter; lines of three trochees. **2** an indecent poem.
[< Latin *īthyphallicus* < Greek *īthyphallikós* < *ithýphallos* the phallic symbol < *ithýs* erect + *phallós* phallus]

itin., itinerary.

i|tin|er|a|cy (ī tin′ər ə sē, i-), *n.* = itinerancy.

i|tin|er|an|cy (ī tin′ər ən sē, i-), *n.* **1** a traveling from place to place. **2** a body of itinerant preachers or judges. **3** official work requiring much travel from place to place, or frequent changes of residence.

i|tin|er|ant (ī tin′ər ənt, i-), *adj., n.* —***adj.*** traveling from place to place, especially in connection with some employment or vocation: *an itinerant judge. In 1739 arrived among us from Ireland the Reverend Mr. Whitefield ... an itinerant preacher* (Benjamin Franklin).
—***n.*** a person who travels from place to place.
[< Late Latin *itinerāns, -antis,* present participle of *itinerārī* to travel < Latin *iter* journey < *īre* to go] —**i|tin′er|ant|ly,** *adv.*

i|tin|er|ar|y (ī tin′ə rer′ē, i-), *n., pl.* **-ar|ies,** *adj.*
—***n.*** **1** a route of travel; plan of travel. **2** a record or journal of travel. **3** a guidebook for travelers.
—***adj.*** **1** of traveling or routes of travel. **2** = itinerant.

i|tin|er|ate (ī tin′ə rāt, i-), *v.i.,* **-at|ed, -at|ing.** to travel from place to place, especially in connection with some employment or vocation. [< Latin *itinerārī* (with English *-ate*[1]); see etym. under **itinerant**]

i|tin|er|a|tion (ī tin′ə rā′shən, i-), *n.* the act of traveling from place to place; tour.

-itious, *combining form.* of or having the nature of: *Fictitious = having the nature of fiction.* [< Latin *-īcius, -icius,* and *-itius*]

-itis, *suffix forming nouns.* **1** inflammation of; inflammatory disease of, as in *appendicitis, tonsillitis, bronchitis.*
2 state of mind or tendency fancifully regarded as a disease, as in *telephonitis.*
[< Greek *-ītis,* feminine of adjective suffix *-ītēs*]

it'll (it′əl), **1** it will: *It'll make too much noise.* **2** it shall.

ITO (no periods) or **I.T.O.,** International Trade Organization.

its (its), *adj. possessive form of* **it.** of it; belonging to it: *The dog wagged its tail.* [< *it* + *-s,* genitive suffix]

it's (its), **1** it is: *It's later than you think.* **2** it has: *It's been a long time.*

it|self (it self′), *pron.* **1** the form of **it** used to make a statement stronger: *The land itself is worth the money, without the house.* **2** the form of **it** used instead of *it, him,* or *her* in cases like: *The horse tripped and hurt itself. The dog saw itself in the mirror.* **3** its normal or usual self: *After a few minor repairs my car was itself again.*

it|sy-bit|sy (it′sē bit′sē), *adj. Informal.* very small; teeny-weeny: *This sort of itsy-bitsy coverage is totally inadequate for such a comprehensive subject* (London Times). [apparently < children's speech]

ITT (no periods), International Telephone and Telegraph Corporation.

it|ty-bit|ty (it′ē bit′ē), *adj.* = itsy-bitsy.

ITU (no periods) or **I.T.U., 1** International Telecommunication Union. **2** International Typographical Union.

ITV[1] (no periods) or **I.T.V.,** Independent Television (the commercial television of Great Britain).

ITV[2] (no periods), **1** industrial television (closed-circuit television used in industry). **2** instructional television: *With certain honorable exceptions, ITV has merely transferred conventional teaching techniques to the screen or served as a conduit for other media: films, slides, etc.* (Saturday Review).

-ity, *suffix forming nouns from adjectives.* the condition, quality, or fact of being ____: *Timidity = the condition of being timid. Sincerity = the condition or quality of being sincere.* Also, **-ty.** [< Old French *-ite* < Latin *-itās*]

It|za (it sä′), *n., pl.* **-za** or **-zas.** a member of a warrior tribe, probably of Toltec origin, that ruled most of Yucatán from the 900's to about 1200.

IU (no periods), international unit.

IUCD (no periods), intrauterine contraceptive device.

IUCN (no periods), International Union for Conservation of Nature and Natural Resources.

IUD (no periods) or **I.U.D.,** intrauterine device (a contraceptive device).

IUE (no periods) or **I.U.E.,** International Union of Electrical Workers.

-ium, *suffix.* chemical element or radical, as in *curium, sodium, ammonium.* [< New Latin *-ium* < Latin *-ium,* a neuter suffix]

IUPAC (no periods), International Union of Pure and Applied Chemistry.

I.U.S., International Union of Students.

i.v., 1 initial velocity. **2** intravenous; intravenously.

IV (no periods) or **I.V.,** intravenous; intravenously.

I've (īv), I have: *I've got nothing to do, and I've been bored stiff.*

-ive, *suffix forming adjectives from nouns.* **1** of or having to do with, as in *interrogative, inductive.* **2** tending to; likely to, as in *appreciative, active, imitative.*

[< Old French *-ive,* feminine of *-if* < Latin *-īvus,* and *-ivus;* or directly < Latin]

i|vied (ī′vēd), *adj.* covered or overgrown with ivy: *Upon an ivied stone Reclined his lanquid head* (Shelley).

I|vo|ri|an (ī′vər ē ən, īv′rə-), *adj., n.* —*adj.* of or belonging to the Ivory Coast, a country in western Africa.
—*n.* a native or inhabitant of the Ivory Coast.

i|vo|ried (ī′vər ēd, īv′rēd), *adj.* finished to resemble ivory: *an ivoried tabletop.*

i|vo|rist (ī′vər ist), *n.* a worker in ivory.

i|vo|ry (ī′vər ē, īv′rē), *n., pl.* **-ries,** *adj.* —*n.* **1a** a hard white substance making up the tusks of elephants or walruses. Ivory is a form of dentin and is used for piano keys, billiard balls, combs, and ornaments. **b** a tusk, such as that of an elephant. **2** a substance like ivory. **3** a creamy white.
—*adj.* **1** made of ivory: *an ivory carving of an elephant.* **2** of or like ivory: *the ivory chill of his look.* **3** creamy-white: *her beautiful ivory-colored complexion.*
ivories, *Slang.* **a** piano keys: *He handles the ivories like a real piano buff.* **b** dice: *The gambler's ivories were loaded.* **c** teeth: *... the swarthy tint, the grinning ivories ... and twinkling little eyes of the immortal governor of Barataria* (G. A. Sala). **d** billiard balls: *On new premises ... where erstwhile the click of ivories was heard* (Sporting Life).
[< Anglo-French *ivorie,* Old North French *ivurie* < Latin *eboreus* of ivory < *ebur, -oris* ivory < Egyptian *āb* elephant]

i|vo|ry-bill (ī′vər ē bil′, īv′rē-), *n.* = ivory-billed woodpecker.

i|vo|ry-billed woodpecker (ī′vər ē bild′, īv′rē-), a woodpecker with an ivory-white bill and flaming red crest, the largest of all North American woodpeckers. It inhabited the forests of the southern United States but is near extinction.

ivory black, 1 a fine black coloring matter made by burning ivory, used in painting. **2** = boneblack.

ivory gull, a small, black-legged, all-white gull of arctic regions.

ivory nut, 1 the nutlike seed of a South American palm tree that is white and very hard when dry. It is used to make buttons, chessmen, and small ornaments. **2** a similar seed obtained from other palms.

ivory palm, a palm tree native to South America with a short trunk, slender, featherlike leaves, and fragrant flowers.

ivory tower, a place or condition of withdrawal from the world of action into a world of ideas and dreams; aloofness: *Administrators with training outside the ivory towers of scholarship are obviously required* (Wall Street Journal). *The land-grant colleges broke with the concept of the ivory tower—scholarship remote from the realities of everyday life and workaday problems* (Fred M. Hechinger).

i|vo|ry-tow|er (ī′vər ē tou′ər, īv′rē-), *adj.* = ivory-towered.

i|vo|ry-tow|ered (ī′vər ē tou′ərd, īv′rē-), *adj.* withdrawn from the world of action; aloof; abstracted: *The scientists ... find refuge in an ivory-towered, secure theoretical world* (Newsweek).

i|vo|ry-tow|er|ish (ī′vər ē tou′ər ish, īv′rē-), *adj.* tending to abstract, speculative, or impractical thought or behavior.

i|vo|ry-tow|er|ism (ī′vər ē tou′ər iz əm, īv′rē-), *n.* the condition of being withdrawn or distant from the world of action.

i|vo|ry|type (ī′vər ē tīp, īv′rē-), *n.* a kind of picture in which a light print, made translucent by varnish and tinted on the back, is placed over a stronger print, so as to give the effect of a photograph in natural colors.

i|vo|ry-white (ī′vər ē hwīt′, īv′rē-), *adj.* having a creamy-white color; of the color of ivory.

I.V.S., International Voluntary Services (a U.S. organization of volunteers who work on farms and in cities of underdeveloped countries).

***i|vy** (ī′vē), *n., pl.* **i|vies. 1** a climbing plant with smooth, shiny, evergreen leaves; English ivy. It belongs to the ginseng family and is grown for ornament on walls and buildings. It is native to Europe and parts of Asia, and bears clusters of greenish-yellow flowers, followed by dark berries. **2** any one of various other climbing plants, such as American ivy, Japanese ivy, or poison ivy. [Old English *īfig*] —**i′vy|like′,** *adj.*

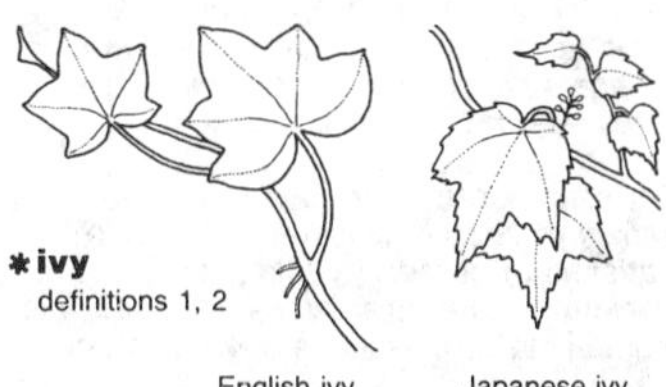

***ivy** definitions 1, 2

I|vy (ī′vē), *adj. Slang.* Ivy League.

ivy bush, 1 a plant or bushy branch of ivy. **2** this plant, or a representation of it, formerly placed outside a tavern as a sign that wine was sold there.

ivy geranium, a trailing geranium with ivylike leaves and purple or pink flowers.

Ivy League, 1 a group of eight old and prestigious universities of the northeastern United States, Brown, Columbia, Cornell, Dartmouth, Harvard, Pennsylvania, Princeton, and Yale. **2** having to do with or characteristic of the Ivy League, especially as traditionally marked by conservatism, restraint, and behavior and attitudes favorable to cultural life of the community. **3** the students or faculty of one or all of these colleges. **4** suitable for or popular in the Ivy League; restrained, as in colors or style: *an Ivy League suit, Ivy League fashions.*

Ivy Leaguer, a student or alumnus of any of the colleges of the Ivy League.

ivy tod, *Archaic.* an ivy bush.

ivy vine, a vinelike plant of the grape family, with heart-shaped leaves, growing in the eastern and central United States.

I.W., Isle of Wight.

i|wan (ē′won), *n.* (in Persian and Islamic architecture) a vaulted hall that is open on one side: *The Congregation Mosque ... consisted of four monumental iwans opening on a central courtyard* (Oleg Grabar). [< Arabic and Persian]

i|wis (i wis′), *adv. Archaic.* certainly; indeed. [Old English *gewis*]

IWW (no periods) or **I.W.W.,** Industrial Workers of the World.

I.X., Jesus Christ (Greek *Iesous Christos.* In the Greek alphabet χ represents a sound that is equated with English *ch,* as in *Christ,* and is so transliterated).

ix|i|a (ik′sē ə), *n.* any one of a group of South African plants of the iris family, having grasslike leaves and spikes of large showy flowers. [< New Latin *Ixia* the genus name < Latin *ixia* a plant whose flowers can change colors < Greek *ixiā* (literally) birdlime (because of its sticky resin)]

Ix|i|on (ik sī′ən), *n. Greek Legend.* the father of the centaurs, who made love to Hera and was punished by Zeus by being bound to an eternally revolving fiery wheel in Hades.

ix|tle (iks′tlē, is′-), *n.* = istle.

I|yar or **Iy|yar** (ē′yär), *n.* the eighth month of the Jewish civil year, and the second month of the ecclesiastical year, beginning in the latter part of April or the first part of May. [< Hebrew *iyyār*]

iz|ar (iz′ər), *n.* **1** an outer garment worn by Moslem women, made of cotton and covering the whole person. **2** a cloth girded round the waist forming part of the ihram (pilgrim's dress). [< Arabic *izār*]

iz|ard (iz′ərd), *n.* an antelope or chamois, found in the Pyrenees. [< French *isard* < Basque *izar* star; white spot on the forehead of the animal < an Iberian stem]

-ization, *suffix.* the act of ___izing or the condition of being ___ized: *Naturalization = the act of naturalizing or the condition of being naturalized.* [< *-ize* + *-ation*]

iz|ba (iz bä′, iz′bə), *n.* = isba.

-ize, *suffix added to adjectives and nouns to form verbs.* **1** make ___: *Legalize = make legal. Apologize = make an apology.*
2 become ___: *Crystallize = become crystal.*
3 engage in or use ___: *Criticize = engage in criticism.*
4 treat or combine with ___: *Oxidize = combine with oxygen.*
5 other meanings, as in *alphabetize, colonize, criticize, memorize. Also,* **-ise.**
[< French *-iser* (< Latin *-izāre*), or < Latin (< Greek *-izein*), or directly < Greek]
▶ **-ize, -ise.** American usage favors the spelling *-ize* for the suffix in words like *apologize, characterize, realize, revolutionize, visualize,* where British usage often calls for *-ise.* A number of words which end in the sound of (-īz), however, do not include the suffix and do not have variant spellings. For instance, *chastise, devise, exercise, supervise,* and *surmise* are spelled only one way in American and British spelling.

I|zod test (ī′zod), a test of the brittleness of a metal or other material, made by measuring the amount of energy absorbed by a test piece into which a notch has been cut when it is fractured by a swinging pendulum. [< E. *Izod,* a British engineer of the 1900's]

iz|zard (iz′ərd), *n. Archaic.* the letter Z.
from A to izzard, from beginning to end: *He has spent his lifetime in the service, and knows from a to izzard every detail of a soldier's needs* (Harper's).
[apparently variant of *zed*]

✱J¹ or **j** (jā), *n., pl.* **J's** or **Js, j's** or **js. 1** the tenth letter of the English alphabet: *Few English words have two j's.* **2** any sound represented by this letter. **3** (used as a symbol for) the tenth (of an actual or possible series): *row J in a theater.*
J² (jā), *n., pl.* **J's.** anything shaped like the letter J: *A spur . . . ran out toward the west and formed a large "J" with the curve facing the south* (Outing).
j (no period), **1** the Roman numeral for 1, chiefly at the end of a series, as in iij, still used in prescriptions. **2** jewel (as in a watch).
j., *Physics.* joule.
J (no period), **1** jet. **2** *Physics.* joule.
J., **1** journal. **2** judge. **3** justice.
ja (yä), *adv., n. German.* yes.
Ja. or **Ja** (no period), January.
JA (no periods) or **J.A.**, **1** joint account. **2** judge advocate. **3** Junior Achievement.
jab (jab), *v.,* **jabbed, jab|bing,** *n.* **—*v.t., v.i.*** **1** to thrust with something pointed; poke: *He jabbed his fork into the potato.* **2** *Boxing.* to hit with a jab.
—*n.* **1** a thrust with something pointed; poke: *She gave him a jab with her elbow.* **2** *Boxing.* a blow in which the arm is extended straight from the shoulder.
[originally Scottish variant of *job,* verb, Middle English *jobben* to poke, jab]
jab|ber (jab′ər), *v., n.* **—*v.i.*** to talk very fast in a confused, senseless way; chatter; prattle: *Demons for fright Jabber and scream about him in the night* (William Butler Yeats). **SYN:** babble, gabble.
—*v.t.* to speak rapidly and indistinctly. **SYN:** babble, gabble.
—*n.* very fast, confused, or senseless talk; chatter.
[probably imitative] **—jab′ber|er,** *n.* **—jab′ber|ing|ly,** *adv.*
jab|ber|wock|y or **Jab|ber|wock|y** (jab′ər wok′ē), *n., adj.* **—*n.*** meaningless writing; nonsensical talk; jabber.
—*adj.* without meaning; having no sense: *the jabberwocky school of modern verse, jabberwocky distortion.*
[< *Jabberwock,* a fabulous animal in Lewis Carroll's *Through the Looking-glass*]
jab|i|ru (jab′ə rü), *n.* **1** a large, white stork of tropical America with long legs and bill and a naked head and neck. It has a wingspread of about 7 feet. **2** any of various similar birds of Africa and Asia.
[< New Latin *jabiru* < Spanish or Portuguese *jabirú* < Tupi or Guarani]
jab|o|ran|di (jab′ə ran′dē), *n., pl.* **-dis. 1** the dried leaflets of a South American shrub of the rue family, containing an alkaloid drug, pilocarpine, and formerly the principal source of it. **2** the plant itself, or any one of various similar plants.
[< Spanish or Portuguese *jaburandí* < Tupi or Guarani]
✱ja|bot (zha bō′; zhab′ō, jab′-), *n.* a ruffle or frill of lace worn at the throat or down the front of a woman's shirt, dress, or blouse. Jabots were formerly worn also on a man's shirt. *A jabot of lace or ruffles was worn at the high neckline* (B. G. Chambers). [< French *jabot* (originally) maw of a bird]

✱jabot

J.A.C., Junior Association of Commerce.
ja|cal (hä käl′), *n.* **1** a native Mexican house or hut whose walls consist of rows of thin vertical poles filled in and plastered with mud. **2** this method of constructing walls and houses. [< Mexican Spanish *jacal* < Nahuatl *xacalli*]
jac|a|mar (jak′ə mär), *n.* any bird of a group of tropical America related to the toucans and woodpeckers, with sharp bills and bright-colored plumage with a metallic sheen.
[< French *jacamar* < Tupi or Guarani *Jacamaciri*]
ja|ça|na (zhä′sə nä′), *n.* a small wading bird of tropical regions having remarkably long toes and nails enabling it to walk on the floating leaves of water plants. It flies poorly but swims well though infrequently.
[< Portuguese *jaçaná,* perhaps < Tupi or Guarani *jasaná*]
jac|a|ran|da (jak′ə ran′də), *n.* **1** any one of a genus of tropical American trees and shrubs of the bignonia family, grown for their finely cut foliage, showy, tubular flowers, and fragrant, ornamental wood. **2** the wood of any one of these trees.
[< Portuguese *jacarandá* < Tupi (Brazil)]
j'ac|cuse (zhȧ kyz′), *French.* **1** I accuse. **2** a strong public accusation: *It is mortifying to observe that one's j'accuse is not summarily followed by redress of the grievances* (Harvey Swados).
ja|cinth (jā′sinth, jas′inth), *n.* **1** a reddish-orange gem, a variety of zircon; hyacinth. **2** any one of several varieties of garnet. [< Old French *jacinte* topaz, hyacinth < Latin *hyacinthus* < Greek *hyákinthos* some kind of flower. See etym. of doublet **hyacinth.**]

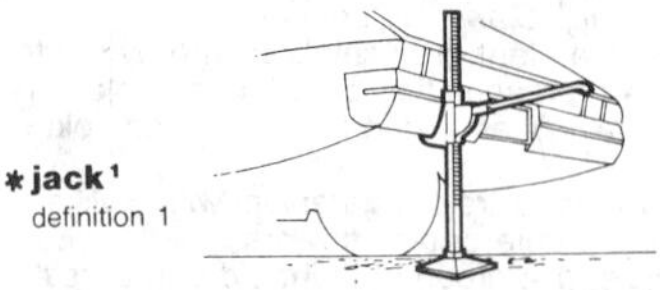
✱jack¹
definition 1

✱jack¹ (jak), *n., v.* **—*n.*** **1** a portable tool or machine for lifting or pushing up heavy weights a short distance: *He lifted the car with a jack to change the flat tire.* **2a** a playing card with a picture of a servant, soldier, or court page on it; knave: *the jack of hearts.* **b** a small six-pointed piece of metal or a pebble tossed up and caught in various ways in the game of jacks; jackstone. **c** *British.* a small ball for players to aim at in lawn bowling: *The object is the same as on the flat green—to place as many bowls as possible nearer to the jack than the opponent's* (London Times). **3** a small flag used on a ship to show nationality or as a signal. **4** a device for turning a spit in roasting meat. **5a** a male donkey; jackass: *He leisurely untied, From head and neck the halter of the jack* (Longfellow). **b** = jack rabbit. **c** the male of various other animals. **d** any one of various edible fishes, such as the pike and the pompano. **6a** a man; boy; fellow: *Every Jack shall have his Jill* (William S. Gilbert). **b** Also, **Jack.** a sailor. **c** a man who does odd jobs: *the house that Jack built.* **7** an electrical device which can receive a plug to make a connection in a circuit. **8** a figure of a man that strikes a bell attached to a clock. **9** a horizontal iron bar or crosstree at the head of a topgallant mast. **10** = bootjack. **11** = jack light. **12** a frame on which wood is sawed; sawhorse. **13** *Slang.* money. **14** *Railroad Slang.* a locomotive.
—*v.t.* **1** to lift or push up with a jack: *to jack a car.* **2** *U.S.* to hunt (game or fish) at night with a jack light. **3** to raise or push; jack up: *Congress happily continued this expansive tradition, jacking the appropriation to $171-million before pausing this year* (Spy Magazine).
—*v.i.* to hunt or fish with a jack light.
every man jack. See under **man jack.**
jacks, a child's game in which pieces of metal or pebbles are tossed up and caught in various ways; jackstones. Each player bounces the ball and picks up the jacks in between bounces. *After supper, Charlotte Loomis would sit on the front stoop . . . playing jacks* (New Yorker).
jack up, a to lift with a jack: *He jacked up the car to change a flat tire. As soon as* [*the bridge*] *reaches its position, it is jacked up* (Scientific American). **b** to raise (as prices, wages, or rates): *Supermarkets have jacked up prices in recent months.* **c** to lift; elevate: *Short men could be jacked up to a more satisfying height by a skilfully corked pair of £25 . . . shoes* (London Times). **d** to enliven; step up: *Editors have . . . reason for jacking up their women's pages* (Newsweek). **e** to give up: [*It*] *took a deal of punishment before he jacked up* (Rolf Boldrewood).
[originally proper name, probably < *Jackie,* variant of *Jankin* (diminutive) < *John*]
jack² (jak), *n.* **1** an East Indian tree of the mulberry family, widely grown for its fruit, resembling the breadfruit but larger and coarser, and for its fine-grained, yellow or brown wood. **2** the fruit of this tree. **3** the wood of this tree.
[earlier *jaca* < Portuguese < Malayalam *chakka*]
jack³ (jak), *n. Archaic.* **1** a sleeveless coat, usually leather, worn for protection by foot soldiers during the Middle Ages. **2** a waxed leather container for holding liquor. [< Old French *jaque* short jacket < Spanish *jaco,* perhaps < Arabic *shakk*]
jack-a-dan|dy (jak′ə dan′dē), *n., pl.* **-dies.** a conceited little fellow; dandy.
jack|al (jak′ôl, -əl), *n., v.* **—*n.*** **1** a wild dog of Asia, Africa, and eastern Europe, about as big as a fox. Jackals hunt in packs at night and feed on small animals, eggs, insects, fruit, and carrion left by large animals. They were formerly supposed to hunt prey for the lion and eat what the lion left. See picture under **dog. 2** *Figurative.* a person who does menial work for another.
—*v.i.* to act as a jackal.
[< Turkish *çakal* < Persian *shaghāl*]
jack|a|napes (jak′ə nāps), *n.* **1** an impertinent, forward person; coxcomb: *a pert jackanapes, full of college petulance and self-conceit* (Tobias G. Smollett). **SYN:** popinjay. **2** a pert, forward child. **3** *Archaic.* a monkey or ape. [variant of Middle English *Jack Napes,* a name applied to William, Duke of Suffolk (1396-1450), whose badge was a clog and chain, such as was used for tame apes]
jack|a|roo (jak′ə rü′), *n., pl.* **-roos.** = jackeroo.
jack|ass (jak′as′, -äs′), *n.* **1** a male donkey. **2** *Figurative.* a very stupid or foolish person: *However, he was a "troublemaker" who insisted on making great men look like jackasses* (Scientific American). **SYN:** fool. **3** *Australian.* = laughing jackass.
[< *jack*¹ + *ass*]
jack|ass|er|y (jak′as′ə rē, -äs′-), *n., pl.* **-ries. 1** great stupidity. **2** a very stupid act; a piece of folly.
jackass penguin, a penguin of the southern coasts of South America and Africa that makes a sound similar to the braying of jackasses.
jack bean, 1 a tropical American plant of the pea family, with purple and white flowers and white seeds, grown especially for forage. **2** its seed.
✱jack|boot (jak′büt′), *n., v.,* **—*n.*** **1** a heavy boot reaching above the knee. **2** a similar boot worn by German soldiers during World War II. **3** *Figurative.* **a** rough, bullying measures; jackboot tactics. **b** a person who uses rough, bullying measures: *a trigger-happy jackboot bent on grabbing full power* (Time).
—*v.t.* to make by using rough, bullying measures: *German* (*Communist*) *troops were jackbooting their way around the northwestern section of Czechoslovakia* (New York Times).
[< *jack*³, or *jack*¹ + *boot*]

✱jackboot
definition 1

jack|boot|ed (jak′bü′tid), *adj.* **1** wearing or worn with jackboots: *a jackbooted soldier, a jackbooted uniform.* **2** *Figurative.* militant; aggressive; violent.
jackboot tactics, rough, bullying measures to achieve compliance or submission.
jack crevalle, a carangoid fish of the eastern coast of tropical America, much valued as a game and food fish.
jack crosstree, = jack¹ (def. 9).
jack|daw (jak′dô′), *n.* **1** a small crow of Europe and North Africa, living in flocks especially around old buildings and towers or in holes in trees; daw.

✱J¹
definition 1

Jj — Script letters look like examples of fine penmanship. They appear in many formal uses, such as invitations to social functions.

Jj *Jj* — Handwritten letters, both manuscript or printed (left) and cursive (right), are easy for children to read and to write.

Jj *Jj* — Roman letters have *serifs* (finishing strokes) adapted from the way Roman stonecutters carved their letters. This is *Times Roman* type.

Jj *Jj* — Sans-serif letters are often called *gothic.* They have lines of even width and no serifs. This type face is called *Helvetica.*

Jj *Jj* — Between roman and gothic, some letters have thick and thin lines with slight flares that suggest serifs. This type face is *Optima.*

J — Computer letters can be sensed by machines either from their shapes or from the magnetic ink with which they are printed.

2 any one of several North American grackles, such as the boat-tailed grackle. 3 *Figurative.* a talkative person.

jack·een (ja kēn′), *n. Irish.* an aggressive city fellow.

jack·er (jak′ər), *n.* one that jacks.

jack·e·roo (jak′ə rü′), *n., pl.* **-roos.** a young apprentice working at a cattle or sheep ranch in the bush of Australia.

jack·et (jak′it), *n., v.* —*n.* **1** a short coat, usually having sleeves. **2** an outer covering. The paper cover for a book, the casing around a steam pipe, the metal covering on a bullet, and the skin of a potato are jackets. **3** a paper or envelope used to cover an official document.
—*v.t.* **1** to put a jacket on; cover with a jacket. **2** *Informal.* to beat; thrash.
dust one's jacket, *British Informal.* to beat someone: *the threat to dust the author's jacket, for the gratification of private malice* (L. J. Jennings).
[< Middle French *jaquet* (diminutive) < Old French *jaque* tunic; see etym. under **jack**[3]]

jack·fish (jak′fish′), *n., pl.* **-fish·es** or (*collectively*) **-fish.** a pike, especially a young or small one.

Jack Frost, frost or freezing weather thought of as a person.

jack·fruit (jak′früt′), *n.* **1** = jack (tree). **2** its fruit. **3** = durian.

jack·ham·mer (jak′ham′ər), *n.* a pneumatic drill used especially on rock and concrete.

jack-in-a-box (jak′in ə boks′), *n., pl.* **-box·es.** **1** = jack-in-the-box (def. 1). **2** a tree of Pacific islands and the East Indies bearing a large nut that rattles in its casing when shaken.

jack-in-the-box (jak′in THə boks′), *n., pl.* **-boxes.** **1** a toy figure that springs up from a box when the lid is opened. **2** *U.S.* = hermit crab.

jack-in-the-pul·pit (jak′in THə pu̇l′pit), *n.* a plant with a greenish, petallike sheath arched over the upright flower stalk; Indian turnip; wake-robin. It is a perennial herb of North America that belongs to the arum family. See picture under **arum family.** [American English < *jack*[1]]

Jack Ketch (kech), a public executioner; hangman. [< *Jack Ketch,* a British executioner around 1670, died 1686]

***jack·knife** (jak′nīf′), *n., pl.* **-knives,** *v.,* **-knifed, -knif·ing,** *adj.* —*n.* **1** a large, strong pocketknife. **2** a kind of dive in which the diver, keeping his knees straight, touches his feet with his hands in midair and straightens out before entering the water. **3** *Theater.* a rolling platform for changing scenery, attached to the stage floor at one place, and pivoted so that it can be rotated on and off stage.
—*v.t.* **1** to double up like a jackknife: *Never jackknife an injured person into a car seat.* **2** to cut with a jackknife.
—*v.i.* **1** to double up like a jackknife. **2** to dive into the water doubled up like this. **3** to turn at a sharp angle like a jackknife: *It has been estimated that . . . an articulated vehicle jackknifes on average once in every 50,000 miles* (New Scientist).
—*adj.* **1** like a jackknife; turning or rotating like a jackknife: *a jackknife bridge, a jackknife stage.* **2** like that of a jackknife or jackknife dive: *By a jackknife motion, a skilful athlete can jump over a bar whilst his centre of gravity is actually below it* (New Scientist).
[American English. Compare dialectal English *jackleg* knife.]

***jackknife**
definition 1

jack·lad·der (jak′lad′ər), *n.* **1** *Nautical.* a ladder having rope sides and wooden or metal rungs; Jacob's ladder. **2** (in lumbering) a gangway.

jack·leg[1] (jak′leg′), *adj., n. U.S.* —*adj.* **1** not skilled or professional; amateur: *a jackleg logger, a jackleg carpenter.* **2** using questionable or dishonest practices; unscrupulous: *a jackleg lawyer.* **3** temporary; makeshift: *a jackleg platform.*
—*n.* a jackleg person or thing.
[< *jack*[1] + (black)*leg*]

jack·leg[2] (jak′leg′), *n.* a device on which a jackhammer is mounted to keep it in line with the advancing hole. [< *jack*(hammer) + *leg*]

jack light, or **jack·light** (jak′līt′), *n. U.S.* a light for hunting or fishing at night, especially one, such as a strong flashlight, that attracts fish or game.

jack-light or **jack·light** (jak′līt′), *v.i. U.S.* to hunt or fish with a light.

jack mackerel, a carangoid food fish similar to the saurel, found on the Pacific coast of the United States.

Jack Mormon, **1** a non-Mormon who is friendly or sympathetic toward Mormons. **2** a Mormon who is not religiously active or observant.

jack of all trades, or **jack-of-all-trades** (jak′əv ôl′trādz′), *n.* **1** a person who can do many different kinds of work fairly well: *a jack of all trades and master of none.* **2** a thing that can be easily adapted to many different uses; something that has versatility: *This jack-of-all-trades is the small private aircraft.*

jack-o'-lan·tern (jak′ə lan′tərn), *n.* **1** a pumpkin hollowed out and cut to look like a face, used as a lantern at Halloween. **2** = will-o'-the wisp.

Jack-o'-Lent (jak′ə lent′), *n. Archaic.* **1** a figure set up to be pelted during Lent. **2** a butt, as of ridicule.

jack pine, a slender pine tree growing in barren or rocky soil in the northeastern and midwestern United States and in Canada.

jack plane, a carpenter's plane used for rough shaving.

jack·pot (jak′pot′), *n., adj.* —*n.* Also, **jack pot.** **1** the stakes that accumulate in a poker game until some player wins with a pair of jacks or something better. **2a** any cumulative pool, such as a large prize, that is competed for regularly and is increased as contestants fail to gain it: *That television quiz show has built up a jackpot of over $100,000.* **b** any large gain.
—*adj.* of or having to do with a jackpot.
hit the (or **a**) **jackpot, a** to win a big prize: *While they might collect on bonds, few Canadians could hit big jackpots in the pools, say the British, because of the expert knowledge of football required* (Maclean's). **b** to have a stroke of very good luck: *When a conductor manages . . . to hit a sort of musical jackpot of rightness, it doesn't take a trained ear to sense the benefits* (Harper's).

jack rabbit, a large hare of western North America, having very long hind legs and long ears: *The jack rabbit . . . is just like any other rabbit except that he is from one-third to twice as large, has longer legs in proportion to his size, and has the most preposterous ears that ever were mounted on any creature but a jackass* (Mark Twain).

jack-raft·er (jak′raf′tər, -räf′-), *n.* a shorter rafter, as in a hip roof.

Jack Russell terrier or **Jack Russell,** a working terrier of an English breed with a short, thick, mainly white coat.
[< *Jack Russell,* an English parson of the 1800's, who introduced the breed]

jacks (jaks), *n.pl.* See under **jack**[1].

jack salmon, = walleyed pike.

jack·screw (jak′skrü′), *n.* a tool or machine for lifting heavy weights short distances, operated by a screw: *You may have seen workmen lift the corner of a house with a large jackscrew* (Beauchamp, Mayfield, and West).

jack·smelt (jak′smelt′), *n., pl.* **-smelts** or (*collectively*) **-smelt.** a silversides of the California coast that grows to a length of 22 inches.

jack·snipe (jak′snīp′), *n.* **1** a very small European snipe; half snipe. **2** a snipe such as Wilson's snipe of America. **3** = pectoral sandpiper.
[< *jack*[1] + *snipe,* noun]

Jack·son Day (jak′sən), *U.S.* January 8, the anniversary of Andrew Jackson's victory at New Orleans in 1815, observed by Democratic Party dinners and political rallies.

Jack·so·ni·an (jak′sō′nē ən), *adj., n.* —*adj.* of or like Andrew Jackson (1767-1845), seventh President of the United States, or his principles: *Andrew Jackson would have been irate had he known how often a vaguely romantic conception of human equality would be defended by calling it Jacksonian* (Newsweek).
—*n.* a follower of Andrew Jackson.

jack-span·iard (jak′span′yərd), *n.* any one of certain paper wasps of the West Indies. [< *jack*[1] + *Spaniard*]

jack·staff (jak′staf′, -stäf′), *n. Nautical.* a short staff, set on the bowsprit or at the bow of a boat or ship, to display a ship's colors.

jack·stay (jak′stā′), *n.* **1** a rope, cable, or iron rod along a yard or gaff, to which the head of a sail is attached. **2** a vertical rod or rope running along the forward side of a mast, on which a yard is raised or lowered.

jack·stone (jak′stōn′), *n.* a small metal object or pebble used in the game of jacks; jack.
jackstones, the game of jacks: *The women . . . amuse themselves with . . . jackstones* (Henry M. Brackenridge).
[altered spelling for variant pronunciation of dialectal *checkstone* or Scottish *chuckstone,* also *chuckie stones*]

jack·straw (jak′strô′), *n.* **1** a straw or strip of wood, bone, or plastic, used in the game of jackstraws. **2** = man of straw.
jackstraws, a child's game played with a set of straws thrown down in a confused pile. Each player tries to pick them up one at a time without moving any of the rest of the pile. *I . . . have no sort of presence of mind* (*not so much as one would use to play at jackstraws*) (Elizabeth Barrett Browning).
[apparently for *Jack*[1] *of straw.* Compare *Jack Straw,* leader of a peasant revolt of 1381.]

Jack Tar or **jack tar,** a sailor: *a jolly warm-hearted Jack Tar* (Charles Lamb). [< *jack*[1] + *tar*[2]]

jack towel, a towel with the ends sewed together, on a roller; roller towel.

jack-up (jak′up′), *n.* **1** *U.S.* an increase: *another jack-up in short-term rates.* **2** a type of rig for offshore oil drilling, on which legs are lowered to the seabed from the operating platform.

jack·y[1] (jak′ē), *n. British Slang.* gin.

jack·y[2] (jak′ē), *n., pl.* **jack·ies.** = sailor.

Jack·y (jak′ē), *n., pl.* **Jack·ies.** = sailor.

jack yard, *Nautical.* **1** a light yard used to extend the head of a square-cut gaff-topsail. **2** a spar to extend the foot of a gaff-topsail beyond the peak.

Ja·cob (jā′kəb), *n.* the son of Isaac and Rebecca and younger twin brother of Esau; Israel. The 12 tribes of Israel traced their descent from Jacob's 12 sons (in the Bible, Genesis 25-50). [< Late Latin *Jacōbus* James, Jacob < Greek *Iákōbos* < Hebrew *ya'ăqōb*]

***Jac·o·be·an** (jak′ə bē′ən), *adj., n.* —*adj.* **1** of King James I of England. **2** of the period of his reign, from 1603 to 1625. Jacobean architecture and furniture are Late English Gothic with a large admixture of Italian forms. Jacobean literature, especially poetry and drama, was at or near its height during this time.
—*n.* a statesman or writer of the time of James I.
[< New Latin *Jacobaeus* (< Late Latin *Jacōbus;* see etym. under **Jacob**) + English *-an*]

***Jacobean**
definition 2

jac·o·be·an lily (jak′ə bē′ən), a spring-blooming, Mexican plant of the amaryllis family, bearing a single crimson flower.
[< New Latin *jacobaea* < Late Latin *Jacōbus* James]

Jac·o·be·than (jak′ə bē′thən, -beth′ən), *adj.* of a style combining or mixing the Jacobean and Elizabethan: *Jacobethan furniture, Jacobethan mansions.* [blend of *Jacobean* and *Elizabethan*]

Ja·co·bi·an (jə kō′bē ən, yä kō′-), *adj., n.* —*adj.* of or having to do with the theories of the German mathematician Karl Gustav J. Jacobi (1804-1851).
—*n. Mathematics.* a determinant of two or more functions in two or more variables.

jac·o·bin (jak′ə bin), *n.* a breed of the domestic pigeon whose neck feathers form a kind of hood.
[< French *Jacobine,* feminine of *Jacobin;* see *Jacobin*]

Jac·o·bin (jak′ə bin), *n., adj.* —*n.* **1** a member of a radical political club organized in 1789 during the French Revolution in the old Convent of Saint James (Jacques) in Paris. **2** an extreme radical, especially in politics. **3** a Dominican friar.
—*adj.* **1** having to do with the revolutionary Jacobins. **2** extremely radical in politics. **3** of or belonging to the Dominican friars.
[< Old French (*frere*) *jacobin* Jacobin (friar) < Medieval Latin *Jacobinus* of James (because the Jacobins' convent was situated near the church of St. Jacques in Paris) < Late Latin *Jacōbus;* see etym. under **Jacobean**]

Jac·o·bin·ic (jak′ə bin′ik), *adj.* of or characteristic of the French Jacobins; radical. —**Jac′o·bin′i·cal·ly,** *adv.*

Jac·o·bin·i·cal (jak′ə bin′ə kəl), *adj.* = Jacobinic.

Jac·o·bin·ism (jak′ə bə niz′əm), *n.* **1** the principles of the French Jacobins. **2** extreme radicalism, especially in politics.

Jac·o·bin·ize (jak′ə bə nīz), *v.t.,* **-ized, -iz·ing.** to make Jacobin; imbue with radical ideas.

Jac·o·bite[1] (jak′ə bīt), *n., adj.* —*n.* a supporter of James II and his descendants (the Stuart family) in their claims to the English throne after the English Revolution of 1688.
—*adj.* of or having to do with the Jacobites: *the*

Pronunciation Key: hat, āge, cãre, fär; let, ēqual, tėrm; it, īce; hot, ōpen, ôrder; oil, out; cup, pu̇t, rüle; child; long; thin; THen; zh, measure;
ə represents **a** in about, **e** in taken, **i** in pencil, **o** in lemon, **u** in circus.

Jacobite rebellions.
[< Late Latin *Jacōbus* James (see etym. under **Jacob**) + English *-ite*[1]]

Jac|o|bite[2] (jak′ə bīt), *n., adj.* —*n.* a member of the Monophysitic Syrian church, governed by the patriarch of Antioch.
—***adj.*** of the Jacobites or their beliefs.
[< Medieval Latin *Jacobita* < *Jacobus* Baradaeus, a monk of Edessa, who revived the Eutychian heresy in the 500's]

Jac|o|bit|ic (jak′ə bit′ik), *adj.* having to do with the British Jacobites.

Jac|o|bit|i|cal (jak′ə bit′ə kəl), *adj.* = Jacobitic.

Jac|o|bit|ism (jak′ə bī′tiz əm), *n.* the principles of the Jacobites; adherence to or sympathy with the cause of the Stuarts.

Ja|cob-Mo|nod (jā′kəb mə nod′; *French* zhà-kôb′mô nō′), *adj.* of or having to do with the theory that genes are controlled by the mechanism called the operon, first advanced by the French scientists François Jacob, born 1920, and Jacques Monod, born 1910.

Jacob's ladder, **1** a ladder to heaven that Jacob saw in a dream (in the Bible, Genesis 28:12). **2** a rope ladder with wooden or metal rungs, used on ships especially by pilots who are boarding or leaving.

Ja|cob's-lad|der (jā′kəbz lad′ər), *n.* **1** a common European garden plant of the same family as the phlox, with blue or white flowers and ladderlike leaves. **2** any one of certain related species. **3** = Jacob's ladder (def. 2).

Ja|cob|son's organ (jā′kəb sənz), either one of the cavities in the roof of the mouth of most vertebrates, which contain branches of the olfactory nerve, undeveloped in man, but highly developed in most reptiles. [< L. L. *Jacobson,* 1783-1843, a Danish anatomist]

Jacob's staff, **1** a support for a surveyor's compass, consisting of a single leg with a steel point to be stuck in the ground, and having at the other end a brass head with a ball-and-socket joint. **2** = cross-staff.

ja|co|bus (jə kō′bəs), *n.* an English gold coin minted under James I, worth originally 20 shillings, later 24. [< Late Latin *Jacōbus* James (I of England, in whose reign it was issued, 1603)]

jac|o|net (jak′ə net), *n.* a soft, light cotton cloth with a smooth finish, originally imported from India. [alteration of *Jagannath,* India, where it was made]

jac|quard or **Jac|quard** (jə kärd′), *n., adj.* —***n.*** a fabric with a figured weave.
—***adj.*** woven on a Jacquard loom: *jacquard cotton.*

Jacquard loom, a loom with an apparatus, more advanced than the heddle, for weaving figured fabrics. [earlier *jacquard engine* < French *jacquard,* or *jacquart* weaving loom < Joseph *Jacquard,* 1752-1834, a French weaver, who invented it]

Jacquard weave, a type of weave, produced on a Jacquard loom, that is a combination of two or more ordinary weaves.

jac|que|rie (zhák rē′), *n.* any revolt of peasants. [< *Jacquerie*]

Jac|que|rie (zhák rē′), *n.* the revolt of the peasants of France against the nobles in 1358. [< Middle French *jacquerie* < *Jacques* (*Bonhomme*)]

jac|ta a|le|a est (jak′tə ā′lē ə est), *Latin.* the die is cast.

jac|ta|tion (jak tā′shən), *n.* **1** a boasting; bragging. **2** *Medicine.* jactitation. [< Latin *jactātiō, -ōnis* < *jactāre* boast of; toss about (frequentative) < *jacere* to throw]

jac|ti|ta|tion (jak′tə tā′shən), *n.* **1** *Law.* a false claim involving harm to another. **2** a boastful declaration; bragging. **3** *Medicine.* a restless and convulsive tossing of the body in disease. [< Medieval Latin *jactitatio, -onis* < Latin *jactitāre* utter in public (frequentative) < *jactāre; see etym.* under **jactation**]

jac|u|late (jak′yə lāt), *v.,* **-lat|ed, -lat|ing.** —***v.t.*** to dart; hurl.
—***v.i.*** to dart forward.
[< Latin *jaculārī* (with English *-ate*[1]) < *jaculum* a dart < *jacere* to throw] —**jac′u|la′tion,** *n.*

Ja|cuz|zi (jə kü′zē), *n.* or **Jacuzzi bath**, a bath in which a device is used to make the water whirl and churn. [< *Jacuzzi,* a trademark for the water-whirling device]

jade[1] (jād), *n., adj.* —***n.*** **1** a hard stone used for jewelry and ornaments; jadeite or nephrite. Most jade is green, but some is whitish. **2** any of various other stones of similar appearance and use. **3** an object or carving made from jade: *a collection of jades.* **4** a light green; jade green.
—***adj.*** light-green; jade-green.
[< French *le jade,* earlier *l'ejade* < Spanish (*piedra de*) *ijada* (stone of) colic; pain in the side (because jade was thought to cure this) < Vulgar Latin *īliata* < *īlia,* flanks, groin] —**jade′like′,** *adj.*

jade[2] (jād), *n., v.,* **jad|ed, jad|ing.** —***n.*** **1** an inferior or worn-out horse. **2** *Figurative.* disreputable or shrewish woman; hussy (used contemptuously or playfully): *a light-minded, jilting jade.*
—***v.t.*** **1** to wear out; tire; weary: *In the second half the Old Boys, now a little jaded, failed to pierce a stubborn defence* (London Times). **SYN:** fatigue, exhaust. **2** to dull by continual use; surfeit; satiate. **3** *Obsolete.* to make a fool of: *I do not now fool myself, to let imagination jade me* (Shakespeare).
—***v.i.*** to become tired or weary; grow dull.
[origin uncertain; perhaps < Scandinavian (compare Old Icelandic *jalda* mare)]

jad|ed (jā′did), *adj.* **1** worn-out; tired; weary: *a jaded horse, a jaded look. Perhaps the fashion writers, . . . at the end of a long season, have grown a little jaded* (London Times). **2** dulled from continual use; surfeited; satiated: *a jaded appetite.* —**jad′ed|ly,** *adv.* —**jad′ed|ness,** *n.*

jade green, the color of jade, a light green.
—**jade′-green′,** *adj.*

jade|ite (jā′dīt), *n.* a rare mineral consisting of a silicate of sodium and aluminum. It is the harder and more highly prized of the two minerals (nephrite and jadeite) commonly called jade, because of its beautiful colors of light green or lilac. [< *jade*[1] + *-ite*[1]]

jad|ish (jā′dish), *adj.* jaded; inferior or worn-out; worthless. —**jad′ish|ly,** *adv.* —**jad′ish|ness,** *n.*

jad|y (jā′dē), *adj.,* **jad|i|er, jad|i|est.** = jadish. —**jad′i|ness,** *n.*

jae|ger (yā′gər, jā′-), *n.* **1** any one of a genus of hawklike sea birds related to the gulls, that pursue weaker birds such as terns and make them disgorge their prey; hunting gull. **2** a German or Swiss hunter. **3** a member of a military unit of German or Austrian sharpshooters. **4** a servant dressed like a hunter. Also **jäger, yager.** [< German *Jäger* hunter]

Ja|el (jā′əl), *n.* the Hebrew woman who killed Sisera (in the Bible, Judges 4:17-22).

jag[1] (jag), *n., v.,* **jagged, jag|ging.** —***n.*** **1** a sharp point sticking out; pointed projection: *a jag of rock.* **2** *Dialect.* a shred, as of cloth. **3** *Dialect.* a prick; jab.
—***v.t.*** **1** to cut or tear unevenly: *to jag cloth.* **2** to make notches in. **SYN:** nick, notch. **3** *Dialect.* to prick; pierce; jab. **4** *Scottish.* to irritate; vex: *Easie Haggart jagged the minister sorely* (James Barrie).

jag[2] (jag), *n.* **1** a period of unrestrained activity: *a crying jag.* **2** *Slang.* **a** a drinking bout or spree. **b** rather more liquor than one can carry. **3** *Dialect.* a small load, especially of hay or wood. Also, **jagg.** [origin unknown]

JAG (no periods) or **J.A.G.**, judge advocate general.

ja|gad|gu|ru (jə gəd gü′rü, -gü rü′), *n.* the title of a widely revered Hindu guru or religious leader. [< Hindustani *jagadgurū* < Sanskrit *jagat* world + *guru* revered]

Jag|an|nath (jug′ə nät, -nôt), *n.* = Juggernaut.

Jag|a|tai (jag′ə tī′), *n.* the branch of the Turkic languages spoken in Turkestan, including Uigur and Uzbek.

jä|ger (yā′gər, jā′-), *n.* = jaeger.

jagg (jag), *n.* = jag[2].

jag|ged (jag′id), *adj.* with sharp points sticking out; unevenly cut or torn; notched: *a jagged streak of lightning. We cut our bare feet on the jagged rocks. Algeria, a land of fertile coastal valleys, jagged mountains, and barren deserts* (Newsweek). **SYN:** serrated. —**jag′ged|ly,** *adv.* —**jag′ged|ness,** *n.*

jag|ger (jag′ər), *n.* **1** a person or thing that jags. **2** a small wheel with a jagged or wavy edge and a handle, for cutting pastry. **3** a toothed chisel.

jag|ger|y (jag′ər ē), *n.* a coarse, dark-brown sugar made in southeastern Asia from the sap of palm trees. [Anglo-Indian < Hindustani *jāgrī* < Sanskrit *çarkara* sugar. Compare etym. under **sugar**.]

jag|gy (jag′ē), *adj.,* **-gi|er, -gi|est.** jagged; notched.

jag|uar (jag′wär, -yü är), *n.* a fierce animal much like a leopard, but more heavily built; panther. It lives in forests in tropical America. Jaguars belong to the same genus as lions, tigers, and leopards. See picture under **leopard**. [< Portuguese *jaguar* < Tupi (Brazil) *jaguara*]

ja|gua|run|di or **ja|gua|ron|di** (jä′gwə run′dē), *n., pl.* **-dis.** a slender, short-legged wildcat, 3 to 4 feet long, found from the southwestern United States south to Argentina; eyra. It occurs in two color phases, gray or reddish-brown. [< a Tupi (Brazil) word]

Jah (jä), *n.* = Yahweh (in the Bible, Psalms 68:4).

Jah|ve or **Jah|veh** (yä′ve), *n.* = Yahweh.

Jah|vism (yä′viz əm), *n.* = Yahwism.

Jah|vist (yä′vist), *n.* = Yahwist.

Jah|vis|tic (yä vis′tik), *adj.* = Yahwistic.

Jah|weh (yä′we), *n.* = Yahweh.

Jah|wis|tic (yä wis′tik), *adj.* = Yahwistic.

***jai a|lai**, or **jai|a|lai** (hī′ə lī′), *n.* a game like handball, played on a walled court with a hard ball, popular in Spain, Latin America, and parts of the United States; pelota. The ball is caught and thrown with a curved wicker basket fastened to the arm. [< Spanish *jai alai* < Basque < *jai* festival + *alai* merry]

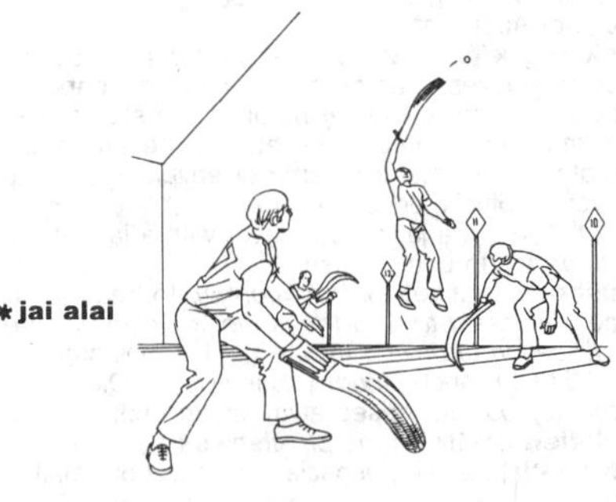

***jai alai**

jail (jāl), *n., v.* —***n.*** a prison, especially one for people awaiting trial or being punished for some small offense. —***v.t.*** to put in jail; keep in jail; imprison: *The police arrested and jailed the suspected thief.* Also, *British,* **gaol.**
break jail, to escape from jail: *A posse has been out after the man who broke jail.*
[< Old French *jaiole,* also *geole* < Vulgar Latin *gaviōla,* for *caveola* (diminutive) < Latin *cavea* coop, cave, cage < *cavus* hollow] —**jail′like′,** *adj.*

jail|bait (jāl′bāt′), *n. U.S. Slang.* a girl who has not reached the legal age of consent and is therefore likely to get a lover or seducer in trouble with the law.

jail|bird (jāl′bėrd′), *n. Informal.* **1** a prisoner in jail. **2** a person who has been in jail many times.

jail|break (jāl′brāk′), *n.* an escape from jail or prison.

jail delivery, **1** an escape from jail or prison. **2** (in English law) the clearing of a jail of prisoners by bringing them to trial.

jail|er or **jail|or** (jā′lər), *n.* **1** the keeper of a jail. **2** a person who keeps someone or something confined. Also, *British,* **gaoler.**

jail|house (jāl′hous′), *n. U.S.* a jail.

jail|mate (jāl′māt′), *n.* a companion in jail; fellow prisoner.

Jain (jīn), *n., adj.* —***n.*** a member of a non-Brahmanic southeast Asian sect resembling Buddhism, and believing, like the Hindus, in transmigration of the soul, established in the 500's B.C.
—***adj.*** of or having to do with the Jains or their religion: *Jain architecture is characterized by horizontal courses.*
[< Hindustani *jaina* of a saint < Sanskrit < *jina* a (Jain) saint; (literally) conqueror]

Jai|na (jī′nə), *n., adj.* = Jain.

Jain|ism (jī′niz əm), *n.* religious system of southeast Asia, established in the 500's B.C., stressing transmigration of the soul, nonviolence, and asceticism; the religious system of the Jains.

jake (jāk), *adj., n. Slang.* —***adj.*** fine, first-rate.
—***n.*** **1** an alcoholic drink made from Jamaica ginger extract as a substitute for whiskey. **2** methylated spirits. [origin uncertain]

jake-leg[1] (jāk′leg′), *n. U.S. Slang.* a paralyzed condition or sensation caused by drinking too much alcoholic liquor. [< *jake* + *leg*]

jake-leg[2] (jāk′leg′), *adj.* unscrupulous: *A sleazy, ambitious, jake-leg lawyer . . .* (Time). [variant of *jackleg*[1]]

jakes (jāks), *n., pl.* **jakes.** *Especially British Dialect.* a privy or toilet. [origin uncertain]

Ja|kob-Creutz|feldt disease (yä′kob kroits′felt, -kop-), = Creutzfeldt-Jakob disease: *It was diagnosed as Jakob-Creutzfeldt disease, and there are few recorded cases of it. Something about a galloping degeneration of the nerve cells. The prognosis for him: up to six months* (William F. Buckley, Jr.).

jal|ap (jal′əp), *n.* **1** a yellow, sweet powder made from the dried roots of a Mexican vine of the morning-glory family, used as a purgative. **2** the plant itself. **3** the roots. [< Spanish *jalapa* < *Jalapa,* a city in Mexico]

ja|lap|ic (jə lap′ik), *adj.* having to do with or consisting of jalap or jalapin.

jal|a|pin (jal′ə pin), *n.,* or **jalap resin**, a glycosidic resin made from jalap roots, used as a purgative.

ja|lop|y (jə lop′ē), *n., pl.* **-lop|ies.** *Informal.* an old automobile or airplane that is in bad condition, or otherwise inferior. [origin uncertain]

***jal|ou|sie** (jal′ə sē, zhal′ə zē′), *n.* **1** a shade or shutter made of adjustable, horizontal slats which may be tilted to let in light and air but keep out sun and rain. **2** a window having a similar function, made of adjustable, horizontal glass louvers set at an angle. [< Middle French *jalousie* (literally) jealousy < *jaloux* jealous]

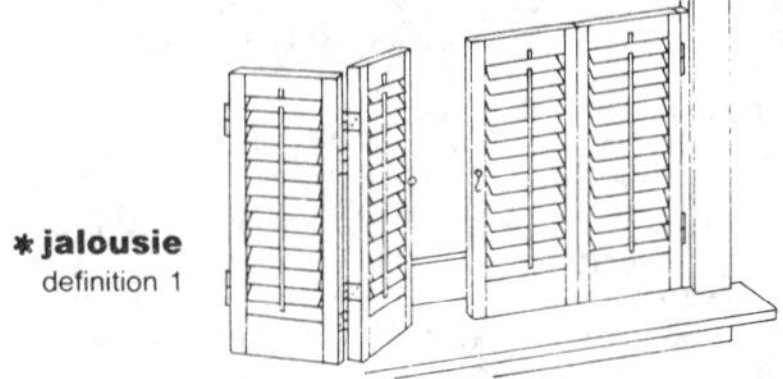

***jalousie**
definition 1

jal|ou|sied (jal′ə sēd, zhal′ə zēd), *adj.* furnished with jalousies.

jam[1] (jam), *v.,* **jammed, jam|ming,** *n.* **—*v.t.*** **1** to press or squeeze tightly between two surfaces: *The ship was jammed between two rocks.* **SYN:** wedge, pack. **2** to bruise or crush by squeezing: *I jammed my fingers in the door.* **3** to press or squeeze (things or people) tightly together: *They jammed us all into one bus.* **SYN:** force, thrust, push, shove. **4** to fill or block up (the way) by crowding: *The river was jammed with logs. Crowds that . . . jam the doors* (Tennyson). **5** to cause to stick, catch, or lock so that it cannot be worked: *The key broke off and jammed the lock.* **6** to push or thrust (a thing) hard (into a place); shove: *to jam one more book into the bookcase. The steersman . . . jammed his helm hard down* (Thomas Hughes). **7** to pull or draw tight, as one does a noose. **8** to make (radio or telephone signals) unintelligible by sending out others of approximately the same frequency: *The broadcasts were jammed by the enemy.*
—*v.i.* **1** to press or push things or persons tightly together: *A crowd jammed into the bus.* **2** to stick or catch so that it cannot be worked: *The window has jammed; I can't open it.* **3** to become unworkable through the sticking, catching, or locking of a movable part. **4** *Slang.* **a** to embellish a jazz composition with lively improvisations. **b** to take part in a jam session.
—*n.* **1** a crush or squeeze; crowded mass: *She was delayed by a traffic jam.* **2** the act of jamming. **3** the condition of being jammed. **4** *Informal.* a difficulty or tight spot: *He was in a jam.* [perhaps imitative] **—jam′ma|ble,** *adj.*

jam[2] (jam), *n.* fruit boiled with sugar until thick: *raspberry jam, plum jam.* [perhaps special use of *jam*[1]] **—jam′like′,** *adj.*

Jam., Jamaica.

Ja|mai|ca (jə mā′kə), *n.* a rum made in Jamaica in the West Indies.

Jamaica ginger, **1** a ginger of high quality that comes mainly from Jamaica. **2** an alcoholic extract of this ginger, used as a flavoring.

Ja|mai|can (jə mā′kən), *adj., n.* **—*adj.*** of or having to do with the island of Jamaica in the West Indies.
—*n.* a native or inhabitant of Jamaica.

Jamaica pepper, = allspice.

Jamaica rum, a rum with a rich flavor and pungent aroma, made in Jamaica.

Jamaica shorts, shorts that end four or five inches above the knee.

ja|mais vu (zhä′me vü′; *French* zhå me vʏ′), the illusion of having never experienced the situation one is in, although it is in fact a familiar situation: *The experience of having been somewhere before—déjà vu—is said to be a purely physical experience which affects the frontal lobe of the brain which provides the impression that one has dreamt the identical situation previously. The same explanation is applied to the opposite feeling—jamais vu—when one momentarily fails to recognize a familiar situation* (Auckland Star, New Zealand). [< French *jamais vu* never seen]

jamb or **jambe** (jam), *n.* **1** the upright piece forming the side of a doorway, window, or fireplace. **2** = jambeau. [< Old French *jambe* (originally) leg < Late Latin *gamba* hock, hoof < Greek *kampē* a bending. Compare etym. under **gam**[2], **gamb.**]

jam|ba|lay|a (jam′bə lī′ə), *n.* **1** a Creole dish, usually consisting of ham or shrimp, rice, tomatoes, and spices. **2** *Informal.* any miscellaneous collection or gathering. [American English, probably < Haitian Creole *jambalaya* < Provençal *jambalaia* a stew made up of rice and fowl]

jam|beau (jam′bō), *n., pl.* **-beaux** (-bōz). a piece of armor for the calf of the leg; greave. [Middle English *jambeau* < Old French *jambe;* see etym. under **jamb**]

jam|bi|ya (jam bē′yə), *n.* a double-edged, inlaid dagger, made in Yemen. [< Arabic]

jam|bo|ree (jam′bə rē′), *n.* **1** a large rally or gathering of Boy Scouts, especially an international one. **2** *Informal.* a noisy party; lively entertainment: *The weekly folk-song jamboree, a Washington Square tradition from late spring to early fall . . .* (New York Times). **3** any large gathering. [American English; perhaps coined from *jam*[1], and patterned after *shivaree*]

James (jāmz), *n.* **1** one of the Apostles of Christ, sometimes called James the Greater (or the Elder). **2** another of the twelve Apostles, sometimes called James the Less (or the Younger). **3** a relative of Jesus (in the Bible, Galatians 1:19, where he is referred to as "the Lord's brother"). **4** a book of the New Testament. *Abbr:* Jas.

James|i|an (jām′zē ən), *adj., n.* **—*adj.*** **1** of or characteristic of the novelist Henry James (1843-1916) or his writings; subtle and intricate. **2** of or like the psychologist and philosopher William James (1842-1910) or his doctrines.
—*n.* a student or follower of Henry or William James.

jam|mer (jam′ər), *n.* a device, or person who uses a device, to jam radio signals.

jam|my (jam′ē), *adj.,* **-mi|er, -mi|est. 1** covered with jam; sticky. **2** *British Informal.* good; easy.

jam-packed (jam′pakt′), *adj. Informal.* filled to absolute capacity; packed tightly.

jam|pan (jam′pan), *n.* a kind of sedan chair carried by four men, used in India. [< Bengali *jhāmpān*]

jams (jamz), *n.pl.* **1** *Informal.* pajamas. **2** swim trunks with a pajamalike drawstring.

jam session, *Slang.* a gathering at which musicians play popular compositions with lively improvisations.

Jam|shid or **Jam|shyd** (jam shēd′), *n. Persian Mythology.* a fairy king who had a cup of the elixir of life and was forced to live as a human being on earth because of his boasts of being immortal. He became a famous Persian ruler.

jam-up (jam′up′), *n.* **1** the act or fact of jamming together: *Such delays have caused a jam-up of vessels waiting for their turn at the docks* (Wall Street Journal). **2** a halting or stopping in the flow of work, sales, or the like; a tie-up.

Jan. or **Jan** (no period), January.

jane (jān), *n. Slang.* a woman or girl.

Jane Crow, *U.S. Slang.* discrimination against women. [patterned after *Jim Crow*]

Jane Doe, fictitious name in legal forms or proceedings for the name of an unknown female.

jan|gle (jang′gəl), *v.,* **-gled, -gling,** *n.* **—*v.i.*** **1** to sound harshly; make a loud, clashing noise: *The pots and pans jangled in the kitchen . . . a jangling noise of words unknown* (Milton). **2** to talk or argue in an angry, quarrelsome manner. **SYN:** wrangle, squabble. **3** *Archaic.* to chatter; babble: *Thy mind is lorn, thou janglest as a jay* (Chaucer).
—*v.t.* **1** to cause to sound harshly: *The children jangled cowbells.* **2** to utter or give forth in an angry, quarrelsome manner.
—*n.* **1** a harsh sound; clashing noise or ring: *the jangle of the telephone.* **2** a quarrel; dispute. [< Old French *jangler,* probably imitative] **—jan′gler,** *n.*

jan|gly (jang′glē), *adj.,* **-gli|er, -gli|est.** jangling; sounding harshly; discordant.

Jan|is|sar|y or **jan|is|sar|y** (jan′ə ser′ē), *n., pl.* **-sar|ies. 1** a Turkish soldier in the Sultan's guard from the 1300's until 1826. Janissaries formed the main fighting force of the Turkish army. **2** any Turkish soldier. **3** = Janizary. [< Middle French *janissaire* < Italian *giannizzero* < Turkish *yeniçeri* < *yeni* new + *çeri* soldiery]

jan|i|tor (jan′ə tər), *n.* **1** a person hired to take care of a building or offices; caretaker: *The janitor swept the floors and locked up the building each night.* **SYN:** custodian. **2** a doorkeeper; porter. [< Latin *jānitor* doorkeeper < *jānua* door < *jānus* arched passageway; originally, Janus]

jan|i|to|ri|al (jan′ə tôr′ē əl, -tōr′-), *adj.* of or having to do with a janitor.

jan|i|tress (jan′ə tris), *n.* a woman janitor.

Jan|i|zar|y or **jan|i|zar|y** (jan′ə zer′ē), *n., pl.* **-zar|ies. 1** a West Indian fish related to the tautog and wrasse. **2** = Janissary.

Jan|sen|ism (jan′sə niz əm), *n.* the doctrine of Cornelius Jansen, 1585-1638, a Dutch theologian, who maintained the perverseness and inability for good of the natural human will, and denied the possibility of resisting divine grace.

Jan|sen|ist (jan′sə nist), *n., adj.* **—*n.*** a believer in Jansenism.
—*adj.* = Jansenistic.

Jan|sen|is|tic (jan′sə nis′tik), *adj.* of, having to do with, or characteristic of Jansenism or the Jansenists.

Jan|son (jan′sən), *n.* a printing type of the old style, based on the design of Anton Janson, a German type founder of the 1600's.

Jan|u|ar|y (jan′yů er′ē), *n., pl.* **-ar|ies.** the first month of the year. It has 31 days. *Abbr:* Jan. [< Latin *Jānuārius* (*mensis*) (the month) of *Jānus* Janus]

jan|u|is clau|sis (jan′yů is klô′zis), *Latin.* with closed doors.

Ja|nus (jā′nəs), *n. Roman Mythology.* the god of gates and doors, and of beginnings and endings, represented with two faces, one looking forward and the other looking backward. [< Latin *Jānus*]

Ja|nus-faced (jā′nəs fāst′), *adj.* **1** two-faced; double-dealing; deceitful. **2** looking two ways: *A friend is Janus-faced: he looks to the past and the future* (Emerson).

Jap (jap), *adj., n. Informal.* Japanese (used in an unfriendly way).

J.A.P. or **JAP** (no periods; *pronounced* jap), *n. U.S. Slang.* Jewish American Princess (used in an unfriendly way to refer to a rich or spoiled Jewish girl or woman): *Q. What do J.A.P.s most often make for dinner? A. Reservations* (Leo Rosten).

Jap., **1** Japan. **2** Japanese.

ja|pan (jə pan′), *n., v.,* **-panned, -pan|ning. —*n.*** **1** a hard, glossy varnish. Black japan is used on wood or metal. **2** articles varnished and ornamented in the Japanese manner. **3** a liquid used to make paint dry faster. **—*v.t.*** to put japan on; varnish with japan or any similar substance. [< *Japan,* where the earliest kind came from]

Japan., Japanese.

Japan clover, a cloverlike plant of the pea family, introduced into the southern United States from Asia, grown for forage and fertilizer.

Japan Current, a strong, warm current that begins near the Philippines and flows northeast past Japan, across the Pacific Ocean; Kuroshio.

Jap|a|nese (jap′ə nēz′, -nēs′), *adj., n., pl.* **-nese.**
—*adj.* of Japan, its people, or their language: *Japanese art, Japanese writings, Japanese customs.*
—*n.* **1** a person born or living in Japan. **2** the language of Japan. Also, **Nipponese.**

Japanese andromeda, an Asian evergreen shrub of the heath family, with large, glossy leaves and clusters of whitish flowers.

Japanese barberry, a compact shrub with yellow flowers, bright red fruit, and smooth-edged leaves, popular as a garden plant.

Japanese beetle, a small green-and-brown beetle that eats fruits, leaves, and flowers. It was brought accidentally from Japan to the United States, where it causes much damage to crops. It is a beetle of the same kind as the scarab.

Japanese chin, = Japanese spaniel.

Japanese clover, = Japan clover.

Japanese crab or **Japanese king crab,** = king crab (def. 2).

Japanese iris, a tall iris with beardless, reddish-purple, yellow, or white flowers.

Japanese ivy, a fast-growing woody vine much used to ornament walls; Boston ivy. Japanese ivy and Virginia creeper belong to a genus of the grape family. See picture under **ivy.**

Japanese Kimona cat, an Asian cat of a rare breed, having black markings on the shoulders and the back that suggest a kimono.

***Japanese lantern,** a lantern of thin, colored paper that can be folded up when not in use; Chinese lantern.

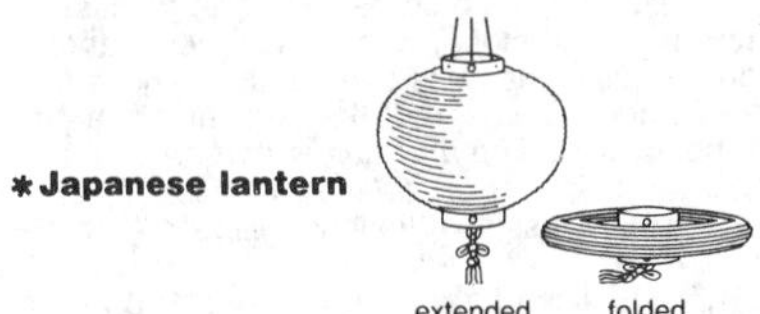

***Japanese lantern**

Japanese macaque, a large monkey of Japan that lives as far north as Honshu Island. It is used for scientific research because of its ability to learn quickly.

Japanese maple, a maple tree of Japan and Korea, with small, purple flowers, cultivated for ornament.

Japanese mink, = China mink.

Japanese persimmon, **1** the edible, orange-colored or red fruit of an Asiatic tree grown in the southern and western United States. **2** the tree itself. Also, **kaki.**

Japanese plum, a very sweet and juicy yellow, red, or purple plum, native to Japan but now grown commercially, especially in California; salicina plum.

Japanese quail, an Asian quail that is believed to be the world's oldest domesticated bird and that is widely used for scientific research.

Japanese quince, an ornamental Asiatic shrub of the rose family, often grown for its showy red, pink, or white flowers; japonica.

Japanese river fever, = scrub typhus.

Japanese snail, a freshwater snail, native to Japan, commonly used in aquariums as a scavenger.

Pronunciation Key: hat, āge, cãre, fär; let, ēqual, tėrm; it, īce; hot, ōpen, ôrder; oil, out; cup, pu̇t, rüle; child; long; thin; ᴛʜen; zh, measure; ə represents **a** in about, **e** in taken, **i** in pencil, **o** in lemon, **u** in circus.

Japanese spaniel, any one of a breed of small dogs with a long, silky, white coat with patches of black, red, or lemon yellow, and a fluffy tail curling up over the back.

Japanese spurge, a low, creeping evergreen plant of the box family. It is a kind of pachysandra and forms a dense ground cover.

Japanese wisteria, a type of wisteria vine that blooms later than most wisterias with violet, pink, or white flowers.

Japanese wood oil, = tung oil.

Japanese yew, an evergreen tree or shrub native to Asia, with flat, dark-green needles and scaly, reddish-brown bark, commonly grown for ornament.

Jap·an·esque (jap′ən esk′), *adj.* in the Japanese style, as of art or decoration.

Jap·an·ize (jap′ə nīz), *v.t.*, **-ized, -iz·ing.** to make Japanese in form, customs, or character. —**Jap′an·i·za′tion,** *n.*

Japan wax, a yellow wax made from the berries of a wax tree, used in making fine candles and in polishing the grain of fine leather.

jape (jāp), *n., v.,* **japed, jap·ing.** —***n.*** **1** a joke; jest; gibe: *Even the old jape about the policeman's knock remains extremely funny* (Listener). **2** a trick: *The japes and mockeries of evil spirits* (Scott).
—***v.t.*** **1** to mock; insult. SYN: deride. **2** to trick; deceive. SYN: beguile. —***v.i.*** to jest; joke; jeer: *I have no mind to jest and jape* (Swinburne). —**jap′er,** *n.*

jap·er·y (jā′pər ē), *n., pl.* **-er·ies. 1** a jest; gibe. **2** *Obsolete.* trickery.

Ja·pheth (jā′fith), *n.* a son of Noah, probably the third son, the legendary ancestor of the so-called Indo-European race (in the Bible, Genesis 5:32, 9:24).

Ja·phet·ic (jə fet′ik), *adj.* **1** of or having to do with Japheth. **2** *Obsolete.* Indo-European.

Jap·lish (jap′lish), *n., adj.* —***n.*** a blend of Japanese and English spoken in Japan.
—***adj.*** of or in Japlish.
[blend of *Japanese* and *English*]

ja·po·nai·se·rie (zhȧ′po nez ə rē′), *n.* a style or work of art or decoration deriving from or suggesting the Japanese tradition: [*The*] *ballet, "Yugen," is a piece of japonaiserie based on a Noh play* (New York Times). [< French *Japonais* Japanese + *-erie* -ery]

ja·pon·i·ca (jə pon′ə kə), *n.* **1** = camellia. **2** a shrub with showy, red, pink, or white flowers; Japanese quince. [< New Latin *japonica,* (originally) feminine adjective, Japanese, probably < French *Japon* Japan]

ja·pyg·id (jə pij′əd), *n.* any one of a group of long, wingless insects with a pair of appendages like forceps at the end of its body and no eyes, found in moss and at the edges of woods. [< New Latin *Japygidae* the family name]

jar[1] (jär), *n.* **1** a deep container made of glass, earthenware, or stone, with a wide mouth and no spout. It sometimes has two handles, and is usually cylindrical in shape. **2** the amount that a jar can hold; jarful: *The boy claims that he can eat a whole jar of jelly at breakfast.* [< Middle French *jarre* earthen vessel < Provençal *jarra* < Arabic *jarrah*]

jar[2] (jär), *v.,* **jarred, jar·ring,** *n.* —***v.t.*** **1** to cause to shake or rattle; vibrate: *Your heavy footsteps jar my table. It* [*music*] *fills the vast pile and seems to jar the very walls* (Washington Irving). **2** to have a harsh, unpleasant effect on; shock: *The children's screams jarred my nerves. The decision will reverberate and will jar the country* (Saturday Review). **3** to injure by concussion. **4** to cause to sound discordantly: *I alone the beauty mar, I alone the music jar* (John Greenleaf Whittier).
—***v.i.*** **1** to make a harsh, grating noise. SYN: scrape, grate. **2** to shake; rattle: *The windows jar when the wind blows.* **3** to clash; quarrel; conflict: *We did not get on well together; our opinions always jarred.* SYN: disagree. **4** to strike with a grating sound, or so as to cause vibration: *a broadsword upon target jarr'd* (Scott). **5** to have a harsh effect (on the ear, nerves, feelings, or other sensibilities): *His laugh jars on one's ear* (Thackeray).
—***n.*** a harsh vibration; shake; rattle: *The violin took an awful jar when it fell to the floor, but didn't break in its case.* **2** a harsh, grating noise: *Bolt and bar Resumed their place with sullen jar* (Scott). **3** a slight shock to the ears, nerves, or feelings; harsh, unpleasant effect: *The crash of the glass window produced a jar in all the passers-by.* **4** *Figurative.* a clash; quarrel; disagreement.
[probably imitative]

jar[3] (jär), *n.* a turn; turning.
on the jar, slightly open; ajar: *I see Mrs. Bardell's street door on the jar* (Dickens).
[variant of *char*[2]]

ja·ra·be ta·pa·tí·o (hä rä′bā tä pä THē′ō), the national dance of Mexico, a folk dance performed by couples who alternately kick out their feet and interlock arms as they swing around. [< Mexican Spanish *jarabe tapatío*]

jar·cha (här′chä, Här′-), *n.* a final verse or refrain added to an Arabic poem in a Mozarabic dialect of Spanish using Arabic or Hebrew characters. Jarchas, which originated in Spain in the 1000's A.D., are the oldest form of lyric poetry in a Romance language. [< Spanish *jarcha*]

jar·di·niere (jär′də nir′), *n.* **1** an ornamental pot or stand for flowers or plants. **2** a garnish of vegetables. [< French *jardinière* < *jardin* garden]

jar·ful (jär′fu̇l), *n., pl.* **-fuls.** as much as a jar will hold.

jar·gon[1] (jär′gən, -gon), *n., v.* —***n.*** **1** confused, meaningless talk or writing; gibberish: *Some of the contributions . . . are so badly written, so muddled and full of jargon, that an editorial attempt to reduce the chaos and translate into English is just not worth while* (Science News). **2** a language that is not understood (used in an unfriendly way): *the jargon of foreigners.* **3** talk containing a mixture of languages, such as pidgin English. **4** the language of a special group, profession, or activity; lingo. Doctors, actors, and sailors have jargons. *surfing jargon.* SYN: cant, argot, slang. **5** = chatter.
—***v.i.*** **1** to talk jargon: . . . *away, and jargon no more in that manner* (Thomas Carlyle). **2** to chatter.
[< Old French *jargon,* probably ultimately imitative]
▶**Jargon** is commonly used to refer to any confused or unintelligible speech or writing: *He spoke such a jargon I couldn't make head or tail of what he said.* Among linguists, *jargon* is a technical word for a dialect composed of the mixture of two or more languages, such as the Chinook jargon of the Pacific Northwest and the Chinese-English jargon, pidgin English.

jar·gon[2] (jär′gon), *n.* a colorless or smoky variety of the mineral zircon, found in Ceylon (Sri Lanka). Also, **jargoon.** [< Middle French *jargon* < Italian *giargone,* perhaps < Portuguese *zarcão* < Arabic *zarqūn* < Persian *zargun.* Compare etym. under **zircon.**]

jar·gon·eer (jär′gə nir′), *n.* = jargonist.

jar·gon·ist (jär′gə nist), *n.* **1** a person who uses a particular jargon or phraseology. **2** a person who studies jargon.

jar·gon·is·tic (jär′gə nis′tik), *adj.* characterized by the use of or expressed in jargon: *Much of what he is looking at is not really science at all but a new kind of . . . jargonistic pseudo-scholarship* (New Yorker).

jar·gon·ize (jär′gə nīz), *v.,* **-ized, -iz·ing.** —***v.i.*** to talk jargon or a jargon.
—***v.t.*** **1** to translate into jargon. **2** to bring or put by means of jargon.

jar·goon (jär gün′), *n.* = jargon[2].

jarl (yärl), *n.* an ancient Scandinavian chief or nobleman. [< Scandinavian (compare Old Icelandic *jarl*)]

jar·o·site (jar′ə sīt, jə rō′-), *n. Mineralogy.* a hydrous sulfate of iron and potassium, occurring in yellowish or brownish crystals. *Formula:* $K_2Fe_6(SO_4)_4(OH)_{12}$ [< Barranco *Jaroso,* an area in Spain + English *-ite*[1]]

jar·o·vize (yär′ə vīz), *v.t.,* **-vized, -viz·ing.** = vernalize. Also, **iarovize, yarovize.** [< Russian *yarovoe* spring grain + English *-ize*]

jar·rah (jär′ə), *n.* a Western Australian eucalyptus tree yielding a weather-resistant timber. [alteration of *Jerrhyl,* the native name]

jar·ring·ly (jär′ing lē), *adv.* in a jarring manner; discordantly.

jar·vey (jär′vē), *n., pl.* **-veys.** *British Informal.* **1** a cabdriver. **2** a cab. **3** the driver of a jaunting car: *I had despatched waiters in different directions for a jarvey* (Charles J. Lever). [< *Jarvis,* or *Jervis,* a proper name]

Jas., James.

ja·sey (jā′zē), *n., pl.* **-seys.** a wig, especially one made of worsted. [perhaps < *Jersey,* one of the Channel Islands; see etym. under **jersey**]

jas·mine or **jas·min** (jas′mən, jaz′-), *n.* **1** a shrub or vine with clusters of fragrant yellow, white, or reddish flowers. Jasmine belongs to the olive family. **2** the essential oil or resin obtained from this plant and used in making perfume. **3** any one of several other plants of other families bearing fragrant flowers, such as the gelsemium and the Madagascar jasmine. Also, **jessamine.** [< French *jasmin* < Arabic *yāsmīn* < Persian]

Ja·son (jā′sən), *n. Greek Legend.* the Greek hero who led the expedition of the Argonauts and secured the Golden Fleece with Medea's help.

jas·per (jas′pər), *n.* **1** an opaque, colored, granular quartz, usually red, yellow, or brown. **2** a green precious stone of ancient times: *And he that sat was to look upon like a jasper and a sardine stone* (Revelation 4:3). [< Old French *jaspre, jaspe* < Latin *iaspis, -idis* < Greek *iaspis, -idos* < a Phoenician word]

jas·per·ize (jas′pə rīz), *v.t.,* **-ized, -iz·ing.** to convert into jasper or a substance like jasper: *jasperized wood.*

jasper ware, a fine porcelain or stoneware invented by Josiah Wedgwood and used by him for his cameo designs.

jas·per·y (jas′pə rē), *adj.* of, like, or containing jasper: *jaspery agate.*

jas·pi·lite (jas′pə līt), *n.* a siliceous rock consisting of interbanded layers of red chert and hematite. [< *jasper* + *-lite*]

Jat (jät, jôt), *n.* one of a people of the Punjab, Sind, and northwestern India. [< Hindi *Jāṭ*]

ja·to (jā′tō), *n. Aeronautics.* a unit consisting of one or more rocket engines, to provide extra jet propulsion for speeding up the take-off of an airplane or for helping it to take off with heavy loads. [< *j*(et) *a*(ssisted) *t*(ake)-*o*(ff)]

jaunce (jôns, jäns), *v.i.,* **jaunced, jaunc·ing.** *Obsolete.* to prance. [origin uncertain]

jaun·dice (jôn′dis, jän′-), *n., v.,* **-diced, -dic·ing.** —***n.*** **1** an unhealthy bodily condition that causes yellowness of the skin, eyes, and body fluids, and disturbed vision; icterus. It is caused by too much bile in the blood. Jaundice is a symptom of some diseases and ailments, such as infectious hepatitis or gallstones. **2** *Figurative.* a disturbed or unnaturally sour mental outlook, due to envy, discontent, or jealousy: *Jealousy, the jaundice of the soul* (John Dryden).
—***v.t.*** **1** to cause jaundice in. **2** *Figurative.* to prejudice the mind and judgment of, by envy, discontent, or jealousy; sour the temper of: *Her perceptions were jaundiced by passion* (Ann Radcliffe). *The envy of wealth jaundiced his soul* (Edward G. Bulwer-Lytton).
[alteration of Middle English *jawnes* < Old French *jaunisse* < *jaune,* earlier *jalne* yellow < Latin *galbinus* greenish-yellow < *galbus* yellow]

jaun·diced (jôn′dist, jän′-), *adj.* **1** affected with or as if with jaundice; yellow-colored: *Koldunov led Lik up a crooked little street, mottled here and there by jaundiced, and also somehow crooked, sunlight* (Vladimir Nabokov). **2** *Figurative.* colored or prejudiced by envy, jealousy, anger, or the like: *The political leaders, with sharp focus on home rule and local patronage, turn a jaundiced eye on such geopolitical thoughts* (New York Times).

jaunt (jônt, jänt), *n., v.* —***n.*** **1** a short journey or excursion, especially for pleasure: *a jaunt to the seashore. My uncle . . . talks of treating us with a jaunt to London* (Tobias Smollett). **2** *Obsolete.* a fatiguing journey: *Fie, how my bones ache! What a jaunt have I had* (Shakespeare).
—***v.i.*** to take a short pleasure trip or excursion: *If the authorities really believe our young service men need to travel, why not give them a free warrant to jaunt round British Railways?* (London Times). [origin uncertain]

* **jaunt·ing car** (jôn′ting, jän′-), a two-wheeled carriage or cart having two seats back to back, used in Ireland.

***jaunting car**

jaun·ty (jôn′tē, jän′-), *adj.,* **-ti·er, -ti·est,** *n., pl.* **-ties.** —***adj.*** **1** easy and lively; carefree; sprightly: *The happy children walked with jaunty steps.* SYN: airy, gay. **2** smart; stylish: *She wore a jaunty little hat.* SYN: elegant. **3** *Obsolete.* genteel.
—***n.*** *Slang.* the person in charge of a ship's police.
[earlier *janty* or *jantée,* apparently < pronunciation of Middle French *gentil* noble, gentle < Old French < Latin *gentīlis.* See etym. of doublets **genteel, gentile, gentle.**] —**jaun′ti·ly,** *adv.* —**jaun′ti·ness,** *n.*

jaunty cart, = jaunting car.

Jav., Javanese.

Ja·va (jä′və, jav′ə), *n.* **1** a kind of coffee obtained from Java and nearby islands. **2** Also, **java.** *Slang.* coffee: *a good cup of java.* **3** any one of a breed of American chicken with solid black or mottled black-and-white plumage, and a long, heavy body.

Java almond, **1** a large tree of Asia with abundant foliage and hard, heavy wood. **2** its hard, oily seed that is eaten or pressed for its oil.

Java man, a very early form of man known from fossil remains found in Java; Pithecanthropus.

Java man lived in the Pleistocene period.

Ja|van (jä′vən, jav′ən), *adj., n.* = Javanese.

Jav|a|nese (jav′ə nēz′, -nēs′), *adj., n., pl.* **-nese.** *—adj.* of Java, its people, or their language. *—n.* **1** a person born or living in Java. **2** the Malayo-Polynesian language of Java.

Java sparrow, a finchlike gray bird native to Java. It is commonly kept as a cage bird.

★jave|lin (jav′lin, jav′ə lin), *n., v.* *—n.* **1** a light spear thrown by hand: *And in his hand a pointed javelin shakes* (Alexander Pope). **2** a wooden or metal spear thrown for distance in track and field contests. It is at least 8 feet 6⅜ inches long and at least 1.761 pounds in weight. *—v.t.* to strike or pierce with or as if with a javelin. [<Middle French *javeline* (diminutive) <Old French *javelot,* perhaps <a Germanic word]

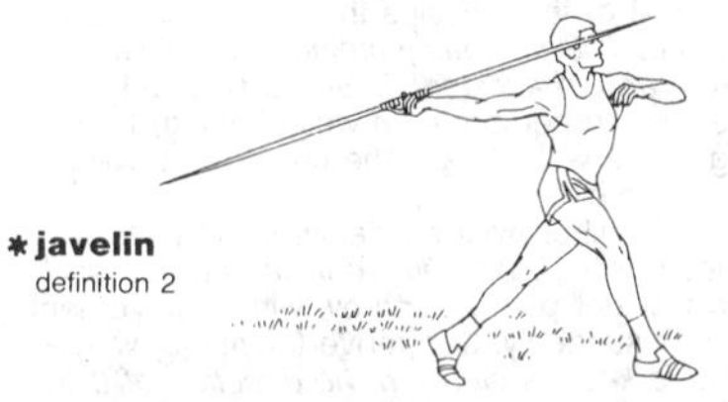

★javelin
definition 2

ja|ve|li|na or **ja|va|li|na** (hä′və lē′nə), *n. Southwestern U.S.* the peccary. [<Spanish *jabalina,* feminine of *jabalin* wild boar]

Ja|vel or **Ja|velle water** (zhə vel′), a solution of sodium or potassium hypochlorite, used as bleach and disinfectant. [<French *eau de Javelle* <*Javelle,* a former town, now included in Paris]

jaw¹ (jô), *n., v.* *—n.* **1** the lower part of the face. **2** the upper or lower bone, or sets of bones, that together form the framework of the mouth; jawbone. The lower jaw is movable. **SYN:** mandible, maxilla. **3** *Slang.* **a** a talk; gossip. **b** impudent talk. *—v.i. Slang.* **1** to go on talking at great length, in a boring way; gossip: *This fellow was leaning against the counter, jawing with the blond waitress* (Guy Endore). **2** to find fault; scold: *Sambo's allers a jawin' at me 'cause I don't pick faster* (Harriet Beecher Stowe). *—v.t. Slang.* to scold or lecture: *I have been jawed for letting you go* (Frederick Marryat). **jaws, a** the mouth with its jawbones and teeth: *The hungry spaniels . . . with greedy jaws* (Edmund Spenser). **b** a narrow entrance to a valley, mountain pass, channel, or the like: *The guide . . . led slowly through the pass's jaws* (Scott). **c** the parts in a tool or machine that bite or grasp. A vise has jaws. **d** *Figurative.* the seizing action or capacity of any devouring agency, as of death or time: *Into the jaws of Death, Into the mouth of Hell Rode the six hundred* (Tennyson). [Middle English *jowe;* perhaps influenced by Middle French *joue* cheek <Latin *gabata* dish, bowl, cheek. Perhaps related to **chew**] **—jaw′er,** *n.* **—jaw′less,** *adj.*

jaw² (jô), *n., v. Scottish.* *—n.* a quantity of water or other liquid dashed, splashed, or thrown out; an outpour of water or other liquid. *—v.t.* to pour or dash (water or other liquid) in waves. *—v.i.* to dash, pour, or splash. [origin unknown]

ja|wan (jə wän′), *n.* a soldier or infantryman of the Indian army. [<Hindi *jawān*]

jaw|bone (jô′bōn′), *n., v.,* **-boned, -bon|ing,** *adj.* *—n.* one of the bones in which the teeth are set, especially the lower jaw. *—v.t., v.i. U.S. Slang.* to lecture, scold, or otherwise try to persuade by talking, especially in an attempt to influence some decision. *—adj.* using or characterized by jawboning.

jaw|bon|ing (jô′bō′ning), *n. U.S. Slang.* strong urging or warning by an influential person to leaders in industry, labor, or other groups, to comply with certain regulations and restraints: *Lecturing business and labor on their responsibilities to hold down prices and wages—jawboning as it was called . . . has been foregone* (Harper's).

jaw|break|er (jô′brā′kər), *n. Informal.* **1** a word that is hard to pronounce. **2** a large, hard piece of candy, usually in the shape of a ball. **3** a machine with powerful jaws for crushing ore.

jaw|break|ing (jô′brā′king), *adj.* hard to pronounce: *In the jawbreaking jargon of geology, the ore was "manganiferous, acid-soluble, in a nonmagnetic amorphous shale gangue"* (Newsweek).

jaw crusher, = jawbreaker (def. 3).

jawed (jôd), *adj.* having a jaw or jaws.

jaw|fish (jô′fish′), *n., pl.* **-fish|es** or (*collectively*) **-fish.** a small fish found near the rocky bottoms of tropical seas, noted for the great length of its upper jaw.

jaw-jaw (jô′jô′), *v., n. Especially British Slang.* *—v.i.* to talk at great length; to engage in a long discussion. *—n.* a drawn-out or lengthy talk; long discussion. [reduplication of *jaw¹* to talk]

jaw|line (jô′līn′), *n.* the outline of a person's or animal's jaw.

jaws (jôz), *n.pl.* See under **jaw¹.**

jay¹ (jā), *n.* **1** any one of various birds of the crow family: **a** a noisy American bird with a crest and blue feathers; blue jay. **b** a noisy European bird with a crest. **c** the Canada jay or the Steller's jay. **2** *Figurative. Slang.* **a** a silly, stupid person; simpleton. **b** someone who is an easy victim. **3** *Figurative.* an impertinent chatterer. [<Old French *jay,* Old North French *gai, gay;* origin uncertain]

jay² (jā), *n. U.S. Slang.* a marijuana cigarette. [<pronunciation of *j* for *joint* (def. 9)]

jay|bird (jā′bėrd′), *n. Dialect.* a jay.

Jay|cee (jā′sē′), *n. U.S. Informal.* **1** a junior chamber of commerce. **2** one of its members. [<pronunciation of *J.C.,* part of the abbreviation of *Junior Chamber of Commerce*]

jay|gee (jā′jē′), *n. U.S. Informal.* a lieutenant junior grade. [<pronunciation of *jg,* abbreviation of *junior grade*]

jay|hawk (jā′hôk′), *v.t. U.S. Slang.* **1** to harry as a jayhawker does; pillage. **2** to carry off. [back formation <*jayhawker*]

jay|hawk|er (jā′hô′kər), *n. U.S.* a plundering guerrilla or irregular soldier, especially a member of the bands in and around Kansas and Missouri before and during the Civil War who combined pillage and guerrilla warfare.

Jay|hawk|er (jā′hô′kər), *n.* a native or inhabitant of Kansas. [<*jayhawker*]

Jayhawk State, a nickname of Kansas.

jay|vee (jā′vē′), *n., adj. U.S. Informal.* *—n.* **1** a junior varsity team. **2** a member of such a team. *—adj.* of or having to do with a jayvee or jayvees. [<pronunciation of *j.v.* for *junior varsity*]

jay|walk (jā′wôk′), *v.i. Informal.* to walk across a street without paying attention to traffic rules. [American English, perhaps <*jay,* in sense of "rustic, ignorant" + *walk*] **—jay′walk′er,** *n.*

jazz (jaz), *n., adj., v.* *—n.* **1a** a kind of music in which the accents fall at unusual places. It is native to the United States, where it developed from ragtime. The players slide from tone to tone, introduce independent tones, and imitate vocal effects with their instruments. **b** a piece of such music. **2** dance music in the style of jazz. **3** *Slang.* liveliness. **4** lively comedy elements introduced into a play or the like. **5** *U.S. Slang.* a worthless or peculiar thing; rubbish; nonsense: . . . *a consignment of Belgian hares or some such jazz* (S. J. Perelman). **6** dancing or a dance performed to jazz music. *—adj.* of or like jazz: *jazz records, jazz rhythms.* *—v.t.* **1** to play (music) as jazz. **2** *Slang.* to make lively. *—v.i.* to play jazz music or dance to jazz. **jazz up,** *Slang.* to make lively; add flavor or interest to: *He jazzed up the New Haven's freight cars with an eye-catching black, white, and Chinese vermilion paint job* (Time). [American English; perhaps variant of earlier *jasm* energy, drive; probably of American Negro origin] **—jazz′er,** *n.*

Jazz Age, 1 a period marked by the great popularity of jazz or the first appearance of jazz. **2** the 1920's, especially in the United States.

jazz loft, *U.S.* an upper floor in a building used as a club or concert hall where jazz, especially experimental jazz, is played.

jazz|man (jaz′man′, -mən), *n., pl.* **-men.** a person who plays jazz; jazz musician.

jazz-rock (jaz′rok′), *n.* a blend of jazz and rock'n'roll rhythms.

jazz tap, tap-dancing to jazz music or rhythms.

jazz|y (jaz′ē), *adj.,* **jazz|i|er, jazz|i|est.** *Informal.* **1** having to do with or suggestive of jazz music. **2** *Slang.* wildly active or lively. **3** *Slang.* fancy; ornate; flashy: *St. John's does not guarantee that the classics make jazzy reading* (Saturday Review). **—jazz′i|ly,** *adv.* **—jazz′i|ness,** *n.*

J.C., 1 Jesus Christ. **2** Julius Caesar.

J.C.B., 1 Bachelor of Canon Law (Latin, *Juris Canonici Baccalaureus*). **2** Bachelor of Civil Law (Latin, *Juris Civilis Baccalaureus*).

J.C.C., Junior Chamber of Commerce.

J.C.D., 1 Doctor of Canon Law (Latin, *Juris Canonici Doctor*). **2** Doctor of Civil Law (Latin, *Juris Civilis Doctor*).

J.C.L., Licenciate in Canon Law (Latin, *Juris Canonici Licentiatus*).

JCS (no periods) or **J.C.S.,** Joint Chiefs of Staff.

jct., junction.

J curve, *Economics.* a curve showing that after devaluation of a country's currency, its trade deficit normally worsens before it improves, reflecting the higher import prices resulting from the devaluation.

J.D., 1 Doctor of Jurisprudence (Latin, *Juris Doctor*). **2** Doctor of Laws (Latin, *Jurum Doctor*). **3** Jordan dinar (the unit of currency of Jordan). **4** *U.S.* Justice Department. **5** juvenile delinquent.

JDL (no periods) or **J.D.L.,** Jewish Defense League.

Je. or **Je** (no period), June.

jeal|ous (jel′əs), *adj.* **1** fearful that a person one loves may love someone else or prefer someone else: *When my brother sees Mother holding the new baby, he becomes jealous. One may be jealous of the person loved or of the rival.* **2** full of envy; envious: *He is jealous of his brother's skill at games.* **SYN:** grudging, resentful. **3** requiring complete loyalty or faithfulness: *"The Lord thy God is a jealous God."* **4** watchful in keeping or guarding something; careful: *Our city is jealous of its rights within the state.* **5** close; watchful; suspicious: *The dog was such a jealous guardian of the little girl that he would not let her cross the street.* **6** *Dialect.* apprehensive of evil; fearful (of). **7** *Obsolete.* doubtful: *That you do love me, I am nothing jealous* (Shakespeare). [<Old French *gelos* (with English *-ous*) <Late Latin *zēlōsus* <Latin *zēlus* zeal <Greek *zêlos.* See etym. of doublet **zealous.**] **—jeal′ous|ly,** *adv.* **—jeal′ous|ness,** *n.*

jeal|ous|y (jel′ə sē), *n., pl.* **-ous|ies. 1** a jealous condition or feeling; dislike or fear of rivals; envy. **2** an instance of jealous feeling.

jean (jēn), *n.* a strong, heavy, twilled cotton cloth, used for overalls and work or play clothes. **jeans,** overalls or trousers made of this cloth: *The cowboy wore blue jeans.* [apparently <Middle English *jeane,* adjective, Genoese <French *Gênes* Genoa (because such cloth was made there)]

jeaned (jēnd), *adj.* wearing jeans: *They're 22, . . . jeaned and meticulously casual; perfectly young* (Maclean's). Also, **bejeaned.**

jeans|wear (jēnz′wãr′), *n.* clothing made out of jeans cloth, especially overalls or trousers for casual wear: *Jeans departments are readying themselves for a flood of related jeanswear which designers are beginning to produce* (New York Times Magazine).

jeb|el (jeb′əl), *n.* = djebel.

Jeb|u|sites (jeb′yə zīts), *n.pl.* the people from whom David captured Mount Zion (in the Bible, II Samuel 5:6-7).

★jeep (jēp), *n., v. Especially U.S.* *—n.* **1** a small but powerful automobile in which power is transmitted to all four wheels, used for many purposes by soldiers, farmers, builders, and others. It was originally designed for use by the United States Army and holds a quarter of a ton. **2 Jeep,** a trademark for any one of certain automobiles for civilian use based on this. **3** a small, light reconnaissance and liaison plane. **4** an escort aircraft carrier. *—v.i.* to ride in a jeep. [American English; reduction of *"Jeepers creepers!"* (the exclamation of Major General George Lynch, Chief of Infantry, U.S. Army, upon the occasion of his first ride in the prototype model of the vehicle in 1939 at Fort Myer, Virginia; coined at the time by Mr. Charles H. Payne, his companion in, and designer of, the vehicle); perhaps later influenced by the initials *G.P.,* for General Purpose, official designation of the vehicle]

★jeep
definition 1

jee|pers (jē′pərz), *interj.* an exclamation of surprise or wonder.

jeep|load (jēp′lōd′), *n.* as much as a jeep can hold or carry.

jeep|ney (jēp′nē), *n., pl.* **-neys** or **-nies.** (in the Philippines) a jeep enlarged to carry about ten passengers, used as a bus or jitney. [<*jeep* + (jit)*ney*]

jeer (jir), *v., n.* *—v.i.* to make fun in a rude or unkind way; scoff; mock: *Do not jeer at the mistakes or misfortunes of others.* **SYN:** See syn. under **scoff.** *—v.t.* to speak to or treat with scornful derision; deride. *—n.* a mocking or insulting remark; gibe; taunt. [origin uncertain] **—jeer′er,** *n.* **—jeer′ing|ly,** *adv.*

jeers (jirz), *n.pl. Archaic Nautical.* heavy tackle for hoisting the lower yards. [origin uncertain]

jeez (jēz), *interj.* an exclamation or mild oath; gosh. Also, **geez.** [alteration of *Jesus*]

je|fe (hā′fā), *n. Spanish.* a chief; leader.

Jef|fer|son Davis's Birthday (jef′ər sən), *U.S.* June 3, the birthday of Jefferson Davis, observed

---

Pronunciation Key: hat, āge, cãre, fär; let, ēqual, tėrm; it, īce; hot, ōpen, ôrder; oil, out; cup, pu̇t, rüle; child; long; thin; ᴛʜen; zh, measure; ə represents **a** in about, **e** in taken, **i** in pencil, **o** in lemon, **u** in circus.

as a legal holiday in various southern states. In Kentucky and Louisiana it is celebrated as Confederate Memorial Day.

Jefferson Day, *U.S.* April 13, the birthday of Thomas Jefferson, sometimes observed by the Democratic Party by holding dinners, usually to raise funds.

Jef|fer|so|ni|an (jef′ər sō′nē ən), *adj., n.* —***adj.*** **1** of or having to do with Thomas Jefferson (1743-1826), third President of the United States, and the first great leader of the Democratic (then called Republican) Party: *Jeffersonian democracy.* **2** of or like the political principles of Thomas Jefferson; democratic.
—***n.*** a follower of Thomas Jefferson.

Jef|fer|so|ni|an|ism (jef′ər sō′nē ə niz′əm), *n.* **1** the political doctrines of Thomas Jefferson, who emphasized the greatest possible individual and local freedom and restrictions of the powers of the national government. **2** adherence to these doctrines.

Jef|frey pine (jef′rē), a pine of the western United States, having long needles and similar to the ponderosa pine; western yellow pine. [< John *Jeffrey,* a Scottish botanist of the 1800's]

je|had (ji häd′), *n.* = jihad.

Je|hosh|a|phat (ji hosh′ə fat, -hos′-), *n., interj.* —***n.*** a son of Asa and a king of Judah from about 873 to 849 B.C. (in the Bible, II Chronicles 17-20). —***interj.*** an exclamation of surprise.

Je|ho|vah (ji hō′və), *n.* one of the names of God in the Old Testament. [modern representation of Hebrew *Yahweh* (originally written without vowels as JHVH), interpreted as meaning "he that is," "the self-existent"; influenced by the vowels of *Adonai*]

Jehovah's Witnesses, a Christian sect, founded by Charles T. Russell in Pennsylvania in the 1870's, adhering to the principle that religious belief is paramount as a rule of life even when in conflict with the regulations of the civil state, and maintaining that the kingdom of God is at hand.

Je|ho|vism (ji hō′viz əm), *n.* = Yahwism.

Je|ho|vist (ji hō′vist), *n., adj.* = Yahwist.

Je|ho|vis|tic (jē′hō vis′tik), *adj.* = Yahwistic.

Je|hu (jē′hyü), *n.* **1** a king of Israel (842 to about 815 B.C.) who overthrew the house of Ahab (in the Bible, II Kings 9-10). **2** a prophet of Judah (9th century B.C.) and chronicler of Jehoshaphat's reign (in the Bible, I Kings 16; II Chronicles 20:34).

je|hu (jē′hyü), *n. Informal.* **1** a fast driver. **2** a coachman. [< *Jehu* (with reference to his furious driving habits)]

je|ju|nal (ji jü′nəl), *adj.* of or having to do with the jejunum.

je|june (ji jün′), *adj.* **1** flat and uninteresting; barren. **2** lacking nourishing qualities; meager. **SYN:** scanty, unsatisfying. [< Latin *jējūnus* (originally) hungry, fasting] —**je|june′ly,** *adv.* —**je|june′ness,** *n.*

je|ju|ni|ty (ji jü′nə tē), *n.* state of being jejune.

je|ju|num (ji jü′nəm), *n. Anatomy.* the middle portion of the small intestine, between the duodenum and the ileum. See diagram under **intestine.** [< New Latin *jejunum* < Latin *jējūnum,* neuter of *jējūnus;* see etym. under **jejune**]

Jek|yll (jek′əl, jē′kəl), *n.* **Dr.,** a good, kind doctor in Robert Louis Stevenson's story *The Strange Case of Dr. Jekyll and Mr. Hyde.* Dr. Jekyll discovered a drug that would change him into a brutal character called Mr. Hyde.

Jek|yll-and-Hyde (jek′əl ən hīd′, jē′kəl-), *adj.* = Jekyll-Hyde.

Jek|yll-Hyde (jek′əl hīd′, jē′kəl-), *adj.* being or embodying both good and evil; having a good and a bad side: *a Jekyll-Hyde personality; . . . the Jekyll-Hyde countenance of automation* (Wall Street Journal).

je|lab or **jel|lab** (jə läb′), *n.* = djellaba.

jell (jel), *v., n.* —***v.i.*** **1** to become jelly; thicken or congeal: *The jelly won't jell* (Louisa M. Alcott). **2** *Informal.* to take definite form; become fixed: *His hunch jelled into a plan.* —***v.t.*** to cause to jell. —***n.*** = jelly. [American English; probably back formation < *jelly*]

jel|la|ba (jə lä′bə), *n.* = djellaba.

jel|lied (jel′ēd), *adj.* **1** turned into jelly; having the consistency of jelly. **2** spread with jelly.

jel|lies (jel′ēz), *n.pl.* = jelly bean shoes: *The exhibit includes everything from "jellies" (transparent, rubbery shoes) to petroleum products* (Newsweek).

jel|li|fy (jel′ə fī), *v.t., v.i.,* **-fied, -fy|ing.** to make or turn into jelly. —**jel′li|fi|ca′tion,** *n.*

Jell-O (jel′ō), *n. Trademark.* a fruit-flavored gelatin dessert.

jel|ly (jel′ē), *n., pl.* **-lies,** *v.,* **-lied, -ly|ing.** —***n.*** **1** a food, soft when hot, but somewhat firm and partly transparent when cold. Jelly can be made by boiling fruit juice and sugar together, or by cooking bones and meat juice, or by using some stiffening preparation like gelatin or pectin. **2** any substance like jelly: *Surface electrodes . . . are applied to the skin with a cushion of a special electrically-conducting jelly* (Science News). **3** a consistency like jelly: (*Figurative.*) *Mademoiselle was nearly crushed to a jelly in a hubbub at the theatre* (Charlotte Brontë). **4** = jellyfish.
—***v.i.*** to become jelly or like jelly; turn into jelly; thicken or congeal; jell: *The strong soup jellied when it was chilled in the refrigerator.* —***v.t.*** **1** to make into jelly. **2** to spread with jelly.
[< Old French *gelee* (originally) frost, past participle of *geler* congeal < Latin *gelāre* < *gelus, -ūs* frost, cold] —**jel′ly|like′,** *adj.*

jelly apple, *U.S.* an apple coated with a glaze of colored sugar syrup and eaten on a stick.

jel|ly|bean (jel′ē bēn′), *n.,* or **jelly bean,** a small candy made of jellied sugar, often shaped like a bean: *pockets sticky with jellybeans.*

jelly bean shoes, jelly shoes, or **jelly sandals.** shoes or sandals made of glossy, molded rubber or plastic in bright colors.

jelly bomb, fire bomb made with jellied gasoline.

jelly doughnut, a round, raised doughnut with a filling of jelly.

jelly|fish (jel′ē fish′), *n., pl.* **-fish|es** or (*collectively*) **-fish. 1** any one of a group of sea animals without a backbone and with a body formed of a mass of almost transparent jellylike tissue; medusa; scyphozoan. Most jellyfish have long, trailing tentacles that may bear stinging hairs or cells. They are free-swimming, marine coelenterates. **2** any similar animal, such as the free-swimming form of a hydrozoan; medusa. **3** *Informal, Figurative.* a person of weak will or character.

jel|ly|roll (jel′ē rōl′), *n.* a layer of sponge cake spread with jelly, rolled up, and often sprinkled with confectioner's sugar.

jel|u|tong (jel′ə tong), *n.* **1** the latex from an Indonesian tree, coagulated with acetic acid and purified by boiling with water, used as a base in chewing gum. **2** the tree, belonging to the dogbane family, from which the latex is obtained. [< Malay *jelutong*]

jem|a|dar (jem′ə där), *n.* in India: **1** any one of certain officials of the police or other government departments. **2** an officer in a sepoy regiment, corresponding in rank to a lieutenant. **3** the chief of a body of servants. [< Hindustani *jama′dār* < Persian *jamā′at* group of men + *dār* holder]

je main|tien|drai (zhə maɴ tyaɴ drā′), *French.* I will maintain (the motto of the Netherlands).

je-m'en-fi|chis|me (zhə mäɴ fē shēz′mə), *n. French.* **1** lack of concern or interest. **2** (literally) "I-don't-care-ism".

jem|my (jem′ē), *n., pl.* **-mies.** *British Slang.* **1** a sheep's head cooked for food. **2** = jimmy. **3** = greatcoat. [< *Jimmy,* nickname for *James*]

je ne sais quoi (zhən sā kwä′), *French.* **1** an indefinable something: *Peppers in a salad add that little je ne sais quoi that makes all the difference.* **2** (literally) I don't know what.

jen min piao (ren′mən pyou′), the official name of the yuan in the People's Republic of China. [< Chinese *jen min piao* people's bank dollar]

jen|net (jen′it), *n.* **1** a small Spanish horse. **2** a female ass. Also, **genet.** [< Middle French *genet,* or *ginet* < Spanish *ginete,* or *jinete* (originally) a Berber horseman; any horseman < Arabic *Zenāta,* a Berber tribe noted for its cavalry]

jen|ny (jen′ē), *n., pl.* **-nies. 1** = spinning jenny. **2a** the female of certain animals or birds: *a jenny wren.* **b** a female donkey. [apparently < *Jenny,* a proper name (diminutive) < *Jane*]

Jen|sen|ism (jen′sə niz əm), *n.* a theory of inheritable intelligence. [< Arthur R. *Jensen,* born 1923, American educational psychologist]

jeop|ard (jep′ərd), *v.t.* = jeopardize. [back formation < *jeopardy*]

jeop|ard|ise (jep′ər dīz), *v.t.,* **-ised, -is|ing.** *Especially British.* jeopardize.

jeop|ard|ize (jep′ər dīz), *v.t.,* **-ized, -iz|ing.** to put in danger; risk; endanger; imperil: *to jeopardize one's fortune by making bad investments. Soldiers jeopardize their lives in war.* **SYN:** hazard.

jeop|ard|y (jep′ər dē), *n.* **1** risk; danger; peril: *The man's life was in jeopardy when the tree suddenly fell.* **2** *Law.* the danger of being convicted and punished when tried for a crime. [Middle English *juparti* a problem (in chess) < Old French *jeu parti* an even or divided game < Medieval Latin *jocus partitus* < Latin *jocus* play, *partīre* to divide < *pars, partis* part]

Jeph|thah (jef′thə), *n.* a judge of Israel who sacrificed his only daughter to fulfill a rash vow (in the Bible, Judges 11:30-40).

je|quir|i|ty (jə kwir′ə tē), *n., pl.* **-ties. 1** a licorice plant of India and Brazil whose scarlet and black seeds are used as beads or weights and in medicine. **2** the seeds themselves. [< French *jéquirity* < Tupi or Guarani *jekiriti*]

Jer., **1** Jeremiah. **2** Jeremy. **3** Jersey.

jer|bo|a (jər bō′ə), *n.* a small, mouselike mammal of the desert regions of northern Africa, and eastern Europe. A jerboa is somewhat like a tiny kangaroo, with a long tail and long hind legs used for jumping. It feeds on insects. [< New Latin *jerboa* < Arabic *yarbū′*]

jer|e|mi|ad (jer′ə mī′ad), *n.* a mournful complaint; lamentation. [< French *jérémiade* < *Jérémie* Jeremiah, supposed author of the *Lamentations of Jeremiah* in the Bible]

Jer|e|mi|ah (jer′ə mī′ə), *n.* **1** a Hebrew prophet (about 626-586 B.C.) who denounced and lamented the evils of his time. **2** a book of the Old Testament containing his prophecies. *Abbr.* Jer. **3** Also, **jeremiah.** a person given to woeful complaining; pessimist.

Jer|e|mi|as (jer′ə mī′əs), *n.* Jeremiah in the Douay Bible.

jerk[1] (jėrk), *n., v.* —***n.*** **1** a sudden, sharp pull, twist, or start: *His old car started with a jerk.* **2** a pull or twist of the muscles that one cannot control; twitch: *The nervous jumping of his knee is a jerk from an old accident.* **3** *Slang.* a stupid or simple-minded person. **4** (in weight lifting) the jerking of the weight from the chest to above the head. [< verb]
—***v.t.*** **1** to pull or twist suddenly: *If the water is unexpectedly hot, you jerk your hand out.* **SYN:** See syn. under **pull. 2** to throw with a movement that stops suddenly. **3** to move (anything) with a jerk: *He jerked his elbow in the direction of the . . . Board School* (Arnold Bennett). **4** to speak or say abruptly. **5** *Informal.* to make (ice-cream sodas, sundaes, and the like) behind a soda fountain. —***v.i.*** **1** to move in a spasmodic manner; twitch. **2** to move with a jerk: *The old wagon jerked along.* [earlier, to lash, strike with a whip; perhaps imitative] —**jerk′er,** *n.*

jerk[2] (jėrk), *v., n.* —***v.t.*** to preserve (meat) by cutting it into long, thin slices and drying it in the sun. The early settlers in America used to jerk beef. —***n.*** jerked meat, especially beef. [American English < American Spanish *charquear* < *charqui* jerked meat < Quechua (Peru)]

***jer|kin** (jėr′kən), *n.* a short coat or jacket, with or without sleeves. Men wore tight leather jerkins in the 1500's and 1600's. *Is not a buff jerkin a most sweet robe of durance* (Shakespeare). [origin uncertain]

***jerkin**

jer|kin-head (jėr′kən hed′), *n.* the end of a roof when shaped like a gable but having the upper portion sloping backward or hipped. [perhaps < *jerking* (< *jerk,* verb) + *head*]

jerk|wa|ter (jėrk′wô′tər, -wot′ər), *n., adj. U.S. Informal.* —***n.*** **1** a train on a branch railway. **2** a place on a railroad where trains stop only or chiefly to get water. **3** a place of slight importance. —***adj.*** **1** insignificant; unimportant. **2** not on the main line: *a jerkwater station.* [American English, supposedly from small localities where train crews had to "jerk" water from streams with a bucket]

jerk|y[1] (jėr′kē), *adj.,* **jerk|i|er, jerk|i|est.** with sudden starts and stops; with jerks; spasmodic. **SYN:** convulsive. [< *jerk*[1] + *-y*[1]] —**jerk′i|ly,** *adv.* —**jerk′i|ness,** *n.*

jerk|y[2] (jėr′kē), *n.* strips of dried meat, usually beef; jerked meat. [< American Spanish *charqui,* see etym. under **jerk[2]**]

Jer|o|bo|am (jer′ə bō′əm), *n.* **1** the first king of the northern kingdom of Israel, from about 933 B.C. to 910 B.C., leader of the northern tribes in revolt against Judah (in the Bible, I Kings 11:26-14:20). **2** the most prosperous of the kings of Israel, who ruled in the 700's B.C. (in the Bible, II Kings 14:23-29).

jer|o|bo|am (jer′ə bō′əm), *n.* **1a** a champagne bottle that holds 104 ounces. **b** the amount that it holds. **2** *British and Scottish.* **a** any large bowl, goblet, or bottle for alcoholic beverages. **b** the contents. [< *Jeroboam,* the first king of the northern kingdom of Israel (because of his valiant nature)]

jer|ri|can (jer′ə kan′), *n.* = jerry can.

jer|ry[1] (jer′ē), ob adj. = jerry-built.

jer|ry[2] or **Jer|ry** (jer′ē), *n., pl.* **-ries.** *Slang.* **1** a German soldier. **2** a German. [perhaps a diminutive < *German*]

jer|ry-build (jer′ē bild′), *v.t.,* **-built, -build|ing.** to build in a cheap, unsubstantial, or shoddy way. —**jer′ry-build′er,** *n.*

jer|ry-built (jer′ē bilt′), *adj.* built quickly, cheaply, or carelessly of poor materials; flimsy. [perhaps

alteration of an earlier *jurybuilt.* Compare etym. under **jury^{2}**, jury-rigged.]
jerry can, a five-gallon container.
jer|sey (jėr′zē), *n., pl.* **-seys. 1** a knitted cloth of wool, cotton, rayon, nylon, or silk with a tight weave. **2** a woman's close-fitting, knitted undergarment. **3** a close-fitting sweater or shirt that is pulled on over the head. [< the island of *Jersey,* where the knitting of worsted was long an industry]
Jer|sey (jėr′zē), *n., pl.* **-seys.** any one of a breed of small, fawn-colored cattle that came originally from the island of Jersey. Jerseys give very rich milk.
Jer|sey|an (jėr′zē ən), *n.* = Jerseyite.
Jersey Black Giant, a large, black American chicken that produces brown-shelled eggs.
jer|seyed (jėr′zid), *adj.* wearing a jersey.
Jer|sey|ite (jėr′zē īt), *n.* a native or inhabitant of New Jersey; New Jerseyite.
Je|ru|sa|lem artichoke (jə rü′sə ləm), **1** a kind of sunflower native to North America that bears edible tubers. **2** its tuber, that tastes somewhat like an artichoke, used as a vegetable. [the use of *Jerusalem* as an alteration of Italian *girasole* sunflower, girasole]
Jerusalem cherry, an ornamental species of nightshade having poisonous orange or scarlet berries.
Jerusalem cricket, a large, yellow long-horned grasshopper with a brown striped body, that digs in sandy soil and is often injurious to plants, found in western North America.
Je|ru|sa|lem|ite (jė rü′sə lə mīt), *n.* a native or inhabitant of Jerusalem, the capital of Israel.
Jerusalem sage, **1** a hairy lungwort having white spotted leaves and blue or purple flowers, grown in Europe as an herb. It belongs to the borage family. **2** a shrub having yellow flowers in a whorl, ovate or oblong leaves, found in southern Europe. It belongs to the mint family.
Jerusalem thorn, = Christ's-thorn.
jess (jes), *n., v.* **—*n.*** a short strap fastened around a falcon's leg, to which a leash can be attached. **—*v.t.*** to put jesses on (a hawk). [< Old French *gies*, earlier, *giez*, nominative of *giet* a throwing; see etym. under **jet^{1}**]
jes|sa|mine (jes′ə min), *n.* = jasmine.
Jes|se (jes′ē), *n.* the father of David (in the Bible, I Samuel 16).
Jesse window, a stained-glass window showing Christ's image. [< *Jesse,* a lineal ancestor of Jesus Christ]
jest (jest), *n., v.* **—*n.* 1** a joke; something said to cause laughter: *With long-ear'd cap, and motley vest, the licensed fool retail'd his jest* (Scott). **2** the act of poking fun; mockery: *a fellow of infinite jest, of most excellent fancy* (Shakespeare). **SYN:** sport, ridicule. **3** a thing to be laughed at or mocked; laughingstock: *Queens may die a jest* (Alexander Pope). **4** a piece of raillery of banter; mocking or jeering speech; taunt; jeer: *Too bitter is thy jest* (Shakespeare). **5** *Obsolete.* **a** a story, tale, or ramance, originally in verse; gest. **b** an exploit; deed.
—*v.i.* 1 to joke. **SYN:** See syn. under **joke. 2** to poke fun (at); make fun: *He jested at other people's ideas. He jests at scars that never felt a wound* (Shakespeare).
—*v.t.* to joke at; ridicule; banter.
in jest, in fun; not seriously: *He spoke in jest. His eyes do drop no tears; his prayers are in jest* (Shakespeare).
[< Old French *geste* (originally) story, exploit, learned borrowing from Latin *gesta* deeds. Compare etym. under **gest^{1}**.] **—jest′ing|ly**, *adv.*
jest|er (jes′tər), *n.* **1** a person who jests. **2** a person who amused the family of a king or nobleman by performing antics similar to those of a clown.
Je|su (jē′zü, -sü), *n.* = Jesus [< Late Latin *Jēsū,* vocative case of *Jēsus* Jesus]
Jes|u|it (jezh′ů it, jez′yů-), *n.* **1** a member of the Society of Jesus, a Roman Catholic religious order of men founded by Saint Ignatius Loyola in 1534. Some of the first explorers in America were Jesuits. **2** a person who is like the conception of Jesuits held by their opponents; a crafty, intriguing, or equivocating person, especially one skilled at subtle reasoning (used in an unfriendly way). [< New Latin *Jesuita* < Late Latin *Jēsus* Jesus]
jes|u|it|ic (jezh′ů it′ik, jez′yů-), *adj.* crafty; scheming; using subtle reasoning.
Jes|u|it|ic (jezh′ů it′ik, jez′yů-), *adj.* of or having to do with the Jesuits. **—Jes′u|it′i|cal|ly**, *adv.*
jes|u|it|i|cal (jezh′ů it′ə kəl, jez′yů-), *adj.* = jesuitic.
Jes|u|it|i|cal (jezh′ů it′ə kəl, jez′yů-), *adj.* = Jesuitic.
jes|u|it|ism (jezh′ů ə tiz′əm, jez′yů-), *n.* **1** crafty or tricky practice; craft; casuistry (used in an unfriendly way). **2** a quibble; very subtle point.
Jes|u|it|ism (jezh′ů ə tiz′əm, jez′yů-), *n.* the system, principles, or practices of the Jesuits.
Jes|u|it|ize (jezh′ů ə tīz, jez′yů-), *v.,* **-ized, -iz|ing.** **—*v.t.*** to make a Jesuit of.
—*v.i.* 1 to become a Jesuit. **2** to be Jesuitical.
Jesuit nut, the fruit of the water chestnut.
Je|sus (jē′zəs), *n.* **1** Also, **Jesus Christ.** the founder of the Christian religion, born between 8 and 4 B.C. and crucified about A.D. 29. **2** the author of Ecclesiasticus, a book of the Apocrypha. [< Late Latin *Iēsus,* or *Jēsus* < Greek *Iēsoûs* < Hebrew *Yēshūa,* earlier *Yəhoshua* (literally) Jehovah is salvation]
▶The paradox that Jesus was born about 4 B.C. is explained by an error in calculation made in the 500's in which the year 1 was placed later than it should have been.
Jesus freak, *U.S. Slang.* one of the Jesus people: *Jesus freaks . . . have blended the counterculture and conservative relation* (Time).
Jesus Movement, a Protestant Christian movement in the United States, consisting chiefly of young people who spread the teachings of Jesus Christ, independent of any of the established churches or denominations.
Jesus people, *U.S.* people belonging to the Jesus Movement.
Jesus shop, a store specializing in popular religious articles used by members of the Jesus Movement, such as posters, buttons, and shirts inscribed with Biblical verses and religious messages.
jet^{1} (jet), *n., adj., v.,* **jet|ted, jet|ting. —*n.* 1a** a stream of water, steam, gas, or any fluid, sent out with force, especially from a small opening: *The fountain sent up a jet of water.* **b** such a shower of solid bodies, such as stones. **2** a spout or nozzle for sending out a jet: *The jet was clogged and the gas could not come out.* **3a** = jet plane. **b** = jet engine.
—*adj.* 1 of, for, or by a jet plane: *a jet airfield, jet speed, jet-powered transports.* **2** resembling or characteristic of the speed or power of jet propulsion: *off to a jet start* (Wall Street Journal).
—*v.i.* 1 to shoot forth in a jet or forceful stream; gush out: *Water jetted from the broken pipe.* **2** to fly by jet plane: *Critic John Crosby . . . jetted to London to see the show* (Newsweek). **3** to fly by jet propulsion: *Airliners would be jetting through the sky at 500 miles an hour* (New York Times).
—*v.t.* 1 to send forth in a stream; shoot out. **2** to take by jet plane: *Doctors and nurses were jetted to the disaster area to help the victims.*
[< Old French *giet* a throwing, a cast < Late Latin *jectus, -ūs,* alteration of Late Latin *jactus, -ūs* < *jacere* to throw]
jet^{2} (jet), *n., adj.* **—*n.* 1** a hard, black kind of coal, glossy when polished, used for making beads, buttons, and ornaments. **2** a deep, glossy black.
—*adj.* 1 made or consisting of jet. **2** deep, glossy black: *Her white dress contrasts with her jet hair.* [< Old French *jaiet* < Latin *gagātēs* < Greek *gagátēs* (*lithos*) (stone) of *Gagas,* a town in Lycia, Asia Minor]
jet age, the present era or period of history, especially as characterized by the development and use of jet propulsion in flight.
jet airplane, = jet plane.
jet|a|va|tor (jet′ə vā′tər), *n.* a steering device on a rocket consisting of vanes or a ring that can be moved against the jet stream to alter the direction of the rocket.
jet|bead (jet′bēd′), *n.* a hardy Japanese shrub of the rose family, grown for its shiny black fruit and showy white flowers.
jet-black (jet′blak′), *adj.* black as jet; very black.
jet|boat (jet′bōt′), *n.* a boat propelled by a jet engine.
jet|borne (jet′bôrn′, -bōrn′), *adj.* carried or transported by jet aircraft: *Today's jetborne businessman . . . often zips in and out of two or three cities in a single day* (Time).
je|té (zhe tā′), *n. French.* (in ballet) a leap from one foot to the other with an outward kick of the leg. See also **grand jeté.**
jet engine, an engine driven by a jet of air or gas; engine using jet propulsion; jet.
jet exhaustion, = jet lag.
jet fatigue, = jet lag.
jet|foil (jet′foil′), *n.* a jet-propelled hydrofoil: *Three times a day, its jetfoil will "fly" down the river from the heart of London to Belgium and back for less than it costs to go by plane* (Listener).
jet helicopter, a helicopter powered by one or more jet engines.
jet-hop (jet′hop′), *v.i.,* **-hopped, hop|ping.** to travel from place to place by jet aircraft.
Jeth|ro (jeth′rō), *n.* a Midianite, the father-in-law of Moses (in the Bible, Exodus 18).
jet injector, an air gun that injects vaccine through the pores of the skin: *A jet injector . . . had been developed by the U.S. Army. Under high pressure it injected a tenth of a millimeter of vaccine into the superficial layers of the skin* (Scientific American).
jet lag, an upset of the body clock, characterized by apathy, fatigue, and other symptoms, caused by traveling in a jet plane through several time zones in twelve hours or less.
jet-lag|ging (jet′lag′ing), *adj.* of or having to do with jet lag: *Right from the jet-lagging start, I was knocked out by the place* (Life).
jet|lin|er (jet′lī′nər), *n.* a large, jet-propelled plane for carrying many passengers; superjet.
jet pilot, a person who operates a jet plane.
jet plane, an airplane that is driven by a jet of air or gas; jet.
jet|port (jet′pôrt), *n.* an airport designed for use by jet planes.
jet-pro|pelled (jet′prə peld′), *adj.* driven in one direction by means of a jet of air or gas that is forced in the opposite direction.
jet propulsion, propulsion in one direction by a jet of air or gas that is forced in the opposite direction. In jet engines such as the ramjet, turbojet, and turboprop, exhaust gases from the combustion of compressed air and fuel shoot backward into space, causing a reaction which drives the engines forward. Various types of jet propulsion are utilized in aircraft and missiles.
jet pump, a pump in which a liquid column moves at high velocity to force other portions of the liquid forward.
jet|sam (jet′səm), *n.* **1** goods which are thrown overboard to lighten a ship in distress and often afterwards washed ashore. **2** *Figurative.* something tossed aside as useless. **SYN:** castoff. [alteration of earlier *jetson,* variant of *jettison*]
jet set, **1** the social group of fashionable people who travel a great deal by jet plane to resorts and to cultural and social events: *The jet set . . . insists on having to its parties at least one Greek shipowner, a Ferrari auto racer, and a cocktail of countesses* (Saturday Evening Post). **2** (originally) young people in the Soviet Union attracted by current fashions of the West.
jet-set (jet′set′), *adj.* of or having to do with the jet set.
jet setter, *U.S. Slang.* a member of the jet set.
jet stream, **1** a current of air traveling at very high speed (usually 100 to 120 miles per hour, but sometimes almost 350) from west to east at altitudes of six to eight miles. The jet stream is often used by airplane pilots to gain extra speed when traveling in an eastward direction. Jet streams are important in weather prediction and aircraft navigation. **2** the exhaust from a jet engine.
jet syndrome, = jet lag.
jet|ted (jet′id), *adj.* ornamented with jet.
jet|ti|son (jet′ə sən, -zən), *v., n.* **—*v.t.* 1** to throw (goods) overboard to lighten a ship or aircraft in distress. **2** *Figurative.* to throw away; discard.
—*n.* 1 the act of throwing goods overboard to lighten a ship or aircraft in distress. **2** the goods thrown overboard; jetsam.
[< Old French *getaison* < Latin *jactātiō, -ōnis;* see etym. under **jactation**] **—jet′ti|son|a|ble**, *adj.*
jet|ton (jet′ən), *n.* a piece of metal, ivory, or other material, used as a counter. [< Old French *jeton* < *jeter* to throw, cast up accounts < Late Latin *jectāre,* alteration of Latin *jactāre;* see etym. under **jactation**]
jet|ty^{1} (jet′ē), *n., pl.* **-ties,** *v.,* **-tied, -ty|ing. —*n.* 1** a wall or similar structure of stones or timbers built out from the shore to break the force of the current or waves or to deepen the channel; breakwater. **SYN:** mole. **2** a landing place; pier. **SYN:** wharf. **—*v.t.*** to furnish with a jetty. [< Old French *jetee* < *jeter* to throw < Late Latin *jectāre;* alteration of Latin *jactāre;* see etym. under **jactation**]
jet|ty^{2} (jet′ē), *adj.* consisting of jet; like the color of jet. [< *jet^{2}* + *-y^{1}*]
jeu (zhœ), *n., pl.* **jeux** (zhœ). *French.* **1** sport; game; entertainment. **2** gambling.
jeu de mots (zhœ′ də mō′), *French.* a play on words; pun.
jeu d'es|prit (zhœ′ des prē′), *French.* **1** a clever remark; witticism; witty piece of writing. **2** (literally) play of wit.
jeune fille (zhœn fē′yə), *French.* a young girl.
jeune pre|mier (zhœn prə myā′), *French.* a juvenile lead (male).
jeune pre|mière (zhœn prə myer′), *French.* a juvenile lead (female).
jeu|nesse do|rée (zhœ nes′ dô rā′), *French.* **1** rich and fashionable young people. **2** (literally) golden youth.
Jew (jü), *n.* **1** a person descended from the Se-

Pronunciation Key: hat, āge, cãre, fär; let, ēqual, tėrm; it, īce; hot, ōpen, ôrder; **oi**l, **ou**t; cup, pu̇t, rüle; **ch**ild; lo**ng**; **th**in; ᴛʜen; **zh**, measure; **ə** represents **a** in about, **e** in taken, **i** in pencil, **o** in lemon, **u** in circus.

mitic people led by Moses, who settled in Palestine, living there from about 1200 B.C. to A.D. 70, and who since then have lived in many countries, including modern Israel; Hebrew; Israelite. **2** a person whose religion is Judaism. **3** a Hebrew of the ancient tribe or kingdom of Judah. [< Old French *gui, jueu* < Latin *Jūdaeus* < Greek *Ioudaîos* < Hebrew *Yəhudi* belonging to the tribe of Judah]

jew (jü), *v.t. Slang.* to bargain with overkeenly; beat (down) in price (used in an unfriendly way).

jew|el (jü′əl), *n., v.,* **-eled, -el|ing** or (*especially British*) **-elled, -el|ling.** —*n.* **1** a precious stone; gem: *The ring was set with several diamond jewels.* **2a** a valuable ornament to be worn, set with precious stones: *Like a rich jewel in an Ethiop's ear* (Shakespeare). **b** any ornament to be worn, such as a ring, bracelet, or necklace. **3** *Figurative.* a person or thing that is very precious; gem: *Good name in man and woman . . . is the immediate jewel of their souls* (Shakespeare). SYN: pearl, treasure. **4** a gem or other hard material used as a bearing in a watch, compass, or other precision instrument; jewel bearing. *Abbr:* j (no period).
—*v.t.* to set or adorn with jewels or with things like jewels: *a jeweled comb. The sky is jeweled with stars.*
[< Old French, *jeul, jouel* < Medieval Latin *jocale* < Latin *jocus* joke, game] —**jew′el|like′,** *adj.*

jewel bearing, a bearing of a precision instrument, such as a watch, in which the pivot is a crystal or some precious stone, such as a ruby.

jewel box, = jewel case.

jewel case, a box or case to hold jewelry.

jew|el|er (jü′ə lər), *n.* a person who makes, sells, or repairs jewels, jeweled ornaments, and watches.

jewelers' rouge, = colcothar.

jew|el|fish (jü′əl fish′), *n., pl.* **-fish|es** or (*collectively*) **-fish.** a small, pink freshwater fish of Africa having green or blue lines on its fins, commonly kept in aquariums.

jew|el|ler (jü′ə lər), *n. Especially British.* jeweler.

jew|el|ler|y (jü′əl rē), *n. Especially British.* jewelry.

jew|el|ly (jü′ə lē), *adj.* **1** jewellike; brilliant. **2** adorned with or as if with jewels.

jew|el|ry (jü′əl rē), *n.* **1** jewels, collectively: *Mother keeps her jewelry in a small locked box.* **2** any ornament to be worn that is like a valuable ornament but is usually set with imitation gems or made of silver or gold-colored metal.

jew|el|weed (jü′əl wēd′), *n.* a plant with yellow or orange-yellow, irregular, hanging flowers with brown spots, and seed pods that snap open at the touch when ripe; touch-me-not. Jewelweed belongs to the same genus as the balsam.

Jew|ess (jü′is), *n.* a Jewish woman or girl. ►See **-ess** for a usage note.

jew|fish (jü′fish′), *n., pl.* **-fish|es** or (*collectively*) **-fish.** **1** a giant sea bass or grouper, such as the California black sea bass or the spotted jewfish. **2** any of various other large fishes of warm seas.

Jew|ish (jü′ish), *adj., n.* —*adj.* **1** of the Jews; belonging to the Jews; characteristic of the Jews; Hebrew: *Jewish religious beliefs.* SYN: Judaic. **2** *Informal.* Yiddish.
—*n. Informal.* Yiddish. —**Jew′ish|ly,** *adv.* —**Jew′ish|ness,** *n.*

Jewish calendar, the calendar used by the Jews, which dates the Creation at 3760 B.C., and divides the year into 12 months of 29 or 30 days, with an extra month of 29 days every second or third year in each 19-year cycle; Hebrew calendar. The civil year begins in September or October and the ecclesiastical year in March or April.

Jewish Princess, *U.S. Slang.* a rich or spoiled Jewish girl or woman; J.A.P. (used in an unfriendly way).

Jew|ry (jü′rē), *n., pl.* **-ries.** **1** Jews as a group; Jewish people. **2** *Archaic.* a district where Jews live; ghetto. **3** *Archaic.* the land of the Jews: *Alexas did revolt, and went to Jewry On affairs of Antony* (Shakespeare). [< Old French *juerie* < *jueu;* see etym. under **Jew**]

***jew's-harp** or **jews'-harp** (jüz′härp′), *n.* a simple musical instrument, held between the teeth and played by striking the free end of a flexible piece of metal with a finger.

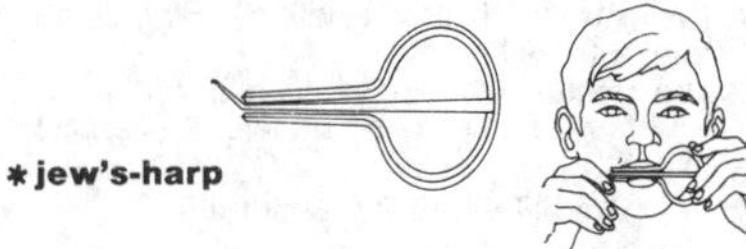

***jew's-harp**

Jez|e|bel (jez′ə bəl), *n.* **1** the wicked wife of Ahab, king of Israel (in the Bible, I Kings 16:31, 21:5-29; II Kings 9:7-10, 30-37). **2** a shameless, immoral woman.

JFK (no periods), John Fitzgerald Kennedy.

j.g. or **jg** (no periods), junior grade (in the United States Navy).

JH (no periods), juvenile hormone.

jha|la (jä′lə), *n.* a heavily cadenced passage ending the second movement of a typical raga. [< Sanskrit *jhala*]

JHS (no periods), the first three letters of the name of Jesus in Greek.

J.H.S., Junior High School.

JHVH or **JHWH** (no periods), the letters used in Hebrew Scripture to represent God, the "ineffable name," replaced in reading by *Adonai.* See also **Jehovah, Yahweh.**

***jib^{1}** (jib), *n.* a triangular sail in front of the mast nearest to the bow.
cut of one's jib. See under **cut^{1}.**
[earlier *gibb.* Perhaps related to **gibbet.**]

***jib^{1}**

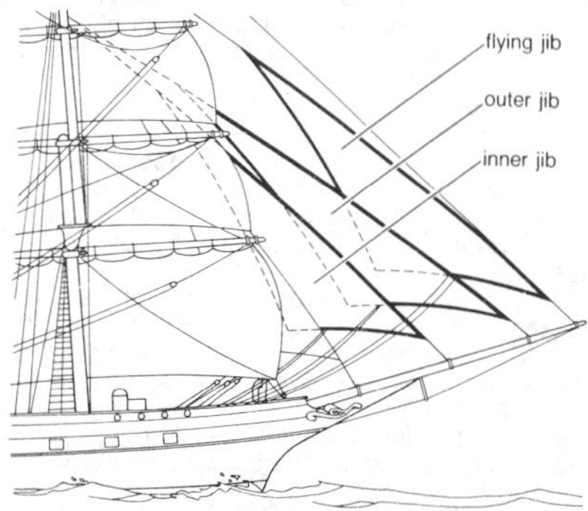

jib^{2} (jib), *v.t., v.i.,* **jibbed, jib|bing.** *n.* = jibe^{1}. [apparently early form of *jibe^{1}*]

jib^{3} (jib), *v.,* **jibbed, jib|bing,** *n.* —*v.i.* to move sidewise or backwards instead of forward; refuse to go ahead; balk.
—*n.* a horse or other animal that jibs.
[origin uncertain] —**jib′ber,** *n.*

jib^{4} (jib), *n.* the projecting arm of a crane or derrick. [probably short for *gibbet*]

ji|ba|ro or **jí|ba|ro** (hē′bä rō), *n., pl.* **-ros.** in Spanish America: **1** a peasant. **2** a country bumpkin.
[< American Spanish *jíbaro*]

jib|bah (jib′ə), *n.* = jubbah.

jib boom, a spar extending out from a ship's bowsprit.

jib crane, a crane with a jib or projection arm that carries a trolley to which the hoisting tackle is attached.

jibe^{1} (jīb), *v.,* **jibed, jib|ing,** *n.* —*v.t.* to cause (a sail or boom) to shift from one side of a ship to another when sailing before the wind.
—*v.i.* **1** to shift itself in this way. **2** to change the course of a ship so that the sails shift in this way.
—*n.* a jibing. Also, **jib.**
[perhaps ultimately < Dutch *gijben,* variant of *gijpen*]

jibe^{2} (jīb), *v.t., v.i.,* **jibed, jib|ing,** *n.* = gibe. —**jib′er,** *n.*

jibe^{3} (jīb), *v.i.,* **jibed, jib|ing.** *Informal.* to be in harmony; agree; fit: *Our opinions jibe; we both have the same ideas. This doesn't jibe with what you said before.* [origin uncertain]

Ji|ca|ril|la (hē kə rē′yə), *n., pl.* **-la** or **-las.** **1** a member of an Apache tribe of northern New Mexico. **2** the language of this tribe.

jiff (jif), *n. Informal.* a jiffy.

jif|fy (jif′ē), *n., pl.* **-fies.** *Informal.* a very short time; moment: *He was on his bike in a jiffy, pedaling down the drive.* SYN: trice, twinkling. [origin unknown]

Jif|fy bag (jif′ē), *Trademark.* an envelope padded with paper stuffing to protect its contents. Also, **jiffy bag.**

jig^{1} (jig), *n., v.,* **jigged, jig|ging.** —*n.* **1** a lively dance, often in triple time: *He danced a jig lively and quick.* **2** music for it or in the same rhythm: *The orchestra played a jig and the audience started to clap in time.* **3** *Slang.* a joke; trick. [probably < verb]
—*v.i.* **1** to dance a jig: *Merry couples jigged across the floor.* **2** to jerk up and down or back and forth; move jerkily.
—*v.t.* **1** to sing or play (music) as a jig or in the style of a jig. **2** to move (anything) with a light, jerky motion: *[He] leaned against the main engine guardrail jigging one shoe and watching the Chief's placid stitching* (Atlantic).
the jig is up, it's all over; there's no more chance: *As soon as the jig was up, he flew off to Prague* (Newsweek).
[< Old French *giguer* to dance < *gigue* leg, fiddle < Germanic (compare Middle High German *gīge*)]

jig^{2} (jig), *n., v.,* **jigged, jig|ging.** —*n.* **1** a fishing lure consisting of a fishhook, or set of fishhooks, weighted with a spoon-shaped piece of bright metal; jigger. It is bobbed up and down or pulled through the water. **2** any one of various mechanical contrivances or devices: **a** a device used to hold a piece of work and guide a drill, file, saw, or other tool toward it; template. **b** an apparatus for washing out waste matter from ore or coal.
—*v.t.* to treat, cut, or form with a jig.
—*v.i.* **1** to fish with a jig. **2** to do work with the aid of a jig.
[origin uncertain; perhaps in some senses < *jig^{1},* verb, in sense of "move with a jerk"]

jig borer, a tool resembling a carpenter's hand drill, used to bore holes in metal plate.

jig|ger^{1} (jig′ər), *n., v.* —*n.* **1** a small set of ropes and pulleys used on a ship. **2** a small sail. **3** = jigger mast. **4** a small fishing boat with a jigger (sail). **5** a machine that operates with a jerky motion. **6** *Informal.* some device, article, or part that one cannot name more precisely; gadget; contraption. **7** a jig used in fishing. **8** *U.S.* **a** a small glass that usually holds 1½ ounces, used to measure liquor. **b** the liquor contained in such a glass. **9** *Golf.* an iron with a narrow blade and a loft between a midiron's and a mashie's, used for low approach shots. **10** a bridge used in billiards and pool. **11** a person who jigs or dances a jig.
—*v.t. Slang.* **1** to interfere with; withhold. **2** to pilfer; filch. **3** to mix up; confuse: *He juggled firm accounts until he had jiggered them completely.*
[< *jig^{2},* verb + *-er^{1}*]

jig|ger^{2} (jig′ər), *n.* **1** a small flea; chigoe. **2** = chigger. [alteration of *chigoe*]

jig|gered (jig′ərd), *adj. Slang.* **1** a word used as a substitute for a profane word: *I'm jiggered if I don't see you home!* (Dickens). **2** intoxicated; drunk.
[origin uncertain]

jigger mast, **1** a mast in the stern of a ship. **2** the mast nearest the stern of a four-masted ship, or the fourth mast from the bow of a ship having five or more masts. See picture under **mast^{1}.**

jig|ger|y (jig′ər ē), *n.* = jiggery-pokery.

jig|ger|y-pok|er|y (jig′ər ē pō′kər ē), *n. Slang.* deception; fraud; hokum.

jig|gle (jig′əl), *v.,* **-gled, -gling,** *n.* —*v.t., v.i.* to shake or jerk slightly: *Don't jiggle the desk when I'm trying to write. The veils and feathers on the women's hats jiggled slightly* (Atlantic).
—*n.* a slight shake; light jerk: *a hearty laugh and many jiggles in the jowls.*
[< *jig^{1},* verb + *-le* (frequentative)]

jig|gly (jig′lē), *adj.,* **-gli|er, -gli|est.** **1** jiggling; jerky: *a jiggly line, a jiggly war dance.* **2** *U.S. Slang.* sexually suggestive or titillating: *ABC's mix of jiggly and blue-collar ingredients retained its successful clout* (John J. O'Connor).

jig|saw (jig′sô′), *n., v.,* **-sawed, -sawed** or **-sawn, -saw|ing,** *adj.* —*n.* **1** a saw with a narrow blade mounted in a frame and worked with an up-and-down motion, used to cut curves or irregular lines. **2** = jigsaw puzzle.
—*v.t.* to cut with a jigsaw.
—*adj.* cut or shaped by or as if by a jigsaw: *a jigsaw pattern.*

jigsaw puzzle, a picture cut into irregular pieces that can be fitted together again.

jig time, the quick, lively rhythm of jig.
in jig time, *Informal.* very quickly; in a jiffy; *They came by and fixed the burner in jig time* (New Yorker).

ji|had (ji häd′), *n.* **1** a religious war of Moslems against unbelievers. **2** *Figurative.* any war against some belief or principle; crusade. Also, **jehad.**
[< Arabic *jihād* (literally) struggle, contest]

jill^{1} or **Jill** (jil), *n.* **1** a woman; girl. **2** a sweetheart; wife: *Our wooing doth not end like an old play; Jack hath not Jill* (Shakespeare). [< *Jill,* a proper name]

jill^{2} (jil), *n.* = gill^{4}.

jil|la|roo (jil ə rü′), *n.* (in Australia) a female jackeroo.

jil|lion (jil′yən), *n., adj. U.S. Slang.* zillion. [< *j* (letter) + (m)*illion*]

jilt (jilt), *v., n.* —*v.t.* to cast off (a lover or sweetheart) after giving encouragement: *He had the mortification of being jilted by a little boarding-school girl* (Washington Irving). SYN: reject
—*n.* a woman who casts off a lover after encouraging him.
[origin uncertain] —**jilt′er,** *n.*

jim|crack (jim′krak′), *n., adj.* = gimcrack.

Jim Crow, *U.S.* **1** discrimination against Negroes. **2** *Slang.* a Negro (used in an unfriendly way). [American English, from a refrain in a Negro minstrel song of about 1835]

Jim-Crow or **jim-crow** (jim′krō′), *adj.* **1** discriminating against Negroes: *a Jim-Crow town.* **2** segregated for use by Negroes only: *a Jim-Crow bus.*

Jim-Crow car, *U.S.* formerly: **1** a separate railroad car for the use of Negroes in some Southern states. **2** any railroad car in which whites and

Negroes were separated.

Jim Crow|ism, or **jim|crow|ism** (jim′krō′iz əm), *n. U.S.* the practice of discriminating against Negroes.

jim-dan|dy (jim′dan′dē), *n., pl.* **-dies**, *adj. U.S. Slang.* **—*n.*** an excellent person: *He is, in fact, a real little jim-dandy of a fellow* (Harper's).
—*adj.* excellent; first-rate: *It's going to be a jim-dandy track* (New Yorker).

jim|jams (jim′jamz), *n.pl. Slang.* **1** delirium tremens. **2** a creepy feeling; fidgets; creeps.

jim|my (jim′ē), *n., pl.* **-mies**, *v.,* **-mied**, **-my|ing**. **—*n.*** a short crowbar used especially by burglars to force open windows, doors, or other things.
—*v.t.* to force open with a jimmy.
[dialectal variant of *jemmy*]

jim|son or **Jim|son weed** (jim′sən), a tall, coarse, bad-smelling weed with large, white or violet, funnel-shaped flowers and poisonous, narcotic leaves and seeds; thorn apple; stramonium. It belongs to the nightshade family. [American English, alteration of earlier *Jamestown weed* < *Jamestown,* Virginia, where it was first found]

jim|son|weed or **jim|son-weed** (jim′sən wēd), *n.* = jimson weed.

jin (jin), *n.* = jinn.

jin|gal (jin′gôl), *n.* a musket or cannon fired from a rest, formerly used in India and China. Also, **gingal**, **gingall**. [< Hindustani *janjāl*]

jing|ko (jing′kō), *n., pl.* **-koes**. = gingko.

jin|gle (jing′gəl), *n., v.,* **-gled**, **-gling**. **—*n.*** **1** a sound like that of little bells, or of coins or keys striking together: *a canvas bag, that gave forth, at a touch, the jingle of gold* (Robert Louis Stevenson). **SYN**: tinkle. **2** a verse or song that has similar sounds repeated in it, or that has a catchy rhyme. "Higgledy, piggledy, my black hen" is a jingle. Mother Goose rhymes are jingles. **3** a covered two-wheeled cart used in Ireland and Australia. [< verb]
—*v.i.* **1** to make a sound like bells, coins, or keys striking together: *The sleigh bells jingle as we ride.* **2** to make jingling verses: *Whene'er my Muse does on me glance, I jingle at her* (Robert Burns). **3** to be full of simple repetitions or catchy rhymes: *a jingling nursery rhyme.*
—*v.t.* to cause (something) to jingle: *to jingle the money in one's pocket.*
[Middle English *gynglen;* imitative] **—jin′gler**, *n.* **—jin′gling|ly**, *adv.*

jin|gle-jan|gle (jing′gəl jang′gəl), *n., v.,* **-gled**, **-gling**. **—*n.*** **1** an alternating jingle of sounds: *the jingle-jangle of spurs.* **2** a verse or sentence characterized by this.
—*v.i.* **1** to jingle with alternation of sounds. **2** to proceed with such simple sounds and repetitions: *Our critics have gone on about Shaw's play in the bumbling and jingle-jangling way of the most amazing of Shaw's doctor-characters, Bloomfield Bonington* (Punch).

Jin|gling Johnny (jing′gling), a jingling device, used especially in military bands; Turkish crescent.

jin|gly (jing′glē), *adj.* like a jingle.

jin|go (jing′gō), *n., pl.* **-goes**, *adj., v.,* **-goed**, **-go-ing**. **—*n.*** **1** a person who favors an aggressive foreign policy that might lead to war with other nations; chauvinist: *. . . a special and welcome breed in contemporary writing—that of unabashed patriot esthetes who somehow manage not to sound like jingoes* (Time). **2** a person who supported Disraeli's aggressive foreign policy in England in 1878.
—*adj.* of jingoes; jingoistic: *A sigh of relief from all parties—the jingo press excluded—has greeted the hopeful news for a final settlement in Cyprus* (Punch).
—*v.i.* to sound of jingoism; express loud or aggressive patriotism: *The flags waved and the speeches jingoed when the United States embarked on its first armed adventure in Asia* (New York Times).
by (or **by the living**) **jingo!** *Informal.* an exclamation used chiefly for emphasis; meaningless oath: *She observed that, by the living jingo, she was all of a muck of sweat* (Oliver Goldsmith).
[< *by Jingo,* phrase in refrain of a music-hall song, which became the "theme song" of Disraeli's supporters in 1878; *jingo,* a magician's term; origin uncertain]

jin|go|ism (jing′gō iz əm), *n.* the attitude of mind, policy or practices of jingoes. **SYN**: chauvinism.

jin|go|ist (jing′gō ist), *n.* = jingo.

jin|go|is|tic (jing′gō is′tik), *adj.* of jingoes; like that of jingoes. **—jin′go|is′ti|cal|ly**, *adv.*

jink (jingk), *v., n. Especially Scottish.* **—*v.i.*** **1** to move nimbly or jerkily; dance. **2** to make a quick, elusive turn; dodge. **—*v.t.*** **1** to elude by dodging; dodge. **2** to cheat; swindle.
—*n.* **1** a quick turn to elude; dodge. **2** a prank or frolic: *He was the star . . . of good company forty years ago. I remember him in the height of his jinks* (Thomas Hardy).
[perhaps imitative of quick motion] **—jink′er**, *n.*

jin|kai sen|jit|su (jin′kī sen jit′sü), the Japanese strategy of throwing waves of men into action. [< Japanese *jinkai-senjutsu*]

jink|er (jing′kər), *n. Australian.* a cart used for moving logs and lumber.

jinn (jin), *n., pl. of* **jinni** *for 1; n. sing., pl.* **jinns**, *for 2. Moslem Mythology.* **1** spirits, lower than the angels, that can appear in human or animal form. Jinn do both good and evil. *The good jinn helped Aladdin when he rubbed his magic lamp.* **2** one of these spirits; jinni: *The jinn turned the stone into gold.* Also, **djin**, **djinn**, **jin**. [< Arabic *jinn,* plural of *jinnī.* Compare etym. under **genie**.]

Jin|ne|stan (jin′ə stan), *n.* = Djinnestan.

jin|ni or **jin|nee** (ji nē′), *n., pl.* **jinn**. one of the jinn; genie. Also, **djinnee**, **djinni**.

***jin|rik|i|sha** or **jin|rick|sha** (jin rik′shə, -shô), *n.* a small, two-wheeled carriage with a folding top, usually pulled by one person. Jinrikishas were once used in Japan, China, and other countries in the Orient. Also, **rickshaw**, **ricksha**. [< Japanese *jinrikisha* < *jin* man + *riki* strength + *sha* cart]

***jinrikisha**

jinx (jingks), *n., v. Informal.* **—*n.*** a person or thing that brings bad luck: *That black cat is a jinx on this house.*
—*v.t.* to bring bad luck to: *This town has jinxed me.* [American English < earlier *jynx, jyng,* (originally) a bird used in magic; a spell < Latin *iynx* < Greek *iynx*]

ji|pi|ja|pa (hē′pi hä′pä), *n.* **1** a palmlike plant of South and Central America. Panama hats are made from its leaves. **2** a panama hat. [< Spanish (*sombrero de*) *jipijapa* panama (hat) < *Jipijapa,* a town in Ecuador]

jit|ney (jit′nē), *n., pl.* **-neys**. *U.S. Slang.* **1** an automobile that carries passengers for a small fare (originally 5 cents). It usually travels along a regular route. **2** any ramshackle automobile. **3** a five-cent piece; nickel. [American English]

jit|ter (jit′ər), *Informal.* **—*v.i.*** to be nervous; act nervously. **—*v.t.*** to say nervously.
[apparently variant of dialectal English *chitter* shiver, tremble, variant of *chatter*]

jit|ter|bug (jit′ər bug′), *n., v.,* **-bugged**, **-bug-ging**. *Informal.* **—*n.*** **1** a lively dance for couples, featuring rapid twirling movements and acrobatic maneuvers, usually done to swing music. It was especially popular in the 1940's. **2** a person who dances the jitterbug. **3** *Informal.* a jittery person: *Meany despised politicians and powerbrokers whose positions seemed to bend with every shift of public opinion or the latest headlines. He dismissed them contemptuously as "jitterbugs"* (Time).
—*v.i.* to dance the jitterbug. [< *jitter,* verb + *bug*]

jit|ters (jit′ərz), *n.pl. Informal.* extreme nervousness: *Republican leaders suffered from a case of jitters last week* (Newsweek). [American English < jitter]

jit|ter|y (jit′ər ē), *adj., Informal.* nervous; jumpy: *The nation is jittery over the Formosa situation* (Wall Street Journal). **—jit′ter|i|ness**, *n.*

jiu|jit|su or **jiu|jut|su** (jü jit′sü), *n.* = jujitsu.

Ji|va|ro (hē′və rō), *n., pl.* **-ro** or **-ros**. **1** a member of a group of Indians of Ecuador and Peru, noted as headshrinkers. **2** their language.

jive (jīv), *n., v.,* **jived**, **jiv|ing**. *Slang.* **—*n.*** **1** = swing music. **2** dancing to swing music. **3** the jargon of swing enthusiasts. **4** the latest slang. **5** misleading or tiresome talk.
—*v.i.* **1** to perform or dance to swing music. **2** to know what is going on; fit in with the others in one's group: *Unless you hear a good old-fashioned hell-fire sermon at least once a week you just don't jive, brother* (Atlantic). **3** to tease playfully; joke: *"You jivin' or you really that ignorant?" Sukie asked* (Louise Meriwether).
—*v.t.* to tease; fool; kid: *"I jive people if I don't trust them, see," he explains* (Time).
[origin uncertain] **—jiv′er**, *n.*

jiv|ey (jī′vē), *adj.,* **jiv|i|er**, **jiv|i|est**. = jivy.

jiv|y (jī′vē), *adj.,* **jiv|i|er**, **jiv|i|est**. *Slang.* like jive: *The dance tunes are sometimes simple and lilting, other times quite jivy* (Wall Street Journal).

jj., **1** judges. **2** justices.

JJ., **1** judges. **2** justices.

JND (no periods) or **j.n.d.**, just noticeable difference (used in scientific experiments to indicate a psychological or physiological threshold).

Jno., John.

Jnr. or **jnr.** or **Jnr** (no period), junior.

►**Jr.** or **jr.** are the usual current forms, especially in the United States. **Jun.** is still used, but with increasingly less frequency. **Jnr.** or **jnr.** or **Jnr** (no period) are mainly British.

jo (jō), *n., pl.* **joes**. *Scottish.* a sweetheart; darling. Also, **joe**. [variant of *joy*]

Jo., (in the Bible) Joel.

Jo|ab (jō′ab), *n.* the commander of David's army (in the Bible, II Samuel 20:23).

jo|an|nes (jō an′ēz), *n., pl.* **-nes**. = johannes.

job[1] (job), *n., adj., v.,* **jobbed**, **job|bing**. **—*n.*** **1** a piece of work: *We had the job of painting the boat.* **2** a definite piece of work undertaken for a fixed price: *If you want your house painted, they will do the job for $500.* **3** work done for pay; employment: *Her brother is hunting for a job. This carpenter has no job now.* **SYN**: See syn. under **position**. **4** anything one has to do: *Washing the dishes is your job, not mine. It'll be a hard job for me to tell her aunt* (George Eliot). **5** *Informal.* affair; matter; business: *to make the best of a bad job.* **6** a piece of public or official business managed dishonestly for private gain: *Who makes a trust of charity a job, and gets an act of parliament to rob* (Alexander Pope). **7a** *U.S. Informal.* an article that is a product of craftsmanship; a skilled piece of work: *His repairing of the window was a good job.* **b** *Informal.* any complex item, such as an automobile, engine, garment, or watch, viewed as a finished product: *By push-button magic, the swank job can be transformed into an open convertible from a closed hardtop* (Wall Street Journal). **8** *Printing.* a small piece of work of a miscellaneous kind, such as the printing of posters, handbills, or cards. **9** *Slang.* a criminal deed, such as a theft or robbery: *His comrades had plotted an orchard to rob, And ask'd him to go and assist in the job* (William Cowper).
—*adj.* done by the job; hired for a particular piece of work: *job printing.*
—*v.t.* **1** to buy (goods) from manufacturers in large quantities and sell to retailers in smaller lots. **2** to let out (work) to different contractors or workmen. **3** to hire or to let out (a horse, vehicle, or coachmen) for a particular job or for a certain time: *She went to the livery-man from whom she jobbed her carriage* (Thackeray). **4** to manage (a public job) for private gain in a dishonest way.
—*v.i.* **1** to work at odd jobs. **2** to manage a public job for dishonest private gain: *I dare say he jobs, as all other people of consequence do, in elections* (Scott). **3** to buy or sell as a jobber.
do a job on, *U.S. Slang.* to damage utterly; smash; crush: (*Figurative*) *In this book he [Hemingway] did a job on Gertrude Stein . . . and Ford Madox Ford* (Atlantic).
on the job, *Informal.* tending to one's work or duty: *She was on the job every minute until the cottage was "on wheels"* (Gertrude Atherton).
[origin uncertain]

job[2] (job), *n., v.t., v.i.,* **jobbed**, **job|bing**. = jab.

Job (jōb), *n.* **1** a very patient man who kept his faith in God in spite of many troubles (in the Bible). **2** a book of the Old Testament that tells about him.

job action, *U.S.* an action by workers, such as a refusal to do a certain type of work, taken to express a grievance or to enforce a demand.

job analysis, the analysis of the various aspects and conditions of a job to determine what qualifications its holder should have, what salary he should receive, and the like.

job bank, a computerized job-placement service: *Job banks . . . produce periodic printout lists of available jobs* (New Scientist).

job|ber (job′ər), *n.* **1** a person who buys goods from manufacturers in large quantities and sells to retail dealers in smaller quantities. **SYN**: middleman. **2** a person who manages public business dishonestly for private gain. **3** a person who works by the job; pieceworker. **4** *British.* a dealer in stocks and bonds.

job|ber|y (job′ər ē), *n.* the dishonest management of public business for private gain.

Job Corps, an agency of the U.S. government established in 1964 to provide training and work for unemployed youths between 16 and 21. **—Job Corpsman**.

job|hold|er (job′hōl′dər), *n.* **1** a person regularly employed: *Most of these taxpayers would receive their benefit via reduced withholding taxes, which means that the average jobholder would find himself with about $1.60 more in his paycheck each week* (Wall Street Journal). **2** an em-

Pronunciation Key: hat, āge, cãre, fär; let, ēqual, tėrm; it, īce; hot, ōpen, ôrder; oil, out; cup, pu̇t, rüle; child; long; thin; ᴛʜen; zh, measure; ə represents **a** in about, **e** in taken, **i** in pencil, **o** in lemon, **u** in circus.

ployee of the United States government.

job-hop (job′hop′), *v.i.*, **-hopped, -hop|ping.** *Informal.* to go from job to job; change jobs frequently: *After leaving Washington in the mid-1950's, he job-hopped, serving briefly as operating vice president of [a company] and later organizing his own law firm in Los Angeles* (Time). —**job′hop′per,** *n.*

job|less (job′lis), *adj.* having no job; unemployed: *Right after the war, many economists glumly predicted 8 million unemployed. The jobless ranks never rose to anywhere near that amount* (Newsweek). —**job′less|ness,** *n.*

job lot, a quantity of goods bought or sold together, often containing several different kinds.

job printer, a printer who does smaller jobs than books, magazines, or newspapers, such as business cards, stationery, and formal invitations.

Job's comforter, 1 a person who increases the misery of the person he pretends to comfort (in the Bible, Job 16:2). **2** a boil (in the Bible, Job 2:7).

job|seek|er (job′sē′kər), *n.* a person who is looking for employment: *The number of June jobseekers usually expands sharply as students enter the labor market* (Wall Street Journal).

Job's-tears (jōbz′tirz′), *n.* **1** the hard, grayish-white seeds of an Asiatic grass, used as beads. **2** the grass itself.

Jo|cas|ta (jō kas′tə), *n. Greek Legend.* the mother of Oedipus, who married him without knowing who he was and killed herself when she learned the truth.

jock¹ (jok), *n. Informal.* **1** jockey: *If a jock lands in a hospital or is set down for illegal riding, why those are days in which he can't win a race* (Time). **2** a disk jockey.

jock² (jok), *n.* **1** = jockstrap. **2** *U.S. Slang.* an athlete, especially at a college. [< dialectal *jock* male genital organs]

Jock (jok), *n. Scottish.* a nickname for a Scotsman.

jock|ette (jo ket′), *n. U.S.* **1** a female jockey. **2** *Slang.* a woman athlete: *Here it [the Olympics] is capsulized into less than two hours, focusing on the most central concerns of myriad wonderful jocks and jockettes* (National Review).

jock|ey (jok′ē), *n., pl.* **-eys,** *v.,* **-eyed, -ey|ing.** —*n.* **1** a person who rides horses in races as an occupation. **2** *U.S. Slang.* the operator of a vehicle or machine: *a truck jockey, a typewriter jockey.* **3** *Especially British.* a crafty bargainer; horse trader: *He is a jockey in trading stocks.* **4** a leather flap on a western saddle, often ornamental, covering the upper parts of the stirrup. **5** *Obsolete.* a strolling minstrel or beggar; vagabond.
—*v.t.* **1** to ride (a horse) in a race. **2** to trick; cheat: *Swindlers jockeyed him into buying some worthless land.* **3** to maneuver so as to get advantage: *The crews were jockeying their boats to get into the best position for the race.*
—*v.i.* **1** to ride as a jockey. **2** to aim at an advantage by skillful maneuvering: *Right now there's feverish jockeying for a favored sales position* (Wall Street Journal). **3** to act in a tricky way; trick; cheat.
[earlier, a boy, lad, (originally) diminutive form of *Jock,* Scottish variant of *Jack*]

Jockey Club, an organization that regulates horse racing.

jock|ey|ship (jok′ē ship), *n.* the skill and quality of a jockey.

jock|o (jok′ō), *n., pl.* **jock|os. 1** = monkey. **2** = chimpanzee. [< French *jocko,* also *enjocko* < *engeco* < *ncheko,* the West African name]

jock|strap (jok′strap′), *n.* an elastic supporter worn by men for athletics.

jo|cose (jō kōs′), *adj.* full of jokes; jesting; humorous; joking: *jocose remarks, to be jocose and pleasant.* SYN: facetious, waggish, playful. [< Latin *jocōsus* < *jocus* jest] —**jo|cose′ly,** *adv.* —**jo|cose′ness,** *n.*

jo|cos|i|ty (jō kos′ə tē), *n., pl.* **-ties. 1** jocose quality. **2** a joking. **3** a joke.

joc|u|lar (jok′yə lər), *adj.* said or done in jest; funny; joking. SYN: jolly, witty. [< Latin *joculāris* < *joculus* (diminutive) < *jocus* jest. Compare etym. under **joke.**] —**jok′u|lar|ly,** *adv.*

joc|u|lar|i|ty (jok′yə lar′ə tē), *n., pl.* **-ties. 1** jocular quality. **2** jocular talk or behavior. **3** a jocular remark or act: *Little jocularities, of which old Joe Bagstock was the perpetual theme* (Dickens).

joc|und (jok′ənd, jō′kənd), *adj.* cheerful; merry; gay: *A poet could not but be gay In such a jocund company* (Wordsworth). SYN: blithe, debonair.
[< Latin *jōcundus,* variant (influenced by *jocus* a jest) of *jūcundus* pleasant < *juvāre* to please] —**joc′und|ly,** *adv.*

jo|cun|di|ty (jō kun′ də tē), *n., pl.* **-ties. 1** merriment; gaiety. **2** a merry remark or act.

***jodh|purs** (jod′pərz, jōd′-), *n.pl.* breeches for horseback riding, loose above the knees and fitting closely below the knees. [< *Jodhpur,* a former state in India]

***jodhpurs**

Jo|do (jō′dō′), *n.* **1** a Japanese Buddhist sect that practices Amidism. **2** Amidism; Pure Land. [< Japanese *jōdo*]

joe¹ (jō), *n. Scottish.* jo (sweetheart).

Joe or **joe²** (jō), *n. U.S. Slang.* **1** a fellow; guy: *. . . the real heroes of combat, those unsung Joes of the ground crew* (New Yorker). **2** coffee: *Boligee's ambassador of good will returned after a year of serving doughnuts and "Joe" to combat soldiers* (Birmingham News).

Joe Blow, *U.S. Slang.* an average American.

Joe College, *U.S. Slang.* a typical college youth: *All study and no attention to diet and exercise can make Joe College a sick boy* (Science News Letter).

Joe Doakes (dōks), *U.S. Slang.* an average man; ordinary citizen.

Jo|el (jō′əl), *n.* **1** a Hebrew prophet of the 300's B.C. **2** a book of the Old Testament containing his prophecies and attributed to him.

Joe Magarac. See **Magarac.**

Joe Miller, an outworn joke. [< *Joe Miller's Jestbook,* a book of jokes published in 1739]

joe-pye weed (jō′pī′), **1** a tall weed of the composite family with pink or purple flowers and whorled leaves. **2** a related plant with similar flowers and stems spotted with purple. [American English, earlier *Joepye,* supposedly from the name of an Indian in Maine who used the plant medicinally]

jo|ey (jō′ē), *n., pl.* **-eys.** *Australian.* **1** a young kangaroo: *A four-month old joey—all kangaroo babies are joeys . . .* (Life). **2** any young animal. **3** a young child. [< Australian dialectal *joè*]

Jo|ey (jō′ē), *n., pl.* **-eys.** a circus clown, especially one who wears whiteface makeup, a white costume with a ruff, and a belled cap. [< diminutive of *Joseph* Grimaldi, 1778-1837, an English clown]

jog¹ (jog), *v.,* **jogged, jog|ging,** *n.* —*v.t.* **1** to shake with a push or jerk: *She jogged my elbow to get my attention.* **2** *Figurative.* to stir up (one's own or another person's memory) with a hint or reminder: *He tied a string around his finger to jog his memory.* **3** to move up and down with a jerk or shaking motion: *The horse trotted along, and jogged me up and down on his back.* **4** to cover (a distance) by jogging: *When it began to rain we jogged the last five miles of our hike.*
—*v.i.* **1** to move up and down with a jerking or shaking motion: *The old horse jogged along. Mr. Boffin jogged to and fro* (Dickens). **2** to run at a slow, regular pace, especially for exercise; engage in jogging: *Father jogs in the park every morning before going to work.* **3** to go forward heavily and slowly; trudge: *The tired boys jogged home.* **4** to get along; carry on; go (on) in a steady or humdrum fashion: *We jogged on together some time till Alfred saw plainly I was no planter* (Harriet Beecher Stowe). **5** to move on or be off: *The door is open, sir; there lies your way; You may be jogging* (Shakespeare).
—*n.* **1** a shake, push, or nudge: *A little breeze . . . which . . . gave them a kind of a jog . . . towards the shore* (Daniel Defoe). **2** *Figurative.* a hint or reminder; an urge: *to give one's memory a jog.* **3** a slow run; trot: *Father goes for a jog every morning.* **4** a short trip or excursion, especially one made by a slow walk: *The supermarkets . . . save the housewife endless jogs to the butcher* (New York Times).
[Middle English *joggen* to prick or spur; perhaps imitative]

jog² (jog), *n.* a part that sticks out or in; unevenness in a line or surface: *We hid behind a jog in the wall.* [American English, variant of *jag*]

jog|ger (jog′ər), *n.* **1** a person or thing that jogs. **2** a device on a printing press or other machine that hits or pushes sheets of paper so as to stack them up with the edges even or aligned.

jog|ging (jog′ing), *n.* the exercise of running at a slow, regular pace, often alternately with walking: *Jogging has become fashionable, and its devotees have adopted "Run for your life" as their slogan* (Charles Marwick).

jog|gle¹ (jog′əl), *v.,* **-gled, -gling,** *n.* —*v.t., v.i.* to shake slightly: *The slow-moving train joggled us to sleep.*
—*n.* a slight shake: *The joggle of the carriage put the baby to sleep.*

jog|gle² (jog′əl), *n., v.,* **-gled, -gling.** —*n.* **1** a projection on one of two joining surfaces, or a notch on the other, to prevent slipping. **2** a joint made in this way.
—*v.t.* to join or fasten with a joggle or joggles. [perhaps related to **jog²**]

joggle post, = king post.

jog trot, 1 a slow, regular trot, such as that of a horse: *Suddenly he slowed his long, effortless jog trot up to the steep road* (Atlantic). **2** *Figurative.* a routine or humdrum way of doing things: *the monotonous jog trot of daily life.*

jog|trot (jog′trot′), *v.,* **-trot|ted, -trot|ting,** *adj.* —*v.i.* to go or move at a jog trot.
—*adj.* routine; humdrum; monotonous: *Honest, jogtrot men who go on smoothly and dully* (Oliver Goldsmith). —**jog′trot′ter,** *n.*

jo|han|nes (jō han′ēz), *n., pl.* **-nes.** a former Portuguese gold coin first issued under John V, worth about $9. Also, **joannes.** [American English < Latin *Joannes* (on the coin), for *John* V, 1703-1750, of Portugal]

Jo|han|nine (jō han′in, -īn), *adj.* of or having to do with John, especially the Apostle John.

john (jon), *n. Slang.* **1** a bathroom or toilet. **2** Also, **John.** the customer of a prostitute. [< the name *John*]

John (jon), *n.* **1** one of the twelve Apostles. According to tradition, he wrote the Gospel of Saint John, the three Epistles of John, and Revelation. He was the disciple "whom Jesus loved." **2** the fourth book of the New Testament, attributed to John (full title: *The Gospel According to Saint John*). **3** = John the Baptist.

John-a-dreams (jon′ə drēmz′), *n. British.* a dreamy, impractical fellow: *A dull and muddy-mettled rascal . . . Like John-a-dreams* (Shakespeare).

John Barleycorn, intoxicating liquor.

john|boat (jon′bōt′), *n. U.S.* a small, light rowboat with a flat bottom and square ends; flat-bottomed skiff: *We passed a landing with a half-sunken johnboat tied to a willow root* (New Yorker).

John Bull, 1 the typical Englishman. **2** the English nation; Englishmen.

John Bullish, typically English: *We can be grateful to our transatlantic cousin for speaking his mind with such John Bullish bluntness* (Atlantic). —**John Bullishness.**

John Bull|ism (bul′iz əm), **1** the typical English character. **2** a typically English act, utterance, or characteristic.

John Doe, a made-up name used in legal forms or proceedings for the name of an unknown person.

John Do|ry (dôr′ē, dōr′-), *pl.* **John Do|rys.** either one of two edible sea fishes of warm seas with high, flat bodies, spiny fins, and a large, black, yellow-ringed spot on each side; dory. [< *John* + *dory²*]

Joh|ne's disease (yō′nəz), a chronic enteritis of cattle, goats, and sheep caused by bacteria; paratuberculosis.
[< Heinrich A. *Johne,* 1839-1910, a German veterinarian who described it]

John Han|cock (han′kok), *U.S. Informal.* a person's signature.
[American English < the signature of *John Hancock,* first signer of the Declaration of Independence]

John Henry, *U.S.* **1** *Informal.* a person's signature. **2** a legendary Negro in American folklore. He is a subject of strength and endurance in ballads and stories.

joh|nin (yō′nin), *n.* a sterile liquid prepared from the proteins or protein products of the bacillus of paratuberculosis, used in the diagnosis of this disease.
[< *John*(e's disease) + *-in*]

John Mark, one of the four Evangelists; Mark.

john|ny (jon′ē), *n., pl.* **-nies.** *Informal.* an idle young man of fashion: *a stage-door johnny.*

John|ny (jon′ē), *n., pl.* **-nies.** *Informal.* **1** a man; boy; fellow. **2** = Johnny Reb.

john|ny|cake (jon′ē kāk′), *n. U.S.* corn bread in the form of a flat cake. It is made of white corn meal, water or milk, and sometimes with eggs. Johnnycakes are cooked on a board before an open fire, on a griddle, or in a pan in an oven.
[American English, variant of *journey cake* a cake to be eaten on a journey]

Johnny collar, a short, upright-standing collar, fitting closely around the neck, and opening at the front. It is usually worn by women as part of a dress, jacket, or cape.

John|ny-come-late|ly (jon′ē kum lāt′lē), *n., pl.* **John|ny-come-late|lies** or **John|nies-come-late|ly,** *adj. Especially U.S. Informal.* —*n.* a late arrival; newcomer: *Man is a mere Johnny-come-*

lately, with a scant million years behind him (Science News Letter).
—*adj.* lately or newly arrived; new; recent.
Johnny darter, a small darter common in the streams of the central United States, the male of which guards eggs which are laid under stones for concealment.
John|ny-jump-up (jon′ē jump′up′), *n. U.S.* **1** a popular name for the wild pansy. **2** any one of various American violets, such as the bird's-foot violet.
Johnny One-Note (wun′nōt′), *U.S. Informal.* a person with a one-track mind; person who adheres to a narrow or one-sided view.
Johnny on the spot, *Informal.* a person who is on hand to perform a duty, seize an opportunity, or act in an emergency; person who is always ready or on the alert.
Johnny Reb, *Informal.* a Confederate soldier in the Civil War. [< *reb*(el)]
John Q. Citizen, *U.S.* = John Q. Public.
John Q. Public, *U.S.* people in general; the public personified: *Traveling political writers in past campaigns have heard it over and over from John Q. Public when asked how he would vote* (Harper's).
John|son|ese (jon′sə nēz′, -nēs′), *n.* a pompous, learned literary style, resembling that of Samuel Johnson.
John|son grass (jon′sən), a tall perennial grass, a variety of sorghum, grown in the southern United States for pasture and hay. [American English < William *Johnson,* an Alabama planter, who introduced it about 1840]
John|so|ni|an (jon sō′nē ən), *adj., n.* —*adj.* **1** of Samuel Johnson or his writings. **2** having a literary style like that of Samuel Johnson (1709-1784); pompous and ponderous: *the Johnsonian balance of rhythmical sentences.* **3** of or having to do with President Lyndon B. Johnson (1908-1973) or his administration.
—*n.* a student or admirer of Samuel Johnson.
John|so|ni|an|ism (jon sō′nē ə niz′əm), *n.* **1** Johnsonian style. **2** a Johnsonian word or expression.
John the Baptist, the Hebrew prophet who foretold the coming of Christ and baptized him; the Baptist. He was beheaded on the order of Herod (in the Bible, Matthew 3; Mark 6:17-29).
joie de vi|vre (zhwȧ′ də vē′vrə), *French.* joy of living; enjoyment of life: *France's advantage is that shopping, nightclubbing, and other joie de vivre items can be worth the price* (Newsweek).
join (join), *v., n.* —*v.t.* **1** to bring or put together; connect, fasten, or clasp: *to join hands, to join an island to the mainland by a bridge, to join two points, to join two pieces of wood with a dowel.* **SYN**: link, couple. **2** to meet and unite with; come together with: *Join us as soon as you can. The stream joins the river just below the mill.* **3** to make one; combine; unite: *The two clubs joined forces during the campaign. But were I join'd with her, Then might we live together as one life* (Tennyson). **4** to become a member of: *to join a church. He joined a boys' club. My uncle has joined the army. He joined a fraternity at college.* **5** to come into the company of: *Go now, and I'll join you later.* **6** to take or return to one's place in: *After a few days on shore the sailor joined his ship.* **7** to be next to; adjoin: *Their farm joins ours.*
—*v.i.* **1** to come together; meet: *The two roads join here.* **2** to become one; combine; unite: *to join in marriage.* **3** to take part with others: *to join in a song.* **4** *Archaic.* to meet in battle or conflict; encounter: *Straight the three bands prepare in arms to join* (Alexander Pope).
—*n.* **1** a point or line where things are joined; seam. **2** a joining or being joined. **3** *Mathematics.* = union (def. 9).
join up, to enlist in the armed forces: *Egbert went and joined up immediately as a private soldier* (D. H. Lawrence).
[< Old French *joindre* < Latin *jungere* join, yoke]
—*Syn. v.t.* **3**, *v.i.* **2 Join, combine, unite** mean to put or come together to form one thing. **Join** emphasizes bringing or coming together, but does not suggest how firm or lasting the association may be: *The two armies joined forces.* **Combine** emphasizes mixing or blending into one for a common purpose: *to combine voices in singing a hymn.* **Unite** emphasizes the oneness of the result and the loss of separate purposes or interests: *His family united to help him.*
▶ **join together**. The *together* is common and historically has been felt necessary by some experienced writers in certain meanings, although strictly speaking it is redundant, for *join* means bring or put together: *These ends must be joined before we go further.* Not: *These ends must be joined together before we go further.* However: *What therefore God hath joined together, let no man put asunder.*
join|der (join′dər), *n.* **1** the act of joining; union: *A contract of eternal bonds of love, Confirm'd by mutual joinder of your hands* (Shakespeare). **2** *Law.* **a** the joining of causes of action in a lawsuit. **b** the joining of parties in a lawsuit. **c** the acceptance by one of the parties to an action of an issue tendered. [< noun use of French *joindre* to join]
join|er (joi′nər), *n.* **1** a person or thing that joins. **2** a skilled carpenter who makes doors, windows, molding, furniture, and other complicated woodwork. **3** *Informal.* a person who joins many clubs, societies, or other organizations: *In a nation of joiners, the convention has become an American social institution* (Newsweek).
join|er|y (joi′nər ē), *n.* **1** the skill or trade of a joiner. **2** woodwork or furniture made by a joiner.
joint (joint), *n., v., adj.* —*n.* **1** the place at which two things or parts are joined. A pocketknife has a joint to fold the blade inside the handle. **2** the way parts are joined: *The square ends of the wood made a perfect joint.* **3a** the part in an animal where two bones move on each other, and the way those parts are put together. **b** the place where parts of an invertebrate's exoskeleton move on each other or the way they are fitted together. **4** one of the parts of which a jointed thing is made up: *the middle joint of the finger.* **5** a part of the stem of a plant from which a leaf or branch grows, especially when thickened, as in grasses, so that it resembles the joint of the knee or elbow; node. **6** a large piece of meat cut for roasting, usually with a bone in it: *Later they will be privileged to watch the two of them at luncheon carving the joint at the sideboard* (Punch). **7** *Slang.* **a** a cheap, low restaurant, bar, hotel, or similar place of entertainment. Joints were formerly for the illegal sale of liquor. **b** any place, building, or establishment. **8** *Geology.* a crack intersecting a mass of rock, usually occurring in sets of parallel planes dividing the mass into blocks. **9** *Slang.* a marijuana cigarette.
—*v.t.* **1** to connect by a joint or joints: *The edges of the tin box were jointed and then soldered together.* **2** to divide at the joints; separate into joints: *Please ask the butcher to joint the chicken.* **3** to form or provide with a joint or joints. **4** to prepare the edge or surface of (a board or stave) for fitting in a joint. **5** to point (brickwork or other masonry).
—*adj.* **1** shared or done by two or more persons: *By our joint efforts, we managed to push the car back on the road.* **2** sharing; joined with another or others: *My brother and I are joint owners of this dog.*
out of joint, **a** moved out of place at the joint: *The fall put his shoulder out of joint.* **b** *Figurative.* out of order; in bad condition: *The time is out of joint: O cursed spite, That ever I was born to set it right!* (Shakespeare).
(**put** or **have**) **one's nose out of joint**. See under **nose**.
[< Old French *joint,* past participle of *joindre;* see etym. under **join**] —**joint′less**, *adj.*
joint account, a bank account owned by two or more persons, each of whom can make deposits or withdrawals.
Joint Chiefs of Staff, the top military advisory board to the President of the United States and the Secretary of Defense, consisting of the chiefs of staff of the Army and Air Force, the chief of naval operations, and sometimes the commandant of the Marine Corps, and headed by its chairman.
joint committee, a committee, especially of a legislature, composed of representatives from various bodies or chambers, appointed to confer together on matters requiring joint action.
joint custody, a legal agreement between divorced or separated parents to share the custody of their offspring: *Where neither of two fit parents wants to be a weekend visitor, the alternative of joint custody cannot be dismissed as "disruptive" when compared with the damage suffered by children in an all-out custody war* (New York Times Magazine).
joint|ed (join′tid), *adj.* having a joint or joints: *a loosely jointed frame, the jointed body of a crayfish.* —**joint′ed|ly**, *adv.* —**joint′ed|ness**, *n.*
jointed glasswort, a showy glasswort which turns birght red in autumn, found on the Pacific and Atlantic coasts of North America.
joint|er (join′tər), *n.* **1** a person who makes joints. **2** a tool or machine used in making joints. **3** a triangular plow attachment, used to cover trash.
joint float, the float of certain Common Market currencies on the monetary market in an attempt to prevent large fluctuations in a single currency by speculation.
joint ill, a bacterial, often fatal, disease of foals and calves, characterized by swollen joints and a high fever.
joint|ly (joint′lē), *adv.* together; as partners; in common: *The two boys owned the boat jointly.*
joint resolution, a resolution passed in identical terms by the two branches of a legislative assembly, which, in the United States, requires the signature of the chief executive before it can become a law.
join|tress (join′tris), *n. Law.* a woman who has a jointure.
joint return, *U.S.* an income-tax report listing the combined earnings of a husband and wife.
joint stock, stock or capital contributed and owned by a number of persons jointly. It is divided into shares and serves as a common fund.
—**joint′-stock′**, *adj.*
joint-stock company (joint′stok′), a company or firm whose capital is owned in shares by stockholders, any one of whom can sell some or all of his shares without the consent of the others.
joint-stock corporation, a corporation whose shares are transferable.
joint stool, a stool made of parts fitted or joined together, as distinguished from one more roughly made, as from planks.
joint tenancy, *Law.* equal ownership of property by two or more persons in which the property goes to the surviving owner.
join|ture (join′chər), *n., v.,* **-tured, -tur|ing.** —*n.* **1** *Law.* property given to a woman at the time of her marriage. It becomes hers to use upon the death of her husband. **2** *Obsolete.* a joining; union. —*v.t. Law.* to make out a jointure to (a wife). [< Old French *jointure* < Latin *junctūra* a joining < *jungere* to join. See etym. of doublet **juncture**.]
joint|weed (joint′wēd′), *n.* any one of a group of North American plants of the buckwheat family, with jointed stems, almost no leaves, and spikelike clusters of small, white or pink flowers.
joint|worm (joint′wėrm′), *n.* the larva of certain insects that damage wheat by feeding on the joints of the stalks.
***joist** (joist), *n., v.* —*n.* **1** one of the parallel beams of timber or steel which support the boards of a floor or ceiling: *They began again on the first floor picking up the top floorboards next to the outer wall, leaving the joists exposed* (Harper's). **2** a scantling larger than a two-by-four.
—*v.t.* to provide with or lay across joists.
[< Old French *giste* beam, noun use of feminine past participle of *gesir* to lie < Latin *jacēre*]

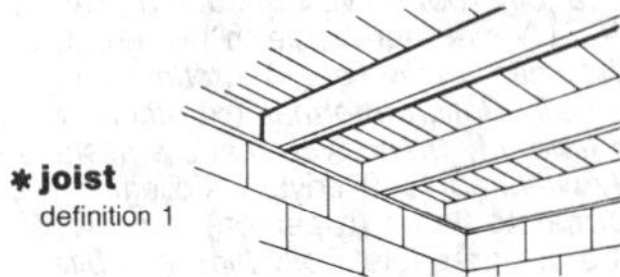
***joist**
definition 1

jo|jo|ba (hō hō′bə, hə-), *n.* a shrub or small tree of the box family, found in Mexico and the southwestern United States. Its seeds are used locally as a substitute for coffee, and yield an oil used in printing ink and polishing waxes. [American English < Mexican Spanish *jojoba*]
joke (jōk), *n., v.,* **joked, jok|ing.** —*n.* **1** something said or done to make somebody laugh; remark that is clever and funny; something funny: *Looking for the hat that was on my head was a good joke on me.* **2** a person or thing laughed at; laughingstock: *I shall be the standing joke of the mess table, until some greater fool than myself can be found* (James Fenimore Cooper). **3** something that is not earnest or actually meant.
—*v.i.* to make jokes; say or do something as a joke; jest. —*v.t.* to laugh at; make fun of; tease: *He disliked any risk of being "joked" about Hetty* (George Eliot). **SYN**: banter, chaff, rally.
no joke, a serious matter: *The loss of my bicycle was no joke.*
[< Latin *jocus* a jest] —**jok′ing|ly**, *adv.*
—*Syn. n.* **1 Joke, jest** mean something said or done to cause amusement or laughter. **Joke** applies to any remark, little story, trick, or mischief said or done in good fun and intended to cause laughter, often noisy laughter. A practical joke is not a real joke because it is not funny and often does harm. **Jest**, more formal, applies chiefly to language, and suggests playful and merry joking, teasing, or poking fun: *Many a truth has been spoken in jest.*
joke|book (jōk′bu̇k′), *n.* a book containing funny stories, sayings, or cartoons; book of jokes.
jok|er (jō′kər), *n.* **1** a person who jokes. **2** an extra playing card used in some games, often counting as the highest trump (as in euchre) or

as a wild card (as in poker). **3** *U.S.* a phrase or sentence hidden away in a law, contract, or other document, to defeat its apparent purpose. **4** a trick for getting the better of someone. **5** *Slang.* **a** a bad-mannered or awkward fellow; clown: *That joker in the blue suit—siddown or get knocked down* (Punch). **b** a fellow; guy.

joke|smith (jōk′smith′), *n. Informal.* a maker or writer of jokes; gagman.

joke|ster (jōk′stər), *n. U.S. Informal.* a person fond of jokes; humorist: ... *the classic telegram perpetrated by a Hollywood jokester who sent a cluster of his friends into a frenzy by wiring each of them: PLEASE DISREGARD PREVIOUS WIRE* (Saturday Review).

jok|ey or **jok|y** (jō′kē), *adj.*, **jok|i|er, jok|i|est.** full of jokes; humorous; jocular: *This section is curiously jokey, a ... playbook, lacking the high seriousness we have come to expect* (Sunday Times). —**jok′i|ly,** *adv.* —**jok′i|ness,** *n.*

Jo|la (jō′lä), *n., pl.* **-la** or **-las. 1** a member of a Negro people of Gambia, living south of the Gambia River near the coast. **2** their language.

jo|lie-laide (zhô lē′led′), *n., adj. French.* —*n.* a plain-looking woman or girl who has charming ways or other attractive features of personality. —*adj.* (of a woman or girl) plain-looking yet charming or attractive; (literally) nice-plain: *Mrs. Bedford, an approachable, jolie-laide woman with exuberant blue eyes* (London Times).

jol|li|fi|ca|tion (jol′ə fə kā′shən), *n.* gay entertainment; merrymaking: *Marriage festivals are usually expensive everywhere and it is hard to limit the price of jollification* (London Times). **SYN:** festivity, revel. [< *jolly* + *-fication*]

jol|li|fy (jol′ə fī), *v.t., v.i.,* **-fied, -fy|ing.** *Informal.* to make or be jolly or merry. [probably back formation < *jollification*]

jol|li|ty (jol′ə tē), *n., pl.* **-ties.** fun; merriment; festivity; gaiety: *All now was turn'd to jollity and game* (Milton). **SYN:** hilarity, mirth.
jollities, jolly festivities: *As a beginning of our jollities, I must remind our leader that my aunt's bedroom awaits him* (Jane Porter).

jol|ly (jol′ē), *adj.,* **-li|er, -li|est,** *adv., v.,* **-lied, -ly|ing,** *n., pl.* **-lies.** —*adj.* **1** very cheerful; full of fun; merry: *And then shook his ears, and was as jolly as ever* (Charles Kingsley). **SYN:** gay, joyful, mirthful, jovial. **2** *Especially British Informal.* **a** pleasant or delightful: *a jolly room. I've got such a jolly pony* (Thackeray). **SYN:** agreeable. **b** big; great: *a jolly fool. They had a jolly fight.* **3** *Archaic.* tipsy.
—*adv. Especially British Informal.* extremely; very: *a jolly good time. My friend, you made a mistake, and you jolly well know it* (Rudyard Kipling).
—*v.t.* **1** *Informal.* to flatter (a person) to make him feel good or agreeable: *Jolly him up a bit.* **2** to tease playfully; banter. —*v.i.* **1** *Informal.* to jolly someone; banter. **2** to make merry.
—*n.* **1** *Informal.* flattering words to make a person feel good or agreeable, often to gain some end. **2** *Informal.* gay entertainment; merrymaking. **3** *British Slang.* a royal marine.
[< Old French *joli* festive, merry, well-dressed, perhaps < a Germanic word] —**jol′li|er,** *n.* —**jol′li|ly,** *adv.* —**jol′li|ness,** *n.*

jolly boat, a small boat carried on a ship, usually at the stern.

***Jolly Rog|er** (roj′ər), a pirates' black flag with a white skull and crossbones on it; black flag; blackjack.

***Jolly Roger**

jolt (jōlt), *v., n.* —*v.t.* **1** to shake up; jar: *The wagon jolted us when the wheel went over the rocks.* **2** *Figurative.* to shock or surprise suddenly. —*v.i.* to move with a shock or jerk: *The car jolted across the rough ground.*
—*n.* **1** a jar, shock, or jerk: *I put the brakes on suddenly and the car stopped with a jolt.* **2** *Figurative.* a sudden surprise or shock: *The loss of so much money gave him a severe jolt.*
[origin uncertain. Related to **jowl**[4] in sense "to butt (with the head)."] —**jolt′er,** *n.* —**jolt′ing|ly,** *adv.*

jolt|y (jōl′tē), *adj.* that jolts; jolting.

Jo|mon (jō′mon, -mən), *adj.* of or belonging to a Japanese culture lasting from about 3000 to 2000 B.C., characterized by pottery and other artifacts made of sea shells. [< Japanese *jōmon*]

Jo|nah (jō′nə), *n.* **1** (in the Bible) a Hebrew prophet who was thrown overboard during a storm because he disobeyed God. He was swallowed by a large fish and later cast up on land alive. **2** a book of the Old Testament that tells about him. **3** a person or thing whose presence is supposed to bring bad luck: *A Jonah must be cast overboard to save the ship* (Cardinal Newman).

Jo|nas (jō′nəs), *n.* Jonah, in the Douay Bible.

Jon|a|than (jon′ə thən), *n.* **1** the son of Saul, and a devoted friend of David (in the Bible, I Samuel 19:1-10). **2** a bright-red apple with a fine flavor, that ripens in the early autumn.

Jones or **jones** (jōnz), *n. U.S. Slang.* **1** Often, **the Jones.** drug addiction: *"Drugs were ruining my life. But then the Brothers got hold of me and wouldn't let me out of their sight. You get a guy on the Jones and that's what you have to do"* (Time). **2** a narcotic, especially heroin: *"Jones" is slang both for heroin and its craving (as in "his jones came on him so bad"). The top ghetto jones-man, as pragmatic as a dumdum bullet, hunts his upstart challengers with stunning, careless cruelty* (Newsweek). [< the proper name *Jones,* perhaps euphemism for *junk*]

Jones|es (jōn′ziz), *n.pl.* the more prosperous or fashionable people of one's neighborhood or social circle; those who represent a desirable status in society, collectively: *to keep up with the Joneses. [At] this place ... there's no living up to the Joneses; there's just a natural desire to help, without any need to make impressions* (Calvin Trillin). [plural form of *Jones,* an ordinary or typical name, as of a neighbor]

jon|gleur (jong′glər; *French* zhôn glœr′), *n.* a wandering minstrel or entertainer in the Middle Ages. [< French *jongleur* < Old French *jogleor* juggler; influenced by *jangleor* chatterer. See etym. of doublet **juggler.**]

jon|quil (jong′kwəl), *n.* **1** a plant with yellow or white flowers and long, slender leaves. It is a kind of narcissus similar to the daffodil and belongs to the amaryllis family. **2** its flower or bulb. [< French *jonquille* < Spanish *junquillo* (diminutive) < *junco* reed < Latin *juncus*]

jor (jôr), *n.* the rhythmic second movement of a typical raga. [< Sanskrit *jor*]

Jor|dan almond (jôr′dən), **1** a choice almond used in making candies. It now comes chiefly from southern Spain. **2** a candy in which the almond is covered with a crunchy coating of smooth sugar. [Middle English *jardyne almaunde* < Old French *jardin* garden; influenced by *Jordan*]

Jordan curve, *Mathematics.* a closed curve which does not intersect itself at any point; simple closed curve. [< M. E. Camille *Jordan,* 1838-1922, a French mathematician]

Jordan curve theorem, *Mathematics.* the theorem that a closed curve in a plane divides the plane into an inside and outside region, so that any point in the inside cannot be joined to another point in the outside region without crossing the curve.

Jor|da|ni|an (jôr dā′nē ən), *adj., n.* —*adj.* of or having to do with Jordan or its people.
—*n.* a native or inhabitant of Jordan.

Jordan machine, a machine that brushes the fibers of paper pulp after it leaves the beater and cuts them to the proper length. [< Joseph *Jordan,* 1859-1960, its American inventor]

jor|na|da (hôr nä′ᴛʜä), *n. Spanish.* **1** the journey or work accomplished in a day. **2** a long expanse of desert in Mexico and the southwestern United States.

jo|ro|po (hō rō′pō), *n.* a lively dance of Venezuela. [< American Spanish *joropo*]

jo|rum (jôr′əm, jōr′-), *n.* **1** a large drinking bowl. **2** its contents: *a jorum of punch.* [probably < *Joram* (II Samuel 8:10), who brought David vessels]

Jos., **1** Joseph. **2** in the Bible: **a** Joshua. **b** Josiah.

Jo|seph (jō′zəf), *n.* **1** the favorite son of Jacob. His jealous brothers sold him into slavery in Egypt, where he finally became governor (in the Bible, Genesis 37,39-41). **2** the husband of Mary, mother of Jesus (in the Bible, Matthew 1:18-25).

jo|seph (jō′zəf), *n.* a long riding cloak with a cape, worn by women in the 1700's. [< *Joseph* (Genesis 39:12)]

Jo|seph|ite (jō′zə fīt), *n.* **1** a member of either of two orders of St. Joseph: the Priests of the Mission of St. Joseph founded about 1640, or a teaching institute founded in Belgium in 1817. **2** a member of the Reorganized Church of Jesus Christ of Latter Day Saints, formed by followers of Joseph Smith, the son of the founder of the Mormon Church. **3** *U.S.* a member of the St. Joseph's Society of the Sacred Heart, founded in 1871 and working in the Negro missions.

Joseph of Ar|i|ma|the|a (ar′ə mə thē′ə) a rich man who put the body of Jesus in his own tomb (in the Bible, Matthew 27:57-60).

Jo|seph's-coat (jō′zəfs kōt′), *n.* an annual plant of the amaranth family having flower clusters and variously colored leaves, growing from two to four feet high. [< *Joseph* (Genesis 37:3)]

Jo|seph|son effect (jō′zəf sən), the effect produced by a Josephson junction: *The Josephson effect, one of the most important in solid state physics, can be used for detecting microwave radiation and low voltages, among other purposes* (London Times). [< Brian D. *Josephson,* an English physicist who predicted this effect in 1962]

Josephson junction, a junction formed by two superconductors separated by a thin insulating layer, across which current flows without resistance and which generates microwaves when subjected to a certain voltage.

josh (josh), *v., n. U.S. Informal.* —*v.t., v.i.* to make good-natured fun of; tease playfully; banter: *You're only joshing me* (Bret Harte).
—*n.* good-natured banter.
[American English, perhaps < *Josh,* nickname for *Joshua*] —**josh′er,** *n.* —**josh′ing|ly,** *adv.*

Josh., (in the Bible) Joshua.

Josh|u|a (josh′ů ə), *n.* **1** the successor of Moses, who led the children of Israel into the Promised Land (in the Bible). **2** a book of the Old Testament. *Abbr:* Josh.

Joshua tree, a small yucca tree that grows in dry or desert regions of the southwestern United States. It belongs to the agave family.

Jo|si|ah (jō sī′ə), *n.* a king of Judah who lived in the 600's B.C. (in the Bible, II Kings 22 and 23).

joss (jos), *n.* **1** the image of a Chinese god; a Chinese idol: *And one called out on a heathen joss and one on the Virgin's Name* (Rudyard Kipling). **2** *Informal.* luck; fortune; chance. [< Chinese Pidgin English form of Javanese *dejos* < Portuguese *deos* god < Latin *deus*]

joss|er (jos′ər), *n. British Slang.* an old fellow.

joss house, a Chinese temple.

joss stick, a slender stick of dried, fragrant paste, burned as incense.

jos|tle (jos′əl), *v.,* **-tled, -tling,** *n.* —*v.t.* to strike, push, or crowd against; elbow roughly; shove: *We were jostled by the big crowd at the entrance to the circus.*
—*v.i.* **1** to be jostled or pushed. **2** *U.S. Slang.* to pick pockets; be a pickpocket.
—*n.* a jostling; push; knock. Also, **justle.**
[< *joust* + *-le* (frequentative)] —**jos′tler,** *n.*

jos|tle|ment (jos′əl mənt), *n.* the act of jostling.

Jos|u|e (jos′yů ē), *n.* Joshua, in the Douay Bible.

jot (jot), *v.,* **jot|ted, jot|ting,** *n.* —*v.t.* to write briefly or in haste: *The clerk jotted down the order.*
—*n.* a little bit; very small amount: *I do not care a jot.* **SYN:** particle, iota, whit.
jot or tittle, the smallest amount; least bit: *I am certain ... that the Secretary of State ... is without any jot or tittle of blame* (Manchester Guardian).
[< Latin *iōta* < Greek *iōta* iota, smallest letter in the Greek alphabet. See etym. of doublet **iota.**]
—**jot′ter,** *n.*

jo|ta or **Jo|ta** (hō′tä), *n.* a lively Spanish dance, accompanied by castanets. [< Spanish *jota;* origin uncertain; perhaps < earlier Spanish *sota* dance < Latin *saltāre* to leap]

jot|ting (jot′ing), *n.* something jotted down; brief note; memorandum.

Jo|tun, Jo|tunn, Jö|tunn, or **jö|tunn** (yô′tůn), *n. Norse Mythology.* one of a race of giants.

Jo|tun|heim, Jo|tunn|heim, or **Jö|tunn|heim** (yô′tůn hām), *n. Norse Mythology.* the home of the giants, at the northwestern edge of the earth.

joual (zhwäl), *n., adj.* —*n.* uneducated or dialectal Canadian French.
—*adj.* of or like joual.
[< Canadian French *joual,* dialectal pronunciation of French *cheval* horse]

joule (joul, jül), *n. Physics.* a measure of the amount of work done. It is equal to ten million ergs in the centimeter-gram-second system, or about 0.7375 foot-pounds, or one newton-meter. *Abbr:* j. [< James P. *Joule,* 1818-1889, a British physicist]

Joule's law (joulz, jülz), *Physics.* a law formulated by James P. Joule, giving the rate at which heat is generated when a current passes through a conductor.

jounce (jouns), *v.,* **jounced, jounc|ing,** *n.* —*v.t., v.i.* to move violently up and down; bounce; bump; jolt: *At every step of the camel, the rider was jounced around. The old car jounced along the rough road.*
—*n.* a bounce; bump; jolt: *She sat down on the bench with a jounce.*
[perhaps related to obsolete *jounce* exercise a horse]

jounc|y (joun′sē), *adj.,* **jounc|i|er, jounc|i|est.** bouncy: *The trolley that gave me the most fun in life was the jouncy open car which ran between Bay Head and Point Pleasant* (Atlantic).

jour., **1** journal. **2** journeyman.

jour|nal (jėr′nəl), *n., adj.* —*n.* **1** a daily record: *During the winter we kept a journal of the temperature, clouds, and rain and snow each day.*

2 an account of what happens or of what one thinks, feels, or notices, such as a diary, a ship's log, or the written account of what happens at each meeting of a society or town meeting: *The ship's journal was a history of its voyage including where it went and what the sailing and weather conditions were.* **3** a newspaper or magazine: *Benjamin Franklin published a successful journal in Philadelphia called the "Pennsylvania Gazette."* **SYN:** gazette, periodical. **4** *Bookkeeping.* **a** a book in which every item of business is written down so that the item can be entered under the proper account or posted later in a general ledger. A special journal is used for each type of transaction that recurs frequently, such as cash receipts, cash disbursements, or sales. Because transactions are first recorded in a journal as they occur, journals are called books of original entry. **b** = daybook. **5** the part of a shaft or axle that turns on a bearing.
—***adj.*** *Obsolete.* diurnal; daily: *ere twice the sun hath made his journal greeting* (Shakespeare).
[< Old French *journal,* adjective, daily < Late Latin *diurnālis* < Latin *diurnus* < *diēs* day. See etym. of doublet **diurnal.**]

journal box, the part in a machine enclosing a journal and its bearings.

jour|nal|ese (jėr′nə lēz′, -lēs′), *n.* a style of writing typical of newspapers and magazines, often characterized as exhibiting careless or roundabout expressions and trite words and phrases or other marks of hurried writing: *It's a clumsy ending and vile journalese* (Rudyard Kipling).

jour|nal in|time (zhür nål aɴtēm′), *French.* private diary.

jour|nal|ise (jėr′nə līz), *v.t., v.i.,* **-ised, -is|ing.** *Especially British.* journalize.

jour|nal|ism (jėr′nə liz əm), *n.* **1** the occupation of writing for, editing, managing, or publishing a newspaper or magazine. **2** the gathering, writing, and editing of material for other news media, such as radio and television: *TV journalism.* **3** writing by journalists: *That article is an example of first-class journalism.* **4** newspapers, magazines, and press or wire services as a group.

jour|nal|ist (jėr′nə list), *n.* **1** a person engaged in journalism. Reporters are journalists. **2** a person who keeps a journal or diary.

jour|nal|is|tic (jėr′nə lis′tik), *adj.* of or like journalism or journalists: *Because of a journalistic blunder, announcement of the foreign-aid program . . . caused a headline hassle* (Time). —**jour′nal|is′ti|cal|ly,** *adv.*

jour|nal|ize (jėr′nə līz), *v.,* **-ized, -iz|ing.** —***v.t.*** to enter or record in a journal.
—***v.i.*** **1** to keep or make entries in a journal. **2** to do the work of a journalist. —**jour′nal|iz′er,** *n.*

jour|ney (jėr′nē), *n., pl.* **-neys,** *v.,* **-neyed, -ney|ing.** —***n.*** **1** a traveling from one place to another; trip: *a journey around the world.* **SYN:** excursion, tour, voyage, jaunt. See syn. under **trip. 2** a distance traveled: *a week's journey.* **3** *Obsolete.* a day's travel: *a place ten journeys from here.*
—***v.i.*** to take a trip; travel: *to journey to Europe. And Abram journeyed, going on still toward the south* (Genesis 12:9).
[< Old French *journee* day's work or travel < Vulgar Latin *diurnāta* events of a day < *diurnum* day, noun use of neuter of Latin *diurnus* of one day < *diēs* day] —**jour′ney|er,** *n.*

jour|ney|man (jėr′nē mən), *n., pl.* **-men. 1** a workman who knows his trade: *The journeyman printer was much more accurate than his young apprentice.* **2** a workman who has completed his apprenticeship and is qualified to practice his trade, but has not become an employer or master workman. **3** *Obsolete.* a workman hired by the day.

jour|ney|work (jėr′nē wėrk′), *n.* the work of a journeyman.

jour|no (jer′nō), *n. Especially British Informal.* a journalist: *Lunch tends to be in a wine bar or pub with fellow journos, talking shop* (Sunday Times).

***joust**

joust** (just, joust, jüst), *n., v.* —n.*** a combat between two knights on horseback, armed with lances, especially as part of a tournament.
[< Old French *jouste* < *jouster,* see verb]
—***v.i.*** **1** to fight with lances on horseback. Knights used to joust with each other for sport. **2** to fight or parry; maneuver: *a company financially stronger, and better able to joust for a bigger slice of the auto market* (Wall Street Journal). Also, **just.**
jousts, a tournament: *Down to the meadow where the jousts were held* (Tennyson).
[< Old French *jouster* < Vulgar Latin *juxtāre* be next to < Latin *juxtā* beside] —**joust′er,** *n.*

Jove (jōv), *n.* **1** *Roman Mythology.* the god Jupiter, ruler of gods and men: *Keep in mind what Jove decrees* (John Dryden). **2** the planet Jupiter: *the moons of Jove* (William Cowper).
by Jove, an exclamation of surprise, pleasure, disgust, or disappointment: *By Jove, I forgot my eyeglasses!*
[< Latin *Jovem,* accusative of *Jupiter* Jupiter]

jo|vi|al (jō′vē əl), *adj.* good-hearted and full of fun; good-humored and merry; jolly; convivial: *Santa Claus is pictured as a jovial old fellow. Be bright and jovial among your guests tonight* (Shakespeare). **SYN:** mirthful. [< *Jovial* (because those born under the sign of the planet Jupiter were supposedly cheerful)] —**jo′vi|al|ly,** *adv.* —**jo′vi|al|ness,** *n.*

Jo|vi|al (jō′vē əl), *adj.* = Jovian.

jo|vi|al|i|ty (jō′vē al′ə tē), *n.* the quality of being jovial; jollity; merriment.

Jo|vi|an (jō′vē ən), *adj.* **1** of or like the god Jove or Jupiter. **2** of the planet Jupiter.

jow (jou, jō), *v., n. Scottish.* —***v.t., v.i.*** to ring or toll (a bell).
—***n.*** a ring or toll, as of a bell.
[variant of *jowl*[4], verb]

jowl[1] (joul, jōl), *n.* **1** the jaw, especially the underjaw: *fat jowls rolling over his collar.* **2** the cheek: *jowls puffed out by a mouthful of popcorn.* [Middle English *chawel,* Old English *ceafl;* perhaps influenced by *jowl*[2], or Old French *joue* cheek]

jowl[2] (joul, jōl), *n.* **1** a fold of flesh hanging from the jaw. **2** the dewlap of cattle. **3** the wattle of a fowl. [alteration of Middle English *cholle,* perhaps related to Old English *ceolur* dewlap, and *ceole* throat]

jowl[3] (joul, jōl), *n.* the head and adjacent parts of a fish, as of the salmon and sturgeon. [Middle English *choll*]

jowl[4] (joul, jōl), *v., n. British and Scottish Dialect.*
—***v.t.*** **1** to strike, knock, bump, or dash: *That skull . . . how the knave jowls it to the ground* (Shakespeare). **2** to shake or jolt. **3** to toll or ring (a bell).
—***v.i.*** **1** to strike; knock; peck. **2** to jolt along. **3** to toll, as a bell does.
—***n.*** **1** a knock; bump. **2** a stroke of a bell.
[Middle English *jollen* (perhaps originally) to slap the cheek or head. Compare etym. under **jowl**[1].]

jowled (jould), *adj.* having a jowl or jowls; jowly.

jowl|y (jou′lē), *adj.,* **jowl|i|er, jowl|i|est.** having large or prominent jowls; having a double chin: *a red-faced Scot of two hundred and fifty pounds, jowly and lugubrious of expression* (Maclean's)
—**jowl′i|ness,** *n.*

joy (joi), *n., v.* —***n.*** **1** a glad feeling; glad behavior; strong feeling of pleasure; happiness: *The little boy jumped for joy when he saw the circus. On with the dance! let joy be unconfined* (Byron). **SYN:** gladness, delight, rapture, bliss. See syn. under **pleasure. 2** something that causes gladness or happiness: *On a hot day, a cool swim is a joy. A thing of beauty is a joy forever* (Keats). **3** the expression of happiness; outward rejoicing: *The joy of Jerusalem was heard even afar off* (Nehemiah 12:43). **4** a state of happiness, especially the bliss of heaven. **5** *Archaic.* glad praise or worship: *Glory and joy and honour to our Lord* (Tennyson).
—***v.i.*** to be joyful: *those cruel potentates of the school, who joy in the smart of their subjects* (Washington Irving). **SYN:** rejoice, delight.
—***v.t.*** **1** *Archaic.* to gladden; delight: *a sight that joys the heart.* **2** *Obsolete.* to enjoy: *I, Who might have lived, and joy'd immortal bliss* (Milton).
[< Old French *joie* < Latin *gaudia,* neuter plural of *gaudium* joy < *gaudēre* rejoice] —**joy′less,** *adj.* —**joy′less|ly,** *adv.* —**joy′less|ness,** *n.*

joy|ance (joi′əns), *n. Archaic.* **1** joy; gladness; gaiety: *With my clear keen joyance Languor cannot be* (Shelley). **2** merrymaking; festive gaiety: *His sports were fair, his joyance innocent* (Edmund Spenser).

Joy|ce|an (joi′sē ən), *adj., n.* —***adj.*** of or characteristic of James Joyce (1882-1941) or his writings: *The novel records, in Joycean confusion but with no trace of Joyce's learning and wit . . .* (Atlantic). —***n.*** a follower or student of the works of James Joyce.

joy|ful (joi′fəl), *adj.* **1** glad; happy: *a joyful heart.* **2** causing joy: *joyful news.* **3** showing joy: *a joyful look.* —**joy′ful|ly,** *adv.* —**joy′ful|ness,** *n.*

joy-juice (joi′jüs′), *n. Slang.* alcoholic liquor.

joy|ous (joi′əs), *adj.* joyful; glad; gay: *a joyous song, a joyous person, a joyous city.* **SYN:** merry, elated. —**joy′ous|ly,** *adv.* —**joy′ous|ness,** *n.*

joy|pop (joi′pop′), *v.i.,* **-popped, -pop|ping.** *Slang.* to use narcotics occasionally, not as an addict does. —**joy′pop′per,** *n.*

joy ride, *Informal.* **1** a ride in an automobile or other vehicle for pleasure, especially when it is driven recklessly or without the owner's permission. **2** a ride for pleasure in any vehicle.

joy-ride (joi′rīd′), *v.i.,* **-rode, -rid|den, -rid|ing.** *Informal.* to take a joy ride. —**joy′-rid′er,** *n.*

joy stick, *Slang.* **1** the control lever of an airplane, usually of a small plane. **2** the control lever of an automobile, submarine, or the like. **3** any similar control lever, as that of a computer game: *The joy stick allows them to rotate the object on the screen* (Kenneth Engel).

JP (no periods), **1** jet pilot. **2** jet propulsion.

J.P., Justice of the Peace.

J particle, = psi particle. [< the letter *J,* because of its resemblance to the Chinese character for (Samuel) *Ting,* a physicist at the Brookhaven National Laboratory who discovered the particle]

Jr. or **jr.,** Junior: *John Parker, Jr., is the son of John Parker, Sr.*
►See **Jnr.** for usage note.

J.R., King James (Latin, *Jacobus Rex*).

J.S.D., Doctor of Juristic Science (Latin, *Juris Scientiae Doctor*).

jt., joint.

Jth., (in the Apocrypha) Judith.

ju|ba (jü′bə), *n.* a characteristic dance of plantation Negroes in the southern United States, performed by one or more dancers, while the spectators clap hands, pat the knee or thigh, stamp with the foot, and sing a refrain in which the word *juba* is frequently repeated. [origin uncertain]

Ju|bal (jü′bəl), *n.* the inventor of musical instruments (in the Bible, Genesis 4:21).

jub|bah (jüb′bə), *n.* a long, coatlike, outer garment with an open front and sleeves, worn by Moslems and Parsees. Also, **jibbah.** [< Arabic *jubba.* See etym. of doublets **jupe, jupon.**]

ju|be (jü′bē), *n.* a rood loft or the entire structure formed by the rood loft and rood screen in a church. [< Latin *jubē* order thou (first word of a prayer read from this platform by the deacon), imperative of *jubēre* to order, command]

ju|bi|lance (jü′bə ləns), *n.* the act or fact of rejoicing; great joy.

ju|bi|lan|cy (jü′bə lən sē), *n.* = jubilance.

ju|bi|lant (jü′bə lənt), *adj.* expressing or showing joy; rejoicing; exulting: *People were jubilant when the war was over. Great organs surged through arches dim Their jubilant floods in praise of him* (James Russell Lowell). **SYN:** joyful, exultant.
[< Latin *jūbilāns, -antis,* present participle of *jūbilāre* shout with joy < *jubilium* wild shout] —**ju′bi|lant|ly,** *adv.*

ju|bi|late (jü′bə lāt), *v.i.,* **-lat|ed, -lat|ing.** to shout for joy; rejoice; exult.
[< Latin *jūbilāre* (with English *-ate*[1]); see etym. under **jubilant**]

Ju|bi|la|te (jü′bə lā′tē, -lä′-), *n.* **1** the 100th Psalm in the Authorized Version or the 99th Psalm in the Douay Version of the Bible. **2** a musical setting of this psalm. **3** the third Sunday after Easter, when the 66th Psalm (65th in the Douay) is used as the introit.
[< Latin *jūbilāte,* imperative of *jūbilāre;* see etym. under **jubilant**]

ju|bi|la|tion (jü′bə lā′shən), *n.* **1** the act or fact of rejoicing. **2** a joyful celebration.

ju|bi|la|to|ry (jü′bə lə tôr′ē, -tōr′-), *adj.* expressing jubilation.

ju|bi|lee (jü′bə lē), *n.* **1** an anniversary thought of as a time of rejoicing. A 25th anniversary is called a silver jubilee; a 50th, a golden jubilee. **2** a time of rejoicing or great joy: *to hold a jubilee over a victory.* **3** rejoicing; great joy: *a day of jubilee. They passed on . . . singing hymns of jubilee* (Washington Irving). **4** (in the Roman Catholic Church) a year in which punishment for sin is remitted, after repentance and the performance of certain acts. Since the 1400's, jubilees have been proclaimed every 25 years. **5** (in Jewish history) a year of emancipation, to be celebrated every 50th year by not cultivating the fields, by setting Hebrew slaves free, and by restoring lands taken from their owners (in the Bible, Leviticus 25).
[< Old French *jubile* < Late Latin *jūbilaeus* < Greek *iōbēlaîos,* adjective < *iôbēlos* jubilee < Hebrew *yobel* (originally) trumpet, ram('s horn)]

ju|co (jü′kō), *n. U.S. Informal.* a junior college.

Jud., **1** (in the Bible) Judges. **2** (in the Apocrypha) Judith.

J.U.D., Doctor of both Canon and Civil Law (Latin, *Juris utriusque Doctor*).

Ju|dae|an (jü dē′ən), *adj., n.* = Judean.

Pronunciation Key: hat, āge, cãre, fär; let, ēqual, tėrm; it, īce; hot, ōpen, ôrder; oil, out; cup, pu̇t, rüle; child; long; thin; ᴛʜen; zh, measure; ə represents **a** in about, **e** in taken, **i** in pencil, **o** in lemon, **u** in circus.

Ju|dae|o-Chris|tian (jü dē′ō kris′chən, -dā′-), *adj., n.* = Judeo-Christian.

Ju|dae|o-Chris|ti|an|i|ty (jü dē′ō kris′chē an′ə-tē, -dā′-), *n.* = Judeo-Christianity.

Ju|dah (jü′də), *n.* **1** the fourth son of Jacob, and ancestor of the tribe of Judah (in the Bible, Genesis 29:35). **2** the most powerful of the twelve tribes of Israel (in the Bible, Numbers 26:19-22). **3** an ancient Hebrew kingdom in southern Palestine, made up of the tribes of Judah and Benjamin. Jerusalem was its capital.

Ju|da|ic (jü dā′ik), *adj.* of or having to do with the Jews or Judaism; Jewish.

Ju|da|i|ca (jü dā′ə kə), *n.pl.* books, documents, art objects, and other cultural artifacts, having to do with Jewish life or Jewish history.

Ju|da|ism (jü′dē iz əm), *n.* **1** the religion of the Jews, based on the teachings of Moses and the prophets as found in the Old Testament, and on the interpretations of the rabbis. Judaism teaches belief in the same God as Christianity, but holds that the Messiah is still to come. *The great prophets of Israel made the search for justice the heart of Judaism* Ogburn and Nimkoff). **2** the observance of this religion or of Jewish rules, customs, and traditions. **3** the culture, religion, history, language, and civilization of the Jewish people. **4** Jews as a group.

Ju|da|ist (jü′dē ist), *n.* **1** an adherent of Judaism. **2** a Jewish Christian in the early church who followed or advocated Jewish rites or practices.

Ju|da|is|tic (jü′dē is′tik), *adj.* of or having to do with Judaism or Judaists: *The Essenes, . . . though they possessed certain doctrines and followed certain practices of their own, were still basically Judaistic* (New Yorker).

Ju|da|ize (jü′dē īz), *v.,* **-ized, -iz|ing.** *—v.i.* to conform to Jewish usages or ideas.
—v.t. to cause to conform to Jewish usages or ideas. **—Ju′da|i|za′tion,** *n.* **—Ju′da|iz′er,** *n.*

Ju|das (jü′dəs), *n.* **1** Judas Iscariot, the disciple who betrayed Jesus Christ for money (in the Bible, Matthew 26:14-50). **2** a person treacherous enough to betray a friend; an utter traitor: *Three Judases, each one thrice worse than Judas* (Shakespeare). **3** Jude, or Saint Judas, one of the Apostles (not Iscariot); Thaddaeus (in the Bible, Luke 6:16). **4** a relative of Jesus (in the Bible, Matthew 13:55, where he is included, with James and Simon, among the "brethren" of Jesus).

Judas goat, a goat used to lead sheep to slaughter.

Judas or **judas hole,** a small opening in a door, especially in a prison cell, through which a person can look without being seen from the other side; peephole.

Judas kiss, an act that appears friendly but is not; kiss of death.

Judas thorn, = Judas tree.

Judas tree, 1 a shrub or small tree of the pea family native to western Asia and southern Europe, having white or purplish flowers before the leaves come out. **2** any related tree, such as the redbud; cercis. [< the belief that *Judas* Iscariot hanged himself on such a tree]

Judas window, = Judas hole.

jud|der (jud′ər), *v., n.* *—v.i.* to jerk and shudder: *The drum must run perfectly true and not judder at its circumference* (New Scientist). *His Jaguar . . . judders to a stop, he pulls up the handbrake* (Punch).
—n. a juddering.
[apparently a blend of *jerk*[1] and *shudder*]

Jude (jüd), *n.* **1** one of the twelve Apostles chosen by Jesus; Saint Judas; Thaddaeus. **2** a book of the New Testament. **3** the author of this book, probably the relative of Jesus referred to in Matthew 13:55.

Ju|de|an (jü dē′ən), *adj., n.* *—adj.* **1** Judea. **2** of the Jews.
—n. **1** a native or inhabitant of Judea. **2** a Jew. Also, **Judaean.**
[< Latin *Jūdaeus* (see etym. under **Jew**) + English *-an*]

Ju|den|rat (yü′den rät), *n. German.* a Jewish council appointed by the Nazis to represent Jews in a ghetto of an occupied territory.

Ju|de|o-Chris|tian (jü dē′ō kris′chən, -dā′-), *adj., n.* *—adj.* both Jewish and Christian, common to Judaism and Christianity: *the Judeo-Christian tradition. The celebrated new chapel with its seventeen spires seems less Judeo-Christian than a sacred shrine of aerospace* (Harper's).
—n. a person who affirms or believes in the teachings and beliefs common to Judaism and Christianity. Also, **Judaeo-Christian.**
[< Latin *Jūdaeus* Jew (< Greek *Ioudaîos*) + English *Christian*]

Ju|de|o-Chris|ti|an|i|ty (jü dē′ō kris′chē an′ə tē, -dā′-), *n.* the concepts and tenets common to Judaism and Christianity; Judeo-Christian teachings and beliefs: *On the face of the record, Judeo-Christianity did more to promote the growth of freedom than did any other of the higher religions* (Harper's). Also, **Judaeo-Chris|tianity.**

Ju|de|o-Span|ish (jü dē′ō span′ish, -dā′-), *n.* = Ladino.

Judg., (in the Bible) Judges

judge (juj), *n., v.,* **judged, judg|ing.** *—n.* **1** a public official appointed or elected to hear and decide cases in a law court: *The judge sentenced the speeding driver to pay a fine and hear a lecture on dangerous driving.* **2** a person chosen to settle a dispute or to decide who wins a race or contest: *Sole judge of truth* (Alexander Pope). **3** a person who can decide on how good a thing is: *a good judge of dogs, a judge of character, a poor judge of poetry.* **4** a ruler in ancient Israel, before the time of the kings.
[< Old French *juge* < Latin *jūdex, -icis* < *jūs* law + *dīcere* say]
—v.t. **1a** to hear and decide (cases) in a law court: *The court was unable to judge the case before all the evidence was put before it.* **b** to decree; order. **2** to settle (a dispute); decide on (in a contest): *The officials of the boys' club judged the races and other sporting events.* **3** to make up one's mind about; form an opinion or estimate about: *to judge the merits of a book, to judge a man innocent until proven guilty.* **4** to think; suppose; conclude; *I judged that you had forgotten to come. Tomorrow, then, I judge a happy day* (Shakespeare). SYN: deem, regard, consider. **5** to criticize; blame: *You had little cause to judge him so harshly. Judge not, that ye be not judged* (Matthew 7:1). SYN: condemn. **6** to govern, as one of the judges of ancient Israel.
—v.i. **1** to act as judge: *God must judge 'twixt man and me* (Robert Browning). **2** to make up one's mind; form an opinion or estimate.
[Middle English *juggen* < Anglo-French *juger,* Old French *jugier* < Latin *jūdicāre* < *jūdex, -icis* < *jūs* law + *dīcere* say] **—judge′like′,** *adj.* **—judg′er,** *n.*

judge advocate, *pl.* **judge advocates** or **judges advocate. 1** *U.S.* an officer who acts as a prosecutor at a court-martial. **2** *British.* a person appointed to manage the proceedings of a court-martial and to advise it on points of law. *Abbr:* JA (no periods) or J.A.

judge advocate general, *pl.* **judge advocate generals, judge advocates general,** or **judges advocate general,** an officer in the armed forces who has general charge of the legal matters of his service.

judge|ment (juj′mənt), *n.* = judgment.

Judg|es (juj′iz), *n.* a book of the Old Testament dealing with the period in Jewish history between the death of Joshua and Saul's accession to the throne, when Israel was ruled by judges or magistrates. *Abbr:* Judg.

judge|ship (juj′ship), *n.* the position, duties, or term of office of a judge: *He handed the Senate his list of nominations for permanent judgeships* (Time).

judg|mat|ic (juj mat′ik), *adj. Informal.* showing good judgment; judicious; discerning: *Each essay is limited to a single page; their range is wide, their elucidation concise and judgmatic* (Atlantic). [< *judge* + *-matic,* as in *pragmatic*] **—judg|mat′i|cal|ly,** *adv.*

judg|mat|i|cal (juj mat′ə kəl), *adj. Informal.* judgmatic: *A judgmatical rap over the head stiffened the lying impostor for a time* (James Fenimore Cooper).

judg|ment (juj′mənt), *n.* **1a** an opinion; estimate: *In my judgment, she is prettier than her sister.* SYN: estimation, belief. **b** the forming of an opinion or conclusion: *To judge rightly of the present, we must oppose it to the past; for all judgment is comparative* (Samuel Johnson). **2** the power to judge well; good sense: *Solomon was a man of judgment. Since she has judgment in such matters, we will ask her. My salad days, when I was green in judgment* (Shakespeare). **3** the act of judging: *Be not faint-hearted when thou sittest in judgment* (Ecclesiasticus 4:9). **4a** a decision, decree, or sentence given by a judge or court. **b** a debt arising from the decision of a judge or court. **c** the official certificate recording such a decision. **5** a decision made by anybody who judges. **6** criticism; condemnation: *Do not pass judgment on your neighbors. I will utter my judgments against them . . . who have forsaken me* (Jeremiah 1:16). **7** a misfortune thought of as a punishment from God: *The neighbors considered his broken leg as a judgment on him for staying away from church.* **8** the final trial of all mankind at the end of the world; Last Judgment. **9** *Archaic,* justice; righteousness: *Learn to do well; seek judgment, relieve the oppressed* (Isaiah 1:17). Also, **judgement.**
the Judgment, = judgment day: *The valley of Cedron . . . where the . . . Judgment shall be* (George Sandys).

judg|men|tal (juj men′təl), *adj.* having to do with judgment: *a judgmental attitude.*

judgment day or **Judgment Day,** the day of God's final judgment of mankind at the end of the world; doomsday.

judgment debt, a debt resulting from a legal decision.

judgment seat, the seat from which judgment is made.

ju|di|ca|ble (jü′də kə bəl), *adj.* capable of being judged; liable to be judged. Also, **judiciable.**
[< Late Latin *jūdicābilis* < Latin *jūdicāre;* see etym. under **judge,** verb]

ju|di|care (jü′də kăr′), *n. U.S.* a government-sponsored program providing free legal services to the poor: *For all the arguments over the pros and cons of judicare, there is agreement that too many of the nation's poor still go without legal help* (Time). [< *judi*(cial) + *care,* patterned on *medicare*]

ju|di|ca|tive (jü′də kā′tiv), *adj.* judicial: *a judicative authority.* [< Latin *jūdicātus,* past participle of *jūdicāre* (see etym. under **judge,** verb)]

ju|di|ca|to|ry (jü′də kə tôr′ē, -tōr′-), *adj., n., pl.* **-ries.** *—adj.* of the administration of justice; judicial: *judicatory authority.*
—n. **1** the administration of justice. **2** a court of justice; tribunal.

ju|di|ca|ture (jü′də kə chůr, -chər), *n.* **1** the administration of justice: *Judicature is nothing else but an interpretation of the law* (Thomas Hobbes). **2** the position, duties, or authority of a judge. **3** the extent of jurisdiction of a judge or court. **4** a group of judges. **5** a court of justice; tribunal.
[< Medieval Latin *judicatura* < Latin *jūdicāre;* see etym. under **judge,** verb]

ju|di|ci|a|ble (jü dish′ē ə bəl), *adj.* = judicable.

ju|di|cial (jü dish′əl), *adj.* **1** of judges; having to do with a law court or the administration of justice: *a judicial decision, judicial districts. The Constitution of the United States provides for the division of government among an executive, legislative, and judicial branch.* **2** of or suited to a judge; impartial; fair: *A judicial mind considers both sides of a dispute fairly before making a decision.* **3** ordered, permitted, or enforced by a judge or court: *a judicial sale. She got a judicial separation from her husband.* **4** forming or expressing a judgment. **5** *Theology.* inflicted by God as a judgment or punishment. [< Latin *jūdiciālis* < *jūdicium* judgment < *jūdex;* see etym. under **judge,** noun] **—ju|di′cial|ly,** *adv.*

judicial astrology, a branch of astrology dealing with the prediction of earthquakes, plagues, wars, and other historical or natural events.

judicial review, *U.S.* the process by which a court or system of courts decide on the constitutionality of a legislative act or an executive order: *Judicial review confines the state and national governments within their constitutional limits* (William G. Carleton).

ju|di|ci|ar|y (jü dish′ē er′ē), *n., pl.* **-ar|ies,** *adj.*
—n. **1** the branch of government that administers justice; system of courts of justice of a country: *organized . . . into legislative, executive, and judiciary* (Thomas Jefferson). **2** the judges of a country, state, or city; judicature.
—adj. of or having to do with courts, judges, or the administration of justice; judicial: *Court cases are judiciary proceedings.*

ju|di|cious (jü dish′əs), *adj.* having, using, or showing good judgment; wise; sensible: *A judicious parent encourages his children to decide many things for themselves. A judicious historian selects and weighs facts carefully and critically.* SYN: prudent, astute, discreet. [< French *judicieux* (with English *-ous*) < Latin *jūdicium* judgment < *jūdex;* see etym. under **judge,** noun] **—ju|di′cious|ly,** *adv.* **—ju|di′cious|ness,** *n.*

Ju|dith (jü′dith), *n.* **1** a Hebrew woman who saved her countrymen by killing the Assyrian general Holofernes. **2** a book of the Apocrypha and of the Douay Version of the Bible that relates her story. *Abbr:* Jth.

***ju|do** (jü′dō), *n.* **1** = jujitsu. **2** a modern form of jujitsu practiced as a sport or as self-defense.
[< Japanese *jūdō* < *jū* softness + *dō* way]

***judo**
definition 2

ju|do|gi (jü dō′gē), *n.* a loose, white cotton jacket and trousers worn by judo wrestlers, with a sash whose color varies with the degree of the wearer's expertness. [< Japanese *jūdōgi* < *jūdō* judo + *ki* clothing]

ju|do|ist (jü′dō ist), *n.* a student of or expert in judo.

ju|do|ka (jü dō′kə), *n., pl.* **-ka** or **-kas.** a person who practices judo; judo wrestler. [< Japanese *jūdōka* < *jūdō* judo + *ka* person]

ju|do|man (jü′dō mən), *n., pl.* **-men.** a judo wrestler; judoka.

Ju|dy (jü′dē), *n.* the wife of Punch in a Punch-and-Judy show.

ju|dy (jü′dē), *n. British Slang.* a girl. [probably < *Judy*]

jug[1] (jug), *n., v.,* **jugged, jug|ging.** —*n.* **1** a container for holding liquids. A jug usually has a spout or a narrow neck and a handle. **2** the contents of a jug; jugful: *a jug of warm water* (Dickens). **3** *Slang.* a prison or jail: *They sentenced me . . . to ten years in the Jug* (James Russell Lowell). **4** *Slang.* the carburetor of an internal-combustion engine.
—*v.t.* **1** *Slang.* to jail; imprison: *He was the justice of the peace that jugged me for a vagrant* (Mark Twain). **2** to stew or boil (especially a rabbit or hare) in a jug.
[probably originally a name, alteration of *Joan*]

jug[2] (jug), *v.i.,* **jugged, jug|ging. 1** to nestle together, as partridges. **2** to collect in a covey.

jug[3] (jug), *n., v.,* **jugged, jug|ging.** —*n.* a sound uttered by the nightingale and some other birds.
—*v.i.* to utter the sound.

ju|gal (jü′gəl), *adj.* of or having to do with the bony arch of the cheek; zygomatic. [< Latin *jugālis* < *jugum* yoke]

jugal bone, 1 the cheekbone in man: *The jugal bone is the principal bone of the cheek.* **2** a corresponding bone in other vertebrate animals.

ju|gate (jü′gāt, -git), *adj., n.* —*adj.* **1** *Biology.* occurring in pairs; connected; yoked, as a pinnate leaf in which the leaflets are in pairs. **2** (of impressions stamped on coins) placed side by side.
—*n.* **1** a jugate impression on a coin. **2** *U.S.* a button pairing the pictures of a presidential candidate and his running mate.
[< Latin *jugātus,* past participle of *jugāre* join < *jugum* yoke]

jug band, *U.S.* a musical band that uses improvised instruments, such as jugs, pans, pots, and washboards, for playing hillbilly music.

jug-eared (jug′ird′), *adj. Slang.* having ears spreading wide from the head.

juge d'in|struc|tion (zhyzh′dan stryk syôn′), *pl.* **juges d'in|struc|tion** (zhyzh′dan stryk syôn′). *French.* an examining magistrate authorized to interrogate witnesses and suspects.

Ju|gend|stil (yü′gənt shtēl′), *n.* the art nouveau of Germany and Austria. [< German *Jugendstil* (literally) youth style]

jug|ful (jug′fu̇l), *n., pl.* **-fuls.** as much as a jug can hold.

jugged hare (jugd), hare stewed or simmered in a jug or casserole.

Jug|ger|naut (jug′ər nôt), *n.* **1** an idol of the Hindu god Krishna, pulled around on a huge car. Devotees of the god are said to have thrown themselves under the wheels to be crushed to death. **2** *Figurative.* Also, **juggernaut. a** something to which a person blindly devotes himself or is cruelly sacrificed: *that remorseless juggernaut—"the needs of man"* (Thomas A. Edison). **b** a frightening, invisible machine, force, or other agent, that destroys anything in its path. **3** *British.* **juggernaut,** a large, heavy vehicle, especially a heavy truck. [< Hindustani *Jagannāth* < Sanskrit *Jagannātha* < *jagat* world + *nātha* lord]

jug|gins (jug′ənz), *n. British Slang.* a simpleton. [origin uncertain]

jug|gle (jug′əl), *v.,* **-gled, -gling,** *n.* —*v.i.* **1** to do tricks that require skill of hand or eye: *He juggled with knives by balancing them on his nose.* **2** *Figurative.* to play tricks; use trickery: *It sidesteps burning issues in order to juggle with words* (London Times). *She never juggles or plays tricks with her understanding* (Charles Lamb).
—*v.t.* **1** to do tricks with: *He can juggle three balls, keeping them in the air at one time.* **2** *Figurative.* to change by trickery or as if by trickery: *The dishonest cashier juggled the store's accounts to hide his thefts.* **3** *Figurative.* to deceive; trick; cheat: *He juggled his brother out of his share of the farm that they had inherited.* **4** *Figurative.* to weigh or balance mentally: *Juggling these imponderables, one guess on the timing would be the last week in September* (Wall Street Journal).
—*n.* **1** the act of juggling. **2** *Figurative.* a trick; deception; fraud: *The Opposition . . . declared the whole transaction to be a mere juggle* (William E. H. Lecky).
[< Old French *jogler* < Latin *joculārī* to joke < *joculus* (diminutive) < *jocus* a jest]

***jug|gler** (jug′lər), *n.* **1** a person who can do juggling tricks: *After dinner comes in a juggler which showed us very pretty tricks* (Samuel Pepys). **2** *Figurative.* a person who uses tricks, deception, or fraud: *The Sophist . . . is proved to be a dissembler and juggler with words* (Benjamin Jowett). [< Old French *jogleor* < Latin *joculātor* joker < *joculārī;* see etym. under **juggle.** See etym. of doublet **jongleur.**]

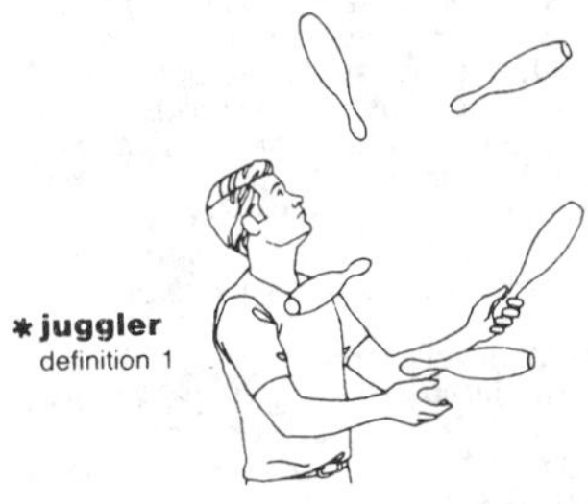

***juggler**
definition 1

jug|gler|y (jug′lər ē), *n., pl.* **-gler|ies. 1** the skill or tricks of a juggler; sleight of hand. **2** *Figurative.* trickery; deception; fraud.

jug|head (jug′hed′), *n. Slang.* a foolish individual; dolt.

ju|glan|da|ceous (jü′glan dā′shəs), *adj.* belonging to the walnut family. [< New Latin *Juglandaceae* the family name (< Latin *jūglāns, -andis* walnut < *Jupiter* Jupiter + *glāns, glandis* acorn) + English *-ous*]

Ju|go|slav or **Ju|go-Slav** (yü′gō släv′, -slav′), *n., adj.* = Yugoslav.

Ju|go|sla|vi|an or **Ju|go-Sla|vi|an** (yü′gō slä′vē-ən, -slav′ē), *adj., n.* = Yugoslavian.

Ju|go|sla|vic (yü′gō slä′vik, -slav′ik), *adj.* = Yugoslavic.

jug|u|lar (jug′yə lər, jü′gyə-), *adj., n.* —*adj.* **1** of the neck or throat: *a jugular vein, a jugular process.* **2** of a jugular vein. **3** *Figurative.* aiming for the jugular vein; cutthroat; murderous: *[He] will not get far in the jugular combat of national politics without a more lionlike approach* (Tom Wicker). *This journalism . . . was gaudy and free-wheeling. The competition was jugular* (Alden Whitman). **4** having the ventral fins at the throat, in front of the pectoral fins
—*n.* **1** = jugular vein. **2** *Figurative.* the most vulnerable point of an opponent: *To the Liberal old guard, he was an apolitical do-gooder, with no instinct for the jugular* (Time).
[< New Latin *jugularis* < Latin *jugulum* collarbone; throat, neck < *jug-,* stem of *jungere* to join]

jugular vein, any one of the four large veins in the head and neck that return blood from the head and neck toward the heart. See picture under **circulation.**

jug|u|late (jug′yə lāt, jü′gyə-), *v.t.,* **-lat|ed, -lat|ing. 1** to stop the course of (a disease or similar process) by extreme measures. **2** to cut the throat of; kill. [< Latin *jugulāre* to kill (with English *-ate*[1]) < *jugulum;* see etym. under **jugular**]

jug|u|lum (jug′yə ləm, jü′gyə-), *n. Zoology.* **1** the lower front part of the neck in birds. **2** a corresponding part in insects. [< New Latin *jugulum* < Latin *jugulum* collarbone; see etym. under **jugular**]

ju|gum (jü′gəm), *n.* **1** *Entomology.* a small projection or lobe on the forewing of certain lepidopterous insects, which extends under the base of the hind wing and holds the two wings together in flight. **2** *Botany.* a pair of leaflets in a pinnate leaf. [< New Latin *jugum* < Latin *jugum* yoke]

juice (jüs), *n., v.,* **juiced, juic|ing.** —*n.* **1** the liquid part of fruits, vegetables, and meats: *the juice of a lemon, meat juice.* **2** a fluid in the body. The juices of the stomach help to digest food. **3** any extracted liquid. **4** *Figurative.* the essence or spirit of anything: *It is not realism which is the juice of Mr. Williams' evening* (Wall Street Journal). **5** *Slang.* electricity: *The one atom-powered electricity-producing operation in the U.S. . . . makes "juice" only on a small scale as a by-product* (Wall Street Journal). **6** *Slang.* gasoline. **7** *U.S. Slang.* **a** alcoholic liquor. **b** a usurious loan or loans. **c** favorable standing; position, power, or influence: *"The important thing now is I got juice as an actor," McQueen went on. "That means you choose your material, you pick your situations"* (New York Times). **d** methadone (because it is usually given with fruit juice): *Don't resort to street slang [such as] "I've got to pick up my juice"* (New Yorker).
—*v.t.* **1** to remove the juice of: *We juiced a dozen oranges.* **2** to add juice to: *to juice a roast, to juice an electric circuit, to juice a car in an automobile race.*
juice up, *Slang.* **a** to brighten up; enliven: *. . . has added a Swiss chef to the payroll to juice up its menus* (Newsweek). **b** to refuel.
stew in one's own juice, *Informal.* to suffer the consequence of one's actions: *As Mr. Smith is immovable and cannot be brought to see reason, so he should be left to stew in his own juice with existing sanctions taking their slow toll* (Sunday Times).
[< Old French *jus* < Latin *jūs, jūris* broth]

juiced (jüst), *adj.* **1** having juice. **2** *U.S. Slang.* drunk.

juice|head (jüs′hed′), *n. U.S. Slang.* a habitual drinker of alcoholic liquor; tippler.

juice|less (jüs′lis), *adj.* lacking juice; dry.

juice man, *U.S. Slang.* a person who lends money at exorbitant interest rates; a loan shark.

juic|er (jü′sər), *n.* **1** a kitchen appliance used to extract juice from fruits and vegetables. **2** *Slang.* an electrician in charge of the lighting of a studio or stage setting. **3** *U.S. Slang.* a heavy drinker of alcoholic liquor.

juic|y (jü′sē), *adj.,* **juic|i|er, juic|i|est. 1** full of juice; having much juice: *a juicy orange.* **2** *Informal, Figurative.* full of interest; lively; spicy: *His quotations are pert and juicy* (Atlantic). **3** *Slang.* (of art) having a rich color or texture. —**juic′i|ly,** *adv.* —**juic′i|ness,** *n.*

ju|jit|su (jü jit′sü), *n.* a Japanese way of wrestling, or of fighting without weapons, that uses the strength and weight of an opponent to his disadvantage; judo. Also, **jiujitsu, jiujutsu, jujutsu.** [< Japanese *jūjutsu* < *jū* gentleness, softness + *jutsu* art]

ju|ju (jü′jü), *n.* **1** an amulet; fetish. **2** among West African native tribes: **a** the magical power of such an object. **b** a ban or spell effected by it. **c** = jujuism. **3** a form of African music influenced by jazz and rock, played with a variety of percussion instruments: *Juju is only the newest—and most exotic—black rhythm to captivate white listeners* (Newsweek).
[< Hausa *dzudzu* fetish, evil spirit]

ju|jube (jü′jüb), *n.* **1** a lozenge or small tablet of gummy candy. **2** an edible, datelike fruit of an Old World shrub or tree of the buckthorn family, used to flavor this candy. **3** a jelly made from this fruit. **4** the shrub or tree which bears this fruit. [< Middle French *jujube,* or < Medieval Latin *jujuba,* ultimately < Latin *zīzyphum* < Greek *zīzyphon*]

ju|ju|ism (jü′jü iz əm), *n.* the system of beliefs connected with jujus.

ju|jut|su (jüjůt′sü), *n.* = jujitsu.

juke (jük), *n., v.,* **juked, juk|ing.** *U.S. Slang.* —*n.* **1** = jukebox. **2** jukebox music.
—*v.t., v.i. Sports.* to fake (a movement or play); fake out.
[back formation < *jukebox*]

juke|box (jük′boks′), *n., adj.* —*n.* an automatic phonograph that plays records for money deposited in the coin slot. The records to be played are selected by pushing a button.
—*adj.* of or like a jukebox: *the jukebox trade.*
[< Gullah *juke* disorderly + English *box*]

juke joint, *U.S. Slang.* **1** a tavern, roadhouse, or cheap cafe where music is furnished by a jukebox. **2** a roadhouse where liquor is sold.

Jukes (jüks), *n.pl.* the fictitious name of a New York family whose history showed a great amount of disease, poverty, and criminality, used in sociological studies.

Jul. or **Jul** (no period), July.

ju|lep (jü′ləp), *n.* **1** *U.S.* a drink made of whiskey or brandy, sugar, crushed ice, and fresh mint; mint julep. **2** (formerly) a sweet drink in which medicine was given. **3** a cold drink flavored with herbs. [< Old French *julep* < Arabic *julāb* rose water < Persion *gulāb* < *gul* rose + *āb* water]

Jul|ia (jül′yə), *n.* a butterfly of tropical America having relatively narrow, dark, reddish-brown wings with black borders.

Jul|ian (jül′yən), *adj.* of Julius Caesar. [< Latin *Jūliānus* < *Jūlius* Julius (Caesar)]

Julian calendar, a calendar in which the average length of a year was 365¼ days with a leap year of 366 days every fourth year. It was introduced by Julius Caesar in 46 B.C. and used in France until 1582, and in Great Britain and its colonies until 1752, when it was replaced by the Gregorian calendar. A year in the Julian calendar was about 11 minutes and 14 seconds longer than a solar year.

ju|li|enne (jü′lē en′), *adj., n.* —*adj.* cut in thin strips or small pieces: *julienne potatoes.*
—*n.* a clear soup containing vegetables cut into thin strips or small pieces.
[< French *julienne,* apparently < *Jules,* or *Julien,* a proper name]

Ju|li|et (jü′lē et, -ət), *n.* **1** the young heroine of Shakespeare's play *Romeo and Juliet.* **2** *U.S.* a code name for the letter *j,* used in transmitting radio messages.

Pronunciation Key: hat, āge, cãre, fär; let, ēqual, tėrm; it, īce; hot, ōpen, ôrder; oil, out; cup, pu̇t, rüle; child; long; thin; ᴛʜen; zh, measure; ə represents **a** in about, **e** in taken, **i** in pencil, **o** in lemon, **u** in circus.

***Juliet cap**, a small cap, often of mesh or lace, worn by women. It is especially used to support a wedding veil.

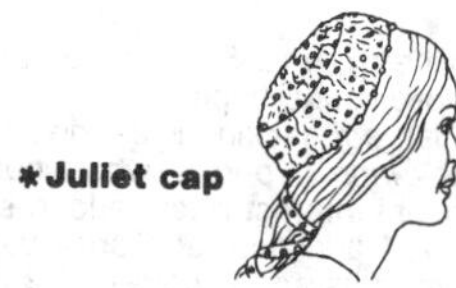
***Juliet cap**

Ju|ly (jů lī′), *n., pl.* -lies. the seventh month of the year. It has 31 days. [Middle English *Julie* < Anglo-French *Juil*, or *Julie* < Latin *Jūlius* Julius Caesar (because he was born in this month)]

Ju|ma|da I (jə mä′də), the fifth month of the Moslem year. It has 30 days. [< Arabic *Jumāda*]

Jumada II, the sixth month of the Moslem year. It has 29 days.

Ju|ma|la (yü′mä lä), *n. Finnish Mythology.* the highest god; god of the air and protector of flocks.

jum|ble[1] (jum′bəl), *v.*, **-bled, -bling,** *n.* **—*v.t.*** **1** to mix or confuse: *She jumbled up everything in her drawer while hunting for her white gloves.* **2** to confuse mentally: *To jumble the innocent and the guilty ... by a general indemnity* (Edmund Burke). **3** to shake up; jolt: *The coach jumbled us insensibly into some sort of familiarity* (Sir Richard Steele).
—*v.i.* **1** to move in a confused manner; flounder; stumble: *They will all meet and jumble together* (Jonathan Swift). **2** to move or travel with jolting: *Trotting Neely ... jumbled off with her cart* (Scott).
—*n.* **1** a muddle; mixed-up mess; state of confusion: *My desk was in such a jumble I couldn't find anything.* **SYN**: medley, hodgepodge. **2** a jolt or jolting.
[perhaps imitative] **—jum′ble|ment,** *n.* **—jum′-bler,** *n.*

jum|ble[2] (jum′bəl), *n.* a cooky with a hole in the middle. [probably variant of earlier *gimbal*, singular of *gimbals* (because it is ring-shaped)]

jumble sale, *British.* a rummage sale.

jum|bo (jum′bō), *adj., n., pl.* **-bos.** *Informal.* **—*adj.*** very big: *a jumbo ice-cream cone.* **—*n.*** **1** a big, clumsy person, animal, or thing; something unusually large of its kind. **2** = jumbo jet. [American English < *Jumbo*, the famous large elephant exhibited by P. T. Barnum, perhaps originally < West African (compare Gullah *jamba* elephant)]

jumbo jet, a large jetliner, capable of carrying over 300 passengers.

jum|buck (jum′buk′), *n. Australian.* a sheep. [< a native name]

jump (jump), *v., n., adv.* **—*v.i.*** **1** to spring from the ground; leap; bound: *to jump up and down. How high can you jump? How far can you jump? Our cat can jump to the table, off the table, and across the path.* **2** to give a sudden start or jerk: *We often jump when a sudden sight, noise, or touch startles us. The film jumped in the projector and flickered on the screen.* **3** *Figurative.* to rise suddenly: *Prices jumped.* **4** to pass over and capture an opponent's piece in checkers. **5** *Figurative.* to come (to) too quickly; arrive (at) too soon; pass abruptly, as if by a leap: *to jump to conclusions.* **6** to make a bid higher than necessary to raise or overcall a previous bid in bridge. **7** to agree; coincide; tally: *For all men live and judge amiss, Whose talents jump not just with his* (Samuel Butler).
—*v.t.* **1a** to leap over: *to jump a stream. The speeding car jumped the curve and crashed.* **b** to go around; by-pass, as an electric circuit: *to jump the ignition of an automobile.* **2** to cause to jump: *to jump a horse over a fence, to jump a child up and down.* **3** to pounce upon; attack: *The old proprietor ... was green, and let the boys ... jump him* (Bret Harte). **4** *Slang.* to evade by running away: *to jump bail, to jump a hotel bill.* **5** *Especially U.S. Slang.* to get on or off (a train or other moving vehicle) by jumping. **6** to skip or pass over. *They jumped the Greek and Latin, and read law, medicine, or sermons, without it* (Emerson). **7** to pass over and capture (an opponent's piece in checkers). **8** to raise (a partner's bid in bridge) by more than one trick. **9** to leave (rails or tracks): *Three cars of the morning express jumped the tracks.* **10** *Obsolete.* to risk; hazard: *Here, upon this bank and shoal of time, We'd jump the life to come* (Shakespeare).
—*n.* **1** a spring from the ground; leap; bound: *The horse made a fine jump.* **2a** a sudden jerk: *a jump in the motion picture film.* **b** the part of a thing that has been passed over, jerked through, or omitted: *The jump in the phonograph record starts after the scratch.* **3** a thing to be jumped over: *The horse cleared all the jumps of the steeplechase.* **4** the distance jumped: *a ten-foot jump.* **5** a contest in jumping for height or distance: *the high jump, the broad jump.* **6** a sudden nervous start or jerk: *He gave a jump at the noise of the gun.* **7** *Figurative.* a sudden rise: *a jump in the cost of living.* **8** a move in the game of checkers made to capture an opponent's piece. **9** *Figurative.* a sudden and abrupt transition from one thing to another: *Their nimble nonsense ... gains remote conclusions at a jump* (William Cowper). **10** an instruction or signal in a computer program which alters the sequence of instructions in the computer. **11** *Slang.* **a** a dance or social event. **b** swing music. **12** *Obsolete.* a venture; risk.
—*adv.* *Obsolete.* exactly; precisely.
get (or **have) the jump on,** *Slang.* to get or have an advantage over: *The alert student can often divine the shape of things to come, thereby getting the jump on his corporate peers* (Harper's). *In the matter of age the town has a jump on most others* (Maclean's).
jump a claim. See under **claim.**
jump at, to accept eagerly and quickly; *to jump at a chance, jump at an offer. He was staggered that the Labour Party leaders had not jumped at it* (London Times).
jump down one's throat. See under **throat.**
jump off, a to start out: *Allied infanty, jumping off at dawn, moved onto "The Yoke," the enemy perimeter at the northern edge of the ridge* (New York Times). **b** *U.S.* to leave: *It was resolved ... to bid a final adieu to the frontier, or in the phraseology of the region, to "jump off"* (Francis Parkman).
jump on, *Slang.* to blame; scold; criticize: *Stop jumping on me every time I make a mistake.*
jumps, Informal, a nervous condition characterized by sudden starts or jerks.
jump the gun. See under **gun.**
jump the track. See under **track.**
on the jump, *Informal.* **a** rushing around; always busy: *Keeping the foe on the jump* (London Daily News). **b** at great speed: *Jake went out the door on the jump* (Mulford and Clay). **c** in a nervous state: *That elderly gentleman was exceedingly "on the jump," as nervous as a man well could be* (F. M. Hueffer).
the jumps, *Informal.* **a** chorea: *The dog was afflicted with the jumps.* **b** delirium tremens: *Alcoholics may get fits of the jumps.*
[probably imitative]
—*Syn.* *v.i.* 1, ***v.t.* 1a Jump, leap** means to spring into or though the air. **Jump** emphasizes the sudden and springing movement of the feet: *He jumped from the roof. He jumped across the puddle.* **Leap** emphasizes springing high into or through the air, or to a point, and suggests more grace, lightness, or liveliness: *I love to watch a ballet dancer leap. The deer leaped lightly to the opposite bank of the stream.*

jump ball, *Basketball.* the toss of the ball between two opposing players by the referee to begin or resume play.

jump bid, a bid higher than necessary to overcall or raise a previous bid in contract bridge.

jump boot, **1** a boot designed for use by parachutists. **2** any similar boot.

jump cables, electric cables used to link a live battery of the same voltage to a dead battery in an automobile or truck to start an internal-combustion engine.

jump cut, an abrupt transition from one motion-picture shot or scene to another.

jump-cut (jump′kut′), *v.i.*, **-cut, -cut|ting.** to intercut motion-picture shots or takes rapidly or abruptly.

jumped-up (jumpt′up′), *adj.* that has risen from a lowly station or position: *a jumped-up bureaucrat.*

jump|er[1] (jum′pər), *n.* **1** a person or thing that jumps. **2** a tool or device that works with a jumping motion, such as a drill to bore holes in rock. **3** *Electricity.* a wire used to cut out an instrument or part of a circuit or to close temporarily a break in a circuit. **4** a kind of sled used for coasting. **5** *U.S.* a small metal chair of tubular construction on which a child may move with a springing motion while sitting down. **6** a Welsh Methodist who jumped in worship. [< *jump*, verb + *-er*[1]]

jump|er[2] (jum′pər), *n,* **1** a sleeveless dress in one piece, worn over a blouse. **2** a loose jacket. Jumpers are worn by workmen to protect their clothes and by sailors as part of a uniform. *Clad in a loose duck jumper and trousers streaked and splashed with red soil* (Bret Harte). **3** a loose blouse reaching to the hips.
jumpers, rompers.
[earlier *jump* short coat, perhaps alteration of Old French *juppe* skirt. Compare etym. under **jupon.**]

jumper cables, = jump cables.

jump|ing bean (jum′ping), the seed of a plant of the spurge family, grown in Central and South America, containing a moth larva whose movements cause the seed to jump; Mexican jumping bean; bronco bean; leaper.

jumping cholla, = cholla.

jumping deer, = mule deer.

jumping gene, *Informal.* = transposon: *Transposons ... are also called jumping genes because they can change their position from one place to another on the chromosomes* (Daniel L. Hartl).

jumping hare, a jerboalike South African rodent, having long, strong hind legs with which it can take long leaps.

jumping jack, **1** a toy man or animal that can be made to jump by pulling a string. **2** *Slang.* a yes man; a fawning hanger-on who curries favor by springing forward eagerly to do his master's bidding (used in an unfriendly way).

jumping mouse, any one of a family of mice with long hind legs and very long tail, which they use for jumping. Jumping mice hibernate in the winter and include a yellow-brown mouse of the wet meadows and grasslands in the northeastern United States and Canada.

jump|ing-off place (jum′ping ôf′, -of′), **1** an out-of-the-way place. **2** a point of departure.

jumping-off point, = jumping-off place.

jumping pit, a pit filled with sawdust, sand, or rubber chips in which a high-jumper or pole-vaulter lands.

jumping rope, = skipping rope.

jumping seed, = jumping bean.

jumping spider, any one of a family of colorful spiders with large eyes and stout front legs, common in the tropics. They have very keen vision and stalk their prey, usually during the day, instead of building a web.

jump-jet (jump′jet′), *n. British.* a jet aircraft designed for vertical take-offs and landings.

jump|mas|ter (jump′mas′tər, -mäs′-), *n. U.S.* an officer who controls the dropping of parachute troops and their equipment from an aircraft.

jump-off (jump′ôf′, -of′), *adj., n.* **—*adj.*** of or for starting or taking off. **—*n.*** **1** a beginning; sudden move; start. **2** a play-off.

jump pass, *Football, Basketball.* a pass made by a player while jumping.

jump-pass (jump′pas′, -päs′), *v.i.*, **-passed, -pass|ing.** to make a jump pass.

jump rope, = skipping rope.

jumps (jumps), *n.pl.* See under **jump.**

jump seat, **1** a collapsible seat hinged to the floor of an automobile directly behind the front seat and in front of the back seat. **2** any similar seat hinged to the floor or wall, especially in an airplane, elevator, or the like.

jump shift, a bid in a new suit exactly one trick higher than needed to overcall partner's last bid in contract bridge.

jump-shoot (jump′shüt′), *v.i.*, **-shot, -shoot|ing** to hunt duck by wading or drfiting downstream in a boat and shooting when the birds flush.

jump shot, *Basketball.* a shot made while jumping, especially at the highest point of the jump.

jump spark, a spark formed when electricity jumps across a permanent gap in a circuit.

jump-start (jump′stärt′), *v., n.* **—*v.t.*** **1a** to start an internal-combustion engine in a car, truck, etc., by connecting cables from an auxiliary storage battery to supplement or replace lost power in the ignition system. **b** to start an internal-combustion engine in a car, truck, etc., by forcing it to turn over while the vehicle is being pushed. **2** *Figurative.* to start some enterprise or process by additional effort or means: *New advertising sections were necessary to jump-start the magazine* (New York Times). **—*n.*** **1** the starting of an internal-combustion engine by auxiliary electric power or by pushing the vehicle the engine is in. **2** *Figurative.* the act or fact of starting some enterprise or process by additional effort or means: *The Los Angeles Times credits a radio talk show with giving a jump-start to baseball salary negotiations in San Diego* (Richard Moony).

***jump suit**
definition 1

***jump suit** or **jump|suit** (jump′süt′), *n.* **1** a one-piece suit used by parachutists. **2** a one-piece garment resembling a parachutist's uniform, used especially for causal wear: *The fashions include jumpsuits for both men and women* (New York Times). *She would own jump suits for everything from skiing to curling up on the fireside rug* (New York Times).

jump-up (jump′up′), *n.* (in the British West Indies and Guyana) an informal dance.
jump-up-and-kiss-me (jump′up ən kis′mē), *n.* = pansy (def. 1).
jump|y (jum′pē), *adj.*, **jump|i|er, jump|i|est.** **1** moving by jumps; making sudden, sharp jerks: *a jumpy puppy.* **2** easily excited or frightened; nervous: *The jumpy little old lady started at every noise.* —**jump′i|ly,** *adv.* —**jump′i|ness,** *n.*
jun (jun), *n., pl.* **jun.** a unit of money in North Korea, equal to 1/100 of a won. [< Korean]
Jun (no period), June.
Jun., **1** June. **2** junior.
▶See **Jnr.** for usage note.
Junc. or **junc.,** junction.
jun|ca|ceous (jung kā′shəs), *adj.* belonging to the family of plants typified by the rush. [< New Latin *Juncaceae* the family name (< Latin *juncus* rush) + English *-ous*]
jun|co (jung′kō), *n., pl.* **-cos.** any one of several small North American finches such as the slate-colored junco or snowbird. One kind is often seen in flocks during the winter. Juncos are related to the sparrows. [< Spanish *junco* a reed, rush < Latin *juncus*]
junc|tion (jungk′shən), *n.* **1** the act or process of joining: *The junction of two rivers resulted in a large flow of water downstream.* **2** the state of being joined. **3** a place of joining or meeting. A junction is a place or point where railroad lines or highways meet or cross. *Motorcyclists: Wear a crash helmet and take particular care at junctions* (News Chronicle). **4** *Electronics.* **a** an area of transition between semiconductors with different electrical properties, such as a p-n junction. **b** a point of contact between two different metals, as in a rectifier. [< Latin *junctiō, -ōnis* < *jungere* join]
junc|tion|al (jungk′shə nəl), *adj.* having to do with or like a junction.
junc|tur|al (jungk′chər əl), *adj.* of or having to do with phonetic juncture: *Languages differ widely in their junctural habits as they do in other ways* (Simeon Potter).
junc|ture (jungk′chər), *n.* **1** a point or line where two things join; joint. **2** a point of time. **3** a state of affairs: *the present political juncture.* **4** a critical state of affairs; crisis. **5a** the act or process of joining. **b** the state of being joined. **6** *Phonetics.* **a** the way in which sounds and sound sequences are joined: *There is a difference in juncture in English between "night rate* (nīt′rāt′)*" and "nitrate* (nī′trāt).*"* **b** any one of the various distinctive types of transition used in a particular language.
at this juncture, when affairs are in this state; at this moment: *The boys were squaring off for a fight, but at this juncture the coach stepped in and cooled everything down.*
[< Latin *junctūra* a joining < *jungere;* see etym. under **join.** See etym. of doublet **jointure.**]
June (jün), *n.* the sixth month of the year. It has 30 days. [ultimately < Latin *Jūnius*]
June beetle, = June bug.
June|ber|ry (jün′ber′ē), *n., pl.* **-ries. 1** the fruit of the shadbush. **2** the tree.
June bug, 1 a large, brown, clumsy beetle of North America that appears in June in the northern parts and in May in the southern; May beetle. June bugs belong to the same group as the chafers. See picture under **beetle**[1]. **2** a large green beetle of the southern United States, very destructive to fruit; fig-eater.
June grass, *U.S.* Kentucky bluegrass.
Jung|i|an (yu̇ng′gē ən), *adj., n.* —*adj.* of or having to do with Carl Gustav Jung (1875-1961) or his teachings.
—*n.* a person who believes in Jung's teachings or follows his technique of psychoanalysis: *Jungians believe that certain kinds of myths are repeated over and over again in all eras and societies, thus furnishing clues to the universal unconscious* (Time).
Jung|i|an|ism (yu̇ng′gē ə niz′əm), *n.* Jungian theories or doctrines.
jun|gle (jung′gəl), *n., adj.* —*n.* **1** wild land thickly overgrown with bushes, vines, and trees. Jungles are hot and humid regions with many kinds of plants and wild animals. *Set off against its cities . . . is the world's largest jungle, the Amazon* (Newsweek). **2** *Figurative.* a tangled mass: *What a world-wide jungle of redtape* (Thomas Carlyle). **3** *Figurative.* a place or situation in which it is difficult to survive because of intense competition, violence, or opposition: *the jungle of a city slum. . . . and with her six brothers and sisters, grew up in the jungle of Manhattan's Lower East Side* (Time). **4** *U.S. Slang.* a camp for tramps.
—*adj.* of or like the jungle; savage; untamed: *jungle calls, jungle towns;* (*Figurative.*) *the jungle life of a city slum.*
[< Hindustani *jangal* < Sanskrit *jangala* desert; thicket, forest] —**jun′gle|like′,** *adj.*
jungle boot, a sturdy, waterproof boot, suitable for use in hot, humid, and overgrown lands: *Jungle boots had to be issued to some of the G.I.'s before they went out on patrol* (New York Times).
jungle cock, the male of the jungle fowl.
jun|gled (jung′gəld), *adj.* covered with jungles.
jungle fever, a severe type of malaria, occurring especially in the East Indies.
jungle fowl, any one of several wild birds of southern Asia and the East Indies that are much like domestic fowl and from which the present-day domestic chicken is probably descended.
***jungle gym,** a framework of steel bars to climb or swing on as a pastime: *Plans for the commons include a basketball court, a slide, a jungle gym* (New York Times). [< *Junglegym,* a trademark]

***jungle gym**

jungle hen, the female of the jungle fowl.
jungle rice, = barnyard grass.
jungle rot, any fungous skin disease aggravated by tropical heat and humidity.
jun|gly (jung′glē), *adj.* of or like a jungle.
jun|ior (jün′yər), *adj., n.* —*adj.* **1** the younger (used of a son having the same name as his father): *John Parker, Junior, is the son of John Parker, Senior, Abbr.* Jr. **2** of or for younger people: *a junior choir, a junior tennis match. The Red Cross offers a junior course in first aid.* **3** of lower position; of less standing than some others; of more recent appointment: *a junior officer, a junior partner.* **4** of or having to do with a third-year student or class in high school or college: *the junior class. Are you going to the Junior Prom?* **5** of or for girls or women with slight figures: *Junior sizes have shorter waists and are a little smaller around.* **6** of later date: *The Cretan civilization was apparently junior to that of the Nile Valley.* **7** *Law.* (of a mortgage, creditor, or the like) more recent in time and therefore second in priority to another.
—*n.* **1** a younger person: *He is his brother's junior by two years.* **2** a person of lower position, rank, or standing; person of more recent appointment. **3** a student in the third year of high school or a four-year college. **4a** the junior size of clothing; junior miss. **b** a girl or woman who wears or can wear junior sizes.
[< Latin *jūnior* (for *juvenior*), comparative of *juvenis* young]
jun|ior|ate (jün′yə rāt), *n.* in the Roman Catholic Church: **1** a preliminary course for Jesuits leading to the deeper study of metaphysics and other philosophical studies. **2** a school for such studies.
junior college, a school giving only the first two years of a regular four-year-college course, or special programs for professional or technical preparation.
junior high school, a school of grades 7, 8, and sometimes 9, attended after an elementary school of six grades. It is followed by high school.
jun|ior|i|ty (jün yôr′ə tē, -yor′-; *especially British* jü′nē ôr′ə tē), *n.* the state or fact of being a junior in age, rank, or standing.
Junior League, any one of the local organizations of the Association of the Junior Leagues of America, Inc., whose members engage in volunteer social work.
Junior Leaguer, a person who is a member of a Junior League.
junior miss, *U.S.* **1** a teen-age girl. **2** the junior size of clothing.
junior school, a school in Great Britain for pupils from 7 to 11 years of age.
jun|ior-sen|ior high school (jün′yər sēn′yər), a school combining junior and senior high school with grades 7 through 12; secondary school.
junior varsity, a high-school or college athletic team that competes on the level next below the varsity.
ju|ni|per (jü′nə pər), *n.* **1** any one of a group of evergreen shrubs or trees with small, brown or bluish, berrylike cones. The cones of one kind of juniper contain an oil used in flavoring gin, in medicine as a diuretic and stimulant, and in fumigating. Junipers belong to the cypress family. **2** *U.S.* any one of various shrubs or trees that resemble the juniper, such as the larch. **3** a tree mentioned in the Bible, having white flowers and rushlike branches; retem. I Kings 19:4. [< Latin *jūniperus.* Compare etym. under **geneva.**]
junk[1] (jungk), *n., v.* —*n.* **1** old metal, paper, rags, or other unwanted articles: *After we cleaned out the collection of junk, the garage looked fairly orderly.* **2** *Informal.* rubbish; trash: *There was a lot of junk stuck to the bottom of the trash barrel.* **3** hard, salted meat eaten by sailors. **4** old rope used especially for making mats, oakum, and gaskets: *The owners of a vessel buy up incredible quantities of "old junk," which the sailors unlay* (Richard Henry Dana). **5** a piece of anything; chunk. **6** *Slang.* a narcotic, such as heroin; dope: *I'd been in contact briefly with some of the scummier elements, including those involved with pot and junk* (New Yorker).
—*v.t.* **1** *Informal.* to throw away or discard as junk: *The whole plan ought to be junked* (Scientific American). **2** to divide into chunks.
[Middle English *jonk* old cable or cordage, perhaps < Portuguese *junco* cordage, rush[2] < Latin *juncus* a rush]
***junk**[2] (jungk), *n.* a Chinese or Japanese sailing ship. Junks have a flat bottom, high stern, low bow, and lug or lateen sails of bamboo matting. Now, a junk often has auxiliary power. [< Portuguese *junco* < Javanese *jong*]

***junk**[2]

junk art, = junk sculpture.
junk artist, = junk sculptor.
junk bond, *U.S.* a high-risk, noncorporate or low-grade corporate bond that is bought at less than face value.
junk dealer, = junkman.
Jun|ker or **jun|ker**[1] (yu̇ng′kər), *n., adj.* —*n.* **1** a member of the former aristocratic, privileged class in Prussia: *The "revolutionary" unification of the Reich was achieved by the reactionary Junker of Prussia* (Harper's). **2** an aristocrat who seeks to retain his social and political privileges.
—*adj.* of or having to do with Junkers.
[< German *Junker* < Middle High German *junchērre* young lord. See related etym. at **younker.**]
junk|er[2] (jung′kər), *n. U.S. Slang.* an old, broken-down automobile or other vehicle or machine. [< *junk*[1] + *-er*[1]]
Jun|ker|dom or **jun|ker|dom** (yu̇ng′kər dəm), *n.* **1** the spirit or policy of the Junkers. **2** the condition or character of a Junker.
Jun|ker|ism or **jun|ker|ism** (yu̇ng′kə riz əm), *n.* the spirit or policy of the Junkers.
jun|ket (jung′kit), *n., v.* —*n.* **1** a pleasure trip, especially one taken by an official at the expense of the government; trip or tour: *The best description of a lecturing junket ever written . . .* (Atlantic). *A junket to Russia comes later* (Wall Street Journal). **2** curdled milk, sweetened and flavored, eaten as a dessert. **3** a feast or picnic. **4** a cream cheese, originally made in a rush basket. **5** *Obsolete.* any dainty candy, cake, or confection; delicacy.
—*v.i.* **1** to go on a pleasure trip, especially at the expense of the government: *He told the House it was senseless to be "sending a lot of Congressmen junketing over in Paris in July"* (New York Times). **2** to hold a feast; join in a picnic.
[earlier, a rush basket, in which creamed curds were prepared and served, probably < Old North French *jonquette* junket, rush basket < Old French *jonc* reed < Latin *juncus*] —**jun′ket|er,** *n.*
junk|et|eer (jung′kə tir′), *n., v.* —*n.* a person who goes on a junket; traveler. —*v.i.* to go on a junket.
junk food, ready-made or quickly prepared food, as that available in vending machines and fast-food establishments.
junk|heap (jungk′hēp′), *n.* **1** = junkyard. **2** *Slang.* a broken-down old automobile.
junk|ie (jung′kē), *n.* **1** *Slang.* **a** a person who uses narcotics; drug addict: *The junkie seeks euphoria. The average citizen seeks happiness* (Harper's). **b** a person who is addicted to anything; devotee or enthusiast; freak: *an art junkie, a sports junkie. He's an egotist and a publicity junkie* (Tom Wolfe). **2** = junkman. Also, **junky.**
junk mail, *U.S.* mail that is third-class bulk advertising matter addressed to no particular person but carrying a specific street address.

Pronunciation Key: **h**a**t**, **ā**ge, **c**ã**re**, **f**ä**r**; **l**e**t**, **ē**qual, **t**ė**rm**; **i**t, **ī**ce; **h**o**t**, **ō**pen, **ô**rder; **oi**l, **ou**t; **c**u**p**, **p**u̇**t**, **r**ü**le**; **ch**ild; lo**ng**; **th**in; **ᴛʜ**en; **zh**, measure;
ə represents **a** in about, **e** in taken, **i** in pencil, **o** in lemon, **u** in circus.

junk|man (jungk′man′), *n., pl.* **-men.** a man who buys and sells old metal, paper, rags, and other unwanted articles or refuse.
junk|pile (jungk′pīl′), *n.* = junkheap.
junk sculptor, an artist who makes junk sculptures; junk artist.
junk sculpture, **1** three-dimensional figures constructed from scrap metal and other discarded material. **2** the art of making such figures; junk art.
junk shop, a shop in which miscellaneous second-hand or discarded articles are sold.
junk|y (jung′kē), *adj.,* **junk|i|er, junk|i|est,** *n., pl.* **junk|ies.** **—*adj.*** of poor quality; like junk.
—*n.* = junkie.
junk|yard (jungk′yärd′), *n.* the place where a junkman stores his items and carries on his business.
Ju|no (jü′nō), *n., pl.* **-nos. 1** *Roman Mythology.* the wife of Jupiter and queen of the gods. She was the goddess of women and marriage. Juno was identified with the Greek goddess Hera. **2** a stately, majestic woman: *Yon Juno of majestic size* (Alexander Pope). **3** an award presented annually in Canada for outstanding achievements in music: *The Junos he has accumulated tell part of the story—three in country categories, two for folk-singer and one for composer of the year* (Maclean's).
Ju|no|esque or **ju|no|esque** (jü′nō esk′), *adj.* like Juno; stately and majestic: *A junoesque dowager in black satin was seating guests like an imperious dinner hostess* (Atlantic).
jun|ta (jun′tə, hůn′tə), *n.* **1a** a political or military group holding power after a revolution: *So far, the junta, with its army and police, has managed to subdue such outbreaks without serious casualties, but this is an impatient country* (Manchester Guardian Weekly). **b** a political faction; group of plotters or partisans. **2** an assembly or council for deliberation or administration, especially in Spain and Latin America. **3** = junto (def. 1). [< Spanish *junta* < Latin *jungere* to join. Compare etym. under **join.**]
jun|to (jun′tō), *n., pl.* **-tos. 1** a group of persons joined for a common purpose; clique; coterie: *At the corners are assembled juntos of village idlers and wise men* (Washington Irving). **2** = junta (def. 1). [alteration of *junta*]
jupe (jüp), *n. Scottish.* **1** a woman's jacket or bodice. **2** a woman's skirt: *a Norman nurse, with a high cap and a red jupe* (Charles Lever). **3** *Obsolete.* a man's jacket or tunic.
jupes, a bodice or stays.
[< Old French *juppe.* See etym. of doublets **jubbah, jupon.**]
***Ju|pi|ter** (jü′pə tər), *n.* **1** *Roman Mythology.* the ruler of the gods and men, identified with the Greek god Zeus; Jove. **2** the largest planet in the solar system. It is the fifth in distance from the sun. See diagram under **solar system.** [< Latin *Jūpiter,* originally vocative of *Diēspiter* (< *diēs* heaven, day) < unrecorded Old Latin *Jou pater* father Jove!]

***Jupiter** definition 2 ♃ symbol

ju|pon (jü′pon, jü pon′), *n.* **1** a plain fabric originally made of silk and wool, now often of wool and cotton or some synthetic fiber, used in making dresses. **2** a close-fitting tunic worn under armor. **3** a sleeveless surcoat worn over armor. **4** a heavy jacket worn under a hauberk. Also, **gipon.** [< Old French *jupon* < *juppe* < Old Provençal *jupa* < Italian *giubba* < Arabic *jubba.* See etym. of doublets **jubbah, jupe.**]
ju|ra (jůr′ə), *n., pl. of* **jus²**. *Latin.* rights; laws.
Ju|ra (jůr′ə), *n. Geology.* Jurassic.
ju|ral (jůr′əl), *adj.* **1** of law; legal. **2** of or having to do with rights and obligations. [< Latin *jūs, jūris* law + English *-al*¹]
ju|ra|men|ta|do (hü′rä men tä′THō), *n., pl.* **-dos** (-THōs). *Spanish.* a Moro or Moslem Malay in the Philippines who has sworn he will die while killing enemies, especially Christians.
Ju|ras|sic (jů ras′ik), *n., adj.* **—*n.*** **1** the middle geological period of the Mesozoic era, after the Triassic and before the Cretaceous, when dinosaurs dominated the earth and birds first appeared. **2** the rocks formed in this period.
—*adj.* of or having to do with this period or its rocks.
[< French *jurassique* < the *Jura* Mountains, patterned on *triassique* Triassic]
ju|rat (jůr′at), *n.* **1** *Law.* a memorandum on an affidavit, noting when, where, and before whom it was sworn. **2** an English official, such as an alderman. **3** *Obsolete.* a person who has taken an oath or who performs some duty on oath; juror. [< Middle French *jurat* < Old Provençal < Medieval Latin *juratus* < Latin *jūrāre* to swear]
ju|ra|to|ry (jůr′ə tôr′ē, -tōr′-), *adj.* of, having to do with, or comprising an oath.
Jur.D., Doctor of Law (Latin, *Juris Doctor*).
ju|re di|vi|no (jůr′ē di vī′nō), *Latin.* by divine right.
ju|re hu|ma|no (jůr′ē hyü mā′nō), *Latin.* by human right.
ju|rel (hü rel′), *n.* any one of various carangoid foods fishes of warm waters, as a kind inhabiting the Atlantic near the West Indies. [< Spanish *jurel,* ultimately (diminutive) < Latin *saurus* < Greek *saûros,* or *saúrā* lizard; the horse mackerel]
ju|rid|ic (jů rid′ik), *adj.* = juridical.
ju|rid|i|cal (jů rid′ə kəl), *adj.* **1** having to do with the administration of justice. **2** of law; having to do with jurisprudence; legal: *juridical powers.* [< Latin *jūridicālis* < *jūridicus,* ultimately < *jūs, jūris* law + *dīcere* say] **—ju|rid′i|cal|ly,** *adv.*
juridical days, days on which the courts are open for the trial of cases
ju|ri|met|ri|cian (jůr′i mə trish′ən), *n.* = jurimetricist.
ju|ri|met|ri|cist (jůr′i met′rə sist), *n.* a person who studies or practices jurimetrics.
ju|ri|met|rics (jůr′i met′riks), *n.* a branch of law using scientific tools and research, such as statistical measurements, to deal with legal matters. [< *juri*(dical) + *metrics;* patterned on *econometrics*]
ju|ris|con|sult (jůr′is kən sult′, -kon′sult), *n.* = jurist. [< Latin *jūriscōnsultus* < *jūs, jūris* law + *cōnsultus* lawyer < *cōnsulere* to consider, consult]
ju|ris|dic|tion (jůr′is dik′shən), *n.* **1** the right or power to give out justice; the giving out of justice: *To live exempt From heaven's high jurisdiction* (Milton). **2** authority; power; control: *The principal has jurisdiction over the teachers in a school.* **3** the things over which authority extends; extent of authority: *A school is the principal's jurisdiction. The judge ruled that the case was not within his jurisdiction.* **4** the territory over which authority extends. **5** either council of the Scottish Rite Masons in the United States; the southern or the northern jurisdiction. [< Latin *jūrisdictiō, -ōnis* < *jūs, jūris* law + *dictiō, -ōnis* a speaking < *dīcere* say]
ju|ris|dic|tion|al (jůr′is dik′shə nəl), *adj.* of or having to do with jurisdiction. **—ju′ris|dic′tion|al|ly,** *adv.*
jurisdictional strike, a strike to determine which of two or more unions shall have jurisdiction over certain work or workers in an area, plant, industry, or profession.
jurisp., jurisprudence.
ju|ris|pru|dence (jůr′is prü′dəns), *n.* **1** the science or philosophy of law. **2** a system of laws. **3** a branch of law. Medical jurisprudence deals with the use of medical knowledge in certain questions of law. **4** knowledge of law. [< Latin *jūrisprūdentia* < *jūs, jūris* law + *prūdentia* knowledge, prudence]
ju|ris|pru|dent (jůr′is prü′dənt), *adj., n.* **—*adj.*** having expert knowledge of the principles of law.
—*n.* an expert in jurisprudence; jurist.
ju|ris|pru|den|tial (jůr′is prü den′shəl), *adj.* having to do with jurisprudence.
ju|rist (jůr′ist), *n.* **1** an expert in law. **2** a learned writer on law. **3** a student or graduate in law. [< Middle French *juriste,* learned borrowing from Medieval Latin *jurista* < Latin *jūs, jūris* law]
ju|ris|tic (jů ris′tik), *adj.* of or having to do with jurists or jurisprudence; relating to law. **—ju|ris′ti|cal|ly,** *adv.*
juristic act, an act intended to have a legal effect, especially on a right.
ju|ris|ti|cal (jů ris′tə kəl), *adj.* = juristic.
ju|ror (jůr′ər), *n.* **1** a member of a jury: *The jurors left the courtroom at the end of the trial to decide the case.* **2** a member of the panel from which the jury is selected. **3** a person who has taken an oath or who has sworn allegiance. [< Anglo-French *jurour,* Old French *jureor* < Latin *jūrātor* a swearer < *jūrāre* to swear < *jūs, jūris* law]
ju|ry¹ (jůr′ē), *n., pl.* **-ries,** *v.,* **-ried, -ry|ing. —*n.*** **1** a group of persons sworn to give a true answer to the question put before it in a court of law, that is, "Is the defendant guilty or not?" or "Is a party at fault or not?" See also **grand jury** and **petit jury. 2** any group of persons chosen to give a judgment or to decide who is the winner in a contest: *The jury of teachers gave her poem the first prize.*
—*v.t.* to select; judge: *About half of the work is by nonmembers, juried by artists from more than 700 submissions* (New York Times).
[< Anglo-French *jurie,* Old French *juree* oath < *jurer* to swear < Latin *jūrāre* < *jūs, jūris* law]
ju|ry² (jůr′ē), *adj. Nautical.* for temporary use on a ship; makeshift. [probably ultimately < Old French *ajurie* help, relief < Latin *adjūtāre* aid. Compare etym. under **adjutant.**]
jury box, the place where the jury sits at a trial.
jury duty, service as a juror.
ju|ry|man (jůr′ē mən), *n., pl.* **-men.** a member of a jury; juror.
jury mast, a temporary mast replacing one that has been broken or carried away.
ju|ry-rig (jůr′ē rig′), *n.* a temporary rig on a ship. [< *jury*² + *rig,* noun]
ju|ry-rigged (jůr′ē rigd′), *adj.* fitted with a temporary rig. [< *jury*² + *rigged*]
jury room, **1** the room where a jury sits while deciding a case before it. **2** the room where prospective jurors wait to be called for serving on a jury.
ju|ry|wom|an (jůr′ē wům′ən), *n., pl.* **-wom|en.** a woman member of a jury.
jus¹ (zhʏ), *n. French.* juice; gravy.
jus² (jus), *n., pl.* **ju|ra.** *Latin.* **1** law; a body of laws; justice. **2** any right or rule as set forth by judicial decision; a law.
jus., justice.
jus ca|no|ni|cum (jus kə non′ə kəm), *Latin.* canon law.
jus ci|vi|le (jus si vī′lē), *Latin.* civil law; Roman law.
jus di|vi|num (jus di vī′nəm), *Latin.* divine law; divine right.
jus gen|ti|um (jus jen′shē əm), *Latin.* the law of nations; international law.
jus na|tu|ra|le (jus nach′ə rā′lē), *Latin.* natural law.
jus post|li|mi|ni|i (jus pōst′li min′ē ī), *Latin.* the law of postliminy.
jus san|gui|nis (jus sang′wə nəs), *Latin.* the right of blood; right of a person to have the nationality of one of his parents, usually the father.
jus|sive (jus′iv), *n., adj. Grammer.* **—*adj.*** expressing a command: *the jussive mood.*
—*n.* a form expressing command. [< Latin *jussus,* past participle of *jubēre* to command + English *-ive*]
jus so|li (jus sō′lī), *Latin.* the right of the soil; right of a person to be a national of the country in which he was born.
just¹ (just), *adv., adj.* **—*adv.*** **1** no more than; only; merely: *We are just an ordinary family, neither rich nor poor. I just have the knack of foreseeing things* (Lord Dunsany). **2** barely: *I just caught the train. The shot just missed the mark.* **3** *Informal.* quite; truly; positively: *The weather is just glorious. I just couldn't refuse.* **4** exactly: *That is just a pound. That is just right. Just as the twig is bent, the tree's inclined* (Alexander Pope). **5** almost exactly: *I saw him just then.* **6** closely; nearly: *See the picture just above.* **7** a very little while ago: *He just left me.*
—*adj.* **1** right; fair: *a just price, a just principal. O just but severe law!* (Shakespeare). **SYN:** impartial, equitable. See syn. under **fair. 2** deserved; merited: *a just reward.* **SYN:** due, rightful, legitimate. **3** having good grounds; well-founded: *just anger, a just opinion.* **4** true; correct; exact: *a just description, just weights, a just scale. Force not my drift beyond its just intent* (William Cowper). **SYN:** precise. **5** in accordance with standards or requirements; proper: *just proportions.* **SYN:** fitting. **6** righteous: *a just life, a just person.* **SYN:** upright, honest. **7** lawful: *a just claim. Our just inheritance* (Milton).
just now, a only a very short time ago: *I saw him just now. My barber told me just now that there is a fellow come to town . . .* (John Ford). **b** exactly at this moment; at present: *The Prince of Devils is just now mustering up all his Legions against me* (John Scott).
[< Middle French *juste,* learned borrowing from Latin *jūstus* upright < *jūs, jūris* right, law] **—just′ness,** *n.*
▶In formal English the limiting word *just* is placed immediately before the word, phrase, or clause it modifies to prevent ambiguity: *The teacher assigned just one chapter for tomorrow.*
just² (just), *n., v.i.* = joust. **—just′er,** *n.*
just., justice.
just-au-corps (zhʏs tō kôr′), *n. French.* a close-fitting, outer garment, especially one reaching to the knees, worn by men in the 1600's and 1700's.
juste mi|lieu (zhʏst mē lyœ′), *French.* the golden mean; the happy medium.
jus|tice (jus′tis), *n.* **1** just conduct; fair dealing: *Judges should have a sense of justice. Justice is the principle and the process by which each man is assured the things that belong to him* (Russell Kirk). **2** the condition of being just; fairness; rightness; correctness: *the justice of a claim, to uphold the justice of our cause.* **3** a well-founded reason; rightfulness; lawfulness: *They complained with justice of the bad treatment they had received.* **4** just treatment; deserved reward or punishment: *Justice consists in giving every man what he deserves. Revenge is a kind of wild jus-*

tice (Francis Bacon). **5** the administration of law; trial and judgment by process of law: *a court of justice.* **6** the exercise of power and authority to maintain what is just and right. **7** = judge. The Supreme Court of the United States consists of nine justices. **8** = justice of the peace.
bring to justice, to punish legally for a crime: *The burglar was brought to justice.*
do justice to, a to treat fairly: *These one-acters, imported from London, are full of bright, quirky lines and notions, but the production doesn't do the plays justice* (New Yorker). **b** to see the good points of; show proper appreciation for: *The crowd's applause did justice to the acrobat's performance. . . . nor dare he do less than justice to the feast prepared for him* (Peter Fleming).
do oneself justice, to do as well as one really can do: *He did not do himself justice on the test. He was too diffident to do justice to himself* (Jane Austen).
[< Old French *justice,* learned borrowing from Latin *jūstitia* < *jūstus* upright, just]

justice of the peace, a local magistrate who tries minor cases, administers oaths, performs civil marriages, and administers other justice; justice. *Abbr:* J.P.

jus|tic|er (jus'tə sər), *n. Archaic.* a judge; magistrate.

jus|tice|ship (jus'tis ship), *n.* the position, duties, or term of office of a justice.

jus|ti|ci|a|bil|i|ty (jus tish'ē ə bil'ə tē), *n.* the quality or fact of being justiciable: *A public demand for justiciability had been created, and the Government wished to amend the constitution accordingly* (London Times).

jus|ti|ci|a|ble (jus tish'ē ə bəl), *adj.* subject to jurisdiction or trial in a court of law: *That offense is not justiciable in a federal court.*

jus|ti|cial (jus tish'əl), *adj.* of or having to do with justice.

Jus|ti|cial|ism (jus tish'ə liz əm), *n.* the governmental program of Juan Perón, former president of Argentina, especially during the period 1946-1955: *Justicialism* [*was*] *Perón's label for his "third position" between capitalism and communism: a kind of welfare state backed by police power which, in Perón's reckoning, adds up to "social justice"* (Time). **—Jus|ti'cial|ist**, *n., adj.*

jus|ti|ci|ar (jus tish'ē ər), *n. British.* **1** a judge in a superior court. **2** the highest judicial and political official under the Norman and Plantagenet kings from William I to Henry III. [< Medieval Latin *justiciarius;* see etym. under **justiciary**]

jus|ti|ci|ar|y (jus tish'ē er'ē), *adj., n., pl.* **-ar|ies**.
—*adj.* of or having to do with the administration of justice.
—*n.* **1** an administrator of justice. **2** = justiciar.
[< Medieval Latin *justiciarius* a judge < Latin *jūstitia;* see etym. under **justice**]

jus|ti|fi|a|bil|i|ty (jus'tə fī'ə bil'ə tē), *n.* the state or quality of being justifiable.

jus|ti|fi|a|ble (jus'tə fī'ə bəl), *adj.* capable of being justified; proper; defensible: *justifiable homicide. An act is justifiable if it can be shown to be just or right.* **—jus'ti|fi'a|ble|ness**, *n.* **—jus'ti|fi'a|bly**, *adv.*

jus|ti|fi|ca|tion (jus'tə fə kā'shən), *n.* **1a** the act or process of justifying: *Their justification of the lie was that they would hurt the innocent.* **b** the state of being justified: *His justification came when he was proved right.* **2** a fact or circumstance that justifies; good reason or excuse: *What is your justification for being so late?* **3** *Theology.* a freeing or being freed from the guilt or penalty of sin.
4 the spacing out or adjusting of type, so that the width of a column or page is filled and the left and right margins are even.

justification by faith, freedom from the penalty of sin through faith in Christ.

jus|ti|fi|ca|tive (jus'tə fə kā'tiv), *adj.* justificatory; affording justification.

jus|ti|fi|ca|to|ry (jus'tə fə kā'tər ē), *adj.* serving to justify; justifying.

jus|ti|fi|er (jus'tə fī'er), *n.* a person or thing that justifies.

jus|ti|fy (jus'tə fī), *v.,* **-fied, -fy|ing.** **—*v.t.*** **1** to give a good reason for: *The fine quality of the cloth justifies its high cost.* **2** to show to be just or right: *Can you justify your act?* SYN: uphold, defend. **3** to clear of blame or guilt; vindicate: *The court ruled that he was justified in hitting the man in self-defense. Woe unto them . . . Which justify the wicked for reward* (Isaiah 5:22-23). SYN: exonerate. **4** *Printing.* to make (lines of type) the right length by proper spacing. **5** *Law.* **a** to show a satisfactory reason or excuse for (something done). **b** to show (oneself) to be acceptable as bail or surety. **c** to prove the truth of (a statement alleged to be defamatory).
—*v.i.* **1** *Printing.* (of lines of type) to fit exactly; be of the required measure. **2** *Law.* **a** to show a satisfactory reason or excuse for something done. **b** to be acceptable as bail or surety.
[< Old French *justifier* < Latin *jūstificāre* < Latin *jūstus* just, right + *facere* do, make]

Jus|tin|i|an Code (jus tin'ē ən), a body of Roman law compiled and annotated at the command of the Emperor Justinian, who reigned from A.D. 527 to 565. It forms the body of civil law and is one of the most important of all monuments of jurisprudence. Also, **Code of Justinian.**

jus|ti|ti|a om|ni|bus (jus tish'ē ə om'nə bəs), *Latin.* justice for all (the motto of the District of Columbia).

jus|tle (jus'əl), *v.t., v.i.,* **-tled, -tling,** *n.* = jostle.

just|ly (just'lē), *adv.* **1** in a just manner; fairly: *to deal justly with others.* **2** with good reason; rightly; properly: *You argue justly.*

jut (jut), *v.,* **jut|ted, jut|ting,** *n.* **—*v.i., v.t.*** to stick out; project; stand out: *The pier jutted out from the shore into the water. The stubborn boy jutted his chin forward in defiance.*
—*n.* a part that sticks out or projects; projection: *Tubal clambered by jut and scar And there he builded a town* (Rudyard Kipling).
[variant of *jet*[1]]

jute (jüt), *n.* **1** a strong, glossy fiber used for making coarse fabrics or rope. Jute is obtained from the bark of certain tropical plants: *Jute from the farms goes into Calcutta factories to make canvas, rope, and rough bags* (Junior Scholastic). **2** any one of these plants. Jute belongs to the basswood family. [< Bengali *jhōto* < Sanskrit *jūta* mat of hair]

Jute (jüt), *n.* a member of a Germanic tribe from Denmark and northern Germany. Some of the Jutes, with the Angles and Saxons, invaded and settled in England in the A.D. 400's and 500's.

Jut|ish (jü'tish), *adj.* of or having to do with the Jutes.

jut|ty (jut'ē), *n., pl.* **-ties,** *v.,* **-tied, -ty|ing.** *Obsolete.* **—*n.*** **1** a projecting part of a wall or building. **2** a jetty, pier, or embankment: *a curious harbor, formed by three stone jutties* (Tobias Smollett).
—*v.i.* to project; jut.
—*v.t.* to project beyond.
[variant of *jetty*[1]]

Ju|tur|na (jü tėr'nə), *n. Roman Mythology.* a nymph of springs and wells, beloved by Jupiter.

juv., juvenile (a book for children).

Ju|ve|na|li|an (jü'və nā'lē ən), *adj.* of, like, or having to do with the Roman poet and satirist Juvenal (A.D. 60?-130?) or his writings.

ju|ve|nes|cence (jü'və nes'əns), *n.* a renewal of youth; youthfulness.

ju|ve|nes|cent (jü'və nes'ənt), *adj.* growing young again; youthful. [< Latin *juvenēscēns, -entis,* present participle of *juvenēscere* < *juvenis* young (person)]

ju|ve|nile (jü'və nəl, -nīl), *adj., n.* **—*adj.*** **1** young; youthful: *He was a blessing to all the juvenile part of the neighborhood* (Jane Austen). SYN: immature, undeveloped. See syn. under **young**. **2** of or for boys and girls: *juvenile books. The picture, done in CinemaScope, is obviously aimed at a juvenile audience* (New Yorker). **3** having never existed on the surface of the earth or in the atmosphere; coming fresh from the earth's interior: *juvenile nitrogen, juvenile water.*
—*n.* **1** a young person; youth: *Tom Sawyer the Pirate looked around upon the envying juveniles about him* (Mark Twain). *Most states in the United States consider anyone under 18 years of age a juvenile. A few states and most of the provinces of Canada consider anyone under 16 a juvenile* (Stanton Wheeler). **2** a book for boys and girls: *There are many juveniles on the shelves of the children's library.* **3** an actor or actress who plays youthful parts. **4** a young bird that is able to fly but has not completely lost its down.
[< Latin *juvenīlis* < *juvenis* young (person)] **—ju've|nile|ly**, *adv.* **—ju've|nile|ness**, *n.*

juvenile court, a law court where cases involving boys and girls are heard.

juvenile delinquency, **1** action or behavior considered a legal offense and committed by a boy or girl under 18 (in some states 16) years of age. **2** the violation of a law by a juvenile.

juvenile delinquent, a boy or girl under 18 (in some states 16) years of age who has committed a legal offense: *Studies show that about one-half of the juvenile delinquents come from homes broken by death, divorce, separation* (Emory S. Bogardus).

juvenile hormone, **1** a hormone, secreted by the corpus allatum (a gland behind the brain of insects), that controls the metamorphosis from the larval to the adult stage: *Juvenile hormones play a regulatory role in the molting process of insects* (Ajay K. Bose). **2** a synthesized form of this hormone, used to prevent development or maturation of insect pests: *Juvenile hormone is a possible DDT substitute in killing insects* (Science Journal).

juvenile officer, a police officer assigned to cases involving juvenile delinquents.

ju|ve|nile-on|set diabetes (jü'və nəl on'set'; -nīl; ôn'-), =insulin-dependent diabetes mellitus.

ju|ve|nil|i|a (jü'və nil'ē ə), *n.pl.* youthful or immature writings or works of art. [< Latin *juvenīlia,* neuter plural of Latin *juvenīlis;* see etym. under **juvenile**]

ju|ve|nil|i|ty (jü'və nil'ə tē), *n., pl.* **-ties**. **1** juvenile quality, condition, or manner: *Cleopatra . . . in her juvenility was always playfully disposed* (Dickens). **2** juveniles; youth.
juvenilities, youthful qualities or actions: *Juvenilities unbecoming the character of old age* (translation of Morvan de Bellegarde).

ju|ve|noc|ra|cy (jü'və nok'rə sē), *n., pl.* **-cies**. **1** government by young people. **2** a country or state having such a government. [< *juven*(ile) + *-ocracy,* as in *democracy*]

ju|vie or **ju|vey** (jü'vē), *n. U.S. Slang.* **1** a juvenile delinquent. **2** a detention home for juvenile delinquents.

jux|ta|pose (juk'stə pōz'), *v.t.,* **-posed, -pos|ing.** to put close together; place side by side.
[< French *juxtaposer* < Latin *juxtā* beside, near + French *poser* to place, pose[1]]

jux|ta|po|si|tion (juk'stə pə zish'ən), *n.* **1** the action of putting close together; a placing side by side: *The juxtaposition of red curtains against yellow walls was startling.* **2** a position close together or side by side: *The twins stood in juxtaposition for their picture.* [< Latin *juxtā* near, beside]

j.v., junior varsity.

JWB (no periods), Jewish Welfare Board (the national association of Jewish Community Centers in the United States, founded in 1917).

J.W.V., Jewish War Veterans.

Jy. or **Jy** (no period), July.

***K^{1}** or **k** (kā), *n., pl.* **K's** or **Ks, k's** or **ks**. **1** the 11th letter of the English alphabet. There are two *k*'s in *kick.* **2** any sound represented by this letter. **3** (used as a symbol for) the 11th or (if *J* is omitted) the 10th (of an actual or possible series): *row K in a theater.*
K^{2} (kā), *n., pl.* **K's**. anything shaped like the letter K.
K^{3} (kā), *n.* **1** *Informal.* thousand; 1000. **2** a unit of memory capacity in a computer equal to a binary thousand or 1024 (2^{10}) bits. [< *K*(ilo-), prefix for 1000]
k (no period), kilo-; 1000.
k., an abbreviation or symbol for:
1 capacity (of an electric circuit or device).
2 *Mathematics.* constant.
3 karat (carat).
4 kilo or kilos.
5 kilogram or kilograms.
6 *Chess.* king or kings.
7 knight.
8 knot.
9 kobo.
10 kopeck or kopecks.
11 krona or kronor or kronur.
12 krone or kronen or kroner.
K (no period), an abbreviation or symbol for:
1 Kaiser.
2 Kelvin (always with a figure, indicating a temperature on the Kelvin scale).
3 *Chess.* king or kings.
4 K-meson; K-particle.
5 kosher.
6 potassium (chemical element).
K., an abbreviation for the following:
1 Kaiser.
2 Kelvin (always with a figure, indicating a temperature on the Kelvin scale).
3 king or kings.
4 knight.
5 Köchel (referring to classification of Mozart's works): *K.82.*
6 makuta: *1 zaire = 100 K.*
ka or **Ka** (kä), *n.* the second self; the soul. The ancient Egyptians believed that a man's ka would inhabit a statue made to look like him, should his body be destroyed. [< Egyptian *k'*]
ka., kathode (cathode).
Kaa|ba (kä'bə), *n.* the most sacred shrine of the Moslems. The Kaaba is a small structure, containing a sacred black stone, in the courtyard of the Great Mosque at Mecca. It is the point toward which Moslems face when praying and the goal of the hajj or pilgrimage. Also, **Caaba**. [< Arabic *ka'ba* (literally) a square house < *ka'b* cube]
kab (kab), *n.* cab, a Hebrew unit of dry measure, about 2 quarts. [< Hebrew *qab*]
Ka|ba|ka or **ka|ba|ka** (kä bä'kä), *n.* the constitutional monarch of the former Ugandan kingdom of Buganda.
kab|a|la (kab'ə lə, kə bä'-), *n.* = cabala.
Ka|bar|di|an (kə bär'dē ən), *n.* the language of a Circassian people who live in northern Caucasia and practice the Moslem religion.
kab|ba|la (kab'ə lə, kə bä'-), *n.* = cabala.
kab|ba|list (kab'ə list), *n.* = cabalist^{1}.
kab|ba|lis|tic (kab'ə lis'tik), *adj.* = cabalistic.
ka|bel|jou (kä'bəl you), *n.* a large, edible, bass-like sciaenoid sea fish found in Mediterranean, African, and Australian waters: *I lost a very large kabeljou while using steel wire for a bait* (Cape Argus). [< Afrikaans *kabeljou* < Dutch *kabeljauw*]
ka|bob (kə bob'), *n.* (in India) roast meat in general. Also, **cabob, kebab.**
kabobs, an Oriental dish of meat cut in small pieces, seasoned with various spices, and roasted on a skewer: *lamb kabobs with rice.* [< Hindustani *kabāb* < Arabic]

***K^{1}**
definition 1

ka|boo|dle (kə bü'dəl), *n.* = caboodle.
Ka|bu|ki or **ka|bu|ki** (kä bü'kē), *n.* a form of Japanese drama with song and dance, a flamboyant style of acting, and rich décor and costuming. It dates from the 1600's. [< Japanese *kabuki* < *ka* song + *bu* dance + *ki* art]
Ka|byle (kə bīl'), *n.* **1** a Berber of Algeria or Tunisia. **2** the Hamitic dialect of these people. [< Arabic *qabā'il,* plural of *qabīla* tribe]
Ka|chin (kə chin'), *n., pl.* **-chin** or **-chins**. **1** a member of a large tribal group living in the mountains of northern Burma. **2** the Tibeto-Burman language of this group.
***ka|chi|na** (kä chē'nə, kə-), *n.* **1** a supernatural rain spirit among the Hopi Indians, representing deceased members of the clan. **2** a masked dancer who personifies a rain spirit in a ritual of the Hopi Indians. **3** a doll, usually carved from a root of a cottonwood tree, decorated to represent the masked dancers impersonating rain spirits and often sold as a souvenir. **4** the ritual or ceremony in which this doll is used. Also, **katchina, katcina.** [American English, perhaps < Zuñi, or Hopi *Katzina*]

***kachina**
definition 3

kad|dish (kä'dish), *n., pl.* **kad|di|shim** (kä dish'-im, kä'di shim'). **1** Also, **Kaddish**. a Hebrew prayer, recited in the synagogue as part of daily service and by a person mourning for a deceased parent, brother, sister, or other close relative: *When the time arrived for him to say his annual kaddish, or memorial prayer, for his dead parents, he came to the Ramaz's synagogue to do it* (New Yorker). **2** *Yiddish.* a son (who will recite the kaddish prayer on the death of his parents). [< Aramaic *qaddīsh* holy]
ka|di (kä'dē, kā'-), *n., pl.* **-dis**. = cadi.
Ka|di|ak bear (kä'dē ak, kad'ē-), = Kodiak bear.
kaf|fee|klatsch or **Kaf|fee|klatsch** (kä'fä-kläch'; kôf'ē kluch', kof'-), *n., pl.* **-klatsch|es, -klät|sche** (-klech'ə). an informal gathering or party at which coffee and pastry are served. [< German *Kaffeeklatsch* < *Kaffee* coffee + *Klatsch* gossip, scandal]
Kaf|fir (kaf'ər), *n., adj.* **—*n.*** **1** a member of the Bantu tribes, especially those of southern Africa. **2** their language. **3** a black person of southern Africa (used in an unfriendly way).
—*adj.* of or having to do with the Kaffirs.
Kaffirs, South African gold-mine shares traded on the London stock exchange: *They dealt in Kaffirs and other mining stocks.*
[< Arabic *kāfir* unbeliever]
kaf|fir (kaf'ər), *n.* = kaffir corn.
Kaffir beer, an alcoholic beverage brewed from corn by Kaffirs in South Africa.
Kaf|fir|boe|tie or **kaf|fir|boe|tie** (kaf'ər bü'tē), *n.* = Kafirboetie.
kaf|fir-boom (kaf'ər büm'), *n.* a South African tree of the pea family: *The kaffir-booms, with their magnificent scarlet flowers, look gorgeous when growing, as they habitually do, among the boulders* (Alice B. Balfour). [< Afrikaans *kaffirboom* < *kaffir* kaffir + *boom* tree < Dutch]
Kaffir cat, a wild cat of Africa, with a light brown or yellowish coat, probably an ancestor of the common domestic cat, but larger and more powerful.
kaffir corn, a grain sorghum with a stout, short-jointed, leafy stalk, grown for grain and forage in dry regions of Africa and elsewhere.
kaffir honeysuckle, a South African climbing shrub of the bignonia family. Kaffir honeysuckle is grown for its showy, yellow or red, trumpet-shaped flowers.
Kaf|firs (kaf'ərz), *n.pl.* See under **Kaffir**.
***kaf|fi|yeh** (kə fē'yə), *n.* the headdress of the desert Arab, consisting of a large folded cloth, often tasseled and with colorful stripes or decoration, bound to the head with a cord. Also, **kafiya, kufiyah.** [< Arabic *kaffīyah,* perhaps < Late Latin *cofia*]

***kaffiyeh**

Kaf|ir^{1} (kaf'ər), *n.* **1** a member of a people of Indo-European speech living in northeastern Afghanistan. **2** = Kaffir (defs. 1 and 2). [< Arabic *kāfir* unbeliever]
Kaf|ir^{2} (kaf'ər), *adj.* of or having to do with South African gold-mine shares. [< *Kaffir*]
Kafir beer, = Kaffir beer.
Kaf|ir|boe|tie (kaf'ər bü'tē), *n.* (in South Africa) a European who objects to the persecution of the Kaffirs by the whites. [< Afrikaans *kafirboetie* < *kafir* Kaffir + *boetie,* diminutive, little brother]
kafir corn, = kaffir corn.
Kaf|irs (kaf'ərz), *n.pl.* See under **Kaffir**.
ka|fi|ya (kə fē'yə), *n.* = kaffiyeh.
Kaf|ka|esque (käf'kä esk'), *adj.* having to do with, characteristic of, or like the Czechoslovak novelist Franz Kafka (1883-1924) or his writings.
kaf|tan (kaf'tən, käf tän'), *n.* = caftan.
ka|go (kä'gō), *n.* a Japanese covered couch made of basketwork and slung on a pole to carry on the shoulders of bearers. [< Japanese *kago*]
ka|gu (kä'gü), *n.* a large, gray bird with a red bill and full, pendent crest, found in New Caledonia. It cannot fly and is probably related to the sun bittern and rails. [< a native Polynesian name]
ka|gu|ra (kä'gü rä), *n.* an ancient, slow, and solemn dance of the Shinto religion of Japan. [< Japanese *kagura*]
kah|lu|a (kä lü'ä), *n.* a sweet Mexican liqueur distilled from coffee. [< Mexican Spanish < Nahuatl]
kahn (kän, kan), *n.* = khan^{1} (def. 2).
ka|hu|na (kä hü'nä), *n. Hawaiian.* **1** a priest or shaman. **2** an expert; master.
kai|ak (kī'ak), *n.* = kayak.
kai|bab squirrel (kī'bab), a color phase of the tassel-eared squirrel, found in a small area north of the Grand Canyon. It is usually black underneath with a solid white tail. [American English < *Kaibab* Forest, an area in Arizona; (originally) an Indian tribe]
ka|id (kä ēd'), *n.* a North African rural chieftain. [< Arabic *qā'id.* Compare etym. under **alcaide**.]
kaif (kīf), *n.* (among the Arabs) easeful or dreamy quiescence as a form of enjoyment. [< Arabic *kayf*]
kail (kāl), *n.* = kale.
kail|yard (kāl'yärd'), *n.* = kaleyard.
kain (kīn), *n.* a kind of colorful skirt worn by Indonesian men and women, similar to a sarong. [< Malay *kain*]
Kain (kān), *n.* = Cain.
ka|i|nite (kä'ə nīt, kī'nīt), *n.* a mineral substance, a combination of sulfates of potassium and magnesium with chloride of magnesium, used as fertilizer. *Formula:* $MgSO_4 \cdot KCl \cdot 3H_2O$ [< German *Kainit* < Greek *kainós* new + German *-it* - ite^{1}]
Kai|ser (kī'zər), *n.* **1** the title of the rulers of Germany, 1871-1918, and of Austria, 1806-1918. **2** the title of the emperors of the Holy Roman Empire, 962-1806. [(def. 1) < German *Kaiser;* (def. 2) Middle English *keiser,* partly < Middle High German, partly Old English *cāsere;* all Germanic forms ultimately < Latin *Caesar*]
kai|ser (kī'zər), *n.* **1** = Kaiser. **2** = emperor: *the old kaisers of Rome* (Scott). [< German *Kaiser*]
kai|ser|in (kī'zə rin), *n.* the wife of a kaiser; an empress. [< German *Kaiserin*]
Kai|ser|ism (kī'zə riz əm), *n.* = Caesarism.
kai|ser|ship (kī'zər ship), *n.* the office of kaiser or emperor.
ka|je|put (kaj'ə pət), *n.* = cajuput.
ka|ka (kä'kə), *n.* an olive-brown parrot of New Zealand, about the size of a crow, marked with red or yellow on various parts of the body and wings. [< Maori *kākā* a parrot]
ka|ka|po (kä'kə pō), *n., pl.* **-pos**. a large nocturnal parrot of New Zealand that seldom uses its wings. [< Maori *kākāpō* < *kākā* parrot + *pō* night]
ka|ke|mo|no (kä'kə mō'nō), *n., pl.* **-nos**. a Japanese picture or writing on silk, paper, or other

Script letters look like examples of fine penmanship. They appear in many formal uses, such as invitations to social functions.

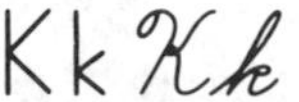
Handwritten letters, both manuscript or printed (left) and cursive (right), are easy for children to read and to write.

Kk *Kk*
Roman letters have *serifs* (finishing strokes) adapted from the way Roman stone-cutters carved their letters. This is *Times Roman* type.

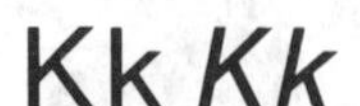
Sans-serif letters are often called *gothic.* They have lines of even width and no serifs. This type face is called *Helvetica.*

Kk *Kk*
Between roman and gothic, some letters have thick and thin lines with slight flares that suggest serifs. This type face is *Optima.*

Computer letters can be sensed by machines either from their shapes or from the magnetic ink with which they are printed.

material that is mounted on a roller and hung vertically. [< Japanese *kakemono* < *kake* hang + *mono* thing]

ka|ki (kä′kē), *n., pl.* **-kis.** = Japanese persimmon. [< Japanese *kaki*]

Ka|ki|e|mon (kä′kē ā′mon) , *n.* a fine grade of Japanese porcelain. [< *Kakiemon,* a Japanese potter of the 1600's]

kak|is|toc|ra|cy (kak′ə stok′rə sē), *n., pl.* **-cies.** government by the worst citizens; a form of government in which the worst persons rule: *His rule was a perfect kakistocracy* (Time). [< Greek *kákistos* worst + *krátos* rule; patterned on English *aristocracy*]

kak|o|to|pi|a (kak′ə tō′pē ə), *n.* a misplanned, ugly, and unhappy place to live in (the opposite of a *utopia*): *A monstrous habitat, in short, in which only monsters could be at home ... it has been a recurrent theme of later technological kakotopia* (Lewis Mumford). Also, **cacotopia.** [< Greek bad + English *utopia*]

kak|o|to|pi|an (kak′ə tō′pē ən), *adj.* of or having to do with a kakotopia.

kal., kalends (calends).

ka|la-a|zar (kä′lä ä zär′), *n.* a tropical disease that causes an enlargement of the spleen and liver, anemia, and a general wasting away. It is a form of leishmaniasis, caused by a parasitic protozoan transmitted to the blood and tissues of the host, usually by the sand fly. [< Hindi *kālā* black + *āzār* disease]

kal|an|cho|e (kal′an kō′ē), *n.* any one of a genus of tropical, chiefly African plants of the same family as the stonecrop, with thick, fleshy leaves and stems and bright yellow, purple, or scarlet blossoms. [< New Latin *Kalanchoe* the genus name, apparently < the Chinese name]

***kale** (kāl), *n.* **1** a plant related to the cabbage, a species of cole, having loose, curled leaves instead of a compact head. Kale looks somewhat like spinach. **2** its leaves, which are eaten as a vegetable. **3** *Scottish.* **a** cabbage or any one of its varieties, such as broccoli or Brussels sprouts. **b** any kind of greens. **c** a broth in which kale or cabbage is the main ingredient. **d** a broth or soup made with various kinds of vegetables. **e** dinner: *I will be back here to my kale against one o'clock* (Scott). **4** *U.S. Slang.* money; cash. Also, **kail.** [Middle English variant of *cole*]

***kale**
definition 1

ka|lei|do|scope (kə lī′də skōp), *n.* **1** a tube containing bits of colored glass and two mirrors. As it is turned, it reflects continually changing patterns. **2** *Figurative.* a continually changing pattern, as of bright colors or colored objects: *This rainbow look'd like hope—Quite a celestial kaleidoscope (Byron).* **3** *Figurative.* anything that changes continually. [< Greek *kalós* beautiful and *eîdos* shape + English *-scope*]

ka|lei|do|scop|ic (kə lī′də skop′ik), *adj.* of or like a kaleidoscope; continually changing: (*Figurative. Maule's well ... was throwing up a succession of kaleidoscopic pictures* (Hawthorne). **—ka|lei′do-scop′i|cal|ly,** *adv.*

kal|en|dar (kal′ən dər), *n., v.t.* = calendar.

kal|ends (kal′əndz), *n.pl.* = calends.

kale|yard (kāl′yärd′), *n. Scottish.* a cabbage plot or kitchen garden, such as is commonly attached to a small cottage. Also, **kailyard.**

kal|i (kal′ē, kā′lē), *n.* = saltwort. [< Arabic *qalī.* Compare etym. under **alkali.**]

Ka|li (kä′lē), *n.* a Hindu goddess who is the wife of Siva, worshiped for the many powers, both good and evil, attributed to her. [< Sanskrit *Kālī*]

kal|ian (käl yän′), *n.* a type of hookah used in Persia. [< Persian *kaliyān* < Arabic *qalyān*]

ka|lif (kā′lif, kal′if), *n.* = caliph.

ka|lif|ate (kā′lə fāt, kal′ə-), *n.* = caliphate.

ka|lim|ba (kə lim′bə), *n.* a Bantu musical instrument, consisting of a small, hollow piece of wood with metal strips that vibrate when played with the thumbs while holding the instrument in both hands with the palms upward. [< a Bantu word; related to *marimba*]

ka|li|um (kā′lē əm), *n.* = potassium. [< New Latin *Kalium* < Arabic *qalī* kali]

kal|li|din (kal′ə din), *n.* either one of two types of polypeptides released by blood plasma globulin, one of which is bradykinin. [irregular < Greek *kállos* beautiful + English *-in*]

Kal|li|kak (kal′ə kak), *n.* the fictitious name of an actual family that was the subject of a famous sociological study, having one branch that showed a high incidence of feeble-mindedness, poverty, disease, and crime, and another that was largely normal and often successful. [coined < Greek *kállos* beauty + *kákos* bad]

kal|li|kre|in (kal′ə krē′ən), *n.* an enzyme that breaks down proteins in blood plasma, pancreatic juice, and other body fluids, thereby releasing kallidins. [< Greek *kallikreas* pancreas (< *kállos* beauty + *kréas* flesh) + English *-in*]

Kal|li|ma (kal′ə mə), *n.* an Asian butterfly that resembles a dead leaf when it folds its wings; leaf butterfly. [< New Latin *Kallima* the genus name < Greek *kállos* beauty]

kal|mi|a (kal′mē ə), *n.* any one of a genus of North American, primarily evergreen shrubs of the heath family, having showy clusters of cup-shaped rose, purple, or white flowers, such as the mountain laurel or calico bush. [American English < New Latin *Kalmia* < Peter *Kalm,* 1715-1779, a Swedish botanist]

Kal|muck or **Kal|muk** (kal′muk), *n.* **1** a member of a group of Mongol tribes living in western China and the southeast Soviet Union. Many of the Kalmucks are Buddhists. *Newspaper stories often identify the Kalmuks as descendants of Genghis Khan's Golden Horde* (Harper's). **2** their Mongolian language. [< Russian *kalmyk* < a Tartar word]

Kal|myk (kal′mik), *n.* = Kalmuck.

ka|long (kä′long), *n.* any large fruit-eating bat of a group up to 20 inches long with a wingspread of five feet, whose flesh is used for food in Malaya; flying fox. [< Javanese *kalong*]

kal|pa (käl′pə), *n.* a cosmic period in Hinduism, consisting of one cycle of creation and destruction of the world. [< Sanskrit *kalpa*]

kal|pac (kal′pak), *n.* = calpac.

kal|pis (kal′pis), *n.* a vase or vessel for water, wine, or other liquid in ancient Greece, a form of the hydria in which the large handle at the back does not rise above the rim. [< Greek *kálpis*]

kal|so|mine (kal′sə mīn, -min), *n., v.t.,* **-mined, -min|ing.** calcimine.

ka|lu|a (kä lü′ä), *adj. Hawaiian.* cooked in an underground oven: *kalua pig.*

Ka|ma (kä′mə), *n.* **1** *Hindu Mythology.* the god of love. **2** (in Hindu literature) sensual desire. [< Sanskrit *kāma* god of love]

ka|ma|ai|na (kä′mä ī′nä), *n. Hawaiian.* a native-born or old resident of Hawaii.

kam|a|cite (kam′ə sīt), *n.* a variety of meteoric iron usually containing nickel. [< German *Kamacit* < Greek *kámax* pole + German *-ite* - ite¹]

ka|ma|graph (kä′mə graf, -gräf). *n.* **1** a type of printing press used in kamagraphy to reproduce exactly an original painting specially made for it. **2** a reproduction of a painting made by a kamagraph: *Each kamagraph looks as though the artist painted it by hand* (Time).

ka|ma|gra|phy (kə mä′grə fē), *n.* a method of reproducing mechanically an original painting that duplicates the color and raised brushstroke of the original on canvas. [< French *kamagraphie,* probably < Sanskrit *kāma* pleasure]

Ka|ma|ku|ra (kä′mə kü′rə), *adj.* of or having to do with Japanese art and architecture from about 1170 until 1350, characterized by the introduction of Zen Buddhist styles. [< *Kamakura,* a town in southeastern Honshu]

ka|ma|la (kə mä′lə, kam′ə lə), *n.* **1** a fine orange powder consisting of the glandular hairs from the fruits of an Asian and Australian tree of the spurge family, used as a yellow dye and formerly used in medicine as a vermifuge. **2** the tree itself. Also, **kamila.** [< Sanskrit *kamala*]

Kam|ba (käm′bə), *n., pl.* **-ba** or **-bas.** **1** a member of a large tribe of central and eastern Kenya. **2** the Bantu language of the Kamba.

kame (kām), *n.* **1** a hill or ridge of glacial detritus; esker. See picture under **glacier.** **2** *Scottish.* comb. [special use of comb¹]

ka|meez (kə mēz′), *n.* a loose shirt of linen, cotton, or silk with tight sleeves, worn with loose trousers in Pakistan and Bangladesh. [< Urdu *kamis* < Arabic *qamīs* < Late Latin *camīsia* shirt]

Ka|me|ha|me|ha Day (kä mā′hä mā′hä), June 11, a holiday in Hawaii, the birthday of Kamehameha I, first king of the Hawaiian Islands.

Ka|me|rad (kä′mə rät′), *n., pl.* **-ra|den** (-rä′dən). comrade; friend (the word used by German soldiers in offering to surrender). [< German *Kamerad* (literally) comrade < French *camarade*]

ka|mi or **Ka|mi** (kä′mē), *n., pl.* **-mi.** (in Shintoism) a deity or deities: *Hence the connotation of the word Kami plainly differs greatly from the God-the-Creator concept of the English word "god" by which Kami is customarily translated* (Atlantic). [< Japanese *kami*]

ka|mi|ka|ze (kä′mē kä′zē), *n., adj.* **—*n.*** **1** a Japanese suicide pilot in World War II, trained to dive an airplane loaded with explosives into a selected target, usually a naval vessel. **2** the plane itself: *Kamikazes plunged out of the sky, their suicidal pilots aiming ... at the destroyers* (Time). **3** a person or thing that acts like a kamikaze: *to run for election as a political kamikaze.*

—*adj.* **1** of or being a kamikaze: *a kamikaze pilot.* **2** *Informal.* extremely reckless: *a kamikaze cabdriver, kamikaze radicals.*
[< Japanese *kamikaze* (originally) "divine wind," a name given to a typhoon which saved Japan from a Mongol invasion in the 1200's < *kami* god + *kaze* wind]

ka|mi|la (kə mē′lə), *n.* = kamala.

kam|pong (käm pong′, käm′pong), *n.* a Malay village, usually consisting of wooden huts on stilts. [< Malay *kampong, kampung* enclosure]

Kam|pu|che|an (kam′pu̇ chē′ən), *adj.* of or having to do with Kampuchea, the official name of Cambodia.

kam|seen (kam sēn′), *n.* = khamsin.

kam|sin (kam′sin, kam sēn′), *n.* = khamsin.

kan (kän, kan), *n.* = khan¹ (def. 2).

Kan., Kansas.

ka|na (kä′nə), *n., pl.* **-na** or **-nas.** a Japanese system of writing consisting of tables of syllables made up of 46 or (formerly) 48 modified Chinese characters. The two types of kana are the common rounded form called hiragana and the square-shaped katakana. [< Japanese *kana* < *ka* borrowed, provisional + *na* characters, syllabics]

Ka|nak|a (kə nak′ə, kan′ə kə), *n.* **1** a native of Hawaii. **2** a native of the South Sea Islands. **3** a plantation worker on many Pacific islands; coolie. [American English < Hawaiian *kanaka* man]

ka|na|ma|ji|ri (kä′nə mä′jə rē, kä′nə mä′-), *n.* the standard Japanese system of writing, which is a combination of kana and kanji. [< Japanese *kanamajiri* < *kanakana* + *majiri* mixture]

kan|a|my|cin (kan′ə mī′sin), *n.* an antibiotic effective against a broad range of bacteria. *Formula:* $C_{18}H_{36}N_4O_{11}$ [< New Latin *kanamyceticus* the species name of the Japanese mold]

Ka|na|rese (kan ə rēz′, -rēs′), *adj., n., pl.* **-rese.**
—*adj.* of or having to do with Kanara, a district of southern India, or its Dravidian inhabitants.
—*n.* **1** a Dravidian of Kanara. **2** the Dravidian language of the Kanarese, closely related to Telugu; Kannada. Also, **Canarese.**

Kan|dy|an (kan′dē ən), *n., pl.* **-an** or **-ans,** *adj.*
—*n.* **1** a member of a Singhalese people of the mountains of Sri Lanka. **2** a native of Kandy, a city in central Sri Lanka.
—*adj.* of or having to do with the Kandyans.

ka|ne (kä′ne), *n.* Hawaiian. a man.

kang (käng), *n.* a structure of brick or other material, with a place for a fire beneath, used in China to sleep on. [< Mandarin *k'ang*]

***kan|ga|roo¹** (kang′gə rü′), *n., pl.* **-roos** or (*collectively*) **-roo.** an animal of Australia, New Guinea, and nearby islands. Kangaroos are mammals with small forelegs and very strong hind legs which give them great leaping power and a heavy tail that gives both balance and support. The female kangaroo has a pouch in front in which she carries her young. The smaller kangaroos are often called wallabies. [probably < a native Australian name]—**kan′ga|roo′like′,** *adj.*

***kangaroo¹**
kangaroo
wallaby

kan|ga|roo² (kang′gə rü′), *adj.* of or having to do with a kangaroo court; unauthorized or irregular; mock: *kangaroo procedures, kangaroo justice.*

kangaroo apple, 1 a leafy shrub 4 to 8 feet high, native to New Zealand, southeastern Australia, and Tasmania, that belongs to the nightshade family. **2** its edible, yellowish egg-shaped berry.

Pronunciation Key: hat, āge, cãre, fär; let, ēqual, tėrm; it, īce; hot, ōpen, ôrder; oil, out; cup, pu̇t, rüle; child; long; thin; ᴛʜen; zh, measure; ə represents a in about, e in taken, i in pencil, o in lemon, u in circus.

kangaroo bear, = koala.

kangaroo court, **1** an unauthorized or unofficial court, usually self-appointed, such as a mock court by prisoners in a jail or a frontier court. **2** an official court that acts in complete disregard of legal rights or procedures: *. . . shot down over North Korea in 1952 and condemned to prison by a Red kangaroo court* (Newsweek).

kangaroo dog, a breed of dog similar to the greyhound, used in Australia for hunting the kangaroo.

kangaroo grass, a tall grass used as fodder, found in Australasia and Africa.

kangaroo mouse, any one of a group of small, jumping, mouselike rodents of the western deserts of the United States, similar to the kangaroo rat but smaller.

kan|ga|roo|paw (kang′gə rü′pô′), *n.* an Australian flower of the amaryllis family, having a bright-green, split perianth that resembles the foot of a kangaroo.

kangaroo rat, **1** any one of a genus of small jumping, burrowing rodents of arid and semiarid regions of North America. Kangaroo rats have cheek pouches and long hind legs and tails. See picture under **rat**. **2** any one of various similar, although not closely related, small rodents of the desert regions of Australia.

kangaroo trial, a trial by a kangaroo court.

kan|ji (kän′jē), *n., pl.* **-ji** or **-jis**. **1** the Japanese system of writing using modified Chinese characters. **2** any of these characters. [< Japanese]

Kan|na|da (kä′nə də, kan′ə-), *n.* a Dravidian language spoken in southern India; Kanarese.

Kans., Kansas.

Kan|sa (kan′sô), *n., pl.* **-sa** or **-sas**. a member of a tribe of Indians of the Siouan linguistic stock, that formerly lived in the vicinity of the Kansas and Missouri rivers.

Kan|sai (kän′sī), *n.* a Japanese dialect spoken in western Honshu, most of Shikoku, and central Kyushu.

Kan|san (kan′zən), *adj., n.* **—*adj.*** **1** of or having to do with the state of Kansas or its inhabitants. **2** of or having to do with the second period of glaciation in North America, beginning about 470,000 years ago, and lasting for 156,000 years. **—*n.*** a person born or living in Kansas.

kan|tar (kän tär′), *n.* a Moslem unit of weight corresponding to the hundred-weight but varying in different localities. Also, **cantar**. [< Arabic *qinṭār*, ultimately < Latin *centēnārium* of 100 < *centum* hundred]

Kant|i|an (kan′tē ən), *adj., n.* **—*adj.*** of or having to do with Immanuel Kant (1724-1804) or his system of philosophy. **—*n.*** a follower of Kant.

Kant|i|an|ism (kan′tē ə niz′əm), *n.* the philosophical doctrines of Immanuel Kant or those developed by his followers.

Kant|ism (kan′tiz əm), *n.* = Kantianism.

KANU (no periods) or **K.A.N.U.**, Kenya African National Union (the leading political party in Kenya).

kan|zu (kan′zü), *n., pl.* **-zu** or **zus**. a long robe, usually white, worn in East Africa chiefly by men. [< Swahili *kanzu*]

ka|o|li|ang (kä′ō lē ang′), *n.* one of a variety of grain sorghums, introduced into the United States from Asia. [< Mandarin *kao liang* (literally) tall millet]

ka|o|lin or **ka|o|line** (kā′ə lin), *n.* a fine white clay used in making porcelain; china clay; porcelain clay. Kaolin is produced by the decomposition of feldspar. It is used chiefly as a filler in paper and, when mixed with ground feldspar and quartz, is used in making ceramics. [< French *kaolin* < Mandarin *Kaoling* (literally) high hill; a mountain in northern China, where it was first obtained]

ka|o|lin|ite (kā′ə lə nīt), *n.* a crystalline, hydrous silicate of aluminum occurring in kaolin. *Formula:* $Al_2O_3{\cdot}2SiO_2{\cdot}2H_2O$

ka|on (kā′on), *n.* = K-meson.

ka|on|ic (kā on′ik), *adj.* containing or producing kaons; K-mesic.

ka|par|ran (kä′pä rän), *n.* (in South Africa) a wooden sandal consisting of a small piece of wood with two slips joined underneath, and a wooden knob on the upper side. Also, **kapparing**. [< Malay or Javanese *gamparan*]

Ka|pel|le (kä pel′ə), *n. German.* **1** a choir or orchestra such as was formerly maintained at German courts. **2** any musical group, such as an orchestra or band.

Ka|pell|meis|ter (kä pel′mīs′tər), *n., pl.* **-ter**. the director of an orchestra, choir, or combination of both. Also, **capellmeister**. [< German *Kapellmeister* < *Kapelle* orchestra + *Meister* master, director]

kaph (käf, kôf), *n.* the eleventh letter of the Hebrew alphabet. Also, **khaph**. [< Hebrew *kaph* (literally) palm (of the hand)]

kap|je (käp′yə), *n.* = kappie. [< Dutch *kapje*]

Kap|lan-type (kap′lən tīp′), *adj.* having blades like a propeller, so that the slant of the blades can be varied according to the load: *a Kaplan-type reaction turbine*. [< *Kaplan* water turbine, a commonly used turbine of this type]

Ka|po or **ka|po** (kä′pō), *n., pl.* **-pos**. a prisoner in a Nazi concentration camp who was put in charge of other prisoners: *The prisoners . . . depended entirely on the whim of the guards and Kapos* (Atlantic). [< German *Kapo* < *Ka*(merad) *Po*(lizei) Comrade Police]

ka|pok (kā′pok, kap′ək), *n.* the silky fibers around the seeds of a tropical tree, used for stuffing pillows, mattresses, and life preservers, and for insulation; silk cotton; ceiba: *Not only is the vegetable wool commonly known as kapok obtained from this tree, but its bark is used in twine manufacture and from its seeds come a light-weight silky wool fiber and a stearine-rich oil* (Science News Letter). [< Malay *kapok*]

kapok tree, the tropical tree from whose seeds kapok is taken; silk-cotton tree; ceiba. The kapok tree belongs to the bombax family.

Ka|po|si's sarcoma (kə pō′sēz, kä′pō shēz), a form of sarcoma characterized by multiple bluish red or brown nodules and plaques, formerly found only in elderly men of Mediterranean descent but now an often fatal disease commonly associated with AIDS. [< Moritz *Kaposi*, 1837-1902, a Hungarian dermatologist, who first described it]

***kap|pa** (kap′ə), *n.* the tenth letter of the Greek alphabet, corresponding to English *k* but often represented by *c* in spelling words of Greek origin. [< Greek *káppa*]

***kappa**	Κ capital letter	κ lower-case letter

kappa particle, a particle containing DNA found in certain strains of paramecia that secretes a toxic substance which kills individuals of sensitive strains.

kap|pa|ring (kä′pä ring), *n.* = kaparran.

kap|pie (kä′pē), *n.* a cloth bonnet worn for protection against the sun in South Africa. Also, **kapje**. [< Afrikaans *kappie* < Dutch *kapje* cap]

ka|pu (kä′pü), *n. Hawaiian.* taboo.

ka|put or **ka|putt** (kə püt′), *adj. Informal.* **1** finished; destroyed; done for: *politically kaput. Their romance is kaput.* **2** out of style; outmoded: *Are westerns now kaput?*

go kaput, to be unsuccessful; fail: *During the recession our business went kaput.*

[< German *kaputt* < French *capot* a winning of all the tricks in piquet by one player]

kar|a|bin|er (kar′ə bē′nər), *n.* (in mountain climbing) an oval-shaped snap link, used for attaching the climbing rope in various ways. [< German *Karabiner* abbreviated form of *Karabinerhaken* carbine hook]

Kar|a|ism (kãr′ə iz əm), *n.* the beliefs and practices of the Karaites.

Kar|a|ite (kãr′ə īt), *n.* a member of a Jewish sect that originated in Persia in the 700's A.D. and rejected the rabbinical tradition and Talmudic authority, basing its tenets on a literal interpretation of the Scriptures. [< Hebrew *qərāīm* scripturalists (< *qārā* to read) + English *-ite*[1]]

kar|a|kul or **kar|a|kule** (kar′ə kəl), *n.* **1** a short, flat, curly fur made from the skin of newborn or very young lambs of a breed of Asian sheep. It is called broadtail, Persian lamb, or caracul, according to the age of the lamb. **2** any one of a breed of robust sheep of Asia, raised for fur or skin. [variant of *caracul*]

Ka|ra|mo|jong (ka rə mō′jong), *n., pl.* **-jong** or **-jongs**. **1** a member of a nomadic, cattle-raising people of northeastern Uganda. **2** their Sudanic language.

kar|at (kar′ət), *n.* = carat. *Abbr:* kt.

***karate**

ka|ra|te** (kə rä′tē), *n., v.,* **-ted, -te|ing**. **—*n. an Oriental method of fighting without weapons by striking with the hands, elbows, knees, and feet at certain parts of the opponent's body.
—*v.t.* to strike or beat with blows used in karate: *A wolf was bugging me, so I . . . karated him, and called the fuzz* (New Yorker).
[< Japanese *karate*]

ka|ra|te-chop (kə rä′tē chop′), *n., v.,* **-chopped, -chop|ping**. **—*n.*** a sharp slanting stroke with the hand used in karate.
—*v.t., v.i.* to strike with a karate-chop.

ka|ra|te|ka (kə rä′tē kä), *n., pl.* **-ka** or **-kas**. an expert in karate; karatist. [< Japanese *karateka*]

Kar|a|thane (kar′ə thān), *n. Trademark.* a chemical used in dusts and sprays for treating mildew and mites on vegetables, fruits, and flowers.

ka|ra|tist (kä rä′tist), *n.* an expert in karate.

ka|ra|ya (kə rä′yə), *n.* a gum derived from the sap of a tropical Asian tree of the sterculia family. It is used in place of tragacanth as a stiffening for textiles, in the production of food and cosmetics, and as a laxative.

ka|ree|boom (kə rē′büm), *n.* a South African tree of the cashew family found growing in the veld near riverbeds and streams. [< Afrikaans *kareeboom*]

Ka|re|li|an (kə rē′lē ən), *adj., n.* **—*adj.*** of or having to do with Karelia (part of a republic of the U.S.S.R. situated east of Finland).
—*n.* **1** a member of an eastern division of the Baltic Finns inhabiting Karelia and eastern Finland. **2** the Finnish dialect of the Karelians.

Ka|ren (kə ren′), *n.* **1** a member of a people living in south and southeast Burma, culturally not related to the native Burmese: *The most serious rebellion against the government is that of the Karens* (Atlantic). **2** any one of various languages of these people spoken in the different districts where they live.

kar|ma (kär′mə), *n.* **1** (in Buddhism and Hinduism) all the acts, words, and thoughts of one life, supposed to determine a person's fate in his next stage of existence. **2** fate; destiny; kismet. **3** quality of good or bad feeling emanating from a person, place, or thing; vibrations: *Disney World alone attracts 1,000,000 visitors a month to its 27,000 acres of fun and games—and school is not even out yet. "It's great karma, man," noted one long-haired California youth* (Time). *Laid back though they are, Los Angelenos can be as touchy as anyone else when the karma feels wrong* (Maclean's). [< Sanskrit *karma* deed]

kar|mic (kär′mik), *adj.* of, having to do with, or determined by karma.

Ka|rok (kə rok′), *n., pl.* **-rok** or **-roks**. **1** a member of a tribe of American Indians of the western United States living along the Klamath River. **2** their Hokan language.

ka|ross (kə ros′), *n.* a cloak or sleeveless jacket made of skins, worn by South African natives. [< Afrikaans *karos*, apparently < Hottentot]

kar|ri (kar′ē), *n.* a very tall eucalyptus tree of western Australia, valuable as a source of lumber. [< the native name]

kar|roo or **ka|roo** (kə rü′), *n., pl.* **-roos**, *adj.* **—*n.*** barren clayey tableland in southern Africa.
—*adj.* **1** of or growing in the karroo: *The waterless desert covered with a species of karoo shrub* (H. Rider Haggard). **2** of or having to do with an important South African series of rocks of Triassic age, chiefly sandstone mixed with volcanic matter.
[< Afrikaans *karo*, probably < Hottentot *karusa* dry]

Kar|roo or **Ka|roo** (kə rü′), *n., pl.* **-roos**, *adj.* = karroo.

karst (kärst), *adj.* of or having to do with limestone topography typified by underground drainage, sinkholes, rolling surfaces, and caverns, as in northern Florida: *karst plains, a karst feature.* [< *Karst*, a desolate region of Yugoslavia]

kart (kärt), *n.* = go-kart.

kart|ing (kär′ting), *n.* = go-karting.

karyo-, *combining form.* cell nucleus: *Karyolysis = dissolution of a cell nucleus.* [< Greek *káryon* nut, kernel]

kar|y|o|ki|ne|sis (kar′ē ō ki nē′sis), *n. Biology.* the division of the cell nucleus, especially in mitosis. [< *karyo-* + Greek *kínēsis* motion < *kīneîn* move]

kar|y|o|ki|net|ic (kar′ē ō ki net′ik), *adj. Biology.* having to do with karyokinesis.

kar|y|ol|o|gy (kar′ē ol′ə jē), *n.* the study of cell nuclei.

kar|y|o|lymph (kar′ē ə limf), *n. Biology.* the more fluid portion of the nucleus of a cell; nuclear sap.

kar|y|ol|y|sis (kar′ē ol′ə sis), *n. Biology.* the dissolution of a cell nucleus.

kar|y|om|i|tome (kar′ē om′ə tōm), *n. Biology.* the network of fibers which forms a constituent of the nucleus of a cell before the process of mitosis begins. [variant of earlier *karyomiton* < *karyo-* + *míton*, neuter of Greek *mítos* thread]

kar|y|o|plasm (kar′ē ə plaz′əm), *n. Biology.* the protoplasm found in the nucleus of a cell; nucleoplasm. [< *karyo-* + (proto)*plasm*]

kar·y·o·plas·ma (kar′ē ə plaz′mə), *n. Biology.* karyoplasm.

kar·y·o·plas·mat·ic (kar′ē ō plaz mat′ik), *adj. Biology.* karyoplasmic.

kar·y·o·plas·mic (kar′ē ə plaz′mik), *adj. Biology.* of or having to do with karyoplasm.

kar·y·o·some (kar′ē ə sōm), *n. Biology.* **1** any one of certain bodies present in the network of chromatin in the nucleus of a cell, similar to but distinguished from the nucleolus or plasmosome. **2** the nucleus of a cell. **3** = chromosome. [< *karyo-* + Greek *sôma* body]

kar·y·o·the·ca (kar′ē ə thē′kə), *n. Biology.* the nuclear membrane of a cell. [< *karyo-* + Greek *thḗkē* case, cover]

kar·y·o·tin (kar′ē ō′tin), *n. Biology.* the part of the nucleus of a cell that will take a stain; chromatin. [< *karyo-* + (chroma)*tin*]

kar·y·o·type (kar′ē ō tīp), *n., v.,* **-typed, -typ·ing.** *Genetics.* **—*n.*** **1** the character of a set of chromosomes as defined by their arrangement, number, size, shape, or other characteristics. **2** a group of chromosome sets having one or more such characteristics in common.
—***v.t., v.i.*** to classify the chromosome sets of (an organism, species, genus, or other grouping) according to their arrangement, number, size, shape, or other characteristics: *Two to six weeks of growth are required before the culture is ready to be karyotyped . . . and examined microscopically to determine the chromosome pattern* (Saturday Review).

kar·y·o·typ·ic (kar′ē ō tip′ik), *adj.* of or having to do with karyotypes or karyotyping.

Kas., Kansas.

Kas·bah (käz′bä), *n.* the native quarter of cities with a large Arab population. Also, **Casbah.**

ka·sha[1] (kä′shə), *n.* coarse grains of buckwheat, barley, wheat, or millet, crushed and cooked, and served as a mush. [< Russian *kasha*]

kash·a[2] (kash′ə), *n.* **1** a soft, twilled woolen fabric: *For sports, he makes a three-quarter length straight coat of ocelot. Red kasha lines the coat and pipes the tailored pockets* (New Yorker). **2 Kasha,** a trademark for this fabric.

ka·sher (kä′shər), *adj., n., v.* **—*adj., n.*** = kosher. —***v.t., v.i.*** **1** to prepare (food) according to Jewish ritual law. **2** to make (utensils) kosher: *Muslim dietary rules resemble the Jewish ones, but there are no professional priests or rabbis in Islam to kasher* (Atlantic). Also, **kosher.**

Kash·mir goat (kash′mir), = Cashmere goat.

Kash·mi·ri (kash mir′ē), *n., pl.* **-ri,** *adj.* **—*n.*** **1** the Indic language of Kashmir. **2** a native or inhabitant of Kashmir.
—***adj.*** of or having to do with Kashmir.

Kash·mir·i·an (kash mir′ē ən), *adj., n.* **—*adj.*** of or having to do with Kashmir or its inhabitants.
—***n.*** a native or inhabitant of Kashmir.

Kashmir shawl, a fine handwoven shawl woven in Kashmir. Also, **Cashmere shawl.**

kash·ruth (käsh rüt′), *n.* **1** the Jewish dietary laws: *The Orthodox emphasize observance of kashruth.* **2** the condition of being kosher. [< Hebrew *kashrūth* (literally) fitness]

Ka·shub (kə shüb′), *n., pl.* **-shubs.** **1** a member of a Slavic people living on the left bank of the lower Vistula River. **2** = Kashubian.

Ka·shu·bi·an (kə shü′bē ən), *n.* the Slavic language of the Kashubs, closely related to Polish.

Kas·kas·ki·a (käs kas′kē ə), *n., pl.* **-ki·a** or **-ki·as.** a member of a tribe of American Indians, once constituting a major part of the Illinois confederacy, who lived in southern Illinois.

Kas·par (kas′pər), *n.* = Gaspar.

Kas·site (ka′sīt), *n.* **1** a member of a tribe of non-Semitic people which conquered and ruled Babylon from about 1600 to about 1100 B.C. and was later absorbed into the Babylonian population. **2** the Elamite language of this tribe.

kat (kät), *n.* **1** a shrub of the staff-tree family native to Arabia and Africa. It is cultivated for its leaves that produce a mild narcotic effect when chewed or used in making tea. **2** its leaf: *Thousands of people in Yemen chew kat.* Also, **khat, qat.** [< Arabic *qat*]

ka·tab·a·sis (kə tab′ə sis), *n., pl.* **-ses** (-sēz). **1** a military retreat, especially that of Cyrus the Younger and the Greeks who fought against Artaxerxes. **2** the act or process of going down. [< Greek *katábasis* a descent < *katabaínein* to go down]

kat·a·bat·ic wind (kat′ə bat′ik), a wind produced by the gravitational flowing of cold, dense air down the slopes of mountains, plateaus, or other elevations; fall wind. [< Greek *katabatikós* < *katabaínein* to go down]

ka·tab·o·lism (kə tab′ə liz əm), *n.* = catabolism.

ka·ta·ka·na (kä′tə kä′ŋə), *n.* one of the two styles of writing the Japanese syllabary of 46 or (formerly) 48 letters (the other being hiragana), consisting of square-shaped characters. [< Japanese *katakana* < *kata* side + *kana* kana]

ka·ta·me·wa·za (kä′tə mə wä′zə), *n.* a form of judo which emphasizes the techniques of pinning or locking an opponent's body. [< Japanese *katamewaza* < *katame* defense + *waza* skilled work]

ka·ta·na (kä tä′nä), *n.* a Japanese sword that has a single edge and is slightly curved toward the point. [< Japanese]

Ka·tan·gan (kə täng′gən, -tang′-), *adj., n.* = Katangese.

Ka·tan·gese (kə täng gēz′, -gēs′), *adj., n., pl.* **-gese.** **—*adj.*** of or having to do with Katanga, a mineral-rich province of Zaire (the former Belgian Congo), in the southeastern part.
—***n.*** a native or inhabitant of Katanga province.

ka·tchi·na or **ka·tci·na** (kä chē′nə, kə-) *n.* = kachina.

katch·up (kech′əp, kach′-), *n.* = ketchup.

Ka·tha·ka·li (kä′tə kä′lē), *n.* a classic religious dance drama of India, performed only by men, in which special costumes and make-up identify each character, dance movements follow fixed patterns, and detailed hand gestures give particular meaning to each word. [< Sanskrit *kathā* story + *kali* play]

ka·tha·rev·ou·sa, ka·tha·rev·u·sa, or **ka·tha·rev·ous·sa** (kä′thə rev′ə sä, -sə; -rev′ü sä), *n.* the literary form of the Greek language of the 1800's and until recently of official documents and modern scientific works. The difference between katharevousa and demotic, the spoken language of today, is largely in grammatical endings. [< New Greek *kathareuousa,* ultimately < Greek *kathareuein* to be pure < *katharós* pure]

ka·thar·sis (kə thär′sis), *n.* = catharsis.

ka·thar·tic (kə thär′tik), *n., adj.* = cathartic.

kath·ode (kath′ōd), *n.* = cathode.

ka·thod·ic (kə thod′ik), *adj.* = cathodic.

kat·i (kat′ē), *n.* = catty[2].

kat·i·on (kat′ī′ən), *n.* = cation.

kat·sup (kech′əp, kat′səp), *n.* = ketchup.

kat·su·ra tree (kät′sər ə), a hardy, shrublike tree of China and Japan, cultivated for ornament. [< Japanese *katsura*]

ka·ty·did (kā′ti did), *n.* any one of various large, green grasshoppers with long antennae. The male makes a shrill noise like its name by rubbing its front wings together. See picture under **grasshopper.** [American English; imitative]

kat·zen·jam·mer (kät′sən yä′mər), *n. Informal.* **1** headache, nausea, or other upset following drunkenness; a hangover: *Our katzenjammer is too severe to yield to aspirin* (Harper's). **2** a caterwauling; uproar; clamor: *the katzenjammer of quarreling neighbors.* [American English < German *Katzenjammer* (literally) cats' wailing]

kau·kau (kou′kou′), *n.* (in Hawaii) food. [< Polynesian *kaukau*]

kau·ri (kou′rē), *n., pl.* **-ris.** **1** a tall evergreen of New Zealand that is the source of a valuable timber and a resin. **2** the wood, used in shipbuilding and for houses and furniture. **3** kauri resin. Also, **kaury.** [< Maori *kauri* the tree; also, its resin]

kauri resin, the resin which exudes from the thick bark of the kauri, used in making varnish and as an amber substitute.

kau·ry (kou′rē), *n., pl.* **-ries.** = kauri.

ka·va (kä′və), *n.* **1** either of two shrubs of the pepper family, growing in Australia and the Pacific Islands, with a pungent, aromatic root from which an alcoholic beverage is prepared. **2** the beverage. Also, **ava.** [apparently < Polynesian (Maori) *kawa* bitter]

ka·va·ka·va (kä′və kä′və), *n.* = kava.

Kaw (kô), *n.* = Kansa.

Ka·wa·sa·ki disease (kä′wə sä′kē), a disease of young children, characterized by acute fever, congested blood vessels, and skin rashes: *Kawasaki disease, . . . whose cause remains unknown, usually affects children under the age of 5* (Jenny Tesar). [< *Kawasaki,* a suburb of Tokyo, Japan, where the disease was first diagnosed]

Kay (kā), *n.* **Sir,** the rude, boastful foster brother of King Arthur in Arthurian legends. Sir Kay was a knight of the Round Table.

***kayak** definition 1

kay·ak** (kī′ak), *n., v.* **—*n. **1** an Eskimo canoe made of animal skins stretched over a light frame of wood or bone, with an opening in the middle for a person: *They and their women built kayaks and from them the men speared fish and harpooned seal and sea lions* (Wall Street Journal). **2** a similar craft of other material: *A single-bladed paddle is used with a canoe, double with a kayak; paddlers sit with their legs forward in kayaks, but kneel in canoes* (New Yorker).
—***v.i.*** to paddle a kayak; travel in a kayak. Also, **kaiak, kyak.** [American English < Eskimo *kayak*]

Ka·yasth (kä′yəst), *n.* a member of one of the upper castes of India, consisting of scribes, clerks, and officials. [< Sanskrit *kāyastha*]

ka·yo (kā′ō′), *v.,* **-yoed, -yo·ing,** *n., pl.* **-yos.** *U.S. Slang.* **—*v.t.*** **1** to hit so hard as to make helpless or unconscious; knock out. **2** to put out of operation; diminish in effect. **—*n.*** *Boxing.* = knockout. [pronunciation of *K.O.*]

Ka·zakh or **Ka·zak** (kä zäk′, -zäн′), *n.* **1** a member of a Turkic people of Central Asia. **2** the Turkic dialect of the Kazakhs.

ka·zatz·ka (kə zäts′kə), *n.* a Slavic folk dance performed by a couple. It includes a part in which the male partner dances in a squatting position. [< Russian *kazachki,* plural of *kazachok* (literally) Cossack dance]

ka·zi (kä′zē, kā′-), *n., pl.* **-zis.** = cadi.

ka·zoo (kə zü′), *n., pl.* **-zoos.** a toy musical instrument made of a tube sealed off at one end with a membrane, which produces a buzzing or vibration when the tube is hummed into. [American English; imitative]

kb (no periods), kilobar.

KB (no periods), **1** kilobyte. **2** *Chess.* king's bishop.

K.B., **1** King's Bench. **2** Knight Bachelor. **3** Knight of the Bath.

kbar (no periods), kilobar.

K.B.E. or **KBE** (no periods), Knight Commander of the British Empire.

Kc (no period), koruna.

kc., kilocycle or kilocycles.

K.C. or **KC** (no periods), **1** Kansas City. **2** Knight Commander. **3** Knights of Columbus.

K.C., King's Counsel.

kcal., kilocalorie or kilocalories.

K.C.B., Knight Commander of the Bath.

KCIA (no periods) or **K.C.I.A.,** Korean Central Intelligence Agency.

K.C.M.G., Knight Commander of Saint Michael and Saint George.

kcps (no periods) or **kc.p.s.,** kilocycles per second.

kc/s or **kcs** (no periods), kilocycles per second.

k.d. or **K.D.,** knocked down (not assembled, especially in various combinations in commerce): *k.d.c.l.* = *knocked down, in carloads.*

ke·a (kä′ə, kē′-), *n.* a large parrot of New Zealand, olive-green in color with red under its wings, having a powerful, hooked bill which it uses to dig out insects and root for food; mountain nestor. It occasionally kills sheep by tearing at their backs to eat the fat around the kidneys. [< Maori *kea;* imitative of the bird's cry]

Keats·i·an (kēt′sē ən), *adj.* of, having to do with, or characteristic of the English poet John Keats, 1795-1821, or his poems.

Keb (keb), *n.* = Geb.

ke·bab (kə bob′), *n.* = kabob.

keb·bie (keb′ē), *n. Scottish.* a staff or stick with a hooked end.

keb·buck or **keb·bock** (keb′ək), *n. Scottish, Irish, or Dialect.* a cheese: *a huge kebbock—a cheese . . . made with ewe-milk mixed with cow's milk* (Scott). [origin uncertain.]

ke·be·le (kə bä′lə), *n.* a unit of local government in Ethiopia, established after the deposition of Emperor Haile Selassie. [< Amharic *kebele*]

Kech·ua (kech′wə), *n.* = Quechua.

Kech·uan (kech′wən), *adj., n.* = Quechuan.

Kech·u·ma·ran (kech′ů mä rän′), *n.* = Quechumaran.

keck (kek), *v.i.* **1** to make a sound as if about to vomit; retch. **2** *Figurative.* to feel or show strong dislike or disgust. [< obsolete *kecke,* interjection; probably imitative]

keck·le[1] (kek′əl), *v.i., v.t.,* **-led, -ling,** *n.* = cackle.

keck·le[2] (kek′əl), *v.t.,* **-led, -ling.** *Nautical.* to cover (a cable or hawser) by winding with something, as to prevent chafing.

ked (ked), *n.* = sheep ked.

ked·dah (ked′ə), *n.* an enclosure, such as a log stockade, built in India to capture wild elephants by driving them into it. Also, **kheda, khedah.** [probably Anglo-Indian < Hindi *khēdā*]

kedge (kej), *v.,* **kedged, kedg·ing,** *n.* **—*v.t.*** to move (a ship or boat) by pulling on a rope attached to an anchor that has been dropped some distance away.
—***v.i.*** **1** to use such a method of moving. **2** (of a ship or boat) to move by being warped with an anchor: *She went to windward as though she were kedging* (Richard Henry Dana).
—***n.*** a small anchor used to kedge a ship or boat

Pronunciation Key: hat, āge, cãre, fär; let, ēqual, tėrm; it, īce; hot, ōpen, ôrder; oil, out; cup, pu̇t, rüle; child; long; thin; ŦHen; zh, measure; ə represents **a** in about, **e** in taken, **i** in pencil, **o** in lemon, **u** in circus.

or keep it clear of its main anchor. [origin uncertain. Compare etym. under **cadge.**]

kedge anchor, = kedge.

kedg|er (kej′ər), *n.* = kedge.

kedg|er|ee (kej′ə rē), *n.* **1** an Indian dish of rice boiled with split peas, onions, eggs, butter, and spices. **2** a European dish made of fish, boiled rice, eggs, and spices, served hot. [< Hindi *khichṛī*]

ke|ef (kē ef′), *n.* = kef.

keek (kēk), *v., n. Scottish or Dialect.* —*v.i.* to peek; peep: *I keeked through a hole in the door* (James M. Barrie).
—*n.* a peek; peep.
[Middle English *kicken.* Compare Middle Low German, Middle Dutch *kīcken.*]

keel¹ (kēl), *n., v.* —*n.* **1** the main timber or steel piece that extends the whole length of the bottom of a ship or boat. The whole ship is built up on the keel. *It has a ballast keel which gives extreme stability and seaworthiness in smooth or choppy water* (Newsweek). **2** the part in an aircraft resembling a ship's keel. **3** *Archaic.* a ship. **4** something that resembles a ship's keel in any way; under surface or lower part. **5** *Biology.* a longitudinal ridge, as on a leaf or the breastbone of a bird, or the two fused lower petals of the flowers of many plants of the pea family; carina. **6** = keelboat.
—*v.t.* to turn over; upset.
—*v.i.* to turn upside down.
keel over, a to turn over or upside down; upset: *The sailboat keeled over in the storm.* **b** to fall or cause to fall over suddenly. **c** *Informal, Figurative.* to faint: *The woman keeled over in the hot sun.*
on an even keel, a with the keel level; horizontal: *The boat sailed on an even keel in good weather.* **b** *Figurative.* calm; steady; unperturbed: *In spite of the fracas, they remained on an even keel.*
[< Scandinavian (compare Old Icelandic *kjölr*); in some senses, translation of Latin *carīna* keel, hull, ship] —**keel′less,** *adj.*

keel² (kēl), *n.* a serious disease of ducks; paratyphoid fever. [apparently special use of *keel¹*, verb]

keel³ (kēl), *n.* **1** a barge or lighter used in Yorkshire, England, for loading coal. **2** the amount of coal carried in a keel. **3** a unit of weight for coal, equal to 47,488 pounds or 21.2 long tons. [apparently < Middle Dutch *kiel*]

keel⁴ (kēl), *n. Scottish.* **1** a red ocher used for marking, as for sheep, stone, and timber; ruddle. **2** a mark made with this. [origin uncertain]

keel⁵ (kēl), *Dialect.* —*v.t.* to cool, especially to cool (a pot about to boil over) by stirring, skimming, or adding cold liquid: *while greasy Joan doth keel the pot* (Shakespeare).
—*v.i.* to become cool or cold.
[Old English *cēlan*]

Keel (kēl), *n.* = Carina.

***keel|boat** (kēl′bōt′), *n. U.S.* a large, shallow barge, with a keel and covered deck, formerly used on the Missouri and other western rivers. [American English, probably < Dutch *kielboot*]

***keelboat**

keeled (kēld), *adj.* having a keel.

keel|er¹ (kē′lər), *n. Dialect.* **1** a vessel for cooling liquids. **2** a shallow tub for various purposes. **3** a shallow box used in dressing mackerel. [< *keel⁵* + *-er¹*]

keel|er² (kē′lər), *n. British.* a sailboat having a keel rather than a centerboard: *846 craft, from centreboard seven-footers to lordly 70 ft. keelers, swept about the seas in ... various races* (London Times). [< *keel¹* + *-er¹*]

keel|hale (kēl′hāl′), *v.t.,* **-haled, -hal|ing.** = keelhaul.

keel|haul (kēl′hôl′), *v.t.* **1** to haul (a person) under the keel of a ship for punishment: *an effigy of Judas which the crew amuse themselves with keelhauling and hanging by the neck from the yard-arms* (Richard Henry Dana). **2** to scold severely; rebuke. [loan translation of Dutch *kielhalen* < *kiel* keel + *halen* to haul]

keel|son (kel′sən, kēl′-), *n.* a beam or line of timbers or iron plates fastened along the top of a ship's keel to strengthen it. Also, **kelson.** [earlier *kelson,* perhaps < Swedish *kölsvin*]

keen¹ (kēn), *adj.* **1** so shaped as to cut well: *a keen blade.* **2** sharp; cutting; piercing; intense: *a keen wind, keen hunger, keen pain,* (*Figurative.*) *keen wit.* **SYN**: penetrating, biting, bitter. **3** strong; vivid: *keen competition.* **4** *Figurative.* able to do its work quickly and exactly; able to perceive well: *a keen mind, a keen sense of smell. She had usually a keen sense of the ludicrous* (Bret Harte). **SYN**: acute. See syn. under **sharp. 5** full of enthusiasm; eager: *He is keen about canoeing. Never did I know a creature ... So keen and greedy to confound a man* (Shakespeare). **SYN**: ardent. See syn. under **eager. 6** *Slang.* wonderful; perfect. [Old English *cēne*] —**keen′ly,** *adv.* —**keen′ness,** *n.*

keen² (kēn), *n., v.* —*n.* a wailing lament for the dead.
—*v.i.* to utter the keen or lamentation for the dead; wail; lament: *I sat on the bed and keened to myself for a moment* (Punch).
—*v.t.* to bewail with keening or wailing: *Isn't it a bitter thing to think of him floating that way ... and no one to keen him but the black hags that do be flying on the sea?* (John M. Synge).
[< Irish *caoine* < *caoinim* I cry] —**keen′er,** *n.*

keen|ing (kē′ning), *n., adj.* —*n.* a wailing lament; keen. —*adj.* wailing; lamenting: *keening widows, a keening song.*

keep (kēp), *v.,* **kept, keep|ing,** *n.* —*v.t.* **1** to have for a long time or forever; continue to hold: *You may keep this book. George Washington kept the interest of the public.* **2** to have and not let go of; retain under one's control: *Can you keep a secret? Some Presidents do not keep the authority of their office.* **3a** to have and take care of; look after; tend: *My aunt keeps two boarders. The hired man kept the farm and a neighbor's bees.* **b** to have in one's service; employ: *to keep a servant.* **4** to take care of and protect; guard: *The bank keeps money for people. The Lord bless thee, and keep thee* (Numbers 6:24). **SYN**: shield. **5** to have; hold, especially for a future occasion; save: *to keep grain for seed. Keep this in mind. Keep a thing, its use will come* (Tennyson). **6** to hold back; restrain; prevent: *Keep the baby from crying. What is keeping her from coming?* **SYN**: detain. **7a** to maintain in good condition: *to keep a garden. A refrigerator keeps food fresh.* **SYN**: preserve. **b** to carry on; manage; run: *I keep a coffee-house* (Sir Richard Steele). *The children played at keeping house* (Tennyson). **8** to cause to continue; cause to stay the same: *The boy kept his progress.* **9** to cause to continue in some stated place, condition, or action; continue to practice or do: *to keep watch, to be kept after school. The blanket keeps the baby warm. Keep the fire burning. They kept the noiseless tenor of their way* (Thomas Gray). *The general kept the field throughout the battle.* **10a** to do the right thing with; observe; celebrate: *to keep Thanksgiving Day as a holiday.* **SYN**: commemorate. **b** to be faithful to: *to keep a promise.* **SYN**: fulfill, implement. **11** to provide for; support: *He is not able to keep himself, much less a family.* **12** to have regularly for sale: *That store keeps canned goods.* **13a** to make regular entries or records in: *to keep books, keep a diary.* **b** to record (transactions or events) regularly: *No record of this conversation was kept.*
—*v.i.* **1** to restrain oneself; refrain: *The little boy couldn't keep from crying when he fell down.* **2** to stay in good condition; preserve: *Milk does not keep long in hot weather.* **3** to stay the same; continue: *to keep cool, to keep at work. Keep along this road for two miles.* **4** to stay in a particular place; remain: *to keep to one's room. Keep off the grass. Keep out. I kept ... within doors* (Daniel Defoe). **5** *U.S. Informal.* to be in session; be held: *one afternoon, when school didn't keep.* **6** *Especially U.S. Informal.* to live; dwell: *Just where she kept in Boston is unknown to history.*
—*n.* **1** food and a place to sleep; maintenance; support: *The money he earns would not pay for his keep.* **2** the strongest part of a castle or fort; central tower; stronghold; donjon: *The walls oppress me, and yon huge keep that hinders half the heaven* (Tennyson). **3** *Archaic.* care or watching; custody: *If from shepherd's keep a lamb strayed far* (Keats). **4** = keep play.
for keeps, a for the winner to keep his winnings: *We, the undersigned, promise not to play marbles for keeps* (The Advance). **b** *Informal.* forever; for good: *I'm through with him for keeps. I'm coming into the business for keeps next fall* (Rudyard Kipling).
in good keep, in good condition: *... as the owner of a fine horse is* [*solicitous*] *to have him appear in good keep* (Charles Lamb).
keep an eye on. See under **eye.**
keep at, to work persistently at; persist in: *By keeping at it all day he is able to get over nearly 2 acres* (Journal of the Royal Agricultural Society).
keep at a distance. See under **distance.**
keep back, a to hold back forcibly; restrain: *She made a brave effort to keep back her tears* (George M. Fenn). **b** *Figurative.* to withhold; conceal: *It really seemed to me as if she were keeping something back* (George Gissing).
keep company (with). See under **company.**
keep down, a to hold in subjection or under control; repress: *to keep down a people's spirits.* **b** to keep low in amount or number; prevent from growing or accumulating: *to keep down the interest on a loan. Employers ... combined to keep down wages* (William Longman). **c** to keep low or subdued: *to keep down a light, to keep down the noise. They hoped the wind would keep down for a while.*
keep in with, *Informal.* to keep acquaintance or friendship with: *Though I do not love him, yet I find it necessary to keep in with him* (Samuel Pepys).
keep on, to continue; go on: *The boys kept on swimming in spite of the rain.*
keep one's distance. See under **distance.**
keep one's eyes open. See under **eye.**
keep one's eyes peeled. See under **eye.**
keep one's hand in. See under **hand.**
keep pace. See under **pace.**
keeps, a game played on the condition that each player retains possession of all that he wins; game played for keeps: *The last five ... are men who do not play keeps* (London Daily Chronicle).
keep to, a to adhere to: *The author has kept very closely to the historical facts. I hope the plan will be kept to.* **b** to abide by: *He has kept to our agreement.*
keep to oneself, a to avoid associating with others: *The hermit keeps to himself.* **b** to keep a secret: *The family kept the scandal to themselves.*
keep under, to hold in subjection or under control; keep down: *She had been accustomed to be kept under all her life* (J. Masterman).
keep up, a to continue; prevent from ending: *We kept up a small fire.* **b** to maintain in good condition: *We must keep up appearances, even though we are poor.* **c** not to fall behind: *If the children can keep up, we will take them with us when we hike into town.* **d** to prevent from sinking or falling; support: *The life preserver kept him up until the boat came.* **e** to bear up; endure under strain: *It is hard to keep up when one feels defeated or depressed.*
keep up with, to go or move as fast as; not fall behind: *You walk so fast that I cannot keep up with you.*
keep up with the Joneses. See under **Joneses.**
[Old English *cēpan* observe]
—*Syn. v.t.* **2 Keep, retain, withhold** mean to hold in one's possession. **Keep** is the general word meaning to have and not let go from one's possession, control, or care: *They were kept in prison.* **Retain,** more formal, emphasizes continuing to keep, especially against efforts to take away or make one let go: *Our team retained a commanding lead.* **Withhold** means to keep or hold back, and suggests some check or obstacle to letting go or, often, refusing to let go: *to withhold part of one's salary. Fear made him withhold the truth.*

keep|a|ble (kē′pə bəl), *adj.* capable of being kept or preserved.

keep|er (kē′pər), *n., v.* —*n.* **1** a person or thing that keeps: *a keeper of secrets or of bees.* **2** a guard; watchman. **3** a guardian; protector: *Am I my brother's keeper?* (Genesis 4:9). **SYN**: warden, custodian. **4** *British.* a gamekeeper. **5** a person who owns or carries on some establishment or business: *the keeper of an inn.* **6** any mechanical device for keeping something in its place, such as a clasp, catch, or loop. **7** a link set across the poles of a magnet to preserve its magnetism when not in use. **8** a fruit or other product that keeps (well or ill). **9** a fish large enough to keep.
—*v.t. British.* to take care of or oversee as a gamekeeper.

keep|er|ing (kē′pər ing), *n. British.* the work of a gamekeeper; gamekeeping.

keep|er|ship (kē′pər ship), *n.* the office or position of a keeper.

keep|ing (kē′ping), *n.* **1** care; charge; maintenance: *The children were left in their uncle's keeping.* **SYN**: custody, guardianship, support. **2** celebration; observance: *The keeping of Thanksgiving Day is an old American custom.* **SYN**: commemoration. **3** agreement; harmony: *Don't trust him; his actions are not in keeping with his promises.* **SYN**: congruity, correspondence. **4** a being kept for future use; preservation. **5** the act or fact of retaining as one's own; retention.

keeping room, *Dialect.* a living room or sitting room: *In the family "keeping room" ... he will remember the staid, respectable old bookcase, with its glass doors* (Harriet Beecher Stowe).

keep play, a football play in which the ball carrier runs with the ball himself.

keeps (kēps), *n.pl.* See under **keep**.

keep|sake (kēp′sāk′), *n.* **1** a thing kept in memory of the giver: *Before my friend went away, he gave me his picture as a keepsake.* **SYN:** remembrance, souvenir, memento. **2** a book of verse, prose, and illustrations designed to be given as a gift, common in the early part of the 1800's.

kees|hond (kās′hond, kēs′-), *n., pl.* **-hond|en** (-hon dən). a dog of a breed developed in the Netherlands, having a dense, gray coat tipped with black and standing about 18 inches high. It is closely related to the Pomeranian and chow. [< Dutch *keeshond* < *kees* terrier + *hond* dog]

keet (kēt), *n.* a young guinea fowl. [imitative]

keeve (kēv), *n.* a large tub or vat. [Old English *cȳf*]

Kee|wa|tin (kē wä′tin), *adj., n.* —*adj.* of or having to do with the earliest period of the Archeozoic era: *Keewatin rocks.*
—*n.* **1** the earliest period of the Archeozoic era, characterized by the first known rock formations and the appearance of the first sea plants, probably algae. **2** its rocks or rock formations.
[< *Keewatin,* an area in Canada in which these rocks were found]

kef (kāf), *n.* **1** drowsiness or dreaminess, such as is produced by a drug. **2** Indian hemp or the like smoked to produce this condition. Also, **keef, kief.** [< Arabic *kef.* colloquial pronunciation of *kayf* well-being, pleasure]

kef|ir (kef′ər), *n.* an effervescent, slightly alcoholic beverage prepared from fermented milk. [< Russian *kefir* < Turkic]

kef|te|des (kef tā′dəs), *n.* a Levantine dish of small, spiced meat balls. [< New Greek *keftèdhes*]

keg (keg), *n.* **1** a small barrel, usually holding less than 10 gallons. **SYN:** cask. **2** as much as a keg can hold: *a keg of beer.* **3** a unit of weight for nails, equal to 100 lbs. **4** *British.* a barrel holding 60 herrings. [variant of Middle English *cag* < Scandinavian (compare Old Icelandic *kaggi*)]

keg|ler (keg′lər), *n. Informal.* a person who bowls; bowler. [< German *Kegler* < Middle High German *kegel* ninepin]

Kei apple (kī), **1** a bushy, thorny tree native to South Africa that bears yellow fruit resembling small apples. **2** the fruit of this tree, used for jam and jelly. [< the *Kei* river, in South Africa]

keit|lo|a (kīt′lō ə), *n.* a large, black South African rhinoceros, having two horns of nearly equal length. [< Sechuana *khetlwa*]

Ke|ku|le's formula (kā′kü lāz), = benzene ring (def. 2). [< Friedrich A. *Kekule,* 1829-1896, a German chemist]

kel|e|be (kel′ə bē), *n.* (in ancient Greece) a large, wide-mouthed vase with a broad, flat rim, and two handles extending from the body to the rim but not above it. [< Greek *kelébē*]

K electron, an electron of the K-shell.

kel|ep (kel′ep), *n.* a carnivorous ant of Central America, that preys on the boll weevil and other insects. [< a native word]

kel|leg (kel′ig), *n.* = killick.

kel|lick (kel′ik), *n.* = killick.

kel|lock (kel′ək), *n.* = killick.

kel|ly[1] (kel′ē), *n., adj.* = kelly green. [probably < *Kelly,* a proper name]

kel|ly[2] (kel′ē), *n., pl.* **-lies.** *U.S. Slang.* a stiff hat, especially a flat-brimmed straw hat.

kel|ly[3] (kel′ē), *n., pl.* **-lies.** a hollow steel tube about 40 feet long with four or six sides that forms the uppermost part of the drill stem of an oil well. [probably < *Kelly,* a proper name]

kelly green, a bright, vivid green.

ke|loid (kē′loid), *n.* a fibrous skin tumor, especially an overgrowth of scar tissue around a cut. Also, **cheloid.** [< French *kéloïde,* variant of *chéloïde,* apparently < Greek *chēlē* crab's claw]

kelp (kelp), *n.* **1** any one of certain large, tough, brown seaweeds. Kelp was formerly burned as a source of potassium and iodine, found in the ashes. Algin is obtained from this seaweed. One of the Pacific giant kelps has stems which can grow more than 150 feet. **2** the ashes of seaweed. It was formerly used as a source of iodine and carbonate of soda, and in the manufacture of soap and glass. [Middle English *culpe;* origin uncertain]

kelp bass, a sea bass of southern California, valued as a game fish.

kel|pie[1] (kel′pē), *n.* (in Scottish folklore) a water spirit, usually in the form of a horse, which haunts rivers and lakes and is supposed to drown people or warn them of drowning. Also, **kelpy.** [apparently < Scottish Gaelic *cailpeach* bullock, heifer, colt]

kel|pie[2] (kel′pē), *n.* a sheepdog of a hardy Australian breed developed from smooth-haired collies imported from Scotland. [< *Kelpie,* the name of one of the first dogs of this breed]

kel|py (kel′pē), *n., pl.* **-pies.** = kelpie[1].

kel|son (kel′sən), *n.* = keelson.

kelt (kelt), *n. Especially Scottish.* a salmon after spawning, before returning to the sea.

Kelt (kelt), *n.* = Celt.

kel|ter (kel′tər), *n. Dialect.* = kilter.

Kelt|ic (kel′tik), *adj., n.* = Celtic.

kel|vin (kel′vin), *n.* the unit of temperature on the Kelvin scale, equal to 1/273.16 of the temperature of the triple point of water.

Kel|vin (kel′vin), *adj.* of, based on, or according to the Kelvin scale. *Abbr:* K.

Kelvin scale, a scale for measuring temperatures on which 273 degrees marks the freezing point of water, 373 degrees marks the boiling point, and 0 marks absolute zero. See picture under **absolute scale.** [< William Thomson, Lord *Kelvin,* 1824-1907, a British physicist and mathematician]

kemb (kem), *v.t.,* **kembed** or **kempt, kemb|ing.** *Dialect.* to comb. [Old English *cemban*]

kemp[1] (kemp), *n., v. Especially Scottish.* —*n.* a mighty warrior; champion.
—*v.i.* **1** to fight or contend in battle with another. **2** to race in doing a piece of work (used especially of a set of reapers striving to finish first). [Old English *cempa*]

kemp[2] (kemp), *n.* a coarse hair occurring in wool or fur. [< Scandinavian (compare Old Icelandic *kampr* beard, whisker)]

kempt (kempt), *adj.* **1** tidy; neat; well-groomed: *The boys are too kempt; their clothes are too pretty; they dope not, neither do they drink* (Sunday Observer). **2** *Archaic.* combed, as the hair. [(def. 1) back formation < *unkempt;* (def. 2) past tense of *kemb*]

ken (ken), *n., v.,* **kenned** or **kent** (kent), **ken|ning.**
—*n.* **1** range of sight or vision: *Then felt I like some watcher of the skies When a new planet swims into his ken* (Keats). **2** range of knowledge: *What happens on Mars is no longer beyond our ken. Much has lain outside our ken* (Thomas Hardy). **SYN:** cognizance.
[< verb]
—*v.t. Scottish.* **1** to know; be acquainted with; be aware of. **2** to recognize; identify; distinguish. **3** to know; understand. **4** *Law.* to recognize (a person) as legal heir. **5** *Obsolete.* to admit to be (genuine, valid, or what is claimed).
—*v.i. Scottish.* to have knowledge.
[Old English *cennan* make a declaration < root of *cann* know, can]

Ken., Kentucky.

ke|naf (kə naf′), *n.* = ambary.

kench (kench), *n. U.S.* a rectangular bin or box used for salting sealskins and fish.

Ken|dal (ken′dəl), *n.* = Kendal green.

Kendal green, **1** a green woolen cloth: *A good archer thou as ever wore Kendal green* (Scott). **2** a shade of green, or the vegetable dye producing it, made from the woadwaxen plant. [< *Kendal,* in Westmorland, where the cloth is made]

ken|do (ken′dō), *n.* a Japanese form of fencing, in which bamboo or wooden sticks are used for swords. [< Japanese *ken* sword + *do* way (of life)]

Ke|nite (kē′nīt), *n.* (in the Bible) a member of a nomadic people who settled with the Jews in Palestine and were later absorbed by them.

ken|nel[1] (ken′əl), *n., v.,* **-neled, -nel|ing** or (*especially British*) **-nelled, -nel|ling.** —*n.* **1** a house for a dog or dogs, or a house for a pack of hounds or sporting dogs: *Our dog lives in a kennel behind the garage.* **2** a pack of hounds or dogs of any kind: *Hurt a dog and the whole kennel will fall on him and worry him* (Scott). **3** a wretched place to live.
—*v.t.* to put into or kept in a kennel.
—*v.i.* **1** to take shelter or lodge in a kennel. **2** (of a fox or other wild beast) to retreat into a lair.
kennels, a place where dogs are bred or boarded: *They put their dog in the kennels when they went on vacation.*
[< unrecorded Old French *kenil* < Vulgar Latin *canīle* < Latin *canis* dog]

ken|nel[2] (ken′əl), *n.* the surface drain of a street; gutter. [variant of Middle English *cannel* bed of a stream < Old North French *canel,* Old French *chanel* < Latin *canālis.* See etym. of dobulets **channel**[1], **canal.**]

ken|nel[3] (ken′əl), *n. Obsolete.* cannel coal.

Ken|nel|ly-Heav|i|side layer (ken′ə lē hev′ē-sīd), the Heaviside layer or E layer. [< Arthur E. *Kennelly,* 1861-1939, an American electrical engineer, and Oliver *Heaviside,* 1850-1925, a British physicist]

ken|nel|man (ken′əl man′, -mən), *n., pl.* **-men.** the owner or keeper of a kennel.

ken|nel|mas|ter (ken′əl mas′tər, -mäs′-), *n.* the keeper of a kennel.

ken|ning[1] (ken′ing), *n.* a descriptive poetical expression used instead of the simple name of a person or thing, especially in Old English and Old Norse poetry. *Examples:* "storm of swords" for "battle," "wave-traveler" for "boat." [< Old Icelandic *kenning* (originally) mark of recognition; doctrine < *kenna vith* to name after]

ken|ning[2] (ken′ing), *n. Scottish.* **1** perception; recognition. **2** just enough to be noticed; a little. [< *ken* + *-ing*[1]]

Ken|ny method or **treatment** (ken′ē), a method of treating infantile paralysis introduced by Elizabeth Kenny, in which hot packs are placed on the muscles and exercise is begun as early as possible. [< Elizabeth *Kenny,* 1886-1952, an Australian nurse]

ke|no (kē′nō), *n.* a gambling game somewhat like lotto, in which the players cover numbers on their cards.
[American English; origin uncertain. Compare French *quine* five numbers needed to win.]

ke|no|gen|e|sis (kē′nə jen′ə sis), *n.* = cenogenesis.

ke|no|ge|net|ic (kē′nə jə net′ik), *adj.* = cenogenetic.

keno gum, = kino[1].

ke|no|sis (ki nō′sis), *n. Theology.* Christ's renunciation of His divine nature in becoming a man. [< Greek *kénōsis* an emptying < *kenoûn* to empty]

ke|not|ic (ki not′ik), *adj.* of or having to do with kenosis.

ken|speck|le (ken′spek′əl), *adj. Scottish.* easily recognizable; conspicuous.

kent[1] (kent), *n. Scottish.* a long staff or pole used for leaping over ditches, brooks, or streams. [origin uncertain. Compare Kentish *quant.*]

kent[2] (kent), *v.* kenned; a past tense and a past participle of **ken.**

***ken|ta** or **ken|te** (ken′tə), *n.* the national dress of Ghana, a toga of brightly colored, handwoven cloth.

***kenta**

Kent|ish (ken′tish), *adj. n.* —*adj.* of Kent, its people, or their language.
—*n.* the Old English dialect spoken in the kingdom of Kent.

kent|ledge (kent′lij), *n. Nautical.* pig iron used as permanent ballast in a ship.

Ken|tuck|i|an (kən tuk′ē ən), *adj., n.* —*adj.* of Kentucky or its people.
—*n.* a person born or living in Kentucky.

Ken|tuck|y bluegrass (kən tuk′ē), a grass common in temperate regions and especially in Kentucky, used for forage and for lawns: *Kentucky bluegrass, the most-used lawn grass in this country, came from Europe, not from Kentucky* (New York Times).

Kentucky coffee beans, the seeds of the Kentucky coffee tree, once used as a substitute for coffee beans.

Kentucky coffee tree, a tall tree of the pea family, found in the Northeastern United States.

Kentucky colonel, a person who is honored in Kentucky by being given the unofficial title of colonel.

Kentucky rifle, a long-barreled, muzzleloading flintlock rifle with a small bore, developed in Pennsylvania and used in the 1700's and early 1800's by the early settlers in Kentucky and Tennessee; Pennsylvania rifle.

Ken|yan (kēn′yən, ken′-), *adj., n.* —*adj.* of or having to do with Kenya, a country in East Africa, or its people.
—*n.* a native or inhabitant of Kenya.

Ken|ya|pi|the|cus (kēn′yə pith′ə kəs, ken′-), *n.* an extinct anthropoid ape of the late Miocene and early Pliocene, whose remains were discovered by the British paleontologist Louis S. B. Leakey near Lake Victoria in Kenya between 1962 and 1967. [< *Kenya* + Greek *píthēkos* ape]

Ke|ogh plan (kē′ō), *U.S.* any of various plans by which self-employed individuals can set aside part of their yearly income as a tax-deferred annuity or retirement fund. Keogh plans permit self-employed people to deduct each year up to 25 per cent of their income, or a maximum of $30,000, without paying taxes on them or on the interest until they retire.
[< Congressman Eugene J. *Keogh,* born 1907, who sponsored a bill for such a plan]

***kep|i** (kep′ē), *n., pl.* **kep|is.** a military cap with a round, flat top and a visor, worn by French soldiers, and by soldiers in the Civil War. [< French *képi* < Swiss German *Käppi* (diminutive) < German *Kappe* cap < Medieval Latin *cappa*]

***kepi**

Kep|le|ri|an (kep lir′ē ən), *adj.* of or having to do with Johannes Kepler (1571-1630) or his laws and theories: *Keplerian laws of planetary motion.*
Kep|ler's law (kep′lərz), any one of three laws, formulated by Johannes Kepler, describing the motions of the planets around the sun.
Ke|pone (kē′pōn), *n. Trademark.* a chlorinated hydrocarbon used as a pesticide, similar to DDT: *The discharging of Kepone into the state's waters has had a crippling effect on Virginia's fishing industry* (C. Brian Kelly)
kept (kept), *v.* the past tense and past participle of **keep**: *He kept the book I gave him. The milk was kept cool.*
ke|ram|ic (kə ram′ik), *adj., n.* = ceramic.
kerat-, *combining form.* the form of **kerato-** before vowels, as in *keratin.*
ker|a|tec|to|my (ker′ə tek′tə mē), *n., pl.* **-mies.** the surgical removal of part of the cornea. [< *kerat-* + *-ectomy*]
ker|a|tin (ker′ə tin), *n.* a complex, insoluble protein, the chief structural constituent of horn, nails, hair, and feathers. Also, **ceratin.** [< Greek *kéras, -atos* horn + English *-in*]
ker|a|tin|ize (ker′ə tə nīz), *v.,* **-ized, -iz|ing.** *—v.i.* to become keratinous.
—v.t. to make keratinous; change into keratin.
—ker′a|tin|i|za′tion, *n.*
ke|rat|i|nous (ke rat′ə nəs), *adj.* having keratin or horn; horny.
ker|a|ti|tis (ker′ə tī′tis), *n.* a painful inflammation of the cornea.
kerato-, *combining form.* **1** horny substance: *Keratosis = a small, horny growth on the skin.* **2** cornea: *Keratitis = inflammation of the cornea.* Also, **kerat-** before vowels. [< Greek *kéras, -atos* horn]
ker|a|to|con|junc|ti|vi|tis (ker′ə tō kən jungk′tə vī′tis), *n.* a serious infection of the cornea and conjunctiva, usually caused by a virus.
ker|a|to|co|nus (ker′ə tō kō′nəs), *n.* a disease of the eye in which the cornea bulges out at its center, creating blurred images that only contact lenses can correct. [< New Latin *keratoconus* < *kerato-* cornea + *conus* conical structure (< Latin *cōnus* cone)]
ker|a|tode (ker′ə tōd), *n., adj.* = keratose.
ker|a|tog|e|nous (ker′ə toj′ə nəs), *adj.* giving rise to horny tissue. [< *kerato-* + *-gen* + *-ous*]
ker|a|toid (ker′ə toid), *adj.* like horn; horny. [< Greek *keratoidês* hornlike < *kéras, -atos* horn + *eîdos* form]
ker|a|to|lyt|ic (ker′ə tə lit′ik), *adj.* having to do with or causing peeling of the skin: *a keratolytic agent.* [< *kerato-* + *lytic*]
ker|a|to|plas|ty (ker′ə tə plas′tē), *n., pl.* **-ties.** plastic surgery on the cornea, especially transplantation of it. [< *kerato-* + Greek *plastós* something formed]
ker|a|tose (ker′ə tōs), *n., adj.* *—n.* a substance like horn, forming part of the skeleton of certain sponges and other invertebrates.
—adj. horny.
[< *kerat-* + *-ose*]
ker|a|to|sis (ker′ə tō′sis), *n., pl.* **-ses** (sēz). **1** any small, horny growth on the skin, such as a callus or a wart. **2** a skin disease marked by such growths. [< *kerat-* + *-osis*]
ker|a|tot|o|my (ker′ə tot′ə mē), *n., pl.* **-mies.** an incision of the cornea by surgery. [< *kerato-* + Greek *-tomiā* a cutting]
ke|rau|no|graph (kə rō′nə graf, -gräf), *n.* = ceraunograph.
kerb (kėrb), *n. Especially British.* curb (of a pavement).
kerb|side (kėrb′sīd′), *n. Especially British.* curbside.
kerb|stone (kėrb′stōn′), *n. Especially British.* curbstone.
ker|chief (kėr′chif), *n.* **1** a piece of cloth worn over the head or around the neck: *She wore a kerchief in the rain to keep her hair dry.* SYN: scarf. **2** = handkerchief. [< Anglo-French *courchief,* Old French *couvre chief* < *couvrir* to cover (< Latin *cooperīre*) + *chief* head < Latin *caput*]
ker|chiefed or **ker|chieft** (kėr′chift), *adj.* wearing a kerchief.
ker|el (ker′əl), *n.* (in South Africa) a fellow: *It does not do . . . for a young kerel like you to wear your thoughts on your face for all the world to read* (Cape Times). [< Afrikaans *kêrel* < Dutch *kerel*]
Ker|e|san (ker′ə sən), *n.* a family of American Indian languages spoken by the Pueblo Indians of north central New Mexico. [< *Keres* the Pueblo Indians of New Mexico who speak this language + *-an*]
kerf (kėrf), *n.* **1** a cut made especially by an ax or saw. **2** a piece or quantity cut off. **3** the place at which a tree or branch is or has been cut across. **4** the act of cutting or carving; cut; stroke. [Old English *cyrf,* related to *ceorfan* carve]
ker|fuf|fle (kər fuf′əl), *n. British Slang.* squabble; scuffle: *The . . . partners, what with all the kerfuffle, thought the best thing was to withdraw* (Observer).
ke|rite (kir′īt), *n.* a substitute for rubber, made by combining asphalt or tar, animal or vegetable oil, and sulfur. It is especially used as an insulating material for electric wires. [< Greek *kērós* wax]
Ker|man (kər män′), *n.* an Oriental rug with elaborate patterns in muted colors, made in Kerman, a province of Iran; Kermanshah. Also, **Kir|man.**
Ker|man|shah (kər män′shä′), *n.* = Kerman.
ker|mes (kėr′mēz), *n.* **1** a scale insect, the females of which live on the twigs of certain kinds of oak trees. **2** a red dyestuff made from the dried bodies of these insects, formerly used in medicine. **3** a small evergreen oak on which these insects live. [< French *kermès* < Arabic *qirmiz* < Sanskrit *krmis* worm, insect. See related etym. at **carmine, cramoisy, crimson.**]
ker|mess (kėr′mis), *n.* = kermis.
ker|messe (kėr′mis), *n. British.* a circuit race for bicycles. [< Flemish *kermesse* kermis (which usually includes such a race)]
ker|mis (kėr′mis), *n.* **1** a fair with games and merrymaking, held in the Netherlands, Belgium, and adjacent regions. **2** any fair or entertainment, usually to raise money for charity. Also, **kirmess.** [< Dutch *kermis* < Middle Dutch *kermisse* < *kerk* church + *mis* Mass]
Ker|mode's bear (kėr′mōdz), = island white bear.
kern[1] or **kerne** (kėrn), *n. Archaic.* **1** an Irish or Scottish foot soldier carrying light weapons. **2** a body or troop of such soldiers. **3** an Irish peasant. [< Middle Irish *ceatharn,* earlier *ceithern* troop of foot soldiers. See related etym. at **cat|er|an.**]
***kern[2]** (kėrn), *n., v., Printing.* *—n.* the part of a letter or type face that projects above the body, as in *h,* or below it, as in *j.*
—v.t. **1** to form or design (a letter or type) with a kern. **2** to smooth the kern of (type).
[< Old North French *carne* edge < Latin *cardō, -inis* hinge. Compare etym. under **cardinal.**]

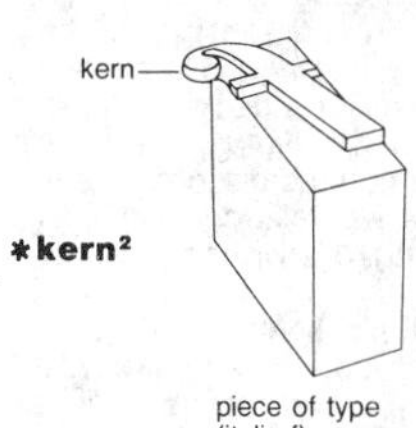

***kern[2]**
piece of type (italic f)

ker|nel (kėr′nəl), *n.* **1** the softer part inside the hard shell of a nut or inside the stone of a fruit: *As brown in hue as hazel nuts and sweeter than the kernels* (Shakespeare). **2** the body of a seed within its coating; embryo, and, when present, the albumen or endosperm. SYN: core, nucleus. **3** a grain or seed like that of wheat or corn. **4** *Figurative.* the central or most important part of anything, around which it is formed or built up; gist: *He does discern clearly wherein lies, for him, the true kernel of the matter* (Thomas Carlyle). **5** a cell nucleus. [Old English *cyrnel* < *corn* seed, grain + *-el,* a diminutive suffix]
ker|neled (kėr′nəld), *adj.* having a kernel.
kernel sentence, (in generative grammar) a simple, declarative sentence from which other, more complex sentences may be generated by transformations.
kern|ite (kėr′nīt), *n.* a colorless or white crystalline mineral, an important ore of boron compounds; rasorite. *Formula:* $Na_2B_4O_7 \cdot 4H_2O$ [< *Kern,* a county in California, where it is found + English *-ite[1]*]
ker|o|gen (ker′ə jən), *n.* the solid bituminous substance found in oil shale, which yields oil when the shale is heated. [< Greek *kērós* wax + English *-gen*]
ker|o|sene or **ker|o|sine** (ker′ə sēn, ker′ə sēn′), *n.* a thin oil made from petroleum, a mixture of hydrocarbons; coal oil. It is used in lamps and stoves, to run tractors and farm machines, as fuel for jet planes, and as a base for insect sprays. *Kerosene is a mixture of hydrocarbons with higher molecular weights. It is therefore more viscous, less volatile, and has a higher flash point than gasoline* (Monroe M. Offner). [American English < Greek *kērós* wax]
ker|plunk (kər plungk′), *interj., adv.* ***—interj.*** imitation of a sudden, loud, heavy sound, as of a fall.
—adv. with such a sound.
Kerr cell (kär, kėr), an electric cell consisting of two electrodes immersed in a liquid such as nitrobenzene, capable of passing a pulse of light of extremely short duration. The Kerr cell is used in recording sound on film, in ultra-high speed photography, and in television. [< John *Kerr,* 1824-1907, a Scottish physicist]
Kerr effect, *Electronics, Physics.* **1** an electrooptical effect in which double refraction is produced in certain transparent substances to which an electric field has been applied. **2** a magnetooptical effect in which a rotation of the plane of polarization of a light beam occurs when the beam is reflected from the surface of magnetic tape or other magnetized material. [< John *Kerr;* see etym. under **Kerr cell**]
ker|rie (ker′ē), *n.* = knobkerrie.
Ker|ry (ker′ē), *n., pl.* **-ries.** any one of a breed of small, black dairy cattle native to County Kerry, Ireland.
Kerry blue terrier, any one of a breed of terriers originating in Ireland, having a short body and long legs and a soft, bluish-gray coat. It weighs 30 to 40 pounds.
[< County *Kerry,* Ireland]
ker|sey (kėr′zē), *n., pl.* **-seys,** *adj.* *—n.* a coarse, ribbed woolen cloth with a cotton warp.
—adj. made of kersey.
kerseys, a trousers made of kersey: *He was dressed in . . . kerseys* (James Payn). **b** makes or varieties of kersey: *The Devonshire kerseys were . . . in great demand* (Tristram Risdon)]
[probably < *Kersey,* a village in Suffolk, England]
ker|sey|mere (kėr′zē mir), *n.* = cassimere.
ke|ryg|ma (kə rig′mə), *n. Theology.* the proclamation of God's revelation in Christ, especially as preached by the Gospels. [< Greek *kḗrygma* (literally) proclamation < *kēŷssein* to proclaim < *kḗryx, -ȳkos* a herald. Compare etym. under **cadu|ceus.**]
ker|yg|mat|ic (ker′ig mat′ik), *adj.* of or contained in the kerygma.
kes|trel (kes′trəl), *n.* a small falcon of Europe, Africa, and Asia, remarkable for its habit of hovering in the air facing into the wind; windhover. It is closely related to the American sparrow hawk. [perhaps < Old French *cresserelle,* or *quercerelle,* ultimately < Latin *crista* crest]
ke|ta (kē′tə), *n.* = chum[2] (def. 2). [< Russian *keta*]
***ketch** (kech), *n.* **1** a small, strongly built sailing ship with two masts, and its sails set fore and aft. It has a large mainmast toward the bow and a smaller mast forward of the sternpost. **2** a former type of sturdy naval sailing ship with two masts and a large mortar on the foredeck where the foremast normally is; bomb ketch. [variant of earlier *catch* or *cache,* probably < *catch,* noun, in sense of "pursuit, chase"]

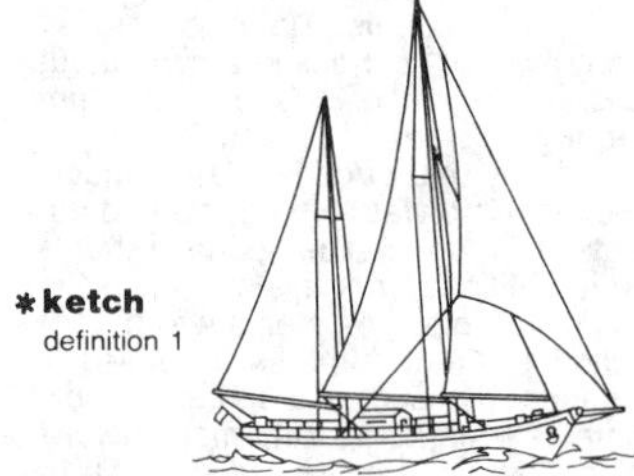
***ketch**
definition 1

ketch|up (kech′əp), *n.* **1** a sauce to use with meat, fish, etc. Tomato ketchup is made of tomatoes, onions, salt, sugar, and spices. **2** a sauce made from mushrooms, walnuts, etc. Also, **catchup, catsup, katchup, katsup.** [< Chinese *kê-tsiap* brine of pickled fish, or < Malay *kĕchap* smack the lips]
ke|ten (kē′ten), *n.* = ketene.
ke|tene (kē′tēn), *n.* **1** a colorless gas with an irritating odor, obtained by decomposing acetone or the anhydride of acetic acid by heat. *Formula:* $CH_2{:}CO$ **2** any one of a class of related compounds having the general formula $R_2C{:}CO$ [< *ket*(one) + *-ene*]

Pronunciation Key: hat, āge, cãre, fär; let, ēqual, tėrm; it, īce; hot, ōpen, ôrder; **oil, out;** cup, pu̇t, rüle; **child;** long; **thin; ᵺen; zh,** measure; **ə** represents **a** in about, **e** in taken, **i** in pencil, **o** in lemon, **u** in circus.

Ke|thu|bim (kə tü′bim; *Hebrew* kə tü′vēm′), *n.pl.* the third and last of the three divisions of the Hebrew Old Testament canon; Hagiographa. [< Hebrew *kethubhim*, plural of *kethabh* writing]

ke|to-e|nol tautomerism (kē′tō ē′nōl, -nol), *Chemistry.* a kind of tautomerism in which the substance reacts both as a ketone and as unsaturated alcohol. [< *keto*(ne) + *enol* (form)]

ke|to form (kē′tō), *Chemistry.* (in a substance exhibiting keto-enol tautomerism) the form having the properties of a ketone.

ke|to|gen|e|sis (kē′tə jen′ə sis), *n.* the production of ketone bodies.

ke|to|gen|ic (kē′tə jen′ik), *adj.* **1** producing ketones. **2** that can be converted into ketones.

ke|to|glu|tar|ic acid (kē′tō glü tar′ik), an acid derived from glutaric acid, important in the metabolism of carbohydrates and proteins.

ke|ton (kē tōn′), *n.* a shirtlike garment worn by the Phoenicians which was later adopted by the Greeks. [< a Phoenician word < Akkadian *kitinnu* or Hebrew *kŭttōneth*]

***ke|tone** (kē′tōn), *n.* any one of a class of organic compounds with the general formula RCOR. Ketones are formed by the oxidation of the secondary alcohols, each consisting of a carbonyl (—CO) radical attached to two univalent hydrocarbon radicals, or to derivatives of either of these, such as acetone. Some ketones are important in perfumes. Others are solvents for plastics, textiles, and paints. *Camphor is a ketone used in certain medicines and for making celluloid.* [< German *Keton*, short for *Aketon* < French *acétone* acetone]

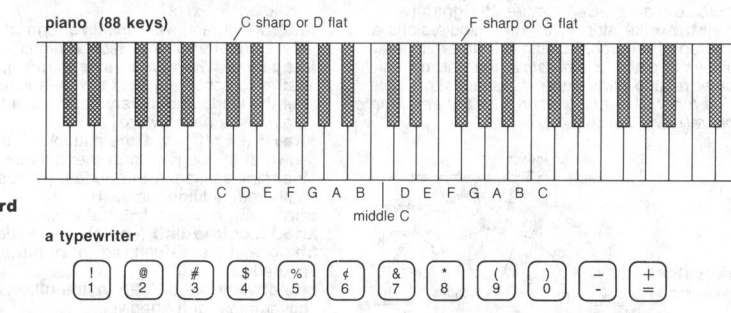

***ketone** R₂C=O (R, R, C=O)

ketone bodies, = acetone bodies.

ke|ton|ic (ki ton′ik), *adj.* of or having to do with ketones.

ke|to|nu|ri|a (kē′tə nu̇r′ē ə, -nyu̇r′-), *n.* = acetonuria.

ke|tose (kē′tōs), *n.* a sugar containing the bivalent —CO radical. [< *ket*(one) + *-ose*²]

ke|to|sis (ki tō′sis), *n.* too much acetone in the body. Ketosis takes place in diabetes and acidosis. [< *ket*(one) + *-osis*]

ke|tos|ter|oid (ki tos′tə roid), *n.* any one of a group of steroid hormones which originate in the adrenal glands and testes. Their presence in urine is used to determine the functioning conditions of these organs. [< *keto*(ne) + *steroid*]

ket|tle (ket′əl), *n.* **1** a metal container for boiling liquids or cooking fruit and vegetables; pot: *The kettle full of soup was boiling on the stove.* SYN: caldron. **2** = teakettle. **3** = kettledrum. **4** = kettle hole. [Old English *cetel*, ultimately < Latin *catillus* (diminutive) < *catīnus* vessel]

ket|tle|drum (ket′əl drum′), *n.* a drum consisting of a hollow hemisphere of brass or copper with parchment stretched across the top; timbal; timpano; tympanum. The top can be tuned to a definite pitch by adjusting the tension. See picture under **drum**¹.

ket|tle|drum|mer (ket′əl drum′ər), *n.* a person who plays a kettledrum; timpanist.

kettle hole, a deep, round cavity in rock or detritus, especially one left in glacial drift by the melting of a mass of ice. See picture at **glacier**.

kettle of fish, **1** an awkward state of affairs; mess; muddle: *Here's a pretty kettle of fish ... you have brought upon us* (Henry Fielding). **2** a thing to be considered; matter; situation: *National politics are a very different kettle of fish from those of the provinces* (London Times).

ke|tu|bah (kə tü′bə), *n.* the Jewish religious marriage contract, signed by a couple before the wedding, which states their marital obligations under Jewish law. [< Hebrew *kethūbhah* (literally) a writing, a written document]

kev or **Kev** (kev), *n.* a thousand electron volts. [< *k*(ilo) *e*(lectron) *v*(olts)]

kev|el (kev′əl), *n. Nautical.* a cleat, peg, or timber to which heavy ropes such as tackle and sheets are fastened; cavel. [< Old North French *keville*, Old French *cheville* < Vulgar Latin *cāvīcula*, for Latin *clāvīcula* (diminutive) < *clāvis* key]

Kev|lar (kev′lär), *n. Trademark.* a strong, lightweight synthetic fiber developed to substitute for steel in automobile tires, cables, and many other products: *Kevlar ... is lighter than nylon and five times as strong as steel* (Newsweek).

Ke|wee|naw|an (kē′wə nô′ən), *adj., n.* —*adj.* of or having to do with the latest period of the Proterozoic era, before the Cambrian and after the Huronian: *the Keweenawan formations.* —*n.* **1** the latest period of the Proterozoic era, before the Cambrian and after the Huronian. It was characterized by the formation of copper-bearing rocks. **2** its rocks or rock formations. [< *Keweenaw*, a promontory on Lake Superior where these rocks are found + *-an*]

kew|pie doll (kyü′pē), **1** a fairy in the form of a fat baby with wings like Cupid's and a topknot of hair. **2** a doll patterned from Rose O'Neill's drawings of these, usually made of celluloid or plastic. **3 Kewpie Doll**, *Trademark.* a name for a doll of this kind. [(apparently diminutive) < *Cupid*]

key¹ (kē), *n., pl.* **keys**, *adj., v.*, **keyed**, **key|ing**. —*n.* **1a** a small metal instrument for fastening and unfastening the lock of a door, a padlock, or any similar device: *the key to a strongbox.* (*Figurative.*) *The love of books, the golden key That opens the enchanted door* (Andrew Lang). **b** anything shaped or used like it: *a key to open a tin can, the key of a clock, a Phi Beta Kappa key.* **2** *Figurative.* **a** an answer to a puzzle or problem: *The key to this puzzle will be published in tomorrow's edition of the newspaper. This does not ... mean, however, that we should try to find the key to the events of our time in the conclusions which these men of another time drew from the events of theirs* (Edmund Wilson). **b** a sheet or book of answers to mathematical or other problems: *a key to a test.* **c** a systematic explanation of abbreviations or symbols in a dictionary or map. The pronunciation key in this dictionary lists all the symbols of the sounds in English that are used in the pronunciations in this book, and also gives examples of words that contain these sounds. **d** an outline map or chart intended to make a full map or chart more intelligible. **3** *Figurative.* a place that commands or gives control of a sea or a district because of its position: *Gibraltar is the key to the Mediterranean.* **4** *Figurative.* an important or essential person or thing: *Hard work is one key to success.* **5a** a pin, bolt, wedge, or other piece put in a hole or space to hold parts together, such as one put between a shaft and a wheel, to lock the wheel to the shaft. **b** a wedge forced into a slot of a canvas stretcher to tighten the surface of a canvas. **c** = keystone. **6a** one of a set of levers pressed down by the fingers in playing some musical instruments, such as a piano, organ, or wind instrument: *Don't hit the keys so hard.* **b** one of a set of levers in a typewriter or similar instrument, pressed by the fingers in the same way as the keys of a piano. **c** = telegraph key. **7** a scale or system of tones in music related to one another in a special way and based on a particular note: *a song written in the key of C.* **8** a device to turn a bolt or nut. Keys were used to wind watches from about 1400 to 1875 and are still used to wind some kinds of clocks. **9** *Figurative.* **a** a tone of voice: *to speak in a shrill key.* **b** a style of thought or expression: *The widow wrote in a sorrowful key.* **10** *Botany.* = key fruit. **11** *Biology.* a guide to the identification of a group of plants or animals, having the outstanding determining characteristics arranged in a systematic way. **12** the matter inserted in an advertisement to determine the quantity of response. —*adj.* very important; controlling; fundamental: *key factors, key executives, the key industries of the nation.* SYN: pivotal. —*v.t.* **1** to fasten or adjust with a key: *The hub is often splined instead of keyed to the shaft.* **2** to regulate the pitch of; tune: *to key a piano in preparation for a concert.* **3** *Figurative.* to adjust (a speech or other written or spoken matter) to give it a particular tone: *The letter was keyed to a tone of defiance.* **4** to lock, especially with a key; lock up. **5** to provide with a key or keys. **6** to put code letters or some other device in (an advertisement) in order to determine the quantity of response, as from a particular periodical or on a particular day. —*v.i.* **1** to tighten a canvas on a stretcher with a wedge: *Stretchers are made about ¼ inch short to allow for keying* (Ralph Mayer). **2** *U.S. Football.* to use the movements of an offensive player to guide a defensive player's movements: *"We —the four defensive linemen—key on him, and we always have a linebacker key on him"* (Gerry Philbin).

key up, **a** *Figurative.* to raise the courage or nerve of (to the point of doing something): *I keyed myself up to ask for a higher salary.* **b** to raise to a higher pitch: *He keyed up the violin for the concert.*

[Old English *cǣg*]

key² (kē), *n., pl.* **keys**. a low island or reef; cay. There are keys in the West Indies and south of Florida. [< Spanish *cayo* < Taino *cayo*, or *caya* small island; influenced by English *key*¹]

key³ (kē), *n., pl.* **keys**. *Slang.* a kilogram of a drug, especially hashish. [< the pronunciation of *ki* in *kilo*]

key bit, the part of a key that enters the lock, cut to correspond with a particular set of notches inside of a lock.

***key|board** (kē′bôrd′, -bōrd′), *n., v.* —*n.* set of keys in a piano, organ, typewriter, calculating machine, or typesetting machine. See picture below. —*v.t.* to feed (information) by the use of an electronic keyboard: *After the encyclopedia, consisting of many volumes, has been keyboarded into the computer, the computer under instruction withdraws the material on a specified subject from its memory storage and sets it up for publication as a separate book or pamphlet* (Scientific American). —*v.i.* to use a keyboard.

key chain, a small chain for attaching keys and other small articles.

key club, *U.S.* a night club that admits only members, who usually receive a key to the premises.

Key or **key deer**, a tiny deer, less than 30 inches high, found in the Florida Keys. It is considered to be a variety of the white-tailed deer.

keyed (kēd), *adj.* **1** having keys: *a keyed flute or trombone.* **2a** pitched in a particular key: *That sonata is keyed in E minor.* **b** stimulated to a particular point: *The contestants were keyed to the highest pitch.* **c** *Figurative.* adjusted; fitted: *A "brain" made essentially of cold cathode trigger tubes, which translate the keyed impulses into each of the 144 output selections* (New Scientist). **3** fastened or strengthened with a key. **4** constructed with a keystone.

keyed-up (kēd′up′), *adj.* agitated: *The police feared the keyed-up crowd would riot.*

key fruit, *Botany.* a dry, winged fruit; samara: *The seeds of the elm, ash, and maple are contained in key fruits.*

key grip, *Theater.* the chief stagehand.

key|hole (kē′hōl′), *n., adj.* —*n.* **1** a small opening in a lock through which a key is inserted to turn the lock. **2** a hole made to receive a peg or key used in carpentry or engineering; keyway. **3** the free throw lane of a basketball court, so named because of its shape. —*adj. Informal.* dealing with private, confidential, or intimate matters: *keyhole news, keyhole journalism. ... keyhole chitchat about "mad, gay, heartbreaking" Hollywood* (Time).

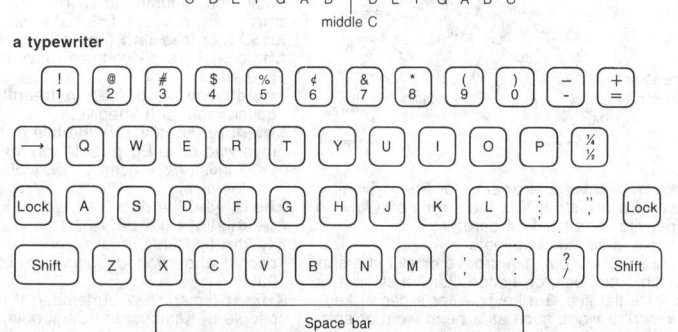

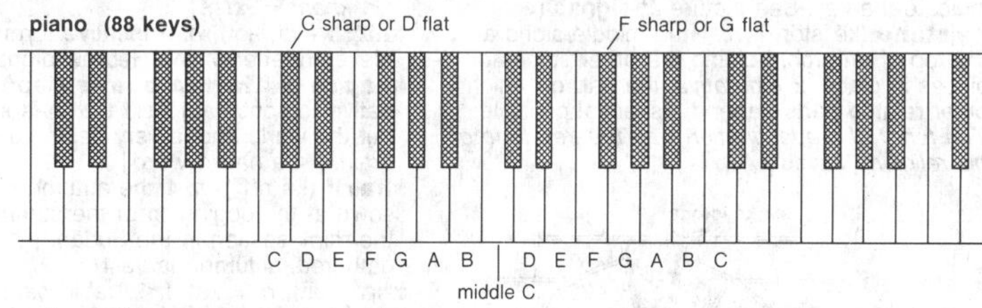

***keyboard**

keyhole saw, = compass saw.

key|less (kē′lis), *adj.* without a key or keys: *a keyless lock.*

key|light (kē′līt′), *n. Photography.* main source of directed light falling on an object, or scene.

key|man (kē′man′), *n., pl.* **-men.** a telegraph operator.

key money, 1 money paid by a prospective tenant for the right to rent: *[He] exploited the housing shortage to extort key money* (London Times). **2** a sum of money deposited by a new tenant as security when he obtains his key.

Keynes|i|an (kān′zē ən), *adj., n.* **—*adj.*** of or having to do with John Maynard Keynes (1883-1946) or his theories of economics: *After 1945, Belgium stood for laissez-faire and orthodox economics, while Holland seemed a model Keynesian economy* (Economist).
—*n.* an advocate of the theories of Keynes.

Keynes|i|an|ism (kān′zē ə niz′əm), *n.* the economic theories of John Maynard Keynes, especially opposition to laissez faire and emphasis on government spending to encourage investment and increase employment.

key|note (kē′nōt′), *n., v.,* **-not|ed, -not|ing. —*n.* 1** the tone on which a scale or system of tones in music is based; tonic. **2** *Figurative.* the main idea; guiding principle: *World peace was the keynote of his speech.*
—*v.t.* 1 to present the keynote address at a convention of (a political campaign, party, or other special group). **2** *Music.* to give the keynote of. **3** *Figurative.* to give the main idea of: *Mr. Gottlieb, the first to speak at the hearings, keynoted the artists' worries* (New York Times).
—*v.i.* to give a keynote address.

keynote address or **speech**, a speech, usually at a political gathering, that presents the principal issues in which those present are interested.

key|not|er (kē′nō′tər), *n.* a person who makes the keynote address of a political campaign, party, or other special group.

keynote speaker, = keynoter.

key|pad (kē′pad′), *n. British.* a small console with a set of buttons for operating an electronic calculator or other machine: *Telephones equipped with a 12-button keypad can be used for data communication or retrieval* (London Times).

key|phone (kē′fōn′), *n. British.* a push-button telephone: *Looking exactly like a conventional instrument, except for its 10-button keypad in place of the rotary dial, the keyphone is being sold to the public as "the phone with the modern touch"* (New Scientist).

key punch, a machine having a keyboard similar to a typewriter, used to code information by punching patterns of holes in cards or tapes.

key|punch (kē′punch′), *v.t.* **1** to punch holes in (a punch card) using a key punch: *Cards are keypunched with index codes describing the record they carry in microfilm* (Scientific American). **2** to record or code (information) by using a key punch: *The same approach applies to literature references, which we keypunch on to IBM cards rather than type* (New Scientist). **—key′-punch′er,** *n.*

key ring, a ring on which keys are kept together.

Keys (kēz), *n.pl.* the body of 24 representatives forming the lower house of the legislature of the Isle of Man.

key signature, *Music.* one or more sharps or flats after the clef at the beginning of a staff to indicate the key. See picture at **signature.**

***key|stone** (kē′stōn′), *n.* **1** the middle stone at the top of an arch, holding the other stones or pieces in place. **2** *Figurative.* the part on which other related parts depend; essential principle: *The tenet of predestination was the keystone of his religion* (Macaulay).

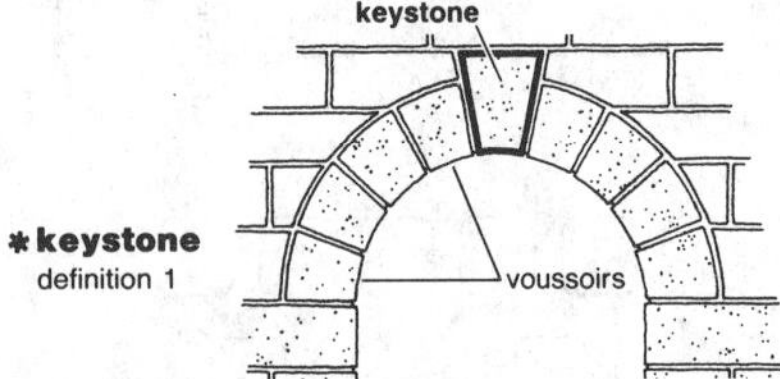

***keystone**
definition 1

Keystone State, a nickname for Pennsylvania.

key|stroke (kē′strōk′), *n.* the stroke of a key on a typewriter or other keyboard.

key tone, a sounded keynote

key|way (kē′wā′), *n.* **1** a groove or slot in a shaft in which a pin, bolt, or wedge fits. **2** a slit in a lock for a flat key. **3** a keyhole for a peg or key.

key word, a word, such as a head word or entry word, that serves as a guide to find other words, articles, or topics, in a list.

kg., **1** keg or kegs. **2** kilogram or kilograms.

K.G., Knight of the Order of the Garter.

KGB (no periods) or **K.G.B.**, the official secret police agency of the Soviet Union, in charge of state security. [< Russian *K(omissija) G(osudarstvennoj) B(ezopasnosti)* Commission of State Security]

kgf (no periods), kilogram-force (a unit of force in the MKS system, used for calibration of specific instruments).

kgm (no periods), kilogram-meter.

Kha (kä), *n., pl.* **Kha** or **Khas.** a member of a tribe inhabiting the valleys of southern Laos.

khad|dar (kud′ər), *n.* ≐ khadi. [< Hindi *khādar*]

***kha|di** (kä′dē), *n.* a very coarse, handloomed, white cotton cloth of India, worn as a garment about the loins and across the shoulder, notably by Gandhi and his followers. [< Hindi *khādī*]

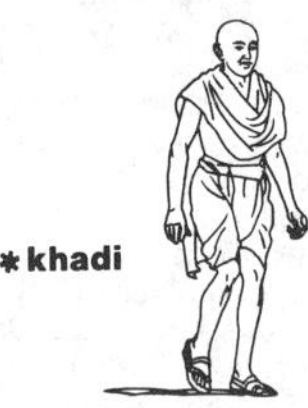
***khadi**

khak|i (kak′ē, kä′kē), *n., pl.* **khak|is,** *adj.* **—*n.* 1** the color of dust; a dull yellowish-brown color. **2** a heavy, twilled cotton cloth of this color, much used for soldiers' uniforms and tents. **3** Also, **khakis. a** a uniform or uniforms made of this cloth, usually worn in the summer: *Khakis will be worn in the parade.* **b** a uniform made of a similar woolen fabric.
—*adj.* 1 dull yellowish-brown: *khaki pants.* **2** made of khaki.
[< Hindi *khākī* (originally) dusty < Persian *khāk* dust]

kha|lee|fate (kā′lə fāt, kal′ə-), *n.* = caliphate.

kha|lif (kā′lif, kal′if), *n.* = caliph.

kha|li|fa (kə lē′fə), *n.* = caliph.

kha|li|fat (kā′lə fat, kal′ə-), *n.* = caliphate.

kha|li|fate (kā′lə fāt, kal′ə-), *n.* = caliphate.

Khal|kha (kal′kə), *n., pl.* **-kha** or **-khas. 1** a member of a Mongolian people constituting the largest population group of the Mongolian People's Republic. **2** the language of this people. It is the official language of their country.

Kham|ba (käm′bə), *n., pl.* **-ba** or **-bas.** a member of a tribe inhabiting the mountains of southeastern Tibet, noted for their resistance to Chinese colonization.

kham|seen (kam sēn′), *n.* = khamsin.

kham|sin (kam′sin, kam sēn′), *n.* an oppressive, hot, southerly wind that blows from the Sahara toward Egypt and Israel at intervals, usually in spring and early summer. Also, **hamsin, kamsin, kamseen.** [< Arabic *khamsīn* < *rih al-khamsīn* (the) wind (of) the fifty (days)]

khan[1] (kän, kan), *n.* **1** the former title of a ruler among Tartar or Mongol tribes, or of the emperor of China during the Middle Ages. **2** a title of respect in Iran, Afghanistan, India, and other parts of central Asia. Also, **kahn, kan.** [< Turkic *khan*]

khan[2] (kän, kan), *n.* an inn without furnishings in Turkey and nearby countries; caravansary. [< Persian *khān*]

khan|ate (kä′nāt, kan′āt), *n.* **1** the territory ruled by a khan. **2** the position or authority of a khan. [< *khan*[1] + *-ate*[3]]

khaph (ʜäf, ʜôf), *n.* a fricative form of *kaph,* the eleventh letter of the Hebrew alphabet.

khap|ra or **Khap|ra beetle** (kap′rə), a beetle native to southeast Asia that has spread throughout the world and is very destructive to stored grain. [< a native word]

kha|rif (kə rēf′), *n.* **1** the autumn crop in India, sown at the beginning of the summer rains. **2** the rainy season in the Sudan. [< Arabic *kharīf* gathered, autumn, harvest]

khat (kät), *n.* = kat. [< Arabic *qat*]

khed|a or **khed|ah** (ked′ə), *n.* = keddah.

khe|di|val (kə dē′vəl), *adj.* of or having to do with a khedive.

khe|di|vate (kə dē′vāt), *n.* the office, authority, or government of a khedive.

khe|dive (kə dēv′), *n.* the title of the Turkish viceroys who ruled Egypt between 1867 and 1914. [< Turkish *hidiv* viceroy of Egypt < Persian *khidīv* ruler]

khe|di|vi|al (kə dē′vē əl), *adj.* = khedival.

khe|di|vi|ate (kə dē′vē āt), *n.* = khedivate.

Khi|tan (kē′tän′), *n.* a member of a Ural-Altaic people who invaded China from Manchuria in A.D. 905.

Khmer (kmer), *n.* **1** a member of the dominant people of Kampuchea (Cambodia), who developed a great civilization under Indian influence in the 800's to 1300's; Kampuchean. **2** the national language of Kampuchea, of Mon-Khmer stock. [< the Khmer word for these people]

Khmer Rouge (kmer′rüzh′), the Communist guerrilla force (and in the mid-1970's the Communist government) of Cambodia (Kampuchea): *Once the Khmer Rouge had captured the country, it became apparent that they were determined to wipe out all vestiges of the preceding regime* (New Yorker). [< French *Khmer Rouge* (literally) Red Khmer]

Khoi|khoi (koi′koi′), *n.* = Hottentot. [< Hottentot *khoikhoi* men of men]

Khoi|san (koi′sän), *n.* a group of African languages, including the Bushman languages and Hottentot, characterized by click sounds.

khot|la (kot′lä), *n.* a meeting place of villagers in Lesotho. [< Sotho *khotla*]

khoum (küm), *n.* a monetary unit of Mauritania, equal to 1/5 of a ougiya. [< an Arabic word]

Khru|shchev|ism (krüsh chôf′iz əm, ʜrüsh-), *n.* Communism practiced by Nikita Khrushchev, Soviet premier from 1958 to 1964, stressing national interests and peaceful coexistence.

khud (kud), *n.* a deep ravine in the East Indies; precipitous cleft or chasm. [< Hindi *khaḍ*]

khur|ta (ku̇r′tä), *n.* a long, loose-fitting, collarless shirt worn in India. Also, **kurta.** [< Hindi *kurtā*]

kHz (no periods), kilohertz.

ki (kē), *n.* = ti[2]. [< Hawaiian *ki*]

KIA (no periods), killed in action (of a member of the U.S. armed forces).

ki|a|boo|ca wood (kī′ə bü′kə), = Amboina wood. [< Malay *kayubuku*]

ki|ang (kē ang′), *n.* a wild ass of Tibet, closely related to the onager but larger and with a narrower stripe along its back. Also, **kyang.** [< Tibetan *kyang*]

kiaugh (kyäʜ), *n. Scottish.* trouble; worry.

kib|ble[1] (kib′əl), *v.,* **-bled, -bling,** *n.* **—*v.t.*** to grind coarsely; crush into small pieces: *kibbled biscuits.* **—*n.*** a small piece, as of compressed meal for dog food. [origin uncertain]

kib|ble[2] (kib′əl), *n., v.,* **-bled, -bling. —*n.*** a large bucket for hoisting ore or debris from a mine.
—*v.t., v.i.* to hoist (ore or debris) in a kibble. [probably < German *Kübel*]

kib|butz (ki büts′), *n., pl.* **-butz|im** (-bü tsēm′). an Israeli communal settlement, especially a farm cooperative. Also, **kibutz.** [< Hebrew *qibbūṭṣ* (literally) gathering]

kib|butz|nik (ki büts′nik), *n.* a member of a kibbutz. [< Yiddish *kibutsnik* < *kibuts* kibbutz + *-nik*]

kibe (kīb), *n.* a chapped or ulcerated sore, inflammation, or swelling, especially on the heel, caused by exposure to cold. [origin uncertain]

kibed (kībd), *adj.* affected by kibes.

Ki|bei (kē′bā′), *n., pl.* **-beis.** a Japanese person born in the United States but educated in Japan. [< Japanese *Kibei* < *ki* return + *bei* the United States]

ki|bit|ka (ki bit′kə), *n.* **1** a Tartar circular tent of collapsible latticework covered with felt. **2** a Russian wagon or sledge with a rounded top or cover. [< Russian *kibitka* < Turkic *kibit*]

kib|itz (kib′its), *v.i. Informal.* **1** to look on as an outsider and also give unasked advice. **2** to watch a card game. [American English, back formation < *kibitzer*]

kib|itz|er (kib′it sər), *n. Informal.* **1** a person who gives unwanted advice; meddler: *The faculties in prep schools now enjoy ... freedom in expressing their views and experimenting with teaching methods without raising outcries from every last local kibitzer* (Newsweek). **2** a person watching a card game, especially one who insists on advising the players. [American English < *kibitzer,* Yiddish form of German *Kiebitz* kibitzer, pewit < dialectal *kiebitschen* visit stealthily]

kib|lah (kib′lə), *n.* **1** the direction, always toward the Kaaba at Mecca, in which Moslems turn when praying. **2** the act of turning to face toward Mecca in praying. [< Arabic *qiblah* that which is opposite]

ki|bosh (kī′bosh, ki bosh′), *n. Slang.* nonsense, humbug. Also, **kybosh.**
put the kibosh on, to finish off; squelch: *The boss put the kibosh on overlong coffee breaks.*

ki|butz (ki büts′), *n., pl.* **-butz|im** (-bü tsēm′). = kibbutz.

kick (kik), *v., n.* **—*v.i.* 1** to strike out with the foot: *That horse kicks when anyone comes near him.* **2** to spring back or recoil when fired: *This shotgun kicks.* **3** *Informal, Figurative.* to grumble; find fault; complain; object.
—*v.t.* 1 to strike with the foot: *to kick a ball. The horse kicked the boy.* **2** to strike with a strong impact: *The gun kicked my shoulder.* **3a** to drive, force, or move (a thing) by or as if by kicking: *to kick a ball along the ground, to kick off one's shoes.* **b** to force or make (one's way) by kicking. **4** to make (a score) by a kick: *to kick a field goal in football.* **5** *Slang, Figurative.* to get rid of; give up; break: *to kick the habit of smoking.*
—*n.* 1 the act of kicking; a blow with the foot: *The horse's kick knocked the boy down.* **2a** the

recoil or backward spring of a gun when it is fired: *The kick of the rifle disconcerts your aim* (James Fenimore Cooper). **b** a jerk or jolt. **3** *Informal, Figurative.* a complaint or a cause for complaint; objection; opposition. **4** *Slang, Figurative.* **a** thrill; excitement: *The children got a kick out of going to the circus.* **b** the intoxicating or stimulating effect of alcohol in a drink, or of a drug. **c** *Slang.* a spree of indulging in something; binge; fad: *to go on a health food kick.* **5** *Slang.* vigor; energy; vim. **6** an indentation in the bottom of a glass bottle, diminishing its capacity. **7** *Slang.* a pocket. **8** a projection on the front of a pocketknife blade to prevent it from going too far when closed.

for kicks, *Slang.* for the pleasure to be derived from something: *He played the game just for kicks.*

kick around (or **about**), *Informal.* **a** to treat roughly or harshly; abuse: *The boys kicked around the old bottle till it broke. "Pretty soon you won't have Johnson to kick around any more"* (New York Times). **b** *Figurative.* to go about aimlessly: *He kicked around for several years before he settled down to work.* **c** *Figurative.* to consider or discuss; toy with: *My book is the first objective, impartial account of jazz. I've been kicking it around for twenty-five years* (New Yorker). **d** to be in danger of being damaged; lie about: *He left his instruments kicking about the office.*

kick back, a *Informal.* to spring back suddenly and unexpectedly: *The gun kicked back with great force.* **b** *Slang.* to return (a stolen item) to its owner: *The thief kicked back the wallet but kept the money.* **c** *Slang.* to return (a portion of money received as a fee), often as the result of coercion or a previous arrangement: *Most of their $5,100-a-year salaries could be kicked back into his million-dollar slush fund* (Newsweek).

kick in, *Slang.* **a** to pay what is due or expected: *The CBC started kicking in $5,000 a day for private detectives to guard employees' homes the clock around* (Maclean's). **b** to die: *Sick and jaded, the old horse finally kicked in.*

kick in the teeth. See under **teeth.**

kick off, a to put a football in play with a kick at the beginning of each half and after a score has been made: *The visiting team kicked off.* **b** *Slang, Figurative.* to begin: *... a farewell dinner and a 30-day European tour to help kick off his life of leisure* (New Yorker). **c** *Slang.* to die: *The general said that he preferred to kick off with his boots on.*

kick oneself, *Informal.* to reproach oneself: *How [he] must have kicked himself for missing an obvious trick like that* (Manchester Guardian Weekly).

kick one's heels. See under **heel**[1].

kick out, *Informal.* to expel or turn out with a kick, or in a humiliating or disgraceful way: *to be kicked out of school.*

kick over, *Informal.* to start to ignite: *The dead battery wouldn't kick over the car's engine. The oil furnace .., would not tick or kick over* (Alistair Cooke).

kick over the traces. See under **trace**[2].

kicks, *Slang.* **a** trousers: *Old Georgy's bang-up togs and kicks ...* (Thomas Moore). **b** shoes: *Let's put on some kicks and go for a walk.*

kick the bucket. See under **bucket.**

kick up, a to raise (dust or some other substance) by or as if by kicking: *The soldiers kicked up a cloud of dust as they rode off.* **b** *Informal, Figurative.* to bring about; start: *to kick up a rumpus.* **c** *Informal, Figurative.* to stir up; excite: *Springfield is so kicked up about the success of its program that it has undertaken to raise another $650,000* (Time).

kick up one's heels. See under **heel**[1].

kick upstairs, *Informal.* to promote (a person) to a higher but less powerful or important position: *In May 1960 Brezhnev was kicked upstairs from the Secretariat to the largely ceremonial chairmanship of the Presidium of the party* (Time).

more kicks than halfpence, more harshness than kindness: *like monkey's allowance ... more kicks than halfpence* (Scott).

[origin uncertain] —**kick'a|ble,** *adj.*

Kick|a|poo (kik'ə pü), *n., pl.* **-poos. 1** a member of a tribe of Algonkian Indians formerly living in Wisconsin and Illinois. **2** the Algonkian language of this tribe. [American English < an Algonkian word meaning "he stands about"]

kick|back (kik'bak'), *n.* **1** *Slang.* the amount or portion returned, especially as a fee. If you were paid $150 a month and paid back $50 a month to your employer, the $50 would be a kickback. *Waterfront Commission continued its investigation into alleged gambling and kickback by longshoremen* (New York Times). **2** *Slang.* a returning of stolen goods. **3** a sudden violent or vigorous reaction, usually unexpected: *Sometimes you don't realize that an apparently simple thing may have a political kickback* (Maclean's). [American English < *kick* + *back*[2]]

kick|ball (kik'bôl'), *n.* a children's game similar to baseball, in which a large ball is kicked instead of being hit with a bat.

kick board, a wood or plastic board used to help a person float while learning to swim.

kick|box|ing (kik'bok'sing), *n.* an Oriental method of boxing in which both gloved hands and the feet are used to deliver blows.

kick|down (kik'doun'), *n.* an automotive device for changing to a lower gear, especially by depressing the accelerator.

kick|er (kik'ər), *n.* **1** a person, animal, or thing that kicks. **2** *Informal, Figurative.* a person who complains; protester; objector. **3** *Slang.* something which gives extra impetus to a device, or acts as a catalyst to a reaction or idea: *The crystals were vaporized, and acted as a kicker for the hot air* (Wall Street Journal). **4** a machine used in tanning to knead oil into hides in order to soften them. **5** *Slang.* an outboard motor. **6** a high card held with a pair on a two-card draw in draw poker. **7** *Cricket.* a thrown or bowled ball which does not bounce straight. **8** a baby's shoe that is used before it can walk.

kick|off (kik'ôf', -of'), *n., adj.* —*n.* **1** a kick that puts a football in play at the beginning of each half and after a score has been made. It is made from the defending team's 40-yard line. **2** *Informal, Figurative.* any move made to begin: *At Nelson's campaign kickoff his grandfather's spirit had been visibly present in the form of the William Cowper bust* (Harper's).
—*adj. Informal.* **1** serving to start off or set in motion: *reported the totals yesterday to 100 persons at a kickoff meeting in City Hall* (New York Times). **2** *Figurative.* introductory: *a kickoff speech, a kickoff TV spectacular.*

kick pleat, a vertical pleat in a skirt which allows greater fullness for walking.

kicks (kiks), *n.pl.* See under **kick.**

kick|shaw (kik'shô'), *n.* **1** a fancy article of food; delicacy: *His mouth was that of an epicure, one who had sampled every vintage and kickshaw of the gourmet's art* (New Yorker). **2** a trifle; trinket. [spelling adaptation of French *quelque chose* something]

kick|shaws (kik'shôz'), *n.* = kickshaw.

kick|stand (kik'stand'), *n.* a metal rod attached to the frame of a bicycle or motorcycle to support the vehicle when not in use.

kick starter or **start,** a self-starter actuated by a downward kick or pressure on a pedal: *a motorcycle kick starter.*

kick turn, a type of skiing turn made while stationary, by lifting one ski to a vertical position, then placing it on the ground in nearly the opposite direction before raising and turning the other ski.

kick|up (kik'up'), *n. Slang.* a disturbance; fuss: *In recent years there have been kickups over many rules, notably those which control publications and societies* (Punch).

kick|y (kik'ē), *adj.,* **kick|i|er, kick|i|est. 1** apt to kick: *a kicky mule.* **2** *Slang.* exciting: *The rock'n'-roll fashion show is the kickiest thing to come along since the trampoline lost its bounce* (Time).

kid[1] (kid), *n., adj., v.,* **kid|ded, kid|ding.** —*n.* **1** a young goat. **2** its flesh, used as food. **3** its skin, used as fur. **4** leather made from the skin of a young goat, used for gloves and shoes; kidskin: *These gloves are of kid.* **5** *Informal.* a child: *I started as an average kid, I finished as a thinkin' man* (Rudyard Kipling). **6** *U.S. Informal.* a person of any age (used especially as a familiar form of address): *Say, kid, I hear you got engaged.*
—*adj.* **1** made of kid leather or other soft leather resembling kid. **2** *Informal.* younger: *She teased her kid brother.*
—*v.i., v.t.* to give birth to (a young goat).
kids, gloves or shoes made of kid: *His great hands ... are encased in lemon-coloured kids* (Thackeray).
[< Scandinavian (compare Old Icelandic *kith*)]

kid[2] (kid), *v.,* **kid|ded, kid|ding,** *n. Slang.* —*v.t., v.i.* **1** to tease playfully; talk in a joking way; banter: *He's always kidding. He had kidded him affectionately ... for giving somebody a promissory note without noticing how much it was for* (Edmund Wilson). **2** to humbug; fool.
—*n.* humbug; fooling.
kid oneself, *Informal.* to deceive oneself; rationalize: *In spite of her acute sense of the ways in which people tell lies, one feels she is kidding herself* (New York Review of Books).
[perhaps < *kid*[1] in sense of "treat as a child"]
—**kid'ding|ly,** *adv.*

kid[3] (kid), *n.* **1** a small tub. **2** a wooden dish in which food was formerly served to sailors. [perhaps variant of *kit*[1]]

kid|der (kid'ər), *n. Slang.* a person who kids.

Kid|der|min|ster (kid'ər min'stər), *n.* a type of carpet made of yarn dyed before weaving. [< *Kidderminster,* a town in Worcestershire]

kid|die (kid'ē), *n.* = kiddy.

kiddie car, = kiddy car.

kid|dle (kid'əl), *n.* **1** a weir or barrier in a stream, fitted with nets or other devices for catching fish. **2** a similar arrangement of stakes and network on a beach. [< Anglo-French *kidel,* Old French *quidel;* origin uncertain]

kid|do (kid'ō), *n., pl.* **-dos** or **-does.** *U.S. Slang.* kid[1] (def. 6): *"Call him yourself, kiddo," said Mr. Hubble* (Harper's).

kid|dush (kid'əsh), *n.* a Hebrew prayer said over a cup of wine or over bread in consecration of the Sabbath or a holiday. [< Hebrew *qiddūsh* sanctification]

kid|dy (kid'ē), *n., pl.* **-dies. 1** *Informal.* a little child. **2** a little kid (young goat).

kiddy car, a small, three-wheeled vehicle that a child can ride while pushing it by his feet on both sides.

kid-glove (kid'gluv'), *adj.* **1** wearing kid gloves. **2** *Informal.* delicate; gentle; careful: *The Communists have given him kid-glove VIP treatment* (Newsweek).

kid-glove orange, a mandarin or a tangerine orange.

kid gloves, gloves made of soft kidskin.
handle with kid gloves, to treat with great care; treat with consideration and delicacy: *The artist was very temperamental, and had to be handled with kid gloves.*

kid|let (kid'lit), *n.* a little kid (young goat).

kid|ling (kid'ling), *n.* = kidlet.

kid|nap (kid'nap), *v.t.,* **-napped, -nap|ping** or **-naped, -nap|ing.** to steal or carry off (anyone, especially a child) by force; seize and hold (a person) against his will by force or by fraud: *Four men kidnapped the boy, but the police soon caught them and rescued the boy.* SYN: abduct. [< *kid*[1] child + *nap* snatch away, early variant of *nab*] —**kid'nap|per, kid'nap|er,** *n.*

***kid|ney** (kid'nē), *n., pl.* **-neys. 1** one of the pair of organs in the body of mammals, birds, amphibians, and reptiles that separate waste matter and water from the blood. The kidneys pass waste matter off through the bladder as urine. **2** the kidney or kidneys of an animal, cooked for food: *beefsteak and kidney pie.* **3** *Figurative.* **a** nature; disposition; temperament: *a man of my kidney ... that am as subject to heat as butter* (Shakespeare). SYN: constitution. **b** kind; sort; class: *We don't like cowards, sneaks, tattletales, or any person of that kidney. He paraded up and down the streets with a crew of hard swearers at his heels ... heroes of his own kidney* (Washington Irving). SYN: stamp. [origin uncertain] —**kid'ney|like',** *adj.*

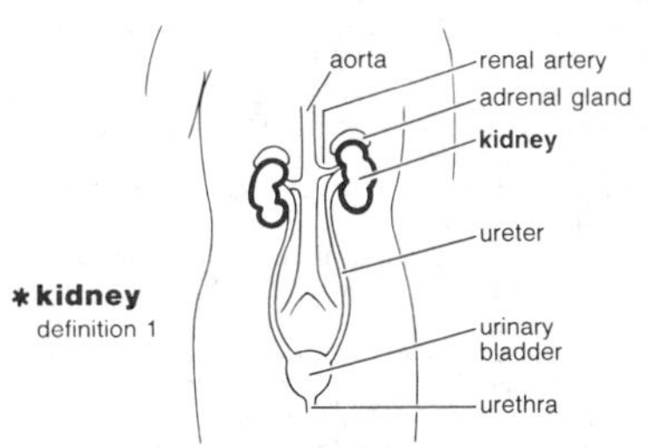

***kidney** definition 1

kidney bean, 1 a large, red bean, shaped like a kidney and used as a vegetable. **2** the plant that it grows on. **3** seed of the scarlet runner.

kidney corpuscle, = renal corpuscle.

kidney machine, a machine used in place of the kidney; hemodialyzer.

kid|ney-shaped (kid'nē shāpt'), *adj.* having the general shape of a long oval indented at one side.

kidney stone, a calculus or concretion that sometimes forms in the kidney.

kidney vetch, a European perennial plant of the pea family, once used for healing wounds.

kidney worm, a nematode worm often entering pigs' livers, moving to other organs, and finally reaching maturity in the kidneys.

kids (kidz), *n.pl.* See under **kid**[1].

kid|skin (kid'skin'), *n., adj.* —*n.* leather made from the skin of young goats, used for gloves and shoes; kid.
—*adj.* made of this leather.

kid stuff, *Informal.* 1 something childish or immature; puerility: *The rumors [were] going around that the Lassie program was going to dump the kid stuff and go adult* (New Yorker). 2 something easy or simple; child's play: *Brahms' Paganini Variations are not kid stuff, either. They are recognized as one of the supreme tests of a pianist* (Harper's).

kid|vid (kid′vid), *n. U.S.* children's television programs as an industry: *In that special region of television land known as kidvid* (New York Times). [< *kid*[1] (def. 5) + *vid*(eo)]

kief (kēf), *n.* = kef.

Kief|fer (kē′fər), *n.* a hybrid variety of pear, grown especially in the southern United States. [< Peter *Kieffer*, 1812-1890, a French-American horticulturist]

kiel|ba|sa (kyel bä′sä), *n. Polish.* a sausage.

kier (kir), *n., v.* —*n.* a large vat in which yarn or cloth is boiled before bleaching or dyeing in order to remove wax, grease, or dirt.
—*v.t.* to boil or treat in a kier: *to kier yarns.* [probably < Scandinavian (compare Old Icelandic *ker* vessel)]

kie|rie (kir′ē), *n.* (in South Africa) a knobkerry.

Kier|ke|gaard|i|an (kēr′kə gär′dē ən), *adj., n.* —*adj.* of or having to do with the Danish philosopher Sören Kierkegaard (1813-1855) or his philosophy of religious existentialism.
—*n.* a student of Kierkegaard or his philosophy.

kie|sel|guhr or **kie|sel|gur** (kē′zəl gůr), *n.* a fine siliceous earth consisting of the fossil remains of diatoms, used as an abrasive, insulator, and filter, and in the manufacture of dynamite as an absorbent for nitroglycerin; diatomaceous earth; diatomite. [< German *Kieselgur* < *Kiesel* gravel + *Gur* earthy sediment, fermentation]

kie|ser|ite (kē′zə rīt), *n.* hydrous magnesium sulfate, usually occurring in fine, granular, white masses, used in making Epsom salts and in the manufacture of potash salts. *Formula:* $MgSO_4 \cdot H_2O$ [< German *Kieserit* < D. G. *Kieser*, former president of Jena Academy in the 1800's]

kif (kif), *n.* hemp, as the source of the narcotic hashish. [variant of *kef*]

ki|fi (kē′fē), *n.* = kif.

Ki|ku|yu (ki kü′yü), *n., pl.* **-yu** or **-yus**, *adj.* —*n.* 1 a member of one of the principal Negro tribes in Kenya. 2 the Bantu language of the Kikuyu.
2 **kikuyu.** = kikuyu grass.
—*adj.* of, having to do with the Kikuyu.

kikuyu grass, a perennial grass, native to Kenya, grown in Australia and elsewhere as a lawn grass and for fodder.

kil., kilometer or kilometers.

kil|am|pere (kil am′pir), *n.* = kiloampere.

kil|der|kin (kil′dər kin), *n.* 1 a unit of dry or liquid measure, equal to ½ of a barrel. 2 a cask holding this amount. 3 an old British unit of measure, equal to about 18 U.S. gallons. [variant of earlier *kinderkin*, apparently < Middle Dutch, variant of *kindeken* fourth of a tun, (diminutive) related to *kintal* < Medieval Latin *quintale* quintal]

kil|erg (kil′ėrg′), *n. Physics.* a unit of work equal to 1,000 ergs. [< *kil*(o)- + *erg*]

Kil|ken|ny cats (kil ken′ē), (in Irish legend) two cats that fought until only their tails remained (used to describe combatants who fight relentlessly). [< *Kilkenny*, a county, and its capital city, in Ireland]

kill[1] (kil), *v., n., adj.* —*v.t.* 1 to put to death; cause the death of; slay; slaughter: *The farmer killed a chicken with his ax.* 2 *Figurative.* to put an end to; get rid of; destroy: *to kill odors, to kill a laugh, to kill faith. As good almost kill a man as kill a good book* (Milton). 3a to cancel (a word, paragraph, item, or the like); delete. b to designate (printing type) as not to be used. 4 to defeat or veto (a legislative bill): *The insurance company's earnings figures were based on a tax gimmick which Congress was about to kill* (Harper's). 5 to destroy or neutralize the active qualities of: *to kill land in farming, to kill grain by overheating in grinding.* 6 *Figurative.* to spoil the effect of: *One color may kill another near it. General laughter killed the speaker's lofty climax.* 7 to use up (time): *We killed an hour at the zoo.* 8 *Informal.* to cause great pain or discomfort to: *My sore foot is killing me.* 9 *Informal, Figurative.* to overcome completely: *His jokes really kill me. Surely that wad touch her heart, Wha kills me wi' disdaining* (Robert Burns). 10 to hit (a ball in tennis and similar games) so hard that it cannot be returned. 11a to stop; stall: *to kill an engine.* b to cut off the electrical connection of (a circuit). 12 *Metallurgy.* to reduce the oxygen content of (a metal, especially steel) by the addition of deoxidizers such as aluminum to the molten metal.
—*v.i.* 1 to cause death; commit murder or slaughter: *"Thou shalt not kill."* 2 to be killed: *Roses may kill in a severe winter.*
—*n.* 1 the act of killing: *The hunter's kill was swift and sure.* 2 an animal or animals killed, especially by sportsmen or by beasts of prey: *If ye plunder his Kill from a weaker, devour not all in thy pride* (Rudyard Kipling). 3a the shooting down or destruction of an enemy missile or aircraft: *Later we discover that the package team came within 10 yards of the target, considered a "kill"* (Christian Science Monitor). b the missile or aircraft so destroyed: *An ace with the record of twenty and one-half kills in Europe in World War II* (New York Times). 4 a ball hit so hard, in tennis and similar games, as to be unreturnable.
—*adj.* killing; lethal: *kill capabilities.*
kill off, a to wipe out; exterminate: *They were being killed off, at the rate of fourteen hundred a year* (Edmund Wilson). b *Slang.* to spend; use up: *A few killings on the printed page is one of man's easiest known methods for killing off a few leisure hours* (Newsweek).
[Middle English *kyllen*, or *cullen*. Perhaps related to **quell**.]—**kill′a|ble**, *adj.*
—*Syn. v.t.* 1 **Kill, murder, slay** mean to cause death. **Kill** is the general word meaning to put to death or in any way cause the death of a person, animal, or plant: *Overwork killed him. Lack of water kills flowers.* **Murder** means to kill a person unlawfully, especially with premeditation: *He murdered his rich uncle.* **Slay**, chiefly literary or journalistic, means to kill a person or animal with violence, in battle, or by murdering: *The dragon was slain by Saint George.*

kill[2] (kil), *n. U.S. Dialect.* a stream, creek, or tributary river (used especially in place names of areas originally settled by the Dutch, such as *Catskill, Schuylkill, Kill Van Kull*). [American English < Dutch *kil*]

kill|dee (kil′dē′), *n., pl.* **-dees** or (*collectively*) **-dee.** = killdeer.

kill|deer (kil′dir′), *n., pl.* **-deers** or (*collectively*) **-deer.** a small wading bird that has a loud, shrill cry and two black bands across its breast. It is the largest and commonest plover of North America. [American English, imitative of its call]

killed (kild), *adj.* (of a vaccine, virus, or bacteria) made powerless to produce disease; inactivated: *The Salk vaccine is a "killed" vaccine, in contrast with the "live," or attenuated, vaccines presently used for diseases such as smallpox and diphtheria* (Wall Street Journal).

kill|er (kil′ər), *n.* 1 a person, animal, or thing that kills. 2 a criminal who recklessly or wantonly kills. SYN: butcher. 3 = killer whale.

killer bee, 1 a black honeybee of Africa, noted for its sensitivity and aggressive reaction to disturbances of its hive. It was imported to Brazil in 1956 and accidentally released to migrate and breed with native bees. 2 any one of numerous hybrid varieties of honeybee, developed from the African killer bee and native South American bees; Brazilian bee. Some varieties are noted for their aggressive behavior.

killer cell, a type of lymphocyte that attacks and destroys foreign or diseased cells.

killer dill|er (dil′ər), *Slang.* something or someone unusual or outstanding: *There is no doubt that the job of being Mayor is a killer diller* (New York Times). [varied reduplication of *killer*]

killer satellite, = hunter-killer satellite.

killer T cell, a type of T cell that destroys viral, bacterial, and other foreign matter in the body, especially with helper T cells.

killer whale, any one of several large mammals, related to the dolphins, that live in northern waters, traveling in schools and killing and eating large fish, seals, and even other whales; grampus. Killer whales are from 20 to 30 feet long and weigh from 3 to 10 tons.

kil|lick (kil′ik), *n.* 1 a small anchor or stone, used for mooring a boat. 2 any anchor. Also, **kelleg, kellick, kellock, killock.** [origin unknown]

kil|lie (kil′ē), *n.* = killifish.

kil|li|fish (kil′i fish′), *n., pl.* **-fish|es** or (*collectively*) **-fish.** any one of various small fishes found in shallow, fresh, brackish, or salt water in North America and used as bait. [probably < Dutch *kille*, earlier form of *kil* stream, kill]

kil|li|kin|ick or **kil|lick|in|ic** (kil′i kə nik′), *n.* = kinnikinick.

kill|ing (kil′ing), *adj., n.* —*adj.* 1 deadly; destructive; fatal: *a killing frost.* SYN: lethal, mortal. 2 overpowering; exhausting: *to work at a killing pace.* 3 *Informal, Figurative.* extremely funny.
—*n.* 1 murder; slaughter. 2 all the game brought down in a hunt; the total kill. 3 *Informal.* a sudden great financial success: *to make a killing in stocks.* —**kill′ing|ly**, *adv.*

killing bottle, a bottle containing poisonous fumes, usually of potassium cyanide or carbon tetrachloride, used for killing specimen insects without damaging their wings or other organs.

kill|joy (kil′joi′), *n.,* adj. —*n.* a person who spoils other people's fun. —*adj.* that destroys joy or pleasure: *killjoy admonitions.*

kil|lock (kil′ək), *n.* = killick.

***kiln** (kil, kiln), *n.,* v. —*n.* 1 a furnace or oven for burning, baking, or drying something. Some lumber is dried in a kiln. Limestone is burned in a kiln to make lime. Bricks are baked in a kiln.
2 a building with a furnace for drying lumber, grain, hops, or tobacco, or for making malt.
—*v.t.* to burn, bake, or dry in a kiln; kiln-dry: *sprouted grain is 'kilned' at a temperature of about 80° C. sufficient to stop germination* (H. J. Bunker).
[Old English *cyln*, or *cylen* < Latin *culīna* kitchen]

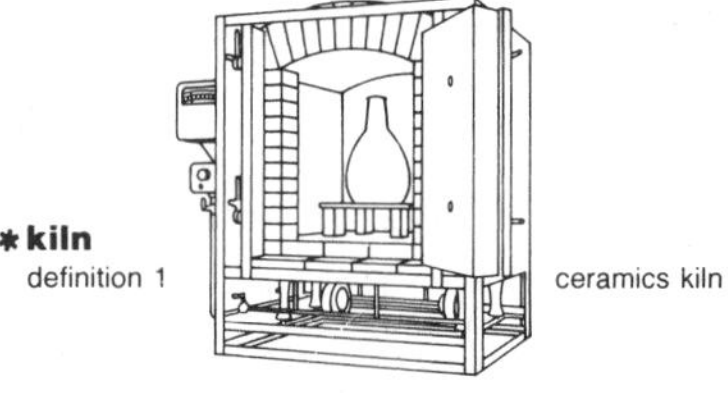

***kiln** definition 1 — ceramics kiln

kiln-dry (kil′drī′, kiln′-), *v.t.,* **-dried, -dry|ing.** to dry in a kiln: *kiln-dried lumber.*

ki|lo (kē′lō, kil′ō), *n., pl.* **-los.** 1 = kilogram. 2 = kilometer. [< French *kilo*]

Ki|lo (kē′lō, kil′ō), *n. U.S.* a code name for the letter *k*, used in transmitting radio messages.

kilo-, *prefix.* one thousand: *Kilogram = one thousand grams. Kilometer = one thousand meters.* [< French *kilo-*, < Greek *chīlioi* a thousand]

kilo., 1 kilogram or kilograms. 2 kilometer or kilometers.

kil|o|am|pere (kil′ō am′pir), *n.* a unit of electric current equivalent to 1,000 amperes.

kil|o|bar (kil′ə bär), *n.* a unit of pressure equal to 14,500 pounds per square inch.

kil|o|bit (kil′ə bit), *n.* a unit of information equal to 1,000 bits or binary digits.

kil|o|byte (kil′ə bīt′), *n.* a unit of computer information equal to one thousand bytes.

kil|o|cal|o|rie or **kil|o|cal|o|ry** (kil′ə kal′ər ē), *n., pl.* **-ries.** *Physics.* = large calorie.

kil|o|cu|rie (kil′ə kyůr′ē), *n.* 1,000 curies.

kil|o|cy|cle (kil′ə sī′kəl), *n.* 1 1,000 cycles. 2 1,000 cycles per second. The term kilocycle has been generally replaced by *kilohertz* as a unit of frequency of radio waves. *Abbr:* kc.

kil|o|dyne (kil′ə dīn′), *n. Physics.* a unit of force equal to 1,000 dynes.

kilog., kilogram or kilograms.

kil|o|gauss (kil′ə gous′), *n. Physics.* a unit of magnetic induction equal to 1,000 gauss.

kil|o|gram (kil′ə gram), *n.* a measure of mass and weight in the metric system equal to 1,000 grams, or 2.2046 pounds avoirdupois. *Abbr:* kg (no period). [< French *kilogramme*]

kilogram calorie, = kilocalorie.

kil|o|gram-me|ter (kil′ə gram mē′tər), *n.* a unit in measuring work or energy, equal to 7.2334 foot-pounds. It is the amount of work done in lifting one kilogram a distance of one meter.

kil|o|hertz (kil′ə hėrts′), *n.* 1,000 hertz, used especially as a replacement for kilocycle in referring to radio frequency. *Abbr:* kHz (no periods).

kil|ohm (kil′ōm′), *n.* a unit of electrical resistance equal to 1,000 ohms.

kil|o|joule (kil′ə joul′, -jül′), *n. Physics.* a unit of work or energy equal to 1,000 joules.

kilol., kiloliter or kiloliters.

kil|o|li|ter (kil′ə lē′tər), *n.* a measure of capacity in the metric system equal to 1,000 liters or one cubic meter; 264.17 U.S. gallons or 1.308 cubic yards. *Abbr:* kl. [< French *kilolitre*]

kilom., kilometer or kilometers.

kil|o|meg|a|cy|cle (kil′ə meg′ə sī′kəl), *n.* a unit of frequency equal to one billion cycles per second.

***kil|o|me|ter** (kə lom′ə tər, kil′ə mē′-), *n.* a measure of length in the metric system equal to 1,000 meters, or 3,280.8 feet (about ⅝ mile). *Abbr:* km (no period). [< French *kilomètre*]

***kilometer**

1 **kilometer** = 3,280.8 feet or 0.62137 statute mile

1 statute mile = 5,280 feet or 1.6093 kilometers

1 international nautical mile = 6,076.1 feet or 1.852 kilometers

kil|o|me|tre (kə lom′ə tər, kil′ə mē′-), *n. Especially British.* kilometer.

kil|o|met|ric (kil′ə met′rik), *adj.* 1 of a kilometer. 2 measured in kilometers.

kil|o|met|ri|cal (kil′ə met′rə kəl), *adj.* = kilometric.

kil|o|par|sec (kil′ə pär′sek), *n.* 1,000 parsecs or 3,262 light-years.

kil|o|rad (kil′ə rad′), *n.* a unit of radiation equal to 1,000 rads.

kil|o|stere (kil′ə stir′), *n.* a unit of volume in the metric system equal to 1,000 steres.

kil|o|ton (kil′ə tun′), *n.* **1** a measure of weight equal to 1,000 tons. **2** a measure of atomic power equivalent to the energy released by 1,000 tons of high explosive, specifically TNT. *Abbr:* kt.

kil|o|tonne (kil′ə tun′), *n. British.* = kiloton.

kil|o|volt (kil′ə vōlt′), *n.* a unit of electromotive force, equivalent to 1,000 volts.

kil|o|volt-am|pere (kil′ə vōlt am′pir), *n.* 1,000 volt-amperes.

kil|o|watt (kil′ə wot′), *n.* a measure of electrical power, equal to 1,000 watts, or 1.34 horsepower. *Abbr:* kw.

kil|o|watt|age (kil′ə wot′ij), *n.* effective electric power, expressed in kilowatts: *Public power groups . . . are arguing for a . . . program of reactor building that will make total kilowattage its final criterion* (Wall Street Journal).

kil|o|watt-hour (kil′ə wot our′), *n.* a unit of electrical energy, equal to the work done by one kilowatt acting for one hour.

kilt** (kilt), *n., v.* **—*n. **1** a pleated skirt, reaching to the knees, worn by men in the Scottish Highlands and some regiments of the British Army. A kilt is usually of tartan cloth. **2** any similar garment worn in other countries. [< verb]
—*v.t.* **1** *Scottish.* to tuck up; fasten up: *The wives maun kilt their coats, and wade into the surf* (Scott). **2** to gather in vertical pleats, fastened at the top only.
[probably < Scandinavian (compare Danish *kilte* tuck up)]

***kilt**
definition 1

kil|ter (kil′tər), *n.* **out of kilter,** *Informal.* out of working order; not in good condition: *Our old radio is so out of kilter that we cannot tune in most stations.* Also, *Dialect,* **kelter.** [origin uncertain]

kim|ber|lite (kim′bər līt), *n.* the peridotite rock in which diamonds occur in South Africa, the Congo, Siberia, and some other areas; hydrated silicate of magnesium. [< *Kimberl* (ey), a city in the Union of South Africa + *ite*[1]]

kim|chi or **kim|chee** (kim′chē), *n.* the national dish of Korea, a highly seasoned mixture of pickled cabbage, onions, and other vegetables. [< Korean *kimch'i*]

kim|mer (kim′ər), *n. Scottish.* cummer.

ki|mo|na (kə mō′nə), *n.* = kimono.

ki|mo|naed (kə mō′nəd), *adj.* = kimonoed.

***ki|mo|no** (kə mō′nə, -nō), *n., pl.* **-nos.** **1** a loose outer garment held in place by a wide sash, worn by men and women in Japan. **2** a woman's loose dressing gown fashioned after this. [< Japanese *kimono* < *ki* wear + *mono* thing]

***kimono**
definition 1

ki|mo|noed (kə mō′nəd, -nōd), *adj.* wearing a kimono: *. . . a group of kimonoed actors performing an ancient Japanese play* (Time).

kin[1] (kin), *n., adj.* **—*n.*** **1** a person's family or relatives; kindred: *All our kin came to the family reunion. One only daughter have I, no kin else* (Shakespeare). SYN: kinsfold. **2** family relationship; connection by birth or marriage: *What kin is she to you?* SYN: consanguinity. **3** a group of persons descended from a common ancestor; stock; clan. **4** *Dialect.* ancestral stock: *from noble kin.* **5** *Archaic.* a kinsman; relative: *Is he thy kin?* (Shakespeare).
—*adj.* related: *Your cousin is also kin to me.*
near of kin, closely related: *The man is near of kin unto us* (Ruth 2:20).
of kin, a related by blood ties: *She is of kin to me.* **b** related in character of qualities; akin: *You are of kin in heart to the prophet-murderers!* (John Cunningham Geikie).
[Old English *cynn.* Compare etym. under **kind**[2].]
—kin′less, *adj.*

kin[2] (kin), *n.* = kine[2].

-kin, *suffix.* little: *Lambkin = a little lamb.* [Middle English *-kin,* probably < Middle Dutch *-kijn,* and *-ken*]

ki|na (kē′nə), *n. pl.* **-na** or **-nas.** the unit of money of Papua New Guinea.

kin|aes|the|sia (kin′əs thē′zhə), *n.* = kinesthesia.

ki|nase (kī′nās, kin′ās), *n. Biochemistry.* an enzyme that activates the inactive form of another enzyme. [< *kin*(etic) + *-ase*]

kind[1] (kīnd), *adj.* **1** doing good rather than harm; friendly; sympathetic: *A kind girl tries to help people and make them happy. Taking a blind man across a street is a kind act. A kind and gentle heart he had* (Oliver Goldsmith). **2** gentle; humane: *Be kind to animals. Be ye kind one to another, tender-hearted, forgiving one another* (Ephesians 4:32). SYN: tender, merciful. **3** showing or characterized by kindness: *kind words.* **4** *Dialect.* affectionate; loving; fond: *styles where we stay'd to be kind, Meadows in which we met* (Tennyson). **5** *Dialect.* having the natural (good) qualities well developed: *a kind crop.* **6** *Obsolete.* natural; native. **7** *Obsolete.* proper; appropriate. [Old English *gecynde* natural < *gecynd* nature, kind[2]]
—*Syn.* **1 Kind, kindly, gracious** mean having or showing a generous, sympathetic, considerate attitude toward others. **Kind** implies that the attitude is genuine, natural, and sincere: *The kind old man helped the young man get a job.* **Kindly** is a milder term and suggests a sympathetic manner or appearance: *The teacher's kindly manner encouraged me to ask for help.* **Gracious** means kindly and courteous in manner, especially to younger people or those of lower position: *The famous singer is a gracious lady.*

kind[2] (kīnd), *n.* **1** a class; sort; type; variety: *He likes many kinds of candy. A kilt is a kind of skirt. What kind of cloth is this?* **2a** a natural group; race: *the rabbit kind* (Oliver Goldsmith). *Snakes belong to the serpent kind. All kinds of animals were in the ark.* **b** a person's, animal's, or plant's own race or species: *France, beloved of every soul that loves or serves its kind!* (Rudyard Kipling). **3** *Archaic.* natural disposition; nature: *The mother bird is gone to sea, As she had changed her kind* (William Cowper). **4** *Archaic.* mode of action; manner; way; fashion: *Mirthful he, but in a stately kind* (Tennyson).
after one's (or **its**) **kind,** *Archaic.* according to one's or its own nature: *God made the beast of the earth after his kind, and cattle after their kind, and every thing that creepth upon the earth after his kind* (Genesis 1:25).
in kind, a in goods or produce, not in money: *to make payments in kind.* **b** in something of the same sort: *He returned their insults in kind by insulting them.* **c** in characteristic quality: *difference in kind, not merely in degree.*
kind of, *Informal.* nearly; almost; somewhat; rather: *The room was kind of dark. This seemed kind of unfair.*
of a kind, a of the same sort; alike: *The cakes were all of a kind—chocolate.* **b** of a poor or mediocre quality: *Two boxes and a plank make a table of a kind.*
[Old English *gecynd*]
—*Syn.* **1 Kind, sort** mean a group of individuals or things alike in some way. **Kind** applies particularly to a group of the same nature or character, having enough closely similar essential qualities in their makeup to put them together as a class or division in some system of classification: *What kind of cake do you like best?* **Sort,** often interchangeable with *kind,* is usually vaguer, and sometimes means only of the same general description: *That sort of action disgusts me.*
▶**kind, sort.** *Kind* and *sort* are both singular nouns in form. In formal English, demonstrative adjectives used to modify them agree with them in number: *This kind of apple is likely to be wormy. That sort of behavior is out of place here.* A plural adjective is used only when *kind* or *sort* is plural: *Those kinds of fish are caught with special tackle.* In informal spoken English the plural idea implied in these words often results in constructions like *those kind of books* and *these sort of ideas.*

kin|der|gar|ten (kin′dər gär′tən), *n.* a school or class for children from about 4 to 6 years old, that educates them by the use of games, exercises, toys, and pleasant occupations. [< German *Kindergarten* < *Kinder* children + *Garten* garden]

kin|der|gart|ner or **kin|der|gar|ten|er** (kin′dər-gärt′nər), *n.* **1** a child who goes to kindergarten. **2** a teacher in a kindergarten.

kind-heart|ed (kīnd′här′tid), *adj.* having or showing a kind heart; kindly sympathetic: *He was by nature a friendly and kind-hearted man* (John Hawkins). **—kind′-heart′ed|ly,** *adv.* **—kind′-heart′ed|ness,** *n.*

kin|dle[1] (kin′dəl), *v.,* **-dled, -dling.** **—*v.t.*** **1** to set fire to; light; ignite: *Light the paper with a match to kindle the wood.* **2** *Figurative.* to stir up; arouse: *His cruelty kindled our anger.* SYN: inflame, excite, rouse, inspire. **3** *Figurative.* to light up; make bright: *Pleasure kindled the child's face.* **—*v.i.*** **1** to catch fire; begin to burn; burst into flame: *This damp wood will never kindle.* **2** *Figurative.* to become stirred up or aroused: *The warrior spirit of the cavaliers kindled at the thoughts* (Washington Irving). **3** *Figurative.* to become eager or animated; light up; brighten: *The boy's face kindled as he told about the circus.* [probably ultimately < Scandinavian (compare Old Icelandic *kynda* kindle) + English *-le*]
—kin′dler, *n.*
—*Syn.* *v.t.* **1 Kindle, ignite** mean to set on fire. **Kindle** means to cause something like wood to burn by setting fire to it, and often suggests some work in getting a fire going: *He kindled a fire in the fireplace.* **Ignite** suggests causing something highly flammable like very dry wood and grass, cleaning fluids, gas, or oil to burst into flame by putting a spark, tiny flame, or great heat to or near it: *Firemen tried to keep flying sparks from igniting the shingles of the house.*

kin|dle[2] (kin′dəl), *v.,* **-dled, -dling,** *n.* **—*v.t., v.i.*** *Dialect.* (of a female animal) to give birth to (young). **—*n.*** **1** a litter of kittens: *It seems only yesterday that they were a mere kindle of kittens* (New Yorker). **2** *Obsolete.* the young of any animal; a young one.
[Middle English *kindlen.* Compare German *Kind* child. See related etym. at **kind**[2].]

kind|less (kīn′dlis), *adj.* **1** without kindness; unkind. **2** *Obsolete.* unnatural. **—kind′less|ly,** *adv.*

kind|li|ness (kīnd′lē nis), *n.* **1** kindly feeling or quality: *These I have loved: . . . The cool kindliness of sheets* (Rupert Brooke). SYN: benevolence. **2** a kindly act: *The old lady thanked the boy for his kindliness when they got across the street.* SYN: favor.

kin|dling (kin′dling), *n.* **1** small pieces of wood for starting a fire. **2** the act of setting fire, exciting, or making bright. **3** a physiological process in which a series of small events, actions, or reactions lead up to, and perhaps stimulate a larger event, such as a seizure or permanent pattern of behavior: *Some scientists believe true kindling represents a kind of learning process and speculate that it may hold clues to the way permanent memories are formed in the brain* (Harold M. Schmeck, Jr.).

kindling temperature, the temperature to which matter must be raised to support active combustion.

kind|ly (kīnd′lē), *adj.,* **-li|er, -li|est,** *adv.* **—*adj.*** **1** kind; friendly; good-natured: *kindly faces, kindly people, kindly criticism.* SYN: See syn. under **kind**[1]. **2** *Figurative.* pleasant; agreeable; genial: *a kindly shower.* **3** *Obsolete.* natural. **4** *Obsolete.* that belongs to one by birth; native; hereditary. [Old English *gecyndelīc* < *gecynde* kind, nature + *-līc* - ly[2]]
—*adv.* **1** in a kind or friendly way; with good nature: *to make criticisms kindly. We thank you kindly for your help.* **2** with pleasure; agreeably; pleasantly: *The cat took kindly to its warm bed. He does not take kindly to criticism.* **3** properly. **4** *Obsolete.* in accordance with nature; naturally; characteristically. [Old English *gecyndelīce* < *gecynde* kind, good + *-līce* - ly[1]]

kind|ness (kīnd′nis), *n.* **1** the quality of being kind; kind nature: *We admire his kindness.* **2** kind treatment: *Thank you for your kindness.* **3** a kind act: *They showed me many kindnesses during my visit.* **4** kind feeling; fondness; affection: *I've a notion that there's a kindness between him and that nice modest girl, Mary Burge* (George Eliot).

kin|dred (kin′drid), *adj., n.* **—*adj.*** **1** like; similar; connected: *We are studying about dew, frost, and kindred facts of nature.* **2** related by birth or descent: *kindred tribes.* SYN: allied, cognate.
—*n.* **1** a person's family or relatives: *In thy seed shall all the kindreds of the earth be blessed* (Acts 3:25). **2** family relationship; connection by birth or marriage; kinship: *Does he claim kindred with you?* **3** *Figurative.* the condition of being alike; resemblance: likeness; agreement: *There is kindred among the words "receive," "receipt,"*

Pronunciation Key: hat, āge, cãre, fär; let, ēqual, tėrm; it, īce; hot, ōpen, ôrder; oil, out; cup, pu̇t, rüle; child; long; thin; ᴛʜen; zh, measure; ə represents **a** in about, **e** in taken, **i** in pencil, **o** in lemon, **u** in circus.

and "reception." **4** any group of people related to each other by blood; clan. SYN: tribe. [Middle English *kynrede* < *kyn* (Old English *cynn*) kin + *-rede* (Old English *rǣden*) condition]

kine[1] (kīn), *n.pl. Archaic or Dialect.* cows or cattle: *A herd of beeves, fair oxen and fair kine* (Milton). *The immemorial sound of the lowing kine was too bucolic to be borne* (Manchester Guardian Weekly). [earlier *kyn* formed on pattern of *oxen* < Old English *cȳ,* plural of cū cow]

kine[2] (kīn), *n. Physics.* the unit of velocity in the centimeter-gram-second system. It is equivalent to a velocity of one centimeter per second. Also, **kin.** [< Greek *kīneîn* move]

kin|e|ma (kin′ə mə), *n. British.* = cinema.

kin|e|mat|ic (kin′ə mat′ik), *adj.* having to do with pure motion or with kinematics. —**kin′e|mat′i|cal|ly,** *adv.*

kin|e|mat|i|cal (kin′ə mat′ə kəl), *adj.* = kinematic.

kinematic link, *Physics.* the structure or device formed when one of the two parts or halves of one kinematic pair is joined by a rigid piece to one of the two parts or halves of another kinematic pair.

kinematic pair, *Physics.* two parts or pieces so connected that they mutually constrain relative motion.

kin|e|mat|ics (kin′ə mat′iks), *n.* **1** the branch of physics that deals with the characteristics of different kinds of pure motion, that is, without reference to mass or to the causes of the motion. **2** this science applied to mechanical contrivances. [spelling alteration of French *cinématique,* noun < Greek *kī́nēma* motion < kīneîn to move]

kin|e|mat|o|graph (kin′ə mat′ə graf, -gräf), *n., v.t., v.i.* = cinematograph

kin|e|ma|tog|ra|phy (kin′ə mə tog′rə fē), *n.* = cinematography.

kin|e|scope (kin′ə skōp), *n., v.,* **-scoped, -scop|ing.** —*n.* **1** a record on film of a television show or other entertainment that may be rebroadcast: *If "canned" television on kinescope is not so good as live video . . .* (New York Times). **2** a cathode-ray tube with a screen at one end on which images are reproduced, used in television; picture tube. **3 Kinescope,** *Trademark.* a name for this kind of tube.
—*v.t.* to record on a kinescope.
[< Greek *kī́nēma* motion + English *-scope*]

ki|ne|sics (ki nē′siks), *n.* gestures, body movements, and facial expressions as a form of communication, especially the study of these as they accompany speech. [< Greek *kī́nēsis* motion + English *-ics*]

ki|ne|si|o|log|i|cal (ki nē′sē ə loj′ə kəl), *adj.* of or having to do with kinesiology.

ki|ne|si|ol|o|gy (ki nē′sē ol′ə jē), *n.* the science which investigates and analyzes human motion. [< Greek *kī́nēsis* motion + English *-logy*]

ki|ne|sis (ki nē′sis), *n., pl.* **-ne|ses** (-nē′sēz). an involuntary movement or reaction as the result of an external stimulus; reflex. [< Greek *kī́nēsis* motion]

kin|es|the|sia (kin′əs thē′zhə), *n.* the sensation of movement in the muscles, joints, and tendons. Also, **kinaesthesia.** [< New Latin *kinaesthesia* < Greek *kīneîn* to move + *aisthēsis* perception < *aisthánesthai* feel, perceive]

kin|es|the|sis (kin′əs thē′sis), *n.* = kinesthesia.

kin|es|thet|ic (kin′əs thet′ik), *adj.* having to do with sensations of motion from the muscles, joints, and tendons. —**kin′es|thet′i|cal|ly,** *adv.*

kin|e|the|od|o|lite (kin′ə thē od′ə līt), *n.* a device consisting of a camera attached to a theodolite, used for tracking missiles and aircraft. [< *kine*(tic) + *theodolite*]

ki|net|ic (ki net′ik), *adj.* **1** of or having to do with motion. **2** caused by or resulting from motion. **3** of or having to do with kinetic art; involving motion or the suggestion of motion produced especially by mechanical parts, colors, and lights. [< Greek *kīnētikós* < *kīneîn* to move] —**ki|net′i|cal|ly,** *adv.*

ki|net|i|cal (ki net′ə kəl), *adj.* = kinetic.

kinetic art, a form of art involving any sort of movement or motion, whether through the use of mobile parts or motor-driven mechanisms, or through the use of light effects, optical illusions, and the like; kineticism.

kinetic artist, a person who produces works of kinetic art: *Kinetic artists . . . try to combine mechanics and art* (Time).

kinetic energy, the energy which a body has because it is in motion. Kinetic energy is equal to one half the product of the mass of a body and the square of its velocity.

ki|net|ic-en|er|gy weapon (ki net′ik en′ər jē), a missile that uses a laser beam to find its target and kinetic energy to produce its destructive effect.

kinetic heat, the heat generated by atmospheric friction at very high speeds.

ki|net|i|cism (ki net′ə siz əm), *n.* = kinetic art.

ki|net|i|cist (ki net′ə sist), *n.* **1** a person who studies kinetics. **2** = kinetic artist.

kinetic kill vehicle, a weapon designed to destroy a nuclear warhead by force of impact: *This system would not employ directed-energy weapons at the outset; instead it would rely on kinetic kill vehicles* (Scientific American).

kinetic potential, *Physics.* the difference between the kinetic energy and potential energy of a dynamic system; Lagrangian function.

ki|net|ics (ki net′iks), *n.* the branch of physics that deals with the effects of forces in causing or changing the motion of objects: *Statics and kinetics are two major branches of the science of mechanics that tells you what happens when a solid material is pushed, pulled, twisted or squashed—when forces are applied to it* (Science News Letter).

kinetic theory of gases, the theory that molecules of a gas are in a state of rapid motion. constantly colliding with the walls of any containing vessel and with one another causing changes in their velocity and direction.

kinetic theory of heat, the theory that the temperature of a body is equivalent to the average kinetic energy of its constituent molecules, and that additional heat results in an increase in this energy.

kinetic theory of matter, the theory that constituent particles of matter are in motion.

ki|ne|tin (kī′nə tin), *n.* an organic compound found in plants and yeast, having a growth-promoting effect on various plant tissues: *Cultured plant cells normally need the hormone kinetin in order to divide and grow* (Walter G. Rosen). *Formula:* $C_{10}H_9N_5O$

ki|ne|to|chore (ki nē′tə kôr, -kōr; -net′ə-), *n.* = centromere. [< Greek *kīnētós* movable + *chorós* place]

ki|ne|to|graph (ki nē′tə graf, -gräf; -net′ə-), *n., v.* —*n.* a motion-picture camera.
—*v.t.* to make a motion picture of.
[< Greek *kīnētós* movable + English *-graph*] —**kin′e|tog′ra|pher,** *n.*

ki|ne|to|graph|ic (ki nē′tə graf′ik, -net′ə-), *adj.* having to do with motion-picture photography.

kin|e|tog|ra|phy (kin′ə tog′rə fē), *n.* motion-picture photography.

ki|net|o|phone (ki net′ə fōn), *n.* a device combining a kinetoscope and a phonograph.

ki|net|o|plast (ki net′ə plast), *n.* a structure at the base of the flagellum in trypanosomes, consisting of a blepharoplast and a larger basal body. [< Greek *kīnētós* movable + English *-plast*]

ki|net|o|scope (ki net′ə skōp), *n.* **1** an early form of motion-picture viewer, a device for presenting to the eye a series of photographs (taken in rapid succession) of moving objects, and thus giving a reproduction of a scene in actual movement. **2** such a device with an eyepiece or peephole for viewing the pictures directly. **3** such a device with an arrangement for projecting the pictures on a screen. [< Greek *kīnētós* movable + English *-scope*]

ki|net|o|scop|ic (ki net′ə skop′ik), *adj.* of or having to do with a kinetoscope.

ki|net|o|some (ki net′ə sōm), *n.* a basal granule in a cell, associated with the formation of cilia, flagella, and certain other motile structures. [< Greek *kīnētós* movable + *sôma* body]

kin|folk (kin′fōk′), *n.pl.* = kinsfolk.

kin|folks (kin′fōks′), *n.pl.* = kinsfolk.

king (king), *n., adj.* —*n.* **1** the man who rules a country and its people; male sovereign, usually with a hereditary position and with either absolute or limited power: *Richard the Lionhearted was king of England. The kings of England do not really rule England now.* **2** *Informal, Figurative.* a person who has great power in industry, business, or sports; very important person: *a steel king, a baseball king.* **3** *Figurative.* something or someone best in its class: *The lion is the king of beasts. He is the king o' gude fellows* (Robert Burns). **4** the highest-ranking piece in the game of chess. It can move one square in any direction. The game is won when the king cannot escape check. **5** a piece that has moved entirely across the board in checkers. It has the power of moving forward or backward, and is usually marked by placing one checker on top of another. **6** a playing card bearing a picture of a king. **7** a king-sized article, such as a cigarette. **8** = chinook salmon. **9** a fully developed male in a colony of termites.
—*adj.* of primary importance or size.
[Old English *cyning*] —**king′less,** *adj.* —**king′like′,** *adj.*

King (king), *n.* God or Christ: *King of kings, King of heaven. Who is this King of glory? The Lord strong and mighty* (Psalms 24:8).

King apple, a winter variety of apple with red stripes.

King Arthur, the hero in a group of medieval legends about the Knights of the Round Table.

king-at-arms (king′ət ärmz′), *n.* = king-of-arms.

king|bird (king′bėrd′), *n.* any one of several American flycatchers, especially a bold, gray-and-white flycatcher of the eastern United States. The kingbird is a quarrelsome bird that catches and eats insects as it flies. [American English]

king|bolt (king′bōlt′), *n.* a main or large bolt in a mechanical structure, especially a vertical bolt connecting the body of a wagon or other vehicle, with the front axle, or the body of a railroad car with a set of wheels; kingpin.

King Charles spaniel, a black-and-tan English toy spaniel.

king cobra, a large, very poisonous cobra found throughout southeastern Asia.

king crab, **1** = horseshoe crab. **2** a large true crab found along the shores of the northern Pacific; Alaskan king crab; Japanese crab. King crabs have extremely long legs and are sold for their meat. See picture under **crab**[1].

king|craft (king′kraft′, -kräft′), *n.* the art of ruling; royal statesmanship.

king|cup (king′kup′), *n.* **1** any one of several common species of buttercup. **2** *Especially British.* the marsh marigold.

king|dom (king′dəm), *n.* **1** a country that is governed by a king or queen; land or territory ruled by one king. England, Denmark, Norway, and Sweden are kingdoms. SYN: monarchy. **2** *Figurative.* a realm, domain, or province: *The mind is the kingdom of thought.* **3** one of the three divisions of the natural world; the animal kingdom, the plant kingdom, or the mineral kingdom. **4** Often, **Kingdom.** *Theology.* the spiritual sovereignty of God or Christ; the domain over which God rules in heaven and on earth: *Jesus went about . . . preaching the gospel of the kingdom* (Matthew 4:23). **5** *Obsolete.* kingly function, power, or position; sovereignty; kingship: *I must be married to my brother's daughter, Or else my kingdom stands on brittle glass* (Shakespeare). [Old English *cyningdōm*]

kingdom come or **Kingdom Come,** heaven or paradise; the next world.

king duck, = king eider.

king eider, a type of eider duck found along the northern coasts of North America and Europe. The adult male has a large orange knob on the forehead.

king|fish (king′fish′), *n., pl.* **-fish|es** or (*collectively*) **-fish. 1** any one of several large food fishes of the Atlantic or Pacific coast. **2** a food fish common along the coasts of California, Australia, and the East Indies. **3** = opah. **4** any one of certain Spanish mackerels, such as the cero, which live in the Atlantic Ocean. **5** *Informal.* the person having uncontested control in a group or community.

king|fish|er (king′fish′ər), *n.* any one of a large group of bright-colored birds having a large head with a crest and a large, strong beak. Kingfishers are found in most parts of the world. The American kingfisher feeds on fish which it captures by diving; some European kingfishers eat insects.

king|head (king′hed′), *n.* = giant ragweed.

king|ing (king′ing), *n.* the condition of being a king or acting like a king.

King James Version, an English translation of the Bible prepared under James I of England and published in 1611, still widely used by English-speaking Protestants; Authorized Version.

king kong, *Slang.* cheap, strong wine or whiskey. [< *King Kong,* a powerful, gigantic ape in a motion picture of the same title]

King Lear, **1** a tragedy by Shakespeare, first printed in 1608. **2** the principal character in this play; Lear.

king|let (king′lit), *n.* **1** a petty king; a king ruling over a small country. **2** any one of certain tiny, olive-green songbirds similar to the warblers, such as the golden-crowned kinglet and the ruby-crowned kinglet of North America.

king|li|ness (king′lē nis), *n.* kingly quality or condition; majesty.

king|ly (king′lē), *adj.,* **-li|er, -li|est,** *adv.* —*adj.* **1** of a king or kings; of royal rank; *the kingly family of Tudor.* SYN: See syn. under **royal. 2** fit for a king; *a kingly crown. Leave kingly backs to cope with kingly cares* (William Cowper). **3** like a king; royal; noble: *kingly pride. I am far better born than is the king . . . more kingly in my thoughts* (Shakespeare). SYN: regal, august, dignified, majestic, kinglike.
—*adv.* as a king does; royally; regally; *Low bow'd the rest, He, kingly, did but nod* (Alexander Pope).

king mackerel, a Spanish mackerel of the western Atlantic Ocean, valued as a game fish.

king|mak|er (king′mā′kər), *n.* **1** a person who makes or establishes kings; power behind the throne. **2** a person of authority who dictates to others, as a politician who is able to force his choice of a candidate for office: *The Democratic convention has begun to sprout more kingmakers* *than candidates* (Wall Street Journal).

king|mak|ing (king′mā′king), *n., adj.* **—*n.*** the activities of a kingmaker: *My mention of Lausche is no exercise in kingmaking* (Newsweek).
—*adj.* like that of a kingmaker: *Chicago's kingmaking Democratic Mayor . . . pressured him off the Democratic ticket* (Wall Street Journal).

king-of-arms or **King-of-Arms** (king′əv ärmz′), *n.* the most important heraldic officer of a country; any of the three chief heralds of the Heralds' College.

king of beasts, = lion.

king penguin, a large penguin similar in appearance to the emperor penguin but slightly smaller. It lives in Patagonia and certain islands of the Antarctic.

king|pin (king′pin′), *n., adj.* **—*n.*** **1** the pin in front or in the center in bowling games. **2** *Informal, Figurative.* the most important person or thing: *Conrad Hilton, U.S. hotel kingpin, reportedly is shopping around for Island property* (Wall Street Journal). **3** the pin connecting a stub axle to the fixed front axle of an automobile. **4** = kingbolt.
—*adj.* *Informal.* important; outstanding; primary: *Okinawa, kingpin bastion of Pacific defenses* (Newsweek).

king post, a vertical post between the apex of a triangular roof truss and a tie beam.

Kings (kingz), *n.pl.* (*sing. in use*). **1** either of two books in the Protestant Old Testament, I Kings or II Kings, containing the history of the reigns of the Hebrew kings in Israel and Judah after David. **2** any one of four books in the Douay Bible that include I and II Samuel and I and II Kings.

King's Bench, *British.* a former court of record and the highest common-law court in England. *Abbr:* K.B. Also, **Queen's Bench.**

King's Birthday, a holiday observed in the Commonwealth on the actual or arbitrarily set birthday of the ruler. Also, **Queen's Birthday.**

King's Color or **Colour,** the Union Jack as an emblem on, or carried with the colors of, a British regiment. Also, **Queen's Color** or **Colour.**

king's counsel, *British.* a barrister or the body of barristers appointed counsel to the Crown. *Abbr:* K.C. Also, **queen's counsel.**

king's English, accepted English, especially correct British usage in speech and writing: *In their "History of English Literature," Professors Emile Legouis and Louis Cazamian . . . defined king's English as that English which was spoken at the Universities of Oxford and Cambridge and at the court* (Listener). Also, **queen's English.**

king's evil, = scrofula (supposed to be cured by the touch of a king).

king's gambit, a series of opening moves in chess starting with the advance of the pawn in front of the king, in which the opening player offers his king's bishop's pawn in return for opportunity for swift attack.

king|ship (king′ship), *n.* **1** the position, rank, or dignity of a king. **2** the rule of a king; government by a king. **3** kingly nature or quality. **4** a title used in referring to a king (with *his*).

king|side (king′sīd′), *n., adj., adv. Chess.* **—*n.*** the side of the board nearest to the king's starting position.
—*adj.* occurring or situated on the kingside.
—*adv.* on the kingside.

king-size (king′sīz′), *adj.* **1** *Informal.* large or long for its kind: *a king-size cigarette.* **2** wider than queen-size; extra wide. A king-size bed is 78 inches wide and 80 inches long.

king-sized (king′sīzd′), *adj. Informal.* **1** larger than normal: *Professor Petro sees compulsory unionism as a king-sized inconsistency in our labor policy* (Wall Street Journal). **2** = king-size.

king snake, 1 a large, harmless colubrine snake that lives in the southern United States. It eats mice and rats and other snakes. It does not hesitate to attack and eat rattlesnakes. **2** any one of various related North American snakes. King snakes are constrictors of the same genus as the milk snakes.

king's proctor, an officer representing the Crown who has the right to intervene in certain divorce and nullity cases. Also, **queen's proctor.**

king's ransom, a very large amount of money.

king's shilling, (in the British Army) a shilling formerly paid a recruit to make his enlistment binding. Also, **queen's shilling.**
take the king's shilling, to enlist: *When war was declared, he took the king's shilling.*

King's speech, a speech read by the king at the opening of the British Parliament, prepared by the ministers of the government to explain domestic and foreign policy. Also, **Queen's speech.**

king's yellow, orpiment or yellow arsenic used as a pigment. *Formula:* As_2S_3

king whiting, = kingfish (def. 1).

king|wood (king′wu̇d), *n.* **1** a Brazilian tree of the pea family whose wood is used in cabinetwork. **2** the wood itself, streaked with violet tints; violet wood.

ki|nin (kī′nən), *n.* any peptide of a group which in plants stimulates cell division and in animals causes dilation of blood vessels and contraction of smooth muscles. [< *kin*(et)*in*]

kink (kingk), *n., v.* **—*n.*** **1** a short twist or curl in a rope, thread, hair, or wire: *a kink in a cable.* **2** a pain or stiffness in the muscles, especially of the neck, back, or leg; crick: *Jackie Robinson didn't start the game because of the kink in his neck* (New York Times). **3** *Informal, Figurative.* a mental twist; queer idea; odd notion; eccentricity; whim: *when a woman gets a kink in her head agin a man* (Harriet Beecher Stowe). SYN: crotchet. **4** a hindrance; difficulty; obstruction: *Some kinks are knotting up auto distribution* (Wall Street Journal).
—*v.i.* to form a kink or kinks; twist or curl stiffly: *The rope kinked as he rolled it up.* **—*v.t.*** to make kinks in: *Don't kink the clothesline.*
[probably < Dutch *kink* twist in a rope]

kin|ka|jou (king′kə jü), *n.* a yellowish-brown mammal of Central America and northern South America, related to and resembling a raccoon but having a long, prehensile tail. It lives in trees and hunts at night. [< French *quincajou;* origin uncertain]

kink|i|ly (king′kə lē), *adv.* **1** twistedly. **2** *Especially British Informal.* oddly; queerly; unconventionally: *kinkily dressed.*

kink|i|ness (king′kē nis), *n.* **1** curliness. **2** *Especially British Informal.* queerness; eccentricity.

kin|kle (king′kəl), *n.* a little or slight kink or twist.

kin|kled (king′kəld), *adj.* having kinkles; finely kinked or curled, as hair.

kink|y (king′kē), *adj.,* **kink|i|er, kink|i|est. 1** full of kinks; twisted; curly: *She has kinky brown hair.* **2** *Especially British Informal.* eccentric; unconventional; whimsical: *kinky clothes, kinky habits. He gets involved in endless kinky-kooky adventures, all set against a mildly distracting mod-baroque-art-nouveau setting* (Maclean's).

kinky boot, *British.* a knee-length or thigh-length boot, especially of black leather or plastic, worn by women.

kin|ni|kin|ick or **kin|ni|kin|ic** (kin′i kə nik′), *n.* **1** a smoking mixture used by the North American Indians, made from dried leaves and bark of the bearberry. **2** = bearberry. Also, **killikinick, killickinic.** [American English < an Algonkian word]

ki|no[1] (kē′nō), *n.* **1** a dark, reddish-brown, dried juice used in medicine and tanning as an astringent, and also in dyeing. **2** the tree of the pea family, growing in North Africa, India, and Ceylon (Sri Lanka), from whose trunk this juice is extracted. [< New Latin *kino* < the West African (Gambia) name of the kind first imported]

ki|no[2] (kē′nō), *n.* a motion-picture theater. [< German *Kino* motion-picture theater]

kins|folk (kinz′fōk′), *n.pl.* a person's family or relatives; kin: *And mark A country for him, kinsfolk, and a home* (Matthew Arnold). Also, **kinfolk.**

kins|folks (kinz′fōks′), *n.pl.* = kinsfolk.

kin|ship (kin′ship), *n.* **1** the state of being kin; family relationship: *His kinship with the owner of the factory helped him to get a job.* **2** relationship. **3** *Figurative.* resemblance.

kinship family, a family unit consisting of several closely related families (as father, mother, sons, their wives, and their children) all living together.

kins|man (kinz′mən), *n., pl.* **-men.** a male relative. Brothers and uncles are kinsmen.

kins|man|ship (kinz′mən ship), *n.* = kinship.

kins|wom|an (kinz′wu̇m′ən), *n., pl.* **-wom|en.** a woman or girl relative.

✱kiosk
definition 1

✱ki|osk (kē osk′; *also, for 1* kī′osk), *n.* **1** a small building with one or more sides open, such as one used as a newsstand, a bandstand, or an opening to a subway: *Down the centre of the concourse are located the seating areas, the main gift shop, and information kiosk* (Manchester Guardian). **2** a light, open summerhouse in Turkey and other Eastern countries: *It was a small kiosk built upon a projecting rock that looked down upon the Bosphorus and the city* (Charles J. Lever). **3** *Especially British.* telephone booth. [< French *kiosque* < Turkish *kösk* pavilion]

Ki|o|wa (kī′ə wə, -wä, -wā), *n., pl.* **-wa** or **-was. 1** a member of a nomadic, warlike Indian tribe of Tanoan stock that once inhabited the plains of the United States. Their descendants now live in Oklahoma. **2** the language of this tribe. [American English < Kiowa *Kiowa* principal people]

Ki|o|wan (kī′ə wən), *adj., n.* **—*adj.*** of or having to do with the Kiowa Indians or their language.
—*n.* = Kiowa.

kip[1] (kip), *n.* **1** the untanned hide of a young or undersized animal. **2** a bundle or group of such hides, containing a definite number. [origin uncertain. Compare Low German *kip,* Middle Dutch *kip,* or *kijp.*]

kip[2] (kip), *n. U.S.* a unit of weight equal to 1,000 lbs. [American English < *ki*(lo-) + *p*(ound)]

kip[3] (kip), *n. Slang.* **1** a cheap lodging house. **2** a lodging or bed in such a house, **3** a bed in general. **4** *Obsolete.* a brothel. [origin uncertain. Compare Danish *kippe.*]

kip[4] (kip), *n.* the basic unit of money in Laos. [< Thai *kip*]

kip[5] (kip), *n. Australian.* a small, flat piece of wood on which the pennies are flipped into the air in the game of two-up.

Kip|ling|esque (kip′ling esk′), *adj.* of, having to do with, or in the style of the English writer and poet Rudyard Kipling (1865-1936).

kip|per (kip′ər), *v., n.* **—*v.t.*** to salt and dry or smoke (herring, salmon, or other fish). [apparently < noun]
—*n.* **1** herring, salmon, or other fish, that has been salted and dried or smoked. **2** the male salmon or sea trout during or after the spawning season. **3** *Slang.* **a** a person. **b** a young person; child.
[Old English *cypera* male salmon]

Kir|di (kir′dē), *n., pl.* **-di** or **-dis.** a member of an African people of western and northern Cameroon. Some Kirdi are nomadic; others are farmers.

Kir|ghiz or **Kir|giz** (kir gēz′), *n., pl.* **-ghiz** or **-giz, -ghiz|es** or **-giz|es. 1** a member of a Mongoloid people widely scattered over the western part of central Asia. **2** their Turkic language.

ki|ri|mon (kir′i mon), *n.* a device representing three leaves of the paulownia tree surmounted by three budding flower stems, used especially as the unofficial or personal badge of the imperial family of Japan, as on the harness of the emperor's horses. [< Japanese *kiri* the paulownia tree + *mon* family crest]

ki|rin (kē′rin), *n.* a mythical animal of a composite form, shown especially in Japanese carvings and procelains. It is the Japanese form of the kylin. *A boxwood carving of a wasp in a rotten pear by Kogetsu made 90 guineas . . . a kirin, the Japanese equivalent of the western unicorn, also carved in ivory, 65 guineas* (London times). [< Japanese *kirin* < Chinese *ch'i lin*]

kirk (kėrk), *n. Scottish.* a church. [probably < Scandinavian (compare Old Icelandic *kirkja*)]

Kirk (kėrk), *n.* **the,** the national church of Scotland; the Presbyterian Church of Scotland as distinguished from the Church of England or the Scottish Episcopal Church (primarily a British use). [< *kirk*]

kirk|man (kėrk′mən), *n., pl.* **-men.** *Scottish.* **1** an ecclesiastic. **2** a member or follower of the Church of Scotland.

Kir|li|an (kir′lē ən), *adj.* having to do with or designating a method of photography in which unexposed film is placed between an electrode and the object to be photographed, so that the finished photograph exhibits a bright glow of different colors that seems to emanate from the photographed object: *Kirlian imagery, the Kirlian process. Soviet parapsychologists believe . . . that all living structures are encompassed by a "bioplasm," or energy field, and that the Kirlian photograph records the surrounding field* (New York Times Magazine). [< Semyon and Valentina *Kirlian,* Russian researchers, who developed this method]

Kir|man (kir män′), *n.* = Kerman.

kir|mess (kėr′mis), *n.* = kermis.

kirsch (kirsh), *n.* a clear, sweet brandy distilled from the fermented juice of wild black cherries, made chiefly in southern Germany, Alsace, and Switzerland. [< French *kirsh* < German *Kirschwasser*]

Kirsch|was|ser (kirsh′väs′ər), *n. German.* kirsch.

kir|sen (kėr′sən), *v.t. Dialect.* to christen.

kir|tle (kėr′təl), *n. Archaic.* **1** a woman's gown, skirt, or outer petticoat: *Ladies . . . were forbidden . . . to go abroad with wide-hooped gowns or kirtles* (James Howell). **2** a man's short coat, usually worn with an outer cloak. [Old English *cyrtel,*

Pronunciation Key: hat, āge, cãre, fär; let, ēqual, tėrm; it, īce; hot, ōpen, ôrder; oil, out; cup, pu̇t, rüle; child; long; thin; ᴛʜen; zh, measure; ə represents **a** in about, **e** in taken, **i** in pencil, **o** in lemon, **u** in circus.

probably <Latin *curtus* short]

Ki|run|di (kə rün′dē), *n.* a Bantu language of Burundi, a country in eastern central Africa. It is one of the official languages of Burundi.

ki|saeng (kē′sang), *n., pl.* **-saeng** or **-saengs.** a Korean singing and dancing girl. [<Korean *kisaeng*]

ki|seng (kē′sang), *n., pl.* **-seng** or **-sengs.** = kisaeng.

kish|ke or **kish|ka** (kish′kə), *n. Jewish Cookery.* a casing of beef or fowl, stuffed with a spicy flour mixture and roasted. It is served as a side dish or as an hors d'oeuvre. [<Yiddish *kishke*]

Kis|lev (kis′lef), *n.* the ninth month of the Jewish ecclesiastical year and the third month of the civil year, corresponding to parts of November and December.
[<Hebrew *kislēv*]

kis|mat (kiz′mət, kis′-), *n.* = kismet.

kis|met (kiz′met, kis′-), *n.* fate; destiny: *The stars or the fates . . . or whatever you like to term your kismet* (Francis M. Crawford). [<Turkish *kismet* <Arabic *qismat* portion]

kiss (kis), *v., n.* **—*v.t.*** **1** to touch with the lips as a sign of love, greeting, or respect: *He kissed his mother good-by.* **2** *Figurative.* to touch gently: *A soft wind kissed the treetops.* **3** to put, bring, or take by kissing: *He kissed away her tears.*
—*v.i.* **1** to give a caress with or as if with the lips: *The two sisters kissed.* **2** *Figurative.* to come into contact or meet with a light touch.
—*n.* **1** a touch with the lips as a sign of love, greeting, or respect: *He gave his mother a kiss good-by.* SYN: osculation. **2** *Figurative.* a gentle touch: *The pebble-paven shore Under the quick, faint kisses of the sea Trembles and sparkles* (Shelley). **3** a piece of candy, usually of chocolate and containing coconut or nuts. **4** a small, fancy cake made of sugar and the whites of egg.
kiss and tell, *Informal.* to betray a secret or trust; break a solemn promise: *A house divided against itself cannot stand, which is why I am not a man to kiss and tell* (Arthur Goldberg).
kiss good-by. See under **good-by.**
kiss off, *U.S. Slang.* to put out of mind; disregard: *You can kiss off that problem, now.*
[Old English *cyssan*] **—kiss′a|ble,** *adj.*

KISS (no periods), *U.S. Informal.* Keep It Simple, Stupid: *She abides by the engineering principle KISS . . . and has the greatest confidence in an immersible [vehicle] with no machine except a human being propelling it* (Science News).

kiss-and-tell (kis′ən tel′), *adj. U.S.* revealing confidential or private matters: *kiss-and-tell books.*

kiss-curl (kis′kėrl′), *n.* a curl of hair drawn over the forehead, twisted in front of the ear, or grown at the nape of the neck: *The kiss-curls of the Empress Eugénie period curve toward [the] ears* (New York Times).

kiss|ee (kis ē′), *n.* a person who is kissed.

kiss|er (kis′ər), *n.* **1** a person who kisses. **2** *U.S. Slang.* the mouth or face.

kiss|ing bug (kis′ing), any one of certain blood-sucking insects, such as some assassin bugs, which sometimes bite persons on the lips.

kissing cousin, a cousin or other relative close enough to kiss in greeting or leave-taking.

kissing disease, = infectious mononucleosis.

kissing kin, 1 a close relative or relatives; kissing cousin or cousins. **2** *Slang.* people or things in harmonious relation with one another.

kiss of death, a seemingly friendly act that leads to betrayal or misfortune.

kiss of life, *British.* **1** mouth-to-mouth resuscitation. **2** *Figurative.* an act that gives back life; something that revitalizes: *The Government's kiss of life for Rolls [-Royce] could be very misleading if it is seen as a sign of a volte face by the Government over propping up ailing companies* (Manchester Guardian Weekly).

kiss-of-life (kis′əv līf′), *adj. British.* mouth-to-mouth: *kiss-of-life respiration.*

kiss of peace, a ceremonial kiss signifying brotherly love; pax. The kiss of peace is given at Mass in the Roman Catholic and Eastern Orthodox churches.

kist[1] (kist), *n. Dialect.* **1** a chest: *attractive kist with packing and drawer space* (Cape Times). **2a** a chest or place in which money is kept; treasury. **b** the store of money itself. [variant of *chest*]

kist[2] (kist), *n.* = cist[2].

kist|vaen (kist′vīn), *n.* = cistvaen.

kis|wa or **kis|wah** (kis′wä), *n.* the traditional holy cloth or carpet covering the Kaaba at Mecca.
[<Arabic *kiswah*]

kit[1] (kit), *n., v.* **—*n.*** **1** the parts of any article to be put together by the buyer: *a radio kit, a model airplane kit.* **2a** an outfit of tools or supplies: *a first-aid kit, a plumber's kit.* **b** a bag, case, or knapsack for carrying such equipment or such an outfit. **3** a person's equipment packed for traveling: *a soldier's kit.* **4** *Informal.* a lot; set; collection: *I'll show a better gentleman than the whole kit of you put together* (Dickens). **5** a small wooden tub or pail.
—*v.t.* *Especially British.* to supply with what is needed; equip; fit (*out* or *up*): *They've press-ganged all these kids from school and kitted them out with bayonets* (Punch).
the whole kit and caboodle, the whole lot; the entire thing: *The whole kit and caboodle was sold off and the store closed.*
[probably <Middle Dutch *kitte* jug]

kit[2] (kit), *n.* a small pocket violin, formerly much used by dancing masters; pochette. [perhaps abbreviation of Greek *cithára* cithara]

kit[3] (kit), *n.* **1** = kitten. **2** any young furry animal, such as a young beaver.

kit|bag (kit′bag′), *n.* a small bag to hold a soldier's or traveler's personal effects: *An exceedingly handy form of knapsack or kitbag* (Westminster Gazette).

kit boat, 1 a boat built from prefabricated parts. Kit boats are less expensive than other boats. **2** the prefabricated parts to be assembled in building such a boat.

kit-cat (kit′kat′), *n.* a particular size of portrait (36 by 28 inches) which is less than half-length but may include the hands. [(originally) *Kit-Cat* Club (because the club members' portraits were limited to this size by the low ceiling of the club's dining room)]

Kit-Cat Club, a political and literary club of London in the early 1700's named for Christopher Cat, who kept the tavern where the club met, and was noted for his mutton pies.

kitch|en (kich′ən), *n., v.* **—*n.*** **1** that room where food is cooked: *The kitchen was filled with the smell of roast lamb cooking.* **2** the cooking department; cuisine. **3** an outfit for cooking, such as one for camping or the like. **4** *Scottish and Irish.* food or drink eaten as relish with bread, potatoes, or other staple fare.
—*v.t.* *Scottish and Irish.* to serve as a relish for or add a relish to.
[Old English *cycene* <unrecorded Medieval Latin *cucina* <Latin *coquīna* <*coquere* to cook]

kitchen cabinet, 1 an article of furniture for the kitchen containing shelves and drawers. **2** *U.S. Informal.* a group of advisers consulted by a President in addition to or rather than his cabinet.

Kitchen Cabinet, a group of advisers to Andrew Jackson who were thought to have more influence with him than his official cabinet.

Kitchen Dutch, = Afrikaans (used in an unfriendly way).

kitch|en|er (kich′ə nər), *n.* **1** a person employed in a kitchen. **2** a person in charge of a kitchen, especially in a monastery: *two most important officers of the convent, the kitchener and refecioner* (Scott). **3** a stove for cooking with various attachments.

kitch|en|ette or **kitch|en|et** (kich′ə net′), *n.* **1** a very small kitchen: *a kitchenette in a small apartment.* **2** a part of a room fitted up as a kitchen.

kitchen garden, a garden where vegetables and fruit for a family are grown.

kitchen Kafir or **Kitchen Kaffir,** a South African pidgin language: *A wonderful langûage is kitchen Kafir, a weird medley of dialects, interspersed with English words* (Cape Argus).

kitchen knave, = scullion.

kitch|en|maid (kich′ən mād′), *n.* a servant who helps a cook.

kitchen match, a wooden match that ignites on friction with any rough surface.

kitchen midden, a mound of shells, bones, and other refuse at a place where prehistoric people lived: *It is from the "kitchen midden" that scientists have gleaned much of the information about our ancestors* (Science News Letter). [translation of Danish *kokkenmodden* <*kokken* kitchen + *modding* dunghill]

kitchen police, 1 a military duty of helping the cooks prepare and serve the food, wash the dishes, and clean up the kitchen. *Abbr:* KP (no periods). **2** soldiers assigned to this duty, often as a punishment for slight offenses.

kitch|en-sink school (kich′ən singk′), a contemporary English group of writers and artists who emphasize drab reality in their work: *Two manifestations of "realism," for example—the so-called "kitchen-sink school" among the painters and a sort of Rodinesque revival among the sculptors* (London Times).

kitch|en|ware (kich′ən wãr′), *n.* kitchen utensils. Pots, kettles, and pans are kitchenware.

kite** (kīt), *n., v.,* **kit|ed, kit|ing.** **—*n. **1** a light frame covered with paper, cloth, or plastic. Kites are flown in the air on the end of a long string, and often have a tail attached to balance them. **2** any one of several hawks with long, pointed wings and usually a notched or forked tail. **3** *Nautical.* any one of the light, small sails, such as a skysail, set high on a ship during calm weather. **4** a type of aircraft pulled by a towline and supported by the force of air currents. **5** *Figurative.* a person who preys upon others; rapacious person; sharper. **6** *Commercial Slang.* a fictitious check, bill of exchange, or other negotiable instrument, representing no actual transaction, used to raise money or to sustain credit. **7** *Slang.* any airplane used in World War II.
—*v.i.* **1** *Informal.* to fly like a kite; move rapidly and easily: *Khrushchev and . . . Bulganin dared to go kiting off to India* (Newsweek). **2** *Commercial Slang.* to obtain money or credit by a kite.
—*v.t.* *Commercial Slang.* to convert into a kite.
fly a kite, a *Slang.* disappear; vanish (used as a command): *"Go fly a kite" an angry housewife snarls at her husband* (Time). **b** to air or issue a proposal, idea, or the like, in a tentative or exploratory manner: *[The] Prime Minister . . . let a kite be flown last week that he was considering holding news conferences* (New York Times).
[Old English *cȳta* a bird of prey]

***kite**
definition 1

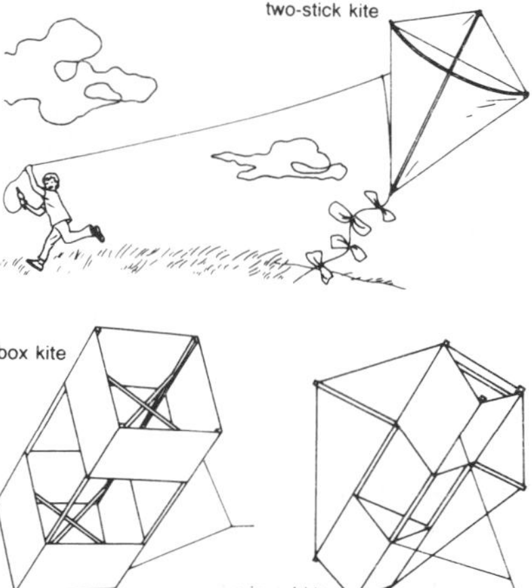

kite balloon, 1 a balloon that can be flown in the manner of a kite. **2** a type of captive sausage-shaped balloon used to elevate men for military observation, and acting more or less like a kite in retaining a fixed and steady position by means of vanes.

kite|mark (kīt′märk′), *n.* the registered certification mark of the British Standards Institution, indicating compliance of a manufactured product with the Institution's standards of performance: *Before a lock can receive the . . . kitemark of approval it must pass tests designed to assess its resistance to the use of force* (London Times). [because it is shaped like a kite]

kit fox, 1 a small, gray or buff-yellow fox of the plains of western North America; desert fox. **2** its fur.
[<*kit*[3] + *fox*]

kith (kith), *n. Archaic.* friends; acquaintances; countrymen; neighbors: *no men of your kith. He is no kith of ours.*
[Old English *cȳthth* native land, kinsfolk <*cunnan* to know]

kith and kin, 1 friends and relatives: *Lancelot's kith and kin so worship him That ill to him is ill to them* (Tennyson). **2** kinsfolk; kin.

kith|a|ra (kith′ər ə), *n.* = cithara.

Kitsch or **kitsch** (kich), *n.* a shallow, pretentious, sentimental artistic production: *. . . conscience forbids them to indulge in the kind of Kitsch that would guarantee a hit* (New Yorker). [<German (colloquial) *Kitsch* trash]

Kitsch|y or **kitsch|y** (kich′ē), *adj.* **Kitsch|i|er** or **kitsch|i|er, Kitsch|i|est** or **kitsch|i|est.** of or like Kitsch; artistically shallow or pretentious.

kit|ten (kit′ən), *n., v.* **—*n.*** **1** a young cat: *The children held the kitten while the mother cat watched them closely.* **2** the young of certain other small animals, such as rabbits.
—*v.t.* to give birth to (kittens); litter. **—*v.i.*** **1** to bring forth a litter of kittens. **2** to act kittenishly.
have a kitten (or **kittens**), *Slang.* to be emotionally upset about something: *She was having kittens from jealousy.*
[apparently <Anglo-French variant of Old French *chitoun,* or *cheton* <*chat* cat <Late Latin *cattus*]

kit|ten|ish (kit′ə nish), *adj.* **1** like a kitten: *a kittenish appetite for milk.* **2** playful or coquettish: *kittenish flirting.* **—kit′ten|ish|ly,** *adv.* **—kit′ten|ish|ness,** *n.*

kit|ti|wake (kit′i wāk), *n., pl.* **-wakes** or (*collectively*) **-wake.** either one of two sea gulls of the North Atlantic and Arctic oceans, with black or red legs, long wings with solid black tips, and a very short or rudimentary hind toe. [earlier *cattiwake;* imitative of its call]

kit|tle (kit′əl), *v.*, **-tled, -tling,** *adj. Scottish.* **—*v.t.*** **1** to tickle. **2** *Figurative.* to excite pleasantly: *Nobody among these brave English cooks can kittle up his Majesty's most sacred palate with our . . . Scottish dishes* (Scott). **3** to puzzle.
 —*adj.* uncertain; risky: (*Figurative.*) *Rob Roy . . . a kittle neighbor to the low country, and particularly obnoxious to his Grace* (Scott).
 [Middle English *kityll;* origin uncertain]

kit|ty¹ (kit′ē), *n., pl.* **-ties.** **1** a kitten. **2** a pet name for a cat. [< *kitt*(en) + *-y*²]

kit|ty² (kit′ē), *n., pl.* **-ties.** **1** the stakes in a poker game. **2** money pooled by the players in other games for some special purpose, such as to pay for refreshments. **3** a fund of money: *The Federal Housing Administration disclosed the reserve kitty . . . had enough money in it* (Wall Street Journal). **4** an extra hand or widow in a card game.
 feed the kitty, to contribute money or chips to a pool: *They had to feed the kitty to ride in my car.*
 [origin uncertain, perhaps special use of dialectal *kitty* jail]

kit|ty-cor|ner (kit′ē kôr′nər), *adj.* = cater-cornered.

kit|ty-cor|nered (kit′ē kôr′nərd), *adj.* = cater-cornered.

ki|va (kē′və), *n.* a large chamber, often wholly or partly underground, in a Pueblo Indian village, used for religious ceremonies and for other purposes. [American English < Shoshonean (Hopi) *kiva* a sacred ceremonial chamber]

Ki|wa|ni|an (ki wä′nē ən), *n., adj.* **—*n.*** a member of a Kiwanis club.
 —*adj.* of or having to do with Kiwanis clubs.

Ki|wa|nis (ki wä′nis), *n.* an international group of clubs of business and professional men, organized to promote civic service and higher ideals in business and professional life. [American English; perhaps < an American Indian word]

***ki|wi** (kē′wē), *n., pl.* **-wis.** **1** a bird of New Zealand that cannot fly; apteryx. The kiwi has a stocky body covered with shaggy, dull-brown feathers and a long, flexible bill. Its relationship to other birds is obscure. **2** *Informal.* a nonflying member of an air service. [< Maori *kiwi*]

***kiwi** definition 1

kiwi fruit, an edible fruit resembling a large gooseberry, produced by a New Zealand vine.

kJ (no periods) or **kj.**, kilojoule.

K.J.V., King James Version.

K.K.K. or **KKK** (no periods), Ku Klux Klan.

K Kt (no periods), *Chess.* king's knight.

kl., kiloliter or kiloliters.

kla|ber|jass (klä′bər yäs), *n.* a card game that is a type of piquet: *An old man joins his friends for a glass of wine and a game of klaberjass behind an ice cream parlor on Augusta Street* (Maclean's). [< German *Klaberjass* < Dutch *klaverjas*]

Kla|math (klam′əth), *n., pl.* **-math** or **-maths.** **1** a tribe of Indians in Oregon and California, along the Klamath River. **2** their language.

Klamath weed, = St.-John's-wort.

Klan (klan), *n.* **1** = Ku Klux Klan. **2** any chapter of the Ku Klux Klan.

Klan|ism (klan′iz əm), *n.* the methods or beliefs of the Ku Klux Klan.

Klans|man (klanz′mən), *n., pl.* **-men.** a member of the Ku Klux Klan.

klatsch or **klatch** (kläch, kluch), *n.* an informal gathering: *. . . sip coffee and laugh and talk at this day's klatch* (Saturday Review). [< German *Klatsch* gossip]

klav|ern (klav′ərn), *n.* **1** the headquarters of a chapter of the Ku Klux Klan. **2** the chapter itself; Klan. [< *Kl*(an) + (c)*avern*]

klax|on (klak′sən), *n.* **1** a kind of horn formerly used in automobiles. **2** a horn with a loud, penetrating sound used as a warning signal: *The Coast Guard klaxon sounded, then the firehouse siren from the town* (New Yorker). [< earlier *Klaxon,* a trademark, apparently coined < Greek *klázein* scream, clang]

klea|gle or **Klea|gle** (klē′gəl), *n.* an official in the present Ku Klux Klan. [American English, perhaps < *kl*(an) + *eagle*]

kleb|si|el|la (kleb′zē el′ə), *n.* a rod-shaped bacterium of the intestinal tract commonly associated with respiratory infections. [< New Latin *Klebsiella* the genus name < Edwin *Klebs,* 1834-1913, a German bacteriologist]

Klebs-Loef|fler or **Klebs-Löf|fler bacillus** (klāps′lœf′lər), the bacterium that causes diphtheria. [< Edwin *Klebs,* 1834-1913, and Friedrich *Löffler,* 1852-1915, German bacteriologists]

klee|nex (klē′neks), *n.* **1** a disposable paper tissue used as a handkerchief, or to remove or apply makeup. **2 Kleenex,** *Trademark.* a name for a paper tissue of this type.

kleft (kleft), *n.* = klepht.

kleig light (klēg), = klieg light.

Klein bottle (klīn), *Geometry.* a continuous, one-sided surface formed by bending the small end of a tapering tube, passing it through one side, and then joining its flared opening to the opening of the wide end. [< Felix *Klein,* 1849-1925, a German mathematician]

Klein|i|an (klī′nē ən), *adj., n.* **—*adj.*** of or having to do with the theories of Melanie Klein (1882-1960), a German pioneer in child psychology.
 —*n.* a follower or supporter of Melanie Klein's theories.

klepht (kleft), *n.* a Greek or Albanian brigand. Also, **kleft.** [< New Greek *kléphtēs* < Greek *kléptēs* thief < *kléptein* to steal]

klep|toc|ra|cy (klep tok′rə sē), *n., pl.* **-cies.** government by thieves. [< Greek *kléptēs* thief + English *-ocracy,* as in *aristocracy*]

klep|to|ma|ni|a (klep′tə mā′nē ə), *n.* an abnormal, irresistible desire to steal, especially things which one does not need or cannot use, or objects of symbolic rather than economic value. Also, **cleptomania.** [< New Latin *kleptomania* < Greek *kléptēs* thief + *maniā* mania]

klep|to|ma|ni|ac (klep′tə mā′nē ak), *n.* a person who has kleptomania. Also, **cleptomaniac.**

klick or **klik** (klik), *n. Slang.* (in southeast Asia) a kilometer. [origin uncertain]

klieg eyes (klēg), **1** eyes inflamed from looking at intense light. **2** an inflammation caused by looking at intense light.

klieg light, a bright, hot arc light, used in taking motion pictures. Also, **kleig light.** [American English < Anton *Kliegl,* 1872-1927, and his brother John, 1869-1959, who invented the lights]

Kline|fel|ter's syndrome (klīn′fel tərz), a hereditary disorder affecting males, characterized by atrophy of the sexual organs and sterility resulting from the presence of an extra female chromosome (XXY instead of XY) in the cells. [< Harry F. *Klinefelter,* Jr., born 1912, an American physician, who first described it]

klip|spring|er (klip′spring′ər), *n.* a small antelope, similar to the chamois in its agility in climbing and leaping, inhabiting the high rocky regions of the east coast and southern part of Africa. [< Afrikaans *klipspringer* < *klip* rock + *springer* one that springs]

klis|ter (klis′tər), *n.* a sticky wax used on skis in wet snow. [< Norwegian *klister*]

***klom|pen** (klom′pən), *n.pl.* wooden shoes worn by the Dutch. [< Dutch *klompen* < Middle Dutch *klompe.* Compare etym. under **clump**]

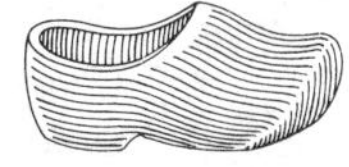
***klompen**

klon|dike (klon′dīk), *n.* one of the forms of solitaire. [< *Klondike,* a region in the Yukon Territory of Canada, where the game was introduced]

Klon|dik|er (klon′dī kər), *n. U.S. and Canadian.* a prospector or pioneer during the Klondike gold rush to the Yukon, 1897-1899.

klong (klong), *n.* a canal in Thailand often lined with buildings that are raised above the surface of the water on stilts.

kloof (klüf), *n.* a narrow valley or ravine among mountains in South Africa; ravine; gorge. [< Afrikaans *kloof* < Dutch, cleft. Compare etym. under **clove⁴**.]

kludge (klüj, kluj), *v.t.,* **kludged, kludg|ing.** *Slang.* to produce (a computer system, design, or the like) by clumsy improvisation. [origin uncertain]

klunk (klungk), *n.* = clunk.

klutz (kluts), *n. U.S. Slang.* a clumsy, awkward person: *"Basically I'm the klutz who makes a terrific entrance to the party and then trips and falls and walks around with food in her hair"* (Time). [< Yiddish *klots* (literally) a block or lump]

klutz|y (klut′sē), *adj.,* **klutz|i|er, klutz|i|est.** *U.S. Slang.* awkward; clumsy: *The sad, klutzy ballerinas of the Music Hall pollute children's first live experience of dance* (New Yorker).

Klux|er (kluk′sər), *n.* = Ku Kluxer.

klys|tron (klīs′tron), *n.* a vacuum tube for producing an ultrahigh-frequency current from a direct current, having several resonators which vary the speed of the electrons and bunch them together; buncher resonator. [perhaps < Greek *klystēr* pipe, syringe (< *klýzein* to wash) + English (elec)*tron*]

km.¹, **1** kilometer or kilometers. **2** kingdom.

km.², square kilometers.

km.³, cubic kilometers.

kmc., kilomegacycle.

K-mes|ic (kā′mes′ik, -mē′sik; -mez′ik, -mē′zik), *adj.* containing or producing heavy mesons; kaonic.

K-mes|on (kā′mes′on, -mē′son; -mez′on, -mē′zon), *n.,* or **K meson,** = heavy meson.

km.p.s., kilometers per second.

km sec (no periods), kilometers per second.

kn., an abbreviation for the following:
 1 krona (Swedish coin).
 2 króna (Icelandic coin).
 3 krone (Danish and Norwegian coin).
 4 krone (former German coin).

knack¹ (nak), *n.* **1** a special skill; the power to do something easily: *That clown has the knack of making very funny faces. Diligence and attention soon gave him the knack of it* (Mark Twain). SYN: aptitude, facility. **2** a trick or habit: *The lady . . . has only, with a very brisk air, a knack of saying the commonest things* (Richard Steele). **3** an adroit or ingenious method of doing something; clever expedient; dodge: *a knack of the trade.* **4** *Obsolete.* a deceitful or crafty device; mean or underhand trick. **5** *Obsolete.* a trinket; trifle; knickknack. [perhaps < *knack²*]

knack² (nak), *n., v.* **—*n.*** a sharp sound such as is made in striking a stone with a hammer; a crack or snap.
 —*v.t.* *Dialect.* to strike together with a sharp, abrupt noise; gnash (the teeth) or snap (the fingers).
 —*v.i.* *Obsolete.* to deal sharp-sounding blows.
 [perhaps imitative]

knack|er (nak′ər), *n.* **1** a person who buys and slaughters useless horses and sells the hides, hoofs, and meat. **2** a person who buys old houses, ships, and the like for their materials. [origin uncertain]

knack|wurst (näk′wėrst, -wůrst; *German* knäk′vůrst′), *n.* a short, thick, highly seasoned sausage. Also, **knockwurst.** [< German *Knackwurst* < *knacken* to crack + *Wurst* sausage]

knag (nag), *n.* **1** = wart. **2** a hook or peg. **3** *Dialect.* a rugged top of a rock or hill. **4** *Obsolete.* one of the projecting points of a deer's antler. [Middle English *knag,* perhaps < Scandinavian (compare Low German *knagge* knot, peg)]

knag|gy (nag′ē), *adj.,* **-gi|er, -gi|est.** knotty; rough; rugged.

knap¹ (nap), *v.,* **knapped** (napt), **knap|ping,** *n.*
 —*v.t., v.i.* **1** to strike with a hard, short sound; knack; knock; rap. **2** to break off; snap. **3** to shape or chip with a hammer, as stone or flint: *An abundance of flint artifacts, mostly scrapers and microlithic blades, were undoubtedly knapped in the tradition of Maglemose* (New Scientist). **4** to bite in a short or abrupt way; snap; nibble.
 —*n.* an abrupt stroke or blow; smart knock.
 [imitative. Compare Low German *knappen.*]
 —knap′per, *n.*

knap² (nap), *n. Dialect.* **1** a hill or hillock. **2** the top of a hill. [Old English *cnæp*]

knap|ping hammer (nap′ing), a hammer for breaking and shaping flints and stones.

***knap|sack** (nap′sak′), *n.* a leather or canvas bag for clothes, equipment, or food, carried on the back; rucksack: *He had walked all over France and Italy with a painter's knapsack on his back* (Henry James). [< Low German *knapsack,* apparently < *knappen* eat + *sack* sack. Compare Dutch *knapzak.*]

***knapsack**

knap|weed (nap′wēd′), *n.* any one of various composite, perennial plants, especially a common weed with a hard, tough stem and light-purple flowers. Various kinds are called knotweed.

Pronunciation Key: hat, āge, cãre, fär; let, ēqual, tėrm; it, īce; hot, ōpen, ôrder; oil, out; cup, pu̇t, rüle; child; long; thin; ᴛʜen; zh, measure; ə represents a in about, e in taken, i in pencil, o in lemon, u in circus.

[Middle English *knopweed* < *knop* knob + *weed*]

knar (när), *n.* a knot in wood. [Middle English *knarre* a rough rock, knot in wood. Compare Low German *knarren* stump, knob.]

knarl (närl), *n. Dialect.* a knot on a tree or in wood; gnarl; knurl. [apparently < *knar.* Compare etym. under **gnarl**[2].]

knave (nāv), *n.* **1** a tricky or dishonest man; rascal; rogue: *The honest dealer is always undone, and the knave gets the advantage* (Jonathan Swift). **SYN:** scoundrel. **2** the jack, a playing card with a picture of a servant or soldier on it. **3** *Archaic.* **a** a boy or lad employed as a servant. **b** a male servant: *What nonsense would the fool thy master prate, When thou, his knave, canst talk at such a rate!* (John Dryden). **4** *Archaic.* a man of humble birth or position. [Old English *cnafa* boy]

knav|er|y (nā′vər ē, nāv′rē), *n., pl.* **-er|ies.** **1** behavior characteristic of a knave or rascal; trickery; dishonesty; roguery: *Why, this is flat knavery, to take upon you another man's name* (Shakespeare). **2** a tricky, dishonest act. **3** *Obsolete.* the playing of tricks; roguishness.

knav|ish (nā′vish), *adj.* tricky; dishonest: *'Tis a knavish piece of work* (Shakespeare). **SYN:** rascally, villainous, fraudulent. **—knav′ish|ly,** *adv.* **—knav′ish|ness,** *n.*

knead (nēd), *v.t.* **1** to work over or work up (moist flour or clay), usually with the hands, into dough or paste: *Machines have been invented to knead bread dough.* **2a** to make or shape by kneading. **b** *Figurative.* to blend, join, or reduce to a common mass, as if by kneading. **3** to press and squeeze with the hands; massage: *Kneading the muscles in a stiff shoulder will take away the stiffness.* [Old English *cnedan*] **—knead′a|ble,** *adj.* **—knead′er,** *n.*

knee** (nē), *n., v.,* **kneed, knee|ing.** **—*n. **1** the joint between the thigh and the lower leg. The knee is formed by the joining of the thighbone and shinbone. It is covered in front by the kneecap. **2** any joint in an animal corresponding to the human knee or elbow, as in the hind leg of a horse, the front or hind leg of an elephant, or the tarsal joint of a bird. **3** anything like a bent knee in shape or position, such as a joint or brace of wood, metal, or other material, with parts that meet at a right angle. **4** the part of a garment covering the knee. **5** a knob on the root of a tree, especially the bald cypress, which shows above the surface of water or wet soil. **—*v.t.*** **1** to strike or touch with the knee. **2** to kneel to, as in reverence. **3** to make (one's way) on the knees: *Fall down and knee The way into his mercy* (Shakespeare).
bring to one's knees, to force to yield: *A very efficacious method of bringing a . . . troublesome class of offenders to their knees* (London Times).
on (or **upon**) **the knees of the gods,** beyond human control: *Such things are yet upon the knees of the gods* (London Daily News).
[Old English *cnēo*] **—knee′like′,** *adj.*

thighbone (femur)
kneecap (patella)
shinbone (tibia)
fibula

***knee**
definition 1

knee action, a method of suspending the front wheels of a motor vehicle, each with its own spring and spindle, so as to have independent vertical movement.

knee|bend (nē′bend′), *n.* an exercise in which a person alternately crouches on the toes and then rises to a standing position.

knee breeches, breeches reaching to or just below the knees.

knee|cap (nē′kap′), *n., v.,* **-capped, -cap|ping.** **—*n.*** **1** the flat movable bone at the front of the knee; patella; kneepan. See diagram under **knee.** **2** a covering to protect the knee, such as an elastic or a knitted cap. **—*v.i.*** to shoot or drill through someone's kneecap as a form of punishment or terrorism: *A man . . . mugs an old lady and gets kneecapped* (Manchester Guardian Weekly).

kneed (nēd), *adj.* having a kneelike joint or bend, as a plant stem; geniculate.

-kneed, *combining form.* having a ___knee or knees: *Weak-kneed = having weak knees.*

knee-deep (nē′dēp′), *adj., adv.* **1** so deep as to reach to the knees: *The snow lay knee-deep.* **2** sunk to the knees: *to wade knee-deep in slush,* (*Figurative.*) *knee-deep in debt or trouble.*

knee drill, (in the Salvation Army) a kneeling to order for prayers.

knee-high (nē′hī′), *adj., adv.* so high as to reach the knees.

knee|hole (nē′hōl′), *n.* a hole or space between the lower drawers of a desk, to make room for the knees.

knee jerk, a sudden, involuntary kick produced by striking the tendon below the kneecap.

knee-jerk (nē′jėrk′), *adj., n.* **—*adj.*** *Informal.* **1** without thought; automatic: *knee-jerk responses.* **2** that reacts without much thought or in a predictable or automatic way: *"What you have here," he said, "is the opposite of the knee-jerk liberal—the knee-jerk conservative"* (Time). **—*n.*** a person whose reactions are predictable or automatic, especially in politics.

kneel (nēl), *v.,* **knelt** or **kneeled, kneel|ing,** *n.* **—*v.i.*** **1** to go down on one's knee or knees: *She knelt down to pull a weed from the flower bed. I kneeled down, and gave God thanks aloud for my recovery from my sickness* (Daniel Defoe). **2** to remain in this position: *They knelt in prayer for half an hour.* **—*n.*** the act or position of kneeling. [Old English *cnēowlian* < *cnēo* knee] **—kneel′er,** *n.*

kneeling bus, *U.S.* a bus with a pneumatic suspension system to lower its body to curb level so that passengers do not have to climb a step: *Pledging that his own administration would be "sensitive to the special needs of the aging," Mr. Koch promised, among other things, . . . the deployment of "kneeling" buses* (Charles Kaiser).

knee|pad (nē′pad′), *n.* a pad worn around the knee for protection.

knee|pan (nē′pan′), *n.* = kneecap.

knee|piece (nē′pēs′), *n.* armor worn on the knee.

knee|room (nē′rüm′, -ru̇m′), *n.* enough room in front of a seat in a vehicle, to keep one's knees in a comfortable position.

knee spavin, a chronic inflammation of the bones of the knee joint in horses.

knee splint, a local bony enlargement near the knee joint of the forelimb in horses.

knee-sprung (nē′sprung′), *adj.* with knees bent from the normal position: *a knee-sprung horse.*

knell (nel), *n., v.* **—*n.*** **1** the sound of a bell rung slowly after a death or at a funeral: *We could hear the knell of the church bell sounding for the dead President.* **2** *Figurative.* something regarded as a sign of death or as telling of a death: *Their refusal rang the knell of our hopes. One dreadful sound could the Rover hear . . . The Devil below was ringing his knell* (Robert Southey). **3** a mournful sound. [< verb]
—*v.i.* **1** (of a bell) to ring slowly, especially for a death or at a funeral; toll: *The sullen, huge oracular bell, Which never knells but for a princely death* (Byron). **2** *Figurative.* to give a warning sign of death, failure, or the like. **3** to make a mournful sound.
—*v.t.* **1** to summon or call by or as if by a knell: *Each matin bell . . . knells us back to a world of death* (Samuel Taylor Coleridge). **2** to proclaim by or as if by a knell: *Its huge clocks had successively knelled three hours after midnight* (Scott). (*Figurative.*) *The surrender knelled the downfall of the tyrant.* **3** *Obsolete.* to ring (a bell), especially to ring slowly and solemnly, as for a death or at a funeral; toll.
[Middle English *knellen,* Old English *cnyllan*]

knelt (nelt), *v.* a past tense and a past participle of **kneel:** *She knelt and prayed.*

Knes|set or **knes|set** (knes′et), *n.* the Israeli parliament: *The Israeli government resigned this morning after last night's votes in the Knesset on motions of no confidence* (London Times). [< Hebrew *Knesset*]

knew (nü, nyü), *v.* the past tense of **know:** *She knew the right answer.*

Knick|er|bock|er (nik′ər bok′ər), *n.* **1** a person descended from the early Dutch settlers of New York. **2** a person living in New York. [< Diedrich *Knickerbocker,* alleged by Washington Irving to be the author of his own *Knickerbocker's History of New York*]

knick|er|bock|ers (nik′ər bok′ərz), *n.pl.* = knickers.

***knickers**
definition 1

***knick|ers** (nik′ərz), *n.pl.* **1** short, loose-fitting trousers gathered in at, or just below, the knee: *old golfing knickers.* **2** a kind of bloomerlike underwear, worn by women. [short for *knickerbockers* < *Knickerbocker* (said to be due to the costume shown in illustrations of Washington Irving's *Knickerbocker's History of New York*)]

knick|knack (nik′nak′), *n.* a pleasing trifle; ornament; trinket: *The old lady surrounded herself with knicknacks.* **SYN:** gimcrack, kickshaw. Also, **nicknack.** [varied reduplication of *knack*[1] a trick]

knick|knack|er|y (nik′nak′ər ē), *n., pl.* **-er|ies.** **1** knickknacks collectively. **2** = knickknack.

knife** (nīf), *n., pl.* **knives,** *v.,* **knifed, knif|ing.** **—*n. **1a** a thin, flat, metal blade fastened in a handle so that it can be used to cut or spread. A table knife is stiff, with no joint; a pocketknife has a joint so that the sharp edge can be folded inside the handle. *Bought a large kitchen knife and half a dozen oyster knives* (Samuel Pepys). **b** any weapon having a short blade with a sharp edge and point, such as a dagger. **2** a sharp blade forming part of a tool or machine: *The knives of a lawn mower cut grass.*
—*v.t.* **1** to cut, strike, or stab with a knife: *The criminal knifed his victim in a rage.* **2** *U.S. Slang., Figurative.* to strike at secretly; try to defeat in an underhand way.
—*v.i.* to move or pass (through) as if with a knife: *A new superhighway . . . knifes through the crowded south of Los Angeles* (Wall Street Journal).
under the knife, *Informal.* undergoing a surgical operation: *While under the knife, the patient was completely unconscious.*
[Old English *cnīf* < Scandinavian (compare Old Icelandic *knīfr*)] **—knife′less,** *adj.* **—knife′like′,** *adj.*

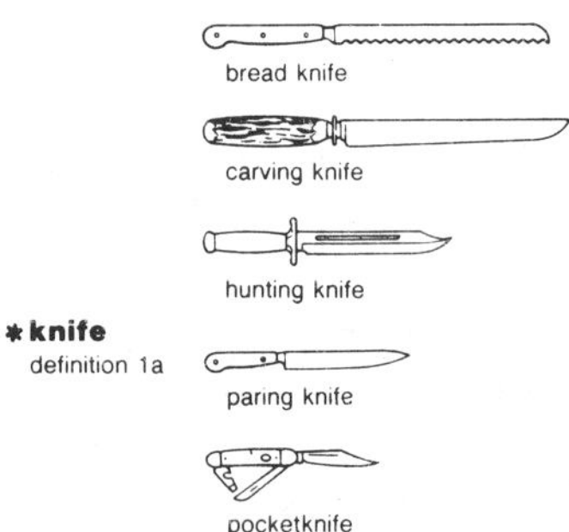

***knife**
definition 1a

knife|board (nīf′bôrd′), *n.* **1** a board on which knives are cleaned and polished. **2** *British.* (formerly) the passenger seat on top of a double-deck bus; a bench placed lengthwise on which passengers sat back to back.

knife edge, **1** the edge of a knife. **2** anything very sharp. **3** a wedge on the fine edge of which a pendulum, scale beam, or the like is hung.

knife-edged (nīf′ejd′), *adj.* having a thin, sharp edge, like a knife.

knife|fish (nīf′fish′), *n., pl.* **-fish|es** or (*collectively*) **-fish.** a transparent, freshwater eel similar to the electric eel, found in Central and South American waters.

knife grinder, **1** a person whose work is grinding or sharpening knives and cutting tools: . . . *a knife grinder working at his wheel* (London Times). **2** a grindstone, emery wheel, or other appliance for grinding tools. **3** = nightjar.

knife money, an ancient Chinese currency consisting of bronze pieces shaped like a knife.

knife|point (nīf′point′), *n.* the point of a knife blade.
at knifepoint, with a knife pointed at a person; under duress: . . . *teachers robbed at knifepoint in their own classrooms* (Harper's).

knife switch, a type of electric switch consisting of one or more metal strips so arranged that they can be inserted between flat springs and thus close a circuit.

knight (nīt), *n., v.* **—*n.*** **1** in the Middle Ages: **a** a man raised to an honorable military rank and pledged to do good deeds. After serving as a page and squire, a man was made a knight by the king or a lord. **b** a military servant of a lord, especially a mounted servant. **2** (in modern times) a man raised to an honorable rank because of great achievement or service. A British knight ranks just below a baronet, and his rank and title are not hereditary. A man named John Smith becomes Sir John Smith, or Sir John, as a knight. *Abbr:* Kt. **3** *Figurative.* a man devoted to the service or protection of a lady: *In all your quarrels Will I be your knight. This I will do, dear damsel, for your sake* (Tennyson). **SYN:** cavalier. **4** a person in ancient history, mythology, or legend, considered to hold a position similar to that of the medieval knight, such as the equites, who were mainly financiers, and were next below senators. **5** a member or holder of a rank or degree in any order or society that bears the official

title of *Knights.* **6** a piece in the game of chess, usually having the figure of a horse's head. It moves two squares horizontally and one square vertically or one square horizontally and two squares vertically from the square it occupies, whether or not any of the intervening squares is occupied. See picture under **chess**[1].
—***v.t.*** to raise to the rank of knight: *He was knighted by the queen. A soldier, by the honour-giving hand Of Coeur-de-lion knighted in the field* (Shakespeare).
[Old English *cniht* boy] —**knight′like′**, *adj.*
▶ See usage note under **Sir**.

knight|age (nī′tij), *n.* **1** the body of knights collectively. **2** a list or register of knights.

knight bachelor, *pl.* **knights bachelors** or **knights bachelor**. **1** a British knight of the lowest but most ancient order. **2** a British subject who has been knighted but not made a member of any special order.

knight-er|rant (nīt′er′ənt), *n., pl.* **knights-errant**. (in the Middle Ages) a knight traveling in search of adventure, especially to exhibit military skill, bravery, and chivalry; a wandering knight.

knight-er|rant|ry (nīt′er′ən trē), *n., pl.* **knight-errant|ries**. **1** conduct or action characteristic of a knight-errant. **2** quixotic conduct or action.

knight|hood (nīt′hůd), *n.* **1** the rank or dignity of a knight: *I would not take a knighthood for my fortune* (Shakespeare). **2** the profession or occupation of a knight: *The champions, all of high degree, Who knighthood lov'd, and deeds of chivalry* (John Dryden). **3** the character or qualities of a knight; chivalrousness: *His knighthood shone as he helped the lady in distress.* **4** knights as a group or class; a company of knights: *All the knighthood of France came to the aid of the king.*

knight|li|ness (nīt′lē nis), *n.* knightly condition or qualities.

knight|ly (nīt′lē), *adj., adv.* —***adj.*** **1** of or like a knight; brave, generous, and courteous; chivalrous: *knightly courage.* **SYN**: noble. **2** belonging to or appropriate to a knight: *a knightly sword, knightly deeds.* **3** consisting or composed of knights: *a knightly company.*
—***adv.*** **1** as a knight should do; in a manner befitting a knight; bravely, generously, and courteously: *His honor knightly shown.* **SYN**: chivalrously, gallantly. **2** like a knight: *Say ... why thou comest thus knightly clad in arms* (Shakespeare).

Knight of the Bath, a member of an order of knighthood in England founded by King George I in 1725.

Knights Hospitalers, a powerful military order of monks of the period of the Crusades and afterward.

Knights of Columbus, a fraternal society of Roman Catholic men to increase the religious and civic usefulness of its members and to encourage benevolence. It was founded in 1882. *Abbr:* K.C.

Knights of Labor, a secret labor organization formed in 1869 to promote the interests of the workingman.

Knights of Malta, **1** the Knights Hospitalers, who ruled on Malta from 1530 to 1798. **2** one of the three highest degrees in the York Rite of Freemasonry.

Knights of Pythias, a fraternal and benevolent society with secret initiation and rites, founded in 1864 in Washington, D.C. *Abbr:* K.P.

Knights of Rhodes, the Knights Hospitalers, who ruled on Rhodes from 1310 to 1522.

Knights of St. John of Jerusalem, the Knights Hospitalers, whose members originally belonged to a monastery in Jerusalem dedicated to Saint John the Baptist.

Knights of the Maccabees, the name of the fraternal society of Maccabees until 1914.

Knight Templar, *pl.* **Knights Templars** *for 1;* **Knights Templar** *for 2.* **1** a member of a religious and military order founded in the Middle Ages to protect the Holy Sepulcher and pilgrims to the Holy Land. **2** a member of an order of Masons in the United States.

knish (knish), *n.* a pastry made of dough, wrapped around a stuffing of potato, cheese, or liver, and often served as an hors d'oeuvre. [< Yiddish *knish*]

knit** (nit), *v.,* **knit|ted** or **knit, knit|ting**, *n.* —v.t.*** **1** to make (cloth or an article of clothing) by looping yarn or thread together with long needles: *She is knitting a sweater.* **2** to form (cloth or an article of clothing) by machinery which forms loops instead of weaving: *Jersey is cloth knitted by machine.* **3** *Figurative.* to join closely and firmly together; connect intimately: *David and Jonathan were knit in friendship. Come, knit hands* (Milton). **4** to draw (the brows) closely together in wrinkles: *She knits her brows when she frowns.* **5** *Figurative.* to make or constitute as if by joining parts: *to knit an agreement or a peace.* **SYN**: cement. **6** *Archaic.* to tie or fasten by or as if by knotting: *I knit my handkercher about your brows* (Shakespeare).
—***v.i.*** **1** to make an article or fabric by looping yarn or thread together with long needles, or by machinery which forms loops instead of weaving: *She knits all day.* **2** to be joined closely and firmly; grow together: *The doctor set my arm so that the broken bone knit in a clean join.* **3** *Figurative.* to become compact, firm, or strong by close consolidation of parts; become consolidated: *Young men, when they knit and shape perfectly, do seldom grow to a further stature* (Francis Bacon). **4** (of the brows) to draw together in wrinkles: *with downcast eyes and knitting brow* (Byron).
—***n.*** **1** the act or process of knitting. **2** a style of knitting. **3** knitted work.
[Old English *cnyttan,* related to *cnotta* a knot] —**knit′ter**, *n.*

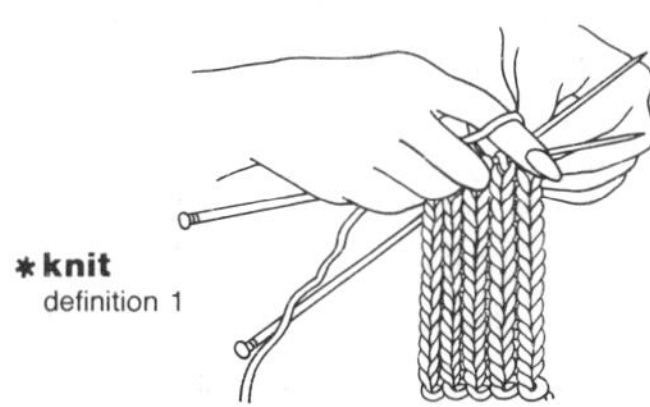

***knit**
definition 1

knit|goods (nit′gůdz′), *n.* = knitwear.

knit|ting (nit′ing), *n.* **1** knitted work: *Her knitting was on the table.* **2** the act or occupation of a person who knits.

knitting machine, a machine designed to make various kinds of knitted fabrics.

knitting needle, one of a pair of long needles used in knitting by hand.

knit|wear (nit′wãr′), *n.* clothing made of knitted fabric.

knives (nīvz), *n.* plural of **knife**.

knob (nob), *n., v.,* **knobbed, knob|bing**. —***n.*** **1** a rounded lump or mass: *A little knob of a nose* (Robert Bridges). **SYN**: knot, protuberance. **2** a rounded part that sticks out: *the knob of a door, the knob of a drawer, the knob of an umbrella, the knob on the dial of a television set.* **3a** an isolated, rounded hill or mountain. **b** any hill. **4** *Architecture.* an ornamental boss, as of carved work. **5** *Slang.* the head.
—***v.t.*** **1** to furnish with a knob or knobs. **2** to free from knobs. **3** to knap (stone in a quarry).
with knobs on, *Slang.* in a noteworthy manner; to a remarkable degree: *Mr. de Vries is a witty writer with knobs on* (Observer).
[Middle English *knobbe.* Compare Middle Low German *knobbe.*] —**knob′like′**, *adj.*

knobbed (nobd), *adj.* having a knob or knobs.

knob|bi|ness (nob′ē nis), *n.* the quality of being knobby.

knob|ble (nob′əl), *v.,* **-bled, -bling**, *n.* —***v.t.*** to remove (knobs) from quarried stone.
—***n.*** a small knob.

knob|bled (nob′əld), *adj.* **1** = knobby. **2** knotty; difficult; rough: *... the Great Siege—the most dramatic single episode in Gibraltar's knobbled past* (New Yorker).

knob|bly (nob′lē), *adj.* = knobby.

knob|by (nob′ē), *adj.,* **-bi|er, -bi|est**. **1** covered with knobs. **2** rounded like a knob.

knob|cone pine (nob′kōn′), a small pine found on the west coast of the United States. It releases its seeds only when the tree burns or dies.

knob|ker|rie or **knob|ker|ry** (nob′ker′ē), *n.,pl.* **-ries**. a short wooden club with a knob at the end, used for striking or throwing by tribesmen in South Africa; kerrie. [half-translation of Afrikaans *knopkirie* < Dutch *knop* knob + Hottentot *kirī* stick, club]

knob|stick (nob′stik′), *n.* = knobkerrie.

knock (nok), *v., n.* —***v.t.*** **1** to give a hard blow or blows to with the fist, knuckles, or anything hard; hit; strike; beat: *He knocked him on the head. The farmer knocked the fence post into the ground with a sledge hammer.* **2** to hit and cause to fall: *The car crashed into a sign and knocked it down.* **3** *Slang, Figurative.* to find fault with; criticize (something): *The critics knocked the new book.*
—***v.i.*** **1** to hit with a noise, as with the fist, knuckles, or something hard; come into a collision with something; rap: *She knocked on the door. His knees knocked together from fright.* **2** to make a noise, especially a rattling or pounding noise: *The old engine is knocking.* **3** *Slang, Figurative.* to find fault; criticize.
—***n.*** **1** a hit; hard stroke or thump: *The hard knock made her cry.* **SYN**: blow. **2** a hit with a noise. **3** the act of knocking. **4** the sound of knocking: *She did not hear the knock at the door.* **5** a sound caused by loose parts or improper burning of fuel: *a knock in the engine.* **6** *Slang, Figurative.* a severe criticism. **7** *British Informal.* (in cricket) an innings.
knock about, *Informal.* **a** to wander from place to place: *The less boys we have knocking about here the better* (Graham Greene). **b** to subject to rough or hard treatment: *She had been knocked about by adversity.*
knock around, to knock about: *They have been knocking around Europe all summer.*
knock back, *Slang.* to eat or drink: *Hurd ... knocks back an unvarying breakfast of eggnog, toast, and coffee* (Time). *About fifty people stood around ... knocking back free liquor* (Punch).
knock down, a to take apart: *We knocked down the bookcases and packed them in the car.* **b** to sell (an article) to the highest bidder at an auction: *It was ... knocked down to the last bidder* (Charles Johnston). **c** to strike down; overcome; vanquish: *Knock him down there* (Shakespeare). **d** *U.S. Slang.* (of a conductor or other collector of fares) to embezzle (money) from passengers' fares: *The driver was accused of knocking down half of each day's intake.*
knock for a loop. See under **loop**[1].
knock off, *Informal.* **a** to take off; deduct: *to knock off 10 dollars from the price.* **b** to stop work: *The men knock off early in hot weather.* **c** to stop; quit (doing something): *Someone will say, "Knock it off, Frank." So I knock it off. I talk about my four kids instead* (New York Times). **d** to accomplish hastily; do quickly: *to knock off a song in 10 minutes.* **e** *Figurative.* to defeat; overcome: [*They*] *astounded rowing fans in the States last summer by knocking off Harvard's varsity* (New Yorker). **f** to kill: *When one of those guys got knocked off, ... the judges were at the funeral* (Harper's).
knock oneself out, to expend all of one's energy; exhaust oneself: *A disillusioned reporter and his photographer knocked themselves out in an effort to invest the ... beauty contest with some spark of interest* (Sunday Times).
knock out, a to hit so hard as to make (someone) helpless or unconscious: *The police feared that he had been knocked out in the accident.* **b** *Figurative.* to drive out of the contest; vanquish: *Two years ago Aston Villa* [*football club*] *knocked out Sunderland* (London Daily News). **c** *Boxing.* to defeat (an opponent) by hitting him so that he falls to the canvas for ten seconds or more.
knock out of the box. See under **box**[1].
knock over, a to overthrow; upset: *The Sampson pitched shell after shell right in among the tents, knocking them over right and left* (William Russell). **b** to overcome: *That evening two of my* [*men*] *... were knocked over by fever* (Frederick Selous). **c** *Slang.* to hold up; rob: [*He*] *arrived to knock over a gas station in Passy one evening* (New York Times).
knock together, to make or put together hastily: *The boys knocked together a sort of raft out of old boards.*
knock up, a to tire out; exhaust: *The much-vaunted steed ... was now nearly knocked up by traveling* (Washington Irving). **b** *Especially British.* to get out of bed by knocking at the door: *You knock up a garage and the proprietor comes down in his pyjamas in the rain* (Punch). **c** *Informal.* to earn: *The little bleeder's still giving me two pounds a week when he's knocking up a fiver* (Atlantic). **d** *British Informal.* to make or put together quickly: *I suspect that if stripped of their brand names they* [*medicines*] *could be knocked up by any backroom pharmacist for a tenth of the retail price* (Punch). **e** *Slang.* to cause to become pregnant.
[Old English *cnocian,* earlier *cnucian*]

knock|a|bout (nok′ə bout′), *n., adj.* —***n.*** **1** a small, easily handled sailboat having one mast, a mainsail, and a jib, but without a bowsprit. **2** something suitable for rough use, such as a car: *He drives an old knockabout.* **3** *British.* **a** a slapstick; horseplay: *There was a distinct note of burlesque in its Restoration knockabout* (Punch). **b** the act of knocking about; a boisterous exchange of words, blows, or ideas: *There was a good party knockabout on pensions on Monday* (Punch).
—***adj.*** **1** suitable for rough use: *A knockabout weekend satchel made of this canvas in tan or navy blue* (New Yorker). **2** rough; boisterous; noisy. **3** (of comic acting or writing) characterized

Pronunciation Key: hat, āge, cãre, fär; let, ēqual, tėrm; it, īce; hot, ōpen, ôrder; oil, out; cup, půt, rüle; **ch**ild; lo**ng**; **th**in; **ᴛʜ**en; **zh**, measure; **ə** represents **a** in about, **e** in taken, **i** in pencil, **o** in lemon, **u** in circus.

by or adept in slapstick and horseplay: *an excellent knockabout comic, a knockabout farce.* **4** characterized by being driven to and fro, or knocking about.
[American English < *knock* + *about*]

knock|down (nok′doun′), *adj., n.* —*adj.* **1** irresistible; overwhelming: *a knockdown bargain.* **2** constructed in separate parts, so as to be easily knocked down or taken apart for storage or moving: *Manufacturers have developed a large and growing business in so-called knockdown kits of precut materials and fastenings* (Christian Science Monitor).
—*n.* **1** a knockdown piece of furniture. **2** the act of knocking down. **3** a blow that knocks down or fells to the ground; overwhelming blow. **4** a stand-up fight.

knock|down-drag-out (nok′doun′drag′out′), *adj. U.S. Slang.* characterized by great violence, especially hand-to-hand; rough; violent; raging: *a knockdown-drag-out fight, a knockdown-drag-out argument.*

knock|er (nok′ər), *n.* **1** a person or thing that knocks: *Who was the knocker at the door?* **2** a hinged knob, ring, or the like, fastened on a door for use in knocking: *The front door ... was ornamented with a gorgeous brass knocker, curiously wrought* (Washington Irving). **3** *British.* a door-to-door salesman.
on the knocker, *British.* from door to door: *Selling gemstones on the knocker will soon become a familiar feature of suburban life* (Sunday Times).

knock|er-up (nok′ər up′), *n., pl.* **knock|ers-up.** *British.* a person who calls the resident of a house to the door in order to prepare the ground for someone else to solicit or canvass: *Three hundred yards away ... the candidate, is canvassing with six knockers-up* (London Times).

knock-knee (nok′nē′), *n.* an inward bending of the legs, so that the knees knock together in walking.
knock-knees, knees that bend like this: *The rider has knock-knees.*

knock-kneed (nok′nēd′), *adj.* having legs bent inward at the knees. The knees of a knock-kneed person hit each other in walking.

knock|off (nok′ôf′, -of′), *n.* **1** the act of knocking off. **2** a device for knocking something off. **3** the point at which something is knocked off. **4** *Slang.* a copy, usually an unauthorized one and often less expensive than the popular original.

knock-on (nok′on′, -ôn′), *v.,* **knocked-on, knock-ing-on,** *n. Rugby, Soccer.* —*v.t., v.i.* to hit (the ball) forward with a hand or arm.
—*n.* an act or instance of knocking-on.

knock|out (nok′out′), *n., adj.* —*n.* **1** the act of knocking out: *The boxer won the fight by a knockout.* **2** the condition of being knocked out. **3** a blow that knocks out. **4** *U.S. Slang.* a very attractive person; overwhelming or striking thing.
—*adj. Slang.* **1** that knocks out; defeating or that can defeat by knocking out: *a knockout blow.* **2** that puts something out of operation or diminishes: *knockout competition. The biggest knockout punch against highway accidents in the state's road history* (Birmingham News). **3** outstanding; stunning; overwhelming: *a knockout performance. ... a knock-out scent to spell tempestuous attraction* (Punch).

knockout drops, any powerful narcotic, often chloral hydrate, used to stupefy an intended victim.

knock|up (nok′up′), *n. Especially British.* warm-up: *The second set lasted no longer than a knockup* (London Times).

knock|wurst (nok′wėrst, -vůrst), *n.* = knackwurst.

knoll[1] (nōl), *n.* a small, rounded hill; mound: *Hills and crags of every size, down to mere hummocks and knolls* (Archibald Geikie). **SYN**: hillock.
[Old English *cnoll*]

knoll[2] (nōl), *n., v. Archaic.* —*n.* **1** the act of tolling a bell. **2** the sound of a large bell.
—*v.t., v.i.* to ring or toll (a bell); knell: *All that night I heard The heavy clocks knolling the drowsy hours* (Tennyson).
[apparently variant of *knell;* perhaps, influenced by *toll*[1]]

knop (nop), *n.* a small, rounded protuberance or knob, as for ornament; boss, stud, button, or tassel. [Middle English *knop, knap,* perhaps related to Old English *cnæp;* see etym. under **knap[2]**. Compare Old Icelandic *knappr* knob, button.]

knopped (nopt), *adj.* having knops; knobbed.

knorr (nôr), *n.* a broad, roomy cargo ship, used by the Vikings between the 700's A.D. and the late 1000's. [< Old Icelandic *knörr* merchant ship]

knosp (nosp), *n.* a budlike ornament, as in architectural work. [< German *Knospe*]

*** knot[1]** (not), *n., v.,* **knot|ted, knot|ting.** —*n.* **1a** a fastening made by tying or twining together pieces of one or more ropes, strings, or cords: *a square knot, a slipknot, a knot in a shoelace.* **b** an accidental tying or twisting of rope, cord, string, cable, or wire, usually drawn tight; tangle. **2** a bow of ribbon or lace, worn as an ornament: *a shoulder knot.* **3a** a group; cluster: *A knot of students stood talking outside the classroom. They had now arrived at the knot of palm trees* (Scott). **SYN**: company. **b** a central, thickened point where lines, nerves, or especially mountain chains are joined. **4a** a hard mass of wood formed in a tree where a branch grows out, which shows as a round, cross-grained piece in a board. **b** any one of several diseases of trees in which large lumps or gnarls are formed. **5** a hard lump. A knot sometimes forms in a tired muscle. **SYN**: knob. **6a** a joint where leaves grow out on the stem of a plant. **b** a node on a stem, especially when of swollen form, such as one of the joints in grasses. **7a** a measure of speed used for ships and aircraft; one nautical mile per hour. A ship with a 20-knot speed can go 20 nautical miles an hour. **b** a nautical mile; 6,076.11549 feet. **c** (formerly) one of the equal divisions on a hand log line to measure the speed of a ship. It is marked by pieces of knotted string. **8** *Figurative.* a difficulty or problem: *Knots worthy of solution, which alone A Deity could solve* (William Cowper). **SYN**: puzzle, perplexity. **9** *Figurative.* **a** a thing that unites closely or intricately; bond; link: *O night and shades! How are ye joined with Hell in triple knot!* (Milton). **b** the bond of wedlock. **10** a design or figure formed of crossing lines, such as an intricate flourish of the pen. **11** *Dialect.* a flower bed of fanciful or intricate design.
—*v.t.* **1** to tie in a knot; fasten with a knot: *He knotted the loose threads together so that they would not tear any further. At his side a wretched scrip was hung, Wide-patch'd and knotted to a twisted thong* (Alexander Pope). **2** to tangle in or as if in knots; entangle. **3** to make knots for (a fringe). **4** *Figurative.* to unite closely in a way that is hard to undo: *The deed knots us together for time and eternity, like the coil of a serpent* (Hawthorne). **SYN**: bind.
—*v.i.* **1** to tangle in knots; be or become tied or twisted into a knot: *My thread has knotted.* **SYN**: snarl. **2** to make a fringe by tying knots. **3** to form into a hard lump.
[Old English *cnotta*] —**knot′less,** *adj.*

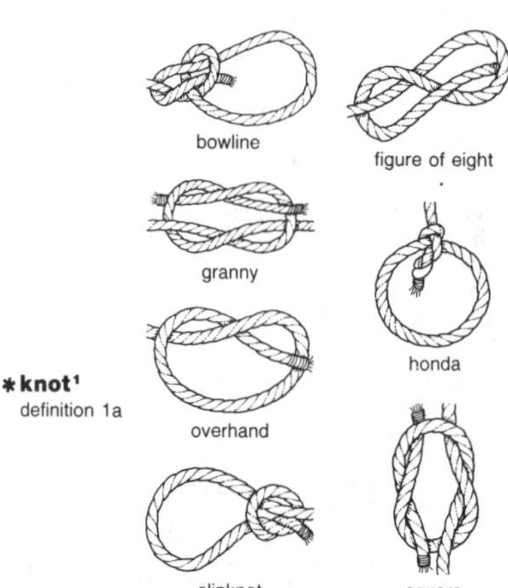

*** knot[1]**
definition 1a

knot[2] (not), *n.* a small shore bird, of the same family as the sandpipers, which breeds in the Arctic and migrates southward in the winter. It has a reddish breast in its spring plumage. [origin uncertain]

knot garden, a flower garden of an intricate or fanciful design; parterre; topiary.

knot|grass (not′gras′, -gräs′), *n.* **1** any one of a group of common weeds of the buckwheat family, whose stems have large joints; knotweed; knotwort. **2** any one of various related or similar plants.

knot|head (not′hed′), *n. U.S. Slang.* a stupid person; blockhead.

knot|hole (not′hōl′), *n.* a hole in a board formed by a knot falling out.

knot stitch, any stitch used in embroidery to form an ornamental knot on the surface of the work.

knot|ted (not′id), *adj.* **1** having a knot or knots; knotty. **2** formed or decorated with knots or the like. **3** *Dialect.* (of a garden) laid out in a fanciful or intricate design.

knot|ter (not′ər), *n.* **1** a person or a machine that ties knots. **2** a person or device that removes knots, as from yarn.

knot|ting (not′ing), *n.* **1** a kind of fancywork made with twisted and knotted threads, and closely imitating some old forms of lace. **2** a solution, as of shellac, to cover knots on wood before painting.

knot|ty (not′ē), *adj.,* **-ti|er, -ti|est. 1** full of knots: *knotty wood. ... the knotty side of an old Pollarel tree* (Keats). *A modern kitchen with knotty pine cabinets and exhaust fans* (New York Times). **SYN**: gnarled. **2** *Figurative.* difficult; puzzling; involved; intricate: *a knotty problem.* **SYN**: complex. —**knot′ti|ness,** *n.*

knot|weed (not′wēd′), *n.* **1** = knotgrass. **2** = knapweed.

knot|work (not′wėrk′), *n.* ornamental work of or representing cords or the like knotted together, intertwined, or interlaced.

knot|wort (not′wėrt′), *n.* = knotgrass.

knout (nout), *n., v.* —*n.* a whip formerly used especially in Russia to inflict punishment: *Shall I weep if ... an infant civilisation be ruled with rod or with knout?* (Tennyson).
—*v.t.* to flog or punish with a knout.
[< French *knout* < Russian *knut* < Scandinavian (compare Swedish, Danish *knut* knot, knout)]

know[1] (nō), *v.,* **knew, known, know|ing,** *n.* —*v.t.* **1** to have the facts of; be skilled in: *He knows arithmetic. An artist must know his art.* **2** to have the facts and be sure they are true; be sure of; have true information about: *We know that 2 and 2 are 4. What is it to be wise? 'Tis but to know how little can be known* (Alexander Pope). **3** to have firmly in the mind or memory: *to know a lesson.* **4** to have an understanding, knowledge, or information of; have experience with: *She knows how to cook.* **5** to be aware of; have seen or heard; have information about: *to know a person's name.* **6** to be acquainted with; be familiar with: *I know her very well, but I don't know her sister. Do you know this road?* **7** to recognize; identify: *You would hardly know him since his illness.* **8** to be able to tell apart from others; distinguish: *You will know our house by the red roof. He knows many kinds of birds.* **9** *Archaic.* to have sexual intercourse with.
—*v.i.* to be sure; have understanding, knowledge, or information: *The doctor does not guess; he knows.*
—*n.* = knowledge.
in the know, *Informal.* having inside or special information: *Few people in the know doubt that he had willingly defected to the Reds* (Newsweek).
let know, to tell; inform: *I'll let him know that we are coming.*
[Old English *cnāwan*] —**know′a|ble,** *adj., n.* —**know′er,** *n.*
—*Syn. v.t.* **1 Know, understand** mean to have a clear understanding of the meaning of something. **Know** is the common and general word for being well acquainted with a subject: *She knows more about Mexico than anyone else at this school.* **Understand** emphasizes having a thorough grasp of both facts and meaning, seeing clearly and fully not only the nature of a fact or idea but also its implications: *to understand the relationship between mathematics and physics.*

know[2] (nou, nō), *n. Scottish.* a knoll; hillock.

know-all (nō′ôl′), *n. U.S. Slang.* a conceited person; a know-it-all.

know-how (nō′hou′), *n. Informal.* the ability to do something, especially something more or less complicated: *Help and know-how on the construction of a French nuclear-powered submarine was offered* (Bulletin of Atomic Scientists).
[American English < *know* + *how*]

know|ing (nō′ing), *adj., n.* —*adj.* **1** having knowledge; well-informed: *I have remarked that your knowing people, who are so much wiser than anybody else, are eternally keeping society in a ferment* (Washington Irving). **SYN**: understanding, intelligent, instructed, enlightened. **2** clever; shrewd: *The knowing fox had slipped away from packs of dogs many times.* **SYN**: sharp, cunning. **3** suggesting shrewd or secret understanding of matters: *His only answer was a knowing look.*
—*n.* **1** acquaintance with a thing or fact; knowledge. **SYN**: cognizance. **2** *Obsolete.* something known. —**know′ing|ly,** *adv.* —**know′ing|ness,** *n.*

know-it-all (nō′it ôl′), *n., adj. U.S. Slang.* —*n.* a person with pretensions to complete or infallible knowledge: *The blasé know-it-all from the large prep school is cynically scornful* (New York Times).
—*adj.* conceited; pretentious: *a know-it-all attitude.*

knowl|edge (nol′ij), *n.* **1** what one knows; range of information: *a hunter's knowledge of guns. If a little knowledge is dangerous, where is the man who has so much as to be out of danger?* (Thomas H. Huxley). **2** all that is known or can be learned; the sum of what is known: *Science is a branch of knowledge. But Knowledge to their eyes her ample page Rich with the spoils of time did ne'er unroll* (Thomas Gray). **3** the fact of knowing: *The knowledge of our victory caused* *great joy.* **4** the act of knowing; familiarity with a thing, person, subject, or place: *a knowledge of the surrounding countryside.* **5** clear and certain mental perception; understanding. **6** *Archaic and Law.* sexual intercourse.

knowledges, a branch of learning: *all the knowledges and skills.*

to (the best of) one's knowledge, as far as one knows; according to one's certain knowledge, or as one actually knows: *This was done twice to my knowledge. I have never met him to the best of my knowledge.*

[Middle English *knowleche,* Old English *cnawlec* acknowledgment, a derivative of *cnāwan* to know]

—knowl′edgelless, *adj.*

—***Syn.*** **1 Knowledge, information** mean what a person knows. **Knowledge** applies to the understanding of an organized body of facts and principles: *scientific knowledge. His knowledge of the subject is limited.* **Information** applies to things one has learned through being told by people or from books or through observation, and often suggests isolated or unrelated facts: *She has acquired much information, but has little real knowledge.*

knowlledgelalbillilty (nol′i jə bil′ə tē), *n.* the quality of being knowledgeable; the possession of useful and thorough information about a particular subject: *This easy knowledgeability—he never lacks for a reference, never loses his sense of perspective* (New Yorker).

knowlledgelalble (nol′i jə bəl), *adj.* well-informed, especially about a particular subject: *His maternal grandfather, knowledgeable on sheep and horses, had come from the New Forest* (Manchester Guardian). **—knowl′edgelalbleness**, *n.* **—knowl′edgelalbly**, *adv.*

knowledge base or **representation**, the basic store of information required by a computer to solve a problem or perform a task: *Until they acquire . . . a knowledge base or knowledge representation, computer systems are going to miss . . . many common, and seemingly simple, writing problems* (Atlantic).

knowlledgles (nol′i jəz), *n.pl.* See under **knowledge**.

known (nōn), *v.* the past participle of **know**: *George Washington is known as the father of his country.*

know-nothling (nō′nuth′ing), *n., adj.* **—*n.*** **1** a person who knows nothing; a very ignorant person; ignoramus. **2** = agnostic.
—*adj.* **1** = ignorant. **2** = agnostic.

Know-Nothling (nō′nuth′ing), *n., adj.* **—*n.*** **1** a member of an American political party, prominent in the 1850's, which wanted to keep control of the government in the hands of native-born citizens. It was originally a secret society whose members pretended to know nothing about it. The Know-Nothings opposed the election of new immigrants and Catholics to political position. **2** the party itself. **3** a member of an earlier native American party, with similar principles.
—*adj.* of or having to do with the Know-Nothings.

Know-Nothlinglism (nō′nuth′ing iz əm), *n.* the doctrines or principles of the Know-Nothings.

known quantity, **1** a quantity, especially an algebraic quantity of a given or fixed value in an equation or analysis. It is often designated by one of the first letters of the alphabet, such as *a, b,* or *c.* **2** *Figurative: Have people become so accustomed to the series idea from television viewing that they go to another Dirty Harry movie because it's a known quantity?* (New Yorker).

know-what (nō′hwot′, -hwut′), *n. Informal.* knowledge of purposes and goals: *In a society shaped by technology . . . know-how takes precedence over know-what* (Harper's).

know-why (nō′hwī′), *n. Informal.* knowledge of reasons and motives: *It has been said that the . . . engineer must combine technical know-how with social know-why* (Atlantic).

Knox Bible or **Version** (noks), a translation of the Latin Vulgate Bible into current English made by Ronald Arbuthnott Knox (1888-1957). It is noted for its literary flavor and is widely used by Roman Catholics.

Knt., knight.

knucklle (nuk′əl), *n., v.,* **-led, -ling.** **—*n.*** **1** a joint in a finger, especially one of the joints between a finger and the rest of the hand. Each finger of a person's hand has three knuckles; the thumbs have two knuckles each. **2** the rounded protuberance formed when a joint is bent. **3** the knee or hock joint of an animal used as food: *boiled pigs' knuckles.* **4** the hollow, circular part at the joint of a hinge, through which a pin is passed. **5a** an angular, rather than curved, junction of two structures or two surfaces of a ship. **b** (formerly) the foremost rib of a wooden ship. **6** something shaped or protruding like a knuckle: *an old ragged wart of an edifice, standing on the knuckle of a hill* (Washington Irving).
—*v.t.* to strike, tap, or touch with the knuckles: *the . . . porter . . . knuckling his forehead as a sign of homage* (Dickens).
—*v.i.* **1** to yield; knuckle down: *When an organization begins thinking about its image, it has finally knuckled to the reality of the twentieth century* (Russell Baker). **2** to put the knuckles on the ground in playing marbles.

knuckle down, a *Informal.* to apply oneself earnestly; work hard: *to knuckle down to a job.* **b** to submit; yield: *He would not knuckle down under their attacks.* **c** to hold the knuckles close to or on the ground in playing marbles: *As happy as we once, to kneel and draw The chalky ring, and knuckle down at taw* (William Cowper).

knuckles, pieces of metal worn over the knuckles as a weapon; brass knuckles: *They wore knuckles during the fight.*

knuckle under, to submit; yield: *Then followed a battle of looks between them; but the captain soon knuckled under* (Robert Louis Stevenson).

near the knuckle, *British Slang.* near the limit of decency; bordering on coarseness or obscenity: *Anyone who didn't know he was an MA might think his conversation was a bit near the knuckle* (Punch).

rap over the knuckles, *Informal.* **a** to criticize or chastise: *It is known that Bilak was criticized in Moscow, that he was rapped over the knuckles for his famous autumn address on international policy* (London Times). **b** an act or instance of criticism or chastisement.

[origin uncertain. Compare Dutch *kneukel* (< *knook* bone), Danish *knokkel.*]

***knuckle ball**, *Baseball.* a slow pitch thrown from the knuckles and the heel of the palm, remarkable for its curving in several directions or dropping abruptly at the end of the delivery: *A knuckle ball does not spin, but floats toward the plate and then either darts to one side or sinks or does both* (New York Times).

***knuckle ball**

knucklelballler (nuk′əl bôl′ər), *n. Baseball.* a pitcher who is adept at throwing a knuckle ball.

knucklelbone (nuk′əl bōn′), *n.* **1** (in man) a bone of a finger which forms part of a knuckle; the rounded end of any one of the bones of the fingers. **2** in animals: **a** a bone corresponding to a finger or toe bone in man, as of a sheep. **b** a leg bone with a ball-like knob at the joint end, or the rounded end of such a bone. **c** a piece of meat including such a bone.

knucklebones, a game like jackstones played with small bones: *Schoolboys still play at the game of knucklebones* (J. Sharman).

knucklelduster (nuk′əl dus′tər), *n.* = knuckles.

knucklelhead (nuk′əl hed′), *n. U.S. Slang.* a stupid, dull, or unthinking person.

knucklelheadled (nuk′əl hed′id), *adj. U.S. Slang.* stupid; bumbling: *. . . an amiable knuckleheaded western about two lumpish modern cowpokes and their love-hate relationship with an obstreperous horse* (Time).

knuckle joint, **1** a joint forming a knuckle. **2** a joint or coupling in which a projection in one part in machinery is inserted into a corresponding recess in another part and held by a transverse pin.

knuckller (nuk′lər), *n.* = knuckle ball.

knuckles (nuk′əlz), *n.pl.* See under **knuckle**.

knuckle-walk (nuk′əl wôk′), *v.i.* to walk as chimpanzees and gorillas do, with the knuckles of the hands touching the ground.

knur or **knurr** (nėr), *n.* a knot or hardened excrescence on the trunk of a tree. [Middle English *knurre* lump, lumpish person, perhaps variant of *knar*]

knurl (nėrl), *n., v.* **—*n.*** **1** a small projection or protuberance; knot, knob, or lump. **2** a small ridge, as on the edge of a coin or thumbscrew. **3** *Dialect.* a thick-set, stumpy person.
—*v.t.* to make knurls on (the edge of a coin, a screwhead, or button); mill.
[apparently diminutive form of *knur*]

knurled (nėrld), *adj.* **1** having knurls or knots; gnarled. **2** having small ridges on the edge or surface; milled.

knurlly (nėr′lē), *adj.,* **knurllier, knurlliest.** = gnarled.

knut (nut), *n. British Slang.* a nut, or idle young man of fashion. [humorous variant of *nut*]

KlO (kā′ō′), *v.,* **KlO'd, KlO'ing,** *n., pl.* **KlO's.** *Slang.* **—*v.t.*** to knock out.
—*n.* a knockout. Also, **kayo.**
[apparently < *k*(nock) *o*(ut)]

KO (no periods), **K.O.**, or **k.o.**, *Boxing.* knockout.

kola (kō′ə), *n.* a valuable Hawaiian tree of the pea family, yielding a beautiful dark wood used in building and cabinetwork. [< Hawaiian *koa*]

***kolalla** (kō ä′lə), *n.* a gray, furry mammal of Australia that has large ears and no tail and looks like a small bear. It lives in trees and eats eucalyptus leaves. The female koala carries her young in a pouch. [< a native Australian name]

***koala**

koan (kō′än), *n.* a short and pithy but illogical statement, intended to free the mind from its rational mode of thought. It forms an important subject for meditation among Zen Buddhists. *We know the sound of two hands clapping. But what is the sound of one hand clapping?—A Zen koan* (J. D. Salinger). [< Japanese *kōan* idea]

kob (kob), *n.* any one of various African antelopes. [< a native name in Senegal]

kolbo (kō′bô), *n., pl.* **-bo.** one hundredth of a naira, the unit of money in Nigeria. [alteration of English *copper*]

kolbold (kō′bold, -bōld), *n.* in German folklore: **1** a mischievous sprite or goblin that does household work. **2** an underground spirit haunting mines or caves; goblin or gnome. [< German *Kobold;* see etym. under **cobalt**]

Koch's postulates (kōHs), the four basic steps bacteriologists follow to establish that a certain bacterium causes a particular disease. [< Robert *Koch,* 1843-1910, a German physician, who formulated the postulates]

Koldalchrome (kō′də krōm), *n. Trademark.* a color film for making 35 millimeter slides and motion pictures.

Koldalcollor (kō′də kul′ər), *n. Trademark.* a color film from which color prints are made.

koldak (kō′dak), *n., v.,* **-daked, -dakling.** **—*n.*** **1** a small camera, with rolls of film on which photographs are taken. **2 Kodak,** *Trademark.* a small camera made by the Eastman Kodak Company.
—*v.t., v.i.* to take photographs (of) with a kodak.
[American English (coined by George Eastman, founder of the Eastman *Kodak* Company)] **—ko′daklèr**, *n.*

Koldel (kō′del), *n. Trademark.* a synthetic polyester fiber similar to Dacron.

Koldilak bear (kō′dē ak), a large brown bear living along the southern coast of Alaska and on nearby islands: *The territory boasts the world's largest carnivorous animal—the Kodiak brown bear, which stands as high as eleven and a half feet and weighs up to sixteen hundred pounds* (New Yorker). Also, **Kadiak bear.** [< *Kodiak,* an island in the North Pacific, where it lives]

kolel (kō′əl), *n.* any one of various cuckoos of India, New Guinea, and Australia. [probably Anglo-Indian < Hindi *kōīl* < Sanskrit *kokila*]

K. of C., Knights of Columbus.

K. of P., Knights of Pythias.

Kolhen (kō′hən, kō′ən), *n., pl.* **Kolhens, Kolhanim** (kō hä′nim), = Cohen.

Kohlilnoor or **Koh-i-noor** (kō′ə nůr), *n.* a very large and famous Indian diamond (108.9 carats), that is now one of the British crown jewels. [< Persian *kōh-i-nūr* (literally) mountain of light]

kohlilnoor (kō′ə nůr), *n.* **1** any large and splendid diamond. **2** *Figurative.* something very beautiful or precious; the most splendid or superb example of something. [< *Kohinoor*]

kohl (kōl), *n.* a powder used in the Orient to darken the eyelids and lashes, usually consisting of finely powdered antimony. [< Arabic *kuhl* metallic powder. Compare etym. under **alcohol.**]

kohllrabi (kōl′rä′bē), *n., pl.* **-bies.** **1** a plant related to the cabbage and having a turnip-shaped stem. Kohlrabi belongs to the mustard family. **2** its stem, which is used as a vegetable and as food for cattle.
[< German *Kohlrabi* < Italian *cavoli rape,* plural; *cavolo* rape, cole < Latin *caulis* cabbage; *rapa* rape < Latin *rāpum* turnip]

Koilne or **koilne** (koi nā′), *n.* **1** the common literary language of the Greeks from the close of classical Attica to the Byzantine era. The New Testament was written in the Koine. **2** = lingua franca. [< Greek (*hē*) *koinē* (*diálektos*) (the) common (language); *koinē*, feminine of *koinós* common]

Ko|jah (kō′jä), *n.* a mutant variety of mink.

ko|kan|ee (kō kan′ē), *n.* a small, landlocked sockeye salmon. [< *Kokanee*, a creek in British Columbia]

ko|ker|boom (kō′kər büm′), *n.* a large aloe of South Africa from whose stem the Bushmen and Hottentots used to make quivers for their arrows. [< Afrikaans *kokerboom* < Dutch *koker* quiver + *boom* tree]

kok-sa|ghyz or **kok-sa|gyz** (kōk′sə gēz′), *n.* a Russian composite plant related to the dandelion, grown for its latex, from which rubber is made. [< Russian *kok-sagyz* < Turkic *kök* root + *sagïz* rubber]

ko|la (kō′lə), *n.* **1** = kola nut. **2** a stimulant or tonic made from kola nuts. **3** the tree on which kola nuts grow. Also, **cola**. [apparently < Temne (West African) *kola*. Compare etym. under **cola**[1].]

ko|lach (kō′läch), *n.* a sweet bun filled with jam or fruit pulp. [< Russian *kolach*]

kola nut, the bitter, red or white nut of a tropical African evergreen tree of the same family as the cacao and grown also in tropical America, and Asia. It contains about 3 percent of caffeine and some theobromine, and is used as an ingredient of soft drinks. Also, **cola nut**.

ko|lin|sky (kə lin′skē), *n., pl.* **-skies**. **1** any one of several varieties of mink that live in Asia; Russian mink. **2** the tawny fur of any of these minks, used to make artists' sable brushes. [< Russian *kolinskij*, adjective < *Kola*, a region of Russia]

kol|khoz (kol koz′; *Russian* kol ʜôz′), *n., pl.* **-khoz|es, -khoz|y** (-ʜô′zē). a Soviet collective farm: *Almost all farms had been collectivized by 1950, resistance being met with mass deportations. There followed the merging of the kolkhozes into the larger collective units, and the third phase, the eradication of the family* (London Times). [< Russian *kolkhoz*, abbreviation of *kollektivnoe khozjajstvo* collective management]

kol|khoz|nik (kol koz′nik; *Russian* kol ʜôz′-), *n., pl.* **-khoz|niks, -khoz|ni|ki** (-ʜôz′nē kē). a member of a kolkhoz.

kolm (kōlm), *n.* a hydrocarbon mineral that contains a high percentage of certain radioactive elements, such as uranium and radium. [< Swedish]

Kol Nid|re (kōl nid′rə), **1** a Jewish prayer of atonement, chanted in the synagogue on the eve of Yom Kippur. **2** the music to which it is sung. [< Aramaic *kōl nidrē* (literally) all vows (the two words which open the prayer)]

ko|lo (kō′lō), *n.* Serbo-Croatian national dance, performed in a circle with intricate steps, foot-stamping, and a fast tempo. [< Serbo-Croatian]

ko|mat|ik (kə mat′ik), *n.* an Eskimo dog sled. [< Eskimo *komatik*]

Kom|in|tern (kom′in tėrn, kom′in tėrn′) *n.* = Comintern.

ko|mi|teh (kō mē tā′), *n.* any of the revolutionary committees with wide police powers formed in Iran after the deposition of the Shah in 1979: The *komitehs summarily tried and executed hundreds of generals and lower-ranking officers* (Paul J. Magnarella). [< Persian *komiteh* < French *comité*]

Kom|man|da|tu|ra (kə man′də tůr′ə), *n.* **1** headquarters of any one of the armies of occupation in Germany and Austria after World War II. **2** a council of the Allied commanders of the occupied zones in Germany or Austria after World War II. [probably alteration of German *Kommandantur*]

***Ko|mo|do dragon** (kə mō′dō), a very large lizard of Indonesia weighing up to 300 pounds; dragon lizard; dragon of Komodo: *Until the year 1912 the Komodo dragons were thought to be legendary monsters. But these specimens of the largest known lizards (up to 12 feet long) are very much alive today* (Sunday Times). [< *Komodo*, island in the Malay archipelago, where this animal is found]

***Komodo dragon**

ko|mon|dor (kō′mon dôr), *n., pl.* **-dors, -do|rok** (-dō′rək). any strong Hungarian dog of an ancient breed with long, dense, woolly, white hair, used to watch over herds. It stands about 30 inches high and weighs about 90 pounds. [< Hungarian]

Kom|so|mol (kom′sə mol), *n.* **1** the Young Communist League, a Soviet organization for young people from 15 to 28 years old. **2** a member of it. Also, **Comsomol**. [< Russian *Komsomol*, abbreviation of *kommunisticheskij sojuz molodëzhi*]

Kon|go (kon′gō), *n.* **1** a member of a Bantu people of West Africa, occupying both banks of the lower Congo River. **2** the Bantu language of this people, spoken in Zaire, Angola, and Congo.

kon|go|ni (kong gō′nē), *n., pl.* **-ni**. a small hartebeest native to East Africa. [< Swahili *kongoni*]

ko|ni|ol|o|gy (kō′nē ol′ə jē), *n.* the study of dust and its components, especially of atmospheric dust. [< Greek *kónis* dust + English *-logy*]

Kon|ka|ni or **Kon|ka|ny** (kon′kə nē), *n.* an Indic language closely related to Mahratti, spoken in Goa and nearby regions of western India.

kon|ta|ki|on (kən tä′kē on; *Greek* kôn tä′kyôn), *n.* in the Greek Church: **1** a short ode or hymn in praise of a saint or on the theme of a festival day. **2** a service book containing only a given liturgy or liturgies. Also, **contakion**. [< Greek *kontákion* essay]

koo|doo (kü′dü), *n., pl.* **-doos**. = kudu.

kook (kük), *n., adj. Slang.* **—*n.*** a kooky person; an odd or crazy individual. **—*adj.*** silly or crazy; kooky: *Bill Bennet, master of all that is kook and strange in British California* (Maclean's).

***kook|a|bur|ra** (kůk′ə bėr′ə, kůk′ə bėr′-), *n.* a large kingfisher of Australia and New Guinea that has a harsh cackling voice; laughing jackass. [< the native Australian name]

***kookaburra**

kook|y or **kook|ie** (kü′kē), *adj.*, **kook|i|er, kook|i|est**. *Slang.* **1** odd or silly: *kooky little polo-neck sweater dresses.* **SYN:** quaint, whimsical. **2** crazy: *kooky about dancing.* [apparently < *cuckoo* crazy] **—kook′i|ness**, *n.*

koo|ra|jong (kü′rə jong), *n.* = currajong.

Koord (kůrd), *n.* = Kurd.

Koo|te|nay (kü′tə nā), *n., pl.* **-nay** or **-nays**. = Kutenai.

kop (kop), *n.* (in South Africa) a hill. [< Afrikaans *kop* < Dutch, head]

ko|peck or **ko|pek** (kō′pek), *n.* a unit of money of the Soviet Union. 100 kopecks make one ruble. Also, **copeck**. [< Russian *kopejka* (originally diminutive) < *kop'ë* spear (kopecks minted from 1535 to 1719 bore a figure of Ivan IV with a lance)]

koph (kōf, kůf), *n.* the 19th letter of the Hebrew alphabet. Also, **qoph**. [< Hebrew *qōph*]

kop|je (kop′ē), *n.* **1** (in South Africa) a small hill: *Soon we were speeding over the plateau, threading our way among its kopjes* (E. K. Lowndes). **2** a hard, chewy candy flavored with coffee. [< Afrikaans *kopje* < Dutch *kopje* little head]

kor (kôr, kōr), *n.* a homer, a Hebrew measure. [< Hebrew *kor*]

Ko|rah|ite (kō′rə īt), *n.* a member of the guild of singers of the Jewish Temple. [< *Korah* the great-grandson of Levi (in the Bible, I Chronicles 6:22) + *-ite*[1])]

Ko|ran (kô rän′, -ran′; kō-), *n.* the sacred book of the Moslems. It consists of revelations of Allah to the prophet Mohammed and is the standard by which Moslems regulate their lives. The book, written in Arabic after Mohammed's death, is divided into 114 chapters. [< Arabic *qur'ān* a recitation. Compare etym. under **Alcoran**.]

Ko|ran|ic (kô ran′ik, kō-), *adj.* of or having to do with the Koran: *Koranic doctrine.*

Ko|re|an (kô rē′ən, kō-), *adj., n.* **—*adj.*** of Korea, its people, or their language. **—*n.*** **1** a person born or living in Korea, a country on a peninsula in eastern Asia, now divided into two republics, North Korea and South Korea. **2** the language of Korea. It is of unknown relationship.

ko|ru|na (kô′rü nä), *n., pl.* **-ru|ny** (-rü nē), **-run** (-rün). the unit of money of Czechoslovakia, equal to 100 halers. [< Czech *koruna* < Latin *corōna* crown]

kos (kōs), *n.* an Indian unit of linear measure, varying from 1½ miles to 3 miles. Also, **coss**. [< Hindi *kōs* < Sanskrit *krosa*]

ko|sher (kō′shər), *adj., v., n.* **—*adj.*** **1** right or clean according to the Jewish law: *kosher meat.* **2** dealing in products that meet the requirements of Jewish law: *a kosher butcher or supermarket.* **3** *Slang, Figurative.* all right; fine; legitimate; proper: *It's not kosher to change the rules while you are playing the game.*
—*v.t.* to prepare (food) or clean (utensils) according to the Jewish law; make kosher.
—*n.* *Informal.* **1** food thus prepared. **2** a shop where kosher food is sold.
[< Hebrew *kåsher* proper, lawful]

kos|mos (koz′məs, -mos), *n.* = cosmos.

ko|to (kō′tō), *n., pl.* **-tos**. a large Japanese zither-like musical instrument with 13 strings, similar to a harp, plucked with the fingers of both hands. [< Japanese *koto*]

ko|tow (kō′tou′), *v.i., n.* = kowtow.

kou|lou|ra (kü′lü rä), *n.* a large doughnut-shaped loaf of bread eaten in Greece. [< New Greek *kouloúra*]

kou|mis, kou|miss, or **kou|myss** (kü′mis), *n.* = kumiss.

kou|prey (kü′prā), *n.* a rare wild ox of northern Kampuchea with long curved horns, small ears, and a large dewlap, first discovered in the 1930's; Indochinese forest ox. It is believed to be an early ancestor of domestic cattle.

kour|bash (kůr′bash), *n., v.t.* = kurbash.

kow|tow (kou′tou′), *v., n.* **—*v.i.*** **1** to kneel and touch the ground with the forehead to show deep respect, submission, or worship. **2** to show slavish respect and obedience: *He doesn't kowtow to win favor* (Newsweek). **—*n.*** the act of kowtowing. **SYN:** obeisance. [< Mandarin *k'o-t'ou* knock (the) head] **—kow′tow′er**, *n.*

KP (no periods), **1** *Chess.* king's pawn. **2** kitchen police.

K.P., **1** Knight of the Order of St. Patrick. **2** Knights of Pythias.

kparsec (no period), kiloparsec.

K-par|ti|cle (kā′pär′tə kəl), *n.*, or **K particle**, = heavy meson.

Kpel|le (kə pel′ə), *n., pl.* **-le** or **-les**. **1** a member of a tribe inhabiting central Liberia. **2** the Mandingo language of this tribe.

kph (no periods), kilometers per hour.

K-point (kā′point′), *n.* the point in the landing area in ski jumping beyond which there is insufficient space for a safe landing: *If someone lands at the K-point, the starting gate is lowered to reduce speed* (Maclean's). [half-translation of German *K-Punkt*, short for *Kritischer Punkt* critical point]

kr (no period), kilorad.

kr., an abbreviation for the following:
1 krona, a Swedish coin.
2 króna, an Icelandic coin.
3 krone, a Danish or Norwegian coin.
4 krone, a former German coin.
5 krone, a former Austrian coin.
6 kroon, a former Estonian coin.

Kr (no period), krypton (chemical element).

KR (no periods), *Chess.* king's rook.

kraal (kräl), *n., v.* in South Africa: **—*n.*** **1a** a village of natives protected by a fence or stockade. **b** the community or social unit of such a village. **2** a pen for cattle or sheep; stockade; fold: *A runaway ox . . . had escaped from the cattle kraals into Hillside suburb* (Cape Times). **3** a pen built in shallow water, in which fishermen keep their catch of sponges, lobsters, or turtles.
—*v.t.* to enclose in a kraal. Also, **craal**.
[< Afrikaans *kraal* < Dutch < Portuguese *curral*, Spanish *corral*. See etym. of doublets **corral**, **crawl**[2].]

krad (no periods), kilorad.

kraft (kraft, kräft), *n.* strong smooth, brown wrapping paper made by boiling wood chips in an alkaline solution. [< German < *Kraft* strength]

krait (krīt), *n.* any one of various very venomous snakes related to the cobra, found in India and adjacent parts of Asia. [< Hindi *karait*]

kra|ken (krä′kən, krā′-), *n.* a mythical sea monster of enormous size, said to appear off the coast of Norway: *Then like a kraken huge and black, She crushed our ribs in her iron grasp* (Longfellow). [< Norwegian *krakjen*]

kran (krän), *n.* an Iranian unit of money or silver coin of 1,000 dinars. [< Persian *qrān*]

krans (kräns), *n.* = krantz.

krantz or **kranz** (kränts), *n.* in South Africa: **1** a wall of rock encircling a mountain or summit. **2** any precipitous or overhanging wall of rocks bordering high ground or hemming in a valley: *The krantz that overhangs the Maraisburg road is in a very dangerous state* (Midland News and Karoo Farmer). [< Afrikaans *krans* < Dutch *krans, krants* corona, chaplet]

***kra|ter** (krā′tər), *n.* a kind of ancient Greek and Roman jar or bowl; crater. [< Greek *krātêr* < *kerannýnai* to mix]

***krater**

K-ra|tion (kā′rash′ən, -rā′shən), *n.*, or **K ration**, *U.S.* one of the army rations issued to troops in the field when other rations are not available, and providing three meals, consisting of highly concentrated or dehydrated portions of food, including meat, beverage, and candy. [*K* < Ancel *Keys,* born 1904, an American physiologist who was the consultant on nutrition to the Secretary of War during World War II]

kraut or **Kraut** (krout), *n. U.S. Slang.* a German (used in an unfriendly way). [< *sauerkraut* (because the Germans were thought to eat quantities of this food)]

Kre|bi|o|zen (krə bī′ə zən), *n. Trademark.* a drug prepared from serum from horse tissue injected with an actinomycete, which has been used experimentally to treat cancer.

Krebs cycle (krebz), a series of chemical reactions important in metabolism, in which acetic acid formed in the body from the partial breakdown of fats, proteins, and carbohydrates is changed to carbon dioxide and water with release of energy; citric acid cycle; tricarboxylic acid cycle. [< Hans A. *Krebs,* born 1900, a British biochemist born in Germany, who discovered the cycle]

KREEP (krēp), *n.* a yellow-brown glassy mineral obtained on the moon, noted for its unusual chemical composition. [< *K* (symbol for potassium), *R*(are)-*E*(arth) *E*(lements), *P* (symbol for phosphorus)]

krem|lin (krem′lən), *n.* the citadel of a Russian city. [< French *kremlin* < Russian *kreml′* citadel]

Krem|lin (krem′lən), *n.* the Soviet government. [< *Kremlin* the citadel of Moscow, where many offices of the Soviet government are located]

Krem|lin|o|log|i|cal (krem′lə nə loj′ə kəl), *adj.* of or having to do with Kremlinology: *He applies the strict Kremlinological method to trace the shifts of power among leaders* (London Times).

Krem|lin|ol|o|gist (krem′lə nol′ə jist), *n.* a Western expert on Soviet policies, leaders, and practices; Sovietologist: *Kremlinologists, those Westerners who read Soviet tea leaves in search of policy trends ...* (Wall Street Journal).

Krem|lin|ol|o|gy (krem′lə nol′ə jē), *n.* the study of the policies, leaders, and practices of the Soviet government; Sovietology: ... *this was "Kremlinology"—an inexact science if ever there was one* (Manchester Guardian Weekly).

kreng (kreng), *n.* the carcass of a whale after its blubber has been removed. [< Dutch *kreng* carcass]

krep|lach (krep′läн, -ləн), *n. Jewish Cookery.* a dish similar to ravioli, consisting of balls of dough filled with meat and boiled, usually served with soup. [< Yiddish *kreplekh* < German *Krapfen* apple fritter]

kreut|zer or **kreu|zer** (kroit′sər), *n.* a former German or Austrian copper coin, worth about half a cent. [< German, Middle High German *kreuzer* < *kreuz* cross, ultimately < Latin *crux, crucis* (because of the cross stamped on them)]

Krieg (krēk), *n. German.* war.

krieg|spiel (krēg′spēl), *n.* a war game; imitation warfare carried out on a map or other surface, with counters or other figures representing armies, guns, fleets, or other forces. It is used in teaching military science. [< German *Kriegsspiel* < *Krieg* war + *Spiel* game]

Kriem|hild (krēm′hild), *n.* the wife of Siegfried in the *Niebelungenlied.* Siegfried was murdered by her brother.

krill (kril), *n., pl.* **krill**. any one of a genus of small, shrimplike crustaceans that feed on plankton and are in turn the staple diet of whales and certain other sea animals. [< Norwegian *kril*]

krim|mer (krim′ər), *n.* a gray lambskin from the Crimean region, dressed as fur, resembling Persian lamb. Also, **crimmer**. [< German *Krimmer* < *Krim* Crimea]

kris (krēs), *n.* = creese. [< Malay *keris*]

Krish|na (krish′nə), *n.* one of the most important Hindu gods, an incarnation of Vishnu. He appears in the sacred text, *Bhagavad-Gita,* as the charioteer and teacher of Arjuna. [< Sanskrit *Kṛṣna* < *kṛṣna* black, dark]

Krish|na|ism (krish′nə iz əm), *n.* the worship of or belief in Krishna.

Kriss Krin|gle (kris′kring′gəl), = Santa Claus. [American English < dialectal German *Christkindl* Christmas gift; (literally) Christ Child]

kro|na (krō′nə), *n., pl.* **-nor** (-nôr). a Swedish unit of money, a silver coin equal to 100 öre. [< Swedish *krona,* ultimately < Latin *corōna* crown]

kró|na (krō′nə), *n., pl.* **-nur** (-nər). an Icelandic unit of money, a coin made of aluminum-bronze, worth 100 aurar. [< Icelandic *krona,* ultimately < Latin *corōna* crown]

kro|ne[1] (krō′ne), *n., pl.* **-ner** (-nər). **1** a Danish and Greenland unit of money, an aluminum-bronze coin worth 100 öre. **2** a Norwegian unit of money, a cupronickel coin worth 100 öre. [< Danish, Norwegian *krone,* ultimately < Latin *corōna* crown]

kro|ne[2] (krō′nə), *n., pl.* **-nen** (-nən). **1** a former German gold coin, worth 100 heller. **2** a former Austrian silver coin, worth 100 heller. **3** a former unit of money of Austria-Hungary. [< German *Krone,* ultimately < Latin *corōna* crown]

Kro|neck|er delta (krō′nek ər), *Mathematics.* a function of two variables that is equal to 1 when the variables have the same value, and equal to 0 when the variables have different values. [< Leopold *Kronecker,* 1823-1891, a German mathematician]

Kro|nos (krō′nos), *n.* = Cronus.

Kron|o|saur|us (kron′ə sôr′əs, krō′nə-), *n., pl.* **-sau|ri** (-sôr′ī). a huge marine reptile of the Cretaceous period whose fossil has been found in Australia: *The 42-foot-long skeleton of the 100-million-year-old Kronosaurus was reconstructed, the only complete skeleton of what was once the largest flesh-eating reptile in the sea* (Science News Letter). [< New Latin *Kronosaurus* the genus name < Greek *Krónos* Cronus + *saûros* lizard]

kroon (krün), *n., pl.* **kroons, kroo|ni** (krü′nē). a former Estonian unit of money. [< Estonian *kroon* < Swedish *krona* krona]

Kru (krü), *n., pl.* **Kru** or **Krus**. **1** a member of a coastal tribe of Liberia and the Ivory Coast. **2** the Kwa language of this tribe.

Kru|ger|rand (krü′gər rand′), *n.* a one-ounce gold coin of South Africa, first struck in 1967. [< Afrikaans *Krugerrand* < Paulus *Kruger* (1824-1904), a South African statesman + *rand*[2]]

krul|ler (krul′ər), *n.* = cruller.

krum|horn or **krumm|horn** (krum′hôrn′), *n.* **1** a medieval wind instrument, having a curved tube and a melancholy tone. **2** = cromorna. Also, **crumhorn**. [< German *Krummhorn* < *krumm* crooked + *Horn* horn]

krutt or **krut** (krut), *n.* a dry cheese made by nomadic tribes in Afghanistan and other regions of central Asia from the milk of camels. [< a native name]

∗**kryp|ton** (krip′ton), *n.* a colorless, inert, gaseous chemical element that forms a very small part of the air. Krypton is used to fill some fluorescent lamps. [< New Latin *krypton* < Greek *kryptón,* neuter of *kryptós* hidden < *krýptein* to hide]

∗krypton

symbol	atomic number	atomic weight
Kr	36	83.80

kryp|ton|ate (krip′tə nāt), *n.* a substance made radioactive by impregnation with an isotope of krypton and used as a tracer.

KS (no periods), Kansas (with postal Zip Code).

Kshat|ri|ya (kshat′rē yə), *n.* a member of the military caste, the second of the four great castes or classes among the Hindus. [< Sanskrit *kṣatriya* ruling ones < *kṣatra* rule, authority]

K-shell (kā′shel′), *n.* the innermost space, or lowest energy level occupied by the orbits of electrons around the nucleus of an atom.

kt., an abbreviation for the following:
1 karat (carat).
2 kiloton.
3 knight.
4 knot.

Kt (no period), *Chess.* knight.

Kt., knight.

K.T., 1 Knight of the Order of the Thistle.
2 Knight Templar.

Ku|ba (kü′bə), *n., pl.* **-ba** or **-bas**, a member of a Bantu-speaking people of the central Congo, known for their woodcarvings and other crafts.

Ku|bla Khan (kü′blə kän′), an unfinished poem by Samuel Taylor Coleridge, published in 1816.

ku|chen (kü′нən), *n.* a coffeecake, originally German, usually made with yeast and topped with fruit, sugar, and cinnamon. [American English < German *Kuchen*]

ku|dos (kyü′dos, kü′-), *n., pl.* **-dos**. *Informal.* praise; fame; prestige; renown: *The kudos of the promise of an exclusive story often beclouds the judgment and influences the course of a correspondent* (Saturday Review). [< Greek *kydos* glory, fame, renown]

▶**Kudos** came into English in the early 1800's as a singular noun: *He received much kudos. This kudos is well deserved.* But because of the final *s,* it was gradually taken in the 1900's as a plural: *He received many kudos. These kudos are well deserved.* The singular form *kudo* derived by back formation, but is not always accepted.

Kud|run (küd′rün, kůтн′-), *n.* = Gudrun.

ku|du (kü′dü), *n., pl.* **-dus** or (*collectively*) **-du**. a large, grayish-brown African antelope with vertical white stripes. It is about four feet to five feet high at the shoulder and is noted for its ability to make great jumps. Also, **koodoo**. [< Bantu *iqudu*]

kud|zu (kůd′zü), *n.* a perennial vine of the pea family native to Japan and China. It is cultivated in the Old and New World for its edible roots, as a hay and ensilage feed, and to curb soil erosion. [< Japanese *kuzu*]

∗**ku|fa** (kü′fə), *n.* a round Iraqi boat of reed covered with animal skins or pitch. Also, **gufa**. [< Arabic *quffa* basket]

∗kufa

Ku|fic (kyü′fik), *n., adj.* **—*n.*** the more formal and angular style of Arabic script, as distinguished from Neskhi: *Islamic writers used Kufic for inscriptions* (Richard Ettinghausen).
—*adj.* of this style of script; Cufic.
[< *Kufa,* variant of *Cufa;* see etym. under **Cufa**]

ku|fi|yah (kə fē′yə), *n.* = kaffiyeh.

Ku-Klux or **Ku-klux** (kü′kluks′, kyü′-), *n.* **1** = Ku Klux Klan. **2** a member of either Ku Klux Klan.

Ku Kluxer, *Informal.* a Klansman.

Ku Klux Klan (kü′kluks′klan′, kyü′), **1** a secret society of white people in the southern United States formed after the Civil War as a social veterans' group to maintain white supremacy. **2** a secret society founded in Georgia in 1915, violently opposed to Negroes, Jews, Catholics, and foreigners. **3** a similar secret society active since the 1960's. Also, **Klan**. [American English, supposedly < Greek *kýklos* circle + English *clan*]

Ku Klux Klan|ner (klan′ər), = Klansman.

kuk|ri (kůk′rē), *n.* a knife with a curved blade broadest toward the point and usually having the sharp edge on the concave side, used by the Gurkhas of India. [< Hindi *kukrī*]

ku|ku|i (kü kü′ē), *n.* the state tree of Hawaii, having long, spreading branches and light green leaves; candlenut. The kukui produces an oil used as fuel and in varnishes. [< Hawaiian *kukui*]

ku|lak (kü läk′), *n.* **1** (formerly in Russia) a well-to-do peasant, farmer, or trader, especially one who opposed Soviet collectivization: *The kulaks and nepmen ... were shipped off by the millions to die in Siberian labor camps* (Harper's). **2** (under the Soviet government) a peasant who owns and tills his land for his own profit. [< Russian *kulak* prosperous peasant; (literally) fist < Turkic]

ku|lak|ism (kü lä′kiz əm), *n.* (under the Soviet government) private ownership and cultivation of land by a peasant for his own profit.

Kul|tur (kůl tür′), *n.* **1** culture, especially the traditional, unchanging spiritual character of a culture: *assertions ... of the insuperable excellencies of German Kultur* (H. G. Wells). **2** the characteristic culture of a time or a people. [< German *Kultur,* ultimately < Latin *cultūra* culture]

Kul|tur|kampf (kůl tür′kämpf′), *n.* the conflict between the German government and the Roman Catholic Church (1872-1886) chiefly over the control of education and ecclesiastical appointments. [< German *Kulturkampf* < *Kultur* culture + *Kampf* conflict, struggle]

ku|miss (kü′mis), *n.* fermented mare's or camel's milk, used as a drink by Asiatic nomads. [< Russian *kumys* < Tartar *kumyz*]

ku|mi|te (kə mə′tā, -tē), *n.* a sparring event or exhibition in karate, in which blows are stopped just short of contact with the oppenent's body: *Free-style combinations of techniques come in kumite, in which two people (karateka) spar with each other* (New Scientist). [< Japanese *kumite* (literally) set hand]

kum|kum (kům′kům′), *n.* **1** a red powder used to make the forehead mark of the Hindu. **2** the mark on the forehead made with this powder. [< Hindi *kunkum*]

küm|mel (kim′əl), *n.* a liqueur flavored especially with caraway seeds, anise, and cumin, first made in Holland in 1575, and since made especially in regions near the Baltic Sea. [< German *Kümmel* < Old High German *kumīn,* or *chumī* < Latin *cumīnum* cumin < Greek *kýmīnon*]

kum|mer|bund (kum′ər bund), *n.* = cummerbund.

kum|quat (kum′kwot), *n.* **1** a yellow or orange fruit somewhat like a small orange. It has a sour pulp and a sweet rind, and is used in preserves and candy. **2** the small tree that it grows on, native to China, now grown in Florida and California. It belongs to the rue family. Also, **cum-**

Pronunciation Key: **h**a**t**, **ā**ge, **c**ã**re**, **fä**r; **l**e**t**, **ē**qual, **tė**rm; **i**t, **ī**ce; **h**o**t**, **ō**pen, **ô**rder; **oi**l, **ou**t; **c**u**p**, **p**ů**t**, **r**ü**le**; **ch**ild; **lo**ng; **th**in; **ᴛʜ**en; **zh**, measure;
ə represents **a** in about, **e** in taken, **i** in pencil, **o** in lemon, **u** in circus.

quat. [< Chinese (Canton) *kam* golden + *kwat* orange]

***kum|san** (küm′sän), *n.* a long cotton shirt reaching to the ankles and gathered at the waist with a wide sash, worn by men in Morocco and other Arab countries. [< Arabic *kumsān*]

***kumsan**

***kung-fu** (kung′fü′), *n.,* or **kung fu**, a Chinese method of fighting without weapons by striking blows at vulnerable places of the body: *"I will make you a master of Chinese kung-fu" promises page one, beside a titillating sketch of a tiny Oriental felling an ox with his left forefinger* (Punch). [< Chinese (Canton) *k'ung fu* (literally) boxing method]

***kung-fu**

kunz|ite (kunts′īt), *n.* a transparent lavender stone, a variety of spodumene found in California and Madagascar, used as a gem. [American English < George F. *Kunz,* 1856-1932, an American mineralogist + *-ite*[1]]

Kuo|min|tang (kwō′min tang′, -täng′), *n.* a Chinese nationalist party organized by Sun Yat-sen in 1911 and now the dominant party of the Chinese Nationalists.

Kuo-yü (kwō′yü′), *n.* the national language of China, based on the form of Mandarin spoken in Peking. [< Chinese (Peking) *kuo* national + *yü* language]

kur|bash (kůr′bash), *n., v. —n.* a whip, usually of the hide of a hippopotamus or rhinoceros, used for punishment in Turkey and Egypt.
—v.t. to flog with a kurbash.
[< Arabic *qurbāsh* < Turkish *qirbāch*]

kur|cha|to|vi|um (kėr′chə tō′vē əm), *n.* the Soviet name for element 104. [< Igor V. *Kurchatov,* a Russian nuclear physicist]

Kurd (kėrd, kůrd), *n.* a member of a nomadic and fiercely independent Moslem people living chiefly in the frontier areas of Iraq, Iran, Turkey, and Syria.

Kurd|ish (kėr′dish, kůr′-), *adj., n. —adj.* of or having to do with the Kurds or their language.
—n. the language of the Kurds, an Iranian dialect.

Kur|di|stan (kėr′də stan, kůr′di stän′), *n.* any one of several types of rugs woven by the Kurds of Iran or Turkey.

kur|gan (kůr gän′), *n.* a prehistoric burial mound in Russia or Siberia. [< Russian *kurgan* < Turkic, stronghold]

Ku|ro|shi|o (kü′rō shē′ō), *n.* = Japan Current.
[< Japanese *kuroshio* < *kuro* black + *shio* tide]

Ku|ro|shi|wo (kü′rō shē′wō), *n.* = Kuroshio.

kur|ra|jong (kur′ə jông), *n.* = currajong.

kur|ta (kėr′tə), *n.* = khurta. [< Hindi]

kur|to|sis (kėr tō′sis), *n. Statistics.* the relative degree of flatness or peakedness in the region about the mode of a curve describing a frequency distribution. [< Greek *kýrtōsis* a bulging, convexity < *kýrtos* bulge, swelling]

ku|ru (kůr′ü), *n.* a fatal disease of the human nervous system similar to scrapie in sheep, occurring especially among members of the Fore tribe of the New Guinea highlands, and characterized by tremors and fits of giggling and other degenerative symptoms; laughing death: *Kuru ... was found to be caused by a virus that persists in the tissues for long periods of time before symptoms appear* (Thomas C. Merigan). [< the native name of the disease, roughly meaning "shivers"]

ku|rus (ků rüsh′), *n., pl.* **-rus**. a Turkish unit of money, a coin worth 1/100 of a lira or Turkish pound. [< Turkish *kurus*]

Kush (kush), *n.* = Cush.

Kush|ite (kush′īt), *n.* = Cushite.

Kush|it|ic (kə shit′ik), *n., adj.* = Cushitic.

Ku|tchin (kü chin′), *n., pl.* **-chin** or **-chins**. **1** a member of a large tribe of American Indians who lived in the Yukon in Canada and were noted for their warlike behavior and caste system. **2** their Athapascan language.

Ku|te|nai (kü′tə nā), *n., pl.* **-nai** or **-nais**. **1** a member of a tribe of Indians living in parts of British Columbia, Montana, and Idaho. **2** the language of this tribe, perhaps of the Algonkian stock. Also, **Kootenay**.

ku|vasz (kü′vôs), *n., pl.* **-va|szok** (-vô sōk) or (*collectively*) **-vasz**. a large white dog of a breed, originally from Tibet, but developed in Hungary as a guard and hunting dog for the nobility. It stands 25 or 26 inches high and weighs about 70 pounds. [< Hungarian *Kuvasz* < Turkish *kavas* armed guard of the nobility]

Ku|wai|ti (kü wā′tē, -wī′-), *adj., n. —adj.* of or having to do with Kuwait, in Arabia.
—n. a native or inhabitant of Kuwait.

kv. or **kv** (no period), kilovolt.

K.V.A., k.v.a., or **kva** (no periods), kilovolt-ampere.

kvass or **kvas** (kväs), *n.* a sour Russian beer, usually made from an infusion of rye or barley flour or bread with malt. Also, **quass**. [< Russian *kvas,* related to *kvasit'* to leaven, make sour]

Kveim test (kvām), a skin test for the diagnosis of sarcoidosis. [< M.A. *Kveim,* a Norwegian physician of the 1900's]

kvetch (kvech), *n., v. U.S. Slang. —n.* a habitual complainer or faultfinder.
—v.i. to whine, complain, or find fault.
[< Yiddish *kvetsh,* noun, *kvetshn,* verb, literally, squeeze]

kw., kilowatt or kilowatts.

Kwa (kwä), *n.* a large group of West African languages, including Fanti, Twi, Ewe, and Ibo. It is a branch of the Niger-Congo language family.

kwa|cha (kwä′chə), *n., pl.* **-cha** or **-chas**. **1** the unit of money of Malawi, equal to 100 tambala. **2** the unit of money of Zambia, equal to 100 ngwee. [< the native name, meaning "dawn"]

Kwa|ki|u|tl (kwä′kē ü′təl), *n.* **1** a member of any one of various American Indian tribes of the northern Pacific coast, known for their shamanism and potlatches. **2** the Wakashan language of this tribe.

kwan|za (kwän′zə), *n., pl.* **-zas**. the unit of money of Angola, equal to 100 lweis: *The Finance Ministry announced the introduction of a new currency, the kwanza (named after the nation's main river), to replace the Portuguese escudo* (Thomas H. Henrikson). [perhaps related to Swahili *kwanza;* see **Kwanza**]

Kwan|za or **Kwan|zaa** (kwän′zə), *n.* an annual Afro-American cultural festival celebrated during the seven-day period from December 26 to January 1. [< Swahili *kwanza,* infinitive of *anza* to begin]

kwa|shi|or|kor (kwä′shē ôr′kôr), *n.* an often fatal condition of infants and young children caused by a protein deficiency in the diet. It occurs among poorer peoples of the world and causes stunted physical and mental growth, loss of hair pigment, and swelling of tissues.
[< West African (Ashanti) *kwashiorkor* (literally) red boy]

K.W.H., kwh., (no period) **kwhr.,** or **kw-hr.,** kilowatt-hour or kilowatt-hours.

KWIC (kwik), *n.* key-word-in-context: *A second type of bibliographic information retrieval device is the key-word-in-context (KWIC) index.* (F. G. Kilgour).

kwt (no period), kilowatt or kilowatts.

Ky., Kentucky.

KY (no periods), Kentucky (with postal Zip Code).

ky|ack (kī′ak), *n. Western U.S.* a packsack that may be hung from either side of a packsaddle. [American English, origin uncertain; perhaps < an American Spanish, or American Indian word]

ky|ak (kī′ak), *n.* = kayak.

kyang (kyang), *n.* = kiang.

ky|a|nite (kī′ə nīt), *n.* = cyanite.

ky|an|ize (kī′ə nīz), *v.t.,* **-ized, -iz|ing**. to treat (wood) with a solution of corrosive sublimate to prevent decay. [< J. H. *Kyan,* who invented the process in 1832 + *-ize*] **—ky′an|i|za′tion,** *n.*

kyat (kyät), *n.* a unit of money of Burma, equal to 100 pyas. [< Burmese *kyat*]

ky|bosh (kī′bosh, ki bosh′), *n.* = kibosh.

ky|lin (kē′lin), *n.* a mythical animal of composite form, commonly figured on Chinese and Japanese pottery. [< Chinese *ch'i lin*]

ky|lix (kī′liks), *n., pl.* **kyl|i|kes** (kil′ə kēz′). = cylix.

ky|loe (kī′lō), *n.* any one of a breed of cattle of the Hebrides and the Scottish Highlands.

ky|mo|gram (kī′mə gram), *n.* the record produced by a kymograph.

ky|mo|graph (kī′mə graf, -gräf), *n.* **1** an instrument by which variations of motion or fluid pressure, such as muscle twitches or the pulse, can be measured and graphically recorded. **2** an instrument which measures variations in the angle made by an airplane in flight in relation to fixed axes in space. Also, **cymograph**. [< Greek *kyma* wave + English *-graph*]

ky|mo|graph|ic (kī′mə graf′ik), *adj.* of or having to do with a kymograph.

Kym|ri or **Kym|ry** (kim′rē), *n.pl.* = Cymry.

Kym|ric (kim′ric), *adj., n.* = Cymric.

kyo|gen (kyō′gen), *n.* a dance drama or comedy performed during intermissions of the classical no dramas of Japan. [< Japanese *kyōgen* play, drama]

ky|phos (kī′fos), *n.* the characteristic hump caused by kyphosis. [< Greek *kȳphós* hunched]

ky|pho|sis (kī fō′sis), *n.* an excessive outward curvature of the spine; humpback; hunchback. [< New Latin *kyphosis* < Greek *kyphōsis* hunchback < *kȳphós* hunched, curved]

ky|phot|ic (kī fot′ik), *adj.* = hunchbacked.

Kyr|i|e (kir′ē ā, -ē ē), *n.* = Kyrie eleison.

Kyrie e|le|i|son (ə lā′ə sən), **1** "Lord have mercy," a prayer in various offices of the Eastern and Roman churches. **2** a response in the Anglican service. **3** a musical setting for either. [< Latin *kyrie eleison* < Greek *kýrie eléēson* Lord have mercy]

kyte (kīt), *n. Scottish.* the belly; stomach; paunch.

K-Z syndrome, a group of symptoms in liberated prisoners of war, including anxiety, insomnia, memory lapse, and guilt for surviving: *It may be that all or part of the K-Z syndrome will show up in the returned Vietnam POW's, but the evidence is inconclusive so far* (Science News). [*K-Z,* from German *Konzentrationslager* concentration camp]